Stanley Gibbons
Simplified Catalogue

Stamps of the World

Stanley Gibbons Simplified Catalogue

Stamps of the World

2012 Edition

Countries **Chile – Georgia**

2

Stanley Gibbons Ltd
London and Ringwood

By Appointment to
Her Majesty The Queen
Stanley Gibbons Limited
London
Philatelists

77th Edition
Published in Great Britain by
Stanley Gibbons Ltd
Publications Editorial, Sales Offices and Distribution Centre
7, Parkside, Christchurch Road,
Ringwood, Hampshire BH24 3SH
Telephone +44 (0) 1425 472363

British Library Cataloguing in
Publication Data.
A catalogue record for this book is available
from the British Library.

Volume 2
ISBN 10: 0-85259-833-5
ISBN 13: 978-0-85259-833-7

Published as Stanley Gibbons Simplified Catalogue from 1934 to 1970, renamed Stamps of the World in 1971, and produced in two (1982-88), three (1989-2001), four (2002-2005) five (2006-2010) and six from 2011 volumes as Stanley Gibbons Simplified Catalogue of Stamps of the World.

Item No. 2881– Set12

Printed and bound in Wales by Stephens & George

Contents – Volume 2

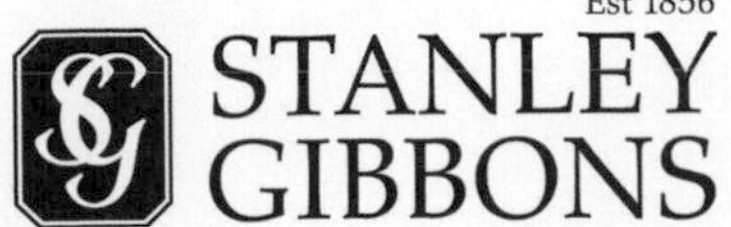

About Us

Our History

Edward Stanley Gibbons started trading postage stamps in his father's chemist shop in 1856. Since then we have been at the forefront of stamp collecting for over 150 years. We hold the Royal Warrant, offer unsurpassed expertise and quality and provide collectors with the peace of mind of a certificate of authenticity on all of our stamps. If you think of stamp collecting, you think of Stanley Gibbons and we are proud to uphold that tradition for you.

399 Strand

Our world famous stamp shop is a collector's paradise, with all of our latest catalogues, albums and accessories and, of course, our unrivalled stockholding of postage stamps.
www.stanleygibbons.com shop@stanleygibbons.com +44 (0)20 7836 8444

Specialist Stamp Sales

For the collector that appreciates the value of collecting the highest quality examples, Stanley Gibbons is the only choice. Our extensive range is unrivalled in terms of quality and quantity, with specialist stamps available from all over the world.
www.stanleygibbons.com/stamps shop@stanleygibbons.com +44 (0)20 7836 8444

Stanley Gibbons Auctions and Valuations

Sell your collection or individual rare items through our prestigious public auctions or our regular postal auctions and benefit from the excellent prices being realised at auction currently. We also provide an unparalleled valuation service.
www.stanleygibbons.com/auctions auctions@stanleygibbons.com +44 (0)20 7836 8444

Stanley Gibbons Publications

The world's first stamp catalogue was printed by Stanley Gibbons in 1865 and we haven't looked back since! Our catalogues are trusted worldwide as the industry standard and we print countless titles each year. We also publish consumer and trade magazines, Gibbons Stamp Monthly and Philatelic Exporter to bring you news, views and insights into all things philatelic. Never miss an issue by subscribing today and benefit from exclusive subscriber offers each month.
www.stanleygibbons.com/shop orders@stanleygibbons.com +44 (0)1425 472 363

Stanley Gibbons Investments

The Stanley Gibbons Investment Department offers a unique range of investment propositions that have consistently outperformed more traditional forms of investment, from capital protected products with unlimited upside to portfolios made up of the world's rarest stamps and autographs.
www.stanleygibbons.com/investment investment@stanleygibbons.com +44 (0)1481 708 270

Fraser's Autographs

Autographs, manuscripts and memorabilia from Henry VIII to current day. We have over 60,000 items in stock, including movie stars, musicians, sport stars, historical figures and royalty. Fraser's is the UK's market leading autograph dealer and has been dealing in high quality autographed material since 1978.
www.frasersautographs.com sales@frasersautographs.com +44 (0)20 7557 4404

stanleygibbons.com

Our website offers the complete philatelic service. Whether you are looking to buy stamps, invest, read news articles, browse our online stamp catalogue or find new issues, you are just one click away from anything you desire in the world of stamp collecting at stanleygibbons.com. Happy browsing!
www.stanleygibbons.com

Introduction

The ultimate reference work for all stamps issued around the world since the very first Penny Black of 1840, now with an improved layout.

Stamps of the World provides a comprehensive, illustrated, priced guide to postage stamps, and is the standard reference tool for every collector. It will help you to identify those elusive stamps, to value your collection, and to learn more about the background to issues. *Stamps of the World* was first published in 1934 and has been updated every year since 1950.

The helpful article 'Putting on a Good Show' provides expert advice on starting and developing a collection, then making the most of its presentation. Also included is a guide to stamp identification so that you can easily discover which country issued your stamp.

Re-designed to provide more colourful, clearer, and easy-to-navigate listings, these volumes continue to present you with a wealth of information to enhance your enjoyment of stamp collecting.

Features:

- Current values for every stamp in the world from the experts
- Easy-to-use simplified listings
- World-recognised Stanley Gibbons catalogue numbers
- A wealth of historical, geographical and currency information
- Indexing and cross-referencing throughout the volumes
- Worldwide miniature sheets listed and priced
- Thousands of new issues since the last edition

For this edition, prices have been thoroughly reviewed for Great Britain up to date, and all Commonwealth countries up to 1970, with further updates for Commonwealth countries which have appeared in our recently-published or forthcoming comprehensive catalogues under the titles *Cyprus, Gibraltar and Malta, Eastern Pacific and St Helena, Ascension and Tristan da Cunha*. Other countries with complete price updates from the following comprehensive catalogues are: *China, Germany, Portugal and Spain and United States of America*. New issues received from all other countries have been listed and priced. The first *Gibbons Stamp Monthly* Catalogue Supplement to this edition is September 2011.

Information for users

Scope of the Catalogue

Stamps of the World contains listings of postage stamps only. Apart from the ordinary definitive, commemorative and air-mail stamps of each country there are sections for the following, where appropriate. Noted below are the Prefixes used for each section (see Guide to Entries for further information):

- postage due stamps – Prefix in listing D
- parcel post or postcard stamps – Prefix P
- official stamps – Prefix O
- express and special delivery stamps - Prefix E
- frank stamps – Prefix F
- charity tax stamps – Prefix J
- newspaper and journal stamps – Prefix N
- printed matter stamps – Prefix
- registration stamps - Prefix R
- acknowledgement of receipt stamps – Prefix AR
- late fee and too late stamps – Prefix L
- military post stamps- Prefix M
- recorded message stamps – Prefix RM
- personal delivery stamps – Prefix P
- concessional letter post – Prefix CL
- concessional parcel post – Prefix CP
- pneumatic post stamps – Prefix PE
- publicity envelope stamps – Prefix B
- bulk mail stamps – Prefix BP
- telegraph used for postage – Prefix PT
- telegraph (Commonwealth Countries) – Prefix T
- obligatory tax – Prefix T
- Frama Labels and Royal Mail Postage Labels No Prefix-

As this is a simplified listing, the following are NOT included:
Fiscal or revenue stamps: stamps used solely in collecting taxes or fees for non-postal purposes. For example, stamps which pay a tax on a receipt, represent the stamp duty on a contract, or frank a customs document. Common inscriptions found include: Documentary, Proprietary, Inter. Revenue and Contract Note.
Local stamps: postage stamps whose validity and use are limited in area to a prescribed district, town or country, or on certain routes where there is no government postal service. They may be issued by private carriers and freight companies, municipal authorities or private individuals.
Local carriage labels and Private local issues: many labels exist ostensibly to cover the cost of ferrying mail from one of Great Britain's offshore islands to the nearest mainland post office. They are not recognised as valid for national or international mail. Examples: Calf of Man, Davaar, Herm, Lundy, Pabay, Stroma.
Telegraph stamps: stamps intended solely for the prepayment of telegraphic communication.
Bogus or "phantom" stamps: labels from mythical places or non-existent administrations. Examples in the classical period were Sedang, Counani, Clipperton Island and in modern times Thomond and Monte Bello Islands. Numerous labels have also appeared since the War from dissident groups as propaganda for their claims and without authority from the home governments. Common examples are the numerous issues for Nagaland.
Railway letter fee stamps: special stamps issued by railway companies for the conveyance of letters by rail. Example: Talyllyn Railway. Similar services are now offered by some bus companies and the labels they issue likewise do not qualify for inclusion in the catalogue.
Perfins ("perforated initials"): stamps perforated with the initials or emblems of firms as a security measure to prevent pilferage by office staff.
Labels: Slips of paper with an adhesive backing. Collectors tend to make a distinction between stamps, which have postal validity and anything else, which has not.

However, Frama Labels and Royal Mail Postage Labels are both classified as postage stamps and are therefore listed in this catalogue.
Cut-outs: Embossed or impressed stamps found on postal stationery, which are cut out if the stationery has been ruined and re-used as adhesives.

Further information on a wealth of terms is in *Philatelic Terms Illustrated*, published by Stanley Gibbons, details are listed under Stanley Gibbons Publications. There is also a priced listing of the postal fiscals of Great Britain in our *Commonwealth & British Empire Stamps 1840-1970* Catalogue and in Volume 1 of the *Great Britain Specialised Catalogue* (5th and later editions). Again, further details are listed under the Stanley Gibbons Publications section (see p.xii).

Organisation of the Catalogue

The catalogue lists countries in alphabetical order with country headers on each page and extra introductory information such as philatelic historical background at the beginning of each section. The Contents list provides a detailed guide to each volume, and the Index has full cross-referencing to locate each country in each volume.

Each country lists postage stamps in order of date of issue, from earliest to most recent, followed by separate sections for categories such as postage due stamps, express stamps, official stamps, and so on (see above for a complete listing).

"Appendix" Countries

Since 1968 Stanley Gibbons has listed in an appendix stamps which are judged to be in excess of true postal needs. The appendix also contains stamps which have not fulfilled all the normal conditions for full catalogue listing. Full catalogue listing requires a stamp to be:

- issued by a legitimate postal authority
- recognised by the government concerned
- adhesive
- valid for proper postal use in the class of service for which they are inscribed
- available to the general public at face value with no artificial restrictions being imposed on their distribution (with the exception of categories as postage dues and officials)

Only stamps issued from component parts of otherwise united territories which represent a genuine political, historical or postal division within the country concerned have a full catalogue listing. Any such issues which do not fulfil this stipulation will be recorded in the Catalogue Appendix only.

Stamps listed in the Appendix are constantly under review in light of newly acquired information about them. If we are satisfied that a stamp qualifies for proper listing in the body of the catalogue it will be moved in the next edition.

"Undesirable Issues"

The rules governing many competitive exhibitions are set by the Federation Internationale de Philatelie and stipulate a downgrading of marks for stamps classed as "undesirable issues".

This catalogue can be taken as a guide to status. All stamps in the main listings are acceptable. Stamps in the Appendix are considered, "undesirable issues" and should not be entered for competition.

Correspondence

We welcome information and suggestions but we must ask correspondents to include the cost of postage for the return of any materials, plus registration where appropriate. Letters and emails should be addressed to Michelle Briggs, 7 Parkside, Christchurch Road, Ringwood, Hampshire BH24 3SH, UK. mrbriggs@stanleygibbons.co.uk. Where information is solicited purely for the benefit of the enquirer we regret we are seldom able to reply.

Identification of Stamps

We regret we do not give opinion on the authenticity of stamps, nor do we identify stamps or number them by our Catalogue.

Thematic Collectors

Stanley Gibbons publishes a range of thematic catalogues (see page xxxix for details) and *Stamps of the World* is ideal to use with these titles, as it supplements those listings with extra information.

Type numbers

Type numbers (in bold) refer to illustrations, and are not the Stanley Gibbons Catalogue numbers.

A brief description of the stamp design subject is given below or beside the illustrations, or close by in the entry, where needed. Where a design is not illustrated, it is usually the same shape and size as a related design, unless otherwise indicated.

Watermarks

Watermarks are not covered in this catalogue. Stamps of the same issue with differing watermarks are not listed separately.

Perforations

Perforations – all stamps are perforated unless otherwise stated. No distinction is made between the various gauges of perforation but early stamp issues which exist both imperforate and perforated are usually listed separately. Where a heading states, "Imperf or perf"or "Perf. or rouletted" this does not necessarily mean that all values of the issue are found in both conditions

Se-tenant Pairs

Se-tenant Pairs – Many modern issues are printed in sheets containing different designs or face values. Such pairs, blocks, strips or sheets are described as being "*se-tenant*" and they are outside the scope of this catalogue, although reference to them may occur in instances where they form a composite design.

Miniature Sheets are now fully listed.

Guide to Entries

A Country of Issue

B Part Number – shows where to find more detailed listings in the Stanley Gibbons Comprehensive Catalogue. Part 6 refers to France and so on – see p. xli for further information on the breakdown of the Catalogue.

C Country Information – Brief geographical and historical details for the issuing country.

D Currency – Details of the currency, and dates of earliest use where applicable, on the face value of the stamps. Where a Colony has the same currency as the Mother Country, see the details given in that country.

E Year Date – When a set of definitive stamps has been issued over several years the Year Date given is for the earliest issue, commeorative sets are listed in chronological order. As stamps of the same design or issue are usually grouped together a list of King George VI stamps, for example, headed "1938" may include stamps issued from 1938 to the end of the reign.

F Stanley Gibbons Catalogue number – This is a unique number for each stamp to help the collector identify stamps in the listing. The Stanley Gibbons numbering system is universally recognized as definitive. The majority of listings are in chronological order, but where a definitive set of stamps has been re-issued with a new watermark, perforation change or imprint date, the cheapest example is given; in such cases catalogue numbers may not be in numerical order.

Where insufficient numbers have been left to provide for additional stamps to a listing, some stamps will have a suffix letter after the catalogue number. If numbers have been left for additions to a set and not used they will be left vacant.

The separate type numbers (in bold) refer to illustrations (see **M**).

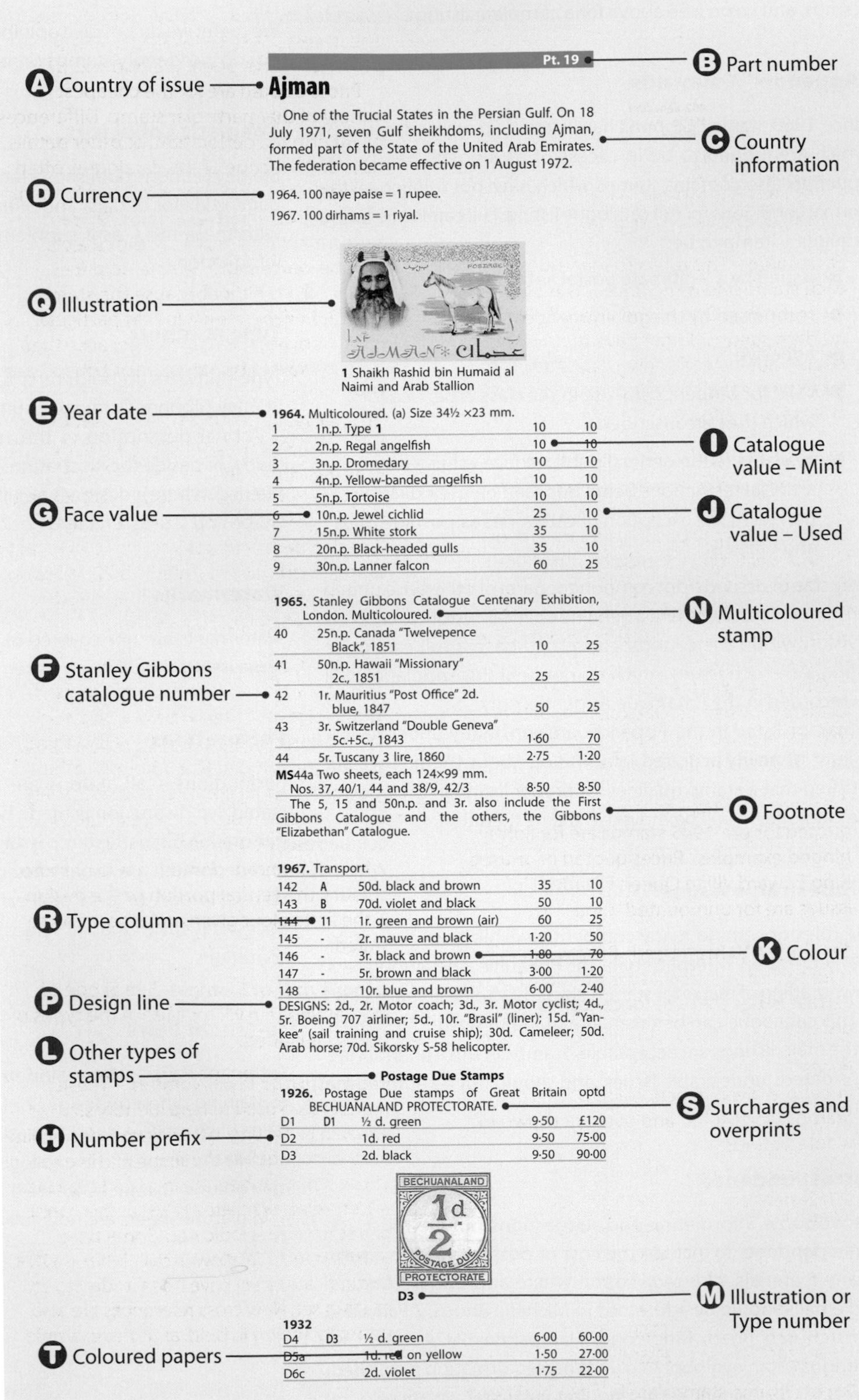

Pt. 19
B Part number
A Country of issue
Ajman
One of the Trucial States in the Persian Gulf. On 18 July 1971, seven Gulf sheikhdoms, including Ajman, formed part of the State of the United Arab Emirates. The federation became effective on 1 August 1972.
C Country information
D Currency
1964. 100 naye paise = 1 rupee.
1967. 100 dirhams = 1 riyal.
Q Illustration
1 Shaikh Rashid bin Humaid al Naimi and Arab Stallion
E Year date
1964. Multicoloured. (a) Size 34½ ×23 mm.
1 1n.p. Type 1 10 10
2 2n.p. Regal angelfish 10 10
3 3n.p. Dromedary 10 10
4 4n.p. Yellow-banded angelfish 10 10
5 5n.p. Tortoise 10 10
6 10n.p. Jewel cichlid 25 10
7 15n.p. White stork 35 10
8 20n.p. Black-headed gulls 35 10
9 30n.p. Lanner falcon 60 25
I Catalogue value – Mint
G Face value
J Catalogue value – Used
1965. Stanley Gibbons Catalogue Centenary Exhibition, London. Multicoloured.
N Multicoloured stamp
40 25n.p. Canada "Twelvepence Black", 1851 10 25
41 50n.p. Hawaii "Missionary" 2c., 1851 25 25
42 1r. Mauritius "Post Office" 2d. blue, 1847 50 25
43 3r. Switzerland "Double Geneva" 5c.+5c., 1843 1·60 70
44 5r. Tuscany 3 lire, 1860 2·75 1·20
MS44a Two sheets, each 124×99 mm. Nos. 37, 40/1, 44 and 38/9, 42/3 8·50 8·50
The 5, 15 and 50n.p. and 3r. also include the First Gibbons Catalogue and the others, the Gibbons "Elizabethan" Catalogue.
F Stanley Gibbons catalogue number
O Footnote
1967. Transport.
142 A 50d. black and brown 35 10
143 B 70d. violet and black 50 10
144 11 1r. green and brown (air) 60 25
145 - 2r. mauve and black 1·20 50
146 - 3r. black and brown 1·80 70
147 - 5r. brown and black 3·00 1·20
148 - 10r. blue and brown 6·00 2·40
DESIGNS: 2d., 2r. Motor coach; 3d., 3r. Motor cyclist; 4d., 5r. Boeing 707 airliner; 5d., 10r. "Brasil" (liner); 15d. "Yankee" (sail training and cruise ship); 30d. Cameleer; 50d. Arab horse; 70d. Sikorsky S-58 helicopter.
R Type column
K Colour
P Design line
L Other types of stamps
Postage Due Stamps
1926. Postage Due stamps of Great Britain optd BECHUANALAND PROTECTORATE.
S Surcharges and overprints
D1 D1 ½ d. green 9·50 £120
D2 1d. red 9·50 75·00
D3 2d. black 9·50 90·00
H Number prefix
BECHUANALAND
1½d
POSTAGE DUE
PROTECTORATE
D3
M Illustration or Type number
1932
D4 D3 ½ d. green 6·00 60·00
D5a 1d. red on yellow 1·50 27·00
D6c 2d. violet 1·75 22·00
T Coloured papers

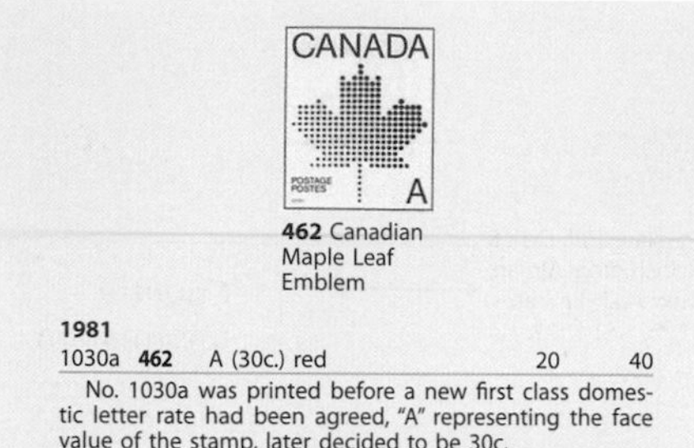

462 Canadian Maple Leaf Emblem

1981

1030a **462** A (30c.) red 20 40

No. 1030a was printed before a new first class domestic letter rate had been agreed, "A" representing the face value of the stamp, later decided to be 30c.

Ⓖ **Face value** – This refers to the value of each stamp and is the price it was sold for at the Post Office when issued. Some modern stamps do not have their values in figures but instead shown as a letter, see for example the entry above for Canada 1030a/Illustration 462.

Ⓗ **Number Prefix** – Stamps other than definitives and commemoratives have a prefix letter before the catalogue number. Such stamps may be found at the end of the normal listing for each country. (See Scope of the Catalogue p.viii for a list of other types of stamps covered, together with the list of the main abbreviations used in the Catalogue).

Other prefixes are also used in the Catalogue. Their use is explained in the text: some examples are A for airmail, E for East Germany or Express Delivery stamps.

Ⓘ **Catalogue Value** – Mint/Unused. Prices quoted for pre-1945 stamps are for lightly hinged examples. Prices quoted of unused King Edward VIII to Queen Elizabeth II issues are for unmounted mint.

Ⓙ **Catalogue Value** – Used. Prices generally refer to fine postally used examples. For certain issues they are for cancelled-to-order.

Prices

Prices are given in pence and pounds. Stamps worth £100 and over are shown in whole pounds:

Shown in Catalogue as	Explanation
10	10 pence
1.75	£1.75
15.00	£15
£150	£150
£2300	£2300

Prices assume stamps are in 'fine condition'; we may ask more for superb and less for those of lower quality. The minimum catalogue price quoted is 10p and is intended as a guide for catalogue users. The lowest price for individual stamps purchased from Stanley Gibbons is £1.

Prices quoted are for the cheapest variety of that particular stamp. Differences of watermark, perforation, or other details, outside the scope of this catalogue, often increase the value. Prices quoted for mint issues are for single examples. Those in *se-tenant* pairs, strips, blocks or sheets may be worth more. Where no prices are listed it is either because the stamps are not known to exist in that particular condition, or, more usually, because there is no reliable information on which to base their value.

All prices are subject to change without prior notice and we cannot guarantee to supply all stamps as priced. Prices quoted in advertisements are also subject to change without prior notice. Due to differing production schedules it is possible that new editions of Parts 2 to 22 will show revised prices which are not included in that year's Stamps of the World.

Ⓚ **Colour** – Colour of stamp (if fewer than four colours, otherwise noted as "multicoloured"– see N below). Colour descriptions are simple in this catalogue, and only expanded to aid identification – see other more comprehensive Stanley Gibbons catalogues for more detailed colour descriptions (see p.xxxix).

Where stamps are printed in two or more colours, the central portion of the design is the first colour given, unless otherwise stated.

Ⓛ **Other Types of Stamps** – See Scope of the Catalogue p.viii for a list of the types of stamps included.

Ⓜ **Illustration or Type Number** – These numbers are used to help identify stamps, either in the listing, type column, design line or footnote, usually the first value in a set. These type numbers are in a bold type face – **123**; when bracketed (**123**) an overprint or a surcharge is indicated. Some type numbers include a lower-case letter – **123a**, this indicates they have been added to an existing set. New cross references are also normally shown in bold, as in the example below.

1990. Small Craft of Canada (2nd series). Early Work Boats. As T **563**. Multicoloured.

Ⓝ **Multicoloured** – Nearly all modern stamps are multicoloured; this is indicated in the heading, with a description of the stamp given in the listing.

Ⓞ **Footnote** – further information on background or key facts on issues

Ⓟ **Design line** – Further details on design variations

Ⓠ **Illustration** – Generally, the first stamp in the set. Stamp illustrations are reduced to 75%, with overprints and surcharges shown actual size.

Ⓡ **Key Type** – indicates a design type (see p. xii for further details) on which the stamp is based. These are the bold figures found below each illustration. The type numbers are also given in bold in the second column of figures alongside the stamp description to indicate the design of each stamp. Where an issue comprises stamps of similar design, the corresponding type number should be taken as indicating the general design. Where there are blanks in the type number column it means that the type of the corresponding stamp is that shown by the number in the type column of the same issue. A dash (–) in the type column means that the stamp is not illustrated. Where type numbers refer to stamps of another country, e.g. where stamps of one country are overprinted for use in another, this is always made clear in the text.

Ⓢ **Surcharges and Overprints** – usually described in the headings. Any actual wordings are shown in bold type. Descriptions clarify words and figures used in the overprint. Stamps with the same overprints in different colours are not listed separately. Numbers in brackets after the descriptions are the catalogue numbers of the non-overprinted stamps. The words "inscribed" or "inscription" refer to the wording incorporated in the design of a stamp and not surcharges or overprints.

Ⓣ **Coloured Papers** – stamps printed on coloured paper are shown – e.g. "brn on yell" indicates brown printed on yellow paper. No information on the texture of paper, e.g. laid or wove, is provided in this catalogue.

Key-Types

Standard designs frequently occuring on the stamps of the French, German, Portuguese and Spanish colonies are illustrated below together with the descriptive names and letters by which they are referred to in the lists to avoid repetition. Please see the Guide to Entries for further information.

French Group

A "Blanc" B "Mouchon" C "Merson" D "Tablet"

INTERNATIONAL COLONIAL EXHIBITION

E F " G H

I "Faidherbe" J "Palms" K "Balay" L "Natives" M "Figure"

German Group

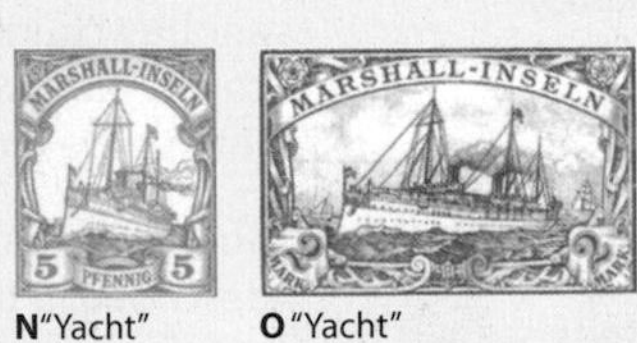

N"Yacht" O "Yacht"

Spanish Group

X "Alfonso XII" Y "Baby" Z "Curly Head"

Portuguese Group

P "Crown" Q "Embossed" R "Figures" S "Carlos" T "Manoel" U Ceres" V "Newspaper" W "Due"

Pt. 20

CHILE

A republic on the W. coast of S. America.

1853. 100 centavos = 1 peso.
1960. 10 milesimos = 1 centesimo; 100 centesimos = 1 escudo.
1975. 100 centavos = 1 peso.

1 Columbus

1853. Imperf.

29	**1**	1c. yellow	43·00	40·00
17	**1**	5c. brown	£170	14·00
37	**1**	5c. red	26·00	6·50
32	**1**	10c. blue	23·00	14·00
33	**1**	20c. green	85·00	37·00

9

1867. Perf.

41	**9**	1c. orange	23·00	2·00
43	**9**	2c. black	23·00	4·00
45	**9**	5c. red	20·00	1·80
46	**9**	10c. blue	17·00	3·50
48	**9**	20c. green	25·00	8·00

10

1877. Roul.

49	**10**	1c. slate	3·00	1·40
50	**10**	2c. orange	15·00	4·00
51	**10**	5c. lake	16·00	75
52	**10**	10c. blue	15·00	2·20
53	**10**	20c. green	16·00	3·75

12 15

1878. Roul.

55	**12**	1c. green	1·20	30
57	**12**	2c. red	1·20	30
58	**12**	5c. red	5·50	25
59a	**12**	5c. blue	1·20	30
60a	**12**	10c. orange	3·75	45
61	**12**	15c. green	3·75	75
62	**12**	20c. grey	3·75	75
63	**12**	25c. brown	3·75	75
64	**12**	30c. red	10·00	5·00
65a	**12**	50c. violet	3·75	2·50
66	**15**	1p. black and brown	29·00	3·75

16

1900. Roul.

82	**16**	1c. green	90	10
83	**16**	2c. red	90	15
84a	**16**	5c. blue	4·50	25
85	**16**	10c. lilac	6·00	60
79	**16**	20c. grey	5·50	1·50
80	**16**	30c. brown	6·25	1·50
81	**16**	50c. brown	7·25	2·00

1900. Surch 5.

86	**12**	5c. on 30c. red	1·20	30

18

1901. Perf.

87	**18**	1c. green	75	10
88	**18**	2c. red	80	10
89	**18**	5c. blue	1·50	10
90	**18**	10c. black and red	2·75	50
91	**18**	30c. black and violet	7·75	1·00
92	**18**	50c. black and red	26·00	4·00

1903. Surch Diez CENTAVOS.

93	**16**	10c. on 30c. brown	2·10	50

20 Huemul (mountain deer)

1904. Animal supporting shield at left without mane and tail. Optd CORREOS in frame.

94	**20**	2c. brown	45	15
95	**20**	5c. red	60	15
96	**20**	10c. olive	2·00	50

1904. As T 20, but animal with mane and tail optd CORREOS in frame and the 1p. also surch CENTAVOS 3 3.

97	2c. brown	6·00	
98	3c. on 1p. brown	50	30
99	5c. red	12·00	
100	10c. green	28·00	

24 Pedro Valdivia

1904. Surch CORREOS in frame and new value.

101	**24**	1c. on 20c. blue	30	20
102	**24**	3c. on 5c. red	46·00	41·00
103	**24**	12c. on 5c. red	1·10	50

26 Christopher Columbus

27 Christopher Columbus

28 Christopher Columbus

1905

104	**26**	1c. green	25	15
105	**26**	2c. red	25	15
106	**26**	3c. brown	80	30
107	**26**	5c. blue	80	15
108	**27**	10c. black and grey	1·30	15
109	**27**	12c. black and lake	6·00	2·75
110	**27**	15c. black and lilac	5·50	30
111	**27**	20c. black and brown	2·75	15
112	**27**	30c. black and green	4·00	35
113	**27**	50c. black and blue	4·00	35
114	**28**	1p. grey and green	20·00	11·00

1910. Optd ISLAS DE JUAN FERNANDEZ or surch also.

115	**27**	5c. on 12c. black & red	55	20
116	**28**	10c. on 1p. grey & green	1·30	30
117	**28**	20c. on 1p. grey & green	1·50	40
118	**28**	1p. grey and green	7·75	2·50

31 Battle of Chacabuco

33 San Martin Monument

1910. Centenary of Independence. Centres in black.

119	-	1c. green	30	15
120	**31**	2c. lake	25	20
121	-	3c. brown	1·20	55
122	-	5c. blue	60	15
123	-	10c. brown	1·20	35
124	-	12c. red	2·75	1·00
125	-	15c. slate	2·40	50
126	-	20c. orange	3·25	85
127	-	25c. blue	4·50	1·30
128	-	30c. mauve	3·50	1·10
129	-	50c. olive	7·75	2·50
130	**33**	1p. yellow	17·00	6·25
131	-	2p. red	17·00	6·25
132	-	5p. green	46·00	20·00
133	-	10p. purple	43·00	19·00

DESIGNS—HORIZ: 1c. Oath of Independence; 3c. Battle of Roble; 5c. Battle of Maipu; 10c. Fight between frigates "Lautaro" and "Esmeralda"; 12c. Capture of the "Maria Isabella"; 15c. First sortie of the liberating forces; 20c. Abdication of O'Higgins; 25c. First Chilean Congress. VERT: 30c. O'Higgins Monument; 50c. Carrera Monument; 2p. General Blanco; 5p. General Zenteno; 10p. Admiral Cochrane.

46 Columbus

47 Valdivia

49 O'Higgins

50 Freire

52 Prieto

57 A. Pinto

64 Admiral Cochrane

65 M. Rengifo

1911. Inscr "CHILE CORREOS".

135	**46**	1c. green	35	10
136	**47**	2c. red	35	10
150	**46**	2c. red	15	10
137	-	3c. sepia	1·20	55
151	-	4c. sepia	20	10
138	**49**	5c. blue	35	10
161	**64**	5c. blue	40	25
152	-	8c. grey	70	15
139	**50**	10c. black and grey	1·20	10
153	**49**	10c. black and blue	70	15
140	-	12c. black and red	1·90	10
154	-	14c. black and red	1·10	15
141	**52**	15c. black and purple	1·70	20
142	-	20c. black and orange	1·40	10
167	-	25c. black and blue	70	15
168	-	30c. black and brown	2·40	15
155	**52**	40c. black and purple	4·00	40
186	**65**	40c. black and violet	90	10
170	-	50c. black and green	2·40	15
156	-	60c. black and blue	9·75	1·20
171	-	80c. black and sepia	2·50	70
188	**57**	1p. black and green	3·25	20
189	-	2p. black and red	6·00	20
190	-	5p. black and olive	12·00	45
190a	-	10p. black and orange	12·00	1·70

PORTRAITS: 3c., 4c. Toro Z. 8c. Freire. 12, 14c. F. A. Pinto. 20c. Bulnes. 25c., 60c. Montt. 30c. Perez. 50c. Errazuriz Z. 80c. Admiral Latorre. 2p. Santa Maria. 5p. Balmaceda. 10p. Errazuriz E.

61 Columbus

62 Valdivia

63 Columbus

1915. Larger Stars.

157	**61**	1c. green	15	10
158	**62**	2c. red	15	10
159	**63**	4c. brown (large head)	20	10
160	**61**	4c. brown (small head)	30	10

67 Chilean Congress Building

1923. Pan-American Conference.

176	**67**	2c. red	20	15
177	**67**	4c. brown	20	40
178	**67**	10c. black and blue	20	15
179	**67**	20c. black and orange	55	15
180	**67**	40c. black and mauve	90	25
181	**67**	1p. black and green	1·10	45
182	**67**	2p. black and red	4·50	50
183	**67**	5p. black and green	15·00	4·00

67a O'Higgins

1927. Air. Unissued stamp surch Correo Aereo and value.

184	**67a**	40c. on 10c. blue & brn	£450	43·00
184a	**67a**	80c. on 10c. blue & brn	70·00	90·00
184b	**67a**	1p.20 on 10c. bl & brn	£450	70·00
184c	**67a**	1p.60 on 10c. bl & brn	£450	70·00
184d	**67a**	2p. on 10c. blue & brn	£450	70·00

1928. Air. Optd CORREO AEREO and bird or surch also.

191	-	20c. blk & orge (No. 141)	55	30
199	**65**	40c. black and violet	75	45
200	**57**	1p. black and green	2·10	65
194	-	2p. black & red (No. 189)	2·75	45
201	**64**	3p. on 5c. blue	70·00	43·00
195	-	5p. black & ol (No. 190)	4·50	1·20
196	**49**	6p. on 10c. black & blue	70·00	37·00
198	-	10p. blk & orge (No. 190a)	18·00	4·75

1928. As Types of 1911, but inscr "CORREOS DE CHILE".

205	**64**	5c. blue	65	20
206	**64**	5c. green	65	20
204	**49**	10c. black and blue	2·75	20
208	**52**	15c. black and purple	2·75	20
209	-	20c. black and orange (As No. 142)	7·25	20
210	-	25c. black and blue (As No. 167)	1·30	20
211	-	30c. black and brown (As No. 168)	90	30
212	-	50c. black and green (As No. 170)	75	20

1929. Air. Nos. 209/12 optd CORREO AEREO and bird.

213a	20c. black and orange	55	20
214	25c. black and blue	65	20
215	30c. black and brown	45	20
216	50c. black and green	55	20

71 Winged Wheel

72 Sower

1930. Centenary of Nitrate Industry.

217	**71**	5c. green	75	55
218	**71**	10c. brown	75	30
219	**71**	15c. violet	75	30
220	-	25c. slate (Girl harvester)	1·90	75
221	**72**	70c. blue	6·50	2·10
222	**72**	1p. green (24½×30 mm)	5·00	1·10

73 Andean Condor and Fokker Super Universal Airplane

75 Ford 4AT Trimotor over Los Cerrillos Airport

1931. Air. Inscr "LINEA AEREA NACIONAL".

223	**73**	5c. green	35	20
224	**73**	10c. brown	35	20
225	**73**	20c. red	35	20
226a	-	50c. sepia	1·10	20
227	**75**	50c. blue	1·70	65
228	-	1p. violet	65	30
229	-	2p. slate	1·40	30
230	**75**	5p. red	3·50	20

DESIGN: 50c. (No. 226a), 1p., 2p. Fokker Super Universal airplane.

76 O'Higgins

1931

231	**76**	10c. blue	1·90	10
232	-	20c. brown (Bulnes)	1·40	10
233	-	30c. mauve (Perez)	2·20	10

79 Mariano Egana

1934. Centenary of Constitution of 1833.

234	**79**	30c. mauve	90	20
235	-	1p.20 blue	1·40	30

PORTRAIT: 1p.20, Joaquin Tocornal (24½×29 mm).

83 Fokker Super Universal Aircraft over Globe

1934. Air. As T 83.

236	10c. green	35	10
237	15c. green	55	30
238	20c. blue	35	10
239	30c. black	35	10
239a	40c. blue	35	10
240	50c. brown	35	10
241	60c. black	35	10
356a	70c. blue	20	10
243	80c. green	35	10
244	1p. grey	35	10
245	2p. blue	35	10
360	3p. brown	20	10
361	4p. brown	20	10
248	5p. red	35	10
249	6p. brown	55	10
250	8p. green	55	30
251	10p. purple	65	30
252	20p. olive	90	30
253	30p. grey	1·00	55
254	40p. violet	1·30	95
255a	50p. purple	1·30	75

DESIGNS—21×25 mm: 10, 15, 20c. Fokker Super Universal over Santiago; 30, 40, 50c. Junkers G.24 over landscape; 60c. Condor in flight; 70c. Airplane and star; 80c. Condor and statue of Caupolican; 25×29 mm: 1, 2p. Type **83**; 3, 4, 5p. Stinson Faucett F.19 seaplane in flight; 6, 8, 10p. Northrop Alpha monoplane and rainbow; 20, 30p. Stylized Dornier Wal flying boat and compass; 40, 50p. Airplane riding a storm.

87 Diego de Almagro

1936. 400th Anniv of Discovery of Chile.

256	-	5c. red	65	30
257	-	10c. violet	45	30
258	-	20c. mauve	45	30
259	-	25c. blue	3·50	85
260	-	30c. green	45	30
261	-	40c. black	3·50	95
262	-	50c. blue	1·80	30
263	-	1p. green	2·00	55
264	-	1p.20 blue	2·20	75
265	**87**	2p. brown	2·20	85
266	-	5p. red	6·00	2·30
267	-	10p. purple	14·50	8·50

DESIGNS: 5c. Atacama desert; 10c. Fishing boats; 20c. Coquito palms; 25c. Sheep. 30c. Coal mines; 40c. Lonquimay forests; 50c. Lota coal port; 1p. "Orduna" (liner), Valparaiso; 1p.20. Mt. Puntiaguda; 5p. Cattle; 10p. Shovelling nitrate.

88 Laja Waterfall

90 "Calbuco" (fishing boat)

1938

268	**88**	5c. purple	20	10
269	-	10c. red	20	10
269a	-	15c. red	20	10
270	-	20c. blue	20	10
271	-	30c. pink	20	10
272	-	40c. green	20	10
273	-	50c. violet	20	10
274	**90**	1p. orange	20	10
275	-	1p.80 blue	75	30
338h	-	2p. red	20	10
278	-	5p. green	1·40	10
338j	-	10p. purple	1·10	10

DESIGNS—As Type **88**: 10c. Rural landscape; 15c. Boldo tree; 20c. Nitrate works; 30c. Mineral spas; 40c. Copper mine; 50c. Petroleum tanks. As Type **90**: 1p.80, Osorno Volcano; 2p. "Conte de Biancamano" (freighter) and "Ponderoso" (tug); 5p. Lake Villarrica; 10p. Steam locomotive No. 908.

92 "Abtao" (armed steamer) and Policarpo Toro

1940. 50th Anniv of Occupation of Easter Island and Local Hospital Fund.

279	**92**	80c.+2p.20 red & green	2·75	2·10
280	-	3p.60+6p.40 green and red	2·75	2·10

DESIGN: 3p.60, "Abtao" and E. Eyraud.

93 Western Hemisphere

1940. 50th Anniv of Pan-American Union.

281	**93**	40c. green	35	10

1940. Air. Surch with winged device above new values.

282	**73**	80c. on 20c. red	75	20
283	**75**	1p.60 on 5p. red	4·75	1·60
284	-	5p.10 on 2p. slate (No. 229)	3·75	1·80

96 Fray Camilo Henriquez

97 Founding of Santiago

1941. 400th Anniv of Santiago.

285	**96**	10c. red	55	20
286	-	40c. green	55	20
287	-	1p.10 red	1·30	1·30
288	**97**	1p.80 blue	1·30	75
289	-	3p.60 blue	5·50	6·50

PORTRAITS—As Type **96**: 40c. P. Valdivia. 1p.10, B. V. MacKenna. 3p.60, D. B. Arana.

98 Potez 56 and Globe

99 Sikorsky S-43 Amphibian and Galleon

1941. Air. No. 304 is dated "1541–1941" and commemorates the 4th Centenary of Santiago.

290		10c. olive	35	20
291		10c. mauve	35	10
316	-	10c. blue	20	10
292	**98**	20c. red	35	20
294	**98**	20c. brown	20	10
318	**98**	20c. green	20	10
295	-	30c. violet	35	20
295a	-	30c. olive	20	10
296	-	40c. brown	35	10
297	-	40c. blue	20	10
324	-	50c. red	20	10
325	-	50c. orange	20	10
299a	-	60c. green	20	10
326	-	60c. orange	20	10
300	-	70c. red	65	30
301	-	80c. blue	3·25	55
302	-	80c. olive	20	20
303a	-	90c. brown	35	20
304	**99**	1p. blue	65	30
304a	**99**	1p. green and blue	35	10
305	-	1p.60 violet	35	20
306	-	1p.80 violet	35	10
307	-	2p. lake	90	30
308	-	2p. brown	65	20
309	-	3p. green	1·30	65
310a	-	3p. violet and yellow	2·75	45
334	-	3p. violet and orange	90	20
311	-	4p. violet and brown	2·00	1·10
335	-	4p. green	90	45
336	-	5p. red	75	30
336a	-	5p. brown	35	20
314	-	10p. green and blue	10·50	6·50
337	-	10p. blue	90	45

DESIGNS: (each incorporating a different type of airplane): 10c. Steeple; 30c. Flag; 40c. Stars; 50c. Mountains; 60c. Tree; 70c. Estuary; 80c. Shore; 90c. Sun rays; 1p.60, 1p.80, Wireless mast; 2p. Compass; 3p. Telegraph wires; 4p. Rainbow; 5p. Factory; 10p. Snow-capped mountain.

See also Nos. 395 etc.

101 V. Letelier

102 University of Chile

103 Coat of arms and Aeroplane

1942. Centenary of Santiago de Chile University.

339	**101**	30c. red (postage)	35	10
340	-	40c. green	35	10
341	-	90c. violet	2·40	1·30
342	**102**	1p. brown	1·50	75
343	-	1p.80 blue	3·75	2·30
344	**103**	100p. red (air)	50·00	32·00

DESIGNS—As Type **101**: 40c. A. Bello; 90c. M. Bulnes; 1p.80, M. Montt.

104 Manuel Bulnes

105 Straits of Magellan

1944. Centenary of Occupation of Magellan Straits.

345	**104**	15c. black	20	10
346	-	30c. red	20	10
347	-	40c. green	20	10
348	-	1p. brown	1·40	45
349	**105**	1p.80 blue	2·00	1·20

PORTRAITS: 30c. J. W. Wilson. 40c. D. D. Almeida. 1p. Jose de los Santos Mardones.

106 "Lamp of Life"

1944. International Red Cross.

350	**106**	40c. black, red and green	35	20
351	-	1p.80 red and blue	1·00	55

DESIGN: 1p.80, Serpent and chalice symbol of Hygiene.

107 O'Higgins (after J. G. de Castro)

108 Battle of Rancagua (after Subercaseaux)

1944. Death Centenary of Bernardo O'Higgins.

367	**107**	15c. black and red	65	30
368	-	30c. black and brown	65	30
369	-	40c. black and green	65	30
370	**108**	1p.80 black and blue	3·00	1·40

DESIGNS—As Type **108**: 30c. Battle of the Maipu; 40c. Abdication of O'Higgins.

109 Columbus Lighthouse, Dominican Republic

1945. 450th Anniv of Discovery of America by Columbus.

371	**109**	40c. green	65	30

110 Andres Bello

1946. 80th Death Anniv of Andres Bello (educationist).

372	**110**	40c. green	35	10
373	**110**	1p.80 blue	35	10

111 Antarctic Territory

1947

374	**111**	40c. red	65	30
375	**111**	2p.50 blue	1·80	55

112 Eusebio Lillo and Ramon Carnicer

1947. Centenary of National Anthem.

376	**112**	40c. green	35	10

113 Miguel de Cervantes

1947. 400th Birth Anniv of Cervantes.

377	**113**	40c. red	35	15

114 Arturo Prat and "Esmeralda" (sail corvette)

1948. Birth Centenary of Arturo Prat.

378	**114**	40c. blue	45	10

115 O'Higgins

1948

379	**115**	60c. black	35	10

1948. No. 272 surch VEINTE CTS. and bar.

380	20c. on 40c. green	35	15

119 "Chiasognathus granti"

1948. Centenary of Publication on Chilean Flora and Fauna. Botanical and zoological designs, as T 119 inscr "CENTENARIO DEL LIBRO DE GAY 1844–1944".

381a/y	60c. blue (postage)	90	45
382a/y	2p.60 green	1·50	1·40
383a/y	3p. red (air)	1·80	1·60

Each value in 25 different designs. Prices are for individual stamps.

120 Airline Badge

1949. Air. 20th Anniv of National Airline.

384	**120**	2p. blue	65	45

121 B. V. Mackenna

1949. Vicuna Mackenna Museum.

385	**121**	60c. blue (postage)	35	20
386	**121**	3p. red (air)	45	20

122 Wheel and Lamp

1949. Cent of School of Arts and Crafts, Santiago.

387	**122**	60c. mauve (postage)	20	20
388	-	2p.60 blue	65	55
389	-	5p. green (air)	1·00	65
390	-	10p. brown	1·80	95

DESIGNS: 2p.60, Shield and book; 5p. Shield, book and factory; 10p. Wheel and column.

123 Heinrich von Stephan

124 Douglas DC-6B and Globe

1950. 75th Anniv of UPU.

391	**123**	60c. red (postage)	35	20
392	**123**	2p.50 blue	65	65
393	**124**	5p. green (air)	35	20
394	**124**	10p. brown	90	55

1950. Air. As T 98/99.

395	20c. brown	35	10
396	40c. violet	35	10
404c	60c. blue	45	10
398	1p. green	10	15
399	2p. brown	35	10
404f	3p. blue	20	10
401	4p. orange	35	10
402	5p. violet	35	10
403	10p. green	45	10
480	20p. brown	45	20
481	50p. green	45	20
482	100p. red	45	20
483	200p. blue	65	20

DESIGNS (each including an aeroplane): 20c. Mountains; 40c. Coastline; 60c. Fishing vessel; 1p. Araucanian pine tree; 2p. Chilean flag; 3p. Dock crane; 4p. River; 5p. Industrial plant; 10p. Landscape; 20p. Aerial railway; 50p. Mountainous coastline; 100p. Antarctic map; 200p. Rock "bridge" in sea.

126 Crossing the Andes (after Y. Prades)

1951. Death Centenary of Gen. San Martin.

405	-	60c. blue (postage)	55	30
406	**126**	5p. purple (air)	1·10	45

PORTRAIT (25×29 mm): 60c. San Martin.

1951. Air. No. 303a surch UN PESO.

407	1p. on 90c. brown	35	20

128 Isabella the Catholic

1952. 500th Birth Anniv of Issabella the Catholic.

408	**128**	60c. blue (postage)	35	10
409	**128**	10p. red (air)	90	75

1952. Surch 40 Ctvs.

410	**115**	40c. on 60c. black	10	10

1952. Air. No. 302 surch 40 Centavos.

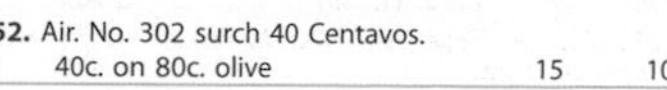

411	40c. on 80c. olive	15	10

116 M. de Toro y Zambrano

1952

379b	**116**	80c. green	35	10
379c	-	1p. turquoise (O'Higgins)	35	10
446	-	2p. lilac (Carrera)	35	10
447	-	3p. blue (R. Freire)	35	10
448	-	5p. sepia (M. Bulnes)	35	10
449	-	10p. violet (F. A. Pinto)	35	10
450	-	50p. red (M. Montt)	55	20

131 Arms of Valdivia

132 Old Spanish Watch-tower

1953. 400th Anniv of Valdivia.

414	**131**	1p. blue (postage)	1·00	30
415	-	2p. violet	1·00	30
416	-	3p. green	1·30	30
417	-	5p. brown	1·30	30
418	**132**	10p. red (air)	3·00	55

DESIGNS—As Type **132**: 2p. Ancient cannons, Corral Fort; 3p. Valdivia from the river; 5p. Street scene (after old engraving).

133 J. Toribio Medina

1953. Birth Centenary of Toribio Medina.

419	**133**	1p. brown	35	10
420	**133**	2p.50 blue	55	10

134 Stamp of 1853

1953. Chilean Stamp Centenary.

421	**134**	1p. brown (postage)	35	10
422	**134**	100p. turquoise (air)	2·00	1·20

135 Map and Graph

1953. 12th National Census.

423	**135**	1p. green	20	10
424	**135**	2p.50 blue	35	20
425	**135**	3p. brown	45	45
426	**135**	4p. red	75	75

136 Aircraft of 1929 and 1954

1954. Air. 25th Anniv of National Air Line.

427	**136**	3p. blue	35	10

137 Arms of Angol

1954. 400th Anniv of Angol City.

428	**137**	2p. red	35	30

138 I. Domeyko

1954. 150th Birth Anniv of Domeyko (educationist and mineralogist).

429	**138**	1p. blue (postage)	35	10
430	**138**	5p. brown (air)	35	20

139 Locomotive "Tiger", 1856

1954. Centenary of Chilean Railways.

431	**139**	1p. red (postage)	45	10
432	**139**	10p. purple (air)	1·40	55

140 Arturo Prat

1954. 75th Anniv of Naval Battle of Iquique.

433	**140**	2p. violet	35	10

141 Arms of Vina del Mar

1955. Int Philatelic Exhibition, Valparaiso.

434	**141**	1p. blue	35	10
435	-	2p. red	35	10

DESIGN: 2p. Arms of Valparaiso.

142 Dr. A. del Rio

1955. 14th Pan-American Sanitary Conference.

436	**142**	2p. blue	35	10

143 Christ of the Andes

1955. Exchange of Visits between Argentine and Chilean Presidents.

437	**143**	1p. blue (postage)	45	10
438	**143**	100p. red (air)	2·20	1·90

144 De Havilland Comet 1

1955. Air.

441a	144	100p. green	65	20
441b	-	200p. blue	75	20
441c	-	500p. red	1·30	30

AIRCRAFT: 200p. Morane Saulnier Paris I. 500p. Douglas DC-6B.

145 M. Rengifo

1955. Death Centenary of Joaquin Prieto (President, 1833–41).

442	145	3p. blue	20	10
443	-	5p. red (Egana)	20	10
444	-	50p. purple (Portales)	2·75	75

For 15p. in similar design see under Compulsory Tax Stamps.

147 Bell Trooper Helicopter and Bridge

1956. Air.

451		1p. red	35	10
452	147	2p. sepia	20	10
455	-	5p. violet	20	10
456	-	10p. green	20	10
456a	-	20p. blue	20	10
456b	-	50p. red	20	10

DESIGNS: 1p. de Havilland Venom FB.4; 5p. Diesel locomotive and Douglas DC-6B; 10p. Oil derricks and Douglas DC-6B; 20p. de Havilland Venom FB.4 and Easter Island monolith; 50p. Douglas DC-2 and control tower.

See also Nos. 524/7.

148 F. Santa Maria

149 Atomic Symbol and Cogwheels

1956. 25th Anniv of Santa Maria Technical University, Valparaiso.

457	148	5p. brown (postage)	35	10
458	149	20p. green (air)	45	20
459	-	100p. violet	1·80	95

DESIGN—As Type **149**: 100p. Aerial view of University.

150 Gabriela Mistral

1958. Gabriela Mistral (poetess, Nobel Prize Winner).

460	150	10p. brown (postage)	35	10
461	150	100p. green (air)	35	20

151 Arms of Osorno

1958. 400th Anniv of Osorno.

462	151	10p. red (postage)	20	10
463	-	50p. green	55	15
464	-	100p. blue (air)	55	20

PORTRAITS: 50p. G. H. de Mendoza. 100p. O'Higgins.

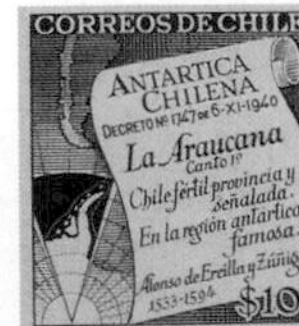
152 "La Araucana" (poem) and Antarctic Map

1958. Antarctic issue.

465	152	10p. blue (postage)	35	10
467	152	20p. violet (air)	35	10
466	-	200p. purple	3·25	2·10
468	-	500p. blue	4·50	1·90

DESIGN: 200p., 500p. Chilean map of 1588.

153 Arms of Santiago de Chile

1958. National Philatelic Exhibition, Santiago.

469	153	10p. purple (postage)	45	30
470	153	50p. green (air)	55	30

154

1958. Cent of Chilean Civil Servants' Savings Bank.

471	154	10p. blue (postage)	35	10
472	154	50p. brown (air)	35	20

155 Antarctic Territory

1958. I.G.Y.

473	155	40p. red (postage)	75	10
474	155	50p. green (air)	90	20

156 Religious Emblems

1959. Air. Human Rights Day.

475	156	50p. red	35	30

157 Bridge, Valdivia

1959. Centenary of German School, Valdivia and Philatelic Exhibition.

477	-	20p. red (air)	35	20
476	157	40p. green (postage)	35	20

DESIGN—VERT: 20p. A. C. Anwandter (founder).

158 Expedition Map

1959. 400th Anniv of Juan Ladrillero's Expedition of 1557.

484	158	10p. violet (postage)	45	10
485	158	50p. green (air)	65	10

159 D. Barros-Arana

1959. 50th Death Anniv of D. Barros-Arana (historian).

486	159	40p. blue (postage)	35	10
487	159	100p. lilac (air)	65	30

160 J. H. Dunant (founder)

1959. Red Cross Commemoration.

488	160	20p. lake & red (postage)	45	10
489	160	50p. black & red (air)	75	30

161 F. A. Pinto

162 Choshuenco Volcano

1960. (a) Portraits as T 161.

490	-	5m. turquoise	35	10
491	161	1c. red	35	10
493	-	5c. blue	35	10

(b) Views as T 162.

492	162	2c. blue	20	10
492a	162	2c. blue (23½×18 mm)	20	10
494	-	10c. green	35	10
495	-	20c. blue	65	10
496	-	1E. turquoise	45	30

DESIGNS—As Type **161**: 5m. M. Bulnes; 5c. M. Montt. As Type **162**: 10c. R. Maule Valley; 20c., 1E. Inca Lake.

163 Martin 4-0-4 Airplane and Dock Crane

1960. Air (Inland).

497		1m. orange	20	20
498		2m. green	20	10
499	163	3m. violet	20	10
500	-	4m. olive	20	10
501	-	5m. turquoise	20	10
502	-	1c. blue	20	10
503	-	2c. brown	45	10
504	-	5c. green	2·75	20
505	-	10c. red	45	10
506	-	20c. blue	55	10

DESIGNS: Airplane over—1m. Araucanian pine; 2m. Chilean flag; 4m. River; 5m. Industrial plant; 1c. Landscape; 2c. Aerial railway; 5c. Mountainous coastline; 10c. Antarctic map; 20c. Rock "bridge" in sea.

164 Refugee Family

1960. World Refugee Year.

507	164	1c. green (postage)	35	10
508	164	10c. violet (air)	45	10

165 Arms of Chile

1960. 150th Anniv of 1st National Government (1st issue).

509	165	1c. brn & red (postage)	20	10
510	165	10c. chestnut & brn (air)	20	10

See also Nos. 512/23.

166 Rotary Emblem and Map

1960. Air. Rotary International S. American Regional Conference, Santiago.

511	166	10c. blue	55	10

167 J. M. Carrera

1960. 150th Anniv of 1st National Government (2nd issue). (a) Postage.

512	-	1c. red and brown	20	10
513	-	5c. turquoise & green	20	10
514	-	10c. purple and brown	55	30
515	-	20c. green and blue	55	30
516	-	50c. red and brown	75	30
517	167	1E. brown and green	1·90	75

DESIGNS—HORIZ: 1c. Palace of Justice; 10c. M. de Toro y Zambrano and M. de Rozas; 20c. M. de Salas and Juan Egana; 50c. M. Rodriguez and J. Mackenna. VERT: 5c. Temple of the National Vow.

(b) Air.

518	2c. violet and red	20	10
519	5c. purple and blue	20	10
520	10c. bistre and brown	35	10
521	20c. violet and blue	55	10
522	50c. blue and green	1·40	30
523	1E. brown and red	1·90	85

DESIGNS—HORIZ: 2c. Palace of Justice; 10c. J. G. Martin and J. G. Argomedo; 20c. J. A. Eyzaguirre and J. M. Infante; 50c. Bishop J. I. Cienfuegos and Fray C. Henriquez. VERT: 5c. Temple of the National Vow. 1E. O'Higgins.

1961. Air (Foreign). As T 147 or 144 (10c. and 50c.), but values in new currency.

524	5m. brown	20	10
525	1c. blue	20	10
526	2c. blue	20	10
527	5c. red	20	10
528	10c. blue	90	10
529	20c. red	1·10	10
530	50c. turquoise	20	10

DESIGNS: 5m. Diesel locomotive and Douglas DC-6B; 1c. Oil derricks and Douglas DC-6B; 2c. De Havilland Venom FB.4 and monolith; 5c. Douglas DC-2 and control tower; 10c. De Havilland Comet 1; 20c. Morane Saulnier Paris I; 50c. Douglas DC-6B.

168 "Population"

1961. National Census. 13th Population Census (5c.); 2nd Housing Census (10c.).

531	168	5c. green	2·75	70
532	-	10c. violet (buildings)	35	10

169 Pedro de Valdivia

1961. Earthquake Relief Fund. Inscr "ESPANA A CHILE".

533	169	5c.+5c. green and pink (postage)	1·40	30
534	-	10c.+10c. violet & buff	1·10	30
535	-	10c.+10c. brown and orange (air)	1·20	30
536	-	20c.+20c. red and blue	1·20	30

PORTRAITS: No. 534, J. T. Medina. No. 535, A. de Ercilla. No. 536, Gabriela Mistral.

170 Congress Building

1961. 150th Anniv of 1st National Congress.

537	170	2c. brown (postage)	90	45
538	170	10c. green (air)	1·30	1·10

171 Footballers and Globe

1962. World Football Championships, Chile.

539	171	2c. blue (postage)	20	10
540	-	5c. green	45	10
541	-	5c. purple (air)	20	10
542	171	10c. lake	45	15

DESIGN—HORIZ: Nos. 540/1, Goalkeeper and stadium.

172 Mother and Child

1963. Freedom from Hunger.

543	172	3c. purple (postage)	35	10
544	-	20c. green (air)	35	20

DESIGN—HORIZ: 20c. Mother holding out food bowl.

173 Centenary Emblem

1963. Red Cross Centenary.

545	173	3c. red & grey (postage)	35	10
546	-	20c. red and grey (air)	35	15

DESIGN—HORIZ: 20c. Centenary emblem and silhouette of aircraft.

174 Fire Brigade Monument

1963. Centenary of Santiago Fire Brigade.

547	174	3c. violet (postage)	35	10
548	-	30c. red (air)	55	30

DESIGN—HORIZ: (39×30 mm): 30c. Fire engine of 1863.

175 Band encircling Globe

1964. Air. "Alliance for Progress" and Pres. Kennedy Commemoration.

549	175	4c. blue	35	10

176 Enrique Molina

1964. Molina Commemoration (founder of Concepcion University).

550	176	4c. bistre (postage)	35	10
551	176	60c. violet (air)	35	20

1965. Casanueva Commemoration. As T 176 but portrait of Mons. Carlos Casanueva, Rector of Catholic University.

552		4c. purple (postage)	35	10
553		60c. green (air)	35	20

177 Battle Scene (after Subercaseaux)

1965. Air. 150th Anniv of Battle of Rancagua.

554	177	5c. brown and green	55	30

178 Monolith

1965. Easter Island Discoveries.

555	178	6c. purple	65	10
556	178	10c. mauve	35	20

179 ITU Emblem and Symbols

1965. Air. Centenary of ITU.

557	179	40c. purple and red	45	30

180 Crusoe on Juan Fernandez

1965. Robinson Crusoe Commemoration.

558	180	30c. red	65	20

181 Skier descending slope

1965. World Skiing Championships.

559	181	4c. green (postage)	45	30
560	-	20c. blue (air)	45	30

DESIGN—HORIZ: 20c. Skier crossing slope.

182 Angelmo Harbour

183 Aviators, Monument

1965. Air.

561	182	40c. brown	35	10
562	183	1E. red	35	10

184 Copihue (National Flower)

1965

563	184	15c. red and green	65	10
563a	184	20c. red and green	35	10

185 A. Bello

1965. Air. Death Centenary of Andres Bello (poet).

564	185	10c. red	45	30

186 Dr. L. Sazie

1966. Death Centenary of Dr. L. Sazie.

565	186	1E. green	90	20

187 Skiers

1966. Air. World Skiing Championships.

566	-	75c. red and lilac	35	10
567	-	3E. ultramarine and blue	75	20
568	187	4E. brown and blue	1·70	45
MS568a		110×140 mm. Nos. 566/7. Imperf. No gum	25·00	

DESIGN—HORIZ: (38×25 mm): 75c., 3E. Skier in slalom race.

188 Ball and Basket

1966. Air. World Basketball Championships.

569	188	13c. red	45	30

189 J. Montt

1966

570	189	30c. violet	35	10
571	-	50c. brown (G. Riesco)	35	10

190 W. Wheelwright and Paddle-steamers "Chile" and "Peru"

1966. 125th Anniv (1965) of Arrival of Paddle-steamers "Chile" and "Peru".

572	190	10c. ultram & bl (postage)	45	30
573	190	70c. blue and green (air)	45	30

191 "Learning"

1966. Education Campaign.

574	191	10c. purple	45	30

192 ICY Emblem

1966. International Co-operation Year (1965).

575	192	1E. brn & green (postage)	1·70	30
576	192	3E. red and blue (air)	65	30
MS576a		111×140 mm. Nos. 575/6. Imperf. No gum	11·00	

193 Chilean Flag and Ships

1966. Air. Antofagasta Centenary.

577	193	13c. purple	45	30

194 Capt. Pardo and "Yelcho" (coastguard vessel)

1967. 50th Anniv of Pardo's Rescue of Shackleton Expedition.

578 **194** 20c. turquoise (postage) 45 30
579 - 40c. blue (air) 55 30

DESIGN: 40c. Capt. Pardo and Antarctic sectoral map.

195 Chilean Family

1967. 8th International Family Planning Congress.

580 **195** 10c. black and purple (postage) 45 30
581 **195** 80c. black and blue (air) 45 30

196 R. Dario (poet)

1967. Air. Birth Centenary of Ruben Dario (Nicaraguan poet).

582 **196** 10c. blue 45 30

197 Pine Forest

1967. National Afforestation Campaign.

583 **197** 10c. green & bl (postage) 45 30
584 **197** 75c. green & brown (air) 45 30

198 Lions Emblem

1967. 50th Anniv of Lions International.

585 **198** 20c. blue & brn (postage) 45 30
586 **198** 1E. violet & yellow (air) 45 30
587 **198** 5E. blue and yellow 1·30 30

199 Chilean Flag

1967. 150th Anniv of National Flag.

589 **199** 50c. red and blue (air) 45 30
588 **199** 80c. red & blue (post) 45 30

200 ITY Emblem

1967. Air. International Tourist Year.

590 **200** 30c. black and blue 45 30

201 Cardinal Caro

1967. Birth Centenary of Cardinal Caro.

591 **201** 20c. lake (postage) 90 55
592 **201** 40c. violet (air) 90 30

202 San Martin and O'Higgins

1968. 150th Anniv of Battles of Chacabuco and Maipu.

MS594a 140×109 mm. Nos. 593/4. Imperf 8·50

594 **202** 2E. violet (air) 45 30
593 **202** 3E. blue (postage) 45 30

203 Farmer and Wife

1968. Agrarian Reform.

595 **203** 20c. black, green and orange (postage) 45 30
596 **203** 50c. black, green and orange (air) 45 30

204 Juan I. Molina (scientist) and "Lamp of Learning"

1968. Molina Commemoration.

597 **204** 2E. purple (postage) 45 30
598 - 1E. green (air) 45 30

DESIGN: 1E. Molina and books.

205 Hand supporting Cogwheel

1968. 4th Manufacturing Census.

599 **205** 30c. red 45 30

206 Map, "San Sebastian" (galleon) and "Alonso de Erckla" (ferry)

1968. "Five Towns" Centenaries.

600 **206** 30c. blue (postage) 45 30
601 - 1E. purple (air) 45 30

DESIGN—VERT: 1E. Map of Chiloe Province.

207 Club Emblem

1968. 40th Anniv of Chilean Automobile Club.

602 **207** 1E. red (postage) 45 30
603 **207** 5E. blue (air) 45 30

208 Chilean Arms

1968. Air. State Visit of Queen Elizabeth II.

604 **208** 50c. brown and green 35 30
605 - 3E. brown and blue 45 30
606 - 5E. purple and plum 55 30

MS607 124×189 mm. Nos. 604/6. Imperf. No gum 28·00

DESIGN—HORIZ: 3E. Royal arms of Great Britain. VERT: 5E. St. Edward's Crown on map of South America.

209 Don Francisco Garcia Huidobro (founder)

1968. 225th Anniv of Chilean Mint.

608 **209** 2E. blue & red (postage) 35 20
609 - 5E. brown and green 35 20
610 - 50c. purple & yell (air) 35 20
611 - 1E. red and blue 35 20

MS612 150×120 mm. Nos. 608/11. Imperf. No gum (sold at 12e.) 13·00

DESIGNS: 50c. First Chilean coin and press; 1E. First Chilean stamp printed by the mint (1915); 5E. Philip V of Spain.

210 Satellite and Dish Aerial

1969. Inauguration of "ENTEL-CHILE" Satellite Communications Ground Station, Longovilo (1st issue).

613 **210** 30c. blue (postage) 45 30
614 **210** 2E. purple (air) 45 30

See also Nos. 668/9.

211 Red Cross Symbols

1969. 50th Anniv of League of Red Cross Societies.

615 **211** 2E. red & violet (postage) 45 30
616 **211** 5E. red and black (air) 45 30

212 Rapel Dam

1969. Rapel Hydro-electric Project.

617 **212** 40c. green (postage) 45 30
618 **212** 3E. blue (air) 45 30

213 Rodriguez Memorial

1969. 150th Death Anniv of Col. Manuel Rodriguez.

620 **213** 30c. brown (air) 45 30
619 **213** 2E. red (postage) 45 30

214 Open Bible

1969. 400th Anniv of Spanish Translation of Bible.

621 **214** 40c. brown (postage) 45 30
622 **214** 1E. green (air) 45 30

215 Hemispheres and ILO Emblem

1969. 50th Anniv of ILO.

623 **215** 1E. grn & blk (postage) 45 30
624 **215** 2E. purple & black (air) 45 30

216 Human Rights Emblem

1969. Human Rights Year (1968).

625 **216** 4E. red and blue (postage) 55 45
626 **216** 4E. red and brown (air) 45 30

MS627 119×140 mm. Nos. 625/6. Imperf. No gum (sold at 12e.) 11·00

217 "EXPO" Emblem

1969. World Fair "EXPO 70", Osaka, Japan.

628 **217** 3E. blue (postage) 45 30
629 **217** 5E. red (air) 45 30

218 Mint, Santiago (18th cent)

1970. Spanish Colonization of Chile.

630 **218** 2E. purple 45 20
631 - 3E. red 45 20
632 - 4E. blue 45 20
633 - 5E. brown 45 20
634 - 10E. green 45 20

MS635 110×140 mm. Nos. 631, 633/4. Imperf. No gum (sold at 25e.) 14·50

DESIGNS—HORIZ: 5E. Cal y Canto Bridge. VERT: 3E. Pedro de Valdivia; 4E. Santo Domingo Church, Santiago; 10E. Ambrosio O'Higgins.

219 Policarpo Toro and Map

1970. 80th Anniv of Seizure of Easter Island.

637 **219** 50c. turquoise (air) 55 30
636 **219** 5E. violet (postage) 55 30

221 Chilean Schooner and Arms

1970. 150th Anniv of Capture of Valdivia by Lord Cochrane.

640	**221**	40c. lake (postage)	55	30
641	**221**	2E. blue (air)	55	30

222 Paul Harris

1970. Birth Centenary of Paul Harris (founder of Rotary International).

643	**222**	1E. red (air)	55	30
642	**222**	10E. blue (postage)	55	30

223 Mahatma Gandhi

1970. Birth Centenary of Gandhi.

644	**223**	40c. green (postage)	5·50	45
645	**223**	1E. brown (air)	55	10

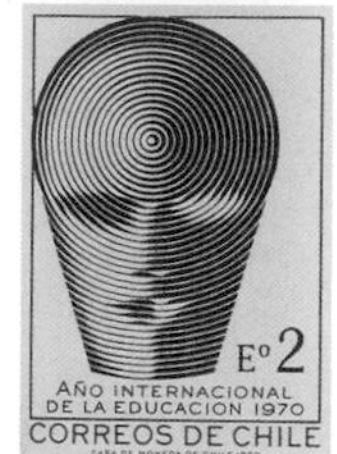

225 Education Year Emblem

1970. International Education Year.

648	**225**	2E. red (postage)	45	30
649	**225**	4E. brown (air)	45	30

226 "Virgin and Child"

1970. O'Higgins National Shrine, Maipu.

650	**226**	40c. green (postage)	45	30
651	**226**	1E. blue (air)	45	30

227 Snake and Torch Emblem

1970. 10th Int Cancer Congress, Houston, U.S.A.

652	**227**	40c. purple & bl (postage)	45	30
653	**227**	2E. brown and green (air)	45	30

228 Chilean Arms and Copper Symbol

1970. Copper Mines Nationalization.

654	**228**	40c. red & brn (postage)	45	30
655	**228**	3E. green & brown (air)	65	30

229 Globe, Dove and Cogwheel

1970. 25th Anniv of United Nations.

656	**229**	3E. vio & red (postage)	55	30
657	**229**	5E. green and red (air)	55	30

1970. Nos. 613/14 surch.

658	**210**	52c. on 30c. blue (postage)	55	30
659	**210**	52c. on 2E. purple (air)	55	30

231 Freighter "Lago Maihue" and Ship's Wheel

1971. State Maritime Corporation.

660	**231**	52c. red (postage)	45	10
661	**231**	5E. brown (air)	65	20

232 Bernardo O'Higgins and Fleet

1971. 150th Anniv of Peruvian Liberation Expedition.

663	**232**	1E. purple & blue (air)	45	20
662	**232**	5E. grn & blue (postage)	45	20

233 Scout Badge

1971. 60th Anniv of Chilean Scouting Association.

665	**233**	5c. green & lake (air)	55	20
664	**233**	1E. brn & grn (postage)	45	20

234 Young People and U.N. Emblem

1971. 1st Latin-American Meeting of UNICEF Executive Council, Santiago (1969).

666	**234**	52c. brn & blue (postage)	45	20
667	**234**	2E. green & blue (air)	45	20

1971. Longovilo Satellite Communications Ground Station (2nd issue). As T 210, but with "LONGOVILO" added to centre inscr and wording at foot of design changed to "PRIMERA ESTACION LATINOAMERICANA".

668	40c. green (postage)	55	20
669	2E. brown (air)	55	30

235 Diver with Harpoon Gun

1971. 10th World Underwater Fishing Championships, Iquique.

670	**235**	1E.15 myrtle and green	55	30
671	**235**	2E.35 ultramarine & blue	45	20

239 Magellan and Caravel

1971. 450th Anniv of Discovery of Magellan Straits.

676	**239**	35c. plum and blue	45	30

240 Dagoberto Godoy and Bristol Monoplane over Andes

1971. 1st Trans-Andes Flight (1918) Commem.

677	**240**	1E.15 green and blue	35	10

241 Statue of the Virgin, San Cristobal

1971. 10th Postal Union of the Americas and Spain Congress, Santiago.

678	**241**	1E.15 blue	65	45
679	-	2E.35 blue and red	65	45
680	-	4E.35 red	65	45
681	-	9E.35 lilac	65	45
682	-	18E.35 mauve	1·00	45

DESIGNS—VERT: 4E.35, St. Francis's Church, Santiago. HORIZ: 2E.35, U.P.A.E. emblem; 9E.35, Central Post Office, Santiago; 18E.35, Corregidor Inn.

242 Cerro el Tololo Observatory

1972. Inauguration of Astronomical Observatory, Cerro el Tololo.

683	**242**	1E.95 blue & dp blue	35	20

243 Boeing 707 over Tahiti

1972. 1st Air Service Santiago–Easter Island–Tahiti.

684	**243**	2E.35 purple and ochre	35	20

244 Alonso de Ercilla y Zuniga

1972. 400th Anniv (1969) of "La Araucana" (epic poem by de Ercilla y Zungia).

685	**244**	1E. brown (postage)	45	20
686	**244**	2E. blue (air)	45	20

245 Antarctic Map and Dog-sledge

1972. 10th Anniv of Antarctic Treaty.

687	**245**	1E.15 black and blue	75	45
688	**245**	3E.50 blue and green	1·20	45

246 Human Heart

1972. World Heart Month.

689	**246**	1E.15 red and black	45	30

247 Text of Speech by Pres. Allende

1972. 3rd United Nations Conference on Trade and Development, Santiago.

690	**247**	35c. green and brown	55	30
691	-	1E.15 violet and blue	35	10
692	**247**	4E. violet and pink	90	55
693	-	6E. blue and orange	35	10

DESIGNS: 1E.15, 6E. Conference Hall Santiago.

Nos. 690 and 692 each include a se-tenant label showing Chilean workers and inscr "CORREOS DE CHILE". The stamp was only valid for postage with the label attached.

248 Soldier and Crest

1972. 150th Anniv of O'Higgins Military Academy.

694	**248**	1E.15 yellow and blue	45	30

249 Copper Miner

1972. Copper Mines Nationalization Law (1971).

695	**249**	1E.15 blue and red	35	10
696	**249**	5E. black, blue and red	65	20

250 Barquentine "Esmeralda"

1972. 150th Anniv of Arturo Prat Naval College.

697	**250**	1E.15 purple	45	30

251 Observatory and Telescope

1972. Inauguration of Cerro Calan Observatory.

698	**251**	50c. blue	45	30

252 Dove with Letter

1972. International Correspondence Week.

699	**252**	1E.15 violet & mauve	45	45

253 Gen. Schneider, Flag and Quotation

1972. 2nd Death Anniv of General Rene Schneider.

700	**253**	2E.30 multicoloured	45	30

254 Book and Students

1972. International Book Year.

701	**254**	50c. black and red	45	30

255 Folklore and Handicrafts

1972. Tourist Year of the Americas.

702	**255**	1E.15 black and red	35	20
703	-	2E.65 purple and blue	35	20
704	-	3E.50 brown and red	35	20

DESIGNS—HORIZ: 2E.65, Natural produce. VERT: 3E.50, Stove and rug.

256 Carrera in Prison

1973. 150th Death Anniv of General J. M. Carrera.

705	**256**	2E.30 blue	65	30

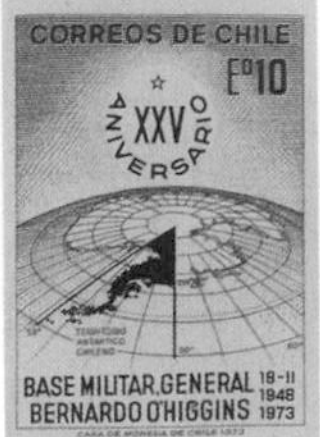

257 Antarctic Map

1973. 25th Anniv of General Bernardo O'Higgins Antarctic Base.

706	**257**	10E. red and blue	65	20

258 "Latorre" (cruiser) and Emblem

1973. 50 Years of Chilean Naval Aviation.

707	**258**	20E. blue and brown	45	30

259 Telescope

1973. Inaug of La Silla Astronomical Observatory.

708	**259**	2E.30 black and blue	45	30

260 Interpol Emblem

1973. 50th Anniv of Interpol.

709	**260**	30E. blue, black & brown	45	45
710	-	50E. black and red	65	45

DESIGN: 50E. Fingerprint superimposed on globe.

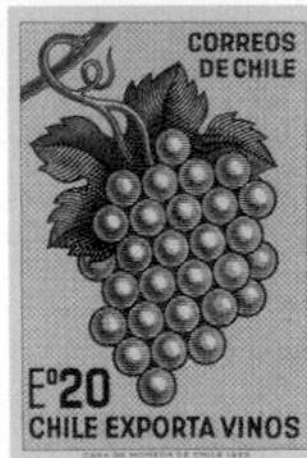

261 Bunch of Grapes

1973. Chilean Wine Exports. Multicoloured.

711		20E. Type **261**	45	20
712		100E. Inscribed globe	45	30

1974. Centenary of World Meteorological Organization. No. 668 surch "Centenario de la Organizacion Meteorologica Mundial IMO-W-MO 1973" and value.

713		27E.+3E. on 40c. green	45	30

263 UPU Headquarters Building, Berne

1974. Centenary of UPU. Unissued stamp surch.

714	**263**	500E. on 45c. green	45	30

264 Bernardo O'Higgins and Emblems

1974. Chilean Armed Forces.

715	**264**	30E. yellow and red	35	10
716	-	30E. lake and red	35	10
717	-	30E. blue and light blue	35	10
718	-	30E. blue and lilac	35	10
719	-	30E. emerald and green	35	10

DESIGNS: No. 716, Soldiers with mortar; No. 717, Naval gunners; No. 718, Air Force pilot; No. 719, Mounted policeman.

1974. 500th Birth Anniv (1973) of Copernicus. No. 683 surch "V Centenario del Nacimiento de Copernico 1473 - 1973" and value.

720	**242**	27E.+3E. on 1E.95 blue and deep blue	55	20

1974. Centenary of Vina del Mar. No. 496 surch "Centenario de la ciudad de Vina del Mar 1874 - 1974" and value.

721		27E.+3E. on 1E. turquoise	45	30

267 Football and Globe

1974. World Cup Football Championships, West Germany.

722	**267**	500E. orange and red	65	30
723	-	1000E. blue & dp blue	75	45

DESIGN—HORIZ: 1000E. Football on stylized stadium.

1974. Various stamps surch.

724	**212**	47E.+3E. on 40c. green	45	30
725	**228**	67E.+3E. on 40c. red and brown	45	30
726	**214**	97E.+3E. on 40c. brown	45	30
727	**223**	100E. on 40c. green	45	30
728	-	300E. on 50c. brown (No. 571)	55	20

269 Police and Gloved Hand

1974. Campaign for Prevention of Traffic Accidents.

729	**269**	30E. brown and green	45	10

270 Manutara and Part of Globe

1974. Inaugural LAN Flight to Tahiti, Fiji and Australia. Each green and brown.

730		200E. Type **270**	90	30
731		200E. Tahitian dancer and part of Globe	90	30
732		200E. Map of Fiji and part of Globe	90	30
733		200E. Eastern grey kangaroo and part of Globe	90	30

271 Core of Globe

1974. International Symposium of Vulcanology, Santiago de Chile.

734	**271**	500E. orange & brown	1·10	20

1974. Inauguration of Votive Temple. No. 650 surch 24 OCTUBRE 1974 INAUGURACION TEMPLO VOTIVO and value.

735	**226**	100E. on 40c. green	45	30

273 Map of Robinson Crusoe Island

1974. 400th Anniv of Discovery of Juan Fernandez Archipelago. Each brown and blue.

736		200E. Type **273**	90	30
737		200E. Chontas (hardwood palm-trees)	90	30
738		200E. Mountain goat	90	30
739		200E. Spiny lobster	90	30

274 O'Higgins and Bolivar

1974. 150th Anniv of Battles of Junin and Ayacucho.

740	**274**	100E. brown and buff	45	30

275 F. Vidal Gormaz and Seal

1975. Centenary of Naval Hydrographic Institute.

741	**275**	100E. blue and mauve	45	30

1975. Surch Revalorizada 1975 and value.

742	**228**	70c. on 40c. red & brown	35	30

277 Dr. Schweitzer

1975. Birth Centenary of Dr. Albert Schweitzer (missionary).

743	**277**	500E. brown and yellow	65	30

278 Lighthouse

1975. 50th Anniv of Valparaiso Lifeboat Service. Each blue and green.

744		150E. Type **278**	90	30
745		150E. Wreck of "Teotopoulis"	90	30
746		150E. "Cap Christiansen" (lifeboat)	90	30
747		150E. Survivor in water	90	30
MS748		110×150 mm. Nos. 744/7. Imperf		15·00

279 Sail/steam Corvette "Baquedano"

1975. 30th Anniv of Shipwreck of Sail Frigate "Lautaro".

749	**279**	500E. black and green	75	30
750	-	500E. black and green	75	30
751	-	500E. black and green	75	30
752	-	500E. black and green	75	30
753	**279**	800E. black and brown	75	30
754	-	800E. black and brown	75	30
755	-	800E. black and brown	75	30
756	-	800E. black and brown	75	30
757	**279**	1000E. black and blue	1·70	55
758	-	1000E. black and blue	1·70	55
759	-	1000E. black and blue	1·70	55
760	-	1000E. black and blue	1·70	55

DESIGNS: Nos. 750, 754, 758, Sail frigate "Lautaro"; Nos. 751, 755, 759, Cruiser "Chacabuco"; Nos. 752, 756, 760, Cadet barquentine "Esmeralda".

280 "The Happy Mother" (A. Valenzuela)

1975. International Women's Year. Chilean Paintings. Multicoloured.

No.	Description	Mint	Used
761	50c. Type **280**	1·10	30
762	50c. "Girl" (F. J. Mandiola)	1·10	30
763	50c. "Lucia Guzman" (P. L. Rencoret)	1·10	30
764	50c. "Unknown Woman" (Magdalena M. Mena)	1·10	30

281 Diego Portales (politician)

1975. Inscr "D. PORTALES".

No.	Type	Description	Mint	Used
765	**281**	10c. green	35	10
765a	**281**	20c. lilac	35	10
765b	**281**	30c. orange	35	10
766	**281**	50c. brown	35	10
767	**281**	1p. blue	35	10
767a	**281**	1p.50 brown	35	10
767b	**281**	2p. black	35	10
767c	**281**	2p.50 brown	35	10
767d	**281**	3p.50 red	45	10
768	**281**	5p. mauve	45	10

For this design inscr "DIEGO PORTALES", see Nos. 901 etc.

282 Lord Cochrane and Fleet, 1820

1975. Birth Bicentenary of Lord Thomas Cochrane. Multicoloured.

No.	Description	Mint	Used
769	1p. Type **282**	65	20
770	1p. Cochrane's capture of Valdivia, 1820	65	20
771	1p. Capture of "Esmeralda", 1820	65	20
772	1p. Cruiser "Cochrane", 1874	65	20
773	1p. Destroyer "Cochrane", 1962	65	20

283 Flags of Chile and Bolivia

1976. 150th Anniv of Bolivia's Independence.

No.	Type	Description	Mint	Used
774	**283**	1p.50 multicoloured	2·20	30

284 Lake of the Incas

1976. 6th General Assembly of Organization of American States.

No.	Type	Description	Mint	Used
775	**284**	1p.50 multicoloured	45	30

285 George Washington

1976. Bicentenary of American Revolution.

No.	Type	Description	Mint	Used
776	**285**	5p. multicoloured	65	30

286 Minerva and Academy Emblem

1976. 50th Anniv of Polytechnic Military Academy.

No.	Type	Description	Mint	Used
777	**286**	2p.50 multicoloured	45	30

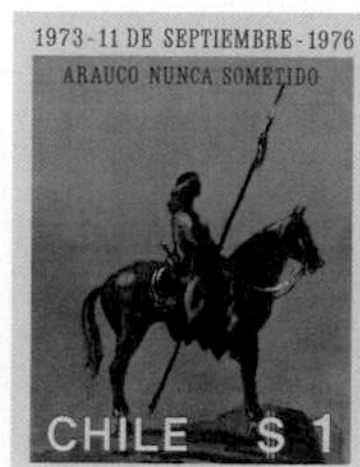

287 Indian Warrior

1976. 3rd Anniv of Military Junta. Multicoloured.

No.	Description	Mint	Used
778	1p. Type **287**	55	20
779	2p. Andean condor with broken chain	55	20
780	3p. Winged woman ("Rebirth of the Country")	55	20

288 Chilean Base, Antarctica

1977. Presidential Visit to Antarctica.

No.	Type	Description	Mint	Used
781	**288**	2p. multicoloured	11·00	65

289 College Emblem and Cultivated Field

1977. Cent of Advanced Agricultural Education.

No.	Type	Description	Mint	Used
782	**289**	2p. multicoloured	2·00	65

290 Statue of Justice

1977. 150th Anniv of Supreme Court.

No.	Type	Description	Mint	Used
783	**290**	2p. brown and grey	2·10	45

291 Globe within "Eye"

1977. 11th Pan-American Ophthalmological Congress.

No.	Type	Description	Mint	Used
784	**291**	2p. multicoloured	2·40	65

292 Police Emblem and Activities

1977. 50th Anniv of Chilean Police Force. Multicoloured.

No.	Description	Mint	Used
785	2p. Type **292**	55	30
786	2p. Mounted carabinero (vert)	55	30
787	2p. Policewoman with children (vert)	55	30
788	2p. Torres del Paine and Osorno Volcano (vert)	55	30

293 "Intelsat" Satellite and Globe

1977. World Telecommunications Day.

No.	Type	Description	Mint	Used
789	**293**	2p. multicoloured	1·10	30

294 Front Page, Press and Schooner

1977. 150th Anniv of Newspaper "El Mercurio de Valparaiso".

No.	Type	Description	Mint	Used
790	**294**	2p. multicoloured	55	20

295 St. Francis of Assisi

1977. 750th Death Anniv of St. Francis of Assisi.

No.	Type	Description	Mint	Used
791	**295**	5p. multicoloured	2·20	30

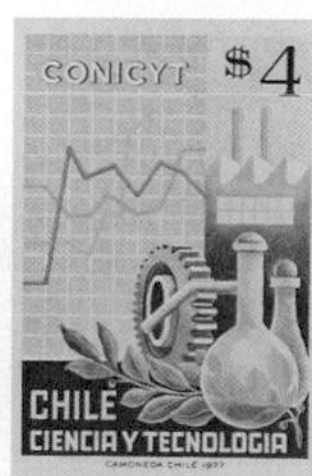

296 "Science and Technology"

1977. Council for Science and Technology.

No.	Type	Description	Mint	Used
792	**296**	4p. multicoloured	65	30

297 Weaving (Mothers' Centres)

1977. 4th Anniv of Government Junta. Welfare Facilities. Multicoloured.

No.	Description	Mint	Used
793	5p. Type **297**	90	20
794	5p. Nurse with cripple (Care of the Disabled)	90	20
795	10p. Children dancing (Protection of Minors) (horiz)	1·70	30
796	10p. Elderly man (Care for the Aged) (horiz)	1·70	30

298 Diego de Almagro (discoverer of Chile)

1977. Columbus Day.

No.	Type	Description	Mint	Used
797	**298**	5p. brown	45	30

299 Boy, Christmas Bell and Post Box

1977. Christmas.

No.	Type	Description	Mint	Used
798	**299**	2p.50 multicoloured	55	30

300 Freighter loading Timber

1978. Timber Export. Multicoloured.

No.	Description	Mint	Used
799	10p. Type **300**	1·70	30
800	20p. As T **300** but inscr "CORREOS" and with ship flying Chilean flag	2·20	55

301 Papal Arms and Globe

1978. World Peace Day.

No.	Type	Description	Mint	Used
801	**301**	10p. multicoloured	1·30	30

302 University

1978. 50th Anniv of Catholic University, Valparaiso.

No.	Type	Description	Mint	Used
802	**302**	25p. multicoloured	2·75	85

303 "Bernardo O'Higgins" (Gil de Castro)

1978. Birth Bicentenary of Bernardo O'Higgins (1st issue).
803 **303** 10p. multicoloured 1·10 45
See also Nos. 804, 806/8 and 816.

304 Chacabuco Victory Monument

1978. Birth Bicentenary of Bernardo O'Higgins (2nd issue), and 5th Anniv of Military Junta.
804 **304** 10p. multicoloured 1·10 45

305 Teacher writing on Blackboard

1978. 10th Anniv and 9th Meeting of Inter-American Council for Education, Science and Culture.
805 **305** 15p. multicoloured 1·30 30

306 "The Last Moments at Rancagua" (Pedro Subercaseaux)

1978. Birth Bicentenary of Bernardo O'Higgins (3rd issue).
806 **306** 30p. multicoloured 3·25 1·10

307 "First National Naval Squadron" (Thomas Somerscales)

1978. Birth Bicentenary of Bernardo O'Higgins (4th issue).
807 **307** 20p. multicoloured 2·75 65

308 Medallion

1978. Birth Bicentenaries of O'Higgins (5th issue) and San Martin.
808 **308** 7p. multicoloured 65 30

309 Council Emblem

1978. 30th Anniv of International Council of Military Sports.
809 **309** 50p. multicoloured 6·50 2·10

310 Three Kings

1978. Christmas. Multicoloured.
810 3p. Type **310** 65 30
811 11p. Virgin and Child 2·00 65

311 Bernardo and Rodulfo Philippi

1978. The Philippi Brothers (scientists and travellers).
812 **311** 3p.50 multicoloured 55 10

1979. No. 765 surch $ 3.50.
813 **281** 3p.50 on 10c. green 45 10

313 Flowers and Flags of Chile and Salvation Army

1979. 70th Anniv of Salvation Army in Chile.
814 **313** 10p. multicoloured 1·70 1·10

314 Pope Paul VI

1979. Pope Paul VI Commemoration.
815 **314** 11p. multicoloured 1·90 1·10

315 Battle of Maipu Monument

1979. Birth Bicentenary of Bernardo O'Higgins (6th issue).
816 **315** 8p.50 multicoloured 2·00 65

316 "Battle of Iquique" (Thomas Somerscales)

1979. Naval Battle Centenaries. Multicoloured.
817 3p.50 Type **316** 90 30
818 3p.50 "Battle of Punta Gruesa" (Alvaro Casanova Zenteno) 90 30
819 3p.50 "Battle of Angamos" (Alvaro Casanova Zenteno) 90 30

317 Diego Portales

1979
820 **317** 1p.50 brown 35 10
821 **317** 2p. grey 35 20
822 **317** 3p.50 red 45 10
823 **317** 4p.50 blue 55 20
824 **317** 5p. red 65 20
825 **317** 6p. green 75 45
826 **317** 7p. yellow 65 45
827 **317** 10p. blue 1·00 45
828 **317** 12p. orange 35 20
The 1p.50, 3p.50, 5p. and 6p. are inscribed "D. PORTALES" and have the imprint "CAMONEDA CHILE". The 2p., 4p.50, 7p. and 10p. are inscribed "DIEGO PORTALES" and have the imprint "CASA DE MONEDA DE CHILE".

318 Horse-drawn Ambulance

1979. 75th Anniv of Chilean Red Cross.
831 **318** 25p. multicoloured 5·00 1·20

319 Monument at Puntas Arenas (Miodrag Zivkovic)

1979. Centenary of Yugoslav Immigration.
832 **319** 10p. multicoloured 1·30 75

320 Children in Playground (Kiochi Kayano Gomez)

1979. International Year of the Child. Mult.
833 9p.50 Type **320** 1·30 75
834 11p. Running girl (Carmed Pizarro Toto) (vert) 1·40 85
835 12p. Children dancing in circle (Ana Pizarro Munizaga) 1·70 1·10

321 Laveredo and Arms of Coyhaique

1979. 50th Anniv of Coyhaique.
836 **321** 20p. multicoloured 2·75 1·60

322 Exhibition Emblem and Posthorn

1979. 3rd World Telecommunications Exhibition, Geneva.
837 **322** 15p. grey, blue & orange 2·10 1·10

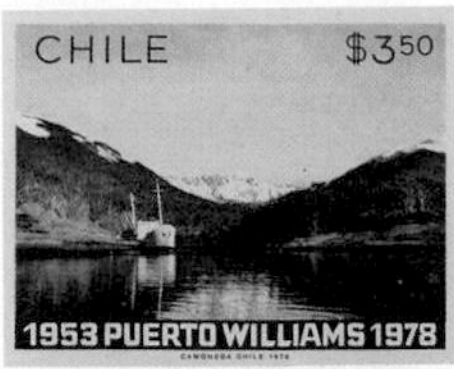

323 Canal

1979. 25th Anniv of Puerto Williams, Navirino Island.
838 **323** 3p.50 multicoloured 55 20

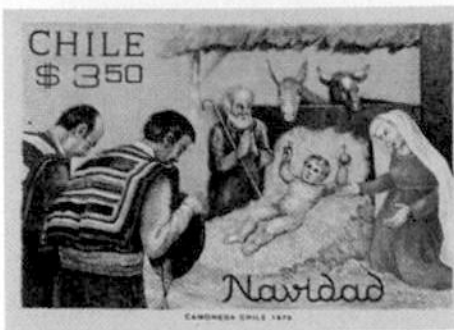

324 Chileans adoring Child Jesus

1979. Christmas.
839 **324** 3p.50 multicoloured 55 30

325 Rafael Sotomayor (Minister of War)

1979. Military Heroes. Each ochre and brown.
840 3p.50 Type **325** 35 30
841 3p.50 General Erasmo Escala (Commander in Chief of Army) 35 30
842 3p.50 Colonel (later General) Emilio Sotomayor (Commander of troops at Battle of Dolores) 35 30
843 3p.50 Colonel Eleuterio Ramirez (Commander of 2nd Line Regiment) 35 30

326 Bell Model 205 Iroquois Rescue Helicopter at Tinguiririca Volcano

1980. 50th Anniv of Chilean Air Force. Mult.
844 3p.50 Type **326** 75 30
845 3p.50 Consolidated Catalina Skua amphibian in Antarctic 75 30
846 3p.50 Northrop Tiger II jet fighter in Andes 75 30

327 Rotary Emblem and Globe

1980. 75th Anniv of Rotary International.
847 **327** 10p. multicoloured 1·30 65

328 "The Death of Bueras" (Pedro Leon Carmona)

1980. Cavalry Charge led by Colonel Santiago Bueras at Battle of Maipu, 1818.

848	**328**	12p. multicoloured	1·30	65

329 "Gen. Manuel Gaquedano" (after Pedro Subercaseaux)

1980. Centenary of Battle of Arica Head. Mult.

849	3p.50 Type **329**	45	10
850	3p.50 Gen. Pedro Largos (43×26 mm)	45	10
851	3p.50 Col. Juan Jose San Martin (43×26 mm)	45	10

330 Freire and Bars of "Ay, Ay, Ay!"

1980. Birth Centenary of Osman Perez Freire (composer).

852	**330**	6p. multicoloured	75	45

331 Mt. Gasherbrum II, Chilean flag and Ice-pick

1980. Chilean Himalayan Expedition (1979).

853	**331**	15p. multicoloured	1·70	85

332 "St Vincent de Paul" (stained glass window, former Mother House)

1980. 125th Anniv of Sisters of Charity in Chile.

854	**332**	10p. multicoloured	2·10	55

333 Andean Condor

1980. 7th Anniv of Military Government.

855	**333**	3p.50 multicoloured	45	30

334 Mummy of Inca Child

1980. 150th Anniv of National History Museum. Multicoloured.

856	5p. Type **334**	90	20
857	5p. Claudio Gay (founder) (after Alejandro Laemlein)	90	20

335 "Pablo Burchard" (Pedro Lira)

1980. Centenary of National Museum of Fine Arts.

858	**335**	3p.50 multicoloured	45	10

336 Emblem and Buildings

1980. "Fisa '80" International Fair, Santiago.

859	**336**	3p.50 multicoloured	45	10

337 "Family and Angels" (Sara Hinojosa Orellana)

1980. Christmas. Multicoloured.

860	3p.50 Type **337**	65	30
861	10p.50 "The Holy Family" (Catalina Imboden Fernandez)	2·40	65

338 Infantryman

1980. Army Uniforms of 1879 (1st series). Multicoloured.

862	3p.50 Type **338**	1·10	30
863	3p.50 Cavalry officer (parade uniform)	1·10	30
864	3p.50 Artillery officer	1·10	30
865	3p.50 Colonel of Engineers (parade uniform)	1·10	30

See also Nos. 887/90.

339 Congress Emblem

1980. 23rd International Congress of Military Medicine and Pharmacy, Santiago.

866	**339**	11p.50 multicoloured	1·80	85

340 Cattle

1981. Eradication of Foot and Mouth Disease from Chile.

867	**340**	9p.50 multicoloured	1·20	30

341 Robinson Crusoe Island

1981. Tourism. Multicoloured.

868	3p.50 Type **341**	1·10	20
869	3p.50 Easter Island monoliths	1·10	20
870	10p.50 Gentoo penguins, Antarctica	3·75	75

342 "Javiera Carrera" (after D. M. Pizarro) and Flag

1981. Birth Bicentenary of Javiera Carrera (creator of first national flag).

871	**342**	3p.50 multicoloured	35	10

343 UPU Emblem

1981. Centenary of UPU Membership.

872	**343**	3p. multicoloured	45	10

344 Unloading Cargo from Lockheed Hercules

1981. 1st Anniv of Lieutenant Marsh Antarctic Air Force Base.

873	**344**	3p.50 multicoloured	1·10	30

345 ITU and W.H.O. Emblems and Ribbons forming Caduceus

1981. World Telecommunications Day.

874	**345**	3p.50 multicoloured	35	10

346 Arturo Prat Antarctic Naval Base

1981. 20th Anniv of Antarctic Treaty.

875	**346**	3p.50 multicoloured	55	20

347 Capt. Jose Luis Araneda

1981. Centenary of Battle of Sangrar.

876	**347**	3p.50 multicoloured	35	10

348 Philatelic Society Yearbook and Medal

1981. 92nd Anniv of Philatelic Society of Chile.

877	**348**	4p.50 multicoloured	45	20

349 "Exchange of Speeches between Minister Recabarren and Indian Chief Conuepan at the Nielol Hill" (Hector Robles Acuna)

1981. Centenary of Temuco City.

878	**349**	4p.50 multicoloured	1·20	30

350 Exports (embroidery by J.L. Gutierrez)

1981. Exports.
879 **350** 14p. multicoloured 1·10 55

351 Moneda Palace (seat of Government)

1981. 8th Anniv of Military Government.
880 **351** 4p.50 multicoloured 65 30

352 St. Vincent de Paul

1981. 400th Birth Anniv of St. Vincent de Paul (founder of Sisters of Charity).
881 **352** 4p.50 multicoloured 55 30

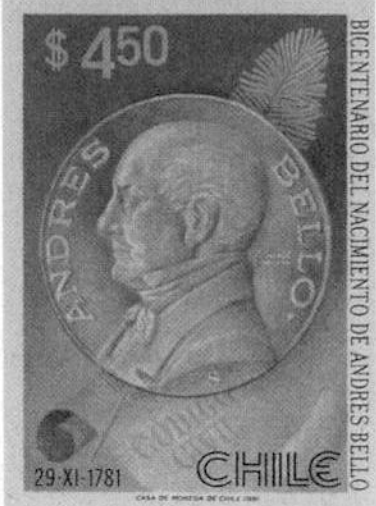

353 Medallion by Rene Thenot, Quill and Law Code

1981. Birth Bicentenary of Andres Bello (statesman, lawyer, and founder of Chile University). Multicoloured.
882 4p.50 Type **353** 55 30
883 9p.50 Profile of Bello and three of his books 1·10 45
884 11p.50 University of Chile arms and Nicanor Plaza's statue of Bello 1·30 65

354 Flag on Map of South America and Police Badge

1981. 2nd South American Uniformed Police Congress, Santiago.
885 **354** 4p.50 multicoloured 55 20

355 FAO and U.N. Emblems

1981. World Food Day.
886 **355** 5p.50 multicoloured 65 30

1981. Army Uniforms of 1879 (2nd series). As T 338. Multicoloured.
887 5p.50 Infantryman 1·10 30
888 5p.50 Military School cadet 1·10 30
889 5p.50 Cavalryman 1·10 30
890 5p.50 Artilleryman 1·10 30

356 Mother and Child

1981. International Year of Disabled Persons.
891 **356** 5p.50 multicoloured 65 3·25

357 "Nativity" (Ruth Tatiana Aguero Eguiliz)

1981. Christmas. Multicoloured.
892 5p.50 Type **357** 65 30
893 11p.50 "The Three Kings" (Ignacio Jorge Manriquez Gonzalez) 1·30 65

358 Dario Salas

1981. Birth Cent of Dario Salas (educationist).
894 **358** 5p.50 multicoloured 65 30

359 Main Buildings of University

1981. 50th Anniv of Federico Santa Maria Technical University, Valparaiso.
895 **359** 5p.50 multicoloured 65 30

360 Fair Emblem

1982. "Fida '82" International Air Fair.
896 **360** 4p.50 multicoloured 55 20

361 Cardinal Caro and Chilean Family

1982. 1st Anniv of New Constitution. Mult.
897 4p.50 Type **361** 65 30
898 11p. Diego Portales and national arms 1·40 55
899 30p. Bernardo O'Higgins and national arms 4·00 1·30

362 Globe on Chilean Flag

1982. 12th Panamerican Institute of Geography and History General Assembly.
900 **362** 4p.50 multicoloured 55 30

363 Pedro Montt (President, 1906–10)

1982. As T 281 but inscr "DIEGO PORTALES" and designs as T 363.

901	**281**	1p. blue	20	10
902	-	1p. blue	20	10
903	**281**	1p.50 orange	20	10
904	**281**	2p. grey	20	10
905	-	2p. lilac	20	10
906	**281**	2p.50 yellow	20	10
907	**363**	4p.50 mauve	55	10
908	-	5p. red	20	10
909	**281**	5p. mauve	45	30
910	-	7p. blue	65	10
911	-	10p. black	65	10

DESIGNS: Nos. 902, 905, 908, 910, 911, Ramon Barros Luco (President, 1911–15).

364 Dassault Mirage IIIC Airplane and Chilean Air Force and American Air Forces Co-operation System Badges

1982. American Air Forces Co-operation System.
916 **364** 4p.50 multicoloured 55 20

365 Trawler and Map

1982. Fisheries Exports.
917 **365** 20p. multicoloured 2·75 1·10

366 Scout Emblems and Brownsea Island

1982. 75th Anniv of Boy Scout Movement and 125th Birth Anniv of Lord Baden-Powell (founder). Multicoloured.
918 4p.50 Type **366** 17·00 5·75
919 4p.50 Lord Baden-Powell and Brownsea Island 17·00 5·75

Nos. 918/19 were printed together, se-tenant, forming a composite design.

367 Capt. Ignacio Carrera Pinto

1982. Centenary of Battle of Concepcion. Mult.
920 4p.50 Type **367** 55 30
921 4p.50 Sub-lieutenant Arturo Perez Canto 55 30
922 4p.50 Sub-lieutenant Julio Montt Salamanca 55 30
923 4p.50 Sub-lieutenant Luis Cruz Martinez 55 30

368 Old Man at Window

1982. World Assembly on Ageing, Vienna.
924 **368** 4p.50 multicoloured 55 30

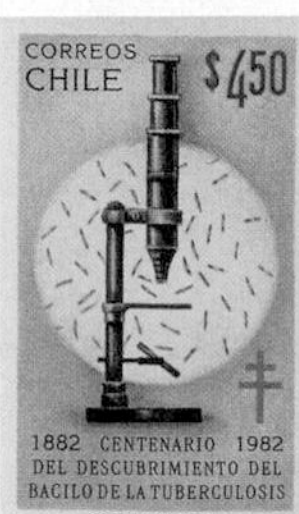

369 Microscope and Bacillus

1982. Centenary of Discovery of Tubercle Bacillus.
925 **369** 4p.50 multicoloured 55 20

370 National Flag and Flame of Freedom

1982. 9th Anniv of Military Government.
926 **370** 4p.50 multicoloured 45 20

1982. Nos. 688/9 surch.
927 **245** 1p. on 3E.50 blue & grn 55 10
928 **246** 2p. on 1E.15 red & black 55 10

372 "Nativity" (Mariela Espinoza Fuetes)

1982. Christmas. Multicoloured.
929 10p. Type **372** 1·10 30
930 25p. "Adoration of the Shepherds" (Jared Jeria Abarca) (vert) 2·20 55

373 "Virgin Mary and Marcellus" (stained-glass window, Sacred Heart of Jesus Church, Barcelona)

1982. 9th World Union of Former Marist Alumni Congress.
931 **373** 7p. multicoloured 1·90 30

374 "El Sur", Quill and Printing Press

1982. Cent of Concepcion's Newspaper "El Sur".
932 **374** 7p. multicoloured 65 30

375 "Steamship Copiapo" (W. Yorke)

1982. 110th Anniv of South American Steamship Company.
933 **375** 7p. multicoloured 75 20

376 Club Badge, Radio Aerial, Dove and Globe

1982. 60th Anniv of Radio Club of Chile.
934 **376** 7p. multicoloured 65 30

377 Arms of Sovereign Military Order

1983. Postal Agreement with Sovereign Military Order of Malta. Multicoloured.
935 25p. Type **377** 2·20 55
936 50p. Arms of Chile 4·50 1·10

378 Badge

1983. 50th Anniv of Criminal Investigation Bureau.
937 **378** 20p. multicoloured 1·80 75

379 Cardinal Samore

1983. Cardinal Antonio Samore Commem.
938 **379** 30p. multicoloured 2·00 75

380 Child watching Railway

1983. Centenary of Valparaiso Incline Railway.
939 **380** 40p. multicoloured 5·50 65

381 Puoko Tangata (carved head from Easter Island)

1983. Tourism. Multicoloured.
940 7p. Type **381** 1·10 45
941 7p. Ruins of Pucar de Quitor, San Pedro de Atacama 1·10 45
942 7p. Rock painting, Rio Ibanez, Aisen 1·10 45
943 7p. Diaguita pot 1·10 45

382 Winged Girl with Broken Chains

1983. 10th Anniv of Military Government. Mult.
944 7p. Type **382** 65 30
945 7p. Young couple with flag 65 30
946 10p. Family with torch 90 30
947 40p. National arms 2·20 95

383 General Francisco Morazan

1983. Famous Hondurans. Multicoloured.
948 7p. Type **383** 35 20
949 7p. Sabio Jose Cecilio del Valle 35 20

384 Central Post Office, Santiago

1983. World Communications Year. Mult.
950 7p. Type **384** 90 20
951 7p. Space Shuttle "Challenger" 90 20

Nos. 950/1 were printed together in se-tenant pairs within the sheet forming a composite design.

385 "Holy Family" (Lucrecia Cardenas Gomez)

1983. Christmas. Children's Paintings. Mult.
952 10p. "Nativity" (Hanny Chacon Scheel) 45 10
953 30p. Type **385** 1·80 45

386 Presidential Coach, 1911

1984. Railway Centenary. Multicoloured.
954 9p. Type **386** 2·75 30
955 9p. Service car and tender 2·75 30
956 9p. Class 80 steam locomotive, 1929 2·75 30

Nos. 954/6 were printed together, se-tenant, forming a composite design.

387 Juan Luis Sanfuentes

1984. (a) Inscr "CORREOS CHILE".
989 **387** 5p. red 10 10
958 **387** 9p. green 45 10
959 **387** 10p. grey 55 10
960 **387** 15p. blue 35 20

(b) Inscr "D.S. No. 20 CHILE".
961 9p. brown 45 10
962 15p. blue 20 10
963 20p. yellow 35 20

388 Piper Pillan Trainer and Flags

1984. 3rd International Aeronautical Fair.
966 **388** 9p. multicoloured 1·30 20

389 Agriculture, Industry and Science

1984. 20th Anniv of Chilean Nuclear Energy Commission.
967 **389** 9p. multicoloured 45 30

1984. Nos. 944/5 surch.
968 9p. on 7p. Type **382** 55 30
969 9p. on 7p. Young couple with flag 55 30

391 Chilean Women's Antarctic Expedition

1984. Chile's Antarctic Territories. Mult.
970 15p. Type **391** 75 55
971 15p. Villa Las Estrellas Antarctic settlement 75 55
972 15p. Scouts visiting Antarctic, 1983 75 55

392 Parinacota Church (Tarapaca Region)

1984. 10th Anniv of Regionalization. Mult.
973 9p. Type **392** 55 30
974 9p. El Tatio geyser (Antofagasta Region) 55 30
975 9p. Copper miners (Atacama Region) 55 30
976 9p. El Tololo observatory (Coquimbo Region) 55 30
977 9p. Valparaiso harbour (Valparaiso Region) 55 30
978 9p. Stone images (Easter Island Province) 55 30
979 9p. St. Francis's Church (Santiago Metropolitan Region) 55 30
980 9p. El Huique Hacienda (Libertador General Bernardo O'Higgins Region) 55 30
981 9p. Hydro-electric dam and reservoir, Machicura (Maule Region) 55 30
982 9p. Sta. Juana de Gaudalcazar Fort (Bio Bio Region) 55 30
983 9p. Araucana woman (Araucania Region) 55 30
984 9p. Church, Guar Island (Los Lagos Region) 55 30
985 9p. South Highway (Aisen del General Carlos Ibanez del Campo Region) 55 30
986 9p. Shepherd (Magallanes Region) 55 30
987 9p. Villa Las Estrellas (Chile Antarctic Territories) 55 30

393 Pedro Sarmiento de Gamboa and Map

1984. 400th Anniv of Spanish Settlements on Straits of Magellan.
988 **393** 100p. multicoloured 6·50 1·50

394 Antonio Varas de la Barra (founder) and Coin

1984. Centenary of State Savings Bank.
990 **394** 35p. multicoloured 1·70 65

395 Flame and Bernardo O'Higgins Monument

1984. 11th Anniv of Military Government.
991 **395** 20p. multicoloured 1·30 45

396 Clown

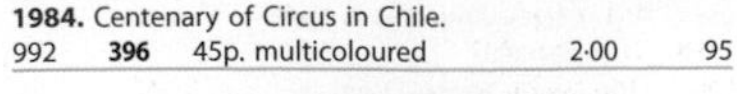

1984. Centenary of Circus in Chile.

992	**396**	45p. multicoloured	2·00	95

397 Blue Whale

1984. Endangered Animals. Multicoloured.

993	9p. Type **397**	7·75	30
994	9p. Juan Fernandez fur seal	7·75	30
995	9p. Chilean guemal	7·75	30
996	9p. Long-tailed chinchilla	7·75	30

398 "Shepherds following Star" (Ruth M. Flores Rival)

1984. Christmas. Multicoloured.

997	9p. Type **398**	20	10
998	40p. "Bethlehem" (Vianka Pastrian Navea)	1·10	55

399 Satellite and Planetarium

1984. Inaug of Santiago University Planetarium.

999	**399**	10p. multicoloured	55	20

400 Andean Hog-nosed Skunk

1985. Flora and Fauna. Multicoloured.

1000	10p. Type **400**	75	55
1001	10p. "Leucocoryne purpurea"	75	55
1002	10p. Black-winged stilt	75	55
1003	10p. Marine otter	75	55
1004	10p. "Balbisia peduncularis"	75	55
1005	10p. Patagonian conure	75	55
1006	10p. Southern pudu	75	55
1007	10p. "Fuchsia magellanica"	75	55
1008	10p. Common diuca finch	75	55
1009	10p. Argentine grey fox	75	55
1010	10p. "Alstroemeria sierrae"	75	55
1011	10p. Austral pygmy owl	75	55

401 Flags and Emblem

1985. 25th Anniv (1986) of American Air forces Co-operation System.

1012	**401**	45p. multicoloured	2·40	1·60

402 Chile and Argentina Flags and Papal Arms

1985. Chilean–Argentinian Peace Treaty.

1013	**402**	20p. multicoloured	3·75	65

403 Kentenich and Schoenstatt Sanctuary, La Florida

1985. Birth Centenary of Father Jose Kentenich (founder of Schoenstatt Movement).

1014	**403**	40p. multicoloured	75	45

404 Landscape and Shrimp

1985. Antarctic Territories and 25th Anniv of Antarctic Treaty. Multicoloured.

1015	15p. Type **404**	85	55
1016	20p. Seismological Station, O'Higgins Base	1·20	70
1017	35p. Earth receiving station, Anvers Island	2·10	1·30

405 "Canis fulvipes"

1985. Endangered Animals. Multicoloured.

1018	20p. Type **405**	2·00	45
1019	20p. James's flamingo	2·00	45
1020	20p. Giant coot	2·00	45
1021	20p. Huidobria otter	2·00	45

406 Doves and "J"

1985. International Youth Year (1022) and 40th Anniv of UNO (1023). Multicoloured.

1022	15p. Type **406**	45	25
1023	15p. U.N. emblem	45	25

407 Farmer with Haycart

1985. Occupations. Each in brown.

1024	10p. Type **407**	35	25
1025	10p. Photographer with plate camera	35	25
1026	10p. Street entertainer	35	25
1027	10p. Basket maker	35	25

408 Carrera and Statue

1985. Birth Bicentenary of Gen. Jose Miguel Carrera (Independence leader and first President).

1028	**408**	40p. multicoloured	1·30	80

409 "Holy Family"

1985. Chilean Art.

1029	**409**	10p. brown and ochre	35	25

410 "Nativity" (Jennifer Gomez)

1985. Christmas. Multicoloured.

1030	15p. Type **410**	85	35
1031	100p. Man with donkey (Esteban Morales Medina) (vert)	4·50	1·50

411 Escort of Light Infantry, 1818

1985. 16th American Armies Conference. Mult.

1032	20p. Type **411**	60	40
1033	35p. Officer of the Hussars of the Grand Guard, 1813	1·10	45

412 Moon, Earth and Comet

1985. Appearance of Halley's Comet.

1034	**412**	45p. multicoloured	90	35
MS1035		90×105 mm. No. 1034 (sold at 180p.)	26·00	26·00

413 Living Trees and Flame

1985. Forest Fires Prevention. Multicoloured.

1036	40p. Type **413**	1·20	70
1037	40p. Burnt trees and flame	1·20	70

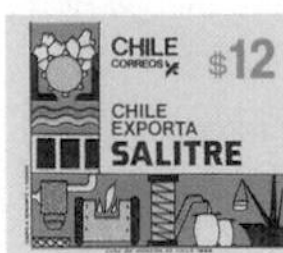

414 Saltpetre

1986. Exports. Each brown and blue.

1038	12p. Type **414**	35	25
1039	12p. Iron	35	25
1040	12p. Copper	35	25
1041	12p. Molybdenum	35	25

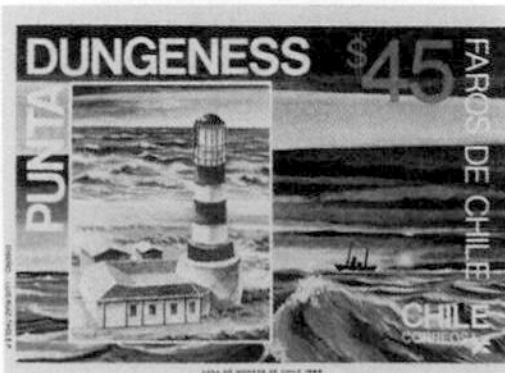

415 Dungeness Point Lighthouse

1986. Chilean Lighthouses. Multicoloured.

1042	45p. Type **415**	1·30	70
1043	45p. Evangelistas lighthouse in storm	1·30	70

416 St. Lucia Hill, Santiago

1986. Death Centenary of Benjamin Vicuna Mackenna (Municipal Superintendent).

1044	**416**	30p. multicoloured	70	35

417 Diego Portales

1986. Unissued stamp surch.

1045	**417**	12p. on 3p.50 mult	60	25

418 National Stadium, Chile, 1962

1986. World Cup Football Championship, Mexico. Multicoloured.

1046	15p. Type **418**	60	30
1047	20p. Azteca Stadium, Mexico, 1970	85	35
1048	35p. Maracana Stadium, Brazil, 1950	1·30	45
1049	50p. Wembley Stadium, England, 1966	1·90	80

419 Birds flying above City

1986. Environmental Protection. Mult.

1050	20p. Type **419**	1·10	35
1051	20p. Fish	1·10	35
1052	20p. Full litter bin in forest	1·10	35

420 "Santiaguillo" (caravel) and flags

1986. 450th Anniv of Valparaiso.

1053	**420**	40p. multicoloured	1·30	70

421 Emblem

1986. 25th Anniv of Inter-American Development Bank.

1054	**421**	45p. multicoloured	1·40	70

422 St. Rosa and Pelequen Sanctuary

1986. 400th Birth Anniv of St. Rosa of Lima.

1055	**422**	15p. multicoloured	95	35

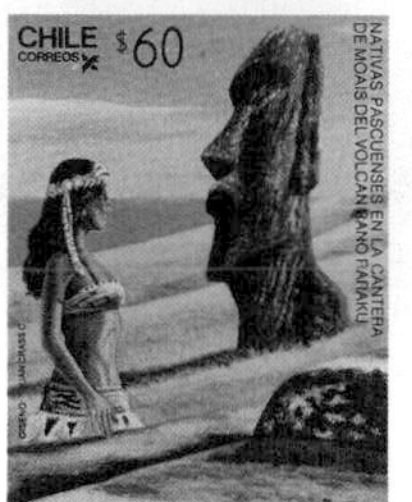

423 Stone Head on Raraku Volcano

1986. Easter Island. Multicoloured.

1056	60p. Type **423**	2·40	90
1057	100p. Tongariki ruins	4·25	1·40
MS1058	Two sheets. (a) 90×104 mm. No. 1056; (b) 104×90 mm. No. 1057 (sold at 420p.)	31·00	31·00

424 Flags, Stamps in Album, Magnifying Glass and Tweezers

1986. "Ameripex '86" International Stamp Exhibition, Chicago.

1059	**424**	100p. multicoloured	3·00	1·40

425 Schooner "Ancud"

1986. Naval Traditions. Multicoloured.

1060	35p. Type **425**	95	55
1061	35p. Brigantine "Aguila"	95	55
1062	35p. Sail corvette "Esmeralda"	95	55
1063	35p. Sail frigate "O'Higgins"	95	55

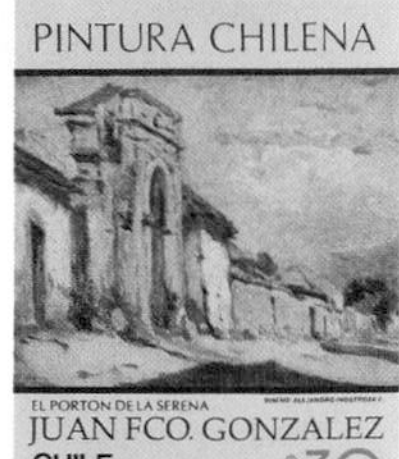

426 "Gate of Serenity"

1986. Paintings by Juan F. Gonzalez. Mult.

1064	30p. "Rushes and Chrysanthemums"	1·10	45
1065	30p. Type **426**	1·10	45

427 Antarctic Terns

1986. Antarctic Fauna. Sea Birds. Mult.

1066	40p. Type **427**	1·40	55
1067	40p. Blue-eyed cormorants	1·40	55
1068	40p. Emperor penguins	1·40	55
1069	40p. Antarctic skuas	1·40	55

428 Pedro de Ona (poet)

1986. Chilean Literature. Multicoloured.

1070	20p. Type **428**	60	35
1071	20p. Vicente Huidobro	60	35

429 Major-General, 1878

1986. Centenary of Military Academy. Mult.

1072	45p. Type **429**	85	55
1073	45p. Major, 1950	85	55

430 Diaguita Art

1986. Indian Art. Multicoloured.

1074	30p. Type **430**	70	35
1075	30p. Mapuche art	70	35

431 "Nativity" (Begona Andrea Orrego Castro)

1986. Christmas. Multicoloured.

1076	15p. Type **431**	70	35
1077	105p. "Shrine and Mountains" (Andrea Maribel Riquelme Labarde)	3·75	90

432 Shepherds looking at Hill Town

1986. Christmas.

1078	**432**	12p. multicoloured	35	25

433 Emblem and Globe

1986. International Peace Year.

1079	**433**	85p. multicoloured	1·70	70

1986. No. 1029 surch.

1080	**409**	12p. on 10p. brown and ochre	35	25

1986. Nos. 1024/7 surch.

1081	12p. on 10p. Farmer with haycart	35	10
1082	12p. on 10p. Photographer with plate camera	35	10
1083	12p. on 10p. Street entertainer	35	10
1084	12p. on 10p. Basket maker	35	10
1085	15p. on 10p. Farmer with haycart	35	10
1086	15p. on 10p. Photographer with plate camera	35	10
1087	15p. on 10p. Street entertainer	35	10
1088	15p. on 10p. Basket maker	35	10

436 Profiles and Flag

1986. Women's Voluntary Organization.

1089	**436**	15p. multicoloured	35	25

437 Virgin of Carmelites

1986. 60th Anniv of Coronation of Virgin of the Carmelites.

1090	**437**	25p. multicoloured	95	35

438 Kitson Meyer Steam Locomotive No. 59

1987. Railways.

1091	**438**	95p. multicoloured	4·25	1·70

439 "The Guitarist of Quinchamali"

1987. Folk Tales. (a) As T 439.

1092	**439**	15p. green	20	10
1093	-	15p. blue	40	10
1094	-	15p. brown	20	10
1095	-	15p. mauve	20	10

(b) Discount stamps. Inscr "D/S No 20" in colour of stamp in right-hand margin and dated "1992".

1092C	15p. As Type **439**	25	10
1093C	15p. As No. 1093	25	10
1094C	15p. As No. 1094	25	10
1095C	15p. As No. 1095	25	10

DESIGNS: No. 1093, "El Caleuche"; 1094, "El Pihuychen"; 1095, "La Lola".

440 Rowing Boat and Storage Tanks

1987. 40th Anniv of Capt. Arturo Prat Antarctic Naval Base. Multicoloured.

1096	100p. Type **440**	3·00	1·40
1097	100p. Buildings and rowing boat at jetty	3·00	1·40

Nos. 1096/7 were printed together, se-tenant, forming a composite design.

441 Pope and "Christ the Redeemer" Statue

1987. Visit of Pope John Paul II. Mult.

1098	20p. Type **441**	45	10
1099	25p. Votive Temple, Maipu	60	25
1100	90p. "Cross of the Seas", Magellan Straits	2·00	90
1101	115p. "Virgin of the Hill" statue, Santiago	2·75	1·50
MS1102	104×90 mm. No. 1101 (sold at 250p.)	7·00	7·00

442 Horse-riding Display

1987. 60th Anniv of Carabineers. Mult.

1103	50p. Type **442**	1·20	55
1104	50p. Sea rescue by Air Police	1·20	55

443 Players and Ball

1987. World Youth Football Cup. Mult.

1105	45p. Type **443**	1·10	55
1106	45p. Player and Concepcion stadium	1·10	55
1107	45p. Player and Antofagasta stadium	1·10	55
1108	45p. Player and Valparaiso stadium	1·10	55
MS1109	89×105 mm. 45p. No. 1105 (sold at 150p.)	4·25	4·25

444 Battleship "Almirante Latorre"

1987. Naval Tradition. Multicoloured.

1110	60p. Type **444**	1·40	80
1111	60p. Cruiser "O'Higgins"	1·40	80

445 Portales and "El Vigia" Newspaper

1987. 150th Death Anniv of Diego Portales (statesman).

1112	**445**	30p. multicoloured	70	35

446 Works Projects

1987. Centenary of Ministry of Public Works.

1113	**446**	25p. multicoloured	85	45

447 School Entrance

1987. Centenary of Infantry School. Mult.

1114	50p. Type **447**	85	35
1115	100p. Soldiers and national flag	1·70	80

448 "Chiasognathus granti"

1987. Flora and Fauna. Multicoloured.

1116	25p. Type **448**	65	35
1117	25p. Sanderling	65	35
1118	25p. Peruvian guemal	65	35
1119	25p. Chilean palm	65	35
1120	25p. "Colias vauthieri" (butterfly)	65	35
1121	25p. Osprey	65	35
1122	25p. Commerson's dolphin	65	35
1123	25p. Mountain cypress	65	35
1124	25p. San Fernandez Island spiny lobster	65	35
1125	25p. Fernandez firecrown	65	35
1126	25p. Vicuna	65	35
1127	25p. Arboreal fern	65	35
1128	25p. Spider-crab	65	35
1129	25p. Lesser rhea	65	35
1130	25p. Mountain viscacha	65	35
1131	25p. Giant cactus	65	35

449 Family

1987. International Year of Shelter for the Homeless.

1132	**449**	40p. multicoloured	95	45

450 Emblem

1987. "fisa'87", 25th International Santiago Fair.

1133	**450**	20p. multicoloured	35	25

451 Condell, Battle of Iquique and Statue

1987. Death Centenary of Admiral Carlos Condell.

1134	**451**	50p. multicoloured	95	35

452 "Holy Family" (Ximena Soledad Rosales Opazo)

1987. Christmas. Multicoloured.

1135	30p. Type **452**	95	35
1136	100p. "Star over Bethlehem" (Marcelo Bordones Meneses)	4·00	1·00

453 Casting

1987. "Cobre '87" International Copper Conference, Vina del Mar.

1137	**453**	40p. multicoloured	85	35

MS1138 88×103 mm. No. 1137 (sold at 150p.) 3·50 3·50

454 "Nativity"

1987. Christmas. (a) Non-discount.

1139	**454**	15p. blue and orange	35	10

(b) Discount stamps. Additionally inscr "D.S. No. 20".

1140	15p. blue and orange	35	10

455 Non-smokers inhaling Smoke

1987. Anti-smoking Campaign.

1141	**455**	15p. blue and orange	35	10

456 "Capitan Luis Alcazar" (supply ship) and Antarctic Landscape

1987. 25th Anniv of National Antarctic Research Commission.

1142	**456**	45p. multicoloured	1·40	80

457 Freire

1987. Birth Bicentenary of General Ramon Freire Serrano (Director, 1823–27).

1143	**457**	20p. red and purple	45	35

458 Violin and Frutillar Church and Lake

1988. 20th Music Weeks, Frutillar.

1144	**458**	30p. multicoloured	60	35

459 St. John with Boy (after C. Di Girolamo)

1988. Death Centenary of St. John Bosco (founder of Salesian Brothers).

1145	**459**	40p. multicoloured	1·20	45

460 Bird, Da Vinci's Glider, Wright's Flyer 1, Junkers Ju 52/3m, De Havilland Vampire and Grumman Tomcat

1988. "Fida'88" 5th International Air Fair.

1146	**460**	60p. blue and deep blue	1·30	90

461 Shot Putting, Pole Vaulting and Javelin Throwing

1988. Olympic Games, Seoul. Multicoloured.

1147	50p. Type **461**	1·70	80
1148	100p. Swimming, cycling and running	3·00	1·60

MS1149 90×105 mm. Nos. 1147/8 (sold at 250p.) 6·00 6·00

1988. Discount stamp. No. 958 surch $20 D.S.No 20.

1150	**387**	20p. on 9p. green	35	25

463 Kava-Kava Head

1988. Easter Island. (a) Inscr "CORREOS" only.

1151	**463**	20p. black and pink	35	25
1152	-	20p. black and pink	35	25

(b) Discount stamps. As T 463 but additionally inscr "D.S.No 20".

1153	**463**	20p. black and yellow	35	25
1154	-	20p. black and yellow	35	25

DESIGN: Nos. 1152, 1154, Tangata Manu bird-man (petroglyph).

464 Medal, Scientist, Bull and Farm Workers

1988. 150th Anniv of National Agricultural Society.

1155	**464**	45p. multicoloured	1·80	55

465 Tending Accident Victim

1988. 125th Anniv of Red Cross.

1156	**465**	150p. multicoloured	2·00	90

466 Gipsy Moth, Boeing 767, Mirage 50 and Merino

1988. Birth Centenary of Commodore Arturo Merino Benitez (air pioneer).

1157	**466**	35p. multicoloured	1·20	35

467 Cadet Barquentine "Esmeralda"

1988. Naval Tradition. Multicoloured.

1158	50p. Type **467**	1·30	80
1159	50p. "Capt. Arturo Prat" (stained glass window, Valparaiso Naval Museum)	1·30	80

468 Vatican City and University Arms

1988. Centenary of Pontifical Catholic University of Chile.

1160	**468**	40p. multicoloured	1·30	35

469 Esslingen Locomotive No. 3331

1988. Railway Anniversaries. Multicoloured.

1161	60p. Type **469** (75th anniv of Arica–La Paz railway)	1·10	70
1162	60p. North British locomotive No. 45 (cent of Antofagasta–Bolivia railway)	1·10	70

MS1163 104×88 mm. Nos. 1161/2 (sold at 180p.) 9·50 9·50

470 Chemistry Student

1988. 175th Anniv of Jose Miguel Carrera National Institute.

1164	**470**	45p. multicoloured	95	45

471 "Chloraea chrysantha"

1988. Flowers. Multicoloured.

1165	30p. Type **471**	70	35
1166	30p. "Lapogeria rosea"	70	35
1167	30p. "Nolana paradoxa"	70	35
1168	30p. "Rhodophiala advena"	70	35
1169	30p. "Schizanthus hookeri"	70	35
1170	30p. "Acacia caven"	70	35
1171	30p. "Cordia decanda"	70	35
1172	30p. "Leontochir ovallei"	70	35

1173		30p. "Alstroemeria pelegrina"	70	35
1174		30p. "Copiapoa cinerea"	70	35
1175		30p. "Salpiglossis sinuata"	70	35
1176		30p. "Leucocoryne coquimbensis"	70	35
1177		30p. "Eucryphia glutinosa"	70	35
1178		30p. "Calandrinia longiscapa"	70	35
1179		30p. "Desfontainia spinosa"	70	35
1180		30p. "Sophora macrocarpa"	70	35

472 Commander Policarpo Toro and "Angamos"

1988. Centenary of Incorporation of Easter Island into Chile. Multicoloured.

1181		50p. Type **472**	1·10	55
1182		50p. Map of Easter Island and globe	1·10	55
1183		100p. Dancers	2·20	1·10
1184		100p. Petroglyphs of bird-men	2·20	1·10
MS1185		105×89 mm. Nos. 1181/4 (sold at 450p.)	10·00	10·00

473 Bleriot XI over Town

1988. 70th Anniv of First National Airmail Service.

1186	**473**	150p. multicoloured	2·50	1·50

474 Pottery

1988. 15th Anniv of Centre for Education of Women. Traditional Crafts. Multicoloured.

1187		25p. Type **474**	45	35
1188		25p. Embroidery	45	35

475 Policeman and Brigade Members

1988. Schools' Security Brigade.

1189	**475**	45p. multicoloured	95	45

476 "Nativity" (Paulette Thiers)

1988. Christmas. Multicoloured.

1190		35p. Type **476**	45	35
1191		100p. "Family going to church" (Jose M. Lamas)	1·40	70

477 Cancelled 1881 2c. Stamp

1988. Centenary of Chile Philatelic Society.

1192	**477**	40p. multicoloured	60	35

478 Child in Manger

1988. Christmas. (a) Non-discount.

1193	**478**	20p. purple and yellow	35	25

(b) Discount stamps. As T 478 but additionally inscr "D.S. No. 20".

1194		20p. purple and yellow	35	25

479 Manuel Bulnes and Battle of Yungay, 1839

1989. Historic Heroes. Multicoloured.

1195		50p. Type **479**	95	35
1196		50p. Soldier and battle scene	95	35
1197		100p. Roberto Simpson and Battle of Casma, 1839	1·90	1·00
1198		100p. Sailor and battle scene	1·90	1·00

480 St. Ambrose's Church, Vallenar (bicentenary)

1989. Town Anniversaries. Multicoloured.

1199		30p. Type **480**	45	35
1200		35p. Craftsman, Combarbala (bicent)	55	35
1201		45p. Laja Falls, Los Angeles (250th anniv)	60	40

See also No. 1306.

1989. Various stamps surch. (a) Surch $25 only.

1202		25p. on 15p. green (1092)	45	25
1203		25p. on 15p. blue (1093)	45	25
1204		25p. on 15p. brown (1094)	45	25
1205		25p. on 15p. mauve (1095)	45	25
1206		25p. on 20p. black and pink (1151)	45	25
1207		25p. on 20p. black and pink (1152)	45	25
1208		25p. on 20p. black and yellow (1153)	45	25
1209		25p. on 20p. black and yellow (1154)	45	25

(b) Surch D.S. No 20 $25.

1210		25p. on 20p. black and pink (1151)	45	25
1211		25p. on 20p. black and pink (1152)	45	25

483 Sister Teresa of the Andes

1989. Beatifications. Multicoloured.

1212		40p. Type **483**	95	45
1213		40p. Laura Vicuna	95	45

484 Christopher Columbus

1989. "Exfina '89" Stamp Exhibition, Santiago. Multicoloured.

1214		100p. Type **484**	2·40	1·10
1215		100p. "Nina", "Santa Maria" and "Pinta"	2·40	1·10
MS1216		90×105 mm. Nos. 1214/15	7·00	7·00

485 Container Ship and Trawler

1989. 50th Anniv of Energy Production Corporation. Multicoloured.

1217		60p. Type **485**	85	55
1218		60p. Tree trunks on trailer and factory	85	55
1219		60p. Telephone tower and pylon	85	55
1220		60p. Coal wagons and colliery	85	55

486 Town and Sketch

1989. Birth Centenary of Gabriela Mistral (writer). Multicoloured.

1221		30p. Type **486**	60	35
1222		30p. Mistral with children	60	35
1223		30p. Mistral writing	60	35
1224		30p. Mistral receiving Nobel Prize	60	35

487 Grapes

1989. Exports. (a) Inscr as T 487.

1225	**487**	5p. blue	35	25
1226	-	5p. red and blue	35	25
1227	**487**	10p. deep blue & blue	35	25
1228	-	10p. red and blue	35	25
1229	**487**	25p. blue and green	45	25
1230	-	25p. red and green	45	25
1350	**487**	45p. blue and mauve	80	25
1351	-	45p. red and mauve	80	25

(b) Discount stamps. As T 487 but additionally inscr "D.S. No. 20".

1231	**487**	25p. blue and yellow	45	25
1232	-	25p. red and yellow	45	25
1352	**487**	45p. blue and yellow	80	25
1353	-	45p. red and yellow	80	25

DESIGNS: Nos. 1226, 1228, 1230, 1232, 1351, 1353, Apple.

488 Battle Scene, Soldiers and "Justice"

1989. 150th Anniv of Army Court of Justice.

1233	**488**	50p. multicoloured	95	45

489 Monument

1989. Frontier Guards' Martyrs' Monument.

1234	**489**	35p. multicoloured	70	35

490 Victoria, Vina del Mar

1989. Transport.

1235	**490**	30p. black and orange	60	25
1236	-	35p. black and blue	60	25
1237	-	40p. black and green	70	25
1238	-	45p. black and green	70	25
1239	-	50p. black and red	85	35
1240	-	60p. black and bistre	1·10	45
1241	-	100p. black and green	1·90	90

DESIGNS—VERT: 35p. Scow, Chiloe Archipelago. HORIZ: 40p. Ox-cart, Cautin; 45p. Raft ferry, Rio Palena; 50p. Lighters, Gen. Carrera Lake; 60p. Valparaiso incline railway; 100p. Santiago funicular.

See also Nos. 1346 and 1458.

491 Scientist and Bearded Penguins

1989. 25th Anniv of Chilean Antarctic Institute.

1245	**491**	150p. multicoloured	3·00	1·40

492 Present Naval Engineers School and "Chacabuco" (first school)

1989. Centenary of Naval Engineering. Mult.

1246		45p. Type **492**	85	35
1247		45p. Sailors in engine room	85	35
1248		45p. Destroyer, Aerospatiale Dauphin 2 helicopter and submarine	85	35
1249		45p. Launch of "Aquiles" (patrol boat)	85	35

493 Globes, Polar Bear and Gentoo Penguins

1989. "World Stamp Expo '89" International Stamp Exhibition, Washington D.C.

1250	**493**	250p. multicoloured	4·75	2·30
MS1251		90×104 mm. No. 1250	8·75	8·75

494 Atacamena Culture

1989. America. Pre-Columbian Cultures. Mult.

1252	30p. Type **494**	95	35
1253	150p. Selk'nam and Onas cultures	3·50	1·30

495 Balls

1989. Christmas. (a) As T 495.

1254	**495**	25p. yellow and green	45	25
1255	-	25p. yellow and green	45	25

(b) Discount stamps. Additionally inscr "D.S. No 20".

1256	**495**	25p. red and green	45	25
1257	-	25p. red and green	45	25

DESIGN: Nos. 1255, 1257, Bells.

496 "Rowing to Church" (Cristina Lopez)

1989. Christmas.

1258	**496**	100p. multicoloured	1·50	70

497 Vicuna, Lauca

1990. National Parks. Multicoloured.

1259	35p. Type **497**	55	35
1260	35p. Chilian flamingo, Salar de Surire	55	35
1261	35p. Cactus, La Chimba	55	35
1262	35p. Guanaco, Pan de Azucar	55	35
1263	35p. Long-tailed meadowlark, Fray Jorge	55	35
1264	35p. Sooty tern, Rapa Nui	55	35
1265	35p. Lesser grison, La Campana	55	35
1266	35p. Torrent duck, Rio Clarillo	55	35
1267	35p. Mountain cypress, Rio de los Cipreses	55	35
1268	35p. Black-necked swan, Laguna de Torca	55	35
1269	35p. Puma, Laguna del Laja	55	35
1270	35p. Araucaria, Villarrica	55	35
1271	35p. "Philesia magellanica", Vicente Perez Rosales	55	35
1272	35p. "Nothofagus pumilio", Dos Lagunas	55	35
1273	35p. Leopard seal, Laguna San Rafael	55	35
1274	35p. Lesser rhea, Torres del Paine	55	35

498 Boot

1990. World Cup Football Championship, Italy. Multicoloured.

1275	50p. Type **498**	95	35
1276	50p. Hand	95	35
1277	50p. Ball in net	95	35
1278	50p. Player	95	35

499 Vickers Wibault I Biplane, 1927–37

1990. Chilean Airforce Airplanes. Multicoloured.

1279	40p. Type **499**	65	35
1280	40p. Curtiss O1E Falcon, 1928–40	65	35
1281	40p. Pitts S-2A (Falcons aerobatic team, 1981–90)	65	35
1282	40p. Extra 33 (Falcons aerobatic team, 1990)	65	35
MS1283	120×115 mm. Nos. 1279/82	4·00	4·00

No. 1282 is inscribed "EXTRA 300". And **MS**1283 is also inscribed for "Fidae'90" international air fair.

500 Inca

1990. 500th Anniv of Discovery of America by Columbus. Multicoloured.

1284	60p. Type **500**	80	35
1285	60p. Spanish officer	80	35

501 Valparaiso

1990. Ports. Multicoloured.

1286	40p. Type **501**	65	35
1287	40p. San Vicente	65	35

502 "Piloto Pardo" (Antarctic supply ship)

1990. Naval Tradition. Multicoloured.

1288	50p. Type **502**	65	35
1289	50p. "Yelcho" (survey ship)	65	35

503 "Sunrise in Chile"

1990. "Democracy in Chile". Multicoloured.

1290	20p. Type **503**	55	35
1291	30p. Dove ("Peace in Chile")	65	40
1292	60p. "ChiLe" ("Rejoicing in Chile")	1·30	45
1293	100p. Star ("Thus Chile pleases me")	2·30	95
MS1294	115×120 mm. Nos. 1290/3	9·25	9·25

504 Child and Slogan

1990. "One Chile for All Chileans".

1295	**504**	45p. multicoloured	95	35
MS1296		90×105 mm. No. 1295	1·90	1·90

505 Sir Rowland Hill

1990. 150th Anniv of the Penny Black.

1297	**505**	250p. multicoloured	5·25	2·40
MS1298		105×90 mm. No. 1297	8·00	8·00

506 Flags

1990. Centenary of Organization of American States.

1299	**506**	150p. multicoloured	2·75	1·20

507 Purplish Scallop and Diver with Net

1990. Fishing. Multicoloured.

1300	40p. Type **507**	65	35
1301	40p. Giant wedge clam and man with net	65	35
1302	40p. Swordfish ("Albacora") and harpooner on "San Antonio" (fishing boat)	65	35
1303	40p. Marine spider crab and fishing boat raising catch	65	35
1304	40p. Chilean hake ("Merluza") and trawler	65	35
1305	40p. Women baiting hooks	65	35

1990. Town Anniversaries. 250th Anniv of San Felipe. As T 480. Multicoloured.

1306	50p. Curimon Convent	95	35

508 Aerosol

1990. Environmental Protection. Each red and black. (a) As T 508.

1307	35p. Type **508**	55	25
1308	35p. Tree and tree stumps	55	25
1309	35p. Factory chimneys emitting smoke	55	25
1310	35p. Oil tanker polluting wildlife and sea	55	25
1311	35p. Deer escaping from burning forest	55	25

(b) Discount stamps. Additionally inscr "D.S. No 20".

1312	35p. Type **508**	55	25
1313	35p. As No. 1308	55	25
1314	35p. As No. 1309	55	25
1315	35p. As No. 1310	55	25
1316	35p. As No. 1311	55	25

See also Nos. 1421/30.

509 Salvador Allende

1990. Presidents.

1317	**509**	35p. black and blue	55	25
1318	-	35p. black and blue	55	25
1319	-	40p. black and green	65	30
1320	-	45p. black and green	80	35
1321	-	50p. black and red	95	40
1322	-	60p. black and red	1·10	45
1323	-	70p. black and blue	1·30	55
1324	-	80p. black and blue	1·50	60
1325	-	90p. black and brown	1·70	70
1326	-	100p. black & brown	1·90	85

DESIGNS: No. 1318, Eduardo Frei; 1319, Jorge Alessandri; 1320, Gabriel Gonzalez; 1321, Juan Antonio Rios: 1322, Pedro Aguirre Cerda; 1323, Juan E. Montero; 1324, Carlos Ibanez; 1325, Emiliano Figueroa; 1326, Arturo Alessandri.

510 Opening Ceremony

1990. Rodeo. Multicoloured.

1327	45p. Type **510**	80	35
1328	45p. Riders saluting crowd	80	35
1329	45p. Rider reining in	80	35
1330	45p. Two riders cornering steer	80	35

511 Chilean Flamingoes

1990. America. The Natural World. Mult.

1331	30p. Type **511**	1·10	35
1332	150p. South American fur seals	4·75	1·20

512 Chilean State Arms and Spanish Royal Arms

1990. State Visit by King Juan Carlos and Queen Sofia of Spain. Multicoloured.

1333	100p. Type **512**	1·90	85
1334	100p. Spanish and Chilean (at right) State Arms	1·90	85

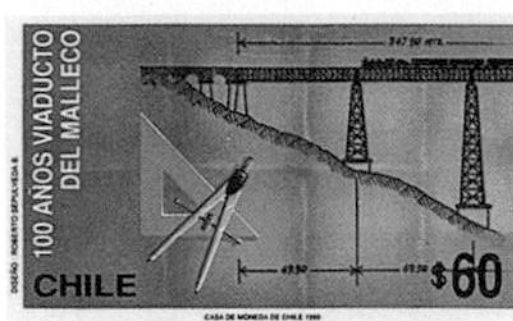

513 Construction Diagram of Viaduct

1990. Centenary of Malleco Viaduct. Mult.

1335	60p. Type **513**	2·00	85
1336	60p. Boy waving to steam train on completed viaduct	2·00	85

Nos. 1335/6 were printed together, se-tenant, forming a composite design.

514 Antarctic Skua, Whale and Supply Ship

1990. 50th Anniv of Chilean Antarctic Territory. Multicoloured.

1337	250p. Type **514**	4·00	1·80
1338	250p. Adelie penguins, Bell Model 206 jet helicopters and tents	4·00	1·80
MS1339	104×89 mm. Nos. 1337/8	13·50	13·50

515 Children decorating Tree

1990. Christmas. (a) As T 515.

1340	**515**	35p. green & emerald	55	25

(b) Discount stamps. Additionally inscr "D.S. No 20".

1341	35p. green and orange	55	25

516 Santa Claus in Space (Carla Levill)

1990. Christmas. Children's drawings. Mult.

1342	35p. Type **516**	95	35
1343	150p. Television on sea bed (Jose M. Lamas)	4·25	1·20

517 Assembly Hall

1990. National Congress. Multicoloured.

1344	100p. Type **517**	1·90	85
1345	100p. Painting above dais	1·90	85

1991. Discount stamp. As No. 1238 but colour changed and additionally inscr "D.S. No 20".

1346	45p. black and yellow	80	35

518 Casa Colorada

1991. 450th Anniv of Santiago. Multicoloured.

1347	100p. Type **518**	1·90	70
1348	100p. City landmarks	1·90	70
MS1349	89×104 mm. Nos. 1347/8	7·25	7·25

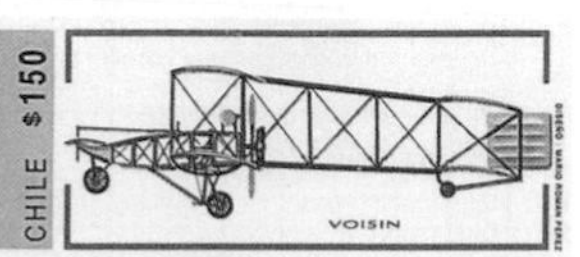

519 Voisin "Boxkite"

1991. Aviation History. Multicoloured.

1354	150p. Type **519**	2·40	1·30
1355	150p. Royal Aircraft Factory S.E.5A	2·40	1·30
1356	150p. Morane Saulnier MS 35	2·40	1·30
1357	150p. Consolidated PBY-5A/OA-10 Catalina amphibian	2·40	1·30

520 Map, Player and Left Half of Ball

1991. America Cup Football Championship. Mult.

1358	100p. Type **520**	1·50	70
1359	100p. Right half of ball and goalkeeper	1·50	70

Nos. 1358/9 were printed together, se-tenant, forming a composite design.

521 Drill and Miner

1991. Coal Mining. Multicoloured.

1360	200p. Type **521**	3·00	1·30
1361	200p. Miners emptying truck	3·00	1·30

522 Youths and Emblem

1991. Centenary of Scientific Society.

1362	**522**	45p. black and green	65	25

523 Dish and Hanging Ornaments

1991. Traditional Crafts. Multicoloured.

1363	90p. Type **523**	1·50	60
1364	90p. Carvings and ceramics	1·50	60

1991. Various stamps surch.

1365	**463**	45p. on 20p. black and yellow	55	25
1366	-	45p. on 20p. black and yellow (1154)	55	25
1367	**487**	45p. on 25p. blue & yell	55	25
1368	-	45p. on 25p. red and yellow (1232)	55	25

525 Santiago Cathedral

1991. National Monuments.

1369	**525**	300p. black, pink & brn	5·50	2·00

526 Dish Aerial and Transmission Masts

1991. World Telecommunications Day.

1370	**526**	90p. multicoloured	1·50	60

527 Pope Leo XIII and Factory Line

1991. Centenary of "Rerum Novarum" (papal encyclical on workers' rights).

1371	**527**	100p. multicoloured	1·50	60

528 Capt. L. Pardo and Sir Ernest Shackleton

1991. Naval Tradition. 75th Anniv of Pardo's Rescue of Shackleton Expedition. Multicoloured.

1372	50p. Type **528**	65	35
1373	50p. "Yelcho" (coast-guard vessel)	65	35
1374	50p. Chilean sailor sighting stranded men on Elephant Island	65	35
1375	50p. "Endurance"	65	35
MS1376	89×109 mm. Nos. 1372/5	4·00	4·00

529 Flags and Globe

1991. 21st General Assembly of Organization of American States, Santiago.

1377	**529**	70p. multicoloured	1·10	45

530 Building and Police Officers

1991. Opening of New Police School.

1378	**530**	50p. Multicoloured	80	35

531 "Maipo" (container ship)

1991. National Merchant Navy Day.

1379	**531**	45p. black and red	65	25

532 Opening Ceremony

1991. 11th Pan-American Games, Havana. Mult.

1380	100p. Type **532**	1·50	70
1381	100p. Cycling, running and basketball competitors	1·50	70

533 Carriage and Building

1991. Bicentenary of Los Andes.

1382	**533**	100p. multicoloured	1·50	70

534 Common Octopus

1991. Marine Life. Multicoloured.

1383	50p. Type **534**	65	35
1384	50p. "Durvillaea antarctica"	65	35
1385	50p. Lenguado	65	35
1386	50p. "Austromegabalanus psittacus"	65	35
1387	50p. Barnacle rock shell ("Concholepas concholepas")	65	35
1388	50p. Crab ("Cancer setosus")	65	35
1389	50p. "Lessonia nigrescens"	65	35
1390	50p. Sea-urchin	65	35
1391	50p. Crab ("Homalaspis plana")	65	35
1392	50p. "Porphyra columbina"	65	35
1393	50p. Loro knife-jaw	65	35
1394	50p. "Chorus giganteus"	65	35
1395	50p. Rock shrimp	65	35
1396	50p. Peruvian anchovy	65	35
1397	50p. "Gracilaria sp."	65	35
1398	50p. "Pyura chilensis"	65	35

535 Nitrate Processing and Jose Balmaceda (President, 1886–91)

1991. Centenary of 1891 Revolution. Pre-Revolution Events. Multicoloured.

1399	100p. Type **535**	1·50	70
1400	100p. Education and Balmaceda	1·50	70

536 "Woman in Red" (Pedro Reszka)

1991. Paintings. Multicoloured.

1401	50p. Type **536**	80	35
1402	70p. "The Traveller" (Camilo Mori)	1·30	45
1403	200p. "Head of Child" (Benito Rebolledo)	3·50	1·30
1404	300p. "Child in Fez" (A. Valenzuela Puelma)	5·50	2·00

537 Map of South American Interests in Antartica

1991. 30th Anniv of Antarctic Treaty. Mult.

1405	80p. Type **537**	2·30	85
1406	80p. Wildlife	2·30	85

538 Globe in Envelope (Guillermo Suarez)

1991. International Letter Writing Week. Children's drawings. Multicoloured.

1407	45p. Type **538**	65	25
1408	70p. Human figures in envelope (Jorge Vargas)	1·10	45

539 Amerindians watching Columbus's Fleet

1991. America. Voyages of Discovery. Mult.

1409	50p. Type **539**	1·10	35
1410	150p. Columbus's fleet and navigator	3·25	95

540 Line Drawing of Neruda

1991. 20th Anniv of Award of Nobel Prize for Literature to Pablo Neruda. Multicoloured, colour of cap given.

1411	**540**	45p. blue	65	25
1412	**540**	45p. red	65	25
MS1413		90×105 mm. Nos. 1411/12	4·25	4·25

Nos. 1411/12 were issued together, se-tenant, the backgrounds of the stamps forming a composite design of one of Neruda's manuscripts.

541 Boy and Stars

1991. Christmas. Multicoloured.

1414	45p. Type **541**	65	35
1415	100p. Girl and stars	1·60	60

542 Postman making Delivery

1991. Christmas. (a) As T 542.

1416	**542**	45p. mauve and violet	65	25
1417	-	45p. mauve and violet	65	25

(b) Discount stamps. Additionally inscr "D.S. No 20" in left-hand margin.

1418	**542**	45p. mauve and violet	65	25
1419	-	45p. mauve and violet	65	25

DESIGN: Nos. 1417, 1419, Starlit town.

1992. No. 1238 surch $60.

1420	60p. on 45p. black & green	80	35

1992. Environmental Protection. As Nos. 1307/16 but values and colours changed. (a) As T 508, each yellow and green.

1421	60p. Type **508**	80	35
1422	60p. As No. 1308	80	35
1423	60p. As No. 1309	80	35
1424	60p. As No. 1310	80	35
1425	60p. As No. 1311	80	35

(b) Discount stamps. Additionally inscr "D.S. No 20". Each orange and green.

1426	60p. Type **508**	80	35
1427	60p. As No. 1308	80	35
1428	60p. As No. 1309	80	35
1429	60p. As No. 1310	80	35
1430	60p. As No. 1311	80	35

544 Houses and Figures

1992. 16th Population and Housing Census.

1431	**544**	60p. blue, orange & blk	80	35

545 Score and Mozart

1992. Death Bicentenary of Wolfgang Amadeus Mozart (composer). Multicoloured.

1432	60p. Type **545**	80	35
1433	200p. Mozart playing harpsichord	2·75	1·20
MS1434	90×104 mm. Nos. 1432/3	5·25	5·25

546 Stylized Jet Fighter

1992. "Fidae '92" International Air and Space Fair.

1435	**546**	60p. multicoloured	80	35

547 Arms and Church, San Jose de Maipo

1992. 200th (80p.) or 250th (others) Anniversaries of Cities. Multicoloured.

1436	80p. Type **547**	1·10	35
1437	90p. Pottery (Melipilla)	1·20	45
1438	100p. Lircunlauta House (San Fernando)	1·30	55
1439	150p. Fruits and woodsman (Cauquenes)	2·00	85
1440	250p. Huilquilemu Cultural Villa (Talca)	3·25	1·40

548 Chilean Pavilion

1992. "Expo '92" World's Fair, Seville. Mult.

1441	150p. Type **548**	1·90	85
1442	200p. Iceberg	2·40	1·20
MS1443	105×90 mm. Nos. 1441/2	6·00	6·00

549 "Morula praecipua", Maculated Conch and Dragon's-head Cowrie

1992. Marine Flora and Fauna of Easter Island. Multicoloured.

1444	60p. Type **549**	80	45
1445	60p. "Codium pocockiae"	80	45
1446	60p. Easter Island swordfish ("Myripristis tiki")	80	45
1447	60p. Seaweed	80	45
1448	60p. Fuentes' wrasse ("Pseudolabrus fuentesi")	80	45
1449	60p. Coral	80	45
1450	60p. Spiny lobster	80	45
1451	60p. Sea urchin	80	45

550 Statues, Liner and Launch

1992. Easter Island Tourism. Multicoloured.

1452	200p. Type **550**	2·40	1·10
1453	200p. Airplane, dancers and hill-carving	2·40	1·10

Nos. 1452/3 were issued together, se-tenant, forming a composite design.

551 Sun shining through Doorway and Handicapped People

1992. National Council for the Handicapped.

1454	**551**	60p. multicoloured	95	35

552 Flags and Emblem

1992. 50th Anniv of National Defence Staff.

1455	**552**	60p. multicoloured	95	35

553 "Simpson" (submarine)

1992. 75th Anniv of Chilean Submarine Fleet. Multicoloured.

1456	150p. Type **553**	2·10	95
1457	250p. Officer using periscope	3·50	1·50

1992. Discount stamp. As No. 1240 but additionally inscr "D/S No 20".

1458	60p. black and bistre	1·20	70

1992. Nos. 1350/3 surch $60.

1459	**487**	60p. on 45p. blue & mve	65	25
1460	-	60p. on 45p. red & mve	65	25
1461	**487**	60p. on 45p. blue & yell	65	25
1462	-	60p. on 45p. red & yell	65	25

1992. Nos. 1416/19 surch $60.

1463	**542**	60p. on 45p. mauve and violet (1416)	65	25
1464	-	60p. on 45p. mauve and violet (1417)	65	25
1465	**542**	60p. on 45p. mauve and violet (1418)	65	25
1466	-	60p. on 45p. mauve and violet (1419)	65	25

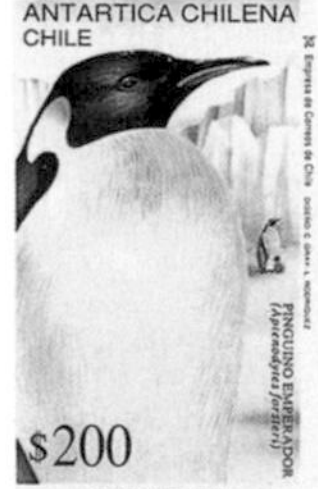

556 Emperor Penguin

1992. The Emperor Penguin. Multicoloured.

1467	200p. Type **556**	3·00	1·10
1468	250p. Adult and chick	3·75	1·30
MS1469	104×90 mm. Nos. 1467/8	9·25	9·25

557 Santiago Central Post Office

1992. National Monuments.

1470	**557**	200p. multicoloured	2·40	1·10

558 Columbus and Navigation Instruments

1992. America. 500th Anniv of Discovery of America by Columbus. Multicoloured.

1471	200p. Type **558**	2·40	1·10
1472	250p. Church, map of Americas and "Santa Maria"	3·00	1·30

559 Presenter at Microphone

1992. 70th Anniv of Chilean Radio.

1473	**559**	250p. multicoloured	3·00	1·30

560 O'Higgins, Flag and Monument

1992. 150th Death Anniv of Bernardo O'Higgins.

1474	**560**	60p. multicoloured	65	35

561 Arrau as a Child

1992. Claudio Arrau (pianist). Multicoloured.

1475	150p. Type **561**	1·90	85
1476	200p. Arrau playing piano	2·50	1·20
MS1477	105×90 mm. Nos. 1475/6	5·25	5·25

562 Statue

1992. 150th Anniv of University of Chile. Mult.

1478	200p. Type **562**	2·30	95
1479	200p. Coat of arms, statues and clock	2·30	95

Nos. 1478/9 were issued together, se-tenant, forming a composite design.

563 Nativity

1992. Christmas. (a) As T 563.

1480	**563**	60p. brown and stone	65	25
1481	-	60p. brown and stone	65	25

(b) Discount stamps. Additionally inscr "DS/20" in right-hand margin.

1482	**563**	60p. red and stone	65	25
1483	-	60p. red and stone	65	25

DESIGN: Nos. 1481, 1483, Nativity (different).

564 Dam

1992. 23rd Ministerial Meeting of Latin-American Energy Organization.
1484 **564** 70p. black and yellow 95 35

565 Hands and Stars

1992. National Human Rights Day.
1485 **565** 100p. multicoloured 1·20 60

566 Achao Church

1993. Churches. (a) As T 566.
1487 **566** 70p. black and pink 95 35
1488 - 70p. black and pink 95 35

(b) Discount stamps. Additionally inscr "DS/20" in left-hand margin.
1489 **566** 70p. black and yellow 95 35
1490 - 70p. black and yellow 95 35
DESIGN: Nos. 1488, 1490, Castro church.
See also Nos. 1507/15.

567 St. Ignatius de Loyola (founder)

1993. 400th Anniv of Jesuits' Arrival in Chile.
1491 **567** 200p. multicoloured 2·40 1·10
MS1492 105×90 mm. No. 1491 3·25 3·25

568 St. Teresa

1993. Canonization of St. Teresa of the Andes.
1493 **568** 300p. multicoloured 3·50 1·70

569 Finger-Puppets

1993. International Theatre Festival.
1494 **569** 250p. multicoloured 3·00 1·30

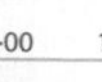

570 Satellite in Orbit

1993. 2nd Pan-American Space Conference.
1495 **570** 150p. multicoloured 1·90 85
MS1496 105×89 mm. No. 1495 4·25 4·25

571 Clotario Blest (Trade Union leader)

1993. Labour Day.
1497 **571** 70p. multicoloured 80 35

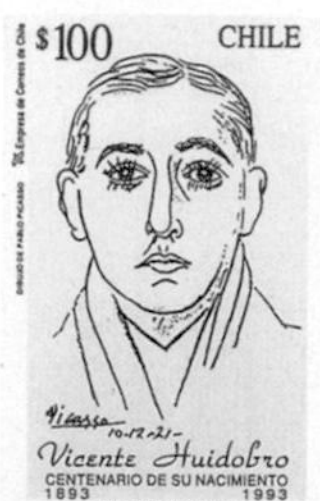

572 Drawing of Huidobro by Picasso

1993. Birth Centenary of Vicente Huidobro (poet). Each black, stone and red.
1498 100p. Type **572** 1·20 45
1499 100p. Drawing of Huidobro by Juan Gris 1·20 45

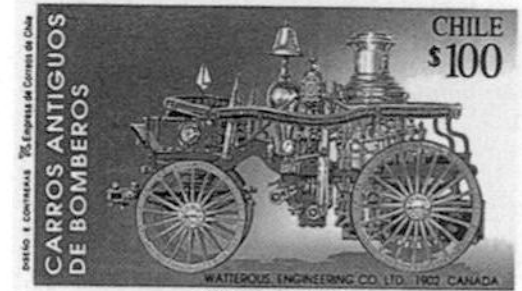

573 Watterous, 1902

1993. Fire Engines (1st series). Multicoloured.
1500 100p. Type **573** 1·30 60
1501 100p. Merryweather, 1872 1·30 60
MS1502 105×89 mm. Nos. 1500/1 4·75 4·75
See also Nos. 1577/80.

574 Douglas B-26 Invader

1993. Aviation and Space. Multicoloured.
1503 100p. Type **574** 1·10 45
1504 100p. Mirage M 50 Pantera 1·10 45
1505 100p. Sanchez Besa biplane 1·10 45
1506 100p. Bell-47 DI helicopter 1·10 45

1993. Churches. (a) As T 566.
1507 10p. black and green 25 10
1508 20p. black and brown 25 10
1509 30p. black and orange 25 10
1510 40p. black and blue 40 20
1511 50p. black and green 55 25
1512 80p. black and buff 95 45
1513 90p. black and green 1·00 55
1514 100p. black and grey 1·20 60

(b) Discount stamp. Additionally inscr "DS/20" at left.
1515 80p. black and lilac 95 45
1516 90p. black and red 1·00 55
1517 100p. black and yellow 1·20 60
CHURCHES: 10p. Chonchi; 20p. Vilupulli; 30p. Llau-Llao; 40p. Dalcahue; 50p. Tenaun; 80p. Quinchao; 90p. Quehui; 100p. Nercon.

575 Nortina

1993. Regional Variations of La Cueca (national dance). Multicoloured.
1525 70p. Type **575** 80 25
1526 70p. Central 80 25
1527 70p. Chilota 80 25

576 "Late Dawn" (Mario Carreno)

1993. Santiago, Iberian-American City of Culture 1993. Paintings. Multicoloured.
1528 80p. Type **576** 95 35
1529 90p. "Summer" (Gracia Barrios) 1·00 40
1530 150p. "Protection" (Roser Bru) (vert) 1·60 70
1531 200p. "Tango, Valparaiso" (Nemesio Antunez) 2·30 95

577 Early Coin Production

1993. 250th Anniv of Chilean Mint.
1532 **577** 250p. multicoloured 2·75 1·30
MS1533 105×90 mm. No. 1523 3·50 3·50

578 Patagonian Conure

1993. America. Endangered Animals. Mult.
1534 150p. Type **578** 1·90 70
1535 200p. Chilean guemal 2·50 95

579 Underground Train

1993. 25th Anniv of Chilean Metro.
1536 **579** 80p. multicoloured 95 35

580 "Ancud" (schooner) off Santa Ana Point

1993. 150th Anniv of Chilean Possession of Strait of Magellan.
1537 **580** 100p. multicoloured 1·80 45

581 Marines in Inflatable Assault Boats

1993. Naval Tradition. Multicoloured.
1538 80p. Type **581** (175th anniv of Marines) 95 45
1539 80p. Sailors making fast patrol boat (125th anniv of Alejandro Navarette Training School) 95 45
1540 80p. "Esmeralda" (cadet barquentine) and cadets in traditional "unloading the cannon" exercise (175th anniv of Arturo Prat Naval College) 95 45
1541 80p. "Sailing of First Squadron" (175th anniv) (painting, Alvaro Casanova Zenteno) 95 45

582 Carved Figures

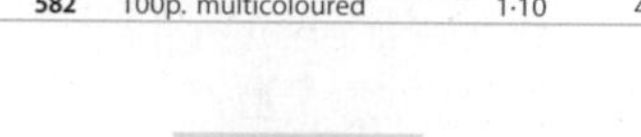

1993. International Year of Indigenous Peoples.
1542 **582** 100p. multicoloured 1·10 45

583 Holy Family

1993. Christmas. (a) Sold at face value.
1543 **583** 70p. lilac and stone 65 35

(b) Discount stamp. Additionally inscribed "DS/20" in right-hand margin.
1544 70p. blue and green 65 35

584 Adelie Penguins

1993. Chilean Antarctic Territory. Mult.
1545 200p. Type **584** 2·40 85
1546 250p. Adelie penguin with young 3·00 1·20
MS1547 105×89 mm. Nos. 1545/6 6·50 6·50

585 Plaza de Armas, Ancud

1993. City Anniversaries. Multicoloured.
1548 80p. Type **585** (225th) 80 35
1549 80p. Matriz church, Curico (250th) 80 35
1550 80p. Corner Pillar House, Rancagua (250th) 80 35

586 Hands

1994. International Year of the Family.

1551	**586**	100p. multicoloured	95	45

587 Violin

1994. 26th Music Weeks, Frutillar. Mult.

1552	150p. Type **587**	1·60	1·40
1553	150p. Cello	1·60	1·40

Nos. 1552/3 were issued together, se-tenant, forming a composite design.

588 Sukhoi Su-30 Flanker

1994. "Fidae '94" International Air and Space Fair. Multicoloured.

1554	300p. Type **588**	2·75	2·40
1555	300p. Vought Sikorsky OS2U3 Kingfisher seaplane	2·75	2·40
1556	300p. Lockheed F-117A Stealth	2·75	2·40
1557	300p. Northrop F-5E Tiger III	2·75	2·40

589 Ears of Grain

1994. 50th Anniv of Chile Agronomical Engineers' College.

1558	**589**	220p. multicoloured	2·30	1·10

1994. Nos. 1092/5 surch $80.

1559	80p. on 15p. green	65	25
1560	80p. on 15p. blue	65	25
1561	80p. on 15p. brown	65	25
1562	80p. on 15p. mauve	65	25

591 Skeletons buried under Cactus

1994. 75th Anniv of Concepcion University. Details of "Latin American Presence" (mural by Jorge Gonzalez Camarena). Multicoloured.

1563	250p. Type **591**	2·30	1·20
1564	250p. Faces	2·30	1·20
1565	250p. Building pyramid from spare parts	2·30	1·20
1566	250p. Cablework in building	2·30	1·20

Nos. 1563/6 were issued together, se-tenant, forming a composite design.

592 Gentoo Penguins and Harbour

1994. 30th Anniv of Chilean Antarctic Institute. Multicoloured.

1567	300p. Type **592**	2·75	1·40
1568	300p. Antarctic base	2·75	1·40

Nos. 1567/8 were issued together, se-tenant, forming a composite design.

593 "Vanessa terpsichore"

1994. Butterflies. Multicoloured.

1569	100p. Type **593**	70	45
1570	100p. "Hypsochila wagenknechti"	70	45
1571	100p. Polydamas swallowtail ("Battus polydamas")	70	45
1572	100p. "Polythysana apollina"	70	45
1573	100p. "Satyridae"	70	45
1574	100p. "Tetraphloebia stellygera"	70	45
1575	100p. "Eroessa chilensis"	70	45
1576	100p. Cloudless sulphur ("Phoebis sennae")	70	45

594 Merryweather Steam Fire Engine, 1869

1994. Fire Engines (2nd series). Mult.

1577	150p. Type **594**	1·40	70
1578	150p. Poniente steam fire engine, 1863	1·40	70
1579	150p. Mieusset steam fire engine, 1905	1·40	70
1580	150p. Merryweather motor fire engine, 1903	1·40	70

595 Bust and Banner

1994. Centenary of Javiera Carrera School for Girls, Santiago.

1581	**595**	200p. multicoloured	2·10	95

596 Door Panels, Porvenir (centenary)

1994. Town Anniversaries. Multicoloured.

1582	90p. Type **596**	85	35
1583	100p. Railway station, Villa Alemana (cent)	1·10	45
1584	150p. Church, Constitucion (bicentenary)	1·50	70
1585	200p. Fountain and church, Linares (bicent)	2·20	95
1586	250p. Steam locomotive and statue, Copiapo (250th)	2·75	1·20
1587	300p. La Serena (450th)	3·25	1·40

597 Painting by Carlos Maturana

1994. 20th International Very Large Data Bases Conference, Santiago.

1588	**597**	100p. multicoloured	1·10	50

1994. Nos. 1487/8 and 1544 surch $80.

1589	**566**	80p. on 70p. blk & pink	95	35
1590	-	80p. on 70p. blk & pink	95	35
1591	**583**	80p. on 70p. blue & grn	95	35

599 First Chilean Mail Van

1994. America. Postal Transport. Mult.

1592	80p. Type **599**	85	50
1593	220p. De Havilland D.H.60G Gipsy Moth (first Chilean mail plane)	2·50	1·10

600 Fr. Hurtado

1994. Beatification of Fr. Alberto Hurtado.

1594	**600**	300p. blue, green & blk	3·00	1·80

601 Madonna and Child

1994. Christmas. (a) Sold at face value.

1595	**601**	80p. multicoloured	85	35

(b) Discount stamp. Additionally inscribed "DS/20" at foot.

1596	80p. multicoloured	85	35

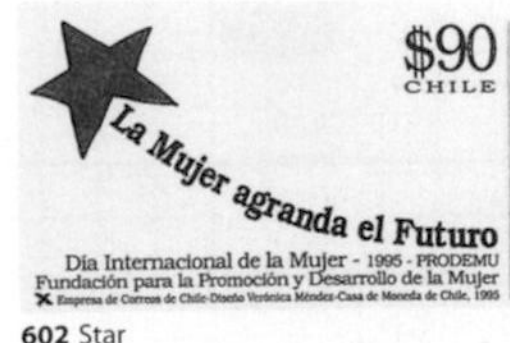

602 Star

1995. International Women's Day. Mult.

1597	90p. Type **602**	95	35
1598	90p. Moon and sun	95	35
1599	90p. Dove	95	35
1600	90p. Earth	95	35

603 "Almirante Williams" (destroyer)

1995. Naval Tradition.

1601	**603**	100p. multicoloured	1·10	50

604 Emblem

1995. United Nations World Summit for Social Development, Copenhagen.

1602	**604**	150p. multicoloured	1·70	75

605 Arms

1995. 150th Anniv of Conciliar Seminary of Ancud.

1603	**605**	200p. multicoloured	2·10	1·00

606 Stained Glass Window, Santiago Cathedral

1995. 400th Anniv of Augustinian Order in Chile.

1604	**606**	250p. multicoloured	2·50	1·20

607 Religious Mask, Limari

1995. Rock Paintings. Multicoloured.

1605	150p. Type **607**	95	60
1606	150p. Herdsmen and llamas, Taira	95	60
1607	150p. Whale, Tal-tal	95	60
1608	150p. Masks, Encanto Valley	95	60

608 Camera and Director's Chair

1995. Centenary of Motion Pictures. Mult.

1609		100p. Type **608**	1·20	50
1610		100p. Advertising poster for "The Kid"	1·20	50
1611		100p. Early cinema advertising poster	1·20	50
1612		100p. Advertising poster for "Valparaiso Mi Amor"	1·20	50

609 Arms and Express Steam Train

1995. Bicentenary of Parral.

1613	**609**	200p. multicoloured	2·50	1·10

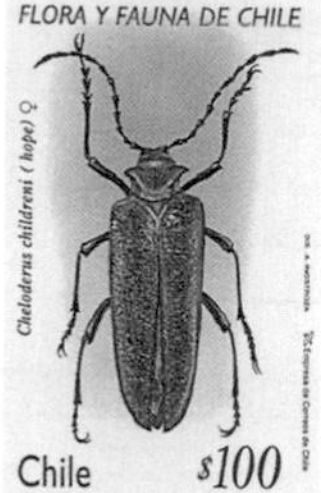

610 "Cheloderus childreni"

1995. Flora and Fauna. Multicoloured.

1614		100p. Type **610**	1·10	50
1615		100p. "Eulychnia acida" (cactus)	1·10	50
1616		100p. "Chiasognathus grantii" (stag beetle)	1·10	50
1617		100p. "Browningia candelaris" (cactus)	1·10	50
1618		100p. "Capiapoa dealbata" (cactus)	1·10	50
1619		100p. "Acanthinodera cummingi" (beetle)	1·10	50
1620		100p. "Neoporteria subgibbosa" (cactus)	1·10	50
1621		100p. "Semiotus luteipennis" (beetle)	1·10	50

611 Congress Emblem

1995. 2nd World Police Congress, Santiago.

1622	**611**	200p. multicoloured	2·50	1·00

612 "Tower of Babel V" (Mario Toral)

1995. 30th Anniv of Ministry of Housing and Town-planning.

1623	**612**	200p. multicoloured	2·50	1·00

613 Bello

1995. 25th Anniv of Andres Bello Agreement (South American co-operation in education, science and culture).

1624	**613**	250p. purple and black	2·75	1·20

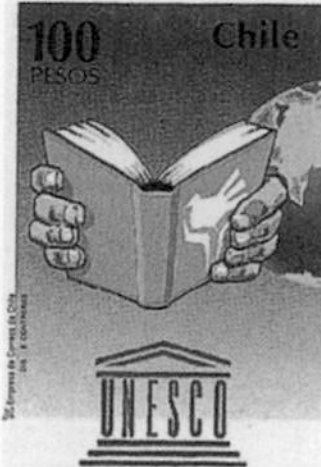

614 Open Book and Emblem

1995. 50th Anniversaries. Multicoloured.

1625		100p. Type **614** (UNESCO)	1·10	50
1626		100p. Globes and handshake (UNO)	1·10	50
1627		100p. Seedling in hand (FAO)	1·10	50

Nos. 1625/7 were issued together, se-tenant, forming a composite design.

615 Farming (M. Cruces)

1995. America. Environmental Protection. Children's Paintings. Multicoloured.

1628		100p. Type **615**	1·20	50
1629		250p. Forestry (E. Munoz) (horiz)	3·00	1·30

616 Sailing Ship and Cape Horn

1995. 51st World Congress of Cape Horn Captains.

1630	**616**	250p. multicoloured	2·50	1·30

617 Crib and Inhabitants of North Chile

1995. Christmas. (a) Sold at face value.

1631	**617**	90p. blue and violet	95	35
1632	-	90p. blue and violet	95	35

(b) Discount stamps. Additionally inscr "DS/20".

1633	**617**	90p. green and purple	95	35
1634	-	90p. green and purple	95	35

DESIGNS: Nos. 1632, 1634, Crib and people of South Chile.

618 Carlos Dittborn (trainer) and Arica Stadium

1995. Centenary of Chile Football Federation. Mult.

1635		100p. Type **618**	1·10	50
1636		100p. Hugo Lepe (player)	1·10	50
1637		100p. Eladio Rojas (player)	1·10	50
1638		100p. Honorino Landa (player)	1·10	50

619 Mistral

1995. 50th Anniv of Award of Nobel Prize for Literature to Gabriela Mistral.

1639	**619**	300p. blue and black	3·00	1·50

620 Penguins

1995. Chilean Antarctic Territory. The Macaroni Penguin. Multicoloured.

1640		100p. Type **620**	1·80	50
1641		250p. Penguins (different)	3·75	1·20
MS1642		105×90 mm. Nos. 1640/1	7·50	7·50

621 Kiwi Fruit and Container Ship

1995. 60th Anniv of Chilean Exports Association. Fruit. Multicoloured.

1643		100p. Type **621**	1·10	50
1644		100p. Grapes and container ship	1·10	50
1645		100p. Peaches and container ship	1·10	50
1646		100p. Apples and container ship	1·10	50
1647		100p. Soft fruit and airplane	1·10	50

622 "Reunion" (Mario Toral)

1995. 50th Anniv of End of Second World War.

1648	**622**	200p. multicoloured	2·10	85

623 Oil Rig

1995. 50th Anniv of Discovery of Oil in Chile. Multicoloured.

1649		100p. Type **623**	95	50
1650		100p. Concon Refinery (grass in foreground)	95	50
1651		100p. Concepcion Refinery	95	50
1652		100p. Rig (different)	95	50

624 Embraer EMB-145

1996. "FIDAE '96" International Air and Space Fair, Santiago. Aircraft. Multicoloured.

1653		400p. Type **624**	4·25	1·80
1654		400p. Mirage M5M Elkan	4·25	1·80
1655		400p. De Havilland D.H.C. 6 Twin Otter	4·25	1·80
1656		400p. Saab JAS-39 Gripen	4·25	1·80

625 School

1996. 175th Anniv of Serena Boys' School.

1657	**625**	100p. multicoloured	1·10	50

626 Old Cordoba Rail Station, Seville

1996. "Espamer" and "Aviation and Space" Spanish and Latin American Stamp Exhibitions, Seville, Spain. Multicoloured.

1658		200p. Type **626**	2·10	1·10
1659		200p. Lope de Vega Theatre, Seville	2·10	1·10

627 Extinguish Matches Properly

1996. Safety Precautions. Multicoloured. (a) Accidents in the Home.

1660		50p. Type **627**	70	25
1661		50p. Do not leave boiling water unattended	70	25
1662		50p. Keep sharp objects away from children	70	25
1663		50p. Protect electrical sockets	70	25
1664		50p. Do not improvise electrical connections	70	25
1665		50p. Do not play the television or radio too loud	70	25
1666		50p. Check gas connections regularly	70	25
1667		50p. Do not overload electrical circuits	70	25
1668		50p. Keep inflammable materials away from fire	70	25
1669		50p. Do not leave toys lying around on the floor	70	25

(b) Road Safety.

1670		50p. Use crossings	70	25
1671		50p. Obey the instructions of the traffic police	70	25
1672		50p. Only cross on the green light	70	25
1673		50p. Wait on the pavement for buses	70	25
1674		50p. Do not cross the road between vehicles	70	25
1675		50p. Do not travel on the step of buses	70	25
1676		50p. Walk on the side of the road facing on-coming traffic	70	25
1677		50p. Look out for drains	70	25
1678		50p. Do not play ball in the road	70	25
1679		50p. Bicyclists should obey the Highway Code	70	25

(c) Safety at School.

1680		50p. Do not panic in emergencies	70	25
1681		50p. Do not run around corners	70	25

1682 50p. Do not play practical jokes 70 25
1683 50p. Do not sit on banisters or railings 70 25
1684 50p. Do not run on the stairs 70 25
1685 50p. Do not drink while walking 70 25
1686 50p. Do not swing on your chair 70 25
1687 50p. Do not play with pointed or sharp objects 70 25
1688 50p. Do not open doors sharply 70 25
1689 50p. Go straight home after school and do not stop to talk to strangers 70 25

(d) Safety in the Workplace.

1690 50p. Wear protective clothing 70 25
1691 50p. Do not work with tools in bad condition 70 25
1692 50p. Keep your attention on your work (man at lathe) 70 25
1693 50p. Always use the proper tools 70 25
1694 50p. Work carefully (man at filing cabinet) 70 25
1695 50p. Do not leave objects on the stairs 70 25
1696 50p. Do not carry so much that you cannot see where you are going 70 25
1697 50p. Check ladders are safe 70 25
1698 50p. Always keep the work-place clean and tidy 70 25
1699 50p. Remove old nails first 70 25

(e) Enjoy Leisure Safely.

1700 50p. Only swim in the permitted areas 70 25
1701 50p. Do not put any part of the body out of the window of a moving vehicle 70 25
1702 50p. Avoid excessive exposure to the sun 70 25
1703 50p. Do not contaminate swimming water with detergents 70 25
1704 50p. Do not throw litter 70 25
1705 50p. Always put out fires before leaving them 70 25
1706 50p. Do not play pranks in water 70 25
1707 50p. Check safety precautions 70 25
1708 50p. Do not fly kites near overhead electrical lines 70 25
1709 50p. Do not run by the side of swimming pools 70 25

(f) Alcohol and Drugs Awareness.

1710 50p. Do not drink and drive 70 25
1711 50p. Do not drink if you are pregnant 70 25
1712 50p. Do not give in to peer pressure 70 25
1713 50p. Being under the influence of alcohol is irresponsible in the workplace 70 25
1714 50p. Do not destroy your family through alcohol 70 25
1715 50p. You do not need drugs to have a good time 70 25
1716 50p. You do not need drugs to succeed 70 25
1717 50p. You do not need drugs to entertain 70 25
1718 50p. Do not abandon your friends and family for drugs 70 25
1719 50p. Without drugs you are free and safe 70 25

628 "Esmeralda" (cadet barquentine) in Dry-dock

1996. Centenary of Dry-dock No. 1, Talcahuano.
1720 **628** 200p. multicoloured 2·20 85

629 "Weather Rose" (Ricardo Mesa)

1996. Modern Sculpture. Multicoloured.
1721 150p. Type **629** 1·70 60
1722 150p. "Friendship" (Francisca Cerda) 1·70 60
1723 200p. "Memory" (Fernando Undurraga) (horiz) 2·10 85
1724 200p. "Andean Airs" (Benito Rojo) (horiz) 2·10 85

630 Addict and Syringe full of Pills

1996. International Day against Drug Abuse.
1725 **630** 250p. multicoloured 3·00 1·30

631 Boxing Glove

1996. Centenary of National Olympic Committee and Modern Olympic Games. Olympic Games, Atlanta. Multicoloured.
1726 450p. Type **631** 4·75 2·10
1727 450p. Running shoe 4·75 2·10
1728 450p. Rollerblade 4·75 2·10
1729 450p. Ball 4·75 2·10

632 School

1996. 150th Anniv of San Fernando School.
1730 **632** 200p. multicoloured 2·30 1·00

633 Polluted Forest

1996. 4th International Congress on Earth Sciences. Multicoloured.
1731 200p. Type **633** 2·10 85
1732 200p. Industrial pollution 2·10 85
1733 200p. Deforestation 2·10 85
1734 200p. Map, camera and cracked earth 2·10 85

Nos. 1731/4 were issued together, se-tenant, forming a composite design.

634 Crookesite and Open-cast Mine

1996. Mining. Multicoloured.
1735 150p. Type **634** 1·50 60
1736 150p. Lapis lazuli and pendant 1·50 60
1737 150p. Bornite and calcium and crates 1·50 60
1738 150p. Azurite and atacamite 1·50 60

635 St. John Leonardi (founder)

1996. 50th Anniv of Order of Mother of God in Chile.
1739 **635** 200p. multicoloured 2·30 1·00

636 German-style Wooden house and Mt. Osorno

1996. 150th Anniv of German Immigration. Multicoloured.
1740 250p. Type **636** 3·00 1·20
1741 300p. "German Fountain" (monument) 3·50 1·50

637 King Penguins

1996. Chilean Antarctic Territory. Mult.
1742 250p. Type **637** 3·00 1·20
1743 300p. Adult and young king penguins 3·50 1·50
MS1744 105×90 mm. Nos. 1742/3 8·25 8·25

638 Lancia Fire Engine, 1937

1996. Centenary of Castro Fire Service. Mult.
1745 200p. Type **638** 1·70 85
1746 200p. Ford V8 fire engine, 1940 1·70 85
1747 200p. Gorlitz G. A. Fischer 4-speed motor pump, 1930s 1·70 85
1748 200p. Lever-action pump, 1907 1·70 85

639 Rafting, Vicente Perez Rosales National Park

1996. National Parks. Multicoloured.
1749 100p. Type **639** 95 50
1750 100p. Horse riding, Torres del Paine National Park 95 50
1751 100p. Cross-country skiing, Puyehue National Park 95 50
1752 100p. Walking, Pan de Azucar National Park 95 50

640 Latorre and "Almirante Latorre" (destroyer)

1996. 150th Birth Anniv of Admiral Juan Jose Latorre.
1753 **640** 200p. multicoloured 2·30 1·00

641 Women with Child

1996. America. Costumes. Multicoloured.
1754 100p. Type **641** 95 50
1755 100p. Men with horse 95 50
1756 250p. Men on horseback 2·75 1·20

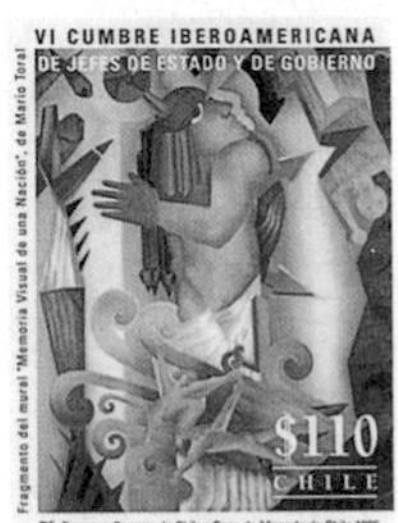

642 "Visual History of a Nation" (Mario Toral) (left-hand detail)

1996. 6th Ibero-Latin American Heads of State Summit, Santiago. Multicoloured.
1757 110p. Type **642** 1·20 60
1758 110p. Right-hand detail of painting 1·20 60

Nos. 1757/8 were issued together, se-tenant, forming a composite design.

643 Beach, Arms and Cathedral, Arica

1996. Cities. 1st Anniv of Arica Law. Multicoloured.
1759 100p. Type **643** 1·10 60
1760 150p. Llamas and Chilean flamingoes, Parinacota Province 1·70 75

644 The Three Kings

1996. Christmas. (a) Face value in black.
1761 **644** 100p. multicoloured 1·10 50

(b) Discount stamp. Additionally inscribed "DS/20" at foot and with face value in orange.
1762 100p. multicoloured 1·10 50

645 Pablo Neruda (poet), Gabriela Mistral (writer) and Nobel Prize Medal

1996. Visit of King and Queen of Sweden.
1763 **645** 300p. multicoloured 3·50 1·50

646 Children, Star and Globe

1996. 50th Anniv of UNICEF.
1764 **646** 200p. multicoloured 2·30 1·00

647 Church

1997. Centenary of Frontera Region. Mult.
1765 110p. Type **647** (centenary of Christian and Missionary Church Alliance) 1·20 60
1766 110p. Mountain valley (cent of Lonquimay Municipality) 1·20 60

648 Base Camp

1997. 50th Anniv of Arturo Prat Antarctic Naval Base.
1767 250p. Type **648** 3·00 1·20
1768 300p. Monument and flags (horiz) 3·50 1·50

649 La Pincoya

1997. Mythology. (a) As T 649.
1769 40p. black and blue 40 35
1770 110p. black and orange 1·20 60

(b) Discount stamp. Additionally inscr "DS/20".
1778 110p. black and green 1·20 60
DESIGN: Nos. 1770, 1778, La Fiura.

650 "Justice" and National Flag

1997. 70th Anniv of Controller General.
1781 **650** 110p. multicoloured 3·00 50

651 Train in Station

1997. Inauguration of Metro Line No. 5.
1782 **651** 200p. multicoloured 2·30 1·00

652 Masonic Symbols and Flags

1997. 50th Anniv of Interamerican Masonic Confederation and 17th Grand General Assembly, Santiago.
1783 250p. Type **652** 3·00 1·20
MS1784 85×105 mm. 1200p. Dividers, set-square and book (48×59 mm) 14·00 14·00

653 Von Stephan

1997. Death Centenary of Heinrich von Stephan (founder of Universal Postal Union).
1785 **653** 250p. multicoloured 3·00 1·20

654 Books

1997. World Books and Copyright Day.
1786 **654** 110p. multicoloured 1·20 60

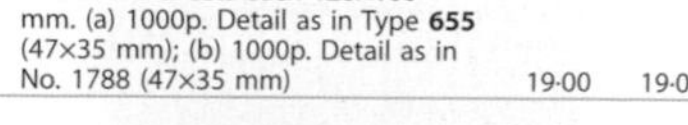

655 "Death to the Invader, Chile"

1997. Birth Centenary of David Alfaro Siqueiros (painter). Designs showing details of his murals in the Mexican School, Chillan, Chile. Multicoloured.
1787 150p. Type **655** 2·30 60
1788 200p. "Death to the Invader, Mexico" 2·75 85
MS1789 Two sheets each 120×100 mm. (a) 1000p. Detail as in Type **655** (47×35 mm); (b) 1000p. Detail as in No. 1788 (47×35 mm) 19·00 19·00

656 Arms and Town Hall

1997. Centenary of Providencia.
1790 **656** 250p. multicoloured 2·50 1·30

657 Pacific Ocean and Mt. Osorno (after Hokusai Katsushika)

1997. Centenary of Chile–Japan Relations.
1791 **657** 300p. multicoloured 3·00 1·70

658 Award, National Flag and "Thumbs-up" Sign

1997. National Centre for Productivity and Quality.
1792 **658** 110p. multicoloured 1·20 60

659 Transmission from University of Chile to "El Mercurio" (newspaper) Offices

1997. 75th Anniv of First Radio Broadcast in Chile.
1793 **659** 110p. multicoloured 1·20 60

660 Postman on Bicycle, 1997

1997. America. The Postman. Multicoloured.
1794 110p. Type **660** 1·20 60
1795 250p. Late 19th-century mounted postman 3·00 1·30

661 Carlo Morelli in "Rigoletto"

1997. Opera Singers. Multicoloured.
1796 120p. Type **661** 1·50 60
1797 200p. Pedro Navia in "La Boheme" 2·50 1·00
1798 250p. Renato Zanelli in "Faust" 3·25 1·50
1799 300p. Rayen Quitral in "The Magic Flute" 3·75 1·60
1800 500p. Ramon Vinay in "Othello" 6·50 2·75

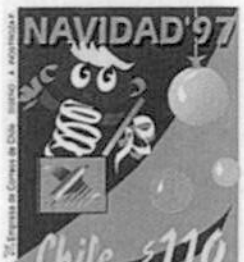

662 Jack-in-a-Box and Baubles on Tree

1997. Christmas. (a) "NAVIDAD '97" in blue.
1801 **662** 110p. multicoloured 1·20 50

(b) Discount stamp. "NAVIDAD '97" in orange and additionally inscr "D/S 20" below face value.
1802 110p. multicoloured 1·20 50

663 Cancelling Letters

1997. 250th Anniv of Postal Service in Chile. Multicoloured.
1803 120p. Type **663** 1·10 60
1804 300p. Man posting letter 3·00 1·50

664 Great Dane

1998. Dogs. Multicoloured. (a) As T 664.
1805 120p. Type **664** 70 60
1806 120p. Dalmatian 70 60

(b) Discount stamps. Additionally inscr "DS/20".
1807 120p. Type **664** 70 60
1808 120p. As No. 1806 70 60

665 Prat and "Esmeralda" (sail corvette)

1998. 150th Birth Anniv of Captain Arturo Prat Chacon.
1809 **665** 120p. multicoloured 1·20 60

666 Summit Emblem

1998. 2nd Summit of the Americas, Santiago. Mult.
1810 150p. Type **666** 1·40 75
MS1811 114×88 mm. 1000p. Summit emblem (26×41 mm) 9·75 9·75

667 Vets treating Horse

1998. Centenary of Army Veterinary Service. Mult.
1812 250p. Type **667** 2·50 1·20
1813 350p. Vet using stethoscope on horse 3·50 1·70

668 "Los Zambos de Calama" (Mauricio Moran)

1998. Paintings. Multicoloured.

1814	350p. Type **668**	3·25	1·70
1815	400p. "Soaking Watermelon" (Roser Bru)	3·50	2·00

669 Monk writing in Book

1998. 150th Anniv of Capuchin Order in Chile. Multicoloured.

1816	150p. Type **669**	1·40	75
1817	250p. Monk treating man's leg	2·30	1·20

670 Players

1998. World Cup Football Championship, France. Multicoloured.

1818	250p. Type **670**	2·30	1·20
1819	350p. Players and trophy	3·00	1·70
1820	500p. Players and map of France	4·75	2·40
1821	700p. Attacker and goalkeeper	6·50	3·25
MS1822	114×89 mm. 1500p. Player with ball (vert)	14·00	14·00

671 Bearded Penguin and Emblem

1998. 25th Meeting of Scientific Committee on Antarctic Research (1823) and 10th Meeting of Council of Managers of National Antarctic Programmes (1824), Concepcion. Multicoloured.

1823	250p. Type **671**	2·50	1·20
1824	350p. Two Gentoo penguins on map of Antarctica and emblem	3·50	1·70

672 Lighthouse

1998. International Year of the Ocean (1st issue). 150th Anniv of General Office for Territorial Waters and the Merchant Navy.

1825	**672**	500p. multicoloured	4·75	2·40

673 Iceberg and Ocean

1998. International Year of the Ocean (2nd issue).

1826	**673**	400p. blue, violet and black	4·25	1·80
1827	-	400p. blue, violet and black	4·25	1·80
1828	-	500p. multicoloured	5·00	2·10

DESIGNS: No. 1827, Compass rose, map of South Chile and ocean; 1828, Easter Island monolith and ocean.

674 Clara Solovera

1998. Composers and Folk Singers. Multicoloured.

1829	200p. Type **674**	1·70	85
1830	250p. Francisco Flores del Campo	2·10	1·00
1831	300p. Victor Jara	2·50	1·30
1832	350p. Violeta Parra	2·75	1·50

675 Delivery to Letter Box and Dog

1998. World Stamp Day.

1833	**675**	250p. multicoloured	2·10	1·00

676 Bilbao

1998. 175th Birth Anniv of Francisco Bilbao (writer).

1834	**676**	250p. purple, blue and orange	2·75	1·20

677 Amanda Labarca (educationist)

1998. America. Famous Women.

1835	**677**	120p. mauve, blue and black	1·10	60
1836	-	250p. yellow, mauve and black	2·30	1·00

DESIGN: 250p. Marta Brunet (writer).

678 "Self-portrait" (Augusto Eguiluz)

1998. Paintings. Multicoloured.

1837	300p. Type **678**	2·30	1·30
1838	450p. "Solitary Tree" (Agustin Abarca) (horiz)	3·50	2·00
MS1839	105×90 mm. 1500p. "Two Nudes" (Henriette Petit)	12·50	12·50

679 Arms and University

1998. 70th Anniv of Valparaiso Catholic University.

1840	**679**	130p. multicoloured	1·10	60

680 Rufous-collared Sparrow

1998. Birds. Multicoloured.

1841	10p. Type **680**	40	10
1842	20p. Austral blackbird	40	10
1845	50p Magellanic woodpecker (vert)	55	20
1849	100p Peregrine falcon (vert)	85	50

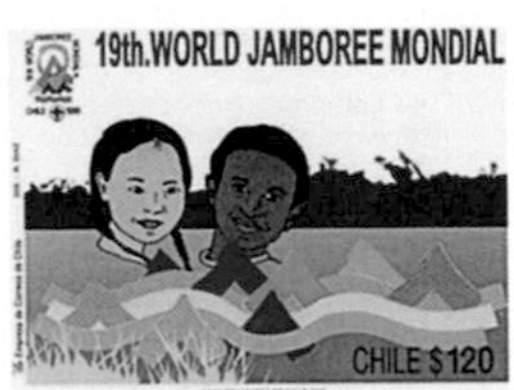

681 Children and Tents

1998. 19th World Scout Jamboree, Picarquin. Mult.

1856	120p. Type **681**	95	50
1857	200p. Lord Baden-Powell (founder of Scout movement)	1·70	85
1858	250p. Tents and doves	2·10	1·00
1859	300p. Scout, tents and globe	2·30	1·30
1860	1000p. Emblem and singsong (vert)	8·25	4·25
MS1861	127×105 mm. 3000p. Jamboree emblems and layout of camp	22·00	22·00

682 Capt. Alberto Larraguibel and Horse

1999. 50th Anniv of World Equestrian High Jump Record.

1862	**682**	200p. multicoloured	1·70	85

683 Fire Engine, 1900

1999. Centenary of Temuco Fire Department. Mult.

1863	140p. Type **683**	95	60
1864	200p. Ford fire engine, 1929	1·50	1·00
1865	300p. Ford K 1800 fire engine, 1955	2·30	1·20
1866	350p. Mercedes Benz fire engine, 1967	2·75	1·50
MS1867	119×100 mm. 1500p. Fireman with boy (vert)	12·50	12·50

684 Chamber

1999. 1000th Session of Chilean Chamber of Deputies.

1868	**684**	140p. multicoloured	1·10	60

685 Facade

1999. 150th Anniv of Sagrados College.

1869	**685**	250p. multicoloured	2·10	1·10

686 Pedro Aguirre Cerda (Chilean President, 1938–41)

1999. 60th Anniv of Economic Development Corporation.

1870	**686**	140p. multicoloured	1·20	60

687 Man with Sphere on Shoulder

1999. Centenary of Chilean Insurance Association.

1871	**687**	140p. multicoloured	1·10	60

1999. Centenary of Barcelona Football Club. Sheet 103×88 mm.

MS1872 **688**	1000p. multicoloured	7·50	7·50

689 Weddell Seal and Blue-eyed Cormorants

1999. Antarctica. Multicoloured.

1873	360p. Type **689**	2·75	1·70
1874	450p. Bearded penguin	3·50	2·20
MS1875	89×105 mm. 1500p. Kerguelen fur seal (35×47 mm)	11·00	11·00

690 Easter Island, Dancers, Ship and Figures

1999. Easter Island.

1876	**690**	360p. multicoloured	2·75	1·70

691 Business and Arts School

1999. 150th Anniv of Santiago University. Mult.

1877	140p. Type **691**	1·10	60
1878	250p. State Technical University	1·90	1·20
1879	300p. Woman using microscope, computer and building	2·50	2·10

692 J. L. Molina (naturalist), Statue of Humboldt, Mountains and Llamas

1999. Bicentenary of Alexander von Humboldt's Exploration of South America. Multicoloured.

1880	300p. Type **692**	2·50	1·50
1881	360p. Rodulfo A. Philippi (medical doctor and naturalist), statue of Humboldt and humboldt penguins	3·00	1·60

693 Cardinal Silva and Crucifix

1999. Cardinal Raul Silva Henrique Commemoration. Multicoloured.

1882	140p. Type **693**	1·20	60
1883	200p. Silva and image of Christ	1·50	85

694 Chinese and Chilean Flags with Pagoda

1999. "China 1999" International Stamp Exhibition, Peking. Multicoloured.

1884	140p. Type **694**	1·10	60
1885	450p. Chinese and Chilean Flags with junk	3·25	2·10
MS1886	120×100 mm. 1500p. Great Wall, China (59×47 mm)	12·00	12·00

695 Our Lady of the Rosary Church Tower, Train and Arms

1999. Centenary of Quilpue City.

1887	**695**	250p. multicoloured	2·20	1·10

696 Nurse and Donor

1999. Red Cross Blood Donation Campaign.

1888	**696**	140p. multicoloured	1·10	60

697 People in Glass Ball

1999. 75th Anniv of Employment Legislation.

1889	**697**	320p. multicoloured	2·30	1·30

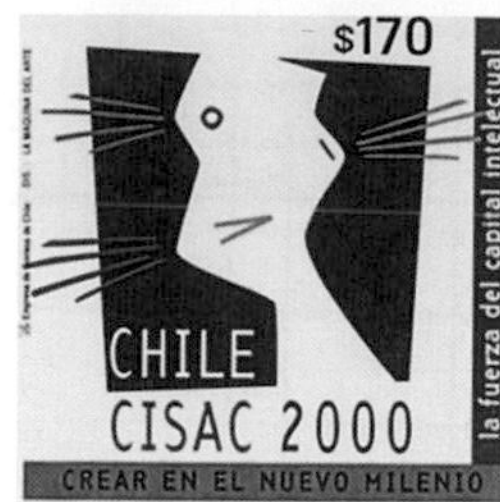

698 Emblem

1999. 42nd International Congress of Confederation of Authors' and Composers' Societies, Santiago.

1890	**698**	170p. multicoloured	1·40	75

699 Elderly Couple watching Children

1999. International Year of Elderly Persons.

1891	**699**	250p. multicoloured	1·90	1·10

700 Post Box, 1854

1999. 125th Anniv of Universal Postal Union. Multicoloured.

1892	300p. Type **700**	2·30	1·20
1893	360p. Gold coloured post box, 1900	2·75	1·50

701 Bomb releasing Doves

1999. America. A New Millennium without Arms. Multicoloured.

1894	140p. Type **701**	1·10	60
1895	320p. Broken bomb	2·30	1·30

702 Felipe Herrera Lane (first President, 1960–71) and Projects

1999. 40th Anniv of Inter-American Development Bank.

1896	**702**	360p. multicoloured	2·75	1·50

703 Globe and Chilean Flag

1999. Holy Year 2000.

1897	**703**	450p. multicoloured	3·25	2·10

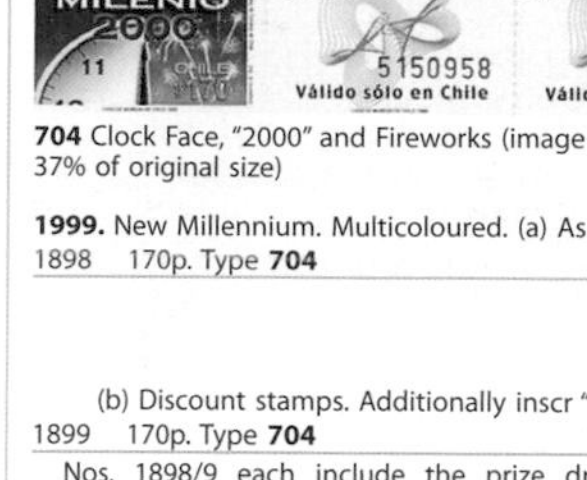

704 Clock Face, "2000" and Fireworks (image scaled to 37% of original size)

1999. New Millennium. Multicoloured. (a) As T 704.

1898	170p. Type **704**	1·40	85

(b) Discount stamps. Additionally inscr "D.S. 20".

1899	170p. Type **704**	1·40	85

Nos. 1898/9 each include the prize draw coupons shown in T **704**.

705 Recabarren and Blest

1999. Trade Union Leaders. Multicoloured.

1900	200p. Type **705**	1·50	1·00
1901	200p. Jimenez and Bustos	1·50	1·00

Nos. 1900/1 were issued together, se-tenant, forming a composite design.

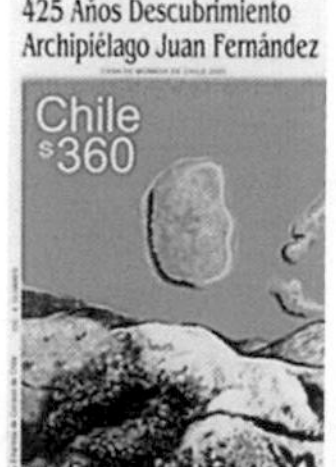

706 Mountains and Map of Islands

2000. Discovery of Juan Fernandez Archipelago. Multicoloured.

1902	360p. Type **706**	2·10	1·80
1903	360p. Mountains and map of islands (different)	2·10	1·80
1904	360p. Fernandez firecrown and mountains	2·10	1·80
1905	360p. *Rhaphythamnus venustus* (plant)	2·10	1·80
1906	360p. Lobster	2·10	1·80
1907	360p. Antennae of lobster and anchored boat	2·10	1·80
1908	360p. Plant and boat	2·10	1·80
1909	360p. *Gavilea insularis* (orchid)	2·10	1·80

Nos. 1902/9 were issued together, se-tenant, forming a composite design.

707 Condorito celebrating

2000. 50th Anniv (1999) of Condorito (cartoon character) by Rene Rios. Multicoloured.

1910	150p. Type **707**	1·10	75
1911	260p. Playing football	1·90	1·30
1912	480p. As a fireman	3·50	2·50
1913	980p. On horseback	7·50	5·25
MS1914	120×100 mm. 2000p. With other characters (47×35 mm)	15·00	15·00

708 Dancer and Local Crafts

2000. Easter Island. Multicoloured.

1915	200p. Type **708**	1·40	1·10
1916	260p. Statue and rock carving	1·80	1·30
1917	340p. Statue and man wearing headdress	2·30	1·80
1918	480p. Dancer and text	3·25	2·40

709 Steam Locomotive and Pot

2000. Centenary of Carahue. Multicoloured.

1919	220p. Type **709**	1·50	1·20
1920	220p. Potato tubers and plant	1·50	1·20

Nos. 1919/20 were issued together, se-tenant, forming a composite design.

710 Iguanodon

2000. Discount stamps. Prehistoric Animals. Mult.

1921	150p. Type **710**	95	75
1922	150p. Plesiosaur	95	75
1923	150p. Titanosaurus	95	75
1924	150p. Milodon	95	75

711 Emblem, Printing Press and Office

2000. Centenary of El Mercurio (newspaper).

1925	**711**	370p. multicoloured	2·50	1·80

712 Emblems

2000. 4th National Masonic Lodge Congress.

1926	**712**	460p. multicoloured	3·25	2·30

713 *Quillaja saponaria*

2000. Medicinal Plants. Multicoloured.

1927	200p. Type **713**	1·40	1·00
1928	360p. *Fabiana imbricata*	2·30	1·80

714 Map and Butterfly

2000. 500th Anniv of Discovery of Brazil. Mult.

1929	260p. Type **714**	2·50	1·30
MS1930	89×99 mm. 1500p. Monkey, child's face and parrots (47×35 mm)	10·50	10·50

715 Man wearing Costume (Bailarin de Diablada Festival, La Tirana)

2000. Religious Festivals. Multicoloured.

1931	150p. Type **715**	1·10	75
1932	200p. Girl wearing costume (San Pedro de Atacama fiesta)	1·40	1·00
1933	370p. Men dancing (La Candelaria Copiapo fiesta)	2·50	1·80
1934	460p. Drummer (Chinese Dance of Andacollo)	3·25	2·30

716 San Martin

2000. 150th Death Anniv of General Jose de San Martin.

1935	**716**	320p. multicoloured	2·50	2·00

717 Emblem, Globe and Weather Symbols

2000. 50th Anniv of World Meteorological Organization.

1936	**717**	320p. multicoloured	2·50	2·00

718 Magellanic Penguin (*Spheniscus magellanicus*)

2000. Antarctica. Multicoloured.

1937	450p. Type **718**	3·00	2·75
1938	650p. Humpback whales (*Megaptera novaeangliae*) (horiz)	4·50	4·00
1939	940p. Killer whale (*Orcinus orca*) (horiz)	6·25	5·50
MS1940	89×104 mm. 2000p. Southern elephant seal (35×47 mm)	17·00	17·00

No. 1937 is inscribed "Sphenis" in error.

719 Tennis, Football, Athletics and Sydney Opera House

2000. Olympic Games, Sydney. Multicoloured.

1941	290p. Type **719**	2·75	1·70
1942	290p. Archery, high jumping, cycling and Australian flag	2·75	3·00

Nos. 1941/2 were issued together, se-tenant, forming a composite design.

720 Native Chileans with Axe and Bow

2000. 450th Anniv of City of Concepcion. Depicting paintings by G. de la Fuente Riojas. Multicoloured.

1943	250p. Type **720**	1·70	1·50
1944	250p. Chileans and Spanish Conquistadors	1·70	1·50
1945	250p. Hand and scenes of destruction	1·70	1·50
1946	250p. Seated woman with shield	1·70	1·50
1947	250p. Horse, locomotive and coal truck	1·70	1·50
1948	250p. Modern Chileans and child	1·70	1·50

Nos. 1943/8 were issued together, se-tenant, forming a composite design.

721 Child's Hand holding Adult's Hand

2000. America. AIDS Awareness Campaign. Multicoloured.

1949	150p. Type **721**	1·20	85
1950	220p. Joined hands showing bones	1·80	1·30

722 Documents and Courtroom

2000. Penal Reform. Multicoloured.

1951	150p. Type **722**	1·20	85
MS1952	119×98 mm. 2000p. Smiling faces and door	17·00	17·00

723 Star

2000. Christmas. Multicoloured. (a) As T 723.

1953	150p. Type **723**	1·10	1·00
1954	150p. Silhouette of sleigh and reindeer above church	1·10	1·00
1955	150p. The Three Wise Men	1·10	1·00
1956	150p. Star on Christmas tree	1·10	1·00
1957	150p. Boy posting letter	1·10	1·00
1958	150p. Boy asleep	1·10	1·00
1959	150p. Man with bowl of fish and hindquarters of oxen	1·10	1·00
1960	150p. Jesus in manger	1·10	1·00
1961	150p. Mary and Joseph	1·10	1·00
1962	150p. Girl decorating tree	1·10	1·00

(b) Discount stamps. As Nos. 1953/62 additionally inscr "D S/20" above (Nos. 1963/7) or below (Nos. 1968/72) face value.

1963	150p. As No. 1953	1·10	1·00
1964	150p. As No. 1954	1·10	1·00
1965	150p. As No. 1955	1·10	1·00
1966	150p. As No. 1956	1·10	1·00
1967	150p. As No. 1957	1·10	1·00
1968	150p. As No. 1958	1·10	1·00
1969	150p. As No. 1959	1·10	1·00
1970	150p. As No. 1960	1·10	1·00
1971	150p. As No. 1961	1·10	1·00
1972	150p. As No. 1962	1·10	1·00

Nos. 1953/62 and Nos. 1963/72 respectively were issued together, se-tenant, forming a composite design.

724 Wild Cat, Gibbon and Ostrich

2001. 75th Anniv of Santiago National Zoo. Multicoloured.

1973	160p. Type **724**	95	85
1974	160p. Lion, elephant and bird	95	85
1975	160p. Polar bears	95	85
1976	160p. Hippopotamus, chameleon and fox	95	85

Nos. 1973/6 were issued together, se-tenant, forming a composite design.

725 Antiguo de Yumbel Church and Statue

2001. San Sebastian de Yumbel Festival.

1977	**725**	210p. multicoloured	2·30	1·20

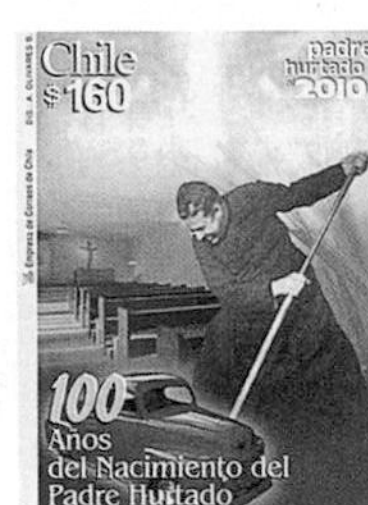

726 Hurtado sweeping and Car

2001. Birth Centenary of Fr. Alberto Hurtado. Multicoloured.

1978	160p. Type **726**	1·20	85
1979	340p. Hurtado and children	2·30	2·00

727 Slender-billed Conure (*Enicognathus leptorhynchus*)

2001. Discount Stamps. Birds. Multicoloured. Inscr "D/S No. 20".

1980	160p. Type **727**	95	85
1981	160p. Moustached turaka (*Pteroptochos megapodius*)	95	85
1982	160p. Chilean mockingbird (*Mimus thenca*)	95	85
1983	160p. Fernandez firecrown (*Sephanoides fernandensis*)	95	85

728 Flag, Globe and Industries

2001. 42nd Annual Reunion of the Governors of Inter-American Development Bank and Inter-American Investments Corporation.

1984	**728**	230p. multicoloured	1·50	1·20

729 Lockheed C-130 Hercules (transport)

2001. Chilean Airforce Anniversaries. Mult.

1985	260p. Type **729** (50th anniv of Chilean Air Force in Antarctica)	1·70	1·50
1986	260p. Flugzeugbau Extra-300 (20th anniv of High Acrobactics Squadron)	1·70	1·50
1987	260p. North American AT-6 Texan (75th anniv of No. 1 Aviation Group)	1·70	1·50
1988	260p. Consolidated PBY-5A/OA-10 Catalina (amphibian) (50th Anniv of first flight to Easter Island)	1·70	1·50

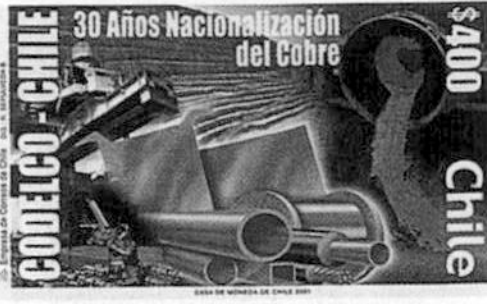

730 Mine, Products and Molten Copper

2001. 30th Anniv of Nationalization of Copper Industry. Multicoloured.

1989	**730**	400p. multicoloured	3·00	2·00
MS1990		118×97 mm. 2000p. Miner and digger	13·00	13·00

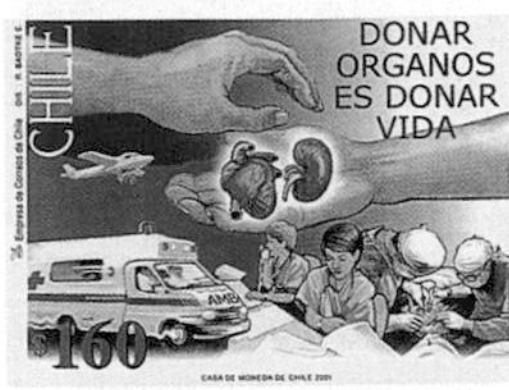

731 Ambulance, Organs and Medical Staff

2001. Organ Donation Campaign.

1991	**731**	160p. multicoloured	1·10	75

732 Pampas Cat (*Lynchailurus colocolo*)

2001. Endangered Species.

1992	**732**	100p. multicoloured	85	50

See also Nos. 2046/7.

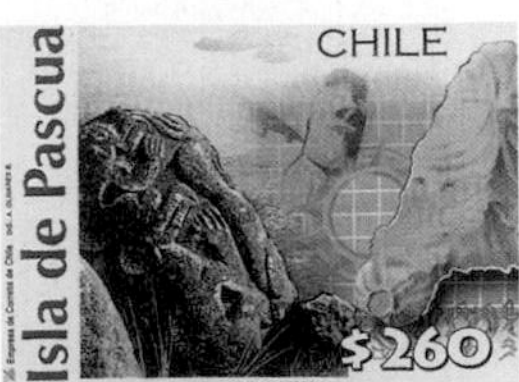

733 Carved Rocks, Head and Island

2001. Easter Island. Multicoloured.

1993	260p. Type **733**	1·70	1·50
1994	260p. Island, seagull, aboriginal and statue	1·70	1·50
MS1995	90×100 mm. 2000p. Carved figure and island	13·00	13·00

Nos. 1993/4 were issued together, se-tenant, forming a composite design.

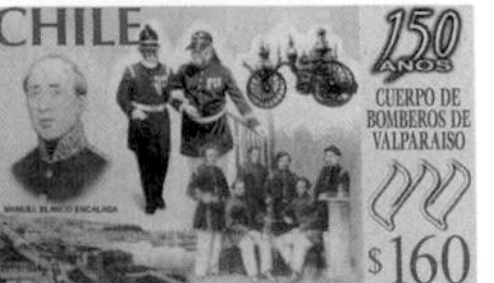

734 Manuel Blanco Encalada (first president), Elderly Firemen and Traditional Appliance

2001. 150th Anniv of Valpariso Fire Brigade. Multicoloured.

1996	160p. Type **734**	1·10	1·00
1997	260p. Traditional appliance, burning building, fireman and modern appliance	1·70	1·50
1998	350p. 1887 firemen	2·30	2·10
1999	490p. Helicopter, modern fire-fighters and tanker lorry	3·25	3·00
MS2000	90×106 mm. 2000p. Fireman, appliance and helicopter	13·00	13·00

735 *Laccata ohiensis*

2001. Fungi. Multicoloured.

2001	300p. Type **735**	2·30	1·70
2002	400p. *Macrolepiota rhacodes*	3·00	2·30

736 Flags, Badge and Soldiers

2001. 24th American Armies Conference.

2003	**736**	350p. multicoloured	2·50	2·00

737 Bernardo O'Higgins and First National Congress

2001. Bernardo O'Higgins Commemoration. 190th Anniv of First National Congress.

2004	**737**	260p. multicoloured	1·90	1·50

738 Scientist and Weddell seal

2001. Antarctica. Multicoloured.

2005	350p. Type **738**	2·50	1·50
2006	700p. Scientists holding Giant petrel	5·00	3·00
MS2007	105×90 mm. 2000p. Snowy sheathbill	13·00	13·00

739 Quinchao Church

2001. America. Cultural Heritage. Multicoloured.

2008	160p. Type **739**	1·10	1·00
2009	230p. Tenuan Church	1·50	1·30

740 "La Araucana" (detail)

2001. 90th Birth Anniv of Roberto Matta (artist).

2010	**740**	300p. multicoloured	1·90	1·70

741 Caldera Station Buildings

2001. 150th Anniv of Chilean Railways. Multicoloured.

2011	200p. Type **741**	1·20	1·10
2012	200p. Steam locomotive and Copiapo station	1·20	1·10
2013	220p. Electric locomotive (45×33 mm)	1·40	1·20

Nos. 2011/12 were issued together, se-tenant, forming a composite design.

742 Schooner

2001. Cape Horn.

2014	**742**	220p. multicoloured	1·70	1·50

743 Three Shepherds

2001. Christmas. Multicoloured. (a) As T 743.

2015	160p. Type **743**	1·10	1·00
2016	160p. Shepherd and cow	1·10	1·00
2017	160p. Mary and Joseph	1·10	1·00
2018	160p. Donkey and King	1·10	1·00
2019	160p. Cow and two Kings	1·10	1·00
2020	160p. Shepherd with raised hands	1·10	1·00
2021	160p. Sheep	1·10	1·00
2022	160p. Jesus in manger	1·10	1·00
2023	160p. Bearded man with staff	1·10	1·00
2024	160p. Sheep facing left	1·10	1·00

(b) Discount stamps. As Nos. 2015/24 additionally inscr "D S/20".

2025	160p. As No. 2015	1·10	1·00
2026	160p. As No. 2016	1·10	1·00
2027	160p. As No. 2017	1·10	1·00
2028	160p. As No. 2018	1·10	1·00
2029	160p. As No. 2019	1·10	1·00
2030	160p. As No. 2020	1·10	1·00
2031	160p. As No. 2021	1·10	1·00
2032	160p. As No. 2022	1·10	1·00
2033	160p. As No. 2023	1·10	1·00
2034	160p. As No. 2024	1·10	1·00

Nos. 2015/24 and 2025/34 respectively were issued together, se-tenant, forming a composite design.

744 Globe, Map of Chile and Monument

2001. Tropic of Capricorn. 75th Anniv of Rotary Club (charitable organization).

2035	**744**	240p. multicoloured	1·70	1·50

745 Austral Thrush (*Turdus falcklandii*)

2002. Discount Stamps. Birds. Multicoloured. Inscr "D/S No. 20".

2036	10p. Type **745**	35	10
2037	20p. Long-tailed meadow lark (*Sturnella loyca*)	35	10

746 Department Emblem

2002. Centenary of Internal Revenue Services.

2038	**746**	180p. multicoloured	1·20	1·10

747 Scull, Black-necked Swans and Spanish Turret

2002. 450th Anniv of Valdivia.

2039	**747**	260p. multicoloured	1·20	1·10

748 Police Officers and Vehicles

2002. 75th Anniv of Police Force.

2040	**748**	250p. multicoloured	1·90	1·70

749 Domeyko and Santiago University, Chile

2002. Birth Bicentenary of Ignacego Domeyko (scientist).

2041	**749**	290p. multicoloured	2·20	2·00

A stamp of the same design was issued by Poland.

750 Town Hall, Arms and Cathedral

2002. 450th Anniv of Villarrica.

2042	**750**	290p. multicoloured	2·20	2·00

751 Town Arms, Road, Peninsula and Church

2002. 400th Anniv of Calbuco.

2043	**751**	230p. multicoloured	1·50	1·30

752 Arms, School Building and Diego Barros Arana (founder)

2002. Centenary of Barros Arana National Boarding School, Santiago.

2044	**752**	250p. multicoloured	1·90	1·70

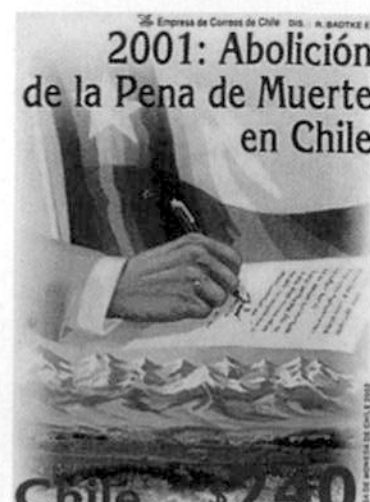

753 Flag and Hand signing Document

2002. 1st Anniv of Abolition of the Death Penalty.

2045	**753**	240p. multicoloured	1·70	1·50

2002. Endangered Species. As T 732. Multicoloured.

2046	10p. Andean mountain cat (*Oreailurus jacobita*)	35	10
2047	20p. Geoffroy's cat (*Oncifelis geoffroyi* (inscr "geoffrovi"))	35	10

754 Moai, Island and Sophora toromiro (extinct tree)

2002. Easter Island. Multicoloured.

2048	250p. Type **754**	1·90	1·70
2049	450p. Common dicua finch, island and man wearing native dress	2·50	2·20
MS2050	89×104 mm. 2000p. *Sophora toromiro*, island and common dicua finch (48×48 mm)	11·00	11·00

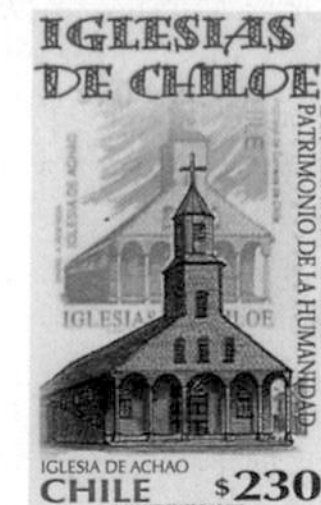

755 Achao Church, Chiloe

2002. UNESCO World Heritage Sites. Churches. Multicoloured.

2051	230p. Type **755**	1·50	1·30
2052	290p. Dalcahue, Chiloe	2·20	2·00

756 Adults and Teacher

2002. America. Education and Literacy Campaign. Multicoloured.

2053	230p. Type **756**	1·50	1·30
2054	450p. Child reading, teacher, computer and boy	2·50	2·20

757 Toy Windmills

2002. Traditional Games. Multicoloured.

2055	290p. Type **757**	2·20	2·00
2056	380p. Kite flying (vert)	2·30	2·10

758 Cerro Tololo Observatory

2002. Observatories. Multicoloured.
2057 450p. Type **758** 2·50 2·20
2058 550p. Paranal 3·00 2·75
MS2059 90×104 mm. 2000p. Cerro Tololo (different) (48×48 mm) 11·00 11·00

759 Hospital Building, Baby, MRI Scanner, Theatre and Doctor

2002. 50th Anniv of University of Chile Clinical Hospital.
2060 **759** 250p. multicoloured 1·90 1·70

760 Trees and Students

2002. 50th Anniv of Forestry Education.
2061 **760** 250p. multicoloured 1·90 1·70

761 Flamingo (*Phoenicoparru andinus*)

2002. 12th Convention on International Trade in Endangered Species (CITIES) Conference, Santiago, Chile. Multicoloured.
2062 300p. Type **761** 2·20 2·00
2063 450p. Vicuna (*Vicugna vicugna*) 2·50 2·20
MS2064 90×104 mm. 2000p. Chinchilla (*Chinchilla lanigera*) (48×48 mm) 11·00 11·00

762 Southern Right Whale (*Eubalaena australis*)

2002. Whales. Multicoloured.
2065 250p. Type **762** 1·90 1·70
2066 500p. Minke whale (*Balaenoptera acutorostrata*) 2·75 2·40
MS2067 90×104 mm. 2000p. Sperm whale (Physeter macrocephalus) (48×48 mm) 11·00 11·00

763 Justice

2002. Campaign to end Violence Against Women.
2068 **763** 230p. multicoloured 1·50 1·30

764 Church, Rose, Chilean and German Flags and Town Emblem

2002. 150th Anniv of Puerto Varas.
2069 **764** 190p. multicoloured 1·20 1·10

765 Magellanic Woodpecker (*Campephilus magellanicus*)

2003. Discount Stamps. Birds. Multicoloured. Inscr "D/S No. 20".
2070 500p. Type **765** 2·75 2·40
2071 1000p. Peregrine falcon (*Falco peregrinus*) 5·50 5·00

766 "Angelmo" (Hardy Wistuba)

2003. 150th Anniv of Puerto Montt.
2072 **766** 240p. multicoloured 1·70 1·50

767 Claudio Arrau

2003. Birth Centenary of Claudio Arrau (musician).
2073 **767** 200p. multicoloured 1·30 1·20

768 1853 5c. Stamp and Postal Building

2003. 150th Anniv of First Stamp. Multicoloured.
2074 300p. Type **768** 2·30 2·00
2075 300p. 1853 10c. stamp and building 2·30 2·00
MS2076 119×100 mm. 2000p. Building facade and stamp (detail) 11·00 11·00
Nos. 2074/5 were issued together, se-tenant, forming a composite design.

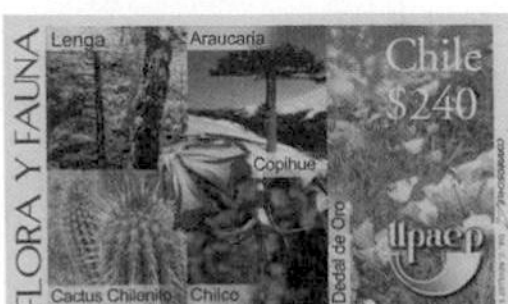

769 Trees, Cacti and Flowers

2003. America. Flora and Fauna. Multicoloured.
2077 240p. Type **769** 1·70 1·50
2078 300p. Frog, butterfly, pudu, fox and parrot 2·30 2·00

770 Decorated Window and Building Façade

2003. 180th Anniv of Supreme Court.
2079 **770** 200p. multicoloured 1·30 1·20

771 Supporters, Nurse and Early Vehicles

2003. Centenary of Chile Red Cross Society.
2080 **771** 200p. black and vermilion 1·30 1·20

772 Nativity

2003. Christmas.
2081 **772** 190p. multicoloured 1·20 1·10

773 Bristol M1C, Wright Flyer, Dagoberto Godoy (Chilean aviation pioneer) and Wright Brothers

2003. Centenary of Powered Flight.
2083 **773** 200p. multicoloured 1·30 1·20

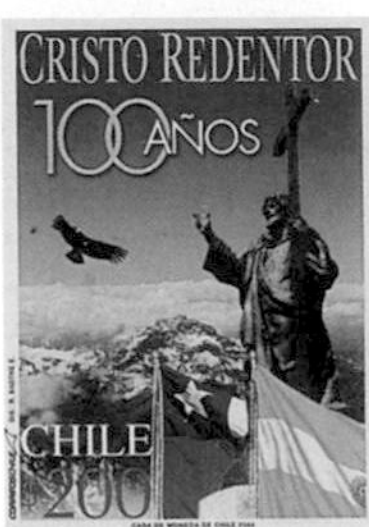

774 Cristo Redentor

2004. Centenary of Cristo Redentor (Christ the Redeemer) (statue commemorating the delineation of Brazil–Chile border).
2084 **774** 200p. multicoloured 1·30 1·20

775 Globe and Emblem

2004. World Conference of Grand Lodges, Santiago.
2085 **775** 190p. multicoloured 1·20 1·10

776 Pablo Neruda

2004. Birth Centenary of Neftali Ricardo Reyes Basoalto (Pablo Neruda) (writer and politician).
2086 **776** 300p. multicoloured 2·30 2·00

777 Flag and People

2004. 80th Anniv of Social Security.
2087 **777** 190p. multicoloured 1·20 1·10

778 Damaged Environment, Lynx and Healthy Environment

2004. America. Environmental Protection. Mult.
2088 100p. Type **778** 70 60
2089 600p. Fox in healthy environment, trucks and chimneys 3·25 3·00

779 School Buildings, Pupils and Mountain

2004. 150th Anniv of German School, Osorno.
2090 **779** 250p. multicoloured 1·90 1·70

780 Magnifying Glass, Tweezers and Stamps

2004. Tematica 2004, National Stamp Exhibition.
2091 **780** 310p. multicoloured 2·30 2·00

781 Ships, Satellite Dish and Flag

2004. Centenary of Naval Communications.
2092 **781** 400p. multicoloured 2·40 2·10

782 Symbols of Power Generation

2004. Cent of Electricity and Power Generation.
2093 **782** 240p. multicoloured 1·70 1·50

783 Emblem and Aircraft (image scaled to 49% of original size)

2005. 75th Anniv of National Air Force.
2094 **783** 230p. multicoloured 1·50 1·30

784 Document and Building

2005. Introduction of Law No. 20,000 (anti-drugs law).

2095	**784**	220p. multicoloured	1·40	1·20

785 Pope John Paul II and Child

2005. Pope John Paul II Commemoration. Multicoloured.

2096	230p. Type **785**	1·50	1·30
2097	230p. Holding staff	1·50	1·30
2098	230p. With raised arm	1·50	1·30

786 Building Facade

2005. Bicentenary of Currency Bureau.

2099	**786**	230p. multicoloured	1·50	1·30

787 Emblem and Mountains

2005. Centenary of Rotary International.

2100	**787**	230p. multicoloured	1·50	1·30

788 Don Quixote

2005. 400th Anniv of "Don Quixote de la Mancha" (novel by Miguel de Cervantes). 120th Anniv of Language Academy (1st series). Each grey.

2101	10p. Type **788**	35	10
2102	10p. Windmill	35	10
2103	20p. Three windmills	35	10
2104	20p. Miguel de Cervantes	35	10

See also Nos. 2126/9.

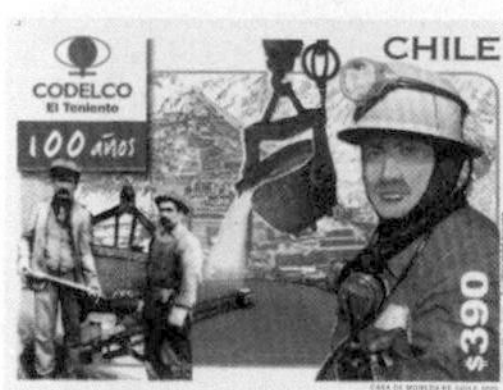

789 Early and Modern Miners

2005. Centenary of CODELCO El Teniente (copper mine).

2105	**789**	390p. multicoloured	2·30	2·10

790 Emblem (image scaled to 49% of original size)

2005. 75th Anniv of Aviation Secretariat.

2106	**790**	400p. multicoloured	2·40	2·10

791 Building Facade

2005. 150th Anniv of Custom House, Valparaiso.

2107	**791**	390p. multicoloured	2·30	2·10

792 Fountains

2005. Bicentenary of Fuente Provincial Municipality, Santiago.

2108	**792**	230p. multicoloured	1·50	1·30

793 Outstretched Hand and Man

2005. America. Struggle against Poverty. Mult.

2109	250p. Type **793**	1·90	1·70
2110	250p. Child and hand	1·90	1·70

Nos. 2109/10 were issued together, se-tenant, forming a composite design.

794 Alberto Hurtado

2005. Canonization of Father Alberto Hurtado Cruchaga.

2111	**794**	390p. multicoloured	2·30	2·10

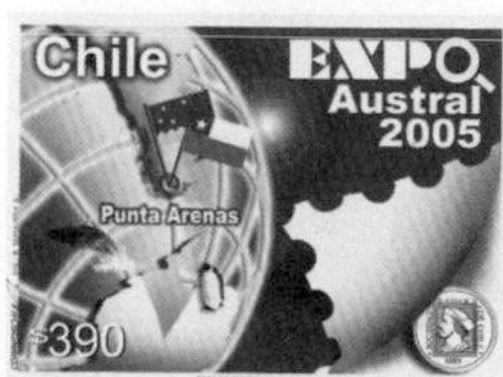

795 Globe, Map, Flags, Perforations and Emblem

2005. EXPO Austral 2005 Stamp Exhibition, Punta Arenas, Magallanes.

2112	**795**	390p. multicoloured	2·30	2·10

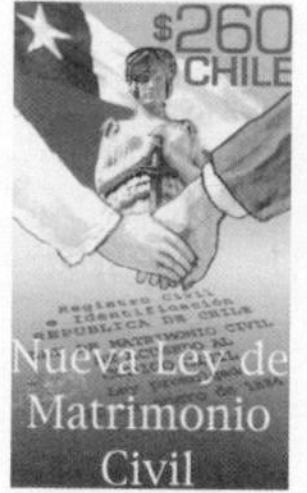

796 Linked Hands

2005. Civil Wedding Law.

2113	**796**	260p. multicoloured	2·00	1·80

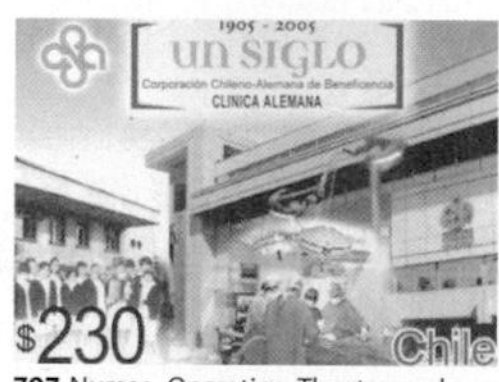

797 Nurses, Operating Theatre and Building

2005. Centenary of Chile-Germany Cooperation. German Clinic.

2114	**797**	230p. multicoloured	1·50	1·30

798 Post Office Building

2005. Restoration of Central Post Office.

2115	**798**	230p. multicoloured	1·50	1·30

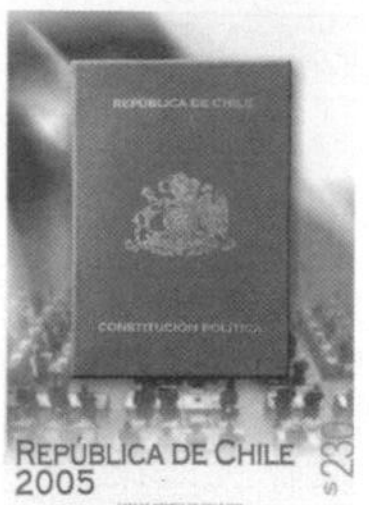

799 Constitution and Assembly

2005. Political Constitution.

2116	**799**	230p. multicoloured	1·50	1·30

800 Uniformed Women

2006. International Woman's Day.

2117	**800**	390p. multicoloured	2·30	2·10

801 "100" and Emblems

2006. Centenary of Departments of Education, Sport and Recreation.

2118	**801**	230p. multicoloured	1·50	1·30

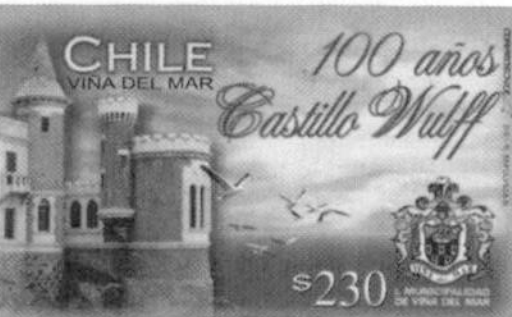

802 Castle, Seabirds and Sea

2006. Centenary of Castle Wulff, Vina del Mar. Multicoloured.

2119	230p. Type **802**	1·50	1·30
2120	390p. Arms, windmill and buildings	2·30	2·10

803 Moro de Arica

2006. Tourism. Each black.

2121	230p. Type **803**	1·50	1·30
2122	230p. Heads, Easter Island	1·50	1·30
2123	230p. Palafitos, Castro	1·50	1·30
2124	230p. Torres del Paine	1·50	1·30
2125	230p. Penguins, Chilean Antarctic	1·50	1·30

2006. 400th Anniv of "Don Quixote de la Mancha" (novel by Miguel de Cervantes). 120th Anniv of Language Academy (2nd series). As T 788. Each grey.

2126	10p. Castle	35	10
2127	10p. Two windmills	35	10
2128	10p. Windmill	35	10
2129	10p. Don Quixote and Sancho Panza	35	10

804 Stone Bridge and Students

2006. 50th Anniv of Catolica del Norte University. Multicoloured.

2130	230p. Type **804**	1·50	1·30
2131	230p. Students and building	1·50	1·30

805 Buildings and Pool

2006. Bicentenary of Plaza de la Ciudadania.

2132	**805**	390p. multicoloured	2·30	2·10

806 Buildings

2006. International Forum on Quality. Mult.

2133	230p. Type **806**	1·50	1·30
2134	230p. Flag	1·50	1·30

Nos. 2133/4 were issued together, se-tenant, forming a composite background.

807 River Valley and Sun (upper left quadrant)

2006. America. Energy Conservation. Multicoloured.

2135	390p. Type **807**	2·30	2·10
2136	390p. Lake and sun (upper right quadrant)	2·30	2·10
2137	390p. Oil installation and sun (lower left quadrant)	2·30	2·10
2138	390p. Wind turbines and sun (lower right quadrant)	2·30	2·10

808 Inscr "Pua IX Region (1906)

2006. Centenary of Adventist University of Chile. Multicoloured.

2139	250p. Type **808**	1·90	1·70
2140	250p. "Chillan VIII Region (1922)"	1·90	1·70
2141	250p. "Chillan VIII Region (1960–70)"	1·90	1·70
2142	250p. "Chillan VIII Region (2006)"	1·90	1·70

809 *Balaenoptera acutorostrata*

2006. Antarctica. Multicoloured.

2143	500p. Type **809**	2·75	2·40
2144	500p. *Aptenodytes forsteri*	2·75	2·40

Stamps of a similar design were issued by Estonia.

810 Map

2006. 160th Anniv of Magellan Straits and Fort Bulnes. Multicoloured.

2145	250p. Type **810**	1·90	1·70
2146	250p. Tower, Fort Bulnes	1·90	1·70

811 Federico Santa María (founder) and Building Facade

2006. 75th Anniv of Federico Santa Maria Technical University, Valparaiso.

2147	**811**	250p. multicoloured	1·90	1·70

812 Factory, San Borja

2006. 150th Anniv of GASCO (gas company). Multicoloured.

2148	250p. Type **812**	1·90	1·70
2149	250p. GASCO building facade	1·90	1·70

813 Carabinieros

2007. 80th Anniv of Carabinieros (national military police). Multicoloured.

2150	250p. Type **813**	1·90	1·70
2151	250p. Family and mounted police	1·90	1·70

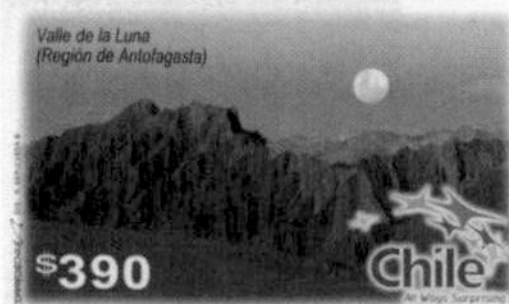

814 Valle de la Luna

2007. Tourism. Multicoloured.

2152	390p. Type **814**	2·30	2·10
2153	390p. Heads, Easter Island	2·30	2·10
2154	390p. Villarrica-Pucon volcano	2·30	2·10
2155	390p. Penguin, Chilean Antarctic	2·30	2·10

815 Parinacota Church

2007. Church Centenaries. Multicoloured.

2156	250p. Type **815**	1·90	1·70
2157	250p. San Pedro de Atacama	1·90	1·70

816 Cardinal Silva Henriquez

2007. Birth Centenary of Cardinal Raul Silva Henriquez (Archbishop of Santiago). Multicoloured.

2158	250p. Type **816**	1·90	1·70
2159	250p. As older man with young men	1·90	1·70
2160	250p. In procession behind horse	1·90	1·70
2161	250p. Addressing crowd	1·90	1·70

817 Marta Colvin and Sculpture

2007. Birth Centenary of Marta Colvin (artist). Multicoloured.

2162	250p. Type **817**	1·90	1·70
2163	250p. Wooden figure	1·90	1·70
2164	250p. Stone abstract	1·90	1·70
2165	250p. Metal abstract	1·90	1·70

818 Buildings at Night

2007. Las Condes Commune.

2166	**818**	330p. multicoloured	2·30	2·00

819 Artequin (interactive museum)

2007. Museums.

2167	**819**	10p. green	35	10
2168	-	20p. black	35	10
2169	-	30p. lilac	40	20
2170	-	50p. vermilion	55	25

DESIGNS: 10p. Type **819**; 20p. Museum of Fine Arts; 30p. Natural History Museum; 50p. Santiago Museum.

820 Ranco Lake

2007. Inauguration of Los Rios Region. Multicoloured.

2171	390p. Type **820**	90	40
2172	390p. Huilo Huilo waterfall	90	40
2173	390p. Pedro de Valdivia bridge	90	40
2174	390p. Choshuenco volcano	90	40

821 Morro de Arica

2007. Inauguration of Arica y Parinacota Region. Multicoloured.

2175	250p. Type **821**	60	30
2176	250p. Parinacota volcano	60	30
2177	250p. Anzota caves	60	30
2178	250p. Vicunas	60	30

822 Post Office, 1747

2007. 260th Anniv of Post in Chile. Multicoloured.

2179	390p. Type **822**	90	40
2180	390p. Modern Post Office	90	40
2181	390p. Outline of early and modern buildings	90	40
MS2182	100×100 mm. 3000p. Cyclist (statue)	6·75	6·75

823 Building Facade

2007. 80th Anniv of Naval Comptroller. Multicoloured.

2183	390p. Type **823**	90	40
2184	390p. Modern headquarters	90	40

Nos. 2183/4 were issued together, se-tenant, forming a composite design.

824 Children and Computer

2007. America. Education for All. Multicoloured.

2185	250p. Type **824**	60	30
2186	250p. Chemistry students	60	30
2187	250p. Runners	60	30
2188	250p. Musicians	60	30
2189	250p. Child and globe	60	30

Nos. 2185/9 were issued together, se-tenant, forming a composite design.

825 Santa, Dog and Fan

2007. Christmas. Multicoloured.

2190	250p. Type **825**	60	30
2191	250p. Santa and sleigh	60	30
2192	250p. Santa in horned car	60	30
2193	250p. Santa in chimney	60	30

826 Sunset

2007. Centenary of Malleco National Reserve. Multicoloured.

2194	250p. Type **826**	60	30
2195	250p. Conifer and puma	60	30
2196	250p. Waterfall	60	30
2197	250p. Forest and coyote	60	30

827 Building and Front Pages

2007. 90th Anniv of La Nation Newspaper. Multicoloured.

2198	250p. Type **827**	1·90	1·70
2199	250p. Machine room and building	1·90	1·70

827a Crowd and Port

2007. Centenary of Massacre of Striking Workers at Santa Maria de Iquique. Multicoloured.

2199a	250p. Type **827a**	1·90	1·70
2199b	250p. Strikers	1·90	1·70
2199c	250p. Victims	1·90	1·70
2199d	250p. Grieving man	1·90	1·70
2199e	250p. Grieving woman	1·90	1·70
MS2199f	102×101 mm. 3000p. Family	14·00	14·00

828 Ahu Koteriku, Rapa Nui National Park

2008. Te Pito o te Henua, Easter Island. Two sheets containing T 828 and similar multicoloured designs.

MS2200	128×161 mm. 390p.×8, Type **828**; Motu Nui and Moto Iti islands; Cave paintings, Ana Kai Tangata cave; Petroglyphs, Mata Ngarau, Orongo; Ceremonial boathouse, Orongo village; Ahu Tahai (archaeological site), Tahai; Anakena beach, North Coast; Volcanic lake, Rano Kau	15·00	15·00
MS2201	99×100 mm. Vert. 1500p.×2, , Male figre and Motu Nui; Female figure and Moto Iti	15·00	15·00

MS2200 was arranged in two columns of four stamps, with a female figure placed centrally over the top four, a male figure over the bottom four stamps and a map outline forming a background design.

The stamps and margins of **MS**2201 form a composite design.

829 Base

2008. International Polar Year. Sheet 131×141 mm containing T 829 and similar horiz designs. Multicoloured.

MS2202	250p.×6, Type **829**; Research vessel; Signpost and helicopter; Supply aircraft unloading; Light aircraft; Two snow mobiles	7·50	7·50

830 Knife Grinder

2008. Street Trades. Multicoloured.
2203 20p. Type **830** 35 10
2204 20p. Road sweeper 35 10
2205 30p. Peanut vendor (Inscr 'Manicero') 35 10
2206 30p. Photographer 35 10
2207 50p. Shoeshine 55 25
2208 50p. Ice cream vendor 55 25
2209 100p. Organ grinder 1·10 55
2210 100p. Inscr 'Palomita' 1·10 55
2211 500p. Newspaper vendor 3·75 3·25
2212 500p. One man band 3·75 3·25

Nos. 2203/4, 2205/6, 2207/8, 2209/10 and 2211/12, respectively, were issued in se-tenant pairs within the sheet.

831 Pablo Neruda (poet) and his House, Isla Negra

2008. Visit of Giorgio Napolitano (Italian president). Multicoloured.
2213 280p. Type **831** 2·10 1·90
2214 280p. Pablo Neruda and his house, Isle of Capri, Italy 2·10 1·90
2215 280p. Pablo Neruda, his house and garden, Isla Negra 2·10 1·90
2216 280p. Pablo Neruda and rocks, Isle of Capri 2·10 1·90

Nos. 2213/16 were issued together, se-tenant, forming a composite design.

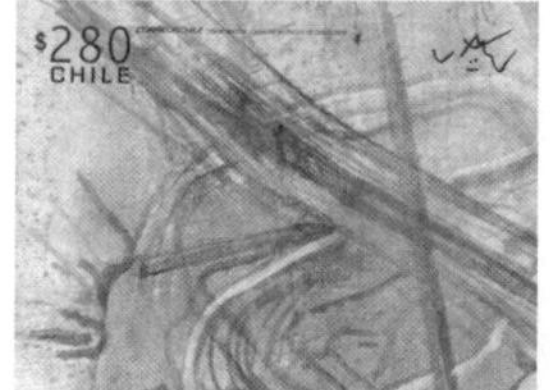

832 *Ensenar la eternidad* (top left)

Enseñar la eternidad

MATTA

833 *Ensenar la eternidad (image scaled to 26% of original size)*

2008. Paintings by Roberto Matta. Four sheets containing horiz designs as T 832 forming overall designs as T 833. Multicoloured.
MS2217 183×147 mm. (a) 280p.×9, Type **833**. (b) 410p.×9, *Foyer du moi*. (c) 410p.×9, *Espejo de Cronos* 40·00 40·00
MS2218 180×127 mm. 410p.×9, *Espejo de Cronos* 22·00 22·00

834 Salvador Allende

2008. Birth Centenary of Salvador Isabelino Allende Gossens (Salvador Allende) (president 1970–1973).
2219 **834** 410p. multicoloured 2·50 2·20

835 Church and Jetties

2008. 150th Anniv of Taltal, Antofagasta.
2220 **835** 280p. multicoloured 2·10 1·90

836 Architecture

2008. Chile–World Leaders. Multicoloured.
2221 280p. Type **836** 2·10 1·90
2222 280p. Art 2·10 1·90
2223 280p. Food production 2·10 1·90
2224 280p. Ceramics 2·10 1·90

Nos. 2221/4 were issued together, se-tenant, forming a composite design around a football enclosing the National stadium.

837 Building and Audience

2008. 50th Anniv of Colegio de Contadores de Chile. Multicoloured.
2225 280p. Type **837** 2·10 1·90
2226 280p. Emblem and map 2·10 1·90

838 Francisco Valdes and Osorno Cathedral

2008. Bishop Francisco Maximiano Valdes Subercaseaux (Capuchin prelate and first Bishop of Osorno) Commemoration. Multicoloured.
2227 280p. Type **838** 2·10 1·90
2228 280p. Francisco Valdes and Cristo del Tromen 2·10 1·90

839 *La vida Allende la muerte* (top left)

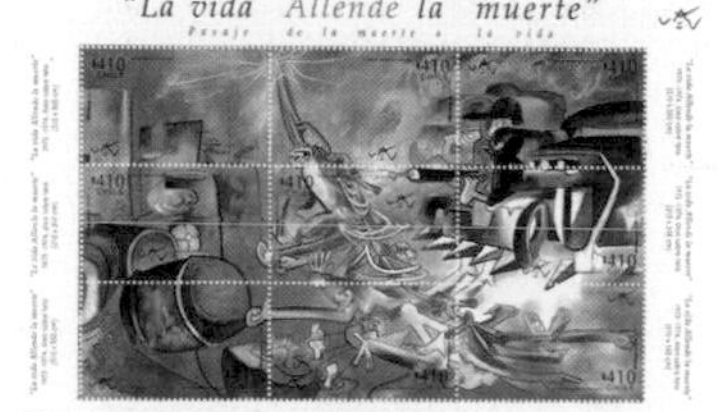

839a *La vida Allende la muerte (image scaled to 26% of original size)*

2008. Death Centenary of Salvador Allende. Painting by Roberto Matta. Sheet 185×130 mm containing horiz designs as T 839 forming overall designs as T 839a. Multicoloured.
MS2229 410p.×9, Type **839** etc 23·00 23·00

The stamps of No. **MS**2229 show parts of the painting, each sheet as a whole showing the complete work.

840 Horse Rider (Cuasimodo)

2008. America. Festivals. T 840 and similar vert designs. Multicoloured.
2230 10p. Type **840** 35 10
2231 200p. Couple crushing grapes (La Vendimia) 1·20 1·10
2232 1000p. Masked dancer (La Tirana) 7·50 6·75
2233 2000p. Couple dancing (Fiestas Parias) 14·00 13·00
2234 5000p Gauchos and cattle (El Rodeo) 25·00 24·00

841 Crags and Wolf

2008. 50th Anniv of Torres del Paine National Park. T 841 and similar horiz designs. Multicoloured.
2235 500p. Type **841** 3·75 3·75
2236 500p. Glacier and puma 3·75 3·75
2237 500p. Paine Grande Mountain and Andean condor 3·75 3·75
2238 500p. Condor and Cuernos del Paine 3·75 3·75
2239 500p. Cuernos del Paine and vicuna 3·75 3·75
2240 500p. South Andean deer (Huemul) and cordillera 3·75 3·75

Nos. 2235/6, 2237/8 and 2239/40, were printed, se-tenant, in horizontal pairs, each pair forming a composite design, within sheets of six stamps.

842 Heart and Emblem

2008. 30th Anniv of Teleton.
2241 **842** 280p. multicoloured 2·10 1·90

843 Underwater Scene

2008. Christmas. T 843 and similar horiz designs. Multicoloured.
2242 280p. Type **843** 2·10 1·90
2243 280p. Postman and envelopes 2·10 1·90
2244 280p. Children, globe and envelopes 2·10 1·90
2245 280p. Girl and Christmas tree 2·10 1·90
2246 280p. Tree decorated with hand prints 2·10 1·90

Nos. 2242/6 were printed, se-tenant, in horizontal strips of five stamps.

844 Street

2008. 450th Anniv of Osorno.
2247 **844** 280p. multicoloured 2·10 1·90

845 Early Building and Students

2008. Centenary of National Police Force College. T 845 and similar horiz design. Multicoloured.
2248 310p. Type **845** 2·10 1·90
2249 310p. Modern students and building 2·10 1·90

Nos. 2248/9 were printed, se-tenant, in horizontal pairs within the sheet.

846 Base Presidente Eduardo Frei Montalva

2009. Expo Antarctica. 50th Anniv of Antarctica Treaty. Multicoloured.
2250 470p. Type **846** 3·25 3·25
MS2251 100×100 mm. 3000p. Villa las Estrellas (horiz) 32·00 32·00

847 Retreating Ice and Emblem (upper)

2009. Preserve Polar Regions and Glaciers. Multicoloured.
2252 470p. Type **847** 3·25 3·25
2253 470p. Retreating ice and emblem (lower) 3·25 3·25
MS2254 80×118 mm. 1500p.×2, Emblem and Arctic; Antarctic and emblem 23·00 23·00

Nos. 2252/3 were printed, se-tenant, forming a composite design.

The stamps and margins of **MS**2254 form a composite design.

848 Oath of Independence

2009. Bicentenary (2010) of Chile. As Type 31 of 1910. Multicoloured.
2255 310p. Type **848** 2·10 1·90
2256 310p. Battle of Chacabuco 2·10 1·90
2257 310p. Battle of Roble 2·10 1·90
2258 310p. Battle of Maipu 2·10 1·90
2259 310p. Frigates *Lautaro* and *Esmeralda* 2·10 1·90
2260 310p. Capture of *Maria Isabella* 2·10 1·90
2261 310p. First sortie of liberating forces 2·10 1·90
2262 310p. Abdication of O'Higgins 2·10 1·90
2263 310p. First Chilean Congress 2·10 1·90
2264 310p. BICENTENARIO CHILE 2010 2·10 1·90
2265 310p. O'Higgins Monument 2·10 1·90
2266 310p. Carrera Monument 2·10 1·90
2267 310p. San Martin Monument 2·10 1·90
2268 310p. General Blanco 2·10 1·90
2269 310p. Jose Ignacio Zenteno del Pozo y Silva (Zenteno) 2·10 1·90
2270 310p. Admiral Thomas Cochrane, 10th Earl of Dundonald, Marquess do Maranhao (Lord Cochrane) 2·10 1·90

849 Monument to Founders (Samuel Roman)

2009. 90th Anniv of University of Concepcion. Multicoloured.

2271	310p. Type **849**	2·10	1·90
2272	310p. Campanile (Enrique San Martin (architect))	2·10	1·90

850 Virgin Mary of the Angels

2009. 50th Anniv of Diocese of Santa Maria de Los Angeles. Multicoloured.

2273	470p. Type **850**	3·25	3·00
2274	470p. Cathedral de Los Angeles	3·25	3·00

851 Condor

2009. Birds. Each black.

2275	10p. Type **851**	25	20
2276	20p. Burrowing parrot ('loro tricahue')	40	30
2277	50p. Chilean flamingo ('Flamenco chileno')	65	50
2278	100p. Humboldt penguin ('pinguino de humboldt')	1·30	1·10
2279	500p. Black-necked swan ('cisne cuello negro')	3·75	3·50

852 Emblem and Congress Building

2009. UPAEP Congress, Santiago.

2280	**852**	500p. multicoloured	3·75	3·75

853 Early Headquarters Building

2009. 90th Anniv of Mutual Insurance. Multicoloured.

2281	310p. Type **853**	2·10	1·90
2282	310p. Modern headquarters building	2·10	1·90

854 Star, Mountains and Buildings (Basic Education)

2009. Winning Designs in Bicentennial Stamp Contest, Chile–2010. Multicoloured designs showing designs from each category.

2283	310p. Type **854**	2·10	1·90
2284	310p. Buildings and multicoloured handprints (Secondary Education)	2·10	1·90
2285	310p. Chilli pepper and colour blocks (Higher Education (University and Technical)) (vert)	2·10	1·90
2286	310p. Celebrations (Visual Artists) (vert)	2·10	1·10

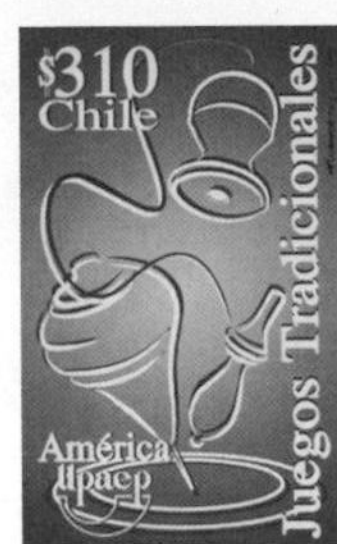

855 Diablo and Spinning Top

2009. America. Games. Multicoloured.

2287	310p. Type **855**	2·10	1·90
2288	470p. Kite flying	3·25	3·00

856 The Nativity

2009. Christmas. Multicoloured.

2289	310p. Type **856**	2·10	1·90
2290	310p. Children drawing Santa Claus	2·10	1·90
2291	310p. Children unwrapping presents	2·10	1·90
2292	310p. Children watching star through window	2·10	1·90

857 Gabriela Mistral

2009. 120th Birth Anniv of Lucila de María del Perpetuo Socorro Godoy Alcayaga (poet, educator, diplomat, feminist and Winner of the 1945 Nobel Prize for Literature) (Gabriela Mistral). Designs showing Gabriela Mistral. Multicoloured.

2293	500p. Type **857**	3·75	3·50
2294	500p. With pink tower in bacjground	3·75	3·50
2295	500p. Facing right	3·75	3·50
2296	500p. Facing left	3·75	3·50

858 Early Letter Card

2010. 120th Anniv of Philatelic Society of Chile

2297	**858**	500p. multicoloured	2·10	1·90

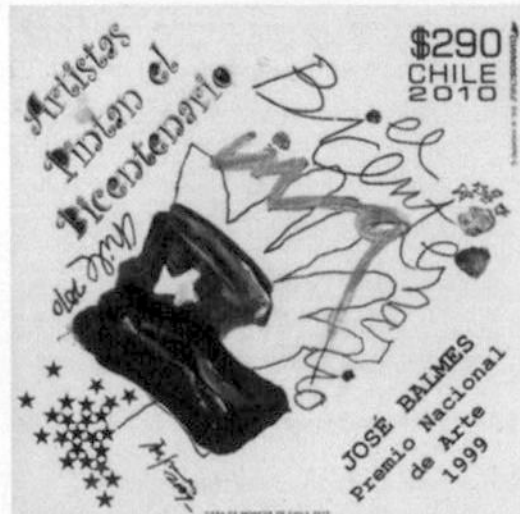

859 Hand, Flag and 'Bicentenario' (José Balmes)

2010. Artists paint the Bicentennial. Multicoloured.

2298	290p. Type **859**	2·10	1·90
2299	290p. 2010 as face (Eugenio Dittborn)	2·10	1·90
2300	290p. Abstract (Guillermo Núnez)	2·10	1·90

860 *Esmeralda* (Chilean tall ship entry)

2010. Bicentennial Regatta. Multicoloured.

2301	430p. Type **860**	2·50	2·20
2302	430p. *Esmeralda* and map of regatta route	2·50	2·20

861 Lockheed C-130 Hercules

2010. 40th Anniv of Eduardo Frei Montalva Antarctic Base. Multicoloured.

2303	500p. Type **861**	3·75	3·00
2304	500p. Buffalo hangar and sign post	3·75	3·00
2305	500p. Lieutenant Rodolfo Marsh aerodrome	3·75	3·00
2306	500p. Bell 412 helicopter	3·75	3·00
2307	500p. de Havilland Canada DHC-6 Twin Otter	3·75	3·00
2308	500p. Villa Estrellas base	3·75	3·00

862 Tower

2010. 105th Anniv of Bauer Tower, Vicuna. Multicoloured.

2309	500p. Type **862**	3·75	3·00
MS2310	100×100 mm. 3000p. Tower (different)	20·00	20·00

863 Flags, Football, Players, Map and Federation Emblem

2010. Centenary of National Football Team. Multicoloured.

2311	500p. Type **863**	3·75	3·00
2312	500p. Flags, football, map enclosing lion, cheetah fur and federation emblem	3·75	3·00

Nos. 2311/12 were printed, *se-tenant*, each pair forming a composite design.

864 Flags and Mount Chajnantor

2010. Inauguration of Mini-TAO Infrared Telescope, Mount Chajnantor (joint effort between Chile and Japan for astronomical research). Multicoloured.

2313	430p. Type **864**	2·50	2·20
MS2314	145×105 mm. 3000p. As Type **864**	20·00	20·00

865 Arco Britanico

2010. Valparaiso World Heritage Site

2315	10p. chocolate	15	10
2316	10p. chocolate	15	10
2317	20p. slate-lilac (horiz)	30	10
2318	20p. slate-lilac (horiz)	30	10
2319	50p. orange	50	30
2320	50p. orange	50	30
2321	100p. green (horiz)	90	45
2322	100p. green (horiz)	90	45

Designs: 10p. Type **865**; 10p. Heroes of Iquitos (statue); 20p. Polanco Palace; 20p. Lyon Palace; 50p. Polanco elevator; 50p. Artilleria elevator; 100p. Trolleybus; 100p. Trolleybus from rear

866 Grupo Bicentenario Emblem, Early Map and Revolutionary Horsemen

2010. Bicentenary of Latin American Freedom from Colonialism

2323	**866**	430p. multicoloured	2·50	2·20

Nos. 2324/5, Type **867** are left for Bicentenary, issued on 15 September 2010, not yet received.

868 *Esmeralda* (cruiser)

2010. Naval Bicentennial Parade, Valparaiso. Multicoloured.

2326	430p. Type **868**	2·50	2·20
2327	430p. *Baquedano* (corvette) in port, 1910	2·50	2·20
2328	430p. National squadron, 2010 (left)	2·50	2·20
2329	430p. National squadron, 2010 (right)	2·50	2·20

Nos. 2328/9, respectively, were printed, *se-tenant*, forming a composite design of the modern fleet.

ACKNOWLEDGEMENT OF RECIEPT STAMP

1894. Portrait of Columbus. Inscr "A.R.". Perf or Imperf.

AR77	5c. brown	2·00	1·60

COMPULSORY TAX STAMPS

T100 Arms of Talca

1942. Talca Bicentenary.

T338	**T100**	10c. blue	10	10

1955. Death Centenary of Pres. Prieto. As T 145.

T445	15p. green	35	30

PORTRAIT: 15p. Pres. Prieto.

1970. Postal Tax. No. 492a and 555 surch E° O,10 Art. 77 LEY 17272.

T638	**162**	10c. on 2c. blue	35	20
T639	**178**	10c. on 6c. purple	35	20

T224 Chilean Arms

1971. Postal Modernization.

T646	**T224**	10c. blue	20	10
T647	**T224**	15c. red	35	15

1971. Postal Modernization. Nos. T646/7 surch.

T673	15c. on 10c. blue	20	10
T674	20c. on 15c. red	20	10
T675	50c. on 15c. red	20	10

OFFICIAL STAMPS

1928. Stamps of 1911 inscr "CHILE CORREOS" optd Servicio del ESTADO.

O190	**49**	10c. black and blue	10·00	2·75
O191	-	20c. (No. 142)	4·75	1·50
O192	-	25c. (No. 167)	11·00	1·50
O193	-	50c. (No. 170)	6·00	1·50
O194	**57**	1p. black and green	7·75	2·30

1930. Stamps inscr "CORREOS DE CHILE" optd Servicio del ESTADO.

O217	**49**	10c. (No. 204)	4·75	2·10
O234	**76**	10c. blue	1·10	75
O219	-	20c. (No. 209)	1·10	75
O235	-	20c. brown (No. 232)	1·10	30
O220	-	25c. (No. 210)	1·10	75
O221	-	50c. (No. 212)	2·20	1·10

1934. Stamps inscr "CORREOS DE CHILE" optd OFICIAL.

O236	**64**	5c. green (No. 206)	90	75
O237	**76**	10c. blue	75	75
O238	-	20c. brown (No. 232)	15·00	75

1939. Optd Servicio del ESTADO.

O279		50c. violet (No. 273)	6·00	3·75
O280	**90**	1p. orange	7·75	5·75

1941. Nos. 269/338j optd OFICIAL.

O281	-	10c. red	2·75	2·75
O282	-	15c. red	1·50	55
O283	-	20c. blue	2·20	85
O284	-	30c. red	1·10	55
O285	-	40c. green	1·10	55
O286	-	50c. violet	6·00	1·10
O339	**90**	1p. orange	3·75	2·10
O288	-	1p.80 blue	15·00	9·00
O442	-	2p. red	1·90	1·10
O383	-	5p. green	5·00	1·90
O443	-	10p. purple	13·00	7·00

1953. No. 379c optd OFICIAL.

O386	1p. turquoise	1·70	75

1956. Nos. 446/450 optd OFICIAL.

O451	2p. lilac	1·90	1·10
O452	3p. blue	10·00	6·50
O453	5p. sepia	2·40	65
O454a	10p. violet	1·40	75
O455	50p. red	8·25	2·30

1958. Optd OFICIAL.

O469	**152**	10p. blue	£275	34·00

1960. No. 493 optd OFICIAL.

O507	5c. blue	4·50	1·80

POSTAGE DUE STAMPS

D18

1895

D98	**D18**	1c. red on yellow	75	40
D99	**D18**	2c. red on yellow	75	40
D100	**D18**	4c. red on yellow	95	40
D101	**D18**	6c. red on yellow	2·10	80
D102	**D18**	8c. red on yellow	95	45
D103	**D18**	10c. red on yellow	75	45
D104	**D18**	20c. red on yellow	75	45
D93	**D18**	40c. red on yellow	3·50	2·30
D94	**D18**	50c. red on yellow	3·50	2·30
D95	**D18**	60c. red on yellow	7·25	3·50
D96	**D18**	80c. red on yellow	7·25	4·50
D109	**D18**	100c. red on yellow	29·00	23·00
D97	**D18**	1p. red on yellow	7·50	5·00

D19

1898

D110	**D19**	1c. red	40	25
D111	**D19**	2c. red	1·00	50
D112	**D19**	4c. red	40	25
D113	**D19**	10c. red	40	25
D114	**D19**	20c. red	40	25

D68

1924

D184	**D68**	2c. red and blue	95	80
D185	**D68**	4c. red and blue	1·20	95
D186	**D68**	8c. red and blue	1·20	95
D187	**D68**	10c. red and blue	1·20	95
D188	**D68**	20c. red and blue	1·20	95
D189	**D68**	40c. red and blue	1·20	95
D190	**D68**	60c. red and blue	1·20	95
D191	**D68**	80c. red and blue	1·20	95
D192	**D68**	1p. red and blue	1·70	1·20
D193	**D68**	2p. red and blue	2·75	2·00
D194	**D68**	5p. red and blue	2·75	2·00

Pt. 17

CHINA

People's Republic in Eastern Asia, formerly an Empire.

CHINESE EMPIRE
1878. 100 candarins = 1 tael.
1897. 100 cents = 1 dollar.

CHINESE REPUBLIC
1912. 100 cents = 1 dollar.
1948. 100 cents = 1 gold yuan.
1949. 100 cents = 1 silver yuan.

CHINESE PEOPLE'S REPUBLIC.
1949. Yuans.
1955. 100 fen = 1 yuan.

CHINA-TAIWAN (FORMOSA).
A. CHINESE PROVINCE
100 sen = 1 yen.
1947. 100 cents = 1 yuan (C.N.C).

CHINESE NATIONALIST REPUBLIC.
1949. 100 cents = 1 silver yuan (or New Taiwan Yuan)

CHINESE CHARACTERS

Simple	Formal	
半	半	= ½
一	壹	= 1
二	貳	= 2
三	叁	= 3
四	肆	= 4
五	伍	= 5
六	陸	= 6
七	柒	= 7
八	捌	= 8
九	玖	= 9
十	拾	= 10
百	佰	= 100
千	仟	= 1,000
萬	萬	= 10,000
	分	= cent
	圓	= dollar

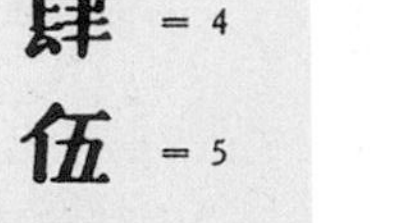

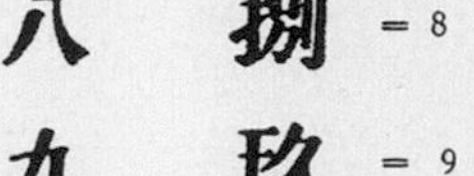

Examples:

十五	= 15
五十	= 50
叁佰圓	= 300 dollars
伍仟圓	= 5,000 dollars

CHINESE EMPIRE

1 Dragon

1878

7	**1**	1ca. green	£550	£550
2	**1**	3ca. red	£950	£300
3	**1**	5ca. orange	£1100	£550

2

1885

13	**2**	1ca. green	30·00	24·00
14	**2**	3ca. mauve	£120	15·00
15	**2**	5ca. yellow	£140	48·00

4

10

1894. Dowager Empress's 60th Birthday.

16	**4**	1ca. orange	30·00	35·00
17	-	2ca. green	40·00	40·00
18	-	3ca. yellow	30·00	10·00
19	-	4ca. pink	£120	£100
20	**4**	5ca. orange	£450	£400
21	-	6ca. brown	40·00	25·00
22	**10**	9ca. green	£250	55·00
23	**10**	12ca. orange	£400	£250
24	-	24ca. red	£600	£300

DESIGNS—VERT: (as Type **4**): 2ca. to 4ca. and 6ca. Dragon. HORIZ: (as Type **10**): 24ca. Junks.

1897. Surch in English and Chinese characters.

78	-	½c. on 3ca. yellow (No. 18)	18·00	20·00
34	**2**	1c. on 1ca. green	50·00	50·00
79	**4**	1c. on 1ca. orange	35·00	12·00
80	-	2c. on 2ca. green (No. 17)	35·00	4·50
35	**2**	2c. on 3ca. mauve	£200	95·00
36	**2**	5c. on 5ca. yellow	£100	45·00
40	-	4c. on 4ca. pink (No. 19)	35·00	15·00
41	-	5c. on 5ca. orange (No. 20)	45·00	15·00
42	-	8c. on 6ca. brown (No. 21)	45·00	15·00
43	-	10c. on 6ca. brown (No. 21)	£120	£200
63	**10**	10c. on 9ca. green	£225	95·00
64	**10**	10c. on 12ca. orange	£550	£150
46	-	30c. on 24ca. red (No. 24)	£750	£300

17

1897. Surch in English and Chinese characters.

88	**17**	1c. on 3c. red	£500	£250
89	**17**	2c. on 3c. red	£500	£250
90	**17**	4c. on 3c. red	£1200	£425
91	**17**	$1 on 3c. red	£5000	£2500
92	**17**	$5 on 3c. red	£70000	£50000

24 **30** Carp **31** Bean Goose

1897. Inscr "IMPERIAL CHINESE POST".

96	**24**	½c. purple	3·25	3·25
97	**24**	1c. yellow	5·00	2·50
98	**24**	2c. orange	5·50	1·25
99	**24**	4c. brown	12·00	2·50
100	**24**	5c. red	18·00	3·50
101	**24**	10c. green	28·00	3·00
102	**30**	20c. lake	75·00	15·00
103	**30**	30c. red	£125	48·00
104	**30**	50c. green	75·00	50·00
105	**31**	$1 red	£650	£250
106	**31**	$2 orange and yellow	£3250	£3500
107	**31**	$5 green and red	£1100	£1800

32 Dragon **33** Carp **34** Bean Goose

1898. Inscr "CHINESE IMPERIAL POST".

121	**32**	½c. brown	2·00	1·00
122	**32**	1c. buff	2·00	1·00
123	**32**	2c. red	3·25	1·00
151	**32**	2c. green	7·50	1·75
152	**32**	3c. green	10·00	1·75
124	**32**	4c. brown	5·00	2·00
153	**32**	4c. red	12·00	2·50
112	**32**	5c. pink	12·00	2·50
126	**32**	5c. orange	30·00	5·50
154	**32**	5c. mauve	15·00	1·50
155	**32**	7c. red	22·00	5·25
127	**32**	10c. green	22·00	1·50
156	**32**	10c. blue	25·00	1·50
157	**33**	16c. green	38·00	12·00
128	**33**	20c. purple	38·00	5·50
115	**33**	30c. red	35·00	9·50
130	**33**	50c. green	55·00	9·50
131	**34**	$1 red and orange	£170	25·00
132	**34**	$2 purple and yellow	£350	50·00
119	**34**	$5 green and orange	£700	£250

36 Temple of Heaven

1909. 1st Year of Reign of Emperor Hsuan T'ung.

165	**36**	2c. green and orange	7·50	5·00
166	**36**	3c. blue and orange	7·50	6·00
167	**36**	7c. purple and orange	8·50	8·50

POSTAGE DUE STAMPS

1904. Stamps of 1898 optd POSTAGE DUE in English and Chinese characters.

D137	**32**	½c. brown	12·00	6·50
D138	**32**	1c. buff	18·00	5·00
D139a	**32**	2c. red	20·00	6·25
D140	**32**	4c. brown	20·00	8·50
D141	**32**	5c. red	30·00	24·00
D142	**32**	10c. green	45·00	25·00

D37

1904

D143	**D37**	½c. blue	5·00	2·25
D144	**D37**	1c. blue	9·50	2·00
D145	**D37**	2c. blue	9·50	2·00
D146	**D37**	4c. blue	12·00	3·25
D147	**D37**	5c. blue	13·00	3·75
D148	**D37**	10c. blue	16·00	6·50
D149	**D37**	20c. blue	42·00	9·50
D150	**D37**	30c. blue	55·00	40·00
D168	**D37**	1c. brown	22·00	10·00
D169	**D37**	2c. brown	35·00	32·00

CHINESE REPUBLIC

1912. Optd vert with four Chinese characters signifying "Republic of China".

192	**32**	½c. brown	2·50	1·00
193	**32**	1c. buff	3·00	75
194	**32**	2c. green	3·25	75
221	**32**	3c. green	3·00	1·00
196	**32**	4c. red	4·50	1·00
197	**32**	5c. mauve	8·00	1·00
198	**32**	7c. lake	9·00	3·50
225	**32**	10c. blue	10·00	1·75
200	**33**	16c. olive	30·00	12·00
227	**33**	20c. red	40·00	3·75
202	**33**	30c. red	38·00	7·25
203	**33**	50c. green	60·00	6·50
204	**34**	$1 red and salmon	£550	30·00
205	**34**	$2 red and yellow	£450	45·00
232	**34**	$5 green and salmon	£750	£650

41 Dr. Sun Yat-sen

1912. Revolution Commemoration.

242	**41**	1c. orange	2·50	3·50
243	**41**	2c. green	2·50	3·50
244	**41**	3c. blue	2·50	2·50
245	**41**	5c. mauve	3·50	5·00
246	**41**	8c. sepia	4·00	5·00
247	**41**	10c. blue	4·00	5·50
248	**41**	16c. olive	15·00	15·00
249	**41**	20c. lake	18·00	12·00
250	**41**	50c. green	48·00	30·00
251	**41**	$1 red	£375	90·00
252	**41**	$2 brown	£1000	£800
253	**41**	$5 slate	£275	£500

1912. As T **41** but portrait of Pres. Yuan Shih-kai, inscr "Commemoration of the Republic".

254	1c. orange	2·00	2·00
255	2c. green	2·00	2·00
256	3c. blue	2·00	1·25
257	5c. mauve	2·00	2·25
258	8c. sepia	5·00	4·25
259	10c. blue	3·50	2·75
260	16c. olive	5·00	6·00
261	20c. lake	4·50	5·00
262	50c. green	25·00	20·00
263	$1 red	£130	70·00
264	$2 brown	£120	£100
265	$5 slate	£750	£700

43 Junk

44 Reaper

45 Entrance Hall of Classics, Peking

1913

287	**43**	½c. sepia	1·00	30
289a	**43**	1½c. purple	2·00	1·25
269	**43**	1c. orange	1·50	40
270	**43**	2c. green	2·25	50
271	**43**	3c. green	5·00	35
292	**43**	4c. red	12·00	30
314	**43**	4c. grey	25·00	65
315	**43**	4c. olive	3·25	35
293	**43**	5c. mauve	5·50	30
294	**43**	6c. grey	12·00	40
317	**43**	6c. red	6·50	40
318	**43**	6c. brown	38·00	3·00
295	**43**	7c. violet	15·00	5·00
296	**43**	8c. orange	9·50	50
297	**43**	10c. blue	8·50	60
298	**44**	13c. brown	7·50	1·00
278	**44**	15c. brown	28·00	7·50
323	**44**	15c. blue	7·50	50
324	**44**	16c. olive	8·00	50
325	**44**	20c. lake	8·00	30
326	**44**	30c. purple	16·00	30
282	**44**	50c. green	48·00	4·25
304	**45**	$1 black and yellow	£100	2·00
328	**45**	$1 sepia and brown	38·00	50
305	**45**	$2 black and blue	£250	5·50
329	**45**	$2 brown and blue	75·00	1·25
306	**45**	$5 black and red	£500	40·00
330	**45**	$5 green and red	£140	8·50
307	**45**	$10 black and green	£850	£375
331	**45**	$10 mauve and green	£475	75·00
308	**45**	$20 black and orange	£6000	£4500
332	**45**	$20 blue and purple	£900	£250

1920. Flood Relief Fund. Surch with new value in English and Chinese characters.

349	**43**	1c. on 2c. green	10·00	3·25
361	**43**	2c. on 3c. green	5·50	50
350	**43**	3c. on 4c. red	10·00	3·75
351	**43**	5c. on 6c. grey	15·00	7·25

47 Curtiss JN-4 "Jenny" over Great Wall of China

I

II

1921. Air. Tail fin of aeroplane as Type I.

352	**47**	15c. black and green	35·00	35·00
353	**47**	30c. black and red	38·00	35·00
354	**47**	45c. black and purple	42·00	48·00
355	**47**	60c. black and blue	45·00	55·00
356	**47**	90c. black and olive	60·00	70·00

For similar stamps in this type but with tail fin as Type II, see Nos. 384a/8.

48 Yen Kung-cho, Pres. Hsu Shih-chang and Chin Yung-peng

1921. 25th Anniv of Chinese National Postal Service.

357	**48**	1c. orange	5·50	2·25
358	**48**	3c. turquoise	5·50	1·50
359	**48**	6c. grey	6·50	3·25
360	**48**	10c. blue	7·50	3·25

53 Temple of Heaven

1923. Adoption of the Constitution.

362	**53**	1c. orange	4·25	1·00
363	**53**	3c. turquoise	4·50	2·25
364	**53**	4c. red	9·50	5·00
365	**53**	10c. blue	15·00	4·25

1925. Surch in English and Chinese characters.

366	**43**	1c. on 2c. green	3·25	30
367	**43**	1c. on 3c. green	2·25	85
369	**43**	1c. on 4c. olive	2·50	30
370	**43**	3c. on 4c. grey	3·50	20

The figures in this surcharge are at the top and are smaller than for the 1920 provisionals.

55 Marshal Chang Tso-lin

1928. Assumption of Title of Marshal of the Army and Navy by Chang Tso-lin.

372	**55**	1c. orange	3·50	3·25
373	**55**	4c. olive	5·50	3·50
374	**55**	10c. blue	10·00	9·00
375	**55**	$1 red	95·00	95·00

56 General Chiang Kai-shek

1929. Unification of China under Gen. Chiang Kai-shek.

376	**56**	1c. orange	4·25	1·25
377	**56**	4c. olive	5·50	1·75
378	**56**	10c. blue	18·00	2·25
379	**56**	$1 red	£140	85·00

57 Mausoleum at Nanking

1929. State Burial of Dr. Sun Yat-sen.

380	**57**	1c. orange	3·25	1·25
381	**57**	4c. olive	5·00	1·25
382	**57**	10c. blue	10·00	2·50
383	**57**	$1 red	£100	65·00

1929. Air. As T 47, but tail fin of airplane as Type II.

384a	**47**	15c. black and green	5·00	1·00
385	**47**	30c. black and red	14·00	3·25
386	**47**	45c. black and purple	20·00	10·00
387	**47**	60c. black and blue	22·00	15·00
388	**47**	90c. black and olive	24·00	28·00

58 Dr. Sun Yat-sen

1931

389	**58**	1c. orange	75	40
396	**58**	2c. olive	40	10
391	**58**	4c. green	1·00	20
398	**58**	5c. green	50	10
399	**58**	15c. green	3·75	1·75
400	**58**	15c. red	75	10
401	**58**	20c. blue	1·00	20
402	**58**	25c. blue	80	10
403a	**58**	$1 sepia and brown	15·00	75
735	**58**	$1 violet	50	2·25
404a	**58**	$2 brown and blue	25·00	1·25
736	**58**	$2 olive	50	3·75
405a	**58**	$5 black and red	40·00	9·50
737	**58**	$20 green	1·25	60
738	**58**	$30 brown	50	55
739	**58**	$50 orange	50	55

59 "Nomads of the Desert"

1932. North-West China Scientific Expedition.

406	**59**	1c. orange	70·00	85·00
407	**59**	4c. olive	70·00	85·00
408	**59**	5c. red	70·00	85·00
409	**59**	10c. blue	70·00	85·00

60 General Teng K'eng

1932. Martyrs of the Revolution.

410	**60**	½c. brown	20	10
508	-	1c. orange	20	20
509	-	2c. blue	20	20
412	**60**	2½c. purple	20	20
511	-	3c. brown	20	20
512	**60**	4c. lilac	20	20
513	-	5c. orange	20	45
514	-	8c. orange	20	20
515	-	10c. purple	2·75	30
516	-	13c. green	20	45
517	-	15c. purple	30	40
417	-	17c. green	50	10
418	-	20c. red	1·00	10
519	-	20c. blue	25	20
520	-	21c. brown	35	25
521	-	25c. purple	25	35
541	-	28c. green	30	70
542	-	30c. purple	45	25
543	-	40c. orange	30	25
544	-	50c. green	30	10

DESIGNS: 1, 25, 50c. Ch'en Ying-shih; 2, 10, 17, 28c. Shung Chiao-jen; 3, 5, 15, 30c. Liao Chung-k'ai; 8, 13, 21c. Chu Chih-hsin; 20, 40c. Gen. Huang Hsing.

61 Junkers F-13 over Great Wall

1932. Air.

422	**61**	15c. green	50	40
556	**61**	25c. orange	40	70
557	**61**	30c. red	40	60
558	**61**	45c. purple	40	1·00
559	**61**	50c. brown	40	55
560	**61**	60c. blue	40	1·00
561	**61**	90c. green	40	1·25
562	**61**	$1 green	55	1·00
563	**61**	$2 brown	1·40	1·40
564	**61**	$5 red	1·10	1·25

62 Tan Yen-kai

1933. Tan Yen-kai Memorial.

440	**62**	2c. olive	3·75	1·25
441	**62**	5c. green	4·50	30
442	**62**	25c. blue	12·00	1·50
443	**62**	$1 red	£120	65·00

63

1936. "New Life" Movement. Symbolic designs as T 63.

444	**63**	2c. olive	2·50	75
445	**63**	5c. green	3·75	50
446	-	20c. blue (various emblems)	10·00	1·00
447	-	$1 red (Lighthouse)	48·00	10·00

66 "Postal Communications."

1936. 40th Anniv of Chinese National Postal Service.

448	**66**	2c. orange	2·00	1·00
449	-	5c. green	2·50	50
450	-	25c. blue	5·00	1·00
451	-	100c. red	32·00	9·50

DESIGNS: 5c. The Bund, Shanghai; 25c. G.P.O., Shanghai; 100c. Ministry of Communications, Nanking.

1936. Surch in figures and Chinese characters.

452	**44**	5c. on 15c. blue	3·25	75
453	**44**	5c. on 16c. olive	4·75	1·00

1937. Surch in figures and Chinese characters.

454	**58**	1 on 4c. green	1·50	30
455	-	8 on 40c. orange (No. 543)	2·25	1·00
456	**58**	10 on 25c. blue	1·75	20

72 Dr. Sun Yat-sen

1938

462	**72**	2c. green	20	20
464	**72**	3c. red	20	20
489B	**72**	5c. green	20	20
492A	**72**	8c. green	50	20
469	**72**	10c. green	20	20
470	**72**	15c. red	3·25	3·25
471	**72**	16c. brown	1·25	75
472	**72**	25c. blue	1·25	1·00
494B	**72**	30c. red	20	20
495B	**72**	50c. blue	50	20
496A	**72**	$1 sepia and brown	3·25	20
497A	**72**	$2 brown and blue	2·50	50
498A	**72**	$5 green and red	2·75	75
499A	**72**	$10 violet and green	6·50	3·25
500A	**72**	$20 blue and purple	18·00	6·50

For dollar values in single colours, see Nos. 666 etc.

For 15c. brown see Japanese Occupation of China: IV Shanghai and Nanking No. 12.

74 Chinese and U.S. Flags and Map of China

1939. 150th Anniv of U.S. Constitution. Flags in red and blue.

501	**74**	5c. green	1·50	1·00
502	**74**	25c. blue	2·25	1·25
503	**74**	50c. brown	3·75	2·25
504	**74**	$1 red	5·00	4·25

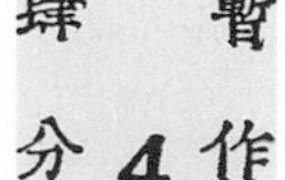

(76)

1940. Surch as T 76.

577	**72**	3c. on 5c. green	2·25	3·25
582	**72**	4c. on 5c. green	1·00	60
619	**72**	7c. on 8c. green	2·25	3·75

77 Dr. Sun Yat-sen

1941

583	**77**	½c. brown	25	35
584	**77**	1c. orange	25	20
585	**77**	2c. blue	30	50
586	**77**	5c. green	30	20
587	**77**	8c. orange	70	1·25
588	**77**	8c. green	60	40
589	**77**	10c. green	35	30
590	**77**	17c. green	12·00	13·00
591	**77**	25c. purple	40	80
592	**77**	30c. red	40	40
593	**77**	50c. blue	40	30
594	**77**	$1 black and brown	50	40
595	**77**	$2 black and blue	75	50
596	**77**	$5 black and red	1·25	85
597	**77**	$10 black and green	5·50	5·00
598	**77**	$20 black and purple	5·50	5·00

78 Industry

1941. Thrift Movement.

599	**78**	8c. green	1·00	1·00
600	**78**	21c. brown	1·25	1·25
601	**78**	28c. olive	1·50	1·50
602	**78**	33c. red	2·00	2·25
603	**78**	50c. blue	2·50	3·25
604	**78**	$1 purple	3·25	4·25
MS605		155×171 mm. Nos. 599/604 in slightly different colours. Imperf. No gum	85·00	£100

中華民國創立
三十週年紀念
三十年十月十日

(79)

1941. 30th Anniv of Republic. Optd with T 79.

606	-	1c. orange (No. 508)	1·25	2·00
607	**72**	2c. green	1·25	2·00
608	**60**	4c. lilac	1·25	2·00
609	**72**	8c. green	1·25	2·00
610	**72**	10c. green	1·25	2·00
611	**72**	16c. brown	1·25	2·00
612	-	21c. brown (No. 520)	1·25	2·00
613	-	28c. green (No. 541)	1·25	2·00
614	**72**	30c. red	1·25	2·00
615	**72**	$1 sepia and brown	3·75	5·25

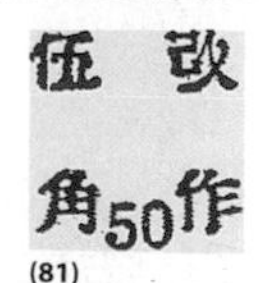

(81)

1942. Provincial surcharges. Surch as T 81.

622	**60**	1c. on ½c. brown	2·00	3·75
624	**77**	1c. on ½c. brown	2·50	3·25
690g	-	20c. on 13c. green (516)	3·25	15·00
691i	**72**	20c. on 16c. brown	2·25	12·00
693e	-	20c. on 17c. green (417)	5·00	15·00
694f	-	20c. on 21c. brown (520)	2·00	15·00
695e	-	20c. on 28c. green (541)	1·50	15·00

625	**72**	40c. on 50c. blue	5·00	6·50
626	-	40c. on 50c. green (544)	10·00	12·00
627	**77**	40c. on 50c. blue	9·50	12·00
689a	-	50c. on 16c. brown	6·50	5·50

82 Dr. Sun Yat-sen

1942

628A	**82**	10c. green	20	1·75
629A	**82**	16c. olive	35·00	48·00
630A	**82**	20c. olive	20	1·25
631A	**82**	25c. purple	20	1·60
632A	**82**	30c. red	20	1·00
642	**82**	30c. brown	35	15·00
633A	**82**	40c. brown	20	1·25
634A	**82**	50c. green	20	20
635A	**82**	$1 red	50	20
636A	**82**	$1 olive	30	30
637A	**82**	$1.50 blue	30	40
638A	**82**	$2 green	30	30
645	**82**	$2 blue	10·00	10·00
646	**82**	$2 purple	20	20
639A	**82**	$3 yellow	30	30
640A	**82**	$4 brown	35	35
641A	**82**	$5 red	30	30
650	**82**	$6 violet	40	45
651	**82**	$10 brown	20	20
652	**82**	$20 blue	20	20
653	**82**	$50 green	10·00	20
654	**82**	$70 violet	5·00	35
655	**82**	$100 brown	20	30

1942. As T 72 but emblem at top redrawn with solid background. Perf, imperf or roul.

666	**72**	$4 blue	60	1·50
667	**72**	$5 grey	1·50	1·10
656	**72**	$10 brown	2·50	1·00
657	**72**	$20 green	2·50	1·00
658	**72**	$20 red	40·00	20·00
659	**72**	$30 purple	1·25	1·00
660	**72**	$40 red	1·50	1·00
661	**72**	$50 blue	2·50	1·25
662	**72**	$100 brown	12·00	5·00

(T **83** Trans. "Surcharge for Domestic Postage Paid")

(83)

1942. Surch as T 83.

688e	**82**	16c. olive	£120	£130

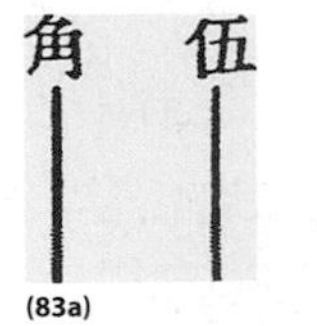

(83a)

1943. No 688e surch as T 83a.

701e	50c. on 16c. olive	10·00	10·00

89 Dr. Sun Yat-sen

1944

702	**89**	40c. red	30	5·50
703	**89**	$2 brown	30	30
704	**89**	$3 red	20	20
705	**89**	$3 brown	75	50
706	**89**	$6 grey	30	35
707	**89**	$10 red	30	30
708	**89**	$20 pink	30	30
709	**89**	$50 brown	5·00	45
710	**89**	$70 violet	45	45

90 War Refugees

1944. War Refugees' Relief Fund. Various frames.

724	**90**	$2+$2 on 50c.+50c. blue	2·50	5·00
725	**90**	$4+$4 on 8c.+8c. green	2·50	5·00
726	**90**	$5+$5 on 21c.+21c. brn	2·50	5·00
727	**90**	$6+$6 on 28c.+28c. olive	3·50	5·50
728	**90**	$10+$10 on 33c.+33c. red	5·00	6·50
729	**90**	$20+$20 on $1+$1 violet	7·50	9·00
MS730		190×100 mm. Nos. 724/9	£100	£100

91 Savings Bank and Money Box

1944

731	**91**	$40 slate	25	65
732	**91**	$50 green	25	20
733	**91**	$100 brown	25	20
734	**91**	$200 green	25	20

92 Dr. Sun Yat-sen

1944. 50th Anniv of Kuomintang.

740	**92**	$2 green	2·50	3·25
741	**92**	$5 brown	2·50	2·50
742	**92**	$6 purple	3·50	4·50
743	**92**	$10 blue	4·50	6·50
744	**92**	$20 red	6·50	10·00

93 Dr. Sun Yat-sen

1945. 20th Death Anniv of Dr. Sun Yat-sen.

746	**93**	$2 green	2·25	3·00
747	**93**	$5 brown	2·50	3·25
748	**93**	$6 blue	3·25	5·00
749	**93**	$10 blue	3·50	5·00
750	**93**	$20 red	5·50	5·50
751	**93**	$30 buff	7·50	7·50

94 Dr. Sun Yat-sen

1945

758	**94**	$2 green	30	1·00
759	**94**	$5 green	30	35
760	**94**	$10 blue	30	35
761	**94**	$20 red	25	35

95 Gen. Chiang Kai-shek

1945. Equal Treaties with Great Britain and U.S.A., abolishing Foreign Concessions. Flags in national colours.

762	**95**	$1 blue	2·25	3·00
763	**95**	$2 green	2·25	3·25
764	**95**	$5 olive	2·50	3·00
765	**95**	$6 brown	2·75	3·00
766	**95**	$10 red	6·50	8·50
767	**95**	$20 red	7·50	9·00

96 Pres. Lin Sen

1945. In Memory of President Lin Sen.

768	**96**	$1 black and blue	2·00	2·75
769	**96**	$2 black and green	2·25	3·00
770	**96**	$5 black and red	2·50	3·25
771	**96**	$6 black and violet	2·75	3·25
772	**96**	$10 black and brown	5·50	5·00
773	**96**	$20 black and olive	6·50	7·50

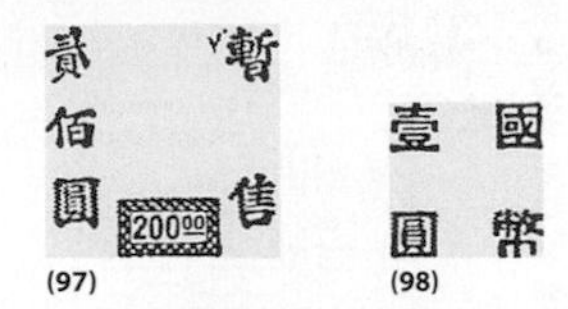

(97) **(98)**

1945. Chinese National Currency (C.N.C.). Various issues surch as T 97 (for Japanese controlled Government at Shanghai and Nanking) and further surch as T 98.

774	**72**	10c. on $20 on 3c. red	20	2·50
775	-	15c. on $30 on 2c. blue (509)	20	2·50
776	**77**	25c. on $50 on 1c. orange	20	1·50
777	**72**	50c. on $100 on 3c. red	20	60
778	**60**	$1 on $200 on 1c. orange (508)	20	20
779	**72**	$2 on $400 on 3c. red	20	30
780	**77**	$5 on $1000 on 1c. orange	20	20

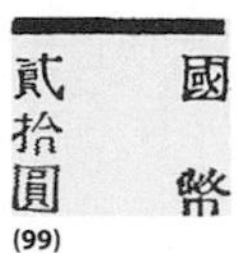

(99)

1945. Kaifeng provisionals. C.N.C. surcharges. Stamps of Japanese Occupation of North China surch as T 99.

781	**60**	$10 on 20c. lake (No. 166)	15·00	30·00
782	**60**	$20 on 40c. orge (No. 168)	40·00	40·00
783	**60**	$50 on 30c. red (No. 167)	23·00	30·00

100 Pres. Chiang Kai-shek

1945. Inauguration of Pres. Chiang Kai-shek. Flag in blue and red.

784	**100**	$2 green	2·25	3·00
785	**100**	$4 blue	2·25	3·00
786	**100**	$5 olive	2·25	3·25
787	**100**	$6 brown	3·00	4·25
788	**100**	$10 grey	6·50	7·50
789	**100**	$20 red	7·50	8·00

101 Pres. Chiang Kai-shek

1945. Victory. Flag in red.

790	**101**	$20 green and blue	50	50
791	**101**	$50 brown and blue	70	70
792	**101**	$100 blue	60	35
793	**101**	$300 red and blue	60	35

(102)

1945. C.N.C. surcharges. Nos. 410, 412, 514, 516/17, 519/20 and 541 surch as T 102 (value tablet at top).

794		$3 on 2½c. purple	15·00	20·00
795		$10 on 15c. purple	20	20
796		$20 on 8c. orange	20	20
797		$20 on 20c. blue	30	80
798		$30 on ½c. brown	30	90
799		$50 on 21c. brown	30	70
806		$70 on 13c. green	20	20
802		$100 on 28c. green	35	1·00

103 Dr. Sun Yat-sen

1945. No gum.

808	**103**	$20 red	15	15
809	**103**	$30 blue	15	20
810	**103**	$40 orange	50	1·00
811	**103**	$50 green	80	30
812	**103**	$100 brown	20	20
813	**103**	$200 brown	20	20

(104)

1946. Air. C.N.C. surcharges. Surch as T 104.

820	**61**	$23 on 30c. red	20	85
821	**61**	$53 on 15c. green	20	85
822	**61**	$73 on 25c. orange	20	1·00
823	**61**	$100 on $2 brown	20	30
824	**61**	$200 on $5 red	20	30

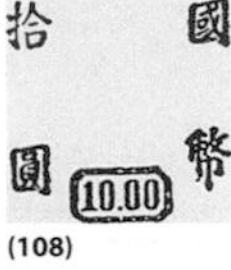

(108)

1946. C.N.C. surcharges. Surch as T 108 (octagonal value tablet at bottom).

898	-	$10 on 1c. orange (508)	20	70
903	**77**	$10 on 1c. orange	40	2·75
896	**72**	$20 on 2c. green	20	1·25
904	**77**	$20 on 2c. blue	30	2·50
897	**72**	$20 on 3c. red	20	1·00
899	-	$20 on 3c. brown (511)	30	1·40
869	**72**	$20 on 8c. green	2·10	2·10
879	-	$20 on 8c. orange (514)	30	2·50
882	**77**	$20 on 8c. orange	2·50	10·00
883	**77**	$20 on 8c. green	30	2·50
900	**60**	$30 on 4c. lilac	30	1·00
876	**72**	$50 on 5c. green	40	30
880	-	$50 on 5c. orange (513)	30	30
884	**77**	$50 on 5c. green	1·10	30

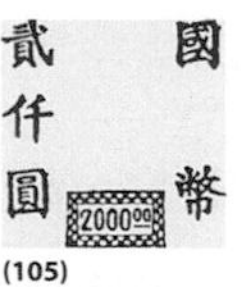

(105)

1946. C.N.C. surcharges. Surch as T 105 (rectangular value tablet at bottom). (a) Box with chequered pattern.

831	**72**	$20 on 3c. red	20	2·50
846	-	$20 on 8c. orange (514)	20	1·00
832	**72**	$50 on 3c. red	20	40
833	**72**	$50 on 5c. green	20	50
847	-	$50 on 5c. orange (513)	20	25
851	**77**	$50 on 5c. green	65	2·25
854	**82**	$50 on $1 green	20	20
848	-	$100 on 1c. orange (508)	20	20
834	**72**	$100 on 3c. red	20	20
842	**72**	$100 on 8c. green	45	30
852	**77**	$100 on 8c. green	40	25
860	**58**	$100 on $1 purple	40	20
868	**107**	$100 on $20 red	45	35
837	**72**	$200 on 10c. green	85	35
861	**58**	$200 on $4 blue	65	25
855	**82**	$250 on $1.50 blue	40	1·50
862	**58**	$250 on $2 green	75	30
863	**58**	$250 on $5 red	75	25
838	**72**	$300 on 10c. green	20	20
853	**77**	$300 on 10c. green	20	1·00
839	**72**	$500 on 3c. red	55	25
864	**58**	$500 on $20 green	20	20
865	**58**	$800 on $30 brown	20	4·25
830	**58**	$1000 on 2c. green	1·00	35
856	**82**	$1000 on $2 green	30	25
857	**82**	$1000 on $2 blue	25	2·00
858	**82**	$1000 on $2 brown	45	40

866	94	$1000 on $2 green	20	4·25
859	82	$2000 on $5 red	35	40
867	94	$2000 on $5 green	15	40

(b) Box with diamond pattern.

978	58	$500 on $20 green	20	20
979	107	$1250 on $70 orange	20	5·50
980	118	$1800 on $350 buff	20	5·50
974	82	$2000 on $3 yellow	50	35
975	82	$3000 on $3 yellow	20	20
976	89	$2000 on $3 red	20	20
977	89	$3000 on $3 brown	20	1·00

107 Dr. Sun Yat-sen

1946

885	107	$20 red	6·50	25
886	107	$30 blue	25	20
887	107	$50 violet	20	15
888	107	$70 orange	26·00	2·50
889	107	$100 red	15	15
890	107	$200 green	15	15
891	107	$500 green	25	15
892	107	$700 brown	15	1·10
893	107	$10000 purple	30	25
894	107	$3000 blue	85	25
895	107	$5000 red and green	85	25

109 Douglas DC-4 over Mausoleum of Dr. Sun Yat-sen

1946. Air. No gum.

905	109	$27 blue	30	1·00

110 Pres. Chiang Kai-shek

1946. President's 60th Birthday.

906A	110	$20 red	40	55
907A	110	$30 green	75	1·00
908A	110	$50 orange	75	1·00
909A	110	$100 green	1·00	1·25
910A	110	$200 yellow	1·00	1·00
911A	110	$300 red	1·25	75

For stamps of this type, but additionally inscribed with four characters around head, see Taiwan Nos. 30/5, or North Eastern Provinces, Nos. 48/53.

111 National Assembly House, Nanking

1946. Opening of National Assembly, Nanking. No gum.

912	111	$20 green	80	1·00
913	111	$30 blue	80	1·00
914	111	$50 brown	80	1·00
915	111	$100 red	80	80

112 Entrance to Dr. Sun Yat-sen Mausoleum

1947. 1st Anniv of Return of Government to Nanking.

942	112	$100 green	80	1·00
943	112	$200 blue	80	1·25
944	112	$250 red	80	1·50
945	112	$350 brown	80	1·50
946	112	$400 purple	80	50

For stamps of this type but additionally inscribed with four characters above numeral of value, see Taiwan, Nos. 36/40, or North Eastern Provinces, Nos. 65/70.

113 Dr. Sun Yat-sen

1947

947	113	$500 olive	50	20
948	113	$1,000 red and green	80	20
949	113	$2,000 lake and blue	80	20
950	113	$5,000 black and orange	90	20

114 Confucius

115 Confucius's Lecture School

116 Tomb of Confucius

1947. Confucius Commem. No gum.

951	114	$500 red	75	1·00
952	115	$800 brown	75	1·25
953	116	$1,250 green	75	1·25
954	116	$1,800 blue	75	1·75

DESIGN—HORIZ: $1,800, Confucian Temple.

118 Dr. Sun Yat-sen and Plum Blossoms

1947. (a) With noughts for cents. No gum.

955	118	$150 blue	20	25·00
956	118	$250 violet	30	5·00
957	118	$500 green	20	10
958	118	$1,000 red	20	10
959	118	$2,000 orange	20	10
960	118	$3,000 blue	20	10
961	118	$4,000 grey	20	20
962	118	$5,000 brown	20	10
963	118	$6,000 purple	20	20
964	118	$7,000 brown	20	20
965	118	$10,000 red and blue	50	10
966	118	$20,000 green and red	1·25	10
967	118	$50,000 blue and green	1·50	10
968	118	$100,000 green & orange	3·75	15
969	118	$200,000 blue and purple	4·25	30
970	118	$300,000 orange & brown	5·25	45
971	118	$500,000 brown & green	6·50	45

(b) Without noughts for cents.

1032	$20,000 red	40	25
1033	$30,000 brown	20	15
1034	$40,000 green	20	15
1035	$50,000 blue	20	15
1036	$100,000 olive	20	15
1037	$200,000 purple	65	15
1038	$300,000 green	3·25	70
1039	$500,000 mauve	1·00	20
1040	$1,000,000 red	65	20
1041	$2,000,000 orange	85	20
1042	$3,000,000 bistre	2·75	45
1043	$5,000,000 blue	6·00	75

119 Map of Taiwan and Chinese Flag

1947. Restoration of Taiwan (Formosa) (1st issue).

972	119	$500 red	1·00	1·25
973	119	$1,250 green	1·00	1·25

See also Nos. 1003/4.

122 Postal Kiosk

1947. Progress of the Postal Service.

981	-	$500 red	80	1·00
982	122	$1,000 violet	1·00	1·00
983	122	$1,250 green	1·00	1·25
984	-	$1,800 blue	1·00	1·25

DESIGN: $500, $1,800, Mobile Post Office.

123 Air, Sea and Rail Transport

124 Postboy and Motor Van

1947. 50th Anniv of Directorate General of Posts.

985	123	$100 violet	40	1·00
986	124	$200 green	40	1·00
987	124	$300 lake	40	1·25
988	-	$400 red	40	1·25
989	-	$500 blue	40	70

DESIGN—As T **123**: $400, $500, Junk and airplane.

126 Book of the Constitution and National Assembly Building

1947. Adoption of the Constitution.

990	126	$2,000 red	75	1·00
991	126	$3,000 blue	75	1·00
992	126	$5,000 green	75	1·00

127 Reproductions of 1947 and 1912 Stamps

1948. Perf or imperf. (a) Nanking Philatelic Exn.

1001	127	$5,000 red	1·00	3·25

(b) Shanghai Philatelic Exhibition.

1002	$5,000 green	1·00	3·25

128 Sun Yat-sen Memorial Hall

1948. Restoration of Taiwan (Formosa) to Chinese Rule (2nd issue).

1003	128	$5,000 lilac	1·00	1·75
1004	128	$10,000 red	1·00	1·75

圓仟肆作改☆ ☆ 400000 ☆☆

(130)

圓仟伍作改 5000.00

(129)

(133)

1948. "Re-valuation" surcharges. (a) Surch as T 130.

1012	118	$4,000 on $100 red	20	48·00
1013	118	$5,000 on $100 red	20	10
1014	118	$8,000 on $700 brown	25	80

(b) Surch as T 129.

1005	82	$5,000 on $1 green	20	20
1007	82	$5,000 on $2 green	20	20
1008	103	$10,000 on $20 red	20	20
1015	82	$15,000 on 50c. green	20	60
1018	82	$15,000 on 10c. green	20	40
1019	82	$15,000 on $4 purple	20	60
1020	82	$15,000 on $6 blue	30	40
1009	82	$20,000 on 10c. green	20	20
1010	82	$20,000 on 50c. green	20	30
1011	82	$30,000 on 30c. red	20	30
1016	82	$40,000 on 20c. olive	20	60
1017	82	$60,000 on $4 brown	25	30

(c) Air. Surch as T 133.

1022	61	$10,000 on 30c. red	20	1·25
1028	109	$10,000 on $27 blue	35	2·00
1023	61	$20,000 on 25c. orange	20	1·25
1024	61	$30,000 on 90c. olive	20	1·50
1025	61	$50,000 on 60c. blue	20	1·50
1026	61	$50,000 on $1 green	20	70

On No. 1028 the Chinese characters read vertically.

135 Great Wall of China

1948. Tuberculosis Relief Fund. Cross in red. Perf or imperf. No gum.

1029	135	$5,000+$2,000 violet	20	2·50
1030	135	$10,000+$2,000 brown	20	2·50
1031	135	$15,000+$2,000 grey	20	2·50

137 "Hai Tien" (freighter) and "Eton" (steamer) of 1872

138 "Kiang Ya" (freighter)

1948. 75th Anniv of China Merchants' Steam Navigation Company. No gum.

1044	137	$20,000 blue	75	3·00
1045	137	$30,000 mauve	75	3·00
1046	138	$40,000 brown	75	3·50
1047	138	$60,000 red	75	3·25

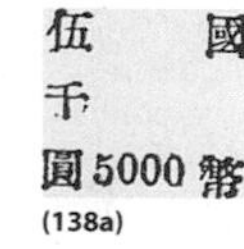

(138a)

1948. C.N.C. surcharge. Surch with T 138a.

1048	107	$5,000 on $100 claret	30·00	85·00

金圓 1/2分 **(139)**

3分 金圓 **(140)**

壹 金 角 10 圓 **(141)**

1948. Gold Yuan surcharges. (a) Surch as T 139 or 140.

1049	82	½c. on 30c. brown	20	8·50
1050	118	½c. on $500 green	20	20
1051	107	1c. on $20 red	20	2·00
1052	82	2c. on $1.50 blue	20	3·25
1053	82	3c. on $5 red	20	3·00
1054	82	4c. on $1 red	20	2·75
1055	82	5c. on 50c. green	20	35

(b) Surch as T 141.

1056	89	5c. on $20 red	20	1·00
1057	103	5c. on $30 blue	20	1·50
1058	72	10c. on 2c. green	20	1·50
1059	60	10c. on 2½c. purple	20	1·25
1061	82	10c. on 25c. brown	20	1·75
1062	89	10c. on 40c. red	20	1·25
1063	82	10c. on $1 green	20	20
1065	89	10c. on $2 brown	20	20
1066	82	10c. on $20 blue	20	20
1067	89	10c. on $20 red	£425	£500
1068	94	10c. on $20 red	20	45
1069	107	10c. on $20 red	75	3·25
1070	103	10c. on $30 blue	20	1·50
1071	89	10c. on $70 violet	20	45
1072	118	10c. on $7,000 brown	1·75	1·75
1073	118	10c. on $20,000 red	20	3·75
1074	89	20c. on $6 purple	20	30
1075	58	20c. on $30 brown	40	5·00

1076	107	20c. on $30 blue	45	4·25
1077	107	20c. on $100 red	20	5·00
1079	60	50c. on ½c. brown	20	45
1081	82	50c. on 20c. green	20	40
1082	82	50c. on 30c. red	20	2·00
1083	82	50c. on 40c. brown	20	80
1084	89	50c. on 40c. red	20	1·00
1085a	82	50c. on $4 purple	20	2·00
1086	82	50c. on $20 blue	20	20
1087	94	50c. on $20 red	40	2·00
1088	107	50c. on $20 red	20	2·25
1089	82	50c. on $70 lilac	25	25
1090a	118	50c. on $6,000 purple	20	1·75
1091	82	$1 on 30c. brown	20	20
1092	82	$1 on 40c. brown	20	20
1093	82	$1 on $1 red	40	2·00
1094	82	$1 on $5 red	45	30
1095	89	$2 on $2 brown	20	20
1096	102	$2 on $20 red	20	20
1097	107	$2 on $100 red	20	20
1098	-	$5 on 17c. green (417)	1·00	1·00
1099	89	$5 on $2 brown	20	20
1100	118	$5 on $30,000 blue	20	2·25
1101	-	$8 on 20c. blue (519)	40	40
1102	118	$8 on $30,000 brown	20	2·25
1103	-	$10 on 40c. orange (543)	95	1·25
1104	89	$10 on $2 brown	20	25
1105	89	$20 on $2 brown	15	15
1106	107	$20 on $20 red	5·00	6·50
1107	82	$50 on 30c. red	20	25
1108	89	$50 on $2 brown	25	20
1109	107	$80 on $20 red	20	1·00
1110	82	$100 on $1 green	20	1·00
1111	89	$100 on $2 brown	30	25
1112	118	$20,000 on $40,000 green	25·00	25·00
1113	118	$50,000 on $20,000 red	1·50	60
1114	118	$50,000 on $30,000 brown	30·00	20·00
1115	118	$100,000 on $20,000 red	22·00	16·00
1116	118	$100,000 on $30,000 brown	2·50	30
1117	118	$200,000 on $40,000 green	20·00	25·00
1118	118	$200,000 on $50,000 blue	20·00	26·00

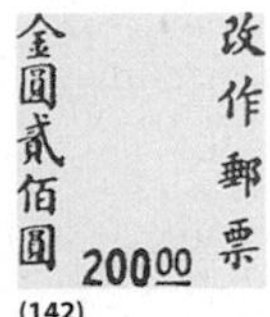

(142)

1949. Gold Yuan surcharges. Parcels Post stamps surch as T 142.

1119	P104	$200 on $3,000 orange	1·00	50
1120	P104	$500 on $5,000 blue	1·25	40
1121	P104	$1,000 on $10,000 vio	1·50	50

143 Liner, Train and Airplane

(144)

1949. Gold Yuan surcharges. Revenue stamps surch. (a) As T 144.

1136	143	50c. on $20 brown	20	45
1137	143	$1 on $15 orange	20	20·00
1127	143	$2 on $50 blue	20	1·50
1144	143	$3 on $50 blue	20	1·00
1138	143	$5 on $500 brown	20	35
1129	143	$10 on $30 mauve	20	45
1140	143	$15 on $20 brown	20	35
1141	143	$25 on $20 brown	20	35
1145	143	$50 on $50 blue	20	35
1147	143	$50 on $300 green	20	45
1130	143	$80 on $50 blue	20	1·25
1146	143	$100 on $50 blue	40	2·00
1124	143	$200 on $50 blue	70	1·00
1125	143	$300 on $50 blue	1·00	1·50
1142	143	$200 on $500 brown	40	50
1134	143	$500 on $30 mauve	50	3·75
1143	143	$500 on $15 orange	1·25	5·50
1135	143	$1,000 on $50 blue	15·00	15·00
1148	143	$1,000 on $100 olive	4·50	10·00
1126	143	$1,500 on $50 blue	1·25	3·25
1151	143	$2,000 on $300 green	40	55

(b) As T 144 but with key pattern inverted at top and bottom.

1183	$50 on $10 green	10·00	20·00
1184	$100 on $10 green	2·00	20·00
1185	$500 on $10 green	1·25	15·00
1186	$1,000 on $10 green	1·00	15·00
1187	$5,000 on $20 brown	50·00	32·00
1188	$10,000 on $20 brown	16·00	15·00
1189	$50,000 on $20 brown	22·00	25·00
1190	$100,000 on $20 brown	28·00	30·00
1191	$500,000 on $20 brown	£650	£325
1192	$2,000,000 on $20 brn	£1300	£550
1193	$5,000,000 on $20 brn	£1800	£1200

145 Dr. Sun Yat-sen

1949

1152	145	$1 orange	25	1·00
1153	145	$10 green	35	1·25
1154	145	$20 purple	15	1·00
1155	145	$50 green	15	75
1156	145	$100 brown	15	50
1157	145	$200 red	15	1·00
1158	145	$500 mauve	15	80
1159	145	$800 red	15	3·75
1160	145	$1,000 blue	25	40
1168	145	$2,000 violet	20	1·50
1169	145	$5,000 blue	20	35
1177	145	$5,000 red	1·00	1·10
1170	145	$10,000 brown	20	35
1171	145	$20,000 green	20	1·40
1179	145	$20,000 orange	1·75	1·50
1172	145	$50,000 pink	20	35
1180	145	$50,000 blue	3·25	6·50
1173	145	$80,000 brown	40	4·25
1174	145	$100,000 green	35	35
1181	145	$200,000 blue	6·00	5·00
1182	145	$500,000 purple	6·75	2·30

For stamps of Type **145** in Silver Yuan currency see Nos. 1348/56.

146 Steam Locomotive

147 Douglas DC-4

148 Postman on Motor Cycle

149 Mountains

1949. No value indicated. Perf or roul.

1211A	146	Orange (Ord. postage)	10·00	3·00
1212A	147	Green (Air Mail)	15·00	30·00
1213A	148	Mauve (Express)	15·00	30·00
1214A	149	Red (Registration)	15·00	25·00

Owing to the collapse of the Gold Yuan the above were sold at the rate for the day for the service indicated.

(154)

1949. Gold Yuan currency. Revenue stamps optd as T 154. No gum.

1232	143	$10 green (B)	60·00	70·00
1233	143	$30 mauve (A)	£170	£130
1234	143	$50 blue (C)	55·00	60·00
1235	143	$100 olive (D)	75·00	£100
1236	143	$200 purple (A)	40·00	25·00
1237	143	$500 green (A)	45·00	35·00

Opt. translation: (A) Domestic Letter Fee. (B) Express Letter Fee. (C) Registered Letter Fee. (D) Air Mail Fee.

(159)

1949. Silver Yuan surcharges. Revenue stamps surch as T 159. No gum.

1312	1c. on $20 brown	£100	£120
1284	1c. on $5,000 brown	10·00	7·50
1285	4c. on $100 olive	6·50	4·00
1286	4c. on $3,000 orange	5·50	2·00
1313	10c. on $20 brown	£110	£130
1287	10c. on $50 blue	10·00	3·25
1288	10c. on $1,000 red	10·00	3·75
1289	20c. on $1,000 red	10·00	4·00
1290	50c. on $30 mauve	25·00	9·00
1291	50c. on $50 blue	35·00	3·25
1292	$1 on $50 blue	25·00	25·00

On Nos. 1312 and 1313 the key pattern is inverted at top and bottom.

169 Tundra Swans over Globe

1949. No gum.

1344	169	$1 orange	12·00	25·00
1345	169	$2 blue	75·00	40·00
1346	169	$5 red	75·00	50·00
1347	169	$10 green	85·00	75·00

1949. Silver Yuan currency.

1348	145	1c. green	60·00	10·00
1349	145	2c. orange	4·00	25·00
1350	145	4c. green	10	1·50
1351	145	10c. lilac	30	1·50
1352	145	16c. red	60	25·00
1353	145	20c. blue	35	6·00
1354	145	50c. brown	1·50	48·00
1355	145	100c. blue	£475	£650
1356	145	500c. red	£500	£750

170 Globe and Doves

1949. 75th Anniv of UPU. Value optd in black. Imperf. No gum.

1357	170	$1 orange	10·00	25·00

171 Buddha's Tower, Peking

172 Bronze Bull

1949. Value optd. Roul.

1358	171	15c. green and brown	15·00	15·00
1359	172	40c. red and green	18·00	18·00

(173) (174)

1949. Silver Yuan surcharges. (a) Chungking issue. Surch as T 173.

1360	145	2½c. on $50 green	2·50	3·00
1361	145	2½c. on $50,000 blue	6·00	3·00
1362	145	5c. on $1,000 blue	6·00	3·25
1363	145	5c. on $20,000 orange	4·50	3·25
1364	145	5c. on $200,000 blue	5·50	3·00
1365	145	5c. on $500,000 purple	3·75	3·00
1366	145	10c. on $5,000 red	10·00	8·50
1367	145	10c. on $10,000 brown	10·00	8·00
1368	145	15c. on $200 red	10·00	25·00
1369	145	25c. on $100 brown	15·00	30·00

(b) Canton issue. Surch as T 174.

1371	1c. on $100 brown	12·00	14·00
1372	2½c. on $500 mauve	14·00	15·00
1374	15c. on $10 green	18·00	30·00
1375	15c. on $20 purple	28·00	40·00

EXPRESS DELIVERY STAMP

E80

1941. Perf. No gum.

E616	E80	(No value) red & yellow	75·00	65·00

This stamp was sold at $2, which included ordinary postage.

MILITARY POST STAMPS

(M85)

1942. Optd variously as Type M 85.

M676	77	8c. orange	£1000	
M682	72	8c. olive	7·50	20·00
M684	77	8c. green	10·00	20·00
M677	82	16c. olive	7·50	15·00
M683	72	16c. olive	75·00	£100
M678	82	50c. green	6·50	15·00
M679	82	$1 red	6·50	16·00
M680	82	$1 olive	6·50	15·00
M681	82	$2 green	8·50	18·00
M687	82	$2 purple	£200	£200

M93 Entrenched Soldiers

1945

M745	M93	(No value) red	1·00	25·00

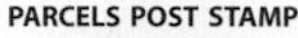
PARCELS POST STAMPS

P90

1944

P711	P90	$500 green	20·00	1·25
P712	P90	$1,000 blue	20·00	1·25
P713	P90	$3,000 red	20·00	1·25
P714	P90	$5,000 brown	£200	60·00
P715	P90	$10,000 purple	£300	£150

P104

1946

P814	P104	$3,000 orange	25·00	1·00
P815	P104	$5,000 blue	35·00	1·00
P816	P104	$10,000 violet	35·00	3·25
P817	P104	$20,000 red	40·00	8·50

P112

1947. Type P 112 and similar design.

P925	$1,000 yellow	10·00	1·50
P926	$3,000 green	10·00	1·50
P927	$5,000 red	10·00	1·50
P928	$7,000 blue	10·00	1·50
P929	$10,000 red	10·00	1·50
P930	$30,000 olive	10·00	2·50
P931	$50,000 black	12·00	2·50
P932	$70,000 brown	12·00	3·00
P933	$100,000 purple	12·00	3·25
P934	$200,000 green	14·00	3·50
P935	$300,000 pink	15·00	5·00
P936	$500,000 plum	15·00	5·00
P937	$3,000,000 blue	17·00	6·00
P938	$5,000,000 lilac	18·00	7·00
P939	$6,000,000 grey	20·00	7·00
P940	$8,000,000 red	22·00	8·50
P941	$10,000,000 olive	22·00	10·00

(P146)

1949. Gold Yuan surcharges. 1947 issue surch as Type P 146.

P1194	$10 on $3,000 green	10·00	1·75
P1195	$20 on $5,000 red	10·00	1·75
P1196	$50 on $10,000 red	10·00	1·75
P1197	$100 on $3,000,000 blue	12·00	2·25
P1198	$200 on $5,000,000 lilac	12·00	2·25
P1199	$500 on $1,000 yellow	14·00	3·00
P1200	$1,000 on $7,000 blue	16·00	3·25

Parcels post stamps were not on sale in unused condition; those now on the market were probably stocks seized by the Communists.

POSTAGE DUE STAMPS

1912. Chinese Empire Postage Due Stamps optd with vertical row of Chinese characters.

D207	**D37**	½c. blue	1·50	1·00
D208	**D37**	1c. brown	2·00	1·00
D209	**D37**	2c. brown	2·00	1·00
D210	**D37**	4c. blue	5·00	4·25
D211	**D37**	5c. blue	£250	£250
D212	**D37**	5c. brown	8·00	8·50
D213	**D37**	10c. blue	10·00	9·00
D214	**D37**	20c. blue	15·00	12·00
D215	**D37**	30c. blue	25·00	26·00

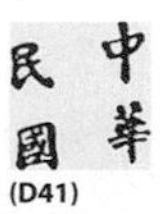

(D41)

1912. Optd with Type D 41.

D233	½c. blue	10·00	9·00
D234	½c. brown	2·50	1·25
D235	1c. brown	2·75	1·50
D236	2c. brown	6·50	6·50
D237	4c. blue	9·50	10·00
D238	5c. brown	15·00	15·00
D239	10c. blue	24·00	28·00
D240	20c. brown	38·00	48·00
D241	30c. blue	75·00	95·00

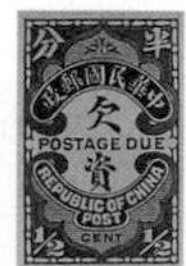
D46

1913

D341	**D46**	½c. blue	1·00	75
D342	**D46**	1c. blue	1·30	25
D343	**D46**	2c. blue	1·30	30
D344	**D46**	4c. blue	1·80	45
D345	**D46**	5c. blue	3·25	80
D346	**D46**	10c. blue	3·50	1·00
D347	**D46**	20c. blue	10·00	1·50
D340	**D46**	30c. blue	25·00	10·00

D62

1932

D432	**D62**	½c. orange	20	25
D433	**D62**	1c. orange	20	25
D434	**D62**	2c. orange	20	25
D435	**D62**	4c. orange	40	25
D569	**D62**	5c. orange	80	40
D570	**D62**	10c. orange	25	40
D571	**D62**	20c. orange	25	40
D572	**D62**	30c. orange	25	40
D573	**D62**	50c. orange	45	55
D574	**D62**	$1 orange	45	85
D575	**D62**	$2 orange	85	85

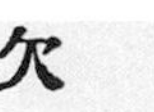

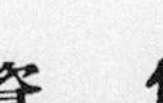

(D75) ("Temporary-use Postage Due")

1940. Optd with Type D 75.

D545	**72**	$1 brown and red	12·00	15·00
D546	**72**	$2 brown and blue	10·00	10·00

D90

1944. No gum.

D717	**D90**	10c. green	25	2·50
D718	**D90**	20c. blue	25	2·50
D719	**D90**	40c. red	25	2·75
D720	**D90**	50c. green	25	2·50
D721	**D90**	60c. blue	25	3·25
D722	**D90**	$1 red	25	1·60
D723	**D90**	$2 purple	25	1·60

D94

1945

D752	**D94**	$2 red	25	2·00
D753	**D94**	$6 red	25	2·00
D754	**D94**	$8 red	25	2·50
D755	**D94**	$10 red	25	1·75
D756	**D94**	$20 red	25	1·60
D757	**D94**	$30 red	55	1·60

D112

1947

D916	**D112**	$50 purple	25	2·25
D917	**D112**	$80 purple	25	2·25
D918	**D112**	$100 purple	25	2·00
D919	**D112**	$160 purple	25	2·50
D920	**D112**	$200 purple	25	2·00
D921	**D112**	$400 purple	25	2·25
D922	**D112**	$500 purple	25	2·00
D923	**D112**	$800 purple	25	2·00
D924	**D112**	$2,000 purple	25	50

圖仟壹作改
1000.00
(D127)

1948. Surch as Type D 127.

D993	**D94**	$1,000 on $20 purple	20	5·00
D994	**D94**	$2,000 on $30 purple	20	3·25
D995	**D94**	$3,000 on $50 purple	20	3·25
D996	**D94**	$4,000 on $100 pur	20	4·25
D997	**D94**	$5,000 on $200 pur	20	1·75
D998	**D94**	$10,000 on $300 pur	20	70
D999	**D94**	$20,000 on $500 pur	20	70
D1000	**D94**	$30,000 on $1,000 pur	20	25

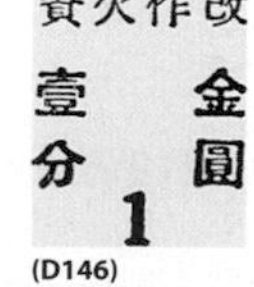

(D146)

1949. Gold Yuan surcharges. Surch as Type D 146.

D1201	**102**	1c. on $40 orange	50	12·00
D1202	**102**	2c. on $40 orange	50	13·00
D1203	**102**	5c. on $40 orange	50	8·50
D1204	**102**	10c. on $40 orange	50	9·00
D1205	**102**	20c. on $40 orange	50	9·50
D1206	**102**	50c. on $40 orange	50	8·00
D1207	**102**	$1 on $40 orange	50	6·00
D1208	**102**	$2 on $40 orange	50	6·00
D1209	**102**	$5 on $40 orange	50	8·50
D1210	**102**	$10 on $40 orange	50	3·75

REGISTRATION STAMP

1941. Roul. No gum.

R617	**E80**	(No value) grn & buff	55·00	40·00

This stamp was sold at $1.50 which included ordinary postage.

CHINESE PROVINCES
Manchuria
A. KIRIN AND HEILUNGKIANG

Stamps of China optd

用貼黑吉限
(1) Stamps of China optd

1927. Stamps of 1913 optd with T 1.

1	**43**	½c. sepia	1·30	25
2	**43**	1c. orange	2·00	25
3	**43**	1½c. purple	2·00	1·40
4	**43**	2c. green	2·00	35
5	**43**	3c. green	2·00	1·00
6	**43**	4c. olive	2·25	2·25
7	**43**	5c. mauve	2·25	2·25
8	**43**	6c. red	2·25	2·00
9	**43**	7c. violet	4·25	2·50
10	**43**	8c. orange	4·25	2·00
11	**43**	10c. blue	3·25	3·25
12	**44**	13c. brown	5·00	4·50
13	**44**	15c. blue	5·50	2·10
14	**44**	16c. olive	6·00	5·00
15	**44**	20c. lake	6·00	4·00
16	**44**	30c. purple	9·00	3·25
17	**44**	50c. green	12·00	4·25
18	**45**	$1 sepia and brown	35·00	8·00
19	**45**	$2 brown and blue	95·00	22·00
20	**45**	$5 green and red	£375	£350

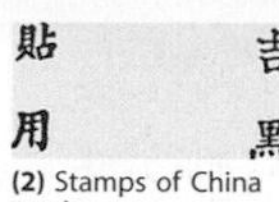

(2) Stamps of China optd

1928. Chang Tso-lin stamps optd with T 2.

21	**55**	1c. orange	5·00	5·00
22	**55**	4c. olive	5·00	4·25
23	**55**	10c. blue	6·50	6·00
24	**55**	$1 red	75·00	65·00

1929. Unification stamps optd as T 2.

25	**56**	1c. orange	4·50	2·50
26	**56**	4c. olive	5·50	3·75
27	**56**	10c. blue	15·00	12·00
28	**56**	$1 red	£140	£120

1929. Sun Yat-sen Memorial stamps optd as T 2.

29	**57**	1c. orange	4·50	4·00
30	**57**	4c. olive	5·50	5·00
31	**57**	10c. blue	10·00	7·50
32	**57**	$1 red	£120	£100

B. NORTH-EASTERN PROVINCES

Issues made by the Chinese Nationalist Government of Chiang Kai-shek.

1 Dr. Sun Yat-sen

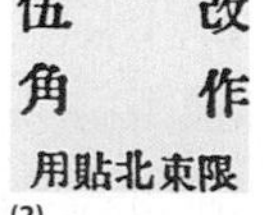

(2)

1946. Surch as T 2.

1	**1**	50c. on $5 red	40	5·50
2	**1**	50c. on $10 green	60	5·50
3	**1**	$1 on $10 green	40	3·25
4	**1**	$2 on $20 purple	40	4·50
5	**1**	$4 on $50 brown	40	3·25

用貼北東限
(3)

1946. Stamps of China optd with T 3 (="Limited for use in North East").

6	-	1c. orange (508)	25	6·00
7	-	3c. brown (511)	25	6·50
8	-	5c. orange (513)	25	3·25
9	**72**	10c. green	25	3·25
11	**72**	20c. blue	25	3·00

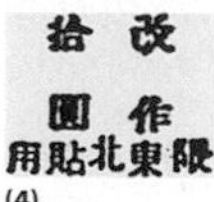

(4)

1946. Stamps of China surch as T 4 but larger.

14	-	$5 on $50 on 21c. brown (No. 799)	£150	£200
15	-	$10 on $100 on 28c. green (No. 802)	£150	£225
16	**91**	$20 on $200 green	£150	£200

5 Dr. Sun Yat-sen

1946

17	**5**	5c. lake	25	3·50
18	**5**	10c. orange	25	3·25
19	**5**	20c. green	25	4·00
20	**5**	25c. brown	25	3·75
21	**5**	50c. orange	25	2·50
22	**5**	$1 blue	25	2·50
23	**5**	$2 purple	25	3·00
24	**5**	$2.50 blue	25	4·25
25	**5**	$3 brown	25	3·00
26	**5**	$4 brown	25	3·75
27	**5**	$5 green	25	3·25
28	**5**	$10 red	25	1·25
29	**5**	$20 olive	25	90
34	**5**	$22 black	£100	£150
35	**5**	$44 red	50·00	85·00
36	**5**	$50 violet	55	1·00
37	**5**	$65 green	£160	£160
38	**5**	$100 green	25	50
39	**5**	$109 green	£120	£150
40	**5**	$200 brown	25	90
41	**5**	$300 green	25	1·80
42	**5**	$500 red	25	50
43	**5**	$1,000 orange	25	45

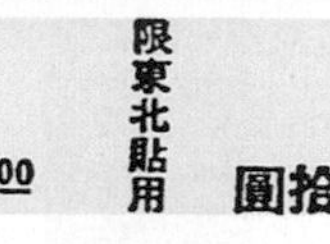
(6)

1946. Nanking National Assembly stamps of China surch as T 6.

44	**111**	$2 on $20 green	50	3·50
45	**111**	$3 on $30 blue	50	4·00
46	**111**	$5 on $50 brown	50	3·50
47	**111**	$10 on $100 red	50	2·50

7 Pres. Chiang Kai-shek (note characters to right of head)

1947. President's 60th Birthday.

54	**7**	$2 red	80	5·00
55	**7**	$3 green	1·00	5·50
56	**7**	$5 red	1·00	6·00
57	**7**	$10 green	1·00	3·50
58	**7**	$20 orange	1·25	3·50
59	**7**	$30 red	1·50	2·75

For other stamps as Types **7** and **9** but with different Chinese characters, see China–Taiwan Types **4** and **5**.

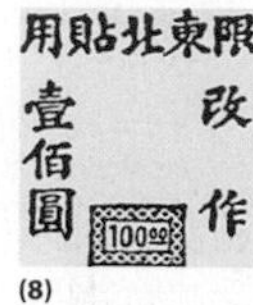
(8)

1947. Stamps of China surch as T 8.

60	**107**	$100 on $1,000 purple	1·00	5·50
61	**107**	$300 on $3,000 blue	1·00	6·00
62	**58**	$500 on $30 brown	50	6·50
63	**107**	$500 on $5,000 red & green	1·25	4·00

9 Entrance to Dr. Sun Yat-sen Mausoleum (note characters above face value)

1947. 1st Anniv of Return of Govt. to Nanking.

64	**9**	$2 green	80	3·25
65	**9**	$4 blue	80	3·50
66	**9**	$6 red	80	3·50
67	**9**	$10 brown	80	2·25
68	**9**	$20 purple	80	1·75

(10)

1948. Surch as T 10.

70	**5**	$1,500 on 20c. green	80	6·50
71	**5**	$3,000 on $1 blue	30	5·00
72	**5**	$4,000 on 25c. brown	30	4·50
73	**5**	$8,000 on 50c. orange	30	4·50
74	**5**	$10,000 on 10c. orange	25	2·75
75	**5**	$50,000 on $109 green	70	6·50
76	**5**	$100,000 on $65 green	65	6·00
77	**5**	$500,000 on $22 black	1·10	5·50

No. 70 has five characters on the left side of the surcharge and No. 77 four characters.

MILITARY POST STAMPS

1946. Military Post stamp of China optd as T 3 but larger.

M13	**M93**	(No value) red	2·50	25·00

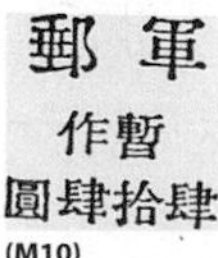

(M10)

1947. Surch with Type M 10.

M69	**5**	$44 on 50c. orange	15·00	45·00

PARCELS POST STAMPS

P11

1948

P78	P11	$500 red	£120	28·00
P79	P11	$1,000 red	£180	55·00
P80	P11	$3,000 olive	£225	70·00
P81	P11	$5,000 blue	£375	£110
P82	P11	$10,000 green	£550	£140
P83	P11	$20,000 blue	£800	£140

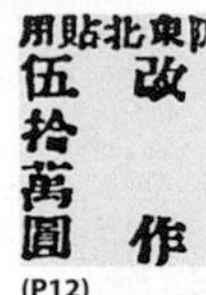

(P12)

1948. Parcels Post stamp of China surch with Type P 12.

P84	$500,000 on $5,000,000 lilac (No. P938)	£500	£225

Parcels Post stamps were not on sale unused.

POSTAGE DUE STAMPS

D7

1947

D48	D7	10c. blue	50	10·00
D49	D7	20c. blue	50	10·00
D50	D7	50c. blue	50	9·00
D51	D7	$1 blue	15	6·50
D52	D7	$2 blue	15	6·50
D53	D7	$5 blue	15	5·00

拾 改

圓 作

(D13)

1948. Surch as Type D 13.

D85	$10 on 10c. blue	25	10·00
D86	$20 on 20c. blue	25	10·00
D87	$50 on 50c. blue	25	10·00

Sinkiang
(Chinese Turkestan)

A province between Tibet and Mongolia. Issued distinguishing stamps because of its debased currency.

The following are all optd on stamps of China.

(1)

1915. 1913 issue optd with T 1.

17	43	½c. sepia	2·00	2·00
2	43	1c. orange	2·75	1·00
49	43	1½c. purple	3·00	4·25
3	43	2c. green	3·25	1·40
4	43	3c. green	3·50	50
5	43	4c. red	5·00	1·25
52	43	4c. grey	5·00	6·50
53	43	4c. olive	5·00	4·25
6	43	5c. mauve	4·50	1·25
55	43	6c. red	10·00	3·25
56	43	6c. brown	38·00	35·00
7	43	6c. grey	8·50	3·75
8	43	7c. violet	9·50	9·50
9	43	8c. orange	7·50	6·50
10	43	10c. blue	7·50	3·25
60	44	13c. brown	10·00	10·00
11	44	15c. brown	8·50	4·50
61	44	15c. blue	15·00	10·00
12	44	16c. olive	14·00	10·00
63	44	20c. lake	12·00	11·00
14	44	30c. purple	18·00	11·00
65	44	50c. green	22·00	12·00
34	45	$1 black and yellow	30·00	15·00
66	45	$1 sepia and brown	28·00	12·00
35	45	$2 black and blue	38·00	22·00
67	45	$2 brown and blue	42·00	17·00
36	45	$5 black and red	£110	55·00
68	45	$5 green and red	£110	38·00
37	45	$10 black and green	£325	£300
69	45	$10 mauve and green	£325	£250
38	45	$20 black and yellow	£1500	£850
70	45	$20 blue and purple	£475	£400

用貼省新限

(3)

1921. 25th Anniv of Chinese National Postal Service stamps optd with T 3.

39	48	1c. orange	3·50	5·00
40	48	3c. turquoise	5·00	6·00
41	48	6c. grey	10·00	10·00
42	48	10c. blue	£100	£100

貼 新 疆 用 省

(4)

1923. Adoption of the Constitution stamps optd with T 4.

43	53	1c. orange	7·50	7·50
44	53	3c. turquoise	8·00	8·00
45	53	4c. red	12·00	12·00
46	53	10c. blue	35·00	35·00

貼 新

用 疆

(5)

1928. Assumption of Title of Marshal of the Army and Navy by Chang Tso-lin. Optd with T 5.

71	55	1c. orange	4·50	4·50
72	55	4c. olive	5·00	5·00
73	55	10c. blue	10·00	8·00
74	55	$1 red	90·00	95·00

1929. Unification of China. Optd as T 5.

75	56	1c. orange	6·50	5·00
76	56	4c. olive	8·00	6·00
77	56	10c. blue	15·00	10·00
78	56	$1 red	£140	£130

1929. Sun Yat-sen State Burial. Optd as T 5.

79	57	1c. orange	4·25	4·00
80	57	4c. olive	5·50	4·75
81	57	10c. blue	10·00	8·00
82	57	$1 red	£120	£110

空航

(6)

1932. Air. Handstamped on Sinkiang issues as T 6 ("By Air Mail").

83	43	5c. mauve (No. 6)	£400	£300
84	43	10c. blue (No. 10)	£400	£225
85	44	15c. blue (No. 61)	£2250	£700
86	44	30c. purple (No. 14)	£1100	£1000

1932. Dr. Sun Yat-sen stamps optd as T 3.

87	58	1c. orange	2·00	4·25
95	58	2c. olive	3·50	3·00
103	58	4c. green	3·25	7·50
104	58	5c. green	3·50	5·50
105	58	15c. green	5·00	10·00
114	58	15c. red	7·50	6·25
115	58	20c. blue	4·75	1·50
107	58	25c. blue	6·50	3·25
108	58	$1 sepia and brown	18·00	22·00
100	58	$2 brown and blue	40·00	40·00
101	58	$5 black and red	55·00	95·00

1933. Tan Yen-kai Memorial. Optd as T 5.

117	62	2c. olive	5·00	5·00
118	62	5c. green	6·50	6·50
119	62	25c. blue	18·00	15·00
120	62	$1 red	£120	£110

1933. Martyrs' issue optd as T 3.

121	60	½c. sepia	50	3·50
122	-	1c. orange	3·25	3·50
167	-	2c. blue	2·00	3·50
123	60	2½c. mauve	75	3·00
124	-	3c. brown	75	4·50
169	60	4c. lilac	20	3·25
125	-	8c. orange	1·75	4·25
126	-	10c. purple	75	4·00
171	-	13c. green	35	4·00
172	-	15c. purple	20	4·25
173	-	17c. olive	75	4·75
137	-	20c. lake	50	9·00
174	-	20c. blue	20	4·25
175	-	21c. sepia	65	4·50
185	-	25c. purple	1·50	7·50
176	-	28c. olive	1·00	4·50
130	-	30c. red	90	6·50
131	-	40c. orange	1·25	6·50
132	-	50c. green	1·50	6·50

1940. Dr. Sun Yat-sen stamps optd as T 3.

139	72	2c. olive	1·25	3·75
140	72	3c. red	40	3·50
141	72	5c. green	40	3·50
143	72	8c. olive	40	2·50
144	72	10c. green	50	2·25
145	72	15c. red	1·50	6·50
146	72	16c. olive	1·25	6·00
147	72	25c. blue	1·50	7·50
156	72	30c. red	1·00	4·00
158	72	50c. blue	1·50	3·75
160	72	$1 brown and red	2·25	9·00
161	72	$2 brown and blue	3·25	10·00
162	72	$5 green and red	3·50	14·00
163	72	$10 violet and green	4·50	14·00
164	72	$20 blue and red	7·50	20·00

用貼省新限

(8)

1942. Air. Air stamps optd with T 8 or larger.

187	61	15c. green	7·50	10·00
197	61	25c. orange	6·50	14·00
198	61	30c. red	9·50	14·00
190	61	45c. purple	14·00	22·00
199	61	50c. brown	10·00	16·00
192	61	60c. blue	12·00	27·00
193	61	90c. olive	65·00	85·00
194	61	$1 green	13·00	25·00
200	61	$2 brown	75·00	70·00
201	61	$5 red	75·00	70·00

1942. Thrift stamps optd as T 8.

221	78	8c. green	10·00	25·00
215	78	21c. brown	10·00	20·00
216	78	28c. olive	10·00	20·00
223	78	33c. red	15·00	28·00
218	78	50c. blue	18·00	22·00
225	78	$1 purple	20·00	32·00
MS220		155×171 mm. China No. **MS**605	£850	£850

1943. Dr. Sun Yat-sen stamps optd as T 3.

227	82	10c. green	1·50	10·00
228	82	20c. olive	2·00	13·00
229	82	25c. purple	50	15·00
230	82	30c. red	75	14·00
231	82	40c. brown	50	11·00
232	82	50c. green	50	11·00
233	82	$1 red	3·50	10·00
234	82	$1 olive	75	12·00
235	82	$1.50 blue	75	18·00
236	82	$2 green	2·50	13·00
237	82	$3 yellow	75	10·00
238	82	$5 red	2·25	10·00

用貼省新限

(9)

1943. Stamps optd with T 9.

239	72	10c. green	22·00	45·00
240	-	20c. blue (No. 519)	22·00	42·00
241	72	50c. blue	22·00	40·00

1944. Dr. Sun Yat-sen stamps optd as T 3.

248	77	$4 blue	2·00	20·00
249	77	$5 grey	3·75	20·00
250	77	$10 brown	4·00	22·00
243	77	$20 red	10·00	25·00
251	77	$20 green	3·75	20·00
253	77	$30 purple	8·50	24·00
245	77	$40 red	9·00	28·00
255	77	$50 blue	7·50	25·00
247	77	$100 brown	18·00	25·00

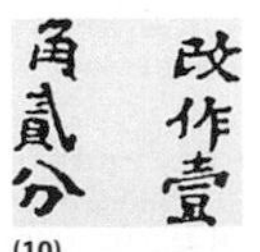

(10)

1944. Nos. 227 and 229 of Sinkiang surch as T 10.

257	82	12c. on 10c. green	12·00	30·00
258	82	24c. on 25c. purple	13·00	30·00

1945. Stamps optd as T 3.

259	89	40c. red	1·00	20·00
260	89	$3 red	1·00	30·00

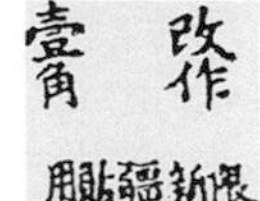

(11)

1949. Silver Yuan surcharges. Sun Yat-sen issues of China surch as T 11.

261	107	1c. on $100 red (No. 889)	35·00	40·00
262	107	3c. on $200 green (No. 890)	40·00	50·00
263	107	5c. on $500 green (No. 891)	45·00	40·00
264	136	10c. on $20,000 red (No. 1032)	48·00	40·00
265	136	50c. on $4,000 grey (No. 961)	£120	£100
266	136	$1 on $6,000 purple (No. 963)	£150	£140

Szechwan

A province of China. Issued distinguishing stamps because of its debased currency.

用貼川四限

(1) Stamps of China optd with T **1**.

1933. Issue of 1913.

1	43	1c. orange	15·00	1·00
2	43	5c. mauve	18·00	1·25
3	44	50c. green	60·00	7·50

1933. Dr. Sun Yat-sen issue.

4	58	2c. olive	2·50	1·00
5	58	5c. green	30·00	2·50
6	58	15c. green	10·00	6·50
7	58	15c. red	18·00	20·00
8	58	25c. blue	12·00	1·75
9	58	$1 sepia and brown	30·00	4·25
10	58	$2 brown and blue	80·00	10·00
11	58	$5 black and red	£160	48·00

1933. Martyrs issue (Nos. 410 etc).

12	60	½c. sepia	1·00	1·00
13	-	1c. orange	2·25	85
14	60	2½c. mauve	4·50	4·50
15	-	3c. brown	5·00	4·00
16	-	8c. orange	2·25	1·75
17	-	10c. purple	6·00	75
18	-	13c. green	6·25	1·00
19	-	17c. olive	8·50	1·40
20	-	20c. lake	10·00	1·00
21	-	30c. red	9·00	1·00
22	-	40c. orange	24·00	1·50
23	-	50c. green	50·00	2·25

Yunnan

A province of China which issued distinguishing stamps because of its debased currency.

用貼省滇限

(1) Stamps of China optd.

1926. Issue of 1913, optd with T 1.

1	43	½c. sepia	1·25	1·00
2	43	1c. orange	2·75	50
3	43	1½c. purple	3·50	4·25
4	43	2c. green	3·75	75
5	43	3c. green	3·25	50
6	43	4c. olive	4·25	60
7	43	5c. mauve	4·50	60
8	43	6c. red	6·50	2·25
9	43	7c. violet	8·50	3·25
10	43	8c. orange	7·50	3·25
11	43	10c. blue	6·50	50
12	44	13c. brown	8·50	8·00
13	44	15c. blue	8·50	6·50
14	44	16c. olive	9·50	5·00
15	44	20c. lake	10·00	5·00
16	44	30c. purple	28·00	18·00
17	44	50c. green	12·00	10·00
18	45	$1 sepia and brown	38·00	15·00
19	45	$2 brown and blue	80·00	25·00
20	45	$5 green and red	£375	£375

(2) Stamps of China optd.

1929. Unification of China. Optd with T 2.

21	56	1c. orange	3·00	3·25
22	56	4c. olive	5·00	5·50
23	56	10c. blue	10·00	10·00
24	56	$1 red	£125	£110

1929. Sun Yat-sen State Burial. Optd as T 2.

25	57	1c. orange	5·00	4·25
26	57	4c. olive	5·00	6·00
27	57	10c. blue	10·00	12·00
28	57	$1 red	£110	£100

用貼省滇限

(3) Stamps of China optd.

1932. Dr. Sun Yat-sen stamps optd with T 3.

29	58	1c. orange	5·00	4·25
30	58	2c. olive	7·50	8·00
44	58	4c. green	14·00	6·50
45	58	5c. green	16·00	6·00
46	58	15c. green	8·50	8·50
47	58	15c. red	9·00	9·00
32	58	20c. blue	5·50	3·25
48	58	25c. blue	10·00	6·50
33	58	$1 sepia and brown	75·00	80·00
34	58	$2 brown and blue	£150	£160
35	58	$5 black and red	£275	£300

1933. Tan Yen-kai Memorial. Optd with T 2.

52	**62**	2c. olive	4·00	4·00
53	**62**	5c. green	6·00	4·00
54	**62**	25c. blue	10·00	8·00
55	**62**	$1 red	£130	£120

1933. Martyrs issue optd as T 3.

56	**60**	½c. sepia	2·00	2·50
57	-	1c. orange	5·00	3·25
58	**60**	2½c. mauve	6·50	5·00
59	-	3c. brown	10·00	5·00
60	-	8c. orange	12·00	11·00
61	-	10c. purple	7·50	7·00
62	-	13c. green	7·00	5·00
63	-	17c. olive	16·00	12·00
64	-	20c. lake	6·50	3·75
65	-	30c. red	16·00	12·00
66	-	40c. orange	70·00	65·00
67	-	50c. green	85·00	70·00

COMMUNIST CHINA

A. East China People's Post

Issues were made by various Communist administrations from 1930 onwards. These had limited local availability and are outside the scope of this catalogue. For details of such issues see Part 17.

In 1946 (North East China) and 1949 these local issues were consolidated into Regional People's Post stamps for those local administrations listed below.

EC105 Methods of Transport

1949. 7th Anniv of Shandong Communist Postal Administration.

EC322	**EC105**	$1 green	25	20
EC323	**EC105**	$2 green	25	20
EC324	**EC105**	$3 red	25	20
EC325	**EC105**	$5 brown	25	20
EC326	**EC105**	$10 blue	25	20
EC327	**EC105**	$13 violet	25	20
EC328	**EC105**	$18 blue	25	20
EC329	**EC105**	$21 red	25	20
EC330	**EC105**	$30 green	25	30
EC331	**EC105**	$50 red	35	50
EC332	**EC105**	$100 green	12·00	10·00

The $5 has an overprinted character obliterating a Japanese flag on the tower.

EC106 Steam Train and Postal Runner

1949. Dated "1949.2.7".

EC333	**EC106**	$1 green	20	50
EC334	**EC106**	$2 green	20	40
EC335	**EC106**	$3 red	20	40
EC336	**EC106**	$5 brown	25	40
EC337	**EC106**	$10 blue	40	70
EC338	**EC106**	$13 violet	25	60
EC339	**EC106**	$18 blue	25	70
EC340	**EC106**	$21 red	25	1·00
EC341	**EC106**	$30 green	30	1·10
EC342	**EC106**	$50 red	30	1·60
EC343	**EC106**	$100 green	65	65

For stamps as Type EC **106**, but dated "1949", see Nos. EC364/71.

EC107 Victorious Troops and Map of Battle

1949. Victory in Huaihai Campaign.

EC344	**EC107**	$1 green	20	20
EC345	**EC107**	$2 green	20	20
EC346	**EC107**	$3 red	20	20
EC347	**EC107**	$5 brown	20	20
EC348	**EC107**	$10 blue	25	20
EC349	**EC107**	$13 violet	25	25
EC350	**EC107**	$18 blue	25	25
EC351	**EC107**	$21 red	25	25
EC352	**EC107**	$30 green	25	25
EC353	**EC107**	$50 red	25	25
EC354	**EC107**	$100 green	2·10	2·10

EC108 Maps of Shanghai and Nanjing

1949. Liberation of Nanjing and Shanghai.

EC355	**EC108**	$1 red	20	30
EC356	**EC108**	$2 green	20	30
EC357	**EC108**	$3 violet	25	25
EC358	**EC108**	$5 brown	25	25
EC359	**EC108**	$10 blue	25	25
EC360	**EC108**	$30 green	25	30
EC361	**EC108**	$50 red	25	55
EC362	**EC108**	$100 green	25	40
EC363	**EC108**	$500 orange	2·75	2·10

1949. As Type EC 106 but dated "1949".

EC364	$10 blue	25	25
EC365a	$15 red	45	30
EC366	$30 green	25	25
EC367	$50 red	25	45
EC368	$60 green	25	65
EC369	$100 green	5·50	45
EC370	$1,600 violet	1·50	3·25
EC371	$2,000 purple	1·40	3·00

EC111 Zhu De, Mao Tse-tung and Troops

1949. 22nd Anniv of Chinese People's Liberation Army.

EC378	**EC111**	$70 orange	20	25
EC379	**EC111**	$270 red	20	25
EC380	**EC111**	$370 green	30	25
EC381	**EC111**	$470 purple	50	40
EC382	**EC111**	$570 blue	25	35

For other values in this design with only three characters in bottom panel, see South West China Nos. SW9/19.

EC112 Mao Tse-tung

1949

EC383	**EC112**	$10 blue	3·75	7·50
EC384	**EC112**	$15 red	4·25	10·00
EC385	**EC112**	$70 brown	25	20
EC386	**EC112**	$100 purple	25	20
EC387	**EC112**	$150 orange	25	25
EC388	**EC112**	$200 green	25	25
EC389	**EC112**	$500 blue	25	25
EC390	**EC112**	$1,000 red	25	25
EC391	**EC112**	$2,000 green	25	75

(EC113) ("Chinese People's Postal Service East China Region")

1949. Stamps of Nationalist China surch as Type EC 113.

EC392	**145**	$400 on $200 red	32·00	1·10
EC393	**145**	$1,000 on $50 green	2·10	65
EC394	**145**	$1,200 on $100 brown	30	1·10
EC395	**145**	$1,600 on $20,000 grn	30	1·80
EC396	**145**	$2,000 on $1,000 blue	30	70

PARCELS POST STAMPS

Stamps of Nationalist China surch

$200 $500 $1,000

$2,000 $5,000 $10,000

(ECP110)

1949. No. 1347 surch as Type ECP 110.

ECP372	**169**	$200 on $10 green	85·00	35·00
ECP373	**169**	$500 on $10 green	85·00	35·00
ECP374	**169**	$1,000 on $10 green	95·00	40·00
ECP375	**169**	$2,000 on $10 green	£100	45·00
ECP376	**169**	$5,000 on $10 green	£110	48·00
ECP377	**169**	$10,000 on $10 green	£160	50·00

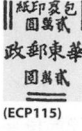

(ECP114)

1949. Nos. 1344/6 and unissued 10c. surch as Type ECP 114.

ECP397	$5,000 on 10c. blue	60·00	40·00
ECP398	$10,000 on $1 orange	70·00	45·00
ECP399	$20,000 on $2 blue	90·00	60·00
ECP400	$50,000 on $5 red	£200	75·00

(ECP115)

1949. Nos. P711/2 and P926/7 surch as Type ECP 115.

ECP401	**P90**	$5,000 on $500 green	25	55·00
ECP402	**P90**	$10,000 on $1 blue	£130	65·00
ECP403	**P112**	$20,000 on $3 green	£130	65·00
ECP404	**P112**	$50,000 on $5 red	2·50	75·00

B. North China People's Post

(NC68) (NC69) (NC70)

1949. Surch "North China People's Postal Administration".

(a) Surch as Type NC 68.

NC258	$5 on $500 orange	48·00	25·00
NC259	$6 on $500 orange	60·00	32·00
NC260	$12 on $200 red	5·00	8·00

(b) Surch as Type NC 69.

NC261	$3 on 2 (20c.) brown	£550	£180
NC262	$3 on 5 (50c.) blue	25·00	15·00
NC263	$5 on 2 (20c.) brown	23·00	15·00
NC264	$5 on 5 (50c.) blue	£600	£250

(c) Surch as Type NC 70.

NC265	$1 on $60 red	28·00	22·00
NC266	$5 on $80 purple	25·00	20·00
NC267	$6 on $2 brown	£150	70·00
NC268	$6 on $40 brown	28·00	15·00
NC269	$6 on $80 purple	£1000	£425

NC71 Infantry

NC72 Industry

1948. Imperf.

NC270	**NC71**	50c. purple	1·00	1·00
NC271	**NC71**	$1 blue	6·50	5·00
NC272	**NC71**	$2 green	1·00	1·00
NC273	**NC71**	$3 violet	1·00	1·00
NC274	**NC71**	$5 brown	1·00	1·00
NC275	**NC72**	$6 purple	1·00	1·00
NC276	**NC71**	$10 green	1·10	1·10
NC277	**NC71**	$12 red	7·50	1·10

The 50c. and $6 have value in Chinese characters only.

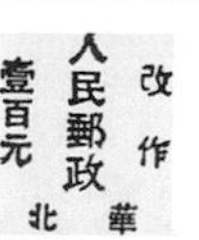

(NC73) "People's Postal Service North China"

1949. Surch as Type NC 73. (a) On stamp of Nationalist China.

NC278	$100* on $100 red	35·00	60

(b) On stamps of North Eastern Provinces.

NC279	**5**	50c. on 5c. red	40	2·20
NC280	**5**	$1 on 10c. orange	40	1·70
NC281	**5**	$2 on 20c. green	85·00	38·00
NC282	**5**	$3 on 50c. orange	40	1·40
NC283	**5**	$4 on $5 green	4·25	1·70
NC284	**5**	$6 on $10 red	1·40	1·70
NC285	**5**	$10 on $300 green	2·75	3·50
NC286	**5**	$12 on $1 blue	1·10	5·00
NC287	**5**	$18 on $3 brown	1·10	1·30
NC288	**5**	$20* on 50c. orange	1·40	1·10
NC290	**5**	$20 on $20 green	2·75	3·50
NC291	**5**	$30 on $2.50 blue	4·25	5·25
NC292	**5**	$40 on 25c. brown	11·00	7·00
NC293	**5**	$50 on $109 green	15·00	3·75
NC294	**5**	$80* on $1 blue	16·00	7·00
NC295	**5**	$100 on $65 green	22·00	2·50

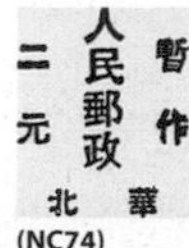

(NC74)

1949. Surch as Type NC 74. (a) On stamps of Nationalist China.

NC296	**107**	$100* on $100 red	85·00	45·00
NC297	**107**	$300* on $700 brown	15·00	10·00
NC298	**118**	$500* on $500 green	10·00	3·00
NC299	**118**	$3,000* on $3,000 blue	18·00	5·00

(b) On stamps of North Eastern Provinces.

NC300a	**5**	$1* on 25c. brown	50	80
NC301	**5**	$2 on 20c. green	1·40	2·50
NC302	**5**	$3 on 50c. orange	70	1·70
NC303	**5**	$4 on $5 green	5·50	3·50
NC305	**5**	$6 on $10 red	4·00	3·50
NC306	**5**	$10* on $300 green	8·75	7·50
NC307	**5**	$12 on $1 blue	1·40	1·40
NC308	**5**	$20* on 50c. orange	20·00	12·00
NC309	**5**	$20* on $20 green	6·00	3·50
NC310	**5**	$40* on 25c. brown	6·00	4·25
NC311	**5**	$50* on $109 green	8·75	10·50
NC312	**5**	$80* on $1 blue	6·00	5·25

*On these stamps the bottom character in the left-hand column of overprints is square in shape.

NC75

1949. Labour Day. Perf or imperf.

NC313A	**NC75**	$20 red	2·25	1·50
NC314A	**NC75**	$40 blue	2·25	1·50
NC315A	**NC75**	$60 brown	2·25	1·50
NC316A	**NC75**	$80 green	2·50	1·75
NC317A	**NC75**	$100 violet	2·75	1·75

NC79 Mao Tse-tung

NC80

1949. 28th Anniv of Chinese Communist Party. Perf or imperf.

NC327A	**NC79**	$10 red	75	55
NC328A	**NC80**	$20 blue	75	55
NC329A	**NC79**	$50 orange	5·00	55
NC330A	**NC80**	$80 green	90	90
NC331A	**NC79**	$100 violet	5·00	90
NC332A	**NC80**	$120 green	65	90
NC333A	**NC79**	$140 purple	5·00	90

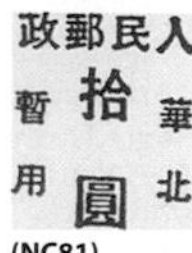

(NC81) ("People's Postal Service North China")

1949. Surch as Type NC 81. (a) On stamp of Nationalist China.

NC334	**118**	$10 on $7,000 brown	20·00	8·00

(b) On stamps of North Eastern Provinces.

NC336	**5**	$10 on $10 red	7·50	3·00
NC337	**5**	$30 on 20c. green	7·50	1·70
NC338	**5**	$50 on $44 red	6·50	90
NC339	**5**	$100 on $3 brown	13·00	3·50
NC341	**5**	$200 on $4 brown	65·00	18·00

NC83 Gate of Heavenly Peace, Peking

1949

NC349	**NC83**	$50 orange	3·25	3·50
NC350	**NC83**	$100 red	30	90
NC351	**NC83**	$200 green	65	90
NC352	**NC83**	$300 purple	12·00	2·10

NC353	**NC83**	$400 blue	13·00	2·10
NC354	**NC83**	$500 brown	13·00	1·10
NC355	**NC83**	$700 violet	5·00	5·00

NC84 Field Workers and Factory

1949

NC356	**NC84**	$1,000 orange	3·00	1·40
NC357	**NC84**	$3,000 blue	30	1·10
NC358	**NC84**	$5,000 red	30	2·20
NC359	**NC84**	$10,000 brown	30	4·25

PARCELS POST STAMPS

Stamps of Nationalist China surch.

(NCP76)

1949. Surch as Type NCP 76.

NCP318	**P112**	$300 on $6,000,000 grey	70·00	
NCP319	**P112**	$400 on $8,000,000 red	75·00	
NCP320	**P112**	$500 on $10,000,000 green	80·00	
NCP321	**P112**	$800 on $5,000,000 lilac	85·00	
NCP322	**P112**	$1 on $3,000,000 blue	90·00	

NC77 Pagoda

(NCP78)

1949. Money Order stamps. Type NC 77 surch as Type NCP 78. No gum.

NCP323	$6 on $5 red	20·00	5·00
NCP324	$6 on $50 grey	20·00	5·00
NCP325	$50 on $20 purple	20·00	5·00
NCP326	$100 on $10 green	20·00	5·00

NCP82 Steam Train

1949

NCP342	**NCP82**	$500 red	50·00	£100
NCP343	**NCP82**	$1,000 blue	£225	£180
NCP344	**NCP82**	$2,000 green	£350	£300
NCP345	**NCP82**	$5,000 green	£400	£350
NCP346	**NCP82**	$10,000 orange	£550	£500
NCP347	**NCP82**	$20,000 red	£850	£800
NCP348	**NCP82**	$50,000 purple	£1400	£1300

C. Port Arthur and Dairen

The Soviet Union obtained facilities in these two ports by treaty in 1945. The Chinese Communists retained the civil administration, but a separate postal authority was established.

(NE6)

1946. Stamps of Japan handstamped "Liaoning Posts" and new value at Type NE 6.

NE8	20c. on 3s. green (No. 316)	25·00	25·00
NE9	$1 on 17s. violet (No. 402)	22·00	25·00
NE11	$5 on 6s. red (No. 242)	35·00	30·00
NE12	$5 on 6s. orange (No. 319)	22·00	22·00
NE13	$15 on 40s. purple (No. 406)	£150	£150

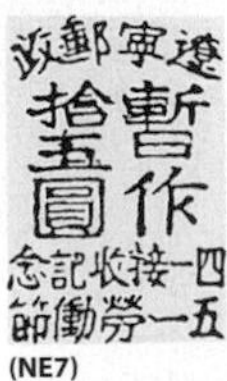

(NE7)

1946. Transfer of Administration on 1 April and Labour Day. Stamps of Manchukuo handstamped as Type NE 7.

NE14	**19**	$1 on 1f. red	25·00	25·00
NE15	-	$5 on 4f. green (No. 84)	30·00	38·00
NE16	**20**	$15 on 30f. brown	60·00	65·00

(NE8)

1946. 9th Anniv of Outbreak of War with Japan. Stamps of Manchukuo surch as Type NE 8.

NE17	$1 on 6f. red (No. 86)	15·00	25·00
NE18	$5 on 2f. green (No. 82)	65·00	95·00
NE19	$15 on 12f. orange (No. 90)	£120	£130

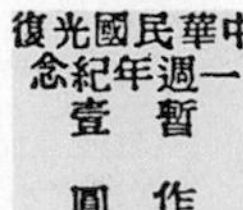

(NE9)

1946. 1st Anniv of Japanese Surrender. Stamps of Manchukuo surch as Type NE 9.

NE20	-	$1 on 12f. orange (No. 90)	35·00	35·00
NE21	**19**	$5 on 1f. red	75·00	65·00
NE22	**13**	$15 on 5f. black	£130	£120

(NE10)

1946. 35th Anniv of Chinese Revolution. Stamps of Manchukuo surch as Type NE 10.

NE23	$1 on 6f. red (No. 86)	55·00	50·00
NE24	$5 on 12f. orange (No. 90)	85·00	75·00
NE25	$15 on 2f. green (No. 82)	£130	£120

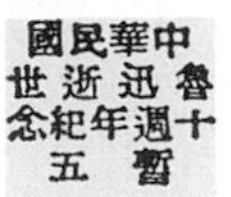

(NE11)

1946. 10th Death Anniv of Lu Xun (author). Stamps of Manchukuo surch as Type NE 11.

NE26	**19**	$1 on 1f. red	75·00	70·00
NE27	-	$5 on 6f. red (No. 86)	£140	£120
NE28	-	$15 on 12f. orange (No. 90)	£150	£140

(NE12)

1947. 29th Anniv of Red Army. Stamps of Manchukuo surch as Type NE 12.

NE29		$1 on 2f. green (No. 82)	£150	£120
NE30		$5 on 6f. red (No. 86)	£300	£250
NE31	**13**	$15 on 13f. brown	£500	£400

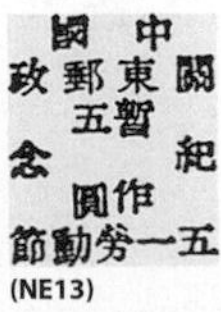

(NE13)

1947. Labour Day. Stamps of Manchukuo surch as Type NE 13.

NE32	-	$1 on 2f. green (No. 82)	35·00	38·00
NE33	-	$5 on 6f. red (No. 86)	£100	95·00
NE34	**20**	$15 on 30f. brown	£160	£150

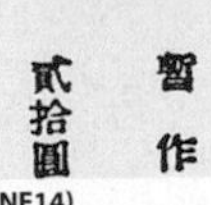

(NE14)

1947. Stamps of Manchukuo surch. "Guandong Postal Service, China" and new value as Type NE 14.

NE35	-	$5 on 2f. green (No. 82)	65·00	50·00
NE36	-	$15 on 4f. green (No. 84)	95·00	85·00
NE37	**20**	$20 on 30f. brown	£150	£150

NE15

1948. 30th Anniv of Red Army. Surch as on Type NE 15.

(a) On stamps of Manchukuo.

NE39	$10 on 2f. green (No. 82)	£300	£300
NE40	$20 on 6f. red (No. 86)	£325	£325

(b) On label (Type NE 15) commemorating 2,600th Anniv of Japanese Empire.

NE41	$100 on (no value) blue and brown	£850	£750

(NE16)

1948. Stamps of Manchukuo surch "Guangdong Postal Administration" and new value as Type NE 16.

NE42	$20 on 2f. green (No. 82)	£650	£550
NE43	$50 on 4f. green (No. 84)	£800	£750
NE44	$100 on 20f. brown (No. 152)	£900	£700

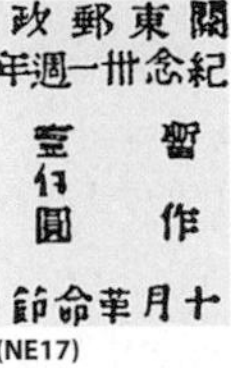

(NE17)

1948. 31st Anniv of Russian October Revolution. Stamps of Manchukuo surch as Type NE 17.

NE45	**19**	$10 on 1f. red	£325	£375
NE46	-	$50 on 2f. green (No. 82)	£550	£700
NE47	-	$100 on 4f. green (No. 84)	£1300	£750

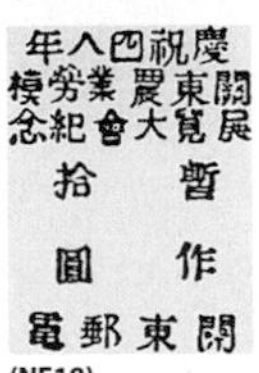

(NE18)

1948. Guangdong Agricultural and Industrial Exhibition Stamps of Manchukuo surch as Type NE 18.

NE48	$10 on 2f. green (No. 82)	£1400	£1300
NE49	$50 on 20f. brown (No. 95)	£1600	£1400

(NE19) **(NE20)**

1948. Stamps of Japan and Manchukuo surch "Chinese Postal Administration: Guangdong Posts and Telegraphs" and new values. (a) No. 316 of Japan surch with Type NE 19.

NE50	$5 on 3s. green	£150	£140

(b) Stamps of Manchukuo surch as Type NE 19.

NE51	$10 on 1f. red (No. 80)	£275	£300
NE52	$50 on 2f. green (No. 82)	£600	£550
NE53	$100 on 4f. green (No. 84)	£950	£950

(c) Stamps of Manchukuo surch as Type NE 20.

NE54	$10 on 2f. green (No. 82)	£375	£225
NE55	$50 on 1f. red (No. 80)	£425	£375

NE21 Peasant and Artisan **NE23** Dalian Port

1949

NE56	**NE21**	$5 green	5·00	10·00
NE57	-	$10 orange	32·00	25·00
NE58	**NE23**	$50 red	22·00	22·00

DESIGN—VERT: $10, "Transport".

For designs as Type NE **23** but with different character in bottom panel, see No. NE62.

NE24 "Labour"

1949. Labour Day.

NE59	**NE24**	$10 red	20·00	25·00

NE25 Mao Tse-tung

1949. 28th Anniv of Chinese Communist Party.

NE61	**NE25**	$50 red	50·00	55·00

1949. Bottom panel inscr "Lushuan and Dalian Post and Telegraphic Administration".

NE62	**NE23**	$50 red	40·00	35·00

NE27 Heroes' Monument, Dalian

1949. 4th Anniv of Victory over Japan and Opening of Dalian Industrial Fair.

NE63	**NE27**	$10 red, blue & lt bl	£225	£200
NE64	**NE27**	$10 red, blue & green	18·00	22·00

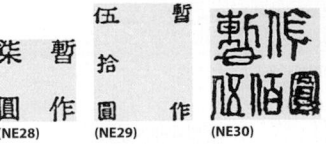

(NE28) **(NE29)** **(NE30)**

1949. Nos. NE56/7 surch as Types NE 28/30.

NE65	**NE28**	$7 on $5 green	55·00	40·00
NE66	**NE29**	$50 on $5 green	£120	75·00
NE67	**NE29**	$100 on $10 orange	£850	£500
NE68	**NE30**	$500 on $5 green	£950	
NE69	**NE29**	$500 on $10 orge	£2250	£2000
NE70	**NE30**	$500 on $10 orge	£1200	£950

NE31 Acclamation of Mao Tse-tung

1949. Founding of Chinese People's Republic.

NE71	**NE31**	$35 red, yellow & bl	25·00	30·00

NE32 Stalin and Lenin

1949. 32nd Anniv of Russian October Revolution.

NE72	**NE32**	$10 green	18·00	25·00

NE33 Josef Stalin

1949. Stalin's 70th Birthday.

NE73	**NE33**	$20 purple	50·00	60·00
NE74	**NE33**	$35 red	50·00	60·00

NE34 Gate of Heavenly Peace, Peking

1950

NE75	**NE34**	$10 blue	35·00	25·00
NE76	**NE34**	$20 green	£225	£120
NE77	**NE34**	$35 red	1·00	10·00
NE78	**NE34**	$50 lilac	2·00	12·00
NE79	**NE34**	$100 mauve	1·50	25·00

All Soviet forces were withdrawn by 26 May 1955 and the stamps of the Chinese People's Republic are now in use.

D. North-East China People's Post

NE48 Mao Tse-tung **NE49** Mao Tse-tung

1946

NE133	**NE48**	$1 violet	25·00	20·00
NE134	**NE49**	$2 red	5·00	5·00
NE135	**NE49**	$5 orange	5·50	5·00
NE136	**NE49**	$10 blue	6·50	6·50

NE50 Map of China with Communist Lion, Japanese Wolf and Chiang Kai-shek

1946. 10th Anniv of Seizure of Chiang Kai-shek at Xi'an.

NE137	**NE50**	$1 violet	2·50	5·00
NE138	**NE50**	$2 orange	2·50	5·00
NE139	**NE50**	$5 brown	8·50	10·00
NE140	**NE50**	$10 green	15·00	20·00

NE51 Railwaymen

1947. 24th Anniv of Massacre of Strikers at Zhengzhou Station.

NE141	**NE51**	$1 red	1·50	4·50
NE142	**NE51**	$2 green	1·50	4·50
NE143	**NE51**	$5 red	3·25	5·00
NE144	**NE51**	$10 green	4·50	6·50

NE52 Women Cheering

1947. International Women's Day.

NE145	**NE52**	$5 red	1·00	5·50
NE146	**NE52**	$10 brown	1·00	5·50

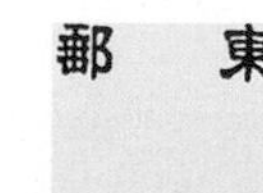

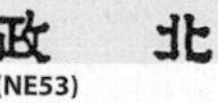

(NE53)

1947. Optd with Type NE 53 ("North East Postal Service").

NE147	**NE53**	$5 red	5·00	10·00
NE148	**NE53**	$10 brown	5·00	10·00

NE54 Children's Troop-comforts Unit

1947. Children's Day.

NE149	**NE54**	$5 red	2·00	5·50
NE150	**NE54**	$10 green	4·50	5·00
NE151	**NE54**	$30 orange	5·50	6·50

NE55 Peasant and Workman

1947. Labour Day.

NE152	**NE55**	$10 red	2·00	4·50
NE153	**NE55**	$30 blue	2·50	5·00
NE154	**NE55**	$50 green	3·75	5·00

NE56 "Freedom"

1947. 28th Anniv of Students' Rebellion, Peking University.

NE155	**NE56**	$10 green	3·25	6·50
NE156	**NE56**	$30 brown	3·75	6·50
NE157	**NE56**	$50 violet	3·75	6·50

(NE57)

1947. Surch as Type NE 57.

NE158	**NE48**	$50 on $1 violet	45·00	60·00
NE159	**NE49**	$50 on $2 red	45·00	60·00
NE160b	**NE48**	$100 on $1 violet	45·00	60·00
NE161	**NE49**	$100 on $2 red	45·00	60·00

NE58 Youths with Banner

1947. 22nd Anniv of Nanjing Road Incident, Shanghai.

NE162	**NE58**	$2 red and mauve	1·50	5·00
NE163	**NE58**	$5 red and green	1·50	5·00
NE164	**NE58**	$10 red & yellow	2·50	5·00
NE165	**NE58**	$20 red & violet	2·50	5·00
NE166	**NE58**	$30 red & brown	3·25	5·00
NE167	**NE58**	$50 red and blue	5·50	5·50
NE168	**NE58**	$100 red & brown	6·50	5·50
MSNE169 218×160 mm. Nos. NE162/8. Imperf			£300	£300

NE59 Mao Tse-tung

1947. 26th Anniv of Chinese Communist Party.

NE170	**NE59**	$10 red	16·00	22·00
NE171	**NE59**	$30 mauve	16·00	23·00
NE172	**NE59**	$50 purple	22·00	25·00
NE173	**NE59**	$100 red	30·00	30·00

NE60 Hand grasping rifle

1947. 10th Anniv of Outbreak of War with Japan.

NE174	**NE60**	$10 orange	6·50	10·00
NE175	**NE60**	$30 green	6·50	12·00
NE176	**NE60**	$50 blue	7·50	12·00
NE177	**NE60**	$100 brown	10·00	13·00
MSNE178 150×110 mm. Nos. NE174/7. Imperf			£325	£325

NE61 Mountains and River

1947. 2nd Anniv of Japanese Surrender.

NE179	**NE61**	$10 brown	8·50	20·00
NE180	**NE61**	$30 green	9·00	20·00
NE181	**NE61**	$50 green	14·00	20·00
NE182	**NE61**	$100 brown	16·00	20·00

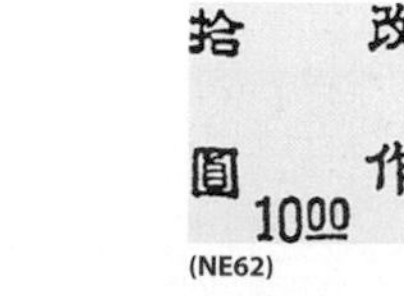

(NE62)

1947. Surch as Type NE 62.

NE183	**NE48**	$5 on $1 violet	48·00	60·00
NE184	**NE49**	$10 on $2 red	48·00	60·00

NE63 Map of Manchuria

1947. 16th Anniv of Japanese Attack on Manchuria.

NE185	**NE63**	$10 green	7·50	15·00
NE186	**NE63**	$20 mauve	7·50	15·00
NE187	**NE63**	$30 brown	12·00	20·00
NE188	**NE63**	$50 red	12·00	20·00

NE64 Mao Tse-tung

1947

NE189	**NE64**	$1 purple	1·40	8·00
NE190	**NE64**	$5 green	2·40	5·00
NE191	**NE64**	$10 green	12·00	25·00
NE192	**NE64**	$15 violet	20·00	25·00
NE193	**NE64**	$20 red	75	2·00
NE194	**NE64**	$30 green	75	2·50
NE195	**NE64**	$50 brown	30·00	27·00
NE213	**NE64**	$50 green	1·00	2·25
NE196	**NE64**	$90 blue	5·00	10·00
NE197	**NE64**	$100 red	65	3·75
NE215	**NE64**	$150 red	2·25	3·00
NE214	**NE64**	$250 lilac	85	3·00
NE228	**NE64**	$300 green	95·00	45·00
NE198	**NE64**	$500 orange	28·00	22·00
NE229	**NE64**	$1,000 yellow	2·00	2·50

For stamps as Type NE **64** but with "YUAN" in top right tablet, see Nos. NE236/40.

NE65 Offices of N.E. Political Council

1947. 35th Anniv of Chinese Republic.

NE199	**NE65**	$10 yellow	65·00	75·00
NE200	**NE65**	$20 red	65·00	75·00
NE201	**NE65**	$100 brown	£110	£120

NE66

1947. 11th Anniv of Seizure of Chiang Kai-shek at Xi'an.

NE202	**NE66**	$30 red	10·00	15·00
NE203	**NE66**	$90 blue	15·00	18·00
NE204	**NE66**	$150 green	20·00	25·00

NE67 Tomb of Gen. Li Zhaolin

1948. 2nd Death Anniv of Gen. Li Zhaolin.

NE205A	**NE67**	$30 green	20·00	25·00
NE206A	**NE67**	$150 lilac	20·00	25·00

NE68 Flag and Globe

1948. Labour Day.

NE207	**NE68**	$50 red	7·25	20·00
NE208	**NE68**	$150 green	2·75	25·00
NE209	**NE68**	$250 violet	2·75	40·00

NE69 Youth with Torch

1948. Youth Day.

NE210	**NE69**	$50 green	12·00	15·00
NE211	**NE69**	$150 brown	15·00	25·00
NE212	**NE69**	$250 red	25·00	30·00

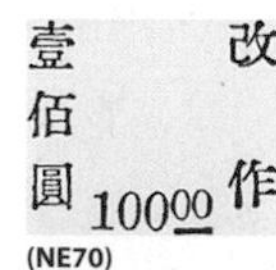

(NE70)

1948. Surch as Type NE 70.

NE217a	**NE64**	$100 on $1 purple	75·00	75·00
NE218	**NE64**	$100 on $15 violet	30·00	32·00
NE219	**NE64**	$300 on $5 green	75·00	50·00
NE220	**NE64**	$300 on $30 green	12·00	20·00
NE221	**NE64**	$300 on $90 blue	13·00	20·00
NE230	**NE49**	$500 on $2 red	15·00	15·00
NE222	**NE64**	$500 on $50 green	40·00	25·00
NE231	**NE49**	$1,500 on $5 orge	15·00	15·00
NE223	**NE64**	$1,500 on $150 red	38·00	35·00
NE232	**NE49**	$2,500 on $10 blue	20·00	20·00
NE224	**NE64**	$2,500 on $300 grn	20·00	25·00

NE71 Crane Operator

1948. All-China Labour Conference.

NE225	**NE71**	$100 red & pink	1·00	2·50
NE226	**NE71**	$300 brown & yell	2·25	3·50
NE227	**NE71**	$500 blue & green	1·50	2·00

NE72 Workman, Soldier and Peasant

1948. Liberation of the North East.

NE233	**NE72**	$500 red	12·00	15·00
NE234	**NE72**	$1,500 green	18·00	20·00
NE235	**NE72**	$2,500 brown	25·00	25·00

1949. As Type NE 64 but "YUAN" at top right.

NE236	$300 green	1·00	2·20
NE237	$500 orange	1·60	1·60
NE238	$1,500 green	40	1·70
NE239	$4,500 brown	40	1·80
NE240	$6,500 blue	40	2·10

NE74 "Production in Field and Industry"

1949

NE241	**NE74**	$5,000 blue	5·00	3·00
NE242	**NE74**	$10,000 orange	30	2·75
NE243	**NE74**	$50,000 green	40	3·75
NE244	**NE74**	$100,000 violet	85	11·00

NE75 Workers and Banners

1949. Labour Day.

NE245	**NE75**	$1,000 red and blue	30	2·50
NE246	**NE75**	$1,500 red and blue	30	2·50
NE247	**NE75**	$4,500 red & brown	45	2·50
NE248	**NE75**	$6,500 brown & grn	45	2·50
NE249	**NE75**	$10,000 purple & bl	55	2·50

NE76 Workers' Procession

1949. 28th Anniv of Chinese Communist Party.

NE250	**NE76**	$1,500 red, vio & bl	45	2·25
NE251	**NE76**	$4,500 red, brn & bl	45	2·50
NE252	**NE76**	$6,500 red, pink & bl	85	2·50

NE77 North-East Heroes, Monument

1949. 4th Anniv of Japanese Surrender.

NE253	**NE77**	$1,500 red	85	2·75
NE254	**NE77**	$4,500 green	85	2·50
NE255	**NE77**	$6,500 blue	1·20	2·50

REPRINTS. The note above No. 1401 of China also refers here to Nos. NE257/60, 261/3, 271/4, 286/89 and 312/4.

NE78 Factory

1949

NE256	**NE78**	$1,500 red	85	1·10

1949. 1st Session of Chinese People's Political Conference. As T 181 of People's Republic but with additional inscr.

NE257	$1,000 blue	20·00	25·00
NE258	$1,500 red	25·00	20·00
NE259	$3,000 green	30·00	30·00
NE260	$4,500 purple	35·00	30·00

1949. World Federation of Trade Unions, Asiatic and Australasian Conference, Peking. As T 182 of People's Republic but with additional inscr.

NE261	$5,000 red	£500	£450
NE262	$20,000 green	£1800	£600
NE263	$35,000 blue	£2200	£1000

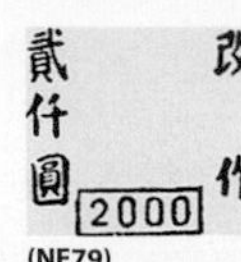

(NE79)

1949. Surch as T NE 79.

NE264	**NE64**	$2,000 on $300 green	32·00	15·00
NE265	**NE64**	$2,000 on $4,500 brown	70·00	50·00
NE266	**NE64**	$2,500 on $1,500 green	65	5·00
NE267	**NE64**	$2,500 on $6,500 blue	30·00	35·00
NE268	**NE78**	$5,000 on $1,500 red	55	1·60
NE269	**NE64**	$20,000 on $4,500 brown	35	8·00
NE270	**NE64**	$35,000 on $300 green	45	10·00

1950. Chinese People's Political Conference. As T 183/4 of People's Republic but with additional inscr.

NE271	$1,000 red	50·00	50·00
NE272	$1,500 blue	65·00	65·00
NE273	$5,000 purple	85·00	80·00
NE274	$20,000 green	£100	£100

1950. As T 185 of People's Republic but with additional four-character inscr.

NE303	**NE34**	$250 brown	85	3·25
NE275	**NE34**	$500 green	1·40	1·30
NE276	**NE34**	$1,000 orange	1·60	50
NE277	**NE34**	$1,000 mauve	5·00	1·30
NE306	**NE34**	$2,000 green	1·80	2·30
NE307	**NE34**	$2,500 yellow	85	2·30
NE300	**NE34**	$5,000 orange	4·25	3·25
NE309	**NE34**	$10,000 brown	1·50	2·30
NE310	**NE34**	$12,500 purple	85	4·00
NE283	**NE34**	$20,000 purple	1·10	1·30
NE301	**NE34**	$30,000 red	1·50	16·00
NE284	**NE34**	$35,000 blue	1·10	2·50
NE285	**NE34**	$50,000 green	20·00	2·50
NE302	**NE34**	$100,000 violet	5·00	25·00

1950. Foundation of People's Republic. Additional inscr at left.

NE286	**188**	$5,000 red, yell & grn	£200	95·00
NE287	**188**	$10,000 red, yell & brn	£250	£180
NE288	**188**	$20,000 red, yell & pur	£375	£225
NE289	**188**	$30,000 red, yell & bl	£500	£325

1950. Peace Campaign. Additional characters below olive branch.

NE290	**191**	$2,500 brown	35·00	30·00
NE291	**191**	$5,000 green	45·00	30·00
NE292	**191**	$20,000 blue	55·00	35·00

1950. 1st Anniv of People's Republic. Additional characters at left. Flag in red, yellow and brown.

NE293	**193**	$1,000 violet	£120	£110
NE294	**193**	$2,500 brown	£150	£130
NE295	**193**	$5,000 green (44×53 mm)	£250	85·00
NE296	**193**	$10,000 green	£325	£250
NE297	**193**	$20,000 blue	£500	£275

1950. 1st All-China Postal Conference. Additional characters at right.

NE298	**194**	$2,500 orange & green	30·00	25·00
NE299	**194**	$5,000 green and red	30·00	25·00

1950. Sino-Soviet Treaty. Additional characters in top right-hand coner.

NE312	**195**	$2,500 red	20·00	20·00
NE313	**195**	$5,000 green	45·00	40·00
NE314	**195**	$20,000 blue	45·00	40·00

PARCELS POST STAMPS

NEP82

1951

NEP316B	**NEP82**	$300,000 purple	£1500
NEP317B	**NEP82**	$500,000 green	£2750
NEP315A	**NEP82**	$1,000,000 violet	£500
NEP318B	**NEP82**	$1,000,000 red	£4000

E. North-West China People's Post

NW25 Mao Tse-tung

NW26 Great Wall

1949. Imperf.

NW97	**NW25**	$50 pink	2·50	5·00
NW98	**NW26**	$100 blue	1·00	1·25
NW99	**NW25**	$200 orange	3·75	4·50

F. South-West China People's Post

SW3 Zhu De, Mao Tse-tung and Troops

1949

SW9	**SW3**	$10 blue	10·00	5·50
SW10	**SW3**	$20 purple	25	3·25
SW11	**SW3**	$30 orange	25	1·50
SW12	**SW3**	$50 green	80	1·00
SW13	**SW3**	$100 red	30	85
SW14	**SW3**	$200 blue	3·25	1·25
SW15	**SW3**	$300 violet	10·00	2·75
SW16	**SW3**	$500 grey	15·00	5·50
SW17	**SW3**	$1,000 purple	20·00	16·00
SW18	**SW3**	$2,000 green	40·00	38·00
SW19	**SW3**	$5,000 orange	50·00	50·00

For other values in this design see East China, Nos. EC378/82.

SW4 Map of China with Flag in S.W.

1950. Liberation of the South West.

SW20	**SW4**	$20 blue	30	1·30
SW21	**SW4**	$30 green	2·50	3·00
SW22	**SW4**	$50 red	40	1·60
SW23	**SW4**	$100 brown	95	1·60

叁仟圓 改作

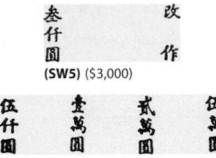

(SW5) ($3,000)

伍仟圓 壹萬圓 贰萬圓 伍萬圓

($5,000) ($10,000) ($20,000) ($50,000)

1950. Surch as Type SW 5 (characters in left-hand column of surcharge differ as indicated in illustrations and footnote).

SW24	$60 on $30 green	28·00	25·00
SW25	$150 on $30 green	28·00	25·00
SW26	$300 on $20 blue	1·50	5·50
SW27	$300 on $100 brown	32·00	12·00
SW28	$1,500 on $100 brown	35·00	20·00
SW29	$3,000 on $50 red	20·00	16·00
SW30	$5,000 on $50 red	5·50	10·00
SW31	$10,000 on $50 red	£100	48·00
SW32	$20,000 on $50 red	4·50	50·00
SW33	$50,000 on $50 red	6·50	70·00

Nos. SW24 and SW26/7 have three characters in left-hand column; Nos. SW25 and SW28 have five.

G. Chinese People's Republic

GUM or NO GUM. Nos. 1401/1891 were issued without gum (except Nos. 1843/5 and 1850/7). From No. 1892 onwards all postage stamps were issued with gum, unless otherwise stated. From 1965 some issues seem to have no gum, though in fact they bear an adhesive substance.

SERIAL MARKINGS. Issues other than definitive issues are divided into two categories: "commemorative" and "special". Figures below the design of each stamp of such issues indicate: (a) serial number of the issue; (b) number of stamps in the issue; (c) number of stamps within the issue; and (d) year of issue (from No. 1557 on). Neither chronological order of issue nor sequence of value is always strictly followed. From No. 2343 these serial markings were omitted until No. 2433.

REPRINTS were later made in replacement of exhausted stocks by the Chinese Postal Administration for sale to stamp collectors and were not available for postal purposes. Nos. 1401/11, 1432/5, 1456/8, 1464/73, 1507/9, 1524/37 and 1543/52. Our prices are for originals. For notes describing the distinguishing features of the reprints, see Stanley Gibbons Part 17 (China) Catalogue.

For other values in the following types see North East China.

181 Celebrations at Gate of Heavenly Peace, Peking

1949. Celebration of First Session of Chinese People's Political Conference.

1401	**181**	$30 blue	5·00	4·50
1402	**181**	$50 red	6·50	5·50
1403	**181**	$100 green	7·50	6·00
1404	**181**	$200 purple	8·50	8·00
NW100	**NW26**	$400 brown	5·00	5·50

182 Globe, Fist and Banner

1949. World Federation of Trade Unions. Asiatic and Australasian Congress, Peking.

1405	**182**	$100 red	20·00	12·00
1406	**182**	$300 green	20·00	12·00
1407	**182**	$500 blue	20·00	13·00

183 Conference Hall **184** Mao Tse-tung

1950. Chinese People's Political Conference.

1408	**183**	$50 red	14·00	10·00
1409	**183**	$100 blue	20·00	8·00
1410	**184**	$300 purple	23·00	12·00
1411	**184**	$500 green	30·00	14·00

185 Gate of Heavenly Peace, Peking

1950

1412	**185**	$200 green	15·00	1·00
1413	**185**	$300 lake	60	1·25
1414	**185**	$500 red	60	35
1415	**185**	$800 orange	£140	20
1420a	**185**	$1,000 lilac	50	40
1417	**185**	$2,000 olive	15·00	2·00
1420b	**185**	$3,000 brown	50	65
1418	**185**	$5,000 pink	30	1·40
1419	**185**	$8,000 blue	30	15·00
1420c	**185**	$10,000 brown	50	35

See also Nos. 1481a/7 and 1493/8.

中國人民郵政
壹佰圓
100

(186)

1950. Surch as T 186. Perf or roul.

1427	**148**	$100 on (–) mauve	75	2·25
1428	**149**	$200 on (–) red	3·50	1·50
1429	**147**	$300 on (–) green	10	2·25
1424	**146**	$500 on (–) orange	25	50
1430	**146**	$800 on (–) orange	4·25	25
1426	**146**	$1,000 on (–) orange	25	60

187 Harvesters and Ox

1950. Unissued stamp of East China surch.

1431	**187**	$20,000 on $10,000 red	£700	65·00

188 Mao Tse-tung, Flag and Parade

1950. Foundation of People's Republic on 1 October 1949.

1432	**188**	$800 red, yellow & green	65·00	12·00
1433	**188**	$1,000 red, yellow & brn	75·00	20·00
1434	**188**	$2,000 red, yellow & pur	95·00	18·00
1435	**188**	$3,000 red, yellow & blue	£120	18·00

(189)

1950. Stamps of North Eastern Provinces surch as T 189.

1436	**5**	$50 on 20c. green	5·00	6·50
1437	**5**	$50 on 25c. brown	4·00	2·40
1438	**5**	$50 on 50c. orange	85	2·00
1439	**5**	$100 on $2.50 blue	1·90	2·00
1440	**5**	$100 on $3 brown	2·50	2·00
1441	**5**	$100 on $4 brown	1·50	10·00
1442	**5**	$100 on $5 green	2·30	1·50
1443	**5**	$100 on $10 red	45·00	10·50
1444	**5**	$400 on $20 green	£100	30·00
1445	**5**	$400 on $44 red	1·20	4·75
1446	**5**	$400 on $65 green	£150	75·00
1447	**5**	$400 on $100 green	30·00	10·00
1448	**5**	$400 on $200 brown	£150	55·00
1449	**5**	$400 on $300 green	£175	50·00

中國人民郵政
壹佰圓
★★ 100
(190)

1950. Nos. 1344/7 and unissued values of Nationalist China (Whistling Swans) surch as T 190.

1450	**169**	$50 on 10c. blue	20	35
1451	**169**	$100 on 16c. green	15	40
1452	**169**	$100 on 50c. green	20	35
1453	**169**	$200 on $1 orange	25	25
1453a	**169**	$200 on $2 blue	10·00	70
1454	**169**	$400 on $5 red	35	35
1455	**169**	$400 on $10 green	35	85
1455a	**169**	$400 on $20 purple	95	2·30

Nos. 1451/2 are imperf.

191 "Peace" (after Picasso)

1950. Peace Campaign (1st issue).

1456	**191**	$400 brown	22·00	8·50
1457	**191**	$800 green	25·00	6·50
1458	**191**	$2,000 blue	28·00	10·00

See also Nos. 1510/12 and 1590/2.

192 Gate of Heavenly Peace, Peking

1950. Clouds redrawn.

1481a	**192**	$100 blue	1·00	1·00
1482	**192**	$200 green	10·00	2·75
1483	**192**	$300 lake	55	3·50
1483a	**192**	$400 green	10·00	1·10
1484	**192**	$500 red	60	1·30
1462	**192**	$800 orange	15·00	25
1485a	**192**	$1,000 violet	75	1·00
1463	**192**	$2,000 olive	3·75	1·50
1486a	**192**	$3,000 brown	60	5·00
1487	**192**	$5,000 pink	60	7·00

193 Flag of People's Republic

1950. 1st Anniv of People's Republic. Flag in red, yellow and brown.

1464	**193**	$100 violet	35·00	10·00
1465	**193**	$400 brown	45·00	10·00
1466	**193**	$800 green (44×53 mm)	55·00	7·50
1467	**193**	$1,000 olive	70·00	18·00
1468	**193**	$2,000 blue	£100	25·00

194 "Communications"

1950. 1st All-China Postal Conference.

1469	**194**	$400 brown and green	30·00	7·50
1470	**194**	$800 green and red	30·00	5·50

195 Stalin greets Mao Tse-tung

1950. Sino-Soviet Treaty.

1471	**195**	$400 red	25·00	10·00
1472	**195**	$800 green	25·00	7·00
1473	**195**	$2,000 blue	35·00	7·50

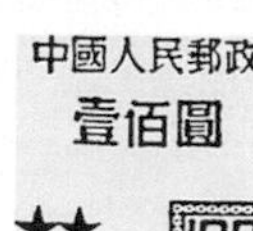

(196)

1950. Nos. EC364/5a, EC367 and EC370/1 of East China People's Post surch as T 196.

1474		$50 on $10 blue	25	25
1475		$100 on $15 red	25	25
1476		$300 on $50 red	1·40	70
1477		$400 on $1,600 purple	2·50	1·00
1478		$400 on $2,000 lilac	95	55

(197)

1950. Stamps of East China surch as T 197.

1479	**EC112**	$50 on $10 blue	20	20
1480	**EC112**	$400 on $15 red	40	20
1481	**EC112**	$400 on $2,000 green	1·50	1·00

198 Temple of Heaven and Ilyushin Il-18

1951. Air.

1488	**198**	$1,000 red	50	50
1489	**198**	$3,000 green	50	30
1490	**198**	$5,000 orange	50	30
1491	**198**	$10,000 green and purple	2·00	50
1492	**198**	$30,000 brn and blue	12·00	8·50

1951. Pink network background.

1493	**185**	$10,000 brown	1·40	25·00
1494	**185**	$20,000 olive	1·40	8·75
1495	**185**	$30,000 green	60·00	70·00
1496	**185**	$50,000 violet	75·00	22·00
1497	**185**	$100,000 red	£3250	£300
1498	**185**	$200,000 blue	£3500	£750

中國人民郵政
貳拾伍圓
25
(200)

1951. Surch as T 200. Perf or roul.

1503	**148**	$5 on (–) mauve	2·10	2·25
1500	**147**	$10 on (–) green	65	1·25
1501	**149**	$15 on (–) red	35	1·25
1506	**146**	$25 on (–) orange	50	2·75

201 Mao Tse-tung

1951. 30th Anniv of Chinese Communist Party.

1507	**201**	$400 brown	12·00	6·50
1508	**201**	$500 green	15·00	4·50
1509	**201**	$800 red	18·00	6·50

202 Dove of Peace, after Picasso

1951. Peace Campaign (2nd issue).

1510	**202**	$400 brown	25·00	7·50
1511	**202**	$800 green	25·00	5·50
1512	**202**	$1,000 violet	25·00	8·50

(203)

1951. Money Order stamps as North China, Type NC 77, surch with T 203. Perf or roul.

1513	$50 on $2 green	3·75	5·00
1515	$50 on $5 orange	1·25	2·50
1517	$50 on $50 grey	20	1·00

204 National Emblem

1951. National Emblem Issue. Yellow network background.

1519	**204**	$100 blue	10·00	6·50
1520	**204**	$200 brown	10·00	6·50
1521	**204**	$400 orange	14·00	5·50
1522	**204**	$500 green	15·00	5·00
1523	**204**	$800 red	15·00	4·50

205 Lu Hsun

1951. 15th Death Anniv of Lu Hsun (author).

1524	**205**	$400 violet	10·00	5·00
1525	**205**	$800 green	15·00	4·25

206 Rebels at Chintien

1951. Centenary of Taiping Rebellion.

1526	**206**	$400 green	12·00	6·50
1527	**206**	$800 red	13·00	5·00
1528	-	$800 orange	16·00	5·00
1529	-	$1,000 blue	18·00	7·50

DESIGN: Nos. 1528/9, Coin and Documents of Taiping "Heavenly Kingdom of Great Peace".

207 Peasants and Tractor

1952. Agrarian Reform.

1530	**207**	$100 red	9·00	4·50
1531	**207**	$200 blue	9·00	4·25
1532	**207**	$400 brown	9·00	3·00
1533	**207**	$800 green	9·00	2·50

208 The Potala, Lhasa

1952. Liberation of Tibet.

1534	**208**	$400 red	15·00	6·50
1535	-	$800 green	15·00	6·50
1536	**208**	$800 red	15·00	4·75
1537	-	$1,000 violet	15·00	6·50

DESIGN: Nos. 1535, 1537 Tibetan ploughing with yaks.

209 "Child Protection"

1952. Int Child Protection Conference, Vienna.

1538	**209**	$400 green	50	30
1539	**209**	$800 blue	60	35

210 Hammer and Sickle

1952. Labour Day. Dated "1952".

1540	**210**	$800 red	35	20
1541	-	$800 green	25	15
1542	-	$800 brown	35	20

DESIGNS: No. 1541, Hand and dove; No. 1542, Hammer, dove and ear of corn.

211 Gymnast

1952. Gymnastics by Radio. As T 211.

1543		$400 red (14–17)	5·00	5·00
1544		$400 deep blue (18–21)	5·00	5·00
1545		$400 purple (22–25)	5·00	5·00
1546		$400 green (26–29)	5·00	5·00
1547		$400 red (30–33)	5·00	5·00
1548		$400 blue (34–37)	5·00	5·00
1549		$400 orange (38–41)	5·00	5·00
1550		$400 violet (42–45)	5·00	5·00
1551		$400 bistre (46–49)	5·00	5·00
1552		$400 pale blue (50–53)	5·00	5·00

DESIGNS: Various gymnastic exercises, the stamps in each colour being arranged in blocks of four throughout the sheet, each block showing four stages of the exercise depicted. Where two stages are the same, the stamps differ only in the serial number in brackets, in the right-hand corner of the bottom margin of the stamp. The serial numbers are shown above after the colours of the stamps.

Prices are for single stamps.

212 "A Winter Hunt" (A.D. 386–580)

1952. "Glorious Mother Country" (1st issue). Tun Huang Mural Paintings.

1553	**212**	$800 sepia	60	25
1554	-	$800 brown	60	25
1555	-	$800 slate	60	25
1556	-	$800 purple	60	25

PAINTINGS: No. 1554, "Benefactor" (A.D. 581–617). No. 1555, "Celestial Flight" (A.D. 618–906). No. 1556, "Tiger" (A.D. 618–906).

See also Nos. 1565/8, 1593/96, 1601/4 and 1628/31.

213 Marco Polo Bridge, Lukouchiao

1952. 15th Anniv of War with Japan.

1557	**213**	$800 blue	60	30
1558	-	$800 green	80	45
1559	-	$800 plum	70	30
1560	-	$800 red	70	25

DESIGNS (dated "1937–1952"): No. 1558, Victory at Pinghsingkwan; No. 1559, Departure of New Fourth Army from Central China; No. 1560, Mao Tse-tung and Chu The.

214 Airman, Sailor and Soldier

1952. 25th Anniv of People's Liberation Army.

1561	**214**	$800 red	35	25
1562	-	$800 green	50	30
1563	-	$800 violet	35	25
1564	-	$800 brown	35	15

DESIGNS—HORIZ: No. 1562, Soldier, tanks and guns; 1563, Sailor and destroyers; 1564, Pilot, Ilyushin Il-4 DB-3 bomber and Mikoyan Gurevich MiG-15 jet fighters.

216 Huai River Barrage

1952. "Glorious Mother Country" (2nd issue).

1565	**216**	$800 violet	30	15
1566	-	$800 red	30	15
1567	-	$800 purple	30	25
1568	-	$800 green	30	25

DESIGNS: No. 1566, Chungking–Chengtu railway viaduct; 1567, Oil refinery; 1568, Tractor, disc harrows and combine drill.

217 Dove of Peace over Pacific Ocean

1952. Asia and Pacific Ocean Peace Conference.

1569	**217**	$400 purple	35	25
1570	-	$800 orange	35	25
1571	**217**	$800 red	35	25
1572	-	$2,500 green	35	25

DESIGNS—HORIZ: Nos. 1570 and 1572, Doves and globe.

218 Peasants collecting food for the Front

1952. 2nd Anniv of Chinese Volunteer Force in Korea.

1573		$800 blue	35	20
1574	**218**	$800 red	35	20
1575	-	$800 violet	35	20
1576	-	$800 brown	35	20

DESIGNS (dated "1950–1952"): HORIZ: No. 1573, Marching troops. No. 1575, Infantry attack. No. 1576, Meeting of Chinese and North Korean soldiers.

220 Textile Worker

1953. International Women's Day.

1578	**220**	$800 red	50	25
1579	-	$800 green	50	25

DESIGN: No. 1579, Woman harvesting grain.

221 Shepherdess

1953

1580		$50 purple	60	20
1581	**221**	$200 green	1·20	25
1582	-	$250 blue	15·00	1·80
1583	-	$800 turquoise	40	20
1584	-	$1,600 grey	60	40
1585	-	$2,000 orange	1·00	25

DESIGNS: $50, Mill girl; $250, Carved lion; $800, Lathe-operator; $1,600, Miners; $2, Old Palace, Peking.

222 Karl Marx

1953. 135th Birth Anniv of Karl Marx.

1586	**222**	$400 brown	65	25
1587	**222**	$800 green	60	25

223 Workers and Flags

1953. 7th National Labour Union Conference.

1588	**223**	$400 blue	60	25
1589	**223**	$800 red	45	25

224 Dove of Peace

1953. Peace Campaign (3rd issue).

1590	**224**	$250 green	95	20
1591	**224**	$400 brown	60	15
1592	**224**	$800 violet	90	15

225 Horseman and Steed (A.D. 386–580)

1953. "Glorious Mother Country" (3rd issue).

1593	**225**	$800 green	75	25
1594	-	$800 orange	40	25
1595	-	$800 blue	45	25
1596	-	$800 red	40	25

PAINTINGS: No. 1594, Court players (A.D. 386–580). No. 1595, Battle scene (A.D. 581–617). No. 1596, Ox-drawn palanquin (A.D. 618–906).

226 Mao Tse-tung and Stalin at Kremlin

1953. 35th Anniv of Russian Revolution.

1597	**226**	$800 green	80	35
1598	-	$800 red	55	25
1599	-	$800 blue	70	25
1600	-	$800 brown	65	25

DESIGNS—HORIZ: No. 1598, Lenin addressing revolutionaries. VERT: No. 1599, Statue of Stalin; No. 1600, Stalin making speech.

227 Compass (300 B.C.)

1953. "Glorious Mother Country" (4th issue). Scientific instruments.

1601	**227**	$800 black	50	25
1602	-	$800 green	35	25
1603	-	$800 slate	40	25
1604	-	$800 brown	40	25

DESIGNS: No. 1602, Seismoscope (A.D. 132); 1603, Drum cart for measuring distances (A.D. 300); 1604, Armillary sphere (A.D. 1437).

228 Rabelais (writer)

1953. Famous Men.

1605	**228**	$250 green	50	25
1606	-	$400 purple	50	30
1607	-	$800 blue	50	25
1608	-	$2,200 brown	50	25

PORTRAITS: $400, Jose Marti (Cuban revolutionary). $800, Chu Yuan (poet). $2,200, Copernicus (astronomer).

229 Flax Mill, Harbin

1954. Industrial Development.

1609	**229**	$100 brown	30	20
1610	-	$200 green	30	20
1611	-	$250 violet	30	20
1612	-	$400 sepia	30	20
1613	-	$800 purple	30	20
1614	-	$800 blue	35	20
1615	-	$2,000 red	30	20
1616	-	$3,200 brown	40	25

DESIGNS: No. 1610, Tangku Harbour; 1611, Tienshui–Lanchow Railway; 1612, Heavy machine works; 1613, Blast furnace; 1614, Open-cast mines, Fuhsin; 1615, North-East Electric power station; 1616, Geological survey team.

230 Gate of Heavenly Peace, Peking

1954

1617	**230**	$50 red	25	20
1618	**230**	$100 blue	25	20
1619	**230**	$200 green	25	20
1620	**230**	$250 blue	4·25	55
1621	**230**	$400 green	30	20
1622	**230**	$800 orange	25	20
1623	**230**	$1,600 grey	25	70
1624	**230**	$2,000 olive	25	35

231 Statue of Lenin and Stalin at Gorki **232** Lenin Speaking

1954. 30th Death Anniv of Lenin.

1625	**231**	$400 green	1·25	30
1626	-	$800 brown	1·00	30
1627	**232**	$2,000 red	2·25	40

DESIGN: (25×37 mm) $800, Lenin (full-face portrait).

233 Painted Pottery (c. 2000 B.C.)

1954. "Glorious Mother Country" (5th issue).

1628	**233**	$800 brown	50	25
1629	-	$800 black	50	25
1630	-	$800 turquoise	50	25
1631	-	$800 lake	50	25

DESIGNS—As Type **233**: No. 1629, Musical stone (1200 B.C.); 1630, Bronze basin (816 B.C.); 1631, Lacquered wine cup and cosmetic tray (403–221 B.C.).

234 Heavy Rolling Mill

1954. Anshan Steel Works.

1632		$400 turquoise	75	35
1633	**234**	$800 purple	75	35

DESIGN: $400, Seamless steel-tubing mill.

235 Statue of Stalin

1954. 1st Death Anniv of Stalin.

1634	**235**	$400 black	1·25	30
1635	-	$800 sepia	75	25
1636	-	$2,000 red	1·25	35

DESIGNS—VERT: $800, Full-face portrait of Stalin (26×37 mm). HORIZ: $2, Stalin and hydro-electric station (42½×25 mm).

236 Exhibition Building

1954. Russian Economic and Cultural Exn, Peking.

1637	**236**	$800 brown on yellow	20·00	10·00

237 The Universal Fixture

1954. Workers' Inventions.

1638	**237**	$400 green	45	20
1639	-	$800 red	45	20

DESIGN: $800, The reverse repeater.

238 Woman Worker

239 Rejoicing Crowds

1954. 1st Session of National Congress.

1640	**238**	$400 purple	25	20
1641	**239**	$800 red	75	25

240 "New Constitution"

1954. Constitution Commemoration.

1642	**240**	$400 brown on buff	45	20
1643	**240**	$800 red on yellow	55	25

241 Pylons

1955. Development of Overhead Transmission of Electricity.

1644	**241**	$800 blue	1·25	40

242 Nurse and Red Cross Worker

1955. 50th Anniv of Chinese Red Cross.

1645	**242**	8f. red and green	14·00	1·75

243 Miner

244 Gate of Heavenly Peace, Peking

1955

1646	**243**	½f. brown	2·50	20
1647	-	1f. purple	2·50	20
1648	-	2f. green	3·00	20
1648a	-	2½f. blue	3·00	20
1649	-	4f. green	3·25	30
1650	-	8f. red	7·50	10
1650b	-	10f. red	25·00	20
1651	-	20f. blue	8·50	25
1652	-	50f. grey	8·50	30
1653	**244**	1y. red	5·00	40
1654	**244**	2y. brown	5·00	40
1655	**244**	5y. grey	4·75	75
1656	**244**	10y. red	9·50	7·50
1657	**244**	20y. violet	15·00	20·00

DESIGNS—As Type **243**: 1f. Lathe operator; 2f. Airman; 2½f. Nurse; 4f. Soldier; 8f. Foundry worker; 10f. Chemist; 20f. Farm girl; 50f. Sailor.

246 Workmen and Industrial Plant

1955. 5th Anniv of Sino–Russian Treaty.

1658	-	8f. brown	8·50	1·00
1659	**246**	20f. olive	9·00	1·75

DESIGN—HORIZ: (37×32 mm): 8f. Stalin and Mao Tse-tung.

247 Chang-Heng (A.D. 78–139, astronomer)

1955. Scientists of Ancient China.

1660	**247**	8f. sepia on buff	3·75	40
1661	-	8f. blue on buff	3·75	40
1662	-	8f. black on buff	3·75	40
1663	-	8f. purple on buff	3·75	40

MS1663a Four sheets, each 63×90 mm. Nos. 1660/3 but printed on white paper. Imperf £225 95·00

PORTRAITS: No. 1661, Tsu Chung-chi (429–500, mathematician). No. 1662, Chang-Sui (683–727, astronomer). No. 1663, Li-Shih-chen (1518–1593, pharmacologist).

248 Foundry

1955. Five Year Plan. Frames in black.

1664	**248**	8f. red and orange	1·10	20
1665	-	8f. brown and yellow	1·10	20
1666	-	8f. yellow and black	1·10	20
1667	-	8f. violet and blue	1·10	20
1668	-	8f. yellow and brown	1·10	20
1669	-	8f. yellow and red	1·10	20
1670	-	8f. grey and blue	1·10	20
1671	-	8f. orange and black	1·10	20
1672	-	8f. yellow and brown	1·10	20
1673	-	8f. red and orange	1·10	20
1674	-	8f. yellow and green	1·10	20
1675	-	8f. red and yellow	1·10	20
1676	-	8f. yellow and grey	1·10	20
1677	-	8f. yellow and blue	1·10	20
1678	-	8f. orange and blue	1·10	20
1679	-	8f. yellow and brown	1·10	20
1680	-	8f. red and brown	1·10	20
1681	-	8f. yellow and brown	1·10	20

DESIGNS—No. 1665, Electricity pylons; No. 1666, Mining machinery; No. 1667, Oil tankers and derricks; No. 1668, Heavy machinery workshop; No. 1669, Factory guard and industrial plant; No. 1670, Textile machinery; No. 1671, Factory workers; No. 1672, Combine-harvester; No. 1673, Dairy herd and farm girl; No. 1674, Dam; No. 1675, Artists decorating pottery; No. 1676, Lorry; No. 1677, Freighter and wharf; No. 1678, Surveyors; No. 1679, Students; No. 1680, Man, woman and child; No. 1681, Workers' rest home.

249 Lenin

1955. 85th Birth Anniv of Lenin.

1682	**249**	8f. blue	10·00	40
1683	**249**	20f. lake	10·00	2·50

250 Engels

1955. 60th Death Anniv of Engels.

1684	**250**	8f. red	10·00	40
1685	**250**	20f. sepia	10·00	2·25

251 Capture of Lu Ting Bridge

1955. 20th Anniv of Long March by Communist Army.

1686	**251**	8f. red	9·50	45
1687	-	8f. blue	10·00	2·25

DESIGN—VERT: (28×46 mm): No. 1687, Crossing the Ta Hsueh Mountains.

252 Convoy of Lorries

1956. Opening of Sikang–Tibet and Tsinghai–Tibet Highways.

1688	**252**	4f. blue	1·00	20
1689	-	8f. brown	1·00	20
1690	-	8f. red	1·00	25

DESIGNS—VERT: (21×42 mm): No. 1689, Suspension bridge: Tatu River. HORIZ: As T **252**: No. 1690, Opening ceremony, Lhasa.

254 Gate of Heavenly Peace

1956. Views of Peking.

1691		4f. red	3·50	25
1692		4f. green	3·50	25
1693	**254**	8f. red	3·50	25
1694	-	8f. blue	3·50	25
1695	-	8f. brown	3·50	25

VIEWS: No. 1691, Summer Palace; 1692, Peihai Park; 1694, Temple of Heaven; 1695, Great Throne Hall, Tai Ho Palace.

255 Salt Production

1956. Archaeological Discoveries at Chengtu.

1696	**255**	4f. green	60	25
1697	-	4f. black	60	25
1698	-	8f. sepia	60	25
1699	-	8f. sepia	60	25

DESIGNS—HORIZ: (Brick carvings of Tung Han Dynasty, A.D. 25–200): No. 1697, Residence; No. 1698, Hunting and farming; No. 1699, Carriage crossing bridge.

256

1956. National Savings.

1700	**256**	4f. buff	7·50	75
1701	**256**	8f. red	8·50	75

257 Gate of Heavenly Peace, Peking

1956. 8th National Communist Party Congress.

1702	**257**	4f. green	10·00	40
1703	**257**	8f. red	10·00	40
1704	**257**	16f. red	12·00	90

258 Dr. Sun Yat-sen

1956. 90th Birth Anniv of Dr. Sun Yat-sen.

1705	**258**	4f. brown	13·00	25
1706	**258**	8f. blue	15·00	1·75

259 Putting the Shot

1955. 1st Chinese Workers' Athletic Meeting, 1955. Inscr "1955". Flower in red and green; inscr in brown.

1707	**259**	4f. lake	2·50	25
1708	-	4f. purple (Weightlifting)	2·50	25
1709	-	8f. green (Sprinting)	2·50	25
1710	-	8f. blue (Football)	2·50	25
1711	-	8f. brown (Cycling)	2·50	25

260 Assembly Line

1957. Lorry Production.

1712		4f. brown	60	25
1713	**260**	8f. blue	75	25

DESIGN: 4f. Changchun motor plant.

261 Nanchang Revolutionaries

1957. 30th Anniv of People's Liberation Army.

1714	**261**	4f. violet	14·00	1·00
1715	-	4f. green	14·00	1·25
1716	-	8f. brown	14·00	80
1717	-	8f. blue	14·00	80

DESIGNS: No. 1715, Meeting of Red Armies at Chinkangshan; No. 1716, Liberation Army crossing the Yellow River; No. 1717, Liberation of Nanking.

262 Congress Emblem

1957. 4th WFTU Congress, Leipzig.

1718	**262**	8f. brown	7·50	40
1719	**262**	22f. blue	7·50	70

263 Yangtse River Bridge

1957. Opening of Yangtse River Bridge, Wuhan.

1720	**263**	8f. red	75	25
1721	-	20f. blue	75	20

DESIGN: 20f. Aerial view of bridge.

264 Fireworks over Kremlin

1957. 40th Anniv of Russian Revolution.

1722	**264**	4f. red	10·00	35
1723	-	8f. sepia	10·00	35
1724	-	20f. green	10·00	35
1725	-	22f. brown	10·00	35
1726	-	32f. blue	10·00	1·10

DESIGNS: 8f. Soviet emblem, globe and broken chains; 20f. Dove of Peace and plant; 22f. Hands supporting book bearing portraits of Marx and Lenin; 32f. Electricity power pylon.

265 Airport Scene

1957. Air.

1727	**265**	16f. blue	15·00	35
1728	-	28f. olive	18·00	35
1729	-	35f. black	20·00	2·00
1730	-	52f. blue	24·00	50

DESIGNS—Lisunov Li-2 over: 28f. mountain highway; 35f. railway tracks; 52f. collier at station.

266 Yellow River Dam and Power Station

1957. Harnessing of the Yellow River.

1731		4f. orange	14·00	1·50
1732	**266**	4f. blue	14·00	2·00
1733	-	8f. lake	14·00	70
1734	-	8f. green	14·00	70

DESIGNS: No. 1731, Map of Yellow River; No. 1733, Yellow River ferry; No. 1734, Aerial view of irrigation on Yellow River.

267 Ploughing

1957. Co-operative Agriculture. Multicoloured.

1735	8f. Farmer enrolling for farm	75	25
1736	8f. Type **267**	75	25
1737	8f. Tree-planting	75	25
1738	8f. Harvesting	75	25

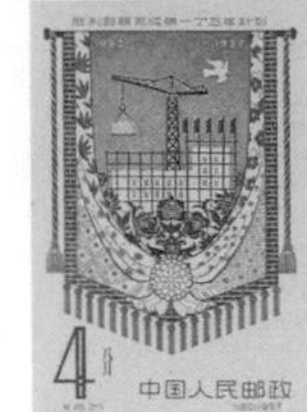

268 "Peaceful Construction"

1958. Completion of First Five Year Plan.

1739	**268**	4f. green and cream	75	25
1740	-	8f. red and cream	75	25
1741	-	16f. blue and cream	75	25

DESIGNS: 8f. "Industry and Agriculture" (grapple and wheat-sheaves); 16f. "Communications and Transport" (steam train on viaduct and ship).

269 High Peak Pagoda, Tenfeng

1958. Ancient Chinese Pagodas.

1742	**269**	8f. brown	3·00	25
1743	-	8f. blue	3·00	25
1744	-	8f. brown	3·00	25
1745	-	8f. green	3·00	25

DESIGNS: No. 1743, One Thousand League Pagoda, Tali; No. 1744, Buddha Pagoda, Yinghsien; No. 1745, Flying Rainbow Pagoda, Hungchao.

270 Trilobite of Hao Li Shan

1958. Chinese Fossils.

1746	**270**	4f. blue	1·25	25
1747	-	8f. sepia	1·25	25
1748	-	16f. green	1·25	25

DESIGNS: 8f. Dinosaur of Lufeng; 16f. "Sinomegaceros pachyospeus" (deer).

271

1958. Unveiling of People's Heroes Monument, Peking.

1749	**271**	8f. red	25·00	2·50
MS1749a 137×87 mm. No. 1749. Imperf			£400	£125

272 Karl Marx (after Zhukov)

1958. 140th Birth Anniv of Karl Marx.

1750	**272**	8f. brown	12·00	1·00
1751	-	22f. myrtle	13·00	2·50

DESIGN: 22f. Marx addressing German workers' Educational Association, London.

273 Cogwheels of Industry

1958. 8th All-China Trade Union Congress, Peking.

1752	**273**	4f. blue	12·00	3·25
1753	**273**	8f. purple	13·00	2·25

274 Federation Emblem

1958. 4th International Democratic Women's Federation Congress, Vienna.

1754	**274**	8f. blue	11·00	25
1755	**274**	20f. green	14·00	3·75

275 Mother and Child

1958. Chinese Children. Multicoloured.

1756	8f. Type **275**	18·00	2·00
1757	8f. Watering sunflowers	18·00	2·00
1758	8f. "Hide and seek"	18·00	2·00
1759	8f. Children sailing boat	18·00	2·00

276 Kuan Han-ching (playwright)

1958. 700th Anniv of Works of Kuan Han-ching.

1760	-	4f. green on cream	20·00	3·25
1761	**276**	8f. purple on cream	22·00	1·00
1762	-	20f. black on cream	25·00	1·00
MS1762a 100×128 mm. Nos. 1760/2 but printed on white paper. Imperf			£500	£200

DESIGNS: Scenes from Han-ching's comedies: 4f. "The Butterfly Dream"; 20f. "The Riverside Pavilion".

277 Peking Planetarium

1958. Peking Planetarium.

1763	**277**	8f. green	10·00	75
1764	-	20f. blue	10·00	1·50

DESIGN: 20f. Planetarium in operation.

278 Marx and Engels

1958. 110th Anniv of "Communist Manifesto".

1765	**278**	4f. purple	14·00	5·25
1766	-	8f. blue	16·00	2·00

DESIGN: 8f. Front cover of first German "Communist Manifesto".

279 Tundra Swan and Radio Pylon

1958. Organization of Socialist Countries' Postal Administrations Conference, Moscow.

1767	**279**	4f. blue	10·00	1·00
1768	**279**	8f. green	10·00	2·50

280 Peony and Doves

1958. International Disarmament Conf, Stockholm.

1769	**280**	4f. red	20·00	1·50
1770	-	8f. green	20·00	9·50
1771	-	22f. brown	20·00	5·50

DESIGNS: 8f. Olive branch; 22f. Atomic symbol and factory plant.

281 Chang Heng's Weather-cock

1958. Chinese Meteorology.

1772	**281**	8f. black on yellow	1·50	25
1773	-	8f. black on blue	1·50	25
1774	-	8f. black on green	1·50	25

DESIGNS: No. 1773. Meteorological balloon; No. 1774, Typhoon signal-tower.

282 Union Emblem within figure "5"

1958. 5th International Students' Union Congress, Peking.

1775	**282**	8f. purple	12·00	65
1776	**282**	22f. green	13·00	1·25

283 Chrysanthemum

1958. Flowers.

1777	-	1½f. mauve (Peony)	10·00	50
1778	-	3f. green (Lotus)	12·00	25
1779	**283**	5f. orange	6·00	25

284 Telegraph Building, Peking

1958. Opening of Peking Telegraph Building.

1780	**284**	4f. olive	4·00	25
1781	**284**	8f. red	4·00	25

285 Exhibition Emblem and Symbols

1958. National Exhibition of Industry and Communications.

1782	**285**	8f. green	12·00	1·00
1783	-	8f. red	12·00	1·00
1784	-	8f. brown	13·00	3·25

DESIGNS: No. 1783, Chinese dragon riding the waves; No. 1784, Horses in the sky.

286 Labourer on Reservoir Site

1958. Inauguration of Ming Tombs Reservoir.

1785	**286**	4f. brown	1·50	25
1786	-	8f. blue	1·50	25

DESIGN: 8f. Ming Tombs Reservoir.

287 Sputnik and ancient Theodolite

1958. Russian Sputnik Commemoration.

1787	**287**	4f. red	5·00	30
1788	-	8f. violet	5·00	30
1789	-	10f. green	5·00	1·50

DESIGNS: 8f. Third Russian sputnik encircling globe; 10f. Three Russian sputniks encircling globe.

288 Chinese and Korean Soldiers

1958. Return of Chinese People's Volunteers from Korea.

1790	**288**	8f. purple	2·00	25
1791	-	8f. brown	2·25	25
1792	-	8f. red	2·50	25

DESIGNS: No. 1791, Chinese soldier embracing Korean woman; No. 1792, Girl presenting bouquet to Chinese soldier.

289 Forest Landscape

1958. Afforestation Campaign.

1793	**289**	8f. green	5·00	1·00
1794	-	8f. slate	5·00	40
1795	-	8f. violet	5·00	40
1796	-	8f. blue	5·00	65

DESIGNS—VERT: No. 1794, Forest patrol. HORIZ: No. 1795, Tree-felling by power-saw. No. 1796, Tree planting.

290 Atomic Reactor

1958. Inauguration of China's First Atomic Reactor.

1797	**290**	8f. blue	15·00	3·25
1798	-	20f. brown	15·00	2·75

DESIGN: 20f. Cyclotron in action.

291 Children with Model Aircraft

1958. Aviation Sports.

1799	**291**	4f. red	1·00	25
1800	-	8f. myrtle	1·00	25
1801	-	10f. sepia	1·00	25
1802	-	20f. slate	1·50	25

DESIGNS: 8f. Gliders. 10f. Parachutists; 20f. Yakovlev Yak-18U trainers.

292 Rooster

1959. Chinese Folk Paper-cuts.

1803		8f. black on violet	15·00	75
1804		8f. black on green	15·00	75
1805	**292**	8f. black on red	15·00	1·20
1806	-	8f. black on blue	15·00	75

DESIGNS: No. 1803, Camel. 1804, Pomegranate; 1806, Actress on stage.

293 Mao Tse-tung and Steel Workers

1959. Steel Production Progress. Inscr "1958".

1807	**293**	4f. red	10·00	1·75
1808	-	8f. purple	10·00	1·75
1809	-	10f. red	12·00	1·75

DESIGNS: 8f. Battery of steel furnaces; 10f. Steel "blowers" and workers.

294 Chinese Women

1959. International Women's Day.

1810	**294**	8f. green on cream	1·75	30
1811	-	22f. mauve on cream	1·75	20

DESIGN: 22f. Russian and Chinese women.

295 Natural History Museum, Peking

1959. Opening of Natural History Museum, Peking.

1812	**295**	4f. turquoise	1·25	25
1813	**295**	8f. sepia	1·25	25

296 Barley

1959. Successful Harvest, 1958.

1814		8f. red (Type **296**)	2·00	30
1815		8f. red (Rice)	2·00	30
1816		8f. red (Cotton)	2·00	30
1817		8f. red (Soya beans, groundnuts and rape)	2·00	30

297 Workers with Marx–Lenin Banner

1959. Labour Day. Inscr "1889–1959".

1818	**297**	4f. blue	12·00	1·50
1819	-	8f. red	12·00	1·50
1820	-	22f. green	12·00	1·50

DESIGNS: 8f. Hands clasping Red Flag; 22f. "5.1" and workers.

298 Airport Building

1959. Inauguration of Peking Airport.

1821	**298**	8f. black on lilac	15·00	1·10
1822	-	10f. black on green	15·00	60

DESIGN: 10f. Ilyushin Il-14P at airport.

299 Students with Banners

1959. 40th Anniv of "May 4th" Students' Rising.

1823	**299**	4f. red, brown and olive	32·00	12·00
1824	-	8f. red, brown & bistre	38·00	8·50

DESIGN: 8f. Workers with banners.

300 F. Joliot-Curie (first President)

1959. 10th Anniv of World Peace Council.

1825	**300**	8f. purple	16·00	3·50
1826	-	22f. violet	14·00	25

DESIGN: 22f. Silhouettes of European, Chinese and Negro.

301 Stamp Printing Works, Peking

1959. Sino-Czech Co-operation in Postage Stamp Production.

1827	**301**	8f. myrtle	15·00	2·50

302

1959. World Table Tennis Championships, Dortmund.

1828	**302**	4f. blue and black	5·00	45
1829	**302**	8f. red and black	5·00	30

303 Moon Rocket

1959. Launching of First Lunar Rocket.

1830	**303**	8f. red, blue & black	22·00	5·00

304 "Prologue"

1959. 1st Anniv of People's Communes.

1831	**304**	8f. red	1·00	35
1832	-	8f. dull purple	1·00	35
1833	-	8f. orange	1·00	35
1834	-	8f. green	1·00	35
1835	-	8f. blue	1·00	35
1836	-	8f. olive	1·00	35
1837	-	8f. blue	1·00	35
1838	-	8f. mauve	1·00	35
1839	-	8f. black	1·00	35
1840	-	8f. green	1·00	35
1841	-	8f. violet	1·00	35
1842	-	8f. red	1·00	35

DESIGNS: No. 1832, Steel worker ("Rural Industries"); No. 1833, Farm girl ("Agriculture"); No. 1834, Salesgirl ("Trade"); No. 1835, Peasant ("Study"); No. 1836, Militiaman ("Militia"); No. 1837, Cook with tray of food ("Community Meals"); No. 1838, Child watering flowers ("Nursery"); No. 1839, Old man with pipe ("Old People's Homes"); No. 1840, Health worker ("Public Health"); No. 1841, Young flautist ("Recreation and Entertainment"); No. 1842, Star-shaped flower ("Epilogue").

305 Mao Tse-tung and Gate of Heavenly Peace, Peking

1959. 10th Anniv of People's Republic. (a) 1st issue. Inscr "1949–1959". With gum.

1843	**305**	8f. red and brown	28·00	7·50
1844	-	8f. red and blue	28·00	4·50
1845	-	22f. red and green	28·00	3·25

DESIGNS: No. 1844, Marx, Lenin and Kremlin; No. 1845, Dove of peace and globe.

306 Republican Emblem

(b) 2nd issue. Emblem in red and yellow; inscriptions in yellow; background colours given.

1846	**306**	4f. turquoise	12·00	5·00
1847	**306**	8f. lilac	12·00	1·00
1848	**306**	10f. blue	12·00	1·00
1849	**306**	20f. buff	12·00	3·00

307 Steel Plant

(c) 3rd issue. Inscr "1949–1959". Frames in purple; centre colours given. With gum.

1850	307	8f. red	1·50	50
1851	-	8f. drab	1·50	50
1852	-	8f. bistre	1·50	50
1853	-	8f. blue	1·50	50
1854	-	8f. salmon	1·50	50
1855	-	8f. green	1·50	50
1856	-	8f. turquoise	1·50	50
1857	-	8f. lilac	1·50	50

DESIGNS: No. 1851, Coal-mine. No. 1852, Steelmill; No. 1853, Double-decked bridge; No. 1854, Combine-harvester; No. 1855, Dam construction; No. 1856, Textile mill; No. 1857, Chemical works.

308 Rejoicing Populace

(d) 4th Issue. Multicoloured.

1858	8f. Type 308	10·00	2·00
1859	10f. Rejoicing people and industrial plant (vert)	10·00	2·00
1860	20f. Tree, banners and people carrying wheat and flowers (vert)	10·00	2·00

309 Mao Tse-tung proclaiming Republic

(e) 5th issue.

1861	309	20f. lake	50·00	22·00

310 Boy Bugler ("Summer Camps")

1959. 10th Anniv of Chinese Youth Pioneers.

1862	-	4f. yellow, red & black	7·50	75
1863	310	4f. red and blue	7·50	75
1864	-	8f. red and brown	7·50	75
1865	-	8f. red and blue	7·50	75
1866	-	8f. red and green	7·50	75
1867	-	8f. red and purple	7·50	75

DESIGNS: No. 1862, Pioneers' emblem; No. 1864, Schoolgirl with flowers and satchel ("Study"); No. 1865, Girl with rain gauge ("Science"); No. 1866, Boy with sapling ("Forestry"); No. 1867, Girl skater ("Athletic Sports").

311 Exhibition Emblem and Symbols of Communication

1959. National Exhibition of Industry and Communications, Peking. Inscr "1949–1959".

1868	311	4f. blue	1·25	50
1869	-	8f. red	1·25	50

DESIGN: 8f. Exn emblem and symbols of industry.

312 Cultural Palace of the Nationalities

1959. Inauguration of Cultural Palace of the Nationalities. Peking.

1870	312	4f. black and red	8·50	1·00
1871	312	8f. black and green	9·50	1·00

313 "Statue of Sport"

1959. 1st National Games, Peking. Multicoloured.

1872	8f. Type 313	4·50	50
1873	8f. Parachuting	4·50	50
1874	8f. Pistol-shooting	4·50	50
1875	8f. Diving	4·50	50
1876	8f. Table tennis	4·50	50
1877	8f. Weightlifting	4·50	50
1878	8f. High jumping	4·50	50
1879	8f. Rowing	4·50	50
1880	8f. Running	4·50	50
1881	8f. Basketball	4·50	50
1882	8f. Fencing	4·50	50
1883	8f. Motor cycling	4·50	50
1884	8f. Gymnastics	4·50	50
1885	8f. Cycling	4·50	50
1886	8f. Horse-racing	4·50	50
1887	8f. Football	4·50	50

314 Wheat (Main Pavilion)

1960. Opening of National Agricultural Exhibition Hall, Peking.

1888	314	4f. black, red & orange	1·50	25
1889	-	8f. black and blue	1·50	25
1890	-	10f. black and brown	1·50	25
1891	-	20f. black and turquoise	1·50	25

DESIGNS: 8f. Meteorological symbols (Meteorological Pavilion); 10f. Cattle (Animal Husbandry Pavilion); 20f. Fishes (Aquatic Products Pavilion).

315 Crossing the Chinsha River

1960. 25th Anniv of Conference during the Long March, Tsunyi, Kweichow.

1892		4f. blue	25·00	1·50
1893		8f. turquoise	25·00	6·50
1894	315	10f. green	35·00	3·50

DESIGNS: 4f. Conference Hall, Tsunyi; 8f. Mao Tse-tung and flags.

316 Clara Zetkin (founder)

1960. 50th Anniv of International Women's Day. Frame and inscriptions black. Centre colours given.

1895	316	4f. blue, black & flesh	4·25	50
1896	-	8f. multicoloured	4·25	50
1897	-	10f. multicoloured	4·25	50
1898	-	22f. multicoloured	4·25	50

DESIGNS: 8f. Mother, child and dove; 10f. Woman tractor-driver; 22f. Women of three races.

317 Chinese and Soviet Workers

1960. 10th Anniv of Sino-Soviet Treaty.

1899	317	4f. brown	15·00	3·50
1900	-	8f. black, yellow & red	15·00	5·00
1901	-	10f. blue	18·00	5·00

DESIGNS: 8f. Flowers and Sino-Soviet emblems; 10f. Chinese and Soviet soldiers.

318 Flags of Hungary and China

1960. 15th Anniv of Hungarian Liberation.

1902	318	8f. multicoloured	22·00	2·50
1903	-	8f. red, black and blue	23·00	7·50

DESIGN: No. 1903, Parliament Building, Budapest.

319 Lenin Speaking

1960. 90th Birth Anniv of Lenin.

1904	319	4f. lilac	14·00	2·50
1905	-	8f. black and red	16·00	5·00
1906	-	20f. brown	32·00	3·75

DESIGNS: 8f. Lenin (portrait); 20f. Lenin talking with Red Guards (after Vasilyev).

320 "Lunik 2"

1960. Lunar Rocket Flights.

1907	320	8f. red	8·50	1·00
1908	-	10f. green ("Lunik 3")	9·50	1·25

321 View of Prague

1960. 15th Anniv of Liberation of Czechoslovakia.

1909		8f. multicoloured	20·00	4·50
1910	321	8f. green	20·00	5·00

DESIGN—VERT: No. 1909, Child pioneers and flags of China and Czechoslovakia.

SERIAL NUMBERS. In this and many later multicoloured sets containing several stamps of the same denomination, the serial number is quoted in brackets to assist identification. This is the last figure in the bottom left corner of the stamp.

322 Narial Bouquet Goldfish

1960. Chinese Goldfish. Multicoloured.

1911	4f. (1) Type 322	50·00	6·50
1912	4f. (2) Black-backed telescopic-eyed goldfish	40·00	6·50
1913	4f. (3) Bubble-eyed goldfish	40·00	6·50
1914	4f. (4) Ranchu goldfish	35·00	5·00
1915	8f. (5) Pearl-scaled goldfish	35·00	6·50
1916	8f. (6) Black moor goldfish	30·00	6·00
1917	8f. (7) Celestial goldfish	35·00	6·50
1918	8f. (8) Oranda goldfish	35·00	5·00
1919	8f. (9) Purple oranda goldfish	£100	8·00
1920	8f. (10) Red-capped goldfish	35·00	9·00
1921	8f. (11) Red-capped oranda goldfish	£100	10·00
1922	8f. (12) Red veil-tailed goldfish	£100	10·00

323 Sow with Litter

1960. Pig-breeding.

1923	323	8f. black and red	30·00	1·50
1924	-	8f. black and green	30·00	1·50
1925	-	8f. black and mauve	30·00	1·50
1926	-	8f. black and olive	30·00	1·50
1927	-	8f. black and orange	40·00	6·00

DESIGNS: No. 1924, Pig being inoculated; No. 1925, Group of pigs; No. 1926, Pig and feeding pens; No. 1927, Pig and crop-bales.

324 "Serving the Workers"

1960. 3rd National Literary and Art Workers' Congress, Peking. Inscr "1960".

1928	324	4f. red, sepia and green	15·00	5·50
1929	-	8f. red, bistre & turq	16·00	5·50

DESIGN: 8f. Inscribed stone seal.

325 N. Korean and Chinese Flags, and Flowers

1960. 15th Anniv of Liberation of Korea.

1930	325	8f. red, yellow and green	28·00	6·50
1931	-	8f. red, indigo and blue	32·00	6·50

DESIGN: No. 1931, "Flying Horse" of Korea.

326 Peking Railway Station

1960. Opening of New Peking Railway Station.

1932	326	8f. multicoloured	15·00	5·00
1933	-	10f. blue, cream & turq	20·00	5·00

DESIGN: 10f. Steam train arriving at station.

327 Chinese and N. Vietnamese Flags, and Children

1960. 15th Anniv of N. Vietnam Republic.

1934	327	8f. red, yellow & black	8·50	3·00
1935	-	8f. multicoloured	9·50	3·00

DESIGN—VERT: No. 1935, "Lake of the Returning Sword", Hanoi.

328 Worker and Spray Fan

1960. Public Health Campaign.

1936	328	8f. black and orange	3·25	40
1937	-	8f. green and blue	3·25	40
1938	-	8f. brown and blue	3·25	40
1939	-	8f. lake and brown	3·25	40
1940	-	8f. blue and turquoise	3·25	40

DESIGNS: No. 1937, Spraying insecticide; No. 1938, Cleaning windows; No. 1939, Medical examination of child; No. 1940, "Tai Chi Chuan" (Chinese physical drill).

329 Facade of Great Hall

1960. Completion of "Great Hall of the People". Multicoloured.

1941		8f. Type **329**	25·00	3·50
1942		10f. Interior of Great Hall	25·00	3·50

330 Dr. N. Bethune operating on Soldier

1960. 70th Birth Anniv of Dr. Norman Bethune (Canadian surgeon with 8th Route Army).

1943	**330**	8f. grey, black and red	5·00	1·00
1944	-	8f. brown	5·00	1·00

PORTRAIT. No. 1943 Dr. N. Bethune.

331 Friedrich Engels

1960. 140th Birth Anniv of Engels.

1945		8f. brown	14·00	5·50
1946	**331**	10f. orange and blue	14·00	5·50

DESIGN: 8f. Engels addressing congress at The Hague.

332 Big "Ju-I"

1960. Chrysanthemums. Background colours given. Multicoloured.

1947	-	4f. blue	30·00	3·50
1948	-	4f. pink	30·00	3·50
1949	-	8f. grey	25·00	1·80
1950	**332**	8f. blue	25·00	1·80
1951	-	8f. green	25·00	1·80
1952	-	8f. violet	22·00	1·80
1953	-	8f. olive	23·00	1·80
1954	-	8f. turquoise	23·00	1·80
1955	-	10f. grey	25·00	1·80
1956	-	10f. brown	20·00	1·50
1957	-	20f. blue	25·00	1·80
1958	-	20f. red	35·00	2·75
1959	-	22f. brown	28·00	6·00
1960	-	22f. red	48·00	9·00
1961	-	30f. green	32·00	5·00
1962	-	30f. mauve	25·00	4·75
1963	-	35f. green	20·00	5·00
1964	-	52f. purple	30·00	10·00

CHRYSANTHEMUMS: No. 1947, "Hwang Shih Pa". No. 1948, "Green Peony". No. 1949, "Er Chiao". No. 1951, "Ju-I" with Golden Hooks. No. 1952, "Golden Peony". No. 1953, "Generalissimo's Banner". No. 1954, "Willow Thread". No. 1955, "Cassia on Salver of Hibiscus". No. 1956, "Pearls on Jade Salver". No. 1957, "Red Gold Lion". No. 1958, "Milky White Jade". No. 1959, "Purple Jade with Fragrant Beads". No. 1960, "Cassia on Ice Salver". No. 1961, "Inky Black Lotus". No. 1962, "Jade Bamboo Shoot of Superior Class". No. 1963, "Smiling Face". No. 1964, "Swan Ballet".

333 "Yue Jin"

1960. 1st Chinese-built Freighter. Launching. No gum.

1965	**333**	8f. blue	9·50	2·00

334 Pantheon, Paris

1961. 90th Anniv of Paris Commune.

1966	**334**	8f. black and red	10·00	2·25
1967	-	8f. sepia and red	10·00	2·25

DESIGN: No. 1967, Proclamation of Commune.

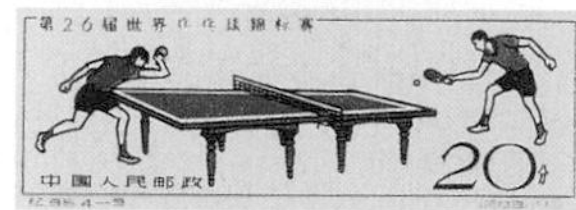

335 Table Tennis Match

1961. 26th World Table Tennis Championships, Peking. Multicoloured.

1968		8f. Championship emblem and jasmine	2·50	75
1969		10f. Table tennis bat and ball and Temple of Heaven	3·00	90
1970		20f. Type **335**	3·50	90
1971		22f. Peking Workers Gymnasium	5·00	1·50

MS1971a 150×100 mm. Nos. 1968/71. No gum £2000 £1200

336 Chan Tien-yu

1961. Birth Centenary of Chan Tien-yu (railway construction engineer).

1972	**336**	8f. black and sage	7·50	1·50
1973	-	10f. brown and sepia	7·50	2·00

DESIGN: 10f. Steam train on Peking-Changchow Railway.

337 Congress Building, Shanghai

1961. 40th Anniv of Chinese Communist Party. Flags, red; frames, gold.

1974	**337**	4f. purple	30·00	2·50
1975	-	8f. green	30·00	3·00
1976	-	10f. brown	30·00	4·00
1977	-	20f. blue	40·00	3·00
1978	-	30f. red	50·00	3·50

DESIGNS: 8f. "August 1" Building, Nanchang; 10f. Provisional Central Govt. Building, Juichin; 20f. Pagoda Hill, Yenan; 30f. Gate of Heavenly Peace, Peking.

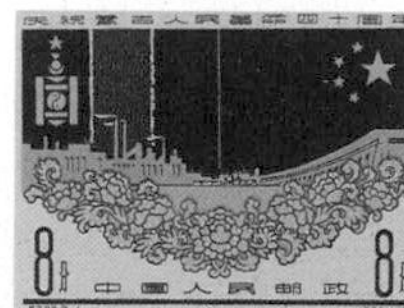

338 Flags of China and Mongolia

1961. 40th Anniv of Mongolian People's Revolution.

1979	**338**	8f. red, blue & yellow	35·00	5·00
1980	-	10f. orange, yellow & grn	40·00	12·00

DESIGN: 10f. Mongolian Government Building.

339 "August I" Building, Nanchang

1961. Size 24×16½ mm. No gum.

1981	**339**	1f. blue	10·00	10
1982	**339**	1½f. red	30·00	10
1983	**339**	2f. green	12·00	30
1984	**A**	3f. violet	40·00	50
1985	**A**	4f. green	3·00	10
1986	**A**	5f. green	3·00	10
1987	**B**	8f. green	3·00	10
1988	**B**	10f. purple	7·50	10
1989	**B**	20f. blue	2·25	10
1990	**C**	22f. brown	1·00	10
1991	**C**	30f. blue	2·00	10
1992	**C**	50f. red	2·00	10

DESIGNS: A, Tree and Sha Chow Pa Building, Juichin; B, Yenan Pagoda; C, Gate of Heavenly Peace, Peking.

For redrawn, smaller, designs see Nos. 2010/21.

340 Military Museum

1961. People's Revolutionary Military Museum.

1993	**340**	8f. brown, green & blue	40·00	1·25
1994	**340**	10f. black, green & brn	45·00	2·25

341 Uprising at Wuhan

1961. 50th Anniv of Revolution of 1911.

1995	**341**	8f. black and grey	25·00	3·25
1996	-	10f. black and brown	35·00	2·25

DESIGN—VERT: 10f. Dr. Sun Yat-sen.

342 Donkey

1961. Tang Dynasty Pottery (618–907 A.D.). Centres multicoloured. Background colours given.

1997	**342**	4f. blue	15·00	1·00
1998	-	8f. green	15·00	1·00
1999	-	8f. purple	18·00	1·00
2000	-	10f. blue	20·00	1·00
2001	-	20f. olive	22·00	2·00
2002	-	22f. turquoise	30·00	5·00
2003	-	30f. red	32·00	10·00
2004	-	50f. slate	38·00	7·50

DESIGNS: No. 1998, Donkey; Nos. 1999/2002, Various horses; Nos. 2003/4, Various camels.

343 Tibetans Rejoicing

1961. "Rebirth of the Tibetan People".

2005	**343**	4f. brown and buff	10·00	1·25
2006	-	8f. brown and turquoise	10·00	1·25
2007	-	10f. brown and yellow	32·00	2·50
2008	-	20f. brown and pink	45·00	5·00
2009	-	30f. brown and blue	70·00	7·50

DESIGNS: 8f. Sower; 10f. Tibetan celebrating "bumper crop"; 20f. "Responsible Citizens"; 30f. Tibetan children.

343a "August I" Building, Nanchang

1962. Size 20½×16½ mm. No gum.

2010	**343a**	1f. blue	50	10
2011	**343a**	2f. green	60	10
2013	**A**	3f. violet	60	10
2014	**343a**	3f. brown	2·50	1·75
2015	**A**	4f. green	85	10
2016	**B**	4f. red	3·25	1·75
2017	**C**	8f. green	1·25	10
2018	**C**	10f. purple	2·00	10
2019	**C**	20f. blue	2·00	10
2020	**B**	30f. blue	2·75	10
2021	**B**	52f. red	2·25	2·25

DESIGNS: A, Tree and Sha Chow Pa Building, Juichin; B, Gate of Heavenly Peace, Peking; C, Yenan Pagoda.

344 Lu Hsun (after Hsieh Chia-seng)

1962. 80th Birth Anniv of Lu Hsun (writer).

2022	**344**	8f. black and red	3·25	50

345 Anchi Bridge, Chaohsien

1962. Ancient Chinese Bridges.

2023	**345**	4f. violet and lavender	3·50	25
2024	-	8f. slate and green	3·50	25
2025	-	10f. sepia and bistre	3·50	40
2026	-	20f. blue and turquoise	4·00	60

BRIDGES: 8f. Paotai, Soochow. 10f. Chupu, Kuanhsien. 20f. Chenyang, Sankiang.

346 Tu Fu

1962. 1250th Birth Anniv of Tu Fu (poet).

2027		4f. black and bistre	60·00	1·00
2028	**346**	8f. black and turquoise	80·00	3·25

DESIGN: 4f. Tu Fu's Memorial, Chengtu.

347 Manchurian Cranes and Trees

1962. "The Sacred Crane". Paintings by Chen Chi-fo. Multicoloured.

2029		8f. Type **347**	20·00	3·25
2030		10f. Two cranes in flight	30·00	4·50
2031		20f. Crane on rock	45·00	5·00

348 Cuban Soldier

1962. "Support for Cuba".

2032	**348**	8f. black and lake	50·00	6·50
2033	-	10f. black and green	75·00	3·50
2034	-	22f. black and blue	£100	30·00

DESIGNS: 10f. Sugar-cane planter; 22f. Militiaman and woman.

349 Torch and Map

1961. "Support for Algeria".

No.	Type	Description	Unused	Used
2035	**349**	8f. orange and brown	1·50	1·00
2036	-	22f. brown and ochre	2·50	1·50

DESIGN: 22f. Algerian patriots.

350 Mei Lan-fang (actor)

1962. "Stage Art of Mei Lan-fang". Multicoloured. Each showing Lan-fang in stage costume with items given below.

No.	Description	Unused	Used
2037	4f. Type **350**	£325	12·00
2038	8f. Drum	£150	10·00
2039	8f. Fan	£150	10·00
2040	10f. Swords	£150	20·00
2041	20f. Bag	£150	15·00
2042	22f. Ribbons (horiz)	£350	35·00
2043	30f. Loom (horiz)	£550	£100
2044	50f. Long sleeves (horiz)	£750	85·00
MS2044a	108×147 mm 3y. multi-coloured	£20000	£10000

351 Han "Flower Drum" Dance

1962. Chinese Folk Dances (1st issue). Multicoloured. No gum.

No.	Description	Unused	Used
2045	4f. Type **351**	1·25	30
2046	8f. Mongolian "Ordos"	2·25	30
2047	10f. Chuang "Catching shrimp"	2·50	35
2048	20f. Tibetan "Fiddle"	3·00	75
2049	30f. Yi "Friend"	3·25	75
2050	50f. Uighur "Tambourine"	4·50	1·20

See also Nos. 2104/15.

352 Soldiers storming the Winter Palace, Petrograd

1962. 45th Anniv of Russian Revolution.

No.	Type	Description	Unused	Used
2051	-	8f. brown and red	40·00	75
2052	**352**	20f. bronze and red	45·00	2·00

DESIGN—VERT: 8f. Lenin leading soldiers.

353 Revolutionary Statue and Map

1962. 50th Anniv of Albanian Independence.

No.	Type	Description	Unused	Used
2053	**353**	8f. sepia and blue	2·50	55
2054	-	10f. multicoloured	3·25	85

DESIGN: 10f. Albanian flag and girl pioneer.

354 Tsai Lun (A.D. ?–121, inventor of paper making process)

1962. Scientists of Ancient China. Multicoloured.

No.	Description	Unused	Used
2055	4f. Type **354**	8·50	35
2056	4f. Paper-making	7·50	30
2057	8f. Sun Szu-miao (581–682, physician)	8·00	30
2058	8f. Preparing medical treatise	9·00	40
2059	10f. Shen Ko (1031–1095, geologist)	9·00	30
2060	10f. Making field notes	10·00	45
2061	20f. Ku Shou-chin (1231–1316, astronomer)	12·00	1·00
2062	20f. Astronomical equipment	14·00	1·00

355 Tank Monument, Havana

1963. 4th Anniv of Cuban Revolution.

No.	Type	Description	Unused	Used
2063	**355**	4f. sepia and red	40·00	2·50
2064	-	4f. black and green	40·00	2·50
2065	-	8f. lake and brown	40·00	3·50
2066	-	8f. lake and brown	85·00	9·50
2067	-	10f. black and buff	85·00	7·50
2068	-	10f. sepia, red and blue	£100	55·00

DESIGNS—As Type **355**: No. 2064, Cuban revolutionaries; No. 2067, Cuban soldier; No. 2068, Castro and Cuban flag. LARGER (48½×27 mm) No. 2065, Crowd in Havana (value on left); No. 2066, Crowd in Peking (value on right).

356 Tibetan Clouded Yellow

1963. Butterflies. Multicoloured. No gum.

No.	Description	Unused	Used
2069	4f. (1) Type **356**	18·00	4·00
2070	4f. (2) Tritailed glory	18·00	1·00
2071	4f. (3) Neumogeni jungle queen	18·00	1·00
2072	4f. (4) Washan swordtail	18·00	1·00
2073	4f. (5) Striped ringlet	18·00	1·00
2074	8f. (6) Green dragontail	20·00	75
2075	8f. (7) Dilunuleted peacock	20·00	75
2076	8f. (8) Yamfly	20·00	75
2077	8f. (9) Golden kaiser-i-hind	20·00	75
2078	8f. (10) Mushaell hair-streak	20·00	75
2079	10f. (11) Yellow orange-tip	20·00	1·20
2080	10f. (12) Great jay	20·00	1·20
2081	10f. (13) Striped punch	20·00	1·20
2082	10f. (14) Beck butterfly	20·00	1·20
2083	10f. (15) Omei skipper	20·00	2·00
2084	20f. (16) Philippine birdwing	18·00	2·75
2085	20f. (17) Keeled apollo	18·00	4·50
2086	22f. (18) Blue-banded king crow	18·00	5·00
2087	30f. (19) Solskyi copper	20·00	5·00
2088	50f. (20) Clipper	30·00	6·00

357 Marx and Engels

1963. 145th Birth Anniv of Karl Marx. No gum.

No.	Type	Description	Unused	Used
2089	-	8f. black, pink & gold	10·00	3·50
2090	-	8f. red and gold	10·00	3·50
2091	**357**	8f. brown and gold	10·00	3·50

DESIGNS: No. 2089, Marx; No. 2090, Slogan "Workers of the World Unite" over cover of 1st edition of "Communist Manifesto".

358 Child with Top

1963. Children. Multicoloured, background colours given. No gum.

No.	Type	Description	Unused	Used
2092	**358**	4f. turquoise	1·25	25
2093	-	4f. brown	1·25	25
2094	-	8f. grey	1·25	25
2095	-	8f. blue	1·25	25
2096	-	8f. beige	1·25	25
2097	-	8f. slate	1·25	25
2098	-	8f. green	1·25	25
2099	-	8f. grey	1·25	25
2100	-	10f. green	2·25	50
2101	-	10f. violet	2·50	50
2102	-	20f. drab	4·50	1·20
2103	-	20f. green	5·00	1·20

DESIGNS (each shows a child): No. 2093, Eating candied hawberries; No. 2094, As "traffic policeman"; No. 2095, With toy windmill; No. 2096, Listening to caged cricket; No. 2097, With toy sword; No 2098, Embroidering; No. 2099, With umbrella; No. 2100, Playing with sand; No. 2101, Playing table tennis; No. 2102, Doing sums; No. 2103, Flying kite.

1963. Chinese Folk Dances (2nd issue). As T 351 but inscr "(261) 1962" to "(266) 1962" in bottom right corner. Multicoloured. No gum.

No.	Description	Unused	Used
2104	4f. Puyi "Weaving Cloth"	1·50	30
2105	8f. Kazakh	1·50	30
2106	10f. Olunchun	2·00	35
2107	20f. Kaochan "Labour"	2·25	50
2108	30f. Miao "Reed-pipe"	3·00	65
2109	50f. Korean "Fan"	4·25	90

1963. Chinese Folk Dances (3rd issue). As T 351 but inscr "(279) 1963" to "(284) 1963" in bottom right corner. Multicoloured. No gum.

No.	Description	Unused	Used
2110	4f. Yu "Wedding Ceremony"	2·25	30
2111	8f. Pai "Encircling Mountain Forest"	2·50	30
2112	10f. Yao "Long Drum"	3·25	35
2113	20f. Li "Third Day of Third Month"	3·25	50
2114	30f. Kava "Knife"	4·50	70
2115	50f. Tai "Peacock"	6·75	1·00

359 Giant Panda eating Apples

1963. Giant Panda. Perf or imperf.

No.	Type	Description	Unused	Used
2116	**359**	8f. black and blue	45·00	3·25
2117	-	8f. black and green	48·00	7·50
2118	-	10f. black and drab	55·00	5·00

DESIGNS—As Type **278**. No. 2117, Giant panda eating bamboo shoots. HORIZ: (52×31 mm): No. 2118, Two giant pandas.

360 Table Tennis Player

1963. 27th World Table-Tennis Championships.

No.	Type	Description	Unused	Used
2119	**360**	8f. grey	25·00	1·70
2120	-	8f. brown	25·00	90

DESIGN: No. 2120, Trophies won by Chinese team.

361 Snub-nosed Monkey

1963. Snub-nosed Monkeys. Multicoloured.

No.	Description	Unused	Used
2121	8f. Type **361**	14·00	1·30
2122	10f. Two monkeys	16·00	1·75
2123	22f. Two monkeys on branch of tree	22·00	6·50

362 Old Pines of Hwangshan

1963. Hwangshan Landscapes. Multicoloured.

No.	Description	Unused	Used
2124	4f. (1) Mount of The Green Jade Screen (vert)	35·00	1·20
2125	4f. (2) The Guest-welcoming Pines (vert)	35·00	1·20
2126	4f. (3) Pines and rocks behind the lake (vert)	35·00	1·40
2127	4f. (4) Terrace of Keeping Cool (vert)	40·00	1·40
2128	8f. (5) Mount of the Heavenly Capital (vert)	50·00	1·50
2129	8f. (6) Mount of Scissors (vert)	50·00	1·50
2130	8f. (7) Forest of Ten Thousand Pines (vert)	50·00	1·50
2131	8f. (8) The Flowering Bush in a Dream (vert)	60·00	1·50
2132	10f. (9) Mount of the Lotus Flower	65·00	1·50
2133	10f. (10) Cumulus Flood Wave of the Eastern Lake	65·00	1·50
2134	10f. (11) Type **362**	70·00	1·50
2135	10f. (12) Cumulus on the Eastern Lake	55·00	1·50
2136	20f. (13) The Stalagmite Mountain Range	£100	7·50
2137	22f. (14) The Apes of the Stone watch the lake below	25·00	10·00
2138	30f. (15) The Forest of Lions	£250	75·00
2139	50f. (16) The Fairy Isles of Peng Lai	£225	25·00

363 Football

1963. "GANEFO" Athletic Games, Jakarta, Indonesia.

No.	Type	Description	Unused	Used
2140	**363**	8f. red & black on lav	35·00	1·50
2141	-	8f. blue & black on buff	35·00	1·50
2142	-	8f. brown & blk on blue	35·00	1·50
2143	-	8f. purple & blk on mve	35·00	1·50
2144	-	10f. multicoloured	35·00	5·00

DESIGNS—As Type **282**: No. 2141, Throwing the discus; No. 2142, Diving; No. 2143, Gymnastics. HORIZ: (48½×27½ mm). No. 2144, Athletes on parade.

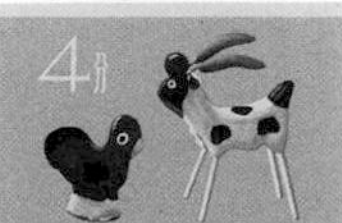

364 Clay Rooster and Goat

1963. Chinese Folk Toys. Multicoloured. No. gum.

No.	Description	Unused	Used
2145	4f. (1) Type **364**	1·00	25
2146	4f. (4) Cloth camel	1·00	25
2147	4f. (7) Cloth tigers	1·00	25
2148	8f. (2) Clay ox and rider	1·00	25
2149	8f. (5) Cloth rabbit, wooden figure and clay cock	1·00	25
2150	8f. (8) Straw cock	1·00	25
2151	10f. (3) Cloth donkey and clay bird	1·00	25
2152	10f. (6) Clay lion	1·00	25
2153	10f. (9) Clay-paper tumbler and cloth tiger	1·10	25

365 Vietnamese Family

1963. "Liberation of South Vietnam". Mult.

2154	8f. Type **365**	7·50	1·50
2155	8f. Vietnamese with flag	7·50	2·50

366 Cuban and Chinese Flags

1964. 5th Anniv of Cuban Revolution. Mult.

2156	8f. Type **366**	30·00	1·50
2157	8f. Boy waving flag	35·00	6·50

367 Woman driving Tractor

1964. "Women of the People's Commune". Multicoloured.

2158	8f. (1) Type **367**	1·00	25
2159	8f. (2) Harvesting	1·00	25
2160	8f. (3) Picking cotton	1·00	25
2161	8f. (4) Picking fruit	1·00	25
2162	8f. (5) Reading book	1·00	25
2163	8f. (6) Holding rifle	1·00	25

368 "Sino-African Friendship"

1964. African Freedom Day.

2164	**368**	8f. multicoloured	1·50	35
2165	-	8f. brown and black	1·50	35

DESIGN: No. 2165, African beating drum.

369 Marx, Engels, Lenin and Stalin

1964. Labour Day.

2166	**369**	8f. black, red & gold	30·00	5·50
2167	-	8f. black, red & gold	20·00	5·50

DESIGN: No. 2167, Workers and banners.

370 History Museum

1964. No gum.

2168	**370**	1f. brown	50	10
2169	**A**	1½f. purple	50	10
2170	**B**	2f. green	50	10
2171	**C**	3f. green	50	10
2172	**370**	4f. blue	50	10
2172a	**A**	5f. purple	1·50	25
2173	**B**	8f. red	1·00	10
2174	**C**	10f. drab	1·25	10
2175	**370**	20f. violet	1·25	10
2176	**A**	22f. orange	2·25	10
2177	**B**	30f. green	3·75	10
2177a	**C**	50f. blue	14·00	2·00

DESIGNS: A, Gate of Heavenly Peace; B, Great Hall of the People; C, Military Museum.

371 Date Orchard, Yenan

1964. "Yenan-Shrine of the Chinese Revolution". Yenan buildings. Multicoloured.

2178	8f. (1) Type **371**	32·00	1·00
2179	8f. (2) Central Auditorium, Yang Chia Ling	20·00	1·00
2180	8f. (3) Mao Tse-tung's Office and Residence at Date Orchard, Yenan	20·00	1·00
2181	8f. (4) Auditorium, Wang Chia Ping	20·00	1·00
2182	8f. (5) Border Region Assembly Hall	30·00	1·00
2183	52f. (6) Pagoda Hill	35·00	3·75

372 Map of Vietnam and Flag

1964. South Vietnam Victory Campaign.

2184	**372**	8f. multicoloured	35·00	7·50

373 "The Alchemist's Glowing Crucible" (peony)

1964. Chinese Peonies. Multicoloured.

2185	4f. (1) Type **373**	20·00	1·20
2186	4f. (2) Night-shining Jade	20·00	1·20
2187	8f. (3) Purple Kuo's Cap	20·00	1·20
2188	8f. (4) Chao Pinks	20·00	1·20
2189	8f. (5) Yao Yellows	20·00	1·20
2190	8f. (6) Twin Beauties	22·00	1·20
2191	8f. (7) Ice-veiled Rubies	24·00	1·40
2192	10f. (8) Gold-sprinkled Chinese Ink	24·00	1·90
2193	10f. (9) Cinnabar Jar	25·00	1·90
2194	10f. (10) Lantien Jade	23·00	2·75
2195	10f. (11) Imperial Robe Yellow	25·00	2·75
2196	10f. (12) Hu Reds	28·00	2·75
2197	20f. (13) Pea Green	65·00	8·00
2198	43f. (14) Wei Purples	48·00	25·00
2199	52f. (15) Intoxicated Celestial Peach	65·00	27·00
MS2199a	77×136 mm. 2y. Glorious Crimson and Great Gold Pink (48×59 mm)	£5000	£1800

374 "Chueh" (wine cup)

1964. Bronze Vessels of the Yin Dynasty (before 1050 B.C.).

2200	**374**	4f. (1) black, grn & yell	18·00	1·50
2201	-	4f. (2) black, grn & yell	18·00	1·50
2202	-	8f. (3) black, grn & yell	20·00	1·50
2203	-	8f. (4) black, blue & grn	22·00	1·50
2204	-	10f. (5) black and drab	22·00	1·50
2205	-	10f. (6) black, grn & yell	20·00	1·50
2206	-	20f. (7) black and grey	25·00	6·50
2207	-	20f. (8) black, bl & yell	25·00	6·50

DESIGNS: No. 2201, "Ku" (beaker); 2202, "Kuang" (wine urn); 2203, "Chia" (wine cup); 2204, "Tsun" (wine vessel); 2205, "Yu" (wine urn); 2206, "Tsun" (wine vessel); 2207, "Ting" (ceremonial cauldron).

375 "Harvesting"

1964. Agricultural Students. Multicoloured.

2208	8f. (1) Type **375**	2·25	25
2209	8f. (2) "Sapling planting"	2·25	25
2210	8f. (3) "Study"	2·25	25
2211	8f. (4) "Scientific experiment"	2·25	25

376 Marx, Engels and Trafalgar Square, London (vicinity of old St. Martin's Hall)

1964. Centenary of "First International".

2212	**376**	8f. red, brown and gold	85·00	30·00

377 Rejoicing People

1964. 15th Anniv of People's Republic. Mult.

2213	8f. (1) Type **377**	35·00	3·50
2214	8f. (2) Chinese flag	35·00	3·50
2215	8f. (3) As T **377** in reverse	35·00	3·50
MS2215a	150×114 mm. Nos. 2213/14 forming a composite design without dividing perfs	£5000	£1600

Nos. 2213/5 were issued in the form of a triptych, in sheets.

378 Oil Derrick

1964. Petroleum Industry. Multicoloured.

2216	4f. Geological surveyors and van (horiz)	£100	6·00
2217	8f. Type **378**	50·00	3·00
2218	8f. Oil-extraction equipment	50·00	3·00
2219	10f. Refinery	£120	3·00
2220	20f. Railway petroleum trucks (horiz)	£200	20·00

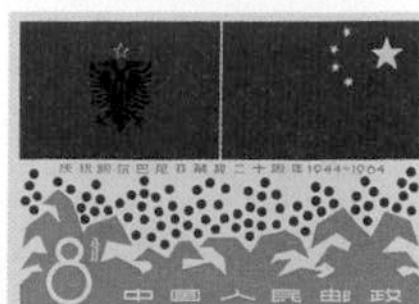

379 Albanian and Chinese Flags and Plants

1964. 20th Anniv of Liberation of Albania.

2221	**379**	8f. multicoloured	25·00	3·50
2222	-	10f. black, red & yellow	30·00	14·00

DESIGN: 10f. Enver Hoxha and Albanian arms.

380 Dam under Construction

1964. Hsinankiang Hydro-electric Power Station. Multicoloured.

2223	4f. Type **380**	£100	3·25
2224	8f. Installation of turbo-generator rotor	40·00	1·25
2225	8f. Main dam	50·00	2·50
2226	20f. Pylon	£200	14·00

381 Fertilisers

1964. Chemical Industry. Main design and inscr in black; background colours given.

2227	**381**	8f. (1) red	3·25	40
2228	-	8f. (2) green	3·25	40
2229	-	8f. (3) brown	3·25	40
2230	-	8f. (4) mauve	3·25	40
2231	-	8f. (5) blue	3·25	40
2232	-	8f. (6) orange	3·25	40
2233	-	8f. (7) violet	3·25	40
2234	-	8f. (8) turquoise	3·25	40

DESIGNS: (2), Plastics; (3), Medicinal drugs; (4), Rubber; (5), Insecticides; (6), Acids; (7), Alkalis; (8), Synthetic fibres.

382 Mao Tse-tung standing in Room

1965. 30th Anniv of Tsunyi Conference. Mult.

2235	8f. (1) Type **382**	85·00	15·00
2236	8f. (2) Mao Tse-tung (vert) (26½×36 mm)	85·00	12·00
2237	8f. (3) "Victory at Loushan Pass"	85·00	12·00

383 Conference Hall

1965. 10th Anniv of Bandung Conference. Mult.

2238	8f. Type **383**	2·00	25
2239	8f. Rejoicing Africans and Asians	2·00	25

384 Lenin

1965. 95th Birth Anniv of Lenin.

No.	Type	Description	Unused	Used
2240	**384**	8f. multicoloured	35·00	10·00

385 Table Tennis Player

1965. World Table Tennis Championships, Peking.

No.	Type	Description	Unused	Used
2241	**385**	8f. (1) multicoloured	1·00	25
2242	-	8f. (2) multicoloured	1·00	25
2243	-	8f. (3) multicoloured	1·00	25
2244	-	8f. (4) multicoloured	1·00	25

DESIGNS: Nos. 2242/4 each show different views of table tennis players.

386 All China T.U. Federation Team scaling Mt. Minya Konka

1965. Chinese Mountaineering Achievements. Each black, yellow and blue.

No.	Description	Unused	Used
2245	8f. (1) Type **386**	10·00	1·25
2246	8f. (2) Men and women's mixed team on slopes of Muztagh Ata	10·00	1·25
2247	8f. (3) Climbers on Mt. Jolmo Lungma	10·00	1·25
2248	8f. (4) Women's team camping on Kongur Tiubie Tagh	10·00	1·25
2249	8f. (5) Climbers on Shishma Pangma	10·00	1·25

387 Marx and Lenin

1965. Organization of Socialist Countries' Postal Administrations Conference, Peking.

No.	Type	Description	Unused	Used
2250	**387**	8f. multicoloured	30·00	10·00

388 Tseping

1965. "Chingkang Mountains – Cradle of the Chinese Revolution". Multicoloured.

No.	Description	Unused	Used
2251	4f. (1) Type **388**	22·00	45
2252	8f. (2) Sanwantsun	22·00	45
2253	8f. (3) Octagonal Building, Maoping	22·00	45
2254	8f. (4) River and bridge at Lungshih	30·00	1·20
2255	8f. (5) Tachingtsun	30·00	1·20
2256	10f. (6) Bridge at Lungyuankou	35·00	60
2257	10f. (7) Hwangyangchieh	35·00	85
2258	52f. (8) Chingkang peaks	50·00	15·00

389 Soldiers with Texts

1965. People's Liberation Army. Mult.

No.	Description	Unused	Used
2259	8f. (1) Type **389**	60·00	7·50
2260	8f. (2) Soldiers reading book	65·00	7·50
2261	8f. (3) Soldier with grenade-thrower	70·00	5·50
2262	8f. (4) Giving tuition in firing rifle	70·00	5·00
2263	8f. (5) Soldiers at rest (vert)	70·00	5·50
2264	8f. (6) Bayonet charge (vert)	70·00	5·50
2265	8f. (7) Soldier with banners (vert)	£120	15·00
2266	8f. (8) Military band (vert)	£100	10·00

390 "Welcome to Peking"

1965. Chinese–Japanese. Youth Meeting, Peking. Multicoloured.

No.	Description	Unused	Used
2267	4f. (1) Type **390**	2·00	20
2268	8f. (2) Chinese and Japanese youths with linked arms	2·00	25
2269	8f. (3) Chinese and Japanese girls	2·00	25
2270	10f. (4) Musical entertainment	3·25	25
2271	22f. (5) Emblem of Meeting	5·00	50

391 Soldier firing Weapon

1965. "Vietnamese People's Struggle".

No.	Type	Description	Unused	Used
2272	**391**	8f. (1) brown and red	3·25	50
2273	-	8f. (2) olive and red	3·25	50
2274	-	8f. (3) purple and red	3·25	50
2275	-	8f. (4) black and red	3·25	50

DESIGNS—VERT: (2) Soldier with captured weapons; (3) Soldier giving victory salute. HORIZ: (48½×26 mm): (4) "Peoples of the world".

392 "Victory"

1965. 20th Anniv of Victory over Japanese.

No.	Type	Description	Unused	Used
2276		8f. (1) multicoloured	48·00	6·75
2277		8f. (2) green and red	35·00	2·50
2278	**392**	8f. (3) sepia and red	35·00	2·50
2279	-	8f. (4) green and red	35·00	2·50

DESIGNS—HORIZ: (50½×36 mm): (1) Mao Tse-tung writing. As Type **392**—HORIZ: (2) Soldiers crossing Yellow River. (4) Recruits in cart.

393 Football

1965. 2nd National Games. Multicoloured.

No.	Description	Unused	Used
2280	4f. (1) Type **393**	25·00	1·25
2281	4f. (2) Archery	25·00	1·25
2282	8f. (3) Throwing the javelin	40·00	1·25
2283	8f. (4) Gymnastics	40·00	1·25
2284	8f. (5) Volleyball	40·00	1·25
2285	10f. (6) Opening ceremony (horiz) (56×35½ mm)	60·00	1·25
2286	10f. (7) Cycling	95·00	1·25
2287	20f. (8) Diving	£120	2·50
2288	22f. (9) Hurdling	30·00	3·25
2289	30f. (10) Weightlifting	30·00	6·50
2290	43f. (11) Basketball	40·00	9·50

394 Textile Workers

1965. Women in Industry. Multicoloured.

No.	Description	Unused	Used
2291	8f. (1) Type **394**	20·00	1·00
2292	8f. (2) Machine building	20·00	1·00
2293	8f. (3) Building construction	20·00	1·00
2294	8f. (4) Studying	20·00	1·00
2295	8f. (5) Militia guard	20·00	5·00

395 Children playing with Ball

1966. Children's Games. Multicoloured.

No.	Description	Unused	Used
2296	4f. (1) Type **395**	75	20
2297	4f. (2) Racing	75	20
2298	8f. (3) Tobogganing	75	20
2299	8f. (4) Exercising	75	25
2300	8f. (5) Swimming	75	25
2301	8f. (6) Shooting	75	25
2302	10f. (7) Jumping with rope	1·25	35
2303	52f. (8) Playing table tennis	2·25	1·20

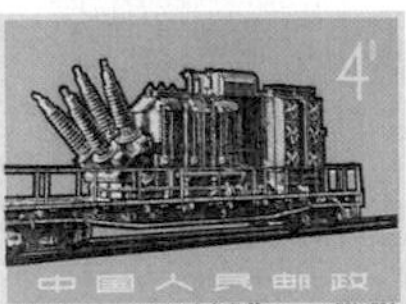

396 Mobile Transformer

1966. New Industrial Machines.

No.	Type	Description	Unused	Used
2304	**396**	4f. (1) black and yellow	25·00	75
2305	-	8f. (2) black and blue	30·00	75
2306	-	8f. (3) black and pink	32·00	75
2307	-	8f. (4) black and olive	35·00	75
2308	-	8f. (5) black and purple	35·00	75
2309	-	10f. (6) black and grey	40·00	3·25
2310	-	10f. (7) black & turq	40·00	5·00
2311	-	22f. (8) black and lilac	55·00	6·50

DESIGNS—VERT: (2), Electron microscope; (4), Vertical boring and turning machine; (6), Hydraulic press; (8), Electron accelerator. HORIZ: (3), Lathe; (5), Gear-grinding machine; (7), Milling machine.

397 Women of Military and Other Services

1966. Women in Public Service. Mult.

No.	Description	Unused	Used
2312	8f. (1) Type **397**	75	25
2313	8f. (2) Train conductress	75	25
2314	8f. (3) Red Cross worker	75	25
2315	8f. (4) Kindergarten teacher	75	25
2316	8f. (5) Roadsweeper	75	25
2317	8f. (6) Hairdresser	75	25
2318	8f. (7) Bus conductress	75	25
2319	8f. (8) Travelling saleswoman	75	25
2320	8f. (9) Canteen worker	75	25
2321	8f. (10) Rural postwoman	75	25

398 "Thunderstorm" (sculpture)

1966. Afro-Asian Writers' Meeting.

No.	Type	Description	Unused	Used
2322	**398**	8f. black and red	10·00	2·50
2323	-	22f. gold, yellow & red	15·00	2·50

DESIGN: 22f. Meeting emblem.

399 Dr. Sun Yat-sen

1966. Birth Centenary of Dr. Sun Yat-sen.

No.	Type	Description	Unused	Used
2324	**399**	8f. sepia and buff	50·00	20·00

400 Athletes with Mao Tse-tung's Portrait

1966. "Cultural Revolution" Games. Multicoloured.

No.	Description	Unused	Used
2325	8f. (1) Type **400**	60·00	12·00
2326	8f. (2) Athletes with linked arms hold Mao texts	60·00	12·00
2327	8f. (3) Two women athletes with Mao texts	70·00	12·00
2328	8f. (4) Athletes reading Mao texts	85·00	13·00

SIZES: No. 2326, As Type **400**, but vert; Nos. 2327/8, 36½×25 mm.

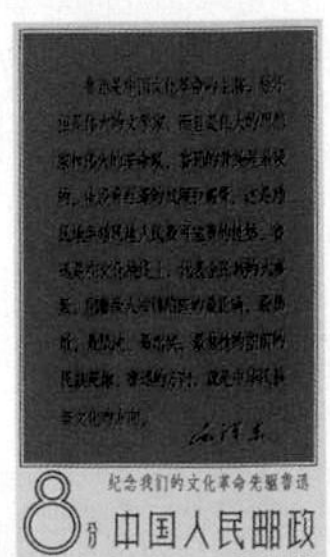

401 Mao's Appreciation of Lu Hsun (patriot and writer)

1966. 30th Death Anniv of Lu Hsun.

No.	Type	Description	Unused	Used
2329	**401**	8f. (1) black & orange	£150	30·00
2330	-	8f. (2) black, flesh & red	65·00	22·00
2331	-	8f. (3) black & orange	85·00	25·00

DESIGNS: (2) Lu Hsun; (3) Lu Hsun's manuscript.

402 "Be Resolute ..." (Mao Tse-tung)

1967. Heroic Oilwell Firefighters.

No.	Type	Description	Unused	Used
2332	**402**	8f. (1) gold, red & black	40·00	22·00
2333	-	8f. (2) black and red	95·00	20·00
2334	-	8f. (3) black and red	65·00	20·00

DESIGNS—HORIZ: (42×27 mm): (2) Drilling Team No. 32111 fighting flames. VERT: (3) Smothering flames with tarpaulins.

403 Liu Ying-chun (military hero)

1967. Liu Ying-chun Commem. Multicoloured.

2335	8f. (1) Type **403**	60·00	18·00
2336	8f. (2) Liu Ying-chun holding book of Mao texts	60·00	15·00
2337	8f. (3) Liu Ying-chun holding horse's bridle	60·00	20·00
2338	8f. (4) Liu Ying-chun looking at film slide	60·00	16·00
2339	8f. (5) Liu Ying-chun lecturing	60·00	16·00
2340	8f. (6) Liu Ying-chun making fatal attempt to stop bolting horse	60·00	20·00

404 Soldier, Nurse, Workers and Banners

1967. 3rd Five-Year Plan. Multicoloured.

2341	8f. (1) Type **404**	95·00	20·00
2342	8f. (2) Armed woman, peasants and banners	95·00	20·00

405 Mao Tse-tung

1967. "Thoughts of Mao Tse-tung" (1st issue). Similar designs showing Mao texts each gold and red. To assist identification of Nos. 2344/53 the total number of Chinese characters within the frames are given. (a) Type 405.

2343	8f. multicoloured	£325	50·00

406 Mao Text (39 characters)

(b) As Type 406. Red outer frames.

2344	8f. Type **406**	£100	50·00
2345	8f. (50 characters)	£100	50·00
2346	8f. (39–in six lines)	£100	50·00
2347	8f. (53)	£100	50·00
2348	8f. (46)	£100	50·00

(c) As Type 406. Gold outer frames.

2349	8f. (41)	£150	80·00
2350	8f. (49)	£150	80·00
2351	8f. (35)	£150	80·00
2352	8f. (22)	£150	80·00
2353	8f. (29)	£150	80·00

See also No. 2405.

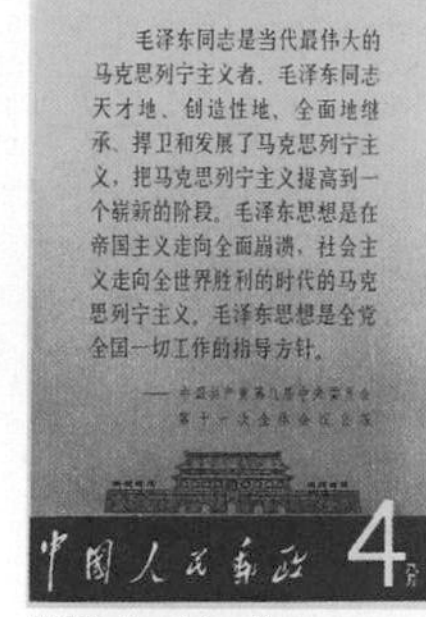

407 Text praising Mao

1967. Labour Day.

2354	**407**	4f. multicoloured	£100	25·00
2355	-	8f. multicoloured	£150	25·00
2356	-	8f. multicoloured	80·00	25·00
2357	-	8f. multicoloured	£150	25·00
2358	-	8f. multicoloured	75·00	25·00

DESIGNS (Mao Tse-tung and): No. 2355, Poem; No. 2356, Multi-racial crowd with texts; No. 2357, Red Guards. (36×50½ mm): Mao with hand raised in greeting.

For stamps similar to No. 2358, see Nos. 2367/9.

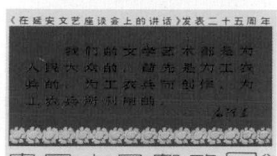

408 Mao Text

1967. 25th Anniv of Mao Tse-tung's "Talks on Literature and Art".

2359	**408**	8f. black, red & yellow	£600	£120
2360	-	8f. black, red & yellow	£400	£120
2361	-	8f. multicoloured	£550	£150

DESIGNS: No. 2360, As Type **408** but different text. (50×36½ mm): No. 2361, Mao supporters in procession.

409 Mao Tse-tung

1967. 46th Anniv of Chinese Communist Party.

2362	**409**	4f. red	40·00	20·00
2363	**409**	8f. red	£325	25·00
2364	**409**	35f. brown	15·00	20·00
2365	**409**	43f. red	20·00	25·00
2366	**409**	52f. red	25·00	20·00

410 Mao Tse-tung and Lin Piao

1967. "Our Great Teacher". Multicoloured.

2367	8f. Type **410**	£325	75·00
2368	8f. Mao Tse-tung (horiz)	£100	50·00
2369	10f. Mao Tse-tung conferring with Lin Piao (horiz)	£500	75·00

For 8f. stamp showing Mao with hand raised in greeting, see No. 2358.

411 Mao Tse-tung as "Sun"

1967. 18th Anniv of People's Republic. Mult.

2370	8f. Type **411**	£140	35·00
2371	8f. Mao Tse-tung with representatives of Communist countries	£120	30·00

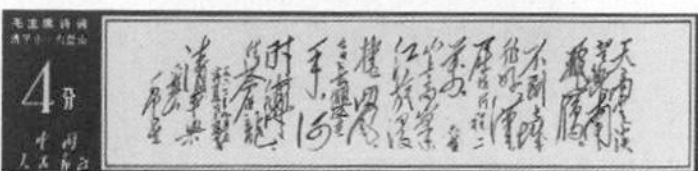

412 "Mount Liupan" (image scaled to 63% of original size)

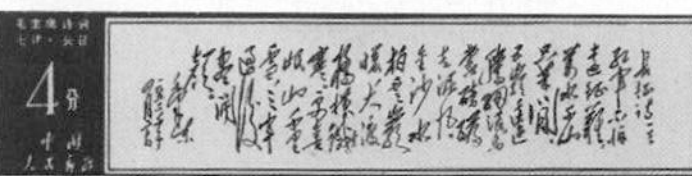

413 "The Long March" (image scaled to 63% of original size)

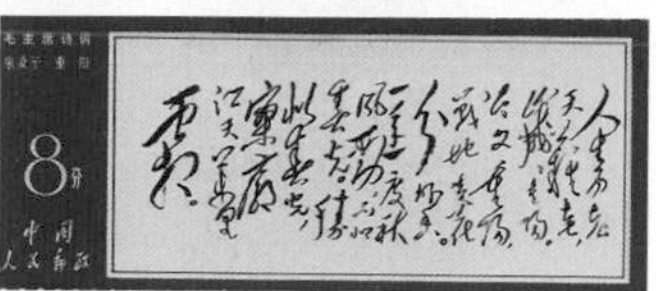

414 "Double Ninth"

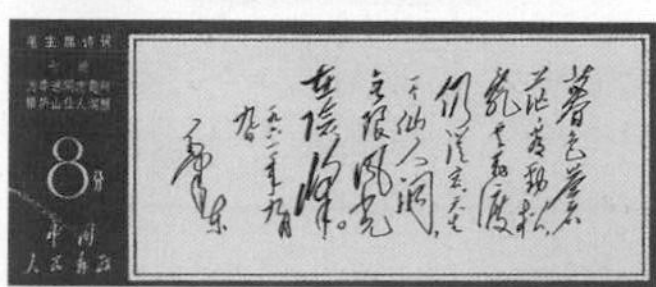

415 "Fairy Cave"

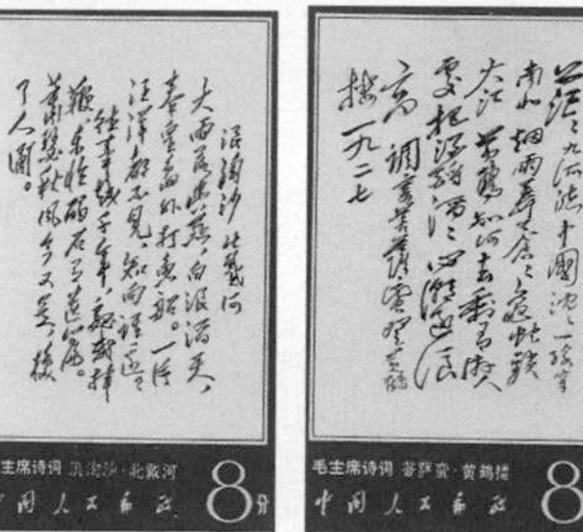

416 "Huichang" **417** "Yellow Crane Pavilion"

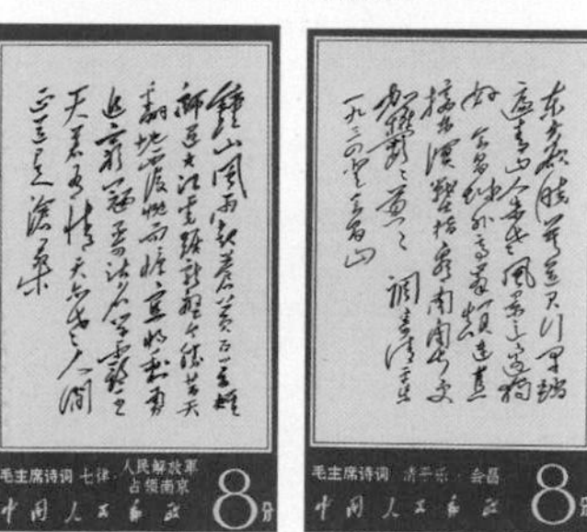

418 "Beidahe" **419** "Swimming"

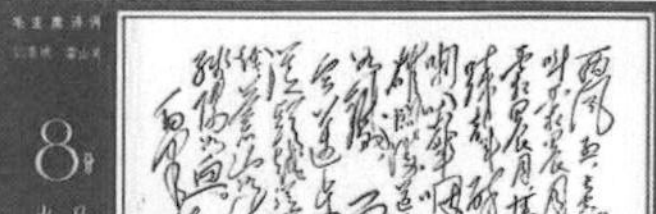

420 "Loushanguan Pass"

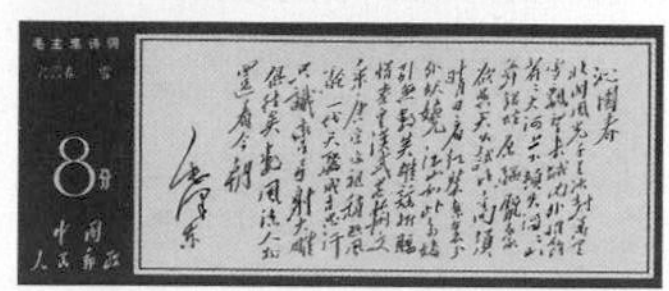

421 "Snow"

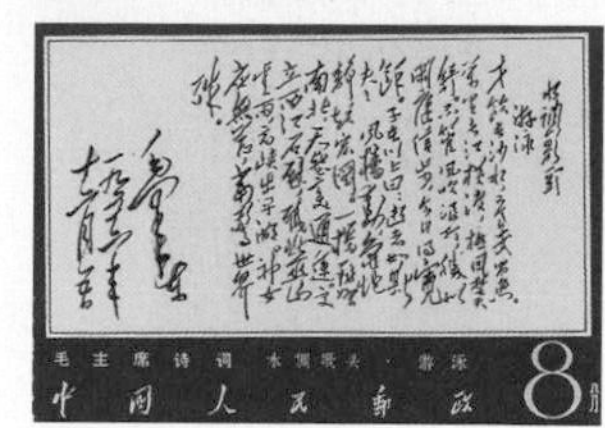

422 "Capture of Nanjing"

423 Mao Writing Poems at Desk

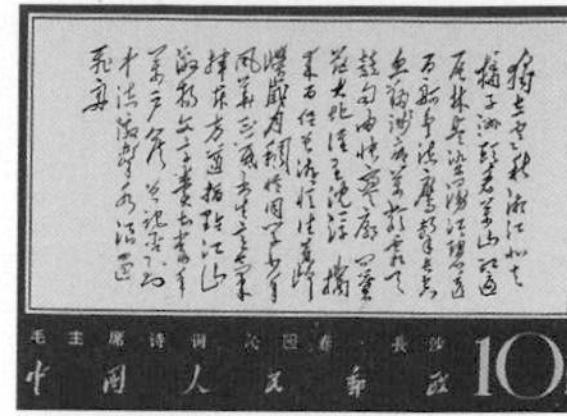

424 "Changsha"

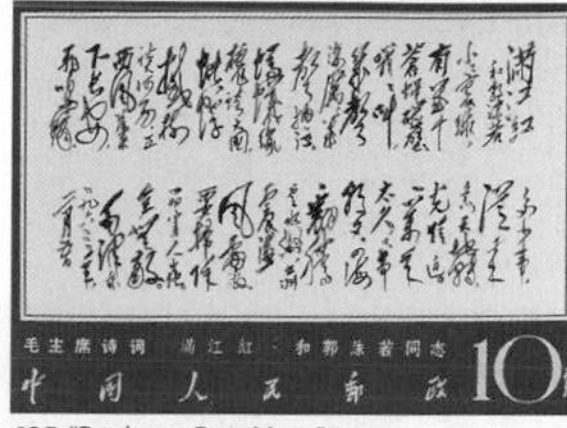

425 "Reply to Guo Moro"

1967. Poems of Mao Tse-tung.

2372	**412**	4f. black, yellow & red	20·00	20·00
2373	**413**	4f. black, yellow & red	22·00	22·00
2374	**414**	8f. black, yellow & red	£150	40·00
2375	**415**	8f. black, yellow & red	£150	40·00
2376	**416**	8f. black, yellow & red	£1400	£300
2377	**417**	8f. black, yellow & red	£750	£200
2378	**418**	8f. black, yellow & red	£700	£200
2379	**419**	8f. black, yellow & red	£750	£225
2380	**420**	8f. black, yellow & red	70·00	35·00
2381	**421**	8f. black, yellow & red	75·00	35·00
2382	**422**	8f. black, yellow & red	£200	60·00
2383	**423**	10f. multicoloured	25·00	20·00
2384	**424**	10f. black, yellow & red	25·00	20·00
2385	**425**	10f. black, yellow & red	25·00	20·00

426 Epigram on Chairman Mao by Lin Piao

1967. Fleet Expansionists' Congress.

2386	**426**	8f. gold and red	38·00	10·00

427 Mao Tse-tung and Procession

1968. "Revolutionary Literature and Art" (1st issue). Multicoloured designs showing scenes from People's Operas.

2387	8f. Type **427**	50·00	12·00
2388	8f. "Raid on the White Tiger Regiment"	£110	12·00
2389	8f. "Taking Tiger Mountain"	75·00	12·00
2390	8f. "On the Docks"	75·00	12·00
2391	8f. "Shachiapang"	75·00	12·00
2392	8f. "The Red Lantern" (vert)	75·00	12·00

428 "Red Detachment of Women" (ballet)

1968. "Revolutionary Literature and Art" (2nd issue). Multicoloured.

2393	8f. Type **428**	£120	20·00
2394	8f. "The White-haired Girl" (ballet)	£120	20·00
2395	8f. Mao Tse-tung, Symphony Orchestra and Chorus (50×36 mm)	£120	20·00

429 Mao Tse-tung ("Unite still more closely")

1968. Mao's Anti-American Declaration.

2396	**429**	8f. brown, gold and red	£500	75·00

430 **431**

432 **433**

434

1968. "Directives of Mao Tse-tung".

2397	**430**	8f. brown, red & yellow	£225	£100
2398	**431**	8f. brown, red & yellow	£225	£100
2399	**432**	8f. brown, red & yellow	£225	£100
2400	**433**	8f. brown, red & yellow	£225	£100
2401	**434**	8f. brown, red & yellow	£225	£100

435 Inscription by Lin Piao. 26 July, 1965

1968. 41st Anniv of People's Liberation Army.

2402	**435**	8f. black, gold and red	30·00	10·00

436 "Chairman Mao goes to Anyuan" (Liu Chunhua)

1968. Mao's Youth.

2403	**436**	8f. multicoloured	85·00	35·00

436a

1968. The Whole Country is Red

2403a	**436a**	8f. multicoloured	£85000	£40000

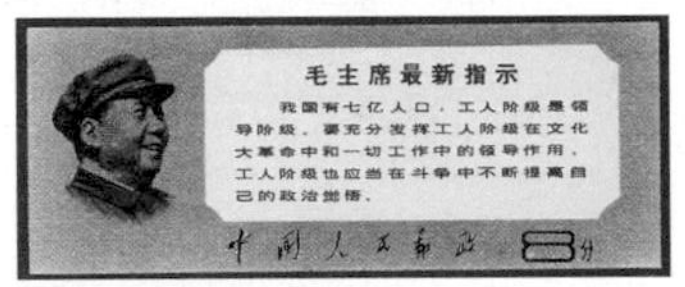

438 Mao Tse-tung and Text

1968. "Thoughts of Mao Tse-tung" (2nd issue).

2405	**438**	8f. brown and red	£120	35·00

439 Displaying "The Words of Mao Tse-tung"

1968. "The Words of Mao Tse-tung". No gum.

2406	**439**	8f. multicoloured	45·00	10·00

440 Yangtse Bridge

1968. Completion of Yangtse Bridge, Nanking. Multicoloured. No gum.

2407	4f. Type **440**	10·00	3·00
2408	8f. Buses on bridge	38·00	10·00
2409	8f. View of end portals	25·00	8·00
2410	10f. Aerial view	10·00	3·25

Nos. 2408/9 are larger, size 49×27 mm.

441 Li Yu-ho singing "I am filled with Courage and Strength"

1969. Songs from "The Red Lantern" Opera. Multicoloured. No gum.

2411	8f. Type **441**	12·00	10·00
2412	8f. Li Ti-mei singing "Hatred in my Heart"	£120	15·00

442 Communist Party Building, Shanghai

1969. No gum.

2413	**442**	1½f. red, brown & lilac	1·00	1·00
2414	-	8f. brown, grn & cream	3·25	3·00
2415	-	8f. red and purple	1·00	40
2416	-	8f. brown and blue	1·50	70
2417	-	20f. blue, purple & red	2·50	1·50
2418	-	50f. brown and green	2·50	1·50

DESIGNS: "Historic Sites of the Revolution"; Size 27×22 mm—No. 2414, Pagoda Hill, Yenan; No. 2415, Gate of Heavenly Peace, Peking; No. 2418. Mao Tse-tung's house, Yenan. Size as T **442**—No. 2416, People's Heroes Monument, Peking; No. 2417, Conference Hall, Tsunyi.

See also Nos. 2455/65.

443 Rice Harvesters

1969. Agricultural Workers. Mult. No gum.

2419	4f. Type **443**	10·00	3·25
2420	8f. Grain harvest	15·00	2·25
2421	8f. Study Group with "Thoughts of Mao"	85·00	12·00
2422	10f. Red Cross worker with mother and child	12·00	3·25

444 Snow Patrol

1969. Defence of Chen Pao Tao in the Ussur River. Multicoloured. No gum.

2423	8f. Type **444**	15·00	6·50
2424	8f. Guards by river (horiz)	15·00	6·50
2425	8f. Servicemen and Militia (horiz)	30·00	8·50
2426	35f. As No. 2424	20·00	10·00
2427	43f. Type **444**	20·00	10·00

445 Farm Worker

1969. "The Chinese People" (woodcuts). No gum.

2428A	**445**	4f. purple and orange	55	45
2429A	-	8f. purple and orange	1·10	60
2430A	-	10f. green and orange	2·10	1·20

DESIGNS: 8f. Foundryman. 10f. Soldier.

446 Chin Hsun-hua in Water

1970. Heroic Death of Chin Hsun-hua in Kirin Border Floods. No gum.

2431	**446**	8f. black and red	35·00	25·00

447 Tractor-driver

1970. No gum.

2432	**447**	5f. black, red & orange	2·25	50
2433	-	1y. black and red	8·50	2·25

DESIGN—HORIZ: 1y. Foundryman.

448 Cavalry Patrol

1970. 43rd Anniv of People's Liberation Army. No gum.

2434	**448**	8f. multicoloured	18·00	9·00

449 "Yang Tse-jung, Army Scout"

1970. "Taking Tiger Mountain" (Revolutionary opera). Multicoloured. No gum.

2435	8f. (1) Type **449**	30·00	12·00
2436	8f. (2) "The patrol sets out" (horiz)	30·00	12·00
2437	8f. (3) "Leaping through the forest"	30·00	12·00
2438	8f. (4) "Li Yung-chi's farewell" (27×48 mm)	30·00	12·00
2439	8f. (5) "Yang Tse-jung in disguise" (27×48 mm)	30·00	12·00
2440	8f. (6) "Congratulating Yang Tse-jung" (horiz)	30·00	12·00

450 Soldiers in Snow

1970. 2nd Anniv of Defence of Chen Pao Tao. No gum.

2441	**450**	4f. multicoloured	3·00	2·20

451 Communard Standard

1971. Cent of Paris Commune. Mult. No gum.

2442	**451**	4f. multicoloured	25·00	12·00
2443	-	8f. brown, pink and red	£120	25·00
2444	-	10f. red, brn and pink	£150	60·00
2445	-	22f. brown, red & pink	25·00	25·00

DESIGNS—HORIZ: 8f. Fighting in Paris, March 1871; 22f. Communards in Place Vendome. VERT: 10f. Commune proclaimed at the Hotel de Ville.

452 Communist Party Building, Shanghai

453 Workers and Great Hall of the People, Peking

1971. 50th Anniv of Chinese Communist Party. Multicoloured. No gum.

2446	4f. (12) Type **452**	12·00	4·25
2447	4f. (13) National Peasant Movement Inst., Canton	12·00	4·25
2448	8f. (14) Chingkang Mountains	12·00	3·25
2449	8f. (15) Conference Building, Tsunyi	12·00	3·25
2450	8f. (16) Pagoda Hill, Yenan	12·00	3·25
2451	22f. (17) Gate of Heavenly Peace, Peking	20·00	8·00
2452	8f. (18) Workers and Industry	20·00	10·00
2453	8f. (19) Type **453**	20·00	10·00
2454	8f. (20) Workers and Agriculture	20·00	10·00

SIZES: As Type **452**. Nos. 2447/2450 and 2451. As Type **453**. Nos. 2452/4.

454 National Peasant Movement Institute, Canton

1971. Revolutionary Sites. Multicoloured. No gum.

2455	1f. Communist Party Building, Shanghai (vert)	40	20
2456	2f. Type **454**	40	20
2457	3f. Site of 1929 Congress, Kutien	40	20
2458	4f. Mao Tse-tung's house, Yenan	40	20
2459	8f. Gate of Heavenly Peace, Peking	50	25
2460	10f. Monument, Chingkang Mountains	50	25
2461	20f. River bridge, Yenan	60	25
2462	22f. Mao's birthplace, Shaoshan	1·00	35
2463	35f. Conference Building, Tsunyi	1·25	40
2464	43f. Start of the Long March, Chingkang Mountains	2·00	50
2465	52f. People's Palace, Peking	3·25	55

455 Welcoming Bouquets

1971. "Afro-Asian Friendship" Table Tennis Tournament, Peking. Multicoloured. No gum.

2466	8f. (22) Type **455**	15·00	4·50
2467	8f. (23) Group of players	15·00	4·50
2468	8f. (24) Asian and African players	15·00	4·50
2469	43f. (21) Tournament badge	20·00	5·00

456 Enver Hoxha making speech

1971. 30th Anniv of Albanian Worker's Party. Multicoloured. No gum.

2470	8f. (25) Type **456**	18·00	10·00
2471	8f. (26) Party Headquarters	12·00	5·00
2472	8f. (27) Albanian flag, rifle and pick	12·00	5·00
2473	52f. (28) Soldier and Worker's Militia (horiz)	22·00	8·00

457 Conference Hall, Yenan

1972. 30th Anniv of Publication of "Yenan Forum's Discussions on Literature and Art". Multicoloured. No gum.

2474	8f. (33) Type **457**	9·50	5·50
2475	8f. (34) Army choir	9·50	5·50
2476	8f. (35) "Brother and Sister"	9·50	5·50
2477	8f. (36) "Open-air Theatre"	9·50	5·50
2478	8f. (37) "The Red Lantern" (opera)	16·00	5·50
2479	8f. (38) "Red Detachment of Women" (ballet)	18·00	5·50

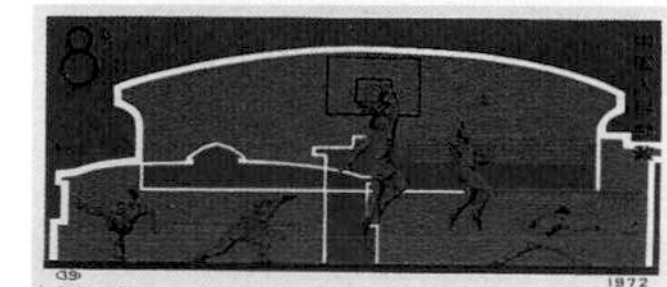
458 Ball Games

1972. 10th Anniv of Mao Tse-tungs's Edict on Physical Culture. Multicoloured. No gum.

2480	8f. (39) Type **458**	18·00	3·50
2481	8f. (40) Gymnastics	18·00	3·50
2482	8f. (41) Tug-of-War	18·00	3·50
2483	8f. (42) Rock-climbing	18·00	3·50
2484	8f. (43) High-diving	18·00	3·50

Nos. 2481/4 are size 26×36 mm.

460 Freighter "Fenglei"

1972. Chinese Merchant Shipping. Multicoloured. No gum.

2485	8f. (29) Type **460**	45·00	10·00
2486	8f. (30) Tanker "Taching No. 30"	45·00	10·00
2487	8f. (31) Cargo-liner "Chang Seng"	45·00	10·00
2488	8f. (32) Dredger "Hsienfeng"	45·00	10·00

461 Championship Badge

1972. 1st Asian Table Tennis Championships, Peking. Multicoloured. No gum.

2489	8f. (45) Type **461**	8·50	1·50
2490	8f. (46) Welcoming crowd (horiz)	8·50	1·50
2491	8f. (47) Game in progress (horiz)	8·50	1·50
2492	22f. (48) Players from three countries	10·00	3·25

462 Wang Chin-hsi, the "Iron Man"

1972. Wang Chin-hsi (workers' hero) Commem. No gum.

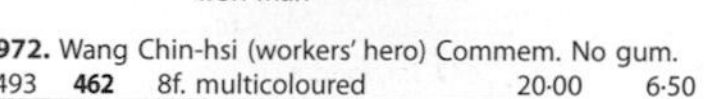

2493	**462**	8f. multicoloured	20·00	6·50

463 Cliff-edge Construction

1972. Construction of Red Flag Canal. Mult.

2494	8f. (49) Type **463**	9·00	3·50
2495	8f. (50) "Youth" tunnel	9·00	3·50
2496	8f. (51) "Taoguan bridge"	9·00	3·50
2497	8f. (52) Cliff-edge canal	9·00	3·50

464 Giant Panda eating Bamboo Shoots

1973. China's Giant Pandas.

2498	**464**	4f. (61) multicoloured	15·00	8·00
2499	-	8f. (59) mult (horiz)	15·00	5·25
2500	-	8f. (60) mult (horiz)	15·00	5·25
2501	-	10f. (58) multicoloured	85·00	15·00
2502	-	20f. (57) multicoloured	45·00	10·00
2503	-	43f. (62) multicoloured	55·00	18·00

DESIGNS: 8f. to 43f. Different brush and ink drawings of pandas.

465 "New Power in the Mines" (Yang Shi-guang)

1973. International Working Women's Day. Mult.

2504	8f. (63) Type **465**	7·50	3·00
2505	8f. (64) "Woman Committee Member" (Tang Hsiaoming)	7·50	3·00
2506	8f. (65) "I am a Sea-gull" (Army telegraph line woman) (Pan Jiajun)	7·50	3·00

466 Girl dancing

1973. Children's Day. Multicoloured.

2507	8f. (86) Type **466**	2·00	1·30
2508	8f. (87) Boy musician	2·00	1·30
2509	8f. (88) Boy with scarf	2·00	1·30
2510	8f. (89) Boy with tambourine	2·00	1·30
2511	8f. (90) Girl with drum	2·00	1·30

467 Badge of Championships

1973. Asian. African and Latin-American Table Tennis Invitation Championships. Multicoloured.

2512	8f. (91) Type **467**	6·50	2·50
2513	8f. (92) Visitors	7·00	2·50
2514	8f. (93) Player	7·00	2·50
2515	22f. (94) Guest players	12·00	3·00

468 "Hsi-erh"

1973. Revolutionary Ballet "Hsi-erh" ("The White-haired Girl"). Multicoloured.

2516	8f. (53) Type **468**	10·00	5·00
2517	8f. (54) Hsi-erh escapes from Huang (horiz)	10·00	5·00
2518	8f. (55) Hsi-erh meets Tachun (horiz)	10·00	5·00
2519	8f. (56) Hsi-erh becomes a soldier	10·00	5·00

469 Fair Building

1973. Chinese Exports Fair, Canton.

2520	**469**	8f. multicoloured	20·00	8·00

470 Mao's Birthplace, Shaoshan

471 Steam and Diesel Trains

1973. No gum.

2521	**470**	1f. green & light green	55	25
2522	-	1½f. red and yellow	55	30
2523	-	2f. blue and green	55	25
2524	-	3f. green and yellow	55	25
2525	-	4f. red and yellow	55	25
2526	-	5f. brown and yellow	55	25
2527	-	8f. purple and flesh	55	25
2528	-	10f. blue and flesh	55	25
2529	-	20f. red and buff	1·30	25
2530	-	22f. violet and yellow	2·00	25
2531	-	35f. purple and yellow	2·75	85
2532	-	43f. brown and buff	3·50	1·40
2533	-	50f. blue and mauve	6·00	2·20
2534	-	52f. brown and yellow	5·50	2·75
2535	**471**	1y. multicoloured	4·00	60
2536	-	2y. multicoloured	4·50	70

DESIGNS—As Type **470**: 1½f. National Peasant Movement Institute, Shanghai. 2f. National Institute, Kwangchow. 3f. Headquarters Building, Nanching uprising. 4f. Great Hall of the People, Peking, 5f. Wen Chia Shih. 8f. Gate of Heavenly Peace, Peking. 10f. Chingkang Mountains. 20f. Kutien Congress building. 22f. Tsunyi Congress building. 35f. Bridge, Yenan. 43f. Hsi Pai Po. 50f. "Fairy Gate", Lushan. 52f. People's Heroes Monument, Peking. As Type **471**: 2y. Trucks on mountain road.

472 "Phoenix" Pot

1973. Archaeological Treasures. Multicoloured.

2537	4f. (66) Type **472**	2·50	1·00
2538	4f. (67) Silver pot	2·50	1·00
2539	8f. (68) Porcelain horse and groom	2·50	75
2540	8f. (69) Figure of woman	2·50	75
2541	8f. (70) Carved pedestals	2·50	75
2542	8f. (71) Bronze horse	2·50	75
2543	8f. (72) Gilded "frog"	2·50	75
2544	8f. (73) Lamp-holder figurine	2·50	75
2545	10f. (74) Tripod jar	2·50	1·25
2546	10f. (75) Bronze vessel	2·50	1·25
2547	20f. (76) Bronze wine vessel	3·00	1·75
2548	52f. (77) Tray with tripod	5·00	3·25

473 Dance Routine

1974. Popular Gymnastics. Multicoloured.

2549	8f. (1) Type **473**	15·00	5·50
2550	8f. (2) Rings exercise	15·00	5·50
2551	8f. (3) Dancing on beam	15·00	5·50
2552	8f. (4) Handstand on parallel bars	15·00	5·50
2553	8f. (5) Trapeze exercise	15·00	5·50
2554	8f. (6) Vaulting over horse	15·00	5·50

474 Lion Dance

1974. Acrobatics. Multicoloured.

2555	8f. (1) Type **474**	12·00	4·50
2556	8f. (2) Handstand on chairs	12·00	4·50
2557	8f. (3) Diabolo team (horiz)	12·00	4·50
2558	8f. (4) Revolving jar (horiz)	12·00	4·50
2559	8f. (5) Spinning plates	12·00	4·50
2560	8f. (6) Foot-juggling with parasol	12·00	4·50

475 Man reading Book

1974. Huhsien Paintings. Multicoloured.

2561	8f. (1) Type **475**	3·25	2·25
2562	8f. (2) Mineshaft (23×57 mm)	3·25	2·25
2563	8f. (3) Workers hoeing field (horiz)	3·25	2·25
2564	8f. (4) Workers eating (horiz)	3·25	2·25
2565	8f. (5) Wheatfield landscape (57×23 mm)	3·25	2·25
2566	8f. (6) Harvesting (horiz)	3·25	2·25

476 Postman

1974. Centenary of UPU. Multicoloured.

2567	8f. (1) Type **476**	7·50	4·00
2568	8f. (2) People of five races	7·50	4·00
2569	8f. (3) Great Wall of China	7·50	4·00

477 Inoculating Children

1974. Country Doctors. Multicoloured.

2570	8f. (1) Type **477**	5·50	2·50
2571	8f. (2) On country visit (vert)	5·50	2·50
2572	8f. (3) Gathering herbs (vert)	5·50	2·50
2573	8f. (4) Giving acupuncture	5·50	2·50

478 Wang Chin-hsi, "The Iron Man"

1974. Chairman Mao's Directives on Industrial and Agricultural Teaching. Multicoloured. (a) "Learning Industry from Taching".

2574	8f. (1) Type **478**	1·75	1·25
2575	8f. (2) Pupils studying Mao's works	1·75	1·25
2576	8f. (3) Oil-workers sinking well	1·75	1·25
2577	8f. (4) Consultation with management	1·75	1·25
2578	8f. (5) Taching oilfield as development site	1·75	1·25

(b) "Learning Agriculture from Tachai".

2579	8f. (1) Tachai workers looking to future	1·75	1·25
2580	8f. (2) Construction workers	1·75	1·25
2581	8f. (3) Agricultural workers making field tests	1·75	1·25
2582	8f. (4) Trucks delivering grain to State granaries	1·75	1·25
2583	8f. (5) Workers going to fields	1·75	1·25

479 National Day Celebrations

1974. 25th Anniv of Chinese People's Republic. Multicoloured. (a) National Day.

2584	8f. Type **479**	9·50	5·00

480 Steel Worker, Taching

(b) Chairman Mao's Directives.

2585	8f. (1) Type **480**	2·00	1·60
2586	8f. (2) Agricultural worker, Tachai	2·00	1·60
2587	8f. (3) Coastal guard	2·00	1·60

481 Fair Building

1974. Chinese Exports Fair, Canton.

2588	**481**	8f. multicoloured	5·00	2·25

482 Revolutionary Monument, Permet

1974. 30th Anniv of Albania's Liberation. Mult.

2589	8f. Type **482**	4·75	2·00
2590	8f. Albanian patriots	4·75	2·00

483 Capital Stadium

1974. Peking Buildings. No gum.

2591	**483**	4f. black and green	1·50	10
2592	-	8f. black and blue	1·50	10

DESIGN: 8f. Hotel Peking.

484 Water-cooled Turbine Generator

1974. Industrial Production. Multicoloured.

2593	8f. (78) Type **484**	95·00	25·00
2594	8f. (79) Mechanical rice sprouts transplanter	95·00	25·00
2595	8f. (80) Universal cylindrical grinding machine	95·00	25·00
2596	8f. (81) Mobile rock drill (vert)	95·00	25·00

485 Congress Delegates

1975. 4th National People's Congress, Peking. Multicoloured.

2597	8f. (1) Type **485**	5·50	2·50
2598	8f. (2) Flower-decked rostrum	5·50	2·50
2599	8f. (3) Farmer, worker, soldier and steel mill	5·50	2·50

486 Teacher Studying

1975. Country Women Teachers. Multicoloured.

2600	8f. (1) Type **486**	18·00	5·00
2601	8f. (2) Teacher on rounds	18·00	5·00
2602	8f. (3) Open-air class	18·00	5·00
2603	8f. (4) Primary class aboard boat	18·00	5·00

487 Broadsword

1975. "Wushu" (popular sport). Multicoloured.

2604	8f. (1) Type **487**	4·50	2·50
2605	8f. (2) Sword exercises	4·50	2·50
2606	8f. (3) "Boxing"	4·50	2·50
2607	8f. (4) Leaping with spear	4·50	2·50
2608	8f. (5) Cudgel exercise	4·50	2·50
2609	43f. (6) Cudgel versus spears (60×30 mm)	15·00	14·00

488 "Mass Revolutionary Criticism"

1975. Criticism of Confucius and Liu Piao. Multicoloured.

2610	8f. (1) Type **488**	12·00	5·00
2611	8f. (2) "Leaders of the production brigade"	12·00	5·00
2612	8f. (3) "The battle continues" (horiz)	12·00	5·00
2613	8f. (4) "Liberated slave – pioneer critic" (horiz)	12·00	5·00

489 Parade of Athletes

1975. 3rd National Games, Peking. Mult.

2614	8f. (1) Type **489**	1·75	1·25
2615	8f. (2) Athletes studying (horiz)	1·75	1·25
2616	8f. (3) Volleyball players (horiz)	1·75	1·25
2617	8f. (4) Athlete, soldier, farmer and worker	1·75	1·25
2618	8f. (5) Various sports (horiz)	1·75	1·25
2619	8f. (6) Ethnic types and horse racing (horiz)	1·75	1·25
2620	35f. (7) Children and divers	6·00	5·00

490 Members of Expedition

1975. Chinese Ascent of Mount Everest. Mult.

2621	8f. (2) Type **490**	1·50	1·00
2622	8f. (3) Mountaineers with flag (horiz)	1·50	1·00
2623	43f. (1) View of Mount Everest (horiz)	2·50	1·50

491 "Studying Together"

1975. National Conference "Learning Agriculture from Tachai". Multicoloured.

2624	8f. (1) Type **491**	6·50	2·25
2625	8f. (2) "Promote Hard Work"	6·50	2·25
2626	8f. (3) Chinese combine- harvester	6·50	2·25

492 Children sticking Posters

1975. "Children's Progress". Multicoloured.

2627	8f. (1) Girl and young boy	1·75	1·25
2628	8f. (2) Type **492**	1·75	1·25
2629	8f. (3) Studying	1·75	1·25
2630	8f. (4) Harvesting	1·75	1·25
2631	52f. (5) Tug-of-war	8·50	5·00

493 Ploughing Paddy Field

1975. Mechanised Farming. Multicoloured.

2632	8f. (1) Type **493**	3·00	1·50
2633	8f. (2) Mechanical rice seedlings transplanter	3·00	1·50
2634	8f. (3) Irrigation pump	3·00	1·50
2635	8f. (4) Spraying cotton field	3·00	1·50
2636	8f. (5) Combine harvester	3·00	1·50

494 Bridge over Canal

1976. Completion of 4th Five-year Plan. Mult.

2637	8f. (1) Harvest scene	5·50	2·25
2638	8f. (2) Type **494**	5·50	2·25
2639	8f. (3) Fertilizer plant	5·50	2·25
2640	8f. (4) Textile factory	5·50	2·25
2641	8f. (5) Iron foundry	5·50	2·25
2642	8f. (6) Steam coal train	5·50	2·25
2643	8f. (7) Hydro-electric power station	5·50	2·25
2644	8f. (8) Shipbuilding	5·50	2·25
2645	8f. (9) Oil industry	5·50	2·25
2646	8f. (10) Pipe-line and harbour	5·50	2·25
2647	8f. (11) Diesel train on viaduct	5·50	2·25
2648	8f. (12) Crystal formation (scientific research)	5·50	2·25
2649	8f. (13) Classroom (rural education)	5·50	2·25
2650	8f. (14) Workers' health centre	5·50	2·25
2651	8f. (15) Workers' flats	5·50	2·25
2652	8f. (16) Department store	5·50	2·25

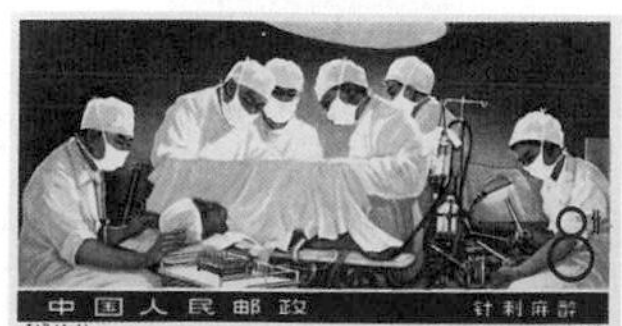

495 Heart Surgery

1976. Medical Services' Achievements. Mult.

2653	8f. (1) Type **495**	6·50	2·00
2654	8f. (2) Restoration of tractor-driver's severed arm	6·50	2·00
2655	8f. (3) Exercise of fractured arm	6·50	2·00
2656	8f. (4) Cataract operation – patient threading needle	6·50	2·00

496 Students studying at "May 7" School

1976. 10th Anniv of Mao's "May 7 Directive". Multicoloured.

2657	8f. (1) Type **496**	3·00	1·40
2658	8f. (2) Students in agriculture	3·00	1·40
2659	8f. (3) Students in production team	3·00	1·40

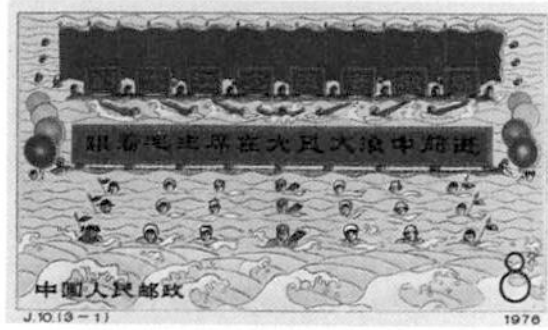

497 Formation of Swimmers

1976. 10th Anniv of Chairman Mao's Swim in Yangtse River. Multicoloured.

2660	8f. (1) Type **497**	2·50	1·40
2661	8f. (2) Swimmers crossing Yangtse	2·50	1·40
2662	8f. (3) Swimmers in surf	2·50	1·40

Nos. 2661/2 are smaller, 35×27 mm.

498 Students with Rosettes

1976. "Going to College". Multicoloured.

2663	8f. (1) Type **498**	3·50	1·40
2664	8f. (2) Study group	3·50	1·40
2665	8f. (3) On-site instructions	3·50	1·40
2666	8f. (4) Students operating computer	3·50	1·40
2667	8f. (5) Return of graduates from college	3·50	1·40

499 Electricity Lineswoman

1976. Maintenance of Electric Power Lines. Multicoloured.

2668	8f. (1) Type **499**	3·50	1·75
2669	8f. (2) Linesman replacing insulator	3·50	1·75
2670	8f. (3) Linesman using hydraulic lift	3·50	1·75
2671	8f. (4) Technician inspecting transformer	3·50	1·75

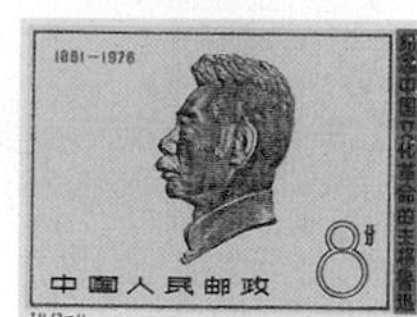

500 Lu Hsun

1976. 95th Birth Anniv of Lu Hsun (revolutionary leader). Multicoloured.

2672	8f. (1) Type **500**	10·00	2·50
2673	8f. (2) Lu Hsun sick, writing in bed	10·00	2·50
2674	8f. (3) Lu Hsun, workers and soldiers	10·00	2·50

501 Peasant arranging Student's Headband

1976. Students and Country Life. Multicoloured.

2675	4f. (1) Type **501**	2·25	1·00
2676	8f. (2) Student teaching farm woman (horiz)	2·25	1·00
2677	8f. (3) Irrigation survey	2·25	1·00
2678	8f. (4) Agricultural student testing wheat (horiz)	2·25	1·00
2679	10f. (5) Student feeding lamb	2·50	1·00
2680	20f. (6) Frontier guards (horiz)	6·50	2·25

502 Mao Tse-tung's Birthplace

1976. Shaoshan Revolutionary Sites. Mult.

2681	4f. (1) Type **502**	2·00	1·00
2682	8f. (2) School building	2·25	1·00
2683	8f. (3) Peasants' Association building	2·25	1·00
2684	10f. (4) Railway station	2·50	1·50

503 Chou En-lai

1977. 1st Death Anniv of Chou En-lai. Mult.

2685	8f. (1) Type **503**	2·75	1·00
2686	8f. (2) Chou En-lai making report	2·75	1·00
2687	8f. (3) Chou meeting "Iron Man" Wang Chin-hsi (horiz)	2·75	1·00
2688	8f. (4) Chou with provincial representatives (horiz)	4·00	1·00

504 Statue of Lui Hu-lan

1977. 30th Death Anniv of Lin Hu-lan (heroine and martyr). Multicoloured.

2689	8f. (1) Type **504**	8·50	3·00
2690	8f. (2) Text by Mao Tse-tung	8·50	3·00
2691	8f. (3) Lin Hu-lan and people	8·50	3·00

505 Revolutionaries and Text

1977. 30th Anniv of 1947 Taiwan Rising. Mult.

2692	8f. Type **505**	2·00	1·00
2693	10f. Three Taiwanese with banner	2·75	1·50

506 Weapon Maintenance

1977. Chinese Militiawomen. Multicoloured.

2694	8f. (1) Type **506**	7·50	3·25
2695	8f. (2) On horseback	7·50	3·25
2696	8f. (3) Directing traffic in tunnel	7·50	3·25

507 Sheep Rearing

1977. Multicoloured.. Multicoloured..

2697	1f. Coal mining	30	30
2698	1½f. Type **507**	30	20
2699	2f. Exports	30	20
2700	3f. Forest and diesel-train	30	20
2701	4f. Hydro-electric power	30	20
2702	5f. Fishing	30	20
2703	8f. Agriculture	30	20
2704	10f. Radio tower and mail-vans	35	25
2705	20f. Steel production	40	25
2706	30f. Road transport	40	25
2707	40f. Textile manufacture	55	25
2708	50f. Tractor assembly	65	25
2709	60f. Oil-rigs and setting sun	75	25
2710	70f. Railway viaduct, Yangtse Gorge	1·20	35

508 Cadre Members

1977. Promoting Tachai-type Developments. Mult.

2711	8f. (1) Type **508**	1·25	95
2712	8f. (2) Modern cultivation	1·25	95
2713	8f. (3) Reading wall newspaper	1·25	95
2714	8f. (4) Reclaiming land for agriculture	1·25	95

509 Party Leader addressing Workers

1977. "Taching-type" Industrial Conference. Mult.

2715	8f. (1) Type **509**	2·25	1·00
2716	8f. (2) Drilling for oil in snowstorm	2·25	1·00
2717	8f. (3) Man with banner over mass formation of workers	2·25	1·00
2718	8f. (4) Smiling workers and industrial scene	2·25	1·00

510 Mongolians Rejoicing

1977. 30th Anniv of Inner Mongolian Autonomous Region. Multicoloured.

2719	8f. Type **510**	80	25
2720	10f. Mongolian industrial scene and iron ore train	90	35
2721	20f. Mongolian pasture	1·75	85

511 Rumanian Flag

1977. Centenary of Rumanian Independence. Mult.

2722	8f. Type **511**	1·10	55
2723	10f. "The Battle of Smirdan" (Grigorescu)	1·25	75
2724	20f. Mihai Viteazu Memorial	2·50	1·60

512 Yenan and Floral Border

1977. 35th Anniv of Yenan Forum on Literature and Art. Multicoloured.

2725	8f. (1) Type **512**	1·25	60
2726	8f. (2) Hammer, sickle and gun	1·25	60

513 Chu Teh, National People's Congress Chairman

1977. 1st Death Anniv of Chu Teh.

2727	**513**	8f. (1) multicoloured	75	35
2728	-	8f. (2) multicoloured	75	35
2729	-	8f. (3) black, bl & gold	75	35
2730	-	8f. (4) black, bl & gold	75	35

DESIGNS—VERT: No. 2728, Chu Teh during his last session of Congress. HORIZ: No. 2729, Chu Teh at his desk. No. 2730, Chu Teh on horseback as Commander of People's Liberation Army.

514 Soldier, Sailor and Airman under Banner of Mao Tse-tung

1977. People's Liberation Army Day. Mult.

2731	8f. (1) Type **514**	2·50	1·00
2732	8f. (2) Soldiers in Ching-kang Mountains	2·50	1·00
2733	8f. (3) Guerrilla fighters returning to base	2·50	1·00
2734	8f. (4) Chinese forces crossing Yangtse River	2·50	1·00
2735	8f. (5) "The Steel Wall" (National Defence Forces)	2·50	1·00

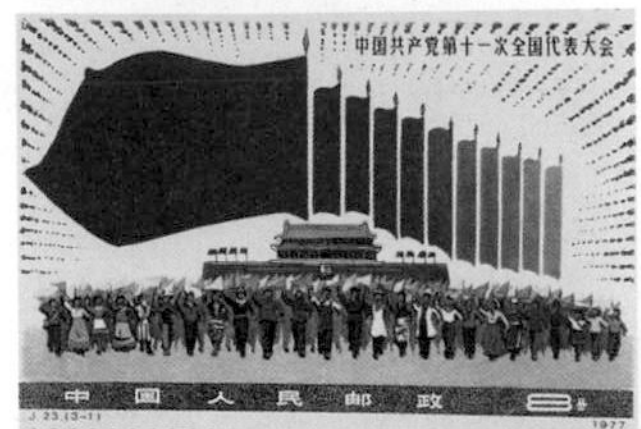

515 Red Flags and Crowd

1977. 11th National Communist Party Congress. Multicoloured.

2736	8f. (1) Type **515**	7·50	3·25
2737	8f. (2) Mao banner and procession	7·50	3·25
2738	8f. (3) Hammer and sickle banner and procession	7·50	3·25

516 Mao Tse-tung

1977. 1st Death Anniv of Mao Tse-tung. Mult.

2739	8f. (1) Type **516**	1·10	80
2740	8f. (2) Mao as young man	1·10	80
2741	8f. (3) Making speech	1·10	80
2742	8f. (4) Mao broadcasting	1·10	80
2743	8f. (5) Mao with Chou En-lai and Chu Teh (horiz)	1·10	80
2744	8f. (6) Reviewing the army	1·10	80

517 Mao Memorial Hall

1977. Completion of Mao Memorial Hall, Peking. Multicoloured.

2745	8f. (1) Type **517**	3·75	1·50
2746	8f. (2) Commemoration text	3·75	1·50

518 Tractors transporting Oil-rig

1978. Development of Petroleum Industry. Mult.

2747	8f. (1) Type **518**	75	45
2748	8f. (2) Clearing wax from oil well	75	45
2749	8f. (3) Laying pipe-line	75	45
2750	8f. (4) Tung Fang Hung oil refinery, Peking	75	45
2751	8f. (5) Loading a tanker, Taching	75	45
2752	20f. (6) Oil-rig and drilling ship "Exploration"	1·60	80

519 Rifle Shooting from Sampan

1978. "Army and People are One Family". Multicoloured.

2753	8f. (1) Type **519**	1·75	1·30
2754	8f. (2) Helping with rice harvest	1·75	1·30

520 Great Banner of Chairman Mao

1978. 5th National People's Congress. Mult.

2755	8f. (1) Type **520**	2·25	1·00
2756	8f. (2) Constitution	2·25	1·00
2757	8f. (3) Emblems of modernization	2·25	1·00

521 "Learn from Comrade Lei Feng" (Inscription by Mao Tse-tung)

1978. Lei Feng (Communist fighter) Commem.

2758	**521**	8f. (1) gold and red	2·50	1·30
2759	-	8f. (2) gold and red	2·50	1·30
2760	-	8f. (3) multicoloured	2·50	1·30

DESIGNS: No. 2759, Inscription by Chairman Hua; No. 2760, Lei Feng reading Mao's works.

522 Hsiang Ching-yu (Women's Movement Pioneer)

1978. International Working Women's Day.

2761	**522**	8f. (1) black, red & gold	1·10	75
2762	-	8f. (2) black, red & gold	1·10	75

DESIGN: No. 2762, Yang Kai-hui (communist fighter).

523 Conference Emblem and Tien on Men Gate, Peking

1978. National Science Conference. Mult.

2763	8f. (1) Type **523**	1·25	80
2764	8f. (2) Flags	1·25	80
2765	8f. (3) Emblem, flag and globe	1·25	80
MS2765a	140×106 mm. Nos. 2763/2765. Imperf	£700	£450

524 Launching a Radio-sonde

1978. Meteorological Services. Multicoloured.

2766	8f. (1) Type **524**	1·00	55
2767	8f. (2) Radar station	1·00	55
2768	8f. (3) Weather forecasting with computers	1·00	55
2769	8f. (4) Commune group observing sky	1·00	55
2770	8f. (5) Cloud-dispersing rockets	1·00	55

525 Galloping Horse

1978. Galloping Horses.

2771	**525**	4f. (1) multicoloured	1·50	75
2772	-	8f. (2) multicoloured	1·50	75
2773	-	8f. (3) multicoloured	1·50	75
2774	-	10f. (4) multicoloured	1·50	75
2775	-	20f. (5) multicoloured	3·75	1·25
2776	-	30f. (6) multicoloured	3·75	1·50
2777	-	40f. (7) mult (horiz)	4·50	2·25
2778	-	50f. (8) mult (horiz)	5·00	2·25
2779	-	60f. (9) mult (horiz)	7·50	3·25
2780	-	70f. (10) mult (horiz)	8·50	5·00
MS2781		148×98 mm. 5y. multicoloured (82×32 mm)	£500	£250

DESIGNS: No. 2772/80, various paintings of horses by Hsu Pei-hung.

526 Football

1978. "Building up Strength for the Revolution". Multicoloured.

2782	8f. (2) Type **526**	75	40
2783	8f. (3) Swimming	75	40
2784	8f. (4) Gymnastics	75	40
2785	8f. (5) Running	75	40
2786	20f. (1) Group exercises	1·25	70

The 20f. is larger, 48×27 mm.

527 Material Feeder

1978. Chemical Industry Development. Fabric Production. Multicoloured.

2787	8f. (1) Type **527**	75	60
2788	8f. (2) Drawing-out threads	75	60
2789	8f. (3) Weaving	75	60
2790	8f. (4) Dyeing and printing	75	60
2791	8f. (5) Finished products	75	60

528 Conference Emblem

1978. National Finance and Trade Conference. Multicoloured.

2792	8f. (1) Type **528**	50	40
2793	8f. (2) Inscription by Mao Tse-tung	50	40

529 Grassland Improvement, Mongolia

1978. Progress in Animal Husbandry. Mult.

2794	8f. (1) Type **529**	1·50	60
2795	8f. (2) Sheep rearing by the Kazakhs	1·50	60
2796	8f. (3) Shearing sheep, Tibet	1·50	60

530 Automated loading of Burning Coke

1978. Iron and Steel Industry. Mult.

2797	8f. (1) Type **530**	1·00	50
2798	8f. (2) Checking molten iron	1·00	50
2799	8f. (3) Pouring molten steel	1·00	50
2800	8f. (4) Steel-rolling mill	1·00	50
2801	8f. (5) Loading steel train	1·00	50

531 Soldier

1978. Army Modernization. Multicoloured.

2802	8f. (1) Type **531**	1·25	50
2803	8f. (2) Soldier firing missile	1·25	50
2804	8f. (3) Amphibious landing	1·25	50

532 Cloth Toy Lion

1978. Arts and Crafts. Multicoloured.

2805	4f. (1) Type **532**	1·00	25
2806	8f. (2) Three-legged pot (vert)	1·00	25
2807	8f. (3) Lacquerware rhinoceros	1·00	25
2808	10f. (4) Embroidered kitten (vert)	1·00	30
2809	20f. (5) Basketware	1·50	50
2810	30f. (6) Cloissone pot (vert)	1·75	65
2811	40f. (7) Lacquerware plate and swan	2·00	85
2812	50f. (8) Boxwood carving (vert)	2·50	1·20
2813	60f. (9) Jade carving	2·75	1·50
2814	70f. (10) Ivory carving (vert)	3·00	1·80
MS2815	139×90 mm. 3y. Lacquerware panel "Flying Fairies" (85×36 mm)	£400	£200

533 Worker, Peasant and Intellectual

1978. 4th National Women's Congress.

2816	**533**	8f. multicoloured	2·25	1·00

534 "Panax ginseng"

1978. Medicinal Plants. Multicoloured.

2817	8f. (1) Type **534**	1·00	25
2818	8f. (2) "Datura metel"	1·00	25
2819	8f. (3) "Belamcanda chinensis"	1·00	25
2820	8f. (4) "Platycodon grandiflorum"	1·00	25
2821	55f. (5) "Rhododendron dauricum"	3·50	1·00

535 Cogwheel, Grain, Rocket and Flag

1978. 9th National Trades Union Congress.

2822	**535**	8f. multicoloured	3·25	1·70

536 Emblem, Open Book and Flowers

1978. 10th National Congress of Communist Youth League.

2823	**536**	8f. multicoloured	3·00	1·10

537 Chinese and Japanese Children exchanging Gifts

1978. Signing of Chinese–Japanese Treaty of Peace and Friendship. Multicoloured.

2824	8f. Type **537**	1·00	35
2825	55f. Great Wall of China and Mt. Fuji	3·00	1·80

538 Hui, Han and Mongolian

1978. 20th Anniv of Ningsia Hui Autonomous Region. Multicoloured.

2826	8f. (1) Type **538**	1·00	80
2827	8f. (2) Coal loading machine, Holan colliery	1·00	80
2828	10f. (3) Irrigation and Ching-tunghsia power station	1·00	80

539 Chinsha River Bridge, West Szechuan

1978. Highway Bridges. Multicoloured.

2829	8f. (1) Type **539**	1·50	35
2830	8f. (2) Hsinghong Bridge, Wuhsi	1·50	35
2831	8f. (3) Chiuhsikou Bridge, Fengdu	1·50	35
2832	8f. (4) Chinsha Bridge	1·50	35
2833	60f. (5) Shangyeh Bridge, Sanmen	6·50	1·30
MS2834	145×70 mm. 2y. Hsingkiang River bridge (horiz, 85×37 mm)	£500	£225

540 Transplanting Rice Seedlings by Machine

1978. Water Country Modernization. Mult.

2835	8f. (1) Type **540**	6·00	2·75
2836	8f. (2) Crop spraying	6·00	2·75
2837	8f. (3) Selecting seeds	6·00	2·75
2838	8f. (4) Canal-side village	6·00	2·75
2839	8f. (5) Delivering and storing grain	6·00	2·75

Nos. 2835/9 were issued together, se-tenant, forming a composite design.

541 Festivities

1978. 20th Anniv of Kwangsi Chuang Autonomous Region. Multicoloured.

2840	8f. (1) Type **541**	2·50	75
2841	8f. (2) Industrial complexes (vert)	2·50	75
2842	10f. (3) River scene (vert)	2·50	90

542 Tibetan Peasant reporting Mineralogical Discovery

1978. Mining Development. Multicoloured.

2843	4f. Type **542**	75	35
2844	8f. Miners with pneumatic drill	85	45
2845	10f. Open-cast mining	1·50	80
2846	20f. Electric mine train	2·00	1·10

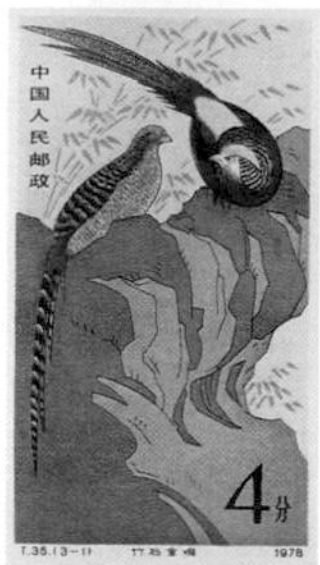

543 Pair of Golden Pheasants on Rock

1979. Golden Pheasants. Multicoloured.

2847	4f. Type **543**	2·50	1·00
2848	8f. Pheasant in flight	3·75	1·00
2849	45f. Pheasant looking for food	6·50	3·50

544 Einstein

1979. Birth Centenary of Albert Einstein (physicist).

2850	**544**	8f. brown, gold & slate	2·75	1·70

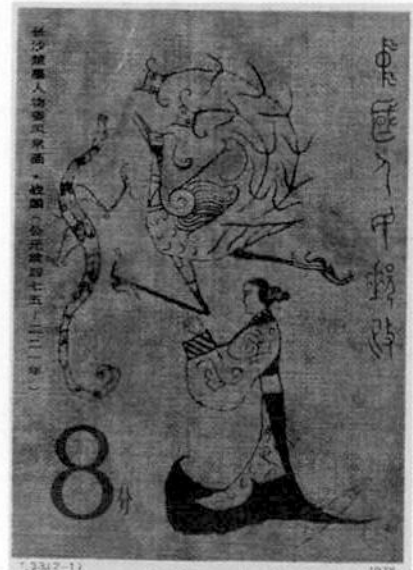

545 Woman, Monster and Phoenix

1979. Silk Paintings from a Tomb of the Warring States Period (475–221 B.C.). Multicoloured.

2851	8f. Type **545**	2·75	1·00
2852	60f. Man riding dragon	4·25	1·90

546 Jing Shan

1979. Peking Scenes. Multicoloured.

2853	1y. Type **546**	1·75	20
2854	2y. Summer Palace	2·50	30
2855	5y. Beihai Park	2·00	50

547 Hammer and Sickle

1979. 90th Anniv of International Labour Day.

2856	**547**	8f. multicoloured	1·25	80

548 Memorial Frieze

1979. 60th Anniv of May 4th Movement. Mult.

2857	8f. (1) Type **548**	1·00	50
2858	8f. (2) Girl and symbols of progress	1·00	50

549 Children of Different Races

1979. International Year of the Child. Mult.

2859	8f. I.Y.C. emblem and children with balloons	3·75	1·50
2860	60f. Type **549**	14·00	6·50

550 Spring over Great Wall

1979. The Great Wall. Multicoloured.

2861	8f. (1) Type **550**	2·50	1·00
2862	8f. (2) Summer over Great Wall	2·50	1·00
2863	8f. (3) Autumn over Great Wall	2·50	1·00
2864	60f. (4) Winter over Great Wall	9·00	6·00
MS2865	139×78 mm. 2y. Shanhaiguan, Great Wall	£275	£130

551 Roaring Tiger

1979. Manchurian Tiger. Paintings by Liu Jiyou. Multicoloured.

2866	4f. Type **551**	1·50	70
2867	8f. Two young tigers	1·50	70
2868	60f. Tiger at rest	6·50	2·25

552 Mechanical Harvester

1979. Trades of the People's Communes. Mult.

2869	4f. (1) Type **552** (Agriculture)	1·50	1·00
2870	8f. (2) Planting a sapling (Forestry)	1·50	1·00
2871	8f. (3) Herding ducks (Stock raising)	1·50	1·00
2872	8f. (4) Basket weaving	1·50	1·00
2873	10f. (5) Fishermen with hand-carts of fish (Fishing)	2·50	1·50

里乔内第31届国际邮票博览会
1979年

(553) (image scaled to 63% of original size)

1979. International Stamp Fair, Riccione. No. MS2865 optd with T 553 and new serial number (J 41 etc), in gold.

MS2874	2y. multicoloured (sold at 2y.50)	£1000	£500

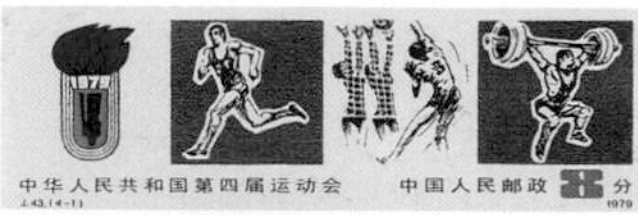

554 Games' Emblem, Running, Volleyball and Weightlifting

1979. 4th National Games.

2875	**554**	8f. (1) multicoloured	65	50
2876	-	8f. (2) multicoloured	65	50
2877	-	8f. (3) black, grn & red	65	50
2878	-	8f. (4) black, red & grn	65	50
MS2879		57×62 mm. 2y. gold, green and vermilion	£130	75·00

DESIGNS: No. 2876, Football, badminton, high jumping and ice dancing. 2877, Fencing, Skiing, gymnastics and diving. 2878, Motor cycling, table tennis, basketball and archery. 21×27 mm—2y. Games emblem.

555 National Flag and Mountains

556 National Emblem

557 National Anthem

558 Dancers and Drummer

559 Tractor and Crop-spraying Antonov An-2

1979. 30th Anniv of People's Republic of China. Multicoloured.

2880	8f. (1) National flag and rainbow	2·50	1·30
2881	8f. (2) Type **555**	2·50	1·30
2882	8f. Type **556**	3·75	1·00
MS2883	67×75 mm. **556** 1y. multicoloured	£130	75·00
2884	8f. Type **557**	5·00	3·25
2885	8f. (1) Type **558**	70	30
2886	8f. (2) Dancers and tambourine player	70	30
2887	8f. (3) Dancers and banjo player	70	30
2888	8f. (4) Dancers and drummer	70	30
2889	8f. (1) Type **559**	80	45
2890	8f. (2) Computer and cogwheels	80	45
2891	8f. (3) Rocket, jet fighter and submarine	80	45
2892	8f. (4) Atomic symbols	80	45

560 Exhibition Emblem

1979. National Exhibition of Juniors' Scientific and Technological Works.

2893	**560**	8f. multicoloured	1·00	60

561 Children with Model Aircraft

1979. Study of Science from Childhood. Mult.

2894	8f. (1) Type **561**	1·00	50
2895	8f. (2) Girls with microscope and test tube	1·00	50
2896	8f. (3) Children with telescope	1·00	50
2897	8f. (4) Boy catching butterflies	1·00	50
2898	8f. (5) Girl noting weather readings	1·00	50
2899	60f. (6) Boys with model boat	3·75	1·60
MS2900	148×90 mm. 2y. Girl with book and space and undersea scenes	£2250	£900

562 Yu Shan

1979. Taiwan Views. Multicoloured.

2901	8f. (1) Type **562**	1·50	1·00
2902	8f. (2) Sun Moon Lake	1·50	1·00
2903	8f. (3) Chikan Tower	1·50	1·00
2904	8f. (4) Suao-Hualien highway	1·50	1·00
2905	55f. (5) Tian Xiang Falls	5·25	1·50
2906	60f. (6) Moonlight over Banping Mountain	6·50	3·00

563 Symbols of Literature and Art

1979. 4th National Congress of Literary and Art Workers. Multicoloured.

2907	4f. Type **563**	75	50
2908	8f. Seals, hammer, sickle, rifle, atomic symbol and flowers	1·30	70

564 "Shaoshan" Type Electric Locomotive

1979. Railway Construction. Multicoloured.

2909	8f. (1) Type **564**	1·25	80
2910	8f. (2) Modern railway viaduct	1·25	80
2911	8f. (3) Goods train crossing bridge	1·25	80

565 "Chrysanthemum Petal"

1979. Camellias of Yunnan. Multicoloured.

2912	4f. (1) Type **565**	1·00	40
2913	8f. (2) "Lion Head"	1·00	40
2914	8f. (3) Camellia "Chrysantha (Hu) Tuyama"	1·00	40
2915	10f. (4) "Small Osmanthus Leaf"	1·00	40
2916	20f. (5) "Baby Face"	2·25	65
2917	30f. (6) "Cornelian"	3·25	85
2918	40f. (7) Peony Camellia	4·00	1·00
2919	50f. (8) "Purple Gown"	4·25	1·20
2920	60f. (9) "Dwarf Rose"	4·50	1·50
2921	70f. (10) "Willow Leaf Spinel Pink"	4·75	1·60
MS2922	135×90 mm. 2y. "Red Jewellery" (85×36 mm)	£400	£200

中华人民共和国邮票展览

J.42 (1-1) 1979

一九七九年 香港

(566) Actual size 91x68 mm. (image scaled to 53% of original size)

1979. People's Republic of China Stamp Exhibition, Hong Kong. No. MS2922 optd in margin with T 566, in gold.

MS2923	2y. multicoloured	£850	£375

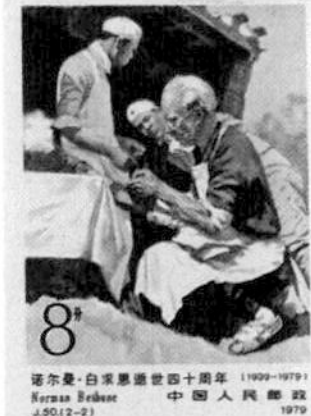

567 Dr. Bethune attending Wounded Soldier

1979. 40th Death Anniv of Dr. Norman Bethune. Multicoloured.

2924	8f. Type **567**	1·30	80
2925	70f. Bethune Memorial, Mausoleum of Martyrs, Shijiazhuang	1·90	1·50

568 Central Archives Hall

1979. International Archives Weeks. Mult.

2926	8f. (1) Type **568**	2·25	40
2927	8f. (2) Gold cabinet containing documents of Ming and Ching dynasties (vert)	2·25	40
2928	60f. (3) Imperial Archives Main Hall	10·00	1·90

569 Waterfall Cave, Home of Monkey King

1979. Scenes from "Pilgrimage to the West" (Chinese classical novel). Multicoloured.

2929	8f. (1) Type **569**	3·50	1·25
2930	8f. (2) Necha, son of Li, fighting Monkey	3·50	1·25
2931	8f. (3) Monkey in Mother Queen's peach orchard	3·50	1·25
2932	8f. (4) Monkey in alchemy furnace	3·50	1·25
2933	10f. (5) Monkey fighting White Bone Demon	6·50	1·50
2934	20f. (6) Monkey extinguishing fire with palm-leaf fan	7·50	2·00
2935	60f. (7) Monkey fighting Spider Demon in Cobweb Cave	16·00	5·00
2936	70f. (8) Monkey on scripture-seeking route to India	18·00	5·00

570 Stalin

1979. Birth Centenary of Stalin.

2937	**570**	8f. (1) brown	1·75	1·00
2938	-	8f. (2) black	1·75	1·00

DESIGN: No. 2038, Stalin appealing for unity against Germany.

571 Peony

1980. Paintings of Qi Baishi.

2939	**571**	4f. (1) multicoloured	2·00	1·00
2940	-	4f. (2) multicoloured	2·00	1·00
2941	-	8f. (3) multicoloured	2·00	1·00
2942	-	8f. (4) black, blue & red	2·00	1·00
2943	-	8f. (5) multicoloured	2·00	1·00
2944	-	8f. (6) black, grey & red	2·00	1·00
2945	-	8f. (7) multicoloured	2·00	1·00
2946	-	8f. (8) multicoloured	2·00	1·00
2947	-	10f. (9) blk, yell and red	2·50	1·25
2948	-	20f. (10) grey, brn & blk	2·50	1·25
2949	-	30f. (11) multicoloured	3·50	1·50
2950	-	40f. (12) multicoloured	4·00	1·75
2951	-	50f. (13) blk, grey & red	5·50	2·00
2952	-	55f. (14) multicoloured	7·50	3·25
2953	-	60f. (15) blk, grey & red	11·00	4·25
2954	-	70f. (16) multicoloured	14·00	6·00
MS2955		120×86 mm. 2y. multicoloured	£275	£120

DESIGNS: No. 2940, Squirrels and grapes; 2941, Crabs and wine; 2942, Tadpoles in mountain spring; 2943, Chicks; 2944, Lotus; 2945, Red plum; 2946, River kingfisher; 2947, Bottle gourds; 2948, "The Voice of Autumn"; 2949, Wisteria; 2950, Chrysanthemums; 2951, Shrimps; 2952, Litchi; 2953, Cabbages and mushrooms; 2954, Peaches. 37×61 mm—**MS**2955, "Evergreen".

572 Meng Liang, "Hongyang Cave"

1980. Facial Make-up in Peking Operas. Mult.

2956	4f. (1) Type **572**	3·25	70
2957	4f. (2) Li Kui, "Black Whirlwind"	3·25	70
2958	8f. (3) Huang Gai, "Meeting of Heroes"	3·25	70
2959	8f. (4) Monkey King, "Havoc in Heaven"	3·25	70
2960	10f. (5) Lu Zhishen, "Wild Boar Forest"	3·25	1·10
2961	20f. (6) Lian Po, "Reconciliation between the General and the Minister"	4·75	2·30
2962	60f. (7) Zhang Fei, "Reed Marsh"	15·00	4·25
2963	70f. (8) Dou Erdun, "Stealing the Emperor's Horse"	20·00	5·50

573 Chinese Olympic Committee Emblem

1980. Winter Olympic Games, Lake Placid. Multicoloured.

2964	8f. (1) Type **573**	1·00	35
2965	8f. (2) Speed skating	1·00	35
2966	8f. (3) Figure skating	1·00	35
2967	60f. (4) Skiing	7·50	1·60

574 Bear Macaque

1980. New Year. Year of the Monkey.

2968	**574**	8f. red, black and gold	£1300	£650

575 Klara Zetkin (journalist and politician)

1980. 70th Anniv of International Working Women's Day.

2969	**575**	8f. black, yellow & brn	1·50	90

576 Orchard

1980. Afforestation. Multicoloured.

2970	4f. Type **576**	45	25
2971	8f. Highway lined with trees	50	25
2972	10f. Aerial sowing by Antonov An-2 biplane	85	40
2973	20f. Factory amongst trees	1·30	65

577 Apsaras (celestial beings)

1980. 2nd National Conference of Chinese Scientific and Technical Association.
2974 **577** 8f. multicoloured 2·25 1·30

578 Freighter

1980. Mail Transport. Multicoloured.
2975 2f. Type **578** 2·25 2·00
2976 4f. Mail bus 2·50 1·50
2977 8f. Travelling post office coach 2·75 1·25
2978 10f. Tupolev Tu-154 airplane 5·00 2·50

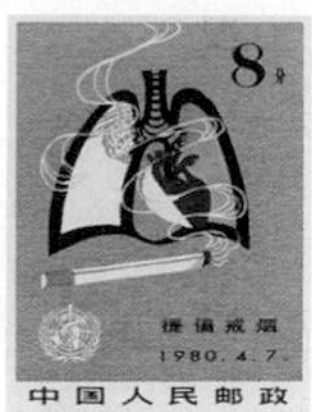
579 Cigarette damaging Heart and Lungs

1980. Anti-smoking Campaign. Multicoloured.
2979 8f. Type **579** 2·50 1·00
2980 60f. Face smoking and face holding flower in mouth, symbolising choice of smoking or health 8·50 4·00

580 Jian Zhen Memorial Hall, Yangzhou

1980. Return of High Monk Jian Zhen's Statue. Multicoloured.
2981 8f. (1) Type **580** 5·00 1·25
2982 8f. (2) Statue of Jian Zhen (vert) 5·00 1·25
2983 60f. (3) Junk in which Jian Zhen travelled to Japan 25·00 8·50

581 Lenin

1980. 110th Birth Anniv of Lenin.
2984 **581** 8f. brown, pink & green 2·00 90

582 "Swallow Chick" Kite

1980. Kites. Multicoloured.
2985 8f. (1) Type **582** 5·00 1·20
2986 8f. (2) "Slender swallow" kite 5·00 90
2987 8f. (3) "Semi-slender swallow" kite 5·00 90
2988 70f. (4) "Dual swallows" kite 18·00 6·00

583 Hare running in Fright

1980. Scenes from "Gu Dong" (Chinese fairy tale). Multicoloured.
2989 8f. (1) Type **583** 1·70 1·40
2990 8f. (2) Hare tells other animals "Gu Dong is coming" 1·70 1·40
2991 8f. (3) Lion asks "What is Gu Dong?" 1·70 1·40
2992 8f. (4) Animals discover sound of "Gu Dong" is made by falling papaya 1·70 1·40

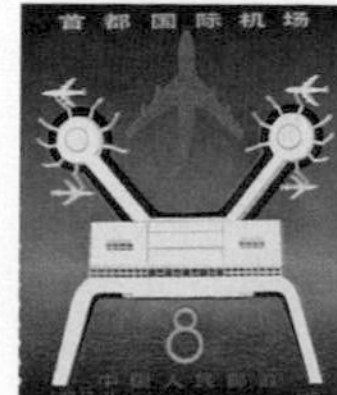
584 Silhouette of Ilyushin Il-86 Jetliner and Plan of Terminal Building

1980. Peking International Airport. Multicoloured.
2993 8f. Type **584** 1·50 80
2994 10f. Airplane and runway lights 2·00 1·30

585 Stag

1980. Sika Deer. Multicoloured.
2995 4f. Type **585** 1·25 95
2996 8f. Doe and fawn 1·25 95
2997 60f. Herd 7·50 4·00

586 "White Lotus"

1980. Lotus Paintings by Yu Zhizhen. Mult.
2998 8f. (1) Type **586** 3·50 90
2999 8f. (2) "Rose-tipped Snow" 3·50 90
3000 8f. (3) "Buddha's Seat" 3·50 90
3001 70f. (4) "Variable Charming Face" 30·00 8·00
MS3002 70×144 mm. 1y. "Fresh Lotus on Rippling Waters" (48×88 mm) £375 £120

587 Returned Pearl Cave and Sword-cut Stone

1980. Guilin Landscapes. Multicoloured.
3003 8f. (1) Type **587** 2·50 1·00
3004 8f. (2) Distant view of three mountains 2·50 1·00
3005 8f. (3) Nine-horse Fresco Hill 2·50 1·00
3006 8f. (4) Egrets around the aged banyan 2·50 1·00
3007 8f. (5) Western Hills at sunset (vert) 2·50 1·00
3008 8f. (6) Moonlight on the Lijiang River (vert) 2·50 1·00
3009 60f. (7) Springhead and ferry (vert) 14·00 3·75
3010 70f. (8) Scenic path at Yangshuo (vert) 15·00 5·00

588 Exhibition Gateway

1980. China Exhibition in United States. Mult.
3011 8f. Type **588** 80 65
3012 70f. Great Wall and emblems of San Francisco, Chicago and New York 7·50 2·75

589 Burebista (founder-king) and Rumanian Flag

1980. 2050th Anniv of Dacian State.
3013 **589** 8f. multicoloured 2·00 1·30

590 "Sea of Clouds" (Liu Haisu)

1980. UNESCO Exhibition of Chinese Paintings and Drawings. Multicoloured.
3014 8f. (1) Type **590** 1·75 60
3015 8f. (2) "Black-naped Oriole and Magnolia" (Yu Feian) (vert) 1·75 60
3016 8f. (3) "Tending Bactrian Camels" (Wu Zuoren) 1·75 60

591 Quzi Tower in Spring

1980. Liu Yuan (Tarrying Garden), Suzhou. Mult.
3017 8f. (1) Type **591** 9·50 3·00
3018 8f. (2) Yuancui Pavilion in Summer 9·50 3·00
3019 10f. (3) Hanbi Shanfang in Autumn 9·50 3·00
3020 60f. (4) Guanyun Peak in Winter 55·00 16·00

592 Xu Guangqi

1980. Scientists of Ancient China. Multicoloured.
3021 8f. (1) Type **592** (agriculturalist and astronomer) 3·50 1·00
3022 8f. (2) Li Bing (hydraulic engineer) 3·50 1·00
3023 8f. (3) Jia Sixie (agronomist) 3·50 1·00
3024 60f. (4) Huang Daopo (textile expert) 18·00 5·00

593 Pistol-shooting

1980. 1st Anniv of Return to International Olympic Committee. Multicoloured.
3025 **593** 4f. (1) brown, yell & mve 75 20
3026 - 8f. (2) brown, yell & grn 1·00 30
3027 - 8f. (3) brown, yell & blue 1·00 30
3028 - 10f. (4) brown, yellow & orange 1·75 55
3029 - 60f. (5) multicoloured 7·50 1·70
DESIGNS: No. 3026, Gymnastics; No. 3027, Diving; No. 3028, Volleyball; No. 3029, Archery.

594 White Flag Dolphin

1980. White Flag Dolphin. Multicoloured.
3030 8f. Type **594** 3·25 40
3031 60f. Two dolphins 5·00 1·60

595 Cock

1981. New Year. Year of the Cock.
3032 **595** 8f. multicoloured 28·00 8·00

596 Early Morning

1981. Scenes of Xishuang Banna. Multicoloured.
3033 4f. (1) Type **596** 1·00 45
3034 4f. (2) Mountain village of Dai nationality 1·00 45
3035 8f. (3) Rainbow over Lanchang River 2·25 60
3036 8f. (4) Ancient Temple (vert) 2·25 60
3037 8f. (5) Moonlit night (vert) 2·25 60
3038 60f. (6) Phoenix tree in bloom (vert) 14·00 3·50

597 Flower Basket Lantern

1981. Palace Lanterns. Multicoloured.
3039 4f. (1) Type **597** 3·50 70
3040 8f. (2) Dragons playing with a pearl 3·50 95
3041 8f. (3) Dragon and phoenix 3·50 95
3042 8f. (4) Treasure bowl 3·50 95
3043 20f. (5) Flower and birds 6·00 2·75
3044 60f. (6) Peony lantern painted with fishes 18·00 9·00

598 Crossing the River

1981. Marking the Gunwale (Chinese fable). Multicoloured.
3045 8f. (1) Chinese text of story 1·20 80
3046 8f. (2) Type **598** 1·20 80
3047 8f. (3) The sword drops in the water 1·20 80
3048 8f. (4) Making mark on gunwale 1·20 80
3049 8f. (5) Diving into river to recover sword 1·20 80

599 Chinese Elm

1981. Miniature Landscapes (dwarf trees). Mult.
3050 4f. (1) Type **599** 1·50 75
3051 8f. (2) Juniper 1·50 75
3052 8f. (3) Maidenhair tree 1·50 75
3053 10f. (4) Chinese Juniper (horiz) 1·50 75
3054 20f. (5) Wild Kaki persimmon (horiz) 2·75 1·25
3055 60f. (6) Single-seed juniper (horiz) 7·50 3·00

600 Vase with Two Tigers (Song Dynasty)

1981. Ceramics from Cizhou Kilns. Multicoloured.

3056	4f. (1) Type **600**	1·00	30
3057	8f. (2) Carved black glazed vase (Jin dynasty) (horiz)	1·25	70
3058	8f. (3) Amphora with apricot blossoms (modern)	1·25	70
3059	8f. (4) Jar with two phoenixes (Yuan dynasty) (horiz)	1·25	70
3060	10f. (5) Flat flask with dragon and phoenix (Yuan dynasty) (horiz)	2·50	70
3061	60f. (6) Vessel with tiger-shaped handles (modern) (horiz)	7·50	3·75

601 Giant Panda "Stamp"

1981. People's Republic of China Stamp Exhibition, Japan. Multicoloured.

3062	8f. Type **601**	75	25
3063	60f. Cockerel and junk "stamps"	2·75	1·30

602 Qinchuan Bull

1981. Cattle. Multicoloured.

3064	4f. (1) Type **602**	1·00	45
3065	8f. (2) Binhu buffalo	1·00	45
3066	8f. (3) Yak	1·00	45
3067	8f. (4) Black and white dairy cattle	1·00	45
3068	10f. (5) Red pasture bull	1·50	60
3069	55f. (6) Simmental crossbreed bull	6·50	2·30

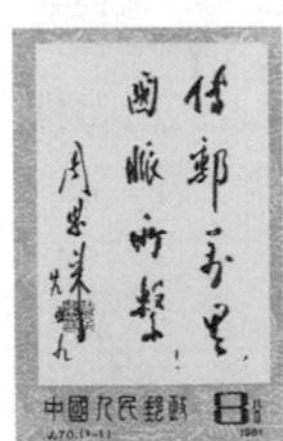

603 Inscription by Chou En-lai

1981. "To Deliver Mail for Ten Thousand Li, Has Bearing on Arteries and Veins of the Country".

3070	**603**	8f. multicoloured	1·00	20

604 ITU and WHO Emblems and Ribbons forming Caduceus

1981. World Telecommunications Day.

3071	**604**	8f. multicoloured	1·00	20

605 Safety in Building Construction

1981. National Safety Month. Multicoloured.

3072	8f. (1) Type **605**	70	45
3073	8f. (2) Mining safety	70	45
3074	8f. (3) Road safety	70	45
3075	8f. (4) Farming and forestry safety	70	45

606 Trunk Call Building

1981

3076	**606**	8f. brown	1·75	25

607 St. Bride Vase (Men's singles)

1981. Chinese Team's Victories at World Table Tennis Championships. Multicoloured.

3077	8f. (3) Type **607**	30	20
3078	8f. (4) Iran Cup (Men's doubles)	30	20
3079	8f. (5) G. Geist Prize (Women's singles)	30	20
3080	8f. (6) W. J. Pope Trophy (Women's doubles)	30	20
3081	8f. (7) Heydusek Prize (Mixed doubles)	30	20
3082	20f. (1) Swathling Cup (Men's team)	1·00	80
3083	20f. (2) Marcel Corbillon Cup (Women's team)	1·00	80

608 Hammer and Sickle

1981. 60th Anniv of Chinese Communist Party.

3084	**608**	8f. multicoloured	1·00	35

609 Five Veterans Peak

1981. Lushan Mountains. Multicoloured.

3085	8f. (1) Type **609**	1·25	75
3086	8f. (2) Hanpo Pass (horiz)	1·25	75
3087	8f. (3) Yellow Dragon Pool and Waterfall	1·25	75
3088	8f. (4) Sunlit Peak (horiz)	1·25	75
3089	8f. (5) Three-layer Spring	1·25	75
3090	8f. (6) Stone and pines (horiz)	1·25	75
3091	60f. (7) Dragon Head Cliff	15·00	5·00

610 Silver Ear ("Tremella fuciformis")

1981. Edible Mushrooms. Multicoloured.

3092	4f. (1) Type **610**	1·00	50
3093	8f. (2) Veiled stinkhorn ("Dictyophora indusiata")	1·25	50
3094	8f. (3) "Hericium erinaceus"	1·25	50
3095	8f. (4) "Russula rubra"	1·25	50
3096	10f. (5) Shii-take mushroom ("Lentinus edodes")	1·75	75
3097	70f. (6) White button mushroom ("Agaricus bisporus")	6·50	2·00

611 Medal

1981. Quality Month.

3098	**611**	8f. (1) silver, black and red	75	45
3099	**611**	8f. (2) gold, brown and red	75	45

612 Huangguoshu Waterfall

1981

3100	-	1f. green	20	20
3101	-	1½f. red	20	20
3102	-	2f. green	20	20
3103	**612**	3f. brown	20	20
3118	-	3f. dp brn, brn & lt brn	30	20
3104	-	4f. violet	20	20
3119	-	4f. mauve and lilac	30	20
3105	-	5f. brown	20	20
3106	-	8f. blue	20	20
3107	-	10f. purple	20	20
3121	-	10f. brown	50	35
3108	-	20f. green	25	20
3122	-	20f. blue	1·00	70
3109	-	30f. brown	30	20
3110	-	40f. black	35	20
3111	-	50f. mauve	45	25
3112	-	70f. black	55	35
3113	-	80f. red	60	45
3114	-	1y. lilac	80	55
3115	-	2y. green	1·30	1·10
3116	-	5y. blue	3·00	2·20

DESIGNS—VERT: 1f. Xishuang Banna. 1½f. Huashan Mountain. 2f. Taishan Mountain. 4f. Palm trees, Hainan. 5f. Pagoda, Huqiu Hill, Suzhou. 8f. Great Wall. 10f. North-east Forest. HORIZ: 20f. Herding sheep on Tianshan Mountain. 30f. Sheep on grassland, Inner Mongolia. 40f. Stone Forest. 50f. Pagodas, Ban Pingshan Mountain, Taiwan. 70f. Mt. Zhumulangma. 80f. Seven Star Grotto, Guangdong. 1y. Gorge, Yangtze River. 2y. Guilin. 5y. Mt. Huangshan.

613 Stone Forest in Autumn

1981. Stone Forest. Multicoloured.

3125	8f. (1) Stone Forest in a mist	1·00	45
3126	8f. (2) Type **613**	1·00	45
3127	8f. (3) Pool in Stone Forest	1·00	45
3128	10f. (4) Dawn over Stone Forest (vert)	1·00	45
3129	70f. (5) Stone Forest by starlight (vert)	7·50	4·75

614 Lu Xun as Youth

1981. Birth Centenary of Lu Xun (writer).

3130	**614**	8f. black, green & yell	70	35
3131	-	20f. blk, brn & dp brn	1·40	95

DESIGN: 20f. Lu Xun in later life.

615 Dr. Sun Yat-sen

1981. 70th Anniv of 1911 Revolution.

3132	**615**	8f. (1) multicoloured	70	35
3133	-	8f. (2) black, grn & yell	70	35
3134	-	8f. (3) black, pk & yell	70	35

DESIGNS: No. 3133, Grave of 72 Martyrs, Huang Hua Gate; No. 3134, Headquarters of Military Government of Hubei Province.

616 "Tree" symbolizing Co-ordination

1981. Asian Conference of Parliamentarians on Population and Development. Multicoloured.

3135	8f. Type **616**	30	25
3136	70f. Design symbolizing Enlightenment	80	65

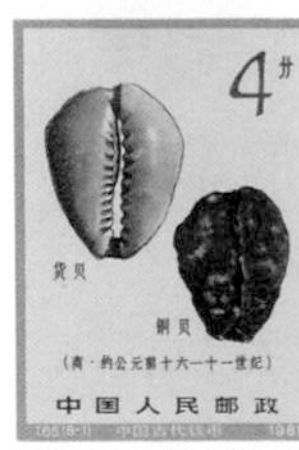

617 Money Cowrie and Cowrie-shaped Bronze Coin

1981. Ancient Chinese Coins (1st series). Minted before 221 B.C. Multicoloured.

3137	4f. (1) Type **617**	75	35
3138	4f. (2) Shovel coin	75	35
3139	8f. (3) Shovel coin inscribed "Li"	1·00	45
3140	8f. (4) Shovel coin inscribed "An Yi Er Jin"	1·00	45
3141	8f. (5) Knife coin inscribed "Qi Fa Ha"	1·00	45
3142	8f. (6) Knife coin inscribed "Jie Mo Zhi Fa Hua"	1·00	45
3143	60f. (7) Knife coin inscribed "Cheng Bai"	3·50	1·10
3144	70f. (8) Circular coin with hole inscribed "Gong"	5·00	1·90

See also Nos. 3162/69.

618 Hands and Globe with IYDP Emblem

1981. International Year of Disabled Persons.

3145	**618**	8f. multicoloured	75	20

619 Daiyu

1981. The Twelve Beauties of Jinling from "A Dream of Red Mansions" by Cao Xueqin. Multicoloured. Designs showing paintings by Liu Danzhai.

3146 4f. (1) Type **619** 2·25 1·00
3147 4f. (2) Baochai chases butterfly 2·25 1·00
3148 8f. (3) Yuanchun visits parents 2·25 1·00
3149 8f. (4) Yingchun reading Buddhist sutras 2·25 1·00
3150 8f. (5) Tanchun forms poetry society 2·25 1·00
3151 8f. (6) Xichun painting 2·25 1·00
3152 8f. (7) Xiangyun picking up necklace 2·25 1·00
3153 10f. (8) Liwan lectures her son 3·75 1·00
3154 20f. (9) Xifeng hatches plot 4·75 1·25
3155 30f. (10) Sister Qiao escapes 6·50 1·50
3156 40f. (11) Keqing relaxing 8·50 3·00
3157 80f. (12) Miaoyu serves tea 15·00 4·50
MS3158 139×78 mm. 2y. Baoyu and Daiyu reading (59×39 mm) £225 £100

620 Volleyball Player

1981. Victory of Chinese Women's Team in World Cup Volleyball Championships. Multicoloured.

3159 8f. Type **620** 30 25
3160 20f. Player holding Cup 70 50

621 Dog

1982. New Year. Year of the Dog.

3161 **621** 8f. multicoloured 6·50 2·10

1982. Ancient Chinese Coins (2nd series). As T 617. Multicoloured.

3162 4f. (1) Guilian ("Monster Mask") 1·00 35
3163 4f. (2) Shu shovel coin 1·00 35
3164 8f. (3) Xia Zhuan shovel coin 1·00 35
3165 8f. (4) Han Dan shovel coin 1·00 35
3166 8f. (5) Pointed-head knife coin 1·00 35
3167 8f. (6) Ming knife coin 1·00 50
3168 70f. (7) Jin Hua knife coin 3·75 1·60
3169 80f. (8) Yi Liu Hua circular coin 5·00 2·10

622 Nie Er and Score of "March of the Volunteers"

1982. 70th Anniv of Nie Er (composer).

3170 **622** 8f. multicoloured 50 25

623 Dripping Water and Children

1982. Int Drinking Water and Sanitation Decade.

3171 **623** 8f. grey, orange & blue 50 25

624 Dr. Robert Koch and Laboratory Equipment

1982. Centenary of Discovery of Tubercle Bacillus.

3172 **624** 8f. multicoloured 75 25

625 Building on Fire, Hoses and Fire Engine

1982. Fire Control. Multicoloured.

3173 8f. (1) Type **625** 75 25
3174 8f. (2) Chemical fire extinguisher 75 25

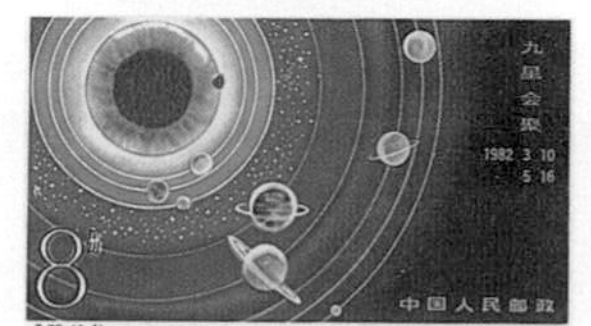

626 Solar System

1982. "Cluster of Nine Planets" (planetary conjunction).

3175 **626** 8f. multicoloured 1·00 25

627 "Hemerocallis flava" and "H. fulva"

1982. Medicinal Plants. Multicoloured.

3176 4f. (1) Type **627** 60 30
3177 8f. (2) "Fritillaria unibracteata" 60 30
3178 8f. (3) "Aconitum carmichaeli" 60 30
3179 10f. (4) "Lilium brownii" 60 30
3180 20f. (5) "Arisaema consanguineum" 1·00 45
3181 70f. (6) "Paeonia lactiflora" 4·00 1·70
MS3182 138×70 mm. 2y. "Iris tectorum" and "Iris" spp. (82×35 mm) 38·00 15·00

628 Soong Ching Ling addressing First Plenary Session

1982. 1st Death Anniv of Soong Ching Ling (former Head of State). Multicoloured.

3183 8f. Type **628** 75 35
3184 20f. Portrait of Soong Ching Ling 2·50 1·30

629 Sable

1982. The Sable. Multicoloured.

3185 8f. Type **629** 1·00 45
3186 80f. Sable running 4·50 2·75

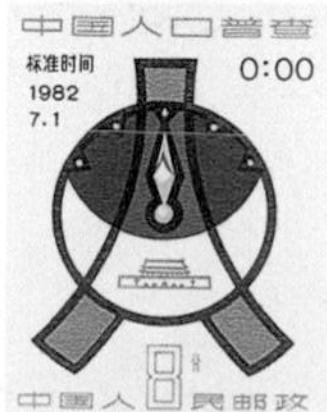
630 Census Emblem

1982. National Census.

3187 **630** 8f. multicoloured 50 20

631 Text, Emblem and Globe

1982. Second U.N. Conference on the Exploration and Peaceful Uses of Outer Space, Vienna.

3188 **631** 8f. multicoloured 50 20

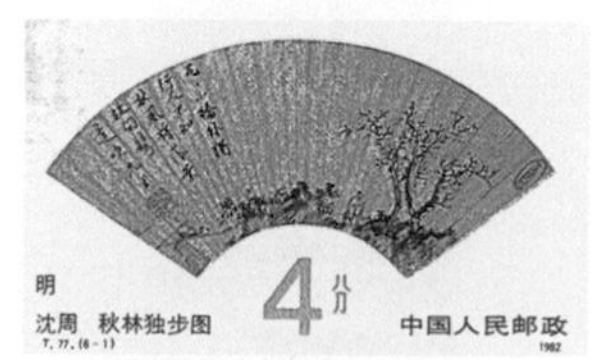

632 "Strolling Alone in Autumn Woods" (Shen Zhou)

1982. Fan Paintings of the Ming and Qing Dynasties. Multicoloured.

3189 4f. (1) Type **632** 1·00 25
3190 8f. (2) "Jackdaw on withered Tree" (Tang Yin) 1·00 50
3191 8f. (3) "Bamboos and Sparrows" (Zhou Zhimian) 1·00 50
3192 10f. (4) "Writing Poem under Pine" (Chen Hongshou and Bai Han) 1·00 50
3193 20f. (5) "Chrysanthemums" (Yun Shouping) 1·75 75
3194 70f. (6) "Masked Hawfinch, Grape Myrtle and Chinese Parasol" (Wang Wu) 5·00 2·40

633 Courier on Horseback (Wei-Jin period tomb mural, Jiayu Pass)

1982. 1st All-China Philatelic Federation Congress. Sheet 136×80 mm.

MS3195 1y. multicoloured 35·00 15·00

634 Society Emblem

1982. 60th Anniv of Chinese Geological Society.

3196 **634** 8f. gold, stone & black 60 20

635 Orpiment

1982. Minerals. Multicoloured.

3197 4f. Type **635** 30 20
3198 8f. Stibnite 30 20
3199 10f. Cinnabar 60 25
3200 20f. Wolframite 1·00 50

636 "12", Hammer and Sickle and Great Hall of the People

1982. 12th National Communist Party Congress.

3201 **636** 8f. multicoloured 75 20

637 Hoopoe

1982. Birds. Multicoloured.

3202 8f. (1) Type **637** 1·50 30
3203 8f. (2) Barn swallow 1·50 30
3204 8f. (3) Black-naped oriole 1·50 30
3205 20f. (4) Great tit 3·25 60
3206 70f. (5) Great spotted woodpecker 7·50 3·00
MS3207 135×79 mm. 2y. Ashy minivet, magpie robin, Daurian redstart, red-flanked bluetail and little cuckoo 60·00 28·00

638 "Plum Blossom" (Guan Shanyue)

1982. 10th Anniv of Normalization of Diplomatic Relations with Japan. Multicoloured.

3208 8f. Type **638** 35 20
3209 70f. "Hibiscus" (Xiao Shufang) 1·00 80

639 Globe, Profiles and Ear of Wheat

1982. World Food Day.

3210 **639** 8f. multicoloured 50 25

640 Guo Moruo

1982. 90th Birth Anniv of Guo Moruo (writer). Multicoloured.

3211	8f. Type **640**	20	20
3212	20f. Guo Moruo writing	40	25

641 Head of Bodhisattva

1982. Sculptures of Liao Dynasty. Mult.

3213	8f. (1) Type **641**	75	35
3214	8f. (2) Bust of Bodhisattva	75	35
3215	8f. (3) Boy on lotus flower	75	35
3216	70f. (4) Bodhisattva	5·50	2·20
MS3217	129×80 mm. 2y. Head of Bodhisattva (different) (36×55 mm)	65·00	20·00

642 Dr. D. S. Kotnis

1982. 40th Death Anniv of Dr. D. S. Kotnis.

3218	**642**	8f. green and black	45	20
3219	-	70f. lilac and black	2·30	1·20

DESIGN: Dr. Kotnis in army uniform.

643 Couple holding Flaming Torch

1982. 11th National Communist Youth League Congress.

3220	**643**	8f. multicoloured	50	20

644 Wine Container

1982. Bronzes of Western Zhou Dynasty. Mult.

3221	4f. (1) Type **644**	1·50	45
3222	4f. (2) Cooking vessel	1·50	45
3223	8f. (3) Food container	1·50	45
3224	8f. (4) Cooking vessel with ox head and dragon design	1·50	45
3225	8f. (5) Ram-shaped wine container	1·50	45
3226	10f. (6) Wine jar	2·50	50
3227	20f. (7) Food bowl	3·50	90
3228	70f. (8) Wine container	12·00	3·00

645 "Pig" (Han Meilin)

1983. New Year. Year of the Pig.

3229	**645**	8f. multicoloured	7·50	3·50

646 Harp

1983. Stringed Musical Instruments.

3230	**646**	4f. (1) green and brown	3·25	60
3231	-	8f. (2) purple, grn & brn	3·25	70
3232	-	8f. (3) multicoloured	3·25	70
3233	-	10f. (4) multicoloured	4·50	85
3234	-	70f. (5) multicoloured	18·00	3·75

DESIGNS—VERT: 8f. (3231), Four string guitar; 10f. Four string lute; 70f. Three string lute. HORIZ: 8f. (3232), Qin.

647 "February 7" Monument, Jiangan

1983. 60th Anniv of Peking–Hankow Railway Workers' Strike.

3235	**647**	8f. (1) yellow, blk & grey	50	35
3236	-	8f. (2) stone, brown and lilac	50	35

DESIGN: No. 3236, "February 7" Memorial tower, Zhengzhou.

648 Zhang Gong attracted by Yingying's Beauty

1983. Scenes from "The Western Chamber" (musical drama) by Wang Shifu.

3237	**648**	8f. (1) multicoloured	3·50	80
3238	**648**	8f. (2) multicoloured	3·50	80
3239	**648**	10f. (3) multicoloured	7·50	1·60
3240	**648**	80f. (4) multicoloured	20·00	4·50
MS3241		130×80 mm. 2y. stone and black	£150	75·00

DESIGNS: As T **648**—No. 3228, Zhang Gong and Yingying listening to music; 3239, Zhang Gong and Yingying's wedding; 3240, Zhang Gong and Yingying parting at Changting Pavilion; 27×48 mm—2y. Interrogation of Hongniang (Yingying's maid) Ming dynasty woodblock.

649 Karl Marx

1983. Death Centenary of Karl Marx.

3242	**649**	8f. grey and black	30	20
3243	-	20f. lilac and black	65	25

DESIGN: 20f. "Marx making Speech" (Wen Guozhang).

650 Tomb, Mt. Qiaoshan, Huangling

1983. Tomb of the Yellow Emperor. Mult.

3244	8f. Type **650**	1·50	40
3245	10f. Hall of Founder of Chinese Culture (horiz)	2·00	40
3246	20f. Xuanyuan cypress	3·25	80

651 Messengers and Globe

1983. World Communications Year.

3247	**651**	8f. multicoloured	55	25

652 Chinese Alligator

1983. Chinese Alligator. Multicoloured.

3248	8f. Type **652**	2·00	45
3249	20f. Alligator and hatching eggs	3·25	75

653 "Scratching" (Wang Yani)

1983. Children's Paintings. Multicoloured.

3250	8f. (1) Type **653**	50	20
3251	8f. (2) "I Love the Great Wall" (Liu Zhong)	50	20
3252	8f. (3) "Kitten" (Tang Axi)	50	20
3253	8f. (4) "The Sun, Birds, Flowers and Me" (Bu Hua)	50	20

654 Congress Hall

1983. 6th National People's Congress. Mult.

3254	8f. Type **654**	50	20
3255	20f. Score of National Anthem	1·50	40

655 Terracotta Soldiers

1983. Terracotta Figures from Qin Shi Huang's Tomb. Multicoloured.

3256	8f. (1) Type **655**	75	50
3257	8f. (2) Heads figures	75	50
3258	10f. (3) Soldiers and horses	1·00	55
3259	70f. (4) Aerial view of excavation	5·75	3·00
MS3260	100×85 mm. 2y. Soldier leading horse (59×39 mm)	£150	50·00

656 Sun Yujiao

1983. Female Roles in Peking Opera. Mult.

3261	4f. (1) Type **656**	1·25	35
3262	8f. (2) Chen Miaochang	1·25	35
3263	8f. (3) Bai Suzhen	1·25	35
3264	8f. (4) Sister Thirteen	1·25	35
3265	10f. (5) Qin Xianglian	1·25	35
3266	20f. (6) Yang Yuhuan	3·50	80
3267	50f. (7) Cui Yingying	8·50	1·70
3268	80f. (8) Mu Guiying	12·00	2·10

657 Li Bai (poet)

1983. Poets and Philosophers of Ancient China. Paintings by Liu Lingcang. Multicoloured.

3269	8f. (1) Type **657**	1·00	25
3270	8f. (2) Du Fu (poet)	1·00	25
3271	8f. (3) Han Yu (philosopher)	1·00	25
3272	70f. (4) Liu Zongyuan (philosopher)	7·50	2·30

658 Woman and Women working

1983. 5th National Women's Congress.

3273	**658**	8f. multicoloured	30	20

659 Games Emblem

1983. 5th National Games. Multicoloured.

3274	4f. (1) Type **659**	45	20
3275	8f. (2) Gymnastics	45	20
3276	8f. (3) Badminton	45	20
3277	8f. (4) Diving	45	20
3278	20f. (5) High jump	1·00	80
3279	70f. (6) Windsurfing	3·25	2·00

660 "One Child per Couple"

1983. Family Planning. Multicoloured.

3280	8f. (1) Type **660**	30	20
3281	8f. (2) "Population, cultivated fields and grain"	30	20

661 Hammer and Cogwheel as "10"

1983. 10th National Trade Union Congress.

3282	**661**	8f. multicoloured	30	20

662 Mute Swan

1983. Swans. Multicoloured.

3283	8f. (1) Type **662**	40	35
3284	8f. (2) Mute swans	40	35
3285	10f. Tundra swans	60	45
3286	80f. (4) Whooper swans in flight	2·75	2·00

663 Liu Shaoqi

1983. 85th Birth Anniv of Liu Shaoqi (former Head of State).

3287	**663**	8f. (1) multicoloured	55	45
3288	-	8f. (2) multicoloured	55	45
3289	-	8f. (3) brown, bl & gold	55	45
3290	-	8f. (4) brown, bl & gold	55	45

DESIGNS: No. 3288, Liu reading a speech; 3289, Liu making a speech; 3290, Liu meeting model worker Shi Chuanxiang.

664 $100 National Emblem Stamp, 1951

1983. National Stamp Exhibition, Peking. Mult.

3291	8f. Type **664**	30	20
3292	20f. North West China $1 Yanan Pagoda stamp, 1946	70	30

665 Mao Tse-tung in 1925

1983. 90th Birth Anniv of Mao Tse-tung.

3293	**665**	8f. (1) multicoloured	30	25
3294	-	8f. (2) stone, brn & gold	30	25
3295	-	10f. (3) grey, brn & gold	70	25
3296	-	20f. (4) multicoloured	1·60	75

DESIGNS: No. 3294, Mao Tse-tung in Yanan, 1945. 3295, Mao Tse-tung inspecting Yellow River, 1952. 3296, Mao Tse-tung in library, 1961.

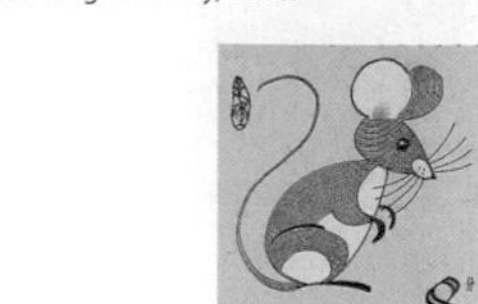

666 "Rat" (Zhan Tong)

1984. New Year. Year of the Rat.

3297	**666**	8f. black, yellow & red	4·25	1·20

667 Young Girl with Ball

1984. Child Welfare. Multicoloured.

3298	8f.+2f. Type **667**	30	25
3299	8f.+2f. Young boy with toy panda	30	25

668 Women with Dog

1984. Tang Dynasty Painting "Beauties wearing Flowers" by Zhou Fang. Details of scroll. Mult.

3300	8f. Type **668**	1·50	35
3301	10f. Women and Manchurian crane	1·50	40
3302	70f. Women, dog and Manchurian crane	8·50	2·30
MS3303	161×39 mm. 2y. Complete scroll (156×35 mm)	£140	70·00

669 "The Spring of Shanghai"

1984. Chinese Roses. Multicoloured.

3304	4f. (1) Type **669**	35	20
3305	8f. (2) "Rosy Dawn of the Pujiang River"	35	20
3306	8f. (3) "Pearl"	35	20
3307	10f. (4) "Black Whirlwind"	40	30
3308	20f. (5) "Yellow Flower in the Battlefield"	80	40
3309	70f. (6) "Blue Phoenix"	2·75	1·20

670 Ren Bishi

1984. 80th Birth Anniv of Ren Bishi (member of Communist Party Secretariat) (1st issue).

3310	**670**	8f. brown, black & pur	30	20

See also Nos. 3361/3.

671 Japanese Crested Ibis

1984. Japanese Crested Ibis. Multicoloured.

3311	8f. (1) Type **671**	75	20
3312	8f. (2) Ibis wading	75	20
3313	80f. (3) Ibis perching	3·25	1·30

672 Red Cross Activities

1984. 80th Anniv of Chinese Red Cross Society.

3314	**672**	8f. multicoloured	30	20

673 Building Dam

1984. Gezhou Dam Project. Multicoloured.

3315	8f. Type **673**	30	20
3316	10f. View of dam and lock gates (vert)	40	30
3317	20f. Freighter in lock	80	65

674 Inverted Image Tower and Yilang Pavilion

1984. Zhuo Zheng Garden, Suzhou. Mult.

3318	8f. (1) Type **674**	1·00	35
3319	8f. (2) Loquat Garden	1·00	35
3320	10f. (3) Water court of Xiao Cang Lang	1·00	35
3321	70f. (4) Yuanxiang Hall and Yiyu Study	3·25	1·40

675 Pistol Shooting

1984. Olympic Games, Los Angeles. Multicoloured.

3322	4f. Type **675**	20	20
3323	8f. High jumping	20	20
3324	8f. Weightlifting	20	20
3325	10f. Gymnastics	25	20
3326	20f. Volley ball	30	25
3327	80f. Diving	1·30	40
MS3328	96×70 mm. 2y. Olympic rings and gymnasts (61×37 mm)	15·00	8·00

676 Calligraphy

1984. Art Works by Wu Changshuo. Mult.

3329	4f. (1) Type **676**	75	25
3330	4f. (2) "Pair of Peaches"	75	25
3331	8f. (3) "Lotus"	75	25
3332	8f. (4) "Wisteria"	75	25
3333	8f. (5) "Peony"	75	25
3334	10f. (6) "Autumn Chrysanthemum"	1·00	45
3335	20f. (7) "Plum Blossom"	1·25	60
3336	70f. (8) Seal and impression	4·25	2·30

677 Tianjin

1984. Luanhe River–Tianjin Water Diversion Project. Multicoloured.

3337	8f. Type **677**	20	20
3338	10f. Locks and canal (horiz)	30	20
3339	20f. Tunnel and sculpture	40	25

678 Chinese and Japanese Pagodas

1984. Chinese–Japanese Youth Friendship Festival. Multicoloured.

3340	8f. Type **678**	20	20
3341	20f. Girls watering shrub	30	20
3342	80f. Young people dancing	75	55

679 Factory Worker

1984. 35th Anniv of People's Republic. Mult.

3343	8f. (1) Type **679**	20	20
3344	8f. (2) Girl and rainbow	20	20
3345	8f. (4) Girl and symbols of science	20	20
3346	8f. (5) Soldier	20	20
3347	20f. (3) Flag and Manchurian cranes (36×50 mm)	45	30

680 Chen Jiageng

1984. 110th Birth Anniv of Chen Jiageng (educationist and patriot). Multicoloured.

3348	8f. Type **680**	30	20
3349	80f. Jimei School	55	35

681 The Maiden's Study

1984. Scenes from "Peony Pavilion" (drama) by Tang Xianzu. Paintings by Dai Dunbang. Multicoloured.

3350	8f. (1) Type **681**	1·00	40
3351	8f. (2) Du Liniang dreaming	1·00	40
3352	20f. (3) Du Liniang drawing self-portrait	1·50	75
3353	70f. (4) Du Liniang and Liu Mengmei married	6·00	3·00
MS3354	136×80 mm. 2y. Du Liniang and her maid, Chun Xiang in garden (85×57 mm)	70·00	20·00

682 Baoguo Temple

1984. Landscapes of Mt. Emei Shan. Mult.

3355	4f. (1) Type **682**	35	20
3356	8f. (2) Leiyin Temple	40	30
3357	8f. (3) Hongchun Lawn	40	30
3358	10f. (4) Elephant Bath Pool	55	35
3359	20f. (5) Woyun Temple	95	75
3360	80f. (6) Shining Cloud Sea, Jinding	4·00	2·40

683 Ren Bishi

1984. 80th Birth Anniv of Ren Bishi (2nd issue).

3361	**683**	8f. brown and purple	20	20
3362	-	10f. black and lilac	30	20
3363	-	20f. black and brown	35	20

DESIGNS: 10f. Ren Bishi reading speech at Communist Party Congress; 20f. Ren Bishi saluting.

684 Flowers in Chinese Vase

1984. Chinese Insurance Industry.

3364	**684**	8f. multicoloured	30	20

685 "Ox" (Yao Zhonghua)

1985. New Year. Year of the Ox.

3365	**685**	8f. multicoloured	1·25	40

686 "Zunyi Meeting" (Liu Xiangping)

1985. 50th Anniv of Zunyi Meeting. Mult.

3366	8f. Type **686**	30	25
3367	20f. "Arrival of the Red Army in Northern Shaanxi" (Zhao Yu)	75	60

687 Lotus of Good Luck

1985. Festival Lanterns. Multicoloured.

3368	8f. (1) Type **687**	50	20
3369	8f. (2) Auspicious dragon and phoenix	50	20
3370	8f. (3) A hundred flowers blossoming	50	20
3371	70f. (4) Prosperity and affluence	2·75	1·20

688 Stylized Dove and Women's Open Hands

1985. United Nations Decade for Women.

3372	**688**	20f. multicoloured	30	20

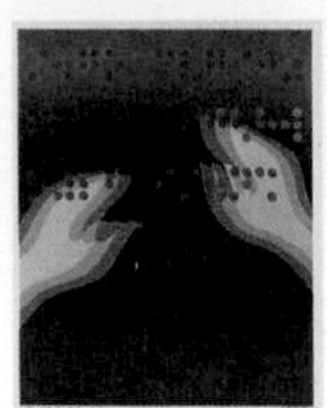
689 Hands reading Braille

1985. Welfare Fund for the Handicapped. Multicoloured.

3373	8f.+2f. (1) Type **689**	1·20	60
3374	8f.+2f. (2) Lips and sign language	1·20	60
3375	8f.+2f. (3) Learning to use artificial limb	1·20	60
3376	8f.+2f. (4) Stylized figure in wheelchair	1·20	60

690 "Green Calyx" Mei

1985. Mei Flowers. Multicoloured.

3377	8f. (1) Type **690**	30	20
3378	8f. (2) "Pendant" mei	30	20
3379	8f. (3) "Contorted dragon" mei	30	20
3380	10f. (4) "Cinnabar" mei	40	20
3381	20f. (5) "Versicolor" mei	55	25
3382	80f. (6) "Apricot" mei	2·50	95
MS3383	130×70 mm. 2y. "Duplicate" mei and "Condensed fragrance" mei (88×48 mm)	45·00	20·00

691 Headquarters

1985. 60th Anniv of All-China Trade Unions Federation.

3384	**691**	8f. multicoloured	30	20

692 Bird and Children

1985. International Youth Year.

3385	**692**	20f. multicoloured	30	20

693 Giant Panda

1985. Giant Panda. Multicoloured.

3386	8f. Type **693**	20	20
3387	20f. Giant panda (different) (horiz)	20	20
3388	50f. Giant panda (different)	45	30
3389	80f. Two giant pandas (horiz)	65	45
MS3390	74×80 mm. 3y. Giant panda and cub (39×58 mm)	4·00	3·00

694 Xian Xinghai (bust, Cao Chongen)

1985. 80th Birth Anniv of Xian Xianghai (composer).

3391	**694**	8f. multicoloured	30	20

695 Agnes Smedley

1985. American Journalists in China.

3392	**695**	8f. brown, stone and ochre	20	20
3393	-	20f. olive, grey and stone	30	20
3394	-	80f. purple, lilac and cream	70	45

DESIGNS: 20f. Anna Louise Strong; 80f. Edgar Snow.

696 Zheng He (navigator)

1985. 580th Anniv of Zheng He's First Voyage to Western Seas. Multicoloured.

3395	8f. (1) Type **696**	40	20
3396	8f. (2) Zheng He on elephant	40	20
3397	20f. (3) Exchanging goods	75	35
3398	80f. (4) Bidding farewell	2·00	65

697 "Self-portrait"

1985. 90th Birth Anniv of Xu Beihong (artist). Multicoloured.

3399	8f. Type **697**	30	20
3400	20f. Xu Beihong at work	70	25

698 Lin Zexu

1985. Birth Bicentenary of Lin Zexu (statesman).

3401	**698**	8f. multicoloured	30	20
3402	-	80f. brown and black	60	25

DESIGN—55×23 mm. 80f. "Burning opium at Humen" (relief).

699 "Prosperity"

1985. 20th Anniv of Tibet Autonomous Region. Multicoloured.

3403	8f. Type **699**	20	20
3404	10f. "Celebration"	30	25
3405	20f. "Harvest	50	45

700 Chinese Army at Lugouqiao

1985. 40th Anniv of Victory over Japan.

3406	**700**	8f. black, brown & red	30	20
3407	-	80f. black, brown & red	30	20

DESIGN: 80f. Defending the Great Wall.

701 Cycling

1985. 2nd National Workers' Games, Peking. Multicoloured.

3408	8f. Type **701**	20	20
3409	20f. Hurdling	30	25

702 Gobi Oasis

1985. 30th Anniv of Xinjiang Uygur Autonomous Region. Multicoloured.

3410	8f. Type **702**	20	20
3411	10f. Oilfield and Lake Tianchi (54×26 mm)	20	20
3412	20f. Tianshan pasture	30	25

703 Athletes and Silhouette of Woman

1985. 1st National Youth Games, Zhengzhou.

3413	**703**	8f. multicoloured	20	20
3414	-	20f. red, blue and black	40	35

DESIGN: 20f. Basketball players and silhouette of man.

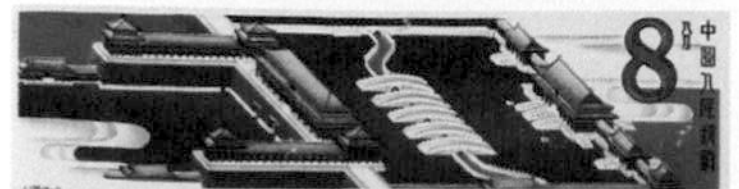
704 Forbidden City (image scaled to 54% of original size)

1985. 60th Anniv of Imperial Palace Museum.

3415	**704**	8f. (1) multicoloured	20	20
3416	-	8f. (2) multicoloured	20	20
3417	-	20f. (3) multicoloured	20	20
3418	-	80f. (4) multicoloured	50	45

DESIGNS: Nos. 3416/18, Different parts of Forbidden City.

705 Zou Taofen

1985. 90th Anniv of Zou Taofen (journalist).

3419	**705**	8f. black, brown & silver	20	20
3420	-	20f. black, green & silver	20	20

DESIGN: 20f. Premier Chou En-lai's inscription in memory of Zou Taofen.

706 Memorial Pavilion

1985. 50th Anniv of December 9th Movement.

3421	**706**	8f. multicoloured	30	20

707 "Tiger"

1986. New Year. Year of the Tiger.

3422	**707**	8f. multicoloured	55	40

708 First Experimental Satellite

1986. Space Research. Multicoloured.

3423	4f. (1) Type **708**	20	20
3424	8f. (2) Mil-Mi8 helicopters recovering satellites	20	20
3425	8f. (3) Underwater launched rocket	20	20
3426	10f. (4) Rocket launched from land	30	20
3427	20f. (5) Dish aerial	30	20
3428	70f. (6) Satellite and diagram of orbit	70	40

709 Dong Biwu

1986. Birth Centenary of Dong Biwu (founder of Chinese Communist Party).

3429	**709**	8f. black and brown	20	20
3430	-	20f. black and brown	30	20

DESIGN: 20f. At meeting for ratification of U.N. Charter, Los Angeles, 1945.

710 Lin Boqu

1986. Birth Centenary of Lin Boqu (politician).

3431	**710**	8f. brown and black	20	20
3432	-	20f. brown and black	30	20

DESIGN: 20f. At Yanan.

711 He Long

1986. 90th Birth Anniv of He Long (politician).

3433	**711**	8f. black and brown	20	20
3434	-	20f. black and brown	30	20

DESIGN: 20f. On horse.

712 Skin Tents, Inner Mongolia

1986. Traditional Houses.

3435	**712**	1f. green, brown & grey	20	20
3436	-	1½f. brown, red & blue	20	20
3437	-	2f. brown and bistre	20	20
3438	-	3f. black and brown	20	20
3439	-	4f. red and black	20	20
3439a	-	5f. black, grey & green	20	20
3440	-	8f. grey, red and black	20	20
3441	-	10f. black and orange	20	20
3441b	-	15f. black, grey & grn	20	20
3442	-	20f. grey, green & blk	20	20
3442b	-	25f. black, grey & pink	30	20
3443	-	30f. lilac, blue & brown	30	20
3444	-	40f. brn, pur & stone	55	25
3445	-	50f. blue, mve & dp bl	55	30
3445b	-	80f. black, grey & blue	50	20
3446	-	90f. black and red	80	50
3447	-	1y. brown and grey	90	60
3448	-	1y.10 blue, blk & brn	90	70
3448a	-	1y.30 blk, grey & red	60	35
3448b	-	1y.60 blue & black	75	35
3448c	-	2y. black, grey & brown	80	35

DESIGNS: 1½f. Tibet. 2f. North-East China. 3f. Hunan. 4f. Jiangsu. 5f. Shandong. 8f. Peking. 10f. Yunnan. 15f. Guangxi. 20f. Shanghai. 25f. Ningxia. 30f. Anhui. 40f. North Shaanxi. 50f. Sichuan. 80f. Shanxi. 90f. Taiwan. 1y. Fujian. 1y.10, Zhejiang, 1y.30, Qinghai. 1y.60, Guizhou. 2y. Jiangxi.

713 Comet and Earth

1988. Appearance of Halley's Comet.

3449	**713**	20f. grey and blue	30	25

714 Cranes

1986. Great White Crane. Multicoloured.

3450	8f. Type **714**	30	20
3451	10f. Crane flying (vert)	30	20
3452	70f. Four cranes (vert)	55	25
MS3453	159×51 mm. 2y. Group of cranes flying (116×27 mm)	15·00	5·00

715 Li Weihan

1986. 90th Birth Anniv of Li Weihan (politician). Each green and black.

3454	8f. Type **715**	20	20
3455	20f. Li Weihan at work	30	25

716 Stylized People on Dove

1986. International Peace Year.

3456	**716**	8f. multicoloured	35	25

717 Mao Dun

1986. 90th Birth Anniv of Mao Dun (writer). Each grey, black and brown.

3457	8f. Type **717**	20	20
3458	20f. Mao Dun and manuscript	30	25

718 Wang Jiaxiang

1986. 80th Birth Anniv of Wang Jiaxiang (first People's Republic ambassador to U.S.S.R.). Multicoloured.

3459	8f. Type **718**	20	20
3460	20f. Wang Jiaxiang at Yan'an	30	25

719 Flowers on Desk

1986. Teachers' Day.

3461	**719**	8f. multicoloured	30	20

720 "Magnolia sinensis"

1986. Magnolias. Multicoloured.

3462	8f. (1) Type **720**	30	30
3463	8f. (2) "Manglietia patungensis"	30	30
3464	70f. (3) "Alcimandra cathcartii"	2·40	2·10
MS3465	131×70 mm. 2y. "Manglietia grandis" and "Manglietiastrum sinicum" (58×48 mm)	11·50	7·00

721 Sun Yat-sen (120th birth anniv)

1986. 75th Anniv of 1911 Revolution. Leaders. Multicoloured.

3466	8f. Type **721**	20	20
3467	10f. Huang Xing (70th death anniv)	30	25
3468	40f. Zhang Taiyan (50th death anniv)	1·00	90

722 Bronze Tiger

1986. 2nd All-China Philatelic Federation Congress. Sheet 129×80 mm.

MS3469	2y. multicoloured	12·00	5·00

723 Dr. Sun Yat-sen

1986. 120th Birth Anniv of Dr. Sun Yat-sen. Sheet 82×136 mm.

MS3470	2y. multicoloured	10·00	6·50

724 Zhu De

1986. Birth Centenary of Marshal Zhu De.

3471	**724**	8f. brown	20	20
3472	-	20f. green	40	25

DESIGN: 20f. Making speech, 1950.

725 Archery

1986. Sport in Ancient China. Each grey, black and red.

3473	8f. (1) Type **725**	75	20
3474	8f. (2) Weiqi (horiz)	75	20
3475	10f. (3) Golf (horiz)	75	25
3476	50f. (4) Football	3·75	1·70

726 "Rabbit"

1987. New Year. Year of the Rabbit.

3477	**726**	8f. multicoloured	35	25

727 Xu Xiake

1987. 400th Birth Anniv of Xu Xiake (explorer). Multicoloured.

3478	8f. Type **727**	45	30
3479	20f. Recording observations in cave	1·90	1·50
3480	40f. Climbing mountain	3·75	2·20

728 Steller's Sea Eagle

1987. Birds of Prey. Multicoloured.

3481	8f. (1) Black kite (horiz)	1·00	25
3482	8f. (2) Type **728**	1·00	25
3483	10f. (3) Himalayan griffon	1·00	25
3484	90f. (4) Upland buzzard (horiz)	6·50	1·00

729 Hawk Kite

1987. Kites. Multicoloured.

3485	8f. (1) Type **729**	50	20
3486	8f. (2) Centipede	50	20
3487	30f. (3) The Eight Diagrams	1·70	80
3488	30f. (4) Phoenix	1·70	80

730 Liao Zhongkai

1987. 110th Birth Anniv of Liao Zhongkai (politician). Multicoloured.

3489	8f. Type **730**	20	20
3490	20f. Liao Zhongkai with wife	30	20

731 "Everywhere Green Hills"

1987. 90th Birth Anniv of Ye Jianying (revolutionary and co-founder of People's Army). Portraits. Multicoloured.

3491	8f. Type **731**	35	30
3492	10f. "Founder of the State"	45	40
3493	30f. "Eventfull Years"	1·70	1·50

732 Worshipping Bodhisattvas (Northern Liang Dynasty)

1987. Dunhuang Cave Murals (1st series). Mult.

3494	8f. Type **732**	75	20
3495	10f. Deer King Jataka (Northern Wei dynasty)	75	25
3496	20f. Heavenly musicians (Northern Wei dynasty)	2·25	60
3497	40f. Flying Devata (Northern Wei dynasty)	3·00	1·10
MS3498	142×93 mm. 2y. Mahasattva Jataka	48·00	18·00

See also Nos. 3553/6, 3682/5, 3811/**MS**3815, 3910/13 and 4131/**MS**4135.

733 "Happy Holiday" (Yan Qinghu)

1987. Children's Day. Childrens' drawings. Mult.

3499	8f. (1) Type **733**	20	20
3500	8f. (2) Children with doves and balloons (Liu Yuan)	30	20

734 Town

1987. Improvements in Rural Areas. Multicoloured.

3501	8f. (1) Type **734**	40	35
3502	8f. (2) Fresh foods (horiz)	40	35
3503	10f. (3) Feeding cattle (horiz)	60	50
3504	20f. (4) Outdoor cinema	1·10	95

735 Emblem

1987. Postal Savings.

3505	**735**	8f. turquoise, yell & red	30	20

736 Globe

1987. Centenary of Esperanto (invented language).

3506	**736**	8f. blue, black & green	25	20

737 Flag over Great Wall

1987. 60th Anniv of People's Liberation Army. Multicoloured.

3507	8f. (1) Type **737**	30	20
3508	8f. (2) Soldier and rocket launcher	30	20
3509	10f. (3) Sailor and submarine	70	30
3510	30f. (4) Pilot and jet fighters	1·40	75

738 Dove above Houses

1987. Int Year of Shelter for the Homeless.

3511	**738**	8f. multicoloured	25	20

739 Chinese Character

1987. China Art Festival, Peking.

3512	**739**	8f. black, red and gold	25	20

740 Pan Gu inventing the Universe

1987. Folk Tales. Multicoloured.

3513	4f. (1) Type **740**	20	20
3514	8f. (2) Nu Wa creating human being	25	20
3515	8f. (3) Yi shooting nine suns	25	20
3516	10f. (4) Chang'e flying to the moon	35	20
3517	20f. (5) Kua Fu chasing the sun	70	30
3518	90f. (6) Jing Wei filling the sea	2·50	1·20

741 Sun rising behind Party Flag

1987. 13th National Communist Party Congress.

3519	**741**	8f. multicoloured	20	20

742 Yellow Crane Tower, Wuhan

1987. Ancient Buildings. Multicoloured.

3520	8f. (1) Type **742**	35	20
3521	8f. (2) Yue Yang Tower	35	30
3522	10f. (3) Teng Wang Pavilion	40	35
3523	90f. (4) Peng Lai Pavilion	3·25	3·25
MS3524	129×93 mm. Nos. 3520/3 (sold at 1y.50)	25·00	12·00

743 Pole Vaulting

1987. 6th National Games, Guangdong Province. Multicoloured.

3525	8f. (1) Type **743**	25	20
3526	8f. (2) Women's softball	25	20
3527	30f. (3) Weightlifting	55	30
3528	50f. (4) Diving	90	50

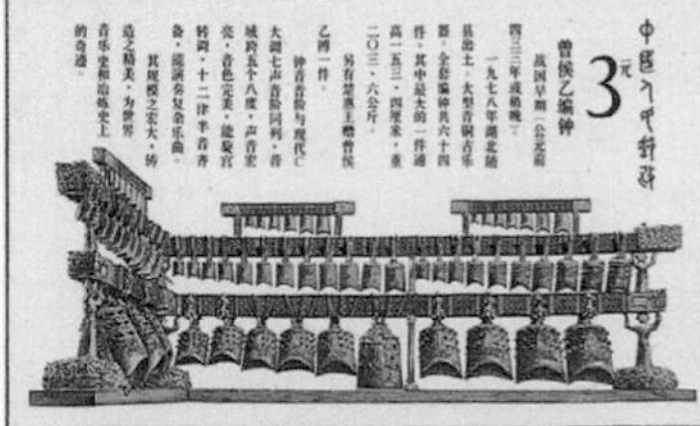
744 Bells (image scaled to 64% of original size)

1987. Warring States Period (430 B.C.) Bronze Chime Bells from Tomb of Marquis Yi Zeng State, Hubei. Sheet 91×165 mm. No gum. Imperf.

MS3529	3y. multicoloured	15·00	6·50

745 Shi Jin practising Martial Arts

1987. Literature. "Outlaws of the Marsh" (1st series). Multicoloured.

3530	8f. Type **745**	35	20
3531	10f. Sagacious Lu uprooting willow tree	45	20
3532	30f. Lin Chon sheltering in temple of mountain spirit	1·50	75
3533	50f. Song Jian helping Chao Gai to escape	2·10	1·60
MS3534	139×87 mm. 2y. Outlaws with captured birthday gift(85×56 mm)	30·00	18·00

See also Nos. 3614/17, 3778/**MS**3782, 3854/7 and **MS**4252.

746 Dragon

1988. New Year. Year of the Dragon.

3535	**746**	8f. multicoloured	35	30

747 Cai Yuanpri

1988. 120th Birth Anniv of Cai Yuanpei (educationist). Multicoloured.

3536	8f. Type **747**	20	20
3537	20f. Cai Yuanpei seated in chair	25	20

748 Tao Zhu

1988. 80th Birth Anniv of Tao Zhu (Communist Party official). Multicoloured.

3538	8f. Type **748**	20	20
3539	20f. Tao Zhu (half-length portrait)	25	20

749 Harvest Festival

1988. Flourishing Rural Areas of China. Mult.

3540	8f. Type **749**	25	20
3541	10f. Couple with fish, flowers and chickens	25	20
3542	20f. Couple making scientific study	45	30
3543	30f. Happy family	70	50

750 Flag and Rainbow

1988. 7th National People's Congress.

3544	**750**	8f. multicoloured	20	20

751 Wuzhi Mountain

1988. Establishment of Hainan Province. Mult.

3545	8f. Type **751**	20	10
3546	10f. Wanquan River	20	20
3547	30f. Beach	20	30
3548	1y.10 Bay and deer	55	45

752 Li Siguang (geologist)

1988. Scientists (1st series). Multicoloured.

3549	8f. Type **752**	20	15
3550	10f. Zhu Kezhen (meteorologist)	20	15
3551	20f. Wu Youxun (physicist)	20	15
3552	30f. Hua Luogeng (mathematician)	25	25

See also Nos. 3702/5 and 3821/4.

1988. Dunhuang Cave Murals (2nd series). As T 732. Multicoloured.

3553	8f. (1) Hunting (Western Wei dynasty)	20	15
3554	8f. (2) Fighting (Western Wei dynasty)	20	15
3555	10f. (3) Farming (Northern Zhou dynasty)	25	15
3556	90f. (4) Building pagoda (Northern Zhou dynasty)	2·00	95

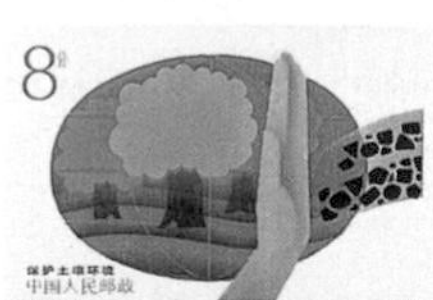

753 Healthy Trees and Hand holding back polluted Soil

1988. Environmental Protection. Multicoloured.

3557	8f. (1) Type **753**	20	15
3558	8f. (2) Doves in clean air and hand holding back polluted air	20	15
3559	8f. (3) Fishes in clean water and hand holding back polluted water	20	15
3560	8f. (4) Peaceful landscape and hand holding back noise waves	20	15

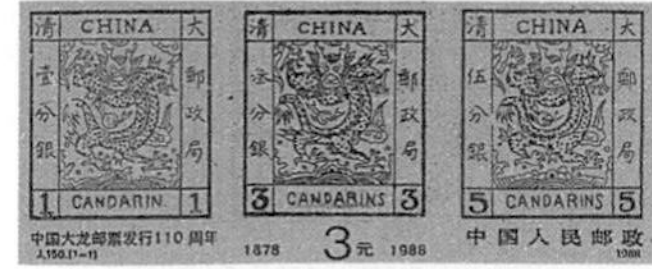

754 Large Dragon Stamps, 1878

1988. 110th Anniv of First Chinese Empire Stamps. Sheet 70×100 mm.

MS3561	3y. multicoloured	10·00	5·00

755 Games Emblem

1988. 11th Asian Games, Peking (1990) (1st issue). Multicoloured.

3562	8f. Type **755**	20	15
3563	30f. Games mascot	20	15

See also Nos. 3653/6 and 3695/3700.

756 Warrior, Longmen Grotto, Henan

1988. Art of Chinese Grottoes.

3564	-	2y. brown & light brown	70	30
3565	**756**	5y. black and brown	1·40	45
3566	-	10y. brown and stone	3·00	95
3567	-	20y. black and brown	6·50	1·90

DESIGNS: 2y. Buddha, Yungang Grotto, Shanxi. 10y. Bodhisattva, Maijishan Grotto, Gansu. 20y. Woman with chickens, Dazu Grotto, Sichuan.

See also No. **MS**3639.

757 Peony

1988. 10th Anniv of Chinese–Japanese Treaty of Peace and Friendship. Multicoloured.

3568	8f. Type **757**	20	10
3569	1y.60 Cherry blossom	85	45

758 Coal Wharf, Quinghuangdao

1988. Achievements of Socialist Construction (1st series). Multicoloured.

3570	8f. Type **758**	20	15
3571	10f. Ethylene works, Shangdong	20	15
3572	20f. Baoshan steel works, Shanghai	25	15
3573	30f. Television centre, Peking	25	25

See also Nos. 3691/22, 3678/81 and 3759/62.

759 Taishan Temple

1988. Mount Taishan Views. Multicoloured.

3574	8f. Type **759**	25	15
3575	10f. Ladder to Heaven	35	25
3576	20f. Daguang Park	70	35
3577	90f. Sun Watching Peak	2·75	1·30

760 Liao Chengzhi

1988. 80th Birth Anniv of Liao Chengzhi (Communist Party leader). Multicoloured.

3578	8f. Type **760**	20	15
3579	20f. Liao Chengzhi at work	20	15

761 Cycling

1988. 1st National Peasant Games. Multicoloured.

3580	8f. Type **761**	20	15
3581	20f. Wushu	20	15

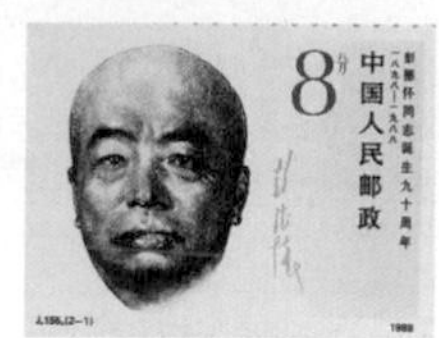

762 Peng Dehuai

1988. 90th Birth Anniv of General Peng Dehuai. Multicoloured.

3582	8f. Type **762**	20	15
3583	20f. In uniform	20	15

763 Battle against Lu Bu

1988. Literature. "Romance of the Three Kingdoms" by Luo Guanzhong (1st series). Multicoloured.

3584	8f. (1) Heroes become sworn brothers (horiz)	30	15
3585	8f. (2) Type **763**	30	25
3586	30f. (3) Fengyi Pavilion (horiz)	80	60
3587	50f. (4) Discussing heroes over wine	1·40	1·00
MS3588	182×65 mm. 3y. Guan Yu and retinue (157×37 mm)	25·00	15·00

See also Nos. 3711/14, 3807/10, 3944/**MS**3948 and 4315/**MS**4319.

764 People in Heart

1988. International Volunteers' Day.

3589	**764**	20f. multicoloured	25	15

765 Stag's Head

1988. Pere David's Deer. Multicoloured.

3590	8f. Type **765**	25	15
3591	40f. Herd	1·20	85

766 Da Yi Pin

1988. Orchids. Multicoloured.

3592	8f. Type **766**	20	15
3593	10f. Dragon	25	25
3594	20f. Large phoenix tail	45	35
3595	50f. Silver-edged black orchid	1·00	85
MS3596	119×85 mm. 2y. Red lotus petal (55×36 mm)	30·00	8·00

767 Snake

1989. New Year. Year of the Snake.

3597	**767**	8f. multicoloured	40	35

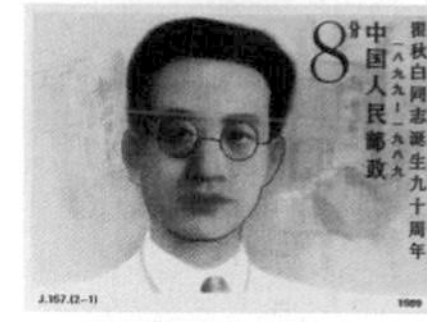

768 Qu Quibai

1989. 90th Birth Anniv of Qu Qiubai (writer). Multicoloured.

3598	8f. Type **768**	20	15
3599	20f. Qu Qiubai (half-length portrait)	25	15

769 Pheasant

1989. Brown Eared-pheasant. Multicoloured.

3600	8f. Type **769**	20	15
3601	50f. Two pheasants	35	35

770 "Heaven" (top section)

1989. Silk Painting from Han Tomb, Mawangdui, Changsha. Multicoloured.

3602	8f. Type **770**	25	15
3603	20f. "Earth" (central section)	25	25
3604	30f. "Underworld" (bottom section)	25	25
MS3605	90×165 mm. 5y. Complete painting. Imperf	4·75	3·00

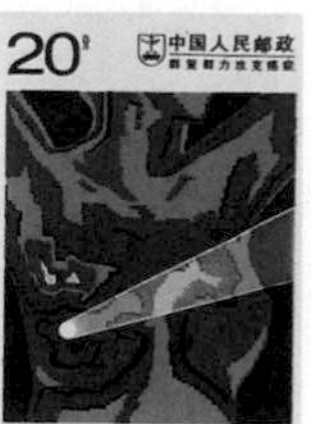

771 Diagnosis by Thermography

1989. Anti-cancer Campaign.

3606	**771**	8f. grey, red & black	25	25
3607	-	20f. multicoloured	25	25

DESIGN: 8f. Crab and red crosses.

772 Memorial Frieze

1989. 70th Anniv of May 4th Movement.

3608	**772**	8f. multicoloured	25	15

773 Children

1989. 40th International Children's Day. Children's paintings. Multicoloured.

3609 8f.+4f. (1) Type **773** 20 15
3610 8f.+4f. (2) Child and penguins 20 15
3611 8f.+4f. (3) Child flying on bird 20 15
3612 8f.+4f. (4) Boy and girl playing ball 20 15

774 Globe, Doves and Lectern

1989. Cent of Interparliamentary Union.

3613 **774** 20f. multicoloured 30 25

1989. Literature. "Outlaws of the Marsh" (2nd series). As T 745. Multicoloured.

3614 8f. Wu Song killing tiger on Jingyang Ridge 20 15
3615 10f. Qin Ming riding through hail of arrows 20 15
3616 20f. Hua Rong shooting wild goose 30 25
3617 1y.30 Li Kui fighting Zhang Shun on sampan 1·50 50

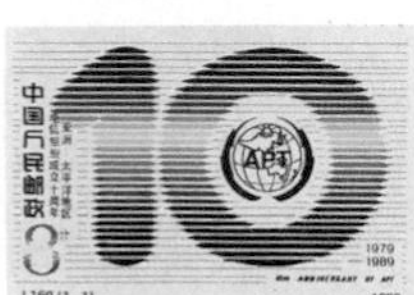

775 Anniversary Emblem

1989. 10th Anniv of Asia–Pacific Telecommunity.

3618 **775** 8f. multicoloured 25 15

1989. Achievements of Socialist Construction (2nd series). As T 758. Multicoloured.

3619 8f. International telecommunications building, Peking (vert) 20 15
3620 10f. Xi Qu coal mine, Gu Jiao 20 15
3621 20f. Long Yang Gorge hydro-electric power station, Qinghai 20 15
3622 30f. Da Yao Shan tunnel on Guangzhou–Heng Yang railway 25 15

776 Five Peaks of Mt. Huashan

1989. Mount Huashan. Multicoloured.

3623 8f. Type **776** 20 10
3624 10f. View from top of Mt. Huashan 20 10
3625 20f. Thousand Foot Precipice 30 15
3626 90f. Blue Dragon Ridge 90 60

777 "Fable of the White Snake" (stage design, Ye Qianyu)

1989. Contemporary Art. Multicoloured.

3627 8f. Type **777** 20 10
3628 20f. "Lijiang River in Fine Rain" (Li Keran) 25 15
3629 50f. "Marching Together" (oxen) (Wu Zuoren) 60 45

778 Doves and 1949 $50 Stamp

1989. 40th Anniv of Chinese People's Political Conference.

3630 **778** 8f. red, blue and black 25 15

779 Lecturing in Temple of Apricot, Qufu

1989. 2540th Birth Anniv of Confucius (philosopher). Multicoloured.

3631 8f. Type **779** 20 15
3632 1y.60 Confucius in ox-drawn cart 75 70
MS3633 74×106 mm. 3y. Confucius. No gum. Imperf 6·50 2·50

780 Ribbons and Gate of Heavenly Peace, Peking

1989. 40th Anniv of People's Republic. Mult.

3634 8f. Type **780** 20 15
3635 10f. Flowers and ribbons 20 15
3636 20f. Stars and ribbons 20 15
3637 40f. Buildings and ribbons 25 15
MS3638 120×84 mm. 3y. Gate of Heavenly Peace, Peking and revellers 5·00 1·60

1989. National Stamp Exhibition, Peking. Sheet 60×109 mm containing No. 3566.

MS3639 10y. sepia and cinnamon 28·00 15·00

781 Woman using Camera

1989. 150th Anniv of Photography.

3640 **781** 8f. multicoloured 25 15

782 Li Dazhao

1989. Birth Centenary of Li Dazhao (co-founder of Chinese Communist Party). Multicoloured.

3641 8f. Type **782** 20 15
3642 20f. Li Dazhao and script 25 25

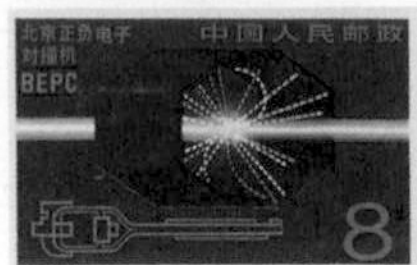

783 Diagram of Collider in Action

1989. Peking Electron-Positron Collider.

3643 **783** 8f. multicoloured 25 15

784 Rockets

1989. National Defence. Multicoloured.

3644 4f. Type **784** 20 15
3645 8f. Rocket on transporter 20 15
3646 10f. Rocket launch (vert) 20 15
3647 20f. Jettison of fuel tank 25 15

785 Spring Morning, Su Causeway

1989. West Lake, Hangzhou. Multicoloured.

3648 8f. Type **785** 20 15
3649 10f. Crooked Courtyard 20 15
3650 30f. Moon over Three Pools 25 25
3651 40f. Snow on Broken Bridge 35 25
MS3652 144×60 mm. 5y. West Lake (85×37 mm) 7·50 2·20

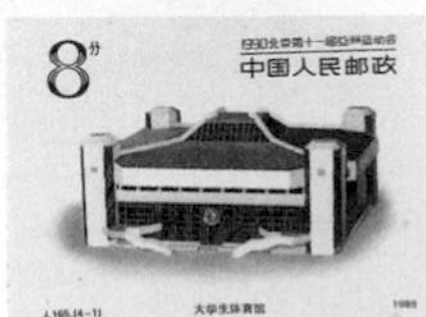

786 Peking College Gymnasium

1989. 11th Asian Games, Peking (1990) (2nd issue). Multicoloured.

3653 8f. Type **786** 20 15
3654 10f. Northern Suburbs swimming pool 20 15
3655 30f. Workers' Stadium 20 15
3656 1y.60 Chaoyang Gymnasium 35 25

787 Horse

1990. New Year. Year of the Horse.

3657 **787** 8f. multicoloured 50 25

788 Narcissi

1990. Narcissi. Multicoloured.

3658 8f. Type **788** 20 15
3659 20f. Natural group of narcissi 20 15
3660 30f. Arrangement of narcissi 20 15
3661 1y.60 Arrangement (different) 50 45

789 Bethune and Medical Team in Canada

1990. Birth Centenary of Norman Bethune (surgeon). Multicoloured.

3662 8f. Type **789** 20 15
3663 1y.60 Bethune and medical team in China 55 45

790 Emblem

1990. 80th International Women's Day.

3664 **790** 20f. red, green and black 30 25

791 Birds flying above Trees

1990. Tree Planting Day. Multicoloured.

3665 8f. Type **791** 20 15
3666 10f. Trees in city 20 15
3667 20f. Great Wall and trees 20 15
3668 30f. Forest and field of wheat 25 15

792 Ban Po Plate

1990. Pottery. Multicoloured.

3669 8f. Type **792** 20 15
3670 20f. Miao Di Gou dish 20 15
3671 30f. Ma Jia Yao jar 20 15
3672 50f. Ma Chang jar 25 15

793 Li Fuchun

1990. 90th Birth Anniv of Li Fuchun (politician). Multicoloured.

3673 8f. Type **793** 20 15
3674 20f. Li Fuchun (different) 25 25

794 Charioteer

1990. 10th Anniv of Discovery of Bronze Chariots in Emperor Qin Shi Huang's Tomb. Multicoloured.

3675 8f. Type **794** 20 10
3676 50f. Horse's head 35 25
MS3677 140×78 mm. 5y. Chariots (115×37 mm) 10·00 3·50

1990. Achievements of Socialist Construction (3rd series). As T 758. Multicoloured.

3678 8f. Second automobile factory 20 15
3679 10f. Yizheng chemical and fibre company 20 15
3680 20f. Shengli oil field 25 15
3681 30f. Qinshan nuclear power station 25 15

1990. Dunhuang Cave Murals (3rd series). Sui Dynasty. As T 732. Multicoloured.

3682 8f. Flying Devatas 20 15
3683 10f. Worshipping Bodhisattva (vert) 20 15
3684 30f. Saviour Avalokitesvara (vert) 45 25
3685 50f. Indra 70 50

795 Snow Leopard

1990. The Snow Leopard. Multicoloured.

3686 8f. Type **795** 25 15
3687 50f. Leopard stalking 25 15

796 West Fujian Communications Bureau (Red Posts) 4p. Stamp

1990. 60th Anniv of Communist China Stamp Issues. Multicoloured.

3688	8f. Type **796**	20	15
3689	20f. Chinese Soviet Republic 1c. stamp	25	15

797 Zhang Wentian

1990. 90th Birth Anniv of Zhang Wentian (revolutionary).

3690	8f. Type **797**	20	15
3691	20f. Zhang Wentian and Zunyi Meeting venue	25	15

798 Emblem

1990. International Literacy Year.

3692	**798**	20f. multicoloured	25	15

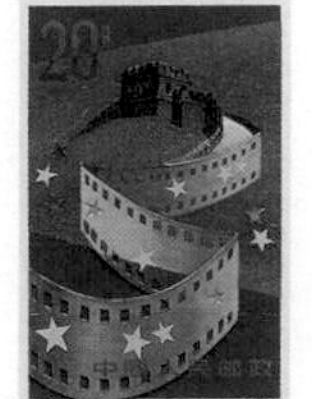

799 Great Wall, Film and Screen

1990. 85th Anniv of Chinese Films.

3693	**799**	20f. multicoloured	25	15

800 Olympic ring "Balloons" carrying Giant Panda

1990. "Sportphilex '90" International Stamp Exhibition, Peking. Sheet 79×110 mm.

MS3694	10y. multicoloured	25·00	12·00

801 Athletics

1990. 11th Asian Games, Peking (3rd issue). Multicoloured.

3695	4f. Type **801**	20	15
3696	8f. Gymnastics	20	15
3697	10f. Martial arts	20	15
3698	20f. Volleyball	20	15
3699	30f. Swimming	25	15
3700	1y.60 Shooting	70	60
MS3701	190×130 mm. Nos. 3562/3, 3653/6 and 3695/3700 (sold at 7y.)	15·00	7·00

802 Zhang Yuzhe (astronomer)

1990. Scientists (2nd series). Multicoloured.

3702	8f. Lin Qiaozhi (gynaecologist)	20	15
3703	10f. Type **802**	20	15
3704	20f. Hou Debang (chemist)	25	15
3705	30f. Ding Ying (agronomist)	25	15

803 Towering Temple

1990. Mount Hengshan, Hunan Province. Mult.

3706	8f. Type **803**	20	15
3707	10f. Aerial view of mountain	20	15
3708	20f. Trees and buildings on slopes	25	15
3709	50f. Zhurong Peak	45	25

804 Gusu Post Office, Suzhou

1990. 3rd All-China Philatelic Federation Congress. Sheet 130×80 mm.

MS3710	2y. multicoloured	8·00	3·75

1990. Literature. "Romance of the Three Kingdoms" by Luo Guanzhong (2nd series). As T 763. Multicoloured.

3711	20f. (1) Cao Cao leading night attack on Wuchao (horiz)	20	15
3712	20f. (2) Liu Bei calling at Zhuge Liang's thatched cottage	20	15
3713	30f. (3) General Zhao rescuing A Dou single-handedly (horiz)	25	25
3714	50f. (4) Zhang Fei repulsing attackers at Changban Bridge	45	25

805 Revellers listening to Music

1990. Painting "Han Xizai's Night Revels" by Gu Hongzhong. Multicoloured.

3715	50f. (1) Type **805**	55	45
3716	50f. (2) Drummer and dancers	55	45
3717	50f. (3) Women attending man with fan and man and women in alcove	55	45
3718	50f. (4) Women playing flutes and couple by painted screen	55	45
3719	50f. (5) Young couple and women attending seated man	55	45

Nos. 3715/19 were printed together, se-tenant, forming a composite design.

806 Sheep

1991. New Year. Year of the Sheep.

3720	**806**	20f. multicoloured	45	25

807 Yuzui (dam at Dujiang)

1991. Dujiangyan Irrigation Project. Mult.

3721	20f. Type **807**	20	10
3722	50f. Feishayan (weir)	35	15
3723	80f. Baopingkou (diversion of part of River Minjiang through new opening in Yulei Mountain)	55	35

808 Wreath on Wall and Last Verse of the "Internationale"

1991. 120th Anniv of Paris Commune.

3724	**808**	20f. multicoloured	25	15

809 Apple

1991. Family Planning. Multicoloured.

3725	20f. Type **809**	20	15
3726	50f. Child's and adult's hands within heart	25	15

810 Saiga

1991. Horned Ruminants. Multicoloured.

3727	20f. Type **810**	20	10
3728	20f. Takin	20	10
3729	50f. Argali	25	15
3730	2y. Ibex	50	35

811 Dancers

1991. 40th Anniv of Chinese Administration of Tibet. Multicoloured.

3731	25f. Type **811**	20	15
3732	50f. Rainbows over mountain road	25	25
MS3733	75×100 mm. 2y. Clouds and cranes around 1952 $400 Lhasa stamp (39×53 mm)	6·50	2·20

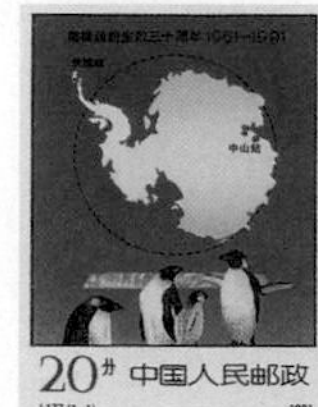

812 Map and Emperor Penguins

1991. 30th Anniv of Implementation of Antarctic Treaty.

3734	**812**	20f. multicoloured	40	25

813 "Rhododendron delavayi"

1991. Rhododendrons. Multicoloured.

3735	10f. Type **813**	20	15
3736	15f. "Rhododendron molle"	20	15
3737	20f. "Rhododendron simsii"	20	15
3738	20f. "Rhododendron fictolacteum"	20	15
3739	50f. "Rhododendron agglutinatum" (vert)	45	25
3740	80f. "Rhododendron fortunei" (vert)	70	45
3741	90f. "Rhododendron giganteum" (vert)	80	50
3742	1y.60 "Rhododendron rex" (vert)	1·30	85
MS3743	135×89 mm. 5y. "Rhododendron wardii"	14·00	6·50

814 Pleasure Boat on Lake Nanhu (venue of first Party congress)

1991. 70th Anniv of Chinese Communist Party. Multicoloured.

3744	20f. Type **814**	20	15
3745	50f. Party emblem	25	25

815 Statue, Xuxian

1991. 2200th Anniv of Peasant Uprising led by Chen Sheng and Wu Guang.

3746	**815**	20f. black, brown and deep brown	25	15

816 Hanging Temple

1991. Mount Hengshan, Shanxi Province. Mult.

3747	20f. Type **816**	20	15
3748	20f. Snow-covered peak	20	15
3749	55f. "Shrine of Hengshan" carved in rock face	45	25
3750	80f. Temples in Flying Stone Grotto	70	45

817 Mammoths and Man

1991. 13th International Union for Quaternary Research Conference, Peking.

3751	**817**	20f. multicoloured	40	25

818 Pine Valley

1991. Chengde Royal Summer Resort. Mult.

3752	15f. Type **818**	20	10
3753	20f. Pavilions around lake	20	10
3754	90f. Maples and pavilions on islet	60	45
MS3755	130×70 mm. 2y. View of resort (88×39 mm)	9·50	3·00

819 Chen Yi

1991. 90th Birth Anniv of Chen Yi (co-founder of People's Army).
3756 20f. Type **819** 20 15
3757 50f. Verse "The Green Pine" written by Chen Yi 25 25

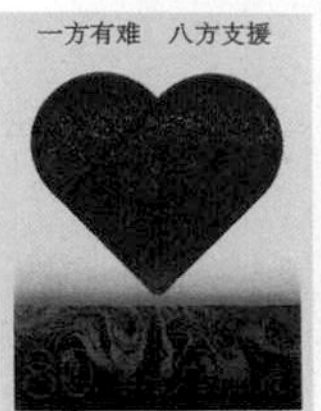

820 Clasped Hands forming Heart

1991. Flood Disaster Relief.
3758 **820** 80f. multicoloured 35 25

The proceeds from the sale of No. 3758 were donated to the International Decade for Natural Disaster Reduction National Committee.

1991. Achievements of Socialist Construction (4th series). As T 758. Multicoloured.
3759 20f. Luoyang glassworks 20 10
3760 25f. Urumchi chemical fertilizer works 20 15
3761 55f. Shenyang–Dalian expressway 20 15
3762 80f. Xichang satellite launching centre 25 25

821 Xu Xilin

1991. 80th Anniv of 1911 Revolution. Mult.
3763 20f. (1) Type **821** 20 15
3764 20f. (2) Qiu Jin 20 15
3765 20f. (3) Song Jiaoren 20 15

822 Wine Pot and Warming Bowl, Song Dynasty

1991. Jingdezhen China. Multicoloured.
3766 15f. (1) Type **822** 20 15
3767 20f. (2) Blue and white porcelain vase, Yuan dynasty 20 15
3768 20f. (3) Covered jar with dragon design, Ming dynasty (horiz) 20 15
3769 25f. (4) Vase with flower design, Qing dynasty 20 15
3770 50f. (5) Modern plate with fish design 25 15
3771 2y. (6) Modern octagonal bowl (horiz) 55 35

823 Tao Xingzhi

1991. Birth Centenary of Tao Xingzhi (educationist). Each blue, grey and red.
3772 20f. Type **823** 20 15
3773 50f. Tao Xingzhi in traditional robes 25 25

824 Xu Xiangqian

1991. 90th Birth Anniv of Xu Xiangqian (revolutionary). Multicoloured.
3774 20f. Type **824** 20 15
3775 50f. In uniform 25 25

825 Emblem

1991. 1st Women's World Football Championship, Guangdong Province. Multicoloured.
3776 20f. Type **825** 20 15
3777 50f. Player 25 25

1991. Literature. "Outlaws of the Marsh" (3rd series). As T 745. Multicoloured.
3778 20f. (1) Dai Zong delivers forged letter from Liangshan Marsh 20 15
3779 25f. (2) Yi Zhangqing captures Stumpy Tiger Wang 20 15
3780 25f. (3) Mistress Gu rescues Xie brothers from Dengzhou jail 20 15
3781 90f. (4) Sun Li gains entrance to Zhu family manor in guise of military magistrate 90 50
MS3782 87×140 mm. 3y. Mount Liangshan warriors raiding execution compound (56×86 mm) 10·00 4·75

826 Monkey

1992. New Year. Year of the Monkey. Paper-cut designs.
3783 **826** 20f. multicoloured 20 15
3784 - 50f. black and red 30 25

DESIGN: 50f. Magpies and plum blossom around Chinese character for monkey.

827 Black Stork

1992. Storks. Multicoloured.
3785 20f. Type **827** 20 15
3786 1y.60 White stork 70 60

828 "Metasequoia glyptostroboides"

1992. Conifers. Multicoloured.
3787 20f. Type **828** 20 15
3788 30f. "Cathaya argyrophylla" 20 15
3789 50f. "Taiwania flousiana" 25 25
3790 80f. "Abies beshanzuensis" 35 25

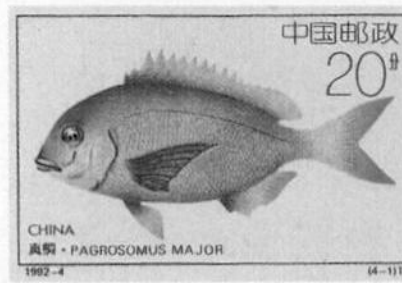

829 Madai Seabream

1992. Offshore Breeding Projects. Multicoloured.
3791 20f. Type **829** 20 15
3792 25f. Prawn 20 15
3793 50f. Farrer's scallops 25 25
3794 80f. "Laminaria japonica" (seaweed) 30 25

830 River Crossing at Yanan

1992. 50th Anniv of Publication of Mao Tse-tung's Talks at the Yanan Forum on Literature and Art.
3795 **830** 20f. black, orange & red 25 15

831 Flower and Landscape on Globe

1992. World Environment Day. 20th Anniv of U. N. Environment Conference, Stockholm.
3796 **831** 20f. multicoloured 30 25

832 Seven-spotted Ladybird

1992. 19th International Entomology Congress, Peking. Insects. Multicoloured.
3797 20f. Type **832** 20 15
3798 30f. "Sympetrum croceolum" (dragonfly) 25 15
3799 50f. "Chrysopa septempunctata" (lacewing) 25 25
3800 2y. Praying mantis 80 45

833 Basketball

1992. Olympic Games, Barcelona. Mult.
3801 20f. Type **833** 20 15
3802 25f. Gymnastics (horiz) 20 15
3803 50f. Diving (horiz) 25 25
3804 80f. Weightlifting 40 35
MS3805 91×68 mm. 5y. Marathon runners (53×36 mm) 3·25 2·10

834 Emblem

1992. International Space Year.
3806 **834** 20f. multicoloured 25 15

1992. Literature. "Romance of the Three Kingdoms" by Luo Guanzhong (3rd series). As T 763. Multicoloured.
3807 20f. Zhuge Liang urging Zhang Zhao to join fight against Cao Cao (horiz) 20 15
3808 30f. Zhuge Liang's sarcastic goading of Sun Quan 20 15
3809 50f. Jiang Gan stealing forged letter from Zhou Yu (horiz) 25 25
3810 1y.60 Zhuge Liang and Lu Su in straw-covered boat under arrow attack 45 35

1992. Dunhuang Cave Murals (4th series). Tang Dynasty. As T 732. Multicoloured.
3811 20f. Bodhisattva (vert) 20 15
3812 25f. Musical performance (vert) 20 15
3813 55f. Flight on a dragon 25 25
3814 80f. Emperor Wudi dispatching his envoy Zhang Qian to the western regions 40 35
MS3815 89×130 mm. 5y. Guanyin, Goddess of Mercy (48×66 mm) 3·00 2·10

835 Manchurian Cranes over Great Wall

1992. 20th Anniv of Normalization of Diplomatic Relations with Japan. Multicoloured.
3816 20f. Type **835** 20 15
3817 2y. Japanese and Chinese girls and dove 80 50

836 Statue of Mazu, Meizhou Islet

1992. Mazu, Sea Goddess.
3818 **836** 20f. brown and blue 25 15

837 Party Emblem

1992. 14th National Communist Party Congress.
3819 **837** 20f. multicoloured 25 15

838 Jiao Yulu

1992. 70th Birth Anniv of Jiao Yulu (Party worker).
3820 **838** 20f. multicoloured 25 15

839 Xiong Qinglai (mathematician) and Formula

1992. Scientists (3rd series). Multicoloured.
3821 20f. Type **839** 20 15
3822 30f. Tang Feifan (microbiologist) and medal 20 15
3823 50f. Zhang Xiaoqian (doctor) and hospital scene 25 15
3824 1y. Liang Sicheng (architect) and plan 30 25

840 Luo Ronghuan in Officer's Uniform

1992. 90th Birth Anniv of Luo Ronghuan (army leader). Multicoloured.

3825 20f. Type **840** 20 15
3826 50f. Luo Ronghuan as young man 25 25

841 State Arms

1992. 10th Anniv of Constitution.

3827 **841** 20f. multicoloured 25 15

842 Liu Bocheng in Officer's Uniform

1992. Birth Centenary of Liu Bocheng (army leader).

3828 **842** 20f. multicoloured 20 15
3829 - 50f. deep green & green 25 25

DESIGN—VERT: 50f. Liu Bocheng as young man.

843 "Spring" (Zhou Baiqi)

1992. Qingtian Stone Carvings. Multicoloured.

3830 10f. Type **843** 20 15
3831 20f. "Chinese Sorghum" (Lin Rukui) 20 15
3832 40f. "Harvest" (Zhang Aiting) 25 15
3833 2y. "Blooming Flowers and Full Moon" (Ni Dongfang) 45 25

844 Cock

1993. New Year. Year of the Cock. Paper-cut designs by Cai Lanying.

3834 **844** 20f. red and black 25 15
3835 - 50f. white, red & black 25 25

DESIGN: 50f. Flowers around Chinese character for rooster.

845 Song Qing-ling

1993. Birth Centenary of Song Qing-ling (Sun Yat-sen's wife). Multicoloured.

3836 20f. Type **845** 20 15
3837 1y. Song Qing-ling with children 40 45

846 Bactrian Camel

1993. Bactrian Camel. Multicoloured.

3838 20f. Type **846** 25 15
3839 1y.60 Adult with young 50 45

847 Flag, Basket of Flowers and Streamers

1993. 8th National People's Congress, Peking.

3840 **847** 20f. multicoloured 25 15

848 Players

1993. Go.

3841 **848** 20f. multicoloured 20 15
3842 - 1y.60 red, black & gold 45 35

DESIGN: 1y.60, "China Vogue" (black) and "linked stars" (white) formations on board.

849 Sportswomen

1993. 1st East Asian Games, Shanghai. Mult.

3843 50f. Type **849** 20 15
3844 50f. Dong dong (mascot) 20 15

Nos. 3843/4 were printed together, se-tenant, forming a composite design of Shanghai Stadium.

850 Li Jishen

1993. Revolutionaries (1st series). Each brown and black.

3845 20f. Type **850** 20 15
3846 30f. Zhang Lan (vert) 20 15
3847 50f. Shan Junru (vert) 20 15
3848 1y. Huang Yanpei 25 15

See also Nos. 3888/91.

851 "Phyllostachys nigra"

1993. Bamboo. Multicoloured.

3849 20f. Type **851** 20 15
3850 30f. "Phyllostachys aureosulcata spectabilis" 20 15
3851 40f. "Bambusa ventricosa" 20 15
3852 1y. "Pseudosasa amabilis" 25 15
MS3853 100×73 mm. 5y. "Phyllostachys heterocycla pubescens" (50×36 mm) 3·25 2·20

1993. Literature. "Outlaws of the Marsh" (4th series). As T 745. Multicoloured.

3854 20f. Yin Tianxi and gang capturing Chai Jin 20 15
3855 30f. Shi Qian stealing Xu Ning's armour 20 15
3856 50f. Xu Ning teaching use of barbed lance 25 25
3857 2y. Shi Xiu saving Lu Junyi from execution 55 45

852 Crater Lake in Winter

1993. Changbai Mountains. Multicoloured.

3858 20f. Type **852** 15 10
3859 30f. Mountain tundra in autumn 20 10
3860 50f. Waterfall in summer 25 15
3861 1y. Forest in spring 40 45

853 Games Emblem and Temple of Heaven

1993. 7th National Games, Peking.

3862 **853** 20f. multicoloured 25 15

854 "Losana", Temple of Ancestors

1993. 1500th Anniv of Longmen Grottoes, Luoyang. Multicoloured.

3863 20f. Type **854** 15 10
3864 30f. "Sakyamuni", Middle Binyang Cave 20 15
3865 50f. "King of Northern Heavens" standing on Yaksha 25 15
3866 1y. "Bodhisattva", Guyang Cave 30 25
MS3867 150×57 mm. 5y. Temple of Ancestors (119×39 mm) 4·00 1·70

855 Queen Bee and Workers on Comb

1993. The Honey Bee. Multicoloured.

3868 10f. Type **855** 20 15
3869 15f. Bee extracting nectar 20 15
3870 20f. Two bees on blossom 20 15
3871 2y. Two bees among flowers 55 70

856 Bowl, New Stone Age

1993. Lacquer Work. Multicoloured.

3872 20f. Type **856** 20 15
3873 30f. Duck-shaped container (from Marquis Yi's tomb), Warring States Period 20 15
3874 50f. Plate decorated with foliage (Zhang Cheng), Yuan Dynasty 25 25
3875 1y. Chrysanthemum-shaped container, Qing Dynasty 30 25

857 Mao Tse-tung in North Shaanxi

1993. Birth Centenary of Mao Tse-tung. Mult.

3876 20f. Type **857** 20 15
3877 1y. Mao in library 25 25
MS3878 83×137 mm. 5y. Mao and Great Wall (48×59 mm) 3·00 2·20

858 Fan Painting of Bamboo and Rock

1993. 300th Birth Anniv of Zheng Banqiao (artist). Multicoloured.

3879 10f. Type **858** 20 15
3880 20f. Orchids 20 15
3881 20f. Orchids, bamboo and rock (scroll) (vert) 20 15
3882 30f. Bamboo (scroll) (vert) 25 15
3883 50f. Chrysanthemum in vase 25 15
3884 1y.60 Calligraphy on fan 55 35

859 Yang Hucheng

1993. Birth Centenary of General Yang Hucheng.

3885 **859** 20f. multicoloured 25 15

860 Dog (folk toy, Hebei)

1994. New Year. Year of The Dog.

3886 **860** 20f. multicoloured 20 15
3887 - 50f. black, red & yellow 25 25

DESIGN: 50f. Dogs and flowers around Chinese character for dog.

861 Ma Xulun

1994. Revolutionaries (2nd series). Each brown and black.

3888 20f. Chen Qiyou (horiz) 20 10
3889 20f. Chen Shutong 20 10
3890 50f. Type **861** 25 15
3891 50f. Xu Deheng (horiz) 25 15

862 Great Siberian Sturgeon

1994. Sturgeons. Multicoloured.

3892 20f. Type **862** 20 15
3893 40f. Chinese sturgeon 20 15
3894 50f. Chinese paddlefish 25 15
3895 1y. Yangtze sturgeon 35 25

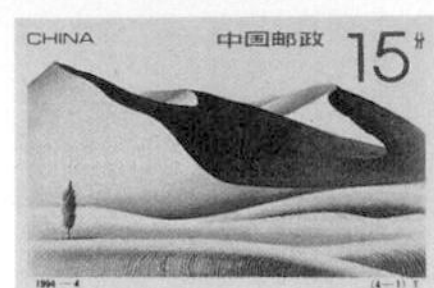

863 Tree in Dunes

1994. "Making the Desert Green". Multicoloured.
3896 15f. Type **863** 15 10
3897 20f. Flower-covered dune 20 10
3898 40f. Forest of poplars 25 15
3899 50f. Oasis 30 25

864 Ming Dynasty Three-legged Round Teapot

1994. Yixing Unglazed Teapots. Multicoloured.
3900 20f. Type **864** 15 10
3901 30f. Qing dynasty four-legged square teapot 20 10
3902 50f. Qing dynasty patterned teapot 20 15
3903 1y. Modern teapot 30 25

865 Entrance Gate

1994. 70th Anniv of Huang-pu Military Academy.
3904 **865** 20f. multicoloured 25 15

866 "100" and Olympic Rings

1994. Centenary of Int Olympic Committee.
3905 **866** 20f. multicoloured 25 15

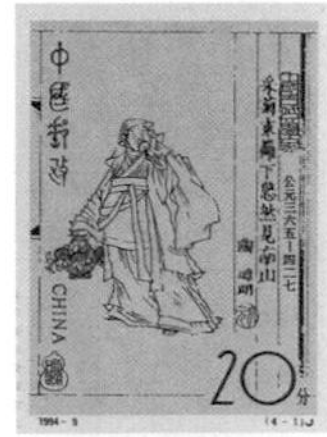

867 Tao Yuanming (poet)

1994. Writers. Each black, brown and red.
3906 20f. Type **867** 15 10
3907 30f. Cao Zhi (poet) 20 15
3908 50f. Sima Qian (historian) 25 15
3909 1y. Qu Yuan (poet) 30 15

1994. Dunhuang Cave Murals (5th series). Tang Dynasty Frescoes in Mogao Caves. As T 732. Multicoloured.
3910 10f. Flying Devata 20 10
3911 20f. Vimalakirti on dais 20 15
3912 50f. Zhang Yichao's forces 25 15
3913 1y.60 Sorceresses 45 25

868 Zhaojun

1994. Marriage of Zhaojun (from Han court) and Monarch of Xiongnu. Multicoloured.
3914 20f. Type **868** 20 15
3915 50f. Journey to Xiongnu 30 20
MS3916 145×80 mm. 3y. Wedding ceremony (85×46 mm) 4·00 2·75

869 Emblem

1994. 6th Far East and South Pacific Games for the Disabled, Peking.
3917 **869** 20f. multicoloured 20 15

870 Heaven's South Gate

1994. UNESCO World Heritage Site. Wulingyuan. Multicoloured.
3918 20f. Type **870** 20 10
3919 30f. Shentangwan 20 15
3920 50f. No. One Bridge (horiz) 25 25
3921 1y. Writing Brush Peak (horiz) 35 35
MS3922 135×80 mm. 3y. Picturesque Corridor (50×36 mm) 4·00 2·50

871 Jade Maiden Peak

1994. Mt. Wuyi. Multicoloured.
3923 50f. (1) Type **871** 25 15
3924 50f. (2) Nine Turns Brook 25 15
3925 50f. (3) Hanging Block 25 15
3926 50f. (4) Elevated Meadow 25 15
Nos. 3923/6 were issued together, se-tenant, forming a composite design.

872 Examining Scroll

1994. Paintings by Fu Baoshi. Multicoloured.
3927 10f. Waterfall and river 20 15
3928 20f. Type **872** 20 15
3929 20f. Tree 20 15
3930 40f. Musicians 20 15
3931 50f. Wooded landscape 25 15
3932 1y. Scholars 30 15

873 Whooping Crane

1994. Cranes. Multicoloured.
3933 20f. Type **873** 25 15
3934 2y. Black-necked crane 45 40

874 UPU Monument

1994. World Post Day. 120th Anniv of Universal Postal Union. Sheet 85×113 mm.
MS3935 3y. multicoloured 4·25 2·20

875 White Emperor's City

1994. Gorges of Yangtse River. Mult.
3936 10f. (1) Type **875** 20 10
3937 20f. (2) River steamer in Qutang Gorge 20 10
3938 20f. (3) Small boat in Wuxia Gorge 20 10
3939 30f. (4) Goddess Peak 20 10
3940 50f. (5) Boats in Xiling Gorge 25 15
3941 1y. (6) Qu Yuan Memorial Hall 30 25
MS3942 140×78 mm. 5y. Panoramic view of river gorges (115×36 mm) 3·75 2·50

876 Rock Formation

1994. 4th All-China Philatelic Federation Congress, Peking. Sheet 120×85 mm.
MS3943 3y. multicoloured 2·20 1·70

1994. Literature. "Romance of the Three Kingdoms" by Luo Guanzhong (4th series). As T 763. Multicoloured.
3944 20f. Cao Cao composing poem with lance in hand (horiz) 15 10
3945 30f. Liu Bei's wedding to sister of Sun Quan 20 10
3946 50f. Ambush at Xiaoyaojin (horiz) 25 15
3947 1y. Lu Xun's forces destroying Liu Bei's camps 80 55
MS3948 182×65 mm. 5y. Battle of Chibi (175×36 mm) 6·50 4·25

877 Shenzhen

1994. Special Economic Zones. Multicoloured.
3949 50f. (1) Type **877** 15 10
3950 50f. (2) Zhuhai 15 10
3951 50f. (3) Shantou 15 10
3952 50f. (4) Xiamen 15 10
3953 50f. (5) Hainan 15 10

878 Dayan Pagoda, Cien Temple, Xian

1994. Pagodas. Each black, lilght brown and brown.
3954 20f. (1) Type **878** 20 15
3955 20f. (2) Zhenguo Pagoda, Kaiyuan Temple, Quanzhou 20 15
3956 50f. (3) Liuhe Pagoda, Kaihua Temple, Hangzhou 20 15
3957 2y. (4) Youguo Temple, Kaifeng 25 15

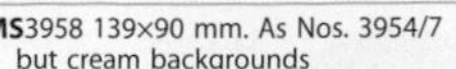
MS3958 139×90 mm. As Nos. 3954/7 but cream backgrounds 9·50 4·75

879 Pig

1995. New Year. Year of the Pig.
3959 **879** 20f. multicoloured 25 15
3960 - 50f. black and red 25 15
DESIGN: 50f. Chinese character ("pig") and pigs.

880 Willows beside River Songhua

1995. Winter in Jilin. Multicoloured.
3961 20f. Type **880** 20 10
3962 50f. Jade tree on hillside (vert) 25 15

881 Relief Map and Tropic of Cancer

1995. Mt. Dinghu. Multicoloured.
3963 15f. (1) Type **881** 20 15
3964 20f. (2) Ravine 20 15
3965 20f. (3) Monastery on hillside and forest-covered slopes 20 15
3966 2y.30 (4) Pair of silver pheasants in forest 40 35

882 Summit Emblem

1995. United Nations World Summit for Social Development, Copenhagen.
3967 **882** 20f. multicoloured 20 10

883 Snowy Owl

1995. Owls. Multicoloured.
3968 10f. Eagle owl 20 15
3969 20f. Long-eared owl 20 15
3970 50f. Type **883** 25 15
3971 1y. Eastern grass owls 35 25

884 "Osmanthus fragrans thunbergii"

1995. Sweet Osmanthus. Multicoloured.
3972 20f. (1) Type **884** 15 10
3973 20f. (2) "Osmanthus fragrans latifolius" 15 10
3974 50f. (3) "Osmanthus fragrans aurantiacus" 25 15
3975 1y. (4) "Osmanthus fragrans semperflorens" 40 35

885 Player

1995. World Table Tennis Championships, Tianjin. Multicoloured.

3976	20f. Type **885**	20	10
3977	50f. Stadium	25	15
MS3978	140×90 mm. Nos. 3976/7 (sold at 700f.)	30·00	16·00

No. **MS**3978 was issued to commemorate Chinese victory in all seven titles contested at the championships.

886 Ladies and Courtiers

1995. "Spring Outing" by Zhang Xuan. Details of the painting. Multicoloured.

3979	50f. (1) Type **886**	25	15
3980	50f. (2) Courtiers on horseback	25	15

Nos. 3979/80 were issued together, se-tenant, forming a composite design.

887 Donglu Play, Shanxi

1995. Shadow Play. Regional characters. Mult.

3981	20f. (1) Type **887**	20	15
3982	40f. (2) Luanxain play, Hebei	20	15
3983	50f. (3) Xiaoyi play, Shanxi	25	15
3984	50f. (4) Dayi play, Sichuan	25	15

888 Siyuan

1995. Motorway Interchanges, Peking. Mult.

3985	20f. Type **888**	15	10
3986	30f. Tianningsi	20	10
3987	50f. Yuting	25	15
3988	1y. Anhui	35	25

890 Asian Elephants at River

1995. 20th Anniv of China–Thailand Diplomatic Relations. Multicoloured.

3990	1y. (1) Type **890**	25	15
3991	1y. (2) Asian elephants at river (face value at left)	25	15

Nos. 3990/1 were issued together, se-tenant, forming a composite design.

891 East and West Dongting Hills

1995. Lake Taihu. Multicoloured.

3992	20f. (1) Type **891**	15	10
3993	20f. (2) Tortoise Islet in spring	15	10
3994	50f. (3) Li Garden in summer	25	15
3995	50f. (4) Jichang Garden in autumn	25	15
3996	230f. (5) Plum Garden in winter	60	50
MS3997	122×81 mm. 500f. Stone tablet on Tortoise Islet inscribed "Beauty that nurtured Wu and Yue" by Liao Lun (88×59 mm)	5·00	2·50

893 Yucheng Post, Jiangsu

1995. "China'96" International Stamp Exhibition, Peking. Ancient Chinese Post Offices. Mult.

3999	20f. Type **893**	20	10
4000	50f. Jimingshan Post, Hebei	25	15

See also No.**MS**4108.

894 Hill Gate

1995. 1500th Anniv of Shaolin Temple, Henan. Multicoloured.

4001	20f. Type **894**	20	15
4002	20f. Pagoda Forest	20	15
4003	50f. Martial arts practice (detail of fresco, White Robe Hall)	20	15
4004	100f. Thirteen monks rescue the Prince of Qin (detail of fresco)	30	25

895 New Stone Age Jar

1995. Tibetan Culture. Multicoloured.

4005	20f. Type **895**	15	10
4006	30f. Helmet (7th century)	20	10
4007	50f. Celestial chart	25	15
4008	100f. Pearl and coral mandala	35	25

896 Koalas in Eucalyptus Tree

1995. Endangered Animals. Multicoloured.

4009	20f. Type **896**	20	10
4010	2y.90 Giant pandas amongst bamboo	1·10	85

897 Japanese Attack in North China, 7 July 1937

1995. 50th Anniv of End of Second World War and of War against Japan. Multicoloured.

4011	10f. (1) Type **897**	15	10
4012	20f. (2) Battle of Taier Village	15	10
4013	20f. (3) Battle at Great Wall	15	10
4014	50f. (4) Guerrillas	20	15
4015	50f. (5) Forces at Mangyo, Burma	20	15
4016	60f. (6) Airplane donated by overseas Chinese	25	15
4017	100f. (7) Liberation of Taiwan, October 1945	30	15
4018	100f. (8) Crew on deck of battleship	30	25

898 Woman's Profile and Flags (equality)

1995. 4th World Conference on Women, Peking. Multicoloured.

4019	15f. Type **898**	15	10
4020	20f. Woman's profile and wheel of colours (development)	15	10
4021	50f. Woman's profile and dove (peace)	25	15
4022	60f. Dove and flower (friendship)	30	25

1995. International Stamp and Coin Exhibition, Peking. Sweet Osmanthus. Sheet 143×85 mm.

MS4023	Nos. 3972/5 (sold at 3y.)	6·50	4·00

899 Great Wall at Jinshanling Hill

1995. The Great Wall of China.

4024	-	5f. turquoise, bl & blk	20	20
4024a	-	10f. black and green	20	20
4024b	-	20f. black and lavender	20	20
4025	-	30f. black and yellow	20	15
4025a	-	40f. black and pink	20	20
4026	-	50f. black, brn & yell	20	10
4027	**899**	60f. black and brown	20	15
4027a	-	60f. black and yellow	20	20
4027b	-	80f. multicoloured	30	20
4028	-	100f. black and red	25	15
4029	-	150f. black and green	45	25
4031	-	200f. black and pink	55	35
4032	-	230f. black and green	60	45
4032a	-	270f. mauve, blk & grn	90	70
4035	-	290f. black and blue	80	60
4036	-	300f. black and green	90	90
4036a	-	320f. mve, blk & lav	1·00	80
4037	-	420f. black and orange	1·20	1·20
4037a	-	440f. light brown, black and brown	1·40	1·40
4038	-	500f. black, brn & bl	1·50	1·00
4038a	-	540f. black and blue	1·50	1·00
4038b	-	10y. multicoloured	3·00	2·00
4038c	-	20y. multicoloured	6·50	4·00
4038d	-	50y. grey, blk & grn	16·00	7·50

DESIGNS: 5f. Hushan section of wall; 10f. Wall at Jiumenkou Pass; 20f. Wall at Shanhaiguan; 30f. Wall at Huangya Pass; 40f. Jinshanling section of wall; 50f. Wall seen from Gubeikou; 60f. (4027a), Huanghua Tower and wall; 80f. Mutianyu section of wall; 100f. Wall seen from Badaling; 150f. Wall at Jurong Pass; 200f. Wall at Zijing Pass; 230f. Wall at Shanhaiguan Pass; 270f. Wall at Pingxingguan Pass; 290f. Laolongtou (end of wall); 300f. Wall at Niangziguan Pass; 320f. Wall at Desheng Pass; 420f. Wall at Pianguan Pass; 440f. Wall at Yanmen Pass; 500f. Bianjing Tower; 540f. Zhenbei Tower; 10y. Huama section; 20y. Wall at Sanguankou Pass; 50y. Wall at Jiayuguan Pass.

900 Dawn on Heavenly Terrace Peak

1995. The Jiuhua Mountains, Anhui. Mult.

4039	10f. (1) Type **900**	15	10
4040	20f. (2) Hall of Meditation (vert)	15	10
4041	20f. (3) Hall of the Mortal Body	15	10
4042	50f. (4) Sunset at Zhiyuan Temple	25	10
4043	50f. (5) Roc listening to Scriptures (rock formation) (vert)	25	10
4044	290f. (6) Phoenix pine	70	45

901 Black and White Film

1995. Centenary of Motion Pictures. Mult.

4045	20f. Type **901**	20	10
4046	50f. Colour film	25	15

902 Flag and New York Headquarters

1995. 50th Anniv of UNO. Multicoloured.

4047	20f. Type **902**	20	10
4048	50f. Anniversary emblem and "flags"	25	15

903 Blessing Spot

1995. Sanqing Mountain. Multicoloured.

4049	20f. Type **903**	15	10
4050	20f. Spring Goddess	15	10
4051	50f. Music charm (vert)	25	15
4052	100f. Supernatural python (rock formation) (vert)	35	35

904 Central Mountain Temple and Huang Gai Peak

1995. Mount Song. Multicoloured.

4053	20f. Type **904**	15	10
4054	50f. Moonrise over Fawang Temple	20	10
4055	60f. Shaolin Temple in snow	25	15
4056	1y. Mountain ridge	35	25

905 Victoria Harbour

1995. Hong Kong. Multicoloured.

4057	20f. Type **905**	20	15
4058	50f. Central Plaza	20	15
4059	60f. Hong Kong Cultural Centre	25	15
4060	290f. Repulse Bay	55	35

906 Sun Zi

1995. "Art of War" (book) by Sun Zi. Mult.

4061	20f. Type **906**	15	10
4062	20f. Elaborating strategies	15	10
4063	30f. Capturing Ying	20	10
4064	50f. Battle at Ailing	25	15
4065	100f. Conference at Huangchi	35	25

907 Rat

1996. New Year. Year of the Rat. Mult.

4066	20f. Type **907**	20	10
4067	50f. Pattern and Chinese character	25	15

908 Speed Skating

1996. 3rd Asian Winter Games, Harbin. Mult.

4068	50f. Type **908**	25	15
4069	50f. Ice hockey	25	15
4070	50f. Figure skating	25	15
4071	50f. Skiing	25	15

Nos. 4068/71 were issued together, se-tenant, forming a composite design.

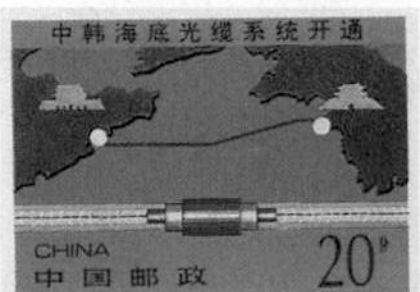

909 Cable Route

1996. Inaug of Korea–China Submarine Cable.

4072	**909** 20f. multicoloured	25	10

910 Palace Complex

1996. Shenyang Imperial Palace. Multicoloured.

4073	50f. Type **910**	25	15
4074	50f. Pagoda and buildings	25	15

Nos. 4073/4 were issued together, se-tenant, forming a composite design.

911 Tianjin Posts Bureau

1996. Cent of Chinese State Postal Service. Mult.

4075	10f. Type **911**	20	15
4076	20f. Former Directorate General of North China Posts building, Peking	20	15
4077	50f. Postal headquarters of Chinese Soviet Republic, Zhongshi, Jiangxi	20	15
4078	100f. Present Peking postal complex	30	25
MS4079	153×83 mm. 1897 surcharged red revenue stamps (89×59 mm)	8·00	4·25

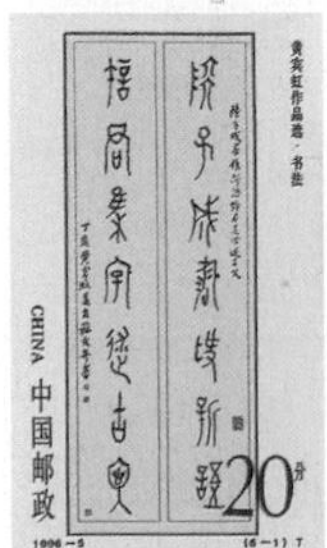

912 Calligraphy

1996. Paintings by Huang Binhong. Mult.

4080	20f. (1) Type **912**	20	15
4081	20f. (2) Mountain landscape	20	15
4082	40f. (3) Mount Qingcheng in rain	45	25
4083	50f. (4) View from Xiling	55	25
4084	50f. (5) Landscape	55	25
4085	230f. (6) Flowers	2·40	1·20

913 Shenyang F-8 Jet Fighter

1996. Chinese Aircraft. Multicoloured.

4086	20f. (1) Type **913**	15	10
4087	50f. (2) Nanchang A-5 jet fighter	25	15
4088	50f. (3) Xian Y-7 transport	25	15
4089	100f. (4) Harbin Y-12 utility plane	35	35

914 Green Scenery of Lijing River

1996. Bonsai Landscapes. Multicoloured.

4090	20f. (1) Type **914**	20	15
4091	20f. (2) Glistening Divine Peak	20	15
4092	50f. (3) Melting snow fills the river	20	15
4093	50f. (4) Eagle Beak Rock	20	15
4094	100f. (5) Memorable Years	30	25
4095	100f. (6) Peaks rising in Rosy Clouds	30	25

915 Sago Cycad ("Cycas revoluta")

1996. Cycads. Multicoloured.

4096	20f. Type **915**	20	10
4097	20f. Panzhihua cycad ("Cycas panzhihuaensis")	20	10
4098	50f. Nepal cycad	25	15
4099	230f. Polytomous cycad	45	45

916 Great Wall of China at Jinshan Ridge

1996. 25th Anniv of China–San Marino Diplomatic Relations. Multicoloured.

4100	100f. Type **916**	40	35
4101	100f. Walled rampart, San Marino	40	35

Nos. 4100/1 were issued together, se-tenant, forming a composite design.

919 Paddy Agricultural Tool

1996. Hemudu Archaeological Site, Yuyao, Zhejiang. Multicoloured.

4104	20f. Type **919**	15	10
4105	50f. Building supports	25	10
4106	100f. Paddles	35	25
4107	230f. Dish engraved with two birds and sun	60	60

920 Bronze Tripod

1996. "China '96" International Stamp Exhibition, Peking (2nd issue). Sheet 77×140 mm.

MS4108	500f. multicoloured	7·50	4·25

921 Children rejoicing

1996. Children. Multicoloured.

4109	20f. Type **921**	15	10
4110	30f. Girls pushing child in wheelchair in rain	20	10
4111	50f. Expedition to Antarctica	25	15
4112	100f. Planting sapling	35	35

922 "The Discus Thrower" (Miron)

1996. Centenary of Modern Olympic Games.

4113	**922** 20f. multicoloured	15	15

923 "Land"

1996. Preserve Land. Designs showing Chinese characters. Multicoloured.

4114	20f. Type **923**	20	10
4115	50f. "Cultivation"	25	15

924 Jinglue Terrace

1996. Jinglue Terrace, Guangxi Zhuang. Mult.

4116	20f. Type **924**	20	10
4117	50f. Structure of Zhenwu Pavilion	25	15

925 Red Flag Car

1996. Motor Vehicles. Multicoloured.

4118	20f. Type **925**	20	15
4119	20f. Dongfeng two-door truck	20	15
4120	50f. Jiefang four-door truck	30	15
4121	100f. Peking four-wheel drive	45	25

926 Banbidian Village, Kaiping District

1996. 20th Anniv of Tangshan Earthquake. Development of New City. Multicoloured.

4122	20f. (1) Type **926**	15	10
4123	50f. (2) East Hebei Cement Works	25	15
4124	50f. (3) Earthquake memorials, Xinhua Road	25	15
4125	100f. (4) Bulk carrier in Jingtang Harbour	35	35

927 Emblem, Globe and "30"

1996. 30th Int Geological Conference, Peking.

4126	**927** 20f. multicoloured	25	15

928 Tianchi Lake

1996. Tianshan Mountains, Xinjiang.

4127	**928** 20f. (1) multicoloured	15	10
4128	- 50f. (2) multicoloured	25	15
4129	- 50f. (3) blue, mve & blk	25	15
4130	- 100f. (4) multicoloured	45	35

DESIGNS—VERT: No. 4128, Waterfalls; 4129, Snow-capped mountain peaks. HORIZ: No. 4130. Mountains and landscape.

1996. Dunhuang Cave Murals (6th series). As T 732. Multicoloured.

4131	10f. Mount Wutai (Five Dynasties) (vert)	15	10
4132	20f. Li Shengtian, King of Khotan (Five Dynasties) (vert)	20	10
4133	50f. Guanyin, Goddess of Mercy, saves boat (Northern Song period)	25	15
4134	100f. Worshipping Bodhisattvas (Western Xia)	35	35
MS4135	95×135 mm. 500f. Goddess of Mercy with 1000 Hands (Yuan dynasty) (45×110 mm)	8·50	5·25

929 Tombs

1996. Emperors' Tombs of Western Xia Dynasty, Yinchuan, Ningxia Hui. Multicoloured.

4136	20f. Type **929**	20	10
4137	20f. Divine Gate ornament	20	10
4138	50f. Stone base from Stele Pavilion	25	15
4139	100f. Piece of stele from Shouling Tomb	40	25

930 Datong–Qinhuangdao Line

1996. Railways. Multicoloured.

4140	15f. Type **930**	15	10
4141	20f. Lanzhou–Xinjiang line	20	10
4142	50f. Peking–Kowloon line	25	15
4143	100f. Peking West railway station	30	25

931 Shang Dynasty Tortoise Shell

1996. Ancient Archives. Multicoloured.
4144 20f. Type **931** 20 10
4145 20f. Han Dynasty wood slip inscribed with divinations on a marriage 20 10
4146 50f. Ming dynasty iron scroll conferring merit on General Li Wen 25 15
4147 100f. Qing dynasty diplomatic credentials (1905) 30 25

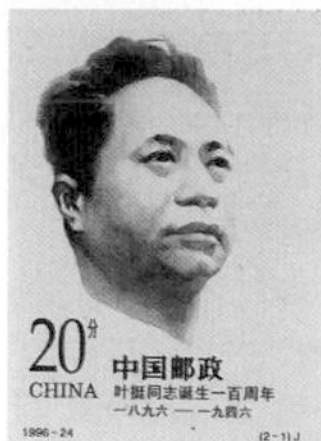

932 Ye Ting

1996. Birth Cent of Ye Ting (revolutionary). Mult.
4148 20f. Type **932** 20 10
4149 50f. Ye Ting in uniform 25 15

933 Emblem

1996. 96th Interparliamentary Union Conference, Peking.
4150 **933** 20f. multicoloured 30 15

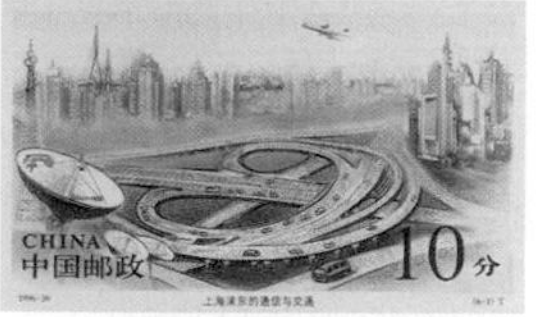

934 Transport and Telecommunications

1996. Pudong Area of Shanghai. Mult.
4151 10f. (1) Type **934** 15 10
4152 20f. (2) People's Bank of China branch, Lujiazui finance and business area 20 10
4153 20f. (3) Jinqiao export centre 20 10
4154 50f. (4) Garden of Advance Science and Technology, Zhangjiang 25 15
4155 60f. (5) Customs House, Waigaoqiao bonded area 25 15
4156 100f. (6) Apartment blocks 30 25
MS4157 161×75 mm. 500f. View of Pudong (89×44 mm) 8·50 5·25

935 Chinese Rocket "Long March"

1996. 47th Congress of International Astronautical Federation. Multicoloured.
4158 20f. Type **935** 20 10
4159 100f. Communications satellite 35 25

936 Singapore

1996. City Scenes. Multicoloured.
4160 20f. Type **936** 20 15
4161 290f. Panmen Gate, Suzhou 80 50

937 Red Army in Marshland

1996. 60th Anniv of Long March by Communist Army. Multicoloured.
4162 20f. Type **937** 35 20
4163 50f. Reunion of three armies 70 35

938 Two Gods

1996. Tianjin Clay Statuettes. Multicoloured.
4164 20f. (1) Type **938** 15 10
4165 50f. (2) Seated man blowing sugar figure 25 15
4166 50f. (3) Woman and child returning from fishing 25 15
4167 100f. (4) Women painting at table 30 25

939 Bank of China

1996. Economic Growth in Hong Kong. Mult.
4168 20f. Type **939** 15 10
4169 40f. Container terminal 20 10
4170 60f. Airplane taking off from Kai Tak Airport 25 15
4171 290f. Stock exchange 50 35

940 Emblem over Farmland

1997. 1st National Agricultural Census.
4172 **940** 50f. multicoloured 25 15

941 "Horse treading on Flying Swallow" (bronze) and Great Wall of China

1997. Tourist Year.
4173 **941** 50f. multicoloured 25 15

942 Chinese Lantern

1997. New Year. Year of the Ox. Mult.
4174 50f. Type **942** 25 15
4175 150f. Ox 45 35

943 "Pine on Mount Huangshan"

1997. Birth Centenary of Pan Tianshou (artist). Multicoloured.
4176 50f. (1) Type **943** 30 15
4177 50f. (2) "Rosy Clouds of Dawn" 30 15
4178 100f. (3) "Clearing Up after Mould Rains" 65 45
4179 100f. (4) "Chrysanthemum and Bamboo" 65 45
4180 150f. (5) "Sleeping Cat" 1·10 60
4181 150f. (6) "Corner of Lingyan Brook" 1·10 60

944 Tea Tree at Lancang, Yunnan

1997. Tea. Multicoloured.
4182 50f. (1) Type **944** 20 10
4183 50f. (2) Statue of Lu Yu (author of "Classic of Tea") 20 10
4184 150f. (3) Tea grinder (Tang dynasty) (horiz) 45 35
4185 150f. (4) "Tea Party at Huishan" (Wen Zhenming) (horiz) 45 35

945 Celebration

1997. 50th Anniv of Autonomous Region of Inner Mongolia. Multicoloured.
4186 50f. (1) Type **945** 20 15
4187 50f. (2) People of different cultures ("Unity") (horiz) 20 15
4188 200f. (3) Galloping horses ("Advance") (horiz) 80 50

946 Lady Amherst's Pheasant

1997. Rare Pheasants. Multicoloured.
4189 50f. Type **946** 20 10
4190 540f. Common pheasant 1·20 95

947 Zengchong Drum Tower

1997. Dong Architecture. Multicoloured.
4191 50f. (1) Type **947** 20 10
4192 50f. (2) Baier drum tower 20 10
4193 150f. (3) Wind and rain bridge over River Nanjiang (horiz) 45 25
4194 150f. (4) Wind and rain shelter in field (horiz) 45 25

948 Buddha and Attendant Bodhisattva (Northern Wei dynasty)

1997. Maiji Grottoes, Gansu Province. Mult.
4195 50f. (1) Type **948** 20 10
4196 50f. (2) Attendant Bodhisattva and disciple (Northern Wei dynasty) 20 10
4197 100f. (3) Maid servant (Western Wei dynasty) 25 15
4198 150f. (4) Buddha (Western Wei dynasty) 35 25
4199 150f. (5) Attendant Bodhisattva (Northern Zhou dynasty) 35 25
4200 200f. (6) Provider (Song dynasty) 45 35

949 Sino-British Joint Declaration and Red Roses

1997. Return of Hong Kong to China. Mult.
4201 50f. Type **949** 30 15
4202 150f. Basic Law and mixed roses 80 50
MS4203 140×95 mm. 800f. Deng Xiaoping (55×46 mm) 2·75 2·20
MS4204 140×95 mm. 50y. As No. **MS**4203 36·00 35·00

950 Taihuai Temple

1997. Ancient Temples, Wutai Mountain. Mult.
4205 40f. (1) Type **950** 20 10
4206 50f. (2) Great Hall, Nanchan Temple 20 10
4207 50f. (3) Eastern Hall, Foguang ("Buddhist Light") Temple 20 10
4208 150f. (4) Bronze Hall, Xiantong ("Revelation") Temple 35 25
4209 150f. (5) Bodhisattva Summit 35 25
4210 200f. (6) Zhenhai Temple 45 35

951 Tanks

1997. 70th Anniv of People's Liberation Army. Multicoloured.
4211 50f. (1) Type **951** 20 10
4212 50f. (2) Frigate flotilla 20 10
4213 50f. (3) Jet fighter 20 10
4214 50f. (4) Ballistic missile 20 10
4215 200f. (5) Tank, destroyer and jet fighters 60 45

952 Scene from "A Dream of Red Mansions" (carved by Jiang Yilin)

1997. Shoushan Stone Carvings. Mult.

4216	50f. (1) Type **952**	20	10
4217	50f. (2) "Rhinoceros basking in Sunshine" (Zhou Jinting)	20	10
4218	150f. (3) "Fragrance and Jade"	45	25
4219	150f. (4) "Li the Cripple, Han Zhongli and Lu Dongbin in drunken Joy" (Lin Fada)	45	25
MS4220	97×97 mm. 800f. Qianlong's chained seals (59×58 mm)	6·50	5·25

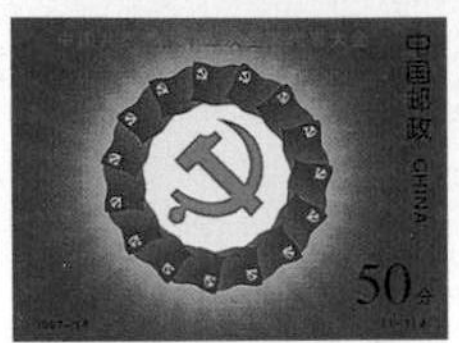

953 Emblem

1997. 15th National Communist Party Congress.

4221	**953**	50f. multicoloured	55	35

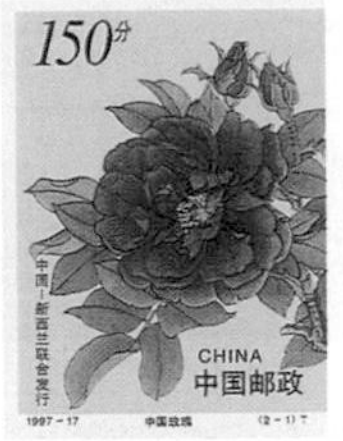

954 "Rosa rugosa"

1997. Roses. Multicoloured.

4222	150f. Type **954**	55	35
4223	150f. "Aotearoa" of New Zealand	85	70

Nos. 4222/3 were issued together, se-tenant, forming a composite design.

955 Putting the Shot and Athletes

1997. 8th National Games, Shanghai. Mult.

4224	50f. Type **955**	20	15
4225	150f. Mascot and stadium	50	45
MS4226	140×90 mm. Nos. 4224/5	7·50	3·50

956 Hall of Prayer for Good Harvests

1997. Temple of Heaven, Peking. Mult.

4227	50f. (1) Type **956**	20	10
4228	50f. (2) Imperial Vault of Heaven	20	10
4229	150f. (3) Circular mound altar	40	25
4230	150f. (4) Hall of Abstinence	40	25

957 Sunrise

1997. Mount Huangshan. Sheet 190×150 mm containing T 957 and similar multicoloured designs.

MS4231	200f. (1) Type **957**; 200f. (2) Xihai (West Sea) Peaks; 200f. (3) Flying Rock in clouds; 200f. (4) Beihai (North Sea) Peaks (vert); 200f. (5) Yuping (Jade Screen) Peak (vert); 200f. (6) Dream of Flowering Brush Peak; 200f	8·00	4·25

958 Archers' Tower, Jar and Gate Tower

1997. Xi'an City Walls. Multicoloured.

4232	50f. (1) Type **958**	20	10
4233	50f. (2) Archers' Tower	20	10
4234	150f. (3) Watchtower	45	35
4235	150f. (4) South-west corner tower	45	35

959 Diversion Canal

1997. Three Gorges Project (damming of Yangtse River). Multicoloured.

4236	50f. Type **959**	20	10
4237	50f. Dam under construction	20	10

Nos. 4236/7 were issued together, se-tenant, forming a composite design.

960 Temple of the Heavenly Queen

1997. Macao. Multicoloured.

4238	50f. Type **960**	20	15
4239	100f. Lianfeng (Lotus Peak) Temple	25	15
4240	150f. Great Sanba Archway (former facade of St. Paul's Church)	35	25
4241	200f. Songshan (Pine Hill) Lighthouse	55	35

961 Metallurgy in Ancient China

1997. Achievement in 1996 of Production of over 100,000,000 Tons of Steel a Year. Multicoloured.

4242	50f. Type **961**	20	15
4243	150f. Modern steel works	50	35

962 Digital Transmission

1997. Telecommunications. Multicoloured.

4244	50f. (1) Type **962**	20	10
4245	50f. (2) Program-controlled switch and computer	20	10
4246	150f. (3) Digital communication	40	35
4247	150f. (4) Mobile communication	40	35

1997. Literature. "Outlaws of the Marsh" (5th series). As T 745. Multicoloured.

4248	40f. (1) Hu Yanzhuo tricks Guan Sheng	25	15
4249	50f. (2) Lu Junyi captures Shi Wengong	25	15
4250	50f. (3) Yan Qing wrestles with Qing Tianzhu	25	15
4251	150f. (4) Hong Tianlei defeats government troops	70	50
MS4252	120×135 mm. 800f. Liangshan Heroes (59×89 mm)	4·00	3·25

963 Cloth Tiger (Guo Qiuying)

1998. New Year. Year of the Tiger. Mult.

4253	50f. Type **963**	20	10
4254	150f. Chinese character	35	25

964 Keyuan Garden

1998. Villas and Gardens in Guangdong. Mult.

4255	50f. Type **964**	20	10
4256	50f. Liangyuan Garden	20	10
4257	100f. Qinghiu Garden	30	25
4258	200f. Yuyin Villa	55	45

965 Deng Xiaoping

1998. 1st Death Anniv of Deng Xiaoping. Mult.

4259	50f. (1) Type **965**	20	10
4260	50f. (2) During Liberation War	20	10
4261	50f. (3) With Mao Tse-tung	20	10
4262	100f. (4) As Chairman of Military Commission	30	25
4263	150f. (5) Making speech	40	35
4264	200f. (6) In south China	55	45

966 Officers and Badge

1998. People's Police. Multicoloured.

4265	40f. (1) Type **966**	20	10
4266	50f. (2) Officers using computer and patrol officers using radio	20	10
4267	50f. (3) Officer and elderly woman	20	10
4268	100f. (4) Officer on traffic control duty	40	25
4269	150f. (5) Officers on fire duty	50	35
4270	200f. (6) Border guards	65	45

967 State Arms

1998. 9th National People's Congress, Peking.

4271	**967**	50f. multicoloured	20	10

968 Chou En-lai on Horseback

1998. Birth Centenary of Chou En-lai.

4272	**968**	50f. black, cream & red	20	10
4273	-	50f. black, cream & red	20	10
4274	-	150f. black, cream & red	50	35
4275	-	150f. multicoloured	50	35

DESIGNS: No. 4273, Walking; 4274, Wearing floral decoration; 4275, Clapping.

969 Fangcao Lake

1998. World Heritage Site. Jiuzhaigou (nine-village valley). Multicoloured.

4276	50f. (1) Type **969**	20	10
4277	50f. (2) Wuhua Lake	20	10
4278	150f. (3) Shuzheng Falls	50	35
4279	150f. (4) Nuorilang Falls	50	35
MS4280	150×85 mm. 800f. Long Lake	3·75	3·25

970 House on Stilts

1998. Dai Architecture, Xishuangbanna. Mult.

4281	50f. (1) Type **970**	20	10
4282	50f. (2) Ornamental well	20	10
4283	150f. (3) Pavilion and streamers	50	35
4284	150f. (4) Pagoda	50	35

971 Haikou

1998. Hainan Special Economic Zone. Mult.

4285	50f. (1) Type **971**	20	10
4286	50f. (2) Yangpu	20	10
4287	150f. (3) Sanya Phoenix International Airport	50	35
4288	150f. (4) Monument, Yalongwan	50	35

972 Yingtian Academy

1998. Ancient Academies. Multicoloured.

4289	50f. (1) Type **972**	20	10
4290	50f. (2) Songyang Academy	20	10
4291	150f. (3) Yuelu Academy	50	35
4292	150f. (4) Bailu Academy	50	35

973 University Buildings

1998. Centenary of Peking University.

4293	**973**	50f. multicoloured	20	10

974 Congress Emblem

1998. 22nd UPU Congress, Peking (1999). Mult.

4294	50f. Type **974**	20	10
4295	540f. Emblem (vert)	1·90	1·20

975 Mountain Peaks

1998. Shennongjia (primitive forest). Mult.

4296	50f. (1) Type **975**	20	10
4297	50f. (2) River gorge	20	10
4298	150f. (3) Forest	50	35
4299	150f. (4) Grasslands	50	35

976 Great Hall of the People of Chongqing

1998. Chongqing. Multicoloured.

4300	50f. Type **976**	20	10
4301	150f. Chongqing port	50	35

977 "Tiger"

1998. Paintings by He Xiangning. Mult.

4302	50f. Type **977**	20	10
4303	100f. "Lion" (vert)	40	25
4304	150f. "Plum Blossom" (vert)	50	35

978 Grasslands

1998. Xilingguole Grasslands, Inner Mongolia. Multicoloured.

4305	50f. (1) Type **978**	20	15
4306	50f. (2) Meadow steppe	20	15
4307	150f. (3) Forest of poplars and birches	65	35
MS4308	140×80 mm. 800f. Xilingguole River	2·50	2·20

979 Baishilazi

1998. Jingpo Lake, Heilonjiang. Multicoloured.

4309	50f. (1) Type **979**	20	10
4310	50f. (2) Pearl Gate	20	10
4311	50f. (3) Mt. Xiaogushan	20	10
4312	50f. (4) Diaoshuilou waterfall	20	10

Nos. 4309/12 were issued together, se-tenant, forming a composite design.

980 Wurzburg Palace, Germany

1998. World Heritage Sites. Multicoloured.

4313	50f. Type **980**	20	10
4314	540f. Puning Temple, Chengde	1·90	1·20

1998. Literature. "The Romance of the Three Kingdoms" by Luo Guanzhong (5th series). As T 763. Multicoloured.

4315	50f. (1) Liu Bei appoints a Guardian for his Heir at Baidi City (horiz)	20	10
4316	50f. (2) Zhuge Liang leads his army home	20	10
4317	100f. (3) Funeral of Zhuge Liang (horiz)	40	25
4318	150f. (4) Three Kingdoms united under the reign of Jin	50	35
MS4319	181×65 mm. 800f. Stratagem of the Empty City	5·25	3·00

981 Wave and Houses

1998. Flood Relief Fund.

4320	**981**	50f. (+50f.) mult	50	45

No. 4320 includes the se-tenant premium-carrying tab shown in Type **981**. The premium was used to help the victims of floods in the Yangtse and Songhuajiang River areas.

982 Louvre Palace, Paris

1998. Ancient Palaces. Multicoloured.

4321	50f. Type **982**	20	10
4322	200f. Imperial Palace, Peking	65	45

983 Face

1998. Rock Paintings, Helan Mountains. Mult.

4323	50f. Type **983**	20	10
4324	100f. Hunting	40	25
4325	150f. Ox	50	35

984 Vase with Five Spouts (Northern Song Dynasty)

1998. Longquan Pottery. Multicoloured.

4326	50f. (1) Type **984**	30	15
4327	50f. (2) Vase with phoenix ears (Southern Song dynasty)	30	15
4328	50f. (3) Double gourd vase (Yuan dynasty)	30	15
4329	150f. (4) Ewer decorated with three fruits (Ming dynasty)	50	35

985 Meridian Gate

1998. Mausoleum of King Yandi, Yanling County, Hunan. Multicoloured.

4330	50f. Type **985**	20	10
4331	100f. Saluting Pavilion	40	25
4332	150f. Tomb	50	35
MS4333	150×80 mm. Nos. 4330/3	2·30	1·90

986 Men discussing Campaign (Yi Rongsheng)

1998. 50th Anniv of Liberation War. Multicoloured.

4334	50f. (1) Type **986**	20	10
4335	50f. (2) Conquering Jinzhou (Ren Mengzhang, Zhang Hongzan, Li Shuji and Guang Tingbo)	20	10
4336	50f. (3) Battle of Huaihai (Chen Qi, Zhao Guangtao, Chen Jian and Wei Chuyu)	20	10
4337	50f. (4) Liberating Peking (Zhang Ruwei, Deng Jiaju, Wu Changjiang and Shen Yaoyi)	20	10
4338	150f. (5) Supporting the Front (Cui Kaixi)	50	35

987 Liu Shaoqi

1998. Birth Centenary of Liu Shaoqi (Chairman of the Republic, 1959–68).

4339	**987**	50f. (1) multicoloured	20	10
4340	-	50f. (2) black, buff and red	20	10
4341	-	50f. (3) multicoloured	20	10
4342	-	150f. (4) multicoloured	50	35

DESIGNS—VERT: No. 4340, Shaoqi at Seventh National Communist Party Congress. HORIZ: No. 4341, Presented with necklace of flowers while on diplomatic mission; 4342, Working at desk.

988 Chillon Castle, Lake Geneva, Switzerland

1998. Lakes. Multicoloured.

4343	50f. Type **988**	20	10
4344	540f. Bridge 24, Slender West Lake, Yangzhou	1·90	1·20

989 Canal Fork

1998. Lingqu Canal. Multicoloured.

4345	50f. Type **989**	20	10
4346	50f. Bridge over canal (vert)	20	10
4347	150f. Lock (vert)	50	35

990 Road into Macao

1998. Macao. Multicoloured.

4348	50f. Type **990**	20	10
4349	100f. Bridge and buildings	40	25
4350	150f. Macao Stadium	50	35
4351	200f. Airport	65	45

991 Deng Xiaoping at Third Plenary Session

1998. 20th Anniv of Third Plenary Session of 11th Central Committee of Chinese Communist Party. Multicoloured.

4352	50f. Type **991**	20	10
4353	150f. Deng Xiaoping Theory and buildings	50	35

992 Emperor Angelfish

1998. 22nd Universal Postal Union Congress and "China '99" International Stamp Exhibition, Peking. Sheet 190×150 mm. containing T 992 and similar multicoloured designs.

MS4354	200f. (1) Type **992**; 200f. (2) Spotted coral grouper; 200f. (3) Blue-spotted butterflyfish; 200f. (4) Ear-spotted angelfish (vert); 200f. (5) Pennant coralfish (vert); 200f. (6) Emperor snapper; 200f. (7) Clown triggerfish; 200f. (8) Regal angelfish	6·75	5·75

993 Ceramic Rabbit (Zhang Chang)

1999. New Year. Year of the Rabbit. Multicoloured.

4355	50f. Type **993**	20	10
4356	150f. Chinese character ("Good Luck")	50	35

994 Ploughing

1999. Stone Carvings of Han Dynasty.

4357	**994**	50f. (1) green, cream and black	20	10
4358	-	50f. (2) brown, cream and black	20	10
4359	-	50f. (3) blue, cream and black	20	10
4360	-	50f. (4) brown, cream and black	50	35
4361	-	150f. (5) green, cream and black	50	35
4362	-	150f. (6) lilac, cream and black	50	35

DESIGNS: No. 4358, Weaving; 4359, Dancing; 4360, Carriage and outriders; 4361, Jing Ke's attempted assassination of Emperor Qinshihuang; 4362, Goddess Chang'e flying to moon.

995 Wine Vessel, Northern Song Dynasty

1999. Ceramics from the Jun Kiln, Henan. Multicoloured.

4363	80f. Type **995**	30	15
4364	100f. Wine vessel, Northern Song Dynasty (different)	40	25
4365	150f. Double-handled stove, Yuan Dynasty	50	35
4366	200f. Double-handled vase, Yuan Dynasty	65	45

996 Peony and Globe

1999. World Horticulture Fair, Kunming. Mult.
4367 80f. Type **996** 30 15
4368 200f. Exhibition halls and tree 65 45

997 Stag

1999. Red Deer. Multicoloured.
4369 80f. (1) Type **997** 30 15
4370 80f. (2) Doe and fawns 30 15

998 Puji Temple

1999. Putuo Mountain, Lianhuayang. Mult.
4371 30f. Type **998** 10 10
4372 60f. Nantian Gate (vert) 20 10
4373 60f. Step beach 20 10
4374 80f. Pantuo Rock 30 15
4375 80f. Fanyin Cave (vert) 30 15
4376 280f. Fayu Temple 95 60

999 Nine Dragon Wall. Beihai (detail)

1999. "China 1999" International Stamp Exhibition, Peking (2nd issue). Sheet 174×68 mm.
MS4377 800f. multicoloured 4·25 2·50

1000 Fang Zhimin (sculpture)

1999. Birth Centenary of Fang Zhimin (revolutionary). Multicoloured.
4378 80y. Type **1000** 40 25
4379 80y. Full-length portrait of Fang Zhimin 40 25

1001 First Congress Building, Berne, Switzerland (1874)

1999. 22nd Universal Postal Union Congress, Peking (3rd issue). Multicoloured (except No. MS4382).
4380 80f. Type **1001** 30 15
4381 540f. 22nd Congress building, Peking 1·90 1·20
MS4382 85×150 mm. 800f. black and brown (Quotation in Chinese characters "Develops modern postal service to satisfy social demands" (by Pres. Jiang Zemin) (51×92 mm) 3·50 3·00

1002 UPU Emblem and Great Wall

1999. 125th Anniv of Universal Postal Union.
4383 **1002** 80f. multicoloured 30 15

1003 Emblem

1999. International Year of the Elderly.
4384 **1003** 80f. multicoloured 30 15

1004 Conference Hall

1999. 50th Anniv of Chinese People's Political Conference. Multicoloured.
4385 60f. Type **1004** 20 10
4386 80f. Mao Tse-tung and emblem (vert) 30 15

1005 Han Couple

1999. 50th Anniv of People's Republic. Ethnic Groups. Couples from different ethnic groups. Multicoloured.
4387 80f. (1) Type **1005** 30 15
4388 80f. (2) Mongolian 30 15
4389 80f. (3) Hui 30 15
4390 80f. (4) Tibetan 30 15
4391 80f. (5) Uygur 30 15
4392 80f. (6) Miao 30 15
4393 80f. (7) Yi 30 15
4394 80f. (8) Zhuang 30 15
4395 80f. (9) Bouyei 30 15
4396 80f. (10) Korean 30 15
4397 80f. (11) Manchu 30 15
4398 80f. (12) Dong 30 15
4399 80f. (13) Yao 30 15
4400 80f. (14) Bai 30 15
4401 80f. (15) Tujia 30 15
4402 80f. (16) Hani 30 15
4403 80f. (17) Kazak 30 15
4404 80f. (18) Dai 30 15
4405 80f. (19) Li 30 15
4406 80f. (20) Lisu 30 15
4407 80f. (21) Va 30 15
4408 80f. (22) She 30 15
4409 80f. (23) Gaoshan 30 15
4410 80f. (24) Lahu 30 15
4411 80f. (25) Sui 30 15
4412 80f. (26) Dongxiang 30 15
4413 80f. (27) Naxi 30 15
4414 80f. (28) Jingpo 30 15
4415 80f. (29) Kirgiz 30 15
4416 80f. (30) Tu 30 15
4417 80f. (31) Daur 30 15
4418 80f. (32) Mulam 30 15
4419 80f. (33) Qiang 30 15
4420 80f. (34) Blang 30 15
4421 80f. (35) Salar 30 15
4422 80f. (36) Maonan 30 15
4423 80f. (37) Gelao 30 15
4424 80f. (38) Xibe 30 15
4425 80f. (39) Achang 30 15
4426 80f. (40) Primi 30 15
4427 80f. (41) Tajik 30 15
4428 80f. (42) Nu 30 15
4429 80f. (43) Uzbek 30 15
4430 80f. (44) Russian 30 15
4431 80f. (45) Ewenki 30 15
4432 80f. (46) De'ang 30 15
4433 80f. (47) Bonan 30 15
4434 80f. (48) Yugur 30 15
4435 80f. (49) Gin 30 15
4436 80f. (50) Tatar 30 15
4437 80f. (51) Derung 30 15
4438 80f. (52) Oroqen 30 15
4439 80f. (53) Hezhen 30 15
4440 80f. (54) Monba 30 15
4441 80f. (55) Lhoba 30 15
4442 80f. (56) Jino 30 15

1006 Mt. Kumgang, North Korea

1999. 50th Anniv of China–North Korea Diplomatic Relations. Multicoloured.
4443 80f. (1) Type **1006** 30 15
4444 80f. (2) Mt. Lushan, China 30 15

1007 Children reading

1999. 10th Anniv of Project Hope (promotion of rural education).
4445 **1007** 80f. multicoloured 30 15

1008 Early Cambrian Chengjiang Biota Fossil

1999. 50th Anniv of Chinese Academy of Sciences. Multicoloured.
4446 80f. (1) Type **1008** 30 15
4447 80f. (2) Underwater robot 30 15
4448 80f. (3) Head and mathematical equation (vert) 30 15
4449 80f. (4) Astronomical telescope (vert) 30 15

1009 Li Lisan

1999. Birth Centenary of Li Lisan (trade unionist). Multicoloured.
4450 80f. Type **1009** 30 15
4451 80f. Li Lisan (different) 30 15

1010 Sino-Portuguese Joint Declaration

1999. Return of Macao to China. Multicoloured.
4452 80f. Type **1010** 30 15
4453 150f. Basic Law of Macao Special Region and Great Wall of China 50 35
MS4454 140×95 mm. 800f. Deng Xiaoping (59×59 mm) 4·25 3·50
MS4455 140×95 mm. 50y. As No. **MS**4454 25·00 21·00

1011 Rongzhen in Uniform

1999. Birth Centenary of Nie Rongzhen (revolutionary). Multicoloured.
4456 80f. Type **1011** 30 15
4457 80f. Rongzhen in chair 30 15

1012 1961 8f. 1911 Revolution Stamp and Dr. Sun Yat-sen

1999. The Twentieth Century. Multicoloured.
4458 60f. (1) Type **1012** 20 10
4459 60f. (2) 1989 8f. May 4th Movement stamp 20 10
4460 80f. (3) 1991 20f. Chinese Communist Party stamp 30 15
4461 80f. (4) 1995 20f. (No. 4013) End of Second World War and of War against Japan stamp 30 15
4462 80f. (5) 1959 20f. People's Republic anniversary stamp and Mao Tse-tung 30 15
4463 200f. (6) 1989 20f. National Defence stamp 65 45
4464 260f. (7) 1996 500f. Pudong Area of Shanghai stamp 75 50
4465 280f. (8) Deng Xiaoping and fireworks (based on 1997 800f. Return of Hong Kong to China stamp) 85 60

1013 Chinese Dragon

2000. New Year. Year of the Dragon. Each black, gold and red.
4466 80f. Type **1013** 20 15
4467 2y.80 "The Sun Rising in the Eastern Sky" and Chinese character for dragon 85 60

1014 Welcoming the Spring Festival

2000. Spring Festival. Multicoloured.
4468 80f. Type **1014** 20 15
4469 80f. Bidding farewell to the outgoing year 20 15
4470 2y.80 Offering sacrifices to the God of Land 85 60
MS4471 124×84 mm. 8y. Family celebrations (90×59 mm) 6·25 5·25

1015 Japanese Crested Ibis

2000. Wildlife. Sheet 146×213 mm containing T 1015 and similar vert designs. Multicoloured.

MS4472	30f. Type **1015**; 60f. Golden Kaiser-i-hind; 80f. Giant panda; 1y. Brown eared-pheasant; 1y.50 Chinese sturgeon; 2y. Snib-nosed monkey; 2y.60 White flag dolphin; 2y.80 Manchurian crane; 3y.70 Tiger; 5y.40 Chinese alligator	7·25	5·25

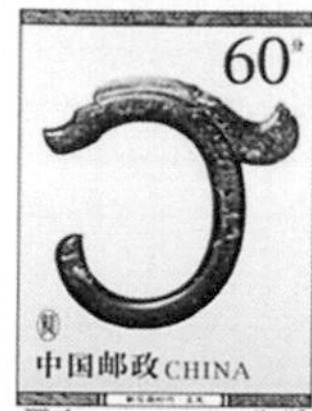

1016 Neolithic Jade Dragon

2000. Chinese Dragon Artefacts. Multicoloured.

4473	60f. (1) Type **1016**	20	15
4474	80f. (2) Dragon-shaped brooch, Warring States	30	15
4475	80f. (3) Eaves tile with carved dragon, Han Dynasty	30	15
4476	80f. (4) Coiled dragon on copper mirror, Tang Dynasty	30	15
4477	80f. (5) Bronze dragon, Jin Dynasty	30	15
4478	2y.80 (6) Dragon decoration from Qing Dynasty Red Sandalwood Throne	85	60

1017 Wanxian Bridge

2000. Road Bridges over the Yangtze River. Mult.

4479	80f. (1) Type **1017**	20	15
4480	80f. (2) Huangshi	20	15
4481	80f. (3) Tongling	20	15
4482	2y.80 (4) Jiangyin	85	60

1018 Cangshan Mountain and Erhai Lake

2000. Landscapes of Dali, Yunnan Province. Mult.

4483	80f. (1) Type **1018**	20	15
4484	80f. (2) Three Pagodas, Chong-sheng Temple	20	15
4485	80f. (3) Jizu Mountain	20	15
4486	2y.80 (4) Shibao Mountain	85	60

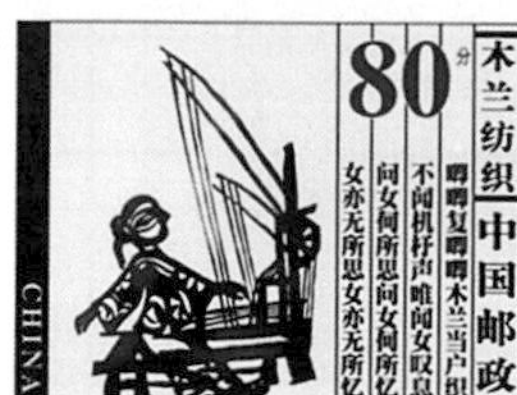

1019 Mulan weaving Cloth

2000. Literature. Mulan (folk tale). Multicoloured.

4487	80f. (1) Type **1019**	30	25
4488	80f. (2) Mulan dressed as male soldier	30	25
4489	80f. (3) Mulan on horseback	30	25
4490	80f. (4) Mulan resuming her female identity	30	25

1020 Good Luck Treasure Pagoda

2000. Taer Lamasery, Qinghai Province. Mult.

4491	80f. (1) Type **1020**	20	15
4492	80f. (2) Big Golden Tile Palace	20	15
4493	80f. (3) Big Scripture Hall	20	15
4494	2y.80 (4) Banqen Residence	85	60

1021 Li Fuchan and Cai Chang

2000. Birth Centenaries of Li Fuchan and Cai Chang (revolutionary couple).

4495	**1021**	80f. black, buff and brown	20	15

1022 "Entering a New Century" (Ling Lifei)

2000. New Millennium. Winning Entries in National Children's "Prospects in the New Century" Stamp Design Competition. Mult.

4496	30f. (1) Type **1022**	10	10
4497	60f. (2) "I Build a Bridge to Connect the Mainland with Taiwan" (Wang Yumeng)	20	15
4498	60f. (3) "Palace in a Tree" (Li Zhao)	20	15
4499	80f. (4) "Protecting the Earth" (Chen Zhuo)	20	15
4500	80f. (5) "Communications in the New Century" (Qin Tian)	20	15
4501	80f. (6) "Space Travel" (Wang Yiru)	20	15
4502	2y.60 (7) "The Earth gets Younger" (Tian Yuan)	75	50
4503	2y.80 (8) "World Peace" (Song Zhili)	85	60

1023 Chen Yun

2000. 95th Birth Anniv of Chen Yun (revolutionary). Multicoloured.

4504	80f. (1) Type **1023**	20	15
4505	80f. (2) Chen Yun wearing white jacket and hat (vert)	20	15
4506	80f. (3) Chen Yun wearing black jacket (vert)	20	15
4507	2y.80 (4) Chen Yun	85	60

1024 He Pot (Chinese wine vessel)

2000. Pots. Multicoloured.

4508	80f. (1) Type **1024**	30	15
4509	80f. (2) Koumiss (fermented mare's milk flask)	30	15

Stamps in similar designs were issued by Kazakhstan.

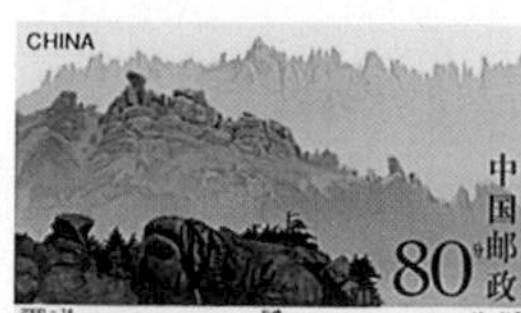

1025 Great Peak

2000. Laoshan Mountain. Multicoloured.

4510	80f. (1) Type **1025**	20	15
4511	80f. (2) Yangkou Bay	20	15
4512	80f. (3) Beijiu Lake	20	15
4513	2y.80 (4) Taiqing Palace	85	60
MS4514	153×82 mm. Nos. 4510/13	6·25	5·25

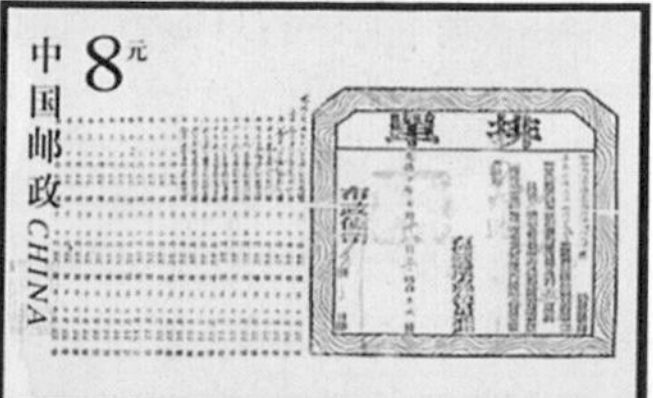

1026 Chinese Characters

2000. 5th Philatelic Federation Congress, Peking. Sheet 130×80 mm.

MS4515	8y. multicoloured	6·25	5·25

1027 Grandma Carp telling a Story

2000. Small Carp Leap Through Dragon Gate (children's story). Multicoloured.

4516	80f. (1) Type **1027**	40	35
4517	80f. (2) Searching for Dragon Gate	40	35
4518	80f. (3) Uncle Crab helping Carp	40	35
4519	80f. (4) Carp leaping through Dragon Gate	40	35
4520	80f. (5) Aunt Swallow delivering a letter	40	35

1028 Financial Central District

2000. Shenzhen Special Economic Zone. Mult.

4526	80f. (1) Type **1028**	30	15
4527	80f. (2) China International New and Hi-Tech Achievement Fair Exhibition Centre	30	15
4528	80f. (3) Yantian Harbour	30	15
4529	80f. (4) Shenzhen Bay	30	15
4530	2y.80 (5) Shekou Industrial District	85	60

1029 "2000" and Olympic Rings (image scaled to 55% of original size)

2000. Olympic Games, Sydney. Sheet 122×82 mm.

MS4531	8y. multicoloured	4·50	3·75

1030 Coconut Forest Bay, Hainan

2000. 40th Anniv of China–Cuba Diplomatic Relations. Multicoloured.

4532	80f. (1) Type **1030**	30	15
4533	80f. (2) Varadero beach, Matanzas, Cuba	30	15

Stamps in similar designs were issued by Cuba.

1031 Puppets

2000. Masks and Puppets. Multicoloured.

4534	80f. (1) Type **1031**	30	15
4535	80f. (2) Carnival masks	30	15

1032 "Eternal Fidelity" Palace Lamp

2000. Relics from Tomb of Liu Sheng. Multicoloured.

4536	80f. (1) Type **1032**	30	15
4537	80f. (2) Bronze pot with dragon design	30	15
4538	80f. (3) Boshan incense burner with gold inlay	30	15
4539	2y.80 (4) Rosefinch-shaped cup	85	60

1033 Confucius

2000. Ancient Thinkers. Each black, red and brown.

4540	60f. (1) Type **1033**	20	15
4541	80f. (2) Mencius	30	15
4542	80f. (3) Lao Zi	30	15
4543	80f. (4) Zhuang Zi	30	15
4544	80f. (5) Mo Zi	30	15
4545	2y.80 (6) Xun Zi	85	60

1034 Launch of *Shenzhou*

2000. Test Flight of Shenzhou (spacecraft). Mult.

4546	80f. Type **1034**	30	25
4547	80f. Orbiting Earth	30	25

1035 Meteorological Satellite

2000. 50th Anniv of World Meteorological Organization. Multicoloured.

4548	80f. (1) Type **1035**	30	15
4549	80f. (2) Meteorological equipment and Qinghai–Tibet plateau	30	15
4550	80f. (3) Computers and numbers	30	15
4551	2y.80 (4) Airplane and wind flow diagram	85	60

1036 Scarlet Kaffir Lily

2000. Flowers. Multicoloured.

4552	80f. (1) Type **1036**	30	15
4553	80f. (2) Noble clivia	30	15
4554	80f. (3) Golden striat kaffir lily	30	15
4555	2y.80 (4) White kaffir lily	85	60
MS4556	145×115 mm. Nos. 4552/5	7·25	6·00

1037 Jingshu Bell, Western Zhou Dynasty

2000. Ancient Bells. Multicoloured.

4557	80f. (1) Type **1037**	30	15
4558	80f. (2) Su chime bell, Spring and Autumn Period	30	15
4559	80f. (3) Jingyun bell, Tang Dynasty	30	15
4560	2y.80 (4) Qianlong bell, Qing Dynasty	85	60

1038 Sun, Moon and Observatory

2001. New Millennium. Multicoloured.

4561	60f. (1) Type **1038**	20	15
4562	80f. (2) Globe and white dove	30	15
4563	80f. (3) Child's hands, leaf and World map (horiz)	30	15
4564	80f. (4) Silhouette of head and circuit board (horiz)	30	15
4565	2y.80 (5) Sun, stars and sundial	85	60

1039 Snake

2001. New Year. Year of the Snake. Multicoloured.

4566	80f. Type **1039**	30	25
4567	2y.80 "Fortune Illuminates all Things" and Chinese character for snake	85	70

1040 Tang Qin

2001. Chou (Clown) Roles in Peking Opera. Multicoloured.

4568	80f. (1) Type **1040**	30	25
4569	80f. (2) Liu Lihua	30	25
4570	80f. (3) Gao Lishi	30	25
4571	80f. (4) Jiang Gan	30	25
4572	80f. (5) Yang Xiangwu	30	25
4573	2y.80 (6) Shi Qian	85	70

1041 Takin

2001. Wildlife (2nd series). Sheet 146×212 mm containing T 1041 and similar vert designs. Multicoloured.

MS4574	30f. Type **1041**; 60f. Chinese paddle-fish; 60f. Pere David's deer; 80f. Yangtze sturgeon; 80f. Ibex; 80f. Steller's sea eagle; 80f. Bactrian camel; 1y. Snow leopard; 2y.60 Sable; 5y.40 Saiga	11·50	9·50

1042 Zhouzhuang, Kunshan

2001. Ancient Towns, Taihu Lake Valley. Multicoloured.

4575	80f. (1) Type **1042**	30	25
4576	80f. (2) Tongli, Wujiang	30	25
4577	80f. (3) Wuzhen, Tongziang	30	25
4578	80f. (4) Nanxun, Huzhou	30	25
4579	80f. (5) Luzhi, Wuxian	30	25
4580	2y.80 (6) Xitang, Jiashan	1·00	85

1043 "Ying Ning"

2001. Classical Literature. Strange Stories from a Chinese Studio by Pu Songling. Multicoloured.

4581	60f. (1) Type **1043**	20	15
4582	80f. (2) "A Bao"	40	35
4583	80f. (3) "Mask of Evildoer"	40	35
4584	2y.80 (4) "Stealing Peach"	1·00	85
MS4585	144×85 mm. 8y. "A Taoist of Laoshan" (86×57 mm)	12·50	10·50

1044 Queen Mother (detail)

2001. Yongle Temple Murals, Shanxi. "Portrait of Paying Homage to Xianyuan Emperor". Multicoloured.

4586	60f. (1) Type **1044**	20	15
4587	80f. (2) Jade Lady presenting treasure	30	25
4588	80. (3) Celestial Worthy of the East	30	25
4589	2y.80 (4) Venus and Mercury	1·00	85

1045 Nanyan Hall in Autumn

2001. Mount Wudang, Hubei Province. Multicoloured.

4590	60f. (1) Type **1045**	20	15
4591	80f. (2) Zixiao Temple in winter	30	25
4592	80f. (3) Taizi slope in summer	30	25
MS4593	150×90 mm. 8y. Golden Crown and buildings in spring (47×72 mm)	9·00	7·50

1046 Pottery Vase

2001. Chinese Pottery. Multicoloured.

4594	80f. (1) Type **1046**	30	25
4595	80f. (2) Teapot	30	25

1047 Dragon Boat Race

2001. Duanwu Dragon Boat Festival. Multicoloured.

4596	80f. (1) Type **1047**	30	25
4597	80f. (2) Vase, mobile and flowers	30	25
4598	2y.80 (3) Dragon's head and expulsion of five poisons	1·00	85

1048 Wang Jinmei

2001. Leaders of the Chinese Communist Party. Multicoloured.

4599	80f. (1) Type **1048**	30	25
4600	80f. (2) Zhao Shiyan	30	25
4601	80f. (3) Deng Enming	30	25
4602	80f. (4) Cai Hesen	30	25
4603	80f. (5) He Shuheng	30	25

1049 Party Flag

2001. 80th Anniv of Chinese Communist Party.

4604	**1049**	80f. red, yellow and black	30	25

1050 Emblem

2001. Choice of Beijing as 2008 Olympic Host City.

4605	**1050**	80f. multicoloured	50	45

1051 Yinlianzhuitan Waterfall

2001. Waterfalls. Multicoloured.

4606	80f. (1) Type **1051**	30	25
4607	80f. (2) Doupotang Waterfall (horiz)	30	25
4608	80f. (3) Dishuitan Waterfall	30	25
MS4609	124×84 mm. 8y. Huangguoshu Waterfall (39×59 mm)	6·25	5·25

1052 Pigeon Nest

2001. Beidaihe Summer Resort. Multicoloured.

4610	60f. (1) Type **1052**	20	15
4611	80f. (2) Umbrellas, Zhonghai Beach	30	25
4612	80f. (3) Sailing dinghies, Lianfeng Hill	30	25
4613	2y.80 Windsurfers, Tiger Stone	1·00	85

1053 "2001" and Emblem

2001. 21st World University Games, Beijing. Multicoloured.

4614	60f. Type **1053**	20	15
4615	80f. "2001" and sports pictograms	30	25
4616	2y.80 "2001" and globes	1·00	85

1054 Water Diversion Canal

2001. Datong River Diversion Project. Mult.

4617	80f. (1) Type **1054**	30	25
4618	80f. (2) Overland pipes, Xianming Gorge	30	25
4619	80f. (3) Canal tunnel	30	25
4620	2y.80 (4) Aqueduct, Zhuanglang River	1·00	85

1055 Wuhu Bridge over Yangtze River

2001. Wuhu Bridge. Multicoloured.

4621	80f. Type **1055**	30	25
4622	2y.80 Road section of Wuhu Bridge	1·00	85

1056 *Paphiopedilum malipoense*

2001. Orchids. Multicoloured.

4623	80f. (1) Type **1056**	30	25
4624	80f. (2) *Paphiopedilum dianthum*	30	25
4625	80f. (3) *Paphiopedilum markianum*	30	25
4626	2y.80 (4) *Paphiopedilum appletonianum*	1·00	85
MS4627	145×95 mm. Nos. 4623/6	7·25	6·00

1057 Mask of San Xing Dui

2001. Golden Masks. Multicoloured.

4628	80f. Type **1057**	40	35
4629	80f. Mask of Tutankhamun	40	35

Stamps in similar designs were also issued by Egypt.

1058 Emblem

2001. 9th Asia Pacific Economic Co-operation Conference, Shanghai.

4630	**1058**	80f. multicoloured	30	25

1059 Ertan Hydroelectric Power Station (image scaled to 54% of original size)

2001. Sheet 150×85 mm.

MS4631	**1059** 8y. multicoloured	3·75	3·25

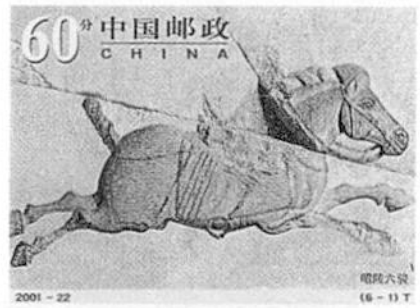

1060 Horse galloping

2001. Six Steeds (relief sculptures), Zhaoling Mausoleum. Multicoloured.

4632	60f. (1) Type **1060**	30	25
4633	80f. (2) Galloping	40	35
4634	80f. (3) Trotting	40	35
4635	80f. (4) With rider	40	35
4636	80f. (5) Trotting	40	35
4637	2y.80 (6) Galloping	1·30	1·00

1061 Chinese Junk

2001. Ancient Sailing Craft. Multicoloured.

4638	80f. Type **1061**	30	25
4639	80f. Portuguese caravel	30	25

Stamps in the same design were issued by Portugal.

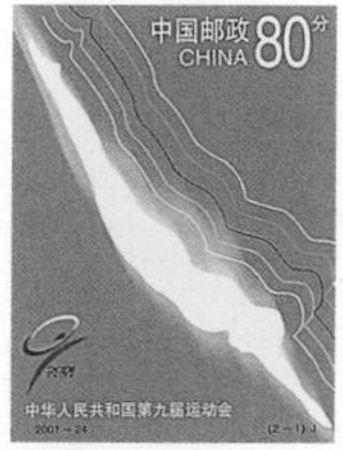

1062 Diving

2001. 9th National Games, Guangzhou. Mult.

4640	80f. Type **1062**	30	25
4641	2y.80 Volleyball	1·30	1·00
MS4642	140×90 mm. Nos. 4640/1	4·75	4·00

1063 Liupanshan Mountains

2001. Liupanshan Mountains. Multicoloured.

4643	80f. (1) Type **1063**	30	25
4644	80f. (2) Forest, Liangdianxia Gorge	30	25
4645	80f. (3) Old Dragon Pool, Jinghe River	30	25
4646	2y.80 (4) Wild Lotus Valley, West Gorge	1·30	1·00

1064 Lending an Umbrella by the Lake

2001. Tale of Xu Xian and the White Snake. Multicoloured.

4647	80f. (1) Type **1064**	30	25
4648	80f. (2) Stealing the Immortal Grass	30	25
4649	80f. (3) Flooding the Jinshan Hill	30	25
4650	2y.80 (4) Meeting at the Broken Bridge	1·30	1·00

1065 Emblem

2001. China's Membership of World Trade Organization.

4651	**1065** 80f. multicoloured	1·60	1·30

1066 Zheng's advancing Fleet

2001. 340th Anniv of Zheng Chenggong's Seizure of Formosa (Taiwan) from Dutch Colonists. Each drab, black and red.

4652	80f. (1) Type **1066**	30	25
4653	80f. (2) Populace offering troops food and water	30	25
4654	2y.80 Zheng viewing island	1·30	1·00

1067 Engineers and Route of Railway (image scaled to 62% of original size)

2001. Construction of the Qinghai--Tibet Railway. Sheet 135×114 mm.

MS4655	**1067** 8y. multicoloured	6·25	5·25

1068 Horse

2002. New Year. Year of the Horse. Multicoloured.

4656	80f. Type **1068**	40	35
4657	2y.80 Chinese character for horse	1·50	1·20

1069 "A Couple of Eagles"

2002. Paintings by Badashanren. Multicoloured.

4658	60f. (1) Type **1069**	30	25
4659	80f. (2) "A Single Pine Tree"	40	35
4660	80f. (3) "Lotus Flowers"	40	35
4661	80f. (4) "Chrysanthemum in a Vase"	40	35
4662	2y.60 (5) "A Couple of Magpies on a Rock"	1·40	1·10
4663	2y.80 (6) "Landscape after Dong Yuan's Style"	1·50	1·20

1070 Forest Protection

2002. Environmental Protection. Multicoloured.

4664	5f. Maintaining low birth rate	10	10
4665	10f. Type **1070**	10	10
4666	30f. Mineral resources protection	20	15
4667	50f. Desert (desertification) control and prevention	20	15
4668	60f. Air pollution prevention	30	25
4670	80f. Water resources protection	40	35
4673	1y.50 Ocean protection	85	70
4674	4y.50 Bird, globe and water (biodiversity protection)	1·40	1·10

1071 Yellow-bellied Tragopan

2002. Birds. Multicoloured.

4674a	40f. Chinese monal pheasant	10	10
4675	80f. Type **1071**	40	35
4676	1y. Biddulph's ground jay	50	45
4676a	1y.20 Taiwan yuhina	20	10
4677	2y. Taiwan blue magpie	1·00	85
4680	4y.20 Przewalski's redstart	2·00	1·70
4682	5y. Yellow bellied tit	1·60	1·30
4683	5y.40 Koslow's bunting	2·50	2·10
4684	6y. Yunnan nuthatch	1·80	1·50

1072 Golden Camellia (*Camellia nitidissima*)

2002. Flowers. Multicoloured.

4690	80f. Type **1072**	40	35
4691	80f. Cannonball tree flower (*Couroupita guianensis*)	40	35

Stamps showing similar subjects were issued by Malaysia.

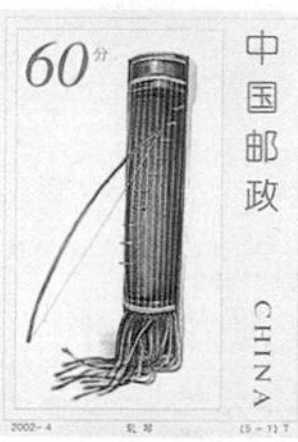

1073 Yaqin

2002. Stringed Musical Instruments. Multicoloured.

4692	60f. (1) Type **1073**	30	25
4693	80f. (2) Erhu	40	35
4694	80f. (3) Banhu	40	35
4695	80f. (4) Satar	40	35
4696	2y.80 (5) Matouqin	1·60	1·30

1074 "The Royal Carriage" (Yan Liben) (image scaled to 34% of original size)

2002. Sheet 160×82 mm.

MS4697	**1074** 8y. multicoloured	3·50	3·00

1075 Wine Vessel

2002. Northern Song Dynasty Ceramics. Mult.

4698	60f. (1) Type **1075**	30	25
4699	80f. (2) Three-legged basin	35	30
4700	80f. (3) Bowl	35	30
4701	2y.80 (4) Dish	1·30	1·00

2001. Classical Literature. Strange Stories from a Chinese Studio by Pu Songling (2nd series). Vert designs as T 1043. Multicoloured.

4702	60f. (1) "Xi Fangping"	30	25
4703	80f. (2) "Pianpian"	35	30
4704	80f. (3) "Tian Qilang"	35	30
4705	2y.80 (4) "Bai Qiulian"	1·30	1·00

1076 Wuliang Taoist Temple

2002. Qianshan Mountain. Views of the mountain. Multicoloured.

4706	80f. (1) Type **1076**	35	30
4707	80f. (2) Maitreya peak	35	30
4708	80f. (3) Longquan temple	35	30
4709	2y.80 (4) "Terrace of the Immortals" (peak)	1·30	1·00

Nos. 4706/9 were issued together, se-tenant, forming a composite design.

1077 Sifang Street

2002. Lijiang City.

4710	**1077**	80f. red	30	25
4711	-	80f. green (vert)	30	25
4712	-	2y.80 blue	1·30	1·00
MS4713	145×101 mm Nos. 4710/12		2·75	2·30

DESIGNS: 80f. Bridges over city river; 2y.80, Traditional Naxi house.

1078 Ruyi (good luck symbol)

2002. Greetings Stamp.

4714	**1078** 80f. multicoloured	50	45

1079 Footballer

2002. World Cup Football Championship, Japan and South Korea. Multicoloured.

4715	80f. Type **1079**	30	25
4716	2y. Players tackling	95	80

1080 Maota Pagoda Lighthouse

2002. Lighthouses.

4717	**1080**	80f. (1) black and green	30	25
4718	-	80f. (2) black and ochre	30	25
4719	-	80f. (3) black and grey	30	25
4720	-	80f. (4) black, brown and orange	30	25
4721	-	80f. (5) black and red	30	25

DESIGNS: 80f. (2) Jianxin pagoda lighthouse; 80f. (3) Hua-niaoshan; 80f. (4) Laotieshan; 80f. (5) Lin'gao.

1081 Lijia Gorge Hydro-electric Power Station

2002. Hydro-electric Power Generation and Water Control on the Yellow River. Multicoloured.

4722	80f. (1) Type **1081**	30	25
4723	80f. (2) Liujia Gorge Hydro-electric Power Station	30	25
4724	80f. (3) Qingtong Gorge dam	30	25
4725	80f. (4) Sanmen Gorge dam	30	25
MS4726	115×96 mm 8y. Xiaolangdi dam (39×59 mm)	3·25	2·75

1082 "Avalokitesvara of the Sun and Moon"

2002. Stone Carvings, Dazu County, Sichuan Province. Multicoloured.

4727	80f. (1) Type **1082**	30	25
4728	80f. (2) Samantabhadra riding elephant, North Mountain	30	25
4729	80f. (3) Three Avatama-saka Sages, Holy Summit Mountain	30	25
4730	80f. (4) Man wearing head-dress (statue), Cave of the Three Emperors, Stone Gate Mountain	30	25
MS4731	130×96 mm 8y. "Avalokitesvara of a Thousand Hands" (39×59 mm)	3·25	2·75

1083 *Ammopiptanthus mongolicus*

2002. Desert Plants. Multicoloured.

4732	80f. (1) Type **1083**	30	25
4733	80f. (2) *Calligonum rubicundum*	30	25
4734	80f. (3) *Hedysarum scoparium*	30	25
4735	2y. (4) *Tamarix leptostachys*	95	80

1084 Emperor Penguins

2002. Antarctica. Multicoloured.

4736	80f. Type **1084**	30	25
4737	80f. Aurora Australis	30	25
4738	2y. Grove mountain, scientists and snowy sheathbill	95	80

1085 Shepherd on Horse-back, Sheep and Lakeside

2002. Qinghai Lake. Multicoloured.

4739	80f. Type **1085**	30	25
4740	80f. Bird island	30	25
4741	2y.80 Lake and mountain	1·30	1·00

1086 Huang Gonglue

2002. Early 20th-century Generals. Multicoloured.

4742	80f. (1) Type **1086**	30	25
4743	80f. (2) Xu Jishen	30	25
4744	80f. (3) Cai Shengxi	30	25
4745	80f. (4) Wei Baqun	30	25
4746	80f. (5) Liu Zhidan	30	25

1087 Bian Que

2002. Early Chinese Scientists.

4747	**1087**	80f. (1) grey and black	30	25
4748	-	80f. (2) grey and black	30	25
4749	-	80f. (3) grey and black	30	25
4750	-	80f. (4) stone and black	30	25

DESIGNS: 80f. (1) Type **1087**; 80f. (2) Lui Hui; 80f. (3) Su Song; 80f. (4) Song Yingxing.

1088 Xianshengmen Gate

2002. Yandang Mountain. Multicoloured.

4751	80f. (1) Type **1088**	30	25
4752	80f. (2) Dalongqiu waterfall and pond	30	25
4753	80f. (3) Beidou cave (horiz)	30	25
4754	80f. (4) Guanyin peak (horiz)	30	25

1089 Large Family Gathering

2002. Mid-autumn Festival. Multicoloured.

4755	80f. (1) Type **1089**	30	25
4756	80f. (2) Food and couple with daughter	30	25
4757	2y. (3) Courting couple with birds perched on knees	85	70

1090 Peng Zhen

2002. Birth Centenary of Peng Zhen (revolutionary leader).

4758	**1090**	80f. brown, cinnamon and black	30	25
4759	-	80f. sepia, cinnamon and black	30	25

DESIGNS: 80f. Type **1090**; 80f. In army uniform.

1091 Bojnice Castle

2002. Castles. Multicoloured.

4760	80f. Type **1091**	30	25
4761	80f. Congtai Pavilion, Handan	30	25

Nos. 4760/1 were issued together, se-tenant, forming a composite design.

Stamps of a similar design were issued by Slovakia.

1092 Immortal Maiden moved by Dong's Filial Love

2002. Tale of Dong Yong and the Seventh Immortal Maiden. Multicoloured.

4762	80f. (1) Type **1092**	30	25
4763	80f. (2) Seventh immortal maiden marrying Dong Yong	30	25
4764	80f. (3) Maiden weaving brocade to buy Dong Yong's freedom	30	25
4765	80f. (4) Everlasting love	30	25
4766	2y. (5) Maiden returned to Heaven leaving Dong Yong behind	85	70

1093 Flowers

2002. Greetings Stamp. Paper with fluorescent fibres.

4767	**1093**	80f. multicoloured	50	45

1094 Waterfalls on the Yellow River

2002. Hukou Waterfalls. Sheet 131×90 mm.

MS4768	**1094**	8y. multicoloured	3·25	2·50

1095 Shanxi History Museum

2002. Museums. Multicoloured.

4769	80f. (1) Type **1095**	30	25
4770	80f. (2) Shanghai	30	25
4771	80f. (3) Henan	30	25
4772	80f. (4) Tibet	30	25
4773	80f. (5) Tianjin Natural History museum	30	25

1096 Kung Fu

2002. Martial Arts. Multicoloured.

4774	80f. (1) Type **1096**	30	25
4775	80f. (2) Tae Kwon Do	30	25

1097 White-handed Gibbon (*Hylobates lar*)

2002. Gibbons. Multicoloured.

4776	80f. (1) Type **1097**	30	25
4777	80f. (2) White-cheeked gibbon (*Hylobates leucogenys*)	30	25
4778	80f. (3) Black gibbon (*Hylobates concolor*)	30	25
4779	2y. (4) Hoolock gibbon (*Hylobates hoolock*)	85	70

1098 Goat

2003. New Year. Year of the Goat. Multicoloured.

4780	80f. Type **1098**	25	20
4781	2y.80 Chinese character for goat	65	50

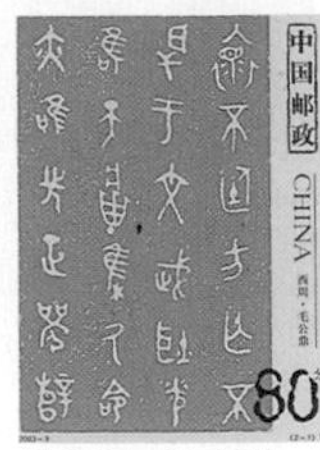

1099 "Five Boys wrestling for a Lotus"

2003. Yangliuqing New Year Pictures (woodcut prints). Multicoloured.

4782	80f. (1) Type **1099**	25	20
4783	80f. (2) "Zhong Kui" (vert)	25	20
4784	80f. (3) "Stealing the Herb of Immortality"	25	20
4785	2y. (4) "Wealth in a Jade Hall" (vert)	65	50

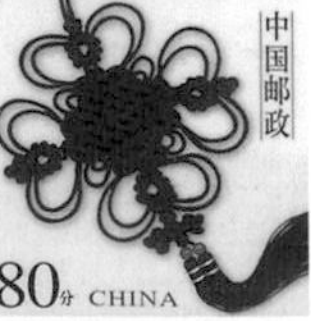

1100 Duke Mao's Tripod (Western Zhou dynasty)

2003. Calligraphy. Seal Characters. Multicoloured.

4786	80f. Type **1100**	30	25
4787	80f. Carvings of Mount Tai (Qin dynasty)	30	25

1101 Knot

2003. Greetings Stamp. Chinese Decorative Knot.
4788 **1101** 80f. multicoloured 30 25

1102 Lily (*Lilium taliense*)

2003. Greetings Stamps. Lilies. Multicoloured.
4789 60f. (1) Type **1102** 20 15
4790 80f. (2) *Lilium lanongense* 25 20
4791 80f. (3) *Lilium distichum* 25 20
4792 2y. (4) *Lilium lophophorum* 65 50
MS4793 140×95 mm. 8y. *Lilium leucanthum* (76×54 mm) 2·50 2·10

1103 Maple Bridge, Suzhou, Jiangsu Province

2003. Ancient Bridges. Multicoloured.
4794 80f. (1) Type **1103** 25 20
4795 80f. (2) Xiaoshang bridge, Linying, Henan province 25 20
4796 80f. (3) Lugouqiao bridge, Beijing 25 20
4797 80f. (4) Double Dragon bridge, Jianshui, Yunnan province 25 20

1104 Bell Tower, Xi'an

2003. Buildings. Multicoloured.
4798 80f. Type **1104** 25 20
4799 80f. Mosque, Isfahan 25 20
Stamps of the same design were issued by Iran.

1105 Giant Buddha (statue, Lingyun mountain, Leshan province)

2003. UNESCO World Heritage Sites. Sheet 145×90 mm.
MS4800 **1105** 8y. multicoloured 2·30 1·90

1106 Eight Diagram Buildings, Gulangyu Island

2003. Gulangyu Island, Fujian Province. Multicoloured.
4801 80f. Type **1106** 25 20
4802 80f. Sunlight rock 25 20
4803 2y. Shuzhuang park 65 50
MS4804 180×80 mm. Nos. 4801/3 1·60 1·30
Nos. 4801/3 were issued together, se-tenant, forming a composite design of the island.

2003. Classical Literature. Strange Stories from a Chinese Studio by Pu Songling (3rd series). As T 1043. Multicoloured.
4805 10f. (1) "Xiang Yu" 20 15
4806 30f. (2) "Tiger of Zhaocheng" 20 15
4807 60f. (3) "Tian Qilang" 20 15
4808 80f. (4) "Ah Xiu" 30 25
4809 1y.50 (5) "Wang Gui'an" 50 45
4810 2y. (6) "Goddess" 65 50

MS4811 144×85 mm. 8y. "Princess of the Dongting Lake" (90×60 mm) 2·50 2·10

1107 "SARS" overprinted with Stop Sign

2003. Campaign to Control Severe Acute Respiratory Syndrome (SARS).
4812 **1107** 80f. multicoloured 20 15

1108 Meteorites descending

2003. Meteorite Shower over Jilin Province, (8 March 1976). Multicoloured.
4813 80f. Type **1108** 20 15
4814 80f. Dispersal 20 15
4815 2y. Meteorite No. 1 (largest ever found) 65 50

1109 Late Spring Cottage

2003. Master-of-Nets Garden, Suzhou. Multicoloured.
4816 80f. (1) Type **1109** 20 15
4817 80f. (2) Pavilion Greeting the Moon and Breeze 20 15
4818 80f. (3) Veranda of Bamboo 20 15
4819 2y. (4) Hall of Ten Thousand Volumes 65 50
Nos. 4816/19 were issued together, se-tenant, forming a composite design.

1110 Antelopes

2003. Endangered Species. Tibetan Antelope (Pantholops hodgsoni). Multicoloured.
4820 80f. Type **1110** 20 15
4821 2y. Female and fawn 65 50

1111 Huangcheng (town)

2003. Kongtong Mountain, Gansu Province. Multicoloured.
4822 80f. (1) Type **1111** 20 15
4823 80f. (2) Playing the Zither Gorge 20 15
4824 80f. (3) Pagoda Courtyard 20 15
4825 2y. (4) Thunder Peak 65 50
Nos. 4822/5 were issued together, se-tenant, forming a composite design.

1112 Junk (sailing ship)

2003. Greetings Stamp. "Plain Sailing".
4826 **1112** 80f. multicoloured 40 35

1113 Concorde

2003. Centenary of Powered Flight.
4827 80f. Type **1113** 20 15
4828 2y. Chinese aircraft 65 50

1114 Ruyi Maid

2003. Painted Statues, Jinci Temple, Shanxi Province. Multicoloured.
4829 80f. (1) Type **1114** 20 15
4830 80f. (2) Maid holding towel 20 15
4831 80f. (3) Maid carrying seal 20 15
4832 2y. (4) Maid smiling 65 50

1115 Dam and Reservoir

2003. Three Gorges Hydroelectric Project on Yangtze River. Multicoloured.
4833 80f. (1) Type **1115** 20 15
4834 80f. (2) Navigation locks 20 15
4835 2y. (3) Electricity pylons 65 50

2003. Regional Traditional Sports. Multicoloured.
4836 80f. (1) Type **1116** 30 25
4837 80f. (2) Archery 30 25
4838 80f. (3) Horse racing 30 25
4839 80f. (4) Swinging 30 25
MS4840 120×80 mm Nos. 4836/40 1·60 1·30

1117 Tian'anmen Gate

2003
4841 **1117** 80f. multicoloured 40 35

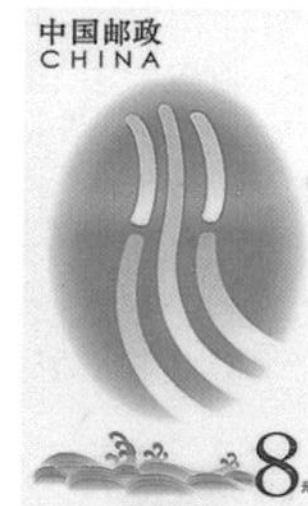

1118 Mother tattooing Back

2003. 900th Birth Anniv of General Yue Fei (Pengju). Multicoloured.
4842 80f. Type **1118** 30 25
4843 80f. Wearing armour 30 25
4844 2y. Reading 65 50

1119 Stylized Water

2003. Inauguration of Water Diversion Project. Sheet 126×80 mm.
MS4845 8y. multicoloured 2·50 2·10

1120 The Book of Zhou Rites

2003. Ancient Books. Multicoloured.
4846 80f. (1) Type **1120** 30 25
4847 80f. The Illuminated Chronicle 30 25
Stamps of a similar design were issued by Hungary.

1121 Climbing Mountain

2003. Double Ninth (ninth day of ninth month) Festival. Multicoloured.
4848 80f. (1) Type **1121** 30 25
4849 80f. (2) Looking at flowers 30 25
4850 2y. Playing chess and drinking tea 65 50

1122 Astronaut and Satellite

2003. 1st Chinese Manned Space Flight. Multicoloured.
4851 80f. Type **1122** 20 15
4852 1y. Astronaut and flag 65 50

1123 Swearing Brotherhood

2003. Folk Tales. Liang Shanbo and Zhu Yingtai. Multicoloured.
4853 80f. (1) Type **1123** 20 15
4854 80f. (2) As classmates 20 15
4855 80f. (3) Saying goodbye 20 15
4856 80f. (4) On terrace 20 15
4857 2y. Turning into butterflies 75 60

1124 Bronze Horse

2003. China 2003, 16th Asia International Stamp Exhibition.
4858 **1124** 80f. multicoloured 30 25

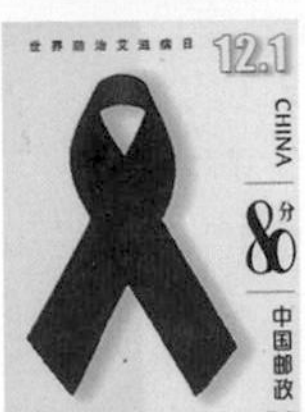

1125 Ribbon

2003. World AIDS Awareness Day.

4859	**1125**	80f. rose and black	30	25

1126 Seated in Deckchair

2003. 110th Birth Anniv of Mao Zedong (Communist Party Chairman). Each brown and black.

4860	80f. (1) Type **1126**	30	25
4861	80f. (2) Wearing coat and hat	30	25
4862	80f. (3) Seated on bench	30	25
4863	80f. (4) Writing	30	25

1127 Rectangular Dish

2003. Eastern Zhou Dynasty Bronze Ware. Multicoloured.

4864	60f. (1) Type **1127**	20	15
4865	60f. (2) Gui (round dish)	20	15
4866	80f. (3) Iron tripod	20	15
4867	80f. (4) Gourd-shaped ladle	20	15
4868	80f. (5) Animal shaped wine vessel (vert)	20	15
4869	80f. (6) Wine vessel (vert)	20	15
4870	1y. Square pot with applied decoration (vert)	40	35
4871	2y. Bronze tripod with dragon-shaped handle (vert)	65	50

1128 Monkey

2004. New Year. "Year of the Monkey".

4872	**1128**	80f. multicoloured	20	15
MS4873		129×182 mm. No. 4872×6	9·50	7·75

1129 "Feelings of Pipa"

2004. Taohuawu New Year Pictures (woodcut prints). Multicoloured.

4874	80f. (1) Type **1129**	20	15
4875	80f. (2) "Kyliin bringing a Son"	20	15
4876	80f. (3) "Liu Hai playing with the Golden Toad"	20	15
4877	2y. (4) "Ten Beauties playing Football"	65	50
MS4878	159×90 mm. Nos. 4874/7	1·40	1·10

1130 Deng Yingchao

2004. Birth Centenary of Deng Yingchao (politician). Multicoloured.

4879	80f. Type **1130**	20	15
4880	80f. Wearing glasses	20	15

1131 "Harmony" Sculpture and Suzhou Industrial Park

2004. 10th Anniv of Suzhou Industrial Park.

4881	**1131**	80f. multicoloured	20	15

A stamp of the same design was issued by Singapore.

1132 Red Crosses

2004. Centenary of China Red Cross Society.

4882	**1132**	80f. rose, black and gold	20	15

1133 "Trying to Learn the Handan Walk"

2004. Idioms. Multicoloured.

4883	80f. (1) Type **1133**	30	25
4884	80f. (2) "Lord Ye's love for Dragon"	30	25
4885	80f. (3) "Filling a Position in Yu Band"	30	25
4886	80f. (4) "When the Snipe and Clam Grapple"	30	25

1134 Peacock

2004. Peafowl. Multicoloured.

4887	80f. Type **1134**	30	25
4888	80f. White peacock (vert)	30	25
MS4889	120×99 mm. 6y. Peahen and peacock with tail displayed (60×40 mm)	1·90	1·60

1135 Mouth of River

2004. Nanxi River, Zhejiang Province. Showing views of the river. Multicoloured.

4890	60f. (1) Type **1135**	20	15
4891	80f. (2) Trees and boat	20	15
4892	80f. (3) Rock and small craft	20	15
4893	2y. (4) Small craft and inlets	50	45

Nos. 4890/3 were issued together, se-tenant, forming a composite design.

1136 Sengmao Peak

2004. Danxia Mountain, Guangdong Province. Views of the mountain. Multicoloured.

4894	60f. (1) Type **1136**	20	15
4895	80f. (2) Xianglong lake	20	15
4896	80f. (3) Chahu peak	20	15
4897	2y. (4) Jinjiang river	50	45

1137 Sky Scrapers

2004. 20th Anniv of Economic and Technological Development Zones.

4898	**1137**	80f. multicoloured	20	15

1138 Xianglong Farm

2004. Returning Emigrants Hometowns. Multicoloured.

4899	80f. (1) Type **1138**	30	25
4900	80f. (2) Jinan university	30	25
4901	80f. (3) Fuqing Rongqiao development zone	30	25
4902	80f. (4) Kaiping hometown	30	25

1139 "Fallen into Water"

2004. "Sima Guang breaking the Vat". Multicoloured.

4903	80f. (1) Type **1139**	20	15
4904	80f. (2) "Breaking the Vat"	20	15
4905	2y. (3) "Rescued"	75	60

1140 Ming Dynasty Decorated Arch, Xidi

2004. Ancient Villages, Anhui Province. Multicoloured.

4906	80f. (1) Type **1140**	30	25
4907	80f. (2) Curved roofs	30	25
4908	80f. (3) Buildings and lake	30	25
4909	80f. (4) Moon, buildings and pond	30	25

1141 "Dragon Princess asking Liu to Deliver Letter"

2004. "Liu Delivers a Letter". Multicoloured.

4910	80f. (1) Type **1141**	20	15
4911	80f. (2) "Delivering letter to Dongting Lake"	20	15
4912	80f. (3) "Family Reunion"	20	15
4913	80f. (4) "Mutual Love"	75	60

1142 "Eight Immortals Crossing the Sea" (⅓-size illustration)

2004. "Eight Immortals Crossing the Sea" (folk tale). Sheet 156×82 mm.

MS4914	6y. multicoloured	1·90	1·60

1143 Temple of Heaven, Beijing

2004. Olympic Games, Athens 2004–Beijing 2008. Multicoloured.

4915	80f. Type **1143**	30	25
4916	80f. Parthenon, Athens	30	25

Stamps of the same design were issued by Greece.

1144 Deng Xiaoping

2004. Birth Centenary of Deng Xiaoping (leader of China, 1978–89). Multicoloured.

4917	80f. Type **1144**	30	25
4918	80f. Saluting (horiz)	30	25
MS4919	90×130 mm. 6y. Seated (50×60 mm)	1·90	1·60

1145 South China Tiger

2004. South China Tiger (Panthera tigris amoyensis). Multicoloured.

4920	80f. Type **1145**	20	15
4921	2y. Mother and cubs	50	45

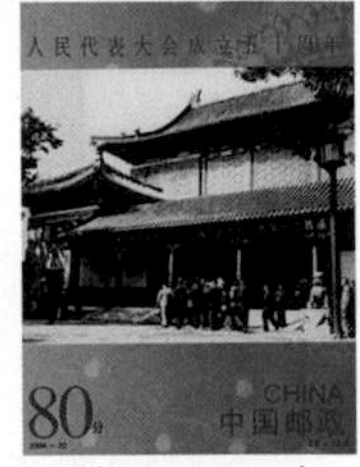

1146 Huairentang and Participants of First Meeting

2004. 50th Anniv of People's Congress. Multicoloured.

4922	80f. Type **1146**	20	15
4923	80f. Auditorium	20	15

1147 Emperor Qianlong's Seal

2004. Bloodstone Seals. Multicoloured.

4924	80f. Type **1147**	20	15
4925	2y. Emperor Jiaquing's seals	50	45

Nos. 4924/5 were issued in se-tenant pairs within the sheet.

1148 *Meconopsis lancifolia*

2004. Meconopsis. Multicoloured.

4926	80f. (1) Type **1148**	20	15
4927	80f. (2) *Meconopsis racemosa*	20	15
4928	80f. (3) *Meconopsis punicea*	20	15
4929	2y. *Meconopsis integrifolia*	50	45

1149 Bronze Age Cucuteni Pot

2004. Cultural Heritage. Multicoloured.

4930	80f. Type **1149**	20	15
4931	80f. Drum supported by phoenixes and tigers	20	15

Stamps of the same design were issued by Romania.

1150 Flag

2004. National Symbols. Multicoloured.

4932	**1150**	80f. scarlet and lemon	20	15
4933	**1150**	80f. multicoloured (vert)	20	15

DESIGN: No. 4933 Emblem.

1151 Forest, Xing'an Mountain

2004. Landscapes. Multicoloured.

4934	80f. (1) Type **1151**	20	15
4935	80f. (2) Yalu river basin	20	15
4936	80f. (3) Reefs, Yellow Sea	20	15
4937	80f. (4) Zhoushan archipelago	20	15
4938	80f. (5) Taiwan coastline	20	15
4939	80f. (6) Xisha Islands	20	15
4940	80f. (7) Lake, trees and mountains, Southern Guangxi	20	15
4941	80f. (8) Rain forest, Southern Yunnan	20	15
4942	80f. (9) Mount Qomolangma	20	15
4943	80f. (10) Pamir mountains	20	15
4944	80f. (11) Badain Jaran desert	20	15
4945	80f. (12) Hulun Buir steppe	20	15
MS4946	230×146 mm. Nos. 4934/45	4·25	3·50

1152 Jinmao Tower, Shanghai

2004. Architecture. Multicoloured.

4947	80f. Type **1152**	20	15
4948	80f. Park Guell, Barcelona	20	15

Stamps of the same design were issued by Spain.

1153 Woodland

2004. "Festival of Brightness on the River". (painting by Zhang Zeduan). Sheet 236×120 mm containing T 1153 and similar horiz designs showing parts of the painting.

MS4949	60f. (1) Type **1153**; 80f. (2) Trees and people on horseback; 80f. (3) Boats at riverbank; 80f. (4) Passenger boats; 80f. (5) Bridge; 80f. (6) Houses and boats on river; 80f. (7) Trees, wagon and buildings; 1y. (8) Tower; 2y. (9) Town crossroads	2·50	2·20

1153a Bird

2004

4949a	**1153a**	80f. multicoloured	20	15

1154 Aiwan Pavilion, Changsha, Hunan Province

2004. Pavilions. Multicoloured.

4950	80f. (1) Type **1154**	20	15
4951	80f. (2) Pipa, Jiujiang, Jiangxi province	20	15
4952	80f. (3) Orchid, Shaoxing, Zhejiang province	20	15
4953	80f. (4) Zuiweng, Chuzhou, Anhui province	20	15

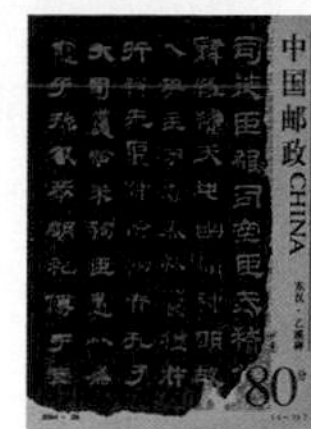
1155 Yi Ying Tablet

2004. Calligraphy. Zuoshu (official script). Showing inscribed tablets. Each black, silver and red.

4954	80f. (1) Type **1155**	20	15
4955	80f. (2) Zhang Qian	20	15
4956	80f. (3) Cao Quan	20	15
4957	80f. (4) Shimen ode	20	15

1156 Rooster

2005. New Year. "Year of the Rooster".

4958	**1156**	80f. multicoloured	30	25

1157 Tower

2005. Completion of Gas Pipeline from Tarim to Baihe. Multicoloured.

4959	80f. Type **1157**	20	15
4960	3y. Pipeline	75	60

1158 North Gate, Taipei

2005. Taiwanese Architecture. Multicoloured.

4961	80f. (1) Type **1158**	20	15
4962	80f. (2) Confucius Temple, Tainan	20	15
4963	80f. (3) Longshan Temple, Lugang	20	15
4964	80f. (4) Erkunshen Fort, Tainan	20	15
4965	1y.50 (5) Matsu Temple, Penghu	40	35

1159 "Door God"

2005. Yangjiabu New Year Pictures (woodcut prints). Multicoloured.

4966	80f. (1) Type **1159**	20	15
4967	80f. (2) "Abundance for Years Running"	20	15
4968	80f. (3) "Good News on New Year's Day"	20	15
4969	80f. (4) "Goddess strewing Flowers from Heaven"	20	15
MS4970	150×90 mm. Nos. 4966/9	1·50	1·20

1160 *Magnolia dennudata*

2005. Magnolias. Multicoloured.

4971	80f. (1) Type **1160**	20	15
4972	80f. (2) *Magnolia delavayi*	20	15
4973	80f. (3) *Magnolia grandiflora*	20	15
4974	80f. (4) *Magnolia liliflora*	20	15

1161 Great Wall

2005

4975	**1161**	80f. multicoloured	15	10

1162 Multicoloured Hands

2005. World Earth Day.

4976	**1162**	80f. multicoloured	15	10

1163 Sunrise

2005. Jigong Mountains. Multicoloured.

4977	80f. (1) Type **1163**	15	10
4978	80f. (2) Garden in the clouds	15	10
4979	80f. (3) Moon pond	15	10
4980	80f. (4) Black Dragon waterfall	15	10

1164 "80"

2005. 80th Anniv of Trade Union Federation.

4981	**1164**	80f. multicoloured	15	10

1165 "Magnolias" (Chen Hongshou)

2005. Paintings. Multicoloured.

4982	80f. Type **1165**	15	10
4983	80f. "Flower Vase in a Window Niche" (Ambrosius Bosschaert)	15	10

Stamps of a similar design were issued by Liechtenstein.

1166 Tiger Beach

2005. Dalian Coast. Multicoloured.

4984	80f. (1) Type **1166**	15	10
4985	80f. (2) Bangchui island	15	10
4986	80f. (3) Golden pebble beach	15	10
4987	80f. (4) Lushunkou	15	10

1167 Emblem

2005. Centenary of Fudan University.

4988	**1167**	80f. multicoloured	15	10

1168 *Emperor's New Clothes*

2005. Birth Bicentenary of Hans Christian Andersen (writer). Multicoloured.

4989	60f. (1) Type **1168**	15	10
4990	80f. (2) *The Little Mermaid*	15	10
4991	80f. (3) *Thumbelina*	15	10
4992	80f. (4) *The Little Match Girl*	15	10
4993	80f. (5) *The Ugly Duckling*	15	10

1169 Zheng He

2005. 600th Anniv of the Voyages of Zheng He (Ma Sanbao). Multicoloured.

4994	80f. (1) Type **1169**	15	10
4995	80f. (2) Map and pavilions	15	10
4996	80f. (3) Navigational instrument	15	10
MS4997	139×80 mm. 6y. Nine-masted "Treasure ship" (71×50 mm)	1·00	1·00

Stamps of a similar design were issued by Hong Kong and Macau.

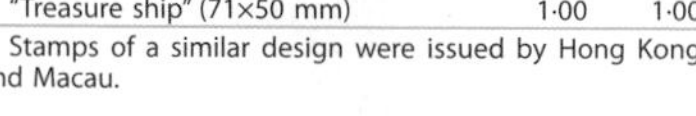

1170 Southern Hall

2005. Centenary of Nantong Museum. Mult.

4998	80f. (1) Type **1170**	15	10
4999	80f. (2) Central Hall	15	10

1171 Red-crowned Crane and Chick

2005. Xianghai Nature Reserve. Multicoloured.

5000	80f. (1) Type **1171**	15	10
5001	80f. (2) Cranes in flight	15	10
5002	80f. (3) Ruddy shelduck	15	10
5003	80f. (4) Golden eagle	15	10

1172 Yang Jingyu

2005. Generals (1st issue). Multicoloured.

5004	80f. (1) Type **1172**	15	10
5005	80f. (2) Zuo Quan	15	10
5006	80f. (3) Peng Xuefeng	15	10
5007	80f. (4) Luo Binghui	15	10
5008	80f. (5) Guan Xiangying	15	10

See also Nos. 5022/31.

1173 Soldiers with Machine Guns

2005. 60th Anniv of End of World War II. Multicoloured.

5009	80f. (1) Type **1173**	15	10
5010	80f. (2) Soldier blowing bugle	15	10
5011	80f. (3) Normandy landings	15	10
5012	80f. (4) Capture of Berlin	15	10
MS5013	81×121 mm. 6p. Dove (vert)	1·00	1·00

1174 Celebration

2005. 40th Anniv of Tibet Autonomous Region.

5014	**1174** 80f. multicoloured	15	10

1175 Early Actor

2005. Centenary of Chinese Cinema.

5015	**1175** 80f. multicoloured	15	10

1176 Chinese Script

2005. "Five Happiness arrive".

5016	**1176** 80f. multicoloured	15	10

1177 Golden Summit

2005. Fanjing Mountain Nature Reserve. Multicoloured.

5017	80f. (1) Type **1177**	15	10
5018	80f. (2) Mushroom Rock	15	10
5019	80f. (3) Broadleaf forest	15	10
5020	80f. (4) Heiwan River	15	10

1178 Waterwheel, China

2005. Waterwheels and Windmills. Multicoloured.

5021	80f. (1) Type **1178**	15	10
5022	80f. (2) Windmill, Netherlands	15	10

Stamps of the same design were issued by Netherlands.

1179 Su Yu

2005. Generals (2nd issue). Each black, grey and red.

5023	80f. (1) Type **1179**	15	10
5024	80f. (2) Xu Haidong	15	10
5025	80f. (3) Huang Kecheng	15	10
5026	80f. (4) Chen Geng	15	10
5027	80f. (5) Tan Zheng	15	10
5028	80f. (6) Xiao Jinguang	15	10
5029	80f. (7) Zhang Yunyi	15	10
5030	80f. (8) Luo Ruiqing	15	10
5031	80f. (9) Wang Shusheng	15	10
5032	80f. (10) Xu Guangda	15	10

1180 Horses

2005. "Goddess of the River Luo" (painting by Gu Kaizhi). Sheet 236×120 mm containing T 1180 and similar horiz designs showing parts of the painting.

MS5033	80f. (1) Type **1179**; 80f. (2) Goddess dancing, Cao Zhi and retinue; 80f. (3) Goddess, banners, hills and trees (60×30 mm.); 80f. (4) Goddess, trees and flowers (40×30 mm.); 80f. (5) Cao Zhi seated with retinue (60×30 mm.); 80f. (6) Goddess with scarf and Cao Zhi (60×30 mm.); 80f. (7) Goddess leaving (60×30 mm.); 80f. (8) Boat; 80f. (9) Cao Zhi seated with two attendants (40×30 mm.); 80f. (10) Cao Zhi leaving	2·20	2·20

1181 Musicians

2005. 50th Anniv of Xinjiang Uygur Autonomous Region. Multicoloured.

5034	80f. (1) Type **1181**	15	10
5035	80f. (2) Dancers	15	10
5036	80f. (3) Women carrying food	15	10

Nos. 5034/6 were issued together, se-tenant, forming a composite design.

1182 Stylized "10"

2005. 10th National Games, Jiangsu Province. Sheet 130×90 mm.

MS5037	**1182** 6y. multicoloured	1·00	1·00

1183 *Panthera pardus*

2005. Carnivores. Multicoloured.

5038	80f. Type **1183**	15	10
5039	80f. Puma concolor	15	10

Stamps of the same design were issued by Canada.

1185 Ceramics

2005. Chengtoushan Archaeological Site.

5041	**1185** 80f. multicoloured	15	10

1187 Emblem

2005. Olympic Games, Beijing. Designs showing games emblem and mascots.

5043	80f. (1) Type **1187**	15	10
5044	80f. (2) Beibei	15	10
5045	80f. (3) Jingjing	15	10
5046	80f. (4) Huanhuan	15	10
5047	80f. (5) Yingying	15	10
5048	80f. (6) Nini	15	10

1188 Dog

2006. New Year. Year of the Dog.

5049	**1188** 80f. multicoloured	25	15

1189 "Being Safe all Year Round"

2006. Wuqiang New Year Pictures (woodcut prints). Multicoloured.

5050	80f. (1) Type **1189**	15	10
5051	80f. (2) "Five blessings approach your door"	15	10
5052	80f. (3) "Flower of prosperity blossoms"	15	10
5053	80f. (4) "Lion rolling embroidered ball"	15	10
MS5054	173×80 mm. Nos. 5050/3	1·00	1·00

1190 Fish Lantern

2006. Chinese Lanterns. Multicoloured.

5055	80f. (1) Type **1190**	15	10
5056	80f. (2) Chinese white cabbage lantern	15	10
5057	80f. (3) Lotus lantern	15	10
5058	80f. (4) Dragon and phoenix lantern	15	10
5059	1w.50 (5) Butterfly lantern	35	20

1191 Rainbow, Field and Animals

2006. Abolition of Agricultural Tax.

5060	**1191** 80f. multicoloured	15	10

1192 Yangdi

2006. Lijiang River. Multicoloured.

5061	80f. (1) Type **1192**	15	10
5062	80f. (2) Langshi	15	10
5063	80f. (3) Huangbu	15	10
5064	80f. (4) Xingping	15	10

Nos. 5061/4 were issued together, se-tenant, forming a composite design.

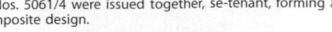

1193 *Ginkgo biloba*

2006. Endangered Species. Trees. Multicoloured.

5065	80f. (1) Type **1193**	15	10
5066	80f. (2) *Glyptostrobus pensilis*	15	10
5067	80f. (3) *Davidia involucrate*	15	10
5068	80f. (4) *Liriodendron chinense*	15	10

1194 Pekinese

2006. Dogs. Multicoloured.

5069	(1) 80f. Type **1194**	15	10
5070	(2) 80f. Pug (vert)	15	10
5071	(3) 80f. Chow chow	15	10
5072	(4) 80f. Tibetan mastiff (vert)	15	10

1195 Gateway

2006. Qingcheng Mountain. Multicoloured.

5073	(1) 60f. Type **1195**	10	10
5074	(2) 80f. Path	15	10
5075	(3) 80f. Temple	15	10
5076	(4) 80f. Spring	15	10

1196 Sakyamuni

2006. Yungang Grottoes. Multicoloured.

5077	(1) 80f. Type **1196**	15	10
5078	(2) 80f. Bodhisattva of Offering	15	10
5079	(3) 80f. Head of Bodhisattva	15	10
5080	(4) 80f. Xieshi Bodhisattva	15	10
MS5081	80×120 mm. 6y. Sakyamuni (40×60 mm)	1·50	1·50

1197 Green Dragon Mountain Stream

2006. Tianzhu Mountain. Multicoloured.

5082	(1) 60f. Type **1197**	10	10
5083	(2) 80f. Terrace	15	10
5084	(3) 80f. Sanzu Temple	15	10
5085	(4) 80f. Qingtian Peak	15	10

2006. Scientists. Multicoloured.

5086	(1) 80f. Type **1198**	15	10
5087	(2) 80f. Mao Yisheng (bridges)	15	10
5088	(3) 80f. Yan Jici (physics)	15	10
5089	(4) 80f. Zhou Peiyuan (physics)	15	10

1199 Dagu Lighthouse

2006. Lighthouses. Multicoloured.

5090	(1) 80f. Type **1199**	15	10
5091	(2) 80f. Guishan	15	10
5092	(3) 80f. Wusongkou	15	10
5093	(4) 80f. Mulantou	15	10

Nos. 5090/3 were issued together, se-tenant, forming a composite design.

1200 Geospace Double Star Exploration

2006. 50th Anniv of Chinese Space Programme. Multicoloured.

5094	(1) 80f. Type **1200**	15	10
5095	(2) 80f. Shenzhou-VI manned space ship	15	10

Nos. 5094/5 were issued together, se-tenant, forming a composite design.

1201 Empire Lasting Forever Gold Cup

2006. Gold and Silver Ware. Multicoloured.

5096	(1) 80f. Type **1201**	15	10
5097	(2) 80f. Baroque tankard	15	10

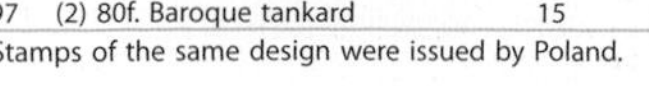

Stamps of the same design were issued by Poland.

1202 Gao Junyu

2006. Early Leaders of Chinese Communist Party. Each black and brown.

5098	(1) 80f. Type **1202**	15	10
5099	(2) 80f. Wang Hebo	15	10
5100	(3) 80f. Su Zhaozheng	15	10
5101	(4) 80f. Peng Pai	15	10
5102	(5) 80f. Deng Zhongxia	15	10

1203 Crossing Kekexili

2006. Opening of Qinghai-Tibet Railway to Traffic. Multicoloured.

5103	(1) 80f. Type **1203**	40	20
5104	(2) 80f. Crossing Danggula mountains	40	20
5105	(3) 80f. Lhasa railway station	40	20

1204 Snow-covered Mountains and Kanasi Lake

2006. Kanasi Nature Reserve. Multicoloured.

5106	(1) 80f. Type **1204**	40	20
5107	(2) 80f. Trees, Crouching Dragon Bend	40	20
5108	(3) 80f. Deer and Celestial Bend	40	20
5109	(3) 80f. Trees in autumn, Moon Bend	40	20

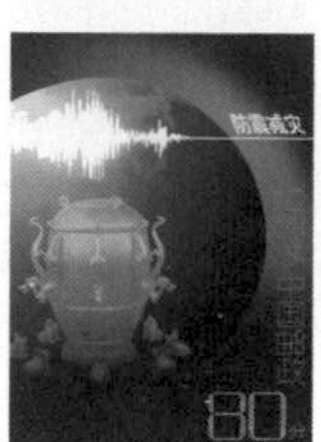

1205 Cheng Heng's Seismometer and Seismograph

2006. Earthquake Awareness and Detection.

5110	**1205** 80f. multicoloured	40	20

1206 Basketball

2006. Olympic Games, Beijing. Multicoloured. Self-adhesive.

5111	60f. Type **1206**	15	10
5112	80f. Fencing	40	20
5113	80f. Sailing	40	20
5114	3y. Gymnastics	80	35

It is reported that designs as Nos. 5111/14 were also issued with ordinary gum.

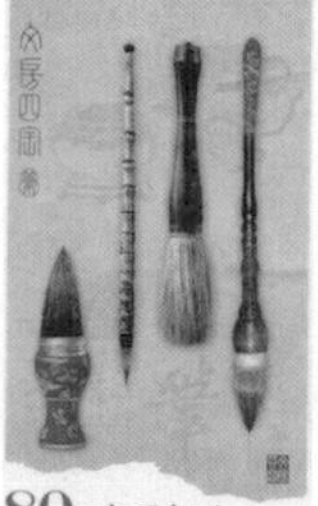

1207 Brushes

2006. Calligraphy. Multicoloured.

5115	(1) 80f. Type **1207**	25	10
5116	(2) 80f. Ink stick	25	10
5117	(3) 80f. Paper and book	25	10
5118	(4) 80f. Ink slab	25	10

1208 Emblem

2006. 50th Anniv of Returned Overseas Chinese Federation.

5119	**1208** 80f. multicoloured	25	10

1209 Piano

2006. Musical Instruments. Multicoloured.

5120	80f. Type **1209**	25	10
5121	80f. Guqin	25	10

Stamps of a similar design were issued by Austria.

1210 "100"

2006. 100th Export Commodities Fair.

5122	**1210** 80f. multicoloured	25	10

1211 Setting Out

2006. 70th Anniv of Long March by Communist Army. Multicoloured.

5123	(1) 80f. Type **1211**	25	10
5124	(2) 80f. Zunyi conference	25	10
5125	(3) 80f. On Luding Bridge	25	10
5126	(4) 80f. Crossing marshy grasslands	25	10
MS5127	120×90 mm. 6y. Joining forces in Jinggangshan (80×50 mm)	1·00	1·00

1212 Flags

2006. 15th Anniv of Diplomatic Relations with Association of Southeast Asian Nations.

5128	**1212** 80f. multicoloured	25	10

1212a Fish

2006. New Year Stamps. Multicoloured.

5129	(1) 80f. Type **1212a**	25	10
5130	(2) 80f. 3y. Greetings	50	30

1213 Emblem

2006. China-Africa Forum.

5131	**1213** 80f. multicoloured	25	10

1214 Home of Sun Yat-sen

2006. 140th Birth Anniv of Sun Yat-sen. Multicoloured.

5132	(1) 80f. Type **1214**	25	10
5133	(2) 80f. Zhongshan Mausoleum	25	10
5134	(3) 80f. Dr.Sun Yat-sen Memorial Hall	25	10
5135	(4) 80f. 1y.50 Zhongshan University	25	10

1214a Chinese monal

2006. Birds. Multicoloured.

5135a	40f. Type **1214a**	15	10
5135b	1y.20 Taiwan	50	30

1215 Boy on Horseback

2006. "Steed" (scroll painting). Design showing parts of the painting. Multicoloured.

5136	(1) 80f. 1y.20 Type **1215**	50	30
5137	(2) 80f. 1y.20 Zhi Dun (monk), scholar and servant	50	30

Nos. 5136/7were issued together, se-tenant, forming a composite design of part of the painting.

1216 Wu Lanfu

2006. Birth Centenary of Wu Lanfu (Vice-Chairman of 5th CPPCC National Committee 1978–83).

5138	**1216** 1y.20 multicoloured	1·00	60

1217 High Speed Locomotive

2006. Railway Expansion. Multicoloured.

5139	(1) 80f. 1y.20 Type **1217**	30	15
5140	(2) 80f. 1y.20 Industrial transport train	30	15
5141	(3) 80f. 1y.20 Agricultural transport truck	30	15
5142	(4) 80f. 1y.20 Dockyard railway	30	15
MS5143	126×76 mm. 6y. High speed train (90×40 mm)	1·50	1·50

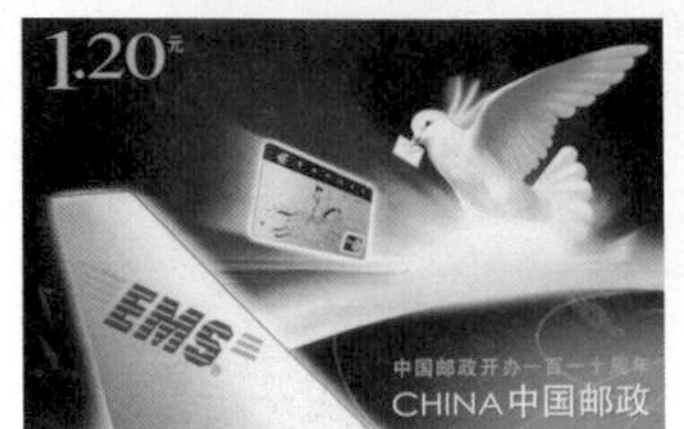

1218 Dove and Emblems

2006. 110th Anniv of Postal Service.

5144	**1218** 1y.20 multicoloured	1·00	60

1219 Pig and Piglets

2007. New Year. Year of the Pig.

5145	**1219** 1y.20 multicoloured	1·00	60

1220 Emblem

2007. Changchun 2007–Asian Winter Games.

5146	**1220** 1y.20 multicoloured	1·00	60

1221 Ta Xue Xun Mei

2007. Shiwan Pottery. Multicoloured.

5147	(1) 80f. 1y.20 Type **1221**	50	30
5148	(2) 80f. 1y.20 Wang Zhaojun Chu Sai	50	30

1222 "Divine Birds of the Sun"

2007. Greetings Stamp.

5149	**1222** 1y.20 multicoloured	25	10

1223 Zuo Zuo Ti Dao

2007. Mianzhu Wood Engravings. Multicoloured.

5150	(1) 80f. 1y.20 Type **1223**	25	10
5151	(2) 80f. 1y.20 Mu Guiying	25	10
5152	(3) 80f. 1y.20 Shuang Xi Tong Zi	25	10
5153	(4) 80f. 1y.20 Zhang Xian She Gou	25	10

1224 Lin Xiangru

2007. Sheng Jue of Beijing Opera. Multicoloured.

5154	(1) 80f. Type **1224**	30	15
5155	(2) 80f. 1y.20 Song Shijie	30	15
5156	(3) 80f. 1y.20 Zhou Yu	30	15
5157	(4) 80f. 1y.20 Xu Xian	30	15
5158	(5) 80f. 1y.20 Gao Chong	30	15
5159	(6) 80f. 1y.20 Ren Tanghui	30	15

1225 Mounted Messenger

2007. Postal Savings Bank.

5160	**1225** 1y.20 multicoloured	1·00	60

1226 "Look on Waterfall under Pine"

2007. Paintings by Li Keran. Multicoloured.

5161	(1) 1y.20 Type **1226**	30	15
5162	(2) 1y.20 "Thousands of Mountains turn Red"	30	15
5163	(3) 1y.20 "Looking on Picture"	30	15
5164	(4) 1y.20 "Setting Crane Free"	30	15
5165	(5) 1y.20 "Grazing Cattle in Pond"	30	15
5166	(6) 1y.20 "Raining in Jiangnan"	30	15

1227 Masks

2007. Centenary of Modern Chinese Theatre.

5167	**1227** 1y.20 multicoloured	1·00	60

1228 He Garden

2007. Yangzhou Gardens. Multicoloured.

5168	(1) 1y.20 Type **1228**	35	20
5169	(2) 1y.20 Ge Garden	35	20
5170	(3) 1y.20 Xu Garden	35	20

1229 Dragon Dance (Indonesia)

2007. Traditional Dances. Multicoloured.

5171	(1) 1y.20 Type **1229**	50	30
5172	(2) 1y.20 Lion dance (China)	50	30

Stamps of a similar design were issued by Indonesia.

1229a Torch Relay Emblem

2007. Personalised Stamp.

5172a	**1229a** 1y.20 multicoloured	1·00	60

1230 Sports

2007. 60th Anniv of Inner Mongolian Autonomous Region. Multicoloured.

5173	(1) 1y.20 Type **1230**	50	30
5174	(2) 1y.20 Women performers	50	30
MS5175	120×70 mm. Nos. 5173/4	1·00	1·00

1231 Zhouling Mausoleum

2007. Qing Dynasty Mausoleums. Multicoloured.

5176	(1) 1y.20 Type **1231**	35	20
5177	(2) 1y.20 Xiaoling	35	20
5178	(3) 1y.20 Tailing	35	20

1232 Emblem

2007. Centenary of Tongji University.

5179	**1232** 1y.20 multicoloured	50	30

1233 Father and Children

2007. Kong Rong and the Pears (tale of unselfishness). Multicoloured. (a) Ordinary gum.

5180	(1) 1y.20 Type **1233**	50	30
5181	(2) 1y.20 Mother and children	50	30

(b) Self-adhesive.

5182	(1) 1y.20 As Type **1233**	50	30
5183	(2) 1y.20 As No. 5181	50	30

Nos. 5180/1 and 5182/3 were each issued together, se-tenant forming a composite design of father, mother and children.

1234 Chongqing

2007. Development of Chongqing. Multicoloured.

5184	(1) 1y.20 Type **1234**	50	30
5185	(2) 1y.20 Road interchange	50	30

Nos. 5184/5 were issued together, se-tenant, forming a composite design.

1235 Heilong Mountain

2007. Wudalianchi National Park. Multicoloured.

5186	(1) 1y.20 Type **1235**	35	20
5187	(2) 1y.20 Sanchi Pool	35	20
5188	(3) 1y.20 Sea of Rock	35	20

1236 Flag, Doves and 'Forever Blooming Bauhinia' (sculpture) (symbol of Hong Kong)

2007. 10th Anniv of Re-unification of Hong Kong and China. Multicoloured.

5189	(1) 1y.20 Type **1236**	35	20
5190	(2) 1y.20 'CEPA'	35	20
5191	(3) 1y.50 Towers and bridge	35	20
MS5191a	110×150 mm. Nos. 5189/91 and No. 1459 of Hong Kong	8·00	8·00

1237 Yang Shangkun

2007. Birth Centenary of Yang Shangkun (president 1988–93). Multicoloured.

5192	(1) 1y.20 Type **1237**	50	30
5193	(2) 1y.20 As older man (*horiz*)	50	30

1238 San Panwei

2007. Nanji Island Nature Reserves. Multicoloured.

5194	(1) 1y.20 Type **1238**	35	20
5195	(2) 1y.20 Longchuan reef	35	20
5196	(3) 1y.50 Da Sha'ao	35	20

1238a Emblem

2007. Personalised Stamp. 80th Anniv of People's Liberation Army (1st issue).

5197	**1238a** 1y.20 multicoloured	1·00	60

See also Nos. 5199/5202.

1239 Western Xia Dynasty Bronze Plate (½-size illustration. Actual size 61×40 mm)

2007. All China Philatelic Federation Congress. Sheet 121×80 mm.

MS5198	6y. multicoloured	1·40	1·40

1240 Soldier, Sailor and Airman

2007. 80th Anniv of People's Liberation Army (2nd issue). Multicoloured.

5199	(1) 1y.20 Type **1240**	25	15
5200	(2) 1y.20 Soldier wearing fatigues	25	15
5201	(3) 1y.20 Soldier wearing helmet and flak jacket	25	15
5202	(4) 1y.20 Women soldiers	25	15

1241 Beibei diving

2007. Olympic Games, Beijing. Showing mascots. Multicoloured.

5203	(1) 1y.20 Type **1241**	30	15
5204	(2) 1y.20 Jingjing shooting	30	15
5205	(3) 1y.20 Yingying pole vaulting (athletics)	30	15
5206	(4) 1y.20 Nini playing volleyball	30	15
5207	(5) 1y.20 Huanhuan riding BMX cycle	30	15
5208	(6) 1y.20 Jingjing weightlifting	30	15

See also Nos. 5043/8.

1242 Hot Sea, Zaotong Valley

2007. Geothermal Volcanoes, Tengcheng. Mult.

5209	(1) 1y.20 Type **1242**	35	20
5210	(2) 1y.20 Group of volcanoes (vert)	35	20
5211	(3) 1y.20 Celestial Pillar Valley (vert)	35	20

1243 Da Chibi

2007. Jin Hu (Golden Lake). Multicoloured.

5212	(1) 1y.20 Type **1243**	50	30
5213	(2) 1y.20 Maoer Mountain	50	30

1244 Emblem

2007. Federation Internationale de Football Association Women's World Cup Football Championships, China.

5214	**1244**	1y.20 multicoloured	1·00	60

1245 Emblem

2007. Special Olympics Summer Games, China.

5215	**1245**	1y.20 multicoloured	1·00	60

1246 Zhang Fei Temple

2007. Historic Sites, Three Gorges. Multicoloured.

5216	(1) 1y.20 Type **1246**	35	20
5217	(2) 1y.20 Pagoda, Shibaozhai Village (vert)	35	20
5218	(3) 1y.20 Archway and street, Old Dachang (vert)	35	20
5219	(4) 1y.20 Quyuan's mausoleum	35	20

1247 First National Congress Site

2007. 17th Chinese Communist Party National Congress. Multicoloured.

5220	(1) 1y.20 Type **1247**	50	30
5221	(2) 1y.20 Site of Second Plenary Session	50	30
MS5222	135×87 mm. 6y. Dove (60×40 mm)	1·40	1·40
MS5222a	171×144 mm. As Nos. 5222/01	1·10	1·10

1247a Happiness

2007. Greetings Stamps. Multicoloured.

5222b	1y.20 Type **1247a**	50	30

Nos. 5222c/d have been left for stamps not yet received.

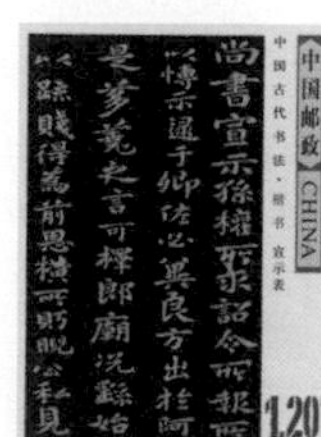

1248 'Proclamation'

2007. Calligraphy. Multicoloured.

5223	(1) 1y.20 Type **1248**	30	15
5224	(2) 1y.20 'Zang Menglong'	30	15
5225	(3) 1y.20 'Sweet Spring at Jiucheng Palace'	30	15
5226	(4) 1y.20 Preface for 'Sacred Religion at Wild Goose Pagoda'	30	15
5227	(5) 1y.20 Yan Qinli stele	30	15
5228	(6) 1y.20 'Mysterious'	30	15

1249 Mount Gongga (China)

2007. Mountains. Multicoloured.

5229	(1) 1y.20 Type **1249**	50	30
5230	(2) 1y.20 Popocatepetl (Mexico)	50	30

Stamps of a similar design were issued by Mexico.

1250 Satellite in Lunar Orbit

2007. Successful Maiden Flight of Cheng E 1.

5231	**1250**	1y.20 multicoloured	1·00	6·00

1251 Emblem

2007. EXPO 2010, Shanghai.

5232	**1251**	(1) 1y.20 emerald, black and yellow	50	30
5233	-	(2) 1y.20 blue, black and ultramarine	50	30

DESIGNS: 5232, Type **1251**; 5233, Mascot.

1252 Agricultural University Gymnasium

2007. Olympic Games, Beijing. Venues. Mult.

5234	(1) 80f. Type **1252**	40	20
5235	(2) 1y.20 Laoshan mountain bike course	40	20
5236	(3) 1y.20 National indoor stadium	40	20
5237	(4) 1y.20 Peking university gymnasium	40	20
5238	(5) 1y.20 National aquatics centre	40	20
5239	(6) 3y. Qingdao Olympic sailing centre	40	20
MS5240	140×85 mm. 6y. National stadium (pentagon) (65×61 mm)	1·60	1·60

See also Nos. 5043/8 and 5203/8.

1253 Rat

2008. New Year. Year of the Rat.

5241	**1253**	1y.20 multicoloured	45	25

1254 *Gate Guardian General Standing with Cane*

2008. Zhuxian New Year Wood Engravings. Multicoloured.

5242	1y.20 Type **1254**	35	20
5243	1y.20 *Give Her Son a Lecture*	35	20
5244	1y.20 *Come Back With Fruitful Result*	35	20
5245	1y.20 *Chivalrous Women*	35	20

1255 Zhang Fei

2008. Jing Roles of Beijing Opera. Multicoloured.

5246	80f. Type **1255**	30	15
5247	1y.20 Xu Yanzhao	35	20
5248	1y.20 Bao Zheng	35	35
5249	1y.20 Lian Po	35	20
5250	1y.20 Cao Cao	35	20
5251	1y.20 Yang Yansi	35	20

1256 *Urocissa caerulea* (Formosan blue magpie)

2008. Birds. Sheet 145×171 mm containing T 1256 and similar vert designs. Multicoloured.

MS5252	1y.20×6, Type **1256**; *Emberiza koslowi* (Koslow's bunting); *Garrulax sukatschewi* (black-fronted laughing thrush); *Tragopan caboti* (Cabot's tragopan); *Chrysolophus pictus* (golden pheasant); *Podoces biddulphi* (Biddulph's ground jay)	1·90	1·90

The stamps and margins of **MS**5252 form a composite design.

1257 Profiles

2008. 11th National People's Congress.

5253	**1257**	1y.20 multicoloured	1·00	60

1258 Huanhuan carrying Torch

2008. Olympic Games, Beijing. Multicoloured.

5254	1y.20 Type **1258**	55	35
5255	3y. Relay torch (vert)	55	35
MS5256	140×90 mm. Nos. 5254/5	1·75	1·75

Nos. 5257/8 have been left for self-adhesive stamps, not yet received.

1259 Bridge

2008. Suzhou-Nantong Bridge over Yangtze River. Multicoloured.

5259	1y.20 Type **1259**	50	35
5260	1y.20 Bridge (right)	50	30

Nos. 5259/60 were issued together, se-tenant, forming a composite design of the bridge.

1260 Dongyu Island

2008. Boao Forum for Asia, Hainan. Multicoloured.
5261 1y.20 Type **1260** 50 30
5262 1y.20 Forum building 50 30

1261 Islands

2008. Qiandao Lake Scenery. Multicoloured.
5263 (1) 1y.20 Type **1261** 50 30
5264 (2) 1y.20 Islands (different) 50 30
MS5265 171×70 mm. Nos. 5263/4 1·00 1·00

Nos. 5263/4 were issued together, se-tenant, forming a composite design.

1262 Emblem

2008. Olympic Expo, Beijing. Multicoloured.
5266 1y.20 Type **1262** 50 30
5267 1y.20 Building, Beijing 50 30

1263 Shiqikong Bridge

2008. Summer Palace. Multicoloured.
5268 (1) 1y. 20 Type **1263** 35 20
5269 (2) 1y. 20 Long Corridor 35 20
5270 (3) 1y. 20 Clear and Peaceful Boat 35 20
5271 (4) 1y. 20 Garden of Harmonious Pleasures 35 20
5272 (5) 1y. 20 Yudai Bridge 35 20
5273 (6) 1y. 20 Houhu Lake 35 20
MS5274 120×91 mm. 6y. Fragrance of the Buddha Tower (50×62 mm) 1·60 1·60

1263a Seismograph Reading and Linked Hearts

2008. Earthquake Relief.
5274a **1263a** 1y.20+1y. vermilion and black 1·00 60

1264 Marking the Water Level on Boat Loaded with Elephant

2008. Cao Chong (child prodigy) Weighs an Elephant using Law of Buoyancy. Multicoloured. (a) Ordinary or self-adhesive gum.
5275 1y.20 Type **1264** 50 30
5276 1y.20 Replacing elephant with weighable objects 50 30

1266 White Horse Temple

2008. Temples. Multicoloured.
5280 1y.20 Type **1266** 50 30
5281 1y.20 Mahabodhi Temple 50 30

1267 Minjiang River

2008. West Side of Taiwan Straits Development. Multicoloured.
5282 (1) 1y.20 Type **1267** 30 15
5283 (2) 1y.20 Xiamen Port 30 15
5284 (3) 1y.20 Exhibition Hall, Xiamen International Conference & Exhibition Centre 30 15
5285 (4) 1y.20 Fujian-Taiwan Kinship Museum 30 15

1268 Slide Rule, Satellite and River Basin (rural area survey)

2008. Second Land Survey. Multicoloured.
5286 1y.20 Type **1268** 50 30
5287 1y.20 Theodolite, slide rule and street plan (urban area survey) 50 30

1269 Bodhisattva

2008. Qiuci Grotto Murals.
5288 (1) 1y.20 Type **1269** 40 20
5289 (2) 1y.20 Caturmaharajakayikas 40 20
5290 (3) 1y.20 Flying Apsaras (horiz) 40 20
5291 (4) 1y.20 Maitreya preaching (horiz) 40 20

1270 Qi Jiguang

2008. 480th Birth Anniv of General Qi Jiguang. Multicoloured.
5292 1y.20 Type **1270** 50 30
5293 1y.20 On horseback 50 50

1271 Symbol of Opening Ceremony

2008. Olympic Games, Beijing. (a) Ordinary gum.
5294 1y.20 Type **1271** 50 30
MS5295 220×149 mm. 60f. As Type **1206**; 80f. As No. 5112; 80f. As No. 5113; 1y.20 As No. 5203;1y.20 As No. 5204;1y.20 As No. 5205;1y.20 As No. 5206;1y.20 As No. 5207;1y.20 As No. 5208; 3y. As No. 5114. 3·00 3·00

(b) Self-adhesive.
5296 1y.20 As Type **1271** 50 30

1272 1896 5l. Stamp of Greece (Type **9**)

2008. Olympex, Olympic Expo, Beijing. Multicoloured.
5297 1y.20 Type **1272** 55 35
5298 1y.20 1928 15c. stamp of Portugal (Type C **81**) 55 35
MS5299 141×96 mm. 6y. 1896 5l. Stamp of Greece, emblems and Olympic coin (56×56 mm circular) 1·70 1·70

1273 Corner Tower of the Forbidden City, Beijing

2008. Handover of Olympic Flag from Beijing to London. Multicoloured. (a) Ordinary or self-adhesive gum.
5300 1y.20 Type **1273** 40 20
5301 1y.20 Tower of London 40 20
5302 1y.20 National Stadium, Beijing 40 20
5303 1y.20 London Eye 40 20

1274 Central TV Building

2008. 50th Anniv of Central Television.
5308 **1274** 1y.20 multicoloured 1·00 1·00

1275 Games Emblem

2008. Paralympic Games. Multicoloured.
5309 1y.20 Type **1275** 50 30
5310 1y.20 Fu Niu Lele (games mascot) 50 30

Nos. 5309/10, each have Braille letters embossed on the surface.

1276 Emblem

2008. 50th Anniv of University of Science and Technology.
5311 **1276** 1y.20 multicoloured 1·00 60

1277 Wind Turbines

2008. 50th Anniv of Ningxia Hui Autonomous Region. Multicoloured.
5312 80f. Type **1277** 30 15
5313 1y.20 Fields 35 20
5314 1y.20 Celebration 35 20

1278 Beijing

2008. International Airports. Multicoloured.
5315 (1) 1y.20 Type **1278** 45 25
5316 (2) 1y.20 Shangai Pudong 45 25
5317 (3) 1y.20 Guangzhou Baiyun 45 25

1278a Blossom of Fortune

2008. Greetings Stamps. Multicoloured.
5317a **1278a** 1y.20 Type **1278a** 50 30
MS5317b 110×177 mm. 1y.20 No. 5317a; 3y. No. 5130 2·75 2·75

1279 Celebrating

2008. 50th Anniv of Guangxi Zhuang Autonomous Region. Multicoloured.
5318 80f. Type **1279** 30 15
5319 1y.20 Centre 50 30
5320 1y.20 Port 50 30

1280 Emblem

2008. ASEM 7, Seventh Asia–Europe Meeting, Beijing.
5321 **1280** 1y.20 multicoloured 1·00 60

1281 Expo Emblem

2008. 500 Days Countdown to Expo 2010, Shanghai.
5322 **1281** 1y.20 black, green and yellow 1·00 60

See also Nos. 5232/3.

1282 Symbols of Modernity

2008. 30th Anniv of Reform. Multicoloured.

5323 1y.20 Type **1282** 1·00 60

MS5324 120×80 mm. 6y. Great Wall and monument (56×56 mm) 2·25 2·25

1283 Ox

2009. Chinese New Year. Year of the Ox.

5325 **1283** 1y.20 multicoloured 50 60

1284 Bo Yibo

2009. Birth Centenary (2008) of Bo Yibo (politician). Multicoloured.

5326 1y.20 Type **1284** 50 30

5327 1y.20 In old age (horiz) 50 30

1285 Lion holding Sword

2009. Zhanghou New Year Wood Engravings. Multicoloured.

5328 1y.20 Type **1285** 45 25

5329 1y.20 Coming Flood of Wealth 45 25

5330 1y.20 Goddess sending Children 45 25

5331 1y.20 Rat marries off It's Daughter 45 25

MS5332 90×160 mm. Nos. 5328/31 2·75 2·75

1286 Games Emblem

2009. Harbin Winter Universiade. Multicoloured.

5333 1y.20 Type **1286** 50 30

5334 1y.20 Dong Dong (games mascot) 50 30

1287 Power Station

2009. Power Production. Multicoloured.

5335 1y.20 Type **1287** 45 25

5336 1y.20 Power lines 45 25

5337 1y.20 Light bulb and city 45 25

1288 *Chaohu Lake*

2009. Art. Paintings by Shi Tao. Multicoloured.

5338 80f. Type **1288** 40 20

5339 1y.20 *Enjoying Fountain Sound* 40 20

5340 1y.20 *Double Chrysanthemums* 40 20

5341 1y.20 *Plum Blossoms and Bamboos* 40 20

5342 1y.20 Man and Horse (pen and ink) 40 20

5343 1y.20 Lotus (pen and ink) 40 20

1289 Vase with Dragon, Phoenix and Peony

2009. China 2009 International Stamp Exhibition, Luoyang. Multicoloured.

5344 1y.20 Type **1289** 50 30

5345 1y.20 Cloisonne enamel vase with decorated shoulders 50 30

MS5346 127×90 mm. Size 40×78 mm. 6y. Peonies (painting) 2·10 2·10

1290 China at Early World Expos

2009. China and World Expo. Multicoloured.

5347 1y.20 (1) Type **1290** 40 20

5348 1y.20 (2) At Expos 1982–1992 40 20

5349 1y.20 (3) At EXPO 99 40 20

5350 1y.20 (4) World Expo 2010, Shanghai 40 20

1291 North Gate

2009. Fenhuang Historic Town. Multicoloured.

5351 1y.20 Type **1291** 40 20

5352 1y.20 (2) Rainbow Bridge 40 20

5353 1y.20 (3) Old Street 30 20

1292 Love for Motherland

2009. International Children's Day. Motherland–Children's Drawings. Multicoloured. (a) Ordinary gum.

5354 80f. Type **1292** 30 20

5355 1y.20 (2) Happy Life (horiz) 40 20

5356 1y.20 (3) Peace Lovers 40 20

5357 1y.20 (4) Enthusiasm for Science (horiz) 40 20

(b) Self-adhesive.

5358 1y.20 (1) As Type **1292** 40 20

5359 1y.20 (2) As No. 5355 (horiz) 40 20

5360 1y.20 (3) As No. 5356 40 20

5361 1y.20 (4) As No. 5357 (horiz) 40 20

1293 Bridge Span

2009. Hangzhou Bay Bridge. Multicoloured.

5362 1y.20 (1) Type **1293** 50 30

5363 1y.20 (2) Marine platform 1·00 60

1294 Li Xiannian

2009. Birth Centenary of Li Xiannian (president 1983–88). Multicoloured.

5364 1y.20 (1) Type **1294** 40 20

5365 1y.20 (2) As older man wearing spectacles 40 20

5366 1y.20 (3) As President 40 20

1295 Emblem

2009. 16th Asian Games–2010, Guangzhou. Multicoloured.

5367 1y.20 (1) Type **1295** 50 30

5368 1y.20 (2) Mascots 50 30

1296 East Gate

2009. Great Hall of the People. Multicoloured.

5369 1y.20 (1) Type **1296** 50 30

5370 1y.20 (2) Grand Auditorium 50 30

1297 Geladandong

2009. Sanjiangyuan Nature Reserve. Multicoloured.

5371 1y.20 (1) Type **1297** 35 20

5372 1y.20 (2) Eling Lake 35 20

5373 1y.20 (3) Dza Chu valley 35 20

1298 Grand Sutra Hall

2009. Labrang Lamasery. Multicoloured.

5374 1y.20 (1) Type **1298** 50 30

5375 1y.20 (2) Gongtang Pagoda 50 30

1298a National Flag

2009. 60th Anniv of National Flag.

5375a **1298a** 1y.20 multicoloured 50 30

1299 Stork Tower

2009. Architecture. Multicoloured.

5376 1y.20 (1) Type **1299** 50 30

5377 1y.20 (2) Golden Gate 50 30

1300 River Valley

2009. Huang Long Scenic Area. Multicoloured.

5378 1y.20 (1) Type **1300** 40 20

5379 1y.20 (2) Waterfall 40 20

5380 1y.20 (3) Lake 40 20

MS5381 150×80 mm. 6y. Five-Colour Ponds (128×46 mm) 2·00 2·00

1301 Ancient Books Library

2009. National Library. Multicoloured.

5382 1y.20 (1) Type **1301** 50 30

5383 1y.20 (2) North headquarters 50 30

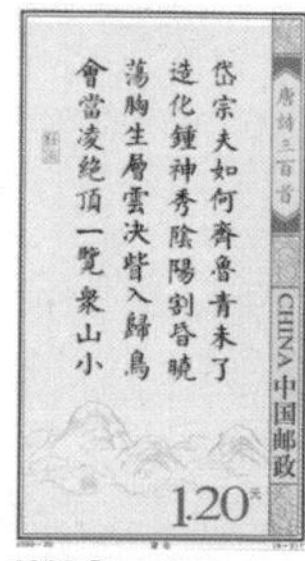

1302 *Downstream to Jiangling* (Li Bai)

2009. 300 Tang Poems. Sheet 150×80 mm containing T 1302 and similar vert designs. Multicoloured.

5383a (1) 1y.20 Type **1302** 50 30

5383b (2) 1y.20 *A View of Taishin* (Du Fu) 50 30

5383c (3) 1y.20 *Song of Pipa Player* (Bai Juyi) 50 30

5383d (4) 1y.50 *Untitled* (Li Shangyin) 60 40

5383e (5) 1y.50 *Looking at the Moon and Thinking of One Far Away* (Zhang Jiuling) 60 40

5383fa (6) 3y. *Ascending the Stork Tower* (Wang Zhihuan) 1·00 90

MS5384 (1) 1y.20 Type **1302**; (2) 1y.20 *A View of Taishin* (Du Fu); (3) 1y.20 *Song of Pipa Player* (Bai Juyi); (4) 1y.20 *Untitled* (Li Shangyin); (5) 1y.50 *Looking at the Moon and Thinking of One Far Away* (Zhang Jiuling); (6) 3y. *Ascending the Stork Tower* (Wang Zhihuan) 3·00 3·00

1303 Emblem

2009. Centenary of Lanzhoui University.

5385	**1303**	1y.20 multicoloured	1·00	60

1304 Emblem

2009. 60th Anniv of Peoples Political Consultative Conference. Multicoloured.

5386	1y.20 (1) Type **1304**	50	30
5387	1y.20 (2) Conference Hall	50	30

1305 Lantern Lighting Pagoda

2009. Beijing–Hangzhou Grand Canal. Multicoloured.

5388	1y.20 (1) Type **1305**	40	20
5389	1y.20 (2) Tianhou Temple and boats	40	20
5390	1y.20 (3) Shanshan Guild Hall	40	20
5391	1y.20 (4) Qingjiang Water Gate	40	20
5392	1y.20 (5) Wenfeng Pagoda	40	20
5393	1y.20 (6) Gongchen Bridge	40	20
MS5394	140×86mm. 6y. Grand Canal (90×50 mm)	2·00	2·00

1305a Caligraphy

2009. Greetings Stamp.

5394a	**1305a**	1y.20 multicoloured	1·00	60

1306 Infantry Group

2009. National Day Parade. Multicoloured.

5395	(1) 1y.20 Type **1306**	40	20
5396	(2) 1y.20 Army and Chinese Second Artillery Groups	40	20
5397	(3) 1y.20 Navy Equipment Group	40	20
5398	(4) 1y.20 Air Group	40	20

1307 Opening Ceremony

2009. 60th Anniv of the Founding of the People's Republic of China. Multicoloured.

5399	(1) 1y.20 Type **1307**	40	20
5400	(2) 1y.20 Parade (reform and opening-up policy)	40	20
5401	(3) 1y.20 Symbols of Hong Kong and Macao (return of Hongkong and Macao)	40	20
5402	(4) 1y.20 Symbols of Olympic Games, Beijing 2008	40	20
MS5403	115×93 mm. 6y. National flag	2·00	2·00

2009. Greetings Stamp.

5404	**1308**	1y.20 multicoloured	1·00	60
MS5404a		105×228 mm. 1y.20 As Type **1308**; 3y. As No. 5222c	2·00	1·20

1309 Games Mascot

2009. National Games. Multicoloured.

5405	1y.20 Type **1309**	50	30
5406	1y.20 Emblem	50	30
MS5407	130× 80 mm. Nos. 5405/6	1·10	70

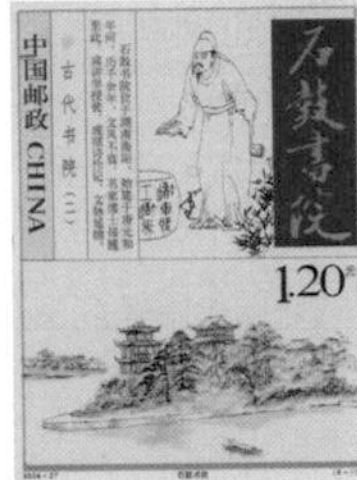
1310 Stone Drum Academy

2009. Ancient Academies. Multicoloured.

5408	(1) 1y.20 Type **1310**	40	20
5409	(2) 1y.20 Anding Academy	40	20
5410	(3) 1y.20 Ehu Academy	40	20
5411	(4) 1y.20 Dongpo Academy	40	20

1311 Guangji Bridge

2009. Guangji Bridge. Multicoloured.

5412	(1) 1y.20 Type **1311**	40	20
5413	(2) 1y.20 Central span and towers	40	20
5414	(3) 1y.20 Right bank	40	20

Nos. 5412/14 were printed, se-tenant, forming a composite design.

1312 Kong Ming Borrows the East Wind

2009. Stage Art of Ma Lianliang (actor). Multicoloured.

5415	(1) 1y.20 Type **1312**	50	30
5416	(2) 1y.20 Zhao the Orphan	50	30

1313 Lotus (symbol of Macau)

2009. 10th Anniv of Return of Macau. Multicoloured.

5417	(1) 1y.20 Type **1313**	40	20
5418	(2) 1y.20 Senado Square	40	20
5419	(3) 1y.50 Symbols of prosperity	40	20

1314 Games Emblem

2009. Asian Games, Guangzhou–2010.

5420	**1314**	1y.20 multicoloured	50	30

1315 Hall

2009. 80th Anniv of Gutian Conference (ninth meeting of the Chinese Communist Party).

5421	**1315**	1y.20 multicoloured	50	30

1315a Dancers

2010. Chinese Ballet–Red Detachment of Women. Multicoloured.

5421a	1y.20 Type **1315a**	50	30
5421b	1y.20 Dancer wearing red	50	30

1316 Tiger

2010. Chinese New Year. Year of the Tiger

5422	**1316**	1y.20 multicoloured	45	25

1317 Song Renqiong

2010. Birth Centenary of Song Renqiong (general in People's Liberation Army). Multicoloured.

5423	1y.20 Type **1317**	50	25
5424	1y.20 In old age	50	25

1318 Expo Centre

2010. Expo 2010 Shanghai Park. Multicoloured.

5425	(1) 80f. Type **1318**	55	35
5426	(2) 1y.20 China Pavillion	55	35
5427	(3) 1y.20 Expo Performance Centre	55	35
5428	(4) 3y. Theme Pavillion	55	35
MS5429	190×174 mm. 6y. Aerial view of Expo Park (30×75 mm)	2·10	2·10

2010. Liangping New Year Woodprints. Multicoloured.

5430	(1) 1y.20 Type **1319**	45	25
5431	(2) 1y.20 Stealing the Immortal Grass	45	25
5432	(3) 1y.20 Peace Leads to Happiness	45	25
5433	(4) 1y.20 Exiting Pass with Stolen Token	45	25
MS5434	150×100 mm. Nos. 5430/3	2·50	2·50

1320 Dove enclosed in Woman's Profile

2010. Centenary of International Women's Day

5435	**1320**	1y.20 multicoloured	50	30

1321 Mountain

2010. Fuchun Mountains. Multicoloured.

5436	1y.20 Type **1321**	60	35
5437	1y.20 Script, valley and hill	60	35
5438	1y.20 Vertical bands and foothills	60	35
5439	1y.20 Ridge	60	35
5440	1y.50 Valley floor	60	95
5441	3y. Tree, lower left and foothills	60	35

Nos. 5436/7 and Nos. 5439/40, respectively, were printed, *se-tenant*, in pairs, each pair forming a composite design, within horizontal strips of three stamps within the sheet.

1322 Ancestor Worship

2010. Tomb Sweeping Festival. Multicoloured.

5442	1y.20 Type **1322**	40	20
5443	1y.20 Spring Outing	40	20
5444	1y.20 Planting Willows	40	20

1323 The Old Man moves a Mountain

2010. Idioms. Multicoloured.

5445	1y.20 Type **1322**	50	30
5446	1y.20 *Sleeping on Brushwood and Tasting Gall*	50	30
5447	1y.20 *Mao Sui recommending Himself*	50	30
5448	1y.20 *Rising Up upon Hearing the Crow of a Rooster to Practise Sword Playing*	50	30

1324 Skyline

2010. Opening of World Expo 2010 Shanghai

5449	**1324**	1y.20 multicoloured	50	30

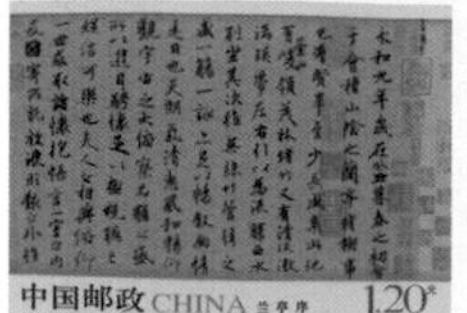
1325 Preface to The Orchid Pavilion

1326

2010. Calligraphy. Multicoloured.

5450	1y.20 (1) Type **1325** (right)	55	35
5451	1y.20 (2) Type **1326** (left)	55	70
5452	1y.20 (3) Poems composed during Cold Food Festival in Huangzhou (right)	55	35
5453	1.20 (3) Poems composed during Cold Food Festival in Huangzhou (right)	55	35
5454	1y.20 (5) Elgiac Lament for My Nephew (right)	55	35
5455	1y.20 (6) Elgiac Lament for My Nephew (left)	55	35

Nos. 5450/1, 5452/3 and 5454/5, respectively, were printed, each pair forming a composite design.

1327 Floral Fantasy

2010. Global Travel and Tourism Summit, Beijing

5456	**1327**	1y.20 multicoloured	1·00	60

1328 Ball kicked into Hole

2010. Wen Yanbo Gets the Ball from Tree Hole. Multicoloured.

5457	1y.20 Type **1328**	50	30
5458	1y.20 Getting ball from tree using water	50	30

1329 Low Carbon Development

2010. Energy and Emmissions Reduction and Environmental Protection. Multicoloured.

5459	1y.20 Type **1329**	50	30
5460	1y.20 Animals and humans protected by umbrella (A Green Future)	50	30

1330 Washing the Silken Gauze

2010. Kunqu Opera. Multicoloured.

5461	1y.20 Type **1330** (1)	40	20
5462	1y.20 *The Peony Pavilion* (2)	40	20
5463	1y.20 *The Palace of Long Life* (3)	40	20

1331 Legend of the Five Goats

2010. Landscapes. Multicoloured.

5464	1y.20 Type **1331**	45	25
5465	1y.20 Guangzhou Grand Theatre	45	25
5466	1y.20 Zhujiang River at night	45	25
5467	1y.20 Guangzhou International Convention and Exhibition Centre	45	25

1332 Loulan Monument

2010. Ancient City of Loulan. Multicoloured.

5468	1y.20 Type **1332**	45	25
5469	1y.20 City ruins	45	25

1333 Dolphin

2010. National Maritime Day

5470	**1333**	1y.20 multicoloured	1·00	60

1334 Johann Sebastian Bach

2010. Composers. Each black, dull green and gold.

5471	1y.20 Type **1334**	45	25
5472	1y.20 Franz Joseph Haydn	45	25
5473	1y.20 Wolfgang Amadeus Mozart	45	25
5474	4y.50 Ludwig van Beethoven	1·70	1·00

1335 Returning Weaving Maids Clothes

2010. The Cowherd and the Weaving Maid. Multicoloured.

5475	1y.20 Type **1335**	45	25
5476	1y.20 Cowherd ploughing, weaving maid weaving	45	25
5477	1y.20 Cowherd carrying their children to retrieve his wife	45	25
5478	1y.20 Meeting once a year	45	25

1336 Games Emblem

2010. Guangzhou 2010, Asian Para Games

5479	**1336**	1y.20 multicoloured	1·00	60

2010. Shangri-la. Multicoloured.

5480	1y.20 Songzanlin Lamasery	2·25	1·40
5481	1y.20 Napa Lake and grassland	45	25
5482	1y.20 Autumn in Pudacuo National Park	45	25
5483	1y.20 Pagoda and tower, Dukezong	45	25

1337 Meri Snow Mountain, Yunnan Province (image scaled to 54% of original size)

2010. Shangri-la. Multicoloured.

MS5484	165×66 mm. 6y. Type **1337** (90×40 mm)	45	25

1338 Dacheng Hall (main hall), Temple of Confucius, Qufu

2010. Architecture associated with Confucius (philosopher). Multicoloured.

5485	1y.20 Type **1338**	45	45
5486	1y.20 Mansion	45	25
5487	3y. Tomb	1·10	65
MS5488	160×80 mm. Nos. 5485/7	3·00	3·00

1339 Nan Wan Reservoir

2010. 60th Anniv of Harnessing of Huai River. Multicoloured.

5489	1y.20 Type **1339**	45	25
5490	1y.20 Linhuai water control project	45	25
5491	1y.20 Huaihe outfall project	45	25
5492	1y.20 Nansi Lake water control project	45	25

1340 Mei (plum blossom)

2010. Mei, Lan, Zhu, Ju (images used to represent highest qualities of mankind in Chinese tradition). Multicoloured.

5493	1y.20 Type **1340**	45	25
5494	1y.20 Lan (orchid)	45	25
5495	1y.20 Zhu (bamboo)	45	25
5496	1y.20 Ju (chrysanthemum)	45	25

1341 Zhu Xi

2010. 880th Birth Anniv of Zhu Xi (Confucian scholar, teacher and calligrapher). Multicoloured.

5497	1y.20 Type **1341**	45	25
5498	1y.20 With student and horse	45	25

1342 A Yi playing Badminton

2010. Opening of Guangzhou 2010 Asian Games. Multicoloured.

5499	1y.20 Type **1342**	45	25
5500	1y.20 Wushu sword play by A He	45	25
5501	1y.20 Le Yangyang hurdling	45	25
5502	1y.20 A He horse jumping	45	25
5503	1y.20 Mascots rowing dragon boat	45	25
5504	3y. A Yi playing Weiqi	1·00	60

1343 Tong Ren Tang

2010. Traditional Chinese Medicine Stores. Multicoloured (shades of brown).

5505	1y.20 Type **1343**	45	25
5506	1y.20 Store front, implements, seated man and woman holding tray (Hu Qing Yu Tang)	45	25
5507	1y.20 Boiling pot, implements, and two men, one seated reading (Lei Yong Shang)	45	25
5508	1y.20 Implements, teapot, couple seated at table and man drinking (Chen Li Ji)	45	25

1344 CRH2 Locomotive (modified E2-1000 Series Shinkansen design from Japan)

2010. China's High Speed Rail Network

5509	**1344**	1y.20 multicoloured	45	25

MILITARY POST STAMPS

M225

1953

M1593	**M225**	$800 yellow, red and orange	£350	£120
M1594	**M225**	$800 yellow, red and purple	£2000	
M1595	**M225**	$800 yellow, red and blue	£160000	

Nos. M1593/5 were issued for the use of the Army, Air Force and Navy respectively.

M892 Armed Forces

1995. No gum.

M3998	**M892**	20f. multicoloured	10·00	1·30

POSTAGE DUE STAMPS

D192

1950

D1459	D192	$100 blue	15	15
D1460	D192	$200 blue	15	15
D1461	D192	$500 blue	15	15
D1462	D192	$800 blue	45·00	15
D1463	D192	$1,000 blue	40	35
D1464	D192	$2,000 blue	40	35
D1465	D192	$5,000 blue	25	50
D1466	D192	$8,000 blue	25	85
D1467	D192	$10,000 blue	60	2·10

D233

1954

D1628	D233	$100 red	2·10	20
D1629	D233	$200 red	60	20
D1630	D233	$500 red	2·10	20
D1631	D233	$800 red	20	20
D1632	D233	$1,600 red	20	20

CHINA - TAIWAN (FORMOSA)

A. CHINESE PROVINCE

The island of Taiwan was ceded by China to Japan in 1895 and was returned to China in 1945 after the defeat of China. From 1949 Taiwan was controlled by the remnants of the National Government under Chiang Kai-shek

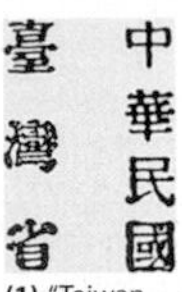

(1) "Taiwan Province, Chinese Republic"

1945. Optd as Type 1. (a) On stamps as Nos. J1/3 of Japanese Taiwan. Imperf.

1	J1	3s. red	1·00	3·25
2	J1	5s. green	1·00	1·25
3	J1	10s. blue	1·75	1·00
4	J1	30s. blue	6·50	6·50
5	J1	40s. purple	7·50	7·50
6	J1	50s. grey	5·00	4·75
7	J1	1y. green	7·50	6·50

(b) On stamps of Japan. Imperf.

8	87	5y. olive (No. 424)	28·00	25·00
9	88	10y. purple (No. 334)	38·00	35·00

(2)

1946. Stamps of China surch as T 2 with two to four characters in lower line denoting value.

10	-	2s. on 2c. blue (No. 509)	20	1·50
11	-	5s. on 5c. orange (No. 513)	20	55
12	60	10s. on 4c. lilac	20	50
13	-	30s. on 15c. pur (No. 517)	20	55
19	107	50s. on $20 red	35	2·00
16	58	65s. on $20 green	50	3·25
15	-	$1 on 20c. blue (No. 519)	20	1·50
17	58	$1 on $30 brown	25	2·50
65	60	$2 on 2½c. red	65	3·00
18	58	$2 on $50 orange	45	55
20	107	$3 on $100 red	20	50
77	103	$5 on $40 orange	1·00	1·50
78	107	$5 on $50 violet	1·00	75
79	107	$5 on $70 orange	1·00	3·25
80	107	$5 on $100 red	1·00	1·00
21	107	$5 on $200 green	20	50
67	82	$10 on $3 yellow	2·25	3·50
82	118	$10 on $150 blue	75	1·25
22	107	$10 on $500 green	25	40
66	72	$20 on 2c. green	90	1·00
71	89	$20 on $3 red	3·00	3·00
83	118	$20 on $250 violet	1·50	1·50
23	107	$20 on $700 brown	80	70
68	82	$50 on 50c. green	3·25	2·00
24	107	$50 on $1,000 red	1·75	1·50
72	89	$100 on $20 pink	1·40	1·00
73	94	$100 on $20 red	£1100	
25	107	$100 on $3,000 blue	3·75	1·00
74	94	$200 on $10 blue	2·25	1·20
70	72	$500 on $30 purple	7·50	3·25
69	82	$800 on $4 brown	7·25	6·50
81	107	$600 on $100 red	14·00	3·75
85	118	$1,000 on $20,000 red	2·75	2·50
75	94	$5,000 on $10 blue	7·50	5·50
76	94	$10,000 on $20 red	14·00	5·00
84	118	$200,000 on $3,000 blue	£850	38·00

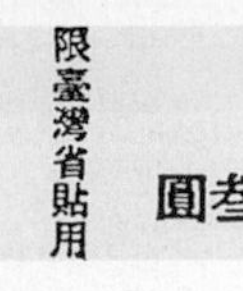

(3)

1946. Opening of National Assembly, Nanking. Issue of China surch as Type 3.

26	111	70s. on $20 green	3·50	6·00
27	111	$1 on $30 blue	4·50	6·50
28	111	$2 on $50 brown	4·50	5·50
29	111	$3 on $100 red	5·00	6·00

4 President Chiang Kai-shek (note characters to right of head)

1947. President's 60th Birthday.

30	4	70s. red	2·25	5·00
31	4	$1 green	3·00	6·50
32	4	$2 red	3·00	6·50
33	4	$3 green	3·25	6·50
34	4	$7 orange	3·25	6·00
35	4	$10 red	4·25	4·25

5 Entrance to Dr. Sun Yat-sen Mausoleum (note characters above face value)

1947. 1st Anniv of Return of Government to Nanking.

36	5	50s. green	2·50	5·00
37	5	$3 blue	2·50	5·50
38	5	$7.50 red	2·50	5·50
39	5	$10 brown	2·50	4·50
40	5	$20 purple	2·50	3·50

For other stamps as Types **4** and **5**, but with different Chinese characters, see N.E. Provinces Types **7** and **9**.

1947. No gum.

41	169	$1 brown	70	1·75
42	169	$2 brown	70	1·50
43	169	$3 green	70	1·50
44	169	$5 orange	70	1·25
45	169	$9 blue	70	2·00
46	169	$10 red	70	1·25
47	169	$20 green	70	1·00
59	169	$25 green	1·00	1·00
48	169	$50 purple	70	75
49	169	$100 blue	70	75
50	169	$200 brown	70	75
60	169	$5,000 orange	12·00	2·25
61	169	$10,000 green	15·00	5·00
62	169	$20,000 brown	15·00	5·00
63	169	$30,000 blue	18·00	2·50
64	169	$40,000 brown	15·00	2·25

6 Sun Yat-sen and Palms

(7)

1948. "Re-valuation" surcharges. Surch as T 7.

51	6	$25 on $100 blue	1·20	2·50
52	6	$300 on $3 green	1·00	50
53	6	$500 on $7.50 orange	1·50	75
54	6	$1,000 on 30c. grey	10·00	10·00
55	6	$1,000 on $3 green	4·25	1·00
56	6	$2,000 on $3 green	3·75	1·00
57	6	$3,000 on $3 green	5·50	1·25
58	6	$3,000 on $7.50 orange	95·00	4·50

1949. No value indicated. Stamps of China optd with five Chinese characters, similar to top line of T 2.

86	146	(-) Orange (Ord. postage)	2·00	50
87	147	(-) Green (Air Mail)	6·50	3·50
88	148	(-) Mauve (Express)	5·00	5·00
89	149	(-) Red (Registration)	5·00	5·00

PARCELS POST STAMPS

1948. As Type P 112 of China, with six Chinese characters in the sky above the lorry.

P65	$100 green	75
P66	$300 red	75
P67	$500 olive	75
P68	$1,000 black	75
P69	$3,000 purple	75

Parcels Post stamps were not on sale in unused condition.

POSTAGE DUE STAMPS

D7

1948

D51	D7	$1 blue	2·50	5·00
D52	D7	$3 blue	2·50	6·50
D53	D7	$5 blue	2·50	5·00
D54	D7	$10 blue	2·50	6·00
D55	D7	$20 blue	2·50	4·50

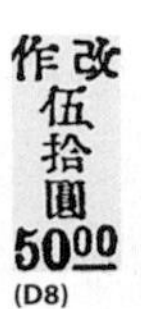

(D8)

1949. "Re-valuation" surcharges. Surch as Type D 8.

D65	$50 on $1 blue	15·00	38·00
D66	$100 on $3 blue	15·00	15·00
D67	$300 on $5 blue	15·00	14·00
D68	$500 on $10 blue	15·00	14·00

(D9)

1949. Handstamped with Type D 9.

D86	6	$1,000 on $3 green (No. 55)	40·00	38·00
D87	6	$3,000 on $3 green (No. 57)	48·00	40·00
D88	6	$5,000 orange (No. 60)	65·00	60·00

B. CHINESE NATIONALIST REPUBLIC.

Silver Yuan Surcharges.

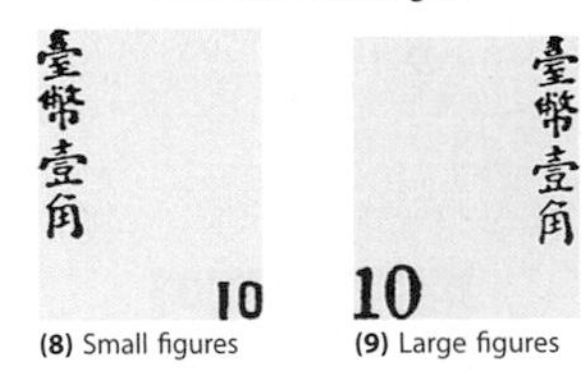

(8) Small figures **(9)** Large figures

1949. Stamps of Taiwan Province surch. (a) With T 8.

90	10c. on $50 purple	75·00	5·00

(b) As T 9 (figures at right).

91	2c. on $30,000 blue	45·00	38·00
92	10c. on $40,000 brown	55·00	35·00

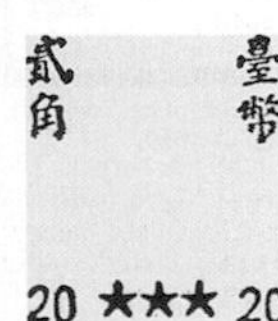

(10)

1949. Stamps of North Eastern Provinces (Manchuria), surch as T 10.

93	5	2c. on $44 red	50·00	10·00
95	5	5c. on $44 red	75·00	20·00
96	5	10c. on $44 red	65·00	3·25
97	5	20c. on $44 red	85·00	1·50
98	5	30c. on $44 red	95·00	27·00
99	5	50c. on $44 red	£100	21·00

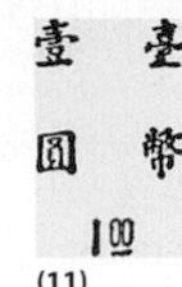

(11)

1950. Surch as T 11 on stamp of China but with no indication of value.

100	169	$1 on (-) green	£140	3·50
101	169	$2 on (-) green	£180	10·00
102	169	$5 on (-) green	£1300	50·00
103	169	$10 on (-) green	£1500	85·00
104	169	$20 on (-) green	£3250	£500

1950. Stamps of China surch. (a) As T 8 (figure "5" at left).

105	118	5c. on $200,000 purple	6·50	2·75

(b) As T 9 (figures at left).

106	3c. on $30,000 brown	7·50	5·00
107	3c. on $40,000 green	12·00	5·50
108	3c. on $50,000 blue	10·00	5·00
108a	10c. on $4,000 grey	38·00	10·00
109	10c. on $6,000 purple	28·00	6·50
110	10c. on $20,000 red	20·00	5·00
110a	10c. on $2,000,000 orge	22·00	4·00
110b	20c. on $500,000 mauve	42·00	6·50
110c	20c. on $1,000,000 red	60·00	6·50
110d	30c. on $3,000,000 bistre	85·00	9·00
110e	50c. on $5,000,000 blue	£130	6·50

GUM. All the following stamps to No. 616 were issued without gum except where otherwise stated.

12 Koxinga

1950. Rouletted. (a) Postage.

111	12	3c. grey	2·75	1·25
112	12	10c. brown	2·00	10
113	12	15c. yellow	15·00	7·50
114	12	20c. green	2·25	10
115	12	30c. red	60·00	20·00
116	12	40c. orange	5·00	10
117	12	50c. brown	8·50	40
118	12	80c. red	16·00	3·25
119	12	$1 violet	12·00	10
120	12	$1.50 green	75·00	8·50
121	12	$1.60 blue	75·00	1·00
122	12	$2 mauve	25·00	25
123	12	$5 turquoise	£130	12·00

(b) Air. With character at each side of head.

124	60c. blue	20·00	15·00

13 Peasant and Ballot Box

1951. Division of Country into Self-governing Districts. Perf or imperf.

125A	13	40c. red	25·00	10
126A	13	$1 blue	35·00	1·75
127A	13	$1.60 purple	40·00	2·75
128A	13	$2 brown	55·00	7·50
MS128Ba		102×71 mm. **13** $2 green. Imperf	£275	£180

1951. Silver Yuan surcharges. As T 169 of China but without value, surch.

129	$5 on (-) green	£100	10·00
130	$10 on (-) green	£375	7·00
131	$20 on (-) green	£850	22·00
132	$50 on (-) green	£900	90·00

15 Peasant and Scroll

1952. Land Tax Reduction. Perf or imperf.

133A	15	20c. orange	15·00	75
134A	15	40c. green	20·00	10
135A	15	$1 brown	30·00	2·50
136A	15	$1.40 blue	40·00	1·50
137A	15	$2 grey	£100	85·00
138A	15	$5 red	£120	2·50

16 President and Rejoicing crowds

1952. 2nd Anniv of Re-election of Pres. Chiang Kai-shek. Flag in red and blue. Eight characters in scroll. Perf or imperf.

139A	**16**	40c. red	20·00	10
140A	**16**	$1 green	25·00	2·25
141A	**16**	$1.60 orange	40·00	75
142A	**16**	$2 blue	60·00	25·00
143A	**16**	$5 purple	95·00	2·25

See also Nos. 151/6.

叁 臺
分 幣
3

(17)

1952. Stamps of China surch. with T 17.

144	**145**	3c. on 4c. grn (No. 1350)	4·25	4·25
145	**145**	3c. on 10c. lilac (No. 1351)	7·50	5·00
146	**145**	3c. on 20c. bl (No. 1353)	5·00	4·50
147	**145**	3c. on 50c. brown (No. 1354)	10·00	10·00

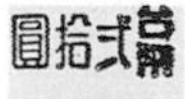

(18)

1953. T 169 of China, but without value, surch as T 18.

148	$10 on (–) green	£225	14·00
149	$20 on (–) green	£500	27·00
150	$50 on (–) green	£1800	£850

1953. 3rd Anniv of Re-election of Pres. Chiang Kai-shek. As T 16 but eleven characters in scroll. Flag in red and blue. Perf or imperf.

151A	10c. orange	18·00	1·00
152A	20c. green	18·00	75
153A	40c. red	20·00	10
154A	$1.40 blue	45·00	3·75
155A	$2 sepia	£100	6·50
156A	$5 purple	£160	18·00

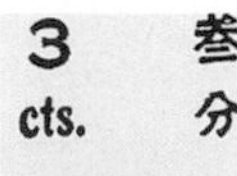

(19)

1953. Surch as T 19.

157	**12**	3c. on $1 violet	1·50	1·50
158	**12**	10c. on 15c. yellow	10·00	1·50
159	**12**	10c. on 30c. red	3·50	1·25
160	**12**	20c. on $1.60 blue	3·50	1·00

20 Doctor, Nurses and Patients

1953. Establishment of Anti-tuberculosis Assn. Cross of Lorraine in red. On paper with coloured network.

161	**20**	40c. brown on stone	20·00	10
162	**20**	$1.60 blue on turquoise	50·00	1·25
163	**20**	$2 green on yellow	65·00	1·25
164	**20**	$5 red on flesh	£110	10·00

21 Pres. Chiang Kai-shek

1953

165	**21**	10c. brown	5·00	10
166	**21**	20c. purple	4·50	10
167	**21**	40c. green	4·00	10
168	**21**	50c. purple	10·00	10
169	**21**	80c. brown	25·00	2·25
170	**21**	$1 green	12·00	10
171	**21**	$1.40 blue	16·00	20
172	**21**	$1.60 red	15·00	10
173	**21**	$1.70 green	25·00	4·25
174	**21**	$2 brown	18·00	10
175	**21**	$3 blue	£250	7·50
176	**21**	$4 turquoise	20·00	1·00
177	**21**	$5 red	22·00	10
178	**21**	$10 green	55·00	1·50
179	**21**	$20 purple	£120	5·00

22 Silo Bridge over River Cho-Shui-Chi

1954. Completion of Silo Bridge. Various frames.

180	**22**	40c. red	30·00	10
181	-	$1.60 blue	£120	75
182	**22**	$3.60 black	£100	2·50
183	-	$5 mauve	£140	3·25

DESIGN: $1.60, $5, Silo Bridge.

23 Sapling, Tree and Plantation

1954. Afforestation Day.

184	**23**	40c. green	25·00	10
185	-	$10 violet	£125	3·25
186	-	$20 red	75·00	75
187	-	$50 blue	£100	2·75

DESIGNS: $10, Tree plantation and houses; $20, Planting seedling; $50, Map of Taiwan and tree.

24 Runner

1954. Youth Day.

188	**24**	40c. blue	30·00	10
189	**24**	$5 red	90·00	10·00

25 Douglas DC-6 over City Gate, Taipeh

1954. Air. 15th Anniv of Air Force Day.

190	**25**	$1 brown	16·00	90
191	-	$1.60 black	15·00	20
192	-	$5 blue	30·00	1·00

DESIGNS: $1.60, Republic F-84G Thunderjets over Chung Shang Bridge, Taipeh. $5, Doves over Chi Kan Lee (Fort Zeelandia) in Tainan City.

26 Refugees crossing Pontoon Bridge

1954. Relief Fund for Chinese Refugees from North Vietnam.

193	**26**	40c.+10c. blue	40·00	10·00
194	**26**	$1.60+40c. purple	£110	45·00
195	**26**	$5+$1 red	£180	£150

27 Junk and Bridge

1954. 2nd Anniv of Overseas Chinese League.

196	**27**	40c. orange	25·00	10
197	**27**	$5 blue	25·00	3·50

28 "Chainbreaker"

1955. Freedom Day.

198	**28**	40c. green	6·50	10
199	-	$1 olive	22·00	5·00
200	-	$1.60 red	20·00	2·50

DESIGNS: $1, Soldier with torch and flag; $1.60, Torch and figures "1.23".

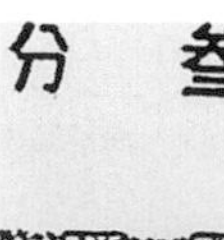

(29)

1955. Surch. as T 29.

201	**12**	3c. on $1 violet	3·25	1·10
202	**12**	20c. on 40c. orange	3·50	75

31 Pres. Chiang Kai-shek and Sun Yat-sen Memorial Building

1955. 1st Anniv of President Chiang Kai-shek's Second Re-election.

203	**31**	20c. olive	5·00	10
204	**31**	40c. green	6·00	10
205	**31**	$2 red	10·00	1·00
206	**31**	$7 blue	16·00	1·75
MS206a 147×104 mm. Nos. 203/6. Imperf			35·00	2·50

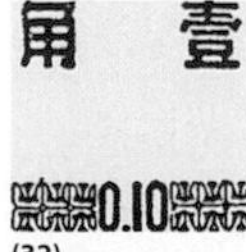

(32)

1955. Nos. 116/18, 120 and 124 surch as T 32. Nos. 212/14 have additional floral ornament below two characters at top.

207	**12**	10c. on 80c. red	3·50	30
208	**12**	10c. on $1.50 green	3·50	50
212	**12**	20c. on 40c. orange	4·00	30
213	**12**	20c. on 50c. brown	4·50	30
214	**12**	20c. on 60c. blue	5·00	1·20

33 Air Force Badge

1955. Armed Forces' Day.

209	**33**	40c. blue	5·00	10
210	**33**	$2 red	22·00	2·10
211	**33**	$7 green	22·00	1·50
MS211a 148×105 mm. Nos. 209/11. Imperf			£500	£300

35 Flags of U.N. and Taiwan

1955. 10th Anniv of UNO.

215	**35**	40c. blue	3·00	10
216	**35**	$2 red	7·50	75
217	**35**	$7 green	10·00	2·00

36 Pres. Chiang Kai-shek

1955. President's 69th Birthday. With gum.

218	**36**	40c. brown, blue and red	6·50	10
219	**36**	$2 blue, green and red	14·00	1·60
220	**36**	$7 green, brown and red	18·00	2·75
MS220a 148×105 mm. Nos. 218/20. Imperf. No gum			£160	90·00

37 Sun Yat-sen's Birthplace

1955. 90th Birth Anniv (1956) of Dr. Sun Yat-sen.

221	**37**	40c. blue	4·00	10
222	**37**	$2 brown	8·50	1·20
223	**37**	$7 red	12·00	2·10

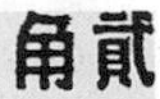

(38)

1956. Nos. 1213 and 1211 of China surch as T 38.

232B	**148**	3c. on (–) mauve	1·00	25
224	**146**	20c. on (–) orange I	55	25
304	**146**	20c. on (–) orange II	75	20

On No. 232 the characters are smaller and there are leaves on either side of the "3".

(I) Surch with Type **38**. (II) The characters are below the figures.

39 Old and Modern Postal Transport

1956. 60th Anniv of Postal Service.

225	**39**	40c. red	1·75	10
226	**39**	$1 blue	3·75	65
227	**39**	$1.60 brown	5·00	45
228	**39**	$2 green	8·00	95
MS228a Two sheets, each 149×103 mm. No. 228 in red and in crimson. Imperf. Set of 2 sheets			17·00	70·00

40 Children at Play

1956. Children's Day.

229	**40**	40c. green	1·50	10
230	**40**	$1.60 blue	3·50	40
231	**40**	$2 red	5·00	95

42 Earliest and Latest Steam Locomotives

1956. 75th Anniv of Chinese Railways.

233	**42**	40c. red	5·00	10
234	**42**	$2 blue	8·50	60
235	**42**	$8 green	10·00	1·50

43 Pres. Chiang Kai-shek

1956. 70th Birthday of President Chiang Kai-shek. Various portraits of President. With gum.

236	**43**	20c. orange	5·00	10
237	-	40c. red	6·50	10
238	-	$1 blue	10·00	15
239	-	$1.60 purple	12·00	10
240	-	$2 brown	18·00	30
241	-	$8 turquoise	35·00	75

SIZES—21½×30 mm: 20c., 40c.; 26½×26½ mm: $1, $1.60; 30×21½ mm: $2, $8.

(44)

1956. No. 1212 of China surch with T 44.

242	**147**	3c. on (–) green	1·00	25

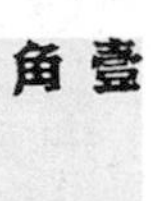
(45)

1956. No. 1214 of China surch with T 45.

243	**149**	10c. on (–) red	1·00	25

46 Telecommunications Symbols

1956. 75th Anniv of Chinese Telegraph Service.

244	**46**	40c. blue	85	10
245	**46**	$1.40 red	1·40	25
246	**46**	$1.60 green	2·40	30
247	**46**	$2 brown	4·50	35

47 Map of China

1957. (a) Printed in one colour.

248	**47**	3c. blue	10	15
249	**47**	10c. violet	1·40	15
250	**47**	20c. orange	1·25	10
251	**47**	40c. red	1·50	10
252	**47**	$1 brown	2·50	10
253	**47**	$1.60 green	5·00	15

(b) With frames in blue.

268	3c. blue	10	15
269	10c. violet	75	15
270	20c. orange	1·00	10
271	40c. red	1·25	10
272	$1 brown	4·25	15
273	$1.60 green	4·50	10

48 Mencius with his Mother

1957. Mothers' Teaching.

254	**48**	40c. green	1·10	10
255	-	$3 brown	1·90	60

DESIGN: $3, Marshal Yueh Fei with his mother.

49 Chinese Scout Badges and Rosettes

1957. 50th Anniv of Boy Scout Movement, Jubilee Jamboree and Birth Centenary of Lord Baden-Powell (Founder).

256	**49**	40c. violet	75	10
257	**49**	$1 green	1·50	45
258	**49**	$1.60 blue	1·90	25

50 Globe, Radio Mast and Microphone

1957. 30th Anniv of Chinese Broadcasting Service.

259	**50**	40c. salmon	35	10
260	**50**	50c. mauve	85	30
261	**50**	$3.50 blue	1·60	60

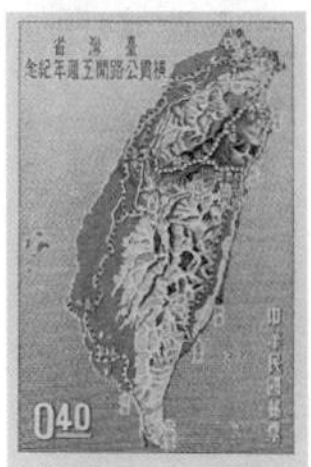
51 Highway Map of Taiwan

1957. 1st Anniv of Taiwan Cross-Island Highway Project.

262	**51**	40c. green	2·50	10
263	**51**	$1.40 blue	5·50	1·50
264	**51**	$2 sepia	7·25	1·80

52 Freighter "Hai Min" and River Vessel "Kiang Foo"

1957. 85th Anniv of China Merchants' Steam Navigation Co.

265	**52**	40c. blue	50	20
266	**52**	80c. purple	1·00	70
267	**52**	$2.80 red	1·80	1·10

53 "Batocera lineolata" (longhorn beetle)

1958. Insects. Multicoloured. With gum.

274	10c. Type **53**	1·25	15
275	40c. "Papilio maraho" (butterfly)	1·25	10
276	$1 Atlas moth	2·50	15
277	$1.40 "Erasmia pulchella" (moth)	4·00	60
278	$1.60 "Cheirotonus macleayi" (beetle)	5·00	15
279	$2 Great mormon (butterfly)	6·50	75

54 "Phalaenopsis amabilis"

1958. Taiwan Orchids. Orchids in natural colours; backgrounds in colours given. With gum.

280	**54**	20c. brown	2·25	10
281	-	40c. violet	2·50	10
282	-	$1.40 purple	4·25	25
283	-	$3 blue	6·25	50

ORCHIDS—VERT: 40c. "Laeliacattleya"; $1.40, "Cycnoches chlorochilon klotzsch". HORIZ: $3, "Dendrobium phalaenopsis".

55 WHO Emblem

1958. 10th Anniv of WHO.

284	**55**	40c. blue	40	10
285	**55**	$1.60 red	65	30
286	**55**	$2 purple	1·20	50

56 Presidential Mansion, Taipeh

1958

290a	**56**	$5 green	10·00	25
290b	**56**	$5.60 violet	10·00	50
290c	**56**	$6 orange	14·00	25
290d	**56**	$10 green	12·00	25
290e	**56**	$20 red	18·00	30
289	**56**	$50 brown	65·00	1·80
290	**56**	$100 blue	90·00	4·50

58 Ploughman

1958. 10th Anniv of Joint Commission on Chinese Rural Reconstruction.

291	**58**	20c. green	95	10
292	**58**	40c. black	1·20	10
293	**58**	$1.40 purple	2·30	25
294	**58**	$3 blue	3·75	65

59 President Chiang Kai-shek Reviewing Troops

1958. 72nd Birthday of President Chiang Kai-shek and National Day Review. With gum.

295	**59**	40c. multicoloured	1·00	10

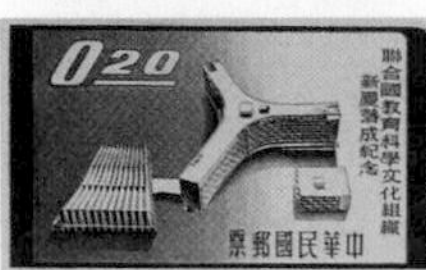
60 UNESCO Headquarters, Paris

1958. Inaug of UNESCO Headquarters.

296	**60**	20c. blue	30	10
297	**60**	40c. green	50	25
298	**60**	$1.40 red	65	35
299	**60**	$3 purple	95	75

1958. 10th Anniv of Declaration of Human Rights.

300	**61**	40c. green	30	10
301	**61**	60c. sepia	35	20
302	**61**	$1 red	55	25
303	**61**	$3 blue	75	50

61 Flame of Freedom encircling Globe

1958. No. 192 surch 350.

305	$3.50 on $5 blue	5·25	2·25

64 The Constitution

1958. 10th Anniv of Constitution.

306	**64**	40c. green	65	10
307	**64**	50c. purple	1·00	25
308	**64**	$1.40 red	1·90	30
309	**64**	$3.50 blue	3·50	85

65 Chu Kwang Tower, Quemoy

1959

310	**65**	3c. orange	30	20
311	**65**	5c. olive	50	25
312	**65**	10c. lilac	35	10
313	**65**	20c. blue	40	10
314	**65**	40c. brown	45	10
315	**65**	50c. turquoise	1·25	20
316	**65**	$1 red	1·25	10
317	**65**	$1.40 green	2·50	20
318	**65**	$2 myrtle	2·50	20
319	**65**	$2.80 mauve	5·50	85
320	**65**	$3 slate	4·25	20

See also Nos. 367/82f.

66 Slaty-backed Gull

1959. Air. With gum.

321	**66**	$8 black, blue and green	5·00	40

67 ILO Emblem and Headquarters, Geneva

1959. 40th Anniv of ILO.

322	**67**	40c. blue	20	10
323	**67**	$1.60 brown	30	20
324	**67**	$3 green	75	30
325	**67**	$5 red	1·20	70

68 Scout Bugler

1959. 10th World Scout Jamboree, Manila.

326	**68**	40c. red	60	10
327	**68**	50c. blue	1·10	25
328	**68**	$5 green	2·20	75

69 Inscribed Rock on Mt. Tai-wu, Quemoy

1959. Defence of Quemoy (Kinmen) and Matsu Islands, 1958.

329	**69**	40c. brown	40	10
330	-	$1.40 blue	70	20
331	-	$2 green	1·70	25
332	**69**	$3 blue	2·10	40

DESIGN—(41×23½ mm): $1.40, $2, Map of Taiwan, Quemoy and Matsu Islands.

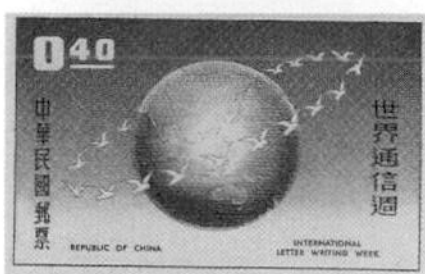

70

1959. International Correspondence Week.

333	**70**	40c. blue	60	10
334	**70**	$1 red	70	30
335	**70**	$2 sepia	85	20
336	**70**	$3.50 red	1·10	70

71 National Science Hall

1959. Inauguration of Taiwan National Science Hall. With gum.

337	**71**	40c. multicoloured	1·20	10
338	-	$3 mult (different view)	2·50	75

72 Confederation Emblem

1959. 10th Anniv of International Confederation of Free Trade Unions.

339	**72**	40c. green	30	10
340	**72**	$1.60 purple	65	35
341	**72**	$3 orange	1·20	65

73 Sun Yat-sen and Abraham Lincoln

1959. 150th Birth Anniv of Lincoln. With gum.

342	**73**	40c. multicoloured	45	10
343	**73**	$3 multicoloured	1·00	40

74 "Bomb Burst" by Thunder Tiger Aerobatic Squadron

1960. Air. Chinese Air Force Commem. With gum.

344	**74**	$1 multicoloured	6·50	45
345	-	$2 multicoloured	5·00	35
346	-	$5 multicoloured	9·00	55

DESIGNS—HORIZ: (Various aerobatics): $2, Loop; $5, Diamond formation flying over jet fighter.

75 Night Delivery

1960. Introduction of "Prompt Delivery" and "Postal Launch" Services.

347	**75**	$1.40 purple	1·50	25
348	**75**	$1.60 blue "Yu-Khi" (postal launch)	2·00	45

76 "Uprooted Tree"

1960. World Refugee Year. With gum.

349	**76**	40c. green, brown & black	25	10
350	**76**	$3 green, orange & black	75	45

77 Cross-Island Highway

1960. Inaug of Taiwan Cross-Island Highway.

351	**77**	40c. green	85	10
352	-	$1 blue	2·50	30
353	-	$2 purple	2·00	30
354	**77**	$3 brown	7·25	65·00
MS354a		144×103 mm. Nos. 352 and 354. Imperf	2·75	40

DESIGN—VERT: $1, $2 Tunnels on Highway.

1960. Visit of Pres. Eisenhower. Nos. 331/2 optd WELCOME U.S. PRESIDENT DWIGHT D. EISENHOWER 1960 in English and Chinese.

355	-	$2 green	1·10	45
356	**69**	$3 blue	1·50	50

79 Winged Tape-reel

1960. Phonopost (tape-recordings) Service.

357	**79**	$2 red	1·50	1·50

80 "Flowers and Red-billed Blue Magpies" (after Hsiao Yung)

1960. Ancient Chinese Paintings from Palace Museum Collection (1st series). With gum.

358	-	$1 multicoloured	4·00	50
359	-	$1.40 multicoloured	9·50	85
360	**80**	$1.60 multicoloured	10·00	1·50
361	-	$2 multicoloured	15·00	3·00

PAINTINGS—HORIZ: $1, "Two Riders" (after Wei Yen). $1.40, "Two Horses and Groom" (after Han Kan). $2, "A Pair of Green-winged Teals in a Rivulet" (after Monk Hui Ch'ung).

See also Nos. 451/4, 577/80 and 716/19.

81 Youth Corps Flag and Summer Activities

1960. Youth Summer Activities.

362	**81**	50c. green	70	25
363	-	$3 brown	1·10	55

DESIGN—HORIZ: $3, Youth Corps Flag and other summer activities.

82 "Forest Cultivation"

1960. 5th World Forestry Congress, Seattle. Multicoloured. With gum.

364		$1 Type **82**	1·75	20
365		$2 "Forest Protection" (trees and sika deer)	2·75	70
366		$3 "Lumber Production" (cable railway)	30·00	19·00
MS366a		100×145 mm. Nos. 364/6 forming a composite design. Imperf. No gum	3·25	50

83 Chu Kwang Tower, Quemoy

1960. As T 65 but redrawn.

367	**83**	3c. brown	10	20
382	**83**	10c. green	2·50	30
368	**83**	40c. violet	40	10
369	**83**	50c. orange	70	10
370	**83**	60c. purple	75	15
371	**83**	80c. green	75	10
372	**83**	$1 green	2·25	10
373	**83**	$1.20 green	1·75	20
374	**83**	$1.50 blue	2·25	20
375	**83**	$2 red	1·75	10
376	**83**	$2.50 blue	2·00	25
377	**83**	$3 green	2·25	20
378	**83**	$3.20 brown	5·50	20
379	**83**	$3.60 blue	6·00	55
382f	**83**	$4 green	14·00	35
380	**83**	$4.50 red	10·00	80

84 Diving

1960. Sports. With gum.

383	**84**	50c. brown, yellow & blue	1·00	10
384	-	80c. violet, yellow & purple	1·00	10
385	-	$2 multicoloured	2·25	25
386	-	$2.50 black and orange	2·50	50
387	-	$3 multicoloured	3·75	60
388	-	$3.20 multicoloured	5·00	75

DESIGNS: 80c. Discus-throwing; $2, Basketball; $2.50, Football; $3, Hurdling; $3.20, Sprinting.

85 Bronze Wine Vase (Shang Dynasty)

1961. Ancient Chinese Art Treasures (1st series). With gum.

389	**85**	80c. multicoloured	3·25	10
390	-	$1 indigo, blue and red	4·25	30
391	-	$1.20 blue, brown & yellow	5·00	45
392	-	$1.50 brown, blue & mauve	5·50	95
393	-	$2 brown, violet and green	6·25	70
394	-	$2.50 black, lilac and blue	10·00	1·20

DESIGNS: $1, Bronze cauldron (Chou); $1.20, Porcelain vase (Sung); $1.50, Jade perforated tube (Chou); $2, Porcelain jug (Ming); $2.50, Jade flower vase (Ming).

See also Nos. 408/13 and 429/34.

86 Farmer and Mechanical Plough

1961. Agricultural Census.

395	**86**	80c. purple	1·00	20
396	**86**	$2 green	3·25	45
397	**86**	$3.20 red	4·75	35

87 Mme. Chiang Kai-shek

1961. 10th Anniv (1960) of Chinese Women's Anti-Aggression League. With gum.

398	**87**	80c. black, red & turquoise	2·50	10
399	**87**	$1 black, red and green	4·25	60
400	**87**	$2 black, red and brown	4·50	65
401	**87**	$3.20 black, red and purple	6·25	1·30

88 Taiwan Lobster

1961. Mail Order Service.

402	**88**	$3 myrtle	4·25	40

89 Jeme Tien-yao and Locomotive

1961. Birth Centenary of Jeme Tien-yao (railway engineer).

403	-	80c. violet	2·25	20
404	**89**	$2 black	3·25	65

DESIGN: 80c. As Type **89** but locomotive heading right.

90 Pres. Chiang Kai-shek

1961. 1st Anniv of Chiang Kai-shek's Third Term Inauguration. Multicoloured. With gum.

405		80c. Map of China (horiz)	3·25	10
406		$2 Type **90**	6·50	1·40
MS406a		139×100 mm. Nos. 405/6. Imperf. No gum	20·00	18·00

91 Convair 880 Jetliner ("The Mandarin Jet"), Biplane and Flag

1961. 40th Anniv of Chinese Civil Air Service. With gum.

407	**91**	$10 multicoloured	4·25	1·40

1961. Ancient Chinese Art Treasures (2nd issue). As T 85. With gum.

408		80c. multicoloured	2·50	25
409		$1 blue, brown and bistre	4·50	50
410		$1.50 blue and salmon	6·00	1·20
411		$2 red, black and blue	9·00	75
412		$4 blue, sepia and red	13·00	1·40
413		$4.50 brown, sepia and blue	23·00	3·00

DESIGNS—VERT: 80c. Palace perfumer (Ching); $1, Corn vase (Warring States); $2, Jade tankard (Sung). HORIZ: $1.50, Bronze bowl (Chou); $4, Porcelain bowl (Southern Sung); $4.50, Jade chimera (Han).

92 Sun Yat-sen and Chiang Kai-shek

1961. 50th National Day. With gum.

414	**92**	80c. brown, blue and grey	2·00	10
415	-	$5 multicoloured	4·50	1·60
MS415a		135×100 mm. Nos. 414/15	15·00	10·00

DESIGN—HORIZ: $5, Map and flag.

93 Lotus Lake

1961. Taiwan Scenery. Multicoloured. With gum.

416		80c. Pitan (Green Lake) (vert)	5·00	20
417		$1 Type **93**	10·00	80
418		$2 Sun-Moon Lake	13·00	60
419		$3.20 Wulai Waterfall (vert)	16·00	1·20

94 Steel Furnace

1961. Taiwan Industries. With gum.

420	-	80c. indigo, brown & blue	2·50	25
421	**94**	$1.50 multicoloured	4·25	75
422	-	$2.50 multicoloured	5·50	70
423	-	$3.20 indigo, brown & blue	7·50	70

DESIGNS—VERT: 80c. Oil refinery. $2.50, Aluminium manufacture. HORIZ: $3.20, Fertilizer plant.

95 Atomic Reactor, National Tsing Hwa University

1961. 1st Taiwan Atomic Reactor Inauguration. Multicoloured. With gum.

424		80c. Type **95**	1·90	20
425		$2 Interior of reactor	5·00	1·50
426		$3.20 Reactor building (horiz)	5·25	1·10

96 Telegraph Wires and Microwave Reflector Pylons

1961. 80th Anniv of Chinese Telecommunications. Multicoloured. With gum.

427		80c. Type **96**	1·25	20
428		$3.20 Microwave parabolic antenna (horiz)	2·75	1·00

1962. Ancient Chinese Art Treasures (3rd issue). As T 85. With gum.

429		80c. brown, violet and red	2·25	25
430		$1 purple, brown and blue	2·50	25
431		$2.40 blue, brown and red	18·00	85
432		$3 multicoloured	20·00	70
433		$3.20 red, green and blue	18·00	70
434		$3.60 multicoloured	28·00	90

DESIGNS—VERT: 80c. Jade topaz twin wine vessel (Chiang). $1, Bronze pouring vase (Warring States). $2.40, Porcelain vase (Ming). $3, Tsun bronze wine vase (Shang). $3.20, Porcelain jar (Ching). $3.60, Jade perforated disc (Han).

97 Postal Segregating, Facing and Cancelling Machine

1962

435	**97**	80c. purple	1·30	40

98 Mt. Yu Weather Station

1962. World Meteorological Day.

436	**98**	80c. brown	65	20
437	-	$1 blue	1·60	40
438	-	$2 green	2·20	85

DESIGNS—HORIZ: $1, Route-map of Typhoon Pamela. VERT: $2, Weather balloon passing globe.

99 Distribution of Milk and U.N. Emblem

1962. 15th Anniv of UNICEF.

439	**99**	80c. red	70	20
440	**99**	$3.20 green	2·10	65
MS440a		135×100 mm. Nos. 439/40. Imperf	15·00	4·00

100 Campaign Emblem

1962. Malaria Eradication. With gum.

441	**100**	80c. red, green and blue	50	20
442	**100**	$3.60 brown, grn & dp brn	1·00	1·40

101 Yu Yu-jen (journalist)

1962. "Elder Reporter" Yu Yu-jen Commemoration. With gum.

443	**101**	80c. sepia and pink	1·80	25

102 Koxinga

1962. Tercentenary of Koxinga's Recovery of Taiwan. With gum.

444	**102**	80c. purple	1·60	25
445	**102**	$2 green	3·00	70

103 Co-operative Emblem

1962. 40th International Co-operative Day.

446	**103**	80c. brown	65	20
447	-	$2 lilac	1·40	60

DESIGN: $2, Global handclasp.

104 UNESCO Symbols

1962. UNESCO Activities Commem.

448	**104**	80c. mauve	55	20
449	-	$2 lake	1·20	50
450	-	$3.20 green	1·30	35

DESIGNS—HORIZ: $2, UNESCO emblem on open book. $3.20, Emblem linking hemispheres.

105 Emperor T'ai Tsu (Ming Dynasty)

1962. Ancient Chinese Paintings from Palace Museum Collection (2nd series). Emperors. Multicoloured. With gum.

451		80c. T'ai Tsung (Tang)	25·00	75
452		$2 T'ai Tsu (Sung)	45·00	6·00
453		$3.20 Genghis Khan (Yuan)	55·00	6·75
454		$4 Type **105**	65·00	18·00

106 "Lions" Emblem and Activities

1962. 45th Anniv of Lions International With gum.

455	**106**	80c. multicoloured	1·20	25
456	**106**	$3.60 multicoloured	2·50	95
MS456a		100×75 mm. Nos. 455/6. Imperf. No gum	22·00	8·00

107 Pole Vaulting

1962. Sports. With gum.

457	**107**	80c. brown, black & blue	1·00	20
458	**107**	$3.20 multicoloured	2·20	55

DESIGN—HORIZ: $3.20, Rifle shooting.

108 Young Farmers

1962. 10th Anniv of Chinese 4-H Clubs.

459	**108**	80c. red	65	20
460	-	$3.20 green	2·00	65
MS460a		135×100 mm. Nos. 459/60. Imperf	23·00	9·75

DESIGN: $3.20, 4-H Clubs emblem.

109 Liner

1962. 90th Anniv of China Merchants' Steam Navigation Co. Multicoloured. With gum.

461		80c. Type **109**	1·80	25
462		$3.60 Freighter "Hai Min" and Pacific route-map (horiz)	4·00	95

110 Harvesting

1963. Freedom from Hunger. With gum.

463	**110**	$10 multicoloured	5·00	95

111 Youth, Girl, Torch and Martyrs Monument, Huang Hua Kang

1963. 20th Youth Day.

464	**111**	80c. purple	75	20
465	**111**	$3.20 green	2·00	60

112 Barn Swallows and Pagoda

1963. 1st Anniv of Asian-Oceanic Postal Union. With gum. Multicoloured.

466	80c. Type **112**	5·00	50
467	$2 Northern gannet	6·50	90
468	$6 Manchurian crane and pine tree (vert)	15·00	2·75

113 Refugee in Tears

1963. Refugees' Flight from Mainland.

469	**113**	80c. black	1·30	20
470	-	$3.20 red	2·75	45

DESIGN—HORIZ: $3.20, Refugees on march.

114 Convair 880 over Tropic of Cancer Monument, Kiai

1963. Air. Multicoloured. With gum.

471	$2.50 Suspension Bridge, Pitan (horiz)	7·50	20
472	$6 Type **114**	12·00	35
473	$10 Lion-head Mountain, Sinchu	15·00	70

115 Red Cross Nurse and Emblem

1963. Red Cross Centenary. With gum.

474	**115**	80c. red and black	5·50	20
475	-	$10 red, green and blue	12·00	2·75

DESIGN: $10, Globe and scroll.

116 Basketball

1963. 2nd Asian Basketball Championships, Taipeh.

476	**116**	80c. mauve	1·25	25
477	-	$2 violet	2·75	75

DESIGN: $2, Hands reaching for inscribed ball.

117 Freedom Torch

1963. 15th Anniv of Declaration of Human Rights.

478	**117**	80c. green	80	40
479	-	$3.20 red	1·60	80

DESIGN—HORIZ: $3.20, Human figures and scales of justice.

118 Country Scene

1963. "Good-People, Good-Deeds" Campaign. Multicoloured. With gum.

480	40c. Type **118**	3·25	30
481	$4.50 Lighting candle	6·75	2·10

119 Dr. Sun Yat-sen and his Book "Three Principles of the People"

1983. 10th Anniv of Land-to-Tillers Programme. With gum.

482	**119**	$5 multicoloured	9·50	1·20

120 Torch of Liberty

1964. 10th Anniv of Liberty Day.

483	**120**	80c. orange	60	20
484	-	$3.20 blue	2·40	45

DESIGN—VERT: $3.20, Hands with broken manacles.

121 Broadleaf Cactus

1964. Taiwan Cacti. Multicoloured. With gum.

485	80c. Type **121**	5·00	25
486	$1 Crab cactus	9·50	1·00
487	$3.20 Nopalxochia	14·00	25
488	$5 Grizzly-Bear cactus	16·00	1·30

122 Wu Chih-hwei (politician)

1964. 99th Birth Anniv of Wu Chih-hwei (politician).

489	**122**	80c. brown	1·60	25

123 Chu Kwang Tower, Quemoy

1964

490	**123**	3c. purple	20	20
491	**123**	5c. green	20	10
492	**123**	10c. green	50	20
493	**123**	20c. green	35	10
494	**123**	40c. red	35	10
495	**123**	50c. purple	60	10
496	**123**	80c. orange	1·00	10
497	**123**	$1 violet	50	10
498	**123**	$1.50 purple	10·00	1·00
499	**123**	$2 purple	1·25	10
500	**123**	$2.50 blue	2·50	20
501	**123**	$3 grey	3·25	25
502	**123**	$3.20 blue	3·50	20
504	**123**	$4 green	4·50	20

125 Weir

1964. Nurses Day.

506	-	80c. violet	1·50	25
507	**124**	$4 red	3·25	70

DESIGN—HORIZ: 80c. Nurses holding candlelight ceremony.

124 Nurse and Florence Nightingale

1964. Inaug of Shihmen Reservoir. With gum. Mult.

508	80c. Type **125**	2·50	20
509	$1 Irrigation channel	3·25	35
510	$3.20 Dam and powerhouse	7·00	50
511	$5 Main spillway	10·00	2·20

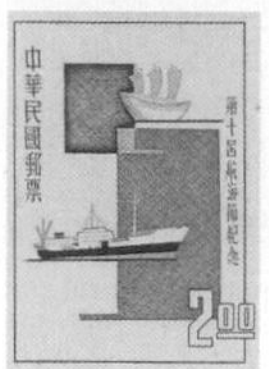

126 Ancient Ship and Modern Freighter

1964. Navigation Day.

512	**126**	$2 orange	75	20
513	**126**	$3.60 green	1·90	50

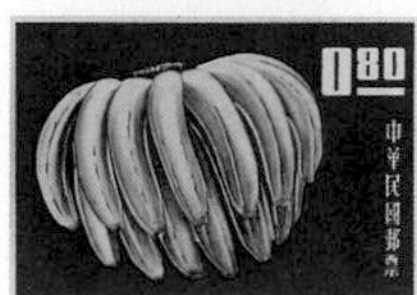

127 Bananas

1964. Taiwan Fruits. Multicoloured. With gum.

514	80c. Type **127**	10·00	10
515	$1 Oranges	18·00	1·25
516	$3.20 Pineapples	23·00	80
517	$4 Water-melons	38·00	2·30

128 Lockheed Starfighters, "Tai Ho", "Tai Choa" and "Tai Tsung" (destroyers) and Artillery

1964. Armed Forces Day.

518	**128**	80c. blue	1·30	20
519	**128**	$6 purple	3·75	65

129 Globe and Flags of Formosa and U.S.A.

1964. New York World's Fair (1st issue). With gum.

520	**129**	80c. multicoloured	2·10	35
521	-	$5 multicoloured	4·75	1·10

DESIGN—HORIZ: $5, Taiwan Pavilion at Fair.

See also Nos. 550/1.

130 Cowman holding Calf

1964. Animal Protection.

522	**130**	$2 purple	1·30	25
523	**130**	$4 blue	3·00	95

131 Cycling

1964. Olympic Games, Tokyo.

524	**131**	80c. blue	1·00	20
525	-	$1 red	1·75	25
526	-	$3.20 green	2·25	40
527	-	$10 violet	4·00	1·80

DESIGNS: $1, Runner breasting tape; $3.20, Gymnastics; $10, High jumping.

132 Hsu Kuang-chi (statesman)

1964. Famous Chinese.

528	**132**	80c. blue	2·40	25

See also Nos. 558/9, 586/7, 599, 606/9, 610, 738/40, 960 and 1072/7.

133 Factory-bench ("Pharmaceutics")

1964. Taiwan Industries. Multicoloured. With gum.

529	40c. Type **133**	2·50	25
530	$1.50 Loom ("Textiles") (horiz)	4·25	1·30
531	$2 Refinery ("Chemicals")	5·50	35
532	$3.60 Cement-mixer ("Cement") (horiz)	8·50	1·20

134 Dr. Sun Yat-sen (founder)

1964. 70th Anniv of Kuomintang.

533	**134**	80c. green	2·20	30
534	**134**	$3.60 purple	4·25	90

135 Mrs. Eleanor Roosevelt and "Human Rights" Emblem

1964. 16th Anniv of Declaration of Human Rights.

535	**135**	$10 brown and violet	1·90	50

136 Law Code and Scales of Justice

1965. 20th Judicial Day.

536	**136**	80c. red	50	20
537	**136**	$3.20 green	95	55

137 Rotary Emblem and Mainspring

1965. 60th Anniv of Rotary International.

538	**137**	$1.50 red	70	20
539	**137**	$2 green	70	25
540	**137**	$2.50 blue	1·30	45

138 "Double Carp"

1965

541	**138**	$5 violet	20·00	60
542	**138**	$5.60 blue	20·00	4·25
543	**138**	$6 brown	20·00	1·30
544	**138**	$10 mauve	28·00	80
545	**138**	$20 red	35·00	1·20
546	**138**	$50 green	50·00	4·00
547	**138**	$100 red	95·00	6·50

See also Nos. 695/698ab.

139 Mme. Chiang Kai-shek

1965. 15th Anniv of Chinese Women's Anti-Aggression League. With gum.

548	**139**	$2 multicoloured	20·00	50
549	**139**	$6 multicoloured	32·00	4·00

140 Unisphere and Taiwan Pavilion, N.Y. Fair

1965. New York World's Fair (2nd issue). Multicoloured. With gum.

550	$2 Type **140**	30·00	85
551	$10 Peacock and various birds ("100 birds paying tribute to Queen Phoenix")	35·00	2·50

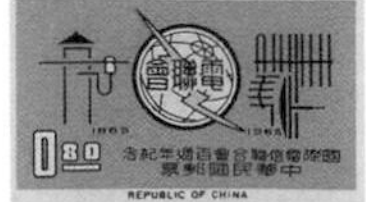

141 ITU Emblem and Symbols

1965. Centenary of ITU. Multicoloured. With gum.

552	80c. Type **141**	80	20
553	$5 ITU emblem and symbols (vert)	2·10	75

142 Madai Seabream

1965. Taiwan Fishes. Mult. With gum.

554	40c. Type **142**	3·00	35
555	80c. Silver pomfret	4·25	40
556	$2 Skipjack tuna (vert)	7·50	1·20
557	$4 Moonfish	13·00	1·70

1965. Famous Chinese. Portraits as T 132.

558	$1 red (Confucius)	4·00	30
559	$3.60 blue (Mencius)	6·00	80

143 ICY Emblem

1965. Int Co-operation Year. Mult. With gum.

560	$2 Type **143**	1·10	25
561	$6 I.C.Y. emblem (horiz)	3·75	1·20

144 Road Crossing

1965. Road Safety.

562	**144**	$1 purple	1·60	40
563	**144**	$4 red	2·50	95

145 Dr. Sun Yat-sen

1965. Birth Centenary of Dr. Sun Yat-sen. Multicoloured. With gum.

564	$1 Type **145**	5·00	25
565	$4 As T **145** but with portrait, etc., on right	10·00	85
566	$5 Dr. Sun Yat-sen and flags (horiz)	14·00	2·20

146 Children with Firework

1965. Chinese Folklore (1st Series). Multicoloured. With gum.

567	$1 Type **146**	6·75	40
568	$4.50 Dragon dance	8·75	1·40

See also Nos. 581/3 and 617.

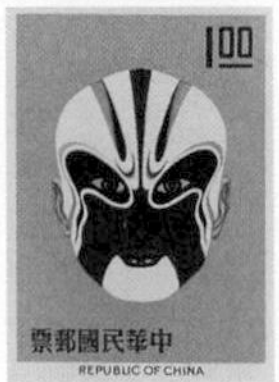

147 Lien Po, "Marshal and Prime Minister Reconciled"

1966. Painted Faces of Chinese Opera. Multicoloured. With gum.

569	$1 Type **147**	15·00	25
570	$3 Kuan Yu, "Reunion at Ku City"	20·00	55
571	$4 Chang Fei, "Long Board Slope"	30·00	85
572	$6 Buddha, "The Flower-scattering Angel"	40·00	3·25

148 Pigeon holding Postal Emblem

1966. 70th Anniv of Chinese Postal Services. Multicoloured. With gum.

573	$1 Type **148**	2·20	25
574	$2 Postman by Chu memorial stone (horiz)	3·25	30
575	$3 Postal Museum (horiz)	3·75	40
576	$4 "Postman climbing"	6·75	1·80

149 "Fishing on a Snowy Day" (After artist of the "Five Dynasties")

1966. Ancient Chinese Paintings from Palace Museum Collection (3rd series). With gum. Multicoloured.

577	$2.50 Type **149**	6·50	45
578	$3.50 "Calves on the Plain"	14·00	65
579	$4.50 "Snowscape"	18·00	1·40
580	$5 "Magpies" (after Lin Ch'un)	22·00	1·80

Nos. 578/9 both after Sung artists.

1966. Chinese Folklore (2nd series). As T 146. With gum. Multicoloured.

581	$2.50 Dragon boat racing (horiz)	16·00	40
582	$4 "Lady Chang O Flying to the Moon" (horiz)	8·50	45
583	$6 Lion Dance	4·75	85

150 Flags of Argentine and Chinese Republics

1966. 150th Anniv of Argentine Republic's Independence. With gum.

584	**150**	$10 multicoloured	3·75	65

151 Lin Sen

1966. Birth Centenary of Lin Sen (statesman).

585	**151**	$1 sepia	1·80	20

1966. Famous Chinese. Portraits as T 132.

586	$2.50 sepia	3·25	35
587	$3.50 red	4·75	65

PORTRAITS: $2.50, General Yueh Fei. $3.50, Wen Tien-hsiang (statesman).

153 Bean Geese

1966

588	**153**	$3.50 brown	1·00	25
589	**153**	$4 red	85	20
590	**153**	$4.50 green	1·60	25
591	**153**	$5 purple	90	20
592	**153**	$5.50 green	1·30	25
593	**153**	$6 blue	5·00	25
594	**153**	$6.50 violet	2·00	30
595	**153**	$7 black	1·20	20
596	**153**	$8 red	1·60	20

154 Pres. Chiang Kai-shek

1966. President Chiang Kai-shek's re-election for 4th Term. With gum. Multicoloured.

597	$1 Type **154**	2·25	30
598	$5 President in Uniform	6·00	1·50

1966. Famous Chinese. Portrait as T 132.

599	$1 blue (Tsai Yuan-Pei, scholar)	1·90	25

155 Various means of Transport

1967. Development of Taiwan Communications. Multicoloured. With gum.

600	$1 Mobile postman and micro-wave station (vert)	1·20	20
601	$5 Type **155**	2·20	80

156 Boeing 727-100 over Chilin Pavilion, Grand Hotel, Taipeh

1967. Air. Multicoloured. With gum.

602	$5 Type **156**	3·25	25
603	$8 Boeing 727-100 over Palace Museum, Taipeh	4·75	55

158 "God of Happiness" (wood carving)

1967. Chiang Kai-shek's 4th Presidential Term. With gum.

604	**157**	$1 multicoloured	1·60	20
605	**157**	$4 multicoloured	3·00	80

1967. Famous Chinese. Poets. Portraits. As T 132.

606	$1 black (Chu Yuan)	1·40	25
607	$2 brown (Li Po)	3·25	30
608	$2.50 brown (Tu Fu)	4·00	50
609	$3 green (Po Chu-i)	6·00	45

1967. Famous Chinese. Portrait as T 132.

610	$1 black (Chiu Ching, female revolutionary)	1·90	25

157 Pres. Chiang Kai-shek

1967. Chinese Handicrafts. Multicoloured. With gum.

611	$1 Type **158**	3·25	45
612	$2.50 Vase and dish	4·00	70
613	$3 Chinese dolls	5·25	1·40
614	$5 Palace lanterns	8·50	3·25

159 "WACL" on World Map

1967. 1st World Anti-Communist League Conference, Taipei.

615	**159**	$1 red	60	20
616	**159**	$5 blue	1·30	70

GUM. From No. 617 all stamps were issued with gum unless otherwise stated.

1967. Chinese Folklore (3rd series). Stilts Pastime. As T 146.

617		$4.50 multicoloured	1·60	40

DESIGN: "The Fisherman and the Wood-cutter" (Chinese play on stilts).

160 Muller's Barbet

1967. Taiwan Birds. Multicoloured.

618		$1 Type **160**	3·50	20
619		$2 Maroon oriole (horiz)	6·50	25
620		$2.50 Japanese green pigeon (horiz)	11·00	75
621		$3 Formosan blue magpie (horiz)	11·00	40
622		$5 Crested serpent eagle	13·00	75
623		$8 Mikado pheasant (horiz)	16·00	75

161 Chung Hsing Pagoda

1967. International Tourist Year. Multicoloured.

624		$1 Type **161**	1·40	20
625		$2.50 Yeh Liu National Park (coastal scene) (horiz)	3·50	45
626		$4 Statue of Buddha (horiz)	4·25	65
627		$5 National Palace Museum, Taipei (horiz)	5·25	85

162 Flags and China Park, Manila

1967. China–Philippines Friendship.

628	**162**	$1 multicoloured	65	20
629	**162**	$5 multicoloured	2·10	55

163 Chungshan Building, Yangmingshan

1968

630	**163**	5c. brown	30	20
631	**163**	10c. green	35	20
632	**163**	50c. purple	30	20
633	**163**	$1 red	35	20
634	**163**	$1.50 green	3·75	55
635	**163**	$2 purple	85	20
636	**163**	$2.50 blue	95	20
637	**163**	$3 blue	1·10	20

For redrawn design see Nos. 791/8.

164 Taroko Gorge

1968. 17th Pacific Area Travel Association Conference, Taipei. Multicoloured.

638		$5 Type **164**	2·00	30
639		$8 Chungshan Building, Yangmingshan	2·50	35

165 Harvesting Sugar-cane

1968. Sugar-cane Technologists Congress, Taiwan.

640	**165**	$1 multicoloured	1·40	20
641	**165**	$4 multicoloured	3·00	55

166 Vice-Pres. Cheng

1968. 3rd Death Anniv of Vice-Pres. Chen Cheng.

642	**166**	$1 multicoloured	1·50	25

167 Bean Geese

1968. 90th Anniv of Chinese Postage Stamps.

643	**167**	$1 red	7·00	25
MS644		75×100 mm. **167** $3 green. Imperf	13·00	4·50

168 Jade Cabbage (Ching Dynasty)

1968. Chinese Art Treasures, National Palace Museum (1st series). Multicoloured.

645		$1 Type **168**	2·25	20
646		$1.50 Jade battle-axe (Warring States period)	3·50	40
647		$2 Lung-ch'uan porcelain flower bowl (Sung dynasty) (horiz)	4·25	20
648		$2.50 Yung Cheng enamelled vase (Ching dynasty)	5·00	55
649		$4 Agate "fingered" flower-holder (Ching dynasty) (horiz)	5·50	55
650		$5 Sacrificial vessel (Western Chou)	6·50	80

See also Nos. 682/7 and 732/7.

169 WHO Emblem on "20"

1968. 20th Anniv of WHO.

651	**169**	$1 green	40	20
652	**169**	$5 red	1·00	55

170 Sun, Planets and "Rainfall"

1968. International Hydrological Decade.

653	**170**	$1 green and orange	45	20
654	**170**	$4 blue and orange	1·20	20

171 "A City of Cathay" (Section of hand-scroll painting)

1968. "A City of Cathay" (Scroll, Palace Museum) (1st series).

655	**171**	$1 (1) multicoloured	1·75	25
656	-	$1 (2) multicoloured	1·75	25
657	-	$1 (3) multicoloured	1·75	25
658	-	$1 (4) multicoloured	1·75	25
659	-	$1 (5) multicoloured	1·75	25
660	-	$5 multicoloured	15·00	2·25
661	-	$8 multicoloured	25·00	3·00

DESIGNS—As Type **171**: Nos. 655/9 together show panorama of the city ending with the palace. LARGER (61×32 mm). $5, City wall and gate; $8, Great bridge.

The five $1 stamps were issued together se-tenant in horiz strips, representing the last 11 feet of the 37 foot scroll, which is viewed from right to left as it is unrolled.

The stamps may be identified by the numbers given in brackets, which correspond to the numbers in the bottom right-hand corners of the stamps.

See also Nos. 699/703.

172 Map and Radio "Waves"

1968. 40th Anniv of Chinese Broadcasting Service.

662	**172**	$1 grey, ultram & blue	50	20
663	-	$4 red and blue	1·10	25

DESIGN—VERT: $4, Stereo broadcast "waves".

173 Human Rights Emblem

1968. Human Rights Year.

664	**173**	$1 multicoloured	55	20
665	**173**	$5 multicoloured	1·40	20

174 Harvesting Rice

1968. Rural Reconstruction.

666	**174**	$1 brown, ochre & yellow	45	20
667	**174**	$5 bronze, green & yellow	1·20	70

175 Throwing the Javelin

1968. Olympic Games, Mexico. Multicoloured.

668		$1 Type **175**	45	20
669		$2.50 Weightlifting	70	20
670		$5 Pole-vaulting (horiz)	1·20	30
671		$8 Hurdling (horiz)	1·80	50

176 President Chiang Kai-shek and Main Gate, Whampoa Military Academy

1968. "President Chiang Kai-shek's Meritorious Services". Multicoloured.

672		$1 Type **176**	1·00	25
673		$2 Reviewing Northern Expedition Forces	1·25	35
674		$2.50 Suppression of bandits	5·00	95
675		$3.50 Marco Polo Bridge and Victory Parade, Nanking, 1945	1·75	50
676		$4 Chinese Constitution	2·00	60
677		$5 National flag	2·75	80

Each stamp bears the portrait of President Chiang Kai-shek as in Type **176**.

177 Cockerel

1968. New Year Greetings. "Year of the Cock".

678	**177**	$1 multicoloured	25·00	60
679	**177**	$4.50 multicoloured	40·00	5·00

178 National Flag

1968. 20th Anniv of Chinese Constitution.

680	**178**	$1 multicoloured	60	20
681	**178**	$5 multicoloured	1·00	60

1969. Chinese Art Treasures, National Palace Museum (2nd series). Multicoloured as T 168.

682		$1 Jade buckle (Ching dynasty) (horiz)	1·75	20
683		$1.50 Jade vase (Sung dynasty)	2·25	30
684		$2 Cloisonne enamel teapot (Ching dynasty) (horiz)	2·00	20
685		$2.50 Bronze sacrificial vessel (Kuei) (horiz)	3·00	45
686		$4 Hsuan-te "heavenly ball" vase (Ming dynasty)	3·25	65
687		$5 "Gourd" vase (Ching dynasty)	4·25	90

179 Servicemen and Savings Emblem

1969. 10th Anniv of Forces' Savings Services.

688	**179**	$1 brown	30	20
689	**179**	$4 blue	90	45

180 Ti (flute)

1969. Chinese Musical Instruments. Mult.

690		$1 Type **180**	70	25
691		$2.50 Sheng (pipes)	1·20	35
692		$4 P'i-p'a (lute)	1·60	60
693		$5 Cheng (zither)	1·80	35

181 Chungshan Building, Yangmingshan

1969. 10th Kuomintang Congress.

694	**181**	$1 multicoloured	65	20

182 "Double Carp"

1969

695ab	**182**	$10 blue	3·25	20
695c	**182**	$14 red	3·25	40
696ab	**182**	$20 brown	5·50	30
697ab	**182**	$50 green	12·00	50
698ab	**182**	$100 red	12·00	1·00

Type **182** is a redrawn version of Type **138**.

1969. "A City of Cathay" (scroll) (2nd series). As T 171. Multicoloured.

699		$1 "Musicians"	1·00	20
700		$1 "Bridal chair"	1·00	20
701		$2.50 Emigrants with ox-cart	2·40	75
702		$5 "Scroll gallery"	4·25	70
703		$8 "Roadside cafe"	7·50	1·00

Nos. 699/70 form a composite picture of a bridal procession.

184 ILO Emblem

1969. 50th Anniv of ILO.

704	**184**	$1 blue	55	20
705	**184**	$8 red	1·40	45

185 "Food and Clothing"

1969. "Model Citizen's Life" Movement.

706	**185**	$1 red	25	20
707	-	$2.50 blue	60	30
708	-	$4 green	75	35

DESIGNS: $2.50, "Housekeeping and Road Safety"; $4, "Schooling and Recreation".

186 Bean Geese over Mountains

1969. Air. Multicoloured.

709		$2.50 Type **186**	2·30	25
710		$5 Bean geese over sea	4·00	45
711		$8 Bean geese over land (horiz)	5·75	60

187 Children and Symbols of Learning

1969. 1st Anniv of Nine-year Free Education System.

712	**187**	$1 red	35	20
713	-	$2.50 green	70	30
714	-	$4 blue	90	35
715	**187**	$5 brown	1·10	50

DESIGNS—VERT: $2.50 and $4, Children and school.

188 "Flowers and Ring-necked Pheasants", Ming dynasty (Lu Chih)

1969. Ancient Chinese Paintings from Palace Museum Collection (4th series). "Birds and Flowers". Multicoloured.

716		$1 Type **188**	2·25	20
717		$2.50 "Bamboos and Ring-necked Pheasants" (Sung dynasty)	3·75	35
718		$5 "Flowers and Birds" (Sung dynasty)	10·00	60
719		$8 "Twin Manchurian Cranes and Flowers" (G. Castiglione, Ching dynasty)	12·00	1·00

189 "Charles Mallerin" Rose

1969. Roses. Multicoloured.

720		$1 Type **189**	1·10	25
721		$2.50 "Golden Sceptre"	3·25	25
722		$5 "Peace"	4·25	30
723		$8 "Josephine Bruce"	3·75	65

190 Launching Missile

1969. 30th Air Defence Day.

724	**190**	$1 purple	1·40	25

191 APU Emblem

1969. 5th Asian Parliamentarians' Union General Assembly. Taipeh.

725	**191**	$1 red	40	20
726	**191**	$5 green	95	30

192 Pekingese Dogs

1969. New Year Greetings. "Year of the Dog".

727	**192**	50c. multicoloured	2·25	25
728	**192**	$4.50 multicoloured	10·00	1·80

193 Satellite and Earth Station

1969. Inauguration of Satellite Earth Station, Yangmingshan.

729	**193**	$1 multicoloured	60	20
730	**193**	$5 multicoloured	1·20	30
731	**193**	$8 multicoloured	2·00	55

1970. Chinese Art Treasures, National Palace Museum (3rd series). As T 168. Multicoloured.

732		$1 Lacquer vase (Ching dynasty)	1·50	20
733		$1.50 Agate grinding-stone (Ching dynasty) (horiz)	2·00	25
734		$2 Jade carving (Ching dynasty) (horiz)	2·25	20
735		$2.50 "Shepherd and Ram" jade carving (Han dynasty) (horiz)	2·75	30
736		$4 Porcelain jar (Ching dynasty)	3·25	40
737		$5 "Bull" porcelain urn (Northern Sung dynasty)	4·00	65

1970. Famous Chinese. Portraits as T 132.

738		$1 red	65	20
739		$2.50 green	95	25
740		$4 blue	1·60	35

PORTRAITS: $1, Hsuan Chuang (traveller). $2.50, Hua To (physician). $4, Chu Hsi (philosopher).

194 Taiwan Pavilion and EXPO Emblem

1970. World Fair "EXPO 70", Osaka, Japan. Multicoloured.

741		$5 Type **194**	75	20
742		$8 Pavilion encircled by national flags	1·50	55

195 Chungshan Building, Yangmingshan

1970

743	**195**	$1 red	50	20

For redrawn design see No. 1039.

196 Rain-cloud, Palm and Recording Apparatus

1970. World Meteorological Day. Mult.

744		$1 Type **196**	40	20
745		$8 "Nimbus 3" satellite (horiz)	95	50

197 Martyrs' Shrine

1970. Revolutionary Martyrs' Shrine. Mult.

746		$1 Type **197**	60	20
747		$8 Shrine gateway	1·70	50

198 General Yueh Fei ("Loyalty")

1970. Chinese Opera. "The Virtues". Opera characters. Multicoloured.

748		$1 Type **198**	1·75	25
749		$2.50 Emperor Shun tortured by stepmother ("Filial Piety")	2·50	40
750		$5 Chin Liang-yu "The Lady General" ("Chastity")	3·75	55
751		$8 Kuan Yu and groom ("Fidelity")	6·50	70

199 Three Horses at Play

1970. "One Hundred Horses" (handscroll by Lang Shih-ning (G. Castiglione)). Multicoloured.

752		$1 (1) Horses on plain	85	25
753		$1 (2) Horses on plain (different)	85	25
754		$1 (3) Horses playing	85	25
755		$1 (4) Horses on river bank	85	25
756		$1 (5) Horses crossing river	85	25
757		$5 Type **199**	10·00	75
758		$8 Groom roping horses	15·00	95

SERIAL NUMBERS. are indicated to aid identification of the above and certain other sets. For key to Chinese numerals see table at the beginning of CHINA.

200 Old Lai-tsu dropping Buckets

1970. Chinese Folk-tales (1st series). Mult.

759		10c. Type **200**	20	15
760		10c. Yien-tsu disguised as a deer	20	15
761		10c. Hwang Hsiang with fan	20	15
762		10c. Wang Shiang fishing	20	15
763		10c. Chu Hsiu-chang reunited with mother	20	15
764		50c. Emperor Wen tasting mother's medicine	35	20
765		$1 Lu Chi dropping oranges	55	25
766		$1 Yang Hsiang fighting tiger	60	30

See also Nos. 817/24, 1000/7, 1064/7, 1210/13 and 1312/15.

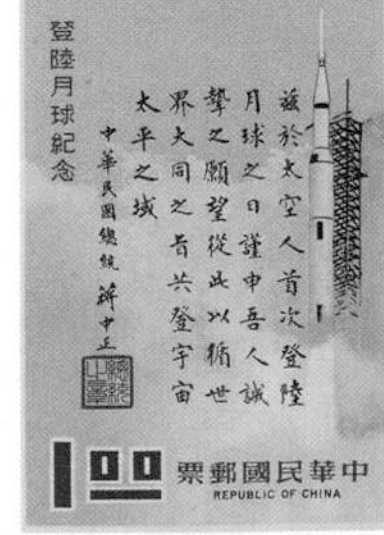

201 Chiang Kai-shek's Moon Message

1970. 1st Man on the Moon. Multicoloured.

767		$1 Type **201**	75	15
768		$5 "Apollo 11" astronauts (horiz)	1·10	35
769		$8 "First step on the Moon"	2·40	55

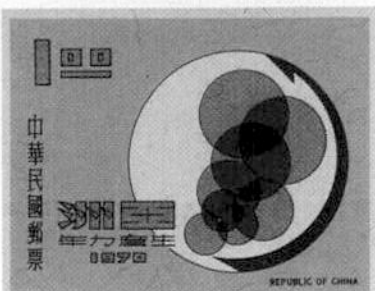

202 Productivity Symbol

1970. Asian Productivity Year.

770	**202**	$1 multicoloured	50	15
771	**202**	$5 multicoloured	1·10	35

203 Flags of Taiwan and United Nations

1970. 25th Anniv of United Nations.

772	**203**	$5 multicoloured	1·60	50

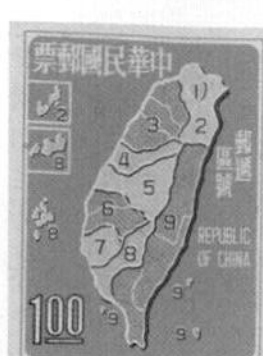

204 Postal Zone Map

1970. Postal Zone Numbers Campaign. Mult.

773	$1 Type **204**	65	15
774	$2.50 Postal Zone emblem (horiz)	1·10	35

205 "Cultural Activities" (10th month)

1970. "Occupations of the Twelve Months" Hanging Scrolls. Multicoloured. (a) "Winter".

775	$1 Type **205**	3·25	40
776	$2.50 "School Buildings" (11th month)	7·50	90
777	$5 "Games in the Snow" (12th month)	12·00	1·10

(b) "Spring".

778	$1 "Lantern Festival" (1st month)	2·50	30
779	$2.50 "Apricots in Blossom" (2nd month)	5·00	65
780	$5 "Purification Ceremony" (3rd month)	8·50	80

(c) "Summer".

781	$1 "Summer Shower" (4th month)	3·00	30
782	$2.50 "Dragon boat Festival" (5th month)	5·50	65
783	$5 "Lotus Pond" (6th month)	8·50	80

(d) "Autumn".

784	$1 "Weaver Festival" (7th month)	3·00	35
785	$2.50 "Moon Festival" (8th month)	6·50	80
786	$5 "Chrysanthemum Blossom" (9th month)	8·50	95

The month numbers are given by the Chinese characters in brackets, which follow the face value on the stamps.

206 "Planned Family"

1970. Family Planning. Multicoloured.

787	$1 Type **206**	60	15
788	$4 "Family excursion" (vert)	1·50	40

207 Toy Pig

1970. New Year Greetings. "Year of the Boar".

789	**207**	50c. multicoloured	2·30	20
790	**207**	$4.50 multicoloured	4·50	70

208 Chungshan Building, Yangmingshan

1971

791	**208**	5c. brown	20	15
792	**208**	10c. green	20	15
793	**208**	50c. red	45	15
794	**208**	$1 red	50	15
795	**208**	$1.50 blue	75	25
796	**208**	$2 purple	1·30	20
797	**208**	$2.50 green	1·80	25
798	**208**	$3 blue	2·10	30

Type **208** is a redrawn version of Type **163**.

209 Shin-bone Tibia

1971. Taiwan Shells. Multicoloured.

799	$1 Type **209**	75	15
800	$2.50 Kuroda's lyria	1·20	35
801	$5 "Conus stupa kuroda"	1·80	70
802	$8 Rumphius's slit shell	2·75	45

210 Savings Book and Certificate

1971. National Savings Campaign. Mult.

803	$1 Type **210**	50	15
804	$4 Hand dropping coin in savings bank	1·50	35

211 Chinese greeting African Farmer

1971. 10th Anniv of Sino-African Technical Co-operation Committee. Multicoloured.

805	$1 Type **211**	45	15
806	$8 Rice-growing (horiz)	1·30	55

212 Red and White Flying Squirrel

1971. Taiwan Animals. Multicoloured.

807	$1 Taiwan macaque (vert)	50	15
808	$2 Type **212**	1·20	25
809	$3 Chinese pangolin	1·50	40
810	$5 Sika deer	2·00	55

213 Pitcher delivering ball

1971. World Little League Baseball Championships, Taiwan. Multicoloured.

811	$1 Type **213**	30	15
812	$2.50 Players at base (horiz)	50	20
813	$4 Striker and catcher	80	25

(214)

1971. Victory of "Tainan Giants" in World Little League Baseball Championships, Williamsport (U.S.A.). Optd with T 214.

814	**163**	$1 red	30	15
815	**163**	$2.50 blue	55	20
816	**163**	$3 blue	45	25

1971. Chinese Folk-tales (2nd series). As T 200. Multicoloured.

817	10c. Yu Hsun and elephant	20	15
818	10c. Tsai Hsun with mulberries	20	15
819	10c. Tseng Sun with firewood	20	15
820	10c. Kiang Keh and bandits	20	15
821	10c. Tsu Lu with sack of rice	20	15
822	50c. Meng Chung gathering bamboo shoots	30	20
823	$1 Tung Yung and wife	70	30
824	$1 Tzu Chien shivering with cold	70	30

215 60th Anniv Emblem and flag

1971. 60th National Day. Multicoloured.

825	$1 Type **215**	50	15
826	$2.50 National anthem, map and flag	85	15
827	$5 Pres. Chiang Kai-shek, constitution and flag	1·00	35
828	$8 Dr. Sun Yat-sen, "Three Principles" and flag	1·20	40

216 AOPU Emblem

1971. Asian-Oceanic Postal Union Executive Committee Session, Taipeh.

829	**216**	$2.50 multicoloured	55	15
830	**216**	$5 multicoloured	85	20

217 "White Frost Hawk"

1971. "Ten Prized Dogs" (paintings on silk by Lang Shih-ning (G. Castiglione)). Multicoloured.

831	$1 Type **217**	1·00	20
832	$1 "Black Dog with Snow-white Claws"	4·50	15
833	$2 "Star-glancing Wolf"	1·50	20
834	$2 "Yellow Leopard"	6·50	30
835	$2.50 "Golden-winged Face"	2·25	55
836	$2.50 "Flying Magpie"	9·50	65
837	$5 "Young Black Dragon"	5·25	60
838	$5 "Heavenly Lion"	12·00	70
839	$8 "Young Grey Dragon"	7·50	70
840	$8 "Mottle-coated Tiger"	16·00	80

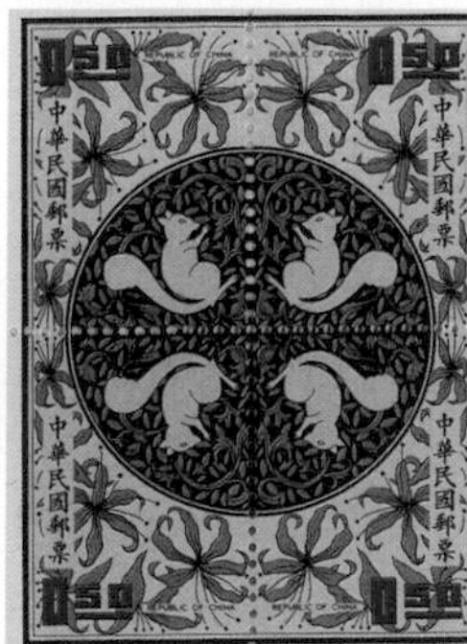

218/221 Squirrels

1971. New Year Greetings. "Year of the Rat".

841	**218**	50c. multicoloured	80	20
842	**219**	50c. multicoloured	80	20
843	**220**	50c. multicoloured	80	20
844	**221**	50c. multicoloured	80	20
845	**218**	$4.50 multicoloured	4·25	50
846	**219**	$4.50 multicoloured	4·25	50
847	**220**	$4.50 multicoloured	4·25	50
848	**221**	$4.50 multicoloured	4·25	50

The four designs in each value were issued together, se-tenant, forming a composite design.

222 Flags of Taiwan and Jordan

1971. 50th Anniv of Hashemite Kingdom of Jordan.

849	**222**	$5 multicoloured	1·50	25

223 Freighter "Hai King"

1971. Centenary of China Merchants Steam Navigation Company. Multicoloured.

850	**223**	$4 blue, red and green	65	30
851	-	$7 multicoloured	1·00	45

DESIGN—VERT: $7. Liner on Pacific.

224 Downhill Skiing

1972. Winter Olympic Games, Sapporo, Japan.

852	**224**	$1 black, yellow and blue	25	15
853	-	$5 black, orange & green	60	20
854	-	$8 black, red and grey	80	25

DESIGNS: $5, Cross-country skiing; $8, Giant slalom.

225 Yung Cheng Vase

1972. Chinese Porcelain. (1st series). Ch'ing Dynasty. Multicoloured.

855	$1 Type **225**	1·00	15
856	$2 Kang Hsi jar	1·75	25
857	$2.50 Yung Cheng jug	2·25	30
858	$5 Chien Lung vase	2·75	30
859	$8 Chien Lung jar	3·25	45

See also Nos. 914/18, 927/31 and 977/81.

226 Doves

1972. 10th Anniv of Asian-Oceanic Postal Union.

860	**226**	$1 black and blue	45	20
861	**226**	$5 black and violet	1·30	35

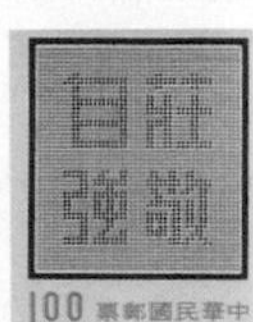

227 "Dignity with Self-Reliance" (Pres. Chiang Kai-shek)

1972

862	**227**	5c. brown and yellow	25	15
863	**227**	10c. blue and orange	3·50	15
863b	**227**	20c. purple and green	25	15
864	**227**	50c. lilac and purple	30	15
865	**227**	$1 red and blue	20	15
866	**227**	$1.50 yellow and blue	35	20
867	**227**	$2 violet, purple & orge	60	20
868	**227**	$2.50 green and red	95	25
869	**227**	$3 red and green	90	25

228 Mounted Messengers

1972. "The Emperor's Procession" (Ming dynasty handscrolls). Multicoloured. (a) First issue.

870	$1 (1) Pagoda and crowds	65	20
871	$1 (2) Seven carriages	65	20
872	$1 (3) Emperor's coach	65	20
873	$1 (4) Horsemen with flags	65	20
874	$1 (5) Horsemen and Emperor	65	20
875	$2.50 Type **228**	2·50	20
876	$5 Guards	3·50	25
877	$8 Imperial sedan chair	4·50	55

(b) Second issue.

878	$1 (1) Three ceremonial barges	8·50	20
879	$1 (2) Sedan chairs	70	20
880	$1 (3) Two ceremonial barges	70	20
881	$1 (4) Horsemen and mounted orchestra	70	20
882	$1 (5) Two carriages	70	20
883	$2.50 City gate	3·50	20
884	$5 Mounted orchestra	4·50	25
885	$8 Ceremonial barge	8·50	50

Nos. 870/4 are numbered from right to left and Nos. 878/82 are numbered from left to right. They were each issued together, se-tenant, forming composite designs showing the departure of the procession from the palace and its return.

Nos. 875/7 and 883/5 show enlarged details from the scrolls.

See also Nos. 937/50 and 1040/7.

229 First Day Covers

1972. Philately Day.

886	**229**	$1 blue	25	15
887	**229**	$2.50 green	30	20
888	**229**	$8 red	55	25

DESIGNS—VERT: $2.50, Magnifying glass and stamps. HORIZ: $8, Magnifying glass, perforation-gauge and tweezers.

(230)

1972. Taiwan's Victories in Senior and Little World Baseball Leagues. Nos. 865/7 and 869 optd with T 230.

889	**227**	$1 red and blue	25	15
890	**227**	$1.50 yellow and blue	40	25
891	**227**	$2 violet, purple & orange	45	20
892	**227**	$3 red and green	45	25

231 Emperor Yao

1972. Chinese Cultural Heroes.

893	**231**	$3.50 blue	55	30
894	-	$4 red	65	15
895	-	$4.50 violet	80	25
896	-	$5 green	75	15
897	-	$5.50 purple	1·10	35
898	-	$6 orange	1·20	30
899	-	$7 brown	1·40	15
900	-	$8 blue	1·60	20

DESIGNS: $4, Emperor Shun; $4.50, Yu the Great; $5, King T'ang; $5.50, King Weng; $6, King Wu; $7, Chou Kung; $8, Confucius.

1972. "ROCPEX" Philatelic Exhibition, Taipeh. Sheet 71×100 mm.

MS901	**227**	Nos. 867 ($2) and 869 ($3)	5·75	2·20

232 Mountaineering

1972. 20th Anniv of China Youth Corps. Multicoloured.

902	$1 Type **232**	30	15
903	$2.50 Winter sport	50	15
904	$4 Diving	70	20
905	$8 Parachuting	1·00	30

233 Microwave Systems and Electronic Sorting Machine

1972. Improvement of Communications.

906	**233**	$1 red	25	15
907	-	$2.50 blue	45	25
908	-	$5 purple	80	40

DESIGNS—HORIZ: $2.50, Boeing 721-100 airliner and "Hai Mou" (container ship); $5, Diesel railcar and motorway.

234 "Eyes" and J.C.I. Emblem

1972. 27th World Congress of Junior Chamber International, Taipeh.

909	**234**	$1 multicoloured	30	15
910	**234**	$5 multicoloured	45	25
911	**234**	$8 multicoloured	60	40

235 Cow and Calf

1972. New Year Greetings. "Year of the Ox".

912	**235**	50c. black and red	2·50	35
913	**235**	$4.50 brown, red & yellow	5·50	90

1973. Chinese Porcelain (2nd series). Ming Dynasty. As T 225. Multicoloured.

914	$1 Fu vase	1·50	15
915	$2 Floral vase	2·00	15
916	$2.50 Ku vase	2·25	30
917	$5 Hu flask	3·00	45
918	$8 Garlic-head vase	3·50	55

236 "Kicking the Shuttlecock"

1973. Chinese Folklore (1st series). Mult.

919	$1 Type **236**	50	15
920	$4 "The Fisherman and the Oyster-fairy" (horiz)	95	20
921	$5 "Lady in a Boat" (horiz)	1·00	20
922	$8 "The Old Man and the Lady"	1·30	40

See also Nos. 982/3 and 1037/8.

237 Bamboo Sampan

1973. Taiwan Handicrafts (1st series). Mult.

923	$1 Type **237**	45	15
924	$2.50 Marble vase (vert)	75	15
925	$5 Glass plate	95	20
926	$8 Aborigine Doll (vert)	1·20	40

See also Nos. 988/91.

1973. Chinese Porcelain (3rd series). Ming Dynasty. Horiz. designs as T 225. Multicoloured.

927	$1 Dragon stem-bowl	1·00	25
928	$2 Dragon pot	1·25	25
929	$2.50 Covered jar with lotus decor	1·75	25
930	$5 Covered jar showing horses	2·25	50
931	$8 "Immortals" bowl	2·75	60

238 Contractors' Equipment

1973. 12th Convention of International Federation of Asian and Western Pacific Contractors' Association.

932	**238**	$1 multicoloured	30	15
933	-	$5 blue and black	65	30

DESIGN—HORIZ: $5, Bulldozer.

239 Pres. Chiang Kai-shek and Flag

1973. Inauguration of Pres. Chiang Kai-shek's 5th Term of Office.

934	**239**	$1 multicoloured	50	25
935	**239**	$4 multicoloured	1·00	50

240 Lin Tse-hsu (statesman)

1973. Lin Tse-hsu Commemoration.

936	**240**	$1 purple	60	20

1973. "Spring Morning in the Han Palace" (Ming dynasty handscroll). As T 228. Mult. (a) First issue.

937	$1 (1) Palace gate	40	20
938	$1 (2) Feeding green peafowl	40	20
939	$1 (3) Emperor's wife	40	20
940	$1 (4) Ladies and pear tree	40	20
941	$1 (5) Music pavilion	40	20
942	$5 Giant rock (vert)	3·50	55
943	$8 Lady musicians (vert)	5·00	95

(b) Second issue.

944	$1 (6) Game with flowers	40	20
945	$1 (7) Leisure room	40	20
946	$1 (8) Ladies with teapots	40	20
947	$1 (9) Artist at work	40	20
948	$1 (10) Palace wall and guards	40	20
949	$5 Playing game at table (vert)	3·50	55
950	$8 Swatting insect (vert)	5·00	95

Nos. 937/41 and 944/8 are numbered from right to left and were each issued together, se-tenant. When the two strips are placed side by side, they form a composite design showing the complete handscroll.

Nos. 942/3 and 949/50 show enlarged details from the scroll.

241 "Bamboo" (Hsiang Te-hsin)

1973. Ancient Chinese Fan Paintings (1st series). Multicoloured.

951	$1 Type **241**	55	15
952	$2.50 "Flowers" (Sun K'O-hung)	95	20
953	$5 "Landscape" (Ch'iu Ying)	1·40	40
954	$8 "Seated Figure and Tree" (Shen Chou)	2·00	50

See also Nos. 1052/5.

243 Emblem of World Series

1973. Little League World Baseball Series. Taiwan Victory in Twin Championships.

955	**243**	$1 blue, red and yellow	65	15
956	**243**	$4 blue, green & yellow	1·40	35

245 Interpol Emblem

1973. 50th Anniv of International Criminal Police Organization (Interpol).

957	**245**	$1 blue and orange	30	15
958	**245**	$5 green and orange	60	25
959	**245**	$8 purple and orange	80	45

1973. Famous Chinese. Portrait as T 132.

960	$1 violet (Ch'iu Feng-chia (poet))	75	25

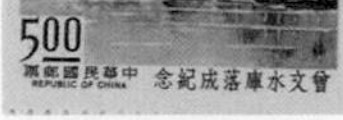

246 Dam and Power Station

1973. Opening of Tsengwen Reservoir. Mult.

961	$1 Upper section of reservoir	25	15
962	$1 Middle section of reservoir	25	15
963	$1 Lower section of reservoir	25	15
964	$5 Type **246** (30×22 mm)	90	50
965	$8 Spillway (50×22 mm)	1·30	45

The $1 values together show complete map of reservoir (each 38×26 mm).

247 "Snow-dotted Eagle"

1973. Paintings of Horses. Multicoloured.

966	50c. Type **247**	70	25
967	$1 "Comfortable Ride"	1·00	25
968	$1 "Red Flower Eagle"	1·00	25
969	$1 "Cloud-running Steed"	1·00	25
970	$1 "Sky-running Steed"	1·00	25
971	$2.50 "Red Jade Steed"	3·25	50
972	$5 "Thunder-clap Steed"	5·50	65
973	$8 "Arabian Champion"	7·50	60
MS974	151×121 mm. Nos. 966/7 and 971/2. Imperf	19·00	11·50

248 Tiger

1973. New Year Greetings. "Year of the Tiger".

975	**248**	50c. multicoloured	1·25	20
976	**248**	$4.50 multicoloured	2·25	50

1974. Chinese Porcelain (4th series). Sung Dynasty. As T 225. Multicoloured.

977	$1 Ko vase	55	15
978	$2 Kuan vase (horiz)	80	20
979	$2.50 Ju bowl (horiz)	1·10	30
980	$5 Kuan incense burner (horiz)	1·30	30
981	$8 Chun incense burner (horiz)	1·40	40

1974. Chinese Folklore (2nd series). As T 236. Multicoloured.

982	$1 Balancing pot	50	15
983	$8 Magicians (horiz)	1·40	20

249 Road Tunnel Taroko Gorge

1974. Taiwan Scenery (1st series). Mult.

984	$1 Type **249**	60	15
985	$2.50 Luce Chapel, Tungai University	85	20
986	$5 Tzu En Pagoda, Sun Moon Lake	1·10	20
987	$8 Goddess of Mercy Statue, Keelung	1·40	25

See also Nos. 992/5.

1974. Taiwan Handicrafts (2nd series). As T 237. Multicoloured.

988	$1 "Fighting Cocks" (brass)	40	15
989	$2.50 "Fruits" (jade)	60	25
990	$5 "Fisherman" (wood-carving) (vert)	85	30
991	$8 "Bouquet of Flowers" (plastic) (vert)	1·50	40

1974. Taiwan Scenery (2nd series). As T 249 but all horiz. Multicoloured.

992	$1 Dr. Sun Yat-Sen Memorial Hall, Taipeh	40	15
993	$2.50 Reaching-Moon Tower, Cheng Ching Lake	65	15
994	$5 Seashore, Lanyu	90	20
995	$8 Inter-island bridge, Penghu	1·20	25

250 Pres. Chiang Kai-shek

1974. 50th Anniv of Chinese Military Academy.

996	**250**	$1 mauve	30	15
997	-	$14 blue	75	45

DESIGN—VERT: $14, Cadets on parade.

251 Long-distance Runner

1974. 80th Anniv of International Olympic Committee.

998	**251**	$1 blue, black & red	30	15
999	-	$8 multicoloured	85	45

DESIGN: $8, Female relay runner.

1974. Chinese Folk tales (3rd series). As T 200. Multicoloured.

1000	50c. Wen Yen-po retrieving ball	25	15
1001	50c. T'i Ying pleading for mercy	25	15
1002	50c. Wang Ch'i in battle	25	15
1003	50c. Wang Hua returning gold	25	15
1004	$1 Pu Shih offering sheep to the emperor	40	25
1005	$1 Szu Ma Kuang saving playmate from water-jar	40	25
1006	$1 Tung Yu at study	40	25
1007	$1 K'ung Yung selecting the smallest pear	40	25

252 "Crape Myrtle" (Wei Sheng)

1974. Ancient Chinese Moon-shaped Fan-paintings (1st series). Multicoloured.

1008	$1 Type **252**	75	15
1009	$2.50 "White Cabbage and Insects" (Hsu Ti)	1·25	25
1010	$5 "Hibiscus and Rock" (Li Ti)	2·25	25
1011	$8 "Pomegranates and Narcissus Fly-catcher" (Wu Ping)	3·00	50

See also Nos. 1068/71 and 1115/1118.

253 "The Battle of Marco Polo Bridge"

1974. Armed Forces' Day.

1012	**253**	$1 multicoloured	35	15
MS1013		108×147 mm. No. 1012 ×8	7·50	6·00

254 Chrysanthemum

1974. Chrysanthemums.

1014	**254**	$1 multicoloured	30	15
1015	-	$2.50 multicoloured	60	30
1016	-	$5 multicoloured	85	30
1017	-	$8 multicoloured	1·30	25

DESIGNS: Nos. 1015/17, various chrysanthemums.

255 Chinese Pavilion

1974. "Expo 74" World Fair, Spokane, Washington. Multicoloured.

1018	$1 Type **255**	30	15
1019	$8 Fairground map	70	45

256 Steel Mill, Kaohsiung

1974. Major Construction Projects (1st series). Chinese inscr in single-line characters, figures of value solid.* Multicoloured.

1020	50c. Type **256**	20	15
1021	$1 Taiwan North link railway	30	15
1022	$2 Petrochemical works, Kaohsiung	20	15
1023	$2.50 TRA trunk line electrification	40	15
1024	$3 Taichung harbour (horiz)	30	15
1025	$3.50 Taoyuan international airport (horiz)	30	15
1026	$4 Taiwan North–south motorway (horiz)	30	15
1027	$4.50 Giant shipyard, Kaohsiung (horiz)	50	35
1028	$5 Su-ao port (horiz)	50	25

*The first series can also be distinguished by the Chinese and English inscr at the foot being in different colours; in the second and third series only one colour is used.

See also Nos. 1122a/1122i and 1145/1153.

257 White Button Mushrooms

1974. Edible Fungi. Multicoloured.

1029	$1 Type **257**	1·25	15
1030	$2.50 Oyster fungus	1·75	20
1031	$5 Veiled stinkhorn	2·25	25
1032	$8 Golden mushrooms	2·75	35

258 Baseball Strikers

1974. Taiwan Triple Championship Victories in World Little League Baseball Series, U.S.A. Multicoloured.

1033	$1 Type **258**	30	15
1034	$8 Player and banners	70	35

259 Chinese Hare

1974. New Year Greetings. "Year of the Hare".

1035	**259**	50c. multicoloured	75	15
1036	**259**	$4.50 multicoloured	2·25	30

1975. Chinese Folklore (3rd series). As T 236. Multicoloured.

1037	$4 Acrobat	75	35
1038	$5 Jugglers with diabolo	1·10	55

260 Chungshan Building, Yangmingshan

1975

1039	**260**	$1 red	50	15

Type **260** is a redrawn version of Type **195**.

1975. "New Year Festivals" (handscroll by Ting Kuan-p'eng). As T 228. Multicoloured.

1040	$1 (1) Greetings	40	15
1041	$1 (2) Entertainer	40	15
1042	$1 (3) Crowd and musicians	40	15
1043	$1 (4) Picnic	40	15
1044	$1 (5) Puppet show	40	15
1045	$2.50 New Year greetings	2·75	35
1046	$5 Children buying fireworks	3·75	55
1047	$8 Entertainer with monkey and dog	5·50	95

Nos. 1040/4 were issued together, se-tenant, forming a composite design.

261 Sun Yat-sen Memorial Hall, Taipeh

1975. 50th Death Anniv of Dr. Sun Yat-sen.

1048	$1 Type **261**	30	15
1049	$4 Sun Yat-sen's handwriting	45	25
1050	$5 Bronze statue of Sun Yat-sen (vert)	65	25
1051	$8 Sun Yat-sen Memorial Hall, St. John's University, U.S.A	90	30

1975. Ancient Chinese Fan Paintings (2nd series). As T 241. Multicoloured.

1052	$1 "Landscape" (Li Liu-fang)	1·00	15
1053	$2.50 "Landscape" (Wen Cheng-ming)	1·25	30
1054	$5 "Landscape" (Chou Ch'en)	1·75	40
1055	$8 "Landscape" (T'ang Yin)	2·50	40

262 "Yuan-chin" Coin (Chou dynasty)

1975. Ancient Chinese Coins (1st series). Mult.

1056	$1 Type **262**	35	15
1057	$4 "Pan-liang" coin (Chin dynasty)	80	20
1058	$5 "Five chu" coin (Han dynasty)	95	20
1059	$8 "Five chu" coin (Liang dynasty)	1·20	25

See also Nos. 1111/14 and 1184/7.

263 "Lohan, the Cloth-bag Monk" (Chang Hung)

1975. Ancient Chinese Figure Paintings. Mult.

1060	$2 Type **263**	1·00	20
1061	$4 "Lao-tzu on buffalo" (Chao Pu-chih)	1·60	25
1062	$5 "Shih-te" (Wang-wen)	2·50	30
1063	$8 "Splashed-ink Immortal" (Liang K'ai)	3·75	40

1975. Chinese Folk-tales (4th series). As T 200. Multicoloured.

1064	$1 Chu-Yin reading by light of fireflies	25	15
1065	$2 Hua Mu-lan going to battle disguised as a man	35	20
1066	$2 Ling Kou Chien living a humble life	45	25
1067	$5 Chou Ch'u defeating the tiger	95	35

1975. Ancient Chinese Moon-shaped Fan Paintings (2nd series). As T 252. Multicoloured.

1068	$1 "Cherry-apple blossoms" (Lin Ch'un)	75	15
1069	$2 "Spring blossoms and a colourful butterfly" (Ma K'uei)	1·00	15
1070	$5 "Monkeys and deer" (I Yuan-chi)	1·50	30
1071	$8 "Tree sparrows among bamboo" (anon.)	3·25	55

1975. Famous Chinese. Martyrs of War against Japan. Portraits as T 132.

1072	$2 red (Gen. Chang Tzu-chung)	25	15
1073	$2 brown (Maj.-Gen. Kao Chih-hang)	25	15
1074	$2 green (Capt. Sha Shih-chiun)	25	15
1075	$5 brown (Maj-Gen. Hsieh Chin-yuan)	35	15
1076	$5 blue (Lt. Yen Hai-wen)	35	15
1077	$5 blue (Lt.-Gen. Tai An-lan)	35	15

264 "Lotus Pond with Willows"

1975. Madame Chiang Kai-shek's Landscape Paintings (1st series). Multicoloured.

1078	$2 Type **264**	2·25	15
1079	$5 "Sun breaks through Mountain Clouds"	2·75	35
1080	$8 "A Pair of Pine Trees"	3·75	45
1081	$10 "Fishing and Farming"	4·75	75

See also Nos. 1139/1142 and 1727/30.

265 Rectangular Cauldron

1975. Ancient Bronzes (1st series). Mult.

1082	$2 Type **265**	30	15
1083	$5 Cauldron with "Phoenix" handles (horiz)	65	20
1084	$8 Flat jar (horiz)	95	25
1085	$10 Wine vessel	1·10	35

See also Nos. 1119/22.

266 Dragon, Nine-Dragon Wall, Peihai

1975. New Year Greetings. "Year of the Dragon".

1086	**266**	$1 multicoloured	50	20
1087	**266**	$5 multicoloured	1·30	60

267 Techi Dam

1975. Completion of Techi Reservoir. Mult.

1088	$2 Type **267**	30	15
1089	$10 Dam and reservoir	60	45

268 Biathlon

1976. Winter Olympic Games, Innsbruck. Mult.

1090	$2 Type **268**	30	15
1091	$5 Luge	50	25
1092	$8 Skiing	70	35

269 "Chin"

1976. Chinese Musical Instruments (1st series). Multicoloured.

1093	$2 Type **269**	35	15
1094	$5 "Se" (string instrument)	55	20
1095	$8 "Standing Kong-ho" (harp)	65	25
1096	$10 "Sleeping Kong-ho" (harp)	85	30

See also Nos. 1156/9.

270 Postman collecting Mail

1976. 80th Anniv of Chinese Postal Service. Multicoloured.

1097	$2 Type **270**	25	15
1098	$5 Mail-sorting systems (vert)	35	20
1099	$8 Mail transport (vert)	85	20
1100	$10 Traditional and modern post deliveries	75	25
MS1101	130×100 mm. Nos. 1097/1100	10·50	6·50

271 Pres. Chiang Kai-shek

1976. 1st Death Anniv of President Chiang Kai-shek. Multicoloured.

1102	$2 Type **271**	25	15
1103	$2 People paying homage (horiz)	25	15
1104	$2 Lying-in-state (horiz)	25	15
1105	$2 Start of funeral procession (horiz)	25	15
1106	$5 Roadside obeisance (horiz)	40	20
1107	$8 Altar, Tzuhu Guest-house (horiz)	50	30
1108	$10 Tzuhu Guest-house (horiz)	65	35

272 Chinese and U.S. Flags

1976. Bicentenary of American Revolution.

1109	**272**	$2 multicoloured	25	15
1110	**272**	$10 multicoloured	70	45

273 "Kung Shou Pu" Coin (Shang/Chou Dynasties)

1976. Ancient Chinese Coins (2nd series). Mult.

1111	$2 Type **273**	50	15
1112	$5 "Chien Tsu Pu" coin (Chao Kingdom)	95	20
1113	$8 "Yuan Tsu Pu" coin (Tsin Kingdom)	1·00	25
1114	$10 "Fang Tsu Pu" coin (Chin/Han Dynasties)	1·50	30

1976. Ancient Chinese Moon-shaped Fan-paintings (3rd series) As T 252. Multicoloured.

1115	$2 "Hibiscus" (Li Tung)	1·00	15
1116	$5 "Lilies" (Lin Chun)	1·50	20
1117	$8 "Two Sika Deer, Mushrooms and Pine" (Mou Chung-fu)	2·00	30
1118	$10 "Wild Flowers and Japanese Quail" (Li An-chung)	4·25	45

1976. Ancient Bronzes (2nd series). As T 265. Multicoloured.

1119	$2 Square cauldron	35	15
1120	$5 Round cauldron	75	15
1121	$8 Wine vessel	1·00	25
1122	$10 Wine vessel with legs	1·20	30

No. 1119 is similar to Type **265**, but has four characters at left only.

1976. Major Construction Projects (2nd series). Designs as Nos. 1020/8, but Chinese inscr in double-lined characters. Figures of value solid. Multicoloured.

1122a	$1 As No. 1021	35	15
1122b	$2 As No. 1023	35	15
1122c	$3 As No. 1024	30	15
1122d	$4 As No. 1026	30	15
1122e	$5 As Type **256**	30	15
1122f	$6 As No. 1025	35	20
1122g	$7 As No. 1027	40	20
1122h	$8 As No. 1022	45	25
1122i	$9 As No. 1028	50	30

See also Nos. 1145/53.

274 Chiang Kai-shek and Mother

1976. 90th Birth Anniv of President Chiang Kai-shek. Multicoloured.

1123	$2 Type **274**	30	15
1124	$5 Chiang Kai-shek	65	20
1125	$10 Chiang Kai-shek and Dr. Sun Yat-sen in railway carriage (horiz)	1·00	45

275 Chinese and KMT Flags

1976. 11th Kuomintang National Congress. Mult.

1126	$2 Type **275**	30	15
1127	$10 President Chiang Kai-shek and Dr. Sun Yat-sen	65	40
MS1128	111×87 mm. No. 1126/7. Perf	5·00	4·25

276 Brazen Serpent

1976. New Year Greetings. "Year of the Snake".

1129	**276**	$1 multicoloured	50	15
1130	**276**	$5 multicoloured	1·60	25

277 "Bird and Plum Blossom" (Ch'en Hung-shou)

1977. Ancient Chinese Paintings. "Three Friends of Winter".

1131	$2 Type **277**	1·25	20
1132	$8 "Wintry Days" (Yang Wei-chen)	2·75	40
1133	$10 "Rock and Bamboo" (Hsia Ch'ang)	4·00	45

278 Black-naped Orioles

1977. Taiwan Birds. Multicoloured.

1134	$2 Type **278**	1·00	15
1135	$8 River kingfisher	1·50	25
1136	$10 Pheasant-tailed jacana	2·25	35

279 Emblems of Industry and Commerce

1977. Industry and Commerce Census.

1137	**279**	$2 multicoloured	25	15
1138	**279**	$10 multicoloured	70	45

280 "Green Mountains rising into Clouds"

1977. Madame Chiang Kai-shek's Landscape Paintings (2nd series). Multicoloured.

1139	$2 Type **280**	1·50	20
1140	$5 "Boat amidst Spring's Beauty"	2·75	40
1141	$8 "Scholar beside the Rivulet"	3·25	40
1142	$10 "Green Water rising to meet the Bridge"	3·75	60

281 WACL Emblem

1977. 10th World Anti-Communist League Conf.

1143	**281**	$2 multicoloured	25	15
1144	**281**	$10 multicoloured	65	45

282 Steel Mill, Kaohsiung

1977. Major Construction Projects (3rd series). Designs as Nos. 1122a/i, but redrawn with double lined figures of value as in T 282. Multicoloured.

1145	$1 Taiwan North link railway	35	15
1146	$2 TRA trunk line electrification	35	15
1147	$3 Taichung harbour (horiz)	30	15
1148	$4 Taiwan North–south highway (horiz)	25	15
1149	$5 Type **282**	30	15
1150	$6 Taoyuan international airport (horiz)	30	20
1151	$7 Giant shipyard, Kaohsiung (horiz)	40	20
1152	$8 Petrochemical works, Kaohsiung	45	25
1153	$9 Su-ao port (horiz)	50	30

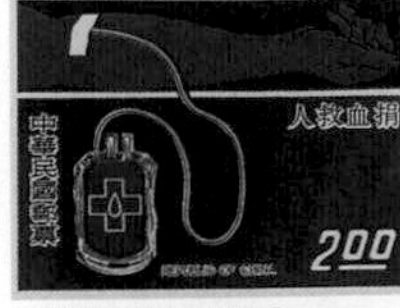

283 "Blood Donation"

1977. Blood Donation Movement.

1154	**283**	$2 red, black and yellow	25	15
1155	-	$10 red and black	70	45

DESIGN—VERT: $10, "Blood Transfusion".

284 San-hsien

1977. Chinese Musical Instruments (2nd series). Multicoloured.

1156	$2 Type **284**	30	15
1157	$5 Tung-hsiao (wind instrument)	45	20
1158	$8 Yang-chin (xylophone)	55	25
1159	$10 Pai-hsiao (pipes)	85	35

285 "Idea leuconoe"

1977. Taiwan Butterflies. Multicoloured.

1160	$2 Type **285**	75	20
1161	$4 Great orange-tip	1·10	30
1162	$6 "Stichophthalma howqua"	1·25	35
1163	$10 "Atrophaneura horishanus"	1·75	30

286 "National Palace Museum"

1977. Children's Drawings. Multicoloured.

1164	$1 Type **286**	25	15
1165	$2 "Festival of Sea Goddess"	30	20
1166	$4 "Boats on Lan-yu"	45	20
1167	$5 "Temple" (vert)	55	25

(287)

1977. Triple Championships of the 1977 Little League World Baseball Series. Nos. 1146 and 1152 optd with Type 287.

1168	$2 multicoloured	25	15
1169	$8 multicoloured	70	30

288 Plate

1977. Ancient Chinese Carved Lacquer Ware (1st series). Multicoloured.

1170	$2 Type **288**	50	20
1171	$5 Bowl	75	20
1172	$8 Box	1·20	25
1173	$10 Three-tiered box	1·30	30

See also Nos. 1206/1209.

289 Lions Club Emblem

1977. 60th Anniv of Lions International.

1174	**289**	$2 multicoloured	25	15
1175	**289**	$10 multicoloured	65	40

290 "Cheng" Government Standard Mark

1977. Standardization Movement.

1176	**290**	$2 multicoloured	55	15
1177	**290**	$10 multicoloured	1·70	30

291 Human Figure and Diagram of Heart

1977. Prevention of Heart Disease Campaign.

1178	**291**	$2 multicoloured	25	15
1179	**291**	$10 multicoloured	65	45

292 White Horse

1977. New Year Greetings. "Year of the Horse". Details from "One Hundred Horses" by Lang Shih-ning (Giuseppe Castiglione). Multicoloured.

1180	$1 Type **292**	75	15
1181	$5 Two Horses (horiz)	1·75	30

293 First Page of Constitution

1977. 30th Anniv of Constitution. Mult.

1182	$2 Type **293**	25	15
1183	$10 President Chiang accepting constitution	65	30

294 "Three-character" Knife (Chi State)

1978. Ancient Chinese Coins (3rd series). Mult.

1184	$2 Type **294**	75	15
1185	$5 Longer sharp-headed knife (Yen State)	1·00	15
1186	$8 Sharp-headed knife (Yet State)	1·25	20
1187	$10 Chao or Ming knife	1·75	30

295 "Dragon" Stamp, 1878

1978. Cent of Chinese Postage Stamp. Mult.

1188	$2 Type **295**	35	15
1189	$5 "Dr. Sun Yat-sen" stamp, 1941	55	25
1190	$10 "Chiang Kai-shek" stamp, 1958	80	40
MS1191	143×101 mm. Nos. 1188/1190	9·00	3·50

296 Dr. Sun Yat-sen Memorial Hall

1978. "Rocpex" Taipeh 1978 Philatelic Exhibition. Multicoloured.

1192	$2 Type **296**	25	15
1193	$10 "Dragon" and 1977 "New Year" stamps	65	35

297 Chiang Kai-shek as a Young Man

1978. 3rd Death Anniv of Pres. Chiang Kai-shek. Multicoloured.

1194	$2 Type **297**	25	15
1195	$5 Chiang on horseback (horiz)	45	25
1196	$8 Chiang making speech (horiz)	60	40
1197	$10 Reviewing armed forces	80	50

298 Section through Nuclear Reactor

1978. Nuclear Power Plant.

1198	**298**	$10 multicoloured	80	20

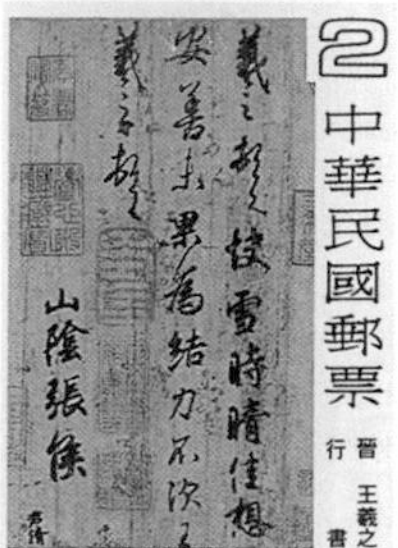

299 Letter by Wang Hsi-chih

1978. Chinese Calligraphy. Multicoloured.

1199	$2 Type **299**	1·25	20
1200	$4 Eulogy of Ni K'uan by Chu Sui-liang	2·25	20
1201	$6 Inscription on poem "Lake Tai" by Wen Cheng-ming	3·00	40
1202	$8 Autobiography by Huai-su	4·25	35
1203	$10 Poem by Ch'ang Piao	6·50	50

300 Human Figure in Polluted Environment

1978. Cancer Prevention.

1204	**300**	$2 green, yellow & red	30	15
1205	**300**	$10 blue, green & dp blue	60	35

1978. Ancient Chinese Carved Lacquer Ware (2nd series). As T 288. Multicoloured.

1206	$2 Square box	30	15
1207	$5 Box on legs	45	15
1208	$8 Round box	60	20
1209	$10 Vase (vert)	85	30

1978. Chinese Folk-tales (5th series). As T 200. Multicoloured.

1210	$1 Tsu Ti brandishing sword	25	15
1211	$2 Pan Ch'ao throwing down pen	50	20
1212	$2 Tien Tan's "Fire Bull Battle"	70	20
1213	$5 Liang Hung-yu as army drummer	1·00	25

1978. Triple Championships of the Little League World Baseball Series. Nos. 1148 and 1150 optd as T 287, but with four lines of characters and dated 1978.

1214	$4 Taiwan North–south highway	25	15
1215	$6 Taoyuan international airport	50	30

302 Yellow Orange-tip

1978. Taiwan Butterflies. Multicoloured.

1216	$2 Type **302**	75	20
1217	$4 Two-brand crow	85	20
1218	$6 Common map butterfly	1·25	30
1219	$10 "Atrophaneura polyeuctes"	2·50	50

303 Jamboree Badge, Camp and Scout Salute

1978. Taiwanese Boy Scouts' 5th Jamboree.

1220	**303**	$2 multicoloured	30	15
1221	**303**	$10 multicoloured	45	30

304 Tropical Tomatoes

1978. Asian Vegetable Research and Development Centre. Multicoloured.

1222	$2 Type **304**	45	20
1223	$10 Tropical tomatoes (different)	1·20	45

305 Aerial View of Bridge

1978. Opening of the Sino-Saudi Bridge. Mult.

1224	$2 Type **305**	40	15
1225	$6 Close-up of bridge	1·10	30

306 National Flag

1978

1226	**306**	$1 red and blue	20	15
1377	**306**	$1 red and blue	25	15
1378	**306**	$1.50 red, blue & yellow	40	15
1227	**306**	$2 red and blue	20	15
1379	**306**	$2 red, blue and yellow	25	15
1297	**306**	$3 red, blue and green	50	15
1380	**306**	$3 red and blue	30	15
1298	**306**	$4 red, blue and brown	55	20
1381	**306**	$4 red, blue and light blue	30	15
1228	**306**	$5 red, blue and green	30	15
1229	**306**	$6 red, blue and orange	35	20
1382	**306**	$5 red, blue and brown	30	15
1300	**306**	$7 red, blue and brown	55	20
1384	**306**	$7 red, blue and green	55	20
1230	**306**	$8 red, blue and green	50	25
1385	**306**	$8 red, blue & deep red	55	20
1386	**306**	$9 red, blue and green	70	20
1231	**306**	$10 red, blue and lt blue	75	30
1387	**306**	$10 red, blue and violet	70	25
1302	**306**	$12 red, blue and mauve	90	30
1389	**306**	$14 red, blue and green	1·30	40

The $1 values differ in the face value, which is printed in colour on No. 1226, whilst on No. 1377 it is white.

Nos. 1377/8, 1379, 1380, 1381, 1382 and the $6 to $14 values are as Type **306** but have solid background panel to face value and inscr.

307 "Imitation of the Three Sheep by Emperor Hsuan-tsung of the Ming Dynasty" (Emperor Kao-tsung)

1978. New Year Greetings. "Year of the Sheep".

1232	**307**	$1 multicoloured	30	20
1233	**307**	$5 multicoloured	1·50	45

308 Boeing 747-100 and Control Building

1978. Completion of Taoyuan International Airport. Multicoloured.

1234	$2 Type **308**	30	15
1235	$10 Passenger terminal building (horiz)	65	45

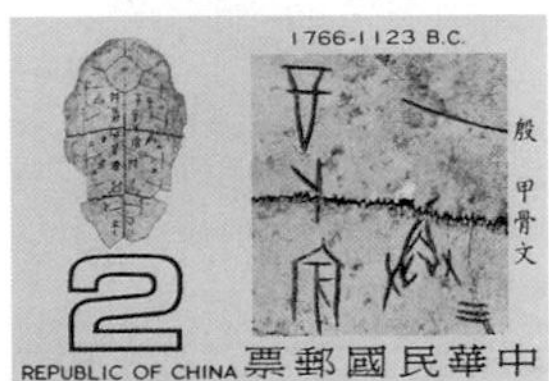

309 Oracle Bones and Inscription (Yin Dynasty)

1979. Origin and Development of Chinese Characters. Multicoloured.

1236	$2 Type **309**	80	15
1237	$5 "Leh-chi" cauldron and inscription (Spring and Autumn period)	1·25	25
1238	$8 Engraved seal and seal-style characters (Western Han dynasty)	2·00	45
1239	$10 Square plain-style characters inscribed on stone (Eastern Han dynasty)	3·25	75

310 Chihkan Tower, Tainan

1979. Tourism. Multicoloured.

1240	$2 Type **310**	30	15
1241	$5 Confucius Temple, Tainan	55	20
1242	$8 Koxinga Shrine, Tainan	80	25
1243	$10 Eternal Castle, Tainan	1·60	35

311/314 "Children Playing Games on a Winter Day" (image scaled to 70% of original size)

1979. Sung Dynasty Painting.

1244	**311**	$5 multicoloured	2·50	45
1245	**312**	$5 multicoloured	2·50	45
1246	**313**	$5 multicoloured	2·50	45
1247	**314**	$5 multicoloured	2·50	45
MS1248		101×145 mm. Nos. 1244/7	23·00	11·50

Nos. 1244/7 were printed together, se-tenant, forming the composite design illustrated.

315 Lu Hao-tung (revolutionary)

1979. Famous Chinese.

1249	**315**	$2 blue	60	15

316 White Jade Brush Washer (Ming dynasty)

1979. Ancient Chinese Jade (1st series). Multicoloured.

1250	$2 Yellow jade brush holder embossed with clouds and dragons (Sung dynasty) (vert)	30	15
1251	$5 Type **316**	85	30
1252	$8 Dark green jade brush washer carved with clouds and dragons (Ch'ing dynasty)	1·10	45
1253	$10 Bluish jade washer in shape of lotus (Ch'ing dynasty)	1·80	60

See also Nos. 1291/4.

317 Plum Blossom

1979

1254	**317**	$10 blue	1·70	20
1255	**317**	$20 brown	2·20	20
1255b	**317**	$40 red	2·20	20
1256	**317**	$50 green	4·50	25
1257	**317**	$100 red	6·25	80
1257b	**317**	$300 red and violet	22·00	3·25
1257c	**317**	$500 red and brown	35·00	5·25

The $300 and $500 are size 25×33 mm.

318 Houses

1979. Environmental Protection. Mult.

1258	$2 Type **318**	25	15
1259	$10 Rural scene (horiz)	85	35

319 Savings Bank Counter

1979. 60th Anniv of Postal Savings Bank. Multicoloured.

1260	$2 Type **319**	25	15
1261	$5 Savings bank queue	35	20
1262	$8 Computer and savings book (horiz)	50	20
1263	$10 Money box and "tree" emblem (horiz)	70	25

320 Steere's Liocichla

1979. Birds. Multicoloured.

1264	$2 Swinhoe's pheasant	50	15
1265	$8 Type **320**	1·10	25
1266	$10 Formosan yuhina	1·40	35

321 Sir Rowland Hill

1979. Death Centenary of Sir Rowland Hill.

1267	**321**	$10 multicoloured	1·00	25

322 Jar with Rope Pattern

1979. Ancient Chinese Pottery. Multicoloured.

1268	$2 Type **322** (Shang dynasty)	35	15
1269	$5 Two handled jar (Shang dynasty)	1·00	20
1270	$8 Red jar with "ears" (Han dynasty)	1·80	20
1271	$10 Green glazed jar (Han dynasty)	2·10	25

323 Children and I.Y.C. Emblem

1979. International Year of the Child.

1272	**323**	$2 multicoloured	30	15
1273	**323**	$10 multicoloured	65	35

324 "Trees on a Winter Plain" (Li Ch'eng)

1979. Ancient Chinese Paintings. Mult.

1274	$2 Type **324** (Sung dynasty)	1·00	20
1275	$5 "Bamboo" (Wen T'ung, Sung dynasty)	1·75	25
1276	$8 "Old Tree, Bamboo and Rock" (Chao Mengfu, Yuan dynasty)	2·75	40
1277	$10 "Twin Pines" (Li K'an, Yuan dynasty)	4·25	45

325 Taiwan Macaque

1979. New Year Greetings. "Year of the Monkey".

1278	**325**	$1 multicoloured	1·00	20
1279	**325**	$6 multicoloured	3·00	50

326 Competition Emblem and Symbols of Ten Trades

1979. 10th National Vocational Training Competition, Taichung.

1280	**326**	$2 multicoloured	25	15
1281	**326**	$10 multicoloured	70	35

327 "75" and Rotary Emblem

1980. 75th Anniv of Rotary International. Multicoloured

1282	$2 Type **327**	30	15
1283	$12 Anniversary emblem and symbols of Rotary's services (vert)	80	40

328 Tunnel of Nine Turns

1980. Tourism. Scenic Spots on the East–West Cross-Island Highway. Multicoloured.

1284	$2 Type **328**	35	15
1285	$8 Mt. Hohuan (horiz)	75	25
1286	$12 Bridge, Tien Hsiang	1·50	35

329 Shih Chien-ju (hero of revolution)

1980. Famous Chinese.

1287	$2 brown	30	15

330 Chung-cheng Memorial Hall

1980. 5th Death Anniv of Chiang Kai-shek. Multicoloured.

1288	$2 Type **330**	25	15
1289	$8 Quotation of Chiang Kai-shek	40	20
1290	$12 Bronze statue of Chiang Kai-shek	55	40

1980. Ancient Chinese Jade (2nd series). As T 316. Multicoloured.

1291	$2 Kuang (cup) decorated with dragons (Sung dynasty) (vert)	45	15
1292	$5 Dark green jade melon-shaped brush washer (Ming dynasty)	85	20
1293	$8 Bluish jade Po Monk's alms bowl (Ch'ing dynasty)	1·20	20
1294	$10 Yellow jade brush washer (Ch'ing dynasty)	1·50	25

331 Tzu-Ch'iang Squadron over Presidential Mansion

1980. Air. Multicoloured.

1303	$5 Type **331**	30	15
1304	$7 Boeing 747-100 airliner and insignia of CAL (state airline)	75	25
1305	$12 National Flag and Boeing 747-100	1·00	35

332 "Wasted Resources"

1980. Energy Conservation.

1306	$2 multicoloured	25	15
1307	$12 multicoloured	75	45

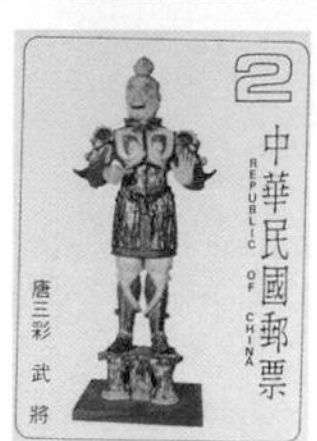

333 Military Official

1980. T'ang Dynasty Tri-coloured Pottery. Multicoloured.

1308	$2 Type **333**	75	15
1309	$5 Chickens	1·25	20
1310	$8 Horse	1·75	20
1311	$10 Camel	2·00	25

1980. Chinese Folk-tales (6th series). As T 200. Multicoloured.

1312	$1 Grinding mortar into a needle	25	15
1313	$2 Returning lost articles	40	20
1314	$2 Wen Tien-hsiang in prison	60	20
1315	$5 Sending coal to poor during snow	1·10	25

334 TRA Trunk Line Electrification

1980. Completion of Ten Major Construction Projects. Multicoloured.

1316	$2 Type **334**	40	15
1317	$2 Taichung Harbour	40	15
1318	$2 Chiang Kai-shek International Airport	40	15
1319	$2 Integrated steel mill	40	15
1320	$2 Sun Yat-sen National Freeway	40	15
1321	$2 Nuclear power plant	40	15
1322	$2 Petrochemical industrial zone in south	40	15
1323	$2 Su-ao Harbour	40	15
1324	$2 Kaohsiung Shipyard	40	15
1325	$2 Taiwan North Link Railway	40	15
MS1326	217×100 mm. Nos. 1316/25	11·50	12·00

335 Money Boxes within Ancient Chinese Coin

1980. 10th National Savings Day. Mult.

1327	$2 Type **335**	40	15
1328	$12 Hand placing coin in money box	1·10	45

336/339 Landscape (image scaled to 70% of original size)

1980. Painting by Ch'iu Ying.

1329	$5 multicoloured	2·30	35
1330	$5 multicoloured	2·30	35
1331	$5 multicoloured	2·30	35
1332	$5 multicoloured	2·30	35
MS1333	101×144 mm. Nos. 1329/32	24·00	16·00

340 Cock

1980. New Year Greetings. "Year of the Cock".

1334	$1 multicoloured	1·00	15
1335	$6 multicoloured	2·75	40
MS1336	77×101 mm. Nos. 1334/5, each ×2	15·00	8·25

341 Heads, Flag and Census Form

1980. Population and Housing Census. Mult.

1337	$2 Type **341**	25	20
1338	$12 Flag and buildings (horiz)	90	45

342 Central Weather Bureau

1981. Completion of Meteorological Satellite Ground Station, Taipei. Multicoloured.

1339	$2 "TIROS-N" weather satellite (vert)	30	15
1340	$10 Type **342**	90	45

343 "Happiness"

344 "Joy"

345 "Wealth"

346 "Longevity"

1981. New Year Calligraphy.

1341	$5 gold, red and black	1·20	20
1342	$5 gold, red and black	1·20	20
1343	$5 gold, red and black	1·20	20
1344	$5 gold, red and black	1·20	20

347 Candle and Siamese Twins

1981. International Year for Disabled Persons.

1345	$2 multicoloured	25	15
1346	$10 multicoloured	75	25

348 Mt. Ali

1981. Tourism. Multicoloured.

1347	$2 Type **348**	35	15
1348	$7 Oluanpi	80	20
1349	$12 Sun Moon Lake	1·40	30

349 "Children on River Bank"

1981. Children's Day. Children's Drawings. Mult.

1350	$1 Type **349**	15	15
1351	$2 "Cable-cars"	25	15
1352	$5 "Lobsters"	30	15
1353	$7 "Village"	35	20

350 Main Gate Chiang Kai-shek Memorial Hall

1981. 6th Death Anniv of Chiang Kai-shek.

1354	20c. violet	25	15
1355	40c. red	25	15
1356	50c. brown	25	15
1712	10c. red	25	15
1714	30c. green	25	15
1717	60c. blue	25	15

351 Brush Washer (Hsuan-te ware)

1981. Ancient Chinese Enamelware (1st series). Ming Dynasty Cloisonne Enamelware. Multicoloured.

1357	$2 Type **351**	45	15
1358	$5 Ritual vessel with ring handles (Chiang-ta'i ware) (vert)	85	20
1359	$8 Plate decorated with dragons (Wan-li ware)	1·10	20
1360	$10 Vase (vert)	1·40	25

352 Electric and First Steam Locomotives

1981. Centenary of Railway. Mult.

1361	$2 Type **352**	75	15
1362	$14 Side views of steam and electric locomotives (horiz)	2·00	45

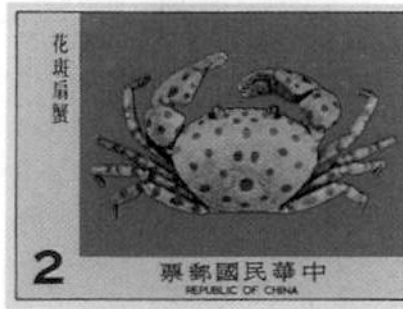

353 "Liagore rubromaculata"

1981. Crabs. Multicoloured.

1363	$2 Type **353**	40	15
1364	$5 "Ranina ranina" (vert)	60	20
1365	$8 "Platymaia wyvillethomsoni"	80	25
1366	$14 "Lambrus nummifera" (vert)	1·30	30

354 Bureau Emblem

1981. 40th Anniv of Central Weather Bureau.

1367	$2 multicoloured	35	15
1368	$14 multicoloured	1·10	45

355 The Cowherd

1981. Fairy Tales. "The Cowherd and the Weaving Maid". Multicoloured.

1369	$2 Type **355**	45	15
1370	$4 The cowherd watching the weaving maid through rushes	70	20
1371	$8 The cowherd and the weaving maid on opposite sides of Heavenly River	1·20	25
1372	$14 The cowherd and the weaving maid meeting on bridge of magpies	2·10	50

356 Laser Display

1981. Lasography Exhibition. Designs showing different laser displays.

1373	$2 multicoloured	25	15

1374	$5 multicoloured	30	20
1375	$8 multicoloured	50	30
1376	$14 multicoloured	1·10	65

357 Goalkeeper catching Ball

1981. Athletics Day. Multicoloured.

1390	$5 Women soccer players	60	20
1391	$5 Type **357**	60	20

358 Officers watching Battle from Mound

1981. 70th Anniv of Founding of Chinese Republic. Multicoloured.

1392	$2 Type **358**	25	15
1393	$2 Officer clenching fist and soldiers awaiting battle	25	15
1394	$2 Officer on horseback saluting	25	15
1395	$2 Attacking buildings	25	15
1396	$3 Attacking fortifications	35	20
1397	$3 Dockside scene	35	20
1398	$8 Chiang Kai-shek	55	30
1399	$14 Sun Yat-sen	1·00	40
MS1400	115×168 mm. Nos. 1392/9	8·00	2·50

359 Chinese Republic Anniv Emblem and "Stamps"

1981. "Rocpex Taipei '81" International Stamp Exhibition.

1401	$2 multicoloured	20	15
1402	$14 multicoloured	65	30

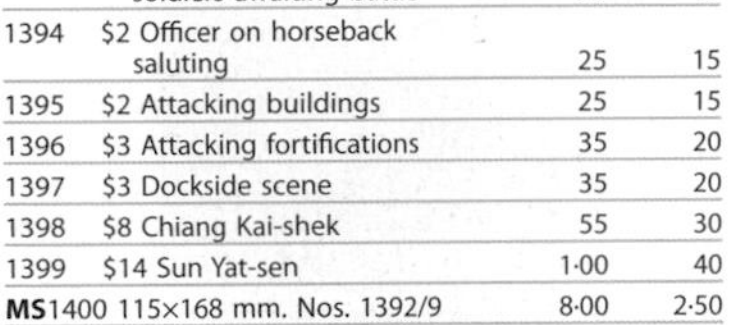

360 Detail of Scroll

1981. Sung Dynasty painting "One Hundred Young Boys". Designs showing details of Scroll.

1403	$2 (1) multicoloured	1·40	25
1404	$2 (2) multicoloured	1·40	25
1405	$2 (3) multicoloured	1·40	25
1406	$2 (4) multicoloured	1·40	25
1407	$2 (5) multicoloured	1·40	25
1408	$2 (6) multicoloured	1·40	25
1409	$2 (7) multicoloured	1·40	25
1410	$2 (8) multicoloured	1·40	25
1411	$2 (9) multicoloured	1·40	25
1412	$2 (10) multicoloured	1·40	25

361 Dog

1981. New Year Greetings. "Year of the Dog".

1413	$1 multicoloured	1·25	15
1414	$10 multicoloured	3·00	45
MS1415	78×102 mm. Nos. 1413/14, each ×2	16·00	3·50

362 Information-using Services and Emblem

1981. Information Week.

1416	$2 multicoloured	45	20

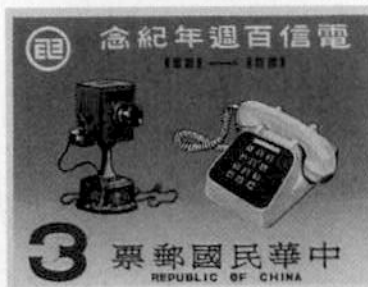

363 Telephones of 1881 and 1981

1981. Centenary of Chinese Telecommunications Service. Multicoloured.

1417	$2 Map and hand holding telephone handset (vert)	25	15
1418	$3 Type **363**	30	20
1419	$8 Submarine cable map	50	20
1420	$18 Computer and telecommunication units (vert)	60	25

364 Arrangement in Basket

1982. Chinese Flower Arrangements. Mult.

1421	$2 Type **364**	25	15
1422	$3 Arrangement in jug	35	20
1423	$8 Arrangement in vase	75	25
1424	$18 Arrangement in holder	1·40	40

365 Kuan Yu leaves for Cheng City

1982. Scenes from "The Ku Cheng Reunion" (opera). Multicoloured.

1425	$2 Type **365**	1·25	15
1426	$3 Chang Fei refuses to open city gates	2·25	20
1427	$4 Chang Fei apologises to Kuan Yu	2·75	25
1428	$18 Liu Pei, Kuan Yu and Chang Fei are reunited	4·25	65

366 Dr. Robert Koch and Tubercle Bacillus

1982. Centenary of Discovery of Tubercle Bacillus.

1429	$2 multicoloured	30	20

367 Chang Shih-liang (revolutionary)

1982. Famous Chinese.

1430	$2 red	25	15

368 "Martyrs' Shrine"

1982. Children's Day. Children's paintings.

1431	$2 Type **368**	45	15
1432	$3 "House Yard"	60	20
1433	$5 "Cattle Herd"	80	20
1434	$8 "A Sacrificial Ceremony for a Plentiful Year"	1·10	25

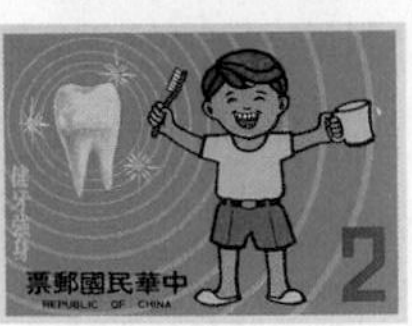

369 Tooth and Child holding Toothbrush and Mug

1982. Dental Health. Multicoloured.

1435	$2 Type **369**	35	15
1436	$3 Methods of cleaning teeth	70	20
1437	$10 Dental check-up	1·40	30

1982. Ancient Chinese Enamelware (2nd series). As T 351. Multicoloured.

1438	$2 Champleve cup and plate (Ch'ien-lung ware)	50	15
1439	$5 Cloisonne duck container (Ch'ien-lung ware) (vert)	95	20
1440	$8 Painted incense burner (K'ang-hsi period)	1·70	20
1441	$12 Cloisonne Tibetan lama milk-tea pot (Ch'ien-lung ware) (vert)	2·50	25

370 "Spring Dawn" (Meng Hao-jan)

1982. Chinese Classical Poetry (1st series). Tang Dynasty Poems. Multicoloured.

1442	$2 Type **370**	3·25	20
1443	$3 "On Looking for a Hermit and not Finding Him" (Chia Tao)	5·50	20
1444	$5 "Summer Dying" (Liu Yu-hsi)	9·00	40
1445	$18 "Looking at the Snow Drifts on South Mountains" (Tsu Yung)	13·00	90

371 Softball

1982. 5th World Women's Softball Championship, Taipeh.

1446	$2 multicoloured	45	15
1447	$18 multicoloured	1·30	45

372 Scouts on Rope Bridge, and Lord Baden-Powell

1982. 75th Anniv of Boy Scout Movement and 125th Birth Anniv of Lord Baden-Powell. Multicoloured.

1448	$2 Type **372**	25	15
1449	$18 Emblem, scouts making frame and camp	80	45

373 Tweezers holding Stamp

1982. Philately Day. Multicoloured.

1450	$2 Type **373**	45	15
1451	$18 Examining stamp album with magnifying glass	1·30	45

374 Carved Lion

1982. Tsu Shih Temple, Sanhsia. Multicoloured.

1452	$2 Type **374**	40	15
1453	$3 Lion brackets (horiz)	55	20
1454	$5 Carved sub-lintels in passageway	90	25
1455	$18 Temple roofs (horiz)	1·80	40

1982. Chinese Folk-tales (7th series). Stories from "36 Examples of Filial Piety" by Wu Yen-huan, As T 200. Multicoloured.

1456	$1 Shao K'ang supporting his mother	30	15
1457	$2 Hsun Kuan leading soldier reinforcements to her father	50	20
1458	$3 Ku Yen-wu refusing to serve Ch'ing dynasty	70	20
1459	$5 Ting Ch'un-liang caring for his paralysed father	1·30	25

375 Riding Horses

1982. 30th Anniv of China Youth Corps. Multicoloured.

1460	$2 Type **375**	15	15
1461	$3 Flag and water sport (vert)	25	15
1462	$18 Mountaineering	80	50

376 Lohan with Boy Attendant and Monkey

1982. Lohan (Buddhist Saint) Scroll Paintings by Liu Sung-nien. Multicoloured.

1463	$2 Type **376**	2·25	20
1464	$3 Monk presenting seated Lohan with scroll	3·50	30
1465	$18 Tribal king paying homage to seated Lohan	9·50	80
MS1466	140×102 mm. Nos. 1463/5	30·00	15·00
MS1467	No. **MS**1466 with vertical overprint in red left and right margins	50·00	35·00

378 Pig

1982. New Year. "Year of the Pig".

1468	$1 multicoloured	2·00	15
1469	$10 multicoloured	3·75	50
MS1470	77×102 mm. Nos. 1468/9, each ×2	18·00	6·00

1983. Ancient Chinese Enamelware (3rd series). Ch'ing Dynasty Enamelware. As T 351. Multicoloured.

1472	$2 Square basin with rounded corners	40	15

1473	$3 Vase decorated with landscape panels (vert)	75	20
1474	$4 Blue teapot with flower pattern	1·20	25
1475	$18 Cloisonne elephant with vase on back (vert)	1·60	40

379 "Wan-hsi-sha" (Yen Shu)

1983. Chinese Classical Poetry (2nd series). Sung Dynasty Lyrical Poems. Multicoloured.

1476	$2 Type **379**	3·75	25
1477	$3 "Ch'ing-yu-an" (Ho Chu)	5·75	35
1478	$5 "Su-mu-che" (Fan Chung-yen)	7·50	40
1479	$11 "Hsing-hsiang-tzu" (Ch'ao Pu-chih)	12·00	60

380 Hsin-hsien Concealed Fall, Wawa Valley

1983. Landscapes. Multicoloured.

1480	$2 Type **380**	75	20
1481	$3 University Pond, Chitou Forest	1·25	30
1482	$18 Mount Jade (horiz)	1·75	45

381 Matteo Ricci and Astrolabe

1983. 400th Anniv of Matteo Ricci's (missionary) Arrival in China. Multicoloured.

1483	$2 Type **381**	40	15
1484	$18 Matteo Ricci and Great Wall	1·20	35

382 Wu Ching-heng (Chairman of development committee)

1983. 70th Anniv of Mandarin Phonetic Symbols. Multicoloured.

1485	$2 Type **382**	40	15
1486	$18 Children studying symbols	1·20	35

383 Hsu Hsien meets Pai Su-chen

1983. Fairy Tales. "Lady White Snake". Multicoloured.

1487	$2 Type **383**	35	15
1488	$3 Pai Su-chen steals Tree of Life	65	20
1489	$3 Confrontation with Fahai at Chin Shan Temple	1·00	30
1490	$18 Pai Su-chen is imprisoned beneath Thunder Peak Pagoda	1·70	50

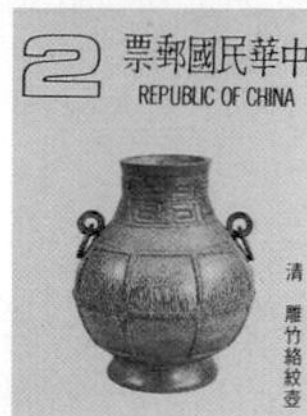

384 Pot with Cord Pattern

1983. Ancient Chinese Bamboo Carvings. Multicoloured.

1491	$2 Type **384**	50	15
1492	$3 Vase with Tao-t'ien motif	80	20
1493	$4 Carved mountain scene with figures	85	25
1494	$18 Brush-holder with relief showing ladies	2·30	40

386 Grouper

1983. World Communications Year. Mult.

1495	$2 Type **385**	40	15
1496	$18 WCY emblem	80	35

1983. Protection of Fishery Resources. Mult.

1497	$2 Type **386**	45	20
1498	$18 Lizardfish	1·70	45

387 T.V. Screen, Antenna and Radio Waves

1983. Journalists' Day.

1499	$2 multicoloured	30	15

388 Yurt

1983. Mongolian and Tibetan Scenes.

1500	$2 Type **388**	50	15
1501	$3 Potala Palace	85	20
1502	$5 Sheep on prairie	1·00	25
1503	$11 Camel caravan	1·40	40

389 Brown Shrike

1983. 2nd East Asian Bird Protection Conference. Multicoloured.

1504	$2 Type **389**	75	20
1505	$18 Grey-faced buzzard-eagle	2·50	45

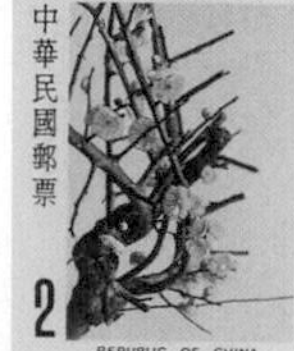

390 Pink Plum Blossom

1983. Plum Blossom. Multicoloured.

1506	$2 Type **390**	25	15
1507	$3 Red plum blossom	40	20
1508	$5 Plum blossom and pagoda	60	20
1509	$11 White plum blossom	1·10	25

391 Congress Emblem

1983. 38th Jaycees International World Congress. Multicoloured.

1510	$2 Type **391**	30	15
1511	$18 Emblems and globe	1·10	45

392 World Map as Heart

1983. 8th Asian-Pacific Cardiology Congress. Mult.

1512	$2 Type **392**	30	15
1513	$18 Heart and electrocardiogram	1·10	45

393 Rat

1983. New Year. "Year of the Rat".

1514	$1 multicoloured	2·00	15
1515	$10 multicoloured	5·00	50
MS1516	78×103 mm. Nos. 1514/15, each ×2	32·00	8·50

394 Mother and Child reading and Chin Ting Prize

1983. National Reading Week. Mult.

1517	$2 Type **394**	30	15
1518	$18 Chin Ting prize (for outstanding publications) books and father and son reading (vert)	1·00	35

395 Boeing 737 over Chiang Kai-shek Airport

1984. Air. 37th Anniv of Civil Aeronautics Administration. Multicoloured.

1519	$7 Type **395**	55	15
1520	$11 Boeing 747 over Chung-cheng Memorial Hall (horiz)	80	30
1521	$18 Boeing 737 over Sun Yat-sen Memorial Hall (horiz)	1·10	45

396 Soldiers with Flags

1984. World Freedom Day. Multicoloured.

1522	$2 Type **396**	30	15
1523	$18 Globe and people of the world	1·30	35

397 "Hsiao-liang-chou" (Kuan Yun-shih)

1984. Chinese Classical Poetry (3rd series). Yuan Dynasty Lyric Poems. Multicoloured.

1524	$2 Type **397**	3·75	25
1525	$3 "A Lady holds a fine fan of silk", "Tien-ching-sha" (Po P'u)	5·50	30
1526	$5 "Picnic under banana leaves "Ch'ing-chiang-yin" (Chang Ko-chin)	8·00	35
1527	$18 "Plum blossoms in the snowbound wilderness "Tien-ching-sha" (Shang Cheng-shu)	11·00	95

398 Forest Scene

1984. Forest Resources. Multicoloured.

1528	$2 Type **398**	80	15
1529	$2 Reservoir and dam	80	15
1530	$2 Camp in forest	80	15
1531	$2 Wooded slopes	80	15

400 Lin Chueh-min (revolutionary)

1984. Famous Chinese.

1536	$2 green	30	15

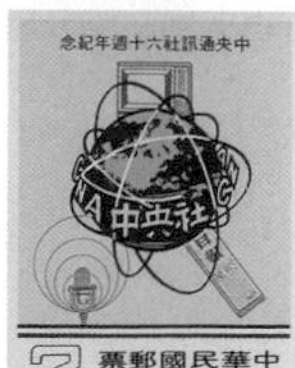

401 Agency Emblem and Broadcasting Equipment

1984. 60th Anniv of Central News Agency. Mult.

1537	$2 Type **401**	25	15
1538	$10 Agency emblem and satellite communications	75	30

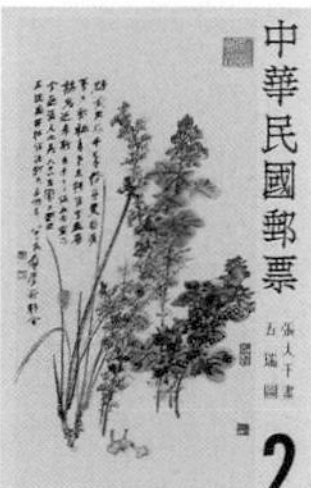

402 "Five Auspicious Tokens"

1984. 85th Birth Anniv of Chang Ta-chien (artist). Multicoloured.

1539	$2 Type **402**	2·00	20
1540	$5 "The God of Longevity"	4·75	20
1541	$18 "Lotus Blossoms in Ink Splash"	6·50	45

1984. Ancient Chinese Enamelware (4th series). Ch'ing Dynasty Enamelware. As T 351. Mult.

1542	$2 Lidded cup and teapot on tray	40	15
1543	$3 Cloisonne wine vessel on phoenix (vert)	60	20
1544	$4 Yellow teapot with pink and blue chrysanthemum decoration	95	25
1545	$18 Cloisonne candle-holder on bird	1·30	40

403 Boeing 747-200 circling Globe

1984. Inauguration of China Airlines Global Service. Multicoloured.

1546	$2 Type **403**	20	15
1547	$7 Globe and Boeing 747-200	35	20
1548	$11 Boeing 747-200 over New York	55	30
1549	$18 Boeing 747-200 over Netherlands	90	50

404 Judo

1984. Olympic Games, Los Angeles. Mult.

1550	$2 Type **404**	25	15
1551	$5 Archery (vert)	40	20
1552	$18 Swimming	95	50

405 Container Ship "Ming Comfort"

1984. 30th Navigation Day. Multicoloured.

1553	$2 Type **405**	75	15
1554	$18 "Prosperity" (tanker)	2·10	40

406 "Gentiana arisanensis"

1984. Alpine Plants. Multicoloured.

1555	$2 Type **406**	95	15
1556	$3 "Epilobium nankotaiza nense"	1·00	20
1557	$5 "Adenophora uehatae"	1·25	30
1558	$18 "Aconitum fukutomei"	3·00	50

1984. Sung Dynasty Painting "The Eighteen Scholars". Multicoloured.

1559	$2 Type **407**	3·50	20
1560	$3 Scholars playing chess	5·00	20
1561	$5 Scholars writing	7·50	25
1562	$18 Scholars painting	15·00	60

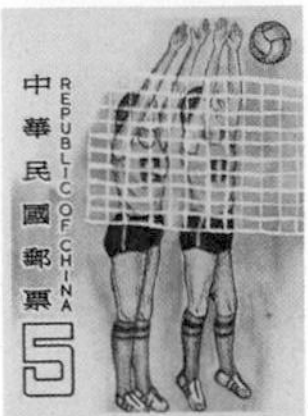

408 Volleyball Players

1984. Athletics Day. Multicoloured.

1563	$5 Type **408**	80	20
1564	$5 Volleyball player	80	20

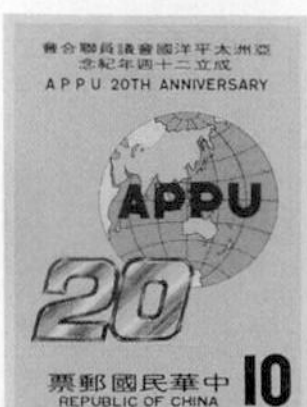

409 Union Emblem

1984. 20th Anniv of Asian-Pacific Parliamentarians' Union.

1565	$10 multicoloured	65	20

410 1965 Confucius $1 Stamp

1984. New Postal Museum Building, Taipeh. Multicoloured.

1566	$2 Type **410**	20	15
1567	$5 1933 Sun Yat-sen 5c. stamp	40	15
1568	$18 New Postal Museum building	1·00	50
MS1569	128×89 mm. Nos. 1566/8	12·00	3·25

411 Flag and Emblem

1984. Grand Alliance for China's Reunification Convention.

1570	$2 multicoloured	40	15

412 Commission Services

1984. 30th Anniv of Vocational Assistance Commission for Retired Servicemen.

1571	$2 multicoloured	40	15

413 Pine Tree

1984. Pine, Bamboo and Plum (1st series). Multicoloured.

1572	$2 Type **413**	25	15
1573	$8 Bamboo	65	20
1574	$10 Plum blossom	75	30

414 Ox

1984. New Year Greetings. "Year of the Ox".

1575	$1 multicoloured	1·25	15
1576	$10 multicoloured	3·25	30
MS1577	78×101 mm. Nos. 1575/6, each ×2	12·00	3·25

415 Legal Code Book and Scales

1985. Judicial Day.

1578	$5 multicoloured	55	20

416 Ku-kang Lake and Pagoda, Quemoy

1985. Scenery of Quemoy and Matsu. Mult.

1579	$2 Type **416**	25	15
1580	$5 Kuang-hai stone, Quemoy	55	20
1581	$8 Sheng-li reservoir, Matsu	95	20
1582	$10 Tung-chu lighthouse, Matsu	1·30	25

416 Ku-kang Lake and Pagoda, Quemoy

1985. 150th Anniv of Sir Robert Hart (founder of Chinese Postal Service).

1583	$2 multicoloured	40	15

418 Lo Fu-hsing

1985. Birth Centenary of Lo Fu-hsing (patriot).

1584	$2 multicoloured	40	15

419 Tsou Jung

1985. 80th Death Anniv of Tsou Jung (revolutionary).

1585	$3 green	40	15

420 Main Gate, Chung-cheng Memorial Hall

1985. 10th Death Anniv of President Chiang Kai-shek. Multicoloured

1586	$2 Type **420**	25	15
1587	$8 Tzuhu, President Chiang's temporary resting place	95	20
1588	$10 President Chiang Kai-shek (vert)	1·20	30

421 Lily

1985. Mothers' Day. Multicoloured.

1589	$2 Type **421**	80	15
1590	$2 Carnation	80	15

422 View of Tunnel

1985. 1st Anniv of Kaohsiung Cross-harbour Tunnel.

1591	$5 multicoloured	60	20

423 Girl Guide saluting

1985. 75th Anniv of Girl Guide Movement.

1592	$2 multicoloured	25	15
1593	$18 multicoloured	1·50	35

424 "Buxom is the Peach Tree..."

1985. Chinese Classical Poetry (4th series). Poems from "Book of Odes", edited by Confucius. Multicoloured.

1594	$2 Type **424**	1·75	20
1595	$5 "Thick grows that tarragon ..."	3·25	30
1596	$8 "Thick grow the rush leaves ..."	5·50	35
1597	$10 "... The snowflakes fly"	7·50	40

425 Wax Jambo

1985. Fruit. Multicoloured.

1598	$2 Type **425**	75	15
1599	$3 Guavas	1·00	20
1600	$5 Carambolas	1·50	20
1601	$8 Lychees	2·25	25

426 Dragon Boat

1985. Ch'ing Dynasty Ivory Carvings. Mult.

1602	$2 Type **426**	35	15
1603	$3 Carved landscape	50	20
1604	$5 Melon-shaped water container	80	25
1605	$18 Brush-holder (vert)	1·00	35

427 Lady of Rank, T'ang Dynasty

1985. 4th Asian Costume Conference. Chinese Costumes (1st series). Multicoloured.

1606	$2 Type **427**	1·25	15
1607	$5 Palace woman, Sung dynasty	2·00	20
1608	$8 Lady of rank, Yuan dynasty	3·25	20
1609	$11 Lady of rank, Ming dynasty	3·75	25

428 Bird feeding Chicks

1985. Social Welfare.

1610	$2 multicoloured	40	15

429 North Gate, Taipeh

1985. Historic Buildings (1st series). Mult.

1611	$2 Type **429**	25	15
1612	$5 San Domingo fort, Tamsui	55	20
1613	$8 Lung Shan Temple, Lukang	75	20
1614	$10 Confucius Temple, Changhua	1·10	25

430 Oak Tree

1985. Bonsai. Multicoloured.

1615	$2 Type **430**	40	15
1616	$5 Five-leaf pine	75	25
1617	$8 Lohan pine	1·00	35
1618	$18 Banyan	1·50	50

431 World Trade Centre and Sports Goods Logo

1985. Trade Shows. Multicoloured.

1619	$2 Type **431**	70	15
1620	$2 Toys and gifts logo (blue and red)	70	15
1621	$2 Electronics logo (blue)	70	15
1622	$2 Machinery logo (black and orange)	70	15

432 Flag, Map and Scenes of Peace

1985. 40th Anniv of Return of Taiwan to China. Multicoloured.

1623	$2 Type **432**	80	15
1624	$18 Chiang Kai-shek and triumphal arch	1·90	45

433 Emblem

1985. 7th Asian Federation for the Mentally Retarded Conference, Taipeh.

1625	$2 multicoloured	40	15
1626	$11 multicoloured	1·20	30

434 Sun Yat-sen

1985. 120th Birth Anniv of Sun Yat-sen.

1627	$2 multicoloured	45	15
1628	$18 multicoloured	1·50	45

435 Tiger

1985. New Year Greetings. "Year of the Tiger".

1629	$1 multicoloured	1·00	15
1630	$10 multicoloured	3·25	35
MS1631	77×101 mm. Nos. 1629/30, each ×2	14·00	2·75

436 Emblem

1985. 50th Anniv of Postal Simple Life Insurance.

1632	$2 multicoloured	40	15

437 Pine Tree

1986. Pine, Bamboo and Plum (2nd series). Multicoloured.

1633	$1 Type **437**	25	15
1634	$11 Bamboo	55	20
1635	$18 Plum blossom	80	20

438 Detail of Scroll

1986. Painting "Hermit Anglers on a Mountain Stream" by T'ang Yin. Designs showing details of the scroll. Multicoloured.

1636	$2 (1) Type **438**	1·60	20
1637	$2 (2) Pavilions on bank	1·60	20
1638	$2 (3) Anglers in boats near waterfall	1·60	20
1639	$2 (4) Pavilions on stilts	1·60	20
1640	$2 (5) Anglers in boat near island	1·60	20

439 Gladioli in Vase

1986. Flower Arrangements (1st series). Mult.

1641	$2 Type **439**	30	20
1642	$5 Roses in double wicker holders	60	20
1643	$8 Roses and fern in pot on stand	75	20
1644	$10 Various flowers in large and small pots	1·10	25

440 Loading and unloading Boeing 747 Mail Plane

1986. 90th Anniv of Post Office. Mult.

1645	$2 Type **440**	25	15
1646	$5 Postman on motorcycle (vert)	30	20
1647	$8 Customer at cash dispenser and clerk at savings bank computer terminal (vert)	50	20
1648	$10 Electronic sorting machine and envelopes circling globe	60	25
MS1649	130×100 mm. Nos. 1645/8	5·25	2·10

441 Chen Tien-hva (revolutionary writer)

1986. Famous Chinese.

1650	$2 violet	25	15

442 Mountain shrouded in Mist

1986. Yushan National Park. Multicoloured.

1651	$2 Type **442**	45	15
1652	$5 People on mountain top	1·10	20
1653	$8 Snow covered mountain peak	1·50	25
1654	$10 Forest on mountain side	2·00	30

443 Hydro-electric Power Station

1986. Power Stations. Multicoloured.

1655	$2 Type **443**	35	15
1656	$8 Thermo-electric power station	65	20
1657	$10 Nuclear power station	95	30

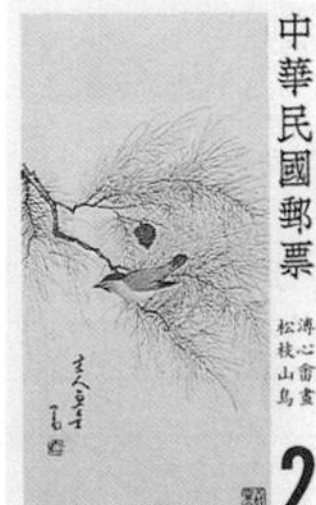
444 Taiwan Firecrest in Tree

1986. Paintings by P'u Hsin-yu. Mult.

1658	$2 Type **444**	2·75	15
1659	$8 Landscape	6·50	25
1660	$10 Woman in garden	6·75	35

445 Emblems

1986. 25th Anniv of Asian Productivity Organization and 30th Anniv of China Productivity Centre.

1661	$2 multicoloured	25	15
1662	$11 multicoloured	90	30

446 Green-winged Macaw

1986. Protection of Intellectual Property.

1663	$2 multicoloured	1·50	20

447 Starck's Damselfish ("Chrysiptera starcki")

1986. Coral Reef Fishes. Multicoloured.

1664	$2 Type **447**	2·30	1·40
1665	$2 Copper-banded butterflyfish ("Chelmon rostratus")	2·30	1·40
1666	$2 Pearl-scaled butterflyfish ("Chaetodon xanthurus")	2·30	1·40
1667	$2 Four-spotted butterflyfish ("Chaetodon quadrimaculatus")	2·30	1·40
1668	$2 Meyer's butterflyfish ("Chaetodon meyeri")	2·30	1·40
1669	$2 Japanese swallow ("Genicanthus semifasciatus") (female)	2·30	1·40
1670	$2 Japanese swallow ("Genicanthus semifasciatus") (male)	2·30	1·40
1671	$2 Blue-ringed angelfish ("Pomacanthus annularis")	2·30	1·40
1672	$2 Harlequin tuskfish ("Lienardella fasciata")	2·30	1·40
1673	$2 Undulate triggerfish ("Balistapus undulatus")	2·30	1·40

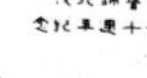
(448)

1986. 60th Anniv of Chiang Kai-shek's Northward Expedition. Nos. 1229 and 1386 surch as T 448.

1674	$2 on $6 red, bl & orge	25	15
1675	$8 on $9 red, bl & grn	50	30

449 Tzu Mu Bridge

1986. Road Bridges. Multicoloured.

1676	$2 Type **449**	45	15
1677	$5 Chang Hung bridge over Hsiu-ku-luan-chi	80	20
1678	$8 Kuan Fu bridge over Hsin-tien River	1·20	20
1679	$10 Kuan Tu bridge over Tanshui River	2·00	25

450 Yingtai and Shanpo going to School

1986. Folk Tales. "Love between Liang Shanpo and Chu Yingtai". Multicoloured.

1680	$5 Type **450**	70	15
1681	$5 Classmates	70	15
1682	$5 Yingtai and Shanpo by lake	70	15
1683	$5 Yingtai telling Shanpo she is to be married	70	15
1684	$5 Ascending to heaven as butterflies	70	15

451 Children playing by Lake and Rainbow

1986. Cleanliness and Courtesy. Mult.

1685	$2 Type **451**	35	20
1686	$8 Children helping others in street	75	25

452 Lady of Warring States Period

1986. Chinese Costumes (2nd series). Mult.

1687	$2 Lady of rank, Shang dynasty	1·25	15
1688	$5 Type **452**	1·75	20
1689	$8 Empress's assembly dress, later Han dynasty	2·25	20
1690	$10 Beribboned dress of lady of rank, Wei and Tsin dynasties	3·25	25

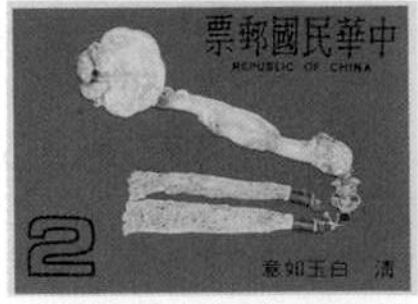

453 White Jade Ju-i Sceptre with Fish Decoration

1986. Ch'ing Dynasty Ju-i (1st series). Mult.

1691	$2 Type **453**	25	15
1692	$3 Coral ju-i sceptre with fungus motif	40	20
1693	$4 Redwood ju-i sceptre inlaid with precious stones	55	25
1694	$18 Gold-painted ju-i sceptre with three abundances (fruit)	1·50	40

454 Chiang Kai-shek and Books

1986. Birth Cent of Chiang Kai-shek. Mult.

1695	$2 Type **454**	45	15
1696	$5 Chiang Kai-shek, flag, map and crowd	75	20
1697	$8 Chiang Kai-shek, emblem and youths	90	20
1698	$10 Chiang Kai-shek, flags on globe and clasped hands	1·10	25
MS1699	120×90 mm. Nos. 1695/8	7·75	2·50

455 Erh-sha-wan Gun Emplacement, Keelung

1986. Historic Buildings (2nd series). Mult.

1700	$2 Chin-kuang-fu House, Pei-pu	35	15
1701	$5 Type **455**	70	20
1702	$8 Hsi T'ai fort	95	25
1703	$10 Matsu Temple, Peng-hu	1·40	30

456 Hare

1986. New Year Greetings. "Year of the Hare".

1704	$1 multicoloured	1·00	15
1705	$10 multicoloured	3·25	30
MS1706	78×102 mm. Nos. 1704/5, each ×2	15·00	2·50

457 Shrubs on Rock Formation

1987. Kenting National Park. Multicoloured.

1707	$2 Type **457**	40	15
1708	$5 Rocky outcrop	80	20
1709	$8 Sandy bay	1·20	20
1710	$10 Rocky bays	1·80	25

458 Glove Puppet

1987. Puppets. Multicoloured.

1721	$2 Type **458**	45	15
1722	$5 String puppet	90	25
1723	$18 Shadow show puppet	1·50	40

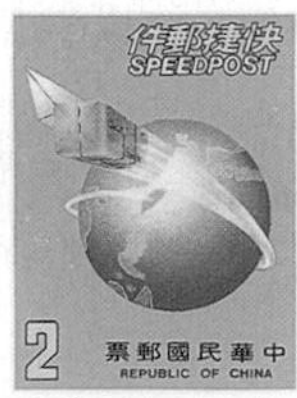

459 Envelope, Parcel and Globe

1987. Speedpost Service.

1724	$2 multicoloured	30	15
1725	$18 multicoloured	1·10	45

460 Wu Yueh (revolutionary)

1987. Famous Chinese.

1726	$2 red	85	15

461 "Singing Creek with Bamboo Orchestra"

1987. Madame Chiang Kai-shek's Landscape Paintings (3rd series). Each black, stone and red.

1727	$2 Type **461**	1·25	15
1728	$5 "Mountains draped in Clouds"	2·00	20
1729	$5 "Vista of Tranquility"	2·75	25
1730	$10 "Mountains after a Snowfall"	3·25	40

462 Bodhisattva Head, Northern Wei Dynasty

1987. Ancient Chinese Stone Carvings. Mult.

1731	$5 Type **462**	65	30
1732	$5 Standing Buddha, Northern Ch'i dynasty	65	30
1733	$5 Bodhisattva head, T'ang dynasty	65	30
1734	$5 Seated Buddha, T'ang dynasty	65	30

1987. Ch'ing Dynasty Ju-i (2nd series). As T 453. Multicoloured.

1735	$2 Silver ju-i sceptre with fungus decoration of pearls and precious stones	50	15
1736	$3 Gold ju-i sceptre with Eight Treasures decoration of pearls and precious stones	90	20
1737	$4 Gilt ju-i sceptre inlaid with precious stones and kingfisher feather	1·40	25
1738	$18 Gilt ju-i sceptre with wirework and inlaid with malachite	3·50	40

463 View of Dam

1987. Feitsui Reservoir Inauguration. Multicoloured.

1739	$2 Type **463**	40	15
1740	$18 View of reservoir	1·60	50

1987. Flower Arrangements (2nd series). As T 439. Multicoloured.

1741	$2 Roses and pine twig in holder	30	15
1742	$5 Flowers in pot	60	20
1743	$8 Tasselled pendant hanging from bamboo in vase	80	20
1744	$10 Pine in flask	95	25

464 Emblem

1987. 70th Lions Clubs International Convention, Taipeh.

1745	$2 multicoloured	35	15
1746	$18 multicoloured	1·30	55

465 Soldiers firing from behind Barricades

1987. 50th Anniv of Start of Sino-Japanese War. Multicoloured.

1747	$1 Type **465**	25	15
1748	$2 Chiang Kai-shek making speech from balcony	35	15
1749	$5 Crowd throwing money onto flag	40	20
1750	$6 Columns of soldiers and tanks on mountain road	50	20
1751	$8 General giving written message to Chiang Kai-shek	75	25
1752	$18 Pres. and Madame Chiang Kai-shek at front of crowd	1·00	40

466 Airplane flying to Left

1987. Air. Multicoloured.

1753	$9 Type **466**	60	30
1754	$14 Airplane	90	45
1755	$18 Airplane flying to right	1·20	55

467 Wang Yun-wu

1987. Birth Centenary (1988) of Wang Yun-wu (lexicographer).

1756	$2 black	30	15

468 Trees on Islands and Fisherman

1987. Painting "After Chao Po-su's 'Red Cliff'" by Wen Cheng-ming. Designs showing details of the scroll. Multicoloured.

1757	$3 (1) Type **468**	80	20
1758	$3 (2) Tree and three figures on island	80	20
1759	$3 (3) House in walled enclosure on island	80	20
1760	$3 (4) Figures in doorway of building and horse in stable	80	20
1761	$3 (5) Cliffs and sea	80	20
1762	$3 (6) Islets, trees and figures on shore	80	20
1763	$3 (7) Trees among cliffs	80	20
1764	$3 (8) People in sampan	80	20
1765	$3 (9) Building surrounded by trees and cliffs	80	20
1766	$3 (10) Cliffs, trees and waterfall	80	20

469 Han Lady of Rank, Early Ch'ing Dynasty

1987. Chinese Costumes (3rd series). Mult.

1767	$1.50 Type **469**	1·25	15
1768	$3 Manchu bannerman's wife, Ch'ing dynasty	1·50	20

1769	$7.50 Woman's Manchu-style Ch'i-p'ao, early Republic period	2·50	25
1770	$18 Jacket and skirt, early Republic period	4·25	40

470 Ta Chen Tian, Confucius Temple, Taichung

1987. International Confucianism and the Modern World Symposium, Taipeh. Multicoloured.

1771	$3 Type **470**	40	20
1772	$18 Confucius and fresco	1·50	70

471 Dragon

1987. New Year Greetings. "Year of the Dragon".

1773	$1.50 multicoloured	1·25	15
1774	$12 multicoloured	3·25	30
MS1775	77×101 mm. Nos. 1773/4, each ×2	13·00	3·25

472 Flag and Emblem as "40"

1987. 40th Anniv of Constitution. Mult.

1776	$3 Type **472**	25	15
1777	$16 "40" in national colours and emblem	1·00	60

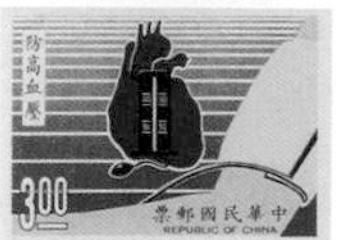

473 Sphygmomanometer

1988. Nat Health. Prevent Hypertension Campaign.

1778	$3 multicoloured	35	15

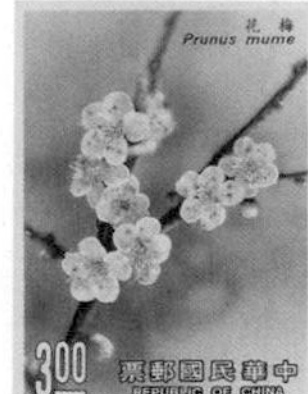

474 Plum

1988. Flowers (1st series). Multicoloured.

1779	$3 Type **474**	1·25	15
1780	$7.50 Apricot	1·75	30
1781	$12 Peach	3·25	45
MS1782	119×80 mm. Nos. 1779/81	24·00	18·00

475 Pine Tree

1988. Pine, Bamboo and Plum (3rd series). Multicoloured.

1783	$1.50 Type **475**	40	15
1784	$7.50 Bamboo	75	20
1785	$16 Plum blossom	1·50	30

476 Modelled Dough Figurines

1988. Traditional Handicrafts. Multicoloured.

1786	$3 Type **476**	65	15
1787	$7.50 Blown sugar fish	1·50	35
1788	$16 Sugar painting	2·30	75

477 Hsu Hsi-lin (revolutionary)

1988. Famous Chinese.

1789	$3 brown	50	20

478 Bio-technology

1988. Science and Technology. Multicoloured.

1790	$1.50 Type **478**	25	15
1791	$3 Surveyors at oil field (energy)	30	15
1792	$7 Syringe piercing letter "B" (hepatitis control)	40	15
1793	$7.50 Mechanised production line (automation)	45	25
1794	$10 Satellite and computer terminal (information)	55	35
1795	$12 Laser (electro-optics)	65	40
1796	$16 Laboratory worker (materials)	85	55
1797	$16.50 Tin of fruit and technician (food technology)	1·10	65

1988. Flowers (2nd series). As T 474. Mult.

1798	$3 Tree peony	1·25	15
1799	$7.50 Pomegranate	1·75	30
1800	$12 East Indian lotus	3·25	45
MS1801	120×80 mm. Nos. 1798/1800	18·00	10·00

479 Policemen on Point Duty and Motor Cycle

1988. Police Day. Multicoloured.

1802	$3 Type **479**	25	15
1803	$12 Communications operator and fire-fighters	70	45

480 Butler's Pigmy Frog

1988. Amphibians. Multicoloured.

1804	$1.50 Type **480**	1·50	15
1805	$3 Taipeh striped slender frog	2·25	25
1806	$7.50 "Microhyla inornata"	3·25	35
1807	$16 Tree frog	4·50	60

481 "60" on Map

1988. 60th Anniv of Broadcasting Corporation of China.

1808	$3 multicoloured	35	15

1988. Flowers (3rd series). As T 474. Mult.

1809	$3 Garden balsam	1·00	15
1810	$7.50 Sweet osmanthus	2·00	30
1811	$12 Chrysanthemum	2·75	45
MS1812	119×80 mm. Nos. 1809/11	16·00	7·00

482 Chiang Kai-shek and Soldiers

1988. 30th Anniv of Kinmen Bombardment. Multicoloured.

1813	$1.50 Type **482**	25	15
1814	$3 Chiang Kai-shek and soldier reporters	35	20
1815	$7.50 Soldiers firing howitzer	55	30
1816	$12 Tank battle	75	45

483 Basketball Player

1988. Sports Day. Multicoloured.

1817	$5 Type **483**	80	20
1818	$5 Two basketball players	80	20
1819	$5 Baseball hitter	80	20
1820	$5 Baseball catcher	80	20

484 Crater

1988. Yangmingshan National Park. Mult.

1821	$1.50 Type **484**	25	15
1822	$3 Lake	40	25
1823	$7.50 Mountains	90	35
1824	$16 Lake and mountains	1·30	50

485-88 "Lofty Mount Lu"

1988. Painting by Shen Chou.

1825	$5 multicoloured	1·40	20
1826	$5 multicoloured	1·40	20
1827	$5 multicoloured	1·40	20
1828	$5 multicoloured	1·40	20

1988. Flowers (4th series). As T 474. Mult.

1829	$3 Cotton rose hibiscus	1·00	15
1830	$7.50 Camellia	2·25	30
1831	$12 Narcissus	3·25	45
MS1832	120×80 mm. Nos. 1829/31	16·00	9·00

1988. Chinese Costumes (4th series). As T 469. Multicoloured.

1833	$2 Nobleman with tall hat, Shang dynasty	1·25	15
1834	$3 Ruler with topknot, Warring States period	2·00	20
1835	$7.50 Male official with writing brush in hair, Wei-chin dynasty	2·25	35
1836	$12 Male court official with hanging brush on hat, late Northern dynasties	3·25	60

489 Snake

1988. New Year Greetings. "Year of the Snake".

1837	$2 multicoloured	2·25	25
1838	$13 multicoloured	5·50	55
MS1839	77×101 mm. Nos. 1837/8, each ×2	16·00	10·50

490 Tai Ch'uan-hsien

1989. Birth Centenary (1990) of Tai Ch'uan-hsien (Civil Service reformer).

1840	$3 black	50	20

491 Pres. Chiang Ching-kuo

1989. 1st Death Anniv of President Chiang Ching-Kuo. Multicoloured.

1841	$3 Type **491**	25	15
1842	$6 Chiang Ching-kuo, political rally and voters	40	25
1843	$7.50 Chiang Ching-kuo at docks	55	35
1844	$16 Chiang Ching-kuo with children	80	55

492 Pine Tree

1989. Pine, Bamboo and Plum (4th series). Multicoloured.

1845	$3 Type **492**	25	15
1846	$16.50 Bamboo	1·20	25
1847	$21 Plum blossom	1·40	35

493 Ni Ying-tien

1989. 79th Death Anniv of Ni Ying-tien (revolutionary).

1848	$3 black	30	15

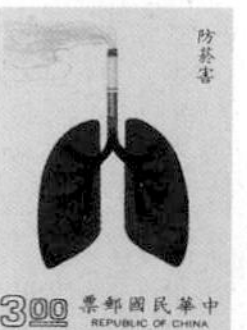

494 Lungs smoking

1989. Anti-smoking Campaign.

1849	$3 multicoloured	30	15

495 Mu Tou Yu Lighthouse

1989. Lighthouses. White panel at foot. Mult.

1850	75c. Type **495**	25	15
1851	$2 Lu Tao lighthouse	25	15
1852	$2.25 Pen Chia Yu lighthouse	25	15
1853	$3 Pitou Chiao lighthouse	35	20
1854	$4.50 Tungyin Tao lighthouse	40	15
1855	$6 Chilai Pi lighthouse	60	25
1856	$7 Fukwei Chiao lighthouse	70	35
1857	$7.50 Hua Yu lighthouse	80	35
1858	$9 Oluan Pi lighthouse	80	25
1859	$10 Kaohsiung lighthouse	95	50
1860	$10.50 Yuweng Tao lighthouse	1·00	35
1861	$12 Tungchu Tao lighthouse	1·20	50
1862	$13 Yeh Liu lighthouse	1·40	50
1863	$15 Tungchi Yu lighthouse	1·70	90
1864	$16.50 Chimei Yu lighthouse	1·60	75

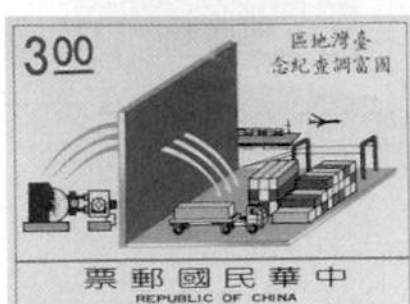

496 Distribution of Industrial Goods

1989. National Wealth Survey.

1865	$3 multicoloured	40	15

497 "I once tended nine Fields of Orchids"

1989. Chinese Classical Poetry (5th series). Poems from "Ch'u Ts'u". Multicoloured.

1866	$3 Type **497**	75	15
1867	$7.50 "No grief is greater than parting"	1·25	40
1868	$12 "...living remote and neglected"	2·50	75
1869	$16 "The horse will not gallop into servitude"	3·00	95

498 Underground Train

1989. Completion of Taipeh Underground Section of Western Railway Line. Multicoloured.

1870	$3 Type **498**	45	15
1871	$16 Train in cutting	1·50	85

499 Blue Triangle

1989. Butterflies (1st series). Multicoloured.

1872	$2 Type **499**	75	15
1873	$3 Great mormon	1·25	20
1874	$7.50 Chequered swallowtail	2·50	25
1875	$9 Common rose	3·00	35

500 Pumpkin Teapot

1989. Teapots (1st series). Multicoloured.

1876	$2 Type **500**	75	15
1877	$3 Clay teapot	1·25	25
1878	$12 "Chopped wood" teapot	2·25	50
1879	$16 Clay pear teapot	2·50	70

501 Fan Chung-yen

1989. Birth Millenary of Fan Chung-yen (civil service reformer).

1880	$12 multicoloured	1·10	55

502 Trees and Right Side of Mountain

1989. Painting "Autumn Colours on the Ch'iao and Hua Mountains" by Ch'iao Mengfu. Designs showing details of the scroll. Multicoloured.

1881	$7.50 (1) Type **502**	1·80	50
1882	$7.50 (2) Left side of mountain and trees	1·80	50
1883	$7.50 (3) Trees and house	1·80	50
1884	$7.50 (4) Mountain, trees and house	1·80	50

503 Insured Groups and Family

1989. Social Welfare.

1885	$3 multicoloured	30	15

504 Liwu River Gorge

1989. Taroko National Park. Multicoloured.

1886	$2 Type **504**	30	15
1887	$3 North Peak of Chilai, Taroko Mountain	35	25
1888	$12 Waterfalls	80	40
1889	$16 Chingshui Cliff	1·00	55

505 Horse

1989. New Year Greetings. "Year of the Horse".

1890	$2 multicoloured	75	20
1891	$13 multicoloured	2·25	60
MS1892	78×102 mm. Nos. 1890/1, each ×2	10·00	2·30

506 Yu Lu

1990. Door Gods. Multicoloured.

1893	$3 Type **506**	1·30	20
1894	$3 Shen Shu	1·30	20
1895	$7.50 Wei-ch'ih Ching-te (facing right)	2·75	45
1896	$7.50 Ch'in Shu-pao (facing left)	2·75	45

507 Lishan

1990. Tourism. Multicoloured.

1897	$2 Type **507**	35	20
1898	$18 Fir tree at Tayuling (vert)	1·70	95

508 Crystal containing Emblem and Industrial Symbols

1990. 40th Anniv of National Insurance.

1899	**508**	$3 multicoloured	45	15

509 Harbour and Tanks

1990. Yung-An Hsiang Liquefied Natural Gas Terminal. Multicoloured.

1900	$3 Type **509**	35	15
1901	$16 Gas tanker and map showing pipeline route (vert)	1·20	60

510 African Monarch

1990. Butterflies (2nd series). Multicoloured.

1902	$2 Orange tiger	75	15
1903	$3 Type **510**	75	25
1904	$7.50 "Pieris canidia"	1·25	35
1905	$9 Peacock	1·50	50

511 Court Official, Northern Wei Period to T'ang Dynasty

1990. Chinese Costumes (5th series). Mult.

1906	$2 Type **511**	50	15
1907	$3 Civil official in winged hat and green robe, Three Kingdoms period to Ming dynasty	75	15
1908	$7.50 Royal guard in bamboo hat, Yuan dynasty	1·75	30
1909	$12 Highest grade civil official in robe decorated with crane bird, Ming dynasty	2·25	60

512 "Spring Song at Midnight"

1990. Chinese Classical Poetry (6th series). Multicoloured.

1910	$3 Type **512**	1·25	25
1911	$7.50 Couple on river bank ("Summer Song at Midnight")	2·00	35
1912	$12 Girl washing clothes in river ("Autumn Song at Midnight")	3·25	50
1913	$16 Snow-bound river scene ("Winter Song at Midnight")	3·50	80

513 Japanese Black Pine

1990. Bonsai. Multicoloured.

1914	$3 Type **513**	35	20
1915	$6.50 "Ehretia microphylla"	55	30
1916	$12 "Buxus harlandii"	85	60
1917	$16 "Celtis sinensis"	1·20	80

514 Bamboo-shaped Glass Snuff Bottle

1990. Snuff Bottles. Multicoloured.

1918	$3 Type **514**	25	15
1919	$6 Glass bottle with peony design	45	30
1920	$9 Melon-shaped amber bottle	70	50
1921	$16 White jade bottle	1·20	90

515 Taiwan Firecrest

1990. Birds. Multicoloured.

1922	$2 Type **515**	50	15
1923	$3 Formosan barwing	60	15
1924	$7.50 White-eared sibia	85	20
1925	$16 Formosan yellow tit	2·00	55

516 Running

1990. Sports. Multicoloured.

1926	$2 Type **516**	25	15
1927	$3 Long jumping	30	20
1928	$7 Pole vaulting	55	30
1929	$16 Hurdling	1·20	60

517 Curtiss Tomahawk II Fighters and Air Crews

1990. 50th Anniv of Arrival of "Flying Tigers" American Volunteer Group.

1930	**517**	$3 multicoloured	80	20

518 Cats

1990. Children's Drawings. Multicoloured.

1931	$2 Type **518**	25	15
1932	$3 Common peafowl	30	20
1933	$7.50 Chickens	60	30
1934	$12 Cattle market	90	50

519 National Theatre

1990. Cultural Buildings in Chiang Kai-shek Memorial Park, Taipeh.

1935	**519**	$3 orange, dp blue & bl	30	15
1936	-	$12 mauve, violet & lilac	1·20	45

DESIGN: $12 National Concert Hall.

520 Cowrie Shells

1990. Ancient Coins. "Shell" Money. Mult.

1937	$2 Type **520**	40	15
1938	$3 Oyster shell	50	20
1939	$6.50 Bone	60	30
1940	$7.50 Bronze	75	35
1941	$9 Jade	1·00	40

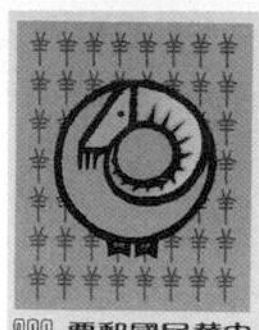
521 Sheep

1990. New Year Greetings. "Year of the Sheep".

1942	**521**	$2 multicoloured	55	15
1943	**521**	$13 multicoloured	2·20	50
MS1944		77×101 mm. Nos. 1942/3, each ×2	10·00	1·80

See also No. 2045.

522 Hu Shih

1990. Birth Centenary of Hu Shih (written Chinese reformer).

1945	**522**	$3 violet	30	15

523 Teapot with Dragon Spout and Handle

1991. Teapots (2nd series). Multicoloured.

1946	$2 Blue and white teapot with phoenix design	30	15
1947	$3 Type **523**	40	25
1948	$9 Teapot with floral design on lid and landscape on body	80	40
1949	$12 Rectangular teapot with passion flower design	1·10	50
1950	$16 Brown rectangular teapot with floral decoration	1·40	80

524 Happiness

1991. Greetings Stamps. Gods of Prosperity. Multicoloured.

1951	$3 Type **524**	50	15
1952	$3 Wealth	50	15
1953	$7.50 Longevity (with white beard)	1·10	35
1954	$7.50 Joy	1·10	35

525 "Petasites formosanus"

1991. Plants (1st series). Multicoloured.

1955	$2 Type **525**	25	15
1956	$3 "Heloniopsis acutifolia"	30	15
1957	$7.50 "Disporum shimadai"	60	30
1958	$9 "Viola nagasawai"	70	35

See also Nos. 1969/72, 1995/8 and 2026/9.

526 Hsiung Cheng-chi (revolutionary)

1991. Famous Chinese.

1959	**526**	$3 blue	25	15

527 Agriculture

1991. 80th Anniv (1992) of Founding of Chinese Republic. Multicoloured.

1960	$3 Type **527**	25	15
1961	$7.50 Industry	50	25
1962	$12 Dancer and leisure equipment	85	45
1963	$16 Transport and communications	1·10	55

528 Bamboo Hobby-horse

1991. Children's Games (1st series). Mult.

1964	$3 Type **528**	30	20
1965	$3 Woven-grass grasshoppers	30	20
1966	$3 Spinning tops	30	20
1967	$3 Windmills	30	20
MS1968	150×100 mm. Nos. 1964/7	5·50	1·70

See also No. 2056/**MS**2060 and 2120/**MS**2124.

1991. Plants (2nd series). As T 525. Mult.

1969	$2 "Gaultheria itoana"	25	15
1970	$3 "Lysionotus montanus"	35	20
1971	$7.50 "Leontopodium microphyllum"	95	25
1972	$9 "Gentiana flavo-maculata"	1·20	35

529 Male Official's Summer Court Dress

1991. Chinese Costumes (6th series). Ch'ing Dynasty. Multicoloured.

1973	$2 Male official's winter court dress with dragon design	40	15
1974	$3 Type **529**	55	20
1975	$7.50 Male official's winter overcoat	1·20	30
1976	$12 Everyday skull-cap, jacket and travelling robe	1·90	45

530 Heart, Pedestrian Crossing and Hand

1991. Road Safety. Multicoloured.

1977	$3 Type **530**	40	15
1978	$7.50 Hand, road and broken bottle ("Don't Drink and Drive")	1·20	35

531 Ch'ing Dynasty Cloisonne Lion

1991. No value expressed. Multicoloured.

1979	(-) Type **531**	60	20
1980	(-) Cloisonne lioness	2·30	70

Nos. 1979/80 were sold at the prevailing rates for domestic ordinary and domestic prompt delivery letters.

532 Strawberries

1991. Fruits. Multicoloured.

1981	$3 Type **532**	30	15
1982	$7.50 Grapes	50	30
1983	$9 Mango	65	35
1984	$16 Sugar apple	1·10	60

533 Formosan Whistling Thrush

1991. River Birds. Multicoloured.

1985	$5 Type **533**	40	20
1986	$5 Brown dipper	40	20
1987	$5 Mandarins	40	20
1988	$5 Black-crowned night herons	40	20
1989	$5 Little egrets	40	20
1990	$5 Plumbeous redstarts	40	20
1991	$5 Little forktail	40	20
1992	$5 Grey wagtail	40	20
1993	$5 River kingfishers	40	20
1994	$5 Pied wagtails	40	20

Nos. 1985/94 were printed together, se-tenant, forming a composite design.

1991. Plants (3rd series). As T 525. Mult.

1995	$3.50 "Rosa transmorrisonensis"	35	15
1996	$5 "Impatiens devolii"	55	20
1997	$9 "Impatiens uniflora"	85	35
1998	$12 "Impatiens taye-monii"	1·10	45

534 Rock Climbing

1991. International Camping and Caravanning Federation Rally, Fulung Beach. Multicoloured.

1999	$2 Type **534**	25	15
2000	$3 Fishing	35	20
2001	$7.50 Bird-watching	65	35
2002	$10 Boys with pail wading in water	95	55

1991. Lighthouses. As Nos. 1851/3 and 1855/64 but with blue panel at foot.

2003	50c. As No. 1863	20	15
2004	$1 As No. 1851	25	20
2005	$3.50 As No. 1855	30	20
2006	$5 As No. 1856	40	25
2007	$7 As No. 1853	45	20
2008	$9 As No. 1858	65	35
2009	$10 As No. 1859	80	45
2010	$12 As No. 1861	85	50
2011	$13 As No. 1852	95	60
2012	$19 As No. 1857	1·40	80
2013	$20 As No. 1862	1·50	80
2014	$26 As No. 1860	1·70	1·00
2015	$28 As No. 1864	2·20	1·20

535 Peacock

1991. "Peacocks" by Giuseppe Castiglione. Designs showing details of painting. Multicoloured.

2020	$5 Type **535**	60	20
2021	$20 Peacock displaying tail	2·40	80
MS2022	138×102 mm. No. 2021	3·50	1·10

536 Monkey

1991. New Year Greetings. "Year of the Monkey".

2023	**536**	$3.50 multicoloured	25	15
2024	**536**	$13 multicoloured	1·20	60
MS2025		78×101 mm. Nos. 2023/4, each ×2	4·75	1·70

See also No. 2046.

1991. Plants (4th series). As T 525. Mult.

2026	$3.50 "Kalanchoe garambiensis"	30	15
2027	$5 "Pieris taiwanensis"	45	20
2028	$9 "Pleione formosana"	70	40
2029	$12 "Elaeagnus oldhamii"	95	45

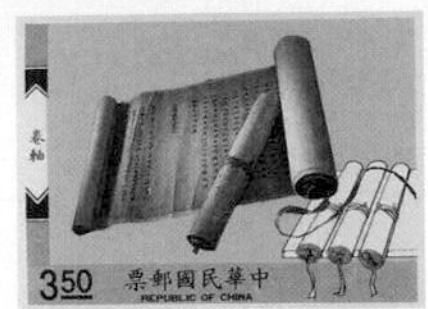

537 Scrolls

1992. International Book Fair, Taipeh. Mult.

2030	$3.50 Type **537**	30	15
2031	$5 Folded-leaves book	45	20
2032	$9 Butterfly-bound books	75	35
2033	$15 Sewn books	1·20	60

538 Peace in the Wake of Firecrackers

1992. Greetings Stamps. Nienhwas (paintings conveying wishes for the coming year). Mult.

2034	$5 Type **538**	35	20
2035	$5 Elephant with riders (Good fortune and satisfaction)	35	20
2036	$12 Children and five "birds" (Five blessings upon the house)	85	55
2037	$12 Children angling for large fish (Abundance for every year)	85	55

1992. Signs of Chinese Zodiac. As previous designs but with additional symbol in top left-hand corner.

2038	**393**	$5 multicoloured	40	15
2039	**414**	$5 multicoloured	40	15
2040	**435**	$5 multicoloured	40	15
2041	**456**	$5 multicoloured	40	15
2042	**471**	$5 multicoloured	40	15
2043	**489**	$5 multicoloured	40	15
2044	**505**	$5 multicoloured	40	15
2045	**521**	$5 multicoloured	40	15
2046	**536**	$5 multicoloured	40	15
2047	**340**	$5 multicoloured	40	15
2048	**361**	$5 multicoloured	40	15
2049	**378**	$5 multicoloured	40	15
MS2050		181×101 mm. Nos. 2038/49	6·50	2·30

Nos. 2038/49 were issued together in se-tenant blocks of 12 stamps within the sheet. The stamps are listed in order from right to left of the block.

539 Taiwan Red Cypress ("Chamaecyparis formosensis")

1992. Forest Resources. Conifers. Mult.

2051	$5 Type **539**	40	10
2052	$5 Taiwan cypress ("Chamaecyparis taiwanensis")	40	10
2053	$5 Taiwan incense cedar ("Calocedrus formosana")	40	10
2054	$5 Ranta fir ("Cunninghamia konishii")	40	10
2055	$5 Taiwania ("Taiwania cryptomerioides")	40	10

Nos. 2051/5 were printed together, se-tenant, forming a composite design.

1992. Children's Games (2nd series). As T 528. Multicoloured.

2056	$5 Walking on tin cans	55	20
2057	$5 Chopstick guns	55	20
2058	$5 Rolling hoops	55	20
2059	$5 Grass fighting	55	20
MS2060	150×101 mm. Nos. 2056/9	4·00	3·25

540 Mother and son (Spring)

1992. Parent–Child Relationships. Mult.

2061	$3.50 Type **540**	35	20
2062	$5 Mother carrying child on back (summer)	55	25
2063	$9 Mother and child pushing toy rabbits (autumn)	75	40
2064	$10 Mother feeding child (winter)	95	45

港 香 一 覽 展 票 郵 華 中

(541) (image scaled to 49% of original size)

1992. Chinese Stamps Exhibition, Hong Kong. Sheet as No. MS2060 but imperf, optd in margin with T 541 in magenta.

MS2065	150×101 mm. Nos. 2056/9	14·00	11·00

542 Vase decorated with Bats and Longevity Characters

1992. Glassware decorated with Enamel. Mult.

2066	$3.50 Type **542**	25	15
2067	$5 Gourd-shaped vase decorated with landscape and children at play	45	20
2068	$7 Vase with peony decoration	65	30
2069	$17 Vase showing mother teaching child to read	1·40	65

543 Lion and Stone Pavilion

1992. Stone Lions from Lugouqiao Bridge.

2070	**543**	$5 blue and brown	50	20
2071	-	$5 green and violet	50	20
2072	-	$12 orange and green	1·10	50
2073	-	$12 violet and black	1·10	50

DESIGNS: No. 2071, Bridge and lioness with cub; 2070, Bridge parapet and lion; 2073, Bridge parapet and lioness with two cubs.

544 "People make Friends and are tied to Each Other as Roots to a Plant"

1992. Chinese Classical Poetry (7th series). Multicoloured.

2074	$3.50 Type **544**	25	15
2075	$5 Couple at window ("Conjugal love will last forever")	55	25
2076	$9 Couple in garden ("Man takes pains to uphold virtue/ Till one's hair turns forever grey")	95	35
2077	$15 "Tartar horses lean toward the north wind"	1·40	55

545 Drummer and Crowd

1992. Temple Fair. Multicoloured.

2078	$5 Type **545**	70	35
2079	$5 Man with basket dancing	70	35
2080	$5 Musicians	70	35
2081	$5 Man pushing cart	70	35
2082	$5 Women and children	70	35

Nos. 2078/82 were printed together, se-tenant, forming a composite design.

546 "Two Birds perched on a Red Camellia Branch"

1992. Ming Dynasty Silk Tapestries. Mult.

2083	$5 Type **546**	50	20
2084	$12 "Two Birds playing on a Peach Branch"	1·50	55
MS2085	111×88 mm. Nos. 2083/4	2·40	75

547 Cart in "The General and the Premier"

1992. Chinese Opera Props. Multicoloured.

2086	$3.50 Type **547**	40	20
2087	$5 Ship in "The Lucky Pearl"	55	25
2088	$9 Horse in "Chao-chun serves as an Envoy"	75	40
2089	$12 Sedan chair in "Escort to the Wedding"	95	50

548 Steam Locomotive and Train

1992. Alishan Mountain Railway. Mult.

2090	$5 Type **548**	45	15
2091	$15 Diesel locomotive and train	1·20	40

549 Chinese River Otter

1992. Mammals. Multicoloured.

2092	$5 Type **549**	55	20
2093	$5 Formosan flying fox	55	20
2094	$5 Formosan clouded leopard	55	20
2095	$5 Formosan black bear	55	20

550 Cock

1992. New Year Greetings. "Year of the Cock". Multicoloured.

2096	$3.50 Type **550**	35	20
2097	$13 Cock (facing left)	1·00	45
MS2098	78×101 mm. Nos. 2096/7, each ×2	3·00	2·40

北臺一覽展票郵賓律菲
PHILIPPINE STAMP EXHIBITION 1992·TAIPEI

(551)

1992. Philippine Stamp Exhibition, Taipeh. No. MS2098 optd in margin with T 551.

MS2099	78×101 mm. Nos. 2096/7, each ×2	3·00	2·40

552 Schall and Astronomical Instruments

1992. 400th Birth Anniv of Johann Adam Schall von Bell (missionary astronomer).

2100	**552**	$5 multicoloured	30	15

553 Satisfaction for Every Year

1993. Greetings Stamps. Nienhwas (paintings conveying wishes for the coming year). Multicoloured.

2101	$5 Type **553**	45	20
2102	$5 Birds and flowers (Joy)	45	20
2103	$12 Butterfly and flowers (Happiness and longevity)	1·10	35
2104	$12 Flowers in vase (Wealth and peace)	1·10	35

554 Applying Enamel and Glass Decoration to Temple Roof

1992. International Traditional Crafts Exhibition, Taipeh. Multicoloured.

2105	$3.50 Type **554**	25	15
2106	$5 Ceremonial lantern	35	20
2107	$9 Pottery jars	65	40
2108	$15 Oil-paper umbrella	95	70

555 Pan Gu creating Universe

1993. The Creation. Multicoloured.

2109	$3.50 Type **555**	30	15
2110	$5 Pan Gu creating animals (horiz)	40	20
2111	$9 Nu Wa creating human beings (horiz)	70	45
2112	$19 Nu Wa mending the sky with smelted stone	1·40	85

556 Mandarins

1993. Lucky Animals (1st series).

2113	556	$3.50 multicoloured	30	15
2114	-	$5 multicoloured	40	25
2115	-	$10 red and black	55	35
2116	-	$15 multicoloured	1·20	80

DESIGNS: $5, Chinese unicorn; $10, Deer; $15, Crane.
See also Nos. 2151/4.

557 Water Lily

1993. Water Plants. Multicoloured.

2117	$5 Type **557**	45	20
2118	$9 Taiwan cow lily	80	40
2119	$12 Water hyacinth	1·00	55

1993. Children's Games (3rd series). As T 528. Multicoloured.

2120	$5 Tossing sandbags	40	20
2121	$5 Bamboo dragonflies	40	20
2122	$5 Skipping	40	20
2123	$5 Duel of strength with rope passed round waists	40	20
MS2124	150×100 mm. Nos. 2120/3	3·00	2·40

北臺——覽展票郵亞利大澳

AUSTRALIAN STAMP EXHIBITION 1993 – TAIPEI
(558) (image scaled to 65% of original size)

1993. Australian Stamp Exhibition, Taipeh. No. MS2124 optd in margin with T 558 in green and black.

MS2125	150×100 mm. Nos. 2120/3	3·25	2·50

國泰——覽展票郵華中
(559)

1993. Chinese Stamp Exhibition, Bangkok, Thailand. No. MS2124 optd with T 559.

MS2126	150×100 mm. Nos. 2120/3	3·25	2·50

560 Ching-Kang-Chang Plateau (source)

1993. Yangtze River. Multicoloured.

2127	$3.50 Type **560**	30	15
2128	$3.50 Turn in river (Chinsha River)	30	15
2129	$5 Roaring Tiger Gorge (white water in narrow ravine)	40	20
2130	$5 Chutang Gorge (calm water in wide gorge)	40	20
2131	$9 Dragon Gate, Pawu and Titsui Gorges	80	45

561 Noise Pollution and Music

1993. Environmental Protection. Children's Drawings. Multicoloured.

2132	$5 Type **561**	40	20
2133	$17 Family looking out over green fields (vert)	1·20	80

562 Cup with Tou-Ts'ai Figures

1993. Ch'eng-hua Porcelain Cups of Ming Dynasty. Multicoloured.

2134	$3.50 Type **562**	30	15
2135	$5 Chicken decoration	40	20
2136	$7 Flowers and fruits of four seasons decoration	60	35
2137	$9 Dragon decoration	75	50

563 Graphic Design

1993. 32nd International Vocational Training Competition, Taipeh. Multicoloured.

2138	$3.50 Type **563**	25	15
2139	$5 Computer technology	30	20
2140	$9 Carpentry	65	40
2141	$12 Welding	80	60

564 Child on Father's Shoulders

1993. Parent–Child Relationships. Mult.

2142	$3.50 Type **564**	30	15
2143	$5 Father playing flute to child	40	20
2144	$9 Child reading to father	75	45
2145	$10 Father pointing at bird	80	50

565 Man carrying Scroll

1993. "Taipeh '93" Asian Stamp Exhibition. Sheet 139×97 mm containing T 565 and similar vert designs showing details of "Enjoying Antiquities" by Tu Chin. Multicoloured.

MS2146	$5 Type **565**; $5 Man examining antiquities; $5 Man sitting by table; $5 Woman tying bundle	2·75	1·30

566 Persimmons

1993. Fruits. Multicoloured.

2147	$5 Type **566**	35	20
2148	$5 Peaches	35	20
2149	$12 Loquats	95	60
2150	$12 Papayas	95	60

1993. Lucky Animals (2nd series). As T 556. Mult.

2151	$1 Blue dragon (representing Spring, wood and the East)	25	15
2152	$2.50 White tiger (Autumn, metal and the West)	35	15
2153	$9 Linnet (Summer, fire and the South)	70	35
2154	$19 Black tortoise (Winter, water and the North)	1·40	80

567 Gymnastics

1993. Taiwan Area Games, Taoyuan. Mult.

2155	$5 Type **567**	35	20
2156	$5 Taekwondo	35	20

568 Stone Lion, New Park, Taipeh

1993. Stone Lions. Multicoloured.

2157	$3.50 Type **568**	25	15
2158	$5 Hsinchu City Council building	40	20
2159	$9 Temple, Hsinchu City	65	35
2160	$12 Fort Providentia, Tainan	95	50

569 Chick

1993. Mikado Pheasant. Multicoloured.

2161	$5 Type **569**	40	25
2162	$5 Mother and chicks	40	25
2163	$5 Immature male and female	40	25
2164	$5 Adults	40	25

Nos. 2161/4 were issued together, se-tenant, forming a composite design.

570 Dog

1993. New Year Greetings. "Year of the Dog". Multicoloured.

2165	$3.50 Type **570**	25	15
2166	$13 Dog (facing left)	1·20	50
MS2167	78×102 mm. Nos. 2165/6, each ×2	2·00	1·10

571 Scientist and Vegetables

1993. 20th Anniv of Asian Vegetable Research and Development Centre. Multicoloured.

2168	$5 Type **571**	35	20
2169	$13 Scientists and fields of crops	1·10	60

念紀展郵光國年二十八
日七十二至日一十二月二十
(572)

1993. "Kuo-kuang" Stamp Exhibition, Kaohsiung. No. MS2167 optd in margin with T 572 in red.

MS2170	78×102 mm. Nos. 2165/6, each ×2	2·30	1·30

573 Courtroom

1994. Inauguration of Taiwan Constitutional Court.

2171	**573**	$5 multicoloured	40	20

574 Cutting Bamboo

1994. Traditional Paper Making. Multicoloured.

2172	$3.50 Type **574**	25	15
2173	$3.50 Cooking bamboo	25	15
2174	$5 Moulding bamboo pulp in wooden panels	45	25
2175	$5 Stacking wet paper for pressing	45	25
2176	$12 Drying paper	95	50

575 "Clivia miniata"

1994. Flowers. Multicoloured.

2177	$5 Type **575**	35	20
2178	$12 "Cymbidium sinense"	95	50
2179	$19 "Primula malacoides"	1·50	90

576 Wind Lion Lord

1994. Kinmen Wind Lion Lords.

2180	**576**	$5 multicoloured	40	20
2181	-	$9 multicoloured	70	35
2182	-	$12 multicoloured	95	45
2183	-	$17 multicoloured	1·20	65

DESIGNS: $9 to $17 Different Lion Lord statues.

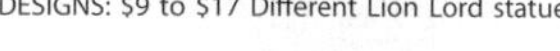

577 Sailing Paper Boats

1994. Children's Games (4th series). Mult.

2184	$5 Type **577**	40	20
2185	$5 Fighting with water-guns	40	20
2186	$5 Throwing paper plane	40	20
2187	$5 Human train	40	20
MS2188	125×80 mm. Nos. 2184/7	1·90	95

578 Playing Chess

1994. Rural Pastimes. Multicoloured.

2189	$5 Type **578**	30	20
2190	$10 Playing the flute	80	35
2191	$12 Telling stories	95	50
2192	$19 Drinking tea	1·50	80

579 Malaysian Night Heron and Chicks

1994. Parent–Child Relationships. Birds with their Young. Multicoloured.

2193	$5 Type **579**	30	20
2194	$7 Little tern (horiz)	55	25
2195	$10 Common noddy (horiz)	85	40
2196	$12 Muller's barbet	1·00	45

580 Book with Hand on Cover

1994. Protection of Intellectual Property Rights. Multicoloured.

2197	$5 Type **580**	40	20
2198	$15 Head with locked computer disk as brain	1·20	60

581 Caring for the Young

1994. International Rotary Clubs Convention, Taipeh. "Towards an Harmonious Society". Multicoloured.

2199	$5 Type **581**	40	20
2200	$17 Caring for the aged	1·40	75

582 Anniversary Emblem and Olympic Rings

1994. Centenary of International Olympic Committee. Multicoloured.

2201	$5 Type **582**	40	20
2202	$15 Running, high jumping and weight-lifting	1·20	60

583 Summit of Dah-pa Mountain

1994. Shei-pa National Park. Multicoloured.

2203	$5 Type **583**	40	20
2204	$7 Shei-san Valley	60	25
2205	$10 Holy Ridge	90	40
2206	$17 Shiah-tsuei Pool	1·30	75

584 Chien Mu

1994. Birth Centenary of Chien Mu (academic).

2207	**584**	$5 multicoloured	40	20

585 Window

1994. International Year of the Family. Mult.

2208	$5 Type **585**	40	20
2209	$15 Globe and house	1·20	60

586 Sueirenjy making Flame

1994. Invention Myths. Multicoloured.

2210	$5 Type **586**	40	20
2211	$10 Fushijy drawing Pa-kua characters	80	35
2212	$12 Shennungjy making pitchfork	95	50
2213	$15 Tsangjier inventing pictorial characters	1·40	75

587 Lin Yutang

1994. Birth Centenary of Dr. Lin Yutang (essayist and lexicographer).

2214	**587**	$5 multicoloured	40	20

588 Cheng Ho's Junk

1994. World Trade Week. Multicoloured.

2215	$5 Type **588**	40	20
2216	$17 Cheng Ho and route map around South Asia	1·20	60

589 Dr. Sun Yat-sen (founder)

1994. Centenary of Kuomintang Party. Mult.

2217	$5 Type **589**	40	20
2218	$19 Modern developments and voter placing slip in ballot box	1·40	70

590 Pig

1994. New Year Greetings. "Year of the Pig". Multicoloured.

2219	$3.50 Type **590**	30	20
2220	$13 Pig (facing left)	1·10	60
MS2221	78×101 mm. Nos. 2219/20, each ×2	2·75	1·60

591 Yen Chia-kan

1994. 1st Death Anniv of Yen Chia-kan (President, 1974–78). Multicoloured.

2222	$5 Type **591**	40	20
2223	$15 Visiting farmers	1·20	60

592 Horse's Back

1995. Traditional Architecture. Roof Styles. Mult.

2224	$5 Type **592**	40	20
2225	$5 Swallow's tail	40	20
2226	$12 Talisman (stove and bowl)	95	50
2227	$19 Cylinder-shaped brick	1·50	90

593 Begonia

1995. Chinese Engravings. Flowers. Mult.

2228	$3.50 Type **593**	25	15
2229	$5 Rose	45	20
2230	$19 Flower	1·50	80
2231	$26 Climbing rose	2·20	1·20

For these designs, but with the characters for the country name in a different order, see Nos. 2480/3.

594 Rotating Wheel of Pipes

1995. Irrigation Techniques from "Tian Gong Kai Wu" (encyclopaedia) by Sung Yin-shing. Multicoloured.

2232	$3.50 Type **594**	25	15
2233	$3.50 Donkey turning wheel to raise water	25	15
2234	$5 Pedal-driven device to raise water	45	25
2235	$12 Man turning wheel to raise water	95	50
2236	$13 Well	1·10	60

595 Courtiers

1995. "Beauties on an Outing" by Lee Gong-lin. Details of the painting. Multicoloured.

2237	$9 Type **595**	75	35
2238	$9 Courtier and beauty with child	75	35
2239	$9 Courtier with two beauties	75	35
2240	$9 Courtier	75	35
MS2241	110×80 mm. Nos. 2238/9	1·80	80

Nos. 2237/40 were issued together, se-tenant, forming a composite design.

596 Emblem and Landscape

1995. Inaug of National Health Insurance Plan.

2242	**596**	$12 multicoloured	95	50

597 Chinese Showy Lily

1995. Bulbous Flowers. Multicoloured.

2243	$5 Type **597**	35	20
2244	$12 Blood lily	80	50
2245	$19 Hyacinth	1·50	90

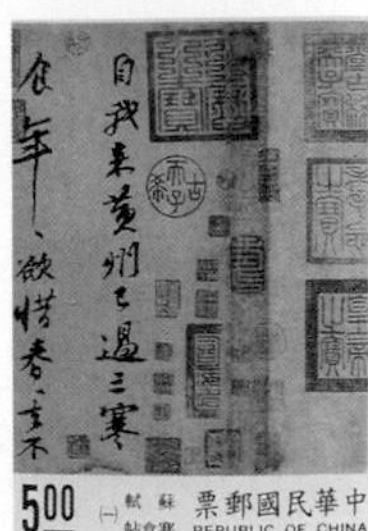
598 Opening Lines

1995. Chinese Calligraphy. "Cold Food Observance" (poem) by Su Shih.

2246	**598**	$5 (1) multicoloured	55	25
2247	-	$5 (2) multicoloured	55	25
2248	-	$5 (3) multicoloured	55	25
2249	-	$5 (4) multicoloured	55	25

Nos. 2246/9 were issued together, se-tenant, forming a composite design; the stamps are numbered in Chinese numerals to the right of the face value, from right to left.

599 Red Peony

1995. Peonies. Paintings by Tsou I-kuei. Self-adhesive. Imperf.

2250	$5 Type **599**	50	20
2251	$5 Pink peony	50	20

600 Hand, Birds and Cracked Symbol

1995. Anti-drugs Campaign. Multicoloured.

2252	$5 Type **600**	40	20
2253	$15 Arm and syringe forming cross	1·10	60

601 Old Hospital Building

1995. Centenary of National Taiwan University Hospital, Taipeh. Multicoloured.

2254	$5 Type **601**	50	20
2255	$19 New building	1·50	80

602 Chichi Bay

1995. Tourism. East Coast National Scenic Area. Multicoloured.

2256	$5 Type **602**	40	20
2257	$5 Shihyuesan (rocky promontory)	40	20
2258	$12 Hsiaoyehlieu (eroded rocks)	1·10	50
2259	$15 Changhong Bridge	1·40	70

603 Mating

1995. The Cherry Salmon. Multicoloured.

2260	$5 Type **603**	40	20
2261	$7 Female digging redd	60	25
2262	$10 Fry hatching	80	45
2263	$17 Fry swimming	1·50	70

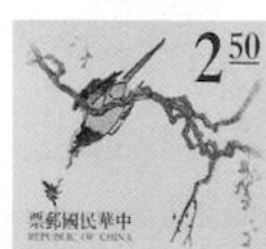

604 Bird feeding on Branch

1995. Chinese Engravings. Birds. Mult.

2264	$2.50 Type **604**	30	20
2265	$7 Bird on branch of peach tree	60	30
2266	$13 Bird preening	1·10	50
2267	$28 Yellow bird	2·50	1·10

For these designs with different face values and the order of the characters in the country name changed, see Nos. 2532/7.

605 "Tubastraea aurea"

1995. Marine Life. Multicoloured.

2268	$3.50 Type **605**	30	20
2269	$3.50 "Chromodoris elizabethina"	30	20
2270	$5 "Spirobranchus giganteus corniculatus"	50	25
2271	$17 "Himerometra magnipinna"	1·40	65

606 Pasteur

1995. Death Cent of Louis Pasteur (chemist).

2272	**606** $17 multicoloured	1·60	65

607 Porcelain Vase

1995. 70th Anniv of National Palace Museum. Multicoloured.

2273	$3.50 "Strange Peaks and Myriad Trees" (painting) (horiz)	25	15
2274	$3.50 Type **607**	25	15
2275	$5 X Fu-K'uei Ting bronze three-fronted vessel	40	20
2276	$26 "The Fragrance of Flowers" (quatrain) (horiz)	2·00	95

608 Soldiers

1995. 50th Anniv of End of Sino-Japanese War. Multicoloured.

2277	$5 Type **608**	45	20
2278	$19 Taiwan flag, map and city	1·50	60
MS2279	78×102 mm. Nos. 2277/8	2·20	95

609 Common Green Turtle ("Chelonia mydas")

1995. Year of the Sea Turtle. Multicoloured.

2280	$5 Type **609**	45	20
2281	$5 Loggerhead turtle ("Caretta caretta")	45	20
2282	$5 Olive ridley turtle ("Lepidochelys olivacea")	45	20
2283	$5 Hawksbill turtle ("Eretmochelys imbricata")	45	20

610 Scientists in Crop Field

1995. Centenary of Taiwan Agricultural Research Institute. Multicoloured.

2284	$5 Type **610**	55	20
2285	$28 Scientists in greenhouse growing anthuriums	2·10	80

611 Rat

1995. New Year Greetings. "Year of the Rat". Multicoloured.

2286	$3.50 Type **611**	25	15
2287	$13 Rat (different)	1·20	45
MS2288	77×101 mm. Nos. 2286/7, each ×2	2·75	1·20

612 Escorting Bride to Ceremony

1996. Traditional Wedding Ceremonies. Mult.

2289	$5 Type **612**	35	15
2290	$12 Honouring Heaven, Earth and ancestors	1·00	40
2291	$19 Nuptial chamber	1·80	75

613 Sharon Fruit

1996. Chinese Engravings of Fruit by Hu Chen-yan.

2292	**613** $9 multicoloured	70	25
2293	- $12 multicoloured	1·10	40
2294	- $15 multicoloured	1·30	50
2295	- $17 multicoloured	1·50	55

DESIGNS: $12 to $17, Different fruits.

For other values with the order of the characters in the country name reversed see Nos. 2580/2.

614-17 "Scenic Dwelling at Chu-Ch'u"

1996. Painting by Wang Meng.

2296	**614** $5 multicoloured	45	20
2297	**615** $5 multicoloured	45	20
2298	**616** $5 multicoloured	45	20
2299	**617** $5 multicoloured	45	20

Nos. 2296/9 were issued together, se-tenant, forming the composite design illustrated.

618 "Bougainvillea spectabilis"

1996. Flowering Vines. Multicoloured.

2300	$5 Type **618**	45	20
2301	$12 Wisteria	1·00	40
2302	$19 Wood rose	1·50	65

619 Postboxes

1996. Centenary of Chinese State Postal Service. Multicoloured.

2303	$5 Type **619**	35	15
2304	$9 Weighing equipment	70	30
2305	$12 Postal transport	90	40
2306	$13 Modern technology	1·00	45
MS2307	78×101 mm. Nos. 2303/6	3·00	1·30

620 Lecture and University

1996. Centenary of National Chiao Tung University.

2308	**620** $19 multicoloured	1·50	60

621 Chimei Giant Lion

1996. Tourism. Penghu National Scenic Area. Multicoloured.

2309	$5 Type **621**	35	15
2310	$5 Chipei beach (sand-spit)	35	15
2311	$12 Tungpan Yu	90	40
2312	$17 Tingkou Yu	1·30	65

622 Hand holding Family (charity)

1996. 30th Anniv of Tzu-Chi Foundation (Buddhist relief organization). Multicoloured.

2313	$5 Type **622**	40	20
2314	$19 Hospital patient in tulip petal (medicine)	1·70	65

623 With National Flag

1996. Inauguration of First Directly-elected President. Designs showing President Lee Teng-Hui and Vice-President Lien Chan. Multicoloured.

2315	$3.50 Type **623**	25	15
2316	$5 Outside Presidential Office building	40	15
2317	$13 Asia-Pacific Operations Hub Project	1·10	45
2318	$15 Meeting public at celebrations	1·20	50
MS2319	124×80 mm. Nos. 2315/18	3·00	1·40

624 Monument

1996. South China Sea Archipelago. Pratas and Itu Aba Islands. Multicoloured.

2320	$5 Type **624**	45	15
2321	$12 Monument (different)	1·40	55
MS2322	78×101 mm. Nos. 2320/1	1·90	70

625 Modern Gymnast and Cyclist

1996. Centenary of Modern Olympic Games. Multicoloured.

2323	$5 Type **625**	45	15
2324	$15 Ancient Greek athletes	1·30	50

626 Feeding Silkworms

1996. Silk Production Techniques from "Tian Gong Kai Wu" (encyclopaedia) by Sung Yin-shing. Multicoloured.

2325	$5 Type **626**	40	15
2326	$5 Picking out cocoons	40	15
2327	$7 Degumming raw silk	50	20
2328	$10 Reeling raw silk	80	40
2329	$13 Weaving silk	1·10	45

627 Bamboo

1996. Chinese Engravings. Plants. Mult.

2330	$1 Type **627**	35	15
2331	$10 Orchid	80	40
2332	$20 Plum tree	1·70	70

628 Tou-kung Bracket

1996. Traditional Architecture. Roof Supports. Multicoloured.

2333	$5 Type **628**	50	20
2334	$5 Chiue-ti bracket	50	20
2335	$10 Bu-tong beam	85	35
2336	$19 Dye-tou structure	1·50	60

629 "Princess Iron Fan" (1941)

1996. Chinese Film Production. Mult.

2337	$3.50 Type **629**	25	15
2338	$3.50 "Chin Shan Bi Xie" (1957)	25	15
2339	$5 "Oyster Girl" (1964)	50	25
2340	$19 "City of Sadness" (1989)	1·50	65

630 Children dancing

1996. Winning Entries in Children's Stamp Design Competition. Multicoloured.

2341	$5 Type **630**	50	20

2342	$5 Children playing in park	50	20
2343	$5 Black and white spotted cat	50	20
2344	$5 Container ship	50	20
2345	$5 Children showering	50	20
2346	$5 Chinese gods and crowd	50	20
2347	$5 Pair of peacocks	50	20
2348	$5 Flying horse and rainbow	50	20
2349	$5 Elephant	50	20
2350	$5 Man and striped animals	50	20
2351	$5 Painting paper lampshades	50	20
2352	$5 Flock of geese	50	20
2353	$5 Children joining hands in garden	50	20
2354	$5 Archer	50	20
2355	$5 Children on ostrich's back	50	20
2356	$5 New Year celebrations	50	20
2357	$5 Butterflies on bamboo plant	50	20
2358	$5 Goatherd	50	20
2359	$5 Water-lilies on pond	50	20
2360	$5 Cats eating fish	50	20

631 "Autumn Scene with Wild Geese"

1996. 10th Asian International Stamp Exhibition, Taipeh. Ancient Paintings from National Palace Museum. Multicoloured.

2361	$5 Type **631**	45	15
2362	$7 "Reeds and Wild Geese"	65	25
2363	$13 "Wild Geese gathering on Shore of Reeds"	1·10	40
2364	$15 "Wild Geese on Bank in Autumn"	1·30	50
MS2365	125×80 mm. Nos. 2361/4	3·50	1·40

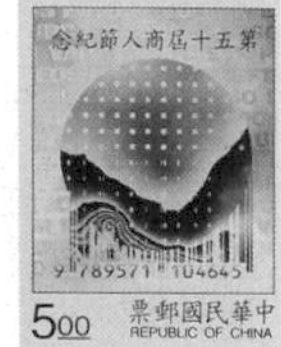

632 Bar Code and Graph

1996. 50th Anniv of Merchants' Day. Mult.

2366	$5 Type **632**	50	20
2367	$26 Line graph and globe	2·30	95

633 Disabled Worker and Open Hands

1996. Caring for the Handicapped. Mult.

2368	$5 Type **633**	55	20
2369	$19 Disabled boy painting, emblems within honeycomb and hands forming heart (employment)	1·50	65

634 Ox

1996. New Year Greetings. "Year of the Ox". Multicoloured.

2370	$3.50 Type **634**	35	20
2371	$13 Ox (different)	1·30	50
MS2372	78×101 mm. Nos. 2370/1, each ×2	3·50	1·40

郵政百週年高雄國際郵展紀念
八十五年十二月二十一日至二十七日

635

1996. Chinese Postal Service Centenary Stamp Exhibition, Kaohsiung. No. **MS**2372 optd in top margin with T 635 in magenta.

MS2373	78×101 mm. Nos. 2370/1, each ×2	3·50	1·40

636 Early Porcelain Production

1997. Porcelain Production Techniques from "Tian Gong Kai Wu" (encyclopaedia) by Sung Yin-shing. Multicoloured.

2374	$5 Type **636**	45	20
2375	$5 Improved shaping	45	20
2376	$7 Painting	65	25
2377	$10 Glazing	85	40
2378	$13 Firing	1·10	55

637 Dragons and Carp (from window, Longsan Temple, Lukang)

1997. (a) T 637.

2379	**637**	$50 red	4·25	1·70
2380	**637**	$60 blue	5·00	2·00
2381	**637**	$70 red	6·00	2·40
2382	**637**	$100 green	8·50	3·50

(b) As T 637 but with outer decorated frame. Size 25×33 mm.

2386	$300 violet and blue	25·00	10·00
2387	$500 red and carmine	39·00	17·00

For $50 and $100 values in different colours and with the characters in the country name in reverse order see Nos. 2573/4.

638 Peace Doves and Memorial

1997. 50th Anniv of 228 Incident (civilian demonstration against government).

2390	**638**	$19 multicoloured	1·50	60

639 "Rhododendron x mucronatum"

1997. Shrubs. Multicoloured.

2391	$5 Type **639**	50	20
2392	$12 "Hibiscus rosa-sinensis"	1·10	40
2393	$19 "Hydrangea macrophylla"	1·60	60

640 River, Trees and Wildlife

1997. Protection of Water Resources. Mult.

2394	$5 Type **640**	45	20
2395	$19 Rivers and trees	1·60	60

641 Decorated Door

1997. Traditional Architecture. Mult.

2396	$5 Type **641**	45	20
2397	$5 Gable wall	45	20
2398	$10 Brick wall-carving	95	40
2399	$19 Verandah	1·50	55

642 "Dorcus formosanus"

1997. Insects. Multicoloured.

2400	$5 Type **642**	40	20
2401	$7 Giant katydid	65	25
2402	$10 Philippine birdwing	90	40
2403	$17 Big-headed stick insect	1·50	60

643 Alunite

1997. Minerals. Multicoloured.

2404	$5 Type **643**	40	20
2405	$5 Aragonite	40	20
2406	$12 Enargite	1·00	40
2407	$19 Hokutolite	1·40	55

644 Nanyashan Coastline

1997. Tourism. North-east Coast National Scenic Area. Multicoloured.

2408	$5 Type **644**	45	20
2409	$5 Pitou Coastline (rocky shore)	45	20
2410	$12 Stone pillar, Nanya	90	35
2411	$19 Tsaoling historic trail	1·20	45

645 Train and Chingshuei Cliffs (northern loop)

1997. Completion of Round-island Railway System. Multicoloured.

2412	$5 Type **645**	50	20
2413	$28 Train leaving tunnel (southern loop)	1·80	60

646 Integrated Circuit and Communications Equipment

1997. Electronic Industry. Multicoloured.

2414	$5 Type **646**	45	20
2415	$26 Circuit board, portable computer, mobile phone and synthesized keyboard	2·30	85

647 Shaolinquan

1997. Martial Arts. Multicoloured.

2416	$5 Type **647**	40	20
2417	$5 Form and will boxing (vert)	40	20
2418	$9 Taijiquan	70	25
2419	$19 Eight diagrams boxing (vert)	1·40	55

648 "Hsi Hsiang Chi" (Wang Shih-fu)

1997. Chinese Classical Opera. Multicoloured.

2420	$5 Type **648**	40	20
2421	$5 "Dan Daw Huei" (Kuan Han-chin)	40	20
2422	$12 "Han Guong Chiou" (Ma Jyi-yuan)	90	35
2423	$15 "Wu Tong Yu" (Bai Pu)	1·20	45

649 Bitan Bridge over River Shindian

1997. Inauguration of Second Northern Freeway. Multicoloured.

2424	$5 Type **649**	40	15
2425	$19 Hsinchu Interchange	1·40	55

650 Badminton

1997. Sports. Multicoloured.

2426	$5 Type **650**	40	20
2427	$12 Bowling	1·00	40
2428	$19 Lawn tennis	1·40	60

651 Palm of Buddha

1997. Classical Literature. "Journey to the West" (Ming dynasty novel). Multicoloured.

2429	$3.50 Type **651**	30	20
2430	$3.50 Pilgrimage of T'ang Monk	30	20
2431	$5 The Flaming Mountain	45	25
2432	$20 The Cobweb Cave	1·40	55

652 Purple-crowned Lory

1997. Birds (1st series). Illustrations from the Ching dynasty Bird Manual. Multicoloured.

2433	$5 Type **652**	40	25
2434	$5 Green magpie (on branch with small orange flowers)	40	25
2435	$5 Blue-crowned hanging parrot (green bird with red throat and rump)	40	25
2436	$5 Niltavas sp. (two birds with orange breasts)	40	25
2437	$5 Red-billed blue magpie (with long blue tail)	40	25
2438	$5 David's laughing thrush (on branch with red flowers)	40	25
2439	$5 Przewalski's rosefinch (on branch with orange-centred white flowers)	40	25
2440	$5 Common rosefinch (on branch with yellow flowers)	40	25
2441	$5 Mongolian trumpeter finch (on branch with white flowers and red hips)	40	25
2442	$5 Long-tailed minivets (two black and red birds)	40	25
2443	$5 Black-naped oriole (on branch with weeping leaves)	40	25

2444	$5 Yellow-headed buntings (two birds on branch with thorns and small pink flowers)	40	25
2445	$5 Bohemian waxwing (on branch with large blue flowers)	40	25
2446	$5 Mongolian trumpeter finches (two birds on branch with large pink flowers)	40	25
2447	$5 Chinese jungle mynah (with "bristles" above beak)	40	25
2448	$5 Java sparrow (with white patch on neck)	40	25
2449	$5 Long-tailed parakeet (on branch with small blue flowers)	40	25
2450	$5 Black-winged starling (by stream)	40	25
2451	$5 Cloven-feathered dove (two green and white birds)	40	25
2452	$5 Wryneck (on ground)	40	25

See also Nos. 2603/6, 2671/4, 2740/3, 2823/6 and 2929/32.

653 Tiger

1997. New Year Greetings. "Year of the Tiger".

2453	**653**	$3.50 multicoloured	25	15
2454	**653**	$13 multicoloured	85	50
MS2455		78×101 mm. Nos. 2453/4, each ×2	2·20	1·20

654 Pres. Chiang

1998. 10th Death Anniv of Chiang Ching-kuo (President 1978–88).

2456	**654**	$5 brown	35	20
2457	-	$19 red	1·10	60

DESIGN—HORIZ: $19 Chiang and applauding crowd.

655 "Abundance"

1998. Wishes for the Coming Year. Mult.

2458	$5 Type **655**	40	15
2459	$5 Flowers springing from lidded bowl ("Harmony")	40	15
2460	$12 Peonies in containers ("Honour and Wealth")	75	30
2461	$12 Flowers in vase and oranges in bowl ("Luck")	75	30

656 "Gaillardia pul-chella var. picta"

1998. Herbaceous Flowers. Multicoloured.

2462	$5 Type **656**	40	15
2463	$12 "Kalanchoe blossfeldiana"	85	40
2464	$19 "Portulaca oleracea var. granatus"	1·90	65

657 Horseman drawing Bow

1998. Painting by Liu Kuan-tao. Mult.

2465	$5 Type **657**	50	25
2466	$19 Kublai Khan and entourage on hunting expedition (63×40 mm)	1·60	60
MS2467	125×170 mm. Nos. 2465/6	2·10	85

658 "A Frog has only One Mouth"

1998. Children's Nursery Rhymes. Mult.

2468	$5 Type **658**	50	25
2469	$5 Mouse and cat ("A Little Mouse climbs an Oil Lamp")	50	25
2470	$12 Children and fireflies ("Fireflies")	85	50
2471	$19 Girl and egret carrying baskets ("Egrets")	1·80	65

659 Cultural Symbols within Human Head

1998. 70th Anniv of Copyright Law.

2472	**659**	$19 multicoloured	1·90	65

660 "Chung K'uei Moving" (Kung Kai)

1998. Ancient Paintings of Chung K'uei (mythological figure). Multicoloured.

2473	$5 Type **660**	50	15
2474	$20 Chung K'uei dancing ("An Auspicious Occasion")	1·60	65

661 Emblem and Cherry Blossom

1998. 125th Anniv of International Law Association and 68th Conference, Taipeh.

2475	**661**	$15 multicoloured	1·30	50

662 Grain Barge

1998. Ships and Vehicles from "Tian Gong Kai Wu" (encyclopaedia) by Sung Yin-shing. Multicoloured.

2476	$5 Type **662**	40	15
2477	$7 Six-oared ferry boat	65	25
2478	$10 One-wheel horse-drawn carriage	85	35
2479	$13 Man pushing one-wheel cart	1·00	50

663 Begonia

1998. Chinese Engravings. Flowers. Designs as Nos. 2228/31 but with values changed and Chinese characters for the country name in reverse order as in T 663. Multicoloured.

2480	$7 Type **663**	50	25
2481	$19 As No. 2229	1·60	65
2482	$20 As No. 2230	1·90	75
2483	$26 As No. 2231	1·90	75

664 Pao-yu visits Garden

1998. Classical Literature. "Red Chamber Dream" (novel) by Tsao Hsueh-Chin. Multicoloured.

2484	$3.50 Type **664**	40	15
2485	$3.50 Tai-yu burying flowers	40	15
2486	$5 Pao-chai playing with butterflies	65	35
2487	$5 Hsiang-yun in drunken sleep	1·20	60

665 Scout Badge

1998. 20th Asia-Pacific and Eighth China National Scout Jamboree, Pingtung University. Multicoloured.

2488	$5 Type **665**	40	15
2489	$5 Tents	40	15

666 Carved Base of Pillar

1998. Traditional Architecture. Multicoloured.

2490	$5 Type **666**	50	25
2491	$5 Carved stone ramp ("spirit way") between staircases	50	25
2492	$10 Carved base (with fishes) of column	85	40
2493	$19 Carved stone drainage spout	1·30	60

1998. Sports. Multicoloured.

2494	$5 Type **667**	40	15
2495	$5 Table tennis player serving	40	15
2496	$7 Rugby player with ball	65	25
2497	$7 Rugby players	65	25

Stamps of the same value were issued together, se-tenant, forming a composite design.

668 "The Fox borrows the Tiger's Ferocity"

1998. Chinese Fables. Multicoloured.

2498	$5 Type **668**	40	25
2499	$5 "A Frog in a Well"	40	25
2500	$12 "Adding Legs to a Drawing of a Snake"	1·00	40
2501	$19 "The Snipe and the Clam at a Deadlock"	1·60	60

670 Taiwushan

1998. Kinmen National Park. Multicoloured.

2508	$5 Type **670**	50	25
2509	$5 Kuningtou Cliff	50	25
2510	$12 Teyueh Tower and Huang Hui-huang's House, Shuitou	1·20	40
2511	$19 Putou beach, Leihyu	1·80	60

671 Hodgson's Hawk Eagle ("Spizaetus nipalensis")

1998. Birds (2nd series). Multicoloured.

2512	$5 Type **671**	40	15
2513	$5 Hodgson's hawk eagle in flight	40	15
2514	$5 Crested serpent eagle ("Spilornis cheela") on branch	40	15
2515	$5 Crested serpent eagle carrying snake	40	15
2516	$10 Black kite ("Milvus migrans") on rock	85	35
2517	$10 Black kite in flight	85	35
2518	$10 Indian black eagle ("Ictinaetus malayensis") on branch	85	35
2519	$10 Indian black eagle in flight	85	35

Nos. 2512/13, 2514/15, 2516/17 and 2518/19 respectively were issued together, se-tenant, each pair forming a composite design.

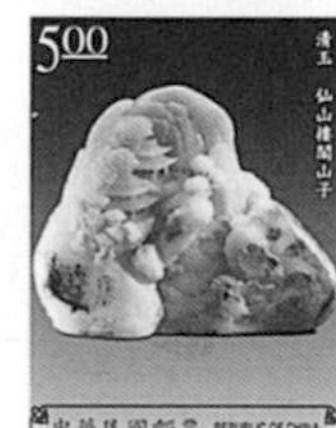

672 Mountain and Pavilions

1998. Ching Dynasty Jade Mountain Carvings. Mult.

2520	$5 Type **672**	40	25
2521	$5 Men working in jade mine (horiz)	40	25
2522	$7 Men washing elephant (horiz)	65	25
2523	$26 Five men on a mountain	2·10	85
MS2524	132×102 mm. Nos. 2520/3	3·50	1·60

673 Rabbit

1998. New Year Greetings. "Year of the Rabbit". Multicoloured.

2525	$3.50 Type **673**	30	15
2526	$13 Rabbit (different)	1·00	50
MS2527	78×102 mm. Nos. 2525/6, each ×2	3·00	1·50

674 Butterfly and Pumpkin ("Many Descendants")

1999. Wishes for the Coming Year. Multicoloured.

2528	$5 Type **674**	50	15
2529	$5 Mandarins (ducks) and lotus flowers ("Good marriage that brings sons")	50	15

2530 $12 Egret ("Prosperity") 1·00 50
2531 $12 Goldfish and flowers ("Abundance") 1·00 50

1999. Chinese Engravings. Birds and Plants. Designs as Nos. 2264/7 and 2330/1 but with values and Chinese characters for the country name in reverse order as in T 663. Multicoloured.

2532 $1 Type **604** 30 15
2533 $3.50 As No. 2265 40 25
2534 $5 As No. 2266 50 35
2535 $10 As No. 2267 85 40
2536 $12 Type **627** 1·30 60
2536a $20 As No. 2482 1·30 60
2537 $28 As No. 2331 1·90 75
2537a $34 As No. 2649 1·90 75

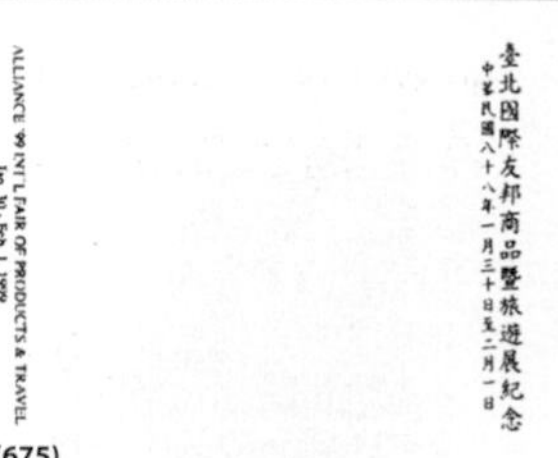

(675)

1999. "Alliance '99" International Products and Travel Fair. No. MS2527 optd in margins with T 675.

MS2538 78×102 mm. Nos. 2525/6, each ×2 3·00 1·50

676 "Gloxinia"

1999. Indoor Flowers. Multicoloured.

2539 $5 Type **676** 40 25
2540 $12 African violet 85 35
2541 $19 Flamingo flower 1·90 65

677 Boy towing Toy Elephant

1999. Illustrations from "Joy in Peacetime" (Ching Dynasty book). Lantern Festival. Multicoloured.

2542 $5 Type **677** 50 25
2543 $5 Women, children and crane 50 25
2544 $7 Children playing with toy animals 85 35
2545 $26 Children playing 2·10 65
MS2546 170×125 mm. Nos. 2542/5 4·50 1·50

678 Hanging Cylinder

1999. Traditional Architecture. Decorative Features. Multicoloured.

2547 $5 Type **678** 50 25
2548 $5 Taishi screen 50 25
2549 $10 Xuanyu (gable decoration) 85 40
2550 $19 Wood carving 1·70 60

679 "Baby Sleeps"

1999. Nursery Rhymes. Multicoloured.

2551 $5 Type **679** 50 25
2552 $5 Mother comforting baby frightened by storm ("Be Brave") 50 25
2553 $12 Mother and baby rocking ("Rock, Rock, Rock") 85 40
2554 $19 Mother, baby, cat and flies ("Buggie Flies") 1·70 60

680 Atayal Ancestor Festival

1999. Taiwan's Aboriginal Culture. Multicoloured.

2555 $5 Type **680** 75 60
2556 $5 Dancers with hip bells (Saisat Festival of the Dwarfs) 75 60
2557 $5 Circle of singers (Bunun Millet Harvest Song) 75 60
2558 $5 Line of singers in red coats (Tsou Victory Festival) 75 60
2559 $5 Dancers and millet biscuits mounted on board (Rukai Harvest Festival) 75 60
2560 $5 Men with bamboo poles (Paiwan Bamboo Festival) 75 60
2561 $5 Procession of men carrying yellow scarves (Puyuma Harvest Ceremony) 75 60
2562 $5 Line of women dancers with white headdresses (Ami Harvest Ceremony) 75 60
2563 $5 Launch of new fishing boat (Yami Boat Ceremony) 75 60

681 Nurses treating Patients

1999. Centenary of International Council of Nurses. Multicoloured.

2564 $5 Type **681** 50 25
2565 $17 Globe and nurse carrying tray 1·40 40

682 "Washing Cotton Yarn" (Liang Chenyu)

1999. Chinese Classical Opera (Legends of the Ming Dynasty). Multicoloured.

2566 $5 Type **682** 50 25
2567 $5 "The Story of a Pipa" (Kaoming) 50 25
2568 $12 "The Story of Hung Fu" (Chang Fengyi) 85 35
2569 $15 "Paiyueh Pavilion" (Shi Hui) 1·30 40
MS2570 139×90 mm. Nos. 2566/9 3·25 1·30

683 Coins

1999. 50th Anniv of Introduction of the Silver Yuan. Multicoloured.

2571 $5 Type **683** 50 25
2572 $25 Banknotes 2·10 1·00

684 Dragons and Carp (from window, Longsan Temple, Lukang)

1999. (a) As Nos. 2379, 2382, 2386 and 2387 but with Chinese characters for the country name in reverse order, as in T 684, and colours changed.

2573 **684** $50 green 4·25 2·50
2574 **684** $100 brown 6·25 5·00

(b) as T 684 but with outer decorated frame. Size 25×33 mm.

2578 $300 red and blue 21·00 12·50
2579 $500 red and brown 47·00 17·00

1999. Chinese Engravings of Fruit by Hu Chen-yan. Designs as Nos. 2292/4 but with Chinese characters for the country name in reverse order, and values changed. Multicoloured.

2580 50c. As Type **613** 30 25
2581 $6 As $12 50 35
2582 $25 As $15 2·10 65

1999. "Taipei" International Stamp Exhibition. As No. MS2570 but additionally inscr "TAIPEI INTERNATIONAL STAMP EXHIBITION 1999" (INVITATIONAL) in English and Chinese and with exhibition emblem.

MS2583 140×90 mm. Nos. 2566/9 3·25 1·30

685 Children giving Present

1999. Fathers' Day. Multicoloured.

2584 $5 Type **685** 50 25
2585 $25 Father teaching boy to ride bike 2·10 1·00

686 Peony Lobster (Taiwanese Cuisine)

1999. Chinese Regional Dishes. Multicoloured.

2586 $5 Type **686** 40 15
2587 $5 Buddha jumps the wall (Fukien) (plate, teapot, jar and cups) 40 15
2588 $5 Flower hors d'oeuvres (Cantonese) 40 15
2589 $5 Dongpo pork (Kiangsu and Chekiang) (plate, bowl and double handled jar) 40 15
2590 $5 Stewed fish jaws (Shanghai) (plate decorated with strawberries) 40 15
2591 $5 Beggar's chicken (Hunan) (with folded napkin) 40 15
2592 $5 Carp jumping over dragon's gate (Szechwan) (on silver platter) 40 15
2593 $5 Peking duck (Peking) (in silver dish) 40 15

687 Scuba Diving

1999. Outdoor Activities. Multicoloured.

2594 $5 Type **687** 40 25
2595 $6 Canoeing 50 35
2596 $10 Surfing 95 40
2597 $25 Windsurfing 2·30 65

688 Stage and Audience

1999. Taiwanese Opera. Multicoloured.

2598 $5 Type **688** 40 25
2599 $6 Preparation in the dressing room 50 35
2600 $10 Two actresses 95 40
2601 $25 Actress as clown 2·30 65

689 Collapsed Buildings

1999. Taiwan Earthquake Victims' Fund. Sheet 124×80 mm containing T 689 and similar horiz design.

MS2602 $25+$25 Type **689**; $25+$25 Hands joined over cracked ground 12·50 10·00

690 Yellow-headed Amazon

1999. Birds (3rd series). Illustrations from the Ching Dynasty Bird Manual. Multicoloured.

2603 $5 Type **690** 40 25
2604 $5 Golden-winged parakeet 40 25
2605 $12 Grey parrot 1·00 40
2606 $25 Chattering lory 2·30 †

691 Dragon

1999. New Year Greetings. "Year of the Dragon". Multicoloured.

2607 $3.50 Type **691** 30 15
2608 $13 Dragon (different) 1·30 50
MS2609 78×102 mm. Nos. 2634/4, each ×2 3·25 1·50

692 ST-1 Communication Satellite over Earth

1999. Year 2000. Multicoloured.

2610 $5 Type **692** (information) 50 25
2611 $5 Deer and river (environmental protection) 50 25
2612 $12 Modern buildings and high-speed train (industry and economy) 1·00 40
2613 $15 Dove and St. Peter's Basilica,Vatican City (peace) 1·40 60
MS2614 102×145 mm. Nos. 2610/13 3·50 1·70

1999. "Taipei 2000" International Stamp Exhibition. As No. MS2614 but additionally inscr "TAIPEI 2000 STAMP EXHIBITION" in English and Chinese and with exhibition emblem in the margin.

MS2615 102×146 mm. Nos. 2610/14 3·50 1·70

693 Emperor Chia-Ching's "Coloured Cloud Dragon" Writing Brushes (Ming Dynasty)

2000. Traditional Chinese Writing Equipment. Mult.

2616 $5 Type **693** 50 25
2617 $5 Emperor Lung Ching's "Imperial Dragon Fragrance" ink stick (Ming Dynasty) (vert) 50 25
2618 $7 "Clear Heart House" (calligraphy, Tsai Hsiang) (Sung Dynasty) (vert) 65 35
2619 $26 "Celadon Toad Inkstone" (Sung Dynasty) 2·50 85

694 Kaoping River Bridge Pylon

2000. Inauguration of Second Southern Freeway. Multicoloured.

2620 $5 Type **694** 65 25
2621 $12 Main junction, Tainan 1·30 40
MS2622 125×60 mm. $25 Road bridge over Kaoping River (79×29 mm) 2·75 90

695 Branch, Fields and Houses

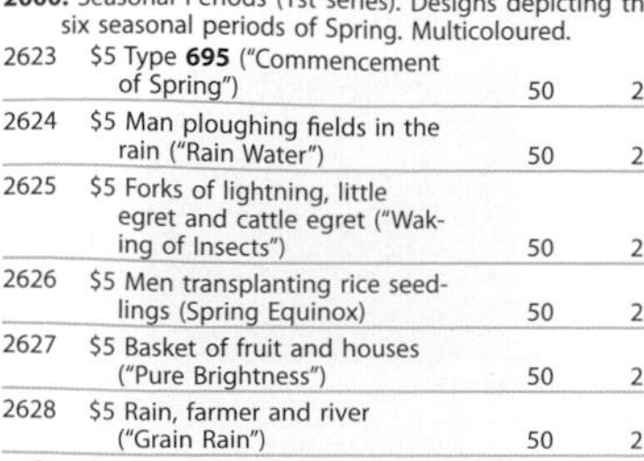

2000. Seasonal Periods (1st series). Designs depicting the six seasonal periods of Spring. Multicoloured.

2623	$5 Type **695** ("Commencement of Spring")	50	25
2624	$5 Man ploughing fields in the rain ("Rain Water")	50	25
2625	$5 Forks of lightning, little egret and cattle egret ("Waking of Insects")	50	25
2626	$5 Men transplanting rice seedlings (Spring Equinox)	50	25
2627	$5 Basket of fruit and houses ("Pure Brightness")	50	25
2628	$5 Rain, farmer and river ("Grain Rain")	50	25

See also Nos. 2636/41, 2652/7 and 2675/80.

696 Shuanghsi River and School Gates, Waishuanghsi Campus

2000. Centenary of Soochow University. Mult.

2629	$5 Type **696**	50	25
2630	$25 Justice statue, Soochow Law School, Taipeh campus and Ansu Hall, Waishuanghsi campus	2·50	1·00

697 Three Heroes at Altar

2000. Classical Literature. Romance of the Three Kingdoms by Luo Guanzhong (1st series). Mult.

2631	$3.50 Type **697**	40	25
2632	$3.50 Guan Yu reading at night	40	25
2633	$5 Couple in cottage receiving guest	65	35
2634	$20 Arrows raining down on sampans	1·70	40
MS2635	140×100 mm. Nos. 2631/4	3·25	1·30

See also Nos. 2797/**MS**2801.

698 Crops and Mountains

2000. Seasonal Periods (2nd series). Designs depicting the six seasonal periods of Summer. Multicoloured.

2636	$5 Type **698** ("Commencement of Summer")	50	25
2637	$5 Water wheel and houses in rain ("Little Fullness")	50	25
2638	$5 Ears of grain and houses ("Husks of Grain")	50	25
2639	$5 Insect on plant and houses (Summer Solstice)	50	25
2640	$5 Palm leaf fan and fields ("Lesser Heat")	50	25
2641	$5 Watermelons ("Great Heat")	50	25

Nos. 2636/41 were issued together, se-tenant, forming a composite design.

699 Chen Shui-bian and Lu Hsiu-lien

2000. Inauguration of Chen Shui-bian as 10th President and Lu Hsiu-lien as Vice-President. Mult.

2642	$5 Type **699**	50	15
2643	$5 Presidential Office building	50	15
MS2644	125×80 mm. Nos. 2642/3, each ×2	2·10	65

700 Hsialiao

2000. Monuments Marking the Tropic of Cancer. Multicoloured.

2645	$5 Type **700**	40	25
2646	$12 Wuho	1·30	50
2647	$25 Chingpu	2·30	90

2000. Chinese Engravings of Fruit by Hu Chen-yan. As No. 2295 but with Chinese characters for the country name in reverse order, as in T 683, and with value (2648) or new design changed.

2648	$32 multicoloured	3·00	2·40
2649	$34 multicoloured	3·25	2·75

701 Taiwan Giant Sacred Tree

2000. Sacred Trees. Multicoloured.

2650	$5 Type **701**	40	25
2651	$39 Sacred Sleeping Moon Tree	3·50	1·40

702 Grain drying

2000. Seasonal Periods (3rd series). Depicting the six seasonal periods of Autumn. Multicoloured.

2652	$5 Type **702** ("Commencement of Autumn")	50	25
2653	$5 Rick and village ("Bounds of Heat")	50	25
2654	$5 Dew covered leaves ("White Dew")	50	25
2655	$5 Red leaves ("Autumn Equinox")	50	25
2656	$5 Bare tree ("Cold Dew")	50	25
2657	$5 Frost on plant ("Descent of Hoar Frost")	50	25

Nos. 2652/57 were issued together, se-tenant. forming a composite design.

2000. No. 1784 surch 350.

2658	$3.50 on $7.50 multicoloured	40	25

704 Red Spider Lily

2000. Poisonous Plants. Multicoloured.

2659	$5 Type **704**	50	25
2660	$5 Odollam erberus-tree (*Cerbera manghas*)	50	25
2661	$12 Rosary pea	1·30	40
2662	$20 Oleander	2·10	75

705 Seismograph and map of Taiwan

2000. Earthquakes. Multicoloured.

2663	$5 Type **705**	40	25
2664	$12 Rescue workers	1·30	40
2665	$25 Earthquake drills	2·75	1·00

706 *Anotogaster sieboldii*

2000. Dragonflies. Multicoloured.

2666	$5 Type **706**	50	25
2667	$5 *Lamelligomphus formosanus* (horiz)	50	25
2668	$12 *Neurothemis ramburii* (horiz)	1·40	40
2669	$12 *Trithemis festiva*	1·40	40
MS2670	135×80 mm. Nos. 2666/9	3·75	1·30

707 White's Thrush

2000. Birds 4th series). Illustrations from the Ching Dynasty Bird Manual. Multicoloured.

2671	$5 Type **707**	50	25
2672	$5 Brambling	50	25
2673	$12 Rothschild's mynah	1·30	40
2674	$25 Southern grackle	2·50	75

708 Lake, Mountains and Bowl

2000. Seasonal Periods (4th series). Designs depicting the six seasonal periods of Winter. Multicoloured.

2675	$5 Type **708** ("Commencement of Winter")	50	25
2676	$5 Trees covered in snow ("Lesser Snow")	50	25
2677	$5 Mountains covered in snow ("Great Snow")	50	25
2678	$5 Rice balls in bowl ("Winter Solstice")	50	25
2679	$5 Houses and tree branch covered in snow ("Lesser Cold")	50	25
2680	$5 Log cabin covered in snow ("Great Cold")	50	25

Nos. 2675/80 were issued together, se-tenant, forming a composite design.

709 Palace Lamp Boulevard and Classrooms

2000. 50th Anniv of Tamkang University. Mult.

2681	$5 Type **709**	50	25
2682	$25 Maritime Museum and "Scroll Plaza" (sculpture)	2·50	1·00

710 Snake

2000. New Year Greetings. "Year of the Snake". Multicoloured.

2683	$3.50 Type **710**	30	25
2684	$13 Snake (different)	1·30	40

(711) (image scaled to 52% of original size)

2000. "Turn of the Century" International Stamp Exhibition, Kaohsiung. As No. MS2685 optd with T 711 in the margin.

MS2685	78×102 mm. 2 ×3.50 multicoloured; 2 ×$13 multicoloured	3·25	1·50

712 Cruise Ship and Buildings

2001. "Three Small Links" (establishment of trade links between Kinmen, Xiamen, Matsu and Foochow). Multicoloured.

2687	$9 Type **712**	85	60
2688	$25 Cruise ship and monument	2·30	1·50

713 Lotus Blossoms ("Marital Bliss")

2001. Wishes for the Coming Year. Multicoloured.

2689	$5 Type **713**	50	35
2690	$5 Loganberries, lichees and walnuts ("Success in one's career")	50	35
2691	$12 Pomegranates ("Producing many offspring")	1·00	75
2692	$12 Peonies and pair of Chinese bulbuls ("Growing old together with wealth and high position")	1·00	75

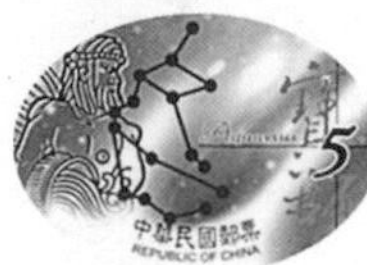

714 Aquarius

2001. Signs of the Western Zodiac (1st series). Air Signs. Multicoloured.

2693	$5 Type **714**	50	25
2694	$12 Gemini	1·20	50
2695	$25 Libra	2·50	1·80

See also Nos. 2708/10, 2726/8 and 2755/7.

715 Apples

2001. Fruits (1st series). Multicoloured.

2696	$5 Type **715**	50	25
2697	$7 Guavas	75	25
2698	$12 Pears	1·20	40
2699	$25 Melons	2·50	75

See also Nos. 2732/5, 2785/8 and 2879/82.

716 Main Peak

2001. Mount Jade. Views of Mount Jade. Mult.

2700	$5 Type **716**	50	35
2701	$5 Western peak	50	35

2702	$12 Northern peak	1·20	85
2703	$25 Eastern peak	2·50	1·70

717 Girls playing with Ball ("Little Ball")

2001. Children's Playtime Rhymes. Multicoloured.

2704	$5 Type **717**	50	35
2705	$5 Children sitting in a circle ("Point to the Water Vat")	50	35
2706	$12 Boys dancing ("Pangolin")	1·20	85
2707	$25 Children playing ("Shake and Stamp")	2·50	1·70

2001. Signs of the Western Zodiac (2nd series). Earth Signs. As T 714. Multicoloured.

2708	$5 Capricorn	50	25
2709	$12 Taurus	1·20	50
2710	$25 Virgo	2·50	1·80

718 Sakyamuni Buddha, Northern Wei Dynasty

2001. Ancient Statues of Buddha. Multicoloured.

2711	$5 Type **718**	50	35
2712	$9 Seated Buddha, Tang Dynasty	75	50
2713	$12 Mahavairocana Buddha, Sung Dynasty	1·30	85
MS2714	102×146 mm. Nos. 2711/13	3·25	2·50

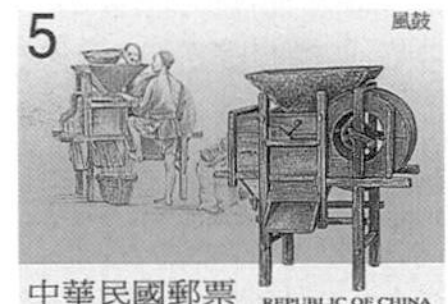
719 Thresher

2001. Early Agricultural Implements. Multicoloured.

2715	$5 Type **719**	50	35
2716	$7 Ox plough	75	50
2717	$10 Bamboo baskets and yoke	95	65
2718	$25 Coir raincoat and hat	2·50	1·70

720 Mackay

2001. Death Centenary of George Leslie Mackay (missionary and educator).

2719	**720**	$25 multicoloured	2·10	1·70

721 Girl dancing, Globe and Emblem

2001. Kiwanis International (community organization) Convention, Taipeh. Multicoloured.

2720	$5 Type **721**	50	25
2721	$25 Mother and child within heart	2·10	1·40

722 Dragon

2001. Kites. Multicoloured.

2722	$5 Type **722**	40	35
2723	$5 Phoenix	40	35
2724	$5 Tiger	40	35
2725	$5 Fish	40	35

2001. Signs of the Western Zodiac (3rd series). Fire Signs. As T 714. Multicoloured.

2726	$5 Aries	50	35
2727	$12 Leo	1·20	65
2728	$25 Sagittarius	2·30	1·50

723 Medium-Capacity Car

2001. Rapid Transit System, Taipeh. Multicoloured.

2729	$5 Type **723**	50	25
2730	$12 Passengers and tickets	1·40	60
MS2731	125×60 mm. $25 Chientan Station, Tamshui Line (84×42 mm)	2·75	1·30

2001. Fruits (2nd series). As T 715. Multicoloured.

2732	$1 Plums	30	15
2733	$3.50 Tangerines	40	25
2734	$20 Longans	1·60	1·00
2735	$40 Grapefruit	3·50	2·40

724 Keeper and Monkeys ("Now Three, Now Four")

2001. Chinese Fables. Multicoloured.

2736	$5 Type **724**	50	35
2737	$5 Man selling weapons ("Selling the All Penetrating Sword and Unyielding Shield")	50	35
2738	$12 Farmer sitting under tree ("Waiting by the Tree for the Rabbit")	1·00	50
2739	$25 Old man and children ("An Old Fool Moves Mountains")	1·90	1·30

725 Japanese Waxwing

2001. Birds (5th series). Showing illustrations from the Ching Dynasty Bird Manual. Multicoloured.

2740	$5 Type **725**	50	35
2741	$5 Siberian rubythroat	50	35
2742	$12 White-rumped munia	1·00	50
2743	$25 Great barbet	1·90	1·30

726 Second Terminal, Chiang Kai-shek International Airport

2001. 90th Anniv of Republic of China. Multicoloured.

2744	$5 Type **726**	50	35
2745	$5 Computer screens, lap top computer, mobile phone and Globe	50	35
2746	$12 Dance, National Theatre	85	50
2747	$15 Dolphins	1·50	90

727 Flame, Karate, Javelin and Table Tennis

2001. National Games, Kaohsiung and Pingtung. Multicoloured.

2748	$5 Type **727**	50	25
2749	$25 Swimming, athletics, weightlifting and map	2·10	1·40

728 Pitcher

2001. 34th World Baseball Championship and 21st Asia Baseball Tournament. Multicoloured.

2750	$5 Type **728**	50	35
2751	$5 Batter	50	35
2752	$12 Catcher	1·00	65
2753	$20 Base runner	1·80	1·20
MS2754	120×85 mm. Nos. 2750/3	4·00	2·50

2001. Signs of the Western Zodiac (4th series). Water Signs. As T 714. Multicoloured.

2755	$5 Pisces	50	35
2756	$12 Cancer	1·20	65
2757	$25 Scorpio	2·30	1·50

729 Mozhaonu holding Fan ("Thunder Storm")

2001. Taiwanese Puppet Theatre. (1st series). Showing puppets. Multicoloured.

2758	$5 Type **729**	50	25
2759	$6 Taiyangau ("Rising Winds, Surging Clouds")	65	35
2760	$10 Kuangdao ("Thunder Crazy Sword")	1·20	65
2761	$25 Chin Chia-chien ("Thunder Golden Light")	2·50	1·30

See also Nos. 2887/90.

730 Old School Building, Shuiyan Road, Taipeh

2001. Centenary of National Defence Medical Centre. Multicoloured.

2762	$5 Type **730**	50	25
2763	$25 New school building and medical staff	2·10	1·40

731 Horse

2001. New Year Greetings. "Year of the Horse". Multicoloured.

2764	$3.50 Type **731**	40	25
2765	$13 Horse (different)	1·30	85
MS2766	78×102 mm. Nos. 2764/5, each ×2	3·25	2·75

732 Yu Pin

2001. Birth Centenary of Yu Pin (religious leader).

2767	**732**	$25 multicoloured	2·30	1·60

MS2768	80×60 mm. $25 As No. 2767	2·30	1·80

733 Carnations

2001. Greetings Stamps. Multicoloured.

2769	$5 Type **733**	40	35
2770	$5 White lilies	40	35
2771	$5 Pink violas	40	35
2772	$5 Orange flowers with yellow centres	40	35
2773	$5 Pink flowers with five petals	40	35
2774	$5 Pink roses	40	35
2775	$5 Christmas tree decorations	40	35
2776	$5 Poinsettia	40	35
2777	$5 Purple ball-shaped flowers	40	35
2778	$5 Sunflowers	40	35

734 Students with Flags

2002. 50th Anniv of Fu Hsing Kang College (military university). Multicoloured.

2779	$5 Type **734**	50	25
2780	$25 University buildings and statue	2·10	1·40

735 Vase containing Lotus Flower and Sweet Osmanthus ("Producing many offspring")

2002. Wishes for the Coming Year. Multicoloured.

2781	$5 Type **735**	50	25
2782	$5 Orchid and osmanthus plants ("Person of high morality")	50	25
2783	$12 Vase containing peonies and flowering crabapple ("Hall full of the rich and famous")	1·30	60
2784	$12 Vase containing roses ("Safe and peaceful in all four seasons")	1·30	60

2002. Fruits (3rd series). As T 715. Multicoloured.

2785	$6 Avocados	50	40
2786	$10 Lychees	85	65
2787	$17 Dates	1·50	1·00
2788	$32 Passionfruit	3·00	2·10

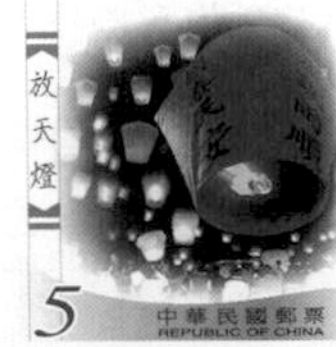
736 Lantern Festival (Pinghsi and Shihfen)

2002. Traditional Folk Festivals (1st series). Multicoloured.

2789	$5 Type **736**	50	35
2790	$5 Fireworks display (Yanshui)	50	35
2791	$10 Matsu (sea goddess) procession (Peikang)	1·00	60
2792	$20 Dragon boat race	2·10	1·30

See also Nos. 2817/20.

737 Mountain in Winter

2002. Mount Hsueh. Views of Mount Hsueh. Multicoloured.

2793	$5 Type **737**	40	35

2794 $5 North ridge 40 35
2795 $12 Slopes in autumn 1·00 75
2796 $25 Glacial cirques (bowl-shaped depressions) 2·10 1·50

738 Three Heroes chasing Lu Bu

2002. Classical Literature. Romance of the Three Kingdoms by Luo Guanzhong (2nd series). Multicoloured.
2797 $3.50 Type **738** 40 25
2798 $3.50 Chao Yun 40 25
2799 $5 Dr. Hua Tuo operating on Guan Yu's arm 50 35
2800 $20 Chu-Ko Liang playing lute to repel invaders 2·10 1·30
MS2801 140×100 mm. Nos. 2797/800 3·50 2·10

739 Chinese Crested Tern (*Thalasseus bernsteini*)

2002. Endangered Species. Chinese Crested Tern. Two sheets, 240×160 mm (**MS**2802a) and 120×60 mm (**MS**2802b) containing T 739 and similar horiz designs. Multicoloured.
MS2802 (a) $5×10, Type **739**; Two Terns in flight; Tern flying (left); Landing on rock; Perched on rock with open beak; Feeding chick; Diving; Flying above rocks; On ground looking left; Adult and chick; On nest (b) $25 Tern in flight (80×30 mm) Set of 2 sheets 6·25 5·00

740 Bowl decorated with Lotus

2002. Ching Dynasty Enamel Porcelain Bowls. Multicoloured.
2803 $5 Type **740** 40 35
2804 $5 Peacock 40 35
2805 $7 Peonies 65 50
2806 $32 Birds and bamboo 3·00 2·00

741 Stock (*Matthiola incana*)

2002. Scented Flowers. Multicoloured.
2807 $5 Type **741** 40 35
2808 $12 Gardenia (*Gardenia jasminoides*) 1·00 85
2809 $25 Banana shrub (*Michelia figo*) 2·10 1·70

742 Bottle-nosed Dolphin (*Tursiops truncates*)

2002. Marine mammals. Multicoloured.
2810 $5 Type **742** 40 35
2811 $5 Humpback whale (*Megaptera novaeangliae*) 40 35
2812 $10 Killer whale (*Orcinus orca*) 85 65
2813 $25 Risso's dolphin (*Grampus griseus*) 2·50 2·00
MS2814 120×80 mm. As Nos. 2810/13 4·25 3·25

743 Player in Wheelchair

2002. International Paralympics Committee World Table Tennis Championships, Taipeh. Multicoloured.
2815 $5 Type **743** 50 35
2816 $5 Player using crutch 50 35

2002. Traditional Folk Festivals (2nd series). As T 736. Multicoloured.
2817 $5 Water lanterns (Keelung) 40 35
2818 $5 Fireworks display (Touchengi) 40 35
2819 $10 Yimin (martyrs) procession (Taoyuan) 95 65
2820 $20 Burning the Prince's boat (Tungkang) 1·80 1·20

744 Republic of China and Vatican City Flags

2002. 60th Anniv of Republic of China—Vatican City Diplomatic Relations ($5). 80th Anniv of First Apostolic Delegate to Republic of China ($17). Multicoloured.
2821 $5 Type **744** 40 35
2822 $17 Celso Costantini (first apostolic delegate) 1·50 1·20

745 Vernal Hanging Parrot

2002. Birds (6th series). Illustrations from the Ching Dynasty Bird Manual. Multicoloured.
2823 $5 Type **745** 40 35
2824 $5 White-rumped munia 40 35
2825 $12 White-headed greenfinch 85 65
2826 $25 Yunnan greenfinch 1·90 1·40

746 Liang Shan-po and Chu Ying-tai (impromptu performance)

2002. Chinese Regional Opera. Multicoloured.
2827 $5 Type **746** 40 35
2828 $6 Hsueh Ting-shan and Fan Li-hua (indoor performance) 50 35
2829 $10 Hsueh Ping-kuei and Wang Pao-chuan (outdoor stage performance) 85 65
2830 $25 The Living Buddha Chikung (modern theatre) 2·10 1·40

747 Mother and Baby Koala

2002. Koalas at Taipei Municipal Zoo. Multicoloured.
2831 $5 Type **747** 40 25
2832 $5 Eating leaf 40 25
2833 $9 Resting 75 50
2834 $21 Mother with baby on back 1·70 1·20
MS2835 85×115 mm. Nos. 2831/4 3·25 2·20

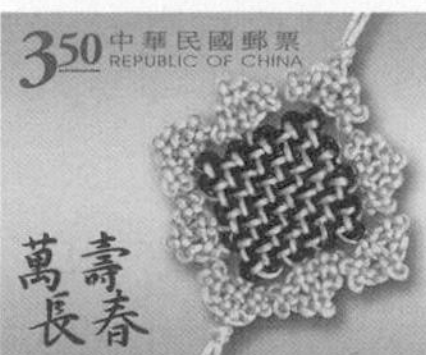

748 Knot

2002. Greetings Stamps. Chinese Decorative Knots. Designs showing various knots (knot colours given). Multicoloured.
2836 $3.50 Type **748** 30 25
2837 $3.50 green, blue and yellow 30 25
2838 $3.50 red and yellow 30 25
2839 $3.50 orange and green 30 25
2840 $3.50 blue and straw 30 25
2841 $3.50 blue, mauve, green, red and yellow 30 25
2842 $3.50 red and yellow (different) 30 25
2843 $3.50 mauve and blue 30 25
2844 $3.50 pink and lavender 30 25
2845 $3.50 yellow and blue 30 25
2846 $5 Type **748** 40 35
2847 $5 As No. 2837 40 35
2848 $5 As 2838 40 35
2849 $5 As 2839 40 35
2850 $5 As 2840 40 35
2851 $5 As 2841 40 35
2852 $5 As 2842 40 35
2853 $5 As 2843 40 35
2854 $5 As 2844 40 35
2855 $5 As 2845 40 35
2856 $25 Type **748** 2·00 1·60
2857 $25 As 2837 2·00 1·60
2858 $25 As 2838 2·00 1·60
2859 $25 As 2839 2·00 1·60
2860 $25 As 2840 2·00 1·60
2861 $25 As 2841 2·00 1·60
2862 $25 As 2842 2·00 1·60
2863 $25 As 2843 2·00 1·60
2864 $25 As 2844 2·00 1·60
2865 $25 As 2845 2·00 1·60

749 Goat

2002. New Year Greetings. "Year of the Goat". Multicoloured.
2866 $3.50 Type **749** 30 25
2867 $13 Goat (different) 1·00 85
MS2868 78×102 mm. Nos. 2866/7, each×2 2·75 2·20

750 "Street Scene on a Summer's Day" (Chen Cheng-po)

2002. Taiwanese Artists (1st series). Multicoloured.
2869 $5 Type **750** 40 35
2870 $5 "Girl in white dress" (Li Mei-shu) (vert) 40 35
2871 $10 "Courtyard with banana trees" (Liao Chi-chun) (vert) 85 65
2872 $20 "Sunrise" (Kuo Po-chuan) 1·70 1·30
See also Nos. 2939/42 and 2964/7.

中華郵政股份有限公司成立紀念
中華民國九十二年一月一日

(751) (image scaled to 49% of original size)

2003. Inauguration of Chunghwa Post Co. (new postal service). No. **MS**2868 optd with T 751 in the margin.
MS2873 78×102 mm. 2 ×$3.50 multicoloured, 2 ×$13 multicoloured 2·75 2·20

752 WTO Emblem, Map and Buildings

2003. 1st Anniv of Membership of World Trade Organisation.
2874 **752** $17 multicoloured 1·40 90

753 Main Peak in Spring

2003. Mount Nanhu. Views of Mount Nanhu. Multicoloured.
2875 $5 Type **753** 40 25
2876 $5 Glacial cirques 40 25
2877 $12 Lake and main peak 95 60
2878 $25 Snow-covered Mount Chungyang Chien 1·90 1·30

2003. Fruits (4th series). As T 715. Multicoloured.
2879 $9 Rose apples 65 50
2880 $13 Kumquats 85 65
2881 $15 Lemons 95 75
2882 $34 Coconuts 2·10 1·70

754 Family

2003. "Caring Heart". Multicoloured.
2883 $5 Type **754** (family life) 40 25
2884 $5 Woman and wheelchair user (volunteers) 40 25
2885 $10 Fields and heart (care for the environment) 85 50
2886 $25 Child and dogs (care for animals) 2·00 1·30

755 Outdoor Performance ("Journey to the West")

2003. Taiwanese Puppet Theatre (2nd series). Multicoloured.
2887 $5 Type **755** 40 25
2888 $5 Television showing hand puppets 40 25
2889 $10 Theatre performance ("Mysteries of the Wolf Castle") 85 50
2890 $25 Film showing hand puppet ("Legend of the Sacred Stone") 2·00 1·30

756 Blue-tailed Bee-eater in Flight

2003. Endangered Species. Blue-tailed Bee-eaters (Merops philippinus). Multicoloured.
2891 $5 Type **756** 40 25
2892 $5 Five birds on branch 40 25
2893 $10 Sunbathing 85 50
2894 $20 Offering food to mate in nest 1·60 1·00
MS2895 135×80 mm. Nos. 2891/4 3·25 1·80

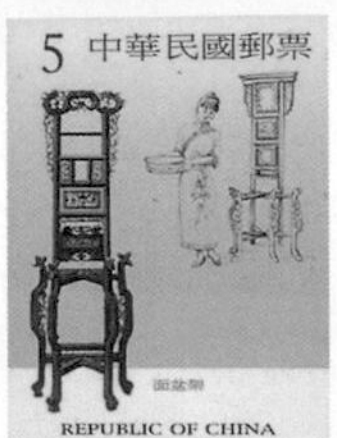

757 Wash Stand

2003. Taiwanese Furniture. Multicoloured.

2896	$5 Type **757**	40	25
2897	$5 Canopied bed	40	25
2898	$12 Taishi chair	95	60
2899	$20 Pahsien table	1·60	1·00

758 Jhang Guo-lao riding Mule

2003. Eight Immortals (1st series). Multicoloured.

2900	$5 Type **758**	40	25
2901	$5 Li Tie-guai riding fish	40	25
2902	$10 Han Jhong-li holding fan	85	50
2903	$25 Lyu Dong-bin wearing sword and carrying flywhisk	2·00	1·20

See also Nos. 2958/61.

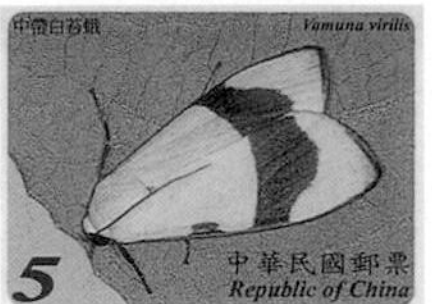

759 *Vamuna virilis*

2003. Moths. Multicoloured.

2904	$5 Type **759**	40	25
2905	$5 *Antitrygodes divisaria perturbata*	40	25
2906	$12 *Sinna extrema*	95	60
2907	$20 *Thyas juno*	1·60	1·00

760 *Sympetrum eroticum ardens*

2003. Dragonflies. Multicoloured.

2908	$5 Type **760**	40	25
2909	$5 *Acisome panorpoides*	40	25
2910	$10 *Anax parthenope Julius* (horiz)	85	50
2911	$17 *Rhyothemis variegata aria* (horiz)	1·40	85
MS2912	80×135 mm. Nos. 2908/11	3·25	1·80

761 Two Cranes

2002. Greetings Stamps. Multicoloured.

2913	$3.50 Type **761**	30	15
2914	$3.50 Carved ducks	30	15
2915	$3.50 Decorative fish	30	15
2916	$3.50 Bamboo	30	15
2917	$3.50 Carved eagle	30	15
2918	$5 Vase and knot	40	25
2919	$5 Type **761**	40	25
2920	$5 As No. 2914	40	25
2921	$5 Three jars	40	25
2922	$5 Flowers in vase	40	25
2923	$5 Carved golden dragon	40	25
2924	$5 As No. 2915	40	25
2925	$5 As No. 2916	40	25
2926	$5 Child riding mythical animal	40	25
2927	$5 As No. 2917	40	25
2928	$12 As No. 2922	95	60

762 White-throated Laughing Thrush

2003. Birds (7th series). Showing illustrations from the Ching Dynasty Bird Manual. Multicoloured.

2929	$5 Type **762**	40	25
2930	$5 Great mynah	40	25
2931	$12 Yellow-legged button quail	95	60
2932	$25 Crested lark	2·00	1·20

763 Chungshan Park, Taichung

2003. Landscapes. Multicoloured.

2933	$5 Type **763**	40	25
2934	$5 Dongshan river, Ilan	40	25
2935	$11 Hills, Tianliao ("Moon-scape")	85	50
2936	$20 Sansiantai coral reef, Chenggong ("Terrace of the Three Immortals")	1·60	1·00

764 Building Central Highway

2003. 25th Anniv of Veteran's Day. Multicoloured.

2937	$5 Type **764**	40	25
2938	$25 Veterans and retirement building	1·90	1·20

765 "Back Yard" (Lu Tie-jhou)

2003. Taiwanese Artists (2nd series). Multicoloured.

2939	$5 Type **765**	40	25
2940	$5 "Jioufen, A Goldmine Town" (Lin Ke-gong)	40	25
2941	$10 "Leisure" (Chen Jin) (horiz)	85	50
2942	$20 "East Gate" (Li Ze-fan) (horiz)	1·70	1·00

766 Monkey

2003. New Year Greetings. "Year of the Monkey". Multicoloured.

2943	$3.50 Type **766**	30	15
2944	$13 Monkey enclosed in heart	1·00	65
MS2945	78×102 mm. Nos. 2943/4, each ×2	2·75	1·60

767 Fumaroles and Spring, Yangmingshan Hot Springs

2003. Thermal Springs. Multicoloured.

2946	$5 Type **767**	40	25
2947	$5 Nanfangao bridge and cold spring, Suao	40	25
2948	$10 Shuei Huo Tang Yuan (water and gas) and hot spring, Guanziling	85	50
2949	$25 Lighthouse and hot spring, Green Island	2·00	1·20
MS2950	102×146 mm. Nos. 2946/9	3·75	2·20

768 Jhonggang Interchange

2004. Completion of National Highway Number Three. Multicoloured.

2951	$5 Type **768**	40	25
2952	$25 Cingshuei service area	1·90	1·20
MS2953	125×60 mm. $20 Cingshuei service area (enlarged) (80×30 mm)	1·70	85

769 *Lilium formosanum*

2004. Flowering Bulbs. Taiwan Flower Expo, Changhua (MS2957). Multicoloured.

2954	$5 Type **769**	40	25
2955	$5 Hippeastrum hybrid	40	25
2956	$12 Freesia hybrid	1·00	60
MS2957	102×146 mm. Nos. 2954/6	1·90	1·10

2004. Eight Immortals (2nd series). As T 758. Multicoloured.

2958	$5 Han Siang-zih playing flute	40	25
2959	$5 He Sian-gu holding lotus blossom	40	25
2960	$10 Cao Guo-jiou holding tablet	85	50
2961	$25 Lan Cai-he holding flower basket	2·00	1·20

770 Stylized People enclosed in Heart

2004. Centenary of Taiwan Red Cross Society. Multicoloured.

2962	$5 Type **770**	40	25
2963	$5 Stylized Red Cross workers	40	25

Nos. 2962/3 were issued together, se-tenant, forming a composite design.

771 "Young Girl from Lu Kai" (Yan Shui-long)

2004. Taiwanese Artists (3rd series). Multicoloured.

2964	$5 Type **771**	40	25
2965	$5 "Old Street in Taipeh" (Yang Sang-lang) (horiz)	40	25
2966	$10 "Farmers" (Lee Shih-chiao) (horiz)	85	50
2967	$20 "Fish Shop" (Liu Chi-hsiang)	1·70	1·00

772 *Parantica sita niphonica*

2004. Butterflies. Multicoloured.

2968	$5 Type **772**	40	25
2969	$5 *Choaspes benjaminii formosanus*	40	25
2970	$17 *Junonia aimana*	1·50	85
2971	$20 *Artipe eryx horiella*	1·70	1·00

773 Outdoor Performance ("Eight General")

2004. Yijhen (folk activities). Multicoloured.

2972	$5 Type **773**	40	25
2973	$5 Martial arts display ("Song Jiang Battle Array")	40	25
2974	$11 Drum dance	85	50
2975	$25 Stilt walking	2·00	1·20

774 President Chen Shui-bian and Vice President Ms. Hsui-lien Annette Lu

2004. Inauguration of President Chen Shui-bian and Vice President Ms. Hsui-lien Annette Lu. Showing the president and vice president. Multicoloured.

2976	$5 Type **774**	40	25
2977	$5 Clasped hands	40	25
2978	$5 Festival	40	25
2979	$5 Train and Taipeh skyline	40	25
MS2980	125×60 mm. $12 Train and Taipeh skyline (different) (80×30 mm)	1·00	60

775 Harry Potter (Daniel Radcliffe) playing Quidditch (game)

2004. Harry Potter and the "Prisoner of Azkaban" (film based on book by J. K. Rowling). Two sheets, each 190×130 mm containing T 775 and similar horiz designs. Multicoloured.

MS2981	(a) $5 ×6, Type **775**; In the storm; Harry and Hermione Granger (Emma Watson) riding Buckbeak the Hippogriff; Harry and Hogwarts towers; Harry repelling Dementors; Harry with wand extended. (b) $5 ×6, Hedwig (Harry's owl) delivering Owl Post; Hedwig; Harry riding Buckbeak; Buckbeak; Harry and *Monster Book of Monsters*; Crookshanks (Hermione's cat)	8·50	5·00

776 Keelung Station

2004. Old Train Stations (1st series). Multicoloured.

2982	$5 Type **776**	40	25
2983	$5 Taipeh	40	25
2984	$15 Hsinchu	1·20	75
2985	$25 Taichung	2·00	1·30

See also Nos. 3062/5.

777 Iron Fort, Nangan

2004. Tourism. Matsu Islands. Multicoloured.

2986	$5 Type **777**	40	25
2987	$5 Cinbi village, Beigan	40	25
2988	$9 Fujheng village, Tungchu	75	50
2989	$25 Lienyuyikeng (virtuous woman's fjord), Tungyin	2·00	1·30

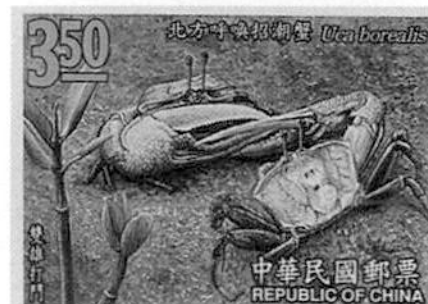

778 *Uca borealis*

2004. Crabs. Multicoloured.

2990	$3.50 Type **778**	30	15
2991	$3.50 *Uca formosensis*	30	15
2992	$5 *Uca arcuata*	40	25
2993	$25 *Uca latea*	2·00	1·30

779 Woman playing Lute (detail)

2004. ROCUPEX'04, International Stamp Exhibition, Taipei. Sheet 80×125 mm containing T 779 and similar vert design. Multicoloured.

MS2994	$5 Type **779**; $25 Seated scholar and standing woman	2·30	1·50

The stamps and margin of **MS**2994 form a composite design of "Listening to the Lute" (painting by Li Sing).

780 Sun Moon Lake

2004. TAIPEH 2005 International Stamp Exhibition. Sheet 103×146 mm containing T 780 and similar horiz design. Multicoloured.

MS2995	$5 Type **780**; $25 Mount Ali	2·30	1·50

781 Children riding Dove, Symbols of Peace and War (Yang Chih-yuan)

2004. International Day of Peace. Winning Design in Lions Club International Peace Poster Competition.

2996	**781**	$15 multicoloured	1·20	75

782 Dear Daniel

2004. 30th Anniv of Hello Kitty (character created by Yamaguchi Yuko). Two sheets, each 130×100 containing T 782 and similar multicoloured designs.

MS2997	(a) $5 Type **782** (boyfriend); $15 Hello Kitty holding teacup. (b) $5 Hello Kitty and bird (60×40 mm); Dear Daniel wearing purple jacket (40×60 mm)	3·25	2·00

The stamps and margins of **MS**2997a form composite designs of a tea table and Taipeh 101 Tower and **MS**2997b a composite design of feeding the birds on the waterfront.

783 Ship

2004. Greetings Stamps. Multicoloured.

2998	$3.50 Type **783** ("Sea of smooth sailing")	30	15
2999	$3.50 Lions ("Two lions bring good fortune")	30	15
3000	$3.50 Goats ("Three suns (goats) of auspiciousness")	30	15
3001	$3.50 Vase of flowers ("Safety in all four seasons")	30	15
3002	$3.50 Stylised bats ("Five blessings at the door")	30	15
3003	$3.50 Fruit ("Six is silky smooth")	30	15
3004	$3.50 Couple ("Married for seven lives")	30	15
3005	$3.50 Embroidered panel and carving ("Eight immortals wish for your longevity")	30	15
3006	$3.50 Dragon ("Nine means success")	30	15
3007	$3.50 Food ("Ten is all round perfection")	30	15
3008	$5 As Type **783**	40	25
3009	$5 As No. 2999	40	25
3010	$5 As No. 3000	40	25
3011	$5 As No. 3001	40	25
3012	$5 As No. 3002	40	25
3013	$5 As No. 3003	40	25
3014	$5 As No. 3004	40	25
3015	$5 As No. 3005	40	25
3016	$5 As No. 3006	40	25
3017	$5 As No. 3007	40	25

784 University Building Facade and Old Medical College Gate

2004. 50th Anniv of Kaohsiung Medical University. Multicoloured.

3018	$5 Type **784**	40	25
3019	$5 Mosquito, snake, scholar and laboratory beaker	40	25

786 Women's Taekwondo

2004. Olympic Games, Athens (2nd series). Medal Winners. Multicoloured.

3024	$5 Type **786** (Chen Shih-hsin) (gold medal)	40	25
3025	$5 Men's Taekwondo (Chu Mu-yen) (gold medal) (horiz)	40	25
3026	$9 Archery team (men's silver medal and women's bronze medal) (horiz)	75	50
3027	$12 Medal winners	95	60

787 Black-billed Spoonbills in Flight

2004. Endangered Species. Black-billed Spoonbill (Platalea minor). Multicoloured.

3028	$2.50 Type **787**	20	15
3029	$2.50 Standing on one leg	20	15
3030	$15 With raised wings	1·30	60
3031	$25 Feeding	2·00	1·20
MS3032	120×60 mm. $20 Six Spoonbills (80×30 mm)	1·70	85

The stamp and margin of No. **MS**3032 form a composite design of Spoonbills and lake.

788 Yen Chai-kan

2004. Birth Centenary of Yen Chai-kan (former president).

3033	**788**	$12 multicoloured	1·00	50

789 Decorated Lantern

2004. New Year Greetings. "Year of the Rooster". Multicoloured.

3034	$3.50 Type **789**	30	15
3035	$13 Lanterns and stylised rooster	1·00	60
MS3036	110×76 mm. $5 Lanterns, rooster, hen and chicks (46×26 mm)	40	25

790 Prefecture Hall, Jhuluo

2004. 300th Anniv of Jhuluo (Chiaya). Multicoloured.

3037	$5 Type **790**	40	25
3038	$5 East Gate	40	25

791 Crane (1st rank)

2005. Cing Dynasty Official Court Dress Designs. Showing bird designs associated with court rank. Multicoloured.

3039	$3.50 Type **791**	20	15
3040	$3.50 Pheasant (2nd rank)	20	15
3041	$5 Peacock (3rd rank)	30	25
3042	$25 Goose (4th rank)	1·80	1·20

792

793

794 **795**

2005. Greetings Stamps. Internet Shorthand.

3043	**792**	$5 multicoloured	30	25
3044	**793**	$5 multicoloured	30	25
3045	**794**	$5 multicoloured	30	25
3046	**795**	$5 multicoloured	30	25

796 Map of Taiwan and Centenary Emblem

2005. Centenary of Rotary International. Mult.

3047	$5 Type **796**	30	25
3048	$12 Dove and emblem	85	60

797 *Kandelia obovata*

2005. Mangroves. Multicoloured.

3049	$3.50 Type **797**	20	15
3050	$3.50 *Rhizophora stylosa*	20	15
3051	$5 *Avicennia marina*	30	25
3052	$5 *Lumnitzera racemosa*	30	25

798 Longshan Temple, Mengjia

2005. Architecture. Multicoloured.

3053	$5 Type **798**	30	25
3054	$5 Lin Ben Yuan's Garden, Banciao	30	25
3055	$13 Chaotian Temple, Beigang	85	65
3056	$15 Anping Fort, Tainan	95	75

799 Ceiling, Lognshan Temple

2005. TAIPEI 2005 International Stamp Exhibition (1st issue). Sheet 102×146 mm containing T 799 and similar multicoloured design.

MS3057	$5 Type **799**; $25 Puppets (horiz)	1·90	1·50

See also Nos. 3074 and **MS**3075.

800 *Rhinomuraena quaesita*

2005. Fish. Multicoloured.

3058	$5 Type **800**	30	25
3059	$5 *Pomacanthus semicirculatus*	30	25
3060	$12 *Forcipiger flavissimus*	75	60
3061	$25 *Pterois volitans*	1·60	1·30

2005. Old Train Stations (2nd series). As T 776. Multicoloured.

3062	$5 Changhua	30	25
3063	$5 Chiayi	30	25
3064	$15 Tainan	95	75
3065	$25 Kaohsiung	1·60	1·30

801 Mayhem in Fengyi Pavilion

2005. Classical Literature. Romance of the Three Kingdoms by Luo Guanzhong (3rd series). Multicoloured.

3066	$3.50 Type **801**	20	15
3067	$3.50 Deterring the enemy	20	15
3068	$5 Releasing Tsao Tsao	30	25
3069	$20 A trick in the bag	1·30	1·00
MS3070	140×100 mm. Nos. 3066/69	2·00	1·60

802 Clasped Hands

2005. Lifeline (telephone counselling service).

3071	**802**	$12 multicoloured	75	60

803 Albert Einstein

2005. Centenary of the Publication of "Special Theory of Relativity" by Albert Einstein.

3072	**803**	$15 multicoloured	95	75

804 Mickey holding Ship's Wheel (*Steamboat Willie*)

2005. Mickey Mouse (character created by Walt Disney). Two sheets, each 140×90 containing T 804 and similar vert designs showing films. Multicoloured.

MS3073 (a) $5 Type **804**; $25 As magician (*Fantasia*). (b) $5 Two Mickeys (*Prince and the Pauper*); $25 Decorating tree (*Twice Upon a Christmas*)		6·25	6·25

2005. TAIPEI 2005 International Stamp Exhibition (2nd issue).

3074	**802**	$15 multicoloured	95	75

2005. TAIPEI 2005 International Stamp Exhibition (3rd issue). Six sheets, each 103×146 mm containing T 803 and similar multicoloured designs.

MS3075 (a) Conservation (circular). $5 Type **803**; $25 Formosan rock monkey. (b) Technology (rectangular). $5 Microscope (29×37 mm); $25 DNA strands (37×29 mm). (c) Flora (triangular). $5 Flowers (52×32 mm); $25 Fruit (52×32 mm). (d) Festivals (rectangular). $5 Ear shooting ceremony (30×40 mm); $25 Dragon boat race (40×30 mm). (e) Cuisine (rectangular). $5 "Buddha jumping over wall" (40×30 mm); $25 Rice cakes (40×30 mm). (f) Ocean life (oval). $5 Angelfish (43×33 mm); $25 Coral (43×33 mm)	1·90	1·90

2005. Classical Literature. Journey to the West (Ming dynasty novel). Multicoloured.

3076	$3.50 Type **804**	20	15
3077	$3.50 Baby in River	20	15
3078	$5 Making pass at Chang E	30	25
3079	$20 Taming Monster of River Flowing Sands	1·30	1·00

See also Nos. 2429/32.

808 "Loyalty and Filial Piety"

2005. Kaohsiung 2005 International Stamp Exhibition. Sheet 102×146 mm containing T 808 and similar multicoloured design.

MS3080 $5 Type **808**; $25 Ruyi sceptre (horiz)	5·00	5·00

809 Triwizard Cup

2005. Harry Potter and The Goblet of Fire (film based on book by J. K. Rowling). Two sheets, each 190×130 mm containing T 809 and similar horiz designs. Multicoloured.

MS3081 (a) $5×6, Type **809**; Harry underwater; Harry and Hungarian Horntail; Harry summons his Firebolt; Golden egg; Harry negotiates the maze. (b) $5×6, Hungarian Horntail; Harry riding his Firebolt; Nagini; Grindylow; Fawkes the phoenix; Merchieftainess	8·50	8·50

810 Siberian Husky

2005. Pets (1st series). Multicoloured.

3082	$3.50 Type **810**	20	15
3083	$5 Golden retriever	30	25
3084	$12 Himalayan cat	1·00	50
3085	$25 Scottish fold cat	1·80	1·20

See also Nos. 3096/99, 3155/58 and 3183/6.

811 Dog

2006. New Year. Year of the Dog. Multicoloured.

3086	$3.50 Type **811**	20	15
3087	$13 Calligraphy and dog	85	65
MS3088	110×76 mm. $12 Three dogs (50×30 mm)	1·20	1·20

812 Preparing Tea Set and Warming Pot

2006. Tea Ceremony. Multicoloured.

3089	$5 Type **812**	40	40
3090	$5 Placing leaves in pot and rinsing	40	40
3091	$5 Pouring hot water over pot and warming cups	40	40
3092	$5 Drying pot and pouring tea	40	40
3093	$5 Smelling and drinking brewed tea	40	40

813 Taipei 101 Tower

2006. Taipei 101 Tower (world's tallest building). Multicoloured.

3094	$5 Type **813**	30	25
3095	$12 Tower at night	75	60

2006. Pets (2nd series). As T 810. Multicoloured.

3096	$2.50 Labrador	15	10
3097	$7 St. Bernard	40	30
3098	$10 Siamese cat	60	50
3099	$32 Persian cat	1·90	1·40

814 Juvenile and Parent

2006. King Penguins (Aptenodytes patagonicus). Multicoloured.

3100	$5 Type **814**	30	25
3101	$5 Courtship	30	25
3102	$9 Swimming and diving (horiz)	55	45
3103	$12 Gliding and preening (horiz)	75	60
MS3104	120×60 mm $15 Five penguins (80×30 mm)	1·50	1·00

815 Storks

2006. Winning Entries in Children's Drawing Competition. Multicoloured.

3105	$5 Type **815**	35	30
3106	$5 Couple wearing striped tops and headdresses	35	30
3107	$5 Pheasants	35	30
3108	$5 Chinese opera characters	35	30
3109	$5 Fishermen	35	30
3110	$5 Giant marrows	35	30
3111	$5 Decorating lanterns	35	30
3112	$5 Bridge	35	30
3113	$5 Steam train	35	30
3114	$5 Sunflowers	35	30
3115	$5 Aborigines	35	30
3116	$5 Children and ladder	35	30
3117	$5 Women wearing feathered headdresses and chickens	35	30
3118	$5 Musicians and dancers	35	30
3119	$5 Mythical animals	35	30
3120	$5 Cats	35	30
3121	$5 Children riding cow	35	30
3122	$5 Whale	35	30
3123	$5 Acrobats	35	30
3124	$5 Coach	35	30

816 *Diaphanes citrinus*

2006. Fireflies. Multicoloured.

3125	$5 Type **816**	35	30
3126	$5 *Pyrocoelia analis*	35	30
3127	$5 *Diaphanes formosus*	35	30
3128	$5 *Diaphanes niveus*	35	30

817 Landscape and Roadway (½-size illustration)

2006. Completion of Nangang—Suao Section of National Highway Number Five. Sheet 125×55 mm.

MS3129 **817** $12 multicoloured	1·20	1·20

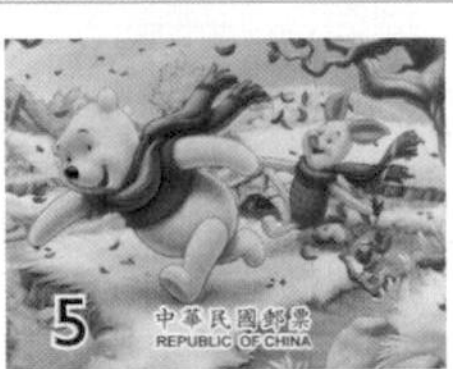

818 Winnie the Pooh and Piglet

2006. Winnie the Pooh (Walt Disney cartoon character (originally created by A. A. Milne)). Two sheets, each 140×90 mm containing T 818 and similar horiz designs. Multicoloured.

MS3130 (a) $5 Type **818**; $25 Pooh and Tigger fishing. (b) $5 Pooh pushing Piglet in wheel barrow; $25 Pooh, Piglet and Tigger floating in rubber ring Set of 2 sheets	3·50	3·50

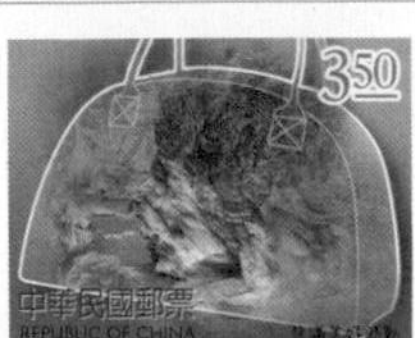

819 Bag Outline containing Coastline

2006. Travel. Multicoloured.

3131	$3.50 Type **819**	20	15
3132	$3.50 Camera outline containing boat	20	15
3133	$3.50 Notebook outline containing bridge	20	15
3134	$3.50 Windsurfer outline containing rock	20	15
3135	$3.50 Heart outline containing steam train	20	15
3136	$5 As Type **819**	30	25
3137	$5 As No. 3132	30	25
3138	$5 As No. 3133	30	25
3139	$5 As No. 3134	30	25
3140	$5 As No. 3135	30	25

820 *Amphiron ocellaris*

2006. Fish. Multicoloured.

3141	$5 Type **820**	30	25
3142	$5 *Zanclus cornutus*	30	25
3143	$12 *Coris gaimard*	30	25
3144	$12 *Oxycirrhites typus*	30	25

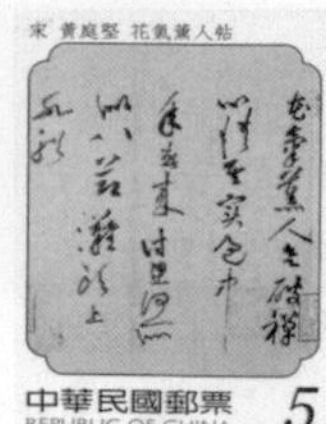

821 Poem in Seven-character Regulated Verse (Huang T'ing-Chien)

2006. Calligraphy and Bird Paintings. Multicoloured.

3145	$5 Type **821**	35	30
3146	$9 Calligraphy on silk (Mi Fu)	60	50
3147	$12 "Magpie and Hare" (detail) (Ts'ui Po)	80	65
3148	$15 "Magpie and Hare" (detail) (different)	1·10	80
MS3149	76×142 mm. $12 As No. 3147; $15 As No. 3148	2·00	2·00

The stamps and margins of **MS**3149 form the painting "Magpie and Hare" (Ts'ui Po).

822 *Crocothemis servilia servilia*

2006. Dragonflies. Multicoloured.

3150	$5 Type **822**	30	25
3151	$5 *Orthetrum pruinosum neglectum* (vert)	30	25
3152	$12 *Diplacodes trivialis* (vert)	75	60
3153	$12 *Orthetrum sabina Sabina*	75	60
MS3154	80×135 mm. As Nos. 3150/3	2·20	2·20

The stamps and margins of **MS**3154 form a composite design of river and meadow.

2006. Pets (3rd series). As T 810. Multicoloured.

3155	$1 Yorkshire terrier	10	10
3156	$9 Pomeranian	55	45
3157	$10 Abyssinian cat	60	50
3158	$32 Norwegian forest cat	1·90	1·40

823 Hang Gliding

2006. Outdoor Activities. Multicoloured.

3159	$3.50 Type **823**	20	15
3160	$3.50 Paragliding (vert)	20	15
3161	$12 Micro-light	75	60
3162	$15 Parasailing (vert)	95	75

824 Fairy Pitta

2006. Fairy Pitta (Pitta nympha). Multicoloured.

3163	$5 Type **824**	35	20
3164	$5 Perched on branch (vert)	35	20
3165	$12 Parent and nestlings	75	60
3166	$12 Catching insect (vert)	75	60
MS3167	135×80 mm. As Nos. 3163/6	2·20	2·20

The stamps and margins of **MS**3167 form a composite design of woodland glade.

2006. Marine Mammals. As T 742. Multicoloured.

3168 $5 *Stenella attenuate* 35 20
3169 $5 *Stenella longirostris* 35 20
3170 $10 *Feresa attenuate* 60 50
3171 $15 *Physter macrocephalus* 60 50
MS3172 135×80 mm. As Nos. 3168/71 1·90 1·90

825 *Ludwigia octovalvis*

2006. Native Flowers. Multicoloured.

3173 $5 Type **825** 35 30
3174 $5 *Hygrophila pogonocalyx* (vert) 35 30
3175 $5 *Titanotrichum oldhamii* (vert) 35 30

826 Jongshan Building, Yangmingshan National Park

2006. Tourism. Multicoloured.

3176 $5 Type **826** 30 25
3177 $5 Taroko Gorge (vert) 30 25
3178 $9 Queen's Head rock, Yeliou (vert) 55 45
3179 $12 Sun Moon Lake 75 60

827 Pig

2006. New Year. Year of the Pig. Multicoloured.

3180 $3.50 Type **827** 20 15
3181 $13 Drums 85 65
MS3182 110×76 mm. $12 Piglets (50×30 mm) 75 75

2006. Pets (4th series). As T 810. Multicoloured.

3183 50c. Border collie 10 10
3184 $13 Beagle 85 65
3185 $17 American shorthair cat 1·00 80
3186 $34 Maine coon cat 2·10 1·90

828 Locomotive 700T

2006. Inauguration of High Speed Railway. Multicoloured.

3187 $12 Type **828** 75 60
3188 $12 Hsinchu Station 75 60

829 *Phaius tankervilleae*

2007. Flowers. Orchids. Multicoloured.

3189 $3.50 Type **829** 20 15
3190 $5 *Spiranthes sinensis* 30 25
3191 $12 *Vanda* 75 60
3192 $25 *Cattleya* 1·60 1·30

830 Earring

2007. Cing Dynasty Jewellery. Multicoloured.

3193 $5 Type **830** 25 20
3194 $5 Gilt hair pin 25 20
3195 $12 Fingernail guard 65 50
3196 $25 Ring 1·30 95

831 Heart and Stylized Couple

2007. St. Valentine's Day.

3197 **831** $5 multicoloured 30 25
3198 **831** $20 multicoloured 1·30 1·00

832 Cilin (1st rank)

2007. Official Cing Dynasty Military Dress Designs. Designs associated with military rank. Multicoloured.

3199 $3.50 Type **832** 20 15
3200 $3.50 Lion (2nd rank) 20 15
3201 $5 Leopard (3rd rank) 30 25
3202 $25 Tiger (4th rank) 1·40 1·10

No. 3203 and Type **833** have been left for 'Memorial Museum' issued on 28 February 2007, not yet received.

834 Kanjin Bridge, Taoyuan

2007. Bridges. Multicoloured.

3204 $5 Type **834** 30 25
3205 $5 Fusing Bridge, Luofu 30 25
3206 $12 MacArthur Second Bridge, Taipei 65 50
3207 $15 Dajhih Bridge, Taipei 80 60

835 Lesser Panda (red panda)

2007. Lesser Panda (Ailurus fulgens). Multicoloured.

3208 $5 Type **835** 30 25
3209 $5 Asleep 30 25
3210 $10 Scratching (vert) 55 40
3211 $10 Foraging (vert) 55 40
MS3212 80×105 mm. $12 Pandas (40×50 mm) 80 80

836 Dharma Drum Monastery

837 Chung Tai Chan Monastery

838 Fo Guang Shan Monastery

839 Tzu Chi Foundation

2007. Buddhist Architecture.

3213 **836** $5 multicoloured 35 30
3214 **837** $5 multicoloured 35 30
3215 **838** $5 multicoloured 35 30
3216 **839** $5 multicoloured 35 30

840 Dahlia

2007. Greetings Stamps. Language of Flowers. Multicoloured.

3217 $3.50 Type **840** (gratitude) 20 15
3218 $3.50 Iris (trust) 20 15
3219 $3.50 Clematis and ladybirds (elegance) 20 15
3220 $3.50 Tung blossom and moths (joy) 20 15
3221 $3.50 Rose (true love) 20 15
3222 $3.50 Sunflower (adoration) 20 15
3223 $3.50 Bird of Paradise (happiness) 20 15
3224 $3.50 Lotus (purity) 20 15
3225 $3.50 Ox-eye daisy (vitality) 20 15
3226 $3.50 Balloon flower and dragon fly (chastity) 20 15
3227 $5 As Type **840** 30 25
3228 $5 As No. 3215 30 25
3229 $5 As No. 3216 30 25
3230 $5 As No. 3217 30 25
3231 $5 As No. 3218 30 25
3232 $5 As No. 3219 30 25
3233 $5 As No. 3220 30 25
3234 $5 As No. 3221 30 25
3235 $5 As No. 3222 30 25
3236 $5 As No. 3223 30 25

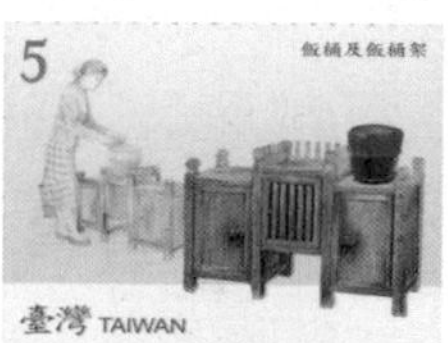

841 Rice Bucket and Shelves

2007. Food Utensils. Multicoloured.

3237 $5 Type **841** 30 25
3238 $5 Wooden steamer 30 25
3239 $12 Rice baskets, rattan and wood 65 50
3240 $12 Bowls, chopsticks and container 65 50

842 *Paphiopedilum*

2007. Orchids. Multicoloured.

3241 $1 Type **842** 15 10
3242 $2.50 *Phalaenopsis Aphrodite* 15 10
3243 $10 *Dendrobium* 60 50
3244 $32 *Oncidium* 1·40 1·10

843 Page, Pen, Flower and Rainbow

2007. 20th Anniv of Lifting of Martial Law.

3245 **843** $12 multicoloured 65 50

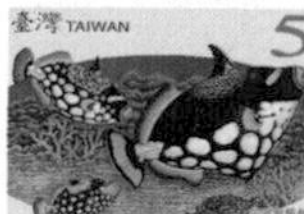

844 *Balistoides conspicillum*

2007. Fish. Multicoloured.

3246 $5 Type **844** 30 25
3247 $5 *Nemateleotris magnifica* 30 25
3248 $12 *Paracanthurus hepatus* 65 50
3249 $25 *Cetoscarus bicolour* 1·40 1·10

845 Chiang Wei-shui

2007. Chiang Wei-shui (politician) Commemoration.

3250 **845** $25 deep brown 1·30 1·10

846 Taipei Tower and Map

2007. 1st Taiwan–African Heads of State Summit.

3251 **846** $12 multicoloured 65 50

847 Horses and Attendants

2007. 'Eighteen Scholars of the T'ang' (painting by Emperor Hui-tsung). Sheet 236×120 mm containing T 847 and similar horiz designs showing parts of the painting.

MS3252 (1) $5 Type **847**; (2) $5 Riders, horses and attendants amongst trees; (3) $5 Laden horse, attendants and scholar; (4) $5 Central figure and three groups of scholars (51×30 mm.); (5) $5 Attendants preparing tea (36×30 mm.); (6) $5 Listening to music (36×30 mm.); (7) $5 Seated around table; (8) $5 Cranes; (9) $5 Raised platform (51×30 mm.); (10) $5 Trees, plants and inscription 2·50 2·50

The stamps of No. **MS**3252 were arranged in two horizontal strips of five stamps, the identification numbers given are from right to left (1/5) upper strip, (6/10) lower strip.

848 Doves and Envelope

2007. 'Feelings'.

3253 **848** $5 gold, silver and vermilion 45 25

849 *Marchia loebbeckei*

2007. Shells. Multicoloured.

3254 $5 Type **849** 30 25
3255 $5 *Harpa major* 30 25
3256 $12 *Cypraea aurantium* 65 50
3257 $12 *Epitonium scalare* 65 50

850 *Ascocentrum*

2007. Orchids. Multicoloured.

No.	Description	Mint	Used
3258	$7 Type **850**	45	35
3259	$9 *Arundina graminifolia*	55	45
3260	$15 *Vanda teres*	85	65
3261	$20 *Epidendrum*	1·10	85

851 *Pericrocotus solaris* (grey-chinned minivet)

2007. Birds. Multicoloured.

No.	Description	Mint	Used
3262	$3.50 Type **851**	20	15
3263	$5 *Parus varius* (varied tit)	30	25
3264	$12 *Luscinia calliope* (Siberian rubythroat)	65	55
3265	$25 *Phoenicurus auroreus* (Daurian redstart)	1·40	1·10

852 Speed Walking

2007. Leisure Sports. Multicoloured.

No.	Description	Mint	Used
3266	$5 Type **852**	30	25
3267	$5 Cycling	30	25
3268	$12 Skate boarding	65	50
3269	$25 In-line skating	1·40	1·10

853 '100', Doves and Emblems

2007. Centenary of Scouting.

No.	Type	Description	Mint	Used
3270	**853**	$12 multicoloured	70	55

854 Rat

2007. New Year. Year of the Rat. Multicoloured.

No.	Description	Mint	Used
3271	$3.50 Type **854**	25	15
3272	$13 Rat (different)	75	60
MS3273	110×76 mm. $12 Decorated rats (64×40 mm)	1·20	1·20

855 Lei Chen

2007. Personalities. Political Reformers.

No.	Type	Description	Mint	Used
3274	**855**	$5 brown	20	15
3275	-	$5 olive	20	15
3276	-	$5 purple	20	15
3277	-	$5 black	20	15

DESIGNS: 3274, Type **855**; 3275, Fu Jheng; 3276, Kuo Yu Sing; 3277, Huang Hsin Chieh.

856 Liou Family Compound in Shangfangliao, Sinpu, Hsinchu County

857 Lin Family Mansion in Banciao, Taipei County

858 Li Teng-fang Compound in Dasi, Taoyuan County

859 Siao Family Compound in Jiadong, Pingtung County

2008. Traditional Houses.

No.	Type	Description	Mint	Used
3278	**856**	$5 multicoloured	25	20
3279	**857**	$5 multicoloured	25	20
3280	**858**	$5 multicoloured	25	20
3281	**859**	$12 multicoloured	65	55

860 *Dicrurus aeneus* (bronzed drongo)

2008. Birds. Multicoloured.

No.	Description	Mint	Used
3282	$1 Type **860**	15	15
3283	$2.50 *Lanius schach* (long-tailed shrike)	15	15
3284	$10 *Dendrocitta formosae* (grey treepie)	60	45
3285	$32 *Pycnonotus sinensis* (light-vented bulbul)	1·50	1·20

861 Mirror Man

2008. Regional Opera–Taiwanese Puppets (The Scholar Knight of Yunjhou).

No.	Description	Mint	Used
3286	$5 Type **861**	20	15
3287	$5 Old Oddball	20	15
3288	$5 Shih Yan-wun	20	15
3289	$5 Dragon Lady of the Bitter Sea	20	15
MS3290	145×88 mm. Nos. 3286/9	95	95

The stamps and margins of **MS**3290 form a composite design.

862 *Plum Blossoms and Solitary Bird* (Pien Wen-Chin)

2008. Taipei 2008–Asian International Stamp Exhibition. Multicoloured.

No.	Description	Mint	Used
3291	$5 Type **862**	30	25
3292	$9 *Apricot Blossoms and Peacocks* (Lu chi)	40	30
3293	$13 *Wild Duck by Brook* (Ch'en Lin)	70	55
3294	$15 *Bamboo and Shrike* (Li An-chung)	80	60
MS3295	145×102 mm. Nos. 3291/4	2·20	1·70

863 *Syrmaticus mikado* (mikado pheasant)

2008

No.	Type	Description	Mint	Used
3296	**863**	$25 multicoloured	1·40	1·10

864 Sheldon

2008. Characters from Finding Nemo (film by Walt Disney/Pixar). Two sheets 140×90 mm containing each T 864 and similar multicoloured designs.

No.	Description	Mint	Used
MS3297	(a) $5×5, Type **864**; Squirt; Tad; Nemo; Peach. (b) $5×5, Turtles; Dory (26×34 mm); Bubbles; Nemo (34×26 mm); Pearl	3·00	3·00

The stamps and margins of **MS**3297a/b, respectively, form composite designs.

865 *Thelocactus bicolor*

2008. Cacti. Multicoloured.

No.	Description	Mint	Used
3298	$5 Type **865**	35	30
3299	$5 *Hylocereus undatus*	35	30
3300	$12 *Rhipsalidopsis gaertneri*	70	55

866 Wurih Bridge

2008. Bridges. Multicoloured.

No.	Description	Mint	Used
3301	$5 Type **866**	30	25
3302	$5 Jilu	30	25
3303	$12 Shueiyun	65	50
3304	$15 Sindong	80	60

867 Pres. Ma Ying-jeou and Vice-Pres. Vincent Siew

2008. Inauguration of President Ma Ying-jeou and Vice-President Vincent Siew. Designs showing President and Vice President. Multicoloured.

No.	Description	Mint	Used
3305	$5 Type **867**	30	25
3306	$5 Wearing casual dress	30	25
3307	$12 With raised fists	60	50
3308	$15 Pres. Ma holding children and Vice Pres. Siew	80	60
MS3309	140×90 mm. Nos. 3305/8	2·00	2·00

868 Yellow Tiger Flag

2008. Centenary of National Museum. Multicoloured.

No.	Description	Mint	Used
3310	$5 Type **868**	30	25
3311	$25 Jheng Cheng-gong	1·40	1·10
MS3312	131×67 mm. Size 34×26 mm. As Nos. 3310/11	1·70	1·10

The stamps and margins of **MS**3312 form a composite design.

869 *Neolucanus swinhoei*

2008. Beetles. Multicoloured.

No.	Description	Mint	Used
3313	$5 Type **869**	30	25
3314	$5 *Dorcus schenklingi*	30	25
3315	$10 *Lucanus datunensis*	55	40
3316	$12 *Cyclommatus asahinai*	65	50

870 *Streptopelia orientalis* (Oriental turtle dove)

2008. Birds. Multicoloured.

No.	Description	Mint	Used
3317	$7 Type **870**	40	30
3318	$15 *Passer montanus* (tree sparrow)	80	60
3319	$20 *Pica pica* (European magpie)	1·10	80
3320	$34 *Zosterops japonicus* (Japanese white-eye)	1·50	1·20

871 *Murex troscheli*

2008. Shells. Multicoloured.

No.	Description	Mint	Used
3321	$5 Type **871**	30	25
3322	$5 *Lambis chiragra*	30	25
3323	$12 *Spondylus regius*	65	50
3324	$12 *Cymatium pyrum*	65	50

872 Blue Magpie

2008. Endangered Species. Blue Magpie (Urocissa caerulea). Multicoloured.

No.	Description	Mint	Used
3325	$5 Type **872**	30	25
3326	$5 Family	30	25
3327	$12 In flight	65	50
3328	$12 Landing	65	50
MS3329	135×80 mm. As Nos. 3325/8	2·00	2·00

The stamps and margins of **MS**3329 form a composite design.

873 Two Hinds

2008. Bailutu (A Hundred Deer) (painting by Ignace Sichelbart). Sheet 236×120 mm containing T 873 and similar horiz designs showing parts of the painting. Multicoloured.

No.	Description	Unused	Used
MS3330	(1) $5 Type **873**; (2) $5 Herd of deer amongst trees (55×38 mm); (3) $5 Several deer in canyon (43×38 mm); (4) $5 Deer swimming in lake (51×30 mm); (5) $5 Stag following hinds from lake and small tree (37×38 mm); (6) $5 Central tree and running deer (43×38 mm); (7) $5 Stags fighting and hinds reaching into tree (43×38 mm); (8) $5 Pines, waterfall and two hinds (64×38 mm)	2·00	2·00

The stamps of No. **MS**3330 were arranged in two horizontal strips of four stamps, the identification numbers given are from right to left (1/4) upper strip, (5/8) lower strip.

The stamps of **MS**3330 form a composite design of the painting.

874 Paiwan Earthenware Pot

2008. Cultural Heritage. Multicoloured.

No.	Description	Unused	Used
3331	$5 Type 874	30	25
3332	$12 Decorated bag (Ami)	65	50
3333	$12 Man's headdress (Rukai)	65	50
3334	$25 Man's chokers (Bunun)	1·40	1·10

875 Lantern Poles

2008. Yimin Festivals. Sheet 128×156 mm containing T 875 and similar multicoloured designs.

No.	Description	Unused	Used
MS3335	$5×4, Type **875**; Sinpu Yimin Temple, Hsinchu (horiz); Pig competition (horiz); Congee (sweet)	1·30	1·30

877 Ox

2008. Chinese New Year. Year of the Ox. Multicoloured.

No.	Description	Unused	Used
3341	$3.50 Type **877**	20	15
3342	$13 Ox	70	55
MS3343	110×76 mm. $10 Ox in water (50×30 mm)	70	70

878 *Rostratula benghalensis* (greater painted snipe)

2009. Birds. Multicoloured.

No.	Description	Unused	Used
3344	50c. Type **878**	10	10
3345	$9 *Turdus poliocephalus* (island thrush)	45	15
3346	$13 *Amauromis phoenicurus* (white-breasted waterhen)	70	55
3347	$17 *Cettia acanthizoides* (yellowish-bellied bush-warbler)	75	60

879 Tuan Tuan

2009. Giant Pandas at Taipei Zoo. Multicoloured.

No.	Description	Unused	Used
3348	$5 Type **879**	35	25
3349	$9 Yuan Yuan	50	35
MS3350	90×70 mm. $25 Both pandas (50×40 mm)	1·40	1·40

880 Gift Basket

2009. Ceremonial Objects. Multicoloured.

No.	Description	Unused	Used
3351	$5 Type **880**	30	25
3352	$5 Wooden carrying box	30	25
3353	$12 Bridal sedan chair	65	50
3354	$12 Candle sticks	65	50

881 *Strombus sinuatus*

2009. Shells. Multicoloured.

No.	Description	Unused	Used
3355	$5 Type **881**	30	25
3356	$5 *Hydatina amplustre*	30	25
3357	$12 *Cymatium hepaticum*	65	50
3358	$12 *Mitra mitra*	65	50

882 *Lantana camara*

2009. Flora. Multicoloured.

No.	Description	Unused	Used
3359	$3.50 Type **882**	20	15
3360	$5 *Murraya paniculata*	30	25
3361	$12 *Tabebuia chrysantha*	60	50
3362	$25 *Hibiscus sabdariffa*	1·40	1·10

883 Central Park Station

2009. Kaohsiung Mass Rapid Transit System. Multicoloured.

No.	Description	Unused	Used
3363	$5 Type **883**	30	25
3364	$25 World Games Station	1·40	1·10

884 Chiang Ching-kuo

2009. Birth Centenary of Chiang Ching-kuo (President 1978–88). Multicoloured.

No.	Description	Unused	Used
3365	$5 Type **884**	30	25
3366	$9 Wearing 'Coolie' hat	45	30
3367	$10 Seated holding cane (horiz)	50	35
3368	$12 As older man holding child (horiz)	65	50
MS3369	125×55 mm. $25 Seated writing and standing with child (80×30 mm)	1·40	1·10

2009. Dragons and Carp (from window Longsan Temple, Lukang). As T 638.

No.	Description	Unused	Used
3370	$50 blue	2·75	1·90

885 *Papilio xuthus*

2009. Butterflies. Sheet 126×92 mm containing T 885 and similar horiz designs. Multicoloured.

No.	Description	Unused	Used
MS3371	$5 Type **885**; $5 *Troides aeacus formosanus*; $12 *Graphium agamemnon*; $12 *Papilio paris nakaharai*	1·90	1·90

886 Kaohsiung Arena

2009. World Games 2009, Kaohsiung. Multicoloured.

No.	Description	Unused	Used
3372	$5 Type **886**	30	25
3373	$12 Main Stadium	65	50
MS3374	155×85 mm. Nos. 3372/3	95	95

887 Gold Gourds

2009. Ancient Art Treasures. Multicoloured.

No.	Description	Unused	Used
3375	$5 Type **887**	30	25
3376	$5 Gold bowl	30	25
3377	$12 Jade covered round urn	65	50
3378	$12 Gilt ewer	65	50
MS3379	140×90 mm. Nos. 3375/7	1·90	1·90

888 Guningtou

2009. Tourism. Kinmen. Multicoloured.

No.	Description	Unused	Used
3380	$5 Type **888**	30	25
3381	$9 Zhaishan Tunnel	45	35
3382	$10 Qingtian Hall	50	40
3383	$10 Lake Taihu	50	40

889 *On the Way Home*

2009. Art. Paintings by Lin Yu-shan. Multicoloured.

No.	Description	Unused	Used
3384	$5 Type **889**	30	25
3385	$25 *Two Cattle*	1·40	1·10

890 *Little Girl and Her Doll*

2009. Folk Rhymes. Multicoloured.

No.	Description	Unused	Used
3386	$5 Type **890**	30	25
3387	$5 Two fish in the rain (*Thunder Shower*) (horiz)	30	25
3388	$5 Boy and rabbit riding toy train (*Train*) (horiz)	30	25
3389	$5 Toy soldiers on horseback (*Kingdom of Dolls*)	30	25

891 Badminton Player and Runner

2009. 21st Summer Deaflympics, Taipei 2009. Multicoloured.

No.	Description	Unused	Used
3390	$5 Type **891**	30	25
3391	$25 Taekwondo and tennis	1·40	1·10

892 Typhoon and Rescuers

2009. Typhoon Morakot Relief Fund. Sheet 125×80 mm containing T 892 and similar horiz designs. Multicoloured.

No.	Description	Unused	Used
MS3392	$25+$25×2, Type **892**; Digger and rescuers	5·25	5·25

The premium was for disaster relief.

893 *Calliandra emarginata*

2009. Flowers. Multicoloured.

No.	Description	Unused	Used
3393	$1 Type **893**	15	10
3394	$2.50 *Bombax ceiba*	20	15
3395	$10 *Delonix regia*	50	35
3396	$32 *Spathodea campanulata*	1·60	1·30

894 Asplenium nidus (bird's-nest fern)

2009. Ferns. Multicoloured.

No.	Description	Unused	Used
3397	$5 Type **894**	30	25
3398	$9 *Cyathea spinulosa* (large spiny tree fern)	45	30
3399	$12 *Cyathea lepifera* (flying spider-monkey tree fern)	65	50
3400	$25 *Cibotium taiwanense*	1·40	1·10
MS3401	145×90 mm. Nos. 3397/400	3·75	2·50

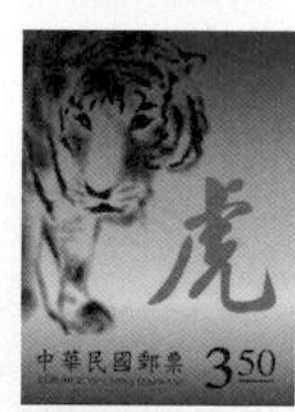

895 Tiger

2009. Chinese New Year

No.	Description	Unused	Used
3402	$5 Type **895**	30	25
3403	$13 Tiger seated	85	65
MS3404	110×76 mm. $12 Multicoloured tiger (64×40 mm)	80	

896 Globe

2009. International Anti-Corruption Day

No.	Description	Unused	Used
3405	$5 multicoloured	20	15

897 Pearl Necklace

2009. Greetings Stamps. Multicoloured.

No.	Description	Mint	Used
3407	$3.50 Type **897**	20	15
3408	$3.50 Presents	20	15
3409	$3.50 Bouquet	20	15
3410	$3.50 Sweets	20	15
3411	$3.50 Balloons	20	15
3412	$3.50 Wine glasses	20	15
3413	$3.50 Hearts	20	15
3414	$3.50 Cake	20	15
3415	$3.50 Sparklers	20	15
3416	$3.50 Four-leafed clover	20	15
3417	$5 As Type **897**	20	15
3418	$5 As No. 3408	30	25
3419	$5 As No. 3409	30	25
3420	$5 As No. 3410	30	25
3421	$5 As No. 3411	30	25
3422	$5 As No. 3412	30	25
3423	$5 As No. 3413	30	25
3424	$5 As No. 3414	30	25
3425	$5 As No. 3415	30	25
3426	$5 As No. 3416	30	25

898 *Michelia champaca*

2010. Flowers. Multicoloured.

No.	Description	Mint	Used
3427	$7 Type **898**	40	30
3428	$15 *Duranta repens*	65	50
3429	$20 *Ixora chinensis*	1·10	80
3430	$34 *Lagerstroemia speciosa*	1·50	1·20

2010. Traditional Houses

No.	Type	Description	Mint	Used
3431	**899**	$5 multicoloured	30	25
3432	**900**	$5 multicoloured	30	25
3433	**901**	$5 multicoloured	30	25
3434	**902**	$12 multicoloured	30	25

No. 3435 is vacant.

903 Little Taiwan, Qimei Islet

2010. Landscapes. Multicoloured.

No.	Description	Mint	Used
3436	$5 Type **903**	30	25
3437	$5 Basalt Rocks, Xiaomen Islet	30	25
3438	$10 Heart Stone Weir, Qimei Islet	55	40
3439	$10 Whale Arch, Xiaomen Islet	55	40

904 Jinde Bridge, Donggang

2010. Bridges. Multicoloured.

No.	Description	Mint	Used
3440	$5 Type **904**	30	25
3441	$5 Qigu River Bridge, Tainan	30	25
3442	$12 Anyi Bridge, Tainan	55	40
3443	$12 Wangyue Bridge, Tainan	55	40

905 *Dictyophora multicolor*

2010. Fungi. Multicoloured.

No.	Description	Mint	Used
3444	$5 Type **905**	30	25
3445	$5 *Pleurotus salmoneostramineus*	30	25
3446	$12 *Pseudocolus fusiformis*	65	50
3447	$12 *Coprinus disseminatus*	65	50
MS3448	80×135 mm. Nos. 3444/7	1·70	1·40

The stamps and margins of No. **MS**3448 form a composite design.

906 *Cardisoma carnifex*

2010. Crabs. Multicoloured.

No.	Description	Mint	Used
3449	$5 Type **906**	30	25
3450	$5 *Scandarma lintou*	30	25
3451	19 *Sesarmops intermedius*	55	40
3452	$25 *Gecarcoidea lalandii*	1·40	1·10

907 Shooting An Arrow at Halberd beside Gate of Camp

2010. Classical Literature. Multicoloured.

No.	Description	Mint	Used
3453	$3.50 Type **907**	25	15
3454	$3.50 Commenting on Heroes over Wine	25	15
3455	$5 Zhou Yu's Anger at being Tricked by Zhuge Liang Three Times	30	25
3456	$20 Holding Meng Huo Captive Seven Times	1·10	80
MS3457	140×100 mm. Nos. 3453/7	1·70	1·20

2010. Flowers. Vert designs as T **898**. Multicoloured.

No.	Description	Mint	Used
3458	50c. *Bauhinia variegata*	10	10
3459	$9 *Euphorbia milii*	45	15
3460	$13 *Brunfelsia hopeana*		
3461	$17 *Plumeria rubra*	75	60

908 *Erythrus formosanus*

2010. Long-horn Beetles. Multicoloured.

No.	Description	Mint	Used
3462	75c. Type **908**	10	10
3463	$2.50 *Rosalia formosa conviva*	10	10
3464	$5 *Aphrodisium faldermannii yuagii*	30	25
3465	$25 *Anoplophora horsfieldi tonkinensis*		

909 Doves and Globe

2010. Centenary of Girlguiding. Multicoloured.

No.	Description	Mint	Used
3466	$5 Type **909**	30	25
3467	$25 Ribbons as hearts and dove	1·40	1·10

910 *Water Buffaloes* by Huang Tu-shui (image scaled to 61% of original size)

2010. Taiwanese Sculpture

No.	Description	Mint	Used
MS3468	$25 multicoloured	1·40	1·10

911 Complete Enlightenment

2010. Classical Literature. Multicoloured.

No.	Description	Mint	Used
3469	$5 Type **911**	30	25
3470	$5 Sun Wukong Wreaks Havoc in Heaven	30	25
3471	$12 Dreaming of Beheading the Jing River Dragon King	65	50
3472	$25 Stealing the Ginseng Fruits	1·40	1·10

912 Chilung Tao Lighthouse

2010. Lighthouses. Multicoloured.

No.	Description	Mint	Used
3473	$5 Type **912**	30	25
3474	$5 Wenkan Tui	30	25
3475	$10 Paisha Chia (horiz)	55	40
3476	$25 Liuchiu Yu (horiz)	1·40	1·10

913 *Bamboo Grove in Early Summer* (Tsai Yun-yan)

2010. Taiwanese Art. Multicoloured.

No.	Description	Mint	Used
3477	$5 Type **913**	30	25
3478	$25 *Pear Espalier* (Lu Yun-sheng)	1·40	1·10

914 Playing Chess

2010. Nine Elders of Mt. Hsiang. Multicoloured.

No.	Description	Mint	Used
MS3479	$5 Type **914**; $25 Two men in bamboo grove; $25 Three standing men and one striking a pose	3·00	3·00

POSTAGE DUE STAMPS

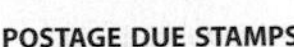
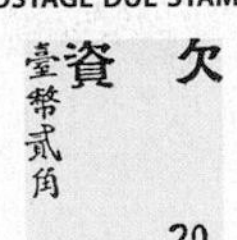

(D12)

1950. Surch as Type D 12.

No.	Type	Description	Mint	Used
D105	6	4c. on $100 blue	20·00	15·00
D106	6	10c. on $100 blue	30·00	20·00
D107	6	20c. on $100 blue	32·00	20·00
D108	6	40c. on $100 blue	48·00	60·00
D109	6	$1 on $100 blue	55·00	65·00

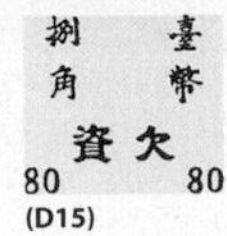

(D15)

1951. No. 524 of China surch as Type D 15.

No.	Description	Mint	Used
D133	40c. on 40c. orange	20·00	25·00
D134	80c. on 40c. orange	20·00	25·00

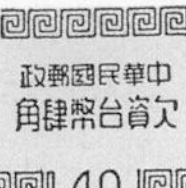

(D19)

1953. Revenue stamps as T 143 of China surch as Type D 19.

No.	Description	Mint	Used
D151	10c. on $50 blue	25·00	15·00
D152	20c. on $100 olive	25·00	6·50
D153	40c. on $20 brown	30·00	4·50
D154	80c. on $500 green	35·00	6·50
D155	100c. on $30 mauve	40·00	14·00

D43

1956

No.	Type	Description	Mint	Used
D236	**D43**	20c. red and blue	1·10	40
D237	**D43**	40c. green and buff	1·60	50
D238	**D43**	80c. brown and grey	3·25	30
D239	**D43**	$1 blue and mauve	3·50	50

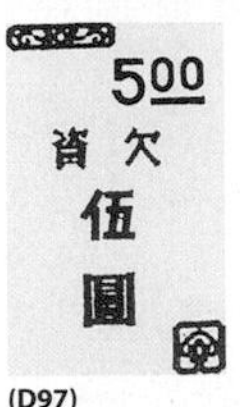

(D97)

1961. Surch with Type D 97.

No.	Type	Description	Mint	Used
D429	**56**	$5 on $20 red	2·75	1·25

1964. Surch as Type D 97.

No.	Type	Description	Mint	Used
D490	**83**	10c. on 80c. green	25	20
D491	**83**	20c. on $3.60 blue	40	20
D492	**83**	40c. on $4.50 red	65	30

D152

1966

No.	Type	Description	Mint	Used
D588	**D152**	10c. brown and lilac	25	20
D589	**D152**	20c. blue and yellow	45	20
D590	**D152**	50c. ultram & blue	75	20
D591	**D152**	$1 violet and flesh	55	20
D592	**D152**	$2 green and blue	70	20
D593	**D152**	$5 red and buff	1·50	35
D594a	**D152**	$10 purple & mauve	12·00	1·00

POSTAGE DUE STAMPS

D399

1984

No.	Description	Mint	Used
D1532a	$1 red and blue	10	10
D1533a	$2 yellow and blue	10	10
D1534	$3 green & mauve	25	20
D1535a	$5 blue and yellow	30	15
D1536	$5.50 mauve & bl	50	35
D1537	$7.50 yellow & vio	60	40
D1538b	$10 yellow and red	30	15
D1539	$20 blue and green	1·70	1·10

D876

2008

No.	Type	Description	Mint	Used
D3336	**D 876**	$1 multicoloured	10	10
D3337	**D 876**	$3 multicoloured	25	20
D3338	**D 876**	$5 multicoloured	30	25
D3339	**D 876**	$10 multicoloured	65	55
D3340	**D 876**	$20 multicoloured	1·30	1·10

Pt. 1

CHINA EXPEDITIONARY FORCE

Stamps used by Indian military forces in China.

12 pies = 1 anna; 16 annas = 1 rupee.

Stamps of India optd **C.E.F.**

1900. Queen Victoria.

C1	**40**	3p. red	40	1·25
C2	**23**	½a. green	75	30
C4	-	1a. purple	4·25	1·50
C11	-	1a. red	45·00	8·00
C3	-	2a. blue	3·00	9·00
C5	-	2a.6p. green	2·75	15·00
C6	-	3a. orange	2·75	16·00
C7	-	4a. green (No. 96)	2·75	8·50
C8	-	8a. mauve	2·75	23·00
C9	-	12a. purple on red	17·00	16·00
C10	**37**	1r. green and red	30·00	38·00

1904. King Edward VII.

C12	**41**	3p. grey	10·00	8·00
C13	-	1a. red (No. 123)	9·00	70
C14	-	2a. lilac	14·00	4·00
C15	-	2a.6p. blue	3·25	5·00
C16	-	3a. orange	3·75	4·00
C17	-	4a. olive	8·50	20·00
C18	-	8a. mauve	8·00	7·50
C19	-	12a. purple on red	11·00	19·00
C20	-	1r. green and red	16·00	32·00

1909. King Edward VII.

C21		½a. green (No. 149)	1·75	1·50
C22		1a. red (No. 150)	4·25	30

1913. King George V.

C23	**55**	3p. grey	8·00	38·00
C24	**56**	½a. green	4·00	6·00
C25	**57**	1a. red	5·00	4·00
C26	**58**	1½a. brown (No. 163)	32·00	£110
C27	**59**	2a. lilac	25·00	80·00
C28	**61**	2a.6p. blue	20·00	28·00
C29	**62**	3a. orange	38·00	£275
C30	**63**	4a. olive	32·00	£200
C32	**65**	8a. mauve	32·00	£425
C33	**66**	12a. red	32·00	£150
C34	**67**	1r. brown and green	90·00	£425

BRITISH RAILWAY ADMINISTRATION

1901. No. 121 of China surch **B.R.A. 5 Five Cents.**

BR133b	**32**	5c. on ½c. brown	£325	£150

Pt. 1

CHRISTMAS ISLAND

Situated in the Indian Ocean about 600 miles south of Singapore. Formerly part of the Straits Settlements and then of the Crown Colony of Singapore, Christmas Island was occupied by the Japanese from 31 March 1942 until September 1945. It reverted to Singapore after liberation but subsequently became an Australian territory on 15 October 1958.

1958. 100 cents = 1 Malayan dollar.
1968. 100 cents = 1 Australian dollar.

1 Queen Elizabeth II

1958. Type of Australia with opt and value in black.

1	**1**	2c. orange	55	80
2	**1**	4c. brown	60	30
3	**1**	5c. mauve	60	50
4	**1**	6c. blue	1·00	30
5	**1**	8c. sepia	1·75	50
6	**1**	10c. violet	1·00	30
7	**1**	12c. red	1·75	1·75
8	**1**	20c. blue	1·00	1·75
9	**1**	50c. green	1·75	1·75
10	**1**	$1 turquoise	1·75	1·75

2 Map

1963

11	**2**	2c. orange	1·25	35
12	-	4c. brown	50	15
13	-	5c. purple	50	20
14	-	6c. blue	30	35
15	-	8c. black	2·50	35
16	-	10c. violet	40	15
17	-	12c. red	40	25
18	-	20c. blue	1·00	20
19	-	50c. green	1·00	20
20	-	$1 yellow	1·75	35

DESIGNS—VERT: 4c. Moonflower; 5c. Robber crab; 8c. Phosphate train; 10c. Raising phosphate. HORIZ: 6c. Island scene; 12c. Flying Fish cove; 20c. Loading cantilever; 50c. Christmas Island frigate bird. LARGER (35× mm): $1 White-tailed tropic bird.

1965. 50th Anniv of Gallipoli Landing. As T 184 of Australia, but slightly larger (22×34½ mm).

21		10c. brown, black and green	30	1·25

12 Golden-striped Grouper

1968. Fishes. Multicoloured.

22	1c. Type **12**	45	45
23	2c. Moorish idol	60	20
24	3c. Long-nosed butterflyfish	60	30
25	4c. Pink-tailed triggerfish	60	20
26	5c. Regal angelfish	60	20
27	9c. White-cheeked surgeonfish	60	40
28	10c. Lionfish	60	20
28a	15c. Saddle butterflyfish	4·50	2·50
29	20c. Ornate butterflyfish	1·50	55
29a	30c. Giant ghost pipefish	4·50	2·50
30	50c. Clown surgeonfish	2·25	2·25
31	$1 Meyer's butterflyfish	2·25	2·25

13 "Angel" (mosaic)

1969. Christmas.

32	**13**	5c. multicoloured	20	30

14 "The Ansidei Madonna" (Raphael)

1970. Christmas. Paintings. Multicoloured.

33	3c. Type **14**	20	15
34	5c. "The Virgin and Child, St. John the Baptist and an Angel" (Morando)	20	15

15 "The Adoration of the Shepherds" (attr to the School of Seville)

1971. Christmas. Multicoloured.

35	6c. Type **15**	30	50
36	20c. "The Adoration of the Shepherds" (Reni)	70	1·00

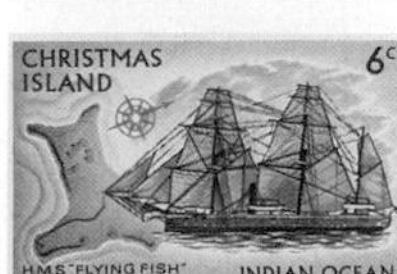

16 H.M.S. "Flying Fish" (survey ship), 1887

1972. Ships. Multicoloured.

37	1c. "Eagle" (merchant sailing ship), 1714	25	60
38	2c. H.M.S. "Redpole" (gunboat), 1890	30	70
39	3c. "Hoi Houw" (freighter), 1959	30	70
40	4c. "Pigot" (sailing ship), 1771	40	75
41	5c. "Valetta" (cargo-liner), 1968	40	75
42	6c. Type **16**	40	75
43	7c. "Asia" (sail merchantman), 1805	40	75
44	8c. "Islander" (freighter), 1929–60	45	80
45	9c. H.M.S. "Imperieuse" (armoured cruiser), 1888	65	70
46	10c. H.M.S. "Hecate" (coast defence turret ship), 1871	50	80
47	20c. "Thomas" (galleon), 1615	50	1·00
48	25c. Royal Navy sail sloop, 1864	50	1·75
49	30c. "Cygnet" (flute), 1688	50	1·00
50	35c. "Triadic" (freighter), 1958	50	1·00
51	50c. H.M.S. "Amethyst" (frigate), 1857	50	1·50
52	$1 "Royal Mary" (warship), 1643	70	1·75

No. 45 is inscribed "H.M.S. Imperious", No. 46 "H.M.S. Egeria" and No. 48 "H.M.S. Gordon", all in error.

17 Angel of Peace

1972. Christmas. Multicoloured.

53	3c. Type **17**	15	40
54	3c. Angel of Joy	15	40
55	7c. Type **17**	20	50
56	7c. As No. 54	20	50

18 Virgin and Child, and Map

1973. Christmas.

57	**18**	7c. multicoloured	25	35
58	**18**	25c. multicoloured	75	1·00

19 Mary and Holy Child within Christmas Star

1974. Christmas.

59	**19**	7c. mauve and grey	25	60
60	**19**	30c. orange, yellow and grey	75	2·50

20 "The Flight into Egypt"

1975. Christmas.

61	**20**	10c. yellow, brown and gold	25	35
62	**20**	35c. pink, blue and gold	75	1·75

21 Dove of Peace and Star of Bethlehem

1976. Christmas.

63	**21**	10c. red, yellow and mauve	15	45
64	-	10c. red, yellow and mauve	15	45
65	**21**	35c. violet, blue and green	20	55
66	-	35c. violet, blue and green	20	55

DESIGNS: Nos. 64 and 66 are "mirror-images" of Type **21**.

22 William Dampier (explorer)

1977. Famous Visitors. Multicoloured.

67	1c. Type **22**	15	80
68	2c. Captain de Vlamingh (explorer)	20	1·00
69	3c. Vice-Admiral MacLear	30	80
70	4c. Sir John Murray (oceanographer)	30	90
71	5c. Admiral Aldrich	30	40
72	6c. Andrew Clunies Ross (first settler)	30	60
73	7c. J. J. Lister (naturalist)	30	40
74	8c. Admiral of the Fleet Sir William May	35	70
75	9c. Henry Ridley (botanist)	40	1·75
76	10c. George Clunies Ross (phosphate miner)	55	55
77	20c. Captain Joshua Slocum (yachtsman)	50	75
78	45c. Charles Andrews (naturalist)	60	45
79	50c. Richard Hanitsch (biologist)	1·00	1·75
80	75c. Victor Purcell (scholar)	50	1·25
81	$1 Fam Choo Beng (educator)	50	1·25
82	$2 Sir Harold Spencer-Jones (astronomer)	55	2·00

23 Australian Coat of Arms on Map of Christmas Island

1977. Silver Jubilee.

83	**23**	45c. multicoloured	45	55

24 "A Partridge in a Pear Tree"

1977. Christmas. "The Twelve Days of Christmas". Multicoloured.

84B	10c. Type **24**	15	25
85A	10c. "Two turtle doves"	10	20
86A	10c. "Three French hens"	10	20
87A	10c. "Four calling birds"	10	20
88A	10c. "Five gold rings"	10	20
89A	10c. "Six geese a-laying"	10	20
90A	10c. "Seven swans a-swimming"	10	20
91A	10c. "Eight maids a-milking"	10	20
92A	10c. "Nine ladies dancing"	10	20
93A	10c. "Ten lords a-leaping"	10	20
94A	10c. "Eleven pipers piping"	10	20
95A	10c. "Twelve drummers drumming"	10	20

25 Abbott's Booby

1978. 25th Anniv of Coronation.

96	-	45c. black and blue	40	60
97	-	45c. multicoloured	40	60
98	**25**	45c. black and blue	40	60

DESIGNS: No. 96, White Swan of Bohun; No. 97, Queen Elizabeth II.

26 "Christ Child"

1978. Christmas Scenes from "The Song of Christmas". Multicoloured.

99	10c. Type **26**	15	20
100	10c. "Herald Angels"	15	20
101	10c. "Redeemer"	15	20
102	10c. "Israel"	15	20
103	10c. "Star"	15	20
104	10c. "Three Wise Men"	15	20
105	10c. "Manger"	15	20
106	10c. "All He Stands For"	15	20
107	10c. "Shepherds Come"	15	20

27 Chinese Children

1979. International Year of the Child. Children of different races. Multicoloured, colours of inscr given.

108	20c. green (Type **27**)	30	45
109	20c. turquoise (Malay children)	30	45
110	20c. lilac (Indian children)	30	45
111	20c. red (European children)	30	45
112	20c. yellow ("Oranges and Lemons")	30	45

28 1958 2c. Definitive

1979. Death Centenary of Sir Rowland Hill. Multicoloured.

113	20c. Type **28**	25	40
114	20c. 1963 2c. map definitive	25	40
115	20c. 1965 50th Anniv of Gallipoli Landing 10c. commemorative	25	40
116	20c. 1964 4c. Pink-tailed triggerfish definitive	25	40
117	20c. 1969 Christmas 5c.	25	40

29 Wise Men following Star

1979. Christmas. Multicoloured.

118	20c. Type **29**	20	30
119	55c. Virgin and Child	45	70

30 9th Green

1980. 25th Anniv of Christmas Island Golf Club. Multicoloured.

120	20c. Type **30**	35	50
121	55c. Clubhouse	40	1·00

31 Surveying

1980. Phosphate Industry (1st series). Multicoloured.

122	15c. Type **31**	15	30
123	22c. Drilling for samples	15	35
124	40c. Sample analysis	20	55
125	55c. Mine planning	25	60

See also Nos. 126/9, 136/9 and 140/3.

1980. Phosphate Industry (2nd series). As T 31. Multicoloured.

126	15c. Jungle clearing	15	15
127	22c. Overburden removal	15	20
128	40c. Open cut mining	20	25
129	55c. Restoration	20	30

32 Angel with Harp

1980. Christmas. Multicoloured.

130	15c. Type **32**	10	25
131	15c. Angel with wounded soldier	10	25
132	22c. Virgin and Child	15	30
133	22c. Kneeling couple	15	30
134	60c. Angel with harp (different)	20	30
135	60c. Angel with children	20	30

1981. Phosphate Industry (3rd series). As T 31. Multicoloured.

136	22c. Screening and Stockpiling	15	15
137	28c. Train loading	20	20
138	40c. Railing	25	25
139	60c. Drying	25	25

1981. Phosphate Industry (4th series). As T 31. Multicoloured.

140	22c. Crushing	20	20
141	28c. Conveying	25	25
142	40c. Bulk storage	30	30
143	60c. "Consolidated Venture" (bulk carrier) loading	35	35

33 "Cryptoblepharus egeriae"

1981. Reptiles. Multicoloured.

144	24c. Type **33**	20	20
145	30c. "Emoia nativitata"	25	25
146	40c. "Lepidodactylus listeri"	30	30
147	60c. "Cyrtodactylus sp. nov."	35	35

34 Scene from Carol "Away in a Manger"

1981. Christmas.

148	**34**	18c. silver, dp blue & bl	30	50
149	-	24c. multicoloured	30	55
150	-	40c. multicoloured	35	65
151	-	60c. multicoloured	40	75

DESIGNS: 24c. to 60c. show various scenes from carol "Away in a Manger".

35 Reef Heron

1982. Birds. Multicoloured.

152	1c. Type **35**	70	30
153	2c. Common noddy ("Noddy")	70	30
154	3c. White-bellied swiftlet ("Glossy Swiftlet")	70	70
155	4c. Christmas Island imperial pigeon ("Imperial Pigeon")	70	70
156	5c. Christmas Island white-eye ("Silvereye")	80	70
157	10c. Island thrush ("Thrush")	70	70
158	25c. Red-tailed tropic bird ("Silver Bosunbird")	1·25	60
159	30c. Emerald dove	80	70
160	40c. Brown booby	80	55
161	50c. Red-footed booby	80	55
162	65c. Christmas Island frigate bird ("Frigatebird")	80	55
163	75c. White-tailed tropic bird ("Golden Bosunbird")	90	65
164	80c. Australian kestrel ("Nankeen Kestrel") (vert)	1·00	2·50
165	$1 Moluccan hawk owl ("Hawk-owl") (vert)	2·00	3·00
166	$2 Australian goshawk ("Goshawk") (vert)	1·50	4·00
167	$4 Abbott's booby (vert)	2·00	3·25

36 Joseph

1982. Christmas. Origami Paper Sculptures. Mult.

168	27c. Type **36**	30	30
169	50c. Angel	35	45
170	75c. Mary and baby Jesus	45	65

37 "Mirror" Dinghy and Club House

1983. 25th Anniv of Christmas Island Boat Club. Multicoloured.

171	27c. Type **37**	20	30
172	35c. Ocean-going yachts	20	35
173	50c. Fishing launch and cargo ship (horiz)	25	40
174	75c. Dinghy-racing and cantilever (horiz)	25	60

38 Maps of Christmas Island and Australia, Eastern Grey Kangaroo and White-tailed Tropic Bird

1983. 25th Anniv of Australian Territory. Mult.

175	24c. Type **38**	60	40
176	30c. Christmas Island and Australian flag	70	70
177	85c. Maps of Christmas Island and Australia, and Boeing 727	1·50	2·25

39 Candle and Holly

1983. Christmas. Candles. Multicoloured.

178	24c. Type **39**	20	20
179	30c. Six gold candles	30	40
180	85c. Candles	70	1·50

40 Feeding on Leaf

1984. Red Land Crab. Multicoloured.

181	30c. Type **40**	25	30
182	40c. Migration	30	40
183	55c. Development stages	30	50
184	85c. Adult females and young	45	70

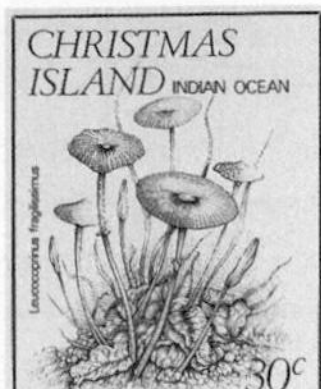

41 "Leucocoprinus fragilissimus"

1984. Fungi. Multicoloured.

185	30c. Type **41**	20	55
186	40c. "Microporus xanthopus"	25	70
187	45c. "Hydropus anthidepes" ("Trogia anthidepas")	30	80
188	55c. "Haddowia longipes"	30	90
189	85c. "Phillipsia domingensis"	35	1·25

42 Run-out

1984. 25th Anniv of Cricket on Christmas Island. Multicoloured.

190	30c. Type **42**	30	85
191	40c. Bowled-out	30	1·10
192	50c. Batsman in action	35	1·50
193	85c. Fielder diving for catch	55	1·75

43 Arrival of Father Christmas

1984. Christmas and "Ausipex" International Stamp Exhibition, Melbourne. Sheet 100×100 mm containing T 43 and similar horiz designs. Multicoloured.

MS194	30c. Type **43**; 55c. Distribution of presents; 85c. Departure of Father Christmas	2·50	3·25

44 Robber Crab

1985. Crabs (1st series). Multicoloured.

195	30c. Type **44**	1·00	70
196	40c. Horn-eyed ghost crab	1·10	1·10
197	55c. Purple hermit crab	1·50	1·60
198	85c. Little nipper	2·25	2·50

1985. Crabs (2nd series). As T 44. Multicoloured.

199	33c. Blue crab	1·25	65
200	45c. Tawny hermit crab	1·40	1·25
201	60c. Red nipper	1·75	2·00
202	90c. Smooth-handed ghost crab	2·50	3·00

1985. Crabs (3rd series). As T 44. Multicoloured.

203	33c. Red crab	1·25	60
204	45c. Mottled crab	1·75	1·40
205	60c. Rock hopper crab	2·50	2·50
206	90c. Yellow nipper	3·00	3·50

45 "Once in Royal David's City"

1985. Christmas Carols. Multicoloured.

207	27c. Type **45**	1·00	1·40
208	33c. "While Shepherds Watched Their Flocks by Night"	1·10	1·50
209	45c. "Away in a Manger"	1·40	1·75
210	60c. "We Three Kings of Orient Are"	1·50	1·90
211	90c. "Hark the Herald Angels Sing"	1·60	2·00

46 Halley's Comet over Christmas Island

1986. Appearance of Halley's Comet. Multicoloured.
212 33c. Type **46** 30 80
213 45c. Edmond Halley 35 1·10
214 60c. Comet and "Consolidated Venture" (bulk carrier) loading phosphate 40 2·25
215 90c. Comet over Flying Fish Cove 50 2·50

47 Ridley's Orchid

1986. Native Flowers. Multicoloured.
216 33c. Type **47** 50 55
217 45c. Hanging flower 30 85
218 60c. Hoya 30 1·50
219 90c. Sea hibiscus 35 2·00

1986. Royal Wedding. As T 112 of Ascension. Multicoloured.
220 33c. Prince Andrew and Miss Sarah Ferguson 45 50
221 90c. Prince Andrew piloting helicopter, Digby, Canada, 1985 95 1·75

48 Father Christmas and Reindeer in Speed Boat

1986. Christmas. Multicoloured.
222 30c. Type **48** 85 60
223 36c. Father Christmas and reindeer on beach 1·00 60
224 55c. Father Christmas fishing 1·50 1·50
225 70c. Playing golf 2·75 3·50
226 $1 Sleeping in hammock 2·75 4·00

49 H.M.S. "Flying Fish" and Outline Map of Christmas Island

1987. Centenary of Visits by H.M.S. "Flying Fish" and H.M.S. "Egeria". Multicoloured.
227 36c. Type **49** 40 75
228 90c. H.M.S. "Egeria" and outline map 70 2·50

50 Blind Snake

1987. Wildlife. Multicoloured.
229 1c. Type **50** 40 90
230 2c. Blue-tailed skink 40 90
231 3c. Insectivorous bat 90 90
232 5c. Grasshopper 1·25 90
233 10c. Christmas Island fruit bat 90 90
234 25c. Gecko 1·00 1·00
235 30c. "Mantis religiosa" (mantid) 1·25 1·25
236 36c. Moluccan hawk owl ("Hawk-owl") 3·00 1·75
237 40c. Bull-mouth helmet 1·75 2·50
237a 41c. Nudibranch ("Phidiana" sp.) 1·25 70
238 50c. Textile or cloth of gold cone 1·75 2·50
239 65c. Brittle stars 1·40 1·25
240 75c. Regal angelfish 1·40 1·75
241 90c. "Appias paulina" (butterfly) 3·00 3·25
242 $1 "Hypolimnas misippus" (butterfly) 3·00 3·25
243 $2 Shrew 3·00 7·00
244 $5 Green turtle 3·25 7·00

51 Children watching Father Christmas in Sleigh

1987. Christmas. Sheet 165×65 mm, containing T 51 and similar multicoloured designs.
MS245 30c. Type **51**; 37c. Father Christmas distributing gifts (48×22 mm); 90c. Children with presents (48×22 mm); $1 Singing carols 4·00 4·00

The stamps within No. **MS**245 form a composite design of a beach scene.

1988. Bicentenary of Australian Settlement. Arrival of First Fleet. As Nos. 1105/9 of Australia, but each inscribed "CHRISTMAS ISLAND Indian Ocean" and "AUSTRALIA BICENTENARY".
246 37c. Aborigines watching arrival of Fleet, Botany Bay 1·50 1·75
247 37c. Aboriginal family and anchored ships 1·50 1·75
248 37c. Fleet arriving at Sydney Cove 1·50 1·75
249 37c. Ship's boat 1·50 1·75
250 37c. Raising the flag, Sydney Cove, 26 January 1788 1·50 1·75

Nos. 246/50 were printed together, se-tenant, forming a composite design.

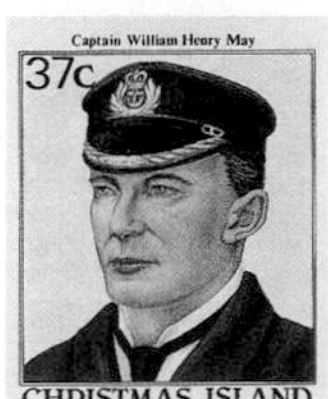

52 Captain William May

1988. Cent of British Annexation. Mult.
251 37c. Type **52** 50 40
252 53c. Annexation ceremony 65 55
253 95c. H.M.S. "Imperieuse" (armoured cruiser) firing salute 1·50 95
254 $1.50 Building commemorative cairn 1·60 1·50

53 Pony and Trap, 1910

1988. Cent of Permanent Settlement. Mult.
255 37c. Type **53** 1·00 40
256 55c. Phosphate mining, 1910 1·25 55
257 70c. Steam locomotive, 1914 1·75 85
258 $1 Arrival of first aircraft, 1957 2·00 1·25

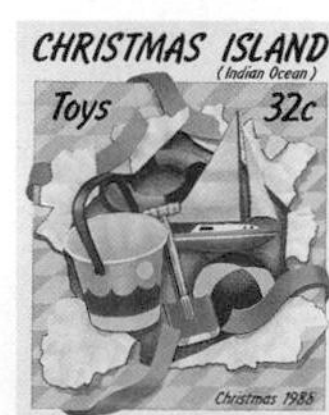

54 Beach Toys

1988. Christmas. Toys and Gifts. Multicoloured.
259 32c. Type **54** 40 35
260 39c. Flippers, snorkel and mask 50 40
261 90c. Model soldier, doll and soft toys 1·10 1·10
262 $1 Models of racing car, lorry and jet aircraft 1·25 1·25

55 Food on Table ("Good Harvesting")

1989. Chinese New Year. Multicoloured.
263 39c. Type **55** 45 40
264 70c. Decorations ("Prosperity") 80 70
265 90c. Chinese girls ("Good Fortune") 1·10 90
266 $1 Lion dance ("Progress Every Year") 1·25 1·00

56 Sir John Murray

1989. 75th Death Anniv of Sir John Murray (oceanographer). Multicoloured.
267 39c. Type **56** 50 50
268 80c. Map of Christmas Island showing Murray Hill 1·25 95
269 $1 Oceanographic equipment 1·50 1·25
270 $1.10 H.M.S. "Challenger" (survey ship), 1872 1·75 1·50

57 Four Children

1989. Malay Hari Raya Festival. Multicoloured.
271 39c. Type **57** 55 50
272 55c. Man playing tambourine 80 70
273 80c. Girl in festival costume 1·25 1·00
274 $1.10 Christmas Island Mosque 1·60 1·40

58 "Huperzia phlegmaria"

1989. Ferns. Multicoloured.
275 41c. Type **58** 75 60
276 65c. "Asplenium polydon" 1·10 85
277 80c. Common bracken 1·40 1·00
278 $1.10 Birds-nest fern 1·60 1·40

59 Virgin Mary and Star

1989. Christmas. Multicoloured.
279 36c. Type **59** 60 40
280 41c. Christ Child in manger 60 45
281 80c. Shepherds and star 1·50 80
282 $1.10 Three Wise Men following star 1·60 1·10

1989. "Melbourne Stampshow '89". Nos. 237a and 242 optd with Stampshow logo.
283 41c. Nudibranch ("Phidiana sp.") 1·75 45
284 $1 "Hypolimnas misippus" (butterfly) 4·00 1·25

61 First Sighting, 1615

1990. 375th Anniv of Discovery of Christmas Island. Multicoloured.
285 41c. Type **61** 1·75 50
286 $1.10 Second sighting and naming, 1643 2·50 1·40

62 Miniature Tractor pulling Phosphate

1990. Christmas Island Transport. Multicoloured.
287 1c. Type **62** 15 20
288 2c. Phosphate train 40 40
289 3c. Diesel railcar No. 8802 (vert) 20 20
290 5c. Loading road train 40 40
291 10c. Trishaw (vert) 30 30
292 15c. Terex truck 65 65
293 25c. Articulated bus 30 30
294 30c. Cable passenger carriage (vert) 30 35
295 40c. Passenger barge (vert) 35 40
296 50c. Kolek (outrigger canoe) 55 55
297 65c. Flying Doctor aircraft and ambulance 3·50 1·50
298 75c. Commercial van 1·25 1·50
299 90c. Vintage lorry 1·25 1·75
300 $1 Water tanker 1·25 1·75
301 $2 Traction engine 1·25 3·00
302 $5 Steam locomotive No. 1 2·00 3·75

63 Male Abbott's Booby

1990. Abbott's Booby. Multicoloured.
303 10c. Type **63** 85 30
304 20c. Juvenile male 1·40 50
305 29c. Female with egg 1·60 55
306 41c. Pair with chick 2·25 70
MS307 122×68 mm. 41c. Male with wings spread; 41c. Male on branch; 41c. Female with fledgling 5·50 3·00

The three stamps within No. **MS**307 form a composite design and are without the WWF logo.

64 1977 Famous Visitors 9c. Stamp

1990. Centenary of Henry Ridley's Visit.
308 41c. Type **64** 55 75
309 75c. Ridley (botanist) in rainforest 85 2·00

1990. "New Zealand 1990" International Stamp Exhibition, Auckland. No. MS307 optd "NZ 1990 WORLD STAMP EXHIBITION AUCKLAND, NEW ZEALAND, 24 AUGUST – 2 SEPTEMBER 1990" in purple on the sheet margins.
MS310 122×68 mm. 41c. Male with wings spread; 41c. Male on branch; 41c. Female with fledgling 7·50 8·50

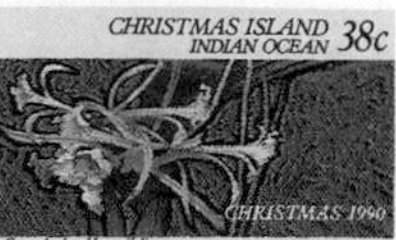

65 "Corymborkus veratrifolia"

1990. Christmas. Flowers. Multicoloured.
311 38c. Type **65** 1·10 70
312 43c. "Hoya aldrichii" 1·25 75

313 80c. "Quisqualis indica" 2·25 2·75
314 $1.20 "Barringtonia racemosa" 2·75 3·50

1990. "Birdpex '90" Stamp Exhibition, Christchurch. No. MS307 optd BIRDPEX '90 NATIONAL PHILATELIC EXHIBITION UNIVERSITY OF CANTERBURY CHRISTCHURCH NZ 6—9 DEC 1990 IN CONJUCTION WITH THE 20TH INTERNATIONAL ORNITHOLOGICAL CONGRESS.

MS315 122×68 mm. 41c. Male with wings spread; 41c. Male on branch; 41c. Female with fledgling 10·00 9·50

66 "Islander" (freighter), 1898

1991. Centenary of First Phosphate Mining Lease. Multicoloured.

316 43c. Type **66** 1·00 90
317 43c. Miners loading tipper wagons, 1908 1·00 90
318 85c. Shay steam locomotive No. 4, 1925 1·40 1·25
319 $1.20 Extracting phosphate, 1951 1·75 1·60
320 $1.70 Land reclamation, 1990 2·00 1·90

Nos. 316/20 were printed together, se-tenant, forming a composite forest design.

67 Teaching Children Road Safety

1991. Christmas Island Police Force. Multicoloured.

321 43c. Type **67** 1·50 1·00
322 43c. Traffic control 1·50 1·00
323 90c. Airport customs 2·25 3·25
324 $1.20 Police launch "Fregata Andrews" towing rescued boat 3·00 3·00
MS325 135×88 mm. Nos. 321/4 7·50 7·50

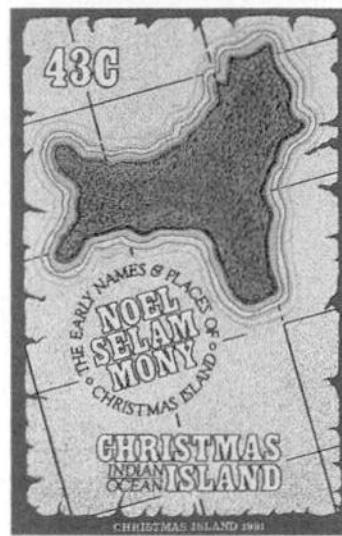

68 Map of Christmas Island, 1991

1991. Maps of Christmas Island. Multicoloured.

326 43c. Type **68** 1·00 65
327 75c. Goos Atlas, 1666 1·75 1·10
328 $1.10 De Manevillette, 1745 2·25 1·60
329 $1.20 Comberford, 1667 2·25 1·90

69 "Bruguiera gymnorrhiza"

1991. Local Trees. Multicoloured.

330 43c. Type **69** 1·00 65
331 70c. "Syzgium operculatum" 1·50 1·00
332 85c. "Ficus microcarpa" 1·75 1·25
333 $1.20 "Arenga listeri" 2·00 1·60

70 "Family round Christmas Tree" (S'ng Yen Luiw)

1991. Christmas. Children's Paintings. Mult.

334 38c. Type **70** 75 55
335 38c. "Opening Presents" (Liew Ann Nee) 75 55
336 38c. "Beach Party" (Foo Pang Chuan) 75 55
337 38c. "Christmas Walk" (Too Lai Peng) 75 55
338 38c. "Santa Claus and Christmas Tree" (Jesamine Wheeler) 75 55
339 43c. "Santa Claus fishing" (Ho Puay Ha) 75 60
340 $1 "Santa Claus in Boat" (Ng Hooi Hua) 1·50 1·50
341 $1.20 "Santa Claus surfing" (Yani Kawi) 1·75 1·75

71 Discussing Evacuation, 1942

1992. 50th Anniv of Partial Evacuation. Mult.

342 45c. Type **71** 1·50 1·50
343 45c. Families waiting to embark 1·50 1·50
344 $1.05 Ferrying evacuees to "Islander" 3·25 3·50
345 $1.20 Departure of "Islander" (freighter) 3·75 4·00

72 Snake's-head Cowrie

1992. Shells. Multicoloured.

346 5c. Tiger cowrie 60 70
347 10c. Type **72** 80 70
348 15c. Scorpion conch 1·25 70
349 20c. Royal oak scallop 1·25 70
350 25c. Striped engina 1·25 70
351 30c. Prickly Pacific drupe 1·25 70
352 40c. Reticulate distorsio 1·25 75
353 45c. Tapestry turban 1·25 75
354 50c. Beautiful goblet 1·25 75
355 60c. Captain cone 1·50 80
356 70c. Layonkaire's turban 1·50 90
357 80c. Chirage spider conch 1·75 1·00
358 90c. Common delphinia 1·75 1·25
359 $1 Ceramic vase 1·75 1·50
360 $2 Partridge tun 1·40 1·75
361 $5 Strawberry drupe 3·50 3·75

73 Torpedoing of "Eidsvold"

1992. 50th Anniv of Sinkings of "Eidsvold" and "Nissa Maru". Multicoloured.

362 45c. Type **73** 2·00 1·25
363 80c. "Eidsvold" sinking 2·75 2·75
364 $1.05 "Nissa Maru" under attack 3·25 4·00
365 $1.20 "Nissa Maru" beached 3·25 4·25

1992. "Kuala Lumpur '92" International Philatelic Exhibition. No. 361 optd with exhibition symbol.

366 $5 Strawberry drupe 9·00 7·00

75 Jungle

1992. Christmas. Multicoloured.

367 40c. Type **75** 90 1·25
368 40c. Red-tailed tropic bird and brown booby over rock 90 1·25
369 45c. Brown boobies on headland 90 1·25
370 $1.05 Red-tailed tropic bird, brown booby and cliffs 1·60 1·75
371 $1.20 Cliffs 1·60 1·75

Nos. 367/71 were printed together, se-tenant, forming a composite coastal design.

76 Abbott's Booby

1993. Seabirds. Multicoloured.

372 45c. Type **76** 60 85
373 45c. Christmas Island frigate bird 60 85
374 45c. Common noddy 60 85
375 45c. White-tailed ("Golden Bosunbird") tropic bird 60 85
376 45c. Brown booby 60 85
MS377 140×70 mm. Nos. 372/6 2·75 4·50

Nos. 372/6 were printed together, se-tenant, forming a composite design.

77 Dolly Beach

1993. Scenic Views of Christmas Island. Mult.

378 85c. Type **77** 1·75 1·75
379 95c. Blow Holes 2·00 2·25
380 $1.05 Merrial Beach 2·25 2·50
381 $1.20 Rainforest 2·25 2·50

78 Turtle on Beach

1993. Christmas. Multicoloured.

382 40c. Type **78** 1·00 70
383 45c. Crabs and wave 1·00 70
384 $1 Christmas Island frigate bird and rainforest 2·25 3·25

79 Map of Christmas Island

1993. 350th Anniv of Naming of Christmas Island.

385 **79** $2 multicoloured 3·00 3·50

80 Pekinese

1994. Chinese New Year ("Year of the Dog"). Multicoloured.

386 45c. Type **80** 1·00 1·40
387 45c. Mickey (Christmas Island dog) 1·00 1·40
MS388 106×70 mm. Nos. 386/7 2·75 3·75

81 Shay Locomotive No. 4

1994. Steam Locomotives. Multicoloured.

389 85c. Type **81** 1·75 1·75
390 95c. Locomotive No. 9 1·75 2·00
391 $1.20 Locomotive No. 1 2·00 2·25

82 "Brachypeza archytas"

1994. Orchids. Multicoloured.

392 45c. Type **82** 1·10 1·40
393 45c. "Thelasis capitata" 1·10 1·40
394 45c. "Corymborkis veratrifolia" 1·10 1·40
395 45c. "Flickingeria nativitatis" 1·10 1·40
396 45c. "Dendrobium crumenatum" 1·10 1·40

83 Angel blowing Trumpet

1994. Christmas. Multicoloured.

397 40c. Type **83** 80 60
398 45c. Wise Man holding gift 80 60
399 80c. Star over Bethlehem 1·75 2·50

84 Pig

1995. Chinese New Year ("Year of the Pig").

400 **84** 45c. multicoloured 75 60
401 - 85c. multicoloured 1·25 1·75
MS402 106×71 mm. Nos. 400/1 2·00 2·50

DESIGN: 85c. Pig (different).

85 Golfer playing Shot

1995. 40th Anniv of Christmas Island Golf Course.

403 **85** $2.50 multicoloured 4·25 4·25

86 Father Christmas with Map on Christmas Island Frigate Bird

1995. Christmas. Multicoloured.

404 40c. Type **86** 80 60
405 45c. Father Christmas distributing presents 80 60
406 80c. Father Christmas waving goodbye 1·75 2·50

87 De Havilland D.H.98 Mosquito on Reconnaissance Mission

1995. 50th Anniv of End of Second World War. Each black, stone and red.

407 45c. Type **87** 95 95
408 45c. H.M.S. "Rother" (frigate) 95 95

88 Lemon-peel Angelfish

1995. Marine Life. Multicoloured.

412	20c. Pink-tailed triggerfish	35	35
413	30c. Japanese inflator-filefish ("Longnose filefish")	50	50
414	45c. Princess anthias	65	50
415	75c. Type **88**	1·00	1·25
416	85c. Moon wrasse	1·25	1·00
417	90c. Spotted boxfish	1·25	1·00
418	95c. Moorish idol	1·25	1·50
419	$1 Emperor angelfish	1·25	1·50
420	$1.20 Glass-eyed snapper ("Glass bigeye")	1·50	2·00

89 Rat with Drum

1996. Chinese New Year ("Year of the Rat"). Multicoloured.

425	45c. Type **89**	1·40	1·75
426	45c. Rat with tambourine	1·40	1·75
MS427	106×70 mm. Nos. 425/6	3·75	4·25

90 Christmas Island White-eye ("White-eye")

1996. Christmas Island Land Birds. Multicoloured.

428	45c. Type **90**	75	50
429	85c. Moluccan hawk owl ("Hawk-owl")	1·75	2·00

91 Three Ships approaching Island

1996. Christmas. "I saw Three Ships" (carol). Multicoloured.

430	40c. Type **91**	90	75
431	45c. Madonna and Child with ships at anchor	90	75
432	80c. Ships leaving	1·75	2·25

1996. 300th Anniv of Willem de Vlamingh's Discovery of Christmas Island. As No. 1665 of Australia.

433	45c. multicoloured	1·25	1·75

92 Ox facing Right

1997. Chinese New Year ("Year of the Ox"). Multicoloured.

434	45c. Type **92**	1·25	1·25
435	45c. Ox facing left	1·25	1·25
MS436	106×70 mm. Nos. 434/5	2·50	3·25

93 Father Christmas reading Letter

1997. Christmas. Multicoloured.

437	40c. Type **93**	90	70
438	45c. Father Christmas carving wooden boat	90	70
439	80c. Father Christmas in sleigh	1·90	2·50

94 Tiger

1998. Chinese New Year ("Year of the Tiger"). Multicoloured.

440	45c. Type **94**	2·00	2·00
441	45c. Tiger with head facing left	2·00	2·00
MS442	106×70 mm. Nos. 440/1	4·00	4·25

95 Christmas Island Frigate Bird

1998. Marine Life. Multicoloured.

443	5c. Type **95**	30	40
444	5c. Four ambon chromis	30	40
445	5c. Three ambon chromis	30	40
446	5c. One pink anemonefish	30	40
447	5c. Three pink anemonefish	30	40
448	10c. Reef heron ("Eastern Reef Egret")	30	40
449	10c. Whitelined cod	30	40
450	10c. Pyramid butterflyfish	30	40
451	10c. Dusky parrotfish	30	40
452	10c. Spotted garden eel	30	40
453	25c. Sooty tern	40	50
454	25c. Stripe-tailed damselfish ("Scissortail sergeant")	40	50
455	25c. Thicklip wrasse	40	50
456	25c. Blackaxil chromis	40	50
457	25c. Orange anthias	40	50
458	45c. Brown booby	45	55
459	45c. Green turtle	45	55
460	45c. Pink anemonefish	45	55
461	45c. Blue sea star	45	55
462	45c. Kunie's chromodoris	45	55

Nos. 443/62 were printed together, se-tenant, with the backgrounds forming a composite design.

96 Orchid Tree

1998. Christmas. Flowering Trees. Multicoloured.

463	40c. Type **96**	60	50
464	80c. Flame tree	1·40	1·40
465	95c. Sea hibiscus	1·40	2·00

97 Leaping Rabbit

1999. Chinese New Year ("Year of the Rabbit"). Multicoloured.

466	45c. Type **97**	1·50	1·75
467	45c. Rabbit with pestle and mortar	1·50	1·75
MS468	106×70 mm. Nos. 466/7	3·00	3·50

98 Carnival Dragon (Fong Jason) (Community Arts Festival)

1999. Festivals. Children's Paintings. Mult.

469	45c. Type **98**	60	60
470	45c. Red crab holding Easter egg (Community Arts Festival, Siti Zanariah Zainal)	60	60
471	85c. Ghost and child (Tan Diana) (Hungry Ghost Festival) (vert)	95	1·10

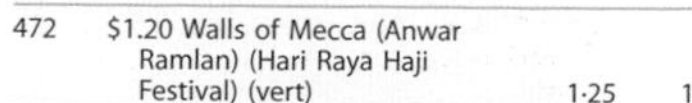

472	$1.20 Walls of Mecca (Anwar Ramlan) (Hari Raya Haji Festival) (vert)	1·25	1·40

99 Santa Claus in Hammock

1999. Christmas. Multicoloured.

473	40c. Type **99**	80	70
474	45c. Santa Claus with Christmas pudding	80	70
475	95c. Santa Claus in sleigh pulled by Abbott's boobies	1·75	2·00

100 Chinese Dragon

2000. Chinese New Year ("Year of the Dragon"). Multicoloured.

476	45c. Type **100**	1·50	1·75
477	45c. Chinese dragon facing left	1·50	1·75
MS478	106×70 mm. Nos. 476/7	3·00	3·50

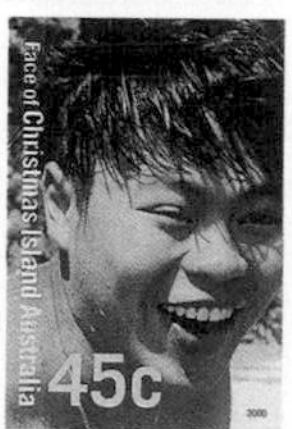

101 Yeow Jian Min

2000. New Millennium. "Face of Christmas Island". Multicoloured.

479	45c. Type **101**	1·25	1·25
480	45c. Ida Chin (schoolgirl)	1·25	1·25
481	45c. Ho Tak Wah (elderly man)	1·25	1·25
482	45c. Thomas Faul and James Neill (young boys)	1·25	1·25
483	45c. Siti Sanniah Kawi (mother of three)	1·25	1·25

102 The Three Kings

2000. Christmas. "We Three Kings" (carol). Mult.

484	40c. Type **102**	65	75
485	40c. Birds with Three Gifts	65	75
486	45c. Crabs with Three Gifts	65	75

103 Green Snake

2001. Chinese New Year ("Year of the Snake"). Mult.

487	45c. Type **103**	1·50	1·25
488	$1.35 Silver snake	2·50	3·00
MS489	106×70 mm. Nos. 487/8	4·00	4·50

104 *Chaetocalathus semisupinus*

2001. International Stamps. Fungi. Multicoloured.

490	$1 Type **104**	1·50	1·25
491	$1.50 *Pycnoporus sanguineus*	2·00	2·25

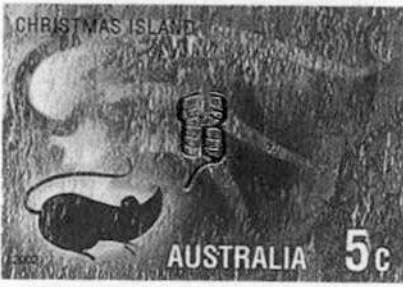

105 Rat

2002. Chinese New Year ("Year of the Horse"). Multicoloured.

492	5c. Type **105**	60	70
493	5c. Ox	60	70
494	5c. Tiger	60	70
495	5c. Rabbit	60	70
496	15c. Dragon	60	70
497	15c. Snake	60	70
498	15c. Horse (gold)	60	70
499	15c. Goat	60	70
500	25c. Monkey	60	70
501	25c. Cock	60	70
502	25c. Dog	60	70
503	25c. Pig	60	70
504	45c. Horse (purple)	90	1·00
505	$1.35 Horse (gold)	1·25	1·50
MS506	106×70 mm. Nos. 504/5	3·25	3·75

106 Imperial Pigeon

2002. Endangered Species. Christmas Island Birds. Multicoloured.

507	45c. Type **106**	1·50	1·50
508	45c. Christmas Island hawk owl	1·50	1·50
509	$1 Goshawk	2·00	2·00
510	$1.50 Thrush	2·50	2·50

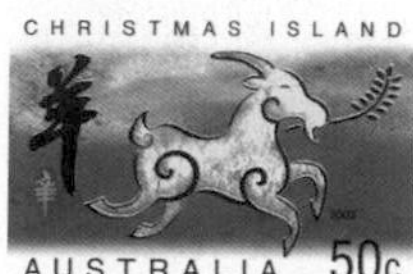

107 Yellow Goat

2003. Chinese New Year ("Year of the Goat"). As T 107 plus designs as Nos. 492/503 with backgrounds in mauve and some values changed. Multicoloured.

511	10c. Type **105**	60	70
512	10c. Ox	60	70
513	10c. Tiger	60	70
514	10c. Rabbit	60	70
515	15c. Dragon	60	70
516	15c. Snake	60	70
517	15c. Horse	60	70
518	15c. Goat (animal in gold)	60	70
519	25c. Monkey	60	70
520	25c. Cock	60	70
521	25c. Dog	60	70
522	25c. Pig	60	70
523	50c. Type **107**	65	70
524	$1.50 Blue goat	1·60	1·90
MS525	105×70 mm. Nos. 523/4	3·25	3·75

Nos. 492/503 have red backgrounds.

108 Santa riding on Whale Shark

2003. Christmas. Multicoloured.

526	45c. Type **108**	1·40	1·40
527	50c. Santa sitting on green turtle and distributing gifts	1·40	1·40

109 Yellow Monkey

2004. Chinese New Year ("Year of the Monkey"). Plus designs as Nos. 492/503 in turquoise and blue with some values changed. Multicoloured.

528	10c. Rat	60	70
529	10c. Ox	60	70
530	10c. Tiger	60	70
531	10c. Rabbit	60	70
532	15c. Dragon	60	70
533	15c. Snake	60	70
534	15c. Horse	60	70
535	15c. Goat	60	70
536	25c. Monkey (animal in gold)	60	70
537	25c. Cock	60	70
538	25c. Dog	60	70
539	25c. Pig	60	70

540	50c. Type **109**	65	75
541	$1.45 Orange-brown monkey	1·60	1·90
MS542	105×70 mm. Nos. 540/1	3·50	4·00

110 Meyer's Butterflyfish

2004. Christmas Island Underwater. Multicoloured.

543	10c. Type **110**	40	50
544	10c. Whale shark	40	50
545	10c. Saddle butterflyfish	40	50
546	10c. Racoon butterflyfish	40	50
547	10c. Green turtles	40	50
548	25c. Clown triggerfish	45	55
549	25c. Pair of Emperor angelfish	45	55
550	25c. False Moorish idols	45	55
551	25c. Emperor angelfish (juvenile)	45	55
552	25c. Pyramid butterflyfish	45	55
553	25c. Bennett's butterflyfish	45	55
554	25c. Parrotfish with blue and yellow stripes	45	55
555	25c. Dotty triggerfish	45	55
556	25c. Divers observing fish	45	55
557	25c. Pair of butterflyfish	45	55
558	50c. Coral cod and powder-blue surgeonfish	65	75
559	50c. Emperor angelfish (adult)	65	75
560	50c. Harlequin filefish	65	75
561	50c. Pink Anemonefish	65	75
562	50c. Nudibranch	65	75

Nos. 543/62 were printed together, se-tenant, with the background forming a composite design showing a coral reef and schools of fish.

111 Rooster

2005. Chinese New Year ("Year of the Rooster"). Designs as Nos. 492/503 with backgrounds in vermilion and yellow with some values changed. Multicoloured.

563	10c. Rat	60	70
564	10c. Ox	60	70
565	10c. Tiger	60	70
566	10c. Rabbit	60	70
567	15c. Dragon	60	70
568	15c. Snake	60	70
569	15c. Horse	60	70
570	15c. Goat	60	70
571	25c. Monkey	60	70
572	25c. Cock (animal in red foil)	60	70
573	25c. Dog	60	70
574	25c. Pig	60	70
575	50c. Type **111**	90	1·00
576	$1.45 Rooster (with right foot raised under body)	1·60	1·75
MS577	105×70 mm. Nos. 575/6	4·00	4·50

2005. Taipei 2005 Internationational Stamp Exhibition. No. MS577 optd Taipei 2005 18th international Stamp Exhibition.

MS578	105×70 mm. Nos. 575/6	3·50	4·00

113 Santa and Decorated Palm Tree

2005. Christmas. Multicoloured.

579	45c. Type **113**	1·25	1·00
580	90c. Santa in sleigh drawn by crabs	2·25	2·50

114 Purple Dog

2006. Chinese New Year ("Year of the Dog"). Multicoloured.

581	10c. Rat	60	70
582	10c. Ox	60	70
583	10c. Tiger	60	70
584	10c. Rabbit	60	70
585	15c. Dragon	60	70
586	15c. Snake	60	70
587	15c. Horse	60	70
588	15c. Goat	60	70
589	25c. Monkey	60	70
590	25c. Cock	60	70
591	25c. Dog (animal in copper foil)	60	70
592	25c. Pig	60	70
593	50c. Type **114**	90	1·00
594	$1.45 Leaping dog (in copper foil)	1·60	1·75
MS595	106×70 mm. Nos. 593/4	2·75	3·25

115 Mosque

2006. Heritage Buildings. Multicoloured.

596	50c. Type **115**	1·40	1·00
597	$1 Tai Pak Kong Temple	2·25	2·50
598	$1 Soon Tian Temple	2·25	2·50
599	$1.45 Tai Jin House	3·00	3·00

116 Orange Pig running

2007. Chinese New Year ('Year of the Pig'). T 116 and similar horiz designs plus designs as Nos. 492/503 with composite backgrounds showing pigs. Multicoloured. (a) Ordinary gum.

600	10c. Rat	60	70
601	10c. Ox	60	70
602	10c. Tiger	60	70
603	10c. Rabbit	60	70
604	15c. Dragon	60	70
605	15c. Snake	60	70
606	15c. Horse	60	70
607	15c. Goat	60	70
608	25c. Monkey	60	70
609	25c. Cock	60	70
610	25c. Dog	60	70
611	25c. Pig (animal in gold foil)	60	70
612	50c. Type **116**	85	90
613	$1.45 Yellow pig standing	1·90	1·90
MS614	106×70 mm. Nos. 612/13	3·75	4·25

(b) Circular sheet 170×170 mm containing designs as Nos. 426, 434, 440, 466, 476, 487, 504, 523, 540, 575, 593 and 612 but smaller, 33×23 mm, with some values changed. Self-adhesive.

MS615 50c.×12 Rat with tambourine; As Type **92**; As Type **94**; As Type **97**; As Type **100**; As Type **103**; Horse (purple); As Type **107**; As Type **109**; As Type **111**; As Type **103**; As Type **116**; $1 — 11·00 12·00

No. **MS**615 commemorates the end of the 12-year cycle of Chinese New Year stamps.

117 Santa arriving by Speedboat

2007. Christmas. Multicoloured. (i) Domestic Mail.

616	45c. Type **117**	1·00	1·00
617	50c. Santa unloading net full of presents	1·10	1·10

(ii) International Post.

618	$1.10 Santa on beach distributing presents	2·50	2·75

118 Rat

2008. Chinese New Year ('Year of the Rat'). Multicoloured.

619	10c. Rat (11.01pm–1.00am) (animal in gold foil)	60	70
620	10c. Ox (1.01–3.00am)	60	70
621	10c. Dragon (7.01am–9.00am)	60	70
622	10c. Snake (9.01am–11.00am)	60	70
623	15c. Tiger (3.01am–5.00am)	60	70
624	15c. Rabbit (5.01am–7.00am)	60	70
625	15c. Horse (11.01am–1.00pm)	60	70
626	15c. Pig (9.01pm–11.00pm)	60	70
627	25c. Goat (1.01pm–3.00pm)	60	70
628	25c. Monkey (3.01pm–5.00pm)	60	70
629	25c. Cock (5.01pm–7.00pm)	60	70
630	25c. Dog (7.01pm–9.00pm)	60	70
631	50c. Type **118**	85	90
632	$1.45 Calligraphy (in gold foil)	1·90	1·90
MS633	136×70 mm. Nos. 631/2	3·00	3·50

119 *Gecarcoidea natalis* (red crab)

2008. 50th Anniv of Christmas Island as an Australian Territory. Multicoloured.

634	50c. Type **119**	1·00	1·10
635	50c. *Papasula abbotti* (Abbott's booby)	1·00	1·10
636	50c. *Asplenium listeri* (Christmas Island spleenwort)	1·00	1·10
637	$1.45 Seal of Union of Christmas Island Workers	2·75	3·00
638	$2.45 Christmas Island flag	4·25	4·50

2008. Olympex the Olympic Expo, Beijing. Sheet 130×90 mm containing designs as Nos. 631/2. Multicoloured.

MS639	50c. Type **118**; $1.45 Calligraphy (in gold foil)	3·25	3·75

120 Christmas Tree with Red Crabs and Seashells

2008. Christmas. Multicoloured. (a) Ordinary gum. (i) Domestic Mail.

640	50c. Type **120**	1·00	1·00

(ii) International Post

641	$1.20 Robber crab stealing Christmas presents	2·50	2·50

(b) Self-adhesive. (i) Domestic Mail

642	50c. As Type **120**	1·10	1·25

(ii) International Post

643	$1.20 As No. 641	2·50	2·75

121 Ox

2009. Chinese New Year ('Year of the Ox'). Multicoloured.

644	10c. Rat	50	60
645	10c. Ox (animal in foil)	50	60
646	10c. Dragon	50	60
647	10c. Snake	50	60
648	20c. Tiger	50	60
649	20c. Rabbit	50	60
650	20c. Horse	50	60
651	20c. Pig	50	60
652	25c. Goat	50	60
653	25c. Monkey	50	60
654	25c. Cock	50	60
655	25c. Dog	50	60
656	55c. Ox	65	65
657	$1.65 Calligraphic symbol for ox	1·90	1·90
MS658	135×70 mm. Nos. 656/7	3·50	3·75

2009. International Post. Christmas. As T 120. Multicoloured.

659	$1.25 Christmas Island frigate bird with presents	2·25	2·25

A souvenir stamp sheet issued on 14 May 2009 for the 23rd Asian International Stamp Exhibition contained stamps as Nos. 644/55 with se-tenant 'HONG KONG 2009' labels. This sheet contained stamps with a face value of $2.20 but was sold at $9.95.

No. 660 is left for self-adhesive $1.25 stamp in same design not yet received.

122 Tiger (animal in gold foil)

2010. Chinese New Year. Year of the Tiger. Multicoloured.

661	10c. Rat (+dragon 'Best-arranged union')	30	20
662	10c. Ox (+rooster 'Stable relationship')	30	20
663	10c. Dragon (+rat 'Highly compatible')	30	20
664	10c. Snake (+rooster 'Love connection')	30	20
665	20c. Tiger (gold foil surround) (+dog 'Harmonic match')	45	40
666	20c. Rabbit (+ram 'Fruitful union')	45	40
667	20c. Horse (+dog 'Mutual love')	45	40
668	20c. Pig (+ram 'Happiest couple')	45	40
669	25c. Ram (+pig 'Best combination')	45	45
670	25c. Monkey (+rat 'Long-lasting relationship')	45	45
671	25c. Rooster (+ox 'Prosperous union')	45	45
672	25c. Dog (+tiger 'Favourable relationship')	45	45
673	55c. Type **122**	1·00	1·00
674	$1.65 Calligraphic symbol for tiger (in gold foil)	3·25	3·25
MS675	136×70 mm. Nos. 673/4	4·25	4·25

123 Male Frigatebird

2010. Endangered Species. Christmas Island Frigate Bird (*Fregata andrewsii*). Multicoloured.

676	60c. Type **123**	1·40	1·50
677	60c. Pair and fledgling	1·40	1·50
678	$1.80 Large fledgling and adult perched on branch	3·25	3·25
679	$1.80 Adult male in flight	1·10	1·10
MS680	150×85 mm. Nos. 676/9	8·00	8·00

124 White-tailed Tropic Bird carrying Christmas Gift

2010. Christmas. Multicoloured.

(a) Ordinary gum

(i) Domestic mail

681	60c. Type **124**	1·40	1·50

(ii) International Post

682	$1.30 Gift bound with vine *Hoya aldrichii* and Ridley's orchid (*Brachypeza archytas*)	2·75	3·00

(b) Self-adhesive

(i) Domestic mail

683 60c. As Type **124** 1·10 1·25

(ii) International mail

684 $1.30 As No. 682 3·25 3·50

125 Rabbit

2011. Chinese New Year. Year of the Rabbit. Multicoloured.

685 15c. Rat-Sagittarius 10 10
686 15c. Ox-Capricorn 10 10
687 15c. Dragon-Aries 10 10
688 15c. Snake-Taurus 10 10
689 20c. Tiger-Aquarius 10 10
690 20c. Rabbit-Pisces (in silver foil disc) 10 10
691 20c. Horse-Gemini 10 10
692 20c. Pig-Scorpio 10 10
693 25c. Goat-Cancer 15 10
694 25c. Monkey-Leo 15 10
695 25c. Rooster-Virgo 15 10
696 25c. Dog-Libra 15 10
697 60c. Type **125** 15 10
698 $1.80 Calligraphic symbol for rabbit 1·10 1·25
MS699 136×70 mm. Nos. 697/8 3·25 3·50

Pt. 16

CILICIA

A district in Asia Minor, occupied and temporarily controlled by the French between 1919 and 20 October 1921. The territory was then returned to Turkey.

40 paras = 1 piastre.

1919. Various issues of Turkey optd CILICIE. A. On No. 726 (surch Printed Matter stamp optd with Star and Crescent).

1 **15** 5pa. on 10pa. green 2·75 4·50

B. On 1901 issue optd with Star and Crescent.

2 **21** 1pi. blue (No. 543) 1·80 1·70
32 **21** 1pi. blue (No. 631) 2·00 3·75

C. On 1909 issue optd with Star and Crescent (No. 7 also optd as T 24).

4 **28** 20pa. red (No. 572) 2·50 3·00
35 **28** 20pa. red (No. 643) 2·00 3·25
7 **28** 1pi. blue (No. 649) £1100 £750
8 **28** 1pi. blue (No. 645) 7·75 9·75

D. On 1913 issue.

36 **30** 20pa. pink 2·00 3·25

E. On Pictorial issue of 1914.

37 **32** 2pa. purple 1·00 2·50
11 - 4pa. brown (No. 500) 1·50 4·25
12 - 6pa. blue (No. 502) 14·00 11·00
13 - 1¾pi. brown and grey (No. 507) 2·30 5·50

F. On Postal Anniv issue of 1916.

14 **60** 5pa. green £130 85·00
15 **60** 20pa. blue 2·30 3·50
40 **60** 1pi. black and violet 2·00 2·40
17 **60** 5pi. black and brown 2·00 4·25

G. On Pictorial issues of 1916 and 1917.

18 **73** 10pa. green 2·50 4·75
19 **76** 50pa. blue 9·25 5·25
41 **69** 5pi. on 2pa. blue (No. 914) 3·00 4·25
21 **63** 25pi. red on buff 2·75 3·50
22 **64** 50pi. red 2·50 4·25
23 **64** 50pi. blue 25·00 37·00

H. On Armistice issue of 1919 optd with T 81 of Turkey.

24 **76** 50pa. blue 10·00 7·75
25 **77** 2pi. blue and brown 3·00 4·75
26 **78** 5pi. brown and blue 15·00 7·25

1919. Various issues of Turkey optd Cilicie. A. On No. 726 (surch Printed Matter stamp optd with Star and Crescent).

46 **15** 5pa. on 10pa. green 1·70 4·25

B. On 1901 issue optd with Star and Crescent.

47 **21** 1pi. blue (No. 543) 1·50 1·70
48 **21** 1pi. blue (No. 631) 2·50 4·75
49 **21** 1pi. blue (No. 669) 95·00 70·00

C. On 1908 issue optd with T 24 and Star and Crescent.

50 **25** 20pa. red 15·00 8·75

D. On 1909 issue optd with Star and Crescent (No. 52 also optd as T 24).

52 **28** 20pa. red (No. 647) 2·20 3·75
52a **28** 20pa. red (No. 643) £160 £130

E. On 1913 issue.

53 **30** 5pa. bistre 4·00 5·50
54 **30** 20pa. pink 1·50 4·25

F. On Pictorial issue of 1914.

55 **32** 2pa. purple 2·00 3·50
56 - 4pa. brown (No. 500) 2·00 2·30

G. On Postal Anniv issue of 1916.

57 **60** 20pa. blue 1·10 2·40
58 **60** 1pi. black and violet 1·10 1·30
59 **60** 5pi. black and brown 2·50 3·75

H. On Pictorial issues of 1916 and 1917.

60 **72** 5pa. orange 3·00 4·75
61 **75** 1pi. blue 2·75 4·25
62 **69** 5pi. on 2pa. blue (No. 914) 8·25 7·75
63 **64** 50pi. green on yellow 55·00 48·00

1919. Various issues of Turkey optd T.E.O. Cilicie. A. On No. 726 (surch Printed Matter stamp optd with Star and Crescent).

69 **15** 5pa. on 10pa. green 2·00 3·25

B. On 1892 issue optd with Star and Crescent and Arabic surch.

70 10pa. on 20pa. red (No. 630) 70 3·25

C. On 1909 issue optd with Star and Crescent.

71 **28** 20pa. red (No. 572) 3·25 4·25
72 **28** 20pa. red (No. 643) 2·50 3·25

D. On 1909 issue optd with Tougra and surch in Turkish.

73 5pa. on 2pa. green (No. 938) 1·00 75

E. On Pictorial stamp of 1914.

74 1pi. blue (No. 505) 1·00 1·20

F. On Postal Anniv issue of 1916.

75 **60** 5pa. green £180 £110
76 **60** 20pa. blue 1·00 1·40
77 **60** 1pi. black and violet 2·50 3·25

G. On Postal Anniv issue of 1916 optd with Star and Crescent.

78 10pa. red (No. 654) 60 1·90

H. On Pictorial issues of 1916 and 1917.

79 **72** 5pa. orange 50 95
80 **73** 10pa. green 1·70 3·25
81 **74** 20pa. red 70 95
82 **77** 2pi. blue and brown 2·20 1·60
83 **78** 5pi. brown and blue 2·50 2·40
84 **69** 5pi. on 2pa. blue 9·50 9·75
85 **63** 25pi. red on buff 9·25 10·50
86 **64** 50pi. green on yellow 90·00 75·00

I. On Charity stamp of 1917.

87 **65** 10pa. purple 2·00 3·75

1920. "Mouchon" key-type of French Levant surch T.E.O. 20 PARAS.

88 **B** 20pa. on 10c. red 2·00 3·50

7

1920. Surch OCCUPATION MILITAIRE Francaise CILICIE and value.

89 **7** 70pa. on 5pa. red 1·50 2·30
90 **7** 3½pi. on 5pa. red 1·70 2·75

1920. Stamps of France surch O.M.F. Cilicie and new value.

100 **11** 5pa. on 2c. red 30 2·30
101 **18** 10pa. on 5c. green 50 1·50
102 **18** 20pa. on 10c. red 70 1·60
103 **18** 1pi. on 25c. blue 80 1·50
104 **15** 2pi. on 15c. green 1·00 1·50
105 **13** 5pi. on 40c. red and blue 1·50 3·00
106 **13** 10pi. on 50c. brown & lav 1·80 3·50
107 **13** 50pi. on 1f. red and green 3·25 5·25
108 **13** 100pi. on 5f. blue & yellow 28·00 37·00

1920. Stamps of France surch O.M.F. Cilicie SAND. EST and new value.

109 **11** 5pa. on 2c. red 4·25
110 **18** 10pa. on 5c. green 5·50
111 **18** 20pa. on 10c. red 3·75
112 **18** 1pi. on 25c. blue 3·25
113 **15** 2pi. on 15c. green 12·00
114 **13** 5pi. on 40c. red and blue 65·00
115 **13** 20pi. on 1f. red and green £110

1921. Air. Nos. 104/5 optd POSTE PAR AVION in frame.

116 **15** 2pi. on 15c. green £9000
117 **13** 5pi. on 40c. red and blue £9000

POSTAGE DUE STAMPS

1919. Postage Due stamps of Turkey optd CILICIE.

D27 **D49** 5pa. brown 3·00 5·75
D28 **D 50** 20pa. red 3·00 5·75
D29 **D 51** 1pi. blue 7·00 9·75
D45 **D 52** 2pi. blue 5·00 7·75

1919. Postage Due stamps of Turkey optd Cilicie.

D64 **D49** 5pa. brown 3·00 4·75
D65 **D 50** 20pa. red 3·00 4·75
D66 **D 51** 1pi. blue 6·00 10·50
D67 **D 52** 2pi. blue 6·00 10·50

1921. Postage Due Stamps of France surch O.M.F. Cilicie and value.

D118 **D11** 1pi. on 10c. brown 8·00 13·00
D119 **D11** 2pi. on 20c. olive 8·00 13·00
D120 **D11** 3pi. on 30c. red 8·00 13·00
D121 **D11** 4pi. on 50c. purple 8·00 13·00

Pt. 1

CISKEI

The Republic of Ciskei was established on 4 December 1981, being constructed from tribal areas formerly part of the Republic of South Africa.

This independence did not receive international political recognition. We are satisfied, however, that the stamps had 'de facto' acceptance for the carriage of mail outside Ciskei.

Ciskei was formally re-incorporated into South Africa on 27 April 1994.

100 cents = 1 rand.

1 Dr. Lennox Sebe, Chief Minister

1981. Independence. Multicoloured.

1 5c. Type **1** 10 10
2 15c. Coat of arms 20 15
3 20c. Flag 30 30
4 25c. Mace 35 25

2 Green Turaco

1981. Birds. Multicoloured.

5 1c. Type **2** 20 15
6 2c. Cape wagtail 20 15
7 3c. White-browed coucal 50 15
8 4c. Yellow-tufted malachite sunbird 20 15
9 5c. Stanley crane 20 15
10 6c. African red-winged starling 20 15
11 7c. Giant kingfisher 20 15
12 8c. Hadada ibis 30 15
13 9c. Black cuckoo 30 15
14 10c. Black-collared barbet 30 15
14a 11c. African black-headed oriole 55 30
14b 12c. Malachite kingfisher 1·10 30
14c 14c. Hoopoe 1·50 30
15 15c. African fish eagle 30 30
15a 16c. Cape puff-back flycatcher 1·00 30
15b 18c. Long-tailed whydah 1·50 30
16 20c. Cape longclaw 40 30
16a 21c. Lemon dove 1·50 60
17 25c. Cape dikkop 30 30
18 30c. African green pigeon 40 40
19 50c. Brown-necked parrot 60 60
20 1r. Narina's trogon 90 1·25
21 2r. Cape eagle owl 1·75 2·50

3 Cecilia Makiwane (first Xhosa nurse)

1982. Nursing. Multicoloured.

22 8c. Type **3** 15 10
23 15c. Operating theatre 30 30
24 20c. Matron lighting nurse's lamp (horiz) 40 40
25 25c. Nurses and patient (horiz) 50 50

4 Boom Sprayer

1982. Pineapple Industry. Multicoloured.

26 8c. Type **4** 10 10
27 15c. Harvesting 20 25
28 20c. Despatch to cannery 25 30
29 30c. Packing for local market 30 35

5 Brown Hare

1982. Small Mammals. Multicoloured.

30 8c. Type **5** 15 15
31 15c. Cape fox 25 25
32 20c. Cape ground squirrel 30 30
33 25c. Caracal 40 40

6 Assegai

1983. Trees (1st series). Multicoloured.

34 8c. Cabbage tree 15 10
35 20c. Type **6** 30 30
36 25c. Cape chestnut 35 35
37 40c. Outeniqua yellowwood 50 55

See also Nos. 52/5.

7 Dusky Shark

1983. Sharks. Multicoloured.

38 8c. Type **7** 15 15
39 20c. Sand tiger ("Ragged-tooth shark") 30 30
40 25c. Tiger shark (57×21 mm) 35 35
41 30c. Scalloped hammerhead (57×21 mm) 40 40
42 40c. Great white shark (57×21 mm) 50 50

8 Lovedale

1983. Educational Institutions.

43 **8** 10c. lt brown, brown & black 10 10
44 - 20c. lt brown, brown & black 20 20
45 - 25c. brown, red and black 25 25
46 - 40c. lt brown, brown & black 40 45

DESIGNS: 20c. Fort Hare; 25c. Healdtown; 40c. Lennox Sebe.

9 White Drill Uniform

1983. British Military Uniforms (1st series). 6th Warwickshire Regiment of Foot, 1821–27. Multicoloured.

47	20c. Type **9**	40	40
48	20c. Light Company privates	40	40
49	20c. Grenadier Company sergeants	40	40
50	20c. Undress blue frock coats	40	40
51	20c. Officer and field officer in parade order	40	40

See also Nos. 64/8 and 95/8.

1984. Trees (2nd series). As T 6. Multicoloured.

52	10c. "Rhus chirindensis"	15	15
53	20c. "Phoenix reclinata"	25	35
54	25c. "Ptaeroxyon obliquum"	30	40
55	40c. "Apodytes dimidiata"	40	55

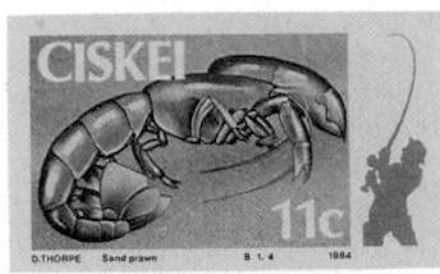

10 Sandprawn

1984. Fish-bait. Multicoloured.

56	11c. Type **10**	20	15
57	20c. Coral worm	30	30
58	25c. Bloodworm	35	35
59	30c. Red-bait	40	40

11 Banded Martin ("Banded Sand Martin")

1984. Migratory Birds. Multicoloured.

60	11c. Type **11**	25	20
61	25c. House martin	50	50
62	30c. Greater striped swallow	60	60
63	45c. Barn swallow ("European Swallow")	80	85

1984. British Military Uniforms (2nd series). Cape Mounted Rifles. As T 9. Multicoloured.

64	25c. (1) Trooper in field and sergeant in undress uniforms, 1830	45	45
65	25c. (2) Trooper and sergeant in full dress, 1835	45	45
66	25c. (3) Officers in undress, 1830	45	45
67	25c. (4) Officers in full dress, 1827–34	45	45
68	25c. (5) Officers in full dress, 1834	45	45

The stamps are numbered as indicated in brackets.

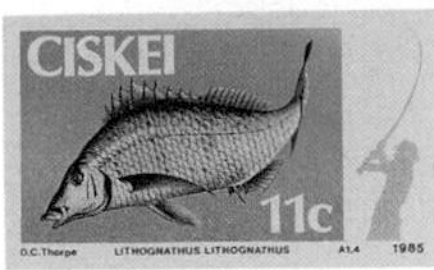

12 White Steenbras

1985. Coastal Angling. Multicoloured.

69	11c. Type **12**	20	15
70	25c. Bronze seabream	30	30
71	30c. Kob	40	45
72	50c. Spotted grunt	70	80

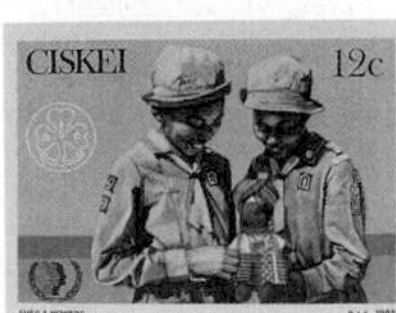

13 Brownies holding Handmade Doll

1985. International Youth Year. 75th Anniv of Girl Guide Movement. Multicoloured.

73	12c. Type **13**	15	15
74	25c. Rangers planting trees	25	25
75	30c. Guides with flag	30	30
76	50c. Guides building fire	60	65

14 Furniture making

1985. Small Businesses. Multicoloured.

77	12c. Type **14**	15	10
78	25c. Dressmaking	30	30
79	30c. Welding	30	30
80	50c. Basketry	60	65

15 "Antelope"

1985. Sail Troopships. Multicoloured.

81	12c. Type **15**	20	15
82	25c. "Pilot"	45	45
83	30c. "Salisbury"	45	45
84	50c. "Olive Branch"	80	85

16 Earth showing Africa

1986. Appearance of Halley's Comet. Mult.

85	12c. (1) Earth showing South America	70	70
86	12c. (2) Type **16**	70	70
87	12c. (3) Stars and Moon	70	70
88	12c. (4) Moon and Milky Way	70	70
89	12c. (5) Milky Way and stars	70	70
90	12c. (6) Earth showing Australia	70	70
91	12c. (7) Earth and meteor	70	70
92	12c. (8) Meteor, Moon and comet tail	70	70
93	12c. (9) Comet head and Moon	70	70
94	12c. (10) Sun	70	70

Nos. 85/94 were issued in sheetlets of 10 stamps forming a composite design of the southern skies in April. Each stamp is inscribed with a number from "A1-10" to "A10-10". The first number is given in brackets in the listing to aid identification.

17 Fifer in Winter Dress

1986. British Military Uniforms (3rd series). 98th Regiment of Foot. Multicoloured.

95	14c. Type **17**	20	15
96	20c. Private in summer dress	30	30
97	25c. Grenadier in full summer dress	35	35
98	30c. Sergeant-major in full winter dress	50	50

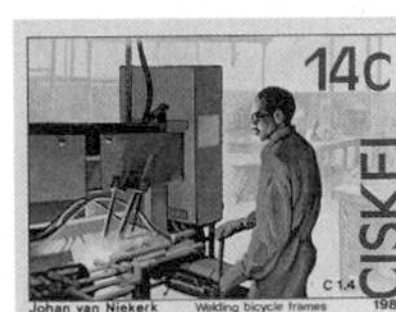

18 Welding Bicycle Frame

1986. Bicycle Factory, Dimbaza. Multicoloured.

99	14c. Type **18**	20	15
100	20c. Spray-painting frame	30	30
101	25c. Installing wheelspokes	35	35
102	30c. Final assembly	50	50

19 President Dr. Lennox Sebe

1986. 5th Anniv of Independence. Multicoloured.

103	14c. Type **19**	15	15
104	20c. National Shrine, Ntaba kaNdoda	20	30
105	25c. Legislative Assembly, Bisho	20	35
106	30c. Automatic telephone exchange, Bisho	25	50

20 "Boletus edulis"

1987. Edible Mushrooms. Multicoloured.

107	14c. Type **20**	25	15
108	20c. "Macrolepiota zeyheri"	40	40
109	25c. "Termitomyces spp"	50	50
110	30c. "Russula capensis"	60	60

21 Nkone Cow and Calf

1987. Nkone Cattle. Multicoloured.

111	16c. Type **21**	20	15
112	20c. Nkone cow	25	30
113	25c. Nkone bull	30	35
114	30c. Herd of Nkone	40	55

22 Wire Windmill

1987. Homemade Toys. Multicoloured.

115	16c. Type **22**	20	15
116	20c. Rag doll	25	30
117	25c. Clay horse (horiz)	30	35
118	30c. Wire car (horiz)	40	55

23 Seven Birds

1987. Folklore (1st series). Sikulume. Mult.

119	16c. Type **23**	20	15
120	20c. Cannibals chasing Sikulume	25	30
121	25c. Sikulume attacking the inabulele	30	35
122	30c. Chief Mangangezulu chasing Sikulume and his bride	40	55

See also Nos. 127/36, 153/6 and 161/4.

24 Bush Lily

1988. Protected Flowers. Multicoloured.

123	16c. Type **24**	20	15
124	30c. Harebell	35	35
125	40c. Butterfly iris	40	40
126	50c. Vlei lily	60	65

25 Numbakatali crying and Second Wife feeding Black Crows

1988. Folklore (2nd series). Mbulukazi. Mult.

127	16c. Type **25**	30	35
128	16c. Numbakatali telling speckled pigeons of her childlessness	30	35
129	16c. Numbakatali finding children in earthenware jars	30	35
130	16c. Broad Breast sees Mbulukazi and brother at river	30	35
131	16c. Broad Breast asking to marry Mbulukazi	30	35
132	16c. Broad Breast and his two wives, Mbulukazi and her half-sister Mahlunguluza	30	35
133	16c. Mahlunguluza pushing Mbulukazi from precipice to her death	30	35
134	16c. Mbulukazi's ox tearing down Mahlunguluza's hut	30	35
135	16c. Ox licking Mbulukazi back to life	30	35
136	16c. Mahlunguluza being sent back to her father in disgrace	30	35

26 Oranges and Grafted Rootstocks in Nursery

1988. Citrus Farming. Multicoloured.

137	16c. Type **26**	20	15
138	30c. Lemons and inarching rootstock onto mature tree	40	40
139	40c. Tangerines and fruit being hand-picked	50	50
140	50c. Oranges and fruit being graded	60	65

27 "Amanita phalloides"

1988. Poisonous Fungi. Multicoloured.

141	16c. Type **27**	75	30
142	30c. "Chlorophyllum molybdites"	1·10	75
143	40c. "Amanita muscaria"	1·40	1·10
144	50c. "Amanita pantherina"	1·60	1·25

28 Kat River Dam

1989. Dams. Multicoloured.

145	16c. Type **28**	35	25
146	30c. Cata dam	55	50
147	40c. Binfield Park dam	65	65
148	50c. Sandile dam	70	80

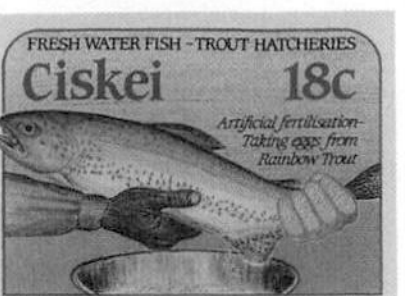

29 Taking Eggs from Rainbow Trout

1989. Trout Hatcheries. Multicoloured.

149	18c. Type **29**	25	15
150	30c. Fertilized eyed trout ova and alevins	45	45
151	40c. Five-week-old fingerlings	55	55
152	50c. Adult male	60	65

30 Lion and Little Jackal killing Eland

1989. Folklore (3rd series). Little Jackal and the Lion. Multicoloured.

153	18c. Type **30**	20	15
154	30c. Little Jackal's children carrying meat to clifftop home	35	35
155	40c. Little Jackal pretending to be trapped	40	40
156	50c. Lion falling down cliff face	45	50

31 Cape Horse-cart

1989. Animal-drawn Transport. Multicoloured.

157	18c. Type **31**	20	15
158	30c. Jubilee spider	35	35
159	40c. Ballantine half-tent ox-drawn wagon	40	40
160	50c. Voortrekker wagon	45	50

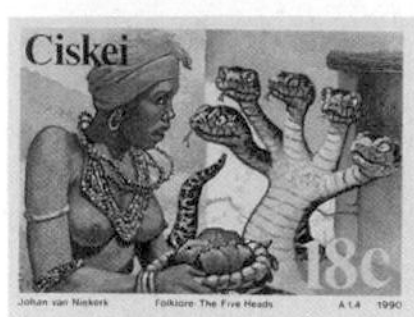

32 Mpunzikazi offering Food to Five Heads

1990. Folklore (4th series). The Story of Makanda Mahlanu (Five Heads). Multicoloured.

161	18c. Type **32**	20	15
162	30c. Five Heads killing Mpunzikazi with his tail	35	35
163	40c. Mpunzanyana offering food to Five Heads	40	40
164	50c. Five Heads transformed into a man	45	50

33 Handweaving on Loom

1990. Handmade Carpets. Multicoloured.

165	21c. Type **33**	30	20
166	35c. Spinning	50	50
167	40c. Dyeing yarn	70	70
168	50c. Knotting carpet	70	70

34 Wooden Beam Plough, 1855

1980. Ploughs. Multicoloured.

169	21c. Type **34**	25	20
170	35c. Triple disc plough, 1895	40	40
171	40c. Reversible disc plough, 1895	50	50
172	50c. "Het Volk" double furrow plough, 1910	60	65

35 Prickly Pear Vendor

1990. Prickly Pear. Multicoloured.

173	21c. Type **35**	30	20
174	35c. Prickly pear bushes	50	50
175	40c. Whole and opened fruits	60	60
176	50c. Bushes in bloom	70	80

36 African Marsh Owl ("Marsh Owl")

1991. Owls. Multicoloured.

177	21c. Type **36**	1·10	40
178	35c. African scops owl ("Scops")	1·40	80
179	40c. Barn owl	1·75	1·00
180	50c. African wood owl ("Wood")	1·90	1·40

37 Sao Bras (now Mossel Bay) on Map, 1500

1991. Stamp Day. D'Ataide's Letter of 1501. Multicoloured.

181	25c. Type **37**	70	70
182	25c. Bartolomeo Dias's ship foundering off Cabo Tormentoso (now Cape of Good Hope) during voyage to India, 1500	70	70
183	25c. Captain Pedro d'Ataide landing at Sao Bras, 1601	70	70
184	25c. D'Ataide leaving letter relating death of Dias on tree	70	70
185	25c. Captain Joao da Nova finding letter, 1501	70	70

The inscriptions at the foot of Nos. 181 and 182 are transposed.

38 Comet Nucleus

1991. The Solar System. Multicoloured.

186	1c. Type **38**	20	15
187	2c. Trojan asteroids	20	15
188	5c. Meteoroids	20	15
189	7c. Pluto	30	15
190	10c. Neptune	30	15
191	20c. Uranus	50	20
192	25c. Saturn	60	20
193	30c. Jupiter	65	30
194	35c. Planetoids in asteroid belt	65	40
195	40c. Mars	80	50
196	50c. The Moon	80	70
197	60c. Earth	80	80
198	1r. Venus	1·00	1·25
199	2r. Mercury	1·60	2·00
200	5r. The Sun	2·25	3·25
MS201	197×93 mm. Nos. 186/200	10·00	10·00

39 Fort Armstrong and Xhosa Warrior

1991. 19th-century Frontier Forts. Multicoloured.

202	27c. Type **39**	30	30
203	45c. Keiskamma Hoek Post and Sir George Grey (governor of Cape Colony, 1854–58)	45	55
204	65c. Fort Hare and Xhosa Chief Sandile	55	70
205	85c. Peddie Cavalry Barracks and cavalryman	75	1·25

40 Cumulonimbus

1992. Cloud Formations. Multicoloured.

206	27c. Type **40**	40	25
207	45c. Altocumulus	55	65
208	65c. Cirrus	65	80
209	85c. Cumulus	75	1·10

41 "Intelsat VI" Communications Satellite

1992. International Space Year. Satellites over Southern Africa. Multicoloured.

210	35c. Type **41**	40	25
211	70c. "G P S Navstar" (navigation)	80	80
212	90c. "Meteosat" (meteorology)	1·10	1·10
213	1r.05 "Landsat VI" (Earth resources survey)	1·25	1·40

42 Universal Disc-harrow, 1914

1992. Agricultural Tools. Multicoloured.

214	35c. Type **42**	40	25
215	70c. Clod crusher and pulveriser, 1914	80	70
216	90c. Self-dump hay rake, 1910	1·10	95
217	1r.05 McCormick hay tedder, 1900	1·10	1·10

43 Mpekweni Sun Marine Resort

1992. Hotels. Multicoloured.

218	35c. Type **43**	40	25
219	70c. Katberg Protea Hotel	80	80
220	90c. Fish River Sun Hotel	1·10	1·10
221	1r.05 Amatola Sun Hotel, Amatole Mountains	1·10	1·25

44 Vasco da Gama, "Sao Gabriel" and Voyage round Cape of Good Hope, 1497

1993. Navigators. Multicoloured.

222	45c. Type **44**	65	30
223	65c. James Cook, H.M.S. "Endeavour" and first voyage, 1768–71	1·10	75
224	85c. Ferdinand Magellan, "Vitoria" and circumnavigation, 1519	1·25	90
225	90c. Sir Francis Drake, "Golden Hind" and circumnavigation, 1577–80	1·25	95
226	1r.05 Abel Tasman, "Heemskerk" and discovery of Tasmania, 1642	1·40	1·25

The ship on No. 222 is wrongly inscribed "San Gabriel", that on No. 224 "Victoria" and that on No. 226 "Heemskerck".

45 Island Canary

1993. Cage Birds. Multicoloured.

227	45c. Type **45**	45	30
228	65c. Budgerigar	70	60
229	85c. Peach-faced lovebirds	90	80
230	90c. Cockatiel	95	85
231	1r.05 Gouldian finch	1·00	1·10

46 Goshen Church (Moravian Mission), Whittlesea

1993. Churches and Missions.

232	**46**	45c. stone, black and red	35	20
233	-	65c. blue, black and red	60	60
234	-	85c. brown, black and red	80	80
235	-	1r.05 yellow, black and red	90	1·00

DESIGNS: 65c. Kamastone Mission Church; 85c. Richie Thompson Memorial Church (Hertzog Mission), near Seymour; 1r.05, Bryce Ross Memorial Church (Pirie Mission), near Dimbaza.

47 Jointed Cactus

1993. Invader Plants. Multicoloured.

236	45c. Type **47**	40	30
237	65c. Thorn apple	70	60
238	85c. Coffee weed	90	80
239	1r.05 Poisonous wild tobacco	1·00	1·00
MS240	98×125 mm. Nos. 236/9	2·75	2·75

48 "Losna" (steamer) (near Fish River), 1921

1994. Shipwrecks. Multicoloured.

241	45c. Type **48**	75	30
242	65c. "Catherine" (barque) (Waterloo Bay), 1846	1·25	60
243	85c. "Bennebroek" (East Indiaman) (near Mtana River), 1713	1·40	90
244	1r.05 "Sao Joao Baptista" (galleon) (between Fish and Kei Rivers), 1622	1·50	1·25

49 "Herman Steyn"

1994. Hybrid Roses. Multicoloured.

245	45c. Type **49**	35	30
246	70c. "Esther Geldenhuys"	60	60
247	95c. "Margaret Wasserfall"	80	80
248	1r.15 "Professor Fred Ziady"	1·00	1·00
MS249	149×114 mm. Nos. 245/8	2·50	2·75

Pt. 1

COCHIN

A state of South West India. Now uses Indian stamps.

6 puttans = 5 annas.
12 pies = 1 anna; 16 annas = 1 rupee.

1 Emblems of State

1892. Value in "puttans".

5a	1	½put. orange	3·50	1·50
2	1	1put. purple	3·50	2·75
3	1	2put. violet	2·25	2·25

3

5

1903. Value in "pies" or "puttans". With or without gum.

16	3	3pies. blue	1·50	10
17	3	½put. green (smaller)	1·25	40
18	5	1put. red	1·75	10
19	3	2put. violet	2·50	50

1909. Surch 2. No gum.

22		2 on 3 pies. mauve	15	50

8 Raja Rama Varma I

1911. Value in "pies" or "annas".

26	8	2p. brown	50	10
27	8	3p. blue	2·50	10
28	8	4p. green	2·75	10
29	8	9p. red	2·25	10
30	8	1a. orange	3·25	10
31	8	1½a. purple	9·50	45
32	8	2a. grey	7·50	40
33	8	3a. red	45·00	42·00

10 Raja Rama Varma II

1916. Various frames.

35b	10	2p. brown	1·60	10
36	10	4p. green	1·00	10
37	10	6p. brown	2·50	10
38	10	8p. brown	2·50	10
39	10	9p. red	26·00	35
40	10	10p. blue	7·50	10
41a	10	1a. orange	12·00	35
42	10	1½a. purple	4·50	20
43	10	2a. grey	4·25	10
44	10	2¼a. green	8·00	3·25
45	10	3a. red	12·00	35

1922. Surch with figure and words.

46	8	2p. on 3p. blue	40	30

1928. Surch ONE ANNA ANCHAL & REVENUE and value in native characters.

50	10	1a. on 2¼a. green	6·00	12·00

1932. Surch in figures and words both in English and in native characters.

51		3p. on 4p. green	1·50	2·00
52		3p. on 8p. brown	2·50	2·75
53		9p. on 10p. blue	1·50	3·25

18 Maharaja Rama Varma III

1933

54	18	2p. brown	1·00	50
55	18	4p. green	60	10
56	18	6p. red	70	10
57	18	1a. orange	1·50	20
58	18	1a.8p. red	3·00	7·50
59	18	2a. grey	7·00	2·00
60	18	2¼a. green	1·75	30
61	18	3a. orange	7·00	1·60
62	18	3a.4p. violet	1·75	1·50
63	18	6a.8p. sepia	1·75	18·00
64	18	10a. blue	3·00	20·00

1934. Surch with figure and words.

65	10	6p. on 8p. brown	75	60
66	10	6p. on 10p. blue	1·75	2·00

1939. Optd ANCHAL.

74	18	1a. orange	75	1·60

1939. Surch in words only.

75		3p. on 1a.8p. red	£325	£120
77		6p. on 1a.8p. red	4·50	24·00

1943. Surch SURCHARGED and value in words.

76		3p. on 1a.8p. red	9·00	13·00
78		1a.3p. on 1a.8p. red	1·00	50
79		3p. on 4p. green	7·00	4·00

1943. Surch ANCHAL SURCHARGED NINE PIES.

84		9p. on 1a. orange	35·00	10·00

1943. Surch ANCHAL and value in words.

81a		6p. on 1a. orange	£190	85·00
82		9p. on 1a. orange	£170	£160

26 Maharaja Kerala Varma II

1943

85	26	2p. brown	6·00	7·00
87a	26	4p. green	3·75	5·50
88	26	6p. brown	5·50	10
89	26	9p. blue	60·00	1·25
90a	26	1a. orange	24·00	70·00
91	26	2¼a. green	32·00	3·75

1944. Surch with value in words only.

93		2p. on 6p. brown	75	4·50
94		3p. on 4p. green	10·00	10
96		3p. on 6p. brown	1·75	20
97		4p. on 6p. brown	7·00	15·00

1944. Surch SURCHARGED and value in words.

92c		1a.3p. on 1a. orange	†	£5500
95		3p. on 4p. green	8·00	10

1944. Surch ANCHAL NINE PIES.

92a		9p. on 1a. orange	9·00	4·75

1944. Surch ANCHAL SURCHARGED NINE PIES.

92b		9p. on 1a. orange	11·00	4·00

28 Maharaja Ravi Varma

1944

98	28	9p. blue	22·00	6·00
99	28	1a.3p. mauve	10·00	9·00
100	28	1a.9p. blue	10·00	16·00

29 Maharaja Ravi Varma

1946. No gum.

101	29	2p. brown	3·25	20
102	29	3p. red	50	30
103	29	4p. green	£3250	85·00
104	29	6p. brown	25·00	9·00
105	29	9p. blue	2·50	10
106	29	1a. orange	10·00	40·00
107	29	2a. black	£150	9·00
108	29	3a. red	95·00	2·50

For No. 106, optd "U.S.T.C." or "T.-C." with or without surch, see Travancore-Cochin.

30 Maharaja Kerala Varma III

1948

109	30	2p. brown	1·75	15
110	30	3p. red	2·75	15
111	30	4p. green	17·00	5·00
112	30	6p. brown	22·00	25
113	30	9p. blue	2·50	60
114	30	2a. black	75·00	2·75
115	30	3a. orange	85·00	1·00
116	30	3a.4p. violet	70·00	£400

31 Chinese Nets

1949

117	31	2a. black	7·50	12·00
118	-	2¼a. green (Dutch palace)	3·00	12·00

SIX PIES

ആറു പൈ

(33)

1949. Surch as T 33.

121	29	3p. on 9p. blue	12·00	24·00
124a	30	3p. on 9p. blue	2·50	50
126	30	6p. on 9p. blue	2·00	40
119	28	6p. on 1a.3p. mauve	7·50	6·00
122	29	6p. on 1a.3p. mauve	20·00	17·00
120	29	1a. on 1a.9p. blue	2·50	1·50
123	29	1a. on 1a.9p. blue	4·50	2·50

1949. Surch SIX PIES or NINE PIES only.

127	29	6p. on 1a. orange	75·00	£180
128	29	9p. on 1a. orange	£120	£180

OFFICIAL STAMPS

1913. Optd ON C G S.

O1	8	3p. blue	£140	10
O2	8	4p. green	12·00	10
O3a	8	9p. red	20·00	10
O4	8	1½a. purple	55·00	10
O5	8	2a. grey	13·00	10
O6	8	3a. red	65·00	45
O7	8	6a. violet	75·00	2·00
O8	8	12a. blue	42·00	7·00
O9	8	1½r. green	35·00	80·00

1919. Optd ON C G S.

O10	10	4p. green	5·00	10
O11	10	6p. brown	17·00	10
O26	10	8p. brown	7·00	10
O13	10	9p. red	80·00	10
O27	10	10p. blue	6·00	10
O15	10	1½a. purple	5·50	10
O28	10	2a. grey	45·00	25
O17	10	2¼a. green	17·00	10
O29	10	3a. red	8·50	20
O19	10	6a. violet	45·00	50
O19a	10	12a. blue	16·00	6·00
O19b	10	1½r. green	27·00	£140

1923. Official stamps surch in figures and words.

O20b	8	8p. on 9p. red	£130	20
O21	10	8p. on 9p. red	70·00	10
O22	10	10p. on 9p. red	85·00	1·00
O23	8	10p. on 9p. red	£1600	15·00
O32	10	6p. on 8p. brown	2·50	10
O33	10	6p. on 10p. blue	4·00	10

1933. Optd ON C G S.

O34	18	4p. green	6·50	10
O35	18	6p. red	5·50	10
O52	18	1a. orange	1·00	10
O37	18	1a.8p. red	1·50	30
O38	18	2a. grey	26·00	10
O39	18	2¼a. green	9·00	10
O53	18	3a. orange	3·25	2·50
O41	18	3a.4p. violet	1·50	15
O42	18	6a.8p. sepia	1·50	20
O43	18	10a. blue	1·50	1·25

1943. Official stamp surch NINE PIES.

O57	10	9p. on 1½a. purple	£850	30·00

1943. Official stamps surch SURCHARGED and value in words.

O63	18	3p. on 4p. green	£200	75·00
O58	18	3p. on 1a.8p. red	6·50	3·50
O66	18	1a.3p. on 1a. orange	£375	£120
O61	18	1a.9p. on 1a.8p. red	2·50	40

1943. Official stamps surch in words.

O59		9p. on 1a.8p. red	£160	35·00
O60		1a.9p. on 1a.8p. red	3·50	3·50
O62		3p. on 4p. green	40·00	14·00
O64		3p. on 1a. orange	3·75	4·00
O65		9p. on 1a. orange	£350	70·00

1944. Optd ON C G S.

O68	26	4p. green	55·00	10·00
O69b	26	6p. brown	1·50	10
O70	26	1a. orange	£5000	70·00
O71	26	2a. black	7·00	1·00
O72	26	2¼a. green	4·25	1·10
O73a	26	3a. red	13·00	40

1944. Official stamps surch SURCHARGED and value in words.

O75		3p. on 4p. green	6·50	50
O78		9p. on 6p. brown	6·00	75
O80		1a.3p. on 1a. orange	4·50	10

1944. Official stamps surch in words.

O74		3p. on 4p. green	4·50	10
O76		3p. on 1a. orange	32·00	10·00
O77		9p. on 6p. brown	14·00	4·50
O79		1a.3p. on 1a. orange	20·00	4·00

1946. Optd ON C G S.

O81	28	9p. blue	3·50	10
O82	28	1a.3p. mauve	1·60	20
O83	28	1a.9p. blue	40	1·00

1948. Optd ON C G S.

O84	29	3p. red	2·00	10
O85	29	4p. green	35·00	8·00
O86	29	6p. brown	20·00	3·00
O87	29	9p. blue	75	10
O88	29	1a.3p. mauve	6·00	1·75
O89	29	1a.9p. blue	7·00	40
O90	29	2a. black	16·00	3·00
O91	29	2¼a. green	28·00	8·00

1949. Optd ON C G S.

O92	30	3p. red	1·25	15
O93	30	4p. green	2·25	40
O94	30	6p. brown	4·00	30
O95	30	9p. blue	4·50	10
O96	30	2a. black	3·50	15
O97	30	2¼a. green	4·50	8·00
O98	30	3a. orange	1·10	1·40
O99	30	3a.4p. violet	55·00	55·00

1949. Official stamps surch as T 33.

O103	30	6p. on 3p. red	1·25	75
O104	30	9p. on 4p. green	75	3·25
O100	28	1a. on 1a.9p. blue	60	70
O101	29	1a. on 1a.9p. blue	26·00	17·00

1949. Optd SERVICE.

O105		3p. on 9p. (No. 125)	60	80

For later issues see **TRAVANCORE-COCHIN**.

Pt. 6

COCHIN-CHINA

A former French colony in the extreme S. of Indo-China, subsequently incorporated into French Indo-China.

100 centimes = 1 franc.

1886. Stamps of French Colonies surch.

2	J	5 on 2c. brown on yellow	26·00	20·00
1	J	5 on 25c. brown on yellow	£170	£130
3	J	5 on 25c. brown on yellow	32·00	18·00
4	J	5 on 25c. black on red	32·00	45·00

Nos. 1 and 4 are surcharged with numeral only; Nos. 2 and 3 are additionally optd **C. CH.**

Pt. 1

COCOS (KEELING) ISLANDS

Islands in the Indian Ocean formerly administered by Singapore and transferred to Australian administration on 23 November 1955.

1963. 12 pence = 1 shilling; 20 shillings = 1 pound.
1966. 100 cents = 1 dollar (Australian).

5 Jukong (sailboat)

6 White Tern

1963

1	-	3d. brown	1·00	1·50
2	-	5d. blue	1·50	80
3	-	8d. red	1·00	1·75
4	-	1s. green	1·00	75
5	5	2s. purple	8·00	2·00
6	6	2s.3d. green	10·00	1·75

DESIGNS—HORIZ (As Type **5**): 3d. Copra industry; 1s. Palms. (As Type **6**): 5d. Lockheed Super Constellation airliner. VERT (As Type **5**): 8d. Map of islands.

1965. 50th Anniv of Gallipoli Landing. As T 184 of Australia, but slightly larger (22x34½ mm).

7	5d. brown, black and green	60	45

With the introduction of decimal currency on 14 February 1966, Australian stamps were used in Cocos Islands until the 1969 issue.

7 Reef Clam

1969. Decimal Currency. Multicoloured.

8	1c. Lajonkaines turbo shell (vert)	30	60
9	2c. Elongate or small giant clam (vert)	75	80
10	3c. Type **7**	40	20
11	4c. Floral blenny (fish)	30	50
12	5c. "Porites cocosensis" (coral)	35	30
13	6c. Atrisignis flyingfish	75	75
14	10c. Buff-banded rail	75	70
15	15c. Java sparrow	75	30
16	20c. Red-tailed tropic bird	75	30
17	30c. Sooty tern	75	30
18	50c. Reef heron (vert)	75	30
19	$1 Great frigate bird (vert)	1·50	75

9 "Dragon", 1609

1976. Ships. Multicoloured.

20	1c. Type **9**	30	40
21	2c. H.M.S. "Juno", 1857 (horiz)	30	40
22	5c. H.M.S. "Beagle", 1836 (horiz)	30	40
23	10c. H.M.A.S. "Sydney", 1914 (horiz)	35	40
24	15c. S.M.S. "Emden", 1914 (horiz)	60	55
25	20c. "Ayesha", 1907 (horiz)	60	65
26	25c. T.S.S. "Islander", 1927	60	75
27	30c. M.V. "Cheshire", 1951	60	75
28	35c. Jukong (sailboat) (horiz)	60	75
29	40c. C.S. "Scotia", 1900 (horiz)	60	75
30	50c. R.M.S. "Orontes", 1929	60	75
31	$1 Royal Yacht "Gothic", 1954	75	1·00

10 Map of Cocos (Keeling) Islands, Union Flag, Stars and Trees

1979. Inauguration of Independent Postal Service and First Statutory Council. Multicoloured.

32	20c. Type **10**	20	40
33	50c. Council seat and jukong (sailboat)	25	85

11 Forceps Fish

1979. Fishes. Multicoloured.

34	1c. Type **11**	30	1·00
35	2c. Ornate butterflyfish	30	30
36	5c. Barbier	50	1·25
37	10c. Meyer's butterflyfish	30	1·25
38	15c. Pink wrasse	30	30
39	20c. Clark's anemonefish	40	30
39a	22c. Undulate triggerfish	45	30
40	25c. Red-breasted wrasse	40	1·25
40a	28c. Guineafowl wrasse	35	35
41	30c. Madagascar butterflyfish	40	45
42	35c. Cocos-Keeling angelfish	40	1·75
43	40c. Coral hogfish	45	1·00
44	50c. Clown wrasse	85	75
45	55c. Yellow-tailed tamarin	50	1·50
45a	60c. Greasy grouper	50	75
46	$1 Palette surgeonfish	60	2·50
47	$2 Melon butterflyfish	70	2·50

12 "Peace on Earth"

1979. Christmas. Multicoloured.

48	25c. Type **12**	25	40
49	55c. Atoll seascape ("Goodwill")	40	70

13 Star, Map of Cocos (Keeling) Islands and Island Landscape

1980. Christmas. Multicoloured.

50	15c. Type **13**	10	10
51	28c. The Three Kings	15	15
52	60c. Adoration	40	40

14 "Administered by the British Government, 1857"

1980. 25th Anniv of Territorial Status under Australian Administration. Multicoloured.

53	22c. Type **14**	15	15
54	22c. Arms of Ceylon	15	15
55	22c. Arms of Straits Settlements	15	15
56	22c. Arms of Singapore	15	15
57	22c. Arms and flag of Australia	15	15

15 "Eye of the Wind" and Map of Cocos (Keeling) Islands

1980. "Operation Drake" (round the world expedition) and 400th Anniv of Sir Francis Drake's Circumnavigation of the World. Multicoloured.

58	22c. Type **15**	25	15
59	28c. Routes map (horiz)	25	15
60	35c. Sir Francis Drake and "Golden Hind"	25	15
61	60c. Prince Charles (patron) and "Eye of the Wind" (brigantine)	45	30

16 Aerial View of Animal Quarantine Station

1981. Opening of Animal Quarantine Station. Multicoloured.

62	22c. Type **16**	15	15
63	45c. Unloading livestock	20	30
64	60c. Livestock in pen	20	35

17 Consolidated Catalina Flying Boat "Guba"

1981. Aircraft. Multicoloured.

65	22c. Type **17**	25	25
66	22c. Consolidated Liberator and Avro Lancastrian	25	25
67	22c. Douglas DC-4 and Lockheed Constellation	25	25
68	22c. Lockheed Electra	25	25
69	22c. Boeing 727-100 airliners	25	25

18 Prince Charles and Lady Diana Spencer

1981. Royal Wedding.

70	18	24c. multicoloured	30	20
71	18	60c. multicoloured	50	60

19 "Angels we have heard on High"

1981. Christmas. Scenes and Lines from Carol "Angels we have heard on High". Multicoloured.

72	18c. Type **19**	10	10
73	30c. "Shepherds why this Jubilee?"	20	20
74	60c. "Come to Bethlehem and see Him"	35	35

20 "Pachyseris speciosa" and "Heliofungia actiniformis" (corals)

1981. 150th Anniv of Charles Darwin's Voyage. Multicoloured.

75	24c. Type **20**	25	15
76	45c. Charles Darwin in 1853 and "Pavona cactus" (coral)	40	30
77	60c. H.M.S. "Beagle", 1832, and "Lobophyllia hemprichii" (coral)	45	35

MS78 130x95 mm. 24c. Cross-section of West Island; 24c. Cross-section of Home Island — 75 85

21 Queen Victoria

1982. 125th Anniv of Annexation of Cocos (Keeling) Islands to British Empire. Multicoloured.

79	24c. Type **21**	15	15
80	45c. Union flag	25	25
81	60c. Captain S. Fremantle (annexation visit, 1857)	30	35

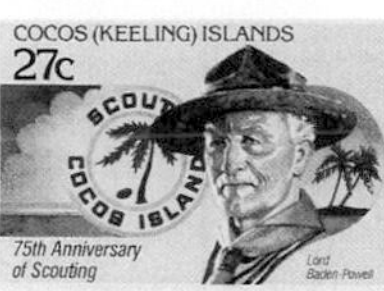

22 Lord Baden-Powell

1982. 75th Anniv of Boy Scout Movement. Multicoloured.

82	27c. Type **22**	25	25
83	75c. "75" and map of Cocos (Keeling) Islands (vert)	60	1·50

23 "Precis villida"

1982. Butterflies and Moths. Multicoloured.

84	1c. Type **23**	1·00	60
85	2c. "Cephonodes picus" (horiz)	40	40
86	5c. "Macroglossom corythus" (horiz)	1·50	70
87	10c. "Chasmina candida"	40	40
88	20c. "Nagia linteola" (horiz)	40	65
89	25c. "Eublemma rivula"	40	75
90	30c. "Eurrhyparodes tricoloralis"	40	65
91	35c. "Hippotion boerhaviae" (horiz)	1·50	75
92	40c. "Euploea core"	40	80
93	45c. "Psara hipponalis" (horiz)	50	80
94	50c. "Danaus chrysippus" (horiz)	60	1·25
95	55c. "Hypolimnas misippus"	60	70
96	60c. "Spodoptera litura"	65	1·75
97	$1 "Achaea janata"	2·75	2·75
98	$2 "Panacra velox" (horiz)	2·00	2·75
99	$3 "Utetheisa pulchelloides" (horiz)	2·75	2·75

24 "Call His Name Immanuel"

1982. Christmas. Multicoloured.

100	21c. Type **24**	25	30
101	35c. "I bring you good tidings"	40	40
102	75c. "Arise and flee into Egypt"	1·00	1·25

25 "God will look after us" (Matt. 1:20)

1983. Christmas. Extracts from New Testament. Multicoloured.

103	24c. Type **25**	30	45
104	24c. "Our baby King, Jesus" (Matthew. 2:2)	30	45
105	24c. "Your Saviour is born" (Luke. 2:11)	30	45
106	24c. "Wise men followed the Star" (Matthew. 2:9–10)	30	45

107 24c. "And worship the Lord" (Matthew. 2:11) 30 45

26 Hari Raya Celebration

1984. Cocos-Malay Culture (1st series). Mult.

108 45c. Type **26** 45 35
109 75c. Melenggok dancing 65 50
110 85c. Cocos-Malay wedding 75 55

See also Nos. 128/31.

27 Unpacking Barrel

1984. 75th Anniv of Cocos Barrel Mail. Multicoloured.

111 35c. Type **27** 40 25
112 55c. Jukong awaiting mail ship 75 50
113 70c. P & O mail ship "Morea" 85 55
MS114 125×95 mm. $1 Retrieving barrel 1·00 1·25

28 Captain William Keeling

1984. 375th Anniv of Discovery of Cocos (Keeling) Islands. Multicoloured.

115 30c. Type **28** 60 40
116 65c. "Hector" 1·25 90
117 95c. Mariner's astrolabe 1·50 1·25
118 $1.10 Map circa 1666 1·60 1·50

29 Malay Settlement, Home Island

1984. "Ausipex" International Stamp Exhibition, Melbourne. Multicoloured.

119 45c. Type **29** 75 50
120 55c. Airstrip, West Island 85 60
MS121 130×95 mm. $2 Jukongs (native craft) racing 2·00 2·00

30 "Rainbow" Fish

1984. Christmas. Multicoloured.

122 24c. Type **30** 50 60
123 35c. "Rainbow" butterfly 1·10 1·40
124 55c. "Rainbow" bird 1·25 2·00

31 Cocos Islanders

1984. Integration of Cocos (Keeling) Islands with Australia. Sheet 90×52 mm, containing T 31 and similar horiz design. Multicoloured.

MS125 30c. Type **31**; 30c. Australian flag on island 1·50 1·25

32 Jukong-building

1985. Cocos-Malay Culture (2nd series). Handicrafts. Multicoloured.

126 30c. Type **32** 75 35
127 45c. Blacksmithing 1·00 55
128 55c. Woodcarving 1·25 65

33 C.S. "Scotia"

1985. Cable-laying Ships. Multicoloured.

129 33c. Type **33** 1·50 40
130 65c. C.S. "Anglia" 2·25 1·60
131 80c. C.S. "Patrol" 2·25 2·25

34 Red-footed Booby

1985. Birds of Cocos (Keeling) Islands. Mult.

132 33c. Type **34** 1·75 2·25
133 60c. Nankeen night heron (juvenile) (horiz) 2·00 2·50
134 $1 Buff-banded rail (horiz) 2·25 2·50

Nos. 132/4 were issued together, se-tenant, forming a composite design.

35 Mantled Top

1985. Shells and Molluscs. Multicoloured.

135 1c. Type **35** 60 1·25
136 2c. Rang's nerite 60 1·25
137 3c. Jewel box 60 1·25
138 4c. Money cowrie 1·00 1·25
139 5c. Purple Pacific drupe 60 1·25
140 10c. Soldier cone 70 1·50
141 15c. Merlin-spike auger 2·00 1·25
142 20c. Pacific strawberry cockle 2·00 1·50
143 30c. Lajonkaire's turban 2·00 1·50
144 33c. Reticulate mitre 2·25 1·50
145 40c. Common spider conch 2·25 1·50
146 50c. Fluted giant clam or scaled tridacna 2·25 1·75
147 60c. Minstrel cowrie 2·25 2·25
148 $1 Varicose nudibranch 3·00 3·25
149 $2 Tesselated nudibranch 3·00 4·25
150 $3 Hamincea cymballum 3·25 4·75

36 Night Sky and Palm Trees

1985. Christmas. Sheet 121×88 mm, containing T 36 and similar horiz designs.

MS151 27c. × 4 multicoloured 2·00 2·75

The stamps within No. **MS**151 show a composite design of the night sky seen through a grove of palm trees. The position of the face value on the four stamps varies. Type **36** shows the top left design. The top right stamp shows the face value at bottom right, the bottom left at top left and the bottom right at top right.

37 Charles Darwin, c. 1840

1986. 150th Anniv of Charles Darwin's Visit. Multicoloured.

152 33c. Type **37** 70 60
153 60c. Map of H.M.S. "Beagle's" route, Australia to Cocos Islands 1·25 2·25
154 $1 H.M.S. "Beagle" 1·75 2·75

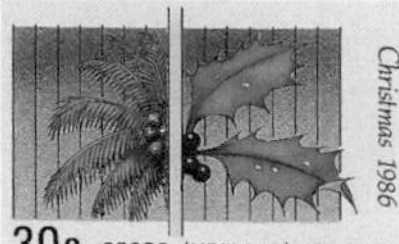

38 Coconut Palm and Holly Sprigs

1986. Christmas. Multicoloured.

155 30c. Type **38** 60 70
156 90c. Nautilus shell and Christmas tree bauble 2·00 3·00
157 $1 Tropical fish and bell 2·00 3·00

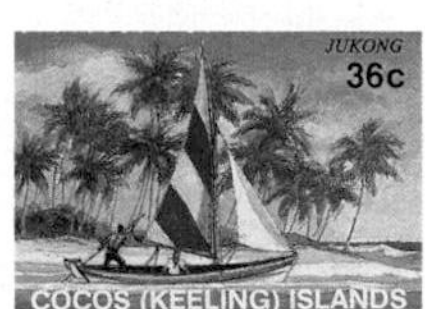

39 Jukong

1987. Sailing Craft. Multicoloured.

158 36c. Type **39** 1·10 1·60
159 36c. Ocean racing yachts 1·10 1·60
160 36c. "Sarimanok" (replica of early dhow) 1·10 1·60
161 36c. "Ayesha" (schooner) 1·10 1·60

Nos. 158/61 were printed together, se-tenant, each strip forming a composite background design.

40 Beach, Direction Island

1987. Cocos Islands Scenes. Multicoloured.

162 70c. Type **40** 1·40 1·40
163 90c. Palm forest, West Island 1·75 2·00
164 $1 Golf course 2·75 3·00

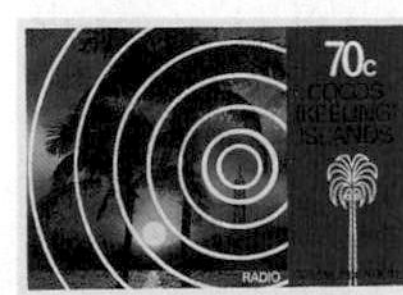

41 Radio Transmitter and Palm Trees at Sunset

1987. Communications. Multicoloured.

165 70c. Type **41** 1·25 1·50
166 75c. Boeing 727-100 airliner at terminal 1·50 1·75
167 90c. "Intelsat 5" satellite 1·75 2·25
168 $1 Airmail letter and globe 2·00 2·25

42 Batik Printing

1987. Cocos (Keeling) Islands Malay Industries. Multicoloured.

169 45c. Type **42** 1·00 1·50
170 65c. Jukong building 1·40 2·00
171 75c. Copra production 1·50 2·25

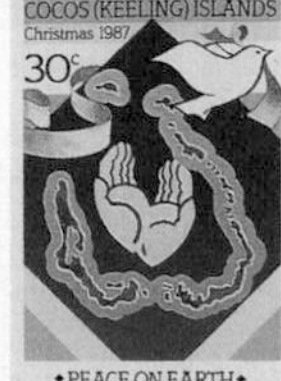

43 Hands releasing Peace Dove and Map of Islands

1987. Christmas. Multicoloured.

172 30c. Type **43** 40 40
173 90c. Local children at Christmas party 1·25 1·90
174 $1 Island family and Christmas star 1·50 1·90

1988. Bicentenary of Australian Settlement. Arrival of First Fleet. As Nos. 1105/9 of Australia but each inscr "COCOS (KEELING) ISLANDS" and "AUSTRALIA BICENTENARY".

175 37c. Aborigines watching arrival of Fleet, Botany Bay 2·00 2·00
176 37c. Aboriginal family and anchored ships 2·00 2·00
177 37c. Fleet arriving at Sydney Cove 2·00 2·00
178 37c. Ship's boat 2·00 2·00
179 37c. Raising the flag, Sydney Cove, 26 January 1788 2·00 2·00

Nos. 175/9 were printed together, se-tenant, forming a composite design.

44 Coconut Flower

1988. Life Cycle of the Coconut. Multicoloured.

180 37c. Type **44** 50 40
181 65c. Immature nuts 75 1·00
182 90c. Coconut palm and mature nuts 1·10 1·75
183 $1 Seedlings 1·25 1·75
MS184 102×91 mm. Nos. 180/3 3·50 4·50

45 Copra 3d. Stamp of 1963

1988. 25th Anniv of First Cocos (Keeling) Islands Stamps. Each showing stamp from 1963 definitive set.

185 **45** 37c. green, black and blue 1·00 1·00
186 - 55c. green, black and brown 1·50 1·50
187 - 65c. blue, black and lilac 1·60 2·25
188 - 70c. red, black and grey 1·60 2·25
189 - 90c. purple, black and grey 1·75 2·50
190 - $1 green, black and brown 1·75 2·50

DESIGNS: 55c. Palms 1s.; 65c. Lockheed Super Constellation airplane 5d.; 70c. Map 8d.; 90c. "Jukong" (sailboat) 2s.; $1 White tern 2s.3d.

46 "Pisonia grandis"

1988. Flora. Multicoloured.

191 1c. Type **46** 50 80
192 2c. "Cocos nucifera" 50 80
193 5c. "Morinda citrifolia" 1·00 90
194 10c. "Cordia subcordata" 70 90
195 30c. "Argusia argentea" 1·00 1·25

196		37c. "Calophyllum inophyllum"	1·50	1·00
197		40c. "Barringtonia asiatica"	1·00	1·25
198		50c. "Caesalpinia bonduc"	1·25	3·00
199		90c. "Terminalia catappa"	1·75	4·00
200		$1 "Pemphis acidula"	1·75	2·50
201		$2 "Scaevola sericea"	2·50	2·50
202		$3 "Hibiscus tiliaceus"	3·50	3·75

1988. "Sydpex '88" National Stamp Exhibition, Sydney. Sheet 78×85 mm. Multicoloured.

MS203		As No. 202	3·75	5·00

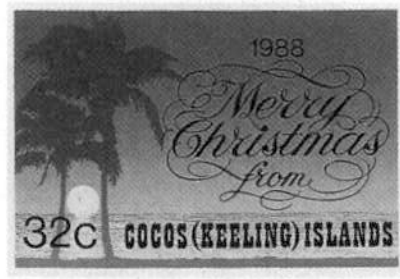

47 Beach at Sunset

1988. Christmas.

204	**47**	32c. multicoloured	80	60
205	**47**	90c. multicoloured	1·50	2·50
206	**47**	$1 multicoloured	1·75	2·50

48 Captain P. G. Taylor

1989. 50th Anniv of First Indian Ocean Aerial Survey.

207	**48**	40c. multicoloured	80	60
208	-	70c. multicoloured	1·75	2·50
209	-	$1 multicoloured	2·00	2·50
210	-	$1.10 blue, lilac and black	2·25	2·75

DESIGNS: 70c. Consolidated Catalina flying boat "Guba" and crew; $1 "Guba" over Direction Islands; $1.10, Unissued Australia 5s. stamp commemorating flight.

49 Jukong and Star

1989. Christmas.

211	**49**	35c. multicoloured	80	60
212	**49**	80c. multicoloured	2·00	2·50
213	**49**	$1.10 multicoloured	2·00	2·50

50 H.M.A.S. "Sydney" (cruiser)

1989. 75th Anniv of Destruction of German Cruiser "Emden". Multicoloured.

214		40c. Type **50**	1·75	1·75
215		70c. "Emden"	2·00	2·00
216		$1 "Emden's" steam launch	2·25	2·25
217		$1.10 H.M.A.S. "Sydney" (1914) and crest	2·25	2·25
MS218		145×90 mm. Nos. 214/7	7·50	7·50

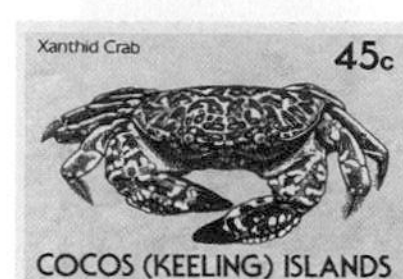

51 Xanthid Crab

1990. Cocos Islands Crabs. Multicoloured.

219		45c. Type **51**	2·00	75
220		75c. Ghost crab	2·75	2·00
221		$1 Red-backed mud crab	3·00	2·25
222		$1.30 Coconut crab (vert)	3·25	3·00

52 Captain Keeling and "Hector", 1609

1990. Navigators of the Pacific.

223	**52**	45c. mauve	2·75	1·25
224	-	75c. mauve and blue	3·00	3·25
225	-	$1 mauve and stone	3·50	3·75
226	-	$1.30 mauve and buff	4·25	5·00
MS227		120×95 mm. As Nos 223/6, but imperf	7·50	9·00

DESIGNS: 75c. Captain Fitzroy and H.M.S. "Beagle", 1836; $1 Captain Belcher and H.M.S. "Samarang", 1846; $1.30, Captain Fremantle and H.M.S. "Juno", 1857.

1990. "New Zealand 1990" International Stamp Exhibition, Auckland. No. 188 optd with logo and NEW ZEALAND 1990 24 AUG 2 SEP AUCKLAND.

228		70c. red, black and grey	4·25	4·25
MS229		127×90 mm. As Nos. 194, 199 and 201, but self-adhesive	8·00	9·00

1990. No. 187 surch $5.

230		$5 on 65c. blue, black and lilac	15·00	15·00

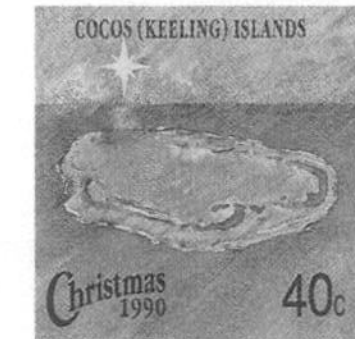

55 Cocos Atoll from West and Star

1990. Christmas. Multicoloured.

231		40c. Type **55**	80	1·25
232		70c. Cocos atoll from south	1·75	2·75
233		$1.30 Cocos atoll from east	3·00	4·00

1990. Nos. 140/1, 143 and 146/7 surch POSTAGE PAID plus additional words as indicated.

235		(43c.) on 10c. Soldier cone (**MAINLAND**)	1·40	2·00
236		(1c.) on 30c. Lajonkaire's turban (**LOCAL**)	2·00	2·75
237		70c. on 60c. Minstrel cowrie (**ZONE 1**)	1·50	2·75
238		80c. on 50c. Fluted giant clam or scaled tridacna (**ZONE 2**)	1·75	3·50
239		$1.20 on 15c. Marlin-spike auger (**ZONE 5**)	2·00	3·75

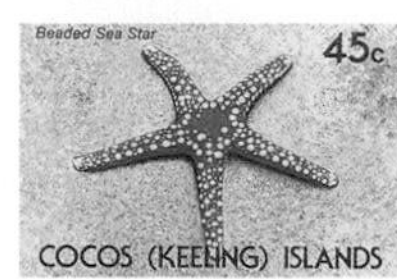

58 Beaded Sea Star

1991. Starfish and Sea Urchins. Multicoloured.

240		45c. Type **58**	1·25	75
241		75c. Feather star	2·00	2·25
242		$1 Slate pencil urchin	2·00	2·25
243		$1.30 Globose sea urchin	2·75	3·25

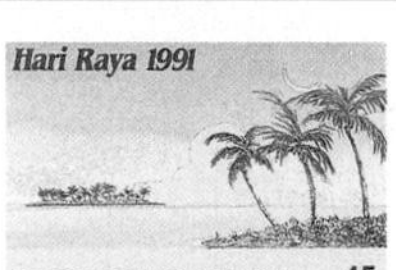

59 Cocos Islands

1991. Malay Hari Raya Festival. Multicoloured.

244		45c. Type **59**	1·00	65
245		75c. Island house	1·75	2·25
246		$1.30 Islands scene	2·50	3·25

60 Child praying

1991. Christmas. Multicoloured.

247		38c. Type **60**	1·25	80
248		43c. Child dreaming of Christmas Day	1·25	80
249		$1 Child singing	2·50	2·50
250		$1.20 Child fascinated by decorations	2·75	4·00
MS251		118×74 mm. 38c., 43c., $1, $1.20, Local children's choir	7·00	8·50

The four values in No. **MS**251 form a composite design.

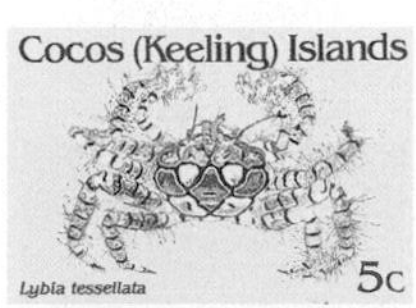

61 "Lybia tessellata"

1992. Crustaceans. Multicoloured.

252		5c. Type **61**	1·00	1·40
253		10c. "Pilodius areolatus"	1·50	1·50
254		20c. "Trizopagurus strigatus"	1·75	1·75
255		30c. "Lophozozymus pulchellus"	2·25	2·25
256		40c. "Thalamitoides quadridens"	2·25	2·25
257		45c. "Calcinus elegans" (vert)	2·25	2·25
258		50c. "Clibarius humilis"	2·50	2·50
259		60c. "Trapezia rufopunctata" (vert)	2·75	2·75
260		80c. "Pylopaguropsis magnimanus" (vert)	3·00	3·25
261		$1 "Trapezia ferruginea" (vert)	3·00	3·25
262		$2 "Trapezia guttata" (vert)	4·00	4·75
263		$3 "Trapezia cymodoce" (vert)	4·50	4·75

62 "Santa Maria"

1992. 500th Anniv of Discovery of America by Columbus.

264	**62**	$1.05 multicoloured	3·75	4·00

63 Buff-banded Rail searching for Food

1992. Endangered Species. Buff-banded Rail. Mult.

265		10c. Type **63**	70	85
266		15c. Banded rail with chick	90	1·10
267		30c. Two rails drinking	1·25	1·40
268		45c. Rail and nest	1·50	1·60
MS269		165×78 mm. 45c. Two rails by pool; 85c. Chick hatching; $1.20, Head of rail	10·00	11·00

64 R.A.F. Supermarine Spitfires on Island Airstrip

1992. 50th Anniv of Second World War. Mult.

270		45c. Type **64**	2·50	1·40
271		85c. Mitsubishi A6M Zero-Sen aircraft bombing Kampong	3·75	3·75
272		$1.20 R.A.F. Short Sunderland flying boat	4·75	5·00

65 Waves breaking on Reef

1992. Christmas. Multicoloured.

273		40c. Type **65**	1·50	80
274		80c. Direction Island	3·25	3·50
275		$1 Moorish idols (fish) and coral	3·25	3·50

66 "Lobophyllia hemprichii"

1993. Corals. Multicoloured.

276		45c. Type **66**	75	55
277		85c. "Pocillopora eydouxi"	1·25	1·75
278		$1.05 "Fungia scutaria"	1·75	2·00
279		$1.20 "Sarcophyton sp"	1·75	2·25

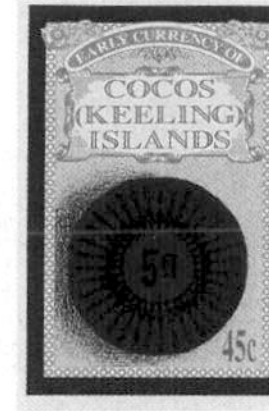

67 Plastic 5r. Token

1993. Early Cocos (Keeling) Islands Currency. Multicoloured.

280		45c. Type **67**	1·60	80
281		85c. 1968 1r. plastic token	2·25	2·50
282		$1.05 1977 150r. commemorative gold coin	2·75	3·00
283		$1.20 1910 plastic token	2·75	3·50

68 Primary School Pupil

1993. Education. Multicoloured.

284		5c. Type **68**	50	85
285		45c. Secondary school pupil	1·25	60
286		85c. Learning traditional crafts	2·25	2·25
287		$1.05 Learning office skills	2·75	3·50
288		$1.20 Seaman training	3·25	3·75

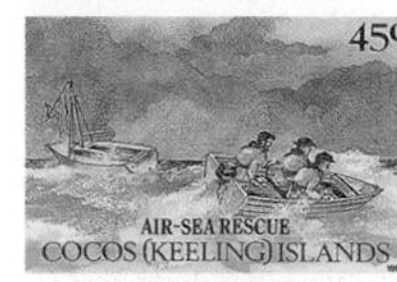

69 Lifeboat and Crippled Yacht

1993. Air-Sea Rescue. Multicoloured.

289		45c. Type **69**	2·50	1·40
290		85c. Israeli Aircraft Industry Westwind Seascan (aircraft)	3·50	3·75
291		$1.05 "R.J. Hawke" (ferry)	4·00	5·00
MS292		135×61 mm. Nos. 289/91	10·00	11·00

70 Peace Doves

1993. Christmas.

293	**70**	40c. multicoloured	1·75	80
294	**70**	80c. multicoloured	3·00	3·50
295	**70**	$1 multicoloured	3·00	3·50

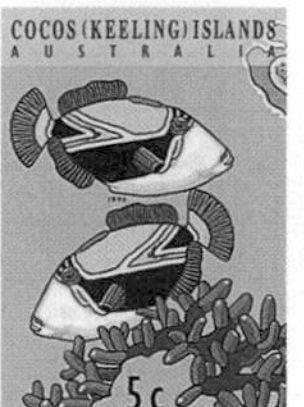

71 Rectangle Triggerfish and Coral

1994. Transfer of Postal Service to Australia Post. Multicoloured.

No.	Description	Mint	Used
296	5c. Type **71**	35	45
297	5c. Three rectangle triggerfish and map section	35	45
298	5c. Two rectangle triggerfish and map section	35	45
299	5c. Two rectangle triggerfish, map section and red coral	35	45
300	5c. Rectangle triggerfish with red and brown corals	35	45
301	10c. Green turtles on beach	35	45
302	10c. Two green turtles	35	45
303	10c. Crowd of young green turtles	35	45
304	10c. Green turtle and map section	35	45
305	10c. Green turtle, pyramid butterflyfish and map section	35	45
306	20c. Three pyramid butterflyfish and map section	55	65
307	20c. Pyramid butterflyfish with brown coral	55	65
308	20c. Two pyramid butterflyfish and coral	55	65
309	20c. Three pyramid butterflyfish and coral	55	65
310	20c. Coral, pyramid butterflyfish and map section	55	65
311	45c. Jukongs with map of airport	60	70
312	45c. Two jukongs with red or blue sails and map section	60	70
313	45c. Jukong in shallows	60	70
314	45c. Two jukongs with red or yellow sails and map section	60	70
315	45c. Two jukongs, one with blue jib, and map section	60	70

Nos. 296/315 were printed together, se-tenant, with the backgrounds forming a composite map.

72 Prabu Abjasa Puppet

1994. Shadow Puppets. Multicoloured.

No.	Description	Mint	Used
316	45c. Type **72**	65	50
317	90c. Prabu Pandu	1·25	1·50
318	$1 Judistra	1·40	1·50
319	$1.35 Abimanju	1·50	2·50

73 Angel playing Harp

1994. Seasonal Festivals. Multicoloured.

No.	Description	Mint	Used
320	40c. Type **73**	50	50
321	45c. Wise Man holding gift	55	50
322	80c. Mosque at night	1·00	1·75

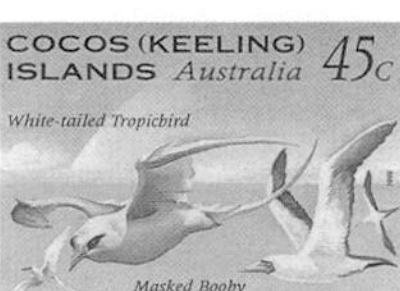

74 White-tailed Tropic Bird and Blue-faced Booby ("Masked Booby")

1995. Sea-birds of North Keeling Island. Multicoloured.

No.	Description	Mint	Used
323	45c. Type **74**	75	50
324	85c. Great frigate bird and white tern	1·00	1·50
MS325	106×70 mm. Nos. 323/4	1·75	2·50

75 Yellow Crazy Ant

1995. Insects. Multicoloured.

No.	Description	Mint	Used
326	45c. Type **75**	1·00	1·25
327	45c. Aedes mosquito	1·00	1·25
328	45c. Hawk moth	1·00	1·25
329	45c. Scarab beetle	1·00	1·25
330	45c. Lauxaniid fly	1·00	1·25
331	$1.20 Common eggfly (butterfly)	1·50	1·75

Nos. 326/30 were printed together, se-tenant, forming a composite design.

76 Saddle Butterflyfish

1995. Marine Life. Multicoloured.

No.	Description	Mint	Used
332	5c. Redspot wrasse	15	20
333	30c. Blue-throated triggerfish ("Gilded triggerfish")	40	45
334	40c. Type **76**	50	55
335	45c. Arc-eyed hawkfish	1·00	1·00
335a	45c. Wideband fusilier	50	55
335b	45c. Striped surgeonfish	50	55
335c	45c. Orangeband surgeonfish	50	55
335d	45c. Indo-Pacific sergeant	50	55
335e	70c. Crowned squirrelfish	75	1·00
336	75c. Orange-pine unicornfish	75	1·00
337	80c. Blue tang	80	80
338	85c. Juvenile twin-spotted wrasse ("Humpback wrasse")	80	80
339	90c. Threadfin butterflyfish	90	1·25
339a	95c. Sixstripe wrasse	1·00	1·00
340	$1 Bluestripe snapper	1·25	1·25
341	$1.05 Longnosed butterflyfish	1·25	1·25
342	$1.20 Freckled hawkfish	1·25	1·25
343	$2 Powder-blue surgeonfish	1·75	2·00
343a	$5 Goldback anthias	3·50	4·25

77 Members of Malay Community

1996. Hari Raya Puasa Festival. Multicoloured.

No.	Description	Mint	Used
344	45c. Type **77**	80	60
345	75c. Beating drums	1·50	1·90
346	85c. Preparing festival meal	1·50	1·90

78 Black Rhinoceros with Calf

1996. Cocos Quarantine Station. Multicoloured.

No.	Description	Mint	Used
347	45c. Type **78**	2·00	1·25
348	50c. Alpacas	1·25	1·50
349	$1.05 Boran cattle	2·00	2·50
350	$1.20 Ostrich with chicks	2·75	3·00

79 Dancers and Tambourine

1997. Hari Raya Puasa Festival. Multicoloured.

No.	Description	Mint	Used
351	45c. Type **79**	65	60
352	75c. Girl clapping and sailing dinghies	1·00	1·60
353	85c. Dancers on beach and food	1·25	1·60

80 "Wrapped Present" (Lazina Brian)

1998. Hari Raya Puasa Festival. Paintings by children. Multicoloured.

No.	Description	Mint	Used
354	45c. Type **80**	85	1·00
355	45c. "Mosque" (Azran Jim)	85	1·00
356	45c. "Cocos Malay Woman" (Kate Gossage)	85	1·00
357	45c. "Yacht" (Matt Harber)	85	1·00
358	45c. "People dancing" (Rakin Chongkin)	85	1·00

81 Preparing Food on Beach

1999. Hari Raya Puasa Festival. Multicoloured.

No.	Description	Mint	Used
359	45c. Type **81**	70	85
360	45c. Woman with child and jukongs on beach	70	85
361	45c. Jukongs and palm fronds	70	85
362	45c. Two men watching jukongs	70	85
363	45c. Jukong and white flowers	70	85

82 Jukong (Cocos sailing boat)

1999. Island Wildlife. Multicoloured.

No.	Description	Mint	Used
364	5c. Type **82**	55	65
365	5c. Bennett's and ornate butterflyfish	55	65
366	5c. Green and hawksbill turtles	55	65
367	5c. Yellow-tailed anemonefish and various butterflyfish	55	65
368	5c. Hump-headed wrasse	55	65
369	10c. Yacht, Direction Island	55	65
370	10c. Black-backed butterflyfish	55	65
371	10c. Moorish idols	55	65
372	10c. "Pseudoanthias cooperi" (fish)	55	65
373	10c. Red-tailed tropic birds	55	65
374	25c. Blue-faced booby	75	85
375	25c. Lesser wanderer (butterfly)	75	85
376	25c. Lesser and greater frigate birds	75	85
377	25c. "Hippotion velox" (moth)	75	85
378	25c. Common eggfly (butterfly)	75	85
379	45c. White tern	85	95
380	45c. Red-tailed tropic bird and great frigate bird	85	95
381	45c. Chinese rose	85	95
382	45c. Meadow argus (butterfly)	85	95
383	45c. Sea hibiscus	85	95

Nos. 364/83 were printed together, se-tenant, with the backgrounds forming a composite design.

83 Ratma Anthoney

2000. New Millennium. "Face of Cocos (Keeling) Islands". Multicoloured.

No.	Description	Mint	Used
384	45c. Type **83**	70	85
385	45c. Nakia Haji Dolman (schoolgirl)	70	85
386	45c. Muller Eymin (elderly man)	70	85
387	45c. Courtney Press (toddler)	70	85
388	45c. Mhd Abu-Yazid (school boy)	70	85

84 Little Nipper (crab)

2000. Endangered Species. Crabs of Cocos (Keeling) Islands. Multicoloured.

No.	Description	Mint	Used
389	5c. Type **84**	50	70
390	5c. Purple crab	50	70
391	45c. Smooth-handed ghost crab	80	95
392	45c. Horn-eyed ghost crab	80	95

85 Loggerhead Turtle

2002. Turtles. Multicoloured.

No.	Description	Mint	Used
393	45c. Type **85**	1·25	1·25
394	45c. Hawksbill turtle	1·25	1·25
395	45c. Leatherback turtle	1·25	1·25
396	45c. Green turtle	1·25	1·25

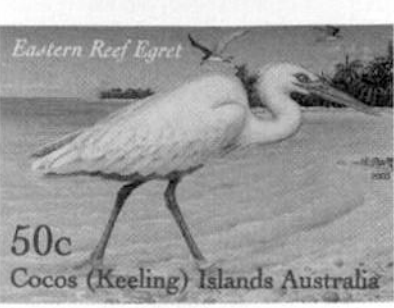

86 Eastern Reef Egret

2003. Shoreline Birds. Multicoloured.

No.	Description	Mint	Used
397	50c. Type **86**	1·75	1·75
398	50c. Sooty tern	1·75	1·75
399	50c. Ruddy turnstone	1·75	1·75
400	50c. Whimbrel	1·75	1·75

Nos. 397/400 were printed together, se-tenant, forming a composite background design of a shoreline.

87 Queen Elizabeth II and Cocos Malay Musicians

2004. 50th Anniv of Royal Tour to Australia. Visit of Queen Elizabeth II to Cocos (Keeling) Islands. Multicoloured.

No.	Description	Mint	Used
401	50c. Type **87**	1·75	1·75
402	50c. Queen and *Gothic* (liner acting as Royal Yacht)	1·75	1·75
403	$1 Queen and Clunies Ross (Oceania) House	2·75	2·75
404	$1.45 Queen and model jukong (Cocos sailing boat)	3·00	3·00
MS405	135×72 mm. Nos. 401/4	8·25	8·75

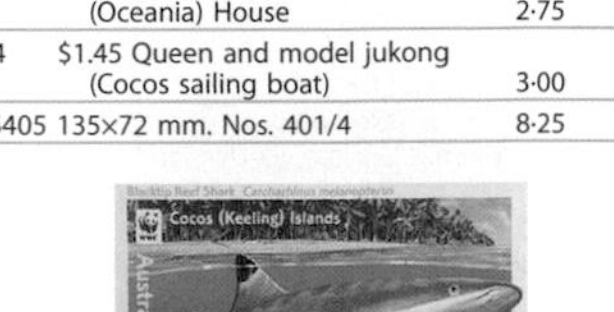

88 Blacktip Reef Shark

2005. Reef Sharks. Multicoloured.

No.	Description	Mint	Used
406	50c. Type **88**	2·00	2·00
407	50c. Two Grey reef sharks	2·00	2·00
408	$1 Two Blacktip reef sharks near atoll	3·25	3·25
409	$1.45 Grey reef shark	3·50	3·50

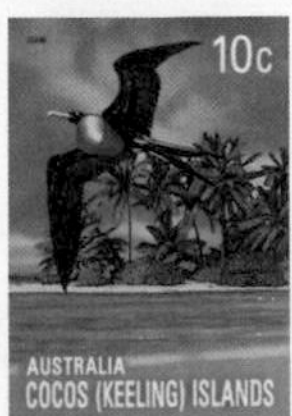

89 Frigate Bird

2006. Coral Reefs. Multicoloured.

No.	Description	Mint	Used
410	10c. Type **89**	60	60
411	10c. Booby	60	60
412	10c. Sooty terns	60	60
413	10c. White terns	60	60
414	10c. Rufous night-heron	60	60

415	25c. Threadfin butterflyfish	75	75
416	25c. Saddle butterflyfish	75	75
417	25c. Orangeband surgeonfish	75	75
418	25c. Manta ray	75	75
419	25c. Scrawled butterflyfish	75	75
420	25c. Blue tang	75	75
421	25c. Picasso triggerfish and wrasse	75	75
422	25c. Turtle	75	75
423	25c. Moorish Idol	75	75
424	25c. Longnose butterflyfish	75	75
425	50c. Seychelles butterflyfish	1·00	1·00
426	50c. Powderblue surgeonfish	1·00	1·00
427	50c. Orange-lined triggerfish and starfish	1·00	1·00
428	50c. Unidentified striped fish	1·00	1·00
429	50c. Bicoloured angelfish	1·00	1·00

Nos. 410/29 were printed together, se-tenant, forming a composite background design showing a coral reef and atoll.

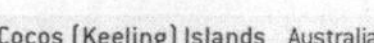

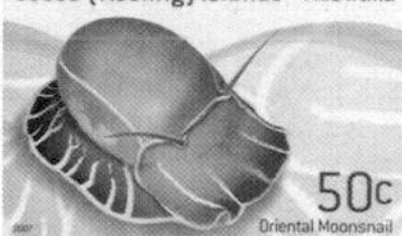

90 Oriental Moonsnail

2007. Living Shells. Multicoloured.

430	50c. Type **90**	1·75	1·75
431	50c. Pearly nautilus	1·75	1·75
432	$1 Partridge tun	2·75	2·75
433	$1.45 Giant clam	3·00	3·00

91 Chinese Pond Heron

2008. Visiting Birds. Multicoloured.

434	50c. Type **91**	1·60	1·60
435	50c. Black-winged stilt	1·60	1·60
436	$1 White-breasted waterhen	2·50	2·50
437	$1.45 Saunders' tern	2·75	2·75

92 Early 17th-century English East Indiaman

2009. 400th Anniv of First European Sighting of Cocos (Keeling) Islands by Captain William Keeling. Multicoloured.

438	55c. Type **92**	1·60	1·60
439	55c. Detail from Darwin's notebooks and sketch of fish (Charles Darwin's visit, 1836)	1·60	1·60
440	$1.10 Coconut labourer	2·50	2·50
441	$1.65 Dugong	3·00	3·00

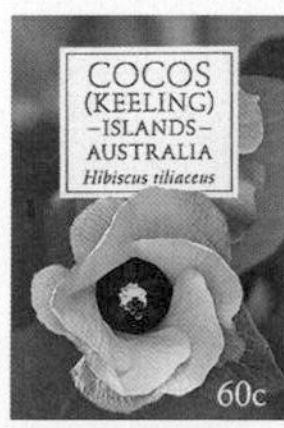

93 *Hibiscus tiliaceus*

2010. Flowers of Cocos (Keeling) Islands. Multicoloured.

442	60c. Type **93**	1·60	1·60
443	60c. *Ipomoea pes-caprae*	1·60	1·60
444	$1.20 *Morinda citrifolia*	3·00	3·00
445	$1.20 *Suriana maritima*	3·00	3·00

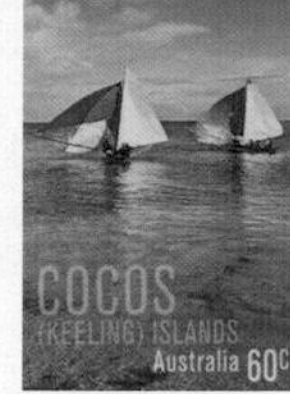

94 Jukongs

2011. Boats. Multicoloured.

446	60c. Type **94**	1·60	1·60
447	$1.20 Dinghy on beach	2·50	2·50
448	$1.80 Glass-bottom boat with canopy	2·75	2·75
449	$3 Catamaran	3·25	3·25

OFFICIAL STAMPS

1991. No. 182 surch OFFICIAL PAID MAINLAND.

O1	(43c.) on 90c. Coconut palm and mature nuts	†	90·00

No. O1 was not sold to the public in unused condition.

Pt. 20

COLOMBIA

A republic in the N.W. of South America. Formerly part of the Spanish Empire, Colombia became independent in 1819. The constituent states became the Granadine Confederation in 1858. The name was changed to the United States of New Granada in 1861, and the name Colombia was adopted later the same year.

100 centavos = 1 peso.

Prices. For the early issues prices in the used column are for postmarked copies, pen-cancellations are generally worth less.

1

1859. Imperf.

1	**1**	2½c. green	£150	£150
2	**1**	5c. blue	£190	£120
8	**1**	5c. slate	80·00	60·00
9	**1**	10c. yellow	80·00	55·00
5	**1**	20c. blue	£150	90·00
6	**1**	1p. red	95·00	£160

3

1861. Imperf.

11	**3**	2½c. black	£1300	£350
12	**3**	5c. yellow	£400	£160
13	**3**	10c. blue	£700	£200
14	**3**	20c. red	£180	55·00
15	**3**	1p. red	£1200	£350

4

1862. Imperf.

16	**4**	10c. blue	£225	£110
17	**4**	20c. red	£4250	£700
18	**4**	50c. green	£225	£150
19	**4**	1p. lilac	£550	£150

5

1862. Imperf.

21	**5**	5c. orange	95·00	60·00
24	**5**	10c. blue	£160	32·00
23	**5**	20c. red	£225	85·00
25	**5**	50c. green	£200	70·00

6

1863. Imperf.

26	**6**	5c. orange	60·00	35·00
27	**6**	10c. blue	50·00	14·50
28	**6**	20c. red	£110	60·00
29	**6**	50c. green	90·00	60·00
30	**6**	1p. mauve	£375	£190

7

8

9

1865. Imperf.

31	**7**	1c. red	9·50	9·00
32	**8**	2½c. black on lilac	19·00	12·50
33	**9**	5c. orange	43·00	19·00
34	**9**	10c. violet	60·00	4·00
35	**9**	20c. blue	60·00	19·00
37	**9**	50c. green	£110	49·00
38	**9**	1p. red	£120	17·00

10

1865. Imperf.

39	**10**	25c. black on blue	80·00	50·00
40	**10**	50c. black on yellow	55·00	75·00
41	**10**	1p. black on red	£160	£120

12

1866. Imperf. Various Arms Designs.

44	**12**	5c. orange	65·00	26·00
45	-	10c. lilac	16·00	5·00
46	-	20c. blue	39·00	20·00
47	-	50c. green	16·00	12·00
48	-	1p. red	85·00	30·00
49	-	5p. black on green	£475	£200
50	-	10p. black on red	£325	£190

19

1868. Arms (various frames) inscr "ESTADOS UNIDOS DE COLOMBIA". Imperf.

51	**19**	5c. yellow	65·00	49·00
52	**19**	10c. lilac	4·00	1·00
54	**19**	20c. blue	2·75	1·20
55	**19**	50c. green	3·25	2·30
57	**19**	1p. red	3·75	3·25

24

1869. Imperf.

58	**24**	2½c. black on violet	4·25	2·40

25 26 27

28

1870. Imperf.

59a	**25**	1c. green	4·75	4·50
60	**25**	1c. red	4·75	4·50
61	**26**	2c. brown	2·20	2·10
62	**27**	5c. orange	2·75	1·80
65a	**28**	10c. mauve	3·25	2·75
67	**28**	25c. black on blue	22·00	18·00
87	**28**	25c. green	44·00	43·00

30

1870. Different frames. Imperf.

69	**30**	5p. black on green	55·00	45·00
71	**30**	10p. black on red	22·00	3·75

See also Nos. 118/19.

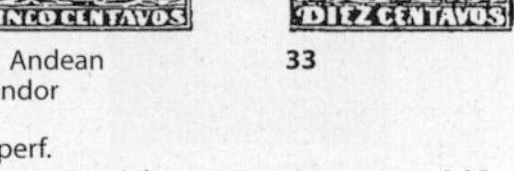

32 Andean Condor 33

1876. Imperf.

84	**32**	5c. violet	9·25	2·75
85	**33**	10c. brown	4·50	1·50
86	-	20c. blue	6·50	3·25

DESIGN: 20c. As Type **33** but with different frame.

35

1881. Imperf.

93	**35**	1c. green	4·50	6·50
99	**35**	2c. red	2·75	2·10
100	**35**	5c. blue	2·20	65
101	**35**	10c. purple	5·50	1·70
97	**35**	20c. black	6·00	2·75

39

1881. Imperf.

102	**39**	1c. black on green	4·50	6·50
103	**39**	2c. black on rose	4·50	6·50
104	**39**	5c. black on lilac	11·00	2·30

40

1883. Inscr "CORREOS NACIONALES DE LOS E.E. U.U. DE COLOMBIA".

106a	**40**	1c. yellow on green	1·30	1·30
107	**40**	2c. red on pink	1·30	1·70
109	**40**	5c. blue on blue	3·25	1·50
111	**40**	10c. orange on yellow	1·70	1·80
112	**40**	20c. mauve on lilac	1·90	1·80
113	**40**	50c. brown on buff	3·75	4·25
114	**40**	1p. red on blue	7·25	2·50
115	**40**	5p. brown on yellow	10·00	9·50
116	**40**	10p. black on red	11·00	11·50

1886. Perf.

118	**30**	5p. brown	13·00	7·50
119	**30**	10p. black on lilac	13·00	7·50

42

43 Gen. Sucre

44 Bolivar

46 Gen. Nerino

1886

120	**42**	1c. green	2·20	95
121	**43**	2c. red on pink	2·75	1·40
124	**44**	5c. blue on blue	2·20	55
125	-	10c. orange (Pres. Nunez)	4·75	95
126	**46**	20c. violet on lilac ("REPULICA")	3·75	1·40
137	**46**	20c. violet on lilac ("REPUBLICA")	2·20	1·70
130	**42**	50c. brown on buff	2·20	2·30
132	**42**	1p. mauve	4·50	2·10
133	**42**	5p. brown	11·00	8·50
134	**42**	5p. black	19·00	13·00
135	**42**	10p. black on pink	28·00	9·00

See also Nos. 162/4a.

48

50

51

1890

143	**48**	1c. green on green	2·40	2·10
144	**51**	2c. red on pink	1·20	1·20
145	**50**	5c. blue on blue	1·80	55
147	**51**	10c. brown on yellow	1·30	55
148	**51**	20c. violet	4·75	5·75

See also Nos. 149, etc.

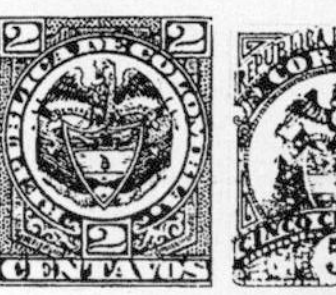

53

54 55

58

1892

149b	**48**	1c. red on yellow	1·10	55
150	**53**	2c. red on rose	55·00	55·00
151a	**53**	2c. green	65	45
152a	**50**	5c. black on brown	17·00	45
153	**54**	5c. brown on brown	1·00	55
155	**51**	10c. brown on red	1·00	55
156	**55**	20c. brown on blue	1·00	55
159	**42**	50c. violet on lilac	1·70	95
161	**58**	1p. blue on green	2·75	1·20
162	**42**	5p. red on pink	11·00	4·25
164	**42**	10p. blue	21·00	4·50

61

1898

171	**61**	1c. red on yellow	90	45
172	**61**	5c. brown on brown	90	45
173	**61**	10c. brown on red	2·75	1·30
174	**61**	50c. blue on lilac	1·80	1·60

For stamps showing map of Panama and inscr "COLOMBIA" see Panama Nos. 5/18.

For provisionals issued at Cartagena during the Civil War, 1899–1902, see list in Stanley Gibbons Stamp Catalogue Part 20 (South America).

75

1902. Arms in various frames. Imperf or perf.

259	**75**	½c. brown	1·40	1·40
260	**75**	1c. green	4·50	4·25
192	**75**	2c. black on red	15	15
261	**75**	2c. blue	1·10	85
193	**75**	4c. red on green	15	15
194	**75**	4c. blue on green	20	20
195	**75**	5c. green on green	15	15
196	**75**	5c. blue on blue	10	10
262	**75**	5c. red	1·20	1·20
197	**75**	10c. black on pink	15	15
263	**75**	10c. mauve	1·40	1·20
198	**75**	20c. brown on brown	15	15
199	**75**	20c. blue on brown	20	20
200	**75**	50c. green on red	45	45
201	**75**	50c. blue on red	1·50	1·50
202	**75**	1p. purple on brown	25	25

82

1903. Imperf or perf.

203	**82**	5p. green on blue	9·00	4·25
204	**82**	10p. green on green	9·00	9·00
205	**82**	50p. orange on red	45·00	42·00
206	**82**	100p. blue on red	38·00	35·00

Nos. 205/6 are larger (31×38 mm).

85 River Magdalena

1902. Imperf or perf.

212A	**85**	2c. green	2·10	2·00
213A	**85**	2c. blue	2·10	2·00
214A	**85**	2c. red	30·00	29·00
215A	-	10c. red	1·40	1·40
216A	-	10c. pink	1·40	1·40
219A	-	10c. orange	17·00	16·00
242A	-	10c. blue on brown	8·25	8·00
243A	-	10c. blue on green	5·00	4·75
245A	-	10c. blue on lilac	5·00	4·75
247A	-	10c. blue on red	5·00	4·75
220A	-	20c. violet	4·75	4·50
221A	-	20c. blue	12·00	11·50
224A	-	20c. red	26·00	26·00

DESIGNS: 10c. Iron Quay, Savanilla, with eagle above; 20c. Hill of La Popa.

88 Gunboat "Cartagena" **89** Bolivar

90 General Pinzon

91

92

1903. Imperf or perf.

225A	**88**	5c. blue	3·50	3·50
226A	**88**	5c. brown	6·00	5·75
227A	**89**	50c. green	6·00	5·75
228A	**89**	50c. brown	6·00	5·75
230A	**89**	50c. orange	5·00	4·75
231	**89**	50c. red	6·00	5·75
233	**90**	1p. brown	2·10	2·00
234	**90**	1p. red	3·25	3·25
235	**90**	1p. blue	3·25	3·25
237	**91**	5p. brown	11·00	10·50
238	**91**	5p. purple	7·25	7·00
239	**91**	5p. green	10·00	9·50
240	**92**	10p. green	10·50	10·00
241	**92**	10p. purple	33·00	32·00

93

1902

248	**93**	1c. green on yellow	45	65
249	**93**	2c. red on pink	45	65
250	**93**	5c. blue	45	65
251	**93**	10c. brown on yellow	45	65
252	**93**	20c. mauve on pink	55	65
253	**93**	50c. red on green	2·75	3·75
254	**93**	1p. black on yellow	6·00	8·50
255	**93**	5p. blue on blue	46·00	45·00
256	**93**	10p. brown on pink	29·00	28·00

96 **97** **98** President Marroquin

1904

270	**96**	½c. yellow	1·10	30
274	**96**	1c. green	1·00	30
278	**96**	2c. red	1·00	30
281	**96**	5c. blue	1·80	30
283	**96**	10c. violet	2·20	3·25
284	**96**	20c. black	2·20	30
286	**97**	1p. brown	24·00	3·75
287	**98**	5p. black and red	75·00	75·00
288	**98**	10p. black and blue	75·00	75·00

102 Camilo Torres **104** Narino demanding Liberation of Slaves

1910. Centenary of Independence.

345	**102**	½c. black and purple	65	45
346	-	1c. green	65	30
347	-	2c. red	65	30
348	-	5c. blue	1·70	55
349	-	10c. purple	10·00	7·50
350	-	20c. brown	19·00	10·00
351	**104**	1p. purple	£110	32·00
352	-	10p. lake	£450	£325

DESIGNS—As Type **102**: 1c. P. Salavarrieta; 2c. Narino; 5c. Bolivar; 10c. Caldas; 20c. Santander. As Type **104**: 10p. Bolivar resigning.

110 C. Torres **113** Arms **111** Boyaca Monument

123 La Sabana Station **112** Cartagena

1917. Portraits as T **110**.

357	**110**	½c. yellow (Caldas)	20	10
358	**110**	1c. green (Torres)	20	10
393	**113**	1½c. brown	1·70	75
359	**110**	2c. red (Narino)	20	10
380	**113**	3c. red on yellow	20	15
394	**113**	3c. blue	75	30
360	**110**	4c. purple (Santander)	1·20	15
395	**110**	4c. blue (Santander)	65	30
361	**110**	5c. blue (Bolivar)	3·75	20
396	**110**	5c. red (Bolivar)	3·75	30
397	**113**	8c. blue	75	30
362	**110**	10c. grey (Cordoba)	3·75	20
398	**110**	10c. blue (Cordoba)	12·00	65
363	**111**	20c. red	2·00	20
399	**113**	30c. bistre (Caldas)	7·75	95
400	**123**	40c. brown	12·00	1·60
364	**112**	50c. red	2·20	30
606	**112**	50c. red (San Pedro Alejandrino)	17·00	7·00
365a	**110**	1p. blue (Sucre)	15·00	30
366	**110**	2p. orange (Cuervo)	18·00	45
367	**110**	5p. grey (Ricaurte)	50·00	14·00
401	**110**	5p. violet (Ricaurte)	12·00	1·20
368	**113**	10p. brown	60·00	15·00
402	**113**	10p. green	20·00	3·25

For similar 40c. see No. 541.

1918. Surch **Especie Provisional** and value.

374	**96**	0.00½c. on 20c. black	1·70	45
376	**96**	0.03c. on 10c. violet	3·75	75

115

1918

378	**115**	3c. red	1·20	20

1918. Air. No. 359 optd **1er Servicio Postal Aereo 6-18-19.**

379	2c. red	£4750	£2250

1920. As T **75**, **96** and **113** but with "PROVISIONAL" added in label across design.

381A	**96**	½c. yellow	1·80	65
382A	**96**	1c. green	1·10	10
383A	**96**	2c. red	75	20
384A	**113**	3c. green	75	20
385A	**96**	5c. blue	1·70	30
386A	**96**	10c. violet	7·75	1·60
387A	**96**	10c. blue	12·00	65
388A	**96**	20c. green	8·75	5·25
389A	**75**	50c. red	11·00	3·75

1921. No. 360 surch **PROVICIONAL $003.**

390	$0.03 on 4c. purple	1·20	20

1921. No. 360 surch **PROVISIONAL $0.03.**

392	$0.03 on 4c. purple	5·00	2·00

124

1924

403	**124**	1c. red	1·10	20
404	**124**	3c. blue	1·20	20

1925. Large fiscal stamps surch **CORREOS 1 CENTAVO** or optd **CORREOS PROVISIONAL**.

405	1c. on 3c. brown	90	20
406	4c. purple	65	20

127

1926

410	**127**	1c. green	65	20
411	**127**	4c. blue	75	20

129 Death of Bolivar (after P. A. Quijano)

1930. Death Centenary of Bolivar.

412	**129**	4c. black and blue	45	20

132 **133** Galleon

1932. Air. Optd **CORREO AEREO**.

413	**132**	5c. yellow	13·00	13·00
414	**132**	10c. purple	2·75	75
415	**132**	15c. green	5·00	5·00
416	**132**	20c. red	2·40	45
417	**132**	30c. blue	2·75	75
418	**132**	40c. lilac	3·25	1·60
419	**132**	50c. olive	5·50	4·75
420	**132**	60c. brown	5·50	4·75
421	**132**	80c. green	22·00	21·00
422	**133**	1p. blue	19·00	15·00
423	**133**	2p. red	50·00	45·00
424	**133**	3p. mauve	£100	85·00
425	**133**	5p. olive	£170	£180

These and similar stamps without the "CORREO AEREO" overprint were issues of a private air company and are not listed in this catalogue.

1932. Nos. 395 and 399 surch.

427	1c. on 4c. blue	20	10
428	20c. on 30c. bistre	13·00	45

137 Oil Wells **138** Coffee Plantation

140 Gold Mining **141** Columbus

1932. 1c. is vert, 8c. is horiz.

429	-	1c. green (Emeralds)	75	20
430	**137**	2c. red (Oil)	75	30
431	**138**	5c. brown (Coffee)	90	30
432	-	8c. blue (Platinum)	6·00	85
485	**140**	10c. yellow (Gold)	3·25	45
486	**141**	20c. blue	13·00	1·60

142 Coffee **143** Gold

1932. Air.

435	**142**	5c. brown and orange	1·00	30
436	-	10c. black and red	1·20	20
437	-	15c. violet and green	65	20
438	-	15c. violet and red	5·00	30
439	-	20c. green and red	1·10	10
440	-	20c. olive and green	5·50	45
441	**142**	30c. brown and blue	3·00	20
442	-	40c. bistre and violet	1·50	20
443	-	50c. brown and green	9·25	2·10
444	-	60c. violet and brown	1·90	20
445	**142**	80c. brown and green	13·00	1·30
446	**143**	1p. bistre and blue	14·50	1·30
447	**143**	2p. bistre and red	22·00	3·75
448	-	3p. green and violet	35·00	9·50
449	-	5p. green and olive	75·00	28·00

DESIGNS—As Type **142**: 10c., 50c. Cattle; 15c., 60c. Oil Wells; 20c., 40c. Bananas. As Type **143**: 3p., 5p. Emeralds.

144 Pedro de Heredia

1934. 400th Anniv of Cartagena.

451	**144**	1c. green	3·75	1·10
452	**144**	5c. brown	5·00	85
453	**144**	8c. blue	3·75	1·10

1934. Air. 4th Centenary of Cartagena. Surch **CARTAGENA 1533 1933** and value.

454	-	10c. on 50c. brown and green (No. 443)	6·00	6·00
455	**142**	15c. on 80c. brn & grn	8·25	8·25
456	**143**	20c. on 1p. bis & bl	8·75	8·75
457	**143**	30c. on 2p. bistre and red	10·00	10·00

147 Oil Wells **148** Coffee Plantation

1934

458	**147**	2c. red	55	30
459	**148**	5c. brown	5·00	10
460	-	10c. orange	33·00	65

DESIGN: 10c. Gold miner facing left.

151 Allegory of 1935 Olympiad

1935. 3rd National Olympiad. Inscr "III OLIMPIADA BARRANQUILLA 1935".

461		2c. orange and green	2·10	65
462		4c. green	2·10	65
463	**151**	5c. yellow and brown	2·10	65
464	-	7c. red	4·00	2·30
465	-	8c. mauve and black	3·25	3·25
466	-	10c. blue and brown	4·75	2·30
467	-	12c. blue	5·50	3·75
468	-	15c. red and blue	4·75	2·30
469	-	18c. yellow and purple	9·25	7·00
470	-	20c. green and violet	11·00	9·00
471	-	24c. blue and green	11·00	8·50
472	-	50c. orange and blue	17·00	14·00
473	-	1p. blue and olive	£150	80·00
474	-	2p. blue and green	£190	£150
475	-	5p. blue and violet	£600	£650
476	-	10p. blue and black	£700	£750

DESIGNS—VERT: 2c. Footballers; 4c. Discus thrower; 1p. G.P.O.; 2p. "Flag of the Race" Monument; 5p. Arms; 10p. Andean condor. HORIZ: 7c. Runners; 8c. Tennis player; 10c. Hurdler; 12c. Pier; 15c. Athlete; 18c. Baseball; 20c. Seashore; 24c. Swimmer; 50c. Aerial view of Barranquilla.

152 Nurse and Patients

1935. Obligatory Tax. Red Cross.

477	**152**	5c. red and green	5·00	10

1935. Surch **12 CENTAVOS**.

478	12c. on 1p. blue (No. 365a)	6·00	1·70

154 Simon Bolivar **155** Tequendama Falls

1937

487	**154**	1c. green	20	10
488	**155**	10c. red	20	10
489	**155**	12c. blue	5·50	1·70

156 Footballer **157** Discus Thrower

1937. 4th National Olympiad.

490	**156**	3c. green	1·40	85
491	**157**	10c. red	5·00	2·30
492	-	1p. black	44·00	34·00

DESIGN: 1p. Runner (20½×27 mm).

159 Exhibition Palace

1937. Barranquilla Industrial Exhibition.

493	**159**	5c. purple	2·75	30
494	-	15c. blue	8·25	5·25
495	-	50c. brown	24·00	9·00

DESIGNS—HORIZ: 15c. Stadium. VERT: 50c. "Flag of the Race" Monument.

161 Mother and Child

1937. Obligatory Tax. Red Cross.

509	**161**	5c. red	3·75	1·20

1937. Surch in figures and words.

510	**156**	1c. on 3c. green	1·30	1·30
511	**155**	2c. on 12c. blue	65	55
512	-	5c. on 8c. blue (No. 432)	65	55
513	-	5c. on 8c. blue (No. 397)	75	85
514	**155**	10c. on 12c. blue	7·25	1·40

164 Entrance to Church of the Rosary **166** "Bochica" (Indian god)

1938. 400th Anniv of Bogota.

515	-	1c. green	35	20
516	**164**	2c. red	35	20
517	-	5c. black	45	30
518	-	10c. brown	1·00	55
519	**166**	15c. blue	5·00	2·00
520	-	20c. mauve	5·00	2·00
521	-	1p. brown	65·00	37·00

DESIGNS—VERT: 1c. "Calle del Arco" ("Street of the Arch") Old Bogota; 5c. Bogota Arms; 10c. G. J. de Quesada. HORIZ (larger): 20c. Convent of S. Domingo; 1p. First Mass on Site of Bogota.

168 Proposed P.O., Bogota

1939. Obligatory Tax. P.O. Rebuilding Fund.

522	**168**	¼c. blue	35	20
564	**168**	¼c. purple	35	20
523	**168**	½c. red	35	20
524	**168**	1c. violet	45	30
567	**168**	1c. orange	2·40	95
525	**168**	2c. green	75	30
526	**168**	20c. brown	6·00	2·00

1939. Air. Surch **5 cts** or **15 cts** and bar.

527	5c. on 20c. (No. 439)	45	20
528	5c. on 40c. (No. 442)	55	20
530	15c. on 30c. (No. 441)	1·10	20
531	15c. on 40c. (No. 442)	1·50	45

171 Bolivar **172** Coffee Plantation

173 Arms of Colombia **174** Columbus **175** Caldas

176 La Sabana Station

1939

533	**171**	1c. green	10	10
535	**172**	5c. brown	20	10
536	**172**	5c. blue	20	10
538	**173**	15c. blue	2·20	10
539	**174**	20c. black	24·00	30
540	**175**	30c. olive	7·25	45
541	**176**	40c. brown	22·00	4·75

For similar 40c. see No. 400.

178 Proposed New P.O., Bogota

1940. Obligatory Tax. P.O. Rebuilding Fund.

542	**178**	¼c. blue	35	15
543	**178**	½c. red	35	15
544	**178**	1c. violet	35	15
545	**178**	2c. green	45	30
546	**178**	20c. brown	1·70	30

179 "Arms and the Law" **180** Bridge at Boyaca

1940. Death Centenary of Gen. Santander.

547	-	1c. olive	35	30
548	**179**	2c. red	65	45
549	-	5c. brown	35	30
550	-	8c. red	2·40	2·30
551	-	10c. yellow	1·10	75
552	-	15c. blue	2·75	1·80
553	-	20c. green	3·75	2·75
554	**180**	50c. violet	8·75	8·00
555	-	1p. red	28·00	27·00
556	-	2p. orange	90·00	85·00

DESIGNS—VERT: 1c. Gen. Santander; 5c. Medallion of Santander by David; 8c. Santander's statue, Cucuta; 15c. Church at Rosario. HORIZ: 10c. Santander's birthplace, Rosario; 20c. Battlefield at Paya; 1p. Death of Santander; 2p. Victorious Army at Zamora.

181 Tobacco Plant **182** Santander **183** Garcia Rovira

184 General Sucre

1940

557	**181**	8c. green and red	1·70	1·90
558	**182**	15c. blue	1·50	30
559	**183**	20c. grey	6·00	65
560	-	40c. brown (Galan)	3·50	65
561	**184**	1p. black	11·00	75
562	**184**	1p. violet	4·00	1·60

185 "Protection"

1940. Obligatory Tax. Red Cross Fund.

563	**185**	5c. red	45	30

186 Pre-Colombian Monument **187** Proclamation of Independence

1941. Air.

568	**186**	5c. grey	10	
691	**186**	5c. yellow	35	10
742	**186**	5c. blue	65	20
747	**186**	5c. red	65	20
569	-	10c. orange	20	10
692	-	10c. red	35	10
743	-	10c. blue	65	30
570	-	15c. red	20	10
693	-	15c. blue	35	10
571	-	20c. green	45	10
694	-	20c. violet	35	10
745	-	20c. blue	1·30	55
749	-	20c. red	1·30	30
572	**186**	30c. blue	45	10
695	**186**	30c. green	45	10
750	**186**	30c. red	2·75	75
573	-	40c. purple	2·00	10
696	-	40c. grey	90	20
574	-	50c. green	2·00	10
697	-	50c. red	1·20	20
575	-	60c. purple	2·00	10
698	-	60c. olive	1·50	20
576	**186**	80c. olive	4·50	30
699	**186**	80c. brown	2·75	30
577	**187**	1p. black and blue	5·00	45
700	**187**	1p. brown and olive	5·50	45
578	-	2p. black and red	11·00	2·10
701	-	2p. blue and green	6·50	1·30
579	**187**	3p. black and violet	22·00	8·50
702	**187**	3p. black and red	14·50	7·00
580	-	5p. black and green	55·00	28·00
703	-	5p. green and sepia	39·00	18·00

DESIGNS: As Type **186**: 10c., 40c. "El Dorado" Monument; 15c., 50c. Spanish Fort, Cartagena; 20c., 60c. Street in Old Bogota. As Type **187**: 2p., 5p. National Library, Bogota.

188 Arms of Palmira

1942. 8th National Agricultural Exn, Palmira.

581	**188**	30c. red	7·25	85

189 Home of Jorge Isaacs (author)

1942. Honouring J. Isaacs.

582	**189**	50c. green	7·25	85

190 Peace Conference Delegates

1942. 40th Anniv of Wisconsin Peace Treaty ending Civil War.

583	**190**	10c. orange	5·00	65

1943. Surch $ 0.0½ MEDIO CENTAVO.

584	**168**	½c. on 1c. violet	35	15
585	**168**	½c. on 2c. green	35	15
586	**168**	½c. on 20c. brown	35	20

1944. Surch **5 Centavos**.

587	5c. on 10c. orge (No. 460)	35	10

193 National Shrine **194** San Pedro, Alejandrino

1944

592	**193**	30c. olive	2·75	1·70
593	**194**	50c. red	2·75	1·70

1944. Surch with new values in figures and words.

594	**172**	1c. on 5c. brn (No. 535)	20	10
595	**172**	2c. on 5c. brn (No. 535)	20	10

195 Banner **196** Viceroy Solis Building

1944. 75th Anniv of General Benefit Institution of Cundinamarca.

596	**195**	2c. blue and yellow	35	30

No.	Type	Description	Mint	Used
597	-	5c. blue and yellow	35	30
598	-	20c. black and green	1·10	1·10
599	-	40c. black and red	5·00	4·75
600	196	1p. black and red	13·00	13·00
MS601		100×87 mm. Nos. 596/600. Imperf	44·00	55·00

DESIGNS: As T **195**: 5c. Arms of the Institution; 20c. Manuel Murillo Toro. As T **196**: 40c. St. Juan de Dios Maternity Hospital.

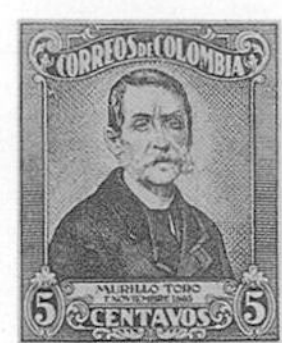

199 Manuel Murillo Toro

1944

No.	Type	Description	Mint	Used
602	199	5c. olive	20	20

201 Proposed P.O., Bogota

1945. Obligatory Tax. P.O. Rebuilding Fund.

No.	Type	Description	Mint	Used
609	201	¼c. blue	35	10
610	201	¼c. brown	35	10
611	201	½c. red	35	10
612	201	½c. mauve	35	10
613	201	1c. violet	35	20
614	201	1c. orange	35	20
615	201	1c. green	35	20
616	201	2c. green	35	20
617a	201	20c. brown	1·00	30

202 Stalin, Roosevelt and Churchill

1945. Victory. Optd with T **202**.

No.	Type	Description	Mint	Used
618	172	5c. brown	55	20

203 Clock Tower, Cartagena

1945

No.	Type	Description	Mint	Used
621	203	50c. green	6·50	2·10

204 Fort San Sebastian Cartagena

1945. Air.

No.	Type	Description	Mint	Used
622	204	5c. grey	35	20
623	-	10c. orange	35	20
624	-	15c. red	35	20
625	204	20c. green	45	30
626	-	30c. blue	45	30
627	-	40c. red	90	30
628	204	50c. green	90	30
629	-	60c. purple	3·75	1·30
630	-	80c. grey	6·00	1·30
631	-	1p. blue	8·75	1·30
632	-	2p. red	12·00	4·25

DESIGNS—As Type **204**: 10c., 30c., 60c. Tequendama Falls; 15c., 40c., 80c. Santa Marta. HORIZ (larger): 1p., 2p. Capitol, Bogota.

207 Sierra Nevada of Santa Maria

1945. 25th Anniv of 1st Air Mail Service in America.

No.	Type	Description	Mint	Used
633	207	20c. green	4·75	1·80
634	-	30c. blue	4·75	1·80
635	-	50c. red	4·75	1·80

DESIGNS: 30c. Junkers F-13 seaplane "Tolima"; 50c. San Sebastian Fortress, Cartagena.

1946. Surch **1** above **UN CENTAVO**.

No.	Type	Description	Mint	Used
636	138	1c. on 5c. brown	10·00	9·50

209 Gen. Sucre

1946

No.	Type	Description	Mint	Used
638	209	1c. blue and brown	35	20
639	209	2c. red and violet	35	20
640	209	5c. blue and olive	35	20
641	209	9c. red and green	1·10	2·10
642	209	10c. orange and blue	90	65
643	209	20c. orange and black	90	65
644	209	30c. green and red	1·10	55
645	209	40c. red and green	1·10	55
646	209	50c. violet and purple	1·10	55

The 5c. to 50c. are larger (23½×32 mm).

1946. Obligatory Tax. Red Cross Fund. Optd with red cross.

No.	Type	Description	Mint	Used
647	172	5c. brown (No. 535)	65	20

211 Map of South America

1946

No.	Type	Description	Mint	Used
648	211	15c. blue	90	65

212 Bogota Observatory

1946

No.	Type	Description	Mint	Used
649	212	5c. brown	45	30
650	212	5c. blue	35	20

213 Andres Bello

1946. 80th Death Anniv of Andres Bello (poet and teacher).

No.	Type	Description	Mint	Used
651	213	3c. brown (postage)	35	10
652	213	10c. orange	90	45
653	213	15c. black	1·00	55
654	213	5c. blue (air)	35	20

214 Joaquin de Cayzedo y Cuero

1946

No.	Type	Description	Mint	Used
655	214	2p. turquoise	8·25	1·70
656	214	2p. green	1·10	20

215 Proposed New P.O., Bogota

1946. Obligatory Tax. P.O. Rebuilding Fund.

No.	Type	Description	Mint	Used
657	215	3c. blue	20	10

1946. 5th Central American and Caribbean Games, Barranquilla. As No. 621 optd **V JUEGOS C. A. Y DEL C. 1946**.

No.	Type	Description	Mint	Used
658		50c. red	2·50	1·60

217 Coffee Plant

1947

No.	Type	Description	Mint	Used
659	217	5c. multicoloured	65	20

218 "Masdevallia Nicterina"

1947. Colombian Orchids. Multicoloured.

No.	Type	Description	Mint	Used
660		1c. Type **218**	35	20
661		2c. "Miltonia vexillaria"	35	10
662		5c. "Cattleya dowiana aurea"	1·30	20
663		5c. "Cattleya chocoensis"	1·30	20
664		5c. "Odontoglossum crispum"	1·30	20
665		10c. "Cattleya labiata trianae"	2·00	30

1947. Obligatory Tax. Optd **SOBRETASA** in fancy letters.

No.	Type	Description	Mint	Used
666	183	20c. grey (No. 559)	7·25	3·75
676	141	20c. blue (No. 486)	44·00	27·00

220 Antonio Narino

1947. 4th Pan-American Press Conf, Bogota.

No.	Type	Description	Mint	Used
667	220	5c. blue on blue (post)	55	20
668	-	10c. brown on blue	55	20
669	-	5c. blue on blue (air)	75	55
670	-	10c. red on blue	1·10	65

PORTRAITS: No. 668, A. Urdaneta y Urdaneta; 669, F. J. de Caldas; 670, M. del Socorro Rodriguez.

222 Arms of Colombia and Cross

1947. Obligatory Tax. Red Cross Fund.

No.	Type	Description	Mint	Used
671	222	5c. lake	35	10
704	222	5c. red	35	10

223 J. C. Mutis and J. J. Triana

224 M. A. Caro and R. J. Cuervo

1947

No.	Type	Description	Mint	Used
673	223	25c. green	55	20
675	224	3p. purple	1·10	55

225 Bogota Cathedral

1948. 9th Pan-American Congress, Bogota. Inscr as in T **225**.

No.	Type	Description	Mint	Used
677	225	5c. brown (postage)	35	20
678	-	10c. orange	90	85
679	-	15c. blue	90	85
MS679a		91×91 mm. 50c. slate. Imperf	2·75	2·75

DESIGNS: 10c. National Capitol; 15c. Foreign Office; 50c. Map of North America and Arms of Bogota.

No.	Type	Description	Mint	Used
680		5c. brown (air)	35	20
681		15c. blue	1·50	1·50
MS681a		91×91 mm. 50c. brown. Imperf	3·50	3·50

DESIGNS: 5c. Chancellery; 15c. Raphael Court, Capitol; 50c. Map of South America and Arms of Colombia.

1948. Obligatory Tax. Savings Bank stamps surch **COLOMBIA SOBRETASA 1 CENTAVO**. Various designs.

No.	Type	Description	Mint	Used
682		1c. on 5c. brown	35	20
683		1c. on 10c. violet	35	20
684		1c. on 25c. red	35	20
685		1c. on 50c. blue	35	20

1948. Optd **C** (= "CORREOS"). No gum.

No.	Type	Description	Mint	Used
686	168	1c. orange	15	10

1948. Optd **CORREOS**.

No.	Type	Description	Mint	Used
687	201	1c. olive	10	10
688	201	2c. green	10	10
689	201	20c. brown	35	10

232 Simon Bolivar

1948

No.	Type	Description	Mint	Used
690	232	15c. green	65	20

233 Proposed New P.O., Bogota

1948. Obligatory Tax. P.O. Rebuilding Fund.

No.	Type	Description	Mint	Used
705	233	1c. red	35	10
706	233	2c. green	35	10
707	233	3c. blue	35	10
708	233	5c. grey	35	10
709	233	10c. violet	35	10

See also Nos. 756 and 758/62.

234 Carlos Martinez Silva

1949

No.	Type	Description	Mint	Used
710	234	40c. red	65	45

235 Julio Garavito Armero

1949. J. G. Armero (mathematician).

No.	Type	Description	Mint	Used
711	235	4c. green	35	10

236 Dr. Juan de Dios Carrasquilla

1949. 75th Anniv of National Agricultural Society.

712	**236**	5c. bistre	35	10

237 Arms of Colombia

238 Allegory of Justice

1949. New Constitution.

713	**237**	15c. blue (postage)	35	10
714	**238**	5c. green (air)	20	10
715	-	10c. orange	20	10

DESIGN: 10c. Allegory of Constitution.

239 Tree and Congress Emblem

1949. 1st Forestry Congress, Bogota.

716	**239**	5c. olive	35	10

240 F. J. Cisneros

1949. 50th Death Anniv of Francisco Javier Cisneros (engineer).

717	**240**	50c. blue and brown	1·70	85
718	**240**	50c. violet and green	1·70	85
719	**240**	50c. yellow and purple	1·70	85

241 Mother and Child

1950. Red Cross Fund. Surch with new value and date as in T 241.

720	**241**	5 on 2c. multicoloured	1·80	55

1950. Obligatory Tax. Optd **SOBRETASA**.

721	**172**	5c. blue	35	20

243 "Masdevallia Chimaera"

244 Santo Domingo Post Office

REPUBLICA DE COLOMBIA

CORREOS ORDINARIO

U.P.U.

1874—1949

50 CENTAVOS 50

244a Globe

1950. 75th Anniv of UPU. (a) Inscr "1874 UPU 1949".

722	**243**	1c. brown (postage)	35	10
723	-	2c. violet	35	
724	-	3c. mauve	55	10
725	-	4c. green	75	10
726	-	5c. orange	1·10	10
727	-	11c. red	3·25	1·90
728	**244**	18c. blue	5·50	75

DESIGNS—VERT: 3c. "Cattleya labiata trianae"; 4c. "Masdevallia nicterina"; 5c. "Cattleya dowiana aurea". HORIZ: 2c. "Odontoglossum crispum"; 11c. "Miltonia vexillaria".

(b) Imperf.

MS728a 90×90 mm. 50c. yellow (postage)		5·50	5·50

(c) Imperf.

MS728b 90×90 mm. 50c. slate (air)		5·50	5·50

245 Antonio Baraya (patriot)

1950

729	**245**	2c. red	20	10

246 Farm

1950

730	**246**	5c. red and buff	35	20
731	**246**	5c. green and turquoise	35	20
732	**246**	5c. blue and light blue	35	20

247 Arms of Bogota

1950

733	**247**	5p. green	4·75	2·10
734	-	10p. orange (Arms of Colombia)	13·00	2·75

248 Map and Badge

1951. 60th Anniv of Colombian Society of Engineers.

735	**248**	20c. red, yellow and blue	65	30

249 Arms of Colombia and Cross

250 Fray Bartolome de Las Casas

1951. Obligatory Tax. Red Cross Fund.

736	**249**	5c. red	45	30
737	**250**	5c. red	45	30
738	**250**	5c. green and red	45	30

251 D. G. Valencia

1951. 8th Death Anniv of D. G. Valencia (poet and orator).

739	**251**	25c. black	1·50	30

1951. Surch **1 centavo**.

740	**233**	1c. on 3c. blue	35	20

1951. Nationalization of Barranca Oilfields. Optd **REVERSION CONCESION MARES 25 Agosto 1951**.

741	**147**	2c. red	35	20

254 Dr. Nicolas Osorio

1952. Colombian Doctors.

751	**254**	1c. blue	15	10
752	-	1c. blue (P. Martinez)	15	10
753	-	1c. bl (E. Uriocoechea)	15	10
754	-	1c. blue (Jose M. Lombana)	15	10

255 Proposed New P.O., Bogota

1952

755	**255**	5c. blue	45	30
756	**233**	20c. brown	13·00	5·75
757	**201**	25c. grey	55·00	55·00
758	**233**	25c. green	1·30	30
759	-	50c. orange	33·00	17·00
760	-	1p. red	3·25	45
761	-	2p. purple	33·00	13·00
762	-	2p. violet	3·75	85

DESIGN: 50c. to 2p. Similar to T **233** but larger, 24½×19 mm.

Owing to a shortage of postage stamps the above obligatory tax types were issued for ordinary postal use.

1952. Obligatory Tax. No. 759 surch.

763		8c. on 50c. orange	35	20

256 Manizales Cathedral

1952. Centenary of Manizales.

764	**256**	23c. black and blue	55	20

1952. 1st Latin-American Congress of Iron Specialists. Surch **1952 1' CONFERENCIA SIDERURGICA LATINO-AMERICANA**. and new value.

765	**223**	15c. on 25c. green (postage)	55	30
766	**186**	70c. on 80c. red (air)	2·40	1·10

258 Queen Isabella and Columbus Monument

1953. 500th Birth Anniv of Isabella the Catholic.

767	**258**	23c. black and blue	1·20	95

1953. Air. Optd **CORREO AEREO** or surch also.

768	**233**	5c. on 8c. blue	10	10
769	**233**	15c. on 20c. brown	45	10
770	**233**	15c. on 25c. green	2·20	10
771	**233**	25c. green	1·30	10

1953. Air. Optd **AEREO**.

772	**155**	10c. red	20	20

EXTRA RAPIDO. Stamps bearing this overprint or inscription were used to prepay the additional cost of air carriage of inland mail handled by the National Postal Service from 1953 to 1964. Subsequently remaining stocks of these stamps were used for other classes of correspondence. Since the 1920s regular air service for inland and foreign mail has been provided by the Air Postal Service, a separate undertaking which is administered by the Avianca airline and for which the regular air stamps are used.

1953. Air. No. 727 surch **CORREO EXTRA RAPIDO 5 5**.

773		5c. on 11c. red	55	55

262

1953. Air. Fiscal stamps optd as in T **262** or surch also.

774	**262**	1c. on 2c. green	20	10
775	**262**	50c. red	20	20

263

1953. Air. Real Estate Tax stamps optd as in T **263**.

776	**263**	5c. red	20	10
777	**263**	20c. brown	35	20

1953. Surch.

778	-	40c. on 1p. red (No. 760)	2·10	30
779	**214**	50c. on 2p. green	2·10	30

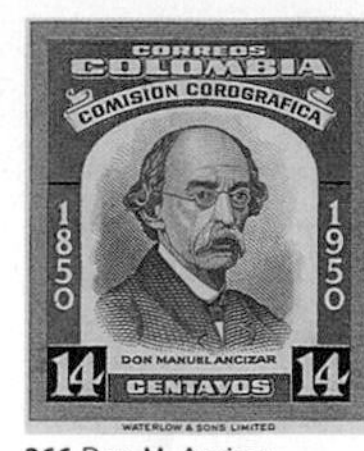

266 Don M. Ancizar

1953. Colombian Chorographical Commission Centenary. Portraits inscr as in T **266**.

780	**266**	14c. red and black	90	85
781	-	23c. blue and black	75	30
782	-	30c. sepia and black	55	30
783	-	1p. green and black	55	30

PORTRAITS: 23c. J. J. Triana; 30c. M. Ponce de Leon; 1p. A. Codazzi.

267 Map of South America

1953. 2nd National Philatelic Exhibition, Bogota. Real Estate Tax stamps surch as in T **267**.

784	**267**	5c. on 5p. mult (post)	55	20
785	-	15c. on 10p. multicoloured (air)	65	55

DESIGN: 15c. Map of Colombia.

1953. Air. Optd **CORREO EXTRA-RAPIDO** or surch also.

786	**233**	2c. on 8c. blue	20	10
787	**233**	10c. violet	20	10

269 Fountain, Tunja

270 Pastelillo Fort, Cartagena

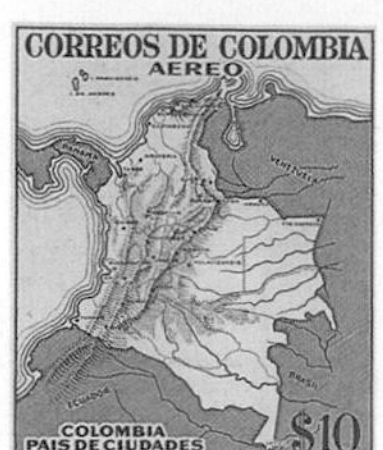

271 Map of Colombia

1954. Air.

788	-	5c. purple	20	10
789	-	10c. black	20	10
790	-	15c. red	20	10
791	-	15c. vermilion	20	10
792	-	20c. brown	20	10
793	-	25c. blue	45	30
794	-	25c. purple	45	30
795	-	30c. brown	35	10
796	-	40c. blue	35	10
797	-	50c. purple	45	10
798	**269**	60c. sepia	55	10
799	-	80c. lake	75	20
800	-	1p. black and blue	4·00	30
801	**270**	2p. black and green	6·00	55
802	-	3p. black and red	13·00	1·80
803	-	5p. green and brown	17·00	4·75
804	**271**	10p. olive and red	22·00	10·00

DESIGNS. As Type **269**—VERT: 5c., 30c. Galeras volcano, Pasto; 15c. red, 50c. Bolivar Monument, Boyaca; 15c. vermilion, 25c. (2) Sanctuary of the Rocks, Narino; 20c., 80c. Nevado del Ruiz Mts., Manizales; 40c. J. Isaacs Monument, Cali. HORIZ: 10c. San Diego Monastery, Bogota. As Type **270**—HORIZ: 1p. Girardot Stadium, Medellin; 3p. Santo Domingo Gateway and University, Popayan. As Type **271**—HORIZ: 5p. Sanctuary of the Rocks, Narino.

1954. Surch.

805	**266**	5c. on 14c. red & black	55	20
806	**256**	5c. on 23c. black & blue	55	20

272 Andean Condor carrying Shield

1954. Air.

807	**272**	5c. purple	1·30	55

273

1954. 400th Anniv of Franciscan Community in Colombia.

808	**273**	5c. brown, green & sepia	55	20

1954. Obligatory Tax. Red Cross Fund. No. 807 optd with cross and bar in red.

809	**272**	5c. purple	2·75	1·20

275 Soldier, Flag and Arms of Republic

1954. National Army Commemoration.

810	**275**	5c. blue (postage)	35	10
811	**275**	15c. red (air)	55	10

276

1954. 7th National Athletic Games, Cali. Inscr "VII JUEGOS ATLETICOS", etc.

812	-	5c. blue (postage)	65	20
813	**276**	10c. red	1·10	20
814	-	15c. brown (air)	1·00	20
815	**276**	20c. green	2·20	45

DESIGN: 5c., 15c. Badge of the Games.

277

1954. 50th Anniv of Colombian Academy of History.

816	**277**	5c. green and blue	35	10

278 Saint's Convent and Cell, Cartagena

1954. Death Tercentenary of San Pedro Claver.

817	**278**	5c. deep green (postage)	20	10
MS818		121×130 mm. No. 817 but printed in green	20·00	16·00
819		15c. deep brown (air)	55	10
MS820		121×130 mm. No. 819 but printed in brown	20·00	16·00

DESIGN: 15c. San Pedro Claver Church, Cartagena.

279 Mercury

1954. 1st International Fair, Bogota.

821	**279**	5c. orange (postage)	75	30
822	**279**	15c. blue (air)	75	30
823	**279**	50c. red ("EXTRA RAPIDO")	75	30

280 Archbishop Mosquera

1954. Air. Death Cent of Archbishop Mosquera.

824	**280**	2c. green	20	20

281 Virgin of Chiquinquira

1954. Air.

825	**281**	5c. mult (brown frame)	10	10
826	**281**	5c. mult (violet frame)	10	10

282 Tapestry presented by Queen Margaret of Austria

1954. Tercentenary of Senior College of Our Lady of the Rosary, Bogota.

827	**282**	5c. black & orge (postage)	55	20
828	-	10c. blue	55	20
829	-	15c. brown	55	20
830	-	20c. brown and black	2·00	20
MS831		125×131 mm. Nos. 827/30 in new colours	12·00	16·00
832	**282**	15c. black & red (air)	65	20
833	-	20c. blue	1·20	20
834	-	25c. brown	1·20	20
835	-	50c. red and black	3·25	1·30
MS836		125×131 mm. Nos. 832/5 in new colours	12·00	16·00

DESIGNS—VERT: Nos. 828, 833, Friar Cristobal de Torres (founder). HORIZ: Nos. 829, 834, Cloisters and statue; 830, 835, Chapel and coat of arms.

283 Paz de Rio Steel Works

1954. Inauguration of Paz del Rio Steel Plant.

837	**283**	5c. black & bl (postage)	20	10
838	**283**	20c. black & green (air)	2·00	75

284 J. Marti

1955. Birth Cent of Marti (Cuban revolutionary).

839	**284**	5c. red (postage)	35	10
840	-	15c. green (air)	45	20

285 Badge, Flags and Korean Landscape

1955. Colombian Forces in Korea.

841	**285**	10c. purple (postage)	20	10
842	**285**	20c. green (air)	75	20

286 Merchant Marine Emblem

1955. Greater Colombia Merchant Marine Commemoration. Inscr as in T **286**.

843	**286**	15c. green (postage)	20	20
844	-	20c. violet	65	20
MS845		125×131 mm. Nos. 810, 841, 843/4 in new colours	13·00	16·00
846	**286**	25c. black (air)	55	20
847	-	50c. green	1·30	55
MS848		125×131 mm. Nos. 125×131 mm. Nos. 811, 842, 846/7 in new colours	13·00	16·00

DESIGN—HORIZ: 20, 50c. "City of Manizales" (freighter) and skyscrapers.

287 M. Fidel Suarez

1955. Air. Birth Centenary of Marco Fidel Suarez (President, 1918–21).

849	**287**	10c. blue	35	20

288 San Pedro Claver feeding Slaves

1955. Obligatory Tax. Red Cross Fund and 300th Anniv of San Pedro Claver.

850	**288**	5c. purple and red	45	30

289 Hotel Tequendama and San Diego Church

1955

851	**289**	5c. blue and light blue (postage)	20	10
852	**289**	15c. lake and pink (air)	55	10

290 Bolivar's Country House

1955. 50th Anniv of Rotary International.

853	**290**	5c. blue (postage)	20	10
854	**290**	15c. red (air)	55	10

291 Belalcazar, De Quesada and Balboa

1955. 7th Postal Union Congress of the Americas and Spain. Inscr as in T **291**.

855	**291**	2c. brn & grn (postage)	65	30
856	-	5c. brown and blue	65	30
857	-	23c. black and blue	75	30
MS858		120×130 mm. Nos. 855/7 in slightly different colours (sold at 50c.)	33·00	33·00
859		15c. black and red (air)	75	30
860		20c. black and brown	1·20	30
MS861		120×130 mm. Nos. 859/60 in slightly different colours (sold at 50c.)	44·00	44·00
862		2c. black and brown ("EXTRA RAPIDO")	65	30
863		5c. sepia and yellow	65	30
864		1p. brown and slate	22·00	10·50
865		2p. black and violet	15·00	8·00

DESIGNS—HORIZ: 2c. (No. 855), Type **291**; 2c. (No. 862), Atahualpa, Tisquesuza, Montezuma; 5c. (No. 856), San Martin, Bolivar and Washington; 5c. (No. 863), King Ferdinand, Queen Isabella and coat of arms; 15c. O'Higgins, Santander and Sucre; 20c. Marti, Hidalgo and Petion; 23c. Colombus, "Santa Maria", "Pinta" and "Nina"; 1p. Artigas, Lopez and Murillo; 2p. Calderon, Baron de Rio Branco and De La Mar.

292 J. E. Caro

1955. Death Cent of Jose Eusebio Caro (poet).

866	**292**	5c. brown (postage)	35	20
867	**292**	15c. green (air)	55	20

293 Salamanca University

1955. Air. 700th Anniv of Salamanca University.

868	**293**	20c. brown	20	10

294 Gold Mining, Narino

1956. Regional Industries. Inscr "DEPARTAMENTO", "PROVIDENCIA" (No. 874), "INTENDENCIA" (2p. to 5p.) or "COMISARIA" (10p.).

869	-	2c. green and red	10	10
870	-	3c. black and purple	10	10
871	-	3c. brown and blue	10	10
872	-	3c. violet and green	10	10
873	-	4c. black and green	10	10
874	-	5c. black and blue	20	10
875	-	5c. slate and red	45	10
876	-	5c. olive and brown	35	10
877	-	5c. brown and olive	35	10
878	-	5c. brown and blue	35	10
879	-	10c. black and yellow	65	10
880	-	10c. brown and green	20	10
881	-	10c. brown and blue	20	10
882	-	15c. black and blue	35	10
883	-	20c. blue and brown	35	10
884	-	23c. red and blue	35	20
885	-	25c. black and olive	35	20
886	**294**	30c. brown and blue	35	10
887	-	40c. brown and purple	35	10
888	-	50c. black and green	35	10
889	-	60c. green and sepia	35	10
890	-	1p. slate and purple	2·40	20
891	-	2p. brown and green	3·50	30
892	-	3p. black and red	4·00	65
893	-	5p. blue and brown	7·75	85
894	-	10p. green and brown	22·00	7·50

DESIGNS—As Type **294**. HORIZ: 2c. Barranquilla naval workshops, Atlantico; 4c. Fishing, Cartagena Port, Bolivar; 5c. (No. 875) View of Port, San Andres; 5c. (No. 876) Cocoa, Cauca; 5c. (No. 877) Prize cattle, Cordoba; 23c. Rice harvesting, Huila; 25c. Bananas, Magdalena; 40c. Tobacco, Santander; 50c. Oil wells of Catatumbo, Norte de Santander; 60c. Cotton harvesting, Tolima. VERT: 3c. (3), Allegory of Industry, Antioquia; 5c. (No. 874) Map of San Andres Archipelago; 5c. (No. 878) Steel plant, Boyaca; 10c. (3), Coffee, Caldas; 15c. Cathedral at Sal Salinas de Zipaquira, Cundinamarca; 20c. Platinum and map, Choco. LARGER (37½×27 mm)—HORIZ: 1p. Sugar factory, Valle del Cauca; 2p. Cattle fording river, Meta; 3p. Statue and River Amazon, Leticia; 5p. Landscape, La Guajira. VERT: 10p. Rubber tapping, Vaupes.

295 Henri Dunant and S. Samper Brush

1956. Obligatory Tax. Red Cross Fund.

895	**295**	5c. brown	65	30

1956. Air. No. 783 optd **EXTRA-RAPIDO**.

896	1p. green and black	55	30

297 Columbus and Lighthouse

1956. Columbus Memorial Lighthouse.

897	**297**	3c. black (postage)	45	30
898	**297**	15c. blue (air)	90	30
899	**297**	3c. green ("EXTRA RAPIDO")	35	20

298 Altar of St. Elisabeth and Sarcophagus of Jimenez de Quesada, Primada Basilica, Bogota

1956. 700th Anniv of St. Elisabeth of Hungary.

900	**298**	5c. purple (postage)	20	10
901	**298**	15c. brown (air)	55	20

299 St. Ignatius of Loyola

1956. 400th Death Anniv of St. Ignatius of Loyola.

902	**299**	5c. blue (postage)	20	10
903	**299**	5c. brown (air)	35	10

300 Javier Pereira

1956. Pereira Commemoration.

904	**300**	5c. blue (postage)	20	10
905	**300**	20c. red (air)	20	10

1957. Air. No. 874 optd **EXTRA-RAPIDO**.

906	5c. black and blue	10·50	4·25

1957. Air. As No. 580 (colours changed) optd **EXTRA-RAPIDO**.

907	5p. black and buff	13·00	10·00

302 Dairy Farm

1957. 25th Anniv of Agricultural Credit Bank.

908	**302**	1c. olive (postage)	10	10
909	-	2c. brown	10	10
910	-	5c. blue	20	10
911	**302**	5c. orange (air)	20	10
912	-	10c. green	1·00	65
913	-	15c. black	55	10
914	-	20c. red	1·40	85
915	-	5c. brown ("EXTRA RAPIDO")	35	10

DESIGNS: 2c., 10c. Farm tractor; 5c. (No. 910), 15c. Emblem of agricultural prosperity; 5c. (No. 915), Livestock; 20c. Livestock.

303 Racing Cyclist

1957. Air. 7th Round Colombia Cycle Race.

916	**303**	2c. brown	20	20
917	**303**	5c. blue	35	30

304 Arms and Gen. Rayes (founder)

1957. 50th Anniv of Military Cadet School.

918	**304**	5c. blue (postage)	20	10
919	-	10c. orange	35	10
MS920		130×120 mm. Nos. 918/19 in slightly different colours	28·00	32·00
921	**304**	15c. red (air)	35	20
922	-	20c. brown	55	30

DESIGN: 10c., 20c. Arms and Military Cadet School.

305 Father J. M. Delgado

1957. Father Delgado Commemoration.

923	**305**	2c. lake (postage)	35	20
924	**305**	10c. blue (air)	35	20

306 St. Vincent de Paul with Children

1957. Centenary of Colombian Order of St. Vincent de Paul.

925	**306**	1c. green (postage)	20	10
926	**306**	5c. red (air)	35	10

307 Signatories to Bogota Postal Convention of 1838, and UPU Monument, Berne

1957. 14th UPU Congress, Ottawa and International Correspondence Week.

927	**307**	5c. green (postage)	20	10
928	**307**	10c. grey	35	10
929	**307**	15c. brown (air)	35	10
930	**307**	25c. blue	35	20

308 Fencer

1957. 3rd S. American Fencing Championships.

931	**308**	4c. purple (postage)	35	10
932	**308**	20c. brown (air)	55	55

309 Discovery of Hypsometry by F. J. de Caldas

1958. International Geophysical Year.

933	**309**	10c. black (postage)	55	10
934	**309**	25c. green (air)	55	20
935	**309**	1p. violet ("EXTRA RAPIDO")	75	30

310 Nurses with Patient, and Ambulance

1958. Obligatory Tax. Red Cross Fund.

936	**310**	5c. red and black	20	10

1958. Nos. 882 and 884 surch.

937	5c. on 15c. black and blue	35	20
938	5c. on 23c. red and blue	35	20

1958. Air. No. 888 optd **AEREO**.

939	50c. black and green	65	20

313 Father R. Almanza and San Diego Church, Bogota

1958. Father Almanza Commemoration.

940	**313**	10c. lilac (postage)	35	20
941	**313**	25c. grey (air)	45	30
942	**313**	10c. green ("EXTRA RAPIDO")	35	20

1958. Nos. 780/2 surch **CINCO** (5c.) or **VEINTE** (20c.).

943	**266**	5c. on 14c. red & black	35	20
944	-	5c. on 30c. sepia & black	35	20
945	-	20c. on 23c. blue & blk	45	20

315 Msr. Carrasquilla and Rosario College, Bogota

1959. Birth Centenary of Msr. R. M. Carrasquilla.

946	**315**	10c. brown (postage)	20	10
947	**315**	25c. red (air)	35	10
948	**315**	1p. blue	1·10	30

1959. Surch **20c.** and ornament.

949	**258**	20c. on 23c. black & bl	45	20

1959. As No. 826 but with "CORREO EXTRA RAPIDO" obliterated.

950	**281**	5c. multicoloured	35	20

1959. No. 794 surch.

951	10c. on 25c. purple	35	20

318 Luz Marina Zuluaga ("Miss Universe 1959")

1959. "Miss Universe 1959" Commemoration.

952	**318**	10c. mult (postage)	1·10	30
953	**318**	1p.20 mult (air)	2·40	1·80
954	**318**	5p. mult ("EXTRA RAPIDO")	65·00	65·00

1959. No. 873 surch.

955	2c. on 4c. black and green	35	20

320 J. E. Gaitan (political leader)

1959. J. E. Gaitan Commem. Nos. 956 and 958 are surch on T **320**.

956	**320**	10c. on 3c. grey	35	20
957	**320**	30c. purple	65	30
958	**320**	2p. on 1p. black ("EXTRA RAPIDO")	2·40	2·00

1959. Air. Surch.

960	**269**	50c. on 60c. sepia	2·40	55

323 Capitol, Bogota **324** Santander

1959

961	**323**	2c. brn & blue (postage)	10	10
962	**323**	3c. violet and black	10	10
963	**324**	5c. brown and yellow	20	10
964	-	5c. ultramarine & blue	20	10
965	-	10c. black and red	20	10
966	**324**	10c. black and green	20	10
967	-	35c. black and grey (air)	45	30

PORTRAIT (as Type **324**): Nos. 964/5, 967, Bolivar.

1959. Air. Unification of Airmail Rates. Optd **UNIFICADO** within outline of aeroplane.

968	**299**	5c. brown	45	45
969	**302**	5c. orange	45	45
970	**306**	5c. red	65	85
971	**155**	10c. red (No. 772)	45	65
972	-	10c. black (No. 789)	35	20
973	**304**	15c. red	35	20
974	-	20c. brown (No. 792)	35	20
975	-	20c. brown (No. 922)	35	20
976	**308**	20c. brown	35	20
977	-	25c. blue (No. 793)	35	20
978	-	25c. purple (No. 794)	35	20
979	**313**	25c. grey	35	20
980	**315**	25c. red	35	20
981	-	30c. brown (No. 795)	35	20
982	**269**	50c. on 60c. sepia (No. 960)	45	30
983	**315**	1p. blue	1·20	30
984	**318**	1p.20 multicoloured	1·80	1·30
985	**270**	2p. black and green	2·40	30
986	-	3p. black & red (No. 802)	6·50	95
987	-	5p. grn & brn (No. 803)	8·75	1·80
988	**271**	10p. olive and red	11·00	3·75

326 Colombian 2½c. stamp of 1859 and Postman with Mule **327** Tete-beche 5c. stamps of 1859

1959. Colombian Stamp Cent. Inscr "1859 1959".

989	**326**	5c. grn & orge (postage)	20	10
990	-	10c. blue and lake	20	10
991	**326**	15c. green and red	55	55
992	-	25c. brown and blue	75	75
993	-	25c. red and brown (air)	65	45
994	-	50c. blue and red	1·70	85
995	-	1p.20 brown and green	3·50	2·10
996	-	10c. lilac and bistre ("EXTRA RAPIDO")	10	10
MS997		74×70 mm. **327** 5c. blue on pink (sold at 5p.)	22·00	27·00

DESIGNS—VERT: Colombian stamps of 1859 (except No. 993): No. 990, 5c. and river steamer; 992, 10c. and steam locomotive "Cordoba"; 993, Postal decree of 1859 and Pres. M. Ospina; 996, 10c. and map of Colombia. HORIZ: No. 994, 20c. and Junkers F-13 seaplane "Colombia"; 995, 1p. and Lockheed Constellation airliner over valley.

328 2c. Air Stamp of 1918, Junkers F-13 "Colombia" and Lockheed Constellation

1959. Air. 40th Anniv of Colombian "AVIANCA" Air Mail Services.

998	**328**	35c. red, black and blue	65	20
999	-	60c. black and green	1·10	1·10
MS1000		90×50 mm. Two 1p. stamps in designs of Nos. 998/9 but in different colours	17·00	17·00
MS1001		Sheets as last but containing two 1p.50 stamps in different colours and inscr "EXTRA RAPIDO"	17·00	17·00

DESIGN: 60c. As Type **328** but without Colombian 2c. stamp.

329 Eldorado Airport, Bogota

1960. Air.

1002	**329**	35c. orange and black	90	30
1003	**329**	60c. red and grey	1·00	65
1004	**329**	1p. blue and grey ("EXTRA RAPIDO")	1·80	95

331 A. von Humboldt (after J. K. Stieler)

1960. Death Centenary of Alexander von Humboldt (naturalist). Animals.

1005	-	5c. brn & turq (postage)	20	10
1006	**331**	10c. sepia and red	35	10
1007	-	20c. purple and yellow	20	10
1008	-	35c. brown (air)	1·90	10
1009	-	1p.30 brown and red	3·50	3·25
1010	-	1p.45 lemon and blue	2·75	2·75

DESIGNS—VERT: 5c. Two-toed sloth; 20c. Long-haired spider monkey. HORIZ: 35c. Giant anteater; 1p.30, Nine-banded armadillo; 1p.45, "Blue" parrotfish.

332 "Anthurium andreanum"

1960. Colombian Flowers.

1011	**332**	5c. mult (postage)	90	30
1013	**B**	5c. multicoloured (air)	35	20
1014	**B**	5c. multicoloured	35	20
1015	**A**	10c. yellow, green & bl	35	20
1023	**D**	10c. multicoloured	35	20
1012	**A**	20c. yellow, green & sep	90	30
1016	**C**	20c. multicoloured	35	20
1017	**D**	25c. multicoloured	45	30
1018	**C**	35c. multicoloured	75	30
1019	**B**	60c. multicoloured	1·50	95
1020	**332**	60c. multicoloured	45	45
1024	**332**	1p. multicoloured	3·50	4·25
1025	**A**	1p. yellow, green & sepia	3·50	4·25
1026	**B**	1p. multicoloured	3·50	4·25
1027	**C**	1p. multicoloured	3·50	4·25
1028	**D**	1p. multicoloured	3·50	4·25
1021	**332**	1p.45 multicoloured	1·80	1·50
1029	**C**	2p. multicoloured	3·50	4·25
1022	**C**	5c. multicoloured ("EXTRA RAPIDO")	35	20

FLOWERS: A, "Espelitia grandiflora"; B, "Passiflora mollissima"; C, Odontoglossum luteo purpureum"; D, "Stanhopea tigrina".

333 Refugee Family

1960. Air. World Refugee Year.

1030a	**333**	60c. grey and green	55	30

1960. Air. 8th Pan-American Highway Congress (1st issue). Sheet 46×56 mm.

MS1031	**339**	2p.50 brown and blue	8·75	8·75

See also Nos. 1056/60.

334 Lincoln Statue, Washington

1960. 150th Birth Anniv of Abraham Lincoln.

1032	**334**	20c. blk & mve (postage)	45	30
1033	**334**	40c. black & brown (air)	2·00	1·40
1034	**334**	60c. black and red	55	10

335 "House of the Flower Vase"

1960. 150th Anniv of Independence.

1035	-	5c. brn & grn (postage)	35	20
1036	**335**	20c. purple and brown	35	20
1037	-	20c. yellow, blue & mve	35	20
1038	-	5c. multicoloured (air)	35	20
1039	-	5c. sepia and violet	35	20
1040	-	35c. multicoloured	35	20
1041	-	60c. green and brown	65	30
1042	-	1p. green and red	1·50	95
1043	-	1p.20 indigo and blue	1·50	95
1044	-	1p.30 black and orange	1·50	95
1045	-	1p.45 multicoloured	1·90	1·50
1046	-	1p.65 brown and green	1·70	1·80
MS1047		90×75 mm. As designs of postage and air stamps but in new colours. 50c. As No. 1037; 50c. As No. 1038; 1p. As No. 1040; 1p. As No. 1035 (Extra Rapido)	9·25	9·00

DESIGNS—VERT: No. 1035, Cartagena coins of 1811–13; 1038, Arms of Cartagena; 1037, Arms of Mompos; 1043, Statue of A. Galan. HORIZ: No. 1039, J. Camacho, J. T. Lozano and J. M. Pey; 1040, 1045, Colombian Flag; 1041, A. Rosillo, A. Villavicencio and J. Caicedo; 1042, B. Alvares and J. Gutierrez; 1044, Front page of "La Bagatela" (newspaper); 1046, A. Santos, J. A. Gomez and L. Mejia.

336 St. Luisa de Marillac and Sanctuary

1960. Obligatory Tax. Red Cross Fund.

1048	**336**	5c. red and brown	45	10
1049	-	5c. red and blue	45	10

DESIGN: No. 1049, H. Dunant and battle scene.

337 St. Isidro Labrador (after G. Vasquez)

1960. St. Isidro Labrador Commem (1st issue).

1050	**337**	10c. mult (postage)	10	10
1051	-	20c. multicoloured	20	10
1052	**337**	35c. multicoloured (air)	35	20
MS1053		90×60 mm. As designs of postage stamps but in slightly different colours. 1p.50 As T **337**; 1p.50 As No. 1051 (Extra Rapido)	14·50	14·50

DESIGN: 20c. "The Nativity" (after Vasquez).

See also Nos. 1126/8.

338 U.N. Headquarters, New York

1960. U.N. Day.

1054	**338**	20c. red and black	35	10
MS1055		55×49 mm. **338** 50c. green and chocolate. Imperf	5·50	5·50

339 Highway Map of Northern Colombia

1961. 8th Pan-American Highway Congress.

1056	**339**	20c. brn & bl (postage)	1·00	85
1057	**339**	10c. purple & green (air)	1·00	85
1058	**339**	20c. red and blue	1·00	85
1059	**339**	30c. black and green	1·00	85
1060	**339**	10c. blue and green ("EXTRA RAPIDO")	1·00	85

340 Alfonso Lopez (statesman)

1961. 75th Birth Anniv of Alfonso Lopez (President, 1934–38 and 1941–45).

1061	**340**	10c. brn & red (postage)	35	20
1062	**340**	20c. brown and violet	35	20
1063	**340**	35c. brown & blue (air)	75	30
1064	**340**	10c. brown and green ("EXTRA RAPIDO")	35	20
MS1065		74×60 mm. **340** 1p. brown and violet	7·75	7·75

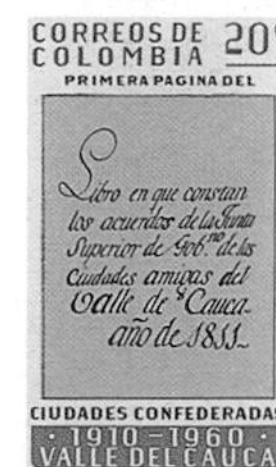

341 Text from Resolution of Confederated Cities

1961. 50th Anniv of Valle del Cauca.

1066	-	10c. mult (postage)	35	20
1067	**341**	20c. brown and black	35	20
1068	-	35c. brown & olive (air)	55	30
1069	-	35c. brown and green	55	30
1070	-	1p.30 sepia and purple	1·50	75
1071	-	1p.45 green and brown	1·50	95
1072	-	10c. brown and olive ("EXTRA RAPIDO")	35	20

DESIGNS—HORIZ: 10c. (No. 1066), La Ermita Church, bridge and arms of Cali; 35c. (No. 1068), St. Francis' Church, Cali; 1p.30, Conservatoire; 1p.45, Agricultural College, Palmira. VERT: 10c. (No. 1072), Aerial view of Cali; 35c. (No. 1069), University emblem.

342 Arms and View of Cucuta

1961. 50th Anniv of North Santander.

1073		20c. mult (postage)	35	15
1074	**342**	20c. multicoloured	35	15
1075	-	35c. green & bistre (air)	1·00	30
1076	-	10c. purple & green ("EXTRA RAPIDO")	35	10

DESIGNS—HORIZ: No. 1073, Arms of Ocana and Pamplona; 1075, Panoramic view of Cucuta. VERT: No. 1076, Villa del Rosario, Cucuta.

1961. Air. Optd **Aereo** (1077) or **AEREO** (others) and airplane or surch also.

1077	**332**	5c. multicoloured	35	10
1078	-	5c. brown & turquoise (No. 1005)	35	10
1079	-	10c. on 20c. purple and yellow (No. 1007)	35	10

345 Arms of Barranquilla

1961. Atlantico Tourist Issue. (a) Postage

1080		10c. mult (postage)	35	10
1081	**345**	20c. red, blue and yellow	35	10
1082	-	20c. multicoloured	35	10
1083	-	35c. sepia and red (air)	75	30
1084	-	35c. red, yellow & green	75	30
1085	-	35c. blue and gold	75	30
1086	-	1p.45 brown and green	75	30
MS1087		90×76 mm. As designs of postage and air stamps but in new colours: 35c. As T **345**; 40c. As No. 1080; 1p. As No. 1084; 1p. As No. 1088	17·00	17·00

"(b) Inscr "EXTRA RAPIDO""

1088		10c. yellow and brown ("EXTRA RAPIDO")	35	10
MS1089		90×76 mm. As designs of postage and air stamps but in new colours: 50c. As No. 1085; 50c. As No. 1083; 50c. As No. 1082; 50c. As No. 1088	17·00	17·00

DESIGNS—VERT: No. 1080, Arms of Popayan; 1082, Arms of Bucaramanga; 1083, Courtyard of Tourist Hotel; 1087, Holy Week procession, Popayan. HORIZ: No. 1084, View of San Gill; 1085, Barranquilla Port; 1086, View of Velez.

346 Nurse M. de la Cruz

1961. Red Cross Fund. Cross in red.

1090	**346**	5c. brown	20	10
1091	**346**	5c. purple	20	10

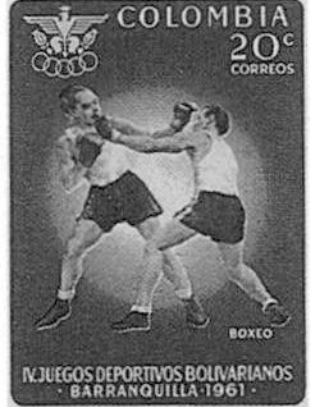

347 Boxing

1961. 4th Bolivarian Games. Inscr as in T **347**. Multicoloured.

1092	20c. Type **347** (postage)	35	15
1093	20c. Basketball	35	15
1094	20c. Running	65	20
1095	25c. Football	35	15
1096	35c. Diving (air)	1·00	30
1097	35c. Tennis	1·00	30
1098	1p.45 Baseball	1·50	85
1099	10c. Statue and flags ("EXTRA RAPIDO")	35	10
1100	10c. Runner with Olympic torch ("EXTRA RAPIDO")	35	10
MS1101	74×106 mm. mult. 50c. Statue and flags; 50c. Baseball; 1p. Football; 1p. Basketball	11·00	11·00

348 "SEM" Emblem and Mosquito

1962. Malaria Eradication.

1102	**348**	20c. red & ochre (post)	35	20
1103	-	50c. blue and ochre	45	20
1104	**348**	40c. red & yellow (air)	35	20
1105	-	1p.45 blue and grey	90	75
1106	-	1p. blue and green ("EXTRA RAPIDO")	6·50	6·50

DESIGN: 50c., 1p., 1p.45, Campaign emblem and mosquito.

349 Society Emblem

1962. 6th National Engineers' Congress, 1961 and 75th Anniv of Colombian Society of Engineers.

1107	**349**	10c. mult (postage)	35	30
1108	-	5c. red and blue (air)	10	10
1109	-	10c. brown and green	20	20
1110	-	15c. brown and purple	65	45
1111	**349**	2p. multicoloured ("EXTRA RAPIDO")	3·25	3·25

DESIGNS: No. 1108, A. Ramos and Engineering Faculty, Cauca University, Popayan; 1109, M. Triana, A. Arroyo and Monserrate cable and funicular railway; 1110, D. Sanchez and first Society H.Q., Bogota.

350 OEA Emblem

1962. 70th Anniv of Organization of American States (OEA). Flags multicoloured; background colours given. (a) Postage

1112	**350**	25c. red & blk (postage)	20	10
MS1113		41×45 mm. **350** 2p.50 yellow and black	7·75	7·75

(b) Air

1114	35c. blue & black (air)	75	10

351 Mother Voting and Statue of Policarpa Salavarrieta

1962. Women's Franchise.

1115	**351**	5c. black, grey and brown (postage)	35	10
1116	**351**	10c. black, grey and blue	20	10
1117	**351**	5c. blk, grey & pink (air)	20	10
1118	**351**	35c. black, grey & buff	35	10
1119	**351**	45c. black, grey & green	55	10
1120	**351**	45c. black, grey & mauve	55	10

353 Scouts in Camp

1962. 30th Anniv of Colombian Boy Scouts and 25th Anniv of Colombian Girl Scouts. As T **353** but without "EXTRA RAPIDO".

1121	**353**	10c. brn & turq (postage)	35	30
1122	**353**	15c. brown & red (air)	45	20
1123	-	40c. lake and red	55	45
1124	-	1p. blue and Salmon	1·10	75
1125	**353**	1p. violet & yellow ("EXTRA RAPIDO")	10·00	8·00

DESIGN: 40c., 1p. Girl Scouts.

354 St. Isidro Labrador (after G. Vasquez)

1962. St. Isidro Labrador Commem (2nd issue).

1126	**354**	10c. multicoloured	35	10
1127	-	10c. mult (air—"EXTRA RAPIDO")	35	10
1128	**354**	2p. multicoloured	6·00	5·75

DESIGN: 10c. (No. 1127), "The Nativity" (after G. Vasquez).

355 Railway Map

1962. Completion of Colombia Atlantic Railway.

1129	**355**	10c. red, green and olive (postage)	35	20
1130	-	5c. myrtle & sepia (air)	35	10
1131	**355**	10c. red, turq & bistre	35	10
1132	-	1p. brown and purple	2·75	30
1133	-	5p. brown, blue & grn ("EXTRA RAPIDO")	6·50	6·50

DESIGNS—HORIZ: 5c. 1854 steam and 1961 diesel locomotives; 1, 5p. Pres. A. Parra and R. Magdalena railway bridge.

356 Posthorn

1962. 50th Anniv of Postal Union of the Americas and Spain.

1134	**356**	20c. gold & bl (postage)	20	10
1135	-	50c. gold & green (air)	55	10
1136	**356**	60c. gold and purple	35	10

DESIGN: 50c. Posthorn, dove and map.

357 Virgin of the Mountain, Bogota

1963. Ecumenical Council, Vatican City.

1137	**357**	60c. mult (postage)	35	10
1138	-	60c. red, yell & gold (air)	55	10

DESIGN: No. 1138, Pope John XXIII.

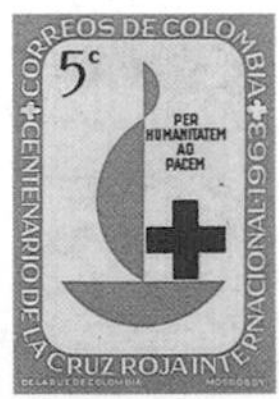

358 Centenary Emblem

1963. Obligatory Tax. Red Cross Centenary.

1139	**358**	5c. red and bistre	35	20

359 Hurdling and Flags

1963. Air. South American Athletics Championships, Cali.

1140	**359**	20c. multicoloured	35	10
1141	**359**	80c. multicoloured	35	10

360 Bolivar Monument

1963. Air. Centenary of Pereira.

1142	**360**	1p.90 brown and blue	35	10

361 Tennis Player

1963. Air. 30th South American Tennis Championships, Medellin.

1143	**361**	55c. multicoloured	35	10

362 Pres. Kennedy and Alliance Emblem

1963. Air. "Alliance for Progress".

1144	**362**	10c. multicoloured	20	10

363 Veracruz Church

1964. Air. National Pantheon, Veracruz Church. Multicoloured.

1145	1p. Type **363**	45	10
1146	2p. "The Crucifixion"	65	30

364 Cartagena

1964. Air. Cartagena Commemoration.

1147	**364**	3p. multicoloured	2·40	1·10

365 Eleanor Roosevelt

1964. Air. 15th Anniv of Declaration of Human Rights.

1148	**365**	20c. brown and olive	35	20

366 A. Castilla (composer and founder) and Music

1964. Air. Tolima Conservatoire Commem.

1149	**366**	30c. turquoise & bistre	20	10

367 Manuel Mejia and Coffee Growers' Flag Emblem

1965. Manuel Mejia Commemoration.

No.	Type	Description	Mint	Used
1150	**367**	25c. brn & red (postage)	20	10
1151	-	45c. sepia & brown (air)	35	10
1152	-	5p. black and green	3·50	30
1153	-	10p. black and blue	5·00	55

DESIGNS: 45c. Gathering coffee-beans; 5p. Mule transport; 10p. Freighter "Manuel Mejia" at Buenaventura Port. Each design includes a portrait of M. Mejia, director of the National Coffee Growers' Association.

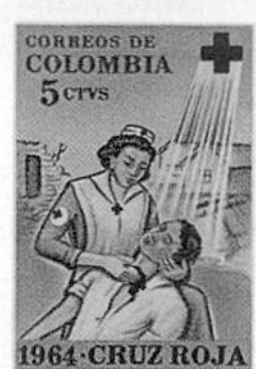

368 Nurse with Patient

1965. Obligatory Tax. Red Cross Fund.

No.	Type	Description	Mint	Used
1154	**368**	5c. blue and red	35	20

369 ITU Emblem and "Waves"

1965. Air. Centenary of ITU.

No.	Type	Description	Mint	Used
1155	**369**	80c. indigo, red and blue	20	10

370 Orchid ("Cattleya trianae")

1965. Air. 5th Philatelic Exhibition, Bogota.

No.	Type	Description	Mint	Used
1156	**370**	20c. multicoloured	1·10	55

371 Satellites, Telegraph Pole and Map

1965. Air. Cent of Colombian Telegraphs. Mult.

No.	Type	Description	Mint	Used
1157		60c. Type **371**	35	20
1158		60c. Statue of Pres. Murrilo Toro, Bogota (vert)	35	20

372 Junkers F-13 Seaplane "Colombia" (1920)

1965. Air. "History of Colombian Aviation". Multicoloured.

No.	Type	Description	Mint	Used
1159		5c. Type **372**	35	10
1160		10c. Dornier Wal Do-J (1924)	35	10
1161		20c. Dornier Do-B Merkur seaplane (1926)	35	10
1162		50c. Ford 5-AT Trimotor (1932)	35	10
1163		60c. De Havilland Gipsy Moth (1930)	55	30
1164		1p. Douglas DC-4 (1947)	1·10	30
1165		1p.40 Douglas DC-3 (1944)	1·30	30
1166		2p.80 Lockheed Constellation (1951)	2·40	1·10
1167		3p. Boeing 720B jet liner (1961)	3·50	1·50

See also No. E1168.

373 Badge, and Car on Mountain Road

1966. Air. 25th Anniv (1965) of Colombian Automobile Club.

No.	Type	Description	Mint	Used
1168	**373**	20c. multicoloured	35	10

374 J. Arboleda (writer)

1966. Julio Arboleda Commemoration.

No.	Type	Description	Mint	Used
1169	**374**	5c. multicoloured	45	10

375 Red Cross and Children as Nurse and Patient

1966. Obligatory Tax. Red Cross Fund.

No.	Type	Description	Mint	Used
1170	**375**	5c.+5c. mult	35	20

376 16th-century Galleon

1966. History of Maritime Mail. Multicoloured.

No.	Type	Description	Mint	Used
1171		5c. Type **376**	55	10
1172		15c. Riohacha brigantine (1850)	55	15
1173		20c. Uraba schooner	55	15
1174		40c. Steamer and barge, Magdalena, 1900	65	20
1175		50c. Modern freighter	1·80	85

377 Hogfish

1966. Fishes. Multicoloured.

No.	Type	Description	Mint	Used
1176		80c. Type **377** (postage)	20	10
1177		10p. Spotted electric ray	12·00	7·50
1178		2p. Pacific flyingfish (air)	75	20
1179		2p.80 Blue angelfish	1·80	1·20
1180		20p. King mackerel	24·00	18·00

378 Arms of Colombia, Venezuela and Chile

1966. Visits of Chilean and Venezuelan Presidents.

No.	Type	Description	Mint	Used
1181	**378**	40c. mult (postage)	20	10
1182	**378**	1p. multicoloured (air)	55	10
1183	**378**	1p.40 multicoloured	45	10

379 C. Torres (patriot)

1967. Famous Colombians.

No.	Type	Description	Mint	Used
1184	**379**	25c. vio & yell (postage)	35	10
1185	-	60c. purple and yellow	35	10
1186	-	1p. green and yellow	55	30
1187	-	80c. blue & yellow (air)	35	20
1188	-	1p.70 black and yellow	55	30

PORTRAITS: 60c. J. T. Lozano (naturalist); 80c. Father F. R. Mejia (scholar); 1p. F. A. Zea (writer); 1p.70, J. J. Casas (diplomat).

380 Map of Signatory Countries

1967. "Declaration of Bogota".

No.	Type	Description	Mint	Used
1189	**380**	40c. mult (postage)	35	10
1190	**380**	60c. multicoloured	35	10
1191	**380**	3p. multicoloured (air)	55	30

381 "Monochaetum" and Bee

1967. National Orchid Congress and Tropical Flora and Fauna Exhibition, Medellin. Multicoloured.

No.	Type	Description	Mint	Used
1192		25c. Type **381** (postage)	45	10
1193		2p. "Passiflora vitifolia" and butterfly	3·00	2·00
1194		1p. "Cattleya dowiana" (vert) (air)	1·20	20
1195		1p.20 "Masdevallia coccinea" (vert)	90	20
1196		5p. "Catasetum macrocarpum" and bee	6·00	1·10
MS1197		100×150 mm. Nos. 1194/6	24·00	24·00

382 Nurse's Cap

1967. Obligatory Tax. Red Cross Fund.

No.	Type	Description	Mint	Used
1198	**382**	5c. red and blue	35	20

383 Lions Emblem

1967. 50th Anniv of Lions International.

No.	Type	Description	Mint	Used
1199	**383**	10p. mult (postage)	4·75	95
1200	**383**	25c. multicoloured (air)	35	10

384 "Caesarean Operation, 1844" (from painting by Grau)

1967. Air. 6th Colombian Surgeons' Congress, Bogota and Centenary of National University.

No.	Type	Description	Mint	Used
1201	**384**	80c. multicoloured	20	10

385 SENA Emblem

1967. 10th Anniv of National Apprenticeship Service.

No.	Type	Description	Mint	Used
1202	**385**	5p. black, gold and green (postage)	2·20	30
1203	**385**	2p. black, gold and red (air)	1·00	20

386 Calima Diadem

1967. Administrative Council of UPU Consultative Commission of Postal Studies. Main design and lower inscr in brown and gold.

No.	Type	Description	Mint	Used
1204	**386**	1p.60 pur (postage)	1·40	30
1205	-	3p. blue	2·00	55
1206	-	30c. red (air)	55	30
1207	-	5p. red	5·00	65
1208	-	20p. violet	24·00	15·00
MS1209		92×92 mm. Nos. 1206/7 but in new colours. Imperf	17·00	17·00

DESIGNS (Colombian archaeological treasures) VERT: 30c. Chief's head-dress; 5p. Cauca breastplate; 20p. Quimbaya jug. HORIZ: 3p. Tolima anthropomorphic figure and postal "pigeon on globe" emblem.

387 Radio Antenna

1968. "21 Years of National Telecommunications Services". Inscr "1947–1968".

No.	Type	Description	Mint	Used
1210	**387**	50c. mult (postage)	20	10
1211	-	1p. multicoloured	55	10
1212	-	50c. mult (air)	20	10
1213	-	1p. yellow, grey & blue	55	10

DESIGNS: No. 1211, Communications network; 1212, Diagram; 1213, Satellite.

388 The Eucharist

1968. 39th International Eucharistic Congress, Bogota (1st issue).

No.	Type	Description	Mint	Used
1214	**388**	60c. mult (postage)	20	10
1215	**388**	80c. multicoloured (air)	20	10
1216	**388**	3p. multicoloured	65	20

389 "St. Augustine" (Vasquez)

1968. 39th International Eucharistic Congress, Bogota (2nd Issue). Multicoloured.

No.	Type	Description	Mint	Used
1217		25c. Type **389** (postage)	10	10
1218		60c. "Gathering Manna" (Vasquez)	10	10
1219		1p. "Betrothal of the Virgin and St. Joseph" (B. de Figueroa)	20	10
1220		5p. "La Lechuga" (Jesuit Statuette)	1·10	10
1221		10p. "Pope Paul VI" (painting by Franciscan Missionary Mothers)	2·20	65
1222		80c. "The Last Supper" (Vasquez) (horiz) (air)	35	10
1223		1p. "St. Francis Xavier's Sermon" (Vasquez)	55	10
1224		2p. "Elijah's Dream" (Vasquez)	65	10
1225		3p. As No. 1220	1·30	10
1226		20p. As No. 1221	7·75	3·75
MS1227		91×90 mm. Nos. 1220/1. Imperf	5·50	5·50

390 Pope Paul VI

1968. Pope Paul's Visit to Colombia. Multicoloured.

1228	25c. Type **390** (postage)	35	10
1229	80c. Reception podium (horiz) (air)	35	20
1230	1p.20 Pope Paul giving Blessing	35	20
1231	1p.80 Cathedral, Bogota	45	30

391 University Arms

1968. Centenary of National University.

1232	**391**	80c. mult (postage)	55	30
1233	-	20c. red, green and yellow (air)	35	20

DESIGN: 20c. Mathematical symbols.

392 Antioquia 2½c. Stamp of 1858

1968. Centenary of First Antioquia Stamps.

1234	**392**	30c. blue and green	55	30
MS1235		59×79 mm. 5p. blue and bistre	4·00	4·00

See also Nos. 1249/50.

393 Institute Emblem and Split Leaf

1969. 25th Anniv (1967) of Inter-American Agricultural Sciences Institute.

1236	**393**	20c. mult (postage)	35	10
1237	**393**	1p. multicoloured (air)	55	30

394 Pen and Microscope

1969. Air. 20th Anniv of University of the Andes.

1238	**394**	5p. multicoloured	1·90	30

395 Von Humboldt and Andes (Quindio Region)

1969. Air. Birth Bicentenary of Alexander von Humboldt (naturalist).

1239	**395**	1p. green and brown	55	30

396 Junkers F-13 Seaplane and Map

1969. Air. 50th Anniv of 1st Colombian Airmail Flight. Multicoloured.

1240	1p. Type **396**	35	10
1241	1p.50 Boeing 720B and globe	55	20
MS1242	93×92 mm. Two 15p. designs as Nos. 1240/1 but colours changed. Imperf	6·00	6·50

See also Nos. 1249/50.

397 Red Cross

1969. Obligatory Tax. Colombian Red Cross.

1243	**397**	5c. red and violet	35	20

398 "The Battle of Boyaca" (J. M. Espinosa)

1969. 150th Anniv of Independence. Mult.

1244	20c. Type **398** (postage)	35	10
1245	30c. "Liberation Army crossing Pisba Pass" (F. A. Caro)	35	10
1246	2p.30 "Entry into Santa Fe" (I. Castillo-Cervantes) (air)	75	30

399 Institute Emblem

1969. Air. 20th Anniv of Colombian Social Security Institute.

1247	**399**	20c. green and black	20	10

400 Cranial Diagram

1969. Air. 13th Latin-American Neurological Congress, Bogota.

1248	**400**	70c. multicoloured	45	15

401 Junkers F-13 Seaplane and Puerto Colombia

1969. Air. 50th Anniv of "Avianca" Airline. Multicoloured.

1249	2p. Type **401**	55	20
1250	3p.50 Boeing 720B and globe	1·10	45
MS1251	93×91 mm. As Nos. 1249/50 but face values changed to 3p.50 and 5p. Imperf	6·00	6·50

402 Child posting Christmas Card

1969. Air. Christmas. Multicoloured.

1252	60c. Type **402**	65	10
1253	1p. Type **402**	65	20
1254	1p.50 Child with Christmas presents	90	20

403 "Poverty"

1970. Colombian Social Welfare Institute and 10th Anniv of Children's Rights Law.

1255	**403**	30c. multicoloured	55	30

404 Dish Aerial and Ancient Head

1970. Air. Opening of Satellite Earth Station, Choconta.

1256	**404**	1p. black, red & green	65	10

405 National Sports Institute Emblem

1970. Air. 9th National Games, Ibague (1st issue).

1257	**405**	1p.50 black, yell & grn	45	30
1258	-	2p.30 multicoloured	65	30

DESIGN: 2p.30, Dove and rings (Games emblem).

See also No. 1265.

406 Exhibition Emblem

1970. Air. 2nd Fine Arts Biennial, Medellin.

1259	**406**	30c. multicoloured	35	10

407 Dr. E. Santos (founder) and Buildings

1970. Air. 30th Anniv (1969) of Territorial Credit Institute.

1260	**407**	1p. black, yellow & grn	35	20

408 U.N. Emblem, Scales and Dove

1970. Air. 25th Anniv of United Nations.

1261	**408**	1p.50 yellow, bl & ultram	35	20

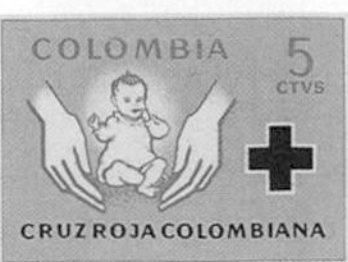

409 Hands protecting Child

1970. Obligatory Tax. Colombian Red Cross.

1262	**409**	5c. red and blue	35	20

410 Theatrical Mask

1970. Latin-American University Theatre Festival. Manizales.

1263	**410**	30c. brown, orange & blk	35	10

411 Postal Emblem, Letter and Stamps

1970. Philatelic Week.

1264	**411**	2p. multicoloured	45	30

412 Discus-thrower and Ibague Arms

1970. 9th National Games, Ibague (2nd issue).

1265	**412**	80c. brown, green & yell	35	10

413 "St. Teresa" (B. de Figueroa)

1970. St. Teresa of Avila's Elevation to Doctor of the Universal Church. No. 1267 optd **AEREO**.

1266	**413**	2p. mult (postage)	65	30
1267	**413**	2p. mult (air)	45	30

414 Int Philatelic Federation Emblem

1970. Air. "EXFILCA 70" Stamp Exhibition, Caracas, Venezuela.

1268	**414**	10p. multicoloured	6·50	30

415 Chicha Maya Dance

1970. Folklore Dances and Costumes. Mult.

1269	1p. Type **415** (postage)	45	30
1270	1p.10 Currulao dance	45	30
1271	60c. Napanga costume (air)	90	15
1272	1p. Joropo dance	75	10
1273	1p.30 Guabina dance	1·00	10
1274	1p.30 Bambuco dance	1·10	30
1275	1p.30 Cumbia dance	75	30

MS1276 Two sheets each 80×110 mm. Face values and colours changed. (a) 2p.50 As No. 1271; 2p.50 As No. 1272; 5p. As No. 1273. (b) 4p. As No. 1270; 4p. As No. 1274; 4p. As No. 1275 Pair 11·00 11·00

In **MS**1276 "AERO" is omitted from the design.

416 Stylized Athlete

1971. Air. 6th Pan-American Games, Cali (1st issue).

1277	**416**	1p.50 multicoloured	1·50	1·10
1278	-	2p. orange, green & blk	1·50	1·10

DESIGN: 2p. Games emblem.

417 G. Alzate Avendano

1971. Air. 10th Anniv of Gilberto Alzate Avendano (politician).

1279	**417**	1p. multicoloured	75	45

418 Priest's House, Guacari

1971. 400th Anniv of Guacari (town).

1280	**418**	1p. multicoloured	35	10

419 Commemorative Medal

1971. Air. Centenary of Bank of Bogota.

1281	**419**	1p. gold, brown & green	75	30

420 Sports Centre

421 Weightlifting

1971. Air. 6th Pan-American Games (2nd issue) and "EXFICALI 71" Stamp Exhibition, Cali. Mult.

1282	1p.30 Type **420** (yellow emblem)	2·00	45
1283	1p.30 Football	2·00	45
1284	1p.30 Wrestling	2·00	45
1285	1p.30 Cycling	2·00	45
1286	1p.30 Volleyball	2·00	45
1287	1p.30 Diving	2·00	45
1288	1p.30 Fencing	2·00	45
1289	1p.30 Type **420** (green emblem)	2·00	45
1290	1p.30 Sailing	2·00	45
1291	1p.30 Show-jumping	2·00	45
1292	1p.30 Athletics	2·00	45
1293	1p.30 Rowing	2·00	45
1294	1p.30 Cali emblem	2·00	45
1295	1p.30 Netball	2·00	45
1296	1p.30 Type **420** (blue emblem)	2·00	45
1297	1p.30 Stadium	2·00	45
1298	1p.30 Baseball	2·00	45
1299	1p.30 Hockey	2·00	45
1300	1p.30 Type **421**	2·00	45
1301	1p.30 Medals	2·00	45
1302	1p.30 Boxing	2·00	45
1303	1p.30 Gymnastics	2·00	45
1304	1p.30 Rifle-shooting	2·00	45
1305	1p.30 Type **420** (red emblem)	2·00	45

422 "Bolivar at Congress" (after S. Martinez-Delgado)

1971. 150th Anniv of Great Colombia Constituent Assembly, Rosario del Cucuta.

1306	**422**	80c. multicoloured	35	10

423 "Battle of Carabobo" (M. Tovar y Tovar)

1971. Air. 150th Anniv of Battle of Carabobo.

1307	**423**	1p.50 multicoloured	1·70	30

424 CIME Emblem

1972. 20th Anniv of Inter-Governmental Committee on European Migration.

1308	**424**	60c. black and grey	45	10

425 ICETEX Symbol

1972. 20th Anniv of Institute of Educational Credit and Technical Training Abroad.

1309	**425**	1p.10 brown and green	35	20

426 Rev. Mother Francisca del Castillo

1972. 300th Birth Anniv of Reverend Mother Francisca J. del Castillo.

1310	**426**	1p.20 multicoloured	35	10

427 Soldier and Frigate "Almirante Padilla"

1972. 20th Anniv of Colombian Troops' Participation in Korean War.

1311	**427**	1p.20 multicoloured	35	10

428 Hat and Ceramics

1972. Colombian Crafts and Products. Mult.

1312	1p.10 Type **428** (postage)	45	10
1313	50c. Woman in shawl (air)	55	10
1314	1p. Male doll	65	10
1315	3p. Female doll	90	20

429 "Maxillaria triloris" (orchid)

1972. 10th National Stamp Exhibition and 7th World Orchid-growers' Congress, Medellin. Mult.

1316	20p. Type **429** (postage)	10·50	65
1317	1p.30 "Mormodes rolfeanum" (orchid) (horiz) (air)	65	10

430 Uncut Emeralds and Pendant

1972. Colombian Emeralds.

1318	**430**	1p.10 multicoloured	1·00	10

431 Pres. Narino's House

1972. 400th Anniv of Leyva (town).

1319	**431**	1p.10 multicoloured	75	30

432 Congo Dance

1972. Air. Barranquilla International Carnival.

1320	**432**	1p.30 multicoloured	75	30

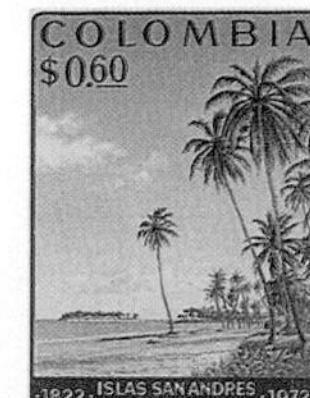

433 Island Scene

1972. 150th Anniv of Annexation of San Andres and Providencia Islands.

1321	**433**	60c. multicoloured	35	10

1972. Air. No. 1142 surch.

1322	**360**	1p.30 on 1p.90 brn and bl	90	30

435 "Pres. Laureano Gomez" (R. Cubillos)

1972. Air. Pres. Gomez Commemoration.

1323	**435**	1p.30 multicoloured	35	10

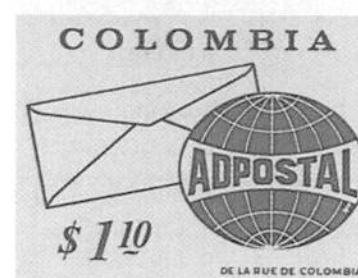

436 Postal Administration Emblem

1972. National Postal Administration.

1324	**436**	1p.10 green	20	10

437 Colombian Family

1972. "Social Front for the People" Campaign.

1325	**437**	60c. orange	35	10

438 Pres. Guillermo Valencia

1972. Air. Pres. Valencia Commemoration.

1326	**438**	1p.30 multicoloured	35	20

439 Benito Juarez

1972. Air. Death Centenary of Benito Juarez (Mexican statesman).

1327	**439**	1p.50 multicoloured	45	20

440 "La Rebeca" Monument

1972. Air. "La Rebeca" Monument, Centenary Park, Bogota.

1328	**440**	80c. multicoloured	90	45
1329	**440**	1p. multicoloured	75	10

441 "350" and Arms of Bucaramanga

1972. Air. 350th Anniv of Bucaramanga (city).

1330	**441**	5p. multicoloured	1·30	30

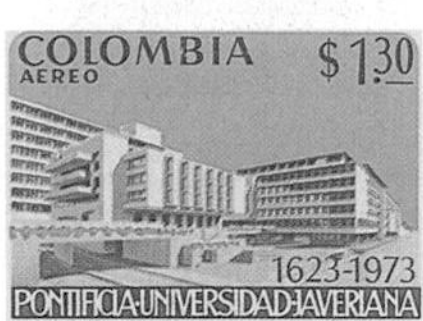

442 University Buildings

1973. Air. 350th Anniv of Javeriana University.

1331	**442**	1p.30 brown and green	45	10
1332	**442**	1p.50 brown and blue	45	10

443 League Emblems

1973. 40th Anniv of Colombian Radio Amateurs League.

1333	**443**	60c. red, dp blue & blue	35	10

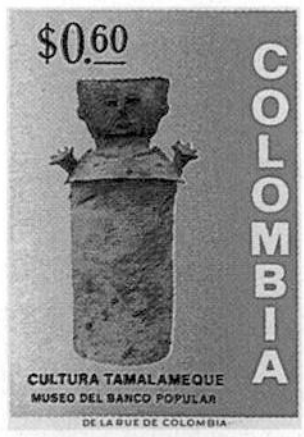

444 Tamalameque Vessel

1973. Inauguration of Museum of Pre-Colombian Antiques, Bogota. Multicoloured.

1334	60c. Type **444** (postage)	55	30
1335	1p. Tairona axe-head	1·10	30
1336	1p.10 Muisca jug	65	30
1337	1p. As No. 1335 (air)	2·40	1·60
1338	1p.30 Sinu vessel	1·20	30
1339	1p.70 Quimbaya vessel	1·30	30
1340	3p.50 Tumaco figurine	2·75	55

445 "Battle of Maracaibo" (M. F. Rincon)

1973. Air. 150th Anniv of Naval Battle of Maracaibo.

1341	**445**	10p. multicoloured	3·25	20

446 Banknote Emblem

1973. Air. 50th Anniv of Republican Bank.

1342	**446**	2p. multicoloured	45	10

1973. Air. No. 1306 optd **AEREO**.

1343	**422**	80c. multicoloured	45	30

448 "Pres. Ospina" (after C. Leudo)

1973. Air. 50th Anniv of Ministry of Communications.

1344	**448**	1p.50 multicoloured	35	20

449 Arms of Toro

1973. Air. 400th Anniv of Toro.

1345	**449**	1p. multicoloured	35	20

450 Bolivar at Bombona

1973. Air. 150th Anniv of Battle of Bombona.

1346	**450**	1p.30 multicoloured	20	10

451 "General Narino" (after J. M. Espinosa)

1973. 150th Death Anniv of General Antonio Narino.

1347	**451**	60c. multicoloured	20	10

452 Young Child

1973. Child Welfare Campaign.

1348	**452**	1p.10 multicoloured	20	10

453 Fiscal Emblem

1974. 50th Anniv of Republic's General Comptrollership.

1349	**453**	80c. black, brown & bl	20	10

454 Copernicus

1974. Air. 500th Birth Anniv of Copernicus.

1350	**454**	2p. multicoloured	75	30

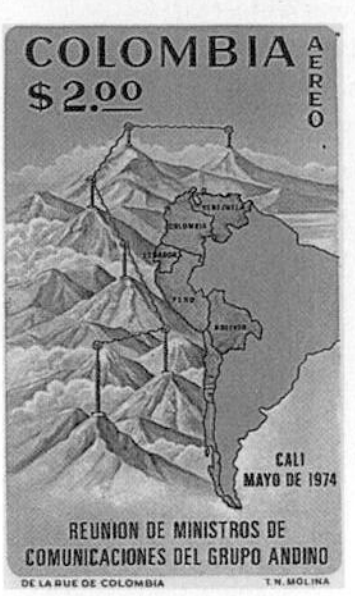

455 Andes Communications and Map

1974. Air. Meeting of Communications Ministers, Andean Group, Cali.

1351	**455**	2p. multicoloured	55	30

456 Laura Montoya and Cross

1974. Birth Centenary of Revd. Mother Laura Montoya (missionary).

1352	**456**	1p. multicoloured	35	10

457 Television Set with Inravision Emblem

1974. Air. 20th Anniv of Inravision (National Institute of Radio and Television).

1353	**457**	1p.30 black, brn & orge	35	10

458 Athlete

1974. 10th National Games, Pereira.

1354	**458**	2p. brown, red & yellow	35	20

459 Rivera and Statue

1974. 50th Anniv of Novel "La Voragine".

1355	**459**	10p. multicoloured	1·70	20

460 Aquatic Emblem

1974. Air. 2nd World Swimming Championships, Cali (1975).

1356	**460**	4p.50 blue, turq & blk	55	20

461 Condor Emblem

1974. Air. Centenary of Bank of Colombia.

1357	**461**	1p.50 multicoloured	35	10

462 Tailplane

1974. Air.

1358	**462**	20c. brown	35	20

463 UPU "Letter"

1974. Air. Centenary of Universal Postal Union (1st issue).

1359	**463**	20p. red, blue & black	4·00	45

See also Nos. 1363/6.

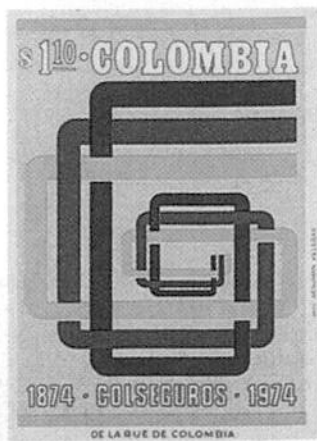

464 General Jose Maria Cordoba

1974. Air. 150th Anniv of Battles of Junin and Ayacucho.

1360	**464**	1p.30 multicoloured	35	10

465 "Progress and Expansion"

1974. Centenary of Colombian Insurance Company.

1361	**465**	1p.10 mult (postage)	35	10
1362	**465**	3p. mult (air)	55	10

466 White-tailed Trogon and U.P.U. "Letter"

1974. Air. Centenary of U.P.U. (2nd issue). Colombian Birds. Multicoloured.

1363	1p. Type **466**	1·50	30
1364	1p.30 Red-billed toucan (horiz)	1·50	30
1365	2p. Andean cock of the rock (horiz)	2·20	30
1366	2p.50 Scarlet macaw	2·20	30

Nos. 1364/6 also depict the U.P.U. "letter".

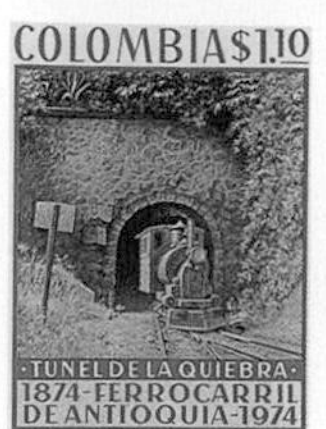

467 La Quiebra Tunnel

1974. Centenary of Antioquia Railway.

1367	**467**	1p.10 multicoloured	2·40	30

468 Boy with Ball

1974. Christmas. Multicoloured.

1368	80c. Type **468**	35	10
1369	1p. Girl with racquet	35	20

469 "Protect the Trees"

1975. Air. Colombian Ecology. Multicoloured.

1370	1p. Type **469**	35	20
1371	6p. "Protect the Amazon"	90	30

470 "Wood No. 1" (R. Roncancio)

1975. Air. Colombian Art. Multicoloured.

1372	2p. Type **470**	1·00	10
1373	3p. "The Market" (M. Diaz Vargas) (vert)	65	10
1374	4p. "Child with Thorn" (G. Vazquez) (vert)	90	30
1375	5p. "The Annunciation" (Santaferena School) (vert)	1·50	55

471 Gold Cat

1975. Pre-Colombian Archaeological Discoveries. Sinu Culture. Multicoloured.

1376	80c. Type **471** (postage)	65	30
1377	1p.10 Gold necklace	65	30
1378	2p. Nose pendant (air)	1·40	30
1379	10p. "Alligator" staff ornament	7·25	1·10

472 Marconi and "Elettra" (steam yacht)

1975. Birth Centenary of Guglielmo Marconi (radio pioneer).

1380	**472**	3p. multicoloured	35	20

473 Santa Marta Cathedral

1975. 450th Anniv of Santa Marta. Multicoloured.

1381	80c. Type **473** (postage)	20	10
1382	2p. "El Rodadero" (sea-front), Santa Marta (horiz) (air)	35	10

474 Maria de J. Paramo (educationalist)

1975. International Women's Year.

1383	**474**	4p. multicoloured	45	10

475 Pres. Nunez

1975. 150th Birth Anniv of President Rafael Nunez.

1384	**475**	1p.10 multicoloured	20	10

476 Arms of Medellin

1975. 300th Anniv of Medellin.

1385	**476**	1p. multicoloured	55	10

See also Nos. 1386, 1388, 1394, 1404, 1419, 1434, 1481/3, 1672/4, 1678/9, 1752, 1758, 1859 and 1876.

1976. Centenary of Reconstruction of Cucuta City. As T **476**.

1386	1p.50 multicoloured	75	30

1976. Surch.

1387	**471**	1p.20 on 80c. mult	35	20

1976. Arms of Cartagena. As T **476**.

1388	1p.50 multicoloured	35	10

479 Sugar Cane

1976. 4th Cane Sugar Export and Production Congress, Cali.

1389	**479**	5p. green and black	1·70	10

480 Bogota

1976. Air. Habitat. U.N. Conference on Human Settlements. Multicoloured.

1390	10p. Type **480**	2·75	1·20
1391	10p. Barranquilla	2·75	1·20
1392	10p. Cali	2·75	1·20
1393	10p. Medellin	2·75	1·20

1976. Arms of Ibague. As T **476**.

1394	1p.20 multicoloured	45	10

481 University Emblem and "90"

1976. Air. 90th Anniv of Colombia University.

1395	**481**	5p. multicoloured	75	30

482 M. Samper

1976. Air. 150th Birth Anniv of Miguel Samper (statesman and writer).

1396	**482**	2p. multicoloured	35	10

483 Early Telephone

1976. Air. Telephone Centenary.

1397	**483**	3p. multicoloured	35	10

484 "Callicore sp."

1976. Colombian Fauna and Flora. Multicoloured.

1398	3p. Type **484**	90	30
1399	5p. "Morpho sp." (butterfly)	1·40	30
1400	20p. Black anthurium (plant)	4·50	1·20

485 Purace Indians, Cauca

1976

1401	**485**	1p.50 multicoloured	20	10

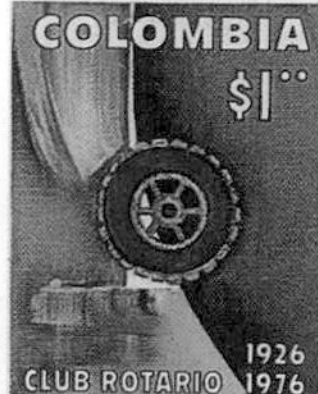

486 Rotary Emblem

1976. 50th Anniv of Colombian Rotary Club.

1402	**486**	1p. multicoloured	20	10

487 Boeing 747 Jumbo Jet

1976. Air. Inaug of Avianca Jumbo Jet Service.

1403	**487**	2p. multicoloured	30	10

1976. 535th Anniv of Tunja City Arms. As T **476**.

1404	1p.20 multicoloured	35	10

488 "The Signing of Declaration of Independence" (left-hand detail of painting, Trumbull)

1976. Bicentenary of American Revolution.

1405	**488**	30p. multicoloured	4·00	2·75
1406	-	30p. multicoloured	4·00	2·75
1407	-	30p. multicoloured	4·00	2·75

DESIGNS: Nos. 1406/7 show different portions of the painting.

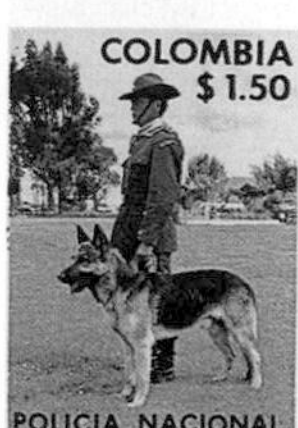

489 Police Handler and Dog

1976. National Police.

1408	**489**	1p.50 multicoloured	35	15

490 Franciscan Convent

1976. Air. 150th Anniv of Panama Congress.

1409	**490**	6p. multicoloured	90	20

491 Head of Columbia

1977. Air. Opening of Philatelic Museum, Medellin. Sheet 130×105 mm.

MS1410	**491**	25p. blue, orange and yellow	18·00	18·00

1977. Surch.

1411	**475**	2p. on 1p.10 mult (postage)	55	10
1412	-	2p. on 1p.20 mult (No. 1404)	20	10
1413	**489**	2p. on 1p.50 mult	20	10
1414	**487**	3p. on 2p. mult (air)	20	10

493 Postal Museum, Bogota

1977. Opening of Postal Museum, Bogota. Sheet 130×106 mm.

MS1415	**493**	25p. multicoloured	4·50	4·50

494 Coffee Plant and Beans

1977. Air. Coffee Production.

1416	**494**	3p. multicoloured	20	10
1416a	**494**	3p.50 multicoloured	20	10

495 Coffee Grower with mule

1977. Air. 50th Anniv of National Federation of Coffee Growers.

1417	**495**	10p. multicoloured	75	20

496 Beethoven and Score of Ninth Symphony

1977. Air. 150th Anniv of Beethoven.

1418	**496**	8p. multicoloured	1·70	30

1977. Arms of Popayan. As T **476**.

1419		5p. multicoloured	65	15

497 Mother feeding Baby

1977. Nutrition Campaign.

1420	**497**	2p. multicoloured	20	10
1420a	**497**	2p.50 multicoloured	2·20	30

498 Wattled Jacana and "Eichhornia crassipes"

1977. Colombian Birds and Plants. Multicoloured.

1421	10p. Type **498** (postage)	2·50	30
1422	20p. Plum-throated cotinga and "Pyrostegia venusta"	4·25	50
1423	5p. Crimson-mantled woodpecker and "Meriania" (air)	1·10	30
1424	5p. American purple gallinule and "Nymphaea"	1·10	30
1425	10p. Pampadour cotinga and "Cochlospermum orinocense"	2·20	50
1426	10p. Northern royal flycatcher and "Jacaranda copaia"	2·20	50

499 Games Emblem

1977. Air. 13th Central American and Caribbean Games, Medellin (1978).

1427	**499**	6p. multicoloured	55	10

500 "La Cayetana" (E. Grau)

1977. Air. 20th Anniv of Female Suffrage. Multicoloured.

1428	8p. Type **500**	90	20
1429	8p. "Nayade" (Beatriz Gonzalez)	90	20

501 "Judge Francisco Antonio Moreno y Escandon" (J. Gutierrez)

1977. Air. Bicentenary of National Library. Mult.

1430	20p. Type **501**	2·40	55
1431	25p. "Viceroy Manuel de Guiror" (unknown artist)	2·75	85

502 "Fidel Cano" (Francisco Cano)

1977. 90th Anniv of "El Espectador" Magazine by Fidel Cano.

1432	**502**	4p. multicoloured	35	10

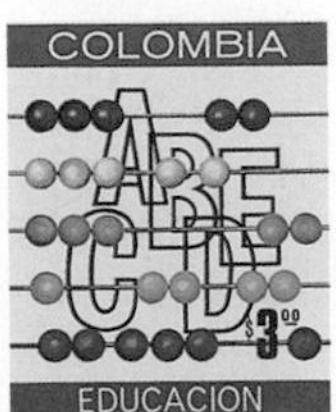

503 Abacus and Alphabet

1977. Popular Education.

1433	**503**	3p. multicoloured	35	10

1977. Arms of Barranquilla. As T **476**.

1434		5p. multicoloured	75	30

504 Dr. F. L. Acosta

1977. Air. Birth Centenary of Dr. Federico Lleras Acosta (veterinary surgeon).

1435	**504**	5p. multicoloured	55	10

505 Cauca University Arms

1977. Air. 150th Anniv of Cauca University.

1436	**505**	5p. multicoloured	55	10

506 "Cudecom" Building, Bogota

1977. Air. 90th Anniv of Society of Colombian Engineers.

1437	**506**	1p.50 multicoloured	20	10

1977. Air. No. 1364 surch **$2.00**.

1438	2p. on 1p.30 multicoloured	90	30

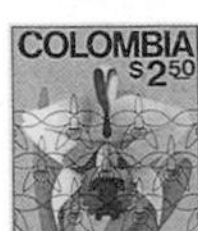

508 "Cattleya triannae"

1978

1439	**508**	2p.50 multicoloured	1·00	30
1439a	**508**	3p. multicoloured	1·00	30

509 Tayronan Lost City

1978. Air.

1440	**509**	3p.50 multicoloured	35	10

510 "Creator of Energy" (A. Betancourt)

1978. Air. 150th Anniv of Antioquia University Law School.

1441	**510**	4p. multicoloured	55	15

511 Column of the Slaves

1978. Air. 150th Anniv of Ocana Convention.

1442	**511**	2p.50 multicoloured	35	10

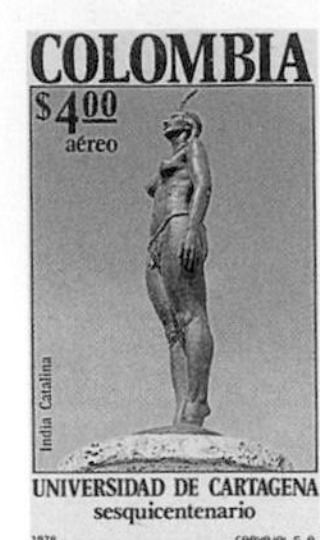

512 "Catalina"

1978. Air. 150th Anniv of Cartagena University.

1443	**512**	4p. multicoloured	55	10

513 Running

1978. 13th Central American and Caribbean Games, Medellin. Multicoloured.

1444	10p. Type **513**	1·70	30
1445	10p. Basketball	1·70	30
1446	10p. Baseball	1·70	30
1447	10p. Boxing	1·70	30
1448	10p. Cycling	1·70	30
1449	10p. Fencing	1·70	30
1450	10p. Football	1·70	30
1451	10p. Gymnastics	1·70	30
1452	10p. Judo	1·70	30
1453	10p. Weightlifting	1·70	30
1454	10p. Wrestling	1·70	30
1455	10p. Swimming	1·70	30
1456	10p. Tennis	1·70	30
1457	10p. Shooting	1·70	30
1458	10p. Volleyball	1·70	30
1459	10p. Water polo	1·70	30

514 "Sigma 2" (A. Herran)

1978. Centenary of Bogota Chamber of Commerce.

1460	**514**	8p. multicoloured	75	30

515 Human Figure from Gold Pendant

1978. Air. Tolima Culture.

1461	**515**	3p.50 multicoloured	55	30

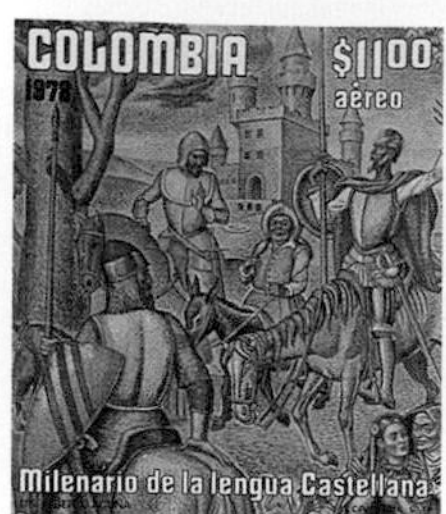

516 "Apotheosis of the Spanish Language" (Left-hand detail of mural, L. A. Acuna)

1978. Air. Millenary of Castilian Language. Multicoloured.

1462	11p. Type **516**	2·00	1·70
1463	11p. Central detail	2·00	1·70
1464	11p. Right-hand detail	2·00	1·70

Nos. 1462/4 were issued together, se-tenant, forming a composite design.

517 Presidential Guard

1978. Air. 50th Anniv of Presidential Guard Battalion.

1465	**517**	9p. multicoloured	75	45

518 Human Figure

1978. Air. Muisca Culture.

1466	**518**	3p.50 multicoloured	55	30

519 General Tomas Cipriano de Mosquera

1978. Death Centenary of General Tomas Cipriano de Mosquera (statesman).

1467	**519**	6p. multicoloured	55	30

520 El Camarin de Carmen, Bogota

1978. Air. "Espamer '78" Stamp Exhibition, Bogota.

1468	**520**	30p. multicoloured	4·00	45
MS1469		126×96 mm. **520** 50p. multicoloured	5·00	5·00

521 Gold Owl Ornament

1978. Air. Calima Culture.

1470	**521**	3p.50 multicoloured	75	30
1470a	**521**	4p. multicoloured	75	30

522 "Virgin and Child" (Gregorio Vasquez)

1978. Air. Christmas.

1471	**522**	2p.50 multicoloured	35	10

523 Church and Bullring

1978. Air. Manizales Fair.

1472	**523**	7p. multicoloured	1·10	30

524 Frog in beaten Gold

1979. Air. Quimbaya Culture.

1473	**524**	4p. multicoloured	75	30

525 Children playing Hopscotch

1979. Air. International Year of the Child. Multicoloured.

1474	8p. Type **525**	65	20
1475	12p. Child in sou'wester and oilskins	90	30
1476	12p. Child at blackboard (horiz)	90	30

526 Anthurium

1979. Anthurium Flowers from Narino. Multicoloured, background colours given.

1477	**526**	3p. light green	45	10
1478	**526**	3p. red	45	10
1479	**526**	3p. green	45	10
1480	**526**	3p. blue	45	10

1979. Arms. As T **476**. Multicoloured.

1481	4p. Sogamoso	1·30	30
1482	10p. Socorro	1·30	30
1483	10p. Santa Cruz y San Gil de la Nueva Baeza	1·30	30

527 Rio Prado Hydro-electric Barrage

1979. Air. Tourism. Multicoloured.

1484	5p. Type **527**	75	10
1485	7p. River Amazon	1·00	20
1486	8p. Tomb, San Agustin Archaeological Park	1·10	30
1487	14p. San Fernando Fort, Cartagena	2·00	95

528 "Jimenez de Quesada" (after C. Leudo)

1979. Air. 400th Death Anniv of Gonzalo Jimenez de Quesada (conquistador).

1488	**528**	20p. multicoloured	4·50	2·10

529 Hill and First Stamps of Great Britain and Colombia

1979. Air. Death Centenary of Sir Rowland Hill.

1489	**529**	15p. multicoloured	1·10	30

530 "Uribe" (after Acevedo Bernal)

1979. 65th Death Anniv of General Rafael Uribe Uribe (statesman).

1490	**530**	8p. multicoloured	65	20

531 "Village" (Leonor Alarcon)

1979. 20th Anniv of Community Works Boards.

1491	**531**	15p. multicoloured	2·20	85

532 Three Kings and Soldiers

1979. Air. Christmas. Multicoloured.

1492	3p. Type **532**	1·90	1·40
1493	3p. Nativity	1·90	1·40
1494	3p. Shepherds	1·90	1·40

533 River Magdalena Bridge and Avianca Emblem

1979. Air. 350th Anniv of Barranquilla and 60th Anniv of Avianca National Airline.

1495	**533**	15p. multicoloured	90	45

534 Gold Nose Pendant

1980. Air. Tairona Culture.

1496	**534**	3p. multicoloured	1·10	30

535 "Boy playing Flute" (Judith Leyster)

1980. Air. 2nd International Music Competition, Ibague.

1497	**535**	6p. multicoloured	65	30

536 Antonio Jose de Sucre

1980. Air. 150th Death Anniv of General Antonio Jose de Sucre.

1498	**536**	12p. multicoloured	75	30

537 "The Watchman" (Edgar Negret)

1980. Air. Modern Sculpture.

1499	**537**	25p. multicoloured	3·25	1·80

538 Television Screen

1980. Inaug of Colour Television in Colombia.

1500	**538**	5p. multicoloured	75	10

539 Bullfighting Poster (H. Courttin)

1980. Tourism. Festival of Cali.

1501	**539**	5p. multicoloured	90	20

540 "Learn to Write"

1980. The Alphabet.

1502	**540**	4p. black, brown & grn	1·10	20
1503	-	4p. multicoloured	1·10	20
1504	-	4p. brown, blk & lt brn	1·10	20
1505	-	4p. multicoloured	1·10	20
1506	-	4p. brown, black & grn	1·10	20

1507	-	4p. black and turquoise	1·10	20
1508	-	4p. black and green	1·10	20
1509	-	4p. mauve, black & grn	1·10	20
1510	-	4p. black and blue	1·10	20
1511	-	4p. black and green	1·10	20
1512	-	4p. green, black & brown	1·10	20
1513	-	4p. multicoloured	1·10	20
1514	-	4p. brown, black & grn	1·10	20
1515	-	4p. multicoloured	1·10	20
1516	-	4p. yellow, black & grn	1·10	20
1517	-	4p. black, brown & yell	1·10	20
1518	-	4p. brown, black & turq	1·10	20
1519	-	4p. brown, black & grn	1·10	20
1520	-	4p. brown, black & grn	1·10	20
1521	-	4p. yellow, black & turq	1·10	20
1522	-	4p. green, black & blue	1·10	20
1523	-	4p. brown, black & grn	1·10	20
1524	-	4p. green, black & lt grn	1·10	20
1525	-	4p. multicoloured	1·10	20
1526	-	4p. multicoloured	1·10	20
1527	-	4p. brown, black & grn	1·10	20
1528	-	4p. multicoloured	1·10	20
1529	-	4p. multicoloured	1·10	20
1530	-	4p. brown, black & grn	1·10	20
1531	-	4p. brown and black	1·10	20

DESIGNS: No. 1503, "a" Eagle; 1504, "b" Buffalo; 1505, "c" Andean Condor; 1506, "ch" Chimpanzee; 1507, "d" Dolphin; 1508, "e" Elephant; 1509, "f" Greater Flamingo; 1510, "g" Seagull; 1511, "h" Hippopotamus; 1512, "i" Iguana; 1513, "j" Giraffe; 1514, "k" Koala; 1515, "l" Lion; 1516, "ll" Llama; 1517, "m" Blackbird; 1518, "n" Otter; 1519, Gnu; 1520, "o" Bear; 1521, "p" Pelican; 1522, "q" Resplendent Quetzal; 1523, "r" Rhinoceros; 1524, "s" Grasshopper; 1525, "t" Tortoise; 1526, "u" Magpie; 1527, "v" Viper; 1528, "w" Wagon with animals; 1529, "x" Fox playing xylophone; 1530, "y" Yak; 1531, "z" Fox.

541 "Miraculous Virgin" (statue, Real del Sarte)

1980. Air. 150th Anniv of Apparition of Holy Virgin to Sister Catalina Labouri Gontard in Paris.

1532	**541**	12p. multicoloured	75	20

542 "Country Scene, San Gil" (painting, Luis Roncancio)

1980. Air. Agriculture.

1533	**542**	12p. multicoloured	90	30

543 Villavicencio Song Festival

1980. Tourism. Festivals. Multicoloured.

1534	5p. Type **543**	65	20
1535	9p. Vallenato festival	65	20

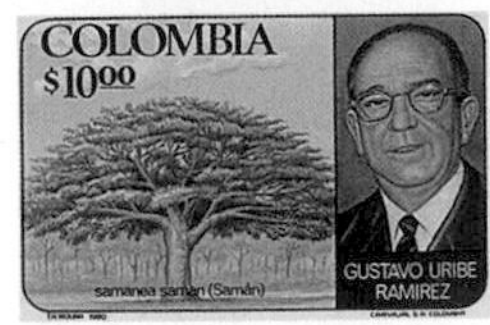

544 Gustavo Uribe Ramirez and "Samanea saman"

1980. 12th Death Anniv of Gustavo Uribe Ramirez (ecologist).

1536	**544**	10p. multicoloured	1·30	30

545 Narino Palace

1980. Narino Palace (Presidential residence).

1537	**545**	5p. multicoloured	90	10

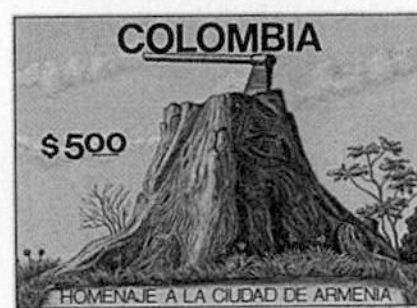

546 Monument to First Pioneers, Armenia

1980. City of Armenia.

1538	**546**	5p. multicoloured	75	10

547 Olaya Herrera (after Miguel Diaz Varges)

1980. Air. Birth Centenary of Dr. Enrique Olaya Herrera (President, 1930–34).

1539	**547**	20p. multicoloured	1·70	30

548 "Simple Simon"

1980. Air. Christmas. Illustrations to stories by Rafael Pombo. Multicoloured.

1540	4p. Type **548**	35	20
1541	4p. "The Cat's Seven Lives"	35	20
1542	4p. "The Walking Tadpole"	35	20

549 Athlete with Torch

1980. 11th National Games, Neiva.

1543	**549**	5p. multicoloured	75	10

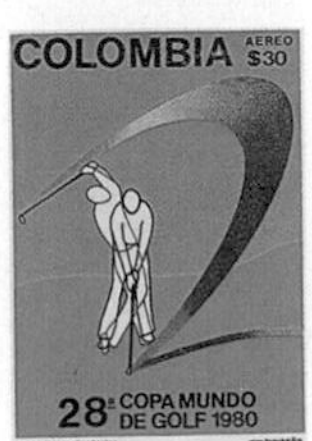

550 Golfers

1980. Air. 28th World Golf Cup, Cajica.

1544	**550**	30p. multicoloured	5·50	3·75

551 Crab pierced by Sword

1980. 20th Anniv of Colombian Anti-cancer League.

1545	**551**	10p. multicoloured	65	20

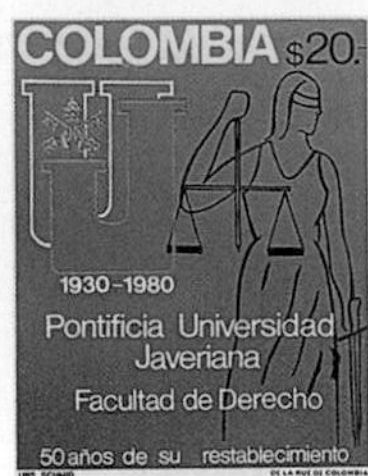

552 "Justice" and University Emblem

1980. 50th Anniv of Refounding of Pontifical Xavier University Law Faculty.

1546	**552**	20p. multicoloured	1·10	45

553 "Bolivar's Last Moments" (Marcos Leon Marino)

1980. 150th Death Anniv of Simon Bolivar. Multicoloured.

1547	25p. Type **553** (postage)	1·50	45
1548	6p. Bolivar and his last proclamation (air)	1·00	30

554 St. Pedro Claver

1981. Air. 400th Birth Anniv of St. Pedro Claver.

1549	**554**	15p. multicoloured	90	45

555 Statue of Bird, San Agustin

1981. Air. Archaeological Discoveries. Mult.

1550	7p. Type **555**	1·10	20
1551	7p. Hypogeum (funeral chamber), Tierradentro	1·10	20
1552	7p. Hypogeum, Tierradentro (different)	1·10	20
1553	7p. Statue of man, San Agustin	1·10	20

556 "Square Abstract" (Omar Rayo)

1981. Air. 4th Biennial Arts Exhibition, Medellin. Multicoloured.

1554	20p. Type **556**	1·80	30
1555	25p. "Flowers" (Alejandro Obregon)	2·00	55
1556	50p. "Child with Hobby Horse" (Fernando Botero)	3·50	95

557 Diver

1981. Air. 8th South American Swimming Championships, Medellin.

1557	**557**	15p. multicoloured	75	30

558 Santamaria Bull Ring

1981. Air. 50th Anniv of Santamaria Bull Ring, Bogota.

1558	**558**	30p. multicoloured	4·50	2·30

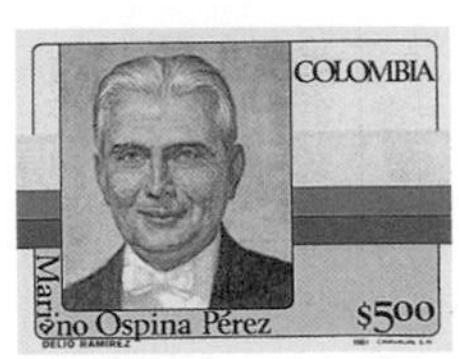

559 Mariano Ospina Perez (after Delio Ramirez)

1981. Presidents of Colombia (1st series). Multicoloured.

1559	5p. Type **559**	90	15
1560	5p. Eduardo Santos (after Ines Acevedo)	90	15
1561	5p. Miguel Abadia Mendez (after Gomez Compuzano)	90	15
1562	5p. Jose Vicente Concha (after Acevedo Bernal)	90	15
1563	5p. Carlos E. Restrepo	90	15
1564	5p. Rafael Reyes (after Acevedo Bernal)	90	15
1565	5p. Santiago Perez	90	15
1566	5p. Manuel Murillo Toro (after Moreno Otero)	90	15
1567	5p. Jose Hilario Lopez	90	15
1568	5p. Jose Maria Obando	90	15

See also Nos. 1569/78, 1579/88, 1599/1608, 1615/24 and 1634/43.

1981. Presidents of Colombia (2nd series). Multicoloured.

1569	7p. Type **559**	6·50	1·10
1570	7p. As No. 1560	6·50	1·10
1571	7p. As No. 1561	6·50	1·10
1572	7p. As No. 1562	6·50	1·10
1573	7p. As No. 1563	6·50	1·10
1574	7p. As No. 1564	6·50	1·10
1575	7p. As No. 1565	6·50	1·10
1576	7p. As No. 1566	6·50	1·10
1577	7p. As No. 1567	6·50	1·10
1578	7p. As No. 1568	6·50	1·10

1981. Presidents of Colombia (3rd series). As T **559**. Multicoloured.

1579	7p. Pedro Alcantara Herran	5·50	75
1580	7p. Mariano Ospina Rodriguez (after Coriolando Leudo)	5·50	75
1581	7p. Tomas Cipriano de Mosquera	5·50	75
1582	7p. Santos Gutierrez	5·50	75
1583	7p. Aquileo Parra (after Constancio Franco)	5·50	75
1584	7p. Rafael Nunez	5·50	75
1585	7p. Marco Fidel Suarez (after Jesus Maria Duque)	5·50	75
1586	7p. Pedro Nel Ospina (after Coriolano Leudo)	5·50	75
1587	7p. Enrique Olaya Herrera (after M. Diaz Vargas)	5·50	75
1588	7p. Alfonso Lopez Pumarejo (after Luis F. Uscategui)	5·50	75

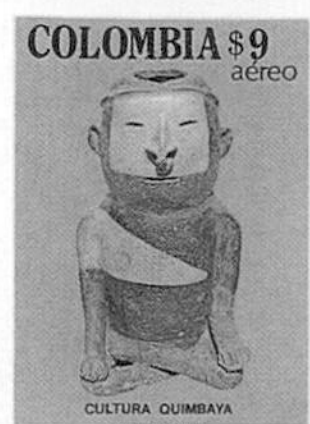

560 Crossed-legged Figure

1981. Air. Quimbaya Culture. Multicoloured.

1589	9p. Type **560**		1·50	20
1590	9p. Seated figure		1·50	20
1591	9p. Printing block and print		1·50	20
1592	9p. Clay pot		1·50	20

561 Fruit

1981. Air. Fruit. Designs showing fruit.

1593	**561**	25p. multicoloured	5·50	3·25
1594	-	25p. multicoloured	5·50	3·25
1595	-	25p. multicoloured	5·50	3·25
1596	-	25p. multicoloured	5·50	3·25
1597	-	25p. multicoloured	5·50	3·25
1598	-	25p. multicoloured	5·50	3·25

Nos. 1593/8 were issued together in se-tenant blocks of six forming a composite design.

1981. Presidents of Colombia (4th series). As T **559**. Multicoloured.

1599	7p. Manuel Maria Mallarino	3·75	55
1600	7p. Santos Acosta	3·75	55
1601	7p. Eustorgio Salgar	3·75	55
1602	7p. Julian Trujillo	3·75	55
1603	7p. Francisco Javier Zaldua (after Francisco Valles)	3·75	55
1604	7p. Jose Eusebio Otalora (after Ricardo Moros)	3·75	55
1605	7p. Miguel Antonio Caro	3·75	55
1606	7p. Manuel A. Sanclemente (after Epifanio Garay)	3·75	55
1607	7p. Laureano Gomez (after Jose Bascones)	3·75	55
1608	7p. Guillermo Leon Valencia (after Luis Angel Rengifo)	3·75	55

562 "Comunero tearing down Edict" (Manuela Beltran)

1981. Air. Bicentenary of Comuneros Uprising.

1609	**562**	20p. multicoloured	1·10	55

563 Jose Maria Villa and West Bridge

1981. West Bridge, Santa Fe de Antioquia.

1610	**563**	60p. multicoloured	1·90	20

564 Restrepo (after R. Acevedo Bernal)

1981. Air. Birth Centenary of Jose Manuel Restrepo (historian).

1611	**564**	35p. multicoloured	1·70	55

565 Anniversary Emblem

1981. 50th Anniv of Caja Agraria (peasants' bank).

1612	**565**	15p. multicoloured	55	30

566 Los Nevados National Park

1981. Los Nevados National Park.

1613	**566**	20p. multicoloured	90	30

567 Andres Bello

1981. Birth Centenary of Andres Bello (poet).

1614	**567**	18p. multicoloured	90	20

1981. Presidents of Colombia (5th series). As T **559**. Multicoloured.

1615	7p. Bartolome Calvo (after Miguel Diaz Vargas)	2·75	45
1616	7p. Sergio Camargo	2·75	45
1617	7p. Jose Maria Rojas Garrido	2·75	45
1618	7p. J. M. Campo Serrano (after H. L. Brown)	2·75	45
1619	7p. Eliseo Payan (after R. Moros Urbina)	2·75	45
1620	7p. Carlos Holguin (after Coriolano Leudo)	2·75	45
1621	7p. Jose Manuel Marroquin (after Rafael Tavera)	2·75	45
1622	7p. Ramon Gonzalez Valencia (after Jose Maria Vidal)	2·75	45
1623	7p. Jorge Holguin (after M. Salas Yepes)	2·75	45
1624	7p. Ruben Piedrahita Arango	2·75	45

568 Squatting Figure

1981. Air. Calima Culture. Multicoloured.

1625	9p. Type **568**	2·20	30
1626	9p. Vessel with two spouts	2·20	30
1627	9p. Human-shaped vessel with two spouts	2·20	30
1628	9p. Pot	2·20	30

569 1c. Stamp of 1881

1981. Air. Centenary of Admission to UPU.

1629	**569**	30p. green and pink	1·40	30
MS1630		100×70 mm. 50p. multicoloured (2, 5, 10 and 20c. stamps of 1881). Imperf	5·50	5·50

570 Girl with Water Jug

1981. Colombian Solidarity.

1631	**570**	30p. brown, blk & orge	2·20	55
1632	-	30p. brown, blk & orge	2·20	55
1633	-	30p. brown, blk & orge	2·20	55

DESIGNS: No. 1632, Baby with basket; 1633, Boy sitting on wheelbarrow.

1982. Presidents of Colombia (6th series). As T **559**. Multicoloured.

1634	7p. Simon Bolivar	1·90	20
1635	7p. Francisco de Paula Santander	1·90	20
1636	7p. Joaquin Mosquera (after C. Franco)	1·90	20
1637	7p. Domingo Caicedo	1·90	20
1638	7p. Jose Ignacio de Marquez (after C. Franco)	1·90	20
1639	7p. Juan de Dios Aranzazu	1·90	20
1640	7p. Jose de Obaldia (after Jesus M. Duque)	1·90	20
1641	7p. Guillermo Quintero Calderon (after Silvano Cuellar)	1·90	20
1642	7p. Carlos Lozano y Lozano (after Helio Ramierz)	1·90	20
1643	7p. Roberto Urdaneta Arbelaez (after Jose Bascones Agneto)	1·90	20

571 Solano Bay, Choco

1982. Air. Tourism. Multicoloured.

1644	20p. Type **571**	75	30
1645	20p. Tota Lake, Boyaca	75	30
1646	20p. Corrales, Boyaca	75	30

572 America Cup Player

1982. Air. World Cup Football Chamoionship, Spain. Sheet 179×150 mm containing T 572 and similar vert designs showing players and badges of Colombian football clubs stadium (h). Multicoloured.

MS1647	9p.×15 (a) Type **572**; (b) Atletico Bucaramanga; (c) Deportivo Cali; (d) Once Caldas; (e) Cucuta Deportivo; (f) Atletico Junior; (g) Independiente Medellin; (h) Barranquilla stadium; (i) Millonarios; (j) Atletico Nacional; (k) Deportivo Pereira; (l) Atletico Quindio; (m) Independiente Santa Fe; (n) Deportes Tolima; (o) Union Magdalena	11·00	11·00

573 Gun Club Emblem

1982. Air. Centenary of Bogota Gun Club.

1648	**573**	20p. multicoloured	90	20

574 Flower Arrangement in Basket

1982. Country Flowers. Designs showing flower arrangements. Multicoloured.

1649	7p. Type **574**	2·20	30
1650	7p. Pink arrangement in basket	2·20	30
1651	7p. Red roses in pot	2·20	30
1652	7p. Lilac and white arrangement in basket	2·20	30
1653	7p. Orange and yellow arrangement in basket	2·20	30
1654	7p. Mixed arrangement in vase	2·20	30
1655	7p. Pink roses in vase	2·20	30
1656	7p. Daisies in pot	2·20	30
1657	7p. Bouquet of yellow roses	2·20	30
1658	7p. Pink and yellow arrangement	2·20	30

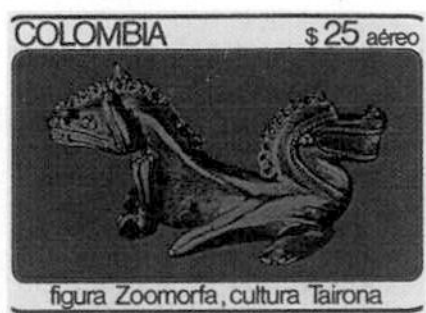

575 Zoomorphic Figure (crocodile)

1982. Air. Tairona Culture.

1659	**575**	25p. gold, black & brown	4·00	1·30
1660	-	25p. gold, black & mve	4·00	1·30
1661	-	25p. gold, black & green	4·00	1·30
1662	-	25p. gold, black & mve	4·00	1·30
1663	-	25p. gold, black & blue	4·00	1·30
1664	-	25p. gold, black & red	4·00	1·30

DESIGNS—VERT: No. 1660, Anthropomorphic figure with crest; 1661, Anthropomorphic figure with two crests; 1662, Anthropozoomorphic figure; 1663, Anthropozoomorphic figure with elaborate headdress; 1664, Pectoral.

576 Capitalization Certificate

1982. 50th Anniv of Central Mortgage Bank.

1665	**576**	9p. green and black	55	20

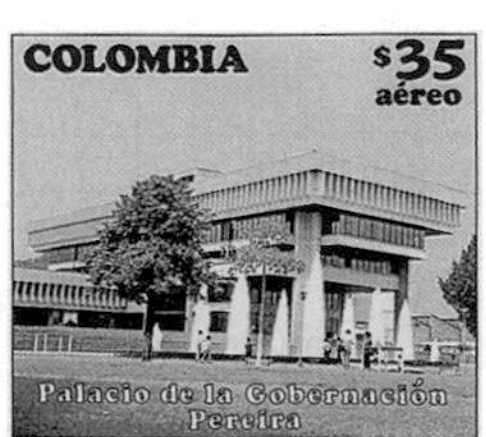

577 State Governor's Palace, Pereira

1982. Air. Pereira City.

1666	**577**	35p. multicoloured	1·50	55

578 Biplane and Badge

1982. Air. American Air Forces Co-operation.

1667	**578**	18p. multicoloured	75	20

579 St. Thomas Aquinas

1982. St. Thomas Aquinas Commemoration.

1668	**579**	5p. multicoloured	35	10

580 St. Theresa of Avila (after Zurbaran)

1982. 400th Death Anniv of St. Theresa of Avila.

1669	**580**	5p. multicoloured	35	10

581 St. Francis of Assisi (after Zurbaran)

1982. 800th Birth Anniv of St. Francis of Assisi.

1670	**581**	5p. multicoloured	35	10

582 Magdalena River

1982. Air. Tourism.

1671	**582**	30p. multicoloured	1·80	1·10

1982. Town Arms. As T **476**. Multicoloured.

1672	10p. Buga	55	10
1673	16p. Rionegro	90	20
1674	23p. Honda	1·00	20

583 Gabriel Garcia Marquez

1982. Award of Nobel Prize for Literature to Gabriel Garcia Marquez.

1675	**583**	7p. grey & grn (postage)	35	20
1676	**583**	25p. grey & blue (air)	90	30
1677	**583**	30p. grey and brown	1·30	45

1983. Town Arms. As T **476**. Multicoloured.

1678	10p. San Juan de Pasto	1·70	55
1679	20p. Santa Fe de Bogota	1·30	35

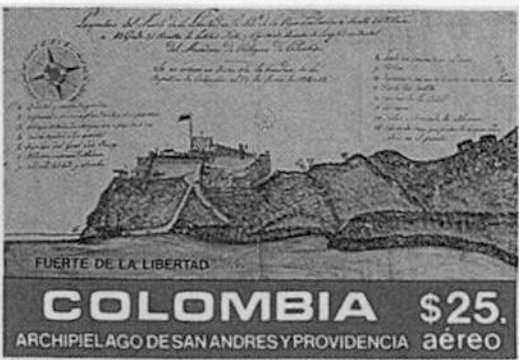

584 "Liberty Fort" (drawing in National Archives)

1983. Air. San Andres Archipelago.

1680	**584**	25p. multicoloured	75	30

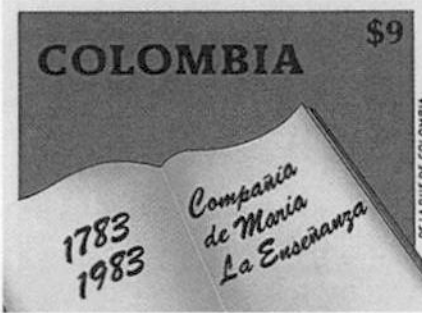

585 Open Book

1983. Bicentenary of First Girls' School, Santa Fe de Bogota.

1681	**585**	9p. grey, black & gold	55	20

586 Sunset

1983. Air. Las Gaviotas Ecological Centre.

1682	**586**	12p. multicoloured	55	20

587 Self-portrait

1983. Death Centenary of Jose Maria Espinosa (artist).

1683	**587**	9p. multicoloured	55	20

588 Radio Bands

1983. Air. 50th Anniv of Radio Amateurs League.

1684	**588**	12p. multicoloured	75	20

589 "Dona Rangel de Cuellas donating Territory" (Marcos L. Marino)

1983. 250th Anniv of Cucuta.

1685	**589**	9p. multicoloured	55	20

590 Bolivar

1983. Birth Bicentenary of Simon Bolivar.

1686	**590**	9p. mult (postage)	55	20
1687	-	30p. yell, bl & red (air)	90	30
1688	-	100p. multicoloured	2·75	2·10

DESIGNS—HORIZ: 30p. Bolivar as national flag. VERT: 100p. Bolivar and flag.

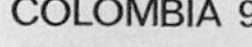

591 Porfirio Barba Jacob (after Frank Linas)

1983. Birth Centenary of Porfirio Barba Jacob.

1689	**591**	9p. brown and black	45	10

592 "Passiflora laurifolia"

1983. Bicentenary of Royal Botanical Expedition from Spain to South America. Multicoloured.

1690	9p. Type **592** (postage)	35	10
1691	9p. "Cinchona lanceifolia"	35	10
1692	60p. "Cinchona cordifolia"	2·20	45
1693	12p. "Cinchona ovalifolia" (air)	55	20
1694	12p. "Begonia guaduensis"	55	20
1695	40p. "Begonia urticae"	2·75	1·80

593 Plaza de la Aduana

1983. Air. 450th Anniv of Cartagena. Mult.

1696	12p. Type **593**	65	20
1697	35p. Cartagena buildings and monuments	1·70	30

594 "Dawn in the Andes" (Alejandro Obregon)

1983

1698	**594**	20p. mult (postage)	90	30
1699	**594**	30p. mult (air)	2·40	55

595 Scout Badge

1983. Air. 75th Anniv of Boy Scout Movement.

1700	**595**	12p. multicoloured	35	20

596 Santander

1984. Francisco de Paula Santander (President of New Granada, 1832–37).

1701	**596**	12p. green	35	20
1702	**596**	12p. blue	35	20
1703	**596**	12p. red	35	20

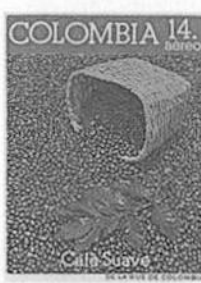

597 Coffee

1984. Air. Exports.

1704	**597**	14p. purple & green	35	10

598 Admiral Jose Prudencio Padilla

1984. Anniversaries. Multicoloured.

1705	10p. Type **598** (birth bicentenary)	45	10
1706	18p. Luis A. Calvo (composer, birth cent)	45	10
1707	20p. Diego Fallon (writer, 150th birth anniv)	45	10
1708	20p. Candelario Obeso (writer, death cent)	45	10
1709	22p. Luis Eduardo Lopez de Mesa (writer, birth centenary)	55	20

599 Rainbow over Countryside

1984. Marandua, City of the Future.

1710	**599**	15p. mult (postage)	45	20
1711	**599**	30p. mult (air)	1·00	30

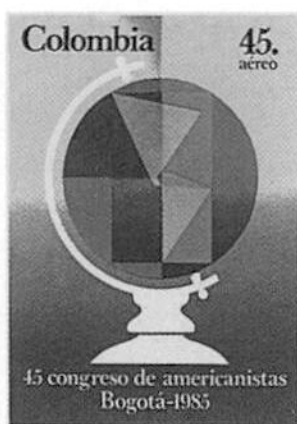

600 Stylized Globe on Stand

1984. Air. 45th Congress of Americanists, Bogota.

1712	**600**	45p. multicoloured	1·10	45

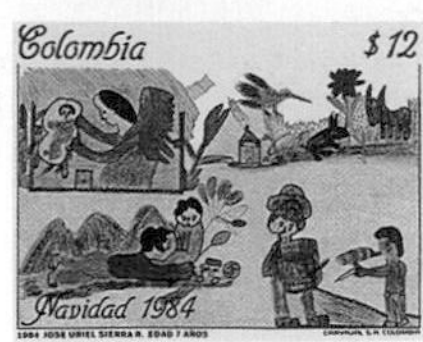

601 Nativity and Children playing

1984. Christmas.

1713	**601**	12p. mult (postage)	45	10
1714	**601**	14p. mult (air)	50	15

602 Maria Concepcion Loperena

1985. 150th Birth Anniv of Maria Concepcion Loperena (Independence heroine).

1715 **602** 12p. multicoloured 35 20

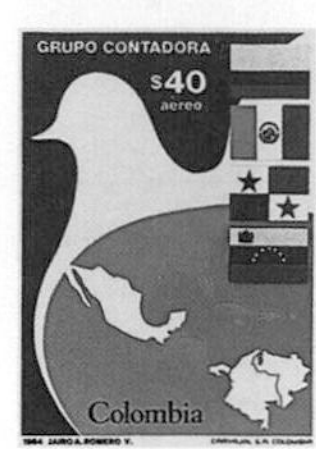

603 Dove, Map and Members' Flags

1985. Air. Contadora Group.

1716 **603** 40p. multicoloured 1·10 45

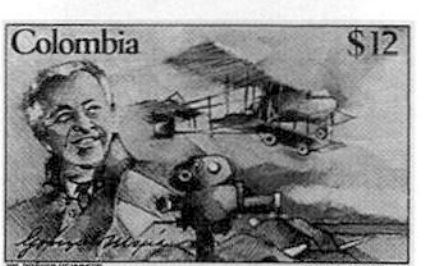

604 Mejia and Farman F.40 Type Biplane

1985. Birth Centenary of Gonzalo Mejia (airport architect).

1717 **604** 12p. multicoloured 55 30

605 "Married Couple" (Pedro nel Gomez)

1985

1718 **605** 37p. mult (postage) 1·00 45

1719 **605** 40p. mult (air) 1·30 95

606 Capybara

607 Straight-billed Woodcreepers

1985. Fauna. Multicoloured. (a) Mammals.

1720 12p. Type **606** (postage) 65 45

1721 15p. Ocelot 65 45

1722 15p. Spectacled bear 65 45

1723 20p. Mountain tapir 1·10 50

(b) Birds.

1724 14p. Lineated woodpeckers (air) 1·00 55

1725 20p. Type **607** 2·00 55

1726 50p. Coppery-bellied pufflegs 4·50 1·40

1727 55p. Blue-crowned motmots 5·50 1·60

608 Scenery and Gardel

1985. 50th Death Anniv of Carlos Gardel (singer).

1728 **608** 15p. multicoloured 35 10

609 "Gloria" (cadet ship), "Caldas" (frigate) and Naval Officer

1985. Air. 50th Anniv of Almirante Padilla Naval College.

1729 **609** 20p. multicoloured 75 30

610 Group of Colombians

1985. Air. National Census.

1730 **610** 20p. multicoloured 55 30

611 Alphabet Tree

1985. National Education Year.

1731 **611** 15p. multicoloured 45 20

612 Boy Playing Flute to Toys

1985. Christmas. Multicoloured.

1732 15p. Type **612** (postage) 55 20

1733 20p. Girl looking at dressed tree (air) 60 25

613 Pumarejo

1986. Air. Birth Centenary of Alfonso Lopez Pumarejo (President, 1934–38 and 1942–45).

1734 **613** 24p. multicoloured 45 20

614 Cyclists and Countryside

1986. Air. "Coffee and Cycling, Pride of Colombia".

1735 **614** 60p. multicoloured 1·50 95

615 Carranza (after Carlos Dupuy)

1986. Eduardo Carranza (poet) Commemoration.

1736 **615** 18p. multicoloured 35 20

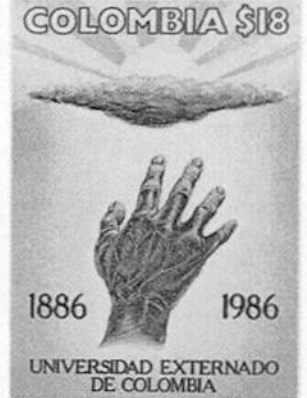

616 Hand reaching for Sun

1986. Centenary of External University.

1737 **616** 18p. multicoloured 45 30

617 Northern Pudu

1986. Air.

1738 **617** 50p. multicoloured 1·70 95

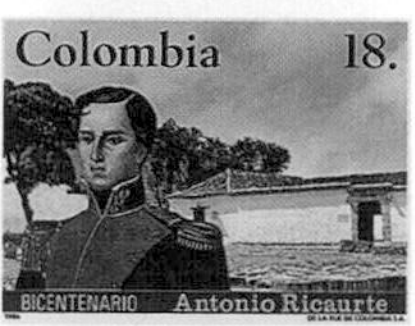

618 Ricaurte and Birth Place, Leiva

1986. Birth Bicentenary of Gen. Antonio Ricaurte (Independence hero).

1739 **618** 18p. multicoloured 35 20

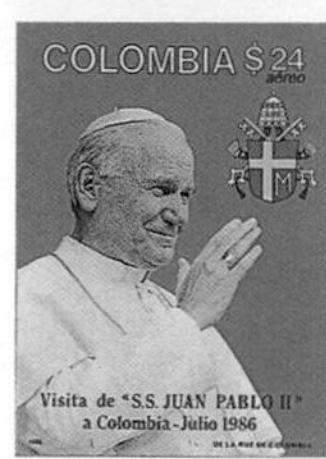

619 Pope and Arms

1986. Air. Visit of Pope John Paul II (1st issue).

1740 **619** 24p. multicoloured 65 20

See also Nos. 1745/**MS**1747.

620 Couple and Satellite

1986. Air. World Communications Day.

1741 **620** 50p. multicoloured 1·10 45

621 Silva and Illustration of "Nocturne"

1986. 90th Death Anniv of Jose Asuncion Silva (poet).

1742 **621** 18p. multicoloured 35 20

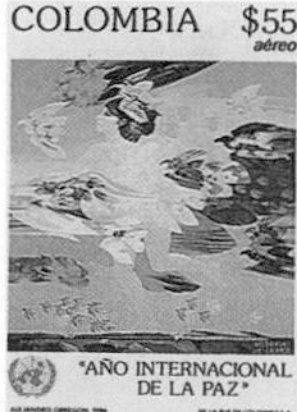

622 Girl and Doves

1986. Air. International Peace Year.

1743 **622** 55p. multicoloured 1·10 65

623 Martinez

1986. 10th Death Anniv of Fernando Gomez Martinez (politician and founder of "El Colombiano" newspaper).

1744 **623** 24p. multicoloured 45 20

624 Pope and Medellin Cathedral

1986. Air. Visit of Pope John Paul II (2nd issue). Multicoloured.

1745 55p. Type **624** 1·10 30

1746 60p. Pope giving blessing in Bogota 1·10 30

MS1747 80×12 mm. 200p. Pope praying before painting "Virgin of Chiquinquira" (49×39 mm) 5·50 4·25

625 Montejo

1986. Air. Birth Centenary of Enrique Santos Montejo (journalist and editor of "El Tiempo").

1748 **625** 25p. multicoloured 45 30

626 Computer Portrait of Bach

1986. Air. Composers' Birth Anniversaries (1985). Multicoloured.

1749 70p. Type **626** (300th anniv) 2·20 55

1750 100p. "The Permanency of Baroque" (300th annivs of Handel and Bach and 400th anniv of H. Schutz) 2·75 85

627 De La Salle (founder) and National Colours

1986. Air. Centenary of Brothers of Christian Schools in Colombia.

1751 **627** 25p. multicoloured 45 30

628 Convent of Mercy

1986. 450th Anniv of Santiago de Cali.

1752 20p. Arms (as T **476**) 35 10

1753 25p. Type **628** 45 25

629 Piece of Coal and National Colours

1986. Air. Completion of El Cerrejon Coal Complex.
1754 **629** 55p. multicoloured 1·50 95

630 Castro Silva

1986. Birth Centenary (1985) of Jose Vincente Castro Silva (Principal of Senior College of the Rosary).
1755 **630** 20p. multicoloured 35 20

631 "The Five Signatories" (detail, R. Vasquez)

1986. Air. Centenary of Constitution. Mult.
1756 25p. Type **631** 45 30
MS1757 120×81 mm. 200p. Rafael Nunez (President 1880s and 1890s), Miguel Antonio Caro (National Council of Delegates chairman, 1886; President 1894–98) and Presidential Palace, Bogota (49×39 mm) 4·00 4·00

1986. Arms of Antioquia. As T **476**.
1758 55p. multicoloured 1·30 30

632 Garcia Lorca

1986. Air. 50th Death Anniv of Federico Garcia Lorca (poet).
1759 **632** 60p. multicoloured 1·20 75

633 Symbolic Prism

1986. Centenary of Fine Art Faculty and 50th Anniv of Architecture Faculty at National University.
1760 **633** 40p. multicoloured 75 55

634 Maya

1986. 6th Death Anniv of Rafael Maya (poet and critic).
1761 **634** 25p. multicoloured 45 25

635 Andean Condor

1986
1762 **635** 20p. blue 45 20
1763 **635** 25p. blue 50 20

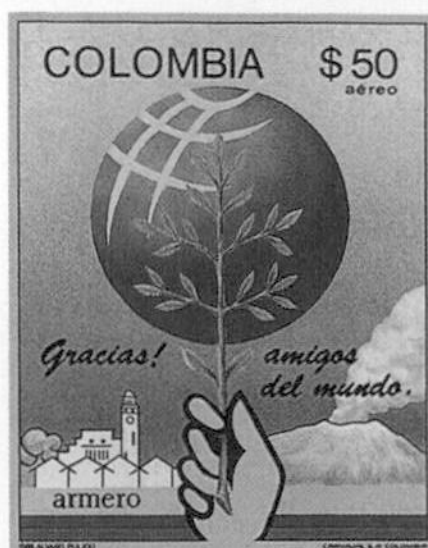

636 "Thanks! Friends of the World"

1986. Air. Thanks for Help after Devastation of Armero by Volcanic Eruption, 1985.
1767 **636** 50p. multicoloured 1·20 95

637 Mestiza Virgin (from crib at Pasto)

1986. Air. Christmas.
1768 **637** 25p. multicoloured 45 20

638 Left-hand Side of Mural

1987. Air. 450th Anniv of Popayan City. "The Apotheosis of Popayan" by Ephram Martinez Zambrano. Multicoloured.
1769 100p. Type **638** 3·25 1·90
1770 100p. Right-hand side of mural 3·25 1·90
Nos. 1769/70 were printed together, se-tenant, forming a composite design.

639 Uribe Mejia

1987. Birth Centenary (1986) of Pedro Uribe Mejia (coffee industry pioneer).
1771 **639** 25p. multicoloured 65 30

640 "Conversion of St. Augustine of Hippo"

1987. Air. 1600th Anniv of Conversion of St. Augustine.
1772 **640** 30p. multicoloured 55 30

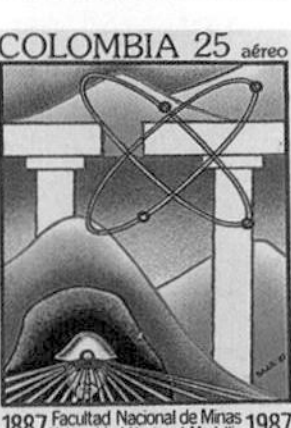

641 Atomic Diagram, Pit Props and Miner in Shaft

1987. Air. Centenary of National Mines Faculty of National University, Medellin.
1773 **641** 25p. multicoloured 45 20

642 St. Barbara's Church

1987. 450th Anniv of Mompox City.
1774 **642** 500p. multicoloured 7·75 2·30

643 Hawk-headed Parrot

1987. Fauna.
1775 **643** 30p. green (postage) 65 20
1776 - 30p. purple 65 20
1777 - 30p. red (air) 65 20
1778 - 35p. brown 65 20
DESIGNS—HORIZ: No. 1776, Boutu; 1778, South American red-lined turtle. VERT: No. 1777, Greater flamingo.
See also Nos. 1807/9, 1815/17, 1823/6 and 1855/8.

644 White Horse

1987. Air. Pure-bred Horses. Multicoloured.
1779 60p. Type **644** 1·70 45
1780 70p. Black horse 1·70 45

645 Mastheads, Fidel Cano (founder), Luis Cano, Luis Gabriel Cano Isaza and Alfonso Cano Isaza (editors)

1987. Air. Cent of "El Espectador" (newspaper).
1781 **645** 60p. multicoloured 1·10 30

646 Isaacs and Scene from "Maria"

1987. 150th Birth Anniv of Jorge Isaacs (writer).
1782 **646** 70p. multicoloured 1·20 30

648 Mutis and Illustration of "Condor"

1987. 33rd Death Anniv of Aurelio Martinez Mutis (poet).
1785 **648** 90p. multicoloured 1·70 75

649 Houses forming House

1987. Air. International Year of Shelter for the Homeless.
1786 **649** 60p. multicoloured 1·30 85

650 Family and Dish Aerial

1987. Social Security and Communications.
1787 **650** 35p. multicoloured 55 30

651 Flags

1987. Air. 1st Meeting of Eight Latin-American Presidents of Contadora and Lima Groups, Acapulco, Mexico.
1788 **651** 80p. multicoloured 1·30 45

652 Nativity Scene in Globe

1987. Air. Christmas.
1789 **652** 30p. multicoloured 55 20

653 Houses, Telephone Wires and Dials

1987. Air. Rural Telephone Network.
1790 **653** 70p. multicoloured 1·10 75

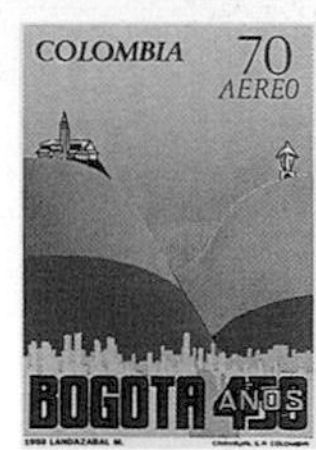

654 Mountain Sanctuaries

1988. Air. 450th Anniv of Bogota (1st issue).
1791 **654** 70p. multicoloured 1·00 55
See also Nos. 1803/4.

655 Flower (Life)

1988. 40th Anniv of Declaration of Human Rights (1st issue).
1792 **655** 30p. green 45 30
1793 - 35p. red 45 30
1794 - 40p. lilac 45 30
1795 - 40p. blue 45 30
DESIGNS—VERT: No. 1793, Road (Freedom of choice). HORIZ: 1794, Circle of children (Freedom of association); 1795, Couple on bench (Communication).
See also Nos. 1840/1.

657 Mask

1988. Air. Gold Museum, Bogota. Multicoloured.
1796 70p. Type **657** 1·10 85
1797 80p. Votive figure 1·30 1·10
1798 90p. Human figure 1·90 1·40

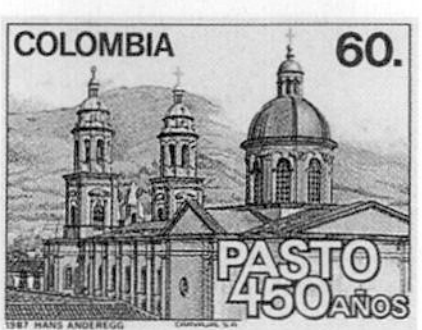

658 Pasto Cathedral

1988. 450th Anniv of Pasto.
1799 **658** 60p. multicoloured 90 55

659 Waterfall

1988. Centenary of Bogota Water Supply and Sewerage Organization.
1800 **659** 100p. multicoloured 1·50 45

660 Score and Composers

1988. Centenary (1987) of National Anthem by Rafael Nunez and Oreste Sindici.
1801 **660** 70p. multicoloured 1·00 30

661 M. Currea de Aya

1988. Birth Centenary of Maria Currea de Aya (women's rights pioneer).
1802 **661** 80p. multicoloured 1·20 30

662 Modern Bogota

1988. Air. 450th Anniv of Bogota (2nd issue). Multicoloured.
1803 80p. Type **662** 1·10 85
1804 90p. Street in old Bogota (horiz) 1·10 85

1988. Fauna. As T **643**.
1807 35p. brown 1·00 30
1808 35p. green 1·00 30
1809 40p. orange 1·00 30
DESIGNS—HORIZ: No. 1807, Crab-eating racoon; 1808, Caribbean monk seal; 1809, Giant otter.

664 College

1988. Centenary of Return of Society of Jesus to St. Bartholomew's Senior College.
1810 **664** 120p. multicoloured 1·70 95

665 Eduardo Santos

1988. Personalities. Multicoloured.
1811 80p. Type **665** (birth centenary) (postage) 1·10 30
1812 90p. Jorge Alvarez Lleras (astronomer) 1·10 30
1813 80p. Zipa Tisquesusa (16th-century Indian chief) (air) 1·10 30

666 Mother and Children

1988. Air. Christmas.
1814 **666** 40p. multicoloured 75 30

1988. Fauna. As T **643**.
1815 40p. grey (postage) 1·10 30
1816 45p. violet 1·10 30
1817 45p. blue (air) 1·10 30
DESIGNS—HORIZ: No. 1815, American manatee; 1816, Masked trogon. VERT: No. 1817, Blue-bellied curassow.

667 Andres Bello College

1988
1818 **667** 115p. multicoloured 1·40 20

668 Building and Nieto Caballero

1989. Air. Birth Centenary of Agustin Nieto Caballero (educationalist).
1819 **668** 100p. multicoloured 1·20 75

669 Gomez

1989. Air. Birth Centenary of Laureano Gomez (President, 1950–53).
1820 **669** 45p. multicoloured 55 30

670 Map

1989. Air. International Coffee Organization.
1821 **670** 110p. multicoloured 1·30 85

671 Modern Flats, Recreation Area and Hands holding Brick

1989. Air. 12th Habitat U.N. Conference on Human Settlements, Cartagena.
1822 **671** 100p. multicoloured 1·20 75

1989. Fauna. As T **643**.
1823 40p. brown (postage) 1·10 20
1824 45p. black 1·10 20
1825 55p. brown 1·10 20
1826 45p. blue (air) 1·10 20
DESIGNS—HORIZ: No. 1823, White-tailed deer; 1824, Harpy eagle; 1826, Blue discus. VERT: No. 1825, False anole.

672 Emblem

1989. 25th Anniv of Adpostal (postal administration).
1827 **672** 45p. multicoloured 55 30

673 Hands

1989. Air. Bicentenary of French Revolution.
1828 **673** 100p. multicoloured 1·20 75

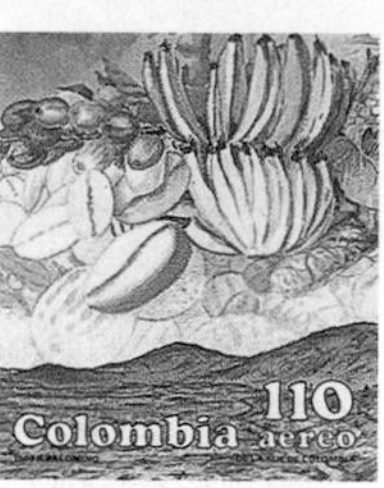

674 Fruit, Coffee Beans and Mountains

1989. Air. Philexfrance 89 International Stamp Exhibition, Paris. Sheet 145×110 mm containing T 674 and similar multicoloured designs.
MS1829 110p. Type **674**; 110p. Fruit, flowers and mountains; 110p. Wildlife and snow-capped mountain peak (41×26 mm); 110p. Man with basket of fruit floating over fields; 110p. River valley; 110p. Gemstones, gold and industry (41×25 mm); 110p. Fishes and seashore (41×26 mm) 17·00 17·00

675 "Simon Bolivar" (Pedro Jose Figueroa)

1989. 170th Anniv of Liberation Campaign. Multicoloured.
1830 40p. Type **675** (postage) 75 30
1831 40p. "Santander" (Figueroa) 75 30
1832 45p. "Bolivar and Santander during the Campaign for the Plains" (J. M. Zamora) (46×37 mm) 90 45
1833 45p. "From Boyaca to Santa Fe" (left-hand detail) (Francisco de P. Alvarez) (29×36 mm) 1·70 65
1834 45p. Right-hand detail (29×36 mm) 1·70 65
1835 45p. Mounted officer and foot soldiers (left-hand detail) (31×51 mm) 1·10 55
1836 45p. Mounted officer (centre detail) (33×51 mm) 1·10 55
1837 45p. Mounted soldiers with flag (right-hand detail) (31×51 mm) 1·10 55
MS1838 119×79 mm. 250p. "The Lancers" (sculpture by R. Arenas Betancur) (49×39 mm) (air) 2·40 1·10
Nos. 1833/4 and 1835/7 (showing details of triptych by A. de Santa Maria) were issued together, se-tenant, each forming a composite design.

676 Founder's House

1989. 450th Anniv of Tunja.
1839 **676** 45p. multicoloured 55 30

1989. Human Rights (2nd issue). As T **655**.
1840 45p. brown (postage) 45 30
1841 55p. green (air) 65 45
DESIGNS—HORIZ: 45p. Musicians (Culture). VERT: 55p. Family.

677 Healthy Children and Shadowy Figures

1989. Air. Anti-drugs Campaign.
1842 **677** 115p. multicoloured 1·30 45

678 Gold Ornaments of Quimbaya, Calima and Tolima

1989. Air. America. Pre-Columbian Crafts. Multicoloured.
1843 115p. Type **678** 1·40 75
1844 130p. Indian making pot and Sinu ceramic figure (horiz) 1·50 95

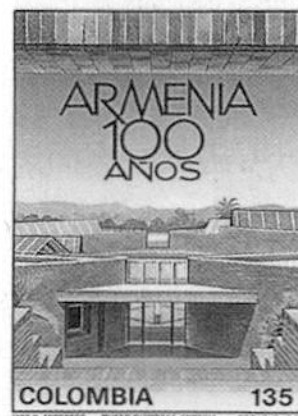

679 Quimbaya Museum

1989. Centenary of Armenia City.
1845 **679** 135p. multicoloured 1·70 1·10

680 Mantilla

1989. Air. 45th Death Anniv of Joaquin Quijano Mantilla (chronicler).

1846	**680**	170p. multicoloured	2·10	85

681 Boeing 767 and Globe

1989. Air.

1847	**681**	130p. multicoloured	1·50	45

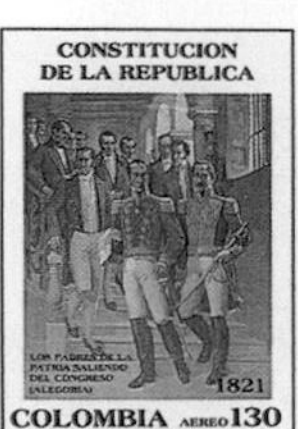

682 "The Fathers of the Fatherland leaving Congress" (R. Acevedo Bernal)

1989. Air. 170th Anniv of Creation of First Republic of Colombia (1851) and 168th Anniv of its Constitution (others). Multicoloured.

1848	130p. Type **682**	1·50	85
1849	130p. "Church of the Rosary, Cucuta" (Carmelo Fernandez)	1·50	85
1850	130p. Republic's arms	1·50	85
1851	130p. "Bolivar at Congress of Angostura" (46×36 mm) (Tito Salas)	1·50	85

683 Nativity (Barro-Raquira clay figures)

1989. Air. Christmas.

1852	**683**	55p. multicoloured	55	20

684 "Plaza de la Aduana" (H. Lemaitre)

1990. Air. Presidential Summit, Cartagena.

1853	**684**	130p. multicoloured	1·00	20

685 Headphones on Marble Head

1990. Air. 50th Anniv of Colombia National Radio.

1854	**685**	150p. multicoloured	2·20	75

1990. Fauna. As T **643**.

1855	50p. grey	75	20
1856	50p. purple	75	20
1857	60p. brown	75	20
1858	60p. brown	75	20

DESIGNS: No. 1855, Grey fox; 1856, Common poison-arrow frog; 1857, Pygmy marmoset; 1858, Sun-bittern.

1990. Air. Velez City Arms. As T **476**.

1859	60p. multicoloured	65	20

686 Cuervo Borda and National Museum

1990. Air. Birth Centenary (1989) of Teresa Cuervo Borda (artist).

1860	**686**	60p. multicoloured	65	20

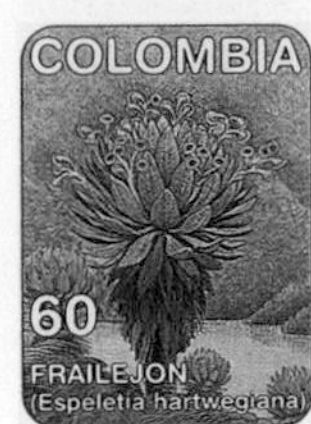

687 "Espeletia hartwegiana"

1990. Multicoloured.. Multicoloured..

1861	60p. Type **687**	55	30
1862	60p. "Ceiba pentandra" (horiz)	55	30
1863	70p. "Ceroxylon quindiuense"	55	30
1864	70p. "Tibouchina lepidota"	55	30

688 Theatrical Masks

1990. Air. 2nd Iberian-American Theatre Festival, Bogota.

1865	**688**	150p. gold, brown & orge	1·20	30

689 Statue, Bogota

1990. 150th Death Anniv of Francisco de Paula Santander (President of New Granada, 1832–37). Multicoloured.

1866	50p. Type **689** (postage)	55	20
1867	60p. Gateway of National Pantheon (air)	55	20
1868	60p. "General Santander with the Constitution" (Jose Maria Espinosa)	55	20
1869	70p. Santander, organizer of public education (after F. S. Guitierrez)	60	20
1870	70p. "The Postal Carrier" (Jose Maria del Castillo) (horiz)	60	20
MS1871	109×89 mm. 5000p. "Santander on Death Bed" (Luis Garcia Hevia) (49×39 mm)	5·50	5·50

690 Postmen

1990. Air. 150th Anniv of the Penny Black.

1872	**690**	150p. multicoloured	1·20	75

691 Cadet, Arms and School

1990. 50th Anniv of General Santander Police Cadets School.

1873	**691**	60p. multicoloured	55	30

692 Cable

1990. Air. Trans-Caribbean Submarine Fibre Optic Cable.

1874	**692**	150p. multicoloured	1·50	75

693 Graph

1990. Air. 50th Anniv of I.F.I.

1875	**693**	60p. multicoloured	55	30

1990. Arms of Cartago. As T **476**.

1876	50p. multicoloured	75	20

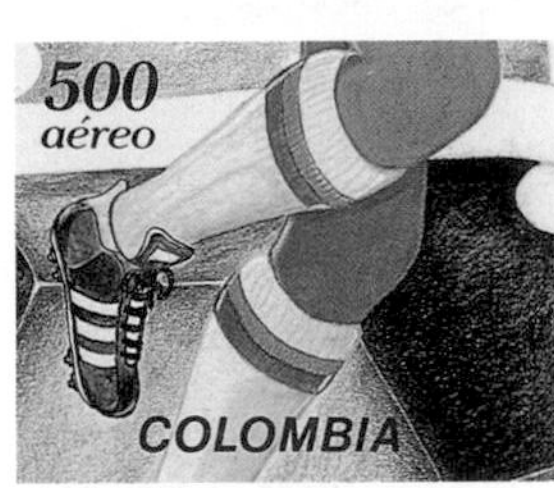

694 Player's Legs

1990. Air. World Cup Football Championship, Italy. Sheet 120×90 mm.

MS1877	**694**	500p. multicoloured	6·00	6·00

695 Map

1990. Air. 100th Anniv of Organization of American States.

1878	**695**	130p. multicoloured	90	30

696 Women on Beach

1990. La Guajira.

1879	**696**	60p. multicoloured	65	20

697 Indian wearing Gold Ornaments

1990. Air. 50th Anniv of Gold Museum, Bogota.

1880	**697**	170p. multicoloured	1·40	85

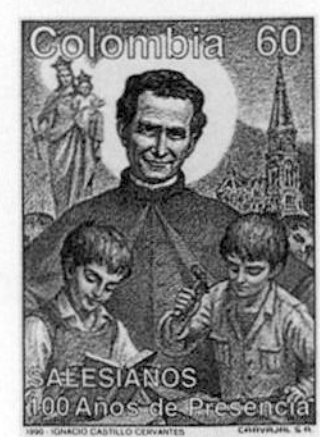

698 St. John Bosco (founder) and Boys

1990. Centenary of Salesian Brothers in Colombia.

1881	**698**	60p. multicoloured	65	20

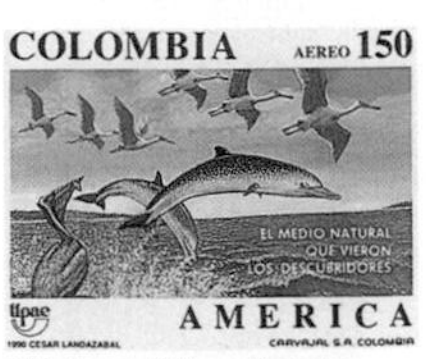

699 Brown Pelican, Roseate Spoonbills and Dolphins

1990. Air. America. Natural World. Multicoloured.

1882	150p. Type **699**	2·75	30
1883	170p. Land animals and Salvin's curassows	2·75	30

700 Christ Child

1990. Air. Christmas.

1884	**700**	70p. multicoloured	65	20

701 Monastery

1990. Air. Monastery of Nostra Senhora de las Lajas, Ipiales.

1885	**701**	70p. multicoloured	65	20

702 Titles and Abstract

1991. Air. Bicentenary of "La Prensa".

1886	**702**	170p. multicoloured	1·40	90

703 Christ of the Miracles, Buga Church

1991
1887 **703** 70p. multicoloured 60 35

704 "Anaea syene"

1991. Butterflies. Multicoloured.
1888 70p. Type **704** (postage) 1·10 35
1889 70p. "Callithea philotima" (horiz) 1·10 35
1890 80p. "Thecla coronata" 1·30 40
1891 80p. "Agrias amydon" (horiz) (air) 1·30 40
1892 170p. "Morpho rhetenor" (horiz) 2·75 45
1893 190p. "Heliconius longarenus ernestus" (horiz) 3·00 50

705 Humpback Whale leaping from Water

1991. Air. Marine Mammals. Multicoloured.
1894 80p. Type **705** 1·80 20
1895 170p. Humpback whale diving 3·75 45
1896 190p. Amazon dolphins (horiz) 4·25 50

706 National Colours

1991. New Constitution.
1897 **706** 70p. multicoloured 60 35
See also No. 1914.

707 Dario Echandia Olaya (after Delio Ramirez)

1991. 2nd Death Anniv of Dario Echandia Olaya.
1898 **707** 80p. multicoloured 65 45

708 Girardot (after Jose Maria Espinosa)

1991. Birth Bicent of Colonel Atanasio Girardot.
1899 **708** 70p. multicoloured 60 35

709 Galan

1991. 2nd Death Anniv of Luis Carlos Galan Sarmiento (politician).
1900 **709** 80p. multicoloured 60 45

710 Stone Statue of God, San Agustin

1991. Pre-Columbian Art. Multicoloured.
1901 80p. Type **710** (postage) 95 35
1902 90p. Burial vessel, Tierradentro 1·20 35
1903 90p. Statue, San Agustin (air) 1·20 35
1904 210p. Gold flyingfish, San Agustin (horiz) 2·50 45

711 Sailfish

1991
1905 **711** 830p. multicoloured 8·75 2·10

712 Cloisters of St. Augustine's, Tunja

1991. Architecture. Multicoloured.
1906 80p. Type **712** (postage) 95 35
1907 90p. Bridge, Chia 1·20 35
1908 90p. Roadside chapel, Pamplona (vert) (air) 1·20 35
1909 190p. Church of the Conception, Santa Fe de Bogota (vert) 2·40 45

713 "Santa Maria"

1991. Air. America. Voyages of Discovery. Mult.
1910 90p. Type **713** 70 45
1911 190p. Amerindians and approaching ship 1·50 90

714 Lleras Camargo (after Rafael Salas)

1991. 1st Death Anniv of Alberto Lleras Camargo (President, 1945–46 and 1958–62).
1912 **714** 80p. multicoloured 60 45

715 Police Officers, Transport, Emblem and Flag

1991. Centenary of Police.
1913 **715** 80p. multicoloured 60 45

1991. Air. New Constitution (2nd issue). As No. 1897 but new value and additionally inscr "SANTAFE DE BOGOTA. D.C. Julio 4 de 1991".
1914 90p. multicoloured 70 50

716 Member Nations' Flags

1991. Air. 5th Group of Rio Presidential Summit, Cartagena.
1915 **716** 190p. multicoloured 1·50 1·00

717 First Government Building, Sogamoso

1991
1916 **717** 80p. multicoloured 60 45

718 "Adoration of the Kings" (Baltazar de Figueroa)

1991. Air. Christmas.
1917 **718** 90p. multicoloured 70 50

719 D. Turbay Quintero

1992. Diana Turbay Quintero (journalist) Commemoration.
1918 **719** 80p. multicoloured 60 45

720 Hand holding Posy of Flowers

1992. Air. 8th U.N. Conference on Trade and Development Session, Cartagena.
1919 **720** 210p. multicoloured 1·80 1·10

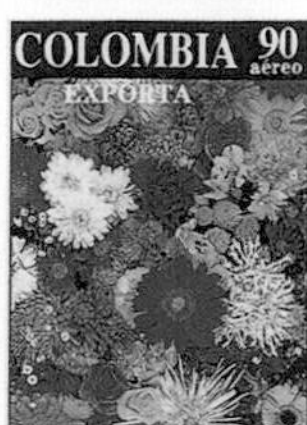

721 Cut Flowers

1992. Air. Exports.
1920 90p. Type **721** 70 50
1921 210p. Fruits and nuts (horiz) 1·70 1·00

722 Statue of General Santander, Barranquilla (R. Verlet)

1992. Birth Bicentenary of General Francisco de Paula Santander. Multicoloured.
1922 80p. Type **722** (postage) 60 45
1923 190p. Francisco de Paula Santander (after Sergio Trujillo Magnenat) (air) 1·50 1·00
MS1924 120×90 mm. 950p. "Battle of Boyaca, 1819" (Martin Tovar) (50×40 mm) 7·75 7·75

723 Music, Book and Paint Brush

1992. Air. Copyright Protection.
1925 **723** 190p. multicoloured 1·50 1·00

725 Lievano Aguirre

1992. 10th Death Anniv of Indalecio Lievano Aguirre (ambassador to United Nations).
1928 **725** 80p. multicoloured 70 50

726 Enrique Low Murtra (1st anniv)

1992. Death Anniversaries of Justice Ministers. Multicoloured.
1929 100p. Type **726** 85 55
1930 110p. Rodrigo Lara Bonilla (8th anniv) 95 55

727 Town Arms and Rings

1992. 14th National Games, Barranquilla.

1931	**727**	110p. multicoloured	95	55

728 Landscape

1992. Air. 2nd U.N. Conference on Environment and Development, Rio de Janeiro. Paintings by Roberto Palomino. Multicoloured.

1932	230p. Type **728**	2·00	1·20
1933	230p. Birds in trees	2·00	1·20

729 Athlete and Olympic Rings

1992. Air. Olympic Games, Barcelona.

1934	**729**	110p. multicoloured	95	55

730 "Discovery of America by C. Columbus" (Dali)

1992. Air. America. Multicoloured.

1935	230p. Type **730**	2·00	1·20
1936	260p. "America Magic, Myth and Legend" (Al. Vivero)	2·20	1·40

731 American Crocodile

1992. Endangered Animals. Multicoloured.

1937	100p. Type **731**	1·80	55
1938	100p. Andean condor (vert)	1·80	55

732 Maria Lopez de Escobar (founder)

1992. 50th Anniv of House of Mother and Child.

1939	**732**	100p. mult (postage)	85	55
1940	**732**	110p. mult (air)	95	55

733 Avianca Colombia McDonnell Douglas MD-83

1992. Air.

1941	**733**	110p. multicoloured	95	55

734 Map of the Americas

1992. Meeting of First Ladies of the Americas and the Caribbean, Cartagena.

1942	**734**	100p. multicoloured	85	55

735 "Zenaida" (Ana Mercedes Hoyos)

1992. 500th Anniv of Discovery of America by Columbus. Paintings.

1943	**735**	100p. mult (postage)	85	55
1944	-	110p. multicoloured	95	55
MS1945		Two sheets. (a) 120×90 mm. 400p. multicoloured; (b) 90×120 mm. 440p. mult	6·00	6·00
1946	-	110p. mult (air)	95	55
1947	-	230p. multicoloured	1·80	1·00
1948	-	260p. green and violet	2·00	1·10

DESIGNS: 110p. (1944), "Study for 1/500" (Beatriz Gonzalez); 110p. (1946), "Blue Eagle" (Alejandro Obregon); 230p. "Cantileo" (Luis Luna); 260p. "Maize" (Antonio Caro); 400p. "Great Curtain" (Luis Caballero); 440p. "Homage to Guatavita" (Alejandro Obegoin).

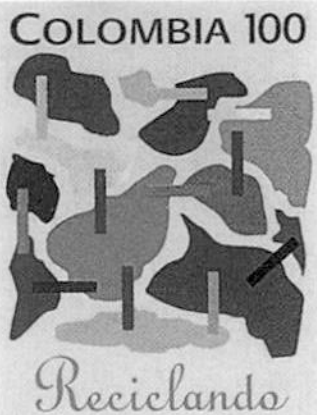

736 Recycling

1992

1949	**736**	100p. multicoloured	85	55

737 Front Curtain

1992. Air. Columbus Theatre.

1950	**737**	230p. multicoloured	1·70	1·00

739 "Nativity" (Carlos Alfonso Mendez)

1992. Christmas. Children's Drawings. Mult.

1952	100p. Type **739** (postage)	85	55
1953	110p. Kings approaching stable (Catalina del Valle) (air)	95	55

740 G. Lara

1992. Air. 10th Death Anniv of Gloria Lara (ambassador to the United Nations).

1954	**740**	230p. multicoloured	1·70	1·00

742 Campaign Emblem

1993. Lions Club International Amblyopia Prevention Campaign.

1956	**742**	100p. multicoloured	85	55

748 Footballers

1993. Air. America Cup Football Championship, Ecuador.

1962	**748**	220p. multicoloured	1·70	1·00

749 Prisoners

1993. Bicentenary of French Declaration of Human Rights. Multicoloured.

1963	150p. Type **749** (postage)	1·20	65
1964	150p. The elderly	1·20	65
1965	200p. The infirm	1·50	90
1966	200p. Children	1·50	90
MS1967	101×88 mm. 800p. Woman releasing dove (29×39 mm)	6·50	6·50
1968	220p. Women (air)	1·80	1·10
1969	220p. The poor	1·80	1·10
1970	460p. Environmental protection	3·50	2·20
1971	520p. Immigrants	4·00	2·40

750 Amerindian (Jose Luis Correal)

1993. Air. International Year of Indigenous Peoples.

1972	**750**	460p. multicoloured	3·25	2·10

751 Emblem and Flags

1993. Air. World Cup Football Championship, U.S.A. (1994) (1st issue).

1973	**751**	220p. multicoloured	2·40	1·00

See also Nos. 2006/9.

752 Green-winged Macaw ("Papagayo")

1993. The Amazon. Multicoloured.

1974	150p. Type **752** (postage)	1·10	65
1975	150p. Anaconda	1·10	65
1976	220p. Water-lilies (air)	1·50	1·00
1977	220p. Ipecacuanha flower	1·50	1·00
MS1978	120×90 mm. 880p. Amerindian on river and detail of map (horiz)	6·50	6·50

753 Cotton-headed Tamarin

1993. Air. America. Endangered Animals. Mult.

1979	220p. Type **753**	1·50	1·00
1980	220p. American purple gallinule	1·50	1·00
1981	460p. Andean cock of the rock	3·25	2·10
1982	520p. American manatee	3·75	2·40

754 Alberto Pumarejo (politician)

1993. Famous Colombians. Multicoloured.

1983	150p. Type **754**	1·10	65
1984	150p. Lorencita Villegas de Santos (First Lady, 1938–42)	1·10	65
1985	200p. Meliton Rodriguez (photographer)	1·40	90
1986	200p. Tomas Carrasquilla (writer)	1·40	90

755 Nativity

1993. Christmas. Multicoloured.

1987	200p. Type **755** (postage)	1·40	90
1988	220p. Shepherd (air)	1·50	1·00

756 San Andres y Providencia

1993. Tourism. Multicoloured.

1989	220p. Type **756**	1·50	1·00
1990	220p. Cocuy National Park	1·50	1·00
1991	220p. La Cocha Lake	1·50	1·00
1992	220p. Waterfall, La Macarena mountains	1·50	1·00
1993	460p. Chicamocha (vert)	3·25	2·10
1994	460p. Sierra Nevada de Santa Marta (vert)	3·25	2·10

1995	520p. Embalse de Penol (vert)	3·75	2·40

See also No. E1996.

757 Museum Entrance

1993. 170th Anniv of National Museum.

1997	**757**	150p. multicoloured	1·10	65

759 Yellow-eared Conure

1994. Birds. Multicoloured.

1999	180p. Type **759** (postage)	1·20	75
2000	240p. Bogota rail	1·70	1·00
2001	270p. Toucan barbets (horiz) (air)	1·90	1·20
2002	560p. Cinnamon teals (horiz)	4·00	2·75

760 Emblem

1994. Air. International Decade for Natural Disaster Reduction. National Disaster Prevention System.

2003	**760**	630p. blue, yellow & red	4·50	3·00

762 Escriva de Balaguer

1994. Air. Beatification of Josemaria Escriva de Balaguer (founder of Opus Dei).

2005	**762**	560p. multicoloured	4·00	2·75

763 Trophy and Player and Emblem on Flag

1994. World Cup Football Championship, U.S.A. (2nd issue). Multicoloured.

2006	180p. Type **763** (postage)	1·20	75
MS2007	121×90 mm. 1110p. Player helping opponent to feet and emblem	8·25	8·25
2008	270p. Match scene, trophy and emblem (air)	1·90	1·20
2009	560p. Trophy, emblem, ball and national colours (vert)	4·00	2·75

764 Flagpoles

1994. Air. 4th Latin American Presidential Summit, Cartagena.

2011	**764**	630p. multicoloured	4·50	3·00

See also No. E2010.

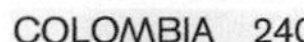

765 "Self-portrait"

1994. Birth Centenary of Ricardo Rendon (painter).

2012	**765**	240p. black	1·70	1·00

766 Biplane and William Knox Martin

1994. Air. 75th Anniv of First Airmail Flight.

2013	**766**	270p. multicoloured	1·90	1·20

767 Emblem

1994. 40th Anniv of Radio and Television Network.

2014	**767**	180p. multicoloured	1·20	75

768 Numbers, Graphs and Pie Chart

1994. 1993 Census.

2015	**768**	240p. multicoloured	1·70	1·00

770 Horse and Bicycle

1994. Air. America. Postal Transport. Mult.

2017	**770**	270p. multicoloured	1·90	1·20

See also No. E2018.

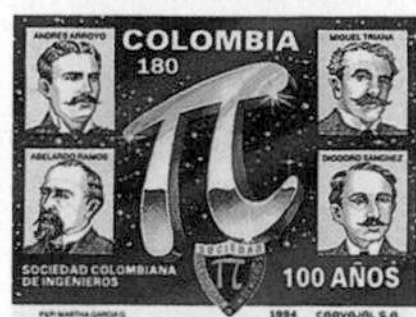

771 Founders and Pi Symbol

1994. Centenary of Colombian Society of Engineers.

2019	**771**	180p. multicoloured	1·20	75

772 Building and Scales

1994. Air. 80th Anniv of National Institute of Legal Medicine and Forensic Sciences.

2020	**772**	560p. multicoloured	4·00	2·75

773 Three Wise Men

1994. Air. Christmas.

2021	**773**	270p. multicoloured	1·90	1·20

See also No. E2022.

774 1921 SCADTA 30c. Stamp

1995. Air. 75th Anniv (1994) of Sociedad Colombo-Alemana de Transportes Aereos (SCADTA) (private air company contracted to carry mail).

2023	**774**	330p. pink, brown & blk	2·40	1·50

775 Common Iguana

1995. Air. Flora and Fauna. Multicoloured.

2024	650p. Type **775**	4·75	3·25
2025	650p. Iguana facing left	4·75	3·25
2026	750p. Forest (left detail)	5·25	3·75
2027	750p. Forest (right detail)	5·25	3·75

Stamps of the same value were issued together in se-tenant pairs, each pair forming a composite design.

776 1920 10c. Stamp

1995. Air. 75th Anniv of Compania Colombiana de Navagacion Aerea (private air company contracted to carry mail).

2028	**776**	330p. multicoloured	2·40	1·50

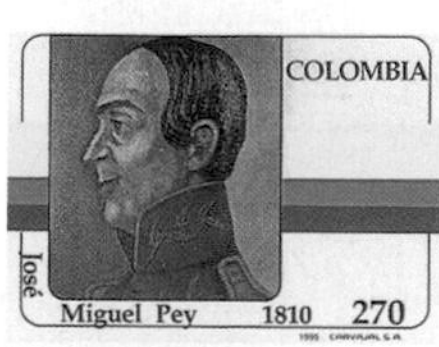

778 Jose Miguel Pey

1995. Colombian Patriots. Multicoloured.

2030	270p. Type **778** (revolutionary)	1·90	1·20
2031	270p. Jorge Tadeo Lozana (zoologist and revolutionary)	1·90	1·20
2032	270p. Antonio Narino (journalist and politician)	1·90	1·20
2033	270p. Camilo Torres (lawyer and revolutionary)	1·90	1·20
2034	270p. Jose Fernandez Madrid (doctor and revolutionary)	1·90	1·20
2035	270p. Jose Maria del Castillo y Rada (lawyer)	1·90	1·20
2036	270p. Custodio Garcia Rovira (revolutionary)	1·90	1·20
2037	270p. Antonio Villavicencio (revolutionary)	1·90	1·20

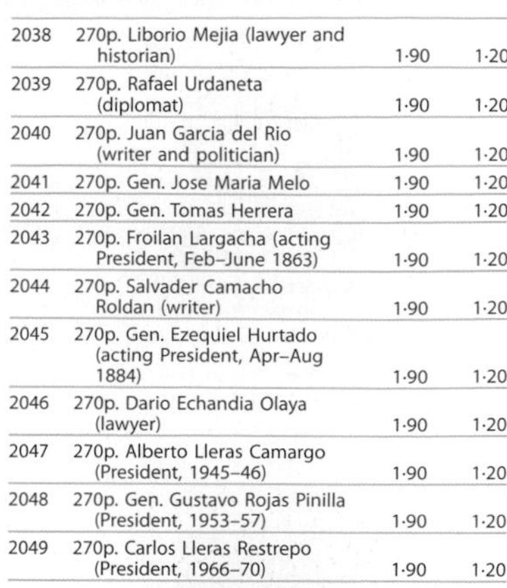

2038	270p. Liborio Mejia (lawyer and historian)	1·90	1·20
2039	270p. Rafael Urdaneta (diplomat)	1·90	1·20
2040	270p. Juan Garcia del Rio (writer and politician)	1·90	1·20
2041	270p. Gen. Jose Maria Melo	1·90	1·20
2042	270p. Gen. Tomas Herrera	1·90	1·20
2043	270p. Froilan Largacha (acting President, Feb–June 1863)	1·90	1·20
2044	270p. Salvader Camacho Roldan (writer)	1·90	1·20
2045	270p. Gen. Ezequiel Hurtado (acting President, Apr–Aug 1884)	1·90	1·20
2046	270p. Dario Echandia Olaya (lawyer)	1·90	1·20
2047	270p. Alberto Lleras Camargo (President, 1945–46)	1·90	1·20
2048	270p. Gen. Gustavo Rojas Pinilla (President, 1953–57)	1·90	1·20
2049	270p. Carlos Lleras Restrepo (President, 1966–70)	1·90	1·20

779 Farmers on Hillside

1995. Air. 50th Anniv of FAO.

2050	**779**	750p. multicoloured	5·25	3·75

780 Bello

1995. Air. 25th Anniv of Andres Bello (scholar and writer). Agreement on Intellectual Co-operation.

2051	**780**	650p. multicoloured	4·75	3·25

781 Fireman

1995. Air. Centenary of Fire Brigade of Bogota.

2052	**781**	330p. multicoloured	2·40	1·50

782 Emblem

1995. Air. 50th Anniv of National Chamber of Commerce.

2053	**782**	330p. multicoloured	2·40	1·50

783 Anniversary Emblem

1995. Air. 50th Anniv of UNO.

2054	**783**	750p. multicoloured	5·25	3·75

784 Emblem

1995. Air. 1st Pacific Ocean Games, Cali.

2055	**784**	750p. multicoloured	5·25	3·75

786 Obando (after Efrain Martinez)

1995. Birth Bicentenary of General Jose Maria Obando.

2057	**786**	220p. multicoloured	1·50	1·00

787 San Filipe de Barajas Castle

1995. Air. 11th Non-aligned Countries' Conference, Cartagena de Indias.

2058	**787**	650p. multicoloured	4·75	3·25

788 Estela Lopez Pomareda in "Maria", Charlie Chaplin and Jackie Coogan

1995. Air. Centenary of Motion Pictures.

2059	**788**	330p. black and brown	2·40	1·50

789 Harvesting Poppies for Opium

1995. Air. World Campaign against Drug Trafficking. Multicoloured.

2060	330p. Type **789**		2·40	1·50
2061	330p. Manacled hands (horiz)		2·40	1·50

790 Anniversary Emblem

1995. Air. 25th Anniv of Andean Development Corporation.

2062	**790**	650p. multicoloured	4·75	3·25

792 Madre-Monte

1995. Air. Myths and Legends (1st issue). Multicoloured.

2065	750p. Type **792**	4·50	3·00
2066	750p. La Llorana	4·50	3·00
2067	750p. El Mohan (river spirit)	4·50	3·00
2068	750p. Alligator man	4·50	3·00

Nos. 2065/8 were issued together, se-tenant, in sheetlets in which the background colour gradually changes down the sheet; each design therefore occurs in four slightly different colours.

See also Nos. 2085/8.

793 Holy Family

1995. Christmas. Stained Glass Windows from Chapel of the Apostles, Bogota School. Mult.

2069	220p. Type **793** (postage)	1·50	1·00
2070	330p. Nativity (air)	2·40	1·50

794 Asuncion Silva

1996. Air. Death Centenary of Jose Asuncion Silva (poet).

2071	**794**	400p. multicoloured	3·00	1·90

795 Painting by Luz Maria Tobon Mesa

1996. Air. Providence Island.

2072	**795**	800p. multicoloured	5·50	4·25

796 Salavarrieta (after Jose Maria Espinosa)

1996. Air. Birth Bicentenary of Policarpa Salavarrieta.

2073	**796**	900p. multicoloured	6·00	4·50

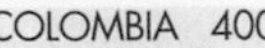

797 De Greiff (Ricardo Rendon)

1996. 1st Death Anniv of Leon De Greiff (poet).

2074	**797**	400p. black	3·00	1·90

799 Santa Maria la Antigua del Darien

1996. Town Arms. Multicoloured.

2076	400p. Type **799**	3·00	1·90
2077	400p. San Sebastian de Mariquita	3·00	1·90
2078	400p. Marinilla	3·00	1·90
2079	400p. Santa Cruz de Mompox	3·00	1·90

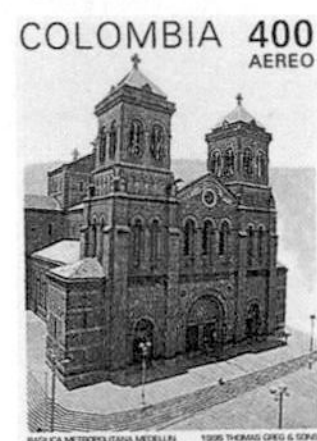

801 Medellin Cathedral

1996. Air.

2081	**801**	400p. multicoloured	3·00	1·90

803 Mosquera Courtyard

1996. 150th Anniv of National Capitol, Bogota.

2083	**803**	400p. multicoloured	3·00	1·90

804 National Archive, Bogota

1996. Air.

2084	**804**	400p. multicoloured	3·00	1·90

1996. Air. Myths and Legends (2nd issue). Multicoloured.

2085	900p. The Creation of Koguin	6·00	4·50
2086	900p. Yonna Wayu	6·00	4·50
2087	900p. Jaguar-man	6·00	4·50
2088	900p. Lord of the Animals	6·00	4·50

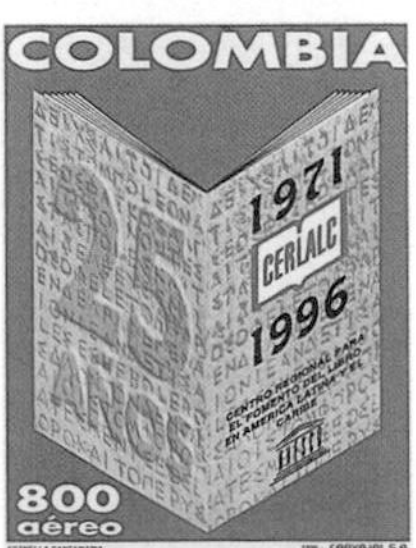

805 Anniversary Emblem

1996. Air. 25th Anniv of Regional Centre for the Development of Books in Latin America and Caribbean.

2089	**805**	800p. brn, blk & dp brn	5·50	4·25

806 Guitar and Notes

1996. 50th Anniv of Society of Colombian Authors and Composers.

2090	**806**	400p. multicoloured	3·00	1·90

807 Jorge Isaacs and Pump

1996. Air. Pioneers of Petroleum Industry. Multicoloured.

2091	800p. Type **807**	4·75	3·25
2092	800p. Francisco Burgos Rubio and refinery (at night)	4·75	3·25
2093	800p. Diego Martinez Camargo and drilling tower	4·75	3·25
2094	800p. Prisciliano Cabrales Lora and drilling platform	4·75	3·25
2095	800p. Manuel Maria Palacio and firefighting tug	4·75	3·25
2096	800p. Roberto de Mares and refinery	4·75	3·25
2097	800p. General Virgilio Barco Maldonado and workmen	4·75	3·25
2098	800p. Workmen and Ecopetrol (state petroleum industry) emblem	4·75	3·25

808 Golf Course

1996. Air. 50th Anniv of Colombian Golf Federation.

2099	**808**	400p. multicoloured	3·00	1·90

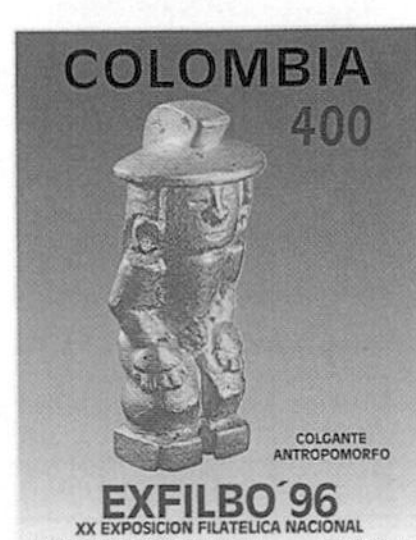

809 Pre-Columban Pendant, Malagana Treasure

1996. "Exfilbo '96" National Stamp Exn, Bogota.

2100	**809**	400p. multicoloured	3·00	1·90

810 Theatre Curtain (detail, Guillermo Vallejo)

1996. 30th Anniv of Founders Theatre, Manizales. Sheet 120×90 mm containing T **810** and similar multicoloured design.

MS2101	4000p. Type **810**; 4000p. Detail showing settlers with animals (horiz)	35·00	35·00

811 Postman delivering Letter

1996. Christmas. The Annunciation. Mult.

2102	400p. Type **811** (postage)	3·00	1·90
2103	400p. Woman reading letter and postman (air)	3·00	1·90

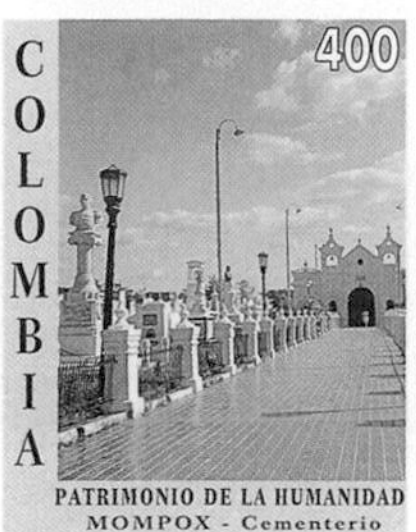

813 Cemetery, Mompox

1996. UNESCO World Heritage Sites. Mult.

2106	400p. Type **813**	3·00	1·90
2107	400p. San Agustin Archaeological Park	3·00	1·90
2108	400p. Palace of the Inquisition, Cartagena	3·00	1·90
2109	400p. Underground tomb, Tierradentro Archaeological Park	3·00	1·90

814 Children holding Hands

1997. Air. Children's Rights.

2110	**814**	400p. multicoloured	3·00	1·90

815 Hurtado

1997. 2nd Death Anniv of Alvaro Gomez Hurtado (lawyer and politician).

2111	**815**	400p. black and blue	3·00	1·90

816 Film Reels and Harbour Tower

1997. Air. Centenary of Colombian Cinema and 53rd International Union of Film Archives Congress, Cartagena de Indias.

2112	**816**	800p. multicoloured	5·50	4·25

817 Emblem

1997. Air. 50th Anniv (1996) of State Social Security.

2113	**817**	400p. multicoloured	3·00	1·90

818 Hand holding Mobile Phone

1997. Air. Centenary (1996) of Ericsson Company in Colombia.

2114	**818**	900p. multicoloured	6·00	4·50

819 Cattle

1997. Air. Cordoba Cattle Fair.

2115	**819**	400p. multicoloured	3·00	1·90

820 "Maria Varilla in the Clouds" (William Vive)

1997. Porro National Festival, San Pelayo.

2116	**820**	400p. multicoloured	3·00	1·90

821 Typewriter

1997. 50th Anniv of Bogota Journalists' Association.

2117	**821**	400p. multicoloured	3·00	1·90

822 Museum Buildings

1997. Air. 1st Anniv of Numismatic Museum at State Mint, Bogota.

2118	**822**	800p. multicoloured	5·50	4·25

823 Palm

1997. Air. Vegetable Ivory Palm Production Project.

2119	**823**	900p. multicoloured	6·00	4·50

824 Barco

1997. Virgilio Barco (President, 1986–90) Commem.

2120	**824**	500p. multicoloured	3·50	2·20

825 Straightening Contorted Tree and Healthy Couple

1997. Air. 50th Anniv of Colombian Society of Orthopaedic Surgery and Traumatology.

2121	**825**	1000p. multicoloured	6·25	4·75

826 Luis Carlos Lopez (poet)

1997. Air. Personalities. Multicoloured.

2122	500p. Type **826**	2·75	1·40
2123	500p. Aurelio Arturo (poet)	2·75	1·40
2124	500p. Enrique Perez Arbelaez (botanist and historian)	2·75	1·40
2125	500p. Jose Maria Gonzalez Benito (mathematician and astronomer)	2·75	1·40
2126	500p. Jose Manuel Rivas Sacconi (philologist and diplomat)	2·75	1·40
2127	500p. Eduardo Lemaitre Roman (historian and journalist)	2·75	1·40
2128	500p. Diojenes Arrieta (journalist and politician)	2·75	1·40
2129	500p. Gabriel Turbay Abunader (politician and diplomat)	2·75	1·40
2130	500p. Guillermo Echavarria Misas (aviation pioneer)	2·75	1·40
2131	500p. Juan Friede Alter (historian)	2·75	1·40
2132	500p. Fabio Lozano Torrijos (diplomat)	2·75	1·40
2133	500p. Lino de Pombo (engineer and diplomat)	2·75	1·40
2134	500p. Cacica Gaitana (Indian resistance leader)	2·75	1·40
2135	500p. Josefa Acevedo de Gomez (writer)	2·75	1·40
2136	500p. Domingo Bioho (Black leader)	2·75	1·40
2137	500p. Soledad Acosta de Samper (historian)	2·75	1·40
2138	500p. Maria Cano Marquez (workers' leader)	2·75	1·40
2139	500p. Manuel Quintin Lame (native leader)	2·75	1·40
2140	500p. Ezequiel Uricoechea (linguist and naturalist)	2·75	1·40
2141	500p. Juan Rodriguez Freyle (chronicler)	2·75	1·40
2142	500p. Gerardo Reichel-Dolmatoff (archaeologist)	2·75	1·40
2143	500p. Ramon de Zubiria (educationist)	2·75	1·40
2144	500p. Esteban Jaramillo (economist)	2·75	1·40
2145	500p. Pedro Fermin de Vargas (economist)	2·75	1·40

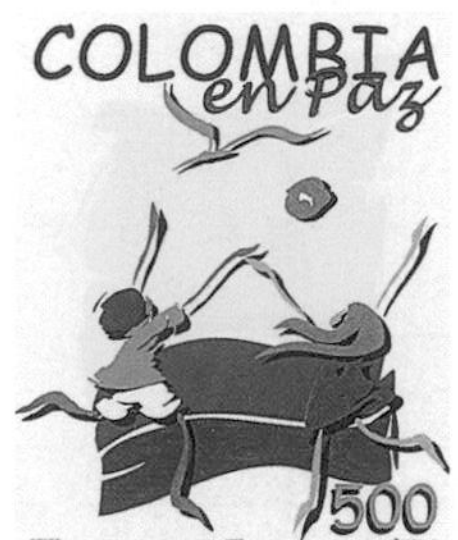

827 National Flag, Dove and Children playing

1997. Peace. Multicoloured.

2146	500p. Type **827** (postage)	3·25	2·00
2147	1100p. Children holding hands in ring (air)	6·00	4·25

828 Postman on Moped

1997. America. The Postman. Multicoloured.

2148	500p. Type **828** (postage)	3·25	2·00
2149	1100p. Postman raising envelope to night sky (air)	6·00	4·25

829 Pregnant Women

1998. Air. 50th Anniv of WHO Safe Motherhood.

2150	**829**	1100p. multicoloured	6·00	4·25

830 Dove Emblem

1998. Air. 4th Bolivarian Stamp Exhibition, Santafe de Bogota.

2151	**830**	1000p. orange and blue	5·75	4·00

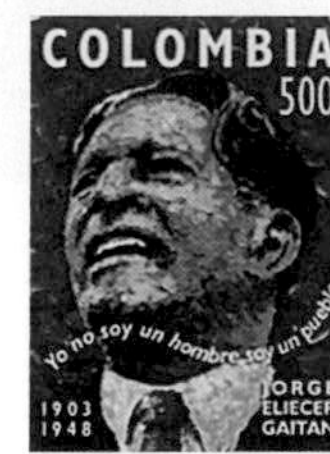

831 Gaitan

1998. 50th Death Anniv of Jorge Eliecer Gaitan.

2152	**831**	500p. multicoloured	3·25	1·20

832 Colombian Flag and Map of the Americas

1998. Air. 50th Anniv of Organization of American States.

2153	**832**	1000p. multicoloured	5·75	4·00

833 Cogs

1998. 50th Anniv of Santander Industrial University.

2154	**833**	500p. multicoloured	3·25	2·00

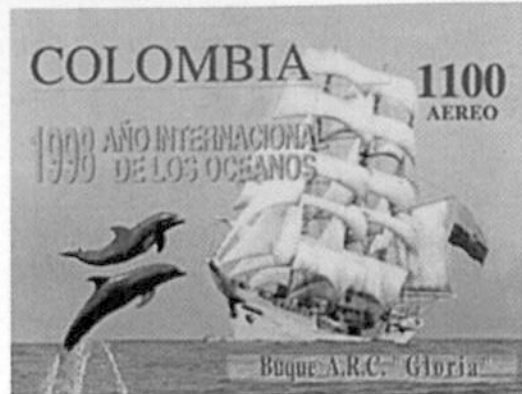

834 "Gloria" (cadet ship) and Dolphins

1998. Air. International Year of the Ocean.

2155	**834**	1100p. multicoloured	6·00	4·25

835 Football Boot

1998. Air. World Cup Football Championship, France. Multicoloured.

2156	1100p. Type **835**	6·00	4·25
2157	1100p. Ball	6·00	4·25
2158	1100p. Goalkeeper's glove	6·00	4·25

Nos. 2156/8 were issued together, se-tenant, forming a composite design.

836 University Arms

1998. 75th Anniv of Colombia Free University.

2159	**836**	500p. black and red	3·25	2·00

837 "Bolivar Condor" (sculpture, R. Arenas Betancur) and Cathedral

1998. 150th Anniv of Manizales.

2160	**837**	500p. multicoloured	3·25	2·00

838 Gold Coin, Tairona Culture

1998. 75th Anniversaries. Multicoloured.

2161	500p. Type **838** (National Bank)	3·25	2·00
2162	500p. Gold sheaf of corn, Malagana Culture (Comptroller-General's Office)	3·25	2·00
2163	500p. Gold mask, Quimbaya Culture (Banking Superintendent's Office)	3·25	2·00

839 Borrero

1998. 1st Death Anniv of Misael Pastrana Borrero (President, 1970–74).

2164	**839**	500p. multicoloured	3·25	2·00

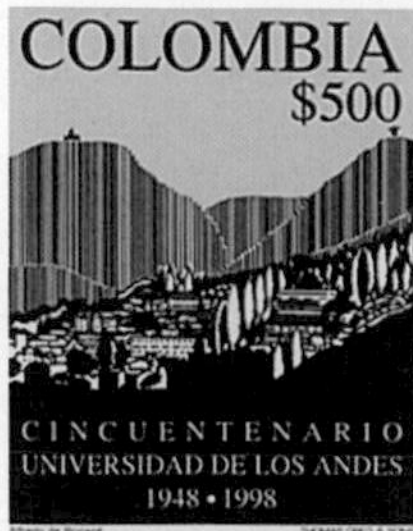

840 The Andes and University Campus

1998. 50th Anniv of University of the Andes, Bogota.

2165	**840**	500p. black and yellow	3·25	2·00

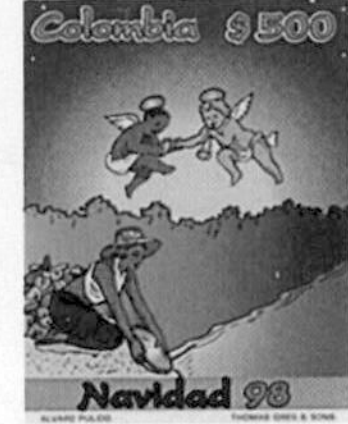

841 Woman panning for Gold, and Cherubs

1998. Christmas. Multicoloured.

2166	500p. Type **841** (postage)	3·25	2·00
2167	1000p. Three kings, camel and star (air)	5·75	4·00
2168	1000p. Nativity	5·75	4·00

Nos. 2167/8 were issued together, se-tenant, forming a composite design.

842 Bochica

1998. Air. Muisca Mythology. Multicoloured.

2169	1000p. Type **842**	5·75	4·00
2170	1000p. Chiminigua	5·75	4·00
2171	1000p. Bachue and Huitica	5·75	4·00

Nos. 2169/71 were issued together, se-tenant, forming a composite design.

843 Academy of Languages Arms

1998. Arms of Colombian Academies. Mult.

2172	500p. Type **843**	3·25	2·00
2173	500p. Medicine	3·25	2·00
2174	500p. Law	3·25	2·00
2175	500p. History	3·25	2·00
2176	500p. Physical and Natural Sciences	3·25	2·00
2177	500p. Economics	3·25	2·00
2178	500p. Ecclesiastical History	3·25	2·00

844 Soledad Roman de Nunez (First Lady, 1880–82 and 1884–94)

1999. America (1998). Famous Women. Mult.

2179	600p. Type **844** (postage)	4·00	2·00
2180	1200p. Bertha Hernandez de Ospina (politician) (air)	6·00	3·25

845 Lopez (after G. Ricci)

1999. Birth Bicentenary of Jose Hilario Lopez (President, 1849–53).

2181	**845**	1000p. multicoloured	5·50	2·75

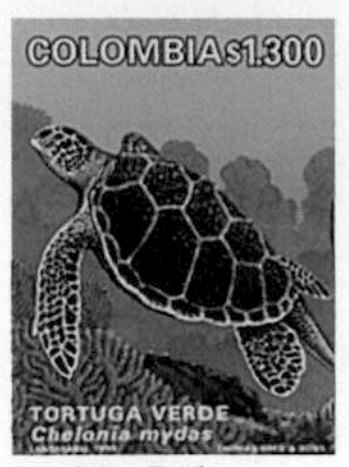

846 Green Turtle

1999. Turtles. Multicoloured.

2182	1300p. Type **846**	6·25	3·50
2183	1300p. Leatherback turtle ("Dermochelys coriacea")	6·25	3·50
2184	1300p. Hawksbill turtle ("Eretmochelys imbricata")	6·25	3·50

Nos. 2182/4 were issued together, se-tenant, forming a composite design.

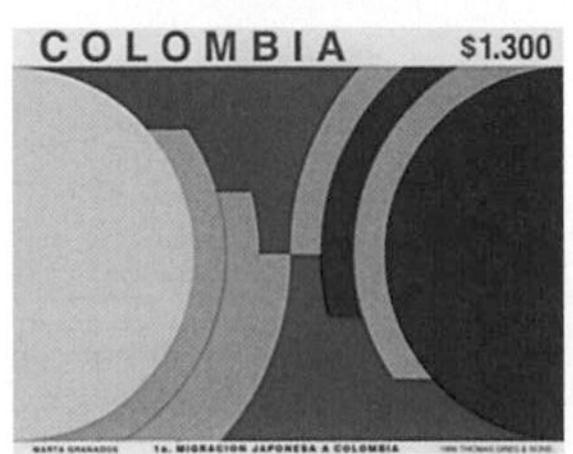

847 Colombian and Japanese Suns across the Pacific

1999. 70 Years of Japanese Emigration to Colombia.

2185	**847**	1300p. multicoloured (yellow sun at left)	6·25	3·50
2186	**847**	1300p. multicoloured (red sun at left)	6·25	3·50

Nos. 2185/6 were issued together, se-tenant, forming a composite design.

848 Medal

1999. 900th Anniv of Sovereign Military Order of Malta.

2187	**848**	1200p. multicoloured	6·00	3·25

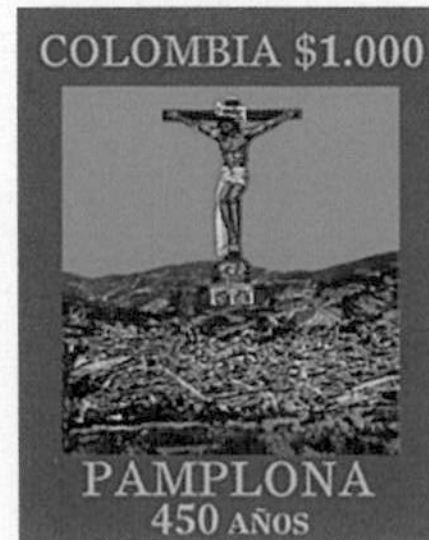

849 Crucifix above Pamplona

1999. 450th Anniv of Pamplona.

2188	**849**	1000p. multicoloured	5·50	2·75

850 Zuleta Angel

1999. Birth Centenary of Eduardo Zuleta Angel (politician and diplomat).

2189	**850**	600p. multicoloured	4·00	2·00

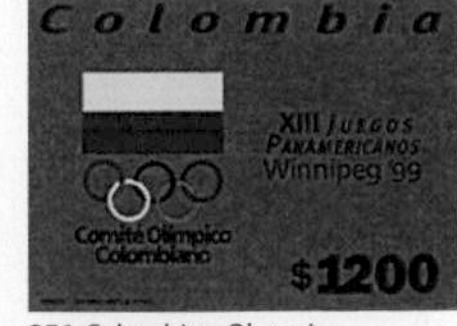

851 Colombian Olympic Committee Emblem

1999. 13th Pan-American Games, Winnipeg. Mult.

2190	1200p. Type **851**	5·75	3·00
2191	1200p. Running (facing right)	5·75	3·00
2192	1200p. Weightlifting (facing left)	5·75	3·00
2193	1200p. Cycling (facing right)	5·75	3·00
2194	1200p. Shooting (facing left)	5·75	3·00
2195	1200p. Roller blading (facing right)	5·75	3·00
2196	1200p. Running (facing left)	5·75	3·00
2197	1200p. Weightlifting (facing right)	5·75	3·00
2198	1200p. Cycling (facing left)	5·75	3·00
2199	1200p. Shooting (facing right)	5·75	3·00
2200	1200p. Roller blading (facing left)	5·75	3·00

852 Robles

1999. 150th Birth Anniv of Luis A. Robles.

2201	**852**	600p. multicoloured	3·75	1·90

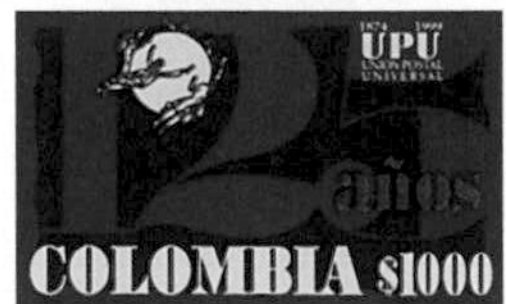

853 "125" and Emblem

1999. 125th Anniv of Universal Postal Union. Each lilac, violet and gold.

2202	1000p. Type **853**	5·00	2·50
2203	1300p. Emblem	6·00	3·25

854 Flowers leaving Hands

1999. America. A New Millennium without Arms. Multicoloured.

2204	1200p. Type **854**	5·75	3·00
2205	1200p. Flowers moving towards hands	5·75	3·00

Nos. 2204/5 were issued together, se-tenant, forming a composite design.

855 Landscape

1999. 40th Anniv of International Development Bank. Multicoloured.

2206 1000p. Type **855** 5·00 2·50

2207 1000p. Landscape, sunbeams and red fruits 5·00 2·50

Nos. 2206/7 were issued together, se-tenant, forming a composite design.

856 Nativity

1999. Christmas. Multicoloured.

2208 600p. Type **856** 3·75 1·90

2209 600p. Angel and Three Wise Men 3·75 1·90

Nos. 2208/9 were issued together, se-tenant, forming a composite design.

857 Emblem

1999. Centenary of Invention of Aspirin (drug).

2210 **857** 600p. multicoloured 3·75 1·90

858 Rainbow, Globe and "2000"

2000. New Millennium. Multicoloured.

2211 1000p. Type **858** 5·00 2·50

2212 1000p. Man with Colombian flag and dove 5·00 2·50

859 University Arms

2000. 50th Anniv of Medellin University.

2213 **859** 1000p. multicoloured 5·00 2·50

860 Faria Bermudez

2000. 20th Death Anniv (1999) of Father Jose Rafael Faria Bermudez.

2214 **860** 1300p. brown and black 6·00 3·25

861 Pianist and Score

2000. Religious Music Festival, Popayan.

2215 **861** 1000p. multicoloured 5·00 2·50

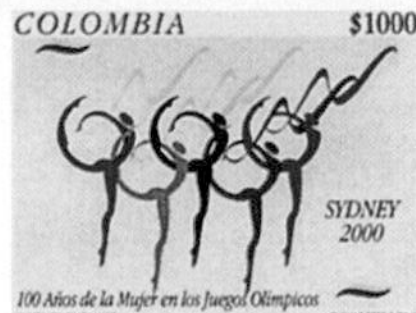

862 Stylized Figures forming Olympic Rings

2000. Olympic Games, Sydney.

2216 **862** 1000p. multicoloured 5·00 2·50

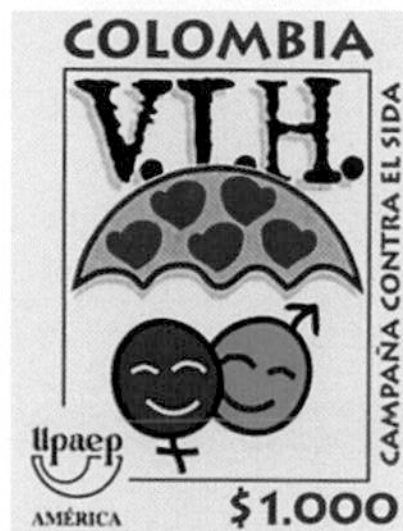

863 Male and Female Symbols under Umbrella

2000. A.I.D.S. Awareness Campaign.

2217 **863** 1000p. multicoloured 5·00 2·50

864 Weather Vane

2000. 50th Anniv of World Meteorological Society.

2218 **864** 1000p. multicoloured 5·00 2·50

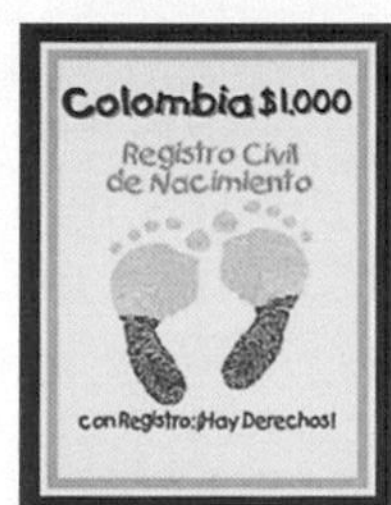

865 Footprints

2000. National Birth Register.

2219 **865** 1000p. multicoloured 5·00 2·50

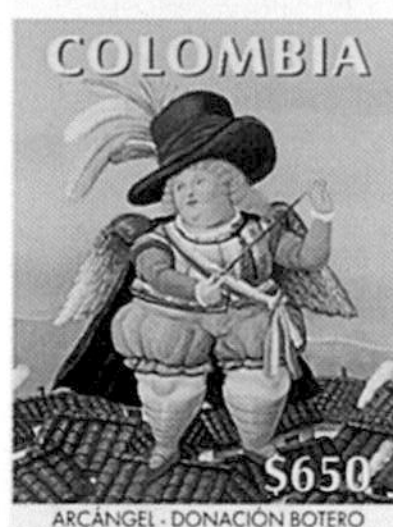

866 "Archangel" (Fernando Botero)

2001. Botero Foundation, Bogota. Multicoloured.

2220 650p. Type **866** 3·75 2·10

2221 650p. "Gypsy with Tamborine" (Jean Baptiste Camille Corot) 3·75 2·10

2222 650p. "Vera Sergine Renoir" (Pierre-Auguste Renoir) 3·75 2·10

2223 650p. "Man on Horse" (Botero) 3·75 2·10

2224 650p. "Mother Superior" (Botero) 3·75 2·10

2225 650p. "Town" (Botero) 3·75 2·10

2226 650p. "Flowers" (Botero) 3·75 2·10

2227 650p. "Cezanne" (Botero) 3·75 2·10

2228 650p. "The Patio" (Botero) 3·75 2·10

2229 650p. "Absinthe Drinker at Grenelle" (Henri Toulouse-Lautrec) 3·75 2·10

2230 650p. "The Pequeno Valley" (Jean Baptiste Camille Corot) 3·75 2·10

2231 650p. "The Studio" (Botero) 3·75 2·10

867 Children enclosed in Circle

2001. Children's Day.

2232 **867** 1100p. multicoloured 5·00 2·75

868 Girl and Dove

2001. 150th Anniv of the Abolition of Slavery.

2233 **868** 1100p. multicoloured 5·00 2·75

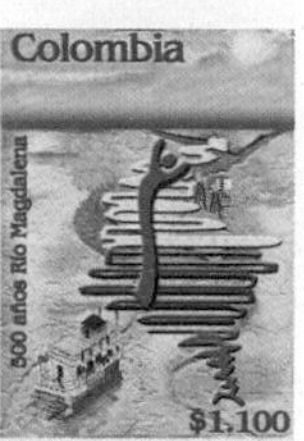

869 Emblem, River Boat and River

2001. 500th Anniv of Discovery of Magdalena River.

2234 **869** 1100p. multicoloured 5·00 2·75

870 Football and Club Emblems

2001. Copa America Football Championships.

2235 **870** 1900p. multicoloured 6·25 4·00

871 Waterfall, Woman and Wildlife

2001. America. Cultural Heritage. Los Katios National Park.

2236 **871** 2100p. multicoloured 6·50 4·00

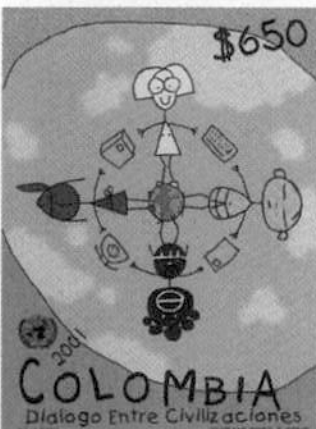

872 Children encircling Globe

2001. United Nations Year of Dialogue among Civilizations.

2237 **872** 650p. multicoloured 3·50 1·90

873 "Reclining Woman" (sculpture, Fernando Botero)

2001

2238 **873** 1100p. multicoloured 5·00 2·75

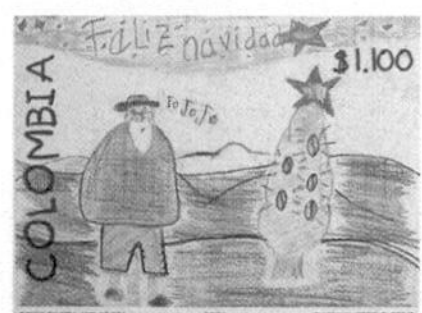

874 Man and Christmas Tree (Diego Rivera)

2001. Christmas.

2239 **874** 1100p. multicoloured 5·00 2·75

875 Cartegna de Indias and Vanessa Mendoza Bustos

2002. Miss Colombia, 2001–2002. Multicoloured.

2240 800p. Type **875** 4·00 2·10

2241 800p. Miss Colombia and St Francis of Assisi church, Quibdo 4·00 2·10

876 Stylized Figures and "BOGOTA 2002"

2002. 7th South American Games, Bogota.

2242 **876** 2100p. red, yellow and black 6·50 4·00

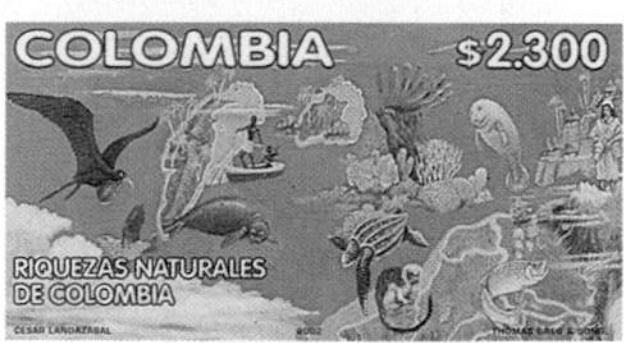

877 Frigate Bird, Islands and Marine Fauna

2002. Nature. Sheet 140×162 mm containing T **877** and similar horiz designs. Multicoloured.

MS2243 2300p.×8, Type **877**; Condors and mountain; Whales, reptiles, birds and cliffs; Horse rider, birds, animals and mountain peak; Monkeys and birds; Macaws; Flamingos and otter; Egret, jaguar, tapir, giant lily pads and manatee 50·00 50·00

No. **MS**2243 forms a composite design.

878 Flower and Girl (Diana Tovar Reyes)

2002. Children's Day.

2244 **878** 1400p. multicoloured 5·75 3·50

879 Postal Emblem

2002. New Emblem of Colombia Post.
2245 **879** 800p. ultramarine, red and yellow 4·00 2·10

880 Ruddy Duck (*Oxyura jamicensis*)

2002
2246 **880** 3900p. multicoloured 9·50 7·00

881 Harlequin Poison Dart Frog (*Dendrobates histrionicus*)

2002. Amphibians. Sheet 120×80 mm containing T **881** and similar horiz design. Multicoloured.
MS2247 7200p.×2, Type **881**; Tree frog (*Hyla crepitans*) 24·00 23·00

882 Flambeau Butterfly (*Dryas iulia*)

2002. Butterflies. Sheet 117×71 mm containing T **882** and similar multicoloured design.
MS2248 13700p.×2, Type **882**; Banded orange heliconian (*Dryadula phaetusa*) (vert) 39·00 38·00

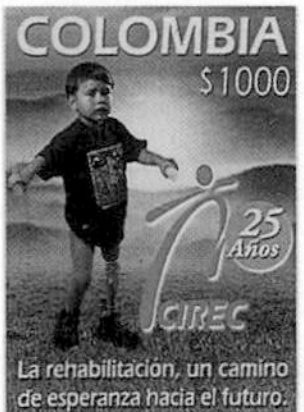

883 Boy wearing Prosthetic Leg

2002. 25th Anniv of Integral Rehabilitation Centre of Colombia (CIREC).
2249 **883** 1000p. multicoloured 4·75 2·50

884 Narino Chest Decoration

2002. Pre-Colombian Art. Multicoloured.
2250 800p. Type **884** 4·00 2·10
2251 800p. Narino disc 4·00 2·10
2252 1400p. Calima diadem with raised decoration 5·50 3·25
2253 1400p. Calima collar 5·50 3·25
2254 2100p. Tairona anthropomorphic chest decoration 6·50 4·00

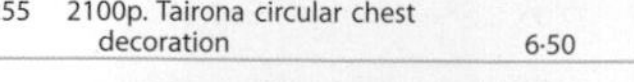
2255 2100p. Tairona circular chest decoration 6·50 4·00

885 Doctors

2002. Centenary of Society of Surgeons, San Jose Hospital, Bogota. Multicoloured.
2256 800p. Type **885** 4·00 2·10
2257 800p. San Jose hospital 4·00 2·10

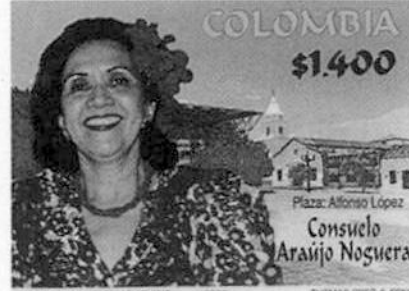

886 Consuelo Araujo Noguera

2002. 1st Death Anniv of Consuelo Araujo Noguera "La Cacica" (journalist and politician).
2258 **886** 1400p. multicoloured 5·50 3·25

887 "End to Violence" and Stylized Woman

2002. Regional Conference of U N I (international trade union organisation), Rio de Janeiro.
2259 **887** 1000p. multicoloured 4·75 2·50

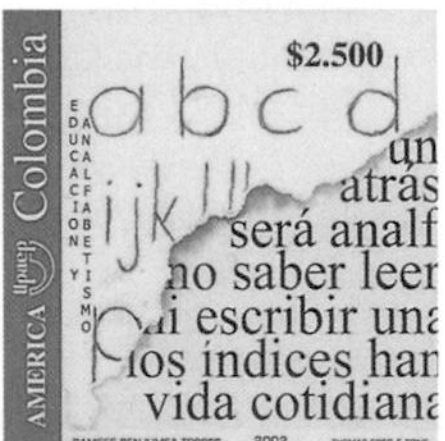

888 Letters and Words

2002. America. Education and Literacy Campaign. Each black, blue and orange.
2260 2500p. Type **888** 6·75 4·50
2261 2500p. Person wearing eye-patch reading 6·75 4·50

889 Nativity

2002. Christmas.
2262 **889** 800p. multicoloured 4·00 2·10

890 "Critical Moments during Independence" (detail, Pedro Nel Gomez)

2002. Centenary of Academy of History. Multicoloured.
2263 800p. Type **890** 3·75 1·90
2264 800p. Horse riders with spears ("Critical Moments during Independence", detail) 3·75 1·90
2265 800p. Slaves, woman feeding baby ("Critical Moments during Independence", detail) 3·75 1·90
2266 800p. Forest ("Cafetal", Gonzalo Ariza) 3·75 1·90
2267 800p. Horse riders ("Battle of Palonegro", Marco Tobon Mejia) 3·75 1·90
2268 800p. "Jaguar hunting" (Noe Leon) 3·75 1·90
2269 800p. Bathers ("I sail across", Pedro Nel Gomez) 3·75 1·90
2270 800p. "Colombia Murdered" (Sebastian Villalaz) 3·75 1·90
2271 800p. "The Women" (Jose Rodriguez) 3·75 1·90
2272 800p. Man with beard ("Santander Plaza" (detail, Juan Cardenas)) 3·75 1·90
2273 800p. Carriage ("Santander Plaza") 3·75 1·90
2274 800p. Horse and couple ("Santander Plaza") 3·75 1·90

Nos. 2263/5 and 2272/4 were respectively issued together, se-tenant, forming a composite design of the painting named.

891 "Marching Soldiers" (Eladio Rubio)

2002. Centenary of Peace Treaty at end of Thousand Days' War.
2275 **891** 1600p. multicoloured 5·25 3·25

892 Man wearing Yellow Hat and Carnival Float

2003. Negros y Blancos Carnival, Pasto. Multicoloured.
2276 1000p. Type **892** 4·25 2·40
2277 1000p. Procession 4·25 2·40
2278 1200p. Float with hands and fish 4·75 2·50

893 Buildings and Buses

2003. TransMilenio (transport system).
2279 **893** 1000p. multicoloured 4·00 2·40

894 City Arms

2003. Departments (1st issue). Caldas. Multicoloured.
2280 1200p. Type **894** 4·25 2·75
2281 1200p. Government building, Manizales (49×39 mm) 4·25 2·75
2282 1200p. "Capesinos" (Alpio Jaramillo) 4·25 2·75
2283 2400p. Parochial Church, Salamina 5·50 4·00
2284 2400p. "Neira" (David Manzur) (49×39 mm) 5·50 4·00
2285 2400p. La Enea Chapel, Manizales 5·50 4·00
2286 2800p. Verde lake, Villamaria 5·75 4·25
2287 2800p. Aguadas (49×39 mm) 5·75 4·25
2288 2800p. Carnival del Diablo 5·75 4·25
2289 4100p. Miner, Marmato 7·75 6·25
2290 4100p. "Mariposa del eje cafetero" (Maripaz Jaramillo) (49×39 mm) 7·75 6·25
2291 4100p. Old town, Pacora 7·75 6·25

See also No. 2295/2306, 2307/18, 2349/60, 2362/73, 2381/92, 2415/26, 2444/56, 2461/72, 2473/84 and 2492/2503.

895 *Montastraea annularis, Acropora cervicornis* and *Diploria strigosa*

2003. Rosario Island. Corals.
2292 **895** 1000p. multicoloured 4·00 2·40

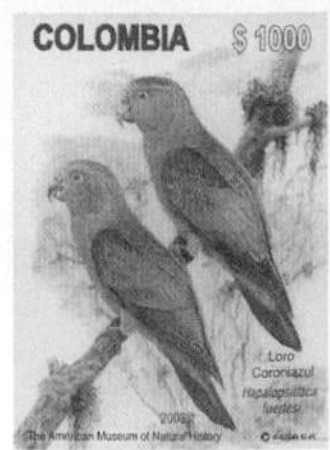

896 *Hapalopsittaca fuertesi* (bird)

2003
2293 **896** 1000p. multicoloured 4·00 2·40

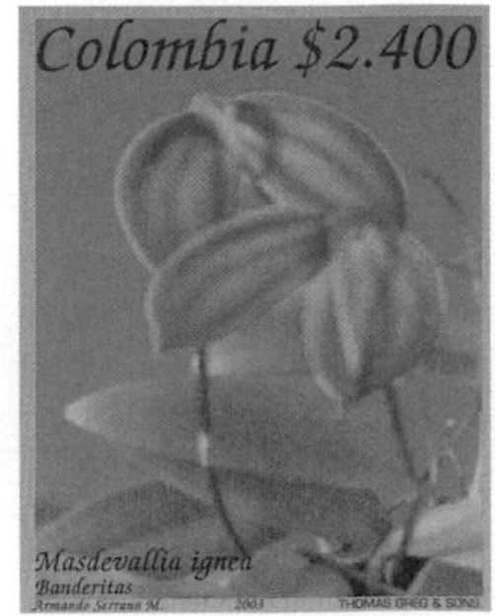

897 *Masdevallia ignea*

2003. Orchids. Four sheets containing T **897** and similar multicoloured designs.
MS2294 (a) 151×120 mm. 2400p. ×2, Type **897**; *Miltoniopisis vexillaria* (56×44 mm); (b) 151×120 mm. 2800p. ×2, *Odontoglossum crispum* (56×44 mm); *Masdevallia macrura*; (c) 99×170 mm. 5000p. ×2, *Cimbidium; Oncidium obryzatum*; (d) 151×120 mm. 7000p. ×2, *Cattleya dowiana; Cattleya trianaei* (50×50 mm) Set of 4 sheets 70·00 70·00

2003. Departments (2nd issue). Huila. As T **894**. Multicoloured.
2295 1000p. Arms 3·25 1·90
2296 1000p. Government building, Neiva (49×39 mm) 3·25 1·90
2297 1000p. "La Gaijana" (Phillippe Massonat) 3·25 1·90
2298 1000p. Bordonnes waterfall, Isnos 3·25 1·90
2299 1000p. San Augustin archaeological park (49×39 mm) 3·25 1·90
2300 1000p. Lavapatas fountain, San Augustin 3·25 1·90
2301 1000p. La Tatacoa desert, Villavieja 3·25 1·90
2302 1000p. Ceiba de La Libertad (49×39 mm) 3·25 1·90
2303 1000p. Hat maker, Suaza 3·25 1·90
2304 1000p. Senora de los Delores, Aipe 3·25 1·90
2305 1000p. "Paisje" (Mario Ayerbe) (49×39 mm) 3·25 1·90
2306 1000p. Dancers 3·25 1·90

2003. Departments (3rd issue). Santander. As T **894**. Multicoloured.
2307 2400p. Historical center, Barichara 4·25 2·75
2308 2400p. Ophthalmic Foundation, Bucaramanga (49×39 mm) 4·25 2·75
2309 2400p. "Quebrada de las Nieves" (Humberto Ballesteros) 4·25 2·75
2310 2400p. International piano festival poster 4·25 2·75

2311 2400p. *Cristo Petrolero* (sculpture), oil refinery, Barrancabermeja (49×39 mm) 4·25 2·75
2312 2400p. Parochial church, San Andres 4·25 2·75
2313 2400p. Gustavo Cote Uribe (writer) 4·25 2·75
2314 2400p. Commercial Club, Bucaramanga (49×39 mm) 4·25 2·75
2315 2400p. "Oriente Colobiano" Carnival, Bucaramanga 4·25 2·75
2316 2400p. Historical centre, Albania 4·25 2·75
2317 2400p. Chicamocha river gorge, Cepita (49×39 mm) 4·25 2·75
2318 2400p. "Entreguerras" (Beatriz Gonzalez) 4·25 2·75

898 Tree and Players

2003. El Tejo (national ball game). Multicoloured.
2319 2400p. Type **898** 4·25 2·75
2320 2400p. Two players 4·25 2·75
2321 2400p. Trophy (40×40 mm) 4·25 2·75
Nos. 2319/20 were issued together, se-tenant, forming a composite design.

899 Hawk, Sloth, Kinkajou, Humming Bird and Anteater

2003. America. Flora and Fauna. Multicoloured.
2322 1600p. Type **899** 3·75 2·10
2323 1600p. Opossum, toucan, leopard, butterfly and armadillo 3·75 2·10

900 Emblem and Building Facade

2003. 117th Anniv of Universad Externado de Colombia. Sheet 120×90 mm containing T **900** and similar horiz design. Multicoloured.
MS2324 1200p. Type **900**; 4100p. Emblem and building (different) 8·50 8·50
The stamps and background of No. **MS**2324 form a composite design.

901 Military Arms

2003. 50th Anniv of End of Korean War. Multicoloured.
2325 1200p. Type **901** 3·75 2·30
2326 1200p. National arms 3·75 2·30
2327 1200p. Navy arms 3·75 2·30
2328 1200p. Air Force arms 3·75 2·30
2329 1200p. Map of Korea 3·75 2·30

902 Fingerprint

2003. 50th Anniv of DAS (security department). Sheet 120×90 mm.
MS2330 4100p. multicoloured 7·00 7·00

903 General Ramon Quinones

2003. General Ramon Arturo Rincon Quinones Commemoration.
2331 **903** 1000p. multicoloured 3·25 1·90

904 Shepherd and Sheep

2003. Christmas. Multicoloured.
2332 1000p. Type **904** 3·25 1·90
2333 1000p. Tree, star, airplane and rabbit 3·25 1·90
2334 1000p. Hares and dog 3·25 1·90
2335 1000p. Sleigh, angel, reindeer and horse 3·25 1·90
2336 1000p. Sheep, child, swan and house 3·25 1·90
2337 1000p. Leaves, cowboy, duck and Red Indian 3·25 1·90

905 El Dorado Ceremony (engraving) (Teodoro de Bry)

2004. Laguna de Guatavita (site of legend of El Dorado (cult of the Muisca Indians)). Multicoloured.
2338 2800p. Type **905** 5·25 4·00
2339 2800p. Laguna de Guatavita (painting) (M. Maria Paz) 5·25 4·00
2340 2800p. Laguna de Guatavita (painting) (Gonzalo Ariza) 5·25 4·00
2341 2800p. Laguna de Guatavita (painting) (A. Humboldt Thibault/F. Schoell) 5·25 4·00
2342 2800p. Laguna de Guatavita 5·25 4·00
2343 2800p. Laguna de Guatavita (engraving) (Eustacio Barreto) 5·25 4·00
MS2344 120×90 mm. 1700p. Prow of Balsa Muisca (gold raft (ritual object found in lake)); 2000p. Stern of raft (vert) 6·50 6·50

906 Locomotive 2-8-2 (painting) (Ferrando Acuna)

2004. Railways. Multicoloured.
2345 1100p. Type **906** 3·25 2·10
2346 1100p. Locomotive 4-8-0 (painting) (Ferrando Acuna) 3·25 2·10
2347 1300p. Locomotive 2-6-2 (painting) (Gustavo Arias de Greiff) 4·00 2·50
2348 1300p. Locomotive 4-6-2 (painting) (Gustavo Arias de Greiff) 4·00 2·50

2004. Departments (4th issue). Tolima. As T **894**. Multicoloured.
2349 2000p. Nevado del Tolima 4·50 3·25
2350 2000p. Arms (25×39 mm) 4·50 3·25
2351 2000p. "Ambalema" (Price) 4·50 3·25
2352 2000p. Pots 4·50 3·25
2353 2000p. Iconozo Waterfall (25×39 mm) 4·50 3·25
2354 2000p. Armita Church, Mariquita 4·50 3·25
2355 2000p. "Matachos" (Jorge Elias Triana) 4·50 3·25
2356 2000p. Panoptico de Ibague (25×39 mm) 4·50 3·25
2357 2000p. Alberto Castilla Conservatory, Ibague 4·50 3·25
2358 2000p. Magdalena river, Pescadores 4·50 3·25
2359 2000p. "Calarca Cheiftain" (painting) (Dario Ortiz Vidales) (25×39 mm) 4·50 3·25
2360 2000p. Tolima Museum of Art, Ibague 4·50 3·25

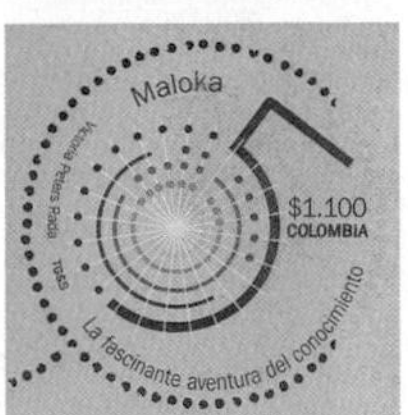

907 Anniversary Emblem

2004. 5th Anniv of Maloka Theme Park.
2361 **907** 1100p. multicoloured 3·50 2·10

2004. Departments (5th issue). Narino. As T **894**. Multicoloured.
2362 1100p. Galeras volcano, San Juan de Pasto 3·50 2·10
2363 1100p. Gen. Antonio Narino (25×39 mm) 3·50 2·10
2364 1100p. Ministry of Interior, San Juan de Pasto 3·50 2·10
2365 1100p. Fields, Catambuco 3·50 2·10
2366 1100p. Our Lady of Lajas Sanctuary, Ipiales (25×39 mm) 3·50 2·10
2367 1100p. Sandona 3·50 2·10
2368 1100p. "Galleria de Espejos" (painting) (Homero Aguilar) 3·50 2·10
2369 1100p. Varnishers (1853) (25×39 mm) 3·50 2·10
2370 1100p. "Palmas Doradas" (painting) (Maria Moran) 3·50 2·10
2371 1100p. El Morro (archaeological site), Tumaco 3·50 2·10
2372 1100p. Virgin de la Playa Sanctuary, San Pablo (25×39 mm) 3·50 2·10
2373 1100p. "Fiesta de negros y blancos" (painting) (Manuel Estrada) 3·50 2·10

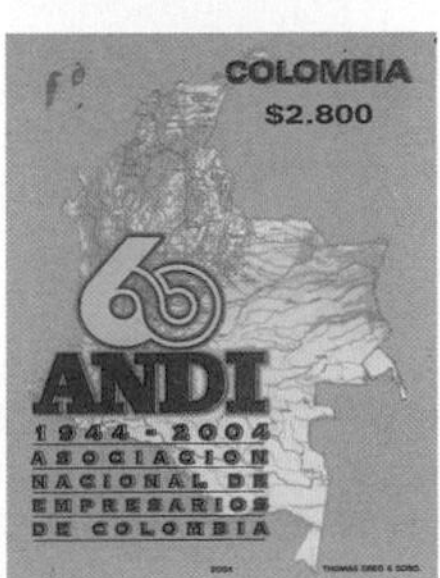

908 Anniversary Emblem and Map

2004. 60th Anniv of ANDI (National Association of Industrialists).
2374 **908** 2800p. bistre, indigo and olive 5·25 3·75
2375 **908** 2800p. indigo and bistre 5·25 3·75

909 Olympic Rings and Flame

2004. Olympic Games, Athens.
2376 **909** 4400p. multicoloured 7·75 6·00

910 Centenary Emblem

2004. Centenary of FIFA (Federation Internationale de Football).
2377 **910** 3500p. multicoloured 6·50 5·00

911 Women

2004. 50th Anniv of Women's Citizenship.
2378 **911** 1500p. multicoloured 4·25 2·75

912 Emblem

2004. 50th Anniv of Federal Commission of Electricity (CFE).
2379 **912** 1300p. multicoloured 4·00 2·50

913 Microphone

2004. 50th Anniv of Colombian Association of Speakers (ACL).
2380 **913** 1700p. multicoloured 4·25 2·75

2004. Departments (6th issue). Choco. As T **894**. Multicoloured.
2381 3000p. Arms 5·75 4·25
2382 3000p. Quibdo (48×38 mm) 5·75 4·25
2383 3000p. Indigenous girls dancing 5·75 4·25
2384 3000p. San Pacho festival 5·75 4·25
2385 3000p. Carasquilla College, Quibdo (48×38 mm) 5·75 4·25
2386 3000p. Woman and child (Manuel Maria Paz) 5·75 4·25
2387 3000p. Boating on San Juan river, Canoa 5·75 4·25
2388 3000p. Women in river (Migdonio Luna Salazar) (48×38 mm) 5·75 4·25
2389 3000p. Our Lady of Rosario Sanctury, Condoto 5·75 4·25
2390 3000p. Utria Cove 5·75 4·25
2391 3000p. Bellavista Church, Bojaya (48×38 mm) 5·75 4·25
2392 3000p. Goldsmith, Acandi 5·75 4·25

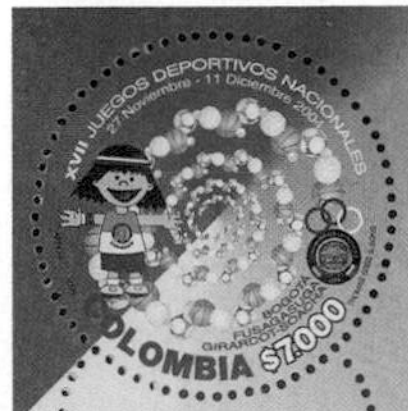

914 Child and Footballs

2004. National Games.
2393 **914** 7000p. multicoloured 10·50 9·25

915 Hammerhead Sharks

2004. America. Environmental Protection. Mult.
2394 5000p. Type **915** 8·50 5·75
2395 5000p. Humpback whale 8·50 5·75

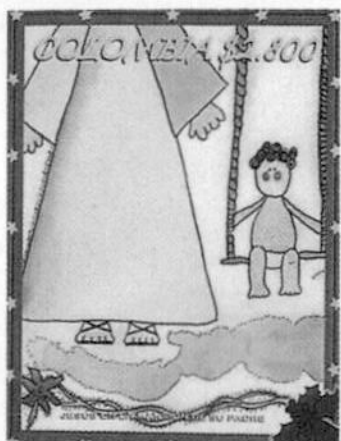

916 Angel and Child on Swing

2004. Christmas. Multicoloured.

2396- 2404 2800p.×9, Type **916**; Angel and Mary; Figure climbing steps in tree; Mary with Halo; Mary holding flowers; Emperor; Joseph and Mary riding donkey; Bethlehem; The Nativity 12·00 12·00

917 Buckle

2005. Pre-Hispanic Gold Artefacts (1st issue). Multicoloured.

2405	1200p. Type **917**	3·75	2·10
2406	1200p. Collar	3·75	2·10

See also Nos. 2408/9.

918 Emblem, Town and Mountains

2005. Centenary of Rotary International.

2407	**918**	3100p. multicoloured	5·75	4·25

2005. Pre-Hispanic Gold Artefacts (2nd issue). As T 917. Multicoloured.

2408	1800p. Articulated collar	4·50	3·00
2409	1800p. Cuff	4·50	3·00

919 Inscr "Protographium tyastes panamensis"

2005. Butterflies. Sheet 138×86 mm containing T **919** and similar horiz designs. Multicoloured.

MS2410 4600p.×3, Type **919**; *Dismorphia zaela*; *Actinote ozomene* 21·00 21·00

The stamps and margins of **MS**2410 form a composite design.

920 Pectoral Decoration (Quinbaya)

2005. 60th Anniv of FENALCO.

2411	**920**	1200p. multicoloured	3·50	2·10

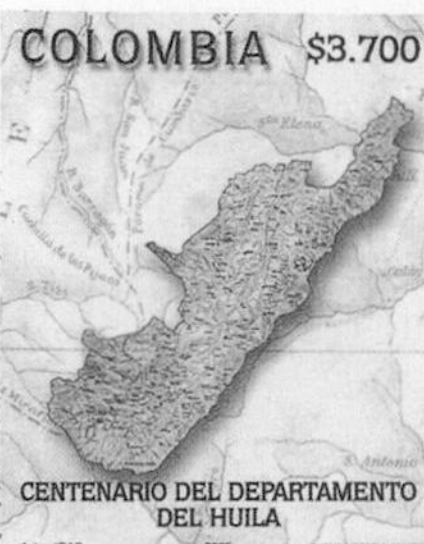

921 Map of Huila

2005. Centenary of Huila Department. Sheet 110×140 mm containing T **921** and similar vert design. Multicoloured.

MS2412 3700p.×2, Type **921**; Map showing position 13·00 13·00

The stamps and margins of **MS**2412 form a composite design.

922 Map of Caldas

2005. Centenary of Caldas Department. Sheet 110×140 mm containing T **922** and similar vert design. Multicoloured.

MS2413 3100p.×2, Type **922**; Map showing position 11·50 11·50

The stamps and margins of **MS**2413 form a composite design.

923 Map of Atlantico

2005. Centenary of Atlantico Department. Sheet 138×86 mm containing T **923** and similar vert design. Multicoloured.

MS2414 4200p.×2, Type **923**; Map showing position 14·00 14·00

The stamps and margins of **MS**2414 form a composite design.

2005. Departments (7th issue). San Andres and Santa Catalina. As T **894**. Multicoloured.

2415	1200p. San Andres archipelago	3·75	2·30
2416	1200p. Arms (48×38 mm)	3·75	2·30
2417	1200p. Johnny cay	3·75	2·30
2418	1200p. Cangrejo cay	3·75	2·30
2419	1200p. Craftsman (48×38 mm)	3·75	2·30
2420	1200p. Cultural Centre, San Andres	3·75	2·30
2421	1200p. Morgan's head, Santa Catalina	3·75	2·30
2422	1200p. Island beach (48×38 mm)	3·75	2·30
2423	1200p. Island architecture	3·75	2·30
2424	1200p. Cove, San Andreas	3·75	2·30
2425	1200p. Bautista Church, San Andreas (48×38 mm)	3·75	2·30
2426	1200p. Panorama	3·75	2·30

924 *Mutisia clematis*

2005. 50th Anniv of Botanical Gardens, Bogota.

2427	**924**	1400p. multicoloured	4·00	2·50

925 Sport (detail) (Guillermo Arriaga)

2005. Bolivarianos Games.

2428	**925**	3500p. multicoloured	6·50	5·00

926 University Building

2005. 50th Anniv of University de los Andes Past Students Association.

2429	**926**	2000p. multicoloured	4·50	3·25

927 Globe

2005. International Ozone Layer Protection Day.

2430	**927**	2000p. multicoloured	4·50	3·25

928 Don Quixote reading

2005. 400th Anniv of "Don Quixote de la Mancha" (novel by Miguel de Cervantes).

2431	1300p. Type **928**	4·00	2·50
2432	1300p. Wearing hat (vert)	4·00	2·50
2433	1300p. Facing right (vert)	4·00	2·50

929 Arms

2005. Facatativa City Arms.

2434	**929**	1800p. multicoloured	4·50	3·00

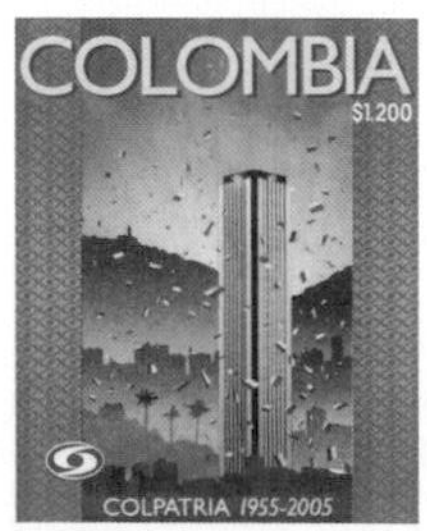

930 Bank Building

2005. 50th Anniv of Colpatria Bank.

2435	**930**	1200p. multicoloured	3·75	2·30

No. 2436 is vacant.

932 Statue

2005. 50th Anniv of Escuela de Lanceros (military training school).

2437	**932**	10000p. multicoloured	35·00	35·00

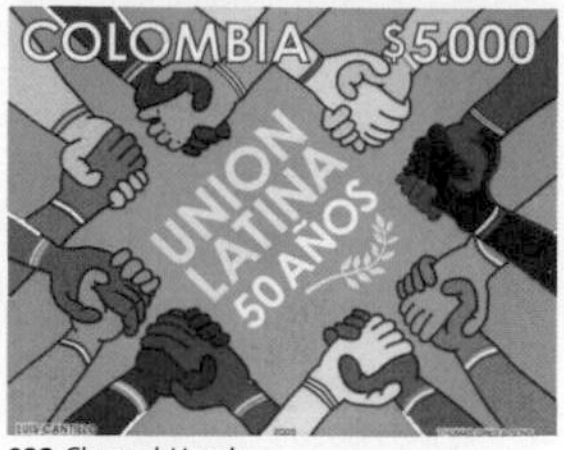

933 Clasped Hands

2005. 50th Anniv of Latin Union.

2438	**933**	5000p. multicoloured	8·75	5·75

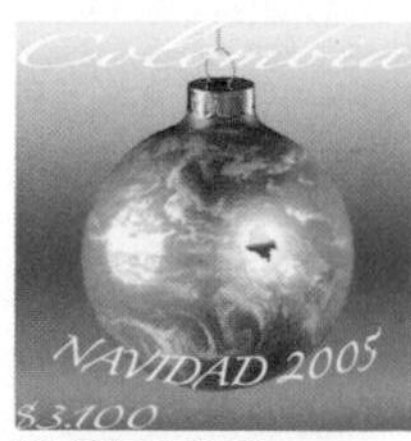

934 Globe as Bauble

2005. Christmas.

2439	**934**	3100p. multicoloured	5·75	4·25

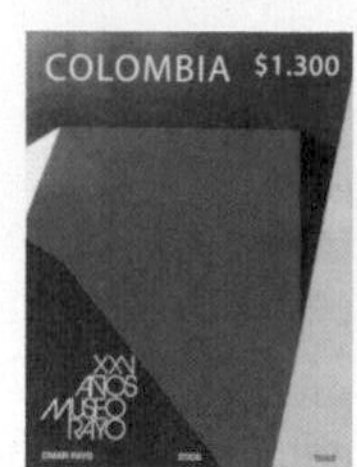

934a Abstract

2006. 25th Anniv of Rayo Museum. Sheet 145×115 mm containing T **934a** and similar vert design showing paintings by Omar Rayo. Multicoloured.

MS2440 1300p. Type **934a**×2; Abstract (different)×2 1·10 1·10

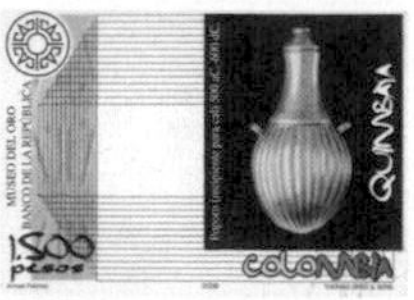

934b Gold Poporo

2006. Gold Museum. Multicoloured.

2441	1500p. Type **934b**	4·50	2·10
2442	1500p. Narrow poporo	4·50	2·10

935 "Impresion de los Derechos del Hombre" (Luis Cancino)

2006. 60th Anniv of Colombian Journalism.

2443	**935**	2000p. multicoloured	4·75	3·25

2006. Department (8th issue) Quindo. As Type **894**. Multicoloured.

2444	3300p. "Paso del Quindio" (painting) (1836) (48×38 mm)	5·50	4·00
2445	3300p. Gold statue (22×38 mm)	5·50	4·00
2446	3300p. Coffee growing, Quimbaya (48×38 mm)	5·50	4·00
2447	3300p. Harvesting coffee, Pijao (48×38 mm)	5·50	4·00
2448	3300p. Valle de Cocora (22×38 mm)	5·50	4·00
2449	3300p. Botanical garden, Calarca (48×38 mm)	5·50	4·00

2450 3300p. Cultural centre, Armenia (48×38 mm) 5·50 4·00
2451 3300p. Statue, Armenia (22×38 mm) 5·50 4·00
2452 3300p. Cemetery, Circasia (48×38 mm) 5·50 4·00
2453 3300p. Panorama (48×38 mm) 5·50 4·00
2454 3300p. San Jose Temple, Genova (22×38 mm) 5·50 4·00
2455 3300p. "Fundacion de Armenia" (painting) (48×38 mm) 5·50 4·00

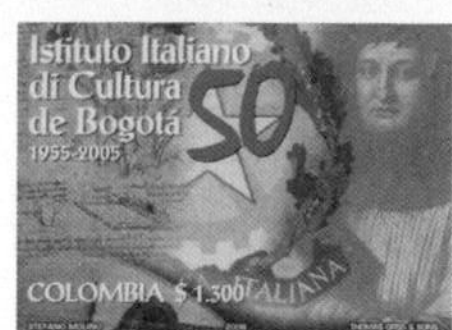

936 "50", Olive Wreath and Face

2006. 50th Anniv (2005) of Italian Cultural Institute, Bogota. Multicoloured.
2457 1300p. Type **936** 4·00 2·50
2458 1300p. "50", olive wreath and face (different) 4·00 2·50

937 Pope John Paul II

2006. Pope John Paul II Commemoration.
2459 **937** 4800p. multicoloured 8·50 5·50

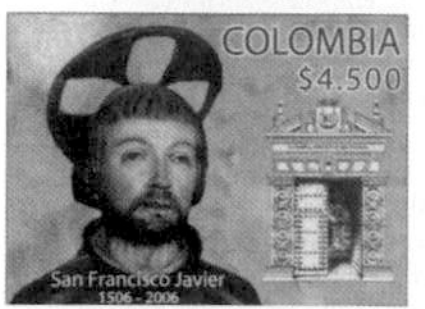

938 Francis Xavier

2006. 500th Birth Anniv of Saint Francis Xavier.
2460 **938** 4500p. multicoloured 7·75 5·25

2006. Department (9th issue). Valle del Cauca. As Type **894**. Multicoloured.
2461 1300p. Landscape (1852) (48×38 mm) 4·00 2·50
2462 1300p. Arms (22×38 mm) 4·00 2·50
2463 1300p. Panorama, Sevilla (48×38 mm) 4·00 2·50
2464 1300p. Lake Calima, El Darién (48×38 mm) 4·00 2·50
2465 1300p. Hermitage, Santiago de Cali. (22×38 mm) 4·00 2·50
2466 1300p. Port, Buenaventura (48×38 mm) 4·00 2·50
2467 1300p. Railway station, Palmira (48×38 mm) 4·00 2·50
2468 1300p. Sugar cane (22×38 mm) 4·00 2·50
2469 1300p. Salsa dancers (48×38 mm) 4·00 2·50
2470 1300p. Museum, El Cerrito (48×38 mm) 4·00 2·50
2471 1300p. Basilica (22×38 mm) 4·00 2·50
2472 1300p. Panorama, Valle del Cauca (48×38 mm) 4·00 2·50

2006. Department (10th issue). Boyaca. As Type **894**. Multicoloured.
2473 2000p. Bolivar Plaza, Tunja (48×38 mm) 4·50 3·25
2474 2000p. Arms (22×38 mm) 4·50 3·25
2475 2000p. Campo de Boyaca (1851) (48×38 mm) 4·50 3·25
2476 2000p. Bolivar monument, Campo de Boyaca (48×38 mm) 4·50 3·25
2477 2000p. Alter, Virgen de Chiquinquira (22×38 mm) 4·50 3·25
2478 2000p. Panorama, Garagoa (48×38 mm) 4·50 3·25
2479 2000p. Los Libertadores Plaza, Duitama (48×38 mm) 4·50 3·25
2480 2000p. Emeralds (22×38 mm) 4·50 3·25
2481 2000p. Plaza, Villa de Leyva (48×38 mm) 4·50 3·25
2482 2000p. Sierra Nevada del Cocuy (48×38 mm) 4·50 3·25
2483 2000p. Temple of the sun, Sogamoso (22×38 mm) 4·50 3·25
2484 2000p. El Salitre Hacienda, Paipa (48×38 mm) 4·50 3·25

939 Fryderyk Chopin

2006. Fryderyk Franciszek (Frederic) Chopin (composer and musician) Commemoration.
2485 **939** 5300p. multicoloured 8·25 5·75

940 Mascot and Emblem

2006. Central American and Caribbean Games.
2486 **940** 2000p. multicoloured 4·50 3·25

941 Alberto Camargo (painting by G. Camacho)

2006. Birth Centenary of Alberto Lleras Camargo (politician and diplomat).
2487 **941** 1300p. multicoloured 4·50 2·30
2488 **941** 3300p. multicoloured 6·00 4·50

942 *Birth of Jesus* (painting attributed to Rubens School)

2006. Christmas.
2489 **942** 1300p. multicoloured 4·50 2·30
2490 **942** 3300p. multicoloured 6·00 4·50

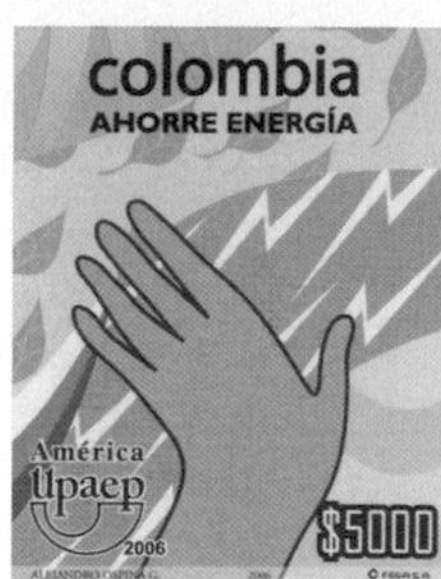

943 Left Hand

2006. America. Energy Conservation. Sheet 120×90 mm containing T 943 and similar vert design. Multicoloured.
MS2491 5000p.×2, Type **943**; Right hand 17·00 17·00

The stamps and margins of **MS**2491 form a composite design.

2007. Department (11th issue). Sucre. As Type **894**. Multicoloured.
2492 3300p. Arms (30×40 mm) 5·75 4·25
2493 3300p. San Francisco de Asis Cathedral, Sincelejo (50×40 mm) 5·75 4·25
2494 3300p. Beach, Tolu (1851) (30×40 mm) 5·75 4·25
2495 3300p. Cattle, Ganaderia (30×40 mm) 5·75 4·25
2496 3300p. Bull fight, Corralejas (50×40 mm) 5·75 4·25
2497 3300p. Parroquial Temple, Corazal (30×40 mm) 5·75 4·25
2498 3300p. Sheet music (30×40 mm)1 5·75 4·25
2499 3300p. La Fandanguera (50×40 mm) 5·75 4·25
2500 3300p. Fisherman, Caimilo (30×40 mm) 5·75 4·25
2501 3300p. Palms, Sincelejo (30×40 mm) 5·75 4·25
2502 3300p. Weaving, Sampues (50×40 mm) 5·75 4·25
2503 3300p. Hammocks, Morroa (30×40 mm) 5·75 4·25

944 General Jose Maria Cordova, Soldiers and Arms

2007. General Jose Maria Cordova Military School.
2504 **944** 10000p. multicoloured 17·00 13·00

944a Emblem

2007. International Spanish Language Congress.
2504a **944a** 5300p. multicoloured 3·00 1·50

945 Robert Baden Powell and Scouts

2007. Centenary of Scouting. Multicoloured.
2505 1500p. Type **945** 4·25 2·30
2506 1500p. Scout camp (21st World Scout Jamboree) 4·25 2·30
2507 1500p. Emblem and Robert Baden Powell 4·25 2·30
2508 1500p. Emblem and badger footprint (75th (2006) anniv of Colombia scouts) 4·25 2·30

946 '120' and Newsvendor

2007. 120th Anniv of El Espectador. Sheet 120×90 mm containing T **946** and similar horiz design. Multicoloured.
MS2509 4500p.×2, Type **946**; Early front page (vert) 16·00 11·50

947 Emblem

2007. Pan American Games.
2510 **947** 3700p. multicoloured 6·75 5·25

No. 2510 was issued together, se-tenant, forming a composite design of a runner when viewed across the sheet.

948 Emblem

2007. International Spanish Language Congress.
2511 **948** 5300p. multicoloured 8·50 5·75

949 Symbols of Welfare

2007. 50th Anniv of CAFAM.
2512 **949** 3500p. multicoloured 6·50 6·50

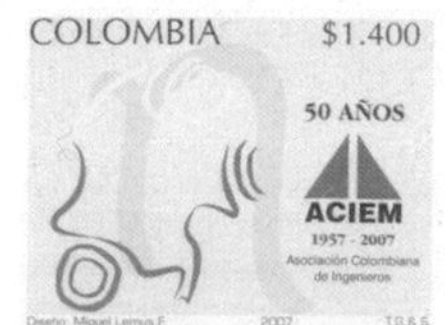

950 Emblems

2007. 50th Anniv of ACIEM Engineering Institute.
2513 **950** 1400p. multicoloured 4·25 4·25

951 Bogota–UNESCO World Book Capital, 2007

2007. Events. Multicoloured.
2514 3700p. Type **951** 6·75 5·25
2515 3700p. Bogota–Leon de Oro, 1990–2006 (architecture award) 6·75 5·25
2516 3700p. Bogota–Ibero-American Capital of Culture, 2007 6·75 5·25

952 Emblem

2007. 50th Anniv of Minuto de Dios Neighbourhood.
2517 **952** 1600p. multicoloured 6·50 5·00

953 The Nativity

2007. Christmas.
2518 **953** 3300p. multicoloured 5·75 4·25

954 Symbols of Education

2007. America. Education for All.
2519 **954** 3500p. multicoloured 6·50 6·50

955 Carlos Lleras

2008. Birth Centenary of Carlos Lleras Restrepo (lawyer and politician).

2520	**955**	1400p. multicoloured	2·50	1·90

956 Emblem

2008. Centenary of Colombia–Japan Friendship.

2521	**956**	5200p. multicoloured	8·50	5·75

957 '472'

2008. 4–72 Postal Network.

2522	**957**	2100p. multicoloured	4·50	3·25

958 Man with Stick

2008. 50th (2005) Anniv of National Institute for the Blind (INCI).

2523	**958**	1400p. multicoloured	4·25	2·75

No. 2523 is embossed with Braille letters.

2008. Department (12th issue). Amazonas. As T **894**. Multicoloured.

2524	1600p. Arms (30×40 mm)	4·25	2·75
2525	1600p. Squirrel monkey, Isla de los Micos (50×40 mm)	4·25	2·75
2526	1600p. *Victoria regia* (water lilies) (30×40 mm)	4·25	2·75
2527	1600p. Butterfly, Puerto Narino (30×40 mm)	4·25	2·75
2528	1600p. Girl (50×40 mm)	4·25	2·75
2529	1600p. Babilla alligator (30×40 mm)	4·25	2·75
2530	1600p. Mask (30×40 mm)	4·25	2·75
2531	1600p. River dolphin (50×40 mm)	4·25	2·75
2532	1600p. Sunset (30×40 mm)		
2533	1600p. Flower (30×40 mm)	4·25	2·75
2534	1600p. Fisherman (50×40 mm)	4·25	2·75
2535	1600p. Market square, Port Leticia (30×40 mm)	4·25	2·75

959 Admiral Jose Padilla

2008. National Navy. 185th Anniv of Battle of Lake Maracaibo.

2536	**959**	3900p. multicoloured	6·75	5·25

960 Emblem

2008. Centenary of Colombia–Switzerland Friendship and Commerce Treaty.

2537	**960**	5200p. multicoloured	9·00	5·75

961 National Stadium, Beijing

2008. Olympic Games, Beijing.

2538	**961**	5000p. multicoloured	8·75	5·75
MS2539		133×114 mm. 10000p. As Type **961**	17·00	17·00

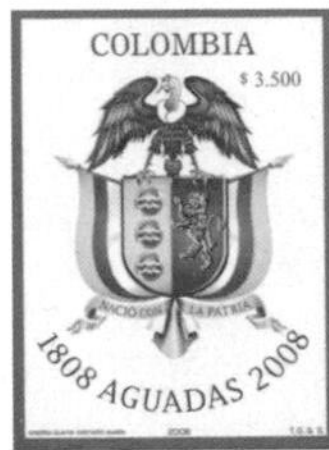

962 Arms

2008. Bicentenary of Aguadas.

2540	**962**	3500p. multicoloured	6·50	5·00

962a Alfonso Lopez Michelsen

2008. Alfonso Lopez Michelsen (president 1974–1978) Commemoration.

2540a	**962a**	5100p. multicoloured	8·75	5·75

2008. Department (13th issue). Antioquia. As T **894**. Multicoloured.

2541	1500p. Medellin (50×40 mm)	4·25	2·30
2542	1500p. Arms (30×40 mm)	4·25	2·30
2543	1500p. Lake, Necocli (500th anniv) (50×40 mm)	4·25	2·30
2544	1500p. Los Silleteros flower parade, Medellin (50×40 mm)		
2545	1500p. Carriel (small leather satchel) (30×40 mm)	4·25	2·30
2546	1500p. Raphael Uribe Palace of Culture (50×40 mm)	4·25	2·30
2547	1500p. Molas (appliqued cloth) (50×40 mm)	4·25	2·30
2548	1500p. *Lipaugus weberi* (Chestnut-capped piha) (30×40 mm)	4·25	2·30
2549	1500p. Waterfall, Tamesis (50×40 mm)	4·25	2·30
2550	1500p. Cups (Carmen Viboral) (50×40 mm))	4·25	2·30
2551	1500p. Santa Fe de Antioquia Church (30×40 mm)	4·25	2·30
2552	1500p. Orquideorama, Botanical Gardens, Medellin (50×40 mm)	4·25	2·30

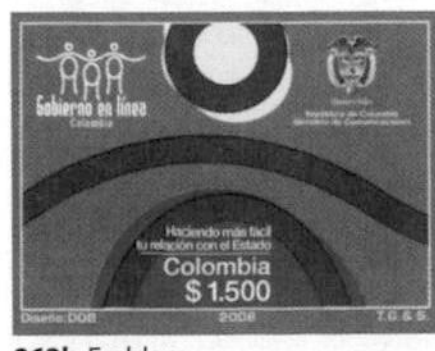

962b Emblem

2008. 85th Anniv of Ministry of Communications. Sheet 150×125 mm containing T **962b** and similar multicoloured designs.

MS2552a	1500p.×4, Type **962b**; Children (vert); 'Internet Sano'; 'Compartel' (vert)	9·50	9·50

962c Arms

2008. Centenary of Episcopal Conference.

2552c	**962b**	1500p. multicoloured	2·50	2·10

963 Mascot and Emblem

2008. National Games.

2553	**963**	1500p. multicoloured	2·30	1·90

964 '50'

2008. 50th Anniv of National Planning Department (DNP).

2554	**964**	1500p. multicoloured	2·30	1·90

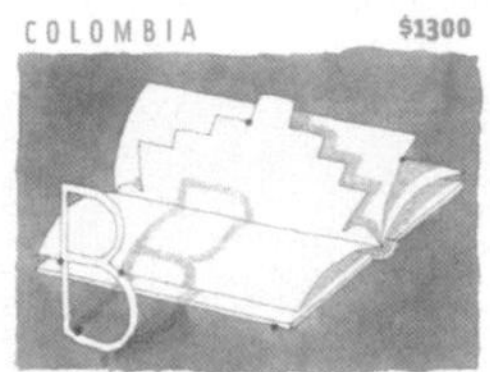

965 'B' and Book

2008. 50th Anniv of Luis Angel Arango Library. Sheet 130×129 mm containing T **965** and similar horiz designs showing letters and open books. Multicoloured.

MS2555	1300p.×4, Type **965**; 'L'; 'a'; 'A'	8·00	8·00

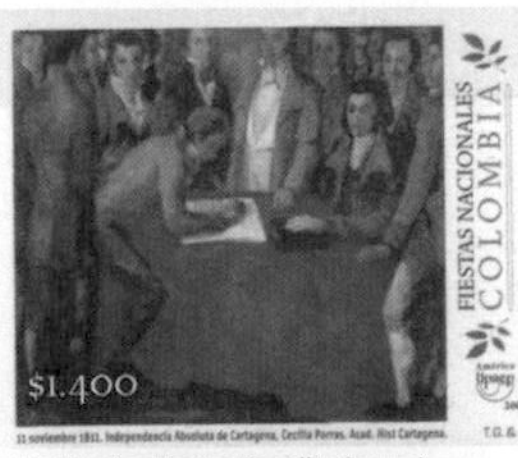

966 Signing Treaty (Cecillia Porras)

2008. America. Festivals. Multicoloured.

2556	1400p. Type **966** (Cartagena Independence)	2·50	2·10
2557	1400p. *Indian Freedom* ('La India de la Liberta') (National Independence) (vert)	2·50	2·10

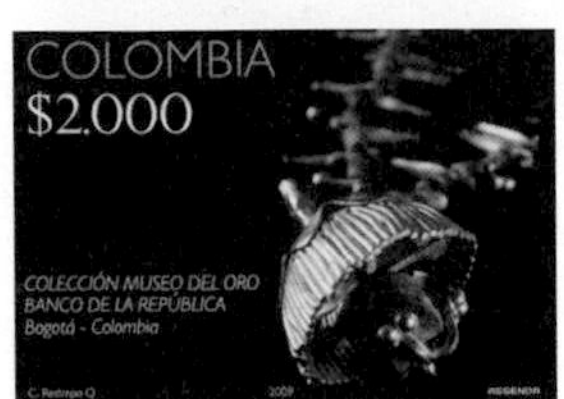

967 Necklace with Flower Pendant, Malagana Period

2009. 70th Anniv of Philatelic Club, Cali. Sheet 135×85 mm containing T **967** and similar multicoloured design.

MS2558	2000p.×2, Type **967**; *Miltoniopsis roezli* ('La Reina del Ville') (vert)	4·50	4·50

968 Globe and '50'

2009. 50th Anniv of Inter-American Development Bank.

2559	**968**	3700p. multicoloured	1·70	1·40

969 Naval Cap and Ships

2009. NCO Naval Academy.

2560	**969**	4000p. multicoloured	7·25	5·50

970 General Rafael Reyes Prieto (founder)

2009. Centenary of Colombia War College

2561	**970**	5500p. multicoloured	4·25	2·75

Nos. 2562/3 are vacant

2009. Department (14th issue). La Guajira. Multicoloured.

2564	1700p. Arms (30×40 mm)	1·40	90
2565	1700p. Francisco el Hombre (mural, Centro Cultural de La Guajira) (50×40 mm)	1·40	90
2566	1700p. Montes de Oca (30×40 mm)	1·40	90
2567	1700p. *Phoenicopterus ruber* (flamingoes) (30×40 mm)	1·40	90
2568	1700p. Domingueka, Kogi village, Sierra Nevada (50×40 mm)	1·40	90
2569	1700p. Cabo de la Vela (30×40 mm)	1·40	90
2570	1700p. Majayuts ('ladies' in Wayuunaiki language) (30×40 mm)	1·40	90
2571	1700p. Riohacha Cathedral (50×40 mm)	1·40	90
2572	1700p. *Cardinalis phoeniceus* (vermilion cardinal) (30×40 mm)	1·40	90
2573	1700p. *Aloe vulgaris*(30×40 mm)	1·40	90
2574	1700p. *Caesalpinia coriaria* (Divi-divi tree) (50×40 mm)	1·40	90
2575	1700p. Woven bags (30×40 mm)	1·40	90

973 Heliconia stricta

2009. Heliconias. Multicoloured.

2576	2000p. Type **973**	1·60	1·00
2577	2000p. *Heliconia rostrata*	1·60	1·00
2578	2000p *Heliconia wagneriana*	1·60	1·00
2579	2000p. *Heliconia orthotricha*	1·60	1·00
2580	2000p. *Heliconia psittacorum*	1·60	1·00

974 1859 2½ cent Stamp

2009. 150th Anniv of First Stamp. Multicoloured.
MS2581 150×130 mm. 4000p.×6, Type **974**; 20 cent stamp; 10 cent stamp; 5 cent stamp; 1 peso stamp; Anniversary emblem 10·50 10·50
MS2582 120×90 mm. 10000p. Anniversary emblem (40×50 mm) 3·75 3·75

976 Rafael Uribe

2009. 150th Birth Anniv of Rafael Uribe (politician)

2485	**976**	1500p. multicoloured	1·10	70

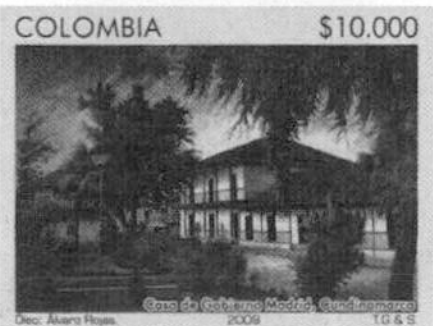
977 Government House, Madrid, Cundinamarca

2009. 450th Anniv of Cundinamarca

2586	**977**	10000p. multicoloured	3·75	3·25

978 *Ada aurantiaca*

2009. Orchids. Multicoloured.

2587	500p. Type **978**	40	25
2588	500p. *Cattleya patinii*	44	25
2589	500p. *Cattleya schreoderae* (inscr 'Cattleya schroderae')	40	25
2590	500p. *Amaliae dracula* (inscr 'Dracula amaliae')	40	25
2591	500p. *Huntleya gustavii*	40	25
2592	500p. *Miltoniopsis phalaenopsis*	40	25
2593	500p. *Masdevallia racemosa* (inscr 'Ada aurantiaca')	40	25
2594	500p. *Pleurothallis casapensis*	40	25
2595	600p. *Anguloa cliftonii* (vert)	45	30
2596	600p. *Cycnoches barthiorum* (vert)	45	30
2597	600p. *Lepanthes telipogoniflora* (vert)	45	30
2598	600p. *Lepanthes calodictyon* (vert)	45	30

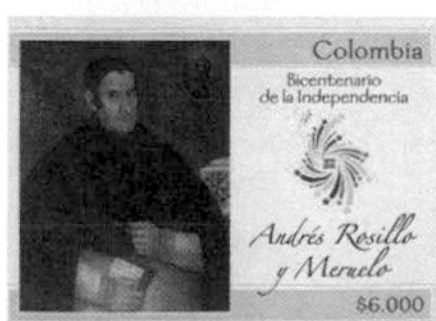
979 Andres Rosillo y Meruelo

2009. Bicentenary of Independence (1st issue). Multicoloured.

2599	6000p. Type **979**	4·00	3·25
2600	6000p. José Félix de Restrepo	4·00	3·25
2601	6000p. Camilo Torres Tenorio	4·00	3·25
2602	6000p. Juan Fernández de Sotomayor	4·00	3·25
2603	6000p. Antonio Villavicencio y Berastegui	4·00	3·25
2604	6000p. Juan de Dios Morales	4·00	3·25
2605	6000p. José María Carbonel	4·00	3·25
2606	6000p. Antonio Morales Galavis	4·00	3·25
2607	6000p. José Ramón de Leyva	4·00	3·25
2608	6000p. Nicholas Mauricio de Omana	4·00	3·25

Nos. 2609/11, Type **980** are left for 150th Anniv of Forst Stamp (2nd issue), issued on 26 November 2009, not yet received.

981 The Holy Family

2009. Christmas

2612	**981**	5000p. multicoloured	4·00	3·25

982 Emblem

2009. For a Mine-free World. Second Review Conference of the Convention on the Prohibition of Anti-personnel Mines, Cartagena
MS2613 multicoloured 8·50 8·50

Nos. 2614/35, Type **983** are left for Presidents, issued on 28 January 2010, not yet received.
Nos. 2636/45, Type **984** are left for Personalities, issued on 28 January 2010, not yet received.

985 Emblem

2010. Medellin 2010, South American Games, Medellin

2646	**985**	5800p. multicoloured	3·75	3·00

986 Pope John Paul II

2010. Pope John Paul II Commemoration

2647	**986**	4400p. multicoloured	3·25	75

987 Crax alberti (blue-billed curassow)

2010. Birds. Multicoloured.
MS2648 1900p.×9, Type **987**; *Ognorhynchus icterotis* (yellow-eared Parrot); *Hapalopsittaca fuertesi* (Fuertes's parrot); *Amazilia castaneiventris* (chestnut-bellied hummingbird); *Rallus semiplumbeus* (Bogotá rail); *Coeligena prunelle* (Prunelle's coeligene); *Grallaria gigantea* (giant antpitta); *Bangsia aureocincta* (gold-ringed tanager); *Hypopyrrhus pyrohypogaster* (red-bellied grackle) 6·00 6·00

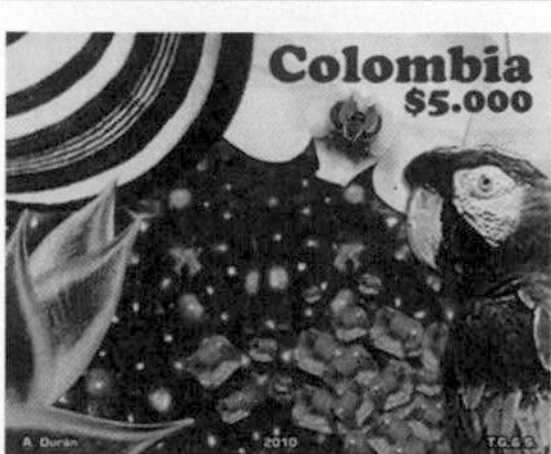
988 Fruit and Scarlet Macaw

2010. Expo 2010, Shanghai
MS2649 multicoloured 3·25 2·75

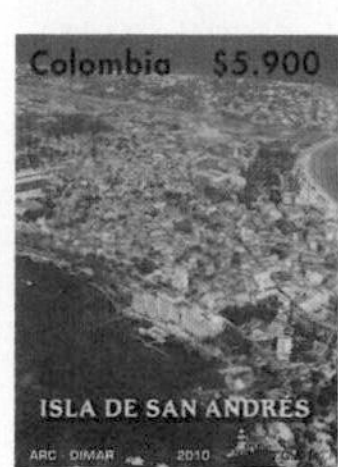
989 San Andreas Island

2010. 500th Anniv of Discovery of San Andreas Archipelago. Multicoloured.

2650	5900p. Type **989**	3·75	3·25
2651	5900p. Island of Providencia and Santa Catlina	3·75	3·25
2652	5900p. Quitasueño Keys	3·75	3·25
2653	5900p. East Southeast Keys (Bolivar Keys)	3·75	3·25
2654	5900p. Roncador Keys	3·75	3·25
2655	5900p. Bajo Nuevo Keys	3·75	3·25
2656	5900p. Serranilla Keys	3·75	3·25
2657	5900p. Serrana Keys	3·75	3·25
2658	5900p. Alberquerque Keys	3·75	3·25

Type **990** is vacant.

2010. Department (15th issue). Atlantico. Multicoloured.

2659	2000p. Arms (30×40 mm)	1·60	1·00
2660	2000p. Palacio de Cultura (50×40 mm)	1·60	1·00
2661	2000p. Petroglyphs (30×40 mm)	1·60	1·00
2662	2000p. *Fluvicola pica* (pied water tyrant) (30×40 mm)	1·60	1·00
2663	2000p. Julio Florez Museum (50×40 mm)	1·60	1·00
2664	2000p. Tocagua swamp (30×40 mm)	1·60	1·00
2665	2000p. Carnival bull mask (30×40 mm)	1·60	1·00
2666	2000p. San Antonio de Padua Temple (50×40 mm)	1·60	1·00
2667	2000p. *Tabebuia rosa* (inscr 'Tabebuya') (national tree) (30×40 mm)	1·60	1·00
2668	2000p. Palm crafts (30×40 mm)	1·60	1·00
2669	2000p. Muelle Port (50×40 mm)	1·60	1·00
2670	2000p. Palacio de la Aduana (30×40 mm)	1·60	1·00

991 Sergeant Luis Alberto Torres Huertas (statue)

2010. National Police Officers School, Gonzalo Jimenez de Quesada

2671	**991**	2000p. multicoloured	1·60	1·00

992 Dancers

2010. 50th Anniv of National Folk Festival and Pageant of Bambuco, Neiva, Huila

2672	**992**	4200p. multicoloured	2·75	2·00

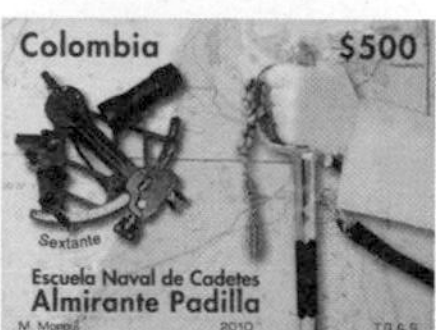
993 Sextant and Sword

2010. Admiral (Almirante) Padilla Naval Cadet School

2673	**993**	500p. multicoloured	40	25

994 Map of Department Area

2010. Centenary of Santander Northern Department. Multicoloured.
MS2674 6000p.×6, Type **994**; Government Building; La Playa de Belen; Cataumbo River; Catedral Santa Ana de Ocana; Catedral Santa Clara de Pamplona 8·00 7·25

The stamps and margins of No. **MS**2674 form a composite design.

2010. Department (16th issue). Guainía. Multicoloured.

2675	600p. Arms (30×40 mm)	45	30
2676	600p. Princess Inirida monument (50×40 mm)	45	30
2677	600p. *Egretta alba* (great egret) (30×40 mm)	45	30
2678	600p. Mavicure hill (30×40 mm)	45	30
2679	600p. Sunset over Inirida river (50×40 mm)	45	30
2680	600p. Basket work made by Curripaco tribe (30×40 mm)	45	30
2681	600p. *Guacamaya superba* (30×40 mm)	45	30
2682	600p. Mouths of Guaviare and Inirida rivers (50×40 mm)	45	30
2683	600p. Remanso community (30×40 mm)	45	30
2684	600p. Cuale stream (30×40 mm)	45	30
2685	600p. Paujil indigenous children (50×40 mm)	45	30
2686	600p. Petroglyphs (30×40 mm)	45	30

995 Teresa Pizarro

2010. Tenth Death Anniv of Teresa Pizarro de Angulo (beauty pageant director and first female farm owner in Cartagena)

2687	**995**	5900p. multicoloured	3·75	3·00

PRIVATE AIR COMPANIES A. "LANSA" (Lineas Aereas Nacionales Sociedad Anonima).

The "LANSA" and Avianca Companies operated inland and foreign air mail services on behalf of the Government and issued the following stamps. Later only the Avianca Company performed this service and the regular air stamps were used on the mail without overprints.

Similar issues were also made by Compania Colombiana de Navegacion Aerea during 1920. These are very rare and will be found listed in the Stanley Gibbons Stamp Catalogue, Part 20 (South America).

1 Wing

1950. Air.

1	**1**	5c. yellow	45	45
2	**1**	10c. red	45	45
3	**1**	15c. blue	75	55
4	**1**	20c. green	1·40	1·30
5	**1**	30c. purple	3·25	3·25
6	**1**	60c. brown	4·50	4·75

With background network colours in brackets.

7	1p. grey (buff)	20·00	21·00
8	2p. blue (green)	22·00	27·00
9	5p. red (red)	85·00	80·00

The 1p. was also issued without the network.

1950. Air. Nos. 691/7 and 700/3 optd L.

10	5c. yellow	35	10
11	10c. red	35	10
12	15c. blue	35	10
13	20c. violet	45	20
14	30c. green	75	20
15	40c. grey	5·50	1·10
16	50c. red	1·70	55
17	1p. purple and green	8·75	5·75

18	2p. blue and green	17·00	8·00
19	3p. black and red	22·00	21·00
20	5p. turquoise and sepia	70·00	70·00

1951. As Nos. 696/703 but colours changed and optd L.

21	40c. orange	2·20	1·30
22	50c. blue	2·50	1·80
23	60c. grey	2·20	1·30
24	80c. red	2·00	1·30
25	1p. red and vermilion	8·25	8·00
26	2p. blue and red	10·00	9·50
27	3p. green and brown	24·00	27·00
28	5p. grey and yellow	65·00	70·00

B. Avianca Company

1950. Air. Nos. 691/703 optd A.

1	5c. yellow	35	10
2	10c. red	35	10
3	15c. blue	35	10
4	20c. violet	45	10
5	30c. green	45	10
6	40c. grey	1·20	20
7	50c. red	1·20	20
8	60c. olive	1·90	30
9	80c. brown	2·75	75
10	1p. purple and green	3·25	95
11	2p. blue and green	9·25	3·25
12	3p. black and red	19·00	16·00
13	5p. turquoise and sepia	55·00	48·00

1951. Air. As Nos. 696/703 but colours changed and optd A.

14	40c. orange	7·75	75
15	50c. blue	22·00	85
16	60c. grey	6·00	75
17	80c. red	1·40	45
18	1p. red and vermilion	9·25	30
19	1p. brown and green	6·50	65
20	2p. blue and red	6·50	95
21	3p. green and brown	12·00	2·75
22	5p. grey and yellow	22·00	2·75

The 60c. also comes with the **A** in the centre.

All values except the 2p. and 3p. exist without the overprint.

ACKNOWLEDGEMENT OF RECEIPT STAMPS

AR60

1894

AR169	**AR60**	5c. red	6·00	7·00

1902. Similar to Type AR **60**. Imperf or perf.

AR265	5c. blue	7·25	7·00
AR211	10c. blue on blue	90	90

1903. No. 197 optd **Habilitado Medellin A R**.

AR258	**75**	10c. black on pink	14·00	13·50

1904. No. 262 optd **A R**.

AR266	5c. red	35·00	34·00

AR100

1904

AR290	**AR100**	5c. blue	5·50	4·50

AR106 A. Gomez

1910

AR354	**AR106**	5c. green & orge	9·25	23·00

AR117 Map of Colombia

1917. Inscr "AR".

AR371	**123**	4c. brown	7·75	8·00
AR372	**AR117**	5c. brown	7·75	5·75

OFFICIAL STAMPS

1937. Optd **OFICIAL**.

O496	-	1c. green (No. 429)	10	10
O497	**137**	2c. red (No. 430)	10	10
O498	-	5c. brown (No. 431)	10	10
O499	-	10c. orge (No. 485)	20	10
O500	**156**	12c. blue	1·40	45
O501	**141**	20c. blue	2·20	1·10
O502	**110**	30c. bistre	2·75	1·30
O503	**123**	40c. brown	2·20	1·10
O504	**112**	50c. red	2·20	1·10
O505	**110**	1p. blue	19·00	7·50
O506	**110**	2p. orange	21·00	7·50
O507	**110**	5p. grey	65·00	70·00
O508	**57**	10p. brown	£140	£160

REGISTRATION STAMPS

R12

1865. Imperf.

R42	**R12**	5c. black	90·00	45·00

1865. Type similar to R **12**, but letter "R" in star. Imperf.

R43	5c. black	£100	48·00

R32

1870. Imperf.

R73	**R32**	5c. black	4·00	3·50

1870. Type similar to R **32** but with "R" in centre and inscr "REJISTRO". Imperf.

R74	5c. black	4·00	3·50

1881. Eagle and arms in oval frame, inscr "RECOMENDADA" at foot. Imperf or pin-perf.

R105	10c. lilac	85·00	70·00

R42

1883. Perf.

R117	**R42**	10c. red on orange	2·75	2·50

R48

1899

R141	**R48**	10c. red	13·00	5·75
R166	**R48**	10c. brown	2·75	2·10

R85

1902. Imperf or perf.

R264	**R85**	10c. purple	7·25	7·00
R207	**R85**	20c. red on blue	80	80
R208	**R85**	20c. blue on blue	1·25	1·25

R94

1902. Perf.

R257	**R94**	10c. purple	29·00	28·00

R99

1904

R289	**R99**	10c. purple	22·00	65

R105 Execution of 24 February, 1810

1910

R353	**R105**	10c. black and red	29·00	70·00

R114 Puerto Colombia

1917

R369	**R114**	4c. blue and green	75	4·50
R370	-	10c. blue	11·00	30

DESIGN: 10c. Tequendama Falls.

R127

1925

R409	**R127**	(10c.) blue	13·00	2·75

1932. Air. Air stamps of 1932 optd **R**.

R426	**132**	20c. red	9·25	6·50
R450	-	20c. green & red (439)	8·25	1·20

SPECIAL DELIVERY STAMPS

E118 Express Messenger

1917

E373	**E118**	5c. green	7·75	7·50

E310

1958. Air.

E936	**E310**	25c. red and blue	75	20

1959. Air. Unification of Air Mail Rates. Optd **UNIFICADO** within outline of airplane.

E989	25c. red and blue	45	30

E361 Boeing 720B on Back of "Express" Letter

1963. Air.

E1143	**E361**	50c. black & red	35	10

1966. Air. "History of Colombian Aviation". As T **372**. Inscr "EXPRESO". Multicoloured.

E1168	80c. Boeing 727 jetliner (1966)	75	30

E647 Numeral

1987

E1783	**E647**	25p. green and red	55	20
E1784	**E647**	30p. green and red	55	20

E663 Sailfish "Istiaphorus amaricanus"

1988. No Value expressed.

E1805	**E663**	(A) blue	1·70	55
E1806	**E663**	(B) blue	5·00	2·10

E724 Black & Chestnut Eagle

1992. No value expressed. Multicoloured.

E1926	B (200p.) Type E **724**	2·50	1·10
E1927	A (950p.) Spectacled bear	13·00	5·00

E738 Postman climbing out of Envelope

1992. World Post Day. No value expressed.

E1951	**E738**	B (200p.) mult	35	20

E741 "Three Musicians"

1993. Fernando Botero (painter) Commemoration. No value expressed.

E1955	**E 741**	B multicoloured	1·80	1·10

E743 Parading "Virgin of the Sorrows"

1993. Popayan Holy Week. No value expressed.

E1957	**E 743**	B multicoloured	1·80	1·10

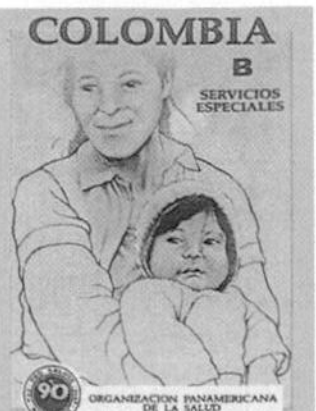
E744 Mother and Child

1993. 90th Anniv of Pan-American Health Organization. No value expressed.

E1958 **E744** B multicoloured 1·80 1·10

E745 Mother House, Pasto

1993. Centenary of Franciscan Convent of Mary Immaculate. No value expressed.

E1959 **E745** B multicoloured 1·80 1·10

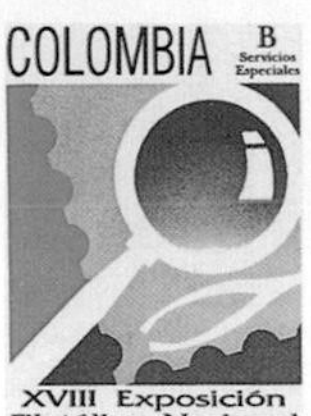

E746 Stamps, Magnifying Glass and Tweezers

1993. 18th National Stamp Exhibition. No value expressed.

E1960 **E 746** B multicoloured 1·80 1·10

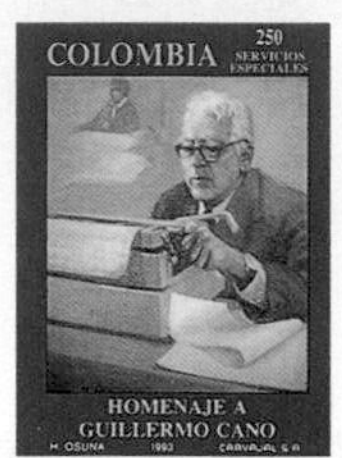

E747 Cano

1993. 7th Death Anniv of Guillermo Cano (newspaper editor).

E1961 **E747** 250p. multicoloured 1·80 1·10

1993. Tourism. As T **756**. Multicoloured.

E1996 250p. Otun Lake (vert) 1·80 1·10

E758 Marie Poussepin (founder)

1994. Order of Sisters of the Presentation.

E1998 **E758** 300p. multicoloured 2·10 1·30

E761 Biplane

1994. 75th Anniv of Air Force.

E2004 **E761** 300p. multicoloured 2·10 1·30

1994. 4th Latin American Presidential Summit, Cartagena. As T **764**. Multicoloured.

E2010 300p. Setting sun over harbour walls 2·10 1·30

E769 Emblem

1994. International Year of The Family.

E2016 **E769** 300p. multicoloured 2·10 1·30

1994. American Postal Transport. As T **770**. Multicoloured.

E2018 300p. Men carrying "stamps" depicting van, ship and aircraft 2·10 1·30

1994. Christmas. As T **773**. Multicoloured.

E2022 300p. Nativity 2·10 1·30

E777 Championship Advertising Poster and Gold Ornament

1995. B.M.X. World Championship, Melgar.

E2029 **E777** 400p. multicoloured 3·00 1·90

E785 Bicycle

1995. World Cycling Championships, Bogota and Boyaca.

E2056 **E785** 400p. multicoloured 3·00 1·90

E791 Hands protecting Lake and Marine Angelfish

1995. America. Environmental Protection. Multicoloured.

E2063 400p. Type E **791** 3·00 1·90

E2064 400p. Hands protecting tree 3·00 1·90

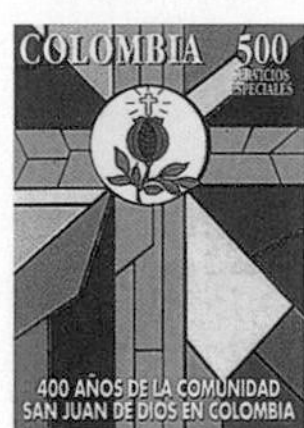

E798 Emblem on Cross

1996. 400th Anniv of Order of St. John of God in Colombia.

E2075 **E798** 500p. multicoloured 3·50 2·20

E800 Trains

1996. Inauguration (1995) of Medellin Underground Railway.

E2080 **E800** 500p. multicoloured 3·50 2·20

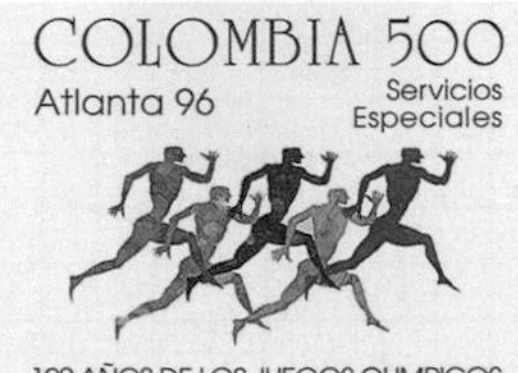

E802 Runners

1996. Olympic Games, Atlanta. Centenary of Modern Olympic Games.

E2082 **E802** 500p. multicoloured 3·50 2·20

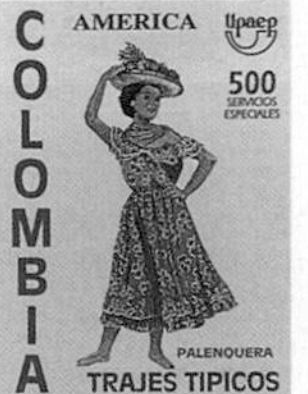

E812 Fruit Seller

1996. America. Traditional Costumes.

E2104 500p. Type E **812** 3·50 2·20

E2105 500p. Fisherman 3·50 2·20

TOO LATE STAMPS

L47

1888. Perf.

L136 **L47** 2½c. black on lilac 5·50 4·25

L59

1892. Perf.

L167 **L59** 2½c. blue on red 5·00 3·50

L86

1902. Imperf or perf.

L209 **L86** 5c. violet on red 45 45

L107

1914. Perf.

L355 **L107** 2c. brown 8·50 6·00

L356 **L107** 5c. green 8·50 6·00

Pt. 6, Pt. 12

COMORO ISLANDS

An archipelago N.W. of Madagascar comprising Anjouan, Great Comoro, Mayotte and Modeli. A French colony from 1891, Mayotte became an Overseas Department of France in December 1974, the remaining islands forming the Independent State of Comoro.

100 centimes = 1 franc.

1 Anjouan Bay

2 Native Woman

6 Mutsamudu Village

1950

1	1	10c. blue (postage)	35	3·75
2	1	50c. green	35	1·10
3	1	1f. brown	85	75
4	2	2f. green	1·50	1·80
5	-	5f. violet	2·00	2·00
6	-	6f. purple	2·00	3·00
7	-	7f. red	2·30	2·30
8	-	10f. green	2·30	1·70
9	-	11f. blue	2·50	3·25
10	-	15f. brown	1·10	1·10
11	-	20f. red	1·30	1·50
12	-	40f. indigo and blue	20·00	15·00
13	6	50f. red and green (air)	4·00	5·00
14	-	100f. brown and red	4·25	5·75
15	-	200f. red, green and violet	36·00	33·00

DESIGNS (as Type **1**)—HORIZ: 7f., 10f., 11f. Mosque at Moroni; 40f. Coelacanth. VERT: 15f., 20f. Ouani Mosque, Anjouan. (As Type **6**)—HORIZ: 100f. Natives and Mosque de Vendredi; 200f. Ouani Mosque, Anjouan (different).

1952. Military Medal Cent. As T 48 of Cameroun.

16		15f. blue, yellow and green	33·00	38·00

1954. Air. 10th Anniv of Liberation. As T 52 of Cameroun.

17		15f. red and brown	23·00	50·00

9 Village Pump

1956. Economic and Social Development Fund.

18	9	9f. violet	1·60	4·50

10 "Human Rights"

1958. 10th Anniv of Declaration of Human Rights.

19	10	20f. green and blue	3·25	13·50

1959. Tropical Flora. As T 58 of Cameroun. Mult.

20		10f. "Colvillea" (horiz)	2·75	4·00

11 Radio Station, Dzaoudzi

1960. Inaug of Comoro Broadcasting Service.

21	11	20f. green, violet and red	1·70	3·75
22	-	25f. green, brown and blue	1·90	3·00

DESIGN: 25f. Radio mast and map.

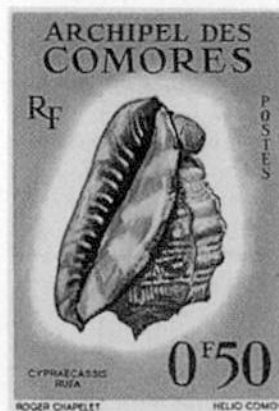

12 Bull-mouth Helmet

1962. Multicoloured. (a) Postage. Sea Shells.

23		50c. Type **12**	75	3·00
24		1f. Common harp	90	3·00
25		2f. Ramose murex	1·80	4·25
26		5f. Giant green turban	2·50	4·75
27		20f. Scorpion conch	7·25	15·00
28		25f. Trumpet triton	9·25	17·00

12a Giant Clam

(b) Air. Marine Plants.

29		100f. Type **12a**	5·50	14·00
30		500f. Stoney coral	18·00	65·00

1962. Malaria Eradication. As T 70 of Cameroun.

31		25f.+5f. red	2·75	10·50

1962. Air. 1st Trans-Atlantic T.V. Satellite Link. As Type F 23 of Andorra.

32		25f. mauve, purple and violet	2·30	2·50

14 Emblem in Hands and Globe

1963. Freedom from Hunger.

33	14	20f. green and brown	3·00	12·00

14a Centenary Emblem

1963. Red Cross Centenary.

34	14a	50f. red, grey and green	3·75	15·00

15 Globe and Scales of Justice

1963. 15th Anniv of Declaration of Human Rights.

35	15	15f. green and red	5·00	10·50

16 Tobacco Pouch

1963. Handicrafts. (a) Postage. As T 17.

36	16	3f. ochre, red and green	2·50	5·00
37	-	4f. myrtle, purple & orange	2·50	6·00
38	-	10f. brown, green & chest	2·40	6·75

(b) Air. Size 27×48 mm.

39		65f. red, brown and green	3·75	8·00
40		200f. pink, red & turq	7·25	13·50

DESIGNS: 4f. Perfume-burner; 10f. Lamp bracket; 65f. Baskets; 200f. Filigree pendant.

16a "Philately"

1964. "PHILATEC 1964" International Stamp Exhibition, Paris.

41	16a	50f. red, green and blue	2·30	11·50

17 Pirogue

1964. Native Craft. Multicoloured.

42		15f. Type **17** (postage)	4·25	5·25
43		30f. Boutre felucca	4·50	8·00
44		50f. Mayotte pirogue (air)	3·25	7·50
45		85f. Schooner	5·25	9·75

Nos. 44/5 are larger, 27×48½ mm.

18 Boxing (Ancient bronze plaque)

1964. Air. Olympic Games, Tokyo.

46	18	100f. green, brown & choc	6·50	21·00

19 Medal

1964. Air. Star of Grand Comoro.

47	19	500f. multicoloured	16·00	43·00

20 "Syncom" Communications Satellite, Telegraph Poles and Morse Key

1965. Air. Centenary of ITU.

48	20	50f. blue, green and grey	9·25	29·00

21 Great Hammerhead

1965. Marine Life.

49	-	1f. green, orange and violet	2·75	4·75
50	21	12f. black, blue and red	3·75	5·75
51	-	20f. red and green	5·50	6·00
52	-	25f. brown, red and green	7·00	4·50

DESIGNS—VERT: 1f. Spiny lobster; 25f. Spotted grouper. HORIZ: 20f. Scaly turtle.

21a Rocket "Diamant"

1966. Air. Launching of 1st French Satellite.

53	21a	25f. lilac, blue and violet	3·75	7·50
54	-	30f. lilac, violet and blue	4·25	8·00

DESIGN: 30f. Satellite "A1".

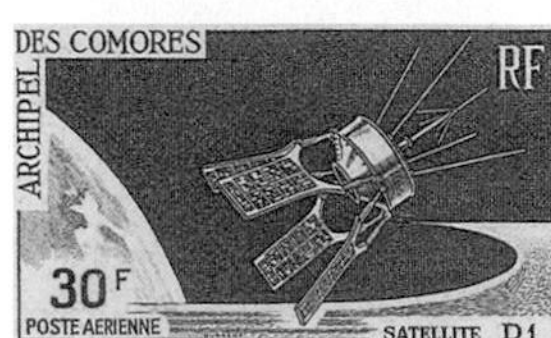

21b Satellite "D1"

1966. Air. Launching of Satellite "D1".

55	21b	30f. purple, green & orange	2·10	3·25

22 Lake Sale

1966. Comoro Views. Multicoloured.

56		15f. Type **22** (postage)	1·70	4·50
57		25f. Itsandra Hotel, Moroni	2·10	2·75
58		50f. The Battery, Dzaoudzi (air)	3·25	5·75
59		200f. Ksar Fort, Mutsamudu (vert)	5·25	10·00

Nos. 58/9 are larger, 48×27 mm and 27×48 mm respectively.

23 Anjouan Sunbird

1967. Birds. Multicoloured.

60		2f. Type **23** (postage)	7·50	6·75
61		10f. Madagascar malachite kingfisher	6·75	8·00
62		15f. Mascarene fody	10·50	10·50
63		30f. Courol	21·00	27·00
64		75f. Madagascar paradise flycatcher (vert) (27×48 mm) (air)	12·00	21·00
65		100f. Blue-cheeked bee eater (vert) (27×48 mm)	13·50	25·00

24 Nurse tending Child

1967. Comoro Red Cross.

66	24	25f.+5f. purple, red & grn	3·50	6·75

25 Slalom Skiing

1968. Air. Winter Olympic Games, Grenoble.

67	**25**	70f. brown, blue and green	5·75	7·00

26 Bouquet, Sun and WHO Emblem

1968. 20th Anniv of WHO.

68	**26**	40f. red, violet and green	1·90	2·75

27 Powder-blue Surgeonfish

1968. Fishes.

69	**27**	20f. bl, yell & red (postage)	5·25	9·25
70	-	25f. blue, orange & turq	6·00	10·00
71	-	50f. ochre, blue & pur (air)	7·50	9·25
72	-	90f. ochre, green & emer	10·50	14·50

DESIGNS—As T **27**: 25f. Emperor angelfish. 48×27 mm: 50f. Moorish idol; 90f. Oriental sweetlips.

28 Human Rights Emblem

1968. Human Rights Year.

73	**28**	60f. green, brown & orange	3·00	6·50

29 Swimming

1968. Air. Olympic Games, Mexico.

74	**29**	65f. multicoloured	3·75	8·50

30 Prayer Mat and Worshipper

1969. Msoila Prayer Mats.

75	**30**	20f. red, green and violet	1·80	4·50
76	-	30f. green, violet and red	2·30	5·25
77	-	45f. violet, red and green	3·75	6·00

DESIGNS: As Type **30**, but worshipper stooping (30f.) or kneeling upright (45f.).

31 Vanilla Flower

1969. Flowers. Multicoloured.

78	10f. Type **31** (postage)	4·00	3·50
79	15f. Ylang-ylang blossom	4·25	3·75
80	50f. "Heliconia" (vert) (air)	4·75	6·25
81	85f. Tuberose (vert)	6·00	10·00
82	200f. Orchid (vert)	10·00	11·50

32 Concorde in Flight

1969. Air. 1st Flight of Concorde.

83	**32**	100f. purple and brown	15·00	34·00

33 ILO Building, Geneva

1969. 50th Anniv of ILO.

84	**33**	5f. grey, green and orange	2·50	3·75

34 Poinsettia

1970. Flowers.

85	**34**	25f. multicoloured	3·75	4·25

1970. New UPU Headquarters Building, Berne. As T 156 of Cameroun.

86		65f. brown, green and violet	4·25	8·25

35 "EXPO" Panorama

1970. Air. World Fair "EXPO 70", Osaka, Japan. Multicoloured.

87	60f. Type **35**	4·25	4·75
88	90f. Geisha and map of Japan	5·25	7·00

36 Chiromani Costume, Anjouan

1970. Comoro Costumes. Multicoloured.

89	20f. Type **36**	3·00	5·00
90	25f. Bouiboui, Great Comoro	3·50	5·75

37 Mosque de Vendredi, Moroni

1970

91	**37**	5f. turquoise, green and red	3·50	4·75
92	**37**	10f. violet, green & purple	3·75	5·25
93	**37**	40f. brown, green and red	4·25	5·50

38 Great Egret

1971. Birds. Multicoloured.

94	5f. Type **38**	3·25	5·00
95	10f. Comoro olive pigeon	3·75	4·50
96	15f. Green-backed heron	4·25	5·25
97	25f. Comoro blue pigeon	4·00	5·25
98	35f. Humblot's flycatcher	5·75	8·00
99	40f. Allen's gallinule	9·00	8·25

39 Sunset, Moutsamoudou (Anjouan)

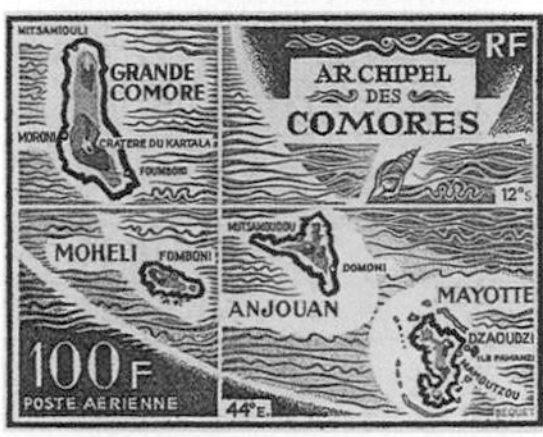

40 Map of Comoro Archipelago

1971. Air. Comoro Landscapes. Multicoloured.

100	**39**	15f. multicoloured	2·50	2·30
101	-	20f. multicoloured	3·00	2·75
102	-	65f. multicoloured	3·50	3·75
103	-	85f. multicoloured	4·00	4·75
104	**40**	100f. brown, green & bl	9·50	9·00

DESIGNS—(As Type **39**): 20f. Sada village (Mayotte); 65f. Ruined palace, Iconi (Great Comoro); 85f. Offshore islands; Moumatchoua (Moheli).

See also Nos. 124/8, 132/6, 157/60 and 168/71.

41 "Pyrostegia venusta"

1971. Tropical Plants. Multicoloured.

105	1f. Type **41** (postage)	2·50	2·75
106	3f. "Allamanda cathartica" (horiz)	3·00	2·75
107	20f. "Plumeria rubra"	5·50	4·00
108	60f. "Hibiscus schizopetalous" (air)	5·25	4·75
109	85f. "Acalypha sanderii"	11·00	9·00

The 60 and 85f. are 27×48 mm.

42 Lithograph Cone

1971. Sea Shells. Multicoloured.

110	5f. Type **42**	3·00	3·25
111	10f. Lettered cone	3·75	4·25
112	20f. Princely cone	4·50	5·50
113	35f. Polished nerite	6·00	3·75
114	60f. Serpent's-head cowrie	13·00	5·75

1971. 1st Death Anniv of Charles de Gaulle. Designs as Nos. 1937 and 1940 of France.

115	20f. black and purple	4·00	7·00
116	35f. black and purple	4·25	7·50

44 Mural, Airport Lounge

1972. Air. Inauguration of New Airport, Moroni.

117	**44**	65f. multicoloured	2·00	3·50
118	-	85f. multicoloured	2·50	4·50
119	-	100f. green, brown & blue	4·50	6·25

DESIGNS: 85f. Mural similar to T **44**; 100f. Airport Buildings.

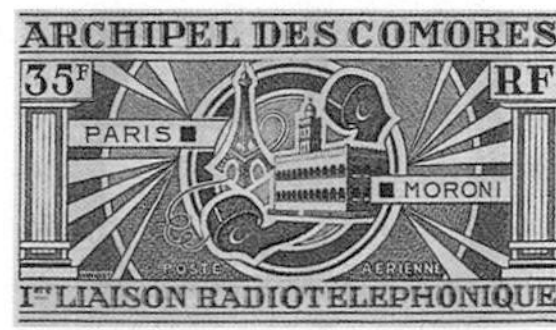

45 Eiffel Tower, Paris and Telecommunications Centre, Moroni

1972. Air. Inauguration of Paris–Moroni Radio-Telephone Link.

120	**45**	35f. red, purple & blue	3·25	2·75
121	-	75f. red, violet and blue	3·50	3·00

DESIGN: 75f. Telephone conversation.

46 Underwater Spear-fishing

1972. Air. Aquatic Sports.

122	**46**	70f. red, green and blue	12·00	11·50

47 Pasteur, Crucibles and Microscope

1972. 150th Birth Anniv of Louis Pasteur.

123	**47**	65f. blue, brown & orange	6·00	9·00

1972. Air. Anjouan Landscapes. (a) As T 39. Multicoloured.

124	20f. Fortress wall, Cape Sima	3·25	3·00
125	35f. Bambao Palace	3·50	3·50
126	40f. Palace, Domoni	3·50	3·50
127	60f. Gomajou Island	3·75	5·75

(b) As T 40.

128	100f. green, blue & brown	11·00	12·50

DESIGN: 100f. Map of Anjouan.

48 Pres. Said Mohamed Cheikh

1973. Air. Said Mohamed Cheikh, President of Comoro Council, Commemoration.

129	**48**	20f. multicoloured	3·25	4·75
130	**48**	35f. multicoloured	3·50	5·00

1973. Air. International Coelacanth Study Expedition. No. 72 surch Mission Internationale pour l'etude du Coelacanthe and value.

131	120f. on 90f. brn, grn & emer	18·00	10·00

1973. Great Comoro Landscapes. (a) Postage. As T 39. Multicoloured.

132	10f. Goulaivoini	4·50	3·00
133	20f. Mitsamiouli	4·75	3·25
134	35f. Foumbouni	5·25	3·75
135	50f. Moroni	6·50	4·75

(b) Air. As Type 40.

136	135f. purple, green & violet	19·00	11·00

DESIGN—VERT: 135f. Map of Great Comoro.

50 Bank

1973. Moroni Buildings. Multicoloured.

137		5f. Type **50**	3·25	4·25
138		15f. Post Office	3·50	4·50
139		20f. Prefecture	4·00	4·75

51 Volcanic Eruption

1973. Air. Karthala Volcanic Eruption (Sept 1972).

140	**51**	120f. multicoloured	16·00	13·00

52 Dr. G. A. Hansen

1973. Air Centenary of Hansen's Identification of Leprosy Bacillus.

141	**52**	100f. green, purple & blue	6·00	6·50

1973. Air. 500th Birth Anniv of Nicolas Copernicus. As T 52.

142		150f. purple, blue & ultram	8·25	9·75

DESIGN: 150f. Copernicus and solar system.

53 Pablo Picasso (artist)

1973. Air. Picasso Commemoration.

143	**53**	200f. multicoloured	21·00	13·00
MS144		100×131 mm. **53** 100f. multicoloured	16·00	17·00

54 Zaouiyat Chaduli Mosque

1973. Mosques. Multicoloured.

145		20f. Type **54**	3·00	4·50
146		35f. Salimata Hamissi Mosque (horiz)	3·75	3·25

55 Star and Ribbon

1974. Air. Order of the Star of Anjouan.

147	**55**	500f. gold, blue & brown	21·00	30·00

56 Said Omar Ben Soumeth (Grand Mufti of the Comoros)

1974. Air. Multicoloured.

148		135f. Type **56**	6·25	5·25
149		200f. Ben Soumeth seated (vert)	10·00	9·50

57 Doorway of Mausoleum

1974. Mausoleum of Shaikh Said Mohamed.

150	**57**	35f. brown, black & green	4·00	5·75
151	-	50f. brown, black & green	4·50	6·00

DESIGN: 50f. Mausoleum.

58 Wooden Combs

1974. Comoro Handicrafts (1st series). Mult.

152		15f. Type **58**	2·00	3·75
153		20f. Three-legged table	3·25	3·75
154		35f. Koran lectern (horiz)	4·50	4·75
155		75f. Sugar-cane press (horiz)	7·00	8·00

See also Nos. 164/7.

59 Mother and Child

1974. Comoros Red Cross Fund.

156	**59**	35f.+10f. brown & red	3·50	5·25

1974. Air. Mayotte Landscapes. (a) As T 39. Multicoloured.

157		20f. Moya beach	3·75	3·75
158		35f. Chiconi	4·00	4·00
159		90f. Mamutzu harbour	7·00	6·25

(b) As T 40.

160		120f. green and blue	9·25	9·25

DESIGN—VERT: 120f. Map of Mayotte.

60 UPU Emblem and Globe

1974. Centenary of Universal Postal Union.

161	**60**	30f. red, brown and green	4·50	4·00

61 Boeing 707 taking off

1975. Inauguration of Direct Moroni–Hahaya–Paris Air Service.

162	**61**	135f. blue, green and red	14·00	14·50

62 Rotary Emblem, Moroni Clubhouse and Map

1975. Air. 70th Anniv of Rotary International and 10th Anniv of Moroni Rotary Club.

163	**62**	250f. multicoloured	17·00	18·00

63 Bracelet

1975. Comoro Handicrafts (2nd series).

164	**63**	20f. brown and purple	4·25	4·75
165	-	35f. brown and green	4·50	5·25
166	-	120f. brown and blue	8·25	9·25
167	-	135f. brown and red	11·50	11·00

DESIGNS: 35f. Diadem; 120f. Sabre; 125f. Dagger.

1975. Moheli Landscapes. (a) Postage. As T 39. Multicoloured.

168		30f. Mohani Village	6·25	5·50
169		50f. Djoezi Village	7·25	6·00
170		55f. Chirazian tombs	9·00	7·25

(b) Air. As T 40.

171		230f. green, blue and brown	26·00	18·00

DESIGN: 230f. Map of Moheli.

64 Coelacanth and Skin-diver

1975. Coelacanth Expedition.

172	**64**	50f. bistre, blue & brown	14·50	11·00

65 Tambourine-player

1975. Folklore Dances. Multicoloured.

173		100f. Type **65**	95·00	95·00
174		150f. Dancers with tambourines	95·00	95·00

66 Athlete and Athens, 1896 Motifs

1976. Olympic Games, Munich (1972) and Montreal (1976). Multicoloured.

175		20f. Type **66** (postage)	10	10
176		25f. Running	30	10
177		40f. Athlete and Paris, 1900 motif	45	20
178		75f. High-jumping	95	50
179		100f. Exercises and World's Fair, St. Louis, 1904 motif (air)	1·00	65
180		500f. Gymnast on bars	5·25	2·75
MS181		91×120 mm. 400f. Olympic stadium, Montreal	4·75	2·75

67 Government House, Flag and Map

1976. 1st Anniv of Independence. Multicoloured.

182	**67**	30f. multicoloured	60	25
183	**67**	50f. multicoloured	1·00	40

68 Agricultural Scene and U.N. Stamp

1976. 25th Anniv of U.N. Postal Services. Multicoloured.

184		15f. Type **68** (postage)	10	10
185		30f. Surgery scene and U.N. W.H.O. stamp	30	10
186		50f. Village scene and UNICEF stamp	55	30
187		75f. Telecommunications satellite and U.N. I.T.U. stamp	80	35
188		200f. Concorde, airship "Graf Zeppelin" and U.N. ICAO stamp (air)	2·20	90
189		400f. Lufthansa jet airliner and U.N. U.P.U. stamp	4·00	2·10
MS190		104×104 mm. 500f. Ring of people with letters on globe (53×35 mm)	4·50	1·80

69 Copernicus, and Rocket on Launch-pad

1976. "Success of Operation Viking", and Bicentenary of American Revolution. Multicoloured.

191		5f. Type **69** (postage)	20	10
192		10f. Einstein, Sagan and Young (horiz)	20	10
193		25f. "Viking" orbiting Mars	35	10
194		35f. Vikings' discovery of America (horiz)	75	25
195		100f. U.S. flag and Mars landing	1·40	50
196		500f. First colour photograph of Martian terrain (horiz) (air)	7·50	2·50
MS197		116×82 mm. 400f. "Viking" on Mars (41×59 mm)	4·50	1·60

70 U.N. Headquarters, New York and Flags

1976. 1st Anniv of Comoro Islands Admission to United Nations.

198	**70**	40f. multicoloured	60	30
199	**70**	50f. multicoloured	85	40

71 President Lincoln and Bombardment of Fort Sumter

1976. Bicentenary of American Revolution. Showing various battle scenes of American Civil War. Multicoloured.

200		10f. Type **71** (postage)	10	10

201	30f. General Beauregard and Bull Run (vert)	35	20
202	50f. General Johnston and Antietam	45	40
203	100f. General Meade and Gettysburg (air)	1·20	60
204	200f. General Sherman and Chattanooga (vert)	1·80	1·10
205	400f. General Pickett and Appomattox	3·75	2·00
MS206 110×76 mm. 500f. Surrender of General Lee to General Grant (59×41 mm)		4·50	2·75

72 Andean Condor

1976. "Endangered Animals" (1st series). Multicoloured.

207	15f. Type **72** (postage)	35	10
208	20f. Tiger cat (horiz)	55	10
209	35f. Leopard	1·00	25
210	40f. White rhinoceros (horiz)	1·30	45
211	75f. Mountain nyala	2·75	55
212	400f. Orang-utan (horiz) (air)	6·75	1·50
MS213 78×100 mm. 500f. Indri (lemur) (38×56 mm)		6·75	1·90

73 Wolf

1977. "Endangered Animals" (2nd series). Mult.

214	10f. Type **73** (postage)	10	10
215	30f. Aye-aye	45	10
216	40f. Banded duiker	95	25
217	50f. Giant tortoise	1·20	25
218	200f. Ocelot (air)	2·75	90
219	400f. Galapagos penguin ("Manchot des Galapagos")	6·00	1·70
MS220 96×76 mm. 500f. Sumatran tiger (56×38 mm)		7·50	1·90

74 Giffard's Dirigible, 1851 and French Locomotive, 1837

1977. History of Communications. Airships and Railways. Multicoloured.

221	20f. Type **74** (postage)	30	10
222	25f. Santos-Dumont's airship "Ballon No. 6" (1906) and Brazilian steam locomotive (19th century)	35	10
223	50f. Russian airship "Astra" (1914) and "Trans-Siberian Express" (1905)	75	25
224	75f. British airship R-34 (1919) and "Southern Belle" pullman express (1910–25)	1·00	30
225	200f. U.S. Navy airship "Los Angeles" (1930) and Pacific locomotive (1930) (air)	2·30	80
226	500f. German airship "Hindenburg", 1933, and "Rheingold" express, 1933	5·75	1·90
MS227 100×80 mm. 500f. Airship "Graf Zeppelin" and locomotive "Nord-Express" (54×35 mm)		5·50	2·10

75 Koch, Morgan, Fleming, Muller and Waksman (medicine)

1977. Nobel Prize Winners. Multicoloured.

228	30f. Type **75** (postage)	50	10
229	40f. Michelson, Bragg, Raman and Zernike (physics)	60	15
230	50f. Tagore, Yeats, Russell and Hemingway (literature)	80	25
231	100f. Rontgen, Becquerel, Planck, Lawrence and Einstein (physics)	2·10	35
232	200f. Ramsey and Marie Curie (chemistry), Banting and Hench (medicine) and Perrin (physics) (air)	2·50	90
233	400f. Dunant, Briand, Schweitzer and Martin Luther King (peace)	5·50	1·70
MS234 94×64 mm. 500f. Alfred Nobel (50×41 mm)		5·50	1·90

The 200f. wrongly attributes the chemistry prize to all those depicted and gives the date 1913 instead of 1911 for Marie Curie. On the 50 and 100f. names are wrongly spelt.

76 "Clara, Ruben's Daughter"

1977. 400th Birth Anniv of Peter Paul Rubens (1st issue). Multicoloured.

235	20f. Type **76** (postage)	25	10
236	25f. "Suzanne Fourment"	30	10
237	50f. "Venus in front of Mirror"	75	25
238	75f. "Ceres"	95	30
239	200f. "Young Girl with Blond Hair" (air)	2·30	75
240	500f. "Helene Fourment in Wedding Dress"	6·25	1·90
MS241 110×86 mm. 500f. "Self-portrait" (31×47 mm)		5·50	2·00

See also Nos. 407/10.

77 Queen Elizabeth II, Westminster Abbey and Guards

1977. Air. Silver Jubilee of Queen Elizabeth II.

242	**77**	500f. multicoloured	5·00	1·80
MS243 114×86 mm. 1000f. multicoloured			9·50	

DESIGN: 1000f. State coach.

79 Swordfish

1977. Fishes. Multicoloured.

256	30f. Type **79** (postage)	45	15
257	40f. Oriental sweetlips	90	20
258	50f. Lionfish	1·30	40
259	100f. Racoon butterflyfish	2·75	70
260	200f. Clown anemonefish (air)	3·75	90
261	400f. Black-spotted puffer	6·75	2·30
MS262 80×100 mm. 500f. Coelacanth (46×37 mm)		6·00	2·10

80 Jupiter Lander

1977. Space Research. Multicoloured.

263	30f. Type **80** (postage)	30	10
264	50f. Uranus probe (vert)	50	10
265	75f. Venus probe	85	30
266	100f. Space shuttle (vert)	1·00	40
267	200f. "Viking 3" (air)	2·10	75
268	400f. "Apollo–Soyuz" link (vert)	4·25	1·60
MS269 101×75 mm. 500f. Allegory of the Sun (50×41 mm)		5·50	1·90

1977. Air. First Paris–New York Commercial Flight of Concorde. No. 188 optd Paris-New-York - 22 nov. 1977.

270	200f. multicoloured	4·25	2·75

82 Allen's Gallinule

1978. Birds. Multicoloured.

271	15f. Type **82** (postage)	30	15
272	20f. Blue-cheeked bee eater	45	20
273	35f. Madagascar malachite kingfisher	65	25
274	40f. Madagascar paradise flycatcher	1·10	35
275	75f. Anjouan sunbird	1·80	40
276	400f. Great egret (air)	8·25	2·00
MS277 76×88 mm. 500f. Mascarene fody (47×33 mm)		6·50	2·10

83 Greek Ball Game and Modern Match

1978. World Cup Football Championship, Argentina. Multicoloured.

278	30f. Type **83** (postage)	30	10
279	50f. Breton football	50	15
280	75f. 14th-century London game	75	30
281	100f. 18th-century Italian game	1·00	40
282	200f. 19th-century English game (air)	2·10	75
283	400f. English cup-tie, 1891	4·25	1·60
MS284 120×70 mm. 500f. English cup-tie final, 1902		5·00	1·90

84 "Oswolt Krel"

1978. 450th Death Anniv of Albrecht Durer (artist) (1st issue). Multicoloured.

286	20f. Type **84** (postage)	10	10
287	25f. "Elspeth Tucher"	30	10
288	50f. "Hieronymus Holzshuher"	60	25
289	75f. "Young Girl"	85	30
290	200f. "Emperor Maximilian I" (air)	2·20	80
291	500f. "Young Girl" (detail)	5·00	1·90
MS292 90×75 mm. 500f. "Self-portrait" (41×50 mm)		5·50	2·00

See also Nos. 411/15.

85 Bach

1978. Composers. Multicoloured.

293	30f. Type **85** (postage)	55	20
294	40f. Mozart	85	20
295	50f. Berlioz	1·00	30
296	100f. Verdi	2·40	50
297	200f. Tchaikovsky (air)	3·25	75
298	400f. Gershwin	5·25	1·70
MS299 100×79 mm. 500f. Beethoven (150th death anniv)		6·75	2·00

Following a revolution on 13 May 1978, it was announced that sets showing Butterflies or commemorating the 25th Anniversary of the Coronation of Queen Elizabeth II, 10th World Telecommunications Day and Aviation History had not been placed on sale in the islands and were not valid for postage there.

86 Rowland Hill, Locomotive "Adler" and Saxony 3pf. Stamp, 1860

1978. Death Centenary of Sir Rowland Hill. Multicoloured.

300	20f. Type **86** (postage)	20	10
301	30f. Penny-farthing and Netherlands 5c. stamp, 1852	40	10
302	40f. Early letter-box and 2d. blue	70	10
303	75f. Pony Express and U.S. stamp, 1847	95	30
304	200f. Airship and French 20c. stamp, 1863 (air)	1·90	65
305	400f. Postman and Basel 2½r. stamp, 1845	4·00	90
MS306 110×79 mm. 500f. Early Comoro Isalnds stamps (53×35 mm)		4·75	2·00

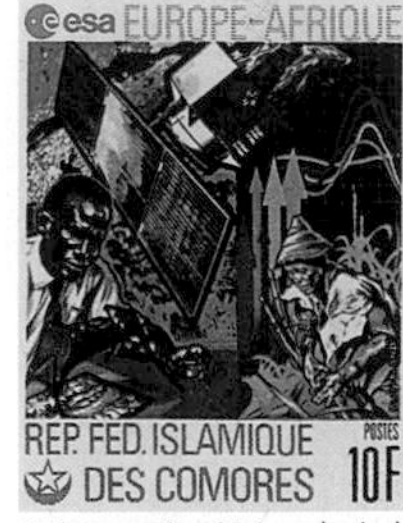

87 Interpreting Meteorological Satellite Photographs

1978. European Space Agency. Multicoloured.

307	10f. Type **87** (postage)	10	10
308	25f. Writing weather forecast	30	10
309	35f. Aiding wrecked ship	35	10
310	50f. Telecommunications as teaching aid	55	20
311	100f. Boeing 727 landing (air)	1·00	30
312	500f. Space shuttle	4·75	1·60
MS313 108×77 mm. 500f. Satellite over map of Africa (59×38 mm)		5·25	2·30

1978. Argentina's Victory in World Cup Football Championship. Nos. 278/284 optd REP. FED. ISLAMIQUE DES COMORES 1 ARGENTINE 2 HOLLANDE 3 BRESIL.

314	**83**	30f. mult (postage)	45	25
315	-	50f. multicoloured	45	40
316	-	75f. multicoloured	55	55
317	-	100f. multicoloured	1·20	1·10
318	-	200f. multicoloured (air)	1·80	45
319	-	400f. multicoloured	3·75	90
MS320 120×70 mm. 500f. multicoloured			4·50	2·50

89 Philidor, Anderssen and Steinitz

1979. Chess Grand Masters. Multicoloured.

321	40f. Type **89** (postage)	45	10
322	100f. Venetian players and pieces	1·00	25
323	500f. Alekhine, Spassky and Fischer (air)	4·75	1·60

90 Galileo and "Voyager 1"

1979. Exploration of the Solar System. Mult.

324	20f. Type **90** (postage)	10	10
325	30f. Kepler and "Voyager 2"	30	10
326	40f. Copernicus and "Voyager 1"	45	20
327	100f. Huygens and "Voyager 2"	1·00	30
328	200f. Herschel and "Voyager 2" (air)	1·80	60
329	400f. Leverrier and "Voyager 2"	3·75	1·20

91 Kayak

1979. Olympic Games, Moscow (1980). Mult.

330	10f. Type **91** (postage)	10	10
331	25f. Swimming	30	10
332	35f. Archery	35	10
333	50f. Pole vault	45	20
334	75f. Long jump	80	35
335	500f. High jump (air)	4·50	1·60

92 "Charaxes defulvata"

1979. Fauna. Multicoloured.

336	30f. Type **92**	1·70	35
337	50f. Courol	3·50	90
338	75f. Blue-cheeked bee eater	5·00	1·60

1979. Optd or surch REPUBLIQUE FEDERALE ISLAMIQUE DES COMORES. (a) Birds, Nos. 271/275.

339	15f. Type **82**	30	25
340	30f. on 35f. Madagascar malachite kingfisher	50	50
341	50f. on 20f. Blue-cheeked bee eater	1·10	1·00
342	50f. on 40f. Madagascar paradise flycatcher	1·10	1·00
343	200f. on 75f. Anjouan sunbird	3·25	3·25

(b) World Cup, Nos. 278/282.

344	1f. on 100f. Italian game (postage)	10	10
345	2f. on 75f. London game	10	10
346	3f. on 30f. Type **83**	10	10
347	50f. Breton football	85	50
348	200f. English game (air)	2·00	1·90

1979. Nos. 293/7 surch or optd Republique Federale Islamique des Comores.

349	-	5f. on 100f. Verdi (post)	55	10
350	**85**	30f. J. S. Bach	1·10	35
351	-	40f. Mozart	1·40	45
352	-	50f. Berlioz	2·30	75
353	-	50f. on 200f. Tchaikovsky (air)	3·25	1·00

94 State Coach

1979. 25th Anniv of Coronation of Queen Elizabeth II. Multicoloured.

354	5f. on 25f. Type **94** (postage)	10	10
355	10f. Drum Major	30	25
356	50f. on 40f. Queen carrying orb and sceptre	65	65
357	100f. St. Edward's Crown	1·40	1·40
358	50f. on 200f. Herald reading Proclamation (air)	1·00	1·00

Nos. 354/8 were only valid for postage overprinted as in Type **94**.

95 "Papilio dardanus-cenea stoll"

1979. Butterflies. Multicoloured.

359	5f. on 20f. Type **95**	30	10
360	15f. "Papilio dardanus–brown"	45	25
361	30f. "Chrysiridia croesus"	65	50
362	50f. "Precis octavia"	1·40	1·10
363	75f. "Bunaea alcinoe"	2·20	1·70

Nos. 359/63 were only valid for postage overprinted as in Type **95**.

96 Otto Lilienthal and Glider

1979. History of Aviation. Multicoloured.

364	30f. Type **96** (postage)	45	45
365	50f. Wright Brothers	65	65
366	50f. on 75f. Louis Bleriot	75	75
367	100f. Claude Dornier	1·40	1·30
368	200f. Charles Lindbergh (air)	2·20	2·10

Nos. 364/8 were only valid for postage overprinted as in Type **96**.

97 Tobogganing

1979. International Year of the Child (1st issue). Multicoloured.

369	20f. Astronauts (postage)	10	10
370	30f. Type **97**	30	10
371	40f. Painting	45	20
372	100f. Locomotive "Rocket", 1829, and toy train	1·00	30
373	200f. Football (air)	1·90	50
374	400f. Canoeing	4·00	1·10

See also Nos. 389/90.

98 Lychees

1979. Fruit. Multicoloured.

375	60f. Type **98**	85	30
376	70f. Papaws	1·00	45
377	100f. Avocado pears	1·30	50
378	125f. Bananas	1·60	80

101 Rotary Emblem and Village Scene

1979. Air. Rotary International.

388	**101**	400f. multicoloured	6·25	3·75

102 Mother and Child on Boat

1979. Air. International Year of the Child (2nd issue). Multicoloured.

389	200f.+30f. Type **102**	3·50	2·75
390	250f. Mother and baby	3·50	2·20

103 Basketball

1979. Indian Ocean Olympic Games.

391	**103**	200f. multicoloured	2·20	1·30

1979. Various stamps optd REPUBLIQUE FEDERALE ISLAMIQUE DES COMORES. (a) Air. Apollo–Soyuz Space Test Project (Appendix).

392	100f. Presidents Brezhnev and Ford with astronauts	1·20	1·20
393	200f. Space link-up	2·40	2·30

(b) Bicentenary of American Revolution (Appendix).

394	25f. Fremont, Kit Carson and dancing Indian	30	25
395	35f. D. Boone, Buffalo Bill and wagon train	40	35
396	75f. H. Wells, W. Fargo and stagecoach ambush	85	80

(c) Winter Olympic Games, Innsbruck (Appendix).

397	35f. Speed skating	40	35

(d) Telephone Centenary (Appendix).

398	75f. Philip Reis	85	80

(e) Air. Olympic Games, Munich and Montreal.

399	100f. multicoloured (No. 179)	1·20	1·20

(f) U.N. Postal Services.

400	75f. mult (No. 187)	85	80

(g) Endangered Animals.

401	35f. mult (No. 209)	40	35
402	40f. mult (No. 210)	45	45

(h) Nobel Prize Winners.

403	100f. mult (No. 231)	1·20	1·20

(i) Rubens.

404	25f. mult (No. 236)	30	25

(j) Durer.

405	25f. mult (No. 287)	30	25
406	75f. mult (No. 289)	85	80

105 "Profile Head of Old Man"

1979. 400th Birth Anniv of Peter Paul Rubens (artist) (2nd issue). Multicoloured.

407	25f. Type **105**	30	10
408	35f. "Young Girl with Flag"	45	10
409	50f. "Isabelle d'Este, Margave of Mantua"	80	15
410	75f. "Philip IV, King of Spain"	95	25

106 "Portrait of Young Girl"

1979. 450th Death Anniv of Albrecht Durer (artist) (2nd issue). Multicoloured.

411	20f. "Self-portrait" (postage)	20	15
412	30f. "Young Man"	30	15
413	40f. Type **106**	45	15
414	100f. "Jerome" (air)	95	25
415	200f. "Jacob Muffel"	2·00	40

107 Satellite and Receiving Station

1979. 10th World Telecommunications Day. Multicoloured.

416	75f. Satellites	85	30
417	100f. Two satellites	1·00	40
418	200f. Type **107**	2·10	90

108 Pirogue

1980. Handicrafts. Multicoloured.

419	60f. Type **108**	95	25
420	100f. Anjouan puppet	1·30	50

109 Sultan Said Ali

1980. Sultans. Multicoloured.

421	40f. Type **109**	50	20
422	60f. Sultan Ahmed	75	25

110 Dimadjou Dispensary

1980. Air. 75th Anniv of Rotary International and 15th Anniv of Moroni Rotary Club (100f.).

423		100f. Type **110**	1·10	50
424		260f. Concorde airplane	2·75	1·20

111 Sherlock Holmes and Sir Arthur Conan Doyle

1980. 50th Death Anniv of Sir Arthur Conan Doyle (writer).

425	**111**	200f. multicoloured	3·75	1·40

112 Grand Mosque and Holy Ka'aba, Mecca

1980. 1350th Anniv of Occupation of Mecca by Mohammed.

426	**112**	75f. multicoloured	85	45

113 Dome of the Rock

1980. Year of the Holy City, Jerusalem.

427	**113**	60f. multicoloured	75	40

114 Kepler, Copernicus

1980. 50th Anniv of Discovery of Pluto.

428	**114**	400f. violet, red & mauve	5·00	2·50

115 Avicenna

1980. Birth Millenary of Avicenna (physician and philosopher).

429	**115**	60f. multicoloured	95	45

116 Mermoz, Dabry, Gimie and Seaplane "Comte da la Vaulx"

1980. 50th Anniv of First South Atlantic Flight.

430	**116**	200f. multicoloured	3·75	2·10

1981. Various stamps surch.

431		15f. on 200f. multicoloured (No. 425) (postage)	30	25
432		20f. on 75f. mult (No. 426)	40	35
433		40f. on 125f. mult (No. 378)	90	90
434		60f. on 75f. mult (No. 338)	1·70	1·20
435		30f. on 200f. multicoloured (No. 430) (air)	70	70

118 Team posing with Shield

1981. World Cup Football Championship, Spain (1982). Multicoloured.

436		60f. Footballers coming on Field (vert)	55	10
437		75f. Type **118**	75	25
438		90f. Captains shaking hands	1·00	25
439		100f. Tackle	1·00	45
440		150f. Players hugging after goal (vert)	1·70	55
MS441		104×80 mm. 500f. Team with cup (vert)	4·50	1·50

119 "Bowls and Pot"

1981. Birth Centenary of Pablo Picasso. Mult.

442		40f. "Dove and Rainbow"	50	10
443		70f. "Still-life on Chest of Drawers"	90	20
444		150f. "Studio with Plaster Head"	1·70	55
445		250f. Type **119**	2·75	80
446		500f. "Red Tablecloth"	5·50	1·60

120 "Apollo" Launch

1981. Conquest of Space. Multicoloured.

447		50f. Type **120**	50	10
448		75f. Space Shuttle launch	65	25
449		100f. Space Shuttle releasing fuel tank	1·00	30
450		450f. Space Shuttle in orbit	4·50	1·50
MS451		104×79 mm. 500f. Space shuttle and carrier aircraft	4·50	1·60

121 Buckingham Palace

1981. British Royal Wedding. Multicoloured.

452		125f. Type **121**	1·20	30
453		200f. Highgrove House	1·80	65
454		450f. Caernarvon Castle	3·75	1·40
MS455		132×97 mm. As Nos. 452/4 but inscriptions and values in magenta	5·00	2·20

1981. Design as Type O 99 but inscr "POSTES 1981".

456		5f. green, black & brn	10	10
457		15f. green, black & yell	10	10
458		25f. green, black & red	30	10
459		35f. green, black & lt grn	45	25
460		75f. green, black & blue	95	40

1981. Various stamps surch.

461	**114**	5f. on 400f. violet, red and mauve (postage)	25	25
462	-	20f. on 90f. mult (No. 438)	45	40
463	-	45f. on 100f. mult (No. 377)	1·20	1·10
464	-	45f. on 100f. mult (No. 420)	1·20	1·10
465	-	10f. on 70f. mult (No. 443) (air)	25	25
466	**110**	10f. on 100f. mult	45	40
467	**102**	50f. on 200f.+30f. mult	1·20	1·10
468	-	50f. on 260f. mult (No. 424)	1·20	1·10

123 Mercedes, 1914

1981. 75th Anniv of French Grand Prix Motor Race. Multicoloured.

469		20f. Type **123**	30	10
470		50f. Delage, 1925	60	15
471		75f. Rudi Caracciola	90	25
472		90f. Stirling Moss	1·00	40
473		150f. Maserati, 1957	1·70	50
MS474		107×86 mm. 500f. Mechanics replacing car tyres (vert)	6·75	1·70

124 Scouts preparing to Sail

1981. 75th Anniv of Boy Scout Movement. Multicoloured.

475		50f. Type **124**	50	25
476		75f. Paddling pirogue	80	40
477		250f. Sailing felucca	2·50	85
478		350f. Scouts looking out to sea from boat	3·50	1·20
MS479		78×102 mm. 500f. Lord Baden-Powell	5·25	1·80

125 Goethe

1982. 150th Death Anniv of Goethe (poet).

480	**125**	75f. multicoloured	75	35
481	**125**	350f. multicoloured	3·50	1·00

126 Princess of Wales

1982. 21st Birthday of Princess of Wales.

482	**126**	200f. multicoloured	1·90	60
483	-	300f. multicoloured	3·00	90
MS484		112×80 mm. 500f. multicoloured	5·00	1·70

DESIGNS: 300, 500f. Different portraits.

1982. Birth of Prince William of Wales. Nos. 452/4 optd NAISSANCE ROYALE 1982.

485		125f. Type **121**	1·30	60
486		200f. Highgrove House	2·10	90
487		450f. Caernarvon Castle	4·00	2·20
MS488		132×97 mm. As Nos. 485/7 but inscriptions and values in magenta	5·75	5·50

1982. World Cup Football Championship Winners. Nos. 436/40 optd.

489		60f. Type **117**	60	25
490		75f. Team posing with shield (horiz)	75	30
491		90f. Captains shaking hands (horiz)	85	45
492		100f. Tackle (horiz)	1·00	45
493		150f. Players hugging after goal	1·50	65
MS494		104×80 mm. 500f. As No. 489	4·50	2·75

OVERPRINTS: 60f., 150f. **ITALIE - ALLEMAGNE (R.F.A.) 3 - 1.**; 75f., 90f., 100f. **ITALIE 3 ALLEMAGNE (R.F.A.) 1.**

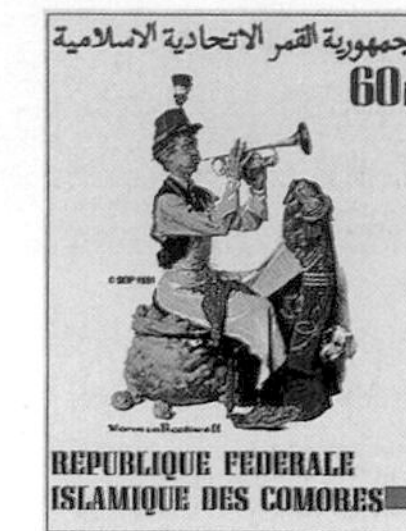

129 Boy playing Trumpet

1982. Norman Rockwell Paintings. Multicoloured.

495		60f. Type **129**	75	25
496		75f. Sleeping porter	75	25
497		100f. Couple listening to early radio	1·20	25
498		150f. Children playing leapfrog	1·70	45
499		200f. Tramp cooking sausages	2·30	55
500		300f. Boy talking to clown	3·25	95

130 Sultan Said Mohamed Sidi

1982. Sultans. Multicoloured.

501		30f. Type **130**	35	10
502		60f. Sultan Ahmed Abdallah	75	10
503		75f. Sultan Salim (horiz)	85	25
504		300f. Sultans Said Mohamed Sidi and Ahmed Abdallah (horiz)	3·25	1·30

131 Montgolfier Brothers' Balloon, 1783

1983. Air. Bicentenary of Manned Flight. Mult.

505	100f. Type **131**	1·20	45
506	200f. Vincenzo Lunardi's balloon over London, 1784	1·80	70
507	300f. Blanchard and Jeffries crossing the Channel, 1785	3·00	95
508	400f. Henri Giffard's steam-powered dirigible airship, 1852 (horiz)	4·25	1·40
MS509	79×103 mm. 500f. Balloon used for carrying post, 1870	5·50	1·70

132 Type "470" Dinghy

1983. Air. Pre-Olympic Year. Multicoloured.

510	150f. Type **132**	1·50	55
511	200f. "Flying Dutchman"	1·80	70
512	300f. Type "470" (different)	3·00	85
513	400f. "Finn" class dinghies	4·25	1·40
MS514	103×80 mm. 500f. Soling yachts	5·25	1·70

133 Lake Ziani

1983. Landscapes. Multicoloured.

515	60f. Type **133**	65	30
516	100f. Sunset	1·00	50
517	175f. Chiromani (vert)	1·70	75
518	360f. Itsandra beach	3·25	1·40
519	400f. Anjouan	4·50	1·80

134 Moheli

1983. Portraits. Multicoloured.

520	30f. Type **134**	35	25
521	35f. "Mask of Beauty"	55	25
522	50f. Mayotte	55	25

135 Pure-bred Arab

1983. Horses. Multicoloured.

523	75f. Type **135**	80	25
524	100f. Anglo-Arab	1·10	30
525	125f. Lipizzan	1·40	50
526	150f. Tennessee	1·60	50
527	200f. Appaloosa	2·00	75
528	300f. Pure-bred English	3·25	1·00
529	400f. Clydesdale	4·25	1·40
530	500f. Andalusian	5·50	1·70

136 "Double Portrait"

1983. 500th Birth Anniv of Raphael. Mult.

531	100f. Type **136**	1·10	45
532	200f. Fresco detail	2·40	80
533	300f. "St. George and the Dragon"	3·50	1·00
534	400f. "Balthazar Castiglione"	4·75	1·40

137 Symbols of Development

1984. Air. International Conference on Development of Comoros.

535	**137**	475f. multicoloured	4·75	2·40

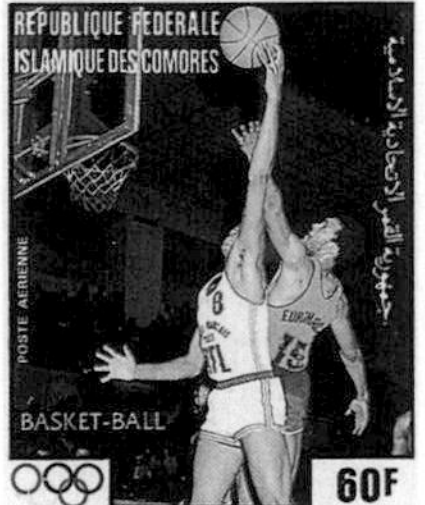

138 Basketball

1984. Air. Olympic Games, Los Angeles. Mult.

536	60f. Type **138**	45	25
537	100f. Basketball (different)	95	40
538	165f. Basketball (different)	1·40	65
539	175f. Baseball (horiz)	1·50	75
540	200f. Baseball (different) (horiz)	1·80	80
MS541	104×80 mm. 500f. Basketball (different) (horiz)	6·00	1·50

139 "William Fawcett"

1984. Transport. Multicoloured. (a) Ships.

542	100f. Type **139**	1·10	40
543	150f. "Lightning"	1·80	60
544	200f. "Rapido"	2·30	90
545	350f. "Sindia"	3·75	1·40

(b) Automobiles.

546	100f. De Dion Bouton and Trepardoux, 1885	1·50	40
547	150f. Benz "Victoria", 1893	2·20	70
548	200f. Colombia electric, 1901	2·75	90
549	350f. Fiat, 1902	4·50	1·40

140 Barn Swallows

1985. Air. Birth Bicentenary of John J. Audubon (ornithologist). Multicoloured.

550	100f. Type **140**	1·00	40
551	125f. Northern oriole	1·30	55
552	150f. Red-shouldered hawk (horiz)	1·60	70
553	500f. Red-breasted sapsucker (horiz)	5·50	2·20

1985. International Exhibitions. Nos. MS451, MS474, MS479, MS509 and MS514 optd.

MS554	Five sheets. (a) 500f. **MOPHILA'85 HAMBOURG**; (b) 500f. **TSUKUBA EXPO '85**; (c) 500f. **ARENTINA'85 BUENOS AIRES**; (d) 500f. **ITALIA '85 ROMA** and emblem; 500f. **OLYMPHILEX '85 LAUSANNE** and emblem	6·75	3·00

142 Harbours

1985. Air. "Philexafrique" Stamp Exhibition, Lome, Togo (1st issue). Multicoloured.

555	200f. Type **142**	2·50	1·60
556	200f. Scouts walking along road	2·50	1·60

See also Nos. 576/7.

143 Victor Hugo (novelist, death centenary)

1985. Anniversaries. Multicoloured.

557	100f. Type **143**	1·30	40
558	200f. Jules Verne (novelist) (80th death anniv)	2·20	80
559	300f. Mark Twain (150th birth anniv)	3·25	1·20
560	450f. Queen Elizabeth, the Queen Mother (85th birth anniv) (vert)	4·50	1·70
561	500f. Statue of Liberty (centenary) (vert)	5·00	2·10

The 200f. and 300f. also commemorate International Youth Year.

144 Map and Flag on Sun

1985. Air. 10th Anniv of Independence.

562	**144**	10f. multicoloured	20	10
563	**144**	15f. multicoloured	30	10
564	**144**	125f. multicoloured	1·80	70
565	**144**	300f. multicoloured	4·25	1·60

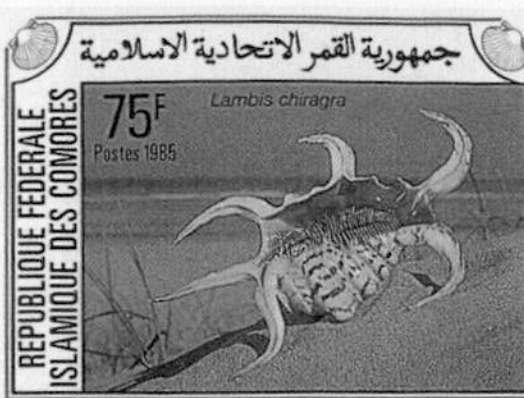

145 Arthritic Spider Conch

1985. Shells. Multicoloured.

566	75f. Type **145**	1·00	30
567	125f. Silver conch	1·50	45
568	200f. Costate tun	2·50	75
569	300f. Elephant's snout	3·75	1·20
570	450f. Orange spider conch	5·50	1·80

146 U.N. Emblem and Map of Islands

1985. 10th Anniv of Membership of UNO.

571	**146**	5f. multicoloured	10	10
572	**146**	30f. multicoloured	20	10
573	**146**	75f. multicoloured	70	30
574	**146**	125f. multicoloured	1·30	50
575	**146**	400f. multicoloured	3·75	1·90

147 Runners ("Youth")

1985. Air. "Philexafrique" Stamp Exhibition, Lome, Togo (2nd issue). Multicoloured.

576	250f. Type **147**	2·50	1·40
577	250f. Earth mover and road construction ("Development")	2·50	1·40

148 Globe, Galleon, Wright Type A Biplane and Rocket Capsule

1985. 20th Anniv of Moroni Rotary Club.

578	**148**	25f. multicoloured	30	10
579	**148**	75f. multicoloured	80	40
580	**148**	125f. multicoloured	1·30	50
581	**148**	500f. multicoloured	4·50	2·30

149 "Astraeus hygrometricus"

1985. Fungi. Multicoloured.

582	75f. "Boletus edulis"	1·20	30
583	125f. "Sarcoscypha coccinea"	1·50	50
584	200f. "Hypholoma fasciculare"	2·50	80
585	350f. Type **149**	3·75	1·30
586	500f. "Armillariella mellea"	5·25	2·10

150 Sikorsky S-43 Amphibian

1985. Air. 50th Anniv of Union des Transports Aeriennes. Multicoloured.

587	25f. Type **150**	25	10
588	75f. Douglas DC-9 airplane and camel	65	30
589	100f. Douglas DC-4, DC-6, Nord 2501 Noratlas and De Havilland Heron 2 aircraft	1·00	55
590	125f. Maintenance	1·30	70
591	1000f. Emblem and Latecoere 28, Sikorsky S-43, Douglas DC-10 and Boeing 747-200 aircraft (35×47 mm)	11·00	5·50
MS592	Two sheets each 131×110 mm. (a) Nos. 587/9; (b) Nos. 590/1	3·25	2·30

151 Edmond Halley, Comet and "Giotto" Space Probe

1986. Air. Appearance of Halley's Comet. Multicoloured.

593	125f. Type **151**	1·20	50
594	150f. Giacobini-Zinner comet, 1959	1·50	65
595	225f. J. F. Encke and Encke comet, 1961	2·30	95
596	300f. Computer enhanced picture of Bradfield comet, 1980	2·75	1·20
597	450f. Halley's comet and "Planet A" space probe	4·50	2·10

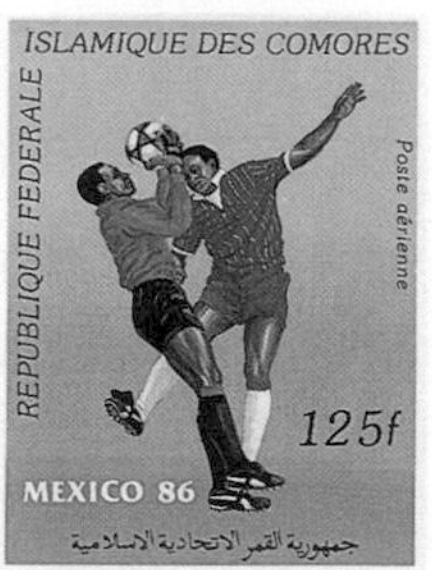

152 Footballers

1986. Air. World Cup Football Championship, Mexico. Designs showing footballers.

598	152	125f. multicoloured	1·20	50
599	-	210f. multicoloured	1·90	90
600	-	500f. multicoloured	4·75	2·20
601	-	600f. multicoloured	5·50	2·50

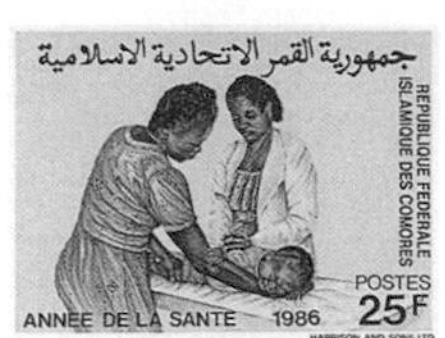

153 Doctor examining Child

1986. World Health Year. Multicoloured.

602	25f. Type **153**	30	10
603	100f. Doctor weighing child	1·00	65
604	200f. Nurse innoculating baby	2·10	1·30

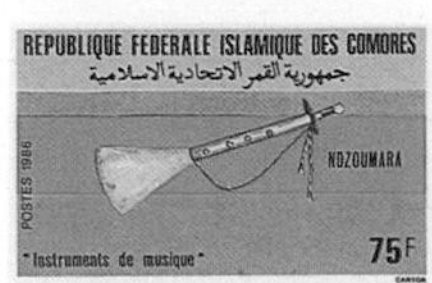

154 Ndzoumara (wind instrument)

1986. Musical Instruments. Multicoloured.

605	75f. Type **154**	80	40
606	125f. Ndzedze (string instrument)	1·20	60
607	210f. Gaboussi (string instrument)	2·00	90
608	500f. Ngoma (drums)	5·00	2·00

155 Server

1987. Air. Tennis as 1988 Olympic Games Discipline. Multicoloured.

609	150f. Type **155**	1·60	55
610	250f. Player preparing shot	2·75	95
611	500f. Player being lobbed	5·00	1·90
612	600f. Players each side of net	6·25	2·30

156 On Tree Branch

1987. Air. Endangered Animals. Mongoose-Lemur. Multicoloured.

613	75f. Type **156**	1·60	40
614	100f. Head of mongoose-lemur with ruff	2·10	55
615	125f. Mongoose-lemur on rock	3·50	90
616	150f. Head of mongoose-lemur without ruff	4·00	1·40

157 Women working in Field

1987. Woman and Development. Multicoloured.

617	75f. Type **157**	80	30
618	125f. Woman picking musk seeds (vert)	1·70	50
619	1000f. Woman making basket	9·50	4·00

158 Men's Downhill

1987. Air. Winter Olympic Games, Calgary (1988). Multicoloured.

620	150f. Type **158**	1·20	55
621	225f. Ski jumping	2·00	90
622	500f. Women's slalom	4·75	2·00
623	600f. Men's luge	5·50	2·50

159 Didier Daurat, Raymond Vanier and "Air Bleu"

1987. Air. Aviation. Multicoloured.

624	200f. Type **159**	2·00	80
625	300f. Letord 4 Lorraine and route map (1st regular airmail service, Paris–Le Mans–St. Nazaire, 1918)	2·75	1·10
626	500f. Morane Saulnier Type H and route map (1st airmail flight, Villacoublay–Pauillac, 1913)	4·75	1·90
627	1000f. Henri Pequet flying Humber-Sommer biplane (1st aerophilately exn, Allahabad) (36×49 mm)	9·50	3·25

160 Ice Skating

1988. Multicoloured. (a) Winter Olympic Games, Calgary.

628	75f. Type **160** (postage)	60	15
629	125f. Speed skating	95	40
630	350f. Two-man bobsleigh	3·00	85
631	400f. Biathlon (air)	3·75	1·10
MS632	116×75 mm. 750f. Slalom	6·75	1·40

(b) Olympic Games, Seoul.

633	100f. Relay (postage)	95	25
634	150f. Showjumping	1·50	45
635	500f. Pole-vaulting	4·50	1·30
636	600f. Football (air)	5·50	1·50
MS637	116×75 mm. 750f. Running	6·75	1·50

161 Kiwanis International Emblem and Hand supporting Figures

1988. Child Health Campaigns. Multicoloured.

638	75f. Type **161**	75	30
639	125f. Kiwanis emblem, wheel-chair and crutch	1·10	50
640	210f. Kiwanis emblem and man with children (country inscr in black)	1·90	85
641	210f. As No. 640 but country inscr in white	2·00	85
642	425f. As No. 639	4·00	1·80
643	425f. As No. 639 but with Lions International emblem	3·75	1·80
644	500f. Type **161**	5·00	2·30
645	500f. As Type **161** but with Rotary emblem	5·00	2·40

162 Throwing the Discus

1988. Olympic Games, Barcelona (1992) (1st issue). Multicoloured.

646	75f. Type **162** (postage)	60	15
647	100f. Rowing (horiz)	95	25
648	125f. Cycling (horiz)	1·20	40
649	150f. Wrestling (horiz)	1·40	55
650	375f. Basketball (air)	3·50	1·00
651	600f. Tennis	5·50	1·20
MS652	90×75 mm. 750f. Marathon See also Nos. 709/MS715	7·25	1·50

See also Nos. 709/14.

163 Columbus and "Santa Maria"

1988. 500th Anniv (1992) of Discovery of America by Columbus. Multicoloured.

653	75f. Type **163** (postage)	60	25
654	125f. Martin Alonzo Pinzon and "Pinta"	1·20	30
655	150f. Vicente Yanez Pinzon and "Nina"	1·40	45
656	250f. Search for gold	2·20	70
657	375f. Wreck of "Santa Maria" (air)	3·50	1·00
658	450f. Preparation for fourth voyage	4·25	1·10
MS659	99×68 mm. 750f. Columbus landing at Samana Cay	7·25	1·50

1988. Nos. 641, 643 and 645 (125 and 400f. with colours changed) surch.

660	75f. on 210f. multicoloured	75	45
661	125f. on 425f. multicoloured	1·00	60
662	200f. on 425f. multicoloured	1·70	80
663	300f. on 500f. multicoloured	2·75	1·20
664	400f. on 500f. multicoloured	3·75	1·90

1988. Olympic Games Medal Winners for Tennis. Nos. 609/12 optd.

665	150f. Optd **Medaille d'or Seoul Miloslav Mecir (Tchec.)**	1·50	70
666	250f. Optd **Medaille d'argent Seoul Tim Mayotte (U.S.A)**	2·50	1·50
667	500f. Optd **Medaille d'or Seoul Steffi Graf (R.F.A.)**	4·50	2·75
668	600f. Optd **Medaille d'argent Seoul Gabriela Sabatini (Argentine)**	5·50	3·50

166 Alberto Santos-Dumont and "14 bis"

1988. Air. Aviation Pioneers.

669	166	100f. purple	1·20	45
670	-	150f. mauve	1·70	60
671	-	200f. black	2·00	80
672	-	300f. brown	2·75	1·50
673	-	500f. blue	4·75	2·40
674	-	800f. green	7·50	3·00

DESIGNS: 150f. Wright Type A and Orville and Wilbur Wright; 200f. Louis Bleriot and Bleriot XI; 300f. Farman Voisin No. 1 bis and Henri Farman; 500f. Gabriel and Charles Voisin and Voisin "Boxkite"; 800f. Roland Garros and Morane Saulnier Type I.

167 Galileo Galilei

1988. Appearance of Halley's Comet. Mult.

675	200f.+10f. Type **167** (postage)	2·00	45
676	200f.+10f. Nicolas Copernicus	2·00	45
677	200f.+10f. Johannes Kepler	2·00	45
678	200f.+10f. Edmond Halley	2·00	45
679	200f.+10f. Japanese "Planet A" space probe	2·00	45
680	200f.+10f. American "Ice" space probe	2·00	45
681	200f.+10f. "Planet A" space probe (different)	2·00	45
682	200f.+10f. Russian "Vega" space probe	2·00	45
MS683	100×75 mm. 750f. Space probe and Halley (41×35 mm) (air)	7·25	1·50

168 Yuri Gagarin (cosmonaut) and Daughters

1988. Personalities. Multicoloured.

684	150f. Type **168** (20th death anniv) (postage)	1·30	40
685	300f. Henri Dunant (founder of Red Cross) (125th anniv of Red Cross Movement)	2·75	85
686	400f. Roger Clemens (baseball player)	3·50	1·10
687	500f. Gary Kasparov (chess player) (air)	5·50	1·10
688	600f. Paul Harris (founder of Rotary International) (birth centenary)	5·50	1·20
MS689	104×84 mm. 750f. John F. Kennedy (American statesman) (25th death anniv) (29×41 mm)	7·25	1·50

169 Alain Prost (racing driver) and Formula 1 Racing Car

1988. Cars, Trains and Yachts. Multicoloured.

690	75f. Type **169** (postage)	1·50	45
691	125f. George Stephenson (railway engineer), "Rocket" and Borsig Class 05 steam locomotive, 1935, Germany	1·30	25
692	500f. Ettore Bugatti (motor manufacturer) and Aravis "Type 57"	4·75	1·10
693	600f. Rudolph Diesel (engineer) and German Class V200 diesel locomotive	5·50	1·30
694	750f. Dennis Conner and "Stars and Stripes" (America's Cup contender) (air)	7·00	1·60
695	1000f. Michael Fay and "New Zealand" (America's Cup contender)	9·25	2·00
MS696	131×85 mm. 1000f. Enzo Ferrari (motor manufacturer) and Formula 1 racing car (50×35 mm)	10·00	1·80

170 "Papilio nireus aristophontes" (female)

1989. Scouts, Butterflies and Birds. Multicoloured.

697	50f. Type **170** (postage)	55	10
698	75f. "Papilio nireus aristophontes" (male)	85	15
699	150f. "Charaxes fulvescens separanus"	1·70	40
700	375f. Bronze mannikin	4·00	70
701	450f. "Charaxes castor comoranus" (air)	4·50	90
702	500f. Madagascar white-eye	5·00	1·10
MS703	116×92 mm. 750f. Red forest fody and "Charaxes paradoxa"	9·00	1·80

171 Aussat "K3" and N. Uphoff (individual dressage)

1989. Satellites and Olympic Games Medal Winners for Equestrian Events. Multicoloured.

704	75f. Type **171** (postage)	70	15
705	150f. "Brasil sat" and P. Durand (individual show jumping)	1·30	40
706	375f. "ECS 4" and J. Martinek (modern pentathlon)	3·50	75
707	600f. "Olympus 1" and M. Todd (cross-country) (air)	5·50	1·40
MS708	97×67 mm. 750f. Satellite and horses	6·75	1·50

172 Running

1989. Olympic Games, Barcelona (1992) (2nd issue). Multicoloured.

709	75f. Type **172** (postage)	75	25
710	150f. Football	1·50	45
711	300f. Tennis	2·75	60
712	375f. Baseball	3·50	80
713	500f. Gymnastics (air)	4·50	1·10
714	600f. Table tennis	5·50	1·40
MS715	90×75 mm. 750f. Show jumping	6·75	1·50

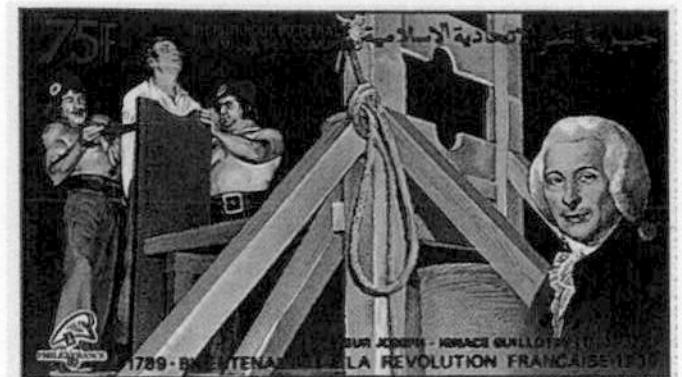

173 Dr. Joseph-Ignace Guillotin and Guillotine

1989. Bicentenary of French Revolution. Mult.

716	75f. Type **173** (postage)	80	25
717	150f. Soldiers with cannon (Battle of Valmy) and Gen. Kellermann	1·70	40
718	375f. Jean Cottereau (Chouan) and Vendeens	3·50	70
719	600f. Invasion of Les Tuileries (air)	5·75	1·60
MS720	113×67 mm. 1000f. Jacques Necker and storming of the Bastille	8·75	2·75

1989. Various stamps surch.

721	25f. on 250f. mult (No. 656) (postage)	35	10
722	150f. on 200f. mult (No. 532)	1·30	55
723	150f. on 200f. mult (No. 558)	1·30	55
724	150f. on 200f. mult (No. 604)	1·30	55
725	5f. on 250f. multicoloured (No. 390) (air)	10	10
726	25f. on 250f. mult (No. 610)	25	20
727	50f. on 250f. mult (No. 576)	45	25
728	50f. on 250f. mult (No. 577)	45	25
729	150f. on 200f. mult (No. 511)	1·40	55
730	150f. on 200f. mult (No. 555)	1·40	55
731	150f. on 200f. mult (No. 556)	1·40	55
732	150f. on 200f. black (No. 671)	1·40	55

175 Airport Pavilion

1990

733	**175**	5f. orange, brown & red	10	10
734	**175**	10f. orange, brown & bl	10	10
735	**175**	25f. orange, brown & grn	10	10
736	-	50f. black and red	45	25
737	-	75f. black and blue	75	25
738	-	150f. black and green	1·40	45

DESIGNS: 50 to 150f. Federal Assembly.

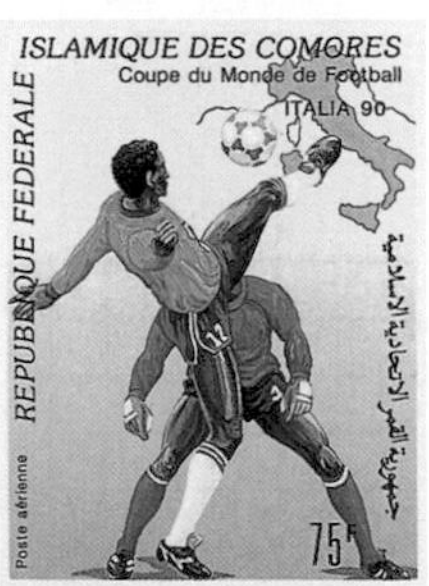

176 Player challenging Goalkeeper

1990. Air. World Cup Football Championship, Italy (1st issue). Multicoloured.

739	75f. Type **176**	95	40
740	150f. Player heading ball	1·50	70
741	500f. Overhead kick	4·25	2·30
742	1000f. Player evading tackle	9·00	2·10

See also Nos. 743/8.

177 Brazilian Player

1990. World Cup Football Championship, Italy (2nd issue). Multicoloured.

743	50f. Type **177** (postage)	45	10
744	75f. English player	75	25
745	100f. West German player	95	30
746	150f. Belgian player	1·40	45
747	375f. Italian player (air)	3·50	1·10
748	600f. Argentinian player	5·50	1·40
MS749	100×80 mm. 750f. Argentine and Italian players	6·75	1·40

178 U.S. Space Telescope

1990. Multicoloured.. Multicoloured..

750	75f. Type **178** (postage)	75	25
751	150f. Pope John Paul II and Mikhail Gorbachev, 1989	1·50	35
752	200f. Kevin Mitchell (San Francisco Giants baseball player)	2·00	45
753	250f. De Gaulle and Adenauer, 1962	2·20	50
754	300f. "Titan 2002" space probe	2·75	70
755	375f. French TGV Atlantique express train and Concorde airplane	3·75	1·00
756	450f. Gary Kasparov (World chess champion) and Anderssen v Steinitz chess match (air)	4·50	1·10
757	500f. Paul Harris (founder of Rotary International) and symbols of health, hunger and humanity	4·50	80
MS758	97×68 mm. 1000f. Lunar module and crew of "Apollo 11" (47×35 mm)	8·75	1·50

179 Edi Reinalter (skiing, 1948)

1990. Winter Olympics, Albertville (1992). Medal Winners at previous Games. Multicoloured.

759	75f. Type **179** (postage)	55	25
760	100f. Canada (ice hockey, 1924)	95	30
761	375f. Baroness Gratia Schimmelpenninck van der Oye (skiing, 1936) (air)	3·25	1·00
762	600f. Hasu Haikki (ski jumping, 1948)	5·50	1·00
MS763	72×87 mm. 750f. Berger and Engelmann (ice skating, 1924) (36×41 mm)	6·75	1·40

180 Dish Aerial, Moroni Volo-volo

1991

764	**180**	75f. multicoloured	85	20
765	**180**	150f. multicoloured	1·60	55
766	**180**	225f. multicoloured	2·20	80
767	**180**	300f. multicoloured	3·00	1·10
768	**180**	500f. multicoloured	4·50	1·40

181 Emblem and Leaves

1991. Indian Ocean Commission Conference.

769	**181**	75f. multicoloured	75	25
770	**181**	150f. multicoloured	1·20	80
771	**181**	225f. multicoloured	2·00	1·20

182 De Gaulle and Battle of Koufra, 1941

1991. 50th Anniv of World War II. Multicoloured.

772	125f. Type **182** (postage)	1·70	30
773	150f. Errol Flynn in "Adventures in Burma"	1·50	50
774	300f. Henry Fonda in "The Longest Day"	3·25	90
775	375f. De Gaulle and Battle of Britain, 1940	3·50	75
776	450f. Humphrey Bogart in "Sahara" (air)	4·50	1·00
777	500f. De Gaulle and Battle of Monte Cassino, 1944	4·50	90
MS778	121×91 mm. 1000f. De Gaulle and "Normandie-Niemen" aircraft, 1943	10·50	2·30

183 Emblem and Stylized View of Exhibition

1991. "Telecom '91" Int Telecommunications Exhibition, Geneva. Multicoloured.

779	75f. Type **183**	1·20	55
780	150f. Emblem (horiz)	1·70	1·30

184 Weather Space Station "Columbus"

1991. Anniversaries and Events. Multicoloured.

781	100f. Type **184** (postage)	1·00	25
782	150f. Gandhi (43rd death anniv)	1·60	40
783	250f. Henri Dunant (founder of Red Cross) (90th anniv of award of Nobel Peace Prize)	2·40	60
784	300f. Wolfgang Amadeus Mozart (composer, death bicentenary)	3·00	70
785	375f. Brandenburg Gate (bicent and second anniv of fall of Berlin Wall)	4·00	95
786	400f. Konrad Adenauer (German Chancellor) signing new constitution (25th death anniv)	4·00	95
787	450f. Elvis Presley (entertainer, 14th death anniv) (air)	5·00	1·00
788	500f. Ferdinand von Zeppelin (airship pioneer, 75th death anniv)	5·00	1·00

185 Cep

1992. Fungi and Shells. Multicoloured.

789	75f. Type **185** (postage)	80	25
790	125f. Textile cone	1·30	45
791	150f. Puff-ball	1·60	55
792	150f. Bull-mouth helmet (shell)	1·60	60
793	500f. Map cowrie (air)	5·75	1·60

794 600f. Scarlet elf cups 5·75 1·10
MS795 100×70 mm. 750f. "Nautilus pompilius" (shell) 8·25 1·80

186 Ham (chimpanzee) on "Mercury" flight, 1960

1992. Space Research. Multicoloured.
796 75f. Type **186** (postage) 90 25
797 125f. "Mars Observer" space probe 1·30 35
798 150f. Felix (cat) and "Veronique" rocket, 1963 1·60 65
799 150f. "Mars Rover" and "Mar-sokod" space vehicles 1·70 70
800 500f. "Phobos" project (air) 5·25 1·40
801 600f. Laika (dog) and "Sputnik 2" flight, 1957 6·25 1·60
MS802 112×80 mm. 1000f. "Viking" space vehicle (29×41 mm) 9·25 2·10

187 "Endeavour" (space shuttle), Capt. James Cook and H.M.S. "Endeavour"

1992. Space and Nautical Exploration. Mult.
803 75f. Type **187** (postage) 90 20
804 100f. "Cariane" space micro-phone, Sir Francis Drake and "Golden Hind" 1·30 25
805 150f. Infra-red astronomical observation device, John Smith and "Susan Constant" 1·70 40
806 225f. Space probe "B", Robert F. Scott and "Discovery" 2·20 70
807 375f. "Magellan" (Venus space probe), Ferdinand Magellan and ship (air) 4·00 95
808 500f. "Newton" (satellite), Vasco da Gama and "Sao Gabriel" 6·25 2·75
MS809 112×77 mm. 1000f. "Hermes-Columbus" (spacescraft), Christopher Columbus and fleet 9·75 2·10

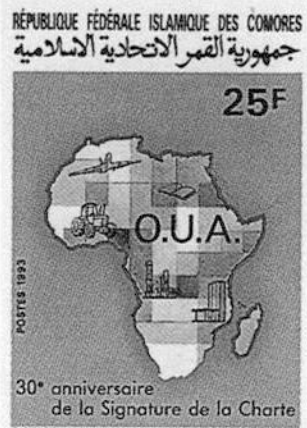

188 Map

1993. 30th Anniv of Organization of African Unity.
810 **188** 25f. multicoloured 10 10
811 **188** 50f. multicoloured 45 25
812 **188** 75f. multicoloured 90 50
813 **188** 150f. multicoloured 1·50 1·10

189 Footballers

1993. World Cup Football Championship, U.S.A. (1994).
814 **189** 25f. multicoloured 30 15
815 **189** 75f. multicoloured 75 25
816 **189** 100f. multicoloured 1·00 40
817 **189** 150f. multicoloured 1·40 55

190 ITU Emblem

1993. World Telecommunications Day. "Telecommunications and Human Development".
818 **190** 50f. multicoloured 45 25
819 **190** 75f. multicoloured 75 25
820 **190** 100f. multicoloured 1·00 40
821 **190** 150f. multicoloured 1·50 80

191 Edaphosaurus

1994. Prehistoric Animals. Multicoloured.
822 75f. Type **191** 55 25
823 75f. Moschops 55 25
824 75f. Kentrosaurus 55 25
825 75f. Compsognathus 55 25
826 75f. Sauroctonus 55 25
827 75f. Ornitholestes 55 25
828 75f. Styracosaurus 55 25
829 75f. Acanthopholis 55 25
830 150f. Edmontonia 85 25
831 150f. Struthiomimus 85 25
832 150f. Diatryma 85 25
833 150f. Uintatherium 85 25
834 450f. Dromiceiomimus 3·00 90
835 450f. Iguanodon 3·00 90
836 525f. Synthetoceras 3·50 90
837 525f. Euryapteryx 3·50 90
MS838 149×106 mm. 1200f. Tyrannosaurus rex (41×59 mm) 9·50 2·75

192 "Hibiscus syriacus"

1994. Plants. Multicoloured.
839 75f. Type **192** 45 25
840 75f. Cashew nut 45 25
841 75f. Butter mushroom 45 25
842 150f. "Pyrostegia venusta" (flower) 95 25
843 150f. Manioc (root) 95 25
844 150f. "Lycogala epidendron" (fungus) 95 25
845 525f. "Allamanda cathartica" (flower) 3·50 1·00
846 525f. Cacao (nut) 3·50 1·00
847 525f. "Clathrus ruber" (fungus) 4·00 1·20

193 Purple-tip ("Colotis zoe")

1994. Insects. Multicoloured.
848 75f. Type **193** 45 25
849 75f. "Charaxes comoranus" (butterfly) 45 25
850 75f. "Hypurgus ova" (beetle) 45 25
851 150f. Death's-head hawk moth ("Acherontia atropos") 95 30
852 150f. "Verdant hawk moth ("Euchloron megaera") 95 30
853 150f. "Onthophagus catta" (beetle) 95 30
854 450f. African monarch ("Danaus chrysippus") (butterfly) 3·50 90
855 450f. "Papilio phorbanta" (butterfly) 3·50 90
856 450f. "Echinosoma bolivari" (beetle) 3·50 90

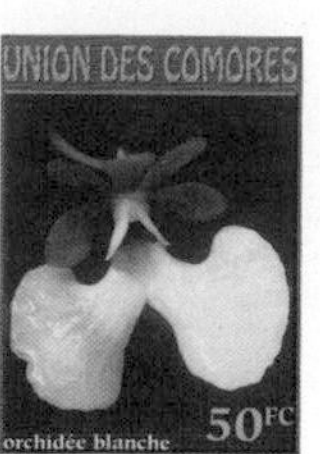

212 Blue and White Orchid

2003. Orchids. Designs showing orchids. Multicoloured.
986 50f. Type **212**
987 75f. Mottled yellow and brown
988 100f. Mauve
989 600f. Red lip and mottled hood

Nos. 857/980 and Types **193**/**210** have been left for surcharges.

Nos. 981/5 and Type **211** have been left for 'Traditional Clothes', issued on 8 April 2002, not yet received.

213 *Cananga odorata* (ylang ylang)

2003. Plants. Multicoloured.
990 50f. Type **213**
991 600f. *Vanilla planifolia* (vanilla)

214 *Peponocephala electra* (melon-headed whale)

2003. Marine Mammals. Multicoloured.
992 75f. Type **214**
993 1000f. *Megaptera novaeangliae* (inscr 'nouaeangliae') (hump-back whale)

215 Door

2003. Crafts. Multicoloured.
994 100f. Type **215**
995 300f. Carved back rest and woven carpet

216 Presidents Azali Assoumani and Hu Jintao (China)

2005. 30th Anniversary of Comoros—China Diplomatic Relations.Multicoloured.
996 125f. Type **216**

Nos. 997/9 have been left for stamps not yet received.

217 Leopold Senghor

2007. Birth Centenary of Léopold Sédar Senghor (poet and president of Senegal (1960–1980)). T 217 and similar multicoloured designs.
1000 125f. Type **217**
1001 125f. Inscription at right and country name at lower margin (horiz)
1002 300f. As No. 1001 (country name at upper margin) (horiz)
1003 300f. As No. 1000 (country name at lower margin)
1004 350f. As Type **217**
1005 500f. As Type **217** (country name at lower margin)

218 *Cymbopogon citratus*

2007. Plants. T 218 and similar vert designs. Multicoloured.
1006 75f. Type **218**
1007 125f. *Ocimum suave*
1008 150f. *Aloe molucaca*
1009 250f. As Type **218**
1010 300f. As No. 1008
1011 500f. As No. 1007

OFFICIAL STAMPS

O99 Comoro Flag

1979
O379 **O99** 5f. grn, blk & azure 10 10
O380 **O99** 10f. grn, blk & grey 10 10
O381 **O99** 20f. grn, blk & stone 10 10
O382 **O99** 30f. green, blk & bl 35 10
O383 **O99** 40f. grn, blk & yell 65 25
O384 **O99** 60f. grn, blk & lt grn 50 25
O384a **O99** 75f. grn, blk & lt grn 45 25
O385 **O99** 100f. grn, blk & yell 1·10 60
O386 - 100f. mult 80 50
O386a - 125f. mult 1·30 70

O387	-	400f. mult	3·50	1·70

DESIGNS: Nos. O386, O386a, O387, Pres. Cheikh.

POSTAGE DUE STAMPS

D9 Mosque in Anjouan

1950

D16	**D9**	50c. green	65	6·75
D17	**D9**	1f. brown	65	6·75

D10 Coelacanth

1954

D18	**D10**	5f. sepia and green	40	7·50
D19	**D10**	10f. violet and brown	4·00	7·50
D20	**D10**	20f. indigo and blue	2·00	9·00

D78 Pineapple

1977. Multicoloured.. Multicoloured..

D244	1f. Hibiscus (horiz)	10	10
D245	2f. Type D **78**	10	10
D246	5f. White butterfly (horiz)	10	10
D247	10f. Chameleon (horiz)	10	10
D248	15f. Banana flower (horiz)	10	10
D249	20f. Orchid (horiz)	10	10
D250	30f. "Allamanda cathartica" (horiz)	40	10
D251	40f. Cashew nuts	70	10
D252	50f. Custard apple	75	10
D253	100f. Breadfruit (horiz)	1·40	40
D254	200f. Vanilla (horiz)	3·25	95
D255	500f. Ylang-ylang flower (horiz)	7·75	2·10

APPENDIX

The following stamps have either been issued in excess of postal needs or have not been available to the public in reasonable quantites at face values. Such stamps may later be given full postal listing if there is evidence of regular postal use.

1975

Various stamps optd **ETAT COMORIEN** or surch also.
Birds issue (No. 60). 10f. on 2f.
Fishes issue (No. 71). Air 50f.
Birds issue (No. 99). 40f.
Comoro Landscapes issue (Nos. 102/4). Air 75f. on 65f., 100f. on 85f., 100f.
Tropical Plants issue (Nos. 105/9). Postage 5f. on 1f., 5f. on 3f.; Air 75f. on 60f., 100f. on 85f.
Seashells issue (No. 114). 75f. on 60f.
Aquatic Sports issue (No. 122). Air 75f. on 70f.
Anjouan Landscapes issue (Nos. 126/8). Air 40f., 75f. on 60f., 100f.
Said Mohamed Cheikh issue (Nos. 129/30). Air 20f., 35f.
Great Comoro Landscapes issue (Nos. 134 and 136). Postage 35f.; Air 200f. on 135f.
Moroni Buildings issue (No. 139). 20f.
Karthala Volcano issue (No. 140). Air 200f. on 120f.
Hansen issue (No. 141). Air 100f.
Copernicus issue (No. 142). Air 400f. on 150f.
Picasso issue (No. 143). Air 200f.
Mosques issue (Nos. 145/6). 15f. on 20f., 25f. on 35f.
Star of Anjouan issue (No. 147). 500f.
Said Omar Ben Soumeth issue (Nos. 148/9). Air 100f. on 135f., 200f.
Shaikh Said Mohamed issue (No. 150). 30f. on 35f.
Handicrafts issue (Nos. 153/5). 20f., 30f. on 35f., 75f.
Mayotte Landscapes issue (Nos. 157/60). Air 10f. on 20f., 30f. on 35f., 100f. on 90f., 200f. on 120f.
UPU Centenary issue (No. 161). 500f. on 30f.
Air Service issue (No. 162). Air 100f. on 135f.
Rotary issue (No. 163). Air 400f. on 250f.
Handicrafts issue (Nos. 164/7). 15f. on 20f., 30f. on 35f., 100f. on 120f., 200f. on 135f.
Moheli Landscapes issue (Nos. 168/71). Postage 30f., 50f., 50f. on 55f.; Air 200f. on 230f.
Coelacanth issue (No. 172). 50f.
Folk-dances issue (Nos. 173/4). 100f., 100f. on 150f.
Apollo-Soyuz Space Test Project. Postage 10, 30, 50f.; Air 100, 200, 400f. Embossed on gold foil. Air 1500f.

1976

Bicent of American Revolution. Postage 15, 25, 35, 40, 75f.; Air 500f. Embossed on gold foil: Air 1000f.
Winter Olympic Games, Innsbruck. Postage 5, 30, 35, 50f.; Air 200, 400f. Embossed on gold foil. Air 1000f.
Children's Stories. Postage 15, 30, 35, 40, 50f.; Air 400f.
Telephone Centenary. Postage 10, 25, 75f.; Air 100, 200, 500f.
Bicentenary of American Revolution (Early Settler and Viking Space Rocket). Embossed on gold foil. Air 1500f.
Bicent of American Revolution (J. F. Kennedy and Apollo). Embossed on gold foil. Air 1500f.

1978

World Cup Football Championship, Argentina. Embossed on gold foil. Air 1000f.
Death Centenary of Sir Rowland Hill. Embossed on gold foil. Air 1500f.
Argentina's World Cup Victory. Optd on World Cup issue. Air 1000f.

1979

International Year of the Child. Embossed on gold foil. Air 1500f.

1988

Rotary International. Embossed on gold foil. Air 1500f.

1989

Scouts, Butterflies and Birds. Embossed on gold foil. Air 1500f.
Satellites and Olympic Winners. Embossed on gold foil. Air 1500f.
Bicentenary of French Revolution. Embossed on gold foil. Air 1500f.

1990

World Cup Football Championship. Embossed on gold foil. Air 1500f.
Winter Olympic Games, Albertville (1992). Embossed on gold foil. Air 1500f.

1991

Birth Centenary of Charles De Gaulle (1990). Embossed on gold foil. Air 1500f.

1992

Olympic Games, Barcelona. Boxing. Embossed on gold foil. Air 1500f.

1997

Diana, Princess of Wales Commemoration. 150×9a. Sheetlet of 9 375f.×6a. Sheetlet of 6
Mother Teresa Commemoration. 200f.

1998

Cats. 200×2, 375, 375.×6a. Sheetlet of 6, 375f.×6a. Sheetlet of 6
Marine Life. 150×9a. Sheetlet of 9, 150f.×9a. Sheetlet of 9, Coelacanth. 200f.×4a. Strip of 4
Classic Cars. 150f.×9a. Sheetlet of 9
Diana, Princess of Wales Commemoration. 250×9a. Sheetlet of 9, 350×9a. Sheetlet of 9, 450×9a. Sheetlet of 9
Personalities. 300×9a. Sheetlet of 9, 500f.×9a. Sheetlet of 9

1999

Birds. 75×2, 150×2,200×2, 375×2, 375×9a. Sheetlet of 9, 375f.×9a. Sheetlet of 9
Fauna. 150f.×8a. Sheetlet of 8, 150f.×8a. Sheetlet of 8, 150f.×8a. Sheetlet of 8
Classic Cars. 150f.×9a. Sheetlet of 9
Fish. 75×2, 150×2, 375f.×2
Endangered Species. 375f.×6a. Sheetlet of 6
Fungi. 375f.×6a. Sheetlet of 6
I Love Lucy. 250×9a. Sheetlet of 9
Cartoons. 300×9a. Sheetlet of 9, 450×9a. Sheetlet of 9

Pt. 22

CONFEDERATE STATES OF AMERICA

Stamps issued by the seceding states in the American Civil War.

100 cents = 1 Dollar

1 Jefferson Davis   2 T. Jefferson

1861. Imperf.

1	**1**	5c. green	£325	£200
3	**2**	10c. blue	£350	£225

3 Jackson

1862. Imperf.

4	**3**	2c. green	£1000	£850
5	**1**	5c. blue	£250	£140
6	**2**	10c. red	£1700	£550

4 Jefferson Davis

1862. Imperf.

7	**4**	5c. blue	17·00	31·00

5 Jackson   6 Jefferson Davis   9 Washington

1863. Imperf or perf (10c.).

9	**5**	2c. red	80·00	£400
10	**6**	10c. blue (TEN CENTS)	£1000	£650
12	**6**	10c. blue (10 CENTS)	17·00	23·00
14	**9**	20c. green	45·00	£450

Pt. 6, Pt. 12

CONGO (BRAZZAVILLE)

Formerly Middle Congo. An independent republic within the French Community.

1 "Birth of the Republic"

1959. 1st Anniv of Republic.

1	**1**	25f. multicoloured	90	40

1960. 10th Anniv of African Technical Co-operation Commission. As T **62** of Cameroun.

2	50f. lake and green	1·20	1·10

1960. Air. Olympic Games. No. 276 of French Equatorial Africa optd with Olympic rings and **XVIIe OLYMPIADE 1960 REPUBLIQUE DU CONGO 250F.**

3	250f. on 500f. blue, black & grn	8·75	8·25

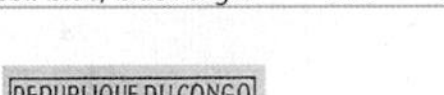

2 Pres. Youlou

1960

4	**2**	15f. green, red and turquoise	45	25
5	**2**	85f. blue and red	1·80	65

3 U.N. Emblem, map and Flag

1961. Admission into UNO.

6	**3**	5f. multicoloured	30	10
7	**3**	20f. multicoloured	45	25
8	**3**	100f. multicoloured	1·90	1·20

4 "Thesium tencio"

1961. Air.

9	-	100f. purple, yellow & green	3·00	1·70
10	-	200f. yellow, turq & brown	5·25	2·50
11	**4**	500f. yellow, myrtle & brown	14·50	6·25

FLOWERS: 100f. "Helicrysum mechowiam"; 200f. "Cogniauxia podolaena".

1961. Air. Foundation of "Air Afrique" Airline. As T **69** of Cameroun.

12	50f. purple, myrtle and green	1·50	80

6 Rainbow Runner

1961. Tropical Fish.

13	**6**	50c. multicoloured	30	10
14	-	1f. brown and green	30	10
15	-	2f. brown and blue	30	15
15a	-	2f. red, brown and green	70	40
16	**6**	3f. green, orange and blue	40	25
17	-	5f. sepia, brown and green	70	40
18	-	10f. brown and turquoise	1·40	40
18a	-	15f. purple, green & violet	2·40	1·40

FISH: 1, 2f. (No. 15), Sloan's viperfish ("Chauliodus sloanei"); 2f. (No. 15a), Fishes pursued by squid; 5f. Giant marine hatchetfish; 10f. Long-toothed fangtooth; 15f. Johnson's deep sea angler.

7 Brazzaville Market

1962

19	**7**	20f. red, green and black	75	45

1962. Malaria Eradication. As T **70** of Cameroun.

20	25f.+5f. brown	95	90

8 "Yang-tse" (freighter) loading Timber, Pointe Noire

1962. Air. International Fair, Pointe Noire.

21	**8**	50f. multicoloured	1·50	1·00

1962. Sports. As T **12** of Central African Republic.

22	20f. sepia, red & blk (postage)	45	30
23	50f. sepia, red and black	95	60
24	100f. sepia, red and black (air)	2·50	1·50

DESIGNS—HORIZ: 20f. Boxing; 50f. Running. VERT: (26×47 mm): 100f. Basketball.

1962. Union of African and Malagasy States. 1st Anniv. As No. 328 of Cameroun.

25	**72**	30f. violet	1·20	75

1962. Freedom from Hunger. As T **76** of Cameroun.

26	25f.+5f. turquoise, brn & bl	95	90

9 Town Hall, Brazzaville and Pres. Youlou

1963. Air.

27	**9**	100f. multicoloured	£170	£140

9a "Costus spectabilis" (K. Schum)

1963. Air. Flowers. Multicoloured.

28		100f. Type **9a**	4·00	2·10
29		250f. "Acanthus montanus T. anders"	7·75	3·75

1963. Air. African and Malagasy Posts and Telecommunications Union. As T **18** of Central African Republic.

30		85f. red, buff and violet	1·50	80

1963. Space Telecommunications. As Nos. 37/8 of Central African Republic.

31		25f. blue, orange and green	75	45
32		100f. violet, brown and blue	1·70	1·30

10 King Makoko's Gold Chain

1963. Folklore and Tourism.

33	**10**	10f. bistre and black	40	25
34	-	15f. multicoloured	55	30

DESIGN: 15f. Kebekebe mask.

See also Nos. 45/6 and 62/4.

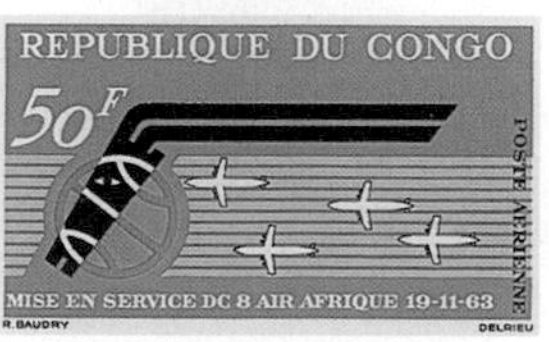

11 Airline Emblem

1963. Air. 1st Anniv of "Air Afrique", and Inaug of DC-8 Service.

35	**11**	50f. multicoloured	95	65

12 Liberty Square, Brazzaville

1963. Air.

36	**12**	25f. multicoloured	85	55

See also No. 56.

1963. Air. European-African Economic Convention. As T **24** of Central African Republic.

37		50f. multicoloured	1·30	90

1963. 15th Anniv of Declaration of Human Rights. As T **26** of Central African Republic.

38		25f. blue, turquoise & brown	80	45

13 Statue of Hathor, Abu Simbel

1964. Air. Nubian Monuments.

39	**13**	10f.+5f. violet & brown	75	45
40	**13**	25f.+5f. brown & turq	95	65
41	**13**	50f.+5f. turquoise & brn	1·90	1·40

14 Barograph

1964. World Meteorological Day.

42	**14**	50f. brown, blue & green	1·00	80

15 Machinist

1964. "Technical Instruction".

43	**15**	20f. brown, mauve & turq	75	45

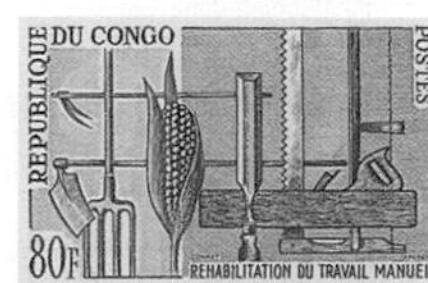

16 Emblem and Implements of Manual Labour

1964. Manual Labour Rehabilitation.

44	**16**	80f. green, red and sepia	1·20	80

17 Diaboua Ballet

1964. Folklore and Tourism. Multicoloured.

45		30f. Type **17**	1·10	55
46		60f. Kebekebe dance (vert)	2·10	1·00

18 Tree-felling

1964. Air.

47	**18**	100f. brown, red and green	2·20	1·00

19 Wood Carving

1964. Congo Sculpture.

48	**19**	50f. sepia and red	1·40	75

20 Students in Classroom

1964. Development of Education.

49	**20**	25f. red, purple and blue	75	45

1964. Air. 5th Anniv of Equatorial African Heads of State Conference. As T **31** of Central African Republic.

50		100f. multicoloured	1·50	90

21 Sun, Ears of Wheat, and Globe within Cogwheel

1964. Air. Europafrique.

51	**21**	50f. yellow, blue and red	1·00	70

22 Stadium, Olympic Flame and Throwing the Hammer

1964. Air. Olympic Games, Tokyo. Sport and flame orange.

52	**22**	25f. violet and brown	55	25
53	-	50f. purple and olive	95	55
54	-	100f. green and brown	2·10	1·10
55	-	200f. olive and red	3·75	2·20
MS55a		191×100 mm. Nos. 52/5	9·50	9·00

DESIGNS—Stadium, Olympic Flame and: VERT: 50f. Weightlifting; 100f. Volleyball. HORIZ: 200f. High-jumping.

1964. 1st Anniv of Revolution and National Festival. As T **12** but inscr "1er ANNIVERSAIRE DE LA REVOLUTION FETE NATIONALE 15 AOUT 1964".

56		20f. multicoloured	55	25

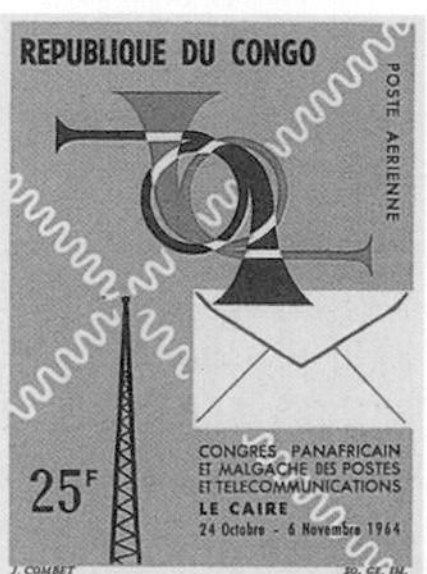

23 Posthorns, Envelope and Radio Mast

1964. Air. Pan-African and Malagasy Posts and Telecommunications Congress, Cairo.

57	**23**	25f. sepia and red	55	40

1964. French, African and Malagasy Co-operation. As T **88** of Cameroun.

58		25f. brown, green and red	75	45

24 Dove, Envelope and Radio Mast

1965. Establishment of Posts and Telecommunications Office, Brazzaville.

59	**24**	25f. multicoloured	55	30

25 Town Hall, Brazzaville and Arms

1965. Air.

60	**25**	100f. multicoloured	1·50	70

26 "Europafrique"

1965. Air. Europafrique.

61	**26**	50f. multicoloured	1·00	70

27 African Elephant

1965. Folklore and Tourism.

62	-	15f. purple, green and blue	1·20	70
63	**27**	20f. black, blue and green	1·20	70
64	-	85f. multicoloured	3·75	4·00

DESIGNS—VERT: 15f. Bushbuck; 85f. Dancer on stilts.

28 Cadran de Breguet's Telegraph and "Telstar"

1965. Air. Centenary of ITU.

65	**28**	100f. brown and blue	2·50	1·10

29 Pres. Massamba-Debat

1965. Portrait in sepia.

66	**29**	20f. yellow, green & brown	30	15
66a	**29**	25f. green, turquoise & brn	45	25
66b	**29**	30f. orange, turq & brn	45	25

30 Sir Winston Churchill

1965. Air. Famous Men.

67	-	25f. on 50f. sepia and red	75	70
68	**30**	50f. sepia and green	1·50	1·40
69	-	80f. sepia and blue	2·40	2·20
70	-	100f. sepia and yellow	3·00	2·75
MS70a		106×145 mm. Nos. 67/70	5·00	5·00

PORTRAITS: 25f. Lumumba; 80f. Pres. Boganda; 100f. Pres. Kennedy.

31 Pope John XXIII

1965. Air. Pope John Commemoration.
71 **31** 100f. multicoloured 2·00 1·40

32 Athletes and Map of Africa

1965. 1st African Games, Brazzaville. Inscr "PREMIERS JEUX AFRICAINS". Mult.
72 25f. Type **32** 55 40
73 40f. Football (34½×34½ mm) 95 45
74 50f. Handball (34½×34½ mm) 95 55
75 85f. Running (34½×34½ mm) 1·30 75
76 100f. Cycling (34½×34½ mm) 1·80 1·40
MS76a 137×169 mm. Nos. 72/6 8·75 8·25

33 Natives hauling Log

1965. Air. National Unity.
77 **33** 50f. brown and green 95 60

34 "World Co-operation"

1965. Air. International Co-operation Year.
78 **34** 50f. multicoloured 1·20 85

35 Arms of Congo

1965
79 **35** 20f. multicoloured 55 25

36 Lincoln

1965. Air. Death Centenary of Abraham Lincoln.
80 **36** 90f. multicoloured 1·50 70

37 Trench-digging

1966. Village Co-operative.
81 **37** 25f. multicoloured 45 25

1966. National Youth Day. As T **37** but showing youth display.
82 30f. multicoloured 55 40

38 De Gaulle and Flaming Torch

1966. Air. 22nd Anniv of Brazzaville Conference.
83 **38** 500f. brown, red & green 34·00 25·00

39 Weaving

1966. World Festival of Negro Arts, Dakar. Multicoloured.
84 30f. Type **39** 75 35
85 85f. Musical Instrument (horiz) 1·90 85
86 90f. Mask 2·00 1·20

40 People and Clocks

1966. Establishment of Shorter Working Day.
87 **40** 70f. multicoloured 1·20 45

41 WHO Building

1966. Inaug of WHO Headquarters, Geneva.
88 **41** 50f. violet, yellow and blue 95 50

42 Satellite "D1" and Brazzaville Tracking Station

1966. Air. Launching of Satellite "D1".
89 **42** 150f. black, red and green 2·75 1·50

43 St. Pierre Claver Church

1966
90 **43** 70f. multicoloured 1·20 60

44 Volleyball

1966. Sports.
91 **44** 1f. brown, bistre and blue 10 10
92 - 2f. brown, green and blue 20 10
93 - 3f. brown, lake and green 30 20
94 - 5f. brown, blue and green 30 20
95 - 10f. violet, turquoise & grn 55 25
96 - 15f. brown, violet and lake 75 35
DESIGNS—VERT: 2f. Basketball; 5f. Sportsmen; 10f. Athlete; 15f. Football. HORIZ: 3f. Handball.

45 Jules Rimet Cup and Globe

1966. World Cup Football Championship, England.
97 **45** 30f. multicoloured 1·00 50

46 Corn, Atomic Emblem and Map

1966. Air. Europafrique.
98 **46** 50f. multicoloured 95 60

47 Pres. Massamba-Debat and Presidential Palace, Brazzaville

1966. Air. 3rd Anniv of Congolese Revolution. Multicoloured.
99 25f. Type **47** 40 25
100 30f. Robespierre and Bastille, Paris 55 25
101 50f. Lenin and Winter Palace, St. Petersburg 1·30 40
MS102 132×160 mm. Nos. 99/101 2·20 2·10

1966. Air. Inauguration of DC-8F Air Services. As T **54** of Central African Republic.
103 30f. yellow, black and violet 75 25

48 Dr. Albert Schweitzer

1966. Air. Schweitzer Commemoration.
104 **48** 100f. multicoloured 2·50 1·20

49 View of School

1966. Inaug of Savorgnan de Brazza High School.
105 **49** 30f. multicoloured 75 30

50 Pointe-Noire Railway Station

1966
106 **50** 60f. red, brown and green 1·30 80

51 Silhouette of Congolese, and UNESCO Emblem

1966. 20th Anniv of UNESCO.
107 **51** 90f. blue, brown & green 1·50 90

52 Balumbu Mask

1966. Congolese Masks.
108 **52** 5f. sepia and red 40 20
109 - 10f. brown and blue 50 20
110 - 15f. blue, sepia & brown 60 25
111 - 20f. multicoloured 95 30
MASKS: 10f. Kuyu; 15f. Bakwele; 20f. Bateke.

53 Cancer "The Crab", Microscope and Pagoda

1966. Air. 9th Int Cancer Congress, Tokyo.
112 **53** 100f. multicoloured 1·70 1·20

54 Sociable Weaver

1967. Air. Birds. Multicoloured.

113	50f. Type **54**	1·60	60
114	75f. European bee eater	3·25	1·10
115	100f. Lilac-breasted roller	3·25	1·10
116	150f. Regal sunbird	4·00	2·30
117	200f. South African crowned crane	7·25	2·75
118	250f. Secretary bird	8·75	3·25
119	300f. Black-billed turaco	13·00	6·00

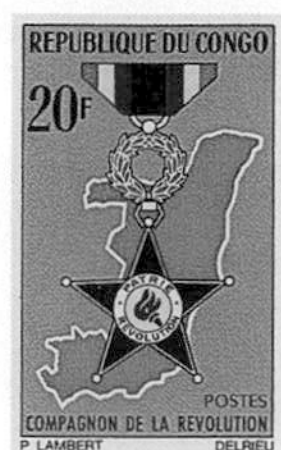

55 Medal, Ribbon and Map

1967. "Companion of the Revolution" Order.

120	**55**	20f. multicoloured	55	35

56 Learning the Alphabet (Educational Campaign)

1967. Education and Sugar Production Campaigns. Multicoloured.

121	25f. Type **56**	75	50
122	45f. Cutting sugar-cane	1·20	60

57 Mahatma Gandhi

1967. Gandhi Commemoration.

123	**57**	90f. black and blue	2·00	80

58 Prisoner's Hands in Chains

1967. Air. African Liberation Day.

124	**58**	500f. multicoloured	10·00	4·00

59 Ndumba, Lady of Fashion

1967. Congolese Dolls. Multicoloured.

125	5f. Type **59**	30	10
126	10f. Fruit seller	45	20
127	25f. Girl pounding saka-saka	50	25
128	30f. Mother and child	60	25

60 Congo Scenery

1967. International Tourist Year.

129	**60**	60f. red, orange and green	95	60

61 "Europafrique"

1967. Europafrique.

130	**61**	50f. multicoloured	95	45

62 "Sputnik 1" and "Explorer 6"

1967. Air. Space Exploration.

131	**62**	50f. blue, violet & brown	75	40
132	-	75f. lake and slate	1·20	55
133	-	100f. blue, red & turquoise	2·00	1·00
134	-	200f. red, blue and lake	3·00	1·90

DESIGNS: 75f. "Ranger 6" and "Lunik 2"; 100f. "Mars 1" and "Mariner 4"; 200f. "Gemini" and "Vostok".

63 Brazzaville Arms

1967. 4th Anniv of Congo Revolution.

135	**63**	30f. multicoloured	75	45

1967. Air. 5th Anniv of African and Malagasy Posts and Telecommunications Union. As T **66** of Central African Republic.

136	100f. green, red and brown	1·50	80

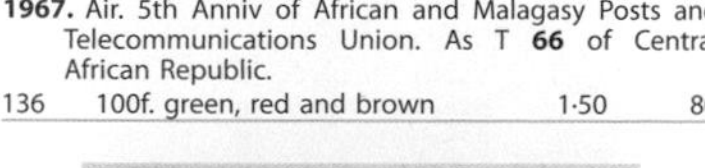

64 Jamboree Emblem, Scouts and Tents

1967. Air. World Scout Jamboree, Idaho.

137	**64**	50f. blue, brown & chestnut	85	30
138	-	70f. red, green and blue	1·30	60

DESIGN: 70f. Saluting hand, Jamboree camp and emblem.

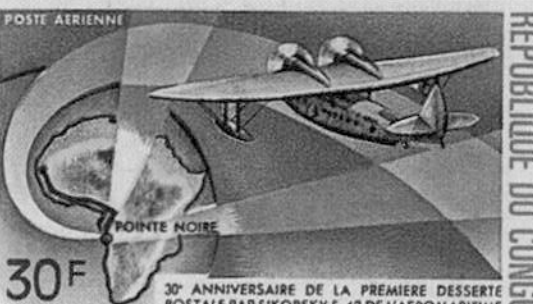

65 Sikorsky S-43 Amphibian and Map

1967. Air. 30th Anniv of Aeromaritime Airmail Link.

139	**65**	30f. multicoloured	75	45

66 Dove, Human Figures and U.N. Emblem

1967. U.N. Day and Campaign in Support of U.N.

140	**66**	90f. multicoloured	1·70	85

67 Young Congolese

1967. 21st Anniv of UNICEF.

141	**67**	90f. black, blue & brown	1·70	85

68 Albert Luthuli (winner of Nobel Peace Prize) and Dove

1968. Luthuli Commemoration.

142	**68**	30f. brown and green	75	50

69 Global Dance

1968. Air. "Friendship of the Peoples".

143	**69**	70f. brown, green & blue	1·00	55

70 Arms of Pointe Noire

1968

144	**70**	10f. multicoloured	50	30

71 "Old Man and His Grandson" (Ghirlandaio)

1968. Air. Paintings. Multicoloured.

145	30f. Type **71**	70	45
146	100f. "The Horatian Oath" (J.-L. David) (horiz)	2·20	1·00
147	200f. "The Negress with Peonies" (Bazille) (horiz)	4·75	3·00

See also Nos. 209/13.

72 "Mother and Child"

1968. Mothers' Festival.

148	**72**	15f. black, blue and red	55	40

73 Diesel Train crossing Mayombe Viaduct

1968

149	**73**	45f. lake, blue and green	2·00	70

74 Beribboned Rope

1968. Air. 5th Anniv of Europafrique.

150	**74**	50f. multicoloured	1·00	50

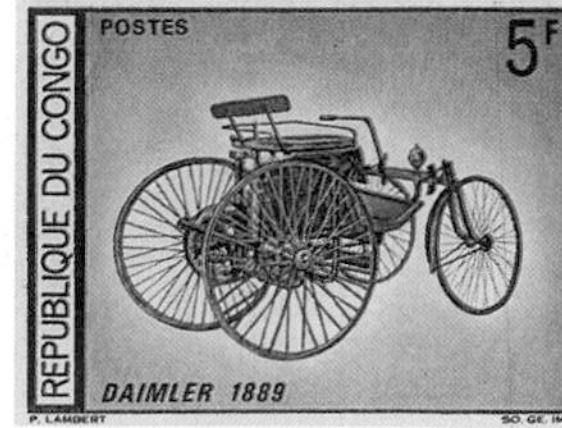

75 Daimler, 1889

1968. Veteran Motor Cars. Multicoloured.

151	5f. Type **75** (postage)	45	25
152	20f. Berliet, 1897	85	45
153	60f. Peugeot, 1898	1·70	70
154	80f. Renault, 1900	2·30	1·10
155	85f. Fiat, 1902	3·25	1·90
156	150f. Ford, 1915 (air)	4·50	2·20
157	200f. Citroen	4·75	2·10

1968. Inauguration of Petroleum Refinery, Port Gentil, Gabon. As T **80** of Central African Republic.

158	30f. multicoloured	95	35

76 Dr. Martin Luther King

1968. Air. Martin Luther King Commemoration.

159 **76** 50f. black, green & emerald 1·20 40

77 "The Barricade" (Delacroix)

1968. Air. 5th Anniv of Revolution Paintings. Multicoloured.

160 25f. Type **77** 1·90 75
161 30f. "Destruction of the Bastille" (H. Robert) 1·90 75

78 Robert Kennedy

1968. Air. Robert Kennedy Commemoration.

162 **78** 50f. black, green and red 95 45

79 "Tree of Life" and WHO Emblem

1968. 20th Anniv of WHO.

163 **79** 25f. red, purple and green 55 40

80 Start of Race

1968. Air. Olympic Games, Mexico.

164 **80** 5f. brown, blue and green 30 10
165 - 20f. green, brown & blue 45 25
166 - 60f. brown, green and red 95 60
167 - 85f. brown, red and slate 2·00 80

DESIGNS—VERT: 20f. Football; 60f. Boxing. HORIZ: 85f. High-jumping.

1968. Air. "Philexafrique" Stamp Exn, Abidjan (1969) (1st issue). As T **86** of Central African Republic.

168 100f. multicoloured 3·00 2·10

DESIGN: 100f. "G. de Gueidan writing" (N. de Largilliere).

1969. Air. "Philexafrique" Stamp Exhibition, Abidjan, Ivory Coast (2nd issue). As T **138** of Cameroun.

169 50f. green, brown & mauve 2·00 1·90

DESIGN: 50f. Pointe-Noire harbour, lumbering and Middle Congo stamp of 1933.

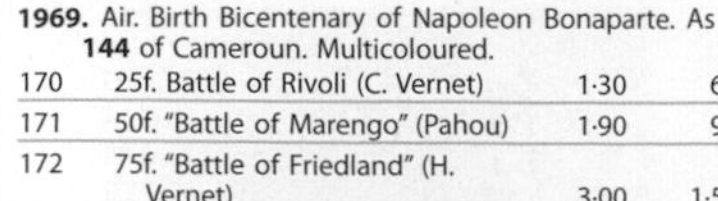

1969. Air. Birth Bicentenary of Napoleon Bonaparte. As T **144** of Cameroun. Multicoloured.

170 25f. Battle of Rivoli (C. Vernet) 1·30 60
171 50f. "Battle of Marengo" (Pahou) 1·90 90
172 75f. "Battle of Friedland" (H. Vernet) 3·00 1·50
173 100f. "Battle of Jena" (Thevenin) 4·50 1·60

81 "Che" Guevara

1969. Air. Ernesto "Che" Guevara (Latin-American revolutionary) Commemoration.

174 **81** 90f. brown, orange & lake 1·20 60

82 Doll and Toys

1969. Air. International Toy Fair, Nuremberg.

175 **82** 100f. slate, mauve & orange 1·70 85

83 Beribboned Bar

1969. Air. Europafrique.

176 **83** 50f. violet, black & turq 85 35

1969. 5th Anniv of African Development Bank. As T **146** of Cameroun.

177 25f. brown, red and green 45 25
178 30f. brown, green and blue 45 25

84 Astronauts

1969. Air. 1st Man on the Moon. Sheet 65×51 mm containing T **84** and similar vert design.

MS179 1000f. Type **84**; 1000f. Lunar module 39·00 39·00

85 Modern Bicycle

1969. Cycles and Motor-cycles.

180 **85** 50f. purple, orange & brn 1·20 45
181 - 75f. black, lake & orange 1·50 45
182 - 80f. green, blue & purple 1·70 70
183 - 85f. green, slate & brown 1·90 90
184 - 100f. multicoloured 2·50 1·00
185 - 150f. brown, red & black 3·50 1·20
186 - 200f. pur, dp grn & grn 5·00 2·00
187 - 300f. green, purple & blk 8·75 3·00

DESIGNS: 75f. "Hirondelle" cycle; 80f. Folding cycle; 85f. "Peugeot" cycle; 100f. "Excelsior Manxman" motor-cycle; 150f. "Norton" motor-cycle; 200f. "Brough Superior" motor-cycle; 300f. "Matchless and N.I.G.-J.A.P.S." motor-cycle.

86 Series ZE Diesel-electric Train entering Mbamba Tunnel

1969. African International Tourist Year. Mult.

188 40f. Type **86** 1·80 60
189 60f. Series ZE diesel-electric train crossing the Mayombe (horiz) 3·00 90

87 Mortar Tanks

1969. Loutete Cement Works.

190 **87** 10f. slate, brown and lake 30 10
191 - 15f. violet, blue & brown 50 20
192 - 25f. blue, brown and red 55 25
193 - 30f. blue, violet & ultram 60 25

MS194 170×101 mm. Nos. 190/3 3·00 3·00

DESIGNS—VERT: 15f. Mixing tower; 25f. Cableway. HORIZ: 30f. General view of works.

1969. 10th Anniv of A.S.E.C.N.A. As T **150** of Cameroun.

195 100f. brown 2·00 90

88 Harvesting Pineapples

1969. 50th Anniv of ILO.

196 **88** 25f. brown, green & blue 40 30
197 - 30f. slate, purple and red 55 30

DESIGN: 30f. Operating lathe.

89 Textile Plant

1970. "SOTEXCO" Textile Plant, Kinsoundi.

198 **89** 15f. black, violet & green 40 25
199 - 20f. green, red and purple 40 25
200 - 25f. brown, blue & lt blue 60 25
201 - 30f. brown, red and slate 60 30

DESIGNS: 20f. Spinning machines; 25f. Printing textiles; 30f. Checking finished cloth.

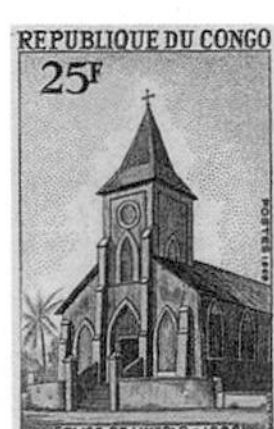

90 Linzolo Church

1970. Buildings.

202 **90** 25f. green, brown & blue 75 25
203 - 90f. brown, green & blue 1·20 40

DESIGN: HORIZ: 90f. Cosmos Hotel, Brazzaville.

91 Artist at work

1970. Air. "Art and Culture".

204 **91** 100f. brown, plum & grn 2·00 70
205 - 150f. plum, lake & green 3·00 1·20
206 - 200f. brown, choc & ochre 4·00 2·10

DESIGNS: 150f. Lesson in wood-carving; 200f. Potter at wheel.

92 Diosso Gorges

1970. Tourism.

207 **92** 70f. purple, brown & grn 1·30 40
208 - 90f. purple, green & brown 2·00 60

DESIGN: 90f. Foulakari Falls.

1970. Air. Paintings. As T **71**. Multicoloured.

209 150f. "Child with Cherries" (J. Russell) 3·75 1·60
210 200f. "Erasmus" (Holbein the younger) 5·50 2·10
211 250f. "Silence" (Bernadino Luini) 5·75 2·50
212 300f. "Scenes from the Scio Massacre" (Delacroix) 7·50 3·50
213 500f. "Capture of Constantinople" (Delacroix) 12·00 4·75

93 Aurichalcite

1970. Air. Minerals. Multicoloured.

214 100f. Type **93** 4·75 1·90
215 150f. Dioptase 6·50 2·50

94 "Volvaria esculenta"

1970. Mushrooms. Multicoloured.

216 5f. Type **94** 65 35
217 10f. "Termitomyces entolomoides" 95 50
218 15f. "Termitomyces microcarpus" 1·50 75
219 25f. "Termitomyces aurantiacus" 2·50 1·10
220 30f. "Termitomyces mamiformis" 4·25 1·70
221 50f. "Tremella fuciformis" 7·00 1·90

95 Laying Cable

1970. Laying of Coaxial Cable, Brazzaville–Pointe Noire.

222 **95** 25f. buff, brown and blue 1·00 45
223 - 30f. brown and green 1·30 75

DESIGN: 30f. Diesel locomotive and cable-laying gang.

1970. New U.P.U. Headquarters Building, Berne. As T **156** of Cameroun.

224 30f. purple, slate and plum 75 45

96 Mother feeding Child

1970. Mothers' Day. Multicoloured.

225	85f. Type **96**	95	40
226	90f. Mother suckling baby	1·20	60

97 U.N. Emblem and Trygve Lie

1970. 25th Anniv of United Nations.

227	**97**	100f. blue, indigo and lake	1·30	90
228	-	100f. lilac, red and lake	1·30	90
229	-	100f. green, turq & lake	1·30	90
MS230 130×100 mm. Nos. 227/9			6·00	5·75

DESIGNS—VERT: No. 228, as Type **97**, but with portrait of Dag Hammarskjold. HORIZ: No. 229, as Type **97**, but with portrait of U Thant and arrangement reversed.

98 Lenin in Cap

1970. Air. Birth Centenary of Lenin.

231	**98**	45f. brown, yellow & grn	1·00	55
232	-	75f. brown, red and blue	1·80	80

DESIGN: 75f. Lenin seated (after Vassiliev).

99 "Brillantaisia vogeliana"

1970. "Flora and Fauna". Multicoloured. (a) Flowers. Horiz designs.

233	1f. Type **99**	60	35
234	2f. "Plectranthus decurrens"	60	35
235	3f. "Myrianthemum mirabile"	45	35
236	5f. "Connarus griffonianus"	1·10	35

(b) Insects. Vert designs.

237	10f. "Sternotomis variabilis"	1·60	55
238	15f. "Chelorrhina polyphemus"	2·50	55
239	20f. "Metopodontus savagei"	2·50	70

100 Karl Marx

1970. Air. Founders of Communism.

240	**100**	50f. brown, green & red	1·30	45
241	-	50f. brown, blue and red	1·30	45

DESIGN: No. 241, Friedrich Engels.

101 Kentrosarus

1970. Prehistoric Creatures. Multicoloured.

242	15f. Type **101**	1·50	65
243	20f. Dinotherium (vert)	3·00	1·00
244	60f. Brachiosaurus (vert)	5·00	1·20
245	80f. Arsinoitherium	6·00	2·50

102 "Mikado 141" Steam Locomotive, 1932

1970. Locomotives of Congo Railways (1st series).

246	**102**	40f. black, green & purple	2·20	1·00
247	-	60f. black, green & blue	2·50	1·20
248	-	75f. black, red and blue	4·00	1·70
249	-	85f. red, green & orange	5·75	2·50

DESIGNS: 60f. Super-Golwe steam locomotive, 1947; 75f. Alsthom Series BB 1100 diesel locomotive, 1962; 85f. Diesel locomotive No. BB BB 302, 1969.

See also Nos. 371/4.

103 Lilienthal's Glider, 1891

1970. Air. History of Flight and Space Travel.

250	**103**	45f. brown, blue and red	85	30
251	-	50f. green and brown	90	45
252	-	70f. brown, red and blue	1·30	60
253	-	90f. brown, olive & blue	1·50	85

DESIGNS: 50f. Lindbergh's "Spirit of St. Louis", 1927; 70f. "Sputnik I"; 90f. First man on the Moon, 1969.

104 "Wise Man"

1970. Air. Christmas. Stained-glass Windows, Brazzaville Cathedral. Multicoloured.

254	100f. Type **104**	1·50	60
255	150f. "Shepherd"	2·00	90
256	250f. "Angels"	3·50	1·60
MS257 152×116 mm. Nos. 254/6		8·00	8·00

105 "Cogniauxia padolaena"

1971. Tropical Flowers. Multicoloured.

258	1f. Type **105**	20	25
259	2f. "Celosia cristata"	30	25
260	5f. "Plumeria acutifolia"	30	25
261	10f. "Bauhinia variegata"	90	40
262	15f. "Euphorbia pulcherrima"	1·30	70
263	20f. "Thunbergia grandiflora"	2·30	60

See also D264/9.

106 Marilyn Monroe

1971. Air. Great Names of the Cinema.

270	**106**	100f. brown, blue & grn	6·50	75
271	-	150f. mauve, blue & pur	6·50	1·00
272	-	200f. brown and blue	6·50	1·30
273	-	250f. plum, blue & green	6·50	1·60

PORTRAITS: 150f. Martine Carol; 200f. Eric K. von Stroheim; 250f. Sergei Eisenstein.

107 "Carrying the Cross" (Veronese)

1971. Air. Easter. Religious Paintings. Mult.

274	100f. Type **107**	1·70	80
275	150f. "Christ on the Cross" (Burgundian School c. 1500) (vert)	2·75	1·00
276	200f. "Descent from the Cross" (Van der Weyden)	3·75	1·20
277	250f. "The Entombment" (Flemish School c. 1500) (vert)	4·50	1·80
278	500f. "The Resurrection" (Memling) (vert)	9·50	3·25

108 Telecommunications Map

1971. Air. Pan-African Telecommunications Network.

279	**108**	70f. multicoloured	95	30
280	**108**	85f. multicoloured	1·30	40
281	**108**	90f. multicoloured	1·80	70

109 Global Emblem

1971. Air. World Telecommunications Day.

282	**109**	65f. multicoloured	95	45

110 Green Night Adder

1971. Reptiles. Multicoloured.

283	5f. Type **110**	45	25
284	10f. African egg-eating snake (horiz)	65	25
285	15f. Flap-necked chameleon	1·10	35
286	20f. Nile crocodile (horiz)	1·80	45
287	25f. Rock python (horiz)	2·20	90
288	30f. Gaboon viper	2·75	90
289	40f. Brown house snake (horiz)	3·25	1·00
290	45f. Jameson's mamba	4·50	1·20

111 Afro-Japanese Allegory

1971. Air. "Philatokyo 1971" Stamp Exn, Tokyo.

291	**111**	75f. black, mauve & violet	1·20	75
292	-	150f. brown, red & purple	1·80	1·10

DESIGN: 150f. "Tree of Life", Japanese girl and African in mask.

112 "Pseudimbrasia deyrollei"

1971. Caterpillars. Multicoloured.

293	10f. Type **112**	80	35
294	15f. "Bunaca alcinoe" (vert)	1·10	50
295	20f. "Epiphora vacuna ploetzi"	1·90	65
296	25f. "Imbrasia eblis"	3·00	1·00
297	30f. "Imbrasia dione" (vert)	4·75	1·50
298	40f. "Holocera angulata"	6·50	1·90

113 Japanese Scout

1971. World Scout Jamboree, Asagiri, Japan (1st issue). On foil.

299	**113**	90f. silver (postage)	3·00	1·90
300	-	90f. silver	3·00	1·90
301	-	90f. silver	3·00	1·90
302	-	90f. silver	3·00	1·90
303	-	1000f. gold (air)	27·00	25·00

DESIGNS—VERT: No. 300, French Scout; 301, Congolese Scout; 302, Lord Baden-Powell. HORIZ: No. 303, Scouts and Lord Baden-Powell.

See also Nos. 306/9.

114 Olympic Torch

1971. Air. Olympic Games, Munich.

304	**114**	150f. red, green & purple	2·00	1·10
305	-	350f. violet, green & brn	5·00	2·50

DESIGN—HORIZ: 350f. Sporting cameos within Olympic rings.

115 Scout Badge, Dragon and Congolese Wood-carving

1971. Air. World Scout Jamboree, Asagiri, Japan (2nd issue).

306	**115**	85f. purple, brown & grn	1·10	30
307	-	90f. brown, violet & lake	1·30	40
308	-	100f. green, red & brown	1·50	60

309 - 250f. brown, red & green 3·00 1·30

DESIGNS—HORIZ: 250f. Congolese mask, geisha and scout badge. VERT: 90f. African and Japanese mask; 100f. Japanese woman and African.

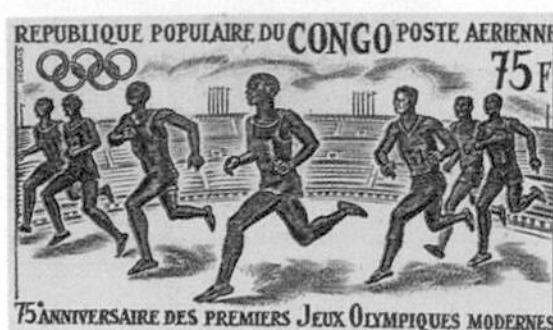

116 Running

1971. Air. 75th Anniv of Modern Olympic Games.

310	**116**	75f. brown, blue and red	85	35
311	-	85f. brown, blue and red	95	45
312	-	90f. brown and violet	1·20	60
313	-	100f. brown and blue	1·50	60
314	-	150f. brown, red & green	2·50	1·00

DESIGNS: 85f. Hurdling; 90f. Various events; 100f. Wrestling; 150f. Boxing.

117 "Cymothae sangaris"

1971. Butterflies. Multicoloured.

315	30f. Type **117**	1·40	60
316	40f. "Papilio dardanus" (vert)	2·50	90
317	75f. "Iolaus timon"	4·00	1·70
318	90f. "Papilio phorcas" (vert)	5·75	2·75
319	100f. "Euchloron megaera"	7·50	3·50

118 African and European Workers

1971. Racial Equality Year.

320 **118** 50f. multicoloured 1·30 45

119 De Gaulle and Congo 1966 Brazzaville Conference Stamp

1971. Air. 1st Death Anniv of General De Gaulle.

321	**119**	500f. brown, green & red	18·00	16·00
322	-	1000f. red & grn on gold	27·00	25·00
323	-	1000f. red & grn on gold	27·00	25·00

DESIGNS—VERT (29×38 mm): No. 322, Tribute by Pres. Ngouabi; 323, De Gaulle and Cross of Lorraine.

1971. Air. 10th Anniv of African and Malagasy Posts and Telecommunications Union. Similar to T **184** of Cameroun. Multicoloured.

324 100f. U.A.M.P.T. H.Q. and Congolese woman 1·50 75

1971. Inauguration of Brazzaville–Pointe Noire Cable Link. Surch **REPUBLIQUE POPULAIRE DU CONGO INAUGURATION DE LA LIAISON COXIALE 18-11-71** and new value.

325	**95**	30f. on 25f. buff, brn & bl	55	40
326	-	40f. on 30f. brown and green (No. 223)	95	50

121 Congo Republic Flag and Allegory of Revolution

1971. Air. 8th Anniv of Revolution.

327 **121** 100f. multicoloured 2·00 70

122 Congolese with Flag

1971. Air. 2nd Anniv of Congolese Workers' Party, and Adoption of New National Flag. Multicoloured.

328	30f. Type **122**	55	25
329	40f. National flag	1·20	45

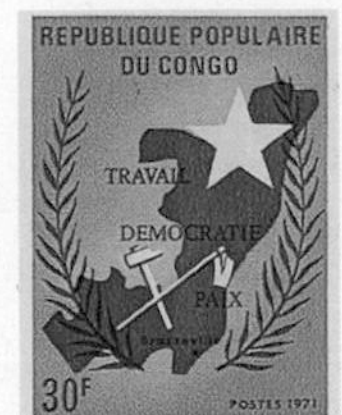

123 Map and Emblems

1971. "Work–Democracy–Peace".

330	**123**	30f. multicoloured	35	25
331	**123**	40f. multicoloured	45	25
332	**123**	100f. multicoloured	1·20	45

124 Lion

1972. Wild Animals.

333	**124**	1f. brown, blue & green	25	10
334	-	2f. brown, green and red	45	10
335	-	3f. brown, orge and red	65	25
336	-	4f. brown, blue & violet	80	30
337	-	5f. brown, green and red	1·00	45
338	-	20f. brown, blue & orge	2·40	75
339	-	30f. green, emer & brn	3·25	90
340	-	40f. black, green and blue	4·75	1·30

DESIGNS—HORIZ: 2f. African elephants; 3f. Leopard; 4f. Hippopotamus; 20f. Potto; 30f. De Brazza's monkey. VERT: 5f. Gorilla; 40f. Pygmy chimpanzee.

125 Book Year Emblem

1972. Air. International Book Year.

341 **125** 50f. green, yellow & red 95 45

126 Team Captain with Cup

1973. Air. Congolese Victory in Africa Football Cup. Multicoloured.

342	100f. Type **126**	1·70	85
343	100f. Congolese team (horiz)	1·70	85

127 Girl with Bird

1973. Air. U.N. Environmental Conservation Conference, Stockholm.

344 **127** 85f. green, blue & orange 2·00 1·10

128 Miles Davis

1973. Air. Famous Negro Musicians.

345	**128**	125f. multicoloured	3·25	1·00
346	-	140f. red, lilac & mauve	3·25	1·00
347	-	160f. green, emer & orge	4·00	1·50
348	-	175f. purple, red & blue	4·00	1·50

DESIGNS: 140f. Ella Fitzgerald; 160f. Count Basie; 175f. John Coltrane.

129 Hurdling

1973. Air. Olympic Games, Munich (1972).

349	**129**	100f. violet and mauve	1·50	70
350	-	150f. violet and green	2·00	1·00
351	-	250f. red and blue	3·50	1·90

DESIGNS—VERT: 150f. Pole-vaulting. HORIZ: 250f. Wrestling.

130 Oil Tanks, Djeno

1973. Air. Oil Installations, Pointe Noire.

352	**130**	180f. indigo, red & blue	3·00	1·70
353	-	230f. black, red and blue	3·75	1·70
354	-	240f. purple, blue & red	4·50	1·90
355	-	260f. black, red and blue	6·75	2·50

DESIGNS—VERT: 230f. Oil-well head; 240f. Drill in operation. HORIZ: 260f. Off-shore oil-rig.

131 Lunar Module and Astronaut on Moon

1973. Air. Moon Flight of "Apollo 17".

356 **131** 250f. multicoloured 4·25 2·20

132 "Telecommunications"

1973. Air. World Telecommunications Day.

357 **132** 120f. multicoloured 2·10 95

133 Copernicus and Solar System

1973. Air. 500th Birth Anniv of Copernicus (astronomer).

358 **133** 50f. green, blue & lt blue 1·00 55

134 Rocket and African Scenes

1973. Air. Centenary of World Meteorological Organization.

359 **134** 50f. multicoloured 1·50 70

135 WHO Emblem

1973. 25th Anniv of WHO. Multicoloured.

360	40f. Type **135**	55	25
361	50f. Design similar to T **135** (horiz)	75	25

136 "Study of a White Horse"

1973. Air. Paintings by Delacroix. Multicoloured.

362	150f. Type **136**	2·75	1·80
363	250f. "Sleeping Lion"	5·25	2·75
364	300f. "Tiger and Lion"	6·25	3·00

See also Nos. 384/6 and 437/40.

137 General View of Brewery

1973. Congo Brewers' Association. Views of Kronenbourg Brewery.

365	**137**	30f. blue, red & lt blue	50	30
366	-	40f. grey, orange & red	55	30
367	-	75f. blue, red and black	1·00	45
368	-	85f. multicoloured	1·50	75
369	-	100f. multicoloured	1·70	1·00
370	-	250f. green, brown & red	3·25	1·90

DESIGNS: 40f. Laboratory; 75f. Regulating vats; 85f. Control console; 100f. Bottling plant; 250f. Capping bottles.

1973. Locomotives of Congo Railways (2nd series). As T **102**. Multicoloured.

371	30f. Golwe steam locomotive c. 1935	1·50	65
372	40f. Diesel-electric locomotive, 1935	2·30	85
373	75f. Whitcomb diesel-electric locomotive, 1946	3·75	1·50
374	85f. Alsthom Series CC200 diesel-electric locomotive, 1973	4·50	1·60

138 Stamp Map, Album, Dancer and Oil Rig

1973. Air. International Stamp Exhibition, Brazzaville and 10th Anniv of Revolution.

375	**138**	30f. grey, lilac & brown	1·20	35
376	-	40f. red, brown & purple	65	40
377	**138**	100f. blue, brown & pur	2·75	1·00
378	-	100f. lilac, purple & red	1·70	1·00

DESIGNS: 40f., 100f. Map, album and Globes.

139 President Marien Ngouabi

1973. Air.

379	**139**	30f. multicoloured	45	10
380	**139**	40f. multicoloured	45	15
381	**139**	75f. multicoloured	1·00	45

1973. Pan-African Drought Relief. No. 236 surch **100F SECHERESSE SOLIDARITE AFRICAINE**.

382	100f. on 5f. multicoloured	1·70	75

1973. 12th Anniv of African and Malagasy Posts and Telecommunications Union. As T **216** of Cameroun.

383	100f. violet, blue and purple	1·50	70

1973. Air. Europafrique. As T **136**. Multicoloured.

384	100f. "Wild Dog"	3·25	1·60
385	100f. "Lion and Leopard"	3·25	1·60
386	100f. "Adam and Eve in Paradise"	3·25	1·60

Nos. 384/6 are details taken from J. Brueghel's "Earth and Paradise".

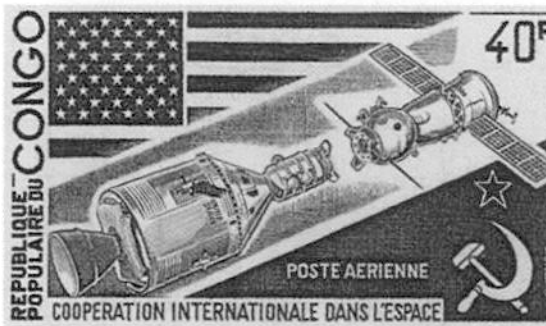

141 "Apollo" and "Soyuz" Spacecraft

1973. Air. International Co-operation in Space.

387	**141**	40f. brown, red & blue	50	35
388	-	80f. blue, red and green	1·10	60

DESIGN: 80f. Spacecraft docked.

142 UPU Monument and Satellite

1973. Air. UPU Day.

389	**142**	80f. blue & ultramarine	1·00	40

1973. Air. "Skylab" Space Laboratory. As T **141**.

390	30f. green, brown and blue	50	25
391	40f. green, red and orange	60	25

DESIGNS: 30f. Astronauts walking outside "Skylab"; 40f. "Skylab" and "Apollo" spacecraft docked.

143 Hive and Bees

1973. "Labour and Economy".

392	**143**	30f. green, blue and red	90	25
393	**143**	40f. green, blue & green	1·30	30

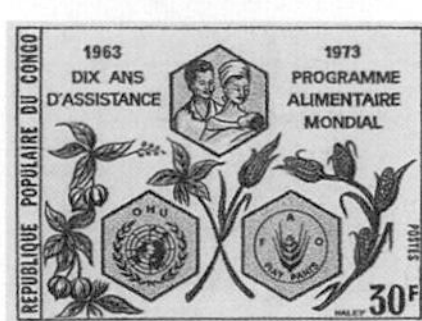

144 Congo Family and Emblems

1973. 10th Anniv of World Food Programme.

394	**144**	30f. brown and red	45	25
395	-	40f. orange, green & blue	60	25
396	-	100f. brown, green & orge	1·20	60

DESIGNS—HORIZ: 40f. Ears of corn and emblems. VERT: 100f. Ear of corn, granary and emblems.

145 Goalkeeper

1973. Air. World Football Cup Championship, West Germany (1974). (1st issue).

397	**145**	40f. green, dp brn & brn	55	25
398	-	100f. green, red & violet	1·70	85

DESIGN: 100f. Forward.

See also Nos. 403 and 408.

146 Runners

1973. Air. 2nd African Games, Lagos, Nigeria.

399	**146**	40f. red, green & brown	60	25
400	**146**	100f. green, red & brown	1·80	85

147 Pres. John F. Kennedy

1973. Air. 10th Death Anniv of President Kennedy.

401	**147**	150f. black, gold & blue	2·00	1·10

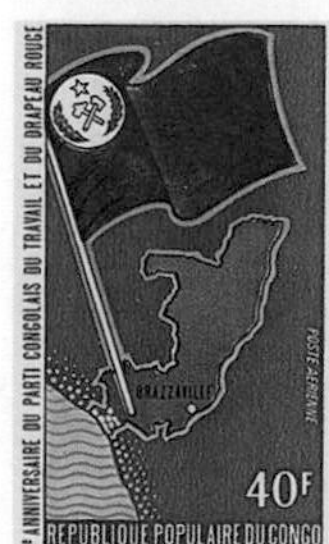

148 Map and Flag

1973. Air. 4th Anniv of Congo Workers' Party.

402	**148**	40f. multicoloured	55	25

149 Players seen through Goalkeeper's Legs

1974. Air. World Cup Football Championship, West Germany (2nd issue).

403	**149**	250f. green, red & brown	3·50	2·20

150 Globe, Flags and Names of Dead Astronauts

1974. Air. Conquest of Space.

404	**150**	30f. brown, blue & red	35	25
405	-	40f. multicoloured	60	40
406	-	100f. brown, blue & red	1·40	90

DESIGNS: 40f. Gagarin and Shepard; 100f. Leonov in space, and Armstrong on Moon.

151 A. Cabral

1974. 1st Death Anniv of Cabral (Guinea-Bissau guerilla leader).

407	**151**	100f. purple, red & blue	1·00	65

1974. Air. West Germany's Victory in World Cup Football Championship. As T **149**.

408	250f. brown, pink and blue	3·75	2·20

DESIGN: Footballers within ball.

152 Spacecraft docking

1974. Air. Soviet-American Space Co-operation.

409	**152**	200f. blue, violet and red	2·30	1·20
410	-	300f. blue, brown & red	3·50	1·70

DESIGN—HORIZ: 300f. Spacecraft on segments of globe.

153 "Sound and Vision"

1974. Air. Centenary of UPU.

411	**153**	500f. black and red	6·75	3·50

154 Felix Eboue and Cross of Lorraine

1974. 30th Death Anniv of Eboue ("Free French" Leader).

412	**154**	30f. multicoloured	75	45
413	**154**	40f. multicoloured	1·20	70

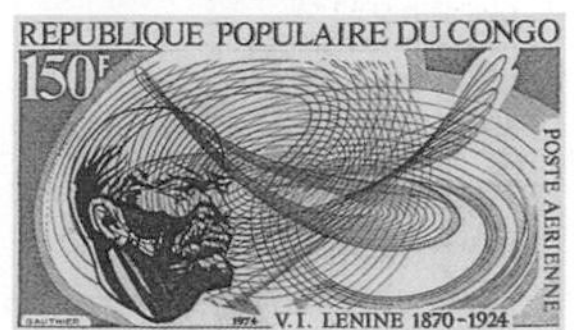

155 Lenin

1974. Air. 30th Death Anniv of Lenin.

414	**155**	150f. orange, red & green	2·20	1·10

1974. Birth Centenary of Churchill. As T **154**. Multicoloured.

415	200f. Churchill and Order of the Garter	2·75	1·50

1974. Birth Centenary of Guglielmo Marconi (radio pioneer). As T **154**. Multicoloured.

416	200f. Marconi and early apparatus	2·50	1·40

1974. Air. Centenary of Berne Convention. No. 411 surch **9 OCTOBRE 1974 300F**.

417	**153**	300f. on 500f. blk & red	3·75	2·20

157 Pineapple

1974. Congolese Fruits. Multicoloured.

418	30f. Type **157**	65	40
419	30f. Bananas	70	45
420	30f. Safous	70	50
421	40f. Avocado pears	1·10	50
422	40f. Mangoes	1·10	50
423	40f. Papaya	1·10	50
424	40f. Oranges	1·10	50

158 Gen. Charles De Gaulle

1974. 30th Anniv of Brazzaville Conference.

425	**158**	100f. brown and green	3·75	2·20

1974. 10th Anniv of Central African Customs and Economic Union. As Nos. 734/5 of Cameroun.

426	40f. mult (postage)	60	25
427	100f. multicoloured (air)	1·20	60

159 George Stephenson (railway pioneer) and Early and Modern Locomotives (image scaled to 62% of original size)

1974. 150th Anniv (1975) of Public Railways.

428	**159**	75f. olive and green	3·00	1·10

160 Irish Setter

1974. Dogs. Multicoloured.

429	30f. Type **160**	1·10	60
430	40f. Borzoi	1·30	60
431	75f. Pointer	2·75	1·10
432	100f. Great Dane	3·75	1·10

1974. Cats. As T **160**. Multicoloured.

433	30f. Havana chestnut	1·10	60
434	40f. Red Persian	1·30	60
435	75f. British blue	2·75	1·10

436 100f. Serval 3·75 1·10

1974. Air. Impressionist Paintings. As T **136**. Mult.

437 30f. "The Argenteuil Regatta" (Monet) 1·70 75
438 40f. "Seated Dancer" (Degas) (vert) 1·80 90
439 50f. "Girl on Swing" (Renoir) (vert) 2·75 1·30
440 75f. "Girl in Straw Hat" (Renoir) (vert) 3·50 1·90

161 National Fair

1974. Air. National Fair, Brazzaville.

441 **161** 30f. multicoloured 85 45

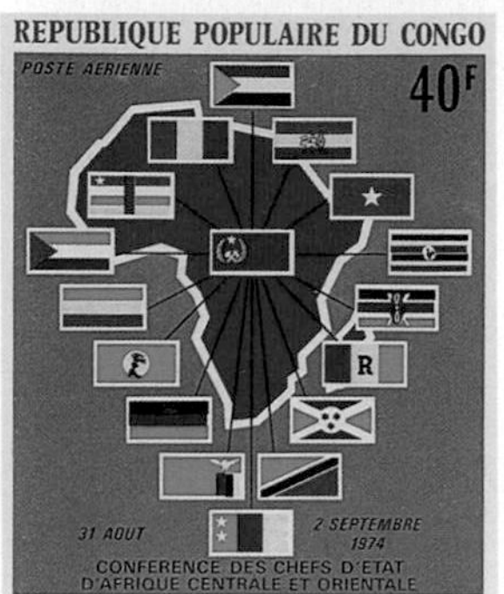

162 African Map and Flags

1974. Air. African Heads-of-State Conference, Brazzaville.

442 **162** 40f. multicoloured 75 45

163 Flags and Dove

1974. 5th Anniv of Congo Labour Party.

443 **163** 30f. red, yellow & green 45 25
444 - 40f. brown, red & yellow 80 30

DESIGN: 40f. Hands holding flowers and hammer.

164 U Thant and U.N. Headquarters Building

1975. 1st Death Anniv of U Thant (U.N. Secretary-General).

445 **164** 50f. multicoloured 75 45

1975. 1st Death Anniv of Paul G. Hoffman (U.N. Programme for Underdeveloped Countries administrator). As T **164**. Multicoloured.

446 50f. Hoffman and U.N. "Laurel Wreath" (vert) 75 45

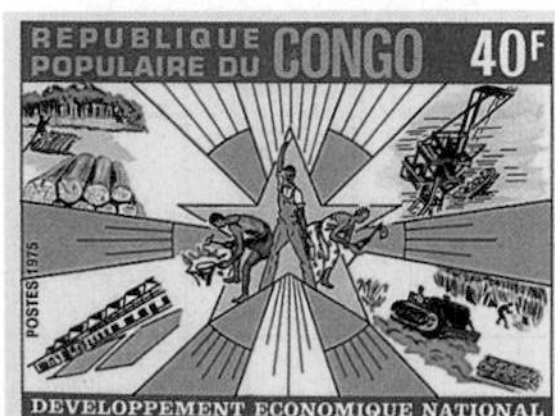

166 Workers and Development

1975. National Economic Development.

447 **166** 40f. multicoloured 60 40

167 Mao Tse-tung and Map of China

1975. 25th Anniv (1974) of Chinese People's Republic.

448 **167** 75f. red, mauve & blue 3·75 1·50

168 Woman with Hoe

1975. 10th Anniv of Revolutionary Union of Congolese Women.

449 **168** 40f. multicoloured 60 30

169 Paris–Brussels Line, 1890 (image scaled to 61% of original size)

1975. Air. Railway History. Multicoloured.

450 50f. Type **169** 1·90 70
451 75f. Santa Fe Line, 1880 3·25 1·00

170 "Five Weeks in a Balloon"

1975. Air. 70th Anniv of Jules Verne (novelist). Multicoloured.

452 40f. Type **170** 1·50 60
453 50f. "Around the World in 80 Days" 1·80 1·10

171 Line-up of Team

1975. Victory of Cara Football Team in Africa Cup. Multicoloured.

454 30f. Type **171** 40 25
455 40f. Receiving trophy (vert) 60 30

172 1935 Citroen and Notre Dame Cathedral, Paris

1975. Veteran Cars. Multicoloured.

456 30f. Type **172** 1·00 50
457 40f. 1911 Alfa Romeo and St. Peter's Rome 1·30 50
458 50f. 1926 Rolls Royce and Houses of Parliament, London 1·60 70
459 75f. 1893 C. F. Duryea and Manhattan skyline, New York 3·00 1·00

173 "Soyuz" Spacecraft

1975. Air. "Apollo–Soyuz" Space Test Project.

460 **173** 95f. black, red & brown 1·10 60
461 - 100f. black, violet & blue 1·30 75

DESIGN: 100f. "Apollo" Spacecraft.

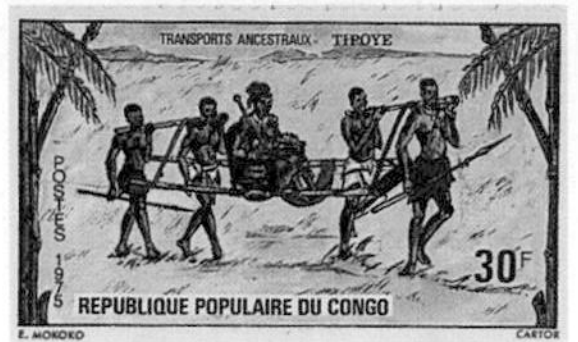

174 Tipoye Carriage

1975. Traditional Congo Transport. Multicoloured.

462 30f. Type **174** 85 45
463 40f. Pirogue 1·00 75

175 "Raising the Flag"

1975. 2nd Anniv of Institutions of Popular Tasks.

464 **175** 30f. multicoloured 55 25

176 Conference Hall

1975. 3rd Anniv of Congolese National Conference.

465 **176** 40f. multicoloured 60 30

177 Fishing with Wooden Baskets

1975. Traditional Fishing. Multicoloured.

466 30f. Type **177** 65 25
467 40f. Fishing with line (vert) 70 35
468 60f. Fishing with spear (vert) 95 35
469 90f. Fishing with net 1·20 80

178 Chopping Firewood

1975. Domestic Chores. Multicoloured.

470 30f. Type **178** 65 30
471 30f. Pounding meal 65 30
472 40f. Preparing manioc (horiz) 90 30

179 "Esanga"

1975. Traditional Musical Instruments. Mult.

473 30f. Type **179** 75 25
474 40f. "Kalakwa" 1·00 35
475 60f. "Likembe" 1·40 60
476 75f. "Ngongui" 1·70 75

180 "Dzeke" Money Cowrie

1975. Ancient Congolese Money.

477 **180** 30f. ochre, brown & red 55 30
478 - 30f. ochre, violet & brn 55 30
478a **180** 35f. orange and brown 80 35
478b - 35f. red, bistre and violet 80 35
479 - 40f. brown and blue 80 30
480 - 50f. blue and brown 95 45
481 - 60f. brown and green 1·10 60
482 - 85f. green and red 1·80 70

DESIGNS: 30, 35 (478b) f. "Okengo" iron money; 40f. Gallic coin (60 B.C.); 50f. Roman coin (37 B.C.); 60f. Danubian coin (2nd century B.C.); 85f. Greek coin (4th century B.C.).

181 Dr. Schweitzer

1975. Birth Centenary of Dr. Albert Schweitzer.

483 **181** 75f. green, mauve & brn 1·50 70

182 "Moschops"

1975. Prehistoric Animals. Multicoloured.

484 55f. Type **182** 1·70 75
485 75f. "Tyrannosaurus" 2·50 75
486 95f. "Cryptocleidus" 4·50 1·10
487 100f. "Stegosauras" 6·00 1·50

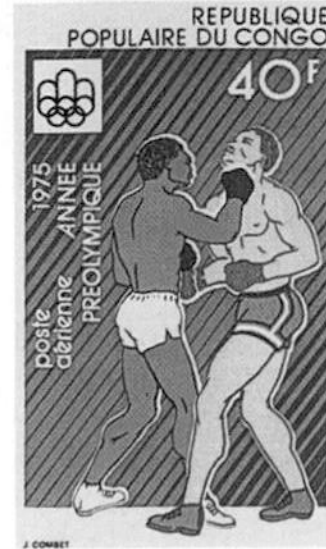

183 Boxing

1975. Air. Olympic Games, Montreal (1976). Multicoloured.

488 40f. Type **183** 45 25
489 50f. Basketball 60 45
490 85f. Cycling (horiz) 1·00 55
491 95f. High jumping (horiz) 1·20 55
492 100f. Throwing the javelin (horiz) 1·50 70
493 150f. Running (horiz) 2·20 95

184 Alexander Fleming (biochemist) (20th Death Anniv)

1975. Celebrities.
494 **184** 60f. black, green and red 1·70 80
495 - 95f. black, blue and red 1·70 80
496 - 95f. green, red and lilac 2·30 1·10
DESIGNS: No. 495, Clement Ader (aviation pioneer) (50th death anniv); 496, Andre Marie Ampere (physicist) (birth bicent).

185 U.N. Emblem with Laurel Wreaths

1975. 30th Anniv of UNO.
497 **185** 95f. blue, red and green 1·30 65

186 Map of Africa and Sportsmen

1975. Air. 10th Anniv of 1st African Games, Brazzaville.
498 **186** 30f. multicoloured 75 35

187 Chained Women and Broken Link

1975. International Women's Year. Multicoloured.
499 35f. Type **187** 65 35
500 60f. Global handclasp 90 50

188 Pres. Ngouabi and Crowd with Flags

1975. 6th Anniv of Congolese Workers' Party. Multicoloured.
501 30f. Type **188** (postage) 55 25
502 35f. "Echo"–P.C.T. "man" with roll of newsprint and radio waves (36×27 mm) 55 25
503 60f. Party members with flag (26×38 mm) (air) 75 45

189 River Steamer "Alphonse Fondere"

1976. Air. Old-time Ships. Multicoloured.
504 5f. Type **189** 20 15
505 10f. Paddle-steamer "Hamburg", 1839 30 15
506 15f. Paddle-steamer "Gomer", 1831 30 15
507 20f. Paddle-steamer "Great Eastern", 1858 45 15
508 30f. Type **189** 55 25
509 40f. As 10f. 70 35
510 50f. As 15f. 95 60
511 60f. As 20f. 1·20 60
512 95f. River steamer "J.M. White II" 1878 1·90 1·00

190 "The Peasant Family" (L. le Nain)

1976. Air. Europafrique. Paintings. Multicoloured.
513 60f. Type **190** 1·40 50
514 80f. "Boy with spinning Top" (Chardin) 1·60 80
515 95f. "Venus and Aeneas" (Poussin) 2·20 80
516 100f. "The Sabines" (David) 2·40 1·00

191 Alexander Graham Bell and Early Telephone

1976. Telephone Centenary.
517 **191** 35f. brown, light brown and yellow (postage) 55 25
518 **191** 60f. red, mve & pink (air) 95 35

192 Fruit Market

1976. Market Scenes. Multicoloured.
519 35f. Type **192** 55 25
520 60f. Laying out produce 1·20 60

193 Congolese Woman

1976. Congolese Women's Hair-styles.
521 **193** 35f. multicoloured 50 25
522 - 60f. multicoloured 85 25
523 - 95f. multicoloured 1·30 40
524 - 100f. multicoloured 1·50 45
DESIGNS: 60f. to 100f. Various Congolese Women's hair-styles.

194 Pole-vaulting

1976. 1st Central African Games, Yaounde. Multicoloured.
525 60f. Type **194** (postage) 75 30
526 95f. Long-jumping 1·30 60
527 150f. Running (air) 1·70 90
528 200f. Throwing the discus 2·75 1·20

195 Kob

1976. Congolese Fauna. Multicoloured.
529 5f. Type **195** 50 10
530 10f. African buffaloes 55 10
531 15f. Hippopotami 85 35
532 20f. Warthog 1·20 45
533 25f. African elephants 1·30 50

196 Saddle-bill Storks ("Jabirus")

1976. Birds. Multicoloured.
534 5f. Type **196** 95 30
535 10f. Shining-blue kingfisher ("Martin-Pecheur") (37×37 mm) 1·50 50
536 20f. Crowned cranes ("Grues Couronnees") (37×37 mm) 2·40 65

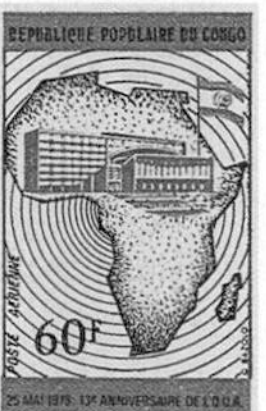

197 OAU Building on Map

1976. Air. 13th Anniv of OAU.
537 **197** 60f. multicoloured 75 35

198 Cycling

1976. Central African Games, Libreville. Mult.
538 35f. Type **198** 35 10
539 60f. Handball 60 25
540 80f. Running 1·00 45
541 95f. Football 1·30 60

199 "Nymphaea micrantha"

1976. Tropical Flowers. Multicoloured.
542 5f. Type **199** 20 10
543 10f. "Heliotrope" 35 10
544 15f. "Strelitzia reginae" 55 20

200 Pioneers' Emblem

1976. National Pioneers Movement.
545 **200** 35f. multicoloured 45 25

201 "Spirit of 76" (detail, A. M. Willard)

1976. Bicent of American Revolution. Mult.
546 100f. Type **201** 1·00 30
547 125f. Destruction of George III's statue 1·20 45
548 150f. Gunners-Battle of Princeton 1·60 60
549 175f. Wartime generals 1·90 70
550 200f. Surrender of Gen. Burgoyne, Saratoga 2·20 90
MS551 114×77 mm. 500f. "Battle of Lexington" (detail, W. Wollen) 5·50 2·20

202 Pirogue Race

1977. Pirogue Racing. Multicoloured.
552 35f. Type **202** 55 25
553 60f. Race in progress 1·00 55

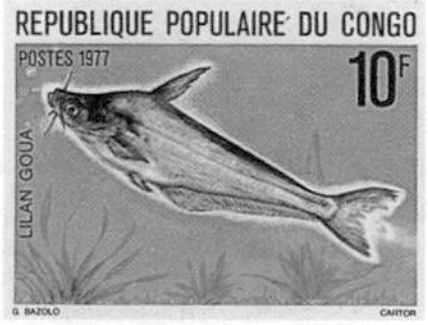

203 Butter Catfish

1977. Freshwater Fishes. Multicoloured.
554 10f. Type **203** 40 10
555 15f. Big-eyed catfish 75 10
556 25f. Citharinid 95 25
557 35f. Mbessi mormyrid 1·30 45
558 60f. "Mongandza" 2·75 70

204 Map of Europe and Africa

1977. Air. Europafrique.
559 **204** 75f. multicoloured 95 60

205 Headdress

1977. Traditional Headdresses. Multicoloured.
560 35f. Type **205** (postage) 45 35
561 60f. Headdress with tail 95 55
562 250f. Two headdresses (air) 3·00 1·80
563 300f. Headdresses with beads 3·50 2·20

206 Wrestling

1977. Bondjo Wrestling.
564 - 25f. multicoloured 45 10
565 **206** 40f. multicoloured 55 25
566 - 50f. multicoloured 75 45
DESIGNS—VERT: 25f., 50f. Different wrestling scenes.

207 "Schwaben", 1911

1977. History of the Zeppelin. Multicoloured.
567 40f. Type **207** (postage) 50 25
568 60f. "Viktoria Luise", 1913 75 45
569 100f. "Bodensee" 1·10 45
570 200f. "Graf Zeppelin" 2·00 70
571 300f. "Graf Zeppelin II" 3·50 1·00
MS572 104×92 mm. 500f. "Graf Zeppelin" LZ127 (different) (air) 6·75 2·20

208 Rising Sun of "Revolution"

1977. 14th Anniv of Revolution.
573 **208** 40f. multicoloured 55 25

209 "Flow of Trade"

1977. Air. GATT Trade Convention, Lome.
574 **209** 60f. black and red 95 45

210 Hugo and Scene from "Hunchback of Notre Dame"

1977. 175th Birth Anniv of Victor Hugo.
575 **210** 35f. brown, red and blue 55 35
576 - 60f. green, drab and blue 85 35
577 - 100f. brown, blue & red 1·50 60
DESIGNS: 60f. Scene from "Les Miserables"; 100f. Scene from "The Toilers of the Sea".

211 Newton and Constellations

1977. Air. 250th Death Anniv of Isaac Newton.
578 **211** 140f. mauve, green & brn 2·20 1·10

212 Mao Tse-tung

1977. 1st Death Anniv of Mao Tse-tung.
579 **212** 400f. gold and red 8·75 6·25

213 Rubens

1977. 400th Birth Anniv of Peter Paul Rubens.
580 **213** 600f. gold and blue 9·50 6·75

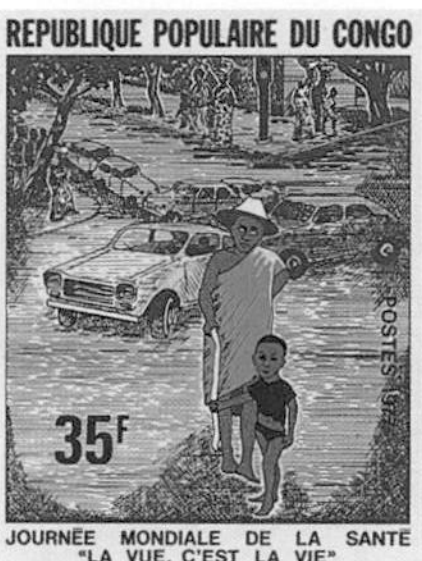

214 Child leading Blind Person

1977. Fight Against Blindness.
581 **214** 35f. multicoloured 60 45

215 Paul Kamba and Records

1977. Paul Kamba (musician) Commemoration.
582 **215** 100f. multicoloured 1·00 60

216 Trajan Vuia and his Vuia No. 1

1977. Aviation History. Multicoloured.
583 60f. Type **216** 55 25
584 75f. Bleriot and Bleriot XI over Channel 70 25
585 100f. Roland Garros and Morane Saulnier Type 1 95 55
586 200f. Lindbergh and "Spirit of St. Louis" 2·20 70
587 300f. Tupolev Tu-144 3·00 90
MS588 116×91 mm. 500f. Lindbergh and "Spirit of St. Louis" over SS "Mauritania" 5·75 2·10

217 General de Gaulle

1977. Historic Personalities, and Silver Jubilee of Queen Elizabeth II. Multicoloured.
589 200f. Type **217** 2·20 45
590 200f. King Baudouin of Belgium 2·50 60
591 250f. Queen and Prince Philip in open car 2·30 90
592 300f. Queen Elizabeth 3·00 95
MS593 110×91 mm. 500f. Royal Family on balcony after Coronation (50×37 mm) (air) 5·50 1·90

218 Ambete Statue

1978. Congolese Sculpture.
594 **218** 35f. lake, brown & green 60 30
595 - 85f. brown, green & lake 1·30 75
DESIGN: 85f. Babembe statue.

219 "The Apostle Simon"

1978. 400th Birth Anniv of Peter Paul Rubens (2nd issue). Multicoloured.
596 60f. Type **219** 95 25
597 140f. "The Duke of Lerma" 1·50 40
598 200f. "Madonna and Saints" 2·20 65
599 300f. "The Artist and his Wife" 3·25 85
MS600 106×123 mm. 500f. "The Farm at Laeken" 6·00 2·10

220 Pres. Ngouabi making Speech

1978. 1st Death Anniv of President Marien Ngouabi.
601 **220** 35f. black, yellow & red 40 25
602 - 60f. multicoloured 55 45
603 - 100f. black, yellow & red 1·00 60
DESIGNS—HORIZ: 60f. Pres. Ngouabi at his desk. VERT: 100f. Portrait of Pres. Ngouabi.

221 Ferenc Puskas (Hungary)

1978. World Cup Football Championship, Argentina. Famous Players. Multicoloured.
604 60f. Type **221** 55 25
605 75f. Giacinto Facchetti (Italy) 75 25
606 100f. Bobby Moore (England) 1·00 45
607 200f. Raymond Kopa (France) 2·30 80
608 300f. Pele (Brazil) 3·25 95
MS609 137×100 mm. 500f. Franz Beckenbauer (West Germany) 6·25 2·10

222 Pearl S. Buck (Literature, 1938)

1978. Nobel Prize Winners. Multicoloured.
610 60f. Type **222** 60 25
611 75f. Fridtjof Nansen and camp scene (Peace) 75 25
612 100f. Henri Bergson and "Elan Vita" (Literature) 1·00 50
613 200f. Alexander Fleming and penicillin (Medicine) 2·00 90
614 300f. Gerhart Hauptmann and hands with book (Literature) 2·75 90
MS615 118×81 mm. 500f. Jean Henri Dunant (Peace, 1901) 6·00 2·75

223 Purple Heron

1978. Air. Birds. Multicoloured.
616 65f. Mallard 1·20 60
617 75f. Type **223** 1·20 60
618 150f. Great reed warbler 3·00 1·10
619 240f. Hoopoe 4·50 1·90

224 Okapi

1978. Endangered Animals. Multicoloured.
620 35f. Type **224** 85 35
621 60f. African buffalo (horiz) 1·70 50
622 85f. Black rhinoceros (horiz) 3·00 60
623 150f. Chimpanzee 4·75 1·10
624 200f. Hippopotamus (horiz) 6·00 1·90
625 300f. Kob 9·25 2·30

225 Clenched Fist, Emblem and Crowd

1978. 11th World Youth and Students Festival, Havana, Cuba.
626 **225** 35f. multicoloured 55 40

226 Pyramids, Egypt

1978. The Seven Wonders of the Ancient World. Multicoloured.

627	35f. Type **226**	45	10
628	50f. Hanging Gardens of Babylon (vert)	45	10
629	60f. Statue of Zeus, Olympia (vert)	60	25
630	95f. Colossos of Rhodes (vert)	80	45
631	125f. Mausoleum, Halicarnassus (vert)	1·20	45
632	150f. Temple of Artemis, Ephesus	1·60	55
633	200f. Pharos, Alexandria (vert)	2·00	60
634	300f. Map showing sites of the Seven Wonders	3·00	90

1978. 25th Anniv of Queen Elizabeth's Coronation. Nos. 591/**MS**593 optd **ANNIVERSAIRE DU COURONNEMENT 1953–1978.** Multicoloured.

635	250f. Queen and Prince Philip in open car	2·50	1·20
636	300f. Queen Elizabeth	3·00	1·50
MS637	110×91 mm. 500f. Royal family on balcony after Coronation	4·50	3·50

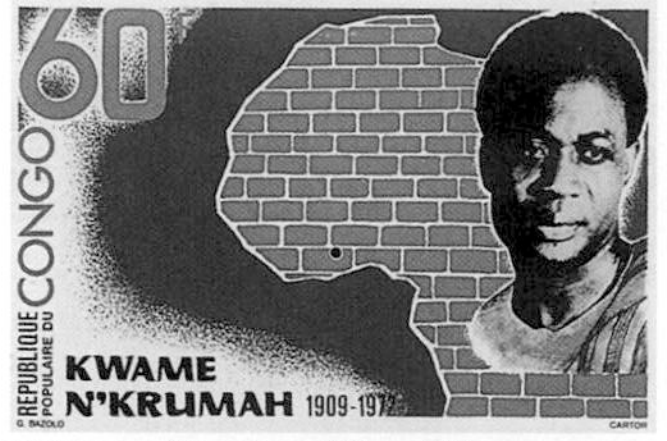

228 Kwame Nkrumah and Map of Africa

1978. Kwame Nkrumah (Ghanaian statesman) Commemoration.
638 **228** 60f. multicoloured 75 45

229 Hunting Wild Pigs

1978. Multicoloured.. Multicoloured..

639	35f. Type **229**	1·50	30
640	50f. Smoking fish	75	45
641	60f. Hunter with kill (vert)	2·30	40
642	140f. Woman hoeing (vert)	1·50	60

1978. Air. "Philexafrique" Stamp Exhibition, Libreville, Gabon (1st issue) and International Stamp Fair, Essen, West Germany. As T **237** of Benin. Multicoloured.

643	100f. Peregrine Falcon and Wurttemberg 1851 1k. stamp	2·00	1·40
644	100f. Leopard and Congo 1978 240f. stamp	2·00	1·40

See also Nos. 668/9.

230 Basket Weaving

1978. Occupations. Multicoloured.

645	85f. Type **230**	85	40
646	90f. Wood sculpture	1·00	60

231 "Kalchreut"

1978. 450th Death Anniv of Albrecht Durer (artist). Multicoloured.

647	65f. Type **231**	65	30
648	150f. "Elspeth Tucher"	1·40	60
649	250f. "Grasses"	2·40	90
650	350f. "Self-portrait"	3·50	1·10

232 Satellites, Antennae and Map of Africa

1978. Air. Pan African Telecommunications.
651 **232** 100f. red, green & orange 1·30 70

1978. World Cup Winners Nos. 604/**MS**609 optd with names of past winners.

652	60f. multicoloured	55	25
653	75f. multicoloured	75	45
654	100f. multicoloured	95	60
655	200f. multicoloured	2·20	80
656	300f. multicoloured	3·00	1·40
MS657	137×100 mm. 500f. multicoloured	5·50	3·50

DESIGNS: 60f. **1962 VAINQUEUR: BRESIL**; 75f. **1966 VAINQUEUR GRANDE BRETAGNE**; 100f. **1970 VAINQUEUR ALLEMAGNE (RFA)**; 300f. **1978 VAINQUEUR ARGENTINA**; 500f. **ARGENTINE-PAYS BAS 3-1 25 juin 1978.**

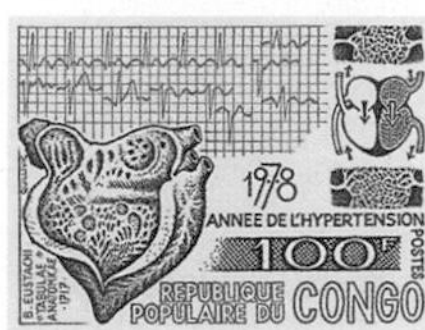

234 Diseased Heart, Blood Pressure Graph and Circulation Diagram

1978. World Hypertension Year.
658 **234** 100f. brown, red & turq 1·20 60

235 Road to the Sun

1978. 9th Anniv of Congolese Workers' Party.
659 **235** 60f. multicoloured 60 25

236 Captain Cook and Native Feast

1979. Death Bicentenary of Captain James Cook. Multicoloured.

660	65f. Type **236**	75	25
661	150f. Easter Island monuments	1·80	40
662	250f. Hawaiian canoes	2·75	80
663	350f. H.M.S. "Resolution" and H.M.S. "Adventure" at anchor	3·75	1·30

237 Pres. Ngouabi

1979. 2nd Anniv of Assassination of President Ngouabi.

664	**237**	35f. multicoloured	35	10
665	**237**	60f. multicoloured	55	25

238 IYC Emblem and Child

1979. International Year of the Child.

666	**238**	45f. multicoloured	45	25
667	**238**	75f. multicoloured	85	30

239 "Solanum torvum" and Earthenware Jars

1979. "Philexafrique" Stamp Exhibition, Libreville, Gabon (2nd issue).

668	**239**	60f. multicoloured	1·40	1·00
669	-	150f. orange, brn & grn	2·75	1·90

DESIGN: 150f. UPU emblem, Concorde airplane, postal runner and diesel locomotive.

240 Rowland Hill, Diesel Locomotive and German 5m. Stamp, 1900

1979. Death Centenary of Sir Rowland Hill. Multicoloured.

670	65f. Type **240**	75	10
671	100f. Steam locomotive and French "War Orphans" stamp of 1917	1·00	45
672	200f. Diesel locomotive and U.S. Columbus stamp of 1893	2·30	65
673	300f. Steam locomotive and England–Australia "First Aerial Post" vignette	3·00	95
MS674	102×77 mm. 500f. Electric locomotive, Concorde and Middle Congo 45c. stamp, 1933	6·00	2·40

241 Pres. Salvador Allende

1979. Salvador Allende (former President of Chile) Commemoration.
675 **241** 100f. multicoloured 1·00 55

242 "The Teller of Legends"

1979. African Folk Tales as Part of Children's Education.
676 **242** 45f. multicoloured 75 45

243 Handball Players

1979. Marien Ngouabi Handball Cup. Mult.

677	45f. Type **243**	50	25
678	75f. Handball players	95	45
679	250f. Cup on map of Africa, player and Marien Ngouabi (vert) (22×37 mm)	2·40	1·20

244 Map of Africa filled with Heads

1979. Air. 5th Pan-African Youth Conference, Brazzaville.

680	**244**	45f. multicoloured	55	25
681	**244**	75f. multicoloured	95	45

245 "Madonna with Joseph and Five Angels" (woodcut)

1979. 450th Death Anniv (1978) of Albrecht Durer (artist) (2nd issue). Sheet 89×115 mm.
MS682 **245** 500f. brown and green 6·25 2·20

246 Congo Map and Flag

1979. 16th Anniv of Revolution.
683 **246** 50f. multicoloured 55 25

247 Abala Peasant Woman

1979. Air.
684 **247** 150f. multicoloured 2·00 1·00

248 IYC Emblem and Child

1979. International Year of the Child (2nd issue). Sheet 110×85 mm.
MS685 **248** 250f. multicoloured 2·75 1·20

249 Bach and Musical Instruments

1979. Personalities. Multicoloured.

686	200f. Type **249**	2·30	90
687	200f. Albert Einstein and astronauts on the Moon	2·30	90

250 Yoro

1979. Yoro Fishing Port. Multicoloured.

688	45f. Type **250**	60	25
689	75f. Yoro at night	95	45

251 Moukoukoulou Dam and Power Station

1979. Moukoukoulou Hydro-electric Power Station.

690	**251**	20f. multicoloured	45	25
691	**251**	45f. multicoloured	95	45

1979. Air. 10th Anniv of "Apollo 11" Moon Landing. Optd **ALUNISSAGE APOLLO XI JUILLET 1969**.

692	-	80f. blue, red and green (No. 388)	90	85
693	**173**	95f. blk, red & crimson	1·00	95
694	-	100f. brown, blue and red (No. 406)	1·00	95
695	-	100f. black, violet and blue (No. 461)	1·00	95
696	-	300f. blue, brown and red (No. 410)	2·75	2·50

253 Fencer

1979. Air. Pre-Olympic Year (1st issue) Multicoloured.

697	65f. Runner, map of Africa and Olympic rings (horiz)	60	10
698	100f. Boxer (horiz)	1·00	45
699	200f. Type **253**	2·00	60
700	300f. Footballer (horiz)	3·00	80
701	500f. Olympic emblem	4·75	1·70

See also Nos. 716/9.

254 ASECNA Emblem and Douglas DC-10

1979. 20th Anniv of ASECNA (African Air Safety Organization).

702	**254**	100f. multicoloured	1·10	60

255 Party Emblem Workers and Flowers

1979. 10th Anniv of Congolese Workers' Party.

703	**255**	45f. multicoloured	55	25

256 Cross-country Skiing

1979. Air. Winter Olympic Games, Lake Placid (1980). Multicoloured.

704	40f. Type **256**	40	10
705	60f. Slalom	70	25
706	200f. Ski-jump	2·00	75
707	350f. Downhill skiing (horiz)	3·50	1·40
708	500f. Skier (vert, 31×46 mm)	4·75	1·90

257 Emblem and Globe

1980. 15th Anniv of National Posts and Telecommunications Office.

709	**257**	45f. multicoloured	45	25
710	**257**	95f. multicoloured	95	35

1980. Air. Winter Olympic Games Medal Winners. Nos. 704/8 optd with names of winners.

711	40f. Cross-country skiing	40	10
712	60f. Slalom	70	25
713	200f. Ski jump	2·00	85
714	350f. Downhill skiing	3·50	1·60
715	500f. Skier	4·75	2·20

OVERPRINTS: 40f. **VAINQUEUR ZIMIATOV U.R.S.S.**; 60f. **VAINQUEUR MOSERPROELL Autriche**; 200f. **VAINQUEUR TOMANEN Finlande**; 350f. **VAINQUEUR STOCK AUTRICHE**; 500f. **VAINQUEURS STENMARK-WENZEL**.

259 Long jump

1980. Air. Olympic Games, Moscow.

716	**259**	75f. multicoloured	85	10
717	-	150f. mult (horiz)	1·50	40
718	-	250f. multicoloured	2·30	60
719	-	350f. multicoloured	3·25	75
MS720		103×78 mm. 500f. multicoloured (horiz)	4·75	2·10

Nos. 717/**MS**720 show different view of the long jump.

260 Pope John Paul II

1980. Papal Visit.

721	**260**	100f. multicoloured	2·00	70

261 Rotary Emblem

1980. 75th Anniv of Rotary International.

722	**261**	150f. multicoloured	1·50	55

262 Glass Works

1980. Pointe Noire Glass Works. Multicoloured.

723	30f. Type **262**	30	25
724	35f. Glass works (different)	55	45

263 Claude Chappe and Semaphore Tower

1980. Claude Chappe Commemoration.

725	**263**	200f. multicoloured	2·50	1·50

264 Real Madrid Stadium

1980. Air. World Cup Football Championship, Spain (1982). Multicoloured.

726	60f. Type **264**	55	10
727	75f. Real Zaragoza	75	25
728	100f. Atletico de Madrid	1·00	45
729	150f. Valencia C.F.	1·40	40
730	175f. R.C.D. Espanol	2·00	45
MS731	104×79 mm. 250f. F.C. Barcelona stadium	2·20	1·10

265 Floating Quay

1980. Port of Mossaka. Multicoloured.

732	45f. Type **265**	45	25
733	90f. Aerial view of port	1·00	55

266 "Crucifixion"

1980. Air. Paintings by Rembrandt. Multicoloured.

734	65f. "Adoration of the Shepherds" (detail) (horiz)	65	25
735	100f. "Entombment" (horiz)	1·00	45
736	200f. "Christ at Emmaus" (horiz)	2·00	60
737	300f. "Annunciation"	3·00	80
738	500f. Type **266**	5·50	1·40

267 Jacques Offenbach (composer)

1980. Air. Death Anniversaries. Multicoloured.

739	100f. Albert Camus (writer) (20th anniv)	1·30	65
740	150f. Type **267** (centenary)	2·20	1·40

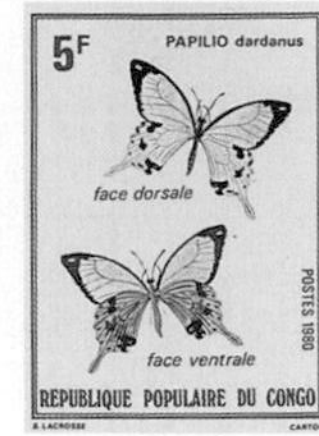

268 "Papilio dardanus"

1980. Butterflies. Multicoloured.

741	5f. Type **268**	45	10
742	15f. "Kallima aethiops"	90	20
743	20f. "Papilio demodocus"	90	25
744	60f. "Euphaedra"	2·40	60
745	90f. "Hypolimnas misippus"	4·50	75
MS746	120×80 mm. 300f. "Charaxes smaragdalis"	15·00	10·00

269 Hospital

1980. "31 July" Hospital.

747	**269**	45f. multicoloured	60	25

270 Man presenting Human Rights Charter

1980. 32nd Anniv of Human Rights Convention. Multicoloured.

748	350f. Type **270**	3·00	1·60
749	500f. Man breaking chains	4·50	2·50

271 Raffia Dancing Skirts

1980. Air. Traditional Dancing Costumes. Mult.

750	250f. Type **271**	3·00	1·10
751	300f. Tam-tam dancers (vert)	3·25	1·70
752	350f. Masks	4·25	2·20

272 Clenched Fists, Flag and Dove

1980. 17th Anniv of Revolution. Multicoloured.

753	75f. Citizens and State emblem (36×23 mm)	75	35
754	95f. Type **272**	95	45
755	150f. Dove carrying state emblem (36×23 mm)	1·40	80

273 Coffee and Cocoa Trees on Map of Congo

1980. Coffee and Cocoa Day. Multicoloured.

756	45f. Type **273**	50	25
757	95f. Coffee and cocoa beans	1·00	60

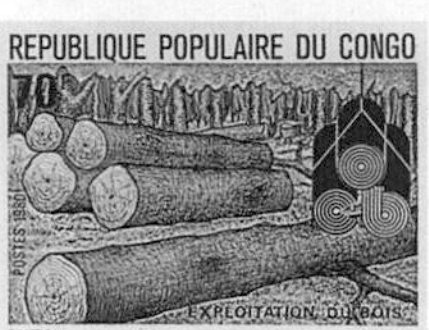

274 Cut Logs

1980. Forest Exploitation. Multicoloured.

758	70f. Type **274**	80	45
759	75f. Lorry with logs	80	45

275 President Neto

1980. 1st Death Anniv of President Neto.

760	**275**	100f. multicoloured	95	45

276 Olive-bellied Sunbird ("Souimanga Olivatre")

1980. Birds. Multicoloured.

761	45f. Type **276**	85	45
762	75f. Red-crowned bishop ("Travailleur a Tete Rouge")	1·00	40
763	90f. Moorhen ("Poule d'Eauafricaine")	1·40	55
764	150f. African pied wagtail ("Alouette Canelle")	2·20	70
765	200f. Yellow-mantled whydah (vert)	3·00	1·40
766	250f. "Geai-bleu" (vert)	3·50	1·60
MS767	148×105 mm. Nos. 761/6	26·00	18·00

277 Conference Emblem

1980. World Tourism Conference, Manila.

768	**277**	100f. multicoloured	95	55

278 Child Writing

1980. Return to School.

769	**278**	50f. multicoloured	55	25

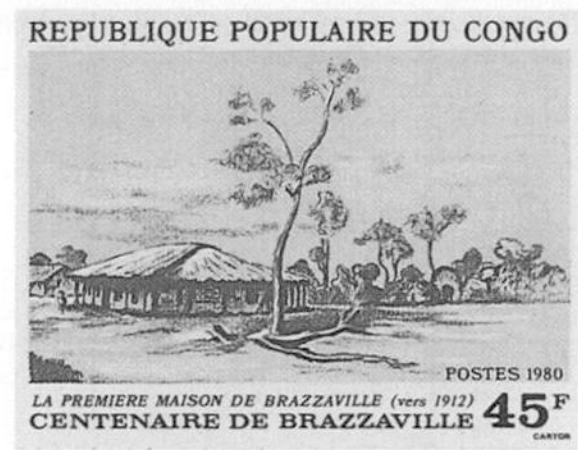

279 The First House

1980. Brazzaville Centenary.

770	**279**	45f. ochre, grey & brown	50	25
771	-	65f. lt brown, brn & orge	75	45
772	-	75f. multicoloured	1·00	60
773	-	150f. multicoloured	1·80	1·20
774	-	200f. multicoloured	2·30	1·70

DESIGNS: 65f. First native village; 75f. The old Town Hall; 150f. Brazzaville from the Bacongo Promontory, 1912; 200f. Meeting between Savorgnan de Brazza (explorer) and Makoko (local chieftain).

280 Cataracts

1980. The River Congo. Multicoloured.

775	80f. Type **280**	1·00	55
776	150f. Bridge at Djoue	1·80	80

1980. Air. Olympic Medal Winners. Nos. 716/19 optd.

777	75f. **DOMBROWSKI (RDA)**	75	45
778	150f. **SANEIEV (URSS)**	1·40	80
779	250f. **SIMEONI (IT)**	2·40	1·20
780	350f. **THOMPSON (GB)**	3·50	1·70
MS781	103×78 mm. 500f. **UUDMAE (URSS)**	4·75	4·25

282 Stadium and Sportsmen

1980. Revolutionary Stadium. Heroes of Congolese Sport.

782	**282**	60f. multicoloured	75	45

283 New Railway Bridge

1980. Realignment of Railway.

783	**283**	75f. multicoloured	95	45

284 Mangoes

1980. Loudima Fruit Station. Multicoloured.

784	10f. Type **284**	30	10
785	25f. Oranges	50	10
786	40f. Lemons	60	25
787	85f. Mandarins	1·10	40

1980. 5th Anniv of African Posts and Telecommunications Union. As T **269** of Benin.

788	100f. multicoloured	95	45

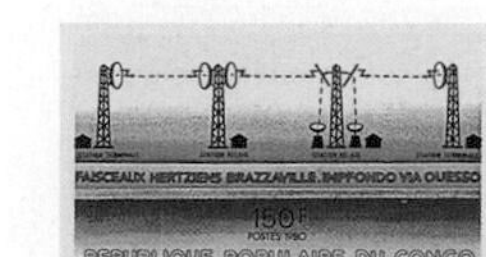

285 Microwave Communication

1980. Communications. Multicoloured.

789	75f. Moungouni Earth Station (36×36 mm)	75	40
790	150f. Type **285**	1·50	55

286 Presentation of Marien Ngouabi Handball Cup

1981. African Handball Champions. Mult.

791	100f. Type **286**	1·30	40
792	150f. Team members	1·50	70

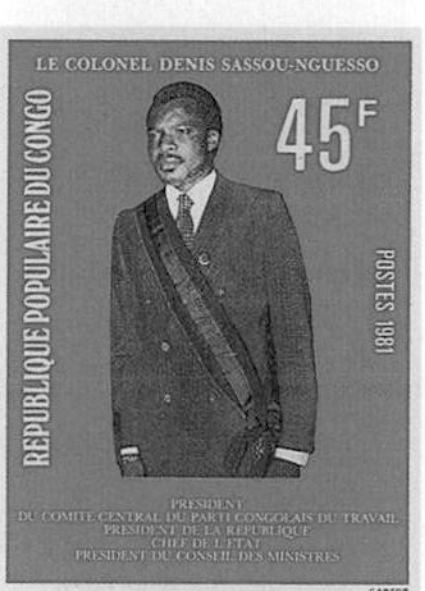

287 Pres. Sassou-Nguesso

1981. President Sassou-Nguesso.

793	**287**	45f. multicoloured	45	20
794	**287**	75f. multicoloured	70	25
795	**287**	100f. multicoloured	95	50

288 Space Shuttle

1981. Conquest of Space. Multicoloured.

796	100f. "Luna 17"	1·00	25
797	150f. Type **288**	1·50	40
798	200f. Satellite and space shuttle	1·90	60
799	300f. Space shuttle approaching landing strip	2·75	85
MS800	103×79 mm. 500f. Space shuttle launch	5·00	1·70

289 Head and Dove

1981. Anti-Apartheid Campaign.

801	**289**	100f. blue	95	40

290 Twin Palm Tree

1981. The Twin Palm Tree of Louingui.

802	**290**	75f. multicoloured	1·00	45

291 Bird approaching Snare

1981. Traditional Snares and Traps. Mult.

803	5f. Type **291**	10	10
804	10f. Bird in snare (vert)	10	10
805	15f. Rodent approaching snare	35	20
806	20f. Rodent in snare	35	20
807	30f. Sprung trap	45	30
808	35f. Deer approaching trap	45	30

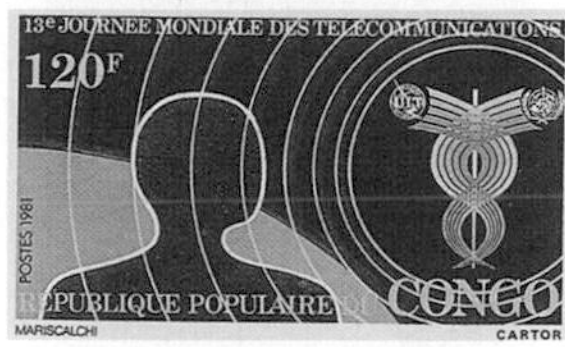

292 Human Figure and Caduceus

1981. World Telecommunications Day.

809	**292**	120f. multicoloured	1·30	40

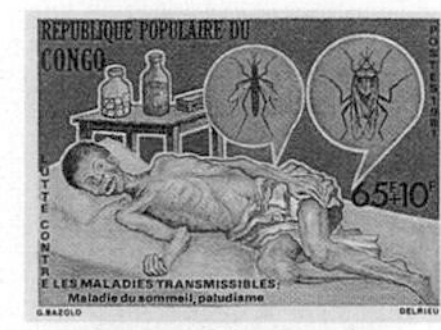

293 Sleeping Sickness and Malaria Victim

1981. Campaign against Transmissible Diseases. Multicoloured.

810	40f.+5f. Doctor, nurse, patients and mosquito	60	25
811	65f.+10f. Type **293**	1·00	60

294 Collecting Rubber

1981. Rubber Extraction. Multicoloured.

812	50f. Tapping rubber tree	60	25
813	70f. Type **294**	95	45

295 Helping a Disabled Person

1981. International Year of Disabled People.

814	**295**	45f. blue, purple & red	45	25
815	-	75f.+5f. multicoloured	95	60

DESIGN: 75f. Disabled people superimposed on globe.

296 "The Studio"

1981. Air. Birth Centenary of Pablo Picasso. Multicoloured.

816	100f. Type **296**	1·20	45
817	150f. "Landscape Land and Sea"	1·80	60
818	200f. "The Studio at Cannes"	2·30	80
819	300f. "Still-life with Water Melon"	4·00	1·20
820	500f. "Large Still-life"	6·50	2·00

297 King Maloango and Mausoleum

1981. Mausoleum of King Maloango. Mult.

821	75f. Mausoleum	75	25
822	150f. Type **297**	1·50	60

298 Prince Charles, Lady Diana Spencer and Coach

1981. Wedding of Prince of Wales. Mult.

823	100f. Type **298**	1·00	50
824	200f. Couple and Landau	1·90	70
825	300f. Couple and horses	3·00	1·10
MS826	103×78 mm. 400f. Couple and ornament	4·00	1·50

299 Preparing Food

1981. World Food Day.

827	**299**	150f. multicoloured	1·70	70

300 Bird carrying Letter

1981. Universal Postal Union Day.

828	**300**	90f. blue, red and grey	95	30

301 Guardsman

1981. Royal Guard.

829	**301**	45f. multicoloured	60	25

302 Spraying Cassava

1981. Campaign for the Control of Cassava Beetle.

830	**302**	75f. multicoloured	1·20	40

303 Bandaging a Patient

1981. Red Cross. Multicoloured.

831	10f. Type **303**	10	10
832	35f. Inoculating a young girl	45	25
833	60f. Nurse and villagers	65	40

304 Brazza's Tree

1981. Tree of Brazza.

834	**304**	45f. multicoloured	85	25
835	**304**	75f. multicoloured	1·10	35

305 Fetish

1981. Fetishes.

836	**305**	15f. multicoloured	10	10
837	-	25f. multicoloured	30	10
838	-	45f. multicoloured	45	10
839	-	50f. multicoloured	60	25
840	-	60f. multicoloured	75	45

DESIGNS: 25f. to 60f. Different fetishes.

306 Bangou Caves

1981. Bangou Caves.

841	**306**	20f. multicoloured	45	25
842	**306**	25f. multicoloured	45	25

307 "Congolese Coiffure"

1982. Ivory Sculptures by R. Engongodzo. Multicoloured.

843	25f. Type **307**	35	10
844	35f. "Congo Coiffure" (different)	40	10
845	100f. "King Makoko, his Queen and Counsellor" (horiz)	1·00	45

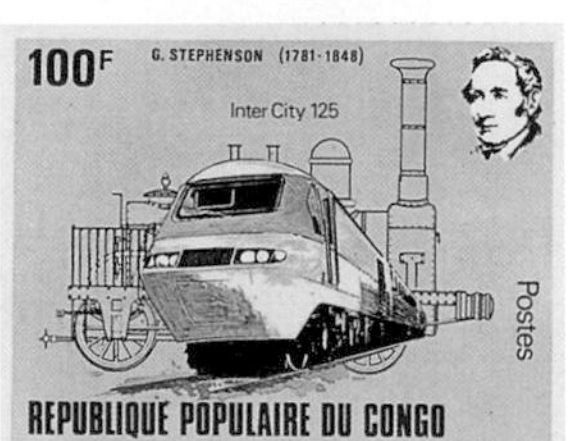

308 "Patentee" and Inter-City 125 Express Train, Great Britain

1982. Birth Bicentenary (1981) of George Stephenson (railway engineer). Multicoloured.

846	100f. Type **308**	1·00	45
847	150f. "Hikari" express train, Japan	1·60	55
848	200f. Advanced Passenger Train (APT), Great Britain	2·20	70
849	300f. TGV 001 locomotive, France	3·25	1·10

309 Scout with Binoculars

1982. 75th Anniv of Boy Scout Movement. Multicoloured.

850	100f. Type **309**	1·00	35
851	150f. Scout reading map	1·50	45
852	200f. Scout talking to village woman	1·90	60
853	300f. Scouts on rope bridge	2·75	80
MS854	96×70 mm. 500f. Scouts (horiz)	5·25	1·50

310 Franklin D. Roosevelt

1982. Anniversaries. Multicoloured.

855	150f. Type **310** (birth cent)	1·60	55
856	250f. George Washington on horseback (250th birth anniv)	2·20	80
857	350f. Johann von Goethe (writer) (150th death anniv)	3·25	1·00

311 Princess of Wales and Candles

1982. 21st Birthday of Princess of Wales. Mult.

858	200f. Type **311**	2·10	60
859	300f. Princess and "21"	2·75	80
MS860	112×80 mm. 500f. Princess within picture frame	4·75	1·50

312 Road Building

1982. Five Year Plan. Multicoloured.

861	60f. Type **312**	85	45
862	100f. Telecommunications	1·20	60
863	125f. Operating theatre equipment	1·50	70
864	150f. Hydro-electric project	2·00	95

313 Dish Antenna

1982. ITU Delegates' Conference, Nairobi.

865	**313**	300f. multicoloured	3·00	1·40

314 Mosque, Medina

1982. Air. 1350th Death Anniv of Mohammed.

866	**314**	400f. multicoloured	4·25	1·90

315 WHO Regional Office

1982. World Health Organization Regional Office, Brazzaville.

867	**315**	125f. multicoloured	1·20	60

316 Mother feeding Baby

1982. Health Campaign.

868	**316**	100f. multicoloured	1·00	55

1982. Birth of Prince William of Wales. Nos. 823/**MS**826 optd **NAISSANCE ROYALE 1982**.

869	100f. multicoloured	95	50
870	200f. multicoloured	1·80	90
871	300f. multicoloured	2·75	1·40
MS872	103×78 mm. 400f. multicoloured	3·75	3·50

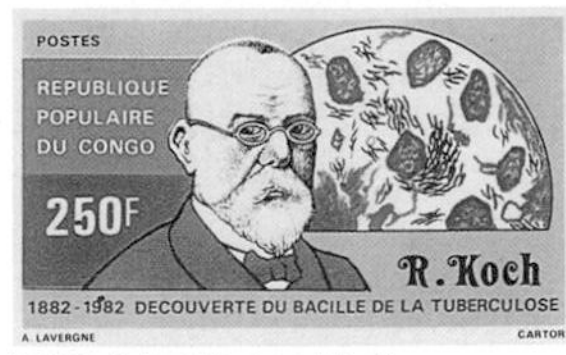

318 Dr. Robert Koch and Bacillus

1982. Centenary of Discovery of Tubercle Bacillus.

873	**318**	250f. multicoloured	3·25	1·40

1982. World Cup Football Championship Results. Nos. 724/28 optd.

874	60f. **EQUIPE QUATRIEME FRANCE**	45	25
875	75f. **EQUIPE TROISIEME POLOGNE**	75	45
876	100f. **EQUIPE SECONDE ALLEMAGNE (RFA)**	1·00	60
877	150f. **EQUIPE VAINQUEUR/ ITALIE**	1·40	70
878	175f. **ITALIE–ALLEMAGNE (RFA) 3 1**	2·00	90
MS879	104×79 mm. 250f. As No. 878	2·50	2·30

320 Pres. Sassou-Ngeusso and Prize

1982. Award of 1980 Simba Prize to Pres. Sassou-Nguesso.

880	**320**	100f. multicoloured	95	45

321 Turtle

1982. Turtles.

881	**321**	30f. multicoloured	50	25
882	-	45f. multicoloured	85	45
883	-	55f. multicoloured	1·00	65

DESIGNS: 45, 55f. Different turtles.

322 Amelia Earhart and "Friendship"

1982. 50th Anniv of Amelia Earhart's Transatlantic Flight.

884	**322**	150f. lt brown, grn & brn	1·80	90

323 "La Malafoutier"

1982

885	**323**	100f. multicoloured	1·20	40

324 Grey Parrots nesting in Hole in Tree

1982. Birds' Nests. Multicoloured.

886	40f. Type **324**	95	25
887	75f. Palm tree and nest	1·60	45
888	100f. Nest hanging from branch	2·40	60

325 Map of Network

1982. Hertzian Wave Network.

889	**325**	45f. multicoloured	45	25
890	**325**	60f. multicoloured	55	25
891	**325**	95f. multicoloured	1·00	40

326 Council Headquarters, Brussels

1983. 30th Anniv of Customs Co-operation Council.

892	**326**	100f. multicoloured	95	45

327 Marien N'Gouabi Mausoleum

1983

893	**327**	60f. multicoloured	1·00	25
894	**327**	80f. multicoloured	85	45

328 Raffia Weaving

1983

895	**328**	150f. multicoloured	1·50	70

329 Chess Pieces

1983. Chess Pieces Carved by R. Engongonzo. Multicoloured.

896	40f. Type **329**	45	25
897	60f. Close-up of white pawn, king, queen and bishop	75	45
898	95f. Close-up of black rook, bishop, queen and king	1·40	70

330 Blacksmiths

1983

899	**330**	45f. multicoloured	55	25

331 Study for "The Transfiguration"

1983. Easter. 500th Birth Anniv of Raphael. Multicoloured.

900	200f. Type **331**	2·30	60
901	300f. "Deposition from the Cross" (horiz)	3·25	85
902	400f. "Christ in his Glory"	4·00	1·20

332 Comb

1983. Traditional Combs. Multicoloured.

903	30f. Type **332**	35	10
904	70f. Comb (different)	90	25
905	85f. Three combs	1·00	60

333 "Pila ovata"

1983. Shells. Multicoloured.

905a	25f. Charonia lampas		
906	35f. Type **333**	90	35
907	65f. True achatina	1·30	50

334 Windsurfing

1983. Air. Pre-Olympic Year.

908	**334**	100f. multicoloured	95	30
909	-	200f. mult (horiz)	1·80	60
910	-	300f. multicoloured	2·75	85
911	-	400f. multicoloured	3·75	1·20
MS912		104×80 mm. 500f. multicoloured (horiz)	4·50	1·50

DESIGNS: 200 to 500f. Various windsurfing scenes.

335 Montgolfier Balloon, 1783

1983. Air. Bicentenary of Manned Flight. Mult.

913	100f. Type **335**	1·50	25
914	200f. Montgolfier balloon "Le Flesselles", 1784	2·50	60
915	300f. Auguste Piccard's stratosphere balloon "F.N.R.S.", 1931	3·25	85
916	400f. Modern hot-air balloon	4·50	1·20
MS917	79×100 mm. 500f. Paris siege balloon, 1870	5·75	1·80

336 Hands holding Gun and Pick

1983. 20th Anniv of Revolution.

918	**336**	60f. multicoloured	45	25
919	**336**	100f. multicoloured	95	45

337 Mgr. A. Carrie and Church of the Sacred Heart, Loango

1983. Centenary of Evangelism. Multicoloured.

920	150f. Type **337**	1·60	70
921	250f. Mgr. Augouard and St. Joseph's Church, Linzolo	2·75	1·20

338 Thunbergia

1984. Flowers. Multicoloured.

922	5f. Type **338**	10	10
923	15f. Bougainvillaea (horiz)	35	10
924	20f. Anthurium	45	10
925	45f. Allamanda (horiz)	80	25
926	75f. Hibiscus	1·20	60

339 "Virgin and Child with St. John"

1984. Air. Christmas. Paintings by Botticelli. Multicoloured.

927	150f. Type **339**	1·50	55
928	350f. "Virgin and Child" (St. Barnabas)	3·25	1·20
929	500f. "Virgin and Child"	5·00	1·70

340 "Vase of Flowers" (Manet)

1984. Air. Paintings. Multicoloured.

930	100f. Type **340**	1·00	35
931	200f. "The Small Holy Family" (Raphael)	1·90	65
932	300f. "La Belle Jardiniere" (detail) (Raphael)	2·75	1·00
933	400f. "The Virgin of Lorette" (Raphael)	3·75	1·40
934	500f. "Richard Wagner" (Giuseppe Tivoli)	4·75	1·70

341 Peace Dove

1984. 34th Anniv of World Peace Council.

935	**341**	50f. multicoloured	45	25
936	**341**	100f. multicoloured	95	45

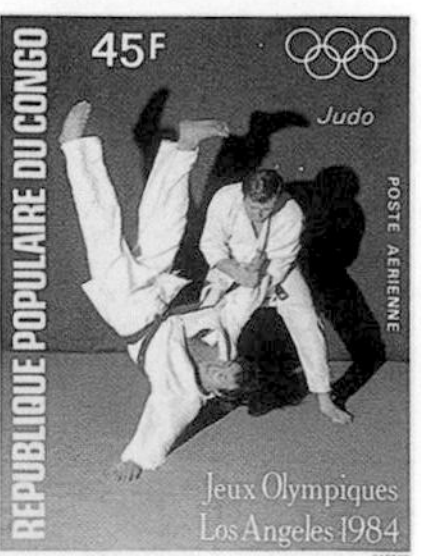

342 Judo

1984. Air. Olympic Games, Los Angeles. Mult.

937	45f. Type **342**	45	10

938	75f. Judo (different) (horiz)	75	25
939	150f. Wrestling (horiz)	1·50	50
940	175f. Fencing (horiz)	1·60	60
941	350f. Fencing (different) (horiz)	3·50	1·20
MS942	103×80 mm. 500f. Boxing	4·75	2·30

343 Mushroom Cloud

1984. Campaign against Weapons of Mass Destruction.

943	**343**	200f. black, brown & orge	1·80	70

344 Rice

1984. Agriculture. Multicoloured.

944	10f. Type **344**	10	10
945	15f. Pineapples	10	10
946	60f. Manioc (vert)	60	25
947	100f. Palms (vert)	1·20	45

345 Congress Palace

1984. Chinese–Congolese Co-operation.

948	**345**	60f. multicoloured	55	25
949	**345**	100f. multicoloured	95	40

346 Loulombo Station

1984. 50th Anniv of Congo Railways. Mult.

950	10f. Type **346**	20	10
951	25f. Chinese workers' camp at Les Bandas	40	30
952	125f. "50" forming bridge and tunnel	1·70	1·00
953	200f. Headquarters building	3·75	1·40

347 Alsthom CC203 Diesel Locomotive

1984. Transport. Multicoloured. (a) Locomotives.

954	100f. Type **347**	1·20	45
955	150f. Alsthom BB 103 diesel	1·80	65
956	300f. Diesel locomotive No. BB BB 301	3·75	1·40
957	500f. BB420 diesel train "L'Eclair"	5·25	2·00

(b) Ships.

958	100f. Pusher tug	1·20	45
959	150f. Pusher tug (different)	1·60	65
960	300f. Buoying boat	3·25	1·40
961	500f. "Saint" (freighter)	5·25	2·10

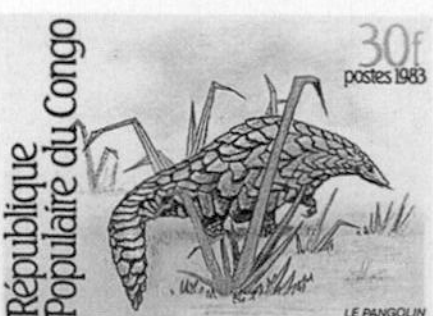

348 Giant Ground Pangolin

1984. Animals. Multicoloured.

962	30f. Type **348**	2·40	70
963	70f. Bat	5·25	1·30
964	85f. African civet	6·75	1·80

Nos. 962/4 are inscribed "1983".

349 Fish in Basket

1984. World Fisheries Year. Multicoloured.

965	5f. Type **349**	35	10
966	20f. Casting nets	50	10
967	25f. Fishes	50	10
968	40f. Men pulling nets in	85	40
969	55f. Boat net and fishes	1·40	55

350 Polio Victims and Hand

1984. Anti-polio Campaign. Multicoloured.

970	250f. Type **350**	2·75	1·20
971	300f. Polio victims within target	3·25	1·70

351 M'bamou Palace Hotel, Brazzaville

1984

972	**351**	60f. multicoloured	45	25
973	**351**	100f. multicoloured	95	25

352 S. van den Berg, Windsurfing

1984. Air. Olympic Games Yachting Gold Medal Winners. Multicoloured.

974	100f. Type **352**	1·00	40
975	150f. U.S.A., "Soling" class (horiz)	1·50	60
976	200f. Spain, "470" dinghy (horiz)	2·00	90
977	500f. U.S.A., "Flying Dutchman" two-man dinghy	4·50	2·00

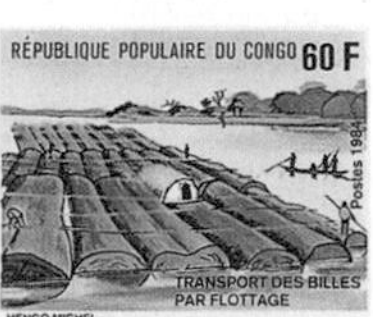

353 Floating Logs

1984. Floating Logs on River Congo. Mult.

978	60f. Type **353**	60	25
979	100f. Logs and boat on river	1·40	55

354 "The Holy Family"

1985. Air. Christmas. Multicoloured.

980	100f. Type **354**	1·00	40
981	200f. "Virgin and Child" (G. Bellini) (horiz)	1·90	85
982	400f. "Virgin and Child with Angels" (Cimabue)	3·75	1·70

355 "Zonocerus variegatus"

1985

983	**355**	125f. multicoloured	1·60	55

1985. International Exhibitions. Nos. **MS**800, **MS**854, **MS**912 and **MS**917 optd.

MS984	(a) 500f. **TSUKUBA EXPO '85**; (b) 500f. **Italia'85 ROME** and emblem; (c) 500f. **OLYMPHILEX '85 LAUSANNE** and emblem; (d) 500f. **MOPHILA '85 HAMBOURG**	5·50	5·50

357 Black-headed Grosbeaks

1985. Air. Birth Bicentenary of John J. Audubon (ornithologist). Multicoloured.

985	100f. Type **357**	1·00	45
986	150f. Scarlet ibis	1·60	65
987	200f. Red-tailed hawk (horiz)	2·30	90
988	350f. Labrador duck	4·00	1·50

358 Funeral Procession

1985. Burial of Teke Chief.

989	**358**	225f. multicoloured	2·30	1·00

359 Mother weighing Child

1985. "Philexafrique" Stamp Exhibition, Lome, Togo (1st issue). Multicoloured.

990	200f. Type **359**	2·75	2·00
991	200f. Boy writing and man ploughing field	2·75	2·00

See also Nos. 1004/5.

360 "Trichoscypha acuminata"

1985. Fruits. Multicoloured.

992	5f. Type **360**	10	10
993	10f. "Aframomum africanum"	10	10
994	125f. "Gambeya lacuurtiana"	1·30	60
995	150f. "Landolphia jumelei"	1·70	80

361 Brazzaville Lions Club Pennant

1985. 30th Anniv of Lions Club.

996	**361**	250f. multicoloured	2·75	1·00

362 Moscow Kremlin, Soldier and Battlefield

1985. 40th Anniv of End of World War II.

997	**362**	60f. multicoloured	60	25

363 Doves forming Heart

1985. Air. 25th Anniv of U.N. Membership.

998	**363**	190f. multicoloured	1·80	85

365 Girl Guide with Yellow-bellied Wattle-eye (International Youth Year)

1985. Anniversaries and Events. Multicoloured.

999	150f. Type **365**	1·60	65
1000	250f. Jacob Grimm (folklorist) and scene from "Snow White and the Seven Dwarfs" (birth bicentenary) (International Youth Year)	2·30	1·10
1001	350f. Johann Sebastian Bach (composer) and organ (300th birth anniv) (European Music Year)	3·00	1·30
1002	450f. Queen Elizabeth, the Queen Mother (85th birthday) (vert)	3·75	1·70
1003	500f. Statue of Liberty (centenary) (vert)	4·75	2·10

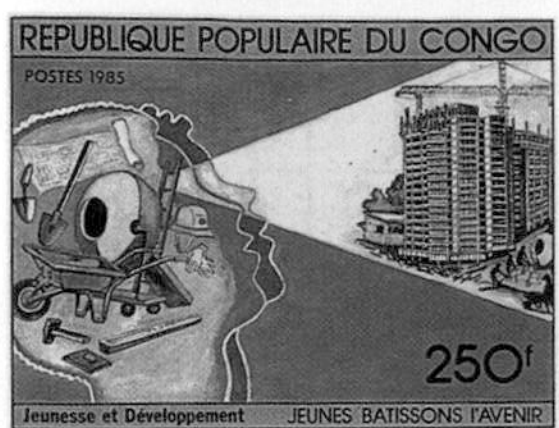

366 Construction Equipment within Heads and Building

1985. "Philexafrique" Stamp Exhibition, Lome, Togo (2nd issue). Multicoloured.

1004	250f. Type **366**		2·75	2·00
1005	250f. Loading mail at airport		2·75	2·00

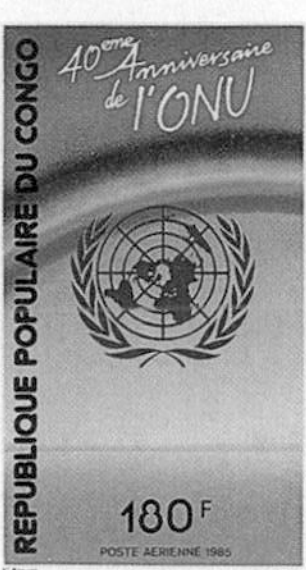

367 Emblem and Rainbow

1985. Air. 40th Anniv of UNO.

1006	**367**	180f. multicoloured	1·80	70

368 "Coprinus"

1985. Fungi. Multicoloured.

1007	100f. Type **368**	1·60	40
1008	150f. "Cortinarius"	2·30	65
1009	200f. "Armillariella mellea"	3·00	75
1010	300f. "Dictyophora"	3·75	1·20
1011	400f. "Crucibulum vulgare"	5·50	1·70

369 "Virgin and Child" (Gerard David)

1985. Air. Christmas. Multicoloured.

1012	100f. Type **369**	1·00	35
1013	200f. "Adoration of the Magi" (Hieronymus Bosch)	1·90	70
1014	400f. "Virgin and Child" (Anthony Van Dyck) (horiz)	3·75	1·60

370 Edmond Halley and Computer Picture of Comet

1986. Air. Appearance of Halley's Comet. Multicoloured.

1015	125f. Type **370**	1·00	45
1016	150f. West's Comet, 1976 (vert)	1·60	55
1017	225f. Ikeya-Seki Comet, 1965 (vert)	2·30	85
1018	300f. "Giotto" space probe and comet trajectory	2·75	1·10
1019	350f. Comet and "Vega" space probe	2·75	1·30

371 President planting Sapling

1986. National Tree Day. Multicoloured.

1020	60f. Type **371**	50	25
1021	200f. Map, tree and production of oxygen and carbon dioxide	2·10	85

372 Boys and Hoops with Handles

1986. Children's Hoop Races. Multicoloured.

1022	5f. Type **372**	10	10
1023	10f. Boy with hoop on string	10	10
1024	60f. Boys racing with hoops (horiz)	75	25
MS1025	150×200 mm. Nos. 1022/4	1·60	1·60

373 Cosmos-Frantel Hotel

1986. Air.

1026	**373**	250f. multicoloured	2·30	1·00

375 Emptying Rubbish into Dustbin

1986. World Environment Day. Multicoloured.

1030	60f. Type **375**	60	25
1031	125f. Woman dumping rubbish in street	1·30	50

376 Woman carrying Basket on Head

1986. Traditional Methods of Carrying Goods. Multicoloured.

1032	5f. Type **376**	10	10
1033	10f. Woman carrying basket at back held by rope from head	10	10
1034	60f. Man carrying wood on shoulder	75	50

377 Footballers

1986. Air. World Cup Football Championship, Mexico.

1035	**377**	150f. multicoloured	1·40	60
1036	-	250f. multicoloured	2·50	1·00
1037	-	440f. multicoloured	4·00	1·70
1038	-	600f. multicoloured	6·25	2·40

DESIGNS: 250f. to 600f. Various football scenes.

378 Sisters tending Patients

1986. Centenary of Sisters of St. Joseph of Cluny Mission.

1039	**378**	230f. multicoloured	2·75	1·50

379 Programme Emblem

1986. International Communications Development Programme.

1040	**379**	40f. multicoloured	45	25
1041	**379**	60f. multicoloured	55	45
1042	**379**	100f. multicoloured	1·00	60

380 Emblem

1986. International Peace Year.

1043	**380**	100f. blue, grn & lt grn	1·00	50

381 Foodstuffs

1986. World Food Day. Multicoloured.

1044	75f. Type **381**	80	45
1045	120f. Woman spoon-feeding child	1·30	60

382 Woman holding Child and Windmill with Medical Symbols

1986. UNICEF Child Survival Campaign. Multicoloured.

1046	15f. Type **382**	10	10
1047	30f. Children (horiz)	30	25
1048	70f. Woman and child	90	50

383 Douglas DC-10 and "25" on Map

1986. Air. 25th Anniv of Air Afrique.

1049	**383**	200f. multicoloured	2·10	95

384 Lenin

1986. 27th U.S.S.R. Communist Party Congress.

1050	**384**	100f. multicoloured	1·40	60

385 Men's Slalom

1986. Air. Winter Olympic Games, Calgary (1988). Multicoloured.

1051	150f. Type **385**	1·40	60
1052	250f. Four-man bobsleigh (vert)	2·50	1·00
1053	440f. Ladies cross-country skiing (vert)	4·00	1·50
1054	600f. Ski-jumping	6·00	2·30

386 "Virgin and Child"

1986. Air. Christmas. Paintings by Rogier van der Weyden. Multicoloured.

1055	250f. Type **386**	2·30	1·00
1056	440f. "Nativity"	4·25	1·70
1057	500f. "Virgin of the Pink"	5·00	1·70

387 "Osteolaemus tetraspis"

1987. Air. Crocodiles. Multicoloured.

1058	75f. Type **387**	1·90	40
1059	100f. "Crocodylus cataphractus"	2·30	60
1060	125f. "Osteolaemus tetraspis" (different)	2·75	75
1061	150f. "Crocodylus cataphractus" (different)	3·25	1·30

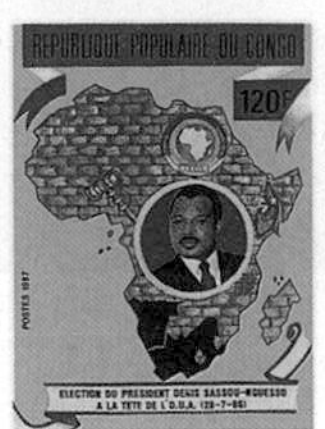

388 Pres. Sassou-Nguesso and Map

1987. Election of Pres. Sassou-Nguesso as Chairman of Organization of African Unity.

1062	**388**	30f. multicoloured	30	10
1063	**388**	45f. multicoloured	45	10
1064	**388**	75f. multicoloured	80	30
1065	**388**	120f. multicoloured	1·30	45

389 Traditional Marriage Ceremony

1987

1066	**389**	5f. multicoloured	10	10
1067	**389**	15f. multicoloured	20	10
1068	**389**	20f. multicoloured	30	10

390 "Sputnik"

1987. Air. 30th Anniv of First Artificial Space Satellite.

1069	**390**	60f. multicoloured	55	25
1070	**390**	240f. multicoloured	2·40	1·40

391 Starting Back-stroke Race

1987. Air. Olympic Games, Seoul (1988) (1st issue). Swimming. Multicoloured.

1071		100f. Type **391**	95	40
1072		200f. Freestyle	1·80	75
1073		300f. Breast-stroke	2·75	1·10
1074		400f. Butterfly	3·75	1·50
MS1075		104×80 mm. 750f. Start of women's race	6·25	4·00

See also Nos. 1121/**MS**1125.

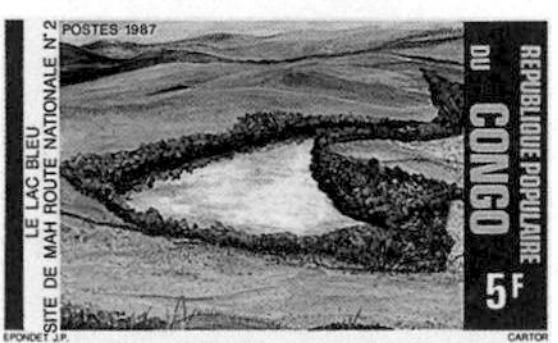

392 Blue Lake, National Route 2

1987

1076	**392**	5f. multicoloured	10	10
1077	**392**	15f. multicoloured	10	10
1078	**392**	75f. multicoloured	1·00	50
1079	**392**	120f. multicoloured	1·50	75

393 Flags and Pres. Ngouabi

1987. 10th Death Anniv of President Marien Ngouabi.

1080	**393**	75f. multicoloured	80	20
1081	**393**	120f. multicoloured	1·30	40

394 "Precis almanta"

1987. Butterflies. Multicoloured.

1082		75f. "Precis epicleli"	1·00	35
1083		120f. "Deilephila nerii"	1·70	55
1084		450f. "Euryphene senegalensis"	5·00	1·70
1085		550f. Type **394**	6·50	2·40

395 Emblem

1987. African Men of Science Congress.

1086	**395**	15f. multicoloured	10	10
1087	**395**	90f. multicoloured	90	60
1088	**395**	230f. multicoloured	2·30	95

396 Fist and Broken Manacle

1987. Anti-Apartheid Campaign. Multicoloured.

1089		60f. Type **396**	60	25
1090		240f. Chain forming outline of map, Nelson Mandela and bars (26×38 mm)	2·50	1·20

397 Hands putting Money into Pot within Map

1987. African Fund.

1091	**397**	25f. multicoloured	30	10
1092	**397**	50f. multicoloured	45	10
1093	**397**	70f. multicoloured	80	25

398 Babies being Vaccinated

1987. National Vaccination Campaign. Mult.

1094		30f. Type **398** (postage)	30	10
1095		45f. Doctor vaccinating child (vert)	75	45
1096		500f. Queue waiting for vaccination (air)	5·25	3·50

399 Handball Player, Map and Runner

1987. 4th African Games, Nairobi.

1097	**399**	75f. multicoloured	80	50
1098	**399**	120f. multicoloured	1·30	75

400 Follereau

1987. 10th Death Anniv of Raoul Follereau (leprosy pioneer).

1099	**400**	120f. multicoloured	1·60	75

401 Coubertin and Greece 1896 1d. Stamp

1987. Air. 50th Death Anniv of Pierre de Coubertin (founder of modern Olympic games). Multicoloured.

1100		75f. Type **401**	80	30
1101		120f. Runners and France 1924 10c. stamp	1·20	45
1102		350f. Congo 1964 100f. stamp and hurdler	3·50	1·40
1103		600f. High jumper and Congo 1968 85f. stamp	5·50	2·30

402 Basket of Produce and Hands holding Ears of Wheat

1987. 40th Anniv of FAO.

1104	**402**	300f. multicoloured	2·75	1·50

403 Hillside Farming and Produce within "2000"

1987. "Food Self-sufficiency by Year 2000".

1105	**403**	20f. multicoloured	30	10
1106	**403**	55f. multicoloured	70	20
1107	**403**	100f. multicoloured	1·00	55

404 Simon Kimbangu

1987. Birth Centenary of Simon Kimbangu (founder of Church of Jesus Christ on Earth). Multicoloured.

1108		75f. Type **404**	75	30
1109		120f. Kimbangu feeding grey parrot	1·20	50
1110		240f. Kimbanguiste Temple, Nkamba (horiz)	2·75	1·50
MS1111		160×100 mm. Nos. 1108/10	5·50	4·25

405 Lenin inspecting Parade in Red Square

1988. 70th Anniv of Russian Revolution.

1112	**405**	75f. multicoloured	1·80	85
1113	**405**	120f. multicoloured	2·40	1·40

406 Writer crossing through "Apartheid"

1988. African Anti-Apartheid Writers.

1114	**406**	15f. multicoloured	10	10
1115	**406**	60f. multicoloured	55	25
1116	**406**	75f. multicoloured	80	45

407 Schweitzer and Hospital

1988. Air. 75th Anniv of Arrival at Lambarene of Dr. Albert Schweitzer (missionary).

1117	**407**	240f. multicoloured	3·00	1·40

408 Samuel Morse

1988. 150th Anniv of Morse Telegraph. Mult.

1118		90f. Type **408**	90	40
1119		120f. Morse and telegraph equipment	1·20	60

409 Banknote and Field within "10"

1988. 10th Anniv of International Agricultural Development Fund.

1120	**409**	240f. multicoloured	2·30	1·10

1988. Air. Olympic Games, Seoul (2nd issue). Modern Pentathlon. As T **391**. Multicoloured.

1121		75f. Swimming	80	30
1122		170f. Cross-country running (vert)	1·80	60
1123		200f. Shooting	2·00	75
1124		600f. Horse-riding	5·50	2·10
MS1125		104×80 mm. 750f. Fencing	7·00	3·00

411 Eucalyptus Plantation, Brazzaville

1988. Anti-desertification Campaign. Mult.

1126		5f. Type **411**	40	10
1127		10f. Stop sign and man chopping down tree	40	10

412 Hands holding Gun and Pick

1988. 25th Anniv of Revolution. Multicoloured.

1128		75f. Type **412**	80	30
1129		75f. People tending crops	80	30
1130		120f. Pres. Sassou-Nguesso holding aubergine	1·00	45

413 Yoro Fishing Village

1988

1131		35f. Type **413**	45	25
1132		40f. Place de la Liberte	45	25

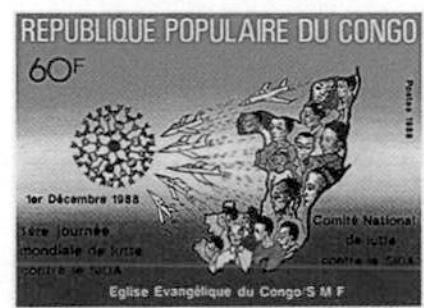

414 People on Map and Jet Fighters attacking Virus

1988. 1st International Day against AIDS.

1133	**414**	60f. multicoloured	45	25
1134	-	75f. multicoloured	75	45
1135	-	180f. black, red & blue	1·80	90

DESIGNS: 75f. Virus consisting of healthy and infected people; 180f. Globe and laurel branches.

415 Pres. Sassou-Nguesso addressing Crowd

1989. 10th Anniv of 5 February Movement. Multicoloured.

1136		75f. Type **415**	80	30
1137		120f. Pres. Sassou-Nguesso and symbols of progress	1·00	55

416 Emblems

1989. 40th Anniv of Declaration of Human Rights.

1138	**416**	120f. multicoloured	1·00	55
1139	**416**	350f. multicoloured	2·75	1·50

417 Bari

1989. Air. World Cup Football Championship, Italy (1990) (1st issue). Multicoloured.

1140		75f. Type **417**	75	30
1141		120f. Rome	1·20	45
1142		500f. Florence	5·00	1·60
1143		550f. Naples	5·50	1·90

See also Nos. 1174/7.

418 "Storming of the Bastille" (detail, J. P. Houel)

1989. Air. "Philexfrance 89" International Stamp Exhibition. Multicoloured.

1144		300f. Type **418** (bicent of French revolution)	3·00	1·30
1145		400f. "Eiffel Tower" (G. Seurat) (centenary of Eiffel Tower (1986))	4·00	1·50

419 Astronaut and Landing Module

1989. Air. 20th Anniv of First Manned Landing on Moon. Multicoloured.

1146		400f. Type **419**	4·00	1·50
1147		400f. Astronaut on lunar surface	4·00	1·50

420 Marien Ngouabi

1989. 50th Birth Anniv (1988) of Marien Ngouabi (President, 1969–77).

1148	**420**	240f. black, yell & mve	2·30	85

421 Henri Dunant (founder), Volunteer with Child and Anniversary Emblem

1989. 125th Anniv (1988) of Red Cross.

1149		75f. Type **421** (postage)	1·00	45
1150		120f. Emblem, Dunant and Congolese Red Cross station (air)	1·20	60

422 Emblem on Dove

1989. 25th Anniv of Organization of African Unity.

1151	**422**	120f. multicoloured	1·20	40

423 "Opuntia phaeacantha"

1989. Cacti. Multicoloured.

1152		35f. Type **423**	35	10
1153		40f. "Opuntia ficus-indica"	50	10
1154		60f. "Opuntia erinacea" (horiz)	75	20
1155		75f. "Opuntia rufida"	1·10	35
1156		120f. "Opuntia leptocaulis" (horiz)	1·50	50
MS1157		55×79 mm. 220f. "Opuntia compresa" (30×39 mm)	3·75	2·30

424 Banknote, Coins and Woman

1989. 25th Anniv of African Development Bank.

1158	**424**	75f. multicoloured	85	45
1159	**424**	120f. multicoloured	1·20	40

425 Ice Dancing

1989. Winter Olympic Games, Albertville (1992) (1st issue). Multicoloured.

1160		75f. Type **425**	60	20
1161		80f. Cross-country skiing	60	30
1162		100f. Speed skating	1·00	35
1163		120f. Luge	1·20	50
1164		200f. Slalom	2·00	65
1165		240f. Ice hockey	2·20	80
1166		400f. Ski jumping	3·75	1·30
MS1167		80×62 mm. 500f. Four-man bobsleigh (31×36 mm)	4·50	2·50

See also Nos. 1245/**MS**1247.

426 Doctor examining Patient

1989. 40th Anniv of WHO. Multicoloured.

1168		60f. Type **426**	80	45
1169		75f. Blood donation (vert)	1·00	70

427 Emblem and People with raised Fists

1989. 20th Anniv of Congolese Workers' Party.

1170	**427**	75f. multicoloured	80	45
1171	**427**	120f. multicoloured	1·30	45

1990. Local Health Campaigns. Nos. 1168/9 optd **NOTRE PLANETE, NOTRE SANTE PENSER GLOBALEMENT AGIR LOCALEMENT.**

1172		60f. multicoloured	80	60
1173		75f. multicoloured	1·00	85

429 Footballers

1990. Air. World Cup Football Championship, Italy (2nd issue). Designs showing footballers.

1174	**429**	120f. multicoloured	1·20	40
1175	-	240f. multicoloured	2·40	90
1176	-	500f. multicoloured	4·50	1·70
1177	-	600f. multicoloured	5·50	2·10

430 Family supporting Open Book

1990. International Literacy Year.

1178	**430**	75f. black, yellow & blue	80	45

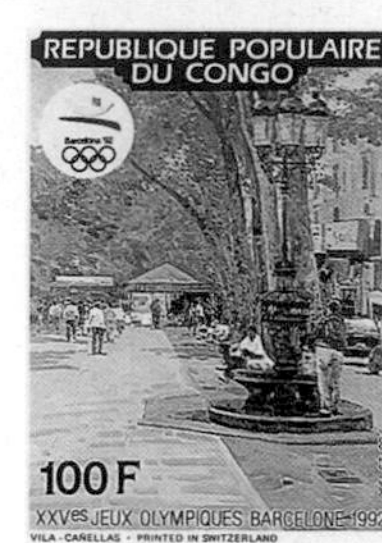

431 Ramblas, Barcelona

1990. Olympic Games, Barcelona (1992) (1st issue). Multicoloured.

1179		100f. Type **431** (postage)	95	35
1180		150f. Yachting (horiz)	1·30	45
1181		200f. Yachting (different) (horiz)	1·90	60
1182		240f. Market stalls, Barcelona (horiz)	2·10	90
1183		350f. Harbour, Barcelona (horiz) (air)	1·40	3·25
1184		500f. Monument, Barcelona	3·25	4·25
MS1185		90×117 mm. 750f. Barcelona Cathedral	6·75	1·70

See also Nos. 1328/**MS**1334.

432 Turtle Dove ("Tourterelle des boris")

1990. Birds. Multicoloured.

1186		25f. Type **432**	35	20
1187		50f. Dartford warbler ("Fauvette Pitchou") (vert)	60	35
1188		70f. Common kestrel ("Faucon Crecerelle") (vert)	1·00	60
1189		150f. Grey parrot ("Perroquet Gris") (vert)	1·90	1·30

433 Mondo Mask

1990. Dance Masks. Multicoloured.

1190		120f. Type **433**	1·20	70

1191	360f. Bapunu mask	3·50	1·50
1192	400f. Kwele mask	4·00	1·70

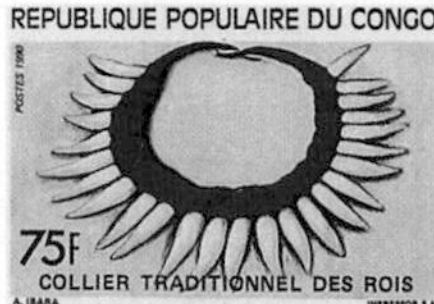

434 Necklace

1990. Traditional Royal Necklaces. Multicoloured.

1193	75f. Type **434**	80	45
1194	100f. Money cowrie necklace	1·10	80

435 Sunflower

1990. Flowers. Multicoloured.

1195	30f. Type **435**	30	10
1196	45f. "Cassia alata" (horiz)	45	25
1197	75f. Opium poppy	80	30
1198	90f. "Acalypha sanderil"	1·00	45

436 Hot-air Balloon dropping Envelopes on Africa

1991. Air. 10th Anniv of Pan-African Postal Union. Multicoloured.

1199	60f. Type **436**	55	40
1200	120f. Envelopes on map of Africa	1·00	60

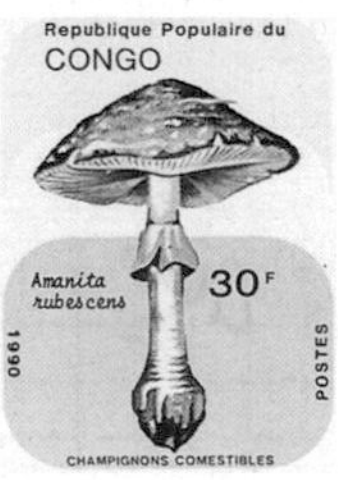

437 The Blusher

1991. Fungi. Multicoloured.

1201	30f. Type **437**	35	10
1202	45f. "Catathelasma imperiale"	45	30
1203	75f. Caesar's mushroom	85	35
1204	90f. Royal boletus	1·00	45
1205	120f. Deer mushroom	1·30	45
1206	150f. "Boletus chrysenteron"	1·80	65
1207	200f. Horse mushroom	2·40	85
MS1208	79×70 mm. 350f. "Boletus versipellis" (39×31 mm)	6·00	2·10

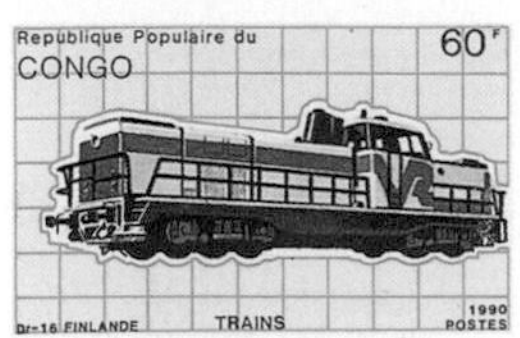

438 Type Dr-16 Diesel Locomotive, Finland

1991. Trains. Multicoloured.

1209	60f. Type **438**	65	20
1210	75f. TGV express, France	75	30
1211	120f. Suburban S-350 electric railcar, Italy	1·30	40
1212	200f. Type DE 24000 diesel locomotive, Turkey	2·20	75
1213	250f. DE 1024 diesel-electric locomotive, Germany	3·25	1·00
MS1214	90×65 mm. 350f. "ETR-450", Italy (31×39 mm)	6·00	1·50

439 Canoe, Palm Tree and Setting Sun

1991. International African Tourism Year. Multicoloured.

1215	75f. Type **439**	80	45
1216	120f. Zebra and map of Africa	1·30	75

440 Congolese Woman

1991

1217	**440**	15f. blue	10	10
1218	**440**	30f. green	30	10
1219	**440**	60f. yellow	35	25
1220	**440**	75f. mauve	55	30
1221	**440**	120f. brown	1·00	50

441 Christopher Columbus (after Sebastian del Pombo)

1991. 500th Anniv (1992) of Discovery of America by Columbus. Multicoloured.

1222	20f. Type **441**	35	10
1223	35f. Christopher Columbus	35	10
1224	40f. Christopher Columbus (different)	45	35
1225	55f. "Santa Maria"	65	35
1226	75f. "Nina"	90	35
1227	150f. "Pinta"	1·70	85
1228	200f. Arms and signature of Columbus	2·20	1·00

442 "Kalanchoe pinnata"

1991. Medicinal Plants. Multicoloured.

1229	15f. "Ocimum viride" (horiz)	10	10
1230	20f. Type **442**	30	10
1231	30f. "Euphorbia hirta" (horiz)	30	10
1232	60f. "Catharantheus roseus"	50	35
1233	75f. "Bidens pilosa"	70	45
1234	100f. "Brillantasia patula"	1·20	60
1235	120f. "Cassia occidentalis"	1·30	95

443 Route Map

1991. Centenary of Trans-Siberian Railway. Mult.

1236	120f. Type **443**	1·50	75
1237	240f. Russian Class N steam locomotive superimposed on map	3·00	1·50

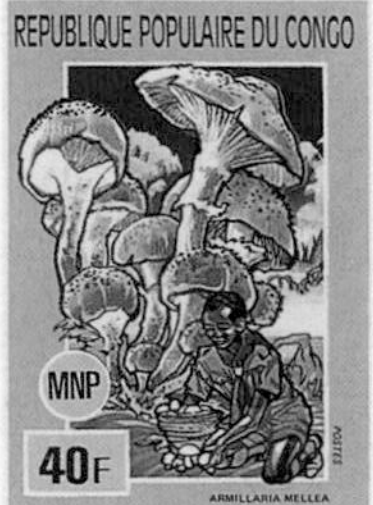

444 Honey fungus

1991. Scouts, Butterflies and Fungi. Mult.

1238	35f. "Euphaedra eusemoides" (butterfly) (postage)	55	35
1239	40f. Type **444**	65	35
1240	75f. "Palla decius" (butterfly)	85	35
1241	80f. "Kallima ansorgei" (butterfly)	1·10	40
1242	500f. "Cortinarius speciocissimus" (fungus) (air)	4·50	1·40
1243	600f. "Graphium illyris" (butterfly)	5·50	1·50
MS1244	99×68 mm. 750f. "Volvariella bombycina" (fungus)	5·75	2·75

445 Ice Hockey

1991. Air. Winter Olympic Games, Albertville (1992) (2nd issue). Multicoloured.

1245	120f. Type **445**	1·50	70
1246	300f. Speed skating	3·25	1·00
MS1247	117×72 mm. 750f. Slalom skiing	7·50	1·80

446 "Telecom 91"

1991. "Telecom 91" World Telecommunications Exhibition, Geneva. Multicoloured.

1248	75f. Type **446**	80	45
1249	120f. Stylized view of exhibition (vert)	1·30	75

447 Beetle and Peanuts

1991. Harmful Insects. Multicoloured.

1250	75f. Type **447**	90	45
1251	120f. Stag beetle (horiz)	1·40	60
1252	200f. Beetle and coffee	2·20	1·00
1253	300f. Goliath beetle	3·25	1·70

448 Woman drinking at Waterfall

1991. "Water is Life".

1254	**448**	75f. multicoloured	80	45

449 Pintail

1991. Wild Ducks. Multicoloured.

1255	75f. Type **449**	95	45
1256	120f. Eider (vert)	1·40	60
1257	200f. Common shoveler (vert)	2·10	1·10
1258	240f. Mallard	2·75	1·40

450 Breaking Chain and Hand holding Dove

1991. 30th Anniv of Amnesty International. Multicoloured.

1259	40f. Candle, barbed wire and sun	45	25
1260	75f. Type **450**	80	45
1261	80f. Boy holding human rights banner and soldiers threatening boy (horiz)	1·00	55

451 1891 5c. on 1c. "Commerce" stamp

1991. Centenary of Congolese Stamps.

1262	**451**	75f. green and brown	80	60
1263	-	120f. dp brn, grn & brn	1·50	1·10
1264	-	240f. multicoloured	2·75	1·90
1265	-	500f. multicoloured	5·00	3·50

DESIGNS: 120f. 1900 1c. "Leopard in ambush" stamp; 240f. 1959 25f. "Birth of the Republic" stamp; 500f. "Commerce", "Leopard" and "Republic" stamps.

452 Ferrari "512 S"

1991. Cars and Space. Multicoloured.

1266	35f. Type **452** (postage)	35	10
1267	40f. Vincenzo Lancia and Lancia "Stratos"	45	10
1268	75f. Airship "Graf Zeppelin", Maybach "Type 12" car and Wilhelm Maybach	85	45
1269	80f. Mars space probe	85	45
1270	500f. "Magellan" space probe over Venus (air)	5·00	1·10
1271	600f. "Ulysses" space probe photographing sun spot	6·25	1·30
MS1272	125×87 mm. 750f. Crew of "Apollo 11" (60×42 mm)	7·25	2·20

453 Small Blue

1991. Butterflies. Multicoloured.

1273	75f. Type **453**	1·00	45
1274	120f. Charaxes	1·30	65
1275	240f. Leaf butterfly (vert)	2·50	1·20
1276	300f. Butterfly on orange (vert)	3·25	2·10

454 General De Gaulle

1991. De Gaulle and Africa. Multicoloured.

1277 75f. Type **454** 1·00 50
1278 120f. De Gaulle, soldiers and Free French flag (vert) 1·30 75
1279 240f. De Gaulle making speech, Brazzaville, 1940 2·50 1·50

455 Bo Jackson (American footballer)

1991. Celebrities and International Organizations. Multicoloured.

1280 100f. Type **455** 1·00 35
1281 150f. Nick Faldo (golfer) 1·50 35
1282 200f. Rickey Henderson and Barry Bonds (baseball players) 2·00 55
1283 240f. Gary Kasparov (World chess champion) 2·75 60
1284 300f. Starving child and Lions International and Rotary International emblems 3·00 70
1285 350f. Wolfgang Amadeus Mozart (composer) 3·75 80
1286 400f. De Gaulle and Churchill visiting the Eastern Front, 1944 4·50 90
1287 500f. Henry Dunant (founder of Red Cross) 5·00 1·10
MS1288 106×74 mm. 750f. President De Gaulle (35×51 mm) 8·75 3·00

456 Painting

1991. Paintings. Multicoloured.

1289 75f. Type **456** 80 40
1290 120f. Couple in silhouette (vert) 1·30 60

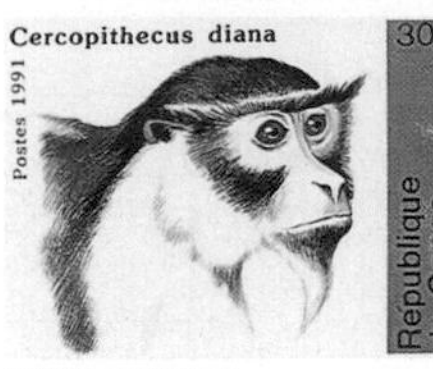

457 Diana Monkey

1991. Primates. Multicoloured.

1291 30f. Type **457** 35 10
1292 45f. Chimpanzee 45 10
1293 60f. Gelada (vert) 85 15
1294 75f. Hamadryas baboon (vert) 1·10 35
1295 90f. Pigtail macaque (vert) 1·40 50
1296 120f. Gorilla (vert) 1·70 50
1297 240f. Mandrill (vert) 3·50 80
MS1298 99×67 mm. 250f. Young gorilla (31×39 mm) 4·00 1·40

458 "Sputnik 2" and Laika (space dog)

1992. Celebrities, Anniversaries and Events. Mult.

1299 50f. Type **458** (35th anniv of space flight) (postage) 85 25
1300 75f. Martin Luther King (Nobel Peace Prize winner, 1964) and Gandhi 85 25
1301 120f. Meteosat "MOP-2" and "ERS-1" satellites, globe and stern trawler ("Europe-Africa") 1·30 40
1302 300f. Konrad Adenauer (German statesman, 25th death anniv) and crowd before Brandenburg Gate (3rd anniv of opening of Berlin Wall) 2·75 75
1303 240f. "Graf Zeppelin", Ferdinand von Zeppelin (75th death anniv) and Maybach Zeppelin motor car (air) 3·00 85
1304 500f. Pope and globe (Papal visit to Africa) 5·50 1·40
MS1305 97×75 mm. 600f. Elvis Presley (entertainer, 15th death anniv) 6·25 2·30

459 Juan de la Cosa and Map

1992. "Genova 92" International Thematic Stamp Exhibition. Multicoloured.

1306 75f. Type **459** 1·10 35
1307 95f. Martin Alonso Pinzon and astrolabe 1·30 35
1308 120f. Alonso de Ojeda and hourglass 2·00 35
1309 200f. Vicente Yanez Pinzon and sun clock 2·75 50
1310 250f. Bartholomew Columbus and quadrant 3·75 60
MS1311 55×81 mm. 400f. Christopher Columbus (40×31 mm) 6·50 1·50

460 Secretary Bird

1992. Birds. Multicoloured.

1312 60f. Type **460** 1·20 35
1313 75f. Saddle-bill stork 1·50 35
1314 120f. Wattled crane 2·00 35
1315 200f. Black-headed heron 3·50 60
1316 250f. Greater flamingo 4·50 85
MS1317 60×84 mm. 400f. South African crowned crane (39×31 mm) 6·75 1·60

461 Lion

1992. Big Cats. Multicoloured.

1318 45f. Type **461** 55 55
1319 60f. Tiger 65 60
1320 75f. Lynx 75 70
1321 95f. Caracal 85 80
1322 250f. Ocelot 2·40 2·20
MS1323 90×64 mm. 400f. Cheetah (31×39 mm) 7·50 1·80

462 "Madonna of the Grand Duke" (Raphael)

1992. Christmas. Multicoloured.

1324 95f. Type **462** 1·20 50
1325 200f. "Madonna of the Book" (Sandro Botticelli) 2·50 90
1326 250f. "Carondelet Madonna" (Fra Bartolommeo) 3·00 1·70
MS1327 59×81 mm. 400f. "Madonna of the Chair" (Raphael) (31×39 mm) 4·50 2·40

No. 1325 is wrongly inscribed "Boticelli" and No. 1326 "Bartolomeo".

463 Baseball and Towers of Church of the Holy Family

1992. Olympic Games, Barcelona (2nd issue). Multicoloured.

1328 75f. Type **463** (postage) 80 20
1329 100f. Running and "The Muses" (Eusebio Arnau) 1·00 35
1330 150f. Hurdling and painted dome (Miguel Barcelo) of Market Theatre 1·50 45
1331 200f. High jumping and Sant Pau hospital 2·20 75
1332 400f. Putting the shot and "Miss Barcelona" (Joan Miro) (air) 3·75 90
1333 500f. Table tennis and "Don Juan of Austria" (galley) 5·00 1·30
MS1334 104×80 mm. 750f. Tennis and Church of the Holy Family (Gaudi) (29×50 mm) 7·25 1·50

464 N. Mishkutienok and A. Dmitriev (Unified Team)

1992. Winter Olympic Games Gold Medal Winners. Multicoloured.

1335 150f. Type **464** (pairs figure skating) (postage) 1·40 35
1336 200f. Austrian team (four-man bobsleighing) 1·80 55
1337 500f. Gunda Niemann (Germany, women's speed skating) (air) 5·00 1·10
1338 600f. Bjorn Daehlie (Norway, 50 km cross-country skiing) 6·25 1·30
MS1339 118×83 mm. 750f. Alberto Tomba (Italy, giant slalom) (35×50 mm) 7·25 1·70

No. 1338 is wrongly inscribed "Blorn Daehlle".

465 African Red-tailed Buzzard ("Charognard")

1993. Birds of Prey. Multicoloured.

1340 45f. Type **465** 90 35
1341 75f. Ruppell's griffon ("Vautour") 1·40 60
1342 120f. Verreaux's eagle ("Aigle") 2·20 1·00

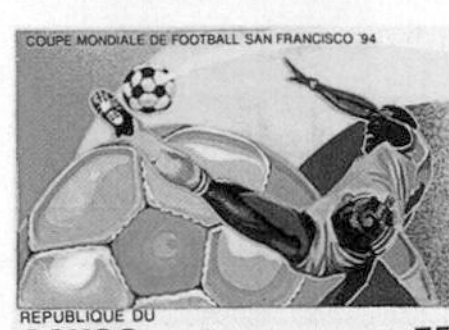

466 Overhead Volley

1993. World Cup Football Championship, U.S.A. (1994).

1343 **466** 75f. multicoloured 1·30 50
1344 - 95f. multicoloured 1·40 75
1345 - 120f. multicoloured 2·20 95
1346 - 200f. multicoloured 3·25 1·40
1347 - 250f. multicoloured 3·75 1·90
MS1348 87×61 mm. 400f. multicoloured 6·75 3·25

DESIGNS: 95f. to 400f. Different footballing scenes.

467 Topi

1993. Animals. Multicoloured.

1349 60f. Type **467** 80 15
1350 75f. Grant's gazelle 1·20 15
1351 95f. Quagga 1·40 30
1352 120f. Leopard 1·90 30
1353 200f. African buffalo 2·75 45
1354 250f. Hippopotamus 3·50 45
1355 300f. Hooded vulture 4·25 45
1356 350f. Lioness and cub 4·75 75

Nos. 1349/56 were issued together, se-tenant, forming a composite design.

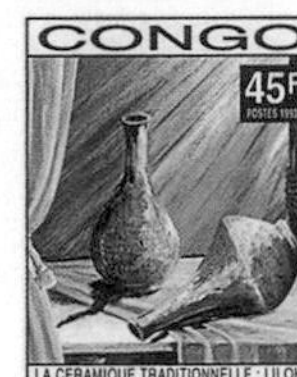

468 Jars from Liloko

1993. Traditional Pottery. Multicoloured.

1357 45f. Type **468** 60 30
1358 75f. Jug from Mbeya 95 50
1359 120f. Jar from Mbeya 1·40 85

470 Show Jumping

1993. Summer Olympic Games, Atlanta (1996) and Winter Olympic Games, Lillehammer, Norway (1994). Multicoloured.

1366 50f. Type **470** (postage) 1·10 30
1367 75f. Cycling 1·10 15
1368 120f. Two-man dinghy 1·10 30
1369 240f. Fencing 2·10 60
1370 300f. Hurdling (air) 2·20 85
1371 400f. Figure skating 2·50 85
1372 500f. Basketball 3·50 1·20
1373 600f. Ice hockey 4·25 1·20
MS1374 Two sheets. (a) 101×71 mm. 750f. Running; (b) 138×101 mm. 750f. Skiing 7·50 1·50

471 "Hibiscus schizopetalus"

1993. Wild Flowers. Multicoloured.

1375 75f. Type **471** 95 25
1376 95f. "Pentas lanceolata" 1·30 45
1377 120f. "Ricinus communis" 2·20 45
1378 200f. "Delonix regia" 3·75 85
1379 250f. "Stapelia gigantea" 4·50 1·40

472 Victor Schoelcher and Slaves

1993. AIR. Personalities. Muulticoloured.

1380	90f. Type **472** (death centenary) (abolition of slavery campaigner)	2·50	1·50
1381	205f. Martin Luther King (25th death anniv) (equal rights campaigner)	4·50	3·00
1382	300f. Claude Chappe (bicentenary of invention of first semaphore telegraph)	7·00	5·00

473 *Choeropsis liberiensis* (pygmy hippopotamus)

1994. Endangered Species. Multicoloured.

1383	50f. Type **473**	50	30
1384	90f. *Hyemoschus aquaticus* (water chevrotain)	1·00	50
1385	205f. *Taurotragus euryceros* (bongo) (vert)	1·80	1·10
1386	300f. *Redunca redunca* (Bohor reedbuck) (vert)	2·50	1·50

474 Woman with Children

1994. International Year of the Family. Multicoloured.

1387	90f. Type **474**	1·00	45
1388	205f. Child's profile in map of Africa	2·30	1·00
1389	300f. Father, mother and child (30×47 mm)	3·25	1·50

475 Warrior, Mbochi

1995. Traditional Costumes. Multicoloured.

1390	90f. Type **475**	1·00	50
1391	205f. Chief seated in chair, Téké	2·30	1·20
1392	500f. Chief seated on platform, Loango	5·25	3·00

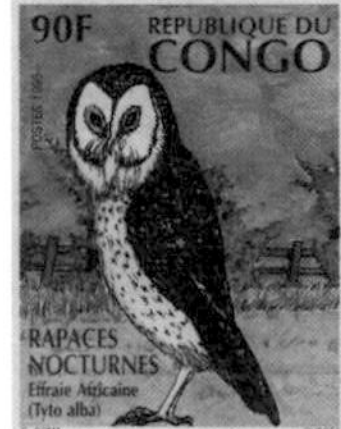

476 *Tyto alba* (barn owl)

1996. African Owls. Multicoloured.

1393	90f. Type **475**	75	40
1394	205f. *Bubo poensis* (Fraser's eagle-owl)	1·80	80
1395	300f. *Scotopelia peli* (Pel's fishing-owl)	2·50	1·10
1396	500f. *Asio capensis* (marsh owl)	4·25	1·80

477 Handshake

1996. World Scout Jamboree, the Netherlands. Multicoloured.

1397	90f. Type **477**	70	35
1398	90f. Scout applying bandages	7·00	35
1399	205f. Life-saving	1·50	80
1400	300f. Robert Baden-Powell (founder)	2·50	1·30

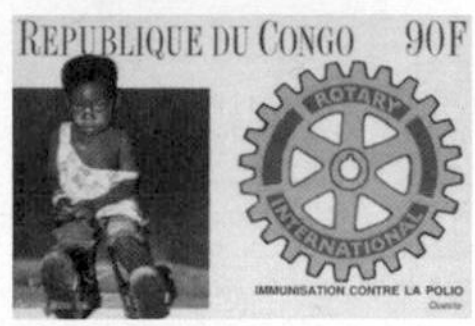

478 Child wearing Calipers

1996. 90th (1995) Anniv of Rotary International. Multicoloured.

1401	90f. Type **478**	60	30
1402	205f. Children eating	1·40	70
1403	205f. Woman playing ball with children	1·40	70
1404	300f. Aid workers carrying polio vaccine	2·00	1·00

479 *Cyrtosperma senegalense* (swamp arum)

1996. Waterplants. Multicoloured.

1405	90f. Type **479**	95	50
1406	205f. *Pistia stratiotes* (inscr 'stratioque') (water lettuce)	2·30	1·20

480 Nile Crocodile

1996. Crocodylia (crocodile like reptiles). Multicoloured.

1407	205f. Type **480**	1·50	65
1408	255f. Gharial (Gavial)	1·60	70
1409	300f. Caiman	2·10	95

481 President Lissouba

1996. Fourth Anniv of President Pascal Lissouba's Investiture (first democratically elected president).

1410	**481**	90f. multicoloured	70	30
1411	**481**	205f. multicoloured	1·60	65

482 Woman carrying Baby

1996. Woman with Basket and Baby

1412	**482**	40f. steel blue	35	15
1413	**482**	50f. brown-purple	40	20
1414	**482**	90f. orange	70	35
1415	**482**	100f. greenish turquoise	80	40
1416	**482**	115f. light grey-black	90	45
1417	**482**	205f. bistre-brown	1·50	80

483 Film Scenes

1996. Anniversaries. Multicoloured.

1418	205f. Rochers de Djeno (20th anniv of OMT) (vert)	1·40	75
1418	90f. Type **483** (centenary of cinema)	60	35
1419	90f. Match (centenary of volleyball) (vert)	60	35
1421	300f. Emblem and '50' (50th anniv of United Nations)	2·00	1·10
1422	300f. Doctor, woman and baby (50th anniv of UNICEF) (vert)	2·00	1·10
1423	300f. Leaves and roots (50th anniv of FAO) (vert)	2·00	1·10

Nos. 1424/75 are left for reported, but not seen, stamps overprinted 'AUTORISE' or 'LEGAL' issued during Civil War.

484 Players (Netherlands 4th place)

1998. World Cup Football Championships, France. Multicoloured.

1476	90f. Type **484**	70	40
1477	205f. Players and head and shoulders of player (Croatia bronze medal)	1·60	85
1478	300f. Three players tackling (Brazil silver medal)	2·40	1·30
1479	500f. Players in goalmouth (France champions)	4·00	2·00

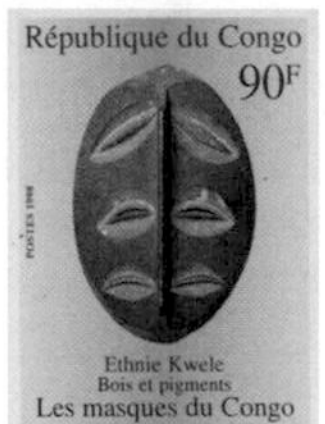

485 Mask, Kwele

1998. Masks. Multicoloured.

1480	90f. Type **485**	80	50
1481	150f. Deer's head mask, Kwele	1·40	80
1482	205f. Incised circular mask, Teke/Tsangui	1·80	1·10
1483	205f. Male head mask, Kuyu	1·80	1·10

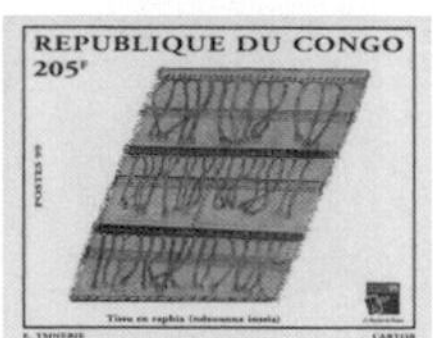

486 Textile (ndzouona inssia)

1999. Traditional Textiles. Multicoloured.

1484	205f. Type **486**	1·60	80
1485	300f. Textile (litsoulou)	2·30	1·20

487 France 1849 20c. Stamp (As Type **1**) and Textile

1999. 150th Anniv of First French Stamp

1486	300f. multicoloured	2·50	1·50

488 Festival Emblem

2001. Pan-African Music Festival, Brazzaville. Multicoloured.

1487	120f. Type **488**	1·10	50
1488	270f. Map of Africa enclosing musicians	2·40	1·20

Nos. 1489/94 and Type **489** are left for Birds issued on 24 October 2001, not yet received.

Nos. 1495/6 and Type **490** are left for 40th Anniv of Independence issued on 15 November 2001, not yet received.

Nos. 1497/502 and Type **491** are left for Wild Fruit issued on 25 June 2002, not yet received.

Nos. 1503/6 and Type **492** are left for Birds issued on 23 July 2002, not yet received.

493 Mammouth

2003. Tusked Mammals

1507	120f. Type **493**	1·00	45
1508	270f. African bush elephant (horiz)	2·30	1·00
1509	350f. Mastodon (horiz)	3·00	1·30
1510	500f. African forest elephant	4·25	1·90

494 Snapdragon (inscr 'Muflier')

2003. Flowering Plants

1511	120f. Type **494**	1·00	45
1512	270f. Peony (inscr 'Pivoine')	2·30	1·00
1513	400f. Petunia	3·25	1·60
1514	600f. Mallow (inscr 'Mauve') (horiz)	5·00	2·50

495 Bark

2005. Medicinal Plants. Multicoloured.

1515	30f. Type **495**	30	20
1516	70f. Root	80	30
1517	90f. Leaves	1·00	45
1518	115f. Seeds	1·10	60
1519	120f. Flowers	1·40	70
1520	360f. Pods	3·50	1·80

Nos. 1521/4 and Type **496** are left for Fruit, issued on 13 July 2005, not yet received.

No. 1525 and Type **497** are left for 50th Death Anniv of Albert Einstein, issued on 17 August 2005, not yet received.

Nos. 1526/7 and Type **498** are left for 125th Anniv of Brazzaville, issued on 3 October 2005, not yet received.

Nos. 1528/9 and Type **499** are left for Pope Benedict XVI, issued on 28 Novemebr 2005, not yet received.

Nos. 1530/3 and Type **500** are left for Coat of Arms, issued on 4 january 2006, not yet received.

501 President Sassou Nguesso

2006. President Sassou Nguesso•Chairman of the African Union

1534	**501**	500f. multicoloured	2·75	1·50

OFFICIAL STAMPS

O68 Arms

1968

O142	**O68**	1f. multicoloured	10	10
O143	**O68**	2f. multicoloured	10	10
O144	**O68**	5f. multicoloured	10	10
O145	**O68**	10f. multicoloured	30	15
O146	**O68**	25f. multicoloured	30	25
O147	**O68**	30f. multicoloured	70	25
O148	**O68**	50f. multicoloured	95	35
O149	**O68**	85f. multicoloured	2·30	90
O150	**O68**	100f. multicoloured	2·50	1·40
O151	**O68**	200f. multicoloured	3·50	2·30

POSTAGE DUE STAMPS

D7 Letter-carrier

1961. Transport designs.

D19	**D7**	50c. bistre, red & blue	10	10
D20	-	50c. bistre, purple & bl	10	10
D21	-	1f. brown, red & green	10	10
D22	-	1f. green, red and lake	10	10
D23	-	2f. brown, green & bl	10	10
D24	-	2f. brown, green & bl	10	10
D25	-	5f. sepia and violet	30	25
D26	-	5f. sepia and violet	30	25
D27	-	10f. brown, blue & grn	75	70
D28	-	10f. brown and green	75	70
D29	-	25f. brown, blue & turq	1·60	1·50
D30	-	25f. black and blue	1·60	1·50

DESIGNS: D20, Holste Broussard monoplane; D21, Hammock-bearers; D22, "Land Rover" car; D23, Pirogue; D24, River steamer of 1932; D25, Cyclist; D26, Motor lorry; D27, Steam locomotive, 1932; D28, Diesel locomotive; D29, Seaplane of 1935; D30, Boeing 707 airliner.

1971. Tropical Flowers. Similar to T 105, but inscr "Timbre-Taxe". Multicoloured.

D264	1f. Stylized bouquet	25	20
D265	2f. "Phaeomeria magnifica"	30	25
D266	5f. "Millettia laurentii"	35	30
D267	10f. "Polianthes tuberosa"	50	45
D268	15f. "Pyrostegia venusta"	80	75
D269	20f. "Hibiscus rosa sinensis"	1·10	1·00

D374 Passion Flower

1986. Flowers and Fruit. Multicoloured.

D1027	5f. Type D **374**	20	20
D1028	10f. Canna lily	40	35
D1029	15f. Pineapple	45	40

APPENDIX

The following stamps have either been issued in excess of postal needs or have not been available to the public in reasonable quantities at face value. Such stamps may later be given full listing if there is evidence of regualr postal use. All embossed on gold foil.

1991

Scout and Butterfly. Air 1500f.
Winter Olympic Games, Albertville (1992). Air 1500f.

1992

Olympic Games, Barcelona. Air 1500f.

Pt. 14

CONGO, DEMOCRATIC REPUBLIC (EX ZAIRE)

In May 1997 Zaire changed its name to the Democratic Republic of Congo after President Mobutu and his Government was overthrown by a rebellion led by Laurent Kabila.

July 1998. 100 cents = 1 Congolese franc.

273 Mother Teresa

1998. 1st Death Anniv of Mother Teresa (founder of Missionaries of Charity).

1494	50000z. Type **273**	1·25	80
MS1495	69×99 mm. 325000z. Praying	7·50	7·50

274 Diana Princess of Wales

1998. 1st Death Anniv of Diana, Princess of Wales. Multicoloured.

1496	50000z. Type **274**	1·10	80
1497	50000z. Wearing white jacket with blue collar	1·10	80
1498	50000z. Wearing large hat	1·10	80
1499	50000z. Wearing white top with blue dots	1·10	80
1500	50000z. Wearing neck scarf	1·10	80
1501	50000z. Wearing pearl necklace	1·10	80
1502	100000z. Wearing tiara	2·10	1·60
1503	100000z. Wearing black top	2·10	1·60
1504	100000z. Resting head on hands	2·10	1·60
1505	100000z. Wearing cream top	2·10	1·60
1506	125000z. Wearing red and black dress	2·50	2·00
1507	125000z. Wearing cream jacket	2·50	2·00
1508	125000z. Profile	2·50	2·00
1509	125000z. Wearing tiara	2·50	2·00
MS1510	Two sheets each 70×100 mm. (a) 400000z. Carrying bouquet; (b) 400000z. Wearing evening dress (31×47 mm)	9·00	9·00

275 Building

1999. Independence. Multicoloured.

1511	25c. Type **275**	50	50
1512	50c. Coat of Arms	95	95
1513	75c. Making speech	1·40	1·40
1514	1f.25 Procession	2·40	2·40
1515	3f. Crowd and man breaking chains	5·50	5·50
MS1516	Two sheets each 90×120 mm. (a) 2f.50 Crossed weapons, handshake and tractor; (b) 3f.50 Crossed weapons, handshake and tractor	10·00	10·00

Nos. 1511/**MS**1516 also exist imperforate.

276 Men fighting in Boat

1999. Outlaws of the Marsh (Chinese literature). Multicoloured.

1517	1f.45 Type **276**	1·10	1·10
1518	1f.45 Men fighting in blacksmith's shop	1·10	1·10
1519	1f.45 Men gathered around tree	1·10	1·10
1520	1f.45 Men writing	1·10	1·10
1521	1f.50 Crowds fighting	1·10	1·25
1522	1f.50 Man pulling tree from ground	1·10	1·25
1523	1f.50 Man threatening other man with sword	1·10	1·25
1524	1f.50 Man climbing over balcony	1·10	1·25
1525	1f.60 Men outside fort	1·25	1·25
1526	1f.60 Man in snow storm	1·25	1·25
1527	1f.60 Man killing tiger	1·25	1·25
1528	1f.60 Man reading writing on wall	1·25	1·25
1529	1f.70 Crowds fighting	1·25	1·40
1530	1f.70 Man drawing sword	1·25	1·40
1531	1f.70 Man jumping from balcony	1·25	1·40
1532	1f.70 Man lifting other man	1·25	1·40
1533	1f.80 Archer on horseback	1·40	1·40
1534	1f.80 Men sitting round table eating	1·40	1·40
1535	1f.80 Joust	1·40	1·40
1536	1f.80 Man tearing scroll	1·40	1·40
MS1537	Four sheets each 110×75 mm. (a) 10f. Man falling into river (83×55 mm); (b) 10f. Men fighting among reeds (83×55 mm); (c) 10f. Horsemen outside burning Fort; (d) 10f. Man dead on floor, horseman and prisoner	16·00	16·00

277 Rat

1999. Chinese Horoscope. Multicoloured.

1538	78c. Type **277**	85	40
1539	78c. Ox	85	40
1540	78c. Tiger	85	40
1541	78c. Rabbit	85	40
1542	78c. Dragon	85	40
1543	78c. Snake	85	40
1544	78c. Horse	85	40
1545	78c. Goat	85	40
1546	78c. Monkey	85	40
1547	78c. Cockerel	85	40
1548	78c. Dog	85	40
1549	78c. Pig	85	40

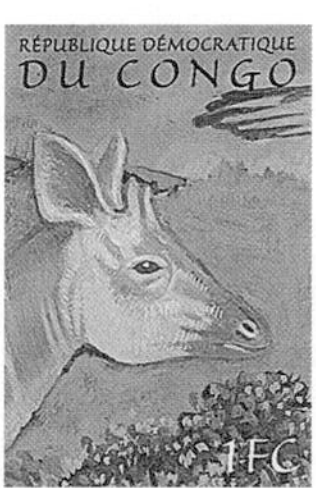

278 Okapi

2000. Flora and Fauna. Multicoloured.

1550	1f. Type **278**	55	55
1551	1f. Common kestrel	55	55
1552	1f. Giraffe and rainbow	55	55
1553	1f. Giraffe	55	55
1554	1f. Mandrill	55	55
1555	1f. Savannah baboon	55	55
1556	1f. Leopard	55	55
1557	1f. Birdwing butterflies	55	55
1558	1f. Hippopotamus	55	55
1559	1f. Hadada ibis	55	55
1560	1f. Water lilies	55	55
1561	1f. Steenbok	55	55
1562	7f.80 Lion (47×34 mm)	3·75	2·75
MS1563	76×106 mm. 10f. Warthog (41×56 mm)	4·00	4·00

Nos. 1550/61 were issued together, se-tenant, forming a composite design.

279 Four-coloured Bush Shrike (*Telophorus quadricolor*)

2000. Flora and Fauna of Africa. Multicoloured.

1564	1f. Type **279**	45	35
1565	1f.50 Leopard (*Panthera pardus*)	70	55
1566	1f.50 Sun	80	80
1567	1f.50 *Pieris citrina* (butterfly)	80	80
1568	1f.50 European bee eater (*Merops apiaster*)	80	80
1569	1f.50 Red-backed shrike (*Lanius collurio*)	80	80
1570	1f.50 Village weaver (*Ploceus cucullatus*)	80	80
1571	1f.50 *Charaxes pelias*	80	80
1572	1f.50 Green charaxes (*Charaxes eupale*)	80	80
1573	1f.50 Giraffe (*Giraffa camelopardalis*)	80	80
1574	1f.50 Bushbaby (*Galago moholi*)	80	80
1575	1f.50 *Strelitzia reginae* (flower)	80	80
1576	1f.50 Thomson's gazelle (*Gazella thomsoni*)	80	80
1577	1f.50 Hoopoe (*Upupa epops*)	80	80
1578	2f. Puku (*Kobus vardoni*)	95	95
1579	2f. Protomedia (*Colotis protomedia*)	95	95
1580	3f. Ground pangolin (*Smutsia temminckii*)	1·40	1·40
1581	3f. *Cararina abyssinica* (flower)	1·40	1·40
MS1582	Two sheets each 106×76 mm. (a) 10f. Cape eland (*Taurotragus oryx*); (b) 10f. Hippopotamus (*Hippopotamus amphibious*)	8·00	8·00

Nos. 1566/1577 were issued together, se-tenant, forming a composite design.

280 Leopard Cat (*Felis bengalensis*)

2000. Wild Cats and Dogs. Multicoloured.

1583	1f.50 Type **280**	80	80
1584	1f.50 African golden cat (*Felis aurata*)	80	80
1585	1f.50 Caracal (*Felis caracal*)	80	80
1586	1f.50 Puma (*Felis concolor*)	80	80
1587	1f.50 Black-footed cat (*Felis nigripes*)	80	80
1588	1f.50 Lion (*Panthera leo*)	80	80
1589	1f.50 Clouded leopard (*Neofelis nebulosa*)	80	80
1590	1f.50 Margay (*Felis wiedii*)	80	80
1591	1f.50 Cheetah (*Acinonyx jubatus*)	80	80
1592	1f.50 Spainsh lynx (*Felis pardina*)	80	80
1593	1f.50 Jaguarundi (*Felis yagouarundi*)	80	80
1594	1f.50 Serval (*Felis serval*)	80	80
1595	2f. Black-backed jackal (*Canis mesomelas*)	1·00	1·00
1596	2f. Bat-eared fox (*Otocyon megalotis*)	1·00	1·00
1597	2f. Bush dog (*Speothos venaticus*)	1·00	1·00
1598	2f. Coyote (*Canis latrans*)	1·00	1·00
1599	2f. Dhole (*Cuon alpinus*)	1·00	1·00
1600	2f. Fennec fox (*Fennecus zerda*)	1·00	1·00
1601	2f. Grey fox (*Urocyon cinereoargenteus*)	1·00	1·00
1602	2f. Wolf (*Canis lupus*)	1·00	1·00
1603	2f. Kit fox (*Vulpes macrotis*)	1·00	1·00
1604	2f. Maned wolf (*Chrysocyon brachyurus*)	1·00	1·00
1605	2f. Racoon-dog (*Nyctereutes procyonoides*)	1·00	1·00
1606	2f. Red fox (*Vulpes vulpes*)	1·00	1·00
MS1607	Two sheets each 106×76 mm. (a) 10f. Leopard (*Panthera pardus*); (b) 10f. Arctic fox (*Alopex lagops*)	8·00	8·00

281 "2000" and Mountains

2000. New Millennium.

1608	**281**	4f.50 multicoloured	1·00	1·00
1609	**281**	9f. multicoloured	1·90	1·90
1610	**281**	15f. multicoloured	3·25	3·25

282 Egyptian Goose (*Alopochen aegyptiacus*)

2000. Birds of the Congo. Multicoloured.

1611	3f. Type **282**	10	10
1612	3f. Ardeola ibis	10	10
1613	4f.50 Black-collared barbet (*Lybius torquatus*)	15	10
1614	4f.50 Namaqua dove (*Oena capensis*)	15	10
1615	9f. Great blue turaco (*Corythaeola cristata*) (inscr "Corythaelo")	30	15
1616	9f. Common kestrel (*Falco tinnunculus*)	30	15

MS1617 Four sheets. (a) 95×97 mm. 9f. ×6, Red bishop (*Euplectes orix*); Red-collared whydah (*Euplectis ardens*); African golden oriole (*Oriolus auratus*); Village weaver (*Ploceus cucullatus*); Zebra waxbill (*Amandava subflava*); Scarlet-chested sunbird (*Nectarina senegalensis*). (b) 95×99 mm. 9f. ×6; Blue-breasted kingfisher (*Halcyon malimbica*) (inscr "Haleyon malimbicus"); *Tachymarptis melba*; African fish eagle (*Haliaeetus vocifer*); Purple heron (*Ardea purpurea*); Whale-headed stork (*Baleaniceps rex*); South African crowned crane (*Balearica regulorum*). (c) 110×85 mm. 15f. African jacana (*Actophilornis africanus*) (horiz). (d) 85×110 mm. 20f. Lesser pied kingfisher (*Ceryle rudis*) (horiz) Set of 4 sheets 4·75 4·75

283 Golden-shouldered Parrot (*Psephotus chrysopterygius*)

2000. Parrots. Multicoloured.

1618	4f.50 Type **283**	15	10
1619	8f. Blue-fronted amazon (*Amazona aestiva*)	15	10
1620	8f.50 *Are nobilis cumanensis*	25	10
1621	9f. Peach-faced lovebird (*Agapornis roseicollis*)	30	15

MS1622 Four sheets. (a) 143×181 mm. 5f. ×9, Scarlet macaw (*Ara macao*); *Neophema elegans*; Vernal hanging parrot (*Loriculus vernalis*); Sun conure (*Aratinga solstialis*); Black-headed caique (*Piontes melanocephala*); *Bolborhynchus lineola*; Chestnut-fronted macaw (*Ara severa*); *Psephotus chrysoptergius dissimilas*; Military macaw (*Ara miltaris*). (b) 143×181 mm. 5f. ×9, *Eos squamata*; Golden conure *Aratinga guarouba*); *Aratinga aurea*; Dusky lory (*Pseudeos fuscata*); Fischer's lovebird (*Agapornis fischeri*); *Aratinga nana*; *Aratinga mitrata*; Rainbow lory (*Trichoglossus haematodus*); Sulphur-crested cockatoo (*Cacatua galerita*). (c) 79×109 mm. 15f. *Opopsitta diophthalma*. (d) 103×74 mm. 15f. Yellow and blue macaw (*Ara ararauna*) (inscr "ararrauna") (horiz) Set of 4 sheets 2·75 2·75

284 White-tailed Goldenthroat (*Polytmus guainumbi*) (inscr "Lophornis ornata")

2000. Hummingbirds. Multicoloured.

1623	8f.50 Type **284**	30	15
1624	9f. Hummingbird (inscr "Polytrus guauvunibi")	30	15

MS1625 Three sheets. (a) 145×103 mm. 4f.50 ×9, White-tipped sicklebill (*Eutoxeres aquila*) (inscr "Ertoxeres"); Long-tailed sylph (*Aglaiocerus kingi*) (inscr "Aglaiolepus kinde"); Ruby-throated hummingbird (*Archilochus colubris*) (inscr "calobris"); Streamertail (*Trochilus polytmus*) (inscr "Trochlus polytaus"); Rainbow bearded thornbill (*Chalcostigma herrani*) (inscr "Chaliostigna"); Sword-billed hummingbird (*Ensifera*); Ruby topaz hummingbird (*Chrysolampis mosquitus*) (inscr "Chrysolampus"); *Phaethornis syrmatophorus* (inscr "Phorethornus"); Bee hummingbird (*Calypte helenae*) (inscr "Calypre hetervare"). (b) 110×84 mm. 15f. Collared Inca (*Coeligena torquata*) (inscr "torgoata"). (c) 111×85 mm. 20f. Violet sabrewing (*Campylopterus hemileucurus*) (inscr "hemileicurus") Set of 3 sheets 2·50 2·50

Nos. 1626/34 are left for surcharges, issued in 2000, not yet seen.

285 Tintin

2001. 70th Anniv of *Tintin in the Congo* (written and illustrated by Herge (Georges Prosper Remi)

1635	190f. Type **285**	2·10	2·10

MS1636 124×88mm. 461f. Tintin driving car with Coco and Snowy (48×38mm) 5·25 5·25

286 President Joseph Kabila

2002. President Joseph Kabila.

1637	**286**	195f. multicoloured	65	65
1638	**286**	350f. multicoloured	1·10	1·10

APPENDIX

The following stamps have either been issued in excess of postal needs or have not been available to the public in reasonable quantities at face value. Such stamps may later be given full listing if there is evidence of regular postal use.

2001

Trains. 1f.; 2f.; 3f.×2; 5f.; 6f.
Butterflies. 5f.; 21.70f.; 45f.; 45.80f.; 50f.; 51f.80
Flowers and Insects. 20f.; 21f.70; 25f.; 45f.80
Ships. 2f.50; 5f.; 20f.; 21f.70; 30f.; 45f.80

2002

Nobel Prize Winners. -250f.×3; 325f.×4; 350fr .; 500f.í--2
Mammals and Scouting.390f.×3
Big Cats. 340f.×3
Fungi. 455f.×3×Birds. 410f.×3Minerals. 480f.×3
Butterflies. 445f.×3

2003

Cars. 325f.; 350f.
Explorers. 410f.×2
Concorde 500f.×2
History of Aviation. 190f.; 250f.×2; 325f.; 375f.
Cycling. 445f.
Space Exploration. 400f.×2; 445f.; 500f.
Trains. 455f.×3

2005

Pope Benedict XVI. 360f.; 500f.
Olympic Games, Athens. 1800f.×2
Death Centenary of Jules Verne. 3000f.×3

2006

Dogs. 475f.; 650f.
Owls. 175f.; 500f.
Cats. 425f.; 500f.
Fungi. 375f.; 800f.
Butterflies. 555f.; 625f.

Pt. 14

CONGO (KINSHASA)

This Belgian colony in Central Africa became independent in 1960. There were separate issues for the province of Katanga (q.v.).

In 1971 the country was renamed ZAIRE and later issues will be found under that heading.

1967. 100 sengi = 1 (li)kuta; 100 (ma)kuta = 1 zaire.

1960. Various stamps of Belgian Congo optd CONGO or surch also. (a) Flowers issue of 1952. Multicoloured.

360	10c. "Dissotis"	20	10
361	10c. on 15c. "Protea"	20	10
362	20c. "Vellozia"	20	10
363	40c. "Ipomoea"	20	10
364	50c. on 60c. "Euphorbia"	20	10
365	50c. on 75c. "Ochna"	20	10
366	1f. "Hibiscus"	20	10
367	1f.50 "Schizoglossum"	20	10
368	2f. "Ansellia"	20	10
369	3f. "Costus"	40	10
370	4f. "Nymphaea"	40	20
371	5f. "Thunbergia"	40	10
372	6f.50 "Thonningia"	60	10
373	8f. "Gloriosa"	80	20
374	10f. "Silene"	1·25	20
375	20f. "Aristolochia"	2·50	55
376	50f. "Eulophia"	14·00	3·75
377	100f. "Cryptosepalum"	24·00	6·25

(b) Wild Animals issue of 1959.

378	10c. brown, sepia and blue	15	10
379	20c. blue and red	15	10
380	40c. brown and blue	15	10
381	50c. multicoloured	15	10
382	1f. black, green & brown	15	10
383	1f.50 black and yellow	20	10
384	2f. black, brown and red	30	10
385	3f.50 on 3f. blk, pur & slate	35	10
386	5f. brown, green and sepia	50	15
387	6f.50 brown, yellow and blue	65	15
388	8f. bistre, violet and brown	80	30
389	10f. multicoloured	1·00	35

(c) Madonna.

390	**102**	50c. brown, ochre & chest	50	50

(d) African Technical Co-operation Commission. Inscr in French or Flemish.

391	**103**	3f.50 on 3f. sal & slate	40	40

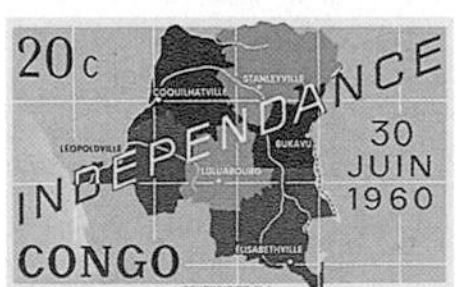

106 Congo Map

1960. Independence Commemoration.

392	**106**	20c. bistre	10	10
393	**106**	50c. red	10	10
394	**106**	1f. green	10	10
395	**106**	1f.50 brown	10	10
396	**106**	2f. mauve	10	10
397	**106**	3f.50 violet	10	10
398	**106**	5f. blue	15	10
399	**106**	6f.50 black	20	10
400	**106**	10f. orange	30	20
401	**106**	20f. blue	50	30

107 Congo Flag and People breaking Chain

1961. 2nd Anniv of Congo Independence Agreement. Flag in yellow and blue.

402	**107**	2f. violet	10	10
403	**107**	3f.50 red	10	10
404	**107**	6f.50 brown	20	10
405	**107**	10f. green	25	15
406	**107**	20f. mauve	45	30

1961. Coquilhatville Conf. Optd CONFERENCE COQUILHATVILLE AVRIL-MAI-1961.

407	**106**	20c. bistre	60	60
408	**106**	50c. red	60	60
409	**106**	1f. green	60	60
410	**106**	1f.50 brown	60	60
411	**106**	2f. mauve	60	60
412	**106**	3f.50 violet	60	60
413	**106**	5f. blue	60	60
414	**106**	6f.50 black	60	60
415	**106**	10f. orange	60	60
416	**106**	20f. blue	60	60

109 Pres. Kasavubu

1961. 1st Anniv of Independence. Inscr as in T 109. Portraits and inscriptions in sepia.

417	**109**	10c. yellow	10	10
418	**109**	20c. red	10	10
419	**109**	40c. turquoise	10	10
420	**109**	50c. salmon	10	10
421	**109**	1f. lilac	10	10
422	**109**	1f.50 brown	10	10
423	**109**	2f. green	10	10
424	-	3f.50 mauve	15	10
425	-	5f. grey	1·75	15
426	-	6f.50 blue	30	10
427	-	8f. olive	35	10
428	-	10f. blue	75	10
429	-	20f. orange	75	15
430	-	50f. blue	1·40	30
431	-	100f. green	2·50	50

DESIGNS—HORIZ: 3f.50 to 8f. Pres. Kasavubu and map of Congo Republic. VERT: 10f. to 100f. Pres. Kasavubu in full uniform and outline map.

1961. Re-opening of Parliament. Optd REOUVERTURE du PARLEMENT JUILLET 1961.

432	**109**	10c. yellow	10	10
433	**109**	20c. red	10	10
434	**109**	40c. turquoise	10	10
435	**109**	50c. salmon	30	20
436	**109**	1f. lilac	30	20
437	**109**	1f.50 brown	80	70
438	**109**	2f. green	80	70
439	-	5f. grey (No. 425)	80	70
440	-	10f. violet (No. 428)	80	85

111 Dag Hammarskjold

1962. Dag Hammarskjold Commemoration.

441	**111**	10c. brown and grey	10	10
442	**111**	20c. blue and grey	10	10
443	**111**	30c. bistre and grey	10	10
444	**111**	40c. blue and grey	10	10
445	**111**	50c. red and grey	10	10
446	**111**	3f. olive and grey	2·50	1·60
447	**111**	6f.50 violet and grey	70	50
448	**111**	8f. brown and grey	80	60

MS448a 65×90 mm. **111** 25f. brown and grey. Imperf 3·75 3·75

112 Campaign Emblem

1962. Malaria Eradication.

449	**112**	1f.50 brown, black & yell	10	10
450	**112**	2f. turq, brown & green	30	15
451	**112**	6f.50 lake, black & blue	15	10

1962. 2nd Anniv of Independence. No. MS448a optd 2 EME ANNIVERSAIRE DE L'INDEPENDANCE, etc. in green.

MS451a 65×90 mm. **111** 25f. brown and grey. Imperf 1·75 1·75

1962. Reorganization of Aboula Ministry. Optd "Paix, Travail, Austerite..., C. ADOULA 11 juillet 1962.

452	**111**	10c. brown and grey	10	10

453	**111**	20c. blue and grey	10	10
454	**111**	30c. bistre and grey	10	10
455	**111**	40c. blue and grey	10	10
456	**111**	50c. red and grey	1·25	50
457	**111**	3f. olive and grey	15	10
458	**111**	6f.50 violet and grey	20	10
459	**111**	8f. brown and grey	30	15

114

1963. 1st Participation in UPU Congress.

460	**114**	2f. violet	1·40	1·00
461	**114**	4f. red	10	10
462	**114**	7f. blue	20	10
463	**114**	20f. green	30	15

115 Emblem, Bears and Tractor

1963. Freedom from Hunger.

464	**115**	5f.+2f. violet & mauve	15	10
465	**115**	9f.+4f. green & yellow	30	20
466	**115**	12f.+6f. violet & blue	35	25
467	**115**	20f.+10f. green & red	1·75	1·60

116 Whale-headed Stork

1963. Protected Birds.

468	-	10c. multicoloured	15	10
469	-	20c. blue, black and red	15	10
470	-	30c. black, brown & grn	15	10
471	-	40c. black, orange & grey	15	10
472	**116**	1f. black, green & brown	30	15
473	-	2f. blue, brown and red	7·00	1·25
474	-	3f. black, pink and green	55	20
475	-	4f. blue, green and red	55	20
476	-	5f. black, red and blue	85	20
477	-	6f. black, bistre & violet	7·00	1·25
478	-	7f. indigo, blue & turq	1·25	20
479	-	8f. blue, yellow & orange	1·40	20
480	-	10f. black, red and blue	1·40	20
481	-	20f. black, red & yellow	2·50	30

BIRDS—VERT: 10c. Eastern white pelicans ("Pelicans"); 30c. African open-bill stork ("Bec-Duvert"); 2f. Marabou stork ("Marabout"); 4f. Congo peafowl ("Paon Congolais"); 6f. Secretary bird ("Serpentaire"); 8f. Sacred ibis ("Ibis Sacre"). HORIZ: 20c. Crested guineafowl ("Pintables de Schouteden"); 40c. Abdim's stork ("Cigoon a Ventre Blanc"); 3f. Greater flamingos ("Flamants Roses"); 5f. Hartlaub's duck ("Canards de Hartlaub"); 7f. Black-casqued hornbill ("Calaos"); 10f. South African crowned cranes ("Grue Caouronnse"); 20f. Saddle-bill stork ("Jabiru d'Afrique").

117 Strophanthus ("S. sarmentosus")

1963. Red Cross Centenary. Cross in red.

482	**117**	10c. green and violet	10	10
483	**A**	20c. blue and red	10	10
484	**117**	30c. red and green	10	10
485	**A**	40c. violet and blue	10	10
486	**117**	5f. lake and olive	10	10
487	**A**	7f. purple and orange	10	10
488	**B**	9f. olive	20	10
489	**B**	20f. violet	1·60	70

DESIGNS—VERT: A, "Cinchona ledgeriana". HORIZ: B, Red Cross nurse.

118 "Reconciliation"

1963. "National Reconciliation".

490	**118**	4f. multicoloured	90	30
491	**118**	5f. multicoloured	10	10
492	**118**	9f. multicoloured	15	10
493	**118**	12f. multicoloured	20	10

119 Kabambare Sewer, Leopoldville

1963. European Economic Community Aid.

494	**119**	20c. multicoloured	10	10
495	**A**	30c. multicoloured	10	10
496	**B**	50c. multicoloured	10	10
497	**119**	3f. multicoloured	90	35
498	**A**	5f. multicoloured	10	10
499	**B**	9f. multicoloured	15	10
500	**A**	12f. multicoloured	15	10

DESIGNS: A, Tractor and bridge on plan; B, Construction of Ituri Road.

120 N'Djili Airport, Leopoldville

1963. "Air Congo" Commemoration.

501	**120**	2f. multicoloured	10	10
502	-	5f. multicoloured	10	10
503	**120**	6f. multicoloured	90	40
504	-	7f. multicoloured	10	10
505	**120**	30f. multicoloured	25	15
506	-	50f. multicoloured	40	25

DESIGN: 5f., 7f., 50f. Mailplane and control tower.

1963. 15th Anniv of Declaration of Human Rights. Optd 10 DECEMBRE 1948 10 DECEMBRE 1963 15e anniversaire DROITS DE L'HOMME.

507	**114**	2f. violet	10	10
508	**114**	4f. red	10	10
509	**114**	7f. blue	20	20
510	**114**	20f. green	20	20

122 Student in Laboratory

1964. 10th Anniv of Lovanium University. Mult.

511		50c. Type **122**	10	10
512		1f.50 University buildings	10	10
513		8f. Atomic and nuclear reactor symbols	1·75	1·60
514		25f. University arms and buildings	20	15
515		30f. Type **122**	20	20
516		60f. As 1f.50	40	30
517		75f. As 8f.	50	50
518		100f. As 25f.	70	60
MS518a		141×70 mm. 20f. (Type **122**), 30f. (As 8f.), 100f. As 25f. Imperf	2·75	2·75

1964. Various stamps surch over coloured metallic panels. (a) Stamps of Belgian Congo surch REPUBLIQUE DU CONGO and value.

519		1f. on 20c. (No. 340)	10	10
520		2f. on 1f.50 (No. 306)	6·25	2·25
521		5f. on 6f.50 (No. 348)	15	15
522		8f. on 6f.50 (No. 311)	60	25

(b) Stamps of Congo (Kinshasa) surch.

523	-	1f. on 20c. (No. 379)	10	10
524	-	1f. on 6f.50 (No. 372)	10	10
525	-	2f. on 1f.50 (No. 367)	10	10
526	-	5f. on 6f.50 (No. 387)	45	20
528	**106**	6f. on 6f.50	30	20
529	**106**	7f. on 20c.	40	25
530	**109**	3f. on 20c.	25	20
531	**109**	4f. on 40c.	25	20

125 Pole-vaulting

1964. Olympic Games, Tokyo.

532	**125**	5f. sepia, grey and red	10	10
533	-	7f. violet, red and green	80	40
534	-	8f. brown, yellow & blue	10	10
535	**125**	10f. purple, blue & purple	10	10
536	-	20f. brown, green & orge	20	10
537	-	100f. brown, mauve & grn	80	20
MS537a		135×85 mm. 21, 31 and 100f. As Nos. 535/7 but new colours. Imperf	4·50	4·50

DESIGNS—VERT: 7f., 20f. Throwing the javelin. HORIZ: 8f., 100f. Hurdling.

OCCUPATION OF STANLEYVILLE. During the occupation of Stanleyville from 5 August to 24 November, 1964, stocks of a number of contemporary issues were overprinted REPUBLIQUE POPULAIRE and issued by the rebel authorities.

126 National Palace

1964. National Palace, Leopoldville.

538	**126**	50c. mauve and blue	10	10
539	**126**	1f. blue and purple	10	10
540	**126**	2f. brown and violet	10	10
541	**126**	3f. green and brown	10	10
542	**126**	4f. orange and blue	10	10
543	**126**	5f. violet and green	10	10
544	**126**	6f. brown and orange	10	10
545	**126**	7f. olive and brown	10	10
546	**126**	8f. red and blue	2·00	35
547	**126**	9f. violet and red	10	10
548	**126**	10f. brown and green	10	10
549	**126**	20f. blue and brown	10	10
550	**126**	30f. red and green	15	10
551	**126**	40f. blue and purple	25	10
552	**126**	50f. brown and green	35	10
553	**126**	100f. black and orange	65	15

127 Pres. Kennedy

1964. Pres. Kennedy Commemoration.

554	**127**	5f. blue and black	10	10
555	**127**	6f. purple and black	10	10
556	**127**	9f. brown and black	10	10
557	**127**	30f. violet and black	30	10
558	**127**	40f. green and black	2·00	60
559	**127**	60f. brown and black	50	25
MS559a		64×76 mm. **127** 150f. grey and red	2·25	2·25

See also No. **MS**630.

128 Rocket and Unisphere

1965. New York World's Fair.

560	**128**	50c. purple and black	10	10
561	**128**	1f.50 blue and violet	10	10
562	**128**	2f. brown and green	10	10
563	**128**	10f. green and red	70	40
564	**128**	18f. blue and brown	10	10
565	**128**	27f. red and green	25	10
566	**128**	40f. grey and red	40	15

129 Football

1965. 1st African Games, Leopoldville.

567	-	5f. black, brown & blue	10	10
568	**129**	6f. red, black and blue	10	10
569	-	15f. black, green & orange	10	10
570	-	24f. black, green & mve	20	10
571	**129**	40f. blue, black & turq	1·25	45
572	-	60f. purple, black & blue	45	15

SPORTS—VERT: 5f., 24f. Basketball; 15f., 60f. Volleyball.

130 Telecommunications Satellites

1965. Centenary of ITU. Multicoloured.

573		6f. Type **130**	10	10
574		9f. Telecommunications satellites (different view)	10	10
575		12f. Type **130**	10	10
576		15f. As 9f.	10	10
577		18f. Type **130**	1·00	30
578		20f. As 9f.	15	10
579		30f. Type **130**	25	10
580		40f. As 9f.	30	10

131 Parachutist and troops landing

1965. 5th Anniv of Independence.

581	**131**	5f. brown and blue	10	10
582	**131**	6f. brown and orange	10	10
583	**131**	7f. brown and green	45	20
584	**131**	9f. brown and mauve	10	10
585	**131**	18f. brown and yellow	15	10

132 Matadi Port

1965. International Co-operation Year.

586	**132**	6f. blue, black & yellow	10	10
587	-	8f. brown, black & blue	10	10
588	-	9f. turq, black & brown	10	10
589	**132**	12f. mauve, black & grey	80	30
590	-	25f. olive, black and red	20	10
591	-	60f. grey, black & yellow	40	10

DESIGNS: 8f., 25f. Katanga mines; 9f., 60f. Tshopo Barrage, Stanleyville.

133 Medical Care

1965. Congolese Army.

592	**133**	2f. blue and red	10	10
593	**133**	5f. brown, red and pink	10	10
594	-	6f. brown and blue	10	10
595	-	7f. green and yellow	10	10
596	-	9f. brown and green	10	10
597	-	10f. brown and green	40	40
598	-	18f. violet and red	15	10
599	-	19f. brown & turquoise	60	40
600	-	20f. brown and blue	15	10
601	-	24f. multicoloured	20	15
602	-	30f. multicoloured	25	10

DESIGNS—HORIZ: 6f., 9f. Feeding child; 7, 18f. Bridge-building. VERT: 10f., 20f. Building construction; 19f. Telegraph line maintenance; 24f., 30f. Soldier and flag.

1966. World Meteorological Day. Nos. 590/1 optd 6e Journee Meteorologique Mondiale / 23.3.66 (on coloured metallic panel) and WMO Emblem.

603		25f. olive, black and red	75	45
604		60f. grey, black and yellow	75	50

135 Carved Stool and Head

1966. World Festival of Negro Arts, Dakar.

605	135	10f. black, red and grey	10	10
606	-	12f. black, green & blue	10	10
607	-	15f. black, blue & purple	15	15
608	-	53f. black, red and blue	1·10	90

DESIGNS—VERT: 12f. Statuettes; 53f. Statuettes of women. HORIZ: 15f. Woman's head and carved goat.

136 Pres. Mobutu and Fish Workers

1966. Pres. Mobutu Commemoration.

609	136	2f. brown and blue	10	10
610	-	4f. brown and red	10	10
611	-	6f. brown and olive	65	60
612	-	8f. brown and turquoise	10	10
613	-	10f. brown and lake	10	10
614	-	12f. brown and violet	10	10
615	-	15f. brown and green	10	10
616	-	24f. brown and mauve	20	15

DESIGNS (Pres. Mobutu and): 4f. Harvesting pyrethrum; 6f. Building construction; 8f. Winnowing maize; 10f. Cotton-picking; 12f. Harvesting fruit; 15f. Picking coffee-beans; 24f. Harvesting pineapples.

137 Pres. Mobutu and Workers rolling up Sleeves ("Retroussons les manches!)

1966

MS617 **137** 128×95 mm. 15f. brown, blue and red (block of four)		75	75

1966. Inaug of WHO Headquarters, Geneva. Nos. 550/3 optd O.M.S. Geneve 1966 and WHO Emblem.

618	126	30f. red and green	70	70
619	126	40f. blue and purple	70	70
620	126	50f. brown and green	75	75
621	126	100f. black and orange	75	75

139 Footballer

1966. World Cup Football Championship.

622	139	10f. green, violet & brown	10	10
623	-	30f. green, violet & purple	25	20
624	-	50f. brown, blue & green	85	80
625	-	60f. gold, sepia & green	45	40

DESIGNS: 30f. Two footballers; 50f. Three footballers; 60f. Jules Rimet Cup and football.

1966. World Cup Football Championship Final. Nos. 622/5 optd FINALE ANGLETERRE - ALLEMAGNE 4 - 2.

626	139	10f. green, violet & brown	25	45
627	-	30f. green, violet & purple	80	1·40
628	-	50f. brown, blue & green	1·25	1·75
629	-	60f. gold, sepia and green	1·40	2·25

141 President Kennedy

1966. Kennedy Commemoration (2nd issue). Two sheets each 65×78 mm.

MS630 **141** 150f. brown; 150f. blue		7·00	7·00

1967. 4th African Unity Organization (O.U.A.) Conf, Kinshasa. Nos. 538/43 surch 4e Sommet OUA KINSHASA du 11 au 14 - 9 - 67 and value.

631	126	1k. on 2f.	10	10
632	126	3k. on 5f.	10	10
633	126	5k. on 4f.	20	15
634	126	6k.60 on 1f.	25	20
635	126	9k.60 on 50c.	40	25
636	126	9k.80 on 3f.	50	40

143 "OUA" Emblem

1967

MS637 **143** 50k. ("0.5z.") red, black and blue (77×80 mm)		2·00	2·00

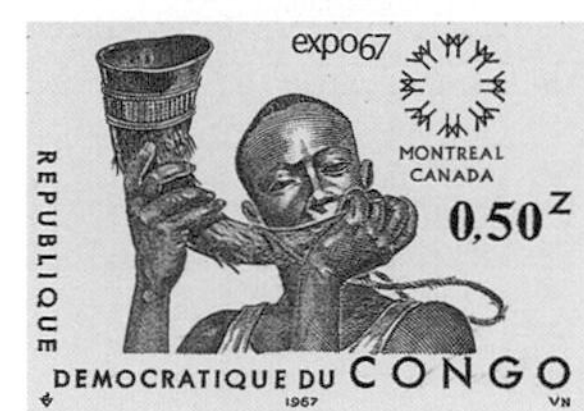

144 Congolese blowing Horn

1967. EXPO 70 World Fair, Montreal. Sheet 90×76 mm.

MS638 **144** 50k. maroon		2·00	2·00

1967. New Constitution. Nos. 609/10 and 592 surch 1967 NOUVELLE CONSTITUTION with coloured metallic panel obliterating old value.

639	136	4k. on 2f.	20	15
640	133	5k. on 2f.	20	15
641	-	21k. on 4f.	90	70

1967. 1st Congolese Games, Kinshasa. Nos. 567 and 569 surch 1ers Jeux Congolais 25/6 au 2/7/67 Kinshasa and value.

642		1k. on 5f.	10	10
643		9.6k. on 15f.	50	50

1967. 1st Flight by Air Congo BAC "One-Eleven". No. 504 surch 1er VOL BAC ONE ELEVEN 14/5/67 and value.

644		9.6k. on 7f.	70	20

1968. World Children's Day (8.10.67). Nos. 586 and 588 surch JOURNEE MONDIALE DE L'ENFANCE 8 - 10 - 67 and new value.

645	132	1k. on 6f.	10	10
646	132	9k. on 9f.	50	50

1968. International Tourist Year (1967). Nos. 538, 541 and 544 surch Annee Internationale du Tourisme 24-10-67 and new value.

647	126	5k. on 50c.	20	20
648	126	10k. on 6f.	40	40
649	126	15k. on 3f.	60	60

1968. (a) No. 540 surch.

650		1k. on 2f.	10	10

(b) Surch (coloured panel obliterating old value, and new value surch on panel. Panel colour given first, followed by colour of new value). (i) Nos. 538 and 542.

651		2k. on 50c. (bronze and black)	10	10
652		2k. on 50c. (blue and white)	10	10
653		9.6k. on 4f. (black and white)	50	45

(ii) No. 609.

654	136	10k. on 2f. (black and white)	55	10

152 Leaping Leopard

1968

655	152	2k. black on green	15	10
656	152	9.6k. black on red	65	15

1968. As Nos. 609, etc, but with colours changed and surch in new value.

657	136	15s. on 2f. brown & blue	10	10
658	-	1k. on 6f. brown & chest	10	10
659	-	3k. on 10f. brown & grn	10	10
660	-	5k. on 12f. brown & orge	20	15
661	-	20k. on 15f. brown & grn	70	50
662	-	50k. on 24f. brown & pur	1·90	1·25

154 Human Rights Emblem

1968. Human Rights Year.

663	154	2k. green and blue	10	10
664	154	9.6k. red and green	40	25
665	154	10k. brown and lilac	40	25
666	154	40k. violet and brown	1·50	1·10

1969. 4th O.C.A.M. (Organization Commune Africaine et Malgache) Summit Meeting, Kinshasa. Nos. 663/6 with colours changed optd 4EME SOMMET OCAM 27-1-1969 KINSHASA and emblem.

667		2k. brown and green	10	10
668		9.60k. green and pink	40	25
669		10k. blue and grey	40	25
670		40k. violet and blue	1·50	1·10

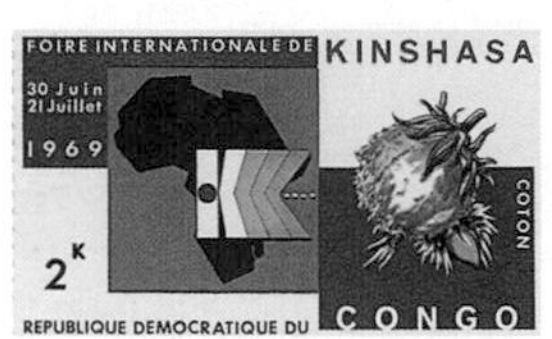

156 Map of Africa and "Cotton"

1969. International Fair, Kinshasa (1st Issue).

671	156	2k. multicoloured	10	10
672	-	6k. multicoloured	30	30
673	-	9.6k. multicoloured	40	20
674	-	9.8k. multicoloured	40	35
675	-	11.6k. multicoloured	50	50

DESIGNS: Map of Africa and: 6k. "Copper"; 9.6k. "Coffee"; 9.8k. "Diamonds"; 11.6k. "Palm-oil".

157 Fair Entrance

1969. Inaug of Int Fair, Kinshasa (2nd issue).

676	157	2k. purple and gold	10	10
677	-	3k. blue and gold	10	10
678	-	10k. green and gold	40	40
679	-	25k. red and gold	1·00	85

DESIGNS: 3k. "Gecomin" (mining company) pavilion; 10k. Administration building; 25k. African Unity Organization pavilion.

158 Congo Arms **159** Pres. Mobutu

1969

680	158	10s. red and black	10	10
681	158	15s. blue and black	10	10
682	158	30s. green and black	10	10
683	158	60s. purple and black	10	10
684	158	90s. bistre and black	10	10
685	159	1k. multicoloured	10	10
686	159	2k. multicoloured	10	10
687	159	3k. multicoloured	15	10
688	159	5k. multicoloured	15	15
689	159	6k. multicoloured	20	15
690	159	9.6k. multicoloured	30	25
691	159	10k. multicoloured	40	30
692	159	20k. multicoloured	80	60
693	159	50k. multicoloured	2·00	1·75
694	159	100k. multicoloured	4·00	3·50

160 "The Well-sinker" (O. Bonnevalle)

1969. 50th Anniv of International Labour Organization. Paintings. Multicoloured.

695	3k. Type **160**	15	15
696	4k. "Cocoa Production" (J. van Noten)	20	15
697	8k. "The Harbour" (C. Meunier) (vert)	70	25
698	10k. "The Poulterer" (H. Evenepoel)	45	35
699	15k. "Industry" (C. Meunier)	85	50

161 "Adoration of the Magi" (Rubens)

1969. Christmas. Sheet 86×85 mm.

MS700 **161** 50k. purple		1·75	1·75

162 Pres. Mobutu, Map and Flag

1970. 10th Anniv of Independence.

701	162	10s. multicoloured	10	10
702	162	90s. multicoloured	10	10
703	162	1k. multicoloured	10	10
704	162	2k. multicoloured	10	10
705	162	7k. multicoloured	25	15
706	162	10k. multicoloured	40	25
707	162	20k. multicoloured	80	50

1970. Surch. (a) National Palace series.

708	126	10s. on 1f.	10	10
709	126	20s. on 2f.	10	10
710	126	30s. on 3f.	10	10
711	126	40s. on 4f.	10	10
712	126	60s. on 7f.	80	75
713	126	90s. on 9f.	80	75
714	126	1k. on 6f.	15	10
715	126	3k. on 30f.	80	75
716	126	4k. on 40f.	15	10
717	126	5k. on 50f.	2·00	1·90
718	126	10k. on 100f.	90	75

(b) Congolese Army series.

719		90s. on 9f. (No. 596)	15	10
720		1k. on 7f. (No. 595)	15	10
721		2k. on 24f. (No. 601)	15	10

(c) Pres. Mobutu series.

722	136	20s. on 2f.	15	10
723	-	40s. on 4f. (No. 610)	15	10
724	-	1k. on 12f. (No. 614)	80	70
725	-	2k. on 24f. (No. 616)	15	10

164 I.T.U. Headquarters, Geneva

1970. United Nations Commemorations.

726	**164**	1k. olive, green and pink	10	10
727	-	2k. grey, green and orange	10	10
728	-	6k.60 red, pink and blue	25	25
729	**164**	9k.60 multicoloured	30	30
730	-	9k.80 sepia, brown and bl	35	35
731	-	10k. sepia, brown and lilac	35	35
732	-	11k. sepia, brown and pink	40	40

DESIGNS AND EVENTS: 1k., 9k.60, (ITU World Day); 2k., 6k.60, New UPU Headquarters, Berne (Inauguration); 9k.80, 10k., 11k. U.N. Headquarters, New York (25th anniversary).

165 Pres. Mobutu and Independence Arch

1970. 5th Anniv of "New Regime".

733	**165**	2k. multicoloured	10	10
734	**165**	10k. multicoloured	45	35
735	**165**	20k. multicoloured	85	80

166 "Apollo 11"

1970. Visit of "Apollo 11" Astronauts to Kinshasa.

736	**166**	1k. blue, black and red	10	10
737	-	2k. violet, black and red	10	10
738	-	7k. black, orange and red	25	25
739	-	10k. black, pink and red	35	35
740	-	30k. black, green and red	1·00	1·00

DESIGNS: 2k. Astronauts on Moon; 7k. Pres. Mobutu decorating wives; 10k. Pres. Mobutu with astronauts; 30k. Astronauts after splashdown.

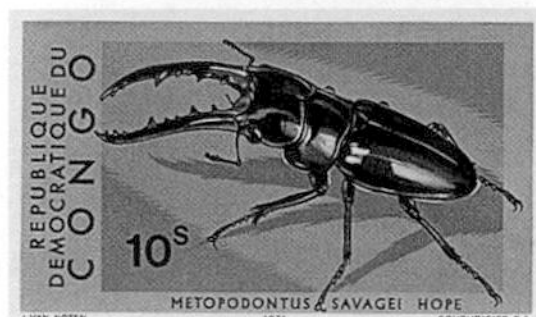

167 "Metopodontus savagei"

1971. Insects. Multicoloured.

741	10s. Type **167**	25	15
742	50s. "Cicindela regalis"	25	15
743	90s. "Magacephala catenulata"	25	15
744	1k. "Stephanorrhina guttata"	25	15
745	2k. "Pupuricenus congoanus"	25	15
746	3k. "Sagra tristis"	50	25
747	5k. "Steraspis subcalida"	1·75	80
748	10k. "Mecosaspis explanata"	2·40	1·25
749	30k. "Goliathus meleagris"	5·75	3·25
750	40k. "Sternotomis virescens"	8·25	4·75

168 "Colotis protomedia"

1971. Butterflies and Moths. Multicoloured.

751	10s. Type **168**	25	15
752	20s. "Rhodophitus simplex"	25	15
753	70s. "Euphaedra overlaeti"	25	15
754	1k. "Argema bouvieri"	25	15
755	3k. "Cymothoe reginae-elisabethae"	50	25
756	5k. "Miniodes maculifera"	1·40	60
757	10k. "Salamis temora"	1·90	90
758	15k. "Eronia leda"	3·75	1·60
759	25k. "Cymothoe sangaris"	5·00	2·50
760	40k. "Euchloron megaera"	8·00	4·50

169 "Four Races" around Globe

1971. Racial Equality Year.

761	**169**	1k. multicoloured	10	10
762	**169**	4k. multicoloured	15	15
763	**169**	5k. multicoloured	20	20
764	**169**	10k. multicoloured	40	40

170 Pres. Mobutu and Obelisk

1971. 4th Anniv of Popular Revolutionary Movement (MPR).

765	**170**	4k. multicoloured	15	15

171 "Hypericum bequaertii"

1971. Tropical Plants. Multicoloured.

766	1k. Type **171**	35	15
767	4k. "Dissotis brazzae"	70	30
768	20k. "Begonia wollast"	3·50	1·50
769	25k. "Cassia alata"	4·50	1·90

172 ITU Emblem (International Telecommunications Day)

1971. "Telecommunications and Space". Mult.

770	1k. Type **172**	10	10
771	3k. Dish aerial (Satellite Earth Station, Kinshasa)	15	15
772	6k. Map of Pan-African telecommunications network	30	30

173 Savanna Monkey

1971. Congo Monkeys. Multicoloured.

773	10s. Type **173**	30	15
774	20s. Moustached monkey (vert)	30	15
775	70s. De Brazza's monkey	45	15
776	1k. Yellow baboon	45	25
777	3k. Pygmy chimpanzee (vert)	75	50
778	5k. Black mangabey (vert)	1·75	1·25
779	10k. Owl-faced monkey	3·25	2·40
780	15k. Diana monkey	5·25	3·50
781	25k. Western black-and-white colobus (vert)	9·00	6·00
782	40k. L'Hoest's monkey (vert)	12·00	8·50

174 Hotel Inter-Continental

1971. Opening of Hotel Inter-Continental, Kinshasa.

783	**174**	2k. multicoloured	10	10
784	**174**	12k. multicoloured	50	50

175 "Reader"

1971. Literacy Campaign. Multicoloured.

785	50s. Type **175**	10	10
786	2k.50 Open book and abacus	20	10
787	7k. Symbolic alphabet	45	35

For later issues see **ZAIRE**.

Pt. 1

COOK ISLANDS

A group of islands in the South Pacific under New Zealand control, including Aitutaki, Niue, Penrhyn and Rarotonga. Granted self-government in 1965.

See also issues for Aitutaki and Penrhyn Island.

1892. 12 pence = 1 shilling; 20 shillings = 1 pound.
1967. 100 cents = 1 dollar.

1

1892

1	**1**	1d. black	30·00	26·00
2	**1**	1½d. mauve	48·00	38·00
3	**1**	2½d. blue	48·00	38·00
4	**1**	10d. red	£140	£130

2 Queen Makea Takau **3** White Tern or Torea

1893

11ba	**3**	½d. blue	5·50	10·00
28	**3**	½d. green	3·00	3·25
12	**2**	1d. blue	5·00	5·50
13	**2**	1d. brown	23·00	21·00
29	**2**	1d. red	4·00	3·00
43	**2**	1½d. mauve	15·00	4·00
15a	**3**	2d. brown	11·00	8·50
16a	**2**	2½d. red	24·00	11·00
32	**2**	2½d. blue	3·75	7·00
9	**2**	5d. black	22·00	15·00
18a	**3**	6d. purple	21·00	26·00
19	**2**	10d. green	18·00	50·00
46	**3**	1s. red	27·00	£100

1899. Surch ONE HALF PENNY.

21	**2**	½d. on 1d. blue	32·00	42·00

1901. Optd with crown.

22	1d. brown	£180	£140

1919. New Zealand stamps (King George V) surch RAROTONGA and value in native language in words.

56	**62**	½d. green	40	1·00
47	**53**	1d. red	1·00	3·50
57	**62**	1½d. brown	50	75
58	**62**	2d. yellow	1·50	1·75
48a	**62**	2½d. blue	2·00	2·25
49a	**62**	3d. brown	2·75	2·00
50c	**62**	4d. violet	1·75	4·25
51a	**62**	4½d. green	1·75	8·00
52a	**62**	6d. red	1·75	5·50
53	**62**	7½d. brown	1·50	5·50
54a	**62**	9d. green	2·25	15·00
55a	**62**	1s. red	2·75	22·00

9 Captain Cook landing **17** Harbour, Rarotonga and Mt. Ikurangi

1920. Inscr "RAROTONGA".

81	**9**	½d. black and green	4·50	8·50
82	-	1d. black and red	6·00	2·25
72	-	1½d. black and blue	8·50	8·50
83	-	2½d. brown and blue	8·00	26·00
73	-	3d. black and brown	2·25	5·50
84	**17**	4d. green and violet	13·00	16·00
74	-	6d. brown and orange	4·00	8·50
75	-	1s. black and violet	6·50	17·00

DESIGNS—VERT: 1d. Wharf at Avarua; 1½d. Captain Cook (Dance); 2½d. Te Po, Rarotongan chief; 3d. Palm tree. HORIZ: 6d. Huts at Arorangi; 1s. Avarua Harbour.

1921. New Zealand stamps optd RAROTONGA.

76	**F4**	2s. blue	27·00	55·00
77	**F4**	2s.6d. brown	19·00	50·00
78	**F4**	5s. green	27·00	70·00
79	**F4**	10s. red	85·00	£140
80	**F4**	£1 red	£140	£250

1926. "Admiral" type of New Zealand optd RAROTONGA.

90	**71**	2s. blue	10·00	40·00
92	**71**	3s. mauve	16·00	48·00

1931. No. 77 surch TWO PENCE.

93	2d. on 1½d. black and blue	9·50	3·25

1931. Arms type of New Zealand optd RAROTONGA.

95	**F6**	2s.6d. brown	11·00	22·00
96	**F6**	5s. green	20·00	55·00
97	**F6**	10s. red	38·00	£100
98	**F6**	£1 pink	£110	£180

20 Captain Cook landing **22** Double Maori Canoe

1932. Inscribed "COOK ISLANDS".

106	**20**	½d. black and green	1·00	4·50
138	-	1d. black and red	2·00	1·75
108	**22**	2d. black and brown	1·50	50
140	-	2½d. black and blue	1·00	2·75
110	-	4d. black and blue	1·50	50
111	-	6d. black and orange	1·75	2·25
105	-	1s. black and violet	17·00	22·00

DESIGNS—VERT: 1d. Captain Cook. HORIZ: 2½d. Natives working cargo; 4d. Port of Avarua; 6d. R.M.S. "Monowai"; 1s. King George V.

1935. Jubilee. As 1932 optd SILVER JUBILEE OF KING GEORGE V. 1910-1935.

113	1d. red	60	1·40
114	2½d. blue	2·75	2·50
115	6d. green and orange	5·50	6·00

1936. Stamps of New Zealand optd COOK ISLANDS.

116	**71**	2s. blue	14·00	45·00
131w	**F 6**	2s.6d. brown	32·00	32·00
117	**71**	3s. mauve	15·00	70·00
132	**F 6**	5s. green	14·00	27·00
133w	**F 6**	10s. red	75·00	£110
134	**F 6**	£1 pink	75·00	£130
135w	**F 6**	£3 green	70·00	£180
98b	**F 6**	£5 blue	£250	£400

1937. Coronation. T 106 of New Zealand optd COOK IS'DS.

124	**106**	1d. red	40	80
125	**106**	2½d. blue	80	1·40
126	**106**	6d. orange	80	60

29 King George VI **30** Native Village

1938

128	**30**	2s. black and brown	21·00	13·00
143	**29**	1s. black and violet	5·50	3·50
145	-	3s. blue and green	42·00	35·00

DESIGN—HORIZ: 3s. Native canoe.

32 Tropical Landscape

1940

No.	Type	Description	Unused	Used
130	**32**	3d. on 1½d. black & purple	75	60

1946. Peace. Peace stamps of New Zealand of 1946 optd COOK ISLANDS.

No.	Type	Description	Unused	Used
146	**132**	1d. green	30	10
147	-	2d. purple	30	50
148	-	6d. brown and red	1·00	1·25
149	**139**	8d. black and red	60	1·25

34 Ngatangiia Channel, Rarotonga

1949

No.	Type	Description	Unused	Used
150	**34**	½d. violet and brown	10	1·50
151	-	1d. brown and green	3·50	3·25
152	-	2d. brown and red	2·00	3·25
153	-	3d. green and blue	4·50	2·00
154	-	5d. green and violet	7·00	1·50
155	-	6d. black and red	5·50	2·75
156	-	8d. olive and orange	55	3·75
157	-	1s. blue and brown	4·25	3·75
158	-	2s. brown and red	5·00	13·00
159	-	3s. blue and green	18·00	30·00

DESIGNS—HORIZ: 1d. Captain Cook and map of Hervey Is; 2d. Rarotonga and Rev. John Williams; 3d. Aitutaki and palm trees; 5d. Rarotonga Airfield; 6d. Penrhyn village; 8d. Native hut. VERT: 1s. Map and statue of Capt. Cook; 2s. Native hut and palms; 3s. "Matua" (inter-island freighter).

1953. Coronation. As Types of New Zealand but inscr "COOK ISLANDS".

No.	Type	Description	Unused	Used
160	**164**	3d. brown	1·00	85
161	**166**	6d. grey	1·25	1·50

1960. No. 154 surch 1/6.

No.	Type	Description	Unused	Used
162		1s.6d. on 5d. green and violet	75	40

45 Tiare Maori

52 Queen Elizabeth II

55 "Tiare Taporo"

1963

No.	Type	Description	Unused	Used
163	**45**	1d. green and yellow	75	65
164	-	2d. red and yellow	30	50
165	-	3d. yellow, green and violet	70	65
166	-	5d. blue and black	8·00	2·25
167	-	6d. red, yellow and green	1·00	60
168	-	8d. black and blue	4·25	1·50
169	-	1s. yellow and green	1·00	60
170	**52**	1s.6d. violet	2·75	2·00
171	-	2s. brown and blue	2·50	1·00
172	-	3s. black and green	2·00	2·25
173	**55**	5s. brown and blue	19·00	6·00

DESIGNS—VERT (As Type **45**): 2d. Fishing god; 8d. Long-tailed tuna. HORIZ (As Type **45**): 3d. Frangipani (plant); 5d. White tern ("Love Tern"); 6d. Hibiscus; 1s. Oranges. (As Type **55**): 2s. Island scene; 3s. Administration Centre, Mangaia.

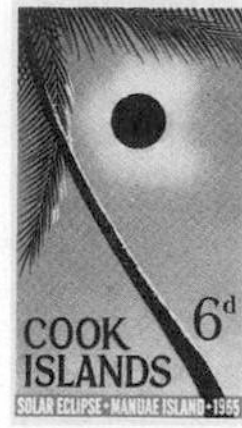

56 Eclipse and Palm

1965. Solar Eclipse Observation, Manuae Island.

No.	Type	Description	Unused	Used
174	**56**	6d. black, yellow and blue	20	10

57 N.Z. Ensign and Map

1965. Internal Self-government.

No.	Type	Description	Unused	Used
175	**57**	4d. red and blue	20	10
176	-	10d. multicoloured	20	15
177	-	1s. multicoloured	20	15
178	-	1s.9d. multicoloured	50	1·25

DESIGNS: 10d. London Missionary Society Church; 1s. Proclamation of Cession, 1900; 1s.9d. Nikao School.

1966. Churchill Commemoration. Nos. 171/3 and 175/7 optd In Memoriam SIR WINSTON CHURCHILL 1874 – 1965.

No.	Type	Description	Unused	Used
179	**57**	4d. red and blue	1·50	30
180	-	10d. multicoloured	2·50	80
181	-	1s. multicoloured	2·75	1·25
182	-	2s. brown and blue	2·75	2·25
183	-	3s. black and green	2·75	2·25
184	**55**	5s. brown and blue	3·00	2·25

1966. Air. Various stamps optd Airmail and Douglas DC-3 airplane or surch in addition.

No.	Type	Description	Unused	Used
185	-	6d. red, yell & grn (No. 167)	1·25	20
186	-	7d. on 8d. blk & bl (No. 168)	2·00	25
187	-	10d. on 3d. green and violet (No. 165)	1·00	15
188	-	1s. yellow and green (No. 169)	1·00	15
189	**52**	1s.6d. violet	2·00	1·25
190	-	2s.3d. on 3s. black and green (No. 172)	1·00	65
191	**55**	5s. brown and blue	1·75	1·50
192	-	10s. on 2s. brown and blue (No. 171)	1·75	14·00
193	-	£1 pink (No. 134)	13·00	17·00

63 "Adoration of the Magi" (Fra Angelico)

1966. Christmas. Multicoloured.

No.	Description	Unused	Used
194a	1d. Type **63**	10	10
195a	2d. "The Nativity" (Memling)	20	10
196a	4d. "Adoration of the Wise Men" (Velazquez)	30	15
197a	10d. "Adoration of the Wise Men" (H. Bosch)	30	20
198a	1s.6d. "Adoration of the Shepherds" (J. de Ribera)	40	35

68 Tennis and Queen Elizabeth II

1967. 2nd South Pacific Games, Noumea. Mult.

No.	Description	Unused	Used
199	½d. Type **68** (postage)	10	10
200	1d. Basketball and Games emblem	10	10
201	4d. Boxing and Cook Islands Team badge	10	10
202	7d. Football and Queen Elizabeth II	20	15
203	10d. Running and Games Emblem (air)	20	15
204	2s.3d. Running and Cook Islands' Team badge	25	65

1967. Decimal currency. Various stamps surch.

No.	Type	Description	Unused	Used
205	**45**	1c. on 1d.	45	1·50
206	-	2c. on 2d. (No. 164)	10	10
207	-	2½c. on 3d. (No. 165)	20	10
209	**57**	3c. on 4d.	15	10
210	-	4c. on 5d. (No. 166)	10·00	30
211	-	5c. on 6d. (No. 167)	15	10
212	**56**	5c. on 6d.	5·00	2·75
213	-	7c. on 8d. (No. 168)	30	10
214	-	10c. on 1s. (No. 169)	15	10
215	**52**	15c. on 1s.6d.	2·00	1·00
216	-	30c. on 3s. (No. 172)	32·00	7·00
217	**55**	50c. on 5s.	4·00	1·75
218	-	$1 and 10s. on 10d. (No. 176)	19·00	5·50
219	-	$2 on £1 (No. 134)	65·00	85·00
220	-	$6 on £3 (No. 135)	£120	£160
221	-	$10 on £5 (No. 98)	£170	£200

75 Village Scene, Cook Islands 1d. Stamp of 1892 and Queen Victoria

1967. 75th Anniv of First Cook Islands Stamps. Multicoloured.

No.	Description	Unused	Used
222	1c. (1d.) Type **75**	10	10
223	3c. (4d.) Post Office, Avarua, Rarotonga and Queen Elizabeth II	15	10
224	8c. (10d.) Avarua, Rarotonga and Cook Islands 10d. stamp of 1892	30	15
225	18c. (1s.9d.) "Moana Roa", (inter-island ship), Douglas DC-3 aircraft, map and Captain Cook	1·40	30
MS226	134×109 mm. Nos. 222/5	1·75	2·75

The face values are expressed in decimal currency and in the Sterling equivalent.

79 Hibiscus

81 Queen Elizabeth and Flowers

1967. Flowers. Multicoloured.

No.	Description	Unused	Used
227A	½c. Type **79**	10	10
228A	1c. "Hibiscus syriacus"	10	10
229A	2c. Frangipani	10	10
230A	2½c. "Clitoria ternatea"	20	10
231B	3c. "Suva Queen"	40	10
232A	4c. Water lily (wrongly inscribed "Walter Lily")	70	1·00
233B	4c. Water lily	2·50	10
234B	5c. "Bauhinia bipinnata rosea"	30	10
235B	6c. Yellow hibiscus	30	10
236B	8c. "Allamanda cathartica"	30	10
237B	9c. Stephanotis	30	10
238B	10c. "Poinciana regia flamboyant"	30	10
239A	15c. Frangipani	40	10
240B	20c. Thunbergia	3·50	1·50
241A	25c. Canna lily	80	30
242A	30c. "Euphorbia pulcherrima poinsettia"	65	50
243A	50c. "Gardinia taitensis"	1·00	55
244B	$1 Queen Elizabeth II	1·25	80
245B	$2 Queen Elizabeth II	2·25	1·50
246A	$4 Type **81**	1·50	4·25
247A	$6 Type **81**	1·75	7·00
247cA	$8 Type **81**	5·00	16·00
248A	$10 Type **81**	3·25	13·00

97 "Ia Orana Maria"

1967. Gauguin's Polynesian Paintings.

No.	Type	Description	Unused	Used
249	**97**	1c. multicoloured	10	10
250	-	3c. multicoloured	15	10
251	-	5c. multicoloured	15	10
252	-	8c. multicoloured	20	10
253	-	15c. multicoloured	35	15
254	-	22c. multicoloured	45	20
MS255		156×132 mm. Nos. 249/54	1·75	1·50

DESIGNS: 3c. "Riders on the Beach"; 5c. "Still Life with Flowers" and inset portrait of Queen Elizabeth; 8c. "Whispered Words"; 15c. "Maternity"; 22c. "Why are you angry?".

98 "The Holy Family" (Rubens)

1967. Christmas. Renaissance Paintings.

No.	Type	Description	Unused	Used
256	**98**	1c. multicoloured	10	10
257	-	3c. multicoloured	10	10
258	-	4c. multicoloured	10	10
259	-	8c. multicoloured	20	15
260	-	15c. multicoloured	35	15
261	-	25c. multicoloured	40	15

DESIGNS: 3c. "The Epiphany" (Durer); 4c. "The Lucca Madonna" (J. van Eyck); 8c. "The Adora-tion of the Shepherds" (J. da Bassano); 15c. "The Nativity" (El Greco); 25c. "The Madonna and Child" (Correggio).

1968. Hurricane Relief. Nos. 231, 233, 251, 238, 241 and 243/4 optd HURRICANE RELIEF PLUS and premium.

No.	Description	Unused	Used
262	3c.+1c. multicoloured	15	15
263	4c.+1c. multicoloured	15	15
264	5c.+2c. multicoloured	15	15
265	10c.+2c. multicoloured	15	15
266	25c.+5c. multicoloured	20	20
267	50c.+10c. multicoloured	25	30
268	$1+10c. multicoloured	35	50

On No. 264 silver blocking obliterates the design area around the lettering.

100 "Matavai Bay, Tahiti" (J. Barralet)

1968. Bicentenary of Captain Cook's First Voyage of Discovery.

No.	Type	Description	Unused	Used
269	**100**	½c. mult (postage)	10	10
270	-	1c. multicoloured	15	10
271	-	2c. multicoloured	30	20
272	-	4c. multicoloured	40	20
273	-	6c. multicoloured (air)	45	25
274	-	10c. multicoloured	45	25
275	-	15c. multicoloured	50	35
276	-	25c. multicoloured	60	55

DESIGNS—VERT: 1c. "Island of Huaheine" (John Cleveley); 2c. "Town of St. Peter and St. Paul, Kamchatka" (J. Webber); 4c. "The Ice Islands" (Antarctica: W. Hodges). HORIZ: 6c. "Resolution" and "Discovery" (J. Webber); 10c. "The Island of Tahiti" (W. Hodges); 15c. "Karakakooa, Hawaii" (J. Webber); 25c. "The Landing at Middleburg" (J. Sherwin).

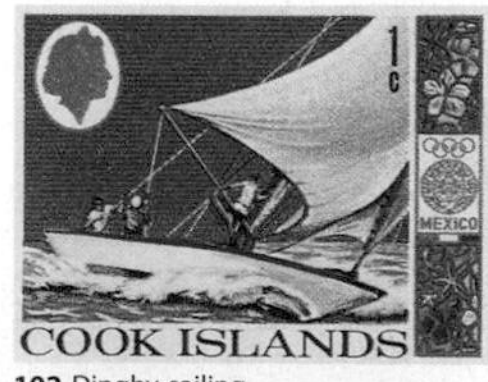

102 Dinghy-sailing

1968. Olympic Games, Mexico. Multicoloured.

No.	Description	Unused	Used
277	1c. Type **102**	10	10
278	5c. Gymnastics	10	10
279	15c. High-jumping	25	10
280	20c. High-diving	25	10
281	30c. Cycling	60	20
282	50c. Hurdling	50	25

103 "Madonna and Child" (Titian)

1968. Christmas. Multicoloured.

283	1c. Type **103**	10	10
284	4c. "The Holy Family of the Lamb" (Raphael)	15	10
285	10c. "The Madonna of the Rosary" (Murillo)	25	10
286	20c. "Adoration of the Magi" (Memling)	40	10
287	30c. "Adoration of the Magi" (Ghirlandaio)	45	10
MS288	114×177 mm. Nos. 283/7	1·25	1·60

104 Campfire Cooking

1969. Diamond Jubilee of New Zealand Scout Movement and 5th National (New Zealand) Jamboree. Multicoloured.

289	½c. Type **104**	10	10
290	1c. Descent by rope	10	10
291	5c. Semaphore	15	10
292	10c. Tree-planting	20	10
293	20c. Constructing a shelter	25	15
294	30c. Lord Baden-Powell and island scene	45	25

105 High Jumping

1969. 3rd South Pacific Games, Port Moresby. Multicoloured.

295	½c. Type **105**	10	40
296	½c. Footballer	10	40
297	1c. Basketball	50	40
298	1c. Weightlifter	50	40
299	4c. Tennis-player	50	50
300	4c. Hurdler	50	50
301	10c. Javelin-thrower	55	50
302	10c. Runner	55	50
303	15c. Golfer	1·75	1·50
304	15c. Boxer	1·75	1·50
MS305	174×129 mm. Nos. 295/304	8·00	7·00

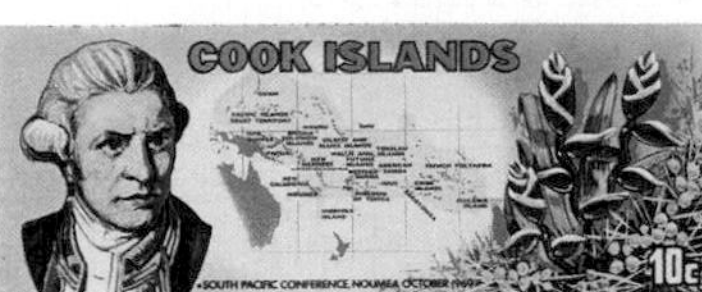

106 Flowers, Map and Captain Cook (image scaled to 68% of original size)

1969. South Pacific Conference, Noumea. Mult.

306	5c. Premier Albert Henry	20	20
307	10c. Type **106**	80	40
308	25c. Flowers, map and arms of New Zealand	30	40
309	30c. Queen Elizabeth II, map and flowers	30	40

107 "Virgin and Child with Saints Jerome and Dominic" (Lippi)

1969. Christmas. Multicoloured.

310	1c. Type **107**	10	10
311	4c. "The Holy Family" (Fra Bartolomeo)	10	10
312	10c. "The Adoration of the Shepherds" (A. Mengs)	15	10
313	20c. "Madonna and Child with Saints" (Robert Campin)	25	20
314	30c. "The Madonna of the Basket" (Correggio)	25	30
MS315	132×97 mm. Nos. 310/14	1·00	1·50

108 "The Resurrection of Christ" (Raphael)

1970. Easter.

316	**108**	4c. multicoloured	10	10
317	-	8c. multicoloured	10	10
318	-	20c. multicoloured	15	10
319	-	25c. multicoloured	20	10
MS320		132×162 mm. Nos. 316/19	1·25	1·25

DESIGNS: "The Resurrection of Christ" by Dirk Bouts (8c.), Altdorfer (20c.), Murillo (25c.).

1970. "Apollo 13". Nos. 233, 236, 239/40, 242 and 245/6 optd KIA ORANA APOLLO 13 ASTRONAUTS Te Atua to Tatou Irinakianga.

321	4c. multicoloured	10	10
322	8c. multicoloured	10	10
323	15c. multicoloured	10	10
324	20c. multicoloured	40	15
325	30c. multicoloured	20	20
326	$2 multicoloured	50	90
327a	$4 multicoloured	1·00	2·75

110 The Royal Family

1970. Royal Visit to New Zealand. Multicoloured.

328	5c. Type **110**	75	30
329	30c. Captain Cook and H.M.S. "Endeavour"	2·25	1·75
330	$1 Royal Visit commemorative coin	3·00	3·00
MS331	145×97 mm. Nos. 328/30	9·50	10·00

1970. 5th Anniv of Self-Government. Nos. 328/30 optd FIFTH ANNIVERSARY SELF-GOVERNMENT AUGUST 1970.

332	**110**	5c. multicoloured	40	15
333	-	30c. multicoloured	80	35
334	-	$1 multicoloured	1·00	90

On No. 332, the opt is arranged in one line around the frame of the stamp.

1970. Surch FOUR DOLLARS $4.00.

335a	**81**	$4 on $8 multicoloured	1·25	1·75
336a	**81**	$4 on $10 multicoloured	1·25	1·50

115 Mary, Joseph, and Christ in Manger

1970. Christmas. Multicoloured.

337	1c. Type **115**	10	10
338	4c. Shepherds and Apparition of the Angel	10	10
339	10c. Mary showing Child to Joseph	15	10
340	20c. The Wise Men bearing Gifts	20	20
341	30c. Parents wrapping Child in swaddling clothes	25	35
MS342	100×139 mm. Nos. 337/41	1·00	1·50

1971. Surch PLUS 20c UNITED KINGDOM SPECIAL MAIL SERVICE.

343	30c.+20c. (No. 242)	30	50
344	50c.+20c. (No. 243)	1·00	1·75

The premium of 20c. was to prepay a private delivery service fee in Great Britain during the postal strike. The mail was sent by air to a forwarding address in the Netherlands. No. 343 was intended for ordinary airmail ½ oz. letters, and No. 344 included registration fee.

117 Wedding of Princess Elizabeth and Prince Philip

1971. Royal Visit of Duke of Edinburgh. Multicoloured.

345	1c. Type **117**	30	50
346	4c. Queen Elizabeth, Prince Philip, Prince Charles and Princess Anne at Windsor	75	1·10
347	10c. Prince Philip sailing	1·25	1·25
348	15c. Prince Philip in polo gear	1·25	1·25
349	25c. Prince Philip in naval uniform, and Royal Yacht, "Britannia"	1·50	2·00
MS350	168×122 mm. Nos. 345/9	6·50	10·00

1971. 4th South Pacific Games, Tahiti. Nos. 238, 241 and 242 optd Fourth South Pacific Games Papeete and emblem or surch also.

351	10c. multicoloured	10	10
352	10c.+1c. multicoloured	10	10
353	10c.+3c. multicoloured	10	10
354	25c. multicoloured	15	10
355	25c.+1c. multicoloured	15	10
356	25c.+3c. multicoloured	15	10
357	30c. multicoloured	15	10
358	30c.+1c. multicoloured	15	10
359	30c.+3c. multicoloured	15	10

The stamps additionally surch 1c. or 3c. helped to finance the Cook Islands' team at the games.

1971. Nos. 230, 233, 236/7 and 239 surch 10c.

360	10c. on 2½c. multicoloured	15	25
361	10c. on 4c. multicoloured	15	25
362	10c. on 8c. multicoloured	15	25
363	10c. on 9c. multicoloured	15	25
364	10c. on 15c. multicoloured	15	25

121 "Virgin and Child" (Bellini)

1971. Christmas.

365	**121**	1c. multicoloured	10	20
366	-	4c. multicoloured	10	20
367	-	10c. multicoloured	25	10
368	-	20c. multicoloured	50	20
369	-	30c. multicoloured	50	40
MS370		135×147 mm. Nos. 365/9	2·00	3·25
MS371		92×98 mm. 50c. + 5c. "The Holy Family in a Garland of Flowers" (Jan Brueghel and Pieter van Avont) (41×41 mm)	75	1·40

DESIGNS: Various paintings of the "Virgin and Child" by Bellini. Similar to Type **121**.

1972. 25th Anniv of South Pacific Commission. No. 244 optd SOUTH PACIFIC COMMISSION FEB. 1947 – 1972.

372	$1 multicoloured	40	75

123 St. John

1972. Easter. Multicoloured.

373	5c. Type **123**	10	10
374	10c. Christ on the Cross	10	10
375	30c. Mary, Mother of Jesus	25	40
MS376	79×112 mm. Nos. 373/5 forming triptych of "The Crucifixion"	1·00	2·25

1972. Hurricane Relief. (a) Nos. 239, 241 and 243 optd HURRICANE RELIEF PLUS and premium.

379	15c.+5c. multicoloured	20	20
380	25c.+5c. multicoloured	20	20
382	50c.+10c. multicoloured	25	25

(b) Nos. 373/5 optd Hurricane Relief Plus and premium.

377	5c.+2c. multicoloured	15	15
378	10c.+2c. multicoloured	15	15
381	30c.+5c. multicoloured	20	20

126/7 Rocket heading for Moon (image scaled to 74% of original size)

1972. Apollo Moon Exploration Flights. Mult.

383	5c. Type **126**	20	15
384	5c. Type **127**	20	15
385	10c. Lunar module and astronaut	20	15
386	10c. Astronaut and experiment	20	15
387	25c. Command capsule and Earth	25	20
388	25c. Lunar Rover	25	20
389	30c. Sikorsky Sea King helicopter	1·00	40
390	30c. Splashdown	1·00	40
MS391	83×205 mm. Nos. 383/90	4·50	6·00

These were issued in horizontal se-tenant pairs of each value, forming one composite design.

1972. Hurricane Relief. Nos. 383/390 surch HURRICANE RELIEF Plus and premium.

392	5c.+2c. multicoloured	10	10
393	5c.+2c. multicoloured	10	10
394	10c.+2c. multicoloured	10	10
395	10c.+2c. multicoloured	10	10
396	25c.+2c. multicoloured	15	15
397	25c.+2c. multicoloured	15	15
398	30c.+2c. multicoloured	25	15
399	30c.+2c. multicoloured	25	15
MS400	83×205 mm. No. **MS**391 surch 3c. on each stamp	2·50	3·50

129 High-jumping

1972. Olympic Games, Munich. Multicoloured.

401	10c. Type **129**	20	10
402	25c. Running	45	15
403	30c. Boxing	45	20
MS404	88×78 mm. 50c. + 5c. Pierre de Coubertin	1·00	2·00
MS405	84×133 mm. Nos. 401/3	1·25	2·00

130 "The Rest on the Flight into Egypt" (Caravaggio)

1972. Christmas. Multicoloured.

406	1c. Type **130**	10	10
407	5c. "Madonna of the Swallow" (Guercino)	25	10
408	10c. "Madonna of the Green Cushion" (Solario)	35	10
409	20c. "Madonna and Child" (di Credi)	55	20
410	30c. "Madonna and Child" (Bellini)	85	30
MS411	141×152 mm. Nos. 406/10	3·25	4·00
MS412	101×82 mm. 50c. + 5c. "The Holy Night" (Correggio) (31×43 mm)	1·00	1·50

131 Marriage Ceremony

1972. Royal Silver Wedding. Each black and silver.

413	5c. Type **131**	25	15
414	10c. Leaving Westminster Abbey	35	25
415	15c. Bride and bridegroom (40×41 mm)	45	50
416	30c. Family group (67×40 mm)	55	75

132 Taro Leaf

1973. Silver Wedding Coinage.

417	**132**	1c. gold, mauve and black	10	10
418	-	2c. gold, blue and black	10	10
419	-	5c. silver, green and black	10	10
420	-	10c. silver, blue and black	20	10
421	-	20c. silver, green and black	30	10
422	-	50c. silver, mauve and black	50	15
423	-	$1 silver, blue and black	75	30

DESIGNS—HORIZ (37×24 mm): 2c. Pineapple; 5c. Hibiscus. (46×30 mm): 10c. Oranges; 20c. White tern; 50c. Striped bonito. VERT: (32×55 mm): $1 Tangaroa.

133 "Noli me Tangere" (Titian)

1973. Easter. Multicoloured.

424	5c. Type **133**	15	10
425	10c. "The Descent from the Cross" (Rubens)	20	10
426	30c. "The Lamentation of Christ" (Durer)	25	10
MS427	132×67 mm. Nos. 424/6	55	1·25

1973. Easter. Children's Charity. Designs as Nos. 424/6 in separate miniature sheets 67×87 mm, each with a face value of 50c. + 5c.

MS428	As Nos. 424/6 Set of 3 sheets	1·00	1·75

134 Queen Elizabeth II in Coronation Regalia

1973. 20th Anniv of Queen Elizabeth's Coronation.

429	**134**	10c. multicoloured	50	90
MS430		64×89 mm. 50c. as 10c.	2·50	2·25

1973. 10th Anniv of Treaty Banning Nuclear Testing. Nos. 234, 236, 238 and 240/2 optd TENTH ANNIVERSARY CESSATION OF NUCLEAR TESTING TREATY.

431	5c. multicoloured	10	10
432	8c. multicoloured	10	10
433	10c. multicoloured	10	10
434	20c. multicoloured	15	15
435	25c. multicoloured	20	15
436	30c. multicoloured	20	15

136 Tipairua

1973. Maori Exploration of the Pacific. Sailing Craft. Multicoloured.

437	½c. Type **136**	10	10
438	1c. Wa'a Kaulua	10	10
439	1½c. Tainui	15	10
440	5c. War canoe	30	15
441	10c. Pahi	40	15
442	15c. Amatasi	60	65
443	25c. Vaka	75	80

137 The Annunciation

1973. Christmas. Scene from a 15th-century Flemish "Book of Hours". Multicoloured.

444	1c. Type **137**	10	10
445	5c. The Visitation	10	10
446	10c. Annunciation to the Shepherds	10	10
447	20c. Epiphany	15	10
448	30c. The Slaughter of the Innocents	20	15
MS449	121×128 mm. Nos. 444/8	55	1·40

See also No. **MS**454.

138 Princess Anne

1973. Royal Wedding. Multicoloured.

450	25c. Type **138**	20	10
451	30c. Captain Mark Phillips	25	10
452	50c. Princess Anne and Captain Phillips	30	15
MS453	119×100 mm. Nos. 450/2	55	35

1973. Christmas. Children's Charity. Designs as Nos. 444/8 in separate miniature sheets 50×70 mm, each with a face value of 50c. + 5c.

MS454	As Nos. 444/8 Set of 5 sheets	75	80

139 Running

1974. British Commonwealth Games, Christchurch. Multicoloured.

455	1c. Diving (vert)	10	10
456	3c. Boxing (vert)	10	10
457	5c. Type 139	10	10
458	10c. Weightlifting	10	10
459	30c. Cycling	40	25
MS460	115×90 mm. 50c. Discobolus	40	55

140 "Jesus carrying the Cross" (Raphael)

1974. Easter. Multicoloured.

461	5c. Type **140**	10	30
462	10c. "The Holy Trinity" (El Greco)	15	20
463	30c. "The Deposition of Christ" (Caravaggio)	25	30
MS464	130×70 mm. Nos. 461/3	1·50	70

1974. Easter. Children's Charity. Designs as Nos. 461/3 in separate miniature sheets 59×87 mm, each with a face value of 50c. + 5c.

MS465	As Nos. 461/3 Set of 3 sheets	70	1·40

141 Grey Bonnet

142 Queen Elizabeth II

1974. Sea Shells. Multicoloured.

466	½c. Type **141**	30	10
467	1c. Common Pacific vase	30	10
468	1½c. True heart cockle	30	10
469	2c. Terebellum conch	30	10
470	3c. Bat volute	45	10
471	4c. Gibbose conch	50	10
472	5c. Common hairy triton	50	10
473	6c. Serpent's head cowrie	50	2·00
474	8c. Granulate frog shell	60	10
475	10c. Fly-spotted auger	60	10
476	15c. Episcopan mitre	70	20
477	20c. Butterfly moon	1·00	20
478	25c. Royal oak scallop	1·00	2·50
479	30c. Soldier cone	1·00	30
480	50c. Textile or cloth of gold cone	8·50	4·50
481	60c. Red-mouth olive	8·50	4·50
482	$1 Type **142**	3·00	4·50
483	$2 Type **142**	1·75	2·25
484	$4 Queen Elizabeth II and sea shells (60×39 mm)	2·50	7·00
485	$6 As $4 (60×39 mm)	18·00	7·00
486	$8 As $4 (60×39 mm)	21·00	9·00
487	$10 As $4 (60×39 mm)	23·00	9·00

143 Footballer and Australasian Map

1974. World Cup Football Championship, West Germany. Multicoloured.

488	25c. Type **143**	20	10
489	50c. Map and Munich Stadium	35	25
490	$1 Footballer, stadium and World Cup	55	45
MS491	89×100 mm. Nos. 488/90	1·00	2·75

144 Obverse and Reverse of Commemorative $2.50 Silver Coin

1974. Bicentenary of Captain Cook's Second Voyage of Discovery.

492	**144**	$2.50 silver, black and violet	11·00	7·00
493	-	$7.50 silver, black and green	16·00	13·00
MS494		73×73 mm. Nos. 492/3	30·00	48·00

DESIGN: $7.50, As Type **144** but showing $7.50 coin.

145 Early Stamps of Cook Islands

1974. Centenary of UPU. Multicoloured.

495	10c. Type **145**	25	15
496	25c. Old landing strip, Rarotonga, and stamp of 1898	35	40
497	30c. Post Office, Rarotonga, and stamp of 1920	40	40
498	50c. UPU emblem and stamps	40	65
MS499	118×79 mm. Nos. 495/8	1·25	1·75

146 "Madonna of the Goldfinch" (Raphael)

1974. Christmas. Multicoloured.

500	1c. Type **146**	10	10
501	5c. "The Sacred Family" (Andrea del Sarto)	20	10
502	10c. "The Virgin adoring the Child" (Correggio)	25	10
503	20c. "The Holy Family" (Rembrandt)	40	20
504	30c. "The Virgin and Child" (Rogier van der Weyden)	50	30
MS505	114×133 mm. Nos. 500/4	1·40	2·25

147 Churchill and Blenheim Palace

1974. Birth Centenary of Sir Winston Churchill. Multicoloured.

506	5c. Type **147**	15	10
507	10c. Churchill and Houses of Parliament	15	10
508	25c. Churchill and Chartwell	25	20
509	30c. Churchill and Buckingham Palace	25	25
510	50c. Churchill and St. Paul's Cathedral	30	50
MS511	108×114 mm. Nos. 506/10	1·25	1·00

1974. Christmas. Children's Charity. Designs as Nos. 500/504 in separate miniature sheets 53×69 mm, each with a face value of 50c. + 5c.

MS512	As Nos. 500/4 Set of 5 sheets	1·00	1·00

148 Vasco Nunez de Balboa and Discovery of Pacific Ocean (1513)

1975. Pacific Explorers. Multicoloured.

513	1c. Type **148**	15	10
514	5c. Fernando de Magellanes and map (1520)	65	20
515	10c. Juan Sebastian del Cano and "Vitoria" (1520)	1·25	20
516	25c. Friar Andres de Urdaneta and ship (1564–67)	2·25	75
517	30c. Miguel Lopez de Legazpi and ship (1564–67)	2·25	80

149 "Apollo" Capsule

1975. "Apollo–Soyuz" Space Project. Mult.

518	25c. Type **149**	45	15
519	25c. "Soyuz" capsule	45	15
520	30c. "Soyuz" crew	50	15
521	30c. "Apollo" crew	50	15
522	50c. Cosmonaut within "Soyuz"	55	25
523	50c. Astronauts within "Apollo"	55	25
MS524	119×119 mm. Nos. 518/23	1·50	1·00

These were issued in horizontal se-tenant pairs of each value, forming one composite design.

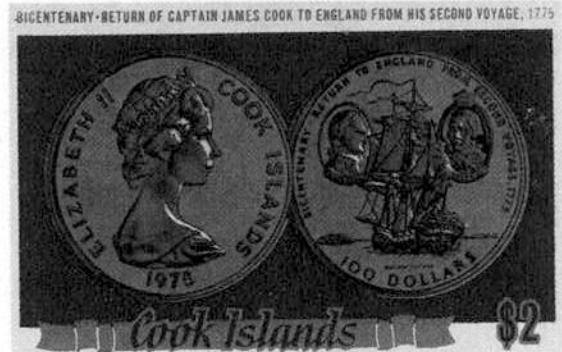

150 $100 Commemorative Gold Coin

1975. Bicentenary of Captain Cook's 2nd Voyage.

525	**150**	$2 brown, gold and violet	2·25	1·50

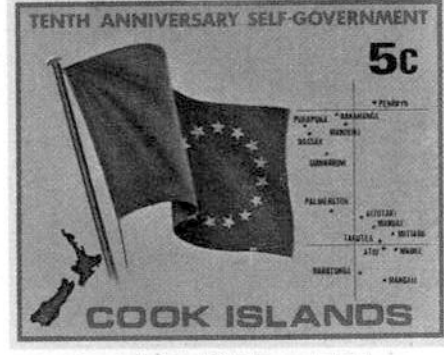

151 Cook Islands' Flag and Map

1975. 10th Anniv of Self-government.

526	5c. Type **151**	40	10
527	10c. Premier Sir Albert Henry and flag (vert)	45	10
528	25c. Rarotonga and flag	80	30

152 "Madonna by the Fireside" (R. Campin)

1975. Christmas. Multicoloured.

529	6c. Type **152**	20	10
530	10c. "Madonna in the Meadow" (Raphael)	20	10
531	15c. "Madonna of the Oak" (att. Raphael)	30	10
532	20c. "Adoration of the Shepherds" (J. B. Maino)	30	15
533	35c. "The Annunciation" (Murillo)	50	20
MS534	110×124 mm. Nos. 529/33	1·25	90

1975. Christmas. Children's Charity. Designs as Nos. 529/33 in separate miniature sheets 53×71 mm, each with a face value of 75c. + 5c.

MS535	As Nos. 529/33 Set of 5 sheets	1·10	1·25

153 "Entombment of Christ" (Raphael)

1976. Easter. Multicoloured.

536	7c. Type **153**	30	10
537	15c. "Pieta" (Veronese)	50	15
538	35c. "Pieta" (El Greco)	75	25
MS539	144×55 mm. Nos. 536/8	1·50	85

1976. Easter. Children's Charity. Designs as Nos. 536/8 in separate miniature sheets 69×69 mm, each with a face value of 60c. + 5c.

MS540	As Nos. 536/8 Set of 3 sheets	1·10	1·40

154 Benjamin Franklin and H.M.S. "Resolution"

1976. Bicent of American Revolution. Mult.

541	$1 Type **154**	6·00	1·50
542	$2 Captain Cook and H.M.S. "Resolution"	8·00	2·50
MS543	118×58 mm. $3 Cook, Franklin and H.M.S. "Resolution" (74×31 mm)	13·00	6·50

1976. Visit of Queen Elizabeth to U.S.A. Nos. 541/2 optd Royal Visit July 1976.

544	**154**	$1 multicoloured	4·00	1·50
545	-	$2 multicoloured	6·00	2·50
MS546		$3 Cook, Franklin and H.M.S. "Resolution"	7·00	5·50

156 Hurdling

1976. Olympic Games, Montreal. Multicoloured.

547	7c. Type **156**	20	10
548	7c. Hurdling (value on left)	20	10
549	15c. Hockey (value on right)	40	15
550	15c. Hockey (value on left)	40	15
551	30c. Fencing (value on right)	40	15
552	30c. Fencing (value on left)	40	15
553	35c. Football (value on right)	40	20
554	35c. Football (value on left)	40	20
MS555	104×146 mm. Nos. 547/54	3·50	2·00

157 "The Visitation"

1976. Christmas. Renaissance Sculptures. Mult.

556	6c. Type **157**	10	10
557	10c. "Adoration of the Shepherds"	10	10
558	15c. "Adoration of the Shepherds" (different)	15	10
559	20c. "The Epiphany"	20	20
560	35c. "The Holy Family"	25	25
MS561	116×110 mm. Nos. 556/60	1·00	1·75

1976. Christmas. Children's Charity. Designs as Nos. 556/60 in separate miniature sheets 66×80 mm, each with a face value of 75c. + 5c.

MS562	As Nos. 556/60 Set of 5 sheets	1·10	1·10

158 Obverse and Reverse of $5 Mangaia Kingfisher Coin

1976. National Wildlife and Conservation Day.

563	**158**	$1 multicoloured	1·00	1·00

159 Imperial State Crown

1977. Silver Jubilee. Multicoloured.

564	25c. Type **159**	30	40
565	25c. The Queen with regalia	30	40
566	50c. Westminster Abbey	40	55
567	50c. Coronation coach	40	55
568	$1 The Queen and Prince Philip	60	75
569	$1 Royal Visit, 1974	60	75
MS570	130×136 mm. As Nos. 564/9 (borders and "COOK ISLANDS" in a different colour)	2·25	2·00

160 "Christ on the Cross"

1977. Easter. 400th Birth Anniv of Rubens. Multicoloured.

571	7c. Type **160**	35	10
572	15c. "Christ on the Cross"	55	15
573	35c. "The Deposition of Christ"	1·10	30
MS574	118×65 mm. Nos. 571/3	1·40	1·60

1977. Easter. Children's Charity. Designs as Nos. 571/3 in separate miniature sheets 60×79 mm, each with a face value of 60c. + 5c.

MS575	As Nos. 571/3 Set of 3 sheets	1·00	1·00

161 "Virgin and Child" (Memling)

1977. Christmas. Multicoloured.

576	6c. Type **161**	25	10
577	10c. "Madonna and Child with Saints and Donors" (Memling)	25	10
578	15c. "Adoration of the Kings" (Geertgen)	35	10
579	20c. "Virgin and Child with Saints" (Crivelli)	45	15
580	35c. "Adoration of the Magi" (16th century Flemish school)	60	20
MS581	118×111 mm. Nos. 576/80	1·40	1·75

1977. Christmas. Children's Charity. Designs as Nos. 576/80 in separate miniature sheets 69×69 mm, each with a face value of 75c. + 5c.

MS582	As Nos. 576/80 Set of 5 sheets	1·00	1·25

162 Obverse and Reverse of $5 Cook Islands Swiftlet Coin

1977. National Wildlife and Conservation Day.

583	**162**	$1 multicoloured	1·00	65

163 Captain Cook and H.M.S. "Resolution" (from paintings by N. Dance and H. Roberts)

1978. Bicent of Discovery of Hawaii. Mult.

584	50c. Type **163**	1·00	60
585	$1 Earl of Sandwich and Cook landing at Owhyhee (from paintings by Thomas Gainsborough and J. Cleveley)	1·40	75
586	$2 Obverse and reverse of $200 coin and Cook monument, Hawaii	1·60	1·25
MS587	118×95 mm. Nos. 584/6	5·00	7·50

164 "Pieta" (Van der Weyden)

1978. Easter. Paintings from the National Gallery, London. Multicoloured.

588	15c. Type **164**	40	25
589	35c. "The Entombment" (Michelangelo)	50	40
590	75c. "The Supper at Emmaus" (Caravaggio)	75	65
MS591	114×96 mm. Nos. 588/90	1·50	2·00

1978. Easter. Children's Charity. Designs as Nos. 588/90 in separate miniature sheets, 85×72 mm, each with a face value of 60c. + 5c.

MS592	As Nos. 588/90 Set of 3 sheets	1·10	1·10

165 Queen Elizabeth II

1978. 25th Anniv of Coronation. Multicoloured.

593	50c. Type **165**	25	35
594	50c. The Lion of England	25	35
595	50c. Imperial State Crown	25	35
596	50c. Statue of Tangaroa (god)	25	35
597	70c. Type **165**	25	35
598	70c. Sceptre with Cross	25	35
599	70c. St. Edward's Crown	25	35
600	70c. Rarotongan staff god	25	35
MS601	103×142 mm. Nos. 593/600*	1·00	1·50

*In No. **MS**601 the designs of Nos. 595 and 599 are transposed.

1978. Nos. 466, 468, 473/4 and 478/82 surch.

602	5c. on 1½c. True heart cockle	60	10
603	7c. on ½c. Type **141**	65	15
604	10c. on 6c. Serpent's-head cowrie	70	15
605	10c. on 8c. Granulate frog shell	70	15
606	15c. on ½c. Type **141**	70	20
607	15c. on 25c. Royal oak scallop	70	20
608	15c. on 30c. Soldier cone	70	20
609	15c. on 50c. Textile or cloth of gold cone	70	20
610	15c. on 60c. Red-mouth olive	70	20
611	17c. on ½c. Type **141**	90	25
612	17c. on 50c. Textile or cloth of gold cone	90	25

1978. 250th Birth Anniv of Captain James Cook. Nos. 584/6 optd 1728 250th ANNIVERSARY OF COOK'S BIRTH 1978.

613	50c. Type **163**	2·00	75
614	$1 Earl of Sandwich and Cook landing at Owhyhee	2·25	1·00
615	$2 $200 commemorative coin and Cook monument, Hawaii	2·50	2·00
MS616	Nos. 613/15	14·00	17·00

168 Obverse and Reverse of Cook Islands Warblers $5 Coin

1978. National Wildlife and Conservation Day.

617	**168** $1 multicoloured	1·00	1·00

169 "The Virgin and Child" (Van Der Weyden)

1978. Christmas. Paintings. Multicoloured.

618	15c. Type **169**	45	15
619	17c. "The Virgin and Child" (Crivelli)	45	20
620	35c. "The Virgin and Child" (Murillo)	80	35
MS621	107×70 mm. Nos. 618/20	1·50	1·50

1979. Christmas. Children's Charity. Designs as Nos. 618/20 in separate miniature sheets 57×87 mm, each with a face value of 75c. +5c.

MS622	As Nos. 618/20 Set of 3 sheets	1·00	1·00

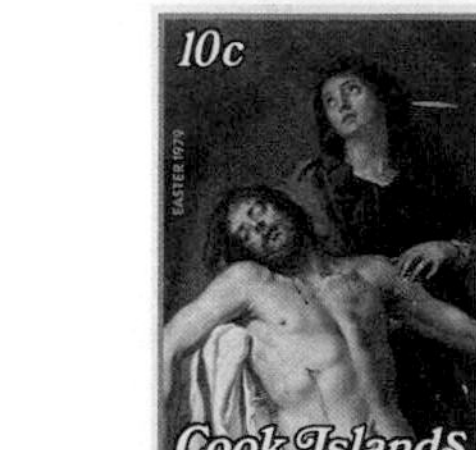

170 Virgin with Body of Christ

1979. Easter. Details of Painting "Descent" by Gaspar de Crayar. Multicoloured.

623	10c. Type **170**	25	10
624	12c. St. John	30	20
625	15c. Mary Magdalene	35	25
626	20c. Weeping angels	45	30
MS627	83×100 mm. As Nos. 623/6, but each with a charity premium of 2c.	65	75

Stamps from No. **MS**627 are slightly smaller, 32×40 mm, and are without borders.

171 "Captain Cook" (James Weber)

1979. Death Bicentenary of Captain Cook. Mult.

628	20c. Type **171**	40	20
629	30c. H.M.S. "Resolution"	50	35
630	35c. H.M.S. "Royal George" (ship of the line)	50	45
631	50c. "Death of Captain Cook" (George Carter)	55	60
MS632	78×112 mm. Nos. 628/31	1·75	1·25

Stamps from No. **MS**632 have black borders.

172 Post-Rider

1979. Death Centenary of Sir Rowland Hill. Mult.

633	30c. Type **172**	15	20
634	30c. Mail coach	15	20
635	30c. Automobile	15	20
636	30c. Diesel train	15	20
637	35c. "Cap-Hornier" (full-rigged ship)	15	20
638	35c. River steamer	15	20
639	35c. "Deutschland" (liner)	15	20
640	35c. "United States" (liner)	15	20
641	50c. Balloon "Le Neptune"	25	25
642	50c. Junkers F13 airplane	25	25
643	50c. Airship "Graf Zeppelin"	25	25
644	50c. Concorde	25	25
MS645	132×104 mm. Nos. 633/44	3·75	4·00

1979. Nos. 466, 468 and 481 surch.

646	6c. on ½c. Type **141**	20	30
647	10c. on 1½c. Cockle shell	25	20
648	15c. on 60c. Olive shell	40	40

174 Brother and Sister

1979. International Year of the Child. Mult.

649	30c. Type **174**	25	25
650	50c. Boy with tree drum	40	40
651	65c. Children dancing	50	50
MS652	102×75 mm. As Nos. 649/51, but each with a charity premium of 5c.	1·00	1·50

Designs for stamps from No. **MS**652 are as Nos. 649/51 but have IYC emblem in red.

175 "Apollo 11" Emblem

1979. 10th Anniv of "Apollo 11" Moon Landing. Multicoloured.

653	30c. Type **175**	40	50
654	50c. "Apollo 11" crew	50	60
655	60c. Neil Armstrong on the Moon	65	80
656	65c. Splashdown recovery	70	90
MS657	119×105 mm. Nos. 653/6	2·50	3·00

176 Obverse and Reverse of $5 Rarotongan Fruit Dove Coin

1979. National Wildlife and Conservation Day.

658	**176** $1 multicoloured	1·25	2·00

177 Glass Christmas Tree Ornaments

1979. Christmas. Multicoloured.

659	6c. Type **177** (postage)	10	10
660	10c. Hibiscus and star	10	10
661	12c. Poinsettia, bells and candle	15	10
662	15c. Poinsettia leaves and Tiki (god)	15	15
663	20c. Type **177** (air)	20	15
664	25c. As No. 660	25	20
665	30c. As No. 661	30	25
666	35c. As No. 662	35	30

1980. Christmas. As Nos. 659/66 but with charity premium.

667	6c.+2c. Type **177** (postage)	10	10
668	10c.+2c. Hibiscus and star	15	15
669	12c.+2c. Poinsettia, bells and candle	15	20
670	15c.+2c. Poinsettia leaves and Tiki (god)	15	20
671	20c.+4c. Type **177** (air)	15	25
672	25c.+4c. As No. 660	15	25
673	30c.+4c. As No. 661	20	30
674	35c.+4c. As No. 662	25	35

178 "Flagellation"

1980. Easter. Illustrations by Gustav Dore. Each gold and brown.

675	20c. Type **178**	25	30
676	20c. "Crown of Thorns"	25	30
677	30c. "Jesus Insulted"	35	35
678	30c. "Jesus Falls"	35	35
679	35c. "The Crucifixion"	40	35
680	35c. "The Descent from the Cross"	40	35
MS681	120×110 mm. As Nos. 675/80, but each with a charity premium of 2c.	1·10	1·75

1980. Easter. Children's Charity. Designs as Nos. 675/80 in separate miniature sheets 60×71 mm, each with a face value of 75c. + 5c.

MS682	As Nos. 675/80 Set of 6 sheets	1·00	1·50

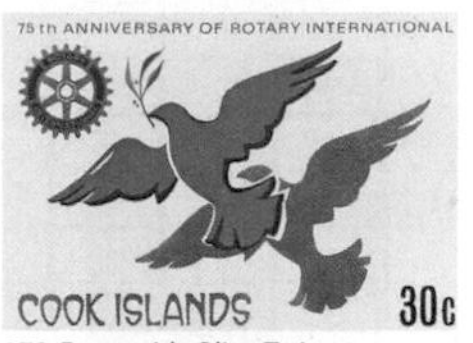

179 Dove with Olive Twig

1980. 75th Anniv of Rotary International. Mult.

683	30c. Type **179**	35	35
684	35c. Hibiscus flower	40	40
685	50c. Ribbons	50	50
MS686	72×113 mm. Nos. 683/5, but each with a charity premium of 3c.	1·10	1·50

1980. "Zeapex 80" International Stamp Exhibition, Auckland. Nos. 633/44 optd ZEAPEX STAMP EXHIBITION—AUCKLAND 1980 and New Zealand 1865 1s. Stamp.

687	30c. Type **172**	35	25
688	30c. Mail coach	35	25
689	30c. Automobile	35	25
690	30c. Diesel train	35	25
691	35c. "Cap-Hornier" (full-rigged ship)	40	30
692	35c. River steamer	40	30
693	35c. "Deutschland" (liner)	40	30
694	35c. "United States" (liner)	40	30
695	50c. Balloon "Le Neptune"	60	35
696	50c. Junkers "F13" airplane	60	35
697	50c. Airship"Graf Zeppelin"	60	35
698	50c. Concorde	60	35
MS699	132×104 mm. Nos. 687/98	6·00	6·00

1980. "Zeapex '80" International Stamp Exhibition, Auckland. As No MS681 but containing stamps without charity premium of 2c. optd "Zeapex '80 Auckland + 10c" in black on gold background.

MS700	120×110 mm. Nos. 675/80 (sold at $1.80)	1·00	1·75

Stamps from No. **MS**700 are unaffected by the overprint which appears on the sheet margin.

181 Queen Elizabeth the Queen Mother

1980. 80th Birthday of the Queen Mother.

701	**181** 50c. multicoloured	1·00	1·00
MS702	64×78 mm. **181** $2 multicoloured	1·25	1·75

182 Satellites orbiting Moon

1980. 350th Death Anniv of Johannes Kepler (astronomer). Multicoloured.

703	12c. Type **182**	50	35
704	12c. Space-craft orbiting Moon	50	35
705	50c. Space-craft orbiting Moon (different)	1·00	80
706	50c. Astronaut and Moon vehicle	1·00	80
MS707	122×122 mm. Nos. 703/6	2·75	2·75

183 Scene from novel "From the Earth to the Moon"

1980. 75th Death Anniv of Jules Verne (author).

708	**183** 20c. multicoloured	45	35
709	- 20c. multicoloured	45	35
710	- 30c. multicoloured (mauve background)	55	45
711	- 30c. multicoloured (blue background)	55	45
MS712	121×122 mm. Nos. 708/11	2·75	2·25

DESIGNS: Showing scenes from the novel "From the Earth to the Moon".

184 "Siphonogorgia"

1980. Corals (1st series). Multicoloured.

713	1c. Type **184**	30	30
714	1c. "Pavona praetorta"	30	30
715	1c. "Stylaster echinatus"	30	30
716	1c. "Tubastraea"	30	30
717	3c. "Millepora alcicornis"	30	30
718	3c. "Junceella gemmacea"	30	30
719	3c. "Fungia fungites"	30	30
720	3c. "Heliofungia actiniformis"	30	30
721	4c. "Distichopora violacea"	30	30
722	4c. "Stylaster"	30	30
723	4c. "Gonipora"	30	30
724	4c. "Caulastraea echinulata"	30	30
725	5c. "Ptilosarcus gurneyi"	30	30
726	5c. "Stylophora pistillata"	30	30
727	5c. "Melithaea squamata"	30	30
728	5c. "Porites andrewsi"	30	30
729	6c. "Lobophyllia bemprichii"	30	30
730	6c. "Palauastrea ramosa"	30	30
731	6c. "Bellonella indica"	30	30
732	6c. "Pectinia alcicornis"	30	30
733	8c. "Sarcophyton digitatum"	30	30
734	8c. "Melithaea albitincta"	30	30
735	8c. "Plerogyra sinuosa"	25	30
736	8c. "Dendropyllia gracilis"	25	30
737	10c. As Type **184**	30	30
738	10c. As No. 714	30	30
739	10c. As No. 715	30	30
740	10c. As No. 716	30	30
741	12c. As No. 717	30	30
742	12c. As No. 718	30	30
743	12c. As No. 719	30	30
744	12c. As No. 720	30	30
745	15c. As No. 721	30	30
746	15c. As No. 722	30	30
747	15c. As No. 723	30	30
748	15c. As No. 724	30	30
749	20c. As No. 725	35	30
750	20c. As No. 726	35	30
751	20c. As No. 727	35	30
752	20c. As No. 728	35	30
753	25c. As No. 729	35	30
754	25c. As No. 730	35	30
755	25c. As No. 731	35	30

756	25c. As No. 732	35	30
757	30c. As No. 733	40	30
758	30c. As No. 734	40	30
759	30c. As No. 735	40	30
760	30c. As No. 736	40	30
761	35c. Type **184**	45	35
762	35c. As No. 714	45	35
763	35c. As No. 715	45	35
764	35c. As No. 716	45	35
765	50c. As No. 717	65	75
766	50c. As No. 718	65	75
767	50c. As No. 719	65	75
768	50c. As No. 720	65	75
769	60c. As No. 721	75	75
770	60c. As No. 722	75	75
771	60c. As No. 723	75	75
772	60c. As No. 724	75	75
773	70c. As No. 725	2·50	75
774	70c. As No. 726	2·50	75
775	70c. As No. 727	2·50	75
776	70c. As No. 728	2·50	75
777	80c. As No. 729	2·50	80
778	80c. As No. 730	2·50	80
779	80c. As No. 731	2·50	80
780	80c. As No. 732	2·50	80
781	$1 As No. 733	3·75	1·00
782	$1 As No. 734	3·75	1·00
783	$1 As No. 735	3·75	1·00
784	$1 As No. 736	3·75	1·00
785	$2 As No. 723	12·00	3·00
786	$3 As No. 720	12·00	3·00
787	$4 As No. 726	4·50	15·00
788	$6 As No. 715	6·00	19·00
789	$10 As No. 734	27·00	42·00

Nos. 761/74 are 30×40 mm, and Nos. 785/9, which include a portrait of Queen Elizabeth II in each design, are 55×35 mm.

See also Nos. 966/94.

185 Annunciation

1980. Christmas. Scenes from 13th-century French Prayer Books. Multicoloured.

801	15c. Type **185**	25	15
802	30c. The Visitation	35	25
803	40c. The Nativity	45	30
804	50c. The Epiphany	60	40
MS805	89×114 mm. Nos. 801/4	1·50	1·50

1981. Christmas. Children's Charity. Designs as Nos. 801/4 in separate miniature sheets 55×68 mm, each with a face value of 75c +5c. Imperf.

MS806	As Nos. 801/4 Set of 4 sheets	1·50	1·50

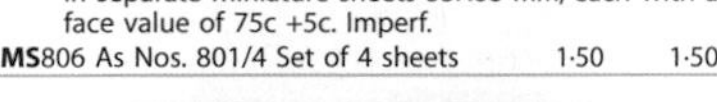

186 "The Crucifixion" (from book of Saint-Amand)

1981. Easter. Illustrations from 12th-century French Prayer Books. Multicoloured.

807	15c. Type **186**	30	30
808	25c. "Placing in Tomb" (from book of Ingeburge)	35	35
809	40c. "Mourning at the Sepulchre" (from book of Ingeburge)	45	45
MS810	72×116 mm. As Nos. 807/9, but each with a charity premium of 2c.	1·00	1·00

1981. Easter. Children's Charity. Designs as Nos. 807/9 in separate miniature sheets 64×53 mm, each with a face value of 75c. + 5c. Imperf.

MS811	As Nos. 807/9 Set of 3 sheets	1·10	1·10

187 Prince Charles

1981. Royal Wedding. Multicoloured.

812	$1 Type **187**	50	1·10
813	$2 Prince Charles and Lady Diana Spencer	60	1·40
MS814	106×59 mm. Nos. 812/13	1·10	2·50

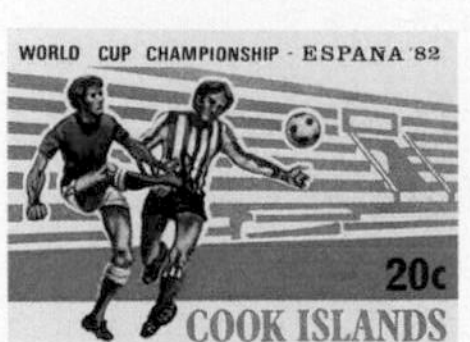

188 Footballers

1981. World Cup Football Championship, Spain (1982). Designs showing footballers. Mult.

815	20c. Type **188**	40	20
816	20c. Figures to right of stamp	40	20
817	30c. Figures to left	50	30
818	30c. Figures to right	50	30
819	35c. Figures to left	50	35
820	35c. Figures to right	50	35
821	50c. Figures to left	65	45
822	50c. Figures to right	65	45
MS823	180×94 mm. As Nos. 815/22, but each with a charity premium of 3c.	6·50	8·50

The two designs of each value were printed together, se-tenant, in horizontal pairs throughout the sheet, forming composite designs.

1981. International Year for Disabled Persons. Nos. 812/13 surch +5c.

824	$1+5c. Type **187**	55	1·75
825	$2+5c. Prince Charles and Lady Diana Spencer	70	2·50
MS826	106×59 mm. $1 + 10c, $2 + 10c. As Nos. 824/5	1·00	4·00

190 "Holy Virgin with Child"

1982. Christmas. Details of Paintings by Rubens. Multicoloured.

827	8c. Type **190**	55	20
828	15c. "Coronation of St. Catherine"	65	25
829	40c. "Adoration of the Shepherds"	90	80
830	50c. "Adoration of the Magi"	1·00	1·00
MS831	86×110 mm. As Nos. 827/30, but each with a charity premium of 3c.	3·75	4·25

1982. Christmas. Children's Charity. Designs as Nos. 827/30 in separate miniature sheets 62×78 mm, each with a face value of 75c. +5c.

MS832	As Nos. 827/30 Set of 4 sheets	3·50	4·00

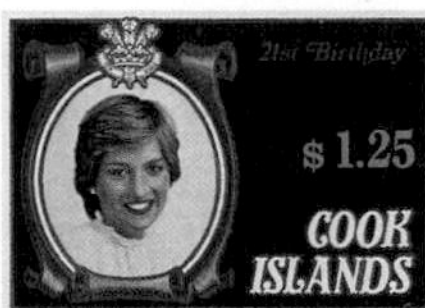

191 Princess of Wales (inscr "21st Birthday")

1982. 21st Birthday of Princess of Wales. Multicoloured.

833	$1.25 Type **191**	2·25	1·50
834	$1.25 As Type **191**, but inscr "1 July 1982"	2·25	1·50
835	$2.50 Princess (inscr "21st Birthday") (different)	3·00	2·25
836	$2.50 As No. 835, but inscr "1 July 1982"	3·00	2·25
MS837	92×72 mm. $1.25, Type **191**; $2.50, As No. 835. Both inscribed "21st Birthday 1 July 1982"	7·00	4·50

1982. Birth of Prince William of Wales (1st issue). Nos. 812/13 optd.

838	$1 Type **187**	1·50	1·25
839	$1 Type **187**	1·50	1·25
840	$2 Prince Charles and Lady Diana Spencer	2·50	2·00
841	$2 Prince Charles and Lady Diana Spencer	2·50	2·00
MS842	106×59 mm. Nos. 812/13 optd **21 JUNE 1982. ROYAL BIRTH**	4·00	4·00

OPTS: Nos. 838 and 840, **ROYAL BIRTH 21 JUNE 1982**; 839 and 841, **PRINCE WILLIAM OF WALES.**

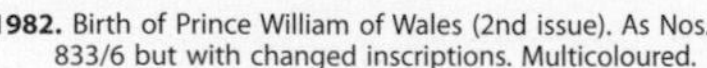

1982. Birth of Prince William of Wales (2nd issue). As Nos. 833/6 but with changed inscriptions. Multicoloured.

843	$1.25 As Type **191**, inscribed "Royal Birth"	1·75	1·00
844	$1.25 As Type **191**, inscribed "21 June 1982"	1·75	1·00
845	$2.50 As No. 835, inscribed "Royal Birth"	1·90	1·50
846	$2.50 As No. 835, inscribed "21 June 1982"	1·90	1·50
MS847	92×73 mm. $1.25, As Type **191**; $2.50, As No. 835. Both inscribed "Royal Birth 21 June 1982".	6·00	2·75

193 "The Accordionist" (inscr "Serenade")

1982. Norman Rockwell (painter) Commemoration. Multicoloured.

848	5c. Type **193**	15	10
849	10c. "Spring" (inscr "The Hikers")	20	15
850	20c. "The Doctor and the Doll"	25	25
851	30c. "Home from Camp"	25	30

194 Franklin D. Roosevelt

1982. Air. American Anniversaries. Multicoloured.

852	60c. Type **194**	1·25	80
853	80c. Benjamin Franklin	1·50	1·00
854	$1.40 George Washington	1·75	2·25
MS855	116×60 mm. Nos. 852/4	4·00	3·00

ANNIVERSARIES: 60c. Roosevelt (birth centenary); 80c. "Articles of Peace" negotiations bicentenary; $1.40, Washington (250th birth anniv).

195 "Virgin with Garlands" (detail, Rubens) and Princess Diana with Prince William

1982. Christmas.

856	**195**	35c. multicoloured	1·75	70
857	-	48c. multicoloured	2·25	1·50
858	-	60c. multicoloured	2·50	2·00
859	-	$1.70 multicoloured	3·50	6·00
MS860		104×83 mm. 60c. × 4. Designs, each 27×32 mm, forming complete painting "Virgin with Garlands"	7·00	8·00

DESIGNS: 48c. to $1.70, Different details from Ruben's painting "Virgin with Garlands".

196 Princess Diana and Prince William

1982. Christmas. Birth of Prince William of Wales. Children's Charity. Sheet 73×59 mm.

MS861	**196** 75c. + 5c. multicoloured	2·75	4·00

No. **MS**861 comes with 4 different background designs showing details from painting "Virgin with Garlands" (Rubens).

197 Statue of Tangaroa

1983. Commonwealth Day. Multicoloured.

862	60c. Type **197**	70	50
863	60c. Rarotonga oranges	70	50
864	60c. Rarotonga Airport	70	50
865	60c. Prime Minister Sir Thomas Davis	70	50

198 Scouts using Map and Compass

1983. 75th Anniv of Boy Scout Movement and 125th Anniv of Lord Baden-Powell (founder). Multicoloured.

866	12c. Type **198**	55	20
867	12c. Hiking	55	20
868	36c. Campfire cooking	80	40
869	36c. Erecting tent	80	40
870	48c. Hauling on rope	1·00	55
871	48c. Using bos'n's chair	1·00	55
872	60c. Digging hole for sapling	1·00	70
873	60c. Planting sapling	1·00	70
MS874	161×132 mm. As Nos. 866/73, but each with a premium of 2c.	3·00	3·50

1983. 15th World Scout Jamboree, Alberta, Canada. Nos. 866/73 optd XV WORLD JAMBOREE (Nos. 875, 877, 879, 881) or ALBERTA, CANADA 1983 (others).

875	12c. Type **198**	60	20
876	12c. Hiking	60	20
877	36c. Campfire cooking	90	40
878	36c. Erecting tent	90	40
879	48c. Hauling on rope	1·10	55
880	48c. Using bos'n's chair	1·10	55
881	60c. Digging hole for sapling	1·25	70
882	60c. Planting sapling	1·25	70
MS883	161×132 mm. As Nos. 875/82, but each with a premium of 2c.	2·75	3·25

1983. Various stamps surch.

884	-	18c. on 8c. mult (No. 733)	75	50
885	-	18c. on 8c. mult (No. 734)	75	50
886	-	18c. on 8c. mult (No. 735)	75	50
887	-	18c. on 8c. mult (No. 736)	75	50
888	-	36c. on 15c. mult (No. 745)	1·25	85
889	-	36c. on 15c. mult (No. 746)	1·25	85
890	-	36c. on 15c. mult (No. 747)	1·25	85
891	-	36c. on 15c. mult (No. 748)	1·25	85
892	-	36c. on 30c. mult (No. 757)	1·25	85
893	-	36c. on 30c. mult (No. 758)	1·25	85
894	-	36c. on 30c. mult (No. 759)	1·25	85
895	-	36c. on 30c. mult (No. 760)	1·25	85
896	184	36c. on 35c. mult	1·25	85
897	-	36c. on 35c. mult (No. 762)	1·25	85
898	-	36c. on 35c. mult (No. 763)	1·25	85
899	-	36c. on 35c. mult (No. 764)	1·25	85
900	-	48c. on 25c. mult (No. 753)	1·50	1·25
901	-	48c. on 25c. mult (No. 754)	1·50	1·25
902	-	48c. on 25c. mult (No. 755)	1·50	1·25
903	-	48c. on 25c. mult (No. 756)	1·50	1·25
904	-	72c. on 70c. mult (No. 773)	2·50	1·75
905	-	72c. on 70c. mult (No. 774)	2·50	1·75

906 - 72c. on 70c. mult (No. 775) 2·50 1·75
907 - 72c. on 70c. mult (No. 776) 2·50 1·75
908 - 96c. on $1.40 multicoloured (No. 854) 2·00 2·00
909 - 96c. on $2 mult (No. 813) 8·50 5·50
910 - 96c. on $2.50 mult (No. 835) 3·00 3·00
911 - 96c. on $2.50 mult (No. 836) 3·00 3·00
912 - $5.60 on $6 mult (No. 788) 23·00 20·00
913 - $5.60 on $10 mult (No. 789) 23·00 20·00

202 Union Flag

1983. Cook Islands Flags and Ensigns. Multicoloured.
914 6c. Type **202** (postage) 70 70
915 6c. Group Federal flag 70 70
916 12c. Rarotonga ensign 85 85
917 12c. Flag of New Zealand 85 85
918 15c. Cook Islands' flag (1973–79) 85 85
919 15c. Cook Islands' National flag 85 85
920 20c. Type **202** (air) 85 85
921 20c. Group Federal flag 85 85
922 30c. Rarotonga ensign 95 95
923 30c. Flag of New Zealand 95 95
924 35c. Cook Islands' flag (1973–1979) 1·00 1·00
925 35c. Cook Islands' National flag 1·00 1·00
MS926 Two sheets, each 132×120 mm. (a) Nos. 914/19. (b) Nos. 920/5. P 13 4·25 4·75

203 Dish Aerial, Satellite Earth Station

1983. World Communications Year.
927 - 36c. multicoloured 80 80
928 - 48c. multicoloured 1·00 1·00
929 **203** 60c. multicoloured 1·40 1·50
930 - 96c. multicoloured 1·90 2·25
MS931 90×65 mm. $2 multicoloured 2·25 2·75
DESIGNS: 36, 48, 96c. Various satellites.

204 "La Belle Jardiniere"

1983. Christmas. 500th Birth Anniv of Raphael. Multicoloured.
932 12c. Type **204** 80 55
933 18c. "Madonna and Child with five Saints" 1·10 70
934 36c. "Madonna and Child with St. John" 1·75 1·75
935 48c. "Madonna of the Fish" 2·25 2·25
936 60c. "Madonna of the Baldacchino" 2·75 3·75
MS937 139×113 mm. As Nos. 932/6, but each with a premium of 3c. 2·00 2·50

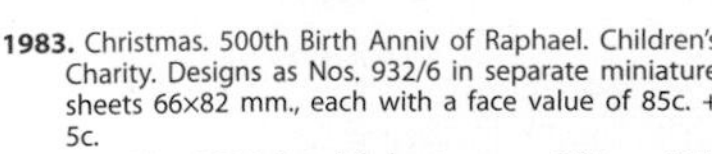

1983. Christmas. 500th Birth Anniv of Raphael. Children's Charity. Designs as Nos. 932/6 in separate miniature sheets 66×82 mm., each with a face value of 85c. + 5c.
MS938 As Nos. 932/6 Set of 5 sheets 5·00 3·75

205 Montgolfier Balloon, 1783

1984. Bicentenary (1983) of Manned Flight. Mult.
939 36c. Type **205** 60 50
940 48c. Ascent of Adorne, Strasbourg, 1784 70 60
941 60c. Balloon driven by sails, 1785 85 90
942 72c. Ascent of man on horse, 1798 1·10 1·40
943 96c. Godard's aerial acrobatics, 1850 1·40 1·60
MS944 104×85 mm. $2.50, Blanchard and Jeffries crossing Channel, 1785 1·50 2·25
MS945 122×132 mm. As Nos. 939/43, but each with a premium of 5c. 1·50 2·25

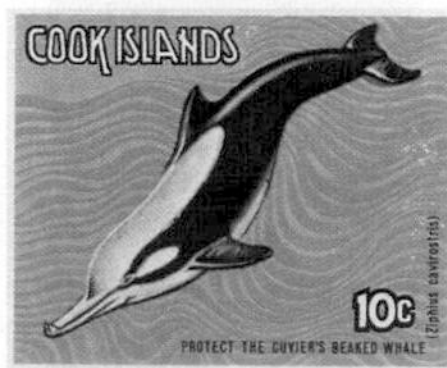

206 Cuvier's Beaked Whale

1984. Save the Whale. Multicoloured.
946 10c. Type **206** 50 50
947 18c. Risso's dolphin 75 75
948 20c. True's beaked whale 75 75
949 24c. Long-finned pilot whale 80 80
950 30c. Narwhal 90 90
951 36c. White whale 1·10 1·10
952 42c. Common dolphin 1·40 1·40
953 48c. Commerson's dolphin 1·60 1·60
954 60c. Bottle-nosed dolphin 1·90 1·90
955 72c. Sowerby's beaked whale 2·00 2·00
956 96c. Common porpoise 2·50 2·50
957 $2 Boutu 3·25 3·25

207 Athens, 1896

1984. Olympic Games, Los Angeles. Multicoloured.
958 18c. Type **207** 60 40
959 24c. Paris, 1900 65 45
960 36c. St. Louis, 1904 75 55
961 48c. London, 1948 85 65
962 60c. Tokyo, 1964 95 75
963 72c. Berlin, 1936 1·00 90
964 96c. Rome, 1960 1·10 1·00
965 $1.20 Los Angeles, 1930 1·25 1·25

208 "Siphonogorgia"

1984. Corals (2nd series). New designs and Nos. 785/9 surch. Multicoloured.
966 1c. Type **208** 30 30
967 2c. "Millepora alcicornis" 30 30
968 3c. "Distichopora violacea" 40 30
969 5c. "Ptilosarcus gurneyi" 45 30
970 10c. "Lobophyllia bemprichii" 50 20
971 12c. "Sarcophyton digitatum" 60 20
972 14c. "Pavona praetorta" 60 20
973 18c. "Junceella gemmacea" 70 20
974 20c. "Stylaster" 70 20
975 24c. "Stylophora pistillata" 70 20
976 30c. "Palauastrea ramosa" 1·00 25
977 36c. "Melithaea albitincta" 1·25 30
978 40c. "Stylaster echinatus" 1·25 30
979 42c. "Fungia fungites" 1·25 35
980 48c. "Gonipora" 1·25 35
981 50c. "Melithaea squamata" 1·75 50
982 52c. "Bellonella indica" 1·75 65
983 55c. "Plerogyra sinuosa" 1·75 70
984 60c. "Tubastraea" 1·90 75
985 70c. "Heliofungia actiniformis" 2·00 90
986 85c. "Caulastraea echinulata" 2·25 1·25
987 96c. "Porites andrewsi" 2·50 1·25
988 $1.10 "Pectinia alcicornis" 2·00 1·60
989 $1.20 "Dendrophyllia gracilis" 2·50 1·75
990 $3.60 on $2 "Gonipora" (55×35 mm) 5·50 4·25
991 $4.20 on $3 "Heliofungia actiniformis" (55×35 mm) 6·00 5·50
992 $5 on $4 "Stylophora pistillata" (55×35 mm) 6·50 6·00
993 $7.20 on $6 "Stylaster echinatus" (55×35 mm) 8·50 9·50
994 $9.60 on $10 "Melithaea albitincta" (55×35 mm) 10·00 11·00

1984. Olympic Gold Medal Winners. Nos. 963/5 optd.
995 72c. Berlin, 1936 (optd **Equestrian Team Dressage Germany**) 60 65
996 96c. Rome, 1960 (optd **Decathlon Daley Thompson Great Britain**) 80 85
997 $1.20 Los Angeles, 1930 (optd **Four Gold Medals Carl Lewis U.S.A.**) 1·00 1·10

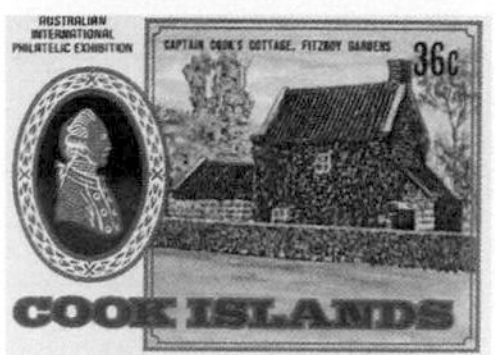

211 Captain Cook's Cottage, Melbourne

1984. "Ausipex" International Stamp Exhibition, Melbourne. Multicoloured.
998 36c. Type **211** 2·00 1·50
999 48c. H.M.S. "Endeavour" careened for Repairs" (Sydney Parkinson) 3·25 2·50
1000 60c. "Cook's landing at Botany Bay" (E. Phillips Fox) 3·50 3·25
1001 $2 "Captain James Cook" (John Webber) 4·25 4·25
MS1002 140×100 mm. As Nos. 998/1001, but each with a face value of 90c. 7·50 7·50

1984. Birth of Prince Henry. Nos. 812 and 833/6 variously optd or surch also (No. 1007).
1003 $1.25 Optd **Commemorating-15 Sept. 1984** (No. 833) 1·75 1·50
1004 $1.25 Optd **Birth H.R.H. Prince Henry** (No. 834) 1·75 1·50
1005 $2.50 Optd **Commemorating-15 Sept. 1984** (No. 835) 2·50 2·75
1006 $2.50 Optd **Birth H.R.H. Prince Henry** (No. 836) 2·50 2·75
1007 $3 on $1 Optd **Royal Birth Prince Henry 15 Sept. 1984** (No. 812) 4·50 5·00

213 "Virgin on Throne with Child" (Giovanni Bellini)

1984. Christmas. Multicoloured.
1008 36c. Type **213** 1·90 40
1009 48c. "Virgin and Child" (anonymous, 15th century) 2·00 60
1010 60c. "Virgin and Child with Saints" (Alvise Vivarini) 2·25 80
1011 96c. "Virgin and Child with Angels" (H. Memling) 2·50 1·60
1012 $1.20 "Adoration of Magi" (G. Tiepolo) 2·75 2·00
MS1013 120×113 mm. As Nos. 1008/12, but each with a premium of 5c. 4·00 4·25

1984. Christmas. Designs as Nos. 1008/12 in separate miniature sheets 62×76 mm, each with a face value of 95c. + 5c.
MS1014 As Nos. 1008/12 Set of 5 sheets 5·50 5·50

214 Downy Woodpecker

1985. Birth Bicentenary of John J. Audubon (ornithologist). Designs showing original paintings. Multicoloured.
1015 30c. Type **214** 2·50 1·25
1016 55c. Black-throated blue warbler 2·75 1·75
1017 65c. Yellow-throated warbler 3·00 2·25
1018 75c. Chestnut-sided warbler 3·25 2·75
1019 95c. Dickcissel 3·25 3·00
1020 $1.15 White-crowned sparrow 3·25 3·50
MS1021 Three sheets, each 76×75 mm. (a) $1.30, Red-cockaded woodpecker. (b) $2.80, Seaside sparrow. (c) $5.30, Zenaida dove Set of 3 sheets 13·00 8·50
No. 1017 is wrongly inscr 'Smooth sea star

215 "The Kingston Flyer" (New Zealand)

1985. Famous Trains. Multicoloured.
1022 20c. Type **215** 25 50
1023 55c. Class 625 locomotive (Italy) 25 85
1024 65c. Gotthard electric locomotive (Switzerland) 30 90
1025 75c. Union Pacific diesel locomotive No. 6900 (U.S.A.) 35 1·10
1026 95c. Canadian National "Super Continental" type diesel locomotive (Canada) 40 1·25
1027 $1.15 TGV express train (France) 40 1·40
1028 $2.20 "The Flying Scotsman" (Great Britain) 40 2·50
1029 $3.40 "Orient Express" 45 3·75
No. 1023 is inscribed "640" in error.

216 "Helena Fourment" (Peter Paul Rubens)

1985. International Youth Year. Multicoloured.
1030 55c. Type **216** 3·50 2·75
1031 65c. "Vigee-Lebrun and Daughter" (E. Vigee-Lebrun) 3·75 3·25
1032 75c. "On the Terrace" (Renoir) 4·00 3·50
1033 $1.30 "Young Mother Sewing" (M. Cassatt) 5·00 7·50
MS1034 103×106 mm. As Nos. 1030/3, but each with a premium of 10c. 9·00 5·50

217 "Lady Elizabeth 1908" (Mabel Hankey)

1985. Life and Times of Queen Elizabeth the Queen Mother. Designs showing paintings. Multicoloured.
1035 65c. Type **217** 40 50
1036 75c. "Duchess of York, 1923" (Savely Sorine) 45 60
1037 $1.15 "Duchess of York, 1925" (Philip de Laszlo) 55 85
1038 $2.80 "Queen Elizabeth, 1938" (Sir Gerald Kelly) 1·40 2·25

MS1039 69×81 mm. $5.30, As $2.80 2·50 3·50

For these designs in a miniature sheet, each with a face value of 55c., see No. **MS**1079.

218 Albert Henry (Prime Minister, 1965–78)

1985. 20th Anniv of Self-government. Mult.

1040 30c. Type **218** 1·00 60

1041 50c. Sir Thomas Davis (Prime Minister, 1978–April 1983 and from November 1983) 1·40 1·25

1042 65c. Geoffrey Henry (Prime Minister, April–November 1983) 1·75 1·75

MS1043 134×70 mm. As Nos. 1040/2, but each with a face value of 55c. 1·75 2·00

219 Golf

1985. South Pacific Mini Games, Rarotonga. Multicoloured.

1044 55c. Type **219** 4·00 3·50

1045 65c. Rugby 4·00 4·00

1046 75c. Tennis 5·50 6·00

MS1047 126×70 mm. Nos. 1044/6, but each with a premium of 10c. 11·00 13·00

220 Sea Horse, Gearwheel and Leaves

1985. Pacific Conference, Rarotonga.

1048 **220** 55c. black, gold and red 1·40 65

1049 - 65c. black, gold and violet 1·50 80

1050 - 75c. black, gold and green 1·75 1·10

MS1051 126×81 mm. As Nos. 1048/50, but each with a face value of 50c. 1·60 2·00

No. 1048 shows the South Pacific Bureau for Economic Co-operation logo and is inscribed "S.P.E.C. Meeting, 30 July–1 August 1985, Rarotonga". No. 1049 also shows the S.P.E.C. logo, but is inscribed "South Pacific Forum, 4–6 August 1985, Rarotonga". No. 1050 shows the Pacific Islands Conference logo and the inscription "Pacific Islands Conference, 7–10 August 1985, Rarotonga".

221 "Madonna of the Magnificat"

1985. Christmas. Virgin and Child Paintings by Botticelli. Multicoloured.

1052 55c. Type **221** 2·50 1·25

1053 65c. "Madonna with Pomegranate" 2·75 1·25

1054 75c. "Madonna and Child with Six Angels" 3·25 1·60

1055 95c. "Madonna and Child with St. John" 3·50 2·00

MS1056 90×104 mm. As Nos. 1052/5, but each with a face value of 50c. 6·50 3·75

1985. Christmas. Virgin and Child Paintings by Botticelli. Square designs (46×46 mm) as Nos. 1052/5 in separate miniature sheets, 50×51 mm, with face values of $1.20, $1.45, $2.20 and $2.75. Imperf.

MS1057 As Nos. 1052/5 Set of 4 sheets 10·00 11·00

222 "The Eve of the Deluge" (John Martin)

1986. Appearance of Halley's Comet. Paintings. Multicoloured.

1058 55c. Type **222** 1·50 1·25

1059 65c. "Lot and his Daughters" (Lucas van Leyden) 1·60 1·40

1060 75c. "Auspicious Comet" (from treatise c. 1857) 1·75 1·75

1061 $1.25 "Events following Charles I" (Herman Saftleven) 2·25 2·50

1062 $2 "Ossian receiving Napoleonic Officers" (Anne Louis Girodet-Trioson) 3·25 3·50

MS1063 130×100 mm. As Nos. 1058/62, but each with a face value of 70c. 7·00 9·00

MS1064 84×63 mm. $4 "Halley's Comet of 1759 over the Thames" (Samuel Scott) 8·50 9·50

223 Queen Elizabeth II

1986. 60th Birthday of Queen Elizabeth II. Designs showing formal portraits.

1065 **223** 95c. multicoloured 1·50 1·50

1066 - $1.25 multicoloured 1·75 1·75

1067 - $1.50 multicoloured 2·00 2·00

MS1068 Three sheets, each 44×75 mm. As Nos. 1065/7, but with face values of $1.10, $1.95 and $2.45 Set of 3 sheets 10·00 11·00

224 U.S.A. 1847 Franklin 5c. Stamp and H.M.S. "Resolution" at Rarotonga

1986. "Ameripex '86" International Exhibition, Chicago. Multicoloured.

1069 $1 Type **224** 5·50 3·75

1070 $1.50 Chicago 3·50 4·25

1071 $2 1975 definitive $2, Benjamin Franklin and H.M.S. "Resolution" 6·50 5·50

225 Head of Statue of Liberty

1986. Centenary of Statue of Liberty. Multicoloured.

1072 $1 Type **225** 75 85

1073 $1.25 Hand and torch of Statue 90 1·10

1074 $2.75 Statue of Liberty 2·00 2·50

226 Miss Sarah Ferguson

1986. Royal Wedding. Multicoloured.

1075 $1 Type **226** 1·25 1·25

1076 $2 Prince Andrew 2·00 2·50

1077 $3 Prince Andrew and Miss Sarah Ferguson (57×31 mm) 2·50 3·50

1986. "Stampex '86" Stamp Exhibition, Adelaide. No. MS1002 optd Stampex 86 Adelaide.

MS1078 90c.×4 multicoloured 6·50 6·50

The "Stampex '86" exhibition emblem is also overprinted on the sheet margin.

1986. 86th Birthday of Queen Elizabeth the Queen Mother. Designs as Nos. 1035/8 in miniature sheet, 91×116 mm, each with a face value of 55c. Multicoloured.

MS1079 55c.×4. As Nos. 1035/8 9·00 9·00

228 "Holy Family with St. John the Baptist and St. Elizabeth"

1986. Christmas. Paintings by Rubens. Mult.

1080 55c. Type **228** 2·25 1·00

1081 $1.30 "Virgin with the Garland" 3·25 3·00

1082 $2.75 "Adoration of the Magi" (detail) 6·50 7·50

MS1083 140×100 mm. As Nos. 1080/2, but each size 36×46 mm with a face value of $2.40 12·00 13·00

MS1084 80×70 mm. $6.40 As No. 1081 but size 32×50 mm 12·00 13·00

1986. Visit of Pope John Paul II to South Pacific. Nos. 1080/2 surch FIRST PAPAL VISIT TO SOUTH PACIFIC POPE JOHN PAUL II NOV 21-24 1986.

1085 55c.+10c. Type **228** 3·25 2·00

1086 $1.30+10c. "Virgin with the Garland" 4·00 2·50

1087 $2.75+10c. "Adoration of the Magi" (detail) 6·00 3·75

MS1088 140×100 mm. As Nos. 1085/7, but each size 36×46 mm with a face value of $2.40 + 10c. 15·00 13·00

MS1089 80×70 mm. $6.40+50c. As No. 1086 but size 32×50 mm 15·00 13·00

1987. Various stamps surch. (a) On Nos. 741/56, 761/76 and 787/8.

1090 10c. on 15c. "Distichopora violacea" 20 20

1091 10c. on 15c. "Stylaster" 20 20

1092 10c. on 15c. "Gonipora" 20 20

1093 10c. on 15c. "Caulastraea echinulata" 20 20

1094 10c. on 25c. "Lobophyllia bemprichii" 20 20

1095 10c. on 25c. "Palauastrea ramosa" 20 20

1096 10c. on 25c. "Bellonella indica" 20 20

1097 10c. on 25c. "Pectinia alcicornis" 20 20

1098 18c. on 12c. "Millepora alcicornis" 25 25

1099 18c. on 12c. "Junceella gemmacea" 25 25

1100 18c. on 12c. "Fungia fungites" 25 25

1101 18c. on 12c. "Heliofungia actiniformis" 25 25

1102 18c. on 20c. "Ptilosarcus gurneyi" 25 25

1103 18c. on 20c. "Stylophora pistillata" 25 25

1104 18c. on 20c. "Melithaea squamata" 25 25

1105 18c. on 20c. "Porites andrewsi" 25 25

1106 55c. on 35c. Type **184** 40 45

1107 55c. on 35c. "Pavona praetorta" 40 45

1108 55c. on 35c. "Stylaster echinatus" 40 45

1109 55c. on 35c. "Tubastraea" 40 45

1110 65c. on 50c. As No. 1098 45 50

1111 65c. on 50c. As No. 1099 45 50

1112 65c. on 50c. As No. 1100 45 50

1113 65c. on 50c. As No. 1101 45 50

1114 65c. on 60c. As No. 1090 45 50

1115 65c. on 60c. As No. 1091 45 50

1116 65c. on 60c. As No. 1092 45 50

1117 65c. on 60c. As No. 1093 45 50

1118 75c. on 70c. As No. 1102 55 60

1119 75c. on 70c. As No. 1103 55 60

1120 75c. on 70c. As No. 1104 55 60

1121 75c. on 70c. As No. 1105 55 60

1122 $6.40 on $4 "Stylophora pistillata" 4·50 4·75

1123 $7.20 on $6 "Stylaster echinatus" 5·00 5·25

(b) On Nos. 812/13.

1124 $9.40 on $1 Type **187** 15·00 16·00

1125 $9.40 on $1 Prince Charles and Lady Diana Spencer 15·00 16·00

(c) On Nos. 835/6.

1126 $9.40 on $2.50 Princess of Wales (inscribed "21st Birthday") 15·00 16·00

1127 $9.40 on $2.50 As No. 1126, but inscribed "1 July 1982" 15·00 16·00

(d) On Nos. 966/8, 971/2, 975, 979/80, 982 and 987/9.

1128 5c. on 1c. Type **208** 20 20

1129 5c. on 2c. "Millepora alcicornis" 20 20

1130 5c. on 3c. "Distichopora violacea" 20 20

1131 5c. on 12c. "Sarcophyton digitatum" 20 20

1132 5c. on 14c. "Pavona praetorta" 25 25

1133 18c. on 24c. "Stylophora pistillata" 15 15

1134 55c. on 52c. "Bellonella indica" 40 45

1135 65c. on 42c. "Fungia fungites" 45 50

1136 75c. on 48c. "Gonipora" 55 60

1137 95c. on 96c. "Porites andrewsi" 70 75

1138 95c. on $1.10 "Pectinia alcicornis" 70 75

1139 95c. on $1.20 "Dendrophyllia gracilis" 70 75

(e) On Nos. 998/1001.

1140 $1.30 on 36c. Type **211** 2·00 2·00

1141 $1.30 on 48c. "The "Endeavour" careened for Repairs" (Sydney Parkinson) 2·00 2·00

1142 $1.30 on 60c. "Cook's landing at Botany Bay" (E. Phillips Fox) 2·00 2·00

1143 $1.30 on $2 "Captain James Cook" (John Webber) 2·00 2·00

(f) On Nos. 1065/7.

1144 **223** $2.30 on 95c. mult 7·00 8·00

1145 - $2.80 on $1.25 mult 7·00 8·00

1146 - $2.80 on $1.50 mult 7·00 8·00

(g) On Nos. 1075/7.

1147 $2.80 on $1 Type **226** 6·00 6·50

1148 $2.80 on $2 Prince Andrew 6·00 6·50

1149 $2.80 on $3 Prince Andrew and Miss Sarah Ferguson (57×31 mm) 6·00 6·50

1987. Various stamps surch.

1150 $2.80 on $2 "Gonipora" (No. 785) 3·00 3·25

1151 $5 on $3 "Heliofungia actiniformis" (No. 786) 5·00 5·50

1152 $9.40 on $10 "Melithaea albitincta" (No. 789) 8·00 9·00

1153 $9.40 on $1 Type **187** (No. 838) 8·00 9·00

1154 $9.40 on $1 Type **187** (No. 839) 8·00 9·00

1155 $9.40 on $2 Prince Charles and Lady Diana Spencer (No. 840) 8·00 9·00

1156 $9.40 on $2 Prince Charles and Lady Diana Spencer (No. 841) 8·00 9·00

MS1157 106×59 mm. $9.20 on $1 Type **187**; $9.20 on $2 Prince Charles and Lady Diana Spencer 12·00 15·00

1987. Hurricane Relief. Various stamps surch HURRICANE RELIEF and premium. (a) On Nos. 1035/8.

1158 65c.+50c. Type **217** 1·00 1·00

1159 75c.+50c. "Duchess of York, 1923" (Savely Sorine) 1·10 1·10

1160 $1.15+50c. "Duchess of York, 1925" (Philip de Laszlo) 1·40 1·50

1161 $2.80+50c. "Queen Elizabeth, 1938" (Sir Gerald Kelly) 2·50 3·25

MS1162 69×81 mm. $5.30 + 50c. As $2.80 + 50c. 5·00 6·50

(b) On Nos. 1058/62.

1163 55c.+50c. Type **222** 85 85

1164 65c.+50c. "Lot and his Daughters" (Lucas van Leyden) 90 90

1165 75c.+50c. "Auspicious Comet" (from treatise c. 1587) 1·10 1·10

1166 $1.50+50c. "Events following Charles I" (Herman Saftleven) 1·40 1·50

1167 $2+50c. "Ossian receiving Napoleonic Officers" (Anne Louis Girodet-Trioson) 2·00 2·50

(c) On Nos. 1065/7.

1168 **223** 95c.+50c. mult 1·25 1·25

1169 - $1.25+50c. mult 1·50 1·50

1170 - $1.50+50c. mult 1·60 1·60

MS1171 Three sheets, each 44×75 mm. As Nos. 1168/70, but with face values of $1.10 + 50c., $1.95 + 50c., $2.45 + 50c. Set of 3 sheets 14·00 16·00

(d) On Nos. 1069/71.

1172 $1+50c. Type **224** 5·50 5·50
1173 $1.50+50c. Chicago 2·25 2·75
1174 $2+50c. 1975 definitive $2, Benjamin Franklin and H.M.S. "Resolution" 6·00 6·00

(e) On Nos. 1072/4.

1175 $1+50c. Type **225** 1·00 1·25
1176 $1.25+50c. Hand and torch of Statue 1·25 1·50
1177 $2.75+50c. Statue of Liberty 2·25 3·00

(f) On Nos. 1075/7.

1178 $1+50c. Type **226** 1·25 1·25
1179 $2+50c. Prince Andrew 2·00 2·25
1180 $3+50c. Prince Andrew and Miss Sarah Ferguson (57×31 mm) 2·75 3·25

(g) On Nos. 1080/2.

1181 55c.+50c. Type **228** 85 85
1182 $1.30+50c. "Virgin with the Garland" 1·50 1·75
1183 $2.75+50c. "The Adoration of the Magi" (detail) 2·50 3·00
MS1184 140×100 mm. As Nos. 1181/3, but each size 36×46 mm with a face value of $2.40 + 50c. 15·00 17·00
MS1185 80×70 mm. $6.40 + 50c. As No. 1182, but size 32×50 mm. 8·50 9·50

(h) On Nos. 1122, 1134/7 and 1150/1.

1186 55c.+25c. on 52c. "Bellonella indica" 90 90
1187 65c.+25c. on 42c. "Fungia fungites" 1·00 1·00
1188 75c.+25c. on 48c. "Gonipora" 1·00 1·00
1189 95c.+25c. on 96c. "Porites andrewsi" 1·25 1·25
1190 $2.80+50c. on $2 "Gonipora" 4·00 4·00
1191 $5+50c. on $3 "Heliofungia actiniformis" 6·00 6·50
1192 $6.40+50c. on $4 "Stylophora pistillata" 7·50 8·50

1987. Royal Ruby Wedding. Nos. 484 and 787 optd ROYAL WEDDING FORTIETH ANNIVERSARY.

1193 $4 Queen Elizabeth II and sea shells 5·50 5·50
1194 $4 Queen Elizabeth II and "Stylophora pistillata" 5·50 5·50

233 "The Holy Family" (Rembrandt)

1987. Christmas. Different paintings of the Holy Family by Rembrandt.

1195 **233** $1.25 multicoloured 2·75 2·50
1196 - $1.50 multicoloured 3·50 3·00
1197 - $1.95 multicoloured 4·75 4·75
MS1198 100×140 mm. As Nos. 1195/7, but each size 47×36 mm with a face value of $115 7·00 8·50
MS1199 70×80 mm. $6 As Nos. 1196, but size 40×31 mm 9·50 11·00

234 Olympic Commemorative $50 Coin

1988. Olympic Games, Seoul. Multicoloured.

1200 $1.50 Type **234** 4·50 2·50
1201 $1.50 Olympic torch and Seoul Olympic Park 4·50 2·50
1202 $1.50 Steffi Graf playing tennis and Olympic medal 4·50 2·50
MS1203 131×81 mm. $10 Combined design as Nos. 1200/2, but measuring 114×47 mm. 11·00 12·00

Nos. 1200/2 were printed together, se-tenant, forming a composite design.

1988. Olympic Tennis Medal Winners, Seoul. Nos. 1200/2 optd.

1204 $1.50 Type **234** (optd **MILOSLAV MECIR CZECHOSLOVAKIA GOLD MEDAL WINNER MEN'S TENNIS**) 4·00 2·25
1205 $1.50 Olympic torch and Seoul Olympic Park (optd **TIM MAYOTTE UNITED STATES GABRIELA SABATINI ARGENTINA SILVER MEDAL WINNERS**) 4·00 2·25
1206 $1.50 Steffi Graf playing tennis and Olympic medal (optd **GOLD MEDAL WINNER STEFFI GRAF WEST GERMANY**) 4·00 2·25
MS1207 131×81 mm. $10 Combined design as Nos. 1200/2, but measuring 114×47 mm (optd **GOLD MEDAL WINNER SEOUL OLYMPIC GAMES STEFFI GRAF – WEST GERMANY**) 12·00 11·00

236 "Virgin and Child"

1988. Christmas.

1208 **236** 70c. multicoloured 3·00 2·00
1209 - 85c. multicoloured 3·25 2·25
1210 - 95c. multicoloured 3·50 2·50
1211 - $1.25 multicoloured 4·25 3·25
MS1212 80×100 mm. $6.40, multicoloured (45×60 mm) 9·50 12·00

DESIGNS: 85c., 95c., $1.25, Various versions of the "Virgin and Child" by Durer.

237 "Apollo 11" leaving Earth

1989. 20th Anniv of First Manned Landing on Moon. Multicoloured.

1213 40c. Type **237** 1·75 1·75
1214 40c. Lunar module over Moon 1·75 1·75
1215 55c. Aldrin stepping onto Moon 2·00 2·00
1216 55c. Astronaut on Moon 2·00 2·00
1217 65c. Working on lunar surface 2·25 2·25
1218 65c. Conducting experiment 2·25 2·25
1219 75c. "Apollo 11" leaving Moon 2·25 2·25
1220 75c. Splashdown in South Pacific 2·25 2·25
MS1221 108×91 mm. $4.20, Astronauts on Moon 5·50 6·50

238 Rarotonga Flycatcher

1989. Endangered Birds of the Cook Islands. Multicoloured.

1222 15c. Type **238** (postage) 2·00 2·00
1223 20c. Pair of Rarotonga flycatchers 2·00 2·00
1224 65c. Pair of Rarotonga fruit doves 2·75 2·75
1225 70c. Rarotonga fruit dove 2·75 2·75
MS1226 Four sheets, each 70×53 mm. As Nos. 1222/5, but with face values of $1, $1.25, $1.50, $1.75 and each size 50×32 mm (air) Set of 4 sheets 12·00 14·00

239 Villagers

1989. Christmas. Details from "Adoration of the Magi" by Rubens. Multicoloured.

1227 70c. Type **239** 1·40 1·40
1228 85c. Virgin Mary 1·60 1·60
1229 95c. Christ Child 1·75 2·00
1230 $1.50 Boy with gift 2·00 3·00
MS1231 85×120 mm. $6.40, "Adoration of the Magi" (45×60 mm) 12·00 14·00

240 Reverend John Williams and L.M.S. Church

1990. Christianity in the Cook Islands. Multicoloured.

1232 70c. Type **240** 85 85
1233 85c. Mgr. Bernardine Castanie and Roman Catholic Church 1·00 1·10
1234 95c. Elder Osborne Widstoe and Mormon Church 1·10 1·40
1235 $1.60 Dr. J. E. Caldwell and Seventh Day Adventist Church 1·90 2·25
MS1236 90×90 mm. As Nos. 1232/5, but each with a face value of 90c. 5·00 6·50

241 "Woman writing a Letter" (Terborch)

1990. 150th Anniv of the Penny Black. Designs showing paintings. Multicoloured.

1237 85c. Type **241** 1·50 1·25
1238 $1.15 "George Gisze" (Holbein the Younger) 1·75 1·75
1239 $1.55 "Mrs. John Douglas" (Gainsborough) 2·25 2·75
1240 $1.85 "Portrait of a Gentleman" (Durer) 2·75 3·25
MS1241 82×150 mm. As Nos. 1237/40, but each with a face value of $1.05 10·00 12·00

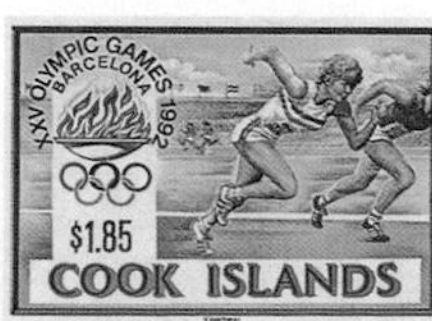

242 Sprinting

1990. Olympic Games, Barcelona, and Winter Olympic Games, Albertville (1992) (1st issue). Multicoloured.

1242 $1.85 Type **242** 6·00 6·00
1243 $1.85 Cook Islands $50 commemorative coin 6·00 6·00
1244 $1.85 Skiing 6·00 6·00
MS1245 109×52 mm. $6.40, As Nos. 1242/4, but size 80×26 mm. 14·00 15·00

See also Nos. 1304/10.

243 Queen Elizabeth the Queen Mother

1990. 90th Birthday of Queen Elizabeth the Queen Mother.

1246 **243** $1.85 multicoloured 6·00 5·00
MS1247 66×101 mm. **243** $6.40, multicoloured 13·00 15·00

244 "Adoration of the Magi" (Memling)

1990. Christmas. Religious Paintings. Mult.

1248 70c. Type **244** 2·00 1·75
1249 85c. "Holy Family" (Lotto) 2·25 1·90
1250 95c. "Madonna and Child with Saints John and Catherine" (Titian) 2·50 2·25
1251 $1.50 "Holy Family" (Titian) 4·00 6·00
MS1252 98×110 mm. $6.40, "Madonna and Child enthroned, surrounded by Saints" (Vivarini) (vert) 12·00 13·00

1990. "Birdpex '90" Stamp Exhibition, Christchurch, New Zealand. No. MS1226 optd Birdpex '90.

MS1253 Four sheets, each 70×53 mm. As Nos. 1222/5, but with face values of $1, $1.25, $1.50, $1.75 and each size 50×32 mm Set of 4 sheets 17·00 19·00

246 Columbus (engraving by Theodoro de Bry)

1991. 500th Anniv (1992) of Discovery of America by Columbus (1st issue).

1254 **246** $1 multicoloured 3·25 3·25

See also No. 1302.

1991. 65th Birthday of Queen Elizabeth II. No. 789 optd 65TH BIRTHDAY.

1255 $10 "Melithaea albitincta" 15·00 16·00

248 "Adoration of the Child" (G. delle Notti)

1991. Christmas. Religious Paintings. Mult.

1256 70c. Type **248** 2·50 1·75
1257 85c. "The Birth of the Virgin" (B. Murillo) 2·75 2·00
1258 $1.15 "Adoration of the Shepherds" (Rembrandt) 3·25 3·25
1259 $1.50 "Adoration of the Shepherds" (L. le Nain) 4·75 7·00
MS1260 79×103 mm. $6.40, "Madonna and Child" (Lippi) (vert) 13·00 15·00

249 Red-breasted Wrasse

1992. Reef Life (1st series). Multicoloured with white borders.

1261 5c. Type **249** 1·00 75

1262	10c. Blue sea star	1·00	75
1263	15c. Bicoloured angelfish ("Black and gold angelfish")	1·25	85
1264	20c. Spotted pebble crab	1·00	75
1265	25c. Black-tipped grouper ("Black-tipped cod")	1·25	1·00
1266	30c. Spanish dancer	1·25	1·00
1267	50c. Regal angelfish	1·25	1·25
1268	80c. Big-scaled soldierfish ("Squirrel fish")	1·50	1·50
1269	85c. Red pencil sea urchin	4·00	4·25
1270	90c. Red-spotted rainbowfish	2·75	4·25
1271	$1 Cheek-lined wrasse	3·50	4·75
1272	$2 Long-nosed butterflyfish	6·00	4·50
1273	$3 Red-spotted rainbowfish	7·00	7·00
1274	$5 Blue sea-star	8·00	8·50
1275	$7 "Pygoplites diacanthus"	13·00	15·00
1276	$10 Spotted pebble crab	16·00	16·00
1277	$15 Red pencil sea urchin	23·00	24·00

The 25, 50c., $1 and $2 include a silhouette of the Queen's head.

For designs in a larger size, 40×30 mm, and with brown borders, see Nos. 1342/52.

250 Tiger

1992. Endangered Wildlife. Multicoloured.

1279	$1.15 Type **250**	2·00	1·25
1280	$1.15 Indian elephant	1·50	1·25
1281	$1.15 Brown bear	1·25	1·25
1282	$1.15 Black rhinoceros	1·50	1·25
1283	$1.15 Chimpanzee	1·25	1·25
1284	$1.15 Argali	1·50	1·25
1285	$1.15 Heaviside's dolphin	1·25	1·25
1286	$1.15 Eagle owl	1·75	1·25
1287	$1.15 Bee hummingbird	1·75	1·25
1288	$1.15 Puma	1·25	1·25
1289	$1.15 European otter	1·25	1·25
1290	$1.15 Red kangaroo	1·25	1·25
1291	$1.15 Jackass penguin	1·75	1·25
1292	$1.15 Asian lion	1·25	1·25
1293	$1.15 Peregrine falcon	1·75	1·25
1294	$1.15 Persian fallow deer	1·25	1·25
1295	$1.15 Key deer	1·25	1·25
1296	$1.15 Alpine ibex	1·25	1·25
1297	$1.15 Mandrill	1·25	1·25
1298	$1.15 Gorilla	1·25	1·25
1299	$1.15 "Vanessa atalanta" (butterfly)	1·25	1·25
1300	$1.15 Takin	1·25	1·25
1301	$1.15 Ring-tailed lemur	1·25	1·25

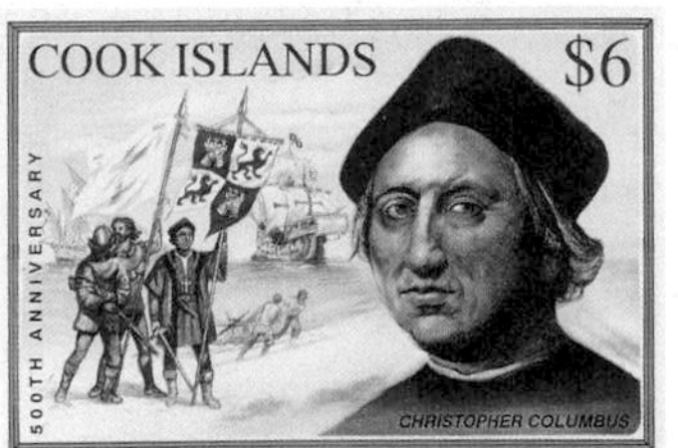

251 Columbus and Landing in New World

1992. 500th Anniv of Discovery of America by Columbus (2nd issue).

1302	**251**	$6 multicoloured	7·50	8·50
MS1303		128×84 mm. $10 As T **251**, but detail of landing party only (40×29 mm)	7·50	9·00

252 Football and $50 Commemorative Coin

1992. Olympic Games, Barcelona (2nd issue). Multicoloured.

1304	$1.75 Type **252**	3·50	3·50
1305	$1.75 Olympic gold medal	3·50	3·50
1306	$1.75 Basketball and $10 coin	3·50	3·50
1307	$2.25 Running	4·50	4·50
1308	$2.25 $10 and $50 coins	4·50	4·50
1309	$2.25 Cycling	4·50	4·50
MS1310	155×91 mm. $6.40, Javelin throwing	15·00	16·00

253 Festival Poster

1992. 6th Festival of Pacific Arts, Rarotonga. Multicoloured.

1311	80c. Type **253**	2·25	2·25
1312	85c. Seated Tangaroa carving	2·25	2·25
1313	$1 Seated Tangaroa carving (different)	2·50	2·50
1314	$1.75 Standing Tangaroa carving	3·25	4·50

1992. Royal Visit by Prince Edward. Nos. 1311/14 optd ROYAL VISIT.

1315	80c. Type **253**	3·50	3·50
1316	85c. Seated Tangaroa carving	3·50	3·50
1317	$1 Seated Tangaroa carving (different)	3·75	3·75
1318	$1.75 Standing Tangaroa carving	6·00	6·00

255 "Worship of Shepherds" (Parmigianino)

1992. Christmas. Religious Paintings by Parmigianino. Multicoloured.

1319	70c. Type **255**	1·40	1·40
1320	85c. "Virgin with Long Neck"	1·60	1·60
1321	$1.15 "Virgin with Rose"	2·00	2·00
1322	$1.90 "St. Margaret's Virgin"	3·75	4·75
MS1323	86×102 mm. $6.40, As 85c. but larger (36×46 mm)	11·00	13·00

256 Queen in Garter Robes

1992. 40th Anniv of Queen Elizabeth II's Accession. Multicoloured.

1324	80c. Type **256**	1·75	1·50
1325	$1.15 Queen at Trooping the Colour	2·00	2·00
1326	$1.50 Queen in evening dress	2·75	3·00
1327	$1.95 Queen with bouquet	3·00	3·50

257 Coronation Ceremony

1993. 40th Anniv of Coronation. Multicoloured.

1328	$1 Type **257**	3·00	2·00
1329	$2 Coronation photograph by Cecil Beaton	4·50	4·00
1330	$3 Royal family on balcony	7·00	6·00

258 "Virgin with Child" (Filippo Lippi)

1993. Christmas. Religious Paintings. Mult.

1331	70c. Type **258**	80	80
1332	85c. "Bargellini Madonna" (Lodovico Carracci)	95	95
1333	$1.15 "Virgin of the Curtain" (Rafael Sanzio)	1·40	1·60
1334	$2.50 "Holy Family" (Agnolo Bronzino)	3·25	3·75
1335	$4 "Saint Zachary Virgin" (Parmigianino) (32×47 mm)	4·00	5·50

259 Skiing, Flags and Ice Skating (image scaled to 51% of original size)

1994. Winter Olympic Games, Lillehammer.

1336	**259**	$5 multicoloured	8·00	8·50

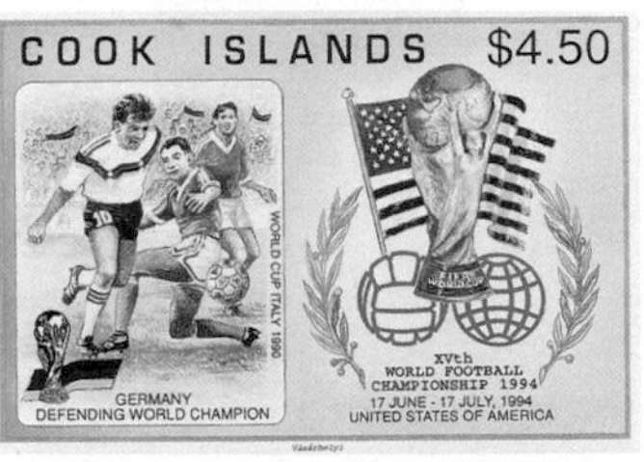

260 Cup on Logo with German and Argentinian Players

1994. World Cup Football Championship, U.S.A.

1337	**260**	$4.50 multicoloured	6·00	7·50

261 Neil Armstrong taking First Step on Moon

1994. 25th Anniv of First Manned Moon Landing. Multicoloured.

1338	$2.25 Type **261**	4·50	4·50
1339	$2.25 Astronaut on Moon and view of Earth	4·50	4·50
1340	$2.25 Astronaut and flag	4·50	4·50
1341	$2.25 Astronaut with reflection in helmet visor	4·50	4·50

1994. Reef Life (2nd series). As Nos. 1261 and 1263/71, but each 40×30 mm and with brown borders.

1342	5c. Type **249**	60	85
1344	15c. Bicoloured angelfish	70	85
1345	20c. Spotted pebble crab	85	90
1346	25c. Black-tipped grouper	90	90
1347	30c. Spanish dancer	90	90
1348	50c. Regal angelfish	1·10	1·10
1349	80c. Big-scaled soldierfish	1·25	1·40
1350	85c. Red pencil sea urchin	1·25	1·40
1351	90c. Red-spotted rainbowfish	1·25	1·40
1352	$1 Cheek-lined wrasse	1·40	1·60

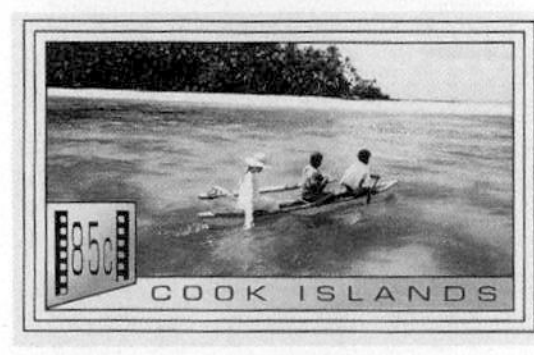

262 Actors in Outrigger Canoe

1994. Release of "The Return of Tommy Tricker" (film shot in Cook Islands). Scenes from film. Multicoloured.

1359	85c. Type **262**	1·40	1·75
1360	85c. Male and female dancers	1·40	1·75
1361	85c. European couple on beach	1·40	1·75
1362	85c. Aerial view of island	1·40	1·75
1363	85c. Two female dancers	1·40	1·75
1364	85c. Cook Islands couple on beach	1·40	1·75
1364a	90c. Type **262**	85	1·25
1364b	90c. As No. 1360	85	1·25
1364c	90c. As No. 1361	85	1·25
1364d	90c. As No. 1362	85	1·25
1364e	90c. As No. 1363	85	1·25
1364f	90c. As No. 1364	85	1·25

263 "The Virgin and Child" (Morales)

1994. Christmas. Religious Paintings. Mult.

1365	85c. Type **263**	2·00	2·00
1366	85c. "Adoration of the Kings" (Gerard David)	2·00	2·00
1367	85c. "Adoration of the Kings" (Foppa)	2·00	2·00
1368	85c. "The Madonna and Child with St. Joseph and Infant Baptist" (Baroccio)	2·00	2·00
1369	$1 "Madonna with Iris" (Durer)	2·00	2·00
1370	$1 "Adoration of the Shepherds" (Le Nain)	2·00	2·00
1371	$1 "The Virgin and Child" (school of Leonardo)	2·00	2·00
1372	$1 "The Mystic Nativity" (Botticelli)	2·00	2·00

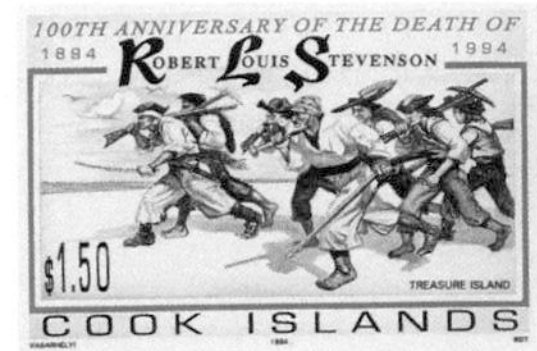

264 Pirates ("Treasure Island")

1994. Death Centenary of Robert Louis Stevenson (author). Multicoloured.

1373	$1.50 Type **264**	3·50	3·50
1374	$1.50 Duel ("David Balfour")	3·50	3·50
1375	$1.50 Mr. Hyde, ("Dr. Jekyll and Mr. Hyde")	3·50	3·50
1376	$1.50 Rowing boat and sailing ship ("Kidnapped")	3·50	3·50

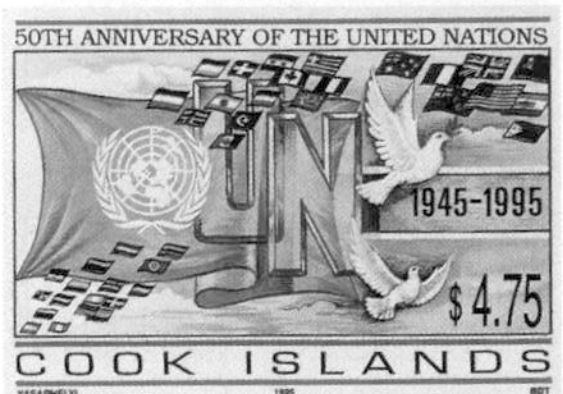

265 U.N. and National Flags with Peace Doves

1995. 50th Anniv of United Nations.

1377	**265**	$4.75 multicoloured	4·75	7·00

266 Queen Elizabeth the Queen Mother and Coat of Arms

1995. 95th Birthday of Queen Elizabeth the Queen Mother.

1378	**266**	$5 multicoloured	11·00	9·00

267 German Delegation signing Unconditional Surrender at Rheims

1995. 50th Anniv of End of Second World War. Multicoloured.
1379 $3.50 Type **267** 9·00 9·00
1380 $3.50 Japanese delegation on U.S.S. "Missouri", Tokyo Bay 9·00 9·00

1995. 50th Anniv of FAO. As T 265. Mult.
1381 $4.50 FAO and U.N. emblems 4·75 7·00

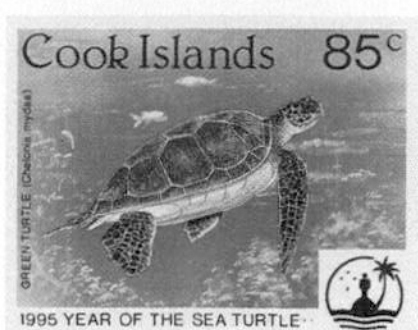

268 Green Turtle

1995. Year of the Sea Turtle. Multicoloured.
1382 85c. Type **268** 2·00 1·75
1383 $1 Hawksbill turtle 2·25 2·00
1384 $1.75 Green turtle on beach 3·25 3·50
1385 $2.25 Young hawksbill turtles hatching 4·25 4·50

269 Emblem and Throwing the Discus

1996. Olympic Games, Atlanta. Multicoloured.
1386 85c. Type **269** 1·50 1·50
1387 $1 Athlete with Olympic Torch 1·75 1·75
1388 $1.50 Running 2·50 2·50
1389 $1.85 Gymnastics 2·75 2·75
1390 $2.10 Ancient archery 3·00 3·00
1391 $2.50 Throwing the javelin 3·00 3·00

270 Queen Elizabeth II

1996. 70th Birthday of Queen Elizabeth II. Multicoloured.
1392 $1.90 Type **270** 3·00 3·00
1393 $2.25 Wearing tiara 3·50 3·50
1394 $2.75 In Garter robes 4·00 4·00
MS1395 103×152 mm. Designs as Nos. 1392/4, but each with a face value of $2.50 16·00 16·00

1997. 28th South Pacific Forum. Nos. 1364a/f optd 28th South Pacific Forum (Nos. 1396, 1399/1400) or 12–22 September 1997 (Nos. 1397/8 and 1401). Multicoloured.
1396 90c. Type **262** 1·25 1·50
1397 90c. As No. 1360 1·25 1·50
1398 90c. As No. 1361 1·25 1·50
1399 90c. As No. 1362 1·25 1·50
1400 90c. As No. 1363 1·25 1·50
1401 90c. As No. 1364 1·25 1·50

272 "Lampides boeticus" (female)

1997. Butterflies. Multicoloured.
1402 5c. Type **272** 45 60
1403 10c. "Vanessa atalanta" 55 60
1404 15c. "Lampides boeticus" (male) 60 50
1405 20c. "Papilio godeffroyi" 60 40
1406 25c. "Danaus hamata" 60 40
1407 30c. "Xois sesara" 60 40
1408 50c. "Vagrans egista" 75 55
1409 70c. "Parthenos sylvia" 90 75
1410 80c. "Hyblaea sanguinea" 75 80
1411 85c. "Melanitis leda" 90 95
1412 90c. "Ascalapha odorata" 1·00 1·00
1413 $1 "Precis villida" 1·10 1·25
1414 $1.50 "Parthenos sylvia" 1·75 1·75
1415 $2 "Lampides boeticus" (female) 2·25 2·25
1416 $3 "Precis villida" 3·50 3·50
1417 $4 "Melanitis leda" 4·00 4·25
1418 $5 "Vagrans egista" 5·00 5·50
1419 $7 "Hyblaea sanguinea" 7·00 8·00
1420 $10 "Vanessa atalanta" 10·00 12·00
1421 $15 "Papilio godeffroyi" 15·00 18·00

The 70c. and $1 include an outline portrait of Queen Elizabeth II. Nos. 1414/21 are larger, 41×25 mm, with the Queen's portrait included on the $4 to $15.

273 Queen Elizabeth and Prince Philip

1997. Golden Wedding of Queen Elizabeth and Prince Philip.
1424 **273** $2 multicoloured 2·75 2·50
MS1425 76×102 mm. **273** $5 multi-coloured 8·00 8·00

274 Diana, Princess of Wales

1998. Diana, Princess of Wales Commemoration.
1426 **274** $1.15 multicoloured 1·25 1·50
MS1427 70×100 mm. $3.50, Princess Diana and guard of honour 2·50 4·50

1998. Children's Charities. No. MS1427 surch +$1 CHILDREN'S CHARITIES.
MS1428 70×100 mm. $3.50 + $1 Princess Diana and guard of honour 2·50 4·50

1999. New Millennium. Nos. 1311/14 optd KIA ORANA THIRD MILLENNIUM.
1429 80c. Type **253** 85 85
1430 85c. Seated Tangaroa carving 90 90
1431 $1 Seated Tangaroa carving (different) 1·25 1·25
1432 $1.75 Standing Tangaroa carving 2·00 2·00

277 Lady Elizabeth Bowes-Lyon

2000. Queen Elizabeth the Queen Mother's 100th Birthday.
1433 **277** $4.50 brown and blue 4·75 4·75
1434 - $4.50 brown and blue 4·75 4·75
1435 - $4.50 multicoloured 4·75 4·75
1436 - $4.50 multicoloured 4·75 4·75
MS1437 73×100 mm. $6 multicoloured 4·75 6·00

DESIGNS: 1434, Lady Elizabeth Bowes-Lyon as young woman; 1435, Queen Mother wearing green outfit; 1436, Queen Mother wearing pearl earrings and necklace; **MS**1437, Queen Mother in blue hat and plum jacket.

278 Ancient Greek Runner on Urn

2000. Olympic Games, Sydney. Multicoloured.
1438 $1.75 Type **278** 1·75 2·00
1439 $1.75 Modern runner 1·75 2·00
1440 $1.75 Ancient Greek archer 1·75 2·00
1441 $1.75 Modern archer 1·75 2·00
MS1442 99×90 mm. $3.90, Olympic torch in Cook Islands 3·00 4·00

2001. Suwarrow Wildlife Sanctuary. Nos. 1279/90 surch 80c SUWARROW SANCTUARY.
1443 80c. on $1.15 Heavisides's dolphin 1·25 1·40
1444 80c. on $1.15 Eagle owl 1·25 1·40
1445 80c. on $1.15 Bee hummingbird 1·25 1·40
1446 80c. on $1.15 Puma 1·25 1·40
1447 80c. on $1.15 European otter 1·25 1·40
1448 80c. on $1.15 Red kangaroo 1·25 1·40
1449 90c. on $1.15 Type **250** 1·25 1·40
1450 90c. on $1.15 Indian elephant 1·25 1·40
1451 90c. on $1.15 Brown bear 1·25 1·40
1452 90c. on $1.15 Black rhinoceros 1·25 1·40
1453 90c. on $1.15 Chimpanzee 1·25 1·40
1454 90c. on $1.15 Argali 1·25 1·40

2002. Christmas. Nos. 1248/51 and 1256/9 optd CHRISTMAS 2002 or surch.
1455 20c. on 70c. Type **244** 60 70
1456 20c. on 70c. Type **248** 60 70
1457 80c. on $1.15 "Adoration of the Shepherds" (Rembrandt) 1·40 1·25
1458 85c. "Holy Family" (Lotto) 1·40 1·60
1459 85c. "The Birth of the Virgin" (B. Murillo) 1·40 1·60
1460 90c. on $1.50 "Adoration of the Shepherds" (L. le Nain) 1·50 1·50
1461 95c. "Madonna and Child with Saints John and Catherine" (Titian) 1·50 1·50
1462 $1 on $1.50 "The Holy Family" (Titian) 1·75 2·00

2003. Nos. 1414/19 surch.
1463 20c. on $1.50 *Parthenos Sylvia* 90 90
1464 80c. on $2 *Lampides boeticus* (female) 2·00 1·75
1465 85c. on $3 *Precis villida* 2·00 2·25
1466 85c. on $4 *Melanitis leda* 2·00 2·25
1467 90c. on $5 *Vagrans egista* 2·00 2·25
1468 90c. on $7 *Hyblaea sanguinea* 2·00 2·25

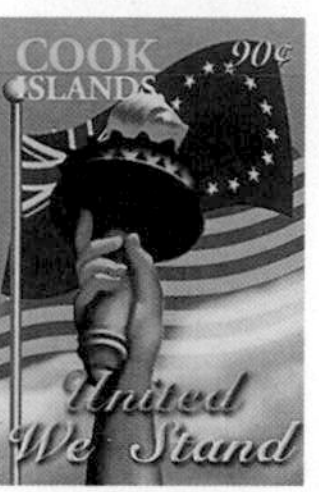

282 Statue of Liberty's Torch and Cook Islands Flag

2003. "United We Stand". Support for Victims of 11 September 2001 Terrorist Attacks.
MS1469 75×109 mm. **282** 90c.×4 multicoloured 4·50 6·00

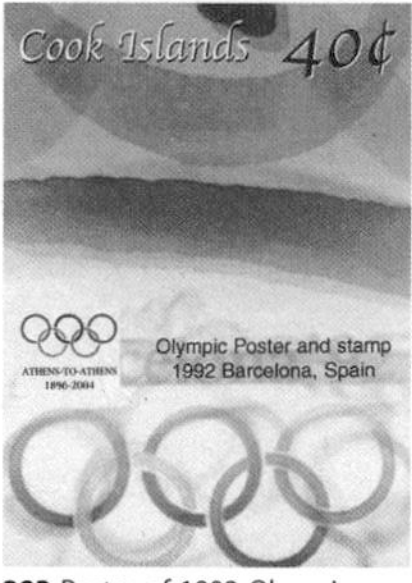

283 Poster of 1992 Olympic Games, Barcelona

2004. Olympic Games, Athens, Greece. Multicoloured.
1470 40c. Type **283** 70 75
1471 60c. "The Pancration" (Greek art) (horiz) 1·10 1·25
1472 $1 Cycling (horiz) 2·50 2·75
1473 $2 Gold medal, Berlin, 1936 3·00 3·50

284 Cook Islands Warbler ("Cook Islands Reed Warbler")

2005. Endangered Birds of the Cook Islands. Four sheets, each 95×132 mm, containing T 284 and similar horiz designs. Multicoloured.
MS1474 (a) 80c.×4 Type **284**. (b) 90c.×4 Mangaia kingfisher. (c) $1.15×4 Rarotonga starling. (d) $1.95×4 Cook Islands swiftlet ("Atiu Swiftlet") 24·00 26·00

285 Pope John Paul II

2005. Pope John Paul II Commemoration.
1475 **285** $1.35 multicoloured 2·25 2·25

2005. Olympic Gold Medal Winners, Athens (2004). Nos. 1470/3 optd.
1476 40c. "Poster of 1992 Olympic Games, Barcelona" (optd with Type A) 75 85
1477 40c. "Poster of 1992 Olympic Games, Barcelona" (optd with Type B) 75 85
1478 40c. "Poster of 1992 Olympic Games, Barcelona" (optd with Type C) 75 85
1479 40c. "Poster of 1992 Olympic Games, Barcelona" (optd with Type D) 75 85
1480 40c. "Poster of 1992 Olympic Games, Barcelona" (optd with Type E) 75 85
1481 60c. "The Pancration" (Greek art) (horiz) (optd with Type A) 90 1·00
1482 60c. "The Pancration" (Greek art) (horiz) (optd with Type B) 90 1·00
1483 60c. "The Pancration" (Greek art) (horiz) (optd with Type C) 90 1·00
1484 60c. "The Pancration" (Greek art) (horiz) (optd with Type D) 90 1·00
1485 60c. "The Pancration" (Greek art) (horiz) (optd with Type E) 90 1·00
1486 $1 Cycling (horiz) (optd with Type A) 2·50 2·75
1487 $1 Cycling (horiz) (optd with Type B) 2·50 2·75
1488 $1 Cycling (horiz) (optd with Type C) 2·50 2·75
1489 $1 Cycling (horiz) (optd with Type D) 2·50 2·75
1490 $1 Cycling (horiz) (optd with Type E) 2·50 2·75
1491 $2 Gold medal, Berlin, 1936 (optd with Type A) 2·75 3·00
1492 $2 Gold medal, Berlin, 1936 (optd with Type B) 2·75 3·00
1493 $2 Gold medal, Berlin, 1936 (optd with Type C) 2·75 3·00
1494 $2 Gold medal, Berlin, 1936 (optd with Type D) 2·75 3·00
1495 $2 Gold medal, Berlin, 1936 (optd with Type E) 2·75 3·00

OVERPRINTS (all with four gold stars): Type A **DWIGHT PHILLIPS Men's LONG JUMP USA 35**; Type B **XING HUI-NA Women's 10,000m CHINA 32**; Type C **IAN THORPE Men's 200m FREESTYLE AUSTRALIA 17**; Type D **MI-ZUKI NOGUCHI Women's Marathon JAPAN** 16; Type E **YVONNE BOENISCH Women's 57kg JUDO GERMANY 14**.

287 Black-lined Maori Wrasse

288 Hawksbill Turtle

289 Red-spot Rainbow Fish, Smooth Sea Star and Black tipped Cod (image scaled to 61% of original size)

2007. Wildlife of the South Pacific. Multicoloured. (a) Size 39×25 mm.
1496 5c. Type **287** 10 15
1497 10c. Pair of blue lorikeets on palm frond 15 20
1498 20c. *Tubastrea aurea* (daisy coral) 30 35

1499	30c. Three ocean sunfish	40	45
1500	40c. *Lampides boeticus* (butterfly) (female)	45	50
1501	50c. Pair of Rarotonga starlings	55	60

(b) Size 48×27 mm. Frames and inscriptions in gold.

1502	80c. Mangaia kingfishers	75	80
1503	80c. Cook Islands reed-warblers	75	80
1504	80c. As No. 1501	75	80
1505	80c. Matiu swiftlet	75	80
1506	90c. *Lampides boeticus* (butterfly) (male)	1·00	1·10
1507	90c. *Vagrans egista* (butterfly)	1·00	1·10
1508	90c. *Melantis leda* (butterfly)	1·00	1·10
1509	90c. As No. 1500	1·00	1·10
1510	$1 As No. 1498	1·10	1·25
1511	$1 *Stylaster elegans* (hydroid coral)	1·10	1·25
1512	$1 *Fromia monilis* (sea star)	1·10	1·25
1513	$1 *Choriaster granulatus* (smooth sea star)	1·10	1·25
1514	$1.10 Black tipped cod	1·40	1·50
1515	$1.10 Red-spot rainbow fish	1·40	1·50
1516	$1.10 As Type **287**	1·40	1·50
1517	$1.10 Longnose butterflyfish	1·40	1·50
1518	$1.20 As No. 1499	1·50	1·75
1519	$1.20 Three ocean sunfish, two feeding on floating weeds	1·50	1·75
1520	$1.20 Diver and ocean sunfish	1·50	1·75
1521	$1.20 Four ocean sunfish, one swimming towards camera with mouth open	1·50	1·75
1522	$2 As No. 1497	2·25	2·40
1523	$2 Two young blue lorikeets in tree hole	2·25	2·40
1524	$2 Pair of blue lorikeets and white hibiscus flowers	2·25	2·40
1525	$2 Pair of blue lorikeets perched on plant	2·25	2·40

(c) Horiz designs as T 288. Multicoloured.

1526	$3 Type **288**	3·50	3·75
1527	$3 Leatherback turtle	3·50	3·75
1528	$3 Green turtle	3·50	3·75
1529	$3 Olive Ridley turtle	3·50	3·75
1530	$5 Sowerby's whale	5·00	5·25
1531	$5 Cuvier's beaked whale	5·00	5·25
1532	$5 Bottle-nosed dolphin	5·00	5·25
1533	$5 Commerson's dolphin	5·00	5·25

(d) Horiz designs as T 289. Multicoloured.

1534	$7.50 Type **289**	9·50	10·00
1535	$10 *Lampides boeticus* (male and female) and *Melantis leda* butterflies	13·00	13·50
1536	$15 Matiu swiftlet, Cook Islands reed-warbler and blue lorikeets	17·00	18·00

No. 1517 is wrongly inscr 'Smooth Sea Star *Choriaster granulatus*'.

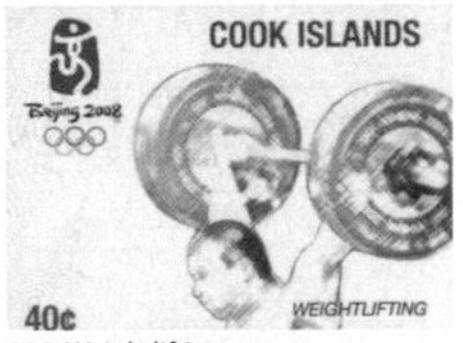

290 Weightlifting

2008. Olympic Games, Beijing. Sheet 150×94 mm containing T 290 and similar horiz designs. Multicoloured.

MS1537	40c. Type **290**; 60c. High jump; $1 Swimming; $1.50 Running	5·00	5·00

291 Shotput and Discus

2009. Pacific Mini Games, Rarotonga. Multicoloured.

1538	20c. Type **291**	45	50
1539	80c. High jump	1·60	1·75
1540	90c. Weightlifting	1·75	2·00
1541	$3 Running	5·25	5·50
MS1542	110×135 mm. Nos. 1538/41	8·25	8·75

DANIEL KILAMA
New Caledonia
27th Sept 2009
Men's Discus Throw

(292)

2009. Pacific Mini Games Gold Medal Winners. Nos. 1538/42 optd.

1543	20c. Mens discus throw (optd **DANIEL KILAMA New Caledonia**)	45	50
1544	80c. High jump (optd **JO-HANNA SUI Tahiti Women's High Jump 24th Sept 2009**)	1·60	1·75
1545	90c. Weightlifting (optd **YUKIO PETER Nauru 85kg Clean & Jerk 1st Oct 2009**)	1·75	2·00
1546	$3 Running (optd **NIKO VEREKAUTA Fiji Men's 100 metres 24th Sept 2009**)	5·25	5·50
MS1547	110×135 mm. Nos. 1543/6	8·25	8·75

OFFICIAL STAMPS

1975. Nos. 228, etc, optd O.H.M.S. or surch also.

O1	1c. multicoloured
O2	2c. multicoloured
O3	3c. multicoloured
O4	4c. multicoloured
O5	5c. on 2½c. multicoloured
O6	8c. multicoloured
O7	10c. on 6c. multicoloured
O8	18c. on 20c. multicoloured
O9	25c. on 9c. multicoloured
O10	30c. on 15c. multicoloured
O11	50c. multicoloured
O12	$1 multicoloured
O13	$2 multicoloured
O14	$4 multicoloured
O15	$6 multicoloured

These stamps were only sold to the public cancelled-to-order and not in unused condition.

1978. Nos. 466/7, 474, 478/81, 484/5, 542 and 568/9 optd O.H.M.S. or surch also.

O16	-	1c. mult (No. 467)	80	10
O17	**141**	2c. on ½c. multicoloured	1·25	10
O18	-	5c. on ½c. multicoloured	1·25	10
O19	-	10c. on 8c. mult (No. 474)	1·00	10
O20	-	15c. on 50c. mult (No. 480)	1·75	10
O21	-	18c. on 60c. mult (No. 481)	1·25	15
O22	-	25c. mult (No. 478)	1·50	20
O23	-	30c. mult (No. 479)	1·50	25
O24	-	35c. on 60c. mult (No. 481)	1·50	30
O25	-	50c. mult (No. 480)	2·00	35
O26	-	60c. mult (No. 481)	2·25	45
O27	-	$1 mult (No. 568)	5·00	65
O28	-	$1 mult (No. 569)	5·00	65
O29	-	$2 mult (No. 542)	7·00	2·25
O30	-	$4 mult (No. 484)	13·00	2·25
O31	-	$6 mult (No. 485)	13·00	3·50

1985. Nos. 786/8, 862/5, 969/74, 976, 978, 981, 984/6 and 988/9 optd O.H.M.S. or surch also.

O32	5c. "Ptilosarcus gurneyi"	50	60
O33	10c. "Lobophyllia bemprichii"	50	60
O34	12c. "Sarcophyton digitatum"	5·00	75
O35	14c. "Pavona praetorta"	5·00	75
O36	18c. "Junceella gemmacea"	5·00	75
O37	20c. "Stylaster"	60	60
O38	30c. "Palauastrea ramosa"	60	60
O39	40c. "Stylaster echinatus"	60	60
O40	50c. "Melithaea squamata"	6·50	90
O41	55c. on 85c. "Caulastraea echinulata"	70	50
O42	60c. "Tubastraea"	70	80
O43	70c. "Heliofungia actiniformis"	6·50	1·10
O46	75c. on 60c. Type **197**	3·00	1·00
O47	75c. on 60c. Rarotonga oranges	3·00	1·00
O48	75c. on 60c. Rarotonga Airport	3·00	1·00
O49	75c. on 60c. Prime Minister Sir Thomas Davis	3·00	1·00
O44	$1.10 "Pectinia alcicornis"	1·60	1·10
O45	$2 on $1.20 "Dendrophyllia gracilis"	3·25	2·00
O50	$5 on $3 "Heliofungia actiniformis"	17·00	5·00
O51	$9 on $4 "Stylophora pistillata"	12·00	13·00
O52	$14 on $6 "Stylaster echinatus"	12·50	14·00
O53	$18 on $10 "Melithaea albitincta"	19·00	19·00

1995. Nos. 1261/6 optd O.H.M.S.

O54	5c. Type **249**	40	75
O55	10c. Blue sea star	40	75
O56	15c. Bicoloured angelfish	50	75
O57	20c. Spotted pebble crab	1·00	80
O58	25c. Black-tipped grouper	80	70
O59	30c. Spanish dancer	1·25	70
O60	50c. Regal angelfish	1·00	80
O61	80c. Big-scaled soldierfish	1·75	1·25
O62	85c. Red pencil sea urchin	1·75	1·25
O63	90c. Red-spotted rainbowfish	1·75	1·25
O64	$1 Cheek-lined wrasse	1·50	1·50
O65	$2 Long-nosed butterflyfish	2·25	2·50
O66	$3 Red-spotted rainbowfish	3·75	4·00
O67	$5 Blue sea star	4·50	5·00
O68	$7 "Pygoplites diacanthus"	7·50	8·50
O69	$10 Spotted pebble crab	8·00	9·50

Pt. 15

COSTA RICA

A republic of Central America. Independent since 1821.

1863. 8 reales = 1 peso.
1881. 100 centavos = 1 peso.
1901. 100 centimos = 1 colon.

1

1863

1	**1**	½r. blue	30	1·00
3	**1**	2r. red	1·50	1·80
4	**1**	4r. green	15·00	15·00
5	**1**	1p. orange	38·00	38·00

1881. Surch.

6	1c. on ½r. blue	2·75	7·75
8	2c. on ½r. blue	3·00	3·50
9	5c. on ½r. blue	6·75	12·50

1882. Surch U.P.U. and value.

10	5c. on ½r. blue	60·00
11	10c. on 2r. red	70·00
12	20c. on 4r. green	£275

8 General P. Fernandez

1883

13	**8**	1c. green	3·00	1·50
14	**8**	2c. red	3·00	1·50
15	**8**	5c. violet	30·00	1·90
16	**8**	10c. orange	£130	12·00
17	**8**	40c. blue	1·90	3·00

14 Pres. Soto

1887

18	**14**	5c. violet	5·75	40
19	**14**	10c. orange	3·25	2·40

1887. Fiscal stamps similar to T 8 and 14 optd CORREOS.

20	1c. red	4·25	3·00
21	5c. brown	5·75	3·00

17 Pres. Soto

1889. Various frames.

22	**17**	1c. brown	35	45
23	**17**	2c. green	35	45
24	**17**	5c. orange	45	35
25	**17**	10c. lake	40	35
26	**17**	20c. green	30	35
27	**17**	50c. red	1·10	85
28	**17**	1p. blue	1·20	85
29	**17**	2p. violet	6·00	4·75
30	**17**	5p. olive	22·00	11·50
31	**17**	10p. black	90·00	60·00

19

1892. Various frames.

32	**19**	1c. blue	30	40
33	**19**	2c. orange	30	40
34a	**19**	5c. mauve	30	25
35	**19**	10c. green	80	35
36	**19**	20c. red	12·00	15
37	**19**	50c. blue	4·00	2·75
38	**19**	1p. green on yellow	95	80
39	**19**	2p. red on grey	2·75	85
40	**19**	5p. blue on blue	1·90	85
41a	**19**	10p. brown on buff	6·50	5·00

29 Juan Santamaria

31 Puerto Limon

1901. Various designs dated "1900".

42	**29**	1c. black and green	3·00	30
43	-	2c. black and red	25	15
52	-	4c. black and purple	1·70	70
44	**31**	5c. black and blue	3·00	30
53	-	6c. black and olive	7·25	4·00
45	-	10c. black and brown	3·00	35
46	-	20c. black and lake	21·00	25
54	-	25c. brown and lilac	16·00	30
47	-	50c. blue and red	5·00	95
48	-	1col. black and olive	£100	3·50
49	-	2col. black and red	15·00	3·00
50	-	5col. black and brown	70·00	3·50
51	-	10col. red and green	27·00	3·00

DESIGNS—VERT: 2c. Juan Mora F; 4c. Jose M. Canas; 6c. Julian Volio; 10c. Braulio (wrongly inscr "BRANLIO") Carrillo; 25c. Eusebio Figueroa; 50c. Jose M. Castro; 1col. Puente de Birris; 2col. Juan Rafael Mora; 5col. Jesus Jimenez. HORIZ: 20c. National Theatre; 10col. Arms.

1905. No. 46 surch UN CENTIMO in ornamental frame.

55	1c. on 20c. black and lake	55	50

43 Juan Santamaria

44 Juan Mora

1907. Dated "1907".

57	**43**	1c. blue and brown	4·00	40
58	**44**	2c. black and green	2·10	30
69	-	4c. blue and red	12·00	2·50
60	-	5c. blue and orange	3·00	30
71	-	10c. black and blue	19·00	1·00
72	-	20c. black and olive	26·00	6·00
63	-	25c. slate and lavender	3·00	3·00
74	-	50c. blue and red	55·00	26·00
75	-	1col. black and brown	21·00	19·00
76	-	2col. green and red	£150	95·00

PORTRAITS: 4c. Jose M. Canas. 5c. Mauro Fernandez. 10c. Braulio Carrillo. 20c. Julian Volio. 25c. Eusebio Figueroa. 50c. Jose M. Castro. 1col. Jesus Jimenez. 2col. Juan Rafael Mora.

53 Juan Santamaria

54 Julian Volio

1910. Various frames.

77	**53**	1c. brown	10	10
78	-	2c. green (Juan Mora F.)	25	10
79	-	4c. red (Jose M. Canas)	30	20
80	-	5c. orange (Mauro Fernandez)	95	10
81	-	10c. blue (B. Carrillo)	25	10
82	**54**	20c. olive	40	20
83	-	25c. purple (Eusebio Figueroa)	12·50	1·20
84	-	1col. brown (Jesus Jimenez)	50	50

1911. Optd 1911 between stars.

85	**29**	1c. black and green	1·90	95
86	**43**	1c. blue and brown	95	40
88	**44**	2c. black and green	1·20	65

1911. Optd Habilitado 1911.

93	4c. black and purple (No. 52)	1·00	10
90	5c. blue and orange (No. 60)	1·50	20
91	10c. black and blue (No. 71)	49·00	5·75

59 Liner "Antilles"

1911. Surch Correos Un centimo or Correos S 5 centimos.

94	**59**	1c. on 10c. blue	35	25
96	**59**	1c. on 25c. violet	35	20
97	**59**	1c. on 50c. brown	50	40
98	**59**	1c. on 1c. brown	50	40
99	**59**	1c. on 5c. red	80	55
100	**59**	1c. on 10c. brown	1·10	70
101	**59**	5c. on 5c. orange	40	25

62

1912. Surch Correos Dos centimos 2.

105	**62**	2c. on 1c. brown	1·30	80
112	**62**	2c. on 2c. red	80	60
102	**62**	2c. on 5c. brown	3·25	2·00
107	**62**	2c. on 5c. green	6·00	3·00
109	**62**	2c. on 10c. blue	95·00	80·00
104	**62**	2c. on 50c. red	44·00	19·00
108	**62**	2c. on 10col. purple	4·75	3·00

67 Plantation and Administration Building

1921. Centenary of Coffee Cultivation.

115	**67**	5c. black and blue	2·75	2·75

68 Simon Bolivar

1921

116	**68**	15c. violet	55	20

69

1921. Cent of Independence of Central America.

117	**69**	5c. violet	90	40

70 Juan Mora and Julio Acosta

1921. Centenary of Independence.

118	**70**	2c. black and orange	1·30	1·30
119	**70**	3c. black and green	1·30	1·30
120	**70**	6c. black and red	2·20	2·20
121	**70**	15c. black and blue	4·00	4·00
122	**70**	30c. black and brown	5·50	5·50

1922. Coffee Publicity. Nos. 77/81 and 116 optd with sack inscr "CAFE DE COSTA RICA".

123	**53**	1c. brown	30	10
124	-	2c. green	30	10
125	-	4c. red	30	10
126	-	5c. orange	1·50	40
127	-	10c. blue	60	40
128	**68**	15c. violet	3·50	2·10

1922. Optd CORREOS 1922.

129	**69**	5c. violet	55	40

1922. Surch with red cross and 5c.

130	5c.+5c. orange (No. 80)	70	30

1923. Optd COMPRE UD. CAFE DE COSTA RICA in circular frame.

131	5c. orange (No. 80)	2·30	70

77 Jesus Jimenez (statesman)

1923. Birth Centenary of J. Jimenez.

132	**77**	2c. brown	30	30
133	**77**	4c. green	35	30
134	**77**	5c. blue	50	30
135	**77**	20c. red	60	40
136	**77**	1col. violet	80	75

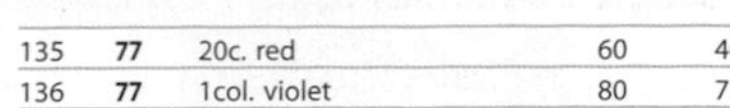

80 National Monument

81 Coffee-growing

1923

137	**80**	1c. purple	15	10
138	**81**	2c. yellow	40	10
139	-	4c. green	70	35
140	-	5c. blue	1·30	10
141	-	5c. green	35	10
142	-	10c. brown	2·50	10
143	-	10c. red	45	10
144	-	12c. red	9·00	2·50
145	-	20c. blue	9·75	65
146	-	40c. orange	10·00	2·30
147	-	1col. olive	2·20	80

DESIGNS—HORIZ: 5c. P.O., San Jose; 10c. Columbus and Isabella I; 12c. "Santa Maria"; 20c. Columbus landing at Cariari; 40c. Map of Costa Rica. VERT: 4c. Banana-growing; 1col. M. Gutierrez.

All the above are inscr "U.P.U. 1923." except the 10c. and 12c. which are inscr "1921 EN COMMEMORACION DEL PRIMER CONGRESO POSTAL", etc.

85 Don R. A. Maldonado y Velasco

1924

148	**85**	2c. green	45	20

For 3c. green see No. 211 and for other portraits as T **85** see Nos. 308/12.

86 Map of Guanacaste

1924. Cent of Province of Nicoya (Guanacaste).

149	**86**	1c. red	35	10
150	**86**	2c. purple	35	10
151	**86**	5c. green	35	10
152	**86**	10c. orange	2·30	50
153	-	15c. blue	80	50
154	-	20c. grey	1·60	85
155	-	25c. brown	2·30	1·50

DESIGN: 15c., 20c., 25c. Church at Nicoya.

88 Discus Thrower

1925. Inscr "JUEGOS OLIMPICOS". Imperf or perf.

156	**88**	5c. green	1·60	2·30
157	-	10c. red	1·60	2·30
158	-	20c. blue	3·50	4·00

DESIGNS—VERT: 10c. Trophy. HORIZ: 20c. Parthenon.

1926. Surch with values in ornamental designs.

159	3c. on 5c. (No. 140)	30	10
160	6c. on 10c. (No. 142)	35	25
161	30c. on 40c. (No. 146)	1·30	35
162	45c. on 1col. (No. 147)	1·50	45

1926. Surch with value between bars.

163	10c. on 12c. red (No. 144)	1·10	30

93 Arms and Curtiss "Jenny"

1926. Air.

164	**93**	20c. blue	2·75	60

94 Heredia Normal School

1926. Dated "1926".

165	-	3c. blue	55	10
166	-	6c. brown	55	20
167	**94**	30c. orange	1·40	35
168	-	45c. violet	3·75	1·40

DESIGNS: 3c. St. Louis College, Cartago; 6c. Chapui Asylum, San Jose; 45c. Ruins of Ujarras.

1928. Lindbergh Good Will Tour of Central America. Surch with aeroplane, LINDBERGH ENERO 1928 and new value.

169		10c. on 12c. red (No. 144)	4·75	4·75

1928. Surch 5 5.

170	**68**	5c. on 15c. violet	20	10

1929. Surch CORREOS and value.

171	**62**	5c. on 2col. red	55	10
173	**62**	13c. on 40c. green	30	15

98 Post Office

1930. Types of 1923 reduced in size and dated "1929" as T 98.

174	-	1c. purple (as No. 137)	20	10
175	**98**	5c. green	20	10
176	-	10c. red (as No. 143)	55	10

1930. Air. No. O178 surch CORREO 1930 AEREO, Bleriot XI airplane and new value.

177	**O95**	8c. on 1col.	70	60
178	**O95**	20c. on 1col.	1·00	65
179	**O95**	40c. on 1col.	2·10	1·60
180	**O95**	1col. on 1col.	3·00	2·00

1930. Air. Optd CORREO AEREO (No. 181) or Correo Aereo (others) or surch also.

181	-	10c. red (No. 143)	1·60	25
182	**62**	5c. on 10c. brown	35	25
183	**62**	20c. on 50c. blue	45	25
184	**62**	40c. on 50c. blue	55	25
185	**62**	1col. orange	1·80	45

103 Juan Rafael Mora

1931

186	**103**	13c. red	55	10

1931. Air. Fiscal stamps (Arms design) inscr "TIMBRE 1929" (or "1930", 3col.), surch Habilitado 1931 Correo Aereo and new value.

190		2col. on 2col. green	36·00	36·00
191		3col. on 5col. brown	36·00	36·00
192		5col. on 10col. black	36·00	36·00

1932. Air. Telegraph stamp optd with wings inscr CORREO CR AEREO.

193	**62**	40c. green	2·50	35

106

1932. 1st National Philatelic Exhibition.

194	**106**	3c. orange	15	10
195	**106**	5c. green	40	25
196	**106**	10c. red	50	25
197	**106**	20c. blue	70	40

See also Nos. 231/4.

107 Ryan Brougham over La Sabana Airport, San Jose

1934. Air.

198	**107**	5c. green	20	20
507	**107**	5c. deep blue	40	20
508	**107**	5c. pale blue	40	20
199	**107**	10c. red	20	20
509	**107**	10c. green	40	20
510	**107**	10c. turquoise	40	20
200	**107**	15c. brown	40	20
511	**107**	15c. red	50	20
201	**107**	20c. blue	40	20
202	**107**	25c. orange	55	20
512	**107**	35c. violet	1·30	20
203	**107**	40c. brown	1·70	20
204	**107**	50c. black	70	20
205	**107**	60c. yellow	1·40	20
206	**107**	75c. violet	2·75	50
207	-	1col. red	1·50	20
208	-	2col. blue	5·75	1·00
209	-	5col. black	5·75	5·00
210	-	10col. brown	8·75	8·50

DESIGN: 1, 2, 5, 10col. Allegory of the Air Mail.

1934

211	**85**	3c. green	15	10

109 Nurse at Altar

1935. Costa Rican Red Cross Jubilee.

212	**109**	10c. red	7·00	25

111 Our Lady of the Angels

1935. 300th Anniv of Apparition of Our Lady of the Angels.

213	-	5c. green	20	20
214	**111**	10c. red	35	20
215	-	30c. orange	50	20
216	-	45c. violet	1·20	60
217	**111**	50c. black	2·00	1·10

DESIGNS: 5c., 30c. Aerial view of Cartago; 45c. Allegory of the Apparition.

112 Cocos Island

1936

218	**112**	4c. brown	35	10
219	**112**	8c. violet	50	20
220	**112**	25c. orange	60	20
221	**112**	35c. brown	80	20
222	**112**	40c. brown	1·10	30
223	**112**	50c. yellow	1·20	60
224	**112**	2col. green	9·75	9·25
225	**112**	5col. green	29·00	23·00

113 Cocos Island and Fleet of Columbus

1936

226	**113**	5c. green	25	20
227	**113**	10c. red	45	20

114 Airplane over Mt. Poas

1937. Air. 1st Annual Fair.

228	**114**	1c. black	40	35
229	**114**	2c. brown	40	35
230	**114**	3c. violet	40	35

1937. 2nd National Philatelic Exhibition. As T 106, but inscr "DICIEMBRE 1937".

231	**106**	2c. purple	35	10
232	**106**	3c. black	35	10
233	**106**	5c. green	35	10
234	**106**	10c. orange	35	10

MS234a 164×101 mm. Nos. 231/4. Imperf 1·10 1·10

115 Tunny

116 Native and Donkey carrying Bananas

117 Puntarenas

1937. National Exhibition, San Jose (1st Issue).

235	**115**	2c. black (postage)	35	10
236	**116**	5c. green	50	10
237	-	10c. red	80	20
238	**117**	2c. black (air)	15	10
239	**117**	5c. green	20	10
240	**117**	20c. blue	30	10
241	**117**	1col.40 brown	2·40	2·40

DESIGN—As Type **116**: 10c. Coffee gathering.

118 Purple Guaria Orchid "Carrleya skinneri"

119 National Bank

1938. National Exhibition, San Jose (2nd Issue).

242	**118**	1c. violet & grn (postage)	50	10
243	**118**	3c. brown	30	10
244	**119**	1c. violet (air)	10	10
245	**119**	3c. red	10	10
246	**119**	10c. red	30	10
247	**119**	75c. brown	2·40	1·80

DESIGN—As Type **118**: 3c. Cocoa-bean.

1938. No. 145 optd 1938.

248		20c. blue	1·40	25

121 La Sabana Airport

1940. Air. Opening of San Jose Airport.

249	**121**	5c. green	20	20
250	**121**	10c. red	20	20
251	**121**	25c. blue	20	20
252	**121**	35c. brown	20	20
253	**121**	60c. orange	40	40
254	**121**	85c. violet	1·20	1·00
255	**121**	2col.35 green	6·00	5·75

1940. No. 168 variously surch 15 CENTIMOS in ornamental frame.

256		15c. on 45c. violet	50	20

There are five distinct varieties of this surcharge.

1940. Pan-American Health Day. Unissued stamps prepared for the 8th Pan-American Child Welfare Congress optd DIA PANAMERICANO DE LA SALUD 2. DICIEMBRE 1940. (a) Postage. Allegorical design.

261		5c. green	25	20
262		10c. red	35	20
263		20c. blue	80	45
264		40c. brown	1·60	1·50
265		55c. orange	3·25	2·50

(b) Air. View of Duran Sanatorium.

266		10c. red	20	20
267		15c. violet	20	20
268		25c. blue	45	40
269		35c. brown	65	55
270		60c. green	1·00	80
271		75c. olive	2·50	2·20
272		1col.35 orange	8·00	6·25
273		5col. brown	42·00	42·00
274		10col. mauve	£140	£110

1940. Air. Pan-American Aviation Day. Surch AERO Aviacion Panamericana Dic. 17 1940 and value.

275		15c. on 50c. yellow	85	85
276		30c. on 50c. yellow	85	85

1941. Surch 15 CENTIMOS 15.

277	**112**	15c. on 25c. orange	45	45
278	**112**	15c. on 35c. brown	45	45
279	**112**	15c. on 40c. brown	45	45
280	**112**	15c. on 2col. green	45	45
281	**112**	15c. on 5col. green	90	90

131 Stadium and Flag

132 Football Match

1941. Central American and Caribbean Football Championship.

282	**131**	5c. green (postage)	65	25
283	**131**	10c. orange	45	25
284	**131**	15c. red	70	35
285	**131**	25c. blue	80	50
286	**131**	40c. brown	3·00	1·20
287	**131**	50c. violet	4·00	1·90
288	**131**	75c. orange	6·25	5·50
289	**131**	1col. red	11·50	11·00
290	**132**	15c. red (air)	80	25
291	**132**	30c. blue	90	25
292	**132**	40c. brown	90	35
293	**132**	50c. violet	1·30	80
294	**132**	60c. green	1·60	90
295	**132**	75c. yellow	2·75	1·50
296	**132**	1col. mauve	4·50	4·50
297	**132**	1col.40 red	9·25	9·25
298	**132**	2col. green	21·00	18·00
299	**132**	5col. black	50·00	40·00

1941. Air. Costa Rica–Panama Boundary Treaty. Optd Mayo 1941 Tratado Limitrofe Costa Rica – Panama or surch also.

300	**107**	5c. on 20c. blue	10	10
301	**107**	15c. on 20c. blue	10	10
302	**107**	40c. on 75c. violet	35	10
303	-	65c. on 1col. red (No. 207)	60	50
304	-	1col.40 on 2col. blue (No. 208)	3·50	3·25
305	-	5col. black (No. 209)	12·00	12·00
306	-	10col. brown (No. 210)	14·50	14·00

1941. As Type 85 but with new portraits.

308		3c. orange	25	10
309		3c. purple	25	10
310		3c. red	25	10
310a		3c. blue	25	10
311		5c. violet	25	10
312		5c. black	25	10

PORTRAITS: 3c. (Nos. 308/10) C. G. Viquez. 3c. (No. 310a) Mgr. B. A. Thiel. 5c. J. J. Rodriguez.

136 New Decree and Restored University

1941. Restoration of National University.

313	-	5c. green (postage)	40	20
314	**136**	10c. orange	40	20
315	-	15c. red	60	20
316	**136**	25c. blue	90	35
317	-	50c. brown	5·75	2·30
318	**136**	15c. red (air)	20	20
319	-	30c. blue	35	20
320	**136**	40c. orange	40	35
321	-	60c. blue	50	40
322	**136**	1col. violet	2·00	2·00
323	-	2col. black	5·00	5·00
324	**136**	5col. purple	16·00	16·00

DESIGN—(Nos. 313, 315, 317, 319, 321 and 323): The original Decree and University.

1941. Surch.

325	5c. on 6c. brn (No. 166)	35	10
326	15c. on 20c. blue (No. 248)	65	20

139 "V", Torch and Flags

1942. War Effort.

327	**139**	5c. red	30	10
328	**139**	5c. orange	30	10
329	**139**	5c. green	30	10
330	**139**	5c. blue	30	10
331	**139**	5c. violet	30	10

140 Francisco Morazan

1942. Portraits and dates.

332	**A**	1c. lilac (postage)	10	10
333	**B**	2c. black	10	10
334	**C**	3c. blue	10	10
335	**D**	5c. turquoise	10	10
336	**D**	5c. green	10	10
337	**140**	15c. red	10	10
338	**E**	25c. blue	60	15
339	**F**	50c. violet	1·80	60
340	**G**	1col. black	3·50	1·70
341	**H**	2col. orange	5·25	3·25
341a	**I**	5c. brown (air)	10	10
342	**A**	10c. red	10	10
342a	**A**	10c. olive	10	10
342b	**J**	15c. violet	10	10
343	**K**	25c. blue	10	45
344	**L**	30c. brown	20	10
345	**D**	40c. blue	25	10
346	**D**	40c. red	25	10
347	**140**	45c. purple	45	25
348	**M**	45c. black	20	10
349	**E**	50c. green	1·70	20
350	**E**	50c. orange	40	20
351	**N**	55c. purple	35	30
352	**F**	60c. blue	60	20
353	**F**	60c. green	20	10
354	**G**	65c. red	90	25
355	**G**	65c. blue	25	20
356	**O**	75c. green	60	35
357	**H**	85c. orange	1·10	45
358	**H**	85c. violet	1·50	60
359	**P**	1col. black	1·50	35
360	**P**	1col. red	60	20
361	**Q**	1col.05 sepia	80	50
362	**R**	1col.15 brown	2·00	1·70
363	**R**	1col.15 green	2·75	1·20
364	**B**	1col.40 violet	3·00	2·30
365	**B**	1col.40 yellow	1·70	1·50
366	**C**	2col. black	4·75	1·20
367	**C**	2col. olive	1·50	45

PORTRAITS: A, J. Mora Fernandez. B, B. Carranza. C, T. Guardia. D, M. Aguilar. E, J. M. Alfaro. F, F. M. Oreamuno. G, J. M. Castro. H, J. R. Mora. I, S. Lara. J, C. Duran. K, A. Esquivel. L, V. Herrera. M, J. R. de Gallegos. N, P. Fernandez. O, B. Soto. P, J. M. Montealegre. Q, B. Carrillo. R, J. Jimenez.

1943. Air. Optd Legislacion Social 15 Setiembre 1943.

368	5col. black (No. 209)	4·50	3·00
369	10col. brown (No. 210)	5·50	3·25

142 San Ramon

143 Allegory of Flight

1944. Centenary of San Ramon.

370	**142**	5c. green (postage)	10	10
371	**142**	10c. orange	10	10
372	**142**	15c. red	30	10
373	**142**	40c. grey	1·20	65
374	**142**	50c. blue	2·20	1·20
375	**143**	10c. orange (air)	10	10
376	**143**	15c. red	10	10
377	**143**	40c. blue	40	10
378	**143**	45c. red	40	35
379	**143**	60c. green	55	40
380	**143**	1col. brown	1·40	85
381	**143**	1col.40 grey	8·75	5·50
382	**143**	5col. violet	24·00	16·00
383	**143**	10col. black	70·00	60·00

1944. Ratification of Costa Rica and Panama Boundary Treaty. Optd La entrevista ... 1944.

384	**139**	5c. orange	15	10
385	**139**	5c. green	15	10
386	**139**	5c. blue	15	10
387	**139**	5c. violet	15	10

1944. Air. No. 207 optd 1944.

388	1col. red	1·80	75

1945. Air. Official Air stamps of 1934 optd 1945 in oblong network frame.

389	**107**	5c. green	75	70
390	**107**	10c. red	75	75
391	**107**	15c. brown	75	75
392	**107**	20c. blue	55	50
393	**107**	25c. orange	75	75
394	**107**	40c. brown	45	45
395	**107**	50c. black	75	75
396	**107**	60c. yellow	1·40	1·20
397	**107**	75c. violet	1·10	1·00
398	-	1col. red (No. O220)	1·10	1·00
399	-	2col. blue (No. O221)	8·50	6·25
400	-	5col. black (No. O222)	9·50	8·50
401	-	10col. brown (No. O223)	15·00	11·50

1945. Air stamps. Telegraph stamps as Type 62 optd CORREO AEREO 1945 and bar.

402	**62**	40c. green	25	10
403	**62**	50c. blue	30	10
404	**62**	1col. orange	90	40

148 Mauro Fernandez

1945. Birth Centenary of Fernandez.

405	**148**	20c. green	30	10

149 Coffee Gathering

1945

406	**149**	5c. black and green	20	10
407	**149**	10c. black and orange	20	10
408	**149**	20c. black and red	40	15

150 Florence Nightingale and Nurse Cavell

1945. Air. 60th Anniv of National Red Cross Society.

409	**150**	1col. black	90	50

1946. Air. Central American and Caribbean Football Championship. As Type 132, but inscribed "FEBRERO 1946".

410	**132**	25c. green	1·10	65
411	**132**	30c. orange	1·10	65
412	**132**	55c. blue	1·40	65

1946. Surch 15 15.

413	**148**	15c. on 20c. green	25	10

152 San Juan de Dios Hospital

1946. Air. Centenary of San Juan de Dios Hospital.

414	**152**	5c. black and green	10	10
415	**152**	10c. black and brown	10	10
416	**152**	15c. black and red	10	10
417	**152**	25c. black and blue	10	10
418	**152**	30c. black and orange	45	25
419	**152**	40c. black and olive	10	10
420	**152**	50c. black and violet	35	25
421	**152**	60c. black and green	65	60
422	**152**	75c. black and brown	50	40
423	**152**	1col. black and blue	65	35
424	**152**	2col. black and brown	1·00	80
425	**152**	3col. black and purple	2·10	2·00
426	**152**	5col. black and yellow	2·50	2·50

153 Ascension Esquivel

1947. Air. Former Presidents.

427	-	2col. black and blue	1·60	1·20
428	**153**	3col. black and red	2·50	1·60
429	-	5col. black and green	4·00	2·10
430	-	10col. black and orange	7·00	5·25

PORTRAITS: 2col. Rafael Iglesias. 5col. Cleto Gonzalez Viquez. 10col. Ricardo Jimenez.

1947. No. O228 optd CORREOS 1947.

431	**57**	5c. green	10	10

1947. Air. Nos. 410/2 surch Habilitado para C 0.15 Decreto No. 16 de 28 abril de 1947.

432	**132**	15c. on 25c. green	1·00	80
433	**132**	15c. on 30c. orange	1·00	80
434	**132**	15c. on 55c. blue	1·00	80

156 Columbus at Cariari

1947. Air.

435	**156**	25c. black and green	25	10
436	**156**	30c. black and blue	30	10
437	**156**	40c. black and orange	40	10
438	**156**	45c. black and violet	55	15
439	**156**	50c. black and red	60	10
440	**156**	65c. black and brown	1·80	90

1947. Air. Stamps of 1942 surch C0.15.

441	**E**	15c. on 50c. orange	30	25
442	**F**	15c. on 60c. green	30	25
443	**O**	15c. on 75c. green	30	25
444	**P**	15c. on 1col. red	45	35
445	**Q**	15c. on 1col.5 sepia	30	25

158 Franklin D. Roosevelt

1947

446	**158**	5c. green (postage)	10	10
447	**158**	10c. red	10	10
448	**158**	15c. blue	15	10
449	**158**	25c. orange	30	25
450	**158**	30c. red	60	35
451	**158**	15c. green (air)	10	10
452	**158**	30c. red	10	10
453	**158**	45c. brown	10	10
454	**158**	65c. orange	25	10
455	**158**	75c. blue	35	10
456	**158**	1col. green	50	35
457	**158**	2col. black	1·40	1·10
458	**158**	5col. red	2·75	2·50

159 Miguel de Cervantes Saavedra

1947. 400th Birth Anniv of Cervantes.

459	**159**	30c. blue	45	10
460	**159**	55c. red	65	40

160 Steam Locomotive "Maria Cecilia"

1947. Air. 50th Anniv of Pacific Electric Railway.

461	**160**	35c. black and green	2·50	55

161 National Theatre

162 Rafael Iglesias

1948. Air. 50th Anniv of National Theatre.

462	**161**	15c. black and blue	20	10
463	**161**	20c. black and red	20	10
464	**162**	35c. black and green	40	10
465	**161**	45c. black and violet	45	15
466	**161**	50c. black and red	45	15
467	**161**	75c. black and purple	1·10	80
468	**161**	1col. black and green	2·10	1·10
469	**161**	2col. black and lake	3·25	1·60
470	**162**	5col. black and yellow	5·25	3·75
471	**162**	10col. black and blue	12·00	7·50

1948. Air. Surch HABILITADO PARA C 0.35.

472	**156**	35c. on 40c. blk & orge	1·20	50

1949. Air. 125th Anniv of Annexation of Guanacaste. Nos. 361, 409, 363 and 365 variously surch 1824-1949 125 Aniversario de la Anexion Guanacaste and value.

473	**Q**	35c. on 1col. 5 sepia	30	10
474	**150**	50c. on 1col. black	50	40
475	**R**	55c. on 1col.15 green	65	55
476	**B**	55c. on 1col.40 yellow	70	50

165 Globe and Dove

1950. Air. 75th Anniv of UPU (1949).

477	**165**	15c. red	10	10
478	**165**	25c. blue	30	30
479	**165**	1col. green	50	40

166 Battle of El Tejar, Cartago

167 Capture of Limon

1950. Air. Inscr "GUERRA DE LIBERACION NACIONAL 1948".

480	**166**	15c. black and red	10	10
481	**167**	20c. black and green	10	10
482	-	25c. black and blue	30	10
483	-	35c. black and brown	35	10
484	-	55c. black and violet	65	10
485	-	75c. black and orange	1·10	35
486	-	80c. black and grey	1·10	50
487	-	1col. black and orange	1·50	60

DESIGNS—VERT: 80c., 1col. Dr. C. L. Valverde. HORIZ: 25c. La Lucha Ranch; 35c. Trench of San Isidro Battalion; 55c., 75c. Observation post.

169 Bull

1950. Air. National Agriculture and Industries Fair. Centres in black.

488	**169**	1c. green	20	20
489	**A**	2c. blue	20	20
490	**B**	3c. brown	20	20
491	**C**	5c. blue	20	20
492	**169**	10c. green	20	20
493	**A**	30c. violet	20	20
494	**D**	45c. orange	20	20
495	**C**	50c. grey	40	20
496	**B**	65c. blue	40	20
497	**D**	80c. red	90	65
498	**169**	2col. orange	2·50	1·70
499	**A**	3col. blue	6·00	4·25
500	**C**	5col. red	7·75	6·50
501	**D**	10col. red	7·75	6·50

DESIGNS—VERT: A, Fishing; B, Pineapple; C, Bananas; D, Coffee.

170 Queen Isabella and Caravels

1952. Air. 500th Anniv of Isabella the Catholic.

502	**170**	15c. red	25	10
503	**170**	20c. orange	50	10
504	**170**	25c. blue	75	10
505	**170**	55c. green	2·50	25
506	**170**	2col. violet	4·75	50

1953. Air. Surch 15 15 within ornaments.

513	**158**	15c. on 30c. red	30	10
514	**158**	15c. on 45c. brown	30	10
515	**158**	15c. on 65c. orange	30	10

1953. Air. Surch HABILITADO PARA CINCO CENTIMOS 1953.

515a	**155**	5c. on 30c. blk & blue	1·50	1·30
516	**155**	5c. on 40c. blk & orge	25	25
517	**155**	5c. on 45c. blk & vio	25	25
518	**155**	5c. on 65c. blk & brn	25	25

173

1953. Fiscal stamps surch as in T 173.

519	**173**	5c. on 10c. green	25	10

174 "Vegetable Oil"

1954. Air. National Industries. Centres in black.

520		5c. red (Type **174**)	15	10
520a		5c. blue (Type **174**)	25	10
521		10c. indigo (Pottery)	20	10
521a		10c. blue (Pottery)	25	10
522		15c. green (Sugar)	15	10
522a		15c. yellow (Sugar)	25	10
523		20c. violet (Soap)	15	10
524		25c. lake (Timber)	20	10
525		30c. lilac (Matches)	55	40
526		35c. purple (Textiles)	25	15
527		40c. black (Leather)	55	35
528		45c. green (Tobacco)	1·00	40
529		50c. purple (Confectionery)	65	15
530		55c. yellow (Canning)	50	15
531		60c. brown (General industries)	1·20	65
532		65c. red (Metals)	1·50	95
533		75c. violet (Pharmaceutics)	2·20	80
533a		75c. red (as No. 533)	50	35
533b		80c. violet (as No. 533)	1·00	80
534		1col. turq (Paper)	65	40
535		2col. mauve (Rubber)	2·10	1·20
536		3col. green (Aircraft)	3·00	1·90
537		5col. black (Marble)	4·50	1·50
538		10col. yellow (Beer)	13·00	9·50

(175)

1955. Fiscal stamps optd for postal use as in T 175.

539	**175**	5c. on 2c. green	15	10
540	**175**	15c. on 2c. green	20	10

176 Rotary Emblem over Central America

1956. Air. 50th Anniv Rotary International.

542	**176**	10c. green	10	10
543	-	25c. blue	10	10
544	-	40c. brown	45	35
545	-	45c. red	30	20
546	-	60c. purple	40	30
547	-	2col. orange	1·10	60

DESIGNS: 25c. Emblem, hand and boy; 40c., 2col. Emblem and hospital; 45c. Emblem, leaves and Central America; 60c. Emblem and lighthouse.

177 Map of Costa Rica

1957. Air. Centenary of War of 1856–67.

548	**177**	5c. blue	20	20
549	-	10c. green	20	20
550	-	15c. orange	20	20
551	-	20c. brown	30	20
552	-	25c. blue	30	20
553	-	30c. violet	45	20
554	-	35c. red	45	20
555	-	40c. black	45	20
556	-	45c. red	50	20
557	-	50c. blue	55	20
558	-	55c. ochre	1·10	20
559	-	60c. red	80	30
560	-	65c. red	1·00	30
561	-	70c. yellow	1·20	35
562	-	75c. green	1·10	35
563	-	80c. sepia	1·30	40
564	-	1col. black	1·50	40

DESIGNS: 10c. Map of Guanacaste; 15c. Wartime inn; 20c. Santa Rosa house; 25c. Gen. D. J. M. Quiros; 30c. Old Presidential Palace; 35c. Minister D. J. B. Calvo; 40c. Dr. Luis Molina; 45c. Gen. D. J. J. Mora; 50c. Gen. D. J. M. Canas; 55c. Juan Santamaria Monument; 60c. National Monument; 65c. A. Vallerriestra; 70c. Pres. R. Castilla Marquesado of Peru; 75c. San Carlos Fortress; 80c. Vice-President D. F. M. Oreamuno of Costa Rica; 1col. Pres. D. J. R. Mora of Costa Rica.

1958. Obligatory Tax. Christmas. Nos. 489 and 521a surch SELLO DE NAVIDAD PRO - CIUDAD DE LOS NINOS 5 5.

565	**A**	5c. on 2c. black & blue	20	20
566	-	5c. on 10c. black & blue	40	20

179 Pres. Gonzalez Viquez

180 Pres. R. J. Oreamuno and Electric Locomotive No. 31

1959. Air. Birth Centenaries of Presidents Gonzalez (1958) and Oreamuno (1959).

567	**179**	5c. blue and pink	15	10
568	-	10c. slate and red	15	10
569	-	15c. black and slate	15	10
570	-	20c. brown and red	40	10
571	-	35c. blue and purple	15	10
572	-	55c. violet and brown	40	15
573	-	80c. blue	50	40
574	**180**	1col. lake and orange	80	50
575	-	2col. lake and black	1·80	1·50

DESIGNS—As Type **179**: 10c. Pres. Oreamuno. As Type **180**: Pres. Gonzalez and: 15c. Highway bridge; 55c. Water pipe-line; 80c. National Library. Pres. Oreamuno and: 20c. Puntarenas Quay; 35c. Post Office, San Jose. 2col. Both presidents and open book inscr "PROBIDAD" ("Honesty").

181 Father Flanagan

1959. Obligatory Tax. Christmas. Inscr "SELLO DE NAVIDAD".

576	**181**	5c. green	55	20
577	-	5c. mauve	55	20
578	-	5c. olive	55	20
579	-	5c. black	55	20

PAINTINGS: No. 577, "Girl with braids" (after Modigliani). No. 578, "Boy with a clubfoot" (after Ribera). No. 579, "The boy blowing on charcoal" (after "El Greco").

182 Goal Attack

1960. Air. 3rd Pan-American Football Games.

580	**182**	10c. blue	25	25
581	-	25c. blue	25	25
582	-	35c. red	30	30
583	-	50c. brown	40	30
584	-	85c. turquoise	1·00	80
585	-	5col. purple	2·30	2·30
MS585a		139×80 mm. 2col. blue (as 35c.). Imperf	5·00	5·00

DESIGNS: 25c. Player heading ball; 35c. Defender tackling forward; 50c. Referee bouncing ball; 85c. Goalkeeper seizing ball; 5col. Player kicking high ball.

183 "Uprooted Tree"

1960. Air. World Refugee Year.

586	**183**	35c. blue and yellow	35	25
587	**183**	85c. black and pink	65	55

184 Prof. J. A. Facio

1960. Birth Centenary of Professor Justo A. Facio.

588	**184**	10c. red	20	20

185 "OEA" and Banner

1960. Air. 6th and 7th Chancellors' Reunion Conference, Organization of American States, San Jose. Multicoloured.

589		25c. Type **185**	15	15
590		35c. "OEA" within oval chains	35	35
591		55c. Clasped hands and chains	50	40
592		5col. Flags in form of flying bird	3·25	3·00
593		10col. "OEA" on map of Costa Rica, and flags	5·25	4·50
MS593a		124×76 mm. 2col. "OEA" and map of Americas. Imperf	3·00	3·00

186 St. Louise de Marillac, Sister of Charity and Children

1960. Air. 300th Death Anniv of St. Vincent de Paul.

594	**186**	10c. green	20	20
595	-	25c. lake	20	20
596	-	50c. blue	20	20
597	-	1col. bistre	40	35
598	-	5col. sepia	2·20	1·70

DESIGNS—HORIZ: St. Vincent de Paul, and: 25c. Two-storey building; 1col. Modern building; 50c. As Type **186**, but scene shows Sister at bedside. VERT: 5col. Stained-glass window picturing St. Vincent de Paul with children.

187 Father Peralta

1960. Obligatory Tax. Christmas. Inscr "SELLO DE NAVIDAD".

599	**187**	5c. brown	50	20
600	-	5c. orange	50	20
601	-	5c. red	50	20
602	-	5c. blue	50	20

DESIGNS: No. 600, "Girl" (after Renoir); No. 601, "The Drinkers" (after Velasquez); No. 602, "Children Singing" (sculpture, after Zuniga).

188 Running

1960. Air. Olympics Game, Rome. Centres and inscriptions in black.

603		1c. yellow (T **188**)	10	10
604		2c. blue (Diving)	10	10
605		3c. red (Cycling)	10	10
606		4c. yellow (Weightlifting)	20	10
607		5c. green (Tennis)	20	10
608		10c. red (Boxing)	20	10
609		25c. turquoise (Football)	20	10

610		85c. mauve (Basketball)	1·20	80
611		1col. grey (Baseball)	1·40	1·10
612		10col. lavender (Pistol-shooting)	11·00	8·00
MS612a		100×65 mm. 5col. multicoloured (27×27 mm) (Romulus and Remus statue)	6·00	6·00

1961. Air. 15th World Amateur Baseball Championships. No. 533a optd XV Campeonato Mundial de Beisbol de Aficionados or surch also.

613		25c. on 75c. black and red	25	15
614		75c. black and red	60	15

190 M. Aguilar

1961. Air. 1st Continental Lawyers' Conference.

615	**190**	10c. blue	25	20
616	-	10c. purple	25	20
617	-	25c. violet	25	20
618	-	25c. sepia	25	20

PORTRAITS: No. 616, A. Brenes. No. 617, A. Gutierrez. No. 618, V. Herrera.

See also Nos. 628/31.

191 Prof. M. Obregon

1961. Air. Birth Centenary of Obregon.

619	**191**	10c. turquoise	30	20

192 Granary (FAO)

1961. Air. United Nations Commemoration.

620	**192**	10c. green	10	10
621	-	20c. orange	10	10
622	-	25c. slate	10	10
623	-	30c. blue	10	10
624	-	35c. red	90	20
625	-	45c. violet	35	15
626	-	85c. blue	70	55
627	-	10col. black	5·25	4·50
MS627a		100×65 mm. 5col. blue	3·25	3·25

DESIGNS: 20c. "Medical Care" (WHO); 25c. Globe and workers (ILO); 30c. Globe and communications satellite "Correo 1B" (ITU); 35c. Compass and rocket (WMO); 45c. "The Thinker" (statue) and open book (UNESCO); 85c. Douglas DC-6 airliner and globe (ICAO); 5col. "United Nations covering the world"; 10col. "Spiderman" on girder (International Bank).

1961. Air. 9th Central American Medical Congress. As T 190 but inscr "NOVENO CONGRESO MEDICO", etc.

628		10c. violet	20	15
629		10c. turquoise	20	15
630		25c. sepia	25	15
631		25c. purple	25	15

PORTRAITS: No. 628, Dr. E. J. Roman. No. 629, Dr. J. M. S. Alfaro. No. 630, Dr. A. S. Llorente. No. 631, Dr. J. J. U. Giralt.

1961. Obligatory Tax. Children's City Christmas issue. No. 522 surch SELLO DE NAVIDAD PRO-CIUDAD DE LOS NINOS 5 5.

632		5c. on 10c. black and green	35	20

1962. Air. Surch in figures.

633		10c. on 15c. black and green (No. 522)	15	10
634		25c. on 15c. black and green (No. 522)	15	15
635		35c. on 50c. black and purple (No. 529)	30	15
636		85c. on 80c. blue (No. 573)	90	75

1962. Air. 2nd Central American Philatelic Convention. Optd II CONVENCION FILATELICA CENTROAMERICANA SETIEMBRE 1962.

637		30c. blue (No. 623)	55	40
638		2col. red and black (No. 575)	1·60	1·20

1962. Air. No. 522 surch C 0.10.

639		10c. on 15c. black & green	15	15

1962. Air. Fiscal stamps as T 175 optd CORREO AEREO and surch with new value for postal use.

640		25c. on 2c. green	10	10
641		35c. on 2c. green	15	15
642		45c. on 2c. green	35	25
643		85c. on 2c. green	65	50

198 "Virgin and Child" (after Bellini)

1962. Obligatory Tax. Christmas.

644	**198**	5c. sepia	65	20
645	**A**	5c. green	65	20
646	**B**	5c. blue	65	20
647	**C**	5c. red	65	20

DESIGNS: A, "Angel with Violin" (after Mellozo); B, Mgr. Ruben Odio; C, "Child's Head" (after Rubens).

See also Nos. 674/7.

199 Jaguar

1963. Air.

648	-	5c. brown and olive	25	15
649	-	10c. blue and orange	25	15
650	**199**	25c. yellow and blue	40	15
651	-	30c. brown and green	65	40
652	-	35c. brown and bistre	1·00	40
653	-	40c. blue and green	1·20	55
654	-	85c. black and green	3·75	55
655	-	5col. brown and green	11·50	4·00

ANIMALS (As Type **199**): 5c. Paca. 10c. Bairds tapir. 30c. Ocelot. 35c. White-tailed deer. 40c. American manatee. 85c. White-throated capuchin. 5col. White-lipped peccary.

200 Arms and Campaign Emblem

1963. Air. Malaria Eradication.

656	**200**	25c. red	15	10
657	**200**	35c. brown	25	15
658	**200**	45c. blue	35	25
659	**200**	85c. green	65	45
660	**200**	1col. blue	1·10	60

1963. Obligatory Tax Fund for Children's Village. Nos. 644/7 surch 1963 10 CENTIMOS.

661	**198**	10c. on 5c. sepia	40	20
662	**A**	10c. on 5c. green	40	20
663	**B**	10c. on 5c. blue	40	20
664	**C**	10c. on 5c. red	40	20

202 Anglo-Costa Rican Bank

1963. Anglo-Costa Rican Bank Centenary.

665	**202**	10c. blue	20	20

203 ½ real Stamp of 1863 and Sail Merchantman "William le Lacheur"

1963. Air. Stamp Centenary.

666	**203**	25c. blue and purple	15	10
667	-	2col. orange and grey	1·80	1·30
668	-	3col. green and ochre	3·00	2·10
669	-	10col. brown and green	10·50	6·00
MS669a		60×100 mm. 5col. blue, brown, green and light brown. Perf or imperf	4·50	4·50

DESIGNS: 2col. 2 reales stamp of 1863 and Postmaster-General R. B. Carrillo; 3col. 4 reales stamp of 1863 and mounted postman and pack-mule of 1839; 5col. ½ real, 2 reales, 4 reales, and 1 pesco stamp of 1863 (as in Nos. 666/9); 10col. 1 peso stamp of 1863 and mule-drawn mail van.

1963. Unissued animal designs as T 199. Surch.

670		10c. on 1c. brown and green	1·10	30
671		25c. on 2c. sepia and brown	1·10	30
672		35c. on 3c. brown and green	1·50	30
673		85c. on 4c. brown and lake	2·75	60

ANIMALS: 1c. Tamandua. 2c. Grey fox. 3c. Nine-banded armadillo. 4c. Giant anteater.

1963. Obligatory Tax. Christmas. As Nos. 644/7 but inscr "1963" and new colours.

674	**198**	5c. blue	45	20
675	**A**	5c. red	45	20
676	**B**	5c. black	45	20
677	**C**	5c. sepia	45	20

205 Pres. Orlich (Costa Rica)

1963. Air. Presidential Reunion, San Jose. Portraits in sepia.

678	**205**	25c. purple	25	20
679	-	30c. mauve	25	20
680	-	35c. ochre	25	20
681	-	85c. blue	45	20
682	-	1col. brown	50	30
683	-	3col. green	2·30	1·60
684	-	5col. slate	3·00	2·30

PRESIDENTS: 30c. Rivera (Salvador). 35c. Ydigoras (Guatemala). 85c. Villeda (Honduras). 1col. Somoza (Nicaragua). 3col. Chiari (Panama). 5col. Kennedy (U.S.A.).

206 Puma (clay statuette)

1963. Air. Archaeological Discoveries.

685	**206**	5c. turquoise and green	20	20
686	-	10c. turquoise and yellow	20	20
687	-	25c. sepia and red	20	20
688	-	30c. turquoise and buff	25	20
689	-	35c. green and salmon	25	20
690	-	45c. brown and blue	25	20
691	-	50c. brown and blue	40	20
692	-	55c. brown and green	55	20
693	-	75c. brown and buff	55	20
694	-	85c. brown and yellow	1·40	1·40
695	-	90c. brown and yellow	1·80	1·80
696	-	1col. brown and blue	1·10	35
697	-	2col. turquoise & yellow	1·60	65
698	-	3col. brown and green	5·50	1·00
699	-	5col. brown & yellow	5·50	5·50
700	-	10col. green and mauve	9·00	9·00

DESIGNS—HORIZ: 10c. Ceremonial stool; 1col. Twin beakers; 2col. Alligator. VERT: 25c. Man (statuette); 30c. Dancer; 35c. Vase; 45c. Deity; 50c. Frog; 55c. "Eagle" bell; 75c. Multi-limbed deity; 85c. Kneeling effigy; 90c. "Bird" jug; 3col. Twin-tailed lizard; 5col. Child; 10col. Stone effigy of woman.

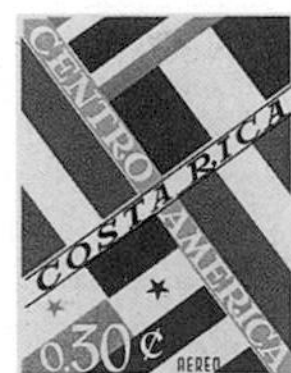

207 Flags

1964. Air. "Centro America".

701	**207**	30c. multicoloured	80	25

1964. Air. Surch.

702	-	5c. on 30c. (No. 688)	55	25
703	**207**	15c. on 30c.	55	25
704	-	15c. on 85c. (No. 694)	55	25

See Nos. 745/9.

1964. Paris Postal Conf. No. 695 surch C 0.15 CONFERENCIA POSTAL DE PARIS - 1864.

705		15c. on 90c. brn & yellow	25	20

210 Mgr. R. Odio and Children

1964. Obligatory Tax. Christmas. Inscr "SELLO DE NAVIDAD", etc.

706	**210**	5c. brown	40	20
707	**A**	5c. blue	40	20
708	**B**	5c. purple	40	20
709	**C**	5c. green	40	20

DESIGNS: A, Teacher and child; B, Children at play; C, Children in class.

211 A. Gonzalez F.

1965. Air. 50th Anniv of National Bank.

710	**211**	35c. green	3·25	25

1965. Air. 75th Anniv of Chapui Hospital. No. 697 surch 75 ANIVERSARIO ASILO CHAPUI 1890–1965.

711		2col. turquoise and yellow	1·40	75

213 Handfuls of Grain

1965. Air. Freedom from Hunger.

712	-	15c. black, grey & brown	25	20
713	**213**	35c. black and buff	25	20
714	-	50c. green and blue	25	20
715	-	1col. silver, black & green	40	25

DESIGNS—HORIZ: 15c. Map and grain silo; 1col. Douglas DC-8 airliner over map. VERT: 50c. Children and population graph.

214 National Children's Hospital

1965. Christmas Charity. Obligatory Tax. Inscr "SELLO DE NAVIDAD", etc.

716	**214**	5c. green	25	20
717	**A**	5c. brown	25	20
718	**B**	5c. red	25	20
719	**C**	5c. blue	25	20

DESIGNS—As Type **214**: A, Father Casiano; B, Poinsettia. DIAMOND: C, Father Christmas with children.

215 L. Briceno B.

1965. Air. Incorporation of Nicoya District.

720	**215**	5c. slate, black & brown	40	20
721	-	10c. slate and blue	40	20
722	-	15c. slate and bistre	40	20
723	-	35c. slate and blue	40	20
724	-	50c. violet and grey	55	20
725	-	1col. slate and ochre	1·20	40

DESIGNS: 10c. Nicoya Church; 15c. Incorporation scroll; 35c. Map of Guanacaste Province; 50c. Provincial dance; 1col. Guanacaste map and produce.

216 Running

1965. Air. Olympic Games (1964). Mult.

No.	Type	Description	Mint	Used
726		5c. Type **216**	15	15
727		10c. Cycling	15	15
728		40c. Judo	15	15
729		65c. Handball	25	15
730		80c. Football	40	15
731		1col. Olympic torches	50	35
MS731a		68×95 mm. No. 731 (×2) in different colours. Perf or imperf	3·25	3·25

217 Pres. John F. Kennedy and "Mercury" Space Capsule encircling Globe

1965. Air. 2nd Death Anniv of Pres. Kennedy. Multicoloured.

No.	Type	Description	Mint	Used
732		45c. Type **217**	25	15
733		55c. Kennedy in San Jose Cathedral (vert)	35	20
734		85c. President with son (vert)	55	40
735		1col. Facade of White House, Washington (vert)	65	45
MS735a		68×94 mm. No. 735 (×2) in different colours. Perf or imperf	1·20	1·20

218 Fire Engine

1966. Air. Centenary of Fire Brigade.

No.	Type	Description	Mint	Used
736	**218**	5c. red and black	35	15
737	-	10c. red and yellow	40	15
738	-	15c. black and red	60	15
739	-	35c. yellow and black	1·00	25
740	-	50c. red and blue	2·10	45

DESIGNS—VERT: 10c. Fire engine of 1866; 15c. Firemen with hoses; 35c. Brigade badge; 50c. Emblem of Central American Fire Brigades Confederation.

219 Angel

1966. Obligatory Tax. Christmas. Inscr "SELLO DE NAVIDAD", etc.

No.	Type	Description	Mint	Used
741	**219**	5c. blue	25	20
742	-	5c. red (Trinkets)	25	20
743	-	5c. green (Church)	25	20
744	-	5c. brown (Reindeer)	25	20

1966. Air. (a) Surch with new value.

No.	Type	Description	Mint	Used
745		15c. on 30c. (No. 688)	15	15
746		15c. on 45c. (No. 690)	15	15
747		35c. on 75c. (No. 693)	20	15
748		35c. on 55c. (No. 733)	20	15
749		50c. on 85c. (No. 734)	40	15

(b) Revenue stamps (as T 175) surch CORREOS DE COSTA RICA AEREO and value.

No.	Type	Description	Mint	Used
750		15c. on 5c. blue	15	10
751		35c. on 10c. red	25	15
752		50c. on 20c. red	40	25

1967. Obligatory Tax. Social Plan for Postal Workers.

No.	Type	Description	Mint	Used
753		10c. blue	25	20

DESIGN—as Type **220**a (34×26 mm.): 10c. Post Office, San Jose.

221 Central Bank, San Jose

1967. Air. 50th Anniv of Central Bank.

No.	Type	Description	Mint	Used
754	**221**	5c. green	25	20
755	**221**	15c. brown	25	20
756	**221**	35c. red	25	20

222 Telecommunications Building, San Pedro

1967. Air. Costa Rican Electrical Industry.

No.	Type	Description	Mint	Used
757	-	5c. black	25	20
758	**222**	10c. mauve	25	20
759	-	15c. orange	25	20
760	-	25c. blue	25	20
761	-	35c. green	25	20
762	-	50c. brown	35	25

DESIGNS—VERT: 5c. Electric pylons; 15c. Central Telephone Exchange, San Jose. HORIZ: 25c. La Garita Dam; 35c. Rio Macho Reservoir; 50c. Cachi Dam.

223 "Chondrorhyncha aromatica"

1967. Air. University Library. Orchids. Mult.

No.	Type	Description	Mint	Used
763		5c. Type **223**	10	10
764		10c. "Miltonia endresii"	40	25
765		15c. "Stanhopea cirrhata"	40	25
766		25c. "Trichopilia suavis"	85	25
767		35c. "Odontoglossum schliepe-rianum"	85	25
768		50c. "Cattleya skinneri"	1·10	25
769		1col. "Cattleya dowiana"	3·00	80
770		2col. "Odontoglossum chir-iquense"	4·50	1·50

224 OEA Emblem and Split Leaf

1967. Air. 25th Anniv of Inter-American Institute of Agricultural Science.

No.	Type	Description	Mint	Used
771	**224**	50c. ultramarine & blue	25	15

225 Madonna and Child

1967. Obligatory Tax. Christmas.

No.	Type	Description	Mint	Used
772	**225**	5c. green	25	20
773	**225**	5c. mauve	25	20
774	**225**	5c. blue	25	20
775	**225**	5c. turquoise	25	20

226 LACSA Emblem

1967. Air. 20th Anniv (1966) of LACSA (Costa Rican Airlines). Multicoloured.

No.	Type	Description	Mint	Used
776		40c. Type **226**	20	15
777		45c. LACSA emblem and jetliner (horiz)	25	15
778		50c. Wheel and emblem	25	20

227 Church of Solitude

1967. Air. Churches and Cathedrals (1st series).

No.	Type	Description	Mint	Used
779	**227**	5c. green	10	10
780	-	10c. blue	10	10
781	-	15c. purple	10	10
782	-	25c. ochre	10	10
783	-	30c. brown	10	10
784	-	35c. blue	25	10
785	-	40c. orange	25	10
786	-	45c. green	25	10
787	-	50c. olive	35	10
788	-	55c. brown	35	10
789	-	65c. mauve	60	25
790	-	75c. sepia	65	35
791	-	80c. yellow	1·20	40
792	-	85c. purple	1·40	40
793	-	90c. green	1·40	65
794	-	1col. slate	1·10	35
795	-	2col. green	5·25	1·80
796	-	3col. orange	7·50	3·00
797	-	5col. blue	7·50	3·00
798	-	10col. red	9·25	4·50

DESIGNS: 10c. Santo Domingo Basilica, Heredia; 15c. Tilaran Cathedral; 25c. Alajuela Cathedral; 30c. Church of Mercy; 35c. Our Lady of the Angels Basilica; 40c. San Rafael Church, Heredia; 45c. Ruins, Ujarras; 50c. Ruins of Parish Church, Cartago; 55c. San Jose Cathedral; 65c. Parish Church, Puntarenas; 75c. Orosi Church; 80c. Cathedral of San Isidro the General; 85c. San Ramon Church; 90c. Church of the Forsaken; 1col. Coronado Church; 2col. Church of St. Teresita; 3col. Parish Church, Heredia; 5col. Carmelite Church; 10col. Limon Cathedral.

See also Nos. 918/33.

228 Scouts in Camp

1968. Air. Golden Jubilee (1966) of Scout Movement in Costa Rica. Multicoloured.

No.	Type	Description	Mint	Used
799		15c. Scout on traffic control (vert)	15	10
800		25c. Scouts tending campfire (vert)	25	15
801		35c. Scout badge and flags (vert)	40	20
802		50c. Type **228**	65	35
803		65c. First scout troop on parade (1916)	80	40

1968. Air. 3rd National Philatelic Exhibition, San Jose. Sheet No. MS669a optd III EXPOSICION FILATELICA NACIONAL 2-4 AGOSTO 1968 COSTA RICA 68 in three lines.

No.	Type	Description	Mint	Used
MS804		60×100 mm. 5col. blue, brown, green and light brown. Perf or imperf	13·50	13·50

229 "Madonna and Child"

1968. Christmas Charity. Obligatory Tax.

No.	Type	Description	Mint	Used
805	**229**	5c. black	25	20
806	**229**	5c. purple	25	20
807	**229**	5c. brown	25	20
808	**229**	5c. red	25	20

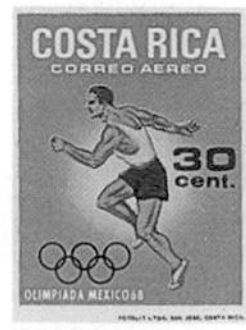

230 Running

1969. Air. Olympic Games, Mexico. Mult.

No.	Type	Description	Mint	Used
809		30c. Type **230**	10	10
810		40c. Woman breasting tape	10	10
811		55c. Boxing	25	15
812		65c. Cycling	35	15
813		75c. Weightlifting	35	15
814		1col. High-diving	40	25
815		3col. Rifle-shooting	1·60	1·00

231 Exhibition Emblem

1969. Air. "Costa Rica 69" Philatelic Exn.

No.	Type	Description	Mint	Used
816	**231**	35c. multicoloured	15	10
817	**231**	40c. multicoloured	15	10
818	**231**	50c. multicoloured	25	15
819	**231**	2col. multicoloured	1·00	55

232 Arms of San Jose

1969. Coats of Arms. Multicoloured.

No.	Type	Description	Mint	Used
820		15c. Type **232**	30	10
821		35c. Cartago	30	10
822		50c. Heredia	35	10
823		55c. Alajuela	35	10
824		65c. Guanacaste	55	25
825		1col. Puntarenas	3·50	35
826		2col. Limon	4·00	55

233 ILO Emblem

1969. Air. 50th Anniv of ILO.

No.	Type	Description	Mint	Used
827	**233**	35c. turquoise and black	25	10
828	**233**	50c. red and black	25	15

234 Map on Football

1969. Air. 4th CONCACAF Football Championships. Multicoloured.

No.	Type	Description	Mint	Used
829		65c. Type **234**	35	15
830		75c. Goalmouth melee	35	20
831		85c. Players with ball	40	35
832		1col. Two players with ball	55	40

235 Madonna and Child

1969. Christmas. Charity. Obligatory Tax.

No.	Type	Description	Mint	Used
833	**235**	5c. turquoise	25	20
834	**235**	5c. lake	25	20
835	**235**	5c. blue	25	20
836	**235**	5c. orange	25	20

236 Stylized Crab

1970. Air. 10th Inter-American Cancer Congress, San Jose.

No.	Type	Description	Mint	Used
837	**236**	10c. black and mauve	25	20
838	**236**	15c. black and yellow	25	20
839	**236**	50c. black and orange	25	20
840	**236**	1col.10 black and green	55	20

238 Costa Rican stamps and Magnifier

1970. Air. "Costa Rica 70" Philatelic Exhibition.

843	**238**	1col. red and blue	1·10	20
844	**238**	2col. mauve and blue	1·20	55

239 Japanese Vase and Flowers

1970. Air. Expo 70. Multicoloured.

845	10c. Type **239**	10	10
846	15c. Ornamental cart (horiz)	10	10
847	35c. Sun tower (horiz)	40	10
848	40c. Tea-ceremony (horiz)	50	10
849	45c. Coffee-picking	50	10
850	55c. View of Earth from Moon	50	10

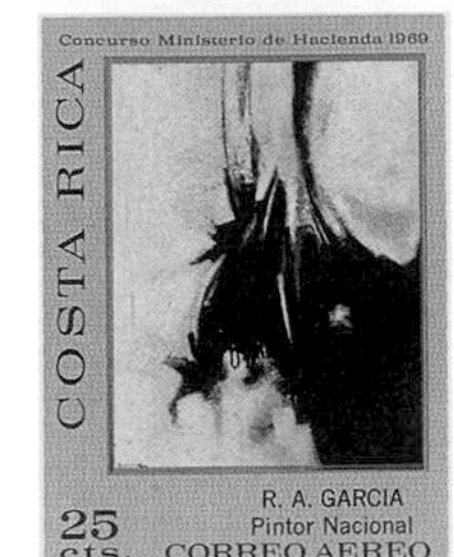

240 "Irazu" (R. A. Garcia)

1970. Air. Costa Rican Paintings. Mult.

851	25c. Type **240**	80	35
852	45c. "Escazu Valley" (M. Bertheau)	80	35
853	80c. "Estuary Landscape" (T. Quiros)	1·30	60
854	1col. "The Other Face" (C. Valverde)	1·30	65
855	2col.50 "Madonna" (L. Daell) (vert)	2·75	2·10

241 "Holy Child"

1970. Christmas Charity. Obligatory Tax.

856	**241**	5c. mauve	35	20
857	**241**	5c. brown	35	20
858	**241**	5c. olive	35	20
859	**241**	5c. violet	35	20

242 Costa Rican Arms of 21 October 1964

1971. Air. Various Costa Rican Coats of Arms (with dates). Multicoloured.

860	5c. Type **242**	40	20
861	10c. 27 November 1906	40	20
862	15c. 29 September 1848	50	20
863	25c. 21 April 1840	50	20
864	35c. 22 November 1824	65	20
865	50c. 2 November 1824	75	20
866	1col. 6 March 1824	80	30
867	2col. 10 May 1823	1·60	85

243 National Theatre, San Jose

1971. Air. OEA General Assembly. San Jose.

868	**243**	2col. purple	40	35

244 J. M. Delgado and M. J. Arce (Salvador)

1971. Air. 150th Anniv of Central American Independence. Multicoloured.

869	5c. Type **244**	20	20
870	10c. M. Larreinaga and M. A. de la Cerda (Nicaragua)	20	20
871	15c. J. C. del Valle and D. de Herrera (Honduras)	20	20
872	35c. P. Alvarado and F. del Castillo (Costa Rica)	20	20
873	50c. A. Larrazabal and P. Molina (Guatemala)	20	20
874	1col. ODECA flag (vert)	20	20
875	2col. ODECA emblem (vert)	40	40

ODECA = Organization of Central American States.

245 Cradle on "PAX"

1971. Christmas Charity. Obligatory Tax.

876	**245**	10c. orange	25	20
877	**245**	10c. brown	25	20
878	**245**	10c. green	25	20
879	**245**	10c. blue	25	20

246 Federation Emblem

1971. Air. 50th Anniv of Costa Rican Football Federation.

880	**246**	50c. multicoloured	35	20
881	**246**	60c. multicoloured	35	20

247 "Children of the World"

1972. Air. 25th Anniv of UNICEF.

882	**247**	50c. multicoloured	25	15
883	**247**	1col.10 multicoloured	40	25

248 Guanacaste Tree

1972. Air. Bicentenary of Liberia City.

884	**348**	green, brown and emerald	40	20
885	–	brown and green	40	20
886	–	brown and black	40	20
887	–	Scarlet, black and buff	40	20

DESIGNS;— HORIZ: 40c. Hermitage, Liberia; 55c. Rincon Brujo Petroglyphs. VERT: 60c. Painted head sculpture.

250 Farmer's Family and Farm

1972. Air. 30th Anniv of OEA Institute of Agricultural Sciences (IICA).

892	**250**	20c. multicoloured	35	20
893	-	45c. multicoloured	35	20
894	-	50c. yellow, green & blk	35	20
895	-	10col. multicoloured	2·75	1·80

DESIGNS—HORIZ: 45c. Cattle. VERT: 50c. Tree-planting; 10col. Agricultural worker and map.

251 Inter-American Stamp Exhibitions

1972. Air. "Exfilbra 72" Stamp Exhibition.

896	**251**	50c. brown and orange	15	15
897	**251**	2col. violet and blue	40	35

252 Madonna and Child

1972. Christmas Charity. Obligatory Tax.

898	**252**	10c. red	25	20
899	**252**	10c. lilac	25	20
900	**252**	10c. blue	25	20
901	**252**	10c. green	25	20

253 First Book printed in Costa Rica

1972. Air. International Book Year. Mult.

902	20c. Type **253**	40	20
903	50c. National Library, San Jose (horiz)	40	20
904	75c. Type **253**	40	20
905	5col. As 50c.	2·00	1·00

254 View near Irazu

1972. Air. American Tourist Year. Mult.

906	5c. Type **254**	35	20
907	15c. Entrance to Culebra Bay	35	20
908	20c. Type **254**	35	20
909	25c. As 15c.	35	20
910	40c. Manuel Antonio Beach	35	20
911	45c. Costa Rican Tourist Institute emblem	35	20
912	50c. Lindora Lake	35	20
913	60c. Post Office Building, San Jose (vert)	35	20
914	80c. As 40c.	40	20
915	90c. As 45c.	40	20
916	1col. As 50c.	40	20
917	2col. As 60c.	75	50

1973. Air. Churches and Cathedrals (2nd series). As Nos. 779/94 but colours changed.

918	**227**	5c. grey	20	20
919	-	10c. green	20	20
920	-	15c. orange	20	20
921	-	25c. brown	20	20
922	-	30c. purple	20	20
923	-	35c. violet	20	20
924	-	40c. green	20	20
925	-	45c. brown	20	20
926	-	50c. red	20	20
927	-	55c. blue	25	20
928	-	65c. black	30	20
929	-	75c. red	30	20
930	-	80c. green	30	20
931	-	85c. lilac	35	25
932	-	90c. red	35	25
933	-	1col. blue	35	25

255 Madonna and Child

1973. Obligatory Tax. Christmas Charity.

934	**255**	10c. red	25	20
935	**255**	10c. purple	25	20
936	**255**	10c. black	25	20
937	**255**	10c. brown	25	20

256 Flame Emblem

1973. Air. 25th Anniv of Declaration of Human Rights.

938	**256**	50c. red and blue	25	20

257 OEA Emblem

1973. Air. 25th Anniv of Organization of American States.

939	**257**	20c. red and blue	25	20

258 J. Vargas Calvo

1974. Air. Costa Rican Composers. Mult.

940	20c. Type **258**	40	20
941	20c. Alejandro Monestel	40	20
942	20c. Julio Mata	40	20
943	60c. Julio Fonseca	40	20
944	2col. Rafael Chaves	90	35
945	5col. Manuel Gutierrez	2·10	1·20

1974. Air. Fiscal stamps as Type 175 (but without surcharge) optd HABILITADO PARA CORREO AEREO.

946	50c. brown	15	10
947	1col. violet	35	15
948	2col. orange	75	40
949	5col. green	1·80	1·60

260 Telephone Centre, San Pedro

1974. Air. 25th Anniv of Costa Rican Electrical Institute. Multicoloured.

950		50c. Type **260**	15	10
951		65c. Control Room, Rio Macho (horiz)	25	15
952		85c. Power house, Rio Macho	35	15
953		1col.25 Cachi Dam, Rio Macho (horiz)	40	20
954		2col. Institute H.Q. building	80	40

261 "Exfilmex" Emblem

1974. Air. "Exfilmex" Stamp Exhibition, Mexico City.

955	**261**	65c. green	15	10
956	**261**	3col. pink	65	40

262 Couple on Map

1974. Air. 25th Anniv of 4-S Clubs.

957	**262**	20c. emerald and green	40	20
958	-	50c. multicoloured	40	20

DESIGN. 50c. Young agricultural workers.

263 Brenes Mesen

1974. Air. Birth Centenary of Roberto Brenes Mesen (educator).

959	**263**	20c. black and brown	15	10
960	-	85c. black and red	25	15
961	-	5col. brown and black	1·60	90

DESIGNS—VERT: 85c. Brenes Mesen's "Poems of Love and Death". HORIZ: 5col. Brenes Mesen's hands.

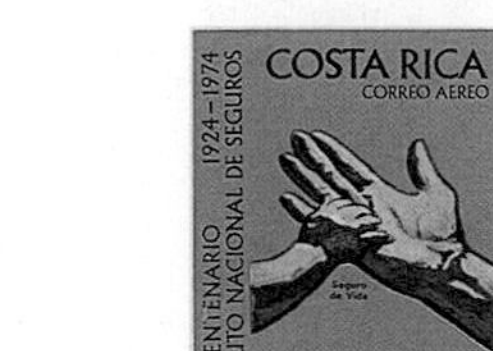

264 Child's and Adult's Hands

1974. Air. 50th Anniv of Costa Rican Insurance Institute.

962		20c. multicoloured	10	10
963		50c. multicoloured	10	10
964	**264**	65c. multicoloured	10	10
965	-	85c. multicoloured	10	10
966	-	1col.25 black and gold	30	10
967	-	2col. multicoloured	55	25
968	-	2col.50 multicoloured	65	40
969	-	20col. multicoloured	4·25	4·25

DESIGNS—HORIZ: 20c. R. Jimenez Oreamuno and T. Soley Guell (founders); 50c. Spade ("Harvest Insurance"). VERT: 85c. Paper boat within hand ("Marine Insurance"); 1col.25, Institute emblem; 2col. Arm in brace ("Workers' Rehabilitation"); 2col.50, Hand holding spanner ("Risks at Work"); 20col. House in protective hands ("Fire Insurance").

265 WPY Emblem

1974. Air. World Population Year.

970	**265**	2col. red and blue	50	25

266 "Boys eating Cakes" (Murillo)

1974. Obligatory Tax. Christmas.

971	**266**	10c. red	30	20
972	-	10c. purple	30	20
973	-	10c. black	30	20
974	-	10c. blue	30	20

DESIGNS: No. 972, "The Beautiful Gardener" (Raphael); No. 973, "Maternity" (J. R. Bonilla); No. 974, "The Prayer" (J. Reynolds).

267 Oscar J. Pinto (football pioneer)

1974. Air. 1st Central American Olympic Games, Guatemala (1973). Each grey and blue.

975		20c. Type **267**	10	10
976		50c. D. A. Montes de Oca (shooting champion)	10	10
977		1col. Eduardo Garnier (promoter of athletics)	50	20

268 "Mormodes buccinator"

1975. Air. 1st Central American Orchids Exhibition. Multicoloured.

978		25c. Type **268**	65	20
979		25c. "Gongora claviodora"	65	20
980		25c. "Masdevallia ephippium"	65	20
981		25c. "Encyclia spondiadum"	65	20
982		65c. "Lycaste skinneri alba"	1·60	20
983		65c. "Peristeria elata"	1·60	20
984		65c. "Miltonia roezelii"	1·60	20
985		65c. "Brassavola digbyana"	1·60	20
986		80c. "Epidendrum mirabile"	2·30	35
987		80c. "Barkeria lindleyana"	2·30	35
988		80c. "Cattleya skinneri"	2·30	35
989		80c. "Sobralia macrantha splendens"	2·30	35
990		1col.40 "Lycaste cruenta"	2·75	40
991		1col.40 "Oncidium obryzatum"	2·75	40
992		1col.40 "Gongora armeniaca"	2·75	40
993		1col.40 "Sievekingia suavis"	2·75	40
994		1col.75 "Hexisea imbricata"	1·60	40
995		2col.15 "Warcewiczella discolor"	1·60	55
996		2col.50 "Oncidium krameri-anum"	2·75	1·10
997		3col.25 "Cattleya dowiana"	3·25	1·40

269 Emblem of Costa Rica Radio Club

1975. Air. 16th Convention of Radio Amateurs Federation of Central America and Panama, San Jose.

998a	**269**	1col. purple and black	45	10
999	-	1col.10 red and blue	75	25
1000	-	2col. blue and black	1·40	40

DESIGNS—VERT: 1col.10, Federation emblem within "V" of Flags. HORIZ: 2col. Federation emblem.

270 Nicoyan Beach

1975. Air. 150th Anniv of Annexation of Nicoya. Multicoloured.

1001		25c. Type **270**	15	10
1002		75c. Cattle-drive	25	20
1003		1col. Colonial church	35	20
1004		3col. Savannah riders (vert)	1·00	85

271 3c. Philatelic Exhibition Stamp of 1932

1975. Air. 6th National Philatelic Exhibition, San Jose.

1005	**271**	2col.20 orange & black	40	35
1006	-	2col.20 green and black	40	35
1007	-	2col.20 red and black	40	35
1008	-	2col.20 blue and black	40	35

DESIGNS: Stamps of 1932. No. 1006, 5c. stamp; No. 1007, 10c. stamp; No. 1008, 20c. stamp.

272 IWY Emblem

1975. Air. International Women's Year.

1009	**272**	40c. red and blue	10	10
1010	**272**	1col.25 blue and black	40	20

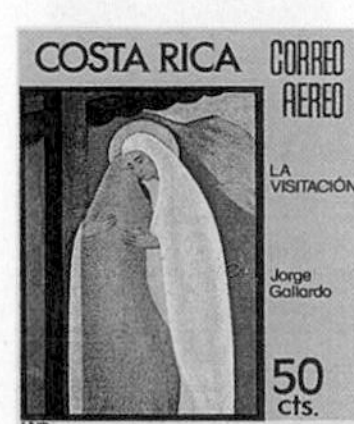

273 U.N. Emblem

1975. Air. 30th Anniv of United Nations.

1011	**273**	10c. blue and black	20	20
1012	-	60c. multicoloured	20	20
1013	-	1col.20 multicoloured	30	20

DESIGNS—HORIZ: 60c. General Assembly. VERT: 1col.20, U.N. Headquarters, New York.

274 "The Visitation"

1975. Air. "The Christmas Tradition". Paintings by Jorge Gallardo. Multicoloured.

1014		50c. Type **274**	35	20
1015		1col. "The Nativity and the Comet"	50	20
1016		5col. "St. Joseph in his workshop"	1·80	75

275 "Children with Tortoise" (F. Amighetti)

1975. Obligatory Tax. Christmas. Children's Village. Multicoloured.

1017	**275**	10c. brown	30	20
1018	-	10c. purple	30	20
1019	-	10c. grey	30	20
1020	-	10c. blue	30	20

DESIGNS: No. 1018, "The Virgin of the Carnation" (Da Vinci); No. 1019, "Happy Dreams" (child in bed—Sonia Romero); No. 1020, "Child with Pigeon" (Picasso).

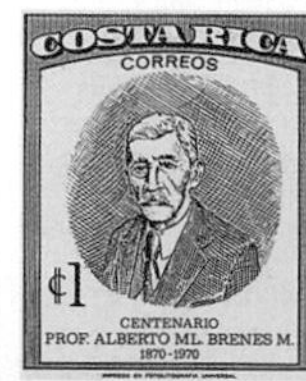

276 Schoolboy and Flags

1976. Air. 20th Anniv of "20–30" Youth Clubs in Costa Rica.

1021	**276**	1col. multicoloured	25	15

277 Prof. A. M. Brenes Mora

1976. Birth Centenary (1970) of Professor A. M. Brenes Mora (botanist).

1022	**277**	1col. violet (postage)	50	20
1023	-	5c. multicoloured (air)	50	20
1024	-	30c. multicoloured	50	20
1025	-	55c. multicoloured	50	20
1026	-	2col. multicoloured	1·00	40
1027	-	10col. multicoloured	4·50	2·75

DESIGNS: 5c. "Quercus breneseii"; 30c. "Maxillaria albertii"; 55c. "Calathea brenesii"; 2col. "Brenesia costaricensis"; 10col. "Philodendron brenesii".

No. 1023 is wrongly inscribed "brenessi".

278 Open Book as "Flower"

1976. Air. Costa Rican Literature. Mult.

1028		15c. Type **278**	20	20
1029		1col.10 Reader with "T.V. eye"	20	20
1030		5col. Book and flag (horiz)	1·00	80

280 Mounted Postman with Pack Mule

1976. Centenary (1974) of UPU.

1032	**280**	20c. black and yellow	35	20
1033	-	50c. multicoloured	35	20
1034	-	65c. multicoloured	35	20
1035	-	85c. multicoloured	35	20
1036	-	2col. black and blue	80	45

DESIGNS—HORIZ: 50c., 5c. UPU stamp of 1882; 65c., 10c. UPU stamp of 1882; 85c., 20c. UPU stamp of 1882. VERT: 2col. UPU Monument, Berne.

281 Early and Modern Telephones

1976. Telephone Centenary.
1037 **281** 1col.60 black and blue 40 20
1038 - 2col. black, brown & grn 50 20
1039 - 5col. black and yellow 1·20 1·00
DESIGNS: 2col. Costa Rica's first telephone; 5col. Alexander Graham Bell.

282 Emblems and Costa Rica 2c. Stamp of 1901 with Centre Inverted

1976. Air. 7th National Philatelic Exhibition.
1040 **282** 50c. multicoloured 15 15
1041 **282** 1col. multicoloured 15 15
1042 **282** 2col. multicoloured 40 15
MS1043 75×60 mm. 5col. As T **282** but with stamp in centre of design. Imperf or perf 2·75 2·75

283 Emblem of Comptroller General

1976. Air. 25th Anniv of Comptroller General.
1044 **283** 35c. blue and black 10 10
1045 - 2col. black, brown & bl 55 40
DESIGN—VERT: 2col. Amadeo Quiros Blanco (1st Comptroller).

284 "Girl in Wide-brimmed Hat" (Renoir)

1976. Obligatory Tax. Christmas.
1046 **284** 10c. lake 30 20
1047 - 10c. purple 30 20
1048 - 10c. slate 30 20
1049 - 10c. blue 30 20
DESIGNS: No 1047, "Virgin and Child" (Hans Memling); No. 1048, "Meditation" (Floria Pinto de Herrero); No. 1049, "Gaston de Mezerville" (Lolita Zeller de Peralta).

285 Nurse tending Child

1976. Air. 5th Pan-American Children's Surgery Congress. Multicoloured.
1050 90c. Type **285** 25 15
1051 1col.10 National Children's Hospital (horiz) 40 25

286 "LACSA" encircling Globe

1976. Air. 30th Anniv of LACSA Airline. Mult.
1052 1col. Type **286** 25 15
1053 1col.20 Route-map of LACSA services 40 20
1054 3col. LACSA emblem and Costa Rican flag 1·10 70

287 Boston Tea Party

1976. Air. Bicent of American Revolution. Mult.
1055 2col.20 Type **287** 40 35
1056 5col. Declaration of Independence 1·00 75
1057 10col. Ringing the Independence Bell (vert) 1·80 1·50

288 Boruca Textile

1977. Air. National Handicrafts Project. Mult.
1058 75c. Type **288** 15 15
1059 1col.50 Decorative handicraft in wood 35 15

289 Tree of Guanacaste

1977. Air. 50th Anniv of Rotary Club, San Jose.
1060 **289** 40c. green, blue and yellow 20 10
1061 - 50c. black, blue and yellow 15 10
1062 - 60c. black, blue and yellow 15 10
1063 - 3col. multicoloured 1·00 60
1064 - 10col. black, blue and yellow 3·50 2·50
DESIGNS—VERT: 50c. Felipe J. Alvarado (founder); 10col. Paul Harris, founder of Rotary International. HORIZ: 60c. Dr. Blanco Cervantes Hospital; 3col. Map of Costa Rica.

290 Juana Pereira

1977. Air. 50th Anniv of Coronation of Our Lady of the Angels (Patron Saint of Costa Rica).
1065 50c. Type **290** 20 20
1066 1col. First church of Our Lady of the Angels (horiz) 20 20
1067 1col.10 Our Lady of the Angels 20 20
1068 1col.25 Our Lady's crown 30 20

291 Alonso de Anguciana de Gamboa

1977. Air. 400th Anniv of Foundation of Esparza.
1069 **291** 35c. purple, mve & blk 10 10
1070 - 75c. brown, red & black 15 10
1071 - 1col. dp bl, bl & blk 35 15
1072 - 2col. green and black 65 40
DESIGNS: 75c. Church of Esparza; 1col. Our Lady of Candelaria, Patron Saint of Esparza; 2col. Diego de Artieda y Chirino.

292 Child

1977. Air. 20 Years of "CARE" in Costa Rica. Multicoloured.
1073 80c. Type **292** 25 15
1074 1col. Soya beans (horiz) 40 15

293 Institute Emblem

1977. Air. 25th Anniv of Hispanic Cultural Institute of Costa Rica. Multicoloured.
1075 50c. Type **293** 50 15
1076 1col.40 First map of the Americas, 1540 (40×30 mm) 1·00 40

294 "Our Lady of Mercy Church" (R. Ulloa)

1977. Air. Mystical Paintings. Multicoloured.
1077 50c. Type **294** 40 20
1078 1col. "Christ" (F. Pinto de Herrero) 40 20
1079 5col. "St. Francis and the Birds" (L. Gonzalez de Saenz) 1·80 75

295 Health Ministry on Map

1977. Air. 50th Anniv of Health Ministry.
1080 **295** 1col.40 multicoloured 40 15

296 "Child's Head" (Rubens)

1977. Obligatory Tax. Christmas.
1081 **296** 10c. red 30 20
1082 - 10c. blue 30 20
1083 - 10c. green 30 20
1084 - 10c. purple 30 20
DESIGNS: No. 1082, "Tenderness" (Cristina Fournier); No. 1083, "Abstraction" (Amparo Cruz); No. 1084, "Mariano Goya" (Francisco de Goya).

297 Weaving

1978. Air. 21st Congress of Confederation of Latin American Tourist Organizations. Multicoloured.
1085 50c. Type **297** 15 15
1086 1col. Picnic 30 15
1087 2col. Beach scene 95 20
1088 5col. Fruit market 1·80 85
1089 10col. Lake scene 2·40 1·90

298 Reader with Book

1978. National Literacy Campaign.
1090 **298** 50c. blue, black & orge 25 20

299 Jose de San Martin

1978. Air. Birth Bicent of Jose de San Martin.
1091 **299** 5col. multicoloured 1·30 80

300 Globe

1978. Air. 50th Anniv of Pan-American Institute of Geography and History.
1092 **300** 5col. blue, gold & lt blue 1·20 65

301 "XXX"

1978. Air. 30th Anniv of Central American University Confederation.
1093 **301** 80c. blue 25 15

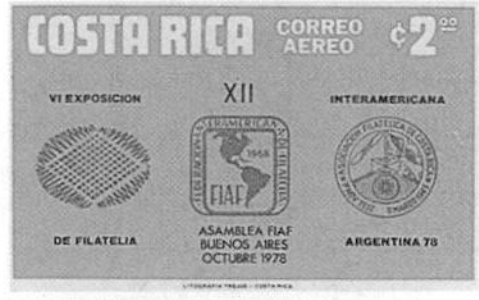

302 Emblems

1978. Air. 6th Inter-American Philatelic Exn, Buenos Aires.
1094 **302** 2col. turq, gold & blk 55 40

1978. Air. 50th Anniv of 1st PanAm Flight in Costa Rica. Nos. 994/6 optd "50 Aniversario del primer vuelo de PAN AM en Costa Rica 1928 – 1978".
1095 1col.75 "Hexisea imbricata" 50 35
1096 2col.15 "Warcewiczella discolor" 65 40
1097 2col.50 "Oncidium krameri-anum" 90 50

1978. Air. 50th Anniv of Lindbergh's Visit to Costa Rica. Nos. 994/6 optd "50 Aniversario de la visita de Lindbergh a Costa Rica 1928 – 1978".
1098 1col.75 "Hexisea imbricata" 1·30 35
1099 2col.15 "Warcewiczella discolor" 1·60 40
1100 2col.50 "Oncidium krameri-anum" 2·00 50

1978. Air. Carlos Maria Ulloa Hospital Centenary. Nos. 964 and 968 surch "Centenario del Asilo Carlos Maria Ulloa 1878 – 1978" and new value.
1101 50c. on 65c. multicoloured 15 15
1102 2col. on 2col.50 mult 55 25

306 Star over Map of Costa Rica

1978. Air. Christmas.
1103 **306** 50c. blue and black 20 15

1104	**306**	1col. mauve and black	20	15
1105	**306**	5col. red and black	1·40	65

1978. Air. Nos. 982/5 and 995/6 surch.

1106	50c. on 65c. "Lycaste skinneri alba"	60	55
1107	50c. on 65c. "Peristeria elata"	60	55
1108	50c. on 65c. "Miltonia roezelii"	60	55
1109	50c. on 65c. "Brassavola digbyana"	60	55
1110	1col.20 on 2col.15 "Warcewiczella discolor"	1·30	55
1111	2col. on 2col.50 "Oncidium kramerianum"	1·30	55

308 "Christmas Winds" (L. F. Chacon)

1978. Obligatory Tax. Christmas. Children's Village.

1112	**308**	10c. slate	30	20
1113	**308**	10c. red	30	20
1114	-	10c. mauve	30	20
1115	-	10c. blue	30	20

DESIGN: Nos. 1114/15, "Girl playing with Kite" (sculpture by Nester Zeledon).

309 "The Flying Men", Chorotega Ritual

1978. Air. 500th Anniv of Gonzalo Fernandez de Oviedo (first chronicler of Spanish Indies).

1116	**309**	85c. multicoloured	20	20
1117	-	1col.20 blue and black	20	20
1118	-	10col. multicoloured	2·10	2·10

DESIGNS—HORIZ: 1col.20, Oviedo giving his "History of Indies" to Duke of Calabria. VERT: 10col. Lord of Oviedo's coat of arms.

310 Domingo Rivas

1978. Air. Centenary of San Jose Cathedral.

1119	**310**	1col. blue and black	15	15
1120	-	20col. multicoloured	3·75	3·75

DESIGN: 20c. San Jose Cathedral.

311 Cocos Island

1979. Air. Presidential Visit to Cocos Island. Mult.

1121	90c. Type **311**	30	15
1122	2col.10 Cocos Island (different)	75	40
1123	3col. Cocos Island (different)	1·10	55
1124	5col. Moon over Cocos Island (vert)	1·80	1·10
1125	10col. Commemorative plaque and people with flag (vert)	3·50	2·75
MS1126	139×102 mm. Nos. 1121/5	12·00	12·00

312 Shrimp

1979. Air. Conservation of Marine Fauna. Multicoloured.

1127	60c. Type **312**	20	20
1128	85c. Mahogany snapper	20	20
1129	1col.80 Yellow corvina	50	20
1130	3col. Lobster	75	40
1131	10col. Frigate mackerel	2·50	2·40

313 Hungry Nestlings (Song Thrushes)

1979. Air. International Year of the Child.

1132	**313**	1col. multicoloured	70	15
1133	**313**	2col. multicoloured	1·60	65
1134	**313**	20col. multicoloured	11·00	5·75

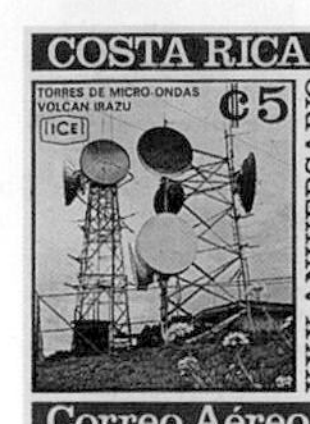

315 Microwave Transmitters, Mt. Hazu

1979. Air. 30th Anniv of Costa Rican Electricity Institute. Multicoloured.

1136	1col. Arenal Dam	20	20
1137	5col. Type **315**	1·10	70

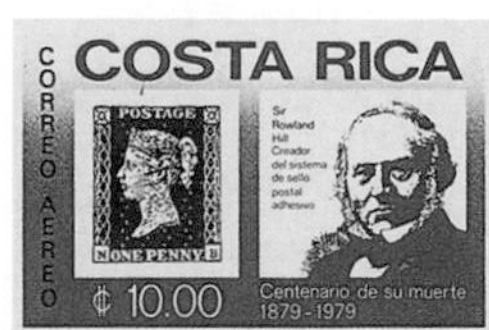

316 Sir Rowland Hill and Penny Black

1979. Air. Death Centenary of Sir Rowland Hill.

1138	-	5col. mauve and blue	1·20	55
1139	**316**	10col. blue and black	2·50	1·20

DESIGN: 5col. Sir Rowland Hill and first Costa Rican stamp.

317 "Waiting" (Hernan Gonzalez)

1979. Air. National Sculpture Competition. Multicoloured.

1140	60c. Type **317**	15	15
1141	1col. "The Heroes of Misery" (Juan Ramon Bonilla)	20	15
1142	2col.10 "Bullocks" (Victor M. Bermudez) (horiz)	55	20
1143	5col. "Chlorite Head" (Juan Rafael Chacon)	1·50	1·10
1144	20col. "Motherhood" (Francisco Zuniga)	5·00	2·50

318 "Danaus plexippus"

1979. Air. Butterflies. Multicoloured.

1145	60c. Type **318**	2·10	35
1146	1col. "Phoebis philea"	4·25	35
1147	1col.80 "Rothschildia sp."	6·50	55
1148	2col.10 "Prepona omphale"	8·50	75
1149	2col.60 "Marpesia marcella"	8·50	1·50
1150	4col.05 "Morpho cypris"	12·50	2·50

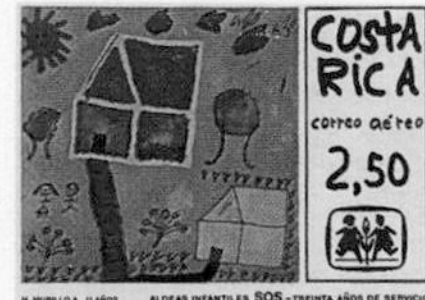

319 "Green House" (M. Murillo)

1979. Air. 30th Anniv of SOS Children's Villages. Children's Paintings. Multicoloured.

1151	2col.50 Type **319**	55	40
1152	5col. "Four houses" (L. Varela)	1·20	65
1153	5col.50 "Blue house" (M. Perez)	1·60	95

320 Jose Joaquin Rodriguez Zeledon

1979. Air. Costa Rican Presidents (1st series).

1154	**320**	10c. blue	10	10
1155	-	60c. purple	15	10
1156	-	85c. red	25	15
1157	-	1col. orange	35	15
1158	-	2col. brown	65	40

DESIGNS: 60c. Rafael Iglesias Castro; 85c. Ascension Esquivel Ibarra; 1col. Cleto Gonzalez Viquez; 2col. Ricardo Jimenez Oreamuno.

See also Nos. 1180/4 and 1256/60.

321 Holy Family

1979. Air. Christmas.

1159	**321**	1col. multicoloured	20	15
1160	**321**	1col.60 multicoloured	50	25

322 Boy leaning on Tree

1979. Obligatory Tax. Christmas. Children's Village.

1161	**322**	10c. blue	25	20
1162	**322**	10c. orange	25	20
1163	**322**	10c. mauve	25	20
1164	**322**	10c. green	25	20

323 Tree

1980. Air. Reafforestation.

1165	**323**	1col. brown, blue & grn	15	15
1166	**323**	3col.40 brown, ol & grn	60	45

324 "Anatomy Lesson" (Rembrandt)

1980. Air. 50th Anniv of Legal Medical Teaching in Costa Rica.

1167	**324**	10col. multicoloured	4·00	1·70

325 Rotary Anniversary Emblem

1980. 75th Anniv of Rotary International.

1168	**325**	2col.10 green, yellow and black	35	25
1169	**325**	5col. multicoloured	95	65

326 Puerto Limon

1980. Air. 14th International Symposium on Remote Sensing of the Environment. Multicoloured.

1170	2col.10 Type **326**	35	25
1171	5col. Gulf of Nicoya, Guanacaste	95	65

327 Football

1980. Air. Olympic Games, Moscow. Mult.

1172	1col. Type **327**	40	15
1173	3col. Cycling	7·75	55
1174	4col.05 Baseball	7·75	75
1175	20col. Swimming	7·75	5·25

328 Poas Volcano

1980. Air. 10th Anniv of National Parks Service.

1176	1col. Type **328**	20	15
1177	2col.50 Beach at Cahuita	50	40

329 Jose Maria Zeledon Brenes (lyric writer)

1980. Air. National Anthem. Multicoloured.

1178	1col. Type **329**	20	15
1179	10col. Manuel Maria Gutierrez (composer)	1·70	1·40

1980. Air. Costa Rican Presidents (2nd series). As T 320.

1180	1col. red	20	10
1181	1col.60 turquoise	35	15
1182	1col.80 brown	40	15
1183	2col.10 green	45	20
1184	3col. lilac	70	45

DESIGNS: 1col. Alfredo Gonzalez; 1col.60, Federico Tinoco; 1col.80, Francisco Aguilar; 2col.10, Julio Acosta; 3col. Leon Cortes.

330 Exhibition Emblem

1980. Air. 8th National Stamp Exhibition.

1185	**330**	5col. multicoloured	85	60
1186	**330**	20col. multicoloured	3·50	2·75

331 Fruit

1980. Air. Costa Rican Produce. Mult.

1187	10c. Type **331**	15	10
1188	60c. Chocolate	20	15
1189	1col. Coffee	35	15
1190	2col.10 Bananas	65	20
1191	3col.40 Flowers	1·10	45
1192	5col. Cane sugar	1·20	65

332 "Giant Poro" (Jorge Carvajal)

1980. Air. Paintings. Multicoloured.

1193	1col. Type **332**	30	15
1194	2col.10 "Secret Look" (Rolando Cubero)	50	25
1195	2col.45 "Consuelo" (Fernando Carballo) (31×32 mm)	65	35
1196	3col. "Volcano" (Lola Fernandez)	75	40
1197	4col.05 "Hearing Mass" (Francisco Amighetti)	1·10	50

333 "Madonna and Child" (Raphael)

1980. Air. Christmas. Multicoloured.

1198	1col. Type **333**	35	25
1199	10col. "Madonna, Jesus and St. John" (Raphael)	2·40	1·80

334 Boy on Swing

1980. Obligatory Tax. Christmas. Children's Village.

1200	**334**	10c. red	25	20
1201	**334**	10c. yellow	25	20
1202	**334**	10c. blue	25	20
1203	**334**	10c. green	25	20

335 New Harbour, Caldera

1980. Air. "Paying your Taxes Means Progress". Multicoloured.

1204	1col. Type **335**	25	15
1205	1col.30 Juan Santamaria International Airport (32×25 mm)	40	15
1206	2col.10 River Frio railway bridge	70	35
1207	2col.60 Highway to Colon City (25×32 mm)	75	40
1208	5col. Regional postal centre, Huetar	1·30	75

336 Harpy Eagle

1980. Air. Fauna. Multicoloured.

1209	2col.10 Type **336**	1·40	35
1210	2col.50 Scarlet macaw	1·90	45
1211	3col. Puma	2·50	55
1212	5col.50 Black-handed spider monkey	5·00	1·10

337 Monge and Magazine "Repertorio Americano"

1980. Air. Birth Centenary of Joaquin Garcia Monge.

1213	**337**	1col.60 blue, yell & red	25	15
1214	**337**	3col. blue, lt bl & red	55	40

338 Arms of Aserri

1981. Air. Cornea Bank.

1215	**338**	1col. multicoloured	20	15
1216	**338**	1col.80 multicoloured	50	20
1217	**338**	5col. blue	1·40	75

DESIGNS: 1col.80, Eye; 5col. Abelardo Rojas (founder).

339 Rodrigo Facio Brenes (rector)

1981. Air. 40th Anniv of University of Costa Rica and 20th Anniv of Medical School.

1218	-	5c. multicoloured	15	10
1219	-	10c. multicoloured	15	10
1220	-	50c. multicoloured	15	10
1221	-	1col.30 multicoloured	20	10
1222	-	3col.40 multicoloured	50	35
1223	**339**	4col.05 grn, bl & dp bl	65	40

DESIGNS: HORIZ: 5c. Medical-surgical clinic; 10c. Physiology lesson; 50c. Medical School and Dr. Antonia Pena Chavarria (first Dean); 1col.30, School of Music and Fine Arts; 3col.40, Carlos Monge Alfaro Library.

340 Ass-drawn Mail Van, 1857

1981. Air. 150th Birth Anniv of Heinrich von Stephan (founder of UPU).

1224	-	1col. lt blue, grn & bl	20	15
1225	**340**	2col.10 yell, red & brn	50	20
1226	-	10col. grey, mve & grn	2·20	1·50

DESIGNS: 1col. Mail carried by mule, 1839; 10col. Carrying mail to Sarapiqui, 1858.

341 ITU and WHO Emblems and Ribbons forming Caduceus

1981. Air. World Telecommunications Day.

1227	**341**	5col. blue and black	1·00	65
1228	**341**	25col. multicoloured	5·00	4·25

342 Sts. Peter and Paul

1981. Air. Centenary of Consecration of Bernardo August Thiel as Bishop of San Jose. Mult.

1229	1col. Type **342**	15	10
1230	1col. St. Vincent de Paul	15	10
1231	1col. Death of St. Joseph	15	10
1232	1col. Archangel St. Michael	15	10
1233	1col. Holy Family	15	10
1234	2col. Bishop Thiel	45	30

343 Juan Santamaria (national hero)

1981. Air. Homage to the Province of Alajuela. Multicoloured.

1235	1col. Type **343** (150th birth anniv)	20	15
1236	2col.45 Alajuela Cathedral	35	30

344 Potter

1981. Air. Banco Popular and the Development of the Community. Multicoloured.

1237	15c. Type **344**	15	10
1238	1col.60 Building construction	20	15
1239	1col.80 Farming	20	15
1240	2col.50 Fishermen	25	15
1241	3col. Nurse and patient	40	15
1242	5col. Rural guard	75	25

345 Leon Fernandez Bonilla (founder)

1981. Air. National Archives. Multicoloured.

1243	1col.40 Type **345**	25	20
1244	2col. Arms of National Archives	35	20
1245	3col. University of Santo Tomas (horiz)	45	35
1246	3col.50 Model of new archives' building (horiz)	55	35

346 Disabled Person in Wheelchair holding Scales of Justice

1981. Air. International Year of Disabled Persons.

1247	-	1col. multicoloured	35	15
1248	**346**	2col.60 deep orange, orange and black	80	15
1249	-	10col. multicoloured	3·50	80

DESIGNS—VERT: 1col. Steps and disabled person in wheelchair. HORIZ: 10col. Healthy person helping disabled towards the sun.

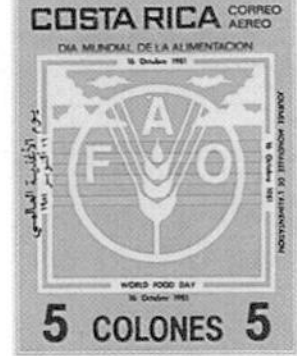

347 FAO Emblem

1981. Air. World Food Day.

1250	**347**	5col. multicoloured	40	25
1251	**347**	10col. multicoloured	80	55

348 Boy in Pedal-car

1981. Obligatory Tax. Christmas. Children's Village.

1252	**348**	10c. red	25	20
1253	**348**	10c. orange	25	20
1254	**348**	10c. blue	25	20
1255	**348**	10c. green	25	20

1981. Air. Costa Rican Presidents (3rd series) As T 320.

1256	1col. red	40	40
1257	2col. orange	40	40
1258	3col. green	50	40
1259	5col. blue	95	65
1260	10col. blue	1·90	1·50

DESIGNS: 1c. Rafael Angel Calderon Guardia; 2col. Teodoro Picado Milchalski; 3col. Jose Figueres Ferrer; 5col. Otilio Ulate Blanco; 10col. Mario Echandi Jimenez.

349 Arms of Bar Association

1982. Air. Centenary of Bar Association.

1261	**349**	1col. blue and black	15	15
1262	-	2col. multicoloured	15	15
1263	-	20col. green and black	2·20	1·40

DESIGNS—VERT: 2col. Eusebio Figueroa (first president of Association). HORIZ: 20col. Bar Association building.

350 Housing

1982. Air. Costa-Rican Progress. Mult.

1264	95col. Type **350**	10	10
1265	1col.15 Farmers' fairs	10	10
1266	1col.45 Grade and high schools	10	10
1267	1col.65 National plan for drinking water	15	10
1268	1col.80 Rural health	15	10
1269	2col.10 Playgrounds	20	10
1270	2col.35 National Theatre Square	30	10
1271	2col.60 Dish aerial (International and national telephone system)	30	10

1272		3col. Electric railway to Atlantic coast	40	10
1273		4col.05 Irrigation at Guanacaste	40	35

351 Fountain, Central Park

1982. Air. Bicentenary of Alajuela. Mult.

1274		5col. Type **351**	50	25
1275		10col. Juan Santamaria Historical and Cultural Museum (horiz)	1·00	45
1276		15col. Christ of Esquipulas Church	1·50	1·10
1277		20col. Mgr. Estevan Lorenzo de Tristan	2·00	1·30
1278		25col. Padre Juan Manuel Lopez del Corral	2·40	1·60

352 Saint's Stone

1982. Air. 50th Anniv of Perez Zeledon County. Multicoloured.

1279		10c. Type **352**	10	10
1280		50c. Monument to Mothers	10	10
1281		1col. Pedro Perez Zeledon	10	10
1282		1col.25 San Isidro Labrador Church	10	10
1283		3col.50 Municipal building (horiz)	30	20
1284		4col.25 County arms	45	20

1982. Air. Nos. 1070 and 1207 surch.

1285		3col. on 75c. red and black	30	20
1286		5col. on 2col.60 mult	50	20

1982. Air. 9th National Stamp Exhibition. Nos. 1005/8 surch IX EXPOSICION FILATELICA - 1982 and new value.

1287	**271**	8col.40 on 2col.20 orange and black	55	40
1288	-	8col.40 on 2col.20 green and black	55	40
1289	-	8col.40 on 2col.20 red and black	55	40
1290	-	8col.40 on 2col.20 blue and black	55	40
1291	**271**	9col.70 on 2col.20 orange and black	65	55
1292	-	9col.70 on 2col.20 green and black	65	55
1293	-	9col.70 on 2col.20 red and black	65	55
1294	-	9col.70 on 2col.20 blue and black	65	55

355 Dr Robert Koch and Cross of Lorraine

1982. Air. Centenary of Discovery of Tubercle Bacillus.

1295		1col.50 red and black	15	15
1296	**355**	3col. grey and black	30	15
1297	-	3col.30 multicoloured	30	15

DESIGNS: 1col.50, Koch and anti-T.B. Campaign emblem; 3col.30, Koch and Ministry of Public Health Building, San Jose.

356 Student at Lathe

1982. Obligatory Tax. Christmas. Children's Village.

1298	**356**	10c. red	25	20
1299	**356**	10c. grey	25	20
1300	**356**	10c. violet	25	20

1301	**356**	10c. blue	25	20

357 Blood Donors Association Emblem

1982. Air. 7th Pan-American Blood Donors Congress. Multicoloured.

1302	**357**	30col. multicoloured	1·90	1·30
1303	-	50col. red, blue & black	3·00	2·00

DESIGN: 50col. Congress emblem.

358 Migration Committee Emblem

1982. Air. 30th Anniv of Intergovernmental Migration Committee.

1304	**358**	8col.40 lt blue, bl & blk	50	20
1305	-	9col.70 blue and black	70	35
1306	-	11col.70 mult	75	35
1307	-	13col.05 bl, blk & grey	90	45

DESIGNS—HORIZ: 11col.70, Emblem and handshake; 13col.05, Emblem within double-headed arrow. VERT: 9col.70, Emblem.

359 "St. Francis" (El Greco)

1983. Air. 800th Birth Anniv (1982) of St. Francis of Assisi.

1308	**359**	4col.80 brown, blk & bl	45	20
1309	-	7col.40 brn, blk & grey	65	20

DESIGN: 7col.40, Portrait of Francis by unknown artist.

360 Pope John Paul II

1983. Air. Papal Visit.

1310	**360**	5col. brown, yell & bl	2·30	20
1311	**360**	10col. brown, grn & bl	2·30	45
1312	**360**	15col. brown, mve & bl	5·25	70

361 WCY Emblem

1983. World Communications Year.

1313	**361**	10c. multicoloured	30	20
1314	**361**	50c. multicoloured	30	20
1315	**361**	10col. multicoloured	1·20	30

362 Egg

1983. 1st World Conference on Human Rights, Alajuela (1982).

1316	**362**	20col. grey and black	2·10	95

363 UPU Monument, Berne, and 1883 2c. Stamp

1983. Centenary of U.P.U. Membership.

1317	**363**	3col. yellow, red & blk	1·10	30
1318	-	10col. yellow, bl & blk	2·20	45

DESIGN: 10col. Central Post Office, San Jose, and 1883 40c. stamp.

364 "Alliance Building, San Jose" (Cristina Fournier)

1983. Centenary of French Alliance (French language-teaching association).

1319	**364**	12col. multicoloured	1·80	55

365 Bolivar (after Francisco Zuniga)

1983. Air. Birth Bicentenary of Simon Bolivar.

1320	**365**	10col. multicoloured	95	20

1983. Nos. 1308/9 surch.

1321		10c. on 4col.80 brown, black and blue	20	20
1321a		50c. on 4col.80 brown, black and blue	20	20
1322		1col.50 on 7col.40 brown, black and grey	20	20
1323		3col. on 7col.40 brown, black and grey	20	20

367 Repairing Wheelchair

1988. Obligatory Tax. Christmas. Children's Village.

1324	**367**	10c. red	25	20
1325	**367**	10c. orange	25	20
1326	**367**	10c. blue	25	20
1327	**367**	10c. green	25	20

368 Three Kings

1983. Christmas. Multicoloured.

1328		1col.50 Type **368**	20	15
1329		1col.50 Holy Family and Shepherds	20	15
1330		1col.50 People bearing gifts	20	15

Nos. 1328/30 were printed together, se-tenant, forming a composite design.

369 Fisherman

1983. Fisheries Development.

1331	**369**	8col.50 multicoloured	80	30

370 Resplendent Quetzal ("Quetzal")

1984. Birds. Multicoloured.

1332		10c. Type **370**	55	20
1333		50c. Red-legged honey-creeper ("Mielero Patirrojo") (horiz)	55	20
1334		1col. Clay-coloured thrush ("Mirlo Pardo") (horiz)	55	20
1335		1col.50 Blue-crowned motmot ("Momotode Diadema Azul")	55	20
1336		3col. Green violetear ("Colibri orejivioloceo verde")	1·40	25
1337		10col. Blue and white swallow ("Golondirina Azul y Blanca") (horiz)	4·75	35

371 Jose Joaquin Mora

1984. 1856 Campaign Heroes. Multicoloured.

1339		50c. Type **371**	10	10
1340		1col.50 Pancha Carrasco	15	10
1341		3col. Juan Santamaria (horiz)	30	20
1342		8col.50 Juan Rafael Mora Porras	95	60

372 Jesus Bonilla Chavarria

1984. Musicians.

1343	**372**	3col. 50 violet and black	30	20
1344	-	5col. red and black	45	30
1345	-	12col. green and black	1·20	90
1346	-	13col. yellow and black	1·30	1·00

DESIGNS: 5col. Benjamin Gutierrez; 12col. Pilar Jimenez; 13col. Jose Daniel Zuniga.

373 Necklace Bead

1984. Jade Museum Artifacts. Multicoloured.

1347		4col. Type **373**	80	25
1348		7col. Seated figure	1·60	40
1349		10col. Ceramic dish (horiz)	2·00	50

374 Basketball Players

1984. Olympic Games, Los Angeles. Mult.

1350		1col. Type **374**	10	10
1351		8col. Swimming	65	15
1352		11col. Cycling	90	40
1353		14col. Running	1·20	65
1354		20col. Boxing	1·60	1·20
1355		30col. Football	2·50	1·50

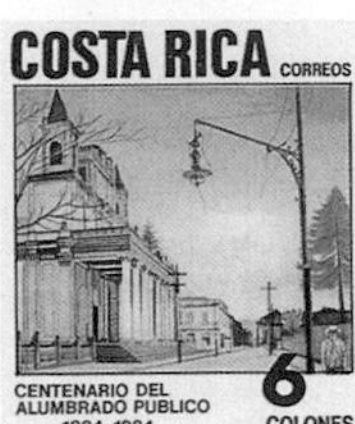

375 Street Scene

1984. Centenary of Public Street Lighting.

1356	**375**	6col. multicoloured	55	40

376 Emblem and National Independence Monument

1984. 10th National Philatelic Exhibition. Mult.

1357		10col. Type **376**	90	55
1358		10col. Emblem and Juan Mora Fernandez statue	90	55
MS1359		116×86 mm. Nos. 1357/8, each ×2	12·00	12·00

377 National Coat of Arms

1984

1360	**377**	100col. blue	8·00	3·75
1361	**377**	100col. yellow	8·00	3·75

378 Child on Tricycle

1984. Obligatory Tax. Christmas. Children's Village.

1362	**378**	10c. violet	25	25

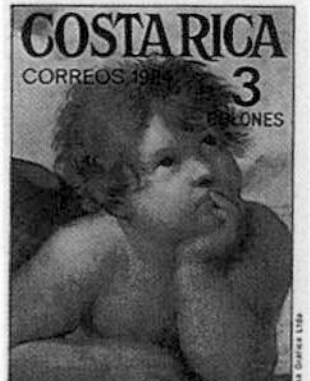

379 "Sistine Virgin" (detail, Raphael)

1984. Christmas. Multicoloured.

1363		3col. Type **379**	25	25
1364		3col. "Sistine Virgin" (detail) (different)	25	25

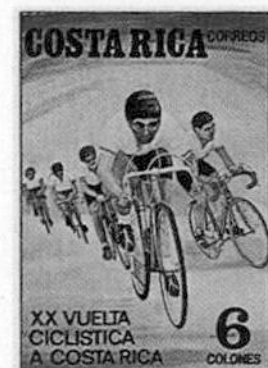

380 Cyclists

1984. 20th Costa Rica Cycle Race.

1365	**380**	6col. multicoloured	55	30

381 Emblem and 1968 Scouting Jubilee Stamp

1985. International Youth Year.

1366	**381**	11col. multicoloured	1·60	55

382 Workers' Monument (Francisco Zuniga)

1985. "National Values".

1367	**382**	6col. mauve and black	80	30
1368	-	11col. yell, blk & bl	1·30	50
1369	-	13col. multicoloured	1·40	55
1370	-	30col. multicoloured	4·50	1·20

DESIGNS—As T **382**. 11col. First printing press (Freedom of speech); 13col. Dove, flag and globe (Neutrality); 65×35 mm—30col. Nos. 1367/9.

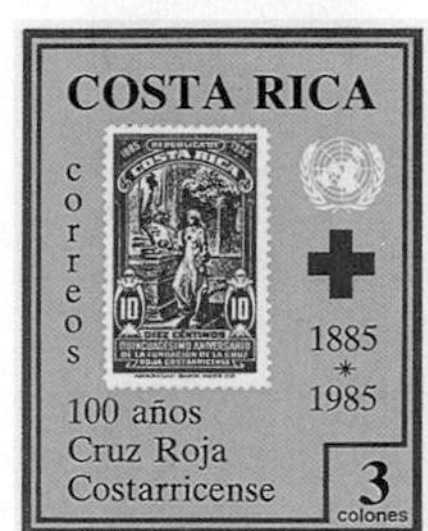

383 U.N. Emblem and 1935 Red Cross Jubilee Stamp

1985. Centenary of Costa Rican Red Cross.

1371	**383**	3col. red, brown & blk	1·60	25
1372	-	5col. black, red and grey	2·40	25

DESIGN: 5col. U.N. Emblem and 1946 Red Cross Society stamp.

384 Hands holding "S"

1985. 50th Anniv of Saprissa Football Club.

1373	**384**	3col. mauve and green	25	15
1374	-	3col. black and mauve	25	15
1375	-	6col. mauve, brn & grn	50	25

DESIGNS: As T **384**—Hands holding football; 34×26 mm—6col. Ricardo Saprissa and Saprissa Stadium.

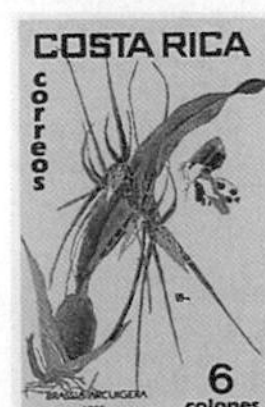

385 "Brassia arcuigera"

1985. Orchids. Multicoloured.

1376		6col. Type **385**	1·30	55
1377		6col. "Encyclia peraltensis"	1·30	55
1378		6col. "Maxillaria especie"	1·30	55
1379		13col. "Oncidium turialbae"	1·50	1·10
1380		13col. "Trichopilia marginata"	1·50	1·10
1381		13col. "Stanhopea ecornuta"	1·50	1·10

386 1940 25c. Stamp and Hand holding Tweezers

1985. 11th National Stamp Exhibition.

1382	**386**	20col. bl, ultram & pink	1·20	55

387 Hands reaching out to Child

1985. Obligatory Tax. Christmas. Children's Village.

1383	**387**	10c. brown	40	25

388 Children looking at Star

1985. Christmas.

1384	**388**	3col. multicoloured	20	10

390 Costa Rica Lyceum

1986. Centenary of Free Compulsory Education.

1390	**390**	3col. brown & lt brown	15	10
1391	**390**	30col. brown and pink	1·60	80

DESIGN: 30col. Mauro Fernandez Acuna (education Minister).

391 Land and Cattle College Project

1986. 27th Annual Inter-American Development Bank Assembly, San Jose. Multicoloured.

1392		10col. Type **391**	50	25
1393		10col. Bank emblem	50	25
1394		10col. Cape Blanco fisherman	50	25

392 Francisco J. Orlich Bolmarcich

1986. Former Presidents of Costa Rica.

1395	**392**	3col. green	40	15
1396	-	3col. green	40	15
1397	-	3col. green	40	15
1398	-	3col. green	40	15
1399	-	3col. green	40	15
1400	-	6col. brown	65	15
1401	-	6col. brown	65	15
1402	-	6col. brown	65	15
1403	-	6col. brown	65	15
1404	-	6col. brown	65	15
1405	-	10col. orange	95	25
1406	-	10col. orange	95	25
1407	-	10col. orange	95	25
1408	-	10col. orange	95	25
1409	-	10col. orange	95	25
1410	-	11col. grey	1·30	40
1411	-	11col. grey	1·30	40
1412	-	11col. grey	1·30	40
1413	-	11col. grey	1·30	40
1414	-	11col. grey	1·30	40
1415	-	13col. brown	1·60	40
1416	-	13col. brown	1·60	40
1417	-	13col. brown	1·60	40
1418	-	13col. brown	1·60	40
1419	-	13col. brown	1·60	40

DESIGNS: Nos. 1395, 1400, 1405, 1410, 1415, Type **392**; 1396, 1401, 1406, 1411, 1416, Jose Joaquin Trejos Fernandez; 1397, 1402, 1407, 1412, 1417, Daniel Oduber Quiros; 1398, 1403, 1408, 1413, 1418, Rodrigo Carazo Odio; 1399, 1404, 1409, 1414, 1419, Luis Alberto Monge Alvarez.

393 Pique (mascot)

1986. World Cup Football Championship. Mexico.

1420	**393**	1col. multicoloured	30	15
1421	-	1col. multicoloured	30	15
1422	-	4col. multicoloured	1·40	15
1423	-	6col. pur, brn & black	2·00	25
1424	-	11col. pur, red & blk	4·00	40

DESIGNS:—VERT: No. 1420, 1422, Type **393**. HORIZ: No. 1421, 1423, Footballs and players; 1424, Footballs and players (different).

394 Emblem and "Peace"

1986. International Peace Year. Each bearing the Year emblem and "Peace" in various languages (first language given in brackets).

1425	**394**	5col. blue and brown (Hoa Binh)	55	25
1426	-	5col. blue and brown (Vrede)	55	25
1427	-	5col. blue and brown (Pace)	55	25

396 Child

1986. Obligatory Tax. Christmas. Children's Village.

1438	**396**	10c. brown	25	25

395 Gold Artefact

1986. Exhibits in Gold Museum. Mult.

1428		6col. Type **395**	40	25
1429		6col. Figure with three-lobed base	40	25
1430		6col. Frog	40	25
1431		6col. Centipede	40	25
1432		6col. Two monkeys in sun	40	25
1433		13col. Figure with dragon-head arms	80	40
1434		13col. Two monkeys	80	40
1435		13col. Animal-shaped figure	80	40
1436		13col. Sun with ball pendant	80	40
1437		13col. Figure within frame	80	40

397 Fork-lift Truck and Airplane (Osvaldo Andres Gonzalez Vega)

1986. Air. 40th Anniv of LACSA (national airline). Children's Drawings. Multicoloured.

1439		1col. Airplane flying over house and van (Adriana Elias Hidalgo)	50	15
1440		7col. Type **397**	3·50	30
1441		16col. Airplane, letters and photographs (David Valverde Rodriguez)	8·00	75

398 Lattice-winged Bat

1986. Flora and Fauna. Bats and Frogs. Multicoloured.

1442		2col. Type **398**	15	15
1443		3col. Common long-tongued bat	30	15
1444		4col. White bat	40	15
1445		5col. Group of white bats	50	15
1446		6col. "Agalychnis callidryas" (frog)	65	25
1447		10col. "Dendrobates pumilio" (frog)	1·10	25
1448		11col. "Hyla ebraccata" (frog)	1·10	40
1449		20col. "Phyllobates lugubris" (frog)	2·00	65
MS1450		60×70 mm. 50 col. "Agalychris callidryas" (frog) on arum flower	1·00	1·00

399 Extracting Snake's Venom (detail of mural, Francisco Amighetti)

1987. National Science and Technology Day.

1451	**399**	8col. multicoloured	3·00	20

400 Statuette

1987. Centenary of National Museum. Pre-Colombian Art. Multicoloured.

1452		8col. Type **400**	40	25
1453		8col. Jug in form of human figure	40	25
1454		8col. Vase in form of human figure	40	25
1455		8col. Stone jar	40	25
1456		8col. Pot with human-type legs and arms	40	25
1457		15col. Bowl (horiz)	65	25
1458		15col. Carving of animal defeating human (horiz)	65	25
1459		15col. Flask (horiz)	65	25

401 Arms of San Jose Province

1987. 250th Anniv of San Jose.

1460	**401**	20col. multicoloured	95	50
1461	-	20col. red, black & bl	95	50
1462	-	20col. red, black & bl	95	50

DESIGNS: Nos. 1461, Donkey cart in cobbled street; 1462, View down street.

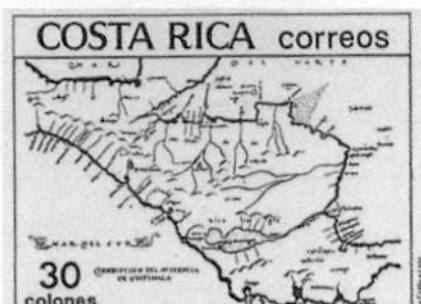

402 16th-century Map of Audiencia, Guatemala

1987. Columbus Day.

1463	**402**	30col. brown and yellow	2·30	65

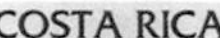

403 Map by Bartholomew Columbus, 1503

1987. 500th Anniv (1992) of Discovery of America by Columbus (1st issue). Each brown and yellow.

1464		4col. Type **403**	25	25
1465		4col. 16th-century map of Costa Rica	25	25

See also Nos. 1480, 1496, 1521 and 1538/40.

404 Cross and Doves

1987. Obligatory Tax. Christmas, Children's Village.

1466	**404**	10c. blue and brown	25	25

405 "Village Scene" (Fausto Pacheco)

1987. International Year of Shelter for the Homeless.

1467	**405**	1col. multicoloured	55	25

406 Pres. Arias and National Flag

1987. Award of Nobel Peace Prize to Pres. Oscar Arias Sanchez.

1468	**406**	10col. multicoloured	1·60	30

407 Green Turtle

1988. 17th Annual General Assembly of International Union for Nature Conservation. Multicoloured.

1469		5col. Type **407**	50	15
1470		5col. Golden toad on leaf	50	15
1471		5col. Emperor (butterfly)	50	15

408 Anniversary Emblem

1988. 125th Anniv of Red Cross.

1472	**408**	30col. red and blue	1·40	65

409 Man with Pen and Radio (Adult Education)

1988. Costa Rica–Liechtenstein Cultural Co-operation.

1473	**409**	18col. red, brown & grn	1·90	25
1474	-	20col. multicoloured	1·90	25

DESIGN: 20col. Headphones on books (radio broadcasts).

410 Symbols of Bank Activities

1988. 125th Anniv of Anglo–Costa Rican Bank.

1475	**410**	3col. blue, red & yellow	25	15

411 Games Emblem

1988. Olympic Games, Seoul. Multicoloured.

1476		25col. Type **411**	80	50
1477		25col. Games mascot	80	50

412 Roman Macava and Curtiss "Robin"

1988. Airmail Pioneers.

1478	**412**	10col. multicoloured	50	15

413 School Courtyard

1988. Centenary of Girls' High School.

1479	**413**	10col. brown & yellow	40	25

414 Amerindian Necklace

1988. 500th Anniv (1992) of Discovery of America by Columbus (2nd issue).

1480	**414**	4col. multicoloured	25	25

415 Dengo and College

1988. Birth Centenary of Omar Dengo (Director of Heredia Teachers' College).

1481	**415**	10col. brown, grey & bl	30	25

416 Former Observation Tower

1988. Cent of National Meteorological Institute.

1482	**416**	2col. multicoloured	30	25

417 "Eschweilera costarricensis"

1989. Flowers. Multicoloured.

1483		5col. Type **417**	25	25
1484		10col. "Heliconia wagneriana"	30	25
1485		15col. "Heliconia lophocarpa"	55	25
1486		20col. "Aechmea magdalenae"	65	25
1487		25col. "Psammisia ramiflora"	80	25
1488		30col. Passion flower	1·10	25

418 Map of France and Costa Rican National Monument

1989. Bicentenary of French Revolution.

1489	**418**	30col. black, blue & red	1·40	50

419 Sugar Mill

1989. 151st Anniv of Grecia County.

1490	**419**	10col. multicoloured	65	25

420 Corn Grinder

1989. America. Pre-Columbian Artefacts. Mult.

1491		50col. Type **420**	2·40	1·20
1492		100col. Granite sphere, 1500 A.D.	4·75	1·80

422 Orchid

1989. "100 Years of Democracy" Presidents' Summit.

1493	**422**	10col. multicoloured	1·50	25

423 Dr. Henri Pittier (first Director)

1989. Centenary of National Geographical Institute.

1494	**423**	18col. multicoloured	65	25

424 Teacher and Children

1989. Obligatory Tax. Christmas. Children's Village.

1495	**424**	1col. blue, green & black	25	25

425 Pre-Columbian Gold Frog and Spanish Coin

1989. 500th Anniv (1992) of Discovery of America by Columbus (3rd issue).

1496	**425**	4col. multicoloured	25	15

426 "Exporting Coffee" (painting in theatre by Jose Villa)

1990. Centenary of National Theatre.

1497	**426**	5col. multicoloured	65	25

427 Football in Cube

1990. World Cup Football Championship, Italy.

1498	**427**	5col. multicoloured	25	15

428 "50 U"

1990. 50th Anniv of University of Costa Rica.

1499	**428**	18col. multicoloured	65	25

429 "Education Democracy Peace"

1990. Patriotic Symbols.

1500	**429**	100col. blue and black	2·10	90
1501	-	200col. multicoloured	4·50	1·40
1502	-	500col. multicoloured	9·75	4·75

DESIGNS: 200col. Map of Costa Rica in national colours; 500col. State arms.

1991. Air. No. 1491 optd LEY 7097 CORREO AEREO.

1503	**420**	50col. multicoloured	1·60	55

431 Painting by Juan Ramirez

1990. Costa Rican Coffee.

1504	**431**	50col. multicoloured	2·10	50

432 Penny Black

1990. 150th Anniv of the Penny Black.

1505	**432**	50col. black and blue	1·80	50

433 Heredia Hospital

1990. Hospital Centenaries.

1506	**433**	50col. blue, orge & grn	1·20	30
1507	-	100col. orange, bl & grn	2·50	65

DESIGN: 100col. National Psychiatric Hospital.

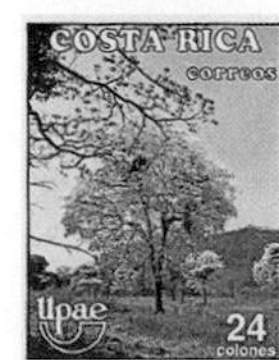

434 Yellow-bark Tree ("Tabebuia ochracea")

1990. America. The Natural World. Mult.

1508		18col. Scarlet macaw ("Ara macao")	55	15
1509		18col. Buffon's macaw ("Ara ambigua")	55	15
1510		24col. Carao tree ("Cassia grandis")	80	40
1511		24col. Type **434**	80	40

1990. Obligatory Tax. Children's Village. No. 1490 optd LEY 7157 PRO-CIUDAD DE LOS NINOS 1990.

1512	**419**	10col. multicoloured	30	25

436 "Banana Picker" (Alleardo Villa, Ceiling of Grand Staircase)

1991. Air. Paintings in National Theatre.

1516	**436**	30col. multicoloured	1·40	40

437 Costa Rica and Panama Flags and Seals

1991. 50th Anniv of Costa Rica–Panama Boundary Treaty.

1517	**437**	10col. multicoloured	25	15
1518	-	10col. black and blue	25	15
1519	-	10col. blue, brown & blk	25	15

DESIGNS: No. 1518. Presidents meeting: 1519, Map.

1991. Air. "Exfilcori '91" National Stamp Exhibition. No. 1501 optd Aereo EXFILCORI '91.

1520		200col. multicoloured	7·00	1·80

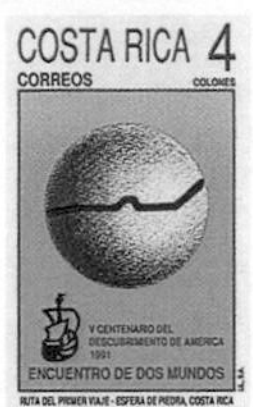

439 Route of First Voyage on Stone Globe

1991. 500th Anniv (1992) of Discovery of America by Columbus (4th issue).

1521	**439**	4col. red, black and blue	80	15

1991. Air. Centenary of Basketball. No. 1474 optd CENTENARIO DEL BALONCESTO CORREO AEREO.

1522		20col. multicoloured	2·75	80

1991. Nos. 1482 and 1342 surch.

1523	**416**	1col. on 2col. mult	30	15
1524	-	3col. on 8col.50 mult	30	15

443 Dr. Rafael Angel Calderon Guardia Hospital

1991. Air. 50th Anniv of Social Security Administration.

1525	**443**	15col. multicoloured	1·30	30

444 Child praying

1991. Obligatory Tax. Christmas. Children's Village.

1526	**444**	10col. blue	90	25

445 "La Poesia" (Vespaciano Bignami)

1992. Air. Paintings in National Theatre.

1527	**445**	35col. multicoloured	3·25	80

446 Benito Serrano Jimenez

1992. Former Presidents of Supreme Court of Justice. Multicoloured.

1528		5col. Type **446**	25	15
1529		5col. Luis Davila Solera	25	15
1530		5col. Fernando Baudrit Solera	25	15
1531		5col. Alejandro Alvarado Garcia	25	15

447 Oxcart

1992. 25th Anniv of National Directorate of Community Development.

1532	**447**	15col. multicoloured	1·50	30

448 Dr. Solon Nunez Frutos (public health pioneer)

1992

1533	**448**	15col. black and red	95	30

449 Total Solar Eclipse

1992. International Space Year. Mult.

1534		45col. Type **449**	1·60	50
1535		45col. Post office building and total eclipse	1·60	50
1536		45col. Partial eclipse	1·60	50

450 Crops

1992. 50th Anniv of Inter-American Institute for Agricultural Co-operation.

1537	**450**	35col. multicoloured	1·40	40

451 "Nina"

1992. Air. 500th Anniv of Discovery of America by Columbus (5th issue). Multicoloured.

1538		45col. Type **451**	80	50
1539		45col. "Santa Maria"	80	50
1540		45col. "Pinta"	80	50

452 Waterfall

1992. 450th Anniv of Discovery of Coco Island. Multicoloured.

1541 2col. Type **452** 20 10
1542 15col. View of cliffs from sea 40 15

453 Drilling

1992. Obligatory Tax. Christmas. Children's Village.

1543 **453** 10col. red 25 15

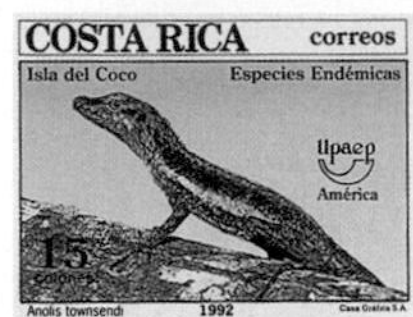

454 American Chameleon

1992. America. Coco Island Fauna. Mult.

1544 15col. Type **454** 1·20 25
1545 35col. Cocos finch 2·75 40

1992. Centenary of Limon. No. 1500 optd CENTENARIO DE LIMON.

1546 **429** 100col. blue and black 2·00 95

456 "Allegory of the Fine Arts" (detail, R. Fontana)

1993. Paintings in National Theatre.

1547 **456** 20col. multicoloured 80 25

457 Emblem

1993. Air. International Arts Festival.

1548 **457** 45col. multicoloured 1·40 50

1993. No. 1494 surch.

1549 **423** 5col. on 18col. mult 40 15

459 Common Dolphin

1993. Dolphins. Multicoloured.

1550 10col. Type **459** 90 25
1551 20col. Striped dolphins 1·80 25

460 Emblem

1993. 40th Anniv of Civil Service Statute.

1552 **460** 5col. multicoloured 30 25

461 Anniversary Emblem

1993. 50th Anniv of Chamber of Industry.

1553 **461** 45col. multicoloured 1·40 90

462 Communication Zone

1993. 25th Anniv of University of Costa Rica School of Communication and Sciences.

1554 **462** 20col. black, red & blue 50 30

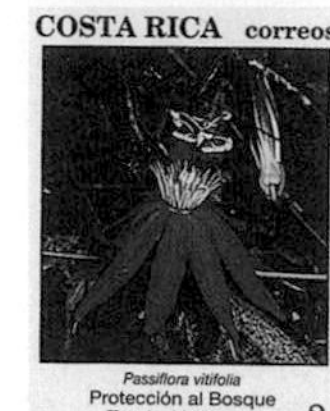

463 "Passiflora vitifolia"

1993. Tropical Rainforest Flora. Mult.

1555 2col. Type **463** 30 15
1556 35col. "Gurania megistantha" 90 55

464 Campaigners

1993. 50th Anniv of Guaranteed Social Rights.

1557 **464** 20col. multicoloured 50 30

465 Association Emblem

1993. 15th International Customs Officers' Associations Congress.

1558 **465** 45col. multicoloured 1·10 75

466 Carpentry

1993. Obligatory Tax. Christmas. Children's Village.

1559 **466** 10col. multicoloured 25 15

467 Dish Aerial

1993. Air. 30th Anniv of Costa Rican Electrical Institute's Responsibility for Development of Telecommunications.

1560 **467** 45col. multicoloured 1·10 75

468 Prof. Castro

1993. Birth Centenary of Miguel Angel Castro Carazo (founder of Commercial School).

1561 **468** 20col. red and blue 65 30

469 Assembly Hall

1993. 150th Anniv of Costa Rica University Faculty of Law.

1562 **469** 20col. multicoloured 50 30

470 "The Dancer" (Adriatico Froli)

1994. National Theatre.

1563 **470** 20col. multicoloured 50 30

471 Mural (Luis Feron)

1994. Air. 150th Anniv of Ministry of Government and Police.

1564 **471** 45col. multicoloured 1·10 75

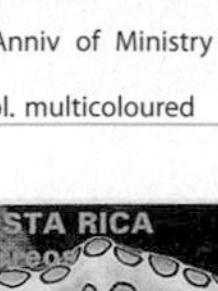

472 Flamingo Tongue

1994. Marine Animals. Multicoloured.

1565 5col. Type **472** 30 15
1566 10col. "Ophioderma rubicundum" 50 15
1567 15col. Black-barred soldierfish 75 25
1568 20col. King angelfish 95 30
1569 35col. Creole-fish 1·60 55
1570 45col. "Tubastraea coccinea" 2·10 75
1571 50col. "Acanthaster planci" 2·40 80
1572 55col. "Ocypode sp." 2·75 90
1573 70col. Speckled balloon-fish 3·75 1·10
MS1574 60×70 mm. 100col. "Thalassoma lucasnum" 4·75 4·75

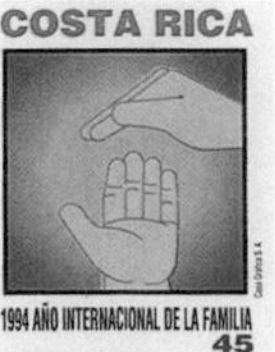

473 Hands forming Shelter

1994. Air. International Year of the Family.

1575 **473** 45col. multicoloured 1·10 1·10

474 Child

1994. Obligatory Tax. Christmas. Children's Village.

1576 **474** 11col. green and lilac 15 15

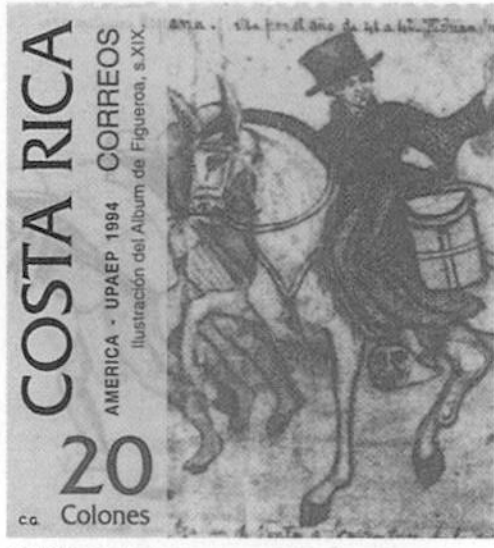

475 Courier

1994. America. Postal Transport. Details of an illustration from "Album de Figueroa". Each orange, light orange and blue.

1577 20col. Type **475** 30 30
1578 20col. Rear of pack ox 30 30

Nos. 1577/8 were issued together in se-tenant pairs with intervening label, each strip forming a composite design.

476 "Federico" (Luis Delgado)

1995. 90th Anniv of Rotary International.

1579 **476** 20col. multicoloured 90 40

477 Antonio Jose de Sucre (President of Bolivia. 1826–28)

1995. Anniversaries. Multicoloured.

1580 10col. Type **477** (birth bicentenary) 25 25
1581 30col. Jose Marti (poet and Cuban revolutionary) (death centenary) 65 65

478 "Rider" (sculpture, Nestor Varela)

1995. 50th Anniv of Guanacaste Institute.

1582 **478** 50col. green, blk & gold 1·10 1·10

1995. No. 1561 surch 5.

1583 **468** 5col. on 20col. red & bl 25 25

480 "The Boy and the Cloud" (Francisco Amighetti)

1995. 50th Anniv of UNO.

1584	**480**	5col. multicoloured	25	25

481 Woman holding Baby

1995. Obligatory Tax. Christmas. Children's Village.

1585	**481**	12col. multicoloured	55	25
MS1586		95×90 mm. No. 1585 plus 5 labels illustrating printing stages	3·50	3·50

482 "January"

1995. 13th National Stamp Exn. Seasonal paintings by Lola Fernandez. Multicoloured.

1587	50col. Type **482**	1·10	1·10
1588	50col. "November"	1·10	1·10

483 Jabiru

1995. America. Environmental Protection. Multicoloured.

1589	30col. Type **483**	65	65
1590	40col. Coastline	90	90
1591	40col. Woodland and lake	90	90
1592	50col. Leaf-cutting ant	1·20	1·20
MS1593	100×70 mm. Nos. 1589/92	6·00	6·00

484 Steam Locomotive

1996. Postcards from Limon. Multicoloured.

1594	30col. Type **484**	65	65
1595	30col. Freighter at quay	65	65
1596	30col. View of Port Moin	65	65
1597	30col. "Fruitsellers" (Diego Villalobos)	65	65
1598	30col. "Calypso" (Jorge Esquivel)	65	65

485 Douglas DC-3

1996. Air. 50th Anniv of LACSA (national airline). Multicoloured.

1599	5col. Type **485**	25	25
1600	10col. Curtiss C-46 Commando	25	25
1601	20col. Beechcraft	40	40
1602	30col. Douglas DC-6B	65	65
1603	35col. B.A.C. One Eleven	75	75
1604	40col. Convair CV 440 Metropolitan	90	90
1605	45col. Lockheed L.188 Electra	95	95
1606	50col. Boeing 727-200	1·10	1·10
1607	55col. Douglas DC-8	1·20	1·20
1608	60col. Airbus Industrie A320	1·30	1·30

486 Mosque, Synagogue and Christian Church

1996. 3000th Anniv of Jerusalem.

1609	**486**	30col. multicoloured	65	45

487 Maria del Milagro Paris and Francisco Rivas

1996. Olympic Games, Atlanta. Costa Rican Swimmers. Multicoloured.

1610	5col. Type **487**	15	10
1611	5col. Sylvia Poll and Federico Yglesias	15	10
1612	5col. Claudia Poll and Alfredo Cruz	15	10

Nos. 1610/12 were issued together, se-tenant, forming a composite design of a swimming pool.

488 Juana del Castillo (wife of Jose Maria Castro)

1996. 175th Anniv of Independence. Mult.

1613	30col. Type **488**	55	40
1614	30col. Juan Mora (President, 1849–59)	55	40
1615	30col. Jose Maria Castro (President, 1847–49 and 1866–68)	55	40
1616	30col. Pacifica Fernandez (wife of Juan Mora)	55	40

489 Water Droplet and Leaves

1996. "Water is Life". 35th Anniv of Aqueducts and Sewers.

1617	**489**	15col. multicoloured	30	25

490 "Christmas Carol" (J. M. Sanchez)

1996. Obligatory Tax. Christmas. Children's Village.

1618	**490**	14col. red and yellow	55	25

491 "Countrywomen" (Gonzalo Morales)

1996. America. Traditional Costumes. Mult.

1619	45col. Type **491**	90	55
1620	45col. "Lemon Black" (Manuel de la Cruz Gonzalez) (horiz)	90	55

492 Procession passing Palm-topped Wall

1997. Entrance of the Saints, San Ramon. Details of a painting by Jorge Carvajal. Multicoloured.

1621	30col. Type **492**	55	30
1622	30col. Church on hill behind procession	55	30
1623	30col. Procession passing beneath tree	55	30

Nos. 1621/3 were issued together, se-tenant, forming a composite design of the painting.

493 Class, 1930s

1997. Centenary of School of Fine Arts.

1624	**493**	50col. multicoloured	1·10	45

494 Child and Man listening to Radio

1997. 50th Anniv of Radio Nederland.

1625	**494**	45col. multicoloured	80	50

495 Postmen

1997. America. The Postman. 14th National Stamp Exhibition.

1626	**495**	30col. multicoloured	40	30

496 Church (Roberto Cambronero)

1997. Bicentenary of Church of the Immaculate Conception, Heredia.

1627	**496**	50col. multicoloured	1·10	60

497 Antonio Obando Chan (bust, Olger Villegas)

1997. Obligatory Tax. Christmas. Children's Village.

1628	**497**	15col. multicoloured	30	30

498 Arche de la Defense and Ball

1998. World Cup Football Championship, France.

1629	**498**	50col. black, blue & red	1·10	80

499 Figueres demolishing Fort Bellavista's Walls

1998. 50th Anniv of Second Republic. Mult.

1630	10col. Type **499**	50	20
1631	30col. Pres. Jose Figueres	75	20
1632	45col. Type **499**	1·10	20
1633	50col. Sledgehammer destroying wall	1·20	30
MS1634	120×91 mm. Nos. 1631 and 1633	1·80	1·80

500 "Caligo memnon"

1998. Butterflies. Multicoloured.

1635	10col. Type **500**	30	20
1636	15col. Emperor	30	30
1637	20col. Orange swallowtail	50	35
1638	30col. Malachite	75	55
1639	35col. Great southern white	90	65
1640	40col. "Parides iphidamas"	95	75
1641	45col. "Smyrna blonfildia"	1·10	80
1642	50col. "Callicore pitheas"	1·20	90
1643	55col. Orion	1·40	1·00
1644	60col. Monarch	1·50	1·20

501 "Generation of Knowledge" (Julio Escamez)

1998. 25th Anniv of National University, Heredia.

1645	**501**	50col. multicoloured	1·20	80

502 Carmen Lyra (writer)

1998. America. Famous Women.

1646	**502**	50col. orange, brown and ochre	65	45

503 Poinsettias

1998. Obligatory Tax. Christmas. Children's Village. Multicoloured (except No. 1649).

1647	16col. Poinsetta (gold background)	40	40
1648	16col. Type **503**	40	40
1649	16col. Berries on branch (green, black and red)	40	40

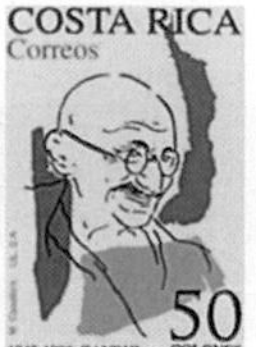
504 Gandhi

1998. 50th Death Anniv of Mahatma Gandhi.

1650	**504**	50col. multicoloured	1·00	60

505 South American Red-lined Turtle

1998. 50th Anniv of International Nature Protection Union. Turtles. Multicoloured.

1651	60col. Type **505**		1·50	1·50
1652	70col. Mexican red turtle ("Rhinoclemmys pulcherrima")		1·60	1·60
1653	70col. Snapping turtle ("Chelydra serpentina")		1·60	1·60

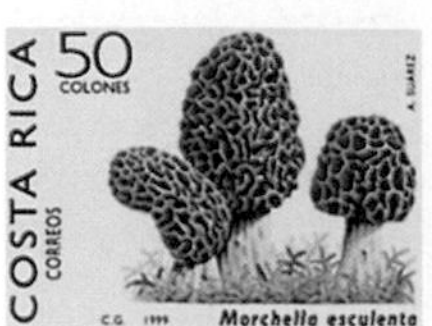

506 Common Morel

1999. Fungi. Multicoloured.

1654	50col. Type **506**		90	90
1655	50col. Cep (*Boletus edulis*)		90	90

507 Boy

1999. 50th Anniv of SOS Children's Villages.

1656	**507**	50col. multicoloured	1·00	55

508 Man minding Cart outside Telephone Box

1999. 50th Anniv of National Electricity Corporation.

1657	**508**	75col. multicoloured	65	45

509 Sanabria Martinez

1999. Birth Centenary of Victor Sanabria Martinez (Archbishop of San Jose).

1658	**509**	300col. violet	2·50	2·10

510 Elderly Woman with Children (poster, Fernando Francia)

1999. International Year of the Elderly.

1659	**510**	50col. multicoloured	40	30

511 Woman helping Children

1999. 50th Anniv of Supreme Elections Tribunal.

1660	**511**	70col. multicoloured	65	45

512 Village and Children

1999. Obligatory Tax. Christmas. Children's Village.

1661	**512**	17col. multicoloured	25	25

513 Granados

1999. Carmen Granados Death Commemoration.

1662	**513**	50col. multicoloured	50	30

514 Woman holding Head

1999. America. A New Millennium without Arms. Multicoloured.

1663	50col. Type **514**		40	30
1664	70col. Man		65	40

515 Globe

1999. 125th Anniv of Universal Postal Union.

1665	**515**	75col. multicoloured	75	45

516 Orchid

1999. "Philexfrance 99" International Stamp Exhibition, Paris. Multicoloured.

1666	300col. Type **516**		2·75	1·80
1667	300col. Orchid and Eiffel Tower		2·75	1·80

517 Jaguar

2000. 50th Anniv of Central Bank of Costa Rica. Multicoloured.

1668	60col. Type **517**		80	60
1669	60col. Scorpion		80	60
1670	60col. Bat		80	60
1671	60col. Crab		80	60
1672	60col. Dragon		80	60
1673	90col. Obverse and reverse of ½-escudo gold coin, 1825		1·40	1·00
1674	90col. Obverse and reverse of ½-unze gold coin, 1850		1·40	1·00
1675	90col. Obverse and reverse of ⅛-peso silver coin, 1850		1·40	1·00
1676	90col. Obverse and reverse of 20 pesos gold coin, 1873		1·40	1·00
1677	90col. Obverse and reverse of 1-colon coin, 1900		1·40	1·00

518 Taekwondo

2000. Olympic Games, Sydney. Multicoloured.

1678	60col. Type **518**		65	40
1679	60col. Cycling		65	40
1680	60col. Swimming		65	40
1681	60col. Football		65	40
1682	70col. Running		75	50
1683	70col. Boxing		75	50
1684	70col. Gymnastics		75	50
1685	70col. Tennis		75	50

Stamps of the same value were issued together, se-tenant, in blocks of four stamps, each block forming the composite design of a map of Australia with the sport appearing within the outline of the map.

519 Rafael Calderon Guardia

2000. Birth Centenary of Rafael Angel Calderon Guardia (politician).

1686	**519**	100col. blue	80	30

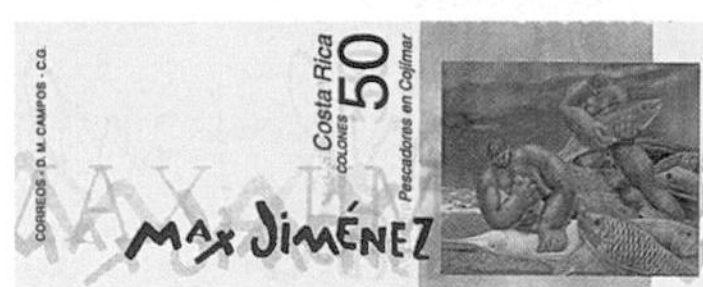

520 "Fisherman in Cojimar"

2000. Birth Centenary of Max Jiminez (artist). Multicoloured.

1687	50col. Type **520**		60	40
1688	50col. "Adamant"		60	40

521 Child's Face

2000. Obligatory Tax. Christmas. Children's Village.

1689	**521**	20col. green	30	30
1690	**521**	20col. red	30	30
1691	**521**	20col. blue	30	30
1692	**521**	20col. brown	30	30

522 Family

2000. AIDS Awareness. Multicoloured.

1693	60col. Type **522**		55	30
1694	90col. Man between blocks of colour		1·10	60

523 Nativity Scene

2000. Christmas.

1695	**523**	100col. multicoloured	1·10	80

524 Cocos Cuckoo (*Coccyzus ferruginous*)

2001. America. UNESCO. World Heritage Sites. Coco Island. Birds. Multicoloured.

1696	95col. Type **524**		1·60	1·20
1697	115col. Cocos finch (*Pinaroloxias inornata*)		1·90	1·60

525 Cart and Windmill

2001. 150th Anniv of Costa Rica–Netherlands Co-operation Treaty.

1698	**525**	65col. multicoloured	65	50

2001. No. 1502 surch.

1699	65col. on 500col. multicoloured	65	55
1700	80col. on 500col. multicoloured	80	70
1701	95co. on 500col. multicoloured	95	80

2001. No. 1602 surch C5.00.

1702	5col. on 30col. multicoloured	25	15

528 Guaria Turrialba (*Cattleya dowiana*)

2001. Spain–Costa Ricen Stamp Exhibition, San Jose. Orchids. Multicoloured.

1703	65col. Type **528**		80	65
1704	65col. "Trichophilia"		80	65

529 Boy pushing Furniture on Barrow

2001. Child Labour Eradication Campaign.

1705	**529**	100col. multicoloured	1·10	80

530 Child holding Stamp and Magnifier

2001. Obligatory Tax. Christmas. Children's Village. Multicoloured, colour of right-hand title panel given.

1706	**530**	21col. violet	30	30
1707	**530**	21col. green	30	30
1708	**530**	21col. red	30	30
1709	**530**	21col. yellow	30	30

531 Steam Locomotive and Tomas Guardia

2001. Tomas Guardia (former President and railway pioneer) Commemoration.

1710	**531**	65col. multicoloured	80	55

2002. No. 1501 surch 65.

1711	65col. on 200col. multicoloured	65	50

534 National Team Members (image scaled to 67% of original size)

2002. World Cup Football Championship, Japan and South Korea.

1712	**534**	65col. multicoloured	65	50

535 Group Emblem

2002. 16th Rio Group Conference, San Jose.

1713	**535**	65col. blue and green	75	50

536 Children and Globe

2002. America. Literacy Campaign. Multicoloured.

1714		65col. Type **536**	75	40
1715		100col. Woman reading Braille	1·10	65

Nos. 1714/15 have Braille letters embossed at lower edge.

537 Bridge

2002. Inauguration of Bridge over River Tempisque.

1716	**537**	95c. multicoloured	1·10	80

538 Two Women and Man

2002. Centenary of Pan American Health Organization. Multicoloured.

1717		10cols. Type **538**	25	10
1718		10cols. Centenary emblem	25	10
1719		10cols. Woman and child	25	10
1720		10cols. Boy and man	25	10
1721		50cols. As No. 1718	55	40

Nos. 1717/20 were issued together, se-tenant, forming a composite design.

539 World Trade Centre, New York, U.S.A.

2002. 1st Anniv of Attack on World Trade Centre, New York.

1722	**539**	110cols. multicoloured	1·20	1·10

No. 1722 has Braille letters embossed at lower edge.

540 *Lirope tetraphylla* (inscr "tetraphyla")

2002. Uvita Island. Multicoloured.

1723		75cols. Type **540**	1·20	1·20
1724		75cols. *Ulva lactuca*	1·20	1·20
1725		75cols. *Cittarium pica*	1·20	1·20
1726		75cols. *Gorgona flabellum*	1·20	1·20

Nos. 1723/6 are embossed with Braille letters.

541 Laughing Child

2002. Obligatory Tax. Christmas. Children's Village. Multicoloured, colour of title panel given.

1727	**541**	22col. violet	30	30
1728	**541**	22col. blue	30	30
1729	**541**	22col. orange	30	30
1730	**541**	22col. green	30	30

542 *Archocentrus sajica*

2003. America. Fauna. Multicoloured.

1731		110col. Type **542**	2·00	1·20
1732		110col. *Asatheros diquis*	2·00	1·20

Nos. 1731/2 are embossed with Braille letters.

543 Small Island

2003. 25th Anniv of Coco Island National Park. Multicoloured.

1733		75c. Type **543**	1·20	75
1734		75c. Bay and coastline	1·20	75

Nos. 1733/4 are embossed with Braille letters.

544 Franklin Ramon Chang-Diaz

2003. Franklin Ramon Chang-Diaz (astronaut). Multicoloured.

1735		75col. Type **544**	1·50	1·10
1736		75col. *Phanaeus changdiazi*	1·50	1·10

Nos. 1735/6 were issued together, se-tenant, each pair forming a composite design. Nos. 1735/6 are embossed with Braille letters.

545 Cocori and Turtle

2003. Cocori (children's story written by Joaquin Gutierrez and illustrated by Hugo Diaz). Multicoloured.

1737		25col. Type **545**	50	30
1738		25col. Cocori looking into water	50	30
1739		25col. Toucan	50	30
1740		25col. Girl and Cocori	50	30
1741		25col. Cocori and bird	50	30
1742		25col. With father and animals	50	30
1743		25col. With monkey and turtle	50	30
1744		25col. Monkey with raised paws, turtle and Cocori	50	30
1745		25col. With mother	50	30
1746		25col. Picking flowers with mother	50	30

Nos. 1737/46 are embossed with Braille letters.

546 Jose Maria Zeledon Brenes (lyricist)

2003. Centenary of National Anthem Lyrics.

1747		75col. Type **546**	1·40	85
1748		75col. Text (50×35 mm)	1·40	85

Nos. 1747/8 were issued together, se-tenant, forming a composite design.

547 Pope John Paul II

2003. 25th Anniv of Pontificate of Pope John Paul II.

1749	**547**	130col. multicoloured	2·50	1·80

548 Children and Star

2003. Obligatory Tacol. Christmas. Children's Village. Multicoloured, colour of title panel given.

1750	**548**	23col. mauve	40	20
1751	**548**	23col. green	40	20
1752	**548**	23col. vermilion	40	20
1753	**548**	23col. yellow	40	20

549 Charles Lindbergh and *Spirit of St. Louis*

2003. 75th Anniv of Charles Lindbergh's Arrival in Costa Rica.

1754	**549**	110col. multicoloured	2·10	1·60

No. 1754 is embossed with Braille letters.

550 Ruins and Wall

2003. Guayabo de Turrialba Archaeological Site.

1755	**550**	110col. multicoloured	2·10	1·60

No. 1755 is embossed with Braille letters.

551 *Tetranema floribundum*

2004. America. Native Fauna and Flora. Trees. Multicoloured.

1756		75col. Type **551**	1·40	85
1757		75col. *Ceiba pentandra*	1·40	85
1758		90col. *Ceiba pentandra* (different)	1·80	1·20
1759		110col. *Tetranema gamboanum*	2·10	1·40

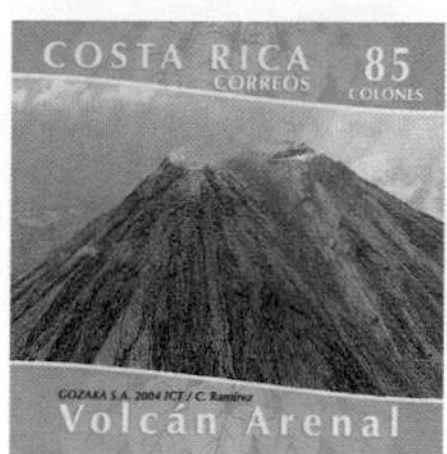

552 Arenal Volcano

2004. Volcanoes. Multicoloured.

1760		85col. Type **552**	1·70	1·00
1761		120col. Irazu	2·40	1·70
1762		140col. Poas	2·50	1·80

554 Miguel Rodriguez and Members Flags

2004. Inauguration of Miguel Angel Rodriguez as President of Organization of American States (OES).

1767	**554**	120col. multicoloured	2·40	1·75

555 Three Kings

2004. Obligatory Tacol. Christmas. Children's Village. Multicoloured, colour of title panel given.

1768	**555**	25col. yellow	50	30
1769	**555**	25col. green	50	30

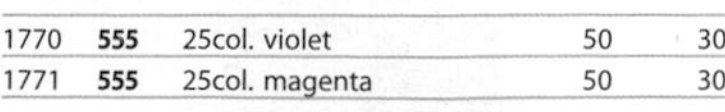

1770	**555**	25col. violet	50	30
1771	**555**	25col. magenta	50	30

556 Centenary Emblem

2004. Centenary of FIFA (Federation Internationale de Football). Multicoloured.

1772		140p. Type **556**	2·50	1·80
1773		140p. Player and ball	2·50	1·80

557 Frog

2005. Centenary of Rotary International. Mult.

1774		140p. Type **557**	2·50	1·80
1775		140p. Centenary emblem	2·50	1·80
1776		140p. Butterfly	2·50	1·80

558 Albert Einstein

2005. International Year of Physics.

1777	**558**	95col. scarlet	1·90	1·30
1778	-	95col. brown	1·90	1·30

DESIGN: No. 1778 Max Planck.

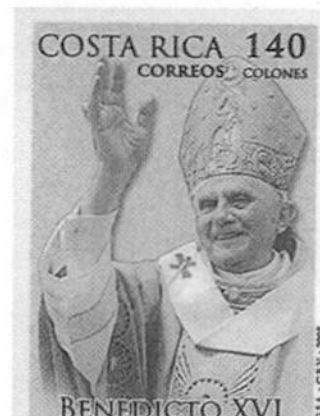

559 Pope Benedict XVI

2005. Pope Benedict XVI and Pope John Paul II. Each brown and ochre.

1779		140p. Type **559**	2·50	1·80
1780		140p. Pope John Paul II	2·50	1·80

560 *Passiflora vitifolia*

2005. National Parks. Multicoloured.

1781		85p. Type **560**	1·70	1·00
1782		85p. *Dryas iulia moderata*	1·70	1·00
1783		85p. *Potos flavus*	1·70	1·00

561 Child using Computer

2005. America. Struggle against Poverty.

1784	**561**	140p. olive and black	2·50	1·80
1785	-	140p. yellow and black	2·50	1·80
1786	-	140p. ochre and black	2·50	1·80

DESIGNS: No. 1785, Carpenter; 1786, Doctor.

562 Children

2005. Obligatory Tax. Christmas. Children's Village. Multicoloured, colour of face value given.

1787	**562**	28col. white	50	30
1788	**562**	28col. ochre	50	30
1789	**562**	28col. brown	50	30
1790	**562**	28col. red	50	30

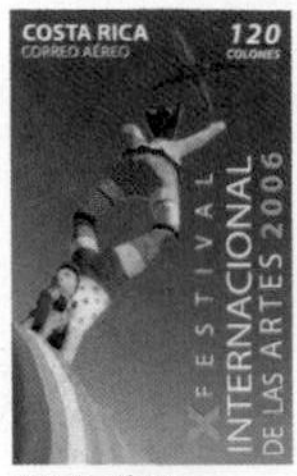

563 Acrobats (sculpture)

2006. Air. International Arts Festival.

1791	**563**	120col. multicoloured	2·40	1·70

564 Players (image scaled to 70% of original size)

2006. Centenary of Club Sport Cartaginees.

1792	**564**	85col. multicoloured	1·70	1·30

565 Juan Raphael Mora (president 1849–59) and National Monument.

2006. 150th Anniv of "National Campaign" (to overthrow William Walker's mercenary army). Sheet 90×182 mm containing T 565 and similar horiz designs. Ochre and brown.

MS1793	85col.×5, Type **565**; Juan Santamaria monument and Meson de Guerra; Map of Central America (49×39 mm); General Jose Maria Cañias and Casa Santa Rosa; Luis Molina (ambassador to Washington) and Joaquin Bernardo Calvo (chancellor)	5·50	5·00

The stamps of **MS**1793 form a composite design.

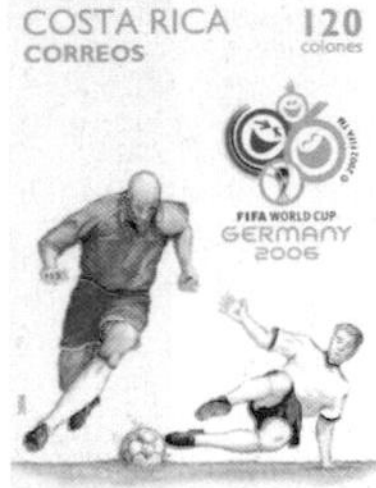

566 Players

2006. World Cup Football Championship, Germany.

1794	**566**	120col. multicoloured	2·40	1·70

567 Globe as Electric Plug

2006. America. Energy Conservation.

1795	**567**	155col. multicoloured	2·70	2·10

568 *Sula sula*

2006. Isla del Coco National Park. Multicoloured.

1796	180col. Type **568**	2·60	2·00
1797	180col. *Mycteroperca olfax*	2·60	2·00
1798	180col. *Zanclus cornutus*	2·60	2·00
1799	180col. *Eretmochelys imbricaas*	2·60	2·00
1800	180col. *Tursiops truncates*	2·60	2·00
1801	180col. *Myripristis berndti*	2·60	2·00
1802	180col. *Dendroica petechia aureola*	2·60	2·00
1803	180col. *Carcharhinus limbatus*	2·60	2·00
1804	180col. *Anous stolidus*	2·60	2·00
1805	180col. *Acarus rubroviolaceus*	2·60	2·00

569 Jose Ferrer

2006. Birth Centenary of Jose Figueres Ferrer (president of Costa Rica, 1948—1949, 1953—1958 and 1970—1974.). Multicoloured.

1806	115col. Type **569**	1·50	1·10
MS1807	89×60 mm. 1000col. As No. 1806. Imperf	12·00	12·00

570 *Bixa orellana*

2006. Forest Fruiting Trees. Multicoloured.

1808	155col. Type **570**	2·50	1·80
1809	155col. *Garcinia intermedia*	2·50	1·80
1810	155col. *Hymenaea courbaril*	2·50	1·80

571 Flag

2006. Centenary of National Symbols. Mult.

1811	155col. Type **571**	2·50	1·80
1812	155col. Arms	2·50	1·80

572 Child

2006. Obligatory Tax. Christmas. Children's Village. Multicoloured, colour of border given.

1813	**572**	32col. bistre	55	35
1814	**572**	32col. ochre	55	35
1815	**572**	32col. green	55	35
1816	**572**	32col. yellow	55	35

573 Francisco Orlich

2007. Birth Centenary of Francisco Jose Orlich Bolmarcich (president, 1962–66).

1817	**573**	115cols. multicoloured	1·50	1·10

574 *Guarianthe skinneri*

2007. Orchids. Multicoloured.

1818	180cols. Type **574**	2·60	2·00
1819	180cols. Inscr 'Galenandra arundinis'	2·60	2·00
1820	180cols. *Encyclia ossenbachiana*	2·60	2·00
1821	180cols. *Dracula inexperata*	2·60	2·00
1822	180cols. *Guarianthe skinneri* (different)	2·60	2·00
1823	180cols. *Kefersteinia retanae*	2·60	2·00
1824	180cols. Inscr 'Corianthes kaiseriana'	2·60	2·00
1825	180cols. *Psychopsis krameriana*	2·60	2·00
1826	180cols. *Chonroscaphe yamilethae*	2·60	2·00
1827	180cols. *Cattleya dowiana*	2·60	2·00
MS1828	90×60 mm.1000cols. *Brassia suavissima*. Imperf	12·00	12·00

575 Giovanni Melchior Bosco (Don Bosco) (founder)

2007. Centenary of the Salesian Society in Costa Rica.

1829	**575**	110cols. multicoloured	1·20	90

576 Frog-shaped Gold Pendant

2007. Pre-Colombian Art. Multicoloured.

1830	155cols. Type **576**	2·50	1·80
1831	155cols. Bird-shaped jade pendant	2·50	1·50
1832	155cols. Carved stone panel (*horiz*)	2·50	1·80
1833	155cols. Ceramic burner with lizard	2·50	1·80
1834	155cols. Male stone figure	2·50	1·80

577 Students and Teacher

2007. America. Education for All. Multicoloured.

1835	115cols. Type **577**	2·50	1·80
1836	155cols. Family	2·50	1·80

578 Space Walk by Ramon Chang-Diaz (Costa Rican born astronaut and plasma specialist)

2007. Plasma Technology. Multicoloured.

1837	240cols. Type **578**	4·75	3·50
1838	240cols. Plasma symbol	4·75	3·50

579 La Negrita (statue)

2007. La Negrita (Costa Rica's patron saint), Basilica Virgin de Los Angeles, Cartago. Multicoloured.

1839	115cols. Type **579**	2·50	1·80
1840	115cols. Enclosed in reliquary	2·50	1·80

Nos. 1839/40 were issued together, *se-tenant*, forming a composite background design.

No. **MS**1841 has been left for miniature sheet not yet received.

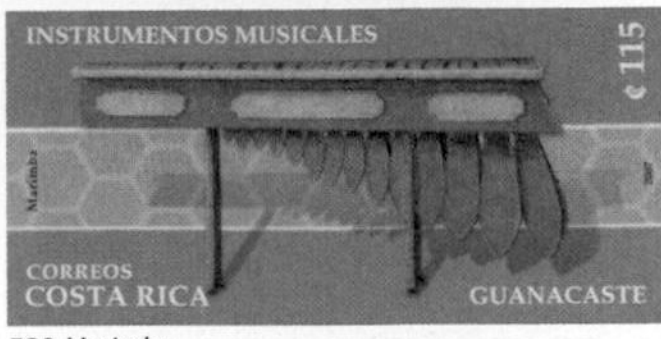

580 Marimba

2007. Musical Instruments. Multicoloured.

MS1841	100×150 mm. 1000cols. Shrine (75×115 mm)	12·00	12·00
1842	115cols. Type **580**	2·50	1·80
1843	115cols. Quijongo (*vert*)	2·50	1·80

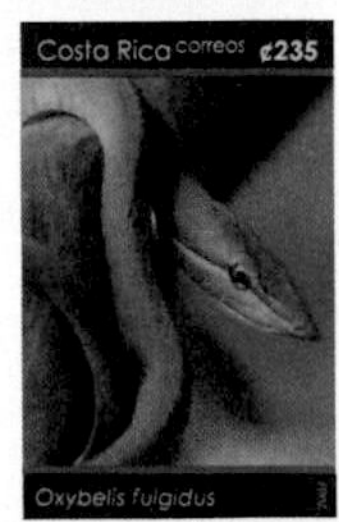

581 *Oxybelis fulgidus* (green vine snake)

2007. National Parks. Multicoloured.

1844	235cols. Type **581**	4·50	3·25
1845	235cols. *Stagmomantis* (praying mantis)	4·50	3·25
1846	235cols. *Heliodoxa jacula* (green-crowned brilliant)	4·50	3·25
1847	235cols. *Pulsatrix perspicillata* (spectacled owl)	4·50	3·25

582 Cyclist

2007. Special Olympic Games, Shanghai. Mult.

1848	240cols. Type **582**	4·75	3·50
1849	240cols. Swimmer	4·75	3·50
1850	240cols. Runner	4·75	3·50

583 *Por qe Tio Conejo las orejas largas* (Why has Tio Conejo such long ears?)

2007. Cuentos de mia Tía Panchita (Tales of My Aunt Panchita) (children's stories by Carmen Lyra (Maria Isabela Carvajal)). Two sheets containing T 583 and similar multicoloured designs.

MS1851	94×40 mm. 100colsx4, Type **583**; *La Mica* (the monkey); *Uvieta* (the grapevine); *Tio Conejo y los caites de su abuela* (Tio Conejo and his grandmother's shoes)	8·00	8·00
MS1852	90×60 mm.1000cols. *De como Tio Conejo salio de un apuro* (Tio Conejo left in a hurry) (79×49 mm.)	12·00	12·00

The stamps and margins of **MS**1851 form a composite design.

584 Ox Cart and Driver

2007. National Heritage. Multicoloured.

1853	180cols. Type **584**		
1854	180cols. Decorated wheel hub	4·25	2·50

585 Child Skateboarding (Genesis Alvarez)

2007. Obligatory Tax. Christmas. Children's Village. Children's Drawings.

1855	35cols. Type **585**	80	50
1856	35cols. Family (Axel Dario Suarez)	80	50
1857	35cols. Pupils (Deryn Arroyo)	80	50
1858	35cols. Children using play equipment (Tiffany Calderon)	80	50

586 Nobel Peace Medal (President Oscar Arias Sanchez)

2007. Esquipulas Peace Agreement. Multicoloured.

1859	135cols. Type **586**	3·25	2·00
1860	135cols. Obverse (Alfred Nobel)	3·25	2·00

587 Dr. Fernando Centeno Güell

2008. Birth Centenary (2007) of Dr. Fernando Centeno Guell.

1861	**587**	115cols. multicoloured	2·75	1·70

588 Ermita Nuestro Señor de la Agonía

2008. Churches. Multicoloured.

1862	230cols. Type **588**	5·50	3·25
1863	230cols. Iglesia de San Francisco	5·50	3·25
1864	230cols. Iglesia Nuestra Senora de la Soledad	5·50	3·25
1865	230cols. Iglesia de Santa Ana	5·50	3·25
1866	230cols. Catedral Nuestra Senora del Carmen	5·50	3·25
1867	230cols. Iglesia de San Bartolome Apostol	5·50	3·25

No. 1868 is left for miniature sheet not yet received.

590 *Megaptera novaeangliae* (humpback whale)

2008. Whales and Dolphins. Multicoloured.

1870	240cols. Type **590**	5·50	3·25
1871	240cols. *Satalia guianensis* (estuarine dolphin)	5·50	3·25
1872	240cols. *Stenella attenuata* (pantropical spotted dolphin)	5·50	3·25
1873	240cols. *Megaptera novaeangliae*	5·50	3·25

591 San Vincente Waterfall

2008. International Year of Planet Earth. Multicoloured.

1874	175cols. Type **591**	4·00	2·40
1875	175cols. Santa Elena penisula	4·00	2·40

592 *La ultima escena* (Rudy Espinoza)

2008. Exhibits from National Museum of Art. Sheet 101×140 mm containing T 592 and similar vert designs. Multicoloured.

MS1876 240cols.×4, Type **592**; *Mujer que avanza* (sculpture) (Cristano Badilla); *Transitoriedad del hombre* (Miguel Hernandez); *Arquetipo* (Lola Fernandez) 21·00 21·00

The stamps of **MS**1870 share a common background design.

593 Two Men

2008. 80th Anniv of Ministry of Labour and Social Security. Sheet 200×70 mm containing T 593 and similar horiz designs. Multicoloured.

MS1877 240cols.×4, Type **593**; Woman carrying fruit and two men; Woman and couple; Women and man carrying sack 21·00 21·00

The stamps and margins of **MS**1877 form a composite design.

594 Mask

2008. America. Festivals. Masquerades. Multicoloured.

1878	115cols Type **594**	2·75	1·70
1879	155cols. Multicoloured mask with large teeth	3·75	2·25

595 Boy and Juguar (DavidMalavassi Zuniga)

2008. Obligatory Tax. Christmas. Children's Village. Children's Drawings. Multicoloured.

1880	40cols. Type **595**	90	60
1881	40cols. Bird and yacht (Valeria Vargas Arias)	90	60
1882	40cols. Woman and stream (Dannia Maria Berrocal Fonseca)	90	60
1883	40cols. Boy with kite (Luis Paulino Murillo Mendez)	90	60

596 Symbols of Recovery (image scaled to 70% of original size)

2009. 25th Anniv of Hogar CREA (drug users rehabilitation programme).

1884	**595**	160cols. multicoloured	3·75	2·25

No. 1885 is vacant.

598 *Tolo el gigante viento norte* (Tolo, giant north wind) (Adela Ferreto de Saenz)

2009. Childrens' Literature. Sheet 120×101 mm containing T 598 and similar vert designs. Multicoloured.

MS1886 65cols.×4, Type **598**; *La nave de las estrellas* (Ship of stars) (Alfredo Cardona Pena); *Cuentos viejos* (Old stories) (Maria Leal de Noguera); *La musica de Paul* (Paul's music) (Lara Rios) 6·50 6·50

599 Albert Marten

2009. Alberto Marten Chavarría (lawyer, economist and founder of Movimiento Solidarista Costarricense) Commemoration.

1887	**599**	135cols. multicoloured	3·25	2·00

600 People and Buildings

2009. 60th Anniv of ICE (telecommunications and electricity provider). Sheet 125×170 mm containing T 600 and similar vert designs. Multicoloured.

MS1888 340cols.×6, Type **600**; Workmen in tunnel; Telephone engineer; Symbols of communication; Alternative energy sources; Environmental education 24·00 24·00

601 Symbols of Switzerland and Costa Rica

2009. Cost Rica–Switzerland Diplomatic Relations.

1889	**601**	225cols. multicoloured	5·25	3·00

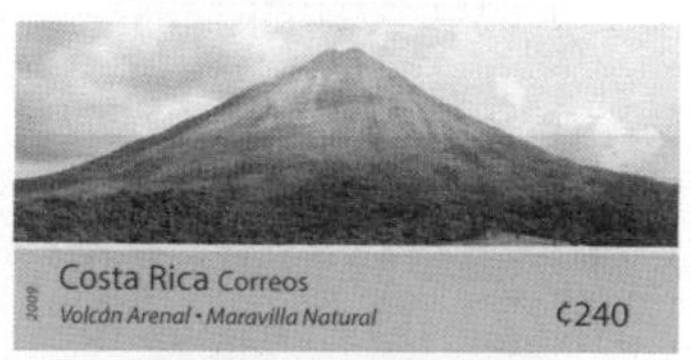

602 Arenal Volcano

2009. Natural Wonders. 30th Anniv of National Parks. Multicoloured.

1890	240cols. Type **602**	5·75	3·50
1891	240cols. Rio Celeste	5·75	3·50
1892	240cols. Cerro Chirripo	5·75	3·50
1893	240cols. Isla del Coco	5·75	3·50
1894	240cols. Biological Reserve, Monteverde	5·75	3·50
1895	240cols. Poas volcano	5·75	3·50
1896	240cols. River, Tortuguero	5·75	3·50

603 Marbles

2009. America. Children's Games. Multicoloured.

1897	135cols. Type **603**	80	50
1898	135cols. Kite flying	80	50

604 Devil

2009. OBLIGATORY TAX

MS1899 Type **604**; Clown riding pantomime cow; Death; Stilt walkers 3·75 3·75

605 Star of David

2009. Holocaust Memorial Day

1900	**605**	$500 multicoloured	8·75	8·75

EXPRESS DELIVERY STAMPS

E237 New UPU Headquarters Building and Emblem

1970. Air. New UPU Headquarters Building.

E841	**E237**	35c. multicoloured	55	25
E842	**E237**	60c. multicoloured	70	25

In Type E **237** "ENTREGA INMEDIATA" is in the form of a perforated tab.

No. E842 has the same main design, but the tab is inscr "EXPRES".

E249 Winged Letter

1972

E888	**E249**	75c. brown & red	35	35
E889	**E249**	75c. green & red	35	35
E890	**E249**	75c. mauve & red	1·60	75
E891	**E249**	1col.50 blue & red	50	40

E279 Concorde

1976

E1031	**E279**	1col. multicoloured	50	40
E1135	-	2col. multicoloured	80	45
E1136	-	2col. multicoloured	75	45
E1137	-	4col. multicoloured	65	40

Nos. E1135/7 is as Type E **279**, but inscribed "EXPRESS".

OFFICIAL STAMPS

Various issues optd OFICIAL except where otherwise stated.

1883. Stamps of 1883.

O35	**8**	1c. green	1·20	55
O36	**8**	2c. red	1·20	50
O22	**8**	5c. violet	7·25	3·00
O23	**8**	10c. orange	9·75	4·00
O38	**8**	40c. blue	1·20	50

1887. Stamps of 1887.

O39	**14**	5c. violet	12·00	3·50
O40	**14**	10c. orange	85	50

1889. Stamps of 1889.

O41	**17**	1c. brown	20	10
O42	**17**	2c. blue	20	10
O43	**17**	5c. orange	20	10
O44	**17**	10c. lake	20	10
O45	**17**	20c. green	30	10
O46	**17**	50c. red	1·30	1·30

1892. Stamps of 1892.

O47	**19**	1c. blue	25	15
O48	**19**	2c. orange	25	15
O49	**19**	5c. mauve	25	15
O50	**19**	10c. green	3·00	1·40
O51	**19**	20c. red	20	10
O52	**19**	50c. blue	60	55

1901. Stamps of 1901 (Nos. 42/48).

O53	1c. black and green	40	40
O54	2c. black and red	40	40
O61	4c. black and purple	1·40	1·30
O55	5c. black and blue	40	30
O62	6c. black and olive	1·60	1·60
O56	10c. black and brown	75	75
O57	20c. black and lake	1·10	1·10
O63	25c. brown and lilac	9·50	9·75
O58	50c. blue and red	7·75	3·75
O59	1col. black and olive	16·00	9·75

1903. Stamp of 1901 optd PROVISORIO OFICIAL.

O60	2c. black & red (No. 43)	2·75	2·75

1908. Stamps of 1907 (Nos. 57/76).

O77	1c. blue and brown	10	10
O78	2c. black and green	10	10
O79	4c. blue and red	10	10
O80	5c. blue and orange	10	10
O81	10c. black and blue	1·20	75
O82	25c. slate and lavender	30	20
O83	50c. blue and red	55	50
O84	1col. black and brown	1·20	1·10

1917. Stamps of 1910 optd OFICIAL 15-VI-1917.

O115	5c. orange (No. 80)	35	35
O116	10c. blue (No. 81)	20	20

1920. No. 82 surch OFICIAL 15 CENTIMOS.

O117	15c. on 20c. olive	55	55

1921. Official stamps of 1908 optd 1921–22 or surch also.

O123	4c. blue & red (No. O79)	40	40
O124	6c. on 1c. blue & brown (No. O77)	50	50
O125	20c. on 25c. slate and lavender (No. O82)	55	50
O126	50c. blue & red (No. O83)	2·40	2·00
O127	1col. black & brn (No. O84)	4·50	3·75

1921. No. O115 surch 10 CTS.

O128	10c. on 5c. orange	45	40

1923. Stamps of 1923.

O137	**77**	2c. brown	10	10
O138	**77**	4c. green	10	10
O139	**77**	5c. blue	30	30
O140	**77**	20c. red	20	20
O141	**77**	1col. violet	45	45

O95

1926

O169	**O95**	2c. black and blue	20	20
O231	**O95**	2c. black and lilac	10	10
O170	**O95**	3c. black and red	20	20
O232	**O95**	3c. black and brown	10	10
O171	**O95**	4c. black and blue	20	20
O233	**O95**	4c. black and red	10	10
O172	**O95**	5c. black and green	20	20
O173	**O95**	6c. black and yellow	10	10
O235	**O95**	8c. black and brown	10	10
O174	**O95**	10c. black and red	20	20
O175	**O95**	20c. black and green	20	20
O237	**O95**	20c. black and blue	10	10
O176	**O95**	30c. black and orange	20	20
O238	**O95**	40c. black and orange	20	20
O177	**O95**	45c. black and brown	20	20
O239	**O95**	55c. black and lilac	30	30
O178	**O95**	1col. black and lilac	35	35
O240	**O95**	1col. black and brown	30	30
O241	**O95**	2col. black and blue	65	65
O242	**O95**	5col. black & yellow	3·00	3·00
O243	**O95**	10col. blue and black	21·00	21·00

1934. Air. Air stamps of 1934.

O211	**107**	5c. green	20	20
O212	**107**	10c. red	20	20
O213	**107**	15c. brown	45	45
O214	**107**	20c. blue	75	75
O215	**107**	25c. orange	75	75
O216	**107**	40c. brown	90	75
O217	**107**	50c. black	90	75
O218	**107**	60c. yellow	1·10	90
O219	**107**	75c. violet	1·10	90
O220	-	1col. red	3·00	1·50
O221	-	2col. blue	6·25	4·50
O222	-	5col. black	8·75	7·75
O223	-	10col. brown	11·00	11·00

1936. Stamps of 1936.

O228	**113**	5c. green	20	20
O229	**113**	10c. red	20	20

POSTAGE DUE STAMPS

D42

1903

D55	**D42**	5c. blue	6·75	1·10
D56	**D42**	10c. brown	6·75	1·00
D57	**D42**	15c. green	3·50	1·80
D58	**D42**	20c. red	4·75	1·80
D59	**D42**	25c. blue	4·75	2·30
D60	**D42**	30c. brown	6·00	2·50
D61	**D42**	40c. olive	6·75	2·50
D62	**D42**	50c. red	6·75	2·40

D64

1915

D115	**D64**	2c. orange	1·20	55
D116	**D64**	4c. blue	1·20	55
D117	**D64**	8c. green	1·20	55
D118	**D64**	10c. violet	1·20	55
D119	**D64**	20c. brown	1·20	55

Pt. 3

CRETE

Former Turkish island in the E. Mediterranean under the joint protection of Gt. Britain, France, Italy and Russia from 1898 to 1908, when the island was united to Greece. This was recognized by Turkey in 1913. Greek stamps now used.

100 lepta = 1 drachma.

1 Hermes

2 Hera

3 Prince George of Greece

4 Talos

1900

1	**1**	1l. brown	55	30
12	**1**	1l. yellow	80	80
2	**2**	5l. green	2·20	30
3	**3**	10l. red	1·70	45
4	**2**	20l. red	5·50	1·10
13	**2**	20l. orange	3·25	85
15	**3**	25l. blue	11·00	55
14	**1**	50l. blue	13·50	13·00
16	**1**	50l. lilac	39·00	27·00
17	**4**	1d. violet	45·00	27·00
18	-	2d. brown	14·50	11·50
19	-	5d. black and green	18·00	13·00

DESIGNS (as Type **4**): 2d. Minos; 5d. St. George and Dragon.

ΠΡΟΣΩΡΙΝΟΝ

(7) ("Provisional")

1900. Optd as T 7.

5A	**3**	25l. blue	1·10	85
6A	**1**	50l. lilac	2·20	1·30
7B	**4**	1d. violet	11·00	6·50
8B	-	2d. brown (No. 18)	29·00	19·00
9B	-	5d. black & green (No. 19)	90·00	85·00

1904. Surch 5 twice.

20	**2**	5 on 20l. orange	3·25	1·10

10 Rhea

12 Prince George of Greece

16 Europa and Jupiter

1905

21	**10**	2l. lilac	1·70	20
22	-	5l. green	2·20	20
23	**12**	10l. red	2·20	1·10
24	-	20l. green	6·25	65
25	-	25l. blue	7·75	1·10
26	-	50l. brown	9·00	3·25
27	**16**	1d. sepia and red	65·00	43·00
28	-	3d. black and orange	39·00	30·00
29	-	5d. black and olive	18·00	17·00

DESIGNS—As Type **10**: 5l. Europa; 20l. Miletus; 25l. Triton; 50l. Ariadne. As Type **16**: 3d. Minos ruins. 44×28½ mm: 5d. Mt. Ida.

19 High Commissioner A. T. A. Zaimis

1907. Various designs.

30	**19**	25l. black and blue	45·00	1·10
31	-	1d. black and green	11·00	7·50

DESIGN—HORIZ: (larger): 1d. Landing of Prince George of Greece at Suda.

21 Hermes

ΕΛΛΑΣ

(22) ("Greece")

1908. Optd as T 22 in various sizes and styles.

32	**1**	1l. brown	65	45
33	**10**	2l. lilac	65	45
34	-	5l. green (No. 22)	65	45
35	**3**	10l. red	1·30	85
36	**21**	10l. red	3·25	85
37	-	20l. green (No. 24)	3·25	1·10
38	**19**	25l. black and blue	9·00	2·20
63	-	25l. blue (No. 25)	3·00	65
39	-	50l. brown (No. 26)	12·50	4·25
40	**16**	1d. sepia and red	£100	65·00
52	-	1d. black & grn (No. 31)	5·50	2·20
41	-	2d. brown (No. 18)	11·00	8·75
42	-	3d. black & orge (No. 28)	39·00	36·00
43	-	5d. black & olive (No. 29)	34·00	32·00

1909. Optd with T 7 and 22 or surch with new value also.

44	**1**	1l. yellow (No. 12)	1·70	1·30
45	**D 8**	1l. red (No. D10)	4·50	4·25
46	**D 8**	2 on 20l. red (No. D73)	1·70	1·30
47	**D 8**	2 on 20l. red (No. D13)	1·70	1·40
48	**2**	5 on 20l. red (No. 4)	£180	£180
49	**2**	5 on 20l. orange (No. 13)	1·70	1·40

OFFICIAL STAMPS

O21

1908

O32	**O21**	10l. red	22·00	1·10
O33	**O21**	30l. blue	45·00	1·10

In the 30l. the central figures are in an oval frame.

1908. Optd with T 22.

O44	10l. red	17·00	1·10
O45	30l. blue	34·00	1·10

POSTAGE DUE STAMPS

D8

1901

D10	**D8**	1l. red	35	30
D11	**D8**	5l. red	55	30
D12	**D8**	10l. red	80	45
D13	**D8**	20l. red	1·10	55
D14	**D8**	40l. red	11·00	11·00
D15	**D8**	50l. red	11·00	11·00
D16	**D8**	1d. red	22·00	22·00
D17	**D8**	2d. red	14·00	11·00

1901. Surch "1 drachma" in Greek characters.

D18	1d. on 1d. red	11·00	9·25

1908. Optd with T 22.

D70	1l. red	45	30

D45	5l. red	65	65
D72	10l. red	1·10	45
D47	20l. red	1·70	1·60
D74	40l. red	11·00	4·75
D75	50l. red	17·00	11·00
D76	1d. red	28·00	27·00
D51	1d. on 1d. red (No. D18)	11·00	8·75
D52	2d. red	18·00	11·00

REVOLUTIONARY ASSEMBLY, 1905

In March a revolt in favour of union with Greece began, organized by Venizelos with headquarters at Theriso, South of Canea. The revolt collapsed in November 1905.

V1

1905. Imperf.

V1	V1	5l. red and green	17·00	8·75
V2	V1	10l. green and red	17·00	8·75
V3	V1	20l. blue and red	17·00	8·75
V4	V1	50l. green and violet	17·00	8·75
V5	V1	1d. red and blue	17·00	8·75

V2 Crete enslaved

1905

V6	V2	5l. orange	90	85
V7	V2	10l. grey	90	85
V8	V2	20l. mauve	90	85
V9	V2	50l. blue	1·70	1·70
V10	-	1d. violet and red	4·50	4·25
V11	-	2d. brown and green	6·75	6·50

DESIGN: 1, 2d. King George of Greece.

Pt. 3

CROATIA

Part of Hungary until 1918 when it became part of Yugoslavia. In 1941 it was proclaimed an independent state but in 1945 it became a constituent republic of the Federal People's Republic of Yugoslavia. In 1991 Croatia became independent.

Croatia.
April 1941. 100 paras = 1 dinar.
Sept 1941. 100 banicas = 1 kuna.
1991. 100 paras = 1 dinar.
1994. 100 lipa = 1 kuna.

Serbian Posts in Croatia.
100 paras = 1 dinar.

NEZAVISNA
DRŽAVA
HRVATSKA
IIIIII

(1)

1941. Stamps of Yugoslavia optd as T **1** ("Independent Croat State").

1	99	50p. orange	3·75	4·25
2	99	1d. green	3·75	4·25
3	99	1d.50 red	4·25	2·20
4	99	2d. mauve	5·00	3·25
5	99	3d. brown	8·25	8·75
6	99	4d. blue	9·75	9·75
7	99	5d. blue	9·75	9·75
8	99	5d.50 violet	11·00	12·00

(2)

1941. Stamps of Yugoslavia optd as T **2**.

9	25p. black	55	65
10	50p. orange	55	65
11	1d. green	55	65
12	1d.50 red	85	65
13	2d. pink	85	65
14	3d. brown	1·10	1·30
15	4d. blue	1·30	1·80
16	5d. blue	2·00	1·80
17	5d.50 violet	2·20	1·80
18	6d. blue	2·75	3·25
19	8d. brown	3·75	3·25
20	12d. violet	5·00	4·25
21	16d. purple	5·50	6·50
22	20d. blue	7·00	7·50
23	30d. pink	10·50	14·00

NEZAVISNA
1
DIN
DRŽAVA
HRVATSKA

(3)

1941. Stamps of Yugoslavia surch as T **3**.

24	1d. on 3d. brown	45	55
25	2d. on 4d. blue	45	55

(4)

1941. Founding of Croatian Army. Nos. 414/26 of Yugoslavia optd with T **4**.

25a	25p. black	38·00	40·00
25b	50p. orange	38·00	41·00
25c	1d. green	38·00	43·00
25d	1d.50 red	43·00	50·00
25e	2d. pink	49·00	50·00
25f	3d. brown	49·00	55·00
25g	4d. blue	38·00	43·00
25h	5d. blue	43·00	45·00
25i	5d.50 violet	43·00	45·00
25j	6d. blue	49·00	50·00
25k	8d. brown	43·00	43·00
25l	12d. violet	43·00	45·00
25m	16d. purple	43·00	50·00
25n	20d. blue	43·00	45·00
25o	30d. pink	49·00	50·00

Sold at double face value.

1941. Stamps of Yugoslavia optd as T **2** but without shield.

26	109	1d.50+1d.50 black	22·00	27·00
27	-	4d.+3d. brown (No. 457)	22·00	27·00

1941. Postage Due stamps of Yugoslavia optd **NEZAVISNA DRZAVA HRVATSKA FRANCO**.

28	D56	50p. violet	55	55
29	D56	2d. blue	1·60	1·60
30	D56	5d. orange	2·20	1·60
31	D56	10d. brown	2·75	2·20

7 Mt. Ozalj

8 Banja Luka

1941

32	7	25b. red	20	10
33	-	50b. green	20	10
34	-	75b. olive	20	10
35	-	1k. green	20	10
36	-	1k.50 green	20	10
37	-	2k. red	20	10
38	-	3k. red	20	10
39	-	4k. blue	20	20
40	-	5k. black	2·75	1·60
41	-	5k. blue	35	20
42	-	6k. olive	35	20
43	-	7k. orange	35	20
44	-	8k. brown	65	35
45	-	10k. violet	1·30	65
46	-	12k. brown	1·70	75
47	-	20k. brown	1·30	55
48	-	30k. brown	1·70	75
49	-	50k. green	3·25	2·20
50	8	100k. violet	5·50	4·50

DESIGNS: 50b. Waterfall at Jajce; 75b. Varazdin; 1k. Mt. Velebit; 1k.50, Zelenjak; 2k. Zagreb Cathedral; 3k. Church at Osijek; 4k. River Drina; 5k. (No. 40), Konjic Bridge; 5k. (No. 41), Modern building at Zemun; 6k. Dubrovnik; 7k. R. Save in Slavonia; 8k. Mosque at Sarajevo; 10k. Lake Plitvice; 12k. Klis Fortress near Split; 20k. Hvar; 30k. Harvesting in Syrmia; 50k. Senj.

9 Croat (Sinj) Costume

1941. Red Cross.

51	9	1k.50+1k.50 blue	1·10	1·30
52	-	2k.+2k. brown	1·10	1·40
53	-	5k.+4k. red	2·75	3·25

COSTUMES: 2k. Travnik. 4k. Turopolje.

10 Emblems of Germany, Croatia and Italy

1941. Eastern Volunteer Fund.

54	10	4k.+2k. blue	3·75	4·25

11 Glider

1942. Aviation Fund. Glider in flight as T **11**.

55	11	2k.+2k. brown (vert)	1·10	1·60
56	-	2k.50+2k.50 green	1·60	1·80
57	-	3 k+3k. red (vert)	2·00	2·20
58	-	4k.+4k. blue	2·75	3·25
MS58a		Two sheets, each 124×110 mm, containing Nos. 55 and 57 but colours changed and with higher premiums (No. 57 also larger). 2k.+8k. blue, 3k.+12k. lake. Imperf or perf	65·00	65·00

DESIGNS—HORIZ: 2k.50, Glider (different); 4k. Seaplane glider. VERT: 3k. Boy with model glider.

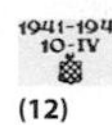

(12)

1942. 1st Anniv of Croat Independence. Optd with T **12**.

59	2k. brown (as No. 37)	55	75
60	5k. red (as No. 40)	85	1·10
61	10k. green (as No. 45)	1·60	2·00

1942. Banja Luka Philatelic Exhibition. Inscr "F.I." in top right corner.

62	8	100k. violet	5·50	6·00

1942. Surch **0.25kn** and bar.

63	0.25k. on 2k. red (No. 37)	55	75

14 Trumpeters

1942. National Relief Fund.

64	14	3k.+1k. red	1·50	1·60
65	-	4k.+2k. brown	2·10	2·20
66	-	5k.+5k. blue	3·00	3·25

DESIGNS—HORIZ: 4k. Procession beneath triumphal archways. VERT: 5k. Mother and child.

15 Sestine (Croatia)

1942. Red Cross Fund. Peasant girls in provincial costumes.

67	15	1k.50+50b. brown	2·00	2·10
68	-	3k.+1k. violet	2·10	2·20
69	-	4k.+2k. blue	2·75	3·00
70	-	10k.+5k. bistre	3·50	3·75
71	15	13k.+6k. red	7·25	7·50

COSTUMES: 3k. Slavonia. 4k. Bosnia. 10k. Dalmatia.

15a Red Cross Sister

1942. Charity Tax. Red Cross Fund. Cross in red.

71a	15a	1k. green	85	90

16 M. Gubec

1942. Croat ("Ustascha") Youth Fund.

72	16	3k.+6k. red	85	1·10
73	-	4k.+7k. brown	85	1·10
MS73a		5k.+20k. blue (perf or imperf)	30·00	35·00

DESIGNS—VERT: Dr. A. Starcevic; 5k. Trumpet and flag.

17

1943. Labour Front. Vert designs showing workers as T 17.

74	17	2k.+1k. brown and olive	5·25	5·50
75	-	3k.+3k. brown & purple	5·25	5·50
76	-	7k.+4k. brown & grey	5·50	6·00

19 Arms of Zagreb

1943. 7th Centenary of Foundation of Zagreb.

77	19	3k.50 (+ 6k.50) blue	5·50	6·00

1943. Pictorial designs as T 8, but with views surrounded by frame line.

78	3k.50 brown	75	1·00
79	12k.50 black	1·10	1·30

DESIGNS: 3k.50, Trakoscan Castle; 12k.50, Veliki Tabor.

21 A. Pavelic

1943. Croat ("Ustascha") Youth Fund.

80	21	5k.+3k. red	65	1·10
81	21	7k.+5k. green	75	1·10
MS81a	21	12k.+8k. blue (perf or imperf)	35·00	40·00

22 Krsto Frankopan

1943. Famous Croats.

82	-	1k. blue	55	55
83	**22**	2k. olive	55	55
84	-	3k.50 red	65	75

PORTRAITS: 1k. Katarina Zrinska. 3k.50, Peter Zrinski.

23 Croat Sailor and Motor Torpedo Boats

1943. Croat Legion Relief Fund.

85	**23**	1k.+50b. green	35	45
86	-	2k.+1k. red	35	45
87	-	3k.50+1k.50 blue	35	45
88	-	9k.+4k.50 brown	35	45
MS88a		1k.+0k.50 blue; 2k.+1k. green; 3k.50+1k.50 blue; 9k.+4k.50 brown (perf or imperf)	7·50	8·25

DESIGNS: 2k. Pilot and Heinkel bomber; 3k.50, Infantrymen; 9k. Mechanized column.

24 St. Mary's Church and Cistercian Monastery, 1650

1943. Philatelic Exhibition, Zagreb.

89	**24**	18k.+9k. blue	7·00	7·50
MS89a		99×132 mm. **24** 18k.+9k. black	20·00	20·00

1943. Return of Sibenik to Croatia. Optd **HRVATSKO MORE 8, IX. 1943.**

90	18k.+9k. blue	14·00	15·00

26 Nurse and Patient

1943. Red Cross Fund.

91	-	1k.+50b. blue	55	75
92	-	2k.+1k. red	55	75
93	-	3k.50+1k.50 blue	55	75
94	**26**	8k.+3k. brown	75	1·10
95	**26**	9k.+4k. green	85	1·10
96	-	10k.+5k. violet	1·20	1·30
97	**26**	12k.+6k. blue	1·40	1·60
98	-	12k.50+6k. brown	1·80	2·00
99	**26**	18k.+8k. orange	3·00	3·25
100	**26**	32k.+12k. grey	4·25	4·50

DESIGN: 1k., 2k., 3k.50, 10k., 12k.50, Mother and children.

26a

1943. Charity Tax. Red Cross Fund. Cross in red.

100a	**26a**	2k. blue	75	90

27 A. Pavelic

1943

101	**27**	25b. red	35	25
105	**27**	50b. blue	35	25
102	**27**	75b. green	35	25
106	**27**	1k. green	35	25
107	**27**	1k.50 violet	35	25
108	**27**	2k. red	35	25
109	**27**	3k. red	35	25
110	**27**	3k.50 blue	35	25
111	**27**	4k. purple	35	25
103	**27**	5k. blue	35	25
112	**27**	8k. brown	35	25
113	**27**	9k. red	35	25
114	**27**	10k. purple	45	35
115	**27**	12k. brown	45	35
116	**27**	12k.50 black	55	35
117	**27**	18k. brown	65	55
104	**27**	32k. brown	1·10	55
118	**27**	50k. green	1·60	55
119	**27**	70k. orange	2·20	1·10
120	**27**	100k. violet	3·25	2·20

The design of the 25b., 75b., 5k., and 32k. is 20½×26 mm, the rest are 22×28 mm.

28 Ruder Boskovic

1943. Honouring Ruder Boskovic (astronomer).

121	**28**	3k.50 red	65	55
122	**28**	12k.50 purple	75	85

29 Posthorn

1944. Postal and Railway Employees' Relief Fund.

123	**29**	7k.+3k.50 brn, red & bis	70	80
124	-	16k.+8k. blue	75	85
125	-	24k.+12k. red	1·00	1·10
126	-	32k.+16k. black & red	1·50	1·60

DESIGNS—VERT: 16k. Dove, airplane and globe; 24k. Mercury. HORIZ: 32k. Winged wheel.

30 St. Sebastian

1944. War Invalids' Relief Fund.

127	**30**	7k.+3k.50 mauve & red	75	85
128	-	16k.+8k. green	1·00	1·10
129	-	24k.+12k. yell, brn & red	1·10	1·30
130	-	32k.+16k. blue	2·00	2·20

DESIGNS—HORIZ: 16k. Blind man and cripple; 32k. Death of Peter Svacic, 1094. VERT: 24k. Mediaeval statuette.

31 The Legion in Action **32** Jure-Ritter Francetic

1944. Croat Youth Fund. No. 134 perf, others imperf.

131	**31**	3k.50+1k.50 brown	15	20
132	-	12k.50+6k.50 blue	15	20
134	**32**	12k.50+287k.50 black	14·00	18·00
133	**32**	18k.+9k. brown	15	20

DESIGN: No. 132, Sentries on the Drina.

33

1944. Labour Front. Inscr "D.R.S.".

135	**33**	3k.50+1k. red	10	20
136	-	12k.50+6k. brown	35	55
137	-	18k.+9k. blue	35	45
138	-	32k.+16k. green	45	55
MS138a		74×100 mm. 32k.+16k. (as No. 138) brown on yellow	5·50	6·50

DESIGNS: 12k.50, Digging; 18k. Instruction; 32k. "On Parade".

34 Bombed Home **35** War Victim

1944. Charity Tax. War Victims.

138b	**34**	1k. green	20	35
138c	**35**	2k. red	20	35
138d	**35**	5k. green	35	45
138e	**35**	10k. blue	55	65
138f	**35**	20k. brown	1·30	1·40

36

1944. Red Cross. Cross in red.

139	**36**	2k.+1k. green	45	55
140	**36**	3k.50+1k.50 red	55	65
141	**36**	12k.50+6k. blue	65	75

37 Storm Division Soldiers

1945. Creation of Croatian Storm Division on 9th October 1944.

142	**37**	50k.+50k. red and grey	£180	£225
143	-	70k.+70k. sepia & grey	£180	£225
144	-	100k.+100k. bl & grey	£180	£225
MS144a		216×134 mm. Nos. 142/4	£2000	£2500

DESIGNS: 70k. Storm Division soldiers in action; 100k. Divisional emblem.

38

1945. Postal Employees' Fund.

145	**38**	3k.50+1k.50 grey	20	35
146	-	12k.50+6k. purple	35	45
147	-	24k.+12k. green	45	55
148	-	50k.+25k. purple	65	85
MS148a		99×110 mm. 100k.+50k. red	11·00	13·00

DESIGNS: 12k.50, Telegraph linesman; 24k. Telephone switchboard; 50k. The postman calls.

39

1945. Labour Day.

149	**39**	3k.50 brown	1·10	2·00

40 Interior of Zagreb Cathedral

1991. Obligatory Tax. Workers' Fund. Mass for Croatia. Perf or imperf.

150	**40**	1d.20 gold and black	75	65

41 Statue of the Virgin and Shrine

1991. Obligatory Tax. Workers' Fund. 700th Anniv of Shrine of the Virgin, Trsat. Perf or imperf.

151	**41**	1d.70 multicoloured	55	55

42 State Arms

1991. Obligatory Tax. Workers' Fund. Rally in Ban Jelacic Square, Zagreb. Perf or imperf.

152	**42**	2d.20 multicoloured	55	55

See also No. 170.

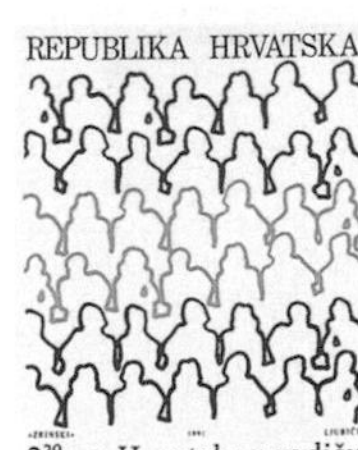

43 Members of Parliament

1991. Obligatory Tax. Workers' Fund. First Multi-party Session of Croatian Parliament, 30 May 1990. Perf or imperf.

153	**43**	2d.20 multicoloured	55	55

44 Sud Aviation Caravelle Jetliner over Zagreb Cathedral and Dubrovnik

1991. Air.

154	**44**	1d. blue, black and red	35	35
155	-	2d. multicoloured	35	35
156	-	3d. multicoloured	35	35

DESIGNS: 2d. Bell tower and ruins of Diocletian's Palace, Split; 3d. Sud Aviation Caravelle jetliner over Zagreb Cathedral and Pula amphitheatre.

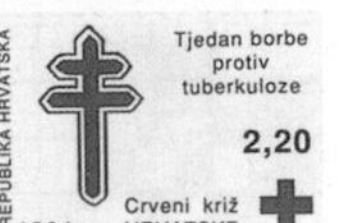

45 Anti-tuberculosis Emblem

1991. Obligatory Tax. Anti-tuberculosis Week.

157	**45**	2d.20 red and blue	35	35

46 Ban Jelacic Statue

1991. Obligatory Tax. Workers' Fund. Re-erection of Ban Josip Jelacic Equestrian Statue, Zagreb. Perf or imperf.

158	**46**	2d.20 multicoloured	55	55

1991. No. 150 surch **4°°** **HPT** and posthorn.

159	**40**	4d. on 1d.20 gold & blk	55	55

48 First Article of Constitution in Croatian

1991. Obligatory Tax. Workers' Fund. 1st Anniv of New Constitution. Multicoloured. Perf or imperf.

160		2d.20 Type **48**	60	55
161		2d.20 Text in English	1·40	1·30
162		2d.20 Text in French	1·40	1·30
163		2d.20 Text in German	1·40	1·30
164		2d.20 Text in Russian	1·40	1·30
165		2d.20 Text in Spanish	1·40	1·30

49 Book of Croatian Independence

1991. Recognition of Independence.

166	**49**	30d. multicoloured	1·30	1·30

50 17th-century Crib Figures, Kosljun Monastery, Krk

1991. Christmas.

167	**50**	4d. multicoloured	85	85

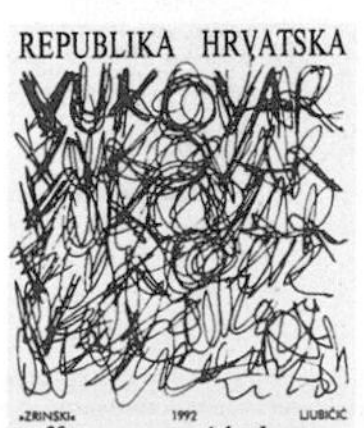

51 "VUKOVAR" and Barbed Wire

1992. Obligatory Tax. Vukovar Refugees' Fund.

168	**51**	2d.20 brown and black	75	75

1992. No. 151 surch **2°°** **HPT** and posthorn.

169	**41**	20d. on 1d.70 mult	6·50	6·50

1992. As No. 152, but redrawn with new value and "HPT" emblem replacing obligatory tax inscr at foot.

170	**42**	10d. multicoloured	45	45

52 Ban Josip Jelacic

1992. Obligatory Tax. Famous Croatians. Multicoloured.

171		4d.+2d. Type **52**	50	50
172		4d.+2d. Dr. Ante Starcevic (founder of Party of the Right)	45	45
173		7d.+3d. Stjepan Radic (founder of Croation Peasant Party)	45	45

53 Olympic Rings

1992. Winter Olympic Games, Albertville, France.

174	**53**	30d. multicoloured	1·00	1·00

54 Osijek Cathedral on Paper Dart

1992. Air.

175	**54**	4d. multicoloured	35	35

55 Knin

1992. Croatian Towns (1st series).

176	**55**	6d. multicoloured	20	20
177	-	7d. multicoloured	35	35
178	-	20d. blue, red and yellow	95	80
179	-	30d. multicoloured	55	55
180	-	45d. multicoloured	65	65
181	-	50d. multicoloured	75	75
182	-	300d. multicoloured	3·25	3·25

DESIGNS: 7d. Von Eltz Castle, Lukovar; 20d. St. Francis's Church, Ilok; 30d. Dr. Ante Starcevic Street, Gospic; 45d. Rector's Palace, Dubrovnik; 50d. St. Jakov's Cathedral, Sibenik; 300d. Sokak houses, Beli Manastir.

See also Nos. 208/14, 382/7, 523/4, 636 and 639.

56 Statue of King Tomislav, Zagreb

1992

183	**56**	10d. green	20	20

57 Red Cross Emblems on Globe

1992. Obligatory Tax. Red Cross Week.

184	**57**	3d. red and black	35	35

58 Map of Croatia on Red Cross

1992. Obligatory Tax. Solidarity Week.

185	**58**	3d. red and black	35	35

59 Central Railway Station, Zagreb

1992. Centenary of Zagreb Central Railway Station.

186	**59**	30d. multicoloured	35	35

60 Society Imprint

1992. 150th Anniv of Matica Hrvatska (Croatian language society).

187	**60**	20d. gold and red	25	25

61 Bishop Josip Strossmayer (patron) and Academy Building

1992. 125th Anniv of Croatian Academy of Sciences and Arts.

188	**61**	30d. multicoloured	35	35

62 Olympic Rings on Computer Pattern

1992. Olympic Games, Barcelona. Mult.

189		40d. Type **62**	35	35
190		105d. Rings and symbolic sports	85	85

63 Bellflowers

1992. Flowers. Multicoloured.

191		30d. Type **63**	30	30
192		85d. Degenia (vert)	75	75

64 Blue Rock Thrush

1992. Environmental Protection. Mult.

193		40d. Type **64**	35	35
194		75d. Red-spot snake	75	75

65 15th-century Carrack, Dubrovnik

1992. Europa. 500th Anniv of Discovery of America by Columbus (1st issue).

195	**65**	30d. multicoloured	55	55
196	-	75d. black and red	1·10	1·10

DESIGN: 75d. "Indian Horseman" (bronze statue in Chicago by Ivan Mestrovic).

See also Nos. 198/9.

66 "Madonna of Bistrica"

1992. Obligatory Tax. Fund for National Shrine to Madonna of Bistrica.

197	**66**	5d. gold and blue	35	35

1992. Europa. 500th Anniv of Discovery of America by Columbus (2nd issue). As Nos. 195/6, but new face values and with additional CEPT posthorns emblem.

198	**65**	60d. multicoloured	1·10	1·10
199	-	130d. black, red and gold (as No. 196)	2·75	2·75

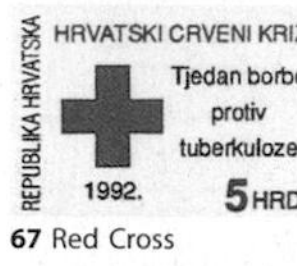

67 Red Cross

1992. Obligatory Tax. Anti-tuberculosis Week.

200	**67**	5d. red and black	45	45

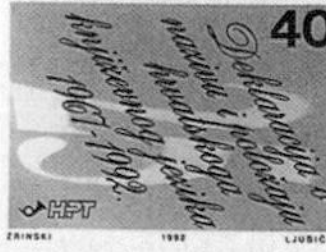

68 "25"

1992. Croatian Language Anniversaries. Mult.

201		40d. Type **68** (25th anniv of Croatian Language Declaration)	35	35
202		130d. "100" (centenary of Croatian "Orthography" by Dr. I. Broz)	55	55

69 Dove and Coat of Arms

1992. 750th Anniv of Grant of Royal City Charter to Samobor.

203	**69**	90d. multicoloured	55	55

70 Remains of Altar Screen from Uzdolje Church

1992. 1100th Anniv of Duke Mucimir's Donation (judgement in ecclesiastical dispute).

204	**70**	60d. multicoloured	35	35

71 St. George and the Dragon

1992. Obligatory Tax. Croatian Anti-cancer League.
205 **71** 15d. multicoloured 35 35

See also No. 255.

72 Seal of King Bela IV

1992. 750th Anniv of Zagreb's Charter from King Bela IV.
206 **72** 180d. multicoloured 70 70

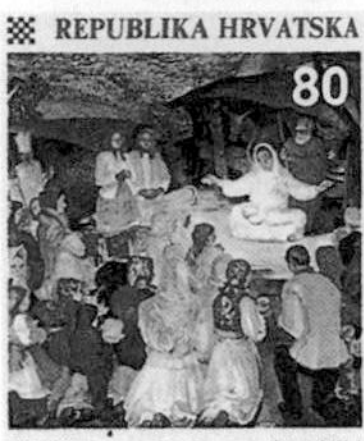

73 "Croatian Christmas" (Ljubo Babic)

1992. Christmas.
207 **73** 80d. multicoloured 45 45

74 Former Town Hall, Vinkovci

1992. Croatian Towns (2nd series). Mult.

208	100d. Type **74**	35	20
209	200d. Castle, Pazin (vert)	45	35
210	500d. Jelacic Square, Slavonski Brod	1·00	85
211	1000d. Town Hall, Jelacic Square, Varazdin	1·40	1·10
212	2000d. Zorin cultural centre, Karlovac	1·60	1·60
213	5000d. St. Donat's Church and St. Stosija's Cathedral belltower, Zadar (vert)	2·40	2·00
214	10000d. Pirovo peninsula and Franciscan monastery, Vis	3·50	3·00

75 Lorkovic

1992. Death Centenary of Blaz Lorkovic (political economist).
218 **75** 250d. multicoloured 85 85

76 Coiled National Colours

1992. 150th Anniv of "Kolo" (literary Magazine).
219 **76** 300d. multicoloured 1·10 1·10

77 Bunic-Vucic

1992. 400th Birth Anniv of Ivan Bunic-Vucic (poet).
220 **77** 350d. multicoloured 1·20 1·20

78 Ljudevit Gaj Square, Krapina

1993. 800th Anniv of Krapina.
221 **78** 300d. multicoloured 85 85

79 Tesla

1993. 50th Death Anniv of Nikola Tesla (physicist).
222 **79** 250d. multicoloured 70 70

80 Quinquerez ("self-portrait")

1993. Death Cent of Ferdo Quiquerez (painter).
223 **80** 100d. multicoloured 35 35

81 Red Deer

1993. Animals of the Kapacki Rit Swamp. Multicoloured.
224 500d. Type **81** 1·20 1·20
225 550d. White-tailed sea eagle 1·30 1·30

82 Sulentic ("self-portrait")

1993. Birth Centenary of Zlatko Sulentic (painter).
226 **82** 350d. multicoloured 60 60

83 Kursalon, Lipik

1993. Centenary of Lipik Spa.
227 **83** 400d. multicoloured 65 65

84 Kovacic (statue, Vojin Bakic)

1993. 50th Death Anniv of Ivan Goran Kovacic (writer).
228 **84** 200d. multicoloured 40 40

85 Minceta Fortress, Dubrovnik

1993. 59th P.E.N. Literary Congress, Dubrovnik.
229 **85** 800d. multicoloured 1·50 1·50

86 Ivan Kakaljevic (writer)

1993. 150th Anniv of First Speech in Croatian Language made to Croatian Parliament.
230 **86** 500d. multicoloured 75 75

87 Mask and Split Theatre

1993. Centenary of Split Theatre.
231 **87** 600d. multicoloured 85 85

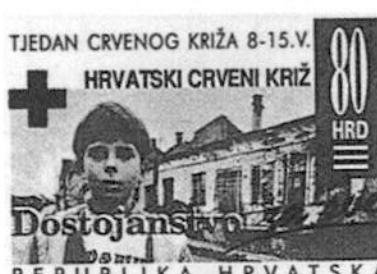

88 Boy and Ruined House

1993. Obligatory Tax. Red Cross Week.
232 **88** 80d. black and red 35 35

89 Pag in 16th Century

1993. 550th Anniv of Refoundation of Pag.
233 **89** 800d. multicoloured 1·00 1·00

90 Dove

1993. 1st Anniv of Croatia's Membership of U.N.
234 **90** 500d. multicoloured 60 60

91 Girl at Window

1993. Obligatory Tax. Solidarity Week.
235 **91** 100d. black and red 35 35

92 "In the Cafe" (Ivo Dulcic)

1993. Europa. Contemporary Art. Mult.

236	700d. Type **92**	1·20	1·20
237	1000d. "The Waiting Room" (Miljenko Stancic)	2·50	2·50
238	1100d. "Two Figures" (Ljubo Ivancic)	3·75	3·75

93 "Homodukt" (Milivoj Bijelic)

1993. 45th Art Biennial, Venice. Mult.

239	250d. Type **93**	35	35
240	600d. "Snails" (Ivo Dekovic)	85	85
241	1000d. "Esa carta de mi flor" (Zeljko Kipke)	1·20	1·20

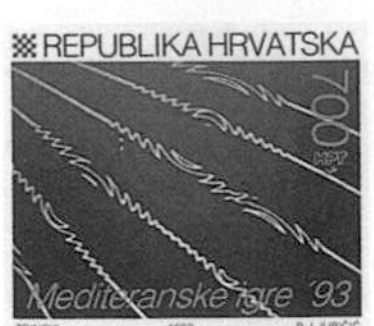

94 Symbolic Running Track

1993. 12th Mediterranean Games, Roussillon (Languedoc), France.
242 **94** 700d. multicoloured 80 80

95 "Slavonian Oaks"

1993. 150th Birth Anniv of Adolf Waldinger (painter).
243 **95** 300d. multicoloured 40 40

96 Battle of Krbava, 1493

1993. Anniversaries of Famous Battles. 16th-century engravings.
244 800d. Type **96** 90 90
245 1300d. Battle of Sisak, 1593 1·50 1·50

97 Krleza (after Marija Ujevic)

1993. Birth Centenary of Miroslav Krleza (writer).
246 **97** 400d. multicoloured 60 60

98 Cardinal Stepinac

1993. Obligatory Tax. Cardinal Stepinac Foundation.
247 **98** 150d. black, mauve & gold 40 40

99 Croatian Postman

1993. 1st Anniv of Croatia's Membership of Universal Postal Union.
248 **99** 1800d. multicoloured 1·40 1·40

100 Paljetak

1993. Birth Centenary of Vlaho Paljetak (singer-songwriter).
249 **100** 500d. multicoloured 55 55

101 Peter Zrinski and Krsto Frankopan

1993. Obligatory Tax. Zrinski-Frankopan Foundation.
250 **101** 200d. blue and grey 40 40

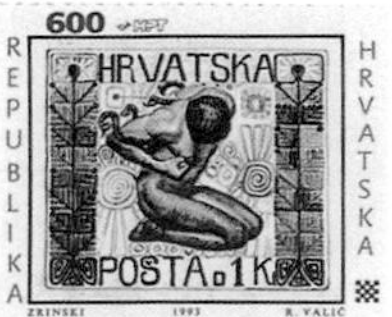
102 "Freedom of Croatia" (central motif of 1918 stamp)

1993. Stamp Day.
251 **102** 600d. multicoloured 70 70

103 Red Cross

1993. Obligatory Tax. Anti-tuberculosis Week.
252 **103** 300d. green, black & red 40 40

104 Antonio Magini's Map of Istria, 1620

1993. 50th Anniv of Incorporation of Istria, Rijeka and Zadar into Croatia.
253 **104** 2200d. multicoloured 1·60 1·60

105 Smiciklas

1993. 150th Birth Anniv of Tadija Smiciklas (historian).
254 **105** 800d. black, gold and red 70 70

1993. Obligatory Tax. Croatian Anti-cancer League.
255 **71** 400d. multicoloured 40 40

106 Allegory of Birth of Croatian History on Shores of the Adriatic

1993. Centenary of National Archaeological Museum, Split.
256 **106** 1000d. multicoloured 80 80

107 Girl In Heart

1993. Obligatory Tax. Save Croatian Children Fund.
257 **107** 400d. red, blue and black 40 40

108 Croatian and French Flags and Soldiers

1993. 50th Anniv of Uprising of 13th Pioneer Battalion, Villefranche-de-Rouergue, France.
258 **108** 3000d. multicoloured 2·00 2·00

109 Tomic

1993. 150th Birth Anniv of Josip Eugen Tomic (writer).
259 **109** 900d. brown, green & red 55 55

110 Astronomical Diagram

1993. 850th Anniv of Publication of "De Essentiis" by Herman Dalmatin.
260 **110** 1000d. multicoloured 55 55

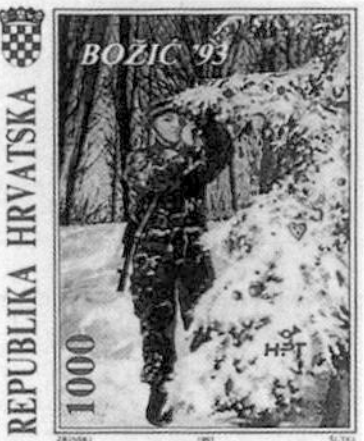
111 Christmas on the Battlefield

1993. Christmas. Multicoloured.
261 1000d. Type **111** 55 55
262 4000d. "Nativity" (fresco, St. Mary's Church, Dvigrad) 2·40 2·40

112 Skiers

1993. Cent of Competitive Skiing in Croatia.
263 **112** 1000d. multicoloured 80 80

113 Decorations and Badge

1993. 125th Anniv of Croatian Militia.
264 **113** 1100d. multicoloured 80 80

114 Printing Press

1994. 500th Anniv of Printing of First Croatian Book (a Glagolitic missal), Senj.
265 **114** 2200d. brown and red 1·10 1·10

115 Skier

1994. Winter Olympic Games, Lillehammer, Norway.
266 **115** 4000d. multicoloured 2·20 2·20

116 Iguanodon

1994. Croatian Dinosaur Fossils from West Istria. Multicoloured.
267 2400d. Type **116** 1·40 1·40
268 4000d. Iguanodon, skeleton and map 2·75 2·75

Nos. 267/8 were issued together, se-tenant, forming a composite design.

117 Masthead

1994. 150th Anniv of "Zora Dalmatinska" (literary periodical).
269 **117** 800d. multicoloured 55 55

118 University, Emperor Leopold I's Seal and Vice-chancellor's Chain

1994. 325th Anniv of Croatian University, Zagreb.
270 **118** 2200d. multicoloured 1·10 1·10

119 Wolf

1994. Planet Earth Day.
271 **119** 3800d. multicoloured 2·00 2·00

120 Safety Signs and Worker wearing Protective Clothing

1994. 75th Anniv of ILO and 50th Anniv of Philadelphia Declaration (social charter).
272 **120** 1000d. multicoloured 70 70

121 Globe and Map

1994. Obligatory Tax. Red Cross Week.
273 **121** 500d. black, stone & red 40 40

122 Flying Man (17th-century idea by Faust Vrancic)

1994. Europa. Inventions. Multicoloured.
274 3800d. Type **122** 4·00 4·00
275 4000d. Quill and pencil writing surname (technical pencil by Slavoljub Penkala, 1906) (32×23 mm) 4·00 4·00

123 Red Cross

1994. Obligatory Tax. Solidarity Week.
276 **123** 50l. red, black and grey 40 40

124 Croatian Iris

1994. Flowers. Multicoloured.

277	2k.40 Type **124**	1·10	1·10
278	4k. Meadow saffron	1·90	1·90

125 Petrovic

1994. 1st Death Anniv of Drazen Petrovic (basketball player).

279	**125**	1k. multicoloured	70	70

126 Plitvice Lakes

1994. 150th Anniv of Tourism in Croatia. Multicoloured.

280	80l. Type **126**	25	25
281	1k. River Krka	40	40
282	1k.10 Kornati Islands	70	70
283	2k.20 Kopacki Trscak ornithological reserve	95	95
284	2k.40 Opatija Riviera	1·40	1·40
285	3k.80 Brijuni Islands	1·60	1·60
286	4k. Trakoscan Castle, Zagorje	2·20	2·20

127 Baranovic at Keyboard

1994. Musical Anniversaries.

287	**127**	1k. multicoloured	55	55
288	-	2k.20 silver, black & red	1·10	1·10
289	-	2k.40 multicoloured	1·20	1·20

DESIGNS—VERT: 1k. Type **127** (birth centenary of Kresimir Baranovic (composer and conductor/director of Croatian National Theatre Opera, Zagreb, 1915–40)); 2k.20, Vatroslav Lisinski (composer, 175th birth anniv). HORIZ: 2k.40, Score and harp player (350th anniv of Pauline song-book).

128 Monstrance

1994. Obligatory Tax. Ludbreg Shrine.

290	**128**	50l. multicoloured	40	40

129 Men dressed in Croatian and American Colours

1994. Centenary of Croatian Brotherhood in U.S.A.

291	**129**	2k.20 multicoloured	2·00	2·00

130 Mother and Children

1994. Obligatory Tax. Save Croatian Children Fund.

292	**130**	50l. multicoloured	40	40

131 Family

1994. International Year of the Family.

293	**131**	80l. multicoloured	70	70

132 St. George and the Dragon

1994. Obligatory Tax. Croatian Anti-Cancer League.

294	**132**	50l. multicoloured	40	40

133 Pope John Paul II and his Arms

1994. Papal Visit.

295	**133**	1k. multicoloured	70	70

134 Franjo Bucar (Committee member, 1920–46)

1994. Cent of International Olympic Committee.

296	**134**	1k. multicoloured	70	70

135 Red Cross on Leaf

1994. Obligatory Tax. Anti-tuberculosis Week.

297	**135**	50l. red, green & black	40	40

136 The Little Prince (book character)

1994. 50th Death Anniv of Antoine de Saint-Exupery (writer).

298	**136**	3k.80 multicoloured	1·90	1·90

137 "Resurrection" (lunette, Gati, Omis)

1994. 13th International Convention on Christian Archaeology, Split and Porec.

299	**137**	4k. multicoloured	2·00	2·00

138 "Still Life with Fruits and Basket" (Marino Tartaglia)

1994. Paintings. Multicoloured.

300	2k.40 Type **138**	1·20	1·20
301	3k.80 "In the Park" (Milan Steiner)	2·00	2·00
302	4k. "Self-portrait" (Vilko Gecan)	2·20	2·20

139 Plan of Fortress

1994. Obligatory Tax. 750th Anniv of Slavonski Brod.

303	**139**	50l. yellow, black & red	40	40

140 IOC Centenary Emblem and Flame

1994. Obligatory Tax. National Olympic Committee. Designs incorporating either the National Olympic Committee emblem or the International Olympic Committee centenary emblem.

304	50l. Type **140**	40	40
305	50l. As T **140** but with National Olympic Committee emblem	40	40
306	50l. Tennis and national emblem (vert)	40	40
307	50l. Football and centenary emblem (vert)	40	40
308	50l. As No. 306 but with centenary emblem (vert)	40	40
309	50l. As No. 307 but with national emblem (vert)	40	40
310	50l. Basketball and centenary emblem (vert)	40	40
311	50l. Handball and national emblem (vert)	40	40
312	50l. As No. 310 but with national emblem (vert)	40	40
313	50l. As No. 311 but with centenary emblem (vert)	40	40
314	50l. Kayaks and national emblem (vert)	40	40
315	50l. Water polo and centenary emblem (vert)	40	40
316	50l. As No. 314 but with centenary emblem (vert)	40	40
317	50l. As No. 315 but with national emblem (vert)	40	40
318	50l. Running and centenary emblem (vert)	40	40
319	50l. Gymnastics and national emblem (vert)	40	40
320	50l. As No. 318 but with national emblem (vert)	40	40
321	50l. As No. 319 but with centenary emblem (vert)	40	40

141 Cover of "Gazophylacium"

1994. 400th Birth Anniv of Ivan Belostenec (lexicographer).

322	**141**	2k.20 multicoloured	1·10	1·10

142 St. Mark's Church and Gas Lamp

1994. 900th Annivs of Zagreb (323/5) and Zagreb Bishopric (326). Multicoloured.

323	1k. Type **142**	40	40
324	1k. Street scene from early film, Maxi Cat (cartoon character) and left side of Zagreb Exchange	40	40
325	1k. Right side of Zagreb Exchange, S. Penkala's biplane and Cibona building	40	40
326	4k. 15th-century bishop's crosier and 17th-century view of Zagreb by Valvasor	1·80	1·80
MS327	79×59 mm. 13k.50 Penkala's biplane and street scene from early film (23×47 mm)	6·50	6·50

Nos. 323/6 were issued together, se-tenant, forming a composite design.

143 "Epiphany" (relief, Vrhovac Church)

1994. Christmas.

328	**143**	1k. multicoloured	70	70

144 "Translation of the Holy House" (Giovanni Battista Tiepolo)

1994. 700th Anniv of St. Mary's Sanctuary, Loreto.

329	**144**	4k. multicoloured	1·90	1·90

145 Modern Tie

1995. Ties. Multicoloured.

330	1k.10 Type **145**	40	40
331	3k.80 English dandy, 1810	1·80	1·80
332	4k. Croatian soldier, 1630	1·90	1·90
MS333	109×88 mm. Nos. 330/2	4·75	4·75

146 St. Catherine's Church and Monastery, Zagreb, and Jesuit

1995. Monasteries. Multicoloured.

334	1k. Type **146** (350th anniv)	55	55
335	2k.40 St. Paul's Monastery, Visovac, and Franciscan monk (550th anniv)	1·40	1·40

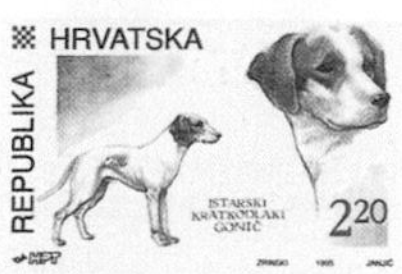

147 Istrian Short-haired Hunting Dog

1995. Dogs. Multicoloured.

336	2k.20 Type **147**	1·40	1·40
337	2k.40 Posavinian hunting dog	1·50	1·50
338	3k.80 Istrian wire-haired hunting dog	2·00	2·00

148 Rowing

1995. Obligatory Tax. National Olympic Committee. Multicoloured.

339	50l. Type **148**	40	40
340	50l. Petanque	40	40
341	50l. Monument to Drazen Petrovic, Olympic Park, Lausanne	40	40
342	50l. Tennis	40	40
343	50l. Basketball	40	40

149 Reconstruction of Emperor Diocletian's Palace

1995. 1700th Anniv of Split. Multicoloured.

344	1k. Type **149**	55	55
345	2k.20 "Split Harbour" (Emanuel Vidovic)	1·20	1·20
346	4k. View of city and bust of Marko Marulic (Ivan Mestrovic)	2·30	2·30
MS347	90×60 mm. 13k.40 Aerial view (23×47 mm)	6·50	6·50

150 Player

1995. World Handball Championship, Iceland.

348	**150**	4k. multicoloured	2·00	2·00

151 Woman's Head

1995. Obligatory Tax. Red Cross Week.

349	**151**	50l. black and red	40	40

152 Storm Clouds and Clear Sky

1995. Europa. Peace and Freedom. Mult.

350	2k.40 Type **152**	2·75	2·75
351	4k. Angel (detail of sculpture, Francesco Robba)	5·50	5·50

153 Shadow behind Cross

1995. 150th Anniv of July Riots (352) and 50th Anniv of Croatian Surrender at Bleiburg (353). Multicoloured.

352	1k.10 Type **153**	80	80
353	3k.80 Sunrise behind cross	1·80	1·80

154 Arms and Hand holding Rose

1995. Independence Day.

354	**154**	1k.10 multicoloured	70	70

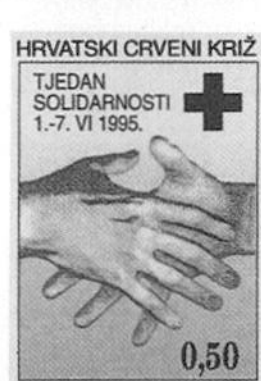

155 Hands

1995. Obligatory Tax. Solidarity Week.

355	**155**	50l. multicoloured	40	40

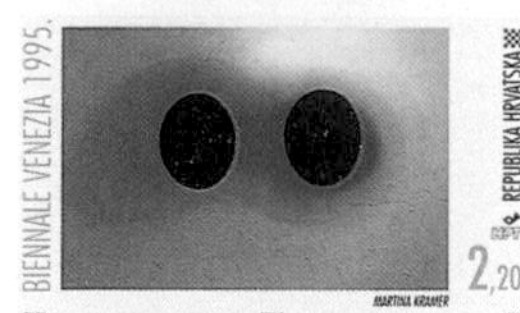

156 "Installation" (detail) (Martina Kramer)

1995. 46th Art Biennale, Venice. Work by Croatian artists. Multicoloured.

356	2k.20 Type **156**	1·20	1·20
357	2k.40 "Paracelsus Paraduchamps" (Mirk Zrinscak) (vert)	1·40	1·40
358	4k. "Shadows/136" (Goran Petercol)	2·30	2·30

157 "St. Antony" (detail of polyptych by Ljubo Babic, St. Antony's Sanctuary, Zagreb)

1995. 800th Birth Anniv of St. Antony of Padua.

359	**157**	1k. multicoloured	55	55

158 Loggerhead Turtle

1995. Animals. Multicoloured.

360	2k.40 Type **158**	1·20	1·20
361	4k. Bottle-nosed dolphin	2·20	2·20

159 Osijek Cathedral

1995. Obligatory Tax. Restoration of Sts. Peter and Paul's Cathedral, Osijek.

362	**159**	65l. multicoloured	40	40

160 "Croatian Pieta"

1995. Obligatory Tax. "Holy Mother of Freedom" War Memorial.

363	**160**	65l. on 50l. blk, red & bl	2·00	2·00
364	-	65l. black, red and blue	70	70
365	-	65l. blue and yellow	70	70

DESIGN: 65l. Projected memorial church.

Nos. 364/5 were not issued without surcharge.

161 Town and Fortress

1995. Liberation of Knin.

366	**161**	1k.30 multicoloured	70	70

162 Electric Power Plant

1995. Centenary of Jaruga Hydro-electric Power Station, River Krka.

367	**162**	3k.60 multicoloured	1·60	1·60

163 Postman

1995. Stamp Day.

368	**163**	1k.30 multicoloured	70	70

165 Suppe and Heroine of "The Fair Galatea" (operetta)

1995. Death Centenary of Franz von Suppe (composer).

370	**165**	6k.50 multicoloured	3·00	3·00

166 Petrinja Fortress (after Valvasor) and Cavalrymen

1995. 400th Anniv of Habsburg Capture of Petrinja.

371	**166**	2k.20 multicoloured	1·40	1·40

167 Ivo Tijardovic

1995. Composers' Anniversaries. Mult.

372	1k.20 Type **167** (birth centenary)	70	70
373	1k.40 Lovro von Matacic (10th death)	80	80
374	6k.50 Jakov Gotovac (birth centenary)	3·25	3·25

168 Herman Bolle (architect, 150th birth)

1995. Anniversaries. Multicoloured.

375	1k.30 Type **168**	95	95
376	2k.40 Izidor Krsnjavi (artist and art administrator, 150th birth)	1·20	1·20
377	3k.60 Gala curtain by Vlaho Bukovac (cent of National Theatre)	2·20	2·20

169 Children in Nest

1995. Obligatory Tax. Save Croatian Children Fund.

378	**169**	65l. multicoloured	40	40

170 Left-hand Detail of Curtain

1995. Obligatory Tax. Centenary of National Theatre, Zagreb. Details of gala curtain by Vlaho Bukovac. Multicoloured.

379	65l. Type **170**	40	40
380	65l. Central detail	40	40
381	65l. Right-hand detail	40	40

Nos. 379/81 were issued together, se-tenant, forming a composite design.

171 Zagrebacka Street, Bjelovar

1995. Croatian Towns (3rd series). Mult.

382	1k. Type **171**	40	40
383	1k.30 St. Peter and St. Paul's Cathedral, Osijek (vert)	70	70
384	1k.40 Castle, Cakovec (vert)	80	80
385	2k.20 Rovinj	1·10	1·10
386	2k.40 Korcula	1·20	1·20
387	3k.60 Town Hall, Zupanja	1·50	1·50

172 "50"

1996. 50th Anniversaries. Multicoloured.

395	3k.60 Type **172** (UNO)	1·60	1·60
396	3k.60 "5" and "FAO" within biscuit forming "50" (FAO)	1·60	1·60

173 Spiro Brusina (zoologist)

1995. Anniversaries. Multicoloured.

397	1k. Type **173** (150th birth)	70	70
398	2k.20 Bogoslav Sulek (philologist, death cent)	1·20	1·20
399	6k.50 Faust Vrancic's "Dictionary of Five European Languages" (400th anniv of publication)	3·00	3·00

174 Birds flying through Sky

1995. Obligatory Tax. Anti-drugs Campaign.

400	**174**	65l. multicoloured	40	40

175 Breast Screening

1995. Obligatory Tax. Croatian Anti-cancer League. Breast Screening Campaign.

401	**175**	65l. multicoloured	40	40

176 Hands reading Braille

1995. Centenary of Institute for Blind Children, Zagreb.

402	**176**	1k.20 red, yellow & black	75	75

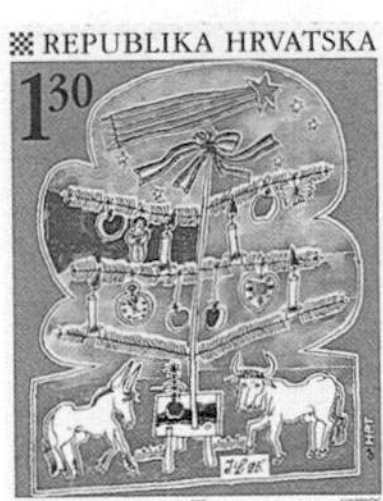

177 Animals under Christmas Tree

1995. Christmas.

403	**177**	1k.30 multicoloured	80	80

178 Polo, Animals in Boat and Court of Kublai Khan

1995. 700th Anniv of Marco Polo's Return from China.

404	**178**	3k.60 multicoloured	1·80	1·80

179 Hrvatska Kostajnica

1995. Liberated Towns. Multicoloured.

405	20l. Type **179**	25	25
406	30l. Slunj	25	25
407	50l. Gracac	40	40
408	1k.20 Drnis (vert)	55	55
409	6k.50 Glina	2·75	2·75
410	10k. Obrovac (vert)	4·00	4·00

180 Lectionary of Bernardin of Split, 1495 (first printed book using Cakavian dialect)

1995. Incunabula. Multicoloured.

420	1k.40 Type **180**	80	80
421	3k.60 Callipers and last page of "Spovid Opcena" (manual for confessors), 1496 (first book printed in Croatia)	2·00	2·00

181 Crucifix

1996. Events and Anniversaries. Mult.

422	1k.30 St. Marko Krizevcanin (detail of mosaic (Ante Starcevic), St. Marko's Church, Zagreb) (canonization)	55	55
423	1k.30 Type **181** (700th anniv of veneration of miraculous crucifix, St. Guido's Church, Rijeka)	55	55
424	1k.30 Ivan Merz (teacher and Catholic youth worker, birth centenary)	55	55

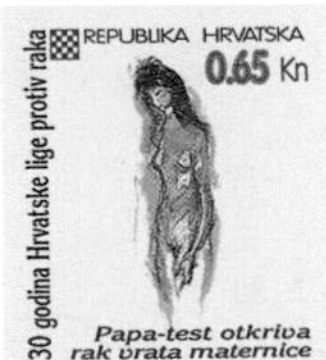

182 Breast Cancer Campaign

1996. Obligatory Tax. 30th Anniv of Anti-cancer League.

425	**182**	65l. multicoloured	40	40

183 Eugen Kvaternik (125th anniv of Rakovica Uprising)

1996. Anniversaries. Multicoloured.

426	1k.20 Type **183**	55	55
427	1k.40 Ante Starcevic (founder of Part of the Right, death centenary) (vert)	70	70
428	2k.20 Stjepan Radic (founder of Croatian Peasant Party) (125th birth anniv and 75th anniv of Peasant Republic constitution) (vert)	1·10	1·10
429	3k.60 Collage (75th anniv of Labin Republic) (vert)	1·80	1·80

184 Madonna and Child and Church

1996. Obligatory Tax. St. Mary of Bistrica Sanctuary.

430	**184**	65l. multicoloured	40	40

185 Julije Domac (founder) and Culture

1996. Centenary of Pharmacology Institute, University of Zagreb.

431	**185**	6k.50 multicoloured	2·75	2·75

186 Score

1996. Music Anniversaries. Multicoloured.

432	2k.20 Type **186** (400th birth anniv of Vinko Jelic, composer)	95	95
433	2k.20 "O" over musical bars (150th anniv of "Love and Malice" (first Croatian opera) by Vatroslav Lisinski)	95	95
434	2k.20 Josip Slavenski (composer, birth cent)	95	95
435	2k.20 "Lijepa nasa domovino" (birth bicent of Antun Mihanovic and 175th birth anniv of Josip Runjanin (composers of National Anthem))	95	95

187 Cvijeta Zuzoric (beauty)

1996. Europa. Famous Women. Mult.

436	2k.20 Type **187**	2·30	2·30
437	3k.60 Ivana Brlic-Mazuranic (writer)	3·75	3·75

188 Olympic Rings

1996. Obligatory Tax. National Olympic Committee.

438	**188**	65l. multicoloured	40	40

189 Nikola Subic Zrinski of Sziget (Ban of Croatia)

1996. 16th and 17th-century Members of Zrinski and Frankopan Families. Multicoloured.

439	1k.30 Type **189**	70	70
440	1k.40 Nikola Zrinski (Ban of Croatia)	70	70
441	2k.20 Petar Zrinski (Ban of Croatia)	1·40	1·40
442	2k.40 Katarina Zrinski (wife of Petar and sister of Fran Krsto Frankopan)	1·50	1·50
443	3k.60 Fran Krsto Frankopan (writer and revolutionary)	1·60	1·60
MS444	117×172 mm. Nos. 439/43	6·00	6·00

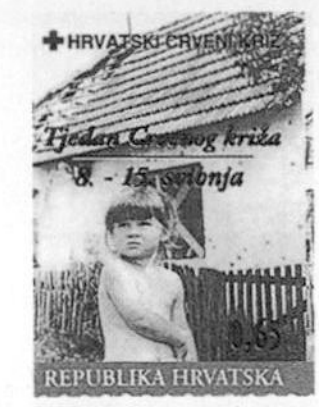

190 Child outside House

1996. Obligatory Tax. Red Cross Fund.

445	**190**	65l. black and red	40	40

191 Soldier carrying Child

1996. 5th Anniv of National Guard.

446	**191**	1k.30 multicoloured	70	70

192 Istrian Bluebell

1996. Flowers. Multicoloured.

447	2k.40 Type **192**	1·10	1·10
448	3k.60 Dubrovnik corn-flower	1·60	1·60

193 Child with Red Cross Parcel

1996. Obligatory Tax. Solidarity Week.

449	**193**	65l. black and red	40	40

194 Football

1996. European Football Championship, England.

450	**194**	2k.20 black and red	1·20	1·20

195 Konscak's Map of California

1996. 250th Anniv of Father Ferdinand Konscak's Expedition to Lower California.

451	**195**	2k.40 multicoloured	1·40	1·40

196 Children sitting outside House

1996. Obligatory Tax. Save Croatian Children Fund.
452 **196** 65l. multicoloured 40 40

197 Anniversary Emblem

1996. Obligatory Tax. 800th Anniv of Osijek.
453 **197** 65l. blue, orange & grey 40 40

198 Man holding Dumb-bell and Falcon

1996. 150th Birth Anniv of Josip Fon (founder of Croatian Falcon gymnastics society).
454 **198** 1k.40 multicoloured 70 70

199 Olympic Colours and Rings

1996. Olympic Games, Atlanta, and Centenary of Modern Olympics.
455 **199** 3k.60 multicoloured 1·80 1·80

200 Cathedral

1996. Obligatory Tax. Restoration of Dakovo Cathedral.
456 **200** 65l. multicoloured 40 40

201 "Church Tower"

1996. Obligatory Tax. 1700th Anniv of Split.
457 **201** 65l. ultramarine and blue 40 40

202 Crucifix

1996. Obligatory Tax. Vukovar.
458 **202** 65l. multicoloured 40 40

203 Lighted Candle, Shell and Lilies

1996. Obligatory Tax. Anti-drugs Campaign.
459 **203** 65l. multicoloured 40 40

204 Tweezers holding Stamp

1996. Stamp Day. 5th Anniv of Issue of First Postage Stamp by Independent Croatia.
460 **204** 1k.30 multicoloured 70 70

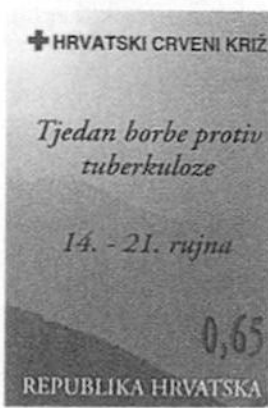
205 Mountains

1996. Obligatory Tax. Anti-tuberculosis Week.
461 **205** 65l. multicoloured 40 40

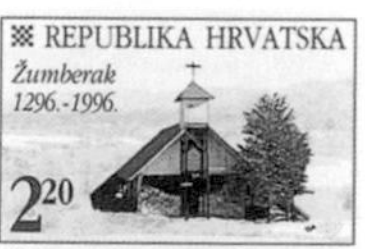
206 St. Elias's Chapel, Zumberak

1996. 700th Anniv of First Written Reference to Zumberak.
462 **206** 2k.20 multicoloured 95 95

207 Illuminated Page

1996. Early Middle Ages. Multicoloured.
463 1k.20 Type **207** (900th anniv of "Vekenega's Book of Gospels") 55 55
464 1k.40 Gottschalk (Benedictine abbot) (1150th anniv of Gottschalk's visit to Duke of Trpimir) 70 70

208 Fishes and Spear

1996. Millenary of First Written Reference to Fishing in Croatia.
465 **208** 1k.30 multicoloured 70 70

209 Gjuro Pilar (geologist, 150th anniv)

1996. Scientists' Birth Anniversaries. Mult.
466 2k.40 Type **209** 95 95
467 2k.40 Frane Bulic (archaeologist, 150th anniv) 95 95
468 2k.40 Ante Sercer (otolaryngologist, cent) 95 95

210 Sir Frederick Banting and Charles Best (discoverers)

1996. Obligatory Tax. Croatian Diabetic Council. 75th Anniv of Discovery of Insulin.
469 **210** 65l. gold, yellow & black 40 40

211 Laws of Dominican Nuns, Zadar

1996. 600th Anniv of Founding of Dominican General High School (university), Zadar.
470 **211** 1k.40 multicoloured 70 70

212 "Rain" (Menci Crncic)

1996. 20th-century Paintings. Multicoloured.
471 1k.30 Type **212** 70 70
472 1k.40 "Peljesac-Korcula Channel" (Mato Medovic) 80 80
473 3k.60 "Pink Dream" (Vlaho Bukovac) 1·60 1·60

213 "Mother of God of Remete", Zagreb

1996. Obligatory Tax.
474 **213** 65l. multicoloured 40 40

214 Children of Different Races

1996. 50th Anniv of UNICEF.
475 **214** 3k.60 multicoloured 1·60 1·60

215 Sts. Peter's and Paul's Cathedral

1996. 800th Anniv of First Written Reference to Osijek. Multicoloured.
476 2k.20 Type **215** 1·10 1·10
477 2k.20 Riverbank and view down street 1·10 1·10

216 Nativity

1996. Christmas.
478 **216** 1k.30 multicoloured 70 70

217 Bond and Bank

1996. Anniversaries. Multicoloured.
479 2k.40 Type **217** (150th anniv of founding of First Croatian Savings Bank, Zagreb) 1·10 1·10
480 3k.60 Frontispiece (bicent of publication of "The Principles of the Corn Trade" by Josip Sipus) 1·80 1·80

218 Mihanovic

1997. Obligatory Tax. Birth Bicentenary (1996) of Antun Mihanovic.
481 **218** 65l. multicoloured 40 40

219 "Professor Baltazar" (Zagreb School of Animated Film)

1997. Centenary of Croatian Films. Mult.
482 1k.40 Oktavijan Miletic (cameraman and director) filming "Vatroslav Lisinski" (first Croatian sound film), 1944 95 95
483 1k.40 Type **219** 95 95
484 1k.40 Mirjana Bohanev-Vidovic and Relja Basic in "Who Sings Means No Harm", 1970 95 95

220 Dr. Ante Starcevic's House

1997. Obligatory Tax.
485 **220** 65l. multicoloured 40 40

221 Don Quixote and Windmill

1997. Birth Anniversaries. Multicoloured.
486 2k.20 Type **221** (450th anniv of Miguel de Cervantes (author of "Don Quixote")) 95 95
487 3k.60 Metal type (600th anniv of Johannes Gutenberg (inventor of printing)) (horiz) 1·60 1·60

222 Woman

1997. Obligatory Tax. Croatian Anti-cancer League.
488 **222** 65l. multicoloured 40 40

223 "Big Joseph" by Vladimir Nazor (illus. Sasa Santel)

1997. Europa. Tales and Legends.
489 - 1k.30 multicoloured 1·40 1·40
490 **223** 3k.60 red, black & gold 3·50 3·50
DESIGNS—HORIZ: 1k.30, Elves from "Stribor's Forest" by Ivana Brlic-Mazuranic (illus. Cvijeta Job).

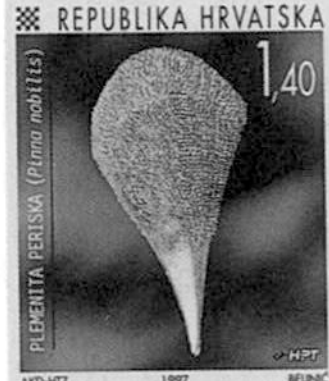

224 Noble Pen Shell

1997. Molluscs and Insects. Multicoloured.
491 1k.40 Type **224** 70 70
492 2k.40 "Radziella styx" (cave beetle) 1·10 1·10
493 3k.60 Giant tun 1·80 1·80

225 Comforting Hand

1997. Obligatory Tax. Red Cross Week.
494 **225** 65l. multicoloured 40 40

226 Pres. Franjo Tudjman

1997. 5th Anniv of Croatia's Membership of United Nations.
495 **226** 6k.50 multicoloured 2·75 2·75

227 Ludwig Zamenhof (inventor)

1997. Croatian Esperanto (invented language) Conference.
496 **227** 1k.20 multicoloured 55 55

228 Congress Emblem

1997. 58th Congress of International Amateur Rugby Federation, Dubrovnik.
497 **228** 2k.20 multicoloured 1·10 1·10

229 "Vukovar" (Zlatko Atac) (image scaled to 70% of original size)

1997. Rebuilding of Vukovar.
498 **229** 6k.50 multicoloured 2·75 2·75

230 King Petar Svacic (1095–97)

1997. Kings of Croatia. Multicoloured.
499 1k.30 Type **230** (900th death anniv) 55 55
500 2k.40 King Stjepan Drzislav (996–97) 95 95

231 16th-century Dubrovnik Courier (after Nicole de Nicolai)

1997. Stamp Day.
501 **231** 2k.30 multicoloured 1·10 1·10

232 Tennis

1997. Olympic Medal Winners. Mult.
502 1k. Type **232** (Goran Ivanisevic—bronze (singles and doubles), Barcelona 1992) 40 40
503 1k.20 Basketball (silver, Barcelona 1992) 55 55
504 1k.40 Water polo (silver, Atlanta 1996) (27×31 mm) 70 70
505 2k.20 Handball (gold, Atlanta 1996) (27×31 mm) 1·10 1·10

233 Turkish Attack on Sibenik, 1647

1997. Defence of Sibenik. Multicoloured.
506 1k.30 Type **233** (350th anniv of defence against the Turks) 55 55
507 1k.30 Air attack on Sibenik, 1991 55 55

234 Frane Petric (philosopher)

1997. Anniversaries. Multicoloured.
508 1k.40 Type **234** (400th death anniv) 70 70
509 1k.40 "Madonna and Child" (detail from the polyptich of St. Michael in Franciscan Church, Cavtat) (500th anniv of first recorded work of Vicko Lovrin (artist)) 70 70
510 1k.40 Frano Krsinic (sculptor, birth cent) 70 70
511 1k.40 Dubravko Dujsin (actor, 50th death anniv) 70 70

235 Parliamentary Session (after Ivan Zasche) and Ivan Kukuljevic (politician)

1997. Anniversaries. Multicoloured.
512 2k.20 Type **235** (150th anniv of promulgation of Croatian as official language) 1·10 1·10
513 3k.60 Zagreb and elevation of school (centenary of Croatian Grammar School, Zadar) 1·60 1·60

236 Primordial Elephant

1997. Palaeontological Finds. Multicoloured.
514 1k.40 Type **236** 55 55
515 2k.40 Fossil of "Viviparus novskaensis" (periwinkle) 95 95

237 "Painter in the Pond" (Nikola Masic)

1997. Paintings. Multicoloured.
516 1k.30 Type **237** 55 55
517 2k.20 "Angelus" (Emanuel Vidovic) 95 95
518 3k.60 "Tree in the Snow" (Slava Raskaj) 1·50 1·50

238 Child Jesus in the Stable

1997. Christmas. Multicoloured.
519 1k.30 Type **238** 55 55
520 3k.60 "Birth of Jesus" (Isidor Krsnjavi) (33×59 mm) 1·40 1·40

239 "Electra" by Sophocles

1997. Literary Anniversaries. Multicoloured.
521 1k. Type **239** (400th anniv of publication of collected translations by Dominko Zlataric) 40 40
522 1k.20 Closed book (300th birth anniv of Filip Grabovac and 250th anniv of publication of his "Best of Folk Speech and the Illyric or Croatian Language") 55 55

240 Ilok

1998. Croatian Towns (4th series).
523 **240** 5k. violet, brown & red 15 15
524 - 10k. brown, violet & red 30 30
DESIGN: 10k. Dubrovnik.

241 Score and Varazdin (Baroque Evenings)

1998. Europa. National Festivals. Mult.
531 1k.45 Type **241** 1·40 1·40
532 4k. Dubrovnik (Summer Festival) 3·50 3·50

242 Olympic Rings and Japanese Red Sun

1998. Winter Olympic Games, Nagano, Japan.
533 **242** 2k.45 multicoloured 1·10 1·10

243 Jelacics Flag and Battle near Moor (lithograph)

1998. Historical Events of 1848. Mult.
534 1k.60 Type **243** 85 85
535 1k.60 "Croatian Assembly in Session" (Dragutin Weingartner) 85 85
536 4k. Ban Josip Jelacic (after Ivan Zasche) (21×31 mm) 2·00 2·00

244 Mimara

1998. Birth Centenary of Ante Topic Mimara (art collector).
537 **244** 2k.65 multicoloured 1·10 1·10

245 Caesar's Mushroom

1998. Fungi. Multicoloured.

538	1k.30 Type **245**	70	70
539	1k.30 Saffron milk cup ("Lactarius deliciosus")	70	70
540	7k.20 "Morchella conica"	3·75	3·75

246 Stepinac

1998. Birth Centenary of Cardinal Alojzije Stepinac (Archbishop of Zagreb).

541	**246**	1k.50 multicoloured	70	70

247 Magnifying Glass over Fingerprint and Dubrovnik

1998. 27th European Regional Conference of Interpol, Dubrovnik.

542	**247**	2k.45 multicoloured	1·10	1·10

248 *Falkusa* (fishing boat)

1998. "Espo '98" World's Fair, Lisbon. Sheet 97×80 mm.

MS543	**248**	14k.85 multicoloured	6·75	6·75

249 Football

1998. World Cup Football Championship, France.

544	**249**	4k. multicoloured	1·80	1·80

250 Title Page of "Slavonic Fairy"

1998. Writers' Anniversaries. Multicoloured.

545	1k.20 Type **250** (450th birth anniv of Juraj Barakovic (poet))	55	55
546	1k.50 Milan Begovic (50th death anniv)	70	70
547	1k.60 Mate Balota (birth centenary)	85	85
548	2k.45 Antun Gustav Matos (125th birth anniv)	1·00	1·00
549	2k.65 Matija Antun Relkovic (death bicentenary)	1·10	1·10
550	4k. Antun Branko Simic (birth centenary)	1·80	1·80

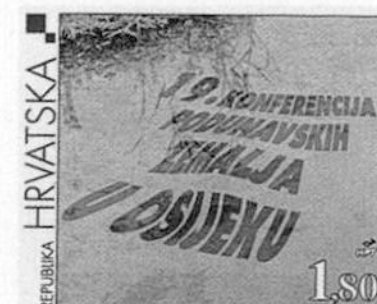

251 Text on Water

1998. 19th Danube Countries Conference, Osijek.

551	**251**	1k.80 multicoloured	70	70

252 Betlheim

1998. Birth Centenary of Dr. Stjepan Betlheim (psychoanalyst).

552	**252**	1k.50 multicoloured	70	70

253 Team Member

1998. Winning of Bronze Medal by Croatia in World Cup Football Championship. Sheet 112×82 mm containing T 253 and similar horiz design. Multicoloured.

MS553	4k. ×4, Composite design of Croatian World Cup Squad	7·00	7·00

254 Liburnian Sewn Boat (1st century B.C.)

1998. Croatian Ships. Multicoloured.

554	1k.20 Type **254**	55	55
555	1k.50 Condura (11th–12th centuries)	65	65
556	1k.60 Ragusan (Dubrovnik) carrack (16th century)	70	70
557	1k.80 Istrian bracera	85	85
558	2k.45 River Neretva sailing barge	1·10	1·10
559	2k.65 Barque	1·30	1·30
560	4k. "Vila Velebita" (sail/steam cadet ship)	1·80	1·80
561	7k.20 "Amorela" (car ferry)	3·50	3·50
562	20k. "King Petar Kresimir IV" (missile corvette)	9·00	9·00

255 Mail Coach and Posthorn

1998. Stamp Day. 150th Anniv of Creation of Croatian Supreme Postal Administration.

563	**255**	1k.50 multicoloured	70	70

256 Font and Cathedral

1998. 700th Anniv of Sibenik Bishopric and Proclamation of Sibenik as a Free Borough.

564	**256**	4k. multicoloured	1·50	1·50

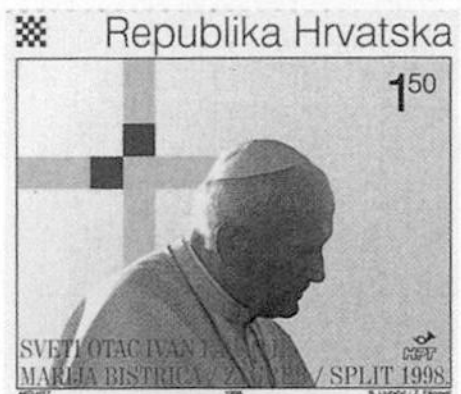

257 Pope John Paul II

1998. 2nd Papal Visit.

565	**257**	1k.50 multicoloured	70	70

258 Horse Tram, Osijek

1998. Transport. Multicoloured.

566	1k.50 Type **258**	70	70
567	1k.50 First motor car in Zagreb, 1901	70	70
568	1k.50 Electric train, Karlovac–Rijeka line (125th anniv)	70	70
569	1k.50 Aerial view of Ostrovica–Delnice section of Zagreb–Rijeka motorway	70	70
570	7k.20 Zagreb funicular railway (19×23 mm)	3·00	3·00

259 "Adoration of the Shepherds" (detail, from breviary "Officinum Virginis" illus by Klovic)

1998. Christmas. 500th Birth Anniv of Julije Klovic (artist).

571	**259**	1k.50 multicoloured	70	70

260 Ibrisimovic

1998. 300th Death Anniv of Father Luka Ibrisimovic (revolutionary).

572	**260**	1k.90 multicoloured	85	85

261 Distorted Tree bound to Stake

1998. 50th Anniv of Universal Declaration of Human Rights.

573	**261**	5k. multicoloured	2·10	2·10

262 "Cypress" (Frano Simunovic)

1998. 20th-century Art. Multicoloured.

574	1k.90 "Paromlin Road" (Josip Vanista) (horiz)	1·00	1·00
575	2k.20 Type **262**	1·10	1·10
576	5k. "Coma" (interactive video installation, Dalibor Martinis)	2·10	2·10

263 Flags

1999. Zagreb Fair.

577	**263**	1k.80 multicoloured	1·00	1·00

264 Haulik

1999. 130th Death Anniv of Cardinal Juraj Haulik (first Archbishop of Zagreb).

578	**264**	5k. multicoloured	2·10	2·10

265 Mljet Island National Park

1999. Europa. Parks and Gardens. Multicoloured.

579	1k.80 Type **265**	2·10	2·10
580	5k. River Lonja Basin Nature Park	5·00	5·00

266 Viper

1999. The Orsini's Viper. Multicoloured.

581	2k.20 Type **266**	1·10	1·10
582	2k.20 Viper on alert	1·10	1·10
583	2k.20 Two vipers	1·10	1·10
584	2k.20 Viper's head	1·10	1·10

267 Anniversary Emblem

1999. 50th Anniv of Council of Europe.

585	**267**	2k.80 multicoloured	1·40	1·40

268 Orlando's Pillar with Mask

1999. 19th Foundation of European Carnival Cities Convention, Dubrovnik.

586	**268**	2k.30 multicoloured	1·10	1·10

269 1 Kreutzer Coin, 1849

1999. 150th Anniv of Minting of Jelacic Kreutzer (587) and Fifth Anniv of Croatian Kuna (588). Multicoloured.

587	2k.30 Type **269**	1·00	1·00
588	5k. One kuna coin	2·10	2·10

270 Vladimir Nazor (writer)

1999. Anniversaries. Multicoloured.
589 1k.80 Type **270** (50th death anniv) 70 70
590 2k.30 Ferdo Livadic (composer, birth bicentenary) 1·00 1·00
591 2k.50 Ivan Rendic (sculptor, 150th birth anniv) 1·10 1·10
592 2k.80 Milan Lenuci (urban planner, 150th birth anniv) 1·30 1·30
593 3k.50 Vjekoslav Klaic (historian, 150th birth anniv) 1·40 1·40
594 4k. Emilij Laszowski (historian, 50th death anniv) 1·70 1·70
595 5k. Antun Kanizlic (religious writer and poet, 300th birth anniv) 2·10 2·10

271 Basilica and Mosaics of Bishop Euphrasius, St. Maurus and Fish

1999. Euphrasian Basilica, Porec.
596 **271** 4k. multicoloured 1·70 1·70

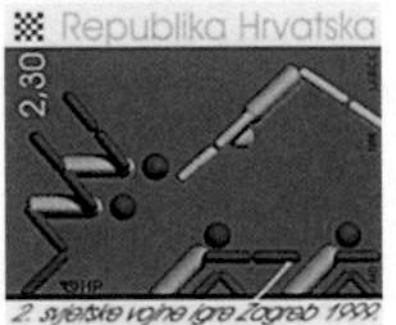

272 Swimming, Diving and Rowing

1999. 2nd World Military Gamzes, Zagreb.
597 **272** 2k.30 multicoloured 85 85

273 Reconstruction of Woman, Skull Fragments and Stone Tools

1999. Centenary of Discovery of Remains of Early Man in Krapina. Multicoloured.
598 1k.80 Type **273** 85 85
599 4k. Dragutin Gorjanovic-Kramberger (palaeontologist and discoverer of remains) and bone fragments 1·70 1·70

Nos. 598/9 were issued together, se-tenant, forming a composite design.

274 UPU Emblem and Clouds

1999. World Post Day. 125th Anniv of Universal Postal Union.
600 **274** 2k.30 multicoloured 1·10 1·10

275 Lace, "Jesus expelling the Merchants from the Temple" (detail of fresco, Ivan Ranger), and Angel, St. Mary's Church

1999. 600th Anniv of Founding of Paulist Monastery of the Blessed Virgin Mary in Lepoglava. Multicoloured.
601 5k. Type **275** 2·20 2·20
602 5k. Altar angel and facade of St. Mary's Church 2·20 2·20
603 5k. St. Elizabeth (statue), detail of choir gallery and lace 2·20 2·20

276 Josip Jelacic, Ban of Croatia (after C. Lanzelli)

1999. 150th Anniv of Composing of the Jelacic March by Johann Strauss, the Elder.
604 **276** 3k.50 multicoloured 1·80 1·80

277 Cloud and Chemical Symbol for Ozone

1999. World Ozone Layer Protection Day.
605 **277** 5k. multicoloured 2·10 2·10

278 Pazin Grammar School

1999. School Anniversaries. Multicoloured.
606 2k.30 Type **278** (centenary) 1·00 1·00
607 3k.50 Pozega Grammar School (300th anniv) 1·50 1·50

279 Hebrang

1999. Birth Cent of Andrija Hebrang (politician).
608 **279** 1k.80 multicoloured 1·10 1·10

280 "Madonna of the Rose- garden" (Blaz Jurjev of Trogir)

1999. "Croats—Christianity, Culture, Art" Exhibition, Vatican City.
609 **280** 5k. multicoloured 2·10 2·10

281 "Nativity for my Children" (plaster relief, Mila Wood)

1999. Christmas.
610 **281** 2k.30 multicoloured 1·10 1·10

282 "Winter Landscape" (Gabrijel Jurkic)

1999. Modern Art. Multicoloured.
611 2k.30 Type **282** 1·00 1·00
612 3k.50 "Klek" (Oton Postruznik) 1·40 1·40
613 5k. "Stone Table" (Ignjat Job) (vert) 2·10 2·10

283 Tudjman

1999. Death Commem of President Franjo Tudjman.
614 **283** 2k.30 black and red 1·00 1·00
615 **283** 5k. blue, black and red 2·10 2·10

284 Angel

2000. Holy Year 2000.
616 **284** 2k.30 multicoloured 1·70 1·70

285 Woman's Face

2000. St. Valentines Day.
617 **285** 2k.30 multicoloured 1·40 1·40

286 Latin Text, Building and Archbishop Stjepan Cosmi (founder)

2000. 300th Anniv of Split Grammar School.
618 **286** 2k.80 multicoloured 2·40 2·40

287 Typewriter

2000. Centenary of Association of Croatian Writers.
619 **287** 2k.30 black and red 2·10 2·10

288 "The Lamentation" (Andrija Medulic)

2000. Anniversaries. Multicoloured.
620 1k.80 Type **288** (artist, 500th birth anniv) 85 85
621 2k.30 Matija Petar Katancic (poet, 250th birth anniv) 1·00 1·00
622 2k.80 Marija Ruzicka-Strozzi (actress, 150th birth anniv) 1·10 1·10
623 3k.50 Statue of Marko Marulic (writer, 550th birth anniv) 1·50 1·50
624 5k. "Madonna with the Child and Saints" (Blaz Jurjev Trogiranin) (artist, 550th death anniv) (47×25 mm) 2·50 2·50

289 Map of Croatia and European Union Stars

2000. Europa. 50th Anniv of Schuman Plan (proposal for pooling the coal and steel industries of France and West Germany). Multicoloured.
625 2k.30 Type **289** 2·10 2·10
626 5k. "Building Europe" (vert) 3·50 3·50

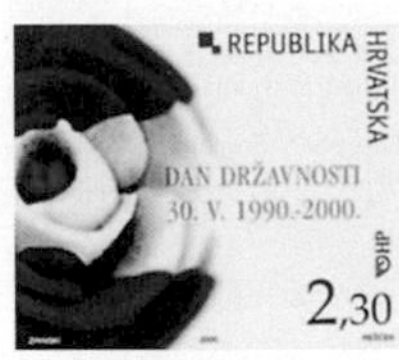

290 Flag

2000. 10th Anniv of Independence.
627 **290** 2k.30 multicoloured 1·70 1·70

291 Pavilion Building

2000. "EXPO 2000" World's Fair, Hanover. Sheet 100×74 mm.
MS628 **291** 14k.40 multicoloured 6·25 6·25

292 *Micromeria croatica*

2000. Flowers. Multicoloured.
629 3k.50 Type **292** 1·50 1·50
630 5k. *Geranium dalmaticum* 2·10 2·10

293 Statute and Postcard of Kastav

2000. 600th Anniv of the Kastav Statute.
631 **293** 1k.80 multicoloured 1·10 1·10

294 Blanusa Gospel and "2000"

2000. World Mathematics Year.

632	294	3k.50 multicoloured	1·80	1·80

295 Angels (fresco), St. George's Church, Purga

2000. 300th Birth Anniv of Ivan Ranger (artist).

633	295	1k.80 multicoloured	1·10	1·10

296 Stone Tablet

2000. 900th Anniv of Baska Stone Tablet (early Croatian written record). Sheet 95×67 mm.

MS634	296	16k.70 multicoloured	7·75	7·75

297 Latin Text

2000. 800th Birth Anniv of Toma, Archdeacon of Split.

635	297	3k.50 black, silver and blue	1·80	1·80

298 Vis

2000. Croatian Towns (5th series).

636	-	2k.30 multicoloured	1·10	1·10
639	298	3k.50 multicoloured	1·80	1·80
639a	-	3k.50 multicoloured	1·80	1·80
640	-	5k. multicoloured	2·75	2·75

DESIGNS: 2k.30, Makarska; 3k.50, Rijeka; 5k. Virovitica.

299 Austrian Empire 1850 9k. Stamp and Postmark

2000. World Post Day. Multicoloured.

641	2k.30 Type **299** (150th anniv of first stamp in territory of Croatia)	1·10	1·10
642	2k.30 Automatic sorting machine (introduction of automatic sorting system)	1·10	1·10

300 Basketball, Football, Handball, Water-polo and Tennis Balls

2000. Olympic Games, Sydney.

643	300	5k. multicoloured	2·75	2·75

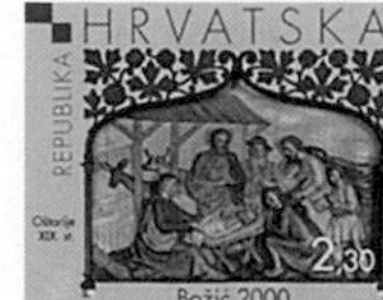

301 "Nativity" (relief, Church of the Blessed Virgin Mary, Ogulin)

2000. Christmas.

644	301	2k.30 multicoloured	1·10	1·10

302 "Korcula" (Vladimir Varlaj)

2000. Paintings (1st series). Multicoloured.

645	1k.80 Type **302**	1·00	1·00
646	2k.30 "Brusnik" (Duro Tiljak)	1·10	1·10
647	5k. "Boats" (Ante Kastelancic)	2·75	2·75

See also Nos. 675/7, 711/13, 746/48, 779/8, 826/8 and 872/4.

303 White Dove, Ship and Village

2001. New Millennium.

648	303	2k.30 multicoloured	1·70	1·70

304 Charles the Great (statue)

2001. 1200th Anniv of the Coronation of Charlemagne as Emperor of the Romans. Sheet 92×78 mm.

MS649	304	14k.40 multicoloured	7·00	7·00

305 Scene from *Radmio and Ljubmir* (poem)

2001. 500th Death Anniv of Dzore Drzic (playwright).

650	305	2k.80 multicoloured	1·50	1·50

306 Black Rider (comic strip character)

2001. Birth Centenary of Andrija Maurovic (comic strip illustrator).

651	306	5k. multicoloured	2·30	2·30

307 Goran Ivanisevic

2001. Croatian Sporting Victories. Multicoloured.

652	2k.50 Type **307** (Wimbledon Men's Champion)	1·80	1·80
653	2k.80 Janica Kostelic (Alpine Skiing World Cup Women's Champion)	2·00	2·00

308 Olive Tree, Kastel Stafilic

2001

654	308	1k.80 multicoloured	90	90

309 Water (green splash to left)

2001. Europa. Water Resources. Multicoloured.

655	3k.50 Type **309**	1·50	1·50
656	5k. Water (blue splash to right)	3·00	3·00

Nos. 655/6 were issued together, se-tenant, forming a composite design.

310 Poster (Mikele Janko)

2001. World No Smoking Day.

657	310	2k.50 multicoloured	1·20	1·20

311 Apollo (*Parnassius apollo*)

2001. Butterflies. Multicoloured.

658	2k.50 Type **311**	1·10	1·10
659	2k.80 Scarce large blue (*Maculinea teleius*)	1·20	1·20
660	5k. False ringlet (*Coenonympha oedippus*)	2·30	2·30

312 Vukovar

2001

661	312	2k.80 multicoloured	1·80	1·80

313 Statues and Flames

2001. Trsteno Arboretum. Sheet 95×76 mm.

MS662	313	14k.40 multicoloured	7·50	7·50

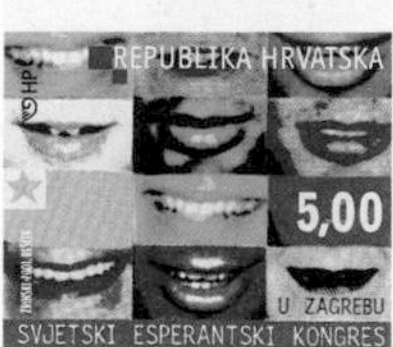

314 Mouths

2001. World Esperanto Congress, Zagreb.

663	314	5k. multicoloured	3·00	3·00

315 Woman and Wall

2001. 50th Anniv of United Nations Commissioner for Refugees (No. 664) and I.O.M. International Organization for Migration (No. 665). Mult.

664	1k.80 Type **315**	1·10	1·10
665	5k. Refugees and 50IOM	2·75	2·75

316 Perforated Blocks of Colour

2001. Stamp Day.

666	316	2k.50 multicoloured	1·10	1·10

317 Croatian Sheep Dog

2001. Dog Breeds. Multicoloured.

667	1k.80 Type **317**	1·10	1·10
668	5k. Dalmatian	2·75	2·75

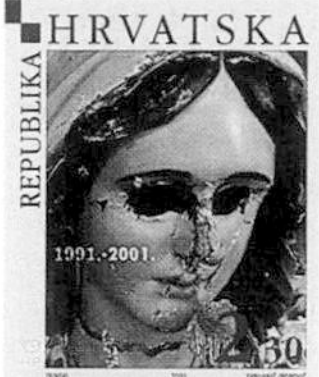

318 Head of "Our Lady of Konavle" (statue)

2001. 10th Anniv of Republic of Croatia.

669	318	2k.30 multicoloured	1·10	1·10

319 Children encircling Globe

2001. U.N. Year of Dialogue among Civilizations.

670	319	5k. multicoloured	2·75	2·75

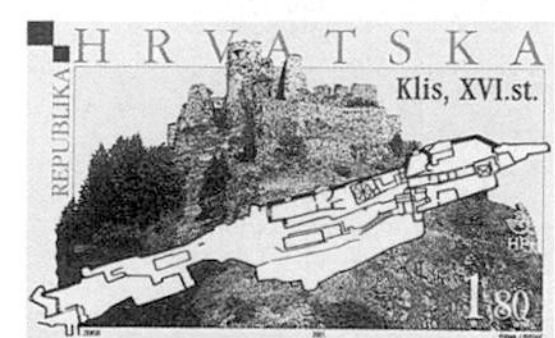

320 Klis (16th-century)

2001. Fortresses (1st series). Multicoloured.

671	1k.80 Type **320**	90	90
672	2k.50 Ston (14th-century)	1·20	1·20
673	3k.50 Sisak (16th-century)	1·70	1·70

See also Nos. 675/7, 705/7, 734/6, 776/8, 817/19, 867/9 and 908/10.

321 Adoration of the Magi (altarpiece), The Visitation of Mary Church, Cucerje

2001. Christmas.
674 **321** 2k.30 multicoloured 1·20 1·20

322 "Amphitheatre Ruins" (Vjekoslav Parac)

2001. Paintings (2nd series). Multicoloured.
675 2k.50 Type **322** 1·20 1·20
676 2k.50 "Maternite du Port-Royal" (Leo Junek) 1·20 1·20
677 5k. "Nude with a Baroque Figure" (Slavko Sohaj) (vert) 2·30 2·30

323 Lavoslav Ruzicka, (Chemistry, 1939)

2001. Nobel Prize Winners. Multicoloured.
678 2k.80 Type **323** 1·50 1·50
679 3k.50 Vladimir Prelog (Chemistry, 1975) 2·30 2·30
680 5k. Ivo Andric (Literature, 1961) 3·00 3·00

323a Emblem

2001. Obligatory Tax. Solidarity Week.
680a **323a** 1k.15 vermilion and black 60 60

324 Ivan Gucetic

2002. Anniversaries. Multicoloured.
681 1k.80 Type **324** (writer, 500th death anniv) 90 90
682 2k.30 Dobrisa Cesaric (writer, birth centenary) 1·10 1·10
683 2k.50 Juraj Rattkay (historian, 350th anniv of publication of *Memoria Regum et Banorum Regnorum Dalmatia, Croatiae et Sclavoniae Ab Origine sua usque ad praesentem Annum 1652 deducta* (history of Croatia)) 1·20 1·20
684 2k.80 Franjo Vranjanin Laurana (sculptor, 500th death anniv) 1·50 1·50
685 3k.50 Augustin Kazotic (Bishop of Zagreb, 300th anniv of beatification) 2·30 2·30
686 5k. Matko Laginja (politician and writer, 150th birth anniv) 3·00 3·00

325 Skier

2002. Winter Olympic Games, Salt Lake City, U.S.A.
687 **325** 5k. multicoloured 3·00 3·00

326 Barcode and "Reaper" (drawing, Robert Franges Mihanovic)

2002. 150th Anniv of Croatian Chamber of Economy.
688 **326** 2k.50 multicoloured 1·50 1·50

327 9th-century Gable bearing Prince Trpimir's Name (detail, altar partition, Rizinice Church)

2002. 1150th Anniv of Prince Trpimir's Deed of Gift of Land to Archbishop of Salona. Sheet 116×59 mm.
MS689 **327** 14k.40 multicoloured 7·50 7·50

328 Kuharic

2002. Cardinal Franjo Kuharic (Archbishop of Zagreb) Commemoration.
690 **328** 2k.30 multicoloured 1·20 1·20

329 "Divan"

2002. 80th Death Anniv of Vlaho Bukovac (artist).
691 **329** 5k. multicoloured 2·50 2·50

A stamp in a similar design was issued by Czech Republic.

330 Arms

2002. 750th Anniv of Royal Borough of Krizevci.
692 **330** 1k.80 multicoloured 90 90

331 Facade

2002. Centenary of Post Office Building, Varazdin.
693 **331** 2k.30 multicoloured 1·20 1·20

332 Clown with Umbrella

2002. Europa. Circus. Multicoloured.
694 **332** 3k.50 multicoloured 1·80 1·80
695 **332** 5k. multicoloured 2·75 2·75

333 Stylised Player and Ball

2002. World Cup Football Championships, Japan and South Korea. Multicoloured.
696 3k.50 Type **333** 1·50 1·50
697 5k. Stylised player ball at right 2·30 2·30

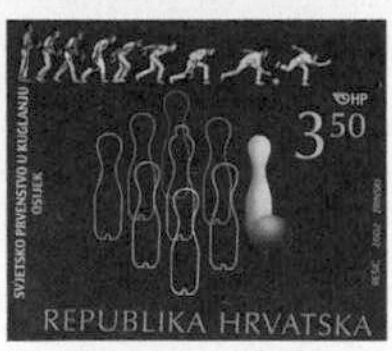

334 Player, Pin and Ball

2002. World Ten-pin Bowling Championship, Osijek.
698 **334** 3k.50 multicoloured 2·30 2·30

335 Common Oak (*Quercus robur*)

2002. Trees. Multicoloured.
699 1k.80 Type **335** 90 90
700 2k.50 Sessile oak (*Quercus petraea*) 1·40 1·40
701 2k.80 Holly oak (*Quercus ilex*) 1·50 1·50

336 Mouse and Moon

2002. 15th World Animated Film Festival, Zagreb.
702 **336** 5k. multicoloured 3·00 3·00

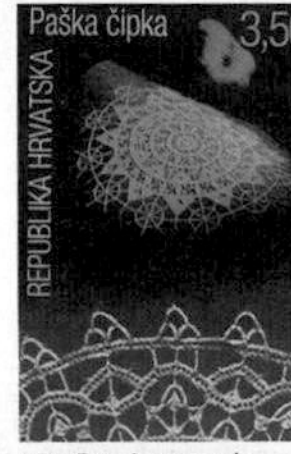

337 Pag Lacework

2002. Lace-making. Multicoloured.
703 3k.50 Type **337** 2·30 2·30
704 5k. Liedekerke lacework and statue of lace-maker 3·00 3·00

Stamps of a similar design were issued by Belgium.

2002. Fortresses (2nd series). As T 320. Multicoloured.
705 2k.50 Skocibuha family summer villa, Sipan (16th-century) 1·40 1·40
706 2k.50 Nehaj (16th-century) 1·40 1·40
707 5k. Veliki Tabor (16th-century) 2·75 2·75

338 Slavonic Script

2002. Centenary of Krk Slavic Academy.
708 **338** 4k. black and red 4·25 4·25

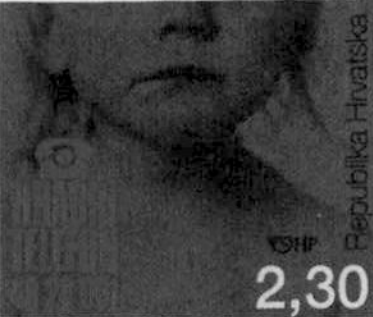

339 Child's Face and Emblem

2002. Children's Telephone Helpline.
709 **339** 2k.30 multicoloured 1·40 1·40

340 "Our Lady and the Saints" (detail) (polyptych, Nikola Bozidarevic), Dance Church, Dubrovnik

2002. Christmas.
710 **340** 2k.30 multicoloured 1·40 1·40

2002. Paintings (3rd series). As T 322.Multicoloured.
711 2k.50 "Girl in the Boat" (Milivoj Uzelac) (vert) 1·40 1·40
712 2k.50 "Flowers on the Window" (Antun Motika) (vert) 1·40 1·40
713 5k. "On the Drava River" (Krsto Hededusic) 2·75 2·75

340a Elderly Woman receiving Red Cross Parcel

2002. Obligatory Tax. Solidarity Week.
713a **340a** 1k.15 multicoloured 70 70

341 Zagreb Cathedral

2002. 150th Anniv of Zagreb Archbishopric.
714 **341** 2k.80 multicoloured 1·40 1·40

342 Pavao Vitezovic

2002. 350th Birth Anniv of Pavao Ritter Vitezovic (writer).
715 **342** 2k.30 multicoloured 1·70 1·70

343 Column Capitals, Bell Tower, St. Mary's Church, Zadar

2002. 900th Anniv of Accession Hungarian King Koloman to Croatian Throne.
716 **343** 3k.50 multicoloured 2·00 2·00

344 Kosjenka (Regoc)

2003. Fairy Stories. Showing characters from stories by Ivana Brlic Mazuranic. Multicoloured.

717 2k.30 Type **344** 1·20 1·20
718 2k.80 Malik Tintilinic (Suma Striborova) 1·40 1·40

345 Heart enclosed in Jigsaw Puzzle

2003. St. Valentine's Day.

719 **345** 2k.30 multicoloured 1·20 1·20

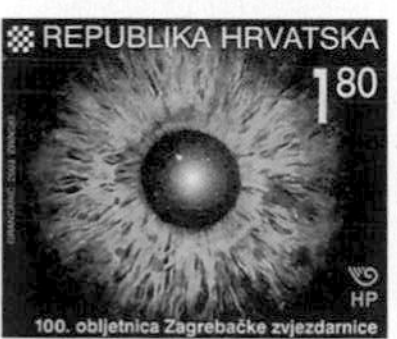

346 Eye

2003. Centenary of Zagreb Astronomical Observatory (1k.80). 150th Anniv of Meteorological Measurements and 50th Anniv of Meteorological Station on Zavizan (3k.50). Multicoloured.

720 1k.80 Type **346** 85 85
721 3k.50 Eye and lightening 1·70 1·70

347 Players and Coach

2003. Croatia, World Handball Champions, Portugal 2003. Sheet 112×83 mm containing T 347 and similar vert designs showing team.

MS722 4k. Type **347**; 4k. Eight players; 4k. Six players; 4k. Four players 7·75 7·75

348 Building Facade and Monks

2003. 500th Anniv of the Paulist (White Friars) Secondary School, Lepoglava.

723 **348** 5k. multicoloured 2·40 2·40

349 Page from Missal

2003. 600th Anniv of Duke Hrvoje's Glagolitic Missal (illuminated book).

724 **349** 5k. multicoloured 2·40 2·40

350 Prosthetic Leg

2003. Anti-Landmine Campaign.

725 **350** 2k.30 multicoloured 1·00 1·00

351 Janica Kostelic

2003. World Cup Alpine Skiing Gold Medallists, St. Moritz 2003. Multicoloured.

726 3k.50 Type **351** 1·50 1·50
727 3k.50 Ivica Kosteli 1·50 1·50

352 Antun Soljan (poet, tenth anniv)

2003. Death Anniversaries. Multicoloured.

728 1k.80 Type **352** 85 85
729 2k.30 Hanibal Lucic (poet, 450th anniv) 1·00 1·00
730 5k. Federiko Benkovic (artist, 250th anniv) 2·20 2·20

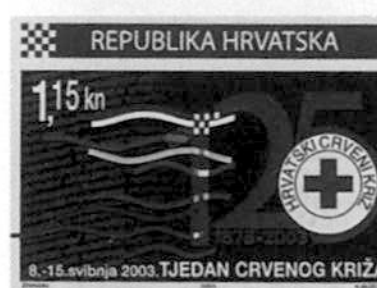

353 St. Jerome

2003. 550th Anniv of St. Jerome Papal Institutions, Rome.

731 **353** 2k.80 multicoloured 1·40 1·40

353a "125"

2003. Obligatory Tax. Red Cross Week. 125th Anniv of Croatian Red Cross.

731a **353a** 1k.15 multicoloured 70 70

354 "Marya Delvard" (Tomislav Krizman)

2003. Europa. Poster Art. Multicoloured.

732 3k.50 Type **354** 2·00 2·00
733 5k. "The Firebird" (Boris Bucan) (35×35 mm) 3·00 3·00

2003. Fortresses (3rd series). As T 320. Multicoloured.

734 1k.80 Kostajnica, (15th-century) 85 85
735 2k.80 Slavonski, Brod (18th-century) 1·40 1·40
736 5k. Minceta, Dubrovnik (15th-century) 2·20 2·20

355 Pope John Paul II

2003. Pope John Paul II's Third Visit to Croatia.

737 **355** 2k.30 multicoloured 1·00 1·00

356 Squirrel (*Sciurus vulgaris*)

2003. Fauna. Multicoloured.

738 2k.30 Type **356** 1·00 1·00
739 2k.80 Dormouse (*Glis glis*) 1·40 1·40
740 3k.50 Beaver (*Castor fiber*) 1·50 1·50

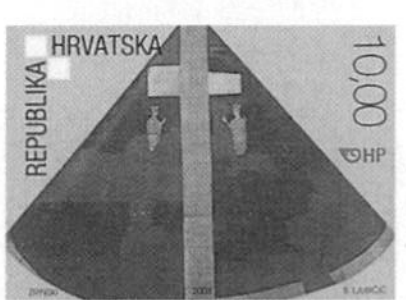

357 Cope

2003. King Ladislaus' Cope (11th-century). Sheet 95×70 mm.

MS741 **357** 1k. multicoloured 4·75 4·75

358 Letter Box, Envelopes and Stamp

2003. Stamp Day. 50th Anniv of Post Museum, Zagreb.

742 **358** 2k.30 multicoloured 1·20 1·20

358a "tjedan borbe protiv TBC"

2003. Obligatory Tax. Anti-Tuberculosis Week.

742a **358a** 1k.15 vermilion and green 70 70

359 Vines and Paths

2003. UNESCO World Heritage Site. Primosten Vineyard. Sheet 110×78 mm.

MS743 **359** 10k. multicoloured 4·75 4·75

360 Mother of Mercy (statue) and Nativity Church, Varazdin

2003. 300th Anniv of Ursuline Religious Order in Croatia.

744 **360** 2k.50 multicoloured 1·20 1·20

361 Three Wise Men

2003. Christmas.

745 **361** 2k.30 multicoloured 1·20 1·20

2003. Paintings (4th series). As T 322. Multicoloured.

746 1k.80 "Flower Girl II" (Slavko Kopac) 90 90
747 3k.50 "Dry Stone Wall" (Oton Gliha) (vert) 1·80 1·80
748 3k.50 "Pont Des Art" (Josip Racic) (vert) 1·80 1·80

362 Ball and Players

2003. 16th Women's World Handball Championships.

749 **362** 5k. multicoloured 3·00 3·00

362a Snow-covered House and Tree

2003. Obligatory Tax. Solidarity Week.

749a **362a** 1k.15 multicoloured 1·00 1·00

363 Josip Hatze

2004. Musical Anniversaries. Multicoloured.

750 5k. Type **363** (125th birth anniv of Josip Hatze (composer)) 3·00 3·00
751 5k. Violin bridge and strings (50th anniv of Zagreb Soloists ensemble) 3·00 3·00

364 Manuscript Page

2004. 600th Anniv of Hval's Manuscript.

752 **364** 2k.30 multicoloured 1·50 1·50

365 Stylized Boxing Ring

2004. European Boxing Championship, Pula.

753 **365** 2k.80 multicoloured 1·70 1·70

366 Adult Heron

2004. Purple Heron (Ardea purourea). Mult.

754	5k. Type **366**	3·00	3·00
755	5k. Adult and chick	3·00	3·00
756	5k. Adults flying	3·00	3·00
757	5k. Adult in reed bed	3·00	3·00

367 Frontispiece of "De Regno Dalmatiae et Croatie"

2004. Anniversaries. Multicoloured.

758	2k.30 Type **367** (writer and historian) (400th birth anniv)	1·70	1·70
759	3k.50 Antun Vrancic (writer) (500th birth anniv)	2·30	2·30
760	3k.50 St. Jerome (sculpture) (Andrija Alesi) (500th death anniv)	2·30	2·30
761	10k. Frontispiece Croatian grammar (Bartol Kasic) (400th anniv of first publication)	6·25	6·25

368 Wild Flowers

2004. Risnjak National Park. Sheet 99×74 mm.

MS762	10k. multicoloured	6·00	6·00

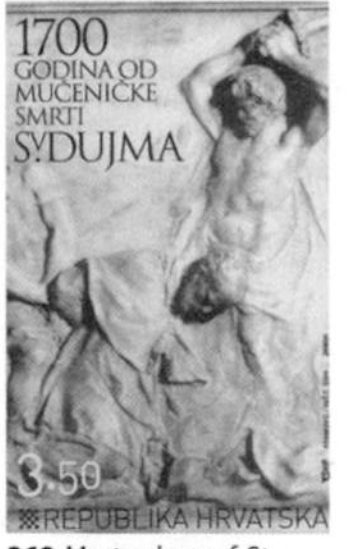

369 Martyrdom of St. Domnius and Ivan Lucic

2004. 700th Anniv of the Martyrdom of St. Domnius.

763	**369**	3k.50 multicoloured	2·30	2·30

369a Elderly man and Child

2004. Obligatory Tax. Red Cross Week.

763a	**369a**	1k.15 multicoloured	1·00	1·00

370 Toboggan, Skater, Ski Poles and Skis

2004. Europa. Holidays. Multicoloured.

764	3k.50 Type **370**	2·20	2·20
765	3k.50 Deck chair, beach ball and sunglasses	2·20	2·20

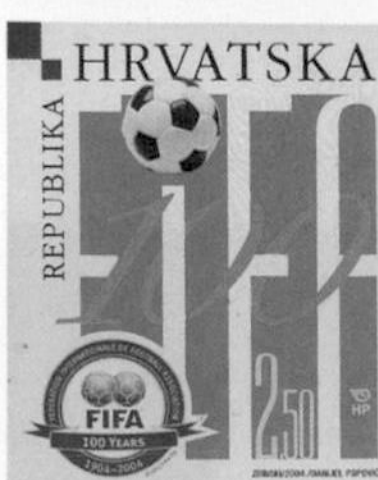

371 Football and Emblem

2004. Centenary of FIFA (Federation Internationale de Football Association).

766	**371**	2k.50 multicoloured	1·50	1·50

372 Dog Rose (*Rosa canina*)

2004. Medicinal Plants. Multicoloured.

767	2k.30 Type **372**	1·70	1·70
768	2k.80 Sweet violet (*Viola odorata*)	2·00	2·00
769	3k.50 Peppermint (*Mentha piperita*)	2·40	2·40

373 Puppets forming "UNIMA"

2004. World UNIMA (puppeteers) Conference, Opatija. International Puppetry Festival, Rijeka.

770	**373**	3k.50 multicoloured	2·30	2·30

374 Multicoloured Football

2004. European Football Championship 2004, Portugal.

771	**374**	3k.50 multicoloured	2·30	2·30

375 Mostar Bridge

2004. Reconstruction of Ottoman Bridge at Mostar.

772	**375**	3k.50 multicoloured	2·30	2·30

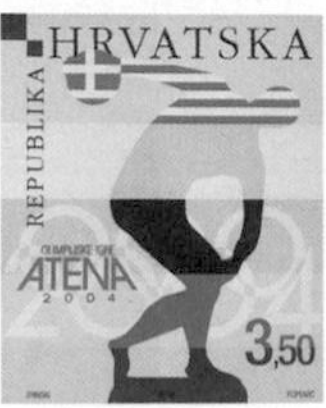

376 Discus Throwing

2004. Olympic Games, Athens.

773	**376**	3k.50 multicoloured	2·30	2·30

377 Building Facade

2004. Centenary of Post Office, Zagreb.

774	**377**	2k.30 multicoloured	1·50	1·50

377a Hand-washing

2004. Obligatory Tax. Anti-Tuberculosis Week.

774a	**377a**	1k.15 multicoloured	1·00	1·00

378 Andrija Miosic

2004. 300th Birth Anniv of Father Andrija Kacic Miosic (writer).

775	**378**	2k.80 multicoloured	1·80	1·80

2004. Fortresses (4th series). As T 320. Multicoloured.

776	3k.50 Dubovac (15th-century)	2·40	2·40
777	3k.50 Valpovo (15th–18th century)	2·40	2·40
778	3k.50 Gripe (17th-century)	2·40	2·40

2004. Paintings (5th series). As T 322. Multicoloured.

779	2k.30 "Parisian Suburb" (Juraj Plancic) (vert)	1·70	1·70
780	2k.30 "Noon in Supetar" (Jerolim Mise) (vert)	1·70	1·70
781	2k.30 "Self-portrait" (Miroslav Kraljevic) (vert)	1·70	1·70

379 Christmas Wheat

2004. Christmas.

782	**379**	2k.30 multicoloured	1·50	1·50

379a Children, Red Cross Parcel and Elderly Woman

2004. Obligatory Tax. Solidarity Week.

782a	**379a**	1k.15 multicoloured	1·00	1·00

380 Antun and Stjepan Radic (founders)

2004. Centenary of Croatian Peoples Peasants' Party (HPSS).

783	**380**	7k.20 turquoise and black	4·25	4·25

381 Halugica

2005. Fairy Stories. Showing characters from stories by Vladimir Nazor. Multicoloured.

784	5k. Type **381**	3·00	3·00
785	5k. Longbeard Mannikin ("Grujo the Pioneer")	3·00	3·00

382 "@" and Circuit Board

2005. World Conferences on Information Technology, Geneva and Tunis.

786	**382**	2k.80 multicoloured	1·80	1·80

383 Livia Drusilla (Oxford—Opuzen Livia) (statue)

2005. Roman Archaeological Site, Narona. Joint British—Croatian Roman Exhibitions, 2004—2005. Sheet 110×71 mm.

MS787	10k. multicoloured	8·00	8·00

384 Circle enclosing Square

2005. EXPO 2005 World Exhibition, Aichi, Japan. Sheet 97×80 mm.

MS788	10k. vermilion and silver	8·00	8·00

385 Pope John Paul II

2005. Pope John Paul II Commemoration.

789	**385**	2k.30 multicoloured	1·50	1·50

386 Keyboard

2005. Croatian Music. Multicoloured.

790	2k.30 Type **386** (Music Biennale (festival), Zagreb)	1·50	1·50
791	2k.30 Stjepan Sulek (composer)	1·50	1·50

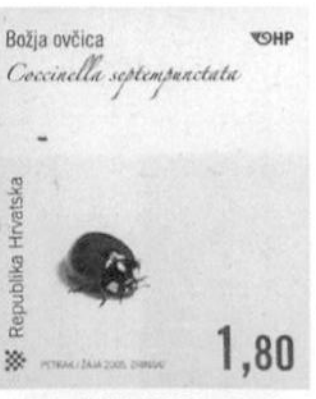

387 Ladybird (*Coccinella septempunctata*)

2005. Insects. Multicoloured.

792	1k.80 Type **387**	1·30	1·30
793	2k.30 *Rosalia alpine*	1·70	1·70
794	3k.50 Stag beetle (*Lucanus cervus*)	2·30	2·30

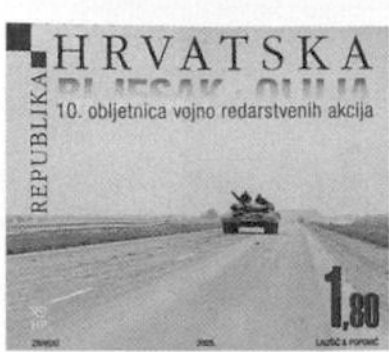
388 Tank

2005. 10th Anniv of Military Action.

795	388	1k.80 multicoloured	1·00	1·00

389 Josip Buturac

2005. Birth Centenary of Josip Buturac (historian and writer).

796	389	2k.80 multicoloured	1·80	1·80

389a Kiss

2005. Obligatory Tax. Red Cross Week.

796a	389a	1k.15 multicoloured	1·00	1·00

390 Bread

2005. Europa. Gastronomy. Multicoloured.

797	3k.50 Type 390	2·00	2·00
798	3k.50 Glass of wine	2·00	2·00

391 Rock, Sea and Cliff

2005. Tourism. Multicoloured.

799	1k.80 Type 391	1·20	1·20
800	1k.80 Branches, cliff and sea	1·20	1·20
801	1k.80 Sea and rock	1·20	1·20
802	1k.80 Canoe, rock and sea	1·20	1·20
803	1k.80 Sea surrounding rock	1·20	1·20
804	3k.50 Trees	2·20	2·20
805	3k.50 Trees and cliff	2·20	2·20
806	3k.50 Cliff and rocks	2·20	2·20
807	3k.50 Cliff and sunken rocks	2·20	2·20
808	3k.50 Rock point and sea	2·20	2·20

392 Kresimir Cosic

2005. 10th Death Anniv of Kresimir Cosic (basketball player).

809	392	3k.50 multicoloured	2·30	2·30

393 Coral surrounding Sponge

2005. Endangered Species.

810	393	3k.50 multicoloured	2·30	2·30

394 Building Facade

2005. Varazdinske Toplice Spa.

811	394	1k.80 multicoloured	1·10	1·10

395 St. Florian (statue)

2005. International Fire Brigade Olympics, Varazdin.

812	395	2k.30 multicoloured	1·50	1·50

2005. 50th Anniv of Europa Stamps. As T 65. Multicoloured.

813	7k.20 As No. 195	4·00	4·00
814	8k. Stylized bird	4·50	4·50
MS815	92×78 mm. Nos. 813/14	60·00	60·00

396 Morse Code Machine

2005. 155th Anniv of First Overhead Telegraph Lines.

816	396	2k.30 multicoloured	1·50	1·50

396a Running

2005. Obligatory Tax. Anti-Tuberculosis Week.

816a	396a	1k.15 multicoloured	1·00	1·00

2005. Fortresses (5th series). As T 320. Multicoloured.

817	1k. Ilok (14th—15th-century)	80	80
818	2k.30 Motovun (13th—15th-century) (vert)	1·60	1·60
819	3k.50 St. Nicholas Fortress, Sibenik (16th-century)	2·20	2·20

397 Adam Baltazar Krcelic (writer) (290th birth anniv)

2005. Personalities. Multicoloured.

820	1k. Type 397	90	90
821	2k.30 Dragutin Tadijanovic (writer) (100th birthday)	1·70	1·70
822	2k.30 Augustin (Tin) Ujevic (writer) (50th death anniv)	1·70	1·70
823	2k.80 "Madonna and Child" (Juraj Culinovic) (400th death anniv (2004))	2·00	2·00

398 "Our Lady with Child and Saints" (detail)

2005. Christmas. Ordinary or self-adhesive gum.

824	398	2k.30 multicoloured	1·00	1·00

2005. Paintings (6th series). As T 322. Multicoloured.

826	1k.80 "Zader" (Edo Mutric)	1·20	1·20
827	5k. "Meander" (Julije Knifer)	3·00	3·00
828	10k. "Drawing" (Miroslav Sutej) (vert)	6·00	6·00

399 Team and Trophy

2005. Croatia—Winner of Davis Cup (tennis championship)—2005.

829	399	5k. multicoloured	3·00	3·00

399a Elderly Man receiving Red Cross Parcel

2005. Obligatory Tax. Solidarity Week.

829a	379a	1k.15 multicoloured	3·00	3·00

400 Boris Papndopulo

2006. Musicians' Birth Centenaries. Multicoloured.

830	1k.80 Type 400	1·00	1·00
831	2k.30 Milo Cipra	1·60	1·60
832	2k.80 Ivan Brkanovic	1·80	1·80

401 Crossed Skies

2006. Winter Olympic Games, Turin.

833	401	3k.50 multicoloured	2·10	2·10

402 "Self-portrait with Velvet Cap with Plume"

2006. 400th Birth Anniv of Rembrandt Harmenszoon Van Rijn (Rembrandt) (artist).

834	402	5k. multicoloured	3·00	3·00

403 Josip Kozarac (writer) (death centenary)

2006. Anniversaries. Multicoloured.

835	1k. Type 403	65	65
836	1k. Andrija Ljudevit Adamic (entrepreneur) (240th birth anniv)	65	65
837	5k. Ljubo Karaman (art historian) (120th birth anniv)	3·00	3·00
838	7k.20 Vanja Radaus (artist and writer) (birth centenary)	4·25	4·25

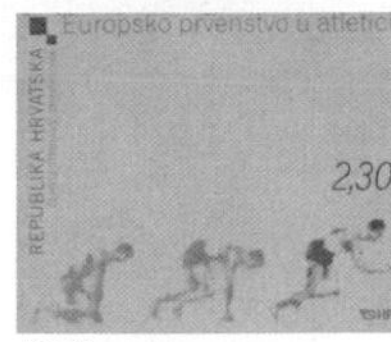
404 Runner

2006. European Athletics Championship, Göteburg.

839	404	2k.30 multicoloured	1·50	1·50

405 Stylized Player

2006. World Cup Football Championship, Germany.

840	405	2k.80 multicoloured	1·80	1·80

406 Crowd and Part of Flag

2006. Tourism. Designs showing parts of the Croatian flag. Multicoloured.

841	1k.80 Type 406	1·00	1·00
842	1k.80 Crowd and part of flag (larger)	1·00	1·00
843	1k.80 Crowd and part of flag (large red square)	1·00	1·00
844	1k.80 Crowd and part of flag (large white square)	1·00	1·00
845	1k.80 Flag and crowd (two raised arms)	1·00	1·00
846	3k.50 Flag creased	2·10	2·10
847	3k.50 Flag (one raised arm)	2·10	2·10
848	3k.50 Flag	2·10	2·10
849	3k.50 Flag and crowd (several raised arms and cap)	2·10	2·10
850	3k.50 Small part of flag and crowd	2·10	2·10

407 Boy carrying Red Cross Bag

2006. Obligatory Tax. Red Cross Week.

851	407	1k.15 multicoloured	1·00	1·00

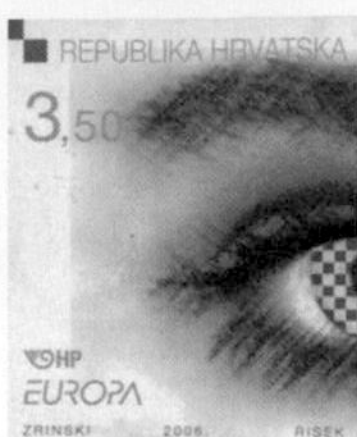

408 Eye containing Squares

2006. Europa. Integration. Multicoloured.

852 3k.50 Type **408** 2·10 2·10

853 3k.50 Eye containing stars 2·10 2·10

Nos. 852/3 were issued together, se-tenant, forming a composite design of an eye.

409 Little Tern

2006. Little Tern (Sterna albifrons). Multicoloured.

854 5k. Type **409** 3·00 3·00

855 5k. Diving 3·00 3·00

856 5k. Facing right 3·00 3·00

857 5k. Sitting on eggs 3·00 3·00

410 Elmore (1905)

2006. Centenary of Croatian Motor Club (HAK).

858 **410** 5k. multicoloured 3·00 3·00

411 *Nymphaea alba*

2006. Flora. Multicoloured.

859 2k.30 Type **411** 1·60 1·60

860 2k.80 *Nuphar lutea* 1·80 1·80

861 3k.50 *Menyanthes trifoliate* 2·30 2·30

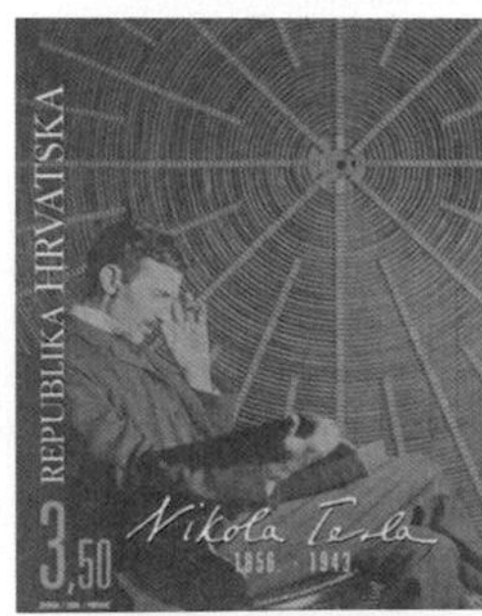

412 Nikola Tesla

2006. 150th Birth Anniv of Nikola Tesla (scientist).

862 **412** 3k.50 multicoloured 2·30 2·30

413 Clock Tower

2006. 250th Anniv of Bjelovar.

863 **413** 2k.80 multicoloured 1·60 1·60

414 Post Box

2006. Statehood.

864 **414** 2k.30 multicoloured 1·40 1·40

415 "Tjedan borbe protiv TBC-a"

2006. Obligatory Tax. Anti-Tuberculosis Week.

865 **415** 1k.15 multicoloured 1·00 1·00

416 Synagogue and Menorah

2006. Bicentenary of Jewish Community, Zagreb.

866 **416** 5k. multicoloured 3·00 3·00

2006. Fortresses (6th series). As T **320**. Mult.

867 1k. Sudurad, Sipan (16th-century) 75 75

868 1k. St Mary of Mercy, Vrboska (16th-century) 75 75

869 7k.20 Francopan Citadel, Ogulin (16th-century) 4·50 4·50

417 "DAN BIJELOG STAPA 2006"

2006. White Stick Day.

869a **417** 1k.80 black and vermilion 1·10 1·10

No. 869a has "White Cane Safety Day" embossed in Braille on its surface.

418 "Nativity" (Pantaleone)

2006. Christmas. Ordinary or self-adhesive gum.

870 **418** 2k.30 multicoloured 1·40 1·40

2006. Paintings (7th series). As T **322**. Mult.

872 1k. "Still Life" (Vladimir Becic) 85 85

873 1k.80 "Composition Tyma 3" (Ivan Picelj) 1·50 1·50

874 10k. "Self Portrait Hunter" (Nasta Rojc) (vert) 6·25 6·25

419 Santa on Skis

2006. Obligatory Tax. Solidarity Week.

875 **419** 1k.15 multicoloured 1·00 1·00

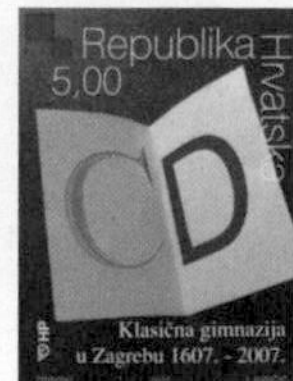

420 Emblem

2007. 400th Anniv of Classical Gymnasium, Zagreb.

876 **420** 5k. multicoloured 3·00 3·00

421 Orko

2007. Fairy Stories. Multicoloured.

877 2k.30 Type **421** 1·30 1·30

878 2k.30 Macic ("Grujo the Pioneer") 1·30 1·30

422 Building Facade

2007. 400th Anniv of National and University Library, Zagreb.

879 **422** 5k. multicoloured 3·00 3·00

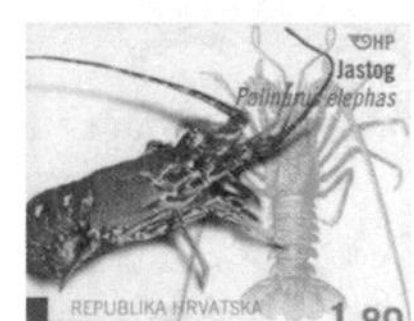

423 *Palinurus elephas*

2007. Fauna. Multicoloured.

880 1k.80 Type **423** 1·20 1·20

881 2k.30 *Nephrops norvegicus* 1·70 1·70

882 2k.80 *Astacus astacus* 1·90 1·90

424 Istrian Ox

2007. Autochthonous Breeds. Multicoloured.

883 2k.80 Type **424** 1·90 1·90

884 3k.50 Posavina horse 2·50 2·50

885 5k. Dalmatian donkey 3·25 3·25

425 Emblem

2007. Europa. Centenary of Scouting. Multicoloured.

886 3k.50 Type **425** 2·10 2·10

887 3k.50 Neckerchief 2·10 2·10

426 Andrija Mohorovicic

2007. Anniversaries. Multicoloured.

888 5k. Type **426** (mathematician and seismologist) (150th birth anniv) 3·00 3·00

889 7k.20 Duro Baglivi (medical scientist) (300th birth anniv) 4·50 4·50

427 Team Members

2007. Croatia–World Water Polo Champions, Melbourne 2007 Sheet 105×68 mm containing T 427 and similar vert designs. Multicoloured.

MS890 5k.×3, Type **427**; Ten team members; Flag and team members 9·25 9·25

The stamps and margins of **MS**890 form a composite design of the winning team and trainers.

428 Red Cross, Red Crescent and Proposed New Emblems

2007. Obligatory Tax. Red Cross Week.

891 **428** 1k.15 multicoloured 1·00 1·00

429 Table and Ball

2007. World Table Tennis Championship, Zagreb–2007.

892 **429** 3k.50 multicoloured 2·30 2·30

430 'China' engraved in Glagolitic Script

2007. 15th Anniv of Croatia–China Diplomatic Relations. Multicoloured.

893 5k. Type **430** 3·00 3·00

894 5k. 'Hrvatska' written in Chinese script 3·00 3·00

431 Women in Window (17th-century Trompe L'Oeil)

2007. Centenary of City Museum, Zagreb.

895 **431** 2k.30 multicoloured 1·50 1·50

432 Lake and Cliff

2007. Red Lake. Sheet 112×72 mm.

MS896 10k. multicoloured 6·25 6·25

The stamp and margins of **MS**896 form a composite design of the Red Lake and surrounding area.

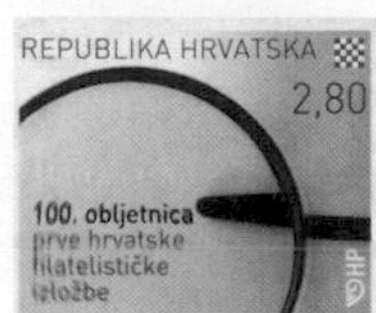

433 Magnifying Glass

2007. Centenary of First National Philatelic Exhibition.

897 **433** 2k.80 multicoloured 1·80 1·80

433a "Tjedan borbe protiv TBC-a"

2007. Obligatory Tax. Anti-Tuberculosis Week.

897a **433a** 1k.15 multicoloured 1·00 1·00

434 Sv. Ivan na pucini (St. John at open sea)

2007. Lighthouses. Multicoloured.

898 5k. Type **434** 3·50 3·50

899 5k. Savudrija 3·50 3·50

900 5k. Porer 3·50 3·50

435 Fragment of Statute

2007. 500th Anniv of Veprinac Statute (oldest Croatian legal document).

901 **435** 2k.70 multicoloured 1·80 1·80

436 Omis

2007. Towns.

902 **436** 1k.80 brown, bistre and vermilion 1·10 1·10

903 - 2k.30 brown, rose and vemilion (horiz) 1·50 1·50

904 - 2k.80 multicoloured 2·00 2·00

DESIGNS: 1k.80 Type **436**; 2k.30 Koprivnica; 2k.80 Krk.

437 Blanka Vlasic

2007. Blanka Vlasic. Women's High Jump World Champion–2007.

905 **437** 2k.30 multicoloured 1·50 1·50

438 Nativity (painting, Bishop's Palace, Pozega)

2007. Christmas. Ordinary or self-adhesive gum.

906 **438** 2k.30 multicoloured 1·60 1·60

439 Marija Zagorka

2007. 50th Death Anniv of Marija Juric Zagorka (writer).

907 **439** 7k.20 multicoloured 4·75 4·75

2007. Paintings (8th series). As T **322**. Mult.

908 2k.80 *Area by the River Sava* (Branko Senoa) 2·50 2·50

909 5k. *Bridgeport* (Ivan Benokovic) 3·50 3·50

910 5k. *Pegasus's Garden* (Ferdinand Kulmer) 3·50 3·50

440 Angel (Vedran Damjanovic Maglica)

2007. New Year.

911 **440** 1k.80 multicoloured 1·30 1·30

441 Gifts

2007. Obligatory Tax. Solidarity Week.

912 **441** 1k.15 multicoloured 1·00 1·00

442 Igor Kuljeric

2008. Croatian Composers. Multicoloured.

913 2k.30 Type **442** (70th birth anniv) 1·60 1·60

914 2k.30 Krsto Odak (120th birth anniv) 1·60 1·60

443 Marija Zagorka

2008. 250th Anniv of Arithmetika Horvatszka (mathematical handbook).

915 **443** 3k.50 multicoloured 2·30 2·30

444 Steam Locomotive MAV 651/JZ 31

2008. Steam Locomotives made by MAV Gepgyar, Budapest. Multicoloured.

916 5k. Type **444** 3·50 3·50

917 5k. MAV 601/JZ 32 3·50 3·50

2008. Towns. As T **436**. Multicoloured .

918 7k.20 St Nicholas Church, Cavtat 4·75 4·75

445 Stylized Athletes

2008. Olympic Games, Beijing.

919 **445** 5k. multicoloured 3·25 3·25

446 *Hellborus niger* (Christmas rose)

2008. Flora. Multicoloured.

920 1k.80 Type **446** 1·40 1·40

921 2k.80 *Onosma stellulata* (star flower) 2·10 2·10

922 3k.50 *Lonicera glutinosa* (honeysuckle) 2·50 2·50

447 Petar Zoranic

2008. Personalities. Multicoloured.

923 2k.30 Type **447** (writer) (500th birth anniv) 1·60 1·60

924 2k.80 Silvije Strahimir Kranjcevic (writer) (death centenary) 1·90 1·90

925 7k.20 Marin Drzic (dramatist) (500th birth anniv) 4·75 4·75

448 Rocks and Water

2008. Tourism. Booklet Stamps. Designs showing parts of Cascades, Plitvice. Multicoloured.

926 3k.50 Type **448** 2·30 2·30

927 3k.50 Rocks and water pouring left 2·30 2·30

928 3k.50 Cascade, central weed covered rock 2·30 2·30

929 3k.50 Rocks and water pouring right 2·30 2·30

930 3k.50 Rocks, water and small tress 2·30 2·30

931 3k.50 Rocks and water pouring left, two rocks central 2·30 2·30

932 3k.50 Cascade, waterweed at left 2·30 2·30

933 3k.50 Cascade, large plume lower right 2·30 2·30

934 3k.50 Water, waterweeds and grass covered rock, lower right 2·30 2·30

935 3k.50 Grass covered rock, lower left and water 2·30 2·30

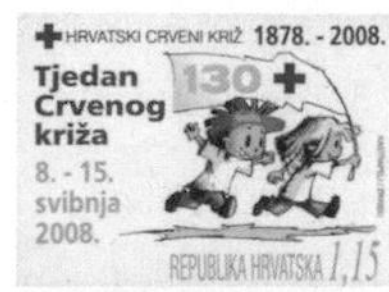

449 Children

2008. Obligatory Tax. 130th Anniv of Croatian Red Cross.

936 **449** 1k.15 multicoloured 1·00 1·00

450 Volkswagen *Beetle*

2008

937 **450** 2k.30 multicoloured 1·60 1·60

451 Envelope sealed with Wax

2008. Europa. The Letter. Multicoloured.

938 3k.50 Type **451** 2·50 2·30

939 5k. Airmail envelope 3·25 3·25

No. 939 has the outline of an aircraft embossed at upper right.

452 Footballs

2008. European Football Championships, Austria and Switzerland.

940 **452** 3k.50 multicoloured 2·30 2·30

453 Sails

2008. Adris.

941 **453** 2k.30 multicoloured 1·60 1·60

454 Ivan Vucetica

2008. 150th Birth Anniv of Ivan Vucetica (fingerprint identification pioneer). Sheet 112× 73 mm.

MS942 **454** 10k. multicoloured 7·00 7·00

The stamp and margins of **MS**942 form a composite design.

455 Water

2008. Zaragoza 2008 International Water and Sustainable Development Exhibition. Sheet 112× 72 mm.
MS943 multicoloured 7·00 7·00

456 Rijeka and Mountains

2008. Bicentenary of Louisiana Road (from Rijeka to Karlovac). Sheet 95× 80 mm containing T 456 and similar vert designs showing map of route. Multicoloured.
MS944 5k.×3, Type **456**; 'Delnice', 'Skrad' and 'Vrbovsko' ; 'Bosiljevo' and 'Karlovac' 10·00 10·00

The stamp and margins of **MS**944 form a composite design.

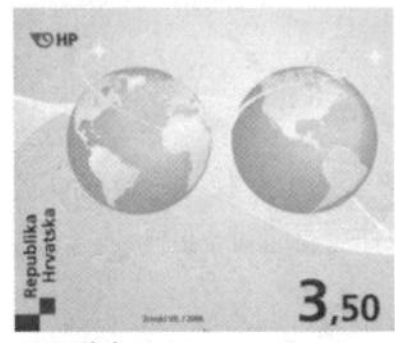

457 Globes

2008. 150th Anniv of Western Union.
945 **457** 3k.50 multicoloured 2·40 2·40

458 Stylized Postmen as Athletes

2008. Post Employees' Sports Meeting.
946 **458** 2k.80 multicoloured 2·00 2·00

459 Pinida

2008. Lighthouses. Multicoloured.

947 5k. Type **459**	3·75	3·75
948 5k. Vnetak	3·75	3·75
949 5k. Zaglav	3·75	3·75

459a

2008. Obligatory Tax. Anti-Tuberculosis Week.
949a **459a** 1k.15 multicoloured 1·00 1·00

460 St Clare Porziuncola (fresco)

2008. 700th Anniv of Order of Poor Clare Sisters in Split.
950 **460** 2k.80 multicoloured 2·00 2·00

461 Embroidered Flowers (Sunja)

2008. Cultural Heritage. Folk Costume Designs. Multicoloured.

951 10l. Type **461**	20	20
952 20l. Beaded strands (Bistra)	30	30
953 50l. Woollen fringes and pierced embroidered cloth (Bizovac)	50	50
954 1k. Fringed cloth (Ravni Kotari)	1·00	1·00
955 10k. Lace (Pag)	6·75	6·75
MS956 118×102 mm. 10l. Type **461**; 20l. Beaded strands (Bistra); 50l. Woollen fringes and pierced embroidered cloth (Bizovac); 1k. Fringed cloth (Ravni Kotari); 10k. Lace (Pag)	8·00	8·00

462 Sun and Skyline

2008. 20th Anniv of Healthy Cities Movement in Europe.
957 **462** 2k.80 multicoloured 2·00 2·00

463 Frontispiece

2008. 550th Anniv of The Book on the Art of Trading by Benedict Kotruljevic.
958 **463** 2k.80 multicoloured 2·00 2·00

464 College Facade

2008. 350th Anniv of Collegium Ragusinum.
959 **464** 7k.20 multicoloured 4·50 4·50

465 Map, Radio Waves and Globe

2008. International Amateur Radio Union Conference, Cavtat.
960 **465** 3k.50 multicoloured 2·50 2·50

466 Boy and Sleigh (Leo Zivica)

2008. New Year. Winning Design in Children's Painting Competition.
961 **466** 1k.80 multicoloured 1·20 1·20

467 *Christmas Interior* (Emanuel Vidovic)

2008. Christmas. Multicoloured.
962 **467** 2k.80 multicoloured 2·00 2·00

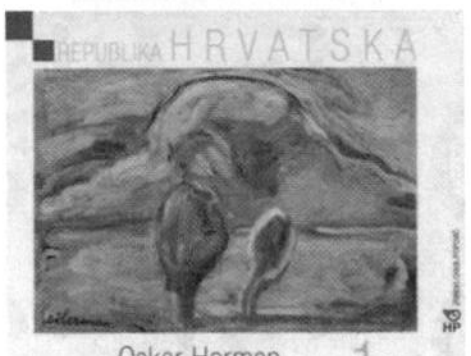

468 *Two Trees at Foot of Hill* (Oskar Herman)

2008. Art. Multicoloured.

963 1k.65 Type **468**	1·20	1·20
964 1k.80 *Carousel* (Nevenka Doroevic)	1·50	1·50
965 6k.50 *Still Life* (Ivo Rezek)	4·50	4·50

469 Zorin dom Karlovac Theatre and Lyre

2008. 150th Anniv of 'Zora' Choral Society.
966 **469** 1k.65 multicoloured 1·20 1·20

469a Child carrying Gifts

2008. Obligatory Tax. Red Cross.
966a **469a** 1k.15 multicoloured 3·50 3·50

470 Ivan Mestrovic

2008. 125th Birth Anniv of Ivan Mestrovic (artist and writer).
967 **470** 5k. multicoloured 3·50 3·50

471 Emblem and Crowd

2009. World Handball Championship, Croatia.
968 **471** 3k.50 multicoloured 2·50 2·50

472 Bruno Bjelinski

2009. Musicians' Birth Centenaries. Multicoloured.

969 1k.80 Type **472**	1·20	1·20
970 3k.50 Josip Andreis	2·50	2·50

2009. Towns. Horiz design as T **436**. Multicoloured.
971 8k. Bridge and street facade, Sisak 5·00 5·00

473 St Tripun (detail) (Statue, 1616)

2009. 1200th Anniv of St Tripun as Patron Saint of Kotor. Multicoloured.

972 3k.50 Type **473**	2·50	2·50
973 3k.50 St Tripun (silver polyptych, Kotor Cathedral)	2·50	2·50

474 Svarozic

2009. Fairy Stories. Multicoloured.

974 1k.65 Type **474**	1·20	1·20
975 1k.65 Bjesomar	1·20	1·20

475 Solar Eclipse

2009. Preserve Polar Regions and Glaciers. Sheet 112×73 mm containing T 475 and similar vert design. Multicoloured.
MS976 5k.×2, Type **475**; Emblem 7·00 7·00

476 Eggs

2009. Easter.

977	**476**	3k.50 multicoloured	2·50	2·50

477 Map and Emblem

2009. Accession to NATO.

978	**477**	8k. multicoloured	5·00	5·00

478 Juraj Sizgoric (500th death anniv)

2009. Writers Anniversaries. Multicoloured.

979	3k.50 Type **478**	3·75	3·75
980	3k.50 Juraj Habdelic (400th birth anniv)	3·75	3·75
981	5k. Petar Segedin (birth centenary)	3·75	3·75
982	5k. Ljudevit Gaj (birth bicentenary)	3·75	3·75

478a Henry Dunant (instigator of campaign resulting in establishment of Geneva Conventions and Red Cross)

2009. Obligatory Tax. 150th Anniv of Battle of Solferino. Red Cross.

982a	**478a**	1k.75 multicoloured	1·00	1·00

479 Universe from Hubble Telescope

2009. Europa. Astronomy. Multicoloured.

983	8k. Type **479**	5·00	5·00
984	8k. Universe (right)	5·00	5·00

Nos. 983/4 were printed, se-tenant, each pair forming a composite design of the universe seen from the Hubble telescope.

480 Franciscan Church, Cakovec

2009. 350th Anniv of Franciscan Order in Cakovec

985	**480**	3k.50 multicoloured	2·00	2·00

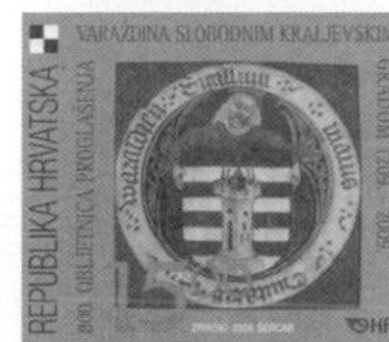

481 City Arms

2009. 800th Anniv of Royal Borough of Varazdin. Sheet 112×73 mm.

MS986	multicoloured	9·50	9·50

482 St. John The Baptist

2009. 500th Death Anniv of Ivan Duknovic (sculptor). Sheet 80×97 mm.

MS987	multicoloured	6·25	6·25

483 Musical Instruments

2009. 50th Anniv of Zagreb Jazz Quartet.

988	**483**	10k.70 multicoloured	6·75	6·75

484 *Acipenser naccarii* (Adriatic sturgeon)

2009. Freshwater Fish. Multicoloured.

989	3k.50 Type **484**	2·20	2·20
990	5k. *Knipowitschia mrakovcici* (Visovac goby)	3·50	3·50
991	5k. *Ballerus sapa* (Danube bream)	3·50	3·50

485 Postmark

2009. 10th Anniv of CP–Croatian Post.

992	**485**	3k.50 multicoloured	2·25	2·25

486 Stazica Lighthouse

2009. Lighthouses. Multicoloured.

993	3k.50 Type **486**	2·25	2·25
994	3k.50 Gruica	2·25	2·25
995	8k. Voscica	5·00	5·00

486a Children

2009. Obligatory Tax. Red Cross. Tuberculosis Week.

995a	**486a**	1k.75 multicoloured	2·25	2·25

487 *St. Francis of Assisi* (Celestin Medovic)

2009. 800th Anniv of Franciscan Order.

996	**487**	3k.50 multicoloured	2·25	2·25

488 Kazun, Pazin

2009. Kazun and Hiska (primitive dry stone buildings). Sheet 112×73 mm containing T 488 and similar horiz design. Multicoloured.

MS997	8k.×2, Type **488**; Hiska, Kopriva na Krasu	10·00	10·00

Stamps of a similar design were issued by Slovenia.

489 Chapel

2009. 800th Anniv of St Martin's Hermit Chapel, Podsused.

998	**489**	3k.50 multicoloured	2·25	2·25

490 Ensemble Lado

2009. 60th Anniv of Ensemble LADO (National Folk Dance Ensemble of Croatia).

999	**490**	3k.50 multicoloured	2·25	2·25

491 Teddy Bear

2009. 50th Anniv of UN Declaration of Rights of the Child and 20th Anniv of UN Convention on the Rights of the Child.

1000	**491**	3k.50 multicoloured	2·25	2·25

492 Snowman (Leonarda Storga)

2009. New Year. (a) Ordinary gum.

1001	**492**	3k.50 multicoloured	2·25	2·25

(b) Self-adhesive.

1002	3k.50 As Type **492**	2·25	2·25

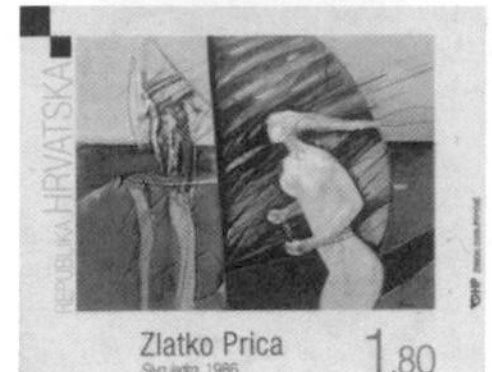

493 *Grey Sail* (Zlatko Prica)

2009. Croatian Modern Art. Multicoloured.

1003	1k.80 Type **493**	1·20	1·20
1004	1k.80 *A Bosom full of Wind* (Nives Kavuric Kurtovic) (vert)	1·20	1·20
1005	1k.80 *Flora* (Ordan Petlevski) (vert)	1·20	1·20

494 *Adoration of the Shepherds* (wood relief, Zminj Parish Church)

2009. Christmas. Multicoloured. (a) Ordinary gum.

1006	3k.50 Type **494**	1·90	1·90
1007	8k. *Adoration of the Shepherds* (detail) (35×35 mm)	4·00	4·00

(b) Self-adhesive.

1008	3k.50 As Type **494**	1·90	1·90

495 Snowman carrying Gifts

2009. Obligatory Tax. Red Cross.

1009	**495**	1k.75 multicoloured	1·10	1·10

496 Arms of Lastovo

2010. 700th Anniv of Statute of Lastovo.
1010 **496** 3k.50 multicoloured 1·90 1·90

497 Emblem

2010. Winter Olympic Games, Vancouver.
1011 **497** 3k.50 multicoloured 1·90 1·90

498 *Paeonia mascula*

2010. Peonies. Multicoloured.
MS1012 Type **498**; *Paeonia officinalis* 3·75 3·75

499 Primorje

2009. Cultural Heritage. Multicoloured.

1013	1k.60 Type **499**	1·10	1·10
1014	3k.10 Medimurje	1·90	1·90
1015	4k.60 Posavina	2·20	2·20
1016	7k.10 Draganic	3·75	3·75
MS1017	144×56 mm. 1k.60 Type **499**; 3k.10 Medimurje; 4k.60 Posavina; 7k.10 Draganic	9·00	9·00

500 Strawberries (*Fragaria vesca*)

2010. Fruit. Multicoloured.

1018	1k. Type **500**	1·00	1·00
1019	4k. Gooseberries (*Ribes uva-crispa*)	2·20	2·20
1020	4k. Grapes (*Vitis vinifera*)	2·20	2·20

Nos. 1018/20 were perforated in a circle around the design, enclosed in an outer perforated rectangle.

501 Christ the King (Ivo Dulcic)

2010. Easter
1021 **501** 3k.10 multicoloured 1·90 1·90

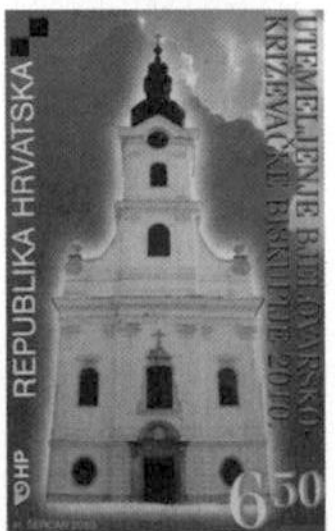

502 Bjelovar Cathedral

2010. Founding of Bjelovar-Krizevci Diocese
1022 **502** 6k.50 multicoloured 3·75 3·75

503 MAV 326/JZ 125 Series Steam Locomotive

2010. 150th Anniv of Croatian Railways. Multicoloured.

1023	7k.10 Type **503**	4·50	4·50
1024	7k.10 SüdB 18 series steam locomotive	4·50	4·50

504 St. Leopold Mandic and Capuchin Monk

2010. 400th Anniv of Capuchin Monks in Croatia
1025 **504** 6k.10 multicoloured 3·50 3·50

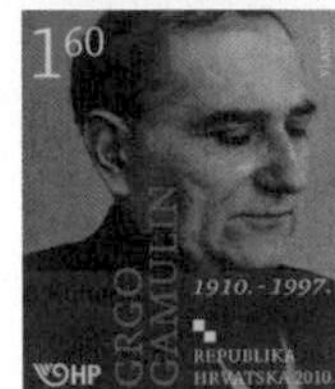

505 Grgo Gamulin

2010. Personalities. Multicoloured.

1026	1k.60 Type **505** (historian and writer)	1·10	1·10
1027	3k.10 Janko Polic Kamov (writer)	1·90	1·90
1028	4k.50 Ivan Matetic Ronjgov (composer)	2·20	2·20
1029	6k.10 Marko Antun de Dominis (theologian and physicist)	2·75	2·75

506 Street Map of Dubrovnik and 'EXPO Shanghai'

2010. Expo 2010, Shanghai
MS1030 multicoloured 6·00 6·00

507 Book, Fairies and Stars

2010. Europa. Multicoloured.

1031	7k.10 Type **507**	4·50	4·50
1032	7k.10 Book, fairies and butterflies	4·50	4·50

Nos. 1031/2 were printed, *se-tenant*, each pair forming a composite design of an open book.

507a Globe, Red Cross, Red Crescent and Red Diamond

2010. OBLIGATORY TAX
1032a **507a** 1k.55 multicoloured

No. 1032a has been re-valued at 1k.55 rather than 1k.75 as originally printed.
No. 1032a was for use from 8th to 15th May.

160
=

507b

2010. Nos. 902 and 823a overprinted as T **507b**

1032b	1k.60 on 1k.80 bistre-brown, bistre and scarlet-vermilion	1·10	1·10
1032c	3k.10 on 3k.50 violet, scarlet vermilion and black	1·90	1·90

Designs:-1k.60 As No. 902; 3k.10 As No. 823a

508 Castle

2010. Lubenice
MS1033 **508** 10k. multicoloured 6·00 6·00

509 Ball and Player's Legs

2010. World Cup Football Championships, South Africa
1034 **509** 4k.50 multicoloured 2·20 2·20

160
=

507b

2010. Surcharges

1035	4k.50 on 5k. multicoloured (horiz)	2·20	2·20
1036	7k.10 on 7k.20 multicoloured (horiz)	4·50	4·50

Designs:- 4k.50 As No. 773a; 7k.10 As No. 918

511 Tajer

2010. Lighthouses. Multicoloured.

1037	3k.10 Type **511**	1·90	1·90
1038	3k.10 Vir	1·90	1·90
1039	3k.10 Veli rat	1·90	1·90

512 Agate, Lepoglava

2010. Minerals. Multicoloured.
MS1040 3k.10×2, Type **512**; Limestone, Brač 2·20 2·20

513 Tram

2010. Dubrovnik Tramway
MS1041 multicoloured 10·50 10·50

514 Adoration of the Shepherds (Josip Biffel) (Franciscan Monastery of St. Anthony, Dubrave, Brcko)

2010. Christmas

(a) Ordinary gum
1042 **514** 3k.10 multicoloured 1·90 1·90

(b) Self-adhesive
1043 **514** 3k.10 multicoloured 1·90 1·90

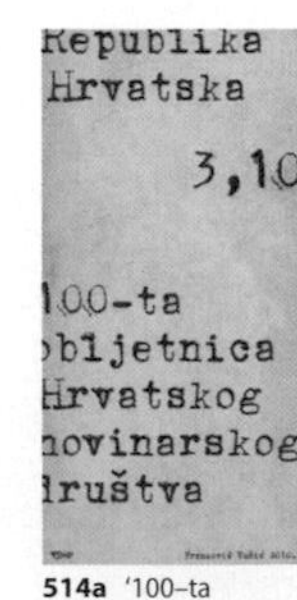

514a '100–ta obljetnica'

2010. Centenary of Journalist Society
1044 **514a** 3k.10 yellow-ochre, black and scarlet-vermilion 1·90 1·90

515 Snow-covered Tree (Marta Bilandžija)

2010. New Year
1045 **515** 1k.60 multicoloured 1·10 1·10

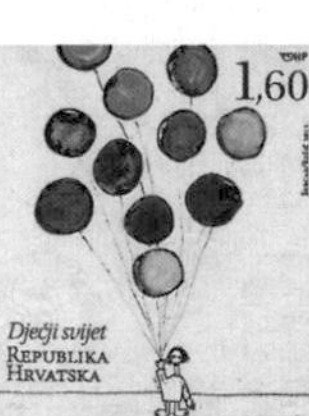

516 Child with Balloons

2011. International Children's Festival in Šibenik
1046 **516** 1k.60 multicoloured 1·10 1·10

517 *Ursos arctos* (brown bear)

2011. Fauna. Multicoloured.

1047	1k.60 Type **517**	1·10	1·10
1048	3k.10 *Falco eleonorae* (Eleonora's falcon)	1·90	1·90
1049	4k.60 *Monachus monachus* (monk seal)	2·20	2·20

OFFICIAL STAMPS

O11

O12

1942

O55A	**O11**	25b. red	20	10
O56A	**O11**	50b. grey	20	10
O57A	**O11**	75b. green	20	10
O58A	**O11**	1k. brown	20	10
O59A	**O11**	2k. blue	20	10
O60A	**O11**	3k. red	20	10
O61A	**O11**	3k.50 red	20	10
O62A	**O11**	4k. purple	20	10
O63A	**O11**	5k. blue	55	65
O64A	**O11**	6k. violet	20	10
O65A	**O11**	10k. green	35	45
O66A	**O11**	12k. red	45	55
O67A	**O11**	12k.50 orange	20	10
O68A	**O11**	20k. blue	55	65
O69A	**O 12**	30k. grey and brown	45	55
O70A	**O 12**	40k. grey and violet	55	65
O71A	**O 12**	50k. grey and red	1·30	1·60
O72A	**O 12**	100k. salmon & black	1·30	1·60

POSTAGE DUE STAMPS

1941. Nos. D259/63 of Yugoslavia optd **NEZAVISNA DRZAVA HRVATSKA** in three lines above a chequered shield.

D26	**D10**	50p. violet	1·10	85
D27	**D10**	1d. red	1·10	85
D28	**D10**	2d. blue	22·00	27·00
D29	**D10**	5d. orange	3·25	2·75
D30	**D10**	10d. brown	16·00	16·00

D9

1941

D51	**D9**	50b. red	55	65
D52	**D9**	1k. red	55	65
D53	**D9**	2k. red	75	1·00
D54	**D9**	5k. red	1·30	1·40
D55	**D9**	10k. red	1·60	2·00

D15

1942

D67	**D15**	50b. olive and blue	45	55
D68	**D15**	1k. olive and blue	55	65
D69	**D15**	2k. olive and blue	55	65
D76	**D15**	4k. olive and blue	35	55
D70	**D15**	5k. olive and blue	55	65
D78	**D15**	6k. olive and blue	35	55
D79	**D15**	10k. blue and indigo	45	75
D80	**D15**	15k. blue and indigo	45	75
D72	**D15**	20k. blue and indigo	2·30	2·40

SERBAIN POSTS IN CROATIA

REPUBLIC OF SRPSKA KRAJINA

Following Croatia's declaration of independence from Yugoslavia on 30 May 1991 fighting broke out between Serb inhabitants, backed by units of the Yugoslav Federal Army, and Croatian forces. By January 1992, when a ceasefire sponsored by the United Nations and the European Community became effective, the Croatian Serbs and their allies controlled 30% of the country organized into the districts of Krajina, Western Slavonia and Eastern Slavonia. These were declared peace-keeping zones under United Nations supervision and the Yugoslav Army withdrew. In 1993 the Serbs proclaimed the Republic of Srpska Krajina, covering all three areas, and elections for a separate president and parliament were held in January 1994.

K1 Stag, Kopacevo Marsh

1993

K1	**K1**	200d. green and yellow	50	50
K2	-	500d. black and red	1·20	1·20
K3	-	1000d. green and yellow	2·30	2·30
K4	-	1000d. green and yellow	2·30	2·30
K5	-	2000d. black and red	4·75	4·75

DESIGNS: No. K2, Krka Monastery; K3, Town walls, Knin; K4, Ruined house, Vukovar; K5, Coat of arms.
For 100000d. in same design as No. K2 see No. K12.

1993. Issued at Knin. Nos. 2594/5 of Yugoslavia surch.

K6	5000d. on 3d. black and red	1·90	1·90
K7	10000d. on 2d. blue and red	1·90	1·90

K3 Coat of Arms

1993

K8	**K 3**	A blue and red	95	95

No. K8 was sold at the internal letter rate.

K4 Citadel, Knin

1993

K9	**K4**	5000d. green and red	50	50
K10	-	10000d. green and red	95	95
K11	-	50000d. blue and red	1·90	1·90
K12	-	100000d. blue and red	2·40	2·40

DESIGNS: 10000d. Heron, Kopacevo Marsh; 50000d. Icon and church, Vukovar; 100000d. Krka Monastery.

Currency Reform

A
(K5)

1993. No. K8 surch with Type K **5** (Cyrillic letter "D").

K13	**K 3**	"D" on A blue and red	1·50	1·50

No. K13 was sold at the new internal letter rate.

1993. Nos. K9/12 surch with Type K **5** (Cyrillic letter "D").

K14	**K 4**	"D" on 5000d. grn & red	50	50
K15	-	"D" on 10000d. green and red	95	95
K16	-	"D" on 50000d. blue and red	4·25	4·25
K17	-	"D" on 100000d. blue and red		

K6 Helmet and Swords

1993

K18	**K 6**	R blue	1·50	1·50

No. K18 was sold at the internal registered letter rate.

K7 St. Simeon

1994. Serb Culture and Tradition. Mult.

K19	50p. Type K **7**	95	95
K20	80p. Krajina coat of arms (vert)	1·90	1·90
K21	1d. "The Vucedol Dove" (carving) (vert)	3·00	3·00

K8 Cup-and-saucer

1994. Climbing Plants. Multicoloured.

K22	30p. Type K **8**	80	80
K23	40p. "Dipladenia"	1·00	1·00
K24	60p. Black-eyed Susan	1·70	1·70
K25	70p. Climbing rose	1·90	1·90

K9 Krka Monastery

1994

K26	**K9**	5p. red	10	10
K27	-	10p. brown	25	25
K28	-	20p. green	50	50
K29	-	50p. red	1·30	1·30
K30	-	60p. violet	1·60	1·60
K31	-	1d. blue	2·75	2·75

DESIGNS: 10p. Carin; 20p. Vukovar; 50p. Monument, Batina; 60p. Ilok; 1d. Lake, Plitvice.

K10 "The Flower of Life" (memorial to Jasenovac Concentration Camp victims)

1995. 50th Anniv of End of Second World War.

K32	**K10**	60p. multicoloured	2·10	2·10

K11 "A" over Mosaic

1995

K33	**K11**	A red	1·00	1·00

No. K33 was sold at the internal letter rate.

K12 Krcic Waterfall, Knin

1995

K34	**K12**	10p. blue	10	10
K35	-	20p. ochre	20	20
K36	-	40p. red	50	50
K37	-	2d. blue	2·50	2·50
K38	-	5d. brown	5·75	5·75

DESIGNS: 20p. Benkovac; 40p. Citadel, Knin; 2d. Petrinja; 5d. Pakrac.

In May 1995 the Croatian army occupied Western Slavonia and in August 1995 the Krajina and these areas were reincorporated into the Republic of Croatia. The only surviving part of the Serbian territories, Eastern Slavonia, was, by agreement, placed under temporary United Nations administration in November 1995 and was subsequently called Sremsko Baranjska Oblast (Srem and Baranya Region).

SREMSKO BARANJSKA OBLAST

K13 Common Cormorant ("Phalocrocorax carbo"), Kopacevo Marsh

1995. Protected Species. Multicoloured.

K39	80p. Type K **13**	3·25	3·25
K40	80p. Chamois, Lika	3·25	3·25

K14 St. Dimitriev's Church, Dalj

1995. Churches (1st series).

K41	**K14**	5p. green	10	10
K42	-	10p. red	20	20
K43	-	30p. mauve	65	65
K44	-	50p. brown	1·20	1·20
K45	-	1d. blue	2·10	2·10

DESIGNS: 10p. St. Peter and St. Paul's Church, Bolman; 30p. St. Nicholas's Church, Mirkovci; 50p. St. Nicholas's Church, Tenja; 1d. St. Nicholas's Church, Vukovar.
See also Nos. K48/53.

K15 Vukovar Marina, River Danube

1996. River Danube Co-operation.

K46	**K15**	1d. multicoloured	3·25	3·25

K16 The Worker's Hall, Vukovar

1996

K47	**K 16**	A red	30	30

No. K47 was sold at the internal letter rate.

K17 Archangel Church, Darda

1996. Churches (2nd series).

K48	**K17**	10p. brown	10	10
K49	-	50p. violet	40	40
K50	-	1d. green	85	85
K51	-	2d. green	1·70	1·70
K52	-	5d. blue	4·25	4·25
K53	-	10d. blue	8·25	8·25

DESIGNS: 50p. St. George's Church, Knezevo; 1 d St. Nicholas's Church, Jagodnjak; 2d. Archangel Gabriel's Church, Brsadin; 5d. St. Stephen's Church, Borovo Selo; 10d. St. Nicholas's Church, Pacetin.

K18 Nikola Tesla

1996. 140th Birth Anniv of Nikola Tesla (inventor).

K54	**K18**	1d.50 multicoloured	3·25	3·25

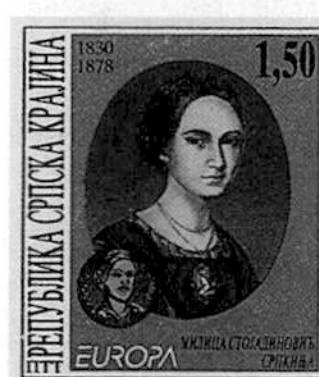
K19 Milica Stojadinovic-Srpkinja (1830–78) (poetess)

1996. Europa, Famous Women, Mult.

K55	1d.50 Type K **19**	26·00	26·00
K56	1d.50 Mileva Marie-Einstein (1875–1948) (mathematician)	26·00	26·00

K20 Jasna Sekaric (Olympic gold medal winner)

1996. Centenary of Modern Olympic Games.

K57	**K20**	1d.50 multicoloured	3·25	3·25

K21 Milutin Milankovic

1996. Milutin Milankovic (geophysicist) Commemoration (1879–1958).

K58	**K21**	1d.50 multicoloured	3·25	3·25

K22 "Madonna and Child" (icon)

1996. Christmas.

K59	**K22**	1d.50 multicoloured	3·25	3·25

K23 Pigeon

1997. Domestic Pets. Multicoloured.

K60	1d. Type K **23**	1·00	1·00
K61	1d. Budgerigar	1·00	1·00
K62	1d. Cat	1·00	1·00
K63	1d. Black labrador	1·00	1·00

1997. No. K18 surch or optd (No. K67) with crosses obliterating former name.

K64	**K6**	10p. on R blue	10	10
K65	**K6**	20p. on R blue	20	20
K66	**K6**	30p. on R blue	40	40
K67	**K6**	R (90p.) blue	1·20	1·20
K68	**K6**	1d. on R blue	1·30	1·30
K69	**K6**	1d.50 on R blue	1·90	1·90
K70	**K6**	2d. on R blue	2·50	2·50
K71	**K6**	5d. on R blue	6·25	6·25
K72	**K6**	10d. on R blue	12·50	12·50
K73	**K6**	20d. on R blue	26·00	26·00

K25 St. Peter and St. Paul's Cathedral, Orolik

1997. Restoration of Orthodox Church, Ilok.

K74	**K25**	50p.+50p. blue	50	50
K75	-	60p.+50p. mauve	60	60
K76	-	1d.20+50p. red	1·00	1·00

DESIGNS: 60p. St. George's Church, Tovarnik; 1d.20, Church, Negoslavci.

K26 Prince Marko and The Turks

1997. Europa. Tales and Legends. Mult.

K77	1d. Type K **26**	6·75	6·75
K78	1d. Emperor Trajan	6·75	6·75

The postal administration of the Srem and Baranya Region was reincorporated into that of the Republic of Croatia on 19 May 1997. Eastern Slavonia was returned to Croatian control on 15 January 1998.

Pt. 15

CUBA

An island in the W. Indies, ceded by Spain to the United States in 1898. A republic under U.S. protection until 1901 when the island became independent. The issues to 1871, except Nos. 13, 14, 19, 20/7, 32, 44 and 48, were for Puerto Rico also.

1855. 8 reales plata fuerte (strong silver reales) = 1 peso.
1866. 100 centimos = 1 escudo.
1871. 100 centimos = 1 peseta.
1881. 100 milesimas = 100 centavos = 1 peso.
1898. 100 cents = 1 U.S. dollar.
1899. 100 centavos = 1 peso.

SPANISH COLONY

1855. Imperf.

6	1	½r. green	9·75	1·20
9	1	½r. blue	5·00	1·20
10	1	1r. green	5·00	1·20
11	1	2r. red	22·00	5·00

Nos. 10/11 optd **HABILITADO POR LA NACION** were issues of Philippines (Nos. 44/5).

1

1855. No. 11a surch Y ¼.

12	Y¼ on 2r. red	£300	£120

5

1862. Imperf.

13	5	¼r. black on buff	30·00	36·00

1864. Imperf.

14	6	¼r. black on buff	23·00	32·00
15	6	½r. green	5·25	1·10
16	6	½r. green on pink	11·50	2·75
17	6	1r. blue on brown	5·00	1·10
18b	6	2r. red	26·00	7·25

1866. Dated "1866". Imperf.

19	7	5c. mauve	48·00	55·00
20	7	10c. blue	5·00	1·10
21	7	20c. green	2·40	1·10
22	7	40c. pink	15·00	10·50

6

1866. No. 14 optd 66. Imperf.

23	6	¼r. black on buff	95·00	£110

7

1867. Dated "1867". Perf.

24	7	5c. mauve	55·00	26·00
25	7	10c. blue	29·00	1·60
26	7	20c. green	18·00	2·50
27	7	40c. pink	18·00	11·50

9

1868. Dated "1868".

28	9	5c. lilac	36·00	16·00
29	9	10c. blue	3·50	1·80
30	9	20c. green	6·75	3·50
31	9	40c. pink	15·00	9·00

1868. Nos. 28/31 optd HABILITADO POR LA NACION.

36	5c. lilac	£140	38·00
37	10c. blue	60·00	36·00
38	20c. green	50·00	36·00
39	40c. pink	70·00	36·00

1869. Dated "1869".

32	5c. pink	60·00	36·00
33	10c. brown	60·00	36·00
34	20c. orange	60·00	36·00
35	40c. lilac	60·00	36·00

1869. Nos. 32/5 optd HABILITADO POR LA NACION.

40		5c. pink	38·00	16·00
41		10c. brown	3·50	1·80
42		20c. orange	6·25	2·30
43		40c. lilac	34·00	11·50
44	11	5c. blue	£180	90·00

11

1870

45	11	10c. green	2·50	90
46	11	20c. brown	2·75	90
47	11	40c. pink	£200	41·00

12

1871. Dated "1871".

48	12	12c. lilac	27·00	11·00
49a	12	25c. blue	2·30	90
50	12	50c. green	2·30	90
51	12	1p. brown	33·00	8·00

13

1873

52	13	12½c. green	39·00	19·00
53	13	25c. grey	2·50	1·10
54	13	50c. brown	2·10	1·10
55	13	1p. brown	£325	55·00

1874. Dated "1874".

56	12	12½c. brown	28·00	14·00
57	12	25c. blue	95	70
58	12	50c. lilac	1·80	85
59	12	1p. red	£325	90·00

14

1875

60	14	12½c. mauve	1·00	1·50
61	14	25c. blue	80	55
62	14	50c. green	80	55
63	14	1p. brown	8·50	5·50

1876. Inscr "ULTRAMAR 1876".

64	15	12½c. green	2·00	1·80
65a	15	25c. lilac	5·50	35
66	15	50c. blue	1·10	35
67	15	1p. black	13·00	7·25

15

1877. Inscr "CUBA 1877".

68	10c. green	35·00	
69	12½c. lilac	8·00	4·50
70	25c. green	80	70
71	50c. black	80	70
72	1p. brown	38·00	16·00

1878. Inscr "CUBA 1878".

73	5c. blue	90	55
74	10c. black	£100	
75a	12½c. bistre	5·50	3·00
76	25c. green	90	20
77	50c. green	90	20
78	1p. red	19·00	5·75

1879. Inscr "CUBA 1879".

79	5c. black	90	35
80	10c. orange	£180	
81	12½c. pink	90	35
82	25c. blue	90	35
83	50c. grey	90	30
84	1p. bistre	19·00	13·50

1880. "Alfonso XII" key-type inscr "CUBA 1880".

85	X	5c. green	80	45
86	X	10c. red	£110	
87	X	12½c. lilac	80	40
88	X	25c. lilac	80	40
89	X	50c. brown	80	40
90	X	1p. brown	5·25	3·00

1881. "Alfonso XII" key-type inscr "CUBA 1881".

91	1c. green	90	30
92	2c. pink	60·00	
93a	2½c. bistre	90	25
94	5c. lilac	90	25
95	10c. brown	90	25
96	20c. brown	5·25	5·25

1882. "Alfonso XII" key-type inscr "CUBA".

97	1c. green	90	35
98	2c. pink	2·40	35
118	2½c. brown	5·00	1·80
119	2½c. mauve	1·50	85
100	5c. lilac	2·40	55
123	5c. grey	2·40	50
101	10c. brown	80	20
126	10c. blue	1·60	85
121	20c. brown	20·00	3·00
122	20c. lilac	20·00	4·25

1883. 1882 issue optd or surch with fancy pattern.

103	5c. lilac	2·50	4·25
106	5 on 5c. lilac	1·70	2·10
104	10c. brown	7·25	8·75
107	10 on 10c. brown	2·75	4·25
105	20c. brown	£225	£200
111	20 on 20c. brown	36·00	30·00

The surcharges exist in four different patterns.

1890. "Baby" key-type inscr "ISLA DE CUBA".

135	Y	1c. brown	25·00	13·00
147	Y	1c. grey	9·00	5·00
159	Y	1c. blue	3·50	55
169	Y	1c. purple	1·00	30
136	Y	2c. blue	8·25	4·00
148	Y	2c. brown	1·70	60
160	Y	2c. pink	44·00	13·00
170	Y	2c. red	9·50	1·00
137	Y	2½c. green	11·50	7·25
149	Y	2½c. orange	55·00	18·00
161	Y	2½c. mauve	3·25	30
171	Y	2½c. pink	70	10
138	Y	5c. grey	95	90
150	Y	5c. green	95	60
172	Y	5c. blue	60	10
139	Y	10c. brown	4·50	1·40
151	Y	10c. pink	2·10	60
173	Y	10c. green	2·50	20
140	Y	20c. purple	95	90
152	Y	20c. blue	23·00	12·50
162	Y	20c. brown	27·00	13·50
174	Y	20c. lilac	18·00	7·25
175	Y	40c. brown	36·00	18·00
176	Y	80c. brown	70·00	26·00

1898. "Curly Head" key-type inscr "CUBA 1898 Y 99".

183	Z	1m. brown	30	10
184	Z	2m. brown	30	10
185	Z	3m. brown	30	10
186	Z	4m. brown	4·25	1·90
187	Z	5m. brown	30	10
188	Z	1c. purple	30	10
189	Z	2c. green	30	10
190	Z	3c. brown	20	10
191	Z	4c. orange	11·00	3·00
192	Z	5c. pink	90	10
193	Z	6c. blue	30	10
194	Z	8c. brown	90	30
195	Z	10c. red	1·00	30
196	Z	15c. grey	4·25	30
197	Z	20c. purple	60	10
198	Z	40c. mauve	2·75	30
199	Z	60c. black	3·25	30
200	Z	80c. brown	18·00	9·75
201	Z	1p. green	18·00	9·75
202	Z	2p. blue	32·00	9·75

OFFICIAL STAMPS

1860. As Nos. O50/3 of Spain but without full points after "OFICIAL" and "ONZAS" or "LIBRA". Imperf.

O12	½o. black on yellow	70·00
O13	1o. black on pink	70·00
O14	4o. black on green	£300
O15	1l. black on blue	£750

The face values of Nos. O12/15 are expressed in onzas (ounces) or libra (pound), referring to the maximum weight for which each value could prepay postage.

PRINTED MATTER STAMPS

All Printed Matter stamps are key-types inscribed "CUBA IMPRESOS".

1888. "Alfonso XII".

P129	X	½m. black	85	20
P130	X	1m. black	85	20
P131	X	2m. black	85	20
P132	X	3m. black	1·10	70
P133	X	4m. black	2·10	1·10
P134	X	8m. black	9·25	4·00

1890. "Baby".

P141	Y	½m. brown	90	70
P142	Y	1m. brown	90	70
P143	Y	2m. brown	1·40	90
P144	Y	3m. brown	1·40	90
P145	Y	4m. brown	10·50	7·25
P146	Y	8m. brown	10·50	7·25

1892. "Baby".

P153	½m. lilac	35	25
P154	1m. lilac	35	25
P155	2m. lilac	35	25
P156	3m. lilac	2·30	35
P157	4m. lilac	4·50	2·10
P158	8m. lilac	10·50	5·00

1894. "Baby".

P163	½m. pink	20	10
P164	1m. pink	70	20
P165	2m. pink	70	20
P166	3m. pink	2·40	90
P167	4m. pink	4·50	1·10
P168	8m. pink	9·00	4·50

1896. "Baby".

P177	½m. green	20	10
P178	1m. green	20	10
P179	2m. green	20	10
P180	3m. green	2·50	80
P181	4m. green	5·50	4·50
P182	8m. green	10·50	7·25

UNITED STATES ADMINISTRATION

1899. Stamps of United States of 1894 surch CUBA and value.

246	1c. on 1c. green (No. 283)	5·75	45
247c	2c. on 2c. red (No. 270)	6·75	45
248a	2½c. on 2c. red (No. 270)	4·75	80
249	3c. on 3c. violet (No. 271)	11·50	2·00
250	5c. on 5c. blue (No. 286)	13·50	2·30
251	10c. on 10c. brown (No. 289)	25·00	7·50

29 Statue of Columbus

1899

307	29	1c. green	5·00	20
308	-	2c. red	5·00	20
303	-	3c. purple	5·75	15
304	-	5c. blue	6·75	15
310	-	10c. brown	16·00	50

DESIGNS: 2c. Palms; 3c. Statue of "La India" (Woman); 5c. Liner "Umbria" (Commerce); 10c. Ploughing Sugar Plantation.

POSTAGE DUE STAMPS

1899. Postage Due stamps of United States of 1894 surch CUBA and value.

D253	D87	1c. on 1c. red	50·00	4·50
D254	D87	2c. on 2c. red	50·00	4·50
D255	D87	5c. on 5c. red	50·00	4·50
D256	D87	10c. on 10c. red	34·00	2·10

SPECIAL DELIVERY STAMP

1899. No. E283 of United States surch CUBA. 10c. de PESO.

E252	E46	10c. on 10c. blue	£225	85·00

INDEPENDENT REPUBLIC

1902. Surch UN CENTAVO HABILITADO OCTUBRE 1902 and figure 1.

306	1c. on 3c. purple (No. 303)	2·00	50

36 Major-General Antonio Maceo

1907

311	36	50c. black and slate	1·20	80
318	36	50c. black and violet	1·70	50

37 B. Maso

1910

312	**37**	1c. violet and green	85	25
320	**37**	1c. green	1·00	25
313	-	2c. green and red	1·50	25
321	-	2c. red	1·00	25
314	-	3c. blue and violet	1·20	25
315	-	5c. green and blue	16·00	85
322	-	5c. blue	2·00	25
316	-	8c. violet and olive	1·20	35
323	-	8c. black and olive	2·00	65
317	-	10c. blue and sepia	7·25	70
319	-	1p. black and slate	8·00	4·25
324	-	1p. black	5·25	2·10

PORTRAITS: 2c. M. Gomez. 3c. J. Sanguily. 5c. I. Agramonte. 8c. C. Garcia. 10c. Mayia. 1p. C. Roloff.

40 Map of W. Indies

1914

325	**40**	1c. green	2·10	25
326	**40**	2c. red	70	25
328	**40**	3c. violet	4·50	35
329	**40**	5c. blue	6·50	25
330	**40**	8c. olive	5·25	65
331	**40**	10c. brown	9·50	35
332	**40**	10c. olive	11·00	50
333	**40**	50c. orange	70·00	9·25
334	**40**	$1 slate	£100	22·00

43 Gertrudis Gomez de Avellaneda

1914. Birth Centenary of Gertrudis Gomez de Avellaneda (poetess).

335	**43**	5c. blue	13·00	4·50

44 Jose Marti

1917

336	**44**	1c. green	75	25
337	-	2c. red (Gomez)	80	25
338	-	3c. violet (La Luz)	85	25
339	-	5c. blue (Garcia)	80	25
349a	-	8c. brown (Agramonte)	3·00	25
341	-	10c. brown (Palma)	2·50	25
342	-	20c. green (Saco)	14·50	1·70
343	-	50c. red (Maceo)	14·50	75
344	-	1p. black (Cespedes)	14·50	75

47

1927. 25th Anniv of Republic.

352	**47**	25c. violet	13·00	3·75

48 PN 9 Flying Boat over Havana Harbour

1927. Air.

353	**48**	5c. blue	3·50	1·70

49 T. Estrada Palma

1928. 6th Pan-American Conference.

354	**49**	1c. green	50	30
355	-	2c. red	50	30
356	-	5c. blue	1·20	45
357	-	8c. brown	2·50	1·10
358	-	10c. brown	1·10	75
359	-	13c. orange	1·70	75
360	-	20c. olive	2·10	90
361	-	30c. purple	4·25	75
362	-	50c. red	6·75	2·75
363	-	1p. black	13·50	6·25

DESIGNS: 2c. Gen. G. Machado; 5c. El Morro, Havana; 8c. Railway Station, Havana; 10c. President's Palace; 13c. Tobacco plantation; 20c. Treasury Secretariat; 30c. Sugar Mill; 50c. Havana Cathedral; 1p. Galician Immigrants' Centre, Havana.

1928. Air. Lindbergh Commemoration. Optd LINDBERGH FEBRERO 1928.

364	**48**	5c. red	3·50	1·50

51 The Capitol, Havana

1929. Inauguration of Capitol.

365	**51**	1c. green	35	30
366	**51**	2c. red	40	30
367	**51**	5c. blue	55	40
368	**51**	10c. brown	1·00	50
369	**51**	20c. purple	3·75	2·40

52 Hurdler

1930. 2nd Central American Games, Havana.

370	**52**	1c. green	60	60
371	**52**	2c. red	60	70
372	**52**	5c. blue	85	70
373	**52**	10c. brown	1·60	1·60
374	**52**	20c. purple	12·50	4·25

1930. Air. Surch CORREO AEREO NACIONAL and value.

375	**47**	10c. on 25c. violet	3·00	1·70

54 Fokker F.10A Super Trimotor over Beach

1931. Air.

376	**54**	5c. green	50	15
377	**54**	8c. red	3·25	1·00
378	**54**	10c. blue	50	15
379	**54**	15c. red	1·10	30
380	**54**	20c. brown	1·10	15
381	**54**	30c. purple	1·70	20
382	**54**	40c. orange	3·75	45
383	**54**	50c. green	4·25	50
384	**54**	1p. black	6·75	1·10

55 Ford "Tin Goose" over Forest

1931. Air.

385	**55**	5c. purple	40	15
386	**55**	10c. black	40	15
387	**55**	20c. red	3·00	90
388	**55**	20c. pink	1·80	50
389	**55**	50c. blue	5·00	95
390	**55**	50c. turquoise	2·50	1·00

56 Mangos of Baragua **57** Battle of Mal Tiempo

1933. 35th Anniv of War of Independence.

391	**56**	3c. brown	1·10	25
392	**57**	5c. blue	1·00	40
393	-	10c. green	2·50	40
394	-	13c. red	2·75	1·00
395	-	20c. black	5·25	3·00

DESIGNS—HORIZ: 10c. Battle of Coliseo; 13c. Maceo, Gomez and Zayas. VERT: 20c. Campaign Monument.

1933. Establishment of Revolutionary Govt. Stamps of 1917 optd GOBIERNO REVOLUCIONARIO 4-9-1933 or surch also.

396A	**44**	1c. green	4·00	25
397A	-	2c. on 3c. vio (No. 338)	4·00	25

59 Dr. Carlos J. Finlay

1934. 101st Birth Anniv of C. J. Finlay ("yellow-fever" researcher).

398	**59**	2c. red	1·00	25
399	**59**	5c. blue	1·90	55

1935. Air. Havana–Miami "Air Train". Surch PRIMER TREN AEREO INTERNACIONAL. 1935 O'Meara y du Pont + 10 cts. Imperf or perf.

400	**54**	10c.+10c. red	4·25	4·25

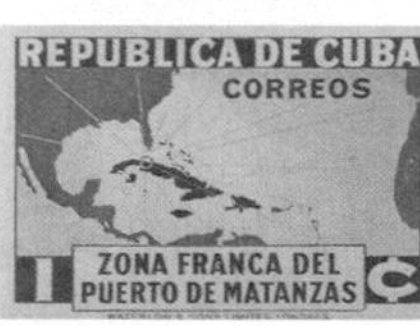

61 Map of Caribbean

1936. Free Port of Matanzas. Inscr as in T 61. Perf or imperf (same prices).

401	**61**	1c. green (postage)	35	25
402	-	2c. red	55	25
403	-	4c. purple	95	25
404	-	5c. blue	1·40	25
405	-	8c. brown	2·50	70
406	-	10c. green	2·75	70
407	-	20c. brown	5·00	2·50
408	-	50c. slate	9·25	3·50
409	-	5c. violet (air)	75	30
410	-	10c. orange	1·00	45
411	-	20c. green	3·50	2·00
412	-	50c. black	8·50	3·50

DESIGNS—POSTAGE: 2c. Matanzas Bay and Free Zone; 4c. "Rex" (liner) in Mantanzas Bay; 5c. Ships in the Free Zone; 8c. Bellamar Caves; 10c. Yumuri Valley; 20c. Yumuri River; 50c. Sailing ship and steamer. AIR: 5c. Aerial panorama; 10c. Airship "Macon" over Concord Bridge; 20c. Airplane "Cuatro Vientos" over Matanzas; 50c. San Severino Fortress.

63 President J. M. Gomez **64** Gen. J. M. Gomez Monument

1936. Inauguration of Gomez Monument.

413	**63**	1c. green	1·20	25
414	**64**	2c. red	1·80	30

65 "Peace and Labour"

66 Maximo Gomez Monument

1936. Inaug of Maximo Gomez Monument.

415	**65**	1c. green (postage)	35	25
416	**66**	2c. red	45	25
417	-	4c. purple	55	25
418	-	5c. blue	3·00	75
419	-	8c. olive	3·50	90
420	-	5c. violet (air)	2·00	1·00
421	-	10c. brown	3·50	1·00

DESIGNS—VERT: 4c. Flaming torch; 8c. Dove of Peace. HORIZ: 5c. (No. 418) Army of Liberation; 5c. (No. 420) Lightning; 10c. "Flying Wing".

68 Caravel and Sugar Cane

1937. 400th Anniv of Cane Sugar Industry.

422		1c. green	1·00	40
423		2c. red	50	25
424	**68**	5c. blue	1·00	40

DESIGNS (each with caravel in upper triangle). HORIZ: 2c. Early sugar mill; 5c. Modern sugar mill.

69 Mountain View (Bolivia) **70** Camilo Henriquez (Chile)

1937. American Writers and Artists Assn.

424a	-	1c. green (postage)	70	70
424b	**69**	1c. green	70	70
424c	-	2c. red	70	70
424d	-	2c. red	70	70
424e	**70**	3c. violet	1·40	1·40
424f	-	3c. violet	1·40	1·40
424g	-	4c. brown	1·50	1·50
424h	-	4c. brown	3·00	3·00
424i	-	5c. blue	1·70	1·70
424j	-	5c. blue	1·70	1·70
424k	-	8c. green	8·00	8·00
424l	-	8c. green	2·50	2·00
424m	-	10c. brown	2·75	2·75
424n	-	10c. brown	2·75	2·75
424o	-	25c. lilac	34·00	28·00
424p	-	5c. red (air)	6·25	6·25
424q	-	5c. red	6·25	6·25
424r	-	10c. blue	6·25	6·25
424s	-	10c. blue	6·25	6·25
424t	-	20c. green	9·00	9·00
424u	-	20c. green	9·00	9·00

DESIGNS—VERT: No. 424a, Arms of the Republic (Argentina); No. 424c, Arms (Brazil); No. 424f, Gen. F. de Paula Santander (Colombia); No. 424g, Autograph of Jose Marti (Cuba); No. 424j, Juan Montalvo (Ecuador); No. 424k, Abraham Lincoln (U.S.A.); No. 4241, Quetzal and scroll (Guatemala); No. 424m, Arms (Haiti); No. 424n, Francisco Morazan (Honduras); No. 424r, Inca gate, Cuzco (Peru); No. 424s, Atlacatl (Indian warrior) (El Salvador); No. 424t, Simon Bolivar (Venezuela); No. 424u, Jose Rodo (Uruguay). HORIZ: No. 424d, River scene (Canada); No. 424h, National Monument (Costa Rica); No. 424i, Columbus Lighthouse (Dominican Republic); No. 424o, Ships of Columbus; No. 424p, Arch (Panama); No. 424q, Carlos Lopez (Paraguay).

1937. Centenary of Cuban Railway. Surch 1837 1937 PRIMER CENTENARIO FERROCARRIL EN CUBA and value either side of an early engine and coach.

425	**47**	10c. on 25c. violet	11·50	3·25

1938. Air. 25th Anniv of D. Rosillo's Overseas Flight from Key West to Havana. Optd 1913 1938 ROSILLO Key West-Habana.

426	**48**	5c. orange	3·50	2·10

74 Pierre and Marie Curie

1938. International Anti-cancer Fund. 40th Anniv of Discovery of Radium.

427	**74**	2c.+1c. red	3·00	1·30
428	**74**	5c.+1c. blue	3·00	1·40

75 Allegory of Child Care

1938. Obligatory Tax. Anti-T.B. Fund.

429	**75**	1c. green	1·60	25

76 Native and Cigar

1939. Havana Tobacco Industry.

430	**76**	1c. green	35	25
431	-	2c. red	45	25
432	-	5c. blue	90	30

DESIGNS: 2c. Cigar, globe and wreath of leaves; 5c. Tobacco plant and box of cigars.

1939. Air. Experimental Rocket Post. Optd EXPERIMENTO DEL COHETE Postal ANO DE 1939.

433	**55**	10c. green	40·00	7·75

80 Calixto Garcia

1939. Birth Centenary of Gen. Calixto Garcia. Perf or imperf.

434	**80**	2c. red	55	25
435	-	5c. blue	90	40

DESIGN: 5c. Garcia on horseback.

82 Nurse and Child

1939. Obligatory Tax. Anti-T.B.

436	**82**	1c. red	90	25

83 Gonzalo de Quesada and Union Flags

1940. 50th Anniv of Pan-American Union.

437	**83**	2c. red	95	40

84 Rotarian Symbol, Flag and Tobacco Plant

1940. Rotary International Convention.

438	**84**	2c. red	1·70	85

85 Lions, Emblem, Flag and Palms

1940. Lions International Convention, Havana.

439	**85**	2c. red	1·70	85

86 Dr. Gutierrez

1940. Centenary of Publication of First Cuban Medical Review.

440	**86**	2c. red	85	40
441	**86**	5c. blue	1·20	40

MS442 127×177 mm. Two each of Nos. 440/1. Imperf (sold at 25c.) 4·75 4·00

See also Nos. **MS**560/1.

87 Sir Rowland Hill and G.B. 1d. of 1840 and Cuba Issues of 1855 and 1899

1940. Air. Centenary of 1st Adhesive Postage Stamps.

443	**87**	10c. brown	3·25	2·10

MS444 128×178 mm. No. 443 in block of four. Imperf (sold at 60c.) 15·00 15·00

88 "Health" protecting Children

1940. Obligatory Tax. Children's Hospital and Anti-T.B. Funds.

445	**88**	1c. blue	90	25

89 Heredia and Niagara Falls

1940. Air. Death Centenary of J. M. Heredia y Campuzaono (poet).

446	-	5c. green	2·25	1·10
447	**89**	10c. grey	2·75	1·60

DESIGN: 5c. Heredia and palms.

90 General Moncada and Sword **91** Moncada riding into Battle

1941. Birth Centenary of H. Moncada.

448	**90**	3c. brown	1·20	45
449	**91**	5c. blue	1·20	45

92 Mother and Child

1941. Obligatory Tax. Anti-T.B.

450	**92**	1c. brown	90	25

95 "Labour, Wealth of America"

1942. American Democracy. Imperf or perf.

451	-	1c. green	25	20
452	-	3c. brown	35	20
453	**95**	5c. blue	55	25
454	-	10c. mauve	1·40	60
455	-	13c. red	2·50	1·00

DESIGNS: 1c. Western Hemisphere; 3c. Cuban Arms and portraits of Maceo, Bolivar, Juarez and Lincoln; 10c. Tree of Fraternity, Havana; 13c. Statue of Liberty.

98 Gen. Ignacio Agramonte Loynaz **99** Rescue of Sanguily

1942. Birth Centenary of Gen. I. A. Loynaz.

456	**98**	3c. brown	85	40
457	**99**	5c. blue	1·70	50

100 "Victory"

1942. Obligatory Tax. Red Cross Fund.

458	**100**	½c. orange	40	25
459	**100**	½c. grey	55	25

1942. Obligatory Tax. Anti-T.B. Fund. Optd 1942.

460	**92**	1c. red	1·00	30

102 "Unmask Fifth Columnists"

1943. Anti-Fifth Column.

461	**102**	1c. green	50	25
462	-	3c. red	95	25
463	-	5c. blue	95	30
464	-	10c. brown	3·25	95
465	-	13c. purple	4·75	2·10

DESIGNS—HORIZ: (45×25 mm.) 5c. Woman in snake's coils ("The Fifth Column is like the Serpent — destroy it"); 10c. Men demolishing column with battering-ram ("Fulfil your patriotic duty by destroying the Fifth Column").

Type **102**. 13c. Woman with monster "Don't be afraid of the Fifth Column. Attack it". VERT: Girl with finger to lips "Be Careful! The Fifth Column is spying on you".

105 Eloy Alfaro, Flags of Ecuador and Cuba and Scroll of Independence

1943. Birth Centenary of E. Alfaro (former President of Ecuador).

466	**105**	3c. green	1·10	40

106 "The Long Road to Retirement"

1943. Postal Employees' Retirement Fund.

467	**106**	1c. green	60	40
470	**106**	3c. red	1·10	50
471	**106**	5c. blue	95	50

107 "Health" Protecting Child

1943. Obligatory Tax. Anti-tuberculosis.

473	**107**	1c. brown	90	25

108 Columbus **109** Discovery of Tobacco

1944. 450th Anniv of Discovery of America.

474	**108**	1c. green (postage)	30	20
475	-	3c. brown	40	20
476	-	5c. blue	65	25
477	**109**	10c. violet	2·75	75
478	-	13c. red	3·75	1·70
479	-	5c. olive (air)	95	40
480	-	10c. grey	2·10	70

DESIGNS—VERT: 3c. Bartolome de las Casas; 5c. (No. 476), Statue of Columbus. HORIZ: 5c. (No. 479) Mountains of Gibara; 10c. (No. 480), Columbus Lighthouse; 13c. Columbus at Pinar del Rio.

110 Carlos Roloff

1944. Birth Centenary of Major-Gen. Roloff.

481	**110**	3c. violet	1·00	30

111 American Continents and Brazilian "Bull's Eyes" stamps

1944. Cent of 1st American Postage stamps.

482	**111**	3c. brown	1·30	55

112 Society Seal **113** Governor Las Casas and Bishop Penalver

1945. 150th Anniv of Economic Society of Friends of Havana.

483	**112**	1c. green	40	20
484	**113**	2c. red	95	30

115 Old Age Pensioners

1945. Postal Employees' Retirement Fund.

485	**115**	1c. green	60	40
487	**115**	2c. red	1·00	40
489	**115**	5c. blue	2·50	40

116 Valdes

1946. Death Centenary of Gabriel de la Concepcion Valdes (poet).

491	**116**	2c. red	1·10	20

117 Manuel Marquez Sterling

1946. Founding of "Manuel Marquez Sterling" Professional School of Journalism.

492	**117**	2c. red	1·80	20

118 Red Cross and Globe

1946. 80th Anniv of International Red Cross.

493	**118**	2c. red	1·20	40

119 Prize Cattle and Dairymaid

1947. National Cattle Show.

494	**119**	2c. red	1·60	50

120 Franklin D. Roosevelt

1947. 2nd Death Anniv of Pres. Roosevelt.

495	**120**	2c. red	1·80	50

121 Antonio Oms and Pensioners

1947. Postal Employees' Retirement Fund.

496	**121**	1c. green	40	40
497	**121**	2c. red	40	40
498	**121**	5c. blue	1·70	70

122 Marta Abreu

1947. Birth Centenary of M. Abreu (philanthropist).

499	**122**	1c. green	50	20
500	-	2c. red	80	20
501	-	5c. blue	1·30	30
502	-	10c. violet	2·75	60

DESIGNS: 2c. Allegory of Charity; 5c. Monument; 10c. Allegory of Patriotism.

123 Dr. G. A. Hansen and Isle of Pines

1948. Int Leprosy Relief Congress, Havana.

503	**123**	2c. red	1·00	30

124 Council of War

1948. Air. 50th Anniv of War of Independence.

504	**124**	8c. black and yellow	1·80	80

1948. Air. American Air Mail Society Convention, Havana. Sheet MS444 optd CONVENCION MAYO 21-22-23 1948 AMERICAN AIR MAIL SOCIETY in blue across block of four.

MS505 128×178 mm. No. 443 in block of four. Imperf (sold at 60c.)		16·00	14·00

125 Woman and Child

1948. Postal Employees' Retirement Fund.

506	**125**	1c. green	40	25
507	**125**	2c. red	45	25
508	**125**	5c. blue	1·20	35

126 Death of Marti

1948. 50th Death Anniv of Jose Marti.

509	**126**	2c. red	80	25
510	-	5c. blue	2·30	40

DESIGN: 5c. Marti disembarking at Playitas.

127 Gathering Tobacco

1948. Havana Tobacco Industry.

511	**127**	1c. green	35	30
512	-	2c. red	50	30
513	-	5c. blue	85	30

DESIGNS: 2c. Girl with box of cigars and flag; 5c. Cigar and shield.

This set comes again redrawn with smaller designs of 21×25 mm.

129 Antonio Maceo

1948. Birth Centenary of Gen. Maceo.

514		1c. green	20	15
515	**129**	2c. red	30	20
516	-	5c. blue	50	20
517	-	8c. brown and black	80	40
518	-	10c. green and brown	80	35
519	-	20c. blue and red	3·00	1·20
520	-	50c. blue and red	5·25	2·75
521	-	1p. violet and black	10·00	4·00

DESIGNS—VERT: 1c. Equestrian statue of Maceo; 5c. Mausoleum at E1 Cacahual. HORIZ: 8c. Maceo and raised swords; 10c. Maceo leading charge; 20c. Maceo at Peralejo; 50c. Declaration at Baragua; 1p. Death of Maceo at San Pedro.

131 Symbol of Medicine

1948. 1st Pan-American Pharmaceutical Congress.

522	**131**	2c. red	1·80	45

132 Morro Castle and Lighthouse

1949. Centenary of El Morro Lighthouse.

523	**132**	2c. red	1·80	45

133 Jagua Castle

1949. Centenary of Newspaper "Hoja Economica" and Bicentenary of Jagua Fortress.

524	**133**	1c. green	70	30
525	**133**	2c. red	1·40	30

134 M. Sanguily

1949. Birth Centenary of Manuel Sanguily y Garritte (poet).

526	**134**	2c. red	60	30
527	**134**	5c. blue	1·90	30

135 Isle of Pines

1949. 20th Anniv of Return of Isle of Pines to Cuba.

528	**135**	5c. blue	2·50	95

136 Ismael Cespedes

1949. Postal Employees' Retirement Fund.

529	**136**	1c. green	70	30
530	**136**	2c. red	70	30
531	**136**	5c. blue	1·70	40

137 Woman and Child

1949. Obligatory Tax. Anti-tuberculosis.

532	**137**	1c. blue	60	25
547	**137**	1c. red	60	25

No. 547 is dated "1950".

138 Enrique Collazo

1950. Birth Centenary of Gen. Collazo.

533	**138**	2c. red	65	20
534	**138**	5c. blue	1·80	40

139 E. J. Varona

1950. Birth Centenary of Varona (writer).

535	**139**	2c. red	40	20
536	**139**	5c. blue	2·00	20

1950. National Bank Opening. No. 512 optd BANCO NACIONAL DE CUBA INAUGURACION 27 ABRIL 1950.

540	2c. red	1·40	30

1950. 75th Anniv of U.P.U. Optd U.P.U. 1874 1949.

541	**127**	1c. green	30	20
542	-	2c. pink (As No. 512)	40	20
543	-	5c. blue (As No. 513)	70	30

142 Balanzategui, Pausa and Railway Crash

1950. Postal Employees' Retirement Fund.

544	**142**	1c. green	1·40	60
545	**142**	2c. red	1·40	60
546	**142**	5c. blue	4·00	95

143 F. Figueredo

1951. Postal Employees' Retirement Fund.

548	**143**	1c. green	1·20	15
549	**143**	2c. red	1·20	15
550	**143**	5c. blue	2·75	15

144 Foundation Stone

1951. Obligatory Tax. P.O. Rebuilding Fund.

551	**144**	1c. violet	90	25

145 Narciso Lopez

1951. Centenary of Cuban Flag.

552	-	1c. red, bl & grn (postage)	55	35
553	**145**	2c. black and red	65	35
554	-	5c. red and blue	1·60	50
555	-	10c. red, blue and violet	2·75	75
556	-	5c. red, blue & olive (air)	1·60	45
557	-	8c. red, blue and brown	2·75	60
558	-	25c. red, blue and black	4·00	1·90

DESIGNS—VERT: 1c. Miguel Teurbe Tolon; 5c. (No. 554) Emilia Teurbe Tolon; 8c. Raising the flag; 10c. Flag; 25c. Flag and El Morro lighthouse. HORIZ: 5c. (No. 556) Lopez landing at Cardenas.

147 Clara Maass, Newark Memorial and Las Animas, Havana, Hospitals

1951. 50th Death Anniv of Clara Maass (nurse).

559	**147**	2c. red	2·10	45

1951. 50th Anniv of Discovery of Cause of Yellow-fever by Dr. Carlos J. Finley, and to honour Martyrs of Science. Sheet MS442 optd 50 ANIVERSARIO DESCUBRIMIENTO AGENTE TRANSMISOR, etc., across block of four.

MS560 127×177 mm. Two each of Nos. 440/1. Imperf (sold at 25c.) (postage) 5·75 5·00

Optd as last but with aeroplane motif and CORREO AERO in addition.

MS561 127×177 mm. Two each of Nos. 440/1 Imperf (sold at 25c.) (air) 11·00 8·50

148 Capablanca (after E. Valderrama)

149 Chessboard showing end of Capablanca v. Lasker

1951. 30th Anniv of Jose Capablanca's Victory in World Chess Championship.

562	**148**	1c. orge & grn (postage)	3·50	70
563	-	2c. brown and red	4·25	1·30
564	**E 150**	5c. blue and black	8·50	2·00
565	**149**	5c. yellow & green (air)	4·75	85
566	-	8c. purple and blue	8·25	1·30
567	**148**	25c. sepia & brown	14·50	3·25

DESIGN—VERT: 2c., 8c. Capablanca playing chess.

151 Dr. A. Guiteras Holmes

152 Morrillo Fortress

1951. 16th Death Anniv of Dr. A. Guiteras Holmes in skirmish at Morrillo.

568	**151**	1c. green (postage)	40	20
569	-	2c. red	70	30
570	**152**	5c. blue	1·40	50
571	**151**	5c. mauve (air)	1·80	1·20
572	-	8c. green	2·50	1·60
573	**152**	25c. black	4·75	3·00

MS574 Two sheets 125×133 mm. each containing Nos. 568/73 (each sold at 60c.)

DESIGNS—HORIZ: 2, 8c. Guiteras framing social laws.

153 Mother and Child

1951. Obligatory Tax. Anti-tuberculosis.

575	**153**	1c. brown	55	25
576	**153**	1c. red	55	25
577	**153**	1c. green	55	25
578	**153**	1c. blue	55	25

154 Christmas Emblems

1951. Christmas Greetings.

579	**154**	1c. red and green	2·75	30
580	**154**	2c. green and red	3·25	60

155 Jose Maceo

1952. Birth Centenary of Gen. Maceo.

581	**155**	2c. brown	55	20
582	**155**	5c. blue	1·20	20

156 General Post Office

1952. Obligatory Tax. P.O. Rebuilding Fund.

583	**156**	1c. blue	40	15
584	**156**	1c. red	75	25

157 Isabella the Catholic

1952. 5th Birth Centenary of Isabella the Catholic.

585	**157**	2c. red (postage)	1·60	40
586	**157**	25c. purple (air)	3·75	1·20

MS587 Two sheets each 108×108 mm containing Nos. 585/6. (a) 2c. indigo and 25c. carmine. (b) 2c. carmine and 25c. indigo 30·00 30·00

1952. As No. 549 surch with new value. (a) Postage.

588	**143**	10c. on 2c. brown	1·70	50

(b) Air. Optd AEREO in addition.

589	5c. on 2c. brown	90	40
590	8c. on 2c. brown	1·80	40
591	10c. on 2c. brown	1·80	40
592	25c. on 2c. brown	2·75	1·40
593	50c. on 2c. brown	9·25	2·50
594	1p. on 2c. brown	21·00	10·00

159 Proclamation of Republic

160 Statue, Havana University

1952. 50th Anniv of Republic.

595	**159**	1c. black & grn (postage)	20	15
596	-	2c. black and red	30	15
597	-	5c. black and blue	40	15
598	-	8c. black and brown	65	15
599	-	20c. black and olive	1·60	40
600	-	50c. black and orange	3·25	90
601	-	5c. green & violet (air)	40	15
602	**160**	8c. green and red	65	15
603	-	10c. green and blue	1·60	40
604	-	25c. green and purple	2·30	1·10

DESIGNS—HORIZ:—POSTAGE: 2c. Estrada Palma and Estevez Romero; 5c. Barnet, Finlay, Guiteras and Nunez; 8c. The Capitol; 20c. Map showing central highway; 50c. Sugar factory. AIR: 5c. Rural school; 10c. Presidential Palace; 25c. Banknote.

162 Curtiss A-1 Seaplane and Route of Flight

1952. Air. 39th Anniv of Florida–Cuba flight by A. Parla.

605	**162**	8c. black	1·40	55
606	-	25c. blue	4·00	1·70

MS607 Four sheets each 111×92 mm. Nos. 605/6 each in blue and in green 65·00 65·00

DESIGN—HORIZ: 25c. Agustin Parla Orduna and Curtiss A-1 seaplane.

164 Coffee Beans

1952. Bicentenary of Coffee Cultivation.

608	**164**	1c. green	55	25
609	-	2c. red	1·00	30
610	-	5c. green and blue	1·70	35

DESIGNS: 2c. Plantation worker and map; 5c. Coffee plantation.

165 Col. C. Hernandez

1952. Postal Employees' Retirement Fund.

611	**165**	1c. green (postage)	35	30
612	**165**	2c. red	55	30
613	**165**	5c. blue	65	30
614	**165**	8c. black	1·70	45
615	**165**	10c. red	1·70	45
616	**165**	20c. brown	6·50	3·50
617	**165**	5c. orange (air)	80	30
618	**165**	8c. green	80	30
619	**165**	10c. brown	1·00	30
620	**165**	15c. green	2·00	70
621	**165**	20c. turquoise	2·50	95
622	**165**	25c. red	2·00	95
623	**165**	30c. violet	5·25	2·30
624	**165**	45c. mauve	5·25	3·25
625	**165**	50c. blue	3·00	2·30
626	**165**	1p. yellow	11·00	4·75

166 A. A. De La Campa

167 Statue, Havana University

168 Dominguez, Estebanez and Capdevila (defence lawyers)

1952. 81st Anniv of Execution of Eight Rebel Medical Students.

627	**166**	1c. black & grn (postage)	30	15
628	-	2c. black and red	60	25
629	-	3c. black and violet	75	25
630	-	5c. black and blue	80	50
631	-	8c. black and sepia	1·60	50
632	-	10c. black and brown	1·30	45
633	-	13c. black and purple	2·50	70
634	-	20c. black and olive	4·00	1·20
635	**167**	5c. blue and indigo (air)	1·40	40
636	**168**	25c. green and orange	4·00	1·40

PORTRAITS: 2c. C. A. de la Torre. 3c. A. Bermudez. 5c. E. G. Toledo. 8c. A. Laborde. 10c. J. De M. Medina. 13c. P. Rodriguez. 20c. C. Verdugo.

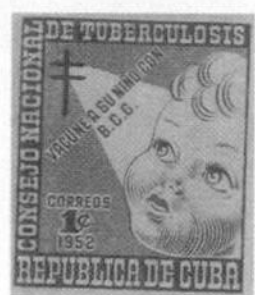

169 Child's Face

1952. Obligatory Tax. Anti- tuberculosis.

637	**169**	1c. orange	90	25
638	**169**	1c. red	90	25
639	**169**	1c. green	90	25
640	**169**	1c. blue	90	25

170 Christmas Tree

1952. Christmas.

641	**170**	1c. red and green	4·75	1·70
642	**170**	3c. green and violet	4·75	1·70

171 Marti's Birthplace

1953. Birth Centenary of Jose Marti.

643	**171**	1c. brn & grn (postage)	40	15
644	-	1c. brown and green	40	15
645	-	3c. brown and violet	45	15
646	-	3c. brown and violet	45	15
647	-	5c. brown and blue	80	15
648	-	5c. brown and blue	80	15
649	-	10c. black and brown	1·60	40
650	-	10c. black and brown	1·60	40
651	-	13c. brown and green	2·75	85
652	-	13c. brown and green	2·75	1·00
653	-	5c. black & red (air)	45	15
654	-	5c. black and red	45	15
655	-	8c. black and green	1·20	15
656	-	8c. black and green	1·20	15
657	-	10c. red and blue	2·75	50
658	-	10c. blue and red	2·75	50
659	-	15c. black and violet	1·90	1·00
660	-	15c. black and violet	1·90	1·00
661	-	25c. red and brown	5·00	1·30
662	-	25c. red and brown	5·00	1·30
663	-	50c. blue and yellow	8·00	2·75

DESIGNS—HORIZ: No. 644, Marti before Council of War; No. 645, Prison wall; No. 647, "El Abra" ranch; No. 652, First edition of "Patria"; No. 656, House of Maximo Gomez, Montecristi; No. 658, Marti as an orator; No. 663, "Fragua Martiana" (modern building). VERT: No. 646, Marti in prison; No. 648, Allegory of Marti's poems; No. 649, Marti and Bolivar Statue, Caracas; No. 650, Marti writing; No. 651, Revolutionaries' meeting-place; No. 653, Marti in Kingston, Jamaica; No. 654, Marti in Ibor City; No. 655, Manifesto of Montecristi; No. 657, Marti's portrait; No. 659, Marti's first tomb; No. 660, Obelisk at Des Rios; No. 661, Monument in Havana; No. 662, Marti's present tomb.

172 Dr. Rafael Montoro

1953. Birth Centenary of Montoro (statesman).

664	**172**	3c. purple	1·60	30

173 Dr. F. Carrera Justiz

1953

665	**173**	3c. red	2·00	30

174 Lockheed Constellation

1953. Air.

666	**174**	8c. brown	1·10	20
667	**174**	15c. red	2·10	65
668	-	2p. brown and green	25·00	9·25
669	-	5p. brown and blue	48·00	16·00
670	-	2p. myrtle and blue	18·00	6·50
671	-	5p. myrtle and red	39·00	15·00

DESIGN: Nos. 668/71, Constellation facing right.

1953. No. 512 surch.

672	3c. on 2c. red	1·60	25

176 Congress Building

1953. 1st Int Accountancy Congress, Havana.

673	**176**	3c. blue (postage)	80	40
674	-	8c. red (air)	2·10	65
675	-	25c. green	3·25	1·10

DESIGNS: 8c. Congress building and "Cuba"; 25c. Aerial view of building and Lockheed Constellation airplane.

177

1953. Obligatory Tax. Anti-T.B.

676	**177**	1c. red	60	25

178 M. Coyula Llaguno

179 Postal Employees' Retirement Association Flag

1954. Postal Employees' Retirement Fund. Inscr "1953".

677	**178**	1c. green (postage)	35	15
678	-	3c. red	35	15
679	**179**	5c. blue	1·00	15
680	-	8c. red	1·90	40
681	-	10c. sepia	3·00	60
682	-	5c. blue (air)	60	25
683	-	8c. purple	80	25
684	-	10c. orange	1·40	30
685	**179**	1p. grey	8·25	6·75

PORTRAITS—VERT: Nos. 678, 680, F.L.C. Hensell; Nos. 681, 683, A. G. Rojas; No. 684, G. H. Saez. HORIZ: No. 682, M. C. Llaguno.

180 Jose Marti

1954. Portraits. Roul. (No. 1180a/b) or perf. (others).

686	**180**	1c. green	35	15
687	-	2c. red (Gomez)	35	15
688	-	3c. violet (de la Luz Caballero)	35	15
689	-	4c. mauve (Aldama)	40	15
690	-	5c. blue (Garcia)	50	15
691	-	8c. lake (Agramonte)	75	15
692	-	10c. sepia (Palma)	75	15
693	-	13c. red (Finlay)	1·10	15
694	-	14c. grey (Sanchez)	1·40	15
695	-	20c. olive (Saco)	2·20	40
696	-	50c. ochre (Maceo)	3·75	40
697	-	1p. orange (Cespedes)	7·25	45
990	**180**	1c. red	50	15
991	-	2c. olive (Gomez)	55	15
1180a	-	3c. orange (Caballero)	1·20	15
1180b	-	13c. brown (Finlay)	1·80	40
1680	**180**	1c. blue	25	10
1681	-	2c. green (Gomez)	25	10
1682	-	20c. violet (Saco)	1·50	50

181 Hauling Sugar and Lockheed Constellation

1954. Air. Sugar Industry.

698		5c. green	40	15
699		8c. brown	1·10	50
700	**181**	10c. green	1·10	50
701	-	15c. brown	2·50	50
702	-	20c. blue	1·10	15
703	-	25c. red	80	15
704a	-	30c. purple	3·00	1·00
705	-	40c. blue	4·25	1·20
706	-	45c. violet	3·50	2·00
707	-	50c. blue	3·50	1·30
708	-	1p. blue	9·25	2·75

DESIGNS—VERT: 5c. Sugar cane; 1p. A. Reinoso. HORIZ: 8c. Sugar harvesting; 15c. Train load of sugar cane; 20c. Modern sugar factory; 25c. Evaporators; 30c. Stacking sugar in sacks; 40c. Loading sugar on ship; 45c. Oxen hauling cane; 50c. Primitive sugar factory.

182 Jose M. Rodriguez

1954. Birth Centenary of Rodriguez.

709	**182**	2c. sepia and lake	80	25
710	-	5c. sepia and blue	2·40	50

DESIGN: 5c. Rodriguez on horseback.

183 View of Sanatorium

1954. General Batista Sanatorium.

711	**183**	3c. blue (postage)	95	45
712	**183**	9c. green (air)	2·10	85

184

1954. Obligatory Tax. Anti-T.B.

713	**184**	1c. red	90	25
714	**184**	1c. green	90	25
715	**184**	1c. blue	90	25
716	**184**	1c. violet	90	25

185 Father Christmas

1954. Christmas Greetings.

717	**185**	2c. green and red	5·75	1·20
718	**185**	4c. red and green	5·75	1·20

186 Maria Luisa Dolz

1954. Birth Centenary of Maria Dolz (educationist).

719	**186**	4c. blue (postage)	95	40
720	**186**	12c. mauve (air)	1·80	70

187 Boy Scouts and Cuban Flag

1954. 3rd National Scout Camp.

721	**187**	4c. green	1·30	40

188 P. P. Harris and Rotary Emblem

1955. 50th Anniv of Rotary International.

722	**188**	4c. blue (postage)	1·60	30
723	**188**	12c. red (air)	1·80	85

189 Major-Gen. F. Carrillo

1955. Birth Centenary of Carrillo.

724	**189**	2c. blue and red	50	25
725	-	5c. sepia and blue	90	40

DESIGN: 5c. Half-length portrait.

190 1855 Stamp and "La Volanta"

1955. Centenary of First Cuban Postage Stamps and 50th Anniv of First Republican Stamps.

726		2c. blue & pur (postage)	75	15
727	**190**	4c. green and buff	1·00	40
728	-	10c. red and blue	3·00	75
729	-	14c. orange and green	6·50	1·80
730	-	8c. green & blue (air)	90	35
731	-	12c. red and green	1·00	35
732	-	24c. blue and red	1·80	1·00
733	-	30c. brown & orange	4·00	1·60

DESIGNS (a) With 1855 stamp: 2c. Old Square and Convent of St. Francis; 10c. Havana in 19th century; 14c. Captain-General's residence and Plaza de Armas; (b) With 1855 and 1905 stamps: 8c. Palace of Fine Arts; 12c. Plaza de la Fraternidad; 24c. Aerial view of Havana; 30c. Plaza de la Republica.

191 Maj.-Gen. Menocal

192 Mariel Bay

1955. Postal Employees' Retirement Fund.

734	**191**	2c. green (postage)	80	15
735	-	4c. mauve	90	25
736	-	10c. blue	1·40	50
737	-	14c. grey	3·25	1·20
738	**192**	8c. green and red (air)	1·20	25
739	-	12c. blue and brown	1·60	70
740	-	1p. ochre and green	9·00	2·75

DESIGNS—As Type **191**: HORIZ: 4c. Gen. E. Nunez; 14c. Dr. A. de Bustamante. VERT: 10c. J. Gomez. As Type **192**: HORIZ: 12c. Varadero Beach; 1p. Vinales Valley.

193 Cuban Academy

1955. Air. Centenary of Tampa, Florida.

741	**193**	12c. brown and red	2·20	60

194 Route of 1914 Flight

1955. Air. 35th Death Anniv of Crocier (aviator).

742	**194**	12c. green and red	90	50
743	-	30c. mauve and green	3·00	75

DESIGN: 30c. Crocier in aircraft cockpit.

195

1955. Obligatory Tax. Anti-T.B.

744	**195**	1c. orange	90	25
745	**195**	1c. yellow	90	25
746	**195**	1c. blue	90	25
747	**195**	1c. mauve	90	25

196 Wright "Flyer 1"

1955. Air. Int Philatelic Exhibition, Havana.

748	**196**	8c. black, red and blue	1·20	60
749	-	12c. black, green and red	2·75	85
750	-	24c. black, violet & red	8·50	3·25
751	-	30c. black, blue & orange	7·25	4·25
752	-	50c. black olive & orange	9·75	5·00
MS753		175×140 mm. Nos. 748/52 in new colours	34·00	34·00

DESIGNS: 12c. Lindbergh's airplane "Spirit of St. Louis"; 24c. Airship "Graf Zeppelin"; 30c. Lockheed Super Constellation airplane; 50c. Convair Delta Dagger airplane.

197 Wild Turkey

1955. Christmas Greetings.

754	**197**	2c. green and red	5·25	2·10
755	**197**	4c. lake and green	5·25	2·20

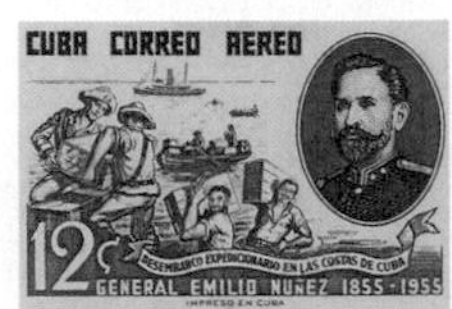

198 Expedition Disembarking

1955. Birth Centenary of General Nunez.

756	-	4c. lake (postage)	1·20	85
757	-	8c. blue and red (air)	1·80	70
758	**198**	12c. green and brown	2·75	1·10

DESIGNS—VERT: (22½×32½ mm.): 4c. Portrait of Nunez. HORIZ: As Type **198**: 8c. "Three Friends" (tug).

199 Bishop P. A. Morell de Santa Cruz

1956. Bicentenary of Cuban Postal Service.

759	-	4c. blue & brn (postage)	1·20	45
760	**199**	12c. green & brown (air)	2·10	50

PORTRAIT: 4c. F. C. de la Vega.

200 J. del Casal

1956. Postal Employees' Retirement Fund.

761	**200**	2c. black & grn (postage)	35	15
762	-	4c. black and mauve	55	15
763	-	10c. black and blue	1·00	15
764	-	14c. black and violet	1·30	15
765	-	8c. black & brown (air)	1·30	15
766	-	12c. black and ochre	2·20	20
767	-	30c. black and blue	4·00	1·50

PORTRAITS: 4c. Luisa Perez de Zambrana. 8c. Gen. J. Sanguily. 10c. J. Clemente Zenea. 12c. Gen. J. M. Aguirre. 14c. J. J. Palma. 30c. Col. E. Fonts Sterling.

201 Victor Munoz

1956. Munoz Commemoration.

768	**201**	4c. brown and green	1·20	45

202 Mother and Baby

1956. Air. Mothers' Day.

769	**202**	12c. blue and red	4·00	35

203 Aerial View of Temple

1956. Masonic Grand Lodge of Cuba Temple, Havana.

770	-	4c. blue (postage)	1·40	45
771	**203**	12c. green (air)	2·75	50

DESIGN: 4c. Ground level view of Temple.

204 Gundlach's Hawk

1956. Air. Birds.

772	-	8c. blue	50	20
773	-	12c. grey	7·50	40
783	-	12c. green	1·50	45
774	**204**	14c. olive	1·70	25
775	-	19c. brown	1·10	55
776	-	24c. mauve	1·30	55
777	-	29c. green	1·90	55
778	-	30c. brown	2·30	85
779	-	50c. slate	4·25	1·10
780	-	1p. red	6·50	2·30
784	-	1p. blue	5·75	5·75
781	-	2p. purple	13·00	4·25
785	-	2p. red	17·00	15·00
782	-	5p. red	35·00	8·75
786	-	5p. purple	37·00	33·00

DESIGNS—HORIZ: 8c. Wood duck; 12c. (2) Plain pigeon; 29c. Goosander; 30c. Northern bobwhite; 2p. (2) Northern jacana. VERT: 19c. Herring gull; 24c. American white pelican; 50c. Great blue heron; 1p. (2) Common caracara; 5p. (2) Ivory-billed woodpecker.

205 H. de Blanck

1956. Air. Birth Centenary of H. De Blanck (composer).

787	**205**	12c. blue	1·80	50

1956. Air. Inaug of Philatelic Club of Cuba Building. No. 776 but colour changed and surch Inauguracion Edificio Club Filatelico de la Republica de Cuba Julio 13 de 1956 and value.

788	8c. on 24c. orange	2·50	85

207 Church of Our Lady of Charity

1956. Inscr "NTRA. SRA. DE LA CARIDAD", etc.

789	-	4c. blue & yell (postage)	1·00	40
790	**207**	12c. green & red (air)	2·10	70
MS791 76×77 mm. Nos. 789/90			12·50	10·50

DESIGN: 4c. Our Lady of Charity over landscape.

208

1956. Air. 250th Birth Anniv of Benjamin Franklin.

792	**208**	12c. brown	2·10	70

209

1956. "Grito de Yara" (War of Independence). Commem.

793	**209**	4c. sepia and green	1·00	40

(210)

1956. Air. 12th Inter-American Press Assn. Meeting. As No. 781 but colour changed and surch with T 210.

794	12c. on 2p. grey	3·00	1·20

211

1956. Obligatory Tax. Anti-T.B.

795	**211**	1c. red	90	25
796	**211**	1c. green	90	25
797	**211**	1c. blue	90	25
798	**211**	1c. brown	90	25

212

1956. Christmas Greetings.

799	**212**	2c. red and green	3·75	1·60
800	**212**	4c. green and red	3·75	1·80

213 Prof. R. G. Menocal

1956. Birth Centenary of Prof. R. G. Menocal.

801	**213**	4c. brown	95	40

214a Martin M. Delgado

1957. Birth Centenary of Delgado (patriot).

802	**214a**	4c. green	95	40

215 Scouts around Camp Fire

1957. Birth Centenary of Lord Baden-Powell.

803	**215**	4c. green & red (postage)	1·30	50
804	-	12c. slate (air)	2·50	95

DESIGN—VERT: 12c. Lord Baden-Powell.

216 "The Art Critics" (Melero)

217 Hanabanilla Falls

1957. Postal Employees' Retirement Fund.

805		2c. green & brn (postage)	60	15
806	**216**	4c. red and brown	1·20	40
807	-	10c. olive and brown	1·80	60
808	-	14c. blue and brown	1·50	45
809	**217**	8c. blue and red (air)	80	15
810	-	12c. green and red	3·25	40
811	-	30c. olive and violet	3·75	65

DESIGNS—HORIZ: As Type **216** (Paintings): 2c. "The Blind" (Vega); 10c. "Carriage in the Storm" (Menocal); 14c. "The Convalescent" (Romanach); As Type **217**: 12c. Sierra de Cubitas; 30c. Puerto Boniato.

218 Posthorn Emblem of Cuban Philatelic Society

1957. Stamp Day. Cuban Philatelic Exn.

812	**218**	4c. bl, brn & red (postage)	95	40
813	-	12c. brn, yell & grn (air)	1·90	50

DESIGN: 12c. Philatelic Society Building, Havana.

219 Juan F. Steegers

1957. Birth Centenary of Steegers (fingerprint pioneer).

814	**219**	4c. blue (postage)	95	40
815	-	12c. brown (air)	1·90	50

DESIGN: 12c. Thumbprint.

220 Baseball Player

1957. Air. Youth Recreation. Centres in brown.

816	**220**	8c. green on green	1·70	50
817	-	12c. lilac on lavender	2·50	60
818	-	24c. blue on blue	3·50	1·70
819	-	30c. flesh on orange	5·25	2·10

DESIGNS—12c. Ballet dancer; 24c. Diver; 30c. Boxers.

221 Nurse Victoria Bru Sanchez

1957. Nurse Victoria Bru Sanchez Commem.

820	**221**	4c. blue	1·20	40

222 J. de Aguero leading Patriots

1957. Joaquin de Aguero (patriot) Commem.

821	**222**	4c. green (postage)	95	40
822	-	12c. blue (portrait) (air)	2·10	50

223 Youth with Dogs and Cat

1957. 50th Anniv of Band of Charity (for prevention of cruelty to animals).

823	**223**	4c. green (postage)	1·80	70
824	-	12c. brown (air)	3·25	70

DESIGN: 12c. Jeanette Ryder (founder).

224 Col. R. Manduley del Rio (patriot)

1957. Col. R. Manduley del Rio. Commem.

825	**224**	4c. green	2·75	2·10

225 J. M. Heredia y Girard

1957. Air. J. M. Heredia y Girard (poet). Commem.

826	**225**	8c. violet	1·10	40

226 Palace of Justice, Havana

1957. Inauguration of Palace of Justice.

827	**226**	4c. grey (postage)	1·30	50
828	**226**	12c. green (air)	2·10	60

227 Army Leaders of 1856

1957. Centenary of Cuban Army of Liberation.

829	**227**	4c. brown and green	95	40
830	**227**	4c. brown and blue	95	40
831	**227**	4c. brown and pink	95	40
832	**227**	4c. brown and yellow	95	40
833	**227**	4c. brown and lilac	95	40

228 J. R. Gregg

1957. Air. Gregg (shorthand pioneer) Commem.

834	**228**	12c. green	2·10	95

229 Cuba's First Publication, 1723

230 Jose Marti Public Library

1957. "Jose Marti" Public Library. Inscr "BIBLIOTECA NACIONAL".

835	**229**	4c. slate (postage)	1·30	50
836	-	8c. blue (air)	60	30
837	**230**	12c. sepia	2·40	60

DESIGN—VERT: As Type **230**: 8c. D. F. Caneda, first Director.

231 U.N. Emblem and Map of Cuba

1957. Air. U.N. Day.

838	**231**	8c. brown and green	1·10	30
839	**231**	12c. green and red	1·60	70
840	**231**	30c. mauve and blue	3·75	1·60

232 Fokker Trimotor "General New" and Map

1957. Air. 30th Anniv of Inaug of Air Mail Services between Havana and Key West, Florida.

841	**232**	12c. blue and purple	2·50	1·00

233

1957. Obligatory Tax. Anti-tuberculosis.

842	**233**	1c. red	90	25
843	**233**	1c. green	90	25
844	**233**	1c. blue	90	25
845	**233**	1c. grey	90	25

235 Courtyard

1957. Centenary of 1st Cuban Teachers' Training College.

846	**235**	4c. brn & grn (postage)	1·30	50
847	-	12c. buff and blue (air)	1·40	50
848	-	30c. sepia and red	2·50	70

DESIGNS—VERT: 12c. School facade. HORIZ: 30c. General view of school.

236 Street Scene, Trinidad

1957. Postal Employees' Retirement Fund.

849	**236**	2c. brown & bl (postage)	30	15
850	-	4c. green and brown	65	15
851	-	10c. sepia and red	1·10	30
852	-	14c. green and red	1·60	25
853	-	8c. black and red (air)	65	30
854	-	12c. black and brown	1·30	40
855	-	30c. brown and grey	2·50	65

DESIGNS—VERT: 4c. Sentry-box on old wall of Havana; 10c. Calle Padre Pico (street), Santiago de Cuba; 12c. Sancti Spiritus Church; 14c. Church and street scene, Camaguey. HORIZ: 8c. "El Viso" Fort, El Caney; 30c. Concordia Bridge, Matanzas.

237 Christmas Crib

1957. Christmas. Multicoloured centres.

856	**237**	2c. sepia	3·00	1·20
857	**237**	4c. black	3·00	1·30

239 Dayton Hedges and Textile Factories

1958. Dayton Hedges (founder of Cuban Textile Industry) Commemoration.

858	**239**	4c. blue (postage)	2·10	1·00
859	**239**	8c. green (air)	2·10	1·00

240 Dr. F. D. Roldan

1958. Dr. Francisco D. Roldan (physiotherapy pioneer) Commemoration.

861	**240**	4c. green	1·30	40

241 "Diario de la Marina" Building

1958. 125th Anniv of "Diario de la Marina" Newspaper.

862	-	4c. olive (postage)	1·00	95
863	**241**	29c. black (air)	3·50	1·60

PORTRAIT—VERT: 4c. J. I. Rivero y Alonso (journalist).

242 Map of Cuba showing Postal Routes of 1756

1958. Stamp Day and National Philatelic Exhibition, Havana. Inscr as in T 242.

864	**242**	4c. myrtle, buff and blue (postage)	95	40
865	-	29c. indigo, buff and blue (air)	3·75	1·40

DESIGN: 29c. Ocean map showing sea-post routes of 1765.

243 Gen. J. M. Gomez

1958. Birth Centenary of Gen. J. M. Gomez.

866	**243**	4c. blue (postage)	1·30	50
867	-	12c. myrtle (air)	2·00	70

DESIGN: 12c. Gomez at Arroyo Blanco.

244 Dr. T. Romay Chacon

1958. Famous Cubans. Portraits as T 244. (a) Doctors. With emblem of medicine.

868	2c. brown and green	70	30
869	4c. black and green	70	30
870	10c. red and green	70	30
871	14c. blue and green	85	30

(b) Lawyers. With emblem of law.

872	2c. sepia and red	70	30
873	4c. black and red	75	30
874	10c. green and red	75	30
875	14c. blue and red	95	30

(c) Composers. With lyre emblem of music.

876	2c. brown and blue	70	30
877	4c. purple and blue	70	30
878	10c. green and blue	80	30
879	14c. red and blue	95	30

PORTRAITS—Doctors: 2c. Type **244**. 4c. A. A. Aballi. 10c. F. G. del Valle. 14c. V. A. de Castro. Lawyers: 2c. J. M. G. Montes. 4c. J. A. G. Lanuza. 10c. J. B. H. Barreiro. 14c. P. G. Llorente. Composers: 2c. N. R. Espadero. 4c. I. Cervantes. 10c. J. White. 14c. B. de Salas.

245 Dr. C. de la Torre

246 Painted Polymita

1958. Birth Cent of De la Torre (archaeologist).

880	**245**	4c. blue (postage)	1·60	50
881	**246**	8c. red, yellow & blk (air)	6·75	40
882	-	12c. sepia on green	9·25	2·30
883	-	30c. green on pink	13·50	2·75

DESIGNS—As Type **246**: 12c. "Megalocnus rodens"; 30c. "Perisphinctes spinatus" (ammonite).

247 Felipe Poey (naturalist)

248 "Papilio caiguanabus" (butterfly)

1958. Poey Commemoration. Designs as T 247/8 inscr "1799–FELIPE POEY–1891".

884		2c. blk & lav (postage)	65	25
885	**247**	4c. sepia	1·00	35
886	**248**	8c. multicoloured (air)	1·60	60
887	-	12c. orange, black & grn	1·80	60
888	-	14c. multicoloured	4·50	90
889	-	19c. multicoloured	5·75	1·20
890	-	24c. multicoloured	6·75	1·20
891	-	29c. blue, brown & black	9·75	1·50
892	-	30c. brown, green & blk	14·00	2·20

DESIGNS—VERT: 2c. Cover of Poey's book; 12c. "Teria gundlachia"; 14c. "Teria ebriola"; 19c. "Nathalis felicia" (all butterflies). HORIZ: 24c. Tobacco fish; 29c. Butter hamlet; 30c. Tattler sea bass (all fishes).

249 Theodore Roosevelt

1958. Birth Centenary of Roosevelt.

893	**249**	4c. green (postage)	1·00	35
894	-	12c. sepia (air)	1·60	45

DESIGN—HORIZ: 12c. Roosevelt leading Rough Riders at San Juan 1898.

250 National Tuberculosis Hospital

1958. Obligatory Tax. Anti-T.B.

895	**250**	1c. brown	45	25
896	**250**	1c. green	45	25
897	**250**	1c. red	45	25
898	**250**	1c. grey	45	25

251 UNESCO Headquarters, Paris

1958. Air. Inaug of UNESCO Headquarters.

899	**251**	12c. green	1·40	45
900	-	30c. blue	2·75	1·50

DESIGN: 30c. Facade composed of letters "UNESCO" and map of Cuba.

252 "Cattleyopsis lindenii" (orchid)

1958. Christmas. Orchids. Multicoloured.

901	2c. Type **252**	3·50	1·20
902	4c. "Oncidium guibertianum"	3·50	1·20

253 "The Revolutionary"

1959. Liberation Day.

903	**253**	2c. black and red	70	30

254 Gen. A. F. Crombet

1959. Gen. Crombet Commemoration.

904	**254**	4c. myrtle	95	35

255 Postal Notice of 1765

1959. Air. Stamp Day and National Philatelic Exhibition, Havana.
905 **255** 12c. sepia and blue 1·40 35
906 - 30c. blue and sepia 2·30 1·30
DESIGN: 30c. Administrative postal book of St. Cristobal, Havana, 1765.

256 Hand Supporting Sugar Factory

1959. Agricultural Reform.
907 **256** 2c.+1c. blue and red (postage) 95 20
908 - 12c.+3c. green and red (air) 2·10 70
DESIGN (42×30 mm.): 12c. Farm workers and factory plant.

257 Red Cross Nurse

1959. "For Charity".
909 **257** 2c.+1c. red 50 25

1959. Air. American Society of Travel Agents Convention, Havana. No. 780 (colour changed) surch CONVENCION ASTA OCTUBRE 17 1959 12c. and bar.
910 12c. on 1p. green 2·40 1·20

259 Teresa Garcia Montes (founder)

1959. Musical Arts Society Festival, Havana.
911 **259** 4c. brown (postage) 1·40 50
912 - 12c. green (air) 2·40 65
DESIGN—HORIZ: 12c. Society Headquarters, Havana.

260 Pres. C. M. de Cespedes

1959. Cuban Presidents.
913 2c. slate (Type **260**) 60 20
914 2c. green (Betancourt) 60 20
915 2c. violet (Calvar) 60 20
916 2c. brown (Maso) 60 20
917 4c. red (Spotorno) 85 30
918 4c. brown (Palma) 85 30
919 4c. black (F. J. de Cespedes) 85 30
920 4c. violet (Garcia) 85 30

261 Rebel Attack at Moncada Barracks

1960. 1st Anniv of Cuban Revolution.
921 **261** 1c. grn, red & bl (postage) 20 15
922 - 2c. green, sepia and blue 95 15
923 - 10c. green, red and blue 2·30 85
924 - 12c. green, purple & blue 3·00 60
925 - 8c. green, red & bl (air) 2·30 40
926 - 12c. green, purple & brn 2·50 35
927 - 29c. red, black & green 4·00 1·20
DESIGNS: 2c. Rebels disembarking from "Granma"; 8c. Battle of Santa Clara; 10c. Battle of the Uvero; 12c. postage, "The Invasion" (Rebel and map of Cuba); 12c. air, Rebel Army entering Havana; 29c. Passing on propaganda ("Clandestine activities in the towns").

1960. Surch HABILITADO PARA and value (No. 932 without PARA).
928 **256** 2c. on 2c.+1c. blue and red (postage) 1·40 30
929 - 2c. on 4c. mve (No. 689) 1·00 50
930 - 2c. on 5c. blue (690) 1·00 50
931 - 2c. on 13c. red (693) 1·00 50
932 - 10c. on 20c. olive (342) 1·80 70
933 - 12c. on 12c.+3c. green and red (908) (air) 2·30 85

1960. Surch in figures.
934 1c. on 4c. (No. 869) (postage) 60 30
935 1c. on 4c. (No. 873) 60 30
936 1c. on 4c. (No. 877) 60 30
937 **245** 1c. on 4c. blue 60 30
938 **245** 1c. on 4c. (No. 902) 80 40
939 **254** 1c. on 4c. myrtle 60 30
940 **260** 1c. on 4c. brown 60 30
941 - 2c. on 14c. (No. 694) 1·20 30
942 **54** 12c. on 40c. orge (air) 2·30 85
943 - 12c. on 45c. (No. 706) 2·30 85

264 Pres. T. Estrada Palma Monument

1960. Postal Employees' Retirement Fund.
944 **264** 1c. brn & blue (postage) 30 15
945 - 2c. green and red 40 15
946 - 10c. brown and red 1·10 30
947 - 12c. green and violet 1·60 60
948 - 8c. grey and red (air) 95 30
949 - 12c. blue and red 1·60 30
950 - 30c. violet and red 3·50 1·60
MONUMENTS—VERT: 2c. "Mambi Victorioso"; 8c. Marti; 10c. Marta Abreu; 12c. (No. 947) Agramonte; 12c. (No. 949) Heroes of Cacarajicara. HORIZ: 30c. Dr. C. de la Torriente.

(265)

1960. Air. Stamp Day and National Philatelic Exn, Havana. Nos. 772/3 in new colours optd with T 265.
951 8c. yellow 85 50
952 12c. red 2·30 85
MS953 128×178 mm. No. 403 in block of four 22·00 22·00

266 Pistol-shooting

1960. Olympic Games.
954 - 1c. vio (Sailing) (postage) 60 30
955 **266** 2c. orange 70 30
956 - 8c. blue (Boxing) (air) 1·00 30
957 - 12c. red (Running) 1·40 60
MS958 79×91 mm. Nos. 954/5 each in blue. Imperf 8·00 8·00

267 C. Cienfuegos and View of Escolar

1960. 1st Death Anniv of Cienfuegos (revolutionary leader). Centre multicoloured.
959 **267** 2c. sepia 1·80 30

268 Air Stamp of 1930, Ford "Tin Goose" Airplane and "Sputnik"

1960. Air. 80th Anniv of National Airmail Service. Centre multicoloured.
960 **268** 8c. violet 4·25 2·50

270 Ipomoea

271 Tobacco Plant and Bars of "Christmas Hymn"

1960. Christmas. Inscr "NAVIDAD 1960–61". (a) T 270.
961 1c. multicoloured 85 85
962 2c. multicoloured 1·10 1·10
963 10c. multicoloured 2·75 3·00

(b) As T 271.
964a/d 1c. multicoloured 2·10 1·80
965a/d 2c. multicoloured 3·50 3·50
966a/d 10c. multicoloured 8·25 8·00
DESIGNS: As T **271** (same for each value) a, T **271**. b, Mariposa. c, Lignum-vitae. d, Coffee plant.
Prices are for single stamps.

272

1960. Sub-industrialized Countries Conference.
967 **272** 1c. black, yellow and red (postage) 30 15
968 - 2c. multicoloured 30 15
969 - 6c. red, black and cream 2·00 70
970 - 8c. multicoloured (air) 70 15
971 - 12c. multicoloured 2·00 15
972 - 30c. red and grey 2·50 85
973 - 50c. multicoloured 3·00 1·10
DESIGNS—HORIZ: 2c. Graph and symbols; 6c. Cogwheels; 12c. Workers holding lever; 30c. Maps. VERT: 8c. Hand holding machete; 50c. Upraised hand.

273 J. Menendez

1961. Jesus Menendez Commemoration.
974 **273** 2c. sepia and green 85 30

274 Jose Marti and "Declaration of Havana"

1961. Air. Declaration of Havana.
975 **274** 8c. red, black and yellow 1·60 1·10
976 **274** 12c. violet, black & buff 2·30 1·80
977 **274** 30c. brown, black & blue 5·25 4·75
MS978 103×80 mm. Nos. 975/7. No gum. Imperf 11·50 11·50
The above were issued with part of background text of the declaration in English, French and Spanish. Prices the same for each language.

275 U.N. Emblem within Dove of Peace

1961. 15th Anniv of U.N.O.
979 **275** 2c. brn & grn (postage) 45 20
980 **275** 10c. green and purple 1·60 60
MS981 102×64 mm. Nos. 979/80. No gum. Imperf 3·50 3·50

982 8c. red and yellow (air) 70 30
983 12c. blue and orange 2·00 60
MS984 102×64 mm. Nos. 982/3. No gum. Imperf 7·50 7·50

276 10c. Revolutionary Label of 1874 and "CUBA MAMBISA" "Postmark"

1961. Stamp Day. Inscr "24 DE ABRIL DIA DEL SELLO".
985 **276** 1c. red, green and black 30 15
986 - 2c. orange, slate & black 40 15
987 - 10c. turq, red & black 1·60 50
DESIGNS: 2c., 50c. stamp of 1907 and "CUBA REPUBLICANA" "postmark"; 10c., 2c. stamp of 1959 and "CUBA REVOLUCIONARIA" "postmark".

1961. May Day. Optd PRIMERO DE MAYO 1961 ESTAMOS VENCIENDO.
988 **273** 2c. sepia and green 1·60 30

278

1961. "For Peace and Socialism".
989 **278** 2c. multicoloured 1·40 30
No. 989 is lightly printed on back with pattern of wavy lines and multiple inscr "CORREOS CUBA" in buff.

1961. Air. Surch HABILITADO PARA 8 cts.
992 **174** 8c. on 15c. red 95 50
993 **54** 8c. on 20c. brown 95 50

1961. 1st Official Philatelic Exhibition. No. 987 optd primera exposicion filatelica oficial oct. 7-17, 1961.
994 10c. turq, red and black 1·90 50

281 Book and Lamp

1961. Education Year.
995 **281** 1c. red, black and green 15 15
996 **281** 2c. red, black and blue 15 15
997 **281** 10c. red, black and violet 90 25
998 **281** 12c. red, black & orange 1·60 60
The 2, 10 and 12c. show the letters "U", "B" and "A" on the book forming the word "CUBA".

282 "Polymita sulfurosa flammulata"

283 "Polymita picta fulminata"

1961. Christmas. Inscr "NAVIDAD 1961–62". Multicoloured.
(a) Various designs as T 282.
999 1c. Type **282** 50 20
1000 2c. Cuban grassquit (vert) 2·10 60
1001 10c. "Othreis toddi" (horiz) 3·00 1·20

(b) Various designs as T 283.
1002a/d 1c. Snails (horiz) 50 20
1003a/d 2c. Birds (vert) 2·10 60
1004a/d 10c. Butterflies (horiz) 3·00 1·20
DESIGNS: No. 1002a, Type **283**; 1002b, "Polymita p. nigrofasciata"; 1002c, "Polymita p. fuscolimbata"; 1002d, "Polymita p. roseolimbata"; 1003a, Cuban macaw; 1003b, Cuban trogon; 1003c, Bee hummingbird; 1003d, Ivory-billed woodpecker; 1004a, "Uranidia boisduvalii"; 1004b, "Phoebis avellaneda"; 1004c, "Phaloe cubana"; 1004d, "Papoilio gundlachianus".
Prices are for single stamps.

284 Castro Emblem

1962. 3rd Anniv of Cuban Revolution. Emblem in yellow, red, grey and blue. Colours of background and inscriptions given.

1005	**284**	1c. grn & pink (postage)	85	40
1006	**284**	2c. black and orange	1·70	50
1007	**284**	8c. brown & blue (air)	85	30
1008	**284**	12c. ochre and green	1·90	60
1009	**284**	30c. violet and yellow	2·50	1·00

285 Hand with Machete

1962. Air. 1st Anniv of Socialist Republic's First Sugar Harvest.

1010	**285**	8c. sepia and red	75	15
1011	**285**	12c. black and lilac	2·00	50

286 Armed Peasant and Tractor

1962. National Militia.

1012	**286**	1c. black and green	30	20
1013	-	2c. black and blue	60	30
1014	-	10c. black and orange	2·10	60

DESIGNS: 2c. Armed worker and welder; 10c. Armed woman and sewing-machinist.

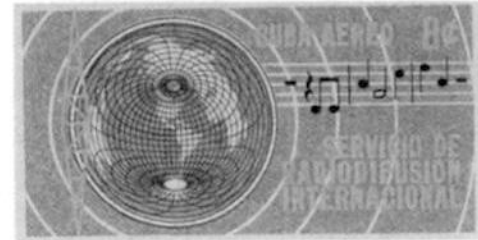
287 Globe and Music Emblem

1962. Air. International Radio Service. Inscr and aerial yellow; musical notation black; lines on globe brown, background colours given.

1015	**287**	8c. grey	95	30
1016	**287**	12c. blue	1·90	60
1017	**287**	30c. green	2·75	1·40
1018	**287**	1p. lilac	5·75	3·75

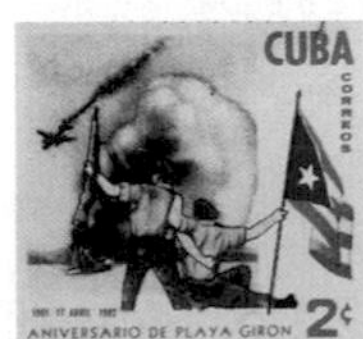

288 Soldiers, Aircraft and Burning Ship

1962. 1st Anniv of "Playa Giron" (Sea Invasion Attempt of Cuban Exiles).

1019	**288**	2c. multicoloured	35	15
1020	**288**	3c. multicoloured	35	20
1021	**288**	10c. multicoloured	2·40	65

289 Arrival of First Mail from the Indies

1962. Stamp Day.

1022	**289**	10c. black and red on cream	3·00	90

290 Clenched Fist Salute

1962. Labour Day.

1023	**290**	2c. black on buff	30	15
1024	**290**	3c. black on red	60	25
1025	**290**	10c. black on blue	2·10	70

291 Wrestling

1962. National Sports Institute (I.N.D.E.R.) Commemoration. As T 291. On cream paper.

1026a/e	1c. brown and red	30	20
1027a/e	2c. red and green	30	20
1028a/e	3c. blue and red	1·20	20
1029a/e	9c. purple and blue	75	30
1030a/e	10c. orange and purple	80	30
1031a/e	13c. black and red	85	45

DESIGNS: No. 1026a, Type **291**; 1026b, Weight-lifting; 1026c, Gymnastics; 1026d, Judo; 1026e, Throwing the discus; 1027a, Archery; 1027b, Roller skating; 1027c, Show jumping; 1027d, Ninepin bowling; 1027e, Cycling; 1028a, Rowing (coxed four); 1028b, Speed boat; 1028c, Swimming; 1028d, Kayak; 1028e, Yachting; 1029a, Football; 1029b, Tennis; 1029c, Baseball; 1029d, Basketball; 1029e, Volleyball; 1030a, Underwater fishing; 1030b, Shooting; 1030c, Model airplane flying; 1030d, Water polo; 1030e, Boxing; 1031a, Pelota; 1031b, Sports stadium; 1031c, Jai alai; 1031d, Chess; 1031e, Fencing.

Prices are for single stamps.

292 A. Santamaria and Soldiers

1962. 9th Anniv of "Rebel Day".

1032	**292**	2c. lake and blue	60	40
1033	-	3c. blue and lake	1·10	60

DESIGN: 3c. Santamaria and children.

293 Dove and Festival Emblem

1962. World Youth Festival, Helsinki.

1034	**293**	2c. multicoloured	85	30
1035	-	3c. multicoloured	1·40	60
MS1036		91×52 mm. Nos. 1034/5. Imperf	5·75	5·75

DESIGN: 3c. As Type **293** but with "clasped hands" instead of dove.

294 Czech 5k. "Praga 1962" stamp of 1961

1962. Air. International Stamp Exn, Prague.

1037	**294**	31c. multicoloured	4·25	1·80
MS1038		150×123 mm. No. 1037	10·50	10·50

295 Rings and Boxing Gloves

1962. 9th Central American and Caribbean Games, Jamaica.

1039	**295**	1c. ochre and red	15	15
1040	-	2c. ochre and blue	15	15
1041	-	3c. ochre and purple	15	15
1042	-	13c. ochre and green	1·90	80

DESIGNS: Rings and: 2c. Tennis rackets; 3c. Baseball bats; 13c. Rapiers and mask.

296 "Cuban Women"

1962. 1st Cuban Women's Federation National Congress.

1043	**296**	9c. red, green and black	95	30
1044	-	13c. black, blue & green	2·10	70

DESIGN—VERT: 13c. Mother and child, and Globe.

297 Running

1962. 1st Latin-American University Games. Multicoloured.

1045	1c. Type **297**	30	15
1046	2c. Baseball	65	20
1047	3c. Netball	1·00	25
1048	13c. Globe	2·00	55

298 Microscope and Parasites

1962. Malaria Eradication. Mult.

1049	1c. Type **298**	45	25
1050	2c. Mosquito and pool	45	25
1051	3c. Cinchona plant and formulae	1·60	40

299 Cuban Boa

300 Cuban Night Lizard

1962. Christmas. Inscr "NAVIDAD 1962–63". Multicoloured.

(a) Various designs as T 299.

1052	2c. Type **299**	50	20
1053	3c. "Cubispa turquino" (vert)	85	70
1054	10c. Jamacian long-tongued bat	3·25	1·70

(b) Various designs as T 300.

1055a/d	2c. Reptiles	50	20
1056a/d	3c. Insects (vert)	85	70
1057a/d	10c. Mammals	3·25	1·70

DESIGNS: No. 1055a, Type **300**; 1055b, Knight anole; 1055c, Wright's ground boa; 1055d, Cuban ground iguana; 1056a, "Chrysis superba"; 1056b, "Essosthutha roberto"; 1056c, "Hortensia conciliata"; 1056d, "Lachnopus argus"; 1057a, Desmarest's hutia; 1057b, Prehensile-tailed hutia; 1057c, Cuban solenodon; 1057d, Desmarest's hutia (white race).

Prices are for single stamps.

301 Titov and "Vostok 2"

1963. Cosmic Flights (1st issue).

1058	-	1c. blue, red and yellow	30	15
1059	**301**	2c. green, purple & yell	60	25
1060	-	3c. violet, red & yellow	60	20

DESIGNS: 1c. Gagarin and "Vostok 1"; 3c. Nikolaev, Popovich and "Vostoks 3 and 4".

See also Nos. 1133/4.

302 Attackers

1963. 6th Anniv of Attack on Presidential Palace.

1061	**302**	9c. black and red	90	15
1062	-	13c. purple and blue	1·10	40
1063	-	30c. green and red	2·75	90

DESIGNS: 13c. Rodriguez, C. Servia, Machado and Westbrook; 30c. J. Echeverria and M. Mora.

303 Baseball

1963. 4th Pan-American Games, Sao Paulo.

1064	**303**	1c. green	1·00	30
1065	-	13c. red (Boxing)	2·75	55

304 "Mask" Letter Box

1963. Stamp Day.

1066	**304**	3c. black and brown	80	25
1067	-	10c. black and violet	2·00	50

DESIGN: 10c. 19th-century Post Office, Cathedral Place, Havana.

305 Revolutionaries and Statue

1963. Labour Day. Multicoloured.

1068	3c. Type **305**	45	15
1069	13c. Celebrating Labour Day	1·80	85

306 Child

1963. Children's Week.

1070	**306**	3c. brown and blue	50	20
1071	**306**	30c. red and blue	2·50	95

307 Ritual Effigy

1963. 60th Anniv of Montane Anthropological Museum.

1072	**307**	2c. brown and salmon	70	20
1073	-	3c. purple and blue	85	30
1074	-	9c. grey and red	1·60	50

DESIGNS—HORIZ: 3c. Carved chair; VERT: 9c. Statuette.

308 "Breaking chains of old regime"

1963. 10th Anniv of "Rebel Day".

1075	**308**	1c. black and pink	20	15
1076	-	2c. purple and lt blue	20	15
1077	-	3c. sepia and lilac	20	15
1078	-	7c. purple and green	30	15
1079	-	9c. purple and yellow	70	40
1080	-	10c. green and ochre	2·00	60
1081	-	13c. blue and buff	3·00	1·10

DESIGNS: 2c. Palace attack; 3c. "The Insurrection"; 7c. "Strike of April 9th" (defence of radio station); 9c. "Triumph of the Revolution" (upraised flag and weapons); 10c. "Agrarian Reform and Nationalization" (artisan and peasant); 13c. "Victory of Giron" (soldiers in battle).

309 Star Apple

1963. Cuban Fruits. Multicoloured.

1082	1c. Type **309**	20	15
1083	2c. Chiromoya	20	15
1084	3c. Cashew nut	30	20
1085	10c. Custard apple	1·90	60
1086	13c. Mango	2·50	1·90

310 "Roof and Window"

1963. 7th Int Architects Union Congress, Havana.

1087	3c. multicoloured	40	20
1088	3c. multicoloured	40	20
1089	3c. black, blue and bistre	40	20
1090	3c. multicoloured	40	20
1091	13c. multicoloured	1·60	70
1092	13c. multicoloured	1·60	70
1093	13c. red, olive and black	1·60	70
1094	13c. multicoloured	1·60	70

DESIGNS—VERT: No. 1087, Type **310**; Nos. 1090/2, Symbols of building construction as Type **310**. HORIZ: Nos. 1089/90 and 1093, Sketches of urban buildings; No. 1094, as Type **310** (girders and outline of house).

311 Hemingway and Scene from "The Old Man and the Sea"

1963. Ernest Hemingway Commemoration.

1095	**311**	3c. brown and blue	55	15
1096	-	9c. turquoise and mauve	1·40	20
1097	-	13c. black and green	2·40	70

DESIGNS—Hemingway and: 9c. Scene from "For Whom the Bell Tolls"; 13c. Residence at San Francisco de Paula, near Havana.

312 "Zapateo" (dance) after V. P. de Landaluze

1964. 50th Anniv of National Museum.

1098	**312**	2c. multicoloured	15	10
1099	-	3c. multicoloured	65	15
1100	-	9c. multicoloured	90	50
1101	-	13c. black and violet	1·90	85

DESIGNS—VERT: (32×42½ mm.): 3c. "The Rape of the Mulattos" (after C. Enriquez); 9c. Greek amphora; 13c. "Dilecta Mea" (bust, after J. A. Houdon).

313 B. J. Borrell (revolutionary)

1964. 5th Anniv of Revolution.

1102	**313**	2c. black, orange & grn	30	15
1103	-	3c. black, orange & red	55	20
1104	-	10c. black, orange & pur	1·00	40
1105	-	13c. black, orange & bl	2·00	85

PORTRAITS: 3c. M. Salado. 10c. O. Lucero. 13c. S. Gonzalez (revolutionaries).

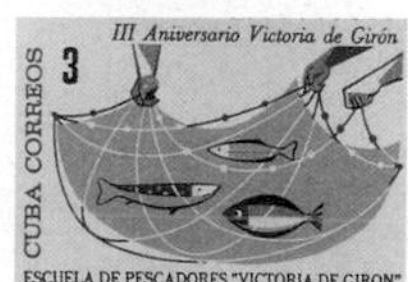

314 Fish in Net

1964. 3rd Anniv of Giron Victory.

1106	**314**	3c. multicoloured	30	15
1107	-	10c. black, grey & bistre	70	40
1108	-	13c. slate, black & orge	2·10	85

DESIGNS—HORIZ: 10c. Victory Monument. VERT: 13c. Fallen eagle.

315 V. M. Pera (1st Director of Military Posts, 1868–71)

1964. Stamp Day.

1109	**315**	3c. blue and brown	40	15
1110	-	13c. green and lilac	2·00	60

DESIGN: 13c. Cuba's first (10c.) military stamp.

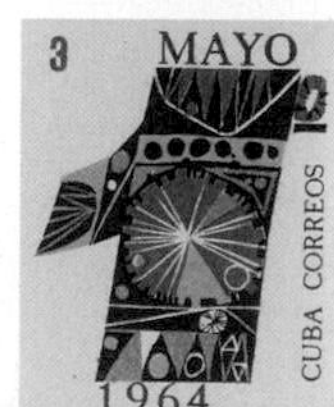

316 Symbolic "1"

1964. Labour Day.

1111	**316**	3c. multicoloured	30	15
1112	-	13c. multicoloured	1·40	70

DESIGN: 13c. As Type **316** but different symbols within "1".

317 Chinese Monument, Havana

1964. Cuban–Chinese Friendship.

1113	**317**	1c. multicoloured	30	15
1114	-	2c. red, olive and black	55	15
1115	-	3c. multicoloured	1·10	20

DESIGNS—HORIZ: 2c. Cuban and Chinese. VERT: 3c. Flags of Cuba and China.

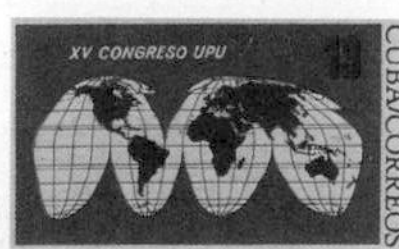

318 Globe

1964. U.P.U. Congress, Vienna.

1116	**318**	13c. brown, green & red	80	30
1117	-	30c. black, bistre & red	1·70	75
1118	-	50c. black, blue and red	3·50	1·20

DESIGNS: 30c. H. von Stephan (founder of U.P.U.); 50c. U.P.U. Monument, Berne.

319 Mutton Snapper

1964. Popular Savings Movement. Mult.

1119	1c. Type **319**	40	15
1120	2c. Cow	60	15
1121	13c. Poultry	2·50	60

320 "Rio Jibacoa"

1964. Cuban Merchant Fleet. Multicoloured.

1122	1c. Type **320**	30	15
1123	2c. "Camilo Cienfuegos"	50	15
1124	3c. "Sierra Maestra"	70	20
1125	9c. "Bahia de Siguanea"	1·70	70
1126	10c. "Oriente"	4·25	1·20

321 Vietnamese Fighter

1964. "Unification of Vietnam" Campaign. Mult.

1127	2c. Type **321**	25	15
1128	3c. Vietnamese shaking hands across map	35	15
1129	10c. Hand and mechanical ploughing	80	20
1130	13c. Vietnamese, Cuban and flags	2·20	60

322 Raul Gomez Garcia and Poem

1964. 11th Anniv of "Rebel Day".

1131	**322**	3c. black, red and ochre	40	15
1132	-	13c. multicoloured	2·40	50

DESIGN: 13c. Inscr "LA HISTORIA ME ABSOLVERA" (Castro's book).

1964. Cosmic Flights (2nd issue). As T 301.

1133	9c. yellow, violet and red	1·20	50
1134	13c. yellow, red and green	3·00	85

DESIGNS: 9c. "Vostok-5" and Bykovksy; 13c. "Vostok-6" and Tereshkova.

323 Start of Race

1964. Olympic Games, Tokyo.

1135	-	1c. yellow, blue and purple	30	15
1136	-	2c. multicoloured	30	15
1137	-	3c. brown, black & red	30	15
1138	**323**	7c. violet, blue and orange	70	20
1139	-	10c. yellow, purple & bl	1·40	70
1140	-	13c. multicoloured	2·75	1·10

DESIGNS—VERT: 1c. Gymnastics; 2c. Rowing; 3c. Boxing. HORIZ: 10c. Fencing; 13c. Games symbols.

325 Satellite and Globe

326 Rocket and part of Globe

1964. Cuban Postal Rocket Experiment. 25th Anniv Various rockets and satellites. (a) Horiz. designs as T 325.

1141	**325**	1c. multicoloured	20	15
1142	-	2c. multicoloured	60	15
1143	-	3c. multicoloured	85	40
1144	-	9c. multicoloured	2·30	85
1145	-	13c. multicoloured	3·00	1·90

(b) Horiz. designs as T 326.

1146a/d	1c. multicoloured	20	15
1147a/d	2c. multicoloured	60	15
1148a/d	3c. multicoloured	85	40
1149a/d	9c. multicoloured	2·30	85
1150a/d	13c. multicoloured	3·00	1·90

(c) Larger 44×28 mm.

1151	50c. green and black	10·50	3·00
MS1152	110×74 mm. As No. 1151 (different)	20·00	20·00

DESIGN: 50c. Cuban Rocket Post 10c. Stamp of 1939.

Nos. 1141 and 1146, 1142 and 1147, 1143 and 1148, 1144 and 1149, 1145 and 1150 were printed together in five sheets of 25, each comprising four stamps as Type **325** plus five se-tenant stamp-size labels inscribed overall "1939 COHETE POSTAL CUBANO 25 ANIVERSARIO 1964" forming a centre cross and four blocks of four different stamps as Type **326** in each corner. The four-stamp design incorporates different subjects, which together form a composite design around a globe.

Prices are for single stamps.

1964. 1st Three-Manned Space Flight. As No. 1151 but colours changed. Optd VOSJOD-1 octubre 12 1964 PRIMERA TRIPULACION DEL ESPACIO and large rocket.

1153	50c. green and brown	4·75	1·80

328 Lenin addressing Meeting

1964. 40th Death Anniv of Lenin.

1154	**328**	3c. black and orange	30	20
1155	-	13c. red and violet	90	35
1156	-	30c. black and blue	1·80	80

DESIGNS—HORIZ: 13c. Lenin mausoleum. VERT: 30c. Lenin and hammer and sickle emblem.

329 Leopard

1964. Havana Zoo Animals. Multicoloured.

1157	1c. Type **329**	30	15
1158	2c. Indian elephant (vert)	30	15
1159	3c. Red deer (vert)	30	15
1160	4c. Eastern grey kangaroo	30	15
1161	5c. Lions	40	15
1162	6c. Eland	35	15
1163	7c. Common zebra	35	15
1164	8c. Striped hyena	65	15
1165	9c. Tiger	65	15
1166	10c. Guanaco	80	15
1167	13c. Chimpanzees	80	15
1168	20c. Collared Peccary	1·10	25
1169	30c. Common racoon (vert)	1·50	55
1170	40c. Hippopotamus	3·00	90
1171	50c. Brazilian tapir	4·00	1·20
1172	60c. Dromedary (vert)	4·50	1·50
1173	70c. American Bison	4·50	1·60

1174	80c. Asiatic black bear (vert)	5·75	1·90
1175	90c. Water buffalo	5·75	2·40
1176	1p. Roe deer at Zoo Entrance	8·25	2·40

330 Jose Marti

1964. "Liberators of Independence". Multicoloured. Each showing portraits and campaigning scenes.

1177	1c. Type **330**	15	15
1178	2c. A. Maceo	35	15
1179	3c. M. Gomez	70	40
1180	13c. C. Garcia	1·90	85

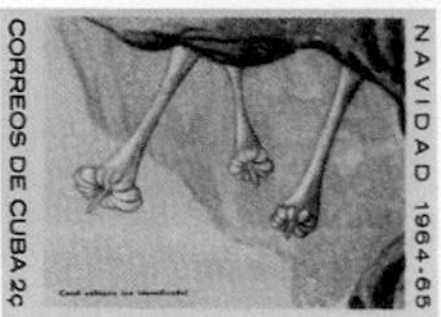

331 Dwarf Cup Coral

332 Small Flower Coral

1964. Christmas. Inscr "NAVIDAD 1964–65". Multicoloured.

(a) As T 331.

1181	2c. Type **331**	65	30
1182	3c. Sea anemone	1·10	60
1183	10c. Stone lily	1·90	1·10

(b) As T 332.

1184a/d	2c. Coral	65	30
1185a/d	3c. Jellyfish	1·10	60
1186a/d	10c. Sea stars and urchins	1·90	1·10

DESIGNS: No. 1184a, Type **332**; 1184b, Elkhorn coral; 1184c, Dense moosehorn coral; 1184d, Yellow brain coral; 1185a, Portuguese man-of-war; 1185b, Moon jellyfish; 1185c, Thimble jellyfish; 1185d, Upside-down jellyfish; 1186a, Big-spined sea-urchin; 1186b, Edible sea urchin; 1186c, Caribbean brittle star; 1186d, Reticulated sea star.

Prices are for single stamps.

333 Dr. Tomas Romay

1964. Birth Bicentenary of Dr. Tomas Romay (scientist).

1187	**333**	1c. black and bistre	40	15
1188	-	2c. sepia and brown	40	15
1189	-	3c. brown and bistre	60	20
1190	-	10c. black and bistre	2·10	50

DESIGNS—VERT: 2c. First vaccination against smallpox. HORIZ: 3c. Dr. Romay and extract from his treatise on the vaccine; 10c. Dr. Romay's statue.

334 Map of Latin America and Part of Declaration

1964. 2nd Declaration of Havana. Mult.

1191	3c. Type **334**	75	50
1192	13c. Map of Cuba and native receiving revolutionary message	2·75	1·60

The two stamps have the declaration superimposed in tiny print across each horiz. row of five stamps, thus requiring strips of five to show the complete declaration.

335 "Maritime Post" (diorama)

1965. Inauguration of Cuban Postal Museum. Mult.

1193	13c. Type **335**	4·25	1·10
1194	30c. "Insurgent Post" (diorama)	3·25	1·80
MS1195	127×76 mm. Two sheets. Nos. 1193/4 but with blue instead of yellow frames. Imperf	9·25	9·25

336 "Sondero" (schooner)

1965. Cuban Fishing Fleet. Multicoloured. Fishing crafts.

1196	1c. Type **336**	15	15
1197	2c. "Omicron"	30	15
1198	3c. "Victoria"	45	15
1199	9c. "Cardenas"	65	30
1200	10c. "Sigma"	3·50	85
1201	13c. "Lambda"	5·75	1·40

337 Lydia Doce

1965. International Women's Day. Multicoloured.

1202	3c. Type **337**	1·00	40
1203	13c. Clara Zetkin	1·60	85

338 Jose Antonio Echeverria University City

1965. "Technical Revolution". Inscr "REVOLUCION TECNICA".

1204	**338**	3c. black, brown and chestnut	90	25
1205	-	13c. multicoloured	4·50	70

DESIGN: 13c. Scientific symbols.

339 Leonov

1965. "Voskhod 2", Space flight.

1206	**339**	30c. brown and blue	2·50	95
1207	-	50c. blue and magenta	4·75	1·90

DESIGN: 50c. Beliaiev, Leonov and "Voskhod 2".

340 "Figure" (after E. Rodrigues)

1965. National Museum Treasures. Mult.

1208	2c. Type **340** (27×42 mm)	30	15
1209	3c. "Landscape with sunflowers" (V. Manuel) (31×42 mm)	50	20
1210	10c. "Abstract" (W. Lam) (42×31 mm)	1·30	50
1211	13c. "Children" (E. Ponce) (39×33½ mm)	2·30	95

341 Lincoln Statue, Washington

1965. Death Centenary of Abraham Lincoln.

1212	-	1c. brown, grey and yellow	15	15
1213	-	2c. ultramarine & blue	30	15
1214	**341**	3c. black, red and blue	95	40
1215	-	13c. black, orange & bl	2·10	70

DESIGNS—HORIZ: 1c. Cabin at Hodgenville, Kentucky (Lincoln's birthplace); 2c. Lincoln Monument, Washington. VERT: 13c. Abraham Lincoln.

342 18th-century Mail Ship and Old Postmarks (bicent of Maritime Mail)

1965. Stamp Day.

1216	**342**	3c. bistre and red	2·50	25
1217	-	13c. red, black and blue	2·50	70

DESIGN: 13c. Cuban; 10c. "Air Train" stamp of 1935 and glider train over Capitol, Havana.

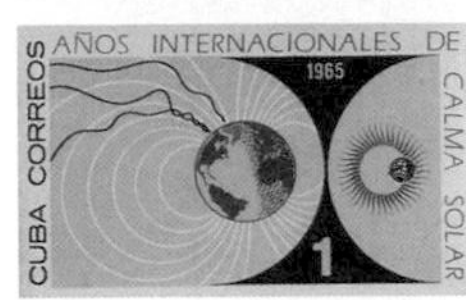

343 Sun and Earth's Magnetic Pole

1965. International Quiet Sun Year. Multicoloured.

1218	1c. Type **343**	30	15
1219	2c. I.Q.S.Y. emblem (vert)	30	15
1220	3c. Earth's magnetic fields	60	15
1221	6c. Solar rays	70	20
1222	30c. Effect of solar rays on various atmospheric layers	2·50	70
1223	50c. Effect of solar rays on satellite orbits	3·25	1·70
MS1224	94×70 mm. No. 1223. Imperf	7·75	7·75

Nos. 1221/3 are larger, 47×20 mm. or 20×47 mm. (30c.).

344 Telecommunications Station

1965. Centenary of I.T.U. Multicoloured.

1225	1c. Type **344**	15	10
1226	2c. Satellite (vert)	15	10
1227	3c. "Telstar"	30	10
1228	10c. "Telstar" and receiving station (vert)	1·10	25
1229	30c. I.T.U. emblem	3·00	1·10

345 Festival Emblem and Flags

1965. World Youth and Students Festival. Multicoloured.

1230	13c. Type **345**	1·40	40
1231	30c. Soldiers of three races and flags	2·75	70

346 M. Perez (pioneer balloonist), Balloon and Satellite

1965. Matias Perez Commemoration.

1232	**346**	3c. black and red	1·80	1·20
1233	-	13c. black and blue	2·75	1·20

DESIGN: 13c. As Type **346**, but with rockets in place of satellite.

347 Rose (Europe)

1965. Flowers of the World. Multicoloured.

1234	1c. Type **347**	15	10
1235	2c. Chrysanthemum (Asia)	30	10
1236	3c. Strelitzia (Africa)	30	10
1237	4c. Dahlia (N. America)	30	10
1238	5c. Orchid (S. America)	1·40	30
1239	13c. "Grevillea banksii" (Oceania)	3·00	1·20
1240	30c. "Brunfelsia nitida" (Cuba)	4·25	2·10

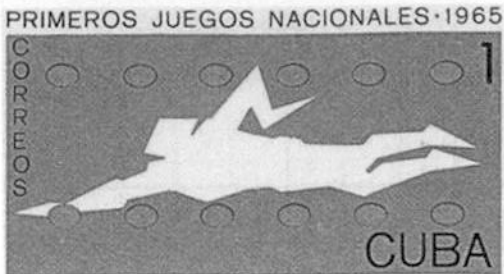

348 Swimming

1965. First National Games.

1241	**348**	1c. multicoloured	20	10
1242	-	2c. multicoloured	30	10
1243	-	3c. black, red and grey	70	30
1244	-	30c. black, red and grey	2·50	95

SPORTS: 2c. Basketball. 3c. Gymnastics. 30c. Hurdling.

349 Anti-tank gun

1965. Museum of the Revolution. Mult.

1245	1c. Type **349**	15	10
1246	2c. Tank	15	10
1247	3c. Bazooka	30	10
1248	10c. Rebel Uniform	95	30
1249	13c. Launch "Granma" and compass	2·75	60

350 C. J. Finlay

1965. 50th Death Anniv of Carlos J. Finlay (malaria researcher).

1250	-	1c. black, green & blue	15	10
1251	-	2c. brown, ochre and black	15	10
1252	**350**	3c. brown and black	30	15
1253	-	7c. black and lilac	40	15
1254	-	9c. bronze and black	70	30
1255	-	10c. black and blue	1·80	40
1256	-	13c. multicoloured	2·75	85

DESIGNS—HORIZ: 1c. Finlay's signature. VERT: 2c. Yellow fever mosquito; 7c. Finlay's microscope; 9c. Dr. C. Delgado; 10c. Finlay's monument; 13c. Finlay demonstrating his theories, after painting by Valderrama.

351 "Anetia numidia" (butterfly)

1965. Cuban Butterflies. Multicoloured.

1257	2c. Type **351**	30	10
1258	2c. "Carathis gortynoides"	30	10
1259	2c. "Hymenitis cubana"	30	10
1260	2c. "Eubaphe heros"	30	10
1261	2c. "Dismorphia cubana"	30	10

1262	3c. "Siderone nemesis"	35	15
1263	3c. "Syntomidopsis variegata"	35	15
1264	3c. "Ctenuchidia virgo"	35	15
1265	3c. "Lycorea ceres"	35	15
1266	3c. "Eubaphe disparilis"	35	15
1267	13c. "Anetia cubana"	1·80	75
1268	13c. "Prepona antimache"	1·80	75
1269	13c. "Sylepta reginalis"	1·80	75
1270	13c. "Chlosyne perezi"	1·80	75
1271	13c. "Anaea clytemnestra"	1·80	75

1965. "Conquest of Space" Philatelic Exhibition, Havana. Sheet 94×65 mm containing stamp as No. 1223 but inscr "EXHIBICION FILATELICA CONQUISTA DEL ESPACIO".

MS1272	50c. multicoloured	14·50	14·50

352 20c. Coin of 1962

1965. 50th Anniv of Cuban Coinage. Mult.

1273	1c. Type **352**	25	10
1274	2c. 1p. coin of 1934	25	10
1275	3c. 40c. coin of 1962	25	15
1276	8c. 1p. coin of 1915	65	25
1277	10c. 1p. coin of 1953	1·50	50
1278	13c. 20p. coin of 1915	2·20	60

353 Oranges

1965. Tropical Fruits. Multicoloured.

1279	1c. Type **353**	20	10
1280	2c. Custard-apples	20	10
1281	3c. Papayas	20	20
1282	4c. Bananas	30	10
1283	10c. Avocado pears	50	15
1284	13c. Pineapples	85	70
1285	20c. Guavas	2·20	70
1286	50c. Mameys	4·50	1·20

354 Northern Oriole **355** Painted Bunting

1965. Christmas. Vert. designs showing bird life. (a) As T 354. Multicoloured.

1287	3c. Type **354**	2·10	1·80
1288	5c. Scarlet tanager	2·30	2·30
1289	13c. Indigo bunting	5·25	4·25

(b) As T 355.

1290a/d	3c. multicoloured	2·10	1·80
1291a/d	5c. multicoloured	2·30	2·30
1292a/d	13c. multicoloured	5·25	4·25

DESIGNS: No. 1290a, Type **355**; 1290b, American redstart; 1290c, Blackburnian warbler; 1290d, Rose-breasted grosbeak; 1291a, Yellow-throated warbler; 1291b, Blue-winged warbler; 1291c, Prothonotary warbler; 1291d, Hooded warbler; 1292a, Blue-winged teal; 1292b, Wood duck; 1292c, Common shoveler; 1292d, Black-crowned night heron.

Prices are for single stamps.

356 Hurdling

1965. 7th Anniv of International Athletics, Havana. Multicoloured.

1293	1c. Type **356**	15	10
1294	2c. Throwing the discus	25	10
1295	3c. Putting the shot	60	15
1296	7c. Throwing the javelin	60	30
1297	9c. High-jumping	85	40
1298	10c. Throwing the hammer	1·70	70
1299	13c. Running	2·30	1·00

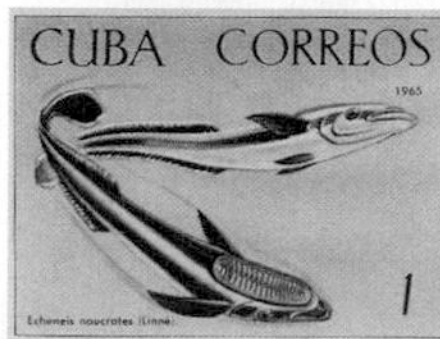

357 Shark-sucker

1965. National Aquarium. Multicoloured.

1300	1c. Type **357**	25	10
1301	2c. Skipjack/Bonito tuna	25	10
1302	3c. Sergeant major	60	10
1303	4c. Sailfish	70	15
1304	5c. Nassau grouper	70	25
1305	10c. Mutton snapper	1·00	40
1306	13c. Yellow-tailed snapper	3·75	1·00
1307	30c. Squirrelfish	5·75	1·70

358 A. Voisin, Cuban and French Flags

1965. 1st Death Anniv of Prof. Andre Voisin (scientist).

1308	**358** 3c. multicoloured	85	30
1309	- 13c. multicoloured	2·10	60

DESIGN: 13c. Similar to Type **358** but with microscope and plant in place of cattle.

359 Skoda Omnibus

1965. Cuban Transport. Multicoloured.

1310	1c. Type **359**	15	10
1311	2c. Ikarus omnibus	15	10
1312	3c. Leyland omnibus	25	10
1313	4c. Russian-built Type TEM-4 diesel locomotive	3·00	55
1314	7c. French-built BB. 69,000 diesel locomotive	3·00	60
1315	10c. Tug "R.D.A."	1·80	40
1316	13c. Freighter "13 de Marzo"	2·75	70
1317	20c. Ilyushin IL-18 airliner	3·00	1·10

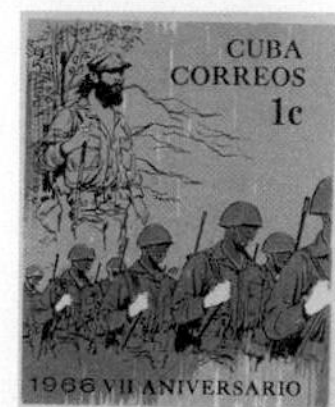

360 Infantry Column

1966. 7th Anniv of Revolution. Mult.

1318	1c. Type **360**	25	10
1319	2c. Soldier and tank	20	10
1320	3c. Sailor and torpedo-boat	85	10
1321	10c. MiG-21 jet fighter	1·80	50
1322	13c. Rocket missile	2·30	85

SIZES—As Type **360**: 2c., 3c. HORIZ: (38½×23½ mm): 10c., 13c.

361 Conference Emblem

1966. Tricontinental Conference, Havana.

1323	**361** 2c. multicoloured	15	10
1324	- 3c. multicoloured	30	15
1325	- 13c. multicoloured	1·70	60

DESIGNS: 3c., 13c. As Type **361** but re-arranged.

362 Guardalabarca Beach

1966. Tourism. Multicoloured.

1326	1c. Type **362**	25	10
1327	2c. La Gran Piedra (mountain resort)	25	15
1328	3c. Guama, Las Villas (country scene)	75	25
1329	13c. Waterfall, Soroa (vert)	3·25	70

363 Congress Emblem and "Treating Patient" (old engraving)

1966. Medical and Stomachal Congresses, Havana. Multicoloured.

1330	3c. Type **363**	55	10
1331	13c. Congress emblem and children receiving treatment	2·75	60

364 Afro-Cuban Doll

1966. Cuban Handicrafts. Multicoloured.

1332	1c. Type **364**	15	10
1333	2c. Sombreros	15	10
1334	3c. Vase	20	10
1335	7c. Gourd lampshades	20	15
1336	9c. Rare-wood lampstand	65	25
1337	10c. "Horn" shark (horiz)	1·00	40
1338	13c. Painted polymita shell necklace and earrings (horiz)	2·00	85

365 "Chelsea College" (after Canaletto)

1966. National Museum Exhibits. Inscr "1966". Multicoloured.

1339	1c. Ming Dynasty vase (vert)	15	10
1340	2c. Type **365**	70	10
1341	3c. "Portrait of a Young Girl" (after Goya) (vert)	60	30
1342	13c. Portrait of Fayum (vert)	2·50	85

366 Cosmonauts in Training

1966. 5th Anniv of 1st Manned Space Flight. Multicoloured.

1343	1c. Tsiolkovsky and diagram (horiz)	15	10
1344	2c. Type **366**	15	10
1345	3c. Gagarin, rocket and globe (horiz)	30	10
1346	7c. Nikolaev and Popovich	50	15
1347	9c. Tereshkova and Bykovsky (horiz)	70	30
1348	10c. Komarov, Feoktistov and Yegorov (horiz)	95	40
1349	13c. Leonov in space (horiz)	1·90	70

367 Tank in Battle

1966. 5th Anniv of Giron Victory.

1350	**367** 2c. black, green and bistre	15	10
1351	- 3c. black, blue and red	70	10
1352	- 9c. black, brown & grey	30	15
1353	- 10c. black, blue and green	1·40	15
1354	- 13c. black, brown and blue	2·40	85

DESIGNS: 3c. "Houston" (freighter) sinking; 9c. Disabled tank and poster-hoarding; 10c. Young soldier; 13c. Operations map.

368 Interior of Postal Museum (1st Anniv)

1966. Stamp Day.

1355	**368** 3c. green and red	1·00	10
1356	- 13c. brown, black & red	2·75	80

DESIGN: 13c. Stamp collector and Cuban 2c. stamp of 1959.

369 Bouquet and Anvil

1966. Labour Day. Multicoloured.

1357	2c. Type **369**	15	10
1358	3c. Bouquet and Machete	30	10
1359	10c. Bouquet and Hammer	70	30
1360	13c. Bouquet and parts of globe and cogwheel	1·90	1·00

370 W.H.O. Building

1966. Inaug of W.H.O. Headquarters, Geneva.

1361	**370** 2c. black, green & yell	15	10
1362	- 3c. black, blue and yellow	60	15
1363	- 13c. black, yellow and blue	2·00	70

DESIGNS (W.H.O. Building on): 3c. Flag; 13c. Emblem.

371 Athletics

1966. 10th Central American and Caribbean Games.

No.	Type	Description	Mint	Used
1364	371	1c. sepia and green	15	10
1365	-	2c. sepia and orange	25	10
1366	-	3c. brown and yellow	35	10
1367	-	7c. blue and mauve	35	15
1368	-	9c. black and blue	65	25
1369	-	10c. black and brown	1·10	25
1370	-	13c. blue and red	2·75	70

DESIGNS—HORIZ: 2c. Rifle-shooting. VERT: 3c. Baseball; 7c. Volleyball; 9c. Football; 10c. Boxing; 13c. Basketball.

372 Makarenko Pedagogical Institute

1966. Educational Development.

No.	Type	Description	Mint	Used
1371	372	1c. black and green	15	10
1372	-	2c. black, ochre & yellow	15	10
1373	-	3c. black, ultram & bl	25	10
1374	-	10c. black, brown & grn	75	25
1375	-	13c. multicoloured	1·90	60

DESIGNS: 2c. Alphabetization Museum; 3c. Lamp (5th anniv of National Alphabetization Campaign); 10c. Open-air class; 13c. "Farmers' and Workers' Education".

373 "Agrarian Reform"

1966. Air. "Conquests of the Revolution". Multicoloured.

No.	Description	Mint	Used
1376	1c. Type **373**	15	10
1377	2c. "Industrialisation"	15	10
1378	3c. "Urban Reform"	40	15
1379	7c. "Eradication of Unemployment"	40	15
1380	9c. "Education"	75	30
1381	10c. "Public Health"	1·70	30
1382	13c. Paragraph from Castro's book, "La Historia me Absolvera"	2·20	50

374 Workers with Flag

1966. 12th Revolutionary Workers' Union Congress, Havana.

No.	Type	Description	Mint	Used
1383	374	3c. multicoloured	1·00	30

375 Flamed Cuban Liguus

1966. Cuban Shells. Multicoloured.

No.	Description	Mint	Used
1384	1c. Type **375**	30	10
1385	2c. Measled cowrie	40	15
1386	3c. West Indian fighting conch	60	25
1387	7c. Rough American scallops	70	30
1388	9c. Crenate liguus	85	30
1389	10c. Atlantic trumpet triton	1·60	50
1390	13c. Archer's Cuban liguus	3·25	1·00

376 Pigeon and Breeding Pen

1966. Pigeon-breeding. Multicoloured.

No.	Description	Mint	Used
1391	1c. Type **376**	40	15
1392	2c. Pigeon and time-clock	40	15
1393	3c. Pigeon and pigeon-loft	40	25
1394	7c. Pigeon and breeder tending pigeon-loft	85	30
1395	9c. Pigeon and pigeon-yard	85	40
1396	10c. Pigeon and breeder placing message in capsule	2·50	60
1397	13c. Pigeons in flight over map of Cuba (44½×28 mm)	4·00	1·00

377 Arms of Pinar del Rio

1966. National and Provincial Arms. Mult.

No.	Description	Mint	Used
1398	1c. Type **377**	15	10
1399	2c. Arms of Havana	25	10
1400	3c. Arms of Matanzas	25	15
1401	4c. Arms of Las Villas	30	15
1402	5c. Arms of Camaguey	60	25
1403	9c. Arms of Oriente	1·00	50
1404	13c. National Arms (26×44 mm)	2·30	60

378 "Queen" and Simultaneous Games

379 Emblem and Chessboard (Capablanca—Lasker game, 1914)

1966. 17th Chess Olympiad, Havana.

No.	Type	Description	Mint	Used
1405	-	1c. black and green	25	10
1406	-	2c. black and blue	25	10
1407	-	3c. black and red	40	15
1408	-	9c. black and ochre	80	30
1409	378	10c. black and mauve	1·90	30
1410	-	13c. black, blue & turq	2·75	85

MS1411 77×61 mm. **379** 30c. black, blue and yellow. Imperf — 12·00 12·00

DESIGNS—VERT: 1c. "Pawn"; 2c. "Rook"; 3c. "Knight"; 9c. "Bishop". HORIZ: 13c. Olympiad Emblem and "King".

380 Lenin Hospital

1966. Cuban–Soviet Friendship. Mult.

No.	Description	Mint	Used
1412	2c. Type **380**	15	10
1413	3c. World map and "Havana" (tanker)	30	10
1414	10c. Cuban and Soviet technicians	1·00	30
1415	13c. Cuban fruit-pickers and Soviet tractor technicians	2·00	95

381 A. Roldan and Music of "Fiesta Negra"

1966. Song Festival.

No.	Type	Description	Mint	Used
1416	381	1c. brown, black & grn	15	10
1417	-	2c. brown, black & mve	25	10
1418	-	3c. brown, black & blue	25	10
1419	-	7c. brown, black & vio	65	15
1420	-	9c. brown, black & yell	65	25
1421	-	10c. brn, blk & orge	2·40	50
1422	-	13c. brown, black & bl	3·25	1·00

CUBAN COMPOSERS AND WORKS: 2c. E. S. de Fuentes and "Tu" (habanera, Cuban dance). 3c. M. Simons and "El Manisero". 7c. J. Ackermann and "El arroyo que murmura". 9c. A. G. Caturla and "Pastoral Lullaby". 10c. E. Grenet and "Ay Mama Ines". 13c. E. Lecuona and "La Comparsa" (dance).

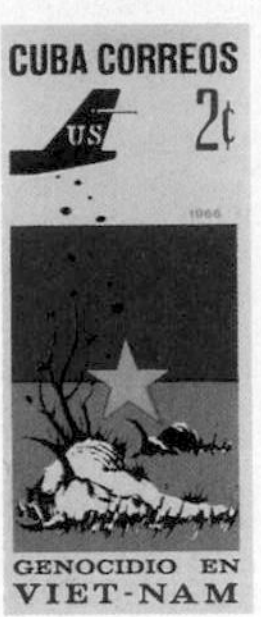

382 Bacteriological Warfare

1966. "Genocide in Viet-Nam". Mult.

No.	Description	Mint	Used
1423	2c. Type **382**	30	10
1424	3c. Gas warfare	50	15
1425	13c. "Conventional" bombing	2·75	70

383 A. L. Fernandez ("Nico") and Beach Landing

1966. 10th Anniv of 1956 Revolutionary Successes. Portrait in black and brown.

No.	Type	Description	Mint	Used
1426	383	1c. brown and green	15	10
1427	-	2c. brown and purple	15	10
1428	-	3c. brown and purple	15	10
1429	-	7c. brown and blue	25	15
1430	-	9c. brown and turquoise	60	15
1431	-	10c. brown and olive	2·10	60
1432	-	13c. brown and orange	2·00	95

HEROES AND SCENES: 2c. C. Gonzalez and beach landing. 3c. J. Tey and street fighting. 7c. T. Aloma and street fighting. 9c. O. Parellada and street fighting. 10c. J. M. Marquez and beach landing. 13c. F. Pais and trial scene.

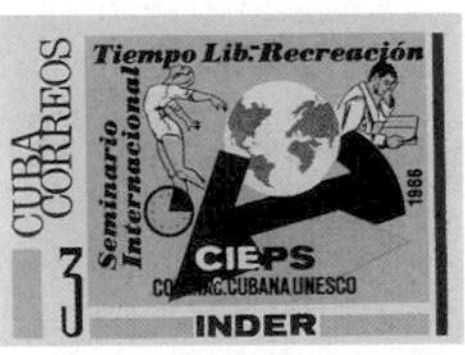

384 Globe and Recreational Activities

1966. International Leisure Time and Recreation Seminar. Multicoloured.

No.	Description	Mint	Used
1433	3c. Type **384**	15	10
1434	9c. Clock, eye and world map	1·40	30
1435	13c. Seminar poster	1·90	70

385 Arrow and Telecommunications Symbols

1966. 1st National Telecommunications Forum. Multicoloured.

No.	Description	Mint	Used
1436	3c. Type **385**	60	10
1437	10c. Target and satellites	3·00	30
1438	13c. Shell and satellites (28½×36 mm)	4·50	85

MS1439 161×116 mm. Nos. 1436/8 (sold at 30c.) — 12·00 12·00

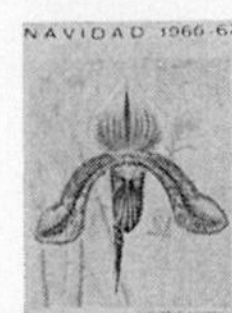

386 "Cypripedium eurilochus"

387 "Cattleya speciosissima"

1966. Christmas. Orchids. Multicoloured. (a) As T 386.

No.	Description	Mint	Used
1440	1c. Type **386**	75	15
1441	3c. "Cypripedium hookerae volunteanum"	1·10	40
1442	13c. "Cypripedium stonei"	4·00	1·60

(b) As T 387.

No.	Description	Mint	Used
1443a/d	1c. multicoloured	75	15
1444a/d	3c. multicoloured	1·10	40
1445a/d	13c. multicoloured	4·00	1·60

DESIGNS: No. 1443a, Type **387**; 1443b, "Cattleya mendelli"; 1443c, "Cattleya trianae"; 1443d, "Cattleya labiata"; 1444a, "Cypripedium morganiae"; 1444b, "Cattleya" "Countess of Derby"; 1444c, "Cattleya gigas"; 1444d, "Cypripedium stonei"; 1445a, "Cattleya mendelli" "Countess of Montrose"; 1445b, "Oncidium macranthum"; 1445c, "Cattleya aurea"; 1445d, "Laelia anceps".

Prices are for single stamps.

388 Flag and Hands ("1959—Liberation")

1966. 8th Anniv of Revolution. Mult.

No.	Description	Mint	Used
1446	3c. Type **388**	25	10
1447	3c. Clenched fist ("1960—Agrarian Reform")	25	10
1448	3c. Hands holding pencil ("1961—Education")	25	10
1449	3c. Hand protecting plant ("1965—Agriculture")	25	10
1450	13c. Head of Rodin's statue, "The Thinker", and arrows ("1962—Planning") (vert)	1·50	50
1451	13c. Hands moving lever ("1963—Organization") (vert)	1·50	50
1452	13c. Hand holding plant within cogwheel ("1964—Economy") (vert)	1·50	50
1453	13c. Hand holding rifle-butt, and part of globe ("1966—Solidarity") (vert)	1·50	50

389 "Spring" (after J. Arche)

1967. National Museum Exhibits. Paintings (1st series). Multicoloured.

No.	Description	Mint	Used
1454	1c. "Coffee-pot" (A. A. Leon) (vert)	30	10
1455	2c. "Peasants" (E. Abela) (vert)	50	15
1456	3c. Type **389**	70	25
1457	13c. "Still Life" (Amelia Pelaez) (vert)	2·10	1·00
1458	30c. "Landscape" (G. Escalante)	5·75	2·10

See also Nos. 1648/54, 1785/91, 1871/7, 1900/6, 2005/11, 2048/54, 2104/9, 2180/5, 2260/5, 2346/51, 2430/5, 2530/5, 2620/5, 2685/90, 2816/21, 3218/23 and 3229/34.

390 Menelao Mora, Jose A. Echeverria and Attack on Presidential Palace

1967. National Events of 13 March 1957.

No.	Type	Description	Mint	Used
1459	390	3c. green and black	15	10
1460	-	13c. brown and black	2·50	85
1461	-	30c. blue and black	2·30	95

DESIGNS (36½×24½ mm.): 13c. Calixto Sanchez and "Corynthia" landing; 30c. Dionisio San Roman and Cienfuegos revolt.

391 "Homo habilis"

1967. "Prehistoric Man". Multicoloured.

1462	1c. Type **391**	30	10
1463	2c. "Australopithecus"	50	10
1464	3c. "Pithecanthropus erectus"	50	15
1465	4c. Peking man	70	25
1466	5c. Neanderthal man	1·00	30
1467	13c. Cro-Magnon man carving ivory tusk	3·50	70
1468	20c. Cro-Magnon man painting on wall of cave	7·25	1·10

392 Victoria

1967. Stamp Day. Carriages. Multicoloured.

1469	3c. Type **392**	30	20
1470	9c. Volanta	1·70	50
1471	13c. Quitrin	2·50	95

393 Cuban Pavilion

1967. "Expo 67", Montreal.

1472	**393**	1c. multicoloured	30	10
1473	-	2c. multicoloured	30	10
1474	-	3c. multicoloured	45	15
1475	-	13c. multicoloured	2·40	95
1476	-	20c. multicoloured	2·75	1·00

DESIGNS: 2c. Bathysphere, satellite and met. balloon ("Man as Explorer"); 3c. Ancient rock-drawing and tablet ("Man as Creator"); 13c. Tractor, ear of wheat and electronic console ("Man as Producer"); 20c. Olympic athletes ("Man in the Community").

394 "Eugenia malaccencis"

1967. 150th Anniv of Cuban Botanical Gardens. Multicoloured.

1477	1c. Type **394**	15	10
1478	2c. "Jacaranda filicifolia"	15	10
1479	3c. "Coroupita guianensis"	35	10
1480	4c. "Spathodea campanulata"	35	15
1481	5c. "Cassia fistula"	75	25
1482	13c. "Plumieria alba"	2·20	70
1483	20c. "Erythrina poeppigiana"	3·75	85

395 "Giselle"

1967. Int Ballet Festival, Havana. Mult.

1484	1c. Type **395**	30	10
1485	2c. "Swan Lake"	30	10
1486	3c. "Don Quixote"	40	15
1487	4c. "Calaucan"	2·20	55
1488	13c. "Swan Lake" (different)	3·25	1·00
1489	20c. "Nutcracker"	3·75	1·40

396 Baseball

1967. 5th Pan-American Games, Winnipeg. Mult.

1490	1c. Type **396**	15	10
1491	2c. Swimming	30	10
1492	3c. Basketball (vert)	40	10
1493	4c. Gymnastics (vert)	70	15
1494	5c. Water-polo (vert)	80	25
1495	13c. Weight-lifting	2·40	50
1496	20c. Hurling the javelin	3·75	95

397 L. A. Turcios Lima, Map and OLAS Emblem

1967. 1st Conference of Latin-American Solidarity Organization (OLAS), Havana.

1497	13c. black, red and blue	1·60	60
1498	13c. black, red and brown	1·60	60
1499	13c. black, red and lilac	1·60	60
1500	13c. black, red and green	1·60	60

DESIGNS: No. 1497, Type **397**; No. 1498, Fabricio Ojidia; No. 1499, L. de La Puente Uceda; No. 1500, Camilo Torres; Martyrs of Guatemala, Venezuela, Peru and Colombia respectively. Each with map and OLAS emblem.

398 "Portrait of Sonny Rollins" (Alan Davie)

1967. "Contemporary Art" (Havana Exn from the Paris "Salon de Mayo"). Various designs showing modern paintings. Sizes given in millimetres. Multicoloured.

1501	1c. Type **398**	25	10
1502	1c. "Twelve Selenites" (F. Labisse) (39×41)	25	10
1503	1c. "Night of the Drinker" (F. Hundertwasser) (53×41)	25	10
1504	1c. "Figure" (Mariano) (48×41)	25	10
1505	1c. "All-Souls" (W. Lam) (45×41)	25	10
1506	2c. "Darkness and Cracks" (A. Tapies) (37×54)	50	15
1507	2c. "Bathers" (G. Singier) (37×54)	50	15
1508	2c. "Torso of a Muse" (J. Arp) (37×46)	50	15
1509	2c. "Figure" (M. W. Svanberg) (57×54)	50	15
1510	2c. "Oppenheimer's Information" (Erro) (37×41)	50	15
1511	3c. "Where Cardinals are Born" (Max Ernst) (37×52)	1·20	25
1512	3c. "Havana Landscape" (Portocarrero) (37×41)	1·20	25
1513	3c. "EG 12" (V. Vasarely) (37×42)	1·20	25
1514	3c. "Frisco" (A. Calder) (37×50)	1·20	25
1515	3c. "The Man with the Pipe" (Picasso) (37×52)	1·20	25
1516	4c. "Abstract Composition" (S. Poliakoff) (36×50)	1·40	65
1517	4c. "Painting" (Bram van Velde) (36×68)	1·40	65
1518	4c. "Sower of Fires" (detail, Matta) (36×47)	1·40	65
1519	4c. "The Art of Living" (R. Magritte) (36×50)	1·40	65
1520	4c. "Poem" (J. Miro) (36×56)	1·40	65
1521	13c. "Young Tigers" (J. Messagier) (50×33)	3·75	2·20
1522	13c. "Painting" (Vieira da Silva) (50×36)	3·75	2·20
1523	13c. "Live Cobra" (P. Alechinsky) (50×35)	3·75	2·20
1524	13c. "Stalingrad" (detail, A. Jorn) (50×46)	3·75	2·20
1525	30c. "Warriors" (E. Pignon) (55×32)	14·00	9·00
MS1526	128×90 mm. 50c. "Cloister" (mural representing the "Salon de Mayo" pictures). Imperf	10·00	10·00

399 Common Octopus

1967. World Underwater Fishing Championships. Multicoloured.

1527	1c. Green moray	15	10
1528	2c. Type **399**	15	10
1529	3c. Great barracuda	15	10
1530	4c. Bull shark	60	15
1531	5c. Spotted Jewfish	1·30	30
1532	13c. Chupare stingray	2·75	95
1533	20c. Green turtle	5·25	1·10

400 "Sputnik 1"

1967. Soviet Space Achievements. Mult.

1534	1c. Type **400**	15	10
1535	2c. "Lunik 3"	15	10
1536	3c. "Venusik"	15	10
1537	4c. "Cosmos"	30	10
1538	5c. "Mars 1"	50	15
1539	9c. "Electron 1, 2"	60	30
1540	10c. "Luna 9"	95	60
1541	13c. "Luna 10"	2·10	85
MS1542	164×132 mm. Nos. 1534/1. Imperf	13·00	13·00

401 "Storming the Winter Palace" (from painting by Sokolov, Skalia and Miasnikova) (image scaled to 72% of original size)

1967. 50th Anniv of October Revolution. Paintings. Multicoloured.

1543	1c. Type **401**	15	10
1544	2c. "Lenin addressing 2nd Soviet Congress" (Serov) (48×36)	15	10
1545	3c. "Lenin in the year 1919" (Nalbandian) (35×37)	35	15
1546	4c. "Lenin explaining the GOELRO Map" (Schmatko) (48×36)	35	25
1547	5c. "Dawn of the Five-Year Plan" construction work (Romas) (50×36)	3·00	45
1548	13c. "Kusnetzkroi steel Furnace No. 1" (Kotov) (36×51)	2·40	70
1549	30c. "Victory Jubilation" (Krivonogov) (50×36)	3·25	1·10

402 Royal Force Castle, Havana

1967. Historic Cuban Buildings. Multicoloured.

1550	1c. Type **402**	15	10
1551	2c. Iznaga Tower, Trinidad (26½×47½)	15	10
1552	3c. Castle of Our Lady of the Angels, Cienfuegos (41½×29)	55	10
1553	4c. Church of St. Francis of Paula, Havana (41½×29)	55	10
1554	13c. Convent of St. Francis, Havana (39×13)	2·75	60
1555	30c. Morro Castle, Santiago de Cuba (43×26)	4·00	1·10

403 Ostrich

404 Golden Pheasant

1967. Christmas. Birds of Havana Zoo. Mult. (a) As T 403.

1556	1c. Type **403**	1·40	70
1557	3c. Hyacinth macaw	1·90	1·10
1558	13c. Greater flamingoes	3·75	2·10

(b) As T 404.

1559a/d	1c. multicoloured	1·40	70
1560a/d	3c. multicoloured	1·90	1·10
1561a/d	13c. multicoloured	3·75	2·10

DESIGNS: No. 1559a, Type **404**; 1559b, White stork; 1559c, Crowned crane; 1559d, Emu; 1560a, Grey parrot; 1560b, Chattering lory; 1560c, Keel-billed toucan; 1560d, Sulphur-crested cockatoo; 1561a, American white pelican, 1561b, Egyptian goose; 1561c, Mandarin; 1561d, Black swan.

Prices are for single stamps.

405 "Che" Guevara

1968. Major Ernesto "Che" Guevara Commem.

1562	**405**	13c. black and red	3·50	60

406 Man and Tree ("Problems of Artistic Creation, Scientific and Technical Work")

1968. Cultural Congress, Havana. Mult.

1563	3c. Chainbreaker cradling flame ("Culture and Independence") (vert)	15	10
1564	3c. Hand with spanner and rifle ("Integral Formation of Man") (vert)	15	10
1565	13c. Demographic emblems ("Intellectual Responsibility") (vert)	1·40	50
1566	13c. Hand with communications emblems ("Culture and Mass-Communications Media") (vert)	1·70	60
1567	30c. Type **406**	2·30	1·10

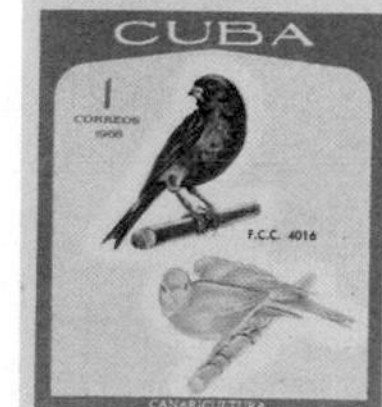

407 Canaries

1968. Canary-breeding.

1568	**407**	1c. multicoloured	15	10
1569	-	2c. multicoloured	15	10
1570	-	3c. multicoloured	30	20
1571	-	4c. multicoloured	30	25
1572	-	5c. multicoloured	60	30
1573	-	13c. multicoloured	3·25	70
1574	-	20c. multicoloured	4·50	95

DESIGNS: Canaries and breeding cycle—mating, eggs, incubation and rearing young.

408 "The Village Postman" (after J. Harris)

1968. Stamp Day. Multicoloured.

1575		13c. Type **408**	2·10	60
1576		30c. "The Philatelist" (after G. Sciltian)	3·00	95

409 Nurse tending Child ("Anti-Polio Campaign")

1968. 20th Anniv of W.H.O.

1577	**409**	13c. black, red and olive	2·10	70
1578	-	30c. black, blue & olive	2·75	1·00

DESIGN: 30c. Two doctors ("Hospital Services").

410 "Children"

1968. International Children's Day.

1579	**410**	3c. multicoloured	1·00	30

411 "Cuatro Vientos" and Route Map

1968. 35th Anniv of Seville–Camaguey Flight by Barberan and Collar. Multicoloured.

1580		13c. Type **411**	2·10	50
1581		30c. Captain M. Barberan and Lieut. J. Collar	2·75	70

412 "Canned Fish"

1968. Cuban Food Products. Multicoloured.

1582		1c. Type **412**	20	15
1583		2c. "Milk Products"	25	15
1584		3c. "Poultry and Eggs"	40	30
1585		13c. "Cuban Rum"	2·50	60
1586		20c. "Canned Shell-fish"	3·00	95

413 Siboney Farmhouse

1968. 15th Anniv of Attack on Moncada Barracks. Multicoloured.

1587		3c. Type **413**	15	10
1588		13c. Map of Santiago de Cuba and assault route	1·90	70
1589		30c. Students and school buildings (on site of Moncada Barracks)	3·00	1·00

414 Committee Members and Emblem

1968. 8th Anniv of Revolutionary Defence Committee.

1590	**414**	3c. multicoloured	1·60	15

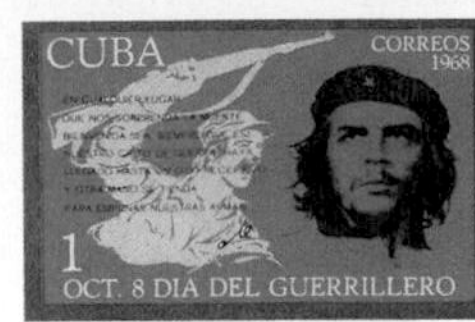

415 Che Guevara and Rifleman

1968. Day of the Guerrillas.

1591	**415**	1c. black, green & gold	15	10
1592	-	3c. black, brown & gold	15	15
1593	-	9c. multicoloured	50	15
1594	-	10c. black, green and gold	1·10	30
1595	-	13c. black, pink & gold	2·10	85

DESIGNS—"Che" Guevara and: 3c. Machine-gunners; 9c. Riflemen; 10c. Soldiers cheering; 13c. Map of Caribbean and South America.

416 C. M. de Cespedes and Broken Wheel

1968. Centenary of Cuban War of Independence. Multicoloured.

1596		1c. Type **416**	15	15
1597		1c. E. Betances and horsemen	15	15
1598		1c. I. Agramonte and monument	15	15
1599		1c. A. Maceo and "The Protest"	15	15
1600		1c. J. Marti & patriots	15	15
1601		3c. M. Gomez and "Invasion"	20	15
1602		3c. J. A. Mella and declaration	20	15
1603		3c. A. Guiteras and monument	20	15
1604		3c. A. Santamaria and riflemen	20	15
1605		3c. F. Pais & graffiti	20	15
1606		9c. J. Echeverria and students	1·00	25
1607		13c. C. Cienfuegos and rebels	2·40	85
1608		30c. "Che" Guevara and Castro addressing meeting	2·75	1·30

417 "The Burning of Bayamo" (J. E. Hernandez Giro)

1968. National Philatelic Exhibition, Bayamo-Manzanillo. Sheet 137×84 mm.

MS1609	**417**	50c. multicoloured	7·75	6·75

418 Parade of Athletes, Olympic Flag and Flame

1968. Olympic Games, Mexico. Multicoloured.

1610		1c. Type **418**	20	10
1611		2c. Basketball (vert)	15	10
1612		3c. Throwing the hammer (vert)	15	10
1613		4c. Boxing	15	10
1614		5c. Water-polo	35	10
1615		13c. Pistol-shooting	2·40	45
1616		30c. Calendar-stone (32½×50 mm)	3·75	70
MS1617		125×84 mm. 50c. Runners and flags (50×30 mm). Imperf	12·00	12·00

419 Crop-spraying

1968. Civil Activities of Cuban Armed Forces. Multicoloured.

1618		3c. Type **419**	15	10
1619		9c. "Che Guevara" Brigade	50	15
1620		10c. Road-building Brigade	80	25
1621		13c. Agricultural Brigade	1·70	70

420 "Manrique de Lara's Family" (J.-B. Vermay)

1968. 150th Anniv of San Alejandro Painting School. Multicoloured.

1622		1c. Type **420**	15	15
1623		2c. "Seascape" (L. Romanach) (48×37)	15	15
1624		3c. "Wild Cane" (A. Rodriguez) (40×48)	35	25
1625		4c. "Self-portrait" (M. Melero) (40×50)	35	25
1626		5c. "The Lottery List" (J. J. Tejada) (48×37)	1·10	35
1627		13c. "Portrait of Nina" (A. Menocal) (40×50)	3·25	55
1628		30c. "Landscape" (E. S. Chartrand) (54×37)	5·00	90
MS1629		63×97 mm. 50c. "The Siesta" (G. Gollazo) (48×37 mm)	7·50	6·50

421 Cuban Flag and Rifles

1969. 10th Anniv of "The Triumph of the Rebellion".

1630	**421**	13c. multicoloured	1·80	60

422 Gutierrez and Sanchez

1969. Cent of Villaclarenos Patriots Rebellion.

1631	**422**	3c. multicoloured	90	20

423 Mariana Grajales, Rose and Statue

1969. Cuban Women's Day.

1632	**423**	3c. multicoloured	1·00	25

424 Cuban Pioneers

1969. Cuban Pioneers and Young Communist Unions. Multicoloured.

1633		3c. Type **424**	30	15
1634		13c. Young Communists	1·80	80

425 Guaimaro Assembly

1969. Centenary of Guaimaro Assembly.

1635	**425**	3c. brown and sepia	90	25

426 "The Postman" (J. C. Cazin)

1969. Cuban Stamp Day. Multicoloured.

1636		13c. Type **426**	2·00	50
1637		30c. "Portrait of a Young Man" (George Romney) (36×44 mm)	3·25	70

427 Agrarian Law, Headquarters, Eviction of Family, and Tractor

1969. 10th Anniv of Agrarian Reform.

1638	**427**	13c. multicoloured	1·90	70

428 Hermit Crab in West Indian Chank

1969. Crustaceans. Multicoloured.

1639		1c. Type **428**	15	10
1640		2c. Spiny shrimp	30	10
1641		3c. Spiny lobster	30	10
1642		4c. Blue crab	40	15
1643		5c. Land crab	40	20
1644		13c. Freshwater prawn	2·75	45
1645		30c. Pebble crab	4·00	80

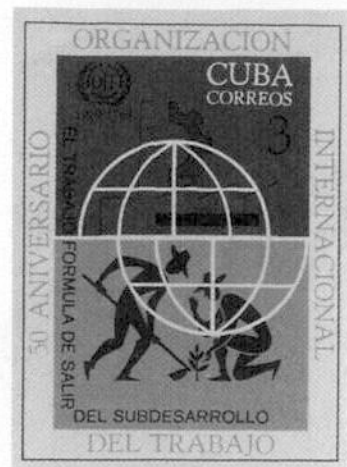

429 Factory and Peasants

1969. 50th Anniv of I.L.O. Mult.

1646 3c. Type **429** 40 15
1647 13c. Worker breaking chain 1·90 70

430 "Flowers" (R. Milian)

1969. National Museum Paintings (2nd series). Multicoloured.

1648 1c. Type **430** 15 10
1649 2c. "The Annunciation" (A. Eiriz) 15 10
1650 3c. "Factory" (M. Pogolotti) 1·00 20
1651 4c. "Territorial Waters" (L. M. Pedro) 25 15
1652 5c. "Miss Sarah Gale" (John Hoppner) 25 15
1653 13c. "Two Women wearing Mantillas" (I. Zuloaga) 1·90 70
1654 30c. "Virgin and Child" (F. Zurbaran) 2·75 90

SIZES—HORIZ: 2c. As No. 1648. VERT: 3c. As No. 1648. 4c. 40×44 mm; 5c. and 30c. 40×46 mm; 13c. 38×42 mm.

431 Television Cameras and Emblem

1969. Cuban Radiodiffusion Institute. Mult.

1655 3c. Type **431** 35 20
1656 13c. Broadcasting tower and "Globe" 1·90 80
1657 1p. TV Reception diagram 4·50 1·70

432 Flamefish

1969. Cuban Pisciculture. Multicoloured.

1658 1c. Type **432** 15 10
1659 2c. Spanish hogfish 15 10
1660 3c. Yellow-tailed damselfish 35 10
1661 4c. Royal gramma 35 20
1662 5c. Blue chromis 55 25
1663 13c. Black-barred soldierfish 3·50 45
1664 30c. Man-of-war fish (vert) 4·75 80

433 "Cuban Film Library"

1969. 10th Anniv of Cuban Cinema Industry. Multicoloured.

1665 1c. Type **433** 15 10
1666 3c. "Documentaries" 25 20
1667 13c. "Cartoons" 2·50 50
1668 30c. "Full-length Features" 2·75 55

434 "Napoleon in Milan". (A. Appiani (the Elder))

1969. Paintings in Napoleonic Museum, Havana. Multicoloured.

1669 1c. Type **434** 15 10
1670 2c. "Hortensia de Beauharnais" (F. Gerard) 20 10
1671 3c. "Napoleon-First Consul" (J. B. Regnault) 20 15
1672 4c. "Elisa Bonaparte" (R. Lefevre) 45 20
1673 5c. "Napoleon planning the Coronation" (J. G. Vibert) 70 30
1674 13c. "Corporal of Cuirassiers" (J. Meissonier) 3·25 65
1675 30c. "Napoleon Bonaparte" (R. Lefevre) 4·00 85

SIZES—VERT: 2c. 42½×55 mm; 3c. 46×56½ mm; 4c., 13c., 44×63 mm; 30c. 45½×60 mm. HORIZ: 5c. 64×47 mm.

435 Baseball Players

1969. Cuba's Victory in World Amateur Baseball Championships, Dominican Republic.

1676 **435** 13c. multicoloured 2·00 50

436 Von Humboldt, Book and American Eel

1969. Birth Bicentenary of Alexander von Humboldt. Multicoloured.

1677 3c. Type **436** 15 10
1678 13c. Night monkey 2·30 75
1679 30c. Andean condors 3·75 65

437 Ancient Egyptians in Combat

1969. World Fencing Championships, Havana. Multicoloured.

1683 1c. Type **437** 15 10
1684 2c. Roman Gladiators 15 10
1685 3c. Norman and Viking 25 10
1686 4c. Medieval tournament 30 15
1687 5c. French musketeers 50 20
1688 13c. Japanese samurai 2·40 45
1689 30c. Mounted Cubans, War of Independence 3·75 70
MS1690 66×98 mm. 50c. Modern fencing. Imperf 10·00 10·00

438 Militiaman

1969. 10th Anniv of National Revolutionary Militias.

1691 **438** 3c. multicoloured 1·00 25

439 Major Cienfuegos and Wreath on Sea

1969. 10th Anniv of Disappearance of Major Camilo Cienfuego.

1692 **439** 13c. multicoloured 2·00 50

440 Strawberries and Grapes

1969. Agriculture and Livestock Projects. Multicoloured.

1693 1c. Type **440** 20 15
1694 1c. Onion and asparagus 20 15
1695 1c. Rice 20 15
1696 1c. Bananas 20 15
1697 3c. Pineapple (vert) 40 40
1698 3c. Tobacco plant (vert) 40 40
1699 3c. Citrus fruits (vert) 40 40
1700 3c. Coffee (vert) 40 40
1701 3c. Rabbits (vert) 40 40
1702 10c. Pigs (vert) 40 25
1703 13c. Sugar-cane 2·30 60
1704 30c. Bull 3·25 85

441 Stadium and Map of Cuba (2nd National Games)

1969. Sporting Events of 1969. Multicoloured.

1705 1c. Type **441** 20 10
1706 2c. Throwing the discus (9th Anniv Games) 20 10
1707 3c. Running (Barrientos commemoration) (vert) 20 10
1708 10c. Basketball (2nd Olympic Trial Games) (vert) 40 25
1709 13c. Cycling (6th Cycle Race) (vert) 3·00 60
1710 30c. Chessmen and Globe (7th Capablanca Int. Chess Tournament, Havana) (vert) 4·25 90

442 "Plumbago capensis" **443** "Petrea volubilis"

1969. Christmas. Flowers. (a) As T 442. Mult.

1711 1c. Type **442** 30 15
1712 3c. "Turnera ulmifolia" 90 25
1713 13c. "Delonix regia" 2·10 90

(b) As T 443.

1714a/d 1c. multicoloured 30 15
1715a/d 3c. multicoloured 90 25
1716a/d 13c. multicoloured 2·10 90

DESIGNS: No. 1714a, Type **443**; 1714b, "Clitoria ternatea"; 1714c, "Duranta repens"; 1714d, "Ruellia tuberosa"; 1715a, "Thevetia peruviana"; 1715b, "Hibiscus elatus"; 1715c, "Allamanda cathartica"; 1715d, "Cosmos sulphureus"; 1716a, "Nerium oleander" (wrongly inscr "Neriun"); 1716b, "Cordia sebestena"; 1716c, "Lochnera rosea"; 1716d, "Jatropha integerrima".

Prices are for single stamps.

444 River Snake

1969. Swamp Fauna. Multicoloured.

1717 1c. Type **444** 10 10
1718 2c. Banana frog 10 10
1719 3c. Giant tropical gar (fish) 15 10
1720 4c. Dwarf hutia (vert) 15 10
1721 5c. Alligator 15 15
1722 13c. Cuban Amazon (vert) 4·25 45
1723 30c. Red-winged blackbird (vert) 5·25 70

445 "Jibacoa Beach" (J. Hernandez)

1970. Tourism. Multicoloured.

1724 1c. Type **445** 10 10
1725 3c. "Trinidad City" (J. Hernandez) 15 15
1726 13c. Santiago de Cuba (A. Alonzo) 1·90 80
1727 30c. Vinales Valley (J. Hernandez) 2·75 95

446 Yamagua

1970. Medicinal Plants. Multicoloured.

1728 1c. Type **446** 25 10
1729 3c. Albahaca Morada 25 10
1730 10c. Curbana 35 15
1731 13c. Romerillo 1·90 70
1732 30c. Marilope 2·50 85
1733 50c. Aguedita 3·50 1·00

447 Weightlifting

1970. 11th Central American and Caribbean Games. Multicoloured.

1734 1c. Type **447** 15 10
1735 3c. Boxing 15 10
1736 10c. Gymnastics 25 15
1737 13c. Athletics 1·90 65
1738 30c. Fencing 2·75 90
MS1739 85×128 mm. 50c. Baseball. Imperf 9·75 9·75

448 "Enjoyment of Life"

1970. "EXPO 70" World Fair, Osaka, Japan. Multicoloured.

1740	1c. Type **448**	15	10
1741	2c. "Uses of nature" (vert)	20	10
1742	3c. "Better Living Standards"	30	25
1743	13c. "International Co-operation" (vert)	2·30	55
1744	30c. Cuban Pavilion	3·25	80

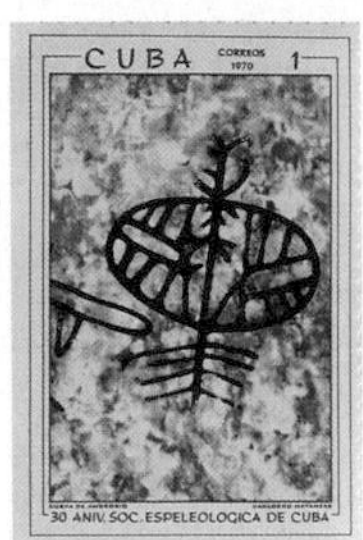

449 Oval Pictograph, Ambrosio Cave

1970. 30th Anniv of Cuban Speleological Society.

1745	**449**	1c. red and brown	10	10
1746	-	2c. black and brown	15	10
1747	-	3c. red and brown	15	10
1748	-	4c. black and brown	20	15
1749	-	5c. black, red and brown	30	25
1750	-	13c. black and brown	1·90	60
1751	-	30c. red and brown	4·00	65

DESIGNS—HORIZ: (42×32½ mm): 2c. Cave 1, Punta del Este, Isle of Pines; 5c. As 2c. (different); 30c. Stylized fish, Cave 2, Punta del Este. VERT: 3c. Stylized mask, Pichardo Cave, Sierra de Cubitas; 4c. Conical complex, Ambrosio Cave, Varadero; 13c. Human face, Garcia Robiou Cave, Catalina de Guines.

450 J. D. Blino, Balloon and Spacecraft

1970. Aviation Pioneers. Multicoloured.

1752	3c. Type **450**	80	15
1753	13c. A. Theodore, balloon and satellite	2·75	70

451 "Lenin in Kazan" (O. Vishniakov) (image scaled to 70% of original size)

1970. Birth Centenary of Lenin. Paintings. Mult.

1754	1c. Type **451**	10	10
1755	2c. "Lenin's Youth" (Prager)	10	10
1756	3c. "The 2nd Socialist Party Congress" (Vinogradov)	15	10
1757	4c. "The First Manifesto" (Golubkov)	25	15
1758	5c. "The First Day of Soviet Power" (Babasiuk)	25	20
1759	13c. "Lenin in the Smolny Institute" (Sokolov)	2·20	50
1760	30c. "Autumn in Gorky" (Varlamov)	2·75	65
MS1761	79×112 mm. 50c. "Lenin and Gorky" (N. Barkakov) (45×43 mm). Imperf	10·50	10·50

SIZES: 4, 5c. As Type **451**: 2, 3, 13, 30c. 70×34 mm.

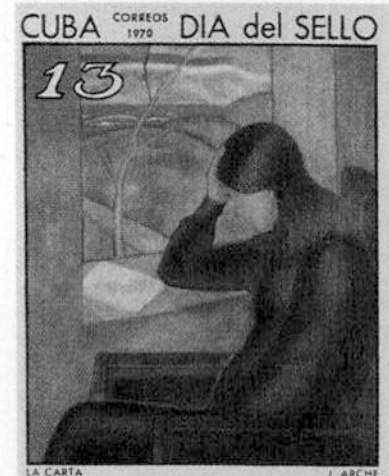

452 "The Letter" (J. Archer)

1970. Cuban Stamp Day. Paintings. Mult.

1762	13c. Type **452**	2·40	50
1763	30c. "Portrait of a Cadet" (anonymous) (35×49 mm)	3·00	65

453 Da Vinci's Anatomical Drawing, Earth and Moon

1970. World Telecommunications Day.

1764	**453**	30c. multicoloured	2·75	50

454 Vietnamese Fisherman

1970. 80th Birthday of Ho Chi Minh (North Vietnamese leader). Multicoloured.

1765	1c. Type **454**	10	10
1766	3c. Cultivating rice-fields	40	10
1767	3c. Two Vietnamese children	40	10
1768	3c. Children entering air-raid shelter	40	10
1769	3c. Camouflaged machine-shop	55	10
1770	3c. Rice harvest	55	15
1771	13c. Pres. Ho Chi Minh	2·75	70

SIZES: Nos. 1766/7, 33×44½ mm, Nos. 1768, 1770, 33½×46 mm, No. 1769, 35×42 mm, No. 1771, 34½×39½ mm.

455 Tobacco Plantation and "Eden" Cigar band

1970. "Cuban Cigar Industry". Multicoloured.

1772	3c. Type **455**	15	10
1773	13c. 19 th century cigar factory and "El Mambi" band	1·70	70
1774	30c. Packing cigars (19th- century) and "Gran Pena" band	2·75	1·00

456 Cane crushing Machinery

1970. Cuban Sugar Harvest Target. "Over 10 million Tons". Multicoloured.

1775	1c. Type **456**	15	10
1776	2c. Sowing and crop-spraying	15	10
1777	3c. Cutting sugar-cane	20	10
1778	10c. Ox-cart and diesel-electric locomotive	4·75	45
1779	13c. Modern cane cutting machine	1·50	25
1780	30c. Cane-cutters and globe (vert)	2·20	70
1781	1p. Sugar warehouse	4·00	1·90

457 P. Figueredo and National Anthem (original version)

1970. Death Centenary of Pedro Figueredo (composer of National Anthem). Multicoloured.

1782	3c. Type **457**	25	15
1783	20c. 18 98 version of anthem	2·20	60

458 Cuban Girl, Flag and Federation Badge

1970. 10th Anniv of Cuban Women's Federation.

1784	**458**	3c. multicoloured	85	50

459 "Peasant Militia" (S. C. Moreno)

1970. National Museum Paintings (3rd series). Multicoloured.

1785	1c. Type **459**	15	15
1786	2c. "Washerwoman" (A. Fernandez)	15	15
1787	3c. "Puerta del Sol, Madrid" (L. P. Alcazar)	15	15
1788	4c. "Fishermen's Wives" (J. Sorolla)	15	15
1789	5c. "Portrait of a Lady" (T. de Keyser)	15	15
1790	13c. "Mrs. Edward Foster" (Lawrence)	2·00	50
1791	30c. "Tropical Gipsy" (V. M. Garcia)	3·25	80

SIZES—HORIZ: 2c., 3c. 46×42 mm. SQUARE. 4c. 41×41 mm. VERT: 5c., 13c., 30c. 39×46 mm.

460 Crowd in Jose Marti Square, Havana (image scaled to 65% of original size)

1970. 10th Anniv of Havana Declaration.

1792	**460**	3c. blue, red & black	60	15

461 C. D. R. Emblem

1970. 10th Anniv of Revolution Defence Committees.

1793	**461**	3c. multicoloured	75	25

462 Laboratory, Emblem and Microscope

1970. 39th A.T.A.C. (Sugar Technicians Assn) Conference.

1794	**462**	30c. multicoloured	2·75	70

463 Helmeted Guineafowl

1970. Wildlife. Multicoloured.

1795	1c. Type **463**	75	15
1796	2c. Black-billed whistling duck	80	15
1797	3c. Common pheasant	1·00	15
1798	4c. Mourning dove	1·10	15
1799	5c. Northern bobwhite	1·20	20
1800	13c. Wild boar	2·10	1·10
1801	30c. White-tailed deer	3·50	1·50

464 "Black Magic Parade" (M. Puente)

1970. Afro-Cuban Folklore Paintings. Mult.

1802	1c. Type **464**	15	10
1803	3c. "Zapateo Hat Dance" (V. L. Landaluze)	30	15
1804	10c. "Los Hoyos Conga Dance" (D. Ravenet)	80	45
1805	13c. "Climax of the Rumba" (E. Abela)	2·20	70

SIZES—HORIZ: 10c. 45×44 mm. VERT: 3, 13c. 37×49 mm.

465 Common Zebra on Road Crossing

1970. Road Safety Week. Multicoloured.

1806	3c. Type **465**	90	15
1807	9c. Prudence the Bear on point duty	1·30	25

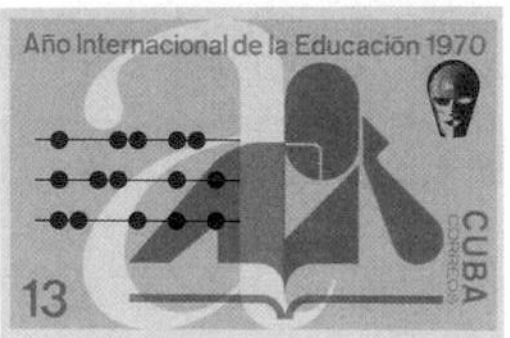

466 Letter "a" and Abacus

1970. International Education Year. Mult.

1808	13c. Type **466**	2·00	25
1809	30c. Microscope and cow	2·75	70

467 Cuban Blackbird

468 Cuban Pygmy Owl

1970. Christmas. Birds. Multicoloured. (a) As T 467.

1810	1c. Type **467**	85	40
1811	3c. Oriente warbler	1·80	60
1812	13c. Zapata sparrow	2·50	1·10

(b) As T 468.

1813a/d	1c. multicoloured	85	40
1814a/d	3c. multicoloured	1·80	60
1815a/d	13c. multicoloured	2·50	1·10

DESIGNS: No. 1813a, Type **468**; 1813b, Cuban tody; 1813c, Cuban green woodpecker; 1813d, Zapata wren; 1814a, Cuban solitaire; 1814b, Blue-grey gnatcatcher; 1814c, Cuban vireo; 1814d, Yellow-headed warbler; 1815a, Hook-billed kite; 1815b, Gundlach's hawk; 1815c, Blue-headed quail dove; 1815d, Cuban conure.

Prices are for single stamps.

469 School Badge and Cadet Colour-party

1970. "Camilo Cienfuegos" Military School.

1816	**469**	3c. multicoloured	1·00	20

470 "Reporter" with Pen

1971. 7th Journalists International Organization Congress, Havana.

1817	**470**	13c. multicoloured	1·80	50

471 Lockheed 8A Sirius

1971. 35th Anniv of Camaguey–Seville Flight by Menendez Pelaez. Multicoloured.

1818	13c. Type **471**	2·40	25
1819	30c. Lieut. Menendez Pelaez and map	2·75	65

472 Meteorological Class

1971. World Meteorological Day. Multicoloured.

1820	1c. Type **472**	10	10
1821	3c. Hurricane map (40×36 mm)	15	10
1822	8c. Meteorological equipment	85	20
1823	30c. Weather radar systems (horiz)	4·00	1·20

473 Games Emblem

1971. 6th Pan-American Games, Cali, Colombia. Multicoloured.

1824	1c. Type **473**	15	10
1825	2c. Athletics	15	10
1826	3c. Rifle-shooting (horiz)	15	10
1827	4c. Gymnastics	15	10
1828	5c. Boxing	15	10
1829	13c. Water-polo (horiz)	2·00	40
1830	30c. Baseball (horiz)	2·50	70

474 Paris Porcelain, 19th-century

1971. Porcelain and Mosaics in Metropolitan Museum, Havana. Multicoloured.

1831	1c. Type **474**	10	10
1832	3c. Mexican pottery bowl, 17th-century	10	10
1833	10c. 19th-century Paris porcelain (similar to T **474**)	30	15
1834	13c. "Colosseum" Italian mosaic, 19th-century	1·80	25
1835	20c. 17th-century Mexican pottery dish (similar to 3c.)	1·80	70
1836	30c. "St. Peter's Square" (Italian mosaic 19th-cent.)	2·30	85

SIZES—VERT: 3c. 46×54 mm. 10c. as Type **474**. 20c. 43×49 mm. HORIZ: 13c., 30c. 50×33 mm.

475 Mother and Child

1971. 10th Anniv of Cuban Infant Centres.

1837	**475**	3c. multicoloured	60	15

476 Cosmonaut in Training

1971. 10th Anniv of First Manned Space Flight. Multicoloured.

1838	1c. Type **476**	15	10
1839	2c. Speedometer test	15	10
1840	3c. Medical examination	15	10
1841	4c. Acceleration tower	15	10
1842	5c. Pressurisation test	25	10
1843	13c. Cosmonaut in gravity chamber	1·80	40
1844	30c. Crew in flight simulator	2·50	85

MS1845 100×63 mm. 50c. Yuri Gagarin. Imperf — 8·25 — 8·25

477 Cuban and Burning Ship

1971. 10th Anniv of Giron Victory.

1846	**477**	13c. multicoloured	2·00	60

478 Sailing Packet "Windsor Castle" attacked by French Privateer Brig "Jeune Richard" (1807)

1971. Stamp Day. Multicoloured.

1847	13c. Type **478**	2·50	60
1848	30c. Mail steamer "Orinoco", 1851	3·75	80

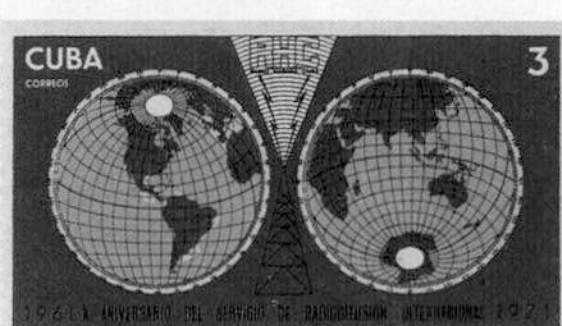

479 Transmitter and Hemispheres

1971. 10th Anniv of Cuban International Broadcasting Services.

1849	**479**	3c. multicoloured	30	15
1850	**479**	50c. multicoloured	3·75	90

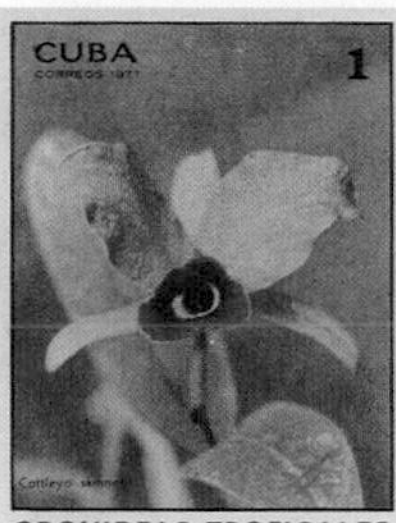

480 "Cattleya skinnerii"

1971. Tropical Orchids (1st series). Mult.

1851	1c. Type **480**	15	10
1852	2c. "Vanda hibrida"	15	10
1853	3c. "Cypripedium callossum"	15	10
1854	4c. "Cypripedium glaucophyllum"	15	10
1855	5c. "Vanda tricolor"	20	10
1856	13c. "Cypripedium mowgh"	2·10	50
1857	30c. "Cypripedium solum"	4·25	95

See also Nos. 1908/14 and 2012/18.

481 Loynaz del Castillo and "Invasion Hymn"

1971. Birth Centenary of Enrique Loynaz del Castillo (composer).

1858	**481**	3c. multicoloured	75	20

482 Larvae and Pupae

1971. Apiculture. Multicoloured.

1859	1c. Type **482**	15	10
1860	3c. Working bee	15	10
1861	9c. Drone	50	15
1862	13c. Defending the hive	2·75	40
1863	30c. Queen bee	4·25	1·00

483 "The Ship" (Lydia Rivera)

1971. Exhibition of Children's Drawings. Havana. Multicoloured.

1864	1c. Type **483**	15	10
1865	3c. "Little Train" (Yuri Ruiz)	75	10
1866	9c. "Sugar-cane Cutter" (Horacio Carracedo)	15	15
1867	10c. "Return of Cuban Fisherman" (Angela Munoz and Lazaro Hernandez)	40	15
1868	13c. "The Zoo" (Victoria Castillo)	1·60	40
1869	20c. "House and Garden" (Elsa Garcia)	2·50	70
1870	30c. "Landscape" (Orestes Rodriguez) (vert)	2·75	1·10

SIZES: 9c., 13c. 45×35 mm, 10c. 45×38 mm, 20c. 47×42 mm, 30c. 39×49 mm.

1971. National Museum Paintings (4th series). As T 459. Multicoloured.

1871	1c. "St. Catherine of Alexandria" (Zurbaran)	10	10
1872	2c. "The Cart" (F. Americo) (horiz)	15	10
1873	3c. "St. Christopher and the Child" (J. Bassano)	15	10
1874	4c. "Little Devil" (R. Portocarrero)	20	10
1875	5c. "Portrait of a Lady" (N. Maes)	30	15
1876	13c. "Phoenix" (R. Martinez)	1·80	50
1877	30c. "Sir William Pitt" (Gainsborough)	2·75	85

SIZES: 1, 3c. 30×56 mm, 2c. 48×37 mm, 4, 5c. 37×49 mm, 13, 30c. 39×49 mm.

485 Bonefish

1971. Sport Fishing. Multicoloured.

1878	1c. Type **485**	25	25
1879	2c. Great amberjack	25	25
1880	3c. Large-mouthed black bass	25	25
1881	4c. Dolphin (fish)	40	25
1882	5c. Atlantic tarpon	50	25
1883	13c. Wahoo	2·50	70
1884	30c. Blue marlin	4·25	1·20

486 Ball within "C"

1971. World Amateur Baseball Championships. Multicoloured.

1885	3c. Type **486**	25	20
1886	1p. Hand holding globe within "C"	5·00	2·00

487 "Dr. F. Valdes Dominguez" (artist unknown)

1971. Centenary of Medical Students' Execution. Multicoloured.

1887	3c. Type **487**	30	15
1888	13c. "Students Execution" (M. Mesa) (62×47 mm)	1·50	50
1889	30c. "Captain Federico Capdevila" (unknown artist)	2·50	70

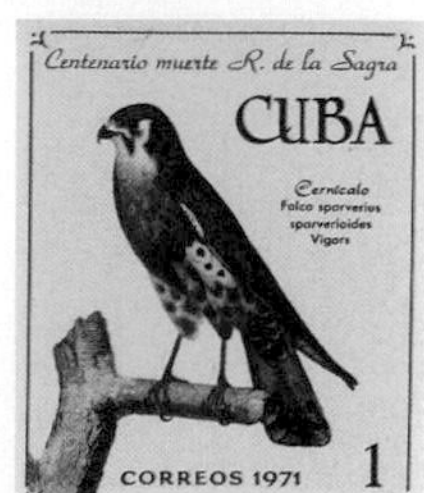

488 American Kestrel

1971. Death Centenary of Ramon de la Sagra (naturalist). Cuban Birds. Multicoloured.

1890	1c. Type **488**	40	15

1891	2c. Cuban pygmy owl	40	15
1892	3c. Cuban trogon	60	15
1893	4c. Great lizard cuckoo	65	25
1894	5c. Fernandina's flicker	85	25
1895	13c. Stripe-headed tanager (horiz)	1·50	45
1896	30c. Red-legged thrush (horiz)	3·00	90
1897	50c. Cuban emerald and ruby-throated hummingbirds (56×30 mm)	6·25	1·80

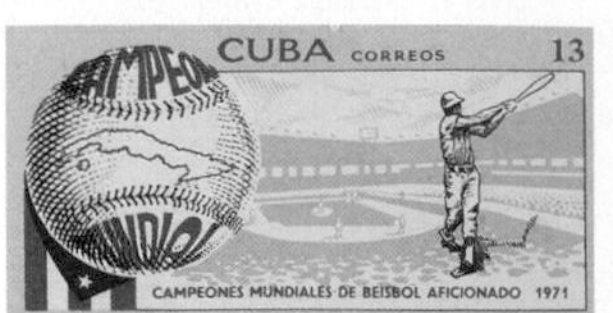

489 Baseball Player and Global Emblem

1971. Cuba's Victory in World Amateur Baseball.

1898	**489**	13c. multicoloured	1·60	70

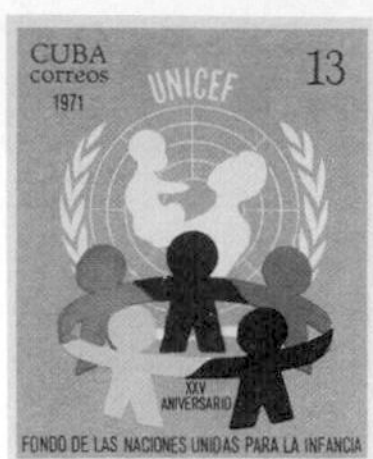

490 "Children of the World"

1971. 25th Anniv of UNICEF.

1899	**490**	13c. multicoloured	2·10	85

1972. National Museum Paintings (5th series). As T 459. Multicoloured.

1900	1c. "The Reception of Ambassadors" (V. Carpaccio)	10	10
1901	2c. "Senora Malpica" (G. Collazo)	15	10
1902	3c. "La Chorrera Fortress (E. Chartrand)	15	10
1903	4c. "Creole Landscape" (C. Enriquez)	15	10
1904	5c. "Sir William Lemon" (G. Romney)	15	10
1905	13c. "La Tajona Beach" (H. Cleenewek)	2·10	50
1906	30c. "Valencia Beach" (J. Sorolla y Bastida)	3·50	1·20

SIZES: 1c., 3c. 51×33 mm, 2c. 28×53 mm, 4c., 5c. 36×44 mm, 13c., 30c. 43×34 mm.

492 "Capitol" Stamp of 1929 (now Natural History Museum)

1972. 10th Anniv of Academy of Sciences.

1907	**492**	13c. purple and yellow	1·80	60

1972. Tropical Orchids (2nd series). As T 480. Multicoloured.

1908	1c. "Brasso Cattleya sindorossiana"	15	10
1909	2c. "Cypripedium doraeus"	15	10
1910	3c. "Cypripedium exul"	15	10
1911	4c. "Cypripedium rosydawn"	15	10
1912	5c. "Cypripedium champolliom"	15	10
1913	13c. "Cypripedium bucolique"	2·20	85
1914	30c. "Cypripedium sullanum"	2·75	1·00

493 "Eduardo Agramonte" (F. Martinez)

1972. Death Centenary of Dr. E. Agramonte (surgeon and patriot).

1915	**493**	3c. multicoloured	50	25

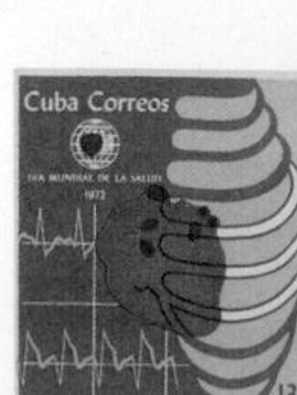

494 Human Heart and Thorax

496 "Vincente Mora Pera" (Postmaster General, War of Independence) (R. Loy)

1972. World Health Day.

1916	**494**	13c. multicoloured	1·60	60

495 "Sputnik 1"

1972. "History of Space". Multicoloured.

1917	1c. Type **495**	25	10
1918	2c. "Vostok 1"	25	10
1919	3c. Valentina Tereshkova in capsule	25	10
1920	4c. A. Leonov in space	25	10
1921	5c. "Lunokhod 1" moon Vehicle	25	10
1922	13c. Linking of "Soyuz" capsules	1·90	40
1923	30c. Dobrovolsky, Volkov and Pataiev, victims of "Soyuz 11" disaster	2·30	70

1972. Stamp Day. Multicoloured.

1924	13c. Type **496**	1·50	60
1925	30c. Mambi Mailcover of 1897 (48×39 mm)	2·40	70

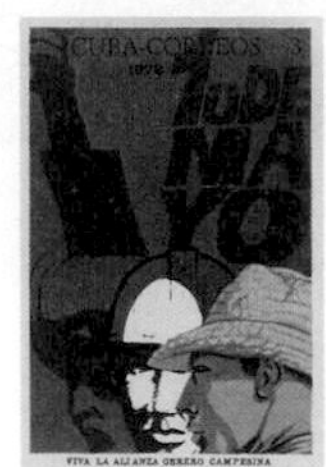
497 Cuban Workers

1972. Labour Day.

1926	**497**	3c. multicoloured	75	30

498 Jose Marti and Ho Chi Minh

1972. 3rd Symposium on Indo-China War. Multicoloured.

1927	3c. Type **498**	30	15
1928	13c. Bombed house (38×29 mm)	1·30	35
1929	30c. Symposium emblem	1·60	45

1972. Paintings from the Metropolitan Museum, Havana (6th series). As T 430. Multicoloured.

1930	1c. "Salvador del Muro" (J. del Rio)	15	10
1931	2c. "Louis de las Casas" (J. del Rio)	15	10
1932	3c. "Christopher Columbus" (anonymous)	15	10
1933	4c. "Tomas Gamba" (V. Escobar)	30	10
1934	5c. "Maria Galarraga" (V. Escobar)	30	10
1935	13c. "Isabella II of Spain" (F. Madrazo)	1·60	40
1936	30c. "Carlos III of Spain" (M. Melero)	2·10	70

SIZES—VERT: (35×44 mm) 1930/34, (34×52 mm) 1935/6.

500 Children in Boat

1972. Children's Song Competition.

1937	**500**	3c. multicoloured	95	30

501 Ilyushin Il-18, Map and Flags

1972. Air. 1st Anniv of Havana–Santiago de Chile Air Service.

1938	**501**	25c. multicoloured	2·50	85

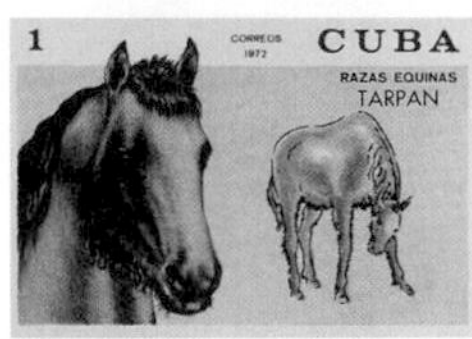

502 Tarpan

1972. Thoroughbred Horses. Multicoloured.

1939	1c. Type **502**	25	10
1940	2c. Kertag	25	10
1941	3c. Creole	25	10
1942	4c. Andalusian	25	10
1943	5c. Arab	25	10
1944	13c. Quarter-horse	2·40	70
1945	30c. Pursang	2·75	1·00

503 Frank Pais

1972. 15th Death Anniv of Frank Pais.

1946	**503**	13c. multicoloured	1·40	60

504 Athlete and Emblem

1972. Olympic Games, Munich.

1947	**504**	1c. orange and brown	25	10
1948	-	2c. purple, blue & orge	25	10
1949	-	3c. green, yellow & blk	25	10
1950	-	4c. bl, yell & brn	25	10
1951	-	5c. red, black & yellow	25	10
1952	-	13c. lilac, green & blue	1·60	40
1953	-	30c. blue, red and green	2·10	70

MS1954	58½×75 mm. 50c. multicoloured. Imperf	5·00	5·00

DESIGNS—HORIZ: 2c. "M" and boxing; 3c. "U" and weight-lifting; 4c. "N" and fencing; 5c. "I" and rifle-shooting; 13c. "C" and running; 30c. "H" and basketball; 50c. Gymnastics.

505 "Landscape with Tree-trunks" (D. Ramos)

1972. International Hydrological Decade. Mult.

1955	1c. Type **505**	15	10
1956	3c. "Cyclone" (T. Lorenzo)	15	10
1957	8c. "Vineyards" (D. Ramos)	65	15
1958	30c. "Forest and Stream" (A. R. Morey) (vert)	2·00	70

506 "Papilio thoas oviedo"

1972. Butterflies from the Gundlach Collection. Multicoloured.

1959	1c. Type **506**	15	10
1960	2c. "Papilio devilliers"	15	10
1961	3c. "Papilio polixenes polixenes"	15	10
1962	4c. "Papilio androgeus epidaurus"	15	10
1963	5c. "Papilio cayguanabus'	20	10
1964	13c. "Papilio andraemon hernandezi"	4·75	1·10
1965	30c. "Papilio celadon"	6·25	1·40

507 "In La Mancha" (A. Fernandez)

1972. 425th Birth Anniv of Cervantes. Paintings by A. Fernandez. Multicoloured.

1966	3c. Type **507**	15	10
1967	13c. "Battle with the Wine Skins" (horiz)	1·80	60
1968	30c. "Don Quixote of La Mancha"	1·90	70
MS1969	76×116 mm. 50c. "Scene from Don Quixote" (J. M. Carbonero) (47×29 mm)	4·00	4·00

508 E. "Che" Guevara and Map of Bolivia

1972. 5th Anniv of Guerrillas' Day. Mult.

1970	3c. Type **508**	15	10
1971	13c. T. "Tania" Bunke and map of Bolivia	1·80	50
1972	30c. G. "Inti" Peredo and map of Bolivia	2·00	60

509 "Abwe" (shakers)

1972. Traditional Musical Instruments. Mult.

1973	3c. Type **509**	15	10
1974	13c. "Bonko enchemiya" (drum)	1·80	60
1975	30c. "Iya" (drum)	1·90	70

510 Cuban 2c. Stamp of 1951

1972. National Philatelic Exhibition, Matanzas. Multicoloured.

1976	13c. Type **510**	2·00	60
1977	30c. Cuban 25c. airmail stamp of 1951	2·40	70

511 Viking Longship

1972. Maritime History. Ships Through the Ages. Multicoloured.

1978	1c. Type **511**	25	10
1979	2c. Caravel (vert)	25	10
1980	3c. Galley	25	10
1981	4c. Galleon (vert)	30	20
1982	5c. Clipper	85	20
1983	13c. Steam packet	4·25	95
1984	30c. Atomic ice-breaker "Lenin" and Adelie penguins (55×29 mm)	7·75	1·70

512 Lion of St. Mark

1972. UNESCO "Save Venice" Campaign. Multicoloured.

1985	3c. Type **512**	15	10
1986	13c. Bridge of Sighs (vert)	1·60	60
1987	30c. St. Mark's Cathedral	2·10	1·20

1972. "Cuba, World Amateur Baseball Champions of 1972".

1988	**513**	3c. violet and orange	1·00	25

513 Baseball Coach (poster)

1972. Sports events of 1972. Posters.

1989	-	1c. multicoloured	25	10
1990	-	2c. multicoloured	25	10
1991	**513**	3c. black, orange & grn	25	10
1992	-	4c. red, black and blue	25	10
1993	-	5c. orge, bl & lt bl	25	10
1994	-	13c. multicoloured	1·40	70
1995	-	30c. vio, blk & bl	2·00	1·00

DESIGNS AND EVENTS: 1c. Various sports (10th National Schoolchildren's Games); 2c. Pole vaulting (Barrientos Memorial Athletics); 3c. As Type **513**, but inscr changed to read "XI serie nacional de beisbol aficionado" and colours changed (11th National Amateur Baseball Series); 4c. Wrestling (Cerro Pelado International Wrestling Championships); 5c. Foil (Central American and Caribbean Fencing Tournament); 13c. Boxing (Giraldo Cordova Boxing Tournament); 30c. Fishes (Ernest Hemingway National Marlin Fishing Contest).

515 Bronze Medal, Women's 100 m

1972. Cuban Successes in Olympic Games, Munich. Multicoloured.

1996	1c. Type **515**	25	10
1997	2c. Bronze (women's 4×100 m relay)	25	10
1998	3c. Gold (boxing, 54 kg)	25	10
1999	4c. Silver (boxing, 81 kg)	25	10
2000	5c. Bronze (boxing, 51 kg)	25	10
2001	13c. Gold (boxing, 67 kg)	1·40	70
2002	30c. Gold (boxing, 81 kg) and Silver Cup (boxing Teofilo Stevenons)	2·00	1·00
MS2003	65×90 mm. 50c. Bronze medal, Basketball. Imperf	5·00	5·00

516 "Gertrude G. de Avellaneda" (A. Esquivel)

1973. Death Centenary of Gertrude Gomez de Avellaneda (poetess).

2004	**516**	13c. multicoloured	1·80	60

1973. National Museum Paintings (6th series). As T 459. Multicoloured.

2005	1c. "Bathers in the Lagoon" (C. Enriquez) (vert)	25	10
2006	2c. "Still Life" (W. C. Heda) (vert)	25	10
2007	3c. "Scene of Gallantry" (V. de Landaluse) (vert)	25	10
2008	4c. "Return at Evening" (C. Troyon) (vert)	25	10
2009	5c. "Elizabetta Mascagni" (F. X. Fabre) (vert)	25	10
2010	13c. "The Picador" (E. de Lucas Padilla)	1·30	70
2011	30c. "In the Garden" (J. A. Morell) (vert)	1·90	1·00

1973. Tropical Orchids (3rd series). As Type 480. Multicoloured.

2012	1c. "Dendrobium" (hybrid)	15	10
2013	2c. "Cypripedium exul. O' Brien"	25	10
2014	3c. "Vanda miss. Joaquin"	25	10
2015	4c. "Phalaenopsis schilleriana Reichb"	25	10
2016	5c. "Vanda gilbert tribulet"	30	10
2017	13c. "Dendrobium" (hybrid) (different)	2·40	60
2018	30c. "Arachnis catherine"	2·75	95

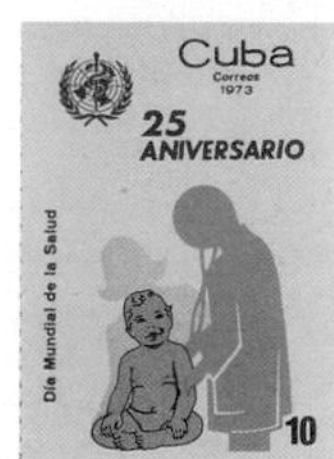

518 Medical Examination

1973. 25th Anniv of W.H.O.

2019	**518**	10c. multicoloured	1·00	40

519 Children and Vaccine

1973. Freedom from Polio Campaign.

2020	**519**	3c. multicoloured	60	30

520 "Soyuz" Rocket on Launch-pad

1973. Cosmonautics Day. Russian Space Exploration. Multicoloured.

2021	1c. Type **520**	25	10
2022	2c. "Luna 1" in moon orbit (horiz)	25	10
2023	3c. "Luna 16" leaving moon	25	10
2024	4c. "Venus 7" probe (horiz)	25	10
2025	5c. "Molniya 1" communications satellite	25	10
2026	13c. "Mars 3" probe (horiz)	1·60	95
2027	30c. Research ship "Kosmonavt Yury Gargarin" (horiz)	4·75	1·20

521 Santiago de Cuba Postmark, 1839

1973. Stamp Day. Multicoloured.

2028	13c. Type **521**	1·80	60
2029	30c. "Havana" postmark, 1760	1·90	70

522 "Ignacio Agramonte" (A. Espinosa)

1973. Death Centenary of Maj.-Gen. Ignacio Agramonte.

2030	**522**	13c. multicoloured	1·30	60

523 Copernicus' Birthplace and Instruments

1973. 500th Birth Anniv of Copernicus. Mult.

2031	3c. Type **523**	15	10
2032	13c. Copernicus and "spaceship"	1·30	60
2033	30c. "De Revolutionibus Orbium Celestium" and Frombork Tower	2·50	85
MS2034	84×78 mm. 50c. Copernicus statue, Warsaw (vert)	5·25	5·00

524 Emblem of Basic Schools

1973. Educational Development.

2035	**524**	13c. multicoloured	1·30	30

525 Jersey Breed

1973. Cattle Breeds. Multicoloured.

2036	1c. Type **525**	25	10
2037	2c. Charolais	25	10
2038	3c. Creole	25	10
2039	4c. Swiss	30	10
2040	5c. Holstein	30	10
2041	13c. St. Gertrude's	1·30	30
2042	30c. Brahman Cebu	2·75	60

526 Festival Emblem

1973. 10th World Youth and Students' Festival, East Berlin.

2043	**526**	13c. multicoloured	1·30	25

527 Siboney Farmhouse

1973. 20th Anniv of Revolution. Mult.

2044	3c. Type **527**	30	30
2045	13c. Moncada Barracks	1·30	40
2046	30c. Revolution Square, Havana	2·10	60

528 Midshipman and Destroyer

1973. 10th Anniv of Revolutionary Navy.

2047	**528**	3c. multicoloured	80	30

529 "Amalia de Sajonia" (J. K. Rossler)

1973. National Museum Paintings (7th series). Multicoloured.

2048	1c. Type **529**	15	10
2049	2c. "Interior" (M. Vicens) (horiz)	15	10
2050	3c. "Margaret of Austria" (J. Pantoja de la Cruz)	20	10
2051	4c. "Syndic of the City Hall" (anon)	20	10
2052	5c. "View of Santiago de Cuba" (J. H. Giro) (horiz)	20	10
2053	13c. "The Catalan" (J. J. Tejada)	1·50	50
2054	30c. "Guayo Alley" (J. J. Tejada)	2·00	60

530 "Spring"

1973. Centenary of World Meteorological Organization. Paintings by J. Madrazo. Mult.

2055	8c. Type **530**	60	15
2056	8c. "Summer"	60	15
2057	8c. "Autumn"	60	15
2058	8c. "Winter"	60	15

531 Weightlifting

1973. 27th Pan-American World Weightlifting Championships, Havana. Designs showing various stages of weightlifting exercise.

2059	**531**	1c. multicoloured	15	10
2060	-	2c. multicoloured	15	10
2061	-	3c. multicoloured	15	10
2062	-	4c. multicoloured	15	10
2063	-	5c. multicoloured	15	10
2064	-	13c. multicoloured	1·30	50
2065	-	30c. multicoloured	2·30	1·00

532 "Erythrina standleyana"

1973. Wild Flowers (1st series). Mult.

2066	1c. Type **532**	15	10
2067	2c. "Lantana camara"	15	10
2068	3c. "Canavalia maritima"	15	10
2069	4c. "Dichromena colorata"	15	10
2070	5c. "Borrichia arborescens"	15	10
2071	13c. "Anguria pedata"	1·60	70
2072	30c. "Cordia sebestena"	2·75	1·00

See also Nos. 2152/6.

533 Congress Emblem

1973. 8th World Trade Union Congress, Varna, Bulgaria.

2073	**533**	13c. multicoloured	1·20	30

534 Ballet Dancers

1973. 25th Anniv of Cuban National Ballet.

2074	**534**	13c. lt blue, bl & gold	1·60	30

535 True Fasciate Liguus

1973. Shells. Multicoloured.

2075	1c. Type **535**	25	10
2076	2c. Guitart's liguus	25	10
2077	3c. Wharton's Cuban liguus	25	10
2078	4c. Angela's Cuban liguus	25	10
2079	5c. Yellow-banded liguus	25	10
2080	13c. "Liguus blainianus"	2·75	95
2081	30c. Ribbon liguus	3·50	1·10

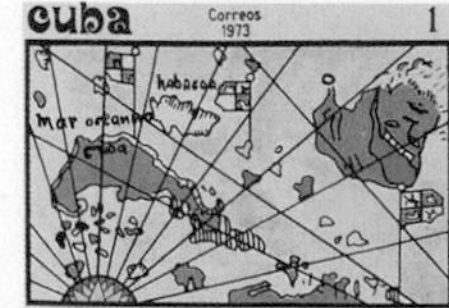

536 Juan de la Cosa's Map, 1502

1973. Maps of Cuba. Multicoloured.

2082	1c. Type **536**	15	10
2083	3c. Ortelius's map, 1572	20	10
2084	13c. Bellini's map, 1762	1·40	20
2085	40c. Cartographic survey map, 1973	1·80	80

537 1c. Stamp of 1960 (No. 921)

1974. 15th Anniv of Revolution. Revolution stamps of 1960. Multicoloured.

2086	1c. Type **537**	15	10
2087	3c. 2c. stamp	25	10
2088	13c. 8c. air stamp	3·75	50
2089	40c. 12c. air stamp	2·10	70

538 "Head of a Woman" (F. Ponce de Leon)

1974. Paintings in Camaguey Museum. Mult.

2090	1c. Type **538**	25	10
2091	3c. "Mexican Children" (J. Arche)	25	10
2092	8c. "Portrait of a Young Woman" (A. Menocal)	30	15
2093	10c. "Mulatto Woman with Coconut" (L. Romanach)	1·00	30
2094	13c. "Head of Old Man" (J. Arburu)	1·60	50

539 A. Cabral

1974. 1st Death Anniv of Amilcar Cabral (Guinea-Bissau guerilla leader).

2095	**539**	13c. multicoloured	1·20	20

540 "Lenin" (after J. V. Kosmin)

1974. 50th Anniv of Lenin's Death.

2096	**540**	30c. multicoloured	2·40	70

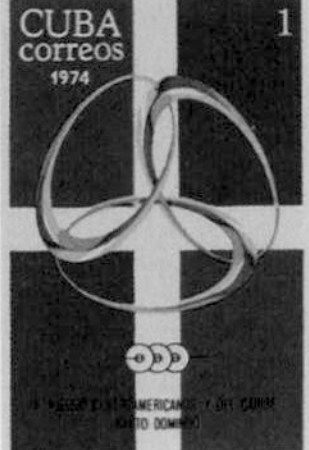

541 Games Emblem

1974. 12th Central American and Caribbean Games, Santo Domingo. Multicoloured.

2097	1c. Type **541**	20	10
2098	2c. Throwing the javelin	20	10
2099	3c. Boxing	20	10
2100	4c. Baseball player (horiz)	20	10
2101	13c. Handball player (horiz)	1·30	25
2102	30c. Volleyball (horiz)	1·90	70

542 "C. M. de Cespedes" (after F. Martinez)

1974. Death Centenary of Carlos M. de Cespedes (patriot).

2103	**542**	13c. multicoloured	1·10	25

543 "Portrait of a Man" (J. B. Vermay)

1974. National Museum Paintings (8th series). Multicoloured.

2104	1c. Type **543**	25	10
2105	2c. "Nodriza" (C. A. Van Loo)	25	10
2106	3c. "Cattle by a River" (R. Morey) (46×32 mm)	25	10
2107	4c. "Village Landscape" (R. Morey) (46×32 mm)	25	10
2108	13c. "Faun and Bacchus" (Rubens)	1·10	30
2109	30c. "Playing Patience" (R. Madrazo)	2·00	70

544 "Comecon" Headquarters Building, Moscow

1974. 25th Anniv of Council for Mutual Economic Aid.

2110	**544**	30c. multicoloured	1·70	70

545 Jose Marti and Lenin

1974. Visit of Leonid Brezhnev (General Secretary of Soviet Communist Party). Multicoloured.

2111	13c. Type **545**	1·60	40
2112	30c. Brezhnev with Castro	1·70	70

546 "Martian Crater"

1974. Cosmonautics Day. Science Fiction paintings by Sokolov. Multicoloured.

2113	1c. Type **546**	20	10
2114	2c. "Fiery Labyrinth"	20	10
2115	3c. "Amber Wave"	20	10
2116	4c. "Space Navigators"	20	15
2117	13c. "Planet in the Nebula"	1·60	20
2118	30c. "The World of the Two Suns"	2·75	60

See also Nos. 2196/201.

547 Cuban Letter of 1874

1974. Centenary of U.P.U.

2119	**547**	30c. multicoloured	2·00	85

1974. Stamp Day. Postal Markings of Pre-Stamp Exhibition. As T 521. Multicoloured.

2120	1c. "Havana" postmark	20	10
2121	3c. "Matanzas" postmark	30	10
2122	13c. "Trinidad" postmark	1·20	25
2123	20c. "Guana Vacoa" postmark	1·80	30

548 Congress Emblem

1974. 18th Sports' Congress of "Friendly Armies".

2124	**548**	3c. multicoloured	70	25

549 "Eumaeus atala atala" (butterfly)

1974. 175th Birth Anniv of Felipe Poey (naturalist). Multicoloured.

2125	1c. Type **549**	25	10
2126	2c. "Pineria terebra" (shell)	25	10
2127	3c. Reef butterflyfish	25	10
2128	4c. "Eurema dina dina" (butterfly)	80	25
2129	13c. "Hemitrochus fuscolabiata" (shell)	2·75	60
2130	30c. Bicoloured damsel-fish	3·50	70
MS2131	92×66 mm. 50c. "Apogon binotatus" (fish). Imperf	6·75	6·75

550 A. Mompo and 'Cello

1974. 50th Anniv of Havana Philharmonic Orchestra. Leading Personalities. Multicoloured.

2132	1c. Type **550**	20	10
2133	3c. C. P. Sentenat and piano	20	10
2134	5c. P. Mercado and trumpet	20	10
2135	10c. P. Sanjuan and emblem	1·10	20
2136	13c. R. Ondina and flute	1·40	30

551 "Heliconia humilis"

1974. Garden Flowers. Multicoloured.

2137	1c. Type **551**	25	10
2138	2c. "Anthurium andraeanum"	25	10
2139	3c. "Canna generalis"	25	10
2140	4c. "Alpinia purpurata"	30	10
2141	13c. "Gladiolus grandifiorus"	1·70	25
2142	30c. "Amomum capitatum"	4·50	85

552 Boxers and Global Emblem

1974. World Amateur Boxing Championships.

2143	**552**	1c. multicoloured	20	15
2144	-	3c. multicoloured	30	15
2145	-	13c. multicoloured	1·30	25

DESIGNS: 3c., 13c. Stages of Boxing matches similar to Type **552**.

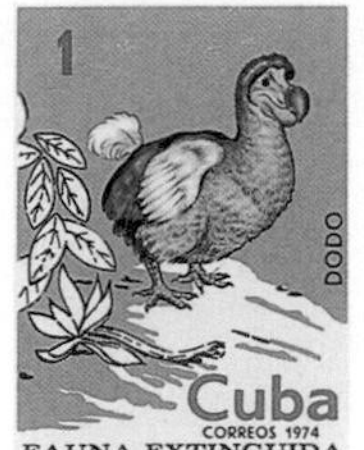

553 Mauritius Dodo ("Dodo")

1974. Extinct Birds. Multicoloured.

2146	1c. Type **553**	35	10
2147	3c. Cuban macaw ("Ara de Cuba")	35	10
2148	8c. Passenger pigeon ("Paloma Migratoria")	75	25
2149	10c. Moa	2·40	45
2150	13c. Great auk ("Gran Alca")	3·00	70

554 Salvador Allende

1974. 1st Death Anniv of Pres. Allende of Chile.

2151	**554**	13c. multicoloured	1·20	50

555 "Suriana maritima"

1974. Wild Flowers. (2nd series). Mult.

2152	1c. Type **555**	25	10
2153	3c. "Cassia ligustrina"	25	10
2154	8c. "Flaveria linearis"	35	20
2155	10c. "Stachytarpheta jamaicensis"	1·90	25
2156	13c. "Bacopa monnieri"	3·25	75

556 Flying Model Airplane

1974. 10th Anniv of Civil Aeronautical Institute. Multicoloured.

2157	1c. Type **556**	25	10
2158	3c. Parachutist	25	10
2159	8c. Glider in flight (horiz)	35	15
2160	10c. Antonov An-2 biplane spraying crops (horiz)	1·10	40
2161	13c. Ilyushin Il-62M in flight (horiz)	1·70	40

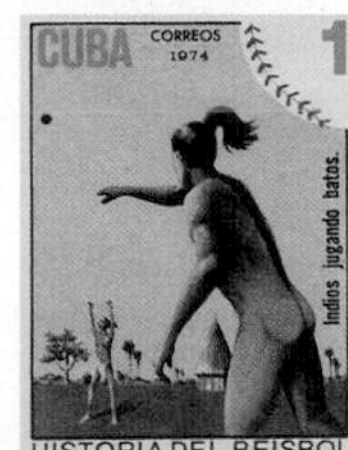

557 Indians playing Ball

1974. History of Baseball in Cuba. Mult.

2162	1c. Type **557**	15	10
2163	3c. Players of 1874 (First official game)	15	10
2164	8c. Emilio Sabourin	30	15
2165	10c. Modern players (horiz) (44×27 mm)	1·00	25
2166	13c. Latin-American Stadium, Havana (horiz) (44×27 mm)	1·60	30

558 Stamp, Cachet and Horseman

1974. Cent of "Mambi" Revolutionary Stamp.

2167	**558**	13c. multicoloured	1·20	25

559 Comecon Headquarters Building, Moscow and Emblem

1974. 16th Socialist Countries' Customs Conference.

2168	**559**	30c. blue and gold	1·70	55

560 Maj. Camilo Cienfuegos (revolutionary)

1974. 15th Anniv of Disappearance of Cienfuegos.

2169	**560**	3c. multicoloured	60	25

561 Miner's Helmet

1974. 8th World Mining Congress.

2170	**561**	13c. multicoloured	1·20	30

562 Oil Refinery

1974. 15th Anniv of Cuban Petroleum Institute.

2171	**562**	3c. multicoloured	60	15

563 Earth Station

1974. Inauguration of "Inter-Sputnik" Satellite Earth Station. Multicoloured.

2172	3c. Type **563**	20	10
2173	13c. Satellite and aerial	1·00	15
2174	1p. Satellite and flags	2·75	1·10

564 Emblems and Magnifying Glass

1974. 10th Anniv of Cuban Philatelic Federation.

2175	**564**	30c. multicoloured	1·90	60

565 "Mercury"

1974. 4th National Stamp Exhibition, Havana. Sheet 85×68 mm.

MS2176	**565** 50c. multicoloured	5·00	5·00

566 F. Joliot-Curie (1st president) (Picasso)

1974. 25th Anniv of World Peace Congress.

2177	**566**	30c. multicoloured	2·40	60

567 R. M. Villena

1974. 75th Birth Anniv of Ruben Martinez Villena (revolutionary).

2178	**567**	3c. red and yellow	55	15

568 Boxing Trophy

1975. Cuban Victories in World Amateur Boxing Championships. Sheet 109×74 mm. Imperf.

MS2179	**568** 50c. multicoloured	5·00	5·00

569 "The Word" (M. Pogolotti)

1975. National Museum Paintings (9th series). Multicoloured.

2180	1c. Type **569**	15	10
2181	2c. "The Silk-Cotton Tree" (H. Cleenewerk)	15	10
2182	3c. "Landscape" (G. Collazo)	15	10
2183	5c. "Still Life" (F. Peralta)	20	10
2184	13c. "Maria Wilson" (F. Martinez) (vert)	1·20	30
2185	30c. "The Couple" (M. Fortunay)	2·20	60

570 Bouquet and Woman's Head

1975. International Woman's Year.

2186	**570**	13c. multicoloured	1·20	30

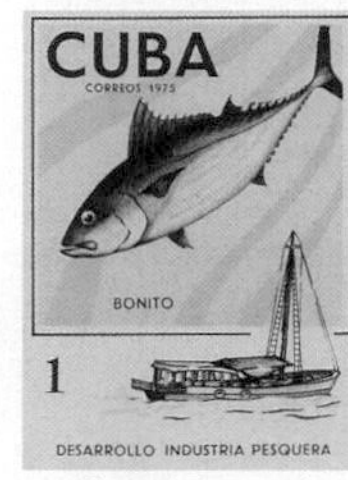

571 Skipjack Tuna and Fishing-boat

1975. Cuban Fishing Industry. Mult.

2187	1c. Type **571**	25	10
2188	2c. Blue-finned tunny	25	10
2189	3c. Nassau grouper	25	10
2190	8c. Silver hake	25	15
2191	13c. Prawn	1·10	60
2192	30c. Lobster	3·25	95

572 Nickel

1975. Cuban Minerals. Multicoloured.

2193	3c. Type **572**	30	15
2194	13c. Copper	1·30	25
2195	30c. Chromium	2·20	60

1975. Cosmonautics Day. Science Fiction paintings. As T 546. Multicoloured.

2196	1c. "Cosmodrome"	15	10
2197	2c. "Exploration craft" (vert)	15	10
2198	3c. "Earth eclipsing the Sun"	15	10
2199	5c. "On the Threshold"	30	10
2200	13c. "Astronauts on Mars"	1·20	20
2201	30c. "Astronauts' view of Earth"	2·00	50

573 Letter and "Correos" Postmark

1975. Stamp Day. Multicoloured.

2202	3c. Type **573**	15	10
2203	13c. Letter and steamship postmark	1·20	25
2204	30c. Letter and "N.A." postmark	1·80	50

574 Hoisting Red Flag over Reichstag, Berlin

1975. 30th Anniv of "Victory over Fascism".

2205	**574**	30c. multicoloured	1·90	50

575 Sevres Vase

1975. National Museum Treasures. Mult.

2206	1c. Type **575**	15	10
2207	2c. Meissen "Shepherdess and Dancers"	15	10
2208	3c. Chinese Porcelain Dish—"Lady with Parasol" (horiz)	20	10
2209	5c. Chinese Bamboo Screen—"The Phoenix"	30	10
2210	13c. "Allegory of Music" (F. Boucher)	1·20	25
2211	30c. "Portrait of a Lady" (L. Toque)	1·70	50
MS2212	61×104 mm. 50c. Park scene—"El Columpio" (H. Roberts) (25×39 mm)	4·75	4·50

576 Coloured Balls and Globe "Man"

1975. International Children's Day.

2213	**576**	3c. multicoloured	40	10

577 Cuban Vireo

1975. Birds (1st series). Multicoloured.

2214	1c. Type **577**	25	10
2215	2c. Cuban screech owl	25	10
2216	3c. Cuban conure	25	10
2217	5c. Blue-headed quail dove	50	15
2218	13c. Hook-billed kite	2·30	50
2219	30c. Zapata rail	3·25	95

See also Nos. 2301/6.

578 View of Centre

1973. 10th Anniv of National Scientific Investigation Centre.

2220	**578**	13c. multicoloured	1·10	20

579 Commission Emblem and Drainage Equipment

1975. Int Commission on Irrigation and Drainage.

2221	**579**	13c. multicoloured	1·10	20

580 "Cedrea mexicana"

1975. Reafforestation. Multicoloured.

2222	1c. Type **580**	15	10
2223	3c. "Swietonia mahagoni"	30	10
2224	5c. "Calophyllum brasiliense"	30	10
2225	13c. "Hibiscus tiliaceus"	90	30
2226	30c. "Pinus caribaea"	1·40	50

581 Women cultivating Young Plants

1975. 15th Anniv of Cuban Women's Federation.

2227	**581**	3c. multicoloured	40	15

582 Conference Emblem and Broken Chains

1975. International Conference on the Independence of Puerto Rico.

2228	**582**	13c. multicoloured	80	25

583 Baseball

1975. 7th Pan-American Games, Mexico. Mult.

2229	1c. Type **583**	20	10
2230	3c. Boxing	20	10
2231	5c. Handball	20	10
2232	13c. High jumping	1·20	30
2233	30c. Weightlifting	1·70	40
MS2234	77×91 mm. 50c. Games emblem and Sun disc. Imperf	4·25	4·25

584 Emblem and Crowd

1975. 15th Anniv of Revolutionary Defence Committees.

2235	**584**	3c. multicoloured	40	15

585 Institute Emblem

1975. 15th Anniv of Cuban "Friendship Amongst the Peoples" Institute.

2236	**585**	3c. multicoloured	25	15

586 Silver 1 Peso Coin, 1913

1975. 15th Anniv of Nationalization of Bank of Cuba. Multicoloured.

2237	13c. Type **586**	90	30
2238	13c. 1 peso banknote, 1934	90	30
2239	13c. 1 peso banknote, 1946	90	30
2240	13c. 1 peso banknote, 1964	90	30
2241	13c. 1 peso banknote, 1973	90	30

587 "La Junta", Cuba's first locomotive, 1837

1975. "Evolution of Railways". Multicoloured.

2242	1c. Type **587**	15	10
2243	3c. Steam locomotive "M. M. Prieto", 1920	25	10
2244	5c. Russian-built Type TEM-4 diesel locomotive	25	10
2245	13c. Hungarian-built Type DVM-9 diesel locomotive	2·50	30
2246	30c. Russian-built Type M-62K diesel locomotive	3·00	60

588 Bobbins and Flag

1975. Textile Industry.

2247	**588**	13c. multicoloured	1·00	20

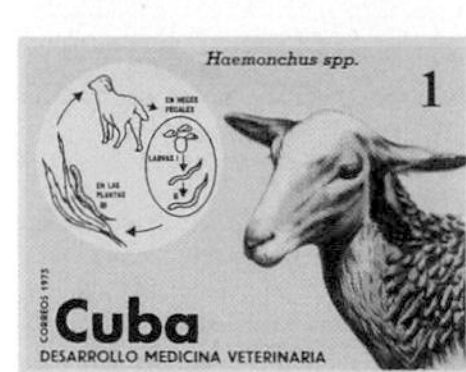

589 Sheep and Diagram

1975. Development of Veterinary Medicine. Animals and Disease Cycles. Multicoloured.

2248	1c. Type **589**	20	10
2249	2c. Dog	20	10
2250	3c. Cockerel	20	10
2251	5c. Horse	20	10
2252	13c. Pig	1·10	30
2253	30c. Ox	2·00	50

590 Manuel Ascunce Domenech

1975. Manuel Domenech Educational Detachment.

2254	**590**	3c. multicoloured	30	15

592 Communists with Flags inside Figure "1"

1975. Agriculture and Water-supply.

2255	**591**	13c. multicoloured	1·00	25

591 "Irrigation"

1976. 1st Cuban Communist Party Congress. Multicoloured.

2256	3c. Type **592**	15	10
2257	13c. Workers with banner (horiz)	90	30
2258	30c. Jose Marti and Cuban leaders (horiz)	1·20	40

593 Pre-natal Exercises

1976. 8th Latin-American Obstetrics and Gynaecology Congress, Havana.

2259	**593**	3c. multicoloured	50	15

594 "Seated Woman" (V. Manuel)

1976. National Museum Paintings (10th series). Multicoloured.

2260	1c. Type **594**	15	10
2261	2c. "Garden" (S. Rusinol) (horiz)	15	10
2262	3c. "Guadalquivir River" (M. Barron y Carrillo) (horiz)	20	10
2263	5c. "Self-portrait" (Jan Steen)	20	10
2264	13c. "Portrait of Woman" (L. M. van Loo)	1·10	20
2265	30c. "La Chula" (J. A. Morell) (27×44 mm)	1·80	40

595 Conference Emblem and Building

1976. Socialist Communications Ministers' Conference, Havana.

2266	**595**	13c. multicoloured	1·10	20

596 American Foxhound

1976. Hunting Dogs. Multicoloured.
2267 1c. Type **596** 20 10
2268 2c. Labrador retriever 20 10
2269 3c. Borzoi 20 10
2270 5c. Irish setter 20 15
2271 13c. Pointer 1·10 25
2272 30c. Cocker Spaniel 2·00 40

597 Flags, Arms and Anthem

1976. Socialist Constitution, 1976.
2273 **597** 13c. multicoloured 1·10 30

598 Ruy Lopez Segura

1976. History of Chess. Multicoloured.
2274 1c. Type **598** 15 10
2275 2c. Francois Philidor 15 10
2276 3c. Wilhelm Steinitz 20 10
2277 13c. Emanuel Lasker 1·50 25
2278 30c. Jose Raul Capablanca 1·60 55

599 Radio Aerial and Map

1976. 15th Anniv of Cuban International Broadcasting Services.
2279 **599** 50c. multicoloured 1·60 70

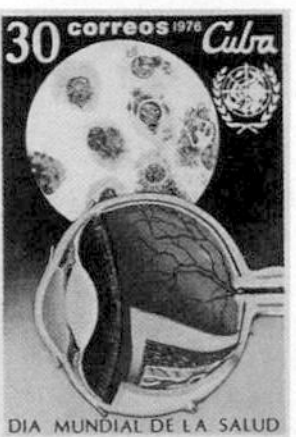

600 Section of Human Eye and Microscope Slide

1976. World Health Day.
2280 **600** 30c. multicoloured 1·20 50

601 Children in Creche

1976. 15th Anniv of Infant Welfare Centres.
2281 **601** 3c. multicoloured 50 15

602 Y. Gagarin in Space-suit

1976. 15th Anniv of First Manned Space Flight. Multicoloured.
2282 1c. Type **602** 15 10
2283 2c. V. Tereshkova and rockets 15 10
2284 3c. Cosmonaut on "space walk" (vert) 20 10
2285 5c. Spacecraft and Moon (vert) 30 10
2286 13c. Spacecraft in manoeuvre (vert) 90 25

2287 30c. Space link 1·40 30

603 Cuban Machine-gunner

1976. 15th Anniv of Giron Victory. Mult.
2288 3c. Type **603** 20 10
2289 13c. Cuban pilot and Stylized fighter aircraft attacking ship 80 25
2290 30c. Cuban soldier wielding rifle (vert) 1·50 45

604 Heads of Farmers

1976. 15th Anniv of National Association of Small Farmers (ANAP).
2291 **604** 3c. multicoloured 50 10

605 Volleyball

1976. Olympic Games, Montreal. Mult.
2292 1c. Type **605** 15 10
2293 2c. Basketball 15 10
2294 3c. Long-jumping 15 10
2295 4c. Boxing 20 10
2296 5c. Weightlifting 20 10
2297 13c. Judo 90 30
2298 30c. Swimming 1·40 50
MS2299 100×80 mm. 50c. Otter emblem. Imperf 3·75 3·75

606 Modern Secondary School

1976. Rural Secondary Schools.
2300 **606** 3c. black and red 50 10

607 Oriente Warbler

1976. Birds (2nd series). Multicoloured.
2301 1c. Type **607** 30 10
2302 2c. Cuban pygmy owl 30 10
2303 3c. Fernandina's flicker 30 20
2304 5c. Cuban tody 85 25
2305 13c. Gundlach's hawk 1·70 40
2306 30c. Cuban trogon 3·50 1·00

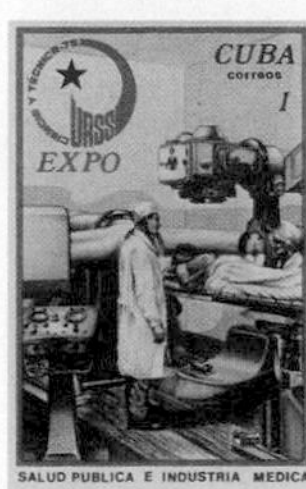

608 Medical Treatment

1976. "Expo", Havana. Soviet Science and Technology. Multicoloured.
2307 1c. Type **608** 15 10
2308 3c. Child and deer ("Environmental Protection") 15 10
2309 10c. Cosmonauts on launch pad ("Cosmos Investigation") 40 30
2310 30c. Tupolev Tu-144 airplane ("Soviet Transport") (horiz) 2·10 60

609 "El Inglesito"

1976. Death Cent of Henry M. Reeve (patriot).
2311 **609** 13c. multicoloured 55 20

610 "G. Collazo" (J. Dabour)

1976. Cuban Paintings. Multicoloured.
2312 1c. Type **610** 15 10
2313 2c. "The Art Lovers" (G. Collazo) (horiz) 15 10
2314 3c. "The Patio" (G. Collazo) 15 10
2315 5c. "Cocotero" (G. Collazo) 15 10
2316 13c. "New York Studio" (G. Collazo) (horiz) 50 20
2317 30c. "Emelinz Collazo" (G. Collazo) (horiz) 1·70 60

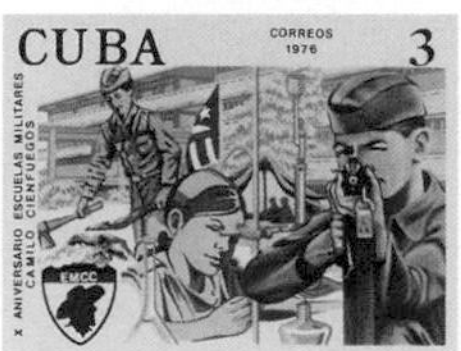

611 School Activities

1976. 10th Anniv of "Camilo Cienfuegos" Military School.
2318 **611** 3c. multicoloured 30 15

612 "Imias" (freighter)

1976. Development of Cuban Merchant Marine. Multicoloured.
2319 1c. Type **612** 30 15
2320 2c. "Comandante Camilo Cienfuegos" (freighter) 30 15
2321 3c. "Comandante Pinares" (cargo liner) 30 15
2322 5c. "Vietnam Heroico" (cargo liner) 60 25
2323 13c. "Presidente Allende" (ore carrier) 1·90 60
2324 30c. "XIII Congreso" (bulk carrier) 3·75 1·00

613 Emblem and part of Cine Film

1976. 8th International Cinematographic Festival of Socialist Countries, Havana.
2325 **613** 3c. multicoloured 30 15

614 Scene from "Apollo"

1976. 5th International Ballet Festival, Havana. Multicoloured.
2326 1c. Type **614** 15 10
2327 2c. "The River and the Forest" (vert) 15 10
2328 3c. "Giselle" 15 10
2329 5c. "Oedipus Rex" (vert) 20 10
2330 13c. "Carmen" (vert) 90 25
2331 30c. "Vital Song" (vert) 1·60 35

615 Soldier and Sportsmen

1976. 3rd Military Games.
2332 **615** 3c. multicoloured 40 15

616 "Granma"

1976. 20th Anniv of "Granma" Landings.
2333 **616** 1c. multicoloured 15 10
2334 - 3c. multicoloured 15 10
2335 - 13c. multicoloured 80 25
2336 - 30c. multicoloured 1·30 55
DESIGNS: 3c. to 30c. Different scenes showing guerrillas.

617 "Cuban Landscape" (F. Cavada)

1976. 5th National Philatelic Exhibition. Sheet 90×100 mm.
MS2337 **617** 50c. multicoloured 5·00 4·75

618 Volleyball

1976. Cuban Victories in Montreal Olympic Games. Multicoloured.
2338 1c. Type **618** 15 10
2339 2c. Hurdling 15 10
2340 3c. Running 15 10
2341 8c. Boxing 20 15
2342 13c. Winning race 65 25
2343 30c. Judo 1·40 50
MS2344 69×101 mm. 50c. As No. 2341 4·00 3·00

619 "Golden Cross Inn" (S. Scott)

1977. National Museum Paintings (11th series). Multicoloured.
2345 1c. Type **619** 15 10
2346 3c. "Portrait of a Man" (J. Verspronck) (vert) 15 10

2347	5c. "Venetian Landscape" (F. Guardi)	15	10
2348	10c. "Valley Corner" (H. Cleenewerck) (vert)	45	15
2349	13c. "F. Xaviera Paula" (anon) (vert)	65	30
2350	30c. "F. de Medici" (C. Allori) (vert)	1·60	50

The vert designs are slightly larger, 27×43 mm.

620 Motor Bus

1977. Rural Transport.

2351	**620**	3c. multicoloured	65	15

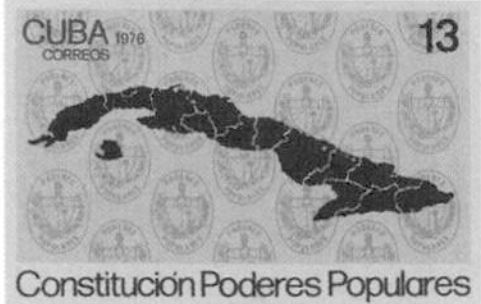

621 Map of Cuba

1977. Constitution of Popular Government.

2352	**621**	13c. multicoloured	55	20

622 Cuban Green Woodpecker

1977. Cuban Birds. Multicoloured.

2353	1c. Type **622**	50	25
2354	4c. Cuban grassquit	60	25
2355	10c. Cuban blackbird	1·20	30
2356	13c. Zapata wren	1·80	35
2357	30c. Bee hummingbird	3·50	85

623 Mechanical Scoop and Emblem

1977. Air. 6th Latin-American and Caribbean Sugar Exporters Meeting, Havana.

2358	**623**	13c. multicoloured	60	20

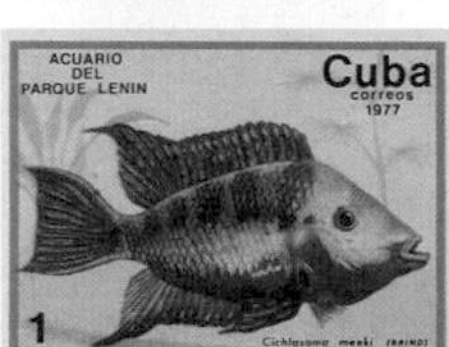

624 Fire-mouthed Cichlid

1977. Fish in Lenin Park Aquarium, Havana. Multicoloured.

2359	1c. Type **624**	15	10
2360	3c. Tiger barb	15	10
2361	5c. Koi carp	15	10
2362	10c. Siamese fightingfish	25	15
2363	13c. Freshwater angelfish (vert)	1·10	20
2364	30c. Buenos Aires tetra	2·30	50

625 "Sputnik 1" and East German Stamp

1977. 20th Anniv of 1st Artificial Satellite. Multicoloured.

2365	1c. Type **625**	20	15
2366	3c. "Luna 16" and Hungarian stamp	20	15
2367	5c. "Cosmos" and North Korean stamp	20	15
2368	10c. "Sputnik 3" and Polish stamp	30	20
2369	13c. Earth, Moon and Yugoslav stamp	95	30
2370	30c. Earth, Moon and Cuban stamp	1·60	50
MS2371	95×76 mm. 50c. "Sputnik 1" and Russian stamp. Imperf	3·75	3·50

626 Antonio Maria Romeu

1977. Cuban Musicians. Multicoloured.

2372	3c. Type **626** (postage)	30	10
2373	13c. Jorge Ankerman (air)	80	25

627 "Hibiscus rosa sinensis"

1977. Birth Centenary of Dr. Juan Tomas Roig (botanist). Cuban Flowers. Multicoloured.

2374	1c. Type **627** (postage)	15	10
2375	2c. "Nerium oleander"	15	10
2376	5c. "Allamanda cathartica"	15	10
2377	10c. "Pelargonium zonale"	30	15
2378	13c. "Caesalpinia pulcherrima" (air)	70	15
2379	30c. "Catharanthus roseus"	1·40	45
MS2380	71×92 mm. 50c. Dr. J. T. Roig (33×40 mm)	3·50	3·00

628 Horse-drawn Fire Engine

1977. Fire Prevention Week. Multicoloured.

2381	1c. Type **628**	15	10
2382	2c. Horse-drawn fire engine (different)	15	10
2383	6c. Early motor fire pump	20	10
2384	10c. Modern motor fire pump	40	15
2385	13c. Turntable-ladder	75	30
2386	30c. Heavy rescue vehicle	1·60	40

629 20th Anniversary Medal

1977. National Decorations.

2387	**629**	1c. mult (postage)	20	10
2388	-	3c. multicoloured	20	15
2389	-	13c. multicoloured (air)	65	20
2390	-	30c. multicoloured	1·20	45

DESIGNS: 3c. to 30c. Various medals and ribbons.

630 "Portrait of Mary"

1977. Painting by Jorge Arche. Mult.

2391	1c. Type **630** (postage)	15	10
2392	3c. "Jose Marti"	15	10
2393	5c. "Portrait of Aristides"	15	10
2394	10c. "Bathers" (horiz)	40	15
2395	13c. "My Wife and I" (air)	50	15
2396	30c. "The Game of Dominoes" (horiz)	1·30	50
MS2397	64×79 mm. 50c. "Self-portrait"	3·25	3·25

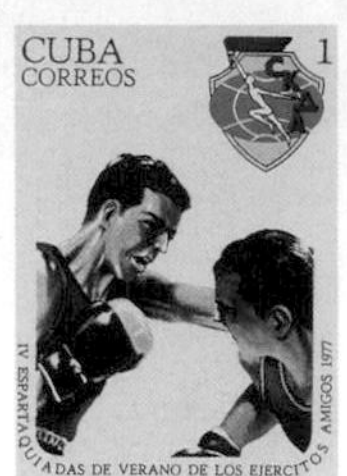

631 Boxing

1977. Military Spartakiad. Multicoloured.

2398	1c. Type **631** (postage)	15	10
2399	3c. Volleyball	15	10
2400	5c. Parachuting	15	10
2401	10c. Running	30	15
2402	13c. Grenade-throwing (air)	50	15
2403	30c. Rifle-shooting (horiz)	1·20	50

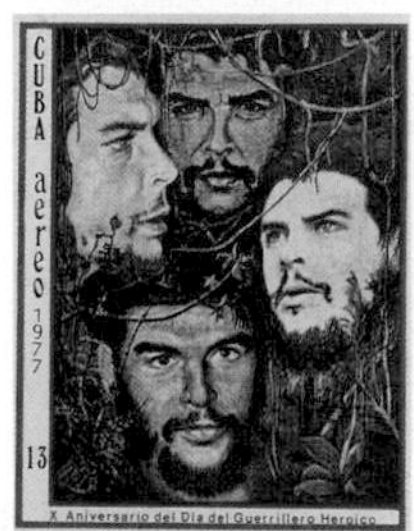

632 Che Guevara

1977. Air. 10th Anniv of Guerrilla Heroes Day.

2404	**632**	13c. multicoloured	80	25

633 Curtiss A-1 Seaplane and Parla Stamp of 1952

1977. 50th Anniv of Cuban Air Mail. Mult.

2405	1c. Type **633** (postage)	15	10
2406	2c. Ford 5-AT trimotor airplane and Havana–Key West cachet	15	10
2407	5c. Flying boat "American Clipper" and first flight cachet	15	10
2408	10c. Douglas DC-4 and Havana–Madrid cachet	45	15
2409	13c. Lockheed L.1049 Super Constellation and Havana–Mexico cachet (air)	80	15
2410	30c. Ilyushin Il-18 and Havana–Prague cachet	1·60	70

634 Cruiser "Aurora"

1977. 60th Anniv of Russian Revolution.

2411	**634**	3c. black, red and gold	15	10
2412	-	13c. black, red and gold	35	20
2413	-	30c. gold, red and black	1·30	50

DESIGNS: 13c. Lenin and flags; 30c. Hammer and sickle with scenes of technology.

635 "The Adoration of the Magi" (detail)

1977. Air. 400th Birth Anniv of Peter Paul Rubens. Sheet 85×115 mm.

MS2414	**635** 50c. multicoloured	3·75	3·75

636 Cat

1977. Felines in Havana Zoo. Multicoloured.

2415	1c. Type **636** (postage)	15	10
2416	2c. Leopard (black race)	15	10
2417	8c. Puma	15	15
2418	10c. Leopard	90	25
2419	13c. Tiger (air)	1·10	25
2420	30c. Lion	1·50	55

637 Cienfuegos Uprising

1977. 20th Anniv of Martyrs of the Revolution. Multicoloured.

2421	3c. Type **637** (postage)	15	10
2422	20c. Attack on the Presidential Palace	80	30
2423	13c. Landing from the "Corynthia" (air)	60	25

638 Clinic, Havana

1977. 75th Anniv of Pan-American Health Organization.

2424	**638**	13c. multicoloured	60	15

639 Map of Cuba and Units of Measurement

1977. International System of Measurement.

2425	**639**	3c. multicoloured	30	10

640 University Building and Coat of Arms

1978. 250th Anniv of Havana University. Multicoloured.

2426	3c. Type **640** (postage)	20	10
2427	13c. University building and crossed sabres (air)	60	25
2428	30c. Student crowd and statue	90	50

641 "Jose Marti" (A. Menocal)

1978. Air. 125th Anniv of Jose Marti (patriot).

2429	**641**	13c. multicoloured	65	15

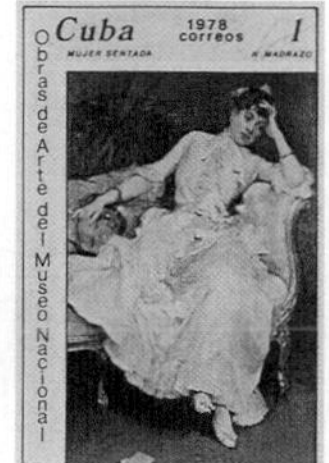
642 "Seated Woman" (R. Madrazo)

1978. National Museum Paintings (12th series). Multicoloured.

2430	1c. Type **642** (postage)	15	10
2431	4c. "Girl" (J. Sorolla)	15	10
2432	6c. "Landscape with Figures" (J. Pilliment) (horiz)	15	10
2433	10c. "The Cow" (E. Abela) (horiz)	50	15
2434	13c. "El Guadalquivir" (M. Barron) (horiz) (air)	85	25
2435	30c. "H. E. Ridley" (J. J. Masqueries)	95	50

643 Patrol Boat, Frontier Guard and Dog

1978. 15th Anniv of Frontier Troops.

2436	**643**	13c. multicoloured	1·30	30

644 Cuban Solitaire

1978. Cuban Birds. Multicoloured.

2437	1c. Type **644** (postage)	45	10
2438	4c. Cuban gnatcatcher	50	10
2439	10c. Oriente warbler	1·30	20
2440	13c. Zapata sparrow (air)	1·50	50
2441	30c. Cuban macaw and ivory-billed woodpecker (vert)	2·30	1·10

645 "Antonio Maceo" (A. Melero)

1978. Air. Centenary of Baragua Protest.

2442	**645**	13c. multicoloured	60	30

646 "Intercosmos" Satellite

1978. Cosmonautics Day. Multicoloured.

2443	1c. Type **646** (postage)	15	10
2444	2c. "Luna 24" (horiz)	15	10
2445	5c. "Venus 9"	30	10
2446	10c. "Cosmos" (horiz)	30	20
2447	13c. "Venus 10" (horiz) (air)	60	15
2448	30c. "Lunokhod 2" (36×46 mm)	1·00	50

647 Smiling Worker and Emblem

1978. 9th World Federation of Trade Unions Congress, Prague.

2449	**647**	30c. red and black	85	45

648 Parliament Building, Budapest and 1919 Hungarian Stamp

1978. Air "Socfilex" Stamp Exhibition, Budapest.

2450	**648**	30c. multicoloured	1·40	55

649 "Melocactus guitarti"

1978. Cactus Flowers. Multicoloured.

2451	1c. Type **649** (postage)	20	10
2452	4c. "Leptocereus wrightii"	20	10
2453	6c. "Opuntia militaris"	20	10
2454	10c. "Cylindropuntia hystrix"	50	20
2455	13c. "Rhodocactus cubensis" (air)	75	30
2456	30c. "Harrisia taetra"	1·20	50

650 Satellite and Globe

1978. Air. World Telecommunications Day.

2457	**650**	30c. multicoloured	1·00	45

651 Africans and O.A.U. Emblem

1978. Air. 15th Anniv of Organization of African Unity.

2458	**651**	30c. multicoloured	85	45

652 "Niven, Wales" (G.H. Russell)

1978. Air. Capex 78 International Philatelic Exhibition, Toronto. Sheet 69×93 mm.

MS2459 **652**	50c. multicoloured	3·00	3·00

653 Clown Barb

1978. Fish in Lenin Park Aquarium, Havana. Multicoloured.

2460	1c. Type **653** (postage)	15	10
2461	4c. Flame tetra	15	10
2462	6c. Guppy	15	10
2463	10c. Dwarf gourami	35	15
2464	13c. Veil-tailed goldfish (air)	70	20
2465	30c. Brown discus	1·40	50

654 Basketball

1978. 13th Central American and Caribbean Games. Multicoloured.

2466	1c. Type **654** (postage)	20	10
2467	3c. Boxing	20	10
2468	5c. Weightlifting	20	10
2469	10c. Fencing (horiz)	35	15
2470	13c. Volleyball (air)	50	25
2471	30c. Running	1·00	45

655 Moncada Fortress

1978. 25th Anniv of Attack on Moncada Fortress. Multicoloured.

2472	3c. Type **655** (postage)	20	10
2473	13c. Soldiers with rifles (air)	40	15
2474	30c. Dove and flags	90	35

656 Prague

1978. 11th World Youth and Students' Festival, Havana. Multicoloured.

2475	3c. Type **656** (postage)	20	10
2476	3c. Budapest	20	10
2477	3c. Berlin	20	10
2478	3c. Bucharest	20	10
2479	3c. Warsaw	20	10
2480	13c. Moscow (air)	55	15
2481	13c. Vienna	55	15
2482	13c. Helsinki	55	15
2483	13c. Sofia	55	15
2484	13c. Berlin	55	15
2485	30c. Havana (46×36 mm)	1·20	30

657 Marching Soldiers with Flag

1978. 5th Anniv of Young Workers Army.

2486	**657**	3c. multicoloured	25	10

658 "Pargo"

1978. Fishing Fleet. Multicoloured.

2487	1c. Type **658** (postage)	15	10
2488	2c. Fish-processing ship	15	10
2489	5c. Shrimp fishing boat	15	10
2490	10c. Stern trawler	40	15
2491	13c. "Mar Carbide" (air)	85	25
2492	30c. Refrigeration and processing ship	1·60	60

659 "Marina" (Venetian fishing vessel) A. Brandeis)

1978. Air. PRAGA 78 International Philatelic Exhibition. Sheet 83×109 mm.

MS2493 **659**	50c. multicoloured	3·00	3·00

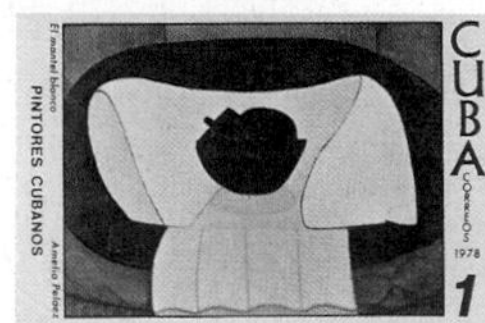
660 "The White Coat" (Pelaez del Casal)

1978. Painting by Amelia Pelaez del Casal. Multicoloured.

2494	1c. Type **660** (postage)	15	10
2495	3c. "Still Life with Flowers"	15	10
2496	6c. "Women"	15	10
2497	10c. "Fish"	35	15
2498	13c. "Flowering Almond" (air)	50	15
2499	30c. "Still Life in Blue"	1·10	45
MS2500	63×80 mm. 50c. "Portrait of Amelia" (L. Romanach)	3·25	3·00

661 Letters, Satellite and Globe

1978. Air 20th Anniv of Organization for Communication Co-operation between Socialist Countries.

2501	**661**	30c. multicoloured	1·00	35

662 Postcard

1978. Air. 6th National Stamp Exhibition. Sheet 105×66 mm. Imperf.

MS2502	662 50c. multicoloured	3·00	3·00

663 Hand

1978. Air. International Anti-Apartheid Year.

2503	663 13c. black, pink & mve	1·30	1·10

664 White Rhinoceros

1978. Animals in Havana Zoo. Multicoloured.

2504	1c. Type **664** (postage)	20	10
2505	4c. Okapi (vert)	20	10
2506	6c. Mandrill	20	10
2507	10c. Giraffe (vert)	50	15
2508	13c. Cheetah (air)	70	30
2509	30c. African elephant (vert)	1·50	65

665 "Grand Pas de Quatre"

1978. 30th Anniv of National Ballet Company. Multicoloured.

2510	3c. Type **665** (postage)	20	10
2511	13c. "Giselle" (air)	65	25
2512	30c. "Genesis"	1·30	40

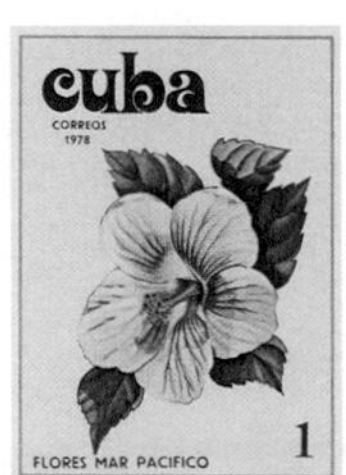

666 Hibiscus

1978. Pacific Flowers.

2513	666	1c. mult (postage)	15	10
2514	-	4c. multicoloured	15	10
2515	-	6c. multicoloured	20	10
2516	-	10c. multicoloured	40	15
2517	-	13c. mult (air)	65	25
2518	-	30c. multicoloured	1·30	40

DESIGNS: 4c. to 30c. Different flowers.

667 Julius and Ethel Rosenberg

1978. Air. 25th Death Anniv of Julius and Ethel Rosenberg (American Communists).

2519	667 13c. multicoloured	50	15

668 Fidel Castro and Soldier

1979. 20th Anniv of Revolution. Mult.

2520	3c. Type **668**	15	15
2521	13c. Symbols of industry	40	15
2522	1p. Flag, flame and globe	2·75	1·10

669 Julio Mella

1979. 50th Death Anniv of J. A. Mella.

2523	669 13c. multicoloured	45	15

670 Blue-headed Quail Dove

1979. Doves and Pigeons. Multicoloured.

2524	1c. Type **670**	35	15
2525	3c. Key West quail dove	40	15
2526	7c. Grey-faced quail dove	40	15
2527	8c. Ruddy quail dove	50	20
2528	13c. White-crowned pigeon	95	25
2529	30c. Plain pigeon	1·90	70

671 "Genre Scene" (D. Teniers)

1979. National Museum Paintings (13th series). Multicoloured.

2530	1c. Type **671**	15	10
2531	3c. "Arrival of Spanish Troops" (J. Meissonier)	15	10
2532	6c. "A Joyful Gathering" (Sir David Wilkie)	25	10
2533	10c. "Capea" (E. de Lucas Padilla)	35	10
2534	13c. "Teatime" (R. Madrazo) (vert)	65	20
2535	30c. "Peasant in front of a Tavern" (Adriaen van Ostade)	1·40	40

672 "Nymphaea capensis"

1979. Aquatic Flowers. Multicoloured.

2536	3c. Type **672**	15	10
2537	10c. "Nymphaea ampla"	30	15
2538	13c. "Nymphaea coerulea"	50	20
2539	30c. "Nymphaea rubra"	1·20	40

673 "20" Flag and Film Frames

1979. 20th Anniv of Cuban Cinema.

2540	673 3c. multicoloured	30	10

674 Rocket Launch

1979. Cosmonautics Day. Multicoloured.

2541	1c. Type **674**	15	10
2542	4c. "Soyuz"	15	10
2543	6c. "Salyut"	30	10
2544	10c. "Soyuz" and "Salyut" link-up	40	10
2545	13c. "Soyuz" and "Salyut"	70	15
2546	30c. Parachute and capsule	1·50	40
MS2547	67×91 mm. 50c. Design similar to 10c	3·00	3·00

675 Hands and Globe

1979. 6th Non-Aligned Countries Summit Conference. Multicoloured.

2548	3c. Type **675**	20	10
2549	13c. "6" ("Against Colonialism")	40	15
2550	30c. Joined coin and globe ("A New Economic Order")	1·10	35

676 Cuna Indian Tapestry, Panama

1979. 20th Anniv of "House of the Americas" Museum.

2551	676 13c. multicoloured	40	20

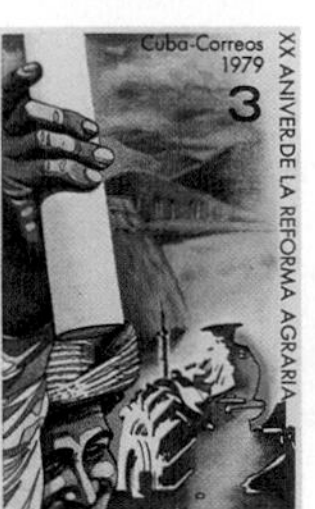

677 Farmer holding Title Deed

1979. 20th Anniv of Agrarian Reform.

2552	677 3c. multicoloured	30	10

678 "The Party" (J. Pascin)

1979. Philaserdica 79 Philatelic Exhibition, Sofia, Bulgaria. Sheet 104×52 mm.

MS2553	678 50c. multicoloured	3·00	3·00

679 "Eulepidotis rectimargo"

1979. Cuban Nocturnal Butterflies. Mult.

2554	1c. Type **679**	15	10
2555	4c. "Othreis materna"	15	10
2556	6c. "Noropsis hieroglyphica"	35	15
2557	10c. "Heterochroma sp."	35	15
2558	13c. "Melanchroia regnatrix"	75	20
2559	30c. "Attera gemmata"	1·80	45

680 Children's Heads

1979. Air. International Year of the Child.

2560	680 13c. multicoloured	80	15

681 "Avenue du Maine, Paris"

1979. 10th Death Anniv of Victor Manuel Garcia (painter). Multicoloured.

2561	1c. Type **681**	15	10
2562	3c. "Portrait of Enmita"	15	10
2563	6c. "Rio San Juan, Matanzas"	15	10
2564	10c. "Landscape with Woman carrying Hay"	25	15
2565	13c. "Still-life with Vase"	35	15
2566	30c. "Street by Night"	1·30	45
MS2567	64×81 mm. 50c. "Self-portrait"	3·00	3·00

682 Clenched Fists, Dove and Bombs

1979. 30th Anniv of World Peace Council.

2568	682 30c. multicoloured	85	35

683 Lighthouse and Fireworks

1979. Air. "Carifesta 79" Festival, Havana.

2569	683 13c. multicoloured	60	15

684 Wrestling

1979. Pre-Olympics, Moscow 1980. Mult.

2570	1c. Type **684**	15	10
2571	4c. Boxing	15	10
2572	6c. Volleyball	15	10
2573	10c. Rifle-shooting	20	15
2574	13c. Weightlifting	45	25
2575	30c. High jump	1·20	35

685 "Rosa eglanteria"

1979. Roses. Multicoloured.

2576	1c. Type **685**	20	10
2577	2c. "Rosa centifolia anemo-noides"	20	10
2578	3c. "Rosa indica vulgaris"	20	10
2579	5c. "Rosa eglanteria var. punicea"	20	10
2580	10c. "Rosa sulfurea"	20	15
2581	13c. "Rosa muscosa alba"	45	15
2582	20c. "Rosa gallica purpurea velutina, Parva"	90	30

686 Council Emblem

1979. 30th Anniv of Council of Mutual Economic Aid.

2583	**686**	13c. multicoloured	40	15

687 Games Emblem and Activities

1979. Air. "Universiada 79" 10th World University Games, Mexico City.

2584	**687**	13c. green, gold & turq	60	15

688 Conventions Palace

1979. Air. 6th Non-Aligned Countries Summit Conference, Havana.

2585	**688**	50c. multicoloured	1·50	95

689 Sir Rowland Hill and Casket containing Freedom of the City of London

1979. Air. Death Centenary of Sir Rowland Hill.

2586	**689**	30c. multicoloured	1·20	30

690 Ford 5-AT Trimotor

1979. 50th Anniv of Cuban Airlines. Mult.

2587	1c. Type **690**	15	10
2588	2c. Sikorsky S-38 flying boat	15	10
2589	3c. Douglas DC-3	30	10
2590	4c. Ilyushin Il-18	30	10
2591	13c. Yakovlev Yak-40	75	25
2592	40c. Ilyushin Il-62M	2·00	50

691 Rumanian "New Constitution" Stamp of 1948

1979. Air. "Socfilex 79" Stamp Exhibition, Bucharest.

2593	**691**	30c. multicoloured	1·10	50

692 Camilo Cienfuegos

1979. 20th Anniv of Disappearance of Camilo Cienfuegos (revolutionary).

2594	**692**	3c. multicoloured	25	10

693 Alvaro Reinoso and Sugar Cane

1979. 15th Anniv of Sugar Cane Institute and 150th Birth Anniv of Alvaro Reinoso.

2595	**693**	13c. multicoloured	60	15

694 Chimpanzees

1979. Young Zoo Animals. Multicoloured.

2596	1c. Type **694**	25	10
2597	2c. Leopards	25	10
2598	3c. Fallow deer	25	10
2599	4c. Lions	25	10
2600	5c. Brown bears	25	10
2601	13c. Eurasian red squirrels	40	25
2602	30c. Giant pandas	95	40
2603	50c. Tigers	1·80	85

695 Ground Receiving Station

1979. Air. 50th Anniv of International Radio Consultative Committee.

2604	**695**	30c. multicoloured	1·10	30

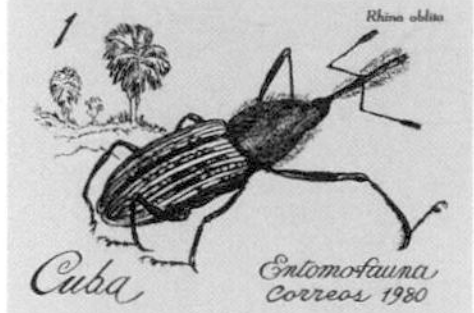

696 "Rhina oblita"

1980. Insects. Multicoloured.

2605	1c. Type **696**	15	10
2606	5c. "Odontocera josemartii" (vert)	15	10
2607	6c. "Pinthocoelium columbi-num"	15	10
2608	10c. "Calosoma splendida" (vert)	35	10
2609	13c. "Homophileurus cubanus" (vert)	75	25
2610	30c. "Heterops dimidiata" (vert)	1·50	65

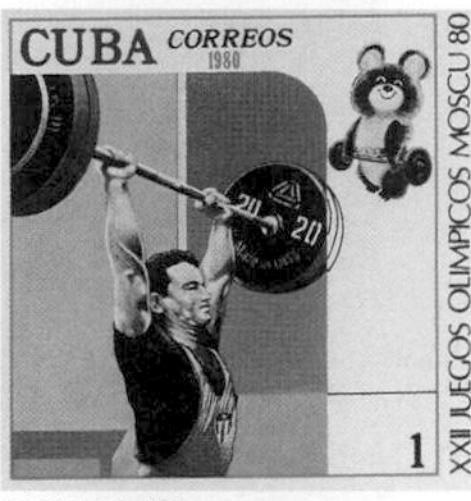

697 Weightlifting

1980. Olympic Games, Moscow. Multicoloured.

2611	1c. Type **697**	15	10
2612	2c. Shooting	15	10
2613	5c. Javelin	15	10
2614	6c. Wrestling	15	10
2615	8c. Judo	20	10
2616	10c. Running	20	15
2617	13c. Boxing	45	25
2618	30c. Volleyball	1·30	60
MS2619	94×79 mm. 50c. Misha the bear (mascot) (27×35 mm)	2·50	2·20

698 "Oak Trees" (Henry Joseph Harpignies)

1980. National Museum Paintings (14th series). Multicoloured.

2620	1c. Type **698**	15	10
2621	4c. "Family Reunion" (Willem van Mieris) (horiz)	15	10
2622	6c. "Poultry" (Melchior de Hondecoeter)	15	10
2623	9c. "Innocence" (Williams A. Bouguereau)	55	15
2624	13c. "Venetian Scene II" (Michele Marieschi) (horiz)	70	25
2625	30c. "Spanish Country-women" (Joaquin Dominguez Bequer)	1·50	55

699 "Malvern Hall" (John Constable)

1980. London 1980 International Stamp Exhibition. Sheet 104×51 mm.

MS2626	**699** 50c. multicoloured	3·00	3·00

700 Intercosmos Emblem

1980. Intercosmos Programme. Mult.

2627	1c. Type **700**	15	10
2628	4c. Satellite and globe (Physics)	15	10
2629	6c. Satellite and dish aerial (Communications)	15	10
2630	10c. Satellite, grid lines and map (Meteorology)	35	15
2631	13c. Staff of Aesculapius, rocket and satellites (Biology and Medicine)	45	25
2632	30c. Surveying Satellite	1·50	55

701 Cuban Stamps of 1955 and 1959 (image scaled to 71% of original size)

1980. 125th Anniv of Cuban Stamps.

2633	**701**	30c. blue, red & lt blue	1·00	50

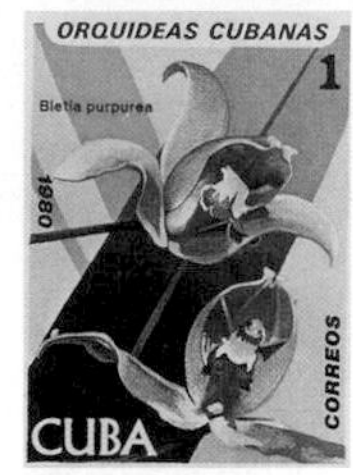

702 "Bletia purpurea"

1980. Orchids. Multicoloured.

2634	1c. Type **702**	20	10
2635	4c. "Oncidium leiboldii"	20	10
2636	6c. "Epidendrum cochieatum"	20	10
2637	10c. "Cattleyopsis lindenii"	50	10
2638	13c. "Encyclia fucata"	90	25
2639	30c. "Encyclia phoenicea"	2·00	60

703 Bottle-nosed Dolphin

1980. Marine Mammals. Multicoloured.

2640	1c. Type **703**	40	10
2641	3c. Humpback whale (vert)	40	10
2642	13c. Cuvier's beaked whale	1·20	15
2643	30c. Caribbean monk seal	3·00	60

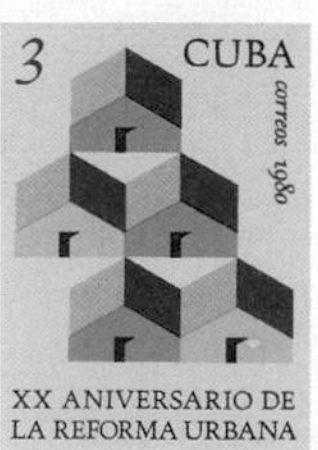

704 Houses

1980. "Moncada" Programme. Mult.

2644	3c. Type **704**	15	10
2645	13c. Refinery	30	15

ANNIVERSARIES: 3c. Urban Reform (20th Anniv). 13c. Foreign industry (20th Anniv).

705 Pitcher

1980. Copper Handicrafts. Multicoloured.

2646		3c. Type **705**	15	10
2647		13c. Wine container (38×26 mm)	55	25
2648		30c. Two handled pitcher	1·10	40

706 Emblem, Flag and Roses

1980. 20th Anniv of Cuban Women's Federation.

2649	**706**	3c. multicoloured	30	15

707 "Clotilde in her Garden" (J. Sorolla y Bastida)

1980. Espamer 80 Stamp Exhibition, Madrid. Sheet 91×53 mm.

MS2650	**707**	50c. multicoloured	3·00	3·00

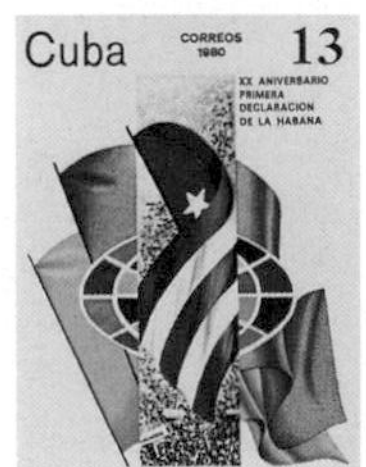

708 Flags

1980. 20th Anniv of 1st Havana Declaration.

2651	**708**	13c. multicoloured	40	25

709 Building Galleon "Nuesta Sra. de Atocha", 1620

1980. Cuban Shipbuilding. Multicoloured.

2652		1c. Type **709**	15	10
2653		3c. Building ship of the line "El Rayo", 1749	15	10
2654		7c. Building ship of the line "Santisima Trinidad", 1769	15	10
2655		10c. "Santisima Trinidad" at sea, 1805 (vert)	45	10
2656		13c. Building steamships "Colon" and "Congreso", 1851	95	15
2657		30c. Cardenas and Chullima shipyards	1·60	60

710 Arnaldo Tamayo

1980. Air. 1st Cuban–Soviet Space Flight.

2658	**710**	13c. multicoloured	40	15
2659	**710**	30c. multicoloured	1·20	40

711 U.N. General Assembly

1980. 20th Anniv of Fidel Castro's First Speech at the United Nations.

2660	**711**	13c. multicoloured	45	15

712 Child being Fed

1980. 20th Anniv of Revolution's Defence Committees.

2661	**712**	3c. multicoloured	25	15

713 "Portrait of a Lady" (Ludger Tom Ring, the younger)

1980. 49th International Philatelic Federation Congress, Essen. Sheet 94×54 mm.

MS2662	**713**	50c. multicoloured	3·00	2·75

714 Inspection Locomotive

1980. Early Locomotives. Multicoloured.

2663		1c. Type **714**	20	10
2664		2c. Inspection locomotive, Chaparra Sugar Company	20	10
2665		7c. Fireless locomotive, San Francisco Sugar Mill	20	10
2666		10c. Saddle-tank locomotive, Australia Estate	40	10
2667		13c. Steam locomotive	70	15
2668		30c. Oil-fired locomotive, 1909, Smith Comas Estate	1·70	55

715 "Roncali" Lighthouse, San Antonio

1980. Lighthouses (1st series). Multicoloured.

2669		3c. Type **715**	15	10
2670		13c. Jagua, Cienfuegos	55	25
2671		30c. Punta Maisi, Guantanamo	1·30	40

See also Nos. 2746/8, 2859/61 and 2920/2.

716 Bronze Medal

1980. Cuban Olympic Medal Winners. Mult.

2672		13c. Type **716**	40	15
2673		30c. Silver medal	90	25
2674		50c. Gold medal	1·80	70

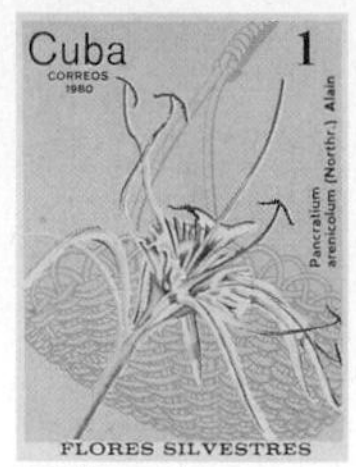

717 "Pancratium arenicolum"

1980. Forest Flowers. Multicoloured.

2675		1c. Type **717**	15	10
2676		4c. "Urechites lutea"	15	10
2677		6c. "Solanum elaegnifolium"	20	10
2678		10c. "Hamelia patens"	45	10
2679		13c. "Morinda royoc"	70	25
2680		30c. "Centrosema virginianum"	1·90	50

718 Locomotive "La Junta", 1840s

1980. 7th National Stamp Exhibition. Sheet 100×49 mm.

MS2681	**718**	50c. multicoloured	3·00	3·00

719 Congress Emblem

1980. 2nd Communist Party Congress. Mult.

2682		3c. Type **719**	15	10
2683		13c. Dish aerial and factories (Industry)	30	15
2684		30c. Gymnast, reader and elderly man resting (Recreation)	90	25

720 "Lady Mayo" (Anton van Dyck)

1981. National Museum Paintings (15th series). Multicoloured.

2685		1c. Type **720**	15	10
2686		6c. "La Hilandera" (Giovanni B. Piazzeta)	15	10
2687		10c. "Daniel Collyer" (Francis Cotes)	40	10
2688		13c. "Gardens of Palma de Mallorca" (Santiago Rusinol) (horiz)	50	25
2689		20c. "Landscape with Road and Houses" (Frederick W. Watts) (horiz)	80	30
2690		50c. "Landscape with Sheep" (Jean F. Millet) (horiz)	1·70	70

721 Short-finned Mako

1981. Fishes. Multicoloured.

2691		1c. Type **721**	20	10
2692		3c. Opah	20	10
2693		10c. Sailfish	40	15
2694		13c. Oceanic sunfish (vert)	1·50	25
2695		30c. Dolphin and flying-fish	95	40
2696		50c. White marlin	1·70	90

722 Saving Ball

1981. World Cup Football Championship, Spain (1982). (1st issue). Multicoloured.

2697		1c. Diving for ball (horiz)	15	10
2698		2c. Passing ball (horiz)	15	10
2699		3c. Running with ball (horiz)	15	10
2700		10c. Type **722**	35	15
2701		13c. Heading ball	35	15
2702		50c. Tackle (horiz)	1·50	85
MS2703		94×55 mm. 1p. Spanish flag and football	4·00	4·00

See also Nos. 2775/**MS**2782.

723 Mother, Child, Boots and Toy Train

1981. 20th Anniv of Kindergartens.

2704	**723**	3c. multicoloured	60	10

724 Jules Verne, Konstantin Tsiolkovsky and Sergei Korolev

1981. 20th Anniv of First Man in Space. Mult.

2705		1c. Type **724**	15	10
2706		2c. Yuri Gagarin (first man in space) (horiz)	15	10
2707		3c. Valentina Tereshkova (first woman in space) (horiz)	15	10
2708		5c. Aleksandr Leonov (first space walker) (horiz)	15	10
2709		13c. Crew of "Voskhod I" (horiz)	35	15
2710		30c. Ryumen and Popov (horiz)	85	40
2711		50c. Tamayo and Romanenko (crew of Soviet–Cuban flight)	1·90	70

725 Jet Fighters and Rocket

1981. 20th Anniv of Defeat of Invasion Attempt by Cuban Exiles. Multicoloured.

2712	3c. Type **725** (Defence and Air Force Day)	15	10
2713	13c. Hand waving machine-pistol (Victory at Giron)	35	25
2714	30c. Book and flags (Proclamation of Revolution's socialist character) (horiz)	85	55

726 Reynold Garcia Garcia (leader of attack), Barracks and Children

1981. 25th Anniv of Attack on Goicuria Barracks.

2715	**726** 3c. multicoloured	40	15

727 Tractor and Women planting Crops

1981. 20th Anniv of National Association of Small Farmers.

2716	**727** 3c. multicoloured	40	15

728 Austrian Stag Stamp, 1959

1981. WIPA 81 International Stamp Exhibition, Vienna. Sheet 103×50 mm.

MS2717	**728** 50c. multicoloured	2·50	2·50

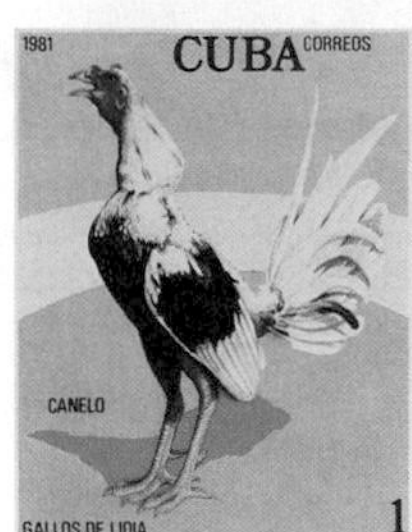

729 Canelo

1981. Fighting Cocks. Multicoloured.

2718	1c. Type **729**	15	10
2719	3c. Cenizo (horiz)	15	10
2720	7c. Blanco	20	10
2721	13c. Pinto	40	10
2722	30c. Giro (horiz)	1·00	40
2723	50c. Jabao	1·80	70

730 Anniversary Emblem

1981. 20th Anniv of Ministry of the Interior.

2724	**730** 13c. multicoloured	30	15

731 "Mother and Child" (wood-engraving by Zlatka Dabov)

1981. 1300th Anniv of Bulgarian State and Bulgaria 81 International Stamp Exhibition. Sheet 58×92 mm.

MS2725	**731** 50c. black, silver and gold	2·20	2·20

732 Tram

1981. Horse-drawn Vehicles. Multicoloured.

2726	1c. Type **732**	15	10
2727	4c. Village bus	15	10
2728	9c. Brake	20	10
2729	13c. Landau	30	10
2730	30c. Phaeton	1·10	45
2731	50c. Hearse	2·00	75

733 "House in the Country" (Maria Cardidad de la O)

1981. International Year of Disabled People.

2732	**733** 30c. multicoloured	1·10	30

734 Sandinista Guerrilla and Map of Nicaragua

1981. 20th Anniv of Sandinista National Liberation Front.

2733	**734** 13c. multicoloured	40	20

735 Gymnasts

1981. 20th Anniv of State Organizations. Mult.

2734	3c. Type **735** (National Sports and Physical Recreation Institute)	15	10
2735	13c. "RHC", radio waves and map (Radio Havana)	35	25
2736	30c. Arrows ("Mincex" Foreign Trade Ministry)	1·10	40

736 Carlos J. Finlay, Mosquito and Theory

1981. Centenary of Biological Vectors Theory.

2737	**736** 13c. multicoloured	80	25

737 Arms of Non-aligned Countries, Manacled Hands and Hands releasing Dove

1981. 20th Anniv of Non-aligned Countries Movement.

2738	**737** 50c. multicoloured	1·70	95

738 White Horse

1981. Horses. Multicoloured.

2739	1c. Type **738**	15	10
2740	3c. Brown horse	15	10
2741	8c. Bucking white horse	15	10
2742	13c. Horse being broken-in	35	25
2743	30c. Black horse	1·10	45
2744	50c. Herd of horses (horiz)	1·70	70

739 "Idyll in a Tea House" (Kitagawa Utamaro)

1981. Philatokyo 81 International Stamp Exhibition. Sheet 92×58 mm.

MS2745	**739** 50c. multicoloured	2·50	2·50

1981. Lighthouses (2nd series). As T 715. Mult.

2746	3c. Piedras del Norte	15	10
2747	13c. Punta Lucrecia	40	15
2748	40c. Guano del Este	1·70	60

740 "Flor de Cuba Sugar Mill"

1981. 80th Anniv of Jose Marti National Library. Lithographs by Eduardo Laplante. Multicoloured.

2749	3c. Type **740**	15	10
2750	13c. "El Progreso Sugar Mill"	30	15
2751	30c. "Santa Teresa Sugar Mill"	1·00	60

741 Pablo Picasso and Cuban Stamp

1981. Birth Centenary of Pablo Picasso (artist).

2752	**741** 30c. multicoloured	1·10	35

742 Sailing Ship

1981. Espamer 81 International Stamp Exhibition, Buenos Aires. Sheet 96×54 mm.

MS2753	**742** 1p. multicoloured	4·00	3·75

743 "Napoleon in Coronation Regalia" (Anon.)

1981. 20th Anniv of Napoleonic Museum. Mult.

2754	1c. Type **743**	15	10
2755	3c. "Napoleon with Landscape" (J. H. Vernet) (horiz)	15	10
2756	10c. "Bonaparte in Egypt" (Eduard Detaille)	30	25
2757	13c. "Napoleon on Horseback" (Hippolyte Bellange) (horiz)	30	25
2758	30c. "Napoleon in Normandy" (Bellange) (horiz)	1·00	50
2759	50c. "Death of Napoleon" (Anon)	1·70	85

744 Revolutionaries

1981. 25th Anniversaries. Multicoloured.

2760	3c. Type **744** (30th November insurrection)	15	10
2761	20c. Soldier (Revolutionary Armed Forces)	35	15
2762	1p. Launch "Granma" (disembarkation of revolutionary forces)	4·00	1·40

745 Cuban Emerald ("Zun-Zun")

1981. Fauna.

2763	**745** 1c. blue	50	10
2764	- 2c. green	70	25
2765	- 5c. brown	15	25
2766	- 20c. red	70	25
2767	- 35c. lilac	1·30	40
2768	- 40c. grey	1·90	60

DESIGNS: 2c. Cuban conure ("Catey"); 5c. Desmarest's hutia; 20c. Cuban solenodon; 35c. American manatee; 40c. Crocodile.

746 Ortiz (after Jorge Arche y Silva)

1981. Birth Centenary of Fernando Ortiz (folklorist). Multicoloured.

2769	3c. Type **746**	15	10
2770	10c. Idol (pendant)	30	15
2771	30c. Arara drum	1·20	45
2772	50c. Thunder god (Chango carving)	1·80	70

747 Conrado Benitez

1981. 20th Anniv of Literacy Campaign. Mult.

2773	5c. Type **747**	25	15
2774	5c. Manuel Ascunce	25	15

748 Goalkeeper

1982. World Cup Football Championship, Spain (2nd issue). Multicoloured.

2775	1c. Type **748**	15	10
2776	2c. Footballers	15	10
2777	5c. Heading ball	15	10
2778	10c. Kicking ball	25	15
2779	20c. Running for ball (horiz)	65	25
2780	40c. Tackle (horiz)	1·30	60
2781	50c. Shooting for goal	1·70	95
MS2782	62×109 mm. 1p. Feet and football (31×39 mm)	4·25	4·25

749 Lazaro Pena (trade union delegate)

1982. 10th World Trade Unions' Congress, Havana.

2783	**749**	30c. multicoloured	95	50

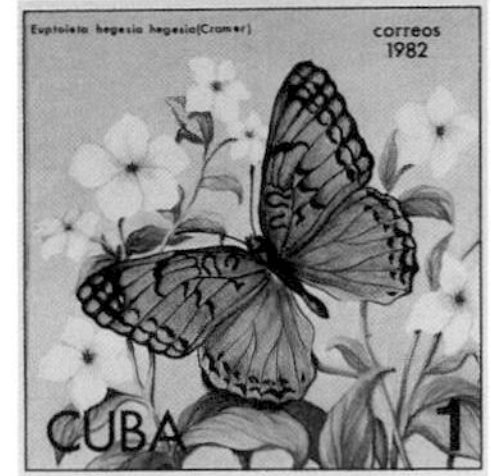

750 "Euptoieta hegesia hegesia"

1982. Butterflies. Multicoloured.

2784	1c. Type **750**	15	10
2785	4c. "Metamorpha stelenes insularis"	15	10
2786	5c. "Helicantus charithanius ramsdeni"	15	10
2787	20c. "Phoebis avellaneda"	1·20	30
2788	30c. "Hamadryas ferox diasia"	1·90	50
2789	50c. "Marpesia eleuchea eleuchea"	3·50	90

751 Lobster

1982. Exports.

2790	-	3c. green	15	10
2791	**751**	4c. red	15	10
2792	-	6c. blue	20	10
2793	-	7c. orange	30	10
2794	-	8c. lilac	30	10
2795	-	9c. grey	30	15
2796	-	10c. lilac	40	15
2797	-	30c. brown	60	25
2798	-	50c. red	1·70	50
2799	-	1p. brown	3·25	1·30

DESIGNS—HORIZ: 3c. Sugar; 6c. Tinned fruit; 7c. Agricultural machinery; 8c. Nickel. VERT: 9c. Rum; 10c. Coffee; 30c. Citrus fruit; 50c. Cigars; 1p. Cement.

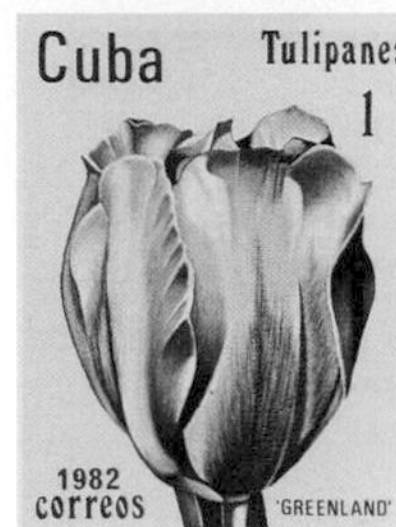

752 "Greenland" (cottage tulip)

1982. Tulips. Multicoloured.

2800	1c. Type **752**	15	10
2801	3c. "Mariette" (Lily-flowered tulip)	20	10
2802	8c. "Ringo" (triumph)	20	15
2903	20c. "Black Tulip" (Darwin)	50	25
2804	30c. "Jewel of Spring" (Darwin hybrid)	1·20	40
2805	50c. "Orange Parrot" (parrot tulip)	1·60	70

753 Youth Activities

1982. 20th Anniv of Communist Youth Union.

2806	**753**	5c. multicoloured	25	15

754 "Mars" Satellite

1982. Cosmonautics Day. Second United Nations Conference on Exploration and Peaceful Uses of Outer Space. Multicoloured.

2807	1c. Type **754**	15	10
2808	3c. "Venera" satellite	15	10
2809	6c. "Salyut-Soyuz" link-up	20	10
2810	20c. "Lunokhod" moon vehicle	40	15
2811	30c. "Venera" with heatshield	1·10	30
2812	50c. "Kosmos" satellite	1·70	60

755 Letter from British Postal Agency, Havana, to Vera Cruz

1982. Stamp Day. Multicoloured.

2813	20c. Type **755**	65	20
2814	30c. Letter from French postal agency, Havana, to Tampico, Mexico	1·10	25

756 Map of Cuba and Wave Pattern

1982. 20th Anniv of Cuban Broadcasting and Television Institute.

2815	**756**	30c. multicoloured	85	25

757 "Portrait of Young Woman" (Jean Greuze)

1982. National Museum Paintings (16th series). Multicoloured.

2816	1c. Type **757**	15	10
2817	3c. "Procession in Brittany" (Jules Breton) (46×36 mm)	15	10
2818	9c. "Landscape" (Jean Piliment) (horiz)	20	15
2819	20c. "Towards Evening" (William Bourgueran)	50	20
2820	30c. "Tiger" (Delacroix) (horiz)	1·00	30
2821	40c. "The Chair" (Wilfredo Lam)	1·60	40

758 Steamship "Louisiane" at St. Nazaire

1982. Philexfrance 82 International Stamp Exhibition, Paris. Sheet 110×60 mm.

MS2822 **758**	1p. multicoloured	4·50	4·50

759 Hurdling and 1930 Sports Stamp

1982. "Deporfilex '82" Stamp and Coin Exhibition, Havana.

2823	**759**	20c. multicoloured	1·20	40

See also No. **MS**2840.

760 Tortoise

1982. Reptiles. Multicoloured.

2824	1c. Type **760**	15	10
2825	2c. Snake	15	10
2826	3c. Cuban crocodile	20	10
2827	20c. Iguana	70	25
2828	30c. Lizard	1·10	35
2829	50c. Snake	2·00	50

761 Georgi Dimitrov

1982. Birth Centenary of Georgi Dimitrov (Bulgarian statesman).

2830	**761**	30c. multicoloured	95	25

762 Dr. Robert Koch and Bacillus

1982. Centenary of Discovery of Tubercle Bacillus.

2831	**762**	20c. multicoloured	1·00	25

763 Baseball

1982. 14th Central American and Caribbean Games, Havana. Multicoloured.

2832	1c. Type **763**	15	10
2833	2c. Boxing	15	10
2834	10c. Water polo	30	15
2835	20c. Javelin	70	35
2836	35c. Weightlifting	1·10	50
2837	50c. Volleyball	1·70	60

764 "Eichornia crassipes"

1982. 20th Anniv of Hydraulic Development Plan.

2838	5c. Type **764**	30	15
2839	20c. "Nymphaea alba"	80	25

765 Crocodile Mascot

1982. Deporfilex 82 Stamp and Coin Exhibition, Havana (2nd issue). Sheet 77×52 mm.

MS2840 **765**	1p. multicoloured	4·25	4·25

766 Hand holding Gun

1982. Namibia Day.

2841	**766**	50c. multicoloured	1·60	95

767 Goal

1982. World Cup Football Championship Finalists. Multicoloured.

2842 5c. Type **767** 15 10
2843 20c. Heading ball 65 35
2844 30c. Tackle 95 40
2845 50c. Saving goal 1·70 80

768 "Devil" (V. P. Landaluse)

1982. 20th Anniv of National Folk Ensemble. Multicoloured.

2846 20c. Type **768** 70 30
2847 30c. "Epiphany festival" (V.P. Landaluze) (horiz) 1·00 50

769 Prehistoric Owl

1982. Prehistoric Animals. Multicoloured.

2848 1c. Type **769** 60 20
2849 5c. "Crocodylus rhombifer" (horiz) 15 10
2850 7c. Prehistoric eagle 2·75 40
2851 20c. "Geocapromys colombianus" (horiz) 60 25
2852 35c. "Megalocnus rodens" 1·00 60
2853 50c. "Nesophontes micrus" (horiz) 1·40 85

770 Che Guevara

1982. 15th Death Anniv of "Che" Guevara (guerrilla fighter).

2854 **770** 20c. multicoloured 80 25

771 Christopher Columbus, "Santa Maria" and Map of Cuba

1982. 490th Anniv of Discovery of America by Columbus. Multicoloured.

2855 5c. Type **771** 95 25
2856 20c. "Santa Maria" (vert) 1·10 35
2857 35c. Caravel "Pinta" (vert) 1·80 65
2858 50c. Caravel "Nina" (vert) 2·20 85

1982. Lighthouses (3rd series). As T 715. Multicoloured.

2859 5c. Cayo Jutias 70 10
2860 20c. Cayo Paredon Grande 1·90 20
2861 30c. Morro, Santiago de Cuba 2·50 50

772 George Washington (anonymous painting)

1982. 250th Birth Anniv of George Washington. Multicoloured.

2862 5c. Type **772** 20 10
2863 20c. Portrait of Washington by Daniel Huntington 65 25

773 Paddle-steamer "Almendares"

1982. 8th National Stamp Exhibition, Ciego de Avila. Sheet 110×60 mm.

MS2864 **773** 1p. multicoloured 4·25 4·25

774 Steam Locomotive (1917) and Boating Lake

1982. 10th Anniv of Lenin Park, Havana.

2865 **774** 5c. multicoloured 50 15

775 Capablanca as Child and Chess King

1982. 40th Death Anniv of Jose Capablanca (chess player). Multicoloured.

2866 5c. Type **775** 20 15
2867 20c. Capablanca and rook 90 25
2868 30c. Capablanca and knight 1·20 45
2869 50c. Capablanca and queen 1·90 70

776 Lenin, Marx, Russian Arms and Kremlin Tower

1982. 60th Anniv of U.S.S.R.

2870 **776** 30c. multicoloured 1·10 20

777 Methods of Communications

1983. World Communications Year (1st issue).

2871 **777** 20c. multicoloured 65 20

See also Nos. 2929/33.

778 Birthplace and Birth Centenary Stamp

1983. 130th Birth Anniv of Jose Marti (writer).

2872 **778** 5c. multicoloured 25 15

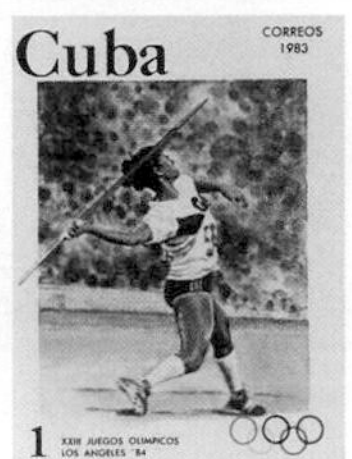

779 Throwing the Javelin

1983. Olympic Games, Los Angeles (1984). Multicoloured.

2873 1c. Type **779** 15 10
2874 5c. Volleyball 20 10
2875 6c. Basketball 20 10
2876 20c. Weightlifting 70 25
2877 30c. Wrestling 1·00 50
2878 50c. Boxing 1·60 70
MS2879 94×54 mm. 1p. Judo (28×36 mm) 4·50 4·50

780 "Che" Guevara and Radio Waves

1983. 25th Anniv of Radio Rebelde.

2880 **780** 20c. multicoloured 60 25

781 Karl Marx

1983. Death Centenary of Karl Marx.

2881 **781** 30c. multicoloured 95 50

782 Charles's Hydrogen Balloon

1983. Bicentenary of Manned Flight. Mult.

2882 1c. Type **782** 15 10
2883 3c. Montgolfier balloon 15 10
2884 5c. Montgolfier balloon "Le Gustave" 15 10
2885 7c. Eugene Godard's quintuple "acrobatic" balloon 30 10
2886 30c. Montgolfier unmanned balloon 1·80 70
2887 50c. Charles Green's balloon "Royal Vauxhall" 2·00 95
MS2888 89×60 mm. 1p. Jose Domingo Blino (first Cuban balloonist) (28×36 mm) 4·00 4·00

783 "Vostok 1"

1983. Cosmonautics Day. Multicoloured.

2889 1c. Type **783** 15 10
2890 4c. French "D1" satellite 20 10
2891 5c. "Mars 2" 25 10
2892 20c. "Soyuz" 65 25
2893 30c. Meteorological satellite 95 45
2894 50c. Intercosmos programme 1·50 70

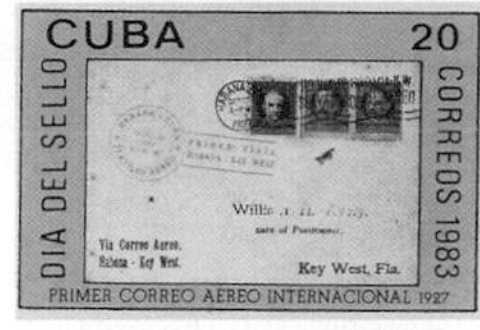

784 Letter sent by First International Airmail Service

1983. Stamp Day. Multicoloured.

2895 20c. Type **784** 65 25
2896 30c. Letter sent by first Atlantic airmail service 1·10 30

785 Weasel

1983. Brasiliana 83 International Stamp Exhibition, Rio de Janeiro. 50th Death Anniv of Santos Dumont (Brazilian aviator). Sheet 101×71 mm.

MS2897 **785** 1p. multicoloured 5·00 5·00

786 Jose Rafael de las Heras

1983. Birth Bicentenary of Simon Bolivar. Mult.

2898 5c. Type **786** 25 15
2899 20c. Simon Bolivar 60 25

787 J. L. Tasende, Abel Santamaria and B. L. Santa Coloma

1983. 30th Anniv of Attack on Moncada Fortress. Multicoloured.

2900 5c. Jose Marti and fortress (horiz) 15 10
2901 20c. Type **787** 65 25
2902 30c. Symbol of Castro's book "History Will Absolve Me" 85 45

788 Santos Dumont's Aircraft "14 bis"

1983. Brasilliana 83 International Stamp Exhibition, Rio de Janeiro. 50th Death Anniv of Santos Dumont (Brazillian auator). Sheet 101×71 mm.

MS2903	**788**	1p. multicoloured	4·50	4·50

789 Weightlifting

1983. 9th Pan-American Games, Caracas. Mult.

2904	1c. Type **789**	15	10
2905	2c. Volleyball	15	10
2906	3c. Baseball	25	10
2907	20c. High jump	65	25
2908	30c. Basketball	95	45
2909	40c. Boxing	1·50	70

790 "Harbour" (Claude Vernet)

1983. Centenary of French Alliance (French language-teaching association).

2910	**790**	30c. multicoloured	2·30	70

791 Salvador Allende and burning Presidential Palace

1983. 10th Death Anniv of Salvador Allende (President of Chile).

2911	**791**	20c. multicoloured	65	25

792 Regional Peasants Committee

1983. 25th Anniv of Peasants in Arms Congress.

2912	**792**	5c. multicoloured	20	10

793 "Portrait of a Young Man"

1983. 500th Birth Anniv of Raphael. Mult.

2913	1c. "Girl with Veil"	15	10
2914	2c. "The Cardinal"	15	10
2915	5c. "Francesco M. della Rovere"	25	10
2916	20c. Type **793**	65	25
2917	30c. "Magdalena Doni"	95	50
2918	50c. "La Fornarina"	1·50	85

794 Quality Seal and Exports

1983. State Quality Seal.

2919	**794**	5c. multicoloured	20	10

1983. Lighthouses (4th series). As T 715. Multicoloured.

2920	5c. Carapachibey, Isle of Youth	15	10
2921	20c. Cadiz Bay	65	35
2922	30c. Punta Gobernadora	1·60	70

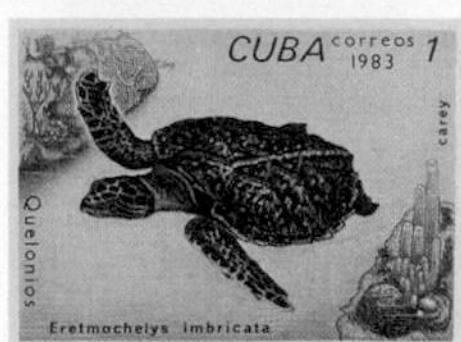

795 Hawksbill Turtle

1983. Turtles. Multicoloured.

2923	1c. Type **795**	15	10
2924	2c. "Lepidochelys kempi"	15	10
2925	5c. "Chrysemys decusata"	20	10
2926	20c. Loggerhead turtle	65	25
2927	30c. Green turtle	1·10	40
2928	50c. "Dermochelys coriacea"	2·20	85

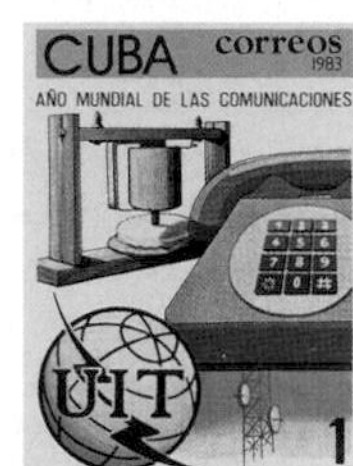

796 Bell's Gallow Frame and Modern Telephones

1983. World Communications Year (2nd issue). Multicoloured.

2929	1c. Type **796**	15	10
2930	5c. Telegram and airmail envelopes and U.P.U. emblem	25	10
2931	10c. Satellite and antenna	35	15
2932	20c. Telecommunications satellite and dish aerial	65	25
2933	30c. Television and Radio Commemorative plaque and tower block	95	40

797 Cuban Stamps of 1933 and 1965

1983. 150th Birth Anniv of Carlos J. Finlay (malaria researcher).

2934	**797**	20c. multicoloured	75	20

798 "Jatropha angustifolia"

1983. Flora and Fauna. Multicoloured. (a) Flowers.

2935	5c. Type **798**	40	15
2936	5c. "Cochlospermum vitifolium"	40	15
2937	5c. "Tabebuia lepidota"	40	15
2938	5c. "Kalmiella ericoides"	40	15
2939	5c. "Jatropha integerrima"	40	15
2940	5c. "Melocactus actinacanthus"	40	15
2941	5c. "Cordia sebestana"	40	15
2942	5c. "Tabernaemontana apoda"	40	15
2943	5c. "Lantana camera"	40	15
2944	5c. "Cordia gerascanthus"	40	15
2945	5c. "Opuntia dillenii"	40	15
2946	5c. "Euphorbia podocarpifolia"	40	15
2947	5c. "Dinema cubincola"	40	15
2948	5c. "Guaiacum officinale"	40	15
2949	5c. "Magnolia cubensis"	40	15

(b) Birds.

2950	5c. Bee hummingbird	40	15
2951	5c. Northern mockingbird	40	15
2952	5c. Cuban tody	40	15
2953	5c. Cuban Amazon	40	15
2954	5c. Zapata wren	40	15
2955	5c. Brown pelican	40	15
2956	5c. Great red-bellied woodpecker	40	15
2957	5c. Red-legged thrush	40	15
2958	5c. Cuban conure	40	15
2959	5c. Eastern meadowlark	40	15
2960	5c. Cuban grassquit	40	15
2961	5c. White-tailed tropic bird	40	15
2962	5c. Cuban solitaire	40	15
2963	5c. Great lizard cuckoo	40	15
2964	5c. Cuban gnatcatcher	40	15
MS2965	Two sheets each 95×55 mm. (a) 1p. "Hedychium coronarium" (flower); (b) 1p. Cuban trogon "Priotelus temnurus"	10·50	10·50

799 Tobacco Flowers

1983. Flowers.

2966	**799**	60c. green	1·90	60
2967	-	70c. red	2·30	70
2968	-	80c. blue	2·50	85
2969	-	90c. violet	3·75	1·10

DESIGNS: 70c. Lily; 80c. Mariposa; 90c. Orchid.

800 Flag and Plan of El Jigue Battlefield

1983. 25th Anniv of Revolution (1st issue). Multicoloured.

2970	5c. Type **800**	15	10
2971	20c. Flag and railway tracks at Santa Clara	3·00	1·00

801 Flag and Revolutionaries

1983. 25th Anniv of Revolution (2nd issue). Multicoloured.

2972	20c. Type **801**	65	30
2973	20c. "25" and star	65	30
2974	20c. Workers and Cuban Communist Party emblem	65	30

802 Lazaro Gonzalez, CTC Emblem and 15th Congress Flag

1984. 45th Anniv of Revolutionary Workers' Union.

2975	**802**	5c. multicoloured	20	15

803 "Ixias balice balice"

1984. Butterflies. Multicoloured.

2976	1c. Type **803**	15	15
2977	2c. "Phoebis avellaneda avellaneda"	15	15
2978	3c. "Anthocaris sara sara"	15	15
2979	5c. "Victorina superba superba"	15	15
2980	20c. "Heliconius cydno cydnides"	80	25
2981	30c. "Parides gundlachianus calzadillae"	1·40	65
2982	50c. "Catagramma sorana sorana"	2·40	90

804 Clocktower and Russian Stamps of 1924–25

1984. 60th Death Anniv of Lenin.

2983	**804**	30c. multicoloured	1·10	20

805 Risso's Dolphin

1984. Whales and Dolphins. Multicoloured.

2984	1c. Type **805**	25	15
2985	2c. Common dolphin	25	15
2986	5c. Sperm whale (horiz)	25	15
2987	6c. Spotted dolphin	25	15
2988	10c. False killer whale (horiz)	80	15
2989	30c. Bottle-nosed dolphin	1·40	30
2990	50c. Humpback whale (horiz)	2·20	60

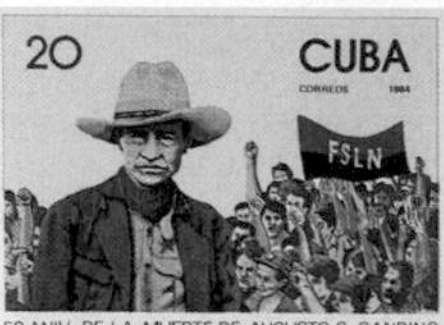

806 Sandino and Crowd holding Banner

1984. 50th Death Anniv of Augusto C. Sandino.

2991	**806**	20c. multicoloured	65	20

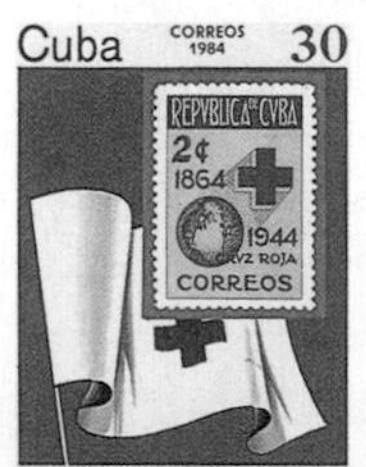

807 Red Cross Flag and Stamp of 1946

1984. 75th Anniv of Cuban Red Cross.

2992	**807**	30c. multicoloured	1·10	30

808 Scene from Cartoon Film

1984. 25th Anniv of Cuban Cinema.

2993	**808**	20c. multicoloured	85	30

809 "Brownea grandiceps"

1984. Caribbean Flowers. Multicoloured.

2994	1c. Type **809**	10	10
2995	2c. "Couroupita guianensis"	10	10
2996	5c. "Triplaris surinamensis"	15	10
2997	20c. "Amherstia nobilis"	85	30
2998	30c. "Plumieria alba"	1·20	50
2999	50c. "Delonix regia"	2·20	90

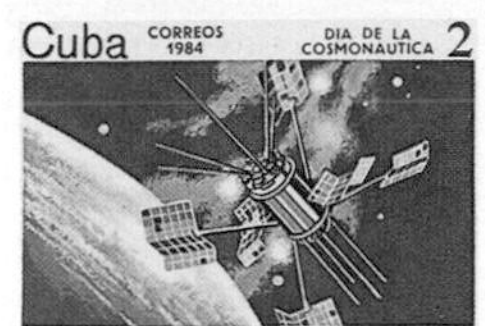

810 "Electron 1"

1984. Cosmonautics Day. Multicoloured.

3000	2c. Type **810**	10	10
3001	3c. "Electron 2"	10	10
3002	5c. "Intercosmos 1"	15	10
3003	10c. "Mars 5"	45	15
3004	30c. "Soyuz 1"	1·20	50
3005	50c. Soviet–Bulgarian space flight, 1979	2·20	90
MS3006	98×53 mm. 1p. "Luna" (vert)	1·70	1·70

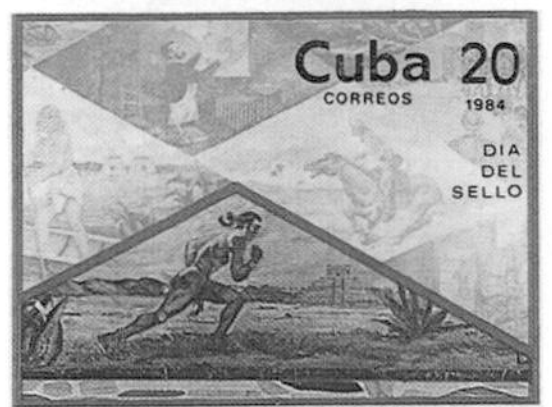

811 Mexican Mail Runner

1984. Stamp Day. Multicoloured.

3007	20c. Type **811**	85	30
3008	30c. Egyptian boatman	1·20	50

Nos. 3007/8 show details of mural by R. R. Radillo in Havana Stamp Museum.

See also Nos. 3097/8, 3170/1, 3336/7 and 3619/20.

812 "Buenos Aires" (mail steamer)

1984. Espana 84 International Stamp Exhibition, Madrid. Sheet 110×64 mm.

MS3009	**812** 1p. multicoloured	4·00	3·50

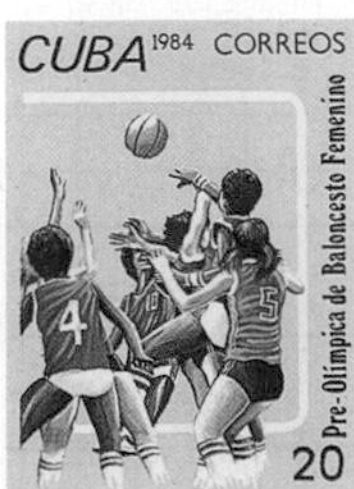

813 Basketball

1984. Pre-Olympics.

3010	**813** 20c. multicoloured	1·10	30

814 Pink Roses

1984. Mothers' Day. Multicoloured.

3011	20c. Type **814**	85	30
3012	20c. Red roses	85	30

815 Workers in Field

1984. 25th Anniv of Land Reform Act.

3013	**815** 5c. multicoloured	35	10

816 Saver and Pile of Coins

1984. 1st Anniv of People's Saving Bank.

3014	**816** 5c. multicoloured	35	10

817 Locomotive

1984. Locomotives. Multicoloured.

3015	1c. Type **817**	15	10
3016	4c. Locomotive No. 73	20	10
3017	5c. Locomotive (different)	25	10
3018	10c. Locomotive (different)	45	15
3019	30c. Locomotive No. 350	1·30	40
3020	50c. Locomotive No. 495	2·20	80

818 Cuban stamp of 1877 1902

1984. 19th Universal Postal Union Congress Philatelic Salon, Hanburg. Sheet 97×67 mm.

MS3021	**818** 1p. multicoloured	4·00	3·50

819 Baron de Coubertin and Runner with Olympic Flame

1984. 90th Anniv of Int Olympic Committee.

3022	**819** 30c. multicoloured	1·20	50

820 Baby with Toy Dog

1984. Children's Day.

3023	**820** 5c. multicoloured	25	10

821 Wrestling

1984. Olympic Games, Los Angeles. Mult.

3024	1c. Type **821**	10	10
3025	3c. Throwing the discus	10	10
3026	5c. Volleyball	15	10
3027	20c. Boxing	85	30
3028	30c. Basketball	1·20	50
3029	50c. Weightlifting	2·20	90
MS3030	76×55 mm. 1p. Baseball	4·75	4·50

822 Emilio Roig de Leuchsenring

1984. 20th Death Anniv of Emilio Roig de Leuchsenring.

3031	**822** 5c. multicoloured	35	10

825 Emu

1984. Friendship Tournament. Mult.

3032	3c. Type **823**	10	10
3033	5c. Women's volleyball	20	10
3034	8c. Water polo	30	10
3035	30c. Boxing	85	30

824 Cow in Pasture

1984. Cattle. Multicoloured.

3036	2c. Type **824**	10	10
3037	3c. Cuban Carib	10	10
3038	5c. Charolaise (vert)	15	10
3039	30c. Cuban Cebu (vert)	1·10	30
3040	50c. White-udder cow	1·90	65

823 Men's Volleyball

1984. Ausipex 84 International Stamp Exhibition, Melbourne. Sheet 57×83 mm.

MS3041	**825** 1p. multicoloured	4·25	4·00

826 Polymita

1984. Cuban Wildlife. Multicoloured.

3042	1c. Type **826**	10	10
3043	2c. Cuban solenodon	10	10
3044	3c. "Alsophis cantherigerus" (snake)	10	10
3045	4c. "Osteopilus septentrionalis" (frog)	15	10
3046	5c. Bee hummingbirds	60	15
3047	10c. Bushy-tailed hutia	35	15
3048	30c. Cuban tody	2·50	95
3049	50c. Peach-faced lovebird	4·00	1·20

827 King Ferdinand and Queen Isabella

1984. "Espamer '85" International Stamp Exhibition, Havana. Multicoloured.

3050	5c. Type **827**	10	10
3051	20c. Columbus departing from Palos de Moguer	1·30	80
3052	30c. "Santa Maria", "Pinta" and "Nina"	1·90	1·40
3053	50c. Columbus arriving in America	1·00	70

828 Balwin tank Locomotive No. 498

1984. 75th Anniv of Havana—Santiago de Cuba Railway and Ninth National Stamp Exhibition, Santiago de Cuba. Sheet 108×75 mm.

MS3054	**828** 1p. multicoloured	4·00	3·25

829 Flag and Soldier

1984. 25th Anniv of National Militia.

3055	**829** 5c. multicoloured	25	10

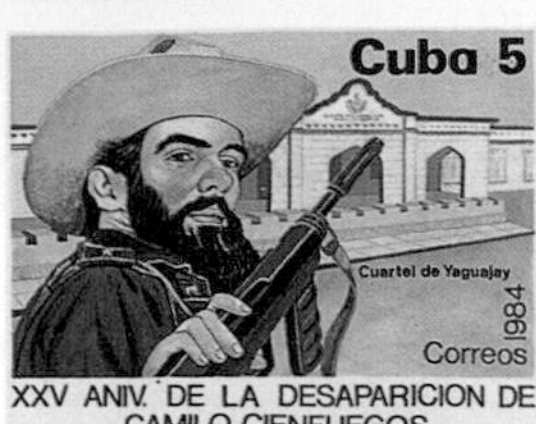

830 Cienfuegos

1984. 25th Anniv of Disappearance of Camilo Cienfuegos (revolutionary).

3056	**830**	5c. multicoloured	35	10

831 Mother breast-feeding Baby

1984. Infant Survival Campaign.

3057	**831**	5c. multicoloured	35	15

832 Morgan, 1909

1984. Cars. Multicoloured.

3058	1c. Type **832**	10	10
3059	2c. Austin, 1922	10	10
3060	5c. Dion-Bouton, 1903	10	10
3061	20c. "T" Ford, 1908	80	15
3062	30c. Karl Benz, 1885	1·30	30
3063	50c. Karl Benz, 1910	2·40	65

833 18th-century Letters and Museum Emblem

1985. 20th Anniv of Cuban Postal Museum.

3064	**833**	20c. multicoloured	65	25

834 Celia Sanchez (after E. Escobedo)

1985. 5th Death Anniv of Celia Sanchez (revolutionary).

3065	**834**	5c. multicoloured	35	15

835 Pigeon

1985. "Porto-1985" International Pigeon Exhibition, Oporto, Portugal.

3066	**835**	20c. multicoloured	1·10	25

836 Chile (1962)

1985. World Cup Football Championship, Mexico (1986) (1st issue). Multicoloured.

3067	1c. Type **836**	10	10
3068	2c. England (1966)	10	10
3069	3c. Mexico (1970)	10	10
3070	4c. West Germany (1974)	15	10
3071	5c. Argentina (1978)	15	15
3072	30c. Spain (1982)	1·20	50
3073	50c. Sweden (1958)	1·90	65
MS3074	84×64 mm. 1p. Footballers (39×31 mm)	3·50	2·75

See also Nos. 3135/**MS**41.

837 Pteranodon

1985. Baconao Valley National Park. Prehistoric Animals (1st series). Multicoloured.

3075	1c. Type **837**	35	15
3076	2c. Brontosaurus	35	15
3077	4c. Iguanodontus	35	15
3078	5c. Estegosaurus	35	15
3079	8c. Monoclonius	50	15
3080	30c. Corythosaurus	1·60	50
3081	50c. Tyrannosaurus	3·00	75

See also Nos. 3264/9.

838 Uruguay 1911 and Argentina 1921 Congress Stamps and Emblem (image scaled to 70% of original size)

1985. 13th Postal Union of the Americas and Spain Congress, Havana.

3082	**838**	20c. multicoloured	2·75	75

839 Indians playing Football

1985. Espamer '85 International Stamp Exhibition, Havana. Multicoloured.

3083	1c. Type **839**	15	15
3084	2c. Indian sitting by fire	15	15
3085	5c. Fishing with nets and spears	45	15
3086	20c. Making pottery	45	25
3087	30c. Hunting with spears	70	40
3088	50c. Decorating canoe and paddle	3·00	80
MS3089	91×51 mm. 1p. Women cooking (25×36 mm)	5·75	5·25

See also Nos. 3264/9.

840 Spaceship circling Moon

1985. Cosmonautics Day. Multicoloured.

3090	2c. Type **840**	10	10
3091	3c. Spaceships	10	10
3092	10c. Cosmonauts meeting in space	35	10
3093	13c. Cosmonauts soldering in space	50	15
3094	20c. "Vostok II" and Earth	60	25
3095	50c. "Lunayod I" crossing moon crater	2·00	65

841 Lenin's Tomb

1985. 12th World Youth and Students' Festival, Moscow.

3096	**841**	30c. multicoloured	70	50

1985. Stamp Day. As T 811. Multicoloured.

3097	20c. Roman soldier and chariot	70	25
3098	30c. Medieval nobleman and monks	95	40

842 Peonies

1985. Mothers' Day. Multicoloured.

3099	1c. Type **842**	10	10
3100	4c. Carnations	10	10
3101	5c. Dahlias	15	10
3102	13c. Roses	45	10
3103	20c. Roses (different)	70	15
3104	50c. Tulips	1·70	55

843 Guiteras and Aponte

1985. 50th Death Anniv of Antonio Guiteras and Carlos Aponte (revolutionaries).

3105	**843**	5c. multicoloured	25	10

844 Star, "40" and Soldier with Flag

1985. 40th Anniv of End of Second World War.

3106	**844**	5c. multicoloured	15	15
3107	-	20c. multicoloured	55	30
3108	-	30c. red, yellow & violet	95	45

DESIGNS: 20c. "40" and Soviet Memorial, Berlin-Treptow; 30c. Dove within "40".

845 Andean Condor

1985. Argentina 85 International Stamp Exhibition, Buenos Aires. Sheet 64×81 mm.

MS3109	**845**	1p. multicoloured	4·25	4·00

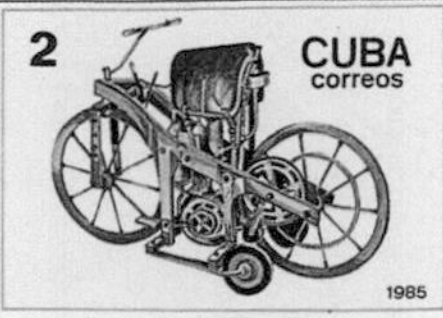

846 Daimler, 1885

1985. Centenary of the Motor Cycle. Multicoloured.

3110	2c. Type **846**	10	10
3111	5c. Kayser tricycle, 1910	15	10
3112	10c. Fanomovil, 1925	35	10
3113	30c. Mars "A 20", 1926	1·10	25
3114	50c. Simson "BSW", 1936	2·00	55

847 La Plata and Hermanos Ameijeiras Hospitals

1985. Development of Health Care since the Revolution.

3115	**847**	5c. multicoloured	25	10

848 Flowers and Soldier with Gun

1985. 25th Anniv of Federation of Cuban Women.

3116	**848**	5c. multicoloured	25	10

849 Athletes and Emblem

1985. World University Games, Kobe, Japan.

3117	**849**	50c. multicoloured	1·50	55

850 Crowd, Flags and Statue

1985. 25th Anniv of First Havana Declaration.

3118	**850**	5c. multicoloured	35	15

851 Roman Cargo Ship

1985. Italia 85 International Stamp Exhibition, Rome. Sheet 97×62 mm.

MS3119	**851**	1p. multicoloured	4·25	3·50

852 Emblem in "25"

1985. 25th Anniv of Committees for Defence of the Revolution.

3120	**852**	5c. multicoloured	25	10

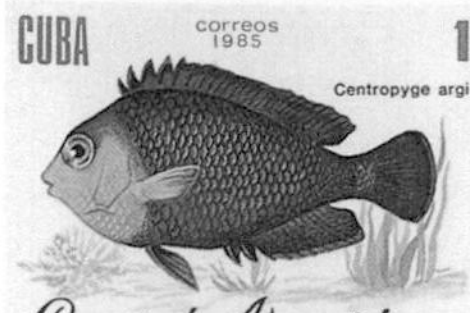

853 Cherub Angelfish

1985. Fishes. Multicoloured.

3121		1c. Type **853**	25	15
3122		3c. Rock beauty	25	15
3123		5c. Four-eyed butterflyfish	25	15
3124		10c. Reef butterflyfish	45	25
3125		20c. Spot-finned butterflyfish	1·00	50
3126		50c. Queen angelfish	2·50	1·60

854 Cuban and Party Flags and Central Committee Building

1985. 20th Anniv of Cuban Communist Party and Third Party Congress.

3127	**854**	5c. multicoloured	35	15

855 Spain 1930 25c. and Cuba 1942 1c. Columbus Stamps

1985. Exfilna 85 International Stamp Exhibition, Madrid. Sheet 99×61 mm.

MS3128	**855**	1p. multicoloured	4·25	3·50

856 U.N. Building, New York, and Emblem

1985. 40th Anniv of U.N.O.

3129	**856**	20c. multicoloured	80	25

857 Old Square and Arms

1985. UNESCO World Heritage. Old Havana. Multicoloured.

3130		2c. Type **857**	20	15
3131		5c. Real Fuerza Castle	20	15
3132		20c. Havana Cathedral	80	25
3133		30c. Captain General's Palace	1·30	40
3134		50c. El Templete	2·10	55

858 Footballers

1986. World Cup Football Championship, Mexico (2nd issue).

3135	**858**	1c. multicoloured	10	10
3136	-	4c. multicoloured	10	10
3137	-	5c. multicoloured	15	10
3138	-	10c. multicoloured	25	15
3139	-	30c. multicoloured	95	30
3140	-	50c. multicoloured	1·50	55
MS3141		94×50 mm. 1p. mult	4·00	3·50

DESIGNS: 4c. to 1p. Various footballing scenes.

859 Red Flags and Emblem

1986. 3rd Cuban Communist Party Congress, Havana. Multicoloured.

3142		5c. Type **859**	10	10
3143		20c. Red and national flags	1·10	25

860 Ministry Emblem

1986. 25th Anniv of Ministry of Interior Trade.

3144	**860**	5c. multicoloured	25	10

861 People practising Sports

1986. 25th Anniv of National Sports Institute.

3145	**861**	5c. multicoloured	25	10

862 "Tecomaria capensis"

1986. Exotic Flowers. Multicoloured.

3146		1c. Type **862**	10	10
3147		3c. "Michelia champaca"	15	10
3148		5c. "Thunbergia grandiflora"	15	10
3149		8c. "Dendrobium phalaenopsis"	25	10
3150		30c. "Allamanda violacea"	95	25
3151		50c. "Rhodocactus bleo"	1·60	40

863 Gundlach and Red-winged Blackbird

1986. 90th Death Anniv of Juan C. Gundlach (ornithologist). Multicoloured.

3152		1c. Type **863**	25	15
3153		3c. Olive-capped warbler	25	15
3154		7c. La Sagra's flycatcher	40	30
3155		9c. Yellow warbler	50	30
3156		30c. Grey-faced quail dove	2·00	1·20
3157		50c. Common flicker	3·50	2·00

864 Pioneers and "25"

1986. 25th Anniv of Jose Marti Pioneers.

3158	**864**	5c. multicoloured	25	10

865 Gomez and Statue

1986. 150th Birth Anniv of Maximo Gomez.

3159	**865**	20c. multicoloured	80	25

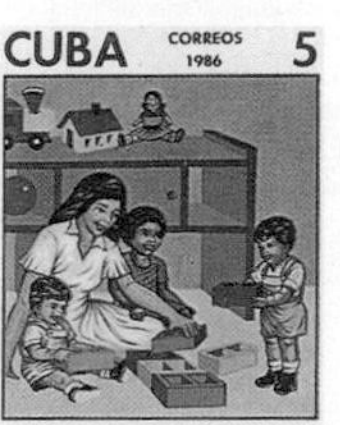

866 Nursery Nurse with Children

1986. 25th Anniv of Children's Day Care Centres.

3160	**866**	5c. multicoloured	35	10

867 "Vostok" and Korolev (designer)

1986. 25th Anniv of First Man in Space. Multicoloured.

3161		1c. Type **867**	10	10
3162		2c. Yuri Gargarin (first man in space) and "Vostok"	10	10
3163		5c. Valentina Tereshkova (first woman in space) and "Vostok"	15	10
3164		20c. "Salyut" space station	50	15
3165		30c. Capsule descending with parachute	70	25
3166		50c. "Soyuz" rocket on launch pad	1·50	55
MS3167		95×70 mm. 100p. Tsoilkovsky (scientist)	4·00	3·25

868 National Flag and 1981 Stamp

1986. 25th Anniv of Socialist State (1959) and Victory at Giron. Multicoloured.

3168		5c. Type **868**	15	10
3169		20c. Flags and arms	95	15

1986. Stamp Day. As T 811 showing details of mural by R. R. Radillo in Havana Stamp Museum. Multicoloured.

3170		20c. Early mail coach	65	15
3171		30c. Express rider	85	25

869 Reels as National Flag and Globe and Tape forming "25"

1986. 25th Anniv of Radio Havana Cuba.

3172	**869**	5c. multicoloured	35	10

870 "Stourbridge Lion", U.S.A., 1829

1986. Expo '86 World's Fair, Vancouver. Railway Locomotives. Multicoloured.

3173		1c. Type **870**	10	10
3174		4c. "Rocket", Great Britain, 1829	10	10
3175		5c. First Russian locomotive, 1845	15	10
3176		8c. Marc Seguin's locomotive, France, 1830	25	15
3177		30c. First Canadian locomotive, 1836	65	30
3178		50c. Steam locomotive, Belgium Grand Central Railway, 1872	1·60	40
MS3179		92×54 mm. 1p. Locomotive "La Junta", 1840s, Cuba	4·25	4·00

871 Hand holding Machete and Farmer ploughing and driving Tractor

1986. 25th Anniv of National Association of Small Farmers.

3180	**871**	5c. multicoloured	35	10

872 Dove and Arms on Coin

1986. International Peace Year.

3181	**872**	30c. multicoloured	85	25

873 Emblem

1986. 25th Anniv of Ministry of the Interior.

3182	**873**	5c. multicoloured	35	15

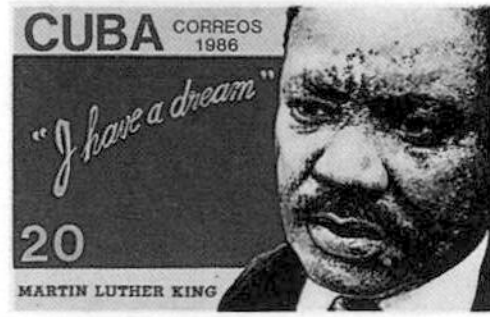

874 King

1986. 18th Death Anniv of Martin Luther King (human rights campaigner).

3183	**874**	20c. multicoloured	85	20

875 Bonifacio Byrne

1986. 50th Death Anniv of Bonifacio Byrne (poet).
3184 **875** 5c. multicoloured 25 10

876 Dove, Pen Nib and Paint Brush

1986. 25th Anniv of National Union of Cuban Writers and Artists.
3185 **876** 5c. multicoloured 25 10

877 Sandino and Pres. Ortega of Nicaragua

1986. 25th Anniv of Sandinista Movement of Nicaragua.
3186 **877** 20c. multicoloured 65 20

878 Tanker, Tupolev Tu-154 and Lorry

1986. 25th Anniv of Ministry of Transport.
3187 **878** 5c. multicoloured 50 25

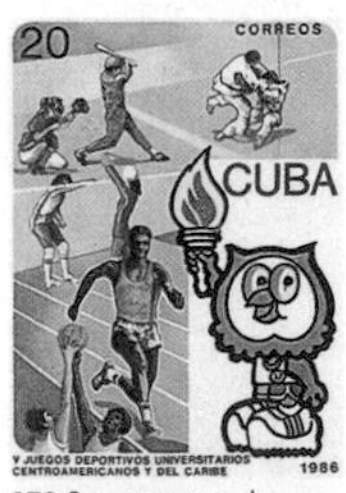

879 Sportsmen and Emblem

1986. 5th Central American and Caribbean University Games, Havana.
3188 **879** 20c. multicoloured 85 20

880 Cuban Revolutionaries' 1897 2c. Stamp

1986. Stockholmia 86 International Stamp Exhibition. Sheet 111×70 mm containing T 880 and similar vert design. Multicoloured.
MS3189 50c. Type **880**; 50c. Sweden 1885 10ore. Stamp 4·00 3·00

881 Map

1986. 25th Anniv of Non-Aligned Countries Movement.
3190 **881** 50c. multicoloured 1·70 40

882 "Cattleya hardyana"

1986. Orchids. Multicoloured.
3191 1c. Type **882** 10 10
3192 4c. "Brassolaeliocattleya" "Horizon Flight" 15 10
3193 5c. "Phalaenopsis" "Margit Moses" 15 15
3194 10c. "Laeliocattleya" "Prism Palette" 25 15
3195 30c. "Phalaenopsis violacea" 95 30
3196 50c. "Disa uniflora" 1·60 50

883 Mayan House and Jade Statue (Belize)

1986. Latin American History. Pre-Columbian Culture (1st series). Multicoloured.
3197 1c. Type **883** 10 10
3198 1c. Inca vessel and Gateway of the Sun, Tiahuanacu (Bolivia) 10 10
3199 1c. Spain 1930 1p. stamp of Columbus and 500th anniv of Columbus's discovery of America emblem 10 10
3200 1c. Diaguitan duck-shaped pitcher and ruins, Pucara de Quitor (Chile) 10 10
3201 1c. Archaeological park, San Augustin and Quimbayan statuette (Columbia) 10 10
3202 5c. Moler memorial and Chorotega decorated earthenware statue (Costa Rica) 15 10
3203 5c. Tabaco idol and typical aboriginal houses (Cuba) 15 10
3204 5c. Spain 1930 40c. stamp of Martin Pinzon and anniversary emblem 15 10
3205 5c. Typical houses and animal shaped seat (Dominica) 15 10
3206 5c. Tolita statue and Ingapirca fort (Ecuador) 15 10
3207 10c. Maya vase and Tikal temple (Guatemala) 25 15
3208 10c. Copan ruins and Maya idol (Honduras) 25 15
3209 10c. Spain 1930 30c. stamp of Vincent Pinzon and anniversary emblem 25 15
3210 10c. Chichen-Itza temple and Zapoteca urn (Mexico) 25 15
3211 10c. Punta de Zapote idols and Ometepe ceramic (Nicaragua) 25 15
3212 20c. Tonosi ceramic and Barrile monolithic sculptures (Panama) 60 25
3213 20c. Machu Picchu ruin and Inca figure (Peru) 60 25
3214 20c. Spain 1930 10p. stamp of Columbus and Pinzon brothers and anniversary emblem 60 25
3215 20c. Typical aboriginal dwellings and triangular stone carving (Puerto Rico) 60 25
3216 20c. Santa Ana female figure and Santo Domingo cave (Venezuela) 60 25

See also Nos. 3276/95, 3371/90, 3458/77, 3563/82, 3666/85 and 3769/88.

884 Medal and Soldier with Rifle

1986. 50th Anniv of Formation International Brigades in Spain.
3217 **884** 30c. multicoloured 80 30

885 "Two Children" (Gutierrez de la Vega)

1986. National Museum Paintings (17th series). Multicoloured.
3218 2c. Type **885** 10 10
3219 4c. "Sed" (Jean-Gorges Vibert) (horiz) 10 10
3220 6c. "Virgin and Child" (Niccolo Abbate) 15 10
3221 10c. "Bullfight" (Eugenio de Lucas Velazquez) (horiz) 25 15
3222 30c. "The Five Senses" (Anon) (horiz) 95 30
3223 50c. "Meeting at Thomops Castle" (Jean Louis Ernest) (horiz) 1·60 55

886 People and "Granma"

1986. 30th Annivs of "Granma" Landings (5c.) and Revolutionary Armed Forces (20c.). Multicoloured.
3224 5c. Type **886** 40 10
3225 20c. Soldier, rifle and flag 1·30 15

887 Scholars and "Che" Guevara

1986. 25th Anniv of Scholarship Programme.
3226 **887** 5c. multicoloured 25 10

888 Man learning to write and Sanmarti

1986. 25th Anniv of Literacy Campaign.
3227 **888** 5c. multicoloured 25 10

889 Map and Revolutionaries

1987. 30th Anniv of Attack on La Plata Garrison.
3228 **889** 5c. multicoloured 25 10

890 "Gitana" (Joaquin Sorolla)

1987. National Museum Paintings (18th series). Multicoloured.
3229 3c. Type **890** 10 10
3230 5c. "Sir Walter Scott" (Sir John W. Gordon) 15 10
3231 10c. "Farm Meadows" (Alfred de Breanski) (horiz) 35 15
3232 20c. "Still Life" (Isaac van Duynen) (horiz) 85 25
3233 30c. "Landscape with Figures" (Francesco Zuccarelli) (horiz) 95 30
3234 40c. "Waffle Seller" (Ignacio Zuloaga) 1·40 50

891 Palace, Delivery Van and Echeverria

1987. 30th Anniv of Attack on Presidential Palace.
3235 **891** 5c. multicoloured 25 10

892 Lazarus Ludwig Zamenhof (inventor) and Russia 1927 14k. Stamp

1987. Centenary of Esperanto (invented language).
3236 **892** 30c. multicoloured 85 30

893 1956 Cuban Postal Service Bicentenary Stamps

1987. 10th National Stamp Exhibition, Holgiun. Sheet 85×61 mm.
MS3237 **893** 1p. multicoloured 1·70 1·70

894 Badge and Slogan

1987. 25th Anniv and 5th Congress of Youth Communist League.
3238 **894** 5c. multicoloured 25 10

895 "Intercosmos I" Satellite

1987. Cosmonautics Day. 20th Anniv of Intercosmos Programme. Multicoloured.
3239 3c. Type **895** 10 10
3240 5c. "Intercosmos II" 15 10
3241 10c. "TD" 25 15
3242 20c. "Cosmos 93" 65 25

3243	30c. "Molniya"	85	30
3244	50c. "Vostok 3"	1·40	55
MS3245	65×85 mm. 1p. Rocket and "Vostok 3" (31×39 mm)	4·00	3·00

896 Cover with Postal Fiscal Stamp, 1890

1987. Stamp Day. Multicoloured.

3246	30c. Type **896**	1·10	25
3247	50c. Cover with bisect, 1869	1·80	50

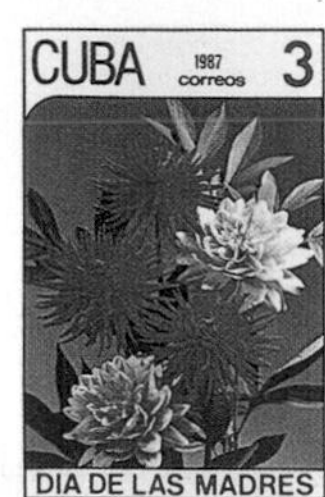

897 Dahlias

1987. Mothers' Day. Multicoloured.

3248	3c. Type **897**	10	10
3249	5c. Roses	15	10
3250	10c. Roses in basket	25	15
3251	13c. Decorative dahlias	35	15
3252	30c. Cactus dahlias	80	25
3253	50c. Roses (different)	1·30	50

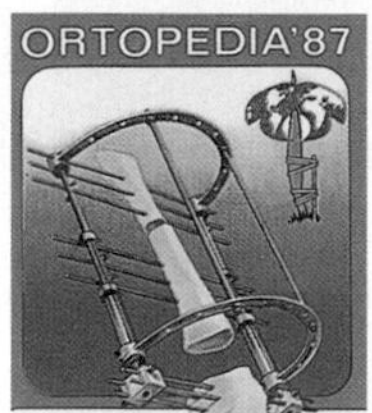

898 Fractured Femur Immobilised in Frame

1987. "Orthopedia '87" Portuguese and Spanish Speaking Countries' Orthopedists Meeting, Havana.

3254	**898**	5c. multicoloured	25	10

899 Emblem

1987. 25th Anniv of Cuban Broadcasting and Television Institute.

3255	**899**	5c. multicoloured	25	10

900 Battle Monument, Sierra Maestra Mountains

1987. 30th Anniv of Battle of El Uvero.

3256	**900**	5c. multicoloured	25	10

901 Messenger with Pack Llamas and 1868 Stamp (Bolivia)

1987. Capex '87 International Stamp Exhibition, Toronto. 19th-century Mail Carriers as depicted on cigarette cards. Multicoloured.

3257	3c. Type **901**	10	10
3258	5c. Postman and motor car and 1900 stamp (France)	15	10
3259	10c. Messenger on elephant and 1883 stamp (Siam)	25	15
3260	20c. Messenger on camel and 1879 stamp (Egypt)	50	25
3261	30c. Mail troika and stamp (Russia)	80	25
3262	50c. Messenger on horseback and stamp (Indo-China)	1·30	50
MS3263	67×71 mm. 1p. Messenger on horseback and stamp (Cuba) (31×39 mm)	4·00	3·75

902 Model of Prehistoric Animal

1987. Prehistoric Valley, Baconao National Park (2nd series). Designs showing various exhibits.

3264	**902**	3c. multicoloured	15	10
3265	-	5c. multicoloured	25	15
3266	-	10c. multicoloured	45	15
3267	-	20c. multicoloured	95	25
3268	-	35c. multicoloured	1·60	30
3269	-	40c. multicoloured	1·70	40

903 Pais and Rafael Maria Mendive Popular University Buildings

1987. 30th Death Anniv of Frank Pais (teacher and student leader).

3270	**903**	5c. multicoloured	25	10

904 Flags and Sportsmen

1987. 10th Pan-American Games, Indianapolis.

3271	**904**	50c. multicoloured	1·50	40

905 Memorial

1987. 30th Anniv of Cienfuegos Uprising.

3272	**905**	5c. multicoloured	25	10

906 "The Post in Denmark, 1887"

1987. Hafnia 87 International Stamp Exhibition, Copenhagen. Sheet 85×60 mm.

MS3273	**906**	1p. multicoloured	4·00	3·00

907 Port of La Coruna

1987. Espamer 87 International Stamp Exhibition, La Coruna, Spain. Sheet 108×70 mm.

MS3274	**907**	1p. multicoloured	4·00	3·25

908 Coins and 1968 Independence War Centenary 30c. Stamp

1987. 20th Anniv of Heroic Guerilla Fighters Day.

3275	**908**	50c. multicoloured	1·30	50

909 Tehuelche Man and Red-crowned Ant-tanager (Argentina)

1987. Latin American History (2nd series). Multicoloured.

3276	1c. Type **909**	15	15
3277	1c. Red-billed toucan and Tibirica man (Brazil)	15	15
3278	1c. Spain 1930 5c. stamp of La Rabida Monastery and 500th anniv of Columbus's discovery of America emblem	15	15
3279	1c. Andean condor and Lautaro man (Chile)	15	15
3280	1c. Calarca man and hoatzin (Colombia)	15	15
3281	5c. Cuban trogon and Hatuey man (Cuba)	45	15
3282	5c. Scaly-breasted ground dove and Enriquillo man (Dominican Republic)	45	15
3283	5c. Spain 1930 30c. stamp of departure from Palos and anniversary emblem	45	15
3284	5c. Toucan barbet and Ruminahui man (Ecuador)	45	15
3285	5c. Resplendent quetzal and Tecum Uman man (Guatemala)	45	15
3286	10c. Anacaona woman and limpkin (Haiti)	70	15
3287	10c. Lempira man and slaty flowerpiercer (Honduras)	70	15
3288	10c. Spain 1930 10p. Columbus stamp and anniversary emblem	70	15
3289	10c. Northern royal flycatcher and Cuauhtemoc woman (Mexico)	70	15
3290	10c. Painted redstart and Nicarao man (Nicaragua)	70	15
3291	20c. Andean cock of the rock and Atahualpa man (Peru)	1·10	40
3292	20c. Atlactl man and red-tailed hawk (El Salvador)	1·10	40
3293	20c. Spain 1930 10p. stamp of arrival in America and anniversary emblem	1·10	40
3294	20c. Abayuba man and red-breasted plantcutter (Uruguay)	1·10	40
3295	20c. Guaycaypuro man and blue and yellow macaw (Venezuela)	1·10	40

910 1950 2c. Train Stamp

1987. 150th Anniv of Cuban Railway. Designs showing Cuban stamps.

3296	**910**	3c. red, brown & black	10	10
3297	-	5c. multicoloured	15	10
3298	-	10c. multicoloured	25	15
3299	-	20c. multicoloured	50	15
3300	-	35c. multicoloured	1·00	30
3301	-	40c. multicoloured	1·20	40
MS3302		Two sheets. (a) 106×67 mm. 1p. multicoloured; (b) 207×165 mm. Nos. 3296/3301. Imperf	4·00	3·75

DESIGNS: 5c. 1965 7c. "BB.69,000" diesel locomotive stamp; 10c. 1975 1c. French-built "La Junta" locomotive stamp; 20c. 1975 3c. M. M. Prieto" locomotive stamp; 35c. 1980 10c. locomotive stamp; 40c. 1980 13c. locomotive stamp.

911 Satellites and Russia 1927 14k. Stamp

1987. 70th Anniv of Russian Revolution.

3303	**911**	30c. multicoloured	85	25

912 "Landscape" (Domingo Ramos)

1988. 170th Anniv of San Alejandro Arts School, Havana. Multicoloured.

3304	1c. Type **912**	10	10
3305	2c. "Portrait of Rodriguez Morey" (Eugenio Gonzalez Olivera)	10	10
3306	3c. "Landscape with Malangas and Palm Trees" (Valentin Sanz Carta)	15	10
3307	5c. "Ox-carts" (Eduardo Morales)	15	15
3308	10c. "Portrait of Elena Herrera" (Armando Menocal) (vert)	35	15
3309	30c. "The Rape of Dejanira" (Miguel Melero) (vert)	75	25
3310	50c. "The Card Player" (Leopoldo Romanach)	1·20	50

913 "Boletus satanas"

1988. Poisonous Mushrooms. Multicoloured.

3311	1c. Type **913**	10	10
3312	2c. "Amanita citrina"	15	10
3313	3c. "Tylopilus felleus"	25	15
3314	5c. "Paxillus involutus"	25	15
3315	10c. "Inocybe patouillardii"	60	25
3316	30c. "Amanita muscaria"	1·60	55
3317	50c. "Hypholoma fasciculare"	2·50	1·10

914 Radio Operator, Satellite and Caribe Ground Station

1988. 30th Anniv of Radio Rebelde.
3318 **914** 5c. multicoloured 25 10

915 Mario Munoz Santiago Monument, de Cuba

1988. 30th Anniv of Mario Munoz Third Front.
3319 **915** 5c. multicoloured 25 15

916 Frank Pais Memorial and Eternal Flame

1988. 30th Anniv of Frank Pais Second Eastern Front.
3320 **916** 5c. multicoloured 25 15

917 Red Roses

1988. Mothers' Day. Multicoloured.

3321	1c. Type **917**	10	10
3322	2c. Pale pink roses	10	10
3323	3c. Daisies	10	10
3324	5c. Dahlias	15	10
3325	13c. White roses	25	15
3326	35c. Carnations	80	25
3327	40c. Pink roses	95	30

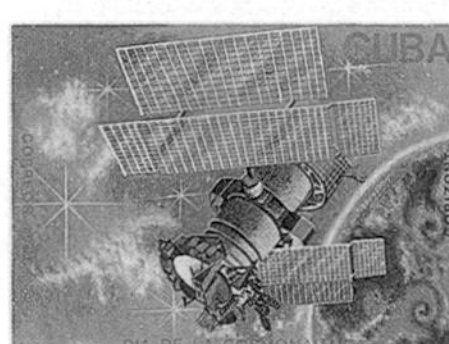

918 "Gorizont" Satellite

1988. Cosmonautics Day. Multicoloured.

3328	2c. Type **918**	10	10
3329	3c. "Mir"–"Kvant" link	10	10
3330	4c. "Signo 3"	10	10
3331	5c. Mars space probe	15	10
3332	10c. "Phobos"	25	15
3333	30c. "Vega" space probe	70	25
3334	50c. Spacecraft	1·20	50
MS3335	95×60 mm. 1p. Spacecraft (different) (31×39 mm)	4·00	3·75

1988. Stamp Day. As T 811. Details of mural by R. R. Radillo in Havana Stamp Museum. Mult.

3336	30c. Telegraphist and mail coach	95	30
3337	50c. Carrier pigeon	1·60	50

919 Storage Tanks, Products, Sugar Cane and Laboratory Equipment

1988. 25th Anniv of ICIDCA (Cuban Institute for Research on Sugarcane Byproducts).
3338 **919** 5c. multicoloured 25 10

920 Havana–Madrid, 1948

1988. Cubana Airlines Transatlantic Flights. Mult.

3339	2c. Type **920**	10	10
3340	4c. Havana–Prague, 1961	10	10
3341	5c. Havana–Berlin, 1972	15	10
3342	10c. Havana–Luanda, 1975	25	15
3343	30c. Havana–Paris, 1983	85	25
3344	50c. Havana–Moscow, 1987	1·50	50

921 "Furst Menschikoff" and 1917 20p. Finnish Stamp

1988. Finlandia 88 International Stamp Exhibition, Helsinki. Sheet 93×51 mm.
MS3345 **921** 1p. multicoloured 3·50 3·25

922 Steam Train (image scaled to 69% of original size)

1988. Postal Union of the Americas and Spain Colloquium on "America" Postage Stamps, Havana.
3346 **922** 20c. multicoloured 1·30 30

923 "Megasoma elephas"

1988. Beetles. Multicoloured.

3347	1c. Type **923**	10	10
3348	3c. "Platycoelia flavoscutellata" (vert)	10	10
3349	4c. "Plusiotis argenteola"	10	10
3350	5c. "Hetersoternus oberthuri"	15	10
3351	10c. "Odontotaenius zodiacus"	35	15
3352	35c. "Chrysophora chrysochlora" (vert)	1·10	30
3353	40c. "Phanaeus leander"	1·40	50

924 Chess Pieces

1988. Birth Centenary of Jose Capablanca (chess master). Multicoloured.

3354	30c. Type **924**	70	30
3355	40c. Juan Corzo, Capablanca and flags (1901 Cuban Championship) (horiz)	95	30
3356	50c. Emanuel Lasker and Capablanca (1921 World Championship) (horiz)	1·00	40
3357	1p. Checkmate in 1921 game with Lasker	2·50	90
3358	3p. "J. R. Capablanca" (E. Valderrama)	7·75	2·40
3359	5p. Chess pieces, flag, globe and Capablanca	14·00	4·50
MS3360	6 sheets, 58×88 mm (b, c) or 89×60 mm (others). (a) 30c. 1951 1c. Capablanca stamp; 30c. As No. 3354 but 29×36 mm; (b) 40c. 1951 5c. chess stamp; 40c. As No. 3355 but 36×27 mm; (c) 50c. 1951 5c. chess stamp; 50c. As No. 3356 but 36×28 mm; (d) 1p. 1951 2c. Capablanca stamp; 1p. As No. 3357 but 29×36 mm; (e) 3p. 1951 25c. Capablanca stamp; 3p. As No. 3358 but 28×36 mm; (f) 5p. 1951 8c. Capablanca stamp; 3p. As No. 3359 but 29×36 mm	60·00	55·00

925 Sun and Fortress

1988. 35th Anniv of Assault on Moncada Fortress.
3361 **925** 5c. red, yellow & black 25 10

926 Czechoslovakia 1920 20h. Stamp

1988. Praga 88 International Stamp Exhibition and 70th Anniv of First Czechoslovak Stamps. Sheet 91×52 mm.
MS3362 **926** 1p. multicoloured 3·50 3·25

927 Camilo Cienfuegos, "Che" Guevara and Map

1988. 30th Anniv of Rebel Invasion Columns.
3363 **927** 5c. multicoloured 15 10

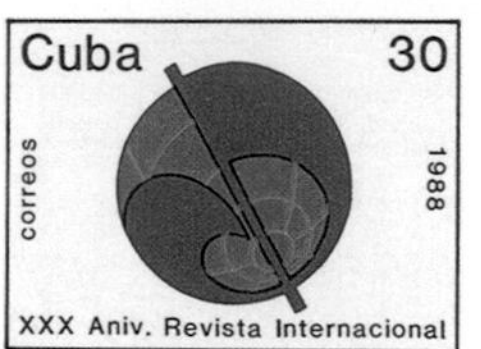

928 Emblem

1988. 30th Anniv of "Revista Internacional" (magazine).
3364 **928** 30c. multicoloured 1·10 30

929 Locomotive "Northumbrian", 1831

1988. Railway Development. Multicoloured.

3365	20c. Type **929**	50	25
3366	30c. Locomotive "E. L. Miller", 1834	1·00	40
3367	50c. "La Junta" (Cuba's first locomotive, 1840s)	2·20	80
3368	1p. Electric railcar	4·00	1·20
3369	2p. Russian-built M-62K diesel locomotive	7·25	2·75
3370	5p. Diesel railcar set	16·00	7·75

930 Arms and Jose de San Martin (Argentina)

1988. Latin-American History (3rd series). Mult.

3371	1c. Type **930**	10	10
3372	1c. Arms and M. A. Padilla (Bolivia)	10	10
3373	1c. 1944 10c. Discovery of America stamp	10	10
3374	1c. Arms and A. de Silva Xavier, "Tiradentes" (Brazil)	10	10
3375	1c. Arms and Bernardo O'Higgins (Chile)	10	10
3376	5c. A. Narino and arms (Colombia)	10	10
3377	5c. Arms and Jose Marti (Cuba)	10	10
3378	5c. 1944 13c. Discovery of America stamp	10	10
3379	5c. Arms and Juan Pablo Duarte (Dominican Republic)	10	10
3380	5c. Arms and Antonio Jose de Sucre (Ecuador)	10	10
3381	10c. Manuel Jose Arce and arms (El Salvador)	25	10
3382	10c. Arms and Jean Jacques Dessalines (Haiti)	25	10
3383	10c. 1944 5c. Discovery of America airmail stamp	25	10
3384	10c. Miguel Hidalgo and arms (Mexico)	25	10
3385	10c. Arms and J. Dolores Estrada (Nicaragua)	25	10
3386	20c. Jose E. Diaz and arms (Paraguay)	35	15
3387	20c. Arms and Francisco Bolognesi (Peru)	35	15
3388	20c. 1944 10c. Discovery of America airmail stamp	35	15
3389	20c. Arms and Jose Gervasio Artigas (Uruguay)	35	15
3390	20c. Simon Bolivar and arms (Venezuela)	35	15

931 Maces and Governor's Palace

1988. 20th Anniv of Havana Museum.
3391 **931** 5c. multicoloured 25 10

932 Ballerinas and Mute Swan

1988. 40th Anniv of National Ballet (3392) and 150th Anniv of Grand Theatre, Havana (3393). Multicoloured.

3392	5c. Type **932**	50	15
3393	5c. Theatre, 1838 and 1988	50	15

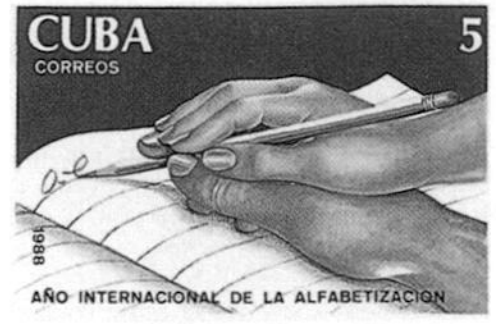

933 Practising Letters

1988. International Literacy Year.
3394 **933** 5c. multicoloured 25 10

934 Emblem

1988. 40th Anniv of Declaration of Human Rights.
3395 **934** 30c. multicoloured 1·10 30

935 Ernesto Che Guevara Plaza

1988. 30th Anniv of Battle of Santa Clara.

3396	**935**	30c. multicoloured	1·10	30

936 National Flag forming "30"

1989. 30th Anniv of Revolution.

3397	**936**	5c. multicoloured	10	10
3398	**936**	20c. multicoloured	55	15
3399	**936**	30c. gold, blue and red	75	25
3400	**936**	50c. gold, blue and red	1·50	50

937 "Pleurotus levis"

1989. Edible Mushrooms. Multicoloured.

3401	2c. Type **937**	10	10
3402	3c. "Pleurotus floridanus"	15	10
3403	5c. "Amanita caesarea"	20	15
3404	10c. "Lentinus cubensis" (horiz)	45	15
3405	40c. "Pleurotus ostreatus" (red)	1·60	40
3406	50c. "Pleurotus ostreatus" (brown)	1·70	50

938 India River Post, 1858

1989. India 89 International Stamp Exhibition, New Delhi. Sheet 91×51 mm.

MS3407	**938**	1p. multicoloured	3·50	3·25

939 1982 30c. Cuban Stamp

1989. 50th Anniv of Revolutionary Workers' Union.

3408	**939**	5c. multicoloured	25	10

940 "Metamorpho dido"

1989. Butterflies. Multicoloured.

3409	1c. Type **940**	10	10
3410	3c. "Callithea saphhira"	10	10
3411	5c. "Papilio zagreus"	15	10
3412	10c. "Mynes sestia"	25	15
3413	30c. "Papilio dardanus"	1·20	30
3414	50c. "Catagranma sorana"	2·10	65

941 Footballer

1989. World Cup Football Championship, Italy (1990).

3415	**941**	1c. multicoloured	10	10
3416	-	3c. multicoloured	10	10
3417	-	5c. multicoloured	10	10
3418	-	10c. multicoloured	15	10
3419	-	30c. multicoloured	85	15
3420	-	50c. multicoloured	1·50	30
MS3421		62×50 mm. 1p. multicoloured (39×31 mm)	3·50	2·75

DESIGNS: 3c. to 1p. Various footballers.

942 "30" and Arms

1989. 30th Anniv of National Revolutionary Police.

3422	**942**	5c. multicoloured	25	15

943 "Zodiac" Rocket and 1934 Australian Cover

1989. Cosmonautics Day. Rocket Post (1st series). Multicoloured.

3423	1c. Type **943**	10	10
3424	3c. Rocket and cover from India to Poland, 1934	10	10
3425	5c. Rocket and 1934 English cover	15	10
3426	10c. "Icarus" rocket and 1935 Dutch cover	20	15
3427	40c. "La Douce France" rocket and 1935 French cover	95	40
3428	50c. Rocket and 1939 Cuban cover	1·20	55

See also Nos. 3516/21.

1989. Stamp Day. As T 811. Details of mural by R. R. Radillo in Havana Stamp Museum. Mult.

3429	30c. Mail coach	70	30
3430	50c. 18th-century sailing packet	5·50	2·00

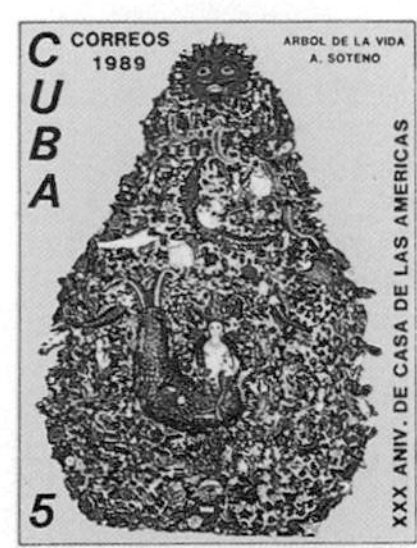

944 "Tree of Life" (A. Soteno)

1989. 30th Anniv of "House of the Americas" Museum, Havana.

3431	**944**	5c. multicoloured	25	10

945 Bulgaria 1l. Stamp

1989. Bulgaria 89 International Stamp Exhibition, Sofia. Sheet 90×50 mm.

MS3432	1p. green, vermillion and black	4·00	2·75

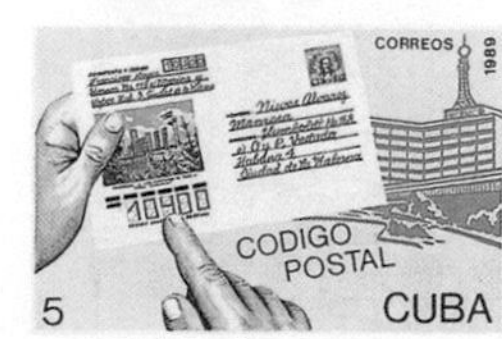

946 Coded Envelope

1989. Post Codes.

3433	**946**	5c. multicoloured	25	10

947 Tobacco Flowers

1989. Mothers' Day. Perfumes and Flowers. Mult.

3434	1c. Type **947**	10	10
3435	3c. Violets	10	10
3436	5c. Mariposa	15	10
3437	13c. Roses	30	15
3438	30c. Jasmine	85	25
3439	50c. Orange-flower	1·50	55

948 Signing Decree

1989. 30th Anniv of Agrarian Reform Law.

3440	**948**	5c. multicoloured	25	10

949 "40" and Headquarters Building, Moscow

1989. 40th Anniv of Council for Mutual Economic Aid.

3441	**949**	30c. multicoloured	1·10	15

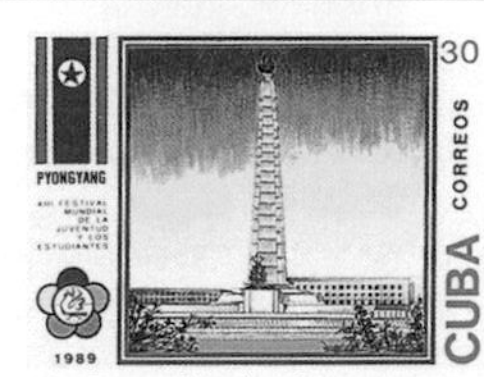

950 Tower of Juche Idea, Pyongyang

1989. 13th World Youth and Students' Festival, Pyongyang.

3442	**950**	30c. multicoloured	1·10	15

951 "Rouger de Lisle singing The Marseillaise" (Pils)

1989. Philexfrance 89 International Stamp Exhibition, Paris. Sheet 96×56 mm.

MS3443	**951**	1p. multicoloured	3·50	2·75

952 Toco Toucan

1989. Brasiliana '89 Stamp Exhibition. Rio de Janeiro. Birds. Multicoloured.

3444	1c. Type **952**	25	10
3445	3c. Chestnut-bellied heron	25	10
3446	5c. Scarlet ibis	35	10
3447	10c. White-winged trumpeter	45	15
3448	35c. Harpy eagle	1·60	50
3449	50c. Amazonian umbrellabird	2·20	75

953 "El Fenix" (galleon)

1989. Cuban Sailing Ships. Multicoloured.

3450	1c. Type **953**	10	10
3451	3c. "Triunfo" (ship of the line)	10	10
3452	5c. "El Rayo" (ship of the line)	15	10
3453	10c. "San Carlos" (ship of the line)	35	15
3454	30c. "San Jose" (ship of the line)	1·30	30
3455	50c. "San Genaro" (ship of the line)	2·10	55

954 Carved Stone and Men in Dugout Canoe

1989. America. Pre-Columbian Cultures. Mult.

3456	5c. Type **954**	25	10
3457	20c. Cave painters	70	30

955 Domingo F. Sarmiento and "Govenia utriculata" (Argentina)

1989. Latin American History (4th series). Multicoloured.

3458	1c. Type **955**	10	10
3459	1c. Machado de Assis and "Laelia grandis" (Brazil)	10	10
3460	1c. El Salvador 1892 1p. Columbus stamp	10	10
3461	1c. Jorge Isaacs and "Cattleya trianae" (Colombia)	10	10
3462	1c. Alejo Carpentier and "Cochleanthes discolor" (Cuba)	10	10
3463	5c. "Oxalis adenophylla" and Pablo Neruda (Chile)	15	10
3464	5c. Pedro H. Urena and "Epidendrum fragrans" (Dominican Republic)	15	10
3465	5c. El Salvador 1893 2p. City of Isabela stamp	15	10
3466	5c. Juan Montalvo and "Miltonia vexillaria" (Ecuador)	15	10
3467	5c. "Odontoglossum rossii" and Miguel A. Asturias (Guatemala)	15	10
3468	10c. "Laelia anceps" and Jose C. del Valle (Honduras)	30	15
3469	10c. "Laelia ancepes alba" and Alfonso Reyes (Mexico)	30	15
3470	10c. El Salvador 1893 5p. Columbus Statue stamp	30	15
3471	10c. "Brassavola acaulis" and Ruben Dario (Nicaragua)	30	15
3472	10c. Belisario Porras and "Pescatorea cerina" (Panama)	30	15
3473	20c. Ricardo Palma and "Coryanthes leucocorys" (Peru)	50	20
3474	20c. Eugenio Maria de Hostos and "Guzmania berteroniana" (Puerto Rico)	50	20
3475	20c. El Salvador 1893 10p. Departure from Palos stamp	50	20
3476	20c. "Cypella herbertii" and Jose E. Rodo (Uruguay)	50	20
3477	20c. "Cattleya mossiae" and Romulo Gallegos (Venezuela)	50	20

956 Cienfuegos and Flag

1989. 30th Anniv of Disappearance of Camilo Cienfuegos (revolutionary).

3478 **956** 5c. multicoloured 25 10

957 Church Tower

1989. 475th Anniv of Trinidad City.

3479 **957** 5c. multicoloured 15 10

958 "Outskirts of Niza" (E. Boudin)

1989. Paintings in National Museum. Mult.

3480 1c. "Family Scene" (Antoine Faivre) 10 10

3481 2c. "Flowers" (Emile J. H. Vernet) 10 10

3482 5c. "Judgement of Paris" (Charles Le Brun) 15 10

3483 20c. Type **958** 75 15

3484 30c. "Portrait of Sarah Bernhardt" (G. J. V. Clairin) (36×46 mm) 95 20

3485 50c. "Fishermen in Harbour" (C. J. Vernet) 1·90 55

959 Archery

1989. 11th Pan-American Games, Havana (1st issue). Multicoloured.

3486 5c. Type **959** 20 10

3487 5c. Shooting 20 10

3488 5c. Fencing 20 10

3489 5c. Cycling 20 10

3490 5c. Water polo 20 10

3491 20c. Lawn tennis (vert) 55 25

3492 30c. Swimming (vert) 95 25

3493 35c. Diving (vert) 1·20 30

3494 40c. Hockey 1·30 30

3495 50c. Basketball (vert) 1·90 65

See also Nos. 3584/93 and 3621/30.

960 Front Page

1989. Centenary of "Golden Age" (children's magazine compiled by Jose Marti).

3496 **960** 5c. blue, black and red 35 10

961 "Almendares" (paddle-steamer)

1990. 25th Anniv of Postal Museum. Mult.

3497 5c. Type **961** 15 10

3498 30c. Mail train 2·75 80

962 Cave Painters (image scaled to 71% of original size)

1990. 50th Anniv of Speleological Society.

3499 **962** 30c. multicoloured 1·70 30

963 Player No. 11 and Colosseum

1990. World Cup Football Championship, Italy. Multicoloured.

3500 5c. Type **963** 10 10

3501 5c. Player No. 10 10 10

3502 5c. Player No. 8 10 10

3503 10c. Goalkeeper 20 10

3504 30c. Player No. 11 and arch 1·10 30

3505 50c. Player 1·80 55

MS3506 94×62 mm. 1p. Goalkeeper catching ball (39×31 mm) 3·00 2·75

964 Baseball

1990. Olympic Games, Barcelona (1992) (1st issue). Multicoloured.

3507 1c. Type **964** 10 10

3508 4c. Running 10 10

3509 5c. Basketball 15 10

3510 10c. Volleyball 40 15

3511 30c. Wrestling (horiz) 95 30

3512 50c. Boxing 1·70 65

MS3513 88×48 mm. 1p. High jumping (39×31 mm) 3·50 2·75

See also Nos. 3604/**MS**3619 and 3692/**MS**3698.

965 Tower of Babel, Dove and Globe

1990. 75th Esperanto Congress, Havana.

3514 **965** 30c. multicoloured 1·10 30

966 Skiing

1990. Winter Olympic Games, Albertville (1992). Sheet 91×50 mm.

MS3515 **966** 1p. multicoloured 4·00 2·75

1990. Cosmonautics Day. Rocket Post (2nd series). As T 943. Multicoloured.

3516 1c. 1932 Austrian Cover and "U12" rocket 10 10

3517 2c. 1933 German cover, rocket and liner 10 10

3518 3c. 1934 Netherlands cover, "NRB" rocket and windmill 15 10

3519 10c. 1935 Belgian cover and rocket 20 15

3520 30c. 1935 Yugoslavian cover and "JUG1" rocket 95 15

3521 50c. 1936 U.S.A. cover and rocket 1·70 55

1990. Stamp Day. As T 811. Showing details of mural by R. R. Radillo in Havana Stamp Museum. Multicoloured.

3522 30c. Russian-built Type TEM-4 diesel locomotive leaving station 2·50 65

3523 50c. de Havilland DH. 10b Comet 1 airplane 1·50 40

967 Flag and Globe

1990. Centenary of Labour Day.

3524 **967** 5c. multicoloured 85 15

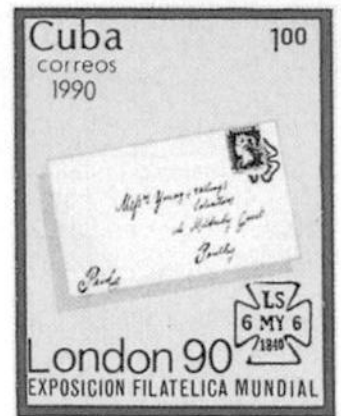

968 Penny Black with Maltese Cross Cancellation

1990. Stamp World London 90 International Stamp Exhibition. Sheet 95×51 mm.

MS3525 **968** 1p. multicoloured 1·40 1·40

969 Hill and Penny Black

1990. 150th Anniv of the Penny Black. Mult.

3526 2c. Type **969** 10 10

3527 3c. Twopenny blue 10 10

3528a 5c. G.B. 1855 4d. stamp 1·10 60

3529 10c. G.B. 1847 1s. embossed stamp 20 15

3530 30c. G.B. paid hand-stamp 1·10 15

3531 50c. Twopenny blues on cover to Malta 1·90 55

970 Celia Sanchez (after O. Yanes)

1990. 70th Birth Anniv of Celia Sanchez Manduley (revolutionary).

3532 **970** 5c. multicoloured 45 15

971 Flags and Ho Chi Minh

1990. Birth Centenary of Ho Chi Minh (Vietnamese leader).

3533 **971** 50c. multicoloured 1·50 40

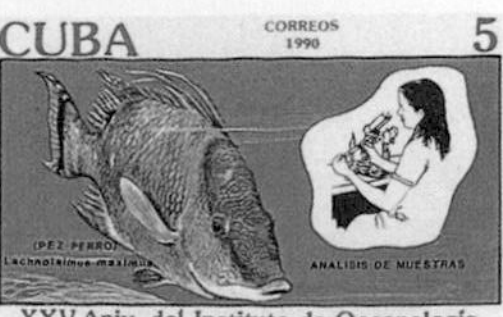

972 Hogfish and Sample Analysis

1990. 25th Anniv of Oceanology Institute. Mult.

3534 5c. Type **972** 10 10

3535 30c. "Arrecife coralino" and research vessel 1·00 30

3536 50c. Lobster and diver collecting samples 1·70 40

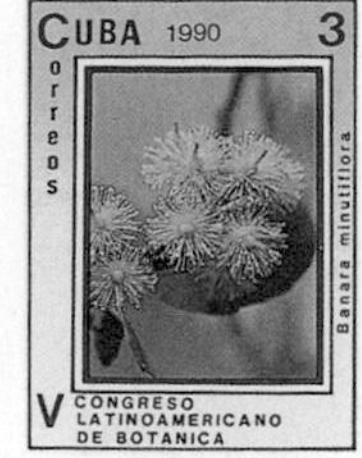

973 "Banara minutiflora"

1990. 5th Latin American Botanical Congress. Multicoloured.

3537 3c. Type **973** 10 10

3538 5c. "Oplonia nannophylla" 10 10

3539 10c. "Jacquinia brunnescens" 40 15

3540 30c. "Rondeletia brachycarpa" 1·20 20

3541 50c. "Rondeletia odorata" 1·90 70

974 Windsurfing

1990. Tourist Sports. Multicoloured.

3542 5c. Type **974** 10 10

3543 10c. Underwater fishing (horiz) 40 20

3544 30c. Sea fishing (horiz) 1·10 20

3545 40c. Shooting 1·80 70

975 "The Flute of Pan" (detail)

1990. Paintings by A. G. Menocal in National Museum. Multicoloured.

3546 5c. Type **975** 20 20

3547 20c. "Shepherd" 65 30

3548 50c. "Ganymede" 1·90 50

3549 1p. "Venus Anadiomena" 2·75 1·10

MS3550 101×128 mm. Nos. 3546/9 6·00 5·75

976 Great Crested Grebe

1990. "New Zealand 90" International Stamp Exhibition, Auckland. Birds. Multicoloured.

3551 2c. Type **976** 20 10

3552 3c. Weka rail 20 10

3553 5c. Kea 20 15

3554 10c. Bush wren 45 20

3555 30c. Grey butcher bird 1·40 40

3556 50c. Parson bird 2·40 85

MS3557 81×55 mm. 1p. Brown Kiwi ("Apteryx australis mantelli") (wrongly inscr "Aptery") (39×31 mm) 5·00 4·75

977 Lighthouse

1990. 8th U.N.O. Congress on Crime Prevention and Treatment of Delinquents.

3558 **977** 50c. red, blue and silver 1·90 50

978 Caravel and Shoreline

1990. America. The Natural World. Mult.

3559	5c. Type **978**	30	20
3560	20c. Christopher Columbus and native village	1·10	40

979 Cameraman

1990. 40th Anniv of Cuban Television.

3561 **979** 5c. multicoloured 40 15

980 Steam Locomotive No. 1712 and Havana Railway Station

1990. 30th Anniv of Nationalization of Railways.

3562 **980** 50c. multicoloured 3·25 1·00

981 Flag and Couple (Argentina)

1990. Latin-American History (5th series). Multicoloured.

3563	1c. Type **981**	10	10
3564	1c. Flag and couple (Bolivia)	10	10
3565	1c. Argentina 1892 5c. Discovery of America stamp	10	10
3566	1c. Flag and couple (Colombia)	10	10
3567	1c. Flag and couple (Costa Rica)	10	10
3568	5c. Flag and couple (Cuba)	20	10
3569	5c. Flag and couple (Chile)	20	10
3570	5c. Dominican Republic 1900 ½c. Columbus stamp	20	10
3571	5c. Flag and couple (Ecuador)	20	10
3572	5c. Flag and couple (El Salvador)	20	10
3573	10c. Flag and couple (Guatemala)	35	15
3574	10c. Flag and couple (Mexico)	35	15
3575	10c. Puerto Rico 1893 3c. Discovery of America stamp	35	15
3576	10c. Flag and couple (Nicaragua)	35	15
3577	10c. Flag and couple (Panama)	35	15
3578	20c. Flag and couple (Paraguay)	65	20
3579	20c. Flag and couple (Peru)	65	20
3580	20c. El Salvador 1894 10p. Columbus stamp	65	20
3581	20c. Flag and couple (Puerto Rico)	65	20
3582	20c. Flag and couple (Venezuela)	65	20

982 Player

1990. 11th World Pelota Championship.

3583 **982** 30c. multicoloured 1·40 50

1990. 11th Pan-American Games, Havana (1991) (2nd issue). As T 959. Multicoloured.

3584	5c. Kayaking	20	10
3585	5c. Rowing	20	10
3586	5c. Yachting	20	10
3587	5c. Judo	20	10
3588	5c. Show jumping	20	10
3589	10c. Table tennis	35	20
3590	20c. Gymnastics (vert)	65	30
3591	30c. Baseball (vert)	1·00	30
3592	35c. Basketball (vert)	1·20	40
3593	50c. Football (vert)	1·80	95

983 Boxing

1990. 16th Central American and Caribbean Games, Mexico. Multicoloured.

3594	5c. Type **983**	10	10
3595	30c. Baseball	1·20	30
3596	50c. Volleyball	2·10	60

984 "Chioides marmorosa"

1991. Butterflies. Multicoloured.

3597	2c. Type **984**	35	10
3598	3c. "Composia fidelissima"	35	10
3599	5c. "Danaus plexippus"	35	10
3600	10c. "Hypolimnas misippus"	55	20
3601	30c. "Hypna iphigenia"	1·80	30
3602	50c. "Hemiargus ammon"	2·75	60

985 Guerra Aguiar and 1966 3c. Stamp

1991. 1st Death Anniv of Jose Guerra Aguiar (founder of Cuban Postal Museum).

3603 **985** 5c. multicoloured 50 20

986 Long Jumping

1991. Olympic Games, Barcelona (1992) (2nd issue). Multicoloured.

3604	1c. Type **986**	10	10
3605	2c. Throwing the javelin	10	10
3606	3c. Hockey	20	10
3607	5c. Weightlifting	20	15
3608	40c. Cycling	1·40	40
3609	50c. Gymnastics	1·90	60
MS3610	59×80 mm. 1p. Torch bearer (31×39 mm)	3·75	3·25

987 Yuri Gagarin and "Vostok"

1991. 30th Anniv of First Man in Space. Mult.

3611	5c. Type **987**	10	10
3612	10c. "Soyuz" and Y. Romanenko	20	10
3613	10c. "Salyut" space station and A. Tamayo	20	10
3614	30c. "Mir" space station (left half)	1·10	20
3615	30c. "Mir" space station (right half)	1·10	20
3616	50c. Launch of "Buran" space shuttle	1·70	60

Nos. 3612/13 and 3614/15 respectively were issued together, se-tenant, forming composite designs.

988 Statue and Flag

1991. 30th Anniversaries. Multicoloured.

3617	5c. Type **988** (proclamation of Socialism)	10	10
3618	50c. Playa Giron (invasion attempt by Cuban exiles)	2·20	95

1991. Stamp Day. Designs as T 811 showing details of mural by R. R. Radillo in Havana Stamp Museum. Multicoloured.

3619	30c. Rocket (vert)	1·10	40
3620	50c. Dish aerial	1·90	50

1991. 11th Pan-American Games, Havana (3rd series). As T 959. Multicoloured.

3621	5c. Volleyball (vert)	10	10
3622	5c. Synchronized swimming (vert)	10	10
3623	5c. Weightlifting (vert)	10	10
3624	5c. Baseball (vert)	10	10
3625	5c. Gymnastics (vert)	10	10
3626	10c. Ten-pin bowling	35	20
3627	20c. Boxing (vert)	65	30
3628	30c. Running	1·00	30
3629	35c. Wrestling	1·20	40
3630	50c. Judo	1·80	60

989 Simon Bolivar and Map

1991. 165th Anniv of Panama Congress.

3631 **989** 50c. multicoloured 2·20 70

990 Dirigible Balloon Design and Jean-Baptiste Meusnier

1991. Espamer '91 Iberia–Latin America Stamp Exhibition, Buenos Aires. Airships. Mult.

3632	5c. Type **990**	20	10
3633	10c. First steam-powered dirigible airship and Henri Giffard	40	20
3634	20c. Paul Hanlein and first airship with gas-powered motor	75	40
3635	30c. "Deutschland" (first airship with petrol motor) and Karl Wolfert	1·00	60
3636	50c. David Schwarz and first rigid aluminium airship	1·80	1·00
3637	1p. Ferdinand von Zeppelin and airship "Graf Zeppelin"	3·50	2·00

No. 3637 is inscr "Hindenburg".

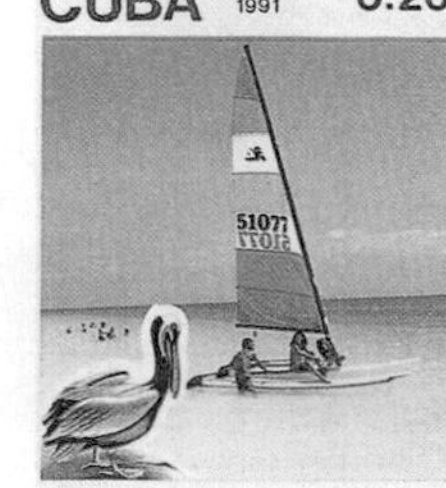

992 Cayo Largo

1991. Tourism. Multicoloured.

3645	20c. Type **992**	65	20
3646	20c. Varadero	65	20
3647	30c. San Carlos de la Cabana Fortress (horiz)	1·10	40
3648	30c. Castillo de los Tres Reyes del Morro (horiz)	1·10	40

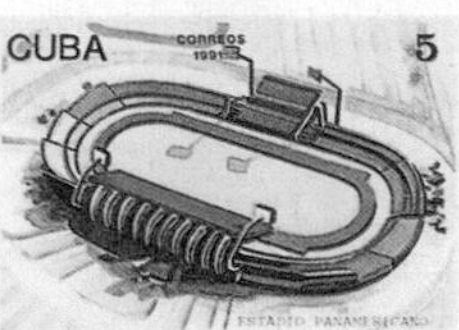

993 Stadium

1991. Panamfilex 1991 Pan-American Stamp Exhibition. Multicoloured.

3649	5c. Type **993**	20	10
3650	20c. Baragua swimming-pool complex	65	40
3651	30c. Ramon Fonst hall	90	60
3652	50c. Reynaldo Paseiro cycle-track	1·70	1·00
MS3653	89×50 mm. 1p. Sports Centre (39×31 mm)	3·75	3·50

994 "Kataoka Dengoemon Takafusa" (Utagawa Kuniyoshi)

1991. Phila Nippon '91 International Stamp Exhibition, Tokyo. Multicoloured.

3654	5c. Type **994**	20	10
3655	10c. "Night Walk" (Hosoda Eishi)	40	20
3656	20c. "Courtesans" (Torii Kiyonaga)	75	40
3657	30c. "Conversation" (Kitagawa Utamaro)	1·00	50
3658	50c. "Inari-bashi Bridge" (Ando Hiroshige)	1·80	95
3659	1p. "On the Terrace" (Torii Kiyonaga)	3·50	2·00

995 Figure Skating

1991. Winter Olympic Games, Albertville. Sheet 60×80 mm.

MS3660 **995** 1p. multicoloured 3·75 3·50

996 Statue of Jose Marti

1991. 4th Cuban Communist Party Congress.

3661	**996**	5c. multicoloured	20	10
3662	-	50c. black, blue and red	1·90	60

DESIGN: 50c. Party emblem.

997 Christopher Columbus and Pinzon Brothers

1991. America. Voyages of Discovery. Mult.

3663		5c. Type **997**	30	10
3664		20c. "Santa Maria", "Nina" and "Pinta"	1·40	30

998 Marti (after F. Martinez)

1991. Centenary of Publication of "The Simple Verses" by Jose Marti.

3665	**998**	50c. multicoloured	2·20	50

999 Julian Aguirre and Charango (Argentina)

1991. Latin-American History (6th series). Music. Multicoloured.

3666		1c. Type **999**	10	10
3667		1c. Eduardo Caba and antara (pipes) (Bolivia)	10	10
3668		1c. Chile 1853 10c. stamp	10	10
3669		1c. Heitor Villalobos and trumpet with gourd resonator (Brazil)	10	10
3670		1c. Guillermo Uribe-Holguin and cununo macho (drum) (Colombia)	10	10
3671		5c. Claves (sticks) and Miguel Failde (Cuba)	20	10
3672		5c. Enrique Soro and Araucanian kultrum (Chile)	20	10
3673		5c. Chile 1903 10c. on 30c. stamp	20	10
3674		5c. Rondador (xylophone) and Segundo L. Moreno (Ecuador)	20	10
3675		5c. Marimba and Ricardo Castillo (Guatemala)	20	10
3676		10c. Vihuela and Carlos Chavez (Mexico)	45	20
3677		10c. Luis A. Delgadillo and maracas (Nicaragua)	45	20
3678		10c. Chile 1906 2c. stamp	45	20
3679		10c. Alfredo de Saint-Malo and mejorana (Panama)	45	20
3680		10c. Jose Asuncion Flores and harp (Paraguay)	45	20
3681		20c. Daniel Alomia and quena (flute) (Peru)	90	30
3682		20c. Cuatro (guitar) and Juan Morell y Campos (Puerto Rico)	90	30
3683		20c. Chile 1905 10c. stamp	90	30
3684		20c. Eduardo Fabini and tambo-ril (drums) (Uruguay)	90	30
3685		20c. Cuatro (guitar) and Juan V. Lecuna (Venezuela)	90	30

1000 Mascot

1991. 1st Jose Marti Pioneers Congress.

3686	**1000**	5p. multicoloured	40	20

1001 Toussaint L'Ouverture (revolutionary leader)

1991. Bicentenary of Haitian Revolution.

3687	**1001**	50c. multicoloured	2·20	50

1002 "35", Stars and Soldier

1991. 35th Anniversaries. Multicoloured.

3688		5c. Type **1002** (Revolutionary Armed Forces)	30	20
3689		50c. Launch "Granma" (disembarkation of revolutionary forces) (vert)	2·20	50

1003 Agramonte (after F. Martinez)

1991. 150th Birth Anniv of Ignacio Agramonte (poet).

3690	**1003**	5c. multicoloured	35	10

1004 Skiing

1992. Winter Olympic Games, Albertville (3rd issue). Sheet 77×63 mm.

MS3691	**1004**	1p. multicoloured	3·75	3·25

1005 Table Tennis and Plan of Montjuic Complex

1992. Olympic Games, Barcelona (3rd issue). Mult.

3692		3c. Type **1005**	10	10
3693		5c. Handball and Vall d'Hebron complex	20	10
3694		10c. Shooting and Badalona complex	35	15
3695		20c. Long jumping and Montjuic complex (vert)	65	20
3696		35c. Judo and Diagonal complex	1·40	50
3697		50c. Fencing and Montjuic complex	1·80	50
MS3698		62×77 mm. 100c. Gymnastics and plan of Barcelona (31×39 mm)	3·75	3·25

1006 Flooded Terraces and Dead Trees

1992. Environmental Protection. Mult.

3699		5c. Type **1006**	30	10
3700		20c. Whale and dead fish in polluted sea	65	30
3701		35c. Satellite picture of ozone levels over Antarctica and gas mask in polluted air	1·40	50
3702		40c. Rainbows, globe, doves and nuclear explosion	1·50	50

1007 Blue Angelfish

1992. Fishes. Multicoloured.

3703		5c. Type **1007**	20	10
3704		10c. Jackknife-fish	20	15
3705		20c. Blue tang	70	20
3706		30c. Sergeant-major	1·20	30
3707		50c. Yellow-tailed damselfish	2·10	60

1008 Boxer

1992. Dogs. Multicoloured.

3708		5c. Type **1008**	10	10
3709		10c. Great dane	20	10
3710		20c. German shepherd	70	20
3711		30c. Short-haired, long-haired and wire-haired dachshunds	1·20	30
3712		35c. Dobermann	1·20	40
3713		40c. Fox terrier	1·50	40
3714		50c. Poodle	1·90	60
MS3715		52×81 mm. 1p. Bichon fries (32×40 mm)	4·50	3·50

1009 Badge

1992. 30th Anniv and Sixth Congress of Youth Communist League.

3716	**1009**	5c. multicoloured	40	15

1010 Jose Marti

1992. Centenary of Cuban Revolutionary Party.

3717	**1010**	5c. multicoloured	30	10
3718	**1010**	50c. multicoloured	1·90	60

1011 Columbus Sighting Land

1992. America. 500th Anniv of Discovery of America by Columbus. Multicoloured.

3719		5c. Type **1011**	35	15
3720		20c. Columbus landing at San Salvador	1·00	30

1012 Alhambra, Sierra Nevada

1992. Granada 92 International Philatelic Exhibition. Designs showing views of the Alhambra. Multicoloured.

3721		5c. Type **1012**	10	10
3722		10c. Sunset	20	10
3723		20c. Doorway and arches	85	20
3724		30c. Courtyard of the Lions	1·40	30
3725		35c. Bedroom	1·70	50
3726		50c. View of Albaicin from balcony	2·30	60

1013 Facade and Plate

1992. 50th Anniv of La Bodeguita del Medio (restaurant).

3727	**1013**	50c. multicoloured	1·90	60

1014 "Cattleya hibrida"

1992. 40th Anniv of Soroa Orchid Garden. Mult.

3728		3c. Type **1014**	20	10
3729		5c. "Phalaenopsis sp."	20	10
3730		10c. "Cattleyopsis lindenii"	20	15
3731		30c. "Bletia purpurea"	1·10	30
3732		35c. "Oncidium luridum"	1·20	40
3733		40c. "Vanda hibrida"	1·50	50

1015 Hummingbird

1992. The Bee Hummingbird. Multicoloured.

3734		5c. Type **1015**	50	20
3735		10c. Perched on twig	70	20

3736	20c. Perched on twig with flowers	1·50	20
3737	30c. Hovering over flower	2·50	40

1016 Guardalavaca Beach

1992. Tourism. Multicoloured.

3738	10c. Type **1016**	35	20
3739	20c. Hotel Bucanero	75	20
3740	30c. View of Havana	1·40	50
3741	50c. Varadero beach	2·00	60

1017 Eligio Sardinas

1992. Olymphilex '92 International Olympic Stamps Exhibition, Barcelona. Designs showing Cuban sportsmen. Multicoloured.

3742	5c. Type **1017**	20	10
3743	35c. Ramon Fonst (fencer)	1·20	40
3744	40c. Sergio "Pipian" Martinez (cyclist)	1·40	50
3745	50c. Martin Dihigo (baseball player)	1·90	70

1018 Columbus before Queen Isabella

1992. Expo 92 World's Fair, Seville. Sheet 95×76 mm.

MS3746	**1018** 1p.50 multicoloured	5·00	4·75

1019 Alvarez Cabral

1992. Genova '92 International Thematic Stamp Exhibition. Explorers and their ships. Multicoloured.

3747	5c. Type **1019**	20	10
3748	10c. Alonso Pinzon	35	20
3749	20c. Alonso de Ojeda	75	20
3750	30c. Amerigo Vespucci	1·20	40
3751	35c. Henry the Navigator	1·40	40
3752	40c. Bartolomeu Dias	1·70	50
MS3753	92×53 mm. 1p. Columbus's fleet (31×39 mm)	4·50	4·25

1020 High Jumping

1992. 6th World Athletics Cup, Havana. Mult.

3754	5c. Type **1020**	20	10
3755	20c. Throwing the javelin	70	20
3756	30c. Throwing the hammer	1·10	30
3757	40c. Long jumping (vert)	1·50	50
3758	50c. Hurdling (vert)	1·90	60
MS3759	64×84 mm. 1p. Relay race (39×31 mm)	3·75	2·75

1021 Men's High Jump (Gold) and Women's Discus (Gold)

1992. Cuban Olympic Games Medal Winners. Multicoloured.

3760	5c. Type **1021**	20	10
3761	5c. Men's 4×400 m relay (silver) and men's discus (bronze)	20	10
3762	5c. Men's 4×100 m relay and women's high jump and 800 m (bronze)	20	10
3763	20c. Baseball (gold)	70	20
3764	20c. Boxing (7 gold and 2 silver)	70	20
3765	20c. Women's volleyball (gold)	70	20
3766	50c. Men's judo (bronze) and women's judo (gold, silver and 2 bronze)	1·90	60
3767	50c. Greco-roman (gold and 2 bronze) and freestyle (gold and bronze) wrestling	1·90	60
3768	50c. Fencing (silver, bronze) and weightlifting (silver)	1·90	60

1022 Christopher Columbus and Queen Isabella the Catholic

1992. Latin-American History (7th series). Multicoloured.

3769	1c. Type **1022**	10	10
3770	1c. Columbus at Rabida Monastery	10	10
3771	1c. Columbus presenting plans to King Ferdinand and Queen Isabella	10	10
3772	1c. Columbus before Salamanca Council	10	10
3773	1c. Departure from Palos	10	10
3774	5c. Fleet stopping off at Canary Islands	20	10
3775	5c. Columbus reassuring crew	20	10
3776	5c. Sighting of land	20	10
3777	5c. Columbus landing	20	10
3778	5c. Columbus's encounter with Amerindians	20	10
3779	10c. "Santa Maria" grounded off Hispaniola	35	20
3780	10c. Arrival of "Nina" at Palos	35	20
3781	10c. Columbus's procession through Barcelona	35	20
3782	10c. Columbus before King and Queen	35	20
3783	10c. Departure from Cadiz on second voyage	35	20
3784	20c. King and Queen welcoming Columbus	85	30
3785	20c. Fleet leaving on third voyage	85	30
3786	20c. Columbus's deportation in chains from Hispaniola	85	30
3787	20c. Fleet embarking on fourth voyage	85	30
3788	20c. Death of Columbus at Valladolid	85	30

1023 Chacon

1992. Birth Centenary of Jose Maria Chacon y Calvo (historian).

3789	**1023** 30c. multicoloured	1·40	50

1024 Sanctuary of Our Lady of Charity, Cobre

1992. Churches. Multicoloured.

3790	5c. Type **1024**	20	10
3791	20c. St. Mary's Church, Rosario	1·00	20
3792	30c. Church of the Holy Spirit, Havana	1·40	30
3793	50c. Guardian of the Holy Angel Church, Pena Pobre, Havana	2·75	40

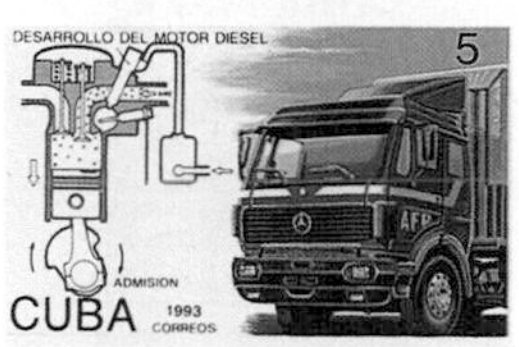

1025 Diagram of Engine and Truck

1993. Development of Diesel Engine. Each showing an engine at a different stage of cycle. Multicoloured.

3794	5c. Type **1025**	10	10
3795	10c. Motor car	20	10
3796	30c. Tug	90	50
3797	40c. Diesel locomotive	3·75	1·40
3798	50c. Tractor	1·50	85
MS3799	81×61 mm. 1p. Rudolph Diesel (80th death anniv) (39×31 mm)	3·75	2·50

1026 Player

1993. Davis Cup Men's Team Tennis Championship. Designs showing tennis players. Multicoloured.

3800	5c. Type **1026**	20	20
3801	20c. Double-handed backhand	65	30
3802	30c. Serve	1·00	50
3803	35c. Stretched forehand (horiz)	1·10	60
3804	40c. Returning drop shot (horiz)	1·40	70
MS3805	50×79 mm. 1p. Forehand (39×31 mm)	3·25	3·00

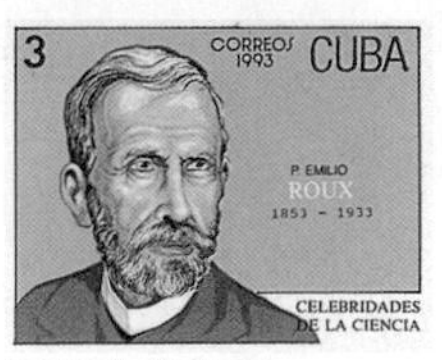

1027 Pedro Emilio Roux

1993. Scientists. Multicoloured.

3806	3c. Type **1027** (bacteriologist)	10	10
3807	5c. Carlos Finlay (biologist)	20	10
3808	10c. Ivan Petrovich Pavlov (physiologist)	35	20
3809	20c. Louis Pasteur (chemist)	65	30
3810	30c. Santiago Ramon y Cajal (histologist)	1·00	50
3811	35c. Sigmund Freud (psychiatrist)	1·10	60
3812	40c. Wilhelm Roentgen (physicist)	1·30	70
3813	50c. Joseph Lister (surgeon)	1·70	85
MS3814	67×52 mm. 1p. Robert Koch (bacteriologist) (vert)	3·25	3·00

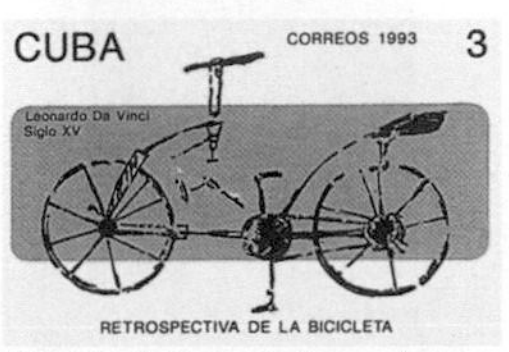

1028 Bicycle Design by Leonardo da Vinci

1993. Bicycles. Multicoloured.

3815	3c. Type **1028**	10	10
3816	5c. Draisiana hobby-horse	20	10
3817	10c. Michaux boneshaker	50	20
3818	20c. Starley penny-farthing	1·00	25
3819	30c. Lawson "Safety" bicycle	1·50	50
3820	35c. Modern bicycle	1·70	60

1029 "Valencian Fishwives"

1993. Paintings by Joaquin Sorolla in the National Museum. Multicoloured.

3821	3c. "Child eating Melon" (vert)	10	10
3822	5c. Type **1029**	20	10
3823	10c. "Regatta"	40	20
3824	20c. "Peasant Girl"	70	30
3825	40c. "Summertime"	1·40	70
3826	50c. "By the Sea"	1·90	85

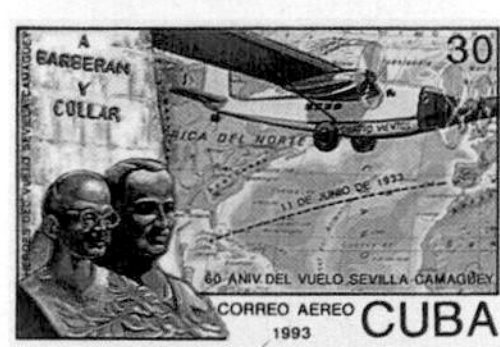

1030 "Four Winds" and Statue of Barberan and Collar

1993. 60th Anniv of Seville (Spain)–Camaguey (Cuba) Flight by Mariano Barberan and Joaquin Collar.

3827	**1030** 30c. multicoloured	1·10	50

1031 Northern Jacana

1993. Brasiliana '93 International Stamp Exhibition, Rio de Janeiro. Water Birds. Multicoloured.

3828	3c. Type **1031**	10	10
3829	5c. Great blue heron (27×44 mm)	20	10
3830	10c. Black-necked stilt	35	20
3831	20c. Black-crowned night heron	65	30
3832	30c. Sandhill crane (27×44 mm)	1·00	50
3833	50c. Limpkin	1·80	85

1032 Fidel Castro and Text

1993. Anniversaries. Multicoloured.

3834	5c. Type **1032** (40th anniv of publication of "History Will Absolve Me")	15	10
3835	5c. Jose Marti (140th birth anniv) and Rafael M. Mendive (vert)	15	10
3836	5c. Carlos M. de Cespedes and broken wheel (125th anniv of Yara Proclamation)	15	10
3837	5c. Moncada Barracks (40th anniv of attack on barracks)	15	10

1033 "Sedum allantoides"

1993. Cienfuegos Botanical Garden. Mult.

3838	3c. Type **1033**	10	10
3839	5c. "Heliconia caribaea"	20	10
3840	10c. "Anthurium andraeanum"	40	20
3841	20c. "Pseudobombax ellipticum"	75	30

3842	35c. "Ixora coccinea"	1·20	60
3843	50c. "Callistemon specious"	2·10	85

1034 Devillier's Swallowtail

1993. Bangkok 1993 International Stamp Exhibition. Butterflies. Multicoloured.

3844	3c. Type **1034**	15	10
3845	5c. Giant brimstone	20	15
3846	20c. Great southern white	75	30
3847	30c. Buckeye	1·10	50
3848	35c. White peacock	1·20	50
3849	50c. African monarch	1·80	85

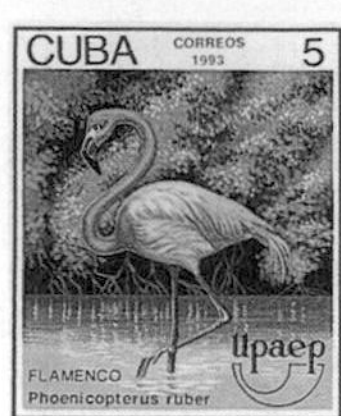

1035 Greater Flamingo

1993. America. Endangered Animals. Mult.

3850	5c. Type **1035**	30	15
3851	50c. Roseate spoonbill	1·90	85

1036 Simon Bolivar

1993. Latin-American Integration. Mult.

3852	50c. Type **1036**	1·50	85
3853	50c. Jose Marti	1·50	85
3854	50c. Benito Juarez	1·50	85
3855	50c. Che Guevara	1·50	85

Nos. 3852/5 were issued together, se-tenant, forming a composite design.

1037 Swimming

1993. 17th Central American and Caribbean Games, Ponce, Puerto Rico. Multicoloured.

3856	5c. Type **1037**	10	10
3857	10c. Pole vaulting	20	15
3858	20c. Boxing	75	30
3859	35c. Gymnastics (parallel bars) (vert)	1·20	50
3860	50c. Baseball (vert)	1·80	85
MS3861	49×80 mm. 1p. Basketball (40×32 mm)	4·25	2·50

1038 Grajales

1993. Death Centenary of Mariana Grajales.

3862	**1038**	5c. multicoloured	35	10

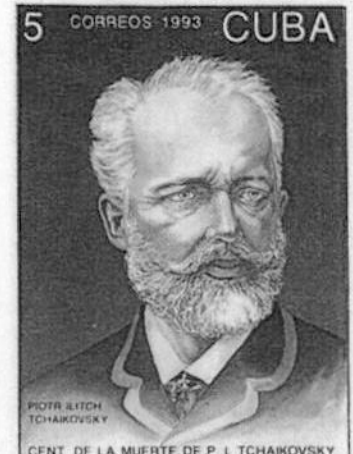

1039 Tchaikovsky

1993. Death Centenary of Pyotr Tchaikovsky (composer). Multicoloured.

3863	5c. Type **1039**	20	10
3864	20c. Ballerina in "Swan Lake"	70	30
3865	30c. Statue of Tchaikovsky	1·00	50
3866	50c. Tchaikovsky Museum (horiz)	1·40	85

1040 Flag, Dove and Broken Chains

1994. 35th Anniv of Revolution.

3867	**1040**	5c. multicoloured	35	10

1041 Players Challenging for Ball

1994. World Cup Football Championship, U.S.A.

3868	**1041**	5c. multicoloured	20	10
3869	-	20c. multicoloured	65	30
3870	-	30c. multicoloured	95	50
3871	-	35c. multicoloured	1·00	50
3872	-	40c. multicoloured	1·40	60
3873	-	50c. multicoloured	1·50	85
MS3874		90×57 mm. 1p. multicoloured (39×31 mm)	3·25	2·50

DESIGNS: 20c. to 1p. Various footballing scenes.

1042 Blue Persian

1994. Cats. Multicoloured.

3875	5c. Type **1042**	20	20
3876	10c. Havana	65	20
3877	20c. Maine coon	95	40
3878	30c. British blue shorthair	1·00	50
3879	35c. Black and white bicolour Persian	1·40	50
3880	50c. Golden Persian	1·50	85
MS3881	49×80 mm. 1p. Abyssinian (39×31 mm)	4·50	2·50

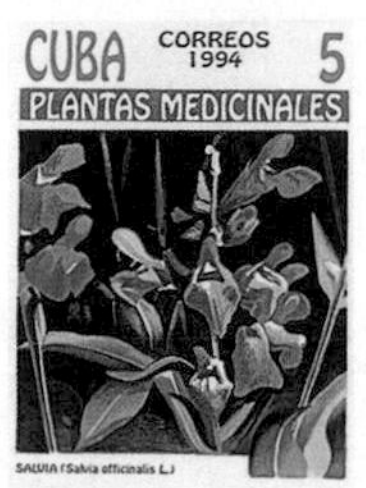

1043 Sage

1994. Medicinal Plants. Multicoloured.

3882	5c. Type **1043**	20	10
3883	10c. Aloe	30	20
3884	20c. Sunflower	70	30
3885	30c. False chamomile	1·00	50
3886	40c. Pot marigold	1·40	60
3887	50c. Large-leaved lime	1·70	85

1044 London Public Transport, 1860

1994. Carriages. Multicoloured.

3888	5c. Type **1044**	20	10
3889	10c. Coach of King Fernando VII and Maria Luisa of Spain	30	20
3890	30c. French Louis XV style coach	1·10	50
3891	35c. Queen Isabel II of Spain's gala-day coach	1·20	50
3892	40c. Empress Catherine II of Russia's summer carriage	1·50	60
3893	50c. Havana cab (68×27 mm)	1·80	85

1045 Caribbean Edible Oyster

1994. Aquaculture. Multicoloured.

3894	5c. Type **1045**	35	20
3895	20c. "Cardisoma guanhumi" (crab)	65	30
3896	30c. Red-breasted tilapia	95	50
3897	35c. "Hippospongia lachne" (sponge)	1·10	50
3898	40c. "Panulirus argus" (crustacean)	1·40	60
3899	50c. Common carp	1·70	85

1046 Ancient Greek Athletes and Olympic Flag

1994. Centenary of International Olympic Committee. Multicoloured.

3900	5c. Type **1046**	20	10
3901	30c. Olympic flag and world map in Olympic colours	95	50
3902	50c. Olympic flag and flame	1·70	85

1047 Michael Faraday (discoverer of electricity)

1994. Scientists. Multicoloured.

3903	5c. Type **1047**	20	10
3904	10c. Marie Sklodowska-Curie (co-discoverer of radium)	30	20
3905	20c. Pierre Curie (co-discoverer of radium)	75	30
3906	30c. Albert Einstein (formulated Theory of Relativity)	1·10	60
3907	40c. Max Planck (physicist)	1·50	60
3908	50c. Otto Hahn (chemist)	1·90	85

1048 "Opuntia dillenii"

1994. Cacti. Multicoloured.

3909	5c. Type **1048**	20	10
3910	10c. "Opuntia millspaughii" (vert)	35	20
3911	30c. "Leptocereus santamarinae"	75	50
3912	35c. "Pereskia marcanoi"	1·20	50
3913	40c. "Dendrocereus nudiflorus" (vert)	1·70	60
3914	50c. "Pilocereus robinii"	1·90	85

1049 Rocket and 1939 10c. Rocket Post Stamp

1994. 2nd Spanish–Cuban Stamp Exhibition. Sheet 51×75 mm.

MS3915	**1049** 1p. multicoloured	3·75	2·50

1050 Rough Collies

1994. Dogs. Multicoloured.

3916	5c. Type **1050**	30	20
3917	20c. American cocker spaniels	75	30
3918	30c. Dalmatians	1·00	50
3919	40c. Afghan hounds	1·50	60
3920	50c. English cocker spaniels	1·80	85

1051 "Carpilius corallinus" (crab)

1994. Cayo Largo. Multicoloured.

3921	15c. Type **1051**	45	20
3922	65c. Shore and Cayman Islands ground iguana (vert)	2·50	1·00
3923	75c. House and brown pelican	2·75	1·20
3924	1p. Fence and common green turtle	3·75	1·70

1052 Cienfuegos

1994. 35th Anniv of Disappearance of Camilo Cienfuegos (revolutionary).

3925	**1052**	15c. multicoloured	90	20

1053 Yellow-edged Grouper

1994. Caribbean Animals. Multicoloured.

3926	10c. Type **1053**	45	20
3927	15c. Spotted eagle ray (vert)	45	20
3928	15c. Sailfish	45	20
3929	15c. Greater flamingoes (vert)	45	20
3930	65c. Bottle-nosed dolphin	2·50	1·00
3931	65c. Brown pelican (vert)	2·50	1·00

1054 Douglas DC-3

1994. 50th Anniv of I.C.A.O.

3932	**1054** 65c. multicoloured	2·20	1·00

1055 Bronze Statues of Deer

1994. 55th Anniv of Havana Zoo. Mult.

3933	15c. Type **1055**	35	20
3934	65c. Green-winged macaw	1·80	1·00
3935	75c. Eurasian goldfinch	2·10	1·20

1056 Boy with Stockbook

1994. 30th Anniv of Cuban Philatelic Federation.

3936	**1056** 15c. multicoloured	55	20

1057 Anole

1994. Reptiles. Multicoloured.

3937	15c. Type **1057**	35	20
3938	65c. Dwarf gecko	1·80	1·00
3939	75c. Curly-tailed lizard	2·00	1·20
3940	85c. Dwarf gecko (different)	2·20	1·40
3941	90c. Anole	2·50	1·60
3942	1p. Dwarf gecko (different)	2·75	1·70

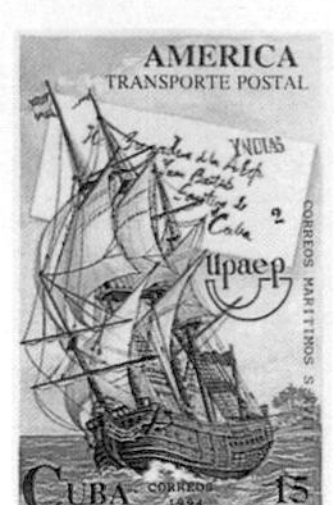

1058 Cover and Spanish Mail Packet (18th-century sea mail)

1994. America. Postal Transport. Mult.

3943	15c. Type **1058**	35	20
3944	65c. Cover and messenger on horseback (19th-century rebel post) (horiz)	1·90	1·00

1059 Cover of "Postal History of Cuba" by Jose Guerra Aguiar

1995. 30th Anniv of Postal Museum.

3945	**1059** 15c. multicoloured	55	20

1060 Jose Marti and Flag

1995. Centenary of War of Independence.

3946	**1060** 15c. multicoloured	55	20

1061 Boxing

1995. 12th Pan-American Games, Mar del Plata, Argentina. Multicoloured.

3947	10c. Type **1061**	20	15
3948	15c. Weightlifting	35	20
3949	65c. Volleyball	1·50	95
3950	75c. Wrestling (horiz)	1·80	1·10
3951	85c. Baseball (horiz)	2·10	1·20
3952	90c. High jumping (horiz)	2·20	1·30

1062 Siboney Cow

1995. 50th Anniv of F.A.O.

3953	**1062** 75c. multicoloured	1·80	1·10

1063 1855 Cuba and Puerto Rico ½r. Stamp

1995. Postal Anniversaries.

3954	**1063** 15c. blue and black	35	20
3955	- 65c. multicoloured	1·50	95

DESIGNS: 15c. Type **1063** (140th anniv of first Cuban postage stamp); 65c. Colonial-style letterbox and letter (140th anniv of domestic postal service).

1064 Queen Angelfish

1995. 35th Anniv of National Aquarium. Mult.

3956	10c. Type **1064**	35	10
3957	15c. Shy hamlet	45	20
3958	65c. Porkfish	1·90	85
3959	75c. Red-spotted hawk-fish	2·20	95
3960	85c. French angelfish	2·75	1·40
3961	90c. Blue tang	2·75	1·40

1065 Portrait of Marti and Death Scene

1995. Death Centenary of Jose Marti (revolutionary). Multicoloured.

3962	15c. Type **1065**	35	15
3963	65c. Marti and Maximo Gomez in boat	1·60	95
3964	75c. Marti and Montecristi Declaration	1·80	1·20
3965	85c. Marti, Antonio Maceo and Gomez	2·20	1·30
3966	90c. Mausoleum and casket (vert)	2·30	1·40

1066 Maceo

1995. Centenary of Battle of Peralejo and 150th Birth Anniv of Antonio Maceo (revolutionary).

3967	**1066** 15c. multicoloured	70	20

1067 Gulf Fritillary

1995. Butterflies. Multicoloured.

3968	10c. Type **1067**	35	10
3969	15c. "Eunica tatila"	35	20
3970	65c. "Melete salacia"	1·60	95
3971	75c. Cuban clearwing	1·80	1·20
3972	85c. Palmira sulphur	2·20	1·30
3973	90c. Cloudless sulphur	2·30	1·40

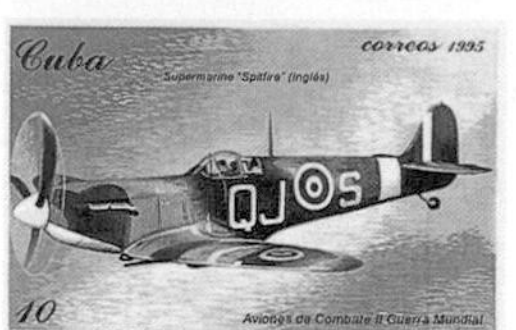

1068 Supermarine Spitfire (Great Britain)

1995. 2nd World War Combat Planes. Mult.

3974	10c. Type **1068**	35	10
3975	15c. Ilyushin Il-2 (Russia)	35	20
3976	65c. Curtiss P-40 (United States)	1·60	95
3977	75c. Messerschmitt ME-109 (Germany)	1·80	1·20
3978	85c. Morane Saulnier 406 (France)	2·20	1·30

1069 Lecuona

1995. Birth Cent of Ernesto Lecuona (composer).

3979	**1069** 15c. multicoloured	55	20

1070 Horse in Stable

1995. Singapore '95 International Stamp Exhibition. Arab Horses. Multicoloured.

3980	10c. Type **1070**	45	10
3981	15c. Two greys (horiz)	45	20
3982	65c. Tethered horse	2·00	95
3983	75c. Horse in field	2·40	1·20
3984	85c. Mare and foal	2·75	1·30
3985	90c. Grey galloping in field	2·75	1·40

1071 China P.R. 1995 20f. Stamp

1995. Beijing 1995 International Stamp and Coin Exhibition. Sheet 89×58 mm.

MS3986	**1071** 50c. multicoloured	1·40	1·20

1072 Wrestling

1995. Olympic Games, Atlanta (1996) (1st issue). Multicoloured.

3987	10c. Type **1072**	25	10
3988	15c. Weightlifting	35	20
3989	65c. Volleyball	1·60	95
3990	75c. Running	1·80	1·20
3991	85c. Baseball	2·20	1·30
3992	90c. Judo	2·30	1·40
MS3993	75×60 mm. 1p. Boxing (31×39 mm)	3·50	2·40

See also Nos. 4052/**MS**4057.

1073 Acana Factory

1995. 400th Anniv of Sugar Production in Cuba. Paintings by Eduardo Laplante. Multicoloured.

3994	15c. Type **1073**	2·75	45
3995	65c. Manaca factory	1·70	85

1074 Flag and Anniversary Emblem

1995. 50th Anniv of U.N.O.

3996	**1074** 65c. multicoloured	1·60	95

1075 Lion

1995. Animals from Havana Zoological Gardens. Multicoloured.

3997	10c. Type **1075**	35	10
3998	15c. Grevy's zebra (horiz)	35	20
3999	65c. Orang-utan	1·60	95
4000	75c. Indian elephant (horiz)	1·80	1·20
4001	85c. Eurasian red squirrel (horiz)	2·20	1·30
4002	90c. Common racoon (horiz)	2·30	1·40

1076 St. Clare of Assisi's Convent

1995. 50th Anniv of UNESCO World Heritage Sites. Multicoloured.

4003	65c. Type **1076**	1·60	95
4004	75c. St. Francis of Assisi's Monastery church	1·80	1·20

1077 "Bletia patula"

1995. Orchids. Multicoloured.

4005	40c. Type **1077**	1·00	65
4006	45c. "Galeandra beyrichii"	1·10	65
4007	50c. "Vanilla dilloniana"	1·30	75
4008	65c. "Macradenia lutescens"	1·60	95
4009	75c. "Oncidium luridum"	1·80	1·20
4010	85c. "Ionopsis utricularioides"	2·30	1·30

1078 Greta Garbo

1995. Centenary of Motion Pictures. Designs showing film stars (except No. 4015). Mult.

4011	15c. Type **1078**	35	15
4012	15c. Marlene Dietrich	35	15
4013	15c. Marilyn Monroe	35	15
4014	15c. Charlie Chaplin	35	15
4015	15c. Lumiere Brothers (inventors of cine camera)	35	15
4016	15c. Vittorio de Sica	35	15
4017	65c. Humphrey Bogart	1·60	95
4018	75c. Rita Montaner	1·80	1·20
4019	85c. Cantinflas	2·20	1·30

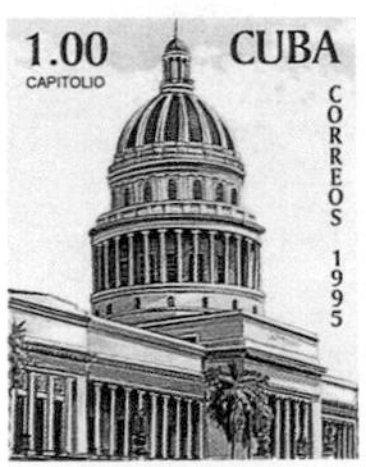

1079 Capitol

1995. 4th Spanish—Cuban Stamp Exhibition. Sheet 90×65 mm.

MS4020	**1079** 1p. multicoloured	3·50	2·40

1080 Great Red-bellied Woodpecker

1995. America. Environmental Protection. Mult.

4021	15c. Type **1080**	40	20
4022	65c. Cuban tody	1·80	95

1081 Alfonso Goulet and Francisco Crombet Ballon

1995. Death Centenaries of Generals killed during War of Independence (1st issue). Mult.

4023	15c. Type **1081**	45	20
4024	15c. Jesus Calvar, Jose Guillermo Moncada and Tomas Jordan	45	20
4025	15c. Francisco Borrero and Francisco Inchaustegui	45	20

Nos. 4023/5 were issued together, se-tenant, forming a composite design of the national flag behind the portraits.

See also Nos. 4089/91 and 4162/3.

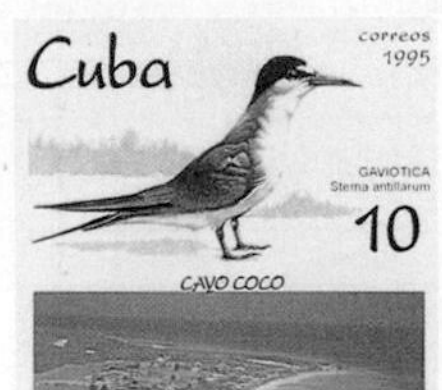

1082 Least Tern and Aerial View

1995. Coco Key. Multicoloured.

4026	10c. Type **1082**	25	10
4027	15c. White ibis and beach	35	20
4028	45c. Stripe-headed tanager and villas	1·10	65
4029	50c. Red-legged thrush and apartments	1·30	75
4030	65c. Northern mocking-bird and villas around pool	1·60	95
4031	75c. Greater flamingo and couple in pool	1·80	1·20

1083 Carlos de Cespedes

1996. Independence Fighters.

4032	-	10c. orange	25	10
4033	**1083**	15c. green	35	20
4034	-	65c. blue	1·60	95
4035	-	75c. red	1·80	1·20
4036	-	85c. green	2·00	1·30
4037	-	90c. brown	2·30	1·40
4040	-	1p.05 mauve	2·75	1·70
4041	-	2p.05 brown	5·50	3·25
4042	-	3p. brown	7·50	4·75

DESIGNS: 10c. Serafin Sanchez; 65c. Jose Marti; 75c. Antonio Maceo; 85c. Juan Gualberto Gomez; 90c. Quintin Bandera; 1p.05, Ignacio Agramonte; 2p.05, Maximo Gomez; 3p. Calixto Garcia.

1084 "Che" Guevara and Emblem

1996. 30th Anniv of Organization of Solidarity of Peoples of Africa, Asia and Latin America.

4043	**1084**	65c. multicoloured	35	20

1085 Leonardo da Vinci

1996. Scientists. Multicoloured.

4046	10c. Type **1085**	25	10
4047	15c. Mikhail Lomonosov (aerodromic machines)	35	20
4048	65c. James Watt (steam engine)	1·60	95
4049	75c. Guglielmo Marconi (first radio transmitter)	1·80	1·20
4050	85c. Charles Darwin (theory of evolution)	2·20	1·30

1086 Athletics

1996. Olympic Games, Atlanta (2nd issue). Multicoloured.

4052	10c. Type **1086**	25	10
4053	15c. Weightlifting	20	10
4054	65c. Judo	1·60	95
4055	75c. Wrestling (horiz)	1·80	1·20
4056	85c. Boxing (horiz)	2·20	1·30
MS4057	59×80 mm. 1p. Baseball (31×39 mm)	3·50	2·40

1087 Cierva C.4 Autogyro

1996. Espamer Spanish–Latin American and "Aviation and Space" Stamp Exhibitions, Seville, Spain. Multicoloured.

4058	15c. Type **1087**	35	20
4059	65c.35 JunkersJu52/3m	1·70	95
4060	75c. C-201 Alcotan airplane	2·00	1·20
4061	85c. CASA C-212 Aviocar	2·30	1·30
MS4062	94×60 mm. 1p. Old Post Office and Gold Tower (40×30 mm)	3·50	2·40

1088 Belted Kingfisher

1996. Death Centenary of Juan Gundlach (ornithologist). Birds. Multicoloured.

4063	10c. Type **1088**	35	10
4064	15c. American redstart	35	20
4065	65c. Common yellowthroat	1·60	95
4066	75c. Painted bunting	1·80	1·20
4067	85c. Cedar waxwing	2·20	1·30
MS4068	90×49 mm. 1p. Cuban vireo ("Vireo gundlachi") (36×28 mm)	3·50	2·40

1089 Yuri Gagarin (cosmonaut)

1996. 35th Anniv of First Man in Space. Mult.

4069	15c. Type **1089**	35	20
4070	65c. Globes and "Vostok I" (spaceship) (horiz)	1·60	95

1090 National Flag and Hand holding Gun

1996. 35th Anniversaries. Multicoloured.

4071	15c. Type **1090** (victory at Giron)	40	20
4072	65c. Flags and "35" (Declaration of Socialist character of the Revolution)	1·80	95

1091 "Bahama"

1996. CAPEX'96 International Stamp Exhibition, Toronto, Canada. 18th-century Ships of the Line built in Cuban Yards. Multicoloured.

4073	10c. Type **1091**	25	10
4074	15c. "Santissima Trinidad"	35	20
4075	65c. "Principe de Asturias"	1·60	95
4076	75c. "San Pedro de Alcantara"	1·80	1·20
4077	85c. "Santa Ana"	2·00	1·30
MS4078	90×50 mm. 1p. "San Genaro" (39×31 mm)	2·50	2·40

1092 Cuban Tody

1996. Caribbean Animals. Multicoloured.

4079	10c. Type **1092**	25	10
4080	15c. Purple-throated carib ("Eulampis jugularis")	35	20
4081	15c. Wood duck ("Aix sponsa")	35	20
4082	15c. Spot-finned butterflyfish	35	20
4083	65c. "Popilio cresphontes" (butterfly)	1·60	95
4084	65c. Indigo hamlet	1·60	95

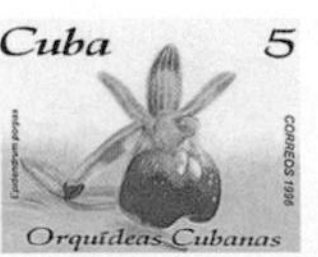

1093 "Epidendrum porpax"

1996. Orchids. Multicoloured.

4085	5c. Type **1093**	25	10
4086	10c. "Cyrtopodlium punctatum"	35	15
4087	15c. "Polyrrhiza lindeni"	35	20

1094 Charging into Battle and Maceo

1996. Death Cent of General Jose Maceo.

4088	**1094**	15c. multicoloured	55	20

1996. Death Centenaries of Generals killed during War of Independence (2nd issue). As T 1081. Multicoloured.

4089	15c. Esteban Tamayo and Angel Guerra	40	20
4090	15c. Juan Fernandez Ruz, Jose Maria Aguirre and Serafin Sanchez	40	20
4091	15c. Juan Bruno Zayas and Pedro Vargas Sotomayor	40	20

Nos. 4089/91 were issued together, se-tenant, forming a composite design.

1095 "Jacaranda arborea" and Coast, Santiago de Cuba

1996. Tourism and Flowers. Multicoloured.

4092	15c. Type **1095**	35	20
4093	65c. "Begonia bissei" and San Pedro de la Roca Fort	1·60	95
4094	75c. "Byrsonima crassifolia" and Baconao Park, Santiago de Cuba (vert)	1·80	1·10

4095 85c. "Pereskia zinniiflora" and Sanctuary, Cobre (vert) 2·00 1·30

1096 Baldwin Locomotive No. 1112, 1878

1996. Steam Railway Locomotives. Mult.

4096 10c. Type **1096** 25 10
4097 15c. American locomotive No. 1302, 1904 35 20
4098 65c. Baldwin locomotive No. 1535, 1906 1·60 95
4099 75c. Rogers locomotive, 1914 1·80 1·10
4100 90c. Baldwin locomotive, 1920 2·20 1·30

1097 Free Negroes, 19th-century

1996. America. Costumes. Multicoloured.

4101 15c. Type **1097** 40 20
4102 65c. Guayabera couple, 20th-century 1·80 95

1098 Children

1996. 50th Anniv of UNICEF.

4103 **1098** 15c. multicoloured 55 20

1099 Capablanca and Pieces

1996. 75th Anniv of Jose Raul Capablanca's First World Championship Victory. Mult.

4104 15c. Type **1099** 35 20
4105 65c. Capablanca and tournament 1·60 95
4106 75c. Globe on king and Capablanca 1·80 1·20
4107 85c. Capablanca as boy playing chess 2·00 1·30
4108 90c. Capablanca playing in tournament 2·20 1·40

1100 Flag and "Granma"

1996. 40th Anniversaries of "Granma" Landings (15c.) and Revolutionary Armed Forces (65c.). Multicoloured.

4109 15c. Type **1100** 35 15
4110 65c. "40", flag and soldier with rifle 2·50 1·40

1101 Monument, Santiago de Cuba

1996. Death Centenary of General Antonio Maceo. Multicoloured.

4111 10c. Type **1101** 25 10
4112 15c. Maceo 45 20
4113 15c. Memorial of Maceo's disembarkation, Duaba (horiz) 45 20
4114 65c. "Fall of Antonio Maceo" (detail, A. Menocal) (horiz) 2·50 1·40
4115 75c. Maceo, Panchito Gomez Toro and monument, San Pedro (horiz) 2·75 1·70

1102 Women's Judo and Gold Medal (Driulis Gonzalez)

1996. Cuban Medal Winners at Olympic Games, Atlanta. Multicoloured.

4116 10c. Type **1102** 25 10
4117 10c. Freestyle wrestling and bronze medal 25 10
4118 15c. Weightlifting and gold medal (Pablo Lara) 45 20
4119 15c. Greco-Roman wrestling and gold medal (Feliberto Aguilera) 45 20
4120 15c. Fencing and silver medal 45 20
4121 15c. Swimming and silver medal 45 20
4122 65c. Women's volleyball and gold medal 2·50 1·40
4123 65c. Boxing and gold medal (Maikro Romero, Hector Vinent, Ariel Hernandez and Felix Savon) 2·50 1·40
4124 65c. Women's running and silver medal 2·50 1·40
4125 65c. Baseball and gold medal 2·50 1·40

1103 Rat

1996. Chinese New Year. Year of the Rat.

4126 **1103** 15c. multicoloured 80 30

1104 Minho Douro, Portugal

1996. Espamer '98 Spanish–Latin American Stamp Exhibition, Havana. Railway Locomotives. Multicoloured.

4127 15c. Type **1104** 45 20
4128 65c. Vulcan Iron Works, Brazil 2·30 1·30
4129 65c. Baldwin, Dominican Republic 2·30 1·30
4130 65c. Alco, Panama 2·30 1·30
4131 65c. Baldwin, Puerto Rico 2·30 1·30
4132 65c. Slaughter Gruning Co, Spain 2·30 1·30
4133 75c. Yorkshire Engine Co, Argentine Republic 2·75 1·50
4134 75c. Porter, Chile 2·75 1·50
4135 75c. Locomotive, Paraguay 2·75 1·50
4136 75c. Locomotive No. 12, Mexico 2·75 1·50
MS4137 105×85 mm. 1p. Baldwin, Cuba (36×29 mm) 3·75 3·50

1105 Seal-point Siamese

1997. Hong Kong '97 International Stamp Exhibition. Cats. Multicoloured.

4138 10c. Type **1105** 35 10
4139 15c. Burmese 45 20
4140 15c. Japanese bobtail (horiz) 45 20
4141 65c. Singapura (horiz) 2·30 1·30
4142 75c. Korat (horiz) 2·75 1·50
MS4143 90×107 mm. 1p. Blue-point Siamese (39×31 mm) 3·50 3·25

1106 "Romance del Palmar", 1938

1997. Centenary of Cuban Films. Mult.

4144 15c. Type **1106** 45 20
4145 65c. "Memorias del Subdesarrollo", 1968 (vert) 2·20 1·20

1107 Dromedary

1997. Zoo Animals. Multicoloured.

4146 10c. Type **1107** 35 10
4147 15c. White rhinoceros 45 20
4148 15c. Giant panda 45 20
4149 75c. Orang-utan 2·40 1·30
4150 90c. European bison 2·75 1·60

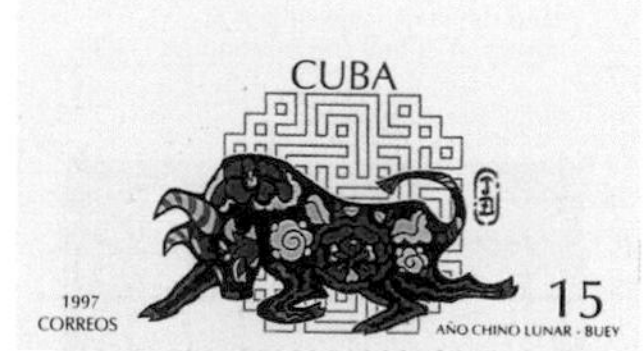

1108 Ox

1997. Chinese New Year. Year of the Ox.

4151 **1108** 15c. multicoloured 65 30

1109 Menelao Mora and Palace

1997. 40th Anniv of Attack on Presidential Palace.

4152 **1109** 15c. multicoloured 85 20

1110 Players

1997. World Cup Football Championship, France (1998).

4153 **1110** 10c. multicoloured 35 10
4154 - 15c. multicoloured (red face value) 45 20
4155 - 15c. multicoloured (mauve face value) 45 20
4156 - 65c. multicoloured 2·40 1·30

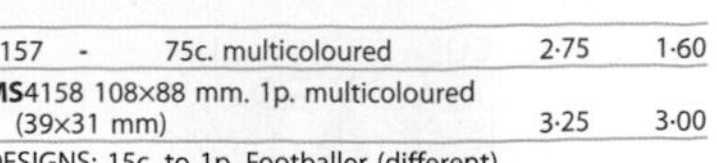
4157 - 75c. multicoloured 2·75 1·60
MS4158 108×88 mm. 1p. multicoloured (39×31 mm) 3·25 3·00

DESIGNS: 15c. to 1p. Footballer (different).

1111 Youths with Flags and Emblem

1997. 35th Anniv of Communist Youth Union.

4159 **1111** 15c. multicoloured 85 20

1112 "Caledonia"

1997. Stamp Day. Postal Services. Mult.

4160 15c. Type **1112** (170th anniv of maritime service) 55 30
4161 65c. Fokker F.10A Super Trimotor airplane (70th anniv of international airmail) 2·20 1·20

1113 Adolfo del Castillo and Enrique del Junco Cruz-Munoz

1997. Death Centenaries of Generals killed during War of Independence (3rd issue).

4162 15c. Type **1113** 45 20
4163 15c. Alberto Rodriguez Acosta and Mariano Sanchez Vaillant 45 20

Nos. 4162/3 were issued together, se-tenant, forming a composite design.

1114 Black-bordered Orange

1997. Butterflies. Multicoloured.

4164 10c. Type **1114** 35 10
4165 15c. Bush sulphur ("Eurema dina") 45 20
4166 15c. Zebra ("Colobura dirce") 45 20
4167 65c. Red admiral 2·20 1·20
4168 85c. "Kricogonia castalia" 2·75 1·30

1115 Luperon

1997. Death Cent of Gen. Gregorio Luperon.

4169 **1115** 65c. multicoloured 2·10 1·20

1116 Royal Palms

1997. 150th Anniv of Chinese Presence in Cuba.
4170 **1116** 15c. multicoloured 1·10 60

1117 National Flag and United Nations Emblem

1997. 50th Anniv of Cuban United Nations Association.
4171 **1117** 65c. multicoloured 2·10 1·20

1118 Rainbow and Dove holding Olive Branch

1997. 14th World Youth and Students Festival, Cuba. Multicoloured.

4172	10c. Type **1118**	30	10
4173	15c. "Alma Mater" (statue)	40	20
4174	15c. Children on play apparatus (vert)	40	20
4175	65c. Che Guevara	2·10	1·20
4176	75c. Statue and tower	2·50	1·30

1119 Pharos of Alexandria

1997. Seven Wonders of the Ancient World. Mult.

4177	10c. Type **1119**	20	10
4178	15c. Egyptian pyramids	40	20
4179	15c. Hanging Gardens of Babylon	40	20
4180	15c. Colossus of Rhodes	40	20
4181	65c. Mausoleum of Halicarnassus	2·10	1·20
4182	65c. Statue of Zeus at Olympia	2·10	1·20
4183	75c. Temple of Artemis at Ephesus	2·30	1·30

1120 Pais and Testamonial of Fidel Castro

1997. 40th Death Anniv of Frank Pais (revolutionary).
4184 **1120** 15c. multicoloured 50 20

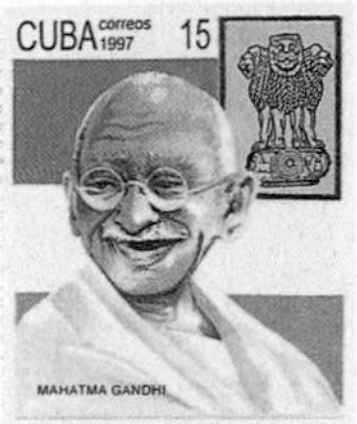

1121 Mahatma Gandhi, Indian Flag and State Arms

1997. 50th Anniv of Indian Independence.
4185 **1121** 15c. multicoloured 50 20

1122 Saffron Finch ("Sicalis flaveola")

1997. Birds of the Caribbean. Multicoloured.

4186	15c. Type **1122**	40	20
4187	15c. Red-headed barbet ("Eubucco bourcierii")	40	20
4188	15c. Cuban Amazon ("Amazona leucocephala")	40	20
4189	15c. Blue-crowned trogon ("Trogon curucui")	40	20
4190	65c. Blue-throated goldentail ("Hylocharis eliciae")	1·90	1·10
4191	65c. Yellow-crowned Amazon ("Amazona ochrocephala")	1·90	1·10
4192	75c. Eurasian goldfinch ("Carduelis carduelis")	2·10	1·20

1123 Franz Liszt and Memorial Stone commemorating his first Concert when Aged Nine

1997. Composers. Multicoloured.

4193	10c. Type **1123**	40	20
4194	15c. Johann Sebastian Bach and original manuscript score of Sonata in G minor for violin	40	30
4195	15c. Frederic Chopin and birthplace, Zelazowa Wola, Poland	40	30
4196	15c. Ludwig van Beethoven and Karntnerther Theatre where he presented the Ninth Symphony Mass in D major	40	30
4197	65c. Ignacio Cervantes and detail of score of "La Solitaria" (dance)	1·10	95
4198	75c. Wolfgang Amadeus Mozart and detail of score of first attempt at choral composition	1·80	1·10

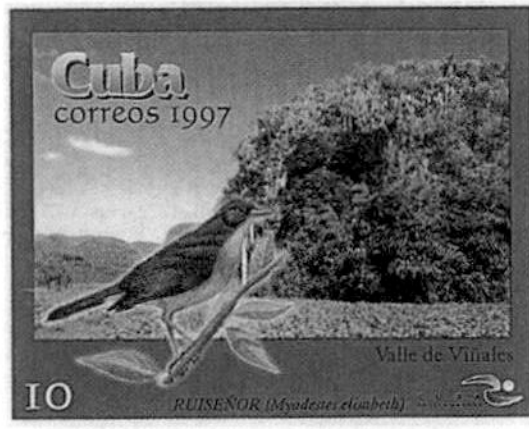

1124 Cuban Solitaire and Valle de Vinales

1997. Tourism. Multicoloured.

4199	10c. Type **1124**	40	20
4200	15c. Cuban crow and Cape Jutia	40	30
4201	65c. Olive-caped warbler and Soroa Falls (vert)	1·70	95
4202	75c. Giant kingbird and San Juan River (vert)	1·80	1·10

1125 "Hibiscus elatus" ("Majagua")

1997. Caribbean Flowers. Multicoloured.

4203	15c. Type **1125**	40	25
4204	15c. Rose periwinkle ("Vicaria")	40	25
4205	15c. Geiger tree ("Vomitel")	40	25
4206	15c. Bur marigold ("Romerillo")	40	25
4207	65c. Minnie root ("Salta perico")	1·70	95
4208	75c. Marilope	1·80	95

1126 Facade

1997. 50th Anniv of Oriente University.
4209 **1126** 15c. multicoloured 50 30

1127 Congress Emblem

1997. 5th Cuban Communist Party Congress and 30th Death Anniv of Ernesto "Che" Guevara (revolutionary). Multicoloured.

4210	15c. Type **1127**	40	25
4211	65c. Che Guevara and letter from Guevara to Fidel Castro	1·70	95
4212	75c. Portrait of Che Guevara	1·80	95

1128 19th-century Post Box and Postman

1997. America. The Postman. Multicoloured.

4213	15c. Type **1128**	40	25
4214	65c. 20th-century post boxes and postman	1·60	85

1129 Australopithecus, South Africa

1997. Prehistoric Man. Multicoloured.

4215	10c. Type **1129**	35	20
4216	15c. Pithecanthropus, Java	45	25
4217	15c. Sinanthropus, China	45	25
4218	15c. Neanderthal man	45	25
4219	65c. Cro-Magnon man	1·80	95
4220	75c. Oberkassel man, Germany	2·00	1·10

1130 Soviet Flag, Lenin and "Aurora" (cruiser)

1997. 80th Anniv of Russian Revolution.
4221 **1130** 75c. multicoloured 2·10 1·20

1131 "John Bull", 1831

1997. Railway Locomotives. Multicoloured.

4222	10c. Type **1131**	25	10
4223	15c. Baldwin steam locomotive, 1910–13	35	20
4224	15c. Locomotive "Old Ironsides", 1832, U.S.A.	35	20
4225	65c. Russian-built Type TEM-4.1 diesel locomotive, 1970	1·60	95
4226	75c. Russian-built Type TE-114k diesel locomotive, 1975	1·80	1·10

No. 4222 is inscribed "1830".

1132 National Flag and Capitol, Havana

1997. 50th Anniv of U.N. Conference on Trade and Employment, Havana.
4227 **1132** 65c. multicoloured 1·60 85

1133 Garcia and 1970 30c. Stamp

1997. Birth Centenary of Victor Manuel Garcia (painter).
4228 **1133** 15c. multicoloured 50 30

1134 Havana Cathedral and Pope John Paul II

1998. Papal Visit. Multicoloured.

4229	65c. Type **1134**	2·40	1·10
4230	75c. Our Lady of Charity Cathedral (vert)	2·75	1·10
MS4231	110×85 mm. 50c. Pres. Fidel Castro meeting Pope on visit to Vatican (31×39 mm); 50c. Pope giving blessing (31×39 mm)	3·50	2·50

1135 Menendez

1998. 50th Death Anniv of Jesus Menendez (labour leader).
4232 **1135** 15c. multicoloured 55 30

1136 Players

1998. World Cup Football Championship, France. Multicoloured.

4233	10c. Type **1136**	50	20
4234	15c. Player in purple shirt lying on ground and player in red and white stripes	80	30
4235	15c. Player in yellow and black strip	80	30
4236	65c. Player in blue shirt tackling player in red and white strip (horiz)	2·50	1·10

4237 65c. Player in red and blue strip fending off player in light blue strip (horiz) 2·50 1·10

MS4238 111×88 mm. 1p. Crowd behind player No. 11 (39×31 mm) 4·00 3·00

1137 Isabel Rubio Diaz

1998. Death Centenary of Captain Isabel Rubio Diaz (founder of mobile military hospital during War of Independence).

4239 **1137** 15c. multicoloured 60 30

1138 Revee

1998. Death Centenary of Brigadier General Vidal Ducasse Revee (revolutionary).

4240 **1138** 15c. multicoloured 60 30

1139 Radio Operator and Che Guevara

1998. Communicators' Day. 40th Anniv of Radio Rebelde.

4241 **1139** 15c. multicoloured 60 30

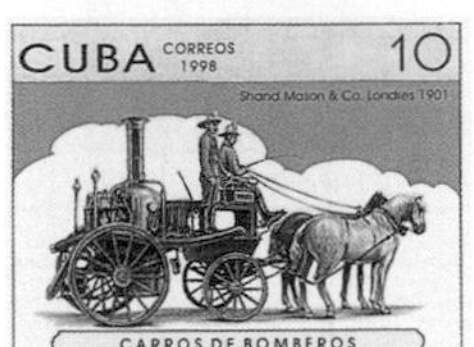

1140 Shand Mason & Co Horse-drawn Fire Engine, 1901 (Havana)

1998. Fire Engines. Multicoloured.

4242 10c. Type **1140** 35 20

4243 15c. Horse-drawn personnel and equipment vehicle, 1905 (Havana Municipal Service) 40 25

4244 15c. American–French Fire Engine Co vehicle, 1921 (Guanabacoa) 50 25

4245 65c. Chevrolet 6400 fire engine, 1952 (used throughout Cuba) 1·60 95

4246 75c. American-French-Foamite Co fire engine, 1956 (Havana) 1·80 1·10

1141 Monument and Antonio Maceo (revolutionary)

1998. 120th Anniv of Baragua Protest (against slavery).

4247 **1141** 15c. multicoloured 60 30

1142 Flags, Soldiers and Tank

1998. 10th Anniv of Victory of Angolan Government and Cuban Forces in Defence of Cuito Cuanavale, Angola.

4248 **1142** 15c. multicoloured 60 30

1143 Tiger

1998. Chinese New Year. Year of the Tiger.

4249 **1143** 15c. multicoloured 60 30

1144 Chihuahua ("Tatiana Vasti de Nino Angelo")

1998. Champion Dogs. Multicoloured.

4250 10c. Type **1144** 30 20

4251 15c. Beagle ("Danco") 40 30

4252 15c. Mexican naked hound ("Xolot del Mictlan") 40 30

4253 65c. German spaniel ("D'Milican Nalut Aiwa") 2·10 1·30

4254 75c. Chow-chow ("Yoki II") 2·50 1·40

1145 Ancestor of Chimpanzee

1998. Evolution of the Chimpanzee. Multicoloured.

4255 10c. Type **1145** 45 20

4256 15c. Head and skull of "Pan troglodytes blumenbach" 50 30

4257 15c. Chimpanzee and hand and foot 50 30

4258 65c. Mother with infant and new-born chimp 2·50 1·40

4259 75c. On branch and distribution map 2·75 1·40

1147 Skate

1998. Deep Sea Fishes. Multicoloured.

4261 15c. Type **1147** 55 30

4262 15c. Gulper ("Eurypharynx pelecanoides") 55 30

4263 65c. "Caulophryne" sp. 2·75 1·30

4264 75c. Sloan's viperfish 3·00 1·40

1148 Garcia Lorca

1998. Birth Cent of Federico Garcia Lorca (poet).

4265 **1148** 75c. multicoloured 3·00 1·40

1149 Crab

1998. International Year of the Ocean. Mult.

4266 65c. Type **1149** 2·40 1·30

4267 65c. Fishes 2·40 1·30

1150 Diana, Princess of Wales

1998. Diana, Princess of Wales Commemoration. Multicoloured.

4268 10c. Type **1150** 40 20

4269 10c. Wearing patterned dress 40 20

4270 10c. Wearing yellow and pink jacket 40 20

4271 15c. Wearing checked jacket 55 30

4272 15c. Wearing red jacket 55 30

4273 65c. Wearing white jacket 2·75 1·30

4274 75c. Wearing purple jacket 3·00 1·40

1151 Abel Santamaria

1998. 45th Anniv of Attack on Moncada Barracks. Multicoloured.

4275 15c. Type **1151** 55 30

4276 65c. Jose Marti 2·75 1·20

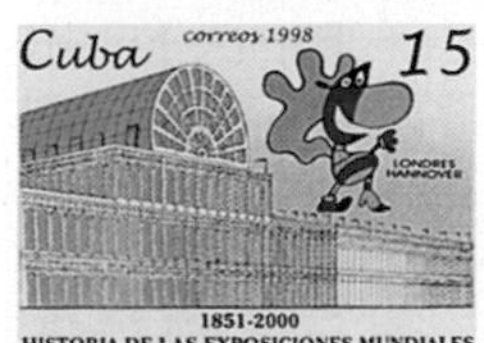

1152 The Crystal Palace, London (Great Exhibition, 1851)

1998. "Expo 2000" World's Fair, Hanover, Germany.

4277 **1152** 15c. multicoloured 55 30

4278 - 15c. multicoloured 55 30

4279 - 15c. multicoloured 55 30

4280 - 15c. black, red & yellow 55 30

4281 - 65c. multicoloured 2·75 1·20

4282 - 75c. multicoloured 3·00 1·40

DESIGNS—HORIZ: No. 4277, Type **1152**; 4278, Atomium, Brussels (International Exhibition, 1958); 4280, Map and flag of Germany; 4282, Twipsy (mascot) on globe and fireworks. VERT: No. 4279, Twipsy; 4281, Eiffel Tower, Paris (Exhibition, 1889).

1153 Baseball

1998. 18th Central American and Caribbean Games, Maracaibo, Venezuela.

4283 **1153** 15c. multicoloured 55 20

1154 Kim Il Sung and Pyongyang Landmarks

1998. 50th Anniv of Korean People's Democratic Republic (North Korea).

4284 **1154** 75c. multicoloured 3·00 1·40

1155 Japanese Bust

1998. Cent of First Japanese Immigrant to Cuba.

4285 **1155** 75c. multicoloured 3·00 1·40

1156 "Coelogyne flaccida"

1998. 30th Anniv of National Botanical Garden. Orchids. Multicoloured.

4286 10c. Type **1156** 40 20

4287 15c. "Dendrobium fimbriatum" 55 30

4288 15c. Bamboo orchid ("Arundina graminifolia") 55 30

4289 65c. "Bletia patula" 2·50 1·10

4290 65c. Nun's orchid ("Phaius tankervilliaea") 2·50 1·10

1157 Buildings and Emblem

1998. 5th Congress of Revolution Defence Committees.

4291 **1157** 15c. multicoloured 55 20

1146 Postman on Bicycle

1998. Juvalex 98 International Youth Stamp Exhibition, Luxembourg. Sheet 111×82 mm.

MS4260 **1146** 1p. multicoloured 4·75 3·75

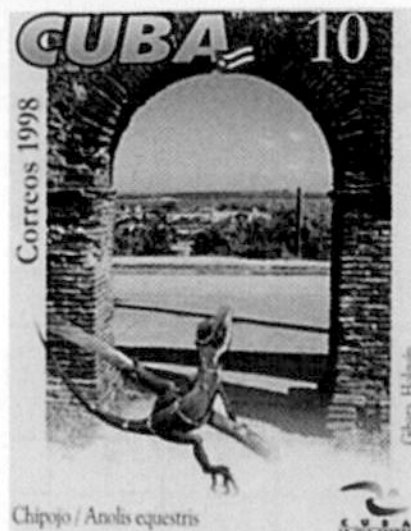

1158 Knight Anole and Archway, Gibara

1998. World Tourism Day. Views of Holguin. Multicoloured.

4292	10c. Type **1158**	40	20
4293	15c. Water lizard, Mirador de Mayabe	55	30
4294	65c. Water chameleon, Guard-alavaca Beach (horiz)	2·50	1·10
4295	75c. Stone lizard, Pinares de Mayari (horiz)	3·00	1·40

1159 Bernarda Toro (Manana)

1998. America. Famous Women. Independence Activists. Multicoloured.

4296	65c. Type **1159**	2·50	1·10
4297	75c. Maria Cabrales	3·00	1·40

1160 Two Conures

1998. The Cuban Conure. Multicoloured.

4298	10c. Type **1160**	40	20
4299	15c. Head of conure	55	30
4300	65c. Conure on branch	2·50	1·10
4301	75c. Conure and leaves	3·00	1·40

1161 "Swan Lake"

1998. 50th Anniv of Cuban National Ballet.

4302	**1161**	15c. blue	55	20
4303	-	65c. multicoloured	2·75	1·20

DESIGN: 65c. "Giselle".

1162 Apartment Building on O'Farrill and Goicuria Streets, Havana, and Victims

1998. 40th Death Anniv of Rogelia Perea, Angel Ameijeiras and Pedro Gutierrez (revolutionaries).

4304	**1162**	15c. multicoloured	55	20

1163 Capt. Braulio Coroneaux (revolutionary) and Tank

1998. 40th Anniv of Battle of Guisa.

4305	**1163**	15c. multicoloured	55	20

1164 Family holding Hands and United Nations Emblem

1998. 50th Anniv of Universal Declaration of Human Rights.

4306	**1164**	65c. multicoloured	2·50	1·20

1165 Garcia Iniguez

1998. Death Centenary of Major-General Calixto Garca Iniguez (independence fighter).

4307	**1165**	65c. multicoloured	2·30	1·20

1166 Varela and San Carlos Seminary, Havana

1998. 145th Death Anniv of Felix Varela (philosopher and Vicar-General of New York).

4308	**1166**	75c. multicoloured	2·30	1·40

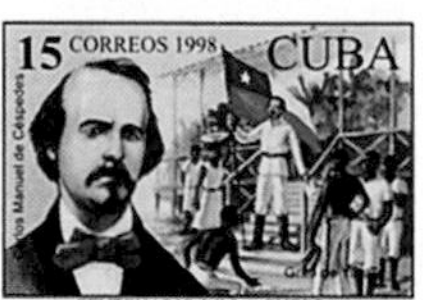

1167 Carlos Manuel de Cespedes

1998. Cent of Cuban War of Independence. Mult.

4309	15c. Type **1167**	40	20
4310	15c. Ignacio Agramonte Loynaz	40	20
4311	15c. Maximo Gomez Baez	40	20
4312	15c. Jose Maceo Grajales	40	20
4313	15c. Salvador Cisneros Betancourt	40	20
4314	15c. Calixto Garcia Iniguez	40	20
4315	15c. Adolfo Flor Crombet	40	20
4316	15c. Serafin Sanchez Valdivia	40	20
4317	65c. Jose Marti Perez	1·40	95
4318	75c. Antonio Maceo Grajales	1·60	95

1168 Revolutionaries and Map

1998. 40th Anniv of Capture of Palma Soriano by Revolutionaries.

4319	**1168**	15c. multicoloured	55	20

1169 "Granma" Landings

1999. 40th Anniv of Revolution. Multicoloured.

4320	65c. Type **1169**	2·10	1·20
4321	65c. Camilo Cienfuegos and Fidel Castro	2·10	1·20
4322	65c. Castro and white doves	2·10	1·20

1170 Police Car and Motor Cycle

1999. 40th Anniv of National Revolutionary Police.

4323	**1170**	15c. multicoloured	60	20

1171 Workers' Rally

1999. 60th Anniv of Revolutionary Workers' Union.

4324	**1171**	15c. multicoloured	55	20

1172 Rabbit

1999. Chinese New Year. Year of the Rabbit.

4325	**1172**	75c. multicoloured	2·10	1·40

1173 Lenin

1999. 75th Death Anniv of Vladimir Ilich Lenin (Russian statesman).

4326	**1173**	75c. multicoloured	2·50	1·40

1174 Ornithosuchus

1999. Prehistoric Animals. Multicoloured.

4327	10c. Type **1174**	40	25
4328	15c. Bactrosaurus	55	30
4329	15c. Saltopus	55	30
4330	65c. Protosuchus	2·30	1·10
4331	75c. Mussaurus	2·50	1·30

1175 Damaso Perez Prado

1999. Cuban Musicians. Multicoloured.

4332	5c. Type **1175**	20	10
4333	15c. Benny More	70	30
4334	15c. Chano Pozo	70	30
4335	35c. Miguelito Valdes	1·40	60
4336	65c. Bola de Nieve	2·75	1·20
4337	75c. Rita Montaner	2·75	1·40

1176 Bolivar

1999. Centenary of Simon Bolivar's Visit to Cuba. Multicoloured.

4338	65c. Type **1176**	2·40	1·20
4339	65c. Simon Bolivar House and statue, Havana	2·40	1·20

1177 Emblem

1999. 40th Anniv of State Security Department of the Ministry of the Interior.

4340	**1177**	65c. multicoloured	2·30	1·20

1178 Giant Panda

1999. China 99 International Stamp Exhibition, Peking. Sheet 109×82 mm.

MS4341	**1178**	1p. multicoloured	4·25	2·10

1179 Postal Rocket

1999. Stamp Day.

4342	15c. Type **1179** (60th anniv)	45	20
4343	65c. Rider on horse (130th anniv of rebel postal service)	2·00	85

1180 Painting by Roberto Matta

1999. 40th Anniv of House of the Americas (cultural organization).

4344	**1180**	65c. multicoloured	2·30	85

1181 Steam Locomotive

1999. iBRA 99 International Stamp Exhibition, Nuremberg. Sheet 86×109 mm.

MS4345	**1181** 1p. multicoloured	1·40	1·40

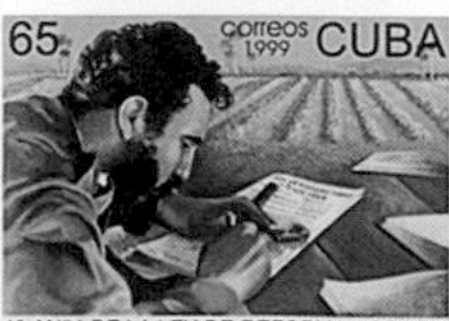

1182 Castro drafting Reform Law

1999. 40th Anniv of Agrarian Reform Law.

4346	**1182** 65c. multicoloured	1·40	85

1183 Royal Gramma

1999. Birth Bicentenary of Felipe Poey (naturalist). Fishes. Multicoloured.

4347	5c. Type **1183**	20	10
4348	15c. Peppermint basslet	45	20
4349	65c. Golden hamlet ("Hypoplectrus gummigutta")	2·00	85
4350	65c. Dusky damselfish ("Stegastes dorsopunicans")	2·00	85
MS4351	84×110 mm. 1p. Poey and shy hamlet ("Hypoplectrus guttavarius") (vert)	4·25	2·10

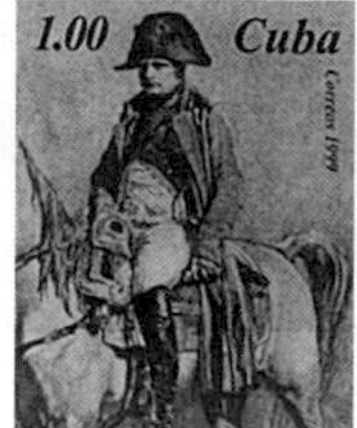

1184 "1814" (engraving, Jean Louis Meissonier)

1999. Philexfrance 99 International Stamp Exhibition, Paris. Sheet 85×110 mm.

MS4352	**1184** 1p. multicoloured	4·25	2·10

1185 Baseball

1999. 13th Pan-American Games, Winnipeg, Canada. Multicoloured.

4353	15c. Type **1185**	40	20
4354	65c. Volleyball (vert)	1·90	85
4355	75c. Boxing	2·20	95

1186 "Victory of Wioming" (Gao Hong)

1999. 50th Anniv of People's Republic of China. Paintings. Multicoloured.

4356	5c. Type **1186**	20	10
4357	15c. "Nanchang Revolt" (Cai Lang)	40	30
4358	40c. "Red Army crossing Marsh" (Gao Quan)	1·30	65
4359	65c. "Occupation of Presidential Palace" (Cheng Yifei and Wei Jingahan)	2·00	1·90
4360	75c. "Founding of the Republic Ceremony" (Dong Xiwen)	2·30	1·30

1187 "Morning Glory" (Qi Baishi)

1999. "China 1999" International Stamp Exhibition, Peking. Chinese Paintings. Multicoloured.

4361	5c. Type **1187**	20	10
4362	5c. "Three Galloping Horses" (Xu Beihong)	20	10
4363	15c. "Hunan Woman" (Fu Baoshi)	45	30
4364	15c. "Village of Luxun" (Wu Guanzhong)	45	30
4365	15c. "Crossing" (Huangzhou)	45	30
4366	40c. "Pine Tree" (He Xiangning)	1·30	70
4367	65c. "Sleeping Woman" (Jin Shangyi)	2·00	95
4368	75c. "Poetic Scene in Xun Yang" (Chen Yifei)	2·20	1·20

1188 Heinrich von Stephan (founder) and Emblem

1999. 125th Anniv of Universal Postal Union.

4369	**1188** 75c. multicoloured	2·10	1·20

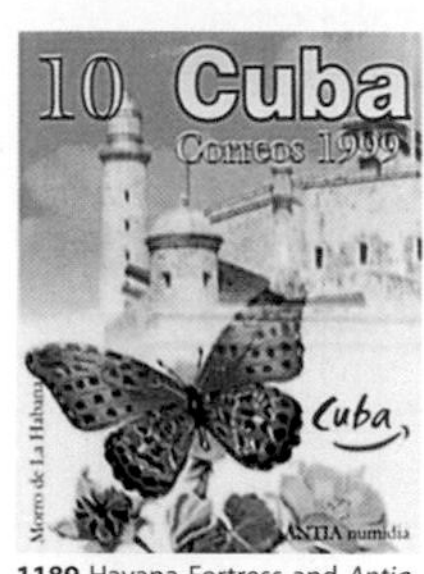

1189 Havana Fortress and *Antia numidia*

1999. World Tourism Day. Butterflies and Views of Havana. Multicoloured.

4370	10c. Type **1189**	30	20
4371	15c. Cathedral and black swallowtail	40	30
4372	65c. St. Francis of Assisi Convent and flambeau	1·90	95
4373	75c. National Senate and *Eueides cleobaea*	2·10	1·20

1190 Map of Germany on Globe

1999. "EXPO 2000" World's Fair, Hanover. Mult.

4374	5c. Type **1190**	20	10
4375	15c. Twipsy (mascot) (vert)	40	30
4376	15c. Exhibition site, Philadelphia, 1876	40	30
4377	15c. Exhibition site, Osaka, 1970	40	30
4378	65c. Exhibition site, Hanover	2·00	95
4379	75c. Exhibition site, Montreal, 1967	2·30	1·20

1191 Fokker F.27 Friendship

1999. 70th Anniv of Cuban Airlines. Multicoloured.

4380	15c. Type **1191**	40	20
4381	15c. Douglas DC-10	40	30
4382	65c. Airbus Industrie A320	1·90	95
4383	75c. Douglas DC-3	2·10	1·20

1192 Atomic Cloud and Feral Rock Pigeon

1999. America. A New Millennium without Arms. Multicoloured.

4384	15c. Type **1192**	40	25
4385	65c. Globe and dove	2·00	1·20

1193 MINFAR Headquarters

1999. 40th Anniversaries. Multicoloured.

4386	15c. Type **1193** (Ministry of Revolutionary Armed Forces)	40	25
4387	65c. Militia members (National Revolutionary Militia)	2·00	1·20

1194 Cienfuegos

1999. 40th Anniv of Disappearance of Major Camilo Cienfuegos (revolutionary).

4388	**1194** 15c. multicoloured	1·20	30

1195 Vieja Plaza

1999. 9th Latin American Summit of Heads of State and Government, Havana. Multicoloured.

4389	65c. Type **1195**	1·90	95
4390	75c. San Francisco de Asis Plaza	2·10	2·10
MS4391	109×85 mm. 1p. Armas Plaza (37×31 mm)	4·75	2·10

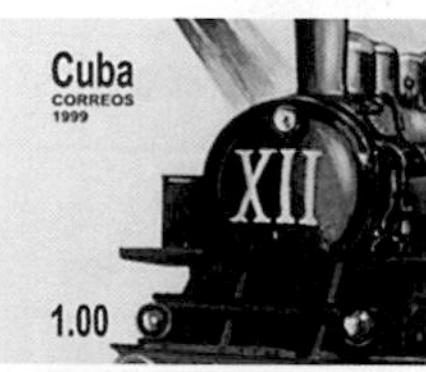

1196 Steam Locomotive

1999. 12th Cuban Philatelic Federation Congress. Sheet 110×85 mm.

MS4392	**1196** 1p. multicoloured	4·25	2·10

1197 Hemingway and Fisherman

1999. Birth Cent of Ernest Hemingway (writer).

4393	**1197** 65c. multicoloured	2·10	95

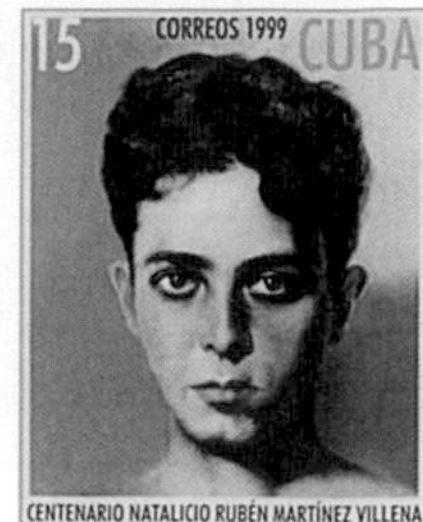

1198 Villena

1999. Birth Centenary of Ruben Martinez Villena (revolutionary).

4394	**1198** 15c. multicoloured	50	30

1199 Romay Chacon

1999. 150th Death Anniv of Tomas Romay Chacon (scientist).

4395	**1199** 65c. multicoloured	2·10	95

1200 Dragon

2000. Chinese New Year. "Year of the Dragon".

4396	**1200** 15c. multicoloured	50	30

1201 "Hot Rumba"

2000. Paintings by Concepcion Ferrant. Mult.

4397	10c. Type **1201**	30	25
4398	15c. "Cachumba"	40	30
4399	65c. "House of the babalao"	1·60	1·20
4400	75c. "Tata Cunengue"	1·80	1·30

1202 *Helcyra superba*

2000. "BANGKOK 2000" International Stamp Exhibition. Butterflies. Multicoloured.

4401	10c. Type **1202**	30	20
4402	15c. *Pantaporia punctata*	40	30
4403	15c. *Neptis themis*	40	30
4404	65c. *Curetis acuta*	1·70	1·20
4405	75c. *Chrysozephyrus ataxus*	2·00	1·40

1203 World Map

2000. Group of 77 South Summit, Havana.

4406 **1203** 75c. multicoloured 2·10 1·40

1204 Lenin

2000. 130th Birth Anniv of Vladimir Ilich Lenin.

4407 **1204** 75c. multicoloured 2·10 1·40

1205 Cuba and Puerto Rico 1855 1r. Stamp

2000. Stamp Day. Multicoloured.

4408 65c. Type **1205** (145th anniv of first Cuba and Puerto Rico stamp) 1·70 1·20

4409 90c. Jaime Gonzalez Crocier (airmail pioneer), Boeing XP-15 and cover (70th anniv of the airmail service) 2·30 1·50

1206 Commander Guevara and Map

2000. 35th Anniv of Visit of "Che" Guevara (guerrilla fighter) to Congo.

4410 **1206** 65c. multicoloured 1·80 1·20

1207 Captain San Luis

2000. 60th Birth Anniv of Eliseo Reyes Rodriguez ("Captain San Luis").

4411 **1207** 65c. multicoloured 1·80 1·20

1208 Baldwin Locomotive, 1882

2000. "Stamp Show 2000" International Stamp Exhibition, London. Steam Locomotives. Mult.

4412 5c. Type **1208** 10 10

4413 10c. Baldwin locomotive, 1895 30 20

4414 15c. Baldwin locomotive, 1912 40 30

4415 65c. Alco locomotive, 1919 1·70 1·20

4416 75c. Alco locomotive, 1925 2·00 1·40

MS4417 104×85 mm. 1p. Henschel locomotive, 1920 (38×28 mm) 3·00 2·20

1209 Henri Giffard and Steam-powered Dirigible Airship

2000. WIPA 2000 International Stamp Exhibition, Vienna. Airship Development. Multicoloured.

4418 10c. Type **1209** 30 20

4419 15c. Albert and Gaston Tissander and airship (vert) 45 30

4420 50c. Charles Renard, Arthur Krebs and *La France* (airship) 1·40 85

4421 65c. Pierre and Paul Lebaudy and airship 1·80 1·20

4422 75c. August von Perseval and airship 2·10 1·40

MS4423 85×108 mm. 1p. Ferdinand von Zeppelin and LZ-1 (first Zeppelin airship) (39×31 mm) 3·00 2·20

1210 Emblem

2000. 2nd World Meeting of "Friendship and Solidarity with Cuba", Havana.

4424 **1210** 65c. multicoloured 1·60 1·40

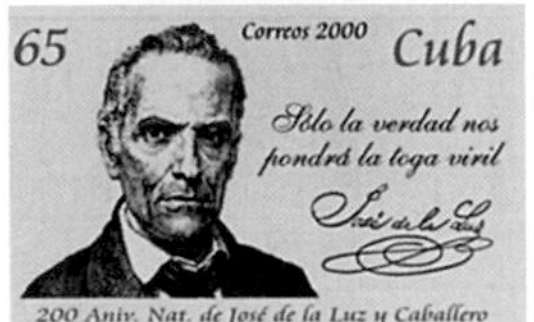

1211 Caballero

2000. Birth Bicentenary of Jose de la Luz y Caballero (educator).

4425 **1211** 65c. multicoloured 1·60 1·40

1212 Music Score, Roldan and Violin

2000. Birth Centenary of Amadeo Roldan (musician and conductor).

4426 **1212** 65c. multicoloured 1·60 1·40

1213 Mother holding Child ("Child of El Senor Don Pomposo")

2000. The Golden Age (children's magazine by Jose Marti). Designs illustrating stories featured in the magazines. Multicoloured.

4427 5c. Type **1213** 10 10

4428 10c. Child with doll ("The Black Doll") 30 20

4429 15c. Child reading ("Mischevious Child") 50 30

4430 50c. "The Nightingale" (Hans Christian Andersen) 1·80 1·20

4431 65c. Frontispiece 2·30 1·40

4432 75c. "The Enchanted Prawn" (Edourd R. L. Laboulaye) 2·75 1·70

MS4433 121×156 mm. As Nos. 4427/32 but smaller (36×29 mm) 5·75 5·25

1214 Members' Flags

2000. 20th Anniv of Latin American Association for Integration (A.L.A.D.I.).

4434 **1214** 65c. multicoloured 1·70 1·40

1215 Touch Bearer

2000. Olymphilex 2000 Stamp Exhibition, Sydney. Sheet 110×86 mm.

MS4435 **1215** 1p. multicoloured 2·50 1·90

1216 Running

2000. Olympic Games, Sydney. Multicoloured.

4436 5c. Type **1216** 10 10

4437 15c. Football 50 30

4438 65c. Baseball 2·30 1·20

4439 75c. Cycling 2·75 1·40

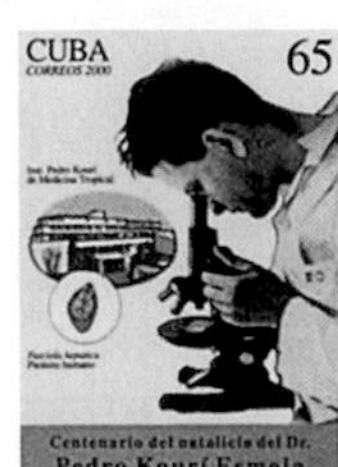

1217 Esmeja using Microscope

2000. Birth Centenary of Dr. Pedro Kouri Esmeja (tropical disease and parasitology pioneer).

4440 **1217** 65c. multicoloured 1·70 1·40

1218 Women and Flag

2000. 40th Anniv of Federation of Cuban Women.

4441 **1218** 15c. multicoloured 50 35

1219 18th-century Sailing Packet

2000. "Espana 2000" World Stamp Exhibition, Madrid. Multicoloured.

4442 10c. Type **1219** 30 20

4443 15c. Statue, La Cibeles Plaza, Madrid and Spain 1850 6c. stamp 50 30

4444 15c. Crystal Palace, Madrid (venue) and 1850 cover 50 30

4445 65c. Palace of Communications, Madrid and set of Spain 1850 stamps 2·30 1·40

4446 75c. Galician Centre, Havana with Cuba and Puerto Rica 1855 ½r. stamp 2·50 1·70

MS4447 111×88 mm. 100c. Queen Isabella II of Spain (31×39 mm) 3·50 3·00

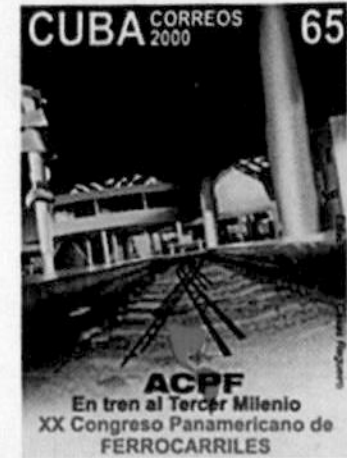

1220 Senen Casas Reguerio Railway Station, Santiago de Cuba

2000. 20th Congress of Pan-American Railways.

4448 **1220** 65c. multicoloured 1·80 1·50

1221 Coconut Forest Bay, Hainan, China

2000. 40th Anniv of Cuba–China Diplomatic Relations. Joint issue with China. Multicoloured.

4449 15c. Type **1221** 50 40

4450 15c. Varadero beach, Matanzas, Cuba 50 40

Nos. 4449/50 were issued together, se-tenant, forming a composite design.

1222 Hawksbill Turtle (*Eretmochelys imbricata*), Guardalavaca

2000. World Tourism Day. Diving Sites. Mult.

4451 10c. Type **1222** 30 20

4452 15c. Nassau grouper (*Epinephelus striatus*), El Colony 40 30

4453 65c. French angelfish (*Pomacanthus paru*), Santa Lucia (horiz) 1·90 1·30

4454 75c. Black margate (*Anisotremus surinamensis*), Maria la Gorda (horiz) 2·10 1·40

1223 House and People Gardening

2000. 40th Anniv of Committees for Defense of the Revolution (CDR).

4455 **1223** 15c. multicoloured 50 35

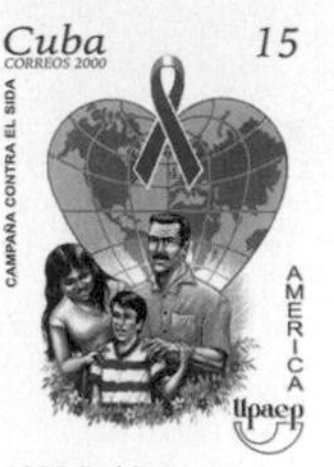

1224 Emblem, Heart-shaped Globe and Family

2000. America. Anti-A.I.D.S. Campaign. Mult.

4456 15c. Type **1224** 50 35

4457 65c. Emblem, heart-shaped globe and couple 2·10 1·40

1225 Soldiers carrying Flags

2000. 25th Anniv of Cuban International Mission to Angola.
4458 **1225** 75c. multicoloured 2·10 1·70

1226 Humboldt and Guesthouse, Trinidad

2000. Bicentennial of Friedrich Wilhelm Heinrich Alexander von Humboldt's Visit to Cuba. Mult.
4459 15c. Type **1226** 50 35
4460 65c. Humboldt, frontispiece of *On the Island of Cuba* (political essay) and Humboldt House, Havana 2·10 1·40

1227 *Polymita picta iolimbata*

2000. New Millennium. Snails. Multicoloured.
4461 65c. Type **1227** 2·10 1·40
4462 65c. *Polymita picta roseolimbata* 2·10 1·40
4463 65c. *Polymita picta picta* 2·10 1·40
4464 65c. *Polymita picta nigrolimbata* 2·10 1·40
4465 65c. *Polymita versicolor* 2·10 1·40

Nos. 4461/4 were issued together, se-tenant, forming a composite design.

1228 Dragon

2001. New Year. Year of the Dragon.
4466 **1228** 15c. multicoloured 85 45

1229 Mandarin Duck (*Aix galericulata*)

2001. Birds. Hong Kong 2001 International Stamp Exhibition. Multicoloured.
4467 5c. Type **1229** 10 10
4468 10c. Golden pheasant (*Chrysolophus pictus*) (inscr "Chryysolophus") 30 20
4469 15c. Grey heron (*Ardea cinerea*) 50 30
4470 65c. Red Jungle-fowl (*Gallus gallus*) 2·30 1·40
4471 75c. Collared dove (*Streptotelia decaocto*) 2·50 1·70

MS4472 111×85 mm. 1p. Common crane (*Grus grus*) (32×40 mm) 3·25 2·30

1230 Sports Centre

2001. 40th Anniv of INDER (National Institute for Sport, Physical Education and Recreation).
4473 **1230** 65c. multicoloured 2·10 1·40

1231 Refugees

2001. 50th Anniv of United Nations High Commissioner for Refugees.
4474 **1231** 65c. multicoloured 2·00 1·30

1232 James Miholland's Locomotive

2001. Steam Locomotives. Multicoloured.
4475 10c. Type **1232** 30 20
4476 15c. Theodore Sheffler's fire-less steam locomotive 40 30
4477 40c. Adams and Price's chain driven locomotive 1·20 75
4478 65c. Peckett and Sons' Bulan 2·00 1·40
4479 75c. W. G. Bagnall's fire-less steam locomotive 2·30 1·70

1233 Anniversary Emblem and Lighthouse 2001

2001. 105th Inter-Parliamentary Union Conference, Havana.
4480 **1233** 65c. multicoloured 2·20 1·40

1234 "Bombardeo del 15 Abril" (Servando Cabrera)

2001. 40th Anniv of Bay of Pigs (Playa Giron).
4481 **1234** 65c. multicoloured 2·10 1·40

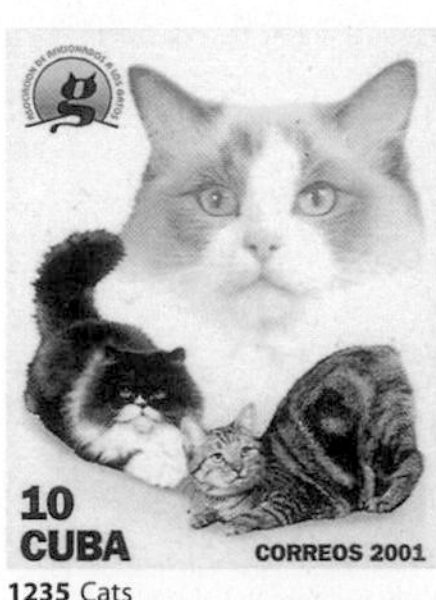

1235 Cats

2001. Cats and Dogs. Showing cats, dogs and animal societies' emblems. Multicoloured.
4482 10c. Type **1235** 30 20
4483 15c. Fighting dogs 40 30
4484 15c. German shepherd, boxer and puppy 40 30
4485 65c. Spaniel and collies 1·90 1·30
4486 75c. Snarling dog, cats, and puppy 2·30 1·40

1236 Anniversary Emblem

2001. 40th Anniv of Radio Havana Cuba.
4487 **1236** 65c. multicoloured 2·00 1·40

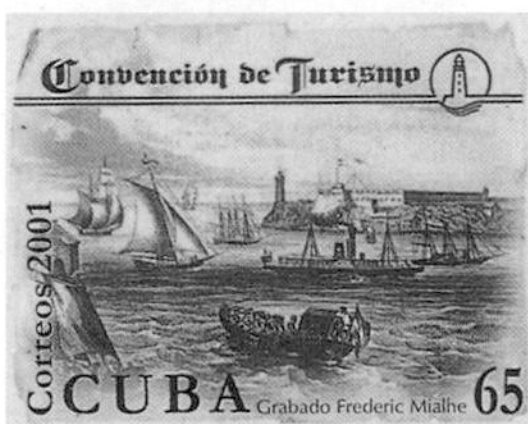

1237 Boats (engraving, Frederic Mialhe)

2001. Cuba 2001 International Tourism Convention, Havana.
4488 **1237** 65c. multicoloured 2·00 1·40

1238 St. Michael's Cathedral, Brussels

2001. Belgica 2001 International Stamp Exhibition, Brussels. Multicoloured.
4489 5c. Type **1238** 20 10
4490 10c. Sablon Church (horiz) 30 20
4491 15c. Royal Palace (horiz) 50 40
4492 65c. Basilica of the Sacred Heart, Koekelberg (horiz) 2·00 1·40
4493 75c. Atomium (model of an iron crystal) Exhibition Centre 2·30 1·70

MS4494 107×83 mm. 100c. Kings Residence, Grand Place, Brussels (32×40 mm) 3·00 2·20

1239 Sniffer Dog and Handler

2001. 40th Anniv of Ministry of Interior.
4495 **1239** 65c. multicoloured 1·80 1·40

1240 Locomotive *JR 500*

2001. Japanese Locomotives. Philanippon '01 International Stamp Exhibition, Tokyo. Multicoloured.
4496 5c. Type **1240** 10 10
4497 10c. Locomotive *JR 700* 30 20
4498 15c. Locomotive *MAX 1* 40 30
4499 65c. Locomotive *MAX 2* 1·90 1·30
4500 75c. Locomotive *300* 2·10 1·40

MS4501 78×110 mm. 100c. Locomotive *Zero* (40×32 mm) 3·00 1·90

1241 Mount Titano and St. Marino (statue)

2001. 1700th Anniv of Founding of San Marino.
4502 **1241** 75c. multicoloured 2·20 1·40

1242 Tench (*Tinca tinca*)

2001. Aquatics Breeding Programme. Multicoloured.
4503 5c. Type **1242** 10 10
4504 10c. Common frog (*Rana temporaria*) 30 20
4505 15c. Blue land crab (*Cardisoma guanhumi*) 40 30
4506 65c. Common mussel (*Mytilus edulis*) 1·90 1·30
4507 75c. Spotted tilapia (*Tilapia mariae*) 2·10 1·40

MS4508 86×111 mm. 1p. White-clawed crayfish (*Potamobius pallipes*) (40×32 mm) 3·00 3·00

1243 Anniversary Emblem and Ernesto "Che" Guevara

2001. 40th Anniv of Recycling.
4509 **1243** 65c. multicoloured 2·00 1·30

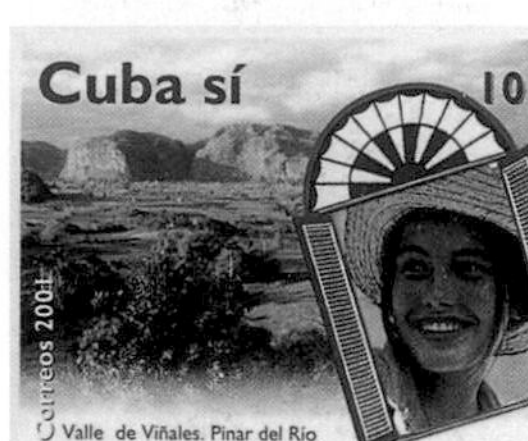

1244 Valle de Vinales, Pinar del Rio

2001. Tourism. Multicoloured.
4510 10c. Type **1244** 25 15
4511 15c. Trindad de Cuba 40 20
4512 65c. Playa Sirena (beach), Cayo Largo del Sur 1·90 1·30
4513 75c. Morro-Cabana (castle), Havana 2·10 1·40

1245 Children encircling Globe

2001. United Nations Year of Dialogue Among Civilizations.
4514 **1245** 65c. multicoloured 2·00 1·40

1246 *Tetramicra malpighiarum* (orchid)

2001. America. UNESCO World Heritage Sites. Desamarco del Granma National Park. Multicoloured.

4515	15c. Type **1246**	40	20
4516	65c. *Liggus vittatus* (shell)	1·90	1·40

1247 Building

2001. Centenary of José Marti National Library.

4517	**1247**	15c. multicoloured	45	30

1248 Torso and Head

2001. 25th Anniv of Cuban Airliner Explosion over Barbados. Showing parts of painting. Multicoloured.

4518	5c. Type **1248**	10	10
4519	10c. Dove	25	15
4520	15c. Pregnant woman	40	20
4521	50c. Stylized birds	1·40	95
4522	65c. Star and houses	1·90	1·30

Nos. 4518/22 were issued together, se-tenant, forming a composite design.

1249 Eduardo Chibas

2001. 50th Death Anniv of Eduardo Chibas (politician).

4523	**1249**	65c. multicoloured	2·00	1·30

1250 Napoleon on Horseback and Map of Battle of Eylau (inscr "Elyeau")

2001. 40th Anniv of Napoleon Museum, Havana. Showing Napoleon and battles maps.

4524	10c. Type **1250**	30	15
4526	10c. Battle of Marengo	30	15
4527	65c. Battle of Waterloo	1·90	1·30
4528	75c. Battle of Abukin	2·10	1·40

1251 Pablo de la Torriente

2001. Birth Centenary of Pablo de la Torriente (writer).

4529	**1251**	75c. multicoloured	2·20	1·40

1252 Mosaic Pigeon (3013-67-HM)

2001. 4th Pigeon Fanciers Federation Congress. Multicoloured.

4530	65c. Type **1252**	1·80	85
4531	65c. Emperor (2241-55-ME)	1·80	85
4532	65c. Bronzed (338-59-HE)	1·80	85
4533	65c. Mosaic (1561-66-HM)	1·80	85
4534	65c. Dark emperor (2021-61-ME)	1·80	85

1253 Tyrone Power

2001. Actors. Multicoloured.

4535	5c. Type **1253**	20	10
4536	10c. Steve McQueen	30	15
4537	10c. Ava Gardner	30	15
4538	15c. Rita Hayworth	40	20
4539	15c. James Dean	40	20
4540	15c. Marilyn Monroe	40	20
4541	65c. Natalie Wood	1·90	85
4542	65c. Rock Hudson	1·90	85
4543	75c. Richard Burton	2·10	1·30
MS4544	150×185 mm. Nos. 4535/43	6·75	5·75

1254 Bamboo and Horse

2002. Year of the Horse.

4545	**1254**	15c. multicoloured	45	30

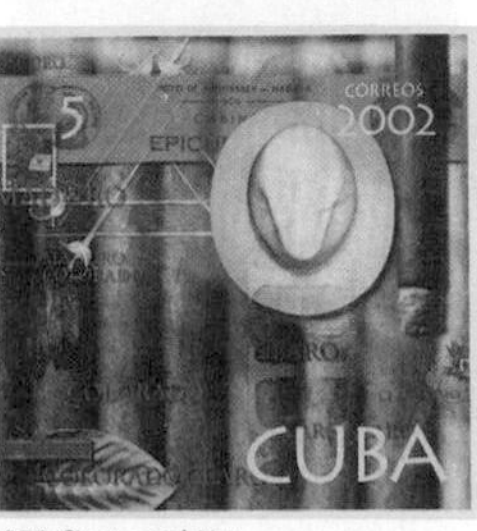

1255 Cigars and Hat

2002. 4th Habano (cigar) Festival, Havana. Multicoloured.

4546	5c. Type **1255**	20	10
4547	10c. Smoking cigar	30	15
4548	15c. Wax seal and map	40	20
4549	65c. Stamps, Punch and crossed swords	1·90	85
4550	75c. Flag, tobacco plants and Alejandro Robaina (5th anniv of "Vegas Robaina" (cigar manufacturer))	2·10	95
MS4551	118×91 mm. 1p. Fidel Castro, map and star (40×32 mm)	3·00	1·90

1256 Profile, Dove holding Envelope and Computer (image scaled to 69% of original size)

2002. 2nd UPAEP Information Technology Workshop.

4552	**1256**	65c. multicoloured	2·10	1·30

1257 Map Reading

2002. Pioneer Explorers (scouts). Multicoloured.

4553	5c. Type **1257**	20	10
4554	15c. Tying knots	40	20
4555	50c. Cooking over campfire	1·40	70
4556	65c. Lighting campfire	1·90	85
4557	75c. Orienteering	2·10	95

1258 Soldiers, Demonstrators, Industry and Computers

2002. 40th Anniv of Young Communists Union.

4558	**1258**	15c. multicoloured	40	30

1259 Two Football Players (Brazil in foreground)

2002. World Cup Football Championships, Japan and South Korea. Showing two players and flag, player in foreground given. Multicoloured.

4559	15c. Type **1259**	40	20
4560	15c. Spain	40	20
4561	15c. France	40	20
4562	15c. Germany	40	20
4563	15c. Korean Republic	40	20
4564	65c. Argentina	1·90	85
4565	75c. Italy	2·10	95
4566	85c. Japan	2·30	1·10

1260 NH Parque Central Hotel, Havana

2002. Spanish–Cuban Philatelic Exhibition, Havana. Sheet 110×84 mm.

MS4567	**1260**	1p. multicoloured	3·00	2·00

1261 Bust and Experimental Agricultural Building, Santiago de las Vegas

2002. 125th Birth Anniv of Juan Thomas Roig (botanist). Multicoloured.

4568	5c. Type **1261**	20	10
4569	10c. Juan Roig's house and bust	30	15
4570	15c. Tobacco plant and Roig	40	20
4571	50c. Roig (sculpture) and *Allophyllum roiggi*	1·40	70
4572	65c. Botanical dictionary and Roig	1·90	85

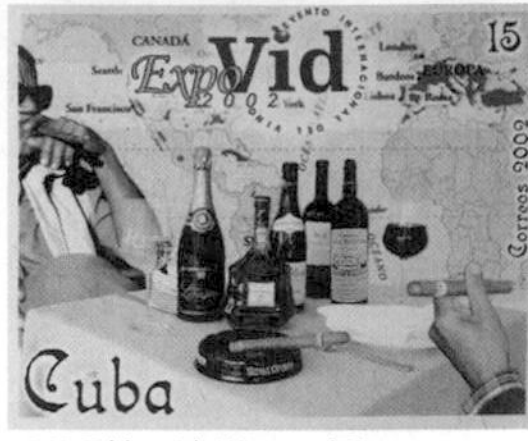

1262 Table with Wine and Cigars

2002. Expovid 2002 International Wine Festival, Havana. Multicoloured.

4573	15c. Type **1262**	20	10
4574	65c. Glass of white wine and barrels	1·90	85
4575	75c. Glass of red wine and vineyard	2·10	95

1263 Hands, Heart and Leaf

2002. 10th Anniv of MediCuba Switzerland (humanitarian organization).

4576	**1263**	75c. multicoloured	2·20	1·40

1264 *Amanita junquillea*

2002. Fungi. Multicoloured.

4577	5c. Type **1264**	20	10
4578	15c. *Lepiota puellaris*	40	20
4579	45c. *Cortinarius cumatillis*	1·20	60
4580	65c. *Pholiota adipose* (inscr "Pholliota")	1·90	85
4581	75c. Shaggy ink cap (*Coprinus comatus*)	2·10	95

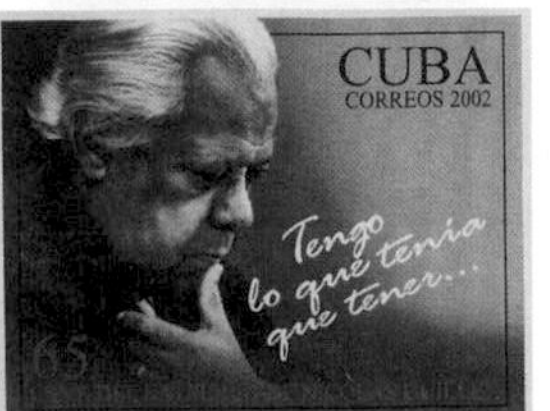

1265 Nicolas Guillen

2002. Birth Centenary of Nicolas Guillen (poet).

4582	**1265**	65c. multicoloured	1·90	1·30

1266 "Dockers" (painting)

2002. Birth Centenary of Marcelo Pogolotti (artist).

4583	**1266** 15c. multicoloured	55	30

1267 Agostinho Neto and Map of Africa

2002. 80th Birth Anniv of Agostinho Neto (first president of independent Angola).

4584	**1267** 65c. multicoloured	1·90	1·30

1268 Grey plover (*Pluvialis squatarola*) (inscr "Calidris minutilla")

2002. Espana 2002 International Stamp Exhibition. Birds. Multicoloured.

4585	5c. Type **1268**	20	10
4586	10c. Greater yellow-legs (*Tringa melanoleuca*) (inscr "mela-noleucas")	30	15
4587	15c. Semi-palmated plover (*Charadius semipalmatus*)	40	20
4588	65c. Least sandpiper (*Calidris minutilla*) (inscr "Pluvialis squatarola")	1·90	95
4589	75c. Ruddy turnstone (*Arenaria interpres*)	2·10	1·30
MS4590	110×87 mm. 1p. Sora crake (*Porzana Carolina*) (40×32 mm)	2·75	1·90

1269 Photographer and War Scene

2002. 3rd International War Correspondents' Conference.

4591	**1269** 65c. multicoloured	1·90	95

1270 Ernesto "Che" Guevara

2002. 35th Death Anniv of Ernesto "Che" Guevara (revolutionary). Multicoloured.

4592	5c. Type **1270**	20	10
4593	10c. Face	30	15
4594	15c. Smoking	50	30
4595	50c. Speaking	1·60	75
4596	65c. Facing left	1·90	85
4597	75c. Seated facing right	2·30	1·10
MS4598	200×161 mm. Nos. 4592/7	6·75	5·25

1271 Emblem, Teacher and Pupil

2002. UPAEP. Literacy Campaign. Multicoloured.

4599	15c. Type **1271**	50	30
4600	65c. School, flag, children and computer	1·90	95

1272 Mercury Monterrey (1957)

2002. Cars. Multicoloured.

4601	5c. Type **1272**	20	10
4602	5c. Pontiac Catalina (1956)	30	15
4603	15c. Cadillac Fleetwood (1959)	50	30
4604	65c. Hudson Hornet (1951)	1·90	95
4605	75c. Chevrolet Bel Air (1957)	2·30	1·20
4606	85c. Mercedes Benz 190 SL (1957)	2·50	1·40

1273 G. Mesa

2002. 15th Intercontinental Cup Baseball Championship. Showing players. Multicoloured.

4607	5c. Type **1273**	20	10
4608	15c. A. Pacheco	50	30
4609	50c. O. Linares	1·60	75
4610	65c. O. Kindelan	1·90	95
4611	75c. L. Ulacia	2·30	1·40

1274 Statuette and Emblem

2002. 4th Havana International Trade Fair.

4612	**1274** 65c. multicoloured	1·90	95

1275 G. and R. Stephenson's *Rocket*

2002. Steam Locomotives. Multicoloured.

4613	5c. Type **1275**	20	10
4614	15c. Early locomotive (inscr "Miller")	50	30
4615	50c. *Vulcan*	1·60	75
4616	65c. *Consolidation*	1·90	95
4617	75c. *Mikado*	2·30	1·40

A brief description of each locomotive is given in the enlarged margin above or below the relevant stamp.

1276 Corp de Ballet

2002. 40th Anniv of Ballet de Camaguey (dance company). Multicoloured.

4618	65c. Type **1276**	1·90	95
4619	75c. Principal dancers	2·30	1·40

1277 Centenary Emblem and Surgeon General Wyman

2002. Centenary of PanAmerican Health Organization.

4620	**1277** 65c. multicoloured	1·90	95

1278 "Emi Cosinca" (painting)

2002. Birth Centenary of Wilfred Lam (artist). Paintings. Multicoloured.

4621	15c. Type **1278**	50	30
4622	45c. "Yo say"	1·60	75
4623	65c. "Retro de H. H."	1·90	95
4624	75c. "Mujer Sentada"	2·30	1·40

1279 Dulce Loynaz

2002. Birth Centenary of Dulce M. Loynaz (writer).

4625	**1279** 65c. multicoloured	1·90	1·30

1280 Bottle-nose Dolphin (*Tursiops truncates*)

2002. National Philately Championship. Sheet 84×111 mm.

MS4626	**1280** 1p. multicoloured	3·00	2·40

1281 Red Deer (*Cervus elaphus*) and Irish Elk (*Megaloceros*) (image scaled to 69% of original size)

2002. Prehistoric Animals. Prehistoric animals and their modern counterparts. Multicoloured.

4627	5c. Type **1281**	20	10
4628	10c. Gelada baboon (*Therop-ithecus gelada*) and baboon (*Papio anubis*)	30	15
4629	15c. Black rhinoceros (*Diceros bicornis*) and woolly rhinoc-eros (*Coelodonta*)	50	30
4630	45c. Dire wolf (*Canis dirus*) and wolf (*Canis lupus*)	1·30	75
4631	65c. Grizzly bear (*Ursus arctos*) and cave bear (*Ursus spelaeus*)	1·90	95
4632	75c. Saber-toothed tiger (*Smilo-don*) and lion (*Panthera leo*)	2·30	1·40
MS4632a	111×65 mm. 1p. "Mam-muthus primagenius"	3·00	2·40

1282 Goat

2003. New Year. "Year of the Goat". Multicoloured.

4633	15c. Type **1282**	50	30
4634	15c. Goat facing left (red background)	50	30

1283 "Flores Amaraillas" (Amelia Pelaez)

2003. 185th Anniv of San Alejandro Art School. Multicoloured.

4635	5c. Type **1283**	20	10
4636	15c. "Harlequin" (Rene Portocar-rero)	40	20
4637	65c. Abstract (Mario Carrreno) (horiz)	1·80	95
4638	75c. Figures (Servando Cabrera)	2·10	1·10

1284 Jose Marti's Birthplace

2003. 150th Birth Anniv of Jose Marti (writer and revolutionary). Multicoloured.

4639	15c. Type **1284**	40	20
4640	65c. "Los Antillos libres…" and clouds (horiz)	1·80	95
4641	65c. Unfinished letter to Manuel Mercado, 18 May 1985	1·80	95
4642	75c. Jose Marti	2·10	1·10
MS4643	84×109 mm. 1p. Jose Marti (40×32 mm)	3·00	2·40

1285 Men seated around Table

2003. Habana (cigar) Festival, Havana. Multicoloured.

4644	15c. Type **1285**	40	20
4644a	15c. Woman with cigar box	40	20

4645 50c. Growing tobacco and hands rolling cigar (46×46 mm) 1·30 75

4646 65c. Building façade (5th anniv of "Trinidad" (cigar manufacturer)) (46×46 mm) 1·80 95

4647 75c. Man seated on stamp, palm and office (46×46 mm) 2·10 1·10

MS4648 125×98 mm. 1p. Aboriginal smoking cigar (32×40 mm) 3·00 2·40

1286 Fidel Castro

2003. 40th Anniv of Radio Rebelde.

4649 **1286** 65c. multicoloured 1·80 95

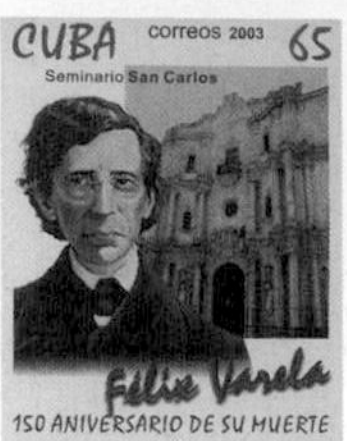

1287 Felix Varela

2003. 150th Death Anniv of Felix Varela (priest and reformer).

4650 **1287** 65c. multicoloured 1·80 95

1288 Mario Munoz

2003. 45th Anniv of Mario Munoz Monroy Third Eastern Front.

4651 **1288** 15c. multicoloured 50 30

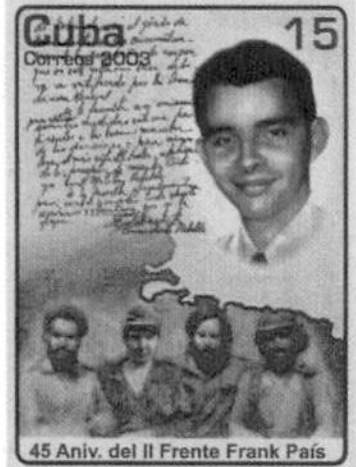

1289 Frank Pais

2003. 45th Anniv of Frank Pais M26J Urban Front.

4652 **1289** 15c. multicoloured 50 30

1290 "El pensamiento" (Manuel Mendive)

2003. 16th World Sexology Congress, Havana.

4653 **1290** 65c. multicoloured 1·80 95

1291 Container Ship

2003. Transport. Multicoloured.

4654 5c. Type **1291** 20 10

4655 10c. Lorry 30 15

4656 15c. Locomotive pulling container truck 40 20

4657 65c. Lorry at airport 1·80 95

4658 75c. Aircraft and lorry 2·10 1·10

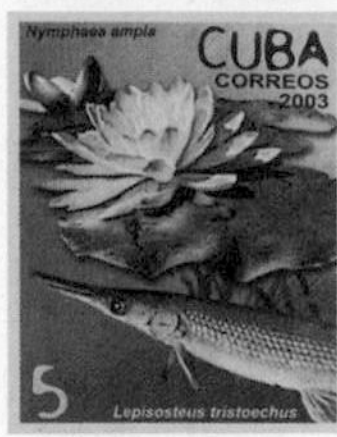

1292 *Nymphaea ampla* and *Lepisosteus tristoechus*

2003. Flora and Fauna. Multicoloured.

4659 5c. Type **1292** 20 10

4660 10c. Stripe-headed tanager (*Spindalis zena pretre*) and *Magnolia grandiflora* 30 15

4661 15c. *Lillium candicum* and *Polymita picta* 40 20

4662 65c. *Stralitzia regale* and *Solenodon cubanus* 1·80 95

4663 75c. *Hibiscus rosa sinesis* and Bee hummingbird (*Mellisuga helenae*) (inscr "Mellysuga") 2·10 1·10

MS4664 112×85 mm. 1p. Woolly mammoth (*Mammuthus primigenius*) (40×32 mm) 3·00 2·40

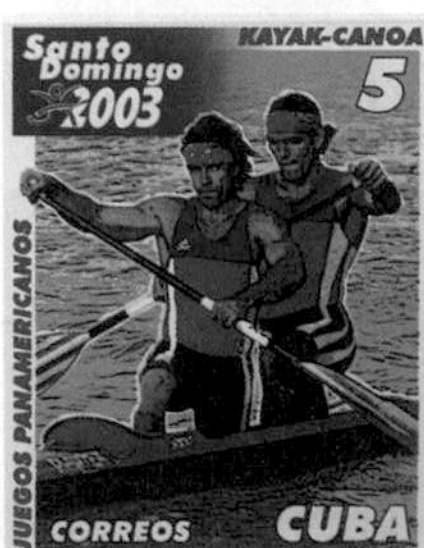

1293 Kayaking

2003. Pan American Games. Multicoloured.

4665 5c. Type **1293** 20 10

4666 15c. Judo 40 20

4667 50c. Athletics 1·30 75

4668 65c. Volleyball 1·80 95

1294 Barrack Facade

2003. 50th Anniv of Assault on Moncada Barracks, Santiago de Cuba. Multicoloured.

4669 15c. Type **1294** 40 20

4670 65c. Fidel Castro 1·80 95

1295 Flat Truck

2003. Railways. Multicoloured.

4671 5c. Type **1295** (Cuba) (c. 1930) 20 10

4672 10c. Crane (USA) (1920) 30 15

4673 15c. General Electric Co. BB120/120E (USA) (1925) 40 20

4674 65c. DVM-9-Ganz (Hungary) (1969) 1·80 95

4675 75c. American Locomotive Co. 2-6-0 (USA) (1905) 2·10 1·10

1296 Flowers in Desert (image scaled to 69% of original size)

2003. United Nations Covention to Combat Desertification (UNCCD) Conference, Havana.

4676 **1296** 65c. multicoloured 2·50 95

1297 Snowy Owl (*Nyctea scandiaca*)

2003. Bangkok 2003 International Stamp Exhibition. Fauna. Multicoloured.

4677 5c. Type **1297** 20 10

4678 10c. Puffin (*Fratercula artica*) 30 15

4679 15c. Gannet (*Sula bassana*) 40 20

4680 65c. Polar bear and cub (*Ursus maritimus*) 1·80 95

4681 75c. Arctic fox (*Alopex lagopus*) 2·10 1·10

MS4682 86×108 mm. 1p. Harp seal pup (*Pagolphilus groenlandicus*) 3·50 3·00

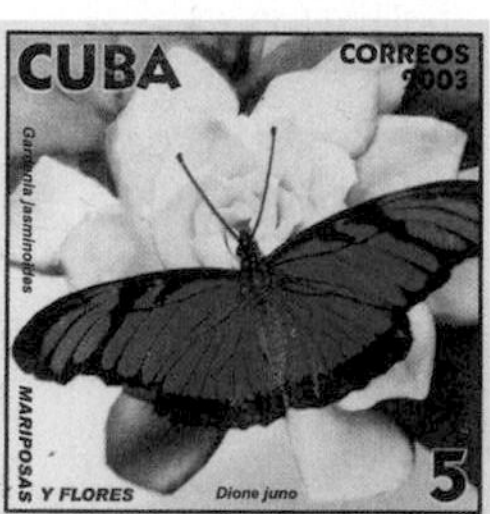

1298 *Gardenia jasminoides* and Silver-spot (*Dione juno*)

2003. Butterflies and Flowers. Multicoloured.

4683 5c. Type **1298** 20 10

4684 15c. *Chrysanthemus sinence* and *Apatura ilia* 40 20

4685 65c. *Hibiscus rosa sinensis* and peacock (*Inachis io*) 1·80 95

4686 75c. *Althea rosea* and *Marpesia iole* 2·10 1·10

MS4687 111×87 mm. 1p. *Zantedeschia aethiopica* and monarch (*Danaus plexippus*) (32×40 mm) 3·50 3·00

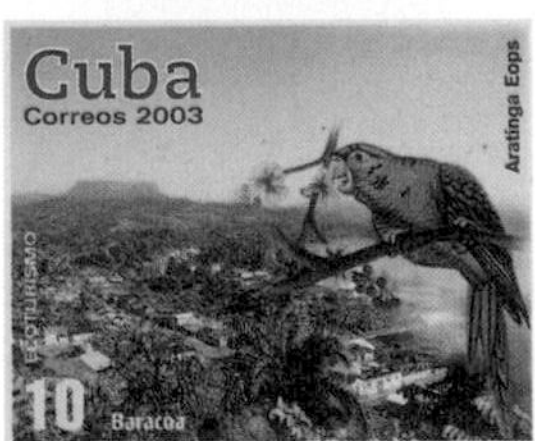

1299 Cuban Conure (*Aratinga euops*) (inscr "eops")

2003. Ecotourism. Multicoloured.

4688 10c. Type **1299** 20 10

4689 15c. Cuban green woodpecker (*Xiphiopicus percussus*) 40 20

4690 65c. Cuban grassquit (*Tiaris canora*) 1·80 95

4691 75c. Cuban trogon (*Priotelus temnurus*) 2·10 1·10

1300 Young Crocodile and Eggs

2003. Crocodiles (Crocodiylus rhombifer). Multicoloured.

4692 15c. Type **1300** 40 20

4693 15c. Adult 40 20

4694 65c. Adult eating bird 1·80 95

4695 75c. Head 2·10 1·10

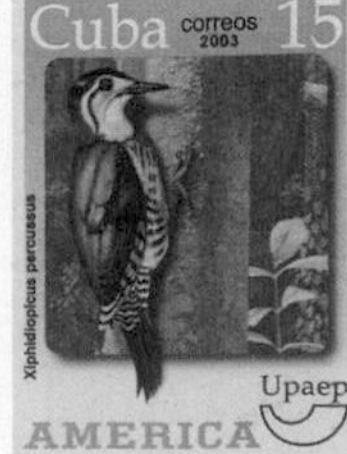

1301 Cuban Green Woodpecker (*Xiphiopicus percussus*)

2003. America. Flora and Fauna. Multicoloured.

4696 15c. Type **1301** 40 20

4697 65c. *Encyclia phoenicea* 2·10 1·10

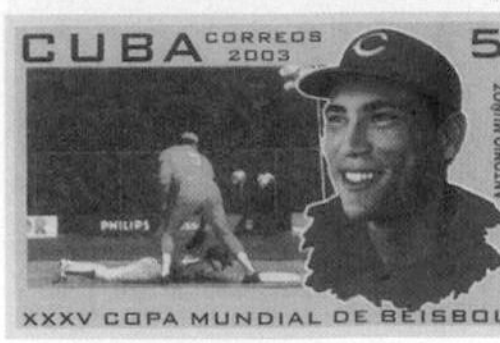

1302 Antonio Munoz

2003. Baseball World Cup Championship—2003, Cuba. Multicoloured.

4698 5c. Type **1302** 20 10

4699 10c. Lourdes Gourriel 20 10

4700 15c. Lazaro Vargas 40 20

4701 15c. Jorge Valdes 40 20

4702 65c. Lazaro Valle 1·80 95

4703 75c. Javier Mendez 2·10 1·10

MS4704 110×86 mm. 1p. Players (32×40 mm) 3·50 3·00

1303 Alicia Alonso as *Giselle*

2003. Ballet Anniversaries. Multicoloured.

4705 65c. Type **1303** (60th anniv of Alicia Alonso's performance as *Giselle*) 2·10 95

4706 65c. National Ballet Company (55th anniv) (horiz) 2·10 95

1304 Wright Brothers and *Wright Flyer*

2003. Centenary of Powered Flight. Multicoloured.

4707 5c. Type **1304** 20 10

4708 15c. Pitcairn PA-5 (1928) 40 20

4709 65c. Estearman C-3MB (1927) 1·80 95

4710 75c. Douglas M-2 (1926) 2·10 1·10

1305 Partisans

2004. 45th Anniv of Revolution.

4711 **1305** 65c. multicoloured 1·60 1·10

1306 Rowing Boats and Emblem (image scaled to 69% of original size)

2004. 15th Anniv of ExpoCuba.

4712	**1306**	65c. multicoloured	1·60	1·10

1307 Baseball and Parthenon (image scaled to 68% of original size)

2004. Olympic Games, Athens. Multicoloured.

4713	10c. Type **1307**	20	10
4714	15c. Early runners (amphora) and modern women runners	30	15
4715	65c. Modern boxers and early athlete	1·80	95
4716	75c. Early charioteer and modern show-jumper	2·10	1·10

1308 Monkey

2004. New Year. Year of the Monkey. Multicoloured, background colour given.

4717	15c. Type **1308** (lilac)	50	30
4718	15c. Monkey (orange)	50	30

1309 Julio Mella

2004. 75th Death Anniv of Julio Antonio Mella (revolutionary).

4719	**1309**	65c. multicoloured	1·60	1·10

1310 San Pablo College and Jose Marti

2004. Jose Marti (writer and revolutionary) Commemoration. Multicoloured.

4720	5c. Type **1310**	20	10
4721	5c. Mariano Marti (father)	20	10
4722	5c. Leonor Perez (mother)	20	10
4723	10c. With Fermin Dominguez	30	15
4724	10c. As young man and Havana jail	30	15
4725	15c. Wearing prison uniform and Fragua Martiana Museum	40	20
4726	15c. "El Abra", Isla de Pinos and Jose Marti	40	20
4727	15c. Guanabacoa Grammar School and Jose Marti seated with his son	40	20
4728	65c. Emperado building and Jose Marti holding son	1·80	95
4729	75c. "La Jatia" and Jose Marti	2·10	1·10

1311 San Juan de Dios Church

2004. 490th Anniv of Santa Maria del Puerto del Principe.

4730	**1311**	15c. multicoloured	50	30

1312 Tram and Conductor

2004. Trams. Multicoloured.

4731	5c. Type **1312**	20	10
4732	10c. Tram No. 276	30	15
4733	15c. Tram with two doors	40	20
4734	65c. Grey tram	1·80	95
4735	75c. Smaller orange tram	2·10	1·10
MS4736	110×81 mm. $1 Green tram (40×32 mm)	3·00	2·40

1313 Mexico Cathedral

2004. Bi-National (Cuba—Mexico) Philatelic Exhibition. Sheet 81×100 mm.

MS4737	**1313**	$1 multicoloured	3·00	2·40

1314 Burgos Pointer

2004. Espana 2004 International Stamp Exhibition. Dogs. Multicoloured.

4738	5c. Type **1314**	20	10
4739	10c. Small Spanish hound	30	15
4740	15c. Malloquin bulldog	40	20
4741	65c. Catalan sheepdog	1·80	95
4742	75c. Pyrenean mastiff	2·10	1·10
MS4743	103×82 mm. $1 Spanish mastiff	2·50	1·90

1315 Cascarita and Julio Cuevas (singers)

2004. 40th Anniv of Egrem Record Company. Singers. Multicoloured.

4744	10c. Type **1315**	30	15
4745	15c. Carlos Puebla	40	20
4746	65c. Benny More	1·80	95
4747	75c. Compay Segundo	2·10	1·10

1316 Police Cars

2004. 45th Anniv of State Security Department.

4748	**1316**	15c. multicoloured	50	30

1317 Children and Fidel Castro playing Chess

2004. National Sports Olympiad. Sheet 111×86 mm.

MS4749	**1317**	$1 multicoloured	2·50	1·90

1318 "Antonio Nunez Jimenez" (Oswaldo Guayasamin)

2004. 10th Anniv of Antonio Nunez Jimenez Foundation for Nature and Man.

4750	**1318**	65c. multicoloured	2·10	1·10

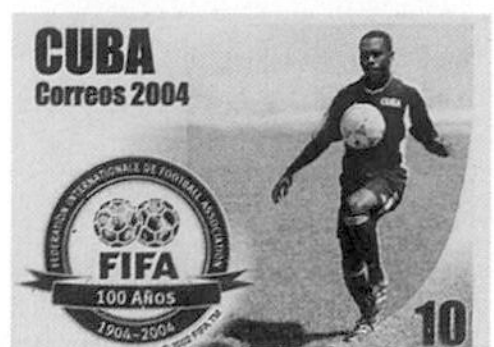
1319 Footballer

2004. Centenary of FIFA (Federation Internationale de Football Association). Multicoloured.

4751	10c. Type **1319**	30	15
4752	15c. Goalkeeper	40	20
4753	65c. No. 10 player	1·80	95
4754	75c. No. 3 player	2·10	1·10

1320 Maria Teresa Mora

2004. 80th Anniv of International Chess Federation. Multicoloured.

4755	15c. Type **1320**	40	20
4756	65c. Jose Raul Capablanca (horiz)	1·80	95
4757	75c. Ernesto "Che" Guevara	2·10	1·10

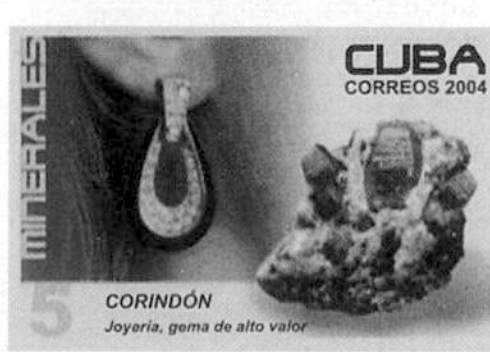
1321 Corundum

2004. Minerals. Multicoloured.

4758	5c. Type **1321**	20	10
4759	10c. Thenardite	30	15
4760	15c. Uranium	40	20
4761	65c. Realgar	1·80	95
4762	75c. Fluoride	2·10	1·10
MS4763	86×112 mm. $1 Copper	3·00	2·40

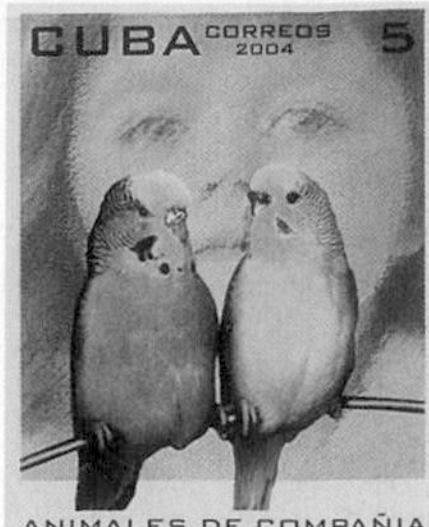
1322 Budgerigars

2004. Pets. Multicoloured.

4764	5c. Type **1322**	20	10
4765	10c. Fish	30	15
4766	15c. Dogs	40	20
4767	65c. Cats	1·80	95
4768	75c. Finches	2·10	1·10
MS4769	105×82 mm. $1 Horse (40×32 mm)	3·50	3·00

1323 Building Facade

2004. 25th Anniv of Convention Centre.

4770	**1323**	65c. multicoloured	2·10	1·20

1324 Lockheed Constellation

2004. 75th Anniv of Cubana Airline. Multicoloured.

4771	15c. Type **1324**	40	20
4772	65c. Ilyushin IL62M	1·80	95
4773	75c. Airbus 330	2·10	1·10

1325 Coastline, Map of Cuba and Tern

2004. America. Environmental Protection. Mult.

4774	15c. Type **1325**	50	30
4775	65c. Fish, reef and map	2·10	1·10

2004. Marine Mammals. Multicoloured.

4776	5c. Type **1326**	20	10
4777	10c. *Lagenorhynchus obliquidens*	30	15
4778	15c. *Stenella attenuate*	40	20
4779	65c. *Grampus griseus*	1·80	95
4780	75c. *Tursiops truncates*	2·10	1·10
MS4781	110×86 mm. $1 *Orcinus orca* (40×32 mm)	3·50	3·00

1327 Camilo Cienfuegos

2004. 45th Anniv of Disappearance of Camilo Cienfuegos (revolutionary).

4782	**1327**	65c. multicoloured	2·10	1·30

1328 Locomotive ALCO No. 48 4-6-0 (Agramonte) (1906)

2004. Centenary of Railway Stations. Multicoloured.

4783	15c. Type **1328**	40	20
4784	65c. BLW No. 57 4-6-0 (Aguacate) (1907)	1·80	95
4785	75c. ALCO No. 7 4-4-0 (Guira De Melina) (1903)	2·10	1·10

1329 Panorama Hotel

2004. Philatelic Congress. 40th Anniv of Cuban Philatelic Federation. Sheet 85×110 mm.

MS4786	**1329** $1 multicoloured	2·50	1·90

1330 El Templete (monument) (site of founding of Havana)

2004. 485th Anniv of San Cristobal de la Habana. Multicoloured.

4787	15c. Type **1330**	40	20
4788	65c. Preaching under ceiba tree (painting)	1·80	95
4789	75c. Founding of Havana (painting)	2·10	1·10

1331 Building Facade

2004. 40th Anniv of Latin American Parliament.

4790	**1331** 65c. multicoloured	1·90	1·20

1332 Ministry Building and Raul Roa (minister 1959—73)

2004. 45th Anniv of Ministry of Foreign Affairs.

4791	**1332** 65c. multicoloured	1·90	1·20

1333 Alejo Carpentier

2004. Birth Centenary of Alejo Carpentier (writer).

4792	**1333** 65c. multicoloured	1·90	1·20

1334 Rey Vicente Anglada

2004. 130th Anniv of Official Baseball Championships. Showing players. Multicoloured.

4793	5c. Type **1334**	20	10
4794	10c. Braudilio Vincent	30	15
4795	15c. Rogelio Garcia	40	20
4796	65c. Luis Casanova	1·80	95
4797	75c. Victor Mesa	2·10	1·10
MS4798	111×87 mm. $1 Martin Dihigo (32×40 mm)	3·00	2·40

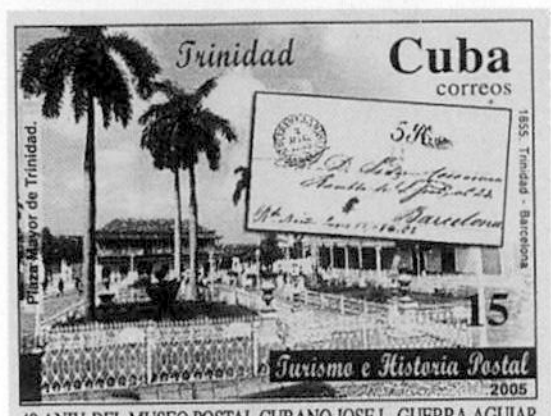

1335 Mayor de Trinidad Plaza and 1865 Trinidad—Barcelona Letter

2005. Tourism and Postal History. 40th Anniv of Postal Museum. Multicoloured.

4799	15c. Type **1335**	40	20
4800	65c. Caridad del Cobre Sanctuary and 1861 El Cobre—Santiago de Cuba letter	2·10	1·10
4801	75c. Matanzas Cathedral and 1848 Matanzas—Havana letter	2·40	1·40

1336 Rooster

2005. New Year. The Year of the Rooster. Multicoloured.

4802	15c. Type **1336**	50	30
4803	15c. Rooster jumping	50	30

1337 Woman, Child and Symbols of Communication (image scaled to 68% of original size)

2005. 5th Anniv of Ministry of Information and Communications.

4804	**1337** 65c. multicoloured	2·10	1·10

1338 Miguel de Cervantes

2005. 400th Anniv of "The Ingenious Hidalgo Don Quixote of La Mancha" (novel written by Miguel de Cervantes y Saavedra).

4805	**1338** 65c. multicoloured	2·10	1·10

1339 Carnotaurus

2005. Pre-Historic Animals. Multicoloured. Litho.

4806	5c. Type **1339**	20	10
4807	10c. Oviraptor	30	15
4808	30c. Parasaurlophus	1·00	50
4809	65c. Sauropelta	2·10	1·10
4810	90c. Iguanodon	2·40	1·20
MS4811	110×86 mm.1p. Velociraptor (40×32 mm)	2·50	1·90

1340 Bacunayagua Bridge

2005. Bridges. Multicoloured.

4812	10c. Type **1340**	30	15
4813	15c. La Concordia	40	20
4814	50c. El Triunfo	1·70	85
4815	65c. Yayabo	2·10	1·10
4816	75c. Canimar	2·40	1·40
MS4817	110×86 mm.1p. Plaza (40×32 mm)	2·50	1·90

1341 *Amazona ochrocephala* and *Amazona leucocephala*

2005. Parrots. Multicoloured.

4818	5c. Type **1341**	20	10
4819	10c. *Agapornis personata* and *Agapornis fischeri*	30	15
4820	15c. *Cactua galerita* and *Cacatua leadbeateri*	40	20
4821	65c. *Psittacula krameri* and *Psittacula himalayana* (vert)	2·10	1·10
4822	75c. *Aratinga guarouba* and *Aratinga euops*	2·40	1·40
MS4823	86×110 mm.1p. *Ara macao* (32×40 mm)	2·50	1·90

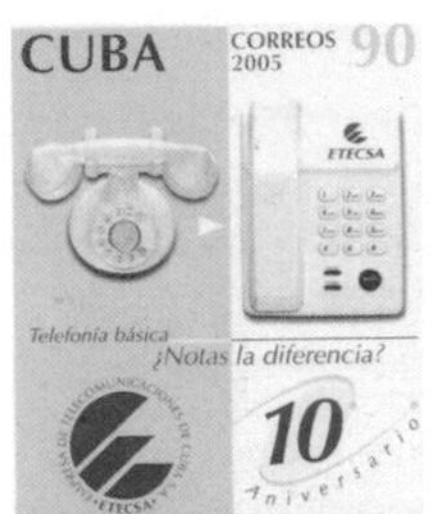

1342 Telephone Handsets

2005. 10th Anniv (2004) of ETECSA.

4824	**1342** 90c. multicoloured	2·50	1·10

1343 Cat

2005. Cats. Multicoloured.

4825	5c. Type **1343**	20	10
4826	10c. Washing (*vert*)	30	15
4827	40c. Hunting	60	30
4828	65c. Two cats	1·80	95
4829	75c. Mother and kitten	2·10	1·10
MS4830	91×100 mm. 1p.Two kittens (32×40 mm)	3·00	2·40

1344 Plaza de la Revolution, Cuba and Canadian Parliamentary Building

2005. 60th Anniv of Cuba–Canada Diplomatic Relations.

4831	**1344** 65c. multicoloured	1·80	95

1345 Manatee (As No. 2767)

2005. Fauna.

4832	**1345**	15c. brown	40	20
4833	-	65c. carmine	1·80	95
4834	-	75c. green	2·10	1·10
4835	-	90c. blue	2·50	1·90

DESIGNS: 15c.Type 1345; 65c. Cuban conure (As No. 2764); 75c. Crocodile (As No. 2768); 90c. Cuban emerald (As Type **745**).

1346 Waterfall

2005. World Water Day.

4836	**1346** 90c. multicoloured	2·50	1·90

1347 Yacht ('Balandro')

2005. Fishing and Merchant Shipping. Multicoloured.

4837	10c. Type **1347**	30	15
4838	20c. Schooner ('Goleta')	35	15
4839	30c. Bonito fishing boat ('Bonitero')	1·00	50
4840	45c. Shrimp boat ('Cameronero')	1·10	55
4841	90c. Lobster boat ('Langostero')	2·50	1·10
MS4842	81×102 mm. 1p. Ferry ('Transbordador') (40×32 mm)	1·50	1·90

1348 1855 ½r. Stamp (No. 1) and San Francisco de Asis Convent

2005. 150th Anniv of First Stamp. Multicoloured.

4843	15c. Type **1348**	40	20
4844	65c. 1855 1r. Stamp (No. 2) and Castillo de los Tres Reyes del Morro, Havana	2·10	1·10
4845	75c. 1855 2r. Stamp (No. 3) and first colonial Postal building	2·40	1·40

1349 People

2005. Social Security for All.

4846	**1349** 65c. multicoloured	2·10	1·10

1350 Locomotive DSB B 40, 1869

2005. Locomotives. Multicoloured.

4847	5c. Type **1350**	20	10
4848	10c. Great Northern locomotive, 1902	20	10
4849	15c. 2-8-2T Minaret locomotive, 1929	40	20
4850	15c. 0-4-2T C. F. White locomotive, 1885	40	20
4851	2p.05 WP FP7A 805D locomotive	4·75	3·75
MS4852	111×86 mm. 1p. Inscr 'XIV No. 4 Krauss & Co, 1884' (40×32 mm)	2·50	1·90

1351 Maximo Gomez

2005. Death Centenary of Maximo Gomez y Baez (military commander).

4853	**1351**	1p.05 multicoloured	2·50	1·90

1352 Castillo del Morro and Flower

2005. 490th (2004) Anniv of Foundation of Santiago de Cuba. Multicoloured.

4854	75c. Type **1352**	2·40	1·40
MS4855	111×86 mm. 1p. Casa de Diego Velaquez de Cuellar (Spanish conquistador, governor of Cuba 1511–1524) (40×32 mm)	2·50	1·90

1353 Elephant

2005. National Zoo. Multicoloured.

4856	10c. Type **1353**	20	10
4857	15c. Cheetah (horiz)	40	20
4858	50c. Water buffalo (horiz)	1·75	85
4859	65c. Giraffe	2·10	1·10
4860	75c. Lion	2·40	1·10
MS4861	111×87 mm. 1p. Zebra (40×32 mm)	2·50	1·90

1354 Flags and Emblem

2005. Venezuela 2005–Festival of Youth and Students.

4862	**1354**	65c. multicoloured	2·10	1·10

1355 Cuban Flag and Son Dancers

2005. National Dances. Multicoloured.

4863	65c. Type **1355**	2·10	1·10
4864	65c. Brazilian flag and Samba dancers	2·10	1·10

Stamps of a similar design were issued by Brazil.

1356 Arnaldo Tamayo Mendez

2005. 25th Anniv of Joint Cuba–Russia Space Flight. Multicoloured.

4865	90c. Type **1356**	2·40	1·20
4866	90c. Yuri Romanenko	2·40	1·20

Nos. 4865/6 were issued together, se-tenant, forming a composite background design.

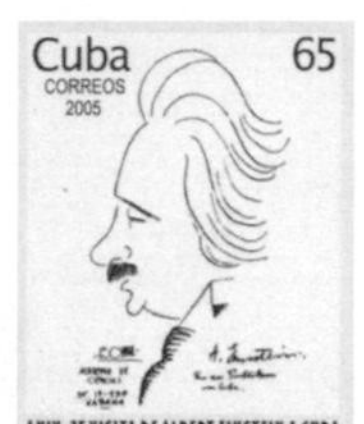
1357 Albert Einstein (sketch)

2005. 25th Anniv of Albert Einstein's Visit to Cuba. Multicoloured.

4867	**1357**	65c. black and yellow	2·10	1·10
4868	-	75c. multicoloured	2·40	1·40

DESIGNS: 65c. Type **1357**; 75c. Einstein writing.

1358 Emblem, Presidential Palace and Fidel Castro (image scaled to 69% of original size)

2005. 45th Anniv of Committee for the Defence of the Revolution.

4869	**1358**	50c. multicoloured	1·70	85

1359 Great Wall, China and Castillo de los Tres Reyes del Morro, Cuba

2005. 45th Anniv of Cuba–China Diplomatic Relations. Multicoloured.

4870	15c. Type **1359**	40	20
4871	15c. Presidents Hu Jintao and Fidel Castro	40	20

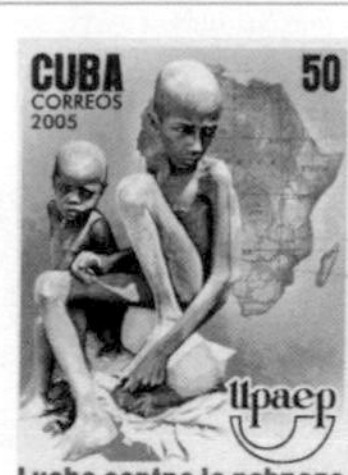
1360 Starving Children

2005. America. Struggle against Poverty. Multicoloured.

4872	50c. Type **1360**	1·75	80
4873	75c. Mother and child	2·40	1·40

1361 Saragossa College and Jose Marti, 1871

2005. Jose Marti (writer and revolutionary) Commemoration. Multicoloured.

4874	5c. Type **1361**	20	10
4875	5c. With Fermin Dominguez and Principal Theatre, Saragossa, 1872	20	10
4876	5c. Central College, Madrid, 1871	20	10
4877	10c. Victor Hugo's house, Paris, 1872	30	15
4878	10c. Moneda No. 12, Mexico City, 1875	30	15
4879	15c. School, Guatemala City, 1876	40	20
4880	15c. Plaza de Guardiola, Mexico City, 1894	40	20
4881	15c. San Idefonso No. 40, Mexico City, 1894	40	20
4882	65c. Plaza Bolivar, Caracas, 1885	2·10	1·10
4883	75c. Santa Maria College, Caracas, 1893	2·40	1·40
MS4884	1121×82 mm. 1p. Speaking to Martinez Ybor's tobacco workers, Tampa, 1892 (40×32 mm)	2·50	1·90

1362 Inscr 'Gelderlander'

2005. Horses. Multicoloured.

4885	10c. Type **1362**	30	15
4886	15c. Inscr 'Arabe'	40	20
4887	50c. Quarter horse	1·70	85
4888	65c. Inscr 'Cimarrones'	2·10	1·10
4889	75c. Lipizzaner	2·40	1·40
MS4890	103×79 mm. 1p. Holstein (32×40 mm)	2·50	1·90

1363 Flag, Emblem, Globe, Computer and Family

2005. World Information Society Summit, Tunis.

4891	**1363**	75c. multicoloured	2·40	1·40

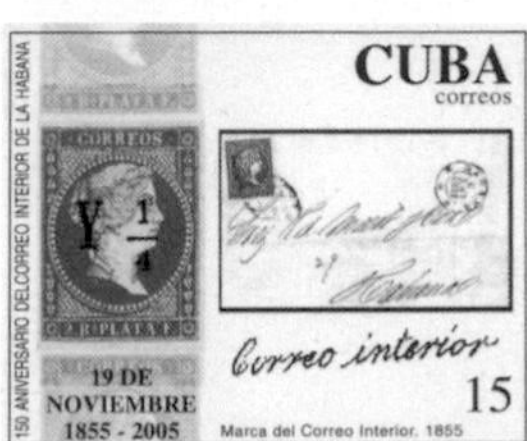
1364 1855 Y¼. Stamp (No. 4) and Cover

2005. 150th Anniv of First Local Delivery, Havana. Multicoloured.

4892	15c. Type **1364**	40	20
4893	65c. 1862 ¼r. Stamp (No. 13) and Colonial mailbox	2·10	1·10

1365 Prisoners

2005

4894	**1365**	65c. multicoloured	2·10	1·10

1366 1962 5p. of Spain Stamp and Castillo de la Real Fuerza

2005. 50th Anniv of Europa Stamps. Multicoloured.

4895	1p.30 Type **1366**	2·90	1·50
4896	2p.05 1961 1p. of Spain and Santisima Trinidad Church	4·75	2·50
4897	2p.55 1968 3p.50 of Spain and Castillo de Morro, Santiago de Cuba	6·00	3·00
4898	3p.90 1964 5p. of Spain and San Cristobal Cathedral, Havana	9·00	4·50
MS4899	121×97 mm. Nos. 4895/8	22·00	16·00

1367 Silver and Ebony Cross

2005. Jewellery. Multicoloured.

4900	5c. Type **1367**	20	10
4901	10c. Silver pendant	30	15
4902	45c. Silver and garnet necklace	1·10	55
4903	65c. Silver and ruby pendant	2·10	1·10
4904	75c. Silver, amber and ebony pendan	2·40	1·40
MS4905	111×86 mm. 1p. Gold, diamond and black enamel pendant (32×40 mm)	2·50	1·90

1368 Institute Building

2005. 45th Anniv of Instituto Cubano de Amistad con los Pueblos (the Cuban Institute for Friendship with the People).

4906	**1368**	1p.05 multicoloured	2·00	1·00

1369 *Clathrus cancellatus*

2005. Fungi and Snails. Multicoloured.

4907	10c. Type **1369**	30	15
4908	20c. *Polymita picta*	60	30
4909	30c. *Lepiota puellaris*	1·00	50
4910	65c. *Polymita muscarum*	2·10	1·10
4911	75c. *Clitocybe infundibuliformis*	2·40	1·40
MS4912	111×86 mm. 1p. *Polymita versicolor* (40×32 mm)	2·50	1·90

1370 Hotel Facade

2005. 130th Anniv of Hotel Inglaterra.

4913	**1370**	65c. multicoloured	2·10	1·10

1371 Pug ('Carlino')

2006. New Year. The Year of the Dog. Multicoloured.

4914	15c. Type **1371**	40	20
4915	15c. Shih Tzu	40	20

1372 Emblems

2006. 40th Anniv of Organizacion de Solidaridad con los Pueblos de Asia, Africa y America Latina (Organization of Solidarity with the People of Asia, Africa and Latin America).

4916	**1372**	65c. multicoloured	2·10	1·10

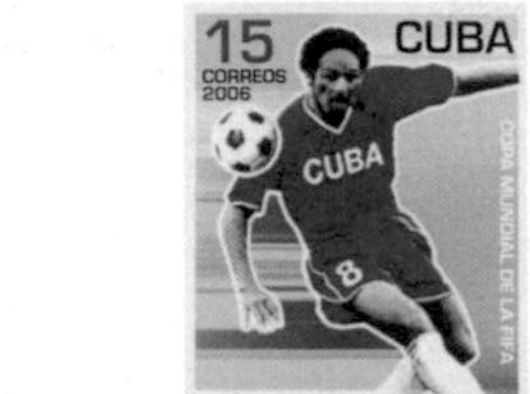

1373 Cuba No. 8 Player

2006. World Cup Football Championships, Germany. Designs showing Cuban footballers. Multicoloured.

4917	15c. Type **1373**	40	20
4918	45c. No. 5 player	1·10	55
4919	65c. Player wearing red and white strip	2·10	1·10
4920	75c. No. 4 player	2·40	1·40

1374 Cover and Post Rider

2006. 250th Anniv of Cuban Postal Service. Multicoloured.

4921	75c. Type **1374**	2·40	1·40
4922	2p.05 Ship and cover	4·75	2·50
MS4923	86×112 mm. 1p. *El Ritmo Cubano* (statue) (F. Gelabert) (Havana 06 International Philatelic Exhibition) (40×32 mm)	2·50	1·90

1375 Maria del Carmen Wastewater Treatment Plant

2006. 30th Anniv of OPEC Development Fund.

4924	**1375**	75c. multicoloured	2·40	1·40

1376 Congregation receiving Mass at Higher Institute of Physical Training, Santa Clara and Pope John Paul II (image scaled to 69% of original size)

2006. 1st Death Anniv of Pope John Paul II. Designs showing Pope John Paul II saying Mass. Multicoloured.

4925	65c. Type **1376**	2·10	1·10
4926	75c. Plaza Ignacio Agramonte, Camaguey (46×30 mm)	2·40	1·40
4927	90c. Plaza Antonio Maceo, Santiago de Cuba (46×30 mm)	2·50	1·10
4928	1p.05 Pope John Paul II and congregation receiving Mass at Plaza Jose Marti, Havana	2·50	1·90

1377 Teodoro Perez's House, Cayo Hueso, 1893

2006. 10th Anniv of Jose Marti Cultural Society. Sheet 111×82 mm.

MS4929	1p. multicoloured	2·50	1·90

1378 Flag, Rifle and Fatigues

2006. 45th Anniv of Bay of Pigs (Playa Giron).

4930	**1378**	65c. multicoloured	2·10	1·10

2006. Jose Marti (writer and revolutionary) Commemoration. As T 1361. Multicoloured.

4931	5c. 116 West Street, New York, Gonzalo de Quesada and Jose Marti, 1893	20	10
4932	5c. Hotel de Madame Griffou, New York, 1890	20	10
4933	10c. 324 Classon Ave, New York and Jose Marti seated with his son, 1885	30	15
4934	10c. Masonic Temple, New York, 1888	30	15
4935	15c. Cajobabo Beach, Oriente and Gomez inscribed on stone	40	20
4936	15c. Marti inscribed on stone and Dos Rios, Oriente	40	20
4937	75c. Hardman Hall, New York, 1891	2·40	1·40
4938	85c. 120 Front Street, New York, 1891	2·50	1·50
4939	90c. Jose Marti seated with Maria Mantilla and Bath Beach, Long Island, 1890	2·50	1·10

Nos. 4935/6 were issued together, se-tenant, forming a composite design.

1379 Yangchuanosaurus

2006. Pre-historic Animals. Multicoloured.

4940	5c. Type **1379**	20	10
4941	10c. Spinosaurus	30	15
4942	30c. Pachycephalosaurus	1·00	50
4943	35c. Muttaburrasaurus	1·20	60
4944	65c. Stegosaurus	2·10	1·10
4945	1p.05 Saichania	2·50	1·90
MS4946	109×88 mm. 1p. Stenonychosaurus (32×40 mm)	2·50	1·90

1380 Statue and Flags

2006. 45th Anniv of Ministry of Interior.

4947	**1380**	75c. multicoloured	2·40	1·40

1381 Chickens

2006. Domesticated Fowl. Multicoloured.

4948	5c. Type **1381**	20	10
4949	15c. Guinea fowl	40	20
4950	15c. Turkeys	40	20
4951	45c. Geese	1·10	55
4952	50c. Golden pheasant	1·70	85
4953	75c. Peacock	2·40	1·40
MS4954	109×88 mm. 1p. Duck (40×32 mm)	2·50	1·50

1382 *Cerro Pelado*

2006. 40th Anniv of Voyage of Cerro Pelado taking Cuban Athletes to Central American and Caribbean Games, Puerto Rico. Multicoloured.

4955	65c. Type **1382**	2·10	1·10
4956	75c. Athletes in cargo crate	2·40	1·40
4957	85c. Disembarking	2·50	1·50

1383 Centre Building

2006. 20th Anniv of Biotech Centre.

4958	**1383**	65c. multicoloured	2·10	1·10

1384 *Pucho y sus Perrerias* (image scaled to 69% of original size)

2006. Cartoons by Virgillo Martinez. Multicoloured.

4959	15c. Type **1384**	40	20
4960	65c. *Cucho*	2·10	1·10

1385 Granville Gee Bee R2

2006. Aircraft. Multicoloured.

4961	10c. Type **1385**	30	15
4962	15c. Comte AC-4 Gentleman	40	20
4963	15c. Bucker Jungmann	40	20
4964	50c. Mustang TF 51	1·70	85
4965	75c. Spitfire Supermarine MK	2·40	1·40
4966	85c. Lavochkin La-9 (Inscr 'Lavochkine')	2·50	1·50
MS4967	111×85 mm. 1p. Bucker Jungmann (different) (40×32 mm). Imperf	2·50	1·90

1386 Bulldog

2006. Dogs. Multicoloured.

4968	5c. Type **1386**	20	10
4969	10c. American cocker spaniel	30	15
4970	15c. Sharpei	40	20
4971	20c. Airedale terrier	60	30
4972	35c. Pomeranian	1·20	60
4973	2p.05 Dalmatian	4·75	2·50
MS4974	86×112 mm. 1p. Whippet (32×40 mm)	2·50	1·90

1387 'Che' Guevara and Emblem

2006. 45th Anniv of Recycling. Multicoloured.

4975	15c. Type **1387**	40	20
4976	65c. Flags and '45'	2·10	1·10

1388 Statue and Cuban Coat of Arms

2006. 7th Cuban–Spanish Philatelic Exhibition. Sheet 86×111 mm containing T 1388 and similar vert design. Multicoloured.

MS4977	50c.×2, Type **1388**; Statue and Spanish coat of arms	3·25	2·10

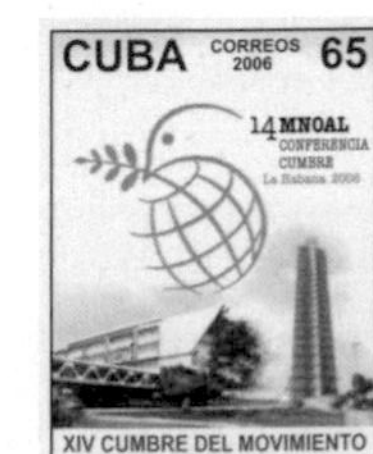

1389 Emblem and Buildings

2006. 14th Non-Aligned Movement Summit.

4978	**1389**	65c. multicoloured	2·10	1·10

1390 Pedro Santacilia (Cuban poet), Casa de Mexico, Habana Vieja and Benito Juarez (image scaled to 69% of original size)

2006. Birth Bicentenary of Benito Juarez.

4979	**1390**	65c. multicoloured	2·10	1·10

1391 Rio Hanabanilla

2006. Espana 06 International Philatelic Exhibition, Malaga. Multicoloured.

4980	5c. Type **1391**	20	10
4981	10c. Laguna Boconao	30	15
4982	15c. Sierra de la Gran Piedra	40	20
4983	20c. Valle de los Ingenios	60	30
4984	50c. Laguno del Tesoro	1·70	85
4985	75c. Sierra Maestra	2·40	1·40
MS4986	111×85 mm. 1p. Villa de Vinales (40×32 mm)	2·50	1·90

1392 Horses

2006. Animals in the Service of Man. Multicoloured.

4987	5c. Type **1392**	20	10

4988	15c. Camels	40	20
4989	30c. Goats	1·00	50
4990	40c. Llamas	1·20	60
4991	50c. Cats	1·70	85
4992	1p.05 Elephants	2·50	1·90
MS4993	111×87 mm. 1p. Dogs (40×32 mm)	2·50	1·90

1393 Solar Panels

2006. America. Energy Conservation. Multicoloured.

4994	65c. Type **1393**	2·10	1·10
4995	65c. Hydro-electric generator	2·10	1·10
4996	65c. Oil field	2·10	1·10
4997	65c. Wind turbines	2·10	1·10

1394 Luis and Sergio Saíz Montes de Oca

2006. 20th Anniv of Saiz Brothers Association of Young Writers and Artists.

4998	**1394**	75c. multicoloured	2·40	1·40

1395 Alicia Alonso and Igor Youskevitch

2006. 20th International Ballet Festival, Havana. Multicoloured.

4999	75c. Type **1395**	2·40	1·40
5000	85c. Alicia Alonso	2·50	1·50

1396 Stephenson's *Rocket* and Inter-city Diesel Electric Locomotive

2006. Belgica 06 International Juvenile Philatelic Exhibition. Locomotives.

5001	5c. Type **1396**	20	10
5002	10c. Turbine locomotive and diesel electric	30	15
5003	15c. *Shinkasen* electric locomotive and *City of Los Angeles* diesel electric	40	20
5004	65c. Steam and diesel locomotives	2·10	1·10
5005	75c. TEE integrated diesel electric locomotive and *TGV*electric	2·40	1·40
5006	85c. Electric monorail locomotive, Brisbane and first monorail, Wuppertal, 1901	2·50	1·50
MS5007	102×94 mm. Size 40×32 mm. 50c.×2,. Steam locomotive; Diesel locomotive	3·25	2·10

1397 Emblem

2006. Telefood.

5008	**1397**	75c. multicoloured	2·40	1·40

1398 Horse-drawn Ambulance, Brazil, 1899

2006. Fire Fighting and Rescue Equipment. Multicoloured.

5009	5c. Type **1398**	20	10
5010	10c. Merry Weather pump, England, 1898	30	15
5011	20c. Laurin & Klement appliance, Czech Republic, 1910	60	30
5012	45c. Motor cycle appliance, UK, 1925	1·10	55
5013	90c. Ladder, Germany, 1930	2·50	1·10
MS5014	87×102 mm. 1p. Fire-fighter (32×40 mm)	2·50	1·90

1399 Frank Pais (revolutionary)

2006. 50th Anniv of Santiago de Cuba Uprising.

5015	**1399**	65c. multicoloured	2·10	1·10

1400 Tank and Medal

2006. 50th Anniversaries. Multicoloured.

5016	65c. Type **1400** (Revolutionary Armed Forces)	2·10	1·10
5017	65c. *Granma* (landing of revolutionary fighters)	2·10	1·10

1401 Flag, Jose Marti and Emblem

2006. 30th Anniv of People Power.

5018	**1401**	75c. multicoloured	2·40	1·40

1402 Globe and Camera

2006. 20th Anniv of Film and Television School.

5019	**1402**	75c. multicoloured	2·40	1·40

1403 Gonzalo de Queseda y Arostegui and Gonzalo De Queseda y Miranda (founder) (image scaled to 69% of original size)

2006. 55th Anniv of Fragua Martiana Museum.

5020	**1403**	90c. multicoloured	2·50	1·10

1404 Students raising Flag

2006. 45th Anniv of Literacy Campaign.

5021	**1404**	65c. multicoloured	2·10	1·10

1405 Birthplace and Ignacio Agramonte y Loinaz

2006. 165th Birth Anniv of Ignacio Agramonte y Loinaz (revolutionary leader).

5022	**1405**	65c. multicoloured	2·10	1·10

1409 Map, Globe and Telephone Handset (image scaled to 68% of original size)

2007. International Information Convention and Exhibition.

5032	**1409**	75c. multicoloured	2·10	2·10

No. 5023 and Type **1406** have been left for '45th Anniv of Special Education', issued on 4 January 2007, not yet received.

Nos. 5024/30 and Type **1407** have been left for 'Trains', issued on 18 January 2007, not yet received.

No. 5031 and Type **1408** have been left for '125th Anniv of Pharmacy', issued on 18 January 2007, not yet received.

1410 Two Kittens

2007. Cats. Multicoloured.

5033	10c. Type **1410**	30	15
5034	15c. Tabby and white kitten	40	20
5035	15c. Ginger tabby	40	20
5036	50c. Ginger and white cat and telephone handset	1·50	80
5037	75c. Black and white cat and ball	2·10	2·10
5038	90c. Silver tabby	2·75	2·20
MS5039	111×87 mm. 1p. Ragdoll. Imperf	3·00	2·40

1411 Pigeon and Emblem

2007. 5th Cuban Pigeon Fanciers Congress.

5040	**1411**	75c. multicoloured	2·10	2·10

1412 Mast Head

2007. 115th Anniv of Patria Newspaper. Sheet 111×87 mm.

MS5041	multicoloured	3·00	2·40

1413 *Ara ararauna* (blue-and-yellow macaw)

2007. National Zoo. Multicoloured.

5042	5c. Type **1413**	20	10
5043	10c. *Testudo elephantopus* (giant land tortoise)	30	15
5044	15c. *Balearica regulorum* (grey crowned crane)	40	20
5045	20c. *Procyon lotor* (raccoon)	50	30
5046	45c. *Panthera pardus* (leopard)	1·10	60
5047	2p.05 *Pongo pygmaeus* (orangutan)	6·00	4·75
MS5048	111×87 mm. 1p. *Giraffa camelopardalis* (giraffe). Imperf	3·00	2·40

1414 Julio Mella, Camilo Cienfuegaos and Ernesto 'Che' Guevera

2007. 45th Anniv of Young Communist Union.

5049	**1414**	75c. multicoloured	2·10	2·10

2007. Jose Marti (writer and revolutionary) Commemoration. As T 1361 Multicoloured.

5050	5c. Liceo Cubano (Cuban high school), Tampa and Jose Marti, 1892	30	15
5051	5c. Casa de los Pedroso, Tampa, 1892	30	15
5052	10c. Hotel Duval, Cayo Hueso, 1891	40	20
5053	10c. Hotel Cherokee, Tampa, 1891	40	20
5054	15c. Tabaqueria Hidalgo Gato, Cayo Hueso, Jose Marti and Valdes Dominguez, 1894	50	30
5055	15c. Jose Marti and Comite Organizador (organizing committee) de Cayo Hueso, 1891 (72×30 mm)	50	30
5056	35c. Club San Carlos, Cayo Hueso, 1893	75	40
5057	40c. Hotel Myrtle Bank, Kingston, 1892	90	50
5058	50c. Jose Marti, Gomez Toro and Sociedad del Pais, Santo Domingo, 1894	1·10	60
5059	65c. Casa de M. Gomez Montecristi, Jose Marti and Maximo Gomez	1·90	95

1415 Raul García

2007. Birth Centenary of Raul Roa Garcia (Foreign Minister 1959–1976).

5060	**1415**	65c. multicoloured	1·90	95

1416 Aguntamiento

2007. Historic Buildings, Cienfuegos. Multicoloured.

5061	15c. Type **1416**	40	20
5062	65c. San Lorenzo College	1·90	95
5063	75c. Tomas Terry Theatre	2·10	2·10
5064	85c. Palacio Ferrer	2·50	2·20
MS5065	111×87 mm. 1p. Jose Marti Park. Imperf	3·00	2·40

1417 Mother and Child

2007. 10th Anniv of National Children's Art Exhibition 'World Food Programme in Action'.

5066 **1417** 65c. multicoloured 1·90 95

1418 Statue

2007. 45th Anniv of Folklore Union.

5067 **1418** 75c. multicoloured 2·10 2·10

1419 Pelican, Cayo Guillermo

2007. Tourism. Islands and Wildlife. Multicoloured.

5068	5c. Type **1419**	40	20
5069	15c. Shells, Cayo Levisa	40	20
5070	15c. Gull, Cayo las Brujas	40	20
5071	20c. Iguana, Cayo Santa Maria	50	30
5072	50c. Plover (chorlito), Cayo Ensenachos	1·10	60
5073	85c. Hawksbill turtle (*Tortuga carey*), Cayo Largo	2·50	2·20
MS5074	111×87 mm. 1p. Carib bean flamingo, Cayo Coco. Imperf	3·00	2·40

1420 Benny More

2007. Son Cubano, Writers and Singers. Multicoloured.

5075	5c. Type **1420**	20	10
5076	10c. Ignacio Pineiro	40	20
5077	30c. Ignacio de Loyola Rodriguez Scull (Arsenio Rodriguez)	80	45
5078	35c. Miguelito Cuni	90	55
5079	65c. Pio Leyva	1·90	90
5080	75c. Ibrahim Ferrer	2·10	2·10
MS5081	111×87 mm. 1p. Miguel Matamoros. Imperf	3·00	2·40

1421 Jose Marti and Crowd, Vegas de Temple Hall, Jamaica

2007. 35th Anniv of Jose Marti Studies Youth Seminar. Sheet 111×87 mm.

MS5082 multicoloured 3·00 2·40

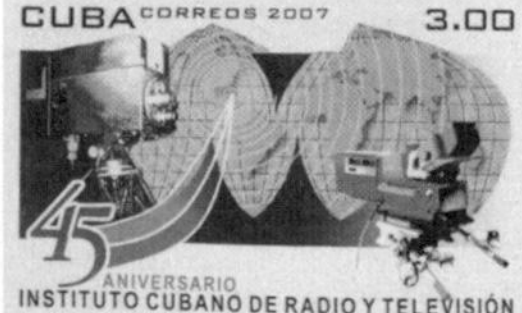

1422 Radio and Television Equipment

2007. 45th Anniv of Radio and Television Institute.

5083 **1422** 3p. multicoloured 9·00 7·25

1423 City Centre

2007. 20th Anniv of Capital Development Group.

5084 **1423** 65c. multicoloured 1·00 95

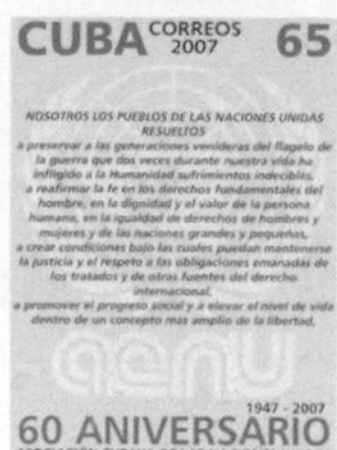

1424 'Nostros los Pueblos...'

2007. 60th Anniv of Cuban United Nations Association.

5085 **1424** 65c. multicoloured 1·90 95

1425 Fencing

2007. Pan American Games, Rio de Janeiro. Multicoloured.

5086	15c. Type **1425**	40	20
5087	15c. Boxing	40	20
5088	20c. Wrestling	55	35
5089	45c. Athletes	80	45
5090	65c. Gymnast	1·90	95
5091	75c. Cycling	2·40	2·40
MS5092	111×87 mm. 1p. Emblem. Imperf	3·00	2·40

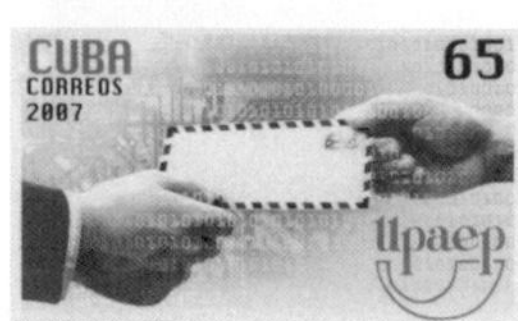

1426 Hands holding Envelope

2007. 3rd Technological Transfer and International Trade Workshop.

5093 **1426** 65c. multicoloured 1·90 95

1427 Frank Pais

2007. 50th Death Anniv of Frank Pais Garcia (revolutionary).

5094 **1427** 65c. multicoloured 1·90 95

1428 The Great Wall

2007. Seven Wonders of the Modern World. Multicoloured.

5095	10c. Type **1428**	30	15
5096	15c. Petra	40	20
5097	20c. *Christ the Redeemer* (statue), Rio de Janeiro	45	25
5098	40c. Machu Picchu, Urubamba Valley, Peru	90	50
5099	65c. Chichen Itza, Yucatan Peninsula, Mexico	1·90	95
5100	75c. Colosseum, Rome	2·10	2·10
5101	85c. Taj Mahal mausoleum, Agra, India	2·40	2·40

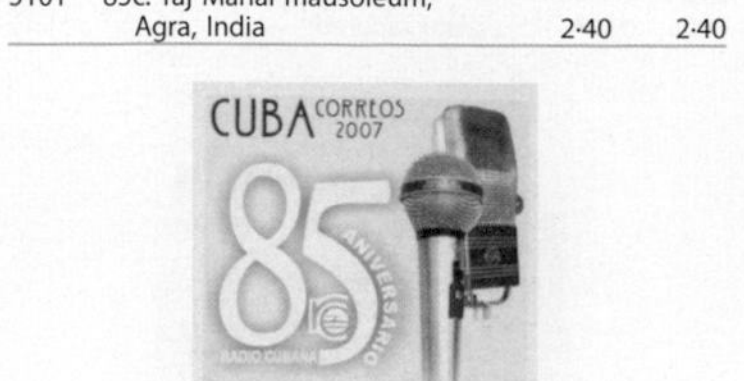

1429 Microphone

2007. 85th Anniv of Radio Cubana.

5102 **1429** 65c. multicoloured 1·90 95

1430 Coco Taxis

2007. Transport. Multicoloured.

5103	10c. Type **1430**	30	15
5104	15c. Lada taxi	40	20
5105	20c. Giron VI bus	50	30
5106	45c. Inscr 'El Camello con cuna international'	1·10	60
5107	65c. DAF articulated bus	1·90	95
5108	75c. Yutong bus	2·10	2·10
MS5109	111×80 mm. 1p. Inscr 'La Gaviota', Fance. Imperf	3·00	2·40

1431 Child and Computer

2007. 20th Anniv of Central Youth Club.

5110 **1431** 65c. multicoloured 1·90 95

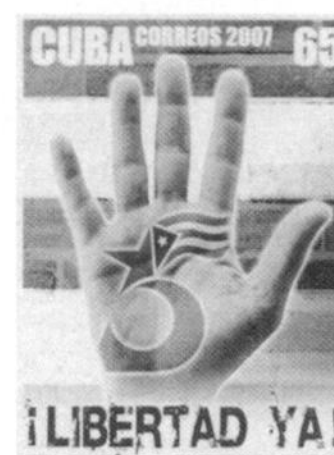

1432 Hand and Flag

2007. Prisoners. Multicoloured.

5111	65c. Type **1432**	1·90	95
5112	65c. Ramon Labanino Salazar	1·90	95
5113	65c. Fernando Gonzalez Llort	1·90	95
5114	65c. Rene Gonzalez Schwerert	1·90	95
5115	65c. Gerardo Hernadez Nordello	1·90	95
5116	65c. Antonio Guerrero Rodriguez	1·90	95

1433 Tree

2007. Tree Planting Campaign.

5117 **1433** 65c. multicoloured 1·90 95

1434 Pink Parfait

2007. Roses. Multicoloured.

5118	5c. Type **1434**	20	10
5119	15c. Alison Wheatcroft	40	20
5120	15c. Prima Ballerina	40	20
5121	45c. Fragrant Cloud	1·10	60
5122	50c. Blue Moon	1·40	1·00
5123	75c. Grandmere Jenny	2·10	2·10
MS5124	112×92 mm. 1p. *Rosa high-downensis*. Imperf	3·00	2·40

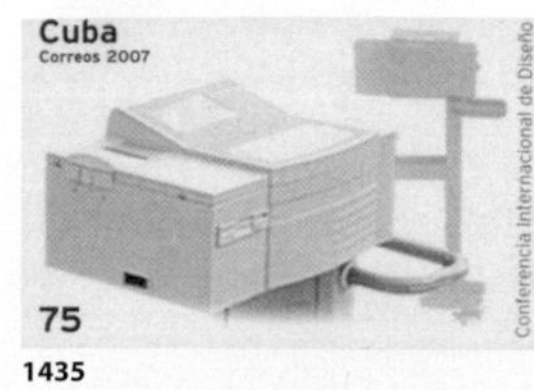

1435

2007. International Design Conference. Multicoloured.

5125 75c. Type **1435** 2·10 2·10

No. 5126 has been left for stamp not yet received.

1436 Ford Trimotor (three engine civil transport aircraft)

2007. 80th Anniv of Airmail from Cuba. National Philatelic Championship. Sheet 111×75 mm.

5127 **1436** 1p. multicoloured 3·00 2·40

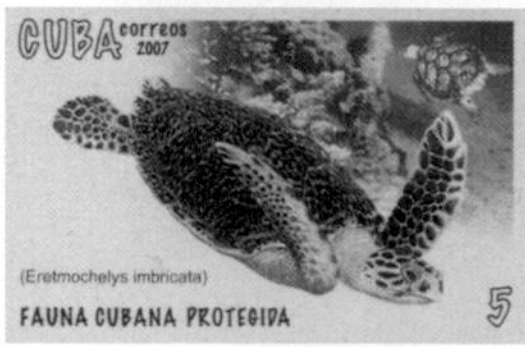

1437 *Eretmochelys imbricata* (hawksbill turtle)

2007. Endangered Species. Multicoloured.

5128	5c. Type **1437**	20	10
5129	10c. *Trichechus manatus* (West Indian manatee)	30	15
5130	20c. *Mesocapromys sanfelipensis* (San Felipe hutia)	50	30
5131	30c. *Mesocapromys nanus* (dwarf hutia)	60	40
5132	45c. *Epinephelus itajara* (Atlantic goliath grouper)	1·10	60
5133	85c. *Balistes vetula* (queen triggerfish)	2·40	2·10
MS5134	112×79 mm. 1p. *Chelonia mydas* (green turtle). Imperf	3·00	2·40

1438 Dancers (Tumba Francesa Society)

2007. 60th Anniv of Cuban UNESCO Commission.

5135 **1438** 65c. multicoloured 1·90 95

1439 Early Locomotive

2007. 170th Anniv of Railways.

5136 **1439** 3p. multicoloured 9·00 7·25

1440 Dancers and Tutor

2007. 40th Anniv of Ballet de Camaguey.
5137 **1440** 75c. multicoloured 2·10 2·10

1441 'infomed'

2007. 15th Anniv of Infomed Health Network.
5138 **1441** 65c. green and black 1·90 95

1442 Crowd and Flag

2007. 85th Anniv of Federation of University Students.
5139 **1442** 65c. multicoloured 1·90 95

1443 Albear Aqueduct

2007. Civil Engineering. Multicoloured.
5140 5c. Type **1443** 20 10
5141 10c. Alcantarillado sewer 30 15
5142 20c. Central Road, Santiago de Cuba 50 30
5143 30c. Harbor tunnel (Tunel de La Bahia) 60 40
5144 85c. Bacunayagua Bridge, Matanzas 2·40 2·10
5145 90c. La Farola viaduct, Guantánamo 2·75 2·50
MS5146 112×87 mm. 1p. FOSCA Building. Imperf 3·00 2·40

1444 Globe and Sun Rays

2007. 20th Anniv of World Ozone Protection Day.
5147 **1444** 65c. multicoloured 1·90 95

1445 *Atlantea perezi*

2007. Turnat 2007—Nature Tourism Congress. Multicoloured.
5148 75c. Type **1445** 2·10 2·10
5149 75c. *Polymita picta* 2·10 2·10
5150 75c. *Eleutherodactylus iberia* 2·10 2·10
5151 75c. *Solenodon cubanus* 2·10 2·10
Nos. 5148/9 and 5150/1, respectively, were each issued together, se-tenant, forming a composite design.

1446 Students and Parade

2007. America. Education for All. Multicoloured.
5152 75c. Type **1446** 2·10 2·10
5153 75c. Artist, students seated and man using computer 2·10 2·10
5154 75c. Teacher, children, students in uniform and girl using computer 2·10 2·10
5155 75c. Students at table and dance students 2·10 2·10
Nos. 5152/3 and 5154/5, respectively, were each issued together, se-tenant, forming a composite design.

1447 With other Guerrillas

2007. 40th Death Anniv of Ernesto 'Che' Guevara (revolutionary). Multicoloured.
5156 65c. Type **1447** 1·90 95
5157 75c. Memorial 2·10 2·10
5158 85c. Che Guevera 2·40 2·10
5159 90c. Protestors 2·75 2·50
MS5160 144×92 mm Nos. 5156/9 8·25 7·75

1448 Hall

2008. 280th Anniv of University of Havana.
5161 **1448** 65c. multicoloured 1·90 95

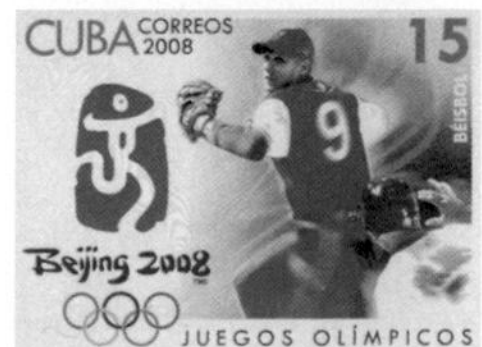

1449 Baseball

2008. Olympic Games, Beijing. Multicoloured.
5162 15c. Type **1449** 40 20
5163 45c. Swimming 1·10 65
5164 65c. Shot putt 1·90 95
5165 75c. Volleyball 2·10 2·10

2008. Jose Marti (writer and revolutionary) Commemoration. As T 1361 showing Jose Marti. Multicoloured.
5166 15c. Twilight Park, 1892 (vert) 40 20
5167 15c. With members of Cuban Revolutionary Party, 1892 (vert) 40 20
5168 30c. With family of Carmen Miyares, 1893 (vert) 60 40
5169 40c. Mausoleum, Cementerio Santa Efigenia, Santiago de Cuba (vert) 95 60
5170 45c. Tomb of Felix Varela and Jose Marti, 1892 (horiz) 1·10 90
5171 50c. Ulpiano Dellunde's House and Jose Marti, 1893 (horiz) 1·30 1·00
5172 65c. Hanabana Massacre Memorial (horiz) 1·90 95
5173 85c. Postal cover, 1889 (horiz) 2·40 2·10

1450 Paris

2008. Underground Railways. Designs showing locomotives and stations. Multicoloured.
5174 15c. Type **1450** 40 20
5175 15c. New York 40 20
5176 30c. Caracas 60 40
5177 65c. Madrid 1·90 95
5178 75c. Mexico 2·10 2·10
5179 1p.05 Tokyo 3·00 2·40
MS5180 112×100 mm. 50c.×2, Steam locomotive, 1866 ; Westminster underground. Imperf 3·00 2·40

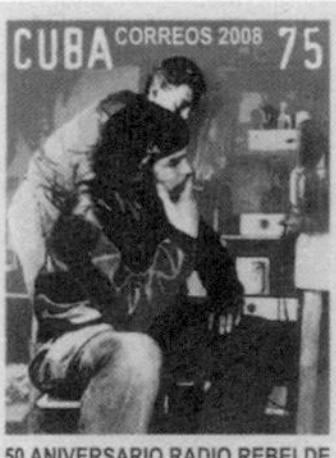

1451 Radio Station

2008. 50th Anniv of Radio Rebelde.
5181 **1451** 75c. multicoloured 2·10 2·10

1452 Helicopter and Soldier

2008. 45th Anniv of Frontier Guards.
5182 **1452** 65c. multicoloured 1·90 95

1452a Monument

2008. 50th Anniv of Frank Pais Second Front.
5182a **1452a** 65c. multicoloured 1·90 95

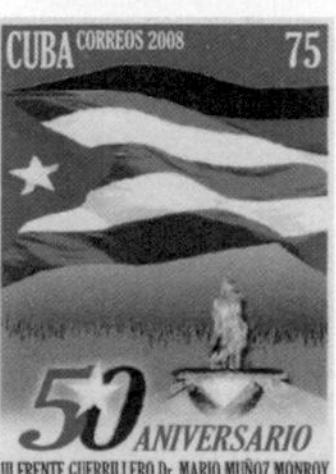

1453 Flag and Flame

2008. 50th Anniv of Mario Munoz Monroy Third Front.
5183 **1453** 75c. multicoloured 2·10 2·10

1454 *Hypophthalmichthys molitrix* (Inscr 'Hypophthalmicthys molitrix')

2008. Aquaculture. Multicoloured.
5184 15c. Type **1454** 40 20
5185 15c. *Cyprinus carpio* 40 20
5186 45c. *Aristichthys nobilis* 1·10 65
5187 65c. *Penaeus vannamei* 1·90 95
5188 75c. *Ctenopharyngodon idella* 2·10 2·10
5189 85c. *Clarias gariepinus* 2·40 2·10
MS5190 112×88 mm. 1p. *Oreochromis aurea*. Imperf 3·00 2·40

1455 Early Cover

2008. 130th Anniv of Postal Service. Sheet 85×105 mm.
MS5191 multicoloured 3·00 2·40

1455a Habana Riviera

2008. Gran Caribe Hotels Anniversaries. Multicoloured.
5192 5c. Type **1455a** (50th anniv) 20 10
5193 10c. Habana Libre (50th anniv) (vert) 30 15
5194 15c. Deauville (50th anniv) (vert) 40 20
5195 50c. Victoria (80th anniv) (vert) 1·30 1·00
5196 65c. Presidente (80th anniv) 1·90 95
MS5197 110×85 mm. 1p. Sevilla (vert). Imperf 3·00 2·40

1455b La Habana

2008. Tourism. Cultural Heritage–Towns and Cities. Multicoloured.
5198 15c. Type **1455b** 40 20
5199 15c. Trinidad 40 20
5200 30c. Sancti Spiritus 60 40
5201 65c. Camaguey 1·90 95
5202 75c. Bayamo 2·10 2·10
5203 85c. Santiago de Cuba 2·40 2·10
MS5204 110×85 mm. 1p. Baracoa. Imperf 3·00 2·40

1456 Front Cover

2008. Centenary of Bohemia Magazine.
5205 **1456** 65c. multicoloured. 1·90 95

1457 Carlos de la Torre and Hand holding Shells

2008. 150th Birth Anniv of Carlos de la Torre (naturalist). Multicoloured.
5206 5c. Type **1457** 20 10
5207 15c. *Polymita picta nigrolimbata* 40 20
5208 50c. *Polymita picta nigrolimbata* (different) 1·30 1·00
5209 65c. *Polymita picta iolimbata* 1·90 95
5210 75c. *Polymita picta nigrolimbata* (different) 2·10 2·10
5211 90c. *Polymita picta fuscolimbata* 2·75 2·50
MS5212 110×85 mm. 1p. *Liguus fasciatus* (39×31 mm). Imperf 3·00 2·40

1458 Tody (inscr 'Cartacuba')

2008. Natural History Museum. Multicoloured.

5213	5c. Type **1458**	10	10
5214	10c. Nightingale (inscr 'Ruisenor')	15	10
5215	15c. Green woodpecker (inscr 'Carpintero verde')	20	10
5216	50c. Tocororo (national bird)	85	50
5217	65c. Parrot (inscr 'Catey') (horiz)	1·00	60
5218	75c. Zapata sparrow (inscr 'Cabrerito de la cienaga') (horiz)	1·40	90
5219	90c. Hummingbird (inscr 'Zunzuncito') (horiz)	1·90	1·10
5220	1p.05 Cuban vireo (inscr 'Juan chivi') (horiz)	2·10	1·30

1459 *Tyto alba* (barn owl) and *Lycaena dispar*

2008. Efiro 2008. Owls and Butterflies. Multicoloured.

5221	15c. Type **1459**	20	10
5222	15c. *Bubo bubo* (Eurasian eagle-owl) and *Loina iolas*	20	10
5223	45c. *Strix nebulosa* (great grey owl) and *Vanessa cardui*	85	50
5224	65c. *Strix aluco* (tawny owl) and *Colias erate*	1·00	60
5225	75c. *Asio otus* (long-eared owl) and *Aporia crataegi*	1·40	90
5226	85c. *Strix uralensis* (Ural owl) and *Colias hecia*	1·70	1·10
MS5227	110×77 mm. 1p. *Anthocharis damone* (horiz). Imperf	2·10	2·10

1460 With his Mother, Rosario, 1928

2008. 80th Birth Anniv of Ernesto 'Che' Guevara. Multicoloured.

5228	65c. Type **1460**	1·00	60
5229	75c. As boy, Villa Nydia, Alta Gracia, Cordoba	1·40	90
5230	85c. As young man and cycling	1·70	1·10
5231	1p.05 With cigar	2·10	1·50
MS5232	132×98 mm. Nos. 5228/31	6·25	6·25

1461 Vilma Espin Guillois

2008. Vilma Lucila Espín Guillois (chemical engineer and revolutionary) Commemoration

5233	**1461** 65c. multicoloured	1·10	65

1462 President Sukarno and Fidel Castro

2008. Visit of President Sukarno of Indonesia, 1960. Multicoloured.

5234	65c. Type **1462**	1·00	60
5235	65c. Pres Sukarno and Che Guevara	1·00	60

1463 *Panthera leo* (lion)

2008. National Zoo. Multicoloured.

5236	5c. Type **1463**	10	10
5237	10c. *Ailurus fulgens* (red panda)	15	10
5238	15c. *Cacatuaa galerita* (cockatoo)	20	15
5239	30c. *Crocodrylus rhomifer* (crocodile)	35	20
5240	40c. *Phoenicopterus ruber* (flamingo)	85	50
5241	2p.05 *Equus burchelli* (zebra)	4·00	2·75
MS5242	110×85 mm. 1p. *Loxodonta africana* (African elephant) (40×32 mm). Imperf	2·10	1·50

1464 Megatherium and Australopithecus afarensis

2008. Paleolithic Hominids and Fauna. Multicoloured.

5243	10c. Type **1464**	10	10
5244	15c. Toxodon and *Australopithecus africanus*	10	10
5245	50c. Bison and *Australopithecus robustus*	85	50
5246	65c. Hipparion (inscr 'Hippioion') and *Homo habilis*	1·00	60
5247	75c. Megantereon and *Homo erectus*	1·40	90
5248	90c. Mammoth and *Neandertal*	1·70	1·10
MS5249	110×77 mm. 1p. Coelodonta. Imperf	2·10	1·50

1465 Joseito Fernandez

2008. Birth Centenary of Jose Fernandez (Joseito) Diaz (singer and songwriter)

5250	**1465** 65c. multicoloured	1·10	65

1466 R. Trevithick, 1802

2008. Early Motorcars. Multicoloured.

5251	15c. Type **1466**	20	10
5252	30c. Gurney, 1829	45	25
5253	40c. Church, 1835	85	50
5254	65c. T. Rikett, 1858	1·40	90
5255	75c. K. Benz, 1890	1·70	1·10
5256	85c. W. Hancock, 1836	1·70	1·10
MS5257	111×79 mm. 1p. Panhard et Levassor, 1958 (inscr 'Panhard-Levassor'). Imperf	2·10	1·50

1467 Neapolitan Mastiff

2008. Dogs. Multicoloured.

5258	10c. Type **1467**	10	10
5259	15c. Golden retriever	15	10
5260	40c. Rottweiler	85	50
5261	65c. Shetland sheepdog	1·00	65
5262	85c. Chow chow	1·70	1·10
5263	90c. Boxer	2·30	1·40
MS5264	100×78 mm. 1p. Chihuahua. Imperf	2·10	1·50

1468 La Vigia

2008. 315th Anniv of Matanza City. Multicoloured.

5265	15c. Type **1468**	20	15
5266	40c. Provincial Museum	85	50
5267	50c. Firestation	90	55
5268	75c. Palace of Justice	1·40	90
5269	85c. Sauto Theatre	1·70	1·10
5270	90c. Government Palace	2·30	1·40
MS5271	100×78 mm. 1p. Monument to the Unknown Soldier. Imperf	2·30	1·40

1469 Broken Wheel and Jose Martin (War of Independence Day)

2008. America. Festivals. Multicoloured.

5272	15c. Type **1469**	25	15
5273	65c. Parade, Fidel Castro and Che Guevara (Liberation day)	1·40	90
5274	75c. Procession, globe, cog and flowers (Workers' day)	1·90	1·20
5275	2p.05 Buildings, flag and gun (National rebellion day)	2·10	1·40
MS5276	145×95 mm. Nos. 5272/5	5·50	3·75

1470 Pas de Deux Swan Lake

2008. 60th Anniv of National Ballet. Multicoloured.

5277	10c. Type **1470**	15	10
5278	15c. Pas de deux, *Giselle*	25	15
5279	50c. Doll and Doctor Coppélius, *Coppélia* (horiz)	85	50
5280	65c. Shakespeare and masks, *Romeo and Juliet* (horiz)	1·00	65
5281	75c. Russian dance , *Nutcracker* (horiz)	1·40	90
5282	85c. Set design, *Sleeping Beauty* (horiz)	1·70	1·10
MS5283	100×78 mm. 1p. Ballet of Havana, international festival opening parade. Imperf	2·10	1·50

1471 Parchment

2008. 400th Anniv of Cuban Literature. Multicoloured.

5284	15c. Type **1471**	35	25
5285	75c. Multicoloured snails leaving trails of text	1·40	90
5286	2p.05 Fireworks as star against red triangle	2·10	1·50

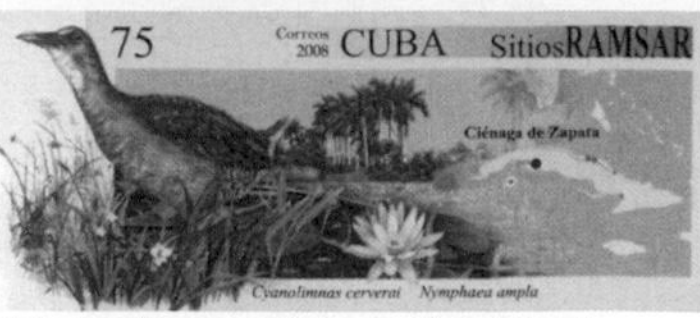

1472 *Cyanolimnas cervai* (Zapata rail) and *Nymphaea ampla* (Illustration reduced. Actual size 72×31 mm) (image scaled to 68% of original size)

2008. Convention on Wetlands of International Importance (Ramsar Convention). Multicoloured.

5287	75c. Type **1472**	1·40	90
5288	75c. *Nelumbo nucifera* and *Porphyrio porphyrio* (purple swamphen)	1·40	90

1473 Playing Chess

2008. 120th Birth Anniv of José Raúl Capablanca y Graupera (world chess champion 1921–1927). Multicoloured.

5289	1p.05 Type **1473**	1·40	90
5290	2p.05 Seated (vert)	2·75	1·90

1474 Carlos Finlay

2008. 175th Birth Anniv of Carlos Juan Finlay (physician, scientist and pioneer in yellow fever research)

5291	**1474** 65c. multicoloured	1·00	60

1475 Fidel Castro and Communist Posters (inscr 'Constitucion Cc del PCC')

2009. 50th Anniv of Revolution (1st issue). Multicoloured.

5292	15c. Type **1475**	45	30
5293	15c. Che Guevara (inscr 'Dia del guerrillero herocico')	45	30
5294	15c. Che Guevara poster (inscr 'Distribucion gratuita del diario del Che')	45	30
5295	15c. PCC congress (inscr '1er congreso del PCC')	45	30
5296	15c. PCC congress (inscr '1er congreso del PCC')	45	30
5297	15c. Teachers and schoolchildren (inscr '1er congreso de education rural')	45	30
5298	15c. Children (inscr 'Se establecio en Cuba dia internacional infancia')	45	30
5299	15c. Early and modern doctors and children (inscr '205 aniv de la vacunacion en Cuba')	45	30
5300	15c. Inscr 'Creacion del MINAZ'	45	30

5301 15c. Factory worker and fishermen (inscr 'Creacion del INP') 45 30
5302 15c. Fishermen (inscr 'Desarollo de la industria pesquera') 45 30
5303 15c. Festival goers (inscr 'XI festival mundial. Juventud y los estudiantes') 45 30
5304 15c. Astronaut (inscr 'El cosmos') 45 30
5305 15c. Researcher using microscope (inscr 'Dia de la cienca Cubana') 45 30
5306 15c. Researcher using electronic scales (inscr 'Dia de la cienca Cubana') 45 30
5307 15c. Doctor and patient (inscr 'Medico y enfermera de la familia') 45 30
5308 15c. Nelson Mandela hugging man (inscr '15 aniv desaparicon del apartheid') 45 30
5309 15c. Boy and soldiers (inscr 'Comienzo de la batalla de ideas') 45 30
5310 15c. Elderly couple, mother and child (inscr 'La seguridad social') 45 30
5311 15c. Boxers (inscr 'Creacion de la EIED') 45 30
5312 15c. Ballet and traditional dancers (inscr 'La cultura nacional') 45 30
5313 15c. Musicians (inscr 'La cultura nacional') 45 30
5314 15c. Nurse and lecturer (inscr 'Programa de la batalla de ideas') 45 30
5315 15c. Students waving flags (inscr 'Programa de la batalla de ideas') 45 30
5316 15c. Castro and revolutionaries (inscr 'Dia de la liberacion') 45 30
5317 15c. Tank and Castro (inscr 'Dia de la liberacion') 45 30
5318 15c. Castro and crowd (inscr 'Llegada de fidel a la Habana') 45 30
5319 15c. Crowd and Castro (inscr '50 aniv 1er desfile y concentracion del pueblo') 45 30
5320 15c. Castro addressing crowd (inscr 'Fidel 1er ministro gobierno revolucionario') 45 30
5321 15c. Camilo Cienfuegos (inscr 'Camilo disuelve el BRAC') 45 30
5322 15c. Che Guevara (inscr 'Declarado el Che ciudadano por nacimiento') 45 30
5323 15c. Castro in Venezuela (inscr '50 aniv viaje del Fidel Castro a Venezuela') 45 30
5324 15c. Revolutionaries (inscr 'Creacion de la PNR') 45 30
5325 15c. Damaged buildings (inscr 'Creacion de la seguridad del estado') 45 30
5326 15c. Gunboat and soldier (inscr 'Creacion de las TGF') 45 30
5327 15c. Farmer and Castro (inscr 'Let de reforma agraria. Dia del campesino') 45 30
5328 15c. Buildings (inscr 'Intervencion de la Cuban Telephone') 45 30
5329 15c. Castro and FMC emblem (inscr 'Creacion de la FMC') 45 30
5330 15c. CDR members (inscr 'Creacion de los CDR') 45 30
5331 15c. Women and students (inscr 'Inicio de la campana de alfabetizacion') 45 30
5332 15c. Woman athlete and stadium (inscr 'Creacion del INDER') 45 30
5333 15c. Equipment and radio waves (inscr 'Llegada de la radio a toda Cuba') 45 30
5334 15c. Che Guevara (inscr 'Designado el che ministro de industria') 45 30
5335 15c. Young people (inscr 'Creacion de la union de Jovenes comunistas') 45 30
5336 15c. Civil defence workers (inscr 'Creacion de la defensa civil') 45 30
5337 15c. Firefighters (inscr 'Creacion del CN de la defensa civil') 45 30
5338 15c. Sugar cane workers (inscr 'Primera zafra del pueblo') 45 30
5339 15c. Che Guevara and UN headquarters (inscr 'Che en la ONU') 45 30
MS5340 100×78 mm. 1p. Flags (inscr '50 aniv de la revolucion Cubana'). Imperf 2·10 1·50
MS5341 100×78 mm. 1p. Castro and marchers (inscr 'Plaza de la Revolucion'). Imperf 2·10 1·50

1476 Che Guevara

2009. 50th Anniv of Revolution (2nd issue)
5342 **1476** 75c. multicoloured 2·10 1·50

1477 Batting

2009. Second World Baseball Classic Championship. Multicoloured.
5343 5c. Type **1477** 20 15
5344 10c. Home run 20 15
5345 15c. Catch 25 15
5346 45c. Throw in 85 50
5347 65c. First stop 1·40 90
5348 75c. Miss 1·70 1·10
MS5349 100×78 mm. 1p. Cuban team. Imperf 2·10 1·50

1478 Lázaro Peña González (General Secretary)

2009. 70th Anniv of Workers' Central Union of Cuba (CTC)
MS5350 105 x 76 mm. **1478** 1p. multicoloured (imperf) 1·60 1·10

1479 Nuestra Senora del Carmen Church

2009. 495th Anniv of Santa María del Puerto del Príncipe (Camagüey)
5351 **1479** 90c. multicoloured 1·40 90

1480 Symbols of Computing

2009. Informática 2009, International Computing Convention and Fair, Havana
MS5352 113×76 mm. **1480** 1p. multicoloured (imperf) 1·60 1·10

1481 Charles Darwin and Mount House, Shrewsbury (birthplace)

2009. Birth Bicentenary of Charles Darwin (evolutionary theorist). 150th Anniv of Publication of *On Origin of Species*. Multicoloured.
5353 10c. Type **1481** 10 85
5354 65c. HMS *Beagle* and route of voyage 50 30
5355 75c. Publication of *On Origin of Species* 1·00 70
5356 85c. Charles Darwin as older man and tree of relationships from his notebook 1·30 80

1482 AVE (Spain)

2009. Rapid Transport. Multicoloured.
5357 15c. Type **1482** 20 10
5358 15c. ACELA Express (USA) 20 15
5359 30c. ATP Eurostar (UK) 50 30
5360 65c. ICE (Germany) 85 50
5361 75c. ICN (Switzerland) 1·10 70
5362 1p.05 TGV (France) 1·70 1·10
MS5363 113×76 mm. 50c.×2, Shinkansen MOD 500 (Japan); Shinkansen MOD 700 (Japan). Imperf 1·60 1·10

1483 Flag, Rifle and Soldier

2009. 50th Anniv of State Security
5364 **1483** 65c. multicoloured 1·40 90

1484 Rachel (*La bella del Alhambra* (directed by Enrique Pineda Barnet))

2009. 30th Anniv of Cuban Institute of Cinematographic Art and Industry (ICAIC). Multicoloured.
5365 10c. Type **1484** 20 10
5366 10c. Reina (*Reina y Rey* (Julio Garcia Espinosa)) 20 10
5367 15c. Elpidio Valdés (*Elpidio Valdés* (Juan Padrón)) 25 15
5368 15c. Three Lucías (*Lucía* (Humberto Solas)) 25 15
5369 45c. Captain (*La primera carga al machete* (Manuel Octavio Gómez)) 70 40
5370 65c. Alberto Delgado (*El hombre de Maisinicú* (Manuel Pérez)) 1·10 90
5371 75c. Ernesto Ardeniz and Nereida (*Clandestinos* (Fernando Pérez)) 1·50 1·00
5372 90c. Teresa (*Retrato de Teresa* (Pastor Vega)) 1·60 1·10
5373 1p.05 Santiago Álvarez Román (founding member of ICAIC) 1·70 1·20
MS5374 105×76 mm. 1p. Diego (*Fresa y Chocolate* (Tomás Gutiérrez Alea and Juan Carlos Tabio)). Imperf 2·10 1·40

1485 Cagiva Mito N1

2009. China 2009 International Stamp Exhibition, Luoyang. Multicoloured.
5375 10c. Type **1485** 20 15
5376 15c. Honda CBR 900 25 15
5377 50c. Hyosung GT 8 70 45
5378 65c. Kawasaki ZX-7R 750cc. 90 55
5379 75c. Gussi MGS 1·10 65
5380 90c. Ducati Monster 900 1·40 90
MS5381 105×76 mm. 1p. Hyosung GT 125 R LD (vert). Imperf 1·40 90

1486 Cat and Kittens

2009. Cats. Multicoloured.
5382 10c. Type **1486** 20 10
5383 15c. Grey and ginger kittens with ball 25 15
5384 40c. Tabby cat and tabby point Siamese 65 50
5385 65c. Tabby and white cats play fighting 85 55
5386 75c. Ginger and white cat 1·10 70
5387 1p.05 Black and white cat eating 1·30 1·80
MS5388 105×74 mm. 1p. Two Siamese cats (vert). Imperf 1·40 90

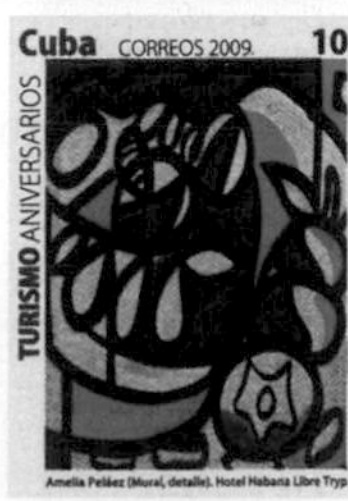

1487 Mural, Hotel Tryp Habana Libre (Amelia Peláez)

2009. Tourism. Multicoloured.
5389 10c. Type **1487** 20 20
5390 10c. Woman's profile enclosed in foliage and bird, Bodeguita del Medio restaurant (René Portocarrero) 20 20
5391 45c. Tree in landscape, Hotel Nacional de Cuba (Domingo Ramos) (horiz) 70 45
5392 65c. Fruit, figures and bird, Hotel Bello Caribe (Mariano Rodriguez) (horiz) 85 50
5393 75c. Seated man, man wearing hat, woman wearing white, woman's face, foliage and rainbow, Hotel Bello Caribe (Raúl Martinez) (horiz) 1·00 60
5394 85c. Vehicle made of everything, Hotel Tryp Habana Libre (Manuel A. Sosabravo) (horiz) 1·40 90
MS5395 105×74 mm. 1p. Mural with central stylized head, Hotel Inglaterra (various artists) (horiz). Imperf 1·50 1·00

1488 Haydee Santamaria Cuadrado (founder)

2009. 50th Anniv of Casa de las Americas (cultural institution)
5396 **1488** 3p. multicoloured 6·50 5·75

1489 Havana

2009. UNESCO World Heritage Sites in Cuba. Multicoloured.
5397 15c. Type **1489** 25 15
5398 45c. Cienfuegos 70 45
5399 50c. Trinidad 80 45
5400 1p.05 Camaguey 1·40 90
MS5401 134×100 mm. Nos. 5397/400 3·25 2·75

1490 Green Macaw, Peru

2009. National Natural History Museum. Multicoloured.

5402	5c. Type **1490**	20	10
5403	10c. Blue-gold macaw, Venezuela	25	15
5404	15c. Red-shouldered macaw, Peru	25	15
5405	20c. Golden-collared macaw, Brazil	35	25
5406	20c. Hyacinth macaw, Brazil	45	30
5407	65c. Scarlet macaw, Mexico	1·20	80
5408	75c. Inscr 'guacamayo frente rojo', Bolivia	1·40	90
5409	90c. Military macaw, Argentina	1·40	1·90

1491 Owls

2009. 25th Anniv of Design Institute

5410	**1491**	65c. multicoloured	1·70	1·10

EXPRESS MAIL STAMPS

E34

1900. As Type E 34, but inscr "immediata".

E306	**E34**	10c. orange	75·00	22·00

1902. Inscr "inmediata".

E307	10c. orange	2·00	1·00

E39 J. B. Zayas

1910

E320	**E39**	10c. blue and orange	13·00	3·50

E41 Bleriot XI and Morro Castle

1914

E352	**E41**	10c. blue	12·50	20

E62 Mercury

1936. Free Port of Matanzas. Inscr as T 61. Perf or imperf (same prices).

E409	**E62**	10c. purple (express)	4·00	1·70
E413	-	15c. blue (air express)	4·00	2·75

DESIGN: 15c. Maya Lighthouse.

E67 "Triumph of the Revolution"

1936. Maximo Gomez Monument.

E422	**E67**	10c. orange	4·50	2·00

E71 Temple of Quetzalcoatl (Mexico)

1937. American Writers and Artists Association.

E424v	**E71**	10c. orange	6·00	6·00
E424w	-	10c. orange	6·00	6·00

DESIGN: No. 424w, Ruben Dario (Nicaragua).

E114

1945

E485	**E114**	10c. brown	3·75	50

E146 Government House, Cardenas

1951. Centenary of Cuban Flag.

E559	**E146**	10c. red, blue & orge	8·00	1·20

E150 Capablanca Club, Havana

1951. 30th Anniv of Jose Capablanca's Victory in World Chess Championship.

E568	**E150**	10c. purple & green	20·00	4·75

1952. As No. 549 surch 10c E. ESPECIAL.

E595	**143**	10c. on 2c. brown	5·50	1·30

E161 National Anthem and Arms

1952. 50th Anniv of Republic.

E605	**E161**	10c. blue & orange	2·75	1·00

1952. Postal Employees' Retirement Fund. Inscr "ENTREGA ESPECIAL".

E627	**165**	10c. olive	5·00	2·20

E176 Roseate Tern

1953

E673	**E176**	10c. blue	4·50	1·30

1954. Postal Employees' Retirement Fund. Portrait of G. H. Saez as No. 684, inscr "ENTREGA ESPECIAL".

E686	10c. olive	4·25	1·10

1955. Postal Employees' Retirement Fund. Vert portrait (F. Varela) as T 191, inscr "ENTREGA ESPECIAL".

E741	10c. lake	3·75	1·10

1956. Postal Employees' Retirement Fund. Vert portrait (J. J. Milanes) as T 200, inscr "ENTREGA ESPECIAL".

E768	10c. black and red	5·50	75

1957. Postal Employees' Retirement Fund. As T 216 but inscr "ENTREGA ESPECIAL".

E812	10c. turquoise & brown	4·00	1·30

PAINTING: 10c. "Yesterday" (Cabrera).

1957. Postal Employees' Retirement Fund. As T 236 but inscr "ENTREGA ESPECIAL".

E856	10c. violet and brown	2·50	1·10

DESIGN—HORIZ: 10c. Statue of Gen. A. Maceo, Independence Park, Pinar del Rio.

E238 Motor-cyclist in Havana

1958

E858	**E238**	10c. blue	2·50	1·00
E954	**E238**	10c. violet	3·00	1·00
E955	**E238**	10c. orange	3·00	95
E859	**E238**	20c. green	2·50	1·00

1958. Poey Commem. As Nos. 890/2 but inscr "ENTREGA ESPECIAL".

E893	10c. multicoloured	5·50	2·75
E894	20c. red, blue and black	18·00	11·50

DESIGNS—HORIZ: Fish: 10c. Black-finned snapper; 20c. Spotted mosquitofish.

1960. Surch HABILITADO ENTREGA ESPECIAL 10c.

E961	**55**	10c. on 20c. pink	2·40	50
E962	**55**	10c. on 50c. turquoise	2·40	50

1962. Stamp Day. As T 289 but inscr "ENTREGA ESPECIAL".

E1023	10c. brown & bl on yell	7·00	1·70

DESIGN: 10c. 18th-century sailing packet.

E991 Great Red-bellied Woodpecker

1991. Birds. Multicoloured.

E3638	45c. Type E **991**	1·80	50
E3639	50c. Cuban solitaire	1·90	60
E3640	2p. Cuban trogon	7·25	2·50
E3641	4p. Cuban grassquit	14·50	4·25
E3642	5p. Ivory-billed woodpecker	18·00	5·25
E3643	10p. Cuban amazon (horiz)	35·00	7·75
E3644	16p.45 Bee hummingbird (horiz)	55·00	16·00

POSTAGE DUE STAMPS

D42

1914

D336	**D42**	1c. red	4·25	85
D338	**D42**	2c. red	6·75	1·00
D340	**D42**	5c. red	7·75	1·20

Pt. 20

CUNDINAMARCA

One of the states of the Granadine Confederation. A Department of Colombia from 1886, now uses Colombian stamps.

100 centavos = 1 peso.

1

2

1870. Imperf.

1	**1**	5c. blue	7·25	7·00
2	**2**	10c. red	22·00	21·00

3

4

1877. Imperf.

5	**3**	10c. red	4·75	4·50
6	**4**	20c. green	10·00	9·50
7	-	50c. mauve	11·00	10·50
8a	-	1p. brown	17·00	16·00

The 50c. and 1p. are in larger Arms designs.

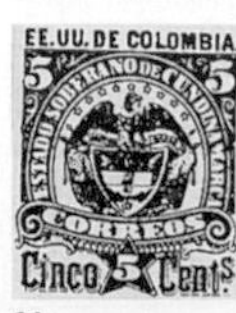
11

1884. Imperf.

14	**11**	5c. blue	1·10	1·10

13

1885. Imperf.

17	**13**	5c. blue	1·10	1·60
18	**13**	10c. red	6·50	6·50
19	**13**	10c. red on lilac	3·50	3·50
20	**13**	20c. green	5·50	5·25
21	**13**	50c. mauve	7·25	7·00
22	**13**	1p. brown	7·75	7·50

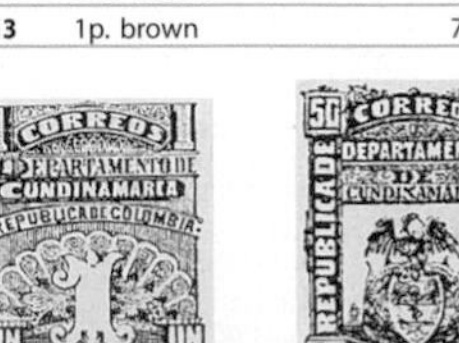
14 15

1904. Imperf or perf. Various frames.

23	**14**	1c. orange	35	30
24	**14**	2c. blue	35	30
35	**14**	2c. grey	1·00	95
25	**15**	3c. red	45	45
26	**15**	5c. green	45	45
27	**15**	10c. brown	45	45
28	**15**	15c. pink	45	45
29	**15**	20c. blue on green	45	45
32	**15**	20c. blue	90	85
42	**15**	40c. blue	90	65
30	**15**	50c. mauve	75	75
31	**15**	1p. green	75	75

The illustrations show the main type. The frames and position of the arms in Type **15** differ for each value.

REGISTRATION STAMP

R17

1904. Imperf or perf.

R46	**R 17**	10c. brown	1·10	1·10

Pt. 4

CURACAO

A Netherlands colony consisting of two groups of islands in the Caribbean Sea, N. of Venezuela. Later part of Netherlands Antilles.

100 cents = 1 gulden.

1

1873

13	1	2½c. green	8·25	14·00
7	1	3c. bistre	80·00	£150
14	1	5c. red	20·00	20·00
26	1	10c. blue	£110	28·00
27	1	12½c. yellow	£225	85·00
22	1	15c. brown	55·00	33·00
23	1	25c. brown	85·00	14·00
24	1	30c. grey	60·00	80·00
17	1	50c. lilac	2·75	2·75
29	1	1g.50 indigo and blue	£160	£140
12	1	2g.50 mauve and bistre	65·00	65·00

2

1889

37	2	1c. grey	2·20	2·20
38	2	2c. mauve	2·20	3·25
39	2	2½c. green	7·75	7·75
40a	2	3c. brown	9·00	9·00
41	2	5c. red	35·00	2·75

1891. Surch 25 CENT.

42	1	25c. on 30c. grey	25·00	22·00

4

1892

43	4	10c. blue	2·20	2·20
44	4	12½c. green	26·00	16·00
45	4	15c. red	5·50	4·50
46	4	25c. brown	£160	7·00
47	4	30c. grey	5·50	11·00

1895. Surch 2½ cent (No. 48) or 2½ CENT (No. 50).

48	1	2½c. on 10c. blue	22·00	17·00
50	1	2½c. on 30c. grey	£225	11·00

1899. 1898 stamps of Netherlands surch CURACAO and value.

51	12	12½c. on 12½c. blue	39·00	14·00
52	12	25c. on 25c. blue and red	2·75	2·75
53	13	1g.50 on 2½g. lilac	31·00	39·00

9

10

11

1903

54	9	1c. olive	2·75	2·75
55a	9	2c. brown	25·00	5·50
56	9	2½c. green	11·00	1·10
57	9	3c. orange	14·00	8·25
58	9	5c. red	14·00	1·70
59	9	7½c. grey	45·00	14·00
60	10	10c. slate	28·00	2·75
61	10	12½c. blue	2·75	1·10
62	10	15c. brown	25·00	20·00
63	10	22½c. olive and brown	25·00	20·00
64	10	25c. violet	31·00	5·50
65	10	30c. brown	60·00	25·00
66	10	50c. brown	50·00	16·00
67	11	1½g. brown	55·00	45·00
68	11	2½g. blue	55·00	50·00

12

13

14

1915

69	12	½c. lilac	2·20	2·20
70	12	1c. olive	55	35
71	12	1½c. blue	55	35
72	12	2c. brown	2·20	2·00
73	12	2½c. green	1·30	55
74	12	3c. yellow	4·00	2·75
75	12	3c. green	4·00	4·00
76	12	5c. red	3·25	55
77	12	5c. green	6·75	4·00
78	12	5c. mauve	3·25	35
79c	12	7½c. bistre	1·90	20
80	13	10c. red	33·00	5·50
81	12	10c. lilac	7·75	8·25
82	12	10c. red	6·75	2·75
83	13	12½c. blue	4·00	1·10
84	13	12½c. red	3·75	2·75
85	13	15c. olive	1·40	2·20
86	13	15c. blue	6·75	4·50
87	13	20c. blue	11·00	4·50
88	13	20c. olive	4·50	3·25
89	13	22½c. orange	4·50	4·50
90	13	25c. mauve	5·50	2·20
91	13	30c. slate	5·50	2·20
92	13	35c. slate and orange	4·50	9·00
93a	14	50c. green	5·50	55
94	14	1½g. violet	25·00	20·00
95	14	2½g. red	36·00	36·00

15

1918

96	15	1c. black on buff	9·75	5·50

1919. Surch 5 CENT.

97	13	5c. on 12½c. blue	5·50	4·00

17 Queen Wilhelmina

1923. Queen's Silver Jubilee.

98	17	5c. green	2·75	4·50
99	17	7½c. green	2·75	4·50
100	17	10c. red	5·50	6·75
101	17	20c. grey	5·50	6·75
102	17	1g. purple	55·00	45·00
103	17	2g.50 black	£120	£275
104	17	5g. brown	£150	£325

1927. Unissued Marine Insurance stamps, as Type M 22 of Netherlands, inscr "CURACAO", surch FRANKEERZEGEL and value.

105		3c. on 15c. green	1·10	1·10
106		10c. on 60c. red	1·10	1·10
107		12½c. on 75c. brown	1·10	1·10
108		15c. on 1g.50 blue	5·50	5·50
109		25c. on 2g.25 brown	13·50	13·50
110		30c. on 4½g. black	14·50	14·50
111		50c. on 7½g. red	13·50	13·50

20

1928

112	20	6c. orange	3·25	55
113	20	7½c. orange	1·10	85
114	20	10c. red	2·20	85
115	20	12½c. brown	2·20	2·00
116	20	15c. blue	2·20	85
117	20	20c. blue	8·25	1·40
118	20	21c. green	14·00	17·00
119	20	25c. purple	5·50	3·00
120	20	27½c. black	20·00	22·00
121	20	30c. green	8·25	1·70
122	20	35c. black	2·75	5·50

1929. Air. Surch LUCHTPOST and value.

123	13	50c. on 12½c. red	22·00	22·00
124	13	1g. on 20c. blue	22·00	22·00
125	13	2g. on 15c. olive	55·00	65·00

1929. Surch 6 ct. and bars.

126	20	6c. on 7½c. orange	2·20	1·70

23

1931. Air.

126a	23	10c. green	25	20
126b	23	15c. slate	60	25
127	23	20c. red	1·40	35
127a	23	25c. olive	2·30	1·20
127b	23	30c. yellow	60	60
128	23	35c. blue	1·70	1·70
129	23	40c. green	1·20	80
130	23	45c. orange	3·00	3·25
130a	23	50c. red	1·70	95
131	23	60c. purple	1·20	60
132	23	70c. black	9·25	3·25
133	23	1g.40 brown	5·75	7·50
134	23	2g.80 bistre	7·00	8·25

1931. Surch.

134a	12	1½ on 2½c. green	5·75	5·75
135	12	2½ on 3c. green	1·70	1·70

24a

1933. 400th Birth Anniv of William I of Orange.

136	24a	6c. orange	3·00	1·70

25 Frederik Hendrik

26 "Johannes van Walbeeck"

1934. 300th Anniv of Dutch Colonization. Inscr "1634 1934".

137	-	1c. black	2·00	2·30
138	-	1½c. mauve	1·50	60
139	-	2c. orange	2·30	3·00
140	25	2½c. green	1·70	2·30
141	25	5c. brown	1·70	2·30
142	25	6c. blue	2·30	60
143	-	10c. red	5·75	2·30
144	-	12½c. brown	13·00	11·50
145	-	15c. blue	4·00	3·00
146	26	20c. black	6·50	5·75
147	26	21c. brown	29·00	20·00
148	26	25c. green	29·00	20·00
149	-	27½c. purple	29·00	29·00
150	-	30c. red	20·00	11·50
151	-	50c. yellow	20·00	17·00
152	-	1g.50 blue	85·00	85·00
153	-	2g.50 green	95·00	£100

PORTRAITS: 1c. to 2c. Willem Usselinx. 10c. to 15c. Jacob Binckes. 27½c. to 50c. Cornelis Evertsen, the younger. 1g.50, 2g.50, Louis Brion.

1934. Air. Surch 10 CT.

154	23	10c. on 20c. red	29·00	23·00

27

1936

155A	27	1c. brown	1·20	30
156A	27	1½c. blue	1·20	30
157A	27	2c. orange	1·20	30
158A	27	2½c. green	1·20	30
159A	27	5c. red	1·20	30

28 Queen Wilhelmina

1936

160	28	6c. purple	1·20	35
161	28	10c. red	1·70	35
162	28	12½c. green	2·30	1·20
163	28	15c. blue	2·30	1·20
164	28	20c. orange	2·30	1·20
165	28	21c. black	5·25	5·75
166	28	25c. red	2·30	1·70
167	28	27½c. brown	4·75	4·75
168	28	30c. bistre	1·20	1·00
169	28	50c. green	5·75	60
170	28	1g.50 brown	26·00	17·00
171a	28	2g.50 red	29·00	29·00

29 Queen Wilhelmina

1938. 40th Anniv of Coronation.

172	29	1½c. violet	60	60
173	29	6c. red	1·20	1·20
174	29	15c. blue	2·30	1·70

30 Dutch Flags and Arms

1941. Air. Prince Bernhard Fund to equip Dutch Forces. Centres in red, blue and orange.

175	30	10c.+10c. red	46·00	41·00
176	30	15c.+25c. blue	46·00	41·00
177	30	20c.+25c. brown	46·00	41·00
178	30	25c.+25c. violet	46·00	41·00
179	30	30c.+50c. orange	46·00	41·00
180	30	35c.+50c. green	46·00	41·00
181	30	40c.+50c. brown	46·00	41·00
182	30	50c.+1g. blue	46·00	41·00

31 Queen Wilhelmina

1941

248	31	6c. violet	2·30	3·00
184a	31	10c. red	4·00	1·70
185	31	12½c. green	4·75	1·70
251	31	15c. blue	2·30	3·50
187	31	20c. orange	4·00	3·00
188	31	21c. grey	17·00	11·50
254	31	25c. red	45	35
255	31	27½c. brown	3·50	3·50
256	31	30c. bistre	3·00	2·00
192	31	50c. green (21×26 mm)	35·00	1·20

257	31	50c. green	3·00	35
193	31	1½g. brown (21×26 mm)	32·00	3·50
194	31	2½g. purple (21×26 mm)	46·00	3·00

See also Nos. 258/61.

33 Aruba

1942

195	-	1c. brown and violet	35	35
196	-	1½c. green and blue	35	35
197	-	2c. brown and black	80	45
198	-	2½c. yellow and green	45	35
199	33	5c. black and red	1·50	35
200	-	6c. blue and purple	1·20	1·20

DESIGNS—HORIZ: 1c. Bonaire. 2c. Saba. 2½c. St. Maarten. 6c. Curacao. VERT: 1½c. St. Eustatius.

34 Queen Wilhelmina and Douglas DC-2 over Atlantic Ocean

1942. Air.

201	34	10c. blue and green	1·20	35
202	-	15c. green and red	1·20	35
203	-	20c. green and brown	1·20	35
204	-	25c. brown and blue	1·20	35
205	-	30c. violet and red	1·20	1·20
206	34	35c. green and violet	1·70	80
207	-	40c. brown and green	2·30	80
208	-	45c. black and red	1·20	35
209	-	50c. black and violet	3·00	35
210	-	60c. blue and brown	4·75	1·70
211	34	70c. blue and brown	4·75	1·70
212	-	1g.40 green and blue	29·00	3·25
213	-	2g.80 blue & ultramarine	41·00	8·75
214	-	5g. green and purple	65·00	29·00
215	-	10g. brown and green	75·00	44·00

DESIGNS: 15, 40c., 1g.40, Fokker airplane "Zilvermeeuw" over coast. 20, 45c., 2g.80, Map of Netherlands West Indies. 25, 50c., 5g. Side view of Douglas DC-2 airplane. 30, 60c., 10g. Front view of Douglas DC-2 airplane.

35 Dutch Royal Family

1943. Birth of Princess Margriet.

216	35	1½c. orange	60	60
217	35	2½c. red	60	60
218	35	6c. black	1·70	1·20
219	35	10c. blue	1·70	1·70

1943. Air. Dutch Prisoners of War Relief Fund. Nos. 212/15 surch Voor Krijgsgevangenen and new value.

220	40c.+50c. on 1g.40 green & bl	11·50	11·50
221	45c.+50c. on 2g.80 blue & ult	11·50	11·50
222	50c.+75c. on 5g. green & pur	11·50	11·50
223	60c.+100c. on 10g. brn & grn	11·50	11·50

37 Princess Juliana

1944. Air. Red Cross Fund. Cross in red; frame in red and blue.

224	37	10c.+10c. brown	3·50	3·50
225	37	15c.+25c. green	3·50	3·50
226	37	20c.+25c. black	3·50	3·50
227	37	25c.+25c. grey	3·50	3·50
228	37	30c.+50c. purple	3·50	3·50
229	37	35c.+50c. brown	3·50	3·50
230	37	40c.+50c. green	3·50	3·50
231	37	50c.+100c. violet	3·50	3·50

38 Map of Netherlands

1946. Air. Netherlands Relief Fund. Value in black.

232	38	10c.+10c. orange & grey	2·30	2·30
233	38	15c.+25c. grey and red	2·30	2·30
234	38	20c.+25c. orange & grn	2·30	2·30
235	38	25c.+25c. grey & violet	2·30	2·30
236	38	30c.+50c. buff & green	2·30	2·30
237	38	35c.+50c. orange & red	2·30	2·30
238	38	40c.+75c. buff & blue	2·30	2·30
239	38	50c.+100c. buff & violet	2·30	2·30

1946. Air. National Relief Fund. As T 38 but showing map of Netherlands Indies and inscr "CURACAO HELPT ONZEOOST". Value in black.

240	10c.+10c. buff & violet	2·30	2·30
241	15c.+25c. buff & blue	2·30	2·30
242	20c.+25c. orange & red	2·30	2·30
243	25c.+25c. buff & green	2·30	2·30
244	30c.+50c. grey & violet	2·30	2·30
245	35c.+50c. orange & grn	2·30	2·30
246	40c.+75c. grey & red	2·30	2·30
247	50c.+100c. orange & grey	2·30	2·30

1947. Size 25×31½ mm.

258	31	1½g. brown	8·75	3·00
259	31	2½g. purple	85·00	41·00
260	31	5g. olive	£170	£250
261	31	10g. orange	£200	£425

40 Aeroplane and Posthorn

41 Douglas DC-2 and Waves

1947. Air.

262	40	6c. black	80	15
263	40	10c. red	80	15
264	40	12½c. purple	1·20	15
265	40	15c. blue	1·20	35
266	40	20c. green	1·40	45
267	40	25c. orange	1·40	25
268	40	30c. violet	1·70	70
269	40	35c. red	1·70	95
270	40	40c. green	1·70	95
271	40	45c. violet	2·00	1·40
272	40	50c. red	2·00	25
273	40	60c. blue	2·75	80
274	40	70c. brown	4·75	2·00
275	41	1g.50 black	3·50	1·20
276	41	2g.50 red	20·00	5·25
277	41	5g. green	41·00	11·00
278	41	7g.50 blue	£160	£120
279	41	10g. violet	£100	46·00
280	41	15g. red	£140	£120
281	41	25g. brown	£140	£120

28 Queen Wilhelmina

1947. Netherlands Indies Social Welfare Fund. Surch NIWIN and value.

282	28	1½c.+2½c. on 6c. purple	1·40	1·40
283	28	2½c.+5c. on 10c. red	1·40	1·40
284	28	5c.+7½c. on 15c. blue	1·40	1·40

43

1948. Portrait of Queen Wilhelmina.

285	43	6c. purple	1·70	1·70
286	43	10c. red	1·70	2·20
287	43	12½c. green	1·70	1·40
288	43	15c. blue	1·70	1·70
289	43	20c. orange	1·70	3·50
290	43	21c. black	1·70	3·50
291	43	25c. mauve	60	35
292	43	27½c. brown	29·00	29·00
293	43	30c. olive	27·00	2·10
294	43	50c. green	24·00	35
295	43	1g.50c. brn (21½×28½ mm)	46·00	11·50

45 Queen Wilhelmina

1948. Golden Jubilee.

296	45	6c. orange	1·20	95
297	45	12½c. blue	1·20	95

46 Queen Juliana

1948. Accession of Queen Juliana.

298	46	6c. red	1·00	80
299	46	12½c. green	1·00	80

47

1948. Child Welfare Fund. Inscr "VOOR HET KIND".

300	47	6c.+10c. brown	3·75	2·50
301	-	10c.+15c. red	3·75	2·50
302	-	12½c.+20c. green	3·75	2·75
303	47	15c.+25c. blue	3·75	2·75
304	-	20c.+30c. brown	4·00	3·00
305	-	25c.+35c. violet	4·00	3·00

DESIGNS—10, 20c. Native boy in straw hat. 12½, 25c. Curly-haired girl.

POSTAGE DUE STAMPS

For stamps as Nos. D42/61 and D96/105 in other colours see Postage Due stamps of Netherlands Indies and Surinam.

D3

1889

D42C	D3	2½c. black and green	2·75	5·50
D43C	D3	5c. black and green	2·75	2·75
D44C	D3	10c. black and green	45·00	45·00
D45C	D3	12½c. black and green	£550	£275
D46C	D3	15c. black and green	33·00	28·00
D47C	D3	20c. black and green	17·00	14·00
D48C	D3	25c. black and green	£275	£225
D49C	D3	30c. black and green	17·00	14·00
D50C	D3	40c. black and green	22·00	14·00
D51C	D3	50c. black and green	55·00	45·00

D5

1892

D52C	D5	2½c. black and green	55	55
D53C	D5	5c. black and green	1·10	1·10
D54C	D5	10c. black and green	2·20	1·70
D55C	D5	12½c. black and green	2·75	1·70
D56C	D5	15c. black and green	4·00	2·20
D57A	D5	20c. black and green	5·50	2·20
D58C	D5	25c. black and green	2·75	1·70
D59A	D5	30c. black and green	45·00	39·00
D60A	D5	40c. black and green	55·00	39·00
D61A	D5	50c. black and green	55·00	39·00

1915

D96a	2½c. green	90	1·10
D97a	5c. green	90	1·10
D98a	10c. green	90	1·10
D99a	12½c. green	1·10	1·70
D100a	15c. green	2·00	2·20
D101a	20c. green	1·10	2·20
D102a	25c. green	35	55
D103a	30c. green	4·00	5·50
D104	40c. green	4·50	4·50
D105a	50c. green	2·75	4·50

For later issues see **NETHERLANDS ANTILLES**.

Pt. 1

CYPRUS

An island in the East Mediterranean. A British colony, which became a republic within the British Commonwealth in 1960.

1880. 12 pence = 1 shilling.
1881. 40 paras = 1 piastre; 180 piastres = 1 pound.
1955. 1000 mils = 1 pound.
1983. 100 cents = 1 pound.
2008. 100 cents = 1 euro.

1880. Stamps of Great Britain (Queen Victoria) optd CYPRUS.

1	7	½d. red	£120	£110
2	5	1d. red	17·00	38·00
3	41	2½d. mauve	4·00	13·00
4	-	4d. green (No. 153)	£140	£225
5	-	6d. grey (No. 161)	£500	£650
6	-	1s. green (No. 150)	£850	£475

1881. Stamps of Great Britain (Queen Victoria) surch with new values.

9	5	½d. on 1d. red	45·00	65·00
10	5	30 paras on 1d. red	£140	85·00

7

1881

31	7	½pi. green	10·00	2·00
40	7	½pi. green and red	4·25	1·25
32	7	30pa. mauve	8·00	11·00
41	7	30pa. mauve and green	2·75	3·00
33	7	1pi. red	15·00	6·50
42	7	1pi. red and blue	8·00	1·25
34	7	2pi. blue	14·00	1·75
43	7	2pi. blue and purple	11·00	1·25
35a	7	4pi. olive	18·00	32·00
44	7	4pi. olive and purple	17·00	11·00
21	7	6pi. grey	65·00	17·00
45	7	6pi. brown and green	18·00	32·00
46	7	9pi. brown and red	22·00	26·00
22	7	12pi. brown	£200	42·00
47	7	12pi. brown and black	22·00	65·00
48	7	18pi. grey and brown	50·00	55·00
49	7	45pi. purple and blue	£100	£160

1882. Surch.

25	½pi. on ½pi. green	£170	7·00
24	30pa. on 1pi. red	£1600	£110

1903. As T 7 but portrait of King Edward VII.

60	5pa. brown and black	1·00	2·00
61	10pa. orange and green	5·50	1·75
50	½pi. green and red	9·00	1·25
51	30pa. violet and green	19·00	4·00
64	1pi. red and blue	9·00	1·00
65	2pi. blue and purple	14·00	1·75
66	4pi. olive and purple	21·00	13·00
67	6pi. brown and green	22·00	15·00
68	9pi. brown and red	50·00	8·50
69	12pi. brown and black	35·00	55·00
70	18pi. black and brown	45·00	14·00
71	45pi. purple and blue	£110	£150

1912. As T 7 but portrait of King George V.

74b	10pa. orange and green	2·25	1·25
86	10pa. grey and yellow	15·00	9·00
75	½pi. green and red	2·75	30
76	30pa. violet and green	3·00	2·25
88	30pa. green	7·50	1·75
77	1pi. red and blue	5·50	1·75
90	1pi. violet and red	3·50	4·00
91	1½pi. yellow and black	12·00	7·00
78	2pi. blue and purple	6·50	2·00
93	2pi. red and blue	15·00	27·00
94	2¾pi. blue and purple	10·00	9·00
79	4pi. olive and purple	4·25	5·00
80	6pi. brown and green	5·50	11·00
81	9pi. brown and red	38·00	26·00
82	12pi. brown and black	23·00	55·00

83		18pi. black and brown	40·00	45·00
84		45pi. purple and blue	£120	£160
100		10s. green and red on yellow	£375	£800
101		£1 purple and black on red	£1300	£2750

13

1924

103	**13**	¼pi. grey and brown	2·00	50
104	**13**	½pi. black	6·00	14·00
118	**13**	½pi. green	2·25	1·00
105	**13**	¾pi. green	4·00	1·00
119	**13**	¾pi. black	4·25	1·00
106	**13**	1pi. purple and brown	2·25	2·00
107	**13**	1½pi. orange and black	3·25	14·00
120	**13**	1½pi. red	5·00	1·50
108	**13**	2pi. red and green	4·00	20·00
121	**13**	2pi. yellow and black	14·00	3·25
122	**13**	2½pi. blue	5·00	1·75
109	**13**	2¾pi. blue and purple	3·25	4·75
110	**13**	4pi. olive and purple	5·00	5·00
111	**13**	4½pi. blk & orge on green	3·50	5·00
112	**13**	6pi. brown and green	5·00	8·50
113	**13**	9pi. brown and purple	8·50	5·50
114	**13**	12pi. brown and black	14·00	60·00
115	**13**	18pi. black and orange	24·00	5·00
116	**13**	45pi. purple and blue	55·00	38·00
117	**13**	90pi. grn & red on yellow	£120	£250
102	**13**	£1 purple & black on red	£300	£850
117a	**13**	£5 black on yellow	£3250	£7500

14 Silver Coin of Amathus, 6th-century B.C.

1928. 50th Anniv of British Rule. Dated "1878 1928".

123	**14**	¾pi. violet	3·50	1·50
124	-	1pi. black and blue	3·50	1·50
125	-	1½pi. red	5·50	2·00
126	-	2½pi. blue	3·75	2·25
127	-	4pi. brown	9·00	9·00
128	-	6pi. blue	12·00	28·00
129	-	9pi. purple	9·50	15·00
130	-	18pi. black and brown	28·00	32·00
131	-	45pi. violet and blue	42·00	50·00
132	-	£1 blue and brown	£225	£300

DESIGNS—VERT: 1pi. Philosopher Zeno; 2½pi. Discovery of body of St. Barnabas; 4pi. Cloister, Abbey of Bella Paise; 9pi. Tekke of Umm Haram; 18pi. Statue of Richard I, Westminster; 45pi. St. Nicholas Cathedral, Famagusta, (now Lala Mustafa Pasha Mosque); £1 King George V. HORIZ: 1½pi. Map of Cyprus; 6pi. Badge of Cyprus.

24 Ruins of Vouni Palace

30 St. Sophia Cathedral, Nicosia (now Selimiye Mosque)

1934

133	**24**	¼pi. blue and brown	1·25	1·00
134	-	½pi. green	1·75	1·00
135	-	¾pi. black and violet	3·25	40
136	-	1pi. black and brown	2·75	2·25
137	-	1½pi. red	3·75	2·00
138	-	2½pi. blue	5·00	1·75
139	**30**	4½pi. black and red	5·00	4·75
140	-	6pi. black and blue	12·00	19·00
141	-	9pi. brown and violet	14·00	8·00
142	-	18pi. black and green	50·00	45·00
143	-	45pi. green and black	£100	80·00

DESIGNS—HORIZ: ½pi. Small Marble Forum, Salamis; ¾pi. Church of St. Barnabas and St. Hilarion, Peristerona; 1pi. Roman theatre, Soli; 1½pi. Kyrenia Harbour; 2½pi. Kolossi Castle; 45pi. Forest scene, Troodos. VERT: 6pi. Bayraktar Mosque, Nicosia; 9pi. Queen's Window, St. Hilarion Castle; 18pi. Buyuk Khan, Nicosia.

The ½pi. to 2½pi. values have a medallion portrait of King George V.

1935. Silver Jubilee. As T 10a of Gambia.

144		¾pi. blue and grey	4·00	1·50
145		1½pi. blue and red	6·00	2·75
146		2½pi. brown and blue	5·00	1·75
147		9pi. grey and purple	23·00	27·00

1937. Coronation. As T 10b of Gambia.

148		¾pi. grey	2·00	1·00
149		1½pi. red	2·50	2·50
150		2½pi. blue	3·00	3·00

36 Map of Cyprus

37 Othello's Tower, Famagusta

38 King George VI

1938

151	-	¼pi. blue and brown	1·75	60
152	-	½pi. green	2·25	50
152a	-	½pi. violet	3·00	75
153	-	¾pi. black and violet	21·00	1·75
154	-	1pi. orange	2·50	40
155	-	1½pi. red	6·00	1·50
155a	-	1½pi. violet	2·50	75
155ab	-	1½pi. green	6·00	1·25
155b	-	2pi. black and red	2·75	40
156	-	2½pi. blue	42·00	2·50
156a	-	3pi. blue	3·25	60
156b	-	4pi. blue	4·50	1·25
157	**36**	4½pi. grey	2·50	40
158	-	6pi. black and blue	3·50	1·00
159	**37**	9pi. black and purple	2·75	75
160	-	18pi. black and olive	14·00	1·75
161	-	45pi. green and black	45·00	4·75
162	**38**	90pi. mauve and black	35·00	8·00
163	-	£1 red and blue	65·00	30·00

DESIGNS: 2pi. Peristerona Church; 3pi., 4pi. Kolossi Castle. All other values except 4½pi., 9pi., 90pi. and £1 have designs as 1934 issue but portrait of King George VI.

1946. Victory. As T 11a of Gambia.

164		1½pi. violet	50	10
165		3pi. blue	50	40

1948. Silver Wedding. As T 11b/c of Gambia.

166		1½pi. violet	1·00	50
167		£1 blue	55·00	75·00

1949. U.P.U. As T 11d/e of Gambia.

168		1½pi. violet	60	1·50
169		2pi. red	1·50	1·50
170		3pi. blue	1·00	1·00
171		9pi. purple	1·00	3·75

1953. Coronation. As T 11h of Gambia.

172		1½pi. black and green	2·00	10

39 Carobs

42 Mavrovouni Copper Pyrites Mine

49 St. Hilarion Castle

53 Arms of Byzantium, Lusignan, Ottoman Empire and Venice

1955

173	**39**	2m. brown	1·00	40
174	-	3m. violet	65	15
175	-	5m. orange	2·50	10
176	**42**	10m. brown and green	2·75	10
177	-	15m. olive and blue	4·50	45
178	-	20m. brown and blue	1·50	15
179	-	25m. turquoise	4·00	60
180	-	30m. black and lake	3·75	10
181	-	35m. brown and turquoise	3·25	40
182	-	40m. green and brown	3·25	60
183	**49**	50m. blue and brown	3·25	30
184	-	100m. mauve and green	13·00	60
185	-	250m. blue and brown	16·00	13·00
186	-	500m. slate and purple	38·00	15·00
187	**53**	£1 lake and slate	30·00	55·00

DESIGNS—As Type **39**: 3m. Grapes; 5m. Oranges. As Type **42**: 15m. Troodos Forest; 20m. Beach of Aphrodite; 25m. 5th-century B.C. coin of Paphos; 30m. Kyrenia; 35m. Harvest in Mesaoria; 40m. Famagusta harbour. As Type **49**: 100m. Hala Sultan Tekke; 250m. Kanakaria Church. As Type **53**: 500m. Coins of Salamis, Paphos, Citium and Idalium.

ΚΥΠΡΙΑΚΗ
ΔΗΜΟΚΡΑΤΙΑ
KIBRIS
CUMHURİYETİ

54 "Cyprus Republic"

1960. Nos. 173/87 optd as T 54 ("CYPRUS REPUBLIC" in Greek and Turkish).

188	**39**	2m. brown	20	75
189	-	3m. violet	20	15
190	-	5m. orange	1·50	10
191	**42**	10m. brown and green	1·00	10
192	-	15m. olive and blue	2·25	40
193	-	20m. brown and blue	1·75	1·50
194	-	25m. turquoise	1·75	1·75
195	-	30m. black and lake	1·75	30
196	-	35m. brown and turquoise	1·75	70
197	-	40m. green and brown	2·00	2·50
198	**49**	50m. blue and brown	2·00	60
199	-	100m. mauve and green	9·00	2·50
200	-	250m. blue and brown	30·00	5·50
201	-	500m. slate and purple	45·00	27·00
202	**53**	£1 lake and slate	48·00	60·00

55 Map of Cyprus

1960. Constitution of Republic.

203	**55**	10m. sepia and green	30	10
204	**55**	30m. blue and brown	65	10
205	**55**	100m. purple and slate	2·00	2·00

56 Doves

1962. Europa.

206	**56**	10m. purple and mauve	10	10
207	**56**	40m. blue and cobalt	20	15
208	**56**	100m. emerald and green	20	20

57 Campaign Emblem

1962. Malaria Eradication.

209	**57**	10m. black and green	15	15
210	**57**	30m. black and brown	30	15

63 St. Barnabas's Church

1962

211	-	3m. brown and orange	10	30
212	-	5m. purple and green	10	10
213	-	10m. black and green	15	10
214	-	15m. black and purple	50	15
215	**63**	25m. brown and chestnut	60	20
216	-	30m. blue and light blue	20	10
217	-	35m. green and blue	35	10
218	-	40m. black and blue	1·25	1·75
219	-	50m. bronze and bistre	50	10
220	-	100m. brown and bistre	3·50	30
221	-	250m. black and brown	15·00	2·25
222	-	500m. brown and green	19·00	10·00
223	-	£1 bronze and grey	17·00	30·00

DESIGNS—VERT: 3m. Iron Age jug; 5m. Grapes; 10m. Bronze head of Apollo; 15m. Selimiye Mosque, Nicosia; 35m. Head of Aphrodite; 100m. Hala Sultan Tekke; 500m. Mouflon. HORIZ: 30m. Temple of Apollo Hylates; 40m. Skiing, Troodos; 50m. Salamis Gymnasium; 250m. Bella Paise Abbey; £1 St. Hilarion Castle.

72 Europa "Tree"

1963. Europa.

224	**72**	10m. blue and black	1·75	20
225	**72**	40m. red and black	6·50	2·00
226	**72**	150m. green and black	20·00	6·00

73 Harvester

1963. Freedom from Hunger.

227	**73**	25c. ochre, sepia and blue	30	25
228	-	75m. grey, black and lake	1·75	1·00

DESIGN: 75m. Demeter, Goddess of Corn.

75 Wolf Cub in Camp

1963. 50th Anniv of Cyprus Scout Movement and 3rd Commonwealth Scout Conference, Platres. Multicoloured.

229	3m. Type **75**	10	20
230	20m. Sea Scout	35	10
231	150m. Scout with Mouflon	1·00	2·50
MS231a	110×90 mm. Nos. 229/31 (sold at 250m.) Imperf	£110	£180

79 Children's Centre, Kyrenia

1963. Centenary of Red Cross. Multicoloured.

232	10m. Nurse tending child (vert)	50	15
233	100m. Type **79**	2·75	3·50

80 "Co-operation" (emblem)

1963. Europa.

234	**80**	20m. buff, blue and violet	1·75	40
235	**80**	30m. grey, yellow and blue	1·75	40
236	**80**	150m. buff, blue and brown	21·00	9·00

1964. U.N. Security Council's Cyprus Resolution, March 1964. Nos. 213 etc. optd with U.N. emblem and 1964.

237	10m. black and green	15	10
238	30m. blue and light blue	20	10
239	40m. black and blue	25	30
240	50m. bronze and bistre	25	10
241	100m. brown and bistre	25	50

82 Soli Theatre

1964. 400th Birth Anniv of Shakespeare. Mult.

242		15m. Type **82**	80	15
243		35m. Curium Theatre	80	15
244		50m. Salamis Theatre	80	15
245		100m. Othello Tower, and scene from "Othello"	1·25	2·25

86 Running

1964. Olympic Games, Tokyo.

246	**86**	10m. brown, black & yell	10	10
247	-	25m. brown, black and slate	20	10
248	-	75m. brown, black and chest	35	65

MS248a 110×90 mm. Nos. 246/8 (sold at 250m.) Imperf 6·00 15·00

DESIGNS—HORIZ: 25m. Boxing; 75m. Charioteers.

89 Europa "Flower"

1964. Europa.

249	**89**	20m. brown and ochre	1·25	10
250	**89**	30m. ultramarine and blue	1·25	10
251	**89**	150m. olive and green	11·00	5·50

90 Dionysus and Acme

1964. Cyprus Wines. Multicoloured.

252		10m. Type **90**	30	10
253		40m. Silenus (satyr) (vert)	65	1·25
254		50m. Commandaria wine (vert)	65	10
255		100m. Wine factory	1·50	2·00

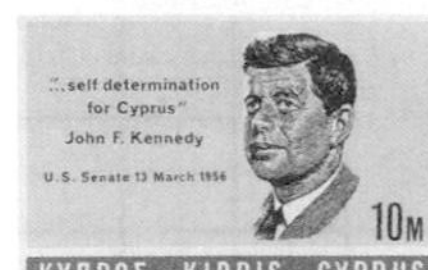

94 President Kennedy

1965. President Kennedy Commemoration.

256	**94**	10m. blue	10	10
257	**94**	40m. green	25	35
258	**94**	100m. red	30	35

MS258a 110×90 mm. Nos. 256/8 (sold at 250m.) Imperf 3·25 8·00

95 "Old Age"

1965. Introduction of Social Insurance Law.

259	**95**	30m. drab and green	15	10
260	-	45m. green, blue and ultramarine	20	10
261	-	75m. brown and flesh	1·25	2·50

DESIGNS—(As Type **95**): 45m. "Accident". LARGER (23×48 mm): 75m. "Maternity".

98 I.T.U. Emblem and Symbols

1965. Centenary of I.T.U.

262	**98**	15m. black, brown & yell	75	20
263	**98**	60m. black, grn & lt grn	7·50	3·25
264	**98**	75m. black, indigo & bl	8·50	4·75

99 I.C.Y. Emblem

1965. International Co-operation Year.

265	**99**	50m. brown and green	75	10
266	**99**	100m. purple and green	1·25	50

100 Europa "Sprig"

1965. Europa.

267	**100**	5m. black, brown & orge	50	10
268	**100**	45m. black, brown & grn	4·00	2·00
269	**100**	150m. black, brn & grey	9·00	4·50

1966. U.N. General Assembly's Cyprus Resolution. Nos. 211, 213, 216 and 221 optd U.N. Resolution on Cyprus 18 Dec. 1965.

270		3m. brown and orange	10	50
271		10m. black and green	10	10
272		30m. blue and light blue	15	15
273		250m. black and brown	80	2·25

102 Discovery of St. Barnabas's Body

1966. 1900th Death Anniv of St. Barnabas.

274	**102**	15m. multicoloured	10	10
275	-	25m. drab, black and blue	15	10
276	-	100m. multicoloured	45	2·00

MS277 110×91 mm. 250m. multicoloured (imperf) 3·50 13·00

DESIGNS—HORIZ: 25m. St. Barnabas's Chapel. VERT: 100m. St. Barnabas (icon). 102×82 mm.: 250m. "Privileges of Cyprus Church".

1966. No. 211 surch 5M.

278		5m. on 3m. brown & orange	10	10

107 General K. S. Thimayya and U.N. Emblem

1966. General Thimayya Commemoration.

279	**107**	50m. black and brown	30	10

108 Europa "Ship"

1966. Europa.

280	**108**	20m. green and blue	40	10
281	**108**	30m. purple and blue	40	10
282	**108**	150m. bistre and blue	3·25	3·00

109 Stavrovouni Monastery

113 Silver Coin of Evagoras I

1966. Multicoloured.. Multicoloured..

283		3m. Type **109**	40	10
284		5m. Church of St. James, Trikomo	10	10
285		10m. Zeno of Citium (marble bust)	15	10
286		15m. Minoan wine ship of 700 B.C. (painting)	15	10
287		20m. Type **113**	1·25	1·00
288		25m. Sleeping Eros (marble statue)	30	10
289		30m. St. Nicholas Cathedral, Famagusta	50	20
290		35m. Gold sceptre from Curium	50	30
291		40m. Silver dish from 7th century	70	30
292		50m. Silver coin of Alexander the Great	90	10
293		100m. Vase, 7th century B.C.	4·00	15
294		250m. Bronze ingot-stand	1·00	40
295		500m. "The Rape of Ganymede" (mosaic)	2·75	70
296		£1 Aphrodite (marble statue)	2·25	6·50

DESIGNS—VERT (As Type **109**): 5m. and 10m. HORIZ (As Type **113**): 15m., 25m. and 50m. VERT (As Type **113**): 30m., 35m., 40m. and 100m.

Nos. 294/6 are as Type **113** but larger, 28×40 mm.

123 Power Station, Limassol

1967. First Development Programme. Mult.

297		10m. Type **123**	10	10
298		15m. Arghaka-Maghounda Dam (vert)	15	10
299		35m. Troodos Highway (vert)	20	10
300		50m. Hilton Hotel, Nicosia (vert)	20	10
301		100m. Famagusta Harbour (vert)	20	1·10

124 Cogwheels

1967. Europa.

302	**124**	20m. olive, grn & lt grn	30	10
303	**124**	30m. violet, lilac and mauve	30	10
304	**124**	150m. sepia, brn chestnut	2·25	2·25

125 Throwing the Javelin

1967. Athletic Games, Thessalonika. Multicoloured.

305		15m. Type **125**	20	10
306		35m. Running	20	35
307		100m. High-jumping	30	1·00

MS308 110×90 mm. 250m. Running (amphora) and Map of Eastern Mediterranean (imperf) 1·25 6·50

127 Ancient Monuments

1967. International Tourist Year. Multicoloured.

309		10m. Type **127**	10	10
310		40m. Famagusta Beach	15	90
311		50m. Hawker Siddeley Comet-4 at Nicosia Airport	15	10
312		100m. Skier and youth hostel	20	95

128 Saint Andrew Mosaic

1967. Centenary of St Andrew's Monastery.

313	**128**	25m. multicoloured	10	10

129 "The Crucifixion" (icon)

1967. Cyprus Art Exhibition, Paris.

314	**129**	50m. multicoloured	10	10

130 The Three Magi

1967. 20th Anniv of UNESCO.

315	**130**	75m. multicoloured	20	20

131 Human Rights Emblem over Stars

1968. Human Rights Year. Multicoloured.

316		50m. Type **131**	10	10
317		90m. Human Rights and U.N. emblems	30	70

MS318 95×75½ mm. 250m. Scroll of Declaration 60 4·75

134 Europa "Key"

1968. Europa.

319	**134**	20m. multicoloured	25	10
320	**134**	30m. multicoloured	25	10
321	**134**	150m. multicoloured	1·00	2·25

135 U.N. Children's Fund Symbol and Boy drinking Milk

1968. 21st Anniv of UNICEF.

322	**135**	35m. brown, red and black	10	10

136 Aesculapius

1968. 20th Anniv of W.H.O.

323	**136**	50m. black, green and olive	10	10

137 Throwing the Discus

1968. Olympic Games, Mexico. Multicoloured.

324	10m. Type **137**	10	10
325	25m. Sprint finish	10	10
326	100m. Olympic Stadium (horiz)	20	1·25

138 I.L.O. Emblem

1969. 50th Anniv of I.L.O.

327	**138**	50m. brown and blue	15	10
328	**138**	90m. brown, black and grey	15	55

139 Mercator's Map of Cyprus, 1554

1969. 1st International Congress of Cypriot Studies.

329	**139**	35m. multicoloured	20	30
330	-	50m. multicoloured	20	10

DESIGN: 50m. Blaeu's map of Cyprus, 1635.

141 Europa Emblem

1969. Europa.

331	**141**	20m. multicoloured	30	10
332	**141**	30m. multicoloured	30	10
333	**141**	150m. multicoloured	1·00	2·00

142 European Roller ("Roller")

1969. Birds of Cyprus. Multicoloured.

334	5m. Type **142**	40	15
335	15m. Audouin's gull	50	15
336	20m. Cyprus warbler	50	15
337	30m. Jay ("Cyprus Jay") (vert)	50	15
338	40m. Hoopoe (vert)	55	30
339	90m. Eleonora's falcon (vert)	1·25	4·50

143 "The Nativity" (12th-century Wall Painting)

1969. Christmas. Multicoloured.

340	20m. Type **143**	15	10
341	45m. "The Nativity" (14th-century wall painting)	15	20
MS342	110×90 mm. 250m. "Virgin and Child between Archangels Michael and Gabriel" (6th–7th-century Mosaic) (imperf)	3·00	12·00

146 Mahatma Gandhi

1970. Birth Centenary of Mahatma Gandhi.

343	**146**	25m. blue, drab and black	50	10
344	**146**	75m. brown, drab and black	75	65

147 "Flaming Sun"

1970. Europa.

345	**147**	20m. brown, yell & orge	30	10
346	**147**	30m. blue, yellow & orge	30	10
347	**147**	150m. purple, yell & orge	1·00	2·50

148 Gladioli

1970. Nature Conservation Year. Multicoloured.

348	10m. Type **148**	10	10
349	50m. Poppies	15	10
350	90m. Giant fennel	50	1·40

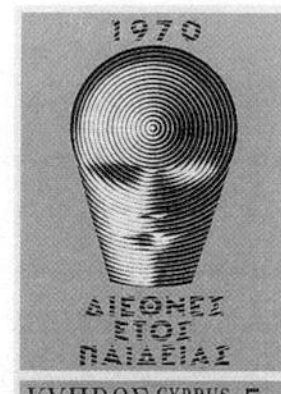

149 I.E.Y. Emblem

1970. Anniversaries and Events.

351	**149**	5m. black and brown	10	10
352	-	15m. multicoloured	10	10
353	-	75m. multicoloured	15	75

DESIGNS AND EVENTS: 5m. International Education Year. HORIZ: 15m. Mosaic (50th General Assembly of International Vine and Wine Office); 75m. Globe, dove and U.N. emblem (25th anniv of United Nations).

152 Virgin and Child

1970. Christmas. Wall-painting from Church of Panayia Podhythou, Galata. Multicoloured.

354	25m. Archangel (facing right)	15	20
355	25m. Type **152**	15	20
356	25m. Archangel (facing left)	15	20
357	75m. Virgin and Child between Archangels (42×30 mm)	15	30

1971. Multicoloured.. Multicoloured..

358	3m. Type **153**	30	35
359	5m. Saint George and Dragon (19th-century bas-relief)	10	10
360	10m. Woman in festival costume	15	50
361	15m. Archaic Bichrome Kylix (cup) (horiz)	20	10
362	20m. A pair of donors (Saint Mamas Church)	35	65
363	25m. "The Creation" (6th-century mosaic)	30	10
364	30m. Athena and horse-drawn chariot (4th-century B.C. terracotta) (horiz)	30	10
365	40m. Shepherd playing pipe (14th-century fresco)	1·00	1·00
366	50m. Hellenistic head (3rd-century B.C.)	80	10
367	75m. "Angel" (mosaic detail), Kanakaria Church	2·00	1·00
368	90m. Mycenaean silver bowl (horiz)	2·00	2·25
369	250m. Moufflon (detail of 3rd-century mosaic) (horiz)	1·50	30
370	500m. Ladies and sacred tree (detail 6th-century amphora) (horiz)	1·00	30
371	£1 Horned god from Enkomi (12th-century bronze statue)	1·75	45

SIZES: 24×37 mm or 37×24 mm 10m. to 90m., 41×28 mm or 28×41 mm 250m. to £1.

154 Europa Chain

1971. Europa.

372	**154**	20m. blue, ultram & blk	25	10
373	**154**	30m. green, myrtle & blk	25	10
374	**154**	150m. yellow, grn & blk	1·10	3·00

155 Archbishop Kyprianos

1971. 150th Anniv of Greek War of Independence. Multicoloured.

375	15m. Type **155**	10	10
376	30m. "Taking the Oath" (horiz)	10	10
377	100m. Bishop Germanos, flag and freedom-fighters	20	50

156 Kyrenia Castle

1971. Tourism. Multicoloured.

378	15m. Type **156**	10	10
379	25m. Gourd on sunny beach (vert)	10	10
380	60m. Mountain scenery (vert)	20	60
381	100m. Church of Saint Evlalios, Lambousa	20	65

157 Madonna and Child in Stable

1971. Christmas. Multicoloured.

382	10m. Type **157**	10	10
383	50m. The Three Wise Men	15	35
384	100m. The Shepherds	20	35

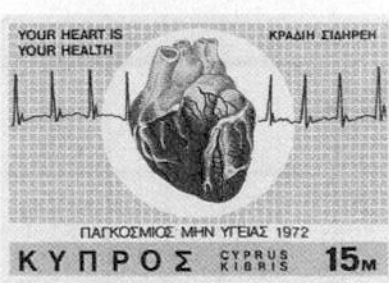

158 Heart

1972. World Heart Month.

385	**158**	15m. multicoloured	10	10
386	**158**	50m. multicoloured	20	45

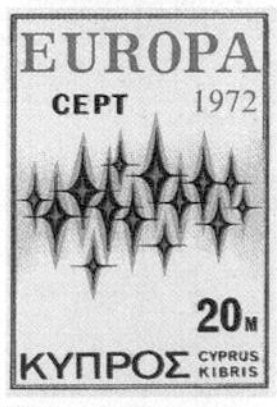

159 "Communications"

1972. Europa.

387	**159**	20m. orange, sepia & brn	40	15
388	**159**	30m. orange, ultram & bl	40	15
389	**159**	150m. orge, myrtle & grn	2·50	4·50

160 Archery

1972. Olympic Games, Munich. Multicoloured.

390	10m. Type **160**	25	10
391	40m. Wrestling	35	15
392	100m. Football	75	1·75

161 Stater of Marion

1972. Ancient Coins of Cyprus (1st series).

393	**161**	20m. blue, black and silver	20	10
394	-	30m. blue, black and silver	20	10
395	-	40m. brown, blk & silver	20	20
396	-	100m. pink, black and silver	60	1·00

COINS: 30m. Stater of Paphos; 40m. Stater of Lapithos; 100m. Stater of Idalion.

See also Nos. 486/9.

162 Bathing the Child Jesus

1972. Christmas. Detail of mural in Holy Cross Church, Agiasmati. Multicoloured.

397	10m. Type **162**	10	10
398	20m. The Magi	10	10
399	100m. The Nativity	15	30
MS400	100×90 mm. 250m. Showing the mural in full (imperf)	1·10	4·50

163 Mount Olympus, Troodos

1973. 29th International Ski Federation Congress. Multicoloured.

401	20m. Type **163**	10	10
402	100m. Congress emblem	25	35

164 Europa "Posthorn"

1973. Europa.

403	**164**	20m. multicoloured	25	10
404	**164**	30m. multicoloured	25	10
405	**164**	150m. multicoloured	1·50	3·50

165 Archbishop's Palace, Nicosia

1973. Traditional Architecture. Multicoloured.

406	20m. Type **165**	10	10
407	30m. House of Hajigeorgajis Cornessios, Nicosia (vert)	10	10
408	50m. House at Gourri, 1850 (vert)	15	10
409	100m. House at Rizokarpaso, 1772	40	85

1973. No. 361 surch 20M.

410	20m. on 15m. multicoloured	15	15

167 Scout Emblem

1973. Anniversaries and Events.

411	**167**	10m. green and brown	20	10
412	-	25m. blue and lilac	20	10
413	-	35m. olive, stone and green	20	25
414	-	50m. blue and indigo	20	10
415	-	100m. brown and sepia	50	80

DESIGNS AND EVENTS—VERT: 10m. (60th anniv of Cyprus Boy Scouts); 50m. Airline emblem (25th anniv of Cyprus Airways); 100m. Interpol emblem (50th anniv of Interpol). HORIZ: 25m. Outlines of Cyprus and the E.E.C. (Association of Cyprus with "Common Market"); 35m. F.A.O. emblem (10th anniv of F.A.O.).

168 Archangel Gabriel

1973. Christmas. Murals from Araka Church. Multicoloured.

416	10m. Type **168**	10	10
417	20m. Madonna and Child	10	10
418	100m. Araka Church (horiz)	40	75

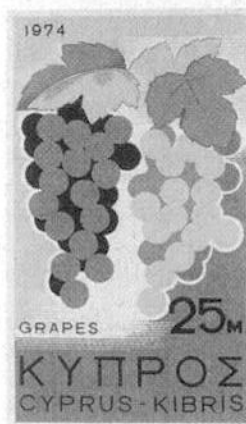

169 Grapes

1974. Products of Cyprus. Multicoloured.

419	25m. Type **169**	10	15
420	50m. Grapefruit	20	70
421	50m. Oranges	20	70
422	50m. Lemons	20	70

170 "The Rape of Europa" (Silver Stater of Marion)

1974. Europa.

423	**170**	10m. multicoloured	15	10
424	**170**	40m. multicoloured	40	30
425	**170**	150m. multicoloured	1·40	2·75

171 Title Page of A. Kyprianos' "History of Cyprus" (1788)

1974. 2nd International Congress of Cypriot Studies. Multicoloured.

426	10m. Type **171**	10	10
427	25m. Solon (philosopher) in mosaic (horiz)	15	10
428	100m. "Saint Neophytos" (wall painting)	60	75
MS429	111×90 mm. 250m. Ortelius' map of Cyprus and Greek Islands, 1584. Imperf	1·25	5·00

1974. Obligatory Tax. Refugee Fund. No. 359 surch REFUGEE FUND in English, Greek and Turkish and 10M.

430	10m. on 5m. multicoloured	10	10

1974. U.N. Security Council Resolution 353. Nos. 360, 365, 366 and 369 optd SECURITY COUNCIL RESOLUTION 353 20 JULY 1974.

431	10m. multicoloured	20	10
432	40m. multicoloured	25	60
433	50m. multicoloured	25	10
434	250m. multicoloured	60	3·00

174 "Refugees"

1974. Obligatory Tax. Refugee Fund.

435	**174**	10m. black and grey	10	10

175 "Virgin and Child between Two Angels", Stavros Church

1974. Christmas. Church Wall-paintings. Mult.

436	10m. Type **175**	10	10
437	50m. "Adoration of the Magi", Ayios Neophytos Monastery (vert)	20	10
438	100m. "Flight into Egypt", Ayios Neophytos Monastery	25	45

176 Larnaca–Nicosia Mail-coach, 1878

1975. Anniversaries and Events.

439	**176**	20m. multicoloured	25	10
440	-	30m. blue and orange	25	60
441	**176**	50m. multicoloured	25	10
442	-	100m. multicoloured	40	1·40

DESIGNS AND EVENTS—HORIZ: 20m., 50m. Centenary of Universal Postal Union. VERT: 30m. "Disabled Persons" (8th European Meeting of International Society for the Rehabilitation of Disabled Persons); 100m. Council flag (25th anniv of Council of Europe).

177 "The Distaff" (M. Kashalos)

1975. Europa. Multicoloured.

443	20m. Type **177**	25	40
444	30m. "Nature Morte" (C. Savva)	25	50
445	150m. "Virgin and Child of Liopetri" (G. P. Georghiou)	40	80

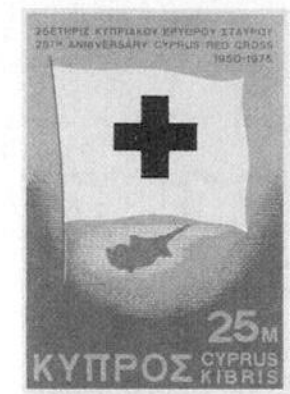

178 Red Cross Flag over Map

1975. Anniversaries and Events. Multicoloured.

446	25m. Type **178**	20	10
447	30m. Nurse and lamp (horiz)	20	10
448	75m. Woman's steatite idol (horiz)	20	90

EVENTS: 25m.25th anniv of Red Cross; 30m. International Nurses' Day; 75m. International Women's Year.

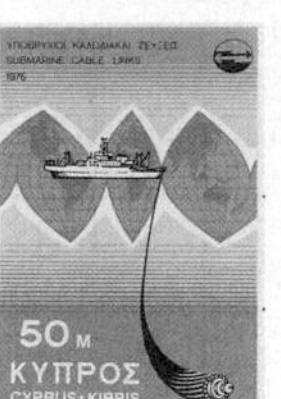

179 Submarine Cable Links

1976. Telecommunications Achievements.

449	**179**	50m. multicoloured	30	10
450	-	100m. yellow, vio & lilac	35	90

DESIGN—HORIZ: 100m. International subscriber dialling.

153 Cotton Napkin

1976. Surch 10M.

451	**153**	10m. on 3m. multicoloured	20	1·00

181 Human-figured Vessel, 19th-century

1976. Europa. Ceramics. Multicoloured.

452	20m. Type **181**	20	10
453	60m. Composite vessel, 2100–2000 B.C.	50	80
454	100m. Byzantine goblet	90	1·75

182 Self-help Housing

1976. Economic Reactivation. Multicoloured.

455	10m. Type **182**	10	10
456	25m. Handicrafts	15	20
457	30m. Reafforestation	15	20
458	60m. BAC One-Eleven (Air communications)	30	55

183 Terracotta Statue of Youth

1976. Cypriot Treasures.

459	**183**	5m. multicoloured	10	80
460	-	10m. multicoloured	10	60
461	-	20m. red, yellow and black	20	60
462	-	25m. multicoloured	20	10
463	-	30m. multicoloured	20	10
464	-	40m. green, brown & blk	30	55
465	-	50m. lt brown, brn & blk	30	10
466	-	60m. multicoloured	30	20
467	-	100m. multicoloured	40	50
468	-	250m. blue, grey and black	50	1·75
469	-	500m. black, brown & grn	60	2·00
470	-	£1 multicoloured	1·00	2·25

DESIGNS—VERT: 10m. Limestone head (23×34 mm); 20m. Gold necklace from Lambousa (24×37 mm); 25m. Terracotta warrior (24×37 mm); 30m. Statue of a priest of Aphrodite (24×37 mm); 250m. Silver dish from Lambousa (28×41 mm); 500m. Bronze stand (28×41 mm); £1 Statue of Artemis (28×41 mm). HORIZ: 40m. Bronze tablet (37×24 mm); 50m. Mycenaean crater (37×24 mm); 60m. Limestone sarcophagus (37×24 mm); 100m. Gold bracelet from Lambousa (As Type **183**).

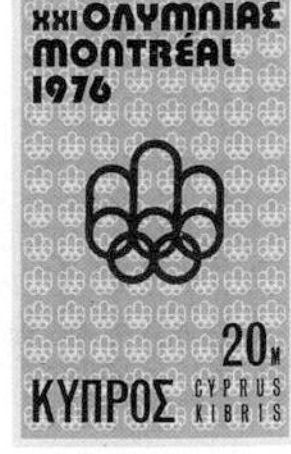

184 Olympic Symbol

1976. Olympic Games, Montreal.

471	**184**	20m. red, black and yellow	10	10
472	-	60m. multicoloured (horiz)	20	30
473	-	100m. multicoloured (horiz)	30	35

DESIGNS: 60m. and 100m. Olympic symbols (different).

185 "George Washington" (G. Stuart)

1976. Bicentenary of American Revolution.

474	**185**	100m. multicoloured	40	30

186 Children in Library

1976. Anniversaries and Events.

475	**186**	40m. multicoloured	15	15
476	-	50m. brown and black	15	10
477	-	80m. multicoloured	30	60

DESIGNS AND EVENTS: 40m. Type **186** (Promotion of Children's books); 50m. Low-cost housing (HABITAT Conference, Vancouver); 80m. Eye protected by hands (World Health Day).

187 Archangel Michael

1976. Christmas. Multicoloured.

478	10m. Type **187**	10	10
479	15m. Archangel Gabriel	10	10
480	150m. The Nativity	45	80

Designs show icons from Ayios Neophytis Monastery.

188 "Cyprus 74" (wood engraving by A. Tassos)

1977. Refugee Fund.

481	**188**	10m. black	20	10

See also Nos. 634 and 892 (after No. 728).

189 "View of Prodhromos" (A. Diamantis)

1977. Europa. Paintings. Multicoloured.

482	20m. Type **189**	20	10
483	60m. "Springtime at Monagroulli" (T. Kanthos)	30	55
484	120m. "Old Port, Limassol" (V. Ioannides)	60	2·40

190 500m. Stamp of 1960

1977. Silver Jubilee.

485	**190**	120m. multicoloured	30	30

191 Bronze Coin of Emperor Trajan

1977. Ancient Coins of Cyprus (2nd series).

486	**191**	10m. black, gold and blue	15	10
487	-	40m. black, silver and blue	30	30
488	-	60m. black, silver & orge	35	35
489	-	100m. black, gold and green	50	95

DESIGNS: 40m. Silver tetradrachm of Demetrios Poliorcetes; 60m. Silver tetradrachm of Ptolemy VIII; 100m. Gold octadrachm of Arsinoe II.

192 Archbishop Makarios in Ceremonial Robes

1977. Death of Archbishop Makarios. Mult.

490	20m. Type **192**	15	10
491	60m. Archbishop in doorway	20	10
492	250m. Head and shoulders portrait	50	1·10

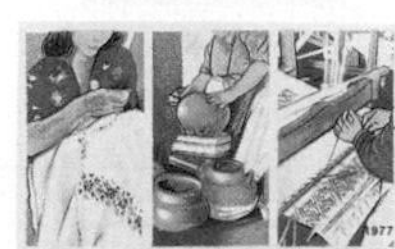

193 Embroidery, Pottery and Weaving

1977. Anniversaries and Events. Multicoloured.

493	20m. Type **193**	10	10
494	40m. Map of Mediterranean	15	20
495	60m. Gold medals	20	20
496	80m. Sputnik	20	85

DESIGNS COMMEMORATE: 20m. Revitalization of handicrafts; 40m. "Man and the Biosphere" Programme in the Mediterranean region; 60m. Gold medals won by Cypriot students in the Orleans Gymnasiade; 80m. 60th anniv of Russian Revolution.

194 "Nativity"

1977. Christmas. Children's Paintings Mult.

497	10m. Type **194**	10	10
498	40m. "The Three Kings"	10	10
499	150m. "Flight into Egypt"	25	80

195 Demetrios Libertis

1978. Cypriot Poets.

500	**195**	40m. brown and bistre	10	10
501	-	150m. grey, black and red	30	80

DESIGN: 150m. Vasilis Michaelides.

196 Chrysorrhogiatissa Monastery Courtyard

1978. Europa. Architecture. Multicoloured.

502	25m. Type **196**	15	10
503	75m. Kolossi Castle	25	35
504	125m. Municipal Library, Paphos	45	1·50

197 Archbishop of Cyprus, 1950–1977

1978. Archbishop Makarios Commem. Mult.

505	15m. Type **197**	15	20
506	25m. Exiled in Seychelles, 9 March 1956–28 March 1957	15	20
507	50m. President of the Republic 1960–1977	20	25
508	75m. "Soldier of Christ"	20	30
509	100m. "Fighter for Freedom"	25	35
MS510	100×80 mm. 300m. "The Great Leader" (imperf)	1·00	2·50

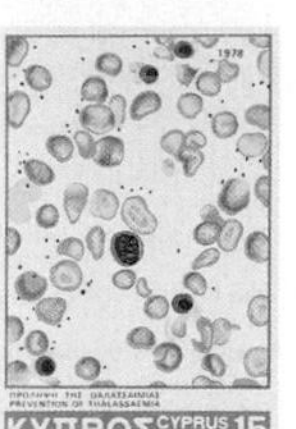

198 Affected Blood Corpuscles (Prevention of Thalassaemia)

1978. Anniversaries and Events.

511	**198**	15m. multicoloured	10	10
512	-	35m. multicoloured	15	10
513	-	75m. black and grey	20	30
514	-	125m. multicoloured	35	80

DESIGNS—VERT: 35m. Aristotle (sculpture) (2300th death anniv). HORIZ: 75m. "Heads" (Human Rights); 125m. Wright brothers and Wright Flyer I (75th anniv of Powered Flight).

199 Icon Stand

1978. Christmas.

515	**199**	15m. multicoloured	10	10
516	-	35m. multicoloured	15	10
517	-	150m. multicoloured	40	60

DESIGNS: 35m., 150m. Different icon stands.

200 Aphrodite (statue from Soli)

1979. Goddess Aphrodite (1st issue). Multicoloured.

518	75m. Type **200**	25	10
519	125m. Aphrodite on shell (detail from Botticelli's "Birth of Venus")	35	25

See also Nos. 584/5.

201 Van, Larnaca–Nicosia Mail-coach and Envelope

1979. Europa. Communications. Multicoloured.

520	25m. Type **201**	20	10
521	75m. Radar, satellite and early telephone	30	20
522	125m. Aircraft, ship and envelopes	85	1·50

202 Peacock Wrasse (*thalassoma pavo*)

1979. Flora and Fauna. Multicoloured.

523	25m. Type **202**	15	10
524	50m. Black partridge (vert)	70	60
525	75m. Cedar (vert)	45	30
526	125m. Mule	50	1·25

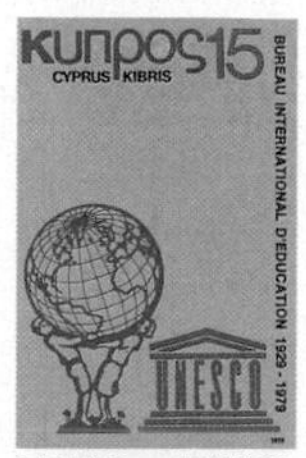

203 I.B.E. and UNESCO Emblems

1979. Anniversaries and Events.

527	**203**	15m. multicoloured	10	10
528	-	25m. multicoloured	10	10
529	-	50m. black, brown and ochre	20	15
530	-	75m. multicoloured	25	10
531	-	100m. multicoloured	30	20
532	-	125m. multicoloured	30	75

DESIGNS AND COMMEMORATIONS—VERT: 15m. Type **203** (50th anniv of International Bureau of Education); 125m. Rotary International emblem and "75" (75th anniv). HORIZ: 25m. Graphic design of dove and stamp album (20th anniv of Cyprus Philatelic Society); 50m. Lord Kitchener and map of Cyprus (Cyprus Survey Centenary); 75m. Child's face (International Year of the Child); 100m. Graphic design of footballers (25th anniv of U.E.F.A. European Football Association).

204 "Jesus" (from Church of the Virgin Mary of Arakas, Lagoudhera)

1979. Christmas. Icons. Multicoloured.

533	15m. Type **204**	10	10
534	35m. "Nativity" (Church of St Nicholas, Famagusta District) (29×41 mm)	10	10
535	150m. "Holy Mary" (Church of the Virgin Mary of Arakas)	25	45

205 1880 ½d. Stamp with "969" (Nicosia) Postmark

1980. Centenary of Cyprus Stamps. Multicoloured.

536	40m. Type **205**	10	10
537	125m. 1880 2½d. stamp with "974" (Kyrenia) postmark	15	20
538	175m. 1880 1s. stamp with "942" (Larnaca) postmark	15	25
MS539	105×85 mm. 500m. 1880 ½d., 1d., 2½d., 4d., 6d. and 1s. stamps (90×75 mm). Imperf	70	85

206 St. Barnabas (patron saint of Cyprus)

1980. Europa. Personalities. Multicoloured.

540	40m. Type **206**	15	10
541	125m. Zeno of Citium (founder of Stoic philosophy)	30	20

207 Sailing

1980. Olympic Games, Moscow. Multicoloured.

542	40m. Type **207**	10	10
543	125m. Swimming	20	20
544	200m. Gymnastics	25	25

208 Gold Necklace, Arsos (7th-century B.C.)

1980. Archaeological Treasures.

545	**208**	10m. multicoloured	30	1·00
546	-	15m. multicoloured	30	1·00
547	-	25m. multicoloured	30	30
548	-	40m. multicoloured	40	75
549	-	50m. multicoloured	40	10
550	-	75m. multicoloured	1·25	1·50
551	-	100m. multicoloured	65	15
552	-	125m. multicoloured	65	1·00
553	-	150m. multicoloured	75	15
554	-	175m. multicoloured	75	1·25
555	-	200m. multicoloured	75	30
556	-	500m. multicoloured	75	1·50
557	-	£1 multicoloured	1·00	1·25
558	-	£2 multicoloured	1·75	2·00

DESIGNS—HORIZ: 15m. Bronze cow, Vouni Palace (5th-cent B.C.); 40m. Gold finger-ring, Enkomi (13th-cent B.C.); 500m. Stone bowl, Khirokitia (6th-millennium B.C.). VERT: 25m. Amphora, Salamis (6th-cent B.C.); 50m. Bronze cauldron, Salamis (8th-cent B.C.); 75m. Funerary stele, Marion (5th-cent B.C.). 100m. Jug (15–14th-cent B.C.); 125m. Warrior (terracotta) (6th–5th-cent B.C.); 150m. Lions attacking bull (bronze relief), Vouni Palace (5th-cent B.C.); 175m. Faience rhyton, Kition (13th-cent B.C.); 200m. Bronze statue of Ingot God, Enkomi (12th-cent B.C.); £1 Ivory plaque, Salamis (7th-cent B.C.); £2 "Leda and the Swan" (mosaic), Kouklia (3rd-cent A.D.).

209 Cyprus Flag

1980. 20th Anniv of Republic of Cyprus. Multicoloured.

559	40m. Type **209**	20	10
560	125m. Signing Treaty of Establishment (41×29 mm)	25	15
561	175m. Archbishop Makarios	35	25

210 Head and Peace Dove

1980. International Day of Solidarity with Palestinian People.

562	**210**	40m. black and grey	20	20
563	-	125m. black and grey	35	35

DESIGN: 125m. Head and dove with olive branch.

211 Pulpit, Tripiotis Church, Nicosia

1980. Christmas. Multicoloured.

564	25m. Type **211**	10	10
565	100m. Holy Doors, Panayia Church Paralimni	15	20
566	125m. Pulpit, Ayios Lazaros Church, Larnaca	15	20

212 Folk Dancing

1981. Europa. Folklore, showing folk-dancing from paintings by T. Photiades.

567	**212**	40m. multicoloured	30	10
568	-	175m. multicoloured	60	50

213 Self-portrait

1981. 500th Anniv of Leonardo da Vinci's Visit. Multicoloured.

569	50m. Type **213**	40	10
570	125m. "The Last Supper" (50×25 mm)	70	40
571	175m. Cyprus lace and Milan Cathedral	95	60

214 "Ophrys kotschyi"

1981. Cypriot Wild Orchids. Multicoloured.

572	25m. Type **214**	40	60
573	50m. "Orchis punctulata"	50	70
574	75m. "Ophrys argolica elegans"	55	80
575	150m. "Epipactis veratrifolia"	65	90

215 Heinrich von Stephan

1981. Anniversaries and Events.

576	**215**	25m. dp green, grn & bl	15	10
577	-	40m. multicoloured	15	10
578	-	125m. black, red and green	30	25
579	-	150m. multicoloured	35	30
580	-	200m. multicoloured	70	80

DESIGNS AND COMMEMORATIONS: 25m. Type **137** (150th birth anniv of Heinrich von Stephan (founder of U.P.U.); 40m. Stylised man holding dish of food (World Food Day); 125m. Stylised hands (International Year for Disabled People); 150m. Stylised building and flower (European Campaign for Urban Renaissance); 200m. Prince Charles, Lady Diana Spencer and St. Paul's Cathedral (Royal Wedding).

216 "The Lady of the Angels" (from Church of the Transfiguration of Christ, Palekhori)

1981. Christmas. Murals from Nicosia District Churches. Multicoloured.

581	25m. Type **216**	20	10
582	100m. "Christ Pantokrator" (Church of Madonna of Arakas, Lagoudera) (vert)	60	20
583	125m. "Baptism of Christ" (Church of Our Lady of Assinou, Nikitari)	70	30

217 "Louomene" (Aphrodite bathing) (statue, 250 B.C.)

1982. Aphrodite (Greek goddess of love and beauty) Commemoration (2nd issue). Mult.

584	125m. Type **217**	55	45
585	175m. "Anadyomene" (Aphrodite emerging from the waters) (Titian)	70	65

218 Naval Battle with Greek Fire, 985 A.D.

1982. Europa. Historic Events. Multicoloured.

586	40m. Type **218**	60	10
587	175m. Conversion of Roman Proconsul Sergius Paulus to Christianity, Paphos, 45 A.D.	80	2·00

219 "XP" (monogram of Christ) (mosaic)

1982. World Cultural Heritage. Multicoloured.

588	50m. Type **219**	20	10
589	125m. Head of priest-king of Paphos (sculpture) (24×37 mm)	40	25
590	225m. Theseus (Greek god) (mosaic)	60	95

1982. No. 550 surch 100.

591	100m. on 75m. Funerary stele, Marion (5th-century B.C.)	50	50

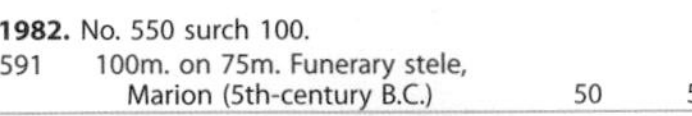

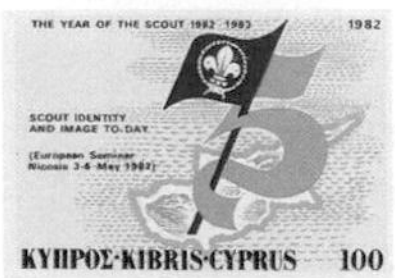

221 Cyprus and Stylised "75"

1982. 75th Anniv of Boy Scout Movement. Multicoloured.

592	100m. Type **221**	35	20
593	125m. Lord Baden-Powell	40	40
594	175m. Camp-site	40	90

222 Holy Communion, The Bread

1982. Christmas.

595	**222**	25m. multicoloured	10	10
596	-	100m. gold and black	30	15
597	-	250m. multicoloured	70	1·50

DESIGN—VERT: 100m. Holy Chalice. HORIZ: 250m. Holy Communion, The Wine.

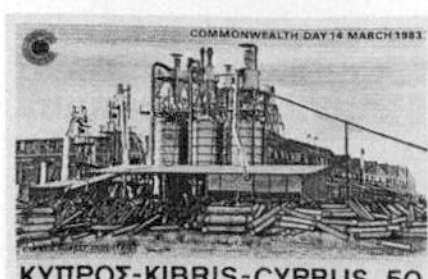

223 Cyprus Forest Industries' Sawmill

1983. Commonwealth Day. Multicoloured.

598	50m. Type **223**	10	10
599	125m. "Ikarios and the Discovery of Wine" (3rd-century mosaic)	20	25
600	150m. Folk-dancers, Commonwealth Film and Television Festival, 1980	25	35
601	175m. Royal Exhibition Building, Melbourne (Commonwealth Heads of Government Meeting, 1981)	25	40

224 Cyprosyllabic Inscription (6th-century B.C.)

1983. Europa. Multicoloured.

602	50m. Type **224**	30	10
603	200m. Copper ore, ingot (Enkomi 1400–1250 B.C.) and bronze jug (2nd century A.D.)	80	2·00

225 *Pararge aegeria*

1983. Butterflies. Multicoloured.

604	60m. Type **225**	25	20
605	130m. "Aricia agestis"	45	25
606	250m. "Glaucopsyche melanops"	85	2·50

1983. Nos. 545/56 surch.

607	1c. on 10m. Type **208**	35	1·00
608	2c. on 15m. Bronze cow, Vouni Palace (5th-century B.C.) (horiz)	35	1·25
609	3c. on 25m. Amphora, Salamis (6th-century B.C.)	35	1·00
610	4c. on 40m. Gold finger-ring, Enkomi (13th-century B.C.) (horiz)	40	1·00
611	5c. on 50m. Bronze cauldron, Salamis (8th-century B.C.)	50	50
612	6c. on 75m. Funerary stele, Marion (5th-century B.C.)	50	1·00
613	10c. on 100m. Jug (15th–14th-century B.C.)	50	40
614	13c. on 125m. Warrior (Terracotta) (6–5th-cent B.C.)	50	50
615	15c. on 150m. Lions attacking bull (bronze relief), Vouni Palace (5th-century B.C.) (horiz)	50	55
616	20c. on 200m. Bronze statue of Ingot God, Enkomi (12th-century B.C.)	50	65
617	25c. on 175m. Faience rhyton, Kition (13th-century B.C.)	55	1·10
618	50c. on 500m. Stone bowl, Khirokitia (6th-millenium B.C.) (horiz)	75	2·00

227 View of Power Station

1983. Anniversaries and Events. Multicoloured.

619	3c. Type **227**	10	20
620	6c. W.C.Y. logo	15	15
621	13c. "Sol Olympia" (liner) and "Polys" (tanker)	30	35
622	15c. Human Rights emblem and map of Europe	20	25
623	20c. Nicos Kazantzakis	20	75
624	25c. Makarios in church	25	75

COMMEMORATIONS: 3c. 30th anniv of Cyprus Electricity Authority; 6c. World Communications Year; 13c. 25th anniv of International Maritime Organization; 15c. 35th anniv of Universal Declaration of Human Rights; 20c. Birth centenary; 25c. 70th birth anniv.

228 St Lazaros Church, Larnaca

1983. Christmas. Church Towers. Multicoloured.

625	4c. Type **228**	15	10
626	13c. St. Varvara Church, Kaimakli, Nicosia	40	35
627	20c. St. Ioannis Church, Larnaca	70	1·50

229 Waterside Cafe, Larnaca

1984. Old Engravings. Each brown and black.

628	6c. Type **229**	15	15
629	20c. Bazaar at Larnaca (39×25 mm)	40	85
630	30c. Famagusta Gate, Nicosia (39×25 mm)	65	1·50
MS631	110×85 mm. 75c. "The Confession" (St. Lazarus Church, Larnaca)	1·50	2·00

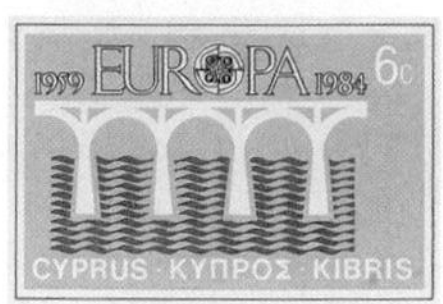

230 C.E.P.T. 25th Anniversary Logo

1984. Europa.

632	**230**	6c. lt green, green & blk	40	10
633	**230**	15c. lt blue, blue & black	70	2·00

1984. Obligatory Tax. Refugee Fund. As T 188 but new value and dated "1984".

634	1c. black	10	10

231 Running

1984. Olympic Games, Los Angeles. Multicoloured.

635	3c. Type **231**	15	10
636	4c. Olympic column	15	20
637	13c. Swimming	35	75
638	20c. Gymnastics	45	1·50

232 Prisoners-of-War

1984. 10th Anniv of Turkish Landings in Cyprus. Multicoloured.

639	15c. Type **232**	40	45
640	20c. Map and burning buildings	50	55

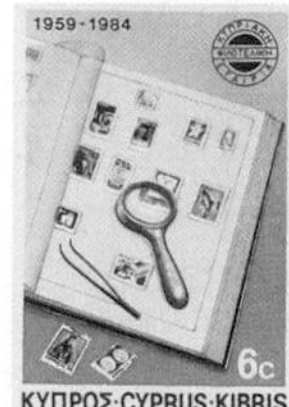

233 Open Stamp Album (25th Anniv of Cyprus Philatelic Society)

1984. Anniversaries and Events. Multicoloured.

641	6c. Type **233**	30	20
642	10c. Football in motion (horiz) (50th anniv of Cyprus Football Association)	45	30
643	15c. "Dr. George Papanicolaou" (medical scientist) (birth centenary)	75	50
644	25c. Antique map of Cyprus and ikon (horiz) (International Symposia on Cartography and Medieval Paleography)	1·10	2·00

234 St. Mark (miniature from 11th-century Gospel)

1984. Christmas. Illuminated Gospels. Mult.

645	4c. Type **234**	25	10
646	13c. Beginning of St. Mark's Gospel	45	50
647	20c. St. Luke (miniature from 11th-century Gospel)	70	2·00

235 Autumn at Platania, Troodos Mountains

1985. Cyprus Scenes and Landscapes. Mult.

648	1c. Type **235**	20	60
649	2c. Ayia Napa Monastery	20	60
650	3c. Phini Village–panoramic view	20	60
651	4c. Kykko Monastery	20	30
652	5c. Beach at Makronissos, Ayia Napa	20	20
653	6c. Village street, Omodhos (vert)	30	20
654	10c. Panoramic sea view	45	30
655	13c. Windsurfing	55	25
656	15c. Beach at Protaras	75	25
657	20c. Forestry for development (vert)	1·00	50
658	25c. Sunrise at Protaras (vert)	1·25	1·00
659	30c. Village house, Pera	1·50	1·25
660	50c. Apollo Hylates Sanctuary, Curium	2·50	1·75
661	£1 Snow on Troodos Mountains (vert)	4·00	3·00
662	£5 Personification of Autumn, House of Dionyssos, Paphos (vert)	14·00	15·00

236 Clay Idols of Musicians (7/6th century B.C.)

1985. Europa. European Music Year. Mult.

663	6c. Type **236**	50	35
664	15c. Violin lute, flute and score from the "Cyprus Suite"	90	2·25

237 Cyprus Coat of Arms (25th Anniv of Republic)

1985. Anniversaries and Events.

665	**237**	4c. multicoloured	15	15
666	-	6c. multicoloured	15	15
667	-	13c. multicoloured	25	1·00
668	-	15c. black, green and orange	1·00	1·25
669	-	20c. multicoloured	30	1·75

DESIGNS—HORIZ (43×30 mm): 6c. "Barn of Liopetri" (detail) (Pol. Georghiou) (30th anniv of EOKA Campaign); 13c. Three profiles (International Youth Year); 15c. Solon Michaelides (composer and conductor) (European Music Year). VERT—(as T **237**): 20c. U.N. Building, New York, and flags (40th anniv of United Nations Organization).

238 "The Visit of the Madonna to Elizabeth" (Lambadistis Monastery, Kalopanayiotis)

1985. Christmas. Frescoes from Cypriot Churches. Multicoloured.

670	4c. Type **238**	20	10
671	13c. "The Nativity" (Lambadistis Monastery, Kalopanayiotis)	50	65
672	20c. "Candlemas-day" (Asinou Church)	70	2·00

239 Figure from Hellenistic Spoon Handle

1986. New Archaeological Museum Fund. Multicoloured.

673	15c. Type **239**	45	45
674	20c. Pattern from early Ionian helmet and foot from statue	60	75
675	25c. Roman statue of Eros and Psyche	65	95
676	30c. Head of statue	75	1·10
MS677	111×90 mm. Nos. 673/6 (sold at £1)	13·00	17·00

No. 676 also commemorates the 50th anniv of the Department of Antiquities.

240 Cyprus Moufflon and Cedars

1986. Europa. Protection of Nature and the Environment. Multicoloured.

678	7c. Type **240**	35	30
679	17c. Greater flamingos ("Flamingos") at Larnaca Salt Lake	1·40	2·75

241 Cat's-paw Scallop (*Manupecten pesfelis*)

1986. Sea Shells. Multicoloured.

680	5c. Type **241**	30	15
681	7c. Atlantic trumpet triton	35	15
682	18c. Purple dye murex	60	70
683	25c. Yellow cowrie	1·00	2·00

1986. Nos. 653 and 655 surch.

684	7c. on 6c. Village street, Omodhos (vert)	40	30
685	18c. on 13c. Windsurfing	1·10	70

243 Globe Outline Map of Cyprus and Barn Swallows (Overseas Cypriots' Year)

1986. Anniversaries and Events. Multicoloured.

686	15c. Type **243**	1·00	45
687	18c. Halley's Comet over Cyprus beach (40×23 mm)	1·25	2·00
688	18c. Comet's tail over sea and Edmond Halley (40×23 mm)	1·25	2·00

Nos. 687/8 were printed together, se-tenant, forming a composite design.

244 Pedestrian Crossing

1986. Road Safety Campaign. Multicoloured.

689	5c. Type **244**	65	30
690	7c. Motor cycle crash helmet	70	30
691	18c. Hands fastening car seat belt	1·50	3·00

245 "The Nativity" (Church of Panayia tou Araka)

1986. Christmas. International Peace Year. Details of Nativity frescoes from Cypriot churches. Multicoloured.

692	5c. Type **245**	30	15
693	15c. Church of Panayia tou Moutoulla	75	30
694	17c. Church of St. Nicholas tis Steyis	90	2·00

246 Church of Virgin Mary, Asinou

1987. Troodos Churches on the World Heritage List. Multicoloured.

695	15c. Type **246**	70	1·10
696	15c. Fresco of Virgin Mary, Moutoulla's Church	70	1·10
697	15c. Church of Virgin Mary, Podithou	70	1·10
698	15c. Fresco of Three Apostles, St. Ioannis Lampadistis Monastery	70	1·10
699	15c. Annunciation fresco, Church of the Holy Cross, Pelentriou	70	1·10
700	15c. Fresco of Saints, Church of the Cross, Ayiasmati	70	1·10
701	15c. Fresco of Archangel Michael and Donor, Pedoula's Church of St. Michael	70	1·10
702	15c. Church of St. Nicolaos, Steyis	70	1·10
703	15c. Fresco of Prophets, Church of Virgin Mary, Araka	70	1·10

247 Proposed Central Bank of Cyprus Building

1987. Europa. Modern Architecture.

704	**247**	7c. multicoloured	40	30
705	-	18c. black, grey and green	85	2·00

DESIGN: 18c. Headquarters complex, Cyprus Telecommunications Authority.

248 Remains of Ancient Ship and Kyrenia Castle

1987. Voyage of "Kyrenia II" (replica of ancient ship). Multicoloured.

706	2c. Type **248**	35	20
707	3c. "Kyrenia II" under construction, 1982–5	45	90
708	5c. "Kyrenia II" at Paphos, 1986	75	20
709	17c. "Kyrenia II" at New York, 1986	1·75	90

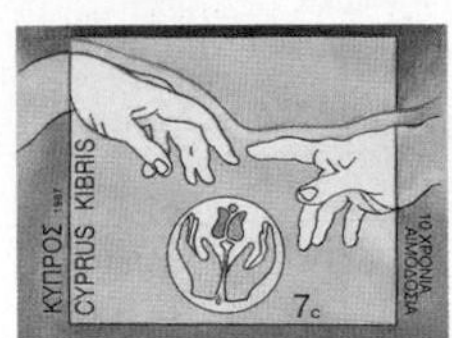

249 Hands (from Michelangelo's "Creation") and Emblem

1987. Anniversaries and Events. Multicoloured.

710	7c. Type **249** (10th anniv of Blood Donation Co-ordinating Committee)	50	25
711	15c. Snail with flowered shell and countryside (European Contryside Campaign)	1·10	40
712	20c. Symbols of ocean bed and Earth's crust ("Troodos '87" Ophiolites and Oceanic Lithosphere Symposium)	1·40	3·00

250 Nativity Crib

1987. Christmas. Traditional Customs. Mult.

713	5c. Type **250**	35	15
714	15c. Door knocker decorated with foliage	1·10	35
715	17c. Bowl of fruit and nuts	1·25	2·00

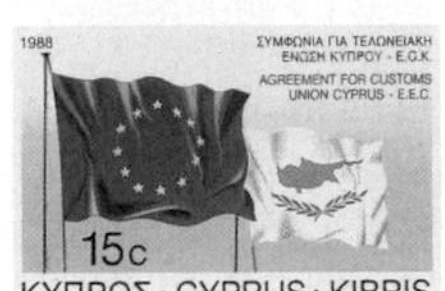

251 Flags of Cyprus and E.E.C.

1988. Cypriot–E.E.C. Customs Union. Mult.

716	15c. Type **251**	90	1·50
717	18c. Outline maps of Cyprus and E.E.C. countries	90	80

252 Intelpost Telefax Terminal

1988. Europa. Transport and Communications. Multicoloured.

718	7c. Type **252**	75	1·25
719	7c. Car driver using mobile telephone	75	1·25
720	18c. Nose of Cyprus Airways airliner and greater flamingos	2·50	3·00
721	18c. Boeing 737 airliner in flight and greater flamingos	2·50	3·00

253 Sailing

1988. Olympic Games, Seoul. Multicoloured.

722	5c. Type **253**	30	20
723	7c. Athletes at start	35	40
724	10c. Shooting	40	70
725	20c. Judo	90	1·50

254 Conference Emblem

1988. Non-Aligned Foreign Ministers' Conference, Nicosia.

726	**254**	1c. black, blue and green	10	10
727	-	10c. multicoloured	45	70
728	-	50c. multicoloured	3·50	2·50

DESIGNS: 10c. Emblem of Republic of Cyprus; 50c. Nehru, Tito, Nasser and Makarios.

255 "Cyprus 74" (wood-engraving by A. Tassos)

1988. Obligatory Tax. Refugee Fund. Variously dated.

892	**255** 1c. black and grey	10	10

1988. No. 651 surch 15c.

730	15c. on 4c. Kykko Monastery	1·75	1·25

256 "Presentation of Christ at the Temple" (Church of Holy Cross tou Agiasmati)

1988. Christmas. Designs showing frescoes from Cypriot churches. Multicoloured.

731	5c. Type **256**	25	20
732	15c. "Virgin and Child" (St. John Lampadistis Monastery)	55	25
733	17c. "Adoration of the Magi" (St. John Lampadistis Monastery)	80	1·75

257 Human Rights Logo

1988. 40th Anniv of Universal Declaration of Human Rights.

734	**257** 25c. lt blue, dp blue & bl	1·00	1·25

258 Basketball

1989. 3rd Small European States' Games, Nicosia. Multicoloured.

735	1c. Type **258**	30	15
736	5c. Javelin	30	15
737	15c. Wrestling	65	20
738	18c. Athletics	85	1·00
MS739	109×80 mm. £1 Angel and laurel wreath (99×73 mm). Imperf	6·00	6·50

259 Lingri Stick Game

1989. Europa. Children's Games. Multicoloured.

740	7c. Type **259**	1·10	1·50
741	7c. Ziziros	1·10	1·50
742	18c. Sitsia	1·25	1·60
743	18c. Leapfrog	1·25	1·60

260 "Universal Man"

1989. Bicentenary of the French Revolution.

744	**260** 18c. multicoloured	1·00	60

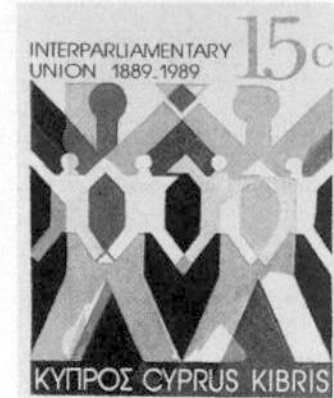

261 Stylized Human Figures

1989. Centenary of Interparliamentary Union (15c.) and 9th Non-Aligned Summit Conference, Belgrade (30c.). Multicoloured.

745	15c. Type **261**	65	40
746	30c. Conference logo	1·10	1·10

262 Worker Bees tending Larvae

1989. Bee-keeping. Multicoloured.

748	3c. Type **262**	30	25
749	10c. Bee on rock-rose flower	70	50
750	15c. Bee on lemon flower	95	50
751	18c. Queen and worker bees	1·10	1·75

263 Outstretched Hand and Profile (aid for Armenian earthquake victims)

1989. Anniversaries and Events. Multicoloured.

752	3c. Type **263**	30	1·25
753	5c. Airmail envelope (Cyprus Philatelic Society F.I.P. membership)	45	10
754	7c. Crab symbol and daisy (European Cancer Year)	75	1·40
755	17c. Vegetables and fish (World Food Day)	1·10	1·40

264 Winter (detail from "Four Seasons")

1989. Roman Mosaics from Paphos. Multicoloured.

756	1c. Type **264**	35	1·50
757	2c. Personification of Crete (32×24 mm)	45	1·50
758	3c. Centaur and Maenad (24×32 mm)	55	1·50
759	4c. Poseidon and Amymone (32×24 mm)	80	1·60
760	5c. Leda	80	20
761	7c. Apollon	90	25
762	10c. Hermes and Dionysos (24×32 mm)	1·25	30
763	15c. Cassiopeia	2·00	45
764	18c. Orpheus (32×24 mm)	2·00	50
765	20c. Nymphs (24×32 mm)	2·25	75
766	25c. Amazon (24×32 mm)	2·25	80
767	40c. Doris (32×24 mm)	3·50	1·75
768	50c. Heracles and the Lion (39×27 mm)	3·50	1·75
769	£1 Apollon and Daphne (39×27 mm)	6·00	3·25
770	£3 Cupid (39×27 mm)	12·00	14·00

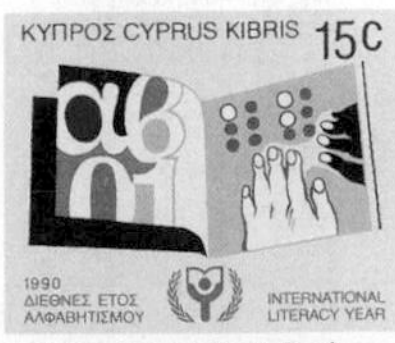

265 Hands and Open Book (International Literacy Year)

1990. Anniversaries and Events. Multicoloured.

771	15c. Type **265**	55	50
772	17c. Dove and profiles (83rd Inter-Parliamentary Conference, Nicosia)	65	90
773	18c. Lions International emblem (Lions Europa Forum, Limassol)	75	90

266 District Post Office, Paphos

1990. Europa. Post Office Buildings. Mult.

774	7c. Type **266**	1·10	25
775	18c. City Centre Post Office, Limassol	1·40	3·00

267 Symbolic Lips (25th anniv of Hotel and Catering Institute)

1990. European Tourism Year. Multicoloured.

776	5c. Type **267**	25	25
777	7c. Bell tower, St. Lazarus Church (1100th anniv)	30	25
778	15c. Butterflies and woman	2·25	45
779	18c. Birds and man	2·50	4·25

268 Sun (wood carving)

1990. 30th Anniv of Republic. Multicoloured.

780	15c. Type **268**	65	45
781	17c. Bulls (pottery design)	75	60
782	18c. Fishes (pottery design)	85	70
783	40c. Tree and birds (wood carving)	2·50	5·50
MS784	89×89 mm. £1 30th Anniversary emblem. Imperf	3·75	6·50

269 *Chionodoxa lochiae*

1990. Endangered Wild Flowers. Book illustrations by Elektra Megaw. Multicoloured.

785	2c. Type **269**	60	1·60
786	3c. "Pancratium maritimum"	60	1·60
787	5c. "Paeonia mascula"	85	20
788	7c. "Cyclamen cyprium"	90	25
789	15c. "Tulipa cypria"	1·75	30
790	18c. "Crocus cyprius"	1·90	3·75

270 "Nativity"

1990. Christmas. 16th-century Icons. Mult.

791	5c. Type **270**	50	20
792	15c. "Virgin Hodegetria"	1·40	30
793	17c. "Nativity" (different)	1·60	3·50

271 Archangel

1991. 6th-century Mosaics from Kanakaria Church. Multicoloured.

794	5c. Type **271**	20	15
795	15c. Christ Child	75	20
796	17c. St. James	1·50	1·75
797	18c. St. Matthew	1·75	2·25

272 *Ulysses* Spacecraft

1991. Europa. Europa in Space. Multicoloured.

798	7c. Type **272**	90	20
799	18c. "Giotto" and Halley's Comet	1·60	2·50

273 Young Cyprus Wheatear

1991. Cyprus Wheatear. Multicoloured.

800	5c. Type **273**	1·00	40
801	7c. Adult bird in autumn plumage	1·10	40
802	15c. Adult male in breeding plumage	1·50	50
803	30c. Adult female in breeding plumage	2·00	4·00

274 Mother and Child with Tents

1991. 40th Anniv of U.N. Commission for Refugees. Each deep brown, brown and silver.

804	5c. Type **274**	25	15
805	15c. Three pairs of legs	90	65
806	18c. Three children	1·10	2·50

1991. Obligatory Tax. Refugee Fund. As T 255 but inscr '1991', '1992', '1993', '1994', '1995', '1996', '1997', '1998', '1999', '2000', '2001', '2002', '2003', '2004', '2005' and '2006'.

807	**255**	1c. black and grey	20	20

275 The Nativity

1991. Christmas. Multicoloured.

808	5c. Type **275**	40	15
809	15c. Saint Basil	80	40
810	17c. Baptism of Jesus	1·10	2·00

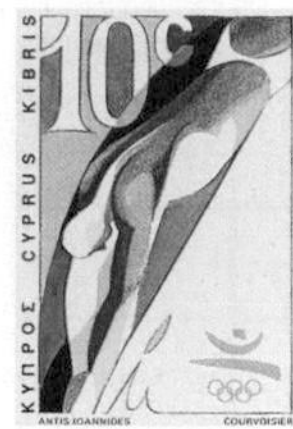

276 Swimming

1992. Olympic Games, Barcelona. Multicoloured.

811	10c. Type **276**	60	35
812	20c. Long jump	1·00	70
813	30c. Running	1·40	1·40
814	35c. Discus	1·60	2·50

277 World Map and Emblem ("EXPO '92" Worlds Fair, Seville)

1992. Anniversaries and Events. Multicoloured.

815	20c. Type **277**	1·60	80
816	25c. European map and football (10th under-16 European Football Championship)	1·75	1·10
817	30c. Symbols of learning (inauguration of University of Cyprus)	1·75	3·00

278 Compass Rose and Map of Voyage

1992. Europa. 500th Anniv of Discovery of America by Columbus. Multicoloured.

818	10c. Type **278**	1·10	1·40
819	10c. "Departure from Palos" (R. Balaga)	1·10	1·40
820	30c. Fleet of Columbus	1·50	2·00
821	30c. Christopher Columbus	1·50	2·00

Nos. 818/19 and 820/1 were each issued together, se-tenant, forming composite designs.

279 *Chamaeleo chamaeleon*

1992. Reptiles. Multicoloured.

822	7c. Type **279**	75	30
823	10c. "Lacerta laevis troodica" (lizard)	95	45
824	15c. "Mauremys caspica" (turtle)	1·40	80
825	20c. "Coluber cypriensis" (snake)	1·60	2·75

280 Minoan Wine Ship of 7th Century B.C. and Modern Tanker

1992. 7th International Maritime and Shipping Conference, Nicosia.

826	**280**	50c. multicoloured	3·00	3·00

281 "Visitation of the Virgin Mary to Elizabeth", Church of the Holy Cross, Pelendri

1992. Christmas. Church Fresco Paintings. Mult.

827	7c. Type **281**	50	15
828	15c. "Virgin and Child Enthroned", Church of Panayia tou Araka	85	45
829	20c. "Virgin and Child", Ayios Nicolaos tis Stegis Church	1·25	2·50

282 School Building and Laurel Wreath

1993. Centenary of Pancyprian Gymnasium (secondary school).

830	**282**	10c. multicoloured	75	60

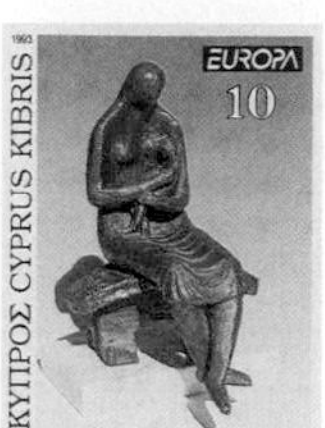

283 "Motherhood" (bronze sculpture, Nicos Dymiotis)

1993. Europa. Comtemporary Art. Multicoloured.

831	10c. Type **283**	75	50
832	30c. "Motherhood" (painting, Christoforos Savva) (horiz)	1·50	2·25

284 Women Athletes (13th European Cup for Women)

1993. Anniversaries and Events. Multicoloured.

833	7c. Type **284**	40	30
834	10c. Scout symbols (80th anniv of Scouting in Cyprus) (vert)	55	40
835	20c. Water-skier, dolphin and gull (Moufflon Encouragement Cup) (inscr "Mufflon")	11·00	11·00
835a	20c. Water-skier, dolphin and seabird (inscr "Moufflon")	95	95
836	25c. Archbishop Makarios III and monastery (80th birth anniv)	1·40	2·00

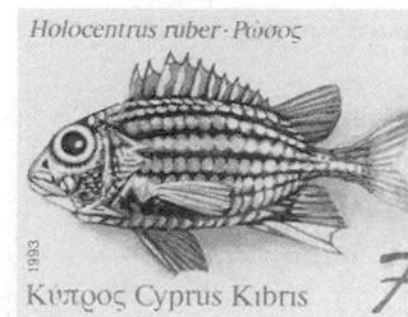

285 Red Squirrelfish

1993. Fish. Multicoloured.

837	7c. Type **285**	50	25
838	15c. Red scorpionfish	75	55
839	20c. Painted comber	85	85
840	30c. Grey triggerfish	1·60	2·50

286 Conference Emblem

1993. 12th Commonwealth Summit Conference.

841	**286**	35c. brown and ochre	1·60	1·90
842	**286**	40c. brown and ochre	1·90	2·40

287 Ancient Sailing Ship and Modern Coaster

1993. "Maritime Cyprus '93" International Shipping Conference, Nicosia.

843	**287**	25c. multicoloured	1·40	1·40

288 Cross from Stavrovouni Monastery

1993. Christmas. Church Crosses. Multicoloured.

844	7c. Type **288**	40	15
845	20c. Cross from Lefkara	1·00	60
846	25c. Cross from Pedoulas (horiz)	1·25	2·50

289 Copper Smelting

1994. Europa. Discoveries. Ancient Copper Industry. Multicoloured.

847	10c. Type **289**	50	35
848	30c. Ingot, ancient ship and map of Cyprus	1·25	2·00

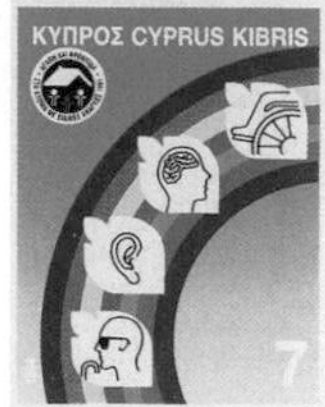

290 Symbols of Disability (Persons with Special Needs Campaign)

1994. Anniversaries and Events. Multicoloured.

849	7c. Type **290**	50	25
850	15c. Olympic rings in flame (Centenary of International Olympic Committee)	75	55
851	20c. Peace doves (World Gymnasiade, Nicosia)	90	80
852	25c. Adults and unborn baby in tulip (International Year of the Family)	1·25	2·25

291 Houses, Soldier and Family

1994. 20th Anniv of Turkish Landings in Cyprus. Multicoloured.

853	10c. Type **291**	50	40
854	50c. Soldier and ancient columns	2·00	3·25

292 Black Pine

1994. Trees. Multicoloured.

855	7c. Type **292**	50	25
856	15c. Cyprus cedar	75	55
857	20c. Golden oak	90	80
858	30c. Strawberry tree	1·40	2·50

293 Boeing 737, Route Map and Emblem

1994. 50th Anniv of I.C.A.O.

859	**293**	30c. multicoloured	2·00	2·00

294 "Virgin Mary" (detail) (Philip Goul)

1994. Christmas. Church Paintings. Multicoloured.

860	7c. Type **294**	60	15
861	20c. "The Nativity" (detail) (Byzantine)	1·40	60
862	25c. "Archangel Michael" (detail) (Goul)	1·60	2·75

295 Woman from Paphos wearing Foustani

1994. Traditional Costumes. Multicoloured.

863	1c. Type **295**	50	1·50
864	2c. Bride from Karpass	65	1·50
865	3c. Woman from Paphos wearing sayia	70	1·50
866	5c. Woman from Messaoria wearing foustani	80	1·50
867	7c. Bridegroom	85	20
868	10c. Shepherd from Messaoria	1·10	40
869	15c. Woman from Nicosia in festive costume	2·00	40
870	20c. Woman from Karpass wearing festive sayia	2·00	50
871	25c. Woman from Pitsillia	2·25	60
872	30c. Woman from Karpass wearing festive doupletti	2·25	70
873	35c. Countryman	2·25	1·50
874	40c. Man from Messaoria in festive costume	2·50	2·00
875	50c. Townsman	2·50	2·50
876	£1 Townswoman wearing festive sarka	4·00	4·50

296 "Hearth Room" Excavation, Alassa, and Frieze

1995. 3rd International Congress of Cypriot Studies, Nicosia. Multicoloured.

877	20c. Type **296**	75	75
878	30c. Hypostyle hall, Kalavasos, and Mycenaean amphora	1·00	1·75
MS879	110×80 mm. £1 Old Archbishop's Palace, Nicosia (107×71 mm). Imperf	3·50	5·00

297 Statue of Liberty, Nicosia (left detail)

1995. 40th Anniv of Start of E.O.K.A. Campaign. Different details of the statue. Multicoloured.

880	20c. Type **297**	1·10	1·40
881	20c. Centre detail (face value at top right)	1·10	1·40
882	20c. Right detail (face value at bottom right)	1·10	1·40

Nos. 880/2 were printed together, se-tenant, forming a composite design.

298 Nazi Heads on Peace Dove over Map of Europe

1995. Europa. Peace and Freedom. Multicoloured.

883	10c. Type **298**	1·00	50
884	30c. Concentration camp prisoner and peace dove	2·25	3·25

299 Symbolic Figure holding Healthy Food

1995. Healthy Living. Multicoloured.

885	7c. Type **299**	30	25
886	10c. "AIDS" and patients (horiz)	70	60
887	15c. Drug addict (horiz)	75	60
888	20c. Smoker and barbed wire	95	1·50

300 European Union Flag and European Culture Month Logo

1995. European Culture Month and "Europhilex '95" International Stamp Exhibition, Nicosia. MS891 blue, yellow and stone or multicoloured (others).

889	20c. Type **300**	55	60
890	25c. Map of Europe and Cypriot church	70	1·25
MS891	95×86 mm. 50c. Peace dove (42×30 mm); 50c. European Cultural Month symbol (42×30 mm)	6·00	7·00

301 Peace Dove with Flags of Cyprus and United Nations

1995. Anniversaries and Events. Multicoloured.

893	10c. Type **301** (50th anniv of United Nations)	50	35
894	15c. Hand pushing ball over net (cent of volleyball) (vert)	95	50
895	20c. Safety pin on leaf (European Nature Conservation Year) (vert)	1·10	80
896	25c. Clay pigeon contestant (World Clay Target Shooting Championship)	1·25	2·25

302 Reliquary from Kykko Monastery

1995. Christmas.

897	**302**	7c. multicoloured	40	15
898	-	20c. multicoloured	90	45
899	-	25c. multicoloured	1·40	2·25

DESIGNS: 20, 25c. Different reliquaries of Virgin and Child from Kykko Monastery.

303 Family (25th anniv of Pancyprian Organization of Large Families)

1996. Anniversaries and Events. Multicoloured.

900	10c. Type **303**	50	35
901	20c. Film camera (centenary of cinema)	1·25	70
902	35c. Silhouette of parent and child in globe (50th anniv of UNICEF)	1·75	1·75
903	40c. "13" and Commonwealth emblem (13th Conference of Commonwealth Speakers and Presiding Officers)	1·75	2·75

304 Maria Synglitiki

1996. Europa. Famous Women. Multicoloured.

904	10c. Type **304**	1·00	30
905	30c. Queen Caterina Cornaro	2·00	2·75

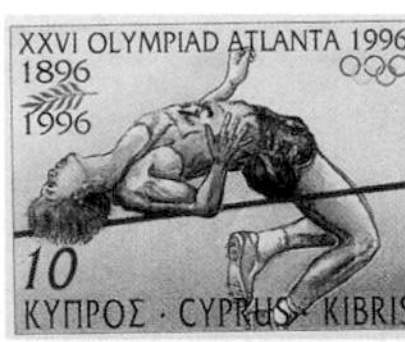

305 High Jump

1996. Centennial Olympic Games, Atlanta. Multicoloured.

906	10c. Type **305**	75	30
907	20c. Javelin	1·25	65
908	25c. Wrestling	1·40	1·10
909	30c. Swimming	1·60	2·50

306 Watermill

1996. Mills. Multicoloured.

910	10c. Type **306**	70	40
911	15c. Olivemill	85	50
912	20c. Windmill	1·00	90
913	25c. Handmill	1·10	2·00

307 Icon of Our Lady of Iberia, Moscow

1996. Cyprus–Russia Joint Issue. Orthodox Religion. Multicoloured.

914	30c. Type **307**	1·75	2·00
915	30c. Stravrovouni Monastery, Cyprus	1·75	2·00
916	30c. Icon of St. Nicholas, Cyprus	1·75	2·00
917	30c. Voskresenskie Gate, Moscow	1·75	2·00

308 "The Nativity" (detail)

1996. Christmas. Religious Murals from Church of The Virgin of Asinou. Multicoloured.

918	7c. Type **308**	60	15
919	20c. "Virgin Mary between the Archangels Gabriel and Michael"	1·50	45
920	25c. "Christ bestowing Blessing" (vert)	1·90	2·75

309 Basketball

1997. Final of European Basketball Cup.

921	**309**	30c. multicoloured	2·25	2·00

310 "The Last Supper"

1997. Easter. Religious Frescoes from Monastery of St. John Lambadestis. Multicoloured.

922	15c. Type **310**	1·00	50
923	25c. "The Crucifixion"	1·25	1·50

311 Kori Kourelleni and Prince

1997. Europa. Tales and Legends. Multicoloured.

924	15c. Type **311**	1·00	40
925	30c. Digenis and Charon	1·75	2·50

312 *Oedipoda miniata* (grasshopper)

1997. Insects. Multicoloured.

926	10c. Type **312**	65	30
927	15c. "Acherontia atropos" (hawk moth)	95	40
928	25c. "Daphnis nerii" (hawk moth)	1·60	1·25
929	35c. "Ascalaphus macaronius" (owl-fly)	1·75	2·50

313 Archbishop Makarios III and Chapel

1997. 20th Death Anniv of Archbishop Makarios III.
930 **313** 15c. multicoloured 1·25 50

314 The Nativity

1997. Christmas. Byzantine Frescos from the Monastery of St. John Lambadestis. Mult.
931 10c. Type **314** 60 15
932 25c. Three Kings following the star 1·75 60
933 30c. Flight into Egypt 1·90 2·75

315 Green Jasper

1998. Minerals. Multicoloured.
934 10c. Type **315** 70 30
935 15c. Iron pyrite 95 45
936 25c. Gypsum 1·40 1·25
937 30c. Chalcedony 1·50 2·50

316 Players competing for Ball

1998. World Cup Football Championship, France.
938 **316** 35c. multicoloured 1·75 1·40

317 Cataclysmos Festival, Larnaca

1998. Europa. Festivals. Multicoloured.
939 15c. Type **317** 1·25 40
940 30c. House of Representatives, Nicosia (Declaration of Independence) 1·75 2·50

318 Mouflon Family Group

1998. Endangered Species. Cyprus Mouflon. Mult.
941 25c. Type **318** 1·25 1·40
942 25c. Mouflon herd 1·25 1·40
943 25c. Head of ram 1·25 1·40
944 25c. Ram on guard 1·25 1·40

319 Flames and Globe Emblem

1998. 50th Anniv of Universal Declaration of Human Rights.
959 **319** 50c. multicoloured 1·25 1·60

320 World "Stamp" and Magnifying Glass

1998. World Stamp Day.
960 **320** 30c. multicoloured 1·60 1·60

321 "The Annunciation"

1998. Christmas. Multicoloured.
961 10c. Type **321** 60 20
962 25c. "The Nativity" 1·40 65
963 30c. "The Baptism of Christ" 1·40 2·50
MS964 102×75 mm. Nos. 961/3 3·00 3·50

322 *Pleurotus eryngii*

1999. Mushrooms of Cyprus. Multicoloured.
965 10c. Type **322** 50 30
966 15c. "Lactarius deliciosus" 80 40
967 25c. "Sparassis crispa" 1·10 90
968 30c. "Morchella elata" 1·40 2·25

323 Pair of Moufflons at Tripylos Reserve

1999. Europa. Parks and Gardens. Multicoloured.
969 15c. Type **323** 1·00 50
970 30c. Turtles on beach at Lara Reserve 1·75 2·25

324 Council of Europe Building, Emblem and Flags

1999. 50th Anniv of Council of Europe.
971 **324** 30c. multicoloured 1·50 1·75

325 Temple of Hylates Apollo, Kourion

1999. Cyprus–Greece Joint Issue. 4000 Years of Greek Culture. Multicoloured.
972 25c. Type **325** 1·40 1·75
973 25c. Mycenaean pot depicting warriors 1·40 1·75
974 25c. Mycenaean crater depicting horse 1·40 1·75
975 25c. Temple of Apollo, Delphi 1·40 1·75

326 Paper Aeroplane Letters and U.P.U. Emblem

1999. 125th Anniv of Universal Postal Union. Multicoloured.
976 15c. Type **326** 1·00 50
977 35c. "125" and U.P.U. emblem 1·50 2·00

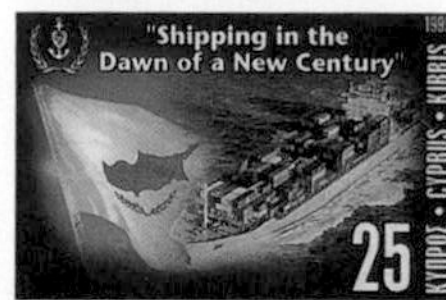

327 Container Ship and Cypriot Flag

1999. "Maritime Cyprus '99" Conference. Sheet 103×80 mm, containing T **327** and similar horiz designs. Multicoloured.
MS978 25c. Type **327**; 25c. Binoculars and chart; 25c. Stern of container ship; 25c. Tanker 3·50 4·00

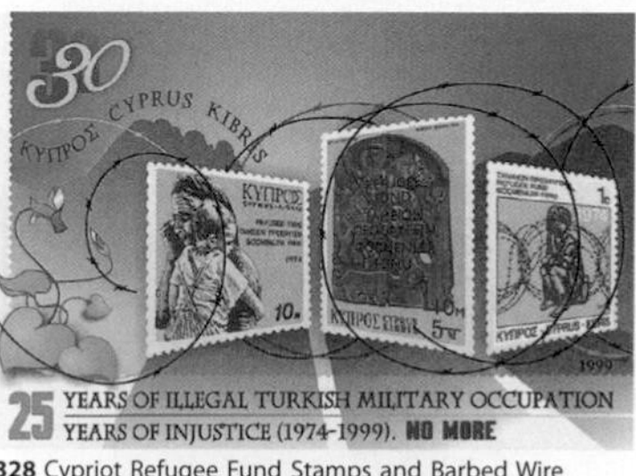

30
CYPRUS KIBRIS
25 YEARS OF ILLEGAL TURKISH MILITARY OCCUPATION
YEARS OF INJUSTICE (1974-1999). NO MORE

328 Cypriot Refugee Fund Stamps and Barbed Wire (image scaled to 44% of original size)

1999. 25th Anniv of Turkish Landings in Cyprus. Sheet 110×75 mm. Imperf.
MS979 **328** 30c. multicoloured 1·50 2·25

329 Angel

1999. Christmas. Multicoloured.
980 10c. Type **329** 60 10
981 25c. The Three Kings 1·40 70
982 30c. Madonna and child 1·50 2·50

330 Woman's Silhouette with Stars and Globe

2000. Miss Universe Beauty Contest, Cyprus. Sheet 80×65 mm, containing T **330** and similar vert design. Multicoloured.
MS983 15c. Type **330**; 35c. Statue of Aphrodite and apple 2·75 2·75

331 Necklace, 4500–4000 B.C.

2000. Jewellery. Multicoloured.
984 10c. Type **331** 45 30
985 15c. Gold earrings, 3rd-cent B.C. 65 40
986 20c. Gold earring from Lampousa, 6th–7th-cent 75 50
987 25c. Brooch, 19th-cent 75 60
988 30c. Gold cross, 6th–7th-cent 95 75
989 35c. Necklace, 18th–19th-cent 1·00 85
990 40c. Gold earring, 19th-cent 1·50 95
991 50c. Spiral hair ring, 4th–5th-cent B.C. 1·60 1·25
992 75c. Gold-plated silver plaques from Gialia, 700–600 B.C. (horiz) 2·25 2·50
993 £1 Gold frontlet from Egkomi, 14th–13th-cent B.C. (horiz) 4·25 3·25
994 £2 Gold necklace from Egkomi, 13th-cent B.C. (horiz) 7·50 7·50
995 £3 Buckles, 19th-cent (horiz) 11·00 12·00

332 "Building Europe"

2000. Europa.
996 **332** 30c. multicoloured 1·75 1·75

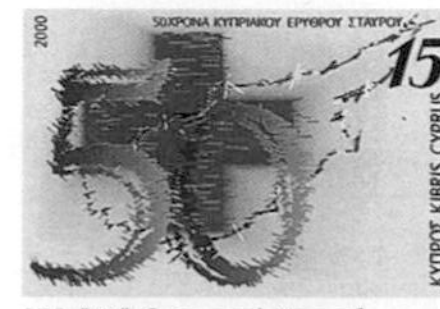

333 "50", Cross and Map of Cyprus

2000. 50th Anniv of Red Cross in Cyprus.
997 **333** 15c. multicoloured 1·75 1·00

334 Flame, Map of Cyprus and Broken Chain

2000. 45th Anniv of Struggle for Independence.
998 **334** 15c. multicoloured 1·75 1·00

335 Weather Balloon, Map and Satellite

2000. 50th Anniv of World Meteorological Organization.
999 **335** 30c. multicoloured 2·25 2·25

336 Monastery of Antifontis, Kalograia

2000. Greek Orthodox Churches in Northern Cyprus.
1000 **336** 10c. brown and red 70 25
1001 - 15c. dp green & green 1·00 45
1002 - 25c. dp violet & violet 1·40 1·10
1003 - 30c. red and grey 1·50 2·50

DESIGNS—VERT: 15c. Church of St. Themonianos, Lysi. HORIZ: 25c. Church of Panagia Kanakaria, Lytrhagkomi; 30c. Church of Avgasida Monastery, Milia.

337 Council of Europe Emblem

2000. 50th Anniv of European Convention of Human Rights.

1004	**337** 30c. multicoloured		2·00	2·00

338 Archery

2000. Olympic Games, Sydney. Multicoloured.

1005	10c. Type **338**	70	25
1006	15c. Gymnastics	90	40
1007	25c. Diving	1·40	1·00
1008	35c. Trampolining	1·60	2·50

339 "The Annunciation"

2000. Christmas. Gold Gospel Covers. Multicoloured.

1009	10c. Type **339**	75	25
1010	25c. "The Nativity"	1·75	70
1011	30c. "The Baptism of Christ"	1·75	2·00

340 "25" and Commonwealth Symbol

2001. 25th Anniv of Commonwealth Day.

1012	**340** 30c. multicoloured	1·75	2·00

341 Silhouette, Dove and Barbed Wire

2001. 50th Anniv of United Nations High Commissioner for Refugees.

1013	**341** 30c. multicoloured	1·75	2·00

342 Pavlos Liasides

2001. Birth Centenary of Pavlos Liasides (poet).

1014	**342** 13c. chocolate, ochre & brown	1·25	60

343 Bridge over River Diarizos

2001. Europa. Cypriot Rivers. Multicoloured.

1015	20c. Type **343**	1·00	50
1016	30c. Mountain torrent, River Akaki	1·75	2·25

344 *Pathenope massena*

2001. Crabs. Multicoloured.

1017	13c. Type **344**	75	20
1018	20c. *Calappa granulata*	1·25	85
1019	25c. *Ocypode cursor*	1·50	1·25
1020	30c. *Pagurus bernhardus*	1·75	2·25

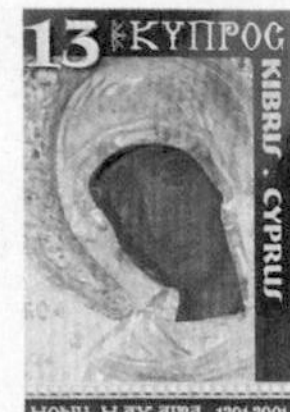
345 Icon of Virgin Mary

2001. Christmas. 800th Anniv of Macheras Monastery. Multicoloured.

1021	13c. Type **345**	55	20
1022	25c. Macheras Monastery	1·50	65
1023	30c. Ornate gold crucifix	1·75	2·25

346 Loukis Akritas

2001. Loukis Akritas (writer) Commemoration.

1024	**346** 20c. green and brown	1·50	1·00

347 Tortoiseshell and White Cat

2002. Cats. Multicoloured.

1025	20c. Type **347**	1·40	1·75
1026	20c. British blue	1·40	1·75
1027	25c. Tortoiseshell and white	1·40	1·75
1028	25c. Red and silver tabby	1·40	1·75

348 Acrobat on Horseback

2002. Europa. Circus. Multicoloured.

1029	20c. Type **348**	1·00	50
1030	30c. Clown on high wire	1·75	2·25

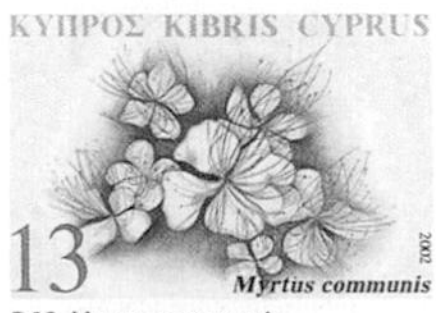
349 *Myrtus communis*

2002. Medicinal Plants. Multicoloured.

1031	13c. Type **349**	75	30
1032	20c. *Lavandula stoechas*	1·25	85
1033	25c. *Capparis spinosa*	1·50	1·25
1034	30c. *Ocimum basilicum*	1·75	2·25

350 Mother Teresa

2002. Mother Teresa (founder of Missionaries of Charity) Commemoration.

1035	**350** 40c. multicoloured	2·75	2·50

351 Blackboard on Easel

2002. International Teachers' Day. Multicoloured.

1036	13c. Type **351**	1·50	1·50
1037	30c. Computer	2·25	2·50

352 Agate Seal-stone (5th century B.C.)

2002. "Cyprus - Europhilex '02", Stamp Exhibition, Nicosia. Cypriot Antiquities showing Europa. Multicoloured.

1038	20c. Type **352**	1·10	1·25
1039	20c. Silver coin of Timochares (5th–4th century B.C.)	1·10	1·25
1040	20c. Silver coin of Stasioikos (5th century B.C.)	1·10	1·25
1041	30c. Clay lamp (green backgound) (2nd century A.D.)	1·50	1·75
1042	30c. Statuette of Europa on the Bull (7th–6th century B.C.)	1·50	1·75
1043	30c. Clay lamp (purple backgound) (1st century B.C.)	1·50	1·75
MS1044	105×71 mm. 50c. Statue of Aphrodite with maps of Crete and Cyprus; 50c. "Europa on the Bull" (painting by Francesco di Giogio)	6·50	7·50

353 "Nativity"

2002. Christmas. Details from "Birth of Christ" (wall painting), Church of Metamorphosis Sotiros, Palechori. Multicoloured.

1045	13c. Type **353**	80	20
1046	25c. "Three Wise Men"	1·50	75
1047	30c. "Birth of Christ" (complete painting) (38×38 mm)	2·25	2·50

354 Triumph Roadster 1800, 1946

2003. International Historic Car Rally. Multicoloured.

1048	20c. Type **354**	1·60	1·75
1049	25c. Ford model T, 1917	1·60	1·75
1050	30c. Baby Ford Y 8hp, 1932	1·60	1·75

355 "POSTER IS ART"

2003. Europa. Poster Art.

1051	**355** 20c. multicoloured	80	50
1052	- 30c. multicoloured	1·40	1·75

356 Mediterranean Horseshoe Bat in Flight

2003. Endangered Species. Mediterranean Horseshoe Bat. Multicoloured.

1053	25c. Type **356**	1·50	1·75
1054	25c. Head of bat (facing forwards)	1·50	1·75
1055	25c. Bats roosting	1·50	1·75
1056	25c. Head of bat (facing sideways, mouth open)	1·50	1·75

357 Stylized Owl

2003. 7th Conference of European Ministers of Education, Nicosia.

1057	**357** 30c. multicoloured	1·75	2·00

358 Eleonora's Falcon

2003. Birds of Prey. Multicoloured.

1058	20c. Type **358**	1·50	1·75
1059	20c. Eleonora's falcon in flight	1·50	1·75
1060	25c. Imperial eagle	1·50	1·75
1061	25c. Imperial eagle in flight	1·50	1·75
1062	30c. Little owl	1·50	1·75
1063	30c. Little owl in flight and eggs in nest	1·50	1·75

359 Constantinos Spyridakis (historian, author and Minister of Education 1965–70)

2003. Birth Centenaries.

1064	**359** 5c. black and drab	50	65
1065	- 5c. blackish olive and green	50	65

DESIGN: 23×31 mm—No. 1065, Tefkros Anthias (poet).

360 Three Angels

2003. Christmas. Multicoloured.

1066	13c. Type **360**	80	20
1067	30c. Three Wise Men	1·50	85
1068	40c. Nativity (37×59 mm)	2·25	2·75

Nos. 1066/7 show details from icon of Nativity in Church of Virgin Mary, Kourdali. No. 1068 shows the complete painting.

361 Stylized Footballer

2004. Centenary of FIFA (Federation Internationale de Football Association).

1069	**361** 30c. multicoloured	1·75	2·00

362 Stylized Footballer

2004. 50th Anniv of UEFA (Union of European Football Associations).

1070	**362** 30c. multicoloured	1·75	2·00

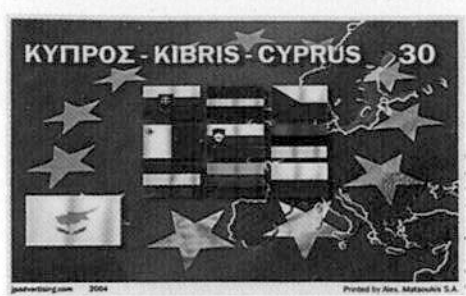
363 Flags of New Member Countries

2004. Enlargement of the European Union.

1071	**363**	30c. multicoloured	1·75	2·00

364 Yiannos Kranidiotis and EU Emblem

2004. 5th Death Anniv of Yiannos Kranidiotis (politician).

1072	**364**	20c. multicoloured	1·25	80

365 Sailing Boat and Ancient Amphitheatre

2004. Europa. Holidays. Multicoloured.

1073	20c. Type **365**	75	50
1074	30c. Family at seaside and statue	1·50	1·75

366 Horse Racing (image scaled to 61% of original size)

2004. Olympic Games, Athens. Ancient Olympic sports. Multicoloured.

1075	13c. Type **366**	65	35
1076	20c. Running	1·00	50
1077	30c. Diving	1·50	1·10
1078	40c. Discus	1·75	2·50

367 Dolphin

2004. Mammals. Multicoloured.

1079	20c. Type **367**	1·25	1·25
1080	20c. Dolphin (blue background)	1·25	1·25
1081	30c. Fox (white background)	1·60	1·60
1082	30c. Fox (green background)	1·60	1·60
1083	40c. Hare (white background)	1·75	1·75
1084	40c. Hare (yellow background)	1·75	1·75

368 Choir of Angels

2004. Christmas. Multicoloured.

1085	13c. Type **368**	85	20
1086	30c. Three Wise Men	1·75	85
1087	40c. Annunciation to the Shepherds (37×60 mm)	2·25	2·50
MS1088	63×84 mm. £1 Virgin and Child (38×38 mm)	5·50	6·00

369 Georgios Philippou Pierides

2004. Intellectual Personalities. Multicoloured.

1089	5c. Type **369**	65	75
1090	5c. Emilios Chourmouzios (wearing tie)	65	75

370 Carolina Pelendritou and Medal

2005. Carolina Pelendritou's Gold Medal for 100 Metres Swimming at Paralympic Games, Athens (2004).

1093	**370**	20c. multicoloured	1·00	70

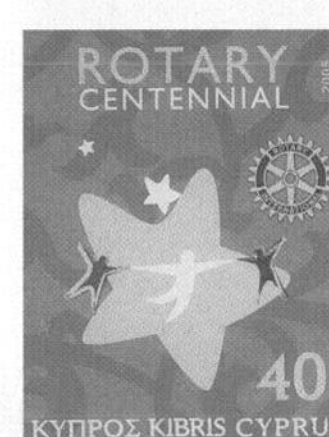
371 Emblem

2005. Centenary of Rotary International.

1094	**371**	40c. multicoloured	1·25	1·60

372 "The Entrance" (Kyriacos Koulli)

2005. 50th Anniv of EOKA Struggle.

1095	**372**	50c. multicoloured	2·00	2·50

373 Table with Fish, Casserole, Wine, Garlic, Tomato and Bread

2005. Europa. Gastronomy. Multicoloured.

1096	20c. Type **373**	75	50
1097	30c. Table with coffee, cheese, cocktail and desserts	1·25	1·50

374 German Shepherd Dog and Police Dog with Handler

2005. Dogs in Man's Life. Multicoloured.

1098	13c. Type **374**	85	30
1099	20c. Hungarian Vizsla and hunter with dog	1·25	85
1100	30c. Labrador and man with guide dog	1·75	1·40
1101	40c. Dalmatian and boy with pet dog	2·00	2·50

375 Angel appearing to Shepherds

2005. Christmas. Multicoloured.

1102	13c. Type **375**	80	20
1103	30c. Holy Family and shepherds	1·60	90
1104	40c. Virgin Mary and Jesus Christ (37×59 mm)	1·90	2·50

Nos. 1102/3 show details from icon "Birth of Christ" and No. 1104 shows icon of the "Virgin Mary Karmiotissa".

376 1964 30c. Flower Stamp

2006. 50th Anniv of First Europa Stamp. Sowing Cyprus Europa stamps. Multicoloured.

MS1105	94×84 mm. 30c. Type **376**; 30c. 1962 40m. doves stamp; 30c. 1963 40m. tree stamp; 30c. 1963 150m. CEPT stamp	4·75	5·50

The stamps within No. **MS**1105 have composite background designs.

377 "25" and Hand Stamp

2006. 25th Anniv of the Postal Museum, Nicosia.

1106	**377**	25c. multicoloured	1·00	1·00

378 Self-portrait and "The Anatomy Lesson of Dr. Nicolaes Tulp"

2006. 400th Birth Anniv of Rembrandt (artist).

1107	**378**	40c. multicoloured	2·50	2·50

379 Footballer kicking Ball

2006. World Cup Football Championship, Germany.

1108	**379**	50c. multicoloured	2·00	2·25

380 Stamna or Kouza (Pitcher) Dance, Cyprus

2006. Folk Dances. Sheet 100×70 mm containing T 380 and similar horiz design. Multicoloured.

MS1109	40c. Type **380**; 40c. Nati dance, Himachal Pradesh, India	3·50	4·50

Stamps in similar designs were issued by India.

381 Stylized Hand and Swallow

2006. Europa. Integration. Multicoloured, background colour given.

1110	**381**	30c. green	1·25	50
1111	**381**	40c. pink	1·50	2·00

382 *Elaeagnus angustifolia* (olive)

2006. Cyprus Fruits. Multicoloured.

1112	20c. Type **382**	1·00	50
1113	25c. *Mespilus germanica* (medlar) (horiz)	1·00	55
1114	60c. *Opuntia ficus barbarica* (prickly pear)	2·75	4·00

383 Flowers and Silhouettes

2006. Transplants.

1115	**383**	13c. multicoloured	75	60

384 Bedford Water Carrier, 1997

2006. Fire Engines. Multicoloured.

1116	13c. Type **384**	1·00	30
1117	20c. Hino fire engine, 1994	1·25	80
1118	50c. Bedford fire engine with turntable ladder, 1959	2·75	3·25

385 Nicos Nicolaides

2006. 50th Death Anniv of Nicos Nicolaides (writer).

1119	**385**	5c. multicoloured	45	35

2006. Christmas. Showing carvings from Agiou Eleftheriou Church, Nicosia. Multicoloured.

1120	13c. Type **386**	70	25
1121	30c. Christ on the Cross from top of iconostasis	1·40	1·25
1122	40c. Stone bas-relief showing cross, spear and sponge	1·60	2·00

387 *Antedon mediterranea* (feather star)

2007. Echinodermata of Cyprus. Multicoloured.

1123	25c. Type **387**	1·50	1·50
1124	25c. *Centrostephanus longispinus* (sea urchin)	1·50	1·50
1125	25c. *Astropecten jonstoni* (starfish)	1·50	1·50
1126	25c. *Ophioderma longicaudum* (brittle star)	1·50	1·50

388 St. Zenon the Postman (image scaled to 64% of original size)

2007. St. Zenon the Postman. Sheet 75 ×65 mm. Imperf.

MS1127	**388** £1 multicoloured	7·00	8·00

389 Triumph Daytona T100R, 1972

2007. Old Motorcycles. Multicoloured.

1128	13c. Type **389**	80	30
1129	20c. Matchless G3L, 1941	1·40	70
1130	40c. BSAWM20, 1940	2·00	1·50
1131	60c. Ariel Red Hunter NH 359, 1939	2·25	3·00

390 Emblem

2007. 50th Anniv of the Treaty of Rome.

1132	**390**	30c. multicoloured	1·10	1·25

391 Ear of Wheat and Scout Badge

2007. Europa. Centenary of Scouting.

1133	**391**	30c. multicoloured	1·25	1·40
1134	**391**	40c. multicoloured	1·50	1·60

392 '50' and Stylized Figures

2007. 50th Anniv of Social Insurance. Multicoloured.

1135	40c. Type **392** (inscr in Greek)	1·50	1·75
1136	40c. Stylized figures (at left) and '50' (inscr '50 YEARS OF SOCIAL INSURANCE' in English)	1·50	1·75

Nos. 1135/6 were issued together, se-tenant, forming a composite design.

393 Pygmy Hippopotamus, 10000 BC

2007. Cyprus through the Ages (1st series). Multicoloured.

1137	25c. Type **393**	1·10	1·25
1138	25c. Stone vessel, 7000 BC	1·10	1·25
1139	25c. Ruins of Choirokoitia settlement of 7000 BC	1·10	1·25
1140	25c. Figurine of a woman, 3000 BC	1·10	1·25
1141	25c. Terracotta vessel, 2000 BC	1·10	1·25
1142	25c. Greek inscription on a bronze skewer, 1000 BC	1·10	1·25
1143	25c. Bird-shaped vessel, 800 BC	1·10	1·25
1144	25c. Map of 1718 showing the ancient Kingdoms of Cyprus in the first millennium BC	1·10	1·25

394 Limassol District Administration Building

2007. Neoclassical Buildings of Cyprus. Multicoloured.

1145	13c. Type **394**	80	75
1146	15c. National Bank of Greece Building, Nicosia	90	80
1147	20c. Archaeological Research Unit's Building, Nicosia	1·10	95
1148	30c. National Art Gallery Building, Nicosia	1·25	1·00
1149	40c. Paphos Municipal Library Building	1·40	1·40
1150	50c. Office Building of A. G. Leventis Foundation, Nicosia	1·75	2·00
1151	£1 Limassol Municipal Library Building	3·75	4·00
1152	£3 Phaneromeni Gymnasium Building, Nicosia	8·50	11·00

395 Virgin Mary and Christ Child

2007. Christmas.Designs showing murals taken from Chapel of St. Themonianus, Lysi. Multicoloured.

1153	13c. Type **395**	65	20
1154	30c. Archangel Gabriel	1·40	1·10
1155	40c. Christ Pantocrater (34×44 mm)	1·75	2·00

396 'Aphrodite' (statue)

2008. Adoption of the Euro Currency. Sheet 100×62 mm containing T 396 and similar square design. Multicoloured.

MS1156	€1 Type **396**; €1 'Sleeping Lady' Statuette of Malta	6·50	7·50

A similar miniature sheet was issued by Malta.

2008. Obigatory Tax. Refugee Fund. Design as T 255 but denominated in cents and euros as T 397. Inscr '2008'.

1157	**255**	2c. black and grey	15	15

398 Pink Anemone

2008. Anemone coronaria. Multicoloured.

1158	26c. Type **398**	80	70
1159	34c. White anemone	1·00	90
1160	51c. Red anemone	1·60	1·60
1161	68c. Mauve anemone	1·90	2·75

399 'CYPRUS' on Letters

2008. Europa. The Letter. Multicoloured.

1162	51c. Type **399**	1·40	1·40
1163	68c. CYPRUS	1·60	1·75

400 Ancient Pottery Vase and Silver Vase

2008. Fourth International Congress of Cypriot Studies, Nicosia. Sheet 75×65 mm.

MS1164	multicoloured	3·00	3·00

401 Windsurfing

2008. Olympic Games, Beijing. Multicoloured.

1165	22c. Type **401**	55	55
1166	34c. High jump	90	90
1167	43c. Volleyball	1·40	1·50
1168	51c. Shooting	1·50	1·75

402 Emblem

2008. 12th Francophone Summit, Quebec.

1169	**402**	85c. multicoloured	2·25	2·50

Nos. 1165/9 were denominated in both euros and Cyprus pounds.

403 Coin, Archaic period (750–480 BC)

2008. Cyprus through the Ages. Multicoloured.

1170	43c. Type **403**	1·25	1·25
1171	43c. Ancient ship, Archaic period (750–780 BC)	1·25	1·25
1172	43c. Statue of Athenian General Kimon and sailing galley, Classical period (480–310 BC)	1·25	1·25
1173	43c. Tombs of the Kings, Hellenistic period (310–30 BC)	1·25	1·25
1174	43c. Coin, Hellenistic period (310–30 BC)	1·25	1·25
1175	43c. St. Paul (missionary to Cyprus, 45 AD)	1·25	1·25
1176	43c. Bronze statue of Roman Emperor Septimus Severus, Roman period (30 BC–324 AD)	1·25	1·25
1177	43c. Granting of privileges to Church of Cyprus, Byzantine period (324–481 AD)	1·25	1·25

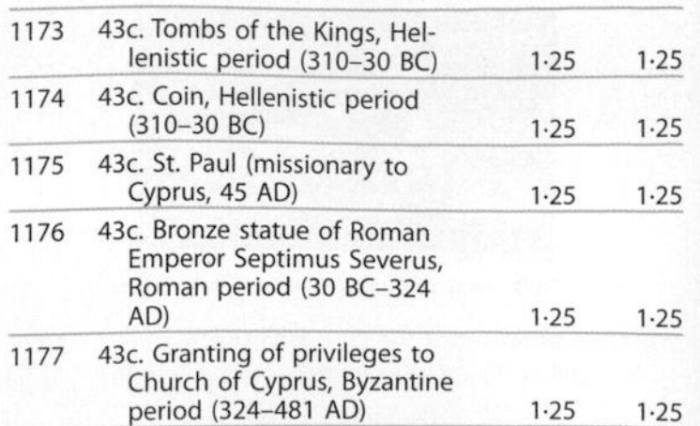

404 Archangel Gabriel

2008. Christmas. Icons from Panagia Catholic Church, Pelendri. Multicoloured.

1178	22c. Type **404**	65	65
1179	51c. Archangel Michael	1·50	1·40
1180	68c. Virgin Mary and Christ Child	2·25	2·50

2009. Obligatory Tax. Refugee Fund. Inscr '2009'.

1181	**397**	2c. black and grey-lilac	20	20

405 Stylized Euro Coin

2009. Tenth Anniv of the Euro. Multicoloured.

1182	51c. Type **405**	1·50	1·50
1183	68c. Euro coin showing map of Europe	2·25	2·25

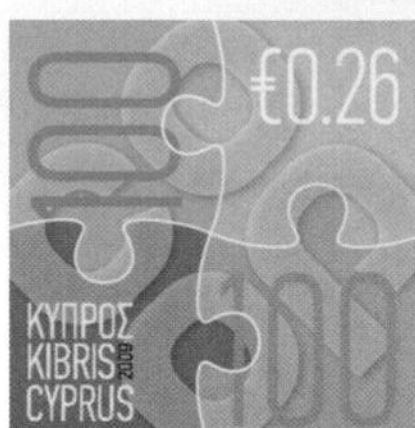

406 Centenary Emblem

2009. Anniversaries. Multicoloured.

1184	26c. Type **406** (Centenary of the Cyprus Co-operative Movement)	75	55
1185	68c. Louis Braille (birth bicentenary)	2·10	2·10

No. 1185 has the face value in Braille.

407 Satellite Image of the Americas

2009. International Year of Planet Earth (2008). Multicoloured.

1186	51c. Type **407**	1·50	1·50
1187	51c. Satellite image of Europe, Asia and North Africa	1·50	1·50

Nos. 1186/7 were printed together, se-tenant, each pair forming a composite design showing the Earth's continents enclosed in a heart.

408 Cassiopeia

2009. Europa. Astronomy. Constellations. Multicoloured.

1188	51c. Type **408**	1·75	2·00
1189	68c. Andromeda	1·75	2·00

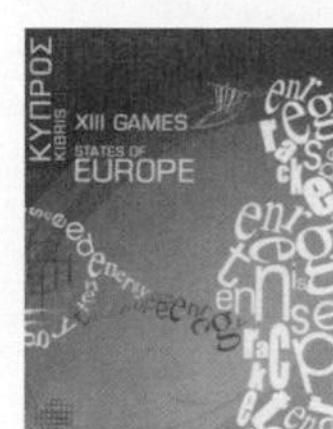

409 Letters forming Player with Racket

2009. 13th Games of the Small States of Europe, Nicosia and Limassol. Multicoloured.

1190	22c. Type **409**	60	60
1191	34c. Letters forming sailor and yacht	1·00	1·00
1192	43c. Letters forming cyclist	1·75	1·75

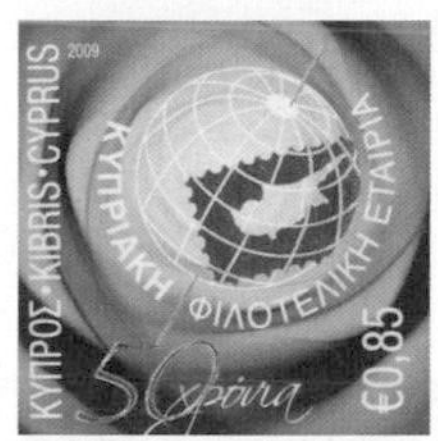

410 Map of Cyprus on Stamp on Globe

2009. 50th Anniv of Cyprus Philatelic Society. Sheet 67×67 mm.

MS1193	67×67 mm. **410** 85c. multi-coloured	2·75	3·00

411 Pigeon

2009. Domestic Fowl. Multicoloured.

1194	22c. Type **411**	65	65
1195	34c. Turkey	1·25	1·25
1196	43c. Cockerel	1·40	1·40
1197	51c. Duck	1·60	1·60

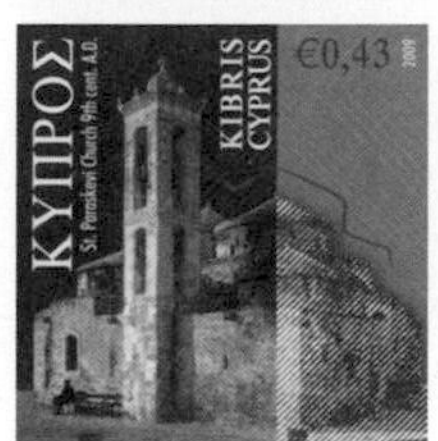

412 St. Paraskevi Church (9th century)

2009. Cyprus through the Ages (3rd series). Multicoloured.

1198	43c. Type **412**	1·40	1·40
1199	43c. Monastery of St. Chrysostomos (1090–1100)	1·40	1·40
1200	43c. Lusignan coat of arms (1192–1489)	1·40	1·40
1201	43c. Chronicle of Machairas (early 15th century)	1·40	1·40
1202	43c. Queen Cornaro passes crown to Venice (1489)	1·40	1·40
1203	43c. Nicosia's Venetian walls (1567–1570)	1·40	1·40
1204	43c. Ottoman siege of Nicosia (1570)	1·40	1·40
1205	43c. Larnaca aqueduct (18th century)	1·40	1·40

413 European Court of Human Rights, Strasbourg

2009. 50th Anniv of European Court of Human Rights, Strasbourg.

1206	**413**	51c. multicoloured	1·50	1·50

414 *Birth of Christ* (16th-century fresco), Church of Archangel Michael, Vyzakia

415 Mauve Star within Silver Star

2009. Christmas. Multicoloured. (a) As Type **414**

1207	22c. Type **414**	60	30

(b) As T **415**.

1208	51c. Type **415**	1·50	1·40
1209	68c. Silver star	2·50	3·00

416 Arms of Cyprus

2010. 50th Anniv of the Republic of Cyprus.

1210	**416**	68c. multicoloured	2·25	2·25
1211	**416**	85c. multicoloured	2·75	2·75

417 Pig

2010. Farm Animals. Multicoloured.

1212	22c. Type **417**	60	60
1213	26c. Sheep	75	75
1214	34c. Goat	1·10	1·10
1215	43c. Cow	1·25	1·25
1216	€1.71 Rabbit	7·25	7·25

418 Emblem and 'Better City Better Life'

2010. Expo 2010, Shanghai, China

1217	**418**	51c. multicoloured	1·50	1·50

419 Football

2010. World Cup Football Championships, South Africa

1218	**419**	€1.71 multicoloured	7·25	7·25

2010. Obligatory Tax. Refugee Fund

1218a	**397**	2c. black and cinnamon	20	20

420 Stack of Books and Flowering Tree

2010. Europa. Multicoloured.

1219	51c. Type **420**	1·50	1·50
1220	51c. Stack of books (at left)	1·50	1·50

Nos. 1219/20 were printed together, *se-tenant*, in horizontal pairs, each pair forming a composite design of a stack of books.

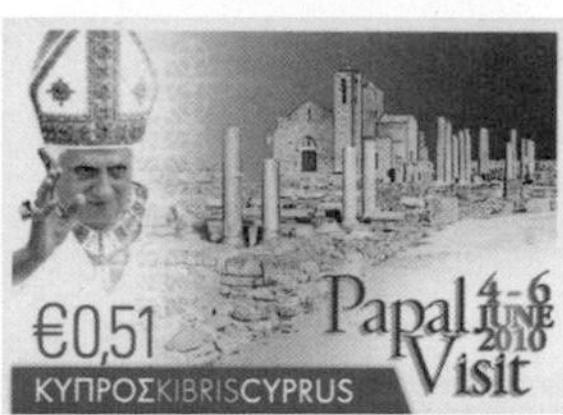

421 Pope Benedict XVI, Ayia Kyriaki Church and Ancient Temple Pillars, Paphos

2010. Visit of Pope Benedict XVI to Cyprus

1221	**421**	51c. multicoloured	1·40	1·40

422 Steam Locomotive

2010. The Cyprus Railway 1905–51. Multicoloured.

1222	43c. Type **422**	1·25	1·25
1223	43c. Steam locomotive (seen from front)	1·25	1·25
MS1224	70×70 mm. 85c. Steam train and map of railway	3·00	3·25

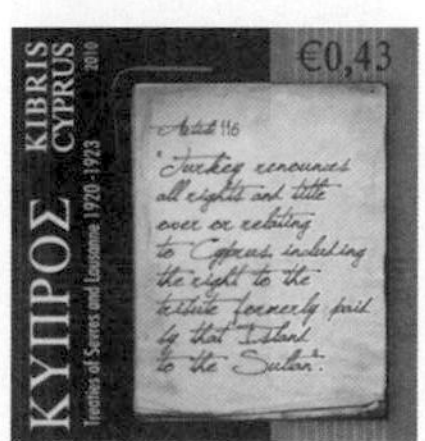

423 Treaties of Sevres, 1920, and Lausanne, 1923

2010. Cyprus through the Ages (4th series). Multicoloured.

1225	43c. Type **423**	1·25	1·25
1226	43c. Burnt Government House, 1931	1·25	1·25
1227	43c. 'Imprisoned Graves' of EOKA fighters, Central Prisons, 1955–9	1·25	1·25
1228	43c. Statue of Gregoris Afxentiou (EOKA second in command), 1957	1·25	1·25
1229	43c. Presidential Palace, 1960	1·25	1·25
1230	43c. *The Black Summer of 1974* (Telemachos Kanthos)	1·25	1·25
1231	43c. Pres. Tassos Papadopoulos signing EU Treaty of Accession, 16 April 2003	1·25	1·25
1232	43c. National flag of Republic of Cyprus	1·25	1·25

424 Birth of Christ (16th-century icon), Church of Agios Nicolas, Klonari)

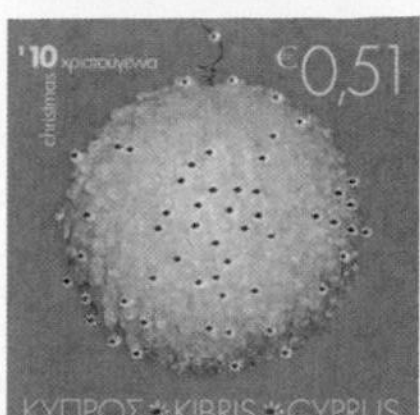

425 White Bauble

2010. Christmas. Multicoloured.

1233	22c. Type **424**	65	65
1234	51c. Type **425**	1·40	1·40
1235	68c. Filigree bauble	2·00	2·00

426 Wine Barrels

2010. Viticulture. Multicoloured.

MS1236	80×60 mm. 51c. Type **426**; 51c. Grapes and decorated ceramic wine jug	3·00	3·00

Stamps in similar designs were issued by Romania.

427 Emblem

2011. Centenary of Anorthosis Ammochostos (football and volleyball club)

1237	**427**	34c. multicoloured	1·10	1·10

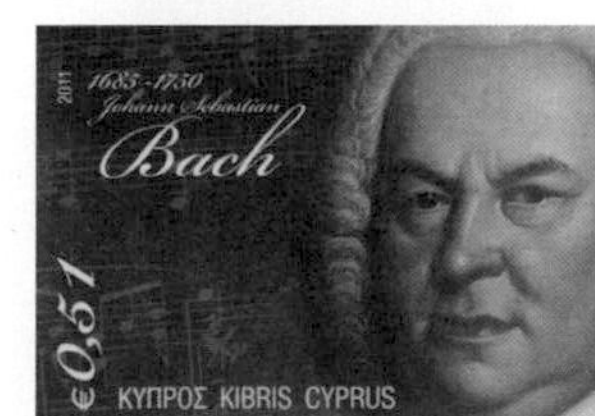

428 Johann Sebastian Bach

2011. Famous 18th-century Composers. Multicoloured.

1238	51c. Type **428**	1·40	1·40
1239	51c. Wolfgang Amadeus Mozart	1·40	1·40
1240	51c. Ludwig van Beethoven	1·40	1·40

429 Embroidery

2011. Cyprus Embroidery. Multicoloured.

1241	26c. Type **429**	75	55
1242	43c. Embroidery (pattern of diamonds)	1·25	1·25

430 Roses

2011. Aromatic Flowers – Roses. Multicoloured.

1243	34c. Type **430**	1·00	1·00
MS1244	75×75 mm. 85c. Roses and rosebuds	2·75	3·00

Nos. 1243/**MS**1244 have a rose scent.

TURKISH CYPRIOT POSTS

After the inter-communal clashes during December 1963, a separate postal service was established on 6 January 1964, between some of the Turkish Cypriot areas, using handstamps inscribed "KIBRIS TURK POSTALARI". During 1964, however, an agreement was reached between representatives of the two communities for the restoration of postal services. This agreement to which the United Nations representatives were a party, was ratified in November 1966 by the Republic's Council of Ministers. Under the scheme postal servcies were provided for the Turkish Cypriot communities in Famagusta, Limassol, Lefka and Nicosia, staffed by Turkish Cypriot employees of the Cypriot Department of Posts.

On 8 April 1970, 5m. and 15m. locally produced labels, originally designated "Social Aid Stamps", were issued by the Turkish Cypriot community and these can be found on commercial covers. These local stamps are outside the scope of this catalogue.

On 29 October 1973 Nos. 1/7 were placed on sale, but were again used only on mail between the Turkish Cypriot areas.

Following the intervention by the Republic of Turkey in July 1974 these stamps replaced issues of the Republic of Cyprus in that part of the island, north and east of the Attila Line, controlled by the Autonomous Turkish Cypriot Administration.

1 50th Anniversary Emblem

1974. 50th Anniv of Republic of Turkey.

1	-	3m. multicoloured	30·00	30·00
2	-	5m. multicoloured	60	40
3	-	10m. multicoloured	50	20
4	1	15m. red and black	2·50	1·50
5	-	20m. multicoloured	70	20
6	-	50m. multicoloured	2·00	1·50
7	-	70m. multicoloured	16·00	16·00

DESIGNS—VERT: 3m. Woman sentry; 10m. Man and woman with Turkish flags; 20m. Ataturk statue, Kyrenia Gate, Nicosia; 50m. "The Fallen". HORIZ: 5m. Military parade, Nicosia; 70m. Turkish flag and map of Cyprus.

1975. Proclamation of the Turkish Federated State of Cyprus. Nos. 3 and 5 surch KIBRIS TURK FEDERE DEVLETI 13.2.1975 and value.

8	30m. on 20m. multicoloured	75	1·00
9	100m. on 10m. multicoloured	1·25	2·00

3 Namik Kemal's Bust, Famagusta

1975. Multicoloured.. Multicoloured..

10	3m. Type **3**	15	40
11	10m. Ataturk Statue, Nicosia	25	10
12	15m. St. Hilarion Castle	35	20
13	20m. Ataturk Square, Nicosia	45	20
14	25m. Famagusta Beach	45	30
15	30m. Kyrenia Harbour	55	10
16	50m. Lala Mustafa Pasha Mosque, Famagusta (vert)	60	10
17	100m. Interior, Kyrenia Castle	80	90
18	250m. Castle walls, Kyrenia	1·00	2·25
19	500m. Othello Tower, Famagusta (vert)	1·50	4·50

See also Nos. 36/8.

4 Map of Cyprus

1975. "Peace in Cyprus". Multicoloured.

20	30m. Type **4**	20	15
21	50m. Map, laurel and broken chain	25	20
22	150m. Map and laurel-sprig on globe (vert)	65	1·40

5 "Pomegranates" (I. V. Guney)

1975. Europa. Paintings. Multicoloured.

23	90m. Type **5**	1·40	1·75
24	100m. "Harvest Time" (F. Direkoglu)	1·40	1·75

1976. Nos. 16/17 surch.

25	10m. on 50m. multicoloured	35	70
26	30m. on 100m. multicoloured	35	80

7 "Expectation" (ceramic statuette)

1976. Europa. Multicoloured.

27	60m. Type **7**	60	80
28	120m. "Man in Meditation"	80	1·75

8 Carob

1976. Export Products. Fruits. Multicoloured.

29	10m. Type **8**	15	10
30	25m. Mandarin	20	10
31	40m. Strawberry	25	25
32	60m. Orange	35	65
33	80m. Lemon	40	2·00

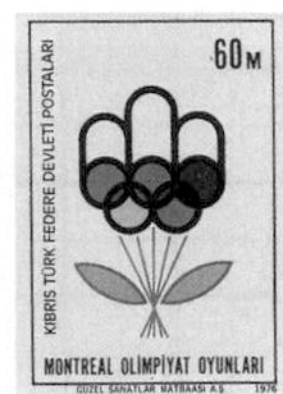

9 Olympic Symbol "Flower"

1976. Olympic Games, Montreal. Multicoloured.

34	60m. Type **9**	25	20
35	100m. Olympic symbol and doves	35	25

10 Kyrenia Harbour

1976. Multicoloured.. Multicoloured..

36	5m. Type **10**	40	15
37	15m. St. Hilarion Castle	40	15
38	20m. Ataturk Square, Nicosia	40	15

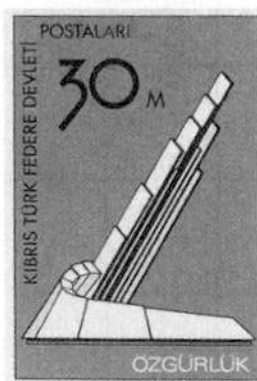

11 Liberation Monument, Karaeglanoglu (Ay Georghios)

1976. Liberation Monument.

47	11	30m. blue, pink and black	15	20
48	-	150m. red, pink and black	35	80

DESIGN: 150m. Liberation Monument (different view).

12 Hotel, Salamis Bay

1977. Europa. Multicoloured.

49	80m. Type **12**	65	95
50	100m. Kyrenia Port	75	95

13 Pottery

1977. Handicrafts. Multicoloured.

51	15m. Type **13**	10	10
52	30m. Pottery (vert)	10	10
53	125m. Basketware	30	50

14 Arap Ahmet Pasha Mosque, Nicosia

1977. Turkish Buildings in Cyprus. Multicoloured.

54	20m. Type **14**	10	10
55	40m. Paphos Castle (horiz)	10	10
56	70m. Bekir Pasha aqueduct (horiz)	15	20
57	80m. Sultan Mahmut library (horiz)	15	25

15 Namik Kemal (bust) and House, Famagusta

1977. Namik Kemal (patriotic poet). Multicoloured.

58	30m. Type **15**	15	15
59	140m. Namik Kemal (portrait) (vert)	35	60

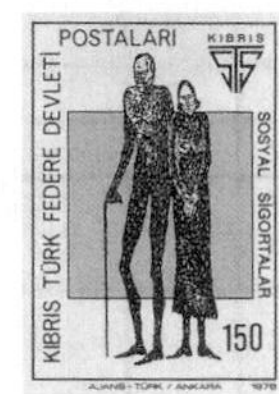

16 Old Man and Woman

1978. Social Security.

60	16	150k. black, yellow and blue	10	10
61	-	275k. black, orange and green	15	15
62	-	375k. black, blue and orange	25	20

DESIGNS: 275k. Injured man with crutch; 375k. Woman with family.

17 Oratory in Buyuk Han, Nicosia

1978. Europa. Multicoloured.

63	225k. Type **17**	85	50
64	450k. Cistern in Selimiye Mosque, Nicosia	1·25	1·50

18 Motorway Junction

1978. Communications. Multicoloured.

65	75k. Type **18**	15	10
66	100k. Hydrofoil	15	10
67	650k. Boeing 720 at Ercan Airport	50	60

19 Dove with Laurel Branch

1978. National Oath.

68	19	150k. yellow, violet and black	10	10
69	-	225k. black, red and yellow	10	10
70	-	725k. black, blue and yellow	20	20

DESIGNS—VERT: 225k. "Taking the Oath". HORIZ: 725k. Symbolic dove.

20 Kemal Ataturk

1978. Ataturk Commemoration.

71	20	75k. turquoise & dp turq	10	10
72	20	450k. pink and brown	15	15
73	20	650k. blue and light blue	20	25

1979. Nos. 30/3 surch.

74	50k. on 25k. Mandarin	10	10
75	1l. on 40m. Strawberry	15	10
76	3l. on 60m. Orange	15	10
77	5l. on 80m. Lemon	35	15

22 Gun Barrel with Olive Branch and Map of Cyprus

1979. 5th Anniv of Turkish Peace Operation in Cyprus. Sheet 72×52 mm. Imperf.

MS78 **22**	15l. black, blue and green	80	1·25

23 Postage Stamp and Map of Cyprus

1979. Europa. Communications. Multicoloured.

79	2l. Type **23**	20	10
80	3l. Postage stamps, building and map	20	10
81	8l. Telephones, Earth and satellite	70	30

24 Microwave Antenna

1979. 50th Anniv of International Consultative Radio Committee.

82	24	2l. multicoloured	20	10
83	24	5l. multicoloured	20	10
84	24	6l. multicoloured	25	15

25 School Children

1979. International Year of the Child. Mult.

85	1½l. Type **25**	25	20
86	4½l. Children and globe (horiz)	40	45

87		6l. College children	60	45

26 Lala Mustafa Pasha Mosque, Magusa

1980. Islamic Commemorations. Multicoloured.

88		2½l. Type **26**	10	10
89		10l. Arap Ahmet Pasha Mosque, Lefkosa	30	15
90		20l. Mecca and Medina	50	20

COMMEMORATIONS: 2½l. 1st Islamic Conference in Turkish Cyprus; 10l. General Assembly of World Islam Congress; 20l. Moslem Year 1400 AH.

27 Ebu-Su'ud Efendi (philosopher)

1980. Europa. Personalities. Multicoloured.

91		5l. Type **27**	20	10
92		30l. Sultan Selim II	80	40

28 Omer's Shrine, Kyrenia

1980. Ancient Monuments.

93	**28**	2½l. blue and stone	10	10
94	-	3½l. green and pink	10	10
95	-	5l. brown on green	15	10
96	-	10l. mauve and green	20	10
97	-	20l. blue and yellow	35	25

DESIGNS: 3½l. Entrance gate, Famagusta; 5l. Funerary monuments (16th-century), Famagusta; 10l. Bella Paise Abbey, Kyrenia; 20l. Selimiye Mosque, Nicosia.

29 Cyprus 1880 6d. Stamp

1980. Cyprus Stamp Centenary.

98	**29**	7½l. black, brown and green	20	10
99	-	15l. brown, dp blue & bl	25	10
100	-	50l. black, red and grey	65	60

DESIGNS—HORIZ: 15l. Cyprus 1960 Constitution of the Republic 30m. commemorative stamp. VERT: 50l. Social Aid local, 1970.

30 Dome of the Rock

1980. Palestinian Solidarity. Multicoloured.

101		15l. Type **30**	30	15
102		35l. Dome of the Rock (horiz)	70	30

31 Extract from World Muslim Congress Statement in Turkish

1981. Day of Solidarity with Islamic Countries.

103	**31**	1l. buff, red and brown	15	75
104	-	35l. light green, black green	55	1·00

DESIGN: 35l. Extract in English.

32 "Ataturk" (F. Duran)

1981. Ataturk Stamp Exhibition, Lefkosa.

105	**32**	10l. multicoloured	25	35

33 Folk-dancing

1981. Europa. Folklore. Multicoloured.

106		10l. Type **33**	40	25
107		30l. Folk-dancing (different)	60	1·00

34 "Kemal Atatürk" (I. Calli)

1981. Birth Centenary of Kemal Atatürk. Sheet 70×95 mm. Imperf.

MS108	**34**	150l. multicoloured	1·10	1·25

35 Wild Convolvulus

1981. Flowers. Multicoloured.

109		1l. Type **35**	10	10
110		5l. Persian cyclamen (horiz)	10	10
111		10l. Spring mandrake (horiz)	10	15
112		25l. Corn poppy	15	20
113		30l. Wild arum (horiz)	15	10
114		50l. Sage-leaved rock rose	20	20
115		100l. "Cistus salviaefolius L."	30	30
116		150l. Giant fennel (horiz)	50	1·00

36 Stylised Disabled Person in Wheelchair

1981. Commemorations. Multicoloured.

117		7½l. Type **36**	25	35
118		10l. Heads of people of different races, peace dove and barbed wire (vert)	35	55
119		20l. People of different races reaching out from globe, with dishes (vert)	50	85

COMMEMORATIONS: 7½l. International Year for Disabled Persons; 10l. Anti-Apartheid publicity; 20l. World Food Day.

37 Turkish Cypriot and Palestinian Flags

1981. Palestinian Solidarity.

120	**37**	10l. multicoloured	45	60

38 Prince Charles and Lady Diana Spencer

1981. Royal Wedding.

121	**38**	50l. multicoloured	1·00	85

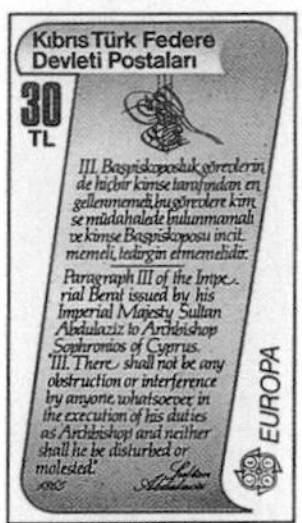

39 Charter issued by Sultan Abdul Aziz to Archbishop Sophronios

1982. Europa (CEPT). Sheet 83×124 mm containing T 39 and similar vert design. Mult.

MS122		30l.×2, Type **39**; 70l.×2, Turkish forces landing at Tuzla, 1571	4·50	5·00

40 Buffavento Castle

1982. Tourism. Multicoloured.

123		5l. Type **40**	10	10
124		10l. Windsurfing (horiz)	15	10
125		15l. Kantara Castle (horiz)	25	15
126		30l. Shipwreck (300 B.C.) (horiz)	60	40

41 "Wedding" (A. Orek)

1982. Art (1st series). Multicoloured.

127		30l. Type **41**	15	30
128		50l. "Carob Pickers" (O. Nazim Selenge) (vert)	30	70

See also Nos. 132/3, 157/8, 176/7, 185/6, 208/9, 225/7, 248/50, 284/5, 315/16, 328/9, 369/70, 436/7, 567/8, 629/30 and 654/5.

42 Cross of Lorraine, Koch and Bacillus (Centenary of Koch's Discovery of Tubercle Bacillus)

1982. Anniversaries and Events. Multicoloured.

129		10l. Type **42**	1·00	40
130		30l. Spectrum on football pitch (World Cup Football Championships, Spain)	1·75	1·10
131		70l. "75" and Lord Baden-Powell (75th Anniv of Boy Scout movement and 125th birth anniv) (vert)	2·25	4·00

43 "Calloused Hands" (Salih Oral)

1983. Art (2nd series). Multicoloured.

132		30l. Type **43**	75	1·40
133		35l. "Malya–Limassol Bus" (Emin Cizenel)	75	1·40

44 Old Map of Cyprus by Piri Reis

1983. Europa. Sheet 82×78 mm containing T 44 and similar horiz design. Multicoloured.

MS134		100l. Type **44**; 100l. Cyprus as seen from "Skylab"	30·00	15·00

45 First Turkish Cypriot 10m. Stamp

1983. Anniversaries and Events. Multicoloured.

135		15l. Type **45**	90	50
136		20l. "Turkish Achievements in Cyprus" (horiz)	90	60
137		25l. "Liberation Fighters"	1·00	80
138		30l. Dish aerial and telegraph pole (horiz)	1·25	1·50
139		50l. Dove and envelopes (horiz)	2·75	3·75

EVENTS: 15, 20, 25l. T.M.T. (25th anniv of Turkish Cypriot Resistance Organization); 30, 50l. World Communications Year.

46 European Bee Eater

1983. Birds of Cyprus. Multicoloured.

140		10l. Type **46**	80	1·25
141		15l. Eurasian goldfinch	1·00	1·25
142		50l. European robin	1·25	1·50
143		65l. Golden oriole	1·40	1·50

1983. Establishment of Republic. Nos. 109, 111/12 and 116 optd Kuzey Kibris Turk Cumhuriyeti 15.11.1983, or surch also.

144		10l. Spring mandrake	20	15
145		15l. on 1l. Type **35**	30	15
146		25l. Corn poppy	40	25
147		150l. Giant fennel	2·25	3·25

48 C.E.P.T. 25th Anniversary Logo

1984. Europa.

148 48 50l. yellow, brown and black 2·25 3·00
149 48 100l. lt blue, blue & black 2·25 3·00

49 Olympic Flame

1984. Olympic Games, Los Angeles. Multicoloured.

150 10l. Type **49** 15 10
151 20l. Olympic events within rings (horiz) 35 25
152 70l. Martial arts event (horiz) 60 1·75

50 Ataturk Cultural Centre

1984. Opening of Ataturk Cultural Centre, Lefkosa.

153 50 120l. stone, black and brown 1·25 1·75

52 Turkish Cypriot Flag and Map

1984. 10th Anniv of Turkish Landings in Cyprus. Multicoloured.

154 20l. Type **52** 50 25
155 70l. Turkish Cypriot flag within book 1·00 2·00

53 Burnt and Replanted Forests

1984. World Forestry Resources.

156 53 90l. multicoloured 1·25 1·75

54 "Old Turkish Houses, Nicosia" (Cevdet Cagdas)

1984. Art (3rd series). Multicoloured.

157 20l. Type **54** 50 40
158 70l. "Scenery" (Olga Rauf) 1·10 2·00

55 Kemal Ataturk, Flag and Crowd

1984. 1st Anniv of Turkish Republic of Northern Cyprus. Multicoloured.

159 20l. Type **55** 50 40
160 70l. Legislative Assembly voting for Republic (horiz) 1·10 2·00

56 Taekwondo Bout

1984. Int Taekwondo Championship, Girne.

161 56 10l. black, brown and grey 40 25
162 - 70l. multicoloured 1·60 2·50

DESIGN: 70l. Emblem and flags of competing nations.

57 "Le Regard"

1984. Exhibition by Saulo Mercader (artist). Multicoloured.

163 20l. Type **57** 30 25
164 70l. "L'equilibre de L'esprit" (horiz) 1·10 2·25

58 Musical Instruments and Music

1984. Visit of Nurnberg Chamber Orchestra.

165 58 70l. multicoloured 1·50 2·25

59 Dr. Fazil Kucuk (politician)

1985. 1st Death Anniv of Dr. Fazil Kucuk (politician). Multicoloured.

166 20l. Type **59** 30 30
167 70l. Dr. Fazil Kucuk reading newspaper 95 2·00

60 Goat

1985. Domestic Animals. Multicoloured.

168 100l. Type **60** 55 30
169 200l. Cow and calf 90 80
170 300l. Ram 1·25 2·00
171 500l. Donkey 2·00 3·25

61 George Frederick Handel

1985. Europa. Composers.

172 61 20l. purple, green & lt grn 2·00 2·50
173 - 20l. purple, brown and pink 2·00 2·50
174 - 100l. purple, blue & lt blue 2·50 3·00
175 - 100l. purple, brn & lt brn 2·50 3·00

DESIGNS: No. 173, Giuseppe Domenico Scarlatti; 174, Johann Sebastian Bach; 175, Buhurizade Mustafa Itri Efendi.

1985. Art (4th series). As T 54. Mult.

176 20l. "Village Life" (Ali Atakan) 60 50
177 50l. "Woman carrying Water" (Ismet V. Guney)) 1·40 2·50

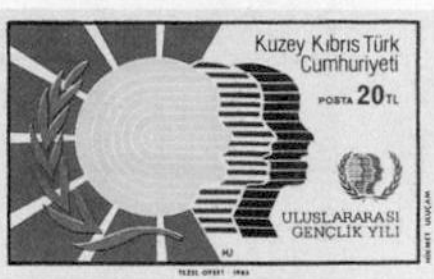

62 Heads of Three Youths

1985. International Youth Year. Multicoloured.

178 20l. Type **62** 75 40
179 100l. Dove and globe 4·00 4·50

63 Parachutist (Aviation League)

1985. Anniversaries and Events.

180 63 20l. multicoloured 1·75 45
181 - 50l. black, brown and blue 2·00 1·25
182 - 100l. brown 1·75 2·75
183 - 100l. multicoloured 1·75 2·75
184 - 100l. multicoloured 2·25 2·75

DESIGNS—VERT: No. 181, Louis Pasteur (Centenary of Discovery of Rabies vaccine); 182, Ismet Inonu (Turkish statesman) (birth centenary (1984)). HORIZ: 183, "40" in figures and symbolic flower (40th anniv of United Nations Organization); 184, Patient receiving blood transfusion (Prevention of Thalassaemia).

1986. Art (5th series). As T 54. Mult.

185 20l. "House with Arches" (Gonen Atakol) 50 30
186 100l. "Ataturk Square" (Yalkin Muhtaroglu) 1·75 1·75

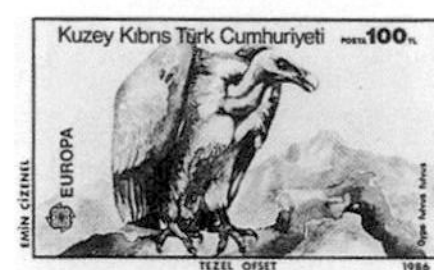

64 Griffon Vulture

1986. Europa. Protection of Nature and the Environment. Sheet 82×76 mm, containing T 64 and similar horiz design. Multicoloured.

MS187 100l. Type **64**; 200l. Litter on Cyprus landscape 10·00 7·50

65 Karagoz Show Puppets

1986. Karagoz Folk Puppets.

188 65 100l. multicoloured 2·25 2·50

66 Old Bronze Age Composite Pottery

1986. Archaeological Artefacts. Cultural Links with Anatolia. Multicoloured.

189 10l. Type **66** 55 20
190 20l. Late Bronze Age bird jug (vert) 95 30
191 50l. Neolithic earthenware pot 1·75 2·00
192 100l. Roman statue of Artemis (vert) 2·25 3·50

67 Soldiers, Defence Force Badge and Ataturk (10th anniv of Defence Forces)

1986. Anniversaries and Events. Multicoloured.

193 20l. Type **67** 1·25 30
194 50l. Woman and two children (40th anniv of F.A.O.) 1·40 1·40
195 100l. Football and world map (World Cup Football Championship, Mexico) (horiz) 3·75 4·25
196 100l. Orbit of Halley's Comet and "Giotto" space probe (horiz) 3·75 4·25

68 Guzelyurt Dam and Power Station

1986. Modern Development (1st series). Mult.

197 20l. Type **68** 1·25 30
198 50l. Low cost housing project, Lefkosa 1·40 1·40
199 100l. Kyrenia Airport 3·25 4·25

See also Nos. 223/4 and 258/63.

69 Prince Andrew and Miss Sarah Ferguson

1986. 60th Birthday of Queen Elizabeth II and Royal Wedding. Multicoloured.

200 100l. Queen Elizabeth II 2·25 3·00
201 100l. Type **69** 2·25 3·00

70 Locomotive No. 11 and Trakhoni Station (image scaled to 40% of original size)

1986. Cyprus Railway. Multicoloured.

202 50l. Type **70** 3·75 2·75
203 100l. Locomotive No. 1 4·25 4·75

1987. Nos. 94, 96/7 and 113 optd Kuzey Kibris Turk Cumhuriyeti or surch also (No. 205).

204 10l. mauve and green 50 80
205 15l. on 3½l. green and pink 50 80
206 20l. blue and yellow 55 85
207 30l. multicoloured 70 1·25

1987. Art (6th series). As T 54. Mult.

208 50l. "Shepherd" (Feridun Isiman) 1·25 1·25
209 125l. "Pear Woman" (Mehmet Uluhan) 1·75 3·00

72 Modern House (architect A. Vural Behaeddin)

1987. Europa. Modern Architecture. Multicoloured.

210 50l. Type **72** 1·00 30

211		200l. Modern house (architect Necdet Turgay)	1·75	3·25

73 Kneeling Folk Dancer

1987. Folk Dancers. Multicoloured.

212		20l. Type **73**	80	20
213		50l. Standing male dancer	90	40
214		200l. Standing female dancer	2·00	1·75
215		1000l. Woman's headdress	4·75	6·50

74 Regimental Colour (1st anniv of Infantry Regiment)

1987. Anniversaries and Events. Multicoloured.

216		50l. Type **74**	1·75	1·00
217		50l. President Denktash and Turgut Ozal (1st anniv of Turkish Prime Minister's visit) (horiz)	1·75	1·00
218		200l. Emblem and Crescent (5th Islamic Summit Conference, Kuwait)	3·00	4·25
219		200l. Emblem and laurel leaves (Membership of Pharmaceutical Federation) (horiz)	3·00	4·25

75 Ahmet Belig Pasha (Egyptian judge)

1987. Turkish Cypriot Personalities.

220	**75**	50l. brown and yellow	65	40
221	-	50l. multicoloured	65	40
222	-	125l. multicoloured	1·50	3·00

DESIGNS: 50l. (No. 221) Mehmet Emin Pasha (Ottoman Grand Vizier); 125l. Mehmet Kamil Pasha (Ottoman Grand Vizier).

76 Tourist Hotel, Girne

1987. Modern Development (2nd series). Mult.

223		150l. Type **76**	1·50	1·50
224		200l. Dogu Akdeniz University	1·75	2·25

1988. Art (7th series). As T 54. Mult.

225		20l. "Woman making Pastry" (Ayhan Mentes) (vert)	50	30
226		50l. "Chair Weaver" (Osman Guvenir)	75	75
227		150l. "Woman weaving a Rug" (Zekai Yesiladali) (vert)	1·75	4·00

77 "Piyale Pasha" (tug)

1988. Europa. Transport and Communications. Multicoloured.

228		200l. Type **77**	2·50	75
229		500l. Dish aerial and antenna tower, Selvilitepe (vert)	3·25	5·00

No. 229 also commemorates the 25th anniv of Bayrak Radio and Television Corporation.

78 Lefkosa

1988. Tourism. Multicoloured.

230		150l. Type **78**	80	80
231		200l. Gazi-Magusa	90	1·00
232		300l. Girne	1·50	2·00

79 Bulent Ecevit

1988. Turkish Prime Ministers. Multicoloured.

233		50l. Type **79**	60	85
234		50l. Bulent Ulusu	60	85
235		50l. Turgut Ozal	60	85

80 Red Crescent Members on Exercise

1988. Civil Defence.

236	**80**	150l. multicoloured	1·75	2·00

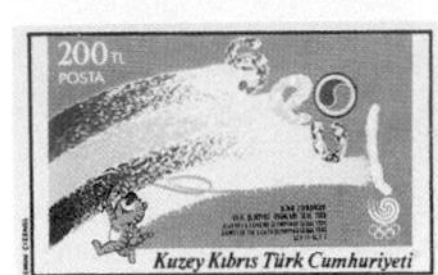

81 Hodori the Tiger (Games mascot) and Fireworks

1988. Olympic Games, Seoul. Multicoloured.

237		200l. Type **81**	1·40	1·00
238		250l. Athletics	1·60	1·25
239		400l. Shot and running track with letters spelling "SEOUL"	2·25	2·00

82 Sedat Simavi (journalist)

1988. Anniversaries and Events.

240	**82**	50l. green	25	25
241	-	100l. multicoloured	75	45
242	-	300l. multicoloured	80	1·00
243	-	400l. multicoloured	2·00	2·00
244	-	400l. multicoloured	1·25	2·00
245	-	600l. multicoloured	2·75	2·75

DESIGNS—HORIZ: No. 241, Stylised figures around table and flags of participating countries (International Girne Conferences); 244, Presidents Gorbachev and Reagan signing treaty (Summit Meeting). VERT: No. 242, Cogwheels as flowers (North Cyprus Industrial Fair); 243, Globe (125th anniv of International Red Cross); 245, "Medical Services" (40th anniv of W.H.O.).

83 "Kemal Atatürk" (I. Calli)

1988. 50th Death Anniv of Kemal Atatürk. Sheet 72×102 mm, containing T 83 and similar vert designs. Multicoloured.

MS246		250l. Type **83**; 250l. "Kemal Atatürk" (N. Ismail); 250l. In army uniform; 250l. In profile	3·25	3·25

84 Abstract Design

1988. 5th Anniv of Turkish Republic of Northern Cyprus. Sheet 98×76 mm. Imperf.

MS247	**84**	500l. multicoloured	2·25	2·25

1989. Art (8th series). As T 54. Mult.

248		150l. "Dervis Pasa Mansion, Lefkosa" (Inci Kansu)	90	60
249		400l. "Gamblers' Inn, Lefkosa" (Osman Guvenir)	1·75	2·25
250		600l. "Mosque, Paphos" (Hikmet Ulucam) (vert)	2·50	3·00

85 Girl with Doll

1989. Europa. Children's Games. Multicoloured.

251		600l. Type **85**	2·25	1·25
252		1000l. Boy with kite	2·50	3·75

86 Meeting of Presidents Vassiliou and Denktash

1989. Cyprus Peace Summit, Geneva, 1988.

253	**86**	500l. red and black	1·25	1·25

87 Chukar Partridge

1989. Wildlife. Multcoloured.

254		100l. Type **87**	65	25
255		200l. Cyprus hare	70	35
256		700l. Black partridge	2·50	2·00
257		2000l. Red fox	3·00	4·00

88 Road Construction

1989. Modern Development (3rd series). Mult.

258		100l. Type **88**	25	15
259		150l. Laying water pipeline (vert)	30	20
260		200l. Seedling trees (vert)	40	30
261		450l. Modern telephone exchange (vert)	1·00	1·00
262		650l. Steam turbine power station (vert)	1·25	1·75
263		700l. Irrigation reservoir	1·50	1·75

89 Unloading "Polly Pioneer" (freighter) at Quayside (15th anniv of Gazi Magusa Free Port)

1989. Anniversaries.

264	**89**	100l. multicoloured	70	20
265	-	450l. black, blue and red	80	80
266	-	500l. black, yellow and grey	80	80
267	-	600l. black, red and blue	2·25	2·25
268	-	1000l. multicoloured	3·50	4·50

DESIGNS—VERT (26×47 mm): 450l. Airmail letter and stylized bird (25th anniv of Turkish Cypriot postal service). HORIZ (as T **89**): 500l. Newspaper and printing press (centenary of "Saded" newspaper); 600l. Statue of Aphrodite, lifebelt and seabird (30th anniv of International Maritime Organization); 1000l. Soldiers (25th anniv of Turkish Cypriot resistance).

90 Erdal Inonu

1989. Visit of Professor Erdal Inonu (Turkish politician).

269	**90**	700l. multicoloured	80	1·00

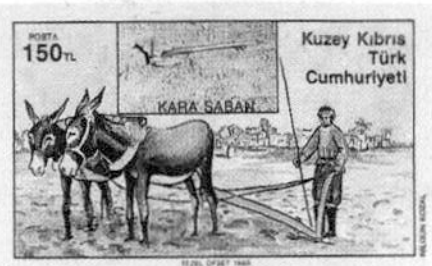

91 Mule-drawn Plough

1989. Traditional Agricultural Implements. Mult.

270		150l. Type **91**	30	25
271		450l. Ox-drawn threshing sledge	75	85
272		550l. Olive press (vert)	90	1·25

92 Smoking Ashtray and Drinks

1990. World Health Day. Multicoloured.

273		200l. Type **92**	1·25	40
274		700l. Smoking cigarette and heart	2·50	3·25

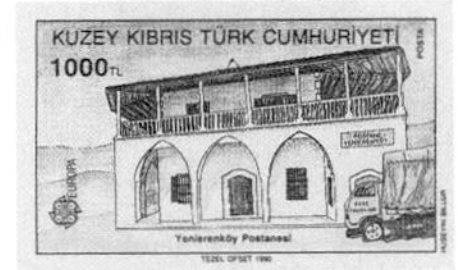

93 Yenierenkoy Post Office

1990. Europa. Post Office Buildings. Mult.

275		1000l. Type **93**	2·00	75
276		1500l. Ataturk Meydani Post Office	2·75	3·75
MS277		105×72 mm. Nos. 275/6 × 2	7·50	8·50

94 Song Thrush

1990. World Environment Day. Birds. Mult.

278		150l. Type **94**	2·75	65
279		300l. Blackcap	3·50	1·00
280		900l. Black redstart	5·50	4·50
281		1000l. Chiff-chaff	5·50	4·50

95 Two Football Teams

1990. World Cup Football Championship, Italy. Multicoloured.

282		300l. Type **95**	75	50
283		1000l. Championship symbol, globe and ball	2·50	3·50

1990. Art (9th series). As T 54. Multicoloured.

284		300l. "Abstract" (Filiz Ankacc)	40	25

285 1000l. Wooden sculpture (S. Tekman) (vert) 1·25 1·50

96 Amphitheatre, Soli

1990. Tourism. Multicoloured.
286 150l. Type **96** 40 20
287 1000l. Swan mosaic, Soli 1·75 2·50

97 Kenan Evren and Rauf Denktash

1990. Visit of President Kenan Evren of Turkey.
288 **97** 500l. multicoloured 1·00 1·00

98 Road Signs and Heart wearing Seat Belt

1990. Traffic Safety Campaign. Multicoloured.
289 150l. Type **98** 1·25 30
290 300l. Road signs, speeding car and spots of blood 1·50 50
291 1000l. Traffic lights and road signs 3·75 4·50

99 Yildirim Akbulut

1990. Visit of Turkish Prime Minister Yildrim Akbulut.
292 **99** 1000l. multicoloured 1·10 1·10

100 "Rosularia cypria"

1990. Plants. Multicoloured.
293 150l. Type **100** 70 20
294 200l. "Silene fraudratrix" 80 30
295 300l. "Scutellaria sibthorpii" 90 35
296 600l. "Sedum lampusae" 1·40 85
297 1000l. "Onosma caespitosum" 1·50 2·25
298 1500l. "Arabis cypria" 2·25 4·00

101 Kemal Ataturk at Easel (wood carving)

1990. International Literacy Year. Multicoloured.
299 300l. Type **101** 1·25 35
300 750l. Globe, letters and books 2·50 3·25

1991. Nos. 189, 212 and 293 surch.
301 **66** 250l. on 10l. multicoloured 1·50 1·50
302 **73** 250l. on 20l. multicoloured 1·50 1·50
303 **100** 500l. on 150l. multicoloured 2·00 2·50

103 "Ophrys lapethica"

1991. Orchids (1st series). Multicoloured.
304 250l. Type **103** 1·25 60
305 500l. "Ophrys kotschyi" 2·25 2·75
See also Nos. 311/14.

104 "Hermes" (projected shuttle)

1991. Europa. Europe in Space. Sheet 78×82 mm, containing T 104 and similar vert design. Multicoloured.
MS306 2000l. Type **104**; 2000l. "Ulysses" (satellite) 9·00 10·00

105 Kucuk Medrese Fountain, Lefkosa

1991. Fountains. Multicoloured.
307 250l. Type **105** 55 15
308 500l. Cafer Pasa fountain, Magusa 75 30
309 1500l. Sarayonu Square fountain, Lefkosa 1·50 1·60
310 5000l. Arabahmet Mosque fountain, Lefkosa 3·75 6·00

1991. Orchids (2nd series). As T 103. Mult.
311 100l. "Serapias levantina" 85 20
312 500l. "Dactylorhiza romana" 2·50 50
313 2000l. "Orchis simia" 4·25 4·50
314 3000l. "Orchis sancta" 4·75 6·00

1991. Art (10th series). As T 54. Mult.
315 250l. "Hindiler" (S. Cizel) (vert) 2·00 50
316 500l. "Dusme" (A. Mene) (vert) 2·50 2·50

106 Symbolic Roots (Year of Love to Yunus Emre)

1991. Anniversaries and Events.
317 **106** 250l. yellow, black and mauve 25 25
318 - 500l. multicoloured 45 60
319 - 500l. multicoloured 45 60
320 - 1500l. multicoloured 5·50 5·50
DESIGNS—VERT: No. 318, Mustafa Cagatay commemoration; 319, University building (5th anniv of Eastern Mediterranean University). HORIZ: No. 320, Mozart (death bicentenary).

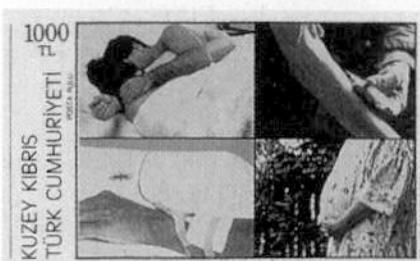
107 Four Sources of Infection

1991. "AIDS" Day.
321 **107** 1000l. multicoloured 2·50 2·00

108 Lighthouse, Gazimagusa

1991. Lighthouses. Multicoloured.
322 250l. Type **108** 2·50 65
323 500l. Ancient lighthouses, Girne harbour 3·25 1·25
324 1500l. Modern lighthouse, Girne harbour 5·50 6·50

109 Elephant and Hippopotamus Fossils, Karaoglanoglu

1991. Tourism (1st series). Multicoloured.
325 250l. Type **109** 2·00 55
326 500l. Roman fish ponds, Lambusa 2·25 80
327 1500l. Roman remains, Lambusa 3·50 5·00
See also Nos. 330/3 and 351/2.

1992. Art (11th series). As T 54, but 31×49 mm. Multicoloured.
328 500l. "Ebru" (A. Kandulu) 1·00 25
329 3500l. "Street in Lefkosa" (I. Tatar) 4·00 5·50

1992. Tourism (2nd series). As T 109. Mult.
330 500l. Bugday Camii, Gazimagusa 80 80
331 500l. Clay pigeon shooting 80 80
332 1000l. Salamis Bay Hotel, Gazimagusa 1·50 1·50
333 1500l. Casino, Girne (vert) 2·50 3·50

110 Fleet of Columbus and Early Map

1992. Europa. 500th Anniv of Discovery of America by Columbus. Sheet 80×76 mm, containing T 110 and similar horiz design. Multicoloured.
MS334 1500l. Type **110**; 3500l. Christopher Columbus and signature 4·00 4·25

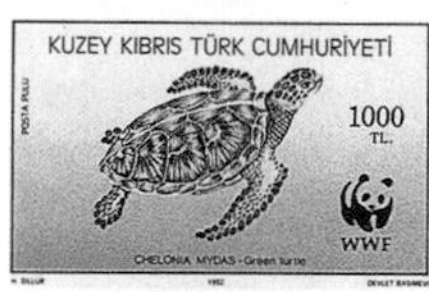
111 Green Turtle

1992. World Environment Day. Sea Turtles. Sheet 105×75 mm, containing T 111 and similar horiz design. Multicoloured.
MS335 1000l. × 2, Type **111**; 1500l. × 2, Loggerhead turtle 6·50 7·00

112 Gymnastics

1992. Olympic Games, Barcelona. Multicoloured.
336 500l. Type **112** 80 90
337 500l. Tennis 80 90
338 1000l. High jumping (horiz) 1·00 1·25
339 1500l. Cycling (horiz) 4·50 4·50

113 New Generating Station, Girne

1992. Anniversaries and Events (1st series). Multicoloured.
340 500l. Type **113** 50 50
341 500l. Symbol of Housing Association (15th anniv) 50 50
342 1500l. Domestic animals and birds (30th anniv of Veterinary Service) 3·75 4·00
343 1500l. Cat (International Federation of Cat Societies Conference) 3·75 4·00

114 Airliner over Runway

1992. Anniversaries and Events (2nd series). Multicoloured.
344 1000l. Type **114** (17th anniv of civil aviation) 2·50 2·50
345 1000l. Meteorological instruments and weather (18th anniv of Meteorological Service) 2·50 2·50
346 1200l. Surveying equipment and map (14th anniv of Survey Department) 3·25 3·50

115 Zubiye

1992. International Conference on Nutrition, Rome. Turkish Cypriot Cuisine. Multicoloured.
347 2000l. Type **115** 1·50 1·50
348 2500l. Cicek Dolmasi 1·75 1·75
349 3000l. Tatar Boregi 2·00 2·25
350 4000l. Seftali Kebabi 2·25 2·50

1993. Tourism (3rd series). As T 109. Mult.
351 500l. St. Barnabas Church and Monastery, Salamis 50 15
352 10000l. Ancient pot 5·50 6·50

116 Painting by Turksal Ince

1993. Europa. Contemporary Art. Sheet 79×69 mm, containing T 116 and similar vert design. Multicoloured.
MS353 2000l. Type **116**; 3000l. Painting by Ilkay Onsoy 1·75 2·50

117 Olive Tree, Girne

1993. Ancient Trees. Multicoloured.
354 500l. Type **117** 45 15
355 1000l. River red gum, Kyrenia Gate, Lefkosa 80 40
356 3000l. Oriental plane, Lapta 1·75 2·00
357 4000l. Calabrian pine, Cinarli 2·00 2·25

118 Traditional Houses

1993. Arabahmet District Conservation Project, Lefkosa. Multicoloured.
358 1000l. Type **118** 1·00 40
359 3000l. Arabahmet street 2·50 3·25

119 National Flags turning into Doves

1993. 10th Anniv of Proclamation of Turkish Republic of Northern Cyprus.

360	**119**	500l. red, black and blue	30	30
361	-	500l. red and blue	30	30
362	-	1000l. red, black and blue	40	30
363	-	5000l. multicoloured	1·75	3·00

DESIGNS—HORIZ: No. 361, National flag forming figure "10"; No. 362, Dove carrying national flag; No. 363, Map of Cyprus and figure "10" wreath.

120 Kemal Ataturk

1993. Anniversaries. Multicoloured.

364	500l. Type **120** (55th death anniv)	30	30
365	500l. Stage and emblem (30th anniv of Turkish Cypriot theatre) (horiz)	30	30
366	1500l. Branch badges (35th anniv of T.M.T. organization) (horiz)	30	50
367	2000l. World map and computer (20th anniv of Turkish Cypriot news agency) (horiz)	1·75	1·75
368	5000l. Ballet dancers and Caykovski'nin (death centenary) (horiz)	5·50	5·50

121 "Soyle Falci" (Goral Ozkan)

1994. Art (12th series). Multicoloured.

369	1000l. Type **121**	30	20
370	6500l. "IV. Hareket" (sculpture) (Senol Ozdevrim)	1·50	2·25

122 Dr. Kucuk and Memorial

1994. 10th Death Anniv of Dr. Fazil Kucuk (politician).

371	**122**	1500l. multicoloured	70	85

123 Neolithic Village, Girne

1994. Europa. Archaeological Discoveries. Sheet 73×79 mm, containing T **123** and similar horiz design. Multicoloured.

MS372	8500l. Type **123**; 8500l. Neolithic man and implements	6·50	7·00

124 Peace Doves and Letters over Pillar Box

1994. 30th Anniv of Turkish Cypriot Postal Service.

373	**124**	50000l. multicoloured	3·00	4·50

125 World Cup Trophy

1994. World Cup Football Championship, U.S.A. Multicoloured.

374	2500l. Type **125**	50	25
375	10000l. Footballs on map of U.S.A. (horiz)	2·00	2·75

126 Peace Emblem

1994. 20th Anniv of Turkish Landings in Cyprus.

376	**126**	2500l. yellow, green and black	40	30
377	-	5000l. multicoloured	60	60
378	-	7000l. multicoloured	80	1·00
379	-	8500l. multicoloured	1·10	1·50

DESIGNS—HORIZ: 5000l. Memorial; 7000l. Sculpture; 8500l. Peace doves forming map of Cyprus and flame.

127 Cyprus 1934 4½ pi. Stamp and Karpas Postmark

1994. Postal Centenary. Multicoloured.

380	1500l. Type **127**	20	20
381	2500l. Turkish Cypriot Posts 1979 Europa 2l. and Gazimagusa postmark	40	30
382	5000l. Cyprus 1938 6pi. and Bey Keuy postmark	70	90
383	7000l. Cyprus 1955 100m. and Aloa postmark	1·00	1·50
384	8500l. Cyprus 1938 18pi. and Pyla postmark	1·25	2·00

128 Trumpet Triton

1994. Sea Shells. Multicoloured.

385	2500l. Type **128**	45	30
386	12500l. Mole cowrie	1·25	1·75
387	12500l. Giant tun	1·25	1·75

1994. Nos. 280, 295, 315 and 317 surch.

388	1500l. on 250l. Type **106**	20	10
389	2000l. on 900l. Black redstart	3·00	90
390	2500l. on 250l. "Hindiler" (Sizel)	40	30
391	3500l. on 300l. "Scutellaria sibthorpii"	2·75	3·00

130 Donkeys on Mountain

1995. European Conservation Year. Multicoloured.

392	2000l. Type **130**	30	20
393	3500l. Coastline	30	30
394	15000l. Donkeys in field	1·50	2·50

131 Peace Dove and Globe

1995. Europa. Peace and Freedom. Sheet 72×78 mm, containing T 131 and similar horiz design. Mult.

MS395	15000l. Type **131**; 15000l. Peace doves over map of Europe	3·75	4·00

132 Sini Katmeri

1995. Turkish Cypriot Cuisine. Multicoloured.

396	3500l. Type **132**	20	20
397	10000l. Kolokas musakka and bullez kizartma	55	65
398	14000l. Enginar dolmasi	90	1·60

133 "Papilio machaon"

1995. Butterflies. Multicoloured.

399	3500l. Type **133**	30	15
400	4500l. "Charaxes jasius"	35	20
401	15000l. "Cynthia cardui"	1·00	1·40
402	30000l. "Vanessa atalanta"	1·75	2·50

134 Forest

1995. Obligatory Tax. Forest Regeneration Fund.

403	**134**	1000l. green and black	3·75	40

135 Beach, Girne

1995. Tourism. Multicoloured.

404	3500l. Type **135**	30	20
405	7500l. Sail boards	50	45
406	15000l. Ruins of Salamis (vert)	1·00	1·25
407	20000l. St. George's Cathedral, Gazimagusa (vert)	1·00	1·25

136 Suleyman Demirel and Rauf Denktash

1995. Visit of President Suleyman Demirel of Turkey.

408	**136**	5000l. multicoloured	60	60

137 Stamp Printing Press

1995. Anniversaries.

409	**137**	3000l. multicoloured	40	40
410	-	3000l. multicoloured	40	40
411	-	5000l. multicoloured	70	70
412	-	22000l. ultram, bl & blk	1·00	1·75
413	-	30000l. multicoloured	1·40	2·25
414	-	30000l. multicoloured	1·40	2·25

DESIGNS—HORIZ: No. 409, Type **137** (20th anniv of State Printing Works); 410, Map of Turkey (75th anniv of Turkish National Assembly); 411, Louis Pasteur (chemist) and microscope (death centenary); 412, United Nations anniversary emblem (50th anniv); 413, Guglielmo Marconi (radio pioneer) and dial (centenary of first radio transmissions). VERT: No. 414, Stars and reel of film (centenary of cinema).

138 Kultegin Epitaph and Sculpture

1995. Centenary of Deciphering of Orhon Epitaphs. Multicoloured.

415	5000l. Type **138**	1·00	50
416	10000l. Epitaph and tombstone	1·75	2·25

139 "Bosnia" (sculpture)

1996. Support for Moslems in Bosnia and Herzegovina.

417	**139**	10000l. multicoloured	1·75	2·00

140 Striped Red Mullet

1996. Fish. Multicoloured.

418	6000l. Type **140**	1·00	30
419	10000l. Peacock wrasse	1·25	45
420	28000l. Common two-banded seabream	2·25	2·50
421	40000l. Dusky grouper	2·75	3·50

141 Palm Trees

1996. Tourism. Multicoloured.

422	100000l. Type **141**	1·25	45
423	150000l. Pomegranate	1·75	1·00
424	250000l. Ruins of Bella Paise Abbey (horiz)	2·25	2·75
425	500000l. Traditional dancers (horiz)	4·75	6·00

142 Beria Remzi Ozoran

1996. Europa. Famous Women. Multicoloured.

426	15000l. Type **142**	1·00	25
427	50000l. Kadriye Hulusi Hacibulgur	2·25	3·50

143 Established Forest

1996. World Environment Day. Sheet 72×78 mm, containing T 143 and similar horiz design. Multicoloured.

MS428 50000l. Type **143**; 50000l. Conifer plantation 8·00 8·00

144 Basketball

1996. Olympic Games, Atlanta. Sheet 105×74 mm, containing T 144 and similar horiz designs. Multicoloured.

MS429 15000l. Type **144**; 15000l. Discus throwing; 50000l. Javelin throwing; 50000l. Volleyball 3·50 4·25

145 Symbolic Footballs

1996. European Football Championship, England. Multicoloured.

430 15000l. Type **145** 1·25 65
431 35000l. Football and flags of participating nations 2·25 3·25

146 Houses on Fire (Auxiliary Fire Service)

1996. Anniversaries and Events. Multicoloured.

432 10000l. Type **146** 1·00 40
433 20000l. Colour party (20th anniv of Defence Forces) (vert) 1·10 55
434 50000l. Children by lake (Nasreddin-Hoca Year) 1·40 1·60
435 75000l. Flowers (Children's Rights) 1·75 3·00

1997. Art (13th series). As T 121. Multicoloured.

436 25000l. "City" (Lebibe Sonuc) (horiz) 1·25 50
437 70000l. "Woman opening Letter" (Ruzen Atakan) (horiz) 2·50 3·25

147 "Amanita phalloides"

1997. Fungi. Multicoloured.

438 15000l. Type **147** 1·00 30
439 25000l. "Morchella esculenta" 1·25 1·50
440 25000l. "Pleurotus eryngii" 1·25 1·50
441 70000l. "Amanita muscaria" 2·50 3·50

148 Flag on Hillside

1997. Besparmak Mountains Flag Sculpture.

442 **148** 60000l. multicoloured 2·00 2·25

149 Mother and Children playing Leapfrog

1997. Europa. Tales and Legends. Multicoloured.

443 25000l. Type **149** 1·50 30
444 70000l. Apple tree and well 3·00 3·50

150 Prime Minister Necmettin Erbakan of Turkey

1997. Visit of the President and the Prime Minister of Turkey.

445 15000l. Type **150** 50 30
446 80000l. President Suleyman Demirel of Turkey (horiz) 2·25 3·25

151 Golden Eagle

1997. Birds of Prey. Multicoloured.

447 40000l. Type **151** 1·75 1·75
448 40000l. Eleonora's falcon 1·75 1·75
449 75000l. Common kestrel 2·50 2·75
450 100000l. Western honey buzzard 2·75 3·00

152 Coin of Sultan Abdulaziz, 1861–76

1997. Rare Coins. Multicoloured.

451 25000l. Type **152** 60 20
452 40000l. Coin of Sultan Mahmud II, 1808–39 80 45
453 75000l. Coin of Sultan Selim II, 1566–74 1·50 1·75
454 100000l. Coin of Sultan Mehmed V, 1909–18 1·75 2·50

153 Open Book and Emblem

1997. Anniversaries.

455 **153** 25000l. multicoloured 75 20
456 - 40000l. multicoloured 1·10 30
457 - 100000l. black, red and stone 2·75 2·50
458 - 150000l. multicoloured 3·50 4·00

DESIGNS—HORIZ: 25000l. Type **153** (centenary of Turkish Cypriot Scouts); 40000l. Guides working in field (90th anniv of Turkish Cypriot Guides); 150000l. Rudolph Diesel and first oil engine (centenary of the diesel engine). VERT: 100000l. Couple and symbols (AIDS prevention campaign).

154 Ahmet and Ismet Sevki

1998. Ahmet and Ismet Sevki (photographers) Commemoration. Multicoloured.

459 40000l. Type **154** 75 25
460 105000l. Ahmet Sevki (vert) 2·00 3·00

155 "Agrion splendens" (dragonfly)

1998. Useful Insects. Multicoloured.

461 40000l. Type **155** 80 25
462 65000l. "Ascalaphus macaronius" (owl-fly) 1·40 40
463 125000l. "Podalonia hirsuta" 2·25 2·75
464 150000l. "Rhyssa persuasoria" 2·50 3·25

156 Wooden Double Door

1998. Old Doors.

465 **156** 115000l. multicoloured 2·25 2·50
466 - 140000l. multicoloured 2·25 2·50

DESIGN: 140000l. Different door.

157 Legislative Assembly Building (Republic Establishment Festival)

1998. Europa. Festivals. Multicoloured.

467 40000l. Type **157** 75 25
468 150000l. Globe, flags and map (Int Children's Folk Dance Festival) (vert) 4·25 4·50

158 Marine Life

1998. International Year of the Ocean.

469 **158** 40000l. multicoloured 1·00 40
470 - 90000l. multicoloured 2·00 2·50

DESIGN: 90000l. Different underwater scene.

159 Prime Minister Mesut Yilmaz of Turkey

1998. Prime Minister Yilmaz's Visit to Northern Cyprus.

471 **159** 75000l. multicoloured 1·75 2·00

160 Pres. Suleyman Demirel of Turkey

1998. President Demirel's "Water for Peace" Project.

472 75000l. Type **160** 1·25 50
473 175000l. Turkish and Turkish Cypriot leaders with inflatable water tank (horiz) 2·50 3·50

161 Victorious French Team

1998. World Cup Football Championship, France. Multicoloured.

474 75000l. Type **161** 1·25 50
475 175000l. World Cup trophy (vert) 2·50 3·50

162 Deputy Prime Minister Bulent Ecevit

1998. Visit of the Deputy Prime Minister of Turkey.

476 **162** 200000l. multicoloured 2·00 2·25

163 Itinerant Tinsmiths

1998. Local Crafts. Multicoloured.

477 50000l. Type **163** 45 25
478 75000l. Basket weaver (vert) 65 35
479 130000l. Grinder sharpening knife (vert) 1·25 1·40
480 400000l. Wood carver 3·50 5·00

164 Stylised Satellite Dish

1998. Anniversaries. Multicoloured (except No. 483).

481 50000l. Type **164** 80 30
482 75000l. Stylised birds and "15" 1·25 1·40
483 75000l. "75" and Turkish flag (red, black and orange) 1·25 1·40
484 175000l. Scroll, "50" and quill pen (vert) 2·00 3·50

MS485 72×78 mm. 75000l. As No. 482; 75000l. Map of Northern Cyprus 2·50 3·00

ANNIVERSARIES: No. 481, 35th anniv of Bayrak Radio and Television; 482, **MS**485, 15th anniv of Turkish Republic of Northern Cyprus; 483, 75th anniv of Turkish Republic; 484, 50th anniv of Universal Declaration of Human Rights.

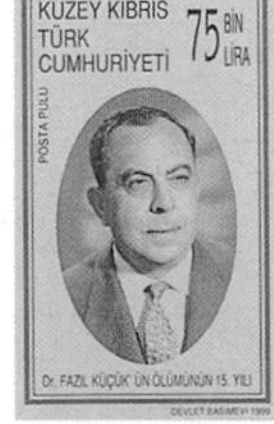

165 Dr. Fazil Kucuk

1999. 15th Death Anniv of Dr. Fazil Kucuk (politician).

486 **165** 75000l. multicoloured 1·50 1·50

166 Otello

1999. Performance of Verdi's Opera Otello in Cyprus. Sheet 78×74 mm, containing T 166 and similar vert design. Multicoloured.

MS487 200000l. Type **166**; 200000l. Desdemona dead in front of fireplace 6·00 6·00

167 "Malpolon monspessulanus insignitus" (Montepellier)

1999. Snakes. Multicoloured.

488	50000l. Type **167**	85	30
489	75000l. "Hierophis jugularis"	1·10	45
490	195000l. "Vipera lebetina lebetina" (levantine viper)	2·00	2·50
491	220000l. "Natrix natrix" (grass snake)	2·00	2·50

168 Entrance to Cave

1999. Europa. Parks and Gardens. Incirli Cave. Multicoloured.

492	75000l. Type **168**	1·25	25
493	200000l. Limestone rocks inside cave (vert)	2·50	3·25

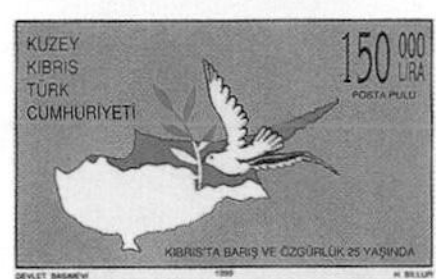
169 Peace Dove and Map of Cyprus

1999. 25th Anniv of Turkish Landings in Cyprus. Multicoloured.

494	150000l. Type **169**	2·00	1·50
495	250000l. Peace dove, map of Cyprus and sun	2·50	3·00

170 Air Mail Envelope and Labels

1999. Anniversaries and Events. Multicoloured.

496	75000l. Type **170** (35th anniv of Turkish Cypriot Posts)	65	25
497	225000l. "125" and U.P.U. emblem (125th anniv of U.P.U.)	1·50	1·75
498	250000l. Total eclipse of the Sun, August 1999	2·00	2·25

171 Turkish Gateway, Limassol

1999. Destruction of Turkish Buildings in Southern Cyprus. Each light brown and brown.

499	75000l. Type **171**	60	25
500	150000l. Mosque, Evdim	85	40
501	210000l. Bayraktar Mosque, Lefkosa	1·10	75
502	1000000l. Kebir Mosque, Baf (vert)	5·00	7·00

172 Mobile Phone

2000. New Millennium. Technology.

503	**172**	75000l. black, green and blue	70	20
504	-	150000l. black and blue	90	35
505	-	275000l. multicoloured	1·60	2·25
506	-	300000l. multicoloured	2·00	2·75

DESIGNS: 150000l. "Hosgeldin 2000"; 275000l. Computer and "internet" in squares; 300000l. Satellite over Earth.

173 Beach Scene

2000. Holidays. Multicoloured.

507	300000l. Type **173**	1·75	2·00
508	340000l. Deck-chair on seashore	1·75	2·00

174 "Building Europe"

2000. Europa. Sheet 77×68 mm, containing T 174 and similar vert design. Multicoloured.

MS509 300000l. Type **174**; 300000l. Map of Europe with flower creating Council of Europe emblem and map of Cyprus 3·50 4·25

175 Bellapais Abbey

2000. 4th International Bellapais Music Festival. Multicoloured.

510	150000l. Type **175**	1·00	60
511	350000l. Emblem (vert)	2·25	3·00

176 Pres. Ahmet Sezer of Turkey

2000. Visit of President Ahmet Sezer of Turkey.

512	**176**	150000l. multicoloured	1·50	1·50

177 Olympic Torch and Rings

2000. Olympic Games, Sydney. Multicoloured.

513	125000l. Type **177**	1·25	50
514	200000l. Runner (horiz)	2·00	2·50

2000. No. 418 surch 50000 LIRA POSTA PULU.

515	50000l. on 6000l. Type **140**	2·50	1·00

179 Grasshopper on Cactus

2000. Nature. Insects and Flowers. Multicoloured.

516	125000l. Type **179**	80	25
517	200000l. Butterfly on flower	1·40	45
518	275000l. Bee on flower	1·50	1·25
519	600000l. Snail on flower	3·00	4·50

180 Traditional Kerchief

2000. Traditional Handicrafts. Kerchiefs.

520	**180**	125000l. multicoloured	70	30
521	-	200000l. multicoloured	1·10	60
522	-	265000l. multicoloured	1·40	1·60
523	-	350000l. multicoloured	2·00	3·00

DESIGNS: 200000l. to 350000l. Different kerchiefs.

181 Lusignan House, Lefkosa

2001. Restoration of Historic Buildings. Mult.

524	125000l. Type **181**	1·25	50
525	200000l. The Eaved House, Lefkosa	2·00	2·50

182 "Cuprum Kuprum Bakir Madeni" (Inci Kansu)

2001. Modern Art. Multicoloured.

526	125000l. Type **182**	1·00	30
527	200000l. "Varolus" (Emel Samioglu)	1·60	45
528	350000l. "Ask Kuslara Ucar" (Ozden Selenge) (vert)	2·25	3·00
529	400000l. "Suyun Yolculugu" (Ayhatun Atesin)	2·25	3·00

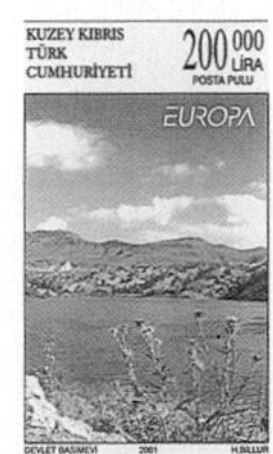
183 Degirmenlik Reservoir

2001. Europa. Water Resources. Multicoloured.

530	200000l. Type **183**	1·25	30
531	500000l. The Waters of Sinar	2·00	2·75

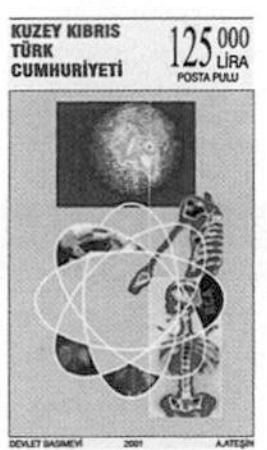
184 Atomic Symbol and X-ray

2001. World Environment Day. Radiation. Mult.

532	125000l. Type **184**	75	20
533	450000l. Radiation symbol and x-ray of hand	2·25	3·00

185 Ottoman Policeman, 1885

2001. Turkish Cypriot Police Uniforms. Multicoloured.

534	125000l. Type **185**	1·25	50
535	200000l. Colonial policeman, 1933	2·00	80
536	500000l. Mounted policeman, 1934	3·00	2·75
537	750000l. Policewoman, 1983	4·00	5·00

186 MG TF Sports Car, 1954

2001. Classic Cars. Multicoloured.

538	175000l. Type **186**	1·00	30
539	300000l. Vauxhall 14, 1948	1·75	75
540	475000l. Bentley, 1922	2·25	2·50
541	600000l. Jaguar XK 120, 1955	2·50	3·25

187 Graduate at Top of Steps and College Names

2001. Anniversaries.

542	**187**	200000l. multicoloured	1·60	1·60
543	-	200000l. black, mauve and brown	1·60	1·60

DESIGNS—HORIZ: No. 542, Type **187** (Centenary of Higher Education). VERT: No. 543, Book cover of *The Genocide Files* by Harry Scott Gibbons (anniversary of publication).

188 Chef mincing Logs into Letters (U. Karsu)

2002. Caricatures. Multicoloured.

544	250000l. Type **188**	1·25	40
545	300000l. Overfed people drinking from inflated cow, and starving children (M. Kayra) (horiz)	1·40	55
546	475000l. Can of cola parachuting down to pregnant African woman (S. Gazi)	1·75	2·00
547	850000l. Artist painting trees in city (M. Tozaki)	2·75	4·50

189 Turtle

2002. Tourism. Underwater Scenes. Multicoloured.

548	250000l. Type **189**	1·25	45
549	300000l. Starfish on rock	1·40	60
550	500000l. Fish in rocks	1·90	1·90
551	750000l. Part of wreck	2·75	4·25

190 Stilt-walker

2002. Europa. Circus. Sheet 79×72 mm, containing T 190 and similar vert design. Multicoloured.

MS552 600000l. Type **190**; 600000l. Child on high wire 4·25 5·00

191 Turkish Football Team

2002. World Cup Football Championship, Japan and Korea (2002). Multicoloured.

553	300000l. Type **191**	1·25	30
554	1000000l. Football Stadium, World Cup Trophy and footballer	3·25	3·75

192 Woman in White Tunic and Trousers

2002. Traditional Costumes. Multicoloured.

555	250000l. Type **192**	1·25	35

556	300000l. Man wearing grey jacket	1·40	55
557	425000l. Man in blue jacket and trousers	2·00	2·00
558	700000l. Woman in yellow tunic	3·50	4·50

193 "Accident by Bridge"

2002. Children's Paintings. Multicoloured.

559	300000l. Type **193**	1·25	60
560	600000l. "Burning House" (vert)	2·50	3·50

194 Sureyya Ayhan (athlete)

2002. Sporting Celebrities. Multicoloured.

561	300000l. Type **194**	1·00	40
562	1000000l. Grand Master Park Jung-tae (taekwon-do)	2·50	3·75

195 Oguz Karayel (footballer) (70th birth anniv)

2002. Celebrities' Anniversaries. Multicoloured.

563	100000l. Type **195**	55	15
564	175000l. Mete Adanir (footballer) (40th birth anniv)	85	40
565	300000l. M. Necati Ozkan (30th death anniv)	1·50	90
566	575000l. Osman Turkay (astronomer) (1st death anniv) (horiz)	2·75	4·50

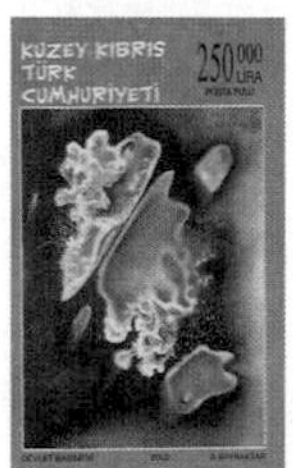

196 Untitled Painting by Salih Bayraktar

2003. Art (14th series). Multicoloured.

567	250000l. Type **196**	1·25	50
568	1000000l. Untitled painting of woman's head (Feryal Suukan)	3·00	4·00

197 Tree containing Meadow and Forest in Polluted Industrial Landscape

2003. Europa. Poster Art. Sheet 78×72 mm, containing T 197 and similar vert design. Multicoloured.

MS569	600000l. Type **197**; 600000l. Question mark containing wildlife in polluted landscape	2·75	3·50

198 Cyprus Wheatear

2003. World Environment Day. Birds. Multi.

570	100000l. Type **198**	90	55
571	300000l. Cyprus warbler	1·75	85
572	500000l. Pygmy cormorant (vert)	2·50	3·00
573	600000l. Greater flamingo (vert)	2·50	3·00

199 Carved Wooden Chest

2003. Wooden Chests. Multicoloured.

574	250000l. Type **199**	50	25
575	300000l. Chest carved with circular designs	60	30
576	525000l. Chest carved with turquoise-blue figures	1·00	1·25
577	1000000l. Chest carved with flower heads and white birds	1·75	3·00

200 *ladiolus triphyllus*

2003. Flowers. Multicoloured.

578	150000l. Type **200**	40	20
579	175000l. *Tulipa cypria*	60	45
580	500000l. *Ranunculus asiaticus*	1·25	1·75
581	525000l. *Narcissus tazetta*	1·25	1·75

201 Kemal Ataturk and Flag of Turkish Republic of Northern Cyprus

2003. Political Anniversaries. Multicoloured.

582	3000000l. Type **201** (20th anniv of proclamation of Turkish Republic of Northern Cyprus)	3·25	4·00
583	3000000l. Kemal Atatürk and Turkish flag (80th anniv of Republic of Turkey)	3·25	4·00

202 Horse-drawn Plough and Modern Farm Machinery

2003. Anniversaries. Multicoloured.

584	300000l. Type **202** (60th anniv of International Federation of Agricultural Producers)	75	40
585	500000l. Emblem (40th anniv of Lions Clubs in Cyprus)	1·25	1·60

203 Post Office and Pillar Box

2004. 40th Anniv of Turkish Cyprus Postal Services. Multicoloured.

586	250000l. Type **203**	40	25
587	1500000l. Globe and winged envelopes	2·00	2·75

204 Beach and Harbour Scenes

2004. Europa. Holidays. Sheet 72×75 mm containing T 204 and similar horiz design. Multicoloured.

MS588	600000l. Type **204**; 600000l. Seated woman with drink and beachside cafe	3·25	3·75

205 Pack Animals and Caravanserai

2004. Silk Road.

589	**205**	300000l. multicoloured	1·00	70

206 *Salvia veneris*

2004. Plants. Multicoloured.

590	250000l. Type **206**	40	25
591	300000l. *Phlomis cypria*	50	30
592	500000l. *Pimpinella cypria*	90	1·00
593	600000l. *Rosularia cypria*	1·10	1·60

207 Inside Stadium

2004. 50th Anniv of UEFA (Union of European Football Associations). Multicoloured.

594	300000l. Type **207**	60	30
595	1000000l. View from top of stadium	1·90	2·50

208 Footballer

2004. Olympic Games, Athens. Multicoloured.

596	300000l. Type **208**	65	75
597	300000l. Boxing and horse riding	65	75
598	500000l. Weight lifting and gymnastics	1·00	1·40
599	500000l. Pole vaulting and tennis	1·00	1·40

Nos. 596/7 and 598/9, respectively, were each printed together, se-tenant, with the backgrounds forming composite designs.

209 Students Celebrating

2005. Anniversaries. Multicoloured.

600	15yhr. Type **209** (25th anniv of Eastern Mediterranean University, Gazimagusa)	35	30
601	30yhr. Eye and outlines of stamps (25th anniv of Cyprus Turkish Philatelic Association)	65	65
602	50yhr. Turtle emblem and outline map (www.studyinnorthcyprus.org)	95	1·25

(New Currency. 100 yeni kurus = 1 yeni lira)

210 Stylized Dinghy

2005. Tourism. Multicoloured.

603	10yhr. Type **210**	20	20
604	1ytl. Temple ruins, setting sun and windsurfer	1·50	2·00

211 Boy and Girl in Orchard (Elmaziye Demirci)

2005. Children's Paintings. Multicoloured.

605	25yhr. Type **211**	55	45
606	50yhr. Couple (Elcim Oztemiz)	1·10	1·40

212 Brick Oven and Table laden with Food

2005. Europa. Gastronomy. Multicoloured.

607	60yhr. Type **212**	80	1·00
608	60yhr. Table laden with food and wine	80	1·00
MS609	113×77 mm. Nos. 607/8, each ×2	2·75	3·50

213 *Dianthus cyprius*

2005. Endemic and Medicinal Plants. Multicoloured.

610	15yhr. Type **213**	35	25
611	25yhr. *Delphinium caseyi*	50	35
612	30yhr. *Brassica hilarionis*	55	50
613	50yhr. *Limonium albidum ssp. Cyprium*	95	1·40

214 Olive Branches and Sun Umbrellas

2005. Cultural and Art Activities. Multicoloured.

614	10yhr. Type **214** (International Olive Festival, Girne)	20	20
615	25yhr. Lala Mustafa Pasa Mosque and musical notes (International Culture and Art Festival, Gazimagusa)	50	35
616	50yhr. Folk dancers and Kyrenia Gate (International Folk Dances Festival, Lefkosa)	85	1·10
617	1ytl. Masks and stage (International Cyprus Theatre Festival)	1·50	2·00

215 Boeing 737 over Ercan Airport

2005. Developments. Multicoloured.

618	50yhr. Type **215**	95	1·10
619	1ytl. Emblem and Middle East Technical University Northern Cyprus Campus, Guzelyurt (horiz)	1·50	2·00

216 Outline Map of Cyprus

2006. 50th Anniv of First Europa Stamp. Multicoloured.

620	1ytl.40 Type **216**	2·00	2·50
621	1ytl.40 View of Cyprus from satellite orbiting Earth	2·00	2·50
MS622	83×78 mm. Nos. 620/1	4·25	5·00

No. **MS**622 also exists imperforate.

217 *Helianthemum obtusifolium*

2006. Wild Flowers. Multicoloured.

623	15yhr. Type **217**	35	25
624	25yhr. *Iris sisyrhinchium* (horiz)	50	35
625	40yhr. *Ranunculus asiaticus* (horiz)	80	1·10
626	50yhr. *Crocus veneris* (horiz)	95	1·25
627	60yhr. *Anemone coronaria* (horiz)	1·00	1·40
628	70yhr. *Cyclamen persicum*	1·10	1·60

218 "Adaption of a Woman's Figure to an Amphora" (ceramic by Semral Oztan)

2006. Art (15th series). Multicoloured.

629	55yhr. Type **218**	1·00	1·40
630	60yhr. "Female Figures" (Mustafa Hasturk)	1·00	1·40

219 Birds (Selma Gürani)

2006. Europa. Integration. Showing winning entries in thematic drawing competition for high school students. Multicoloured.

631	70ykr. Type **219**	1·25	1·50
632	70ykr. Pregnant woman and flags of many nations (Suzan Özcan)	1·25	1·50
MS633	78×72 mm. Nos. 631/2. Perf or imperf	2·50	3·00

220 Dr. Fazil Kucuk

2006. Birth Centenary of Dr. Fazil Kucuk (Deputy President (1959–73) of Republic of Cyprus).

634	**220**	40ykr. multicoloured	1·25	1·00

221 Mustafa Kemal Ataturk

2006. 125th Birth Anniv of Mustafa Kemal Ataturk (first President (1923–38) of Turkey).

635	1ytl. Multicoloured	2·00	2·25

222 World Cup Trophy and Map of Germany

2006. World Cup Football Championship, Germany. Multicoloured.

636	50ykr. Type **222**	75	1·25
637	1ytl. Football, player and Brandenburg Gate, Berlin	1·50	1·75

223 Lapwing

2006. Birds. Multicoloured.

638	40ykr. Type **223**	1·25	80
639	50ykr. Mallard	1·40	1·00
640	60ykr. Kingfisher	1·75	1·60
641	1ytl. Black-winged stilt	2·75	3·25

224 Trees ("Protect our Forests against Fire")

2006. Anniversaries and Events. Multicoloured.

642	50ykr. Type **224**	1·00	75
643	1ytl.50 Yachts (Eastern Mediterranean Yacht Rally)	2·25	3·00

225 Naci Talat

2006. 15th Death Anniv of Naci Talat (former General Secretary of Turkish Cypriot Republican Turkish Party).

644	**225**	70ykr. multicoloured	1·00	1·00

226 Skeletal Leaf

2007. International Conference on Environment: Survival and Sustainability, Lefkosa. Mult.

645	50ykr. Type **226**	1·00	75
646	80ykr. Red globe and parched ground	1·40	1·75

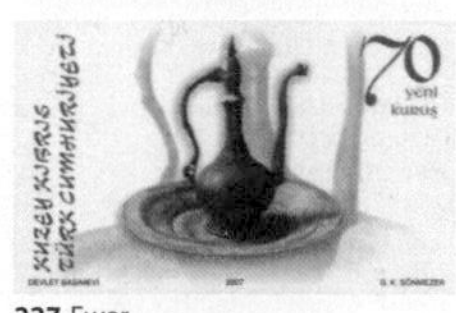

227 Ewer

2007. Antique Household Utensils. Multicoloured.

647	70ykr. Type **227**	1·00	1·00
648	80ykr. Coal iron	1·40	1·50
649	1ytl.50 Oil lamp (vert)	2·25	2·75
650	2ytl. Coffee pot on stove (vert)	3·50	4·00

228 Scout and Camp in Countryside

2007. Europa. Centenary of Scouting. Multicoloured.

651	80ykr. Type **228**	2·25	2·25
652	80ykr. Three scouts playing music	2·25	2·25
MS653	79×73 mm. Nos. 651/2. Imperf	4·50	4·50

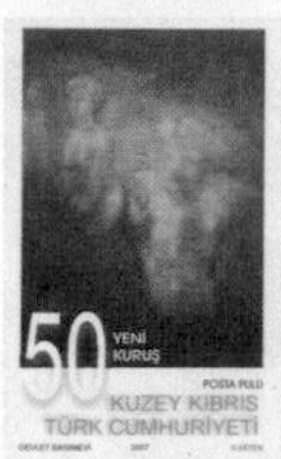

229 Painting by Osman Keten

2007. Art (16th series). Multicoloured.

654	50ykl. Type **229**	1·00	80
655	70ykl. 'FRAGMENT CITY INTEGRI CITY' (Senih Cavusoglu) (horiz)	1·25	1·25

230 Chair-caner

2007. Crafts. Multicoloured.

656	40ykr. Type **230**	70	70
657	65ykr. Barrow man	90	1·25
658	70ykr. Cobbler	1·00	1·25
659	1ytl. Shoeshine man	1·75	2·00

231 Post Pigeon and Pigeon carrying Letter

2007. Post Office Past and Present. Multicoloured.

660	50ykr. Type **231**	1·00	80
661	60ykr. Mounted postman and early motor vehicles	1·25	1·00
662	1ytl. Postman on bicycle and wall letterbox (horiz)	2·00	2·50
663	1ytl.25 Modern postman on moped and postbox (horiz)	2·25	3·00

232 *Asphodelus aestivus*

2008. Wild Flowers. Multicoloured.

664	25ykr. Type **232**	50	40
665	50ykr. *Ophrys fusca ssp. iricolor*	1·00	80
666	60ykr. *Bellis perennis*	1·50	90
667	70ykr. *Ophrys sphegodes*	1·50	1·25
668	80ykr. *Dianthus strictus*	1·75	1·75
669	1ytl.60 *Ophrys argolica* ssp. *elegans*	2·50	2·25
670	2ytl.20 *Crocus cyprius*	4·00	3·50
671	3ytl. *Limodorum abortivum*	6·00	6·00
672	5ytl. *Carlina pygmaea*	9·00	9·50
673	10ytl. *Ophrys kotschyi*	18·00	20·00

233 Woman writing Letter

2008. Europa. The Letter. Multicoloured.

674	80ykr. Type **233**	1·75	2·00
675	80ykr. World map and fragments of printed paper	1·75	2·00

234 Diver

2008. Olympic Games, Beijing. Sheet 78×73 mm containing T 234 and similar vert design. Multicoloured.

MS676	65ykr. Type **234**; 65ykr. Gymnast	4·25	4·25

No. **MS**676 also exists imperforate.

235 Anniversary Emblem

2008. 50th Anniv of Turk Mukavemet Teskilati'nin (Turkish resistance organization). Sheet containing T 235 and similar horiz design. Multicoloured.

MS677	1ytl. Type **235**; 1ytl. Monument	6·25	6·25

236 Council Buildings

2008. Anniversaries and Events. Multicoloured.

678	55ykr. Type **236** (50th anniv of Lefkosa Turkish Municipality)	1·40	1·10
679	80ykr. Gateway and emblems (Inner Wheel)	2·50	2·00
680	1ytl. Airliner (35th anniv of Cyrus Turkish Airlines) (horiz)	2·75	2·75
681	1ytl.50 Landing of Turkish forces, 1974 (32nd anniv of Turkish Federated State of Northern Cyprus)	3·50	3·50

237 Coin

2008. 25th Anniv of the Establishment of the Turkish Republic of Northern Cyprus.

682	**237**	1ytl. multicoloured	2·75	2·75

238 Halit Karabina (upholsterer)

2008. The Masters and the Craftsmen. Multicoloured.

683	60ykr. Type **238**	1·50	1·25
684	70ykr. Burhan Bardak (oil miller)	1·75	1·75
685	80ykr. Kemal Kose (bicycle repairer)	2·00	2·00
686	2ytl. Kemal Sah (circumciser)	5·00	6·00

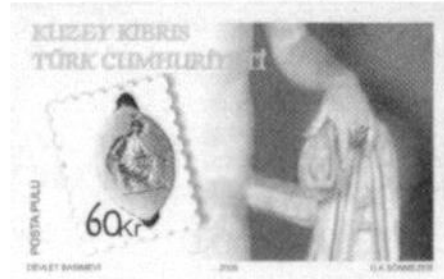

239 Gold Brooch

2009. The Golden Leaves of Soli Exhibition, Museum of Archaeology and Nature, Guzelyurt. Multicoloured.

687	60ykr. Type **239**	1·50	1·10
688	2ytl. Golden leaves	5·50	6·00

240 Galaxy and Comet

2009. Europa. Astronomy. Multicoloured.

689	80ykr. Type **240**	2·25	2·25
690	80ykr. Solar system	2·25	2·25

241 *Cistus creticus*

2009. Medicinal Plants. Multicoloured.

691	50ykr. Type **241**	1·50	1·00
692	60ykr. *Capparis spinosa*	1·60	1·25
693	70ykr. *Pancratium maritimum*	1·90	1·75
694	1ytl. *Passiflora caerulea*	3·00	3·50

242 *Agama stellio*

2009. Fauna. Multicoloured.

695	80ykr. Type **242**	2·75	2·75
696	1ytl.50 *Bufo viridis*(toad)	4·75	5·00

243 Control Tower and Aircraft

2009. 'Our Institutions and Foundations'. Multicoloured.

697	65ykr. Type **243** (CTATCA Cyprus Turkish Air Traffic Controllers)	2·00	1·50
698	1ytl. Open door leading to globe and ktto emblems (Turkish Cypriot Chamber of Commerce) (vert)	3·00	3·00
699	1ytl.50 Ziya Rizki (Ziya Rizki Vakfi) (vert)	4·50	4·50

244 Islamic Architecture, Emblem, Flag and Outline Map

2010. 34th Anniv of Representation of Turkish Cyprus at Organization of Islamic Conference. Multicoloured.

700	70ykr. Type **244**	2·25	2·25
701	1ytl. Arch, emblem and minaret	3·00	3·00

245 Girls reading (Nadide Keles)

2010. Europa. Children's Books. Multicoloured.

702	80ykr. Type **245**	2·25	2·25
703	80ykr. Girl reading with book characters at her shoulders (Afet Deniz)	2·25	2·25

246 *Larus audouinii*

2010. Endangered Species. Seagulls. Multicoloured.

704	25ykr. Type **246**	1·00	70
705	25ykr. *Larus melanocephalus*	1·00	70
706	30ykr. *Larus ridibundus*	1·25	1·00
707	30ykr. *Larus genei*	1·25	1·00

247 World Cup Trophy and Crowd

2010. World Cup Football Championship, South Africa. Multicoloured.

708	50kyr. Type **247**	1·50	1·00
709	2ytl. Footballer, South African flag, elephants and mascot	6·00	6·00

250 Kemal Asik

2010. Journalists. Multicoloured.

709a	60ykr. Type **247a**	1·50	1·25
709b	70ykr. Abdi Ipekçi	1·75	1·75
709c	80ykr. Adem Yavuz	2·50	2·00
709d	1ytl. Sedat Simavi	2·75	2·75

248 *Bozcaada* (ferry) and Temple Ruins

2010. Passenger Ships which Sail to Cyprus. Multicoloured.

710	1ytl.50 Type **248**	4·50	4·50
711	2ytl. *Yesilada* (ferry)	6·00	6·00

249 Özdemir Sennaroglu

2010. Personalities. Multicoloured.

712	50ykr. Type **249**	1·75	1·25
713	60ykr. Osman Örek	2·25	2·25
714	70ykr. Salih Miroglu	2·50	2·50
715	80ykr. Özker Özgür	2·75	2·75

250 University Building and Arms

2010. 25th Anniv of Girne American University

716	**250**	1ytl. multicoloured	3·00	3·00

251 Dr. Niyazi Manyera

2011. Turkish Cypriot Vice President and Government Ministers. Multicoloured.

717	80ykr. Type **251** (Minister of Health 1963–74)	2·25	2·25
718	1ytl.10 Mustafa Fazil Plümer (Agriculture Minister, Republic of Cyprus, 1960–3)	3·25	3·50
719	2ytl. Osman Örek (Prime Minister of Northern Cyprus, 1978)	5·50	6·00
720	2ytl.20 Dr. Fazil Küçük (Vice President, Republic of Cyprus, 1960–3)	6·50	6·75

252 Ayios Philon Church

2011. Tourism. Multicoloured.

721	50ykr. Type **252**	1·75	1·25
722	80ykr. Ruins of Salamis (vert)	2·75	2·75
723	1ytl.10 Ruins	3·00	3·00
724	2ytl. Apostolos Andreas Monastery and Karpaz Peninsula (vert)	6·75	6·75

Pt. 8

CYRENAICA

Part of the former Italian colony of Libya, N. Africa. Allied Occupation, 1942–49. Independent Administration, 1949–52. Then part of independent Libya.

Stamps optd **BENGASI** formerly listed here will be found under Italian P.O.s in the Turkish Empire, Nos. 169/70.

100 centesimi = 1 lira.

Stamps of Italy optd CIRENAICA

1923. Tercent of Propagation of the Faith.

1	**66**	20c. orange and green	6·50	37·00
2	**66**	30c. orange and red	6·50	37·00
3	**66**	50c. orange and violet	2·10	43·00
4	**66**	1l. orange and blue	2·10	48·00

1923. Fascist March on Rome stamps.

5	**77**	10c. green	7·25	16·00
6	**77**	30c. violet	7·25	16·00
7	**77**	50c. red	7·25	16·00
8	**74**	1l. blue	7·25	43·00
9	**74**	2l. brown	7·25	55·00
10	**75**	5l. black and blue	7·25	75·00

1924. Manzoni stamps (Nos. 155/60).

11	**77**	10c. black and purple	6·50	37·00
12	-	15c. black and green	6·50	37·00
13	-	30c. black	6·50	27·00
14	-	50c. black and brown	6·50	37·00
15	-	1l. black and blue	60·00	£275
16	-	5l. black and purple	£650	£2500

1925. Holy Year stamps.

17		20c.+10c. brown & green	3·50	27·00
18	**81**	30c.+15c. brown & choc	3·50	27·00
19	-	50c.+25c. brown & violet	3·50	27·00
20	-	60c.+30c. brown and red	3·50	32·00
21	-	1l.+50c. purple and blue	3·75	37·00
22	-	5l.+2l.50 purple and red	3·75	50·00

1925. Royal Jubilee stamps.

23	**82**	60c. red	86	8·50
24	**82**	1l. blue	1·30	8·50
24a	**82**	1l.25 blue	4·00	21·00

1926. St. Francis of Assisi stamps.

25	**83**	20c. green	2·50	16·00
26	-	40c. violet	2·50	16·00
27	-	60c. red	2·50	21·00
28	-	1l.25 blue	2·50	32·00
29	-	5l.+2l.50 olive (as No. 196)	5·75	65·00

6

1926. Colonial Propaganda.

30	**6**	5c.+5c. brown	1·10	7·50
31	**6**	10c.+5c. olive	1·10	7·50
32	**6**	20c.+5c. green	1·10	7·50
33	**6**	40c.+5c. red	1·10	7·50
34	**6**	60c.+5c. orange	1·10	7·50
35	**6**	1l.+5c. blue	1·10	13·00

1927. 1st National Defence stamps of Italy optd CIRENAICA.

36	**89**	40+20c. black & brown	2·40	32·00
37	-	60+30c. brown and red	2·40	32·00
38	-	1l.25+60c. black & blue	2·40	55·00
39	-	5l.+2l.50 black & green	4·75	75·00

1927. Volta Centenary stamps of Italy optd Cirenaica.

40	**90**	20c. violet	8·00	32·00
41	**90**	50c. orange	12·00	21·00
42	**90**	1l.25 blue	19·00	55·00

8

1928. 45th Anniv of Italian-African Society.

43	**8**	20c.+5c. green	2·75	10·50
44	**8**	30c.+5c. red	2·75	10·50
45	**8**	50c.+10c. violet	2·75	16·00
46	**8**	1l.25+20c. blue	2·75	21·00

Stamps of Italy optd **CIRENAICA**. Colours changed in some instances.

1929. 2nd National Defence stamps.

47	**89**	30c.+10c. black & red	4·25	21·00
48	**89**	50c.+20c. grey & lilac	4·25	21·00
49	**89**	1l.25+50c. blue & brown	6·50	43·00
50	-	5l.+2l. black & green	6·50	65·00

1929. Montecassino stamps (No. 57 optd Cirenaica).

51	**104**	20c. green	6·00	17·00
52	-	25c. red	6·00	17·00
53	-	50c.+10c. red	6·00	21·00
54	-	75c.+15c. brown	6·00	10·00
55	**104**	1l.25+25c. purple	12·00	37·00
56	-	5l.+1l. blue	12·00	43·00
57	-	10l.+2l. brown	12·00	65·00

1930. Marriage of Prince Humbert and Princess Marie Jose stamps.

58	**109**	20c. green	1·70	5·25
59	**109**	50c.+10c. red	1·30	6·50
60	**109**	1l.25+25c. red	1·30	19·00

1930. Ferrucci stamps (optd Cirenaica).

61	**114**	20c. violet	3·00	4·25
62	-	25c. green	3·00	4·25
63	-	50c. black	3·00	10·50
64	-	1l.25 blue	3·00	16·00
65	-	5l.+2l. red	9·50	30·00

1930. 3rd National Defence stamps.

66	**89**	30c.+10c. turq & grn	24·00	32·00
67	-	50c.+10c. purple & green	24·00	48·00
68	-	1l.25+30c. lt brown & brn	24·00	£6530
69	-	5l.+1l.50 green and blue	80·00	£150

13

1930. 25th Anniv (1929) of Italian Colonial Agricultural Institute.

70	**13**	50c.+20c. brown	3·00	19·00
71	**13**	1l.25+20c. blue	3·00	19·00
72	**13**	1l.75+20c. green	3·00	21·00
73	**13**	2l.55+50c. violet	6·50	37·00
74	**13**	5l.+1l. red	6·50	55·00

1930. Virgil Bimillenary stamps optd CIRENAICA.

75	**118**	15c. violet	90	6·50
76	-	20c. brown	90	3·25
77	-	25c. green	90	3·25
78	-	30c. brown	90	3·25
79	-	50c. purple	90	3·25
80	-	75c. red	90	4·25
81	-	1l.25 blue	90	8·50
82	-	5l.+1l.50 purple	6·50	43·00
83	-	10l.+2l.50 brown	6·50	75·00

1931. St. Anthony of Padua stamps optd Cirenaica (75c., 5l.) or CIRENAICA (others).

84	**121**	20c. brown	2·20	15·00
85	-	25c. green	2·20	6·50
86	-	30c. brown	2·20	6·50
87	-	50c. purple	2·20	6·50
88	-	75c. grey (as No. 308)	2·20	17·00
89	-	1l.25 blue	2·20	34·00
90	-	5l.+2l.50 brn (as No. 310)	6·75	75·00

1932. Air stamps of Tripolitania optd Cirenaica.

91	**18**	50c. red	1·70	1·10
92	**18**	60c. orange	6·50	16·00
93	**18**	80c. purple	6·50	27·00

1932. Air stamps of Tripolitania of 1931 optd CIRENAICA and bars.

94	50c. red	2·10	9·50
95	80c. purple	6·50	24·00

17 Columns of Leptis

1932. Air.

96	-	50c. violet	5·25	10
97	-	75c. red	7·50	10·50
98	-	80c. blue	7·50	21·00
99	**17**	1l. black	3·75	10
100	**17**	2l. green	3·75	10·50
101	**17**	5l. red	5·25	24·00

DESIGN—VERT: 50c. to 80c. Arab on Camel.

18 "Graf Zeppelin"

1933. Air. "Graf Zeppelin". Inscr "CROCIERA ZEPPELIN".

102	**18**	3l. brown	9·50	£120
103	-	5l. violet	9·50	£120
104	-	10l. green	9·50	£225
105	-	12l. blue	9·50	£225
106	**18**	15l. red	9·50	£225
107	-	20l. black	9·50	£275

DESIGNS: 5l., 12l. "Graf Zeppelin" and Roman galley; 10l., 20l. "Graf Zeppelin" and giant archer.

19 Air Squadron

1933. Air. Balbo Transatlantic Mass Formation Flight by Savoia Marchetti S-55X Flying Boats.

108	**19**	19l.75 blue and green	19·00	£600
109	**19**	44l.75 blue and red	19·00	£600

1934. Air. Rome–Buenos Aires Flight. T 17 (new colours) optd with Savoia Marchetti S-71 airplane and 1934-XII PRIMO VOLO DIRETTO ROMA = BUENOS-AYRES TRIMOTORE "LOMBARDI-MAZZOTTI" or surch also.

110	**17**	2l. on 5l. brown	4·25	65·00
111	**17**	3l. on 5l. green	4·25	65·00
112	**17**	5l. brown	4·25	70·00
113	**17**	10l. on 5l. pink	4·25	70·00

21 Arab Horseman

1934. 2nd International Colonial Exn, Naples.

114	**21**	5c. brn & grn (postage)	5·50	17·00
115	**21**	10c. black and brown	5·50	17·00
116	**21**	20c. blue and red	5·50	17·00
117	**21**	50c. brown and violet	5·50	17·00
118	**21**	60c. blue and brown	5·50	24·00
119	**21**	1l.25 green and blue	5·50	35·00
120	-	25c. orange & blue (air)	2·75	9·00
121	-	50c. blue and green	5·50	17·00
122	-	75c. orange and brown	5·50	17·00
123	-	80c. green and brown	5·50	17·00
124	-	1l. green and red	5·50	29·00
125	-	2l. brown and blue	5·50	35·00

DESIGNS: 25 to 75c. Arrival of Caproni Ca 101 mail plane; 80c. to 2l. Caproni Ca 101 mail plane and Venus of Cyrene.

22

1934. Air. Rome–Mogadiscio Flight.

126	**22**	25c.+10c. green	4·75	13·00
127	**22**	50c.+10c. brown	4·75	13·00
128	**22**	75c.+15c. red	4·75	13·00
129	**22**	80c.+15c. black	4·75	13·00
130	**22**	1l.+20c. brown	4·75	13·00
131	**22**	2l.+20c. blue	4·75	13·00
132	**22**	3l.+25c. violet	24·00	80·00
133	**22**	5l.+25c. orange	24·00	80·00
134	**22**	10l.+30c. purple	24·00	80·00
135	**22**	25l.+2l. green	24·00	80·00

OFFICIAL AIR STAMP

1934. Optd SERVIZIO DI STATO and crown.

O136	25l.+2l. red	£3500	£4000

For stamps of British Occupation see under British Occupation of Italian Colonies.

Pt. 5

CZECH REPUBLIC

Formerly part of Czechoslovakia, a federation dissolved on 31 December 1992 when the constituent republics became separate states.

100 haleru = 1 koruna.

1 State Arms

1993

1	**1**	3k. multicoloured	25	20

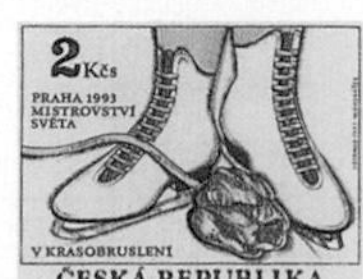

2 Skater's Boots and Tulip

1993. Ice Skating Championships, Prague.

2	**2**	2k. multicoloured	20	15

3 Pres. Vaclav Havel

1993

3	**3**	2k. purple, blue & mauve	10	15
3a	**3**	3k.60 violet, mauve & blue	30	15

4 St. John and Charles Bridge, Prague

1993. 600th Death Anniv of St. John of Nepomuk (patron saint of Bohemia).

4	**4**	8k. multicoloured	85	45

5 "Hladovy Svaty I" (Mikulas Medek)

1993. Europa. Contemporary Art.

5	**5**	14k. multicoloured	7·50	2·40

6 Church of Sacred Heart, Prague

1993

6	**6**	5k. multicoloured	1·50	45

See also No. 45.

7 Brevnov Monastery

1993. UNESCO World Heritage Site. Millenary of Brevnov Monastry, Prague.

7	**7**	4k. multicoloured	40	25

8 Weightlifter

1993. Junior Weightlifting Championships, Cheb.

8	**8**	6k. multicoloured	55	35

9 Town Hall Tower and Cathedral of St. Peter and St. Paul

1993. 750th Anniv of Brno.

9	**9**	8k. multicoloured	1·90	70

10 Sts. Cyril and Methodius

1993. 1130th Anniv of Arrival of Sts. Cyril and Methodius in Moravia.

10	**10**	8k. multicoloured	75	30

11 State Arms

1993. Sheet 76×90 mm.

MS11 **11**	8k. ×2 multicoloured	2·75	2·75

12 Ceske Budejovice

1993. Towns.

12	**12**	1k. brown and red	10	10
13	-	2k. red and blue	10	10
14	-	3k. blue and red	15	10
15	-	3k. blue and red	25	20
16	-	5k. green and brown	50	15
17	-	6k. green and yellow	60	30
18	-	7k. brown and green	60	35
20	-	8k. violet and yellow	40	30
21	-	10k. green and red	55	35
23	-	20k. red and blue	1·10	90
26	-	50k. brown and green	30	1·60

DESIGNS—VERT: 2k. Usti nad Labem; 3k. (15) Brno; 5k. Pilsen; 6k. Slanyi; 7k. Antonin Dvorak Theatre, Ostrava; 8k. Olomouc; 10k. Hradec Kralove; 20k. Prague; 50k. Opava. HORIZ: 3k. (14) Cesky Krumlov (UNESCO World Heritage Site).

13 Rower

1993. World Rowing Championships, Racice.

27	**13**	3k. multicoloured	25	30

14 August Sedlacek (historian, 150th anniv)

1993. Birth Anniversaries.

28	**14**	2k. buff, blue and green	15	15
29	-	3k. buff, blue and violet	30	20

DESIGN: 3k. Eduard Cech (mathematician, centenary).

15 Pedunculate Oak

1993. Trees. Multicoloured.

30		5k. Type **15**	35	20
31		7k. Hornbeam	50	30
32		9k. Scots pine	70	45

16 "Composition" (Joan Miro)

1993. Art (1st series). Multicoloured.

33		11k. Type **16**	2·10	1·25
34		14k. "Green Corn Field with Cypress" (Vincent van Gogh)	3·50	1·50

See also Nos. 62/4, 116/18, 140/2, 174/6, 200/1, 221/2, 252/4, 282/4, 312/14, 350/2, 385/7, 393, 416/18, 449/451, 457, 485/7, 521/3, 564/**MS**566 and 575/b.

17 St. Nicholas

1993. Christmas.

35	**17**	2k. multicoloured	25	10

18 "Strahov Madonna"

1993. Christmas.

36	**18**	9k. multicoloured	3·00	90

19 "Family" (C. Littasy-Rollier)

1994. International Year of the Family.

37	**19**	2k. multicoloured	10	10

20 Kubelik

1994. 54th Death Anniv of Jan Kublik (composer and violinist).

38	**20**	3k. yellow and black	25	10

21 Voltaire (writer, 300th anniv)

1994. Birth Anniversaries.

39	**21**	2k. purple, grey & mauve	15	25
40	-	6k. black, blue and green	45	25

DESIGN: 6k. Georg Agricola (mineralogist, 500th anniv).

22 Athletes

1994. Winter Olympic Games, Lillehammer, Norway.

41	**22**	5k. multicoloured	40	30

23 Marco Polo and Fantasy Animal

1994. Europa. Discoveries. Marco Polo's Journeys to the Orient. Multicoloured.

42		14k. Type **23**	1·10	1·25
43		14k. Marco Polo and woman on fantasy animals	1·10	1·25

24 Benes

1994. 110th Birth Anniv of Edvard Benes (President of Czechoslovakia 1935–38 and 1945–48).

44	**24**	5k. violet and purple	40	20

25 Cubist Flats by Josef Chochol, Prague

1994. UNESCO World Heritage Sites. Mult.

45		8k. Market place, Telc	1·10	60
46		9k. Type **25**	1·25	75

No. 45 is similar to Type **6**.

26 Crayon Figures

1994. For Children.

47	**26**	2k. multicoloured	10	10

27 "Stegosaurus ungulatus"

1994. Prehistoric Animals. Multicoloured.

48		2k. Type **27**	20	10
49		3k. "Apatosaurus excelsus"	30	10
50		5k. "Tarbosaurus bataar" (vert)	50	30

28 Statue of Liberty holding Football

1994. World Cup Football Championship, U.S.A.

51	**28**	8k. multicoloured	75	45

29 Flag of Prague Section

1994. 12th Sokol (sports organization) Congress, Prague.

52	**29**	2k. multicoloured	10	15

30 Olympic Flag and Flame

1994. Centenary of Int Olympic Committee.

53	**30**	7k. multicoloured	60	40

31 Stylized Carrier Pigeons

1994. 120th Anniv of Universal Postal Union.

54	**31**	11k. multicoloured	90	80

32 Common Stonechat

1994. Birds. Multicoloured.

55		3k. Type **32**	20	15
56		5k. Common rosefinch	30	25
57		14k. Bluethroat	1·25	75

33 NW, 1900

1994. Racing Cars. Multicoloured.

58		2k. Type **33**	15	15
59		3k. L & K, 1908	25	15
60		9k. Praga, 1912	70	45

34 Angel

1994. Christmas.

61	**34**	2k. multicoloured	10	10

1994. Art (2nd series). As T 16.

62		7k. black and buff	50	55
63		10k. multicoloured	95	10
64		14k. multicoloured	1·60	1·10

DESIGNS—VERT: 7k. "The Old Man and the Woman" (Lucas van Leyden); 10k. "Moulin Rouge" (Henri de Toulouse-Lautrec); 14k. "Madonna of St. Vitus".

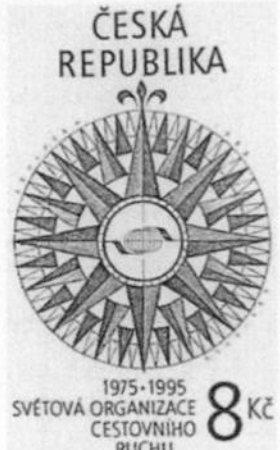

35 Emblem

1995. 20th Anniv of World Tourism Organization.

65	**35**	8k. blue and red	70	45

36 E.U. and Czech Republic Flags

1995. Association Agreement with European Union.

66	**36**	8k. multicoloured	70	45

37 Engraver's Transposition of 1918 Czechoslovakia 2h. Newspaper Stamp

1995. Czech Stamp Production.

67	**37**	3k. blue, grey and red	25	20

38 Johannes Marcus Marci

1995. Birth Anniversaries.

68	**38**	2k. sepia, stone & brown	20	10
69	-	5k. multicoloured	35	30
70	-	7k. purple, grey & mauve	70	35

DESIGNS: 2k. Type **38** (academic, 400th anniv); 5k. Ferdinand Peroutka (journalist and dramatist, centenary); 7k. Premysl Pitter (founder of Youth Care Centre, centenary).

39 Jiri Voskovec (actor and dramatist)

1995. 90th Birth Anniversaries of Members of the Liberated Theatre, Prague. Caricatures from posters by Adolf Hoffmeister.

71	**39**	3k. black, yellow & orange	25	10
72	-	3k. black, yellow & green	25	10
73	-	3k. black, yellow & blue	25	10

DESIGNS: No. 72, Jan Werich (dramatist and actor); 73, Jaroslav Jezek (composer) (anniv 1996).

40 Church and Buildings

1995. Townscapes.

75	**40**	40h. brown and pink	10	10
76	-	60h. brown and stone	10	10

DESIGN: 60h. Buildings, church and archway.

41 Buff-tailed Bumble Bee

1995. European Nature Conservation Year. Endangered Insects. Multicoloured.

84		3k. Type **41**	25	10
85		5k. Praying mantis	40	30
86		6k. Banded agrion	55	30

42 Sandstone Arch, Labske Piskovce

1995. Rock Formations. Multicoloured.

87		8k. Stone Organ (basalt columns), Central Bohemia	85	60
88		9k. Type **42**	85	70

43 Rose and Women's Profiles

1995. Europa. Peace and Freedom. Multicoloured.

89		9k. Type **43**	85	40
90		14k. Butterfly, girl and profiles of ageing woman	1·10	70

44 Cat

1995. For Children.

91	**44**	3k.60 multicoloured	40	25

45 Early Steam Train leaving Chocen Tunnel

1995. 150th Anniv of Olomouc–Prague Railway.

92	**45**	3k. black, brown & blue	35	10
93	-	9k.60 black, brown & red	70	40

DESIGN: 9k.60. Crowd welcoming arrival of first train at Prague.

46 Wrestlers

1995. World Greco-Roman Wrestling Championship, Prague.

94	**46**	3k. brown, stone and red	40	10

47 Violinist and Washerwoman (Vladimir Rencin)

1995. Cartoons. Cartoons by named artists. Multicoloured.

95		3k. Type **47**	20	10
96		3k.60 Angel and naked man (Vladimir Jiranek)	30	10
97		5k. Champagne cork flying through ringmaster's hoop (Jiri Sliva)	40	30

48 Voskovec, Wencih and Jezek (poster, Adolf Hoffmeister)

1995. 70th Anniv of the Liberated Theatre, Prague, and 90th Birth Anniv of Founding Members (2nd issue). Sheet 61×81 mm.

MS98	**48**	22k. yellow and black	1·75	1·60

49 Houses around smiling Sun

1995. 25th Anniv of SOS Children's Villages.

99	**49**	3k. multicoloured	25	10

50 Gothic Window

1995. Architectural Styles.

101	**50**	2k.40 red and green	10	10
102	-	3k. green and blue	25	10
103	-	3k.60 violet and green	35	10
104	-	4k. blue and red	30	15
105	-	4k.60 mauve and green	40	10
107	-	9k.60 blue and mauve	70	45
108	-	12k.60 brown and blue	85	45
109	-	14k. green and mauve	1·25	55

DESIGNS: 3k. Secession window; 3k.60, Roman window; 4k. Classicist doorway; 4k.60, Rococo window; 9k.60, Renaissance doorway; 12k.60, Cubist window; 14k. Baroque doorway.

51 Rontgen and X-Ray Tube

1995. Centenary of Discovery of X-Rays by Wilhelm Rontgen.

113	**51**	6k. buff, black & violet	55	25

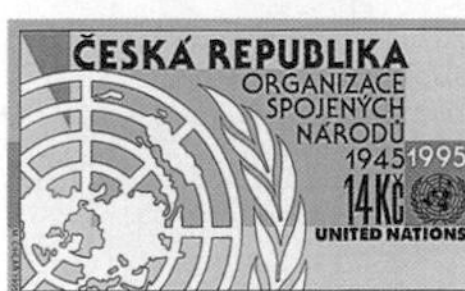

52 Emblem

1995. 50th Anniv of U.N.O.

114	**52**	14k. multicoloured	1·25	65

53 Christmas Tree

1995. Christmas.

115	**53**	3k. multicoloured	25	20

1995. Art (3rd series). As T 16.

116		6k. black, blue and buff	45	45
117		9k. multicoloured	75	60
118		14k. multicoloured	1·25	90

DESIGNS: 6k. "Parisienne" (Ludek Marold); 9k. "Bouquet" (J. K. Hirschely); 14k. "Portrait of the Sculptor Josef Malinsky" (Antonin Machek).

54 Allegory of Music

1996. Cent of Czech Philharmonic Orchestra.

119	**54**	3k.60 multicoloured	30	30

55 Stamp Design by Jaroslav Benda

1996. Tradition of Czech Stamp Production.

120	**55**	3k.60 multicoloured	30	20

56 Mencikova and Chessmen

1996. 90th Birth Anniv of Vera Mencikova (chess champion).

121	**56**	6k. black, buff and red	50	30

57 Woman with Bowl of Easter Eggs

1996. Easter.

122	**57**	3k. multicoloured	25	20

58 Sudek and Camera

1996. Birth Cent of Josef Sudek (photographer).

123	**58**	9k.60 buff, black & grey	80	45

59 Jiri Guth-Jarkovsky (first President of National Olympic Committee) and Stadium

1996. Centenary of Modern Olympic Games.

124	**59**	9k.60 multicoloured	80	45

60 Jan (John the Blind)

1996. Bohemian Kings of the Luxembourg Dynasty.

125	**60**	14k. blue, grey & purple	1·25	90
126	-	14k. green, grey & purple	1·25	90
127	-	14k. green, grey & purple	1·25	90
128	-	14k. blue, grey & purple	1·25	90

DESIGNS: No. 126, Karel (Charles IV, Holy Roman Emperor); 127, Vaclav IV; 128, Sigismund.

61 Garden Dormouse

1996. Nature Conservation. Mammals. Sheet 119×138 mm containing T 61 and similar vert designs. Multicoloured.

MS129		3k.60 Type **61**; 5k. ×2 Forest dormouse; 6k. ×2 European souslik; 8k. ×2 Northern birch mouse	1·75	2·25

62 Ema Destinnova (singer)

1996. Europa. Famous Women.

130	**62**	8k. lilac, black & mauve	70	50

63 Entering Stage as Pierrot

1996. Birth Bicentenary of Jean Gasparde Deburau (mime actor).

131	**63**	12k. multicoloured	90	50

64 Throwing the Javelin

1996. Olympic Games, Atlanta.

132	**64**	3k. multicoloured	25	10

65 Boy and Girl on Cat

1996. For Children.

133	**65**	3k. multicoloured	25	10

66 St. John of Nepomuk's Church, Zelena Hora

1996. Tourist Sites. Multicoloured.

134		8k. Type **66** (UNESCO World Heritage Site)	65	50
135		9k. Prague Loretto	75	60

67 Boy playing Flute and Flowers forming Butterfly

1996. 50th Anniv of UNICEF.
136 **67** 3k. multicoloured 2·25 10

68 Black Horse

1996. Kladruby Horses. Multicoloured.
137 3k. Type **68** 25 10
138 3k. White horse 25 10

69 Havel

1996. 60th Birthday of President Vaclav Havel. Sheet 79×100 mm.
MS139 **69** 6k. ×2 blue and red 95 95

1996. Art (4th series). As T 16. Multicoloured.
140 9k. "Eden" (Josef Vachal) 65 60
141 11k. "Breakfast with Egg" (Georg Flegel) (vert) 90 75
142 20k. "Baroque Chair" (Endre Nemes) (vert) 1·50 1·10

70 Brahe

1996. 450th Birth Anniv of Tycho Brahe (astronomer).
143 **70** 5k. multicoloured 40 30

71 Letov S-1

1996. Biplanes. Multicoloured.
144 7k. Type **71** 55 15
145 8k. Aero A-11 65 20
146 10k. Avia BH-21 80 35

72 Nativity

1996. Christmas.
147 **72** 3k. multicoloured 25 10

73 Czechoslovakia 1920 Stamp Design of V. Brunner

1997. Czech Stamp Production.
148 **73** 3k.60 blue and red 25 10

74 Easter Symbols

1997. Easter.
149 **74** 3k. multicoloured 25 10

75 Dog's-tooth Violet

1997. Endangered Plants. Multicoloured.
150 3k.60 Type **75** 25 10
151 4k. Bog arum 35 10
152 5k. Lady's slipper 35 10
153 8k. Dwarf bearded iris 70 30

76 Girl and Cats ("Congratulations")

1997. Greetings Stamp.
154 **76** 4k. multicoloured 30 10

77 St. Adalbert

1997. Death Millenary of St. Adalbert (Bishop of Prague).
155 **77** 7k. lilac 55 40

78 Prince Bruncvik, Neomenie and Lion

1997. Europa. Tales and Legends. Multicoloured.
156 8k. Type **78** 65 50
157 8k. King Wenceslas IV watching Zito the Magician in cart pulled by cocks 65 50

79 Ark of the Torah, Old-New Synagogue (east side)

1997. Jewish Monuments in Prague. Each black, blue and red.
158 8k. Type **79** 70 50
159 10k. Grave of Rabbi Loew (Chief Rabbi of Prague), Old Jewish Cemetery 75 60

80 Objects d'Art from Rudolf II's Collection

1997. "Rudolf II and Prague" Exhibition, Prague. Sheet 117×91 mm containing T 80 and similar vert design. Each black, red and green.
MS160 6k. Type **80**; 8k. Rudolf IV and Muses; 10k. Arcimboldo (court painter) 1·60 1·50

81 Rakosnicek (cartoon character) and Rowan Berries

1997. For Children.
161 **81** 4k.60 multicoloured 40 10

82 Krizik and Arc Lamp

1997. 150th Birth Anniv of Frantisek Krizik (electrical engineer).
162 **82** 6k. pink, blue and red 45 20

83 Swimmer

1997. European Swimming and Diving Championships, Prague.
163 **83** 11k. black, buff & blue 75 40

84 Mrs. Muller and Svejk in Wheelchair

1997. 110th Anniv of "Fortunes of the Good Soldier Svejk" (novel by Jaroslav Hasek). Illustrations by Josef Lada. Multicoloured.
164 4k. Type **84** 35 15
165 4k.60 Lt. Lukas and Col. Kraus von Zillergut with stolen dog 35 15
166 6k. Svejk smoking pipe 40 35

85 Prague Castle

1997. "Praga 1998" International Stamp Exhibition. Multicoloured.
167 15k. Type **85** 1·00 75
168 15k. View of Prague Old Town 1·00 75
MS169 99×119 mm. Nos. 167/8 plus two half stamp-size labels 2·00 2·40
See also No. **MS**182.

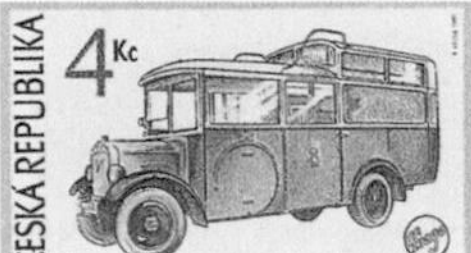

86 Post Bus, 1928

1997. Historic Service Vehicles. Multicoloured.
170 4k. Type **86** 30 10
171 4k.60 Skoda Sentinel lorry, 1924 30 20
172 8k. Tatra fire engine, 1933 60 45

87 Carp, Candle, Fir, Apple and Nut

1997. Christmas.
173 **87** 4k. multicoloured 30 10

1997. Art (5th series). As T 16.
174 7k. multicoloured 35 15
175 12k. green and black 1·00 75
176 16k. multicoloured 1·10 1·10
DESIGNS—HORIZ: 7k. "Landscape with Chateau in Chantilly" (Antonin Chittussi). VERT: 12k. "The Prophets came out of the Desert" (Frantisek Bilek); 16k. "Parisian Second-hand Booksellers" (T. F. Simon).

88 Olympic Rings and Ice Hockey Puck

1998. Winter Olympic Games, Nagano, Japan.
177 **88** 7k. multicoloured 45 25

89 Jakub Obrvrovsky's 1920 Design

1998. Czech Stamp Production.
178 **89** 12k.60 brown and green 90 50

90 Pres. Vaclav Havel

1998
179 **90** 4k.60 green and red 40 10
179a **90** 5k.40 blue and brown 40 10
179b **90** 6k.40 agate and blue 30 15

91 Cupid and Heart

1998. St. Valentine's Day.
180 **91** 4k. multicoloured 30 10

92 Slalom

1998. World Skibob Championships, Spindleruv Mlyn.
181 **92** 8k. multicoloured 60 30

93 Vysehrad (1938 stamp design)

1998. "Praga 1998" International Stamp Exhibition (2nd issue). 50th Anniv of First Prague Stamp Exhibition. Sheet 149×105 mm.
MS182 **93** 2 ×30k. blue 4·00 3·75

94 Chick in Egg Shell

1998. Easter.
183 **94** 4k. multicoloured 30 10

95 Observatory Building and Telescope Dome

1998. Centenary of Ondrejov Observatory.
184 **95** 4k.60 yellow, black & red 40 30

96 Hands forming Arch and Seal

1998. 650th Anniv of Charles University and New Town, Prague. Sheet 120×92 mm containing T 96 and similar vert designs. Each black, red and blue.
MS185 15k. Type **96**; 22k. Charles IV (Holy Roman Emperor and King of Bohemia) and plan of Prague; 23k. Groin vault, St. Vitus's Cathedral 4·00 3·25

97 Player celebrating

1998. Czech Gold Medal for Ice Hockey, Winter Olympic Games, Nagano. Sheet 106×88 mm.
MS186 **97** 23k. multicoloured 1·75 1·50

98 Grey Partridge

1998. Endangered Species. Multicoloured.
187 4k.60 Type **98** 40 30
188 4k.60 Black grouse ("Lyrurus tetrix") 40 60
189 8k. White deer ("Cervus elphus") 50 30
190 8k. Elk ("Alces alces") 50 45

99 Book and Copyright Symbol

1998. World Book and Copyright Day.
191 **99** 10k. multicoloured 75 30

100 The King's Ride, Moravia

1998. Europa. National Festivals. Multicoloured.
192 11k. Type **100** 75 55
193 15k. Carnival masks 1·10 70

101 Devil Musicians

1998. For Children. Multicoloured.
194 4k. Type **101** 30 10
195 4k.60 Water sprite riding catfish 35 10

102 Frantisek Kmoch (composer)

1998. Anniversaries. Multicoloured.
196 4k. Type **102** (150th birth anniv) 30 10
197 4k.60 Frantisek Palacky (historian, birth bicent) 40 30
198 6k. Rafael Kubelik (conductor, 2nd death anniv) 45 30

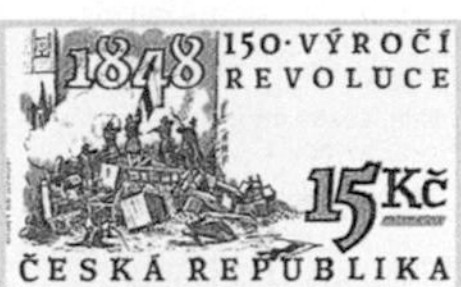

103 Prague Barricades, June 1848

1998. 150th Anniv of 1848 Revolutions.
199 **103** 15k. multicoloured 1·10 60

1998. Art (6th series). As T 16. Multicoloured.
200 22k. "Amorpha-Two-coloured Fugue" (Frantisek Kupka) 1·50 1·10
201 23k. "Flight" (Paul Gauguin) 1·50 1·25

104 St. Barbara's Cathedral, Kutna Hora

1998. World Heritage Sites. Multicoloured.
202 8k. Type **104** 60 30
203 11k. Chateau Valtice 90 45

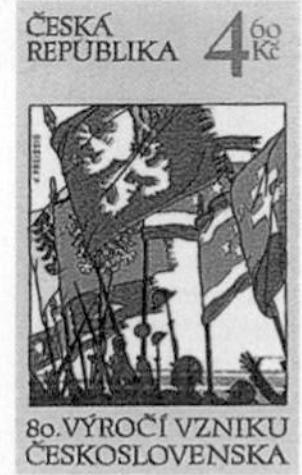

105 Soldiers with Flags

1998. 80th Anniv of Founding of Czechoslovak Republic. Paintings by Vojtech Preissig. Mult.
204 4k.60 Type **105** 40 10
205 5k. Soldiers marching 40 30
206 12k.60 Flags in Mala Street, Prague 1·00 60

106 Capricorn

1998. Signs of the Zodiac.
206a - 40h green, brown & blk 10 10
207 **106** 1k. yellow, red and black 10 10
208 - 2k. black, lilac and blue 10 10
209 - 5k. red, black and yellow 40 10
210 - 5k.40 green, black & brn 40 10
211 - 8k. red, black & purple 50 30
212 - 9k. green, black & orge 60 30
213 - 10k. yellow, blue & black 75 30
214 - 12k. orange, blue & black 85 50
216 - 17k. multicoloured 75 45
217 - 20k. violet, black & brn 1·40 70
218 - 26k. multicoloured 1·10 65

DESIGNS: 40h. Pisces; 2k. Virgo; 5k. Taurus; 5k.40; Scorpio; 8k. Cancer; 9k. Libra; 10k. Aquarius; 12k. Leo; 17k. Gemini; 20k. Sagittarius; 26k. Aries.

107 People following Star

1998. Christmas. Multicoloured.
219 4k. Type **107** 25 15
220 6k. Angel with trumpet over village (vert) 50 90

1998. Art (7th series). As T 16. Multicoloured.
221 15k. Section of "The Greater Cycle" (Jan Preisler) 1·10 90
222 16k. "Spinner" (Josef Navratil) (vert) 1·40 1·00

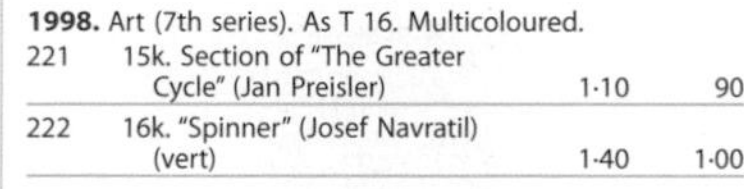

108 1929 2k.50 Prague Stamp

1999. Czech Stamp Production.
223 **108** 4k.60 multicoloured 40 20

109 Cat

1999. Cats. Multicoloured.
224 4k.60 Type **109** 35 15
225 5k. Cat with kitten 35 25
226 7k. Two cats 60 30

110 Ornate Cockerel

1999. Easter.
227 **110** 3k. multicoloured 25 10

111 Hoopoe

1999. Nature Conservation. Multicoloured.
228 4k.60 Type **111** 40 25
229 4k.60 European bee eater ("Merops apiaster") 40 40
230 5k. "Euphydryas maturna" 40 25
231 5k. Rosy underwing ("Catocala electa") 40 25

112 Emblem

1999. Admission of Czech Republic into North Atlantic Treaty Organization.
232 **112** 4k.60 blue and red 40 20

113 Emblem and Sky

1999. 50th Anniv of Council of Europe.
233 **113** 7k. multicoloured 55 20

114 Josef Rossler-Orovsky (co-founder)

1999. Centenary of Czech Olympic Committee.
234 **114** 9k. multicoloured 65 40

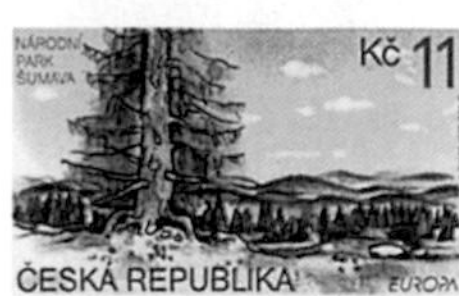

115 Sumava National Park

1999. Europa. Parks and Gardens. Multicoloured.
235 11k. Type **115** 85 50
236 17k. Podyji National Park 1·25 75

116 "Ferda the Ant, Pytlik the Beetle and The Proud Ladybird"

1999. For Children. Birth Centenary of Ondrej Sekora (children's writer).
237 **116** 4k.60 multicoloured 30 10

117 Chain Bridge, Stadlec

1999. Bridges. Multicoloured.

238	8k. Type **117**	60	40
239	11k. Wooden bridge, Cernvir (horiz)	85	55

118 King Wenceslas I handing over Grant and Miners

1999. 750th Anniv of Granting of Jihlava Mining Rights.

240	**118**	8k. multicoloured	60	30

119 "UPU", Globe and Emblem

1999. 125th Anniv of Universal Postal Union.

241	**119**	9k. black, blue and green	60	45

120 Barrande and Trilobites

1999. Birth Bicentenary of Joachim Barrande (French geologist and palaeontologist). Sheet 106×77 mm containing T 120 and similar horiz design. Each green, brown and black.

MS242 13k. Type **120**; 31k. *Deiphon forbesi*, *Ophioceras simplex* and *Carolincrinus barrandei* (trilobites)	3·00	2·00

121 Priessnitz and Treatments

1999. Birth Bicent of Vincenc Priessnitz (folk healer).

243	**121**	4k.60 multicoloured	30	10

122 Woman

1999. Folk Art. Beehives. Multicoloured.

244	4k.60 Type **122**	20	15
245	5k. St. Joseph with Infant Jesus	35	25
246	7k. Sweeper	65	25

123 Clown Doctor and Laughing New-born Baby

1999. Graphic Humour of Miroslav Bartak. Multicoloured.

247	4k.60 Type **123**	25	10
248	5k. Dog disobeying No Smoking and No Dogs sign	40	30
249	7k. Night sky seeping in under window	65	30

124 "Mother of God" (altar painting)

1999. Beuron School (art movement). Sheet 108×166 mm containing T 124 and similar vert design showing paintings in St. Gabriel's Church, Prague. Multicoloured.

MS250 11k. Type **124**; 13k. "Jesus the Pantocrater" (painting in vault of apse)	1·75	1·40

125 Baby Jesus with Sheep and Lamb

1999. Christmas.

251	**125**	3k. multicoloured	25	10

1999. Art (8th series). As T 16. Multicoloured.

252	13k. "Red Orchid" (Jindrich Styrsky) (vert)	90	70
253	17k. "Landscape with Marsh" (Julius Marak) (vert)	1·25	95
254	26k. "Monument" (Frantisek Hudecek) (vert)	1·60	1·40

126 Brmo, 1593 (after Willenberg)

2000. "Brno 2000" Stamp Exhibition. Multicoloured.

255	5k. Type **126**	35	25
MS256	80×100 mm. 50k. St. James's Church (vert)	3·25	2·40

127 Czechoslovakia 1938 1k.+50h. Child Welfare Stamp

2000. Czech Stamp Production.

257	**127**	5k.40 multicoloured	40	25

128 Kutna Hora Coat of Arms and 14th-century Miners

2000. 700th Anniv of Granting of Royal Mining Rights to Kutn Hora.

258	**128**	5k. multicoloured	40	25

129 Masaryk

2000. 150th Birth Anniv of Tomas Masaryk (President of Czechoslovakia, 1918–35). Sheet 60×85 mm.

MS259 **129** 17k. blue, ultramarine and red	1·25	1·00

130 Animal-shaped Cake and Painted Eggs

2000. Easter.

260	**130**	5k. multicoloured	40	30

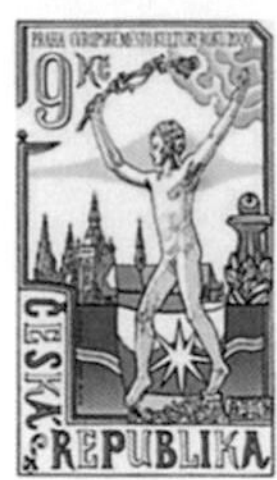

131 "Winner" (statue, Stursa) and Prague Castle Tower)

2000. Prague, European City of Culture. Sheet 166×109 mm containing T 131 and similar multicoloured designs.

MS261 9k. Type **131**; 11k. King David (wooden statue), Na Karlove Church; 17k. King Charles IV statue and Prague Castle (50×40 mm)	2·50	3·00

132 Vitezslav Nezval (poet) (centenary)

2000. Birth Anniversaries.

262	**132**	5k. blue, lilac and violet	40	25
263	-	8k. mauve, red and violet	50	35

DESIGN: 8k. Gustav Mahler (composer, 140th anniv).

133 Steam Locomotive, 1900

2000. Conference of European Ministers of Transport, Prague. Railways. Sheet 114×112 mm containing T 133 and similar horiz design. Multicoloured.

MS264 8k. Type **133**; 15k. T371 electric locomotive, 2000	1·60	1·50

134 "Building Europe"

2000. Europa.

265	**134**	9k. multicoloured	60	40

135 Alarm Clock and Bird

2000. International Children's Day.

266	**135**	5k.40 multicoloured	40	25

136 Fermat's Great Theorem

2000. World Mathematics Year.

267	**136**	7k. multicoloured	45	40

137 *Geastrum pouzarii*

2000. Endangered Fungi. Multicoloured.

268	5k. Type **137**	20	25
269	5k. Devil's boletus (*Boletus satanas*)	20	25
270	5k.40 *Verpa bohemica*	30	30
271	5k.40 *Morchella pragensis*	30	30

138 Old Town Bridge Tower

2000. Historic Buildings. Multicoloured.

272	9k. Type **138**	35	55
273	11k. St. Nicolas's Church	45	55
274	13k. Municipal Hall	55	65

139 Leaves

2000. Annual International Monetary Fund and World Bank Group Meeting, Prague.

275	**139**	7k. multicoloured	55	40

140 Chariot Racing (detail from amphora)

2000. Olympic Games, Sydney.

276	**140**	9k. red, black and green	60	50
277	-	13k. multicoloured	90	65

DESIGN: 13k. Canoeing and Czech flag.

141 Northern Goshawk and Common Pheasant (Autumn)

2000. Hunting and Gamekeeping. Multicoloured.

278	5k. Type **141**	20	30
279	5k. Deer (winter)	20	45
280	5k.40 Mallard and ducklings (spring)	25	30
281	5k.40 Deer (summer)	25	30

2000. Art (9th series). As T 16. Multicoloured.

282	13k. "St. Luke the Evangelist" (Master Theodoricus) (vert)	90	65
283	17k. "Simon with the Infant Jesus" (Petr Jan Brandl) (vert)	1·10	75
284	26k. "Brunette" (Alfons Mucha) (vert)	1·60	1·40

142 Nativity

2000. Christmas.

285	**142**	5k. multicoloured	40	25

143 Cat

2000. Old and New Millennia. Multicoloured.

286	9k. Type **143**	60	50
287	9k. Magician pulling rabbit from hat	60	50

144 Czechoslovakia 1951 5c. Stamp

2001. Czech Stamp Production. 150th Birth Anniv of Alois Jirasek (writer).

288	**144**	5k.40 multicoloured	40	25

145 Jan Amos Komensky (Comenius) (philosopher)

2001

289	**145**	9k. black, red and brown	60	50

146 Cockerel and Woman

2001. Easter.

290	**146**	5k.40 multicoloured	40	25

147 Church, Jakub u Kutne Hory

2001. Czech Architecture. Sheet 113×85 mm containing T 147 and similar vert designs. Each orange, green and black.

MS291	13k. Type **147**; 17k. Bucovice Chateau; 31k. The Dancing House, Prague	4·25	3·25

148 "Allegory of Art" (fresco, Vaclav Vavincec Reiner)

2001. Baroque Art. Sheet 146×117 mm.

MS292 **148**	50k. multicoloured	3·25	3·00

149 Pond

2001. Europa. Water Resources.

293	**149**	9k. lilac and black	60	45

150 Players

2001. Men's European Volleyball Championship, Ostrava.

294	**150**	12k. multicoloured	1·00	65

151 Maxipes Fik riding Bicycle

2001. International Children's Day. Vecernicek (cartoon created by Rudolf Cechura).

295	**151**	5k.40 multicoloured	1·00	25

152 Frantisek Skroup (composer)

2001. Birth Anniversaries. Multicoloured.

296	5k.40 Type **152** (bicentenary)	35	25
297	16k. Frantisek Halas (poet, centenary)	1·10	60

153 Cats

2001. Greetings Stamp. "Congratulations".

298	**153**	5k.40 multicoloured	40	25

154 West Highland White Terrier

2001. Dogs. Multicoloured.

299	5k.40 Type **154**	35	25
300	5k.40 Beagle	35	25
301	5k.40 Golden retriever	35	25
302	5k.40 German shepherd	35	25

155 Fennec Fox (*Fennecus zerda*)

2001. Zoo Animals. Multicoloured.

303	5k.40 Type **155**	35	25
304	5k.40 Lesser panda (*Ailurus fulgens*)	35	25
305	5k.40 Siberian tiger (*Panthera tigris altaica*)	35	25
306	5k.40 Orang-utan (*Pongo pygmaeus*)	35	25

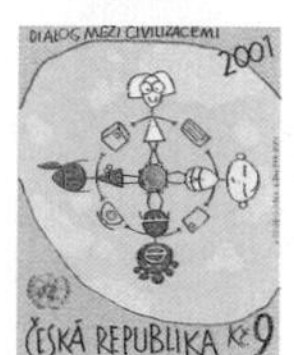

156 Emblem

2001. "Dialogue between Civilizations".

307	**156**	9k. multicoloured	60	40

157 Windmill, Kuzelov

2001. Mills. Multicoloured.

308	9k. Type **157**	50	50
309	14k.40 Water mill, Strehom	80	70

158 Kromeriz Chateau

2001. UNESCO World Heritage Sites. Mult.

310	12k. Type **158**	75	60
311	14k. Holasovice village	70	70

2001. Art (10th series). As T 16.

312	12k. black, buff and blue	80	75
313	17k. multicoloured	1·25	90
314	26k. multicoloured	1·90	1·50

DESIGNS—VERT: 12k. "The Annunciation of the Virgin Mary" (Michael Jindrich Rentz); 17k. "Sans-Souci Bar in Nimes" (Cyril Bouda); 26k. "The Goose Keeper" (Vaclav Brozik).

159 Christmas Tree and Half Moon carrying Gifts

2001. Christmas.

315	**159**	5k.40 multicoloured	40	25

160 1938 2k. Stamp

2002. 40th Death Anniv of Max Svabinsky (stamp designer).

316	**160**	5k.40 multicoloured	40	30

161 Skier

2002. Winter Paralympic Games, Salt Lake City, U.S.A.

317	**161**	5k.40 multicoloured	40	25

162 Ski Jumper

2002. Winter Olympic Games, Salt Lake City, U.S.A.

318	**162**	12k. multicoloured	80	65

163 Girl with Easter Egg and Boy with Easter Sticks

2002. Easter.

319	**163**	5k.40 multicoloured	25	15

164 Jaromir Vejvoda, Josef Poncar and Karel Vacek

2002. Composers' Birth Centenaries.

320	**164**	9k. black, red and violet	40	25

2002. No. 318 optd ALES VALENTA ZLATA MEDAILE.

321	**162**	12k. multicoloured	50	30

166 "Divan" (Vlaho Bukovac)

2002

322	**166**	17k. multicoloured	70	45

A stamp in a similar design was issued by Croatia.

167 Circus Tent, Clown and Lion

2002. Europa. Circus.

323	**167**	9k. multicoloured	40	25

168 "Piano Keys–Lake" (Frantisek Kupka)

2002. Art. Sheet 148×105 mm, containing T 168 and similar vert design. Multicoloured.

MS324 23k. Type **168**. 31k. "Man with Broken Nose" (bust) (Auguste Rodin) 2·10 2·10

169 Mole and Butterfly

2002. For Children.

325	**169**	5k.40 multicoloured	25	15

170 Pearl Oysters

2002. Nature Conservation.

326	**170**	9k. multicoloured	40	25

171 Hus

2002. Jan Hus (clergyman and preacher) Commemoration.

327	**171**	9k. multicoloured	40	25

172 *Maculinea nausithous*

2002. Endangered Species. Butterflies. Sheet 109×65 mm, containing T 172 and similar horiz designs. Multicoloured.

MS328 5k.40, Type **172**; 5k.40, *Maculinea alcon*; 9k. *Maculinea teleius*; 9k. *Maculinea arion* 1·10 70

173 Pansy

2002. Flowers.

329		50h. Cornflower	10	10
335	**173**	6k.40 multicoloured	30	15
336	**173**	6k.50 Dahlia	25	15

174 Zatopek

2002. 80th Birth Anniv of Emil Zatopek (athlete).

340	**174**	9k. multicoloured	45	25

175 Chateau, Litomysl, Bohemia

2002. UNESCO World Heritage Sites. Mult.

341		12k. Type **175**	50	30
342		14k. Holy Trinity Column, Olumouc, Moravia (vert)	60	35

176 Angel, St. Nicholas with Basket of Gifts, and Devil

2002. St Nicholas.

343	**176**	6k.40 multicoloured	30	15

177 Star and Christmas Tree

2002. Christmas.

344	**177**	6k.40 multicoloured	30	15

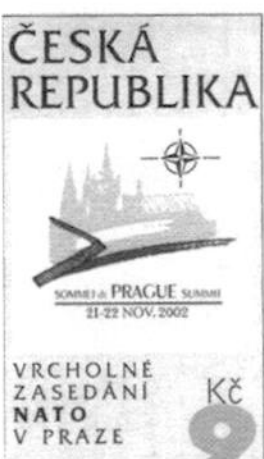

178 Emblem

2002. North Atlantic Treaty Organization Summit Meeting, Prague.

345	**178**	9k. azure, red and blue	40	25

179 17th-century Armchair

2002. Antique Furniture. Multicoloured.

346		6k.40 Type **179**	30	15
347		9k. Sewing table, 1820	40	25
348		12k. Thonet dressing table, 1860	50	30
349		17k. Armchair, 1923	75	45

2002. Art (11th series). As T 16.

350		12k. black and blue	50	30
351		20k. multicoloured	85	50
352		26k. multicoloured	1·10	65

DESIGNS—HORIZ: 12k. "Forlorn Woman" (Jarsolav Panuska). VERT: 20k. "St. Wenceslas" (stained glass window) (Mikolas Ales); 26k. "Young Man with Lute" (Jan Peter Molitor).

180 Lion (statue, Josef Max)

2003. 10th Anniv of Czech Republic. Sheet 78×118 mm.

MS353 25k. brown, blue and red 1·10 1·10

181 Czechoslovakia 1937 2k.50 Stamp

2003. Czech Stamp Production. Jan C. Vondrous (stamp designer) and K. Seizinger (engraver) Commemoration.

354	**181**	6k.40 multicoloured	30	15

182 Jaroslav Vrchlicky

2003. 150th Birth Anniversaries. Multicoloured.

355		6k.40 Type **182** (writer)	30	15
356		8k. Josef Thomayer (physician and writer)	35	20

183 Easter Egg

2003. Easter.

357	**183**	6k.40 multicoloured	25	15

184 Rose and Prague

2003

358	**184**	6k.40 multicoloured	25	15

185 18th-century netted Lace

2003. Traditional Crafts. Lace.

359	**185**	6k.40 multicoloured	25	15
360	-	9k. red, deep blue and blue	35	20

DESIGN: 9k. Bobbin lace.

186 Poster for film *La Dolce Vita* (Karel Vaca)

2003. Europa. Poster Art.

361	**186**	9k. multicoloured	35	20

187 Dragon Rocks and Trosky Castle, North-eastern Bohemia

2003. Natural Heritage. Multicoloured.

362		12k. Type **187**	50	30
363		14k. Punkva river caves, Brno	60	35

188 Jonathon (dog), Mach, Sebestova and Telephone (illustration from *The Boy Mach and the Girl Sebestova* (book) (Milos Maourek))

2003. For Children.

364	**188**	6k.40 multicoloured	25	15

189 Stone Tower, Klet, South Bohemia

2003. Viewing Towers. Multicoloured.

365		6k.40 Type **189**	25	15
366		6k.40 Metal tower, Slovanka, Jablonec and Nisou	25	15

190 Electric Train

2003. Centenary of First Tabor–Bechyne Electric Railway.

367	**190**	10k. multicoloured	45	30

191 Marksman with Rifle

2003. European Marksmanship Championships, Plzen and Brno.

368	**191**	9k. multicoloured	35	20

192 Josef Dubrovsky

2003. 250th Birth Anniv of Josef Dubrovsky (linguist).

369	**192**	9k. multicoloured	35	20

193 President Vaclav Klaus

2003. (1st issue).
370 **193** 6k.40 stone, blue and mauve 25 15

See also No. 384, 424 and 542.

194 Siamese Fighting Fish (*Betta splendens*)

2003. Aquarium Fish. Sheet 176×115 mm containing T 194 and similar multicoloured designs.
MS371 12k. Type **194**; 14k. Freshwater angelfish (*Pterophyllum scalare*); 16k. Goldfish (*Carassius auratus*) (55×46 mm); 20k. Blue discus (*Symphysodon aequifasciatus*) (55×46 mm) 2·75 1·60

195 19th-century Anatolian Prayer Carpet

2003. Oriental Carpets. Multicoloured.
372 9k. Type **195** 35 20
373 12k. 18th-century Islamic carpet 50 30

196 Carving, Porta Coeli Monastery, Predklasteri

2003. Brno 2005 International Stamp Exhibition.
374 **196** 6k.50 multicoloured 25 15

197 Red Kite (*Milvus milvus*)

2003. Birds of Prey. Multicoloured.
375 6k.50 Type **197** 25 15
376 8k. Peregrine falcon (*Falco peregrinus*) 35 20
377 9k. Booted eagle (*Hieraaetus pennatus*) 35 20

198 Wooden Fire Engine (1822)

2003. Fire Engines. Multicoloured.
378 6k.50 Type **198** 25 15
379 9k. Engine (1933) 35 20
380 12k. CSA 8/AVIA Daewoo (2002) 50 30

2003. As T 184 but with colour changed.
381 **184** 6k.50 multicoloured 25 15

199 Hand-made Metal Lantern, Novy Svet, Prague

2003
382 **199** 9k. multicoloured 35 20

200 Snow-covered Christmas Tree

2003. Christmas.
383 **200** 6k.50 multicoloured 25 15

2003. President Vaclav Klaus (2nd issue). As T 193.
384 **193** 6k.50 blue and lilac 25 15

2003. Art (12th series). As T 16. Multicoloured.
385 17k. "Poor Countryside" (Max Svabinsky) 70 45
386 20k. "Autumn in Veltrusy" (Antonin Slavícek) (vert) 85 50
387 26k. "Eleonore from Toledo" (Angola Brozino) (vert) 1·10 65

201 Czechoslovakia 1970 1k.80 Stamp

2004. Czech Stamp Production. Jivi Svengsbir (designer and engraver) Commemoration.
388 **201** 6k.50 multicoloured 25 15

202 Water-powered Hammer, Lniste

2004. Iron Works. Multicoloured.
389 6k.50 Type **202** 25 15
390 17k. Iron furnace, Stara Hut u Adamova 75 45

203 Assumption of the Virgin Mary Church, Brno

2004
391 **203** 17k. multicoloured 70 45

204 Family

2004. Easter.
392 **204** 6k.40 multicoloured 25 15

2004. Art (13th series). As T 16. Multicoloured.
393 26k. multicoloured 1·10 65
DESIGNS—VERT: 26k. "Prometheus" (Antonin Prochazka).

205 Players

2004. World Ice Hockey Championship, Prague and Ostrava.
394 **205** 12k. multicoloured 50 30

206 Stars

2004. Accession to European Union.
395 **206** 9k. blue, yellow and deep blue 35 20

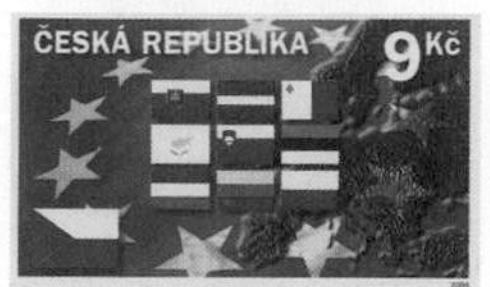

207 New Members Flags and EU Stars

2004. Enlargement of European Union.
396 **207** 9k. multicoloured 40 25

208 Bedrich Smetana

2004. Operatic Composers' Anniversaries. Multicoloured.
397 6k.50 Type **208** 25 15
398 8k. Antoniin Dvorak (death centenary) 35 20
399 10k. Leos Janacek (150th birth) 45 25

209 Family by River

2004. Europa. Holidays.
400 **209** 9k. multicoloured 35 20

210 Toad (illustration from *The Wind in the Willows* (children's book, Kenneth Graham)

2004. For Children.
401 **210** 6k.50 multicoloured 30 20

211 Radegast (sculpture) (Albin Polsek)

2004. Brno 2005 International Stamp Exhibition (2nd issue).
402 **211** 6k.50 multicoloured 60 35

212 Svata Hora (Holy Mountain), Pribram

2004. Tourism. Places of Pilgrimage. Multicoloured.
403 12k. Type **212** 55 35
404 14k. Svaty Hostyn, Bystrice Pod Hostynem 60 35

213 Athlete holding Javelin

2004. Paralympic Games, Athens 2004.
405 **213** 6k.50 multicoloured 30 20

214 Cyclist

2004. Olympic Games, Athens 2004.
406 **214** 9k. multicoloured 40 25

215 Petrarch

2004. 700th Birth Anniv of Francesco Petrarca (Petrarch) (poet).
407 **215** 14k. multicoloured 60 35

216 Tree in Winter

2004. Tree Conservation. Multicoloured.
408 6k.50 Type **216** 30 20
409 8k. Tree in leaf 35 20

217 Budgerigars (*Melopsittacus undulates*)

2004. Parrots. Sheet 115×168 mm containing T 217 and similar horiz designs. Multicoloured.
MS410 12k. Type **217**; 14k. Masked lovebird (*Agapornis personata*); 16k. Rose-ringed parakeet (*Psittacula krameri*); Green-winged macaw (*Ara chloroptera*) 2·00 2·00

218 18th-century Music Teacher and Child

2004. 230th Anniv of Introduction of Compulsory Education.
411 **218** 6k.50 ochre, black and vermilion 30 20

219 Perambulator (1880)

2004. Early Perambulators. Multicoloured.
412 12k. Type **219** 55 35
413 14k. Pram (1890) 60 35
414 16k. Pram (1900) 70 40

220 Apple, Candle and Leaves

2004. Christmas.
415 **220** 6k.50 multicoloured 30 20

2004. Art (14th series). As T 16. Multicoloured.
416 20k. "On the Outskirts of Cesky Raj" (Alois Bubak) 85 60
417 22k. "The Long, the Broad and the Sharpsight" (Hanus Schwaiger) (vert) 90 65
418 26k. "Spring" (Vojtech Hynais) (vert) 1·20 70

221 Czechoslovakia 1960 60h. Stamp

2005. Czech Stamp Production. Jaroslav Svab (stamp designer) and Jan Mracek (engraver) Commemorations.
419 **221** 6k.50 multicoloured 30 20

222 "Moon Landscape" (drawing)

2005. 60th Death Anniv of Petr Ginz (artist and Auschwitz victim). First Anniv of Colombia Space Shuttle Accident. Sheet 76×116 mm.
MS420 **222** 31k. multicoloured 1·40 1·40

223 Gate with Peacock and Trumpeter

2005
421 **223** 7k.50 multicoloured 35 20

224 Lily

2005
422 **224** 7k.50 multicoloured 35 20

225 "Granny"

2005. Babicka (The Grandmother) novel by Bozena Nemcova.
423 **225** 7k.50 multicoloured 35 20

2005. President Vaclav Klaus (3rd issue). As T 193.
424 **193** 7k.50 brown and magenta 35 20

226 Easter Egg

2005. Easter.
425 **226** 7k.50 multicoloured 35 20

227 Fuchsia

2005. Flower.
426 **227** 19k. multicoloured 90 60

228 St. Prokop's Basilica, Trebic

2005. Tourism. Multicoloured.
427 14k. Type **228** 60 35
428 16k. Tugendhaft Villa, Brno (horiz) 70 40

229 Bohuslav Brauner

2005. Birth Anniversaries. Multicoloured.
429 7k.50 Type **229** (150th) (chemist) 35 20
430 12k. Adalbert Stifter (200th) (artist and writer) 55 35
431 19k. Mikulas Dacicky (450th) (writer) 90 60

230 Roast Duck, Dumplings and Glass of Beer

2005. Europa Gastronomy.
432 **230** 9k. multicoloured 35 15

231 Peace Monument and Napoleon I

2005. Bicentenary of Battle of Austerlitz. Brno 2005 International Stamp Exhibition. Multicoloured.
433 19k. Type **231** 90 60
MS434 141×112 mm. 30k. "Napoleon I before the Battle of Austerlitz" (L. F. Lejune) (55×45 mm) 1·30 1·30

232 Kremilek and Vochomurka (cartoon characters)

2005. For Children.
435 **232** 7k.50 multicoloured 30 20

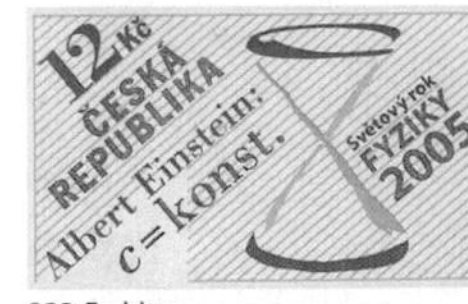

233 Emblem

2005. International Year of Physics.
436 **233** 12k. multicoloured 55 35

234 Player

2005. European Baseball Championships.
437 **234** 9k. multicoloured 40 30

235 Butterfly and Flowers (*Viola lutea sudetica* and *Hedysarum hedysaroides*)

2005. Endangered Species. Krkonose Mountains Fauna and Flora. Sheet 114×170 mm containing T 235 and similar multicoloured designs.
MS438 12k. Type **235**; 14k.White-throated dipper (*Cinclus cinclus*) and *Leucojum vernum*; 15k. *Salamandra salamandra, Primula minima* and Alpine shrew (*Sorex alpinus*) (44×55 mm); 22k. *Pneumonanthe asclepiadea, Aeschna coerulea* and Bluethroat (*Luscinia svecica svecica*) (44×55 mm) 3·00 3·00
The stamps and margin of No. **MS**438 were printed together, se-tenant, forming a composite design.

236 Franciscan Monastery Bell, Benesov and Assumption of Virgin Mary Church Bell, Havlickuv Brod

2005. Bells.
439 **236** 7k.50 multicoloured 35 20
440 - 9k. green and black 40 30
441 - 12k. violet and black 55 35
DESIGNS: Type **236**; 9k. St. Jon and St. Paul Church, Dobrs; 12k. St Wenceslas Cathedral, Olomouc.

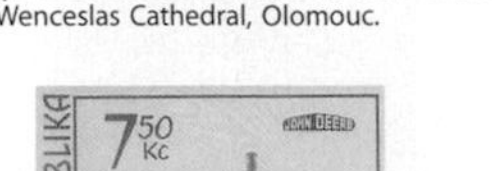

237 John Deere (1923)

2005. Tractors. Multicoloured.
442 7k.50 Type **237** 35 20
443 9k. Lanz Bulldog (1921) 40 30
444 18k. Skoda (1937) 85 55

238 Emblem

2005. World Information Society Summit, Tunis.
445 **238** 9k. orange and violet 40 30

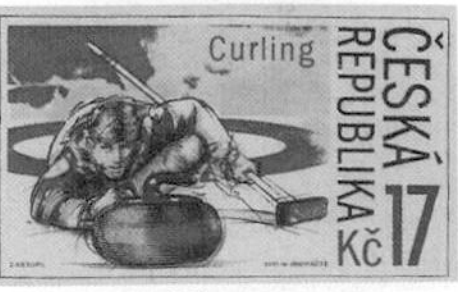

239 Stone and Player

2005. Curling.
446 **239** 17k. multicoloured 80 50

240 The Nativity

2005. Christmas. Multicoloured.
447 7k.50 Type **240** 35 20
448 9k. Three Magi (horiz) 40 30

2005. Art (15th series). As T 16. Multicoloured.
449 22k. "Summer Landscape" (Adolf Kosarek) 1·00 65
450 25k. "Deinotherium" (Zdenek Burian) 1·20 70
451 26k. "Poplars near Velke Nemcice" (Alois Kalvoda) 1·20 70

241 Prague Castle (Czechoslovakia 1968 30h. Stamp)

2005. Czech Stamp Production. Jaroslav Lukavsky (stamp designer) and Ladislav Jirka (engraver) Commemoration.
452 **241** 7k.50 multicoloured 35 20

242 Bouquet

2005. Greetings Stamps.
453 **242** 10k. multicoloured 45 35

243 Hibiscus

2005
454 **243** 11k. multicoloured 55 35

244 Ice Hockey Players

2006. Winter Paralympic Games, Turin.
455 **244** 7k.50 multicoloured 35 20

245 Women Skiers

2006. Winter Olympic Games, Turin.
456 **245** 9k. multicoloured 1·20 70

2006. Art (16th series). As T 16. Multicoloured.
457 25k. multicoloured 1·20 70
DESIGN: 25k. "Madonna of Zbraslav" (icon) (40×50 mm).

246 Frantisek Josef Gerstner (mathematician) (250th birth anniv)

2006. Anniversaries. Multicoloured.
458 11k. Type **246** 55 35
459 12k. Jaroslav Jezek (composer) (birth centenary) 55 35
460 19k. Sigmund Freud (psychoanalyst) (150th birth anniv) 80 50

246a Glass and Grapes

2006. Still Life.
460a **246a** 12k. multicoloured 55 35

247 Daffodil

2006
461 **247** 24k. multicoloured 1·10 65

2006. K. Neumannova–Gold Medallist–Winter Olympic Games, Turin. No. 456 optd K. NEUMANNOVA ZLATA MEDALLE.
462 **248** 9k. multicoloured 40 30

249 Chicken and Easter Egg

2006. Easter.
463 **249** 7k.50 multicoloured 35 20

250 Monastery, Osek

2006. Tourism. Multicoloured.
464 12k. Type **250** 55 35
465 15k. Rock formation, Kokorinsko 70 40

251 Rose as Violinist

2006. Greetings Stamp.
466 **251** 7k.50 multicoloured 35 20

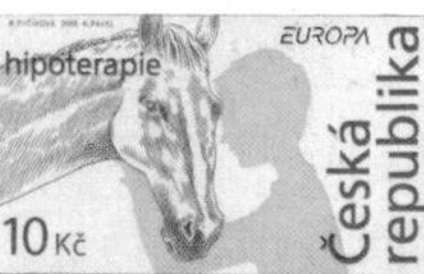

252 Horse and Silhouette

2006. Europa. Integration. Multicoloured.
467 10k. Type **252** (hippotherapy) 45 35
468 20k. Dog and silhouette (canistherapy) 90 70

253 Rumcajs and Family

2006. Rumcajs (cartoon by Vaclav Ctvrtek).
469 **253** 7k.50 multicoloured 1·10 65

254 Premysl Otakar I

2006. Premyslid Dynasty Hereditary Kings. Sheet 112×165 mm containing T 254 and similar vert designs. Each claret, purple and slate.
MS470 12k. Type **254**; 14k. Vaclav (Wenceslas) I; 15k. Premysl Otakar II; 22k. Vaclav (Wenceslas) II; 28k Vaclav (Wenceslas) III 13·00 13·00

255 Gilded Brooch (1904)

2006. Bohemian Jewellery. Multicoloured.
471 15k. Type **255** 2·10 1·40
472 18k. Garnet encrusted pendant (1930) 2·40 1·50

256 Kamenice River Narrows

2006. Czech-Switzerland National Park.
473 **256** 19k. multicoloured 2·60 1·50

257 *Gymnocalycium denudatum*

2006. Cacti. Multicoloured.
474 7k.50 Type **257** 1·10 65
475 7k.50 *Obregonia denegrii* 1·10 65
476 10k. *Astrophytum asterias* 1·40 75
477 10k. *Cintia knizei* 1·40 75

258 Prague Castle (mosaic) (Giovanni Castrucci) (image scaled to 60% of original size)

2006. PRAGA 2008 (1st issue). Sheet 105×141 mm.
MS478 **258** 35k. multicoloured 4·75 4·75

See also No. 481, 488, 498, 502, **MS**512, 526, 536, 542, **MS**550, 555 and **MS**559.

259 Multicoloured Tree

2006. Ecology.
479 **259** 7k.50 multicoloured 1·10 65

260 Robin and Candle

2006. Christmas Congratulations.
480 **260** 7k.50 multicoloured 1·10 65

261 Statue and Railings, Vrtbovska Gardens

2006. PRAGA 2008 International Stamp Exhibition (2nd issue).
481 **261** 7k.50 multicoloured 1·10 65

262 Church of the Virgin Mary, Broumov

2006. Folk Architecture. Churches.
482 7k.50 Type **262** 1·10 65
483 19k. Church of St. Andrew, Hodslavice 2·60 1·50

263 The Nativity

2006. Christmas.
484 **263** 7k.50 multicoloured 1·10 65

2006. Art (17th series). As T 16. Multicoloured.
485 22k. multicoloured 3·50 2·10
486 22k. multicoloured 3·50 2·10
487 22k. multicoloured 3·50 2·10
DESIGNS: 22k. "Still Life with Fruit" (Jan Davidz de Heem) (40×50 mm); 25k. "Montenegrin Madonna" (Jaroslav Cermak) (40×50 mm); 28k. "Pod suchym skalim" (Frantisek Kavan).

264 Exhibition Emblem

2006. PRAGA 2008 International Stamp Exhibition (3rd issue).
488 **264** 7k.50 magenta and ultramarine 1·10 65

265 Frana Sramek

2007. Personalities. Multicoloured.
489 7k.50 Type **265** (writer) (130th birth anniv) 1·10 65
490 19k. Kerl Slavoj Amerling (scientist) (birth bicentenary) 2·60 1·50

266 Emblem

2007. 300th Anniv of Technical University, Prague.
491 **266** 9k. multicoloured 1·20 70

267 Josef Slavik (violinist) (As Type **227**)

2007. Czech Stamp Production. Josef Liesler (stamp designer) Commemoration.
492 **267** 7k.50 multicoloured 1·10 65

268 Angel with Infected Wing and Cancer Cell

2007. Oncological Disease Prevention.
493 **268** 7k.50 multicoloured 1·10 65

269 Snake

2007. 2nd Prize Winner in Design-a-Stamp Competition.
494 **269** 12k. multicoloured 1·90 1·10

270 "Girl with a Puppet" (Utagawa Kunisada)

2007. Asian Art. Multicoloured.
495 12k. Type **270** 1·20 70
496 24k. "Siva, Parvati and Ganesa" (under painting on glass) 3·75 2·50

271 Pieta

2007. Easter.
497 **271** 7k.50 multicoloured 1·10 65

272 Langweil's Model of Prague

2007. Praga International Stamp Exhibition (4th issue). 750th Anniv of Lesser Prague.
498 **272** 7k.50 multicoloured 1·10 65

273 Bouquet

2007. Congratulations.
499 **273** 11k. multicoloured 1·75 95

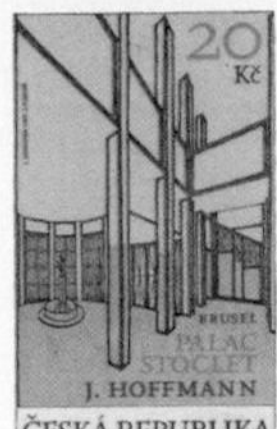

274 Hall (J. Hoffman (architect))

2007. Stoclet Palace, Brussels. Multicoloured.
500 20k. Type **274** 2·75 1·60
501 35k. Palace exterior 4·75 3·25

275 Emblem

2007. Praga International Stamp Exhibition (5th issue).
502 **275** 11k. multicoloured 1·75 95

276 Jurkovic House, Luhacovice

2007. Tourism. Spa Resorts. Multicoloured.
503 12k. Type **276** 1·90 1·10
504 15k. Gocar Pavilion, Bohdanec 2·10 1·40

277 Cyclamen

2007. Flowers. Multicoloured.
505 1k. Type **277** 20 10
506 23k. Geranium 3·50 2·10

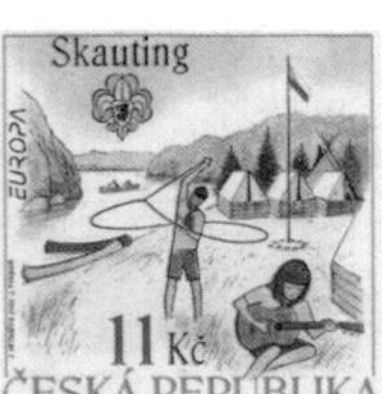

278 Scouts

2007. Europa. Centenary of Scouting.
507 **278** 11k. multicoloured 1·75 95

279 Fast Arrows

2007. For Children. Birth Centenary of Jaroslav Foglar (creator of Fast Arrows (children's cartoon series)).
508 **279** 7k.50 multicoloured 1·10 65

280 Gothic Stove

2007. Traditional Stoves. Multicoloured.
509 7k.50 Type **280** 1·10 65
510 12k. Renaissance stove 1·75 1·10

281 Vaclav Hollar (Jan Meyssens)

2007. 400th Birth Anniv of Wenceslaus Hollar Bohemus (Vaclav Hollar) (artist). Sheet 116×121 mm.
MS511 35k. multicoloured 5·00 5·00

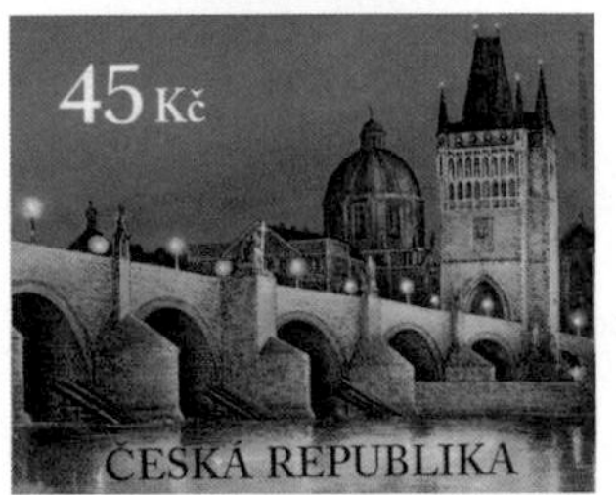

282 Charles Bridge, Prague

2007. Praga 2008, International Stamp Exhibition (6th issue). 650th Anniv of Charles Bridge, Prague. Sheet 155×101 mm.
MS512 45k. multicoloured 6·25 6·25

The stamp and margins of **MS**512 form a composite design of Charles Bridge.

283 Film Projection (Victor Ponrepo's Blue Pike Cinema)

2007. Centenary of First Cinema, Prague.
513 **283** 7k.50 multicoloured 1·10 65

284 *Ophrys holosericea*

2007. Nature Protection. White Carpathian Mountains and Orchid Meadows—UNESCO Biosphere Reservation. Sheet 166×114 mm containing T 284 and similar multicoloured designs.
MS514 9k. Type **284** 10k.*Colias myrmidone* and *Anacamptis pyramidalis*; 11k.*Ophrys apifera*; 12k. *Coracias garrulus* and *Gymnadenia densiflora* (54×44 mm) 6·00 6·00

The stamps and margins of **MS**514 form a composite design of a mountain meadow.

285 Teacher and Pupil

2007. 350th Anniv of Opera Didactica Omnia (educational treatise by Jan Amos Komensky).
515 **285** 12k. gold, black and magenta 1·75 1·10

286 Indian Cress

2007
516 **286** 15k. multicoloured 2·10 1·30

287 Water Tower, Karvina

2007. Water Towers. Multicoloured.
517 7k.50 Type **287** 1·10 65
518 18k. Water tower, Pilsen 3·25 1·90

288 Emil Holub

2007. 160th Birth Anniv of Emil Holub (explorer).
519 **288** 11k. green and carmine 1·75 1·10

289 The Nativity

2007. Christmas.
520 **289** 7k.50 multicoloured 1·20 75

2007. Art (18th series). As T 16. Multicoloured.
521 22k. multicoloured 3·50 2·10
522 25k. multicoloured 4·25 3·50
523 28k. multicoloured 4·75 2·75

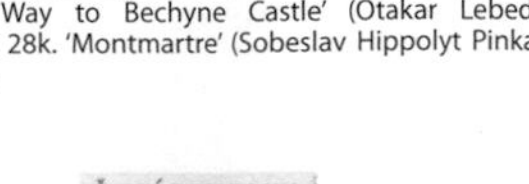

DESIGNS: 22k. 'Vrbicany Castle' (Amalie Manesova) (50×40 mm); 25k. 'Way to Bechyne Castle' (Otakar Lebeda) (40×50 mm); 28k. 'Montmartre' (Sobeslav Hippolyt Pinkas) (50×40 mm).

290 Gaillardia

2007
524 **290** 2k.50 multicoloured 1·00 60

291 Traffic Lights

2007. Entry of Czech Republic into Schengen Area (European Union area without border controls)–21 December 2007.
525 **291** 10k. multicoloured 1·60 95

292 Emblem

2007. Praga International Stamp Exhibition (7th issue).

526	**292**	18k. green and blue	3·00	1·80

293 *Zbraslav* Steam Locomotive (As No. 946)

2008. Czech Stamp Production. Frantisek Hudecek (stamp designer) and Bohdan Roule (engraver) Commemoration.

527	**293**	10k. multicoloured	1·60	95

294 Karel Klosterman

2008. Personalities. Multicoloured.

528	11k. Type **294** (writer) (160th birth anniv)	1·75	1·10
529	14k. Josef Kajetan (playwright and writer) (birth bicentenary)	1·90	1·10

223 Gate with Peacock and Trumpeter

2008. Greetings Stamp.

530	**223**	10k. multicoloured	1·50	90

295 Rose

2008

531	**295**	10k. multicoloured	1·50	90

295a Glass and Grapes

2008. Greetings Stamp.

532	**295a**	17k. multicoloured	2·40	1·50

296 King Jiri

2008. 550th Anniv of Election of Jiri of Podebrady as King of Bohemia.

533	**296**	12k. plum, blue and ultramarine	1·75	1·10

297 Globe as Tree

2008. International Year of Planet Earth.

534	**297**	18k. multicoloured	3·00	1·80

298 *Mourning Christ*

2008. Easter.

535	**298**	10k. multicoloured	1·50	90

299 *Bath Servant Suzanna carrying King Wenceslas IV over River Vltava* (J. Navratil)

2008. Praga 2008 International Stamp Exhibition (8th issue).

536	**299**	10k. multicoloured	1·50	90

300 Gerbera

2008. Flowers.

537	**300**	21k. multicoloured	2·75	1·60

301 Azalea

2008. Flowers.

538	**301**	3k. multicoloured	1·00	60

302 Decorated Globe

2008. 350th Anniv of Orbis Pictus (World in Pictures) (children's encyclopedia) by Jan Amos Komensky.

539	**302**	10k. multicoloured	1·50	90

303 TV Tower and Hotel Jested

2008. Tourism. Multicoloured.

540	12k. Type **303**	1·60	95
541	15k. Hradec Kralove	2·50	1·50

2008. President Vaclav Klaus (4th issue). As T 193.

542	10k. indigo, blue and magenta	1·50	90

304 Astronomical Theodolite (made by Reichenbach Ertel), c.1830

2008. Centenary of National Technical Museum. Multicoloured.

543	10k. Type **304**	1·50	90
544	14k. JAWA 750 sports car (designed for 1000 Czechoslovak Miles Competion), 1935 (horiz)	1·90	1·10
545	18k. Siegfried Marcus petrol combustion engine (made by Märky, Bromovsky-Schultz works, Adamov), 1889	3·00	1·80

305 Early and Modern Player

2008. Centenary of Czechoslovak Ice Hockey.

546	**305**	17k. multicoloured	2·40	1·50

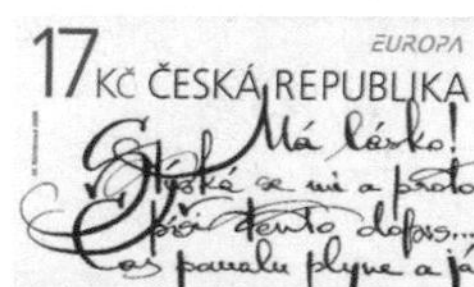

306 Script

2008. Europa. The Letter.

547	**306**	17k. indigo, black and vermilion	2·40	1·50

307 Doggy and Kitty

2008. For Children. The Doggy and Kitty's Tales, How They Kept Their House and About Many Other Things by Josef Capek.

548	**307**	10k. multicoloured	1·60	95

308 *Alcedo atthis* (kingfisher)

2008. Nature Protection. Trebonsko–UNESCO Biosphere Reservation. Sheet 167×116 mm containing T 308 and similar multicoloured designs.

MS549 10k. Type **308**; 12k. *Lutra lutra* (otter) and *Spirea salicifolia* (willowleaf meadowsweet) (54×44 mm); 14k. *Haliaeetus albicilla* (white-tailed eagle) (54×44 mm); 18k. *Netta rufina* (red-crested pochard) and *Nymphaea alba* (water lily) (54×44 mm)	8·00	8·00

The stamps and margins of **MS**549 form a composite design of a pond and its inhabitants.

309 Pavilion, Ledeburk Garden, Prague

2008. Praga 2008 International Stamp Exhibition (9th issue). Sheet 150×114 mm.

MS550 51k. multicoloured	3·75	3·75

The stamp and margins of **MS**550 form a composite design of the gardens.

310 Archer

2008. Paralympic Games, Beijing.

551	**310**	10k. multicoloured	1·90	1·10

311 Ferdinand Stolicka

2008. Travellers' Anniversaries. Multicoloured.

552	12k. Type **311** (geologist and paleontologist) (170th birth anniv)	2·25	1·40
553	21k. Alois Musil (geographer and orientalist) (140th birth anniv)	4·00	2·40

312 Discus

2008. Olympic Games, Beijing.

554	**312**	18k. multicoloured	3·50	2·10

313 Emauzy Monastery and St. Cosmas and Damian Church, Prague

2008. Praga 2008 International Stamp Exhibition (10th issue).
555 **313** 10k. multicoloured 6·50 4·00

314 Landscape

2008. Summer Day. Illustration by Josef Palecek, from Das Lied vom Apfelbaum written by Jaroslav Seifert.
556 **314** 10k. multicoloured 1·75 1·10

315 Vase

2008. Centenary of Applied Art Designers' Association (Artel).
557 **315** 26k. multicoloured 16·00 9·50

316 Express Mail (detail) (painting by K. Schorpfeil)

2008. Praga 2008 International Stamp Exhibition (11th issue). Sheet 120×80 mm.
MS558 **316** 35k. multicoloured 6·50 4·00
Stamp of the same design was issued by Austria.

317 Karel Plicka

2008. Karel Plicka (photographer and film maker) Commemoration. Sheet 109×81 mm.
MS559 **317** 35k. multicoloured 6·50 6·50

2008. Traditional Stoves. As T 280. Multicoloured.
560 10k. Baroque stove, Sternberk Castle 1·75 1·10
561 17k. Rococo stove, Archbishop's Palace 2·75 1·70

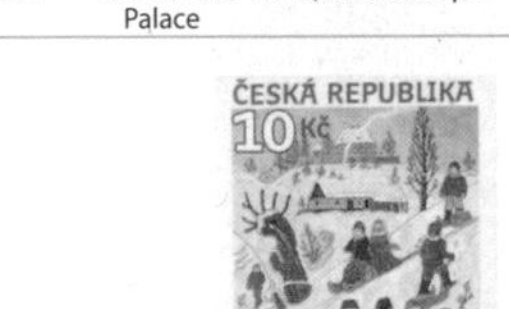

318 *Children in Winter* (Josef Lada)

2008
562 **318** 10k. multicoloured 6·50 4·00

319 Christmas Fruit

2008. Christmas.
563 **319** 10k. multicoloured 1·75 1·10

DESIGNS: 23k.*Vltava River near Klecany* (Zdenka Braunerova) (53×43 mm); 26k.*Autumn Road* (Otakar Nejedly) (43×53 mm); 30k. *Allegory of Water* (Jan Jakub Hartmann) (53×43 mm).

2008. Art (19th series). As T 16.
564 23k. multicoloured 4·25 2·50
565 26k. multicoloured 4·75 2·75

MS566 167×115 mm. 30k. multicoloured 5·50 5·50

320 Bethlehem (detail)

2008. Trebechovice Bethlehem (23 feet long, ten feet high and eight feet deep wooden scene, containing more than 2,000 figures moved by gears of oak, depicting the New Testament from the birth of Christ to the crucifixion and resurrection. Sheet 155×112 mm.
MS567 **320** 30k. multicoloured 5·50 5·50

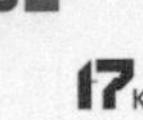

321 'EU2009.CZ'

2008. Czech Republic's Presidency of European Union.
568 **321** 17k. multicoloured 2·75 1·70

322 Louis Braille (inventor of Braille writing for the blind)

2009. Birth Bicentenaries.
569 10k. new blue, blue and black 1·40 85
570 17k. multicoloured 1·90 1·10
DESIGNS: 10k. Type **322**; 17k. Charles Darwin (naturalist and evolutionary theorist).

323 Child eating Pastry (As No. 1153 of Czechoslovakia)

2009. Czech Stamp Production. Anna Podzemna (stamp designer) and Jiri Svengsbir (engraver) Commemoration.
571 **323** 10k. multicoloured 1·50 90

324 Skier

2009. Nordic Skiing World Championships, Liberec.
572 **324** 18k. multicoloured 2·75 1·70

325 Emperor Penguins

2009. Preserve Polar Regions and Glaciers. Sheet 152×108 mm.
MS573 **325** 35k. multicoloured 1·60 1·60

326 Easter Hare carrying Egg

2009. Easter.
574 **326** 10k. multicoloured 1·60 95

2009. Art (20th series). Asian Art. As T 16.
575 18k. multicoloured 3·00 1·80
576 24k. multicoloured 4·00 2·40
DESIGNS: 18k. *Immortal Lu Tung-Pin* (44×54 mm); 24k. *Mythological Scene* (44×54 mm).

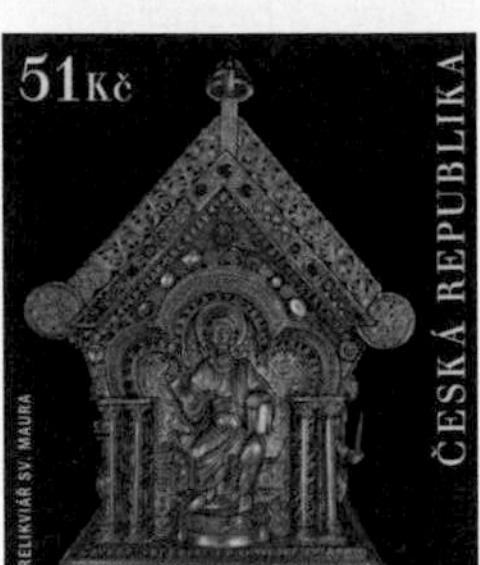

327 Reliquary

2009. Saint Maur's Reliquary, Becov Nad Teplou. Sheet 110×165 mm.
MS577 **327** 51k. multicoloured 3·75 3·75

328 Building Facade

2009. 75th Anniv of Ministry of Industry and Trade Building, Prague.
578 **328** 10k. multicoloured 1·60 95

329 Locomotive IIa SNDVB

2009. 150th Anniv of Pardubice—Liberec Railway Line.
579 **329** 10k. multicoloured 1·60 95

330 Cistercian Monastery, Vyssi Brod

2009. Cultural Heritage. Multicoloured.
580 12k. Type **330** 1·60 95
581 14k. Chateau, Horsovsky Tyn 1·90 1·10

331 Johannes Kepler

2009. Europa. Astronomy. 400th Anniv of Astronoma Nova (Kepler's Laws).
582 **331** 17k. multicoloured 2·40 1·50

332 Spejbl and Hurvinek (marionettes designed by Josef Skupa)

2009. For Children.
583 **332** 10k. multicoloured 1·80 1·30

333 Rabbi Judah Loew

2009. 400th Birth Anniv of Rabbi Judah Loew ben Bezalel.
584 **333** 21k. multicoloured 3·50 2·60

334 Firefighters

2009. CTIF International Fire Brigades Competitions, Ostrava.
585 **334** 17k. multicoloured 3·00 2·30

335 Hands

2009. 400th Anniv of Rudolf II's Majesty Letter (granting religious freedom).
586 **335** 26k. multicoloured 4·50 3·50

336 *Eudia pavonia*

2009. Nature Protection. Krivoklatsko Region–UNESCO Biosphere Reserve. Sheet 114×172 mm containing T 336 and similar multicoloured designs.
MS587 10k. Type **336**; 12k. *Aglia tau* (Tau emperor moth) and *Cervus elaphus* (red deer) (45×55 mm); 14k. *Bubo bubo* (Eurasian eagle owl) and *Ciconia nigra* (black stork) (45×55 mm); 17k. *Tyto alba* (barn owl) (45×55 mm) 30·00 30·00

337 Brnikov Village

2009. Stredohori Uplands–Tertiary Volcanic Region. Sheet 145×96 mm.
MS588 **337** 43k. multicoloured 25·00 25·00

338 Ruprechtov

2009. Windmill (589) and Watermill (590).

589	10k. Type **338**	5·75	4·25
590	12k. Hoslovice (horiz)	7·25	5·50

339 Czech Lion and Linden Twig

2009. 175th Anniv of *Where is my Home* (song which became national anthem in 1993).

591	**339**	10k. multicoloured	1·50	1·10

340 Empire Style, c. 1810

2009. Traditional Stoves. Multicoloured.

592	10k. Type **340**	2·00	1·50
593	14k. Beidermeir style, c. 1835	2·25	1·70

341 Barbora Eliasova

2009. 135th Birth Anniv of Barbora Marketa Eliasova (professional traveler).

594	**341**	18k. multicoloured	3·00	2·30

342 Bell enclosing Winter Landscape

2009. Christmas.

595	**342**	10k. multicoloured	1·50	1·10

343 '17.11''1939' '1989'

2009. 1939, beginning of Oppression—17 November 1989, beginning of Freedom.

596	**343**	14k. ultramarine, scarlet and black	2·30	1·70

2008. Art (21st series). Designs as T 16.

597	24k. multicoloured	4·00	3·00
598	26k. multicoloured	4·25	3·25
MS599	167×115 mm. 34k. multicoloured	5·50	5·50

DESIGNS. 24k.*Canal Lock in Moret* (Alfred Sisley) (53×43 mm); 26k. *An Alley* (Alfred Justitz) (54×44 mm); 34k. *Oldrich and Bozena* (Frantisek Zenisek) (54×44 mm).

344 Medici Vase (As No. 2344 of Czechoslovakia)

2010. Czech Stamp Production. Vladimir Kovarik (stamp designer) Commemoration.

600	**344**	10k. multicoloured	1·80	1·30

345 Magdalena Rettigova

2010. Magdalena Dobromila Rettigova (cookery writer) Commemoration.

601	**345**	12k. multicoloured	2·00	1·50

346 Skier

2010. Winter Paralympics, Vancouver.

602	**346**	18k. multicoloured	3·00	2·30

347 Speed Skater

2010. Winter Olympic Games, Vancouver.

603	**347**	18k. multicoloured	3·00	2·30

348 Exhibition Pavillion

2010. Expo 2010, Shanghai, China. Sheet 110×95 mm.

MS604	**348**	35k. multicoloured	6·00	6·00

349 Children carrying Easter Eggs and Whips

2010. Easter.

605	**349**	10k. multicoloured	1·80	1·30

350 Karel Hynek Macha

2010. Birth Bicentenary of Karel Hynek Macha (poet). Sheet 108×78 mm.

MS606	**350**	43k. multicoloured	7·25	7·25

350a Hands holding Medal

2010. Martina Sablikova, Speed Skating Gold Medallist, Winter Olympic Games, Vancouver

606a	**350a**	10k. multicoloured	1·80	1·30

350b Kasim Ushag Carpet

2010. Transcaucasian Carpets. Multicoloured.

606b	21k. Type **350b**	4·00	3·00
606c	24k. Chndzoresk carpet	3·75	3·25

350c Enrique Stanko Vraz

2010. 150th Birth Anniv of Enrique Stanko Vraz (traveller)

606d	**350c**	24k. multicoloured	4·00	3·00

350d Fifinka

2010. Fifinka (character from *Ctyrlistek* comic book by Jaroslav Nemcek)

606e	**350d**	A (10k.) multicoloured	1·80	1·30

351 Charles Bridge and Prague Castle (image scaled to 73% of original size)

2010. Prague Castle on Stamps Exhibition.

607	**351**	17k. purple-brown	3·50	3·50

352 Dasenka from Puppy to Adult

2010. Europa. Children's Books. *Dasenka* by Karel Capek.

608	**352**	17k. carmine-vermilion, black and new blue	3·00	2·30

353 Pitrysek (character from *Putovani za svestkovou vuni* written by Ludvik Askenazy and illustrated by Helena Zmatlikova)

2010. For Children. Helena Zmatlikova (illustrator) Commemoration

609	**353**	10k. multicoloured	1·80	1·30

354 Sarah Bernhard as *Gismonda*

2010. 150th Birth Anniv of Alphonse (Alfons) Maria Mucha. Multicoloured

610	E (17k.) Type **354**	3·50	2·75
611	Z (18k.) *Zodiac* (43×55 mm)	3·75	3·00

355 Zarské Hills

2010. Nature Conservation

612	**355**	10k. multicoloured	1·80	1·30

356 Klatovy

2010. Tourism. Multicoloured.

613	12k. Type **356**	2·00	1·50
614	14k. Stramberk	2·20	1·70

357 John of Luxembourg and Elisabeth of Bohemia

2010. 700th Anniv of Accession of House of Luxembourg to Czech Throne

615	**357**	17k. multicoloured	3·00	2·30

A stamp of a similar design was issued by Luxembourg.

358 Astronomical Clock at Night

2010. 600th Anniv of Astronomical Clock, Prague

616	**358**	21k. multicoloured	3·50	3·50

359 Bobík (pig), Fifinka (dog), Pinda (rabbit) and Myšpulín (cat)

2010. Characters from *Ctyrlistek* (comic book by Jaroslav Nemcek)

617 **359** A (10k.) multicoloured 1·80 1·30

360 *Tichodroma muraria* (wallcreeper) and *Papilio machaon* (Old World swallowtail)

2010. Lower Morava, UNESCO Biosphere Reserve

MS618 119×170 mm. 10k. Type **360**; 12k. *Saga pedo* (bush cricket) (40×23 mm); 14k. *Lacerta viridis* (Eastern green lizard) (40×23 mm); 18k. *Upupa epops* (hoopoe) 9·25 9·25

361 Children and Stamp Album

2010. Philately. Multicoloured.

619 A (10k.) Type **361** 1·80 1·30

620 E (17k.) Boy holding magnifier and stamp 2·75 1·70

362 Players and Basket

2010. FIBA Women's Basketball Championships, Czech Republic

621 **362** 17k. multicoloured 3·00 2·30

363 Iris

2010. Flowers. Multicoloured.

622 25k. Type **363** 3·75 2·50

623 30k. Tulip 5·75 3·25

364 Anemone

2010. Flowers

624 **364** 4k. multicoloured 1·00 1·00

365 Postal Elves and Early Austrian Postal Administration Shield

2010. Postal Museum

625 **365** A (10k.) multicoloured 1·00 1·00

366 Adolf Branold

2010. Birth Centenaries. Multicoloured.

626 10k. Type **366** (writer and playwright) 1·80 1·30

627 12k. Karel Zeman (film director, graphic designer, puppeteer and animator) 2·00 1·40

367 Myšpulín

2010. Characters from *Ctyrlistek* (comic book by Jaroslav Nemcek)

628 A (10k.) multicoloured 1·80 1·30

368 Ústi nad Labem Cable Stay Bridge

2010. Technical Monuments

629 10k. azure, new blue and indigo 1·80 1·30

630 12k. pale green, pale turquoise and slate-green 2·00 1·40

Designs: 10k. Type **368**; 12k. Pisek Stone Bridge (oldest bridge in Czech Republic).

369 Stove

2010. Traditional Stoves. Art Deco Period. Multicoloured.

631 10k. Type **369** 1·80 1·30

632 20k. Stove with arched over mantle, green curved pillars and top 3·50 2·50

370 The Nativity (illustration from hymnal)

2009. Christmas

633 **370** 10k. multicoloured 1·80 1·30

2010. Art (22nd series)

634 24k. multicoloured 4·00 2·50

635 26k. multicoloured 4·75 3·75

636 30k. multicoloured 5·25 4·25

Designs:—24k. *Paris and Helena* (Karel Skréta) (40×50 mm); 26k. *Piskari* (sand bargeman) (Milos Jiránek) (40×50 mm); 30k. *Jaro* (spring) (Karel Spilar) (50×40 mm)

371 Digital Pictogram of Census

2011. Census 2011

637 **371** 10k. bright apple green and black 1·80 1·30

372 Kaspar Maria von Sternberk

2011. Kaspar Maria von Sternberk (19th-century natural scientist) Commemoration

MS638 81×110 mm. **372** 43k. black, olive-green and bright crimson 8·75 6·50

373 Mail Coach on Charles Bridge

2011. Czech Stamp Production

639 **373** 10k. multicoloured 1·80 1·30

374 St. Agnes

2011. 800th Birth Anniv of St. Agnes of Bohemia (princess who lived a life of charity and piety)

640 **374** 12k. multicoloured 2·00 1·50

375 Pinda (rabbit)

2011. Character from *Ctyrlistek* (comic book by Jaroslav Nemcek)

641 **375** A (10k.) multicoloured 1·80 1·30

376 Imperial Fortress Chapel, St. Nicolas Church and Half-timbered House (950th anniv of Cheb)

2011. Cultural Heritage. Multicoloured.

642 12k. Type **376** 2·00 1·50

643 14k. Entrance portal and Black Madonna, Black Madonna House, Prague (cubist architecture) 2·30 1·70

377 Coat of Arms

2011. 500th Birth Anniv of Jiri Melantrich of Aventino (Renaissance printer and publisher)

644 **377** 30k. black, vermilion and new blue 5·50 4·00

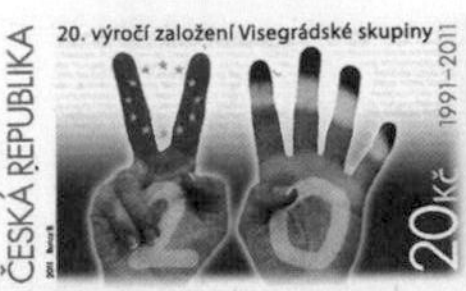

378 Hands inscribed '20

2011. 20th Anniv of Visegrad Group (regional alliance of Czech Republic, Hungary, Poland and Slovakia)

645 **378** 20k. multicoloured 3·75 2·75

379 South, North and West Bohemian Gables

2011. Folk Architecture

646 A (10k.) black, azure and new blue 1·80 30

647 E (20k.) black, pink and olive-bistre 3·75 2·75

Designs:- 646, Type **379**; 647, North Bohemian gable, Central Bohemian gateway, Wallachian cottage and South Bohemian gable.

380 Peter Vok and Vilem of Rozmberk

2011. 400th Death Anniv of Petr Vok of Rozmberk (ruler and philanthropist) and Vilem of Rozmberk (ruler, politician and leader of moderate Catholics) Commemoration

MS648 120×110 mm. **380** 49k. sepia, claret and olive-green 8·50 8·50

381 Chicks in Nest and Spring Flowers

2011. Easter

649 **381** A (10k.) multicoloured 1·80 1·30

382 Vlasta Burian

2011. Josef Vlastimil (Vlasta) Burian (actor and comedian) Commemoration

650 **382** 10k. black, rosine and dull ultramarine 1·80 1·30

383 Dancer

2011. Bicentenary of Prague Conservatory

651	**383**	10k. multicoloured	1·80	1·30

384 Bobik

2011. Character from *Ctyrlistek* (comic book by Jaroslav Nemcek)

652	**384**	A (10k.) multicoloured	1·80	1·30

385 River and Alluvial Forest

2011. Europa

653	**385**	20k. multicoloured	3·75	2·75

386 Little Witch and Raven

2011. For Children

654	**386**	10k. multicoloured	1·80	1·30

387 Jan Kašpar and Aircraft

2011. Centenary of Jan Kašpar's First Public Flight

655	**387**	21k. multicoloured	4·00	3·00

388 Bodies in Old Town Square

2011. 390th Anniv of Execution of 27 Protestant Leaders in Old Town Square, Prague

656	**388**	26k. black and rosine	4·75	3·75

Pt. 5

CZECHOSLOVAK ARMY IN SIBERIA

During the War of 1914–18 many Czech and Slovak soldiers in the Austro-Hungarian armies surrendered to the Russian Army. After the war many of these formed an army in Siberia and fought the Bolshevists. They issued stamps for their own postal service and these were also sold to the public on the Siberian Railway.

100 kopeks = 1 rouble.

1 Church in Irkutsk

3 Sentry

1919. Imperf.

1	**1**	25k. red	15·00	22·00
2	-	50k. green	40·00	40·00
3	**3**	1r. red	40·00	45·00

DESIGN: 50k. Armoured train "Orlik".

1920. Perf.

4	**1**	25k. red	15·00	15·00
5	-	50k. green (as No. 2)	35·00	38·00
6	**3**	1r. brown	40·00	38·00

4 Lion of Bohemia

1919

7	**4**	(25k.) red and blue	2·75

1920. No. 7 optd 1920.

8	(25k.) red and blue	7·00

1920. No. 8 surch.

9	2(k.) red and blue	20·00
10	3(k.) red and blue	20·00
11	5(k.) red and blue	20·00
12	10(k.) red and blue	20·00
13	15(k.) red and blue	20·00
14	25(k.) red and blue	20·00
15	35(k.) red and blue	20·00
16	50(k.) red and blue	20·00
17	1r. red and blue	20·00

Pt. 5

CZECHOSLOVAKIA

Formed in 1918 by the Czechs of Bohemia and Moravia and the Slovaks of northern Hungary (both part of Austro–Hungarian Empire). Occupied by Germany in 1939 (see note after No. 393c); independence restored 1945.

On 31 December 1992 the Czech and Slovak Federative Republic was dissolved, the two constituent republics becoming independent as the Czech Republic and Slovakia.

100 haleru = 1 koruna.

1

1918. Roul.

1	**1**	10h. blue	13·50	15·00
2	**1**	20h. red	13·50	15·00

2 Hradcany, Prague

1918. (a) Imperf.

4	**2**	3h. mauve	10	10
9	**2**	30h. olive	25	10
10	**2**	40h. orange	25	10
12	**2**	100h. brown	65	10
14	**2**	400h. violet	1·40	25

(b) Imperf or perf.

5		5h. green	10	10
6		10h. red	10	10
7		20h. green	10	10
8		25h. blue	10	10
13		200h. blue	1·10	10

3

1919. Imperf or perf.

3	**3**	1h. brown	10	10
38	**3**	5h. green	10	10
39	**3**	10h. green	10	10
40	**3**	15h. red	10	10
41	**3**	20h. red	10	10
28	**3**	25h. purple	10	10
49	**3**	30h. mauve	10	10
11	**3**	50h. purple	25	10
30	**3**	50h. blue	25	10
50	**3**	60h. orange	25	10
32	**3**	75h. green	65	10
33	**3**	80h. green	1·10	10
34	**3**	120h. black	1·10	40
35	**3**	300h. green	3·50	40
36	**3**	500h. brown	2·10	35
37	**3**	1000h. purple	11·50	80

6 7

1919. 1st Anniv of Independence and Czechoslovak Legion Commemoration.

61	**6**	15h. green	10	10
62	**6**	25h. brown	10	10
63	**6**	50h. blue	10	10
64	**7**	75h. grey	10	10
65	**7**	100h. brown	10	10
66	**7**	120h. violet on yellow	10	10

1919. Charity. Stamps of Austria optd POSTA CESKOSLOVENSKA 1919. A. Postage stamp issue of 1916.

67	**49**	3h. violet	10	40
68	**49**	5h. green	10	40
69	**49**	6h. orange	50	60
70	**49**	10h. purple	60	90
71	**49**	12h. blue	60	60
72	**60**	15h. red	10	10
73	**60**	20h. green	10	10
75	**60**	25h. blue	10	25
76	**60**	30h. violet	10	25
77	**51**	40h. green	10	25
78	**51**	50h. green	10	25
79	**51**	60h. blue	10	25
80	**51**	80h. brown	10	25
81	**51**	90h. purple	45	60
82	**51**	1k. red on yellow	35	40
83aa	**52**	2k. blue	1·40	2·10
85aa	**52**	3k. red	6·00	7·00
87a	**52**	4k. green	14·00	14·00
89a	**52**	10k. violet	£325	£300

B. Air stamps of 1918 optd FLUGPOST or surch also.

91		1k.50 on 2k. mauve	£150	80·00
92		2k.50 on 3k. yellow	£150	£110
93		4k. grey	£600	£500

C. Newspaper stamp of 1908. Imperf.

94	**N43**	10h. red	£1500	£1500

D. Newspaper stamps of 1916. Imperf.

95	**N53**	2h. brown	10	25
96	**N53**	4h. green	25	35
97	**N53**	6h. blue	25	30
98	**N53**	10h. orange	3·50	4·50
99	**N53**	30h. red	1·75	1·50

E. Express Newspaper stamps of 1916.

100	**N54**	2h. red on yellow	29·00	25·00
101	**N54**	5h. green on yellow	£1400	£900

F. Express Newspaper stamps of 1917.

102	**N61**	2h. red on yellow	10	15
103	**N61**	5h. green on yellow	10	15

G. Postage Due stamps of 1908.

104	**D44**	2h. red	£5250	£3500
105	**D44**	4h. red	28·00	21·00
106	**D44**	6h. red	11·00	8·00
108	**D44**	14h. red	55·00	4·00
109	**D44**	25h. red	35·00	32·00
110	**D44**	30h. red	£350	£275
111	**D44**	50h. red	£1100	£700

H. Postage Due stamps of 1916.

112	**D55**	5h. red	10	10
113	**D55**	10h. red	15	20
114	**D55**	15h. red	15	20
115	**D55**	20h. red	1·90	2·40
116	**D55**	25h. red	1·10	1·50
117	**D55**	30h. red	45	80
118	**D55**	40h. red	1·10	1·50
119	**D55**	50h. red	£550	£250
120	**D56**	1k. blue	10·50	7·00
121	**D56**	5k. blue	45·00	30·00
122	**D56**	10k. blue	£425	£250

I. Postage Due stamps of 1916 (optd PORTO or surch 15 also).

123	**36**	1h. black	27·00	17·00
124	-	15h. on 2h. violet	£130	85·00

J. Postage Due stamps of 1917 (surch PORTO and value).

125	**50**	10h. on 24h. blue	70·00	75·00
126	**50**	15h. on 36h. violet	45	60
127	**50**	20h. on 54h. orange	70·00	90·00
128	**50**	50h. on 42h. brown	50	65

1919. Various stamps of Hungary optd POSTA CESKOSLOVENSKA 1919. A. Postage stamp issue of 1900 ("Turul" type).

129	**7**	1f. grey	£2250	£1600
130	**7**	2f. yellow	4·00	5·25
131	**7**	3f. orange	50·00	25·00
132	**7**	6f. olive	4·75	5·25
133	**7**	50f. lake on blue	60	60
134	**7**	60f. green on red	50·00	35·00
135	**7**	70f. brown on green	£2750	£1600

B. Postage stamp issue of 1916 ("Harvester" and "Parliament" types).

136	**18**	2f. brown (No. 245)	10	10
137	**18**	3f. red	10	10
138	**18**	5f. green	10	10
139	**18**	6f. blue	50	60
140	**18**	10f. red (No. 250)	1·00	1·25
141	**18**	10f. red (No. 243)	£400	£200
142	**18**	15f. purple (No. 251)	10	25
143	**18**	15f. purple (No. 244)	£200	£110
144	**18**	20f. brown	8·00	9·00
145	**18**	25f. blue	60	60
146	**18**	35f. brown	8·00	10·50
147	**18**	40f. green	2·10	2·00
148	**19**	50f. purple	55	65
149	**19**	75f. green	50	50
150	**19**	80f. green	1·10	1·10
151	**19**	1k. red	1·25	1·25
152	**19**	2k. brown	7·75	10·50
153	**19**	3k. grey and violet	38·00	35·00
154	**19**	5k. lt brown & brown	£130	65·00
155	**19**	10k. mauve and brown	£1600	£850

C. Postage stamp issue of 1918 ("Charles" and "Zita" types).

156	**27**	10f. red	10	10
157	**27**	20f. brown	25	30
158	**27**	25f. blue	1·75	1·10
159	**28**	40f. green	3·00	2·50
160	**28**	50f. purple	45·00	26·00

D. War Charity stamps of 1916.

161	**20**	10+2f. red	30	60
162	-	15+2f. lilac (No. 265)	50	90
163	**22**	40+2f. red	6·75	3·75

E. Postage stamps of 1919 ("Harvester" type inscr "MAGYAR POSTA").

164	**30**	10f. red (No. 305)	8·75	9·00
165	**30**	20f. brown	£6500	£6500

F. Newspaper stamp of 1900.

166	**N9**	2f. orange (No. N136)	10	30

G. Express Letter stamp of 1916.

167	**E18**	2f. olive & red (No. E245)	10	30

H. Postage Due stamps of 1903 with figures in black.

168	**D9**	12f. green	£5500	£4000
170	**D9**	1f. green (No. D170)	£1400	£1000
172	**D9**	50f. green	£325	£225
173	**D9**	2f. green	£900	£550
174	**D9**	5f. green	£1800	£1100

I. Postage Due stamps of 1915 with figures in red.

176		1f. green (No. D190)	£160	£110
177		2f. green	70	50
178		5f. green	10·50	14·00
179		6f. green	1·75	1·75
180		10f. green	35	45
181		12f. green	2·10	2·40
182		15f. green	6·00	9·00
183		20f. green	80	1·10
184		30f. green	35·00	38·00

9 President Masaryk

1920

185	**9**	125h. blue	70	20
186	**9**	500h. black	3·00	2·00
187	**9**	1000h. brown	5·25	4·25

10 **11** Allegories of Republic **12** Hussite

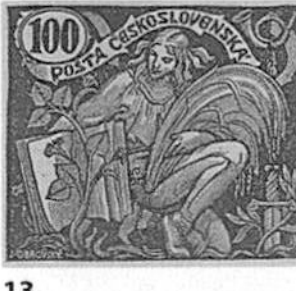

13

1920

188	**10**	5h. blue	10	10
189	**10**	5h. violet	10	10
190	**10**	10h. green	10	10
191	**10**	10h. olive	10	10
192	**10**	15h. brown	10	10
193b	**10**	20h. orange	10	10
196	**11**	20h. red	10	10
194a	**10**	25h. green	15	10
197	**11**	25h. brown	10	10
195	**10**	30h. purple	4·00	10
198	**11**	30h. purple	10	10
199	**11**	40h. brown	10	10
200	**11**	50h. red	10	10
201	**11**	50h. green	10	10
202	**11**	60h. blue	10	10
203	**12**	80h. violet	10	25
204	**12**	90h. sepia	35	50
205	**13**	100h. green	45	10
206	**11**	100h. brown	45	10
227	**13**	100h. red on yellow	2·00	10
207	**11**	150h. red	3·50	70
208	**11**	185h. orange	1·40	20
209	**13**	200h. purple	80	10
228	**13**	200h. blue on yellow	7·00	10
210	**11**	250h. green	2·75	45
211	**13**	300h. red	1·75	10
229	**13**	300h. purple on yellow	5·25	10
212	**13**	400h. brown	4·75	55
213	**13**	500h. green	6·00	55
214	**13**	600h. purple	8·00	55

1920. Air. Surch with airplane and value. Imperf or perf.

215	**2**	14k. on 200h. blue (No. 13)	18·00	25·00
216	**3**	24k. on 500h. brn (No. 36)	45·00	38·00
220	**3**	28k. on 1000h. pur (No. 37)	45·00	32·00

1920. Red Cross Fund. Surch with new value in emblem.

221	**2**	40h.+20h. yellow	80	95
222	**3**	60h.+20h. green	80	95
223	**9**	125h.+25h. blue	2·25	2·75

1922. Surch with airplane and value.

224	**13**	50 on 100h. green	1·75	2·25
225	**13**	100 on 200h. purple	4·25	3·75
226	**13**	250 on 400h. brown	7·00	8·00

18 President Masaryk, after portrait by M. Savatimsky

1923. 5th Anniv of Republic.

230	**18**	50h. (+50h.) green	1·00	65
231	**18**	100h. (+100h.) red	1·40	1·10
232	**18**	200h. (+200h.) blue	7·00	6·50
233	**18**	300h. (+300h.) brown	8·50	8·00

20

1925

234	**20**	40h. orange	85	20
235	**20**	50h. green	1·75	10
236	**20**	60h. purple	1·90	10
237	**18**	1k. red	1·90	10
238	**18**	2k. blue	1·00	30
245	**18**	3k. brown	6·75	10
240	**18**	5k. green	1·75	30

The 1, 2 and 3k. (which with the 5k. differ slightly in design from the haleru values) come in various sizes, differing in some cases in the details of the designs.

1925. International Olympic Congress. Optd CONGRES OLYMP. INTERNAT. PRAHA 1925.

246	50h. (+50h.) green	6·00	10·00
247	100h. (+100h.) red	9·25	14·00
248	200h. (+200h.) blue	55·00	90·00

1926. 8th All-Sokol Display, Prague. Optd VIII. SLET VSESOKOLSKY PRAHA 1926.

249	50h. (+50h.) green	4·75	6·00
250	100h. (+100h.) red	4·75	6·00
251	200h. (+200h.) blue	23·00	21·00
252	300h. (+300h.) brown	35·00	45·00

23a

1926

254b	**23a**	50h. green	10	10
254c	**23a**	60h. purple	60	10
254d	**23a**	1k. red	25	10

25 Karluv Tyn Castle **26** Strahov **27** Pernstyn Castle

28 Orava Castle **30** Hradcany, Prague

1926. Perf or imperf × perf.

267	**25**	20h. red	25	10
268	**27**	30h. green	15	10
258	**28**	40h. brown	50	10
259	**25**	1k.20 purple	35	45
270	**26**	1k.20 purple	35	10
271	**25**	1k.50 red	35	10
263	**30**	2k. blue	90	10
272	**27**	2k. green	25	10
273	**25**	2k.50 blue	5·25	25
273a	-	2k.50 blue	35	10
264a	**30**	3k. red	1·75	10
273b	**28**	3k. brown	45	10
265	-	4k. purple	6·25	65
277	-	5k. green	9·00	1·10

DESIGNS—As T **25/28**: 2k.50 (No. 273a), Statue of St. Wenceslas, Prague. As T **30**: 4, 5k. Upper Tatra.

32 Hradek Castle **33** Pres. Masaryk

1928. 10th Anniv of Independence.

278	**32**	30h. black	10	10
279	-	40h. brown	10	10
280	-	50h. green	15	15
281	-	60h. red	15	25
282	-	1k. red	25	20
283	-	1k.20 purple	40	65
284	-	2k. blue	45	65
285	-	2k.50 blue	1·40	1·75
286	**33**	3k. sepia	1·10	1·25
287	-	5k. violet	1·40	2·25

DESIGNS—HORIZ: 40h. Town Hall, Levoca; 50h. Telephone Exchange, Prague; 60h. Village of Jasina; 1k. Hluboka Castle; 1k.20, Pilgrim's House, Velehrad; 2k.50, The Grand Tatra. VERT: 2k. Brno Cathedral; 5k. Town Hall, Prague.

34 National Arms

1929. Perf or imperf × perf.

287a	**34**	5h. blue	10	10
287b	**34**	10h. brown	10	10
288	**34**	20h. red	10	10
289	**34**	25h. green	10	10
290	**34**	30h. purple	10	10
291a	**34**	40h. brown	10	10

35 St. Wenceslas on Horseback

1929. Death Millenary of St. Wenceslas.

293	**35**	50h. green	15	10
294	-	60h. violet	30	10
295	-	2k. blue	75	35
296	-	3k. brown	1·10	25
297	-	5k. purple	4·00	2·50

DESIGNS: 2k. Foundation of St. Vitus's Church; 3k., 5k. Martyrdom of St. Wenceslas.

36 Brno Cathedral

1929

298	**36**	3k. brown	1·10	10
299	-	4k. blue	4·00	60
300	-	5k. green	3·00	35
301	-	10k. violet	8·75	3·00

DESIGNS: 4k. Tatra Mountains; 5k. Town Hall, Prague; 10k. St. Nicholas Church, Prague.

38

1930

302a	**38**	50h. green	10	10
303	**38**	60h. purple	50	10
304	**38**	1k. red	10	10

See also No. 373.

39

1930. 80th Birthday of President Masaryk.

305	**39**	2k. green	80	35
306	**39**	3k. red	1·25	35
307	**39**	5k. blue	3·25	2·40
308	**39**	10k. black	7·00	4·75

40 Fokker F.IXD **41** Smolik S.19

1930. Air.

394	**40**	30h. violet	10	10
309	**40**	50h. green	10	20
310	**40**	1k. red	25	30
311	**41**	2k. green	55	70
312	**41**	3k. purple	1·40	95
313	-	4k. blue	85	90
314	-	5k. brown	2·75	1·90
315	-	10k. blue	4·00	5·25
316	-	20k. violet	5·00	5·00

DESIGNS—As Type **41**: 4, 5k. Smolik S.19 with tree in foreground; 10, 20k. Fokker F.IXD over Prague.

43 Krumlov

1932. Views.

317	-	3k.50 purple (Krivoklat)	1·40	1·00
318	-	4k. blue (Orlik)	1·60	60
319	**43**	5k. green	2·75	60

44 Dr. Miroslav Tyrs

1932. Birth Centenary of Dr. Tyrs, founder of the "Sokol" Movement.

320	**44**	50h. green	30	10
321	**44**	1k. red	80	10
322	-	2k. blue	5·00	40
323	-	3k. brown	8·00	50

On the 2k. and 3k. the portrait faces left.

46 Dr. M. Tyrs

1933

324	**46**	60h. violet	10	10

47 Church and Episcopal Palace, Nitra

1933. 1100th Anniv of Foundation of 1st Christian Church at Nitra.

325	**47**	50h. green	30	10
326	-	1k. red (Church gateway)	3·25	25

49 Frederick Smetana

1934. 50th Death Anniv of Smetana.

327	**49**	50h. green	10	10

50 Consecrating Colours at Kiev

1934. 20th Anniv of Czechoslovak Foreign Legions.

328	**50**	50h. green	20	10
329	-	1k. red	25	10
330	-	2k. blue	1·75	25
331	-	3k. brown	2·25	30

DESIGNS—HORIZ: 1k. French battalion enrolling at Bayonne. VERT: 2k. Standard of the Russian Legion; 3k. French, Russian and Serbian legionaries.

52 Antonin Dvorak

1934. 30th Death Anniv of Dvorak.

332	**52**	50h. green	10	10

53 "Where is my Fatherland?"

1934. Centenary of Czech National Anthem.

333	**53**	1k. purple	35	20
334	**53**	2k. blue	90	40

54 Autograph portrait of Pres. Masaryk **55**

1935. 85th Birthday of President Masaryk.

335	**54**	50h. green	15	10
336	**54**	1k. red	30	10
337	**55**	2k. blue	1·00	35
338	**55**	3k. brown	2·10	50

See also No. 374.

56 Czech Monument, Arras

1935. 20th Anniv of Battle of Arras.

339	**56**	1k. red	40	10
340	**56**	2k. blue	95	45

57 Gen. M. R. Stefanik

1935. 16th Death Anniv of Gen. Stefanik.

341	**57**	50h. green	10	10

58 St. Cyril and St. Methodius

1935. Prague Catholic Congress.

342	**58**	50h. green	15	10
343	**58**	1k. red	25	10
344	**58**	2k. blue	1·10	45

59 J. A. Komensky (Comenius) **60** Dr. Edward Benes **60a** Gen. M. R. Stefanik

61 Pres. Masaryk

1935

345	**59**	40h. blue	10	10
346	**60**	50h. green	10	10
390	**60a**	50h. green	10	10
347	**60a**	60h. violet	10	10
391	**60a**	60h. blue	7·00	14·00
348	**61**	1k. purple	10	10
395	**61**	1k. purple	10	10

No. 390 differs from No. 341 in having an ornament in place of the word "HALERU".

No. 348 has "I Kc" in value tablets, No. 395 "I K".

62 Symbolic of Infancy

1936. Child Welfare.

349	-	50h.+50h. green	25	35
350	**62**	1k.+50h. red	40	55
351	-	2k.+50h. blue	1·10	1·50

DESIGN: 50h., 2k. Grandfather, mother and child from centre of Type **62** (enlarged).

63 K. H. Macha

1936. Death Centenary of Macha (poet).

352	**63**	50h. green	10	10
353	**63**	1k. red	30	10

64 Banska Bystrica **65** Podebrady

1936

354	-	1k.20 purple	10	10
355	**64**	1k.50 red	10	10
355a	-	1k.60 olive	10	10
356	-	2k. green	10	10
357	-	2k.50 blue	10	10
358	-	3k. brown	10	10
359	-	3k.50 violet	70	45
360	**65**	4k. violet	30	10
361	-	5k. green	30	10
362	-	10k. blue	55	45

DESIGNS—As Type **64**: 1k.20, Palanok Castle; 1k.60, St. Barbara's Church, Kutna Hora; 2k. Zvikov (Klingden Berg) Castle; 2k.50, Strecno Castle; 3k. Hruba Skala Castle (Cesky Raj); 3k.50, Slavkov Castle; 5k. Town Hall, Olomouc (23½×29½ mm). As Type **65**: 10k. Bratislava and Danube.

66 President Benes

1937

363	**66**	50h. green	10	10

67 Mother and Child

68 "Lullaby"

1937. Child Welfare.

364	**67**	50h.+50h. green	30	50
365	**67**	1k.+50h. red	45	65
366	**68**	2k.+1k. blue	90	1·50

69 Czech Legionaries

1937. 20th Anniv of Battle of Zborov.

367	**69**	50h. green	15	10
368	**69**	1k. red	15	10

70 Prague

1937. 16th Anniv of Founding of Little Entente.

369	**70**	2k. green	45	10
370	**70**	2k.50 blue	70	50

71 J. E. Purkyne

1937. 150th Birth Anniv of J. E. Purkyne (physiologist).

371	**71**	50h. green	10	10
372	**71**	1k. red	15	10

1937. Mourning for Pres. Masaryk. As T 38 and 55, but panels of T 55 dated "14.IX.1937".

373	**38**	50h. black	10	10
374	**55**	2k. black	25	10

1937. Labour Congress, Prague. Optd B.I.T. 1937.

375	**66**	50h. green	15	30
376	**64**	1k.50 red	15	30
377	-	2k. green (No. 356)	40	60

72a Gen. Stefanik Memorial

1937. Philatelic Exhibition, Bratislava. (a) Sheet 150×110 mm.

MS377a 50h. blue (Poprad Lake, Tatra Mountains); 1k. red (as T **72a**) 1·50 2·25

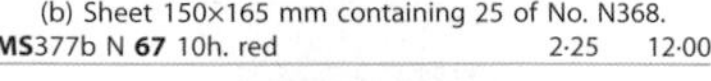

(b) Sheet 150×165 mm containing 25 of No. N368.

MS377b N **67** 10h. red 2·25 12·00

73 Peregrine Falcon

1938. 10th International Sokol Display, Prague.

378	**73**	50h. green	30	10
379	**73**	1k. red	30	10

74 Pres. Masaryk and Slovak Girl

1938. Child Welfare and Birthday of Late President Masaryk.

380	**74**	50h.+50h. green	35	50
381	**74**	1k.+50h. red	45	65

MS381a 71×91 mm. Memorial sheet **74**; 2k.+3k. black. Imperf 2·40 3·50

75 Czech Legionaries at Bachmac

1938. 20th Anniv of Battles in Russia, Italy and France. Inscr "1918 1938".

382	**75**	50h. green	20	10
383	-	50h. green	10	10
384	-	50h. green	10	10

DESIGNS: Czech Legionaries at Doss Alto (No. 383) and at Vouziers (No. 384).

76 J. Fugner

1938. 10th Sokol Summer Games.

385	**76**	50h. green	10	10
386	**76**	1k. red	10	10
387	**76**	2k. blue	15	10

77 Armament Factories, Pilsen

1938. Provincial Economic Council Meeting, Pilsen.

388	**77**	50h. green	10	10

77a Vysehrad

1938. Prague Philatelic Exhibition.

MS388a 148×105 mm. 50h. blue (T **77a**); 1k. red (Hradcany, Prague) 3·25 3·50

78 St. Elizabeth's Cathedral, Kosice

1938. Kosice Cultural Exhibition.

389	**78**	50h. green	10	10

79 "Peace"

1938. 20th Anniv of Czech Republic.

392	**79**	2k. blue	15	10
393	**79**	3k. brown	35	10

MS393a 71×90 m. 2k. (+8k.) blue (T **79**) 2·25 3·50

1939. Inauguration of Slovak Parliament. No. 362 surcharged Otvorenie slovenskeho snemu 18.1.1939 and 300 h between bars.

393b	300h. on 10k. blue	60	3·00

No. 393b was only issued in Slovakia but was withdrawn prior to the establishment of the Slovak state. The used price is for cancelled to order stamps.

80 Jasina

1939. Inaug of Carpatho-Ukrainian Parliament.

393c	**80**	3k. blue	10·00	65·00

The used price is for cancelled-to-order.

From mid-1939 until 1945, Czechoslovakia was divided into the German Protectorate of Bohemia and Moravia and the independent state of Slovakia. Both these countries issued their own stamps. Germany had already occupied Sudetenland where a number of unauthorized local issues were made at Asch, Karlsbad, Konstantinsbad, Hiklasdorf, Reichenberg-Maffersdorf and Rumburg. Hungary occupied Carpatho-Ukraine and the stamps of Hungary were used there. In 1945, upon liberation, stamps of Czechoslovakia were once again issued.

81 Clasped Hands

82 Arms and Soldier

1945. Kosice Issue. Imperf.

396	**81**	1k.50 purple	1·75	2·00
397	**82**	2k. red	20	25
398	**82**	5k. green	2·00	1·75
399	**82**	6k. blue	45	40
400	**81**	9k. red	25	35
401	**81**	13k. brown	65	70
402	**81**	20k. blue	1·60	1·40

MS402a 132×120 mm. Nos. 397/9 3·50 4·25

83 Arms and Linden Leaf

1945. Bratislava Issue. Imperf.

403	**83**	50h. green	10	10
404	**83**	1k. purple	10	10
405	**83**	1k.50 red	10	10
406	**83**	2k. blue	10	10
407	**83**	2k.40 red	30	30
408	**83**	3k. brown	10	10
409	**83**	4k. green	15	10
410	**83**	6k. violet	15	10
411	**83**	10k. brown	30	20

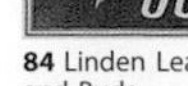

84 Linden Leaf and Buds

85 Linden Leaf and Flower

1945. Prague Issue.

412	**84**	10h. black	10	10
413	**84**	30h. brown	10	10
414	**84**	50h. green	10	10
415	**84**	60h. blue	10	10
416	**85**	60h. blue	10	10
417	**85**	80h. red	10	10
418	**85**	120h. red	10	10
419	**85**	300h. purple	10	10
420	**85**	500h. green	10	10

86 Pres. Masaryk

1945. Moscow Issue. Perf.

421	**86**	5h. violet	10	10
422	**86**	10h. yellow	10	10
423	**86**	20h. brown	10	10
424	**86**	50h. green	10	10
425	**86**	1k. red	10	10
426	**86**	2k. blue	10	10

87 Staff Capt. Ridky

1945. War Heroes.

427	**87**	5h. grey	10	10
428	-	10h. brown	10	10
429	-	20h. red	10	10
430	-	25h. red	10	10
431	-	30h. violet	15	10
432	-	40h. brown	10	10
433	-	50h. green	10	10
434	-	60h. violet	15	10
435	**87**	1k. red	10	10
436	-	1k.50 red	10	10
437	-	2k. blue	10	10
438	-	2k.50 violet	10	10
439	-	3k. brown	10	10
440	-	4k. mauve	10	10
441	-	5k. green	10	10
442	-	10k. blue	15	10

PORTRAITS: 10h., 1k.50, Dr. Novak. 20h., 2k. Capt. O. Jaros. 25h., 2k.50, Staff Capt. Zimprich. 30h., 3k. Lt. J. Kral. 40h., 4k. J. Gabcik (parachutist). 50h., 5k. Staff Capt. Vasatko. 60h., 10k. Fr. Adamek.

88 Allied Flags

89 Russian Soldier and Slovak Partisan

1945. 1st Anniv of Slovak Rising.

443	**88**	1k.50 red	10	10
444	-	2k. blue	10	10
445	**89**	4k. brown	20	25
446	-	4k.50 violet	20	25
447	-	5k. green	25	40

MS447a 148×210 mm. Nos. 443/7 32·00 42·00

DESIGNS—VERT: 2k. Banska Bystrica. HORIZ: 4k.50, Sklabina; 5k. Strecno and partisan.

90 Pres. Masaryk

91 Pres. Benes

1945

452	-	30h. purple	10	10
448	**90**	50h. brown	10	10
453	**91**	60h. blue	15	10
449	-	80h. green	10	10
454	-	1k. orange	10	10
455	**90**	1k.20 red	15	10
456	**90**	1k.20 mauve	10	10
450	**91**	1k.60 green	15	10
457	-	2k.40 red	15	10
458	**91**	3k. purple	20	10
459	**90**	4k. blue	15	10
460	**90**	5k. green	20	10
461	**91**	7k. black	25	10
462	-	10k. blue	55	10
451	**90**	15k. purple	50	10
462a	-	20k. brown	85	10

PORTRAIT: 30h., 80h., 1k., 2k.40, 10k., 20k. Gen. M. R. Stefanik.

92

1945. Students' World Congress, Prague.
463 **92** 1k.50+1k.50 red 10 10
464 **92** 2k.50+2k.50 blue 20 20

93 J. S. Kozina Monument

1945. Execution of Jan Stadky Kozina, 1695.
465 **93** 2k.40 red 15 10
466 **93** 4k. blue 20 25

94 St. George and Dragon

1946. Victory.
467 **94** 2k.40+2k.60 red 15 15
468 **94** 4k.+6k. blue 20 15
MS468a 79×91 mm. T **94** 4k.+6k. blue 90 1·00

94a Lockheed L.049 Constellation over Charles Bridge, Prague

1946. Air. 1st Prague–New York Flight.
468b **94a** 24k. blue on buff 90 85
See also Nos. 475/6.

95 Capt. F. Novak and Westland Lysander

96 Lockheed L.049 Constellation over Bratislava

1946. Air.
469 **95** 1k.50 red 15 10
470 **95** 5k.50 blue 35 15
471 **95** 9k. purple 60 20
472 **96** 10k. green 50 35
473 **95** 16k. violet 80 30
474 **96** 20k. blue 80 50
475 **94a** 24k. red 1·00 75
476 **94a** 50k. blue 2·00 1·25

97 K. H. Borovsky

1946. 90th Death Anniv of Borovsky (Independence advocate).
477 **97** 1k.20h. grey 10 10

98 Brno

1946
478 **98** 2k.40 red 40 15
479 - 7k.40 violet (Hodonin) (horiz) 20 10
MS479a 69×89 mm. No. 478 90 70

100 Emigrants

1946. Repatriation Fund.
480 1k.60+1k.40 brown 55 55
481 **100** 2k.40+2k.60 red 20 25
482 - 4k.+4k. blue 30 45
DESIGNS: 1k.60, Emigrants' departure; 4k. Emigrants' return.

101 President Benes

1946. Independence Day.
483 **101** 60h. blue 10 10
484 **101** 1k.60 green 10 10
485 **101** 3k. purple 10 10
486 **101** 8k. purple 20 10

102 Flag and Symbols of Transport, Industry, Agriculture and Learning

1947. "Two Year Plan".
487 **102** 1k.20 green 10 10
488 **102** 2k.40 red 10 10
489 **102** 4k. blue 50 20

103 St. Adalbert

1947. 950th Death Anniv of St. Adalbert (Bishop of Prague).
490 **103** 1k.60 black 45 45
491 **103** 2k.40 red 65 60
492 **103** 5k. green 1·00 40

104 "Grief"

105 Rekindling Flame of Remembrance

1947. 5th Anniv of Destruction of Lidice.
493 **104** 1k.20 black 30 30
494 **104** 1k.60 black 45 45
495 **105** 2k.40 mauve 55 45

106 Congress Emblem

1947. Youth Festival.
496 **106** 1k.20 purple 45 25
497 **106** 4k. grey 45 15

107 Pres. Masaryk

1947. 10th Death Anniv of Pres Masaryk.
498 **107** 1k.20 black on buff 15 10
499 **107** 4k. blue on cream 25 25

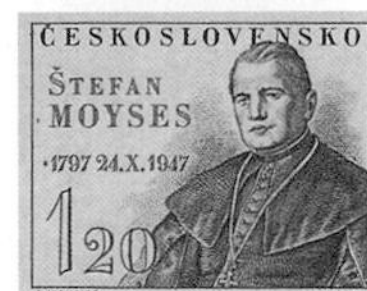
108 Stefan Moyses

1947. 150th Birth Anniv of Stefan Moyses (Slavonic Society Organizer).
500 **108** 1k.20 purple 15 10
501 **108** 4k. blue 25 25

109 "Freedom"

1947. 30th Anniv of Russian Revolution.
502 **109** 2k.40 red 30 15
503 **109** 4k. blue 50 15

110 Pres. Benes

1948
504 **110** 1k.50 brown 10 10
505 **110** 2k. purple (19×23 mm) 10 10
506 **110** 5k. blue (19×23 mm) 15 10

111 "Athletes paying Homage to Republic"

1948. 11th Sokol Congress, Prague. (a) 1st issue.
507 **111** 1k.50 brown 10 10
508 **111** 3k. red 15 10
509 **111** 5k. blue 40 10

115 Dr. J. Vanicek

(b) 2nd issue. Inscr "XI. VSESOKOLSKY SLET V PRAZE 1948".
515 **115** 1k. green 10 10
516 - 1k.50 brown 15 10
517 - 2k. blue 15 10
518 **115** 3k. purple 20 10
PORTRAIT: 1k.50, 2k. Dr. J. Scheiner.

112 Charles IV

113 St. Wenceslas and Charles IV

1948. 600th Anniv of Charles IV University, Prague.
510 **112** 1k.50 brown on buff 10 10
511 **113** 2k. brown on buff 15 10
512 **113** 3k. red on buff 15 10
513 **112** 5k. blue on buff 20 20

114 Insurgents

1948. Centenary of Abolition of Serfdom.
514 **114** 1k.50 black 10 10

117 Fr. Palacky and Dr. F. L. Rieger

1948. Cent of Constituent Assembly at Kromeriz.
519 **117** 1k.50 violet on buff 10 10
520 **117** 3k. purple on buff 15 10

118 J. M. Hurban

1948. Centenary of Slovak Insurrection.
521 **118** 1k.50 brown 10 10
522 - 3k. red (L. Stur) 10 10
523 - 5k. blue (M. Hodza) 20 20

119 President Benes

1948. Death of President Benes.
524 **119** 8k. black 10 10

120 "Independence"

1948. 30th Anniv of Independence.
525 **120** 1k.50 blue 15 10
526 **120** 3k. red 20 15

1948
526a **121** 1k. green 20 10
527 **121** 1k.50 brown 20 10
528b **121** 3k. red 30 10
529 **121** 5k. blue 55 10
530 **121** 20k. violet (23×30 mm) 60 10
MS530a 66×99 mm. 30k. red (T **121**) 3·50 3·25
772 **121** 15h. green 35 10
773 **121** 20h. brown 45 10
774 **121** 1k. lilac 1·10 10
775 **121** 3k. black 80 10
See also No. 538.

122 Czech and Russian Workers

1948. 5th Anniv of Russian Alliance.
531 **122** 3k. red 10 10

1948. 30th Anniv of First Czechoslovak Stamps. Imperf.
MS531a 70×90 mm. 10k. blue (T **2**) 2·00 1·75

123 Girl and Birds

1948. Child Welfare.

532	-	1k.50+1k. purple	30	10
533	-	2k.+1k. blue	15	10
534	**123**	3k.+1k. red	25	10

DESIGNS: 1k.50, Boy and birds; 2k. Mother and child.

124 V. I. Lenin

1949. 25th Death Anniv of Lenin.

535	**124**	1k.50 purple	30	10
536	**124**	5k. blue	30	25

125 Pres. Gottwald Addressing Rally

1949. 1st Anniv of Gottwald Government.

537	**125**	3k. brown	10	10

1949. As T 121 (23×30 mm) but inscr "UNOR 1948".

538	**121**	10k. green	35	25

126 P. O. Hviezdoslav

1949. Poets.

539	**126**	50h. purple	10	10
540	-	80h. red	10	10
541	-	1k. green	10	10
542	-	2k. blue	30	10
543	-	4k. purple	30	10
544	-	8k. black	45	10

PORTRAITS: 80h. V. Vancura. 1k. J. Sverma. 2k. J. Fucik. 4k. J. Wolker. 8k. A. Jirasek.

127 Mail Coach and Steam Train

1949. 75th Anniv of U.P.U.

545	**127**	3k. red	1·00	1·00
546	-	5k. blue	60	35
547	-	13k. green	1·60	40

DESIGNS: 5k. Mounted postman and mail van; 13k. Sailing ship and Douglas DC-2 airliner.

128 Girl Agricultural Worker **130** Industrial Worker

1949. 9th Meeting of Czechoslovak Communist Party.

548	**128**	1k.50 green	45	50
549	-	3k. red	25	25
550	**130**	5k. blue	45	50

DESIGN—HORIZ: 3k. Workers and flag.

131 F. Smetana and National Theatre, Prague

1949. 125th Birth Anniv of Smetana (composer).

551	**131**	1k.50 green	15	10
552	**131**	5k. blue	65	30

132 A. S. Pushkin

1949. 150th Birth Anniv of A. S. Pushkin (poet).

553	**132**	2k. green	25	25

133 F. Chopin and Warsaw Conservatoire

1949. Death Centenary of Chopin (composer).

554	**133**	3k. red	45	25
555	**133**	8k. purple	45	50

134 Globe and Ribbon

1949. 50th Sample Fair, Prague.

556	**134**	1k.50 purple	25	25
557	**134**	5k. blue	80	75

135 Zvolen Castle

1949

558	**135**	10k. lake	60	10

1949. Air. Nos. 469/76 surch.

559	**95**	1k. on 1k.50 red	15	10
560	**95**	3k. on 5k.50 blue	25	10
561	**95**	6k. on 9k. purple	40	10
562	**95**	7k.50 on 16k. violet	50	25
563	**96**	8k. on 10k. green	50	55
564	**96**	12k.50 on 20k. blue	90	45
565	**94a**	15k. on 24k. red	2·25	75
566	**94a**	30k. on 50k. blue	1·75	75

137 Mediaeval Miners **138** Modern Miner

1949. 700th Anniv of Czechoslovak Mining Industry and 150th Anniv of Miners' Laws.

567	**137**	1k.50 violet	50	40
568	**138**	3k. red	5·25	1·90
569	-	5k. blue	4·00	1·50

DESIGN—HORIZ: 5k. Miner with cutting machine.

139 Carpenters

1949. 2nd T.U.C., Prague. Inscr 1949".

570	**139**	1k. green	3·00	1·25

571	-	2k. purple (Mechanic)	1·90	50

140 Dove and Buildings

1949. Red Cross Fund. Inscr "CS CERVENY KRIZ".

572	**140**	1k.50h.+50h. red	3·50	1·60
573	-	3k.+1k. red	3·50	1·60

DESIGN—VERT: 3k. Dove and globe.

141 Mother and Child

1949. Child Welfare Fund. Inscr "DETEM 1949".

574	**141**	1k.50+50h. grey	3·25	1·10
575	-	3k.+1k. red	4·75	1·75

DESIGN: 3k. Father and child.

142 Joseph Stalin

1949. 70th Birth Anniv of Joseph Stalin.

576	**142**	1k.50 green on buff	75	40
577	-	3k. purple on buff	4·00	1·50

PORTRAIT: 3k. Stalin facing left.

143 Skier **144** Efficiency Badge

1950. Tatra Cup Ski Championship.

578	**143**	1k.50 blue	2·75	1·00
579	**144**	3k. red and buff	2·75	1·00
580	**143**	5k. blue	1·90	85

145 V. Mayakovsky

1950. 20th Death Anniv of Mayakovsky (poet).

581	**145**	1k.50 purple	2·10	1·10
582	**145**	3k. red	1·75	80

146 Soviet Tank Driver and Hradcany, Prague

1950. 5th Anniv of Republic (1st issue).

583	**146**	1k.50 green	25	20
584	-	2k. purple	95	80
585	-	3k. red	20	10
586	-	5k. blue	40	20

DESIGNS: 2k. "Hero of Labour" medal; 3k. Workers and Town Hall; 5k. "The Kosice Programme" (part of text).

147 Factory and Workers

1950. 5th Anniv of Republic (2nd issue).

587	**147**	1k.50 green	1·40	75
588	-	2k. brown	1·75	65
589	-	3k. red	90	35
590	-	5k. blue	90	30

DESIGNS: 2k. Crane and Tatra Mts; 3k. Labourer and tractor; 5k. Three workers.

148 S. K. Neumann

1950. 75th Birth Anniv of S. K. Neumann (writer).

591	**148**	1k.50 blue	25	10
592	**148**	3k. purple	1·10	85

149 Bozena Nemcova

1950. 130th Birth Anniv of Bozena Nemcova (authoress).

593	**149**	1k.50 blue	1·25	80
594	**149**	7k. purple	25	20

150 "Liberation of Colonial Nations"

1950. 2nd International Students' World Congress, Prague. Inscr "II KONGRES MSS".

595	**150**	1k.50 green	15	10
596	-	2k. purple	1·50	1·25
597	-	3k. red	20	25
598	-	5k. blue	40	50

DESIGNS—HORIZ: 2k. Woman, globe and dove ("Fight for Peace"); 3k. Group of students ("Democratisation of Education"); 5k. Students and banner ("International Students, Solidarity").

151 Miner, Soldier and Farmer

1950. Army Day.

599	**151**	1k.50 blue	90	75
600	-	3k. red	25	35

DESIGN: 3k. Czechoslovak and Russian soldiers.

152 Z. Fibich

1950. Birth Centenary of Fibich (composer).

601	**152**	3k. red	1·40	1·40
602	**152**	8k. green	25	15

153 "Communications"

1950. 1st Anniv of League of Postal, Telephone and Telegraph Employees.

603	153	1k.50 brown	25	15
604	153	3k. red	65	65

154 J. G. Tajovsky

1950. 10th Death Anniv of J. Gregor Tajovsky (writer).

605	154	1k.50 brown	85	70
606	154	5k. blue	85	55

155 Reconstruction of Prague

1950. Philatelic Exhibition, Prague.

607	155	1k.50 blue	35	20
608	155	3k. red	60	55
MS608a 120×101 mm. No. 607 in imperf block of four			27·00	20·00

156 Czech and Russian Workers

1950. Czechoslovak–Soviet Friendship.

609	156	1k.50 brown	55	25
610	156	5k. blue	75	50

157 Dove (after Picasso)

1951. Czechoslovak Peace Congress.

611	157	2k. blue	5·00	2·75
612	157	3k. red	3·00	1·60

158 Julius Fucik

1951. Peace Propaganda.

613	158	1k.50 grey	50	35
614	158	5k. blue	1·90	1·75

159 Mechanical Hammer

1951. Five Year Plan (heavy industry).

615	159	1k.50 black	10	10
616	-	3k. brown	15	10
617	159	4k. blue	65	50

DESIGN—HORIZ: 3k. Installing machinery.

160 Industrial Workers

1951. International Women's Day.

618	160	1k.50 olive	25	10
619	-	3k. red	2·40	65
620	-	5k. blue	50	10

DESIGNS: 3k. Woman driving tractor; 5k. Korean woman and group.

161 Karlovy Vary

1951. Air. Spas.

621	161	6k. green	2·25	75
622	-	10k. purple	2·25	95
623	-	15k. blue	5·50	75
624	-	20k. brown	7·00	2·25

DESIGNS—Ilyushin Il-12 airplane over: 10k. Piestany; 15k. Marianske Lazne; 20k. Silac.

162 Miners

1951. Mining Industry.

625	162	1k.50 black	1·00	60
626	162	3k. purple	10	15

163 Ploughing

1951. Agriculture.

627	163	1k.50 brown	50	65
628	-	2k. green (Woman and cows)	1·75	1·40

164 Tatra Mountains

1951. Recreation Centres. Inscr "ROH".

629	164	1k.50 green	20	10
630	-	2k. brown	90	70
631	-	3k. red	25	10

DESIGNS: 2k. Beskydy Mts; 3k. Krkonose Mts.

165 Partisan and Soviet Soldier

1951. 30th Anniv of Czechoslovak Communist Party. Inscr "30 LET" etc.

635	-	1k.50 grey	95	25
632	-	2k. brown	25	10
633	165	3k. red	30	10
636	-	5k. blue	1·90	90
634	-	8k. black	70	30

DESIGNS—HORIZ: 1k.50, 5k. Gottwald and Stalin; 8k. Marx, Engels, Lenin and Stalin. VERT: 2k. Factory militiaman.

167 Dvorak

1951. Prague Musical Festival.

637	167	1k. brown	25	10
638	-	1k.50 grey (Smetana)	1·25	55
639	167	2k. brown	1·25	60
640	-	3k. purple (Smetana)	25	15

168 Gymnast

1951. 9th Sokol Congress.

641	168	1k. green	55	20
642	-	1k.50 brown (Woman discus thrower)	55	25
643	-	3k. red (Footballers)	1·25	25
644	-	5k. blue (Skier)	3·25	1·25

1951. 10th Death Anniv of Bohumir Smeral. As T 154, but portrait of Smeral.

645	1k.50 grey	45	40
646	3k. purple	45	15

170 Scene from "Fall of Berlin"

1951. International Film Festival, Karlovy Vary. Inscr "SE SOVETSKYM FILMEM", etc.

647	170	80h. red	35	25
648	-	1k.50 grey	35	25
649	170	4k. blue	1·10	75

DESIGN: 1k.50, Scene from "The Great Citizen".

1951. 30th Death Anniv of J. Hybes (politician). As T 154, but portrait of Hybes.

650	1k.50 brown	10	10
651	2k. red	1·00	35

172 A. Jirasek

173 "Fables and Fates" (M. Ales)

1951. Birth Centenary of Jirasek (author).

652	172	1k.50 black	40	10
653	173	3k. red	40	10
654	-	4k. black	40	10
655	172	5k. blue	1·90	1·10

DESIGN—As Type **173**: 4k. "The Region of Tabor" (M. Ales).

174 Miner and Pithead

1951. Miner's Day.

656	174	1k.50 brown	15	10
657	-	3k. red (miners drilling)	15	10

658	174	5k. blue	1·25	95

176 Soldiers Parading

1951. Army Day. Inscr "DEN CS ARMADY 1951".

659	176	80h. brown	25	20
660	-	1k. green	25	25
661	-	1k.50 black	40	25
662	-	3k. purple	40	25
663	-	5k. blue	1·60	60

DESIGNS—VERT: 1k. Gunner and field-gun; 1k.50, Pres. Gottwald; 3k. Tank driver and tank; 5k. Two pilots and aircraft.

178 Stalin and Gottwald

1951. Czechoslovak–Soviet Friendship.

664	178	1k.50 black	10	10
665	-	3k. red	15	10
666	178	4k. blue	1·25	45

DESIGN (23½×31 mm): 3k. Lenin, Stalin and Russian soldiers.

179 P. Jilemnicky

1951. 50th Birth Anniv of Jilemnicky (writer).

667	179	1k.50 purple	20	15
668	179	2k. blue	70	35

180 L. Zapotocky

1952. Birth Centenary of Zapotocky (socialist pioneer).

669	180	1k.50 red	10	15
670	180	4k. black	1·00	35

181 J. Kollar

1952. Death Centenary of Kollar (poet).

671	181	3k. red	10	10
672	181	5k. blue	1·00	50

182 Lenin Hall, Prague

1952. 40th Anniv of 6th All-Russian Party Conference.

673	182	1k.50 red	10	25
674	182	5k. blue	1·00	60

183 Dr. E. Holub and Negro

1952. 50th Death Anniv of Dr. Holub (explorer).

675	**183**	3k. red	40	25
676	**183**	5k. blue	2·00	1·40

184 Electric Welding

1952. Industrial Development.

677	**184**	1k.50 black	35	15
678	-	2k. brown	1·40	50
679	-	3k. red	15	10

DESIGNS: 2k. Foundry; 3k. Chemical plant.

185 Factory-worker and Farm-girl

1952. International Women's Day.

680	**185**	1k.50 blue on cream	1·00	40

186 Young Workers

1952. International Youth Week.

681	**186**	1k.50 blue	10	10
682	-	2k. green	15	10
683	**186**	3k. red	1·60	65

DESIGN: 2k. Three heads and globe.

187 O. Sevcik

1952. Birth Centenary of Sevcik (musician).

684	**187**	2k. brown	70	45
685	**187**	3k. red	15	15

188 J. A. Komensky (Comenius)

1952. 360th Birth Anniv of Komensky (educationist).

686	**188**	1k.50 brown	1·25	50
687	**188**	11k. blue	25	10

189 Anti-fascist

1952. "Fighters Against Fascism" Day.

688	**189**	1k.50 brown	10	10
689	**189**	2k. blue	1·00	50

190 Woman and Children

1952. Child Welfare.

690	**190**	2k. purple on cream	1·25	1·10
691	**190**	3k. red on cream	15	15

191 Combine Harvester

1952. Agriculture Day.

692	**191**	1k.50 blue	1·90	1·10
693	**191**	2k. brown	25	25
694	-	3k. red (Combine drill)	25	25

192 May Day Parade

1952. Labour Day.

695	**192**	3k. red	30	35
696	**192**	4k. brown	1·40	80

193 Russian Tank and Crowd

1952. 7th Anniv of Liberation.

697	**193**	1k.50 red	60	50
698	**193**	5k. blue	1·75	1·40

194 Boy Pioneer and Children

1952. International Children's Day.

699	**194**	1k.50 brown	10	10
700	**194**	2k. green	1·40	70
701	-	3k. red (Pioneers and teacher)	15	10

195 J. V. Myslbek

1952. 30th Death Anniv of Myslbek (sculptor).

702	**195**	1k.50 brown	10	10
703	**195**	2k. brown	1·10	1·00
704	-	8k. green	15	10

DESIGN: 8k. "Music" (statue).

196 Beethoven

1952. International Music Festival, Prague. No. 706 inscr "PRAZSKE JARO 1952", etc.

705	**196**	1k.50 brown	30	25
706	-	3k. lake	30	25
707	**196**	5k. blue	1·60	90

DESIGN—HORIZ: 3k. The House of Artists.

197 "Rebirth of Lidice"

1952. 10th Anniv of Destruction of Lidice.

708	**197**	1k.50 black	10	10
709	**197**	5k. blue	90	55

198 Jan Hus

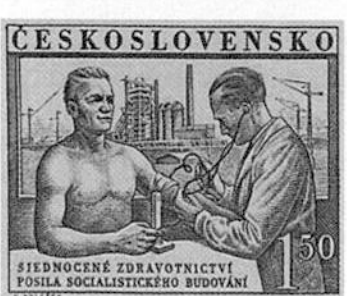

199 Bethlehem Chapel, Prague

1952. Renovation of Bethlehem Chapel and 550th Anniv of Installation of Hus as Preacher.

710	**198**	1k.50 brown	10	10
711	**199**	3k. brown	10	10
712	**198**	5k. black	1·10	75

200 Testing Blood-pressure

1952. National Health Service.

713	**200**	1k.50 brown	1·10	80
714	-	2k. violet	30	10
715	**200**	3k. red	50	10

DESIGN—HORIZ: 2k. Doctor examining baby.

201 Running

1952. Physical Culture Propaganda.

716	**201**	1k.50 brown	70	35
717	-	2k. green (Canoeing)	2·00	85
718	-	3k. brown (Cycling)	50	45
719	-	4k. blue (Ice hockey)	3·25	2·25

202 F. L. Celakovsky

1952. Death Centenary of Celakovsky (poet).

720	**202**	1k.50 sepia	20	10
721	**202**	2k. green	1·60	85

203 M. Ales

1952. Birth Centenary of Mikulas Ales (painter) (1st issue).

722	**203**	1k.50 green	60	20
723	**203**	6k. brown	2·25	1·75

See also Nos. 737/8.

204 Mining in 17th Century

1952. Miner's Day.

724	**204**	1k. brown	1·25	70
725	-	1k.50 blue	10	1·00
726	-	2k. black	10	10

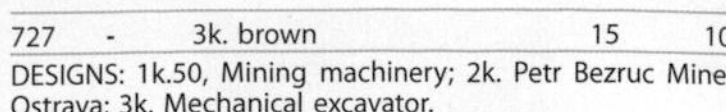

727	-	3k. brown	15	10

DESIGNS: 1k.50, Mining machinery; 2k. Petr Bezruc Mine, Ostrava; 3k. Mechanical excavator.

205 Jan Zizka

206 "Fraternization" (after Pokorny)

1952. Army Day.

728	**205**	1k.50 red	15	10
729	**206**	2k. brown	15	10
730	-	3k. red	15	10
731	**205**	4k. black	1·75	70

DESIGNS: 3k. Soldiers marching with flag.

207 R. Danube, Bratislava

1952. National Philatelic Exhibition, Bratislava.

732	**207**	1k.50 brown	10	10

MS732a 100×75 mm. 2k. red (Partisan Memorial); 3k. blue (Soviet Army Memorial) 95·00 26·00

208 Lenin, Stalin and Revolutionaries

1952. 35th Anniv of Russian Revolution.

733	**208**	2k. brown	1·25	80
734	**208**	3k. red	10	10

209 Nurses and Red Cross Flag

1952. 1st Czechoslovak Red Cross Conference.

735	**209**	2k. brown	1·25	55
736	**209**	3k. red	15	10

210 Matej Louda z Chlumu (Hussite Warrior)

1952. Birth Centenary of Mikulas Ales (2nd issue).

737	**210**	2k. brown	25	10
738	-	3k. black	65	10

DESIGN: 3k. "Trutnov" (warrior fighting dragon).

211 Flags

1952. Peace Congress, Vienna.

739	**211**	3k. red	20	10
740	**211**	4k. blue	1·40	70

212 "Dove of Peace" (after Picasso)

1953. 2nd Czechoslovak Peace Congress, Prague.

741	**212**	1k.50 sepia	10	10
742	-	4k. blue	55	35

DESIGN: 4k. Workman, woman and child (after Lev Haas).

213 Smetana Museum, Prague

1953. 75th Birth Anniv of Prof. Z. Nejedly (museum founder).

743	**213**	1k.50 brown	10	10
744	-	4k. black	1·40	65

DESIGN: 4k. Jirasek Museum, Prague.

214 Marching Soldiers

1953. 5th Anniv of Communist Govt.

745	**214**	1k.50 blue	15	10
746	-	3k. red	15	10
747	-	8k. brown	2·00	80

DESIGNS—VERT: 3k. Pres. Gottwald addressing meeting. HORIZ: 8k. Stalin, Gottwald and crowd with banners.

215 M. Kukucin

1953. Czech Writers and Poets.

748	**215**	1k. grey	10	10
749	-	1k.50 brown	10	10
750	-	2k. lake	10	10
751	-	3k. brown	50	40
752	-	5k. blue	1·90	75

PORTRAITS—VERT: 1k.50, J. Vrchlicky. 2k. E. J. Erben. 3k. V. M. Kramerius. 5k. J. Dobrovsky.

216 Torch and Open Book

1953. 10th Death Anniv of Vaclavek (writer).

753	**216**	1k. brown	1·50	50
754	-	3k. brown (Vaclavek)	15	10

217 Woman Revolutionary

1953. International Women's Day.

755		1k.50 blue	15	10
756	**217**	2k. red	1·00	50

DESIGN—VERT: 1k.50, Mother and baby.

218 Stalin

1953. Death of Stalin.

757	**218**	1k.50 black	35	20

219 Pres. Gottwald

1953. Death of President Gottwald.

758	**219**	1k.50 black	20	10
759	**219**	3k. black	20	10
MS759a		67×100 mm. 5k. black (T **219**)	2·75	2·25

220 Pecka, Zapotocky and Hybes

1953. 75th Anniv of 1st Czech Social Democratic Party Congress.

760	**220**	2k. brown	25	10

221 Cyclists

1953. 6th International Cycle Race.

761	**221**	3k. blue	60	30

222 1890 May Day Medal

223 Marching Crowds

1953. Labour Day.

762	**222**	1k. brown	1·75	85
763	-	1k.50 blue	10	10
764	**223**	3k. red	20	10
765	-	8k. green	25	10

DESIGNS—As Type **222**: 1k.50, Lenin and Stalin; 8k. Marx and Engels.

224 Hydro-electric Barrage

1953

766	**224**	1k.50 green	95	40
767	-	2k. blue	20	10
768	-	3k. brown	20	10

DESIGNS—VERT: 2k. Welder and blast furnaces, Kuncice. HORIZ: 3k. Gottwald Foundry, Kuncice.

225 Seed-drills

1953

769	**225**	1k.50 brown	20	10
770	-	7k. green (Combine harvester)	1·60	1·10

226 President Zapotocky

229

1953

776	**226**	30h. blue	60	10
777	**226**	60h. red	30	10
780	**229**	30h. blue	55	10
781	**229**	60h. pink	1·10	10

227 J. Slavik

1953. Prague Music Festival. (a) 120th Death Anniv of Slavik (violinist).

778	**227**	75h. blue	60	10

228 L. Janacek

(b) 25th Death Anniv of Janacek (composer).

779	**228**	1k.60 brown	1·25	10

230 Charles Bridge, Prague

1953

782a	**230**	5k. grey	4·50	10

231 J. Fucik

232 Book, Carnation and Laurels

1953. 10th Death Anniv of Julius Fucik (writer).

783	**231**	40h. black	20	10
784	**232**	60h. mauve	50	25

233 Miner and Banner

1953. Miner's Day.

785	**233**	30h. black	20	10
786	-	60h. purple	1·25	50

DESIGN: 60h. Miners and colliery shafthead.

234 Volley ball

1953. Sports.

787	**234**	30h. red	2·10	1·40
788	-	40h. purple	3·75	70
789	-	60h. purple	3·75	70

DESIGNS—HORIZ: 40h. Motor cycling. VERT: 60h. Throwing the javelin.

235 Hussite Warrior

1953. Army Day.

790	**235**	30h. sepia	25	10
791	-	60h. red	30	20
792	-	1k. red	1·75	1·25

DESIGNS: 60h. Soldier presenting arms; 1k. Czechoslovak Red Army soldiers.

236 "Friendship" (after T. Bartfay)

1953. Czechoslovak–Korean Friendship.

793	**236**	30h. sepia	2·50	1·10

237 Hradcany, Prague and Kremlin, Moscow

1953. Czechoslovak–Soviet Friendship: Inscr "MESIC CESKOSLOVENSKO SOVETSKEHO", etc.

794	**237**	30h. black	1·00	55
795	-	60h. brown	1·25	75
796	-	1k.20 blue	2·50	1·40

DESIGNS: 60h. Lomonosov University, Moscow; 1k.20, "Stalingrad" tug, Lenin Ship-Canal.

238 Ema Destinnova (Opera Singer)

239 National Theatre, Prague

1953. 70th Anniv of National Theatre, Prague.

797	**238**	30h. black	95	80
798	**239**	60h. brown	25	10
799	-	2k. sepia	2·25	80

PORTRAIT—As Type **238**: 2k. E. Vojan (actor).

240 J. Manes (painter)

1953

800	**240**	60h. lake	25	10
801	**240**	1k.20 blue	1·50	95

241 Vaclav Hollar (etcher)

1953. Inscr "1607 1677".

802	**241**	30h. black	25	10
803	-	1k.20 black	1·25	55

PORTRAIT: 1k.20, Hollar and engraving tools.

242 Leo Tolstoy

1953. 125th Birth Anniv of Tolstoy (writer).

804	**242**	60h. green	15	10
805	**242**	1k. brown	1·40	40

243 Class 498.0 Steam Locomotive

1953

806	**243**	60h. blue and brown	65	25
807	-	1k. blue and brown	1·60	90

DESIGN: 1k. Lisunov Li-2 (30th anniv of Czech airmail services).

244 Lenin (after J. Lauda)

245 Lenin Museum, Prague

1954. 30th Death Anniv of Lenin.

808	**244**	30h. sepia	45	10
809	**245**	1k.40 brown	1·75	1·25

246 Gottwald Speaking

1954. 25th Anniv of 5th Czechoslovak Communist Party Congress. Inscr "1929 1954".

810	**246**	60h. brown	30	10
811	-	2k.40 lake	3·75	1·40

DESIGN: 2k.40, Revolutionary and flag.

See also No. **MS**2917.

247 Gottwald Mausoleum, Prague

248 Gottwald and Stalin (after relief by O. Spaniel)

1954. 1st Anniv of Deaths of Stalin and Gottwald.

812	**247**	30h. sepia	25	20
813	**248**	60h. blue	30	10
814	-	1k.20h. lake	1·75	85

DESIGN—HORIZ: As Type **247**: 1k.20h. Lenin-Stalin Mausoleum, Moscow.

249 Girl and Sheaf of Corn

1954

815		15h. green	25	10
816		20h. lilac	30	10
817		40h. brown	45	10
818		45h. blue	45	10
819		50h. green	30	10
820		75h. blue	30	10
821		80h. brown	30	10
822	**249**	1k. green	65	10
823	-	1k.20 blue	30	10
824	-	1k.60 black	2·25	10
825	-	2k. brown	1·90	10
826	-	2k.40 blue	2·25	10
827	-	3k. red	1·50	10

DESIGNS: 15h. Labourer; 20h. Nurse; 40h. Postwoman; 45h. Foundry worker; 50h. Soldier; 75h. Metal worker; 80h. Mill girl; 1k.20, Scientist; 1k.60, Miner; 2k. Doctor and baby; 2k.40 Engine-driver; 3k. Chemist.

250 Athletics

1954. Sports.

828	**250**	30h. sepia	2·25	85
829	-	80h. green	6·50	3·50
830	-	1k. blue	1·40	60

DESIGNS—HORIZ: 80h. Hiking. VERT: 1k. Girl diving.

251 Dvorak

1954. Czechoslovak Musicians. Inscr as in T 251.

831	**251**	30h. brown	1·00	25
832	-	40h. red (Janacek)	1·40	25
833	-	60h. blue (Smetana)	80	15

252 Prokop Divis (physicist)

1954. Bicentenary of Invention of Lightning Conductor by Divis.

834	**252**	30h. black	25	10
835	**252**	75h. brown	1·25	40

253 Partisan

1954. 10th Anniv of Slovak National Uprising. Inscr "1944–29. 8–1954".

836	**253**	30h. red	20	10
837	-	1k.20 bl (Woman partisan)	1·10	90

254 A. P. Chekhov

1954. 50th Death Anniv of Chekhov (playwright).

838	**254**	30h. green	20	10
839	**254**	45h. brown	1·25	50

255 Soldiers in Battle

1954. Army Day. 2k. inscr "ARMADY 1954".

840	**255**	60h. green	20	10
841	-	2k. brown	1·25	1·10

DESIGN: 2k. Soldier carrying girl.

256 Farm Workers in Cornfield

1954. Czechoslovak–Russian Friendship.

842	**256**	30h. brown	15	10
843	-	60h. blue	25	10
844	-	2k. salmon	1·75	1·40

DESIGNS: 60h. Factory workers and machinery; 2k. Group of girl folk dancers.

257 J. Neruda

1954. Czechoslovak Poets.

845	**257**	30h. blue	50	15
846	-	60h. red	1·50	30
847	-	1k.60 purple	40	15

PORTRAITS—VERT: 60h. J. Jesensky. 1k.60 J. Wolker.

258 Ceske Budejovice

1954. Czechoslovak Architecture. Background in buff.

848		30h. black (Telc)	90	10
849		60h. brown (Levoca)	45	10
850	**258**	3k. blue	1·75	1·40

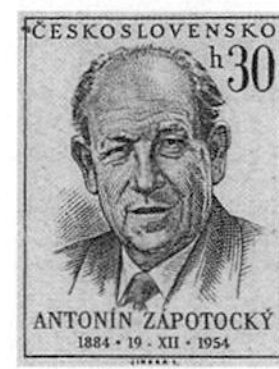

259 President Zapotocky

1954. 70th Birthday of Zapotocky.

851	**259**	30h. sepia	45	10
852	**259**	60h. blue	20	10
MS852a		65×100 mm 2k. red (as T **259**)	8·00	4·75

See also Nos. 1006/7.

260 "Spirit of the Games"

1955. 1st National Spartacist Games (1st issue). Inscr as in T 260.

853	**260**	30h. red	1·50	40
854	-	45h. black & blue (Skier)	4·25	30

See also Nos. 880/2.

261 University Building

1955. 35th Anniv of Comenius University, Bratislava. Inscr as in T 261.

855	**261**	60h. green	30	10
856	-	75h. brown	1·75	55

DESIGN: 75h. Comenius Medal (after O. Spaniel).

262 Cesky Krumlov

1955. Air.

857	**262**	80h. green	1·10	20
858	-	1k.55 sepia	1·50	35
859	-	2k.35 blue	1·50	15
860	-	2k.75 purple	2·75	30
861	-	10k. blue	5·25	1·25

DESIGNS: 1k.55, Olomouc; 2k.35, Banska Bystrica; 2k.75, Bratislava; 10k. Prague.

263 Skoda Motor Car

1955. Czechoslovak Industries.

862	**263**	45h. green	70	50
863	-	60h. blue	15	10
864	-	75h. black	25	10

DESIGNS: 60h. Shuttleless jet loom; 75h. Skoda Machine-tool.

264 Russian Tank-driver

1955. 10th Anniv of Liberation. Inscr as in T 264.

865		30h. blue	25	10
866	**264**	35h. brown	1·25	55
867	-	60h. red	25	10
868	-	60h. black	25	10

DESIGNS—VERT: 30h. Girl and Russian soldier; No. 867, Children and Russian soldier. HORIZ: No. 868, Stalin Monument, Prague.

265 Agricultural Workers

1955. 3rd Trades' Union Congress. Inscr as in T 265.

869		30h. blue	15	10
870	**265**	45h. green	1·25	55

DESIGN: 30h. Foundry worker.

266 "Music and Spring"

1955. International Music Festival, Prague. Inscr as in T 266.

871	**266**	30h. indigo and blue	35	10
872	-	1k. blue and pink	1·25	1·25

DESIGN: 1k. "Music" playing a lyre.

267 A. S. Popov (60th anniv of radio discoveries)

1955. Cultural Anniversaries. Portraits.

873		20h. brown	20	10
874		30h. black	20	10
875		40h. green	70	15
876		60h. black	45	10
877	**267**	75h. purple	1·40	50
878	-	1k.40 black on yellow	35	25
879	-	1k.60 blue	35	20

PORTRAITS: 20h. Jakub Arbes (writer). 30h. Jan Stursa (sculptor). 40h. Elena Marothy-Soltesova (writer). 60h. Josef V. Sladek (poet). 1k.40 Jan Holly (poet). 1k.60 Pavel J. Safarik (philologist).

268 Folk Dancers

1955. 1st National Spartacist Games (2nd issue). Inscr as in T 268.

880		20h. blue	85	40
881	**268**	60h. green	25	10
882	-	1k.60 red	90	25

DESIGNS: 20h. Girl athlete; 1k.60, Male athlete.

269 "Friendship"

1955. 5th World Youth Festival, Warsaw.

883	**269**	60h. blue	35	10

270 Ocova Woman, Slovakia

1955. National Costumes (1st series).

884	**270**	60h. sepia, rose and red	10·00	7·00
885	-	75h. sepia, orange & lake	5·75	5·00
886	-	1k.60 sepia, blue & orge	10·00	5·50
887	-	2k. sepia, yellow and red	13·00	5·50

DESIGNS: 75h. Detva man, Slovakia; 1k.60, Chodsko man, Bohemia; 2k. Hana woman, Moravia.
See also Nos. 952/5 and 1008/11.

271 Swallowtail

1955. Animals and Insects.

888		20h. black and blue	55	10
889		30h. brown and red	55	10
890		35h. brown and buff	1·10	15
891	**271**	1k.40 black and yellow	5·25	1·90
892	-	1k.50 black and green	55	15

DESIGNS: 20h. Common carp; 30h. Stag beetle; 35h. Grey partridge; 1k.50, Brown hare.

272 Tabor

1955. Towns of Southern Bohemia.

893	**272**	30h. purple	20	10
894	-	45h. red	75	55
895	-	60h. green	20	10

TOWNS: 45h. Prachatice; 60h. Jindrichuv Hradec.

273 Motor Cyclists and Trophy

1955. 30th Int Motor Cycle Six-Day Trial.

896	**273**	60h. purple	2·40	25

273a Round Chapel

1955. Prague International Philatelic Exhibition. Sheets 145×111 mm.

MS896a 30h. black (T **273a**); 45h. black (Brick tower); 60h. lake (fountain); 75h. lake (Winter Palace); 1k.60 black (Hradcany, 50×31 mm)	27·00	27·00
MS896b As above but imperf	65·00	65·00

274 Soldier and Family

1955. Army Day. Inscr as in T 274.

897	**274**	30h. brown	25	10
898	-	60h. grn (Tank attack)	1·75	1·25

275 Hans Andersen

1955. Famous Writers. Vert portraits.

899	**275**	30h. red	15	10
900	-	40h. blue (Schiller)	2·10	80
901	-	60h. purple (Mickiewicz)	25	10
902	-	75h. blk (Walt Whitman)	50	10

276 Railway Viaduct

1955. Building Progress. Inscr "STAVBA SOCIALISMU".

903	**276**	20h. green	30	25
904	-	30h. brown	30	10
905	-	60h. blue	30	10
906	-	1k.60 red	55	10

DESIGNS: 30h. Train crossing viaduct; 60k. Train approaching tunnel; 1k.60, Housing project, Ostrava.

277 "Electricity"

1956. Five Year Plan. Inscr "1956–1960".

907	**277**	5h. brown	25	10
908	-	10h. black	25	10
909	-	25h. red	25	10
910	-	30h. green	25	10
911	-	60h. blue	35	10

DESIGNS—HORIZ: 10h. "Mining"; 25h. "Building"; 30h. "Agriculture"; 60h. "Industry".

278 Karlovy Vary

1956. Czechoslovak Spas (1st series).

912	**278**	30h. green	1·40	25
913	-	45h. brown	1·25	35
914	-	75h. purple	6·25	3·50
915	-	1k.20 blue	90	15

SPAS: 45h. Marianske Lazne; 75h. Piestany; 1k.20, Vysne Ruzbachy, Tatra Mountains.

279 Jewellery

1956. Czechoslovak Products.

916	**279**	30h. green	25	10
917	-	45h. blue (Glassware)	4·75	2·75
918	-	60h. purple (Ceramics)	1·00	10
919	-	75h. black (Textiles)	25	10

280 "We serve our People" (after J. Cumpelik)

1956. Defence Exhibition.

920	**280**	30h. brown	35	10
921	-	60h. red	35	10
922	-	1k. blue	5·50	3·25

DESIGNS: 60h. Liberation Monument, Berlin; 1k. "Tank Soldier with Standard" (after T. Schor).

281 Cyclists

282 Discus Thrower, Hurdler and Runner

1956. Sports Events of 1956.

923	**281**	30h. green and blue	2·75	20
924	-	45h. blue and red	1·10	20
925	-	60h. blue and buff	1·50	45
926	**282**	75h. brown and yellow	1·00	20
927	-	80h. purple & lavender	1·00	20
928	**282**	1k.20 green & orange	95	35

DESIGNS—As Type **281**. VERT: 30h. T **281** (9th International Cycle Race); 45h. Basketball players (5th European Women's Basketball Championship, Prague). HORIZ: 60h. Horsemen jumping (Pardubice Steeplechase); 80h. Runners (International Marathon, Kosice). T **282**: 75h., 1k.20, (16th Olympic Games, Melbourne).

283 Mozart

1956. Bicentenary of Birth of Mozart and Prague Music Festival. Centres in black.

929	**283**	30h. yellow	1·00	70
930	-	45h. green	14·50	9·50
931	-	60h. purple	55	10
932	-	1k. salmon	1·60	45
933	-	1k.40 blue	2·75	90
934	-	1k.60 lemon	1·00	15

DESIGNS: 45h. J. Myslivecek; 60h. J. Benda; 1k. "Bertramka" (Mozart's villa); 1k.40, Mr. and Mrs. Dushek; 1k.60, Nostic Theatre.

284

1956. 1st National Meeting of Home Guard.

935	**284**	60h. blue	90	20

285 J. K. Tyl

1956. Czech Writers (1st issue).

936	-	20h. purple (Stur)	70	10
937	-	30h. blue (Sramek)	35	10
938	**285**	60h. black	25	10
939	-	1k.40 pur (Borovsky)	4·50	2·40

See also Nos. 956/9.

286 Naval Guard

1956. Frontier Guards' Day.

940	**286**	30h. blue	1·10	40
941	-	60h. green	15	10

DESIGN: 60h. Military guard and watchdog.

287 Picking Grapes

1956. National Products.

942	**287**	30h. lake	25	10
943	-	35h. green	30	25
944	-	80h. blue	60	15
945	-	95h. brown	1·50	1·60

DESIGNS—VERT: 35h. Picking hops. HORIZ: 80h. Fishing; 95h. Logging.

288 "Kladno", 1855

1956. European Freight Services Timetable Conference. Railway engines.

946		10h. brown	1·25	10
947	288	30h. black	75	10
948	-	40h. green	3·50	15
949	-	45h. purple	19·00	9·50
950	-	60h. blue	75	10
951	-	1k. blue	1·25	15

DESIGNS—VERT: 10h. "Zbraslav", 1846. HORIZ: 40h. Class 534, 1945; 45h. Class 556.0, 1952; 60h. Class 477.0, 1955; 1k. Class E499.0 electric locomotive, 1954.

1956. National Costumes (2nd series). As T 270.

952	30h. sepia, red and blue	2·25	70
953	1k.20 sepia, blue and red	2·25	15
954	1k.40 brown, yellow & red	4·00	1·90
955	1k.60 sepia, green & red	2·40	30

DESIGNS: 30h. Slovacko woman; 1k.20, Blata woman; 1k.40, Cicmany woman, 1k.60, Novohradsko woman.

1957. Czech Writers (2nd issue). As T 285. On buff paper.

956	15h. brown (Olbracht)	30	10
957	20h. green (Toman)	30	10
958	30h. sepia (Salda)	30	10
959	1k.60 blue (Vansova)	55	10

289 Forestry Academy, Banska Stiavnica

1957. Towns and Monuments Anniversaries.

960	-	30h. blue	20	10
961	289	30h. purple	20	10
962	-	60h. red	40	10
963	-	60h. brown	40	10
964	-	60h. green	30	10
965	-	1k.25 black	3·50	1·40

DESIGNS: No. 960, Kolin; 962, Uherske Hradiste; 963, Charles Bridge, Prague; 964, Karlstejn Castle; 965, Moravska Trebova.

290 Girl Harvester

1957. 3rd Collective Farming Agricultural Congress, Prague.

966	290	30h. turquoise	70	10

291 Komensky's Mausoleum

292 J. A. Komensky (Comenius)

1957. 300th Anniv of Publication of Komensky's "Opera Didactica Omnia".

967	291	30h. brown	40	10
968	-	40h. green	40	10
969	292	60h. brown	1·90	1·10
970	-	1k. red	55	10

DESIGNS: As Type 291: 40h. Komensky at work; 1k. Illustration from "Opera Didactica Omnia".

293 Racing Cyclists

1957. Sports Events of 1957.

971	293	30h. purple and blue	35	10
972	293	60h. green and bistre	1·60	1·40
973	-	60h. violet and brown	35	10
974	-	60h. purple and brown	35	10
975	-	60h. black and green	35	10
976	-	60h. black and blue	1·00	10

DESIGNS—HORIZ: Nos. 971/2 (10th Int Cycle Race); 973, Rescue squad (Mountain Rescue Service); 975, Archer (World Archery Championships, Prague). VERT: 974, Boxers (European Boxing Championships, Prague); 976, Motor Cyclists (32nd Int Motor Cycle Six-Day Trial).

294 J. B. Foerster

1957. Int Music Festival Jubilee. Musicians.

977		60h. violet (Stamic)	25	10
978		60h. black (Laub)	25	10
979		60h. blue (Ondricek)	25	10
980	294	60h. sepia	25	10
981	-	60h. brown (Novak)	90	10
982	-	60h. turquoise (Suk)	25	10

295 J. Bozek (founder)

1957. 250th Anniv of Polytechnic Engineering Schools, Prague.

983	295	30h. black	15	10
984	-	60h. brown	35	10
985	-	1k. purple	35	15
986	-	1k.40 violet	50	15

DESIGNS—VERT: 60h. F. J. Gerstner; 1k. R. Skuhersky. HORIZ: 1k.40, Polytechnic Engineering Schools Building, Prague.

296 Young Collector Blowing Posthorn

1957. Junior Philatelic Exn, Pardubice.

987	296	30h. orange and green	50	10
988	-	60h. blue and brown	2·10	1·25

DESIGN: 60h. Girl sending letter by pigeon.

297 "Rose of Friendship and Peace"

1957. 15th Anniv of Destruction of Lidice.

989		30h. black	35	10
990	297	60h. red and black	1·00	35

DESIGN: 30h. Veiled woman.

298 Karel Klic and Printing Press

1957. Czech Inventors.

991	298	30h. black	15	10
992	-	60h. blue	35	10

DESIGN: 60h. Joseph Ressel and propeller.

299 Chamois

1957. Tatra National Park.

993	299	20h. black and green	65	45
994	-	30h. brown and blue	65	10
995	-	40h. blue and brown	1·25	30
996	-	60h. green and yellow	50	10
997	-	1k.25 black and ochre	1·25	1·25

DESIGNS—VERT: 30h. Brown bear. HORIZ: 40h. Gentian; 60h. Edelweiss; 1k.25 (49×29 mm), Tatra Mountains.

300 Marycka Magdonova

1957. 90th Birthday of Petr Bezruc (poet).

998	300	60h. black and red	50	10

301 Worker with Banner

1957. 4th World T.U.C., Leipzig.

999	301	75h. red	50	15

302 Tupolev Tu-104A and Paris–Prague–Moscow Route

1957. Air. Opening of Czechoslovak Airlines.

1000	302	75h. blue and red	80	10
1001	-	2k.35 blue and yellow	95	10

DESIGN: 2k.35, "Prague–Cairo–Beirut–Damascus".

303 Television Tower and Aerials

1957. Television Development.

1002	303	40h. blue and red	25	10
1003	-	60h. brown and green	30	10

DESIGN: 60h. Family watching television.

304 Youth, Globe and Lenin

1957. 40th Anniv of Russian Revolution.

1004	304	30h. red	20	10
1005	-	60h. blue	35	10

DESIGN: 60h. Lenin, refinery and Russian emblem.

1957. Death of President Zapotocky. As T 259 but dated "19 XII 1884–13 XI 1957".

1006	30h. black	10	10
1007	60h. black	25	10
MS1007a	70×100 mm. 2k. black (as 1006). Imperf	2·40	2·00

1957. National Costumes (3rd series). As T 270.

1008	45h. sepia, red and blue	2·75	1·25
1009	75h. sepia, red and green	1·90	80
1010	1k.25 sepia, red & yellow	2·75	65
1011	1k.95 sepia, blue and red	3·25	2·10

DESIGNS—VERT: 45h. Pilsen woman; 75h. Slovacko man; 1k.25, Hana woman; 1k.95, Tesin woman.

305 Artificial Satellite ("Sputnik 2")

1957. International Geophysical Year. Showing globe and dated "1957–1958".

1012	-	30h. brown and yellow	1·40	45
1013	-	45h. brown and blue	30	25
1014	305	75h. red and blue	2·00	65

DESIGNS—HORIZ: 30h. Radio-telescope and observatory. VERT: 45h. Lomnicky Stit meteorological station.

306 Figure Skating (European Championships, Bratislava)

1958. Sports Events of 1958.

1015	306	30h. purple	90	20
1016	-	40h. blue	30	20
1017	-	60h. brown	30	10
1018	-	80h. violet	1·40	65
1019	-	1k.60 green	50	15

EVENTS: 40h. Canoeing (World Canoeing Championships, Prague); 60h. Volleyball (European Volleyball Championships, Prague); 80h. Parachuting (4th World Parachute-jumping Championship, Bratislava); 1k.60, Football (World Cup Football Championship, Stockholm).

307 Litomysl Castle (birthplace of Nejedly)

1958. 80th Birthday of Nejedly (musician).

1020	307	30h. green	20	10
1021	-	60h. brown	20	10

DESIGN—HORIZ: 60h. Bethlehem Chapel, Prague.

308 Soldiers guarding Shrine of "Victorious February"

1958. 10th Anniv of Communist Govt.

1022		30h. blue and yellow	25	10
1023	308	60h. brown and red	25	10
1024	-	1k.60 green and orange	35	10

DESIGNS—VERT: 30h. Giant mine-excavator. HORIZ: 1k.60, Combine-harvester.

309 Jewellery

1958. Brussels International Exhibition. Inscr "Bruxelles 1958".

1025	**309**	30h. red and blue	25	10
1026	-	45h. red and lilac	60	10
1027	-	60h. violet and green	25	10
1028	-	75h. blue and orange	1·10	80
1029	-	1k.20 green and red	60	10
1030	-	1k.95 brown and blue	70	15

DESIGNS—VERT: 45h. Toy dolls; 60h. Draperies; 75h. Kaplan turbine; 1k.20, Glassware. HORIZ: (48½×29½ mm), 1k.95, Czech pavilion.

310 George of Podebrady and his Seal

1958. National Exhibition of Archive Documents. Inscr as in T 310.

1031	**310**	30h. red	35	10
1032	-	60h. violet	35	10

DESIGN: 60h. Prague, 1628 (from engraving).

311 Hammer and Sickle

1958. 11th Czech Communist Party Congress and 15th Anniv of Czech–Soviet Friendship Treaty. 45h. inscr as in T 311 and 60h. inscr "15. VYROCI UZAVRENI".

1033	**311**	30h. red	20	10
1034	-	45h. green	20	10
1035	-	60h. blue	20	10

DESIGNS: 45h. Map of Czechoslovakia, with hammer and sickle; 60h. Atomic reactor, Rez (near Prague).

312 "Towards the Stars" (after sculpture by G. Postnikov)

1958. Cultural and Political Events. 45h. inscr "IV. KONGRES MEZINARODNI", etc, and 60h. inscr "I. SVETOVA ODBOROVA", etc.

1036	**312**	30h. red	70	40
1037	-	45h. purple	20	25
1038	-	60h. blue	20	10

DESIGNS—VERT: 45h. Three women of different races and globe (4th Int Democratic Women's Federation Congress, Vienna). HORIZ: 60h. Boy and girl with globes (1st World T.U. Conference of Working Youth, Prague). Type **312** represents the Society for the Dissemination of Cultural and Political Knowledge.

313 Pres. Novotny

1958

1039	**313**	30h. violet	45	10
1039a	**313**	30h. purple	3·50	1·00
1040	**313**	60h. red	45	10

314 Telephone Operator

1958. Communist Postal Conference, Prague. Inscr as in T 314.

1041	**314**	30h. sepia and brown	30	10
1042	-	45h. black and green	30	30

DESIGN: 45h. Aerial mast.

315 Karlovy Vary (600th Anniv)

1958. Czech Spas (2nd series).

1043	**315**	30h. lake	10	10
1044	-	40h. brown	10	10
1045	-	60h. green	15	10
1046	-	80h. sepia	30	10
1047	-	1k.20 blue	45	15
1048	-	1k.60 violet	1·10	65

SPAS: 40h. Podebrady; 60h. Marianske Lazne (150th Anniv); 80h. Luhacovice; 1k.20, Strbske Pleso; 1k.60, Trencianske.

316 "The Poet and the Muse" (after Max Svabinsky)

1958. 85th Birthday of Dr. Max Svabinsky (artist).

1049	**316**	1k.60 black	3·25	80

317 S. Cech

1958. Writers' Anniversaries.

1050	-	30h. red (Julius Fucik)	25	10
1051	-	45h. violet (Gustav K. Zechenter)	1·25	45
1052	-	60h. blue (Karel Capek)	15	10
1053	**317**	1k.40 black	50	10

318 Children's Hospital, Brno

1958. National Stamp Exn, Brno. Inscr as in T 318.

1054	**318**	30h. violet	20	10
1055	-	60h. red	20	10
1056	-	1k. sepia	45	10
1057	-	1k.60 myrtle	1·60	1·50

DESIGNS: 60h. New Town Hall, Brno; 1k. St. Thomas's Church, Red Army Square; 1k.60, (50×28½ mm), Brno view.

319 Parasol Mushroom

1958. Mushrooms.

1058	**319**	30h. buff, green & brown	40	20
1059	-	40h. buff, red & brown	45	20
1060	-	60h. red, buff and black	55	25
1061	-	1k.40 red, green & brn	65	35
1062	-	1k.60 red, green & blk	5·25	2·00

DESIGNS—VERT: 40h. Cep; 60h. Red cap; 1k.40, Fly agaric; 1k.60, Boot-lace fungus.

320 Children sailing

1958. Inauguration of UNESCO Headquarters Building, Paris. Inscr "ZE SOUTEZE PRO UNESCO".

1063	**320**	30h. red, yellow & blue	20	10
1064	-	45h. red and blue	50	10
1065	-	60h. blue, yellow & brn	20	10

DESIGNS: 45h. Mother, child and bird; 60h. Child skier.

321 Bozek's Steam Car of 1815

1958. Czech Motor Industry Commemoration.

1066	**321**	30h. violet and yellow	65	10
1067	-	45h. brown and green	50	10
1068	-	60h. green and orange	65	10
1069	-	80h. red and green	50	10
1070	-	1k. brown and green	50	10
1071	-	1k.25 green & yellow	1·60	75

DESIGNS: 45h. "President" car of 1897; 60h. Skoda "450" car; 80h. Tatra "603" car; 1k. Skoda "706" motor coach; 1k.25, Tatra "III" and Praga "VS 3" motor trucks in Tibet.

322 Garlanded Woman ("Republic") with First Czech Stamp

1958. 40th Anniv of 1st Czech Postage Stamps.

1072	**322**	60h. blue	25	10

323 Ice Hockey Goalkeeper

1959. Sports Events of 1959.

1073	-	20h. brown and grey	30	10
1074	-	30h. brown & orange	30	10
1075	**323**	60h. blue and green	30	10
1076	-	1k. lake and yellow	30	10
1077	-	1k.60 violet and blue	45	10
1078	-	2k. brown and blue	1·60	1·25

DESIGNS: 20h. Ice hockey player (50th anniv of Czech Ice Hockey Association); 30h. Throwing the javelin; 60h. (Type **323**) World Ice Hockey Championships, 1959; 1k. Hurdling; 1k.60, Rowing; 2k. High jumping.

324 U.A.C. Emblem

1959. 4th National Unified Agricultural Co-operatives Congress, Prague.

1079	**324**	30h. lake and blue	20	10
1080	-	60h. blue and yellow	40	10

DESIGN: 60h. Artisan shaking hand with farmer.

325 "Equal Rights"

1959. 10th Anniv of Declaration of Human Rights.

1081	**325**	60h. green	15	10
1082	-	1k. sepia	25	10
1083	-	2k. blue	1·40	55

DESIGNS: 1k. "World Freedom" (girl with Dove of Peace); 2k. "Freedom for Colonial Peoples" (native woman with child).

326 Girl with Doll

1959. 10th Anniv of Young Pioneers' Movement.

1084	**326**	30h. blue and yellow	30	10
1085	-	40h. black and blue	30	25
1086	-	60h. black and purple	30	10
1087	-	80h. brown and green	30	25

DESIGNS: 40h. Boy hiker; 60h. Young radio technician; 80h. Girl planting tree.

327 F. Joliot-Curie (scientist)

1959. 10th Anniv of Peace Movement.

1088	**327**	60h. purple	1·40	40

328 Man in outer space and Moon Rocket

1959. 2nd Czech Political and Cultural Knowledge Congress, Prague.

1089	**328**	30h. blue	90	35

329 Pilsen Town Hall

1959. Centenary of Skoda Works and National Stamp Exhibition, Pilsen. Inscr "PLZEN 1959".

1090	**329**	30h. brown	15	10
1091	-	60h. violet and green	15	10
1092	-	1k. blue	25	20
1093	-	1k.60 black & yellow	1·25	1·00

DESIGNS: 60h. Part of steam turbine; 1k. St. Bartholomew's Church, Pilsen; 1k.60, Part of SR-1200 lathe.

330 Congress Emblem and Industrial Plant

1959. 4th Trades Union Congress, Prague.

1094	**330**	30h. red and yellow	20	10
1095	-	60h. olive and blue	20	10

DESIGN: 60h. Dam.

331 Zvolen Castle

1959. Slovak Stamp Exhibition, Zvolen.

1096	**331**	60h. olive and yellow	35	10

332 F. Benda (composer)

1959. Cultural Anniversaries.

1097	**332**	15h. blue	20	10
1098	-	30h. red	20	10
1099	-	40h. green	30	10
1100	-	60h. brown	30	10
1101	-	60h. black	55	10
1102	-	80h. violet	30	10
1103	-	1k. brown	30	10
1104	-	3k. brown	1·40	1·10

PORTRAITS: 30h. Vaclav Klicpera (dramatist); 40h. Aurel Stodola (engineer); 60h. (1100) Karel V. Rais (writer); 60h. (1101) Haydn (composer); 80h. Antonin Slavicek (painter); 1k. Petr Bezruc (poet). 3k. Charles Darwin (naturalist).

333 "Z" Pavilion

1959. Int Fair, Brno. Inscr "BRNO 6-20. IX. 1959".

1105		30h. purple & yellow	15	10
1106		60h. blue	15	10
1107	**333**	1k.60 blue & yellow	45	10

DESIGNS: 30h. View of Fair; 60h. Fair emblem and world map.

334 Revolutionary (after A. Holly)

1959. 15th Anniv of Slovak National Uprising and 40th Anniv of Republic. Inscr "1944 29.8.1959".

1108	**334**	30h. black & mauve	15	10
1109	-	60h. red	20	10
1110	-	1k.60 blue & yell	40	10

DESIGNS—VERT: 60h. Revolutionary with upraised rifle (after sculpture "Forward" by L. Snopka). HORIZ: 1k.60, Factory, sun and linden leaves.

335 Moon Rocket

1959. Landing of Russian Rocket on Moon.

1111	**335**	60h. red and blue	1·25	25

336 Lynx

1959. 10th Anniv of Tatra National Park. Inscr "1949 TATRANSKY NARODNY PARK 1959".

1112	-	30h. black and grey	65	10
1113	-	40h. brown & turquoise	65	10
1114	**336**	60h. red & yellow	90	10
1115	-	1k. brown & blue	2·00	75
1116	-	1k.60 brown	1·75	10

DESIGNS—HORIZ: 30h. Alpine marmots; 40h. European bison; 1k. Wolf; 1k.60, Red deer.

337 Stamp Printing Works, Peking

1959. 10th Anniv of Chinese People's Republic.

1117	**337**	30h. red and green	25	10

338 Bleriot XI Monoplanes at First Czech Aviation School

1959. Air. 50th Anniv of 1st Flight by Jan Kaspar.

1118	**338**	1k. black and yellow	15	10
1119	-	1k.80 black & blue	75	10

DESIGN: 1k.80, Jan Kaspar and Bleriot XI in flight.

339 Great Spotted Woodpecker

1959. Birds.

1120	**339**	20h. multicoloured	85	15
1121	-	30h. multicoloured	85	15
1122	-	40h. multicoloured	2·10	1·10
1123	-	60h. multicoloured	85	15
1124	-	80h. multicoloured	85	20
1125	-	1k. red, blue & black	85	20
1126	-	1k.20 brn, blue & blk	1·10	40

BIRDS: 30h. Blue tit; 40h. Eurasian nuthatch; 60h. Golden oriole; 80h. Eurasian goldfinch; 1k. Northern bullfinch; 1k.20, River kingfisher.

340 Tesla and Electrical Apparatus

1959. Radio Inventors.

1127	**340**	25h. black and red	1·10	20
1128	-	30h. black and brown	15	10
1129	-	35h. black and lilac	20	10
1130	-	60h. black and blue	25	10
1131	-	1k. black and green	20	10
1132	-	2k. black and bistre	80	85

INVENTORS (each with sketch of invention): 30h. Aleksandr Popov; 35h. Edouard Branly; 60h. Guglielmo Marconi; 1k. Heinrich Hertz; 2k. Edwin Armstrong.

341 Exercises

1960. 2nd National Spartacist Games (1st issue). Inscr as in T 341.

1133	**341**	30h. brown and red	1·10	10
1134	-	60h. blue & light blue	45	25
1135	-	1k.60 brown & bistre	70	30

DESIGNS: 60h. Skiing; 1k.60, Basketball.
See also Nos. 1160/2.

342 Freighter "Lidice"

1960. Czech Ships.

1136		30h. green and red	80	15
1137		60h. red and turquoise	25	10
1138		1k. violet and yellow	80	25
1139	**342**	1k.20 purple and green	1·75	90

SHIPS: 30h. Dredger "Praha Liben"; 60h. Tug "Kharito Latjev"; 1k. River boat "Komarno".

343 Ice Hockey

1960. Winter Olympic Games. Inscr as in T 343.

1140	**343**	60h. sepia and blue	45	25
1141	-	1k.80 black & green	4·00	2·10

DESIGN: 1k.80, Skating pair.
See also Nos. 1163/5.

344 Trencin Castle

1960. Czechoslovak Castles.

1142	-	5h. blue	15	10
1143	-	10h. black (Bezdez)	15	10
1144	-	20h. orange (Kost)	25	10
1145	-	30h. green (Pernstejn)	25	10
1146	-	40h. brn (Kremnica)	25	10
1146a	-	50h. black (Krivoklat)	25	10
1147	-	60h. red (Karestejn)	45	10
1148	-	1k. purple (Smolenice)	30	10
1149	-	1k.60 blue (Kokorin)	65	10

345 Lenin

1960. 90th Birth Anniv of Lenin.

1150	**345**	60h. olive	85	25

346 Soldier and Child

1960. 15th Anniv of Liberation.

1151	**346**	30h. lake and blue	30	10
1152	-	30h. green and lavender	25	10
1153	-	30h. red and pink	25	10
1154	-	60h. blue and buff	25	10
1155	-	60h. purple and green	25	10

DESIGNS—VERT: No. 1152, Solider with liberated political prisoner; 1153, Child eating pastry. HORIZ: No. 1154, Welder; 1155, Tractor-driver.

347 Smelter

1960. Parliamentary Elections.

1156	**347**	30h. red and grey	15	10
1157	-	60h. green and blue	20	10

DESIGN: 60h. Country woman and child.

348 Red Cross Woman with Dove

1960. 3rd Czechoslovak Red Cross Congress.

1158	**348**	30h. red and blue	10	10

349 Fire-prevention Team with Hose

1960. 2nd Firemen's Union Congress.

1159	**349**	60h. blue and pink	35	10

1960. 2nd National Spartacist Games (2nd issue). As T 341.

1160	30h. red and green	40	10
1161	60h. black and pink	40	10
1162	1k. blue and orange	60	25

DESIGNS: 30h. Ball exercises; 60h. Stick exercises; 1k. Girls with hoops.

1960. Olympic Games, Rome. As Type 343.

1163	1k. black and orange	50	25
1164	1k.80 black and red	1·25	25
1165	2k. black and blue	2·50	85

DESIGNS: 1k. Sprinting; 1k.80, Gymnastics; 2k. Rowing.

350 Czech 10k. Stamp of 1936

1960. National Philatelic Exn, Bratislava (1st issue).

1166	-	60h. black and yellow	40	10
1167	**350**	1k. black and blue	90	10

DESIGN: 60h. Hand of philatelist holding stamp Type **350**.
See also Nos. 1183/4.

351 Stalin Mine, Ostrava-Hermanice

1960. 3rd Five Year Plan (1st issue).

1168	**351**	10h. black and green	25	10
1169	-	20h. lake and blue	25	10
1170	-	30h. blue and red	25	10
1171	-	40h. green and lilac	25	10
1172	-	60h. blue and yellow	25	10

DESIGNS: 20h. Hodonin Power Station; 30h. Klement Gottwald Iron Works, Kuncice; 40h. Excavator; 60h. Naphtha refinery.

See also Nos. 1198/1200.

352 V. Cornelius of Vsehra (historian)

1960. Cultural Anniversaries.

1173	**352**	10h. black	20	10
1174	-	20h. brown	30	10
1175	-	30h. red	40	10
1176	-	40h. green	45	10
1177	-	60h. violet	50	10

PORTRAITS: 20h. K. M. Capek Chod (writer); 30h. Hana Kvapilova (actress); 40h. Oskar Nedbal (composer); 60h. Otakar Ostricil (composer).

353 Zlin Zr22b Trener 6 flying upside-down

1960. 1st World Aviation Aerobatic Championships, Bratislava.

1178	**353**	60h. violet and blue	90	25

354 "New Constitution"

1960. Proclamation of New Constitution.

1179	**354**	30h. blue and red	25	10

355 Worker with "Rude Pravo"

1960. Czechoslovak Press Day (30h.) and 40th Anniv of Newspaper "Rude Pravo".

1180	-	30h. blue and orange	10	10
1181	**355**	60h. black and red	20	10

DESIGN—HORIZ: (inscr "DEN TISKU"): 30h. Steel-workers with newspaper.

356 Globes

1960. 15th Anniv of W.F.T.U.

1182	**356**	30h. blue and bistre	25	10

357 Mail Coach and Ilyushin Il-18B

1960. Air. National Philatelic Exhibition, Bratislava (2nd issue).

1183	**357**	1k.60 blue and grey	2·50	1·40
1184	-	2k.80 green & cream	4·00	2·00

DESIGN: 2k.80, Mil Mi-4 helicopter over Bratislava.

358 Mallard

1960. Water Birds.

1185		25h. black and blue	50	10
1186		30h. black and green	1·10	20
1187		40h. black and blue	70	20
1188		60h. black and pink	80	20
1189		1k. black and yellow	1·25	20
1190	**358**	1k.60 black and lilac	2·75	1·60

BIRDS—VERT: 25h. Black-crowned night heron; 30h. Great crested grebe; 40h. Northern lapwing; 60h. Grey heron. HORIZ: 1k. Greylag goose.

359 "Doronicum clusii tausch"

1960. Flowers. Inscr in black.

1191	**359**	20h. yellow, orge & grn	50	10
1192	-	30h. red and green	65	20
1193	-	40h. yellow and green	65	20
1194	-	60h. pink and green	70	20
1195	-	1k. blue, violet & green	1·00	35
1196	-	2k. yellow, green & pur	3·00	1·25

FLOWERS: 30h. "Cyclamen europaeum L"; 40h. "Primula auricula L"; 60h. "Sempervivum mont L"; 1k. "Gentiana clusil perr, et song"; 2k. "Pulsatilla slavica reuss".

360 A. Mucha (painter and stamp designer)

1960. Stamp Day and Birth Centenary of Mucha.

1197	**360**	60h. blue	70	10

361 Automatic Machinery

1961. 3rd Five Year Plan (2nd issue).

1198	**361**	20h. blue	10	10
1199	-	30h. red	20	10
1200	-	60h. green	20	10

DESIGNS: 30h. Turbo-generator and control desk; 60h. Excavator.

362 Motor Cyclists (Int Grand Prix, Brno)

1961. Sports Events of 1961.

1201	**362**	30h. blue and mauve	20	10
1202	-	30h. red and blue	20	10
1203	-	40h. black and red	35	10
1204	-	60h. purple and blue	35	10
1205	-	1k. blue and yellow	35	10
1206	-	1k.20 green & salmon	35	10
1207	-	1k.60 brown and red	1·60	1·00

DESIGNS—VERT: 30h. (No. 1202), Athletes with banners (40th anniv of Czech Physical Culture); 60h. Figure skating (World Figure Skating Championships, Prague); 1k. Rugger (35th anniv of rugby football in Czechoslovakia); 1k.20, Football (60th anniv of football in Czechoslovakia); 1k.60, Running (65th anniv of Bechovice–Prague Marathon Race). HORIZ: 40h. Rowing (European Rowing Championships, Prague).

363 Exhibition Emblem

1961. "PRAGA 1962" Int Stamp Exn (1st issue).

1208	**363**	2k. red and blue	2·00	20

See also Nos. 1250/6, 1267/70, 1297/1300 and 1311/15.

364 "Sputnik 3"

1961. Space Research (1st series).

1209	-	20h. red and violet	50	10
1210	**364**	30h. blue and buff	50	10
1211	-	40h. red and green	45	15
1212	-	60h. violet and yellow	30	10
1213	-	1k.60 blue and green	50	10
1214	-	2k. purple and blue	1·50	1·00

DESIGNS—VERT: 20h. Launching cosmic rocket; 40h. Venus rocket. HORIZ: 60h. "Lunik 1"; 1k.60, "Lunik 3" and Moon; 2k. Cosmonaut (similar to T **366**).

See also Nos. 1285/90 and 1349/54.

365 J. Mosna

1961. Cultural Anniversaries.

1215	**365**	60h. green	30	10
1216	-	60h. black	40	10
1217	-	60h. blue	40	10
1218	-	60h. red	30	10
1219	-	60h. brown	30	10

PORTRAITS: No. 1216, J. Uprka (painter); 1217, P. O. Hviezdoslav (poet); 1218, A. Mrstik (writer); 1219, J. Hora (poet).

366 Man in Space

1961. World's 1st Manned Space Flight.

1220	**366**	60h. red and turquoise	55	10
1221	**366**	3k. blue and yellow	2·00	50

367 Kladno Steel Mills

1961

1222	**367**	3k. red	85	10

368 "Instrumental Music"

1961. 150th Anniv of Prague Conservatoire.

1223	**368**	30h. sepia	30	10
1224	-	30h. red	35	10

1225	-	60h. blue	30	10

DESIGNS: No. 1224, Dancer; 1225, Girl playing lyre.

369 "People's House" (Lenin Museum), Prague

1961. 40th Anniv of Czech Communist Party.

1226	**369**	30h. brown	25	10
1227	-	30h. blue	25	10
1228	-	30h. violet	25	10
1229	-	60h. red	25	10
1230	-	60h. myrtle	25	10
1231	-	60h. red	25	10

DESIGNS—HORIZ: No. 1227, Gottwald's Museum, Prague. VERT: No. 1228, Workers in Wenceslas Square, Prague; 1229, Worker, star and factory plant; 1230, Woman wielding hammer and sickle; 1231, May Day procession, Wenceslas Square.

370 Manasek Doll

1961. Czech Puppets.

1232	**370**	30h. red and yellow	20	10
1233	-	40h. sepia & turquoise	20	10
1234	-	60h. blue and salmon	20	10
1235	-	1k. green and blue	20	10
1236	-	1k.60 red and blue	1·25	35

PUPPETS: 40h. "Dr. Faustus and Caspar"; 60h. "Spejbl and Hurvinek"; 1k. Scene from "Difficulties with the Moon" (Askenazy); 1k.60, "Jasanek" of Brno.

371 Gagarin waving Flags

1961. Yuri Gagarin's (first man in space) Visit to Prague.

1237	**371**	60h. black and red	25	10
1238	-	1k.80 black and blue	45	10

DESIGN: 1k.80, Yuri Gagarin in space helmet, rocket and dove.

372 Woman's Head and Map of Africa

1961. Czecho-African Friendship.

1239	**372**	60h. red and blue	25	10

373 Map of Europe and Fair Emblem

1961. Int Trade Fair, Brno. Inscr "M.V.B. 1961".

1240	**373**	30h. blue and green	15	10
1241	-	60h. green & salmon	25	10
1242	-	1k. brown and blue	25	10

DESIGNS—VERT: 60h. Horizontal drill. HORIZ: 1k. Scientific discussion group.

374 Clover and Cow

1961. Agricultural Produce.

1243		20h. purple and blue	15	10
1244	**374**	30h. ochre and purple	15	10
1245	-	40h. orange and brown	15	10
1246	-	60h. bistre and green	20	10
1247	-	1k.40 brown & choc	40	10
1248	-	2k. blue and purple	1·40	50

DESIGNS: 20h. Sugar beet, cup and saucer; 40h. Wheat and bread; 60h. Hops and beer; 1k.40, Maize and cattle; 2k. Potatoes and factory.

375 Prague

1961. 26th Session of Red Cross Societies League Governors' Council, Prague.

1249	**375**	60h. violet and red	1·00	10

376 Orlik Dam

1961. "Praga 1962" International Stamp Exhibition (2nd and 3rd issues).

1250	**376**	20h. black and blue	75	30
1251	-	30h. blue and red	45	10
1252	-	40h. blue and green	75	30
1253	-	60h. slate and bistre	75	30
1267	-	1k. purple and green	55	50
1254	-	1k.20 green and pink	90	45
1268	-	1k.60 brown and violet	95	65
1269	-	2k. black and orange	1·50	1·10
1255	-	3k. blue and yellow	1·60	45
1256	-	4k. violet and orange	2·25	1·25
1270	-	5k. multicoloured	22·00	17·00

DESIGNS—As Type **376**: 30h. Prague; 40h. Hluboka Castle from lake; 60h. Karlovy Vary; 1k. Pilsen; 1k.20, North Bohemian landscape; 1k.60, High Tatras; 2k. Iron-works, Ostrava-Kuncice; 3k. Brno; 4k. Bratislava. (50×29 mm): 5k. Prague and flags.

377 Orange-tip

1961. Butterflies and Moths. Multicoloured.

1257	15h. Type **377**	35	10
1258	20h. Southern festoon	50	10
1259	30h. Apollo	90	25
1260	40h. Swallowtail	90	25
1261	60h. Peacock	1·10	25
1262	80h. Camberwell beauty	1·25	25
1263	1k. Clifden's nonpareil	1·25	25
1264	1k.60 Red admiral	1·40	40
1265	2k. Brimstone	2·75	1·90

378 Congress Emblem and World Map

1961. 5th W.F.T.U. Congress, Moscow.

1266	**378**	60h. blue and red	45	10

379 Racing Cyclists (Berlin–Prague–Warsaw Cycle Race)

1962. Sports Events of 1962.

1271	**379**	30h. black and blue	25	10
1272	-	40h. black and yellow	20	10
1273	-	60h. grey and blue	30	10
1274	-	1k. black and pink	30	10
1275	-	1k.20 black and green	30	10
1276	-	1k.60 black and green	1·40	55

DESIGNS: 40h. Gymnastics (15th World Gymnastics Championships, Prague); 60h. Figure Skating (World Figure Skating Championships, Prague); 1k. Bowling (World Bowling Championships, Bratislava); 1k.20, Football (World Cup Football Championship, Chile); 1k.60, Throwing the discus (7th European Athletic Championships, Belgrade).

See also No. 1306.

380 K. Kovarovic (composer, centenary of birth)

1962. Cultural Celebrities and Anniversaries.

1277	**380**	10h. brown	10	10
1278	-	20h. blue	10	10
1279	-	30h. brown	10	10
1280	-	40h. purple	15	10
1281	-	60h. black	15	10
1282	-	1k.60 myrtle	40	10
1283	-	1k.80 blue	50	10

DESIGNS—As Type **380**: 20h. F. Skroup (composer); 30h. Bozena Nemcova (writer); 60h. Rod of Aesculapius and Prague Castle (Czech Medical Association Cent); 1k.60, L. Celakovsky (founder, Czech Botanical Society). HORIZ: (41×22½ mm): 40h. F. Zaviska and K. Petr; 1k.80, M. Valouch and J. Hronec. (These two commemorate Czech Mathematics and Physics Union Cent).

381 Miner holding Lamp

1962. 30th Anniv of Miners' Strike, Most.

1284	**381**	60h. blue and red	25	10

382 "Man Conquers Space"

1962. Space Research (2nd series).

1285	**382**	30h. red and blue	25	10
1286	-	40h. blue and orange	25	10
1287	-	60h. blue and pink	25	10
1288	-	80h. purple and green	60	10
1289	-	1k. blue and yellow	25	25
1290	-	1k.60 green and yellow	1·40	60

DESIGNS—VERT: 40h. Launching of Soviet rocket; 1k. Automatic station on Moon. HORIZ: 60h. "Vostok-II"; 80h. Multi-stage automatic rocket; 1k.60, Television satellite station.

383 Indian and African Elephants

1962. Animals of Prague Zoos.

1291		20h. black & turquoise	55	10
1292		30h. black and violet	55	10
1293		60h. black and yellow	65	10
1294	**383**	1k. black and green	95	10
1295	-	1k.40 black and mauve	1·00	25
1296	-	1k.60 black and brown	2·10	1·10

ANIMALS—VERT: 20h. Polar bear; 30h. Chimpanzee; 60h. Bactrian camel. HORIZ: 1k.40, Leopard; 1k.60, Wild horses.

384 Dove and Nest

1962. Air. "Praga 1962" International Stamp Exhibition (4th issue).

1297	**384**	80h. multicoloured	50	25
1298	-	1k.40 red, blue & black	2·00	2·75
1299	-	2k.80 multicoloured	3·25	2·75
1300	-	4k.20 multicoloured	4·75	2·75

DESIGNS: 1k.40, Dove; 2k.80, Flower and bird; 4k.20, Plant and bird. All designs feature "Praga 62" emblem. The 80h. and 2k.80 are inscr in Slovakian and the others in Czech.

385 Girl of Lidice

1962. 20th Anniv of Destruction of Lidice and Lezaky.

1301	**385**	30h. black and red	35	10
1302	-	60h. black and blue	35	10

DESIGN: 60h. Flowers and Lezaky ruins.

386 Klary's Fountain, Teplice

1962. 1200th Anniv of Discovery of Teplice Springs.

1303	**386**	60h. green and yellow	45	10

387 Campaign Emblem

1962. Malaria Eradication.

1304	**387**	60h. red and black	15	10
1305	-	3k. blue and black	1·25	65

DESIGN: 3k. Campaign emblem and dove (different).

1962. Czechoslovakia's Participation in World Cup Football Championship Final, Chile. As No. 1275 but inscr "CSSR VE FINALE" and new value.

1306	1k.60 green and yellow	1·25	20

388 Swimmer with Rifle

1962. 2nd Military Spartacist Games. Inscr as in T 388.

1307	**388**	30h. myrtle and blue	15	10
1308	-	40h. violet and yellow	20	10
1309	-	60h. brown and green	25	10
1310	-	1k. blue and red	30	10

DESIGNS: 40h. Soldier mounting obstacle; 60h. Footballer; 1k. Relay Race.

389 "Sun" and Field (Socialized Agriculture)

1962. "Praga 1962" Int Stamp Exn (5th issue).

1311	**389**	30h. multicoloured	3·00	1·10
1312	-	60h. multicoloured	80	25
1313	-	80h. multicoloured	3·50	2·40
1314	-	1k. multicoloured	3·50	2·75
1315	-	1k.40 multicoloured	3·50	2·75

MS1315a 96×75 mm. 5k. multicoloured (View of Prague with Exhibition emblem) (perf or imperf) 16·00 16·00

DESIGNS—VERT: 60h. Astronaut in "spaceship"; 1k.40, Children playing under "tree". HORIZ: 80h. Boy with flute, and peace doves; 1k. Workers of three races. All have "Praga 62" emblem.

390 Swallow, "Praga 62" and Congress Emblems

1962. F.I.P. Day (Federation Internationale de Philatelie).

1316	**390**	1k.60 multicoloured	4·75	4·00

391 Zinkovy Sanatorium and Sailing Dinghy

1962. Czech Workers' Social Facilities.

1317	-	30h. black and blue	20	10
1318	**391**	60h. sepia and ochre	25	10

DESIGN—HORIZ: 30h. Children in day nursery, and factory.

392 Cruiser "Aurora"

1962. 45th Anniv of Russian Revolution.

1319	**392**	30h. sepia and blue	10	10
1320	**392**	60h. black and pink	25	10

393 Astronaut and Worker

1962. 40th Anniv of U.S.S.R.

1321	**393**	30h. red and blue	25	10
1322	-	60h. black and pink	30	10

DESIGN—VERT: 60h. Lenin.

394 Crane ("Building Construction")

1962. 12th Czech Communist Party Congress, Prague.

1323	**394**	30h. red and yellow	25	10
1324	-	40h. blue and yellow	25	10
1325	-	60h. black and pink	25	10

DESIGNS—VERT: 40h. Produce ("Agriculture"). HORIZ: 60h. Factory plants ("Industry").

395 Stag Beetle

1962. Beetles. Multicoloured.

1326	20h. Caterpillar-hunter (horiz)	25	10
1327	30h. Cardinal beetle (horiz)	25	10
1328	60h. Type **395**	25	10
1329	1k. Great dung beetle (horiz)	85	10
1330	1k.60 Alpine longhorn beetle	1·25	35
1331	2k. Blue ground beetle	3·00	1·40

396 Table Tennis (World Championships, Prague)

1963. Sports Events of 1963.

1332	**396**	30h. black and green	25	10
1333	-	60h. black and orange	25	10
1334	-	80h. black and blue	25	10
1335	-	1k. black and violet	30	10
1336	-	1k.20 black and brown	30	20
1337	-	1k.60 black and red	90	20

DESIGNS: 60h. Cycling (80th Anniv of Czech Cycling); 80h. Skiing (1st Czech Winter Games); 1k. Motor-cycle dirt track racing (15th Anniv of "Golden Helmet" Race, Pardubice); 1k.20, Weightlifting (World Championships, Prague); 1k.60, Hurdling (1st Czech Summer Games).

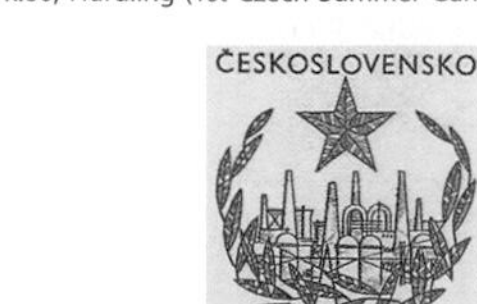

397 Industrial Plant

1963. 15th Anniv of "Victorious February" and 5th T.U. Congress.

1338	**397**	30h. red and blue	15	10
1339	-	60h. red and black	15	10
1340	-	60h. black and red	15	10

DESIGNS—VERT: No. 1339, Sun and campfire. HORIZ: No. 1340, Industrial plant and annual "stepping stones".

398 Guild Emblem

1963. Cultural Anniversaries.

1341	**398**	20h. black and blue	10	10
1342	-	30h. red	10	10
1343	-	30h. red and blue	10	10
1344	-	60h. black	15	10
1345	-	60h. purple and blue	15	10
1346	-	60h. myrtle	15	10
1347	-	1k.60 brown	45	10

DESIGNS—VERT: No. 1341 (Artist's Guild cent); 1342, E. Urx (journalist); 1343, J. Janosik (national hero); 1344, J. Palkovic (author); 1346, Woman with book, and children (cent of Slovak Cultural Society, Slovenska Matice); 1347, M. Svabinsky (artist, after self-portrait). HORIZ: 1345, Allegorical figure and National Theatre, Prague (80th anniv).

399 Young People

1963. 4th Czech Youth Federation Congress, Prague.

1348	**399**	30h. blue and red	25	10

1963. Space Research (3rd series). As T 364 but inscr "1963" at foot.

1349	30h. purple, red & yellow	15	10
1350	50h. blue and turquoise	25	10
1351	60h. turquoise & yellow	25	10
1352	1k. black and brown	55	10
1353	1k.60 sepia and green	40	10
1354	2k. violet and yellow	1·60	75
MS1354a	84×70 mm. 3k. orange and green (Spacecraft and Mars). Imperf	7·00	4·00

DESIGNS—HORIZ: 30h. Rocket circling Sun; 50h. Rockets and Sputniks leaving Earth; 60h. Spacecraft and Moon; 1k. "Mars 1" rocket and Mars; 1k.60, Rocket heading for Jupiter; 2k. Spacecraft returning from Saturn.

400 TV Cameras and Receiver

1963. 10th Anniv of Czech Television Service. Inscr as in T 400.

1355	**400**	40h. blue and orange	20	10
1356	-	60h. red and blue	20	10

DESIGN—VERT: 60h. TV transmitting aerial.

401 Broadcasting Studio and Receiver

1963. 40th Anniv of Czech Radio Service. Inscr as in T 401.

1357	**401**	30h. purple and blue	15	10
1358	-	1k. purple & turquoise	25	10

DESIGN—VERT: 1k. Aerial mast, globe and doves.

402 Ancient Ring and Moravian Settlements Map

1963. 1100th Anniv of Moravian Empire.

1359	**402**	30h. black and green	20	10
1360	-	1k.60 black and yellow	40	10

DESIGN: 1k.60, Ancient silver plate showing falconer with hawk.

403 Tupolev Tu-104A

1963. 40th Anniv of Czech Airlines.

1361	**403**	80h. violet and blue	80	20
1362	-	1k.80 blue and green	1·50	45

DESIGN: 1k.80, Ilyushin Il-18B.

404 Singer

1963. 60th Anniv of Moravian Teachers' Singing Club.

1363	**404**	30h. red	35	10

405 Nurse and Child

1963. Centenary of Red Cross.

1364	**405**	30h. blue and red	35	10

406 Wheatears and Kromeriz Castle

1963. National Agricultural Exhibition.

1365	**406**	30h. green and yellow	35	10

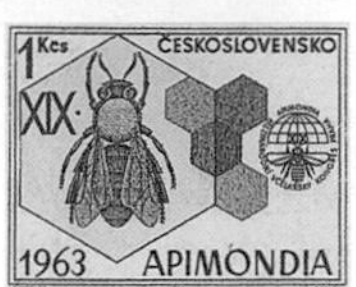

407 Honey Bee, Honeycomb and Congress Emblem

1963. 19th International Bee-keepers' Congress ("Apimondia '63").

1366	**407**	1k. brown and yellow	45	10

408 "Vostok 5" and Bykovsky

1963. 2nd "Team" Manned Space Flights.

1367	**408**	80h. pink and blue	35	10
1368	-	2k.80 blue and purple	2·25	25

DESIGN: 2k.80, "Vostok 6" and Valentina Tereshkova.

409 "Modern Fashion"

1963. Liberec Consumer Goods Fair.

1369	**409**	30h. black and mauve	35	10

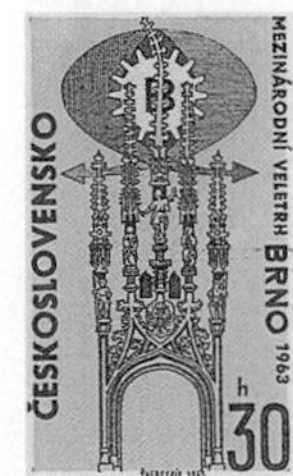

410 Portal of Brno Town Hall

1963. Brno International Fair.

1370	**410**	30h. purple and blue	25	10
1371	-	60h. blue and salmon	30	10

DESIGN: 60h. Tower of Brno Town Hall.

411 Cave and Stalagmites

1963. Czech Scenery. (a) Moravia.

1372	**411**	30h. brown and blue	25	10
1373	-	80h. brown and pink	40	10

(b) Slovakia.

1374	30h. blue and green	30	10
1375	60h. blue, green & yellow	30	10

DESIGNS: No. 1373, Macocha Chasm; 1374, Pool, Hornad Valley; 1375, Waterfall, Great Hawk Gorge.

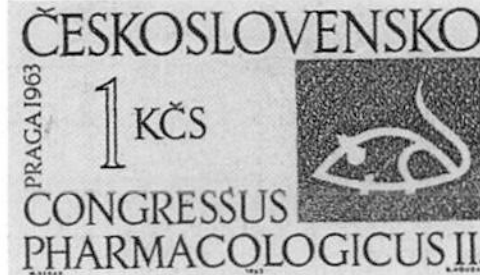

412 Mouse

1963. 2nd International Pharmacological Congress, Prague.

1376	**412**	1k. red and black	45	10

413 Blast Furnace

1963. 30th International Foundry Congress, Prague.

1377	**413**	60h. black and blue	25	10

414 "Aid for Farmers Abroad"

1963. Freedom from Hunger.

1378	**414**	1k.60 sepia	45	10

415 Dolls

1963. UNESCO. Folk Art. Multicoloured.

1379	60h. Type **415**	15	10
1380	80h. Rooster	25	10
1381	1k. Vase of flowers	35	20
1382	1k.20 Detail of glass-painting "Janosik and his Men"	35	10
1383	1k.60 Stag	35	20
1384	2k. Horseman	2·75	1·10

416 Canoeing

1963. Olympic Games, Tokyo, 1964, and 50th Anniv of Czech Canoeing (30h.).

1385	**416**	30h. blue and green	30	10
1386	-	40h. brown and blue	30	10
1387	-	60h. lake and yellow	25	10
1388	-	80h. violet and red	30	20
1389	-	1k. blue and red	30	20
1390	-	1k.60 ultram & blue	1·50	70

DESIGNS: 40h. Volleyball; 60h. Wrestling; 80h. Basketball; 1k. Boxing; 1k.60, Gymnastics.

417 Linden Tree

1963. 20th Anniv of Czech–Soviet Treaty of Friendship.

1391	**417**	30h. brown and blue	15	10
1392	-	60h. red and green	15	10

DESIGN: 60h. Hammer and sickle, and star.

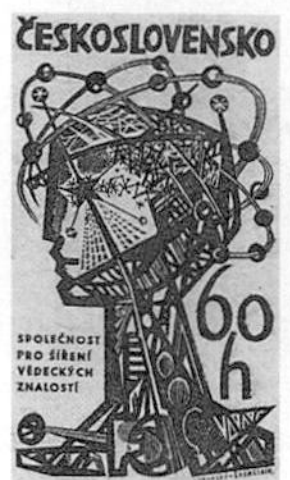

418 "Human Reason and Technology."

1963. Technical and Scientific Knowledge Society Congress.

1393	**418**	60h. violet	35	10

419 Chamois

1963. Mountain Animals.

1394	**419**	30h. multicoloured	65	15
1395	-	40h. multicoloured	65	30
1396	-	60h. sepia, yellow & grn	1·00	35
1397	-	1k.20 multicoloured	1·00	15
1398	-	1k.60 multicoloured	1·40	40
1399	-	2k. brown, orge & grn	4·00	2·25

ANIMALS: 40h. Ibex; 60h. Mouflon; 1k.20, Roe deer; 1k.60, Fallow deer; 2k. Red deer.

420 Figure Skating

1964. Sports Events of 1964.

1400	**420**	30h. violet and yellow	15	10
1401	-	80h. blue and orange	15	10
1402	-	1k. brown and lilac	80	20

DESIGNS—VERT: 30h. Type **420** (Czech Students' Games); 1k. Handball (World Handball Championships). HORIZ: 80h. Cross-country skiing (Students' Games).

421 Ice Hockey

1964. Winter Olympic Games, Innsbruck.

1403	**421**	1k. purple and turquoise	75	30
1404	-	1k.80 green & lavender	1·00	55
1405	-	2k. blue and green	2·50	2·10

DESIGNS—VERT: 1k.80, Tobogganing. HORIZ: 2k. Ski jumping.

422 Belanske Tatra Mountains, Skiers and Tree

1964. Tourist Issue.

1406	**422**	30h. purple and blue	20	10
1407	-	60h. blue and red	30	10
1408	-	1k. brown and olive	55	10
1409	-	1k.80 green and orange	1·00	35

DESIGNS: 60h. Telc (Moravia) and motorcamp; 1k. Spis Castle (Slovakia) and angler; 1k.80, Cesky Krumlov (Bohemia) and sailing dinghies. Each design includes a tree.

423 Magura Hotel, Zdiar, High Tatra

1964. Trade Union Recreation Hotels.

1410	**423**	60h. green and yellow	20	10
1411	-	80h. blue and pink	20	10

DESIGN: 80h. "Slovak Insurrection" Hotel, Lower Tatra.

424 Statuary (after Michelangelo)

1964. UNESCO Cultural Anniversaries.

1412	**424**	40h. black and green	20	10
1413	-	60h. black and red	20	10
1414	-	1k. black and blue	45	15
1415	-	1k.60 black and yellow	45	10

DESIGNS—HORIZ: 40h. Type **424** (400th death anniv of Michelangelo); 60h. Bottom, "Midsummer Night's Dream" (400th birth anniv of Shakespeare); 1k.60, King George of Podebrady (500th anniv of his mediation in Europe). VERT: 1k. Galileo Galilei (400th birth anniv).

425 Yuri Gagarin

1964. "Space Exploration". On cream paper.

1416	**425**	30h. blue and black	55	15
1417	-	60h. red and green	30	10
1418	-	80h. violet and lake	55	20
1419	-	1k. violet and blue	85	25
1420	-	1k.20 bronze and red	55	25
1421	-	1k.40 turq & black	1·25	55
1422	-	1k.60 turq & violet	3·75	1·25
1423	-	2k. red and blue	85	25

ASTRONAUTS—HORIZ: 60h. Titov; 80h. Glenn; 1k.20, Popovich and Nikolaev. VERT: 1k. Carpenter; 1k.40, Schirra; 1k.60, Cooper; 2k. Tereshkova and Bykovsky.

426 Campanula

1964. Wild Flowers.

1424	**426**	60h. purple, orge & grn	1·50	10
1425	-	80h. multicoloured	1·50	10
1426	-	1k. blue, pink & green	1·50	40
1427	-	1k.20 multicoloured	60	30
1428	-	1k.60 violet & green	80	40
1429	-	2k. red, turq & violet	4·75	1·90

FLOWERS: 80h. Musk thistle; 1k. Chicory; 1k.20, Yellow iris; 1k.60, Marsh gentian; 2k. Common poppy.

427 Miner of 1764

1964. Czech Anniversaries.

1430		30h. black and yellow	25	10
1431		60h. red and blue	50	10
1432	**427**	60h. sepia and green	25	10

DESIGNS—HORIZ: (30½×22½ mm): 30h. Silesian coat of arms (stylized) (150th Anniv of Silesian Museum, Opava). (41½×23 mm): 60h. (No. 1431), Skoda ASC-16 fire engine (Centenary of Voluntary Fire Brigades); 60h. (No. 1432), (Bicentenary of Banska Stiavnica Mining School).

428 Cine-film "Flower"

1964. 14th Int Film Festival, Karlovy Vary.

1433	**428**	60h. black, blue & red	1·60	10

429 Hradcany, Praque and Black-headed Gulls

1964. 4th Czech Red Cross Congress, Prague.

1434	**429**	60h. violet and red	45	10

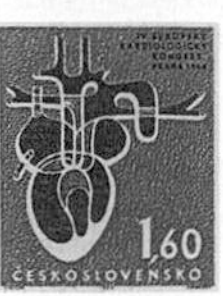

430 Human Heart

1964. 4th European Cardiological Congress, Prague.

1435	**430**	1k.60 red and blue	1·00	10

431 Slovak Girl and Workers

1964. 20th Anniv of Slovak Rising and Dukla Battles.

1436	**431**	30h. red and brown	10	10
1437	-	60h. blue and red	10	10
1438	-	60h. sepia and red	10	10

DESIGNS: No. 1437, Armed Slovaks; 1438, Soldiers in battle at Dukla Pass.

432 Hradcany, Prague

1964. Millenary of Prague.

1439	**432**	60h. brown & mauve	45	10
MS1439a		76×99 mm. 5k. red (Charles Bridge and City). Imperf	2·75	2·40

433 Cycling

1964. Olympic Games, Tokyo. Multicoloured.

1440	60h. Type **433**	40	20
1441	80h. Throwing the discus and pole vaulting (vert)	45	20
1442	1k. Football (vert)	45	20
1443	1k.20 Rowing (vert)	55	35
1444	1k.60 Swimming	90	35
1445	2k.80 Weightlifting	4·00	2·40

433a "Voskhod", Astronauts and Globe

1964. Three-manned Space Flight of October 12–13.

MS1445a	**433a** 3k. blue and lilac	5·75	4·25

434 Common Redstart

1964. Birds. Multicoloured.

1446	30h. Type **434**	35	10
1447	60h. Green woodpecker	65	10
1448	80h. Hawfinch	90	25
1449	1k. Black woodpecker	90	30
1450	1k.20 European robin	90	35
1451	1k.60 Eurasian roller	1·40	90

435 Brno Engineering Works (150th Anniv)

1964. Czech Engineering.

1452	**435**	30h. brown	10	10
1453	-	60h. green and salmon	25	10

DESIGN: 60h. Class T334.0 diesel-hydraulic shunter.

436 "Dancing Girl"

1965. 3rd National Spartacist Games.

1454	**436**	30h. red and blue	10	10

See also Nos. 1489/92.

437 Mountain Rescue Service (10th Anniv)

1965. Sports Events of 1965.

1455	**437**	60h. violet and blue	20	10
1456	-	60h. lake and orange	20	10
1457	-	60h. green and red	20	10
1458	-	60h. green and yellow	20	10

SPORTS: No. 1456, Exercising with hoop (1st World Artistic Gymnastics Championships, Prague); 1457, Cycling (World Indoor Cycling Championships, Prague); 1458, Hurdling (Czech University Championships, Brno).

438 Domazlice

1965. 700th Annivs of Six Czech Towns, and 20th Anniv of Terezin Concentration Camp (No. 1465).

1459	**438**	30h. violet and yellow	20	10
1460	-	30h. violet and blue	20	10
1461	-	30h. blue and olive	20	10
1462	-	30h. sepia and olive	20	10
1463	-	30h. green and buff	20	10
1464	-	30h. slate and drab	20	10
1465	-	30h. red and black	20	10

TOWNS: No. 1460, Beroun; 1461, Zatec; 1462, Policka; 1463, Lipnik and Becvou; 1464, Frydek-Mistek; 1465, Terezin concentration camp.

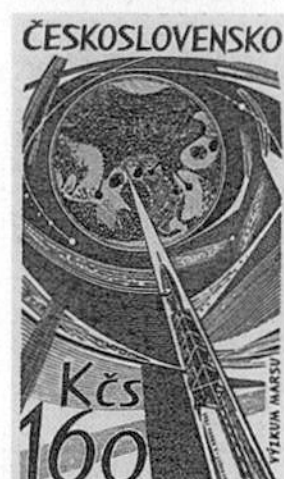

439 Exploration of Mars

1965. Int Quiet Sun Years and Space Research.

1466		20h. purple and red	25	10
1467		30h. yellow and red	25	10
1468		60h. blue and yellow	25	10
1469		1k. violet & turquoise	50	10
1470		1k.40 slate and salmon	50	25
1471	**439**	1k.60 black and pink	50	25
1472	-	2k. blue & turquoise	1·40	1·25

DESIGNS—HORIZ: 20h. Maximum sun-spot activity; 30h. Minimum sun-spot activity ("Quiet Sun"); 60h. Moon exploration; 1k.40, Artificial satellite and space station; 2k. Soviet "Kosmos" and U.S. "Tiros" satellites. VERT: 1k. Spaceships rendezvous.

440 Horse Jumping (Amsterdam, 1928)

1965. Czechoslovakia's Olympic Victories.

1473	**440**	20h. brown and gold	20	10
1474	-	30h. violet and green	20	10
1475	-	60h. blue and gold	20	10
1476	-	1k. brown and gold	40	20
1477	-	1k.40 green and gold	85	55
1478	-	1k.60 black and gold	85	55
1479	-	2k. red and gold	85	25

DESIGNS (each with city feature): 30h. Throwing the discus (Paris, 1900); 60h. Marathon (Helsinki, 1952); 1k. Weightlifting (Los Angeles, 1932); 1k.40, Gymnastics (Berlin, 1936); 1k.60, Rowing (Rome, 1960); 2k. Gymnastics (Tokyo, 1964).

441 Leonov in Space

1965. Space Achievements.

1480	**441**	60h. purple and blue	15	20
1481	-	60h. blue and mauve	15	20
1482	-	3k. purple and blue	1·40	1·10
1483	-	3k. blue and mauve	1·40	1·10

DESIGNS: No. 1481, Grissom, Young and "Gemini 3"; 1482, Leonov leaving spaceship "Voskhod 2"; 1483, "Gemini 3" on launching pad at Cape Kennedy.

442 Soldier

1965. 20th Anniv of Liberation. Inscr "20 LET CSSR".

1484	**442**	30h. olive, black & red	20	10
1485	-	30h. violet, blue & red	20	10
1486	-	60h. black, red & blue	25	10
1487	-	1k. violet, brown & orge	50	20
1488	-	1k.60 multicoloured	85	40

DESIGNS: 30h. (No. 1485), Workers; 60h. Mechanic; 1k. Building worker; 1k.60, Peasant.

443 Children's Exercises

1965. 3rd National Spartacist Games.

1489	**443**	30h. blue and red	15	10
1490	-	60h. brown and blue	20	10
1491	-	1k. blue and yellow	30	10
1492	-	1k.60 red and brown	35	25

DESIGNS: 60h. Young gymnasts; 1k. Women's exercises; 1k.60, Start of race.

444 Slovak "Kopov"

1965. Canine Events.

1493	**444**	30h. black and red	40	10
1494	-	40h. black & yellow	40	10
1495	-	60h. black and red	50	10
1496	-	1k. black and red	95	10
1497	-	1k.60 black & yellow	60	25
1498	-	2k. black and orange	2·10	1·10

DOGS: 30h. Type **444**; 1k. Poodle (Int Dog-breeders' Congress, Prague); 40h. German sheepdog; 60h. Czech "fousek" (retriever), (both World Dog Exn, Brno); 1k.60, Czech terrier; 2k. Afghan hound (both Plenary Session of F.C.I.—Int Federation of Cynology, Prague).

445 U.N. Emblem

1965. U.N. Commem and Int Co-operation Year.

1499	**445**	60h. brown & yellow	20	10
1500	-	1k. blue and turquoise	45	10
1501	-	1k.60 red and gold	45	30

DESIGNS: 60h. T **445** (The inscr reads "Twentieth Anniversary of the signing of the U.N. Charter"); 1k. U.N. Headquarters ("20th Anniv of U.N."); 1k.60, I.C.Y. emblem.

446 "SOF" and Linked Rings

1965. 20th Anniv of World Federation of Trade Unions.

1502	**446**	60h. red and blue	35	10

447 Women of Three Races

1965. 20th Anniv of International Democratic Women's Federation.

1503	**447**	60h. blue	35	10

448 Children's House

1965. Prague Castle (1st series). Inscr "PRAHA HRAD".

1504	**448**	30h. green	20	10
1505	-	60h. sepia	25	10

DESIGN—VERT: 60h. Mathias Gate.

See also Nos. 1572/3, 1656/7, 1740/1, 1827/8, 1892/3, 1959/60, 2037/8, 2103/4, 2163/4, 2253/4, 2305/6, 2337/8, 2404/5, 2466/7, 2543/4, 2599/2600, 2637/8, 2685/6, 2739/40, 2803/4, 2834/5, 2878/9, 2950/1, 2977/8 and 3026/7.

449 Marx and Lenin

1965. 6th Organization of Socialist Countries' Postal Ministers Conference, Peking.

1506	**449**	60h. red and gold	25	10

450 Jan Hus

1965. Various Anniversaries and Events (1st issue).

1507	**450**	60h. black and red	25	10
1508	-	60h. blue and red	25	10
1509	-	60h. lilac and gold	25	10
1510	-	1k. blue and orange	30	10

DESIGNS—VERT: No. 1507, T **450** (reformer, 550th death anniv); 1508, G. J. Mendel (publication cent in Brno of his study of heredity). HORIZ: (30½×23 mm): No. 1509, Jewellery emblems ("Jablonec 65" Jewellery Exn); 1510, Early telegraph and telecommunications satellite (I.T.U. cent).

451 "Lady at her Toilet" (after Titian)

1965. Culture. Sheet 75×99 mm.

MS1511	**451**	5k. multicoloured	3·50	3·00

1965. Various Anniversaries and Events (2nd issue). As T 450.

1512	30h. black and green	15	10
1513	30h. black and brown	15	10
1514	60h. black and red	20	10
1515	60h. brown on cream	20	10
1516	1k. black and orange	20	10

DESIGNS—As Type **450**. HORIZ: No. 1512, L. Stur (nationalist, 150th birth anniv); 1513, J. Navratil (painter, death cent). VERT: No. 1514, B. Martinu (composer, 75th birth anniv). LARGER—VERT: (23½×30½ mm): No. 1515, Allegoric figure (Academia Istropolitana, Bratislava, 500th anniv). HORIZ: (30×22½ mm): No. 1516, Emblem (IUPAC Macromolecular Symposium, Prague).

452 "Fourfold Aid"

1965. Flood Relief.

1517	**452**	30h. blue	15	10
1518	-	2k. black and olive	70	40

DESIGN—HORIZ: 2k. Rescue by boat.

453 Dotterel

1965. Mountain Birds. Multicoloured.

1519	30h. Type **453**	60	10
1520	60h. Wallcreeper (vert)	60	10
1521	1k.20 Redpoll	65	30
1522	1k.40 Golden eagle (vert)	1·10	35
1523	1k.60 Ring ousel	90	40
1524	2k. Spotted nutcracker (vert)	2·00	1·50

454 Levoca

1965. Czech Towns. (a) Size 23×19 mm.

1525	**454**	5h. black and yellow	10	10
1526	-	10h. blue and bistre	20	10
1527	-	20h. sepia and blue	10	10
1528	-	30h. blue and green	20	10
1529	-	40h. sepia and blue	20	10
1530	-	50h. black and buff	25	10
1531	-	60h. red and blue	30	10
1532	-	1k. violet and green	35	10

(b) Size 30½×23½ mm.

1533	1k.20 olive and blue	30	10
1534	1k.60 blue and yellow	55	10
1535	2k. bronze and green	70	10
1536	3k. purple & yellow	85	10
1537	5k. black and pink	1·60	10

TOWNS: 10h. Jindrichuv Hradec; 20h. Nitra; 30h. Kosice; 40h. Hradec Kralove; 50h. Telc; 60h. Ostrava; 1k. Olomouc; 1k.20, Ceske Budejovice; 1k.60, Cheb; 2k. Brno; 3k. Bratislava; 5k. Prague.

455 Coltsfoot

1965. Medicinal Plants. Multicoloured.

1538	30h. Type **455**	25	10
1539	60h. Meadow saffron	45	10
1540	80h. Common poppy	50	10
1541	1k. Foxglove	60	15
1542	1k.20 Arnica	1·00	25
1543	1k.60 Cornflower	75	35
1544	2k. Dog rose	3·00	1·50

456 Panorama of "Stamps"

1965. Stamp Day.

1545	**456**	1k. red and green	3·75	3·50

457 "Music"

1966. 70th Anniv of Czech Philharmonic Orchestra.

1546	**457**	30h. black and gold	55	25

458 Pair Dancing

1966. Sports Events of 1966. (a) European Figure Skating Championships, Bratislava.

1547	**458**	30h. red and pink	15	10
1548	-	60h. emerald and green	20	10
1549	-	1k.60 brown & yellow	40	20
1550	-	2k. blue and turquoise	2·50	35

DESIGNS: 60h. Male skater leaping; 1k.60, Female skater leaping; 2k. Pair-skaters taking bows.

(b) World Volleyball Championships, Prague.

1551	60h. red and buff	20	10
1552	1k. violet and blue	25	10

DESIGNS—VERT: 60h. Player leaping to ball; 1k. Player falling.

459 S. Sucharda (sculptor)

1966. Cultural Anniversaries.

1553	**459**	30h. green	15	10
1554	-	30h. blue	15	10
1555	-	60h. red	20	10
1556	-	60h. brown	20	10

PORTRAITS: No. 1553, Type **459** (birth centenary); 1554, Ignac J. Pesina (veterinary surgeon, birth bicentenary); 1555, Romain Rolland (writer, birth centenary); 1556, Donatello (sculptor, 500th death anniv).

460 "Ajax", 1841, Austria

1966. Railway Locomotives.

1557	**460**	20h. brown on cream	40	10
1558	-	30h. violet on cream	40	10
1559	-	60h. purple on cream	40	15
1560	-	1k. blue on cream	75	15
1561	-	1k.60 blue on cream	80	15
1562	-	2k. red on cream	4·00	1·25

LOCOMOTIVES: 30h. "Karlstejn", 1865; 60h. Class 423.0 steam locomotive, 1946; 1k. Class 498.0 steam locomotive, 1946; 1k.60, Class S699.0 electric locomotive, 1964; 2k. Class T699.0 diesel locomotive, 1964.

461 Dancer

1966. Centenary of Bedrich Smetana's "Bartered Bride" (opera). Sheet 84×106 mm.

MS1563	**461**	3k. red, blue and deep blue	3·00	2·40

462 Brown Trout

1966. World Angling Championships, Svit. Mult.

1564	30h. Type **462**	30	10
1565	60h. Eurasian perch (horiz)	50	10
1566	1k. Common (Mirror) carp (horiz)	65	10
1567	1k.20 Northern pike (horiz)	65	15
1568	1k.40 European grayling (horiz)	1·00	25
1569	1k.60 European eel (horiz)	3·00	1·00

463 "Solidarity of Mankind"

1966. 20th Anniv of UNESCO.

1570	**463**	60h. black and yellow	25	10

464 W.H.O. Building

1966. Inaug of W.H.O. Headquarters, Geneva.

1571	**464**	1k. ultramarine and blue	45	10

465 Belvedere Palace

1966. Prague Castle (2nd series).

1572	**465**	30h. blue	20	10
1573	-	60h. black and yellow	35	20
MS1574		75×97½ mm. 5k. multicoloured	2·75	3·00

DESIGN: 60h. Wood triptych, "Virgin and Child" (St. George's Church).

See also Nos. 1656/**MS**1658 and 1740/**MS**1742.

467 Scarce Swallowtail

1966. Butterflies and Moths. Multicoloured.

1575	30h. Type **467**	40	10
1576	60h. Moorland clouded yellow	70	10
1577	80h. Lesser purple emperor	70	20
1578	1k. Apollo	70	25
1579	1k.20 Scarlet tiger moth	1·40	35
1580	2k. Cream-spot tiger moth	4·50	1·90

468 Flags

1966. 13th Czechoslovakian Communist Party Congress.

1581	**468**	30h. red and blue	20	10
1582	-	60h. red and blue	20	10
1583	-	1k.60 red and blue	65	10

DESIGNS: 60h. Hammer and sickle; 1k.60, Girl.

469 Indian Village

1966. "North American Indians". Centenary of Naprstek's Ethnographic Museum, Prague.

1584	**469**	20h. blue and orange	20	10
1585	-	30h. black and brown	20	10
1586	-	40h. sepia and blue	20	10
1587	-	60h. green and yellow	25	10
1588	-	1k. purple and green	35	10
1589	-	1k.20 blue and mauve	50	20
1590	-	1k.40 multicoloured	1·25	60

DESIGNS—VERT: 30h. Tomahawk; 40h. Haida totem poles; 60h. Katchina, "good spirit" of Hopi tribe; 1k.20, Dakote calumet (pipe of peace); 1k.40, Dakota Indian chief. HORIZ: 1k. Hunting American bison.

470 Atomic Symbol

1966. Centenary of Czech Chemical Society.

1591	**470**	60h. black and blue	35	10

471 "Guernica", after Picasso (image scaled to 63% of original size)

1966. 30th Anniv of International Brigade's War Service in Spain.

1592	**471**	60h. black and blue	1·75	1·75

472 Pantheon, Bratislava

1966. Cultural Anniversaries.

1593	**472**	30h. lilac	20	10
1594	-	60h. blue	25	10
1595	-	60h. green	25	10
1596	-	60h. brown	25	10

DESIGNS: Type **472** (21st anniv of liberation of Bratislava); 1594, L. Stur (Slovak leader) and Devin Castle; 1595, Nachod (700th anniv); 1596, Arms, globe, books and view of Olomouc (400th anniv of State Science Library).

473 Fair Emblem

1966. Brno International Fair.

1597	**473**	60h. black and red	25	10

474 "Atomic Age"

1966. Jachymov (source of pitch-blende).

1598	**474**	60h. black and red	35	10

475 Olympic Coin

1966. 70th Anniv of Olympic Committee.

1599	**475**	60h. black and gold	20	10
1600	-	1k. blue and red	85	20

DESIGN: 1k. Olympic flame and rings.

476 Missile Carrier, Tank and Mikoyan Gurevich MiG-21D Fighter

1966. Military Manoeuvres.

1601	**476**	60h. black and yellow	35	10

477 Moravian Silver Thaler (reverse and obverse)

1966. Brno Stamp Exhibition.

1602	**477**	30h. black and red	30	10
1603	-	60h. black and orange	30	10
1604	-	1k.60 black and green	85	30
MS1605		75×100 mm. 5k. multicoloured	3·25	3·25

DESIGNS—HORIZ: 60h. "Mercury"; 1k.60, Brno buildings and crest.

479 First Space Rendezvous

1966. Space Research.

1606	**479**	20h. violet and green	30	10
1607	-	30h. green and orange	30	10
1608	-	60h. blue and mauve	30	10
1609	-	80h. purple and blue	30	10
1610	-	1k. black and violet	30	10
1611	-	1k.20 red and blue	1·40	55

DESIGNS: 30h. Satellite and "back" of Moon; 60h. "Mariner 4" and first pictures of Mars; 80h. Satellite making "soft" landing on Moon; 1k. Satellite, laser beam and binary code; 1k.20, "Telstar", Earth and tracking station.

480 Eurasian badger

1966. Game Animals. Multicoloured.

1612	30h. Type **480**	20	10
1613	40h. Red deer (vert)	25	10
1614	60h. Lynx	30	10
1615	80h. Brown hare	40	25
1616	1k. Red fox	50	25
1617	1k.20 Brown bear (vert)	50	30
1618	2k. Wild boar	3·75	1·10

481 "Spring" (V. Hollar)

1966. Art (1st series).

1619	**481**	1k. black	5·50	2·25
1620	-	1k. multicoloured	3·25	2·25
1621	-	1k. multicoloured	3·50	2·75
1622	-	1k. multicoloured	3·25	2·25
1623	-	1k. multicoloured	28·00	20·00

PAINTINGS: No. 1620, "Mrs. F. Wussin" (J. Kupecky); 1621, "Snowy Owl" (K. Purkyne); 1622, "Bouquet" (V. Spale); 1623, "Recruit" (L. Fulla).

See also Nos. 1669, 1699/1703, 1747, 1753, 1756, 1790/4, 1835/8, 1861/5, 1914/18, 1999/2003, 2067/71, 2134/9, 2194/8, 2256/60, 2313/16, 2375/9, 2495/9, 2549/53, 2601/5, 2655/9, 2702/6, 2757/61, 2810/14, 2858/62, 2904/8, 2954/6, 3000/2, 3044/7, 3077/81 and 3107/9.

482 "Carrier Pigeon"

1966. Stamp Day.

1624	**482**	1k. blue and yellow	1·10	90

483 "Youth" (5th Czech Youth Federation Congress)

1967. Czech Congresses.

1625	**483**	30h. red and blue	20	10
1626	-	30h. red and yellow	20	10

DESIGN: No. 1626, Rose and T.U. emblem (6th Trade Union Congress).

484 Distressed Family

1967. "Peace for Viet-Nam".

1627	**484**	60h. black and salmon	25	10

485 Jihlava

1967. International Tourist Year.

1628	**485**	30h. purple	15	10
1629	-	40h. red	15	10
1630	-	1k.20 blue	40	30
1631	-	1k.60 black	1·90	50

DESIGNS—As Type **485**: 40h. Brno. (76×30 mm): 1k.20, Bratislava; 1k.60, Prague.

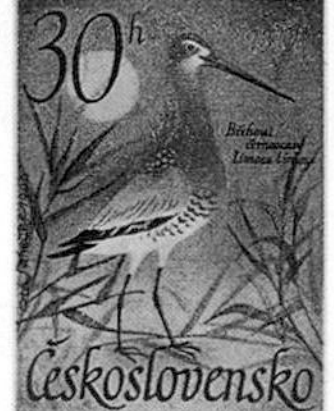

486 Black-tailed Godwit

1967. Water Birds. Multicoloured.

1632	30h. Type **486**	25	10
1633	40h. Common shoveler (horiz)	35	10
1634	60h. Purple heron	35	10
1635	80h. Penduline tit	70	25
1636	1k. Pied avocet	70	25
1637	1k.40 Black stork	1·50	40
1638	1k.60 Tufted duck (horiz)	2·75	1·75

487 Sun and Satellite

1967. Space Research.

1639	**487**	30h. red and yellow	15	10
1640	-	40h. blue and grey	15	10
1641	-	60h. green and violet	25	10
1642	-	1k. blue and mauve	25	10
1643	-	1k.20 black and blue	40	25
1644	-	1k.60 lake and grey	1·75	45

DESIGNS: 40h. Space vehicles in orbit; 60h. "Man on the Moon" and orientation systems; 1k. "Exploration of the planets"; 1k.20, Lunar satellites; 1k.60, Lunar observatory and landscape.

488 Gothic Art (after painting by Theodoric)

1967. World Fair, Montreal. Multicoloured.

1645	30h. Type **488**	15	10
1646	40h. Jena Codex—ancient manuscript, "Burning of John Hus"	15	10
1647	60h. Lead crystal glass	20	10
1648	80h. "The Shepherdess and the Chimney Sweep" (Andersen's Fairy Tales), after painting by J. Trnka	30	10
1649	1k. Atomic diagram ("Technical Progress")	35	25
1650	1k.20 Dolls by P. Rada ("Ceramics")	1·75	95
MS1651	95×75 mm. 3k. Montreal skyline	3·00	2·75

489 Bicycle Wheels and Dove

1967. Sports Events of 1967.

1652	**489**	60h. black and red	20	10
1653	-	60h. black & turquoise	20	10
1654	-	60h. black and blue	20	10
1655	-	1k.60 black and violet	1·50	45

DESIGNS—HORIZ: Type **489** (20th Warsaw–Berlin–Prague Cycle Race): No. 1654, Canoeist in kayak (5th World Canoeing Championships). VERT: No. 1653, Basketball players (World Women's Basketball Championships); 1655, Canoeist (10th World Water-slalom Championships).

1967. Prague Castle (3rd series). As Type 465.

1656	30h. lake	20	10
1657	60h. slate	50	10
MS1658	75×95 mm. 5k. multicoloured	2·00	3·00

DESIGNS: 30h. "Golden Street"; 60h. St. Wenceslas' Hall. SMALLER (30½×50 mm)—5k. "The Glory of Christ" (Bohemian 11th-century illuminated manuscript).

490 "PRAZSKE 1967"

1967. Prague Music Festival.

1659	**490**	60h. violet and green	25	10

491 Synagogue Curtain (detail)

1967. Jewish Culture.

1660	**491**	30h. red and blue	20	10
1661	-	60h. black and green	25	10
1662	-	1k. blue and mauve	35	10
1663	-	1k.20 red and brown	50	10
1664	-	1k.40 black and yellow	50	10
1665	-	1k.60 green and yellow	4·50	2·75

DESIGNS: 60h. Printers' imprint (1530); 1k. Mikulov jug (1801); 1k.20, "Old-New" Synagogue, Prague (1268); 1k.40, Jewish memorial candelabra, Pinkas Synagogue (1536) (The memorial is for Czech victims of Nazi persecution); 1k.60, David Gans' tombstone (1613).

492 Lidice Rose

1967. 25th Anniv of Destruction of Lidice.

1666	**492**	30h. black and red	25	10

493 "Architecture"

1967. 9th Int Architects' Union Congress, Prague.

1667	**493**	1k. black and gold	35	10

494 Petr Bezruc

1967. Birth Centenary of Petr Bezruc (poet).

1668	**494**	60h. black and red	25	10

1967. Publicity for "Praga 68" Stamp Exhibition. As Type 481. Multicoloured.

1669	2k. "Henri Rousseau" (self-portrait)	2·40	1·40

495 Skalica

1967. Czech Towns.

1670	**495**	30h. blue	20	10
1671	-	30h. lake (Presov)	20	10
1672	-	30h. green (Pribram)	20	10

496 Thermal Fountain and Colonnade, Karlovy Vary

1967. Postal Employees' Games.

1673	**496**	30h. violet and gold	25	10

497 Ondrejov Observatory and Universe

1967. 13th Int Astronomic Union Congress, Prague.

1674	**497**	60h. silver, blue & purple	1·75	35

498 "Miltonia spectabilis"

1967. Botanical Garden Flowers. Multicoloured.

1675	20h. Type **498**	25	10
1676	30h. Cup and saucer plant	25	10
1677	40h. "Lycaste deppei"	25	15
1678	60h. "Glottiphyllum davisii"	40	10
1679	1k. Painter's palette	60	25
1680	1k.20 "Rhodocactus bleo"	60	40
1681	1k.40 "Dendrobium phalaenopsis"	2·40	65

499 Eurasian Red Squirrel

1967. Fauna of Tatra National Park.

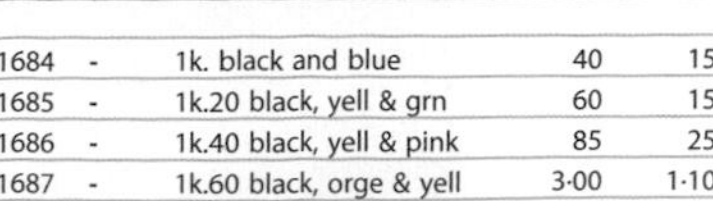

1682	**499**	30h. black, orge & yell	35	10
1683	-	60h. black and buff	35	10
1684	-	1k. black and blue	40	15
1685	-	1k.20 black, yell & grn	60	15
1686	-	1k.40 black, yell & pink	85	25
1687	-	1k.60 black, orge & yell	3·00	1·10

DESIGNS: 60h. Wild cat; 1k. Stoat; 1k.20, Hazel dormouse; 1k.40, West European hedgehog; 1k.60, Pine marten.

500 Military Vehicles

1967. Army Day.

1688	**500**	30h. green	25	10

501 Prague Castle ("PRAGA 62")

1967. Air. "PRAGA 1968" Int Stamp Exhbition (1st issue).

1689	**501**	30h. multicoloured	15	10
1690	-	60h. multicoloured	25	20
1691	-	1k. multicoloured	25	20
1692	-	1k.40 multicoloured	35	25
1693	-	1k.60 multicoloured	35	35
1694	-	2k. multicoloured	55	25
1695	-	5k. multicoloured	2·50	2·10

DESIGNS (Sites of previous Int Stamp Exns): 60h. Selimiye Mosque, Edirne ("ISTANBUL 1963"); 1k. Notre Dame, Paris ("PHILATEC 1964"); 1k.40, Belvedere Palace, Vienna ("WIPA 1965"); 1k.60, Capitol, Washington ("SIPEX 1965"); 2k. Amsterdam ("AMPHILEX 1967"). (40×55 mm): 5k. Prague ("PRAGA 1968").

See also Nos. 1718/20, 1743/8, 1749/54 and 1756.

502 Cruiser "Aurora"

1967. 50th Anniv of October Revolution.

1696	**502**	30h. red and black	10	10
1697	-	60h. red and black	15	10
1698	-	1k. red and black	15	10

DESIGNS—VERT: 60h. Hammer and sickle emblems; 1k. "Reaching hands".

1967. Art (2nd series). As T 481. Multicoloured.

1699	60h. "Conjurer with Cards" (F. Tichy)	25	25
1700	80h. "Don Quixote" (C. Majernik)	25	25
1701	1k. "Promenade in the Park" (N. Grund)	55	55
1702	1k.20 "Self-Portrait" (P. J. Brandl)	55	55
1703	1k.60 "Epitaph to Jan of Jeren" (Czech master)	4·25	4·25

All in National Gallery, Prague.

503 Pres. Novotny

1967

1704	**503**	2k. green	1·25	10
1705	**503**	3k. brown	1·75	10

504 Letov L-13 Glider

1967. Czech Aircraft. Multicoloured.

1706 30h. Type **504** 15 10
1707 60h. Letov L-40 Meta-Sokol 20 10
1708 80h. Letov L-200 Morava 20 10
1709 1k. Letov Z-37 Cmelak crop-sprayer 45 10
1710 1k.60 Zlin Z-526 Trener Master 55 10
1711 2k. Aero L-29 Delfin jet trainer 1·75 65

505 Czech Stamps of 1920

1967. Stamp Day.

1712 **505** 1k. lake and silver 1·75 1·40

506 "CESKOSLOVENSKO 1918–1968"

1968. 50th Anniv of Republic (1st issue).

1713 **506** 30h. red, blue & ultram 70 25

See also Nos. 1780/1.

507 Skater and Stadium

1968. Winter Olympic Games, Grenoble.

1714 **507** 60h. black, yell & ochre 15 10
1715 - 1k. brown, bistre & blue 30 10
1716 - 1k.60 black, grn & lilac 55 10
1717 - 2k. black, blue & yellow 1·10 50

DESIGNS: 1k. Bobsleigh run; 1k.60, Ski jump; 2k. Ice hockey.

508 Charles Bridge, Prague, and Charles's Hydrogen Balloon

1968. Air. "PRAGA 1968" International Stamp Exhibition (2nd issue). Multicoloured.

1718 60h. Type **508** 45 15
1719 1k. Royal Summer-house, Belvedere, and William Henson's "Aerial Steam Carriage" 70 25
1720 2k. Prague Castle and airship 80 55

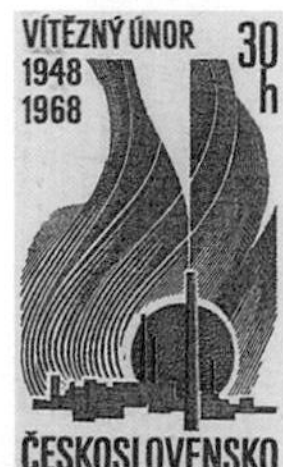

509 Industrial Scene and Red Sun

1968. 20th Anniv of "Victorious February".

1721 **509** 30h. red and blue 10 10
1722 - 60h. red and blue 15 10

DESIGN: 60h. Workers and banner.

510 Battle Plan

1968. 25th Anniv of Sokolovo Battles.

1723 **510** 30h. red, blue & green 45 10

511 Human Rights Emblem

1968. Human Rights Year.

1724 **511** 1k. red 1·10 30

512 Liptovsky Mikulas (town) and Janko Kral (writer)

1968. Various Commemorations.

1725 **512** 30h. green 25 10
1726 - 30h. blue and orange 25 10
1727 - 30h. red and gold 25 10
1728 - 30h. purple 25 10
1729 - 1k. multicoloured 40 10

DESIGNS—VERT: No. 1726, Allegorical figure of woman (150th anniv of Prague National Museum); 1727, Girl's head (cent of Prague National Theatre); 1728, Karl Marx (150th anniv of birth); 1729, Diagrammatic skull (20th anniv of W.H.O.).

513 "Radio" (45th anniv)

1968. Czech Radio and Television Annivs.

1730 **513** 30h. black, red and blue 20 10
1731 - 30h. black, red and blue 20 10

DESIGN: No. 1731, "Television" (15th anniv).

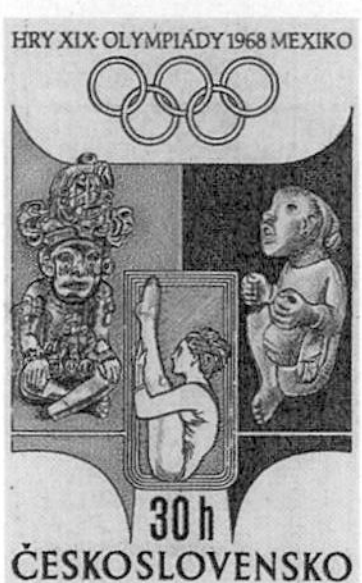

514 Athlete and Statuettes

1968. Olympic Games, Mexico. Multicoloured.

1732 30h. Type **514** 15 10
1733 40h. Runner and seated figure (Quetzalcoatl) 20 10
1734 60h. Netball and ornaments 25 10
1735 1k. Altar and Olympic emblems 35 10
1736 1k.60 Football and ornaments 50 20
1737 2k. Prague Castle and key 1·75 55

515 Pres. Svoboda

1968

1738 **515** 30h. blue 10 10
1738a **515** 50h. green 10 10
1739 **515** 60h. red 25 10
1739a **515** 1k. red 30 10

1968. Prague Castle (4th series). As Type 465.

1740 30h. multicoloured 25 10
1741 60h. black, green & red 25 10
MS1742 75×95 mm. 5k. multicoloured 2·50 2·50

DESIGN: 30h. "Bretislav I" (from tomb in St. Vitus' Cathedral); 60h. Knocker on door of St. Wenceslas' Chapel. SMALLER (30½×51 mm)—5k. "St. Vitus" (detail of mosaic).

516 "Business" (sculpture by O. Gutfreund)

1968. "PRAGA 1968" Int Stamp Exn (3rd Issue). Multicoloured.

1743 30h. Type **516** 20 10
1744 40h. Broadcasting building, Prague 20 10
1745 60h. Parliament Building 20 20
1746 1k.40 "Prague" (Gobelin tapestry by Jan Bauch) 50 25
1747 2k. "The Cabaret Artiste" (painting by F. Kupka) (size 40×50 mm) 1·90 1·40
1748 3k. Presidential standard 50 45

1968. "PRAGA 1968" Int Stamp Exn (4th issue).

1749 30h. green, yellow & grey 20 10
1750 60h. violet, gold & green 20 10
1751 1k. indigo, pink and blue 30 20
1752 1k.60 multicoloured 55 25
1753 2k. multicoloured 1·10 90
1754 3k. black, blue, pink & yell 1·25 35

DESIGNS—As Type **516**: 30h. St. George's Basilica, Prague Castle; 60h. Renaissance fountain; 1k. Dvorak's Museum; 1k.60, "Three Violins" insignia (18th-cent house); 3k. Prague emblem of 1475. As Type **481**: 2k. "Josefina" (painting by Josef Manes, National Gallery, Prague).

517 View of Prague

1968. "PRAGA 1968" (5th issue—50th Anniv of Czechoslovak Stamps). Sheet 73×111½ mm.

MS1755 **517** 10k. multicoloured 4·00 4·25

1968. "PRAGA 1968" (6th issue—F.I.P. Day). As T 481.

1756 5k. multicoloured 4·25 3·50

DESIGN: 5k. "Madonna of the Rosary" (detail from painting by Albrecht Durer in National Gallery, Prague).

518 Horse-drawn Coach on Rails "Hannibal" (140th Anniv of Ceske-Budejovice–Linz Railway)

1968. Railway Anniversaries.

1757 **518** 60h. multicoloured 30 15
1758 - 1k. multicoloured 85 25

DESIGN: 1k. Early steam locomotive "Johann Adolf" and modern electric locomotive (centenary of Ceske-Budejovice–Pilsen Railway).

519 Symbolic "S"

1968. 6th Int Slavonic Congress, Prague.

1759 **519** 30h. red and blue 55 10

520 Adrspach Rocks and "Hypophylloceras bizonatum" (ammonite)

1968. 23rd Int Geological Congress, Prague.

1760 **520** 30h. black and yellow 20 10
1761 - 60h. black and mauve 20 10
1762 - 80h. black, pink & lav 25 10
1763 - 1k. black and blue 35 10
1764 - 1k.60 black and yellow 1·40 55

DESIGNS: 60h. Basalt columns and fossilised frog; 80h. Bohemian "Paradise" and agate; 1k. Tatra landscape and "Chlamys gigas" shell; 1k.60, Barrandien (Bohemia) and limestone.

521 M. J. Hurban and Standard-bearer

1968. 120th Anniv of Slovak Insurrection and 25th Anniv of Slovak National Council.

1765 **521** 30h. blue 10 10
1766 - 60h. red 10 10

DESIGN: 60h. Partisans (120th anniv of Slovak Insurrection).

522 "Man and Child" (Jiri Beutler, aged 10)

1968. Munich Agreement. Drawings by children in Terezin concentration camp. Multicoloured.

1767 30h. Type **522** 20 10
1768 60h. "Butterflies" (Kitty Brunnerova, aged 11) 30 10
1769 1k. "The Window" (Jiri Schlessinger, aged 10) 45 10

The 1k. is larger (40×22 mm).

523 Banska Bystrica

1968. Arms of Czech Regional Capitals (1st series). Multicoloured.

1770 60h. Type **523** 20 10
1771 60h. Bratislava 20 10
1772 60h. Brno 20 10
1773 60h. Ceske Budejovice 20 10
1774 60h. Hradec Kralove 20 10
1775 60h. Kosice 20 10
1776 60h. Ostrava 20 10
1777 60h. Pilsen 20 10
1778 60h. Usti nad Labem 20 10
1779 1k. Prague (vert) 75 10

See also Nos. 1855/60, 1951/6, 2106/8 and 2214/15.

524 National Flag

1968. 50th Anniv of Republic (2nd issue).

1780 **524** 30h. deep blue & blue 20 10
1781 - 60h. multicoloured 20 10
MS1782 76×100 mm. 5k. red 3·00 3·25

DESIGN: 60h. Prague and Bratislava within outline "map" 5k. As T **6**.

525 Ernest Hemingway

1968. UNESCO. "Cultural Personalities of the 20th century in Caricature" (1st series).

1783	525	20h. black and red	15	10
1784	-	30h. multicoloured	15	10
1785	-	40h. red, black & lilac	15	10
1786	-	60h. black, green & bl	15	10
1787	-	1k. black, brn & yell	45	10
1788	-	1k.20 black, vio & red	50	20
1789	-	1k.40 black, brn & orge	1·40	45

PERSONALITIES: 30h. Karel Capek (dramatist); 40h. George Bernard Shaw; 60h. Maxim Gorky; 1k. Picasso; 1k.20, Taikan Yokoyama (painter); 1k.40, Charlie Chaplin.
See also Nos. 1829/34.

1968. Art (3rd series). As T 481. Paintings in National Gallery, Prague. Multicoloured.

1790	60h. "Cleopatra II" (J. Zrzavy)	50	30
1791	80h. "The Black Lake" (J. Preisler)	70	50
1792	1k.20 "Giovanni Francisci as a Volunteer" (P. Bohun)	1·40	1·10
1793	1k.60 "Princess Hyacinth" (A. Mucha)	90	45
1794	3k. "Madonna and Child" (altar detail, Master Paul of Levoca)	4·00	3·50

526 "Cinder Boy"

1968. Slovak Fairy Tales. Multicoloured.

1795	30h. Type **526**	15	10
1796	60h. "The Proud Lady"	25	10
1797	80h. "The Knight who ruled the World"	30	10
1798	1k. "Good Day, Little Bench"	40	15
1799	1k.20 "The Enchanted Castle"	45	15
1800	1k.80 "The Miraculous Hunter"	2·00	50

527 5h. and 10h. Stamps of 1918

1968. Stamp Day and 50th Anniv of 1st Czech Stamps.

1801	527	1k. gold and blue	1·40	1·25

528 Red Crosses forming Cross

1969. 50th Anniv of Czech Red Cross and League of Red Cross Societies.

1802	528	60h. red, gold and sepia	25	10
1803	-	1k. red, blue and black	45	20

DESIGN: 1k. Red Cross symbols within heart-shaped "dove".

529 I.L.O. Emblem

1969. 50th Anniv of Int Labour Organization.

1804	529	1k. black and grey	25	10

530 Wheel-lock Pistol, c. 1580

1969. Early Pistols. Multicoloured.

1805	30h. Type **530**	15	10
1806	40h. Italian horse-pistol, c. 1600	20	10
1807	60h. Kubik wheel-lock carbine, c. 1720	20	10
1808	1k. Flint-lock pistol, c. 1760	30	10
1809	1k.40 Lebeda duelling pistols, c. 1830	50	20
1810	1k.60 Derringer pistols, c. 1865	1·60	35

531 University Emblem and Symbols (50th Anniv of Brno University)

1969. Anniversaries.

1811	531	60h. black, blue & gold	20	10
1812	-	60h. blue	20	10
1813	-	60h. multicoloured	20	10
1814	-	60h. black and red	20	10
1815	-	60h. red, silver & blue	20	10
1816	-	60h. black and gold	20	10

DESIGNS and ANNIVERSARIES: No. 1812, Bratislava Castle, open book and head of woman (50th Anniv Comenius University, Bratislava); 1813, Harp and symbolic eagle (50th Anniv Brno Conservatoire); 1814, Theatrical allegory (50th Anniv Slovak National Theatre (1970); 1815, Arms and floral emblems (Slovak Republican Council, 50th Anniv); 1816, Grammar school and allegories of Learning (Zniev Grammar School. Cent).

532 Veteran Cars of 1900–05

1969. Motor Vehicles. Multicoloured.

1817	30h. Type **532**	40	10
1818	1k.60 Veteran Cars of 1907	70	20
1819	1k.80 Prague Buses of 1907 and 1967	1·75	85

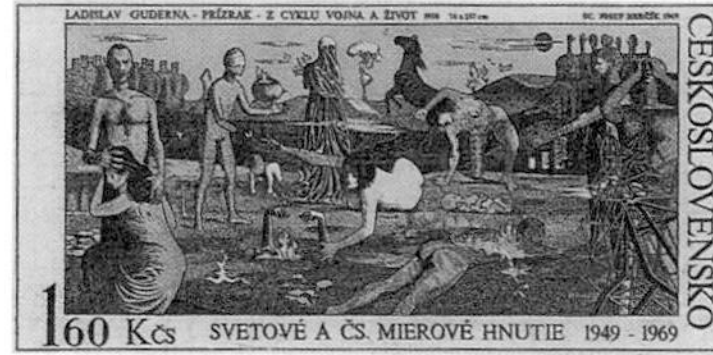

533 "Peace" (after L. Guderna) (image scaled to 69% of original size)

1969. 20th Anniv of Peace Movement.

1820	533	1k.60 multicoloured	55	25

534 Engraving by H. Goltzius

1969. Horses. Works of Art.

1821	534	30h. sepia on cream	25	10
1822	-	80h. purple on cream	25	10
1823	-	1k.60 slate on cream	40	20
1824	-	1k.80 black on cream	40	25
1825	-	2k.40 mult on cream	2·50	65

DESIGNS—HORIZ: 80h. Engraving by M. Merian. VERT: 1k.60, Engraving by V. Hollar; 1k.80, Engraving by A. Durer; 2k.40, Painting by J. E. Ridinger.

535 Dr. M. R. Stefanik as Civilian and Soldier

1969. 50th Death Anniv of General Stefanik.

1826	535	60h. red	35	10

536 "St. Wenceslas" (mural detail, Master of Litomerice, 1511)

1969. Prague Castle (5th series). Multicoloured.

1827	3k. Type **536**	2·10	1·40
1828	3k. Coronation Banner of the Czech Estates, 1723	2·10	1·40

See also Nos. 1892/3, 1959/60, 2037/8, 2103/4, 2163/4, 2253/4, 2305/6, 2337/8, 2404/5, 2466/7, 2543/4, 2599/600 and 2637/8.

1969. UNESCO. "Cultural Personalities of the 20th Century in Caricature" (2nd series). Designs as Type 525.

1829	30h. black, red and blue	10	10
1830	40h. black, violet & blue	15	10
1831	60h. black, red & yellow	15	10
1832	1k. multicoloured	30	10
1833	1k.80 black, blue & orge	40	10
1834	2k. black, yellow & green	2·00	60

DESIGNS: 30h. P. O. Hviezdoslav (poet); 40h. G. K. Chesterton (writer); 60h. V. Mayakovsky (poet); 1k. Henri Matisse (Painter); 1k.80, A. Hrdlicka (anthropologist); 2k. Franz Kafka (novelist).

537 "Music"

1969. "Woman and Art". Paintings by Alfons Mucha. Multicoloured.

1835	30h. Type **537**	30	10
1836	60h. "Painting"	35	10
1837	1k. "Dance"	50	10
1838	2k.40 "Ruby and Amethyst" (40×51 mm)	2·00	1·10

538 Astronaut, Moon and Aerial View of Manhattan

1969. Air. 1st Man on the Moon. Multicoloured.

1839	60h. Type **538**	20	10
1840	3k. "Eagle" module and aerial view of J. F. Kennedy Airport, New York	2·40	1·10

539 Soldier and Civilians

1969. 25th Anniv of Slovak Rising and Battle of Dukla.

1841	539	30h. bl & red on cream	10	10
1842	-	30h. grn & red on cream	10	10

DESIGN: No. 1842, General Svoboda and partisans.

540 Ganek (image scaled to 65% of original size)

1969. 20th Anniv of Tatra National Park.

1843	540	60h. purple	15	10
1844	-	60h. blue	15	10
1845	-	60h. green	15	10
1846	-	1k.60 multicoloured	1·75	45
1847	-	1k.60 multicoloured	45	15
1848	-	1k.60 multicoloured	45	15

DESIGNS: No. 1844, Mala Valley; 1845, Bielovodska Valley. (SMALLER 40×23 mm): 1846, Velka Valley and gentian; 1847, Mountain stream, Mala Valley and gentian; 1848, Krivan Peak and autumn crocus.

541 Bronze Belt Fittings (8th–9th century)

1969. Archaeological Discoveries in Bohemia and Slovakia. Multicoloured.

1849	20h. Type **541**	15	10
1850	30h. Decoration showing masks (6th–8th century)	15	10
1851	1k. Gold Earrings (8th–9th century)	25	10
1852	1k.80 Metal Crucifix (obverse and reverse) (9th century)	50	25
1853	2k. Gilt ornament with figure (9th century)	1·75	50

542 "Focal Point"—Tokyo

1969. 16th U.P.U. Congress, Tokyo.

1854	542	3k.20 multicoloured	1·60	1·00

1969. Arms of Czech Regional Capitals (2nd series). As T 523. Multicoloured.

1855	50h. Bardejov	20	10
1856	50h. Hranice	20	10
1857	50h. Kezmarok	20	10
1858	50h. Krnov	20	10
1859	50h. Litomerice	20	10
1860	50h. Manetin	20	10

1969. Art (4th series). As T 481. Multicoloured.

1861	60h. "Great Requiem" (F. Muzika)	55	50
1862	1k. "Resurrection" (Master of Trebon)	55	50
1863	1k.60 "Crucifixion" (V. Hloznik)	55	50
1864	1k.80 "Girl with Doll" (J. Bencur)	55	75
1865	2k.20 "St. Jerome" (Master Theodoric)	2·75	2·10

543 Emblem and "Stamps"

1969. Stamp Day.

1866	**543**	1k. purple, gold & blue	1·50	1·10

544 Ski Jumping

1970. World Skiing Championships, High Tatras. Multicoloured.

1867	50h. Type **544**	20	10
1868	60h. Cross-country skiing	20	10
1869	1k. Ski jumper "taking off"	20	10
1870	1k.60 Woman skier	1·10	35

545 J. A. Comenius (300th Death Anniv)

1970. UNESCO. Anniversaries of World Figures.

1871	**545**	40h. black	15	10
1872	-	40h. grey	25	10
1873	-	40h. brown	25	10
1874	-	40h. red	15	10
1875	-	40h. red	15	10
1876	-	40h. brown	15	10

DESIGNS: No. 1872, Ludwig van Beethoven (composer, birth bicent); 1873, Tosef Manes (artist, 150th birth anniv); 1874, Lenin (birth cent); 1875, Friedrich Engels (150th birth anniv); 1876, Maximilian Hell (astronomer, 250th birth anniv).

546 Bells

1970. World Fair, Osaka, Japan. "Expo 70". Multicoloured.

1877	50h. Type **546**	15	10
1878	80h. Heavy Machinery	25	10
1879	1k. Beehives (folk sculpture)	25	10
1880	1k.60 "Angels and Saints" (17th-century icon)	45	35
1881	2k. "Orlik Castle, 1787" (F. K. Wolf)	50	35
1882	3k. "Fujiyama" (Hokusai)	2·40	80

Nos. 1880/2 are larger, 51×37 mm.

547 Town Hall, Kosice

1970. 25th Anniv of Kosice Reforms.

1883	**547**	60h. blue, gold & red	35	10

548 "Autumn, 1955"

1970. Paintings by Joseph Lada. Multicoloured.

1884	60h. Type **548**	20	10
1885	1k. "The Magic Horse" (vert)	40	10
1886	1k.80 "The Water Demon" (vert)	45	20
1887	2k.40 "Children in Winter, 1943"	2·00	55

549 Lenin

1970. Birth Centenary of Lenin.

1888	**549**	30h. red and gold	10	10
1889	-	60h. black and gold	10	10

DESIGN: 60h. Lenin (bareheaded).

550 Prague Panorama and Hand giving "V" Sign

1970. 25th Anniv of Prague Rising and Liberation of Czechoslovakia.

1890	**550**	30h. purple, gold & blue	20	10
1891	-	30h. green, gold & red	20	10

DESIGN: No. 1891, Soviet tank entering Prague.

1970. Prague Castle. Art Treasures (6th series). As Type 536. Multicoloured.

1892	3k. "Hermes and Athena" (painting by B. Spranger)	1·90	1·75
1893	3k. "St. Vitus" (bust)	1·90	1·75

551 Compass and "World Capitals" (image scaled to 67% of original size)

1970. 25th Anniv of United Nations.

1894	**551**	1k. multicoloured	45	25

552 Thirty Years War Cannon and "Baron Munchausen"

1970. Historic Artillery. Multicoloured.

1895	30h. Type **552**	15	10
1896	60h. Hussite bombard and St. Barbara	15	10
1897	1k.20 Austro-Prussian War field-gun and Hradec Kralove	45	10
1898	1k.80 Howitzer (1911) and Verne's "Colombiad"	75	25
1899	2k.40 Mountain-gun (1915) and "Good Soldier Schweik"	1·50	50

553 "Rude Pravo"

1970. 50th Anniv of "Rude Pravo" (newspaper).

1900	**553**	60h. red, drab & black	20	10

554 "Golden Sun", Bridge-tower, Prague

1970. Ancient Buildings and House-signs from Prague, Brno and Bratislava. Multicoloured.

1901	40h. Type **554**	15	10
1902	60h. "Blue Lion" and Town Hall tower, Brno	25	10
1903	1k. Gothic bolt and Town Hall tower, Bratislava	25	10
1904	1k.40 Coat of arms and Michael Gate, Bratislava	1·90	35
1905	1k.60 "Moravian Eagle" and Town Hall gate, Brno	40	20
1906	1k.80 "Black Sun", "Green Frog" and bridge-tower, Prague	60	20

555 World Cup Emblem and Flags

1970. World Cup Football Championship, Mexico. Multicoloured.

1907	20h. Type **555**	10	10
1908	40h. Two players and badges of Germany and Uruguay	15	10
1909	60h. Two players and badges of England and Czechoslovakia	20	10
1910	1k. Three players and badges of Rumania and Czechoslovakia	30	10
1911	1k.20 Three players and badges of Brazil and Italy	50	10
1912	1k.80 Two players and badges of Brazil and Czechoslovakia	1·75	30

556 "S.S.M." and Flags

1970. 1st Congress of Czechoslovak Socialist Youth Federation.

1913	**556**	30h. multicoloured	35	10

1970. Art (5th series). As T 481. Multicoloured.

1914	1k. "Mother and Child" (M. Galanda)	25	25
1915	1k.20 "The Bridesmaid" (K. Svolinsky)	50	35
1916	1k.40 "Walk by Night" (F. Hudecek)	50	40
1917	1k.80 "Banska Bystrica Market" (detail, D. Skutecky)	65	45
1918	2k.40 "Adoration of the Kings" (Vysehrad Codex)	2·10	2·40

557 Dish Aerial

1970. "Intercosmos". Space Research Programme. Multicoloured.

1919	20h. Type **557**	10	10
1920	40h. Experimental satellite	15	10
1921	60h. Meteorological satellite	20	10
1922	1k. Astronaut ("medical research")	25	10
1923	1k.20 Solar research	30	10
1924	1k.60 Rocket on Launch-pad	1·25	40

558 "Adam and Eve with Archangel Michael" (16th-century)

1970. Slovak Icons. Multicoloured.

1925	60h. Type **558**	20	25
1926	1k. "Mandylon" (16th-century) (horiz)	30	30
1927	2k. "St. George slaying the Dragon" (18th-century) (horiz)	50	50
1928	2k.80 "St. Michael the Archangel" (18th-century)	2·50	2·10

559 Czech 5h. Stamps of 1920

1970. Stamp Day.

1929	**559**	1k. red, black & green	90	85

560 "Songs from the Walls" (frontispiece, K. Stika)

1971. Czechoslovak Graphic Art (1st series).

1930	**560**	40h. brown	15	10
1931	-	50h. multicoloured	20	10
1932	-	60h. grey	20	10
1933	-	1k. grey	25	10
1934	-	1k.60 black & cream	45	10
1935	-	2k. multicoloured	1·75	50

DESIGNS: 50h. "The Fruit Trader" (C. Bouda); 60h. "Moon searching for Lilies-of-the-valley" (J. Zrzavy); 1k. "At the End of the Town" (K. Sokol); 1k.60, "Summer" (V. Hollar); 2k. "Shepherd and Gamekeeper, Orava Castle" (P. Bohun).

See also Nos. 2026/30, 2079/82, 2147/50 and 2202/5.

561 Saris Church

1971. Regional Buildings.

1936		50h. multicoloured	10	10
1936a		1k. black, red & blue	20	10
1937	**561**	1k.60 black, vio & grn	45	10
1938	-	2k. multicoloured	55	10
1939	-	2k.40 multicoloured	55	10
1940	-	3k. multicoloured	70	10
1941	-	3k.60 multicoloured	85	10
1942	-	5k. multicoloured	95	10
1943	-	5k.40 multicoloured	95	10
1944	-	6k. multicoloured	1·40	10
1945	-	9k. multicoloured	2·10	10
1946	-	10k. multicoloured	1·75	15
1947	-	14k. multicoloured	2·25	10
1948	-	20k. multicoloured	3·00	50

DESIGNS—HORIZ: 50h., 3k.60, Church, Chrudimsko; 2k.40, House, Jicinsko, 5k.40, Southern Bohemia baroque house, Posumavi; 10k. Wooden houses, Liptov; 14k. House and belfry, Valassko; 20k. Decorated house, Cicmany. (22×19 mm): 3k. Half-timbered house, Melnicko; 6k. Cottages, Orava; 9k. Cottage, Turnovsko. VERT: (19×22 mm): 1k. Ornamental roofs, Horacko; 2k. Bell-tower, Hornsek; 5k. Watch-tower, Nachodsko.

562 "The Paris Commune" (allegory) (image scaled to 66% of original size)

1971. UNESCO. World Annivs. Multicoloured.

1949	1k. Type **562**	30	25
1950	1k. "World Fight against Racial Discrimination" (allegory)	30	25

1971. Arms of Czech Regional Capitals (3rd series). As Type 523. Multicoloured.

1951	60h. Ceska Trebova	15	10
1952	60h. Karlovy Vary	15	10
1953	60h. Levoca	15	10
1954	60h. Trutnov	15	10
1955	60h. Uhersky Brod	15	10
1956	60h. Zilina	15	10

563 Chorister

1971. 50th Annivs. Multicoloured.
1957 30h. Type **563** (Slovak Teachers' Choir) 20 10
1958 30h. Edelweiss, ice-pick and mountain (Slovak Alpine Organisation) (19×48 mm) 20 10

1971. Prague Castle (7th series). Art Treasures. As Type 536. Multicoloured.
1959 3k. brown, buff and black 2·10 1·90
1960 3k. multicoloured 2·10 1·90
DESIGNS: No. 1959, "Music" (16th-century wall painting); 1960, Head of 16th-century crozier.

564 Lenin

1971. 50th Anniv of Czech Communist Party.
1961 30h. Type **564** 10 10
1962 40h. Hammer and sickle emblems 10 10
1963 60h. Clenched fists 15 10
1964 1k. Emblem on pinnacle 20 10

565 "50" Star Emblem

1971. 14th Czech Communist Party Congress. Multicoloured.
1965 30h. Type **565** 10 10
1966 60h. Clenched fist, worker and emblems (vert) 15 10

566 Common Pheasant

1971. World Hunting Exn, Budapest. Mult.
1967 20h. Type **566** 45 10
1968 60h. Rainbow trout 15 10
1969 80h. Mouflon 20 10
1970 1k. Chamois 20 10
1971 2k. Red deer 45 20
1972 2k.60 Wild boar 3·00 65

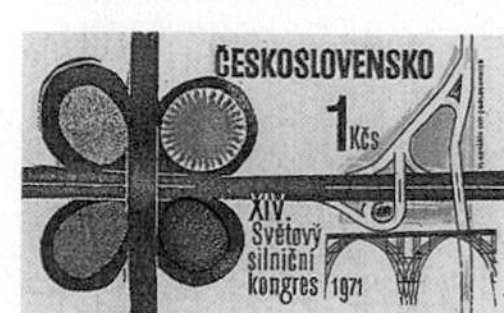

567 Motorway Junction (diagram)

1971. World Road Congress.
1973 **567** 1k. multicoloured 25 10

568 Class T478.3 Diesel Locomotive

1971. Cent of Prague C.K.D. Locomotive Works.
1974 **568** 30h. black, red & blue 10 10

569 Gymnasts

1971. 50th Anniv of Proletarian Physical Federation.
1975 **569** 30h. multicoloured 10 10

570 "Procession" (from "The Miraculous Bamboo Shoot" by K. Segawa)

1971. Biennial Exhibition of Book Illustrations for Children, Bratislava. Multicoloured.
1976 60h. "Princess" (Chinese Folk Tales, E. Bednarova) (vert) 20 10
1977 1k. "Tiger" (Animal Fairy Tales, Hanak) (vert) 20 10
1978 1k.60 Type **570** 55 25

571 Coltsfoot and Canisters

1971. International Pharmaceutical Congress, Prague. Medicinal Plants and Historic Pharmaceutical Utensils. Multicoloured.
1979 30h. Type **571** 10 10
1980 60h. Dog rose and glass jars 15 10
1981 1k. Yellow pheasant's-eye and hand scales 25 10
1982 1k.20 Common valerian, pestle and mortar 40 10
1983 1k.80 Chicory and crucibles 55 20
1984 2k.40 Henbane and grinder 1·40 50

573 "Co-operation in Space"

1971. "Intersputnik" Day.
1997 **573** 1k.20 multicoloured 35 10

574 "The Krompachy Revolt" (J. Nemcik) (image scaled to 62% of original size)

1971. 50th Anniv of The Krompachy Revolt.
1998 **574** 60h. multicoloured 35 10

1971. Art (6th issue). As Type 481. Multicoloured.
1999 1k. "Waiting" (I. Weiner-Kral) 40 35
2000 1k.20 "The Resurrection" (unknown 14th century artist) 40 35
2001 1k.40 "Woman with Jug" (M. Bazovsky) 55 40
2002 1k.80 "Woman in National Costume" (J. Manes) 70 50
2003 2k.40 "Festival of the Rosary" (Durer) 2·40 2·50

575 Wooden Dolls and Birds

1971. 25th Anniv of UNICEF. Czech and Slovak Folk Art. Multicoloured.
2004 60h. Type **575** (frame and UNICEF emblem in bl) 15 10
2005 60h. Type **575** (frame and UNICEF emblem in black) 2·75 1·40
2006 80h. Decorated handle 20 10
2007 1k. Horse and rider 20 10
2008 1k.60 Shepherd 35 20
2009 2k. Easter eggs and rattle 50 25
2010 3k. Folk hero 2·10 60

576 Ancient Greek Runners

1971. 75th Anniv of Czechoslovak Olympic Committee and 1972 Games at Sapporo and Munich. Multicoloured.
2011 30h. Type **576** 10 10
2012 40h. High Jumper 10 10
2013 1k.60 Skiers 50 10
2014 2k.60 Discus-throwers, ancient and modern 1·75 65

577 Posthorns

1971. Stamp Day.
2015 **577** 1k. multicoloured 35 10

578 Figure Skating

1972. Winter Olympic Games, Sapporo, Japan. Multicoloured.
2016 40h. Type **578** 10 10
2017 50h. Skiing 15 10
2018 1k. Ice hockey 50 10
2019 1k.60 Bobsleighing 1·10 45

579 Sentry

1972. 30th Annivs.
2020 - 30h. black and brown 10 10
2021 - 30h. black, red & yellow 10 10
2022 **579** 60h. multicoloured 20 10
2023 - 60h. black, red & yellow 20 10
ANNIVERSARIES: No. 2020, Child and barbed wire (Terezin Concentration Camp); 2021, Widow and buildings (Destruction of Lezaky); 2022, Type **579** (Czechoslovak Unit in Russian Army); 2023, Hand and ruined building (Destruction of Lidice).

580 Book Year Emblem

1972. International Book Year.
2024 **580** 1k. black and red 35 10

581 Steam Locomotive No. 2 and Class E499.0 Electric Locomotive

1972. Centenary of Kosice–Bohumin Railway.
2025 **581** 30h. multicoloured 35 10

1972. Czechoslovak Graphic Art (2nd series). As Type 560. Multicoloured.
2026 40h. "Pasture" (V. Sedlacek) 10 10
2027 50h. "Dressage" (F. Tichy) 15 10
2028 60h. "Otakar Kubin" (V. Fiala) 20 15
2029 1k. "The Three Kings" (E. Zmetak) 30 25
2030 1k.60 "Toilet" (L. Fulla) 1·40 1·25

582 Cycling

1972. Olympic Games, Munich. Multicoloured.
2031 50h. Type **582** 10 10
2032 1k.60 Diving 35 20
2033 1k.80 Kayak-canoeing 40 25
2034 2k. Gymnastics 1·25 45

583 Players in Tackle

1972. World and European Ice Hockey Championships, Prague. Multicoloured.
2035 60h. Type **583** 25 10
2036 1k. Attacking goal 45 10

1972. Prague Castle (8th series). Roof Decorations. As T 536. Multicoloured.
2037 3k. Bohemian Lion emblem (roof boss), Royal Palace 1·00 80
2038 3k. "Adam and Eve" (bracket), St. Vitus Cathedral 2·50 2·50

1972. Czech Victory in Ice Hockey Championships. Nos. 2035/6 optd.
2039 **583** 60h. multicoloured 7·00 7·00
2040 - 1k. multicoloured 7·00 7·00
OVERPRINTS: 60h. **CSSR MISTREM SVETA**. 1k. **CSSR MAJSTROM SVETA**.

585 Frantisek Bilek (sculptor, birth centenary)

1972. Cultural Anniversaries.
2041 **585** 40h. multicoloured 10 10
2042 - 40h. multicoloured 10 10
2043 - 40h. green, yellow & blue 10 10
2044 - 40h. multicoloured 10 10
2045 - 40h. violet, blue & green 10 10
2046 - 40h. green, brown & orge 10 10
DESIGNS: No. 2042, Antonin Hudecek (painter, birth cent); 2043, Janko Kral (poet, 150th birth anniv); 2044, Ludmila Podjavorinska (writer, birth cent); 2045, Andrej Sladkovic (painter, death cent); 2046, Jan Preisler (painter, birth cent).

586 Workers with Banners

1972. 8th Trade Union Congress, Prague.
2047 **586** 30h. violet, red & yellow 10 10

587 Wire Coil and Cockerel

1972. Slovak Wireworking. Multicoloured.

2048	20h. Type **587**	10	10
2049	60h. Aeroplane and rosette	15	10
2050	80h. Dragon and gilded ornament	20	10
2051	1k. Steam locomotive and pendant	55	10
2052	2k.60 Owl and tray	75	55

588 "Jiskra" (freighter)

1972. Czechoslovak Ocean-going Ships. Mult.

2053	50h. Type **588**	25	10
2054	60h. "Mir" (freighter)	30	10
2055	80h. "Republika" (freighter)	35	10
2056	1k. "Kosice" (tanker)	40	10
2057	1k.60 "Dukla" (freighter)	60	10
2058	2k. "Kladno" (freighter)	1·60	40

Nos. 2056/8 are size 49×30 mm.

589 "Hussar" (ceramic tile)

1972. "Horsemanship". Ceramics and Glass. Multicoloured.

2059	30h. Type **589**	10	10
2060	60h. "Turkish Janissary" (enamel on glass)	15	10
2061	80h. "St. Martin" (painting on glass)	25	10
2062	1k.60 "St. George" (enamel on glass)	45	10
2063	1k.80 "Nobleman's Guard, Bohemia" (enamel on glass)	55	10
2064	2k.20 "Cavalryman, c. 1800" (ceramic tile)	1·60	50

590 Revolutionary and Red Flag

1972. 55th Anniv of Russian October Revolution and 50th Anniv of U.S.S.R.

2065	**590**	30h. multicoloured	10	10
2066	-	60h. red and gold	15	10

DESIGN: 60h. Soviet star emblem.

1972. Art (7th issue). As T 481.

2067	1k. multicoloured	70	45
2068	1k.20 multicoloured	95	55
2069	1k.40 brown and cream	95	65
2070	1k.80 multicoloured	1·00	1·00
2071	2k.40 multicoloured	2·10	2·25

DESIGNS: 1k. "Nosegay" (M. Svabinsky); 1k.20, "St. Ladislav fighting a Nomad" (14th century painter); 1k.40, "Lady with Fur Cap" (V. Hollar); 1k.80, "Midsummer Night's Dream" (J. Liesler); 2k.40, "Self-portrait" (P. Picasso).

591 Warbler feeding young European Cuckoo

1972. Songbirds. Multicoloured.

2072	60h. Type **591**	40	15
2073	80h. European cuckoo	50	15
2074	1k. Black-billed magpie	50	15
2075	1k.60 Northern bullfinch (30×23 mm)	65	25
2076	2k. Eurasian goldfinch (30×23 mm)	1·10	35
2077	3k. Song thrush (30×23 mm)	5·00	1·40

592 "Thoughts into Letters"

1972. Stamp Day.

2078	**592**	1k. black, gold & pur	45	40

1973. Czechoslovak Graphic Art (3rd series). As Type 560. Multicoloured.

2079	30h. "Flowers in the Window" (J. Grus)	10	10
2080	60h. "Quest for Happiness" (J. Balaz)	15	10
2081	1k.60 "Balloon" (K. Lhotak)	45	20
2082	1k.80 "Woman with Viola" (R. Wiesner)	1·50	25

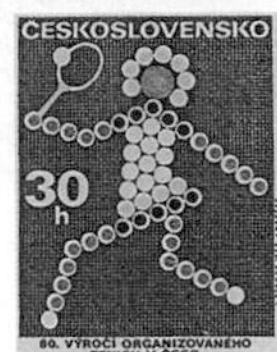

593 "Tennis Player"

1973. Sports Events. Multicoloured.

2083	30h. Type **593**	35	10
2084	60h. Figure skating	20	10
2085	1k. Spartakaid emblem	35	10

EVENTS: 30h. 80th anniv of lawn tennis in Czechoslovakia; 60h. World Figure Skating Championships, Bratislava; 1k. 3rd Warsaw Pact Armies Summer Spartakiad.

594 Red Star and Factory Buildings

1973. 25th Anniv of "Victorious February" and People's Militia (60h.).

2086	**594**	30h. multicoloured	10	10
2087	-	60h. blue, red & gold	15	10

DESIGN: 60h. Militiaman and banners.

595 Jan Nalepka and Antonin Sochar

1973. Czechoslovak Martyrs during World War II.

2088	**595**	30h. black, red and gold on cream	10	10
2089	-	40h. black, red and green on cream	15	10
2090	-	60h. black, red and gold on cream	15	10
2091	-	80h. black, red and green on cream	15	10
2092	-	1k. black, pink and green on cream	20	10
2093	-	1k.60 black, red and silver on cream	1·25	50

DESIGNS: 40h. Evzen Rosicky and Mirko Nespor; 60h. Vlado Clementis and Karol Smidke; 80h. Jan Osoha and Josef Molak; 1k. Marie Kuderikova and Jozka Jaburkova; 1k.60, Vaclav Sinkule and Eduard Urx.

596 Russian "Venera" Space-probe

1973. Cosmonautics' Day. Multicoloured.

2094	20h. Type **596**	10	10
2095	30h. "Cosmos" satellite	10	10
2096	40h. "Lunokhod" on Moon	10	10
2097	3k. American astronauts Grissom, White and Chaffee	1·00	70
2098	3k.60 Russian cosmonaut Komarov, and crew of "Soyuz II"	1·10	1·40
2099	5k. Death of Yuri Gagarin (first cosmonaut)	4·25	4·00

Nos. 2094/6 are size 40×23 mm.

597 Radio Aerial and Receiver

1973. Telecommunications Annivs. Multicoloured.

2100	30h. Type **597**	10	10
2101	30h. T.V. colour chart	10	10
2102	30h. Map and telephone	10	10

ANNIVERSARIES: No. 2100, 50th anniv of Czech broadcasting; 2101, 20th anniv of Czechoslovak television service; 2102, 20th anniv of nationwide telephone system.

1973. Prague Castle (9th series). As Type 536. Multicoloured.

2103	3k. Gold seal of Charles IV	1·75	2·00
2104	3k. Rook showing Imperial Legate (from "The Game and Playe of Chesse" by William Caxton)	90	60

598 Czechoslovak Arms

1973. 25th Anniv of May 9th Constitution.

2105	**598**	60h. multicoloured	10	10

1973. Arms of Czech Regional Capitals (4th series). As T 523.

2106	60h. multicoloured (Mikulov)	20	10
2107	60h. multicoloured (Smolenice)	20	10
2108	60h. black and gold (Zlutice)	20	10

599 "Learning."

1973. 400th Anniv of Olomouc University.

2109	**599**	30h. multicoloured	10	10

600 Tulip

1973. Olomouc Flower Show. Multicoloured.

2110	60h. Type **600**	95	55
2111	1k. Rose	75	25
2112	1k.60 Anthurium	35	20
2113	1k.80 Iris	40	25
2114	2k. Chrysanthemum	1·75	2·25
2115	3k.60 Boat orchid	1·10	30

Nos. 2112/13 and 2115 are smaller, size 23×50 mm.

601 Irish Setter

1973. 50th Anniv of Czechoslovak Hunting Organization. Hunting Dogs. Multicoloured.

2116	20h. Type **601**	10	10
2117	30h. Czech whisker	10	10
2118	40h. Bavarian mountain bloodhound	10	10
2119	60h. German pointer	15	10
2120	1k. Golden cocker spaniel	20	10
2121	1k.60 Dachshund	2·00	60

602 "St. John the Baptist" (M. Svabinsky)

1973. Birth Centenary of Max Svabinsky (artist and designer).

2122	**602**	20h. black and green	10	10
2123	-	60h. black and yellow	20	10
2124	-	80h. black	25	25
2125	-	1k. green	25	25
2126	-	2k.60 multicoloured	2·10	1·90

DESIGNS: 60h. "August Noon"; 80h. "Marriage of True Minds"; 1k. "Paradise Sonata 1"; 2k.60, "The Last Judgement" (stained glass window).

603 Congress Emblem

1973. 8th World Trade Union Congress, Varna, Bulgaria.

2127	**603**	1k. multicoloured	10	10

604 Tupolev Tu-104A over Bitov Castle

1973. 50th Anniv of Czechoslovak Airlines. Multicoloured.

2128	30h. Type **604**	10	10
2129	60h. Ilyushin Il-62 and Bezdez Castle	15	10
2130	1k.40 Tupolev Tu-134A and Orava Castle	40	10
2131	1k.90 Ilyushin Il-18 and Veveri Castle	55	20
2132	2k.40 Ilyshin Il-14P and Pernstejn Castle	2·75	60
2133	3k.60 Tupolev Tu-154 and Trencin Castle	70	25

1973. Art (8th series). As Type 481.

2134	1k. multicoloured	1·75	1·60
2135	1k.20 multicoloured	1·75	1·60
2136	1k.80 black and buff	65	50
2137	2k. multicoloured	75	65
2138	2k.40 multicoloured	90	75
2139	3k.60 multicoloured	1·10	1·25

DESIGNS: 1k. "Boy from Martinique" (A. Pelc); 1k.20, "Fortitude" (M. Benka); 1k.80, Self-portrait (Rembrandt); 2k. "Pierrot" (B. Kubista); 2k.40, "Ilona Kubinyiova" (P. Bohun); 3k.60, Madonna and Child" (unknown artist, c. 1350).

605 Mounted Postman

1973. Stamp Day.

2140	**605**	1k. multicoloured	25	25

606 "CSSR 1969–1974"

1974. 5th Anniv of Federal Constitution.

2141	**606**	30h. red, blue and gold	10	10

607 Bedrich Smetana (composer) (150th birth anniv)

1974. Celebrities' Birth Anniversaries.

2142	607	60h. multicoloured	20	10
2143	-	60h. multicoloured	20	10
2144	-	60h. brown, blue & red	20	10

DESIGNS AND ANNIVERSARIES: No. 2143, Josef Suk (composer, birth anniv); 2144, Pablo Neruda (Chilean poet, 70th birth anniv).

608 Council Building, Moscow

1974. 25th Anniv of Communist Bloc Council of Mutual Economic Assistance.

2145	608	1k. violet, red & gold	10	10

609 Exhibition Allegory

1974. "BRNO 74" National Stamp Exhibition (1st issue).

2146	609	3k.60 multicoloured	80	25

1974. Czechoslovak Graphic Art (4th series). As T 560. Inscr "1974". Multicoloured.

2147	60h. "Tulips" (J. Broz)	20	10
2148	1k. "Structures" (O. Dubay)	30	10
2149	1k.60 "Golden Sun-Glowing Day" (A. Zabransky)	55	15
2150	1k.80 "Artificial Flowers" (F. Gross)	1·50	35

610 Oskar Benes and Vaclav Prochazka

1974. Czechoslovak Partisan Heroes. Mult.

2151	30h. Type **610**	10	10
2152	40h. Milos Uher and Anton Sedlacek	10	10
2153	60h. Jan Hajecek and Marie Sedlackova	15	10
2154	80h. Jan Sverma and Albin Grznar	20	10
2155	1k. Jaroslav Neliba and Alois Hovorka	30	10
2156	1k.60 Ladislav Exnar and Ludovit Kukorelli	1·50	25

611 "Water—Source of Energy"

1974. International Hydrological Decade. Mult.

2157	60h. Type **611**	55	30
2158	1k. "Water for Agriculture"	55	30
2159	1k.20 "Study of the Oceans"	55	30
2160	1k.60 Decade emblem	60	30
2161	2k. "Keeping water pure"	1·75	2·00

612 "Telecommunications"

1974. Inauguration of Czechoslovak Satellite Telecommunications Earth Station.

2162	612	30h. multicoloured	25	10

1974. Prague Castle (10th series). As Type 536. Multicoloured.

2163	3k. "Golden Cockerel", 17th-century enamel locket	1·75	1·90
2164	3k. Bohemian glass monstrance, 1840	1·75	1·90

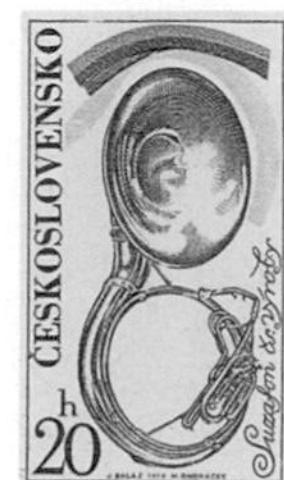
613 Sousaphone

1974. Musical Instruments. Multicoloured.

2165	20h. Type **613**	15	10
2166	30h. Bagpipes	15	10
2167	40h. Benka violin	20	10
2168	1k. Sauer pyramid piano	30	15
2169	1k.60 Hulinsky tenor quinton	1·25	30

614 Child and Flowers (book illustration)

1974. 25th International Children's Day.

2170	614	60h. multicoloured	10	10

615 "Stamp Collectors"

1974. "BRNO 74" National Stamp Exhibition (2nd issue). Multicoloured.

2171	30h. Type **615**	10	10
2172	6k. "Rocket Post"	2·00	1·25

616 Slovak Partisan

1974. Czechoslovak Anniversaries. Multicoloured.

2173	30h. Type **616**	15	10
2174	30h. Folk-dancer	15	10
2175	30h. Actress holding masks	15	10

EVENTS: No. 2173, 30th anniv of Slovak Uprising; 2174, 25th anniv of Slovak SLUK Folk Song and Dance Ensemble; 2175, 25th anniv of Bratislava Academy of Music and Dramatic Arts.

617 "Hero and Leander"

1974. Bratislava Tapestries. "Hero and Leander" (1st series). Multicoloured.

2176	2k. Type **617**	1·50	1·25
2177	2k.40 "Leander Swimming across the Hellespont"	1·50	1·75

See also Nos. 2227/8 and 2281/2.

618 "Soldier on Guard"

1974. Old Shooting Targets. Multicoloured.

2178	30h. Type **618**	15	10
2179	60h. "Pierrot and Owl", 1828	20	15
2180	1k. "Diana awarding Marksman's Crown", 1832	30	15
2181	1k.60 "Still Life with Guitar", 1839	45	40
2182	2k.40 "Stag", 1834	70	60
2183	3k. "Turk and Giraffe", 1831	2·75	2·75

619 U.P.U. Emblem and Postilion

1974. Centenary of Universal Postal Union. Mult.

2184	30h. Type **619**	10	10
2185	40h. Early mail coach	10	10
2186	60h. Early railway carriage	35	10
2187	80h. Modern mobile post office	25	10
2188	1k. Ilyushin Il-14m mail plane	60	10
2189	1k.60 Dish aerial, earth station	1·00	35

620 Posthorn and Old Town Bridge Tower, Prague

1974. Czechoslovak Postal Services.

2190	620	20h. multicoloured	10	10
2191	-	30h. red, blue & brn	10	10
2192	-	40h. multicoloured	10	10
2193	-	60h. orange, yell & bl	15	10

DESIGNS: 30h. P.T.T. emblem within letter; 40h. Postilion; 60h. P.T.T. emblem on dove's wing.

See also No. 2900.

1974. Art (9th series). As Type 481. Multicoloured.

2194	1k. "Self-portrait" (L. Kuba)	80	70
2195	1k.20 "Frantisek Ondricek" (V. Brozik)	80	70
2196	1k.60 "Pitcher with Flowers" (O. Khubin)	80	70
2197	1k.80 "Woman with Pitcher" (J. Alexy)	80	70
2198	2k.40 "Bacchanalia" (K. Skreta)	2·00	2·40

621 Stylized Posthorn

1974. Stamp Day.

2199	621	1k. multicoloured	25	10

622 Winged Emblem

1975. Coil Stamps.

2200	622	30h. blue	10	10
2201	622	60h. red	15	10

1975. Czechoslovak Graphic Art (5th series). Engraved Hunting Scenes. As T 560.

2202	60h. brown & cream	25	10
2203	1k. brown and cream	30	15
2204	1k.60 brown & green	45	25
2205	1k.80 brown & lt brown	1·75	50

DESIGNS: 60h. "Still Life with Hare" (V. Hollar); 1k. "The Lion and the Mouse" (V. Hollar); 1k.60, "Deer Hunt" (detail, P. Galle); 1k.80, "Grand Hunt" (detail, J. Callot).

623 "Woman"

1975. International Women's Year.

2206	623	30h. multicoloured	10	10

624 Village Family

1975. 30th Anniv of Razing of 14 Villages. Multicoloured.

2207	60h. Type **624**	20	10
2208	1k. Women and flames	25	10
2209	1k.20 Villagers and flowers	40	10

625 "Little Queens" (Moravia)

1975. Czechoslovak Folk Customs. Multicoloured.

2210	60h. Type **625**	60	60
2211	1k. Shrovetide parade, Slovakia	60	60
2212	1k.40 "Maid Dorothea" (play)	60	60
2213	2k. "Morena" effigy, Slovakia	1·40	1·40

1975. Arms of Czech Regional Capitals (5th series). As T 523.

2214	60h. black, gold and red	25	10
2215	60h. multicoloured	25	10

ARMS: No. 2214, Nymburk. 2215, Znojmo.

626 Partisans at Barricade (image scaled to 67% of original size)

1975. Czechoslovak Anniversaries.

2216	626	1k. multicoloured	30	20
2217	-	1k. sepia and cream	30	20
2218	-	1k. multicoloured	30	20

DESIGNS and ANNIVERSARIES: No. 2216, Type **626** (30th anniv of Czech Rising); 2217, Liberation celebrations (30th anniv of Liberation by Soviet Army); 2218, Czech–Soviet fraternity (5th anniv of Czech–Soviet Treaty).

627 Youth Exercises

1975. National Spartacist Games.

2219	**627**	30h. purple, bl & pink	10	10
2220	-	60h. red, lilac & yellow	15	10
2221	-	1k. violet, red & yell	25	20

DESIGNS: 60h. Children's exercises; 1k. Adult exercises.

628 Siamese Tigerfish and Lined Seahorse

1975. Aquarium Fishes. Multicoloured.

2222	60h. Type **628**	15	10
2223	1k. Siamese fighting fish and freshwater angelfish	30	10
2224	1k.20 Veil-tailed goldfish	65	15
2225	1k.60 Clown anemone-fish and butterflyfish	75	25
2226	2k. Yellow-banded angelfish, palette surgeonfish and semicircle angelfish	3·50	65

1975. Bratislava Tapestries. "Hero and Leander" (2nd series). As T 617. Multicoloured.

2227	3k. "Leander's Arrival"	90	70
2228	3k.60 "Hermione"	2·25	2·40

629 "Pelicans" (N. Charushin)

1975. Biennial Exhibition of Book Illustrations for Children, Bratislava. Multicoloured.

2229	20h. Type **629**	10	10
2230	30h. "Sleeping Hero" (L. Schwarz)	10	10
2231	40h. "Horseman" (V. Munteau)	15	10
2232	60h. "Peacock" (K. Ensikat)	20	10
2233	80h. "The Stone King" (R. Dubravec)	70	35

630 "CZ-150" Motor Cycle (1951)

1975. Czechoslovak Motor Cycles. Multicoloured.

2234	20h. Type **630**	15	10
2235	40h. "Jawa 250", 1945	20	10
2236	60h. "Jawa 175", 1935	25	10
2237	1k. Janatka "ITAR", 1921	30	15
2238	1k.20 Michl "Orion", 1903	25	10
2239	1k.80 Laurin and Klement, 1898	1·60	40

631 "Solar Radiation"

1975. Co-operation in Space Research.

2240	**631**	30h. violet, yellow & red	15	10
2241	-	60h. red, lilac & yellow	20	10
2242	-	1k. purple, yell & blue	25	10
2243	-	2k. multicoloured	55	10
2244	-	5k. multicoloured	3·00	2·75

DESIGNS—HORIZ: 60h. "Auroa Borealis"; 1k. Cosmic radiation measurement; 2k. Copernicus and solar radiation. VERT (40×50 mm): 5k. "Apollo-soyuz" space link.

632 President Gustav Husak

1975

2245	**632**	30h. blue	10	10
2246	**632**	60h. red	15	10

633 Oil Refinery

1975. 30th Anniv of Liberation. Multicoloured.

2247	30h. Type **633**	15	10
2248	60h. Atomic power complex	15	10
2249	1k. Underground Railway, Prague	40	10
2250	1k.20 Laying oil pipelines	30	15
2251	1k.40 Combine-harvesters and granary	30	20
2252	1k.60 Building construction	1·10	35

1975. Prague Castle. Art Treasures (11th series). As T 536. Multicoloured.

2253	3k. Late 9th-century gold earring	95	75
2254	3k.60 Leather Bohemian Crown case, 1347	1·90	2·00

634 General Svoboda

1975. 80th Birthday of General Ludvik Svoboda. Sheet 76×96 mm.

MS2255 **634**	10k. multicoloured	11·50	11·50

1975. Art (10th series). As T 481.

2256	1k. red, brown and black	75	75
2257	1k.40 multicoloured	75	75
2258	1k.80 multicoloured	75	75
2259	2k.40 multicoloured	1·10	1·25
2260	3k.40 multicoloured	1·75	1·60

PAINTINGS—VERT: 1k. "May" (Z. Sklenar); 1k.40, "Girl in National Costume" (E. Nevan); 2k.40, "Fire" (J. Capek); 3k.40, "Prague, 1828" (V. Morstadt). HORIZ: 1k.80, "Liberation of Prague" (A. Cermakova).

635 Posthorn Motif

1975. Stamp Day.

2261	**635**	1k. multicoloured	35	25

636 Frantisek Halas (poet)

1976. Celebrities' Anniversaries.

2262	**636**	60h. multicoloured	15	10
2263	-	60h. multicoloured	15	10
2264	-	60h. multicoloured	30	10
2265	-	60h. blue, red & yellow	15	10
2266	-	60h. multicoloured	15	10

DESIGNS AND ANNIVERSARIES—HORIZ: No. 2262, Type **636** (75th birth anniv); 2266, Ivan Krasko (poet, birth cent). VERT: No. 2263, Wilhelm Pieck (German statesman, birth cent); 2264, Frantisek Lexa (Egyptologist, birth cent); 2265, Jindrich Jindrich (ethnographer, birth cent).

637 Ski Jumping

1976. Winter Olympic Games, Innsbruck. Mult.

2267	1k. Type **637**	20	10
2268	1k.40 Figure skating	30	20
2269	1k.60 Ice hockey	1·25	30

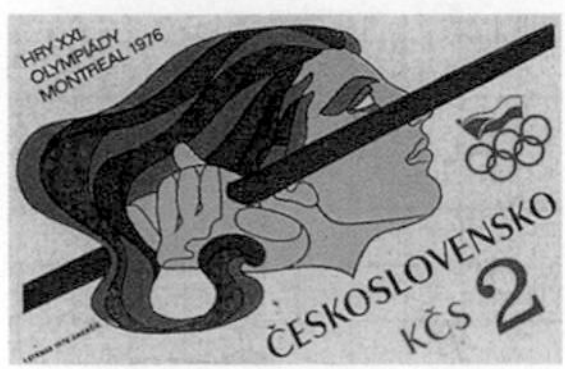

638 Throwing the Javelin

1976. Olympic Games, Montreal. Multicoloured.

2270	2k. Type **638**	45	20
2271	3k. Relay-racing	80	30
2272	3k.60 Putting the shot	3·00	1·10

639 Table Tennis Player

1976. European Table Tennis Championships, Prague and 50th Anniv of Organized Table Tennis in Czechoslovakia.

2273	**639**	1k. multicoloured	35	10

640 Star Emblem and Workers

1976. 15th Czechoslovak Communist Party Congress, Prague. Multicoloured.

2274	30h. Type **640**	10	10
2275	60h. Furnace and monolith	15	10

641 Microphone and Musical Instruments

1976. Cultural Events and Anniversaries.

2276	**641**	20h. multicoloured	10	10
2277	-	20h. multicoloured	10	10
2278	-	20h. multicoloured	10	10
2279	-	30h. multicoloured	10	10
2280	-	30h. violet, red & blue	10	10

DESIGNS—HORIZ: No. 2276, Type **641** (50th anniv of Czechoslovak Radio Symphony Orchestra); 2278, Stage revellers (30th anniv of Nova Scena Theatre, Bratislava); 2279, Folk dancers, Wallachia (International Folk Song and Dance Festival, Straznice). VERT: No. 2277, Ballerina, violin and mask (30th anniv of Prague Academy of Music and Dramatic Art); 2280, Film "profile" (20th Film Festival, Karlovy Vary).

1976. Bratislava Tapestries. "Hero and Leander" (3rd series). As T 617. Multicoloured.

2281	3k. "Hero with Leander's body"	2·00	1·25
2282	3k.60 "Eros grieving"	85	60

642 Hammer, Sickle and Red Flags

1976. 55th Anniv of Czechoslovak Communist Party.

2283	**642**	30h. blue, gold and red	15	10
2284	-	60h. multicoloured	20	10
MS2285		100×90 mm. 6k. multicoloured	2·75	3·00

DESIGN—VERT: (23×40 mm) 60h. Hammer and Sickle on flag. HORIZ (50×30 mm)—6k. Flag and commemorative inscription.

643 Manes Hall, Czechoslovakia Artists' Union

1976. Air. "PRAGA 78" International Stamp Exhibition (1st issue). Prague Architecture. Multicoloured.

2286	60h. Type **643**	35	10
2287	1k.60 Congress Hall, Julius Fucik Park	40	20
2288	2k. Powder Tower, Old Town (vert)	70	25
2289	2k.40 Charles Bridge and Old Bridge Tower	55	25
2290	4k. Old Town Square and Town Hall (vert)	85	30
2291	6k. Prague Castle and St. Vitus Cathedral (vert)	3·50	1·00

See also 2313/16, 2326/30, 2339/42, 2349/52, 2358/62, 2389/93, 2407/12, 2413/17, 2420/3 and **MS**2424/5.

644 "Warship" (Frans Huys)

1976. Ship Engravings.

2292	**644**	40h. blk, cream & drab	35	10
2293	-	60h. blk, cream & grey	35	10
2294	-	1k. black, cream & grn	60	10
2295	-	2k. black, cream & blue	1·25	45

DESIGNS: 60h. "Dutch Merchantman" (V. Hollar); 1k. "Ship at Anchor" (N. Zeeman); 2k. "Galleon under Full Sail" (F. Chereau).

645 "UNESCO" Plant

1976. 30th Anniv of UNESCO.

2296	**645**	2k. multicoloured	95	55

646 "Protected Child"

1976. European Security and Co-operation Conference, Helsinki. Sheet 114×167 mm containing two stamps as T 646.
MS2297 6k. ×2 blue, yellow and red 5·00 5·00

647 Merino Ram

1976. "Bountiful Earth" Agricultural Exhibition, Ceske Budejovice. Multicoloured.
2298 30h. Type **647** 15 10
2299 40h. Berna-Hana Cow 15 10
2300 1k.60 Kladruby stallion 45 10

648 "Stop Smoking"

1976. W.H.O. Campaign against Smoking.
2301 **648** 2k. multicoloured 90 40

649 Postal Code Emblem

1976. Coil Stamps. Postal Code Campaign.
2302 **649** 30h. green 10 10
2303 - 60h. red 15 10
DESIGN: 60h. Postal map.

650 "Guernica 1937" (I. Weiner-Kral)

1976. 40th Anniv of International Brigades in Spanish Civil War.
2304 **650** 5k. multicoloured 1·25 55

1976. Prague Castle. Art Treasures (12th series). As T 536. Multicoloured.
2305 3k. "Prague Castle, 1572" (F. Hoogenberghe) 2·00 1·90
2306 3k.60 "Satyrs" (relief from summer-house balustrade) 60 70

651 Common Zebra with Foal

1976. Dvurkralove Wildlife Park. Multicoloured.
2307 10h. Type **651** 15 10
2308 20h. African elephant, calf and cattle egret (vert) 50 15
2309 30h. Cheetah 15 10
2310 40h. Giraffe and calf (vert) 15 10
2311 60h. Black rhinoceros 20 10
2312 3k. Bongo with offspring (vert) 2·50 65

1976. "PRAGA 1978" International Stamp Exhibition (2nd series). Art (11th series). As T 481. Multicoloured.
2313 1k. "Flowers in Vase" (P. Matejka) 80 55
2314 1k.40 "Oleander Blossoms" (C. Bouda) 1·10 80
2315 2k. "Flowers in Vase" (J. Brueghel) 1·75 1·40
2316 3k.60 "Tulips and Narcissi" (J. R. Bys) 80 80

652 Postilion, Postal Emblem and Satellite

1976. Stamp Day.
2317 **652** 1k. blue, mauve & gold 25 10

653 Ice Hockey

1977. 6th Winter Spartakiad of Warsaw Pact Armies. Multicoloured.
2318 60h. Type **653** 25 10
2319 1k. Rifle shooting (Biathlon) 30 10
2320 1k.60 Ski jumping 1·40 45
2321 2k. Slalom 50 25

654 Arms of Vranov

1977. Coats of Arms of Czechoslovak Towns (1st series). Multicoloured.
2322 60h. Type **654** 15 10
2323 60h. Kralupy and Vltavou 15 10
2324 60h. Jicin 15 10
2325 60h. Valasske Mezirici 15 10
See also Nos. 2511/14, 2612/15, 2720/3, 2765/7, 2819/21 and 3017/20.

655 Window, Michna Palace

1977. "PRAGA 78" International Stamp Exhibition (3rd issue). Historic Prague Windows. Multicoloured.
2326 20h. Type **655** 10 10
2327 30h. Michna Palace (different) 10 10
2328 40h. Thun Palace 10 10
2329 60h. Archbishop's Palace 15 10
2330 5k. Church of St. Nicholas 2·25 65

656 Children Crossing Road

1977. 25th Anniv of Police Aides Corps.
2331 **656** 60h. multicoloured 10 10

657 Cyclists at Warsaw (starting point)

1977. 30th Anniv of Peace Cycle Race. Mult.
2332 30h. Type **657** 15 10
2333 60h. Cyclists at Berlin 20 10
2334 1k. Cyclists at Prague (finishing point) 85 25
2335 1k.40 Cyclists and modern buildings 40 15

658 Congress Emblem

1977. 9th Trade Unions Congress.
2336 **658** 30h. gold, red & carmine 10 10

1977. Prague Castle (13th series). As T 536.
2337 3k. multicoloured 1·10 1·25
2338 3k.60 green, gold & black 1·90 1·60
DESIGNS: 3k. Onyx cup, 1350 (St. Vitus Cathedral); 3k.60, Bronze horse, 1619 (A. de Vries).

659 French Postal Rider, 19th-century

1977. "PRAGA 78" International Stamp Exhibition (4th issue). Multicoloured.
2339 60h. Type **659** 15 10
2340 1k. Austrian postal rider, 1838 30 10
2341 2k. Austrian postal rider, c. 1770 50 25
2342 3k.60 German postal rider, 1700 2·25 80

660 Coffee Pots

1977. Czechoslovak Porcelain.
2343 **660** 20h. multicoloured 10 10
2344 - 30h. multicoloured 10 10
2345 - 40h. multicoloured 15 10
2346 - 60h. multicoloured 20 10
2347 - 1k. blue, grn & violet 25 10
2348 - 3k. blue, gold and red 2·10 60
DESIGNS: 30h. Vase; 40h. Amphora; 60h. Jug, beaker, cup and saucer; 1k. Plate and candlestick; 3k. Coffee pot, cup and saucer.

661 Mlada Boleslav Headdress

1977. "PRAGA 78" International Stamp Exhibition (5th issue). Regional Headdresses. Multicoloured.
2349 1k. Type **661** 75 80
2350 1k.60 Vazek 3·50 3·50
2351 3k.60 Zavadka 75 80
2352 5k. Belkovice 1·25 1·10

662 V. Bombova's Illustrations of "Janko Gondashik and the Golden Lady"

1977. 6th Biennial Exhibition of Children's Book Illustrators, Bratislava. Multicoloured.
2353 40h. Type **662** 10 10
2354 60h. "Tales of Amur" (G. Pavlishin) 15 10
2355 1k. "Almgist et Wiksel" (U. Lofgren) 25 10
2356 2k. "Alice in Wonderland" and "Through the Looking Glass" (Nicole Claveloux) 75 25
2357 3k. "Eventyr" (J. Trnka) 2·25 65

663 Airships LZ-5 and LZ-127 "Graf Zeppelin"

1977. Air. "PRAGA 1978" International Stamp Exhibition (6th issue). Early Aviation. Mult.
2358 60h. Type **663** 15 10
2359 1k. Clement Ader's monoplane "Eole", Etrich Holubice and Dunne D-8 30 10
2360 1k.60 Jeffries and Blanchard balloon, 1785 40 15
2361 2k. Lilienthal biplane glider, 1896 50 15
2362 4k.40 Jan Kaspar's Bleriot XI over Prague 3·50 85

664 UNESCO Emblem, Violin and Doves

1977. Congress of UNESCO International Music Council.
2363 **664** 60h. multicoloured 10 10

665 "Peace"

1977. European Co-operation for Peace. Mult.
2364 60h. Type **665** 15 30
2365 1k.60 "Co-operation" 40 45
2366 2k.40 "Social Progress" 1·50 60

666 Yuri Gagarin

1977. Space Research. Multicoloured.
2367 20h. S. P. Koroliov (space technician, launch of first satellite) 10 10
2368 30h. Type **666** (first man in space) 10 10
2369 40h. Aleksei Leonov (first space walker) 10 10
2370 1k. Neil Armstrong (first man on the Moon) 25 10
2371 1k.60 "Salyut" and "Skylab" space stations 1·25 35

667 Revolutionaries and Cruiser "Aurora"

1977. 60th Anniv of Russian Revolution, and 55th Anniv of U.S.S.R. Multicoloured.
2372 30h. Type **667** 15 10
2373 30h. Russian woman, Kremlin, rocket and U.S.S.R. arms 15 10

668 "Wisdom"

1977. 25th Anniv of Czechoslovak Academy of Science.

2374	**668**	3k. multicoloured	70	30

1977. Art (12th series). As Type 481.

2375	2k. multicoloured	75	80
2376	2k.40 multicoloured	2·50	2·75
2377	2k.60 stone and black	2·10	1·60
2378	3k. multicoloured	1·00	1·00
2379	5k. multicoloured	1·00	1·00

DESIGNS: 2k. "Fear" (J. Mudroch); 2k.40, "Portrait of Jan Francis" (P. M. Bohun); 2k.60, "Self Portrait" (V. Hollar); 3k. "Portrait of a Girl" (L. Cranach); 5k. "Cleopatra" (Rubens).

669 "Bratislava, 1574" (G. Hoefnagel)

1977. Historic Bratislava (1st series). Mult.

2380	3k. Type **669**	1·90	2·00
2381	3k.60 Bratislava Arms, 1436	1·10	80

See also Nos. 2402/3, 2500/1, 2545/6, 2582/3, 2642/3, 2698/9, 2736/7, 2793/4, 2842/3, 2898/9, 2952/3, 2997/8 and 3034/5.

670 Posthorn and Stamps

1977. Stamp Day.

2382	**670**	1k. multicoloured	25	10

671 Z. Nejedly (historian)

1978. Cultural Anniversaries. Multicoloured.

2383	30h. Type **671** (birth cent)	10	10
2384	40h. Karl Marx (160th birth anniv)	10	10

672 Civilians greeting Armed Guards

1978. 30th Annivs of "Victorious February" and National Front. Multicoloured.

2385	1k. Type **672**	20	10
2386	1k. Intellectual, peasant woman and steel worker	20	10

1978. Soviet–Czechoslovak Space Flight. No. 2368 optd SPOLECNY LET SSSR*CSSR.

2387	30h. red	20	15
2388	3k.60 blue	4·25	4·50

674 Modern Coins

1978. 650th Anniv of Kremnica Mint and "PRAGA 1978" International Stamp Exhibition (7th issue). Multicoloured.

2389	20h. Type **674**	10	10
2390	40h. Culture medal, 1972 (Jan Kulich)	10	10
2391	1k.40 Charles University Medal, 1948 (O, Spaniel)	2·40	35
2392	3k. Ferdinand I medal, 1563 (L. Richter)	80	40
2393	5k. Gold florin of Charles Robert, 1335	95	50

675 Tyre Marks and Ball

1978. Road Safety.

2394	**675**	60h. multicoloured	10	10

676 Hands supporting Globe

1978. 9th World Federation of Trade Unions Congress, Prague.

2395	**676**	1k. multicoloured	25	10

677 Putting the Shot

1978. Sports.

2396	-	30h. multicoloured	15	10
2397	**677**	40h. multicoloured	15	10
2398	-	60h. multicoloured	70	15
2399	-	1k. multicoloured	35	10
2400	-	2k. yellow, blue & red	55	25
2401	-	3k.60 multicoloured	1·75	85

DESIGNS AND EVENTS—HORIZ: 70th anniv of bandy hockey: 30h. Three hockey players, World Ice Hockey Championships; 60h. Tackle in front of goal; 2k. Goal-mouth scrimmage. VERT: European Athletics Championships, Prague: 1k. Pole vault; 3k.60, Running.

1978. Historic Bratislava (2nd series). As T 669.

2402	3k. green, violet and red	1·25	1·40
2403	3k.60 multicoloured	2·75	2·50

DESIGNS: 3k. "Bratislava" (Orest Dubay); 3k.60, "Fishpond Square, Bratislava" (Imro Weiner-Kral).

1978. Prague Castle (14th series). As T 536.

2404	3k. yellow, black & green	95	80
2405	3k.60 multicoloured	3·25	2·50

DESIGNS: 3k. Memorial to King Premysl Otakar II, St. Vitus Cathedral; 3k.60, Portrait of King Charles IV (Jan Ocka).

678 Ministry of Posts, Prague

1978. 14th COMECON Meeting, Prague.

2406	**678**	60h. multicoloured	10	10

679 Palacky Bridge

1978. "PRAGA 78" International Stamp Exhibition (8th issue). Prague Bridges. Multicoloured.

2407	20h. Type **679**	10	10
2408	40h. Railway bridge	55	10
2409	1k. Bridge of 1st May	25	10
2410	2k. Manes Bridge	45	15
2411	3k. Svatopluk Cech Bridge	55	30
2412	5k.40 Charles Bridge	3·50	95

680 St. Peter and other Apostles

1978. "PRAGA 78" International Stamp Exhibition (9th issue). Prague Town Hall Astronomical Clock. Multicoloured.

2413	40h. Type **680**	15	10
2414	1k. Astronomical clock face	20	15
2415	2k. Centre of Manes's calendar	35	15
2416	3k. "September" (grape harvest)	2·10	70
2417	3k.60 "Libra" (sign of the Zodiac)	1·25	25
MS2418	89×125 mm. 10k. Manes's calendar (48×38 mm)	10·50	12·50

681 Dancers

1978. 25th Vychodna Folklore Festival.

2419	**681**	30h. multicoloured	10	10

682 Gottwald Bridge

1978. "PRAGA 78" International Stamp Exhibition (10th issue). Modern Prague. Multicoloured.

2420	60h. Type **682**	65	10
2421	1k. Powder Gate Tower and Kotva department store	25	10
2422	2k. Ministry of Posts	55	25
2423	6k. Prague Castle and flats	2·10	1·10

683 "Old Prague and Charles Bridge" (V. Morstadt)

1978. "PRAGA 1978" International Stamp Exhibition (11th issue). Sheet 96×74 mm.

MS2424	**683** 20k. multicoloured	10·50	12·50

684 Detail of "The Flaying of Marsyas" (Titian)

1978. "PRAGA 1978" International Stamp Exhibition (12th issue). Sheet 108×165 mm containing T 684 and similar vert design showing detail of painting.

MS2425	10k. Type **684**; 10k. King Midas	11·50	13·00

685 Fair Buildings

1978. 20th International Engineering Fair, Brno.

2426	**685**	30h. multicoloured	10	10

686 "Postal Newspaper Service" (25th Anniv)

1978. Press, Broadcasting and Television Days.

2427	**686**	30h. green, blue & orge	10	10
2428	-	30h. multicoloured	10	10
2429	-	30h. multicoloured	10	10

DESIGNS: No. 2428, Microphone, newspapers, camera and Ministry of Information and Broadcasting; 2429, Television screen and Television Centre, Prague (25th anniv of Czechoslovak television).

687 Horses falling at Fence

1978. Pardubice Steeplechase. Multicoloured.

2430	10h. Type **687**	10	10
2431	20h. Sulky racing	10	10
2432	30h. Racing horses	15	10
2433	40h. Passing the winning post	15	10
2434	1k.60 Jumping a fence	40	20
2435	4k.40 Jockey leading a winning horse	2·50	90

688 Woman holding Arms of Czechoslovakia

1978. 60th Anniv of Independence.

2436	**688**	60h. multicoloured	10	10

689 "Still Life with Flowers" (J. Bohdan)

1978. 30th Anniv of Slovak National Gallery, Bratislava. Multicoloured.

2437	2k.40 Type **689**	80	55
2438	3k. "Dream in a Shepherd's Hut" (L. Fulla) (horiz)	80	70
2439	3k.60 "Apostle with Censer" (detail, Master of the Spis Chapter)	3·75	3·50

690 Violinist and Bass Player (J. Konyves)

1978. Slovak Ceramics.

No.	Type	Description	Mint	Used
2440	**690**	20h. multicoloured	10	10
2441	-	30h. blue and violet	10	10
2442	-	40h. multicoloured	10	10
2443	-	1k. multicoloured	20	10
2444	-	1k.60 multicoloured	1·60	25

DESIGNS: 30h. Horseman (J. Franko); 40h. Man in Kilt (M. Polasko); 1k. Three girl singers (I. Bizmayer); 1k.60, Miner with axe (F. Kostka).

691 Alfons Mucha and design for 1918 Hradcany Stamp

1978. Stamp Day.

No.	Type	Description	Mint	Used
2445	**691**	1k. multicoloured	25	10

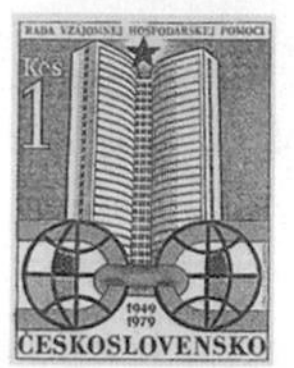

692 Council Building, Moscow

1979. Anniversaries.

No.	Type	Description	Mint	Used
2446	-	30h. brown, grn & orge	10	10
2447	-	60h. multicoloured	15	10
2448	**692**	1k. multicoloured	20	10

DESIGNS—HORIZ: 30h. Girl's head and ears of wheat (30th anniv of Unified Agricultural Co-operatives); 60h. Czechoslovakians and doves (10th anniv of Czechoslovak Federation). VERT: 1k. Type **692** (30th anniv of Council of Economic Mutual Aid).

693 "Soyuz 28"

1979. 1st Anniv of Russian–Czech Space Flight. Multicoloured.

No.	Type	Description	Mint	Used
2449		30h. Type **693**	15	10
2450		60h. A. Gubarev and V. Remek (vert)	15	10
2451		1k.60 J. Romanenko and G. Grechko	45	10
2452		2k. "Salyut 6" space laboratory	1·90	40
2453		4k. "Soyuz 28" touch down (vert)	85	40
MS2454		75×95 mm. 10k. Gubarev and Remek waving (38×54 mm)	5·00	5·00

694 "Campanula alpina"

1979. 25th Anniv of Mountain Rescue Service. Multicoloured.

No.	Type	Description	Mint	Used
2455		10h. Type **694**	10	10
2456		20h. "Crocus scepusiensis"	10	10
2457		30h. "Dianthus glacialis"	10	10
2458		40h. Alpine hawkweed	15	10
2459a		3k. "Delphinium oxysepalum"	1·25	50

695 Stylized Satellite

1979. Anniversaries.

No.	Type	Description	Mint	Used
2460	**695**	10h. multicoloured	10	10
2461	-	20h. multicoloured	10	10
2462	-	20h. blue, orge & lt bl	10	10
2463	-	30h. blue, gold & red	10	10
2464	-	30h. red, blue & blk	10	10
2465	-	60h. multicoloured	15	10

DESIGNS AND EVENTS—HORIZ: No. 2460, Type **695** 30th anniv of Telecommunications Research. 46×19 mm: (No. 2461), Artist and model (30th anniv of Academy of Fine Arts, Bratislava); 2462, Student and technological equipment (40th anniv of Slovak Technical University, Bratislava); 2463, Musical instruments and Bratislava Castle (50th anniv of Radio Symphony Orchestra, Bratislava); 2464, Pioneer's scarf and I.Y.C. emblem (30th anniv of Young Pioneer Organization and International Year of the Child); 2465, Adult and child with doves (30th anniv of Peace Movement).

1979. Prague Castle (15th series). As T 536. Multicoloured.

No.	Type	Description	Mint	Used
2466		3k. Burial crown of King Premysl Otakar II	2·40	2·40
2467		3k.60 Portrait of Miss B. Reitmayer (Karel Purkyne)	1·25	1·00

696 Arms of Vlachovo Brezi

1979. Animals in Heraldry. Multicoloured.

No.	Type	Description	Mint	Used
2468		30h. Type **696**	10	10
2469		60h. Jesenik (bear and eagle)	15	10
2470		1k.20 Vysoke Myto (St. George and the dragon)	30	10
2471		1k.80 Martin (St. Martin on horseback)	1·60	40
2472		2k. Zebrak (half bear, half lion)	40	10

697 Healthy and Polluted Forests

1979. Man and the Biosphere. Multicoloured.

No.	Type	Description	Mint	Used
2473		60h. Type **697**	15	15
2474		1k.80 Clear and polluted water	45	30
2475		3k.60 Healthy and polluted urban environment	2·50	85
2476		4k. Healthy and polluted pasture	95	40

698 Numeral and Printed Circuit

1979. Coil Stamps.

No.	Type	Description	Mint	Used
2477	-	50h. red	15	10
2478	**698**	1k. brown	20	10
2478a	-	2k. green	50	25
2478b	-	3k. purple	80	35

DESIGNS: Numeral and—50h. Dish aerial; 2k. Airplane; 3k. Punched tape.

699 Industrial Complex

1979. 35th Anniv of Slovak Uprising.

No.	Type	Description	Mint	Used
2479	**699**	30h. multicoloured	10	10

700 Illustration by Janos Kass

1979. International Year of the Child and Biennial Exhibition of Children's Book Illustrations, Bratislava. Designs showing illustrations by artists named. Multicoloured.

No.	Type	Description	Mint	Used
2480		20h. Type **700**	10	10
2481		40h. Rumen Skorcev	15	10
2482		60h. Karel Svolinsky	15	10
2483		1k. Otto S. Svend	30	10
2484		3k. Tatyana Mavrina	1·90	45

701 Modern Bicycles

1979. Historic Bicycles. Multicoloured.

No.	Type	Description	Mint	Used
2485		20h. Type **701**	15	10
2486		40h. Bicycles, 1910	15	10
2487		60h. "Ordinary" and tricycle, 1886	15	10
2488		2k. "Bone-shakers", 1870	45	25
2489		3k.60 Drais cycles, 1820	2·50	65

702 Bracket Clock (Jan Kraus)

1979. Historic Clocks. Multicoloured.

No.	Type	Description	Mint	Used
2490		40h. Type **702**	10	10
2491		60h. Rococo clock	15	10
2492		80h. Classicist clock	1·60	35
2493		1k. Rococo porcelain clock (J. Kandler)	25	10
2494		2k. Urn-shaped clock (Dufaud)	45	25

1979. Art (13th series). As T 481.

No.	Type	Description	Mint	Used
2495		1k.60 multicoloured	65	55
2496		2k. multicoloured	75	60
2497		3k. multicoloured	1·00	70
2498		3k.60 multicoloured	2·75	2·75
2499		5k. yellow and black	1·10	1·25

DESIGNS: 1k.60, "Sunday by the River" (Alois Moravec); 2k. "Self-portrait" (Gustav Mally); 3k. "Self-portrait" (Ilja Jefimovic Repin); 3k.60, "Horseback Rider" (Jan Bauch); 5k. "Village Dancers" (Albrecht Durer).

1979. Historic Bratislava (3rd issue). As T 669. Multicoloured.

No.	Type	Description	Mint	Used
2500		3k. "Bratislava, 1787" (L. Janscha)	1·10	90
2501		3k.60 "Bratislava, 1815" (after stone engraving by Wolf)	2·50	2·40

703 Postmarks, Charles Bridge and Prague Castle

1979. Stamp Day.

No.	Type	Description	Mint	Used
2502	**703**	1k. multicoloured	25	10

704 Skiing

1980. Winter Olympic Games, Lake Placid.

No.	Type	Description	Mint	Used
2503	**704**	1k. multicoloured	25	10
2504	-	2k. red, pink & blue	1·60	40
2505	-	3k. multicoloured	1·00	55

DESIGNS: 2k. Ice skating; 3k. Four-man bobsleigh.

705 Basketball

1980. Olympic Games, Moscow. Multicoloured.

No.	Type	Description	Mint	Used
2506		40h. Type **705**	15	10
2507		1k. Swimming	25	10
2508		2k. Hurdles	2·40	40
2509		3k.60 Fencing	85	35

706 Marathon

1980. 50th International Peace Marathon, Kosice.

No.	Type	Description	Mint	Used
2510	**706**	50h. multicoloured	10	10

1980. Arms of Czech Towns (2nd series). As T 654.

No.	Type	Description	Mint	Used
2511		50h. blue, black and gold	15	10
2512		50h. black and silver	15	10
2513		50h. multicoloured	15	10
2514		50h. gold, black and blue	15	10

DESIGNS: No. 2511, Bystrice nad Pernstejnem; 2512, Kunstat; 2513, Rozmital pod Tremsinem; 2514, Zlata Idka.

707 Bratislava Opera House and Bakovazena as King Lear

1980. 60th Anniv of Slovak National Theatre, Bratislava.

No.	Type	Description	Mint	Used
2515	**707**	1k. blue, yellow & orange	25	10

708 Tragic Mask

1980. 50th Anniv of Theatrical Review "Jiraskuv Hronov".

No.	Type	Description	Mint	Used
2516	**708**	50h. multicoloured	10	10

709 Mouse in Space

1980. "Intercosmos" Space Programme.

No.	Type	Description	Mint	Used
2517	**709**	50h. blue, black and red	15	10
2518	-	1k. multicoloured	30	10
2519	-	1k.60 violet, blk & red	2·25	50
2520	-	4k. multicoloured	1·00	35
2521	-	5k. blue, black & purple	1·50	50
MS2522		75×94 mm. 10k. multicoloured	5·00	5·00

DESIGNS—VERT: 1k. Weather map and satellite; 1k.60, "Inter-sputnik" T.V. transmission; 4k. Survey satellite and camera. HORIZ: 5k. Czech-built satellite station; 10k. "Intercosmos" emblem.

710 Police Parade Banner

1980. 35th Anniv of National Police Corps.

2523	**710**	50h. gold, red & blue	10	10

711 Lenin

1980. 110th Birth Anniv of Lenin and 160th Birth Anniv of Engels.

2524	**711**	1k. brown, red & grey	20	10
2525	-	1k. blue and brown	20	10

DESIGN: No. 2525, Engels.

712 Flag, Flowers and Prague Buildings

1980. Anniversaries. Multicoloured.

2526	50h. Type **712**	15	10
2527	1k. Child writing "Mir" (peace)	20	10
2528	1k. Czech and Soviet arms	20	10
2529	1k. Flowers, flags and dove	20	10

ANNIVERSARIES: No. 2526, 35th anniv of May uprising; 2527, 35th anniv of Liberation; 2528, 10th anniv of Czech–Soviet Treaty; 2529, 25th anniv of Warsaw Pact.

713 Gymnast

1980. National Spartakiad.

2530	-	50h. black, red & blue	10	10
2531	**713**	1k. multicoloured	20	10

DESIGN—HORIZ: 50h. Opening parade of athletes.

714 U.N. Emblem

1980. 35th Anniv of United Nations. Sheet 109×165 mm.

MS2532 **714** 4k. ×2 multicoloured	3·50	3·50

715 "Gerbera jamesonii"

1980. Olomuc and Bratislava Flower Shows. Multicoloured.

2533	50h. Type **715**	15	15
2534	1k. "Aechmea fasciata"	1·75	40
2535	2k. Bird of paradise flower	35	25
2536	4k. Slipper orchid	85	40

716 "Chod Girl"

1980. Graphic Cut-outs by Cornelia Nemeckova.

2537	**716**	50h. multicoloured	15	10
2538	-	1k. mauve, brown & red	25	10
2539	-	2k. multicoloured	45	25
2540	-	4k. multicoloured	2·50	70
2541	-	5k. blue, mauve & lt bl	1·10	50

DESIGNS: 1k. "Punch with his dog"; 2k. "Dandy cat with Posy"; 4k. Lion and Moon ("Evening Contemplation"); 5k. Dancer and piper ("Wallacchian Dance").

717 Map of Czechoslovakia and Family

1980. National Census.

2542	**717**	1k. multicoloured	25	10

1980. Prague Castle (16th series). As T 536. Multicoloured.

2543	3k. Gateway of Old Palace	2·40	2·75
2544	4k. Armorial lion	1·10	75

1980. Historic Bratislava (4th issue). As T 669. Multicoloured.

2545	3k. "View across the Danube" (J. Eder)	2·40	2·75
2546	4k. "The Old Royal Bridge" (J. A. Lantz)	1·10	75

718 Heads

1980. 10th Anniv of Socialist Youth Federation.

2547	**718**	50h. blue, orange & red	10	10

1980. "Essen '80" International Stamp Exhibition. Sheet 129×78 mm containing No. 2365 ×2 optd DEN CSSR / 3 / MEZINARODNI VELETRH ZNAMEK / ESSEN 80 / TSCHECHOSLOWAKISCHER TAG and 80 / 3. Internationale / Briefmarken-Messe / Essen / 1980 with Exhibition emblems in red.

MS2548 1k.60 ×2 multicoloured	17·00	17·00

1980. Paintings (14th series). As T 481.

2549	1k. buff, blue and brown	1·25	1·00
2550	2k. multicoloured	2·00	2·10
2551	3k. red, brown and green	55	45
2552	4k. multicoloured	65	55
2553	5k. green, buff and black	85	80

DESIGNS—VERT: 1k. "Pavel Jozef Safarik" (Jozef B. Klemens); 2k. "Peasant Revolt" (mosaic, A. Podzemma); 3k. Bust of Saint from Lucivna Church; 5k. "Labour" (sculpture, Jan Stursa). HORIZ: 4k. "Waste Heaps" (Jan Zrzavy).

719 Carrier Pigeon

1980. Stamp Day.

2554	**719**	1k. black, red & blue	25	10

720 Five Year Plan Emblem

1981. 7th Five Year Plan.

2555	**720**	50h. multicoloured	10	10

721 Invalid and Half-bare Tree

1981. International Year of Disabled Persons.

2556	**721**	1k. multicoloured	25	10

722 Landau, 1800

1981. Historic Coaches in Postal Museum.

2557	**722**	50h. yellow, black & red	20	10
2558	-	1k. yellow, black & grn	30	10
2559	-	3k.60 lt blue, blk & bl	2·00	40
2560	-	5k. stone, black & red	1·25	35
2561	-	7k. yellow, black & blue	1·50	65

DESIGNS: 1k. Mail coach, c. 1830–40; 3k.60, Postal sleigh, 1840; 5k. Mail coach and four horses, 1860; 7k. Coupe carriage, 1840.

723 Jan Sverma (partisan)

1981. Celebrities' Anniversaries. Multicoloured.

2562	50h. Type **723** (80th birth anniv)	25	10
2563	50h. Mikulas Schneider-Trnavsky (composer) (birth cent)	35	10
2564	50h. Juraj Hronec (mathematician) (birth cent)	25	10
2565	50h. Josef Hlavka (architect) (150th birth anniv)	25	10
2566	1k. Dimitri Shostakovich (composer) (75th birth anniv)	60	10
2567	1k. George Bernard Shaw (dramatist) (125th birth anniv)	60	10
2568	1k. Bernardo Bolzano (philosopher) (birth bicent)	1·50	25
2569	1k. Wolfgang Amadeus Mozart (composer) (225th birth anniv)	75	15

724 Yuri Gagarin

1981. 20th Anniv of First Manned Space Flight. Sheet 108×165 mm.

MS2570 **724** 6k. ×2 multicoloured	5·00	5·00

725 Party Member with Flag

1981. 60th Anniv of Czechoslovak Communist Party. Multicoloured.

2571	50h. Type **725**	10	15
2572	1k. Symbols of progress and hands holding flag	20	15
2573	4k. Party member holding flag bearing symbols of industry (vert)	80	40

726 Hammer and Sickle

1981. 16th Czechoslovak Communist Party Congress. Multicoloured.

2574	50h. Type **726**	10	10
2575	1k. "XVI" and Prague buildings	25	10

1981. "WIPA 1981" International Stamp Exhibition, Vienna. Sheet 150×104 mm.

MS2576 No. 2561×4	21·00	21·00

727 Fallow-plough

1981. 90th Anniv of Agricultural Museum.

2577	**727**	1k. multicoloured	25	10

728 Man, Woman and Dove

1981. Elections to Representative Assemblies.

2578	**728**	50h. red, stone & blue	10	10

729 "Uran" (Tatra Mountains) and "Rudy Rijen" (Bohemia)

1981. Achievements of Socialist Construction (1st series). Multicoloured.

2579	80h. Type **729** (Trade Union recreational facilities)	25	10
2580	1k. Prague–Brno–Bratislava expressway	30	10
2581	2k. Jaslovske Bohunice nuclear plant	50	25

See also Nos. 2644/6, 2695/7, 2753/5 and 2800/2.

1981. Historic Bratislava (5th issue). As T 669. Multicoloured.

2582	3k. "Bratislava, 1760" (G. B. Probst)	2·75	2·75
2583	4k. "Grassalkovichov Palace, 1815" (C. Bschor)	80	70

730 "Guernica" (image scaled to 73% of original size)

1981. 45th Anniv of International Bridges in Spain and Birth Centenary of Pablo Picasso (artist). Sheet 90×76 mm.

MS2584 **730** 10k. multicoloured	3·75	3·75

731 Puppets

1981. 30th National Festival of Amateur Puppetry Ensembles, Chrudim.

2585	**731**	2k. multicoloured	45	30

732 Map

1981. National Defence. Multicoloured.

2586	40h. Type **732** (Defence of borders)	10	10
2587	50h. Emblem of Civil Defence Organization (30th Anniv) (vert)	15	10
2588	1k. Emblem of Svazarm (Organization for Co-operation with Army, 30th anniv) (28×23 mm)	25	10

733 Edelweiss, Climbers and Lenin

1981. 25th International Youth Climb of Rysy Peaks.

2589	**733**	3k.60 multicoloured	85	40

734 Illustration by Albin Brunovsky

1981. Biennial Exhibition of Book Illustrations for Children, Bratislava. Multicoloured.

2590	50h. Type **734**	15	15
2591	1k. Adolf Born	30	20
2592	2k. Vive Tolli	60	25
2593	4k. Etienne Delessert	90	40
2594	10k. Suekichi Akaba	3·00	1·25

735 Gorilla Family

1981. 50th Anniv of Prague Zoo. Multicoloured.

2595	50h. Type **735**	30	10
2596	1k. Lion family	35	15
2597	7k. Przewalski's horses	2·75	1·50

736 Skeletal Hand removing Cigarette

1981. Anti-smoking Campaign.

2598	**736**	4k. multicoloured	1·75	85

1981. Prague Castle (17th series). As T 536. Multicoloured.

2599	3k. Fragment of Pernstejn terracotta from Lobkovic Palace (16th century)	90	45
2600	4k. St. Vitus Cathedral (19th century engraving by J. Sembera and G. Dobler)	2·25	2·75

1981. Art (15th series). As T 481.

2601	1k. multicoloured	3·50	3·25
2602	2k. brown	60	50
2603	3k. multicoloured	80	65
2604	4k. multicoloured	90	70
2605	5k. multicoloured	1·10	1·60

DESIGNS: 1k. "View of Prague from Petrin Hill" (V. Hollar); 2k. "Czech Academy of Arts and Sciences Medallion" (Otakar Spaniel); 3k. South Bohemian embroidery (Zdenek Sklenar); 4k. "Peonies" (A. M. Gerasimov); 5k. "Figure of a Woman Standing" (Picasso).

737 Eduard Karel (engraver)

1981. Stamp Day.

2606	**737**	1k. yellow, red and blue	25	10

738 Lenin

1982. 70th Anniv of 6th Russian Workers' Party Congress, Prague.

2607	**738**	2k. red, gold and blue	55	25
MS2608		107×83 mm. No. 2607×4	6·50	6·50

739 Player kicking Ball

1982. World Cup Football Championship, Spain. Multicoloured.

2609	1k. Type **739**	20	15
2610	3k.60 Heading ball	75	40
2611	4k. Saving goal	2·50	65

740 Hrob

1982. Arms of Czech Towns (3rd series). Multicoloured.

2612	50h. Type **740**	20	10
2613	50h. Mlada Boleslav	20	10
2614	50h. Nove Mesto and Metuji	20	10
2615	50h. Trencin	20	10

See also Nos. 2720/3, 2765/7, 2819/21 and 3017/20.

741 Conference Emblem

1982. Tenth World Federation of Trade Unions Congress, Havana.

2616	**741**	1k. multicoloured	25	10

742 Workers and Mine

1982. 50th Anniv of Great Strike at Most (coalminers' and general strike).

2617	**742**	1k. multicoloured	25	10

743 Locomotives of 1922 and 1982

1982. 60th Anniv of International Railways Union.

2618	**743**	6k. multicoloured	1·75	70

744 Worker with Flag

1982. 10th Trade Unions Congress, Prague.

2619	**744**	1k. multicoloured	25	10

745 Georgi Dimitrov

1982. Birth Centenary of Georgi Dimitrov (Bulgarian statesman).

2620	**745**	50h. multicoloured	10	10

746 Girl with Flowers

1982. 10th International Exhibition of Children's Art, Lidice. Sheet 165×108 mm.

MS2621	**746**	2k. ×6 multicoloured	14·00	14·00

747 "Euterpe" (Crispin de Passe)

1982. Engravings with a Music Theme.

2622	**747**	40h. black, gold & brown	15	10
2623	-	50h. black, gold & red	20	10
2624	-	1k. black, gold & brown	30	15
2625	-	2k. black, gold & blue	50	25
2626	-	3k. black, gold & green	2·40	70

DESIGNS: 50h. "The Sanguine Man" (Jacob de Gheyn); 1k. "The Crossing of the Red Sea" (Adriaen Collaert); 2k. "Wandering Musicians" (Rembrandt); 3k. "Beggar with Viol" (Jacques Callot).

748 Girl with Doves

1982. Second Special Session of United Nations General Assembly on Disarmament, New York. Sheet 165×108 mm.

MS2627	**748**	6k. ×2 multicoloured	12·50	12·50

749 Child's Head, Rose and Barbed Wire (Lidice)

1982. 40th Anniv of Destruction of Lidice and Lezaky. Multicoloured.

2628	1k. Type **749**	30	10
2629	1k. Hands and barbed wire (Lezaky)	30	10

750 Memorial and Statue of Jan Zizka

1982. 50th Anniv of National Memorial, Prague.

2630	**750**	1k. multicoloured	25	10

751 Satellite Orbits around Earth

1982. Second United Nations Conference on Research and Peaceful Uses of Outer Space, Vienna. Sheet 165×108 mm.

MS2631	**751**	5k. ×2 multicoloured	12·50	12·50

752 Krivoklat Castle

1982. Castles. Multicoloured.

2632	50h. Type **752**	20	10
2633	1k. Interior and sculptures at Krivoklat Castle	35	15
2634	2k. Nitra Castle	65	30
2635	3k. Archaeological finds from Nitra Castle	1·00	40
MS2636	105×125 mm. Nos. 2632/5	3·00	3·00

1982. Prague Castle (18th series). As T 536.

2637	3k. brown and green	2·40	70
2638	4k. multicoloured	1·25	95

DESIGNS: 3k. "St. George" (statue by George and Martin of Kluz, 1372); 4k. Tomb of Prince Vratislav I, Basilica of St. George.

753 Ferry "Kamzik" in Bratislava Harbour

1982. Danube Commission. Multicoloured.

2639	3k. Type **753**	80	30
2640	3k.60 "TR 100" tug at Budapest	1·00	40
MS2641	Two sheets, each 127×127 mm. (a) No. 2639 ×4; (b) No. 2640 ×4	20·00	20·00

1982. Historic Bratislava (6th issue). As T 669.

2642	3k. black and red	1·90	85
2643	4k. multicoloured	2·10	1·25

DESIGNS: 3k. "View of Bratislava with Steamer"; 4k. "View of Bratislava with Bridge".

754 Agriculture

1982. Achievements of Socialist Construction (2nd series). Multicoloured.

2644	20h. Type **754**	10	10
2645	1k. Industry	35	10
2646	3k. Science and technology	95	45

See also Nos. 2695/7, 2753/5 and 2800/2.

755 "Scientific Research"

1982. 30th Anniv of Academy of Sciences.

2647	**755**	6k. multicoloured	1·10	55

756 Couple with Flowers and Silhouette of Rider

1982. 65th Anniv of October Revolution and 60th Anniv of U.S.S.R. Multicoloured.

2648	50h. Type **756**	15	10
2649	1k. Cosmonauts and industrial complex	20	10

757 "Jaroslav Hasek" (writer) (Jose Malejovsky)

1982. Sculptures. Multicoloured.

2650	1k. Type **757**	30	10
2651	2k. "Jan Zrzavy" (patriot) (Jan Simota)	55	25
2652	4k.40 "Leos Janacek" (composer) (Milos Axman)	1·10	55
2653	6k. "Martin Kukucin" (patriot) (Jan Kulich)	1·50	75
2654	7k. "Peaceful Work" (detail) (Rudolf Pribis)	3·00	1·25

1982. Art (16th series). As T 481. Multicoloured.

2655	1k. "Revolution in Spain" (Josef Sima)	1·60	95
2656	2k. "Woman drying Herself" (Rudolf Kremlicka)	2·50	2·25
2657	3k. "The Girl Bride" (Dezider Milly)	1·60	90
2658	4k. "Oil Field Workers" (Jan Zelibsky)	1·60	1·25
2659	5k. "The Birds Lament" (Emil Filla)	1·75	1·50

758 Jaroslav Goldschmied (engraver) and Engraving Tools

1983. Stamp Day.

2660	**758**	1k. multicoloured	25	10

759 President Husak

1983. 70th Birthday of President Husak.

2661	**759**	50h. blue	10	10

See also No. 2911.

760 Jaroslav Hasek (writer)

1983. Celebrities' Anniversaries.

2662	**760**	50h. green, blue & red	15	15
2663	-	1k. brown, blue & red	25	15
2664	-	2k. multicoloured	45	25
2665	-	5k. black, blue & red	1·40	50

DESIGNS: Type **760** (birth centenary); 1k. Julius Fucik (journalist) (80th birth and 40th death annivs); 2k. Martin Luther (church reformist) (500th birth anniv); 5k. Johannes Brahms (composer) (150th birth anniv).

761 Armed Workers

1983. Anniversaries. Multicoloured.

2666	50h. Type **761** (35th anniv of "Victorious February")	15	10
2667	1k. Family and agriculture and industrial landscapes (35th anniversary of National Front)	25	15

762 Radio Waves and Broadcasting Emblem

1983. Communications. Multicoloured.

2668	40h. Type **762** (60th anniv of Czech broadcasting)	15	10
2669	1k. Television emblem (30th anniv of Czech television)	20	10
2670	2k. W.C.Y. emblem and "1983" (World Communications Year) (40×23 mm)	45	25
2671	3k.60 Envelopes, Aero A-10 aircraft and mail vans (60th anniv of airmail and 75th anniv of mail transport by motor vehicles) (49×19 mm)	1·00	50

763 Ski Flyer

1983. 7th World Ski Flying Championships, Harrachov.

2672	**763**	1k. multicoloured	25	10

764 A. Gubarev and V. Remek

1983. 5th Anniv of Soviet-Czechoslovak Space Flight. Sheet 109×165 mm.

MS2673	**764** 10k. ×2 multicoloured	14·00	14·00

765 Emperor Moth and "Viola sudetica"

1983. Nature Protection. Multicoloured.

2674	50h. Type **765**	20	10
2675	1k. Water lilies and edible frogs	40	15
2676	2k. Red crossbill and cones	1·60	40
2677	3k.60 Grey herons	1·60	50
2678	5k. Lynx and "Gentiana asclepiadea"	1·50	45
2679	7k. Red deer	3·25	1·50

766 Ivan Stepanovich Kbnev

1983. Soviet Army Commanders. Multicoloured.

2680	50h. Type **766**	15	10
2681	1k. Andrei Ivanovich Yeremenko	25	15
2682	2k. Rodion Yakovlevich Malinovsky	55	25

767 Dove

1983. World Peace and Life Congress, Prague.

2683	**767**	2k. multicoloured	45	40
MS2684		108×83 mm. No. 2683 ×4	9·25	9·25

768 "Rudolf II" (Adrian de Vries)

1983. Prague Castle (19th series).

2685	**768**	4k. multicoloured	1·40	1·00
2686	-	5k. orange, blk & red	85	1·00

DESIGN: 5k. Kinetic relief with timepiece by Rudolf Svoboda.

769 Mounted Messenger (Oleg K. Zotov)

1983. 9th Biennial Exhibition of Book Illustration for Children.

2687	**769**	50h. multicoloured	15	10
2688	-	1k. multicoloured	25	10
2689	-	4k. multicoloured	95	40
2690	-	7k. red and black	1·40	55
MS2691		115×133 mm. Nos. 2687/90	4·50	4·00

DESIGNS: 1k. Boy looking from window at birds in tree (Zbigniew Rychlicki); 4k. "Hansel and Gretel" (Lisbeth Zwerger); 7k. Three young negroes (Antonio P. Domingues).

770 Ilyushin Il-62m and Globe

1983. World Communications Year and 60th Anniv of Czechoslovak Airlines.

2692	**770**	50h. red, purple & pink	15	10
2693	-	1k. purple, red & pink	30	10
2694	-	4k. purple, red & pink	1·90	85

DESIGNS—VERT: 1k. Ilyushin Il-62m and envelope. HORIZ: 4k. Ilyushin Il-62m and Aero A-14 biplane.

1983. Achievements of Socialist Construction (3rd series). As T 754.

2695	50h. Surveyor	15	10
2696	1k. Refinery	30	10
2697	3k. Hospital and operating theatre	75	50

1983. Historic Bratislava (7th series). As T 669.

2698	3k. green, red and black	1·75	70
2699	4k. multicoloured	1·75	70

DESIGNS: 3k. Sculptures by Viktor Tilgner; 4k. "Mirbachov Palace" (Julius Schubert).

771 National Theatre, Prague

1983. Czechoslovak Theatre Year.

2700	**771**	50h. brown	15	10
2701	-	2k. green	55	25

DESIGN: 2k. National Theatre and Tyl Theatre, Prague.

1983. Art (17th series), showing works from the National Theatre, Prague. As Type 481.

2702	1k. multicoloured	1·25	90
2703	2k. multicoloured	2·75	90
2704	3k. yellow, black and blue	1·00	60
2705	4k. multicoloured	1·00	60
2706	5k. multicoloured	1·00	60

DESIGNS: 1k. "Zalov" (lunette detail by Mikolas Ales); 2k. "Genius" (stage curtain detail, Vojtech Hynais); 3k. "Music" and "Lyrics" (ceiling drawings, Frantisek Zenisek); 4k. "Prague" (detail from President's box, Vaclav Brozik); 5k. "Hradcany Castle (detail from President's box, Julius Marak).

772 "Soldier with Sword and Shield" (Hendrik Goltzius)

1983. Period Costume from Old Engravings. Multicoloured.

2707	40h. Type **772**	15	10
2708	50h. "Warrior with Sword and Lance" (Jacob de Gheyn)	15	10
2709	1k. "Lady with Muff" (Jacques Callot)	30	10
2710	4k. "Lady with Flower" (Vaclav Hollar)	1·10	40
2711	5k. "Gentleman with Cane" (Antoine Watteau)	2·25	80

773 Karel Seizinger (stamp engraver)

1983. Stamp Day.

2712	**773**	1k. multicoloured	25	10

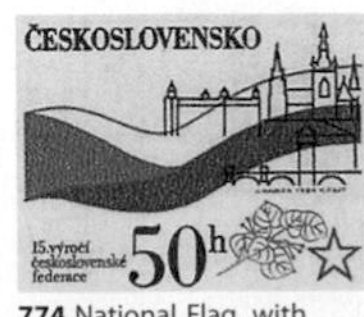

774 National Flag, with Bratislava and Prague Castles

1984. 15th Anniv of Czechoslovak Federation.

2713	**774**	50h. multicoloured	10	10

775 Council Emblem

1984. 35th Anniv of Council for Mutual Economic Aid.

2714	**775**	1k. multicoloured	25	25

776 Cross-country Skiing

1984. Winter Olympic Games, Sarajevo. Mult.

2715	2k. Type **776**	45	25
2716	3k. Ice hockey	70	40
2717	5k. Biathlon	1·50	65
MS2718	110×99 mm. No. 2716 ×4	8·00	8·00

777 Olympic Flag, Ancient Greek Athletes and Olympic Flame

1984. 90th Anniv of International Olympic Committee.

2719	**777**	7k. multicoloured	1·25	55

1984. Arms of Czech Towns (4th series). As T 740. Multicoloured.

2720	50h. Turnov	30	10
2721	50h. Kutna Hora	30	10
2722	1k. Milevsko	45	25
2723	1k. Martin	45	25

778 "Soyuz" and Dish Aerials

1984. "Interkosmos" International Space Flights. Multicoloured.

2724	50h. Type **778**	20	10
2725	1k. "Salyut"–"Soyuz" complex	35	15
2726	2k. Cross-section of orbital station	55	25
2727	4k. "Salyut" taking pictures of Earth's surface	75	50
2728	5k. "Soyuz" returning to Earth	1·00	65

779 Vendellin Opatrny

1984. Anti-fascist Heroes.

2729	**779**	50h. black, red & blue	20	10
2730	-	1k. black, red & blue	30	10
2731	-	2k. black, red & blue	55	25
2732	-	4k. black, red & blue	1·10	40

DESIGNS: 1k. Ladislav Novomesky; 2k. Rudolf Jasiok; 4k. Jan Nalepka.

780 Musical Instruments

1984. Music Year.

2733	**780**	50h. lt brown, gold & brn	20	10
2734	-	1k. multicoloured	25	10

DESIGN: 1k. Organ pipes.

781 Telecommunications Building

1984. Central Telecommunications Building, Bratislava.

2735	**781**	2k. multicoloured	55	25

1984. Historic Bratislava (8th series). As T 669. Multicoloured.

2736	3k. Arms of Vintners' Guild	1·25	85
2737	4k. Painting of 1827 Skating Festival	1·25	85

782 Doves, Globes and U.P.U. Emblem

1984. 110th Anniv of Universal Postal Union. Sheet 165×108 mm.

MS2738 **782** 5k. ×4 multicoloured	16·00	16·00

1984. Prague Castle (20th series). As T 768. Multicoloured.

2739	3k. Weather cock, St. Vitus Cathedral	75	80
2740	4k. King David playing psaltery (initial from Roudnice Book of Psalms)	1·40	1·25

783 Jack of Spades (16th century)

1984. Playing Cards. Multicoloured.

2741	50h. Type **783**	20	10
2742	1k. Queen of Spades (17th century)	35	10
2743	2k. Nine of Hearts (18th century)	50	25
2744	3k. Jack of Clubs (18th century)	85	35
2745	5k. King of Hearts (19th century)	1·25	55

784 Family and Industrial Complex

1984. 40th Anniv of Slovak Uprising.

2746	**784**	50h. multicoloured	10	10

785 Soldiers with Banner

1984. 40th Anniv of Battle of Dukla Pass.

2747	**785**	2k. multicoloured	45	25

786 High Jumping

1984. Olympic Games, Los Angeles. Mult.

2748	1k. Type **786**	30	15
2749	2k. Cycling	50	25
2750	3k. Rowing	70	40
2751	5k. Weightlifting	1·10	55
MS2752	107×95 mm. Nos. 2748/51	5·00	5·00

1984. Achievements of Socialist Construction (4th series). As T 754. Multicoloured.

2753	1k. Telephone handset and letters (Communications)	40	10
2754	2k. Containers on railway trucks and river barge (Transport)	75	30
2755	3k. Map of Transgas pipeline	65	45
MS2756	157×105 mm. No. 2755 ×3	5·00	5·00

1984. Art (18th series). As T 481. Multicoloured.

2757	1k. "Milevsky River" (Karel Stehlik)	1·25	75
2758	2k. "Under the Trees" (Viktor Barvitius)	1·25	90
2759	3k. "Landscape with Flowers" (Zolo Palugyay)	1·25	60
2760	4k. Illustration of king from Vysehrad Codex	1·60	80
2761	5k. "Kokorin" (Antonin Manes)	2·00	95

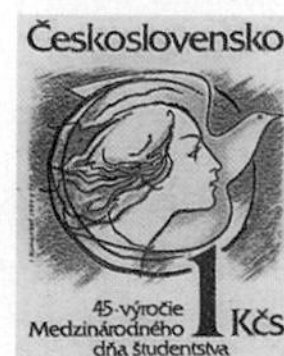

787 Dove and Head of Girl

1984. 45th Anniv of International Students Day.

2762	**787**	1k. multicoloured	25	10

788 Zapotocky

1984. Birth Centenary of Antonin Zapotocky (politician).

2763	**788**	50h. multicoloured	10	10

789 Bohumil Heinz (engraver) and Hands engraving

1984. Stamp Day.

2764	**789**	1k. multicoloured	25	25

1985. Arms of Czech Towns (5th series). As T 740. Multicoloured.

2765	50h. Kamyk nad Vltavou	30	10
2766	50h. Havirov	30	10
2767	50h. Trnava	30	10

790 "Art and Pleasure" (Jan Simota)

1985. Centenary of Prague University of Applied Arts.

2768	**790**	3k. multicoloured	60	40

791 View of Trnava

1985. 350th Anniv of Trnava University.

2769	**791**	2k. multicoloured	35	20

792 Helmet, Mail Shirt and Crossbow

1985. Exhibits from Military Museum. Mult.

2770	50h. Type **792**	15	10
2771	1k. Cross and star of Za vitezstvi order	30	10
2772	2k. Avia B-534 airplane and "Soyuz 28" (horiz)	70	25

793 Lenin reading

1985. 115th Birth Anniv of Lenin.

MS2773 **793** 2k. ×6 multicoloured	4·50	3·00

794 U.N. Emblem and Stylized Dove

1985. 40th Anniv of United Nations Organization and International Peace Year (1986).

MS2774 **794** 6k. ×4 multicoloured	14·00	14·00

795 State Arms and Crowd

1985. 40th Anniv of Kosice Reforms.

2775	**795**	4k. multicoloured	70	40

796 State Arms and Soldiers with National Flag

1985. 40th Anniv of National Security Forces.

2776	**796**	50h. multicoloured	10	10

797 Automatic Optical Platform and Comet Trajectory

1985. Space Project "Vega" (research into Venus and Halley's Comet). Sheet 106×96 mm.

MS2777 **797** 5k. ×2 multicoloured	10·50	10·50

798 Emblem and Ice Hockey Players

1985. World and European Ice Hockey Championships, Prague.

2778	**798**	1k. multicoloured	25	10

799 Pieces on Chessboard

1985. 80th Anniv of Czechoslovak Chess Organization.

2779	**799**	6k. multicoloured	1·50	70

800 Freedom Fighters and Prague

1985. Anniversaries. Multicoloured.

2780	1k. Type **800** (40th anniv of May uprising)	20	10
2781	1k. Workers shaking hands, flags and industrial motifs (15th anniv of Czechoslovak–Soviet Treaty)	20	10
2782	1k. Girl giving flowers to soldier, Prague Castle and tank (40th anniv of liberation)	20	10
2783	1k. Soldiers and industrial motifs (30th anniv of Warsaw Pact)	20	10

1985. Czechoslovak Victory in Ice Hockey Championships. No. 2778 optd CSSR MISTREM SVETA.

2784	**798**	1k. multicoloured	5·25	5·00

802 Tennis

1985. National Spartakiad. Multicoloured.

2785	50h. Type **802**	15	10
2786	1k. Gymnasts performing with ribbons (48×19 mm)	20	10

803 Study for "Fire" and "Republic" (Josef Capek)

1985. Anti-fascist Artists. Multicoloured.

2787	50h. Type **803**	15	10
2788	2k. "Geneva Conference on Disarmament" and "Prophecy of Three Parrots" (Frantisek Bidlo)	45	25
2789	4k. "Unknown Conscript" and "The almost peaceful Dove" (Antonin Pelc)	70	40

804 Girl holding Dove and Olive Branch

1985. 10th Anniv of European Security and Co-operation Conference, Helsinki. Sheet 107×135 mm.

MS2790	**804** 7k. ×4 multicoloured	11·50	11·50

805 Moscow Buildings and Young People holding Doves

1985. 12th World Youth and Students' Festival, Moscow.

2791	**805**	1k. multicoloured	25	10

806 Figures on Globe

1985. 40th Anniv of World Federation of Trade Unions.

2792	**806**	50h. multicoloured	10	10

1985. Historic Bratislava (9th series). As T 669.

2793	3k. lt brown, green & brown	70	75
2794	4k. black, green and red	1·00	1·10

DESIGNS: 3k. Tapestry (Elena Holeczyova); 4k. Pottery.

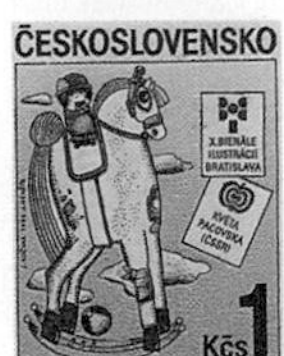

807 Rocking Horse (Kveta Pacovska)

1985. 10th Biennial Exhibition of Book Illustrations for Children, Bratislava. Mult.

2795	1k. Type **807**	20	10
2796	2k. Elves (Gennady Spirin)	35	20
2797	3k. Girl, butterfly and flowers (Kaarina Kaila)	65	30
2798	4k. Boy shaking hands with hedgehog (Erick Ingraham)	80	40
MS2799	95×128 mm. Nos. 2795/8	5·00	5·00

1985. Achievements of Socialist Construction (5th series). As T 754. Multicoloured.

2800	50h. Mechanical excavator	10	10
2801	1k. Train and map of Prague underground railway	30	15
2802	2k. Modern textile spinning equipment	35	25

808 Gateway to First Courtyard

1985. Prague Castle (21st series).

2803	**808**	2k. black, blue & red	50	30
2804	-	3k. multicoloured	1·10	40

DESIGN: 3k. East side of Castle.

809 Jug (4th century)

1985. Centenary of Prague Arts and Crafts Museum. Glassware. Multicoloured.

2805	50h. Type **809**	10	10
2806	1k. Venetian glass container (16th century)	20	10
2807	2k. Bohemian glass with hunting scene (18th century)	40	25
2808	4k. Bohemian vase (18th century)	65	40
2809	6k. Bohemian vase (c. 1900)	1·40	65

1985. Art (19th series). As T 481. Multicoloured.

2810	1k. "Young Woman in Blue Dress" (Josef Ginovsky)	1·60	1·00
2811	2k. "Lenin on Charles Bridge" (Martin Sladky)	1·60	1·00
2812	3k. "Avenue of Poplars" (Vaclav Rabas)	1·60	1·00
2813	4k. "Beheading of St. Dorothea" (Hans Baldung Grien)	1·60	1·00
2814	5k. "Jasper Schade van Westrum" (Frans Hals)	1·60	1·00

810 Bohdan Roule (engraver) and Engraving Plate

1985. Stamp Day.

2815	**810**	1k. multicoloured	25	10

811 Peace Dove and Olive Twig

1986. International Peace Year. Multicoloured.

2816	**811**	1k. multicoloured	25	10

812 Victory Statue Prague

1986. 90th Anniv of Czech Philharmonic Orchestra.

2817	**812**	1k. black, brown & vio	25	10

813 Zlin Z-50LS Airplane, Locomotive "Kladno" and Rock Drawing of Chariot

1986. "Expo '86" International Transport and Communications Exhibition, Vancouver.

2818	**813**	4k. multicoloured	70	40

1986. Arms of Czech Towns (6th series). As T 740. Multicoloured.

2819	50h. Vodnany	25	10
2820	50h. Zamberk	25	10
2821	50h. Myjava	25	10

814 Banner, Industry and Hammer and Sickle

1986. 17th Communist Party Congress, Prague. Multicoloured.

2822	50h. Type **814**	10	10
2823	1k. Buildings, hammer and sickle and star	25	10

815 Couple, Banner and Star

1986. 65th Anniv of Czechoslovakian Communist Party. Multicoloured.

2824	50h. Type **815**	10	10
2825	1k. Workers, banner and hammer and sickle	25	10

816 Map and Stylized Man

1986. National Front Election Programme.

2826	**816**	50h. multicoloured	10	10

817 Emblem and Crest on Film

1986. 25th Int Film Festival, Karlovy Vary.

2827	**817**	1k. multicoloured	25	10

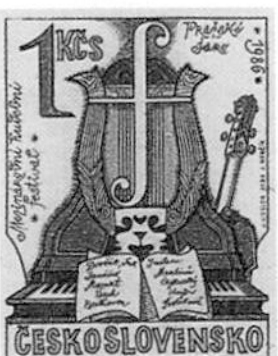

818 Musical Instruments

1986. 40th Anniv of Prague Spring Music Festival.

2828	**818**	1k. multicoloured	25	10

819 Ilyushin Il-86 and Airspeed A.S.6 Envoy II

1986. 50th Anniv of Prague–Moscow Air Service.

2829	**819**	50h. multicoloured	10	10

820 Sports Pictograms

1986. 90th Anniv of Czechoslovak Olympic Committee.

2830	**820**	2k. multicoloured	45	25

821 Map and Goalkeeper

1986. World Cup Football Championship, Mexico.

2831	**821**	4k. multicoloured	80	55

822 Globe, Net and Ball

1986. Women's World Volleyball Championship, Prague.

2832	**822**	1k. multicoloured	35	10

823 Emblem

1986. "Praga '88" Stamp Exhibition, Prague (1st issue) and 60th Anniv of International Philatelic Federation. Sheet 110×82 mm containing T 823 and two labels.

MS2833	**823** 20k. multicoloured	14·00	14·00

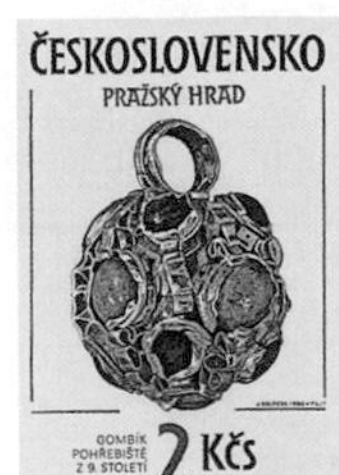

824 Funeral Pendant

1986. Prague Castle (22nd series).

2834	**824**	2k. multicoloured	55	50
2835	-	3k. orange, brown & bl	65	65

DESIGN: 3k. "Allegory of Blossoms" (sculpture, Jaroslav Horejc).

825 Wooden Cock, Slovakia

1986. 40th Anniv of UNICEF. Toys. Mult.

2836	10h. Type **825**	10	10
2837	20h. Wooden soldier on hobby horse, Bohemia	10	10
2838	1k. Rag doll, Slovakia	15	10
2839	2k. Doll	35	10
2840	3k. Mechanical bus	50	25

826 Registration Label and Mail Coach

1986. Centenary of Registration Label.

2841	**826**	4k. multicoloured	60	30

1986. Historic Bratislava (10th series). As T 669.

2842	3k. black, red and blue	60	55
2843	4k. black, red and green	75	70

DESIGNS: 3k. Sigismund Gate, Bratislava Castle; 4k. "St. Margaret with a Lamb" (relief from Castle).

827 Eagle Owl

1986. Owls. Multicoloured.

2844	50h. Type **827**	25	10
2845	2k. Long-eared owl	55	25
2846	3k. Tawny owl	55	40
2847	4k. Barn owl	70	50
2848	5k. Short-eared owl	1·50	60

828 Curtain of D 37 Theatre (Vladimir Sychra)

1986. 50th Anniv of Formation of International Brigades in Spain. Sheet 165×108 mm.

MS2849 **828** 5k. ×2 multicoloured		14·00	14·00

See also Nos. 2880/4, **MS**2833, 2900, **MS**2903, 2923/**MS**2927, 2929, **MS**2933, 2934/**MS**2938, 2940/**MS**2944, **MS**2945, **MS**2946, **MS**2947, **MS**2948 and **MS**2949.

829 Type "Kt8" Articulated Tram and 1920s' Prague Tram

1986. Rail Vehicles. Multicoloured.

2850	50h. Type **829**	20	10
2851	1k. Series E 458.1 electric shunting engine and 1882–1913 steam locomotive	30	10
2852	3k. Series T 466.2 diesel locomotive and 1900–24 steam locomotive	70	35
2853	5k. Series M 152.0 railcar and 1930–35 railbus	95	60

830 "The Circus Rider" (Jan Bauch)

1986. Circus and Variety Acts on Paintings. Multicoloured.

2854	1k. Type **830**	1·25	25
2855	2k. "The Ventriloquist" (Frantisek Tichy)	1·50	35
2856	3k. "In the Circus" (Vincent Hloznik)	1·45	55
2857	6k. "Clown" (Karel Svolinsky)	1·75	1·25

1986. Art (20th series). As T 481. Multicoloured.

2858	1k. "The Czech Lion, May 1918" (Vratislav H. Brunner)	1·50	65
2859	2k. "Boy with Mandolin" (Jozef Sturdik)	1·40	75
2860	3k. "The Metra Building" (Frantisek Gross)	80	80
2861	4k. "Maria Maximiliana of Sternberk" (Karel Skreta)	80	95
2862	5k. "Adam and Eve" (Lucas Cranach)	1·10	1·10

831 Brunner and Stamps of 1920

1986. Stamp Day. Birth Centenary of Vratislav Hugo Brunner (stamp designer).

2863	**831**	1k. multicoloured	25	10

832 Bicyclists

1987. World Cross-country Cycling Championships, Mlada Boleslav.

2864	**832**	6k. multicoloured	95	55

833 Pins and Ball

1987. 50th Anniv of Czechoslovakian Bowling Federation.

2865	**833**	2k. multicoloured	35	25

834 Gold Stars of Heroes of C.S.S.R. and of Socialist Labour

1987. State Orders and Medals.

2866	**834**	50h. red, black & gold	10	10
2867	-	2k. multicoloured	30	25
2868	-	3k. multicoloured	55	40
2869	-	4k. multicoloured	70	55
2870	-	5k. multicoloured	95	60

DESIGNS: 2k. Order of Klement Gottwald; 3k. Order of the Republic; 4k. Order of Victorious February; 5k. Order of Labour.

835 Poplar Admiral

1987. Butterflies and Moths. Multicoloured.

2871	1k. Type **835**	20	10
2872	2k. Eyed hawk moth	45	25
2873	3k. Large tiger moth	75	40
2874	4k. Viennese emperor moth	1·00	40

836 Emblem

1987. Nuclear Power Industry.

2875	**836**	5k. multicoloured	80	55

837 Emblem

1987. 11th Trades Union Congress, Prague.

2876	**837**	1k. multicoloured	10	10

1987. 20th Anniv of "Interkosmos" Space Programme. Sheet 165×104 mm.

MS2877 **838** 10k. ×2 multicoloured		5·00	5·00

839 Stained Glass Window, St. Vitus's Cathedral (Frantisek Sequens)

1987. Prague Castle (23rd series). Multicoloured.

2878	2k. Type **839**	45	40
2879	3k. Arms (mural), New Land Rolls Hall, Old Royal Palace	75	55

See also Nos. 2950/1 and 2977/8.

840 Telephone, 1894

1987. "Praga 88" Int Stamp Exhibition (2nd issue). Technical Monuments. Multicoloured.

2880	3k. Type **840**	45	35
2881	3k. Mail Van, 1924	45	35
2882	4k. Tank locomotive "Archduke Charles" 1907	90	35
2883	4k. Prague tram, 1900	90	35
2884	5k. Steam roller, 1936	90	55

See also Nos. 2900, 2923/6, 2929/32 2934/7 and 2940/3.

841 "When the Fighting Ended" (Pavel Simon)

1987. 45th Anniv of Destruction of Lidice and Lezaky. Multicoloured.

2885	1k. Type **841**	25	10
2886	1k. "The End of the Game" (Ludmila Jirincova)	25	10

842 Prague Town Hall Clock and Theory of Functions Diagram

1987. 125th Anniv of Union of Czech Mathematicians and Physicists. Multicoloured.

2887	50h. Type **842**	10	10
2888	50h. J. M. Petzval, C. Strouhal and V. Iarnik	10	10
2889	50h. Trajectory of Brownian motion and earth fold diagram	10	10

843 Chickens in Kitchen (Asun Balzola)

1987. 11th Biennial Exhibition of Book Illustrations for Children, Bratislava. Designs showing illustrations by artists named. Multicoloured.

2890	50h. Type **843**	35	15
2891	1k. Cranes with egg at railway points (Frederic Clement)	45	15
2892	2k. Birds on nest (Elzbieta Gaudasinska)	35	25
2893	4k. Couple looking over rooftops (Marija Lucija Stupica)	35	30
MS2894 97×130 mm. No. 2892 ×2 plus label		1·60	1·60

844 Barbed Wire, Flames and Menorah

1987. 40th Anniv of Terezin Memorial.

2895	**844**	50h. multicoloured	10	10

845 "OSS" and Communications Equipment

1987. 30th Anniv of Organization of Socialist Countries' Postal Administrations.

2896	**845**	4k. multicoloured	70	10

846 Purkyne and Microtome

1987. Birth Bicentenary of Jan Evangelista Purkyne (physiologist).

2897	**846**	7k. multicoloured	1·25	70

1987. Historic Bratislava (11th series). As T 669.

2898	3k. buff, black and blue	50	50
2899	4k. black and brown	1·00	1·00

DESIGNS: 3k. Detail of projecting window by Vyzdoby; 4k. "View of Bratislava" (engraving, Hans Mayer).

848 Postilion

1987. "Praga '88" International Stamp Exhibition (3rd issue).

2900	**848**	1k. multicoloured	25	10

849 Symbols of Industry, Lenin and Red Flag

1987. 70th Anniv of Russian Revolution (2901) and 65th Anniv of USSR (2902). Multicoloured.

2901	50h. Type **849**	15	10
2902	50h. Hammer and sickle	15	10

848 Postilion

1987. "Praga '88" International Stamp Exhibition (4th issue). Sheet 101×100 mm.

MS2903 **838** 10k. ×4 multicoloured		14·50	14·50

1987. Art (21st series). As T 481.

2904	1k. multicoloured	70	25
2905	2k. multicoloured	90	70
2906	3k. multicoloured	1·25	75
2907	4k. black, blue and red	90	90
2908	5k. multicoloured	1·25	1·00

DESIGNS: 1k. "Enclosure of Dreams" (Kamil Lhotak); 2k. "Tulips" (Ester Simerova-Martincekova); 3k. "Bohemian Landscape" (triptych, Josef Lada); 4k. "Accordion Player" (Josef Capek); 5k. "Self-portrait" (Jiri Trnka).

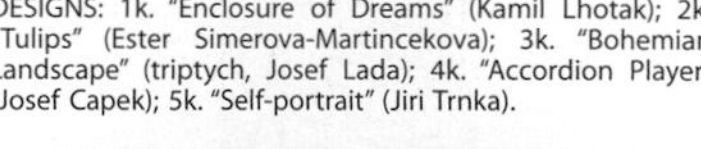

850 Obrovsky and Detail of 1919 Stamp

1987. Stamp Day. 105th Birth Anniv of Jakub Obrovsky (designer).

2909	**850**	1k. multicoloured	10	10

851 "Czechoslovakia", Linden Tree and Arms

1988. 70th Anniv of Czechoslovakia.

2910	**851**	1k. multicoloured	10	10

1988. 75th Birthday of President Husak.

2911	**759**	1k. brown and red	10	10

852 Ski Jumping and Ice Hockey

1988. Olympic Games, Calgary and Seoul. Mult.

2912	50h. Type **852**	10	10
2913	1k. Basketball and football	15	10
2914	6k. Throwing the discus and weightlifting	90	40

853 Red Flags and Klement Gottwald Monument, Pecky

1988. 40th Annivs of "Victorious February" (2915) and National Front (2916). Multicoloured.

2915	50h. Type **853**	10	10
2916	50h. Couple and detail of "Czech Constitution, 1961" (Vincent Hloznik)	10	10
MS2917	87×99 mm. 50h. ×2 multicoloured (Type **853**); 60h. ×2 sepia (Type **246**)	2·50	2·50

854 Laurin and Klement Car, 1914

1988. Historic Motor Cars. Multicoloured.

2918	50h. Type **854**	10	10
2919	1k. Tatra "NW" type B, 1902	15	10
2920	2k. Tatra "NW" type E, 1905	40	20
2921	3k. Tatra "12 Normandie", 1929	55	25
2922	4k. "Meteor", 1899	75	40

855 Praga Post Office and Velka Javorina T.V. Transmitter

1988. "Praga '88" International Stamp Exhibition (5th issue) and 70th Anniv of Postal Museum. Multicoloured.

2923	50h. Type **855**	10	10
2924	1k. Mlada Boleslav telecommunications centre and Carmelite Street post office, Prague	30	10
2925	2k. Prague 1 and Bratislava 56 post offices	45	25
2926	4k. Malta Square, Prague, and Prachatice post offices	90	40
MS2927	108×80 mm. Nos. 2924/5 each ×2	3·50	3·50

856 Woman with Linden Leaves as Hair and Open Book

1988. 125th Anniv of Slovak Cultural Society.

2928	**856**	50h. multicoloured	10	10

857 Strahov Monastery

1988. "Praga '88" International Stamp Exhibition (6th issue). National Literature Memorial, Strahov Monastery. Multicoloured.

2929	1k. Type **857**	15	10
2930	2k. Open book and celestial globe	35	20
2931	5k. Illuminated initial "B", scrolls and decorative binding	80	50
2932	7k. Astrological signs, Strahov, illuminated book and globe	1·50	1·10
MS2933	125×79 mm. Nos. 2929/32	4·00	4·00

858 Waldstein Garden Fountain

1988. "Praga '88" International Stamp Exhibition (7th issue). Prague Fountains.

2934	**858**	1k. black, lilac & blue	15	10
2935	-	2k. multicoloured	35	20
2936	-	3k. black, orange & lilac	55	35
2937	-	4k. black, orange & grn	65	45
MS2938		79×125 mm. Nos. 2934/7	3·50	3·50

DESIGNS: 2k. Old Town Square; 3k. Charles University; 4k. Courtyard, Prague Castle.

859 Washington Capitol and Moscow Kremlin

1988. Soviet–American Strategic Arms Limitation Talks, Moscow. Sheet 110×106 mm.

MS2939 **859**	4k. multicoloured	2·40	2·40

1988. "Praga '88" (8th issue). Thematic Philately Day. As No. MS2903 but inscr "DEN NAMETOVE FILATELIE" at top.

MS2940 **838**	10k. ×4 multicoloured	10·00	10·00

860 Trade Unions Central Recreation Centre

1988. "Praga '88" International Stamp Exhibition (9th issue). Present-day Prague. Multicoloured.

2941	50h. Type **860**	10	10
2942	1k. Koospol foreign trade company	20	10
2943	2k. Motol teaching hospital	40	10
2944	4k. Palace of Culture	75	25
MS2945	Two sheets, each 148×96 mm. (a) Nos. 2941 ×2 and 2944 ×2; (b) Nos. 2942/3 each ×2	1·60	1·60

861 Alfons Mucha (designer of first stamps)

1988. "Praga '88" International Stamp Exhibition (10th issue). 70th Anniv of First Czechoslovak Stamps. Sheet 82×96 mm.

MS2946 **861**	5k. ×2 multicoloured	2·40	2·40

862 "Turin, Monte Superag" (detail, Josef Navratill)

1988. "Praga '88" International Stamp Exhibition (11th issue). Postal Museum. Sheet 108×165 mm.

MS2947 **862**	5k. ×2 multicoloured	3·25	3·25

863 Ariadne

1988. "Praga '88" (12th issue). Prague National Gallery. Sheet 108×165 mm containing T 863 and similar vert design showing details of "Bacchus and Ariadne" by Sebastian Ricci.

MS2948	10k. Type **863**; 10k. Bacchus	5·00	5·00

864 King George

1988. "Praga '88" International Stamp Exhibition (13th issue). King George of Podebrady's Religious Peace Plans. Sheet 106×133 mm.

MS2949 **864**	1k.60 ×4 black and yellow	5·00	5·00

1988. Prague Castle (24th series). As T 839. Multicoloured.

2950	2k. 17th-century pottery jug	30	35
2951	3k. "St. Catherine" (Paolo Veronese)	45	55

1988. Historic Bratislava (12th series). As T 669. Multicoloured.

2952	3k. Hlavne Square (detail of print by R. Alt-Sandman)	45	40
2953	4k. Ferdinand House	50	55

1988. Art (22nd series). As T 481.

2954	2k. multicoloured	40	40
2955	6k. brown, black and blue	1·25	1·10
2956	7k. multicoloured	1·75	1·50

DESIGNS: 2k. "Field Workers carrying Sacks" (Martin Benka); 6k. "Woman watching Bird" (Vojtech Preissig); 7k. "Leopard attacking Horseman" (Eugene Delacroix).

865 Benda and Drawings

1988. Stamp Day. 106th Birth Anniv of Jaroslav Benda (stamp designer).

2957	**865**	1k. multicoloured	10	10

866 Emblem

1989. 20th Anniv of Czechoslovak Federal Socialist Republic.

2958	**866**	50h. multicoloured	10	10

867 Globe and Truck

1989. Paris–Dakar Rally. Multicoloured.

2959	50h. Type **867**	10	10
2960	1k. Globe and view of desert on truck side	15	10
2961	2k. Globe and truck (different)	30	15
2962	4k. Route map, turban and truck	50	25

868 Taras G. Shevchenko

1989. Birth Anniversaries.

2963	**868**	50h. multicoloured	15	10
2964	-	50h. multicoloured	15	10
2965	-	50h. brown and green	15	10
2966	-	50h. brown and green	15	10
2967	-	50h. black, brn & dp brn	15	10
2968	-	50h. multicoloured	15	10

DESIGNS: No. 2963, Type **868** (Ukrainian poet and painter, 175th anniv); 2964, Modest Petrovich Musorgsky (composer, 150th anniv); 2965, Jan Botto (poet, 160th anniv); 2966, Jawaharlal Nehru (Indian statesman, cent); 2967, Jean Cocteau (writer and painter, centenary); 2968, Charlie Chaplin (actor, centenary).

869 "Republika" (freighter)

1989. Shipping.

2969	**869**	50h. grey, red and blue	15	10
2970	-	1k. multicoloured	20	10
2971	-	2k. multicoloured	25	10
2972	-	3k. grey, red and blue	35	20
2973	-	4k. multicoloured	40	25
2974	-	5k. multicoloured	45	35

DESIGNS: 1k. "Pionyr" (trawler); 2k. "Brno" (tanker); 3k. "Trinec" (container ship); 4k. "Orlik" (container ship); 5k. "Vltava" (tanker) and communications equipment.

870 Dove and Pioneers

1989. 40th Anniv of Young Pioneer Organization.

2975	**870**	50h. multicoloured	10	10

1989. Art (23rd series). Sheet 110×86 mm containing vert designs as T 481 showing details of "Festival of Rose Garlands" by Albrecht Durer.

MS2976	10k. ×2 multicoloured	3·50	3·50

1989. Prague Castle (25th series). As T 839.

2977	2k. brown, yellow and red	20	20
2978	3k. multicoloured	40	35

DESIGNS: 2k. King Kard of Bohemia (relief by Alexandra Colin from Archduke Ferdinand I's mausoleum); 3k. "Self-portrait" (V. V. Reiner).

871 Bastille, Crowd and Flag

1989. Bicentenary of French Revolution. Sheet 73×98 mm.

MS2979 **871**	5k. black, red and blue	80	80

872 White-tailed Sea Eagle

1989. Endangered Species.

2980	**872**	1k. multicoloured	15	25

873 Fire-bellied Toads

1989. Endangered Amphibians. Multicoloured.

2981	2k. Type **873**	30	25
2982	3k. Yellow-bellied toad	45	35
2983	4k. Alpine newts	85	55
2984	5k. Carpathian newts	1·10	60

874 Dancers

1989. 40th Anniv of Slovak Folk Art Collective.
2985 **874** 50h. multicoloured 10 10

875 Horsemen and Mountains

1989. 45th Anniv of Slovak Rising.
2986 **875** 1k. multicoloured 10 10

876 "Going Fishing" (Hannu Taina)

1989. 12th Biennial Exhibition of Book Illustrations for Children. Multicoloured.
2987 50h. Type **876** 10 10
2988 1k. "Donkey Rider" (Aleksandur Aleksov) 15 10
2989 2k. "Animal Dreams" (Jurgen Spohn Zapadny) 25 15
2990 4k. "Scarecrow" (Robert Brun) 40 25
MS2991 100×143 mm. No. 2990 ×2 1·25 1·25

877 "Nolanea verna"

1989. Poisonous Fungi.
2992 **877** 50h. brown, deep brown and green 10 10
2993 - 1k. multicoloured 20 10
2994 - 2k. green and brown 35 25
2995 - 3k. brown, yellow & red 45 35
2996 - 5k. multicoloured 65 55
DESIGNS: 1k. Death cap; 2k. Destroying angel; 3k. "Cortinarius orellanus"; 5k. "Galerina marginata".

1989. Historic Bratislava (13th series). As T 669.
2997 3k. multicoloured 35 40
2998 4k. black, red and green 55 50
DESIGNS: 3k. Devin Fortress and flower; 4k. Devin Fortress and pitcher.

878 Jan Opletal (Nazi victim)

1989. 50th Anniv of International Students Day.
2999 **878** 1k. multicoloured 10 10

1989. Art (24th series). As T 481. Multicoloured.
3000 2k. "Nirvana" (Anton Jasusch) 25 25
3001 4k. "Dusk in the Town" (Jakub Schikaneder) (horiz) 50 50
3002 5k. "Bakers" (Pravoslav Kotik) (horiz) 80 70

879 Bearded Falcon Stamp, Pens and Bouda

1989. Stamp Day. 5th Death Anniv of Cyril Bouda (stamp designer).
3003 **879** 1k. brown, yellow & red 10 10

880 Practising Alphabet

1990. International Literacy Year.
3004 **880** 1k. multicoloured 10 10

881 Tomas Masaryk (first President)

1990. Birth Anniversaries. Multicoloured.
3005 50h. Type **881** (140th anniv) 10 10
3006 50h. Karel Capek (writer, centenary) 10 10
3007 1k. Vladimir Ilyich Lenin (120th anniv) 15 10
3008 2k. Emile Zola (novelist, 150th anniv) 30 15
3009 3k. Jaroslav Heyrovsky (chemist, centenary) 35 20
3010 10k. Bohuslav Martinu (composer, centenary) 1·10 65

882 Pres. Vaclav Havel

1990
3011 **882** 50h. ultram, bl & red 10 10

883 Players

1990. Men's World Handball Championship.
3012 **883** 50h. multicoloured 10 10

884 Snapdragon

1990. Flowers. Multicoloured.
3013 50h. Type **884** 10 10
3014 1k. "Zinnia elegans" 15 10
3015 3k. Tiger flower 35 25
3016 5k. Madonna lily 55 40

1990. Arms of Czech Towns (7th series). As T 740. Multicoloured.
3017 50h. Bytca 10 10
3018 50h. Podebrady 10 10
3019 50h. Sobeslav 10 10
3020 50h. Prostejov 10 10

885 Pope John Paul II

1990. Papal Visit.
3021 **885** 1k. brown, yellow & red 10 10

886 Woman holding Flags

1990. 45th Anniv of Liberation.
3022 **886** 1k. multicoloured 10 10

887 Twopenny Blue

1990. 150th Anniv of Penny Black. Sheet 102×94 mm.
MS3023 **887** 7k. multicoloured 1·25 1·25

888 Footballers

1990. World Cup Football Championship, Italy.
3024 **888** 1k. multicoloured 10 10

889 Victory Signs

1990. Free General Election.
3025 **889** 1k. multicoloured 10 10

1990. Prague Castle (26th series). As T 824.
3026 2k. multicoloured 50 40
3027 3k. green, dp green & red 70 65
DESIGNS: 2k. Jewelled glove (from reliquary of St. George); 3k. Seal of King Premysl Otakar II of Bohemia.

890 Map of Europe and Branch

1990. 15th Anniv of European Security and Co-operation Conference, Helsinki.
3028 **890** 7k. multicoloured 80 55

891 Milada Horakova

1990. 40th Anniv of Execution of Milada Horakova.
3029 **891** 1k. multicoloured 10 10

892 Poodles

1990. "Inter Canis" Dog Show, Brno. Mult.
3030 50h. Type **892** 10 10
3031 1k. Afghan hound, Irish wolfhound and greyhound 15 10
3032 4k. Czech terrier, bloodhound and Hanoverian bearhound 40 30
3033 7k. Cavalier King Charles, cocker and American cocker spaniels 65 50

1990. Historic Bratislava (14th series). As T 669.
3034 3k. black and red 40 35
3035 4k. multicoloured 65 55
DESIGNS: 3k. Coin; 4k. "M. R. Stefanik" (J. Mudroch).

893 Horses jumping

1990. Centenary of Pardubice Steeplechase. Mult.
3036 50h. Type **893** 10 10
3037 4k. Horses galloping 45 35

894 Alpine Marmot

1990. Mammals. Multicoloured.
3038 50h. Type **894** 10 10
3039 1k. European wild cat 10 10
3040 4k. Eurasian beaver 45 30
3041 5k. Common long-eared bat 60 40

895 European Flag

1990. Helsinki Pact Civic Gathering, Prague.
3042 **895** 3k. blue, yellow & gold 35 30

896 Snow-covered Church

1990. Christmas.
3043 **896** 50h. multicoloured 10 10

1990. Art (25th series). As T 481. Multicoloured.
3044 2k. multicoloured 40 35
3045 3k. black, brown & blue 50 40
3046 4k. multicoloured 60 60
3047 5k. multicoloured 70 75
DESIGNS—HORIZ: 2k. "Krucemburk" (Jan Zrzavy). VERT: 3k. "St. Agnes" (detail of sculpture, Josef Vaclav Myslbek); 4k. "Slovene in his Homeland" (detail, Alfons Mucha); 5k. "St. John the Baptist" (detail of sculpture, Auguste Rodin).

897 Karel Svolinsky (stamp designer) and "Czechoslovakia"

1990. Stamp Day.
3048 **897** 1k. purple, lilac & blue 10 10

898 Judo Throw

1991. European Judo Championships, Prague.
3049 **898** 1k. multicoloured 10 10

899 Svojsik

1991. 80th Anniv of Czechoslovak Scout Movement and 115th Birth Anniv of A. B. Svojsik (founder).
3050 **899** 3k. multicoloured 35 10

900 Jan Hus preaching

1991. Anniversaries.

3051	**900**	50h. brown, stone & red	10	10
3052	-	1k. multicoloured	10	10
3053	-	5k. multicoloured	60	30

DESIGNS AND EVENTS: 50h. Type **900** (600th anniv of Bethlehem Chapel, Prague); 40×23 mm: 1k. Estates Theatre, Prague (re-opening) and Mozart (death bicent); 49×20 mm: 5k. Paddle-steamer "Bohemia" (150th anniv of boat excursions in Bohemia).

901 Alois Senefelder

1991. Birth Anniversaries.

3054	**901**	1k. green, brown & red	20	10
3055	-	1k. black, green & red	20	10
3056	-	1k. blue, mauve & red	20	10
3057	-	1k. violet, blue and red	20	10
3058	-	1k. brown, orange & red	20	10

DESIGNS: No. 3054, Type **901** (inventor of lithography, 220th anniv); 3055, Andrej Kmet (naturalist, 150th anniv); 3056, Jan Masaryk (politician, 105th anniv); 3057, Jaroslav Seifert (composer, 90th anniv); 3058, Antonin Dvorak (composer, 150th anniv).

902 "Magion II" Satellite and Earth

1991. Europa. Europe in Space.

3059	**902**	6k. blue, black & red	70	50

903 Exhibition Pavilion, 1891

1991. Cent of International Exhibition, Prague.

3060	**903**	1k. blue, grey & mauve	10	10

904 Bearded Penguins, Map and Flag

1991. 30th Anniv of Antarctic Treaty.

3061	**904**	8k. multicoloured	90	55

905 Blatna Castle

1991. Castles. Multicoloured.

3062		50h. Type **905**	10	1·00
3063		1k. Bouzov	10	10
3064		3k. Kezmarok	40	25

906 Jan Palach

1991. Jan Palach Scholarship.

3065	**906**	4k. black	35	30

907 Rip

1991. Beauty Spots.

3066	**907**	4k. red, blue & yellow	45	40
3067	-	4k. purple, green & blk	45	40

DESIGN: No. 3067, Krivan.

908 "The Frog King" (Binette Schroeder)

1991. 13th Biennial Exhibition of Book Illustrations for Children. Multicoloured.

3068		1k. Type **908**	10	10
3069		2k. "Pinocchio" (Stasys Eidrigevicius)	25	15

909 Hlinka

1991. 53rd Death Anniv of Father Andrej Hlinka (Slovak nationalist).

3070	**909**	10k. black	1·25	55

910 "Prague Jesus Child" (Maria-Victoria Church)

1991. Prague and Bratislava. Multicoloured.

3071		3k. Type **910**	45	40
3072		3k. St. Elisabeth's Church, Bratislava	45	40

911 "Gagea bohemica"

1991. Nature Protection. Flowers. Multicoloured.

3073		1k. Type **911**	10	10
3074		2k. "Aster alpinus"	20	20
3075		5k. "Fritillaria meleagris"	55	40
3076		11k. "Daphne eneorum"	1·25	75

1991. Art (26th series). As T 481. Multicoloured.

3077	2k. "Family at Home" (Max Ernst)	20	20
3078	3k. "Milenci" (Auguste Renoir)	30	30
3079	4k. "Christ" (El Greco)	75	40
3080	5k. "Coincidence" (Ladislav Guderna)	85	55
3081	7k. "Two Japanese Women" (Utamaro)	1·10	80

912 Boys in Costume

1991. Christmas.

3082	**912**	50h. multicoloured	10	10

913 Martin Benka (stamp designer) and Slovakian 1939 Stamp

1991. Stamp Day.

3083	**913**	2k. red, black & orange	35	10

914 Biathlon

1992. Winter Olympic Games, Albertville.

3084	**914**	1k. multicoloured	10	10

915 Comenius

1992. 400th Birth Anniv of Jan Komensky (Comenius) (educationist). Sheet 63×76 mm.

MS3085 **915**	10k. multicoloured	1·75	1·75

916 Player

1992. World Ice Hockey Championship, Prague and Bratislava.

3086	**916**	3k. multicoloured	35	35

917 Traffic Lights

1992. Road Safety Campaign.

3087	**917**	2k. multicoloured	45	20

918 Tower, Seville Cathedral

1992. "Expo '92" World's Fair, Seville.

3088	**918**	4k. multicoloured	25	25

919 Amerindian, "Santa Maria" and Columbus

1992. Europa. 500th Anniv of Discovery of America by Columbus.

3089	**919**	22k. multicoloured	2·50	1·90

920 J. Kubis and J. Gabcik

1992. Free Czechoslovak Forces in World War II. Multicoloured.

3090	1k. Type **920** (50th anniv of assassination of Reinhard Heydrich)	10	10
3091	2k. Supermarine Spitfires (air battles over England, 1939–45)	20	10
3092	3k. Barbed wire and soldier (Tobruk, 1941)	25	15
3093	6k. Soldiers (Dunkirk, 1944–45)	90	25

921 Tennis Player

1992. Olympic Games, Barcelona.

3094	**921**	2k. multicoloured	35	10

922 Nurse's Hats and Red Cross

1992. Red Cross.

3095	**922**	2k. multicoloured	25	10

923 Player

1992. European Junior Table Tennis Championships, Topolcany.

3096	**923**	1k. multicoloured	10	10

924 Crawling Cockchafer

1992. Beetles. Multicoloured.

3097	1k. Type **924**	10	10
3098	2k. "Ergates faber"	20	10
3099	3k. "Meloe violaceus"	25	10
3100	4k. "Dytiscus latissimus"	30	45

925 Troja Castle

1992

3101	**925**	6k. multicoloured	60	45
3102	-	7k. black and lilac	70	60
3103	-	8k. multicoloured	90	75

DESIGNS—VERT: 7k. "St. Martin" (sculpture, G. R. Donner), Bratislava Cathedral. HORIZ: 8k. Lednice Castle.

926 Double Head and Posthorns

1992. Post Bank.

3104	**926**	20k. multicoloured	1·75	70

927 Anton Bernolak and Georgius Fandly

1992. Bicentenary of Slovak Education Assn.

3105	**927**	5k. multicoloured	55	30

928 Cesky Krumlov

1992

3106	**928**	3k. brown and red	35	10

1992. Art (27th series). As T 481.

3107	6k. black and brown	50	50
3108	7k. multicoloured	65	70
3109	8k. multicoloured	1·00	90

DESIGNS—VERT: 6k. "The Old Raftsman" (Koloman Sokol); 8k. "Abandonned" (Toyen). HORIZ: 7k. "Still Life with Grapes" (Georges Braque).

929 Organ

1992. Christmas.

3110	**929**	2k. multicoloured	10	10

930 Jindra Schmidt (engraver)

1992. Stamp Day.

3111	**930**	2k. multicoloured	10	10

NEWSPAPER STAMPS

N4

1918. Imperf.

N24	**N4**	2h. green	10	10
N25	**N4**	5h. green	10	10
N26	**N4**	6h. red	10	10
N27	**N4**	10h. lilac	10	10
N28	**N4**	20h. blue	10	10
N29	**N4**	30h. brown	10	10
N30	**N4**	50h. orange	10	10
N31	**N4**	100h. brown	45	10

1925. Surch with new value and stars.

N249	5 on 2h. green	60	55
N250	5 on 6h. red	35	85

1926. Newspaper Express stamps optd NOVINY or surch also.

N251	**E4**	5h. on 2h. pur on yell	10	10
N253	**E4**	5h. green on yellow	45	25
N254	**E4**	10h. brown on yellow	10	10

1934. Optd O.T.

N332	**N4**	10h. lilac	10	10
N333	**N4**	20h. blue	10	10
N334	**N4**	30h. brown	15	10

N67 Dove

1937. Imperf.

N364	**N67**	2h. brown	10	10
N365	**N67**	5h. blue	10	10
N366	**N67**	7h. orange	10	10
N367	**N67**	9h. green	10	10
N368	**N67**	10h. lake	10	10
N369	**N67**	12h. blue	10	10
N370	**N67**	20h. green	10	10
N371	**N67**	50h. brown	10	10
N372	**N67**	1k. olive	10	10

N94 Messenger

1946. Imperf.

N467	**N94**	5h. blue	10	10
N468	**N94**	10h. red	10	10
N469	**N94**	15h. green	10	10
N470	**N94**	20h. green	10	10
N471	**N94**	25h. purple	10	10
N472	**N94**	30h. brown	10	10
N473	**N94**	40h. red	10	10
N474	**N94**	50h. brown	10	10
N475	**N94**	1k. grey	10	10
N476	**N94**	5k. blue	10	10

EXPRESS NEWSPAPER STAMPS

E4

1918. Imperf. On yellow or white paper.

E24	**E4**	2h. purple	10	10
E25	**E4**	5h. green	10	10
E26	**E4**	10h. brown	45	45

OFFICIAL STAMPS

O92

1945

O463	**O92**	50h. green	10	10
O464	**O92**	1k. blue	10	10
O465	**O92**	1k.20 purple	15	10
O466	**O92**	1k.50 red	10	10
O467	**O92**	2k.50 blue	15	10
O468	**O92**	5k. purple	20	30
O469	**O92**	8k. red	30	45

O103

1947

O490	**O103**	60h. red	10	10
O491	**O103**	80h. olive	10	10
O492	**O103**	1k. blue	10	10
O493	**O103**	1k.20 purple	10	10
O494	**O103**	2k.40 red	10	10
O495	**O103**	4k. blue	15	10
O496	**O103**	5k. purple	15	30
O497	**O103**	7k.40 violet	20	30

PERSONAL DELIVERY STAMPS

P66

1937. For Prepayment. "V" in each corner.

P363	**P66**	50h. blue	20	35

1937. For Payment on Delivery. "D" in each corner.

P364	50h. red	20	35

P95

1946

P469	**P95**	2k. blue	20	20

POSTAGE DUESTAMPS

D 4

1919. Imperf.

D24	**D4**	5h. olive	10	10
D25	**D4**	10h. olive	10	10
D26	**D4**	15h. olive	10	10
D27	**D4**	20h. olive	10	10
D28	**D4**	25h. olive	10	10
D29	**D4**	30h. olive	25	10
D30	**D4**	40h. olive	25	25
D31	**D4**	50h. olive	25	10
D32	**D4**	100h. brown	1·25	10
D33	**D4**	250h. orange	6·00	1·10
D34	**D4**	400h. red	8·25	1·10
D35	**D4**	500h. green	3·00	25
D36	**D4**	1000h. violet	3·00	35
D37	**D4**	2000h. blue	16·00	75

1922. Postage stamps surch DOPLATIT and new value. Imperf or perf.

D229	**2**	10 on 3h. mauve	10	10
D224a	**2**	20 on 3h. mauve	10	10
D230	**2**	30 on 3h. mauve	10	10
D257	**3**	30 on 15h. red	1·75	30
D231	**2**	40 on 3h. mauve	10	10
D258	**3**	40 on 15h. red	35	25
D225	**3**	50 on 75h. green	25	25
D262	**3**	60 on 50h. purple	3·00	1·50
D263	**3**	60 on 50h. blue	3·50	1·90
D232	**3**	60 on 75h. green	40	10
D226	**3**	60 on 80h. green	35	10
D227	**3**	100 on 80h. green	30	10
D233	**3**	100 on 120h. black	90	10
D264	**2**	100 on 400h. violet	55	10
D265	**3**	100 on 1000h. purple	1·10	30
D228	**2**	200 on 400h. violet	55	25

1924. Postage Due stamp surch.

D249	**D4**	10 on 5h. olive	10	10
D250	**D4**	20 on 5h. olive	10	10
D251	**D4**	30 on 15h. olive	10	10
D252	**D4**	40 on 15h. olive	10	10
D253	**D4**	50 on 250h. orange	60	10
D234	**D4**	50 on 400h. red	55	10
D254	**D4**	60 on 250h. orange	90	20
D235	**D4**	60 on 400h. red	2·10	60
D255	**D4**	100 on 250h. orange	1·25	25
D236	**D4**	100 on 400h. red	1·25	25
D256	**D4**	200 on 500h. green	3·00	1·75

1926. Postage stamps optd DOPLATIT or surch also.

D266	**13**	30 on 100h. green	10	10
D279	**11**	40 on 185h. orange	10	10
D267	**13**	40 on 200h. purple	10	10
D268	**13**	40 on 300h. red	1·10	25
D280	**11**	50 on 20h. red	10	10
D281	**11**	50 on 150h. red	25	10
D269	**13**	50 on 500h. green	55	10
D282	**11**	60 on 25h. brown	25	25
D283	**11**	60 on 185h. orange	25	10
D270	**13**	60 on 400h. brown	45	10
D278	**11**	100h. brown	55	20
D284	**11**	100 on 25h. brown	60	10
D271	**13**	100 on 600h. purple	1·75	35

D34

1928

D285	**D34**	5h. red	10	10
D286	**D34**	10h. red	10	10
D287	**D34**	20h. red	10	10
D288	**D34**	30h. red	10	10
D289	**D34**	40h. red	10	10
D290	**D34**	50h. red	10	10
D291	**D34**	60h. red	10	10
D292	**D34**	1k. blue	10	10
D293	**D34**	2k. blue	35	10
D294	**D34**	5k. blue	60	10
D295	**D34**	10k. blue	1·25	10
D296	**D34**	20k. blue	2·40	10

D94

1946

D467	**D94**	10h. blue	10	10
D468	**D94**	20h. blue	10	10
D469	**D94**	50h. blue	15	10
D470	**D94**	1k. red	30	10
D471	**D94**	1k.20 red	35	10
D472	**D94**	1k.50 red	40	10
D473	**D94**	1k.60 red	45	10
D474	**D94**	2k. red	60	10
D475	**D94**	2k.40 red	65	10
D476	**D94**	3k. red	1·00	10
D477	**D94**	5k. red	1·60	10
D478	**D94**	6k. red	2·25	10

D257

D258

1954

D845	**D257**	5h. green	10	10
D846	**D257**	10h. green	10	10
D860	**D257**	30h. green	10	10
D861	**D257**	50h. green	15	10
D849	**D257**	60h. green	15	10
D850	**D257**	95h. green	35	10
D863	**D258**	1k. violet	25	10
D864	**D258**	1k.20 violet	30	10
D865	**D258**	1k.50 violet	45	10
D854	**D258**	1k.60 violet	40	10
D855	**D258**	2k. violet	75	10
D866	**D258**	3k. violet	1·50	30
D867	**D258**	5k. violet	2·00	45

D572 Stylized Plant

1971

D1985	-	10h. pink and blue	10	10
D1986	-	20h. blue & purple	10	10
D1987	-	30h. pink & green	10	10
D1988	-	60h. green & pur	15	10
D1989	-	80h. blue & orange	20	10
D1990	-	1k. green & red	25	10
D1991	-	1k.20 orange & grn	30	10
D1992	-	2k. red and blue	55	20
D1993	-	3k. yellow & black	95	20
D1994	-	4k. blue & brown	1·10	30
D1995	**D572**	5k.40 lilac and red	1·60	35
D1996	-	6k. yellow and red	2·00	45

DESIGNS: Various stylized plants as Type D **572**.

Pt. 6, Pt. 12

DAHOMEY

A French colony on the W. Coast of Africa, incorporated in French West Africa in 1944. In 1958 it became an autonomous republic within the French Community, and in 1960 was proclaimed fully independent. The area used the issues of French West Africa from 1944 until 1960.

100 centimes = 1 franc.

1899. "Tablet" key-type inscr "DAHOMEY ET DEPENDANCES".

1	**D**	1c. black and red on blue	90	1·10
2	**D**	2c. brown & blue on buff	1·00	90
3	**D**	4c. brown & blue on grey	1·80	1·70
4	**D**	5c. green and red	2·75	1·80
5	**D**	10c. red and blue	4·50	2·30
6	**D**	15c. grey and red	6·00	1·50
7	**D**	20c. red & blue on green	16·00	16·00
8	**D**	25c. black & red on pink	9·25	5·50
9	**D**	25c. blue and red	14·00	13·00
10	**D**	30c. brown & bl on drab	14·50	18·00
11	**D**	40c. red & blue on yellow	14·00	12·00
12	**D**	50c. brown & red on blue	23·00	50·00
13	**D**	50c. brown & blue on blue	43·00	16·00
14	**D**	75c. brown & red on orge	75·00	80·00
15	**D**	1f. green and red	32·00	55·00
16	**D**	2f. violet and red on pink	90·00	£110
17	**D**	5f. mauve & blue on blue	£100	£120

1906. "Faidherbe", "Palms" and "Balay" key-types inscr "DAHOMEY".

18	**I**	1c. grey and red	1·70	1·20
19	**I**	2c. brown and red	1·50	75
20	**I**	4c. brown & red on blue	2·30	1·80
21	**I**	5c. green and red	7·25	90
22	**I**	10c. pink and blue	28·00	2·30
23	**J**	20c. black & red on blue	12·00	12·00
24	**J**	25c. blue and red	9·25	7·25
25	**J**	30c. brown & red on pink	11·00	28·00
26	**J**	35c. black & red on yellow	65·00	10·00
27	**J**	45c. brown & red on green	14·00	29·00
28	**J**	50c. violet and red	11·00	17·00
29	**J**	75c. green & red on orange	20·00	29·00
30	**K**	1f. black and red on blue	24·00	50·00
31	**K**	2f. blue and red on pink	£110	£120
32	**K**	5f. red & blue on yellow	£100	£120

1912. Surch in figures.

33A	05 on 2c. brown & blue on buff	1·60	1·30
34A	05 on 4c. brown & blue on grey	1·50	1·20
35A	05 on 15c. grey and red	1·60	1·50
36A	05 on 20c. red & blue on green	1·40	1·80
37A	05 on 25c. blue and red	1·60	2·10
38A	05 on 30c. brown & bl on drab	1·40	1·60
39A	10c. on 40c. red & bl on yellow	1·40	1·30
40A	10c. on 50c. brn & bl on blue	2·20	3·00
40Aa	10c. on 50c. brn & red on blue	£900	£950
41A	10c. on 75c. brown and red on orange	6·00	14·00

6 Native Climbing Palm

1913

42	**6**	1c. black and violet	10	35
43	**6**	2c. pink and brown	10	40
44	**6**	4c. brown and black	45	70
45	**6**	5c. green and light green	2·50	70
60	**6**	5c. violet and purple	45	50
46	**6**	10c. pink and red	2·40	60
61	**6**	10c. green and lt green	1·20	95
75	**6**	10c. green and red	30	30
47	**6**	15c. purple and brown	60	35
48	**6**	20c. brown and grey	1·00	1·70
76	**6**	20c. green	40	2·50
77	**6**	20c. black and mauve	45	40
49	**6**	25c. blue & ultramarine	3·00	1·60
62	**6**	25c. orange and purple	85	25
50	**6**	30c. violet and brown	5·00	7·00
63	**6**	30c. carmine and red	2·00	7·75
78	**6**	30c. violet and yellow	75	70
79	**6**	30c. green and olive	35	70
51	**6**	35c. black and brown	1·30	2·50
80	**6**	35c. green and turquoise	1·30	6·50
52	**6**	40c. orange and black	1·00	70
53	**6**	45c. blue and grey	85	3·50
54	**6**	50c. brown & chocolate	5·00	8·25
64	**6**	50c. blue & ultramarine	1·30	2·75
81	**6**	50c. blue and red	45	40
82	**6**	55c. brown and green	85	4·00
83	**6**	60c. violet on pink	2·00	6·75
84	**6**	65c. green and brown	45	1·40
55	**6**	75c. violet and blue	1·20	1·20
85	**6**	80c. blue and brown	1·10	5·50
86	**6**	85c. pink and blue	1·40	6·00
87	**6**	90c. red and carmine	1·30	2·75
87a	**6**	90c. red and brown	1·70	7·50
56	**6**	1f. black and green	1·20	1·90
88	**6**	1f. light blue and blue	1·40	1·50
89	**6**	1f. red and brown	90	55
90	**6**	1f. red and light red	3·25	4·25
91	**6**	1f.10 brown and violet	4·25	10·00
92	**6**	1f.25 brown and blue	14·00	17·00
93	**6**	1f.50 light blue and blue	2·75	2·50
94	**6**	1f.75 orange and brown	5·00	3·50
94a	**6**	1f.75 ultramarine & blue	1·50	2·30
57	**6**	2f. brown and yellow	1·20	1·00
95	**6**	3f. mauve on pink	3·75	3·50
58	**6**	5f. blue and violet	3·00	4·00

1915. Surch 5c and red cross.

59	10c.+5c. pink and red	1·50	2·40

1922. Surch in figures and bars.

65	25c. on 2f. brown & yellow	1·40	6·50
66	60 on 75c. violet on pink	90	3·00
67	65 on 15c. purple & brown	2·30	8·75
68	85 on 15c. purple & brown	2·30	8·25
69	90c. on 75c. red and carmine	2·50	5·25
70	1f.25 on 1f. lt blue & blue	90	4·00
71	1f.50 on 1f. lt blue & blue	2·00	1·80
72	3f. on 5f. red and green	8·25	9·50
73	10f. on 5f. brown & blue	4·50	6·00
74	20f. on 5f. green and red	3·75	6·00

1931. "Colonial Exhibition" key-types inscr "DAHOMEY".

96	**E**	40c. green	6·00	12·00
97	**F**	50c. mauve	6·00	12·00
98	**G**	90c. red	6·00	12·00
99	**H**	1f.50 blue	6·00	12·00

1937. Paris Int Exn. As T **58a** of Guadeloupe.

100	20c. violet	1·70	5·25
101	30c. green	1·70	6·00
102	40c. red	1·40	6·00
103	50c. brown	1·40	2·75
104	90c. red	1·40	3·50
105	1f.50 blue	1·40	2·30
MS105a	120×100 mm. 3f. blue and agate (as T **16**). Imperf	12·00	32·00

1938. Int Anti-cancer Fund. As T **58b** of Guadeloupe.

106	1f.75+50c. blue	9·75	34·00

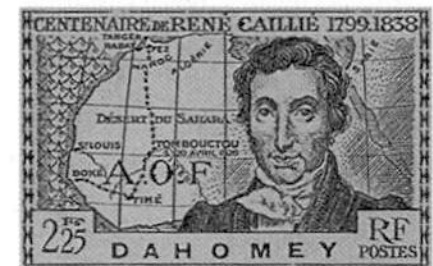

11 Rene Caillie

1939. Death Centenary of R. Caillie (explorer).

107	**11**	90c. orange	65	2·10
108	**11**	2f. violet	1·20	5·25
109	**11**	2f.25 blue	1·40	5·50

1939. New York World's Fair. As T **58c** of Guadeloupe.

110	1f.25 red	2·30	3·75
111	2f.25 blue	2·30	5·25

1939. 150th Anniv of French Revolution. As T **58d** of Guadeloupe.

112	45c.+25c. green	8·25	28·00
113	70c.+30c. brown	8·25	28·00
114	90c.+35c. orange	8·25	28·00
115	1f.25+1f. red	8·25	28·00
116	2f.25+2f. blue	8·25	28·00

12 African Landscape

1940. Air.

117	**12**	1f.90 blue	1·40	5·75
118	**12**	2f.90 red	90	6·50
119	**12**	4f.50 green	1·20	6·25
120	**12**	4f.90 olive	1·00	6·00
121	**12**	6f.90 orange	1·30	6·25

13 Native Poling Canoe

1941

122	**13**	2c. red	40	2·50
123	**13**	3c. blue	40	3·75
124	**13**	5c. violet	95	7·50
125	**13**	10c. green	50	6·25
126	**13**	15c. black	35	4·00
127	-	20c. brown	85	3·75
128	-	30c. violet	85	4·25
129	-	40c. red	70	5·25
130	-	50c. green	1·20	4·50
131	-	60c. black	90	3·75
132	-	70c. mauve	2·10	6·00
133	-	80c. black	2·30	5·50
134	-	1f. violet	70	70
135	-	1f.30 violet	2·30	7·25
136	-	1f.40 green	2·40	5·00
137	-	1f.50 red	1·70	3·75
138	-	2f. orange	1·70	6·75
139	-	2f.50 blue	2·75	4·25
140	-	3f. red	1·60	2·75
141	-	5f. green	1·40	3·00
142	-	10f. brown	1·30	5·25
143	-	20f. black	1·80	9·50

DESIGNS—HORIZ: 20c. to 70c. Village on piles. VERT: 80c. to 2f. Sailing pirogue on Lake Nokoue; 2f.50 to 20f. Dahomey warrior.

1941. National Defence Fund. Surch SECOURS NATIONAL and value.

143a	**6**	+1f. on 50c. blue & red	5·25	12·00
143b	**6**	+2f. on 80c. blue & brn	9·00	14·50
143c	**6**	+2f. on 1f.50 lt blue & bl	11·50	21·00
143d	**6**	+3f. on 2f. brown & yell	12·00	20·00

14b Village on Piles and Marshal Petain

1942. Marshal Petain Issue.

143e	**14b**	1f. green	65	3·75
143f	**14b**	2f.50 blue	1·10	6·50

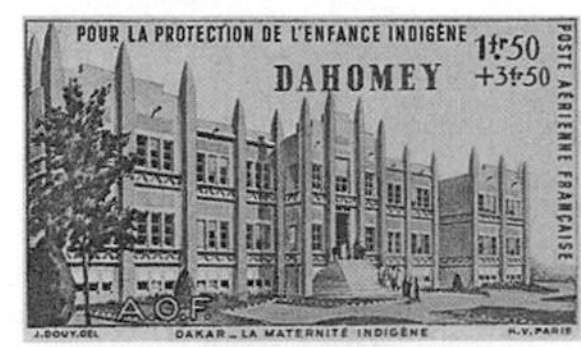

14c Maternity Hospital, Dakar

1942. Air. Colonial Child Welfare Fund.

143g	**14c**	1f.50+3f.50 green	1·20	6·25
143h	-	2f.+6f. brown	1·20	6·25
143i	-	3f.+9f. red	1·20	6·25

DESIGNS: 2f. Dispensary, Mopti. (48½×27 mm): 3f. "Child welfare".

14d "Vocation"

1942. Air. "Imperial Fortnight".

143j	**14d**	1f.20+1f.80 blue & red	1·40	6·00

14e Camel Caravan

1942. Air.

143k	**14e**	50f. blue and green	5·00	11·00

15 Ganvie Village

1960

144	**15**	25f. brn, red & bl (postage)	75	35
145	-	100f. brown, ochre & bl (air)	3·25	3·00
146	-	500f. red, bistre & green	9·25	7·50

DESIGNS: 100f. Somba fort; 500f. Royal Court, Abomey.

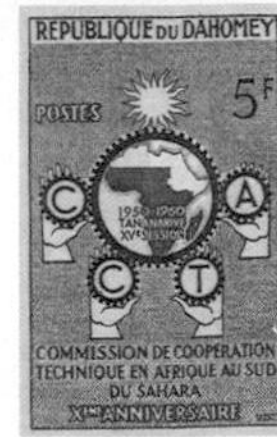

15a CCTA Emblem

1960. 10th Anniv of African Technical Co-operation Commission.

147	**15a**	5f. blue and purple	1·40	2·75

16 Conseil de l'Entente Emblem

1960. 1st Anniv of Conseil de l'Entente.

148	**16**	25f. multicoloured	1·60	3·75

17 Prime Minister Maga

1960. Independence Proclamation.

149	**17**	85f. purple and sepia	1·60	85

18 Weaver

1961. Artisans.

150	**18**	1f. purple and orange	10	10
151	-	2f. chocolate and brown	10	10
152	-	3f. orange and green	30	10
153	-	4f. lake and bistre	30	10
154	**18**	6f. red and lilac	45	10
155	-	10f. myrtle and blue	55	45
156	-	15f. violet and purple	85	45
157	-	20f. turquoise and blue	1·00	55

DESIGNS—VERT: 2f., 10f. Wood-carver. HORIZ: 3f., 15f. Fisherman casting net; 4f., 20f. Potter.

1961. 1st Anniv of Independence. No. 149 surch 100 F President de la Republique.

158	**17**	100f. on 85f. pur & sepia	3·25	3·25

20 Doves and U.N. Emblem

1961. 1st Anniv of Admission into U.N.O.

159	**20**	5f. multicoloured (postage)	40	25
160	**20**	60f. multicoloured	1·30	90
161	**20**	200f. multicoloured (air)	3·50	2·50
MS161a 120×85 mm. Nos. 159/61			7·00	7·00

1961. Abidjan Games. Optd JEUX SPORTIFS D'ABIDJAN 24 AU 31 DECEMBRE 1961.

162	**15**	25f. brown, red and blue	75	45

20a European, African and Boeing 707 Airliners

1962. Air. Foundation of "Air Afrique" Airline.

163	**20a**	25f. blue, brown & black	95	45

1962. Malaria Eradication. As T 55a of French Somali Coast.

164	25f.+5f. brown	80	75

22 Wrecked Car and Fort

1962. 1st Anniv of Portuguese Evacuation from Fort Ouidah.

165	**22**	30f. multicoloured	60	40
166	**22**	60f. multicoloured	1·00	50

1962. 1st Anniv of Union of African and Malagasy States. As T 38 of Gabon.

167	**72**	30f. multicoloured	1·30	75

23 Map, Nurses and Patients

1962. Red Cross.

168	**23**	5f. red, blue and purple	35	15
169	**23**	20f. red, blue and green	60	45
170	**23**	25f. red, blue and sepia	80	45
171	**23**	30f. red, blue and brown	95	75

24 Peuhl Herd-boy

1963. Dahomey Tribes.

172	**A**	2f. violet and blue	10	10
173	**B**	3f. black and blue	10	10
174	**24**	5f. green, brown & black	55	25
175	**C**	15f. brown, chest & turq	55	25
176	**D**	20f. black, red & green	45	15
177	**E**	25f. turquiose, brown & bl	55	25
178	**D**	30f. brown, mauve & red	70	45
179	**E**	40f. blue, brown, & green	1·20	40
180	**C**	50f. brown, black & green	1·70	55
181	**24**	60f. orange, red & purple	3·00	1·10
182	**B**	65f. brown and red	2·20	85
183	**A**	85f. brown and blue	3·25	1·20

DESIGNS—VERT: A, Ganvie girl in pirogue; B, Bariba chief of Nikki; C, Ouidah witch-doctor and python; D, Nessoukoue witch-doctors of Abomey. HORIZ: E, Dahomey girl.

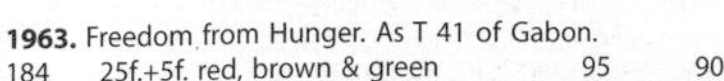

1963. Freedom from Hunger. As T 41 of Gabon.

184	25f.+5f. red, brown & green	95	90

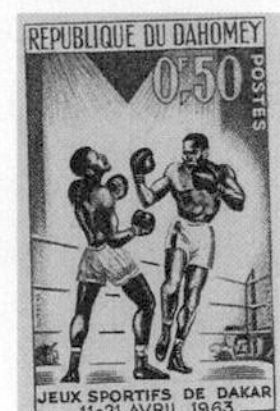

25 Boxing

1963. Dakar Games.

185	**25**	50c. black and green	10	10
186	-	1f. black, bistre & brown	10	10
187	-	2f. brown, blue & bronze	10	10
188	-	5f. black, red & brown	25	10
189	**25**	15f. purple and violet	50	35
190	-	20f. black, green & red	95	65

DESIGNS—HORIZ: 1f., 20f. Football. VERT: 2f., 5f. Running.

27 U.A.M. Palace

1963. Air. Meeting of Heads of State of African and Malagasy Union.

191	**27**	250f. multicoloured	5·00	2·75

28 Presidential Palace, Cotonou

1963. 3rd Anniv of Independence.

192	**28**	25f. multicoloured	55	25

1963. Air. African and Malagasy Posts and Telecommunications Union. As T 44 of Gabon.

193	25f. red, buff, brown & blue	75	50

29 Boeing 707 Airliner

1963. Air.

194	**29**	100f. bistre, green & violet	2·40	60
195	-	200f. violet, brown & grn	4·25	1·60
196	-	300f. purple, grn and blue	6·25	2·50
197	-	500f. purple, brown & blue	11·00	3·25

DESIGNS: 200f. Aerial views of Boeing 707; 300f. Cotonou Airport; 500f. Boeing 707 in flight.

30 Toussaint L'Ouverture

1963. 150th Death Anniv of Toussaint L'Ouverture (Haitian statesman).

198	**30**	25f. multicoloured	50	25
199	**30**	30f. multicoloured	75	30
200	**30**	100f. multicoloured	1·60	95

31 Flame on U.N. Emblem

1963. 15th Anniv of Declaration of Human Rights. Multicoloured. Background colours given.

201	**31**	4f. blue	10	10
202	**31**	6f. brown	30	25
203	**31**	25f. green	55	25

32 Sacred Boat of Isis, Philae

1964. Air. Nubian Monuments Preservation.

204	**32**	25f. brown and violet	2·00	1·10

33 Somba Dance (Taneka Coco)

1964. Native Dances.

205	**33**	2f. black, red and green	10	10
206	-	3f. red, green and blue	30	10
207	-	10f. black, red & violet	45	25
208	-	15f. sepia, lake & green	50	25
209	-	25f. blue, brown and orge	1·00	35
210	-	30f. red, orange & brown	1·20	45

DANCES—HORIZ: 3f. Nago (Pobe-Ketou). 15f. Nago (Ouidah). 30f. Nessou houessi (Abomey). VERT: 10f. Baton (Paysbariba). 25f. Sakpatassi (Abomey).

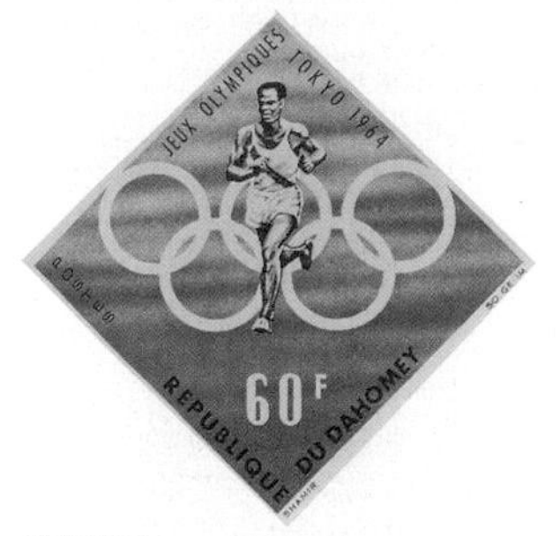

34 Running

1964. Olympic Games, Tokyo.

211	**34**	60f. green and brown	2·00	90
212	-	85f. purple and blue	3·00	1·20

DESIGN: 85f. Cycling.

1964. French, African and Malagasy Co-operation. As T 58 of Gabon.

213	25f. brown, violet & orange	95	30

35 Mother and Child

1964. 18th Anniv of UNICEF.

214	**35**	20f. black, green & red	45	25
215	-	25f. black, blue & red	60	45

DESIGN: 25f. Mother and child (different).

36 Satellite and Sun

1964. International Quiet Sun Year.

216	**36**	25f. green and yellow	65	25
217	-	100f. yellow and purple	2·40	1·00

DESIGN: 100f. Another satellite and Sun.

37 "Weather"

1965. Air. World Meteorological Day.

218	**37**	50f. multicoloured	95	60

38 Rug Pattern

1965. Abomey Rug-weaving. Multicoloured.

219	20f. Bull, tree, etc. (vert)	95	30
220	25f. Witch-doctor, etc. (vert)	1·00	45
221	50f. Type **38**	1·70	90
222	85f. Ship, tree, etc	3·00	1·20
MS222a 195×100 mm. Nos. 219/22		8·75	8·75

39 Baudot's Telegraph and Ader's Telephone

1965. Centenary of I.T.U.

223	**39**	100f. black, purple & orge	2·75	1·50

40 Sir Winston Churchill

1965. Air. Churchill Commemoration.

224	**40**	100f. multicoloured	2·75	1·50

41 Heads of Three Races within I.C.Y. Emblem

1965. Air. International Co-operation Year.

225	**41**	25f. lake, green & violet	60	25
226	**41**	85f. lake, green & blue	1·20	80

42 Lincoln

1965. Air. Death Centenary of Abraham Lincoln.
227 **42** 100f. multicoloured 2·00 1·20

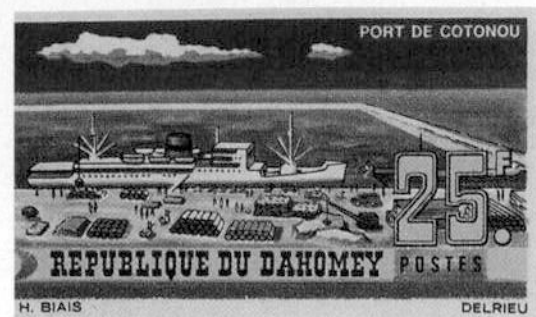

43 Cotonou Port

1965. Inaug of Cotonou Port. Multicoloured.
228 25f. Type **43** 95 35
229 100f. Cotonou Port 2·50 1·30

The two stamps joined together form a complete design and were issued se-tenant in the sheets.

44 Spanish Mackerel

1965. Fishes.
230 **44** 10f. black, turquoise & bl 55 25
231 - 25f. orange, grey & blue 95 60
232 - 30f. blue and turquoise 1·80 85
233 - 50f. grey, orange & blue 2·75 1·10

FISHES: 25f. Sama seabream. 30f. Sailfish. 50f. Tripletail.

45 Independence Monument

1965. 2nd Anniv of 28th October Revolution.
234 **45** 25f. red, grey and black 45 25
235 **45** 30f. red, blue and black 60 30

1965. No. 177 surch 1f.
236 1f. on 25f. turq, brn & bl 35 10

47 Arms and Pres. Kennedy

1965. Air. 2nd Death Anniv of Pres. Kennedy.
237 **47** 100f. brown and green 3·00 2·10

48 Dr. Schweitzer and Hospital Scene

1966. Air. Schweitzer Commemoration.
238 **48** 100f. multicoloured 3·00 1·50

49 Porto-Novo Cathedral

1966. Dahomey Cathedrals.
239 **49** 30f. purple, blue & green 55 30
240 - 50f. brown, blue & purple 85 50
241 - 70f. purple, blue & green 1·30 80

DESIGNS—VERT: 50f. Ouidah Church (old Pro-Cathedral). HORIZ: 70f. Cotonou Cathedral.

50 Beads, Bangles and Anklets

1966. World Festival of Negro Arts, Dakar.
242 **50** 15f. purple and black 45 25
243 - 30f. red, purple & blue 75 45
244 - 50f. blue and brown 1·30 60
245 - 70f. lake and black 2·50 90

DESIGNS: 30f. Building construction; 50f. Craftsman; 70f. Religious carvings.

1966. 5th Anniv of France–Dahomey Treaty. Nos. 228/9 surch ACCORD DE COOPERATION FRANCE - DAHOMEY 5e Anniversaire - 24 Avril 1996.
246 **43** 15f. on 25f. mult 75 45
247 - 15f. on 100f. mult 75 45

52 W.H.O. Building and Emblem

1966. Inaug of W.H.O. Headquarters, Geneva.
248 **52** 30f. multicoloured (post) 75 35
249 - 100f. multicoloured (air) 1·90 1·40

DESIGN (48×27 mm): 100f. W.H.O. building (different view) and emblem.

53 African Pygmy Goose

1966. Air. Birds. Multicoloured.
250 50f. Type **53** 2·30 80
251 100f. Fiery-breasted bush shrike 2·75 1·30
252 500f. Iris glossy starling 16·00 6·50

See also Nos. 271/2.

54 Industrial Emblems

1966. Air. "Europafrique".
253 **54** 100f. multicoloured 1·80 90

55 Pope Paul and St. Peter's

1966. Air. Pope Paul's Visit to U.N.
254 **55** 50f. red, brown & green 95 45
255 - 70f. red, green and blue 1·20 65
256 - 100f. purple and blue 2·00 1·30
MS257 180×100 mm. Nos. 254/6 5·75 5·75

DESIGNS—HORIZ: 70f. Pope Paul and New York. VERT: (36×48 mm); 100f. Pope Paul and U.N. General Assembly.

1966. Air. Inauguration of DC-8F Air Services. As T 84 of Gabon.
258 30f. grey, black and purple 80 45

56 Scout signalling with flags

1966. Scouting.
259 **56** 5f. red, ochre and brown 10 10
260 - 10f. mauve, green & black 35 25
261 - 30f. orange, red & violet 90 50
262 - 50f. brown, green & blue 1·50 60
MS263 171×100 mm. Nos. 259/62 3·25 3·25

DESIGNS—VERT: 10f. Tent-pole and banners; 30f. Scouts, camp-fire and map. HORIZ: 50f. Constructing bridge.

57 Scientific Emblem

1966. Air. 20th Anniv of UNESCO.
264 **57** 30f. plum, blue & purple 50 25
265 - 45f. lake and green 90 70
266 - 100f. blue, lake & black 2·10 1·10
MS267 170×100 mm. Nos. 264/6 4·75 4·75

DESIGNS—VERT: 45f. Cultural Emblem; HORIZ: 100f. Educational emblem.

58 "The Nativity" (15th-cent. Beaune Tapestry)

1966. Air. Christmas. Multicoloured.
268 50f. Type **58** 3·00 2·30
269 100f. "The Adoration of the Shepherds" (after Jose Ribera) 5·25 3·75
270 200f. "Madonna and Child" (after A. Baldovinetti) 10·50 5·50

See also Nos. 311/14, 348/51, 384/7 and 423/6.

59 African Broad-billed Roller

1967. Air. Birds. Multicoloured.
271 200f. Type **59** 9·50 2·75
272 250f. African Emerald cuckoo 9·50 4·25

60 "Clappertonia ficifolia"

1967. Flowers. Multicoloured.
273 1f. Type **60** 10 10
274 3f. "Hewittia sublobata" 35 10
275 5f. "Clitoria ternatea" 50 10
276 10f. "Nymphaea micrantha" 90 35
277 15f. "Commelina forskalaei" 1·20 50
278 30f. "Eremomastax speciosa" 2·10 85

1967. Nos. 182/3 surch.
279 30f. on 65f. brown & red 1·00 65
280 30f. on 85f. brown & blue 1·00 65

62 Bird bearing Lions Emblem

1967. 50th Anniv of Lions International.
281 **62** 100f. blue, green & violet 2·75 1·10

63 "Ingres" (self-portrait)

1967. Air. Death Centenary of Ingres (painter). Multicoloured.
282 100f. Type **63** 3·75 1·80
283 100f. "Oedipus and the Sphinx" (after Ingres) 3·75 1·80

See also Nos. 388/90, 429/30, 431/2 and 486/7.

64 "Suzanne" (barque)

1967. Air. French Sailing ships. Multicoloured.
284 30f. Type **64** 1·30 80
285 45f. "Esmeralda" (schooner) (vert) 1·50 95
286 80f. "Marie Alice" (schooner) (vert) 2·75 1·50
287 100f. "Antonin" (barque) 3·75 2·10

1967. Air. 50th Birth Anniv of Pres. Kennedy. Nos. 227 and 237 surch 29 MAI 1967 50e Anniversaire de la naissance de John F. Kennedy.
288 **42** 125f. on 100f. mult 2·75 1·40
289 **47** 125f. on 100f. brn & grn 2·75 1·40

66 "Man in the City" Pavilion

1967. World Fair, Montreal.
290 **66** 30f. brn & grn (postage) 80 25
291 - 70f. red and green 1·60 65
292 - 100f. blue & brown (air) 1·90 85
MS293 150×100 mm. Nos. 290/2 4·75 4·75

DESIGNS—HORIZ: 70f. "New Africa" pavilions. VERT: (27×48 mm): 100f. "Man Examines the Universe".

67 Dr. Konrad Adenauer (from painting by O. Kokoschka)

1967. Air. Dr. Adenauer Commemoration.
294 **67** 70f. multicoloured 2·00 1·10
MS295 140×160 mm. No. 294×4 8·75 8·75

68 "Economic Association"

1967. Europafrique.

296	**68**	30f. multicoloured	70	25
297	-	45f. multicoloured	1·20	45

69 Scouts Climbing

1967. World Scout Jamboree, Idaho.

298	**69**	30f. ind, brn & bl (postage)	90	30
299	-	70f. purple, green & blue	2·10	85
300	-	100f. pur, grn & bl (air)	1·90	1·20
MS301		150×100 mm. Nos. 298/300	5·25	5·25

DESIGNS—HORIZ: 70f. Scouts with canoe. VERT: (27×48 mm): 100f. Jamboree emblem, rope and map.

1967. Air. Riccione Stamp Exhibition. No. 270 surch RICCIONE 12-29 Aout 1967 and value.

302	150f. on 200f. mult	3·75	3·00

71 Rhone at Grenoble

1967. Winter Olympic Games, Grenoble.

303	**71**	30f. blue, brown & green	75	45
304	-	45f. blue, green & brown	1·00	60
305	-	100f. purple, green & blue	2·30	1·30
MS306		130×100 mm. Nos. 303/5	4·50	4·50

DESIGNS—VERT: 45f. View of Grenoble. HORIZ: 100f. Rhone Bridge, Grenoble, and Pierre de Coubertin.

1967. Air. 5th Anniv of U.A.M.P.T. As T 104 of Gabon.

307	100f. green, red & purple	1·80	1·00

72 Currency Tokens

1967. 5th Anniv of West African Monetary Union.

308	**72**	30f. black, red & green	80	50

73 Pres. de Gaulle

1967. Air. "Homage to General de Gaulle". President Soglo of Dahomey's visit to Paris.

309	**73**	100f. multicoloured	4·00	2·40
MS310		140×160 mm. No. 309 in block of four	18·00	18·00

74 "The Adoration" (Master of St. Sebastian)

1967. Air. Christmas. Religious paintings. Mult.

311	30f. "Virgin and Child" (M. Grunewald) (vert)	75	50
312	50f. Type **74**	1·50	70
313	100f. "The Adoration of the Magi" (Ulrich Apt the Elder) (vert)	2·50	1·30
314	200f. "The Annunciation" (M. Grunewald) (vert)	5·75	2·20

75 Venus de Milo and "Mariner 5"

1968. Air. "Exploration of the Planet Venus". Multicoloured.

315	70f. Type **75**	1·90	80
316	70f. Venus de Milo and "Venus 4"	1·90	80
MS317	105×95 mm. Nos. 315/16	4·00	4·00

76 African Buffalo

1968. Fauna (1st series). Multicoloured.

318	15f. Type **76**	55	30
319	30f. Lion	85	45
320	45f. Kob	1·60	60
321	70f. Crocodile	3·00	75
322	100f. Hippopotamus	5·25	2·00

See also Nos. 353/7.

77 W.H.O. Emblem

1968. 20th Anniv of W.H.O.

323	**77**	30f. brown, blue & ultram	60	35
324	**77**	70f. multicoloured	1·50	80

78 Gutenberg Memorial, Strasbourg

1968. Air. 500th Death Anniv of Johann Gutenberg.

325	**78**	45f. green and orange	1·00	50
326	-	100f. deep blue & blue	2·00	1·30
MS327		130×100 mm. Nos. 325/6	4·25	4·25

DESIGNS: 100f. Gutenberg statue, Mainz, and printing-press.

79 Dr. Martin Luther King

1968. Air. Martin Luther King Commemoration.

328		30f. black, brown & yellow	80	50
329		55f. multicoloured	1·30	80
330	**79**	100f. multicoloured	1·80	1·00
MS331		150×115 mm. Nos. 328/30	4·25	4·25

DESIGNS: 55f. Dr. King receiving Nobel Peace Prize. LARGER (25×46 mm): 30f. Inscription "We must meet hate with creative love" (also in French and German).

80 Schuman

1968. Air. 5th Anniv of Europafrique.

332	**80**	30f. multicoloured	55	35
333	-	45f. purple, olive & orge	95	50
334	-	70f. multicoloured	1·50	65

DESIGNS: 45f. De Gasperi; 70f. Dr. Adenauer.

81 "Battle of Montebello" (Philippoteaux)

1968. Air. Red Cross. Paintings. Multicoloured.

335	30f. Type **81**	1·10	60
336	45f. "2nd Zouaves at Magenta" (Riballier)	1·40	85
337	70f. "Battle of Magenta" (Charpentier)	3·25	1·40
338	100f. "Battle of Solferino" (Charpentier)	4·00	1·90

82 Mail Van

1968. Air. Rural Mail Service. Multicoloured.

339	30f. Type **82**	85	50
340	45f. Rural Post Office and mail van	1·10	55
341	55f. Collecting mail at river-side	1·70	80
342	70f. Loading mail on train	3·25	1·10

83 Aztec Stadium

1968. Air. Olympic Games, Mexico.

343	**83**	30f. green and purple	80	30
344	-	45f. lake and blue	1·50	40
345	-	70f. brown and green	2·30	80
346	-	150f. brown and red	3·00	1·50
MS347		239×104 mm. Nos. 343/6	8·00	8·00

DESIGNS—VERT: 45f. "Pelota-player" (Aztec figure); 70f. "Uxpanapan wrestler" (Aztec figure). HORIZ: 150f. Olympic Stadium.

1968. Air. Christmas. Paintings by Foujita. As T 74. Multicoloured.

348	30f. "The Nativity" (horiz)	95	60
349	70f. "The Visitation"	1·70	80
350	100f. "Virgin and Child"	2·00	1·30
351	200f. "Baptism of Christ"	4·00	2·75

1968. Air. "Philexafrique" Stamp Exhibition, Abidjan (Ivory Coast, 1969). As T 125 of Gabon. Multicoloured.

352	100f. "Diderot" (L. M. Vanloo)	4·00	4·00

84 Warthog

1969. Fauna (2nd series). Multicoloured.

353	5f. Type **84**	35	10
354	30f. Leopard	95	45
355	60f. Spotted hyena	1·80	70
356	75f. Olive baboon	3·25	90
357	90f. Hartebeest	4·75	1·30

1969. Air. "Philexafrique" Stamp Exn, Abidjan, Ivory Coast (2nd issue). As T 127 of Gabon.

358	50f. violet, sepia and blue	2·30	2·30

DESIGN: 50f. Cotonou harbour and stamp of 1941.

85 Heads and Globe

1969. 50th Anniv of I.L.O.

359	**85**	30f. multicoloured	55	35
360	**85**	70f. multicoloured	1·60	80

86 "The Virgin of the Scales" (C. da Sesto-Da Vinci School)

1969. Air. Leonardo da Vinci Commem. Mult.

361	100f. Type **86**	2·00	1·00
362	100f. "The Virgin of the Rocks" (Da Vinci)	2·00	1·00

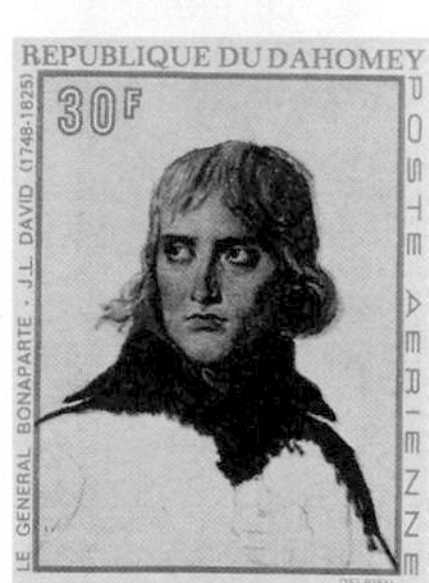

87 "General Bonaparte" (J. L. David)

1969. Air. Birth Bicentenary of Napoleon Bonaparte. Multicoloured.

363	30f. Type **87**	1·70	1·50
364	60f. "Napoleon I in 1809" (Lefevre)	3·00	1·80
365	75f. "Napoleon at the Battle of Eylau" (Gros) (horiz)	3·50	2·50
366	200f. "General Bonaparte at Arcola" (Gros)	8·25	4·75

88 Arms of Dahomey

1969

367	**88**	5f. multicoloured (postage)	45	35
368	**88**	30f. multicoloured	1·80	60
369	**88**	50f. multicoloured (air)	80	45

89 "Apollo 8" over Moon

1969. Air. Moon flight of "Apollo 8". Embossed on gold foil.

370	89	1,000f. gold	22·00	22·00

1969. Air. 1st Man on the Moon (1st issue). Nos. 315/6 surch ALUNISSAGE APOLLO XI JUILLET 1969, lunar module and value.

371	75	125f. on 70f. (No. 315)	2·75	1·90
372	-	125f. on 70f. (No. 316)	2·75	1·90

91 Bank Emblem and Cornucopia

1969. 5th Anniv of African Development Bank.

373	91	30f. multicoloured	80	50

92 Kenaf Plant and Mill, Bohicon

1969. "Europafrique". Multicoloured.

374	30f. Type **92** (postage)	1·10	45
375	45f. Cotton plant & mill, Parakou	1·30	75
376	100f. Coconut and palm-oil plant, Cotonou (air)	2·40	1·30
MS377	108×148 mm. Nos. 374/6	5·75	5·75

93 Dahomey Rotary Emblem

1969. Air. Rotary International Organization.

378	93	50f. multicoloured	95	40

1969. Air. No. 250 surch.

379	53	10f. on 50f. multicoloured	2·75	25

95 Sakpata Dance

1969. Dahomey Dances. Multicoloured.

380	10f. Type **95** (postage)	70	45
381	30f. Guelede dance	1·40	70
382	45f. Sato dance	2·00	85
383	70f. Teke dance (air)	2·75	1·00

1969. Air. Christmas. Paintings. As T 58. Mult.

384	30f. "The Annunciation" (Van der Stockt)	55	45
385	45f. "The Nativity" (15th-cent. Swabian School)	95	60
386	110f. "Virgin and Child" (Masters of the Gold Brocade)	2·50	1·40
387	200f. "The Adoration of the Magi" (Antwerp School, c. 1530)	4·25	2·20

1969. Air. Old Masters. As T **63**. Multicoloured.

388	100f. "The Painter's Studio" (G. Courbet)	2·30	1·30
389	100f. "Self-portrait with Gold Chain" (Rembrandt)	2·30	1·30
390	150f. "Hendrickje Stoffels" (Rembrandt)	3·75	1·80

96 F. D. Roosevelt

1970. Air. 25th Death Anniv of Franklin D. Roosevelt.

391	96	100f. black, green & bl	1·90	80

97 Rocket and Men on Moon

1970. Air. 1st Man on the Moon (2nd issue). Multicoloured.

392	30f. Type **97**	80	25
MS393	121×160 mm. 30f. Type **97**; 50f. Astronauts astride rocket; 70f. Preparing to land on Moon; 110f. Raising the Stars and Stripes	9·00	9·00

98 "U.N. in War and Peace"

1970. 25th Anniv of U.N.

394	98	30f. indigo, blue & red	75	40
395	98	40f. green, blue & brown	1·00	50

99 Walt Whitman and African Village

1970. Air. 150th Birth Anniv of Walt Whitman (American poet).

396	99	100f. brown, blue & grn	1·40	75

1970. Air. Space Flight of "Apollo 13". No. 392 surch 40F APOLLO 13 SOLIDARITE SPATIALE INTERNATIONALE.

397	97	40f. on 30f. multicoloured	1·30	85

101 Footballers and Globe

1970. Air. World Cup Football Championship, Mexico. Multicoloured.

398	40f. Type **101**	1·00	35
399	50f. Goalkeeper saving goal	1·00	55
400	200f. Player kicking ball	4·00	1·40

1970. 10th Anniv (1969) of Aerial Navigation Security Agency for Africa and Madagascar (A.S.E.C.N.A.). As T **147** of Gabon.

401	40f. red and purple	1·00	30

103 Mt. Fuji and "EXPO" Emblem

1970. World Fair "EXPO 70", Osaka, Japan. Multicoloured.

402	5f. Type **103** (postage)	45	20
403	70f. Dahomey Pavilion (air)	1·20	60
404	120f. Mt. Fuji and temple	1·90	90

104 "La Justice" and "La Concorde" (French warships)

1970. 300th Anniv of Ardres Embassy to Louis XIV of France.

405	104	40f. brown, blue & green	75	35
406	-	50f. red, brown & green	1·00	50
407	-	70f. brown, slate & bistre	1·60	75
408	-	200f. brown, blue & red	4·25	1·60

DESIGNS: 50f. Matheo Lopes; 70f. King Alkemy of Ardres; 200f. Louis XIV of France.

1970. Air. Brazil's Victory in World Cup Football Championship. No. 400 surch BRESIL–ITALIE 4 – 1 and value.

409	100f. on 200f. multicoloured	2·10	1·00

106 Mercury

1970. Air. Europafrique.

410	106	40f. multicoloured	85	45
411	106	70f. multicoloured	1·50	75

107 Order of Independence

1970. 10th Anniv of Independence.

412	107	30f. multicoloured	60	35
413	107	40f. multicoloured	85	35

108 Bariba Horseman

1970. Bariba Horsemen. Multicoloured.

414	1f. Type **108**	10	10
415	2f. Two horsemen	35	10
416	10f. Horseman facing left	50	25
417	40f. Type **108**	1·70	45
418	50f. As 2f.	2·10	65
419	70f. As 10f.	2·50	1·00

109 Beethoven

1970. Air. Birth Bicentenary of Beethoven.

420	109	90f. violet and blue	1·50	45
421	109	110f. brown and green	1·80	70

110 Emblems of Learning

1970. Air. Laying of Foundation Stone, Calavi University.

422	110	100f. multicoloured	1·60	80

111 "The Annunciation"

1970. Air. Christmas. Miniatures of the Rhenish School c. 1340. Multicoloured.

423	40f. Type **111**	60	45
424	70f. "The Nativity"	1·20	60
425	110f. "The Adoration of the Magi"	2·75	1·30
426	200f. "The Presentation in the Temple"	4·50	2·30

112 De Gaulle and Arc de Triomphe

1971. Air. 1st Death Anniv of Gen. Charles de Gaulle. Multicoloured.

427	40f. Type **112**	90	65
428	500f. De Gaulle and Notre Dame, Paris	3·50	1·80

1971. Air. 250th Death Anniv of Watteau. Paintings. As T 63. Multicoloured.

429	100f. "The Dandy"	3·50	1·90
430	100f. "Girl with Lute"	3·50	1·90

1971. Air. 500th Birth Anniv of Durer. As T 63. Multicoloured.

431	100f. Self-portrait, 1498	2·75	1·30
432	200f. Self-portrait, 1500	5·00	2·50

113 Hands supporting Heart

1971. Racial Equality Year.
433 **113** 40f. red, brn & green 1·70 55
434 - 100f. red, blue & green 3·50 1·50
DESIGN—HORIZ: 100f. "Heart" on Globe.

114 "The Twins" (wood-carving) and Lottery Ticket

1971. 4th Anniv of National Lottery.
435 **114** 35f. multicoloured 90 35
436 **114** 40f. multicoloured 1·20 50

115 Kepler, Earth and Planets

1971. Air. 400th Birth Anniv of Johannes Kepler (astronomer).
437 **115** 40f. black, pur and blue 90 65
438 - 200f. green, red & blue 3·50 1·80
DESIGN: 200f. Kepler, globe, satellite and rocket.

116 Boeing 747 Airliner linking Europe and Africa

1971. Air. Europafrique.
439 **116** 50f. orge, blue & black 1·40 70
440 - 100f. multicoloured 2·00 1·10
DESIGN: 100f. "General Mangin" (liner) and maps of Europe and Africa.

117 Cockerel and Drum (King Ganyehoussou)

1971. Emblems of Dahomey Kings. Multicoloured.
441 25f. Leg, saw and hatchet (Agoliagbo) 50 30
442 35f. Type **117** 90 45
443 40f. Fish and egg (Behanzin) (vert) 1·30 55
444 100f. Cow, tree and birds (Guezo) (vert) 2·30 80
445 135f. Fish and hoe (Ouegbadja) 2·75 1·20
446 140f. Lion and sickle (Glele) 4·50 1·80

1971. Air. 10th Anniv of U.A.M.P.T. As T **166** of Gabon. Multicoloured.
447 100f. U.A.M.P.T. H.Q., Brazzaville and Arms of Dahomey 1·90 85

119 "Adoration of the Shepherds" (Master of the Hausbuch)

1971. Air. Christmas. Paintings. Multicoloured.
448 40f. Type **119** 1·20 50
449 70f. "Adoration of the Magi" (Holbein) 1·80 65
450 100f. "Flight into Egypt" (Van Dyck) (horiz) 2·50 85
451 200f. "Birth of Christ" (Durer) (horiz) 6·00 2·20

120 "Prince Balthazar" (Velazquez)

1971. Air. 25th Anniv of UNICEF. Paintings of Children. Multicoloured.
452 40f. Type **120** 1·50 65
453 100f. "The Maids of Honour" (detail, Velazquez) 2·10 1·00

1972. No. 395 surch in figures.
454 **98** 35f. on 40f. green, bl & brn 80 45

122 Cross-country Skiing

1972. Winter Olympic Games, Sapporo, Japan.
455 **122** 35f. purple, brown and green (postage) 2·30 1·00
456 - 150f. purple, blue and brown (air) 3·50 1·70
DESIGN: 150f. Ski-jumping.

123 Scout taking Oath

1972. Air. International Scout Seminar, Cotonou. Multicoloured.
457 35f. Type **123** 55 25
458 40f. Scout playing "xylophone" 95 45
459 100f. Scouts working on the land (26×47 mm) 1·40 65
MS460 151×115 mm. As Nos. 457/9 but colours changed 4·50 4·50

124 Friedrich Naumann and Institute Building

1972. Air. Laying of Foundation Stone for National Workers Education Institute. Multicoloured.
461 100f. Type **124** 1·60 75
462 250f. Pres. Heuss of West Germany and Institute 3·50 1·50

125 Stork with Serpent

1972. Air. UNESCO. "Save Venice" Campaign. Mosaics in St. Mark's Basilica. Multicoloured.
463 35f. Type **125** 1·30 65
464 40f. Cockerels carrying fox 1·60 90
465 65f. Noah releasing dove 3·00 1·50

126 Exhibition Emblem and Dancers

1972. Air. 12th International Philatelic Exhibition, Naples.
466 **126** 100f. multicoloured 1·70 80

127 Running

1972. Air. Olympic Games, Munich.
467 **127** 20f. brown, grn & blue 50 25
468 - 85f. brown, blue & green 1·30 70
469 - 150f. brown, blue & grn 2·75 1·20
MS470 131×100 mm. Nos. 467/9 5·50 5·50
DESIGNS: 85f. High-jumping; 150f. Putting the shot.

128 Louis Bleriot and Bleriot XI

1972. Air. Birth Centenary of Louis Bleriot (pioneer airman).
471 **128** 100f. blue, violet & red 3·25 1·60

129 Brahms, and Clara Schumann at Piano

1972. 75th Death Anniv of Johannes Brahms (composer).
472 - 30f. black, brn & violet 2·20 1·00
473 **129** 65f. black, violet & lake 5·00 2·10
DESIGN—VERT: Brahms and opening bars of "Soir d'Ete".

130 "The Hare and the Tortoise"

1972. Fables of Jean de La Fontaine.
474 **130** 10f. grey, blue & lake 1·60 75
475 - 35f. blue, lake & purple 3·25 1·20
476 - 40f. indigo, blue & purple 4·50 1·80
DESIGNS—VERT: 35f. "The Fox and the Stork". HORIZ: 40f. "The Cat, the Weasel and the Little Rabbit".

131 "Adam" (Cranach)

1972. Air. 500th Birth Anniv of Lucas Cranach (painter). Multicoloured.
477 150f. Type **131** 2·75 1·50
478 200f. "Eve" (Cranach) 4·25 1·90

132 Africans and 500f. Coin

1972. 10th Anniv of West African Monetary Union.
479 **132** 40f. brown, grey & yell 65 25

133 "Pauline Borghese" (Canova)

1972. Air. 150th Death Anniv of Antonio Canova.
480 **133** 250f. multicoloured 5·50 2·10

1972. Air. Olympic Medal Winners. Nos. 467/9 optd as listed below.
481 **127** 20f. brown, blue & grn 45 25
482 - 85f. brown, blue & green 1·30 60
483 - 150f. brown, blue & grn 2·75 1·30
MS484 131×100 mm. Nos. 481/3 5·50 5·50
OVERPRINTS: 20f. **5.000m. – 10.000m. VIREN 2 MEDAILLES D'OR.** 85f. **HAUTEUR DAMES MEYFARTH MEDAILLE D'OR.** 150f. **POIDS KOMAR MEDAILLE D'OR.**

135 Pasteur and Apparatus

1972. Air. 150th Birth Anniv of Louis Pasteur (scientist).
485 **135** 100f. pur, violet & grn 2·75 95

1972. Air. Paintings by G. de la Tour. As T **63**. Multicoloured.
486 35f. "Hurdy-gurdy Player" (vert) 90 50
487 150f. "The New-born Child" 3·00 1·60

136 "The Annunciation" (School of Agnolo Gaddi)

1972. Air. Christmas. Religious Paintings. Mult.
488 35f. Type **136** 80 30
489 125f. "The Nativity" (Simone dei Crociffissi) 1·90 75
490 140f. "The Adoration of the Shepherds" (P. di Giovanni) 2·40 1·10
491 250f. "Adoration of the Magi" (Giotto) 4·00 1·80

137 Dr. Hansen, Microscope and Bacillus

1973. Centenary of Identification of Leprosy Bacillus by Hansen.
492 **137** 35f. brown, purple & blue 50 35
493 - 85f. brown, orange & grn 1·20 80

DESIGN: 85f. Dr. Gerhard Armauer Hansen.

138 Statue and Basilica, Lisieux

1973. Air. Birth Centenary of St. Theresa of Lisieux. Multicoloured.

494		40f. Type **138**	85	50
495		100f. St. Theresa of Lisieux (vert)	2·40	1·00

139 Arms of Dahomey

1973

496	**139**	5f. multicoloured	10	10
497	**139**	35f. multicoloured	45	15
498	**139**	40f. multicoloured	60	25

140 Scouts in Pirogue

1973. Air. 24th World Scouting Congress, Nairobi, Kenya.

499	**140**	15f. purple, green & blue	55	35
500	-	20f. blue and brown	65	35
501	-	40f. blue, green & brown	95	45
MS502 181×100 mm. 15f. chocolate, green and ultramarine; 20f. ultramarine, chocolate and blue; 40f. blue, green and chocolate			3·00	3·00

DESIGNS—VERT: 20f. Lord Baden-Powell. HORIZ: 40f. Bridge-building.

141 Interpol Badge and "Communications"

1973. 50th Anniv of International Criminal Police Organization (Interpol).

503		35f. brown, green & red	60	30
504	**141**	50f. green, brown & red	1·20	60

DESIGN—HORIZ: 35f. Interpol emblem and web.

142 "Education in Nutrition"

1973. 25th Anniv of World Health Organization. Multicoloured.

505		35f. Type **142**	60	35
506		100f. Pre-natal examination	1·40	70

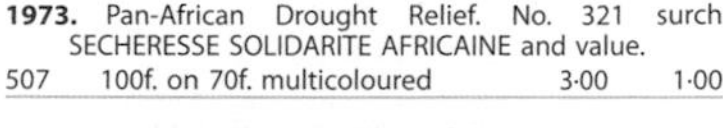

1973. Pan-African Drought Relief. No. 321 surch SECHERESSE SOLIDARITE AFRICAINE and value.

507		100f. on 70f. multicoloured	3·00	1·00

144 Copernicus, "Venera" and "Mariner" Probes and Plane of Solar System

1973. Air. 500th Birth Anniv of Copernicus.

508	**144**	65f. black, purple & yell	1·90	75
509	-	125f. green, blue & purple	3·25	1·10

DESIGN—VERT: 125f. Copernicus.

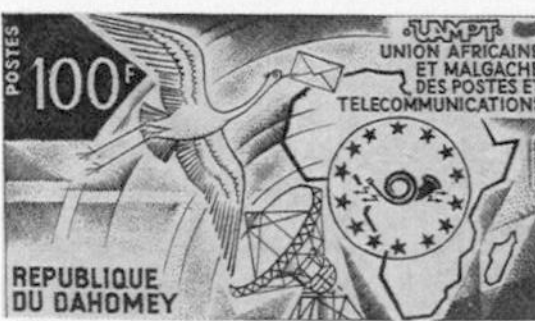

144a Crane with Letter and Telecommunications Emblem

1973. U.A.M.P.T.

510	**144a**	100f. violet, red & black	1·30	65

1973. Air. African Fortnight, Brussels. As No. 696 of Cameroun.

511		100f. black, green & blue	1·30	60

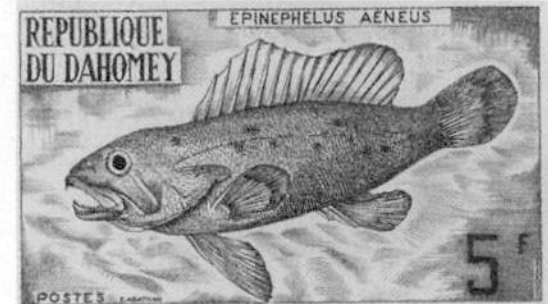

145 White Grouper

1973. Fishes.

512	**145**	5f. dp blue and blue	85	35
513	-	15f. black and blue	1·30	50
514	-	35f. lt brn, brn & grn	3·25	95

DESIGNS: 15f. African spadefish; 35f. Blue-pointed porgy.

148 W.M.O. Emblem and World Weather Map

1973. Air. Centenary of I.M.O./W.M.O.

515	**148**	100f. brown and green	1·40	1·20

149 "Europafrique"

1973. Air. Europafrique.

516	**149**	35f. blue, green & yell	55	30
517	-	40f. brown, ultram & bl	65	35

DESIGN: 40f. Europafrique, plant and cogwheels.

150 President John F. Kennedy

1973. Air. 10th Death Anniv of President Kennedy.

518	**150**	200f. grn, violet & grn	3·00	3·00
MS519 140×110 mm. **150** 200f. brown, crimson and blue			5·75	5·50

151 Footballers

1973. Air. World Football Championship Cup.

520	**151**	35f. green, brn & bistre	65	30
521	-	40f. brown, blue & orange	95	30
522	-	100f. green, brown & blue	1·50	65

DESIGNS: 40f., 100f. Football scenes similar to Type **151**.

152 Chameleon

1973. 1st Anniv of 26th October Revolution. Multicoloured.

523		35f. Type **152**	95	35
524		40f. Arms of Dahomey (vert)	70	30

153 "The Annunciation" (Dirk Bouts)

1973. Air. Christmas. Multicoloured.

525		35f. Type **153**	75	35
526		100f. "The Nativity" (Giotto)	1·50	65
527		150f. "The Adoration of the Magi" (Botticelli)	2·75	1·10
528		200f. "The Adoration of the Shepherds" (Bassano) (horiz)	3·25	1·90

1974. Air. "Skylab". No. 515 surch OPERATION SKYLAB 1973-1974 and value.

529	**148**	200f. on 100f. brn & grn	2·30	1·30

155 "The Elephant, the Chicken and the Dog"

1974. Dahomey Folk Tales. Multicoloured.

530		5f. Type **155**	65	45
531		10f. "The Sparrowhawk and the Dog"	65	20
532		25f. "The Windy Tree" (horiz)	85	35
533		40f. "The Eagle, the Snake and the Chicken" (horiz)	1·30	45

156 Snow Crystal and Skiers

1974. Air. 50th Anniv of Winter Olympic Games.

534	**156**	100f. blue, brn and vio	1·90	1·10

157 Alsatian

1974. Breeds of Dogs. Multicoloured.

535		40f. Type **157**	1·70	50
536		50f. Boxer	1·90	75
537		100f. Saluki	3·50	1·50

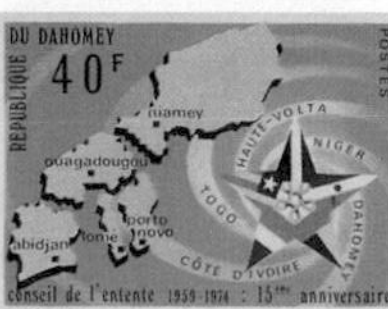

158 Map of Member Countries

1974. 15th Anniv of Council of Accord.

538	**158**	40f. multicoloured	80	25

159 Lenin (50th Death Anniv)

1974. Air. Celebrities' Anniversaries.

539	**159**	50f. purple and red	2·30	1·00
540	-	125f. brn & green	2·40	90
541	-	150f. blue & purple	2·40	1·50

DESIGNS AND ANNIVERSARIES: 125f. Marie Curie (40th death anniv); 150f. Sir Winston Churchill (birth cent).

160 18th-century Persian Bishop

1974. Air. 21st Chess Olympiad, Nice. Mult.

542		50f. Type **160**	2·30	1·10
543		200f. 19th-century Siamese queen	6·50	2·75

161 Beethoven and opening bars of the "Moonlight" Sonata

1974. Air. Famous Composers.

544	**161**	150f. red and black	3·75	1·70
545	-	150f. red and black	3·75	1·70

DESIGN: No. 545, Chopin.

162 Earth seen through Astronaut's Legs

1974. Air. 5th Anniv of 1st Manned Moon Landing.

546	**162**	150f. brn, blue & red	2·50	1·20

Sets commemorating the World Cup, U.P.U. Centenary, Treaty of Berne, Space Exploration and West Germany's World Cup Victory appeared in 1974. Their status is uncertain.

1974. Air. 11th Pan-Arab Scout Jamboree, Batroun, Lebanon. Nos. 499/500 surch XIe JAMBOREE PANARABE DE BATROUN – LIBAN and value.

547	**140**	100f. on 15f. purple, green and blue	1·30	60
548	-	140f. on 20f. bl & brn	1·80	90

1974. Air. West Germany's Victory in World Cup Football Championships. Nos. 521/2 surch R F A 2 HOLLANDE 1 and value.

549		100f. on 40f. brn, bl & orge	1·20	65
550		150f. on 100f. grn, brn & bl	1·60	1·00

165 U.P.U. Emblem and Globe

1974. Air. Centenary of U.P.U.

551	**165**	35f. violet and red	80	40
552	-	65f. blue and red	1·40	80
553	-	125f. green, blue & lt bl	2·50	1·60
554	-	200f. blue, yellow & brn	3·25	2·10

DESIGNS: 65f. Concorde in flight over African village; 125f. French mobile post office, circa 1860; 200f. Drummer and mail van.

166 "Lion of Belfort"

1974. Air. 70th Death Anniv of F. Bartholdi (sculptor).

555	**166**	100f. brown	2·75	1·20

1974. Air. 30th Death Anniv of Philippe de Champaigne (painter). As T **153**. Mult.

556	250f. "Young Girl with Falcon"	4·00	2·50

167 Locomotive No. 3.1102, 1911, France

1974. Steam Locomotives.

557	**167**	35f. multicoloured	90	50
558	-	40f. grey, black & red	1·70	50
559	-	100f. multicoloured	2·50	1·50
560	-	200f. multicoloured	5·00	2·50

DESIGNS: 40f. Goods locomotive, 1877; 100f. Crampton Type 210 locomotive, 1849; 200f. Stephenson locomotive "Aigle", 1846, France.

168 Rhamphorhynchus

1974. Air. Prehistoric Animals. Multicoloured.

561	35f. Type **168**	1·60	85
562	150f. Stegosaurus	5·25	2·10
563	200f. Tyrannosaurus	6·75	2·50

169 Globe, Notes and Savings Bank

1974. World Savings Day.

564	**169**	35f. brown, myrtle & grn	60	35

170 Europafrique Emblem on Globe

1974. Air. Europafrique.

565	**170**	250f. multicoloured	3·50	2·30

1974. Air. Christmas. Paintings by Old Masters. As T **153**. Multicoloured.

566	35f. "The Annunciation" (Schongauer)	50	35
567	40f. "The Nativity" (Schongauer)	65	40
568	100f. "The Virgin of the Rose Bush" (Schongauer)	1·90	65
569	250f. "The Virgin, Infant Jesus and St. John the Baptist" (Botticelli)	3·75	1·90

171 "Apollo" and "Soyuz" Spacecraft

1975. Air. "Apollo–Soyuz" Space Link. Mult.

570	35f. Type **171**	50	30
571	200f. Rocket launch and flags of Russia and U.S.A.	2·75	1·30
572	500f. "Apollo" and "Soyuz" docked together	5·75	3·25

172 Dompago Dance, Hissi

1975. Dahomey Dances and Folklore. Mult.

573	10f. Type **172**	55	10
574	25f. Fetish dance, Vaudou-Tchinan	1·20	35
575	40f. Bamboo dance, Agbehoun	1·50	70
576	100f. Somba dance, Sandoua (horiz)	2·75	90

173 Flags on Map of Africa

1975. "Close Co-operation with Nigeria". Multicoloured.

577	65f. Type **173**	75	25
578	100f. Arrows linking maps of Dahomey and Nigeria (horiz)	1·00	55

174 Community Emblem and Pylons

1975. Benin Electricity Community. Mult.

579	40f. Type **174**	70	50
580	150f. Emblem and pylon (vert)	1·90	1·00

C.E.B. = "Communaute Electrique du Benin".

175 Head of Ceres

1975. Air. "Arphila 75" International Stamp Exhibition, Paris.

581	**175**	100f. purple, ind & blue	1·50	75

176 Rays of Light and Map

1975. "New Dahomey Society".

582	**176**	35f. multicoloured	45	25

1975. Air. "Apollo–Soyuz" Space Test Project. Nos. 570/1 surch RENCONTRE APOLLO-SOYOUZ 17 Juil. 1975 and value.

583	**171**	100f. on 35f. mult	1·50	75
584	-	300f. on 200f. mult	3·75	1·60

178 Dr. Schweitzer

1975. Birth Centenary of Dr. Albert Schweitzer.

585	**178**	200f. olive, brown & green	5·50	1·70

179 "The Holy Family" (Michelangelo)

1975. Air. Europafrique.

586	**179**	300f. multicoloured	4·25	2·20

180 Woman and I.W.Y. Emblem

1975. International Women's Year.

587	**180**	50f. blue and violet	90	45
588	-	150f. orange, brn & grn	2·50	1·30

DESIGN: 150f. I.W.Y. emblem within ring of bangles.

181 Continental Infantry

1975. Air. Bicent of American Revolution.

589	**181**	75f. lilac, red & green	1·00	50
590	-	135f. brown, pur & bl	1·80	1·00
591	-	300f. brown, red & blue	3·00	2·00
592	-	500f. brown, red & grn	6·00	2·75

DESIGNS: 135f. "Spirit of 76"; 300f. Artillery battery; 500f. Cavalry.

182 Diving

1975. Air. Olympic Games, Montreal.

593	**182**	40f. brown, bl and vio	60	35
594	-	250f. brown, grn & red	2·50	1·50

DESIGN: 250f. Football.

183 "Allamanda cathartica"

1975. Flowers. Multicoloured.

595	10f. Type **183**	40	35
596	35f. "Ixora coccinea"	1·20	50
597	45f. "Hibiscus rosa-sinensis"	1·40	70
598	60f. "Phaemeria magnifica"	1·90	1·10

184 "The Nativity" (Van Leyden)

1975. Air. Christmas. Multicoloured.

599	40f. Type **184**	1·00	50
600	85f. "Adoration of the Magi" (Rubens) (vert)	1·60	80
601	140f. "Adoration of the Shepherds" (Le Brun)	2·75	1·10
602	300f. "The Virgin of the Blue Diadem" (Raphael) (vert)	5·50	2·50

For later issues see BENIN.

PARCEL POSTAGE STAMPS

1967. Surch COLIS POSTAUX and value.

P271	**18**	5f. on 1f. (postage)	30	25
P272	-	10f. on 2f. (No. 151)	45	45
P273	**18**	20f. on 6f.	80	80
P274	-	25f. on 3f. (No. 152)	1·00	95
P275	-	30f. on 4f. (No. 153)	1·00	95
P276	-	50f. on 10f. (No. 155)	1·60	1·60
P277	-	100f. on 20f. (No. 157)	3·25	3·25
P278	-	200f. on 200f. (No. 195) (air)	6·50	4·50
P279	**29**	300f. on 100f.	6·50	5·25
P280	-	500f. on 300f. (No. 196)	13·50	9·75
P281	-	1000f. on 500f. (No. 197)	27·00	£110
P282	-	5000f. on 100f. (No. 145)	£100	£100

POSTAGE DUE STAMPS

1906. "Natives" key-type inscr "DAHOMEY" in blue (10, 30c.) or red (others).

D33	L	5c. green	2·50	1·30
D34	L	10c. red	4·00	2·50
D35	L	15c. blue on blue	4·50	3·75
D36	L	20c. black on yellow	4·25	5·25
D37	L	30c. red on cream	4·75	8·75
D38	L	50c. violet	14·00	48·00
D39	L	60c. black on buff	9·25	39·00
D40	L	1f. black on pink	37·00	75·00

1914. "Figure" key-type inscr "DAHOMEY".

D59	M	5c. green	30	4·25
D60	M	10c. red	45	3·50
D61	M	15c. grey	45	3·25
D62	M	20c. brown	90	4·25
D63	M	30c. blue	1·10	6·25
D64	M	50c. black	1·30	7·75
D65	M	60c. orange	1·70	3·50
D66	M	1f. violet	2·30	4·50

1927. Surch in figures.

D96	2f. on 1f. mauve	2·00	7·00
D97	3f. on 1f. brown	3·00	10·50

D14 Native Head

1941

D143	**D14**	5c. black	1·10	6·50
D144	**D14**	10c. red	50	6·25
D145	**D14**	15c. blue	35	5·25
D146	**D14**	20c. green	40	6·25
D147	**D14**	30c. orange	1·20	7·25
D148	**D14**	50c. brown	1·70	8·25
D149	**D14**	60c. green	1·90	8·25
D150	**D14**	1f. red	2·30	8·75
D151	**D14**	2f. yellow	2·50	9·00
D152	**D14**	3f. purple	2·50	10·00

D26 Panther attacking African

1963

D191	**D26**	1f. red and green	20	20
D192	**D26**	2f. green & brown	40	35
D193	**D26**	5f. blue and orange	40	35
D194	**D26**	10f. black and purple	80	80
D195	**D26**	20f. orange & blue	1·30	1·30

D72 Pirogue

1967

D308	**D72**	1f. plum, blue & brn	10	10
D309	**A**	1f. brown, bl & plum	10	10
D310	**B**	3f. green, orge & brn	20	20
D311	**C**	3f. brown, orge & grn	20	20
D312	**D**	5f. purple, blue & brn	45	40
D313	**E**	5f. brown, blue & pur	45	40
D314	**F**	10f. green, vio & brn	60	60
D315	**G**	10f. brown, grn & vio	60	60
D316	**H**	30f. violet, red & bl	1·20	1·20
D317	**I**	30f. blue, red & vio	1·20	1·20

DESIGNS: A, Heliograph; B, Old morse receiver; C, Postman on cycle; D, Old telephone; E, Renault ABH diesel railcar; F, Citroen "2-CV" mail van; G, Radio station; H, Douglas DC-8-10/50CF airliner; I, "Early Bird" satellite.

Pt. 11

DANISH WEST INDIES

A group of islands in the West Indies formerly belonging to Denmark and purchased in 1917 by the United States, whose stamps they now use. Now known as the United States Virgin Islands.

1855. 100 cents = 1 dollar.
1905. 100 bit = 1 franc.

1

1855. Imperf.

4	**1**	3c. red	42·00	70·00

1872. Perf.

6		3c. red	80·00	£225
7		4c. blue	£225	£450

2

1873

31	**2**	1c. red and green	11·50	23·00
32	**2**	3c. red and blue	10·00	16·00
33	**2**	4c. blue and brown	16·00	13·00
19	**2**	5c. brown and green	24·00	23·00
21	**2**	7c. yellow and purple	28·00	£100
25	**2**	10c. brown and blue	44·00	70·00
27	**2**	12c. green and purple	55·00	£140
28	**2**	14c. green and lilac	£800	£1400
29	**2**	50c. lilac	£190	£275

1887. Handstamped 1 CENT.

37		1c. on 7c. yellow & purple	90·00	£200

1895. Surch 10 CENTS 1895.

38		10c. on 50c. lilac	36·00	60·00

1900

39	**5**	1c. green	2·75	2·75
40	**5**	2c. red	8·50	23·00
41	**5**	5c. blue	18·00	26·00
42	**5**	8c. brown	30·00	45·00

1902. Surch 2 (or 8) CENTS 1902.

43	**2**	2c. on 3c. red and blue	9·00	23·00
47	**2**	8c. on 10c. brown & blue	11·00	13·50

5

1905. Surch 5 BIT 1905.

48		5b. on 4c. blue & brown	25·00	55·00
49	**5**	5b. on 5c. blue	19·00	40·00
50	**5**	5b. on 8c. brown	19·00	40·00

10 King Christian IX

11 Charlotte Amalie Harbour and Training ship "Ingolf"

1905

51	**10**	5b. green	6·25	3·25
52	**10**	10b. red	6·25	3·25
53	**10**	20b. blue and green	12·00	7·00
54	**10**	25b. blue	12·00	9·25
55	**10**	40b. grey and red	12·00	7·00
56	**10**	50b. grey and yellow	15·00	11·00
57	**11**	1f. blue and green	22·00	39·00
58	**11**	2f. brown and red	34·00	55·00
59	**11**	5f. brown and yellow	85·00	£250

14 King Frederik VIII

1907

60	**14**	5b. green	3·00	1·90
61	**14**	10b. red	2·75	1·90
62	**14**	15b. brown and violet	4·75	4·50
63	**14**	20b. blue and green	34·00	25·00
64	**14**	25b. blue	2·40	2·50
65	**14**	30b. black and red	60·00	49·00
66	**14**	40b. grey and red	7·50	9·00
67	**14**	50b. brown and yellow	7·25	13·00

15 King Christian X

1915

68	**15**	5b. green	5·75	4·25
69	**15**	10b. red	5·75	44·00
70	**15**	15b. brown and lilac	5·75	44·00
71	**15**	20b. blue and green	5·75	44·00
72	**15**	25b. blue	5·75	12·00
73	**15**	30b. black and red	5·75	75·00
74	**15**	40b. grey and red	6·50	75·00
75	**15**	50b. brown and yellow	5·75	75·00

POSTAGE DUE STAMPS

D6

1902

D43	**D6**	1c. blue	5·50	23·00
D44	**D6**	4c. blue	17·00	27·00
D45	**D6**	6c. blue	28·00	55·00
D46	**D6**	10c. blue	28·00	55·00

D12

1905

D60	**D12**	5b. grey and red	6·25	7·00
D61	**D12**	20b. grey and red	10·00	13·00
D62	**D12**	30b. grey and red	9·00	13·00
D63	**D12**	50b. grey and red	7·75	32·00

Pt. 7

DANZIG

A Baltic seaport, from 1920–1939 (with the surrounding district) a free state under the protection of the League of Nations. Later incorporated in Germany. Now part of Poland.

1920. 100 pfennige = 1 mark.
1923. 100 pfennige = 1 Danzig gulden.

Stamps of Germany inscr "DEUTSCHES REICH" optd or surch.

1920. Optd Danzig horiz.

1	**10**	5pf. green	40	65
2	**10**	10pf. red	40	40
3	**24**	15pf. brown	40	40
4	**10**	20pf. blue	40	1·40
5	**10**	30pf. black & orge on buff	40	40
6	**10**	40pf. red	40	40
7	**10**	50pf. black & pur on buff	55	40
8	**12**	1m. red	55	75
9	**12**	1m.25 green	55	75
10	**12**	1m.50 brown	1·10	2·10
11	**13**	2m. blue	3·75	8·50
12	**13**	2m.50 red	3·75	5·75
13	**14**	3m. black	7·50	15·00
14	**10**	4m. red and black	5·00	7·50
15a	**15**	5m. red and black	3·25	4·75

1920. Surch Danzig horiz and large figures of value.

16	**10**	5 on 30pf. black and orange on buff	30	30
17	**10**	10 on 20pf. blue	30	30
18	**10**	25 on 30pf. black and orange on buff	30	30
19	**10**	60 on 30pf. black and orange on buff	85	1·40
20	**10**	80 on 30pf. black and orange on buff	85	1·40

1920. Optd Danzig diagonally and bar.

21	**24**	2pf. grey	£130	£250
22	**24**	2½pf. grey	£180	£375
23	**10**	3pf. brown	12·50	21·00
24	**10**	5pf. green	65	95
25	**24**	7½pf. orange	48·00	70·00
26	**10**	10pf. red	4·25	8·50
27	**24**	15pf. violet	85	95
28	**10**	20pf. blue	85	95
29	**10**	25pf. blk & red on yell	85	95
30	**10**	30pf. blk & orge on buff	65·00	£120
31	**10**	40pf. black and red	2·75	3·25
32	**10**	50pf. blk & pur on buff	£200	£375
32a	**10**	60pf. mauve	£1500	£2750
33	**10**	75pf. black and green	85	95
34	**10**	80pf. blk & red on pink	3·00	5·25
34a	**12**	1m. red	£1500	£2750

1920. Optd DANZIG three times in semicircle.

34b	**13**	2m. blue	£1500	£2750

1920. No. 5 of Danzig surch MARK 1 MARK and Types of Germany with burelage added surch with new value and DANZIG (36/37), Danzig (38, 40f) or DANZIG and flag (40e).

35A	**10**	1m. on 30pf. black and orange on buff	1·10	1·90
36A	**10**	1¼m. on 3pf. brown	1·30	1·90
37A	**24**	2m. on 35pf. brown	1·90	1·90
38A	**24**	3m. on 7½pf. orange	1·30	1·90
39A	**24**	5m. on 2pf. grey	1·30	2·75
40Af	**24**	10m. on 7½pf. orange	1·60	2·75

1920. Air. No. 6 of Danzig surch with airplane or wings and value.

41	**10**	40 on 40pf. red	1·60	3·75
42	**10**	60 on 40pf. red	1·60	3·75
43	**10**	1m. on 40pf. red	1·60	3·75

13 Hanse Kogge

1921. Constitution of 1920.

44	**13**	5pf. purple and brown	20	20
45	**13**	10pf. violet and orange	20	20
46	**13**	25pf. red and green	65	85
55	**13**	40pf. red	65	1·10
48	**13**	80pf. blue	55	65
49	-	1m. grey and red	2·10	2·75
50	-	2m. green and blue	6·25	6·25
51	-	3m. green and black	2·75	3·75
52	-	5m. red and grey	2·75	3·75
53	-	10m. brown and green	3·25	5·75

The mark values are as Type **13**, but larger.

15

16 Sabaltnig PIII over Danzig

1921. Air.

57	**15**	40pf. green	30	55
58	**15**	60pf. purple	30	55
59	**15**	1m. red	30	55
60	**15**	2m. brown	30	55
116	**16**	5m. violet	75	1·30
117	**16**	10m. green	75	1·30
118	**16**	20m. brown	75	1·30
119	**15**	25m. blue	55	95
120	**16**	50m. orange	55	95
121	**16**	100m. red	55	95
122	**16**	250m. brown	85	95
123	**16**	500m. red	85	95

Nos. 120 to 123 are similar to Type **16**, but larger.

1921. No. 33 of Danzig surch 60 and bars.

63	**10**	60 on 75pf. black & green	1·30	1·10

18

1921

64	**18**	5pf. orange	20	20
65	**18**	10pf. brown	20	20
66	**18**	15pf. green	20	20
67	**18**	20pf. grey	20	20
68	**18**	25pf. green	20	20
69	**18**	30pf. red and blue	20	20
70	**18**	40pf. red and green	20	20
71	**18**	50pf. red and green	20	20
72	**18**	60pf. red	55	55
73	**18**	75pf. purple	30	30
74	**18**	80pf. red and black	40	55
75	**18**	80pf. green	30	30
76	**18**	1m. red and orange	65	55
77	**18**	1.20m. blue	1·60	1·60
78	**18**	1.25m. red and purple	30	30
79	**18**	1.50m. grey	20	55
80	**18**	2m. red and grey	3·75	6·75
81	**18**	2m. red	30	30
82	**18**	2.40m. red and brown	1·40	2·75
83	**18**	3m. red and purple	10·50	12·50
84	**18**	3m. red	20	55
106	**18**	4m. blue	20	55
86	**18**	5m. green	20	40
87	**18**	6m. red	20	40
88	**18**	8m. blue	65	2·10
89	**18**	10m. orange	20	40
90	**18**	20m. brown	20	40
110	**18**	40m. blue	30	75
111	**18**	80m. red	30	75

19

1921. Rouletted.

91	**19**	5m. green, black and red	1·60	3·75
91b	**19**	9m. orange and red	3·75	10·50
92	**19**	10m. blue, black and red	1·60	3·75
93	**19**	20m. black and red	1·60	3·75

20

1921. Tuberculosis Week.

93b	**20**	30pf.(+30pf.) grn & orge	55	1·30
93c	**20**	60pf.(+60pf.) red & yell	1·60	2·10
93d	**20**	1.20m.(+1.20m.) bl & orge (25×29½ mm)	2·75	3·00

21

1922

94ba	**21**	50m. red and gold	2·75	6·75
95a	**21**	100m. red and green	4·25	7·50

1922. Surch in figures.

96	**18**	6 on 3m. red	40	75
97	**18**	8 on 4m. blue	40	1·10
98	**18**	20 on 8m. blue	40	75

25

26

1923

99	**25**	50m. red and blue	20	55
136	**25**	50m. blue	30	75
100	**25**	100m. red and green	20	55
137	**25**	100m. green	30	75
101	**25**	150m. red and purple	20	55
138	**25**	200m. orange	30	75
102	**26**	250m. red and purple	55	55
103	**26**	500m. red and grey	55	55
104	**26**	1000m. pink and brown	55	55
105	**26**	5000m. pink and silver	2·10	8·00
139	**26**	10000m. red and orange	85	85
140	**26**	20000m. red and blue	85	1·40
141	**26**	50000m. red and green	85	1·40

28

1923. Poor People's Fund.

123b	**28**	50+20m. red	30	85
123c	**28**	100+30m. purple	30	85

29

1923

124	**29**	250m. red and purple	30	75
125	**29**	300m. red and green	30	55
126	**29**	500m. red and grey	30	75
127	**29**	1000m. brown	30	75
128	**29**	1000m. red and brown	30	55
129	**29**	3000m. red and violet	30	75
130	**29**	5000m. pink	20	55
131	**29**	20000m. blue	20	55
132	**29**	50000m. green	20	55
133	**29**	100000m. blue	20	55
134	**29**	250000m. purple	20	55
135	**29**	500000m. grey	20	55

1923. Surch with figure of value and Tausend (T) or Million or Millionen (M).

142	**25**	40T. on 200m. orange	1·10	2·75
143	**25**	100T. on 200m. orange	1·10	2·75
144	**25**	250T. on 200m. orange	8·00	17·00
145	**25**	400T. on 100m. green	75	55
146	**29**	500T. on 50000m. green	55	55
147	**29**	1M. on 10000m. orange	4·75	8·00
148	**29**	1M. on 10000m. red	30	55
149	**29**	2M. on 10000m. red	30	55
150	**29**	3M. on 10000m. red	30	55
151	**29**	5M. on 10000m. red	40	55
152	**29**	10M. on 10000m. lavender	55	95
158	**26**	10M. on 1000000m. orge	55	1·60
153	**29**	20M. on 10000m. lavender	55	95
154	**29**	25M. on 10000m. lavender	20	95
155	**29**	40M. on 10000m. lavender	20	95
156	**29**	50M. on 10000m. lavender	20	95
159	**29**	100M. on 10000m. lav	20	95
160	**29**	300M. on 10000m. lav	20	95
161	**29**	500M. on 10000m. lav	20	95

1923. Surch 100000 and bar.

157	**26**	100000 on 20000m. red and blue	1·10	8·00

35 Etrich/Rumpler Taube

1923. Air.

162	**35**	250,000m. red	40	1·60
163	**35**	500,000m. red	40	1·60

1923. Surch in Millionen.

164	2m. on 100,000m. red	40	1·60
165	5m. on 50,000m. red	40	1·60

1923. Surch with new currency, Pfennige or Gulden.

166	**25**	5pf. on 50m. red	65	55
167	**25**	10pf. on 50m. red	65	55
168	**25**	20pf. on 100m. red	65	55
169	**25**	25pf. on 50m. red	4·75	10·50
170	**25**	30pf. on 50m. red	4·75	2·25
171	**25**	40pf. on 100m. red	3·00	2·75
172	**25**	50pf. on 100m. red	3·00	3·75
173	**25**	75pf. on 100m. red	10·50	21·00
174	**26**	1g. on 1000000m. red	5·75	8·00
175	**26**	2g. on 1000000m. red	16·00	21·00
176	**26**	3g. on 1000000m. red	30·00	80·00
177	**26**	5g. on 1000000m. red	34·00	85·00

39

1924. Arms

177b	**39**	3pf. brown	1·60	1·90
268	**39**	5pf. orange	1·10	2·75
178e	**39**	7pf. green	2·10	3·75
178f	**39**	8pf. green	2·10	8·00
270	**39**	10pf. green	1·10	2·75
180	**39**	15pf. grey	5·25	85
180b	**39**	15pf. red	5·75	1·40
181	**39**	20pf. red and carmine	21·00	85
182	**39**	20pf. grey	2·10	3·25
183	**39**	25pf. red and grey	32·00	4·75
272	**39**	25pf. red	2·75	16·00
185	**39**	30pf. red and green	19·00	1·10
186	**39**	30pf. purple	2·10	5·25
186a	**39**	35pf. blue	5·75	1·90
187	**39**	40pf. blue and indigo	16·00	1·30
188	**39**	40pf. red and brown	8·50	16·00
189	**39**	40pf. blue	2·10	4·75
274	**39**	50pf. red and blue	2·75	£170
190b	**39**	55pf. red and purple	10·50	19·00
191	**39**	60pf. red and green	8·50	23·00
192	**39**	70pf. red and green	2·75	9·50
193	**39**	75pf. red and purple	12·50	10·50
194	**39**	80pf. red and brown	2·75	9·50

40

1924. Air. Etrich/Rumpler Taube

195	**40**	10pf. red	29·00	4·75
196	**40**	20pf. mauve	2·75	2·10
197	**40**	40pf. brown	4·00	2·75
198	**40**	1g. green	4·00	3·75
199	-	2½g. purple (22×40 mm)	23·00	44·00

42 Oliva

1924

200	**42**	1g. black and green	26·00	60·00
275	**42**	1g. black and orange	8·50	£150
201	-	2g. black and purple	60·00	£140
206	-	2g. black and red	4·75	10·50
202	-	3g. black and blue	6·25	6·25
203	-	5g. black and lake	6·25	10·50
204	-	10g. black and brown	26·00	£140

DESIGNS—HORIZ: 2g. Krantor and River Mottlau; 3g. Zoppot. VERT: 5g. St. Mary's Church; 10g. Town Hall and Langemarkt.

44 Fountain of Neptune

1929. Int Philatelic Exhibition. Various frames.

207	**44**	10pf.(+10pf.) blk & grn	3·25	2·10
208	**44**	15pf.(+15pf.) blk & red	3·25	2·10
209	**44**	25pf.(+25pf.) blk & bl	10·50	17·00

1930. 10th Anniv of Constitution of Free City of Danzig. Optd 1920 15. November 1930.

210	**39**	5pf. orange	3·25	4·75
211	**39**	10pf. green	4·25	5·75
212	**39**	15pf. red	7·50	13·50
213	**39**	20pf. red and carmine	3·75	7·50
214	**39**	25pf. red and grey	5·25	13·50
215	**39**	30pf. red and green	10·50	32·00
216	**39**	35pf. blue	42·00	£130
217	**39**	40pf. blue and indigo	13·50	48·00
218	**39**	50pf. red and blue	42·00	£110
219	**39**	75pf. red and purple	42·00	£120
220	**42**	1g. black and orange	42·00	£110

1932. Danzig Int Air Post Exn ("Luposta"). Nos. 200/4 surch Luftpost-Ausstellung 1932 and value.

221		10pf.+10pf. on 1g. black and green	11·50	30·00
222	-	15pf.+15pf. on 2g. black and purple	11·50	30·00
223	-	20pf.+20pf. on 3g. black and blue	11·50	30·00
224	-	25pf.+25pf. on 5g. black and lake	11·50	30·00
225	-	30pf.+30pf. on 10g. black and brown	11·50	30·00

1934. "Winter Relief Work" Charity. Surch 5 W.H.W. in Gothic characters.

226	**39**	5pf.+5pf. orange	11·50	26·00
227	**39**	10pf.+5pf. green	30·00	65·00
228	**39**	15pf.+5pf. red	17·00	48·00

1934. Surch.

229	6pf. on 7pf. green	1·10	2·10
230b	8pf. on 7pf. green	1·10	3·25
231	30pf. on 35pf. blue	12·50	32·00

50 Junkers F-13

51

1935. Air.

233	**50**	10pf. red	2·10	1·10
234	**50**	15pf. yellow	2·10	1·60
235	**50**	25pf. green	2·10	2·10
236	**50**	50pf. blue	10·50	12·50
237	**51**	1g. purple	4·25	17·00

52 Stockturm, 1346

1935. Winter Relief Fund.

238	**52**	5pf.+5pf. orange	85	2·10
239	-	10pf.+5pf. green	1·50	3·25
240	-	15pf.+10pf. red	3·50	4·75

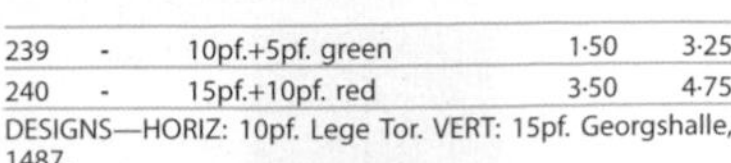

DESIGNS—HORIZ: 10pf. Lege Tor. VERT: 15pf. Georgshalle, 1487.

54 Brosen War Memorial

1936. 125th Anniv of Brosen. Inscr "125 JAHRE OSTSEEBAD BROSEN".

241		10pf. green	1·30	1·60
242		25pf. red	1·70	3·00
243	**54**	40pf. blue	3·00	5·75

DESIGNS—HORIZ: 10pf. Brosen Beach; 25pf. Zoppot end of Brosen Beach.

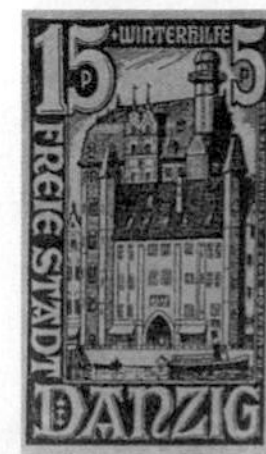

55 Frauentor and Observatory

1936. Winter Relief Fund.

244	-	10pf.+5pf. blue	2·10	6·25
245	**55**	15pf.+5pf. green	2·10	8·50
246	-	25pf.+10pf. red	3·25	12·50
247	-	40pf.+20pf. brn & red	4·25	15·00
248	-	50pf.+20pf. blue	7·50	21·00

DESIGNS—VERT: 10pf. Milchkannenturm; 25pf. Krantor. HORIZ: 40pf. Langgartertor; 50pf. Hohestor.

56 D(anziger) L(uftschutz) B(und)

1937. Air Defence League.

249	**56**	10pf. blue	75	1·60
250	**56**	15pf. purple	2·10	3·25

57 Marienkriche, Danzig

1937. 1st National Philatelic Exhibition, Danzig. Sheets 147×104 mm.

MS251 **57** 50pf. blue-green/toned (postage)	4·25	85·00
MS252 **57** 50pf. blue/toned (air)	4·25	£110

57a Danziger Dorf, Magdeburg

1937. Foundation of Danzig Community, Magdeburg.

253	**57a**	25pf. (+25pf.) red	3·75	7·50
254	-	40pf. (+40pf.) red & bl	3·75	7·50

DESIGN—HORIZ: 40pf. Village and Arms of Danzig and Magdeburg.

1937. Danzig Productivity Show. Sheet 146×105 mm.

MS254a Nos. 253/4 (sold for 1g.50)	65·00	£325

58 Madonna and Child

1937. Winter Relief Fund. Statues.

255	**58**	5pf.+5pf. violet	3·25	10·50
256	-	10pf.+5pf. brown	3·25	8·00
257	-	15pf.+5pf. orange & blue	3·25	11·50
258	-	25pf.+10pf. green & blue	4·25	16·00
259	-	40pf.+25pf. blue & red	7·50	21·00

DESIGNS: 10pf. Mercury; 15pf. The "Golden Knight"; 25pf. Fountain of Neptune; 40pf. St. George and Dragon.

59 Schopenhauer

1938. 150th Birth Anniv of Schopenhauer (philosopher). Portraits inscr as in T 59.

260		15pf. blue (as old man)	1·90	3·25
261		25pf. brown (as youth)	4·50	10·50
262	**59**	40pf. red	1·90	4·25

60 Yacht "Peter von Danzig" (1936)

1938. Winter Relief Fund. Ships.

276	**60**	5pf.+5pf. green	1·80	2·30
277	-	10pf.+5pf. brown	1·80	4·75
278	-	15pf.+10pf. olive	2·10	4·25
279	-	25pf.+10pf. blue	3·00	6·25
280	-	40pf.+15pf. purple	4·25	9·50

DESIGNS: 10pf. Dredger "Fu Shing"; 15pf. Liner "Columbus"; 25pf. Liner "Hansestadt Danzig"; 40pf. Sailing ship "Peter von Danzig" (1472).

61 Teutonic Knights

1939. 125th Anniv of Prussian Annexation. Historical designs.

281	**61**	5pf. green	75	2·75
282	-	10pf. brown	1·10	3·25
283	-	15pf. blue	1·60	3·75
284	-	25pf. purple	2·10	5·25

DESIGNS: 10pf. Danzig–Swedish treaty of neutrality, 1630; 15pf. Danzig united to Prussia, 2.1.1814; 25pf. Stephen Batori's defeat at Weichselmunde, 1577.

62 Gregor Mendel

1939. Anti-cancer Campaign.

285	**62**	10pf. brown	85	1·10
286	-	15pf. black (Koch)	85	2·75
287	-	25pf. green (Rontgen)	1·60	3·75

OFFICIAL STAMPS

1921. Stamps of Danzig optd D M.

O94	**18**	5f. orange	30	20
O95	**18**	10pf. brown	30	20
O96	**18**	15pf. green	30	20
O97	**18**	20pf. grey	30	20
O98	**18**	25pf. green	30	20
O99	**18**	30pf. red and blue	75	75
O100	**18**	40pf. red and green	30	20
O101	**18**	50pf. red and green	30	20
O102	**18**	60pf. red	30	20
O103	**18**	75pf. purple	20	55
O104	**18**	80pf. red and black	1·10	1·10
O105	**18**	80pf. green	20	3·50
O106	**18**	1m. red and orange	30	20
O107	**18**	1m.20 blue	1·60	1·60
O108	**18**	1m.25 red and purple	20	55
O109	**18**	1m.50 grey	40	65
O110	**18**	2m. red and grey	21·00	15·00
O111	**18**	2m. red	20	55
O112	**18**	2m.40 red and brown	1·60	3·50
O113	**18**	3m. red and purple	12·50	15·00
O114	**18**	3m. red	40	65
O122	**18**	4m. blue	30	65
O116	**18**	5m. green	40	65
O117	**18**	6m. red	40	65
O118	**18**	10m. orange	40	65
O119	**18**	20m. brown	40	65

1922. Stamps of Danzig optd D M.

O120a	**19**	5m. green, black and red (No. 91)	4·25	8·50
O126a	**25**	50m. red and blue	30	65
O142	**25**	50m. blue	30	1·10
O127a	**25**	100m. red and green	30	65
O143	**25**	100m. green	30	1·10
O144	**25**	200m. orange	30	1·10
O145	**29**	300m. red and green	30	65
O146	**29**	500m. red and grey	30	1·10
O147	**29**	1000m. red and brown	30	1·10

1922. No. 96 optd D M.

O121	**18**	6 on 3m. red	40	1·10

1924. Optd Dienst-marke.

O195	**39**	5pf. orange	2·75	4·25
O196	**39**	10pf. green	2·75	4·25
O197	**39**	15pf. grey	2·75	4·25
O198	**39**	15pf. red	23·00	12·50
O199	**39**	20pf. red and carmine	2·75	2·75
O200	**39**	25pf. red and black	23·00	34·00
O201	**39**	30pf. red and green	3·75	4·75
O202	**39**	35f. blue	65·00	65·00
O203	**39**	40pf. blue and indigo	8·50	10·50
O204	**39**	50pf. red and blue	26·00	55·00
O205	**39**	75pf. red and purple	48·00	£150

POSTAGE DUE STAMPS

D20

1921. Value in "pfennig" (figures only).

D94	**D20**	10pf. purple	40	65
D95	**D20**	20pf. purple	40	65
D96	**D20**	40pf. purple	40	65
D97	**D20**	60pf. purple	40	65
D98	**D20**	75pf. purple	40	65
D99	**D20**	80pf. purple	40	65
D112	**D20**	100pf. purple	1·10	1·10
D100	**D20**	120pf. purple	40	65
D101	**D20**	200pf. purple	40	1·40
D102	**D20**	240pf. purple	25	1·10
D114	**D20**	300pf. purple	1·10	1·10
D115	**D20**	400pf. purple	1·10	1·10
D116	**D20**	500pf. purple	1·10	1·40
D117	**D20**	800pf. purple	1·80	5·25

Value in "marks" ("M" after figure).

D118a	**D 20**	10m. purple	1·10	1·10
D119a	**D 20**	20m. purple	1·10	1·10
D120a	**D 20**	50m. purple	1·10	1·10
D121	**D 20**	100m. purple	1·10	1·40
D122	**D 20**	500m. purple	1·10	1·40

1923. Surch with figures and bar.

D162	1000 on 100m. pur	£160	
D163	5000 on 50m. purple	55	1·10
D164	10000 on 20m. pur	55	1·10
D165	50000 on 500m. pur	55	1·10
D166	100000 on 20m. pur	1·10	1·60

D39

1924

D178	**D39**	5pf. blue and black	1·10	1·10
D179	**D39**	10pf. blue and black	55	1·10
D180	**D39**	15pf. blue and black	1·60	2·10
D181	**D39**	20pf. blue and black	1·70	2·75
D182	**D39**	30pf. blue and black	10·50	2·75
D183	**D39**	40pf. blue and black	3·00	4·25
D184	**D39**	50pf. blue and black	3·00	3·25
D185	**D39**	60pf. blue and black	16·00	25·00
D186	**D39**	100pf. blue and black	23·00	13·50
D187	**D39**	3g. blue and red	11·50	65·00

1932. Surch in figures over bar.

D226	**D 39**	5 on 40pf. blue & blk	3·75	9·50
D227	**D 39**	10 on 60pf. bl & blk	42·00	12·50
D228	**D 39**	20 on 100pf. bl & blk	3·50	9·50

Pt. 6

DEDEAGATZ

Former French Post Office, closed in August 1914. Dedeagatz was part of Turkey to 1913, then a Bulgarian town.

25 centimes = 1 piastre.

1893. Stamps of France optd Dedeagh or surch also in figures and words.

59	**10**	5c. green	7·00	11·00
60	**10**	10c. black on lilac	32·00	28·00
62a	**10**	15c. blue	26·00	27·00
63	**10**	1pi. on 25c. black on red	50·00	17·00
64	**10**	2pi. on 50c. red	55·00	50·00
65	**10**	4pi. on 1f. olive	75·00	60·00
66	**10**	8pi. on 2f. brn on blue	85·00	85·00

1902. "Blanc", "Mouchon" and "Merson" key-types inscr "DEDEAGH". Some surch in figures and words.

67a	**A**	5c. green	2·75	6·00
68	**B**	10c. red	1·40	2·00
70	**B**	15c. orange	3·25	4·00
71	**B**	1pi. on 25c. blue	3·75	4·00
72	**C**	2pi. on 50c. brown & lav	5·50	14·50
73	**C**	4pi. on 1f. red and green	8·75	9·25
74	**C**	8pi. on 2f. lilac & yellow	11·00	12·00

Pt. 11

DENMARK

A kingdom in N. Europe, on a peninsula between the Baltic and the North Sea.

1851. 96 rigsbank skilling = 1 rigsdaler.
1875. 100 ore = 1 krone.

1

2

1851. Imperf.

3	**1**	2r.b.s. blue	£2750	£1000
4	**2**	4r.b.s. brown	£650	37·00

4

1854. Dotted background. Brown burelage. Imperf.

8	**4**	2sk. blue	65·00	55·00
9b	**4**	4sk. orange	£500	9·75
12	**4**	8sk. green	£275	75·00
13	**4**	16sk. lilac	£450	£190

5

1858. Background of wavy lines. Brown burelage. Imperf.

15	**5**	4sk. brown	70·00	9·75
18	**5**	8sk. green	£650	£110

1863. Brown burelage. Roul.

20		4sk. brown	£110	14·00
21	**4**	16sk. mauve	£1300	£600

7

1864. Perf.

22	**7**	2sk. blue	60·00	35·00
25	**7**	3sk. mauve	80·00	65·00
28	**7**	4sk. red	41·00	7·50
29	**7**	8sk. bistre	£300	£130
30a	**7**	16sk. green	£475	£130

8

1870. Value in "skilling".

37	**8**	48sk. lilac and brown	£425	£225
39	**8**	2sk. blue and grey	50·00	25·00
42	**8**	3sk. purple and grey	90·00	85·00
44	**8**	4sk. red and grey	43·00	7·50
46	**8**	8sk. brown and grey	£190	65·00
48	**8**	16sk. green and grey	£225	£140

1875. As T 8, but value in "ore".

56	5ore blue and red	28·00	55·00
72	20ore grey and red	95·00	26·00
80	3ore grey and blue	4·00	2·40
81	4ore blue and grey	4·25	40
82	8ore red and grey	4·25	40
83	12ore purple and grey	5·00	3·25
84	16ore brown and grey	17·00	3·25
85	25ore green and grey	9·00	3·50
86	50ore purple and brown	27·00	17·00
87	100ore orange and grey	27·00	10·00

10

1882

96	**10**	1ore orange	70	50
97	**10**	5ore green	4·25	20
98	**10**	10ore red	3·50	20
99	**10**	15ore mauve	11·50	1·10
100	**10**	20ore blue	18·00	3·00
101	**10**	24ore brown	6·75	4·25

1904. No. 82 and 101 surch.

102	**8**	4ore on 8ore red & grey	2·30	3·75
103	**10**	15ore on 24ore brown	3·50	5·75

14 King Christian IX

1904

104	**14**	10ore red	1·70	35
105	**14**	20ore blue	14·50	1·90
106	**14**	25ore brown	17·00	4·25
107	**14**	50ore lilac	60·00	60·00
108	**14**	100ore brown	9·00	33·00
119	**14**	5ore green	2·75	20

15

1905. Solid background.

173	**15**	1ore orange	30	25
174	**15**	2ore red	2·75	30
175	**15**	3ore grey	4·00	35
176	**15**	4ore blue	5·75	40
177	**15**	5ore brown	90	25
178	**15**	5ore green	2·20	25
179	**15**	7ore green	4·00	5·00
180	**15**	7ore violet	18·00	3·25
181	**15**	8ore grey	7·25	2·20
114	**15**	10ore pink	4·25	25
182	**15**	10ore green	1·20	25
183	**15**	10ore brown	3·00	25
184	**15**	12ore lilac	25·00	6·00
115	**15**	15ore mauve	14·00	70
116	**15**	20ore blue	28·00	75

For stamps with lined background but without hearts, see Nos. 265/76k.

17 King Frederik VIII

1907

121	**17**	5ore green	1·00	20
122	**17**	10ore red	2·50	20
124	**17**	20ore blue	9·25	1·70
125	**17**	25ore brown	22·00	80
127	**17**	35ore orange	3·50	3·00
128	**17**	50ore purple	22·00	4·25
130	**17**	100ore brown	75·00	2·75

1912. (a) Nos. 84 and 72 surch 35 ORE.

131	**8**	35ore on 16ore brn & grey	9·75	31·00
132	**8**	35ore on 20ore grey and red	18·00	44·00

(b) No. O98 surch 35 ORE FRIMAERKE.

133	**O9**	35ore on 32ore green	17·00	55·00

20 G.P.O., Copenhagen

1912

134	**20**	5k. red	£200	90·00

21 King Christian X

22

1913

135	**21**	5ore green	85	20
136	**21**	7ore orange	2·00	80
137	**21**	8ore grey	6·75	3·25
138	**21**	10ore red	1·30	20
139	**21**	12ore grey	5·25	5·75
141a	**21**	15ore mauve	1·50	20
142	**21**	20ore blue	7·75	35
143	**21**	20ore brown	1·00	25
144	**21**	20ore red	1·40	25
145	**21**	25ore brown	9·50	40
146	**21**	25ore black and brown	55·00	4·25
147	**21**	25ore red	3·50	80
148	**21**	25ore green	3·25	40
149	**21**	27ore black and red	20·00	32·00
150	**21**	30ore black and green	39·00	1·60
151	**21**	30ore orange	3·25	1·20
152	**21**	30ore blue	1·60	40
153	**21**	35ore yellow	15·00	2·40
154	**21**	35ore black and yellow	5·00	3·25
155	**21**	40ore black and violet	12·00	2·40
156	**21**	40ore blue	4·00	80
157	**21**	40ore yellow	1·40	80
158	**21**	50ore purple	25·00	3·25
159	**21**	50ore black and purple	43·00	80
160a	**21**	50ore grey	6·75	40
161	**21**	60ore blue and brown	36·00	3·25
162	**21**	60ore blue	6·75	75
163	**21**	70ore green and brown	17·00	2·40
164	**21**	80ore green	30·00	8·75
165	**21**	90ore red and brown	10·50	2·40
166	**22**	1k. brown	65·00	80
167	**21**	1k. blue and brown	34·00	1·20
168	**22**	2k. black	95·00	4·75
169	**21**	2k. purple and grey	45·00	11·50
170	**22**	5k. violet	10·50	5·75
171	**21**	5k. brown and mauve	5·75	4·00
172	**21**	10k. green and red	£180	24·00

1915. (a) No. O94 surch DANMARK 80 ORE POSTFRIM.

186	**O9**	80ore on 8ore red	28·00	80·00

(b) No. 83 surch 80 ORE.

187	**8**	80ore on 12ore pur & grey	27·00	75·00

1918. Newspaper stamps surch POSTFRIM. ORE 27 ORE DANMARK.

197	**N18**	27ore on 1ore green	2·75	6·50
198	**N18**	27ore on 5ore blue	7·00	14·50
199	**N18**	27ore on 7ore red	2·75	6·50
200	**N18**	27ore on 8ore green	4·00	8·00
201	**N18**	27ore on 10ore lilac	2·75	5·75
202	**N18**	27ore on 20ore green	4·00	8·00
203	**N18**	27ore on 29ore orge	2·75	5·75
204	**N18**	27ore on 38ore orge	23·00	60·00
205	**N18**	27ore on 41ore brn	6·50	29·00
194	**N18**	27ore on 68ore brn	5·50	16·00
206	**N18**	27ore on 1k. pur & grn	2·50	6·50
195	**N18**	27ore on 5k. grn & pk	5·00	13·50
196	**N18**	27ore on 10k. bl & stone	5·50	18·00

1919. No. 135 surch 2 ORE.

207	**21**	2ore on 5ore green	£950	£650

27 Castle of Kronborg, Elsinore

29 Roskilde Cathedral

1920. Recovery of Northern Schleswig.

208	**27**	10ore red	4·00	25
209	**27**	10ore green	7·50	35
210	**-**	20ore slate	3·50	25
211	**29**	40ore brown	11·50	3·50
212	**29**	40ore blue	43·00	6·50

DESIGN—HORIZ: 20ore Sonderborg Castle.

1921. Nos. 136 and 139 surch 8 8.

217	**21**	8 on 7ore orange	1·70	2·40
213	**21**	8 on 12ore green	1·70	5·25

1921. Red Cross. Nos. 209/10 surch with figure of value between red crosses.

214	**27**	10ore+5ore green	17·00	40·00
215	**-**	20ore+10ore grey	20·00	44·00

1921. No. 175 surch 8.

216	**15**	8 on 3ore grey	2·75	2·40

33 King Christian IV

34 King Christian X

1924. 300th Anniv of Danish Post. A. Head facing to left.

218A	**33**	10ore green	6·50	4·75
221A	**34**	10ore green	6·50	4·75
219A	**33**	15ore mauve	6·50	4·75
222A	**34**	15ore mauve	6·50	4·75
220A	**33**	20ore brown	6·50	4·75
223A	**34**	20ore brown	6·50	4·75

B. Head facing to right.

218B	**33**	10ore green	6·50	4·75
221B	**34**	10ore green	6·50	4·75
219B	**33**	15ore mauve	6·50	4·75
222B	**34**	15ore mauve	6·50	4·75
220B	**33**	20ore brown	6·50	4·75
223B	**34**	20ore brown	6·50	4·75

35

1925. Air.

224	**35**	10ore green	28·00	34·00
225	**35**	15ore lilac	55·00	55·00
226	**35**	25ore red	39·00	55·00
227	**35**	50ore grey	£110	£120
228	**35**	1k. brown	£110	£120

1926. Surch 20 20.

229	**21**	20 on 30ore orange	4·00	10·00
230	**21**	20 on 40ore blue	4·50	11·50

38

39

1926. 75th Anniv of First Danish stamps.

231	**38**	10ore olive	85	40
232	**39**	20ore red	1·40	40
233	**39**	30ore blue	5·00	1·40

1926. Various stamps surch.

234	**15**	7 on 8ore grey	1·40	2·75
235	**21**	7 on 20ore red	55	1·40
236	**21**	7 on 27ore black & red	3·50	10·00
237	**21**	12 on 15ore lilac	2·40	3·25

1926. Official stamps surch DANMARK 7 ORE POSTFRIM.

238	**O9**	7ore on 1ore orange	4·00	10·50
239	**O9**	7ore on 3ore grey	9·00	19·00
240	**O9**	7ore on 4ore blue	4·00	10·00
241	**O9**	7ore on 5ore green	45·00	75·00
242	**O9**	7ore on 10ore green	4·00	10·50
243	**O9**	7ore on 15ore lilac	4·25	10·50
244	**O9**	7ore on 20ore blue	19·00	43·00

40 Caravel

1927. Solid background.

246	**40**	15ore red	4·50	20
247	**40**	20ore grey	10·00	1·80
248	**40**	25ore blue	80	35
249	**40**	30ore yellow	1·00	35
250	**40**	35ore red	17·00	1·00
251	**40**	40ore green	16·00	35

For stamps with lined background see Nos. 277b, etc.

41

1929. Danish Cancer Research Fund.

252	**41**	10ore (+5ore) green	4·25	5·50
253	**41**	15ore (+5ore) red	8·25	10·50
254	**41**	25ore (+5ore) blue	31·00	37·00

42 King Christian X

1930. 60th Birthday of King Christian X.

255	**42**	5ore green	2·75	20
256	**42**	7ore violet	6·75	3·00
257	**42**	8ore grey	23·00	20·00
258	**42**	10ore brown	4·25	15
259	**42**	15ore red	8·00	15
260	**42**	20ore grey	23·00	5·75
261	**42**	25ore blue	7·25	1·20
262	**42**	30ore yellow	9·00	1·90
263	**42**	35ore red	10·00	3·50
264	**42**	40ore green	9·00	1·10

43 Numeral

1933. Lined background.

265	**43**	1ore green	20	20
266	**43**	2ore red	20	20
267	**43**	4ore blue	35	20
268	**43**	5ore green	1·10	25
268c	**43**	5ore purple	20	15
268d	**43**	5ore orange	20	15
268e	**43**	6ore orange	30	20
269	**43**	7ore violet	1·80	25
269a	**43**	7ore green	1·60	45
269b	**43**	7ore brown	30	25
270	**43**	8ore grey	50	20
270a	**43**	8ore green	30	20
271	**43**	10ore orange	8·75	25
271b	**43**	10ore brown	6·50	15
271c	**43**	10ore violet	60	20
271d	**43**	10ore green	20	15
272	**43**	12ore green	30	25
272a	**43**	15ore green	25	15
272c	**43**	20ore blue	20	15
272e	**43**	25ore green	40	15
272f	**43**	25ore blue	25	15
273	**43**	30ore green	20	15
273a	**43**	30ore orange	25	15
273c	**43**	40ore orange	25	15
273d	**43**	40ore purple	20	20
274	**43**	50ore brown	20	15
274d	**43**	60ore green	1·40	40
274e	**43**	60ore grey	60	55
275	**43**	70ore red	75	20
275a	**43**	70ore green	30	20
275d	**43**	80ore green	35	20
275e	**43**	80ore brown	50	30
276	**43**	100ore green	45	20
276a	**43**	100ore blue	40	15
276b	**43**	125ore brown	55	25
276c	**43**	150ore green	55	30
276ca	**43**	150ore violet	45	30
276d	**43**	200ore green	50	20
276e	**43**	230ore green	95	40
276f	**43**	250ore green	95	30
276g	**43**	270ore green	75	35
276h	**43**	300ore green	90	20
276i	**43**	325ore green	1·20	65
276j	**43**	350ore green	1·10	40
276k	**43**	375ore green	1·10	30
276l	**43**	400ore green	75	45

45 King Christian X

1933. T 40 with lined background.

277b	**40**	15ore red	2·75	20
277de	**40**	15ore green	5·75	60
278a	**40**	20ore grey	3·75	20
278b	**40**	20ore red	90	50
279	**40**	25ore blue	75·00	19·00
279ab	**40**	25ore brown	95	25
280a	**40**	30ore orange	65	20
280b	**40**	30ore blue	1·60	20
281	**40**	35ore violet	65	25
282	**40**	40ore green	3·75	20
282b	**40**	40ore blue	1·30	20
283	**45**	50ore grey	1·40	20
283a	**45**	60ore green	2·75	20
283b	**45**	75ore blue	50	25
284	**45**	1k. brown	4·00	20
284a	**45**	2k. red	5·75	85
284b	**45**	5k. violet	10·00	2·40

1934. Nos. 279 and 280a surch.

285	**40**	4 on 25ore blue	65	40
286	**40**	10 on 30ore orange	2·75	2·20

47 Fokker FVIIa over Copenhagen

1934. Air.

287	**47**	10ore orange	85	1·10
288	**47**	15ore red	3·25	4·50
289	**47**	20ore green	3·75	5·00
290	**47**	50ore green	3·75	5·00
291	**47**	1k. brown	13·00	17·00

49 Hans Andersen

1935. Centenary of Hans Andersen's Fairy Tales.

292	**-**	5ore green	4·25	20
293	**49**	7ore violet	3·00	2·75
294	**-**	10ore orange	6·50	20
295	**49**	15ore red	15·00	20
296	**49**	20ore grey	15·00	1·10
297	**49**	30ore blue	2·75	35

DESIGNS: 5ore "The Ugly Duckling"; 10ore "The Little Mermaid".

51 St. Nicholas's Church, Copenhagen

52 Hans Tausen

53 Ribe Cathedral

1936. 400th Anniv of Reformation.

298	**51**	5ore green	1·40	20
299	**51**	7ore mauve	1·70	3·00
300	**52**	10ore brown	2·10	20
301	**52**	15ore red	3·00	20
302	**53**	30ore blue	15·00	95

54 Dybbol Mill

1937. H. P. Hanssen (North Schleswig patriot) Memorial Fund.

303	**54**	5ore+5ore green	70	1·10
304	**54**	10ore+5ore brown	3·25	5·75
305	**54**	15ore+5ore red	3·25	5·75

56 King Christian X

1937. Silver Jubilee of King Christian X.

306	-	5ore green	1·40	20
307	**56**	10ore brown	1·40	20
308	-	15ore red	1·40	20
309	**56**	30ore blue	20·00	1·90

DESIGNS—HORIZ: 5ore Marselisborg Castle and "Rita" (King's yacht); 15ore Amalienborg Castle.

1937. Copenhagen Philatelic Club's 50th Anniv Stamp Exhibition. No. 271b optd K.P.K. 17.-26. SEPT. 19 37 (="Kobenhavns Philatelist Klub").

310	**43**	10ore brown	1·40	1·60

58 Emancipation Monument

1938. 150th Anniv of Abolition of Villeinage.

311	**58**	15ore red	70	20

59 B. Thorvaldsen

1938. Centenary of Return of Sculptor Thorvaldsen to Denmark.

312	**59**	5ore purple	30	20
313	-	10ore violet	45	20
314	**59**	30ore blue	1·90	60

DESIGN: 10ore Statue of Jason.

61 Queen Alexandrine

1939. Red Cross Charity. Cross in red.

314a	**61**	5ore+3ore purple	30	35
315	**61**	10ore+5ore violet	30	20
316	**61**	15ore+5ore red	35	40

1940. Stamps of 1933 (lined background) surch.

317	**43**	6 on 7ore green	25	25
318	**43**	6 on 8ore grey	25	20
319a	**40**	15 on 40ore green	95	95
320	**40**	20 on 15ore red	1·20	20
321	**40**	40 on 30ore blue	1·10	25

65 Queen Ingrid (when Princess) and Princess Margrethe

1941. Child Welfare.

322	**65**	10ore+5ore violet	30	25
323	**65**	20ore+5ore red	30	25

66 Bering's Ship "Sv. Pyotr"

1941. Death Bicent of Vitus Bering (explorer).

324	**66**	10ore violet	30	20
325	**66**	20ore brown	65	25
326	**66**	40ore blue	50	35

67 King Christian X

1942

327	**67**	10ore violet	20	15
328	**67**	15ore green	25	15
329	**67**	20ore red	30	15
330	**67**	25ore brown	50	30
331	**67**	30ore orange	40	15
332	**67**	35ore purple	40	30
333	**67**	40ore blue	50	15
333a	**67**	45ore olive	50	20
334	**67**	50ore grey	75	20
335	**67**	60ore green	55	20
335a	**67**	75ore blue	75	25

68 Round Tower of Trinity Church

1942. Tercentenary of the Round Tower.

336	**68**	10ore violet	30	20

69 Focke-Wulf Fw 200 Condor

1943. 25th Anniv of D.D.L. Danish Airlines.

337	**69**	20ore red	30	20

1944. Red Cross. No. 336 surch 5 and red cross.

338	**68**	10ore+5ore violet	30	20

70 Osterlars Church

1944. Danish Churches.

339	-	10ore violet	30	20
340	**70**	15ore green	30	25
341	-	20ore red	25	15

DESIGNS: 10ore Ejby Church; 20ore Hvidbjerg Church.

71 Ole Romer

1944. Birth Tercent of Romer (astronomer).

342	**71**	20ore brown	30	20

72 King Christian X

1945. King Christian's 75th Birthday.

343	**72**	10ore mauve	20	15
344	**72**	20ore red	30	15
345	**72**	40ore blue	55	25

73 Arms

1946

346	**73**	1k. brown	65	15
346a	**73**	1k.10 purple	4·00	1·30
346b	**73**	1k.20 grey	2·40	20
346c	**73**	1k.20 blue	1·20	25
346d	**73**	1k.25 orange	2·40	20
346e	**73**	1k.30 green	90	20
346f	**73**	1k.50 purple	1·30	15
346g	**73**	2k. red	1·30	15
347	**73**	2k.20 orange	2·00	20
347a	**73**	2k.50 olive	1·40	25
347b	**73**	2k.80 grey	1·70	25
347c	**73**	2k.80 olive	95	55
347d	**73**	2k.80 green	85	45
347e	**73**	2k.90 purple	3·25	25
347f	**73**	3k. green	80	15
347g	**73**	3k.10 purple	4·50	25
347h	**73**	3k.30 red	95	55
347i	**73**	3k.50 purple	1·50	25
347j	**73**	3k.50 blue	2·30	2·20
347k	**73**	4k. grey	1·00	25
347l	**73**	4k.10 brown	4·50	25
347m	**73**	4k.30 brown	3·00	3·25
347n	**73**	4k.30 green	3·75	3·75
347o	**73**	4k.50 brown	3·75	25
347p	**73**	4k.60 grey	3·00	3·25
347q	**73**	4k.70 purple	2·75	3·50
348	**73**	5k. blue	1·00	35
348a	**73**	5k.50 blue	2·00	75
348b	**73**	6k. black	1·40	15
348c	**73**	6k.50 green	1·70	45
348d	**73**	6k.60 green	3·00	3·25
348e	**73**	7k. mauve	1·70	20
348f	**73**	7k.10 purple	2·10	1·80
348g	**73**	7k.30 green	3·50	3·50
348h	**73**	7k.50 green	2·00	1·90
348i	**73**	7k.70 purple	2·75	1·30
348j	**73**	8k. orange	1·90	30
348k	**73**	9k. brown	2·00	20
348l	**73**	10k. yellow	2·20	25
348la	**73**	10k.50 blue	3·25	85
348m	**73**	11k. brown	3·75	1·60
348ma	**73**	11k.50 blue	3·00	2·10
348n	**73**	12k. brown	3·25	45
348o	**73**	14k. brown	4·00	55
348p	**73**	16k. red	4·25	45
348q	**73**	17k. red	6·00	95
348r	**73**	18k. brown	7·00	85
348s	**73**	20k. blue	4·50	45
348t	**73**	22k. red	5·00	1·00
348u	**73**	23k. green	6·50	1·10
348v	**73**	24k. green	6·50	85
348w	**73**	25k. green	5·75	30
348x	**73**	26k. green	8·25	1·40
348z	**73**	50k. red	11·50	1·80

74 Tycho Brahe

1946. 400th Birth Anniv of Tycho Brahe (astronomer).

349	**74**	20ore red	35	20

75 Symbols of Freedom

1947. Liberation Fund.

350	**75**	15ore+5ore green	50	30
351	-	20ore+5ore red (Bombed railways)	50	30
352	-	40ore+5ore blue (Flag)	1·00	90

77 Class H Steam Goods Train

1947. Centenary of Danish Railways.

353		15ore green	50	20
354	**77**	20ore red	70	20
355	-	40ore blue	2·75	1·30

DESIGNS—HORIZ: 15ore First Danish locomotive "Odin"; 40ore Diesel-electric train "Lyntog" and train ferry "Fyn".

79 I. C. Jacobsen

1947. 60th Death Anniv of Jacobsen and Centenary of Carlsberg Foundation for Promotion of Scientific Research.

356	**79**	20ore red	30	10

80 King Frederick IX

1948

357a	**80**	15ore green	85	20
358	**80**	15ore violet	50	15
359a	**80**	20ore red	55	15
360	**80**	20ore brown	30	15
361	**80**	25ore brown	1·00	15
362	**80**	25ore red	3·25	15
362a	**80**	25ore blue	70	25
362b	**80**	25ore violet	25	20
363	**80**	30ore orange	9·25	30
363b	**80**	30ore red	40	25
364	**80**	35ore green	40	30
365	**80**	40ore blue	3·25	60
366	**80**	40ore grey	75	15
367	**80**	45ore bistre	1·20	15
368	**80**	50ore grey	1·20	15
369	**80**	50ore blue	2·20	20
369a	**80**	50ore green	40	25
370	**80**	55ore brown	20·00	1·40
371a	**80**	60ore blue	50	25
371b	**80**	65ore grey	40	20
372	**80**	70ore green	1·70	15
373	**80**	75ore purple	1·10	15
373a	**80**	80ore orange	70	25
373b	**80**	90ore bistre	2·75	25
373c	**80**	95ore orange	60	25

81 "The Constituent Assembly of the Kingdom" (after Constantin Hansen)

1949. Centenary of Danish Constitution.

374	**81**	20ore brown	35	20

82 Globe

1949. 75th Anniv of U.P.U.

375	**82**	40ore blue	50	40

83 Kalundborg Transmitter

1950. 25th Anniv of State Broadcasting.

376	**83**	20ore brown	35	20

84 Princess Anne-Marie

1950. National Children's Welfare Assn.

377	**84**	25ore+5ore red	55	55

85 "Fredericus Quartus" (warship)

1951. 250th Anniv of Naval Officers' College.

378	**85**	25ore red	55	30
379	**85**	50ore blue	3·00	60

86 H. C. Oersted (after C. A. Jensen)

1951. Death Centenary of Oersted (physicist).

380	**86**	50ore blue	1·20	55

87 Mail Coach

1951. Danish Stamp Centenary.

381	**87**	15ore violet	50	25
382	**87**	25ore red	50	25

88 Hospital Ship "Jutlandia"

1951. Danish Red Cross Fund.

383	**88**	25ore +5ore red	60	60

89 "Life-Saving" (relief, H. Solomon)

1952. Centenary of Danish Life-Saving Service.

384	**89**	25ore red	40	30

1953. Netherlands Flood Relief Fund. Surch NL+10.

385	**80**	30ore+10ore red	1·10	1·00

91 Memorial Stone, Skamlings-banken

1953. Danish Border Union Fund.

386	**91**	30ore+5ore red	1·10	1·10

92 Runic Stone at Jelling

1953. 1,000 years of Danish Kingdom. Inscr "KONGERIGE i 1000 AR". (a) 1st series.

387	**92**	10ore green	25	20
388	-	15ore lilac	25	20
389	-	20ore brown	25	20
390	-	30ore red	25	20
391	-	60ore blue	35	20

DESIGNS: 15ore Vikings' camp, Trelleborg; 20ore Kalundborg Church; 30ore Nyborg Castle; 60ore Goose Tower, Vordinborg.

(b) 2nd series.

392	10ore green	25	15
393	15ore lilac	25	15
394	20ore brown	25	15
395	30ore red	25	15
396	60ore blue	55	20

DESIGNS: 10ore Spottrup Castle; 15ore Hammershus Castle; 20ore Copenhagen Stock Exchange; 30ore King Frederik V statue; 60ore Soldier's Statue (H. V. Bissen).

93 Telegraph Table, 1854

1954. Telecommunications Centenary.

397	**93**	30ore brown	30	25

94 Head of Statue of King Frederik V at Amalienborg

1954. Bicent of Royal Academy of Fine Arts.

398	**94**	30ore red	50	35

1955. Liberty Fund. Nos. 350/1 surch.

399	**75**	20+5 on 15ore +5ore grn	50	35
400	-	30+5 on 20ore +5ore red	1·10	1·10

1955. Nos. 268e, 269b, 359a and 362 surch.

401	**43**	5ore on 6ore orange	1·10	1·10
402	**43**	5ore on 7ore brown	15	15
403	**80**	30ore on 20ore red	15	15
404	**80**	30ore on 25ore red	50	30

98 S. Kierkegaard (philosopher)

1955. Death Centenary of Kierkegaard.

405	**98**	30ore red	30	20

99 Ellehammer 11 Aircraft

1956. 50th Anniv of 1st Flight by J. C. H. Ellehammer.

406	**99**	30ore red	45	20

100 Whooper Swans

1956. Northern Countries' Day.

407	**100**	30ore red	1·50	15
408	**100**	60ore blue	1·20	70

1957. Danish Red Cross Hungarian Relief Fund. No. 373c surch Ungarns-hjaelpen 30 + 5.

409	**80**	30ore+5ore on 95ore orange	50	45

102 National Museum

1957. 150th Anniv of National Museum.

410	**102**	30ore red	65	15
411	-	60ore blue	70	50

DESIGN: 50ore "Sun-God's Chariot" (bronze age model).

103 Harvester

1958. Centenary of Danish Royal Veterinary and Agricultural College.

412	**103**	30ore red	25	20

1959. Greenland Fund. No. 363b surch Gronlands-fonden + 10.

413	**80**	30ore+10ore red	75	70

The Greenland Fund was devoted to the relatives of the crew and passengers of the "Hans Hedtoft", the Greenland vessel lost at sea on 30 January 1959.

105 King Frederik IX

1959. 60th Birthday of King Frederik IX.

414	**105**	30ore red	30	15
415	**105**	35ore purple	40	25
416	**105**	60ore blue	40	25

106 Margrethe Schanne in "La Sylphide"

1959. Danish Ballet and Music Festival, 1959.

417	**106**	35ore purple	25	20

See also Nos. 445 and 467.

107

1959. Centenary of Red Cross.

418	**107**	30ore+5ore red	50	45
419	**107**	60ore+5ore red & blue	65	60

1960. World Refugee Year. Surch 30 Verdensflygtningearet 1959-60 and uprooted tree.

420	**80**	30ore on 15ore violet	20	15

109 Sowing Machine

1960. 1st Danish Food Fair.

421	**109**	12ore green	20	15
422	-	30ore red	25	15
423	-	60ore blue	50	35

DESIGNS: 30ore Combine-harvester; 60ore Plough.

110 King Frederik and Queen Ingrid

1960. Royal Silver Wedding.

424	**110**	30ore red	35	15
425	**110**	60ore blue	50	45

111 Ancient Bascule Light

1960. 400th Anniv of Danish Lighthouse Service.

426	**111**	30ore red	30	20

112 N. Finsen

1960. Birth Cent of Niels R. Finsen (physician).

427	**112**	30ore red	25	20

113 Mother and Child

1960. W.H.O. 10th European Regional Committee Meeting.

428	**113**	60ore blue	50	40

113a Conference Emblem

1960. Europa.

429	**113a**	60ore blue	65	55

114 Queen Ingrid

1960. 25th Year of Queen Ingrid's Service in Girl Guides.

430	**114**	30ore+10ore red	1·00	95

115 Douglas DC-8

1961. 10th Anniv of Scandinavian Airlines System (SAS).

431	**115**	60ore blue	75	35

116 Coastal Scene

1961. 50th Anniv of Society for Preservation of Danish National Amenities.

432	**116**	30ore red	20	20

117 King Frederik IX

1961

433	**117**	20ore brown	35	15
434	**117**	25ore brown	25	15
435	**117**	30ore red	45	15
436	**117**	35ore green	55	35
437	**117**	35ore red	25	15
438	**117**	40ore grey	1·00	15
438a	**117**	40ore brown	25	15
439	**117**	50ore turquoise	45	15
439a	**117**	50ore red	70	15
439b	**117**	50ore brown	55	15
440	**117**	60ore blue	80	15
440a	**117**	60ore red	55	20
441	**117**	70ore green	1·00	20
442	**117**	80ore orange	1·00	15
442a	**117**	80ore blue	70	45
442b	**117**	80ore green	55	15
443	**117**	90ore olive	3·50	20
443a	**117**	90ore blue	55	30
444	**117**	95ore purple	80	65

1962. Danish Ballet and Music Festival, 1962. As T 106 but inscr "15–31 MAJ".

445	60ore blue	25	20

118 Borkop Watermill

1962. "Dansk Fredning" (Preservation of Danish Natural Amenities and Ancient Monuments) and Centenary of Abolition of Mill Monopolies.

446	**118**	10ore brown	20	20

119 African Mother and Child

1962. Aid for Under-developed Countries.

447	**119**	30ore+10ore red	85	85

120 "Selandia"

1962. 50th Anniv of Freighter "Selandia".

448	**120**	60ore blue	1·50	1·10

121 "Tivoli"

1962. 150th Birth Anniv of George Carstensen (founder of Tivoli Pleasure Gardens, Copenhagen).

449	**121**	35ore purple	25	20

122 Cliffs, Island of Mon

1962. "Dansk Fredning" (Preservation of Danish Natural Amenities and Ancient Monuments).

450	**122**	20ore brown	20	15

123 Wheat

1963. Freedom from Hunger.

451	**123**	35ore red	20	20

124 Rail and Sea Symbols

1963. Opening of Denmark–Germany Railway ("Bird-flight Line").

452	**124**	15ore green	25	20

125 19th-century Mail Transport

1963. Centenary of Paris Postal Conference.

453	**125**	60ore blue	35	30

126 Hands

1963. Danish Cripples Foundation Fund.

454	**126**	35ore+10ore red	85	85

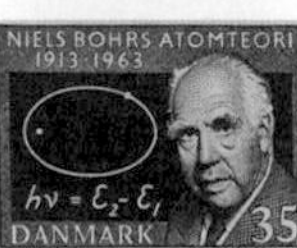

127 Prof. Niels Bohr

1963. 50th Anniv of Bohr's Atomic Theory.

455	**127**	35ore red	25	15
456	**127**	60ore blue	65	30

128 Ancient Bridge, Immervad

1964. Danish Border Union Fund.

457	**128**	35ore+10ore red	60	75

129 "Going to School" (child's slate)

1964. 150th Anniv of Institution of Primary Schools.

458	**129**	35ore brown	20	15

130 Princesses Margrethe, Benedikte and Anne-Marie

1964. Danish Red Cross Fund.

459	**130**	35ore+10ore red	50	45
460	**130**	60ore+10ore blue & red	85	85

131 "Exploration of the Sea"

1964. International Council for the Exploration of the Sea Conference, Copenhagen.

461	**131**	60ore blue	35	30

132 Danish Stamp "Watermarks, Perforations and Varieties"

1964. 25th Anniv of Stamp Day.

462	**132**	35ore pink	35	20

133 Landscape, R. Karup

1964. "Dansk Fredning" (Preservation of Danish Natural Amenities and Ancient Monuments).

463	**133**	25ore brown	20	20

134 Office Equipment

1965. Centenary of 1st Commercial School.

464	**134**	15ore green	20	20

135 Morse Key, Teleprinter Tape and I.T.U. Emblem

1965. Centenary of I.T.U.

465	**135**	80ore blue	40	25

136 C. Nielsen

1965. Birth Centenary of Carl Nielsen (composer).

466	**136**	50ore red	20	20

1965. Danish Ballet and Music Festival, 1965. As T 106 but inscr "15-31 MAJ".

467	50ore red	20	15

137 Child in Meadow

1965. Child Welfare.

468	**137**	50ore+10ore red	60	60

138 Bogo Windmill

1965. "Dansk Fredning" (Preservation of Danish Natural Amenities and Ancient Monuments).

469	**138**	40ore brown	20	15

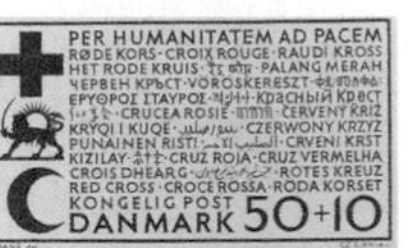

139 Titles of International Red Cross Organizations

1966. Danish Red Cross Fund.

470	**139**	50ore+10ore red	50	60
471	**139**	80ore+10ore bl & red	75	85

140 Heathland

1966. Centenary of Danish Heath Society.

472	**140**	25ore green	20	20

141 C. Kold

1966. 150th Birth Anniv of Christen Kold (educationist).

473	**141**	50ore red	20	15

142 Almshouses, Copenhagen

143 Trees at Bregentved

1966. "Dansk Fredning" (Preservation of Danish Natural Amenities and Ancient Monuments).

474	**142**	50ore red	20	20
475	**143**	80ore blue	35	30

144 G. Jensen

1966. Birth Cent of Georg Jensen (silversmith).

476	**144**	80ore blue	60	30

145 Fund Emblem

1966. "Refugee 66" Fund.

477	**145**	40ore+10ore brown	65	70
478	**145**	50ore+10ore red	60	65
479	**145**	80ore+10ore blue	1·10	1·10

146 Barrow in Jutland

1966. "Dansk Fredning" (Preservation of Danish Natural Amenities and Ancient Monuments).

480	**146**	1k.50 green	70	25

147 Musical Instruments

1967. Cent of Royal Danish Academy of Music.

481	**147**	50ore red	20	15

148 Cogwheels

1967. European Free Trade Assn.

482	**148**	80ore blue	75	25

149 Old City and Windmill

1967. 800th Anniv of Copenhagen.

483	**149**	25ore green	25	20
484	-	40ore brown	25	20
485	-	50ore brown	25	20
486	-	80ore blue	85	65

DESIGNS: 40ore Old bank and ship's masts; 50ore Church steeple and burgher's house; 80ore Building construction.

150 Princess Margrethe and Prince Henri de Monpezat

1967. Royal Wedding.

487	**150**	50ore red	30	20

151 H. C. Sonne

1967. 150th Anniv of Hans Sonne (founder of Danish Co-operative Movement).

488	**151**	60ore red	25	20

152 "Rose"

1967. The Salvation Army.

489	**152**	60ore+10ore red	55	55

153 Porpoise and Cross-anchor

1967. Centenary of Danish Seamen's Church in Foreign Ports.

490	**153**	90ore blue	45	35

154 Esbjerg Harbour

1968. Cent of Esbjerg Harbour Construction Act.

491	**154**	30ore green	20	15

155 Koldinghus Castle

1968. 700th Anniv of Koldinghus Castle.

492	**155**	60ore red	20	15

156 "The Children in the Round Tower" (Greenlandic legend)

1968. Greenlandic Child Welfare.

493	**156**	60ore+10ore red	60	60

157 Shipbuilding

1968. Danish Industries.

494	**157**	30ore green	20	15
495	-	50ore brown	20	15
496	-	60ore red	20	20
497	-	90ore blue	80	75

INDUSTRIES: 50ore Chemicals, 60ore Electric power, 90ore Engineering.

158 "The Sower"

1969. Bicentenary of Danish Royal Agricultural Society.

498	**158**	30ore green	20	15

159 Viking Ships (from old Swedish coin)

1969. 50th Anniv of Northern Countries' Union.

499	**159**	60ore red	70	30
500	**159**	90ore blue	1·10	1·10

160 King Frederik IX

1969. King Frederik's 70th Birthday.

501	**160**	50ore brown	25	25
502	**160**	60ore red	35	30

161 Colonnade

1969. Europa.

503	**161**	90ore blue	85	70

162 Kronborg Castle

1969. 50th Anniv of "Danes Living Abroad" Association.

504	**162**	50ore brown	20	15

163 Fall of Danish Flag

1969. 750th Anniv of "Danish Flag Falling from Heaven".

505	**163**	60ore red, blue & black	25	20

164 M. A. Nexo

1969. Birth Cent of Martin Andersen Nexo (poet).

506	**164**	80ore green	40	20

165 Niels Stensen (geologist)

1969. 300th Anniv of Stensen's "On Solid Bodies".

507	**165**	1k. sepia	40	20

166 "Abstract"

1969. "Non-figurative" stamp.

508	**166**	60ore red, rose and blue	25	20

167 Symbolic "P"

1969. Birth Cent of Valdemar Poulsen (inventor).

509	**167**	30ore green	20	15

168 Princess Margrethe, Prince Henri and Prince Frederik (baby)

1969. Danish Red Cross.

510	**168**	50ore+10ore brn & red	55	60
511	**168**	60ore+10ore brn & red	55	60

169 "Postgiro"

1970. 50th Anniv of Danish Postal Giro Service.

512	**169**	60ore and orange	20	15

170 School Safety Patrol

1970. Road Safety.

513	**170**	50ore brown	30	30

171 Child appealing for Help

1970. 25th Anniv of Save the Children Fund.

514	**171**	60ore+10ore red	55	55

172 Candle in Window

1970. 25th Anniv of Liberation.

515	**172**	50ore black, yellow & bl	45	20

173 Red Deer in Park

1970. 300th Anniv of Jaegersborg Deer Park.

516	**173**	60ore brown, red & grn	20	15

174 Ship's Figurehead ("Elephanten")

1970. 300th Anniv of "Royal Majesty's Model Chamber" (Danish Naval Museum).

517	**174**	30ore multicoloured	20	15

175 "The Reunion"

1970. 50th Anniv of North Schleswig's Reunion with Denmark.

518	**175**	60ore violet, yellow & grn	20	15

176 Electromagnetic Apparatus

1970. 150th Anniv of Oersted's Discovery of Electromagnetism.

519	**176**	80ore green	40	20

177 Bronze-age Ship (from engraving on razor)

1970. Danish Shipping.

520	**177**	30ore purple and brown	25	15
521	-	50ore brn and purple	25	15
522	-	60ore brown and green	25	15
523	-	90ore blue and green	95	90

DESIGNS: 50ore Viking shipbuilders (Bayeux Tapestry); 60ore "Emanuel" (schooner); 90ore "A. P. Moller" (tanker).

178 Strands of Rope

1970. 25th Anniv of United Nations.

524	**178**	90ore red, green & blue	95	90

179 B. Thorvaldsen from self-portrait

1970. Birth Bicentenary of Bertel Thorvaldsen (sculptor).

525	**179**	2k. blue	65	45

180 Mathilde Fibiger (suffragette)

1971. Centenary of Danish Women's Association ("Kvindesamfund").

526	**180**	80ore green	40	25

181 Refugees

1971. Aid for Refugees.

527	**181**	50ore brown	30	20
528	**181**	60ore red	30	20

182 Danish Child

1971. National Children's Welfare Association.

529	**182**	60ore+10ore red	60	60

183 Hans Egede

1971. 250th Anniv of Hans Egede's Arrival in Greenland.

530	**183**	1k. brown	40	20

184 Swimming

1971. Sports.

531	**184**	30ore green and blue	25	20
532	-	50ore dp brown & brown	25	15
533	-	60ore yellow, blue & grey	50	20
534	-	90ore violet, green & bl	75	55

DESIGNS: 50ore Hurdling; 60ore Football; 90ore Yachting.

185 Georg Brandes

1971. Centenary of First Lectures by Georg Brandes (writer).

535	**185**	90ore blue	40	30

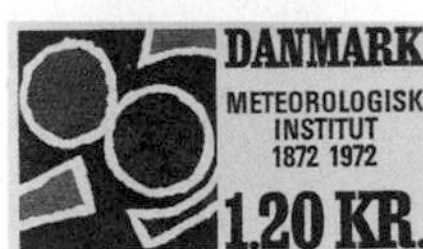

186 Beet Harvester

1972. Centenary of Danish Sugar Production.

536	**186**	80ore green	40	20

187 Meteorological Symbols

1972. Cent of Danish Meteorological Office.

537	**187**	1k.20 brown, blue & pur	65	60

188 King Frederik IX

1972. King Frederik IX-In Memoriam.

538	**188**	60ore red	20	15

189 "N. F. S. Grundtvig" (pencil sketch, P. Skovgaard)

1972. Death Centenary of N. F. S. Grundtvig (poet and clergyman).

539	**189**	1k. brown	50	45

190 Locomotive "Odin", Ship and Passengers

1972. 125th Anniv of Danish State Railways.

540	**190**	70ore red	30	20

191 Rebild Hills

1972. Nature Protection.

541	**191**	1k. green, brown & blue	45	25

192 Marsh Marigold

1972. Centenary of "Vanforehjemmet" (Home for the Disabled).

542	**192**	70ore+10ore yellow & bl	75	85

193 "The Tinker" (from Holberg's satire)

1972. 250th Anniv of Theatre in Denmark and of Holberg's Comedies.

543	**193**	70ore red	30	20

194 W.H.O. Building, Copenhagen

1972. Inauguration of World Health Organization Building, Copenhagen.

544	**194**	2k. black, blue and red	75	50

195 Little Belt Bridge

1972. Danish Construction Projects.

545	**195**	40ore green	25	20
546	-	60ore brown	30	20
547	-	70ore red	30	20
548	-	90ore green	45	40

DESIGNS: 60ore Hanstholm port; 70ore Limfjord Tunnel; 90ore Knudshoved port.

196 House, Aeroskobing

1972. Danish Architecture.

549	**196**	40ore black, brown & red	25	20
550	-	60ore blue, green & brn	25	20
551	-	70ore brown, red & verm	25	20
552	-	1k.20 grn, brn & dp brn	80	75

DESIGNS—28×21 mm: 60ore Farmhouse, East Bornholm; 37×21 mm: 1k.20, Farmhouse, Hvide Sande; 21×37 mm: 70ore House, Christanshavn.

197 Johannes Jensen

1973. Birth Cent of Johannes Jensen (writer).

553	**197**	90ore green	35	15

198 Cogwheels and Guardrails

1973. Centenary of 1st Danish Factory Act.

554	**198**	50ore brown	20	15

199 P. C. Abildgaard (founder)

1973. Bicentenary of Royal Veterinary College, Christianshavn.

555	**199**	1k. blue	45	35

200 "Rhododendron impeditum"

1973. Cent of Jutland Horticultural Society.

556	**200**	60ore violet, green & brn	45	20
557	-	70ore pink, green & red	45	20

DESIGN: 70ore "Queen of Denmark" rose.

201 Nordic House, Reykjavik

1973. Nordic Countries' Postal Co-operation.

558	**201**	70ore multicoloured	60	30
559	**201**	1k. multicoloured	1·30	1·10

202 Stella Nova and Sextant

1973. 400th Anniv of Tycho Brahe's "De Nove Stella" (book on astronomy).

560	**202**	2k. blue	60	25

203 "St. Mark the Evangelist" (Book of Dalby)

1973. 300th Anniv of Royal Library.

561	**203**	1k.20 multicoloured	70	65

204 Heimaey Eruption

1973. Aid for Victims of Heimaey Eruption, Iceland.

562	**204**	70ore+20ore red and blue	65	65

205 "Devil and Scandalmongers" (Fanefjord Church)

1973. Church Frescoes. Each red, turquoise and yellow on cream.

563		70ore Type **205**	1·10	30
564		70ore "Queen Esther and King Xerxes" (Tirsted Church)	1·10	30
565		70ore "The Harvest Miracle" (Jetsmark Church)	1·10	30

566		70ore "The Crowning with Thorns" (Biersted Church)	1·10	30
567		70ore "Creation of Eve" (Fanefjord Church)	1·10	30

206 Drop of Blood and Donors

1974. Blood Donors Campaign.

568	**206**	90ore red and violet	35	20

207 Queen Margrethe

1974

569	**207**	60ore brown	35	30
570	**207**	60ore orange	35	25
571	**207**	70ore red	25	15
572	**207**	70ore brown	25	20
573	**207**	80ore green	40	20
574	**207**	80ore brown	35	20
575	**207**	90ore purple	40	15
576	**207**	90ore red	40	15
577	**207**	90ore olive	40	25
577a	**207**	90ore grey	2·00	2·00
578	**207**	100ore blue	45	25
579	**207**	100ore grey	45	25
580	**207**	100ore red	45	20
580a	**207**	100ore brown	40	15
580b	**207**	110ore orange	60	40
580c	**207**	110ore brown	45	25
581	**207**	120ore grey	65	40
581b	**207**	120ore red	35	15
582	**207**	130ore blue	1·40	1·40
582a	**207**	130ore red	40	15
582b	**207**	130ore brown	45	40
582c	**207**	140ore orange	1·50	1·70
582d	**207**	150ore blue	70	55
582e	**207**	150ore red	55	50
582f	**207**	160ore blue	70	70
582g	**207**	160ore red	50	15
582h	**207**	180ore green	50	25
582i	**207**	180ore blue	95	90
582j	**207**	200ore blue	80	55
582k	**207**	210ore grey	1·60	1·80
582l	**207**	230ore green	70	30
582m	**207**	250ore green	85	60

208 Theatre Facade

1974. Centenary of Tivoli Pantomime Theatre, Copenhagen.

583	**208**	100ore blue	40	25

209 Hverringe

1974. Provincial Series.

584	**209**	50ore multicoloured	35	30
585	-	60ore grn, dp grn & mve	50	45
586	-	70ore multicoloured	45	45
587	-	90ore multicoloured	35	15
588	-	120ore grn, red & orge	50	45

DESIGNS—HORIZ: 60ore Carl Nielsen's birthplace, Norre Lyndelse; 70ore Hans Christian Andersen's birthplace, Odense; 1k.20, Hindsholm. VERT: 90ore Hessselagergaard.

210 Orienteering

1974. World Orienteering Championships.

589	**210**	70ore brown and blue	55	50
590	-	80ore blue and brown	25	25

DESIGN: 80ore Compass.

211 "Iris spuria"

1974. Cent of Botanical Gardens, Copenhagen.

591	**211**	90ore blue, green & brn	30	15
592	-	120ore red, green and blue	55	50

DESIGN: 120ore "Dactylorhiza purpurella" (orchid).

212 Mail-carriers of 1624 and 1780

1974. 350th Anniv of Danish Post Office.

593	**212**	70ore bistre and purple	35	30
594	-	90ore green and purple	35	25

DESIGN: 90ore Johan Colding's mail balloon (1808) H.M.S. "Edgar" and H.M.S. "Dictator".

213 Pigeon with Letter

1974. Centenary of U.P.U.

595	**213**	120ore blue	40	25

214 Stamp Essay (Arms)

1975. "Hafnia 76" Stamp Exhibition (1st issue). Sheet 67×93 mm containing T 214 and similar vert designs.

MS596		70ore grey and green; 80ore grey and green; 90ore brown and green; 100ore brown and green (sold at 5k.)	6·75	6·75

DESIGNS: 80ore King Frederik VII; 90ore King Frederik VII (different); 100ore Mercury.

See also Nos. **MS**617 and 629/**MS**630.

215 Radio Equipment of 1925

1975. 50th Anniv of Danish Broadcasting.

597	**215**	90ore pink	40	20

216 Queen Margrethe and I.W.Y. Emblem

1975. International Women's Year.

598	**216**	90ore+20ore red	80	80

217 Floral Decorated Plate

1975. Danish Porcelain.

599	**217**	50ore green	20	15
600	-	90ore red	40	15
601	-	130ore blue	85	85

DESIGNS: 90ore Floral decorated tureen; 130ore Floral decorated vase and tea-caddy.

218 Moravian Brethren Church Christiansfeld

1975. European Architectural Heritage Year.

602	**218**	70ore brown	50	45
603	-	120ore green	55	45
604	-	150ore blue	45	30

DESIGNS—HORIZ: 120ore Farmhouse, Lejre. VERT: 150ore Anna Queenstraede (street), Helsingore.

219 "Numskull Jack" (V. Pedersen)

1975. 170th Birth Anniv of Hans Christian Andersen.

605	**219**	70ore grey and brown	65	60
606	-	90ore brown and red	80	15
607	-	130ore brown and blue	1·30	1·50

DESIGNS: 90ore Hans Andersen (from photograph by G. E. Hansen); 130ore "The Marshking's Daughter" (L. Frolich).

220 Watchman's Square, Aabenraa

1975. Provincial series. South Jutland.

608	**220**	70ore multicoloured	40	30
609	-	90ore brown, red & blue	30	20
610	-	100ore multicoloured	40	25
611	-	120ore blue, black & grn	50	30

DESIGNS—VERT: 90ore, Haderslev Cathedral. HORIZ: 100ore, Mogeltonder Polder; 120ore, Estuary of Vidaaen at Hojer floodgates.

221 River Kingfisher

1975. Danish Endangered Animals.

612	**221**	50ore blue	40	30
613	-	70ore brown	40	30
614	-	90ore brown	40	15
615	-	130ore blue	1·10	95
616	-	200ore black	60	25

DESIGNS: 70ore West European hedgehog; 90ore Cats; 130ore Pied avocets; 200ore European otter.

The 90ore also commemorates the centenary of the Danish Society for the Prevention of Cruelty to Animals.

1975. "Hafnia 76" Stamp Exhibition (2nd issue). Sheet 69×93 mm containing vert designs similar to T 214 showing early Danish stamps.

MS617		50ore brown and buff; 70ore blue, brown and buff; 90ore blue, brown and buff; 130ore brown, olive and buff (sold at 5k.)	3·00	4·00

DESIGNS: 50ore 1851 4 R.B.S. stamp; 70ore 1851 2 R.B.S. stamp; 90ore 1864 2sk. stamp; 130ore 1870 8sk. stamp with inverted frame.

222 Viking Longship

1976. Bicentenary of American Revolution.

618	**222**	70ore+20ore brown	65	75
619	-	90ore+20ore red	65	75
620	-	100ore+20ore green	65	75
621	-	130ore+20ore blue	80	85

DESIGNS: 90ore Freighter "Thingvalla"; 100ore Liner "Frederik VIII"; 130ore Cadet full-rigged ship "Danmark".

223 "Humanity"

1976. Centenary of Danish Red Cross.

622	**223**	100ore+20ore black and red	40	45
623	**223**	130ore+20ore black, red and blue	55	60

224 Old Copenhagen

1976. Provincial Series. Copenhagen.

624	**224**	60ore multicoloured	35	25
625	-	80ore multicoloured	35	25
626	-	100ore red & vermilion	35	20
627	-	130ore grn, dp brn & brn	1·30	1·20

DESIGNS—VERT: 80ore View from the Round Tower; 100ore Interior of the Central Railway Station. HORIZ: 130ore Harbour buildings.

225 Handicapped Person in Wheelchair

1976. Danish Foundation for the Disabled.

628	**225**	100ore+20ore black and red	50	45

226 Mail Coach Driver (detail from "A String of Horses outside an Inn" (O. Bache))

1976. "Hafnia 76" Stamp Exhibition.

629	**226**	130ore multicoloured	1·00	95
MS630		103×82 mm. **226** 130ore multicoloured	9·50	11·00

227 Prof. Emil Hansen

1976. Centenary of Carlsberg Foundation.

631	**227**	100ore red	35	20

228 Moulding Glass

1976. Danish Glass Industry.

632	**228**	60ore green	25	25
633	-	80ore brown	25	20
634	-	130ore blue	75	70
635	-	150ore red	40	25

DESIGNS: 80ore Removing glass from pipe; 130ore Cutting glass; 150ore Blowing glass.

229 Five Water Lilies

1977. Northern Countries Co-operation in Nature Conservation and Environment Protection.

636	**229**	100ore multicoloured	40	30
637	**229**	130ore multicoloured	1·40	1·20

230 "Give Way"

1977. Road Safety.

638	**230**	100ore brown	45	20

231 Mother and Child

1977. 25th Anniv of Danish Society for the Mentally Handicapped.

639	**231**	100ore+20ore green, blue and brown	80	75

232 Allinge

1977. Europa.

640	**232**	1k. brown	45	15
641	-	1k.30 blue	4·50	3·25

DESIGN: 1k.30, Farm near Ringsted.

233 Kongeaen

1977. Provincial Series. South Jutland.

642	**233**	60ore green and blue	1·10	95
643	-	90ore multicoloured	60	45
644	-	150ore multicoloured	60	40
645	-	200ore grn, pur & emer	60	40

DESIGNS: 90ore Skallingen; 150ore Torskind; 200ore Jelling.

234 Hammers and Horseshoes

1977. Danish Crafts.

646	**234**	80ore brown	35	20
647	-	1k. red	35	20
648	-	1k.30 blue	85	50

DESIGNS: 1k. Chisel, square and plane; 1k.30, Trowel, ceiling brush and folding rule.

235 Globe Flower

1977. Endangered Flora.

649	**235**	1k. green, yellow & brn	45	20
650	-	1k.50 green, ol & brn	1·00	95

DESIGN: 1k.50, "Cnidium dubium".

236 Handball Player and Emblem

1978. Men's Handball World Championship.

651	**236**	1k.20 red	50	20

237 Christian IV on Horseback

1978. Centenary of National History Museum, Frederiksborg.

652	**237**	1k.20 brown	50	15
653	-	1k.80 black	65	25

DESIGN: 1k.80, North-west aspect of Frederiksborg Castle.

238 Jens Bang's House, Aalborg

1978. Europa.

654	**238**	1k.20 brown	45	20
655	-	1k.50 blue and dp blue	1·30	80

DESIGN: 1k.50, Plan and front elevation of Frederiksborg Castle, Copenhagen.

239 Kongenshus Memorial Park

1978. Provincial Series. Central Jutland.

656	**239**	70ore multicoloured	40	25
657	-	1k.20 multicoloured	50	25
658	-	1k.50 multicoloured	90	65
659	-	1k.80 blue, brn & grn	60	45

DESIGNS: 1k.20, Post office, Aarhus Old Town; 1k.50, Lignite fields, Soby; 1k.80, Church wall, Stadil Church.

240 Boats in Harbour

1978. Fishing Industry.

660	**240**	70ore green	40	30
661	-	1k. brown	45	25
662	-	1k.80 black	55	30
663	-	2k.50 brown	95	40

DESIGNS: 1k. Eel traps; 1k.80, Fishing boats on the slipway; 2k.50, Drying ground.

241 Campaign Emblem

1978. 50th Anniv of Danish Cancer Campaign.

664	**241**	120ore+20ore red	75	75

242 Common Morel

1978. Mushrooms.

665	**242**	1k. brown	75	45
666	-	1k.20 red	75	25

DESIGN: 1k.20, Satan's mushroom.

243 Early and Modern Telephones

1979. Centenary of Danish Telephone System.

667	**243**	1k.20 red	65	20

244 Child

1979. International Year of the Child.

668	**244**	1k.20+20ore red & brn	75	75

245 University Seal

1979. 500th Anniv of Copenhagen University.

669	**245**	1k.30 red	40	15
670	-	1k.60 black	55	40

DESIGN: 1k.60, Pentagram representing the five faculties.

246 Letter Mail Cariole

1979. Europa.

671	**246**	1k.30 red	90	30
672	-	1k.60 blue	2·40	85

DESIGN: 1k.60, Morse key and sounder.

247 Pendant

1979. Viking "Gripping Beast" Decorations.

673	**247**	1k.10 brown	35	25
674	-	2k. green	80	35

DESIGN: 2k. Key.

248 Mols Bjerge

1979. Provincial Series. North Jutland.

675	**248**	80ore green, ultram & brown	40	25
676	-	90ore multicoloured	1·40	1·20
677	-	200ore grn, orge & red	75	25
678	-	280ore slate, sepia & brn	90	60

DESIGNS. 90ore Orslev Kloster; 200ore Trans; 280ore Bovbjerg.

249 Silhouette of Oehlenschlager

1979. Birth Bicentenary of Adam Oehlenschlager (poet).

679	**249**	1k.30 red	50	20

250 Music, Violin and Dancers (birth cent of Jacob Gade (composer))

1979. Anniversaries.

680	**250**	1k.10 brown	40	30
681	-	1k.60 blue	60	45

DESIGN: 1k.60, Dancer at bar (death centenary of August Bournonville (ballet master)).

251 Royal Mail Guards' Office, Copenhagen (drawing, Peter Klaestrup)

1980. Bicentenary of National Postal Service.

682	**251**	1k.30 red	50	20

252 Stylized Wheelchair

1980. 25th Anniv of Foundation for the Disabled.

683	**252**	130ore+20ore red	75	55

253 Karen Blixen (writer)

1980. Europa.

684	**253**	1k.30 red	50	20
685	-	1k.60 blue	1·50	75

DESIGN: 1k.60, August Krogh (physiologist).

254 Symbols of Employment, Health and Education

1980. U.N. Decade for Women World Conference.

686	**254**	1k.60 blue	75	50

255 Lindholme Hoje

1980. Provincial Series. Jutland North of Limfjorden. Multicoloured.

687	80ore Type **255**	45	35
688	110ore Skagen lighthouse (vert)	60	35
689	200ore Borglum	65	25
690	280ore Fishing boats at Vorupor	1·50	1·20

256 Silver Pitcher, c. 1641

1980. Nordic Countries Postal Co-operation.

691	**256**	1k.30 black and red	50	20
692	-	1k.80 blue & dp blue	1·10	85

DESIGN: 1k.80, Bishop's bowl.

257 Earliest Danish Coin, Hedeby (c. 800)

1980. Coins from the Royal Collection.

693	**257**	1k.30 red and brown	55	25
694	-	1k.40 olive and green	1·00	85
695	-	1k.80 blue and grey	90	80

DESIGNS: 1k.40, Silver coin of Valdemar the Great and Bishop Absalon (1152–82); 1k.80, Christian VII gold current ducat (1781).

258 Lace Pattern

1980. Lace Patterns. Various designs showing lace.

696	258	1k.10 brown	55	40
697	-	1k.30 red	50	25
698	-	2k. green	55	25

259 Children Playing in Yard

1981. National Children's Welfare Association.

699	259	1k.60+20ore red	80	70

260 Original Houses, 1631

1981. 350th Anniv of Nyboder (Naval Barracks), Copenhagen.

700	260	1k.30 red and yellow	70	55
701	-	1k.60 red and yellow	55	20

DESIGN: 1k.60, 18th-century terraced houses.

261 Tilting at a Barrel (Shrovetide custom)

1981. Europa.

702	261	1k.60 red	60	20
703	-	2k. blue	1·40	60

DESIGN: 2k. Midsummer bonfire.

262 Soro

1981. Provincial Series. Zealand and Surrounding Islands.

704	262	100ore blue and brown	40	25
705	-	150ore black and green	60	40
706	-	160ore brown and green	60	25
707	-	200ore multicoloured	80	45
708	-	230ore blue and brown	90	45

DESIGNS: 150ore N. F. S. Grundtvig's childhood home, Udby; 160ore Kaj Munk's childhood home, Opager; 200ore Gronsund; 230ore Bornholm.

263 Rigensgade District, Copenhagen

1981. European Urban Renaissance Year.

709	263	1k.60 red	50	20

264 Decaying Tree

1981. International Year for Disabled Persons.

710	264	2k.+20ore blue	1·10	1·10

265 Ellehammer II at Lindholm, 1906

1981. History of Aviation.

711	265	1k. green and black	55	40
712	-	1k.30 brown & dp brn	80	55
713	-	1k.60 vermilion & red	55	20
714	-	2k.30 blue & dp blue	80	60

DESIGNS: 1k.30, Captain P.A. Botved's Fokker C.VE biplane R-1 (Copenhagen–Tokyo, 1926); 1k.60, Hojriis Hillig's Bellanca J-300 Special NR-797 "Liberty" (U.S.A.–Denmark, 1931); 2k.30. Douglas DC-7C "Seven Seas" (first Polar flight, 1957).

266 Queen Margrethe II

1982

715	266	1k.60 red	50	20
716	266	1k.60 green	2·75	2·50
717	266	1k.80 brown	60	40
718	266	2k. red	65	15
719	266	2k.20 green	2·20	1·90
720	266	2k.30 violet	85	85
721	266	2k.50 red	75	20
722	266	2k.70 blue	90	40
723	266	2k.70 red	75	20
724	266	2k.80 red	90	20
725	266	3k. violet	75	20
726	266	3k. red	75	20
727	266	3k.20 violet	85	50
727a	266	3k.20 red	1·00	15
728	266	3k.30 black	1·30	45
729	266	3k.40 green	2·20	2·40
730	266	3k.50 blue	1·00	25
730a	266	3k.50 purple	1·10	55
730b	266	3k.50 red	1·00	20
731	266	3k.70 blue	1·00	40
732	266	3k.75 green	1·50	1·40
733	266	3k.80 blue	1·10	50
734	266	3k.80 purple	1·60	1·70
735	266	4k.10 blue	1·60	25
736	266	4k.20 violet	2·20	1·60
737	266	4k.40 blue	1·50	40
738	266	4k.50 purple	1·90	1·60
739	266	4k.75 blue	1·80	25

267 Revenue Cutter "Argus"

1982. 350th Anniv Customs Service.

740	267	1k.60 red	50	15

268 Skater

1982. World Figure Skating Championships, Copenhagen.

741	268	2k. blue	60	35

269 Villein (Abolition of adscription, 1788)

1982. Europa.

742	269	2k. brown	1·00	30
743	-	2k.70 blue	2·10	65

DESIGN: 2k.70, Procession of women (Enfranchisement of women, 1915).

270 Distorted Plant

1982. 25th Anniv of Danish Multiple Sclerosis Society.

744	270	2k.+40ore red	1·80	1·50

271 Dairy Farm at Hjedding and Butter Churn

1982. Centenary of Co-operative Dairy Farming.

745	271	1k.80 brown	70	45

272 Hand holding Quill Pen

1982. 400th Anniv of Record Office.

746	272	2k.70 green	1·00	35

273 Blicher (after J. V. Gertner)

1982. Birth Bicent of Steen Steensen Blicher (poet).

747	273	2k. red	75	15

274 Odense Printing Press, 1482

1982. 500th Anniv of Printing in Denmark.

748	274	1k.80 brown	80	55

275 Petersen and the Number Men

1982. Birth Centenary of Robert Storm Petersen (cartoonist).

749	275	1k.50 red and blue	55	30
750	-	2k. green and red	80	30

DESIGN—HORIZ: 2k. Peter and Ping with dog.

276 Library Seal

1982. 500th Anniv University Library.

751	276	2k.70 brown and black	95	40

277 "Interglobal Communications"

1983. World Communications Year.

752	277	2k. orange, red & blue	85	25

278 Nurse tending Patient

1983. Red Cross.

753	278	2k.+40ore blue & red	1·40	1·60

279 Clown and Girl with Balloon

1983. 400th Anniv of Dyrehavsbakken Amusement Park.

754	279	2k. multicoloured	75	15

280 Lene Koppen

1983. World Badminton Championships.

755	280	2k.70 blue	1·00	35

281 Burin and Engraving of lore Numeral Stamp

1983. 50th Anniv of Danish Recess-printed Stamps.

756	281	2k.50 red	80	15

282 Egeskov Castle

1983. Nordic Countries Postal Co-operation. "Visit the North".

757	282	2k.50 dp brown & brn	75	20
758	-	3k.50 dp blue & blue	1·10	65

DESIGN: 3k.50, Troldkirken long barrow, North Jutland.

283 Kildeskovshallen Recreation Centre, Copenhagen

1983. Europa.

759	283	2k.50 red and brown	1·20	15
760	-	3k.50 dp blue & blue	1·50	65

DESIGN: 3k.50, Sallingsund Bridge.

284 Weights and Measures

1983. 300th Anniv of Weights and Measures Ordinance.

761	284	2k.50 red	80	15

285 Title Page of Law

1983. 300th Anniv of King Christian V's Danish Law (code of laws for Norway).

762	285	5k. dp brown & brown	1·80	60

286 Crashed Car and Hand with Eye (Police)

1983. Life-saving Services.

763	**286**	1k. brown	45	25
764	-	2k.50 red	80	20
765	-	3k.50 blue	1·30	65

DESIGNS: 2k.50 Ladder, stretcher and fire-hose (ambulance and fire services); 3k.50 Lifebelt and lifeboat (sea-rescue services).

287 Family Group

1983. The Elderly in Society.

766	**287**	2k. green	65	45
767	-	2k.50 red	85	15

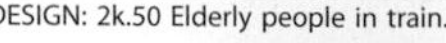
DESIGN: 2k.50 Elderly people in train.

288 Grundtvig (after Constantin Hansen)

1983. Birth Bicentenary of Nicolai Frederik Severin Grundtvig (writer).

768	**288**	2k.50 brown	80	30

289 Perspective Painting

1983. Birth Bicentenary of Christoffer Wilhelm Eckersberg (painter).

769	**289**	2k.50 red	75	25

290 Spade and Sapling

1984. Plant a Tree Campaign.

770	**290**	2k.70 yellow, red and green	1·00	25

291 Billiards

1984. World Billiards Championships.

771	**291**	3k.70 green	1·20	40

292 Athletes

1984. Olympic Games, Los Angeles.

772	**292**	2k.70+40ore mult	1·90	2·00

293 Compass Rose

1984. Bicentenary of Hydrographic Department (2k.30) and 300th Anniv of Pilotage Service (2k.70).

773	**293**	2k.30 green	95	65
774	-	2k.70 red	80	25

DESIGN: 2k.70, Pilot boat.

294 Parliament Emblem

1984. 2nd Direct Elections to European Parliament.

775	**294**	2k.70 yellow and blue	1·00	30

295 Girl Guides

1984. Scout Movement.

776	**295**	2k.70 multicoloured	95	25

296 Bridge

1984. Europa. 25th Anniv of European Post and Telecommunications Conference.

777	**296**	2k.70 red	1·50	25
778	**296**	3k.70 blue	2·40	1·30

297 Anchor (memorial to Danish Sailors)

1984. 40th Anniv of Normandy Invasion.

779	**297**	2k.70 purple	1·30	30

298 Prince Henrik

1984. 50th Birthday of Prince Henrik.

780	**298**	2k.70 brown	1·00	25

299 Old Danish Inn

1984

781	**299**	3k. multicoloured	1·10	80

300 Shoal of Fish (research)

1984. Danish Fisheries and Shipping.

782	**300**	2k.30 blue and green	1·30	1·40
783	-	2k.70 blue and red	90	30
784	-	3k.30 blue and violet	1·30	1·40
785	-	3k.70 blue & ultramarine	1·20	1·20

DESIGNS: 2k.70, Ships (sea transport); 3k.30, "Bettina" (deep sea fishing boat); 3k.70, Deck of trawler "Jonna Tornby".

301 Heart and Cardiograph

1984. Heart Foundation.

786	**301**	2k.70+40ore red	1·90	1·60

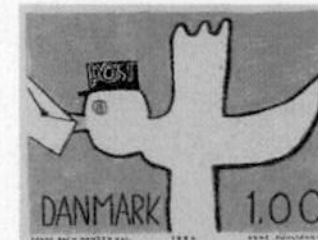

302 Bird with Letter

1984

787	**302**	1k. multicoloured	50	15

303 "Holberg meeting Officer and Dandy" (Wilhelm Marstrand)

1984. 300th Birth Anniv of Ludvig Holberg (historian and playwright).

788	**303**	2k.70 black, stone & red	1·00	15

304 Woman and Sabbath Candles

1984. 300th Anniv of Jewish Community.

789	**304**	3k.70 multicoloured	1·20	75

305 "Ymer sucking Milk from the Cow Odhumble" (Nicolai Abildgaard)

1984. Paintings. Multicoloured.

790		5k. "Carnival in Rome" (Christoffer Wilhelm Eckersberg) (horiz)	2·40	1·90
791		10k. Type **305**	4·00	3·50

306 Gothersgade Reformed Church, Copenhagen

1985. 300th Anniv of French and German Reformed Church in Denmark.

792	**306**	2k.80 red	1·00	15

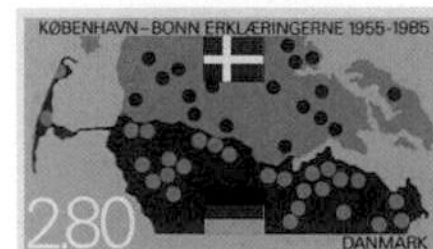

307 Flags and Border

1985. 30th Anniv of Copenhagen–Bonn Declarations.

793	**307**	2k.80 multicoloured	1·30	40

308 Flag, Girl and Boy

1985. International Youth Year.

794	**308**	3k.80 multicoloured	1·10	80

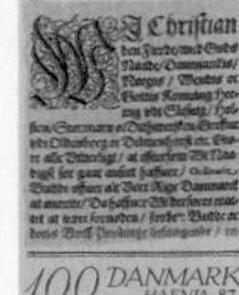

309 Statue on Postmen

1985. "Hafnia 87" International Stamp Exhibition, Copenhagen (1st issue). Sheet 70×95 mm containing T 309 and similar vert designs, each black, ochre and red.

MS795	200ore Type **309**; 250ore 1711 mandate on disinfection of letters; 280ore 1775 decree granting postal monopoly to Danish Post Office; 380ore 1851 title page of *Law on Postal Mail* (sold at 15k.)	4·75	4·75

See also Nos. **MS**817, **MS**836 and 851/**MS**852.

310 Music Score

1985. Europa. Music Year.

796	**310**	2k.80 yell, red & verm	1·60	40
797	-	3k.80 black, bl & grn	2·50	1·30

DESIGN: 3k.80, Music score (different).

311 Flames and Houses

1985. 40th Anniv of Liberation.

798	**311**	2k.80+50ore mult	1·80	1·60

The surtax was for the benefit of Resistance veterans.

312 Queen Ingrid and "Chrysanthemum frutescens" "Sofieri"

1985. 50th Anniv of Queen Ingrid's Arrival in Denmark.

799	**312**	2k.80 multicoloured	1·00	25

313 Faro Bridges

1985. Inauguration of Faro Bridges.

800	**313**	2k.80 multicoloured	1·00	25

314 St. Canute and Lund Cathedral

1985. 900th Anniv of St. Canute's Deed of Gift to Lund.

801	**314**	2k.80 black and red	85	25
802	-	3k. black and red	1·80	1·30

DESIGN: 3k. St. Canute and Helsingborg.

315 Gymnastics

1985. Sports. Multicoloured.

803	2k.80 Type **315**	1·10	15
804	3k.80 Canoeing	1·40	65
805	6k. Cycling	2·00	95

316 Woman Cyclist

1985. United Nations Women's Decade.
806 **316** 3k.80 multicoloured 1·20 95

317 Kronborg Castle

1985. 400th Anniv of Kronborg Castle, Elsinore.
807 **317** 2k.80 multicoloured 1·00 25

318 Dove and U.N. Emblem

1985. 40th Anniv of U.N.O.
808 **318** 3k.80 multicoloured 1·20 80

319 Niels and Margrethe Bohr

1985. Birth Centenary of Niels Bohr (nuclear physicist).
809 **319** 2k.80 multicoloured 1·20 1·20

320 Tapestry (detail) by Caroline Ebbesen

1985. 25th Anniv of National Society for Welfare of the Mentally Ill.
810 **320** 2k.80+40ore mult 1·60 1·20

321 "D" in Sign Language

1985. 50th Anniv of Danish Association of the Deaf.
811 **321** 2k.80 brown & black 1·10 30

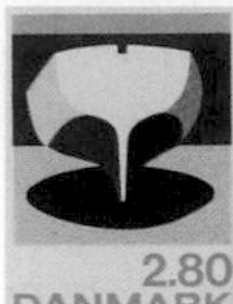

322 Stern of Boat

1985
812 **322** 2k.80 multicoloured 1·00 30

323 "Head"

1985
813 **323** 3k.80 multicoloured 2·50 2·00

324 Leaves and Barbed Wire

1986. 25th Anniv of Amnesty International.
814 **324** 2k.80 multicoloured 1·00 15

325 Girl with Bird

1986
815 **325** 2k.80 multicoloured 1·20 95

326 Reichhardt as Papageno in "The Magic Flute"

1986. 1st Death Anniv of Poul Reichhardt (actor).
816 **326** 2k.80+50ore mult 1·50 1·50

327 Holstein Carriage, 1840

1986. "Hafnia 87" International Stamp Exhibition, Copenhagen (2nd issue). Sheet 70×94 mm containing T 327 and similar vert designs. Multicoloured.
MS817 100ore Type **327** 250ore Ice boat, 1880; 280ore Mail van, 1908; 380ore Friedrichshafen FF-49 seaplane, 1919 (sold at 15k.) 7·00 7·00

328 Hands reading Braille

1986. 75th Anniv of Danish Society for the Blind.
818 **328** 2k.80+50ore red, brown and black 1·50 1·50

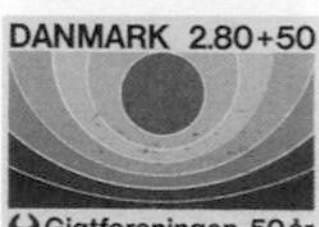

329 Bands of Colour

1986. 50th Anniv of Danish Arthritis Association.
819 **329** 2k.80+50ore mult 1·50 1·50

330 Changing the Guard at Barracks

1986. Bicentenary of Royal Danish Life Guards Barracks, Rosenborg.
820 **330** 2k.80 multicoloured 1·00 25

331 Academy and Arms

1986. 400th Anniv of Soro Academy.
821 **331** 2k.80 multicoloured 1·00 25

332 Hands reaching out

1986. International Peace Year.
822 **332** 3k.80 multicoloured 1·20 80

333 Prince Frederik

1986. 18th Birthday of Crown Prince Frederik.
823 **333** 2k.80 black and red 1·30 30

334 Station

1986. Inaug of Hoje Tastrup Railway Station.
824 **334** 2k.80 black, bl & red 1·00 25

335 Aalborg

1986. Nordic Countries Postal Co-operation. Twinned Towns.
825 **335** 2k.80 black 1·10 25
826 - 3k.80 blue and red 1·30 50
DESIGN: 3k.80, Thisted.

336 Common Raven

1986. Birds. Multicoloured.
827 2k.80 Type **336** 1·60 55
828 2k.80 Common starling ("Sturnus vulgaris") 1·60 55
829 2k.80 Mute swan ("Cygnus olor") 1·60 55
830 2k.80 Northern lapwing ("Vanellus vanellus") 1·60 55
831 2k.80 Eurasian skylark ("Alauda arvensis") 1·60 55

337 Post Box, Wires and Telephone

1986. 19th International Postal Telegraph and Telephone Congress, Copenhagen.
832 **337** 2k.80 multicoloured 1·00 25

338 Sports Pictograms

1986. 125th Anniv of Danish Rifle, Gymnastics and Sports Clubs.
833 **338** 2k.80 multicoloured 1·00 25

339 Roadsweeper

1986. Europa.
834 **339** 2k.80 red 1·50 30
835 - 3k.80 blue 2·10 75
DESIGN: 3k.80, Refuse truck.

340 Stagecoach, 1840

1986. "Hafnia 87" International Stamp Exhibition, Copenhagen (3rd issue). Sheet 70×94 mm containing T 340 and similar vert design. Multicoloured.
MS836 100ore Type **340**; 250ore Postmaster, 1840; 280ore Postman, 1851; 380ore Rural Postman, 1893 (sold at 15k.) 7·00 7·00

341 Man fleeing

1986. Aid for Refugees.
837 **341** 2k.80 blue, brown & blk 1·00 25

342 Cupid

1986. Bicentenary of First Performance of "The Whims of Cupid and the Ballet Master" by V. Galeotti and J. Lolle.
838 **342** 3k.80 multicoloured 1·20 55

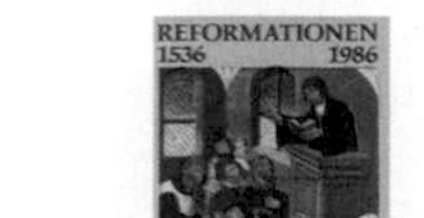

343 Lutheran Communion Service in Thorslunde Church

1986. 450th Anniv of Reformation.
839 **343** 6k.50 multicoloured 2·30 95

344 Graph of Danish Economic Growth and Unemployment Rate

1986. 25th Anniv of Organization of Economic Co-operation and Development.
840 **344** 3k.80 multicoloured 1·70 1·40

345 Abstract

1987
841 **345** 2k.80 multicoloured 1·00 15

346 Price Label through Magnifying Glass

1987. 40th Anniv of Danish Consumer Council.
842 **346** 2k.80 black and red 1·00 15

347 Fresco

1987. Ribe Cathedral. Multicoloured.
843 3k. Type **347** 1·00 45
844 3k.80 Stained glass window (detail) 1·40 95
845 6k.50 Mosaic (detail) 2·40 1·60

348 Cog and Oscillating Waves

1987. 50th Anniv of Danish Academy of Technical Sciences.
846 **348** 2k.50 black and red 1·30 1·00

349 Gentofte Central Library

1987. Europa. Architecture.
847 **349** 2k.80 red 1·60 30
848 - 3k.80 blue 2·40 1·00
DESIGN—HORIZ: 3k.80, Hoje Tastrup Senior School.

350 Ball and Ribbons

1987. 8th Gymnaestrada (World Gymnastics Show), Herning.
849 **350** 2k.80 multicoloured 1·00 15

351 Pigs

1987. Centenary of First Co-operative Bacon Factory, Horsens.
850 **351** 3k.80 multicoloured 1·20 80

352 1912 5k. Stamp, Steam Locomotive and Mail Wagon

1987. "Hafnia 87" International Stamp Exhibition, Copenhagen.
851 **352** 280ore multicoloured 1·30 95
MS852 70×95 mm. No. 851 (sold at 45k.) 22·00 22·00

353 Single Scull

1987. World Rowing Championships, Bagsvaerd Lake.
853 **353** 3k.80 indigo and blue 1·20 70

354 Abstract

1987
854 **354** 2k.80 multicoloured 1·00 15

355 Waves

1987. 25th Anniv of Danish Epileptics Association.
855 **355** 2k.80+50ore blue, red and green 1·80 1·40

356 Rask

1987. Birth Bicentenary of Rasmus Kristjan Rask (philologist).
856 **356** 2k.80 red and brown 1·00 15

357 Association Badge

1987. 125th Anniv of Clerical Association for Home Mission in Denmark.
857 **357** 3k. brown 1·00 20

358 Lions supporting Monogram

1988. 400th Anniv of Accession of King Christian IV.
858 **358** 3k. gold and blue 1·00 15
859 - 4k.10 multicoloured 1·30 45
DESIGN: 4k.10, Portrait of Christian IV by P. Isaacsz.

359 Worm and Artefacts

1988. 400th Birth Anniv of Ole Worm (antiquarian).
860 **359** 7k.10 brown 2·10 1·60

360 St. Canute's Church

1988. Millenary of Odense.
861 **360** 3k. brown, black & green 1·00 15

361 African Mother and Child

1988. Danish Church Aid.
862 **361** 3k.+50ore mult 1·80 1·50

362 Sirens, Workers and Emblem

1988. 50th Anniv of Civil Defence Administration.
863 **362** 2k.70 blue and orange 85 80

363 Blood Circulation of Heart

1988. 40th Anniv of W.H.O.
864 **363** 4k.10 red, blue and black 1·30 85

364 Postwoman on Bicycle

1988. Europa. Transport and Communications. Multicoloured.
865 3k. Type **364** 1·60 35
866 4k.10 Mobile telephone 3·00 95

365 "King Christian VII riding past Liberty Monument" (C. W. Eckersberg)

1988. Bicentenary of Abolition of Villeinage.
867 **365** 3k.20 multicoloured 1·10 80

366 "Men of Industry" (detail, P. S. Kroyer)

1988. 150th Anniv of Federation of Danish Industries.
868 **366** 3k. multicoloured 1·00 35

367 Speedway Riders

1988. World Speedway Championships.
869 **367** 4k.10 multicoloured 1·30 55

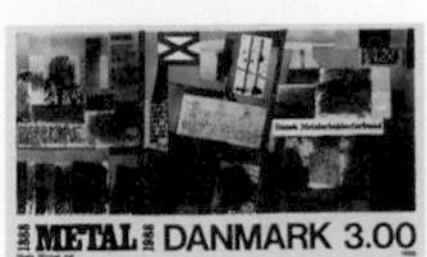

368 Glass Mosaic (Niels Winkel)

1988. Centenary of Danish Metalworkers' Union.
870 **368** 3k. multicoloured 1·00 25

369 College

1988. Bicent of Tonder Teacher Training College.
871 **369** 3k. brown 1·00 25

370 "Tribute to Leon Degand" (Robert Jacobsen)

1988. Franco-Danish Cultural Co-operation.
872 **370** 4k.10 red and black 2·50 2·40

371 Emblem

1988. 5th Anniv of National Council for the Unmarried Mother and Her Child.
873 **371** 3k.+50ore red 1·80 1·50

372 Lumby Windmill

1988. Mills.
874 **372** 3k. black, red & orange 1·00 15
875 - 7k.10 black, ultramarine and blue 2·20 1·70
DESIGN: 7k.10, Veistrup water mill.

373 "Bathing Boys 1902" (Peter Hansen)

1988. Paintings. Multicoloured.
876 4k.10 Type **373** 2·75 2·40
877 10k. "Hill at Overkoerby. Winter 1917" (Fritz Syberg) 5·25 4·75

374 "The Little Mermaid" (statue, Edvard Eriksen), Copenhagen

1989. Centenary of Danish Tourist Association.

878	**374**	3k.20 green	1·20	15

375 Army Members in Public House

1989. 102nd Anniv of Salvation Army in Denmark.

879	**375**	3k.20+50ore mult	2·10	1·60

376 Footballer

1989. Centenary of Danish Football Association.

880	**376**	3k.20 red, blk & lt red	1·10	15

377 Emblem

1989. 40th Anniv of N.A.T.O.

881	**377**	4k.40 bl, cobalt & gold	1·50	80

378 "Valby Woman"

1989. Nordic Countries' Postal Co-operation. Traditional Costumes. Engravings by Christoffer Wilhelm Eckersberg. Multicoloured.

882	3k.20 Type **378**	1·00	15
883	4k.40 "Pork Butcher"	1·60	1·00

379 "Parliament Flag

1989. 3rd Direct Elections to European Parliament.

884	**379**	3k. blue and yellow	1·20	95

380 Lego Bricks

1989. Europa. Children's Toys. Multicoloured.

885	3k.20 Type **380**	1·60	15
886	4k.40 Wooden guardsmen by Kay Bojesen	2·40	95

381 Tractor, 1917

1989. Centenary of Danish Agricultural Museum.

887	**381**	3k.20 red	1·10	15

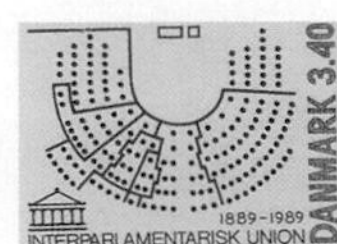

382 Diagram of Folketing (Parliament) Chamber

1989. Centenary of Interparliamentary Union.

888	**382**	3k.40 red and black	2·30	2·00

383 Chart and Boat Identity Number

1989. Centenary of Danish Fishery and Marine Research Institute.

889	**383**	3k.20 multicoloured	1·20	25

384 "Ingemann" (after J. V. Gertner)

1989. Birth Bicentenary of Bernhard Severin Ingemann (poet).

890	**384**	7k.70 green	2·20	95

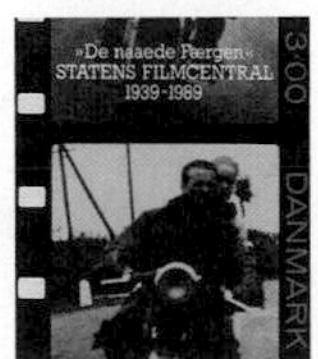

385 Scene from "They Caught the Ferry" (50th anniv of Danish Government Film Office)

1989. Danish Film Industry.

891	**385**	3k. blue, black & orge	1·10	75
892	-	3k.20 pink, blk & orge	1·00	35
893	-	4k.40 brown, blk & orge	1·30	55

DESIGNS: 3k.20, Scene from "The Golden Smile" (birth cent of Bodil Ipsen, actress); 4k.40, Carl Th. Dreyer (director, birth cent).

386 Stamps

1989. 50th Stamp Day.

894	**386**	3k.20 salmon, orge & brn	1·10	25

387 "Part of Northern Citadel Bridge" (Christen Kobke)

1989. Paintings. Multicoloured.

895	4k.40 Type **387**	2·10	1·60
896	10k. "A Little Girl, Elise Kobke, with Cup" (Constantin Hansen)	4·25	3·50

388 Silver Coffee Pot (Axel Johannes Kroyer, 1726)

1990. Centenary of Museum of Decorative Art, Copenhagen.

897	**388**	3k.50 black and blue	1·10	20

389 Andrew Mitchell's Steam Engine

1990. Bicent of Denmark's First Steam Engine.

898	**389**	8k.25 brown	2·50	1·50

390 Queen Margrethe II

1990

910	**390**	3k.50 red	1·10	15
911	**390**	3k.75 green	2·75	2·40
912	**390**	3k.75 red	1·10	25
913	**390**	4k. brown	1·10	55
914	**390**	4k.50 violet	1·30	90
915	**390**	4k.75 blue	1·30	40
916	**390**	4k.75 violet	1·40	85
917	**390**	5k. blue	1·40	40
918	**390**	5k.25 black	1·60	80
919	**390**	5k.50 green	1·80	1·70

391 Royal Monogram over Door of Haderslev Post Office

1990. Europa. Post Office Buildings.

930	**391**	3k.50 yellow, red & blk	2·40	25
931	-	4k.75 multicoloured	3·25	60

DESIGN: 4k.75, Odense Post Office.

392 Main Guardhouse, Rigging Crane and Ships (after C. O. Willars)

1990. 300th Anniv of Nyholm.

932	**392**	4k.75 black	1·50	55

393 Covered Ice Dish

1990. Bicentenary of Flora Danica Banquet Service. Multicoloured.

933	3k.50 Type **393**	1·50	1·20
934	3k.50 Sauce boat	1·50	1·20
935	3k.50 Lidded ice pot	1·50	1·20
936	3k.50 Serving dish	1·50	1·20

394 Marsh Mallow

1990. Endangered Flowers. Multicoloured.

937	3k.25 Type **394**	1·10	95

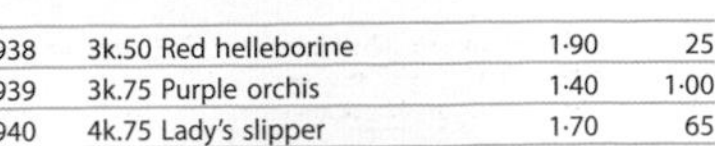

938	3k.50 Red helleborine	1·90	25
939	3k.75 Purple orchis	1·40	1·00
940	4k.75 Lady's slipper	1·70	65

395 Insulin Crystals

1990. 50th Anniv of Danish Diabetes Association.

941	**395**	3k.50+50ore mult	2·50	2·10

396 Gjellerup Church

1990. Jutland Churches. Each brown.

942	3k.50 Type **396**	1·10	20
943	4k.75 Veng Church	1·30	55
944	8k.25 Bredsten Church (vert)	2·50	1·20

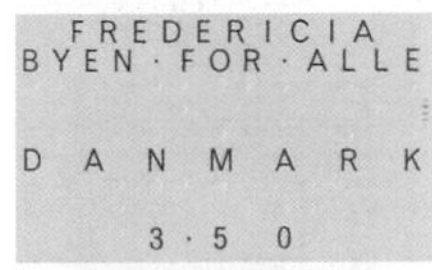

397 Slogan and Braille

1990. Fredericia: "Town for Everybody" (access for the handicapped project).

945	**397**	3k.50 red and black	1·10	45

398 "Tordenskiold and Karlsten's Commandant" (Otto Bache)

1990. 300th Birth Anniv of Admiral Tordenskiold (Peter Wessel).

946	**398**	3k.50 multicoloured	1·20	20

399 Bicycle (Bicycle stealing)

1990. Campaigns.

947	**399**	3k.25 multicoloured	1·20	80
948	-	3k.50 black, bl & mve	1·10	20

DESIGN: 3k.50, Glass and car (Drunken driving).

400 IC3 Diesel Passenger Train, 1990

1991. Railway Locomotives.

949	**400**	3k.25 blue, red & green	1·30	95
950	-	3k.50 black and red	1·10	20
951	-	3k.75 brown & dp brn	1·50	95
952	-	4k.75 black and red	1·30	80

DESIGNS: 3k.50, Class A steam locomotive, 1882; 3k.75, Class MY diesel-electric locomotive, 1954; 4k.75, Class P steam locomotive, 1907.

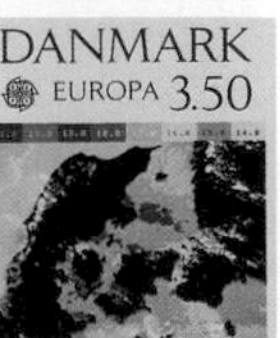

401 Satellite Picture of Denmark's Water Temperatures

1991. Europa. Europe in Space. Mult.

953	3k.50 Type **401**	2·50	30

954 4k.75 Denmark's land temperatures 3·50 80

402 First Page of 1280s Manuscript

1991. 750th Anniv of Jutland Law.
955 **402** 8k.25 multicoloured 2·75 1·70

403 Fano

1991. Nordic Countries' Postal Co-operation. Tourism. Multicoloured.
956 3k.50 Type **403** 1·30 20
957 4k.75 Christianso 1·60 65

404 Child using Emergency Helpline

1991. 15th Anniv of Living Conditions of Children (child welfare organization).
958 **404** 3k.50+50ore blue 1·70 1·70

405 Stoneware Vessels (Christian Poulsen)

1991. Danish Design. Multicoloured.
959 3k.25 Type **405** 1·10 80
960 3k.50 Chair, 1949 (Hans Wegner) (vert) 1·10 25
961 4k.75 Silver cutlery, 1938 (Kay Bojesen) (vert) 1·50 80
962 8k.25 "PH5" lamp, 1958 (Poul Henningsen) 2·75 2·40

406 Man cleaning up after Dog

1991. "Keep Denmark Clean".
963 **406** 3k.50 red 1·10 25
964 - 4k.75 blue 1·30 80
DESIGN: 4k.75, Woman putting litter into bin.

407 Nordic Advertising Congress 1947 (Arne Ungermann)

1991. Posters. Multicoloured.
965 3k.50 Type **407** 1·10 20
966 4k.50 Poster Exhibition, Copenhagen Zoo, 1907 (Valdemar Andersen) 2·00 1·70
967 4k.75 Douglas DC-3 of D.D.L. (Danish Airlines, 1945) (Ib Andersen) 1·50 95
968 12k. Casino's "The Sinner", 1925 (Sven Brasch) 4·00 2·75

408 "Lady at Her Toilet" (Harald Giersing)

1991. Paintings. Multicoloured.
969 4k.75 Type **408** 2·30 2·20
970 14k. "Road through Wood" (Edvard Weie) 5·50 5·25

409 Skarpsalling Earthenware Bowl

1992. Re-opening of National Museum, Copenhagen. Exhibits from Prehistoric Denmark Collection.
971 **409** 3k.50 brown and lilac 1·10 25
972 - 4k.50 green and blue 2·00 1·40
973 - 4k.75 black & brown 1·50 80
974 - 8k.25 purple & green 2·75 2·00
DESIGNS: 4k.50, Grevensvaenge bronze figure of dancer; 4k.75, Bottom plate of Gundestrup Cauldron; 8k.25, Hindsgavl flint knife.

410 Aspects of Engineering

1992. Centenary of Danish Society of Chemical, Civil, Electrical and Mechanical Engineers.
975 **410** 3k.50 red 1·10 30

411 Queen Margaret I (detail, Vastra Sallerup Church fresco)

1992. "Nordia 94" International Stamp Exhibition, Arhus. Sheet 70×94 mm containing T 411 and similar vert design, each brown, slate and red.
MS976 3k.50, Type **411**; 4k.75 Alabaster bust of Queen Margaret I (attr. Johannes Junge) (sold at 12k.) 5·75 5·75

412 Potato Plant

1992. Europa. 500th Anniv of Discovery of America by Columbus.
977 **412** 3k.50 green & brown 1·30 30
978 - 4k.75 green & yellow 4·50 1·30
DESIGN: 4k.75, Head of maize.

413 Royal Couple in 1992 and in Official Wedding Photograph

1992. Silver Wedding of Queen Margrethe and Prince Henrik.
979 **413** 3k.75 multicoloured 1·50 95

414 Hare, Eurasian Sky Lark and Cars

1992. Environmental Protection. Multicoloured.
980 3k.75 Type **414** 1·10 20
981 5k. Atlantic herrings and sea pollution 1·50 60
982 8k.75 Felled trees and saplings (vert) 2·50 1·60

415 Celebrating Crowd

1992. Denmark, European Football Champion.
983 **415** 3k.75 multicoloured 1·90 30

416 Danish Pavilion

1992. "Expo '92" World's Fair, Seville.
984 **416** 3k.75 blue 1·10 25

417 "Word"

1992. 50th Anniv of Danish Dyslexia Association.
985 **417** 3k.75+50ore mult 2·20 2·20

418 "A Hug"

1992. Danish Cartoon Characters.
986 **418** 3k.50 purple, red & gold 1·60 70
987 - 3k.75 violet and red 1·20 25
988 - 4k.75 black and red 2·00 1·50
989 - 5k. blue and red 1·50 50
DESIGNS: 3k.75, "Love Letter"; 4k.75, "Domestic Triangle"; 5k. "The Poet and his Little Wife".

419 Abstract

1992. European Single Market.
990 **419** 3k.75 blue and yellow 1·20 35

420 "Jacob's Fight with the Angel" (bible illustration by Bodil Kaalund)

1992. Publication of New Danish Bible.
991 **420** 3k.75 multicoloured 1·10 20

421 "Landscape from Vejby, 1843" (Johan Thomas Lundbye)

1992. Paintings. Multicoloured.
992 5k. Type **421** 1·90 1·90
993 10k. "Motif from Halleby Brook, 1847" (Peter Christian Skovgaard) 3·75 3·75

422 Funen Guldgubber

1993. Danish Treasure Trove. Guldgubber (anthropomorphic gold foil figures). Mult.
994 3k.75 Type **422** 1·10 20
995 5k. Bornholm guldgubber (vert) 1·50 55

423 Small Tortoiseshell

1993. Butterflies. Multicoloured.
996 3k.75 Type **423** 1·20 20
997 5k. Large blue 1·60 60
998 8k.75 Marsh fritillary 3·25 2·40
999 12k. Red admiral 3·50 2·75

424 Untitled Painting (Troels Worsel)

1993. Europa. Contemporary Art. Mult.
1000 3k.75 Type **424** 1·20 65
1001 5k. "The 7 Corners of the Earth" (Stig Brogger) (vert) 1·90 90

425 "Pierrot" (Thor Bogelund, 1947)

1993. Nordic Countries' Postal Co-operation. Tourism. Publicity posters for Tivoli Gardens, Copenhagen. Multicoloured.
1002 3k.75 Type **425** 1·10 30
1003 5k. Child holding balloons (Wilhelm Freddie, 1987) (vert) 1·50 60

426 "Danmark"

1993. Training Ships. Multicoloured.
1004 3k.75 Type **426** 1·20 25
1005 4k.75 "Jens Krogh" (25×30 mm) 2·30 2·20
1006 5k. "Georg Stage" 1·80 80
1007 9k.50 "Marilyn Anne" (36×26 mm) 4·00 3·50

427 Map

1993. Inauguration of Denmark–Russia Submarine Cable and 500th Anniv of Friendship Treaty.

1008	**427**	5k. green	1·80	45

428 Prow of Viking Ship

1993. Children's Stamp Design Competition.

1009	**428**	3k.75 multicoloured	1·10	20

429 Emblem

1993. 75th Anniv of Social Work of Young Men's Christian Association.

1010	**429**	3k.75+50ore green, red and black	1·50	1·30

430 "If you want a Letter... Write one Yourself"

1993. Letter-writing Campaign.

1011	**430**	5k. ultram, bl & blk	1·60	75

431 Silver Brooch and Chain, North Falster

1993. Traditional Jewellery. Multicoloured.

1012	3k.50 Type **431**	1·30	80
1013	3k.75 Gilt-silver brooch with owner's monogram, Amager	1·30	30
1014	5k. Silver buttons and brooches, Laeso	1·70	45
1015	8k.75 Silver buttons, Romo	3·25	2·30

432 "Assemblage" (Vilhelm Lundstrom)

1993. Paintings. Multicoloured.

1016	5k. Type **432**	2·20	2·10
1017	15k. "Composition" (Franciska Clausen)	5·25	5·00

433 Duck

1994. Save Water and Energy Campaign.

1018	**433**	3k.75 multicoloured	1·10	20
1019	-	5k. green, red & black	1·40	50

DESIGN: 5k. Spade (in Danish "spar" = save) and "CO2".

434 Marselisborg Castle, Aarhus

1994. Royal Residences.

1020	**434**	3k.50 dp brn, grn & brn	1·10	75
1021	-	3k.75 multicoloured	1·10	20
1022	-	5k. grn, dp brn & brn	1·80	65
1023	-	8k.75 dp brn, grn & brn	3·00	2·30

DESIGNS: 3k.75, Amalienborg Castle, Copenhagen; 5k. Fredensborg Castle, North Zealand; 8k.75, Graasten Castle, South Jutland.

435 "Danmark" and Wegener's Weather Balloon, Danmarkshavn

1994. Europa. Discoveries. "Danmark" Expedition to North-East Greenland, 1906–08.

1024	**435**	3k.75 purple	1·30	30
1025	-	5k. black	1·80	55

DESIGN: 5k. Johan Peter Koch and theodolite.

436 Copenhagen Tram No. 2, 1911

1994. Trams. Multicoloured.

1026	3k.75 Type **436**	1·00	30
1027	4k.75 Aarhus tram, 1928	2·00	1·60
1028	5k. Odense tram, 1911 (vert)	1·80	95
1029	12k. Copenhagen horse tram "Honen", 1880 (37×21 mm)	4·75	4·00

437 Prince Henrik

1994. Danish Red Cross Fund. 60th Birthday of Prince Henrik, the Prince Consort.

1030	**437**	3k.75+50ore mult	1·50	1·50

438 Kite

1994. Children's Stamp Design Competition.

1031	**438**	3k.75 multicoloured	1·20	45

439 Emblem

1994. 75th Anniv of I.L.O.

1032	**439**	5k. multicoloured	1·50	50

440 House Sparrows

1994. Protected Animals. Multicoloured.

1033	3k.75 Type **440**	1·00	30
1034	4k.75 Badger	2·30	2·10
1035	5k. Red squirrel (vert)	1·60	65
1036	9k.50 Pair of black grouse	4·25	3·75
1037	12k. Black grass snake (36×26 mm)	4·25	3·75

441 Teacher

1994. 150th Anniv of Folk High Schools.

1038	**441**	3k.75 multicoloured	1·20	30

442 Study for "Italian Woman with Sleeping Child" (Wilhelm Marstrand)

1994. Paintings. Multicoloured.

1039	5k. Type **442**	1·70	1·70
1040	15k. "Interior from Amaliegade with the Artist's Brothers" (Wilhelm Bendz)	4·75	4·50

443 The Red Building (architect's drawing, Hack Kampmann)

1995. 800th Anniv of Aarhus Cathedral School.

1041	**443**	3k.75 multicoloured	1·20	30

444 Anniversary Emblem

1995. 50th Anniv of United Nations Organization. U.N. World Summit for Social Development, Copenhagen.

1042	**444**	5k. multicoloured	1·50	45

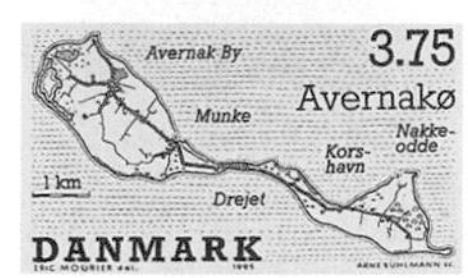
445 Avernako

1995. Danish Islands. Each brown, blue and red.

1043	3k.75 Type **445**	1·10	20
1044	4k.75 Fejo	1·90	1·80
1045	5k. Fur	1·50	65
1046	9k.50 Endelave	3·00	3·00

446 Field-Marshal Montgomery and Copenhagen Town Hall

1995. Europa. Peace and Freedom. Mult.

1047	3k.75 Type **446**	1·10	30
1048	5k. White coaches (repatriation of Danes from German concentration camps) (horiz)	1·50	65
1049	8k.75 Dropping of supplies from Lockheed C-130 Hercules (horiz)	2·50	1·90
1050	12k. Jews escaping by boat to Sweden (horiz)	4·50	4·00

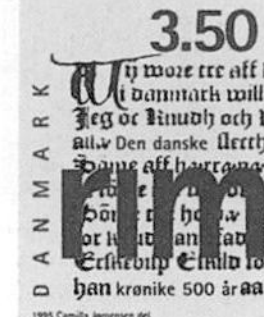
447 Detail of Page

1995. 500th Anniv of "The Rhymed Chronicle" by Friar Niels (first book printed in Danish).

1051	**447**	3k.50 multicoloured	1·10	65

448 Stage

1995. Nordic Countries' Postal Co-operation. Music Festivals. Multicoloured.

1052	3k.75 Type **448** (25th anniv of Roskilde Festival)	1·10	30
1053	5k. Violinist (21st anniv of Tonder Festival) (20×38 mm)	1·70	80

449 Broken Feather

1995. 50th Anniv of National Society of Polio and Accident Victims.

1054	**449**	3k.75+50ore red	1·80	1·70

450 "Midsummer Eve" (Jens Sondergaard)

1995. Paintings. Multicoloured.

1055	10k. Type **450**	3·50	3·50
1056	15k. "Landscape at Gudhjem" (Niels Lergaard)	5·75	5·50

451 Sextant

1995. 450th Birth Anniv of Tycho Brahe (astronomer). Multicoloured.

1057	3k.75 Uraniborg (Palace Observatory)	1·10	25
1058	5k.50 Type **451**	1·80	1·50

452 TEKNO Model Vehicles

1995. Danish Toys. Multicoloured.

1059	3k.75 Type **452**	1·10	20
1060	5k. Edna (celluloid doll), Kirstine (china doll) and Holstebro teddy bear	1·40	60
1061	8k.75 Toy bin-plate locomotives and rolling stock	2·30	2·00
1062	12k. Glud & Marstrand horse-drawn fire engine and carriage	3·50	3·75

453 The Round Tower

1996. Copenhagen, European Cultural Capital. Multicoloured.

1063	3k.75 Type **453**	1·10	30
1064	5k. Christiansborg	1·50	65
1065	8k.75 Dome of Marble Church as hot-air balloon	2·50	1·90
1066	12k. "The Little Mermaid" on stage	3·50	3·25

454 Disabled Basketball Player

1996. Sport. Multicoloured.

1067	3k.75 Type **454**	1·10	20
1068	4k.75 Swimming	1·50	1·30
1069	5k. Yachting	1·50	65
1070	9k.50 Cycling	3·00	2·40

455 Businessmen

1996. Cent of Danish Employers' Confederation.

1071	**455**	3k.75 multicoloured	1·10	50

456 Asta Nielsen (actress)

1996. Europa. Famous Women.

1072	-	3k.75 brown & dp brn	1·20	50
1073	**456**	5k. grey and blue	1·70	80

DESIGN: 3k.75, Karin Blixen (writer).

457 Roskilde Fjord Boat

1996. Wooden Sailing Boats.

1074	**457**	3k.50 brn, bl & red	1·20	95
1075	-	3k.75 lilac, grn & red	1·10	30
1076	-	12k.25 blk, brn & red	4·50	4·50

DESIGNS—As T **457**: 12k.25, South Funen Archipelago smack; 20×38 mm: 3k.75, Limfjorden skiff.

458 Fornaes

1996. Lighthouses. Multicoloured.

1077	3k.75 Type **458**	1·20	30
1078	5k. Blavandshuk	1·50	60
1079	5k.25 Bovbjerg	1·60	1·40
1080	8k.75 Mon	2·50	1·90

459 Ribbons forming Hearts within Star

1996. AIDS Foundation.

1081	**459**	3k.75+50ore red & blk	1·80	1·60

460 Vase

1996. 150th Birth Anniv of Thorvald Bindesboll (ceramic artist). Multicoloured.

1082	3k.75 Type **460**	1·10	30
1083	4k. Portfolio cover	1·30	95

461 "At Lunch" (Peder Kroyer)

1996. Paintings. Multicoloured.

1084	10k. Type **461**	3·25	2·50
1085	15k. "Girl with Sunflowers" (Michael Ancher)	4·00	3·75

462 Queen Margrethe waving to Children

1997. Silver Jubilee of Queen Margrethe. Mult.

1086	3k.50 Queen Margrethe and Prince Henrik	1·00	75
1087	3k.75 Queen Margrethe and Crown Prince Frederik	1·20	30
1088	4k. Queen Margrethe at desk	1·10	1·00
1089	5k.25 Type **462**	1·60	1·30

463 Queen Margrethe

1997

1092	**463**	3k.75 red	1·10	45
1093	**463**	4k. green	1·10	65
1094	**463**	4k. red	1·10	25
1095	**463**	4k.25 brown	1·40	1·30
1096	**463**	4k.50 blue	1·40	95
1097	**463**	4k.75 brown	1·60	1·50
1098	**463**	5k. violet	1·40	45
1099	**463**	5k.25 blue	1·50	55
1100	**463**	5k.50 red	1·40	1·20
1101	**463**	5k.75 blue	1·50	1·00
1104	**463**	6k.75 green	1·60	1·60

464 Karlstrup Post Mill, Zealand

1997. Centenary of Open Air Museum, Lyngby. Construction Drawings by B. Ehrhardt.

1111	**464**	3k.50 brown & purple	1·10	85
1112	-	3k.75 lilac and green	1·20	30
1113	-	5k. green and lilac	1·50	65
1114	-	8k.75 green & brown	2·50	1·60

DESIGNS: 3k.75, Ellested water mill, Funen; 5k. Fjellerup Manor Barn, Djursland; 8k.75, Toftum farm, Romo.

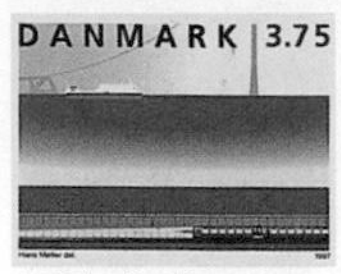

465 The East Tunnel

1997. Inauguration of Railway Section of the Great Belt Link. Multicoloured.

1115	3k.75 Type **465**	1·00	30
1116	4k.75 The West Bridge	1·40	1·30

466 Sneezing

1997. Asthma Allergy Association.

1117	**466**	3k.75+50ore mult	1·90	1·80

467 Electric Trains under New Carlsberg Bridge

1997. 150th Anniv of Copenhagen–Roskilde Railway. Multicoloured.

1118	3k.75 Type **467**	1·10	30
1119	8k.75 Steam train under original Carlsberg bridge (after H. Holm)	2·50	1·60

468 King Erik and Queen Margrete I

1997. 600th Anniv of Kalmar Union (of Denmark, Norway and Sweden). Multicoloured.

1120	4k. Type **468**	1·30	1·10
1121	4k. The Three Graces	1·30	1·10

Nos. 1120/1 were issued, se-tenant, forming a composite design of a painting by an unknown artist.

469 Post Office Cars on Great Belt Ferry

1997. Closure of Travelling Post Offices.

1122	**469**	5k. multicoloured	1·40	60

470 "The Tinder-box"

1997. Europa. Tales and Legends by Hans Christian Andersen.

1123	**470**	3k.75 dp brn & brn	1·10	30
1124	-	5k.25 red, dp grn & grn	1·50	1·20

DESIGN: 5k.25, "Thumbelina".

471 "Dust dancing in the Sun" (Vilheim Hammershoi)

1997. Paintings. Multicoloured.

1125	9k.75 Type **471**	3·25	2·75
1126	13k. "Woman Mountaineer" (Jens Willumsen)	4·25	3·75

472 Faaborg Chair (Kaare Klint)

1997. Danish Design. Multicoloured.

1127	3k.75 Type **472**	1·10	25
1128	4k. Margrethe bowls (Sigvard Bernadotte and Acton Bjorn)	1·10	1·00
1129	5k. The Ant chairs (Arne Jacobsen) (horiz)	1·70	40
1130	12k.25 Silver bowl (Georg Jensen)	3·75	3·50

473 Workers

1998. Centenary of Danish Confederation of Trade Unions. Multicoloured.

1131	3k.50 Type **473** (General Workers' Union in Denmark)	1·10	75
1132	3k.75 Crowd at meeting (Danish Confederation of Trade Unions)	1·20	30
1133	4k.75 Nurse (Danish Nurses' Organization)	1·50	1·40
1134	5k. Woman using telephone (Union of Commercial and Clerical Employees in Denmark)	1·60	65

474 Roskilde Cathedral and Viking Longship

1998. Millenary of Roskilde.

1135	**474**	3k.75 multicoloured	1·10	40

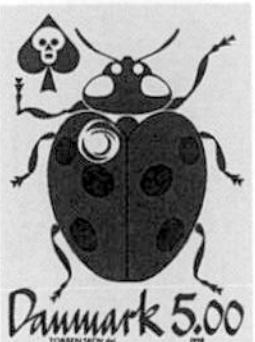

475 Seven-spotted Ladybird

1998. Environmental Issues. Gardening Without Chemicals.

1136	**475**	5k. red and black	1·30	50

476 Postman, 1922

1998. Post and Tele Museum, Copenhagen. Mult.

1137	3k.75 Type **476**	1·10	30
1138	4k.50 Morse operator, 1910	1·30	1·00
1139	5k.50 Telephonist, 1910	1·80	1·30
1140	8k.75 Postman, 1998	3·00	2·00

477 The West Bridge

1998. Inauguration of Road Section of the Great Belt Link. Each blue, black and red.

1141	5k. Type **477**	1·30	75
1142	5k. The East Bridge	1·30	75

478 Harbour Master

1998. Nordic Countries' Postal Co-operation. Shipping. Multicoloured.

1143	6k.50 Type **478**	2·10	1·50
1144	6k.50 Sextant and radar image of Copenhagen harbour	2·10	1·50
MS1145	106×75 mm. Nos. 1143/4	6·25	6·00

Nos. 1143/4 were issued together, se-tenant, forming a composite design.

479 Horse (Agriculture Show)

1998. Europa. National Festivals. Mult.

1146	3k.75 Type **479**	1·10	50
1147	4k.50 Aarhus Festival Week	1·40	1·20

480 Reaching Hand

1998. Anti-cancer Campaign.

1148	480	3k.75+50ore red, orange and black	1·60	1·50

481 "Danish Autumn" (Per Kirkeby)

1998. Philatelic Creations. Multicoloured.

1149	3k.75 Type **481**	1·20	1·30
1150	5k. "Alpha" (Mogens Andersen) (vert)	1·80	1·50
1151	8k.75 "Imagery" (Ejler Bille) (vert)	3·00	2·20
1152	19k. "Celestial Horse" (Carl-Henning Pedersen)	6·00	4·75

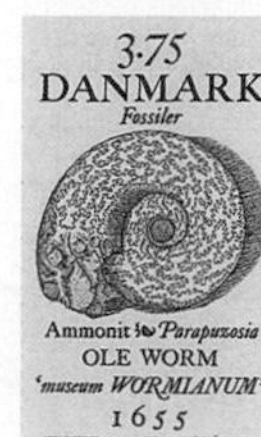

482 Ammonite (from "Museum Wormianum" by Ole Worm)

1998. Fossils. Designs reproducing engravings from geological works. Each black and red on cream.

1153	3k.75 Type **482**	1·10	50
1154	4k.50 Shark's teeth (from "De Solido" by Niels Stensen)	1·60	1·30
1155	5k.50 Sea urchin (from "Stevens Klint" by Soren Abildgaard)	1·70	1·50
1156	15k. Pleurotomariida (from "Den Danske Atlas" by Erich Pontoppidan)	4·00	3·75
MS1157	114×142 mm. Nos. 1153/6	8·25	8·00

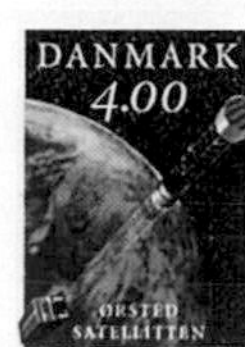

483 Satellite and Earth

1999. Launch of "Orsted" Satellite (Danish research satellite).

1158	483	4k. multicoloured	1·10	25

484 Beech

1999. Deciduous Trees. Multicoloured.

1159	4k. Type **484**	1·20	35
1160	5k. Ash (vert)	1·60	1·10
1161	5k.25 Small-leaved lime (vert)	1·70	65
1162	9k.25 Pendunculate oak	2·75	1·80

485 Home Guard

1999. 50th Anniv of Home Guard.

1163	485	3k.75 multicoloured	1·20	1·10

486 Northern Lapwing and Eggs

1999. Harbingers of Spring. Multicoloured.

1164	4k. Type **486**	1·10	25
1165	5k.25 Greylag goose with chicks	1·50	55
MS1166	99×82 mm. Nos. 1164/5	3·75	3·75

487 Emblem and Lockheed Martin F-16 Fighting Falcon

1999. 50th Anniv of North Atlantic Treaty Organization.

1167	487	4k.25 multicoloured	1·30	1·10

488 Vejlerne

1999. Europa. Parks and Gardens. Multicoloured.

1168	4k.50 Type **488**	1·10	1·00
1169	5k.50 Langli Island	1·80	1·40

489 Anniversary Emblem

1999. 50th Anniv of Council of Europe.

1170	489	9k.75 blue	2·50	2·00

490 "g" and Paragraph Sign

1999. 150th Anniv of Danish Constitution.

1171	490	4k. red and black	1·10	35

491 Kjeld Petersen and Dirch Passer

1999. 150th Anniv of Danish Revue.

1172	491	4k. red	1·10	40
1173	-	4k.50 black	1·60	1·40
1174	-	5k.25 blue	1·70	1·10
1175	-	6k.75 mauve	1·50	2·00

DESIGNS: 4k.50, Osvald Helmuth; 5k.25, Preben Kaas and Jorgen Ryg; 6k.75, Liva Weel.

492 Emblem

1999. Alzheimer's Disease Association.

1176	492	4k.+50ore. red and blue	1·20	1·10

493 The "Black Diamond"

1999. Inauguration of Royal Library Extension, Copenhagen.

1177	493	8k.75 black	3·25	2·75

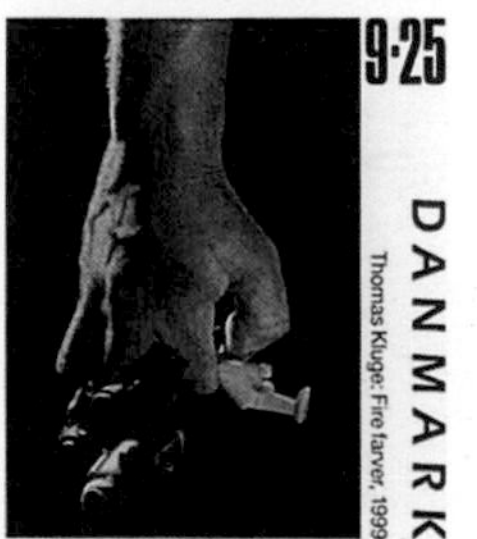

494 "Four Colours" (Thomas Kluge)

1999. Paintings. Multicoloured.

1178	9k.25 Type **494**	2·20	1·90
1179	16k. "Boy" (Lise Malinovsky)	4·25	3·75

495 Barn Swallows

1999. Migratory Birds. Multicoloured.

1180	4k. Type **495**	1·20	35
1181	5k.25 Greylag geese with goslings	1·60	70
1182	5k.50 Eiders	1·80	1·20
1183	12k.25 Arctic tern feeding chick	3·25	2·50
MS1184	Two sheets, each 116×72 mm. (a) Nos. 1180/1. (b) Nos. 1182/3	8·00	7·75

496 Hearts

1999. New Millennium. Multicoloured.

1185	4k. Type **496**	1·10	40
1186	4k. Horizontal wavy lines	1·10	40

497 Johan Henrik Deuntzer (Prime Minister) on Front Page of *Aftenposten* (newspaper)

2000. The Twentieth Century (1st series).

1187	497	4k. black and cream	1·10	40
1188	-	4k.50 multicoloured	1·30	1·30
1189	-	5k.25 multicoloured	1·40	1·10
1190	-	5k.75 multicoloured	1·80	1·20

DESIGNS—4k. Type **497** (Venstre (workers') party victory in election, 1901); 4k.50, Caricature of Frederik Borgbjerg (party member, Alfred Schmidt) (first Social Democrat Lord Mayor in Denmark, 1903); 5k.25, Asta Nielson and Poul Reumert (actors) in scene from *The Abyss* (film), 1910; 5k.75, Telephone advertising poster, 1914.

See also Nos. 1207/10, 1212/15 and 1221/4.

498 Queen Margrethe II (Pia Schutzmann)

2000. 60th Birthday of Queen Margrethe II.

1191	498	4k. black and red	1·00	45
1192	498	5k.25 black and blue	1·40	55
MS1193		63×60 mm. Nos. 1191/2	2·75	2·75

499 Queen Margrethe II

2000

1194	499	4k. red	1·10	20
1195	499	4k.25 blue	1·70	1·60
1195a	499	4k.25 red	1·10	20
1196a	499	4k.50 red	7·25	20
1196b	499	4k.75 brown	1·10	20
1196d	499	4k.75 rosine	1·40	1·10
1197	499	5k. green	1·40	1·00
1198	499	5k.25 blue	1·40	45
1199	499	5k.50 violet	1·70	55
1199a	499	5k.50 red	2·25	1·50
1200	499	5k.75 green	1·70	85
1201	499	6k. brown	1·70	1·10
1201a	499	6k.25 green	1·70	1·60
1201b	499	6k.50 green	2·30	1·60
1201c	499	6k.50 blue	2·50	1·60

1202	499	6k.75 red	2·00	1·50
1203	499	7k. purple	2·00	1·60
1203a	499	7k.25 brown	2·00	1·90
1203b	499	7k.50 ultramarine	2·00	1·90
1203c	499	7k.75 agate	3·25	2·10
1203d	499	8k. black	1·80	1·70
1203e	499	8k.25 blue	2·50	2·00
1204	499	8k.50 blue	2·75	2·10
1204a	499	8k.50 blue	4·00	2·60
1204b	499	9k. blue	4·75	3·00

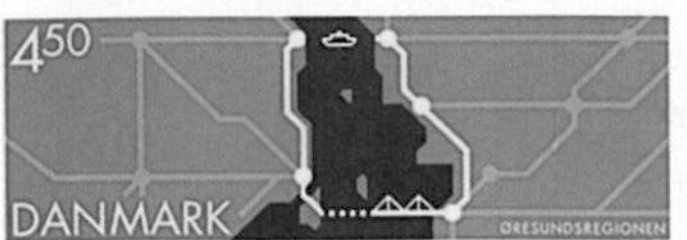

500 Map of Oresund Region

2000. Inauguration of Oresund Link (Denmark–Sweden road and rail system).

1205	500	4k.50 blue, white & blk	1·40	1·10
1206	-	4k.50 blue, green & blk	1·40	1·10

DESIGN: No. 1206, Oresund Bridge.

501 Suffragette on Front Page of *Politiken* (newspaper)

2000. The Twentieth Century (2nd series).

1207	501	4k. red, blk & cream	1·10	30
1208	-	5k. multicoloured	1·40	1·10
1209	-	5k.50 multicoloured	1·60	1·10
1210	-	6k.75 multicoloured	2·00	1·60

DESIGNS—4k. Type **501** (women's suffrage, 1915); 5k. Caricature of Thorvald Stauning (Prime Minister 1924–26 and 1929–42) (Herluf Jensenius) (The Kanslergade Agreement (economic and social reforms)), 1933; 5k.50, Poster for *The Wheel of Fortune* (film), 1927; 6k.75, Front page of *Radio Weekly Review* (magazine), 1925.

502 "Building Europe"

2000. Europa.

1211	502	9k.75 multicoloured	2·75	2·20

503 Front Page of *Kristeligt Dagblad* (newspaper), 5 May 1945

2000. The Twentieth Century (3rd series).

1212	503	4k. black and cream	1·10	20
1213	-	5k.75 multicoloured	1·70	85
1214	-	6k.75 multicoloured	2·00	1·60
1215	-	12k.25 multicoloured	3·00	2·50

DESIGNS—4k. Type **503** (Liberation of Denmark); 5k.75, Caricature of Princess Margrethe (Herlif Jenserius) (adoption of new constitution, 1953); 6k.75, Ib Schonberg and Hvid Moller (actors) in a scene from *Cafe Paradise* (film), 1950; 12k.25, Front cover of brochure for Danish Arena televisions, 1957.

504 Linked Hands

2000. Cerebral Palsy Association.

1216	504	4k.+50ore blue and red	1·40	1·30

505 Lockheed C-130 Hercules Transport Plane

2000. 50th Anniv of Royal Danish Air Force.

1217	505	9k.75 black and red	2·50	2·10
MS1218		116×60 mm. No. 1217	3·00	3·00

506 "Pegasus" (Kurt Trampedach)

2000. Paintings. Multicoloured.

1219	4k. Type **506**	1·40	1·10
1220	5k.25 "Untitled" (Nina Sten-Knudsen)	1·70	1·30

507 Front Page of *Berlingske Tidende* (newspaper), 3 October 1972

2000. The Twentieth Century (4th series).

1221	507	4k. red, blk & cream	1·10	55
1222	-	4k.50 multicoloured	1·40	1·10
1223	-	5k.25 blk, red & cream	1·70	1·10
1224	-	5k.50 multicoloured	2·00	1·30

DESIGNS: 4k. Type **507** (referendum on entry to European Economic Community); 4k.50, Caricature from *Blaeksprutten* (magazine), 1969 (The Youth Revolt); 5k.25, Poster for *The Olsen Gang* (film, 1968); 5k.50, Web page (development of the internet).

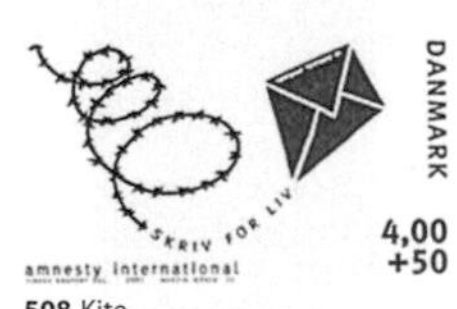

508 Kite

2001. 40th Anniv of Amnesty International.

1225	508	4k.+50 ore blk & red	1·40	1·10

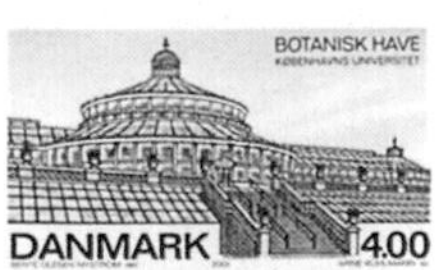

509 Palm House

2001. 400th Anniv of Copenhagen University Botanical Gardens. Multicoloured.

1226	4k. Type **509**	1·10	55
1227	6k. Lake (28×21 mm)	1·40	85
1228	12k.25 Giant lily-pad (28×21 mm)	2·75	3·00

510 "a", Text and Flowers

2001. Reading. Danish Children's Book "ABC" (first reader) by Halfdan Rasmussen. Multicoloured.

1229	4k. Type **510**	1·10	55
1230	7k. "Z" and text	1·70	1·60

511 Martinus William Ferslew (designer and engraver)

2001. 150th Anniv of First Danish Stamp. Each black, red and brown.

1231	4k. Type **511**	1·10	55
1232	5k.50 Andreas Thiele (printer)	1·40	1·10
1233	6k. Frantz Christopher von Jessen (Copenhagen postmaster)	1·70	1·30
1234	10k.25 Magrius Otto Sophus (Postmaster-General)	2·40	2·30

512 Hands catching Water

2001. Europa. Water Resources. Multicoloured.

1235	4k.50 Type **512**	1·40	1·10
1236	9k.75 Woman in shower	2·75	2·75

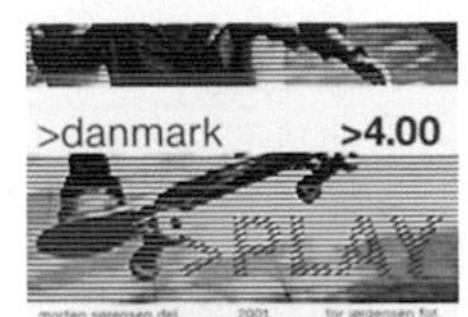

513 Skateboarder

2001. Youth Culture. Multicoloured.

1237	4k. Type **513**	1·10	35
1238	5k.50 Couple kissing	1·50	1·30
1239	6k. Mixing records	1·60	1·40
1240	10k.25 Pierced tongue	2·75	2·50
MS1241	121×70 mm. Nos. 1237/40	7·75	7·50

514 "Missus" (Jorn Larsen)

2001. Paintings.

1242	514	18k. black and red	4·50	3·75
1243	-	22k. multicoloured	5·75	5·50

DESIGN: 22k. "Postbillede" (Henning Damgaard-Sorensen).

515 Queen Margrethe II with 1984 Prince Henrik and 1994 Marselisborg Castle Stamps

2001. "HAFNIA '01" International Stamp Exhibition, Copenhagen. Multicoloured.

1244	4k. Type **515**	1·10	65
1245	4k.50 King Frederik IX with 1985 Queen Ingrid and 1994 Graasten Castle stamps	1·20	85
1246	5k.50 King Christian X with 1994 Amalienborg Castle and 1939 Queen Alexandrine stamps	1·50	1·40
1247	7k. King Christian IX with 1994 Fredensborg Castle and 1907 King Frederick VIII stamps	2·00	1·90
MS1248	90×100 mm. Nos. 1244/7	6·75	6·50

516 *Bukken-Bruse*

2001. Ferries.

1249	516	3k.75 black, green and emerald	1·00	65
1250	-	4k. black, brown and green	1·10	75
1251	-	4k.25 black, green and blue	1·20	85
1252	-	6k. grey, black and red	1·70	1·60

DESIGNS: 4k. *Ouro*; 4k.25, *Hjarno*; 6k. *Barsofargen*.

517 Rasmus Klump (Vilhelm Hansen)

2002. Danish Cartoons. Multicoloured.

1253	4k. Type **517**	1·10	30
1254	5k.50 Valhalla (Peter Madsen)	1·20	1·30
1255	6k.50 Jungo and Rita (Flemming Quist Moller)	1·50	1·50
1256	10k.50 Cirkleen (Hanne and Jannik Hastrup)	2·30	2·30
MS1257	142×80 mm. Nos. 1253/6	7·50	7·25

518 Back View

2002. Nordic Countries' Postal Co-operation. Modern Art. Showing "The Girls in the Airport" (sculpture, Hanne Varming). Each black, bronze on cream.

1258	4k. Type **518**	1·10	55
1259	5k. Front view	1·50	1·30

519 Face

2002. L.E.V. National Association (mental health foundation).

1260	519	4k. +50ore brown, agate on cream	1·40	1·30

520 Clown (Luna Ostergard)

2002. Europa. Circus. Winning Entries in Stamp Design Competition. Multicoloured.

1261	4k. Type **520**	1·10	55
1262	5k. Clown (different) (Camille Wagner Larsen)	1·40	1·10

521 Jon's Chapel, Bornholm

2002. Landscape Photographs by Kirsten Klein.

1263	521	4k. black and brown	1·10	40
1264	-	6k. black	1·60	1·10
1265	-	6k.50 deep green and green	1·70	1·30
1266	-	12k.50 black and blue	3·00	2·75

DESIGNS: 6k. Trees, Vestervig; 6k.50, Woods, Karskov, Langeland; 12k.50, Cliffs and beach, Stenbjerg, West Jutland.

522 1953 Nimbus Motorcycle and Sidecar

2002. Postal Vehicles. Multicoloured.

1267	4k. Type **522**	1·10	40
1268	5k.50 1962 Bedford CA van	1·40	1·10
1269	10k. 1984 Renault 4 van	2·50	1·60
1270	19k. 1998 Volvo FH12 lorry	5·00	4·25

523 *Dana* (marine research ship) and Atlantic Cod

2002. Centenary of International Council for the Exploration of the Sea. Multicoloured.

1271	4k. Type **523**	1·10	40
1272	10k. Hirtshals lighthouse and atlantic cod	3·00	2·50
MS1273	186×61 mm. 4k. Type **523**; 10k.50 Lighthouse and atlantic cod	4·25	4·00

Stamps of a similar design were issued by Faroe Islands and Greenland.

524 "Children's Corner" (Jens Birkemose)

2002. Paintings.

1274	**524**	5k. red and blue	1·60	1·50
1275	-	6k.50 multicoloured	2·00	1·90

DESIGN: 6k.50 "Maleren og modellen" (Frans Kannik).

525 Underground Train

2002. Inauguration of Copenhagen Metro.

1276	**525**	5k.50 black, green and brown on cream	1·70	1·30

526 Dianas Have, Horsholm (Vandkunsten Design Studio)

2002. Domestic Architecture (1st series). Multicoloured.

1277	4k. Type **526**	90	45
1278	4k.25 Bapistry, Long House and Gate (Poul Ingemann) Blangstedgard, Odense	1·10	1·10
1279	5k.50 Dansk Folkeferie, Karrebaeksminde (Stephan Kappel)	1·40	1·30
1280	6k.50 Terrasser, Fredensborg (Jorn Utzon)	1·50	1·50
1281	9k. Soholm, Klampenborg (Arne Jacobsen)	2·30	2·20

See also Nos. 1296/1300, 1369/73 and 1398/1402.

527 Football

2003. Youth Sports. Multicoloured.

1282	4k.25 Type **527**	1·00	30
1283	5k.50 Swimming	1·40	1·10
1284	8k.50 Gymnastics	2·00	1·70
1285	11k.50 Basketball	3·25	2·75

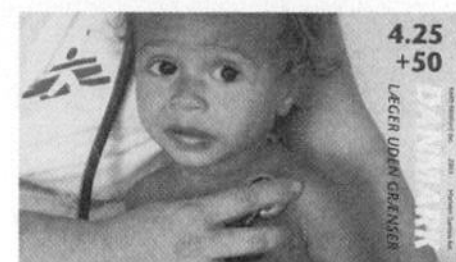

528 Child and Doctor

2003. Medicins sans Frontieres (medical charity).

1286	**528**	4k.25+50ore multicoloured	1·40	1·10

529 Expedition Members

2003. Centenary of the Danish Literary Expedition to Greenland.

1287	**529**	4k.25 blue	1·10	40
1288	-	7k. brown, green and blue (60×22 mm)	2·30	1·90
MS1289		167×61 mm. Nos. 1287/81	2·75	2·75

DESIGN: 7k. Tents and mountains.

Stamps of a similar design were issued by Greenland.

530 Mayfly (*Ephemera danica*)

2003. Insects. Multicoloured.

1290	4k.25 Type **530**	1·00	40
1291	6k.50 Water beetle (*Dysticus latissimus*)	1·70	1·30
1292	12k. Dragonfly (*Cordulegaster boltoni*) (20×39 mm)	3·25	3·00
MS1293	80×76 mm. Nos. 1290/2	6·75	6·00

531 "Fools" Festival Poster' (Ole Flick)

2003. Europa. Poster Art.

1294	**531**	4k.25 multicoloured	1·00	40
1295	-	5k.50 black	1·40	75

DESIGN: 5k.50, "Thorvaldsen's Museum" (Ole Woldbye).

2003. Domestic Architecture (2nd series). As T 526. Multicoloured.

1296	4k. Bellahoj, Copenhagen (Tage Nielsen and Mogens Irming)	1·00	85
1297	4k.25 Anchersvej Christiansholm Fort, Klampenborg (Mogens Lasen)	1·10	45
1298	5k.25 Gerthasminde, Odense (Anton Rosen)	1·50	1·10
1299	9k. Solvang, Vallekilde (Anton Bentsen)	2·50	2·20
1300	15k. Stenbrogard, Brorup (Peder Holden Hansen)	4·00	3·25

532 "Baering" (Sys Hindsbo)

2003. Paintings. Multicoloured.

1301	5k.50 Type **532**	1·70	1·40
1302	19k. "The Forgotten Land" (Poul Anker Bech)	5·00	4·75

533 Thyra's Stone

2003. UNESCO World Heritage Site. Royal Jelling Open Air Museum.

1303	**533**	4k.25 black, sepia and brown	1·00	40
1304	-	5k.50 black, brown and sepia	1·50	1·10
1305	-	8k.50 black and bistre	2·30	1·90
1306	-	11k.50 black and deep olive	3·25	2·20

DESIGNS: Type **533**; 5k.50, Gorm's cup; 8k.50, Harald's stone; 11k.50, Jelling church.

534 "Towards the Light" (statue, Rudolph Tegner)

2003. Centenary of Niels Finsen's Nobel Prize for Physiology and Medicine.

1307	**534**	6k.50 indigo	1·70	1·40

2004. Arms. As T 73.

(a) Ordinary gum

1307a		10k. bistre	2·30	2·20
1307b		10k.50 carmine	2·50	2·30
1308	**73**	12k.50 indigo	3·00	2·75
1309	**73**	13k. orange	3·25	3·00
1310	**73**	13k.50 green	3·50	3·25
1311	**73**	15k. blue	3·75	3·25
1311a	**73**	16k. green	5·75	5·50
1312	**73**	16k.50 brown	4·25	4·00
1313	**73**	17k. green	4·50	4·25
1314	**73**	17k.50 purple	5·25	5·00
1315	**73**	20k. ultramarine	5·50	5·25
1315a	**73**	20k.50 lilac	10·25	10·00
1316	**73**	22k. maroon	5·75	5·50

(b) Self-adhesive gum

1331		10k. pale olive-bistre	5·50	3·50
1332		15k. blue	6·50	4·50
1333		20k. dull ultramarine	15·00	13·00
1333a		25k. deep blue-green (26.10.10)	7·00	6·25
1317	**73**	30k. chesnut (24.3.2010)	7·50	6·50
1334		30k. chestnut	13·50	11·00
1335		50k. pale carmine	25·00	22·00

535 Butterfly and Caterpillar

2004. Centenary of Children's Aid Day (fund raising charity).

1368	**535**	4k.25+50ore multicoloured	1·30	1·10

2004. Domestic Architecture (3rd series). As T 526. Multicoloured.

1369	4k.50 Spurveskjul, Virum Copenhagen (Nicolai Abildgaard)	1·10	85
1370	6k. Liselund, Møn (Andreas Kirkerup)	1·50	1·30
1371	7k. Kampmann's Yard, Varde (Hans Ollgaard)	1·80	1·60
1372	12k.50 Harsdorff's House, Copenhagen (Caspar Harsdorff)	3·00	2·75
1373	15k. Nyso, Praesto (Jens Lauridsen)	3·75	3·25

536 Heimdal carrying Gjallar Horn on Bifrost Bridge

2004. Nordic Mythology. Each sepia, blue and black.

1374	4k.50 Type **536**	1·10	60
1375	6k. Gefion ploughing Sealand out of Sweden	1·50	1·30
MS1376	105×71 mm. Nos. 1374/5	2·75	2·75

Stamps of a similar theme were issued by Aland Islands, Faroe Islands, Finland, Greenland, Iceland, Norway and Sweden.

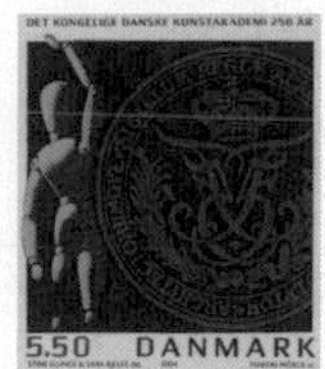

537 Artist's Wooden Figure and Academy Seal

2004. 250th Anniv of Academy of Fine Arts, Copenhagen.

1377	**537**	5k.50 multicoloured	1·50	1·20

538 Fountain viewed through Doorway

2004. 300th Anniv of Frederiksberg Palace. Multicoloured.

1378	4k.25 Type **538**	1·10	90
1379	4k.50 Courtyard viewed through arch	1·10	50
1380	6k.50 Aerial view of palace (57×33 mm)	1·80	1·50
MS1381	125×78 mm. Nos. 1378/80	4·00	3·75

539 Prince Frederik and Mary Donaldson

2004. Marriage of Crown Prince Frederik and Mary Elizabeth Donaldson. Multicoloured.

1382	4k.50 Type **539**	1·20	90
1383	4k.50 As No. 1382 but with design reversed	1·20	90
MS1384	130×65 mm. Nos. 1382/3	2·75	2·50

Stamps of same design were issued by Faroe Islands and Greenland.

540 Prince Henrik

2004. 70th Birthday of Prince Henrik.

1385	**540**	4k.50 multicoloured	1·10	50

541 Cycling

2004. Europa. Holidays. Multicoloured.

1386	6k. Type **541**	1·50	1·30
1387	9k. Sailing	2·30	2·10

542 Trial Sailing of Skuldelev Reconstruction

2004. Viking Ship Museum, Roskilde. Multicoloured.

1388	4k.50 Type **542**	1·10	50
1389	5k.50 Reconstructed hull	1·50	1·10
1390	6k.50 Exhibition	1·80	1·30
1391	12k.50 Excavation	3·00	2·75

543 "Senses the Body Landscape" (Lars Ravn)

2004. Paintings. Multicoloured.

1392	13k. Type **543**	3·25	3·00
1393	21k. "The Dog Bites" (Lars Norgard)	5·25	5·00

544 Kestrel (*Falco tinnunculus*)

2004. Birds of Prey. Multicoloured.

1394	4k.50 Type **544**	1·10	50
1395	5k.50 Northern sparrow hawk (*Accipter nisus*)	1·50	1·10
1396	6k. Common buzzard (*Buteo buteo*)	1·60	1·40
1397	7k. Western marsh harrier (*Circus aeruginosus*)	1·90	1·60

2005. Domestic Architecture (4th series). As T 526. Multicoloured.

1398	4k.25 Hjarup Manse, Vamdrup	1·10	90
1399	4k.50 Ejdersted Farm, South-West Schleswig (Adriaen Alberts Hauwert)	1·20	50
1400	7k.50 Provstegade, Randers	1·90	1·60
1401	9k.50 Smith's Yard, Kirkestræde, Koge	2·30	2·10
1402	16k.50 Carmelite Monastery, Elsinore	4·25	3·50

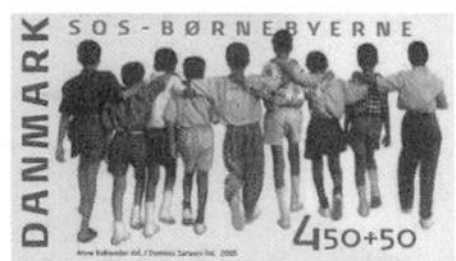

545 Boys

2005. SOS Children's Villages.

1403	**545**	4k.50 +50 ore multicoloured	1·30	1·20

546 Hans Christian Andersen

2005. Birth Bicentenary of Hans Christian Andersen (writer).

1404	**546**	4k.50 black	1·20	55
1405	-	5k.50 multicoloured (23×38 mm)	1·50	1·20
1406	-	6k.50 multicoloured (23×38 mm)	1·80	1·50
1407	-	7k.50 multicoloured (23×38 mm)	2·00	1·80

DESIGNS: 5k.50 Paper cut-out; 6k.50 Duckling, script, quill and ink pot; 7k.50 Boots.

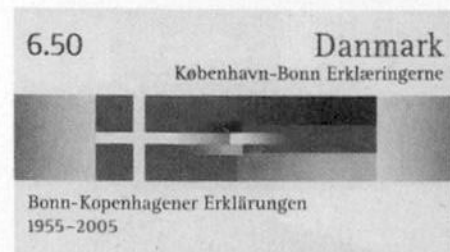

547 Danish and German Flags

2005. 50th Anniv of Copenhagen—Bonn Declarations (tolerance for minorities).

1408	**547**	6k.50 multicoloured	1·80	1·70

548 August Bournonville

2005. Birth Bicentenary of August Bournonville (choreographer).

1409	**548**	4k.50 blue, deep blue and black	1·00	95
1410	-	5k.50 yellow, claret and black	1·30	1·20
MS1411		106×70 mm. Nos. 1409/10	2·30	2·20

DESIGN: 5k.50, Pas de Deux.

549 Ships at Sea

2005. 60th Anniv of End of World War II.

1412	**549**	4k.50 blackish brown	1·00	95
1413	-	7k.50 greenish black	1·70	1·60

DESIGN: 7k.50, Unloading.

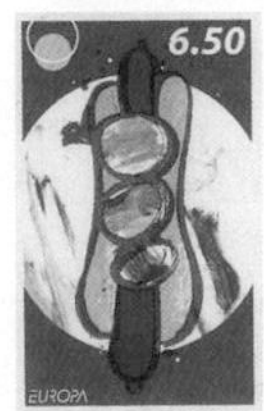

550 Hotdog

2005. Europa. Gastronomy. Multicoloured.

1414	6k.50 Type **550**	1·40	1·40
1415	9k.50 Fish	2·20	2·10

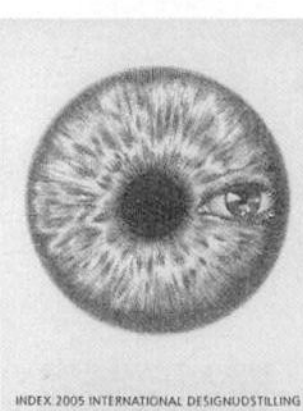

551 Iris containing Eye

2005. Index 2005 International Design Exhibition, Copenhagen.

1416	**551**	4k.50 black	1·10	1·00

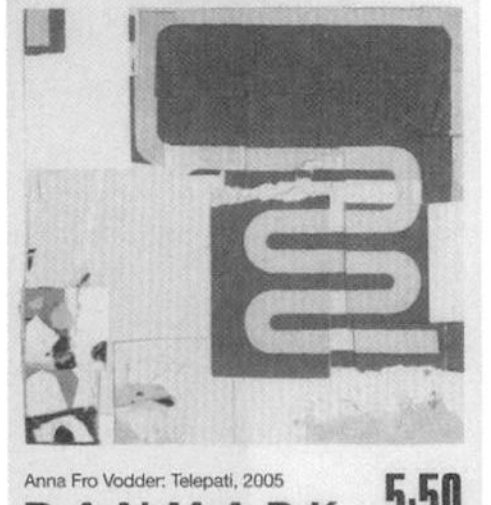

552 "Telepathy" (Anna Fro Vodder)

2005. Paintings. Multicoloured.

1417	5k.50 Type **552**	1·30	1·20
1418	6k.50 "Home Again" (Kaspar Bonnen)	1·40	1·40
1419	7k.50 "Unrest" (John Korner)	1·70	1·60
1420	12k.50 "Palace in the Morning" (Tal R) (horiz)	2·75	2·75

553 Numeral

2005. Centenary of Wavy Line.

(a) Ordinary gum

1421	**553**	25ore indigo	10	10
1422	**553**	50ore brown	15	15
1423	**553**	100ore blue	25	20
1424	**553**	200ore green	50	45
1425	**553**	450ore green	1·10	1·00
1425a	**553**	500ore green	2·50	2·50

(b) Self-adhesive gum

1431	50ö brown	30	20
1432	100ö blue	50	35
1433	200ö deep blue-green	85	70
1433a	300ö deep reddish lilac	95	60
1434	300ö pale orange	1·90	1·40
1435	400ö grey-lilac	2·10	1·50
1436	500ö light green	2·40	1·70

554 Harbour Seal (*Phoca vitulina*)

2005. Seals.

1450	**554**	4k.50 black, brown and indigo	1·00	95
1451	-	5k.50 black and indigo	1·30	1·20
MS1452		105×70 mm. Nos. 1450/1	2·30	2·20

DESIGNS: Type **554**; 5k.50 Grey seal (*Halichoerus grypus*).

555 *Galanthus nivalis*

2006. Spring Flowers. Multicoloured.

1453	4k.75 Type **555**	1·10	50
1454	5k.50 *Eranthis hyemalis*	1·20	1·20
1455	7k. *Crocus vernus*	1·60	1·30
1456	8k. *Anemone nemorosa*	1·80	1·60

556 Refugees

2006. Danish Refugee Council.

1457	**556**	4k.75+50ore brown and black	1·30	1·20

557 Castle

2006. 400th Anniv of Rosenborg Castle. Multicoloured.

1458	4k.75 Type **557**	1·10	50
1459	5k.50 Thrones and silver lion	1·30	1·20
1460	13k. Ceiling decoration	3·25	3·00

558 Elf Mound, Elf King and Elvish Women

2006. Nordic Mythology. Multicoloured.

1461	4k.75 Type **558**	1·10	50
1462	7k. Werewolves, hel-horse, incubi, gnome and troll	1·60	1·30
MS1463	105×70 mm. Nos. 1461/2	2·75	2·50

Stamps of a similar theme were issued by Aland Islands, Greenland, Faröe Islands, Finland, Iceland, Norway and Sweden.

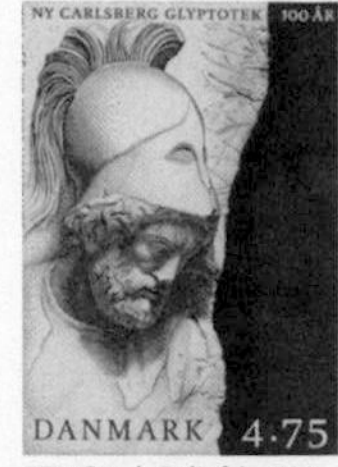

559 Greek Relief (c. 330 BC)

2006. Centenary of New Carlsberg Glyptotek (museum). Multicoloured.

1464	**559**	4k.75 green and black	1·00	50
1465	-	5k.50 drab and black	1·30	1·20
1466	-	8k. bistre and black	1·80	1·60
MS1467		105×70 mm. Nos. 1464/6	4·00	4·00

DESIGNS: 4k.75 Type **559**; 5k.50 Conservatory dome; 8k. "Dancer looking at the Sole of her Right Foot" (Edgar Degas).

560 Alfa Dana Midget and SWEBE-JAP

2006. Vintage Race Cars. Multicoloured.

1468	4k.75 Type **560**	1·10	55
1469	5k.50 Alfa Romeo GTA, Ford Cortina GT and Austin Cooper S	1·30	1·20
1470	10k. Volvo P 1800 and Jaguar E-Type	2·30	1·90
1471	17k. Renault Alpine A 110 and Lotus Elan	3·50	3·00

561 Ellehammer, 1906

2006. Vintage Aircraft. Multicoloured.

1472	4k.50 Type **561**	1·70	90
1473	4k.75 KZ 11, 1946	1·80	1·00
1474	5k.50 KZ IV, 1944	2·50	1·70
1475	13k. KZ V11 Lark, 1947	6·00	3·50

562 Faces (Rikke Veber Rasmussen)

2006. Europa. Integration. Winning designs in Children's Drawing Competition.

1476	**562**	4k.75 multicoloured	1·80	1·20
1477	-	7k. black and green	3·00	2·00

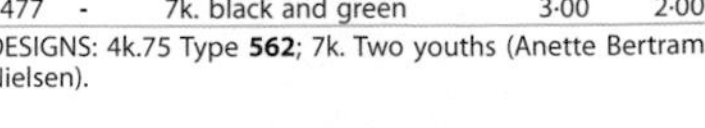
DESIGNS: 4k.75 Type **562**; 7k. Two youths (Anette Bertram Nielsen).

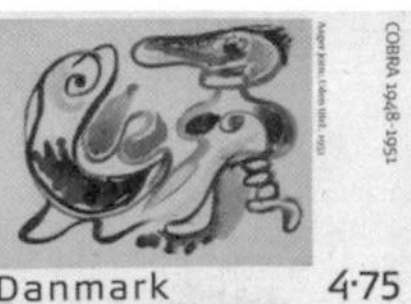

563 'Untitled' (Asger Jorn)

2006. CoBrA (artistic movement). Multicoloured.

1478	4k.75 Type **563**	1·90	1·20
1479	5k.50 "Landscape of the Night" (Else Alfelt) (vert)	2·50	1·70
1480	7k. "New Skin" (Pierre Alechinsky)	3·00	2·00
1481	8k. "The Olive Eater" (Asger Jorn) (vert)	3·50	2·50

Stamps of similar design were issued by Belgium.

563a Askov Windmill (1891)

2007. Windmills.

1482	**563a**	4k.50 agate	1·70	90
1483	-	4k.75 crimson	1·90	1·20
1484	-	6k. green	2·50	1·70
1485	-	8k.50 blue	4·00	3·00

DESIGNS: 4k.50 Type **563a**; 4k.75 Gedser (1957); 6k. Bogø (1989); 8k.50 Middlegrunden (2000).

564 Emblem and Eye

2007. 50th Anniv of Danish United Nations Soldiers.

1486	**564**	4k.75 blue, vermilion and black	2·00	1·30

565 Royal Family

2007. Charity Stamp.

1487	**565**	4k.75+50ore maroon and black	2·30	1·50

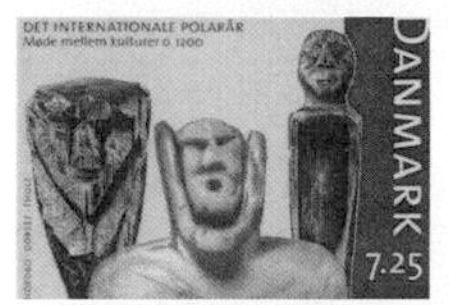

566 Carved Figures

2007. International Polar Year. Multicoloured.

1488	7k.25 Type **566**	2·75	2·00
1489	13k.50 de Havilland Canada DH-6 Twin Otter research plane	5·50	3·75
MS1490	100×70 mm. Nos. 1488/9	8·25	6·50

567 Globe of Fish

2007. Galathea 3 Scientific Research Voyage. Multicoloured.

1491	4k.75 Type **567**	2·00	1·30
1492	7k.25 Route	3·00	2·25
MS1493	106×70 mm. Nos. 1491/2	5·00	3·75

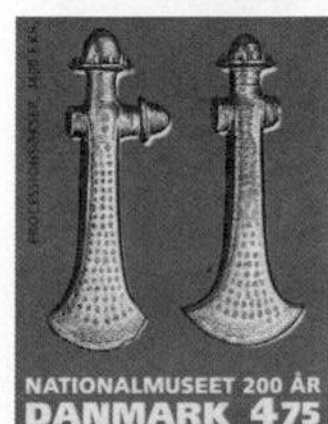

568 Ceremonial Axe Heads, Vendsyssel

2007. Bicentenary of National Museum.

1494	**568**	4k.75 blue and black	2·00	1·30
1495	-	6k. brown and black	2·50	1·70
1496	-	8k.25 yellow and black	3·50	2·75
1497	-	10k.25 blue, black and yellow	5·25	4·00

DESIGNS: 4k.75 Type **568**; 6k. Funen aquamanile; 8k.25 Armillary sphere, Germany; 10k.25 Mask, Borneo.

569 Scouts

2007. Europa. Centenary of Scouting. Multicoloured.

1498	4k.75 Type **569**	2·00	1·30
1499	7k.25 Campfire and tent	3·00	2·25

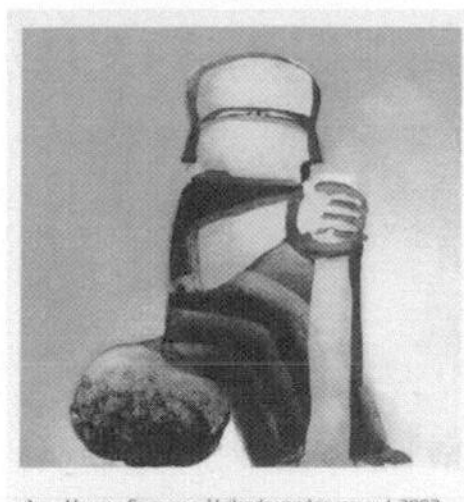

570 *The Traveller* (Arne Haugen Sorensen)

2007. Art. Multicoloured.

1500	4k.75 Type **570**	2·00	1·30
1501	8k.25 Trionfale (Seppo Mattinen)	3·50	2·75

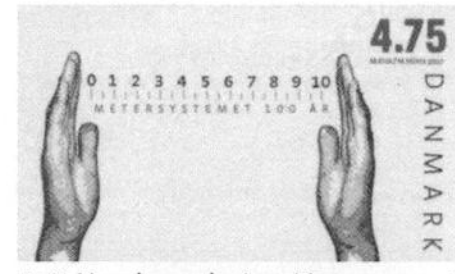

571 Hands enclosing Measurement

2007. Centenary of Metric System.

1502	**571**	4k.75 black and rose	2·10	1·30

572 Niobe Fritillary Butterfly

2007. Rabjerg Dune's Flora and Fauna. Multicoloured.

1503	4k.75 Type **572**	2·20	1·30
1504	6k. Northern dune tiger beetle	2·50	1·70
1505	7k.25 Sand lizard	3·25	2·25
1506	13k.50 Seaside pansy	6·25	4·25
MS1507	151×71 mm. Nos. 1503/6	13·00	10·50

573 Poul Henningsen

2007. Personalities.

1508	**573**	4k.75 carmine, red and black	2·20	1·70
1509	-	6k. blue and black	2·50	1·90
1510	-	7k.25 green, rosine and black	3·25	2·25
1511	-	8k.25 violet and black	3·75	2·75

DESIGNS: 4k.75 Type **573** (designer and social commentator) and 'Artichoke' lamp; 6k. Victor Borge (entertainer) and piano; 7k.25 Arne Jacobsen (architect and designer) and 'Egg' chair; 8k.25 Piet Hein (designer, artist, poet and mathematician) and 'superellipse'.

574 Old Stage Theatre, Kongens Nytorv

2008. Inauguration of New Royal Danish Playhouse, Royal Theatre Complex. Multicoloured.

1512	5k.50 Type **574**	3·00	2·20
1513	6k.50 Playhouse Theatre, Kvæsthusbroen	3·25	2·50
1514	7k.75 Opera House, Holmen, Copenhagen	4·00	3·00

575 Woman

2008. Breast Cancer Awareness Campaign. Danish Cancer Society.

1515	**575**	5k.50+50ore vermilion and black	3·00	2·20

576 Lindholm High

2008. Norse Mythology. Mythical Places. Each black.

1516	5k.50 Type **576**	3·00	2·20
1517	7k.75 Feggeklit	3·50	2·75
MS1518	105×70 mm. Nos. 1516/17	7·50	7·50

577 Gala Uniform

2008. 350th Anniv of Royal Life Guards. Multicoloured.

1519	5k.50 Type **577**	3·00	2·20
1520	10k. On parade	4·50	3·75
MS1521	106×71 mm. Nos. 1519/20	7·50	7·50

578 Allotment, Hjelm, Aabenraa

2008. Centenary of Allotment Association. Multicoloured.

1522	5k.50 Type **578**	2·50	1·90
1523	6k.50 Summer house, Vennelyst, Klovermarken	3·25	2·75

579 Boy and Symbols of Letter Writing

2008. Europa. The Letter. Multicoloured.

1524	5k.50 Type **579**	2·50	1·90
1525	7k.75 Girl and symbols of letter writing	4·00	3·00

580 *The Old Villa, Figures in Landscape* (Roy Lichtenstein) and *I am in You* (video installation) (Doug Aitken)

2008. 50th Anniv of Louisiana Museum of Modern Art. Multicoloured.

1526	5k.50 Type **580**	2·00	1·10
1527	7k.50 *I am in You* (different), glass corridor and *A Closer Grand Canyon* (David Hockney)	3·25	2·50
1528	8k.75 *Reclining Figure* (Henry Moore), *Walking Man* and *Big Head* (Alberto Giacometti) and *Slender Ribs* (Alexander Calder)	4·50	3·50
1529	16k. *Slender Ribs* (different), children and concert hall	8·25	7·00

Although not se-tenant Nos. 1526/7 and 1528/9, respectively, each form a composite design.

581 Halfdan Rasmussen

2008. Personalities. Multicoloured.

1530	5k. claret and black	2·20	1·70
1531	5k.50 blue, green and black	3·00	2·20
1532	6k.50 red, mauve and black	3·75	2·75
1533	10k. mauve, indigo and black	5·00	4·25

DESIGNS: 5k. Type **581** (poet); 5k.50 Eric Balling (film director); 6k.50 Bodil Kjer (actor); 10k. Neils-Henning Orsted Pedersen (musician).

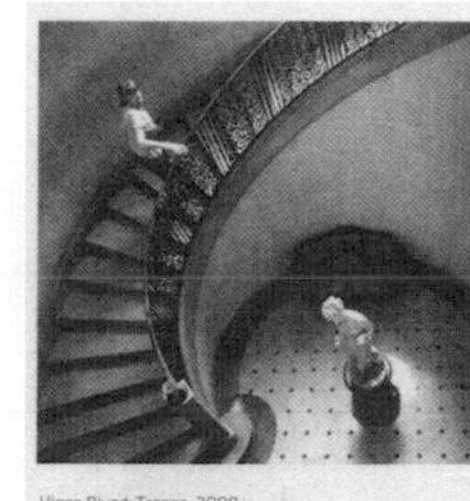

582 *Trappe* (Viggo Raval)

2008. Art Photographs. Both black.

1534	5k.50 Type **582**	2·75	1·70
1535	7k.75 *Berlin* (Krass Clement) (horiz)	4·25	3·25

583 Holly Berries (*Ilex aquifolium*)

2008. Winter Flora. Multicoloured.

1536	5k.50 Type **583**	2·10	1·30
1537	6k.50 Christmas rose (*Hellebore niger*)	2·75	1·90
1538	7k.75 Yew berries (*Taxus baccata*)	4·00	3·00
1539	8k.75 Snowberries (*Symphoricarpos rivularis*)	5·25	4·25

No. 1540 is left for miniature sheet not yet received.

584 Mintmaster's Mansion and Town Drummer

2009. Centenary of Old Town, Aarhus (open air museum). Multicoloured.

1540	5k.50 Type **584**	2·10	1·30
1541	6k.50 Mayor's House	2·75	1·90
1542	8k. Clocks and Watches Museum	3·75	3·00
1543	10k.50 Kertminde School	5·50	4·75
MS1544	151×70 mm. Nos. 1540/3	12·50	12·50

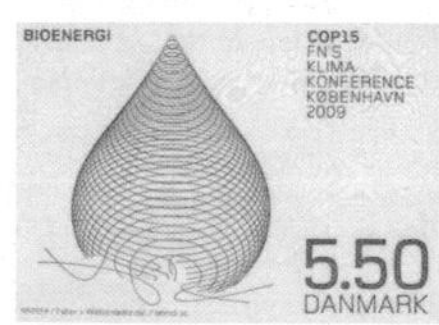

585 Bioenergy

2009. COP15—United Nations Climate Change Conference, Copenhagen. Each indigo.

1545	5k.50 Type **585**	2·10	1·30
1546	9k. Low energy building	5·25	4·25

586 Prince Henrik

2009. World Wildlife Fund. 75th Birth Anniv of Prince Henrik (president of Danish World Wildlife Fund).

1547	**586**	5k.50 + 50 multicoloured	3·00	2·20

1547	**586**	5k.50 + 50 multicoloured	3·00	2·20

The premium is for the World Wildlife Fund.

587 *Anacamptis pyramidalis* (pyramidal orchid)

2009. Flora and Fauna of Mons Klint. Multicoloured.

1548	5k. Type **587**	2·40	1·50
1549	5k.50 *Falco peregrinus* (peregrine)	3·00	1·80
1550	8k. *Zygaena purpuralis* (transparent burnet)	4·50	2·75
1551	17k. *Mosasaurus lemonnieri* (fossil)	10·50	10·50
MS1552	151×71 mm. Nos. 1549/51	20·00	20·00

588 Round Towers

2009. Europa. Astronomy. Multicoloured.

1553	5k.50 Type **588**	3·25	2·00
1554	8k. Tyco Brahe Planetarium	4·75	2·75

589 Rhinoceros

2009. 150th Anniv of Copenhagen Zoo. Multicoloured.

1555	5k.50 Type **589**	2·75	1·70
1556	6k.50 Elephants	3·50	2·10
1557	8k. Red-eyed tree frog and flamingoes	4·50	3·25
1558	9k. Royal python and golden lion tamarin	5·25	3·25

590 First Official Map of Denmark, 1841

2009. Early Maps. Multicoloured.

1559	5k.50 Type **590**	2·40	1·50
1560	6k.50 Map by Johannes Mejer, 1650 (24×40 mm)	6·75	4·00
1561	12k. Map by Marcus Jordan, 1585 (24×40 mm)	6·75	4·00
1562	18k. First printed map of Denmark by Abraham Ortelius, 1570 (24×40 mm)	9·00	5·50

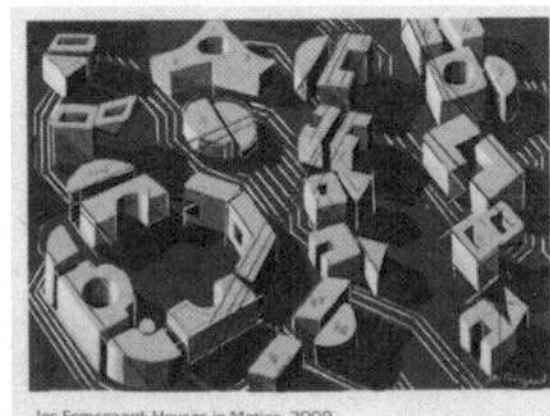

591 *Houses in Motion* (Jes Fomsgaard)

2009. Art.

1563	**591**	5k.50 multicoloured	3·25	2·00

592 Hans Scherfig and Metropolitanskole Building, Fiolstraede, Frue Plads c.1816

2009. Metropolitanskole (Metropolitan School), Copenhagen.

1564	5k.50 black and carmine	2·75	1·70
1565	6k.50 black and bottle-green	4·25	2·50

DESIGNS: 5k.50 Type **592**; 6k.50 Modern Metropolitanskole building, Struenseegade.

2009. COP15—United Nations Climate Change Conference, Copenhagen (2nd issue). As T 585. Indigo.

1566	5k.50 Fuel cell	3·25	2·00
1567	8k.50 Wind turbine	4·50	2·75

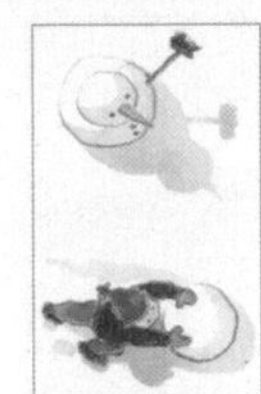

593 Making Snowman

2009. Playing in Snow. Multicoloured. (a) Self-adhesive.

1568	5k.50 Type **593**	2·75	1·70
1569	6k.50 Sledging	4·00	2·40
1570	8k. Snowball fight	4·50	2·75
1571	9k. Making snow angels	5·75	3·50

(b) Sheet 150×70 mm. Ordinary gum.

MS1572	As Nos. 1568/70	17·00	17·00

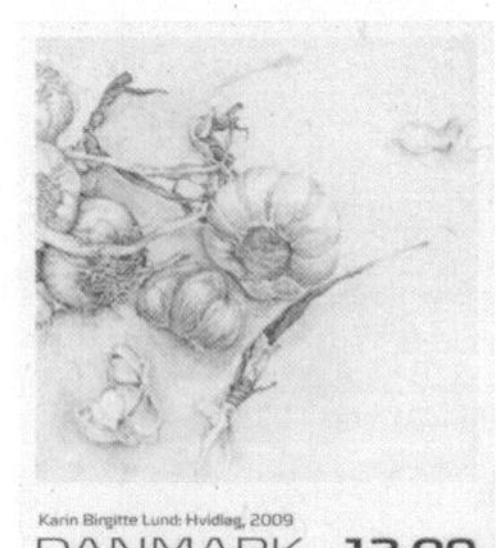

594 *Garlic* (Karin Birgitte Lund)

2009. Art.

1573	**594**	12k. multicoloured	7·00	4·25

597 70th Birthday Portrait of Queen Margrethe II

2010. Queen Margrethe II

1581	**597**	5k.50 bright red and black	2·75	1·70
1581a		6k. bright deep turquoise-green and black	4·00	2·50
1582	**73**	6k.50 bright deep turquoise-green and black	4·25	2·50
1582a		8k. bright red and black	4·50	2·75
1583	**73**	8k.50 deep bright apple green and black	4·75	2·75
1583a		9k. deep bright apple green and black	5·75	3·50
1584		9k.50 dull ultramarine and black	5·25	4·25
1585		11k. deep ultramarine and black	5·25	4·25

Numbers have been left for additions to this series.

598 Royal Family

2010. 70th Birth Anniv of Queen Margrethe II

1590	**598**	5k.50 multicoloured	2·75	1·70

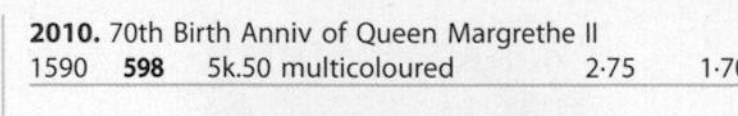

599 Ribe Cathedral

2010. 1300th Anniv of Ribe. Each black.

1591	5k.50 Type **599**	2·75	1·70
1592	6k.50 Queen Dagmar (statue)	4·25	2·50

600 Lindø Shipyard

2010. Life at the Coast. Multicoloured.

(a) Self-adhesive

1593	5k.50 Type **600**	2·75	1·70
1594	8k.50 Aarhus Port	4·50	2·75

(b) Miniature sheet. Ordinary gum

MS1595	105×70 mm. As Nos. 1593/4	7·25	4·75

Stamps of a similar theme were issued by Aland, Greenland, Faröe Islands, Finland, Iceland, Norway and Sweden.

601 Gasolin 3 (painting by Tage Hansen)

2010. 50th Anniv of P4 Radio Station

1596	**601**	5k.50 multicoloured	3·50	2·25

602 Flower and Posthorn

2010. Greetings Stamps. Multicoloured.

1597	5k.50 Type **602**	2·75	1·70
1598	5k.50 Parcel	2·75	1·70
1599	5k.50 'Tillykke' (congratulations)	2·75	1·70
1600	5k.50 Flag	2·75	1·70
1601	5k.50 Heart	2·75	1·70

603 *Iver Huitfeldt* (frigate)

2010. 500th Anniv of Royal Danish Navy. Each rosine and black, ship's colour given.

1602	5k.50 Type **603**	2·75	1·70
1603	6k.50 *Niels Iuel* (artillery ship) (black)	4·00	2·25
1604	8k.50 *Tordenskjold* (ironclad warship) (rosine)	4·50	2·75
1605	9k.50 *Jylland* (screw frigate) (black)	5·75	3·50
1606	16k. *Maria* (caravel) (rosine)	9·00	7·00

604 Sporge Jorgen

2010. Europa. Children's Books. Multicoloured.

1607	5k.50 Type **604** (*Spørge Jørgen* written by Kamma Laurents, illustrated by Robert Storm Petersen)	3·25	2·00
1608	8k.50 Orla Frø-Snapper (*Orla Frø-Snapper* written and illustrated by Ole Lund Kirkegard) (vert)	4·50	2·75

605 Race Horses

2010. Centenary of Copenhagen Racecourse. Multicoloured.

1609	5k.50 Type **605**	4·25	2·75
1610	24k. Derby Day race-goers and race horse	18·75	16·00

606 Cyclist

2011. Post Danmark Rundt Bicycle Race. Multicoloured.

MS1611	5k.50×10, Type **606**; Racing on country road; Group of cyclists, head and shoulders, striped helmets; Two cyclists; Side view of large group of cyclists; Single cyclist wearing white outfit with red inserts; Cyclist, wearing red; Large group of cyclist, facing front; Three cyclists, facing left; Cyclist with arms raised in celebration	28·00	28·00

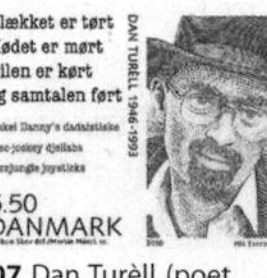

607 Dan Turèll (poet, lecturer, essayist and crime writer)

2010. Personalities

1612	5k.50 dull violet, bright carmine and black	2·75	1·70
1613	6k.50 bright carmine, new blue and black	4·25	2·50
1614	9k.50 deep magenta, apple green and black	5·75	3·50
1615	12k.50 carmine-lake and black	6·75	4·00

Designs:- 5k.50 Type **607**; 6k.50 Tove Ditlevsen (writer); 9k.50 Henry Heerup (painter, sculptor and graphic artist);12k.50 Dea Trier Mørch (writer and visual artist)

608 Two Roses (Inge Ellegaard)

2010. Art. Multicoloured.

1616	5k.50 Type **608**	2·75	1·70
1617	18k.50 *Night Flower* (Kirstine Roepstorff) (horiz)	12·00	9·00

609 Lonely Girl

2010. Winter Stamps. Multicoloured.

(a) Self-adhesive

1618	5k.50 Type **609**	2·75	1·70
1619	6k.50 Lonely girl embracing snowman	4·25	2·50
1620	8k.50 Lonely girl kissing snowman	4·50	2·50
1621	12k.50 Ice man with black and white dog offering lonely girl flowers	7·00	4·25

(b) Miniature sheet. Ordinary gum

MS1622	150×70 mm. As Nos. 1618/21	19·00	19·00

610 'One in Eight'

2010. Danish Rheumatism Association

1623	**610**	5k.50+50ö. black and scarlet-vermilion	3·50	2·20

MILITARY FRANK STAMPS

1917. Nos. 135 and 138 optd S F (= "Soldater Frimaerke").

M188	**21**	5ore green	13·00	34·00
M189	**21**	10ore red	13·00	34·00

NEWSPAPER STAMPS

N18

1907

N131	**N18**	1ore green	11·00	3·00
N132	**N18**	5ore blue	27·00	10·50
N133	**N18**	7ore red	15·00	1·20
N188	**N18**	8ore green	35·00	2·00
N134	**N18**	10ore lilac	34·00	2·75
N135	**N18**	20ore green	25·00	1·60
N191	**N18**	29ore orange	42·00	3·25
N136	**N18**	38ore orange	34·00	1·90
N193	**N18**	41ore brown	50·00	3·50
N137	**N18**	68ore brown	85·00	24·00
N138	**N18**	1k. purple & green	25·00	2·10
N139	**N18**	5k. green and pink	£160	24·00
N140	**N18**	10k. blue and stone	£170	28·00

OFFICIAL STAMPS

O9

1871. Value in "skilling".

O51a	**O9**	2sk. blue	£130	90·00
O52	**O9**	4sk. red	50·00	18·00
O53	**O9**	16sk. green	£350	£180

1875. Value in "ore".

O185	1ore orange	90	1·20
O100	3ore lilac	1·20	85
O186	3ore grey	3·75	6·50
O101	4ore blue	1·80	1·40
O188	5ore green	1·00	40
O189	5ore brown	5·25	21·00
O94	8ore red	8·75	2·40
O104	10ore red	2·50	1·20
O191	10ore green	3·50	4·25
O192	20ore lilac	13·50	28·00
O193	20ore blue	19·00	9·50
O98	32ore green	25·00	23·00

PARCEL POST STAMPS

1919. Various types optd POSTFAERGE.

P208	**21**	10ore red	39·00	60·00
P209	**15**	10ore green	32·00	12·00
P210	**15**	10ore brown	23·00	9·50
P211	**21**	15ore lilac	19·00	28·00
P212	**21**	30ore orange	17·00	25·00
P213	**21**	30ore blue	5·00	5·50
P214	**21**	50ore black & purple	£225	£225
P215a	**21**	50ore grey	25·00	16·00
P216	**22**	1k. brown	£110	£150
P217	**21**	1k. blue and brown	70·00	32·00
P218	**21**	5k. brown & mauve	1·80	1·90
P219	**21**	10k. green and red	75·00	75·00

1927. Stamps of 1927 (solid background) optd POSTFAERGE.

P252	**40**	15ore red	18·00	9·75
P253	**40**	30ore yellow	13·50	16·00
P254	**40**	40ore green	23·00	11·50

1936. Stamps of 1933 (lined background) optd POSTFAERGE.

P491	**43**	5ore purple	40	40
P299	**43**	10ore orange	18·00	15·00
P300	**43**	10ore brown	1·40	1·30
P301	**43**	10ore violet	25	25
P302	**43**	10ore green	60	30
P303a	**40**	15ore red	55	1·30
P304	**40**	30ore blue	4·50	4·50
P305	**40**	30ore orange	55	65
P306	**40**	40ore green	4·50	5·25
P307	**40**	40ore blue	45	85
P308	**45**	50ore grey	90	1·00
P309	**45**	1k. brown	1·00	85

1945. Stamps of 1942 optd POSTFAERGE.

P346	**67**	30ore orange	2·75	1·40
P347	**67**	40ore blue	1·30	1·30
P348	**67**	50ore grey	1·50	1·30

1949. Stamps of 1946 and 1948 optd POSTFAERGE.

P376	**80**	30ore orange	3·75	1·60
P377	**80**	30ore red	1·50	1·40
P378	**80**	40ore blue	3·00	1·60
P379	**80**	40ore grey	1·50	1·40
P380	**80**	50ore grey	17·00	3·25
P381	**80**	50ore green	1·50	1·40
P382	**80**	70ore green	1·50	1·40
P383	**73**	1k. brown	1·90	1·30
P384	**73**	1k.25 orange	6·75	8·25
P495	**73**	2k. red	2·50	2·40
P496	**73**	5k. blue	6·25	5·75

1967. Optd POSTFAERGE.

P488	**117**	40ore brown	65	65
P492	**117**	50ore brown	45	40
P489	**117**	80ore blue	80	75
P493	**117**	90ore blue	1·00	85

1975. Optd POSTFAERGE.

P597	**207**	100ore blue	1·50	1·30

POSTAGE DUE STAMPS

1921. Stamps of 1905 and 1913 optd PORTO.

D214	**15**	1ore orange	2·30	1·70
D215	**21**	5ore green	4·50	2·00
D216	**21**	7ore orange	3·50	2·00
D217	**21**	10ore red	20·00	9·75
D218	**21**	20ore blue	17·00	5·75
D219	**21**	25ore black and brown	23·00	2·75
D220	**21**	50ore black & purple	10·00	3·50

D32

1921. Solid background.

D221	**D32**	1ore orange	70	80
D222	**D32**	4ore blue	1·70	2·75
D223	**D32**	5ore brown	2·30	1·20
D224	**D32**	5ore green	1·70	80
D225	**D32**	7ore green	11·50	19·00
D226	**D32**	7ore violet	28·00	32·00
D227	**D32**	10ore green	2·30	80
D228	**D32**	10ore brown	1·70	80
D229	**D32**	20ore blue	1·10	95
D230	**D32**	20ore grey	2·30	2·00
D231	**D32**	25ore red	2·75	1·60
D232	**D32**	25ore lilac	2·75	2·75
D233	**D32**	25ore blue	4·50	3·25
D234	**D32**	1k. blue	70·00	6·50
D235	**D32**	1k. blue and brown	8·50	4·75
D236	**D32**	5k. violet	17·00	7·25

For stamps with lined background see Nos. D285/97.

1921. Military Frank stamp optd PORTO.

D237	**21**	10ore red (No. M189)	8·00	5·75

1934. Lined background.

D285	**D32**	1ore grey	25	15
D286	**D32**	2ore red	25	15
D287	**D32**	5ore green	25	15
D288	**D32**	6ore green	35	15
D289	**D32**	8ore mauve	2·20	2·00
D290	**D32**	10ore orange	25	15
D291	**D32**	12ore blue	45	25
D292	**D32**	15ore violet	45	30
D293	**D32**	20ore grey	25	15
D294	**D32**	25ore blue	35	15
D295	**D32**	30ore green	55	25
D296	**D32**	40ore purple	65	50
D297	**D32**	1k. brown	55	15

1934. Surch PORTO 15.

D298	**15**	15 on 12ore lilac	4·50	4·50

SPECIAL FEE STAMPS

1923. No. D227 optd GEBYR GEBYR.

S218	**D32**	10ore green	10·00	3·25

S36

1926. Solid background.

S229	**S36**	10ore green	6·75	95
S230	**S36**	10ore brown	8·50	95

1934. Lined background.

S285	5ore green	20	20
S286	10ore orange	20	20

Pt. 1

DHAR

A state of Central India. Now uses Indian stamps.

4 pice = 1 anna.

1

1897. Imperf.

1	**1**	½pice black on red	3·50	3·25
3	**1**	¼a. black on orange	3·75	6·50
4	**1**	½a. black on mauve	4·75	7·00
5	**1**	1a. black on green	8·50	19·00
6	**1**	2a. black on yellow	35·00	65·00

2

1898. Perf.

7b	**2**	½a. red	4·50	6·00
8	**2**	1a. purple	6·00	8·00
10	**2**	2a. green	10·00	28·00

Pt. 6

DIEGO-SUAREZ

A port in N. Madagascar. A separate colony till 1896, when it was incorporated with Madagascar.

100 centimes = 1 franc.

1890. Stamps of French Colonies (Type J Commerce), surch 15 sideways.

1	**J**	15 on 1c. black on blue	£190	85·00
2	**J**	15 on 5c. green	£500	85·00
3	**J**	15 on 10c. black on lilac	£225	85·00
4	**J**	15 on 20c. red on green	£500	85·00
5	**J**	15 on 25c. black on red	£120	28·00

3

1891

10	**3**	5c. black	£150	£100

1891. Stamps of French Colonies. (Type J Commerce) surch 1891 DIEGO-SUAREZ 5 c.

13	**J**	5c. on 10c. black on lilac	£160	£110
14	**J**	5c. on 20c. red on green	£170	75·00

2

1890. Various designs.

6	**2**	1c. black	£450	£120
7	**2**	5c. black	£450	£110
8	**2**	15c. black	£130	46·00
9	**2**	25c. black	£140	60·00

1892. Stamps of French Colonies (Type J Commerce) optd DIEGO-SUAREZ.

15	1c. black on blue	48·00	25·00
16	2c. brown on buff	48·00	27·00
17	4c. brown on grey	44·00	18·00
18	5c. green on green	£120	75·00
19	10c. black on lilac	55·00	46·00
20	15c. blue on blue	34·00	18·00
21	20c. red on green	32·00	18·00
22	25c. black on pink	30·00	23·00
23	30c. brown on drab	£900	£750
24	35c. black on orange	£900	£750
25	75c. red on pink	85·00	50·00
26	1f. green	85·00	65·00

1892. "Tablet" key-type inscr "DIEGO-SUAREZ ET DEPENDANCES".

38	**D**	1c. black on blue	3·50	5·75
39	**D**	2c. brown on buff	3·00	2·00
40	**D**	4c. brown on grey	1·00	7·25
41	**D**	5c. green on green	3·00	8·75
42	**D**	10c. black on lilac	6·00	17·00
43	**D**	15c. blue	5·00	25·00
44	**D**	20c. red on green	8·25	12·00
45	**D**	25c. black on pink	5·00	10·00
46	**D**	30c. brown on drab	8·75	32·00
47	**D**	40c. red on yellow	30·00	32·00
48	**D**	50c. red on pink	17·00	32·00
49	**D**	75c. brown on yellow	65·00	60·00
50	**D**	1f. green	80·00	65·00

1894. "Tablet" key-type inscr "DIEGO-SUAREZ".

51	1c. black on blue	45	3·50
52	2c. brown on buff	3·25	4·50
53	4c. brown on grey	2·00	5·25
54	5c. green on green	4·50	11·00
55	10c. black on lilac	7·50	10·50
56	15c. blue	3·50	7·75
57	20c. red on green	11·50	36·00
58	25c. black on pink	5·25	4·50
59	30c. brown on drab	13·00	10·00
60	40c. red on yellow	7·25	6·00
61	50c. red on pink	4·75	13·00
62	75c. brown on yellow	2·00	8·25
63	1f. green	12·50	13·50

POSTAGE DUE STAMPS

D4

1891

D11	**D4**	5c. violet	£100	32·00
D12	**D4**	50c. black on yellow	£110	60·00

1892. Postage Due stamps of French Colonies overprinted DIEGO-SUAREZ.

D27	1c. black	£130	70·00
D28	2c. black	£130	60·00
D29	3c. black	£130	70·00
D30	4c. black	£130	80·00
D31	5c. black	£130	80·00
D32	10c. black	40·00	29·00
D33	15c. black	46·00	32·00
D34	20c. black	£180	£130
D35	30c. black	£120	70·00
D36	60c. black	£900	£650
D37	1f. brown	£2500	£1100

Pt. 6

DJIBOUTI

A port in French Somaliland S. of the Red Sea, later capital of French Territory of the Afars and the Issas.

100 centimes = 1 franc.

1893. "Tablet" key-type stamp of Obock optd DJ.

83	D	5c. green & red on green	£130	£130

1894. Same type surch in figures and DJIBOUTI.

85	25 on 2c. brn & bl on buff	£325	£225
86	50 on 1c. blk & red on blue	£375	£250

1894. Triangular stamp of Obock optd DJIBOUTI or surch 1 also.

87	5	1f. on 5f. red	£650	£425
88	5	5f. red	£1800	£1500

12x 12 Djibouti (The apparent perforation is part of the design.)

13x 13 "Pingouin" (French gunboat)

14x 14 Crossing the Desert

1894. Imperf.

89	12	1c. red and black	1·40	1·40
90	12	2c. black and red	1·40	90
91	12	4c. blue and brown	4·50	3·75
92	12	5c. red and green	3·75	1·80
93	12	5c. green	3·25	6·00
94	-	10c. green and brown	6·50	1·80
95	-	15c. green and lilac	3·75	2·10
96	-	25c. blue and red	10·00	2·30
97	-	30c. red and brown	5·50	4·25
98	-	40c. blue and yellow	60·00	50·00
99	-	50c. red and blue	25·00	8·25
100	-	75c. orange and mauve	50·00	25·00
101	-	1f. black and olive	25·00	14·00
102	-	2f. red and brown	£110	80·00
103	13	5f. blue and red	£200	£130
104	14	25f. blue and red	£900	£950
105	14	50f. red and blue	£700	£700

DESIGNS— As Type **12**: 10 to 75c. Different views of Djibouti; 1, 2f. Port of Djibouti.

1899. As last, surch.

108	-	0.05 on 75c. orge & mve	70·00	50·00
109	-	0.10 on 1f. blk & olive	£100	60·00
106	12	0.40 on 4c. blue & brown	£3500	14·00
110	-	0.40 on 2f. red & brown	£500	£375
111	13	0.75 on 5f. blue and red	£500	£400

1902. Rectangular stamp of Obock surch 0.05.

107	6	0.05 on 75c. lilac & orange	£1300	£1000

1902. Triangular stamps of Obock surch.

112	7	5c. on 25f. blue and brown	60·00	70·00
113	7	10c. on 50f. green & red	90·00	75·00

1902. Nos. 98/9 surch.

114	5c. on 40c. blue and yellow	3·25	1·80
115	10c. on 50c. red and blue	28·00	23·00

1902. Stamps of Obock surch DJIBOUTI and value.

120	6	5c. on 30c. yellow & grn	7·25	10·00
116	6	10c. on 25c. black & blue	7·25	8·75
118	7	10c. on 2f. orange & lilac	60·00	60·00
119	7	10c. on 10f. lake and red	34·00	32·00

For later issues see **FRENCH SOMALI COAST, FRENCH TERRITORY OF THE AFARS AND THE ISSAS** and **DJIBOUTI REPUBLIC**.

Pt. 12

DJIBOUTI REPUBLIC

Formerly French Territory of the Afars and the Issas.

100 centimes = 1 franc.

112 Map and Flag

1977. Independence. Multicoloured.

685	45f. Type **112**	1·30	1·00
686	65f. Map of Djibouti (horiz)	2·10	1·20

1977. Various stamps of the French Territory of the Afars and the Issas optd REPUBLIQUE DE DJIBOUTI or surch also. (a) Sea Shells.

687	81	1f. on 4f. mult	1·30	35
688	-	2f. on 5f. brown, mauve and violet (629)	1·30	35
689	-	20f. brown & grn (633)	2·75	95
690	-	30f. brn, pur & grn (634)	2·75	1·00
691	-	40f. brown & grn (635)	3·25	1·60
692	-	45f. brn, grn & bl (636)	3·50	1·60
693	-	60f. black & brn (638)	5·25	2·40
694	-	70f. brn, bl & blk (639)	6·00	3·00

(b) Flora and Fauna.

695	103	5f. on 20f. multicoloured	45	45
696	106	45f. multicoloured	5·00	1·70
697	-	50f. multicoloured (675)	5·75	2·40
698	107	70f. multicoloured	4·50	3·25
699	-	100f. multicoloured (653)	8·00	4·00
700	-	150f. multicoloured (676)	8·75	5·00
701	-	300f. multicoloured (654)	11·00	10·50

(c) Buildings.

702	99	8f. grey, red & bl (postage)	45	45
703	109	500f. mult (air)	13·50	12·50

(d) Celebrities.

704	111	55f. red, grey & grn (air)	2·50	1·60
705	-	75f. red, brn & grn (682)	5·00	3·25
706	104	200f. blue, green and orange (postage)	5·75	5·50

(e) Sport.

707	108	200f. multicoloured	6·25	6·00

115 Headrest

1977. Local Art. Multicoloured.

708	10f. Type **115**	35	10
709	20f. Water cask (vert)	65	20
710	25f. Washing jar (vert)	1·00	35

116 Ostrich

1977. Birds. Multicoloured.

711	90f. Type **116**	4·50	1·60
712	100f. Vitelline masked weaver	5·25	2·10

117 "Glossodoris"

1977. Sea Life. Multicoloured.

713	45f. Type **117**	1·30	45
714	70f. Turtle	1·70	55
715	80f. Catalufa	2·30	80

118 Map, Dove and U.N. Emblem

1977. Air. Admission to the United Nations.

716	118	300f. multicoloured	6·50	3·75

119 Crabs "Uca lactea"

1977. Fauna. Multicoloured.

717	15f. Type **119**	75	10
718	50f. Klipspringer	1·70	55
719	150f. Dolphin (fish)	4·50	2·00

120 President Hassan Gouled Aptidon and Flag

1978

720	120	65f. multicoloured	1·30	70

121 Marcel Brochet MB 101

1978. Air. Djibouti Aero Club. Multicoloured.

721	60f. Type **121**	1·30	75
722	85f. de Havilland D.H.82A Tiger Moth	1·90	1·00
723	200f. Morane Saulnier MS892 Rallye Commodore	4·00	2·00

122 "Charaxes hansali"

1978. Butterflies. Multicoloured.

724	5f. Type **122**	20	10
725	20f. "Colias electo"	1·00	30
726	25f. "Acraea chilo"	1·40	65
727	150f. "Junonia hierta"	5·50	2·00

123 "Head of an Old Man"

1978. Air. 400th Birth Anniv of Rubens. Mult.

728	50f. Type **123**	1·50	50
729	500f. "The Hippopotamus Hunt" (detail)	12·00	4·75

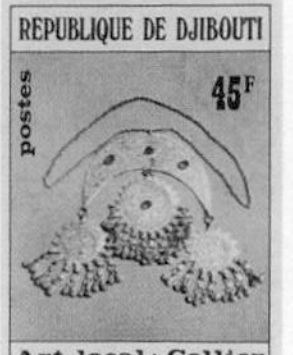

124 Necklace

1978. Native Handicrafts. Multicoloured.

730	45f. Type **124**	1·30	60
731	55f. Necklace	1·60	65

125 Player with Cup

1978. Air. World Cup Football Championship, Argentina. Multicoloured.

732	100f. Type **125**	2·00	65
733	300f. World Cup, footballer and map of Argentina	6·25	1·80

126 "Bougainvillea glabra"

1978. Flowers. Multicoloured.

734	15f. Type **126**	60	10
735	35f. "Hibiscus schizopetalus"	1·10	25
736	250f. "Caesalpinia pulcherrima"	6·50	1·20

1978. Air. Argentina's Victory in World Cup Football Championship. Nos. 722/3 optd.

737	100f. Type **125**	2·75	90
738	300f. World Cup, footballer and map of Argentina	6·75	2·20

OVERPRINTS: 100f. **ARGENTINE CHAMPION 1978**; 300f. **ARGENTINE HOLLANDE 3–1**.

128 "The Hare" (Albrecht Durer)

1978. Air. Paintings. Multicoloured.

739	100f. "Tahitian Women" (Paul Gauguin) (horiz)	3·00	80
740	250f. Type **128**	7·00	2·75

129 Knobbed Triton

1978. Sea Shells. Multicoloured.

741	10f. Type **129**	1·00	40
742	80f. Trumpet triton	3·75	1·00

130 Copper-banded Butterflyfish

1978. Fishes. Multicoloured.

743	8f. Type **130**	65	10
744	30f. Yellow tang	1·40	25
745	40f. Harlequin sweetlips	2·40	45

1978. Air. "Philexafrique" Exhibition, Libreville, Gabon (1st issue) and Int. Stamp Fair, Essen, W. Germany. As T **262** of Gabon. Multicoloured.

746	90f. Jay and Brunswick 1852 3sqr. stamp	3·00	2·10
747	90f. African spoonbill and Djibouti 1977 optd 300f. stamp	3·00	2·10

131 Dove and U.P.U. Emblem

1978. Air. Centenary of Paris U.P.U. Congress.

748	**131**	200f. green, brn & turq	4·00	2·00

132 Alsthom BB 1201 Diesel Locomotive

1979. Djibouti–Addis Ababa Railway. Mult.

749	40f. Type **132**	1·00	25
750	55f. Pacific locomotive No. 231	1·20	25
751	60f. Steam locomotive No. 130	1·70	40
752	75f. Alsthom CC 2001 diesel-electric locomotive	2·00	50

133 Children learning to Count

1979. International Year of the Child. Multicoloured.

753	20f. Type **133**	50	15
754	200f. Mother and child	4·25	1·70

134 de Havilland DHC-6 Twin Otter 100 over Crater

1979. Ardoukoba Volcano. Multicoloured.

755	30f. Sud Aviation SE 3130 Alouette II helicopter over crater	1·20	55
756	90f. Type **134**	2·75	1·00

135 Sir Rowland Hill and 300f. Stamp, 1977

1979. Death Centenary of Sir Rowland Hill. Multicoloured.

757	25f. Type **135**	45	10
758	100f. Letters with 1894 50f. and 1977 45f. stamps	2·00	65
759	150f. Loading mail on ship	3·00	1·00

136 Junkers Ju 52/3m and Dewoitine D-338 Trimotor

1979. Air. 75th Anniv of Powered Flight. Multicoloured.

760	140f. Type **136**	3·25	1·10
761	250f. Potez 63-11 bomber and Supermarine Spitfire Mk. VII	4·75	2·20
762	500f. Concorde and Sikorsky S-40 flying boat "American Clipper"	10·50	3·75

137 Djibouti, Local Woman and Namaqua Dove

1979. "Philexafrique 2" Exhibition, Gabon (2nd issue). Multicoloured.

763	55f. Type **137**	3·00	1·70
764	80f. U.P.U. emblem, map, Douglas DC-8-60 "Super Sixty", Alsthom diesel-electric train and postal runner	3·50	1·70

138 "Opuntia"

1979. Flowers. Multicoloured.

765	2f. Type **138**	10	10
766	8f. "Solanacea" (horiz)	30	10
767	15f. "Trichodesma" (horiz)	50	15
768	45f. "Acacia etbaica" (horiz)	1·00	25
769	50f. "Thunbergia alata"	1·30	30

139 "The Washerwoman"

1979. Air. Death Centenary of Honore Daumier (painter).

770	**139**	500f. multicoloured	12·50	3·75

140 Basketball

1979. Pre-Olympic Year. Multicoloured.

771	70f. Type **140**	1·60	45
772	120f. Running	2·40	80
773	300f. Football	4·00	1·20

141 Bull-mouth Helmet

1979. Shells. Multicoloured.

774	10f. Type **141**	25	10
775	40f. Arthritic spider conch	1·20	25
776	300f. Ventral harp	6·75	1·80

142 Winter Sports Equipment and Mosque

1980. Air. Winter Olympic Games, Lake Placid.

777	**142**	150f. multicoloured	3·00	90

143 Lions Club Banner and Steam Locomotive

1980. Djibouti Clubs. Multicoloured.

778	90f. Rotary Club banner and Morane Saulnier MS 892 Rallye Commodore (75th anniv of Rotary International)	2·20	90
779	100f. Type **143**	2·30	1·00

144 "Colotis danae"

1980. Butterflies. Multicoloured.

780	5f. Type **144**	55	45
781	55f. "Danaus chrysippus"	2·75	1·20

145 Boeing 737

1980. Air. Foundation of "Air Djibouti".

782	**145**	400f. multicoloured	8·75	2·75

1980. Air. Winter Olympic Games. No. 777 surch with names of Medal Winners.

783	**142**	80f. on 150f.	1·60	60
784	**142**	200f. on 150f.	4·25	1·70

OVERPRINTS: 80f. **A.M. MOSER-PROEL AUTRICHE DESCENT DAMES MEDAILLE D'OR**. 200f. **HEIDEN USA 5 MEDAILLES D'OR PATINAGE DE VITESSE**.

147 Basketball

1980. Olympic Games, Moscow. Multicoloured.

785	60f. Type **147**	1·30	30
786	120f. Football	2·30	70
787	250f. Running	4·50	1·30

148 "Apollo XI" Moon Landing

1980. Air. Conquest of Space. Multicoloured.

788	200f. Type **148**	4·25	95
789	300f. "Apollo-Soyuz" link-up	6·50	1·40

149 Samisch v Romanovsky Game, Moscow, 1925

1980. Founding of International Chess Federation, 1924. Multicoloured.

790	20f. Type **149**	1·20	25
791	75f. "Royal Chess Party" (15th-century Italian book illustration)	2·75	65

150 Satellite and Earth Station

1980. Air. Inauguration of Satellite Earth Station.

792	**150**	500f. multicoloured	10·50	2·75

151 Sieve Cowrie

1980. Shells. Multicoloured.

793	15f. Type **151**	65	20
794	85f. Chambered nautilus	2·50	65

152 Sir Alexander Fleming and Penicillin

1980. Anniversaries. Multicoloured.

795	20f. Type **152**	95	30
796	130f. Jules Verne and space capsules	3·25	90

ANNIVERSARIES: 20f. Discovery of penicillin, 25th anniv. 130f. Jules Verne, 75th death anniv.

153 "Graf Zeppelin" and Sphinx

1980. Air. 80th Anniv of First Zeppelin Flight. Multicoloured.

797	100f. Type **153**	2·75	80
798	150f. Ferdinand von Zeppelin	3·50	1·10

154 Capt. Cook and H.M.S. "Endeavour"

1980. Death Bicentenary (1979) of Captain James Cook. Multicoloured.

799	55f. Type **154**	1·30	80
800	90f. Cook's ships and map of voyages	2·50	1·10

155 "Voyager" and Saturn

1980. Air. Space Exploration.
801 **155** 250f. multicoloured 5·75 1·50

156 Saving a Goal

1981. Air. World Cup Football Eliminators. Multicoloured.
802 80f. Type **156** 1·60 50
803 200f. Tackle 4·00 1·00

157 Transport

1981. Air European–African Economic Convention.
804 **157** 100f. multicoloured 3·25 1·00

158 Yuri Gagarin and "Vostok 1"

1981. Air. Space Anniversaries and Events. Multicoloured.
805 75f. Type **158** (20th anniv of first man in space) 1·60 55
806 120f. "Viking" exploration of Mars (horiz) 2·50 75
807 150f. Alan Shepard and "Freedom 7" (20th anniv of first American in space) 3·25 85

159 Arabian Angelfish

1981. Djibouti Tropical Aquarium. Mult.
808 25f. Type **159** 1·60 40
809 55f. Moorish idol 3·00 60
810 70f. Golden trevally 4·00 1·30

160 Caduceus, Satellite and Rocket

1981. World Telecommunications Day.
811 **160** 140f. multicoloured 2·75 80

161 German 231 and American RC4 Diesel Locomotives

1981. Locomotives. Multicoloured.
812 40f. Type **161** 1·20 35
813 55f. George Stephenson, "Rocket" (1829) and Djibouti locomotive 1·60 40
814 65f. French TGV and Japanese "Hikari" high speed trains 2·10 50

162 Antenna on Globe and Morse Key

1981. Djibouti Amateur Radio Club.
815 **162** 250f. multicoloured 5·00 1·50

163 Prince Charles and Lady Diana Spencer

1981. Royal Wedding. Multicoloured.
816 180f. Type **163** 3·75 1·30
817 200f. Prince Charles and Lady Diana in wedding dress 4·25 1·50

164 Admiral Nelson and H.M.S. "Victory"

1981. Admiral Nelson Commemoration. Mult.
818 100f. Type **164** 2·00 75
819 175f. Nelson and stern view of H.M.S. "Victory" 3·25 1·30

165 Tree Hyrax and Scout tending Camp-fire

1981. 28th World Scouting Congress, Dakar, and Fourth Panafrican Scouting Conference, Abidjan. Multicoloured.
820 60f. Type **165** 2·50 65
821 105f. Scouts saluting, map reading and greater kudu 3·25 90

166 "Football Players" (Picasso)

1981. Air. Paintings. Multicoloured.
822 300f. Type **166** 7·25 2·10
823 400f. "Portrait of a Man in a Turban" (Rembrandt) 8·00 3·00

167 Launch

1981. Air. Space Shuttle. Multicoloured.
824 90f. Type **167** 1·90 60
825 120f. Space Shuttle landing 2·50 85

168 19th-century Chinese Pawn and Knight

1981. Chess Pieces. Multicoloured.
826 50f. 13th-century Swedish pawn and queen (horiz) 1·70 55
827 130f. Type **168** 3·50 1·10

169 Aerial View

1981. Inauguration of Djibouti Sheraton Hotel.
828 **169** 75f. multicoloured 1·70 65

1981. 2nd Flight of Space Shuttle "Columbia". Nos. 824/5 optd.
829 90f. Type **167** 1·90 75
830 120f. Space Shuttle landing 2·50 1·20
OPTS: 90f. **COLUMBIA 2eme VOL SPATIAL 12 NOVEMBRE 1981**. 120f. **JOE ENGLE et RICHARD TRULY 2eme VOL SPATIAL—12 Nov. 1981.**

171 "Clitoria ternatea"

1981. Flowers. Multicoloured.
831 10f. Type **171** 35 10
832 30f. "Acacia mellifera" (horiz) 80 20
833 35f. "Punica granatum" (horiz) 1·10 25
834 45f. Malvacee 1·40 45

1981. World Chess Championship, Merano (1st issue). Nos. 826/7 optd.
835 50f. multicoloured 1·50 75
836 130f. multicoloured 3·25 1·40
OPTS: 50f. **Octobre-Novembre 1981 ANATOLI KARPOV VICTOR KORTCHNOI MERANO (ITALIE)**. 130f. **ANATOLI KARPOV Champion du Monde 1981**.
See also Nos. 843/4.

173 Saving Goal

1982. Air. World Cup Football Championship, Spain. Multicoloured.
837 110f. Type **173** 2·20 80
838 220f. Footballers 4·75 1·60

174 John H. Glenn

1982. Air. Space Anniversaries. Mult.
839 40f. "Luna 9" (15th anniv of first unmanned moon landing) 80 25
840 60f. Type **174** (20th anniv of flight) 1·30 50
841 180f. "Viking 1" (5th anniv of first Mars landing) (horiz) 3·50 1·30

175 Dr. Robert Koch, Bacillus and Microscope

1982. Centenary of Robert Koch's Discovery of Tubercle Bacillus.
842 **175** 305f. multicoloured 7·00 2·30

176 14th-century German Bishop and 18th-century Marie de Medici Bishop

1982. World Chess Championship, Merano (2nd issue). Multicoloured.
843 125f. Type **176** 3·50 1·00
844 175f. Late 19th-century queen and pawn from Nuremberg 4·25 1·40

177 Princess of Wales

1982. Air. 21st Birthday of Princess of Wales. Multicoloured.
845 120f. Type **177** 2·20 1·20
846 180f. Princess of Wales (different) 3·75 1·30

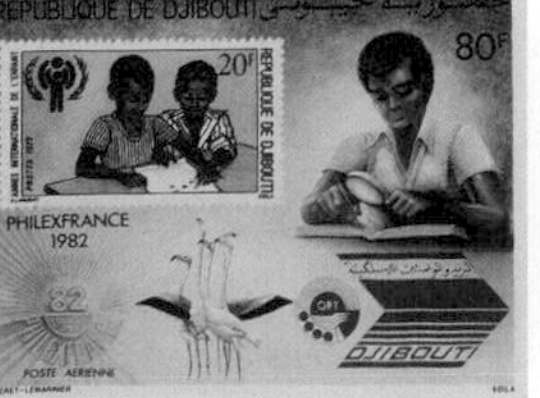

178 I.Y.C. Stamp, Collector, Greater Flamingoes and Emblems

1982. "Philexfrance" International Stamp Exhibition, Paris. Multicoloured.

847 80f. Type **178** 2·30 1·20

848	140f. Rowland Hill stamp Exhibition Centre and U.P.U. emblem	3·00	1·50

179 Microwave Antenna

1982. World Telecommunications Day.

849	**179**	150f. multicoloured	2·50	1·00

180 Mosque, Medina

1982. Air. 1350th Death Anniv of Mohammed.

850	**180**	500f. multicoloured	9·50	3·50

181 Lord Baden-Powell

1982. Air. 125th Birth Anniv of Lord Baden-Powell. Multicoloured.

851	95f. Type **181**	1·80	75
852	200f. Saluting Scout and camp	4·00	1·60

182 Bus and Jeep

1982. Transport. Multicoloured.

853	20f. Type **182**	55	25
854	25f. Ferry and dhow	65	30
855	55f. Boeing 727-100 airliner and Alsthom Series BB 500 diesel locomotive and train	1·50	70

1982. Air. World Cup Football Championship winners. Nos. 837/8 optd.

856	110f. Type **173**	2·20	90
857	220f. Footballers	4·25	1·90

OPTS: 110f. **ITALIE RFA 3-1 POLOGNE FRANCE 3-2.** 220f. **ITALIE RFA 3-1 2 RFA 3 POLOGNE.**

1982. Air. Birth of Prince William of Wales. Nos. 845/6 optd.

858	120f. Type **177**	2·20	1·10
859	180f. Princess of Wales (different)	3·75	1·40

OPTS: 120f. **21 JUIN 1982 WILLIAM-ARTHUR-PHILIPPE-LOUIS PRINCE DES GALLES.** 180f. **21ST JUNE 1982 WILLIAM-ARTHUR-PHILIP-LOUIS PRINCE OF WALES.**

185 Satellite, Dish Aerial and Conference

1982. Air. Second U.N. Conference on the Exploration and Peaceful Uses of Outer Space, Vienna.

860	**185**	350f. multicoloured	7·00	2·40

186 Franklin D. Roosevelt

1982. Air. 250th Birth Anniv of George Washington and Birth Centenary of Franklin D. Roosevelt. Multicoloured.

861	115f. Type **186**	2·20	75
862	250f. George Washington	4·50	1·50

187 Red Sea Cowrie

1982. Shells. Multicoloured.

863	10f. Type **187**	30	10
864	15f. Sumatran cone	45	25
865	25f. Lovely cowrie	75	30
866	30f. Engraved cone	95	40
867	70f. Heavy bonnet	2·10	90
868	150f. Burnt cowrie	4·00	1·30

188 Dove perched on Gun

1982. Palestinian Solidarity Day.

869	**188**	40f. multicoloured	80	30

189 Montgolfier's Balloon, 1783

1983. Air. Bicentenary of Manned Flight. Mult.

870	35f. Type **189**	95	30
871	45f. Henri Giffard's balloon "Le Grand Ballon Captif", 1878	1·50	55
872	120f. Balloon "Double Eagle II", 1978	3·00	1·30

190 Volleyball

1983. Air. Olympic Games, Los Angeles (1984). Multicoloured.

873	75f. Type **190**	1·50	65
874	125f. Wind-surfing	3·00	1·40

191 Bloch 220 Gascogne

1983. Air. 50th Anniv of Air France. Mult.

875	25f. Type **191**	50	30
876	100f. Douglas DC-4	2·00	1·20
877	175f. Boeing 747-200	3·50	1·30

1983. Flowers. As T **171**. Multicoloured.

878	5f. Ipomoea	10	10
879	50f. Moringa (horiz)	1·20	40
880	55f. Cotton flower	1·40	1·10

192 Martin Luther King

1983. Air. Celebrities. Multicoloured.

881	180f. Type **192** (15th death anniv)	3·50	1·30
882	250f. Alfred Nobel (150th birth anniv)	4·50	1·90

193 W.C.Y. Emblem

1983. World Communications Year.

883	**193**	500f. multicoloured	9·00	3·75

194 Yacht and Rotary Club Emblem

1983. Air. International Club Meetings. Mult.

884	90f. Type **194**	2·40	1·40
885	150f. Minaret and Lions Club emblem	2·75	1·10

195 Renault, 1904

1983. Air. Early Motor Cars. Multicoloured.

886	60f. Type **195**	1·80	55
887	80f. Mercedes Knight, 1910 (vert)	2·75	65
888	100f. Lorraine-Dietrich, 1912	3·00	1·20

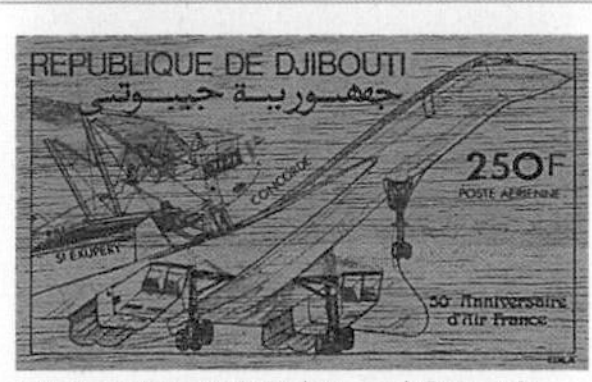

196 Saint-Exupery's Biplane and Concorde

1983. Air. 50th Anniv of Air France. Sheet 121×91 mm.

MS889	250f. multicoloured	27·00	27·00

197 "Vostok VI"

1983. Air. Conquest of Space. Multicoloured.

890	120f. Type **197**	2·20	1·00
891	200f. "Explorer I"	3·75	1·70

198 Development Projects

1983. Donors Conference.

892	**198**	75f. multicoloured	1·50	75

199 Red Sea Marginella

1983. Shells. Multicoloured.

893	15f. Type **199**	50	10
894	30f. Jickeli's cone	1·00	25
895	55f. MacAndrew's cowrie	1·50	60
896	80f. Cuvier's cone	2·00	75
897	100f. Tapestry turban	2·50	90

200 "Colotis chrysonome"

1984. Butterflies.

898	5f. Type **200**	25	15
899	20f. "Colias erate"	60	25
900	30f. "Junonia orithyia"	1·00	45
901	75f. "Acraea doubledayi"	3·25	1·10
902	110f. "Byblia ilithya"	4·00	1·70

201 Speed Skating

1984. Air. Winter Olympic Games, Sarajevo. Mult.

903	70f. Type **201**	1·50	60
904	130f. Ice dancing	2·75	1·10

202 Cable Ship

1984. Air. Agreement to construct Marseille—Singapore Submarine Cable. Sheet 127×96 mm.

MS905	**202** 250f. multicoloured	8·75	8·75

203 Microlight

1984. Air. Microlight Aircraft. Multicoloured.

906	65f. Type **203**	1·30	45
907	85f. Powered hang-glider "Jules"	1·70	55
908	100f. Microlight (different)	2·50	80

1984. Air. Winter Olympic Games Medal Winners. Nos. 903/4 optd.

909	70f. **1000 METRES HOMMES OR: BOUCHER (CANADA) ARGENT: KHLEBNIKOV (URSS) BRONZE: ENGEL-STADT (NORV.)**	1·50	75
910	130f. **DANSE OR: TORVILL-DEAN (G.B.) ARGENT: BESTEMIANOVA-BUKIN (URSS) BRONZE: KLIMOVA-PONOMARENKO (URSS)**	2·75	1·30

205 "Marguerite Matisse with Cat"

1984. Air. 30th Death Anniv of Matisse and Birth Centenary of Modigliani. Multicoloured.

911	150f. Type **205**	3·50	1·60
912	200f. "Mario Varvogli" (Modigliani)	5·00	2·20

206 Randa

1984. Landscapes. Multicoloured.

913	2f. Type **206**	15	10
914	8f. Ali Sabieh	15	10
915	10f. Lake Assal	25	10
916	15f. Tadjoura	30	10
917	40f. Alaili Dada (vert)	80	25
918	45f. Lake Abbe	95	55
919	55f. Obock	1·70	85
920	125f. Presidential Palace	3·25	1·60

207 Marathon

1984. Air. Olympic Games, Los Angeles. Mult.

921	50f. Type **207**	1·00	55
922	60f. High jump	1·20	65
923	80f. Swimming	1·60	80

208 Battle of Solferino

1984. Air. 125th Anniv of Battle of Solferino and 120th Anniv of Red Cross.

924	**208**	300f. multicoloured	6·25	2·75

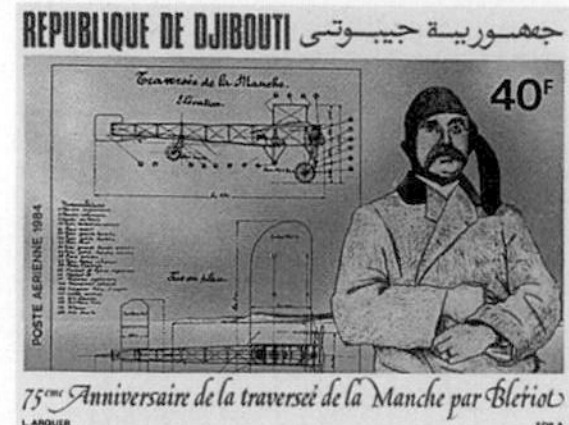

209 Bleriot and Diagram of Bleriot XI

1984. Air. 75th Anniv of Louis Bleriot's Cross-Channel Flight. Multicoloured.

925	40f. Type **209**	85	50
926	75f. Bleriot and Bleriot XI and Britten Norman Islander aircraft	1·50	1·00
927	90f. Bleriot and Boeing 727 airliner	1·80	1·20

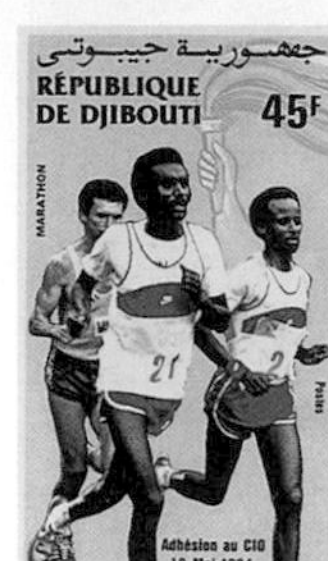

210 Marathon

1984. Membership of International Olympic Committee.

928	**210**	45f. multicoloured	95	50

211 U.S.A. Attack-pumper Fire Engine

1984. Fire Fighting. Multicoloured.

929	25f. Type **211**	95	30
930	95f. French P.P.M. rescue crane	3·00	85
931	100f. Canadair CL-215 fire-fighting amphibian	3·00	1·40

212 Men on Moon, Telescope and Planets

1984. Air. 375th Anniv of Galileo's Telescope. Multicoloured.

932	120f. Type **212**	2·50	1·10
933	180f. Galileo, telescope and planets	3·50	1·80

213 Football Teams (Europa Cup)

1984. Air. European Football Championship and Olympic Games, Los Angeles. Multicoloured.

934	80f. Type **213**	2·40	90
935	80f. Football teams (Olympic Games)	2·40	90

214 Motor Carriage, 1886

1984. 150th Birth Anniv of Gottlieb Daimler (automobile designer). Multicoloured.

936	35f. Type **214**	95	45
937	65f. Canstatt-Daimler cabriolet, 1896	1·50	80
938	90f. Daimler "Phoenix", 1900	2·20	1·10

215 Pierre Curie

1985. Pierre and Marie Curie (physicists). Mult.

939	150f. Type **215** (150th birth anniv)	3·25	1·50
940	150f. Marie Curie (50th death anniv)	3·25	1·50

216 White-throated Bee Eater

1985. Birth Bicentenary of John J. Audubon. Multicoloured.

941	5f. Type **216**	50	25
942	15f. Chestnut-bellied sand-grouse	1·90	80
943	20f. Yellow-breasted barbet	2·20	85
944	25f. European roller	2·75	1·00
MS945	100×120 mm. 200f. Osprey (air)	13·00	13·00

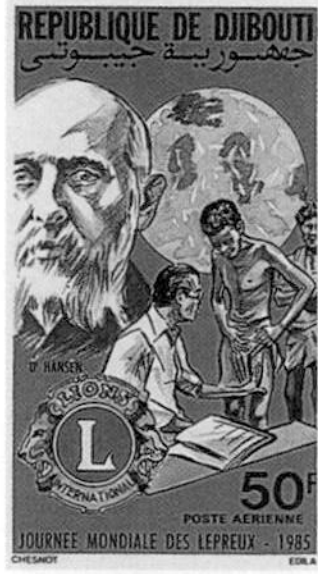

217 Dr. Hansen, Bacilli, Lepers and Lions Emblem

1985. Air. International Organizations. Mult.

946	50f. Type **217** (World Leprosy Day)	1·20	65
947	60f. Rotary International emblem and pieces on chessboard	1·90	85

218 Globe and Pictograms

1985. International Youth Year.

948	**218**	10f. multicoloured	15	15
949	**218**	30f. multicoloured	65	40
950	**218**	40f. multicoloured	80	55

219 Steam Locomotive No. 29, Addis Ababa–Djibouti Railway

1985. Railway Locomotives. Multicoloured.

951	55f. Type **219**	1·70	80
952	75f. "Adler", 1835 (150th anniv of German railways)	2·30	1·10

220 Planting Sapling

1985. Foundation of Djibouti Scouting Association. Multicoloured.

953	35f. Type **220**	95	45
954	65f. Childcare	1·90	80

221 Victor Hugo (novelist)

1985. Writers. Multicoloured.

955	80f. Type **221**	1·70	1·00
956	100f. Arthur Rimbaud (poet)	1·90	1·20

222 Dish Aerials, Off-shore Oil Rigs and Building

1985. Air. "Philexafrique" Stamp Exhibition, Lome (1st issue). Multicoloured.

957	80f. Type **222**	2·30	1·50
958	80f. Carpenter, girl at micro-scope and man at visual display unit	2·30	1·50

See also Nos. 969/70.

1985. Shells. As T **199**. Multicoloured.

959	10f. Twin-blotch cowrie	30	10
960	15f. Thrush cowrie	45	20
961	30f. Vice-Admiral cowrie	1·20	30
962	40f. Giraffe cone	1·40	55
963	55f. Terebra cone	2·10	90

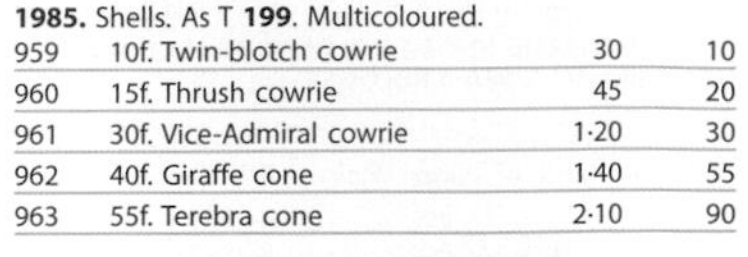

223 Team Winners on Rostrum

1985. 1st Marathon World Cup, Hiroshima. Multicoloured.

964	75f. Type **223**	1·30	85

965 100f. Finishing line and officials 2·00 1·30

224 Launch of "Ariane"

1985. Air. Telecommunications Development. Mult.

966 50f. International Transmission Centre 95 50

967 90f. Type **224** 1·70 95

968 120f. "Arabsat" satellite 2·20 1·40

225 Windsurfing and Tennis

1985. Air. "Philexafrique" Stamp Exhibition, Lome, Togo (2nd issue). Multicoloured.

969 100f. Type **225** 2·75 1·60

970 100f. Construction of Tadjoura road 2·75 1·60

226 Edmond Halley, Bayeux Tapestry and Comet

1986. Appearance of Halley's Comet. Multicoloured.

971 85f. Type **226** 1·50 65

972 90f. Solar system, comet trajectory and space probes "Giotto" and "Vega 1" 1·90 1·00

227 Footballers

1986. Air. World Cup Football Championship, Mexico. Multicoloured.

973 75f. Type **227** 1·50 85

974 100f. Players and stadium 1·90 1·10

228 Runners on Shore

1986. "ISERST" Solar Energy Project. Mult.

975 50f. Type **228** 95 55

976 150f. "ISERST" building 2·75 1·50

229 "Santa Maria"

1986. Historic Ships of Columbus, 1492. Multicoloured.

977 60f. Type **229** 2·20 1·10

978 90f. "Nina" and "Pinta" 3·00 1·80

230 Statue of Liberty, Eiffel Tower and French and U.S. Flags

1986. Air. Centenary of Statue of Liberty.

979 **230** 250f. multicoloured 4·50 2·00

231 Rainbow Runner

1986. Red Sea Fish. Multicoloured.

980 20f. Type **231** 60 25

981 25f. Sehel's grey mullet 85 40

982 55f. Blubber-lipped snapper 1·80 80

232 People's Palace

1986. Public Buildings. Multicoloured.

983 105f. Type **232** 2·00 1·00

984 115f. Ministry of the Interior, Posts and Telecommunications 2·20 1·30

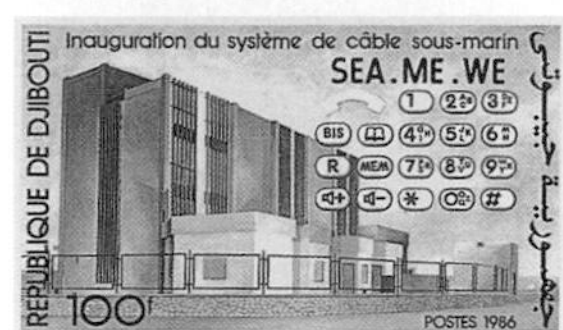

233 Transmission Building and Keyboard

1986. Inauguration of Sea-Me-We Submarine Communications Cable.

985 **233** 100f. multicoloured 1·90 95

MS986 125×95 mm. **233** 250f. multicoloured 9·75 9·75

1986. Air. World Cup Football Championship Winners. Nos. 973/4 optd. Multicoloured.

987 75f. **FRANCE-BELGIQUE 4-2** 1·50 90

988 100f. **3-2 ARGENTINA-RFA** 1·90 1·10

235 Javanese Bishop, Knight and Queen

1986. Air. World Chess Championship, London and Leningrad. Multicoloured.

989 80f. Type **235** 2·00 90

990 120f. German rook, pawn and king 3·25 1·30

1986. 5th Anniv of Inaug of Djibouti Sheraton Hotel. No. 828 surch 5e ANNIVERSAIRE.

991 **169** 55f. on 75f. mult 1·30 80

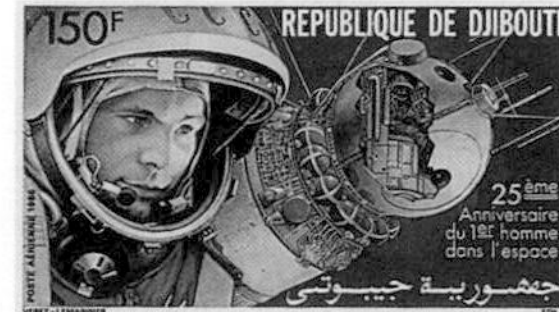

237 Gagarin and Space Capsule

1986. Air. 25th Anniv of First Man in Space and 20th Anniv of "Gemini 8"–"Agena" Link-up. Multicoloured.

992 150f. Type **237** 3·00 1·10

993 200f. "Gemini 8" and "Agena" craft over Earth 4·25 1·60

238 Amiot 370

1987. Air. Flight Anniversaries and Events. Multicoloured.

994 55f. Type **238** (45th anniv of first Istres-Djibouti flight) 1·30 45

995 80f. "Spirit of St Louis" and Charles Lindbergh (60th anniv of first solo flight across North Atlantic) 1·60 65

996 120f. Dick Rutan, Jeana Yeager and "Voyager" (first non-stop flight around the world) 2·50 1·10

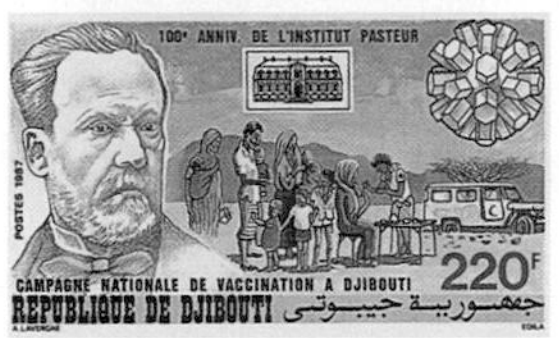

239 Louis Pasteur and Vaccination Session

1987. Centenary of Pasteur Institute. National Vaccination Campaign in Djibouti.

997 **239** 220f. multicoloured 5·00 1·60

240 Follereau and Hansen

1987. Air. Anti-leprosy Campaign. 75th Death Anniv of Gerhard Hansen (discover of bacillus) and 10th Death Anniv of Raoul Follereau (leprosy pioneer). Sheet 110×99 mm.

MS998 **240** 500f. multicoloured 20·00 20·00

241 "Macrolepiota imbricata"

1987. Fungi. Multicoloured.

999 35f. Type **241** 1·10 75

1000 50f. "Lentinus squarrosulus" 1·70 95

1001 95f. "Terfezia boudieri" 3·00 1·50

242 Hare

1987. Wild Animals. Multicoloured.

1002 5f. Type **242** 20 10

1003 30f. Young dromedary with mother 85 40

1004 140f. Cheetah 3·75 1·30

243 President Hassan Gouled Aptidon, Map, Flag and Crest

1987. Air. 10th Anniv of Independence.

1005 **243** 250f. multicoloured 4·50 1·90

244 Pierre de Coubertin (founder of modern Games) and Athlete lighting Flame

1987. Olympic Games, Calgary and Seoul (1st issue) (1988). Multicoloured.

1006 85f. Type **244** 1·50 70

1007 135f. Ski-jumper 2·40 1·10

1008 140f. Runners and spectators 2·75 1·20

See also No. 1021.

245 "Telstar" Satellite

1987. Air. Telecommunications Anniversaries. Multicoloured.

1009 190f. Type **245** (25th anniv) 3·50 1·60

1010 250f. Samuel Morse and morse key (150th anniv of morse telegraph) 4·50 2·10

246 Djibouti Creek and Quay, 1887

1987. Air. Centenary of Djibouti City.

1011 **246** 100f. agate and stone 2·00 85

1012 - 150f. multicoloured 3·00 1·20

MS1013 118×87 mm. 250f. multicoloured 5·50 5·50

DESIGNS: 150f. Aerial view of Djibouti, 1978; 250f. Postmarks and 1894–1902 stamps.

247 Comb

1988. Traditional Djibouti Art. Multicoloured.

1014 30f. Type **247** 60 25

1015 70f. Water pitcher 1·30 65

249 Anniversary Emblem

1988. Air. 125th Anniv of Red Cross.

1017 **249** 300f. multicoloured 6·00 2·75

250 Rabat and Footballers

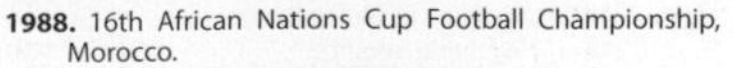

1988. 16th African Nations Cup Football Championship, Morocco.

1018	**250**	55f. multicoloured	1·20	50

251 Ski Jumping

1988. Winter Olympic Games, Calgary.

1019	**251**	45f. multicoloured	95	45

252 Doctor examining Child

1988. UNICEF. "Universal Vaccinations by 1990" Campaign.

1020	**252**	125f. multicoloured	2·50	1·00

253 Runners and Stadium

1988. Air. Olympic Games, Seoul (2nd issue).

1021	**253**	105f. multicoloured	3·00	1·20

1988. Air. Paris–Djibouti–St. Denis (Reunion) Roland Garros Air Race. No. 994 surch PARIS-DJIBOUTI-ST DENIS LA REUNION RALLYE ROLAND GARROS 70 F.

1022	**238**	70f. on 55f. mult	2·20	1·10

255 Animals at Water Trough

1988. Anti-drought Campaign.

1023	**255**	50f. multicoloured	1·30	50

256 Djibouti Post Offices of 1890 and 1977

1988. Air. World Post Day.

1024	**256**	1000f. multicoloured	19·00	6·25

257 Combine Harvester, Tractor and Ploughman with Camel

1988. 10th Anniv of International Agricultural Development Fund.

1025	**257**	135f. multicoloured	2·50	1·00

258 de Havilland Tiger Moth, 1948, and Socata TB-100 Tobago, 1988

1988. 40th Anniv of Michel Lafoux Air Club.

1026	**258**	145f. multicoloured	2·00	1·10

1988. 1st Djibouti Olympic Medal Winner. No. 1021 optd AHMED SALAH 1re MEDAILLE OLYMPIQUE.

1027	**253**	105f. multicoloured	2·20	1·20

260 "Lobophyllia costata"

1989. Underwater Animals. Multicoloured.

1028		90f. Type **260**	2·00	50
1029		160f. Giant spider conch	4·25	1·50

261 "Colotis protomedia"

1989

1030	**261**	70f. multicoloured	5·00	1·40

1989. Nos. 849 and 913 surch 70f.

1031	**206**	70f. on 2f. mult	1·90	60
1032	**179**	70f. on 150f. mult	1·90	60

263 Dancers

1989. Folklore. Multicoloured.

1033		30f. Type **263**	55	25
1034		70f. Dancers with parasol	1·40	65

264 Pale-bellied Francolin ("Francolin de Djibouti")

1989

1035	**264**	35f. multicoloured	2·20	45

265 Arrows and Dish Aerials

1989. Air. World Telecommunications Day.

1036	**265**	150f. multicoloured	2·75	1·20

266 "Calotropis procera"

1989

1037	**266**	25f. multicoloured	50	25

267 Emblem, Declaration and People

1989. Air. "Philexfrance 89" International Stamp Exhibition, Paris, and Bicentenary of Declaration of Rights of Man.

1038	**267**	120f. multicoloured	2·50	95

268 Emblem and State Arms

1989. Cent of Interparliamentary Union.

1039	**268**	70f. multicoloured	1·40	50

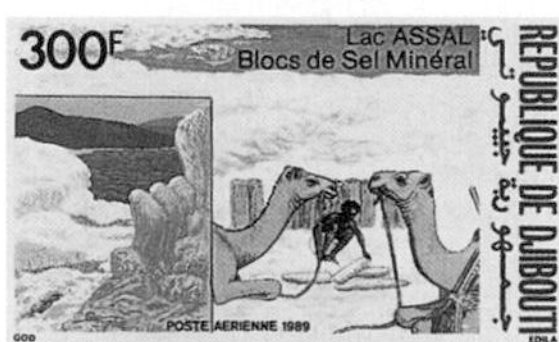

269 Collecting Salt

1989. Air. Lake Assal.

1040	**269**	300f. multicoloured	6·00	1·70

270 Child going to School

1989. International Literacy Year.

1041	**270**	145f. multicoloured	2·75	1·10

271 Tourka Maddw Cave Painting

1989

1042	**271**	5f. multicoloured	45	35

272 Traditional Ornaments

1989

1043	**272**	55f. multicoloured	1·20	50

1990. Nos. 914 and 916/17 surch.

1044		30f. on 8f. multicoloured	55	25
1045		50f. on 40f. mult	1·60	50
1046		120f. on 15f. mult	2·40	80

274 Water-storage Drums and Arid Landscape

1990. Anti-drought Campaign.

1047	**274**	120f. multicoloured	2·30	80

275 Basketry

1990. Traditional Crafts. Multicoloured.

1048		30f. Type **275**	60	35
1049		70f. Jewellery (vert)	1·60	50

275a Blue-spotted Stingray

1990. Multicoloured, colour of face-value box given.

1049b	**275a**	70f. yellow		
1049c	**275a**	100f. green		

276 "Commiphora sp."

1990

1050	**276**	30f. multicoloured	70	45

277 Footballers

1990. World Cup Football Championship, Italy.

1051	**277**	100f. multicoloured	1·90	75

278 Athlete

1990. Djibouti 20 km Race.

1052	**278**	55f. multicoloured	1·20	45

279 Queue of Patients

1990. Vaccination Campaign.

1053	**279**	300f. multicoloured	4·75	2·20

280 De Gaulle

1990. Birth Centenary of Charles de Gaulle (French statesman).

1054	**280**	200f. multicoloured	4·00	1·70

281 Technology in Developed Countries

1990. United Nations Conference on Less Developed Countries.

1055	**281**	45f. multicoloured	1·00	50

282 Mammoth and Fossilized Remains

1990

1056	**282**	90f. multicoloured	4·25	1·70

283 Hamadryas Baboon

1990

1057	**283**	50f. multicoloured	1·40	55

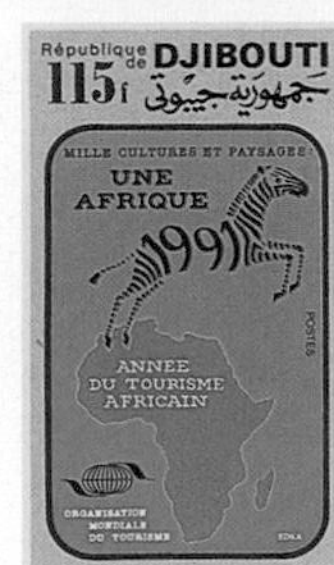
284 Emblem and Map

1991. African Tourism Year.

1058	**284**	115f. multicoloured	2·50	1·20

285 "Acropora"

1991. Corals. Multicoloured.

1059	40f. Type **285**	1·00	50
1060	45f. "Seriatopora hytrise"	1·10	50

286 Pink-backed Pelican

1991. Birds. Multicoloured.

1061	10f. Type **286**	40	15
1062	15f. Western reef heron	90	30
1063	20f. Goliath heron (horiz)	1·10	35
1064	25f. White spoonbill (horiz)	1·30	40

287 Osprey

1991

1065	**287**	200f. multicoloured	4·50	2·50

288 Traditional Game

1991

1066	**288**	250f. multicoloured	5·25	2·50

289 Diesel Locomotive

1991. Djibouti–Ethiopia Railway (1st issue).

1067	**289**	85f. multicoloured	3·00	1·10

See also No. 1076.

290 Hands holding Earth above Polluted Sea

1991. World Environment Day.

1068	**290**	110f. multicoloured	2·50	90

291 Windsurfers and Islets

1991. "Philexafrique" Stamp Exhibition.

1069	**291**	120f. multicoloured	3·00	1·20

292 Handball

1991. Olympic Games, Barcelona (1992) (1st issue).

1070	**292**	175f. multicoloured	4·00	1·80

See also No. 1079.

293 Harvesting Crops

1991. World Food Day.

1071	**293**	105f. multicoloured	2·50	1·00

294 Route-map, Woman using Telephone and Cable-laying Ship

1991. Inauguration of Marseilles–Djibouti–Singapore Submarine Cable.

1072	**294**	130f. multicoloured	2·75	1·30

295 Columbus and Ships

1991. 500th Anniv (1992) of Discovery of America by Columbus (1st issue).

1073	**295**	145f. multicoloured	3·00	1·60

See also No. 1080.

296 Rimbaud, Ship and Serpent

1991. Death Centenary of Arthur Rimbaud (poet). Multicoloured.

1074	90f. Type **296**	2·50	1·10
1075	150f. Rimbaud, camel train and map	3·00	1·30

297 Camel Driver and Diesel Train

1992. Djibouti—Ethiopia Railway (2nd issue). Multicoloured.

1076	70f. Type **297**	2·40	90
MS1077	114×109 mm. 205f. Steam locomotive and route map from Djibouti to Addis Ababa (48×36 mm)	5·50	5·50

298 Boys Playing Game

1992. Traditional Games.

1078	**298**	100f. multicoloured	2·00	80

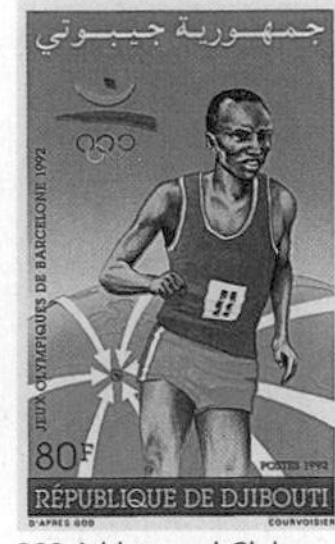
299 Athlete and Globe

1992. Olympic Games, Barcelona (2nd issue).

1079	**299**	80f. multicoloured	1·90	85

300 Caravel crossing Atlantic

1992. 500th Anniv of Discovery of America by Columbus (2nd issue).

1080	**300**	125f. multicoloured	2·50	1·10

301 Crushing Grain

1992. Traditional Methods of Preparing Food. Multicoloured.

1081	30f. Type **301**	90	45
1082	70f. Winnowing	1·30	80

302 Players, Map of Africa and Final Result

1992. 18th African Nations Cup Football Championship, Senegal.

1083	**302**	15f. multicoloured	45	35

303 "Ariane" Rocket and Satellite

1992. International Space Year. Multicoloured.

1084	120f. Type **303**	2·50	80
1085	135f. Satellite and astronaut (horiz)	2·75	1·20

304 Salt's Dik-dik

1992

1086	**304**	5f. multicoloured	85	40

305 Loggerhead Turtle

1992

1087	**305**	200f. multicoloured	4·00	1·60

306 Preparing Mofo

1992. Mofo. Multicoloured.

1088	45f. Type **306**		
1089	75f. Cooking mofo		

307 Nomadic Girl

1993. Traditional Costumes. Multicoloured.

1090	70f. Type **307**	1·70	75
1091	120f. Nomadic girl with headband	2·75	90

308 White-eyed Gull ("Geoland a Iris Blanc")

1993

1092	**308**	300f. multicoloured	5·50	2·40

309 Amin Salman Mosque

1993

1093	**309**	500f. multicoloured	55·00	6·00

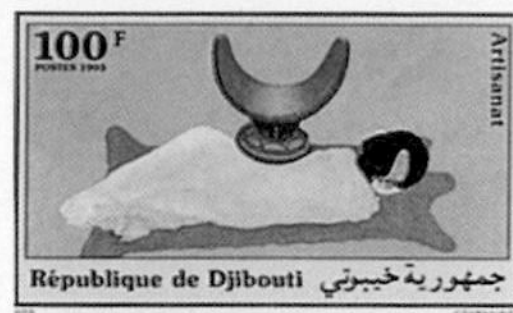

310 Headrest

1993. Crafts. Multicoloured.

1094	100f. Type **310**	1·20	1·20
1095	125f. Flask	1·60	1·60

311 Savanna Monkey

1993

1096	**311**	150f. multicoloured	£110	1·80

312 Flags of Member Countries

1993. 30th Anniv of Organization of African Unity.

1097	**312**	200f. multicoloured	£110	2·40

313 Woman carrying Water on Back

1993. Water Carriers. Multicoloured.

1098	30f. Type **313**	40	35
1099	50f. Man carrying water on yoke	65	65

314 Plants and Spacecraft

1993. Space.

1100	**314**	90f. multicoloured	1·10	1·10

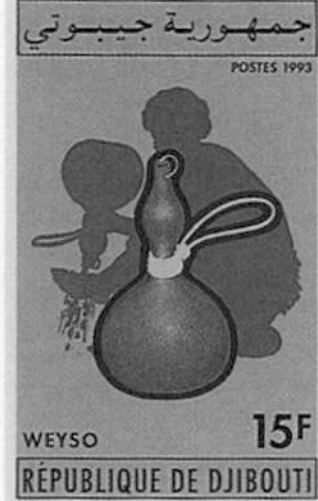

315 Water Jar

1993. Utensils. Multicoloured.

1101	15f. Type **315**	45	35
1102	20f. Hangol (agricultural tool)	80	35
1103	25f. Comb	1·00	55
1104	30f. Water-skin	1·20	3·00

316 Pipes

1993. Musical Instruments. Multicoloured.

1105	5f. Type **316**	50	40
1106	10f. Hand-held drum and lines of women	65	35

317 Royal Couple at Wedding Ceremony

1994. Wedding (1993) of Crown Prince Naruhito of Japan and Masako Owada. Sheet 120×100 mm.

MS1107 **316**	500f. blue, orange and black	20·00	20·00

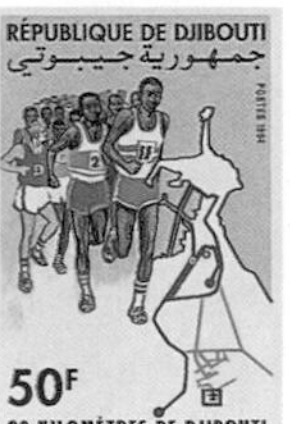

318 Runners and Route Map

1994. Djibouti 20 km Race.

1108	**318**	50f. multicoloured	1·90	90

319 Mother with Children

1994. UNICEF. Breast-feeding Campaign. Multicoloured.

1109	40f. Type **319**	1·90	90
1110	45f. Woman breast-feeding baby	1·90	90

320 Stadium

1994. Hassan Gouled Aptidon Stadium.

1111	**320**	70f. multicoloured	2·20	1·20

321 Spinner Dolphins

1994

1112	**321**	120f. multicoloured	2·40	2·00

322 Houses encircling Globe

1994. World Housing Day.

1113	**322**	30f. multicoloured	45	45

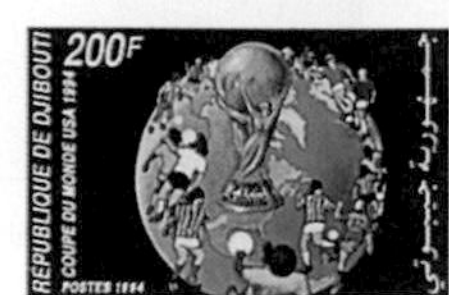

323 White-bellied Bustards

1994

1114	**323**	10f. multicoloured		

324 Trophy, Globe and Players

1994. World Cup Football Championship, U.S.A.

1115	**324**	200f. multicoloured	£190

325 Nomadic Man

1994. Traditional Costumes. Multicoloured.

1116	100f. Type **325**	2·75	1·70
1117	150f. Town dress	2·50	2·50

326 Golden Jackals

1994

1118	**326**	400f. multicoloured	£140

327 Walkers

1994. World Walking Day.

1119	**327**	75f. multicoloured

328 Book Rests

1994. Traditional Crafts.
1120 **328** 55f. multicoloured

329 Traditional Dancers

1994. Folklore.
1121 **329** 35f. multicoloured

330 Camel, Ostrich and Net

1995. Centenary of Volleyball.
1122 **330** 70f. multicoloured

331 U.N. Flag tied around Cracked Globe

1995. 50th Anniv of U.N.O.
1123 **331** 120f. multicoloured

332 Drawing Water from Well

1995. Drought Relief Campaign.
1124 **332** 100f. multicoloured

333 Greater Flamingo

1995. Birds. Multicoloured.
1125 30f. Type **333**
1126 50f. Sacred ibis

334 Camel Rider

1995. Telecommunications Day.
1127 **334** 125f. multicoloured 55·00 1·40

335 Spotted Hyena

1995
1128 **335** 200f. multicoloured 10·50 1·60

336 Council held under Tree

1995
1129 **336** 150f. multicoloured 65·00

337 Nomads

1995. Nomadic Life.
1130 **337** 45f. multicoloured 65·00

338 Palm Tree, Map and Emblem

1995. 50th Anniv of F.A.O.
1131 **338** 250f. multicoloured 65·00

339 Development Project and Emblem

1995. 30th Anniv of African Development Bank.
1132 **339** 300f. multicoloured 65·00

340 Traditional Costume

1995
1133 **340** 90f. multicoloured

341 Trophy on Map and Football

1996. Africa Cup Football Championship.
1134 **341** 70f. multicoloured £190

342 Leopard

1996. Wildlife. Multicoloured.
1135 70f. Type **342**
1136 120f. Ostrich (vert)

343 Woman wearing Amber Necklace

1996. Traditional Crafts.
1137 **343** 30f. multicoloured

344 Olympic Flag

1996. Olympic Games, Atlanta.
1138 **344** 105f. multicoloured £130

345 "Commicarpus grandiflorus"

1996
1139 **345** 350f. multicoloured 65·00

346 Women's Rite

1996. Folklore.
1140 **346** 95f. multicoloured

347 The Lion and the Three Bullocks

1996. Stories and Legends.
1141 **347** 95f. multicoloured £140

348 Children with Flags

1996. National Children's Day.
1142 **348** 130f. multicoloured 65·00

349 Fox and Tortoise

1997. Stories and Legends. The Tortoise and the Fox. Multicoloured.
1143 60f. Type **349**
1144 60f. Fox running away from tortoise
1145 60f. Tortoise winning race

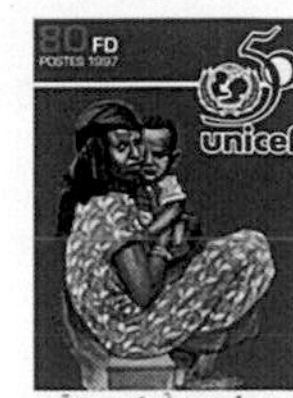
350 Mother and Child

1997. 50th Anniv of UNICEF. Multicoloured.
1146 80f. Type **350**
1147 90f. Arms cradling globe of children

351 Dancers

1997. Folklore.
1148 **351** 70f. multicoloured 75·00

352 Using Necklace as Pendulum

1997. Local Fortune Telling. Multicoloured.
1149 200f. Type **352**
1150 300f. Using pebbles

353 Woman weaving Basket

1997. Women's Day.
1151 **353** 250f. multicoloured £190

354 Writing Board

1997. Traditional Implements. Multicoloured.
1152 30f. Type **354**
1153 400f. Bowl and spoon (vert)

355 Arta Post Office

1997. 20th Anniv of Independence. Multicoloured.

1154 30f. Type **355**

1155 100f. Telecommunications station

1156 120f. Undersea cable, route map and cable ship (horiz)

356 Goats in Tree

1997

1157 **356** 120f. multicoloured

357 Diana, Princess of Wales

1998. Diana, Princess of Wales Commemoration.

1158	**357**	125f. multicoloured	2·50	1·50
1159	**357**	130f. multicoloured	2·50	1·50
1160	**357**	150f. multicoloured	3·00	1·60

358 Paradise Tanager

1998. International Year of the Ocean. Mult.

1161	75c. Type **358**	1·50	90
1162	75c. Red-eyed tree frog ("Agalychnis callidryas")	1·50	90
1163	75c. Common dolphin ("Delphinus delphis") and humpback whale ("Megaptera novaeangliae")	1·50	90
1164	75c. Savanna monkey ("Cercopithecus aethiops")	1·50	90
1165	75c. Great hammerhead ("Sphyrna mokarran") and yellow-lipped sea snakes ("Laticaudia colubrina")	1·50	90
1166	75c. Long-horned cowfish ("Lactoria cornuta") and common dolphin ("Delphinus delphis")	1·50	90
1167	75c. Common dolphins ("Delphinus delphis")	1·50	90
1168	75c. Striped mimic blenny ("Aspidontus taeniatus") and foxface ("Lovulpinus")	1·50	90
1169	75c. Big-fin reef squid ("Sepioteuthis lessoniana)	1·50	90
1170	75c. Ornate butterflyfish ("Chaetodon ornatissimus) and blue shark ("Prionace glauca")	1·50	90
1171	75c. Hermit crab ("Eupagurus bernherdus")	1·50	90
1172	75c. Common octopus ("Octopus vulgaris")	1·50	90

Nos. 1161/72 were issued together, se-tenant, forming a composite design.

359 Gandhi

1998. 50th Death Anniv of Mahatma Gandhi (Indian patriot).

1173 **359** 250f. multicoloured 65·00

360 Vase

1998. Traditional Art.

1174 **360** 30f. multicoloured £140

361 Woman carrying Basket on Back and Road-crossing Officer

1998. Women's Rights and International Peace.

1175 **361** 70f. multicoloured 39·00

362 Water Pump and Donkey carrying Water Containers

1998. World Water Day.

1176 **362** 45f. multicoloured 65·00

363 Football, Trophy and Eiffel Tower

1998. World Cup Football Championship, France.

1177 **363** 200f. multicoloured £170

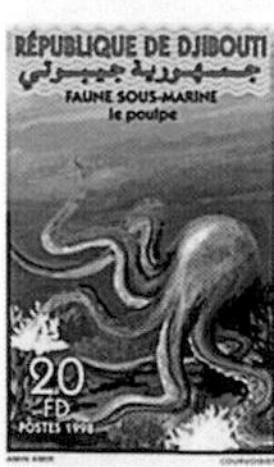
364 Octopus

1998. Marine Life. Multicoloured.

1178 20f. Type **364**

1179 25f. Shark (horiz)

365 Catmint and Cats

1998

1180 **365** 120f. multicoloured £140

366 Globe using Mobile Phone and Computer

1998. World Telecommunications Day.

1181 **366** 150f. multicoloured

367 National Bank

1998. Public Buildings.

1182 **367** 100f. multicoloured £140

368 Flags of Member States and Emblem

1998. Inter-Governmental Authority on Development.

1183 **368** 85f. multicoloured 40·00

369 Boys playing Goos

1998. Traditional Games.

1184 **369** 110f. multicoloured 65·00

370 Fishing Harbour

1998. Public Buildings.

1185 **370** 100f. multicoloured £120

371 Gulls sp. and Maskali Island

1998. Tourist Sites.

1186 **371** 500f. multicoloured £150

372 Mother Teresa

1998. Mother Teresa (founder of Missionaries of Charity) Commemoration.

1187 **372** 130f. multicoloured 2·50 1·50

377 Mother and Piglets

2000. Endangered Species. Eritrean Warthog (Phacochoerus africanus aeliani). Multicoloured.

1192	100f. Type **377**	1·90	1·40
1193	100f. Facing front	1·90	1·40
1194	100f. Head	1·90	1·40
1195	100f. Running	1·90	1·40

No. 1188 and Type **373** have been left for 'Telecommunications', issued on 8 February 1999, not yet received.

No. 1189 and Type **374** have been left for 'Gazelle', issued on 16 March 1999, not yet received.

No. 1190 and Type **375** have been left for 'Fish', issued on 6 May 1999, not yet received.

No. 1191 and Type **376** have been left for '50th Anniv of Djibouti', issued in 1999, not yet received.

378 Flamingo

2000. Fauna. Sheet 190×103 mm containing T 378 and similar horiz designs. Multicoloured.

MS1196 100f.×8, Type **378**; Ostrich; Sifaka; Yellow-billed stork; Scarlet macaw; Dwarf puff adder; Toucan; Whooping cranes 4·75 4·75

The stamps of **MS**1196 form a composite design.

379 *Doxocopa cherubina*

2000. Butterflies. Three sheets containing T 379 and similar multicoloured designs.

MS1197 156×134 mm. 100f.×6, Type **379**; *Heliconius charitonius; Cantonephelenumili; Danus gilippus; Morpho peleides; Heliconius doris* 15·00 15·00

MS1198 Two sheets, each 70×100 mm. Size 57×42 mm. (a) 250f. *Agraulis vanilla.e* (b) 250f. *Strymon melinus* 9·50 9·50

The stamps and margins of **MS**1197 form a composite design.

380 Pouring Water

2000. NABAD Conference.

1199 **380** 500f. multicoloured 11·50 7·25

381 Class QI 2-10-2 (China)

2000. Locomotives. Multicoloured.

1200	5f. Type **381**	30	25
1201	15f. Glacier Express (Switzerland)	30	25
1202	25f. Eurostar (France/Britain)	45	40
1203	35f. Class WP 4-6-2 (India)	50	50
1204	40f. Diesel set	50	50
1205	110f. Nord Chapelon Pacific (France)	2·20	1·60
1206	110f. Class 23 2-6-2 (Germany)	2·20	1·60
1207	110f. Class GS-4 4-8-4 (USA)	2·20	1·60
1208	110f. Class A4 4-6-2 (Britain)	2·20	1·60
1209	110f. Pacific 4-6-2 (South Africa)	2·20	1·60
1210	110f. Class HP (India)	2·20	1·60
1211	120f. VT 601 (Germany)	1·90	1·20

1212	120f. ICII Bo-Bo EMU (Netherlands)	1·90	1·20
1213	120f. TGV (France)	1·90	1·20
1214	120f. ETR 450 (Italy)	1·90	1·20
1215	120f. AVE (Spain)	1·90	1·20
1216	120f. Bullet train (Japan)	1·90	1·20
MS1217	Two sheets, each 100×75 mm. (a) 250f. GM *Warbonnet* (USA). (b) 250f. Class 8 Pacific (Britain)	4·75	4·75

382 Dancers

2000

1218	**382**	75f. multicoloured	1·90	1·40

383 *Dendrochirus biocellatus*

2000. Marine Fauna. Multicoloured.

1219	55f. Type **383**	1·10	80
1220	55f. *Hippocampus*	1·10	80
1221	55f. *Amphiprion percula*	1·10	80
1222	55f. *Periclimenes imperator*	1·10	80
1223	55f. *Pomacnetradae*	1·10	80
1224	55f. *Octopus vulgaris*	1·10	80
MS1225	Two sheets, each 206×189 mm. (a) 50f.×12, *Cephalopholis miniata; Ptereleatris hanae; Sphyraena genie; Tripterygion segmentatum; Odontosididae; Cirrhitidae; Amphiprion; Capros aper; Balistidae; Trygonorhina fasciata; Cephalopholis; Corythoichthys ocellatus.* (b) 60f.×12, *Lutjanus kasmira;Chaetodon fasciata; Epinphelinae; Hypoplectrus gutavarius; Loligo opalescens; Diodontinae; Coelenterata; Sargcentron xantherythrum; Thalassoma lunare; Hemichromis bimaculatus; Dasyatis; Fromia monilis* (all horiz)	11·50	11·50
MS1226	76×106 mm. 250f. *Eschrichtius robustus* (horiz)	4·75	4·75
MS1227	106×76 mm. 250f. *Cheloniidae* (horiz)	4·75	4·75

The stamps and margins of Nos. **MS**1225a/b, respectively form a composite design.

384 Blacksmith

2000

1228	**384**	100f. multicoloured	2·40	1·80

385 *Thomas W. Lawson* (1902)

2000. Ships. A Millennium of Navigation. Multicoloured.

1229	10f. Type **385** (seven-masted, steel-hulled schooner)	45	25
1230	15f. BT *Global Challenge* (2000)	1·40	30
1231	20f. *Reliance* and *Shamrock* (1903) (yachts)	2·40	35
1232	25f. *Archibald Russell* (1905) (four-masted steel barque)	3·25	45
1233	50f. 8th century Greek merchantman	4·25	90
1234	130f. Norman warship (1066)	2·50	1·60
1235	130f. Hanseatic cog (c. 1300)	2·50	1·60
1236	130f. *Santa Maria* (1492) (carrack)	2·50	1·60
1237	130f. *Mary Rose* (1510) (carrack)	2·50	1·60
1238	130f. *Golden Hind* (1577) (galleon)	2·50	1·60
1239	130f. *Sovereign of the Seas* (1637) (three decked warship)	2·50	1·60
1240	135f. HMB *Endeavour* (1768) (bark) (inscr 'HMS')	2·50	1·60
1241	135f. USS *Constitution* (1797) (three-masted heavy frigate)	2·50	1·60
1242	135f. *Chasse Maree* (1800) (three-masted lugger)	2·50	1·60
1243	135f. Baltimore clipper (1812)	2·50	1·60
1244	135f. *Lightning* (1853) (clipper)	2·50	1·60
1245	135f. *Bluenose* (1921) (schooner)	2·50	1·60
MS1246	Two sheets, each 81×96 mm. (a) 250f. HM Yacht *Britannia* (1893). (b) 250f. *Herzogin Cecilie* (1902) (four-masted steel barque)	9·50	9·50

386 Camel milking

2000

1247	**386**	35f. multicoloured	95	70

387 '2000'

2000. Millennium.

1248	**387**	125f. multicoloured	2·75	1·80

388 *Lanius excubitor* (great grey shrike)

2000. Birds. Multicoloured.

1249	5f. Type **388**	55	35
1250	10f. *Phoenicopterus minor* (lesser flamingo)	55	35
1251	15f. *Eupodotis senegalensis* (inscr 'Eupodatis') (white-bellied bustard)	55	35
1252	40f. *Noephron percnopterus* (inscr 'perchopterus') (Egyptian vulture)	55	35
1253	50f. *Pterocles lichtensteinii* (Lichtenstein's sandgrouse)	55	35

389 Apollo 11 Service Module (1969)

2000. Space Exploration. Five sheets containing T 389 and similar multicoloured designs.

MS1254	Two sheets, each 143×111 mm. (a) 100f.×6, Type **389**; Telstar (1962); Ariane 4 (1988); Apollo 11 Lunar Module *Eagle* (1969); First moon walk by Neil Armstrong (1969); Apollo 11 Command Module. (b) 100f.×6, John Glenn and Space Capsule; Soyuz 19 (docking of Apollo 18 and Soyuz 19) (1975); Hubble telescope (1990); Apollo 18 (docking of Apollo 18 and Soyuz 19) (1975); John Glenn elected senator (1974); Space shuttle *Columbia*	4·75	4·75
MS1255	Three sheets, each 110×85 mm. (a) 200f. Moonwalk (incorrectly inscr '1986 Space Shuttle Challenger'). (b) 250f. Space shuttle *Challenger*. (c) 250f. Neil Armstrong and Edwin 'Buzz' Aldrin on the moon (horiz)	4·75	4·75

The stamps and margins of **MS**1254a/b form composite designs.

POSTAGE DUE STAMPS

D248 Milking Bowl

1988. Traditional Djibouti Art.

D1016	**D248**	60f. multicoloured	1·20	85

Pt. 8

DODECANESE ISLANDS

A group of islands off the coast of Asia Minor occupied by Italy in May 1912 and ceded to her by Turkey in 1920. The islands concerned are now known as Kalimnos, Kasos, Kos, Khalki, Leros, Lipsoi, Nisiros, Patmos, Tilos (Piskopi), Rhodes (Rodos), Karpathos, Simi and Astipalaia. Castelrosso came under the same administration in 1921.

In 1944 the Dodecanese Islands were occupied by British forces (see **BRITISH OCCUPATION OF ITALIAN COLONIES**). In 1947 they were transferred to Greek administration, since when Greek stamps have been used.

100 centesimi = 1 lira.

B. Greek Military Administration.
100 lepta = 1 drachma.

A. ITALIAN OCCUPATION

A. Italian Occupation.

1912. Stamps of Italy optd EGEO.

1	39	25c. blue	55·00	37·00
2	-	50c. violet	55·00	37·00

1912. Stamps of Italy optd, or surch also, for the individual islands (all in capitals on Nos. 6 and 10, in upper and lower case on others). A. Calimno.

3A	31	2c. brown	9·25	6·50
4A	37	5c. green	2·75	6·50
5A	37	10c. red	55	6·50
6A	41	15c. grey	55·00	17·00
7A	37	15c. grey	12·00	48·00
8A	41	20c. on 15c. grey	26·00	32·00
10A	41	20c. orange	12·00	48·00
11A	39	25c. blue	17·00	6·50
12A	39	40c. brown	55	6·50
13A	39	50c. violet	55	11·50

B. Caso.

3B	31	2c. brown	9·25	6·50
4B	37	5c. green	5·00	6·50
5B	37	10c. red	55	6·50
6B	41	15c. grey	55·00	17·00
7B	37	15c. grey	8·00	48·00
8B	41	20c. on 15c. grey	4·00	27·00
10B	41	20c. orange	8·00	48·00
11B	39	25c. blue	55	6·50
12B	39	40c. brown	55	6·50
13B	39	50c. violet	55	11·50

C. Cos.

3C	31	2c. brown	9·25	8·50
4C	37	5c. green	£110	8·50
5C	37	10c. red	4·75	8·50
6C	41	15c. grey	55·00	17·00
7C	37	15c. grey	8·00	65·00
8C	41	20c. on 15c. grey	2·75	27·00
10C	41	20c. orange	8·00	48·00
11C	39	25c. blue	65	6·50
12C	39	40c. brown	65	6·50
13C	39	50c. violet	65	11·50

D. Karki.

3D	31	2c. brown	9·25	6·50
4D	37	5c. green	3·25	6·50
5D	37	10c. red	55	6·50
6D	41	15c. grey	55·00	17·00
7D	37	15c. grey	4·00	32·00
8D	41	20c. on 15c. grey	4·00	32·00
10D	41	20c. orange	8·00	48·00
11D	39	25c. blue	65	6·50
12D	39	40c. brown	65	6·50
13D	39	50c. violet	65	11·50

E. Leros.

3E	31	2c. brown	9·25	6·50
4E	37	5c. green	2·75	6·50
5E	37	10c. red	65	6·50
6E	41	15c. grey	£100	17·00
7E	37	15c. grey	8·00	43·00
8E	41	20c. on 15c. grey	26·00	32·00
9E	41	20c. orange	80·00	£170
11E	39	25c. blue	40·00	6·50
12E	39	40c. brown	6·50	6·50
13E	39	50c. violet	65	11·50

F. Lipso.

3F	31	2c. brown	4·00	6·50
4F	37	5c. green	4·00	6·50
5F	37	10c. red	2·00	6·50
6F	41	15c. grey	55·00	17·00
7F	37	15c. grey	8·00	43·00
8F	41	20c. on 15c. grey	2·75	32·00
10F	41	20c. orange	8·00	48·00
11F	39	25c. blue	55	6·50
12F	39	40c. brown	2·00	6·50
13F	39	50c. violet	55	11·50

G. Nisiros.

3G	31	2c. brown	9·25	6·50
4G	37	5c. green	2·75	6·50
5G	37	10c. red	55	6·50
6G	41	15c. grey	55·00	16·00
7G	37	15c. grey	40·00	48·00
8G	41	20c. on 15c. grey	2·75	32·00
10G	41	20c. orange	£140	£130
11G	39	25c. blue	2·75	6·50
12G	39	40c. brown	1·30	6·50
13G	39	50c. violet	8·00	11·50

H. Patmos.

3H	31	2c. brown	9·25	6·50
4H	37	5c. green	1·30	6·50
5H	37	10c. red	1·30	6·50
6H	41	15c. grey	55·00	17·00
7H	37	15c. grey	8·00	48·00
8H	41	20c. on 15c. grey	26·00	43·00
9H	41	20c. orange	£160	£180
11H	39	25c. blue	55	6·50
12H	39	40c. brown	2·75	6·50
13H	39	50c. violet	1·30	11·50

I. Piscopi.

3I	31	2c. brown	9·25	6·50
4I	37	5c. green	3·25	6·50
5I	37	10c. red	65	6·50
6I	41	15c. grey	55·00	17·00
7I	37	15c. grey	26·00	45·00
8I	41	20c. on 15c. grey	2·75	32·00
10I	41	20c. orange	75·00	90·00
11I	39	25c. blue	55	6·50
12I	39	40c. brown	55	6·50
13I	39	50c. violet	55	11·50

J. Rodi.

3J	31	2c. brown	1·30	5·25
4J	37	5c. green	2·75	5·25
5J	37	10c. red	1·30	5·25
6J	41	15c. grey	60·00	21·00
7J	37	15c. grey	£225	£140
8J	41	20c. on 15c. grey	£190	£170
10J	41	20c. orange	10·50	21·00
11J	39	25c. blue	4·00	5·25
12J	39	40c. brown	10·00	5·25
13J	39	50c. violet	1·30	13·00

K. Scarpanto.

3K	31	2c. brown	9·25	6·50
4K	37	5c. green	2·75	6·50
5K	37	10c. red	55	6·50
6K	41	15c. grey	50·00	17·00
7K	37	15c. grey	26·00	37·00
8K	41	20c. on 15c. grey	2·75	32·00
10K	41	20c. orange	75·00	55·00
11K	39	25c. blue	9·25	6·50
12K	39	40c. brown	55	6·50
13K	39	50c. violet	2·75	11·50

L. Simi.

3L	31	2c. brown	9·25	6·50
4L	37	5c. green	3·25	6·50
5L	37	10c. red	55	6·50
6L	41	15c. grey	80·00	17·00
7L	37	15c. grey	£170	75·00
8L	41	20c. on 15c. grey	17·00	27·00
10L	41	20c. orange	£100	43·00
11L	39	25c. blue	4·00	6·50
12L	39	40c. brown	55	6·50
13L	39	50c. violet	55	11·50

M. Stampalia.

3M	31	2c. brown	9·25	6·50
4M	37	5c. green	55	6·50
5M	37	10c. red	55	6·50
6M	41	15c. grey	65·00	17·00
7M	37	15c. grey	18·00	32·00
8M	41	20c. on 15c. grey	2·75	27·00
10M	41	20c. orange	65·00	55
11M	39	25c. blue	1·30	6·50
12M	39	40c. brown	4·00	6·50
13M	39	50c. violet	55	11·50

1916. Optd Rodi.

14	33	20c. orange	10·50	21·00
15	39	85c. brown	£100	£110
16	34	1l. brown & green	6·50	

1 Rhodian Windmill

2 Knight kneeling before the Holy City

1929. King of Italy's Visit.

17B	1	5c. purple	2·00	30
18B	-	10c. brown	2·00	30
19B	-	20c. red	2·00	30
20B	-	25c. green	2·00	30
21B	2	30c. blue	2·00	30
22B	-	50c. brown	2·00	30
23B	-	1l.25 blue	2·00	30
24B	2	5l. purple	2·00	5·00
25B	2	10l. green	4·00	4·25

DESIGNS—As Type **1**: 10c. Galley of Knights of St. John; 20c., 25c. Knight defending Christianity; 50c., 1l.25, Knight's tomb.

1930. 21st Hydrological Congress. Nos. 17/25 optd XXI Congresso Idrologico.

26	5c. purple	20·00	19·00
27	10c. brown	22·00	19·00
28	20c. red	37·00	19·00
29	25c. green	46·00	19·00
30	30c. blue	22·00	19·00
31	50c. brown	£700	65·00
32	1l.25 blue	£475	95·00
33	5l. purple	£250	£400
34	10l. green	£250	£450

1930. Ferrucci issue of Italy (colours changed) optd for each individual island, in capitals. A. CALINO; B. CASO; C. COO; D. CALCHI; E. LERO; F. LISSO; G. NISIRO; H. PATMO; I. PISCOPI; J. RODI; K. SCARPANTO; L. SIMI; M. STAMPALIA.

35	114	20c. violet	6·50	8·50
36	-	25c. green	6·50	8·50
37	-	50c. black	6·50	16·00
38	-	1l.25 blue	6·50	16·00
39	-	5l.+2l. red	10·00	30·00

Same prices for each of the 13 islands.

1930. Air. Ferrucci air stamps of Italy (colours changed) optd ISOLE ITALIANE DELL'EGEO.

40	117	50c. purple	10·00	21·00
41	117	1l. blue	10·00	21·00
42	117	5l.+2l. red	20·00	60·00

1930. Virgil stamps of Italy optd ISOLE ITALIANE DELL'EGEO.

43	-	15c. violet (postage)	3·25	10·50
44	-	20c. brown	3·25	10·50
45	-	25c. green	3·25	4·25
46	-	30c. brown	3·25	4·25
47	-	50c. purple	3·25	4·25
48	-	75c. red	3·25	10·50
49	-	1l.25 blue	3·25	16·00
50	-	5l+1l.50 purple	3·25	32·00
51	-	10l.+2l.50 brown	3·25	32·00
52	119	50c. green (air)	4·00	19·00
53	119	1l. red	4·00	21·00
54	119	7l.70+1l.30 brown	8·00	27·00
55	119	9l.+2l. grey	8·00	43·00

1931. Italian Eucharistic Congress. Nos. 17/25 optd 1931 CONGRESSO EUCARISTICO ITALIANO.

56	5c. red	8·25	16·00
57	10c. brown	8·00	16·00
58	20c. red	8·00	21·00
59	25c. green	8·00	21·00
60	30c. blue	8·00	21·00
61	50c. brown	65·00	55·00
62	1l.25 blue	55·00	90·00

1932. St. Antony of Padua stamps of Italy optd ISOLE ITALIANE DELL'EGEO.

63	121	20c. purple	33·00	19·00
64	-	25c. green	33·00	19·00
65	-	30c. brown	33·00	23·00
66	-	50c. purple	33·00	16·00
67	-	75c. red	33·00	29·00
68	-	1l.25 blue	33·00	32·00
69	-	5l.+2l.50 orange	33·00	£130

1932. Dante stamps of Italy optd ISOLE ITALIANE DELL'EGEO.

70		10c. green (postage)	2·00	6·50
71		15c. violet	2·00	6·50
72		20c. brown	2·00	6·50
73		25c. green	2·00	6·50
74		30c. red	2·00	6·50
75		50c. purple	2·00	2·10
76		75c. red	2·00	8·50
77		1l.25 blue	2·00	4·25
78		1l.75 sepia	2·75	6·50
79		2l.75 red	2·75	6·50
80		5l.+2l. violet	4·00	10·50
81	124	10l.+2l.50 brown	4·00	16·00
82	125	50c. red (air)	2·00	6·50
83	-	1l. green	2·00	6·50
84	-	3l. purple	2·00	8·50
85	-	5l. red	2·00	8·50
86	125	7l.70+2l. sepia	4·00	21·00
87	-	10l.+2l.50 blue	4·00	32·00
88	127	100l. olive and blue	25·00	85·00

No. 88 is inscribed instead of optd.

1932. Garibaldi issue of Italy (colours changed) optd for each individual island in capital letters. A. CALINO; B. CASO; C. COO; D. CARCHI; E. LERO; F. LIBO; G. NISIRO; H. PATMO; I. PISCOPI; J. RODI; K. SCARPANTO; L. SIMI; M. STAMPALIA.

89	-	10c. sepia	20·00	21·00
90	128	20c. brown	20·00	21·00
91	-	25c. green	20·00	21·00
92	128	30c. black	20·00	21·00
93	-	50c. lilac	20·00	21·00
94	-	75c. red	20·00	21·00
95	-	1l.25 blue	20·00	21·00
96	-	1l.75+25c. sepia	20·00	21·00
97	-	2l.55+50c. red	20·00	21·00
98	-	5l.+1l. violet	20·00	21·00

Same prices for each of the 13 islands.

1932. Air. Garibaldi air stamps of Italy optd ISOLE ITALIANE DELL'EGEO.

99	130	50c. green	60·00	85·00
100	-	80c. red	60·00	85·00
101	130	1l.+25c. blue	60·00	85·00
102	-	2l.+50c. brown	60·00	85·00
103	-	5l.+1l. black	60·00	85·00

8

1932. 20th Anniv of Italian Occupation of Dodecanese Islands.

106	8	5c. red, black and green	13·00	21·00
107	8	10c. red, black and blue	13·00	16·00
108	8	20c. red, black and yellow	13·00	16·00
109	8	25c. red, black and violet	13·00	16·00
110	8	30c. red, black and red	13·00	16·00
111	-	50c. red, black and blue	13·00	16·00
112	-	1l.25 red, purple & blue	13·00	32·00
113	-	5l. red and blue	40·00	85·00
114	-	10l. red, green and blue	£110	£150
115	-	25l. red, brown and blue	£550	£1300

DESIGN—VERT: 50c. to 25l. Arms on map of Rhodes.

10 Airship "Graf Zeppelin"

1933. Air. "Graf Zeppelin".

116	10	3l. brown	75·00	£110
117	10	5l. purple	75·00	£110
118	10	10l. green	75·00	£170
119	10	12l. blue	75·00	£180
120	10	15l. red	75·00	£180
121	10	20l. black	75·00	£180

1933. Air. Balbo Mass Formation Flight issue of Italy optd ISOLE ITALIANE DELL'EGEO.

122	135	5l.25+19l.75 red, green and blue	55·00	£110
123	136	5l.25+44l.75 red, green and blue	55·00	£110

11 Wing from Arms of Francesco Sans

1934. Air.

124	11	50c. black and yellow	55	20
125	11	80c. black and red	8·00	3·50
126	11	1l. black and green	5·25	20
127	11	5l. black and mauve	13·00	7·75

1934. World Football Championship stamps of Italy (some colours changed) optd ISOLE ITALIANE DELL'EGEO.

128	142	20c. red (postage)	95·00	75·00
129	-	25c. green	95·00	75·00
130	-	50c. violet	£375	43·00
131	-	1l.25 blue	95·00	£130
132	-	5l.+2l.50 blue	95·00	£300
133	-	50c. brown (air)	13·00	32·00
134	-	75c. red	13·00	32·00
135	-	5l.+2l.50 orange	45·00	65·00
136	-	10l.+5l. green	45·00	£110

1934. Military Medal Centenary stamps of Italy (some colours changed) optd ISOLE ITALIANE DELL'EGEO.

157	146	10c. grey (postage)	60·00	70·00
158	-	15c. brown	60·00	70·00
159	-	20c. orange	60·00	70·00
160	-	25c. green	60·00	70·00
161	-	30c. red	60·00	70·00
162	-	50c. green	60·00	70·00
163	-	75c. red	60·00	70·00
164	-	1l.25 blue	60·00	70·00
165	-	1l.75+1l. violet	46·00	43·00
166	-	2l.55+2l. red	46·00	43·00
167	-	2l.75+2l. brown	46·00	43·00
168	-	25c. green (air)	75·00	85·00
169	-	50c. grey	75·00	85·00
170	-	75c. red	75·00	85·00
171	-	80c. brown	75·00	85·00
172	-	1l.+50c. green	55·00	85·00
173	-	2l.+1l. blue	55·00	85·00
174	-	3l.+2l. violet	55·00	85·00

16

1935. Holy Year.

177	16	5c. orange	20·00	16·00
178	16	10c. brown	20·00	16·00
179	16	20c. red	20·00	19·00
180	16	25c. green	20·00	19·00
181	16	30c. purple	20·00	19·00
182	16	50c. brown	20·00	19·00
183	16	1l.25 blue	20·00	65·00

1938. Augustus the Great stamps of Italy (colours changed) optd ISOLE ITALIANE DELL'EGEO.

186	163	10c. brown (postage)	5·25	8·50
187	-	15c. violet	5·25	8·50
188	-	20c. brown	5·25	8·50
189	-	25c. green	5·25	8·50
190	-	30c. purple	5·25	8·50
191	-	50c. green	5·25	16·00
192	-	75c. red	5·25	16·00
193	-	1l.25 blue	5·25	16·00
194	-	1l.75+1l. orange	8·00	27·00
195	-	2l.55+2l. brown	8·00	27·00
196	-	25c. violet (air)	6·50	8·50
197	-	50c. green	6·50	8·50
198	-	80c. blue	6·50	27·00
199	-	1l.+1l. purple	9·25	32·00
200	164	5l.+1l. red	13·00	65·00

1938. Giotto stamps of Italy optd ITALIANE ISOLE DELL'EGEO.

201	1l.25 blue (No. 527)	1·30	2·10
202	2l.75+2l. brown (530)	3·25	8·50

19 Dante House, Rhodes

1940. Colonial Exhibition. Inscr as in T **19**.

203	-	5c. brown (postage)	55	2·10
204	-	10c. orange	55	2·10
205	19	25c. green	2·00	3·25
206	-	50c. violet	2·00	3·25
207	-	75c. red	2·00	4·25
208	19	1l.25 blue	2·00	4·25
209	-	2l.+75c. red	2·00	27·00

DESIGNS—VERT: 5c., 50c. Roman Wolf statue; 10c., 75c., 2l. Crown and Maltese Cross.

210	50c. brown (air)	2·75	4·25
211	1l. violet	2·75	4·25
212	2l.+75c. blue	2·75	10·50
213	5l.+2l.50 brown	2·75	16·00

DESIGNS—HORIZ: Savoia Marchetti S.M.75 airplane over: 50c., 2l. statues, Rhodes Harbour; 1, 5l. Government House, Rhodes.

1943. Aegean Relief Fund. Nos. 17/25 surch PRO ASSISTENZA EGEO and value.

214	1	5c.+5c. purple	2·00	1·10
215	-	10c.+10c. brown	2·00	1·10
216	-	20c.+20c. red	2·00	1·10
217	-	25c.+25c. green	2·00	1·10
218	2	30c.+30c. blue	2·75	1·10
219	-	50c.+50c. brown	2·75	2·10
220	-	1l.25+1l.25 blue	5·25	3·25
221	2	5l.+5l. purple	£150	£110

1944. War Victims' Relief. Nos. 17/20 and 22/23 surch PRO SINISTRATI DI GUERRA, value and stag symbol.

224	1	5c.+3l. purple	2·75	3·25
225	-	10c.+3l. brown	2·75	3·25
226	-	20c.+3l. red	2·75	3·25
227	-	25c.+3l. green	4·00	3·25
228	-	50c.+3l. brown	4·00	3·25
229	-	1l.25+5l. blue	40·00	43·00

1944. Air. War Victims Relief. Surch PRO SINISTRATI DI GUERRA and value.

232	11	50c.+2l. blk & yellow	13·00	6·50
233	11	80c.+2l. black and red	17·00	10·50
234	11	1l.+2l. black & green	23·00	13·00
235	11	5l.+2l. black & mauve	85·00	£110

1945. Red Cross Fund. Nos. 24/5 surch FEBBRAIO 1945 + 10 and Cross.

236	+10l. on 5l. purple	13·00	6·50
237	+10l. on 10l. green	13·00	6·50

EXPRESS STAMPS

1932. Air. Garibaldi Air Express stamps of Italy optd ISOLE ITALIANE DELL'EGEO.

E104	E3	2l.25+1l. red & blue	75·00	95·00
E105	E3	4l.50+1l.50 grey and yellow	75·00	95·00

1934. Air. As Nos. E442/3 of Italy, but colours changed, optd ISOLE ITALIANE DELL'EGEO.

E175	2l.+1l.25 blue	55·00	85·00
E176	4l.50+2l. green	55·00	85·00

E17

1935

E184	E17	1l.25 green	2·75	3·25
E185	E17	2l.50 orange	4·00	5·25

1943. Aegean Relief Fund. Surch PRO ASSISTENZA EGEO and value.

E222	1l.25+1l.25 green	55·00	43·00
E223	2l.50+2l.50 orge	80·00	55·00

1944. Nos. 19/20 surch ESPRESSO and value.

E230	1l.25 on 25c. green	55	1·10
E231	2l.50 on 50c. red	55	1·10

PARCEL POST STAMPS

P12

1934

P137	P12	5c. orange	4·75	5·25
P138	P12	10c. red	4·75	5·25
P139	P12	20c. green	4·75	5·25
P140	P12	25c. violet	4·75	5·25
P141	P12	50c. blue	4·75	5·25
P142	P12	60c. black	4·75	5·25
P143	-	1l. orange	4·75	5·25
P144	-	2l. red	4·75	5·25
P145	-	3l. green	4·75	5·25
P146	-	4l. violet	4·75	5·25
P147	-	10l. blue	4·75	5·25

DESIGN: 1l. to 10l. Left half: Stag as in Type E **17**; Right half: Castle.

POSTAGE DUE STAMPS

D14 Badge of the Knights of St. John

D15 Immortelle

1934

D148	D14	5c. orange	4·50	3·25
D149	D14	10c. red	4·50	3·25
D150	D14	20c. green	4·50	2·10
D151	D14	30c. violet	4·50	2·10
D152	D14	40c. blue	4·50	5·25
D153	D 15	50c. orange	4·50	2·10
D154	D 15	60c. red	4·50	10·50
D155	D 15	1l. green	4·50	8·50
D156	D 15	2l. violet	4·50	5·25

B. GREEK MILITARY ADMINISTRATION

1947. Stamps of Greece optd with characters as in Type G 1.

G1	-	10d. on 2000d. blue (No. 623)	55	1·10
G3	89	50d. on 1d. grn (No. 642)	55	1·10
G4	89	250d. on 3d. brn (No. 643)	55	1·10

(G1)

1947. Stamps of Greece surch as Type **G1**.

G5	-	20d. on 500d. brown (No. 582)	1·00	1·60
G6	-	30d. on 5d. green (No. 574)	1·00	1·60
G7	106	50d. on 2d. brown	1·00	1·60
G8	-	250d. on 10d. brown (No. 510)	1·30	2·10
G9	-	400d. on 15d. green (No. 511)	2·00	3·25
G10	-	1000d. on 200d. blue (No. 581)	1·70	2·75

Pt. 1

DOMINICA

Until 31 December 1939 one of the Leeward Islands, but then transferred to the Windward Islands. Used Leeward Island stamps concurrently with Dominican issues from 1903 to above date.

1874. 12 pence = 1 shilling; 20 shillings = 1 pound.
1949. 100 cents = 1 West Indian dollar.

1

1874

13	1	½d. yellow	4·50	10·00
20	1	½d. green	3·00	5·50
5	1	1d. lilac	10·00	3·00
22a	1	1d. red	3·25	10·00
15	1	2½d. brown	£140	3·00
23	1	2½d. blue	3·75	5·50
7	1	4d. blue	£120	3·00
24	1	4d. grey	4·50	7·50
8	1	6d. green	£160	20·00
25	1	6d. orange	17·00	75·00
9	1	1s. mauve	£120	50·00

1882. No. 5 bisected and surch with a small ½.

10	½(d.) on half 1d. lilac	£225	55·00

1882. No. 5 bisected and surch with large ½.

11	½(d.) on half 1d. lilac	32·00	19·00

1883. No. 5 bisected and surch **HALF PENNY** vert.

12	½d. on half 1d. lilac	70·00	30·00

1886. Nos. 8 and 9 surch in words and bar.

17	½d. on 6d. green	7·00	8·00
18	1d. on 6d. green	£35000	£10000
19	1d. on 1s. mauve	17·00	20·00

9 "Roseau from the Sea" (Lt. Caddy)

10

1903

27	9	½d. green	4·00	3·25
38	9	1d. grey and red	2·00	40
29	9	2d. green and brown	2·50	5·00
30	9	2½d. grey and blue	7·50	4·00
31	9	3d. purple and black	8·00	3·25
32	9	6d. grey and brown	9·00	18·00
43	9	1s. mauve and green	3·75	55·00
34	9	2s. black and purple	27·00	30·00
45	9	2s.6d. green and orange	24·00	70·00
46	10	5s. black and brown	60·00	60·00

1908

48w	9	1d. red	1·50	40
64	9	1½d. orange	3·00	16·00
65	9	2d. grey	2·75	3·25
66	9	2½d. blue	2·00	12·00
51	9	3d. purple on yellow	3·00	3·75
52a	9	6d. purple	3·50	18·00
53	9	1s. black on green	3·00	2·75
53b	9	2s. purple and blue on blue	25·00	85·00
70	9	2s.6d. black and red on blue	38·00	£120

1914. As T **10**, but portrait of King George V.

54	5s. red and green on yellow	60·00	95·00

1916. No. 37 surch **WAR TAX ONE HALFPENNY**.

55	½d. on ½d. green	3·00	75

1918. Optd **WAR TAX**.

57	½d. green	15	50
58	3d. purple on yellow	4·00	4·00

1919. Surch WAR TAX 1½D.

59	1½d. on 2½d. orange	15	55

1920. Surch 1½D.

60	1½d. on 2½d. orange	6·00	4·50

16

1923

71	16	½d. black and green	1·75	60
72	16	1d. black and violet	4·75	1·75
73	16	1d. black and red	16·00	1·00
74	16	1½d. black and red	5·00	65
75	16	1½d. black and brown	15·00	70
76	16	2d. black and grey	3·50	50
77	16	2½d. black and yellow	3·00	9·00
78	16	2½d. black and blue	7·50	2·00
79	16	3d. black and blue	3·00	14·00
80	16	3d. black and red on yellow	3·25	1·00
81	16	4d. black and brown	3·75	5·50
82	16	6d. black and mauve	3·75	7·00
83	16	1s. black on green	2·75	3·00
84	16	2s. black and blue on blue	15·00	26·00
85	16	2s.6d. black and red on blue	20·00	26·00
86	16	3s. black and purple on yellow	3·25	12·00
87	16	4s. black and red on green	18·00	29·00
90	16	5s. black and green on yellow	9·00	55·00
91	16	£1 black and purple on red	£225	£350

1935. Silver Jubilee. As T **10a** of Gambia.

92	1d. blue and red	1·50	30
93	1½d. blue and grey	5·50	3·00
94	2½d. brown and blue	5·50	4·50
95	1s. grey and purple	5·50	11·00

1937. Coronation. As T **10b** of Gambia.

96	1d. red	40	10
97	1½d. brown	40	10
98	2½d. blue	60	1·75

17 Fresh Water Lake

1938

99	17	½d. brown and green	10	15
100	-	1d. black and red	25	25
101	-	1½d. green and purple	45	70
102	-	2d. red and black	50	2·25
103a	-	2½d. purple and blue	20	2·25
104	-	3d. olive and brown	30	50
104a	-	3½d. blue and mauve	2·25	2·00
105	17	6d. green and violet	1·75	1·50
105a	17	7d. green and brown	2·25	1·50
106	-	1s. violet and olive	5·00	1·50
106a	-	2s. grey and purple	9·50	12·00
107	17	2s.6d. black and red	18·00	5·50
108	-	5s. blue and brown	14·00	10·00
108a	-	10s. black and orange	20·00	23·00

DESIGNS—As Type **17**: 1d., 3d., 2s., 5s. Layou River; 1½d., 2½d., 3½d. Picking Limes; 2d., 1s., 10s. Boiling Lake.

21 King George VI

1940

109a	21	¼d. brown	10	1·00

1946. Victory. As T **11a** of Gambia.

110	1d. red	20	10
111	3½d. blue	20	10

1948. Silver Wedding. As T **11b/c** of Gambia.

112	1d. red	15	10
113	10s. brown	24·00	30·00

1949. U.P.U. As T **11d/g** of Gambia.

114	5c. blue	20	15
115	6c. brown	1·25	2·75
116	12c. purple	45	2·00
117	24c. olive	30	30

1951. Inauguration of B.W.I. University College. As T **43a/b** of Grenada.

118	3c. green and violet	50	1·25
119	12c. green and red	75	40

23 Drying Cocoa

1951. New Currency.

120	-	½c. brown	10	30
121	23	1c. black and red	10	30
122	-	2c. brown and green	10	40
123	-	3c. green and purple	25	3·50
124	-	4c. orange and sepia	70	3·75
125	-	5c. black and red	85	30
126	-	6c. olive and brown	1·00	30
127	-	8c. green and blue	3·00	1·50
128	-	12c. black and green	70	1·25
129	-	14c. blue and purple	1·25	3·50
130	-	24c. purple and red	75	40
131	-	48c. green and orange	4·50	13·00
132	-	60c. red and black	3·75	9·00
133	-	$1.20 green and black	7·50	6·50
134	-	$2.40 orange and black	27·00	55·00

DESIGNS: ½c. As Type **21**, but with portrait as Type **23**. HORIZ (as Type **23**): 2c., 60c. Carib baskets; 3c., 48c. Lime plantation; 4c. Picking oranges; 5c. Bananas; 6c. Botanical Gardens; 8c. Drying vanilla beans; 12c., $1.20, Fresh Water Lake; 14c. Layou River, 24c. Boiling Lake. VERT: $2.40, Picking oranges.

1951. New Constitution. Stamps of 1951 optd **NEW CONSTITUTION 1951**.

135	3c. green and violet	15	70
136	5c. black and red	15	1·60
137	8c. green and blue	15	15
138	14c. blue and violet	1·75	20

1953. Coronation. As T **11h** of Gambia.

139	2c. black and green	20	10

1954. As Nos 120/34 but with portrait of Queen Elizabeth II.

140	½c. brown	10	1·25
141	1c. black and red	30	20
142	2c. brown and green	1·25	2·75
143	3c. green and purple	1·50	40
144	3c. black and red	3·75	2·50
145	4c. orange and brown	30	10
146	5c. black and red	3·50	1·00
147	5c. blue and brown	13·00	1·00
148	6c. green and brown	50	10
149	8c. green and blue	1·75	10
150	10c. green and brown	6·00	3·50
151	12c. black and green	60	10
152	14c. blue and purple	60	10
153	24c. purple and red	60	10
154	48c. green and orange	3·00	16·00
155	48c. brown and violet	2·50	3·00
156	60c. red and black	4·25	1·00
157	$1.20 green and black	20·00	7·00
158	$2.40 orange and black	20·00	14·00

DESIGNS (New)—HORIZ: Nos. 144, 155, Mat making; 147, Canoe making; 150, Bananas.

1958. British Caribbean Federation. As T **47a** of Grenada.

159	3c. green	45	10
160	6c. blue	60	1·25
161	12c. red	70	15

40 Seashore at Rosalie

1963

162	40	1c. green, blue and sepia	10	85
163	-	2c. blue	30	10
164	-	3c. brown and blue	1·75	1·25
165	-	4c. green, sepia and violet	10	10
166	-	5c. mauve	30	10
167	-	6c. green, bistre and violet	10	80
168	-	8c. green, sepia and black	30	20
169	-	10c. sepia and pink	10	20
170	-	12c. green, blue and sepia	1·00	10
171	-	14c. multicoloured	70	10
204	-	15c. yellow, green and brown	70	10
173	-	24c. multicoloured	9·00	20
174	-	48c. green, blue and black	75	1·00
175	-	60c. orange, green and black	1·00	70
176	-	$1.20 multicoloured	6·50	1·00
177	-	$2.40 blue, turq & brn	3·50	4·00
178	-	$4.80 green, blue and brown	20·00	28·00

DESIGNS—VERT: 2c., 5c. Queen Elizabeth II (after Annigoni); 14c. Traditional costume; 24c. Imperial amazon ("Sisserou Parrot"); $2.40, Trafalgar Falls; $4.80, Coconut palm. HORIZ: 3c. Sailing canoe; 4c. Sulphur springs; 6c. Road making; 8c. Dug-out canoe; 10c. Crapaud (frog); 12c. Scott's Head; 15c. Bananas; 48c. Goodwill; 60c. Cocoa tree; $1.20, Coat of Arms.

1963. Freedom from Hunger. As T **21a** of Gambia.

179	15c. violet	15	10

1963. Centenary of Red Cross. As T **21b** of Gambia.

180	5c. red and black	20	40
181	15c. red and blue	40	60

1964. 400th Birth Anniv of Shakespeare. As T **35a** of Gambia.

182	15c. purple	10	10

1965. Centenary of I.T.U. As T **45** of Gibraltar.

183	2c. green and blue	10	10
184	48c. turquoise and grey	45	20

1965. I.C.Y. As T **46** of Gibraltar.

185	1c. purple and turquoise	10	20
186	15c. green and lavender	50	10

1966. Churchill Commemoration. As T **47** of Gibraltar.

187	1c. blue	10	1·60
188	5c. green	40	10
189	15c. brown	85	10
190	24c. violet	95	20

1966. Royal Visit. As T **49** of Grenada.

191	5c. black and blue	75	30
192	15c. black and mauve	1·00	30

1966. World Cup Football Championship. As T **48** of Gibraltar.

193	5c. multicoloured	25	15
194	24c. multicoloured	85	15

1966. Inauguration of W.H.O. Headquarters, Geneva. As T **54** of Gibraltar.

195	5c. black, green and blue	15	15
196	24c. black, purple and ochre	30	15

1966. 20th Anniv of UNESCO. As T **56a/c** of Gibraltar.

197	5c. red, yellow and orange	20	15
198	15c. yellow, violet and olive	50	10
199	24c. black, purple and orange	60	15

56 Children of Three Races

1967. National Day. Multicoloured.

205	5c. Type **56**	10	10
206	10c. The "Santa Maria" and motto	40	15
207	15c. Hands holding motto ribbon	15	15
208	24c. Belaire dancing	15	20

57 John F. Kennedy

1968. Human Rights Year. Multicoloured.

209	1c. Type **57**	10	30
210	10c. Cecil E. A. Rawle	10	10
211	12c. Pope John XXIII	50	15
212	48c. Florence Nightingale	35	25
213	60c. Albert Schweitzer	35	30

1968. Associated Statehood. Nos. 162 etc, optd **ASSOCIATED STATEHOOD**.

214	1c. green, blue and sepia	10	10
215	2c. blue	10	10
216	3c. brown and blue	10	10
217	4c. green, sepia and violet	10	10
218	5c. mauve	10	10
219	6c. green, bistre and violet	10	10
220	8c. green, sepia and black	10	10

221	10c. sepia and pink	55	10
222	12c. green, blue and brown	10	10
224	14c. multicoloured	10	10
225	15c. yellow, green and brown	10	10
226	24c. multicoloured	4·25	10
227	48c. green, blue and black	55	2·50
228	60c. orange, green and black	1·00	70
229	$1.20 multicoloured	1·00	3·25
230	$2.40 blue, turquoise and brown	1·00	2·50
231	$4.80 green, blue and brown	1·25	8·50

1968. National Day. Nos. 162/4, 171 and 176 optd **NATIONAL DAY 3 NOVEMBER 1968.**

232	1c. green, blue and sepia	10	10
233	2c. blue	10	10
234	3c. brown and blue	10	10
235	14c. multicoloured	10	10
236	$1.20 multicoloured	55	40

60 Forward shooting at Goal

1968. Olympic Games, Mexico. Multicoloured.

237	1c. Type **60**	10	10
238	1c. Goalkeeper attempting to save ball	10	10
239	5c. Swimmers preparing to dive	10	10
240	5c. Swimmers diving	10	10
241	48c. Javelin-throwing	15	15
242	48c. Hurdling	15	15
243	60c. Basketball	90	25
244	60c. Basketball players	90	25

61 "The Small Cowper Madonna" (Raphael)

1968. Christmas.

245	**61**	5c. multicoloured	10	10

62 "Venus and Adonis" (Rubens)

1969. 20th Anniv of World Health Organization.

246	**62**	5c. multicoloured	20	10
247	-	15c. multicoloured	30	10
248	-	24c. multicoloured	30	10
249	-	50c. multicoloured	50	40

DESIGNS: 15c. "The Death of Socrates" (J.-L. David); 24c. "Christ and the Pilgrims of Emmaus" (Velasquez); 50c. "Pilate washing his Hands" (Rembrandt).

66 Picking Oranges

1969. Tourism. Multicoloured.

250	10c. Type **66**	15	10
251	10c. Woman, child and ocean scene	15	10
252	12c. Fort Yeoung Hotel	50	10
253	12c. Red-necked amazon	50	10
254	24c. Calypso band	30	15
255	24c. Women dancing	30	15
256	48c. Underwater life	30	25
257	48c. Skin-diver and turtle	30	25

67 "Strength in Unity" Emblem and Fruit Trees

1969. 1st Anniv of C.A.R.I.F.T.A. (Caribbean Free Trade Area). Multicoloured.

258	5c. Type **67**	10	10
259	8c. Hawker Siddeley H.S.748 aircraft, emblem and island	30	20
260	12c. Chart of Caribbean Sea and emblem	30	25
261	24c. Steamship unloading, tug and emblem	40	25

71 "Spinning" (J. Millet)

1969. 50th Anniv of International Labour Organization. Multicoloured.

262	15c. Type **71**	10	10
263	30c. "Threshing" (J. Millet)	15	15
264	38c. "Flax-pulling" (J. Millet)	15	15

72 Mahatma Gandhi weaving and Clock Tower, Westminster

1969. Birth Cent of Mahatma Gandhi. Mult.

265	6c. Type **72**	45	10
266	38c. Gandhi, Nehru and Mausoleum	65	15
267	$1.20 Gandhi and Taj Mahal	1·00	1·00

All stamps are incorrectly inscribed "Ghandi".

75 "Saint Joseph"

1969. National Day. Multicoloured.

268	6c. Type **75**	10	10
269	8c. "Saint John"	10	10
270	12c. "Saint Peter"	10	10
271	60c. "Saint Paul"	30	50

79 Queen Elizabeth II **80** Purple-throated Carib ("Humming Bird") and Flower

1969. Centres multicoloured; colours of "D" given.

272a	**79**	½c. black and silver	30	1·75
273	**80**	1c. black and yellow	1·00	3·00
274	-	2c. black and yellow	15	10
275a	-	3c. black and yellow	3·50	1·50
276a	-	4c. black and yellow	3·50	1·50
277a	-	5c. black and yellow	2·75	1·75
278a	-	6c. black and brown	2·75	2·75
279	-	8c. black and brown	20	10
280	-	10c. black and yellow	20	10
281	-	12c. black and yellow	20	10
282	-	15c. black and blue	20	10
283	-	25c. black and red	30	10
284a	-	30c. black and olive	1·50	70
285	-	38c. black and purple	10·00	1·75
286	-	50c. black and brown	50	45
287	-	60c. black and yellow	55	1·50
288	-	$1.20 black and yellow	1·25	1·75
289	-	$2.40 black and gold	1·00	4·00
290	-	$4.80 black and gold	1·25	7·00

DESIGNS—HORIZ (As Type **80**): 2c. Poinsettia; 3c. Redneck pigeon ("Ramier"); 4c. Imperial amazon ("Sisserou"); 5c. "Battus polydamas" (butterfly); 6c. "Dryas julia" (butterfly); 8c. Shipping bananas; 10c. Portsmouth Harbour; 12c. Copra processing plant; 15c. Straw workers; 25c. Timber plant; 30c. Pumice mine; 38c. Grammar school and playing fields; 50c. Roseau Cathedral. (38×26½ mm): 60c. Government Headquarters. (40×27 mm): $1.20, Melville Hall airport. (39½×26 mm): $2.40, Coat of arms. VERT: (26×39 mm): $4.80, As Type **79**, but larger.

99 "Virgin and Child with St. John" (Perugino)

1969. Christmas. Paintings. Multicoloured.

291	6c. "Virgin and Child with St. John" (Lippi)	10	10
292	10c. "Holy Family with Lamb" (Raphael)	10	10
293	15c. Type **99**	10	10
294	$1.20 "Madonna of the Rose Hedge" (Botticelli)	35	40
MS295	89×76 mm. Nos. 293/4. Imperf	75	1·00

101 Astronaut's First Step onto the Moon

1970. Moon Landing. Multicoloured.

296	½c. Type **101**	10	10
297	5c. Scientific experiment on the Moon and flag	15	10
298	8c. Astronauts collecting rocks	15	10
299	30c. Module over Moon	30	15
300	50c. Moon plaque	40	25
301	60c. Astronauts	40	30
MS302	116×112 mm. Nos. 298/301. Imperf	2·00	2·25

107 Giant Green Turtle

1970. Flora and Fauna. Multicoloured.

303	6c. Type **107**	30	20
304	24c. Atlantic flyingfish	40	45
305	38c. Anthurium lily	50	65
306	60c. Imperial and red-necked amazons	2·75	5·50
MS307	160×111 mm. Nos. 303/6	5·50	7·50

108 18th-century National Costume

1970. National Day. Multicoloured.

308	5c. Type **108**	10	10
309	8c. Carib basketry	10	10
310	$1 Flag and chart of Dominica	30	40
MS311	150×85 mm. Nos. 308/10	50	1·75

109 Scrooge and Marley's Ghost

1970. Christmas and Death Centenary of Charles Dickens. Scenes from "A Christmas Carol". Multicoloured.

312	2c. Type **109**	10	10
313	15c. Fezziwig's Ball	20	10
314	24c. Scrooge and his Nephew's Party	20	10
315	$1.20 Scrooge and the Ghost of Christmas Present	65	90
MS316	142×87 mm. Nos. 312/15	1·00	3·75

110 "The Doctor" (Sir Luke Fildes)

1970. Centenary of British Red Cross. Multicoloured.

317	8c. Type **110**	10	10
318	10c. Hands and Red Cross	10	10
319	15c. Flag of Dominica and Red Cross emblem	15	10
320	50c. "The Sick Child" (E. Munch)	50	45
MS321	108×76 mm. Nos. 317/20	1·00	3·00

111 Marigot School

1971. International Education Year. Multicoloured.

322	5c. Type **111**	10	10
323	8c. Goodwill Junior High School	10	10
324	14c. University of West Indies (Jamaica)	10	10
325	$1 Trinity College, Cambridge	35	30
MS326	85×85 mm. Nos. 324/5	50	1·25

112 Waterfall

1971. Tourism. Multicoloured.

327	5c. Type **112**	15	10
328	10c. Boat-building	15	10
329	30c. Sailing	25	10
330	50c. Yacht and motor launch	40	30
MS331	130×86 mm. Nos. 327/30	85	1·00

113 UNICEF Symbol in "D"

1971. 25th Anniv of UNICEF.

332	**113**	5c. violet, black and gold	10	10
333	**113**	10c. yellow, blk & gold	10	10
334	**113**	38c. green, blk & gold	10	10
335	**113**	$1.20 orange, blk & gold	30	45
MS336		84×79 mm. Nos. 333 and 335	50	1·75

Both No. 340 and the $1 value from the miniature sheet show the national flag of the Dominican Republic in error.

"Dominica" on the scout's shirt pocket is omitted on the $1 value from the miniature sheet.

114 German Boy Scout

1971. World Scout Jamboree, Asagiri, Japan. Various designs showing Boy Scouts from the nations listed. Multicoloured.

337	20c. Type **114**	15	20
338	24c. Great Britain	20	20
339	30c. Japan	25	25
340	$1 Dominica	50	2·25
MS341	114×102 mm. Nos. 339/40	1·00	2·25

115 Groine at Portsmouth

1971. National Day. Multicoloured.

342	8c. Type **115**	10	10
343	15c. Carnival scene	10	10
344	20c. Carifta Queen (vert)	10	10
345	50c. Rock of Atkinson (vert)	20	25
MS346	63×89 mm. $1.20, As 20c.	50	70

116 Eight Reals Piece, 1761

1972. Coins.

347	**116**	10c. black, silver and violet	10	10
348	-	30c. black, silver and green	15	15
349	-	35c. black, silver and blue	15	20
350	-	50c. black, silver and red	25	1·75
MS351		86×90 mm. Nos. 349/50	50	1·25

DESIGNS—HORIZ: 30c. Eleven and three bitt pieces, 1798. VERT: 35c. Two reals and two bitt pieces, 1770; 50c. Mocos, pieces-of-eight and eight reals-eleven bitts piece, 1798.

117 Common Opossum

1972. U.N. Conference on the Human Enviroment, Stockholm. Multicoloured.

352	½c. Type **117**	10	10
353	35c. Brazilian agouti (rodent)	30	15
354	60c. Orchid	2·00	50
355	$1.20 Hibiscus	1·25	1·60
MS356	139×94 mm. Nos. 352/5	5·00	9·50

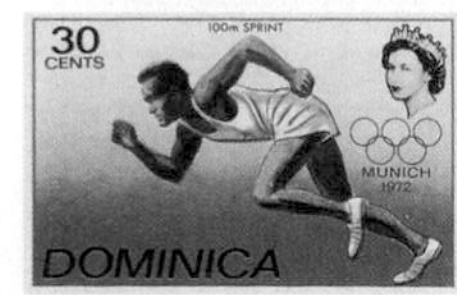

118 Sprinter

1972. Olympic Games, Munich. Multicoloured.

357	30c. Type **118**	10	10
358	35c. Hurdler	15	15
359	58c. Hammer-thrower (vert)	20	20
360	72c. Long-jumper (vert)	40	40
MS361	98×96 mm. Nos. 359/60	75	1·00

119 General Post Office

1972. National Day. Multicoloured.

362	10c. Type **119**	10	10
363	20c. Morne Diablotin	10	10
364	30c. Rodney's Rock	15	15
MS365	83×96 mm. Nos. 363/4	50	70

1972. Royal Silver Wedding. As T **98** of Gibraltar, but with Bananas and Imperial Parrot in background.

366	5c. green	20	10
367	$1 green	60	40

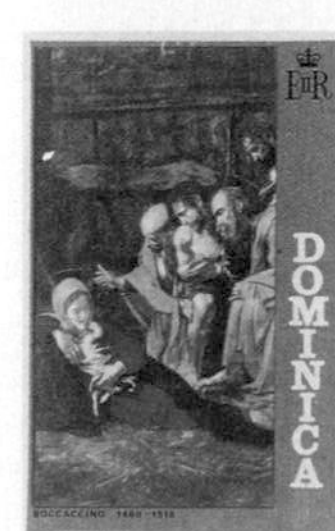

121 "The Adoration of the Shepherds" (Caravaggio)

1972. Christmas. Multicoloured.

368	8c. Type **121**	10	10
369	14c. "The Myosotis Virgin" (Rubens)	10	10
370	30c. "Madonna and Child with St Francesca Romana" (Gentileschi)	15	10
371	$1 "Adoration of the Kings" (Mostaert)	50	1·75
MS372	102×79 mm. Nos. 370/1. Imperf	60	80

122 Launching of Weather Satellite

1973. Centenary of I.M.O./W.M.O. Multicoloured.

373	½c. Type **122**	10	20
374	1c. Nimbus satellite	10	20
375	2c. Radiosonde balloon	10	20
376	30c. Radarscope (horiz)	15	15
377	35c. Diagram of pressure zones (horiz)	20	20
378	50c. Hurricane shown by satellite (horiz)	30	35
379	$1 Computer weather-map (horiz)	60	65
MS380	90×105 mm. Nos. 378/9	70	1·75

123 Going to Hospital

1973. 25th Anniv of W.H.O. Multicoloured.

381	½c. Type **123**	10	10
382	1c. Maternity care	10	10
383	2c. Smallpox inoculation	10	10
384	30c. Emergency service	30	15
385	35c. Waiting for the doctor	30	15
386	50c. Medical examination	30	25
387	$1 Travelling doctor	40	60
MS388	112×110 mm. Nos. 386/7	75	1·25

124 Cyrique Crab

1973. Flora and Fauna. Multicoloured.

389	½c. Type **124**	10	10
390	22c. Blue land-crab	30	10
391	25c. Bread fruit	30	15
392	$1.20 Sunflower	55	2·00
MS393	91×127 mm. Nos. 389/2	1·00	4·00

125 Princess Anne and Captain Mark Phillips

1973. Royal Wedding.

394	**125**	25c. multicoloured	10	10
395	-	$2 multicoloured	30	30
MS396		79×100 mm. 75c. as 25c. and $1.20 as $2	40	30

DESIGN: $2 As Type **125**, but with different frame.

126 "Adoration of the Kings" (Brueghel)

1973. Christmas. Religious Paintings. Multicoloured.

397	½c. Type **126**	10	10
398	1c. "Adoration of the Magi" (Botticelli)	10	10
399	2c. "Adoration of the Magi" (Durer)	10	10
400	12c. "Mystic Nativity" (Botticelli)	20	10
401	22c. "Adoration of the Magi" (Rubens)	25	10
402	35c. "The Nativity" (Durer)	25	10
403	$1 "Adoration of the Shepherds" (Giorgione)	60	55
MS404	122×98 mm. Nos. 402/3	85	1·10

127 Carib Basket-weaving

1973. National Day. Multicoloured.

405	5c. Type **127**	10	10
406	10c. Staircase of the Snake	10	10
407	50c. Miss Caribbean Queen (vert)	15	15
408	60c. Miss Carifta Queen (vert)	15	15
409	$1 Dance group (vert)	25	30
MS410	95×127 mm. Nos. 405/6 and 409	40	65

128 University Centre, Dominica

1973. 25th Anniv of West Indies University. Multicoloured.

411	12c. Type **128**	10	10
412	30c. Graduation ceremony	10	10
413	$1 University coat of arms	25	35
MS414	97×131 mm. Nos. 411/13	30	55

129 Dominica 1d. Stamp of 1874 and Map

1974. Stamp Centenary. Multicoloured.

415	½c. Type **129**	10	10
416	1c. 6d. stamp of 1874 and posthorn	10	10
417	2c. 1d. stamp of 1874 and arms	10	10
418	10c. Type **129**	20	10
419	50c. As 1c.	40	30
420	$1.20 As 2c.	50	70
MS421	105×121 mm. Nos. 418/20	1·00	1·50

130 Footballer and Flag of Brazil

1974. World Cup Football Championship, West Germany. Multicoloured.

422	½c. Type **130**	10	10
423	1c. West Germany	10	10
424	2c. Italy	10	10
425	30c. Scotland	50	10
426	40c. Sweden	50	10
427	50c. Netherlands	55	35
428	$1 Yugoslavia	90	90
MS429	89×87 mm. Nos. 427/8	70	80

131 Indian Hole

1974. National Day. Multicoloured.

430	10c. Type **131**	10	10
431	40c. Teachers' Training College	10	10
432	$1 Bay Oil distillery plant, Petite Savanne	50	45
MS433	96×143 mm. Nos. 430/2	60	65

132 Churchill with "Colonist"

1974. Birth Centenary of Sir Winston Churchill. Multicoloured.

434	½c. Type **132**	10	10
435	1c. Churchill and Eisenhower	10	10
436	2c. Churchill and Roosevelt	10	10
437	20c. Churchill and troops on assault-course	15	10
438	45c. Painting at Marrakesh	20	10
439	$2 Giving the "V" sign	50	1·00
MS440	126×100 mm. Nos. 438/9	70	1·50

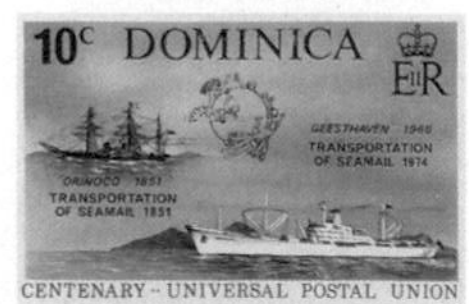

133 Mailboats "Orinoco" (1851) and "Geesthaven" (1974)

1974. Centenary of U.P.U. Multicoloured.

441	10c. Type **133**	20	10
442	$2 de Haviland D.H.4 (1918) and Boeing 747-100 (1974)	80	1·00
MS443	107×93 mm. $1.20 as 10c. and $2.40 as $2	1·00	1·40

Nos. 442 and **MS**443 are inscr "De Haviland".

134 "The Virgin and Child" (Tiso)

1974. Christmas. Multicoloured.

444	½c. Type **134**	10	10
445	1c. "Madonna and Child with Saints" (Costa)	10	10
446	2c. "The Nativity" (school of Rimini, 14th-century)	10	10
447	10c. "The Rest on the Flight into Egypt" (Romanelli)	20	10
448	25c. "The Adoration of the Shepherds" (da Sermoneta)	35	10
449	45c. "The Nativity" (Guido Reni)	45	10
450	$1 "The Adoration of the Magi" (Caselli)	65	40
MS451	114×78 mm. Nos. 449/50	60	1·00

135 Queen Triggerfish

1975. Fishes. Multicoloured.

452	½c. Type **135**	10	20
453	1c. Porkfish	10	15
454	2c. Sailfish	10	15
455	3c. Swordfish	10	15
456	20c. Great barracuda	50	25
457	$2 Nassau grouper	1·40	2·75
MS458	104×80 mm. No. 457	1·90	6·00

136 "Myscelia antholia"

1975. Dominican Butterflies. Multicoloured.

459	½c. Type **136**	10	60
460	1c. "Lycorea ceres"	10	60
461	2c. "Anaea marthesia" ("Siderone nemesis")	15	60
462	6c. "Battus polydamas"	50	1·00
463	30c. "Anartia lytrea"	60	70
464	40c. "Morpho peleides"	60	75
465	$2 "Dryas julia"	1·00	6·50
MS466	108×80 mm. No. 465	1·25	4·75

137 "Yare" (cargo liner)

1975. "Ships tied to Dominica's History". Mult.

467	½c. Type **137**	20	35
468	1c. "Thames II" (liner), 1890	20	35
469	2c. "Lady Nelson" (cargo liner)	20	35
470	20c. "Lady Rodney" (cargo liner)	40	35
471	45c. "Statesman" (freighter)	60	55
472	50c. "Geestcape" (freighter)	60	80
473	$2 "Geeststar" (freighter)	1·00	4·50
MS474	78×103 mm. Nos. 472/3	1·50	5·00

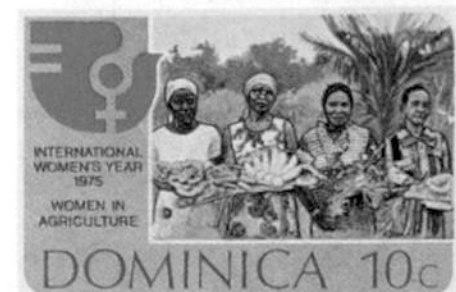

138 "Women in Agriculture"

1975. International Women's Year. Multicoloured.

475	10c. Type **138**	10	10
476	$2 "Women in Industry and Commerce"	40	60

139 Miss Caribbean Queen, 1975

1975. National Day. Multicoloured.

477	5c. Type **139**	10	10
478	10c. Public library (horiz)	10	10
479	30c. Citrus factory (horiz)	10	10
480	$1 National Day Trophy	25	50
MS481	130×98 mm. Nos. 478/80. Imperf	50	1·40

140 "Virgin and Child" (Mantegna)

1975. Christmas. "Virgin and Child" paintings by artists named. Multicoloured.

482	½c. Type **140**	10	10
483	1c. Fra Filippo Lippi	10	10
484	2c. Bellini	10	10
485	10c. Botticelli	15	10
486	25c. Bellini	25	10
487	45c. Correggio	30	10
488	$1 Durer	55	50
MS489	139×85 mm. Nos. 487/88	1·00	1·50

141 Hibiscus

1975. Multicoloured.. Multicoloured..

490	½c. Type **141**	10	1·00
491	1c. African tulip	15	1·00
492	2c. Castor-oil tree	15	1·00
493	3c. White cedar flower	15	1·00
494	4c. Egg plant	15	1·00
495	5c. Needlefish ("Gare")	20	1·00
496	6c. Ochro	20	1·10
497	8c. Zenaida dove ("Mountain Dove")	3·00	1·10
498	10c. Screw pine	20	15
499	20c. Mango longue	30	15
500	25c. Crayfish	35	15
501	30c. Common opossum	90	80
502	40c. Bay leaf groves	90	80
503	50c. Tomatoes	40	50
504	$1 Lime factory	55	65
505	$2 Rum distillery	1·00	3·50
506	$5 Bay Oil distillery	1·00	5·00
507	$10 Queen Elizabeth II (vert)	1·40	15·00

Nos. 502/7 are larger, 28×44 mm ($10) or 44×28 (others).

142 American Infantry

1976. Bicentenary of American Revolution. Mult.

508	½c. Type **142**	10	10
509	1c. British three-decker, 1782	10	10
510	2c. George Washington	10	10
511	45c. British sailors	30	10
512	75c. British ensign	40	40
513	$2 Admiral Hood	60	1·25

MS514	105×92 mm. Nos. 512/13	1·00	3·00

143 Rowing

1976. Olympic Games, Montreal. Multicoloured.

515	½c. Type **143**	10	10
516	1c. Shot putting	10	10
517	2c. Swimming	10	10
518	40c. Relay	15	10
519	45c. Gymnastics	15	10
520	60c. Sailing	20	20
521	$2 Archery	55	80
MS522	90×140 mm. Nos. 520/1	85	75

144 Ringed Kingfisher

1976. Wild Birds. Multicoloured.

523	½c. Type **144**	10	75
524	1c. Mourning dove	15	75
525	2c. Green-backed heron ("Green Heron")	15	75
526	15c. Blue-winged hawk (vert)	60	35
527	30c. Blue-headed hummingbird (vert)	65	55
528	45c. Bananaquit (vert)	70	60
529	$2 Imperial amazon ("Imperial Parrot") (vert)	1·25	12·00
MS530	133×101 mm. Nos. 527/9	2·75	14·00

1976. West Indian Victory in World Cricket Cup. As T **223a** of Grenada.

531	15c. Map of the Caribbean	75	1·25
532	25c. Prudential Cup	75	1·75

145 Viking Spacecraft System

1976. Viking Space Mission. Multicoloured.

533	½c. Type **145**	10	10
534	1c. Landing pad (horiz)	10	10
535	2c. Titan IIID and Centaur DII	10	10
536	3c. Orbiter and lander capsule	10	10
537	45c. Capsule, parachute unopened	15	15
538	75c. Capsule, parachute opened	20	70
539	$1 Lander descending (horiz)	25	75
540	$2 Space vehicle on Mars (horiz)	35	2·00
MS541	104×78 mm. Nos. 539/40	1·10	2·25

146 "Virgin and Child with Saints Anthony of Padua and Roch" (Giorgione)

1976. Christmas. "Virgin and Child" paintings by artists named. Multicoloured.

542	½c. Type **146**	10	10
543	1c. Bellini	10	10
544	2c. Mantegna	10	10
545	6c. Mantegna (different)	10	10
546	25c. Memling	15	10
547	45c. Correggio	20	10
548	$3 Raphael	1·00	1·00
MS549	104×85 mm. 50c. as No. 547 and $1 as No. 548	1·00	1·10

147 Island Craft Co-operative

1976. National Day. Multicoloured.

550	10c. Type **147**	10	10
551	50c. Harvesting bananas	15	10
552	$1 Boxing plant	30	35
MS553	96×122 mm. Nos. 550/2	50	1·00

148 American Giant Sundial

1976. Shells. Multicoloured.

554	½c. Type **148**	10	10
555	1c. Flame helmet	10	10
556	2c. Mouse cone	10	10
557	20c. Caribbean vase	30	10
558	40c. West Indian fighting conch	40	25
559	50c. Short coral shell	40	25
560	$3 Apple murex	1·00	3·25
MS561	101×55 mm. $2 Long-spined star shell	1·10	1·40

149 The Queen Crowned and Enthroned

1977. Silver Jubilee. Multicoloured.

562	½c. Type **149**	10	10
563	1c. Imperial State Crown	10	10
564	45c. The Queen and Princess Anne	15	10
565	$2 Coronation Ring	25	30
566	$2.50 Ampulla and Spoon	30	40
MS567	104×97 mm. $5 Queen Elizabeth and Prince Philip	75	1·25

150 Joseph Haydn

1977. 150th Death Anniv of Ludwig van Beethoven. Multicoloured.

568	½c. Type **150**	10	10
569	1c. Scene from "Fidelio"	10	10
570	2c. Maria Casentini (dancer)	10	10
571	15c. Beethoven and pastoral scene	30	10
572	30c. "Wellington's Victory"	30	10
573	40c. Henriette Sontag (singer)	30	10
574	$2 The young Beethoven	75	2·00
MS575	138×93 mm. Nos. 572/4	1·10	3·25

151 Hiking

1977. Caribbean Scout Jamboree, Jamaica. Mult.

576	½c. Type **151**	10	10
577	1c. First-aid	10	10
578	2c. Camping	10	10
579	45c. Rock climbing	25	15

580	50c. Canoeing	30	20
581	$3 Sailing	1·40	1·75
MS582	111×113 mm. 75c. Map-reading; $2 Campfire sing-song	1·00	1·25

152 Holy Family

1977. Christmas. Multicoloured.

583	½c. Type **152**	10	10
584	1c. Angel and Shepherds	10	10
585	2c. Holy Baptism	10	10
586	6c. Flight into Egypt	15	10
587	15c. Three Kings with gifts	15	10
588	45c. Holy Family in the Temple	30	10
589	$3 Flight into Egypt (different)	80	1·10
MS590	113×85 mm. 50c. Virgin and Child; $2 Flight into Egypt (different)	60	75

1977. Royal Visit. Nos. 562/66 optd **ROYAL VISIT W.I. 1977.**

591	½c. Type 149	10	10
592	1c. Imperial State Crown	10	10
593	45c. The Queen and Princess Anne	15	10
594a	$2 Coronation Ring	30	30
595a	$2.50 Ampulla and Spoon	35	35
MS596	104×79 mm. $5 Queen Elizabeth and Prince Philip	1·00	1·50

154 "Sousouelle Souris"

1978. "History of Carnival". Multicoloured.

597	½c. Type **154**	10	10
598	1c. Sensay costume	10	10
599	2c. Street musicians	10	10
600	45c. Douiette band	15	10
601	50c. Pappy Show wedding	15	10
602	$2 Masquerade band	45	60
MS603	104×88 mm. $2.50, No. 602	60	65

155 Colonel Charles Lindbergh and "Spirit of St. Louis"

1978. Aviation Anniversaries. Multicoloured.

604	6c. Type **155**	20	60
605	10c. "Spirit of St. Louis", New York, 20 May, 1927	25	10
606	15c. Lindbergh and map of Atlantic	35	10
607	20c. Lindbergh reaches Paris, 21 May, 1927	45	10
608	40c. Airship LZ-1, Lake Constance, 1900	55	20
609	60c. Count F. von Zeppelin and Airship LZ-2, 1906	65	30
610	$3 Airship "Graf Zeppelin", 1928	1·40	2·25
MS611	139×108 mm. 50c. Ryan NYP Special "Spirit of St. Louis" in mid-Atlantic; $2 Airship LZ-127 "Graf Zeppelin", 1928	1·60	1·10

The 6, 10, 15, 20 and 50c. values commemorate the 50th anniversary of first solo transatlantic flight by Col. Charles Lindbergh; the other values commemorate anniversaries of various Zeppelin airships.

156 Queen receiving Homage

1978. 25th Anniv of Coronation. Multicoloured.

612	45c. Type **156**	15	10
613	$2 Balcony scene	30	30
614	$2.50 Queen and Prince Philip	40	40
MS615	76×107 mm. $5 Queen Elizabeth II	75	75

157 Wright Flyer III

1978. 75th Anniv of First Powered Flight. Mult.

616	30c. Type **157**	15	15
617	40c. Wright Type A, 1908	20	20
618	60c. Wright "Flyer I"	25	30
619	$2 Wright "Flyer I" (different)	85	1·25
MS620	116×89 mm. $3 Wilbur and Orville Wright	1·00	1·00

158 "Two Apostles"

1978. Christmas. Paintings by Rubens. Mult.

621	20c. Type **158**	10	10
622	45c. "Descent from the Cross"	15	10
623	50c. "St Ildefonso receiving the Chasuble"	15	10
624	$3 "Assumption of the Virgin"	35	80
MS625	113×83 mm. $2 "The Holy Family" (Sebastiano del Piombo*)	75	75

*This painting was incorrectly attributed to Rubens on the stamp.

159 Map showing Parishes

1978. Independence. Multicoloured.

626	10c. Type **159**	75	40
627	25c. "Sabinea carinalis" (national flower)	55	15
628	45c. New National flag	1·25	30
629	50c. Coat of arms	60	30
630	$2 Prime Minister Patrick John	70	3·00
MS631	113×90 mm. $2.50, Type **159**	1·00	1·25

1978. Nos. 490/507 optd **INDEPENDENCE 3rd NOVEMBER 1978.**

632	½c. Type **57**	40	60
633	1c. African tulip	45	60
634	2c. Castor-oil tree	45	50
635	3c. White cedar flower	50	50
636	4c. Egg plant	50	50
637	5c. Needlefish ("Gare")	50	50
638	6c. Ochro	50	50
639	8c. Zenaida dove	3·50	60
640	10c. Screw pine	50	15
641	20c. Mango longue	60	40
642	25c. Crayfish	70	40
643	30c. Common opossum	70	40
644	40c. Bay leaf groves	70	25
645	50c. Tomatoes	80	30
646	$1 Lime factory	80	65
647	$2 Rum distillery	1·00	1·00
648	$5 Bay Oil distillery	1·00	2·25
649	$10 Queen Elizabeth II	1·50	4·50

161 Sir Rowland Hill

1979. Death Centenary of Sir Rowland Hill.

650	**161**	25c. multicoloured	10	10
651	-	45c. multicoloured	15	15
652	-	50c. black, violet and mauve	15	10
653	-	$2 black, mauve and yellow	35	65
MS654		186×96 mm. $5 black and red	1·00	1·25

DESIGNS: 45c. Great Britain 1840 2d. blue; 50c. 1874 1d. stamp; $2 Maltese Cross cancellations; $5 Penny Black.

162 Children and Canoe

1979. International Year of the Child. Multicoloured.

655	30c. Type **162**	25	15
656	40c. Children with bananas	25	45
657	50c. Children playing cricket	1·25	80
658	$3 Child feeding rabbits	1·75	2·00
MS659	117×85 mm. $5 Child with catch of fish	1·00	1·50

163 Nassau Grouper

1979. Marine Wildlife. Multicoloured.

660	10c. Type **163**	40	15
661	30c. Striped dolphin	70	35
662	50c. White-tailed tropic-bird	1·75	65
663	60c. Brown pelican	1·75	1·50
664	$1 Long-finned pilot whale	2·00	1·75
665	$2 Brown booby	2·25	4·50
MS666	120×94 mm. $3 Elkhorn coral	1·25	1·40

No. 661 is inscr "SPOTTED DOLPHIN" in error.

164 H.M.S. "Endeavour"

1979. Death Bicent of Captain Cook. Mult.

667	10c. Type **164**	65	30
668	50c. H.M.S. "Resolution" (Second Voyage)	80	1·00
669	60c. H.M.S. "Discovery" (Third Voyage)	80	1·50
670	$2 Detail of Cook's chart of New Zealand, 1770	80	2·75
MS671	97×90 mm. $5 Captain Cook and signature	1·25	2·00

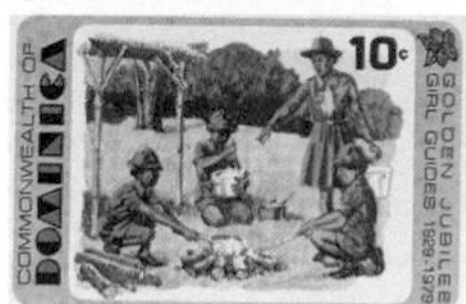

165 Cooking at Campfire

1979. 50th Anniv of Girl Guide Movement in Dominica. Multicoloured.

672	10c. Type **165**	20	10
673	20c. Pitching emergency rain tent	25	10
674	50c. Raising Dominican flag	35	10
675	$2.50 Singing and dancing to accordion	90	80
MS676	110×86 mm. $3 Guides of different age-groups	75	1·25

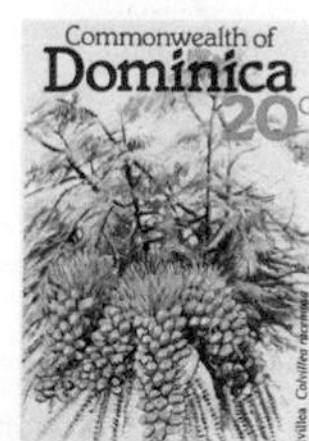

166 Colvillea

1979. Flowering Trees. Multicoloured.

677	20c. Type **166**	15	10
678	40c. "Lignum vitae"	20	15
679	60c. Dwarf poinciana	25	15
680	$2 Fern tree	50	75
MS681	114×89 mm. $3 Perfume tree	75	1·10

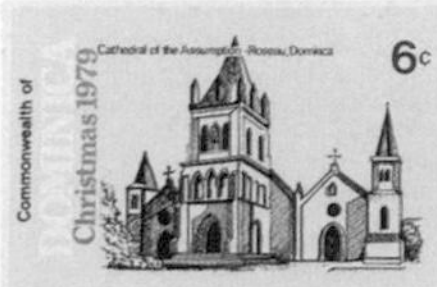

167 Cathedral of the Assumption, Roseau

1979. Christmas. Cathedrals. Multicoloured.

682	6c. Type **167**	10	10
683	45c. St. Paul's, London (vert)	15	10
684	60c. St. Peter's, Rome	15	10
685	$3 Notre Dame, Paris (vert)	55	60
MS686	113×85 mm. 40c. St. Patrick's, New York; $2 Cologne Cathedral (both vert)	50	80

1979. Hurricane Relief. Nos. 495, 502 and 506/7 optd **HURRICANE RELIEF.**

687	5c. Gare	10	10
688	40c. Bay leaf groves	10	10
689	$5 Bay Oil distillery	1·00	1·25
690	$10 Queen Elizabeth II	1·25	1·75

169 Mickey Mouse and Octopus playing Xylophone

1979. International Year of the Child. Walt Disney Cartoon Characters. Multicoloured.

691	½c. Type **169**	10	10
692	1c. Goofy playing guitar on rocking-horse	10	10
693	2c. Mickey Mouse playing violin and Goofy on bagpipes	10	10
694	3c. Donald Duck playing drum with a pneumatic drill	10	10
695	4c. Minnie Mouse playing saxophone	10	10
696	5c. Goofy one-man band	10	10
697	10c. Horace Horsecollar blowing Dale from french horn	10	10
698	$2 Huey, Dewey and Louie playing bass	1·00	2·00
699	$2.50 Donald Duck at piano and Huey playing trumpet	1·00	2·25
MS700	127×102 mm. $3 Mickey Mouse playing piano	2·50	3·00

170 Hospital Ward

1980. 75th Anniv of Rotary International. Mult.

701	10c. Type **170**	10	10
702	20c. Electro-cardiogram	15	10
703	40c. Mental hospital site	20	15
704	$2.50 Paul Harris (founder)	55	90
MS705	128×113 mm. $3 Interlocking cogs of Rotary emblem and globe	60	80

1980. "London 1980" International Stamp Exhibition. Optd **LONDON 1980.**

706	**161**	25c. multicoloured	25	10
707	-	45c. multicoloured	30	15
708	-	50c. brown, blue and red	30	15
709	-	$2 brown, red and yellow	80	60

171 Shot Putting

1980. Olympic Games, Moscow. Multicoloured.

710	30c. Type **171**	15	10
711	40c. Basketball	60	15
712	60c. Swimming	35	20
713	$2 Gymnastics	60	65

MS714	114×86 mm. $3 The marathon	70	90

172 "Supper at Emmaus" (Caravaggio)

1980. Famous Paintings. Multicoloured.

715	20c. Type **172**	20	10
716	25c. "Portrait of Charles I Hunting" (Van Dyck) (vert)	20	10
717	30c. "The Maids of Honour" (Velasquez) (vert)	25	10
718	45c. "The Rape of the Sabine Women" (Poussin)	25	10
719	$1 "Embarkation for Cythera" (Watteau)	35	35
720	$5 "Girl before a Mirror" (Picasso) (vert)	1·00	1·50
MS721	114×111 mm. $3 "The Holy Family" (Rembrandt) (vert)	60	80

173 Scene from "Peter Pan"

1980. Christmas. Scenes from "Peter Pan". Multicoloured.

722	½c. Type **173** (Tinker Bell)	10	10
723	1c. Wendy sewing back Peter's shadow	10	10
724	2c. Peter introduces the mermaids	10	10
725	3c. Wendy and Peter with lost boys	10	10
726	4c. Captain Hook, Pirate Smee and Tiger Lily	10	10
727	5c. Peter with Tiger Lily and her father	10	10
728	10c. Captain Hook captures Peter and Wendy	10	10
729	$2 Peter fights Captain Hook	2·25	1·50
730	$2.50 Captain Hook in crocodile's jaws	2·25	1·75
MS731	124×98 mm. $4 Peter Pan	4·25	3·50

174 Queen Elizabeth the Queen Mother in Doorway

1980. 80th Birthday of the Queen Mother.

732a	**174**	40c. multicoloured	15	15
733a	**174**	$2.50 multicoloured	45	60
MS734		85×66 mm. $3 multicoloured	75	2·00

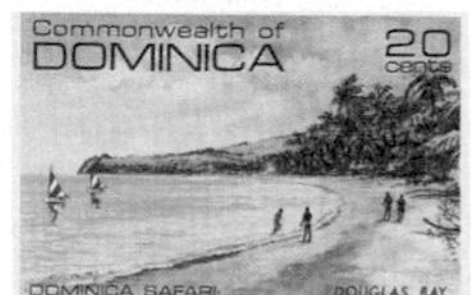

175 Douglas Bay

1981. "Dominica Safari". Multicoloured.

735	20c. Type **175**	10	10
736	30c. Valley of Desolation	10	10
737	40c. Emerald Pool (vert)	10	10
738	$3 Indian River (vert)	75	1·10
MS739	84×104 mm. $4 Trafalgar Falls (vert)	1·10	1·40

1981. Walt Disney's Cartoon Character, Pluto. As T **169**. Multicoloured.

740	$2 Pluto and Fifi	1·00	1·50
MS741	128×102 mm. $4 Pluto in scene from film "Pluto's Blue Note"	1·25	1·50

176 Forest Thrush

1981. Birds. Multicoloured.

742	20c. Type **176**	55	30
743	30c. Wied's crested flycatcher	65	35
744	40c. Blue-hooded euphonia	75	45
745	$5 Lesser Antillean pewee	3·50	4·75
MS746	121×95 mm. $3 Imperial Amazon	2·75	1·75

177 Windsor Castle

1981. Royal Wedding. Multicoloured.

747	40c. Prince Charles and Lady Diana Spencer	10	10
748	60c. Type **177**	15	15
749a	$4 Prince Charles flying helicopter	30	50
MS750	96×82 mm. $5 Westland HU Mk 5 Wessex helicopter of Queen's Flight	1·00	90

178 Lady Diana Spencer

1981. Royal Wedding. Multicoloured.

751	25c. Type **178**	20	35
752	$2 Prince Charles	50	1·00
753	$5 Prince Charles and Lady Diana Spencer	1·75	2·50

1981. Christmas. Scenes from Walt Disney's cartoon film "Santa's Workshop". As T **169**.

754	½c. multicoloured	10	10
755	1c. multicoloured	10	10
756	2c. multicoloured	10	10
757	3c. multicoloured	10	10
758	4c. multicoloured	15	10
759	5c. multicoloured	15	10
760	10c. multicoloured	20	10
761	45c. multicoloured	1·25	30
762	$5 multicoloured	3·00	5·50
MS763	129×103 mm. $4 multicoloured	4·00	3·50

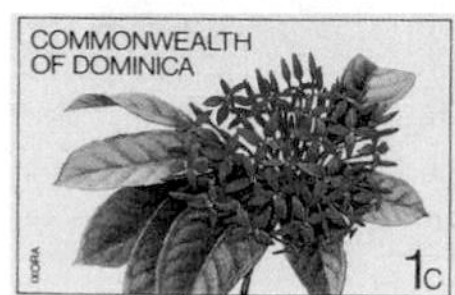

179 Ixora

1981. Plant Life. Multicoloured.

764A	1c. Type **179**	10	75
765A	2c. Flamboyant	10	80
766A	4c. Poinsettia	15	80
767A	5c. Bois caribe (national flower of Dominica)	15	70
768A	8c. Annatto or roucou	20	1·00
769A	10c. Passion fruit	30	20
770A	15c. Breadfruit or yampain	55	20
771A	20c. Allamanda or buttercup	40	20
772A	25c. Cashew nut	40	20
773A	35c. Soursop or couassol	45	30
774A	40c. Bougainvillea	45	30
775A	45c. Anthurium	50	35
776A	60c. Cacao or cocoa	1·25	70
777A	90c. Pawpaw tree or papay	70	1·50
778A	$1 Coconut palm	1·50	1·75
779A	$2 Coffee tree or cafe	1·00	3·50
780B	$5 Heliconia or lobster claw	3·25	5·50
781A	$10 Banana fig	1·75	12·00

Nos. 769, 770, 776, 778, 780 and 781 come with or without imprint date.

180 Curb Slope for Wheelchairs

1981. International Year for Disabled People. Multicoloured.

782	45c. Type **180**	40	15
783	60c. Bus with invalid step	50	20
784	75c. Motor car controls adapted for handicapped	60	30
785	$4 Bus with wheelchair ramp	1·00	2·50
MS786	82×96 mm. $5 Specially designed elevator control panel	4·25	3·00

181 "Olga Picasso in an Armchair"

1981. Birth Centenary of Picasso. Multicoloured.

787	45c. Type **181**	35	15
788	60c. "Bathers"	40	15
789	75c. "Woman in Spanish Costume"	40	25
790	$4 "Detail of Dog and Cock"	1·00	2·25
MS791	140×115 mm. $5 "Sleeping Peasants" (detail)	2·50	3·50

1982. World Cup Football Championship, Spain. Walt Disney Cartoon Characters. As T **169**. Mult.

792	½c. Goofy chasing ball with butterfly net	10	10
793	1c. Donald Duck with ball in beak	10	10
794	2c. Goofy as goalkeeper	10	10
795	3c. Goofy looking for ball	10	10
796	4c. Goofy as park attendant puncturing ball with litter spike	10	10
797	5c. Pete and Donald Duck playing	10	10
798	10c. Donald Duck after kicking rock instead of ball	15	10
799	60c. Donald Duck feeling effects of a hard game and Daisy Duck dusting ball	1·50	1·25
800	$5 Goofy hiding ball under his jersey from Mickey Mouse	5·50	6·50
MS801	132×105 mm. $4 Dale making off with ball	4·00	3·25

182 "Gone Fishing"

1982. Norman Rockwell (painter) Commemoration. Multicoloured.

802	10c. Type **182**	10	10
803	25c. "Breakfast"	20	10
804	45c. "The Marbles Champ"	30	30
805	$1 "Speeding Along"	55	65

No. 802 is inscribed "Golden Days" and No. 803 " The Morning News".

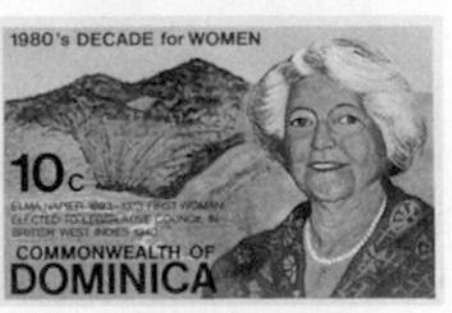

183 Elma Napier (first woman elected to B.W.I. Legislative Council)

1982. Decade for Women. Multicoloured.

806	10c. Type **183**	10	10
807	45c. Margaret Mead (anthropologist)	30	30
808	$1 Mabel (Cissy) Caudeiron (folk song composer and historian)	55	55
809	$4 Eleanor Roosevelt	2·25	2·25
MS810	92×83 mm. $3 Florence Nightingale	2·00	3·00

184 George Washington and Independence Hall, Philadelphia

1982. 250th Birth Anniv of George Washington and Birth Centenary of Franklin D. Roosevelt. Multicoloured.

811	45c. Type **184**	25	25
812	60c. Franklin D. Roosevelt and Capitol, Washington D.C.	30	35
813	90c. Washington at Yorktown (detail "The Surrender of Cornwallis" by Trumbull)	40	55
814	$2 Construction of dam (from W. Groppers' mural commemorating Roosevelt's) "New Deal"	70	1·60
MS815	115×90 mm. $5 Washington and Roosevelt with U.S.A. flags of 1777 and 1933	2·00	3·25

185 "Anaea dominicana"

1982. Butterflies. Multicoloured.

816	15c. Type **185**	1·50	35
817	45c. "Heliconius charithonia"	2·50	65
818	60c. "Hypolimnas misippus"	2·75	1·75
819	$3 "Biblis hyperia"	5·50	6·00
MS820	77×105 mm. $5 "Marpesia petreus"	7·00	5·00

186 Prince and Princess of Wales

1982. 21st Birthday of Princess of Wales. Multicoloured.

821	45c. Buckingham Palace	20	10
822	$2 Type **186**	50	70
823	$4 Princess of Wales	1·10	1·25
MS824	103×75 mm. $5 Princess Diana (different)	2·50	2·25

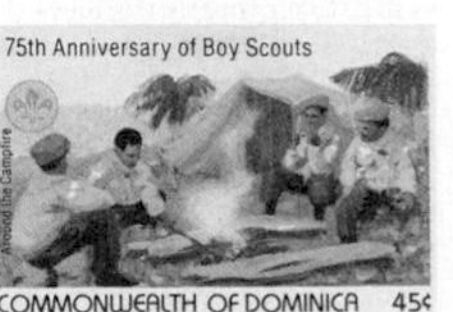

187 Scouts around Campfire

1982. 75th Anniv of Boy Scouts Movement. Mult.

825	45c. Type **187**	1·25	50
826	60c. Temperature study, Valley of Desolation	1·75	1·25
827	75c. Learning about native birds	2·25	1·50
828	$3 Canoe trip along Indian River	4·25	5·50
MS829	99×70 mm. Dominican scouts saluting the flag (vert)	1·50	3·25

1982. Birth of Prince William of Wales. Nos. 821/3 optd **ROYAL BABY 21.6.82.**

830	45c. Buckingham Palace	30	30
831	$2 Type **186**	80	1·10
832	$4 Princess of Wales	1·40	1·90
MS833	103×75 mm. $5 Princess Diana (different)	2·00	2·75

188 "Holy Family of Francis I"

1982. Christmas. Raphael Paintings. Multicoloured.

834	25c. Type **188**	15	10
835	30c. "Holy Family of the Pearl"	15	10
836	90c. "Canigiani Holy Family"	30	35
837	$4 "Holy Family of the Oak Tree"	1·25	1·50
MS838	95×125 mm. $5 "Holy Family of the Lamp"	1·25	2·00

189 Cuvier's Beaked Whale

1983. Save the Whales. Multicoloured.

839	45c. Type **189**	2·00	65
840	60c. Humpback whale	2·25	1·75
841	75c. Black right whale	2·25	2·25
842	$3 Melon-headed whale	4·50	6·50
MS843	99×72 mm. $5 Pygmy sperm whale	4·00	4·00

190 Banana Export

1983. Commonwealth Day. Multicoloured.

844	25c. Type **190**	15	15
845	30c. Road building	15	20
846	90c. Community nursing	30	45
847	$3 Tourism-handicrafts	75	1·50

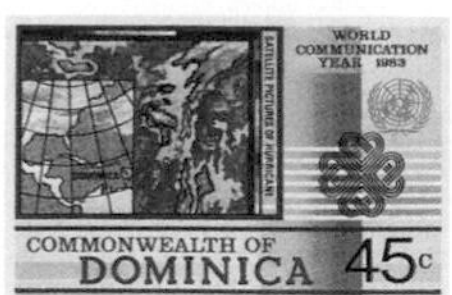

191 Map and Satellite Picture of Hurricane

1983. World Communications Year. Multicoloured.

848	45c. Type **191**	20	25
849	60c. Aircraft-to-ship transmission	25	35
850	90c. Satellite communications	30	45
851	$2 Shortwave radio	75	1·00
MS852	110×85 mm. $5 Communications satellite	1·25	2·75

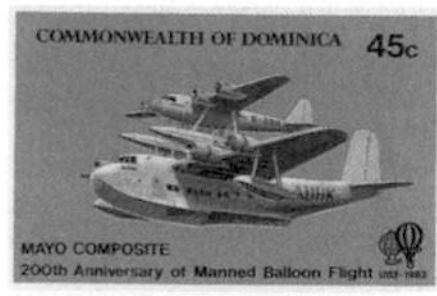

192 Short-Mayo Composite

1983. Bicentenary of Manned Flight. Mult.

853	45c. Type **192**	50	30
854	60c. Macchi M.39 Schneider Trophy seaplane	60	65
855	90c. Fairey Swordfish torpedo bomber	70	1·50
856	$4 Airship LZ-3	1·25	4·75
MS857	105×79 mm. $5 "Double Eagle II" (balloon)	1·25	2·75

193 Duesenberg "SJ", 1935

1983. Classic Motor Cars. Multicoloured.

858	10c. Type **193**	25	15
859	45c. Studebaker "Avanti", 1962	35	25
860	60c. Cord "812"	40	35
861	75c. MG "TC", 1945	45	50
862	90c. Camaro "350 SS", 1967	50	60
863	$3 Porsch "356", 1948	1·00	1·60
MS864	110×75 mm. $5 Ferrari "312 T", 1975	1·50	2·75

194 "Charity"

1983. Christmas. 500th Birth Anniv of Raphael. Multicoloured.

865	45c. Type **194**	30	30
866	60c. "Hope"	30	30
867	90c. "Faith"	40	60
868	$4 "The Cardinal Virtues"	1·00	3·25
MS869	101×127 mm. $5 "Justice"	1·25	2·75

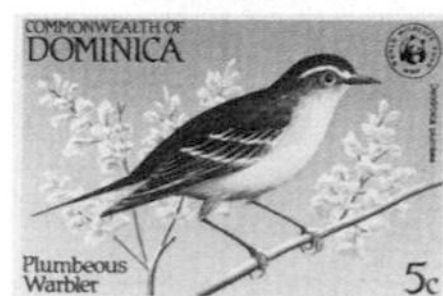

195 Plumbeous Warbler

1984. Birds. Multicoloured.

870	5c. Type **195**	2·50	1·10
871	45c. Imperial amazon ("Imperial Parrot")	5·00	75
872	60c. Blue-headed hummingbird	5·50	3·25
873	90c. Red-necked amazon ("Red-necked Parrot")	6·50	6·00
MS874	72×72 mm. $5 Greater flamingos	4·00	4·50

196 Donald Duck

1984. Easter. Multicoloured.

875	½c. Type **196**	10	10
876	1c. Mickey Mouse	10	10
877	2c. Tortoise and Hare	10	10
878	3c. Brer Rabbit and Brer Bear	10	10
879	4c. Donald Duck (different)	10	10
880	5c. White Rabbit	10	10
881	10c. Thumper	10	10
882	$2 Pluto	3·25	2·75
883	$4 Pluto (different)	4·50	4·00
MS884	126×100 mm. $5 Chip and Dale	3·50	4·00

197 Gymnastics

1984. Olympic Games, Los Angeles. Multicoloured.

885	30c. Type **197**	20	25
886	45c. Javelin-throwing	30	35
887	60c. High diving	40	45
888	$4 Fencing	1·50	2·50
MS889	104×85 mm. $5 Equestrian event	3·25	3·25

198 "Atlantic Star"

1984. Shipping. Multicoloured.

890	45c. Type **198**	1·75	75
891	60c. "Atlantic" (liner)	2·00	1·25
892	90c. Carib fishing boat	2·50	2·50
893	$4 "Norway" (liner)	6·00	9·00
MS894	106×79 mm. $5 "Santa Maria", 1492	3·25	5·50

1984. U.P.U. Congress, Hamburg. Nos. 769 and 780 optd **19th UPU CONGRESS HAMBURG**.

895	10c. Passion fruit	10	10
896	$5 Heliconia or lobster claw	2·75	4·00

200 "Guzmania lingulata"

1984. "Ausipex" International Stamp Exhibition, Melbourne. Bromeliads. Multicoloured.

897	45c. Type **200**	30	35
898	60c. "Pitcairnia angustifolia"	40	55
899	75c. "Tillandsia fasciculata"	50	75
900	$3 "Aechmea smithiorum"	2·00	3·50
MS901	75×105 mm. $5 "Tillandsia utriculata"	2·25	4·25

201 "The Virgin and Child with Young St. John" (Correggio)

1984. 450th Death Anniv of Correggio (painter). Multicoloured.

902	25c. Type **201**	30	20
903	60c. "Christ bids Farewell to the Virgin Mary"	40	40
904	90c. "Do not Touch Me"	50	80
905	$4 "The Mystical Marriage of St Catherine"	80	3·50
MS906	89×60 mm. $5 "The Adoration of the Magi"	1·75	3·50

202 "Before the Start" (Edgar Degas)

1984. 150th Birth Anniv of Edgar Degas (painter). Multicoloured.

907	30c. Type **202**	30	25
908	45c. "Race on the Racecourse"	35	35
909	$1 "Jockeys at the Flagpole"	55	1·25
910	$3 "Racehorses at Longchamp"	80	3·75
MS911	89×60 mm. $5 "Self-portrait" (vert)	2·00	3·75

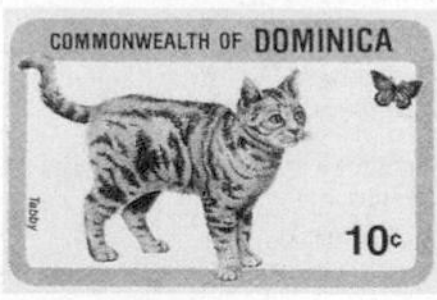

203 Tabby

1984. Cats. Multicoloured.

912	10c. Type **203**	20	15
913	15c. Calico shorthair	25	15
914	20c. Siamese	35	15
915	25c. Manx	35	20
916	45c. Abyssinian	50	30
917	60c. Tortoise-shell longhair	55	65
918	$1 Cornish rex	60	1·00
919	$2 Persian	80	3·00
920	$3 Himalayan	80	4·00
921	$5 Burmese	1·00	7·00
MS922	105×75 mm. $5 Grey Burmese, Persian and American shorthair	3·50	7·00

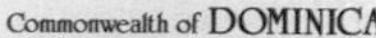

204 Hawker Siddeley H.S.748

1984. 40th Anniv of International Civil Aviation Organisation. Multicoloured.

923	30c. Type **204**	1·00	50
924	60c. de Havilland Twin Otter 100	1·75	50
925	$1 Britten Norman Islander	2·00	1·60
926	$3 de Havilland Twin Otter 100 (different)	3·00	6·50
MS927	102×75 mm. $5 Boeing 747–200	2·50	3·50

205 Donald Duck, Mickey Mouse and Goofy with Father Christmas

1984. Christmas. Walt Disney Cartoon Characters. Multicoloured.

928	45c. Type **205**	1·25	30
929	60c. Donald Duck as Father Christmas with toy train	1·50	70
930	90c. Donald Duck as Father Christmas in sleigh	2·00	1·75
931	$2 Donald Duck and nephews in sledge	3·25	3·75
932	$4 Donald Duck in snow with Christmas tree	4·25	6·00
MS933	127×102 mm. $5 Donald Duck and nephews opening present	3·50	4·00

206 Mrs. M. Bascom presenting Trefoil to Chief Guide Lady Baden-Powell

1985. 75th Anniv of Girl Guide Movement. Mult.

934	35c. Type **206**	60	30
935	45c. Lady Baden-Powell inspecting Dominican brownies	80	35
936	60c. Lady Baden-Powell with Mrs. M. Bascom and Mrs. A. Robinson (guide leaders)	1·00	65
937	$3 Lord and Lady Baden-Powell (vert)	2·50	3·75
MS938	77×105 mm. $5 Flags of Dominica and Girl Guide Movement	3·50	4·00

206a Clapper rail ("King Rail")

1985. Birth Bicentenary of John J Audubon (ornithologist) (1st issue). Multicoloured.

939	45c. Type **206a**	1·10	30
940	$1 Black and white warbler (vert)	2·00	1·50
941	$2 Broad-winged hawk (vert)	2·75	3·00
942	$3 Ring-necked duck	3·50	4·00
MS943	101×73 mm. $5 Reddish egret	3·50	3·75

See also Nos. 1013/**MS**17.

207 Student with Computer

1985. Duke of Edinburgh's Award Scheme. Multicoloured.

No.	Description		
944	45c. Type **207**	50	30
945	60c. Assisting doctor in hospital	1·75	40
946	90c. Two youths hiking	1·90	80
947	$4 Family jogging	3·50	6·50
MS948	100×98 mm. $5 Duke of Edinburgh	2·75	3·00

208 The Queen Mother visiting Sadlers Wells Opera

1985. Life and Times of Queen Elizabeth the Queen Mother. Multicoloured.

No.	Description		
949	60c. Type **208**	1·75	60
950	$1 Fishing in Scotland	1·75	70
951	$3 On her 84th birthday	2·25	3·25
MS952	56×85 mm. $5 Attending Garter ceremony, Windsor Castle	3·25	3·00

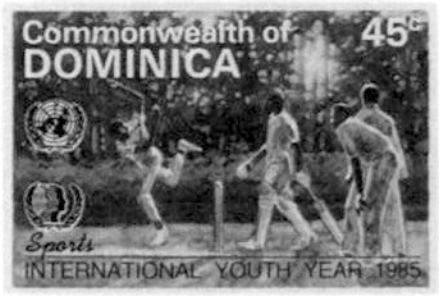

209 Cricket Match ("Sports")

1985. International Youth Year. Multicoloured.

No.	Description		
953	45c. Type **209**	4·25	1·50
954	60c. Bird-watching ("Environmental Study")	4·25	2·25
955	$1 Stamp collecting ("Education")	4·25	3·50
956	$3 Boating ("Leisure")	5·50	8·00
MS957	96×65 mm. $5 Young people linking hands	2·75	4·00

1985. 300th Birth Anniv of Johann Sebastian Bach (composer). As T **309a** of Grenada. Antique musical instruments.

No.	Description		
958	45c. multicoloured	1·50	40
959	60c. multicoloured	1·75	60
960	$1 multicoloured	2·25	1·00
961	$3 multicoloured	4·00	3·50
MS962	199×75 mm. $5 black	3·00	4·50

DESIGNS: 45c. Cornett; 60c. Coiled trumpet; $1 Piccolo; $3 Violoncello piccolo; $5 Johann Sebastian Bach.

1985. Royal Visit. As T **310a** of Grenada. Mult.

No.	Description		
963	60c. Flags of Great Britain and Dominica	75	50
964	$1 Queen Elizabeth II (vert)	75	1·25
965	$4 Royal Yacht "Britannia"	1·75	5·50
MS966	111×83 mm. $5 Map of Dominica	3·50	4·00

209a "The Glorious Whitewasher"

1985. 150th Birth Anniv of Mark Twain (author). Walt Disney cartoon characters in scenes from "Tom Sawyer". Multicoloured.

No.	Description		
967	20c. Type **209a**	75	30
968	60c. "Aunt Polly's home dentistry"	1·50	75
969	$1 "Aunt Polly's pain killer"	2·00	1·25
970	$1.50 Mickey Mouse balancing on fence	2·50	3·00
971	$2 "Lost in the cave with Becky"	2·75	3·50
MS972	126×101 mm. $5 Mickey Mouse as pirate	5·50	7·00

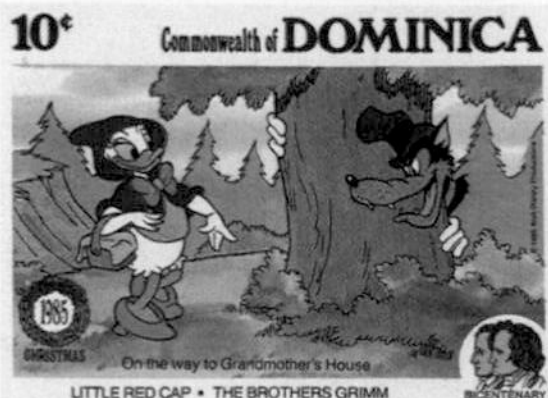

209b Little Red Cap (Daisy Duck) meeting the Wolf

1985. Birth Bicentenaries of Grimm Brothers (folklorists). Walt Disney cartoon characters in scenes from "Little Red Cap". Multicoloured.

No.	Description		
973	10c. Type **209b**	30	20
974	45c. The Wolf at the door	85	30
975	90c. The Wolf in Grandmother's bed	1·75	1·75
976	$1 The Wolf lunging at Little Red Cap	2·00	1·75
977	$3 The Woodsman (Donald Duck) chasing the Wolf	3·75	5·00
MS978	126×101 mm. $5 The Wolf falling into cooking pot	5·00	5·50

1985. 40th Anniv of United Nations Organization. Designs as T **311a** of Grenada showing United Nations (New York) stamps. Multicoloured.

No.	Description		
979	45c. Lord Baden-Powell and 1984 International Youth Year 35c.	70	50
980	$2 Maimonides (physician) and 1966 W.H.O. Building 11c.	1·50	3·25
981	$3 Sir Rowland Hill (postal reformer) and 1976 25th anniv of U.N. Postal Administration 13c.	1·50	3·50
MS982	110×85 mm. $5 "Apollo" spacecraft	2·75	3·25

210 Two Players competing for Ball

1986. World Cup Football Championship, Mexico. Multicoloured.

No.	Description		
983	45c. Type **210**	1·75	40
984	60c. Player heading ball	2·00	1·50
985	$1 Two players competing for ball (different)	2·25	1·75
986	$3 Player with ball	4·50	6·00
MS987	114×84 mm. $5 Three players	8·00	10·00

211 Police in Rowing Boat pursuing River Pirates, 1890

1986. Centenary of Statue of Liberty. Mult.

No.	Description		
988	15c. Type **211**	2·75	65
989	25c. Police patrol launch, 1986	2·75	85
990	45c. Hoboken Ferry Terminal c. 1890	2·50	85
991	$4 Holland Tunnel entrance and staff, 1986	5·00	7·50
MS992	104×76 mm. $5 Statue of Liberty (vert)	4·00	5·00

211a Nasir al Din al Tusi (Persian astronomer) and Jantal Mantar Observatory, Delhi

1986. Appearance of Halley's Comet (1st issue). Multicoloured.

No.	Description		
993	5c. Type **211a**	40	50
994	10c. Bell XS-1 Rocket Plane breaking sound barrier for first time, 1947	45	50
995	45c. Halley's Comet of 1531 (from "Astronomicum Caesareum", 1540)	1·00	30
996	$4 Mark Twain and quotation, 1910	3·75	4·25
MS997	104×71 mm. $5 Halley's Comet over Dominica	3·00	3·50

See also Nos. 1032/6.

1986. 60th Birthday of Queen Elizabeth II. As T **151b** of Gambia.

No.	Description		
998	2c. multicoloured	10	15
999	$1 multicoloured	70	80
1000	$4 multicoloured	2·00	3·00
MS1001	120×85 mm. $5 black and brown	4·00	4·25

DESIGNS: 2c. Wedding photograph, 1947; $1 Queen meeting Pope John Paul II, 1982; $4 Queen on royal visit, 1982; $5 Princess Elizabeth with corgis, 1936.

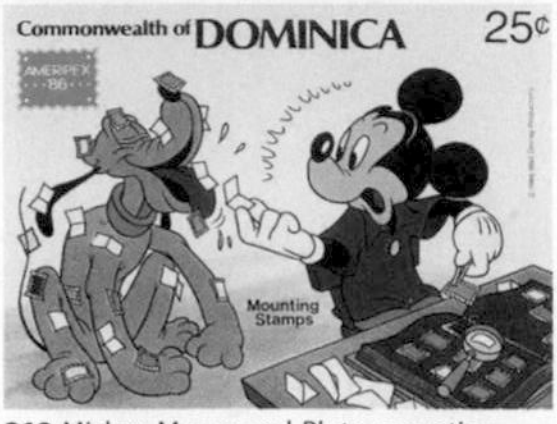

212 Mickey Mouse and Pluto mounting Stamps in Album

1986. "Ameripex" International Stamp Exhibition, Chicago. Showing Walt Disney cartoon characters. Multicoloured.

No.	Description		
1002	25c. Type **212**	60	40
1003	45c. Donald Duck examining stamp under magnifying glass	80	65
1004	60c. Chip n' Dale soaking and drying stamps	1·10	1·50
1005	$4 Donald Duck as scoutmaster awarding merit badges to Nephews	3·50	6·00
MS1006	127×101 mm. $5 Uncle Scrooge conducting stamp auction	4·00	8·00

213 William I

1986. 500th Anniv (1985) of Succession of House of Tudor to English Throne. Multicoloured.

No.	Description		
1007	10c. Type **213**	40	40
1008	40c. Richard II	80	80
1009	50c. Henry VIII	90	90
1010	$1 Charles II	1·00	1·75
1011	$2 Queen Anne	1·50	3·00
1012	$4 Queen Victoria	2·00	4·50

1986. Birth Bicentenary (1985) of John J. Audubon (ornithologist) (2nd issue). As T **312b** of Grenada showing original paintings. Multicoloured.

No.	Description		
1013	25c. Black-throated diver	1·50	50
1014	60c. Great blue heron (vert)	2·00	1·50
1015	90c. Yellow-crowned night heron (vert)	2·00	2·25
1016	$4 Common shoveler ("Shoveler Duck")	4·50	6·50
MS1017	73×103 mm. $5 Canada goose ("Goose")	10·00	12·00

1986. Royal Wedding. As T **153b** of Gambia. Multicoloured.

No.	Description		
1018	45c. Prince Andrew and Miss Sarah Ferguson	35	30
1019	50c. Prince Andrew	45	45
1020	$4 Prince Andrew climbing aboard aircraft	2·00	3·00
MS1021	88×88 mm. $5 Prince Andrew and Miss Sarah Ferguson (different)	4·25	4·75

1986. World Cup Football Championship Winners, Mexico. Nos. 983/6 optd **WINNERS Argentina 3 W. Germany 2**.

No.	Description		
1022	45c. Type **210**	1·50	55
1023	60c. Player heading ball	1·75	1·50
1024	$1 Two players competing for ball	2·25	2·50
1025	$3 Player with ball	5·00	7·00
MS1026	114×84 mm. $5 Three players	8·50	11·00

214 "Virgin at Prayer"

1986. Christmas. Paintings by Durer. Multicoloured.

No.	Description		
1027	45c. Type **214**	1·00	35
1028	60c. "Madonna and Child"	1·50	1·25
1029	$1 "Madonna of the Pear"	2·00	2·25
1030	$3 "Madonna and Child with St. Anne"	5·50	8·50
MS1031	76×102 mm. $5 "The Nativity"	8·00	11·00

214a

1986. Appearance of Halley's Comet (2nd issue). Nos. 993/6 optd as T **214a**.

No.	Description		
1032	5c. Nasir al Din al Tusi (Persian astronomer) and Jantal Mantar Observatory, Delhi	15	15
1033	10c. Bell XS-1 Rocket Plane breaking sound barrier for first time, 1947	20	15
1034	45c. Halley's Comet of 1531 (from "Astronomicum Caesareum", 1540)	55	30
1035	$4 Mark Twain and quotation, 1910	2·50	3·50
MS1036	104×71 mm. $5 Halley's Comet over Dominica	3·25	3·50

215 Broad-winged Hawk

1987. Birds of Dominica. Multicoloured.

No.	Description		
1037	1c. Type **215**	20	1·00
1038	2c. Ruddy quail dove	20	1·00
1039	5c. Red-necked pigeon	30	1·00
1040	10c. Green-backed heron ("Green Heron")	30	20
1041	15c. Moorhen ("Common Gallinule")	40	30
1042	20c. Ringed kingfisher	40	30
1043	25c. Brown pelican	40	20
1044	35c. White-tailed tropic bird	40	30
1045	45c. Red-legged thrush	50	30
1046	60c. Purple-throated carib	65	45
1047	90c. Magnificent frigate bird	70	70
1048	$1 Brown trembler ("Trembler")	80	80
1049	$2 Black-capped petrel	1·25	4·50
1050	$5 Barn owl	3·00	7·00
1051	$10 Imperial amazon ("Imperial Parrot")	5·00	12·00

1987. America's Cup Yachting Championships. As T **321b** of Grenada. Multicoloured.

No.	Description		
1052	45c. "Reliance", 1903	60	30
1053	60c. "Freedom", 1980	70	55
1054	$1 "Mischief", 1881	80	90
1055	$3 "Australia", 1977	1·25	3·00
MS1056	113×83 mm. $5 "Courageous", 1977 (horiz)	3·00	3·50

1987. Birth Centenary of Marc Chagall (artist). As T **156** of Gambia. Multicoloured.

No.	Description		
1057	25c. "Artist and His Model"	50	25
1058	35c. "Midsummer Night's Dream"	60	25
1059	45c. "Joseph the Shepherd"	70	25
1060	60c. "The Cellist"	80	30
1061	90c. "Woman with Pigs"	1·00	55
1062	$1 "The Blue Circus"	1·10	75
1063	$3 "For Vava"	2·00	2·00
1064	$4 "The Rider"	2·25	2·25
MS1065	Two sheets, each 110×95 mm. (a) $5 "Purim" (104×89 mm). (b) $5 "Firebird" (stage design) (104×89 mm) Set of 2 sheets	6·00	6·50

216 Poulsen's Triton

1987. Sea Shells.

No.	Type	Description		
1066	**216**	35c. multicoloured	20	20
1067	-	45c. violet, black and red	25	25
1068	-	60c. multicoloured	30	40
1069	-	$5 multicoloured	2·40	4·25
MS1070		109×75 mm. $5 multicoloured	3·25	5·50

DESIGNS—VERT: 45c. Elongate janthina; 60c. Banded tulip; $5 Deltoid rock shell. HORIZ: $5 (**MS**1070) Junonia volute.

No. 1066 is inscribed "TIRITON" in error.

217 "Cantharellus cinnabarinus"

1987. "Capex '87" International Stamp Exhibition, Toronto. Mushrooms of Dominica. Multicoloured.

1071	45c. Type **217**	1·50	50
1072	60c. "Boletellus cubensis"	2·00	1·25
1073	$2 "Eccilia cystiophorus"	4·25	4·50
1074	$3 "Xerocomus guadelupae"	4·50	5·00
MS1075	85×85 mm. $5 "Gymnopilus chrysopellus"	10·00	11·00

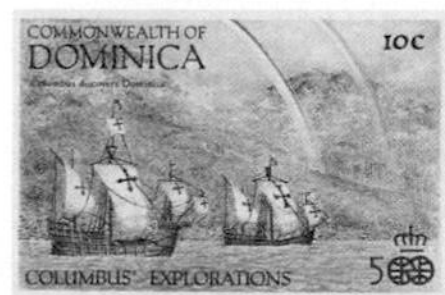

218 Discovery of Dominica, 1493

1987. 500th Anniv (1992) of Discovery of America by Columbus (1st issue). Multicoloured.

1076	10c. Type **218**	40	25
1077	15c. Caribs greeting Columbus's fleet	50	30
1078	45c. Claiming the New World for Spain	65	35
1079	60c. Wreck of "Santa Maria"	80	60
1080	90c. Fleet leaving Spain	1·00	1·00
1081	$1 Sighting the New World	1·10	1·25
1082	$3 Trading with Indians	1·75	3·00
1083	$5 Building settlement	2·75	4·00
MS1084	Two sheets, each 109×79 mm. (a) $5 Fleet off Dominica, 1493. (b) $5 Map showing Columbus's route, 1493 Set of 2 sheets	8·00	11·00

See also Nos. 1221/5, 1355/63, 1406/14, 1547/53 and 1612/13.

1987. Milestones of Transportation. As T **168** of Gambia. Multicoloured.

1085	10c. H.M.S. "Warrior" (first ironclad warship, 1860)	50	50
1086	15c. "MAGLEV-MLU 001" (fastest train), 1979	60	60
1087	25c. "Flying Cloud" (fastest clipper passage New York–San Francisco) (vert)	70	70
1088	35c. First elevated railway, New York, 1868 (vert)	80	80
1089	45c. Peter Cooper's locomotive "Tom Thumb" (first U.S. passenger locomotive), 1829	80	80
1090	60c. "Spray" (Slocum's solo, circumnavigation), 1895–98 (vert)	90	90
1091	90c. "Sea-Land Commerce" (fastest Pacific passage), 1973 (vert)	1·25	1·25
1092	$1 First cable cars, San Francisco, 1873	1·40	1·40
1093	$3 "Orient Express", 1883	3·00	3·50
1094	$4 "Clermont" (first commercial paddle-steamer), 1807	3·25	3·75

219 "Virgin and Child with St. Anne" (Durer)

1987. Christmas. Religious Paintings. Mult.

1095	20c. Type **219**	30	15
1096	25c. "Virgin and Child" (Murillo)	30	15
1097	$2 "Madonna and Child" (Foppa)	1·50	2·25
1098	$4 "Madonna and Child" (Da Verona)	2·75	4·25
MS1099	100×78 mm. $5 "Angel of the Annunciation" (anon, Renaissance period)	2·50	3·75

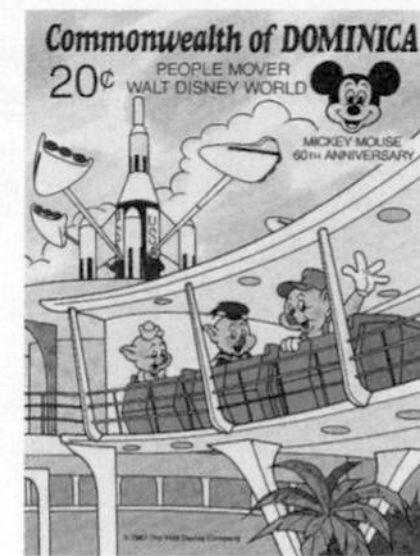

220 Three Little Pigs in People Mover, Walt Disney World

1987. 60th Anniv of Mickey Mouse (Walt Disney cartoon character). Cartoon characters in trains. Multicoloured.

1100	20c. Type **220**	45	35
1101	25c. Goofy driving horse tram, Disneyland	45	35
1102	45c. Donald Duck in "Roger E. Broggie", Walt Disney World	75	65
1103	60c. Goofy, Mickey Mouse, Donald Duck and Chip 'n Dale aboard "Big Thunder Mountain" train, Disneyland	85	75
1104	90c. Mickey Mouse in "Walter E. Disney", Disneyland	1·40	1·25
1105	$1 Mickey and Minnie Mouse, Goofy, Donald and Daisy Duck in monorail, Walt Disney World	1·50	1·40
1106	$3 Dumbo flying over "Casey Jr"	3·25	3·75
1107	$4 Daisy Duck and Minnie Mouse in "Lilly Belle", Walt Disney World	3·75	4·50
MS1108	Two sheets, each 127×101 mm. (a) $5 Seven Dwarfs in Rainbow Caverns Mine train, Disneyland (horiz). (b) $5 Donald Duck and Chip n'Dale on toy train (from film "Out of Scale" (horiz) Set of 2 sheets	5·50	7·00

1988. Royal Ruby Wedding. As T **330a** of Grenada.

1109	45c. multicoloured	70	30
1110	60c. brown, black and green	80	50
1111	$1 multicoloured	1·00	1·00
1112	$3 multicoloured	2·00	3·75
MS1113	102×76 mm. $5 multicoloured	3·00	3·75

DESIGNS: 45c. Wedding portrait with attendants, 1947; 60c. Princess Elizabeth with Prince Charles, c. 1950; $1 Princess Elizabeth and Prince Philip with Prince Charles and Princess Anne, 1950; $3 Queen Elizabeth; $5 Princess Elizabeth in wedding dress, 1947.

221 Kayak Canoeing

1988. Olympic Games, Seoul. Multicoloured.

1114	45c. Type **221**	60	25
1115	60c. Taekwon-do	80	60
1116	$1 High diving	85	1·00
1117	$3 Gymnastics on bars	1·75	3·75
MS1118	81×110 mm. $5 Football	2·50	3·50

222 Carib Indian

1988. "Reunion '88" Tourism Programme. Mult.

1119	10c. Type **222**	10	10
1120	25c. Mountainous interior (horiz)	10	15
1121	35c. Indian River	10	15
1122	60c. Belaire dancer and tourists	15	30
1123	90c. Boiling Lake	20	60
1124	$3 Coral reef (horiz)	60	2·00
MS1125	112×82 mm. $5 Belaire dancer	1·75	4·50

1988. Stamp Exhibitions. Nos. 1092/3 optd.

1126	$1 First cable cars, San Francisco, 1873 (optd **FINLANDIA 88**, Helsinki)	1·00	75
1127	$3 "Orient Express", 1883 (optd **INDEPENDENCE 40**, Israel)	2·75	2·75
MS1128	Two sheets, each 109×79 mm. (a) $5 Fleet off Dominica, 1493 (optd **OLYMPHILEX '88, Seoul**). (b) $5 Map showing Columbus's route, 1493 (optd **Praga '88, Prague**) Set of 2 sheets	4·25	5·50

223 White-tailed Tropic Bird

1988. Dominica Rain Forest Flora and Fauna. Multicoloured.

1129	45c. Type **223**	65	50
1130	45c. Blue-hooded euphonia ("Blue-throated Euphonia")	65	50
1131	45c. Smooth-billed ani	65	50
1132	45c. Scaly-breasted thrasher	65	50
1133	45c. Purple-throated carib	65	50
1134	45c. "Marpesia petreus" and "Strymon maesites" (butterflies)	65	50
1135	45c. Brown trembler ("Trembler")	65	50
1136	45c. Imperial amazon ("Imperial Parrot")	65	50
1137	45c. Mangrove cuckoo	65	50
1138	45c. "Dynastes hercules" (beetle)	65	50
1139	45c. "Historis odius" (butterfly)	65	50
1140	45c. Red-necked amazon ("Red-necked Parrot")	65	50
1141	45c. Tillandsia (plant)	65	50
1142	45c. Bananaquit and "Polystacha luteola" (plant)	65	50
1143	45c. False chameleon	65	50
1144	45c. Iguana	65	50
1145	45c. "Hypolimnas misippus" (butterfly)	65	50
1146	45c. Green-throated carib	65	50
1147	45c. Heliconia (plant)	65	50
1148	45c. Agouti	65	50

Nos. 1129/48 were printed together, se-tenant, forming a composite design.

224 Battery Hens

1988. 10th Anniv of International Fund for Agricultural Development. Multicoloured.

1149	45c. Type **224**	50	30
1150	60c. Pig	70	65
1151	90c. Cattle	95	1·25
1152	$3 Black belly sheep	2·25	4·00
MS1153	95×68 mm. $5 Tropical fruits (vert)	2·25	3·75

225 Gary Cooper

1988. Entertainers. Multicoloured.

1154	10c. Type **225**	35	25
1155	35c. Josephine Baker	40	25
1156	45c. Maurice Chevalier	45	25
1157	60c. James Cagney	60	30
1158	$1 Clark Gable	80	50
1159	$2 Louis Armstrong	1·40	1·00
1160	$3 Liberace	1·60	1·75
1161	$4 Spencer Tracy	2·00	2·25
MS1162	Two sheets, each 105×75 mm. (a) $5 Humphrey Bogart. (b) $5 Elvis Presley Set of 2 sheets	8·50	6·50

1988. Flowering Trees. As T **339** of Grenada. Multicoloured.

1163	15c. Sapodilla	10	10
1164	20c. Tangerine	10	10
1165	25c. Avocado pear	10	10
1166	45c. Amherstia	20	25
1167	90c. Lipstick tree	40	55
1168	$1 Cannonball tree	45	55
1169	$3 Saman	1·25	1·75

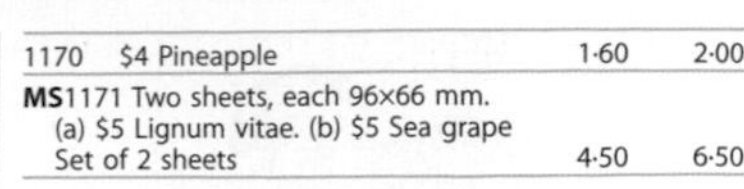

1170	$4 Pineapple	1·60	2·00
MS1171	Two sheets, each 96×66 mm. (a) $5 Lignum vitae. (b) $5 Sea grape Set of 2 sheets	4·50	6·50

1988. 500th Birth Anniv of Titian (artist). As T **166a** of Gambia. Multicoloured.

1172	25c. "Jacopo Strada"	15	15
1173	35c. "Titian's Daughter Lavinia"	20	15
1174	45c. "Andrea Navagero"	20	15
1175	60c. "Judith with Head of Holoferenes"	25	15
1176	$1 "Emilia di Spilimbergo"	40	50
1177	$2 "Martyrdom of St. Lawrence"	70	1·25
1178	$3 "Salome"	1·00	2·00
1179	$4 "St. John the Baptist"	1·25	2·25
MS1180	Two sheets, each 110×95 mm. (a) $5 "Self Portrait". (b) $5 "Sisyphus" Set of 2 sheets	6·00	7·00

226 Imperial Amazon

1988. 10th Anniv of Independence. Multicoloured.

1181	20c. Type **226**	1·50	40
1182	45c. Dominica 1874 1d. stamp and landscape (horiz)	90	30
1183	$2 1978 Independence 10c. stamp and landscape (horiz)	1·50	2·75
1184	$3 Carib wood (national flower)	1·75	3·25
MS1185	116×85 mm. $5 Government Band (horiz)	2·25	3·75

227 President and Mrs. Kennedy

1988. 25th Death Anniv of John F. Kennedy (American statesman). Multicoloured.

1186	20c. Type **227**	10	10
1187	25c. Kennedy sailing	10	10
1188	$2 Outside Hyannis Port house	80	1·50
1189	$4 Speaking in Berlin (vert)	1·60	2·50
MS1190	100×71 mm. $5 President Kennedy (vert)	2·10	3·75

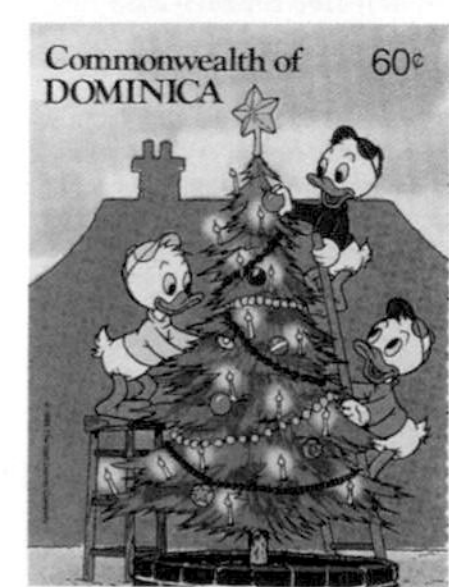

228 Donald Duck's Nephews decorating Christmas Tree

1988. Christmas. "Mickey's Christmas Mall". Walt Disney Cartoon Characters. Multicoloured.

1191	60c. Type **228**	55	65
1192	60c. Daisy Duck outside clothes shop	55	65
1193	60c. Winnie the Pooh in shop window	55	65
1194	60c. Goofy with parcels	55	65
1195	60c. Donald Duck as Father Christmas	55	65
1196	60c. Mickey Mouse contributing to collection	55	65
1197	60c. Minnie Mouse	55	65
1198	60c. Chip n' Dale with peanut	55	65
MS1199	Two sheets, each 127×102 mm. (a) $6 Mordie Mouse with Father Christmas. (b) $6 Mickey Mouse at West Indian market Set of 2 sheets	6·50	8·00

Nos. 1191/8 were printed together, se-tenant, forming a composite design.

229 Raoul Wallenberg (diplomat) and Swedish Flag

1988. 40th Anniv of Universal Declaration of Human Rights. Multicoloured.
1200 $3 Type **229** 2·00 2·50
MS1201 92×62 mm. $5 Human Rights Day logo (vert) 3·00 3·50

230 Greater Amberjack

1988. Game Fishes. Multicoloured.
1202 10c. Type **230** 20 15
1203 15c. Blue marlin 20 15
1204 35c. Cobia 35 30
1205 45c. Dolphin (fish) 45 30
1206 60c. Cero 60 55
1207 90c. Mahogany snapper 85 95
1208 $3 Yellow-finned tuna 2·00 2·75
1209 $4 Rainbow parrotfish 2·75 3·50
MS1210 Two sheets, each 104×74 mm. (a) $5 Manta. (b) $5 Tarpon Set of 2 sheets 11·00 11·00

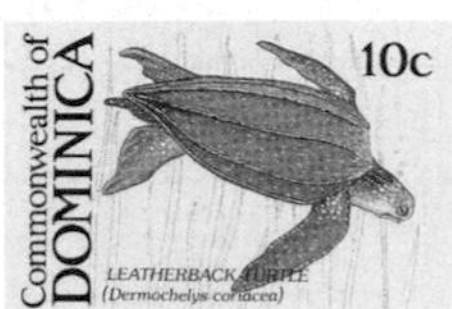

231 Leatherback Turtle

1988. Insects and Reptiles. Multicoloured.
1211 10c. Type **231** 45 35
1212 25c. "Danaus plexippus" (butterfly) 1·25 75
1213 60c. Green anole (lizard) 1·60 1·25
1214 $3 "Mantis religiosa" (mantid) 4·00 6·50
MS1215 119×90 mm. $5 "Dynastes hercules" (beetle) 3·00 4·50

1989. Olympic Medal Winners, Seoul. Nos. 1114/17 optd.
1216 45c. Type **221** (optd **Men's C-1, 500m O. Heukrodt DDR**) 20 25
1217 60c. Taekwon-do (optd **Women's Flyweight N. Y. Choo S. Korea**) 25 35
1218 $1 High diving (optd **Women's Platform Y. Xu China**) 40 60
1219 $3 Gymnastics on bars (optd **V. Artemov USSR**) 1·25 2·25
MS1220 81×110 mm. $5 Football (optd **USSR defeated Brazil 3–2 on penalty kicks after a 1–1 tie**) 3·50 4·00

1989. 500th Anniv (1992) of Discovery of America by Columbus (2nd issue). Pre-Columbian Carib Society. As T **97a** of Grenadines of Grenada but horiz. Multicoloured.
1221 20c. Carib canoe 20 20
1222 35c. Hunting with bows and arrows 30 20
1223 $1 Dugout canoe making 70 90
1224 $3 Shield contest 1·75 3·00
MS1225 87×71 mm. $6 Ceremonial dress 2·75 4·00

233 Map of Dominica, 1766

1989. "Philexfrance '89" International Stamp Exhibition, Paris. Multicoloured.
1226 10c. Type **233** 1·00 55
1227 35c. French coin of 1653 (horiz) 1·00 40
1228 $1 French warship, 1720 (horiz) 1·75 1·25
1229 $4 Coffee plant (horiz) 2·25 3·50
MS1230 98×98 mm. $5 Exhibition inscription (horiz) (black, grey and yellow) 3·00 4·00

1989. Japanese Art. Paintings by Taikan. As T **178a** of Gambia, but vert. Multicoloured.
1231 10c. "Lao-tzu" (detail) 10 10
1232 20c. "Red Maple Leaves" (panels 1 and 2) 10 10
1233 45c. "King Wen Hui learns a Lesson from his Cook" (detail) 20 25
1234 60c. "Red Maple Leaves" (panels 3 and 4) 25 35
1235 $1 "Wild Flowers" (detail) 45 50
1236 $2 "Red Maple Leaves" (panels 5 and 6) 85 1·10
1237 $3 "Red Maple Leaves" (panels 7 and 8) 1·00 1·60
1238 $4 "Indian Ceremony of Floating Lamps on the River" (detail) 1·25 2·00
MS1239 Two sheets. (a) 78×102 mm. $5 "Innocence" (detail). (b) 101×77 mm. $5 "Red Maple Leaves" (detail) Set of 2 sheets 4·75 5·75

234 "Papilio homerus"

1989. Butterflies. Multicoloured.
1255 10c. Type **234** 40 30
1256 15c. "Morpho peleides" 45 30
1257 25c. "Dryas julia" 65 30
1258 35c. "Parides gundlachianus" 70 30
1259 60c. "Danaus plexippus" 1·00 75
1260 $1 "Agraulis vanillae" 1·25 1·25
1261 $3 "Phoebis avellaneda" 2·75 3·25
1262 $5 "Papilio andraemon" 3·75 5·00
MS1263 Two sheets. (a) 105×74 mm. $6 "Adelpha cytherea". (b) 105×79 mm. $6 "Adelpha iphicala" Set of 2 sheets 8·00 9·00

235 "Oncidium pusillum"

1989. Orchids. Multicoloured.
1264 10c. Type **235** 35 30
1265 35c. "Epidendrum cochleata" 70 30
1266 45c. "Epidendrum ciliare" 75 40
1267 60c. "Cyrtopodium andersonii" 1·00 80
1268 $1 "Habenaria pauciflora" 1·25 1·25
1269 $2 "Maxillaria alba" 2·00 2·25
1270 $3 "Selenipedium palmifolium" 2·50 2·75
1271 $4 "Brassavola cucullata" 3·25 3·75
MS1272 Two sheets, each 108×77 mm. (a) $5 "Oncidium lanceanum". (b) $5 "Comparettia falcata" Set of 2 sheets 8·00 9·00

236 "Apollo 11" Command Module in Lunar Orbit

1989. 20th Anniv of First Manned Landing on Moon. Multicoloured.
1273 10c. Type **236** 30 30
1274 60c. Neil Armstrong leaving lunar module 70 70
1275 $2 Edwin Aldrin at Sea of Tranquility 1·60 2·00
1276 $3 Astronauts Armstrong and Aldrin with U.S. flag 2·00 2·50
MS1277 62×77 mm. $6 Launch of "Apollo 11" (vert) 4·50 6·00

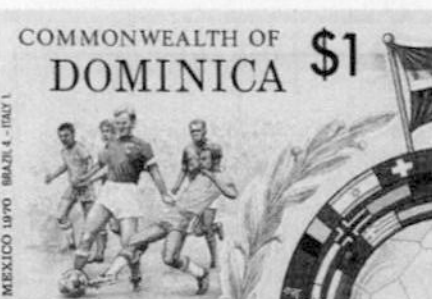

237 Brazil v Italy Final, 1970

1989. World Cup Football Championship, Italy (1st issue). Multicoloured.
1278 $1 Type **237** 2·00 2·25
1279 $1 England v West Germany, 1966 2·00 2·25
1280 $1 West Germany v Holland, 1974 2·00 2·25
1281 $1 Italy v West Germany, 1982 2·00 2·25
MS1282 106×86 mm. $6 Two players competing for ball 4·00 4·75

Nos. 1278/81 were printed together, se-tenant, forming a composite central design of a football surrounded by flags of competing nations.

See also Nos. 1383/7.

238 George Washington and Inauguration, 1789

1989. "World Stamp Expo '89" International Stamp Exhibition, Washington. Bicentenary of U.S. Presidency. Multicoloured.
1283 60c. Type **238** 90 80
1284 60c. John Adams and Presidential Mansion, 1800 90 80
1285 60c. Thomas Jefferson, Graff House, Philadelphia and Declaration of Independence 90 80
1286 60c. James Madison and U.S.S. "Constitution" defeating H.M.S. "Guerriere", 1812 90 80
1287 60c. James Monroe and freed slaves landing in Liberia 90 80
1288 60c. John Quincy Adams and barge on Erie Canal 90 80
1289 60c. Millard Fillmore and Perry's fleet off Japan 90 80
1290 60c. Franklin Pierce, Jefferson Davis and San Xavier Mission, Tucson 90 80
1291 60c. James Buchanan, "Buffalo Bill" Cody carrying mail and Wells Fargo Pony Express stamp 90 80
1292 60c. Abraham Lincoln and U.P.U. Monument, Berne 90 80
1293 60c. Andrew Johnson, polar bear and Mount McKinley, Alaska 90 80
1294 60c. Ulysses S. Grant and Golden Spike Ceremony, 1869 90 80
1295 60c. Theodore Roosevelt and steam shovel excavating Panama Canal 90 80
1296 60c. William H. Taft and Admiral Peary at North Pole 90 80
1297 60c. Woodrow Wilson and Curtis "Jenny" on first scheduled airmail flight, 1918 90 80
1298 60c. Warren G. Harding and airship U.S.S. "Shenandoah" at Lakehurst 90 80
1299 60c. Calvin Coolidge and Lindbergh's "Spirit of St Louis" on trans-Atlantic flight 90 80
1300 60c. Mount Rushmore National Monument 90 80
1301 60c. Lyndon B. Johnson and Earth from Moon as seen by "Apollo 8" crew 90 80
1302 60c. Richard Nixon and visit to Great Wall of China 90 80
1303 60c. Gerald Ford and "Gorch Fock" (German cadet barque) at Bicentenary of Revolution celebrations 90 80
1304 60c. Jimmy Carter and President Sadat of Egypt with Prime Minister Begin of Israel 90 80
1305 60c. Ronald Reagan and space shuttle "Columbia" 90 80
1306 60c. George Bush and Grumman TBF Avenger (fighter-bomber) 90 80

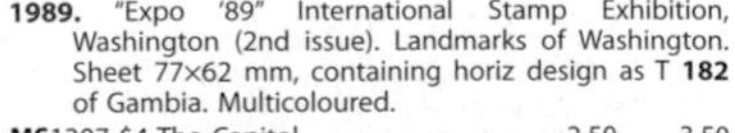

1989. "Expo '89" International Stamp Exhibition, Washington (2nd issue). Landmarks of Washington. Sheet 77×62 mm, containing horiz design as T **182** of Gambia. Multicoloured.
MS1307 $4 The Capitol 2·50 3·50

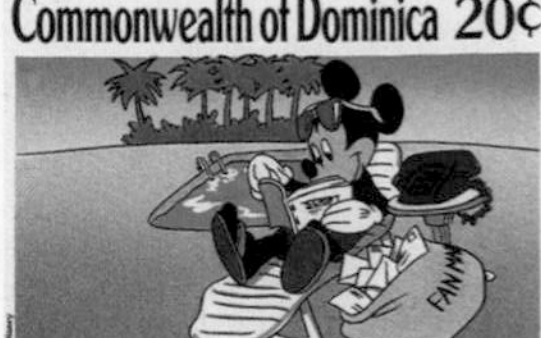

239 Mickey Mouse reading Script

1989. Mickey Mouse in Hollywood (Walt Disney cartoon character). Multicoloured.
1308 20c. Type **239** 45 40
1309 35c. Mickey Mouse giving interview 60 55
1310 45c. Mickey and Minnie Mouse with newspaper and magazines 70 65
1311 60c. Mickey Mouse signing autographs 80 75
1312 $1 Trapped in dressing room 1·40 1·25
1313 $2 Mickey and Minnie Mouse with Pluto in limousine 2·25 2·50
1314 $3 Arriving at Awards ceremony 2·50 2·75
1315 $4 Mickey Mouse accepting award 2·50 2·75
MS1316 Two sheets, each 127×102 mm. (a) $5 Mickey Mouse leaving footprints at cinema. (b) $5 Goofy interviewing Set of 2 sheets 7·50 9·50

1989. Christmas. Paintings by Botticelli. As T **352a** of Grenada. Multicoloured.
1317 20c. "Madonna in Glory with Seraphim" 40 30
1318 25c. "The Annunciation" 40 30
1319 35c. "Madonna of the Pomegranate" 55 40
1320 45c. "Madonna of the Rose-garden" 65 45
1321 60c. "Madonna of the Book" 80 60
1322 $1 "Madonna under a Baldachin" 1·00 90
1323 $4 "Madonna and Child with Angels" 2·50 4·50
1324 $5 "Bardi Madonna" 2·75 4·75
MS1325 Two sheets, each 71×96 mm. (a) $5 "The Mystic Nativity". (b) $5 "The Adoration of the Magi" Set of 2 sheets 7·00 9·00

240 Lady Olave Baden-Powell and Agatha Robinson (Guide leaders)

1989. 60th Anniv of Girl Guides in Dominica. Multicoloured.
1326 60c. Type **240** 1·00 1·00
MS1327 70×99 mm. $5 Doris Stockmann and Judith Pestaina (horiz) 3·50 4·00

241 Jawaharal Nehru

1989. Birth Centenary of Jawaharal Nehru (Indian statesman). Multicoloured.
1328 60c. Type **241** 1·50 1·25
MS1329 101×72 mm. $5 Parliament House, New Delhi (horiz) 3·50 4·00

242 Cocoa Damselfish

1990. Tropical Fishes. Multicoloured.
1330 45c. Type **242** 45 55
1331 45c. Stinging jellyfish 45 55
1332 45c. Dolphin (fish) 45 55

1333 45c. Atlantic spadefish and queen angelfish 45 55
1334 45c. French angelfish 45 55
1335 45c. Blue-striped grunt 45 55
1336 45c. Porkfish 45 55
1337 45c. Great hammerhead 45 55
1338 45c. Atlantic spadefish 45 55
1339 45c. Great barracuda 45 55
1340 45c. Southern stingray 45 55
1341 45c. Black grunt 45 55
1342 45c. Spot-finned butterflyfish 45 55
1343 45c. Dog snapper 45 55
1344 45c. Band-tailed puffer 45 55
1345 45c. Four-eyed butterflyfish 45 55
1346 45c. Lane snapper 45 55
1347 45c. Green moray 45 55

Nos. 1330/47 were printed together, se-tenant, forming a composite design.

243 St. Paul's Cathedral, London, c. 1840

1990. 150th Anniv of the Penny Black and "Stamp World London 90" International Stamp Exhibition.

1348 **243** 45c. green and black 55 25
1349 - 50c. blue and black 75 35
1350 - 60c. blue and black 75 45
1351 - 90c. green and black 1·40 85
1352 - $3 blue and black 3·50 3·50
1353 - $4 blue and black 3·50 3·50
MS1354 Two sheets. (a) 103×79 mm. $5 ochre and black. (b) 85×86 mm. $5 red and brown Set of 2 sheets 6·50 7·50

DESIGNS: 50c. British Post Office "accelerator" carriage, 1830; 60c. St. Paul's and City of London; 90c. Travelling post office, 1838; $3 "Hen and chickens" delivery cycle, 1883; $4 London skyline; $5 (a) Type **243**; (b) Motor mail van, 1899.

1990. 500th Anniv (1992) of Discovery of America by Columbus (3rd issue). New World Natural History—Seashells. As T **354a** of Grenada. Mult.

1355 10c. Reticulated cowrie-helmet 30 30
1356 20c. West Indian chank 40 40
1357 35c. West Indian fighting conch 50 35
1358 60c. True tulip 75 60
1359 $1 Sunrise tellin 1·00 1·00
1360 $2 Crown cone 1·75 2·75
1361 $3 Common dove shell 2·50 3·50
1362 $4 Common or Atlantic fig shell 2·75 3·50
MS1363 Two sheets, each 103×70 mm. (a) $5 King helmet. (b) $6 Giant tun Set of 2 sheets 6·50 8·00

244 Blue-headed Hummingbird

1990. Birds. Multicoloured.

1364 10c. Type **244** 35 35
1365 20c. Black-capped petrel 45 45
1366 45c. Red-necked amazon ("Red-necked Parrot") 65 40
1367 60c. Black swift 80 70
1368 $1 Troupial 1·25 1·25
1369 $2 Common noddy ("Brown Noddy") 2·00 2·50
1370 $4 Lesser Antillean pewee 3·25 3·50
1371 $5 Little blue heron 3·75 4·25
MS1372 Two sheets, each 103×70 mm. (a) $6 Imperial amazon. (b) $6 House wren Set of 2 sheets 7·00 8·50

244a Queen Elizabeth the Queen Mother

1990. 90th Birthday of Queen Elizabeth the Queen Mother. As T **244a**.

1373 **244a** 20c. multicoloured 20 15
1374 - 45c. multicoloured 35 25
1375 - 60c. multicoloured 60 60
1376 - $3 multicoloured 2·25 3·00
MS1377 80×90 mm. $5 multicoloured 2·75 3·75

DESIGNS: 45c. to $5, Recent photographs of Queen Mother.

1990. Olympic Games, Barcelona (1992) (1st issue). As T **195a** of Gambia. Multicoloured.

1378 45c. Tennis 1·25 40
1379 60c. Fencing 1·25 50
1380 $2 Swimming 2·00 3·25
1381 $3 Yachting 2·50 3·75
MS1382 100×70 mm. $5 Boxing 4·25 6·00

See also Nos. 1603/11.

245 Barnes, England

1990. World Cup Football Championship, Italy (2nd issue). Multicoloured.

1383 15c. Type **245** 40 30
1384 45c. Romario, Brazil 70 30
1385 60c. Franz Beckenbauer, West Germany manager 85 70
1386 $4 Lindenberger, Austria 3·25 5·00
MS1387 Two sheets, each 105×90 mm. (a) $6 McGrath, Ireland (vert). (b) $6 Litovchenko, Soviet Union (vert) Set of 2 sheets 7·50 10·00

246 Mickey Mouse riding Herschell-Spillman Frog

1990. Christmas. Walt Disney cartoon characters and American carousel animals. Multicoloured.

1388 10c. Type **246** 40 20
1389 15c. Huey, Dewey and Louie on Allan Herschell elephant 50 25
1390 25c. Donald Duck on Allan Herschell polar bear 60 30
1391 45c. Goofy on Dentzel goat 90 30
1392 $1 Donald Duck on Zalar giraffe 1·25 1·00
1393 $2 Daisy Duck on Herschell-Spillman stork 2·00 2·75
1394 $4 Goofy on Dentzel lion 3·25 4·50
1395 $5 Daisy Duck on Stein and Goldstein palomino stander 3·50 4·50
MS1396 Two sheets, each 127×101 mm. (a) $6 Mickey, Morty and Ferdie Mouse on Philadelphia Toboggan Company swan chariot (horiz). (b) $6 Mickey and Minnie Mouse with Goofy on Philadelphia Toboggan Company winged griffin chariot Set of 2 sheets 12·00 14·00

246a Steam locomotive, Glion-Roches De Naye Rack Railway, 1890

1991. Cog Railways.

1397 10c. Type **246a** 65 40
1398 35c. Electric railcar, Mt. Pilatus rack railway 1·00 30
1399 45c. Schynige Platte rack railway train 1·10 30
1400 60c. Steam train on Bugnli Viaduct, Furka–Oberalp rack railway (vert) 1·40 55
1401 $1 Jungfrau rack railway train, 1910 1·75 1·25
1402 $2 Testing Pike's Peak railcar, Switzerland, 1983 2·25 2·25
1403 $4 Brienz–Rothorn railway locomotive, 1991 2·75 3·25
1404 $5 Steam locomotive, Arth-Rigi, 1890 2·75 3·25
MS1405 Two sheets. (a) 100×70 mm. $6 Swiss Europa stamps of 1983 showing Riggenbach's locomotive of 1871 (50×37 mm). (b) 90×68 mm. $6 Brunig line train and Sherlock Holmes (50×37 mm) Set of 2 sheets 9·50 10·00

1991. 500th Anniv (1992) of Discovery of America by Columbus (4th issue). History of Exploration. As T **363a** of Grenada. Multicoloured.

1406 10c. Gil Eannes sailing south of Cape Bojador, 1433–34 25 25
1407 25c. Alfonso Baldaya sailing south to Cape Blanc, 1436 35 35
1408 45c. Bartolomeu Dias round the Southern Tip of Africa, 1487 45 35
1409 60c. Vasco da Gama on voyage to India, 1497–99 55 50
1410 $1 Vallarte the Dane off African coast 75 90
1411 $2 Aloisio Cadamosto in Cape Verde Islands, 1456–58 1·40 2·00
1412 $4 Diogo Gomes on River Gambia, 1457 2·75 3·75
1413 $5 Diogo Cao off African coast, 1482–85 3·25 4·00
MS1414 Two sheets, each 105×71 mm. (a) $6 Green-winged macaw and bow of "Santa Maria". (b) $6 Blue and yellow macaw and caravel Set of 2 sheets 7·50 8·50

1991. "Phila Nippon '91" International Stamp Exhibition, Tokyo. As T **198c** of Gambia. Mult.

1415 10c. Donald Duck as Shogun's guard (horiz) 60 20
1416 15c. Mickey Mouse as Kabuki actor (horiz) 70 25
1417 25c. Minnie and Mickey Mouse as bride and groom (horiz) 85 25
1418 45c. Daisy Duck as geisha 1·00 25
1419 $1 Mickey Mouse in Sokutai court dress 2·00 1·00
1420 $2 Goofy as Mino farmer 2·50 2·75
1421 $4 Pete as Shogun 3·75 4·00
1422 $5 Donald Duck as Samurai (horiz) 3·75 4·25
MS1423 Two sheets, each 127×112 mm. (a) $6 Mickey Mouse as Noh actor. (b) $6 Goofy as Kabubei-jishi dancer Set of 2 sheets 14·00 14·00

247 "Craterellus cornucopioides"

1991. Fungi. Multicoloured.

1424 10c. Type **247** 25 25
1425 15c. "Coprinus comatus" 50 25
1426 45c. "Morchella esculenta" 50 25
1427 60c. "Cantharellus cibarius" 60 30
1428 $1 "Lepista nuda" 80 70
1429 $2 "Suillus luteus" 1·40 1·75
1430 $4 "Russula emetica" 2·25 2·75
1431 $5 "Armillaria mellea" 2·25 2·75
MS1432 Two sheets, each 100×70 mm. (a) $6 "Fistulina hepatica". (b) $6 "Lactarius volemus" Set of 2 sheets 8·00 9·00

1991. 65th Birthday of Queen Elizabeth II. As T **198a** of Gambia. Multicoloured.

1433 10c. Queen and Prince William on Buckingham Palace Balcony, 1990 40 20
1434 60c. The Queen at Westminster Abbey, 1988 95 50
1435 $2 The Queen and Prince Philip in Italy, 1990 2·00 2·00
1436 $5 The Queen at Ascot, 1986 3·00 3·00
MS1437 68×90 mm. $5 Separate portraits of Queen and Prince Philip 4·00 4·50

1991. 10th Wedding Anniv of Prince and Princess of Wales. As T **198a** of Gambia. Multicoloured.

1438 15c. Prince and Princess of Wales in West Germany, 1987 80 30
1439 40c. Separate photographs of Prince, Princess and sons 1·50 50
1440 $1 Separate photographs of Prince William and Prince Henry 2·25 2·50
1441 $4 Prince Charles at Caister and Princess Diana in Thailand 5·00 4·50
MS1442 68×90 mm. $5 Prince Charles, and Princess Diana with sons on holiday 8·75 7·00

1991. Death Centenary (1990) of Vincent van Gogh (artist). As T **200b** of Gambia. Multicoloured.

1443 10c. "Thatched Cottages" (horiz) 65 30
1444 25c. "The House of Pere Eloi" (horiz) 90 30
1445 45c. "The Midday Siesta" (horiz) 1·10 30
1446 60c. "Portrait of a Young Peasant" 1·40 35
1447 $1 "Still Life: Vase with Irises against Yellow Background" 2·00 1·10
1448 $2 "Still Life: Vase with Irises" (horiz) 2·50 2·75
1449 $4 "Blossoming Almond Tree" (horiz) 3·25 4·00
1450 $5 "Irises" (horiz) 3·25 4·00
MS1451 Two sheets. (a) 77×102 mm. $6 "Doctor Gachet's Garden in Auvers". (b) 102×77 mm. $6 "A Meadow in the Mountains: Le Mas de Saint-Paul" (horiz). Imperf Set of 2 sheets 11·00 12·00

247a Ariel, Flounder and Sebastian (horiz)

1991. International Literacy Year (1990). Scenes from Disney cartoon film "The Little Mermaid". Multicoloured.

1452 10c. Type **247a** 30 25
1453 25c. King Triton (horiz) 45 30
1454 45c. Sebastian playing drums (horiz) 60 30
1455 60c. Flotsam and Jetsam taunting Ariel (horiz) 85 55
1456 $1 Scuttle, Flounder and Ariel with pipe (horiz) 1·25 1·00
1457 $2 Ariel and Flounder discovering book (horiz) 2·00 2·00
1458 $4 Prince Eric and crew (horiz) 3·25 3·50
1459 $5 Ursula the Sea Witch (horiz) 3·50 4·00
MS1460 Two sheets, each 127×102 mm. (a) $6 Ariel without tail (horiz). (b) $6 Ariel and Prince Eric dancing Set of 2 sheets 8·50 10·00

248 Empire State Building, New York

1991. World Landmarks. Multicoloured.

1461 10c. Type **248** 40 30
1462 25c. Kremlin, Moscow (horiz) 40 30
1463 45c. Buckingham Palace, London (horiz) 70 30
1464 60c. Eiffel Tower, Paris 85 60
1465 $1 Taj Mahal, Agra (horiz) 3·75 1·75
1466 $2 Opera House, Sydney (horiz) 5·00 3·25
1467 $4 Colosseum, Rome (horiz) 3·75 4·25
1468 $5 Pyramids, Giza (horiz) 4·25 4·50
MS1469 Two sheets, each 100×68 mm. (a) $6 Galileo on Leaning Tower, Pisa (horiz). (b) $6 Emperor Shi Huang and Great Wall of China (horiz) Set of 2 sheets 14·00 14·00

249 Aichi D3A "VAL" bomber leaving Carrier "Akagi"

1991. 50th Anniv of Japanese Attack on Pearl Harbor. Multicoloured.

1470 10c. Type **249** 65 50

1471 15c. U.S.S. "Ward" (destroyer) and Consolidated Catalina PBY-5 flying boat attacking midget submarine 70 40
1472 45c. Second wave of Mitsubishi A6M Zero-Sen aircraft leaving carriers 95 35
1473 60c. Japanese Mitsubishi M6M Zero-Sen aircraft attacking Kaneche naval airfield 1·25 50
1474 $1 U.S.S. "Breeze", "Medusa" and "Curtiss" (destroyers) sinking midget submarine 1·40 90
1475 $2 U.S.S. "Nevada" (battleship) under attack 1·75 1·75
1476 $4 U.S.S. "Arizona" (battleship) sinking 2·50 3·00
1477 $5 Mitsubishi A6M Zero-Sen aircraft 2·50 3·00
MS1478 Two sheets, each 118×78 mm. (a) $6 Mitsubishi A6M Zero-Sen over anchorage. (b) $6 Mitsubishi A6M Zero-Sen attacking Hickam airfield Set of 2 sheets 8·00 8·50

250 "Eurema venusta"

1991. Butterflies. Multicoloured.
1479 1c. Type **250** 40 80
1480 2c. "Agraulis vanillae" 40 80
1481 5c. "Danaus plexippus" 60 80
1482 10c. "Biblis hyperia" 60 15
1483 15c. "Dryas julia" 70 15
1484 20c. "Phoebis agarithe" 70 20
1485 25c. "Junonia genoveva" 70 20
1486 35c. "Battus polydamas" 80 30
1487 45c. "Leptotes cassius" 80 30
1487a 55c. "Ascia monuste" 1·10 55
1488 60c. "Anaea dominicana" 90 35
1488a 65c. "Hemiargus hanno" 1·10 55
1489 90c. "Hypolimnas misippus" 1·25 55
1490 $1 "Urbanus proteus" 1·25 60
1490a $1.20 "Historis odius" 1·40 1·50
1491 $2 "Phoebis sennae" 2·00 2·25
1492 $5 "Cynthia cardui" ("Vanessa cardui") 3·00 4·75
1493 $10 "Marpesia petreus" 6·00 8·00
1494 $20 "Anartia jatrophae" 11·00 14·00

250a De Gaulle in Uniform

1991. Birth Centenary (1990) of Charles De Gaulle (French statesman).
1495 **250a** 45c. brown 1·75 75
MS1496 70×100 mm. $5 brown and blue 4·75 5·50
DESIGN: $5 De Gaulle in uniform.

251 Symbolic Cheque

1992. 40th Anniv of Credit Union Bank.
1497 **251** 10c. grey and black 40 30
1498 - 60c. multicoloured 1·40 95
DESIGN—HORIZ: 60c. Credit Union symbol.

252 "18th-Century Creole Dress" (detail) (Agostino Brunias)

1991. Creole Week. Multicoloured.
1499 45c. Type **252** 80 25
1500 60c. Jing Ping band 1·00 60
1501 $1 Creole dancers 1·40 1·90
MS1502 100×70 mm. $5 "18th-century Stick-fighting Match" (detail) (Agostino Brunias) (horiz) 4·25 6·00

253 Island Beach

1991. Year of Environment and Shelter. Mult.
1503 15c. Type **253** 25 15
1504 60c. Imperial amazon 3·50 1·50
MS1505 Two sheets. (a) 100×70 mm. $5 River estuary. (b) 70×100 mm. $5 As 60c. Set of 2 sheets 14·00 14·00

1991. Christmas. Religious Paintings by Jan van Eyck. As T **200c** of Gambia. Multicoloured.
1506 10c. "Virgin Enthroned with Child" (detail) 70 30
1507 20c. "Madonna at the Fountain" 85 30
1508 35c. "Virgin in a Church" 1·00 30
1509 45c. "Madonna with Canon van der Paele" 1·10 30
1510 60c. "Madonna with Canon van der Paele" (detail) 1·75 60
1511 $1 "Madonna in an Interior" 2·00 1·00
1512 $3 "The Annunciation" 3·25 4·50
1513 $5 "The Annunciation" (different) 4·50 7·00
MS1514 Two sheets, each 102×127 mm. (a) $5 "Virgin and Child with Saints and Donor". (b) $5 "Madonna with Chancellor Rolin" Set of 2 sheets 13·00 14·00

1992. 40th Anniv of Queen Elizabeth II's Accession. As T **202a** of Gambia. Multicoloured.
1515 10c. Coastline 20 20
1516 15c. Mountains overlooking small village 20 20
1517 $1 River estuary 1·00 70
1518 $5 Waterfall 4·00 4·00
MS1519 Two sheets, each 74×97 mm. (a) $6 Roseau. (b) $6 Mountain stream Set of 2 sheets 8·00 8·50

254 Cricket Match

1992. Centenary (1991) of Botanical Gardens. Multicoloured.
1520 10c. Type **254** 2·00 70
1521 15c. Scenic entrance 40 20
1522 45c. Traveller's tree 40 25
1523 60c. Bamboo House 55 30
1524 $1 The Old Pavilion 80 70
1525 $2 "Ficus benjamina" 1·40 2·00
1526 $4 Cricket match (different) 5·50 3·75
1527 $5 Thirty-five Steps 3·00 3·75
MS1528 Two sheets, each 104×71 mm. (a) $6 Past and present members of national cricket team. (b) $6 The Fountain Set of 2 sheets 8·00 9·00

1992. Easter. Religious Paintings. As T **204a** of Gambia. Multicoloured.
1529 10c. "The Supper at Emmaus" (Van Honthorst) 20 20
1530 15c. "Christ before Caiaphas" (Van Honthorst) (vert) 25 25
1531 45c. "The Taking of Christ" (De Boulogne) 40 30
1532 60c. "Pilate washing his Hands" (Preti) (vert) 55 45
1533 $1 "The Last Supper" (detail) (Master of the Church of S. Francisco d'Evora) 75 75
1534 $2 "The Three Marys at the Tomb" (detail) (Bouguereau) (vert) 1·50 2·00
1535 $3 "Denial of St. Peter" (Terbrugghen) 1·75 2·50
1536 $5 "Doubting Thomas" (Strozzi) 2·75 3·75
MS1537 Two sheets, each 72×102 mm. (a) $6 "The Crucifixion" (detail) (Grünewald) (vert). (b) $6 "The Resurrection" (detail) (Caravaggio) (vert) Set of 2 sheets 7·50 8·50

1992. "Granada '92" International Stamp Exhibition, Spain. Art of Diego Rodriguez Velasquez. As T **481a** of Ghana. Mult.
1538 10c. "Pope Innocent X" (detail) 15 10
1539 15c. "The Forge of Vulcan" (detail) 20 10
1540 45c. "The Forge of Vulcan" (different detail) 40 25
1541 60c. "Queen Mariana of Austria" (detail) 50 30
1542 $1 "Pablo de Valladolid" 80 70
1543 $2 "Sebastian de Morra" 1·25 1·60
1544 $3 "King Felipe IV" (detail) 1·60 2·25
1545 $4 "King Felipe IV" 1·75 2·40
MS1546 Two sheets, each 120×95 mm. (a) $6 "The Drunkards" (110×81 mm). (b) $6 "Surrender of Breda" (110×81 mm). Imperf Set of 2 sheets 7·00 8·00

255 Columbus and "Dynastes hercules" (beetle)

1992. 500th Anniv of Discovery of America by Columbus (5th issue). World Columbian Stamp "Expo '92", Chicago. Multicoloured.
1547 10c. Type **255** 75 30
1548 25c. Columbus and "Leptodactylus fallax" (frog) 1·40 25
1549 75c. Columbus and red-necked amazon (bird) 3·50 1·00
1550 $2 Columbus and "Ameiva fuscata" (lizard) 2·25 2·25
1551 $4 Columbus and royal gramma (fish) 2·50 3·25
1552 $5 Columbus and "Rosa sinensis" (flower) 2·50 3·25
MS1553 Two sheets, each 100×67 mm. (a) $6 Ships of Columbus (horiz). (b) $6 "Mastophyllum scabricolle" (katydid) (horiz) Set of 2 sheets 7·00 8·00

1992. "Genova '92" International Thematic Stamp Exhibition. Hummingbirds. As T **370a** of Grenada. Multicoloured.
1554 10c. Female purple-throated carib 80 25
1555 15c. Female rufous-breasted hermit 80 25
1556 45c. Male Puerto Rican emerald 1·25 30
1557 60c. Female Antillean mango 1·50 45
1558 $1 Male green-throated carib 1·75 85
1559 $2 Male blue-headed hummingbird 2·25 2·25
1560 $4 Female eastern streamertail 3·00 3·25
1561 $5 Female Antillean crested hummingbird 3·00 3·25
MS1562 Two sheets, each 105×72 mm. (a) $6 Jamaican Mango ("Green Mango"). (b) $6 Vervain hummingbird Set of 2 sheets 10·00 11·00

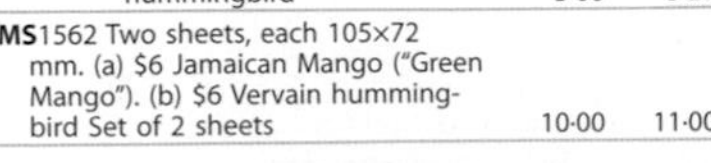

255a Head of Camptosaurus

1992. Prehistoric Animals. Multicoloured.
1563 10c. Type **255a** 80 30
1564 15c. Edmontosaurus 85 30
1565 25c. Corythosaurus 95 30
1566 60c. Stegosaurus 1·60 40
1567 $1 Torosaurus 2·00 1·00
1568 $3 Euoplocephalus 2·50 3·00
1569 $4 Tyrannosaurus 3·00 3·25
1570 $5 Parasaurolophus 3·00 3·25
MS1571 Two sheets, each 100×70 mm. (a) $6 As 25c. (b) $6 As $1 Set of 2 sheets 7·50 8·50

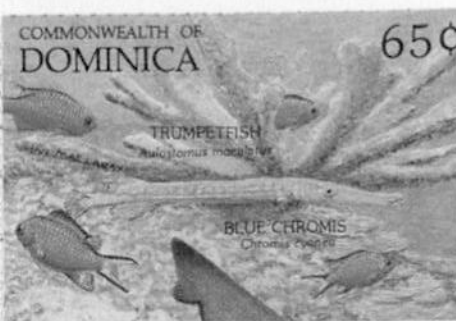

256 Trumpetfish and Blue Chromis

1992. Marine Life. Multicoloured.
1572- 65c.×30. As Type **256**
1601 14·00 15·00
MS1602 Two sheets, each 73×105 mm. (a) $6 multicoloured (Harlequin bass). (b) $6 multicoloured (Flamefish) Set of 2 sheets 9·50 11·00

1992. Olympic Games, Barcelona (2nd issue). As T **372** of Grenada. Multicoloured.
1603 10c. Archery 30 25
1604 15c. Two-man canoeing 35 25
1605 25c. Men's 110 m hurdles 40 25
1606 60c. Men's high jump 70 30
1607 $1 Greco-Roman wrestling 1·00 65
1608 $2 Men's gymnastics—rings 1·50 2·00
1609 $4 Men's gymnastics—parallel bars 2·75 3·25
1610 $5 Equestrian dressage 3·50 3·50
MS1611 Two sheets, each 100×70 mm. (a) $6 Women's platform diving. (b) $6 Men's hockey Set of 2 sheets 8·50 10·00

1992. 500th Anniv of Discovery of America by Columbus (6th issue). Organization of East Caribbean States. T **372a** of Grenada. Multicoloured.
1612 $1 Columbus meeting Amerindians 65 65
1613 $2 Ships approaching island 1·10 1·25

1992. Hummel Figurines. As T **501a** of Ghana. Multicoloured.
1614 20c. Angel playing violin 40 15
1615 25c. Angel playing recorder 40 15
1616 55c. Angel playing lute 65 30
1617 65c. Seated angel playing trumpet 75 35
1618 90c. Angel on cloud with lantern 1·00 65
1619 $1 Angel with candle 1·10 70
1620 $1.20 Flying angel with Christmas tree 1·25 1·25
1621 $6 Angel on cloud with candle 3·75 6·00
MS1622 Two sheets, each 97×127 mm. (a) Nos. 1614/17. (b) Nos. 1618/21 Set of 2 sheets 8·00 9·00

257 Brass "Reno" Locomotive, Japan (1963)

1992. Toy Trains from Far Eastern Manufacturers. Multicoloured.
1623 15c. Type **257** 65 35
1624 25c. Union Pacific "Golden Classic" locomotive, China (1992) 75 35
1625 55c. L.M.S. third class brake carriage, Hong Kong (1970s) 1·25 40
1626 65c. Brass Wabash locomotive, Japan (1958) 1·40 50
1627 75c. Pennsylvania "Duplex" type locomotive, Korea (1991) 1·50 1·00
1628 $1 Streamlined locomotive, Japan (post 1945) 1·60 1·00
1629 $3 Japanese National Railways Class "C62" locomotive, Japan (1960) 2·50 3·00
1630 $5 Tinplate friction driven trains, Japan (1960s) 3·00 3·75
MS1631 Two sheets, each 119×87 mm. (a) $6 "Rocket's" tender, Japan (1972) (multicoloured) (51½×40 mm). (b) $6 American model steam train presented to Emperor of Japan, 1854 (black, blackish olive and flesh) (40×51½ mm). Set of 2 sheets 10·00 10·00

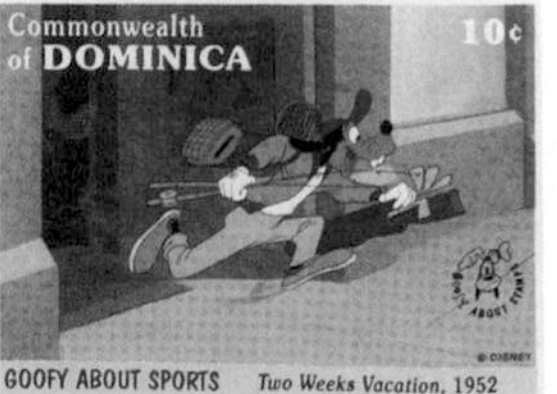

258 Goofy in "Two Weeks Vacation", 1952

1992. 60th Anniv of Goofy (Disney cartoon character). Designs showing sports from cartoon films. Multicoloured.
1632 10c. Type **258** 70 30
1633 15c. "Aquamania", 1961 80 30

1634 25c. "Goofy Gymnastics", 1949 95 20

1635 45c. "How to Ride a Horse", 1941 1·25 25

1636 $1 "Foul Hunting", 1947 2·00 85

1637 $2 "For Whom the Bulls Toil", 1953 2·75 3·00

1638 $4 "Tennis Racquet", 1949 3·50 4·00

1639 $5 "Double Dribble", 1946 3·50 4·00

MS1640 Two sheets, each 128×102 mm. (a) $6 "The Goofy Sports Story", 1956 (vert). (b) $6 "Aquamania", 1961 (different) (vert) Set of 2 sheets 11·00 12·00

259 "Graf Zeppelin", 1929

1992. Anniversaries and Events. Multicoloured.

1641 25c. Type **259** 75 40

1642 45c. Elderly man on bike 1·50 45

1643 45c. Elderly man with seedling 40 30

1644 45c. Elderly man and young boy fishing 40 30

1645 90c. Space Shuttle "Atlantis" 1·00 60

1646 90c. Konrad Adenauer (German statesman) 60 60

1647 $1.20 Sir Thomas Lipton and "Shamrock N" (yacht) 1·50 1·75

1648 $1.20 Snowy egret (bird) 2·75 1·75

1649 $1.20 Wolfgang Amadeus Mozart 3·25 1·75

1650 $2 Pulling fishing net ashore 2·00 2·50

1651 $3 Helen Keller (lecturer) 2·25 2·75

1652 $4 Eland (antelope) 3·50 4·00

1653 $4 Map of Allied Zones of Occupation, Germany, 1949 4·50 4·00

1654 $4 Earth resources satellite 3·50 4·00

1655 $5 Count von Zeppelin 3·50 4·00

MS1656 Five sheets. (a) 100×70 mm. $6 Airship propeller. (b) 100×70 mm. $6 "Mir" Russian space station with "Soyuz". (c) 70×100 mm. $6 Cologne Cathedral. (d) 100×70 mm. $6 Rhinoceros hornbill (bird). (e) 100×70 mm. $6 Monostatos from "The Magic Flute" Set of 5 sheets 24·00 25·00

ANNIVERSARIES AND EVENTS: Nos. 1641, 1655, **MS**1656a, 75th death anniv of Count Ferdinand von Zeppelin; 1642/4, International Day of the Elderly; 1645, 1654, **MS**1656b, International Space Year; 1646, 1653, **MS**1656c, 25th death anniv of Konrad Adenauer; 1647, Americas Cup Yachting Championship; 1648, 1652, **MS**1656d, Earth Summit '92, Rio; 1649, **MS**1656e, Death bicent of Mozart; 1650, International Conference on Nutrition, Rome; 1651, 75th anniv of International Association of Lions Clubs.

No. **MS**1656b is inscribed "M.I.R." and No. **MS**1656d "Rhinocerus Hornbill", both in error.

1993. Bicentenary of the Louvre, Paris. As T **209b** of Gambia. Multicoloured.

1657 $1 "Madonna and Child with St. Catherine and a Rabbit" (left detail) (Titian) 70 70

1658 $1 "Madonna and Child with St. Catherine and a Rabbit" (right detail) (Titian) 70 70

1659 $1 "Woman at her Toilet" (Titian) 70 70

1660 $1 "The Supper at Emmaus" (left detail) (Titian) 70 70

1661 $1 "The Supper at Emmaus" (right detail) (Titian) 70 70

1662 $1 "The Pastoral Concert" (Titian) 70 70

1663 $1 "An Allegory, perhaps of Marriage" (detail) (Titian) 70 70

1664 $1 "An Allegory, perhaps of Marriage" (different detail) (Titian) 70 70

MS1665 70×100 mm. $6 "The Ship of Fools" (Bosch) (52×85 mm) 4·00 4·50

260 Elvis Presley

1993. 15th Death Anniv of Elvis Presley (singer). Multicoloured.

1666 $1 Type **260** 1·10 90

1667 $1 Elvis with guitar 1·10 90

1668 $1 Elvis with microphone 1·10 90

261 Plumbeous Warbler

1993. Birds. Multicoloured.

1669 90c. Type **261** 1·50 1·25

1670 90c. Black swift 1·50 1·25

1671 90c. Blue-hooded euphonia 1·50 1·25

1672 90c. Rufous-throated solitaire 1·50 1·25

1673 90c. Ringed kingfisher 1·50 1·25

1674 90c. Blue-headed hummingbird 1·50 1·25

1675 90c. Bananaquit 1·50 1·25

1676 90c. Brown trembler ("Trembler") 1·50 1·25

1677 90c. Forest thrush 1·50 1·25

1678 90c. Purple-throated carib 1·50 1·25

1679 90c. Ruddy quail dove 1·50 1·25

1680 90c. Least bittern 1·50 1·25

MS1681 Two sheets, each 100×70 mm. (a) $6 Imperial amazon. (b) $6 Red-necked amazon Set of 2 sheets 9·50 9·50

Nos. 1669/80 were printed together, se-tenant, forming a composite design.

262 School Crest

1993. Cent of Dominica Grammar School. Mult.

1682 25c. Type **262** 20 15

1683 30c. V. Archer (first West Indian headmaster) 25 20

1684 65c. Hubert Charles (first Dominican headmaster) 45 50

1685 90c. Present school buildings 65 80

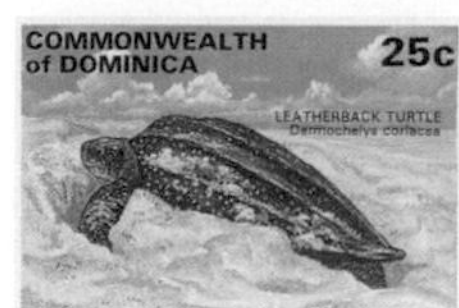

263 Leatherback Turtle on Beach

1993. Turtles. Multicoloured.

1686 25c. Type **263** 50 15

1687 55c. Hawksbill turtle swimming 70 40

1688 65c. Atlantic ridley turtle 80 50

1689 90c. Green turtle laying eggs 1·00 70

1690 $1 Green turtle swimming 1·00 70

1691 $2 Hawksbill turtle swimming (different) 1·50 2·00

1692 $4 Loggerhead turtle 2·25 3·00

1693 $5 Leatherback turtle swimming 2·25 3·00

MS1694 Two sheets, each 99×70 mm. (a) $6 Green turtle hatchling. (b) $6 Head of hawksbill turtle Set of 2 sheets 8·50 10·00

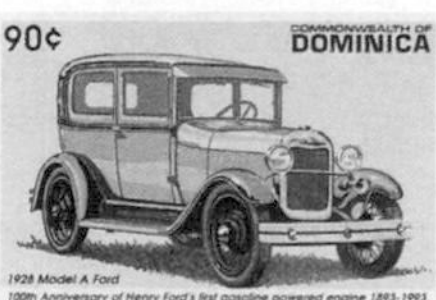

264 Ford "Model A", 1928

1993. Centenaries of Henry Ford's First Petrol Engine (90c., $5) and Karl Benz's First Four-wheeled Car (others). Multicoloured.

1695 90c. Type **264** 75 45

1696 $1.20 Mercedes Benz car winning Swiss Grand Prix, 1936 1·00 55

1697 $4 Mercedes Benz car winning German Grand Prix, 1935 2·50 3·25

1698 $5 Ford "Model T", 1915 2·50 3·25

MS1699 Two sheets, each 99×70 mm. (a) $3 Benz "Viktoria", 1893; $3 Mercedes Benz sports coupe, 1993. (b) $6 Ford "G.T.40", Le Mans, 1966 (57½×48 mm) Set of 2 sheets 7·50 8·50

1993. 40th Anniv of Coronation. As T **215a** of Gambia.

1700 20c. multicoloured 80 1·00

1701 25c. brown and black 80 1·00

1702 65c. multicoloured 1·10 1·25

1703 $5 multicoloured 4·25 4·50

MS1704 71×101 mm. $6 multicoloured 6·50 7·00

DESIGNS: 20c. Queen Elizabeth II at Coronation (photograph by Cecil Beaton); 25c. Queen wearing King Edward's Crown during Coronation ceremony; 65c. Coronation coach; $5 Queen and Queen Mother in carriage. (28½×42½ mm)—$6 "Queen Elizabeth II, 1969" (detail) (Norman Hutchinson).

265 New G.P.O. and Duke of Edinburgh

1993. Anniversaries and Events. Each brown, deep brown and black (Nos. 1707, 1717) or multicoloured (others).

1705 25c. Type **265** 45 40

1706 25c. "Bather with Beach Ball" (Picasso) (vert) 45 40

1707 65c. Willy Brandt and Pres. Eisenhower, 1959 55 40

1708 90c. As Type **265** but portrait of Queen Elizabeth II 85 60

1709 90c. "Portrait of Leo Stein" (Picasso) (vert) 85 60

1710 90c. Monika Holzner (Germany) (speed skating) (vert) 85 60

1711 90c. "Self-portrait" (Marian Szczyrbula) (vert) 85 60

1712 90c. Prince Naruhito and engagement photographs 85 60

1713 $1.20 16th-century telescope (vert) 1·50 1·25

1714 $3 "Bruno Jasienski" (Tytus Czyzewski) (vert) 2·00 2·50

1715 $3 Modern observatory (vert) 2·75 3·00

1716 $4 Ray Leblanc and Tim Sweeney (U.S.A.) (ice hockey) (vert) 3·50 3·75

1717 $5 "Wilhelm Unde" (Picasso) (vert) 3·00 3·75

1718 $5 Willy Brandt and N. K. Winston at World's Fair, 1964 3·00 3·75

1719 $5 Masako Owada and engagement photographs 3·00 3·75

1720 $5 Pres. Clinton and wife applauding 3·00 3·75

MS1721 Seven sheets, each 105×75 mm (a, c and f) or 75×105 mm (others). (a) $5 Copernicus (vert). (b) $6 "Man with Pipe" (detail) (Picasso) (vert). (c) $6 Willy Brandt, 1972. (d) $6 Toni Nieminen (Finland) (120 metre ski jump) (vert). (e) $6 "Miser" (detail) (Tadeusz Makowski) (vert). (f) $6 Masako Owada (vert). (g) $6 Pres. W. Clinton (vert) Set of 7 sheets 20·00 23·00

ANNIVERSARIES AND EVENTS: Nos. 1705, 1708, Opening of New General Post Office Building; 1706, 1709, 1717, **MS**1721b, 20th death anniv of Picasso (artist); 1707, 1718, **MS**1721c, 80th birth anniv of Willy Brandt (German politician); 1710, 1716, **MS**1721d, Winter Olympic Games '94, Lillehammer; 1711, 1714, **MS**1721e, "Polska '93" International Stamp Exhibition, Poznan; 1712, 1719, **MS**1721f, Marriage of Crown Prince Naruhito of Japan; 1713, 1715, **MS**1721a, 450th death anniv of Copernicus (astronomer); 1720, **MS**1721g, Inauguration of U.S. President William Clinton.

No. 1714 is inscribed "Tyrus" in error.

266 Hugo Eckener in New York Parade, 1928

1993. Aviation Anniversaries. Multicoloured.

1722 25c. Type **266** 1·25 40

1723 55c. English Electric Lightning F.2 (fighter) 2·25 50

1724 65c. Airship "Graf Zeppelin" over Egypt, 1929 2·25 65

1725 $1 Boeing 314A (flying boat) on transatlantic mail flight 2·50 1·10

1726 $2 Astronaut carrying mail to the Moon 3·00 3·00

1727 $4 Airship "Viktoria Luise" over Kiel harbour, 1912 4·00 4·50

1728 $5 Supermarine Spitfire (vert) 4·00 4·50

MS1729 Three sheets, each 99×70 mm. (a) $6 Hugo Eckener (42½×57 mm). (b) $6 Royal Air Force crest (42½×57 mm). (c) $6 Jean-Pierre Blanchard's hot air balloon, 1793 (vert) Set of 3 sheets 13·00 13·00

ANNIVERSARIES: Nos. 1722, 1724, 1727, **MS**1729a, 125th birth anniv of Hugo Eckener (airship commander); 1723, 1728, **MS**1729b, 75th anniv of Royal Air Force; 1725/6, **MS**1729c, Bicentenary of first airmail flight.

267 Maradona (Argentina) and Buchwald (Germany)

1993. World Cup Football Championship, U.S.A. (1994) (1st issue). Multicoloured.

1730 25c. Type **267** 80 20

1731 55c. Ruud Gullit (Netherlands) 1·10 40

1732 65c. Chavarria (Costa Rica) and Bliss (U.S.A.) 1·10 45

1733 90c. Diego Maradona (Argentina) 1·60 90

1734 90c. Leonel Alvares (Colombia) 1·60 90

1735 $1 Altobelli (Italy) and Yong-hwang (South Korea) 1·60 90

1736 $2 Stopyra (France) 2·75 2·75

1737 $5 Renquin (Belgium) and Yaremtchuk (Russia) 3·75 4·50

MS1738 Two sheets. (a) 73×103 mm. $6 Nestor Fabbri (Argentina). (b) 103×73 mm. $6 Andreas Brehme (Germany) Set of 2 sheets 7·50 8·50

See also Nos. 1849/56.

268 Ornate Chedi, Wat Phra Boromathat Chaiya

1993. Asian International Stamp Exhibitions. Multicoloured. (a) "Indopex '93", Surabaya, Indonesia.

1739 25c. Type **268** 30 30

1740 55c. Temple ruins, Sukhothai 50 30

1741 90c. Prasat Hin Phimai, Thailand 70 45

1742 $1.65 Arjuna and Prabu Gilling Wesi puppets 1·00 1·00

1743 $1.65 Loro Blonyo puppet 1·00 1·00

1744 $1.65 Yogyanese puppets 1·00 1·00

1745 $1.65 Wayang gedog puppet, Ng Setro 1·00 1·00

1746 $1.65 Wayang golek puppet 1·00 1·00

1747 $1.65 Wayang gedog puppet, Raden Damar Wulan 1·00 1·00

1748 $5 Main sanctuary, Prasat Phanom Rung, Thailand 2·25 2·50

MS1749 105×136 mm. $6 Sculpture of Majaphit noble, Pura Sada 3·25 3·75

(b) "Taipei '93", Taiwan.

1750 25c. Aw Boon Haw Gardens, Causeway Bay 30 30

1751 65c. Observation building, Kenting Park 50 30

1752 90c. Tzu-en pagoda on lake-shore, Taiwan 70 45

1753 $1.65 Chang E kite 1·00 1·00

1754 $1.65 Red Phoenix and Rising Sun kite 1·00 1·00

1755 $1.65 Heavenly Judge kite 1·00 1·00

1756 $1.65 Monkey King kite 1·00 1·00

1757 $1.65 Goddess of Luo River kite 1·00 1·00

1758 $1.65 Heavenly Maiden kite 1·00 1·00

1759 $5 Villa, Lantau Island 2·25 2·50

MS1760 105×136 mm. $6 Jade sculpture of girl, Liao Dynasty 3·25 3·75

(c) "Bangkok '93", Thailand.

1761 25c. Tugu Monument, Java 30 30

1762 55c. Candi Cangkuang mon, West Java 50 30

1763 90c. Merus, Pura Taman Ayun, Mengwi 70 45

1764 $1.65 Hun Lek puppets of Rama and Sita 1·00 1·00

1765 $1.65 Burmese puppet 1·00 1·00

1766 $1.65 Burmese puppets 1·00 1·00

1767 $1.65 Demon puppet at Wat Phra Kaew 1·00 1·00

1768 $1.65 Hun Lek puppet performing Khun Chang 1·00 1·00

1769 $1.65 Hun Lek puppets performing Ramakien 1·00 1·00

1770 $5 Stone mosaic, Ceto 2·25 2·50

MS1771 105×136 mm. $6 Thai stone carving 3·25 3·75

No. 1753 is inscribed "Chang E Rising Up th the Moon" in error.

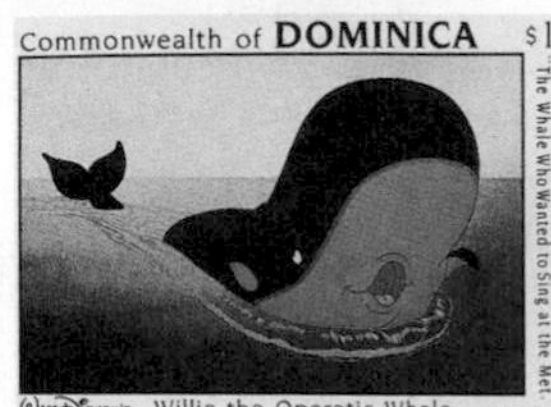

269 Willie

1993. "Willie the Operatic Whale". Scenes from Walt Disney's cartoon film. Multicoloured.

1772	$1 Type **269**	1·40	1·10
1773	$1 Willie's pelican friend	1·40	1·10
1774	$1 Willie singing to seals	1·40	1·10
1775	$1 Willie singing "Lucia"	1·40	1·10
1776	$1 Willie in "Pagliacci"	1·40	1·10
1777	$1 Willie as Mephistopheles	1·40	1·10
1778	$1 Tetti Tatti searching for Willie	1·40	1·10
1779	$1 Whalers listening to Willie	1·40	1·10
1780	$1 Tetti Tatti with harpoon gun	1·40	1·10
MS1781	Two sheets. (a) 130×102 mm. $6 Seals listening to Willie. (b) 97×118 mm. $6 Willie in Heaven (vert) Set of 2 sheets	7·00	8·00

270 "Adoration of the Magi" (detail) (Durer)

1993. Christmas. Religious Paintings. Each black, yellow and red (Nos. 1782/5) or multicoloured (others).

1782	25c. Type **270**	35	20
1783	55c. "Adoration of the Magi" (different detail) (Durer)	55	30
1784	65c. "Adoration of the Magi" (different detail) (Durer)	65	35
1785	90c. "Adoration of the Magi" (different detail) (Durer)	80	75
1786	90c. "Madonna of Foligno" (detail) (Raphael)	80	75
1787	$1 "Madonna of Foligno" (different detail) (Raphael)	90	75
1788	$3 "Madonna of Foligno" (different detail) (Raphael)	2·00	3·25
1789	$5 "Madonna of Foligno" (different detail) (Raphael)	2·75	4·50
MS1790	Two sheets, each 105×130 mm. (a) $6 "Adoration of the Magi" (different detail) (Dürer) (horiz). (b) $6 "Madonna of Foligno" (different detail) (Raphael) Set of 2 sheets	7·00	8·50

1994. "Hong Kong '94" International Stamp Exhibition (1st issue). As T **222a** of Gambia. Multicoloured.

1791	65c. Hong Kong 1988 Peak Tramway 50c. stamp and skyscrapers	1·25	1·25
1792	65c. Dominica 1991 Cog Railways $5 stamp and Hong Kong Peak tram	1·25	1·25

Nos. 1791/2 were printed together, se-tenant, forming a composite design.

See also Nos. 1793/8.

1994. "Hong Kong '94" International Stamp Exhibition (2nd issue). Tang Dynasty Jade. As T **222b** of Gambia, but vert. Multicoloured.

1793	65c. Horse	85	85
1794	65c. Cup with handle	85	85
1795	65c. Vase with birthday peaches	85	85
1796	65c. Vase	85	85
1797	65c. Fu Dog with puppy	85	85
1798	65c. Drinking cup	85	85

271 Male "Dynastes hercules" (beetle)

1994. Endangered Species. Birds and Insects. Multicoloured.

1799	20c. Type **271**	20	15
1800	25c. Male "Dynastes hercules" (different)	20	15
1801	65c. Male "Dynastes hercules" (different)	45	35
1802	90c. Female "Dynastes hercules"	60	55
1803	$1 Imperial Amazon ("Imperial Parrot")	90	75
1804	$2 "Marpesia petreus" (butterfly)	1·50	2·00
1805	$3 "Hypolimnus misippus" (butterfly)	2·00	2·50
1806	$5 Purple-throated carib	2·75	3·50
MS1807	Two sheets, each 98×70 mm. (a) $6 Blue-headed hummingbird. (b) $6 "Libytheana fulvescens" (butterfly) Set of 2 sheets	8·00	9·00

Nos. 1803/7 do not carry the W.W.F. Panda emblem.

272 "Laelio-cattleya"

1994. Orchids. Multicoloured.

1808	20c. Type **272**	35	15
1809	25c. "Sophrolaelio cattleya"	35	15
1810	65c. "Odontocidium"	70	45
1811	90c. "Laelio-cattleya" (different)	90	75
1812	$1 "Cattleya"	1·00	75
1813	$2 "Odontocidium" (different)	1·50	2·00
1814	$3 "Epiphronitis"	2·00	2·75
1815	$4 "Oncidium"	2·00	2·75
MS1816	Two sheets, each 100×70 mm. (a) $6 "Cattleya" (different). (b) $6 "Schombo cattleya" Set of 2 sheets	7·50	8·50

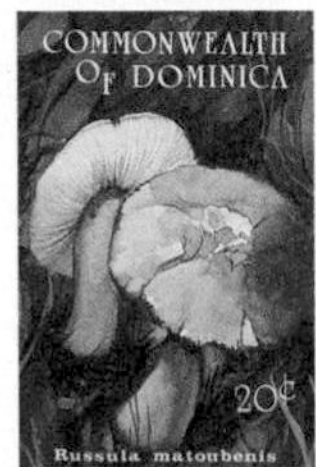

273 "Russula matoubenis"

1994. Fungi. Multicoloured.

1817	20c. Type **273**	40	25
1818	25c. "Leptonia caeruleocapitata"	40	25
1819	65c. "Inocybe littoralis"	60	35
1820	90c. "Russula hygrophytica"	70	55
1821	$1 "Pyrrhoglossum lilaceipes"	80	70
1822	$2 "Hygrocybe konradii"	1·25	1·75
1823	$3 "Inopilus magnificus"	1·75	2·25
1824	$5 "Boletellus cubensis"	2·25	2·75
MS1825	Two sheets, each 110×85 mm. (a) $6 "Lentinus strigosus". (b) $6 "Gerronema citrinum" Set of 2 sheets	7·50	7·50

274 "Appias drusilla"

1994. Butterflies. Multicoloured.

1826	20c. Type **274**	35	15
1827	25c. "Didonis biblis"	35	15
1828	55c. "Eurema daira"	70	45
1829	65c. "Hypolimnas misippus"	75	45
1830	$1 "Phoebis agarithe"	1·00	75
1831	$2 "Marpesia petreus"	1·50	2·00
1832	$3 "Libytheana fulvescens"	1·75	2·75
1833	$5 "Precis evarete"	2·50	3·50
MS1834	Two sheets, each 100×70 mm. (a) $6 "Chlorostrymon maesites". (b) $6 "Vanessa cardui" Set of 2 sheets	9·00	9·50

275 Dachshund

1994. Chinese New Year ("Year of the Dog"). Multicoloured.

1835	20c. Type **275**	30	25
1836	25c. Beagle	30	25
1837	55c. Greyhound	50	30
1838	90c. Jack Russell terrier	70	55
1839	$1 Pekingese	80	70
1840	$2 Wire fox terrier	1·25	1·50
1841	$4 English toy spaniel	2·25	2·75
1842	$5 Irish setter	2·25	2·75
MS1843	Two sheets, each 102×72 mm. (a) $6 Welsh corgi. (b) $6 Labrador retriever Set of 2 sheets	8·00	8·00

1994. Royal Visit. Nos. 1700/4 optd **ROYAL VISIT FEBRUARY 19, 1994**.

1844	20c. multicoloured	1·50	1·40
1845	25c. brown and black	1·50	1·40
1846	65c. multicoloured	2·25	2·25
1847	$5 multicoloured	4·00	4·25
MS1848	71×101 mm. $6 multicoloured	7·00	7·50

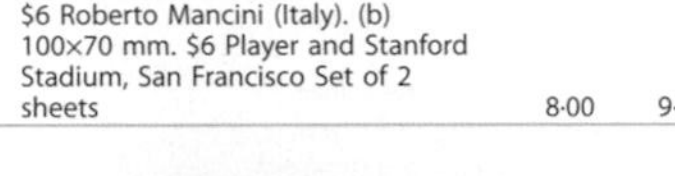

277 Des Armstrong (U.S.A.)

1994. World Cup Football Championship, U.S.A. (2nd issue). Multicoloured.

1849	25c. Jefferey Edmund (Dominica)	50	25
1850	$1 Type **277**	75	80
1851	$1 Dennis Bergkamp (Netherlands)	75	80
1852	$1 Roberto Baggio (Italy)	75	80
1853	$1 Rai (Brazil)	75	80
1854	$1 Cafu (Brazil)	75	80
1855	$1 Marco van Basten (Netherlands)	75	80
MS1856	Two sheets. (a) 70×100 mm. $6 Roberto Mancini (Italy). (b) 100×70 mm. $6 Player and Stanford Stadium, San Francisco Set of 2 sheets	8·00	9·00

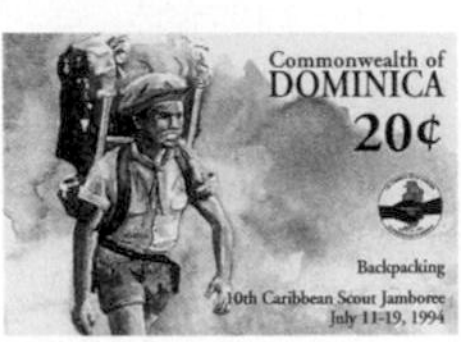

278 Scout Backpacking

1994. 10th Caribbean Scout Jamboree. Multicoloured.

1857	20c. Type **278**	35	15
1858	25c. Cooking over campfire	35	15
1859	55c. Erecting tent	60	30
1860	65c. Serving soup	70	45
1861	$1 Corps of drums	1·00	75
1862	$2 Planting tree	1·50	2·00
1863	$4 Sailing dinghy	2·25	2·50
1864	$5 Saluting	2·25	2·50
MS1865	Two sheets, each 100×70 mm. (a) $6 Early scout troop. (b) $6 Pres. Crispin Sorhaindo (chief scout) (vert) Set of 2 sheets	8·50	9·00

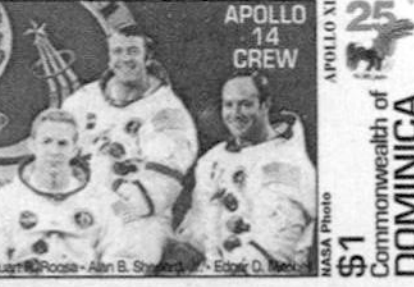

278a Crew of "Apollo 14"

1994. 25th Anniv of First Manned Moon Landing. Multicoloured.

1866	$1 Type **278a**	1·25	1·00
1867	$1 "Apollo 14" mission logo	1·25	1·00
1868	$1 Lunar module "Antares" on Moon	1·25	1·00
1869	$1 Crew of "Apollo 15"	1·25	1·00
1870	$1 "Apollo 15" mission logo	1·25	1·00
1871	$1 Lunar crater on Mt. Hadley	1·25	1·00
MS1872	99×106 mm. $6 "Apollo 11" logo and surface of Moon	4·50	5·00

1994. Centenary of International Olympic Committee. Gold Medal Winners. As T **227b** of Gambia. Multicoloured.

1873	55c. Ulrike Meyfarth (Germany) (high jump), 1984	75	40
1874	$1.45 Dieter Baumann (Germany) (5000 m), 1992	1·75	2·00
MS1875	106×76 mm. $6 Ji Hoon Chae (South Korea) (500 metres speed skating), 1994	3·50	4·00

1994. Centenary (1995) of First English Cricket Tour to the West Indies. As T **397a** of Grenada. Multicoloured.

1876	55c. David Gower (England) (vert)	80	45
1877	90c. Curtly Ambrose (West Indies) and Wisden Trophy	1·25	90
1878	$1 Graham Gooch (England) (vert)	1·25	1·00
MS1879	76×96 mm. $3 First English touring team, 1895	3·75	3·25

1994. 50th Anniv of D-Day. As T **227c** of Gambia. Multicoloured.

1880	65c. American Waco gliders	85	45
1881	$2 Airspeed Horsa glider	1·75	1·75
1882	$3 Airspeed glider and troops attacking Pegasus Bridge	2·00	2·25
MS1883	107×77 mm. $6 British Hadrian glider	3·25	3·75

279 Pink Bird and Red Flowers Screen Painting

1994. "Philakorea '94" International Stamp Exhibition, Seoul. Multicoloured.

1884	55c. Type **279**	30	40
1885	55c. Bird with yellow, pink and red flowers	30	40
1886	55c. Pair of birds and yellow flowers	30	40
1887	55c. Chickens and flowers	30	40
1888	55c. Pair of birds and pink flowers	30	40
1889	55c. Ducks and flowers	30	40
1890	55c. Blue bird and red flowers	30	40
1891	55c. Common pheasant and flowers	30	40
1892	55c. Stork and flowers	30	40
1893	55c. Deer and flowers	30	40
1894	65c. P'alsang-jon Hall (38×24 mm)	40	40
1895	90c. Popchu-sa Temple (38×24 mm)	50	55
1896	$2 Uhwajong Pavillion (38×24 mm)	1·10	1·50
MS1897	100×70 mm. $4 Spirit Post Guardian (38×24 mm)	2·25	3·00

280 Dippy Dawg

1994. 65th Anniv (1993) of Mickey Mouse. Walt Disney Cartoon Characters. Multicoloured.

1898	20c. Type **280**	60	25
1899	25c. Clarabelle Cow	60	25
1900	55c. Horace Horsecollar	90	35
1901	65c. Mortimer Mouse	1·00	45
1902	$1 Joe Piper	1·50	85
1903	$3 Mr. Casey	2·75	3·00
1904	$4 Chief O'Hara	3·00	3·25
1905	$5 Mickey and The Blot	3·00	3·25
MS1906	Two sheets, each 127×102 mm. (a) $6 Minnie Mouse with Tanglefoot. (b) $6 Minnie and Pluto (horiz) Set of 2 sheets	10·00	11·00

281 Marilyn Monroe

1994. Entertainers. Multicoloured.
1907 20c. Sonia Lloyd (folk singer) 40 25
1908 25c. Ophelia Marie (singer) 40 25
1909 55c. Edney Francis (accordion player) 60 30
1910 65c. Norman Letang (saxophonist) 70 35
1911 90c. Edie Andre (steel-band player) 80 55
1912 90c. Type **281** 1·10 1·25
1913 90c. Marilyn Monroe wearing necklace 1·10 1·25
1914 90c. In yellow frilled dress 1·10 1·25
1915 90c. In purple dress 1·10 1·25
1916 90c. Looking over left shoulder 1·10 1·25
1917 90c. Laughing 1·10 1·25
1918 90c. In red dress 1·10 1·25
1919 90c. Wearing gold cluster earrings 1·10 1·25
1920 90c. In yellow dress 1·10 1·25
MS1921 Two sheets, each 106×76 mm. (a) $6 Marilyn Monroe with top hat. (b) $6 With arms above head Set of 2 sheets 7·50 8·50
No. 1907 is inscribed "Llyod" in error.

1994. Christmas. Religious Paintings. As T **230a** of Gambia. Multicoloured.
1922 20c. "Madonna and Child" (Luis de Morales) 30 10
1923 25c. "Madonna and Child with Yarn Winder" (De Morales) 30 10
1924 55c. "Our Lady of the Rosary" (detail) (Zurbaran) 50 30
1925 65c. "Dream of the Patrician" (detail) (Murillo) 65 55
1926 90c. "Madonna of Charity" (El Greco) 90 45
1927 $1 "The Annunciation" (Zurbaran) 1·00 60
1928 $2 "Mystical Marriage of St. Catherine" (Jusepe de Ribera) 1·50 2·25
1929 $3 "The Holy Family with St. Bruno and Other Saints" (detail) (De Ribera) 1·75 3·00
MS1930 Two sheets. (a) 136×97 mm. $6 "Adoration of the Shepherds" (detail) (Murillo). (b) 99×118 mm. $6 "Vision of the Virgin to St. Bernard" (detail) (Murillo) Set of 2 sheets 7·50 8·50

281a Sir Shridath Ramphal

1994. First Recipients of Order of the Caribbean Community. Multicoloured.
1931 25c. Type **281a** 20 10
1932 65c. William Demas 50 50
1933 90c. Derek Walcott 1·00 80

1995. 18th World Scout Jamboree, Netherlands. Nos. 1860 and 1863/4 optd **18th World Scout Jamboree Mondial, Holland, May 6, 1995.**
1934 65c. Serving soup 60 35
1935 $4 Sailing dinghy 2·25 2·75
1936 $5 Saluting 2·25 2·75
MS1937 Two sheets, each 100×70 mm. (a) $6 Early scout troop. (b) $6 Pres. Crispin Sorhaindo (chief scout) (vert) Set of 2 sheets 7·50 8·50

283 Wood Duck

1995. Water Birds. Multicoloured.
1938 25c. Type **283** 1·10 30
1939 55c. Mallard 1·25 40
1940 65c. Blue-winged teal 1·25 55
1941 65c. Cattle egret (vert) 1·25 1·10
1942 65c. Snow goose (vert) 1·25 1·10
1943 65c. Peregrine falcon (vert) 1·25 1·10
1944 65c. Barn owl (vert) 1·25 1·10
1945 65c. Black-crowned night heron (vert) 1·25 1·10
1946 65c. Common grackle (vert) 1·25 1·10
1947 65c. Brown pelican (vert) 1·25 1·10
1948 65c. Great egret (vert) 1·25 1·10
1949 65c. Ruby-throated humming-bird (vert) 1·25 1·10
1950 65c. Laughing gull (vert) 1·25 1·10
1951 65c. Greater flamingo (vert) 1·25 1·10
1952 65c. Moorhen ("Common Morehen") (vert) 1·25 1·10
1953 $5 Red-eared conure ("Blood eared parakeet") 3·25 4·00
MS1954 Two sheets, each 105×75 mm. (a) $5 Trumpeter swan (vert). (b) $6 White-eyed vireo Set of 2 sheets 8·00 9·00
Nos. 1941/5 were printed together, se-tenant, forming a composite design.
No. 1946 is inscribed "Common Gralkle" in error.

284 Pig's Head facing right

1995. Chinese New Year ("Year of the Pig"). Multicoloured.
1955 25c. Type **284** 40 40
1956 65c. Pig facing to the front 45 45
1957 $1 Pig facing left 50 50
MS1958 101×50 mm. Nos. 1955/7 1·25 1·50
MS1959 105×77 mm. Two pigs (horiz) 1·25 1·50

284a German Panther Tank in the Ardennes

1995. 50th Anniv of End of Second World War in Europe. Multicoloured.
1960 $2 Type **284a** 1·25 1·25
1961 $2 Republic P-47 Thunderbolt American fighter-bomber 1·25 1·25
1962 $2 American mechanized column crossing the Rhine 1·25 1·25
1963 $2 Messerschmitt Me 163B Komet and Allied bombers Boeing B-17 1·25 1·25
1964 $2 V2 rocket on launcher 1·25 1·25
1965 $2 German U-boat surrendering 1·25 1·25
1966 $2 Heavy artillery in action 1·25 1·25
1967 $2 Soviet infantry in Berlin 1·25 1·25
MS1968 106×76 mm. $6 Statue and devastated Dresden (56½×42½ mm) 4·50 4·75

285 Paul Harris (founder) and Emblem

1995. 90th Anniv of Rotary International.
1969 **285** $1 brown, purple & blk 75 75
MS1970 70×100 mm. $6 red and black 2·75 3·25
DESIGN: $6 Rotary emblems.

1995. 50th Anniv of End of Second World War in the Pacific. As T **284a**. Multicoloured.
1971 $2 Mitsubishi A6M Zero-Sen torpedo-bomber 1·50 1·25
1972 $2 Aichi D3A "Val" dive bomber 1·50 1·25
1973 $2 Nakajima B5N "Kate" bomber 1·50 1·25
1974 $2 "Zuikaku" (Japanese aircraft carrier) 1·50 1·25
1975 $2 "Akagi" (Japanese aircraft carrier) 1·50 1·25
1976 $2 "Ryuho" (Japanese aircraft carrier) 1·50 1·25
MS1977 108×76 mm. $6 Mitsubishi A6m Zero-Sen torpedo-bomber at Pearl Harbor 4·50 4·50

286 Boxing

1995. Olympic Games, Atlanta (1996). (1st issue). Multicoloured.
1978 15c. Type **286** 40 25
1979 20c. Wrestling 45 25
1980 25c. Judo 55 25
1981 55c. Fencing 60 30
1982 65c. Swimming 70 35
1983 $1 Gymnastics (vert) 90 80
1984 $2 Cycling (vert) 2·50 2·25
1985 $5 Volleyball 2·75 3·50
MS1986 Two sheets, each 104×74 mm. (a) $6 Show jumping. (b) $6 Football (vert) Set of 2 sheets 8·00 9·00
See also Nos. 2122/45 and 2213.

286a Signatures and U.S Delegate

1995. 50th Anniv of United Nations. Multicoloured.
1987 65c. Type **286a** 50 45
1988 $1 U.S. delegate 75 75
1989 $2 Governor Stassen (U.S. delegate) 1·25 1·50
MS1990 100×71 mm. $6 Winston Churchill 3·25 3·50
Nos. 1987/9 were printed together, se-tenant, forming a composite design.

287 Market Customers

1995. 50th Anniv of Food and Agriculture Organization. T **287** and similar multicoloured designs.
MS1991 110×74 mm. 90c., $1, $2 Panorama of Dominican market 1·60 1·90
MS1992 101×71 mm. $6 Women irrigating crops (horiz) 2·50 3·00

1995. 95th Birthday of Queen Elizabeth the Queen Mother. As T **239a** of Gambia.
1993 $1.65 brown, lt brown & blk 1·10 1·25
1994 $1.65 multicoloured 1·10 1·25
1995 $1.65 multicoloured 1·10 1·25
1996 $1.65 multicoloured 1·10 1·25
MS1997 103×126 mm. $6 multicoloured 4·50 4·75
DESIGNS: No. 1993, Queen Elizabeth the Queen Mother (pastel drawing); 1994, Holding bouquet of flowers; 1995, At desk (oil painting); 1996, Wearing blue dress; **MS**1997, Wearing ruby and diamond tiara and necklace.

288 Monoclonius

1995. "Singapore '95" International Stamp Exhibition. Prehistoric Animals. Multicoloured.
1998 20c. Type **288** 65 30
1999 25c. Euoplocephalus 65 30
2000 55c. Head of coelophysis 75 30
2001 65c. Head of compsognathus 80 35
2002 90c. Dimorphodon 85 75
2003 90c. Ramphorynchus 85 75
2004 90c. Head of giant alligator 85 75
2005 90c. Pentaceratops 85 75
2006 $1 Ceratosaurus (vert) 85 75
2007 $1 Comptosaurus (vert) 85 75
2008 $1 Stegosaur (vert) 85 75
2009 $1 Camarasaurus (vert) 85 75
2010 $1 Baronyx (vert) 85 75
2011 $1 Dilophosaurus (vert) 85 75
2012 $1 Dromaeosaurids (vert) 85 75
2013 $1 Deinonychus (vert) 85 75
2014 $1 Dinicthys (terror fish) (vert) 85 75
2015 $1 Head of carcharodon (Giant-toothed shark) (vert) 85 75
2016 $1 Nautiloid (vert) 85 75
2017 $1 Trilobite (vert) 85 75
MS2018 Two sheets. (a) 95×65 mm. $5 Sauropelta. (b) 65×95 mm. $6 Triceratops (vert) Set of 2 sheets 7·50 8·50

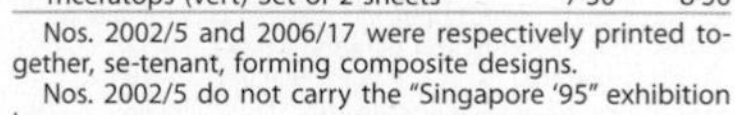
Nos. 2002/5 and 2006/17 were respectively printed together, se-tenant, forming composite designs.
Nos. 2002/5 do not carry the "Singapore '95" exhibition logo.

289 Oscar Sanchez (1987 Peace)

1995. Centenary of Nobel Prize Trust Fund. Mult.
2019 $2 Type **289** 1·50 1·50
2020 $2 Ernst Chain (1945 Medicine) 1·50 1·50
2021 $2 Aage Bohr (1975 Physics) 1·50 1·50
2022 $2 Jaroslav Seifert (1984 Literature) 1·50 1·50
2023 $2 Joseph Murray (1990 Medicine) 1·50 1·50
2024 $2 Jaroslav Heyrovsky (1959 Chemistry) 1·50 1·50
2025 $2 Adolf von Baeyer (1905 Chemistry) 1·50 1·50
2026 $2 Eduard Buchner (1907 Chemistry) 1·50 1·50
2027 $2 Carl Bosch (1931 Chemistry) 1·50 1·50
2028 $2 Otto Hahn (1944 Chemistry) 1·50 1·50
2029 $2 Otto Diels (1950 Chemistry) 1·50 1·50
2030 $2 Kurt Alder (1950 Chemistry) 1·50 1·50
MS2031 76×106 mm. $2 Emil von Behring (1901 Medicine) 1·40 1·60

1995. Christmas. Religious Paintings. As T **245a** of Gambia. Multicoloured.
2032 20c. "Madonna and Child with St. John" (Pontormo) 25 20
2033 25c. "The Immaculate Conception" (Murillo) 25 20
2034 55c. "The Adoration of the Magi" (Filippino Lippi) 45 30
2035 65c. "Rest on the Flight into Egypt" (Van Dyck) 55 35
2036 90c. "The Holy Family" (Van Dyck) 75 50
2037 $5 "The Annunciation" (Van Eyck) 2·75 4·00
MS2038 Two sheets, each 102×127 mm. (a) $5 "Madonna and Child Reading" (detail) (Van Eyck). (b) $6 "The Holy Family" (detail) (Ribera) Set of 2 sheets 6·50 7·50

289a Florida Panther

1995. Centenary (1992) of Sierra Club (environmental protection society). Endangered Species. Multicoloured.
2039 $1 Type **289a** 60 60
2040 $1 Manatee 60 60
2041 $1 Sockeye salmon 60 60
2042 $1 Key deer facing left 60 60
2043 $1 Key deer doe 60 60
2044 $1 Key deer stag 60 60
2045 $1 Wallaby with young in pouch 60 60
2046 $1 Wallaby feeding young 60 60
2047 $1 Wallaby and young feeding 60 60
2048 $1 Florida panther showing teeth (horiz) 60 60
2049 $1 Head of Florida panther (horiz) 60 60
2050 $1 Manatee (horiz) 60 60
2051 $1 Pair of manatees (horiz) 60 60
2052 $1 Pair of sockeye salmon (horiz) 60 60
2053 $1 Sockeye salmon spawning (horiz) 60 60
2054 $1 Pair of southern sea otters (horiz) 60 60
2055 $1 Southern sea otter with front paws together (horiz) 60 60
2056 $1 Southern sea otter with front paws apart (horiz) 60 60

290 Street Scene

1995. "A City of Cathay" (Chinese scroll painting). Multicoloured.

2057	90c. Type **290**	60	70
2058	90c. Street scene and city wall	60	70
2059	90c. City gate and bridge	60	70
2060	90c. Landing stage and junk	60	70
2061	90c. River bridge	60	70
2062	90c. Moored junks	60	70
2063	90c. Two rafts on river	60	70
2064	90c. Two junks on river	60	70
2065	90c. Roadside tea house	60	70
2066	90c. Wedding party on the road	60	70
MS2067	Two sheets, each 106×77 mm. (a) $2 City street and sampan; $2 Footbridge. (b) $2 Stern of sampan (vert); $2 Bow of sampan (vert) Set of 2 sheets	4·25	4·75

291 "Bindo Altoviti" (Raphael)

1995. Paintings by Raphael. Multicoloured.

2068	$2 Type **291**	1·75	1·75
2069	$2 "Pope Leo with Nephews"	1·75	1·75
2070	$2 "Agony in the Garden"	1·75	1·75
MS2071	110×80 mm. $6 "Pope Leo X with Cardinals Giulio de Medici and Luigi dei Rossi" (detail)	4·00	4·75

292 Rat

1996. Chinese New Year ("Year of the Rat").

2072	**292**	25c. black, violet and brown	35	40
2073	-	65c. black, red and green	60	70
2074	-	$1 black, mauve and blue	70	80
MS2075		100×50 mm. Nos. 2072/4	1·25	1·50
MS2076		105×77 mm. $2 black, green and violet (two rats)	1·25	1·50

DESIGNS: 65c., $1, $2, Rats and Chinese symbols (different).

293 Mickey and Minnie Mouse (Year of the Rat)

1996. Chinese Lunar Calendar. Walt Disney Cartoon Characters. Multicoloured.

2077	55c. Type **293**	65	70
2078	55c. Casey Jones (Year of the Ox)	65	70
2079	55c. Tigger, Pooh and Piglet (Year of the Tiger)	65	70
2080	55c. White Rabbit (Year of the Rabbit)	65	70
2081	55c. Dragon playing flute (Year of the Dragon)	65	70
2082	55c. Snake looking in mirror (Year of the Snake)	65	70
2083	55c. Horace Horsecollar and Clarabelle Cow (Year of the Horse)	65	70
2084	55c. Black Lamb and blue birds (Year of the Ram)	65	70
2085	55c. King Louis reading book (Year of the Monkey)	65	70
2086	55c. Cock playing lute (Year of the Cock)	65	70
2087	55c. Mickey and Pluto (Year of the Dog)	65	70
2088	55c. Pig building bridge (Year of the Pig)	65	70
MS2089	Two sheets. (a) 127×102 mm. $3 Basil the Great Mouse Detective (Year of the Rat). (b) 102×127 mm. $6 Emblems for 1996, 1997 and 2007 Set of 2 sheets	7·00	8·00

294 Steam Locomotive "Dragon", Hawaii

1996. Trains of the World. Multicoloured.

2090	$2 Type **294**	1·25	1·40
2091	$2 Class 685 steam locomotive "Regina", Italy	1·25	1·40
2092	$2 Class 745 steam locomotive, Calazo to Padua line, Italy	1·25	1·40
2093	$2 Mogul steam locomotive, Philippines	1·25	1·40
2094	$2 Class 23 and 24 steam locomotives, Germany	1·25	1·40
2095	$2 Class BB-15000 electric locomotive "Stanislaus", France	1·25	1·40
2096	$2 Class "Black Five" steam locomotive, Scotland	1·25	1·40
2097	$2 Diesel-electric locomotive, France	1·25	1·40
2098	$2 LNER class A4 steam locomotive "Sir Nigel Gresley", England	1·25	1·40
2099	$2 Class 9600 steam locomotive, Japan	1·25	1·40
2100	$2 "Peloponnese Express" train, Greece	1·25	1·40
2101	$2 Porter type steam loco- motive, Hawaii	1·25	1·40
2102	$2 Steam locomotive "Holand", Norway	1·25	1·40
2103	$2 Class 220 diesel-hydraulic locomotive, Germany	1·25	1·40
2104	$2 Steam locomotive, India	1·25	1·40
2105	$2 East African Railways Class 29 steam locomotive	1·25	1·40
2106	$2 Electric trains, Russia	1·25	1·40
2107	$2 Steam locomotive, Austria	1·25	1·40
MS2108	Two sheets, each 103×73 mm. (a) $5 L.M.S. steam locomotive "Duchess of Hamilton", England. (b) $6 Diesel locomotives, China Set of 2 sheets	7·50	8·00

295 Horse-drawn Gig, 1965

1996. Traditional Island Transport. Multicoloured.

2109	65c. Type **295**	1·10	35
2110	90c. Early automobile, 1910	1·25	55
2111	$2 Lorry, 1950	2·00	2·00
2112	$3 Bus, 1955	2·50	3·00

296 Giant Panda

1996. "CHINA '96" 9th Asian International Stamp Exhibition, Peking. Giant Pandas. Multicoloured.

2113	55c. Type **296**	70	70
2114	55c. Panda on rock	70	70
2115	55c. Panda eating bamboo shoots	70	70
2116	55c. Panda on all fours	70	70
MS2117	Two sheets. (a) 90×125 mm. $2 Huangshan Mountain, China (50×75 mm). (b) 160×125 mm. $3 Panda sitting (50×37 mm) Set of 2 sheets	3·75	3·75

296a Queen Elizabeth II

1996. 70th Birthday of Queen Elizabeth II. Multicoloured.

2118	$2 Type **296a**	1·25	1·40
2119	$2 Queen in robes of Order of St. Michael and St. George	1·25	1·40
2120	$2 Queen in blue dress with floral brooch	1·25	1·40
MS2121	103×125 mm. $6 Queen at Trooping the Colour	4·50	4·75

297 Moscow Stadium, 1980

1996. Olympic Games, Atlanta (2nd issue). Multicoloured.

2122	20c. Type **297**	35	25
2123	25c. Hermine Joseph (running) (vert)	35	25
2124	55c. Zimbabwe women's hockey team, 1980	1·00	40
2125	90c. Jerome Romain (long jump) (vert)	70	75
2126	90c. Sammy Lee (diving), 1948 and 1952 (vert)	70	75
2127	90c. Bruce Jenner (decathalon), 1976 (vert)	70	75
2128	90c. Olga Korbut (gymnastics), 1972 (vert)	70	75
2129	90c. Steffi Graf (tennis), 1988 (vert)	70	75
2130	90c. Florence Griffith-Joyner (track and field), 1988 (vert)	70	75
2131	90c. Mark Spitz (swimming), 1968 and 1972 (vert)	70	75
2132	90c. Li Ning (gymnastics), 1984 (vert)	70	75
2133	90c. Erika Salumae (cycling), 1988 (vert)	70	75
2134	90c. Abebe Bikila (marathon), 1960 and 1964 (vert)	70	75
2135	90c. Ulrike Meyfarth (high jump), 1972 and 1984 (vert)	70	75
2136	90c. Pat McCormick (diving), 1952 and 1956 (vert)	70	75
2137	90c. Takeichi Nishi (equestrian), 1932 (vert)	70	75
2138	90c. Peter Farkas (Greco-Roman wrestling), 1992 (vert)	70	75
2139	90c. Carl Lewis (track and field), 1984, 1988 and 1992 (vert)	70	75
2140	90c. Agnes Keleti (gymnastics), 1952 and 1956 (vert)	70	75
2141	90c. Yasuhiro Yamashita (judo), 1984 (vert)	70	75
2142	90c. John Kelly (single sculls), 1920 (vert)	70	75
2143	90c. Naim Suleymanoglu (weightlifting), 1988 and 1992 (vert)	70	75
2144	$1 Polo (vert)	70	75
2145	$2 Greg Louganis (diving), 1976, 1984 and 1988	70	75
MS2146	Two sheets, each 105×75 mm. (a) $5 Joan Benoit (marathon), 1984 (vert). (b) $5 Milt Campbell (discus) Set of 2 sheets	6·00	7·50

Nos. 2126/34 and 2135/43 respectively were printed together, se-tenant, the backgrounds forming composite designs.

297a Child and Globe

1996. 50th Anniv of UNICEF. Multicoloured.

2147	20c. Type **297a**	25	15
2148	55c. Child with syringe and stethoscope	40	35
2149	$5 Doctor and child	2·75	3·50
MS2150	74×104 mm. $5 African child (vert)	2·75	3·50

297b Shrine of the Book, Israel Museum

1996. 3000th Anniv of Jerusalem. Multicoloured.

MS2151	114×95 mm. 90c. Type **297b**; $1 Church of All Nations; $2 The Great Synagogue	2·50	2·50
MS2152	104×74 mm. $5 Hebrew University, Mount Scopus	4·00	4·00

1996. Centenary of Radio. Entertainers. As T **259a** of Gambia. Multicoloured.

2153	90c. Artie Shaw	60	50
2154	$1 Benny Goodman	65	55
2155	$2 Duke Ellington	1·25	1·40
2156	$4 Harry James	2·25	2·50
MS2157	70×99 mm. $6 Tommy and Jimmy Dorsey (horiz)	3·50	4·00

298 Irene Peltier in National Dress

1996. Local Entertainers. Multicoloured.

2158	25c. Type **298**	25	20
2159	55c. Rupert Bartley (steel-band player)	40	35
2160	65c. Rosemary Cools-Lartigue (pianist)	50	40
2161	90c. Celestine 'Orion' Theophile (singer)	65	65
2162	$1 Cecil Bellot (band master)	70	80

299 Humphrey Bogart as Sam Spade

1996. Centenary of Cinema. Screen Detectives. Multicoloured.

2163	$1 Type **299**	1·25	90
2164	$1 Sean Connery as James Bond	1·25	90
2165	$1 Warren Beatty as Dick Tracy	1·25	90
2166	$1 Basil Rathbone as Sherlock Holmes	1·25	90
2167	$1 William Powell as the Thin Man	1·25	90
2168	$1 Sidney Toler as Charlie Chan	1·25	90
2169	$1 Peter Sellers as Inspector Clouseau	1·25	90
2170	$1 Robert Mitchum as Philip Marlowe	1·25	90
2171	$1 Peter Ustinov as Hercule Poirot	1·25	90
MS2172	105×75 mm. $6 Margaret Rutherford as Miss Marple	4·00	4·50

300 Scribbled Filefish

1996. Fishes. Multicoloured.

2173	1c. Type **300**	25	10
2174	2c. Lionfish	25	10
2175	5c. Porcupinefish	40	10
2176	10c. Powder-blue surgeon fish	50	10
2177	15c. Red hind	60	10
2178	20c. Golden butterflyfish	65	15
2179	25c. Copper-banded butterflyfish	65	20
2180	35c. Pennant coralfish	70	20
2181	45c. Spotted drum	75	30
2182	55c. Blue-girdled angelfish	80	30
2183	60c. Scorpionfish	80	35
2184	65c. Harlequin sweetlips	80	40
2185	90c. Flame angelfish	1·25	50
2186	$1 Queen triggerfish	1·40	55
2187	$1.20 Spotlight parrotfish	1·75	65
2188	$1.45 Black durgon	2·00	80
2189	$2 Glass-eyed snapper	2·50	1·10
2190	$5 Balloonfish	4·50	5·50
2191	$10 Creole wrasse	8·50	9·50
2192	$20 Sea bass	13·00	16·00

For these designs size 24×21 mm, see Nos. 2374/91.

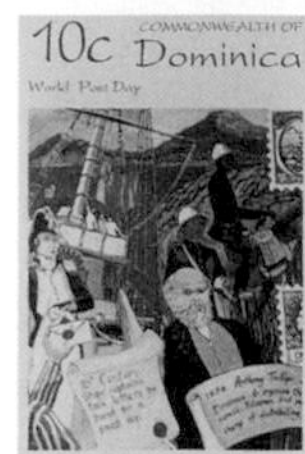

301 Anthony Trollope and Postal Scenes

1996. World Post Day. Multicoloured.

2193	10c. Type **301**	25	15
2194	25c. Anthony Trollope and Dominican postmen	30	20
2195	55c. "Yare" (mail streamer)	60	35
2196	65c. Rural post office	60	40
2197	90c. Postmen carrying mail	90	50
2198	$1 Grumman Goose (seaplane) and 1958 Caribbean Federation 12c. stamp	1·00	80
2199	$2 Old and new post offices and 1978 Independence 10c. stamp	1·40	1·75
MS2200	74×104 mm. $5 18th-century naval officer	3·75	4·00

302 "Enthroned Madonna and Child" (S. Veneziano)

1996. Christmas. Religious Paintings. Mult.

2201	25c. Type **302**	30	20
2202	55c. "Noli Me Tangere" (Fra Angelico)	55	35
2203	65c. "Madonna and Child Enthroned" (Angelico)	65	40
2204	90c. "Madonna of Corneto Tarquinia" (F. Lippi)	80	50
2205	$2 "The Annunciation" and "The Adoration of the Magi" (School of Angelico)	1·50	1·75
2206	$5 "Madonna and Child of the Shade" (Angelico)	3·00	3·75
MS2207	Two sheets. (a) 76×106 mm. $6 "Coronation of the Virgin" (Angelico). (b) 106×76 mm. $6 "Holy Family with St. Barbara" (Veronese) (horiz) Set of 2 sheets	7·50	8·50

303 "Herdboy playing the Flute" (Li Keran)

1997. Lunar New Year ("Year of the Ox"). Paintings by Li Keran. Multicoloured.

2208	90c. Type **303**	60	70
2209	90c. "Playing Cricket in the Autumn"	60	70
2210	90c. "Listening to the Summer Cicada"	60	70
2211	90c. "Grazing in the Spring"	60	70
MS2212	76×106 mm. $2 "Return in Wind and Rain" (34×51 mm).	1·00	1·25
MS2212a	135×80 mm. 55c. × 4. Designs as Nos. 2208/11	1·00	1·25

304 Lee Lai-shan (Gold Medal – Windsurfing, 1996)

1997. Olympic Games, Atlanta (3rd issue). Mult.

2213	$2 Type **304**	1·50	1·75
MS2214	97×67 mm. $5 Lee Lai-shan wearing Gold medal (37×50 mm)	3·00	3·50

305 "Meticella metis"

1997. Butterflies. Multicoloured.

2215	55c. Type **305**	50	55
2216	55c. "Coeliades forestan"	50	55
2217	55c. "Papilio dardanus"	50	55
2218	55c. "Mylothris chloris"	50	55
2219	55c. "Poecilmitis thysbe"	50	55
2220	55c. "Myrina silenus"	50	55
2221	55c. "Bematistes aganice"	50	55
2222	55c. "Euphaedra neophron"	50	55
2223	55c. "Precis hierta"	50	55
2224	90c. "Coeliadas forestan" (vert)	60	65
2225	90c. "Spialia spio" (vert)	60	65
2226	90c. "Belenois aurota" (vert)	60	65
2227	90c. "Dingana bowkom" (vert)	60	65
2228	90c. "Charaxes jasius" (vert)	60	65
2229	90c. "Catacroptera cloanthe" (vert)	60	65
2230	90c. "Colias electo" (vert)	60	65
2231	90c. "Junonia archesia" (vert)	60	65
MS2232	Two sheets, each 102×71 mm. (a) $6 "Eurytela dryope". (b) "Acraea natalica" Set of 2 sheets	8·00	9·00

No. 2230 is inscribed "Collas electo" in error.

Nos. 2215/23 and 2224/31 respectively were printed together, se-tenant, with the backgrounds forming a composite design.

1997. 50th Anniv of UNESCO. As T **273a** of Gambia. Multicoloured.

2233	55c. Temple roof, China	50	35
2234	65c. The Palace of Diocletian, Split, Croatia	60	40
2235	90c. St. Mary's Cathedral, Hildesheim, Germany	70	50
2236	$1 The Monastery of Rossanou, Mount Meteora, Greece	70	70
2237	$1 Carved face, Copan, Honduras (vert)	70	75
2238	$1 Cuzco Cathedral, Peru (vert)	70	75
2239	$1 Church, Olinda, Brazil (vert)	70	75
2240	$1 Canaima National Park, Venezuela (vert)	70	75
2241	$1 Galapagos Islands National Park, Ecuador (vert)	70	75
2242	$1 Church ruins, La Santisima Jesuit Missions, Paraguay (vert)	70	75
2243	$1 San Lorenzo Fortress, Panama (vert)	70	75
2244	$1 Fortress, National Park, Haiti (vert)	70	75
2245	$2 Scandola Nature Reserve, France	1·40	1·75
2246	$4 Church of San Antao, Portugal	2·50	3·25
MS2247	Two sheets, each 127×102 mm. (a) $6 Chengde Lakes, China. (b) $6 Pavilion, Kyoto, Japan Set of 2 sheets	7·50	8·50

No. 2234 is inscr "DICELECIAN" in error.

306 Tanglefoot and Minnie

1997. Disney Sweethearts. Multicoloured.

2248	25c. Type **306**	45	20
2249	35c. Mickey and Minnie kissing on ship's wheel	55	20
2250	55c. Pluto and kitten	70	30
2251	65c. Clarabelle Cow kissing Horace Horsecollar	70	35
2252	90c. Elmer Elephant and tiger	85	55
2253	$1 Minnie kissing Mickey in period costume	95	70
2254	$2 Donald Duck and nephew	1·60	1·75
2255	$4 Dog kissing Pluto	2·50	3·50
MS2256	Three sheets. (a) 126×100 mm. $5 Simba and Nala in "The Lion King". (b) 133×104 mm. $6 Mickey covered in lipstick and Minnie (horiz). (c) 104×124 mm. $6 Mickey and Pluto Set of 3 sheets	9·50	10·00

307 Afghan Hound

1997. Cats and Dogs. Multicoloured.

2257	20c. Type **307**	45	25
2258	25c. Cream Burmese	45	25
2259	55c. Cocker spaniel	55	35
2260	65c. Smooth fox terrier	60	40
2261	90c. West highland white terrier	70	75
2262	90c. St. Bernard puppies	70	75
2263	90c. Boy with grand basset	70	75
2264	90c. Rough collie	70	75
2265	90c. Golden retriever	70	75
2266	90c. Golden retriever, Tibetan spaniel and smooth fox terrier	70	75
2267	90c. Smooth fox terrier	70	75
2268	$1 Snowshoe	75	75
2269	$2 Sorrell Abyssinian	1·40	1·50
2270	$2 British bicolour shorthair	1·40	1·50
2271	$2 Maine coon and Somali kittens	1·40	1·50
2272	$2 Maine coon kitten	1·40	1·50
2273	$2 Lynx point Siamese	1·40	1·50
2274	$2 Blue Burmese kitten and white Persian	1·40	1·50
2275	$2 Persian kitten	1·40	1·50
2276	$5 Torbie Persian	3·25	3·75
MS2277	Two sheets, each 106×76 mm. (a) $6 Silver tabby. (b) $6 Shetland sheepdog Set of 2 sheets	8·00	9·00

Nos. 2262/7 and 2270/5 respectively were printed together, se-tenant, with the backgrounds forming composite designs.

308 "Oncidium altissimum"

1997. Orchids of the Caribbean. Multicoloured.

2278	20c. Type **308**	50	25
2279	25c. "Oncidium papilio"	50	25
2280	55c. "Epidendrum fragrans"	60	35
2281	65c. "Oncidium lanceanum"	70	40
2282	90c. "Campylocentrum micranthum"	90	50
2283	$1 "Brassavola cucculata" (horiz)	1·00	1·10
2284	$1 "Epidendrum ibaguense" (horiz)	1·00	1·10
2285	$1 "Ionopsis utricularioides" (horiz)	1·00	1·10
2286	$1 "Rodriguezia lanceolata" (horiz)	1·00	1·10
2287	$1 "Oncidium cebolleta" (horiz)	1·00	1·10
2288	$1 "Epidendrum ciliare" (horiz)	1·00	1·10
2289	$4 "Pogonia rosea"	2·75	3·00
MS2290	Two sheets, each 106×76 mm. (a) $5 "Oncidium ampliatum" (horiz). (b) $5 "Starhopea grandiflora" (horiz) Set of 2 sheets	7·00	7·50

Nos. 2283/8 were printed together, se-tenant, with the backgrounds forming a composite design.

309 "Mary, Mary Quite Contrary"

1997. 300th Anniv of Mother Goose Nursery Rhymes. Sheet 72×102 mm.

MS2291	**309** $6 multicoloured	3·25	3·50

1997. 10th Anniv of Chernobyl Nuclear Disaster. As T **276b** of Gambia. Multicoloured.

2292	$2 As Type **276b** of Gambia	1·25	1·40
2293	$2 As Type **276b** of Gambia but inscribed "CHABAD'S CHILDREN OF CHERNOBYL" at foot	1·25	1·40

1997. 50th Death Anniv of Paul Harris (founder of Rotary International). As T **276c** of Gambia. Multicoloured.

2294	$2 Paul Harris and irrigation project, Honduras	1·25	1·50
MS2295	78×107 mm. $6 Paul Harris with Rotary and World Community Service emblems	3·25	4·00

1997. Golden Wedding of Queen Elizabeth and Prince Philip. As T **276d** of Gambia. Multicoloured.

2296	$1 Queen Elizabeth II	80	80
2297	$1 Royal Coat of Arms	80	80
2298	$1 Queen Elizabeth and Prince Philip in shirt sleeves	80	80
2299	$1 Queen Elizabeth and Prince Philip in naval uniform	80	80
2300	$1 Buckingham Palace	80	80
2301	$1 Prince Philip	80	80
MS2302	100×71 mm. $6 Queen Elizabeth and Prince Philip with flower arrangement	4·00	4·25

1997. "Pacific '97" International Stamp Exhibition, San Francisco. Death Centenary of Heinrich von Stephan (founder of the U.P.U.). As T **276e** of Gambia.

2303	$2 violet	1·25	1·40
2304	$2 brown	1·25	1·40
2305	$2 brown	1·25	1·40
MS2306	82×119 mm. $6 blue and grey	3·50	3·75

DESIGNS: No. 2303, Kaiser Wilhelm II and Heinrich von Stephan; 2304, Heinrich von Stephan and Mercury; 2305, Early Japanese postal messenger; **MS**2306, Heinrich von Stephan and Russian postal dog team, 1895.

310 "Ichigaya Hachiman Shrine"

1997. Birth Centenary of Hiroshige (Japanese painter). "One Hundred Famous Views of Edo". Multicoloured.

2307	$1.55 Type **310**	1·40	1·40
2308	$1.55 "Blossoms on the Tama River Embankment"	1·40	1·40
2309	$1.55 "Kumano Junisha Shrine, Tsunohazu"	1·40	1·40
2310	$1.55 "Benkei Moat from Soto-Sakurada to Kojimachi"	1·40	1·40
2311	$1.55 "Kinokuni Hill and View of Akasak Tameike"	1·40	1·40
2312	$1.55 "Naito Shinjuku, Yotsuya"	1·40	1·40
MS2313	Two sheets, each 102×127 mm. (a) $6 "Sanno Festival Procession at Kojimachi I-chome". (b) $6 "Kasumigaseki" Set of 2 sheets	8·50	9·00

1997. 175th Anniv of Brothers Grimm's Third Collection of Fairy Tales. The Goose Girl. As T **277a** of Gambia. Multicoloured.

2314	$2 Goose girl with horse	1·50	1·60

2315 $2 Geese in front of castle 1·50 1·60
2316 $2 Goose girl 1·50 1·60
MS2317 124×96 mm. $6 Goose girl (horiz) 4·00 4·25

311 Hong Kong Skyline at Dusk

1997. Return of Hong Kong to China. Multicoloured.
2318 65c. Type **311** 60 70
2319 90c. Type **311** 70 80
2320 $1 Type **311** 75 85
2321 $1 Hong Kong at night 75 85
2322 $1.45 Hong Kong by day 1·00 1·25
2323 $2 Hong Kong at night (different) 1·25 1·75
2324 $3 Type **311** 1·50 2·00

312 Yukto Kasaya (Japan) (ski jump), 1972

1997. Winter Olympic Games, Nagano, Japan (1998). Multicoloured.
2325 20c. Type **312** 50 25
2326 25c. Jens Weissflog (Germany) (ski jump), 1994 50 25
2327 55c. Anton Maier (Norway) (100 m men's speed skating), 1968 60 45
2328 55c. Ljubov Egorova (Russia) (women's 5 km cross-country skiing), 1994 60 45
2329 65c. Swedish ice hockey, 1994 80 45
2330 90c. Bernhard Glass (Germany) (men's single luge), 1980 85 60
2331 $1 Type **312** 90 1·00
2332 $1 As No. 2326 90 1·00
2333 $1 As No. 2327 90 1·00
2334 $1 Christa Rethenburger (Germany) (women's 100 m speed skating), 1988 90 1·00
2335 $4 Frank-Peter Roetsch (Germany) (men's biathlon), 1988 2·50 3·00
MS2336 Two sheets, each 106×76 mm. (a) $5 Charles Jewtraw (U.S.A.) (men's 500 m speed skating), 1924. (b) $5 Jacob Tullin Thams (Norway) (ski jumping), 1924 Set of 2 sheets 6·00 7·00

1997. World Cup Football Championship, France (1998). As T **283a** of Gambia. Multicoloured (except Nos. 2343/4, 2348, 2350, 2353/4).
2337 20c. Klinsmann, Germany (vert) 50 25
2338 55c. Bergkamp, Holland (vert) 70 35
2339 65c. Ravanelli, Italy (vert) 70 75
2340 65c. Wembley Stadium, England 70 75
2341 65c. Bernabeu Stadium, Spain 70 75
2342 65c. Maracana Stadium, Brazil 70 75
2343 65c. Stadio Torino, Italy (black) 70 75
2344 65c. Centenary Stadium, Uruguay (black) 70 75
2345 65c. Olympiastadion, Germany 70 75
2346 65c. Rose Bowl, U.S.A. 70 75
2347 65c. Azteca Stadium, Mexico 70 75
2348 65c. Meazza, Italy (black) 70 75
2349 65c. Matthaus, Germany 70 75
2350 65c. Walter, West Germany (black) 70 75
2351 65c. Maradona, Argentina 70 75
2352 65c. Beckenbaur, Germany 70 75
2353 65c. Moore, England (black) 70 75
2354 65c. Dunga, Brazil (black) 70 75
2355 65c. Zoff, Italy 70 75
2356 90c. Klinkladze, Georgia 70 75
2357 $2 Shearer, England (vert) 1·40 1·60
2358 $4 Dani, Portugal (vert) 2·50 3·00
MS2359 Two sheets. (a) 102×126 mm. $5 Mario Kempes, Argentina (vert). (b) 126×102 mm. $6 Ally McCoist, Scotland (vert) Set of 2 sheets 7·00 8·00

313 Joffre Robinson (former Credit Union President)

1997. 40th Anniv of Co-operative Credit Union League.
2360 **313** 25c. blue and black 25 20
2361 - 55c. green and black 45 40
2362 - 65c. purple and black 55 55
2363 - 90c. multicoloured 65 70
MS2364 94×106 mm. $5 multicoloured 3·00 3·50
DESIGNS—As T **313**: 55c. Sister Alicia (founder); 65c. Lorrel Bruce (first Credit Union President). 30×60 mm: $5 Sister Alicia, Joffre Robinson and Lorrel Bruce.

314 Louis Pasteur

1997. Medical Pioneers.
2365 **314** 20c. brown 50 25
2366 - 25c. pink and red 50 25
2367 - 55c. violet 70 35
2368 - 65c. red and brown 75 45
2369 - 90c. yellow and olive 85 55
2370 - $1 blue and ultramarine 1·00 80
2371 - $2 black 1·60 1·75
2372 - $3 red and brown 1·90 2·25
MS2373 Two sheets, each 70×100 mm. (a) $5 multicoloured. (b) $6 multicoloured Set of 2 sheets 8·00 8·50
DESIGNS: 25c. Christiaan Barnard (first heart transplant); 55c. Sir Alexander Fleming (discovery of penicillin); 65c. Camillo Golgi (neurologist); 90c. Jonas Salk (discovery of polio vaccine); $1 Har Gobind Khorana (genetics); $2 Elizabeth Black (first woman doctor); $3 Sir Frank MacFarlane Burnet (immunologist); $5 (**MS**2373a), Sir Alexander Fleming (different); $6 (**MS**2373b), Louis Pasteur (different).

1997. Fishes. As Nos. 2175/92, but smaller, 24×21 mm.
2374 5c. Porcupinefish 55 60
2375 10c. Powder-blue surgeonfish 55 60
2376 15c. Red hind 75 60
2377 20c. Golden butterflyfish 75 30
2378 25c. Copper-banded butterflyfish 75 30
2379 35c. Pennant coralfish 90 35
2380 45c. Spotted drum 90 30
2381 55c. Blue-girdled angelfish 1·00 40
2382 60c. Scorpionfish 1·00 40
2383 65c. Harlequin sweetlips 1·00 40
2384 90c. Flame angelfish 1·40 60
2385 $1 Queen triggerfish 1·50 85
2386 $1.20 Spotlight parrotfish 1·75 1·50
2387 $1.45 Black durgon 2·00 2·00
2388 $2 Glass-eyed snapper 2·75 3·50
2389 $5 Balloonfish 4·25 4·75
2390 $10 Creole wrasse 6·00 7·00
2391 $20 Seabass 10·00 12·00

315 Diana, Princess of Wales

1997. Diana, Princess of Wales Commemoration. Multicoloured.
2392 $2 Type **315** 1·25 1·40
2393 $2 Wearing diamond-drop earrings 1·25 1·40
2394 $2 Resting head on hand 1·25 1·40
2395 $2 Wearing tiara 1·25 1·40
MS2396 76×106 mm. $5 Diana, Princess of Wales 3·50 3·50

316 "Echo et Narcisse" (Toile)

1997. Christmas. Paintings.
2397 20c. Type **316** 35 15
2398 55c. "The Archangel Raphael leaving the Family of Tobias" (Rembrandt) 55 35
2399 65c. "Seated Nymphs with Flute" (Francois Boucher) 65 40
2400 90c. "Angel" (Rembrandt) 80 50
2401 $2 "Dispute" (Raphael) 1·50 1·75
2402 $4 "Holy Trinity" (Raphael) 2·50 3·25
MS2403 Two sheets, each 114×104 mm. (a) $6 "The Annunciation" (Botticelli) (horiz). (b) $6 "Christ on the Mount of Olives" (El Greco) (horiz) Set of 2 sheets 8·00 9·00
No. **MS**2403a is inscribed "Study (of the) Muse" in error.

317 "Tiger" (Gao Qifeng)

1998. Chinese New Year ("Year of the Tiger"). Multicoloured.
2404 55c. Type **317** 50 40
2405 65c. "Tiger" (Zhao Shao'ang) 60 45
2406 90c. "Tiger" (Gao Jianfu) 70 55
2407 $1.20 "Tiger" (different) (Gao Jianfu) 85 1·00
MS2408 95×65 mm. $3 "Spirit of Kingship" (Gao Jianfu) (48×40 mm) 1·75 2·00

318 Akira Kurosawa

1998. Millennium Series. Famous People of the Twentieth Century. Multicoloured (except Nos. 2411, 2414/15 and **MS**2417). (a) Japanese Cinema Stars.
2409 $1 Type **318** 80 85
2410 $1 "Rashomon" directed by Kursawa (56×42 mm) 80 85
2411 $1 Toshiro Mifune in "Seven Samurai" (black and grey) (56×42 mm) 80 85
2412 $1 Toshiro Mifune 80 85
2413 $1 Yasujiro Ozu 80 85
2414 $1 "Late Spring" directed by Ozu (black and grey) (56×42 mm) 80 85
2415 $1 Sessue Hayakawa in "Bridge on the River Kwai" (brown, deep brown and black) (56×42 mm) 80 85
2416 $1 Sessue Hayakawa 80 85
MS2417 110×80 mm. $6 Akira Kurosawa (brown, red and black) 5·75 6·00

(b) Sporting Record Holders. Multicoloured.
2418 $1 Jesse Owens (winner of four Olympic gold medals, Berlin, 1936) 80 85
2419 $1 Owens competing at Berlin (56×42 mm) 80 85
2420 $1 Isaac Berger competing (56×42 mm) 80 85
2421 $1 Isaac Berger (weightlifter) 80 85
2422 $1 Boris Becker (Wimbledon champion) 80 85
2423 $1 Boris Becker on court (56×42 mm) 80 85
2424 $1 Ashe with Wimbledon trophy (56×42 mm) 80 85
2425 $1 Arthur Ashe (1st African-American Wimbledon singles champion, 1975) 80 85
MS2426 $6 Franz Beckenbauer (captain of German football team) (horiz) 4·25 4·50

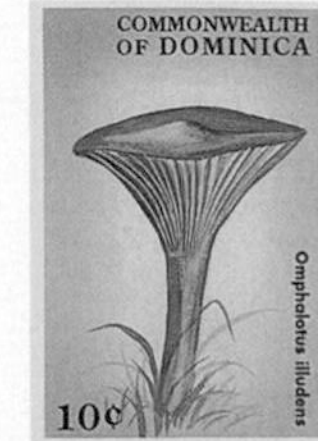

319 "Omphalotus illudens"

1998. Fungi of the World. Multicoloured.
2427 10c. Type **319** 40 50
2428 15c. "Inocybe fastigiata" 40 40
2429 20c. "Marasmius plicatulus" 40 40
2430 50c. "Mycena lilacifolia" 55 40
2431 55c. "Armillaria straminea" and "Calastrina argiolus" (butterfly) 55 40
2432 90c. "Tricholomopsis rutilans" and "Melitaea didyma" (butterfly) 70 50
2433 $1 "Lepiota naucina" 75 75
2434 $1 "Cortinarius violaceus" 75 75
2435 $1 "Boletus aereus" 75 75
2436 $1 "Tricholoma aurantium" 75 75
2437 $1 "Lepiota procera" 75 75
2438 $1 "Clitocybe geotropa" 75 75
2439 $1 "Lepiota acutesquamosa" 75 75
2440 $1 "Tricholoma saponaceum" 75 75
2441 $1 "Lycoperdon gemmatum" 75 75
2442 $1 "Boletus ornatipes" 75 75
2443 $1 "Russula xerampelina" 75 75
2444 $1 "Cortinarius collinitus" 75 75
2445 $1 "Agaricus meleagris" 75 75
2446 $1 "Coprinus comatus" 75 75
2447 $1 "Amanita caesarea" 75 75
2448 $1 "Amanita brunnescens" 75 75
2449 $1 "Amanita muscaria" 75 75
2450 $1 "Morchella esculenta" 75 75
MS2451 76×106 mm. $6 "Cortinarius violaceus" 4·00 4·25
Nos. 2433/41 and 2442/50 respectively were printed together, se-tenant, with the backgrounds forming composite designs.

320 Topsail Schooner

1998. History of Sailing Ships. Multicoloured.
2452 55c. Type **320** 50 50
2453 55c. "Golden Hind" (Drake) 50 50
2454 55c. "Moshulu" (barque) 50 50
2455 55c. "Bluenose" (schooner) 50 50
2456 55c. Roman merchant ship 50 50
2457 55c. "Gazela Primiero" (barquentine) 50 50
2458 65c. Greek war galley 50 40
2459 90c. Egyptian felucca 65 60
2460 $1 Viking longship 70 75
2461 $2 Chinese junk 1·25 1·50
MS2462 Two sheets, each 106×76 mm. (a) $5 "Pinta" (Columbus). (b) $5 Chesapeake Bay skipjack Set of 2 sheets 7·00 7·50
No. 2457 is inscribed "GAZELA PRIMERIRO", and both Nos. 2458/9 "EGPYTIAN FELUCCA", all in error.

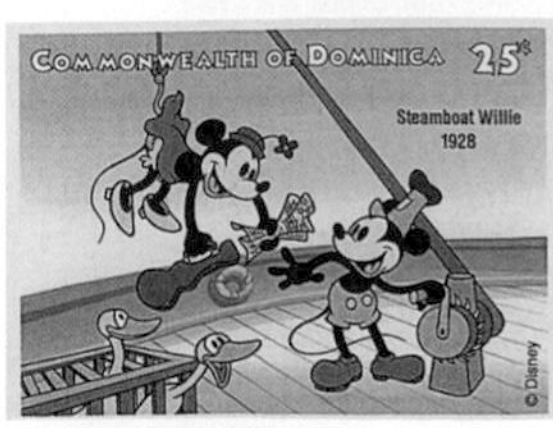

321 "Steamboat Willie", 1928

1998. 70th Anniv of Mickey and Minnie Mouse. Multicoloured.
2463 25c. Type **321** 80 85
2464 55c. "The Brave Little Tailor", 1938 95 1·10
2465 65c. "Nifty Nineties", 1941 1·00 1·25

2466 90c. "Mickey Mouse Club", 1955 1·25 1·40
2467 $1 Mickey and Minnie at opening of Walt Disney World, 1971 1·25 1·40
2468 $1.45 "Mousercise Mickey and Minnie", 1980 1·40 1·60
2469 $5 "Runaway Brain", 1995 (97×110 mm) 2·75 3·00
MS2470 Two sheets, each 130×104 mm. (a) $5 Walt Disney with Mickey and Minnie Mouse. (b) $5 Mickey and Minnie at 70th birthday party with Donald and Daisy Duck, Goofy and Pluto. Imperf Set of 2 sheets 9·00 9·50

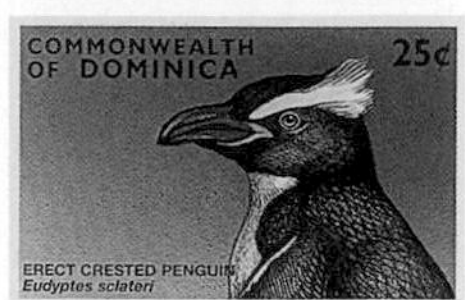

322 Big-crested Penguin ("Erect Crested Penguin")

1998. Sea Birds. Multicoloured.
2471 25c. Type **322** 60 40
2472 65c. Humboldt penguin 75 40
2473 90c. Red knot 80 75
2474 90c. Greater crested tern 80 75
2475 90c. Franklin's gull 80 75
2476 90c. Australian pelican 80 75
2477 90c. Fairy prion 80 75
2478 90c. Andean gull 80 75
2479 90c. Blue-eyed cormorant ("Imperial Shag") 80 75
2480 90c. Grey phalarope ("Red Phalarope") 80 75
2481 90c. Hooded grebe 80 75
2482 90c. Least aucklet 80 75
2483 90c. Little grebe 80 75
2484 90c. Pintado petrel ("Cape Petrel") 80 75
2485 90c. Slavonian grebe ("Horned Grebe") 80 75
2486 $1 Audubon's shearwater 80 70
MS2487 Two sheets, each 100×70 mm. (a) $5 Blue-footed booby. (b) $5 Fulmar Set of 2 sheets 7·50 8·00

Nos. 2474/85 were printed together, se-tenant, with the backgrounds forming a composite design.

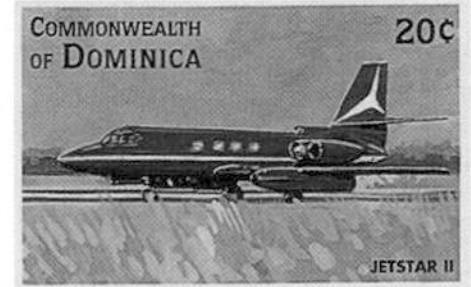

323 Lockheed Jetstar II

1998. Modern Aircraft. Multicoloured.
2488 20c. Type **323** 65 50
2489 25c. Antonov AN 225 65 50
2490 55c. de Havilland DHC-8 Dash-8 75 35
2491 65c. Beech Model, Beech-99 75 40
2492 90c. American Airlines Eagle 80 50
2493 $1 Lockheed SR 71 "Blackbird" spy plane 80 75
2494 $1 Northrop B-2A Spirit 80 75
2495 $1 Northrop YF-23 80 75
2496 $1 Grumman F-14A Tomcat 80 75
2497 $1 Boeing F-15 Eagle S 80 75
2498 $1 MiG 29 Fulcrum 80 75
2499 $1 Europa X5 80 75
2500 $1 Camion 80 75
2501 $1 E 400 80 75
2502 $1 CL-215 C-GKDN amphibian 80 75
2503 $1 Piper PA-46 Malibu Meridian 80 75
2504 $1 Beech Model 390 Premier 80 75
2505 $1 Lockheed F-22 Raptor 80 75
2506 $1 Piper Seneca V 80 75
2507 $1 CL-215 amphibian 80 75
2508 $1 Vantase 80 75
2509 $2 Hansa HFB 320 14·00 1·40
MS2510 Two sheets. (a) 88×69 mm. $6 F1 Fighter. (b) 69×88 mm. $6 Sea Hopper seaplane Set of 2 sheets 8·50 9·00

1998. 50th Anniv of Organization of American States. As T **454b** of Grenada. Multicoloured.
2511 $1 Stylised Americas 75 75

1998. 25th Death Anniv of Pablo Picasso (painter). As T **291a** of Gambia. Multicoloured.
2512 90c. "The Painter and his Model" 60 50
2513 $1 "The Crucifixion" 70 70
2514 $2 "Nude with Raised Arms" (vert) 1·25 1·50
MS2515 122×102 mm. $6 "Cafe at Royan" 3·50 4·00

1998. Birth Centenary of Enzo Ferrari (car manufacturer). As T **564a** of Ghana. Mult.
2516 55c. 365 GT 2+2 80 40
2517 90c. Boano/Ellena 250 GT 1·10 85
2518 $1 375 MM coupe 1·25 1·40
MS2519 104×70 mm. $5 **212** (91×34 mm) 4·00 4·25

1998. 19th World Scout Jamboree, Chile. As T **454c** of Grenada. Multicoloured.
2520 65c. Scout saluting 50 35
2521 $1 Scout handshake 70 70
2522 $2 International scout flag 1·50 1·50
MS2523 76×106 mm. $5 Lord Baden-Powell 3·50 3·75

324 Mahatma Gandhi

1998. 50th Death Anniv of Mahatma Gandhi. Multicoloured.
2524 90c. Type **324** 1·00 75
MS2525 106×75 mm. $6 Gandhi spinning thread 4·25 4·25

1998. 80th Anniv of Royal Air Force. As T **292a** of Gambia. Multicoloured.
2526 $2 H.S. 801 Nimrod MR2P (reconnaissance) 1·50 1·60
2527 $2 Lockheed C-130 Hercules (transport) 1·50 1·60
2528 $2 Panavia Tornado GR1 1·50 1·60
2529 $2 Lockheed C-130 Hercules landing 1·50 1·60
MS2530 Two sheets, each 90×68 mm. (a) $5 Bristol F2B fighter and Golden eagle (bird). (b) $6 Hawker Hart and EF-2000 Euro-fighter Set of 2 sheets 7·50 8·50

No. 2529 is inscribed "Panavia Tornado GR1" in error.

325 Fridman Fish

1998. International Year of the Ocean. Multicoloured.
2531 25c. Type **325** 45 35
2532 55c. Hydrocoral 55 35
2533 65c. Feather-star 60 35
2534 90c. Royal angelfish 70 50
2535 $1 Monk seal 70 75
2536 $1 Galapagos penguin 70 75
2537 $1 Manta ray 70 75
2538 $1 Hawksbill turtle 70 75
2539 $1 Moorish idols 70 75
2540 $1 Nautilius 70 75
2541 $1 Giant clam 70 75
2542 $1 Tubeworms 70 75
2543 $1 Nudibranch 70 75
2544 $1 Spotted dolphins 70 75
2545 $1 Atlantic sailfish 70 75
2546 $1 Sailfin flying fish 70 75
2547 $1 Fairy basslet 70 75
2548 $1 Atlantic spadefish 70 75
2549 $1 Leatherback turtle 70 75
2550 $1 Blue tang 70 75
2551 $1 Coral-banded shrimp 70 75
2552 $1 Rock beauty 70 75
MS2553 Two sheets, each 110×85 mm. (a) $5 Humpback whale and calf (56×41 mm). (b) $6 Leafy sea-dragon (56×41 mm) Set of 2 sheets 7·50 8·00

Nos. 2535/43 and 2544/52 respectively were printed together, se-tenant, with the backgrounds forming composite designs.

1998. Save the Turtles Campaign. Nos. 1686/7, 1689/90 and 1692 optd **Save the Turtles.**
2554 25c. Type **263** 35 30
2555 55c. Hawksbill turtle swimming 50 30
2556 90c. Green turtle laying eggs 65 45
2557 $1 Green turtle swimming 70 65
2558 $4 Loggerhead turtle 2·75 3·25

327 Common Cardinal ("Northern Cardinal")

1998. Christmas. Birds. Multicoloured.
2559 25c. Type **327** 40 25
2560 55c. Eastern bluebird 50 25
2561 65c. Carolina wren 55 30
2562 90c. Blue jay 70 50
2563 $1 Evening grosbeak 80 75
2564 $2 Bohemian waxwing 1·50 1·75
MS2565 Two sheets, each 70×97 mm. (a) $5 Northern Parula. (b) $6 Painted bunting Set of 2 sheets 7·50 8·00

328 "Magpies and Hare" (Ts'ui Pai)

1999. Chinese New Year ("Year of the Rabbit").
2566 **328** $1.50 multicoloured 1·40 1·60

329 "Broughtonia sanguinea"

1999. Orchids of the Caribbean. Multicoloured.
2567 55c. Type **329** 60 35
2568 65c. "Cattleyonia Keith Roth" "Roma" 70 40
2569 90c. "Comparettia falcata" 80 50
2570 $1 "Dracula erythiochaete" 80 75
2571 $1 "Lycasle aromatica" 80 75
2572 $1 "Masdevallia marguerile" 80 75
2573 $1 "Encyclia marlae" 80 75
2574 $1 "Laelia gouldiana" 80 75
2575 $1 "Huntleya meleagris" 80 75
2576 $1 "Galeandria baueri" 80 75
2577 $1 "Lycale deppei" 80 75
2578 $1 "Anguloa clowesii" 80 75
2579 $1 "Lemboglossum cervantesii" 80 75
2580 $1 "Oncidium cebolleta" 80 75
2581 $1 "Millonia" 80 75
2582 $1 "Pescatorea lehmannll" 80 75
2583 $1 "Sophronitis coccinea" 80 75
2584 $1 "Pescatorea cerina" 80 75
2585 $1 "Encyclia vitellina" 80 75
2586 $2 "Cochleanthes discolor" 1·40 1·40
MS2587 Two sheets, each 76×89 mm. (a) $5 "Lepanthes ovalis". (b) $5 "Encyclia cochleata" Set of 2 sheets 7·00 8·00

330 County Donegal Petrol Rail Car No. 10, Ireland

1999. "Australia '99" International Stamp Exhibition, Melbourne. Diesel and Electric Trains. Multicoloured.
2588 $1 Type **330** 75 75
2589 $1 Canadian Pacific rail car, Canada 75 75
2590 $1 Class WDM locomotive, India 75 75
2591 $1 Bi-polar locomotive, No. E-2, U.S.A. 75 75
2592 $1 Class X locomotive, Australia 75 75
2593 $1 Class "Beijing" locomotive, China 75 75
2594 $1 Class E428 locomotive, Italy 75 75
2595 $1 Class 581 twelve-car train, Japan 75 75
2596 $1 Class 103.1 locomotive, West Germany 75 75
2597 $1 Class 24 Trans-Pennine train, Great Britain 75 75
2598 $1 Amtrak Class GG1, No. 902, U.S.A. 75 75
2599 $1 Class LRC train, Canada 75 75
2600 $1 Class EW train, New Zealand 75 75
2601 $1 Class SS1 Shao-Shani, China 75 75
2602 $1 Gulf, Mobile and Ohio train, U.S.A. 75 75
2603 $1 Class 9100 locomotive, France 75 75
MS2604 Two sheets, each 106×76 mm. (a) $5 X-2000 tilting express train, Sweden (vert). (b) $6 Class 87 locomotive, Great Britain (vert) Set of 2 sheets 7·00 8·00

No. 2589 is inscribed "USA - RDC Single Rail Car" in error.

331 Hypacrosaurus

1999. Prehistoric Animals. Multicoloured.
2605 25c. Tyrannosaurus (vert) 50 40
2606 65c. Type **331** 75 40
2607 90c. Sauropelta 80 50
2608 $1 Barosaurus 80 75
2609 $1 Rhamphorhynchus 80 75
2610 $1 Apatosaurus 80 75
2611 $1 Archaeopteryx 80 75
2612 $1 Diplodocus 80 75
2613 $1 Ceratosaurus 80 75
2614 $1 Stegosaurus 80 75
2615 $1 Elaphrosaurus 80 75
2616 $1 Vulcanodon 80 75
2617 $1 Psittacosaurus 80 75
2618 $1 Pteranodon 80 75
2619 $1 Ichthyornis 80 75
2620 $1 Spinosaurus 80 75
2621 $1 Parasaurolophus 80 75
2622 $1 Ornithomimus 80 75
2623 $1 Anatosaurus 80 75
2624 $1 Triceratops 80 75
2625 $1 Baryonx 80 75
2626 $2 Zalambdalestes 1·40 1·40
MS2627 Two sheets, each 106×80 mm. (a) $5 Yangchuanosaurus. (b) $6 Brachiosaurus (vert) Set of 2 sheets 7·50 8·00

Nos. 2608/16 and 2617/25 respectively were each printed together, se-tenant, with the backgrounds forming composite designs.

332 Miss Sophie Rhys-Jones

1999. Royal Wedding.
2628 **332** $3 blue and black 1·75 2·00
2629 - $3 multicoloured 1·75 2·00
2630 - $3 blue and black 1·75 2·00
MS2631 78×108 mm. $6 multicoloured 3·50 4·00

DESIGNS: No. 2629 and **MS**2631, Miss Sophie Rhys-Jones and Prince Edward; 2630, Prince Edward.

1999. "iBRA '99" International Stamp Exhibition, Nuremberg. As T **299a** of Gambia. Multicoloured.
2632 65c. "Eendracht" (Dirk Hartog) with Cameroons Expeditionary Force 1915 2d. and 3d. surcharges 60 35
2633 90c. "Eendracht" with Kamerun 1900 10pf. and 25pf. stamps 70 50
2634 $1 Early German railway locomotive with Kamerun 1900 5m. stamp 80 75
2635 $2 Early German railway locomotive with Kamerun 1890 overprinted 50pf. stamp 1·50 1·75
MS2636 138×109 mm. $6 Exhibition emblem and Kamerun 5m. stamp postmarked 1913 3·50 4·00

1999. 150th Death Anniv of Katsushika Hokusai (Japanese artist). As T **299b** of Gambia. Multicoloured.

2637	$2 "Pilgrims at Kirifuri Waterfall"	1·25	1·40
2638	$2 "Kakura-Sato" (rats pulling on rope)	1·25	1·40
2639	$2 "Travellers on the Bridge by Ono Waterfall"	1·25	1·40
2640	$2 "Fast Cargo Boat battling the Waves"	1·25	1·40
2641	$2 "Kakura-Sato" (rats with barrels)	1·25	1·40
2642	$2 "Buufinfinh and Weeping Cherry"	1·25	1·40
2643	$2 "Cuckoo and Azalea"	1·25	1·40
2644	$2 "Soldiers" (with lamp)	1·25	1·40
2645	$2 "Lovers in the Snow"	1·25	1·40
2646	$2 "Ghost of Koheiji"	1·25	1·40
2647	$2 "Soldiers" (with hand on hip)	1·25	1·40
2648	$2 "Chinese Poet in Snow"	1·25	1·40
MS2649	Two sheets, each 101×72 mm. (a) $5 "Empress Jito". (b) $6 "One Hundred Poems by One Hundred Poets" Set of 2 sheets	6·50	7·00

1999. 10th Anniv of United Nations Rights of the Child Convention. As T **299c** of Gambia. Multicoloured.

2650	$3 Small girl (vert)	1·25	1·40
2651	$3 Small boy (vert)	1·25	1·40
2652	$3 Small boy and girl (vert)	1·25	1·40
MS2653	85×110 mm. $6 Peace dove	3·50	4·00

Nos. 2650/2 were printed together, se-tenant, forming a composite design which continues onto the sheet margins.

1999. "PhilexFrance '99" International Stamp Exhibition, Paris. Railway Locomotives. Two sheets, each containing horiz designs as T **299d** of Gambia. Multicoloured.

MS2654	Two sheets, each 106×81 mm. (a) $5 Steam locomotive "L'Aigle", 1855. (b) $6 Mainline diesel locomotive, 1963 Set of 2 sheets	7·00	7·00

1999. 250th Birth Anniv of Johann von Goethe (German writer). As T **299e** of Gambia.

2655	$2 multicoloured	1·25	1·25
2656	$2 blue, purple and black	1·25	1·25
2657	$2 multicoloured	1·25	1·25
MS2658	76×100 mm. $6 grey, black and brown	3·50	4·00

DESIGNS—HORIZ: No. 2655, Faust and astrological sign; 2656, Von Goethe and Von Schiller; 2657, Faust tempted by Mephistopheles. VERT: No. **MS**2658, Johann von Goethe.

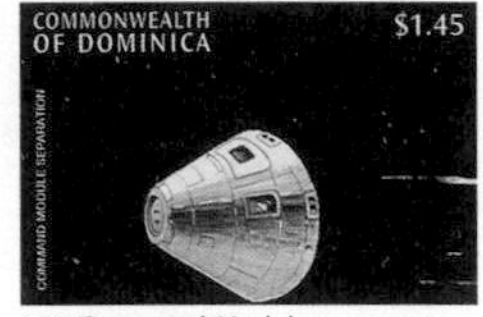

333 Command Module

1999. 30th Anniv of First Manned Landing on Moon. Multicoloured.

2659	$1.45 Type **333**	1·10	1·25
2660	$1.45 Service module	1·10	1·25
2661	$1.45 Booster separation	1·10	1·25
2662	$1.45 Lunar and command modules	1·10	1·25
2663	$1.45 Tracking telescope	1·10	1·25
2664	$1.45 Goldstone radio telescope	1·10	1·25
MS2665	106×76 mm. $6 "Apollo 11" after splashdown	3·50	4·00

1999. "Queen Elizabeth the Queen Mother's Century". As T **305a** of Gambia.

2666	$2 black and gold	1·40	1·40
2667	$2 black and gold	1·40	1·40
2668	$2 multicoloured	1·40	1·40
2669	$2 multicoloured	1·40	1·40
MS2670	153×157 mm. $6 multicoloured	4·00	4·25

DESIGNS: No. 2666, Queen Elizabeth, 1939; 2667, Queen Mother in Australia, 1958; 2668, Queen Mother in blue hat and coat, 1982; 2669, Queen Mother laughing, 1982. (37×50 mm)—No. **MS**2670, Queen Mother in 1953.

334 Female Dancer and "DOMFESTA"

1999. 21st Anniv of Dominica Festivals Commission. Multicoloured.

2671	25c. Type **334**	40	25
2672	55c. "21st BIRTHDAY" logo	55	30
2673	65c. Carnival Development Committee emblem	60	40
2674	90c. World Creole music emblem	70	55
MS2675	90×90 mm. $5 "21st BIRTHDAY" logo (different) (33×48 mm)	3·25	3·75

335 Family

1999. International Year of the Elderly. Sheet 90×50 mm, containing T **335** and similar vert designs. Multicoloured.

MS2676	25c. Type **335**; 65c. Parents and grandparents; 90c. Family around elderly woman in chair	1·50	1·75

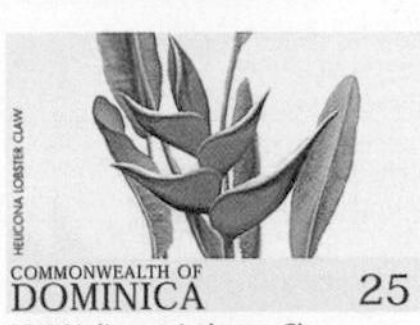

336 Helicona Lobster Claw

1999. Flora and Fauna. Multicoloured.

2677	25c. Type **336**	40	25
2678	65c. Broad-winged hawk	75	50
2679	90c. White-throated sparrow	80	70
2680	90c. Blue-winged teal	80	70
2681	90c. Racoon	80	70
2682	90c. Alfalfa butterfly	80	70
2683	90c. Foot bridge	80	70
2684	90c. Whitetail deer	80	70
2685	90c. Grey squirrel	80	70
2686	90c. Banded-purple butterfly	80	70
2687	90c. Snowdrops	80	70
2688	90c. Bullfrog	80	70
2689	90c. Mushrooms	80	70
2690	90c. Large-blotched ensatina	80	70
2691	$1 Anthurium	80	70
2692	$1.55 Blue-headed hummingbird	1·25	1·10
2693	$2 Bananaquit	1·40	1·25
2694	$4 Agouti	2·50	2·50
MS2695	Two sheets, each 100×70 mm. (a) $5 Eastern chipmunk. (b) $6 Black-footed ferret Set of 2 sheets	6·50	7·50

Nos. 2679/90 were printed together, se-tenant, with the backgrounds forming a composite design.

337 Yellow-crowned Parrot

1999. Christmas. Birds. Multicoloured.

2696	25c. Type **337**	45	35
2697	55c. Red bishop	60	40
2698	65c. Troupial	70	40
2699	90c. Puerto Rican woodpecker	1·00	55
2700	$2 Mangrove cuckoo	1·40	1·40
2701	$3 American robin	2·00	2·50
MS2702	76×98 mm. $6 "Mary with Child beside the Wall" (Dürer) (drab, black and cream)	3·50	4·00

No. 2699 is inscribed "PUERTO RECAN WOODPECKER" and No. **MS**2702 "MARYWITH", both in error.

337a Leonardo Fibonacci (mathematician, 1202)

1999. New Millennium. People and Events of the Thirteenth Century (1200–50). Multicoloured.

2703	55c. Type **337a**	55	55
2704	55c. St. Francis of Assisi (founder of Franciscan Order, 1207)	55	55
2705	55c. Mongol horsemen (Conquest of China, 1211)	55	55
2706	55c. Children with banner (Children's Crusade, 1212)	55	55
2707	55c. King John signing Magna Carta, 1215	55	55
2708	55c. University class (foundation of Salamanca University, 1218)	55	55
2709	55c. Snorre Sturlusson (author of the "Edda", 1222)	55	55
2710	55c. Ma Yuan (Chinese painter) in garden (died 1224)	55	55
2711	55c. Genghis Khan (Mongol Emperor) (died 1227)	55	55
2712	55c. Student and Buddha (establishment of Zen Buddhism in Japan, 1227)	55	55
2713	55c. Galleys (The Sixth Crusade, 1228)	55	55
2714	55c. Seals (Lubeck–Hamburg Treaty, 1230)	55	55
2715	55c. Cardinal and angel (Holy Inquisition, 1231)	55	55
2716	55c. Palace interior (conquest of Cordoba, 1236)	55	55
2717	55c. San Marino (town founded, 1243)	55	55
2718	55c. Maimonides (Jewish philosopher) (died 1204) (59×39 mm)	55	55
2719	55c. Notre Dame Cathedral, Paris (completed 1250)	55	55

338 Bombing of Pearl Harbor, 1941

1999. New Millennium. People and Events of the Twentieth Century (1940–49). Multicoloured.

2720	55c. Type **338**	60	55
2721	55c. Sir Winston Churchill (British Prime Minister, 1940)	60	55
2722	55c. Children in front of set (start of television broadcasting in U.S.A., 1940)	60	55
2723	55c. Anne Frank (Holocaust, 1942)	60	55
2724	55c. Troops wading ashore (D-Day, 1944)	60	55
2725	55c. Churchill, Roosevelt and Stalin (Yalta Conference, 1945)	60	55
2726	55c. U.N. Headquarters, New York (United Nations Organization, 1945)	60	55
2727	55c. American G.I. and concentration camp (Surrender of Germany, 1945)	60	55
2728	55c. Hoisting the Red Flag on the Reichstag (Fall of Berlin, 1945)	60	55
2729	55c. "Eniac" (first operational computer, 1946)	60	55
2730	55c. Indian with flag (Independence of India, 1947)	60	55
2731	55c. Early transistor, 1947	60	55
2732	55c. Mahatma Gandhi assassinated, 1948	60	55
2733	55c. Israelis with flag (Establishment of Israel, 1948)	60	55
2734	55c. Aircraft and children (Berlin Airlift, 1948)	60	55
2735	55c. Atomic bomb test, New Mexico, 1948 (59×39 mm)	60	55
2736	55c. Great Wall of China (People's Republic established, 1949)	60	55

No. 2732 is inscribed "Ghandi" in error.

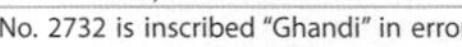

339 "Dragon flying in the Mist" (Chen Rong)

2000. Chinese New Year ("Year of the Dragon"). Multicoloured.

2737	$1.50 Type **339**	1·00	1·10
MS2738	80×60 mm. $4 Red dragon (horiz)	2·25	2·50

340 European Shorthair

2000. Cats and Dogs of the World. Multicoloured.

2739	$1 Type **340**	70	70
2740	$1 Devon rex	70	70
2741	$1 Chartreux	70	70
2742	$1 Bengal	70	70
2743	$1 American wirehair	70	70
2744	$1 Siberian	70	70
2745	$1 Burmese	70	70
2746	$1 American shorthair	70	70
2747	$1 Asian longhair	70	70
2748	$1 Burmilla	70	70
2749	$1 Snowshoe	70	70
2750	$1 Pekeface Persian	70	70
2751	$1 Himalayan Persian	70	70
2752	$1 Japanese bobtail	70	70
2753	$1 Seychelles longhair	70	70
2754	$1 Exotic shorthair	70	70
2755	$1 Jack Russell puppy (vert)	70	70
2756	$1 Shar pei puppies (vert)	70	70
2757	$1 Basset hound puppy (vert)	70	70
2758	$1 Boxer puppies (vert)	70	70
2759	$1 Wire-haired terrier (cross) puppy (vert)	70	70
2760	$1 Golden retriever puppies (vert)	70	70
MS2761	Three sheets, each 101×81 mm. (a) $6 Sleeping cat. (b) $6 Grey cat with yellow eyes. (c) $6 Beagle puppy (vert) Set of 3 sheets	9·00	10·00

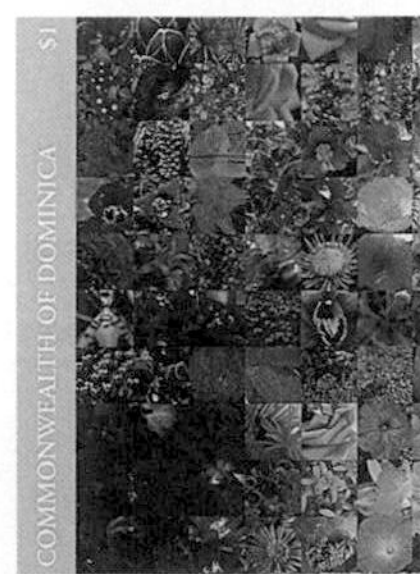

341 Flowers forming Top of Head

2000. Faces of the Millennium: Diana, Princess of Wales. Designs showing collage of miniature flower photographs. Multicoloured.

2762	$1 Type **341** (face value at left)	65	70
2763	$1 Top of head (face value at right)	65	70
2764	$1 Ear (face value at left)	65	70
2765	$1 Eye and temple (face value at right)	65	70
2766	$1 Cheek (face value at left)	65	70
2767	$1 Cheek (face value at right)	65	70
2768	$1 Blue background (face value at left)	65	70
2769	$1 Chin (face value at right)	65	70

Nos. 2762/9 were printed together, se-tenant, in sheetlets of 8 with the stamps arranged in two vertical columns separated by a gutter also containing miniature photographs. When viewed as a whole, the sheetlet forms a portrait of Diana, Princess of Wales.

342 Giant Swallowtail

2000. Butterflies. Multicoloured.

2770	$1.50 Type **342**	90	90
2771	$1.50 Tiger pierid	90	90
2772	$1.50 Orange theope butterfly	90	90
2773	$1.50 White peacock	90	90
2774	$1.50 Blue tharops	90	90
2775	$1.50 Mosaic	90	90
2776	$1.50 Banded king shoemaker	90	90
2777	$1.50 Figure-of-eight butterfly	90	90
2778	$1.50 Grecian shoemaker	90	90
2779	$1.50 Blue night butterfly	90	90
2780	$1.50 Monarch	90	90
2781	$1.50 Common morpho	90	90
2782	$1.50 Orange-barred sulphur	90	90
2783	$1.50 Clorinde	90	90
2784	$1.50 Small flambeau	90	90
2785	$1.50 Small lace-wing	90	90
2786	$1.50 Polydamas swallowtail	90	90
2787	$1.50 The atala	90	90

MS2788 Three sheets, each 100×70 mm. (a) $6 Polydamas swallowtail (vert). (b) $6 Blue-green reflector (vert). (c) $6 Sloane's urania (vert) Set of 3 sheets 9·00 10·00

343 Passion Flower

2000. Flowers. Multicoloured. (a) Size 28×42 mm.

2789 65c. Type **343** 50 30
2790 90c. Spray orchid 1·50 60
2791 $1 Peach angels trumpet 70 65
2792 $4 Allamanda 2·25 2·25

(b) Size 32×48 mm.

2793 $1.65 Bird of paradise 85 90
2794 $1.65 Lobster claw heliconia 85 90
2795 $1.65 Candle bush 85 90
2796 $1.65 Flor de San Miguel 85 90
2797 $1.65 Hibiscus 85 90
2798 $1.65 Oleander 85 90
2799 $1.65 Anthurium 85 90
2800 $1.65 Fire ginger 85 90
2801 $1.65 Shrimp plant 85 90
2802 $1.65 Sky vine thumbergia 85 90
2803 $1.65 Ceriman 85 90
2804 $1.65 Morning glory 85 90
MS2805 Two sheets, each 76×106 mm. (a) $6 Bird of Paradise and butterfly (38×50 mm). (b) $6 Hibiscus and hummingbird (38×50 mm) Set of 2 sheets 7·00 7·50

Nos. 2793/8 and 2799/804 were each printed together, se-tenant, with the backgrounds forming composite designs.

2000. 400th Birth Anniv of Sir Anthony Van Dyck (Flemish painter). As T **312a** of Gambia. Multicoloured.

2806 $1.65 "The Ages of Man" (horiz) 85 90
2807 $1.65 "Portrait of a Girl as Ermina accompanied by Cupid" (horiz) 85 90
2808 $1.65 "Cupid and Psyche" (horiz) 85 90
2809 $1.65 "Vertumnus and Pomona" (horiz) 85 90
2810 $1.65 "The Continence of Scipio" (horiz) 85 90
2811 $1.65 "Diana and Endymion surprised by a Satyr" (horiz) 85 90
2812 $1.65 "Ladies-in-Waiting" (horiz) 85 90
2813 $1.65 "Thomas Wentworth, Earl of Strafford, with Sir Philip Mainwaring" (horiz) 85 90
2814 $1.65 "Dorothy Rivers Savage, Viscountess Andover, and her sister Lady Elizabeth Thimbleby" (horiz) 85 90
2815 $1.65 "Mountjoy Blount, Earl of Newport, and Lord George Goring with a Page" (horiz) 85 90
2816 $1.65 "Thomas Killigrew and an Unidentified Man" (horiz) 85 90
2817 $1.65 "Elizabeth Villiers, Lady Dalkeith, and Cecilia Killigrew" (horiz) 85 90
2818 $1.65 "Lady Jane Goodwin (Mrs. Arthur)" 85 90
2819 $1.65 "Philip Herbert, Earl of Pembroke" 85 90
2820 $1.65 "Philip, Lord Wharton" 85 90
2821 $1.65 "Sir Thomas Hammer" 85 90
2822 $1.65 "Olivia Porter" 85 90
2823 $1.65 "Sir Thomas Chaloner" 85 90
MS2824 Three sheets, each 128×103 mm. (a) $5 "Archilles and the Daughters of Lycomedes" (vert). (b) $5 "Amaryllis and Mirtilo" (vert). (c) $6 "Aletheia, Countess of Arundel" (vert) Set of 3 sheets 8·00 9·00

No. 2813 is inscribed "Wenthworth" in error.

343a In Skiing Gear

2000. 18th Birthday of Prince William. Multicoloured.

2825 $1.65 Type **343a** 1·00 1·00
2826 $1.65 In red jumper 1·00 1·00
2827 $1.65 Holding order of service 1·00 1·00
2828 $1.65 Prince William laughing 1·00 1·00
MS2829 100×80 mm. $6 Prince William with Prince Harry (37×50 mm) 4·00 4·25

2000. "EXPO 2000" World Stamp Exhibition, Anaheim. Space Satellites. As T **582a** of Ghana. Multicoloured.

2830 $1.65 "Essa 8" 85 90
2831 $1.65 "Echo 1" 85 90
2832 $1.65 "Topex Poseidon" 85 90
2833 $1.65 "Diademe" 85 90
2834 $1.65 "Early Bird" 85 90
2835 $1.65 "Molyna" 85 90
2836 $1.65 "Explorer 14" 85 90
2837 $1.65 "Luna 16" 85 90
2838 $1.65 "Copernicus" 85 90
2839 $1.65 "Explorer 16" 85 90
2840 $1.65 "Luna 10" 85 90
2841 $1.65 "Arybhattan" 85 90
MS2842 Two sheets, each 106×76 mm. (a) $6 "Eole". (b) $6 "Hipparcos" 7·00 7·50

Nos. 2830/5 and 2836/41 were printed together, se-tenant, with the backgrounds forming composite designs.

2000. 25th Anniv of "Apollo–Soyuz" Joint Project. As T **582b** of Ghana. Multicoloured.

2843 $3 Saturn 1B ("Apollo" launch vehicle) 1·75 1·90
2844 $3 "Apollo 18" command module 1·75 1·90
2845 $3 Donald Slayton ("Apollo 18" crew) 1·75 1·90
MS2846 88×71 mm. $6 Spacecraft about to dock (horiz) 3·75 4·00

No. 2843 is inscribed "Vechicle" in error.

2000. 50th Anniv of Berlin Film Festival. As T **582c** of Ghana. Multicoloured.

2847 $1.65 Satyajit Ray (director of Ashani Sanket) 85 90
2848 $1.65 *Mahanagar*, 1964 85 90
2849 $1.65 *La Tulipe*, 1952 85 90
2850 $1.65 *Le Salaire de la Peur*, 1953 85 90
2851 $1.65 *Les Cousins*, 1959 85 90
2852 $1.65 *Hon Dansade en Sommar*, 1952 85 90
MS2853 97×103 mm. $6 *Buffalo Bill and the Indians*, 1976 3·75 4·00

2000. 175th Anniv of Stockton and Darlington Line (first public railway). As T **582d** of Ghana. Multicoloued.

2854 $3 George Stephenson and *Locomotion No. 1*, 1875 2·25 2·25
2855 $3 John B. Jervis's *Brother Jonathan*, 1832 2·25 2·25

No. 2855 is inscribed "Jonathon" in error.

2000. 250th Death Anniv of Johann Sebastian Bach (German composer). Sheet 77×88 mm, containing vert portrait as T **312c** of Gambia.

MS2856 $6 brown and black 4·50 4·75

2000. Election of Albert Einstein (mathematical physicist) as Time Magazine "Man of the Century". Sheet 117×91 mm, containing vert portrait as T **312d** of Gambia.

MS2857 $6 multicoloured 3·75 4·00

344 Count Ferdinand von Zeppelin

2000. Centenary of First Zeppelin Flight. Mult.

2858 $1.65 Type **344** 1·00 1·00
2859 $1.65 LZ-1 at Lake Constance, 1900 1·00 1·00
2860 $1.65 LZ-10 *Schwaben*, over flock of sheep, 1911 1·00 1·00
2861 $1.65 LZ-6 and LZ-7 *Deutschland* in hangar, Friedrichshafen 1·00 1·00
2862 $1.65 LZ-4 at Luneville, 1913 1·00 1·00
2863 $1.65 LZ-11 *Viktoria-Luise* over Kiel Harbour 1·00 1·00
MS2864 93×115 mm. $6 As No. 2859 4·00 4·25

No. 2861 is inscribed "Friedrichshrfed" in error.

2000. Olympic Games, Sydney. As T **582f** of Ghana. Multicoloured.

2865 $2 Jesse Owens (athletics), Berlin (1936) 1·25 1·25
2866 $2 Pole-vaulting 1·25 1·25
2867 $2 Lenin Stadium, Moscow (1980) and U.S.S.R. flag 1·25 1·25
2868 $2 Ancient Greek discus-thrower 1·25 1·25

2000. West Indies Cricket Tour and 100th Test Match at Lord's. As T **472a** of Grenada. Multicoloured.

2869 $4 Norbert Phillip 3·00 3·25
MS2870 121×104 mm. $6 Lord's Cricket Ground (horiz) 5·50 6·00

No. 2869 is inscribed "Phillp" in error.

2000. 80th Birthday of Pope John Paul II. As T **341**, showing collage of miniature religious photographs. Multicoloured.

2871 $1 Top of head (face value at left) 1·00 85
2872 $1 Top of head (face value at right) 1·00 85
2873 $1 Ear (face value at left) 1·00 85
2874 $1 Forehead (face value at right) 1·00 85
2875 $1 Neck (face value at left) 1·00 85
2876 $1 Cheek (face value at right) 1·00 85
2877 $1 Shoulder (face value at left) 1·00 85
2878 $1 Hands (face value at right) 1·00 85

Nos. 2871/8 were printed together, se-tenant, in sheetlets of 8 with the stamps arranged in two vertical columns separated by a gutter also containing miniature photographs. When viewed as a whole, the sheetlet forms a portrait of Pope John Paul.

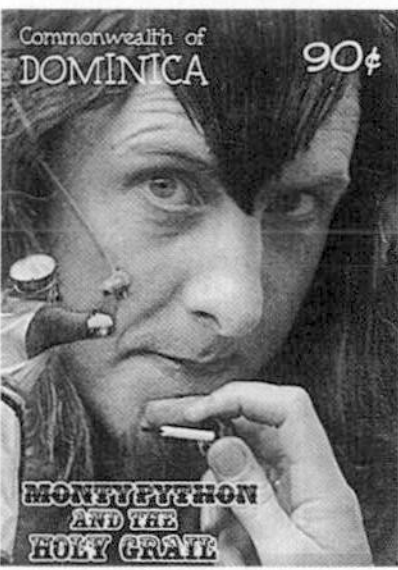

345 Roger the Shrubber

2000. Monty Python and the Holy Grail (comedy film). Multicoloured.

2879 90c. Type **345** 75 65
2880 90c. Three-headed giant 75 65
2881 90c. Attacking the castle 75 65
2882 90c. King Arthur and knight 75 65
2883 90c. Headless knight 75 65
2884 90c. Limbless Black Knight 75 65

346 Member of The Crystals

2000. Famous Girl Pop Groups. The Crystals. Mult.

2885 90c. Type **346** 65 65
2886 90c. Group member with long hair (blue background in top right corner) 65 65
2887 90c. Group member with long hair (yellow background in top right corner) 65 65
2888 90c. Group member with short hair 65 65

Nos. 2885/8 were printed together, se-tenant, forming a composite design.

347 Bob Hope singing

2000. Bob Hope (American entertainer).

2889 **347** $1.65 black, blue and lilac 85 90
2890 - $1.65 multicoloured 85 90
2891 - $1.65 black, blue and lilac 85 90
2892 - $1.65 multicoloured 85 90
2893 - $1.65 black, blue and lilac 85 90
2894 - $1.65 multicoloured 85 90

DESIGNS: No. 2890, Entertaining troops; 2891, As English comic character; 2892, In 50th birthday cake; 2893, Making radio broadcast; 2894, With Man in the Moon.

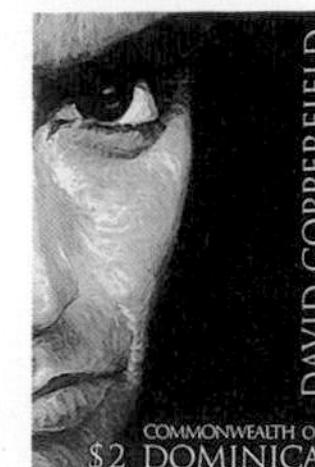

348 David Copperfield

2000. David Copperfield (conjurer).

2895 **348** $2 multicoloured 1·25 1·25

2000. Monarchs of the Millennium. As T **314a** of Gambia.

2896 $1.65 multicoloured 1·00 1·00
2897 $1.65 black, stone and brown 1·00 1·00
2898 $1.65 multicoloured 1·00 1·00
2899 $1.65 black, stone and brown 1·00 1·00
2900 $1.65 multicoloured 1·00 1·00
2901 $1.65 black, stone and brown 1·00 1·00
MS2902 115×135 mm. $6 multicoloured 5·00 5·50

DESIGNS: No. 2896, King Edward IV of England; 2897, Tsar Peter the Great of Russia; 2898, King Henry VI of England; 2899, King Henry III of England; 2900, King Richard III of England; 2901, King Edward I of England; **MS**2902, King Henry VIII of England.

2000. Popes of the Millennium. As T **314b** of Gambia. Each black, yellow and green.

2903 $1.65 Clement X 1·00 1·00
2904 $1.65 Innocent X 1·00 1·00
2905 $1.65 Nicholas V 1·00 1·00
2906 $1.65 Martin V 1·00 1·00
2907 $1.65 Julius III 1·00 1·00
2908 $1.65 Innocent XII 1·00 1·00
MS2909 115×135 mm. $6 Clement XIV (brown, yellow and black) 5·00 5·50

2000. Christmas and Holy Year. As T **491** of Grenada. Multicoloured.

2910 25c. Angel in blue robe 25 15
2911 65c. Young angel 45 30
2912 90c. Angel with drapery 70 40
2913 $1.90 As 25c. 1·00 1·25
2914 $1.90 As 65c. 1·00 1·25
2915 $1.90 As 90c. 1·00 1·25
2916 $1.90 As $5 1·00 1·25
2917 $5 Head and shoulders of angel 2·50 3·00
MS2918 110×120 mm. $6 Angel's face (as 25c.) 3·75 4·00

348c Couple with hawk (Minnesangers in Germany, 1350)

2000. New Millennium. People and Events of the Fourteenth Century (1350–1400). Multicoloured.

2919 65c. Type **348c** 55 55
2920 65c. Acamapitzin, first King of the Aztecs, 1352 55 55
2921 65c. Rat (end of Black Death, 1353) 55 55
2922 65c. Giotto's *Campanile* (completed by Francesco Talenti, 1355) 55 55
2923 65c. First French franc, 1360 55 55
2924 65c. Emperor Hung-wu (foundation of Ming Dynasty, 1360) 55 55
2925 65c. Tamerlane (foundation of Timurid Empire, 1369) 55 55
2926 65c. "Triumph of Death" (Francis Traini), 1370 55 55
2927 65c. Robin Hood (first appearance in English legends, 1375) 55 55
2928 65c. "The Knight" (The Canterbury Tales by Geoffrey Chaucer, 1387) 55 55
2929 65c. Mounted samurai (disputed succession in Japan, 1392) 55 55
2930 65c. Refugees (Jews expelled from France, 1394) 55 55
2931 65c. Temple of the Golden Pavilion, Kyoto (constructed, 1394) 55 55
2932 65c. Carving, Strasbourg Cathedral (completed, 1399) 55 55
2933 65c. Alhambra Palace, Granada (completed, 1390) (60×40 mm) 55 55
2934 65c. Ife Bronzes produced in Nigeria, 1400 55 55

No. 2929 is inscribed "SUDDESSION" in error.

348d "Eight Prize Steeds" (Guiseppe Castiglione)

2000. New Millennium. Two Thousand Years of Chinese Paintings. Multicoloured.

2935	55c. Type **348d**	40	45
2936	55c. "Oleanders" (Wu Hsi Tsai)	40	45
2937	55c. "Mynah and Autumn Flowers" (Chang Hsiung)	40	45
2938	55c. "Hen and Chicks beneath Chrysanthemums," (Chu Ch'ao)	40	45
2939	55c. "Long Living Pine and Crane" (Xugu)	40	45
2940	55c. "Flowers and Fruits" (Chu Lien)	40	45
2941	55c. "Lotus and Willow" (Pu Hua)	40	45
2942	55c. "Kuan-Yin" (Ch'ien Hui-an)	40	45
2943	55c. "Human Figures" (Jen Hsun)	40	45
2944	55c. "Han-Shan and Shih-Te" (Ren Yi)	40	45
2945	55c. "Landscape and Human Figure" (Jen Yu)	40	45
2946	55c. "Poetic Thoughts while Walking with a Staff" (Wangchen)	40	45
2947	55c. "Peony" (Chen Heng-ko)	40	45
2948	55c. "Plum and Orchid" (Wu Chang-shih)	40	45
2949	55c. "Monkey" (Kao Chi-feng)	40	45
2950	55c. "Grapes and Locust" (Chi Pai-shih); and "Galloping Horse" (Xu Beihong) (60×40 mm)	40	45
2951	55c. "The Beauty" (Lin Fengmian)	40	45

No. 2937 is inscribed "YNAH" and No. 2948 "ORCHIS", both in error.

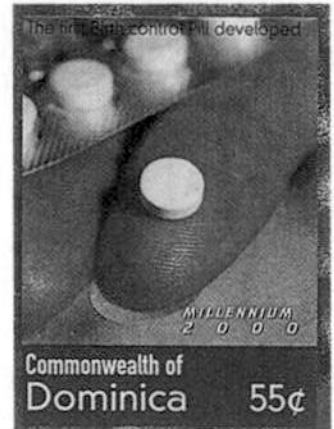

349 First Birth-control Pill, 1961

2000. New Millennium. People and Events of Twentieth Century (1960–69). Multicoloured.

2952	55c. Type **349**	70	60
2953	55c. Yuri Gagarin (first man in Space), 1961	70	60
2954	55c. Fans with The Beatles tickets, 1962	70	60
2955	55c. Funeral of President John F. Kennedy, 1963	70	60
2956	55c. Martin Luther King's "I Have a Dream" speech, 1963	70	60
2957	55c. Betty Friedan (author of *The Feminist Mystique*), 1963	70	60
2958	55c. Duke of Edinburgh and Jomo Kenyatta (independence of Kenya), 1963	70	60
2959	55c. Anti-smoking poster, 1964	70	60
2960	55c. Civil Rights demonstrators (U.S. Civil Rights Act), 1964	70	60
2961	55c. Troops outside Saigon (U.S. involvement in Vietnam), 1965	70	60
2962	55c. Ernesto "Che" Guevara (Cuban revolutionary) killed in Peru, 1965	70	60
2963	55c. Dr. Christiaan Barnard (first heart transplant operation), 1967	70	60
2964	55c. General Moshe Dayan addressing Arabs ("Six-Day" War), 1967	70	60
2965	55c. Death of Ho Chi Minh (North Vietnamese leader), 1969	70	60
2966	55c. Neil Armstrong on the Moon, 1969	70	60
2967	55c. Couple at Berlin Wall, 1961 (60×40 mm)	70	60
2968	55c. Woodstock Festival, 1969	70	60

350 Ancient Star Signs

2000. New Millennium. Inventions. Multicoloured.

2969	55c. Type **350**	60	60
2970	55c. Precision tools	60	60
2971	55c. Astral chart	60	60
2972	55c. Growth of medicine	60	60
2973	55c. Exchange of medical information	60	60
2974	55c. Monastic chapterhouse	60	60
2975	55c. Water alarm clock	60	60
2976	55c. Weighted clock	60	60
2977	55c. Spring-loaded miniature clock movement	60	60
2978	55c. Glass blowing	60	60
2979	55c. Early screws	60	60
2980	55c. Wood lathe	60	60
2981	55c. Ship building	60	60
2982	55c. Interchangeable rifle parts	60	60
2983	55c. Study of movement	60	60
2984	55c. The Industrial Revolution (60×40 mm)	60	60
2985	55c. Concept of efficiency	60	60

351 "Snake in the Wilderness" (Hwa Yan)

2001. Chinese New Year. "Year of the Snake".

2986	**351** $1.20 multicoloured	1·00	1·00

352 Female Green-throated Carib

2001. Hummingbirds. Multicoloured.

2987	$1.25 Type **352**	1·00	1·00
2988	$1.25 Male bee hummingbird ("Mellisuga helenae")	1·00	1·00
2989	$1.25 Male bee hummingbird ("Russelia eqoisetiformis")	1·00	1·00
2990	$1.25 Female bahama woodstar	1·00	1·00
2991	$1.25 Antillean mango	1·00	1·00
2992	$1.25 Female blue-headed hummingbird	1·00	1·00
2993	$1.65 Male streamertail	1·10	1·10
2994	$1.65 Purple-throated carib	1·10	1·10
2995	$1.65 Vervain hummingbird	1·10	1·10
2996	$1.65 Bahama woodstar	1·10	1·10
2997	$1.65 Puerto Rican emerald	1·10	1·10
2998	$1.65 Antillean crested hummingbird	1·10	1·10
MS2999	Two sheets. (a) $5 Unidentified hummingbird. (b) $6 Hispaniolan emerald Set of 2 sheets	8·00	8·50

Nos. 2987/92 and 2993/8 were each printed together, se-tenant, with the backgrounds forming composite designs.

No. 2987 is inscribed "Fehale Greentrriroated Carib", No. 2990 "Tenale", No. 2994 "Trivoated", No. 2998 "Cresteo" and No. **MS**2999b "Hispaniolian", all in error.

No. 2989 carries the inscription "Russelia eqoisetiformis". This should read "Russelia equisetiformis", and refers to the plant (commonly known as a Firecracker Plant) at the bottom of the stamp, not the hummingbird.

353 Puerto Rican Crested Toad

2001. Caribbean and Latin-American Fauna. Mult.

3000	15c. Type **353**	40	25
3001	20c. Axolotl	40	25
3002	$1.45 St. Vincent amazon ("St. Vincent Parrot")	1·10	1·10
3003	$1.45 Indigo macaw	1·10	1·10
3004	$1.45 Guianian cock of the rock ("Cock of the Rock")	1·10	1·10
3005	$1.45 Cuban solenodon	1·10	1·10
3006	$1.45 Cuban hutia	1·10	1·10
3007	$1.45 Chinchilla	1·10	1·10
3008	$1.45 Chilian flamingo ("South American Flamingo")	1·10	1·10
3009	$1.45 Golden conure	1·10	1·10
3010	$1.45 Ocelot	1·10	1·10
3011	$1.45 Giant armadillo	1·10	1·10
3012	$1.45 Margay	1·10	1·10
3013	$1.45 Maned wolf	1·10	1·10
3014	$1.90 Panamanian golden frog	1·10	1·10
3015	$2.20 Manatee	1·10	1·10
MS3016	Two sheets, each 106×71 mm. (a) $6 Hawksbill turtle. (b) $6 Anteater Set of 2 sheets	8·00	9·00

Nos. 3002/7 and 3008/13 were each printed together, se-tenant, with the backgrounds forming composite designs.

2001. Characters from "Pokemon" (children's cartoon series). As T **332a** of Gambia. Multicoloured.

3017	$1.65 "Butterfree No. 12"	85	90
3018	$1.65 "Bulbasaur No. 01"	85	90
3019	$1.65 "Caterpie No. 10"	85	90
3020	$1.65 "Charmander No. 04"	85	90
3021	$1.65 "Squirtle No. 07"	85	90
3022	$1.65 "Pidgeotto No. 17"	85	90
MS3023	75×105 mm. $6 "Nidoking No. 34"	3·75	4·00

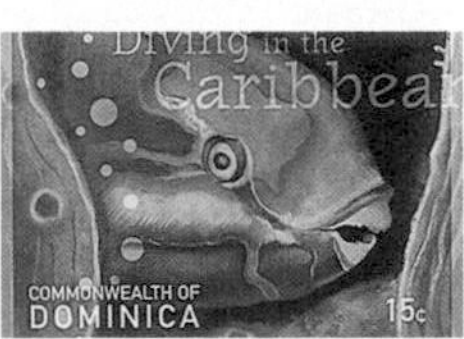

354 Large Blue and Green Fish

2001. Diving in the Caribbean. Depicting marine life. Multicoloured.

3024	15c. Type **354**	20	15
3025	65c. Ray	45	30
3026	90c. Octopus	60	40
3027	$2 Shark	1·10	1·25
3028	$2 Starfish	1·10	1·25
3029	$2 Seahorse	1·10	1·25
3030	$2 Pink anemonefish	1·10	1·25
3031	$2 Crab	1·10	1·25
3032	$2 Moray eel	1·10	1·25
3033	$3 Pink anemonefish	1·60	1·75
MS3034	78×57 mm. $5 Young turtle	3·25	3·50

355 Banded Sea-snake

2001. Caribbean Marine Life. Multicoloured.

3035	15c. Type **355**	20	15
3036	25c. Soldierfish	25	15
3037	55c. False moorish idol ("Banner Fish")	45	25
3038	90c. Crown of Thorns starfish	60	40
3039	$1.65 Red sponge and shoal of anthias	85	90
3040	$1.65 Undulate triggerfish ("Orange-Striped Trigger Fish")	85	90
3041	$1.65 Coral hind ("Coral Grouper") and soft tree coral	85	90
3042	$1.65 Peacock fan-worms and Gorgonian sea fan	85	90
3043	$1.65 Sweetlips and sea fan	85	90
3044	$1.65 Giant clam and golden cup coral	85	90
3045	$1.65 White-tipped reef shark, lionfish and sergeant majors	85	90
3046	$1.65 Blue-striped snappers	85	90
3047	$1.65 Great hammerhead shark, stovepipe sponge and pink vase sponge	85	90
3048	$1.65 Hawaiian monk seal and bluetube coral	85	90
3049	$1.65 False clown anemonefish ("Common Clown Fish"), chilka seahorse and red feather star coral	85	90
3050	$1.65 Bat starfish and brown octopus	85	90
MS3051	Two sheets, each 88×83 mm. (a) $5 Regal anglefish. (b) $5 Pink anenomefish Set of 2 sheets	6·00	6·50

Nos. 3039/44 and 3045/50 were each printed together, se-tenant, with the backgrounds forming composite designs.

No. 3045 is inscribed "Sargent" and 3049 "Cconn", both in error.

356 Prince Albert in Military Uniform

2001. Death Centenary of Queen Victoria. Multicoloured.

3052	$2 Type **356**	1·25	1·25
3053	$2 Young Queen Victoria wearing crown	1·25	1·25
3054	$2 Young Queen Victoria wearing tiara	1·25	1·25
3055	$2 Prince Albert in evening dress	1·25	1·25
MS3056	106×122 mm. $6 Queen Victoria in 1897 (38×50 mm)	3·75	4·00

357 Mao Tse-tung in 1945

2001. 25th Death Anniv of Mao Tse-tung (Chinese leader). Portraits. Multicoloured.

3057	$2 Type **357**	1·10	1·25
3058	$2 Mao in 1926	1·10	1·25
3059	$2 Mao in 1949	1·10	1·25
MS3060	135×110 mm. $3 Mao Tse-tung with farm workers in 1930	1·50	1·75

358 "The Lake at Argenteuil"

2001. 75th Death Anniv of Claude-Oscar Monet (French painter). Multicoloured.

3061	$2 Type **358**	1·25	1·40
3062	$2 "Bridge at Argenteuil"	1·25	1·40
3063	$2 "Railway bridge at Argenteuil"	1·25	1·40
3064	$2 "Seine bridge at Argenteuil"	1·25	1·40
MS3065	139×111 mm. $6 "Woman with Parasol – Madame Monet and her Son" (vert)	3·75	4·00

359 Queen Elizabeth at Coronation

2001. 75th Birthday of Queen Elizabeth II. Multicoloured.

3066	$1.20 Type **359**	85	85
3067	$1.20 Queen Elizabeth wearing yellow hat	85	85
3068	$1.20 Bare-headed portrait after Annigoni	85	85

No.	Description	Mint	Used
3069	$1.20 Queen Elizabeth wearing fur hat	85	85
3070	$1.20 With Prince Andrew as a baby	85	85
3071	$1.20 Wearing white hat and pearl necklace	85	85
MS3072	78×102 mm. $6 Queen Elizabeth in Guards uniform taking salute at Trooping the Colour	4·25	4·50

360 Verdi as a Young Man

2001. Death Centenary of Giuseppe Verdi (Italian composer). Multicoloured.

No.	Description	Mint	Used
3073	$2 Type **360**	1·50	1·50
3074	$2 "Lady Macbeth"	1·50	1·50
3075	$2 Orchestra	1·50	1·50
3076	$2 Score for Verdi's *Macbeth* (opera)	1·50	1·50
MS3077	76×105 mm. $6 Verdi as an old man	6·00	6·00

Nos. 3073/6 were printed together, se-tenant, with the backgrounds forming a composite design.

361 "Daruma" (Tsuji Kako)

2001. "Philanippon '01" International Stamp Exhibition, Tokyo. Japanese Paintings. Multicoloured.

No.	Description	Mint	Used
3078	25c. Type **361**	20	15
3079	55c. "Village by Bamboo Grove" (Takeuchi Seiho)	40	25
3080	65c. "Mountain Village in Spring" (Suzuki Hyakunen)	50	30
3081	90c. "Gentleman amusing Himself" (Domoto Insho)	65	40
3082	$1 "Calmness of Spring Light" (Takeuchi Seiho)	70	45
3083	$1.65 "Thatched Cottages in Willows" (Tsuji Kako)	85	90
3084	$1.65 "Joy in the Garden" (Tsuji Kako)	85	90
3085	$1.65 "Azalea and Butterfly" (Kikuchi Hobun)	85	90
3086	$1.65 "Pine Grove" (Tsuji Kako)	85	90
3087	$1.65 "Woodcutters talking in an Autumn Valley" (Kubota Beisen)	85	90
3088	$1.65 "Waterfowl in Snow" (Tsuji Kako)	85	90
3089	$1.65 "Heron and Willow" (Tsuji Kako)	85	90
3090	$1.65 "Crow and Cherry Blossoms" (Kikuchi Hobun)	85	90
3091	$1.65 "Chrysanthemum Immortal" (Yamamoto Shunkyo)	85	90
3092	$1.65 "Cranes of Immortality" (Tsuji Kako)	85	90
3093	$2 "Su's Embankment on a Spring Morning" (Tomioka Tessai)	1·10	1·25
MS3094	Three sheets. (a) 95×118 mm. $6 "Girl" (Suzuki Harunobu) (38×50 mm). (b) 105×90 mm. $6 "Kamo Riverbank in the Misty Rain" (Tsuji Kakō) (38×50 mm). (c) 125×91 mm. $6 "Diamond Gate" (Tsuji Kakō) (38×50 mm) Set of 3 sheets	8·50	9·50

No. **MS**3094c is inscribed "DIAMON GATE" in error.

362 "Two Women Waltzing"

2001. Death Centenary of Henri de Toulouse-Lautrec (French painter). Multicoloured.

No.	Description	Mint	Used
3095	$2 Type **362**	1·10	1·25
3096	$2 "The Medical Inspection"	1·10	1·25
3097	$2 "Two Girlfriends"	1·10	1·25
3098	$2 "Woman pulling up her Stockings"	1·10	1·25
MS3099	66×86 mm. $6 "Self-portrait"	3·75	4·00

363 *Cantharellus cibarius*

2001. Fungi of the World. Multicoloured.

No.	Description	Mint	Used
3100	15c. Type **363**	20	15
3101	25c. *Hygrocybe pratensis*	25	15
3102	55c. *Leccinum aurantiacum*	40	25
3103	90c. *Caesar's amanita* (horiz)	65	70
3104	90c. *Agaricus augustus* (horiz)	65	70
3105	90c. *Clitocybe nuda* (horiz)	65	70
3106	90c. *Hygrocybe plavescens* (horiz)	65	70
3107	90c. *Stropharia kaufmanii* (horiz)	65	70
3108	90c. *Hygrophorus speciosus* (horiz)	65	70
3109	$2 *Marasmiellus candidus*	1·10	1·25
3110	$2 *Calostoma cinnabarina*	1·10	1·25
3111	$2 *Cantharellus infundibuliformis*	1·10	1·25
3112	$2 *Hygrocybe punicea*	1·10	1·25
3113	$2 *Dictyophora indusiata*	1·10	1·25
3114	$2 *Agrocybe praecox*	1·10	1·25
3115	$3 *Mycena haematopus*	1·50	1·60
MS3116	Two sheets. (a) 76×54 mm. $5 Gymnophilus spectabilis (horiz). (b) 54×76 mm. $5 Amanita muscaria (horiz) Set of 2 sheets	6·50	7·00

364 St. Vincent Amazon ("St. Vincent Parrot")

2001. Caribbean Fauna. Multicoloured.

No.	Description	Mint	Used
3117	$1.45 Type **364**	85	90
3118	$1.45 Painted bunting	85	90
3119	$1.45 Jamaican giant anole	85	90
3120	$1.45 White-fronted capuchin monkey	85	90
3121	$1.45 Strand racerunner	85	90
3122	$1.45 Agouti	85	90
3123	$2 Cook's tree boa	1·10	1·25
3124	$2 Tamandua	1·10	1·25
3125	$2 Common iguana	1·10	1·25
3126	$2 Solenodon	1·10	1·25
MS3127	Four sheets. (a) 63×92 mm. $5 American purple gallinule. (b) 63×92 mm. $5 Rufous-tailed jaramar. (c) 92×63 mm. $5 Ruby-throated hummingbird (horiz). (d) 73×52 mm. $5 Bottlenose dolphins (horiz) Set of 4 sheets	11·00	12·00

365 Yellow Warbler

365a Baltimore ("Northern" Oriole)

2001. Birds. Multicoloured. (a) Design as T 365.

No.	Description	Mint	Used
3128	5c. Type **365**	35	50
3129	10c. Palm chat	40	40
3130	15c. Snowy cotinga	50	40
3131	20c. Blue-grey gnatcatcher	50	40
3132	25c. Belted kingfisher	50	40
3142b	50c Design as T **365a**	1·00	60
3133	55c. Red-legged thrush	70	40
3134	65c. Bananaquit	80	45
3135	90c. Yellow-bellied sapsucker	1·00	70
3136	$1 White-tailed tropicbird	1·10	1·00
3137	$1.45 Ruby-throated hummingbird	1·50	1·50
3138	$1.90 Painted bunting	1·75	1·75
3139	$2 Great frigate bird	1·75	1·75
3140	$5 Brown trembler	3·75	4·00
3141	$10 Red-footed booby	6·00	7·00
3142	$20 Sooty tern	10·00	12·00

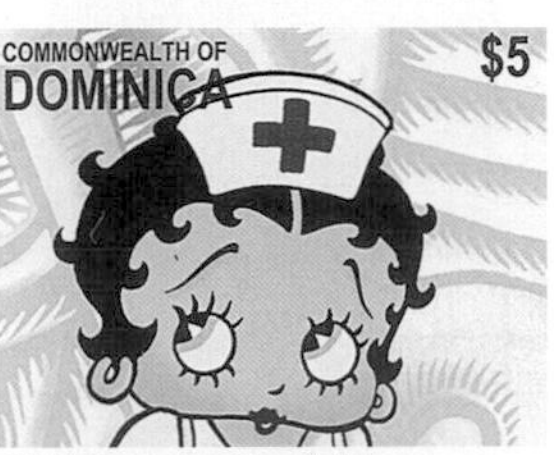

366 Betty wearing Nurse's Hat

2001. Betty Boop (cartoon character). Four sheets, each 87×138 mm, containing horiz designs as T **366**. Multicoloured.

No.	Description	Mint	Used
MS3143	(a) $5 Type **366**. (b) $5 Betty as film star. (c) $5 Betty in front of foliage. (d) $5 Betty in front of roses. Set of 4 sheets	9·50	10·00

367 Larry, Moe and Curly in Overalls

2001. Scenes from The Three Stooges (American T.V. comedy series). Multicoloured.

No.	Description	Mint	Used
3144	$1 Type **367**	60	65
3145	$1 Larry, Moe and Curly with woman in floral dress	60	65
3146	$1 Larry, Moe and Curly under table	60	65
3147	$1 Larry, Moe and Curly attacking singer in red dress	60	65
3148	$1 Larry, Moe and Curly with pony in cot	60	65
3149	$1 Larry in naval uniform, being arrested	60	65
3150	$1 Larry in evening dress (face value at top left)	60	65
3151	$1 Curly in green shirt	60	65
3152	$1 Moe in evening dress (face value at top right)	60	65
MS3153	Two sheets. (a) 126×95 mm. $5 Larry with pony in cot. (b) 95×126 mm. $5 Moe and Larry in radio studio Set of 2 sheets	6·00	6·50

368 Queen Elizabeth II

2001. Golden Jubilee.

No.	Description	Mint	Used
3154	$1 multicoloured	1·00	1·00

No. 3154 was printed in sheetlets of 8, containing two vertical rows of four, separated by a large illustrated central gutter. Both the stamp and the illustration on the central gutter are made up of a collage of miniature flower photographs.

369 United States Team, Brazil, 1950

2001. World Cup Football Championship, Japan and Korea (2002). Multicoloured.

No.	Description	Mint	Used
3155	$2 Type **369**	1·10	1·25
3156	$2 Publicity poster, Switzerland, 1954	1·10	1·25
3157	$2 Publicity poster, Sweden, 1958	1·10	1·25
3158	$2 Zozimo (Brazil), Chile, 1962	1·10	1·25
3159	$2 Gordon Banks (England), England, 1966	1·10	1·25
3160	$2 Pele (Brazil), Mexico, 1970	1·10	1·25
3161	$2 Daniel Passarella (Argentina), Argentina, 1978	1·10	1·25
3162	$2 Paolo Rossi (Italy), Spain, 1982	1·10	1·25
3163	$2 Diego Maradona (Argentina), Mexico, 1986	1·10	1·25
3164	$2 Publicity poster, Italy, 1990	1·10	1·25
3165	$2 Seo Jungulon (South Korea), U.S.A., 1994	1·10	1·25
3166	$2 Jürgen Klinsmann (Germany), France, 1998	1·10	1·25
MS3167	Two sheets, each 88×75 mm. (a) $5 Detail of Jules Rimet Trophy, Uruguay, 1930. (b) $5 Detail of World Cup Trophy, Japan/Korea, 2002 Set of 2 sheets	6·00	6·50

370 "Madonna and Child" (Giovanni Bellini)

2001. Christmas. Paintings by Giovanni Bellini. Multicoloured.

No.	Description	Mint	Used
3168	25c. Type **370**	25	15
3169	65c. "Madonna with Child"	45	30
3170	90c. "Baptism of Christ"	65	40
3171	$1.20 "Madonna with Child" (different)	80	85
3172	$4 "Madonna with Child" (different)	2·25	2·50
MS3173	136×76 mm. $6 "Madonna with Child and Sts. Catherine and Mary Magdalene"	3·75	4·00

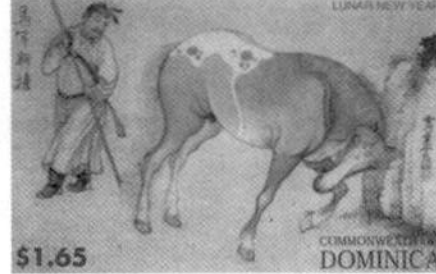

371 Horse and Groom

2001. Chinese New Year ("Year of the Horse"). Paintings by Lum Mei. Multicoloured.

No.	Description	Mint	Used
3174	$1.65 Type **371**	85	90
3175	$1.65 Two horses grazing	85	90
3176	$1.65 Groom with sick horse	85	90
3177	$1.65 Two horses galloping	85	90

2002. Golden Jubilee (2nd issue). As T **507** of Grenada. Multicoloured.

No.	Description	Mint	Used
3178	$2 Queen Elizabeth in blue hat and coat	1·25	1·25
3179	$2 Queen Elizabeth presenting Prince Philip with polo trophy	1·25	1·25
3180	$2 Queen Elizabeth in evening dress	1·25	1·25
3181	$2 Queen Elizabeth in pink hat and coat	1·25	1·25
MS3182	76×108 mm. $6 Princess Elizabeth and Duke of Edinburgh, 1948.	4·00	4·25

2002. "United We Stand". Support for Victims of 11 September 2001 Terrorist Attacks. As T **506** of Grenada.

No.	Description	Mint	Used
3183	$2 U.S. Flag as Statue of Liberty and Dominica flag	1·25	1·40

2002. Shirley Temple in Just Around the Corner. As T **519** of Grenada showing film scenes. Mult.

No.	Description	Mint	Used
3184	$1.90 With maid and dogs (horiz)	1·00	1·10
3185	$1.90 Penny (Shirley Temple) with father and Lola (horiz)	1·00	1·10

3186 $1.90 With father in study (horiz) 1·00 1·10
3187 $1.90 Carving turkey (horiz) 1·00 1·10
3188 $1.90 Talking to S. G. Henshaw (horiz) 1·00 1·10
3189 $1.90 Collecting money from crowd (horiz) 1·00 1·10
3190 $2 Frowning at boy 1·10 1·25
3191 $2 Pretending to shoot with Gus the chauffeur 1·10 1·25
3192 $2 Penny wearing apron and talking to father 1·10 1·25
3193 $2 Cutting boy's hair 1·10 1·25
MS3194 106×75 mm. $6 Dancing in the rain 3·50 3·75

372 "Courtesan Tsukioka" (Ichirakutei Eisui)

2002. Japanese Art. Multicoloured.
3195 $1.20 Type **372** 65 70
3196 $1.20 "Woman and Servant in the Snow" (Eishosai Choki) 65 70
3197 $1.20 "Courtesan Shiratsuyu" (Chokosai Eisho) 65 70
3198 $1.20 "Ohisa of the Takashima-Ya" (Utagawa Toyokuni) 65 70
3199 $1.20 "Woman and Cat" (Utagawa Kunimasa) 65 70
3200 $1.20 "Genre Scenes of Beauties" (detail) (Keisai Eisen) 65 70
3201 $1.65 "Women inside and outside a Mosquito Net" (Suzuki Harushige) 85 90
3202 $1.65 "Komachi at Shimizu" (Suzuki Harushige) 85 90
3203 $1.65 "Women viewing Plum Blossoms" (Suzuki Harunobu) 85 90
3204 $1.65 "Women cooling themselves at Shijogawara in Kyoto" (Utagawa Toyohiro) 85 90
3205 $1.65 "Women reading a Letter" (Kitagawa Utamaro) 85 90
3206 $1.65 "Women dressed for Kashima Dance at Niwaka Festival" (Kitagawa UTamaro) 85 90
3207 $1.90 "Iwai Kiyotaro" (Kunimasa) 95 1·00
3208 $1.90 "Otani Hiriji III and Arashi Ryuzo" (Toshusai Sharaku) 95 1·00
3209 $1.90 "Ichikawa Komazo II" (Katsukawa Shunko) 95 1·00
3210 $1.90 "Ichikawa Yaozo III and Sakata Hangoro III" (Sharaku) 95 1·00
3211 $1.90 "Tanimura Torazo" (Sharaku) 95 1·00
3212 $1.90 "Iwai Kiyotaro as Oishi" (Toyokuni) 95 1·00
MS3213 Three sheets. (a) 85×125 mm. $5 "Iwai Hanshiro IV and Sawamura Sojuro III" (Torii Kyonaga) (horiz). (b) 85×110 mm. $5 "Actor Nakamura Riko" (Katsukawa Shunsho). (c) $6 "Daughter of the Motoyanagi-Ya" (Suzuki Harunobu) 8·50 9·00

372a Mount Everest

2002. International Year of Mountains. Multicoloured.
3214 $2 Type **372a** 1·25 1·25
3215 $2 Mount Kilimanjaro 1·25 1·25
3216 $2 Mount McKinley 1·25 1·25

373 Waterfall and "Detective H2O"

2002. U.N. Year of Ecotourism. Each including a member of the Eco Squad (cartoon characters). Multicoloured.
3217 45c. Type **373** 30 25
3218 50c. Waterfall and "Factman" 35 25
3219 55c. River and "B.B." 35 25
3220 60c. Sea cliffs and "Stanley the Starfish" 35 30
3221 90c. River and "Toxi" 50 50
3222 $1.20 Forest and "Adopt" 65 70
MS3223 117× 96 mm. $6 Park and "Litterbit" 3·75 4·00

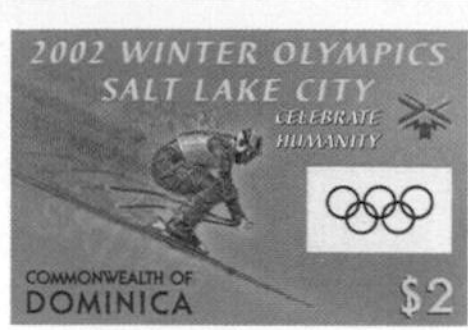

373a Downhill Skiing

2002. Winter Olympic Games, Salt Lake City. As T **482**. Multicoloured.
3224 $2 Type **373a** 1·25 1·40
3225 $2 Two man bobsleigh 1·25 1·40
MS3226 84×114 mm. Nos. 3218/19 2·50 2·75

374 Colonel Baden-Powell in Military Uniform

2002. 20th World Scout Jamboree, Thailand. Mult.
3227 $3 Type **374** 1·60 1·75
3228 $3 Agnes Baden-Powell (founder of Girl Guides) 1·60 1·75
3229 $3 Maceo Johnson 1·60 1·75
MS3230 80×99 mm. $6 Lord Baden-Powell in Scout uniform 3·75 4·00

374a Charles Lindbergh and *The Spirit of St. Louis* (aircraft)

2002. 75th Anniv of First Solo Transatlantic Flight. Multicoloured.
3231 $3 Type **374a** 1·90 1·90
3232 $3 Charles and Anne Lindbergh in flying kit 1·90 1·90
MS3233 117×83 mm. $6 Charles Lindbergh and the *Spirit of St. Louis* 4·50 4·75

375 Olive Oyl in Rowing Boat

2002. "Popeye " (cartoon character) in New York. Multicoloured.
3234 $1 Type **375** 60 65
3235 $1 Brutus with oar 60 65
3236 $1 Sweet Pea 60 65
3237 $1 Wimpy 60 65
3238 $1 Jeep 60 65
3239 $1 Popeye with telescope 60 65
3240 $1.90 Popeye and Olive Oyl at Bronx Zoo 95 1·00
3241 $1.90 Popeye and Olive Oyl on ferry passing Statue of Liberty 95 1·00
3242 $1.90 Popeye and Olive Oyl by Empire State Building 95 1·00
3243 $1.90 Popeye skating at Rockefeller Centre 95 1·00
3244 $1.90 Popeye pitching at baseball game 95 1·00
3245 $1.90 Popeye holding hose 95 1·00
MS3246 Two sheets, each 83×114 mm. (a) $6 Popeye and Olive Oyl dancing (horiz). (b) $6 Popeye flexing muscles 6·50 7·00

No. 3243 is inscribed "ROCKERFELLER" in error.

376 Brown Trembler

2002. Fauna. Multicoloured designs.
3247 $1.50 Type **376** 1·00 1·00
3248 $1.50 Snowy cotinga 1·00 1·00
3249 $1.50 Bananaquit 1·00 1·00
3250 $1.50 Painted bunting 1·00 1·00
3251 $1.50 Belted kingfisher 1·00 1·00
3252 $1.50 Ruby-throated hummingbird 1·00 1·00
3253 $1.50 Field cricket 1·00 1·00
3254 $1.50 Migratory grasshopper 1·00 1·00
3255 $1.50 Honey bee 1·00 1·00
3256 $1.50 Hercules beetle 1·00 1·00
3257 $1.50 Black ant 1·00 1·00
3258 $1.50 Cicada 1·00 1·00
3259 $1.50 Carolina sphinx 1·00 1·00
3260 $1.50 White-lined sphinx 1·00 1·00
3261 $1.50 Orizaba silkmoth 1·00 1·00
3262 $1.50 Hieroglyphic moth 1·00 1·00
3263 $1.50 Hickory tussock moth 1·00 1·00
3264 $1.50 Diva moth 1·00 1·00
3265 $1.50 Sei whale 1·00 1·00
3266 $1.50 Killer whale 1·00 1·00
3267 $1.50 Blue whale 1·00 1·00
3268 $1.50 White whale 1·00 1·00
3269 $1.50 Pygmy whale 1·00 1·00
3270 $1.50 Sperm whale 1·00 1·00
MS3271 Four sheets, each 100×70 mm. (a) $6 Yellow-bellied sapsucker (horiz). (b) $6 Bumble bee (horiz). (c) $6 Ornate moth (horiz). (d) $6 Grey whale (horiz) 15·00 17·00

Nos. 3241/6 (birds), 3247/52 (insects), 3253/8 (moths) and 3259/64 (whales) were each printed together, se-tenant, with the backgrounds forming composite designs.

Nos. 3248 and 3259 are inscribed "Ctinga" or "Carilina", both in error.

377 Willem Einthoven (Medicine, 1924)

2002. "Amphilex '02", International Stamp Exhibition, Amsterdam. (a) Dutch Nobel Prize Winners.
3272 **377** $1.50 black and green 90 90
3273 - $1.50 black and orange 90 90
3274 - $1.50 black and violet 90 90
3275 - $1.50 black and salmon 90 90
3276 - $1.50 black and sepia 90 90
3277 - $1.50 black and green 90 90

DESIGNS: No. 3273, Economics Prize medal; 3274, Peter Debye (Chemistry, 1935); 3275, Frits Zernike (Physics, 1953); 3276, Jan Tinbergen (Economics, 1969); 3277, Simon van de Meer (Physics, 1984).

(b) Dutch Lighthouses. Multicoloured.
3278 $1.50 Marken lighthouse 1·25 1·00
3279 $1.50 Harlingen lighthouse 1·25 1·00
3280 $1.50 Den Oever lighthouse 1·25 1·00
3281 $1.50 De Ven lighthouse 1·25 1·00
3282 $1.50 Urk lighthouse 1·25 1·00
3283 $1.50 Oosterleek lighthouse 1·25 1·00

(c) Dutch Women's Traditional Costumes. Multicoloured. Each 37×51 mm.
3284 $3 Lace cap from Zuid Holland 2·00 2·00
3285 $3 Winged headdress from Zeeland 2·00 2·00
3286 $3 Scarf and shawl from Limburg 2·00 2·00

377a Elvis Presley

2002. 25th Death Anniv of Elvis Presley (American entertainer).
3287 **377a** $1.50 black 1·25 1·00

378 Compass

2002. 550th Birth Anniv of Amerigo Vespucci (explorer). Multicoloured.
3288 $3 Type **378** 2·00 2·00
3289 $3 Studying chart 2·00 2·00
3290 $3 Rolled chart 2·00 2·00
MS3291 98×78 mm. $5 Amerigo Vespucci and Spanish soldier (30×42 mm) 3·25 3·50

379 Princess Diana

2002. 5th Death Anniv of Diana, Princess of Wales. Multicoloured.
3292 $1.90 Type **379** 1·00 1·10
3293 $1.90 Princess Diana carrying rose spray 1·00 1·10
3294 $1.90 Wearing white yoked dress 1·00 1·10
3295 $1.90 In lace top 1·00 1·10
MS3296 98×66 mm. $5 Princess Diana wearing tiara fur coat 2·50 2·75

380 John F. Kennedy in Navy Uniform

2002. Presidents John F. Kennedy and Ronald Reagan Commemoration. Multocoloured.
3297 $1.90 Type **380** 90 1·00
3298 $1.90 Wearing brown suit (face value in red) 90 1·00
3299 $1.90 Wearing brown suit (face value in blue) 90 1·00
3300 $1.90 In fawn suit 90 1·00
3301 $1.90 John F. Kennedy smiling 90 1·00
3302 $1.90 John F. Kennedy frowning 90 1·00
3303 $1.90 Looking up 90 1·00
3304 $1.90 With hand on chin 90 1·00
3305 $1.90 Ronald Reagan in film role as deputy marshal 90 1·00
3306 $1.90 Wearing green T-shirt 90 1·00
3307 $1.90 In red pullover 90 1·00

3308	$1.90 Wearing blue T-shirt	90	1·00
3309	$1.90 Nancy and Ronald Reagan (wearing blue shirt) (horiz)	90	1·00
3310	$1.90 Nancy Reagan (horiz)	90	1·00
3311	$1.90 Ronald Reagan (horiz)	90	1·00
3312	$1.90 Nancy and Ronald Reagan (wearing pink shirt) (horiz)	90	1·00

381 Elizabeth "Ma Pampo" Israel

2003. 128th Birthday of Elizabeth "Ma Pampo" Israel (world's oldest person).

3313	**381**	90c. multicoloured	1·00	80

382 Rams

2003. Chinese New Year ("Year of the Ram").

3314	**382**	$1.65 multicoloured	85	90

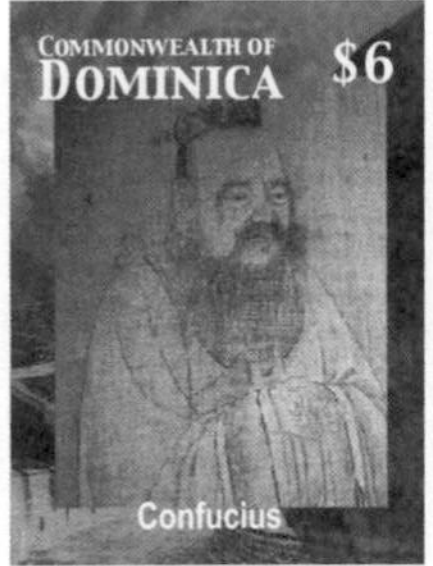

383 Confucius (Chinese philosopher)

2003. Science Fiction. Six sheets, each 145×100 mm, containing T **383** and similar vert designs. Multicoloured.

MS3315	Six sheets. (a) $6 Type **383**. (b) $6 Nazca Lines, Peru. (c) $6 Atlas carrying Globe. (d) $6 Zoroaster. (e) $6 Mayan calendar. (f) $6 Presidents Franklin D. Roosevelt and John F. Kennedy (both deaths predicted by Edgar Cayce)	16·00	18·00

No. **MS**3315(e) is inscribed "Calender" in error.

384 Queen Elizabeth II in Pale Grey Dress

2003. 50th Anniv of Coronation. Multicoloured.

MS3316	155×93 mm. $3 Type **384**; $3 Queen in Garter robes; $3 Queen wearing diadem	4·00	4·00
MS3317	75×105 mm. $6 Queen wearing diadem	4·00	4·25

384a Teddy Bear wearing Black T-shirt and Blue Jeans

2003. Centenary of the Teddy Bear. Multicoloured.

MS3318	90×166 mm. $1.65 Type **384a**; $1.65 Wearing conical party hat and carrying streamers; $1.65 Carrying party blower; $1.65 Wearing black bowler hat, t-shirt and jeans; $1.65 Wearing mauve bowler hat, black t-shirt and green jeans; $1.65 Holding birthday cake (all 27×41 mm)	5·50	6·00
MS3319	165×127 mm. $2×2 Teddy bear wearing jumper, hat and mittens; $2×2 Father Christmas teddy bear	4·25	4·50

385 Bobby Moore

2003. World Cup Football Championship, Japan and Korea (2002). Multicoloured.

MS3320	165×84 mm. $1.45 Type **385**; $1.45 Roger Hunt; $1.45 Gordon Banks; $1.45 Bobby Charlton; $1.45 Alan Ball; $1.45 Geoff Hurst	3·75	4·00
MS3321	165×84 mm. $1.45 Danny Mills; $1.45 Paul Scholes; $1.45 Darius Vassell; $1.45 Michael Owen; $1.45 Emile Heskey; $1.45 Rio Ferdinand	3·75	4·00
MS3322	Five sheets, each 84×84 mm. (a) $3 Ashley Cole; $3 David Seaman. (b) $3 Franz Beckenbauer; $3 Oliver Kahn. (c) $3 Charlton, Ball, Hunt; $3 Nobby Stiles. (d) $3 Sven-Goran Eriksson; $3 Nikki Butt. (e) $3 Robbie Fowler; $3 Sol Campbell Set of 5 sheets	14·00	15·00

385a Prince William wearing Blue-collared Shirt

2003. 21st Birthday of Prince William of Wales. Multicoloured.

MS3323	148×78 mm. $3 Type **385a**; $3 Wearing blue jacket and tie; $3 Playing polo	5·00	5·50
MS3324	68×98 mm. $6 In school uniform	3·75	4·00

386 Model A Runabout (1903)

2003. Centenary of General Motors Cadillac. Multicoloured.

MS3325	120×170 mm. $2 Type **386**; $2 Model 30 (1912); $2 Type 57 Victoria Coupe (1918); $2 Lasalle Convertible Coupe (1927)	4·25	4·50
MS3326	120×84 mm. $5 355-C V8 Sedan (1933)	2·50	2·75

387 Corvette (1953)

2003. Centenary of General Motors Chevrolet Corvette. Multicoloured.

MS3327	120×170 mm. $2 Type **387**; $2 Corvette (1956); $2 Corvette (1957); $2 Corvette (1962)	4·25	4·50
MS3328	120×84 mm. $5 Corvette (1959)	2·50	2·75

388 "Sputnik I" (first orbiting satellite, 1957)

2003. Centenary of Powered Flight. Multicoloured.

MS3329	180×110 mm. $2 Type **388**; $2 Yuri Gagarin (first man in space, 1961); $2 Neil Armstrong (first man on the Moon, 1969); $2 "Skylab 1" (1973)	4·25	4·50
MS3330	104×74 mm. $6 Westland Wallace over Mount Everest (1933)	3·00	3·25

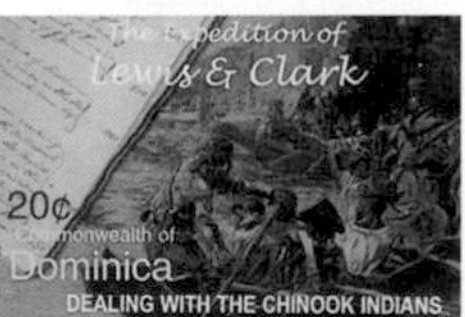

389 Expedition Canoe and Chinook Indians

2003. Bicentenary (2004) of Lewis and Clark's Expedition to the American West and Pacific North West. Multicoloured.

3331	20c. Type **389**	25	20
3332	50c. Lewis and Clark and expedition compass	40	25
3333	55c. Lewis and Clark with map and telescope	40	25
3334	65c. Medal presented to Indians (vert)	40	30
3335	90c. Expedition members and grizzly bear	55	50
3336	$1 Lewis and Clark with Sacagawea (Indian interpreter)	65	65
3337	$2 Captain Meriwether Lewis (vert)	1·25	1·40
3338	$4 Statue of Lewis and Clark (vert)	2·25	2·50
MS3339	Two sheets, each 80×115 mm. (a) $5 Captain Meriwether Lewis (vert). (b) $5 Lieutenant William Clark (vert) Set of 2 sheets	5·00	5·50

389a Firmin Lambot (1919)

2003. Centenary of Tour de France Cycle Race. Showing past winners. Multicoloured.

MS3340	160×100 mm. $2 Type **389a**; $2 Phillipe Thys (1920); $2 Leon Scieur (1921); $2 Firmin Lambot (1922)	4·50	4·50
MS3341	100×70 mm. $6 Francois Faber	3·25	3·50

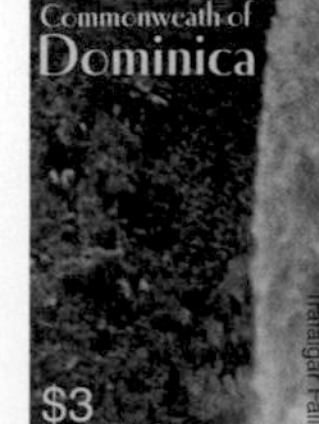

390 Trafalgar Falls, Dominica

2003. International Year of Freshwater. Multicoloured.

MS3342	96×146 mm. $3 Type **390**; $3 YS Falls, Jamaica; $3 Dunn's River, Jamaica	4·25	4·50
MS3343	70×100 mm. $6 Annandale Falls, Grenada	3·25	3·50

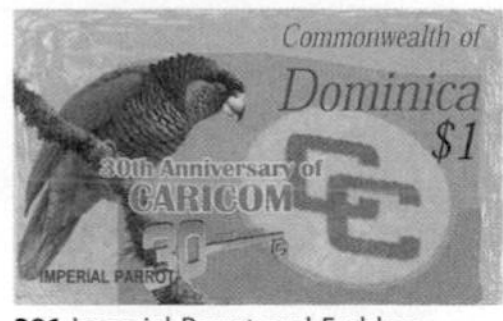

391 Imperial Parrot and Emblem

2003. 30th Anniv of CARICOM.

3344	**391**	$1 multicoloured	1·00	75

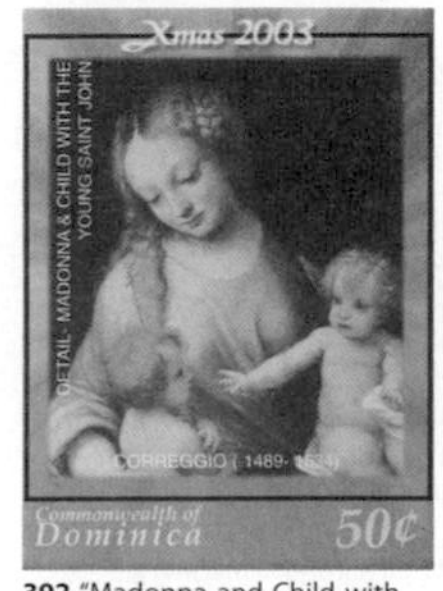

392 "Madonna and Child with the Young St. John" (detail) (Correggio)

2003. Christmas. Multicoloured.

3345	50c. Type **392**	30	25
3346	90c. "Madonna in Glory with the Christ Child and the Saints Frances and Alvise with the Donor" (detail) (Titian)	55	40
3347	$1.45 "Madonna and Child with Angels playing Musical Instruments" (detail) (Correggio)	80	75
3348	$3 "Madonna of the Cherries" (detail) (Titian)	1·75	2·00
MS3349	75×97 mm. $6 "Holy Family with St. John the Baptist" (Andrea del Sarto)	3·25	3·50

No. **MS**3349 also commemorates the 300th anniversary of St. Petersburg.

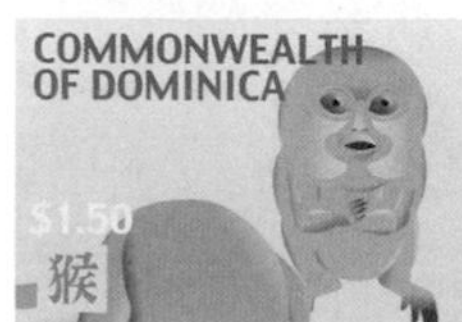

393 Small Orange Marmoset

2004. Chinese New Year ("Year of the Monkey"). Sheet 143×116 mm containing T **393** and similar horiz designs. Multicoloured.

MS3350	$1.50 Type **393**; $1.50 Monkey; $1.50 Baboon drinking; $1.50 Baboon with blue face	3·00	3·25

394 *Epidendrum pseudepidendrum*

2004. Orchids. Multicoloured.

3351	25c. Type **394**	50	25
3352	55c. *Aspasia epidendroides*	80	35
3353	$1.50 *Cochleanthes discolor*	1·40	1·10
3354	$4 *Brassavola nodosa*	3·00	3·50
MS3355	116×132 mm. $1.90 *Laelia anceps*; $1.90 *Caularthron bicornutum*; $1.90 *Cattleya velutina*; $1.90 *Cattleya warneri*; $1.90 *Oncidium splendidum*; $1.90 *Psychlis atropurpurea*	7·50	8·00

MS3356	96×66 mm. $5 *Maxillaria cuculata* (vert)	3·50	3·75

395 Dwight D. Eisenhower

2004. 25th Death Anniv (2003) of Norman Rockwell (artist). Type 395 and similar vert designs. Multicoloured.

MS3357	160×186 mm. $2 Type **395**; $2 John F. Kennedy; $2 Lyndon B. Johnson; $2 Richard M. Nixon	4·50	5·00
MS3358	55×78 mm. $5 Abraham Lincoln. Imperf	3·00	3·25

396 "Portrait of Manuel Pallares , 1909"

2004. 30th Death Anniv (2003) of Pablo Picasso (artist). T **396** and similar multicoloured designs.

MS3359	171×142 mm. $1 Type **396**; $1 "Woman with Vase of Flowers, 1909"; $1 "Woman with a Fan (Fernande), 1908"; $1 "Portrait of Clovis Sagot, 1909"	2·25	2·50
MS3360	95×74 mm. $5 "Brick Factory at Torosa (The Factory), 1909". Imperf	3·00	3·25

397 "Village Tahitien, Avec La Femme En Marche"

2004. Death Centenary of Paul Gauguin (artist). T **397** and similar vert designs. Multicoloured.

MS3361	165×116 mm. $2 Type **397**; $2 "La Barriere"; $2 "Bonjour, Monsieur Gauguin"; $2 "Vegetation Tropicale"	4·25	4·50
MS3362	60×78 mm. $5 "Petites Bretonnes Devant La Mer". Imperf	3·00	3·25

398 Small Flambeau

2004. Butterflies. Multicoloured.

3363	50c. Type **398**	45	25
3364	90c. Tiger pierid	75	55
3365	$1 White peacock	90	90
3366	$2 Cramer's mesene	1·60	1·75
MS3367	116×133 mm. $2 Figure-of-eight; $2 Orange theope; $2 Clorinde; $2 Grecian shoemaker; $2 Orange-barred sulphur; $2 Common Morpho	8·50	9·00
MS3368	66×96 mm. $5 Giant swallowtail (vert)	3·50	3·75

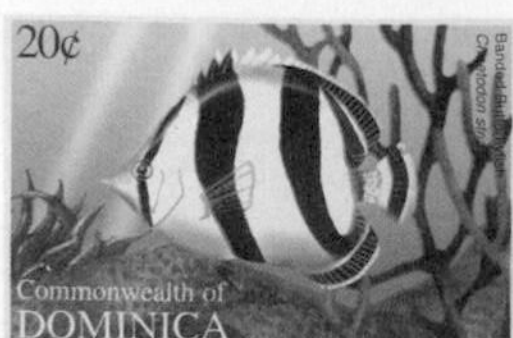

399 Banded Butterflyfish

2004. Tropical Fish. Multicoloured.

3369	20c. Type **399**	30	20
3370	25c. Queen angelfish	30	20
3371	55c. Porkfish	60	35
3372	$5 Redband parrotfish	3·00	3·50
MS3373	116×133 mm. $2 Beaugregory; $2 Two porkfish; $2 Bicolor cherubfish; $2 Rock beauty; $2 Blackfin snapper; $2 Blue tang	7·00	8·00
MS3374	96×66 mm. $5 Indigo hamlet	3·25	3·50

400 "Symphony in White No. 3"

2004. Birth Bicentenary of James McNeill Whistler (artist). Multicoloured.

3375	50c. Type **400**	30	25
3376	$1 "The Artists Studio" (vert)	55	55
3377	$1.65 "The Thames in Ice" (vert)	85	90
3378	$2 "Arrangement in Black: Portrait of F.R. Leyland" (vert)	1·10	1·25
MS3379	168×122 mm. $2 "Arrangement in Brown and Black: Portrait of Miss Rosa Corder" (36×72 mm); $2 "Harmony in Red; Lamplight" (36×72 mm); $2 "Symphony in Flesh Color and Pink: Portrait of Mrs Frances Leyland" (36×72 mm); $2 "Arrangement in Yellow and Grey: Effie Deans" (36×72 mm)	5·50	6·00
MS3380	71×103 mm. $5 "Harmony in Grey and Green: Miss Cicely Alexander". Imperf	3·00	3·25

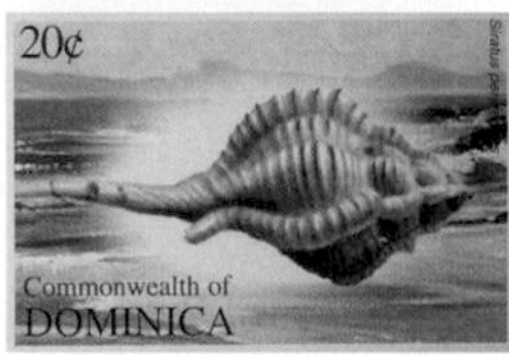

401 *Siratus perelegans*

2004. Sea Shells. Multicoloured.

3381	20c. Type **401**	30	20
3382	90c. *Polystira albida*	70	45
3383	$1.45 *Cypraea cervus*	1·10	1·10
3384	$2 *Strombus gallus*	1·50	1·60
MS3385	116×133 mm. $1.90 *Strombus pugilis*; $1.90 *Cittarium pica*; $1.90 *Distorsio clathrata*; $1.90 *Melongeria morio*; $1.90 *Prunum labiata*; $1.90 *Chione paphia*	6·50	7·50
MS3386	96×66 mm. $5 *Strombus alatus*	3·00	3·25

402 E. Robinson (Amsterdam, 1928)

2004. Olympic Games, Athens. Multicoloured.

3387	20c. Type **402**	25	20
3388	25c. K. Takacs (London, 1948)	25	20
3389	55c. B. Beamon (Mexico, 1968)	45	25
3390	65c. M. Didrikson (Los Angeles, 1932)	50	30
3391	$1 V. Ritola (Paris, 1924)	75	55
3392	$1.65 A. Hajos (Guttman) (Athens, 1896)	1·10	1·25
3393	$2 P. Nurmi (Antwerp, 1920)	1·40	1·50
3394	$4 N. Nadi (Antwerp, 1920)	2·50	3·00

403 Santa Fe Train

2004. Bicentenary of Steam Trains. Multicoloured.

MS3395	Three sheets each 147×153 mm. (a) $1 Type **403**; $1 ViaRail Canada; $1 Conrail 6435; $1 Strasburg Rail Road 90; $1 Deltic diesel-electric engine; $1 *Brighton Belle*. (b) $1 Canadian Pacific freight train; $1 Queensland Rail IMU Railcar; $1 Shinkansen (green and white); $1 Amtrak; $1 Shinkansen (blue and white); $1 Passenger carriage. (c) $1 Three early steam engines; $1 Green locomotive; $1 Baldwin 2-D-D; $1 Southern Engine No. 20; $1 Electric locomotive; $1 Roaring Camp and Big Trees railroad Set of 3 sheets	13·00	14·00
MS3396	Three sheets each 98×68 mm. (a) $6 Shinkansen (blue, yellow and white). (b) $6 Southern Pacific steam locomotive. (c) $6 Golsdorf two-cylinder compound engine Set of 3 sheets	13·00	14·00

404 Eddie Hannath M.B.E. (7th Battalion, Hampshire Regiment)

2004. 60th Anniv of D-Day Landings.

3397	**404**	$1 multicoloured	1·00	70
3398	-	$4 multicoloured	3·00	3·25
MS3399		177×107 mm. $2 blue and black; $2 brown and black; $2 blue and black; $2 brown and black	4·50	4·75
MS3400		101×69 mm. $6 purple and black	3·50	3·75

DESIGNS: No. 3397 Type **403**; No. 3398 Franklin D. Roosevelt; No. **MS**3399 Rangers at the cliffs of Pointe du Hoc; Rangers climbing cliffs; British troops advancing towards Sword Beach; AVRE Petard tank on Sword Beach; No. **MS**3400 British troops on Sword Beach.

405 Marilyn Monroe

2004. Marilyn Monroe Commemoration. Sheet 125×125 mm containing T **405** and similar vert designs. Each red and carmine.

MS3401	$2 Type **405**; $2 Wearing drop earrings and off the shoulder top; $2 Close up of face; $2 Wearing pearl necklace	4·25	4·75

406 George Herman Ruth Jr.

2004. Centenary of Baseball World Series. Sheet 127×178 mm containing T **406** and similar vert designs showing George Herman Ruth Jr. ("Babe Ruth"). Multicoloured.

MS3402	$2 Type **406**; $2 Poised to hit ball; $2 Holding three bats; $2 With hands on hip and knee	4·00	4·50

407 Jode Luis Villalonga

2004. European Football Championship 2004, Portugal. Commemoration of Match between Spain and USSR (1964). Multicoloured designs as T **407**.

MS3403	148×86 mm. $2 Type **407**; $2 Lev Yashin; $2 Marcelino Martinez; $2 Santiago Bernabeu	4·25	4·75
MS3404	97×86 mm. $6 Spanish team, 1964 (51×38 mm)	3·25	3·50

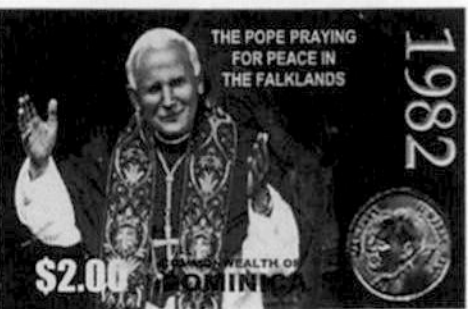

408 Pope John Paul II

2004. 25th Anniv of the Pontificate of Pope John Paul II. Sheet 166×154 mm containing horiz designs as T **408**. Multicoloured.

MS3405	$2 Type **408**; $2 Facing lines of people, Croatia; $2 With hands clasped; $2 With Franciscan monks; $2 Remembering the Holocaust	5·00	5·50

409 Mother Teresa

2004. United Nations International Year of Peace. Sheet 137×77 mm containing horiz designs as T **409**. Multicoloured.

MS3406	$2 Type **409**; $2 Mother Teresa with feeding utensils; $2 Peace dove carrying olive branch	4·75	5·00

410 Deng Xiaoping meeting with Chairman Mao

2004. Birth Centenary of Deng Xiaoping (Chinese politician). Sheet 96×67 mm.

MS3407	$6 multicoloured	3·00	3·25

411 Princess Juliana, 1925

2004. Queen Juliana of the Netherlands Commemoration.

3408	**411**	$2 multicoloured	1·10	1·25

412 Players

2004. National Football Team.

3409	**412**	90c. multicoloured	70	70

413 Ferenc Puskas

2004. Centenary of FIFA (Federation Internationale de Football Association). Multicoloured.

MS3410	192×97 mm. $2 Type **413**; $2 Rivaldo (Brazil); $2 Carsten Jancker (Germany); $2 Johan Cruyff (Holland)	4·25	4·50
MS3411	107×87 mm. $6 George Best (Ireland)	3·25	3·50

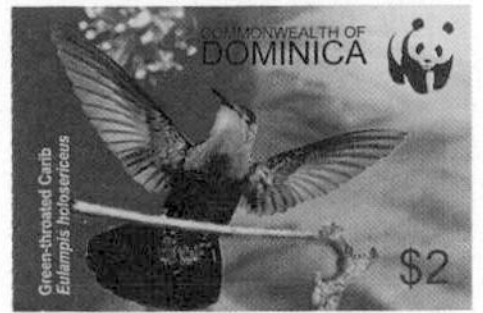

414 Green-throated Carib

2005. Endangered Species. Hummingbirds. Multicoloured.

3412	$2 Type **414**	1·25	1·25
3413	$2 Purple-throated carib on nest	1·25	1·25
3414	$2 Green-throated carib on nest	1·25	1·25
3415	$2 Purple-throated carib on branch	1·25	1·25
MS3416	205×130 mm. Nos. 3412/15, each×2	8·50	9·50

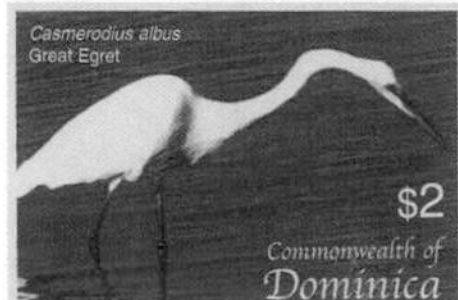

415 Great Egret

2005. Birds, Mushrooms and Flowers. Multicoloured.

3417	25c. Brown booby	40	25
3418	90c. Brown pelican	75	55
3419	$1 Red-billed tropic bird	85	70
3420	$4 Northern gannet	3·00	3·25
MS3421	135×105 mm. $2 Type **415**; $2 Black-necked grebe; $2 Turkey vulture; $2 Everglade kite ("Snail Kite")	4·75	5·00
MS3422	$2 *Cortinarius mucosus*; $2 *Cortinarius splendens*; $2 *Cortinarius rufo-olivaceus*; $2 *Inocybe erubescens*	4·75	5·00
MS3423	$2 Sweetshrub; $2 Pink turtleheads; $2 Flowering quince; $2 Water lily	3·50	4·00
MS3424	Three sheets. (a) 65×95 mm. $6 Red Knot. (b) 97×66 mm. $6 *Inocybe rimosa*. (c) 65×97 mm. $6 Glory-of-the-Snow (vert). Set of 3 sheets	13·00	14·00

416 Mammuthus columbi

2005. Prehistoric Animals. Multicoloured.

MS3425	138×101 mm. $2 Type **416**; $2 Spinosaurus; $2 Ankylosaurus; $2 Mammuthus primigenius	4·50	4·75
MS3426	152×111 mm. $2 Pterodactylus; $2 Pteranodon; $2 Sordes; $2 Caudipteryx zoui	4·50	4·75
MS3427	138×101 mm. $2 Tyrannosaurus rex; $2 Velociraptor; $2 Stegosaurus; $2 Psittacosaurus	4·50	4·75
MS3428	Three sheets, each 100×70 mm. (a) $3 Compsongnathus. (b) $5 Archaeopteryx. (c) $6 Mammuthus primigenius. Set of 3 sheets	9·50	10·00

417 Rooster

2005. Chinese New Year ("Year of the Rooster"). Multicoloured.

MS3429	$1 Type **417**×4	2·00	2·25
MS3430	100×70 mm. $4 Three roosters (60×40 mm)	2·00	2·25

418 Elvis Presley

2005. 70th Birth Anniv of Elvis Presley. Multicoloured.

3431	$1 Type **418**	75	75
3432	$1 Guitar and signature	75	75
3433	$1 Elvis Presley (wearing red shirt)	75	75
3434	$1 Guitar and drawing of Elvis Presley	75	75

419 Pope John Paul II with Princess Diana

2005. Pope John Paul II Commemoration.

3435	**419**	$3 multicoloured	2·75	2·75

420 Italian Team, 1934

2005. 75th Anniv of First World Cup Football Championship, Uruguay. Scenes from World Cup, Italy, 1934. Multicoloured.

3436	$2 Type **420**	1·10	1·10
3437	$2 Final between Italy and Czechoslovakia	1·10	1·10
3438	$2 Flaminio Stadium	1·10	1·10
3439	$2 Angelo Schiavio	1·10	1·10
MS3440	115×90 mm. $6 Victorious Italian team carrying coach Vittorio Pozzo	3·25	3·50

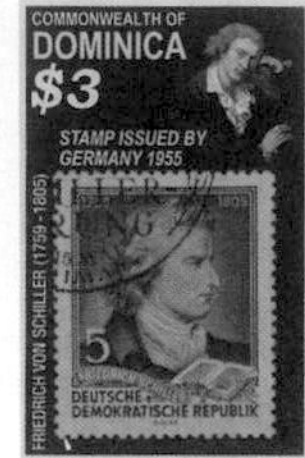

421 East Germany 5pf. Stamp

2005. Death Bicentenary of Frederick von Schiller (poet and dramatist). Showing stamps of 1955 issued by German Democratic Republic for 150th Death Anniv (Nos. 3441/3). Multicoloured.

3441	$3 Type **421**	1·75	1·90
3442	$3 10pf. Stamp	1·75	1·90
3443	$3 20pf. Stamp	1·75	1·90
MS3444	70×100 mm. $6 Von Schiller and statue (horiz)	3·25	3·50

422 Scene depicting Weightlessness in *From the Earth to the Moon*

2005. Death Centenary of Jules Verne (writer). Multicoloured.

3445	$2 Type **422**	1·10	1·10
3446	$2 Astronauts inside shuttle	1·10	1·10
3447	$2 Nautilus crew observing marine life in *Twenty Thousand Leagues under the Sea*	1·10	1·10
3448	$2 Submarine	1·10	1·10
MS3449	100×70 mm. $6 Jules Verne	3·25	3·50

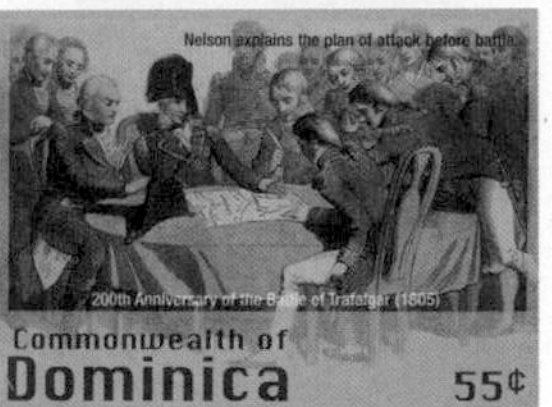

423 Nelson explaining Plan of Attack before Battle

2005. Bicentenary of the Battle of Trafalgar. Multicoloured.

3450	55c. Type **423**	55	40
3451	65c. *L'Orient* explodes, Battle of the Nile (vert)	65	45
3452	$1 Nelson leading boarding party onto *San Nicolas*, Battle of Cape St. Vincent (vert)	1·00	85
3453	$2 HMS *Agamemnon* in battle with Ca Ira	1·75	1·90
MS3454	70×100 mm $6 HMS *Victory* and British fleet	4·00	4·25

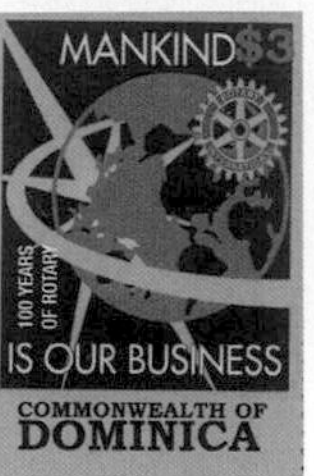

424 Centenary Emblem

2005. Centenary of Rotary International. Mult.

3455	$3 Type **424**	1·75	1·90
3456	$3 Rotary emblem and "100 Years"	1·75	1·90
3457	$3 Women with children	1·75	1·90

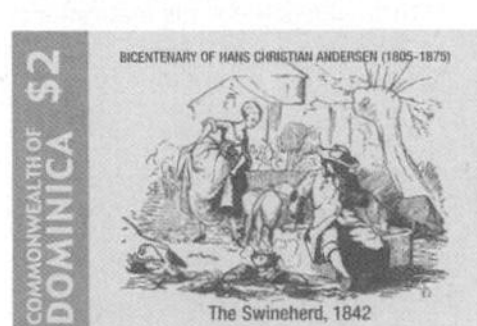

425 *The Swineherd*

2005. Birth Bicentenary of Hans Christian Andersen (writer). Multicoloured.

3458	$2 Type **425**	1·10	1·10
3459	$2 *The Nightingale*	1·10	1·10
3460	$2 *The Fir Tree*	1·10	1·10
MS3461	100×70 mm. $6 *The Ugly Duckling* (50×38 mm)	3·25	3·50

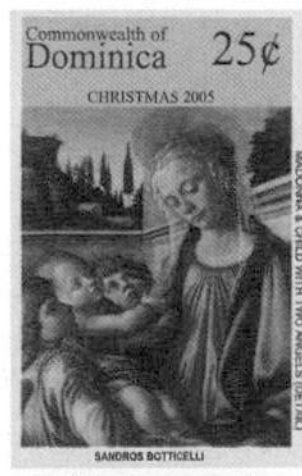

426 "Madonna and Child with Two Angels" (detail) (Botticelli)

2005. Christmas. Multicoloured.

3462	25c. Type **426**	20	15
3463	50c. "Madonna and Child with Angels" (detail) (Botticelli)	35	30
3464	65c. "Madonna and Child" (detail) (Pietro Lorenzetti)	50	30
3465	90c. "Madonna del Roseto" (detail) (Botticelli)	70	50
3466	$1.20 "Adoration of the Magi" (detail) (Pietro Lorenzetti)	90	90
3467	$3 "Madonna in Glory with the Seraphim" (detail) (Botticelli)	1·90	2·25
MS3468	70×100 mm. $5 "Madonna of Frari" (Titian) (horiz)	3·00	3·25

427 Pope Benedict XVI

2005. Election of Pope Benedict XVI.

3469	**427**	$2 multicoloured	1·40	1·40

428 Spaniel

2006. Chinese New Year ("Year of the Dog"). Designs showing china dogs. Multicoloured.

3470	$2 Type **428**	1·25	1·25
3471	$2 Walking dog	1·25	1·25
3472	$2 Staffordshire dog (sitting on plinth)	1·25	1·25

429 Elton Brand, Los Angeles Clippers

2006. US National Basketball Association Players. Multicoloured.

3473	90c. Los Angeles Clippers emblem	50	55
3474	90c. Type **429**	50	55
3475	90c. Denver Nuggets emblem	50	55
3476	90c. Kenyon Martin, Denver Nuggets	50	55
3477	90c. Jason Richardson, Golden State Warriors	50	55
3478	90c. Golden State Warriors emblem	50	55
3479	90c. Phoenix Suns emblem	50	55
3480	90c. Amare Stoudemire, Phoenix Suns	50	55
3481	90c. Orlando Magic emblem	50	55
3482	90c. Hedo Turkoglu, Orlando Magic	50	55
3483	90c. Miami Heat emblem	50	55
3484	90c. Antoine Walker, Miami Heat	50	55

430 Leopold Senghor

2006. Birth Centenary of Leopold Sedar Senghor (first President (1960–80) of Senegal).

3485	**430**	$2 multicoloured	1·00	1·10

431 Yugoslavia 1984 Winter Olympics 23d.70 Ski-jumping Stamp

2006. Winter Olympic Games, Turin. Multicoloured.

3486	75c. Type **431**	50	35
3487	90c. Poster for Winter Olympic Games, Sarajevo, 1984 (vert)	60	55
3488	$2 Japan 1998 Winter Olympics 80y. curling stamp (vert)	1·10	1·10

3489	$3 Poster for Winter Olympic Games, Nagano, 1998 (vert)	1·40	1·60

432 Duchess of York with Baby Princess Elizabeth

2006. 80th Birthday of Queen Elizabeth II. Multicoloured.

3490	$2 Type **432**	1·25	1·25
3491	$2 Princess Elizabeth as young girl	1·25	1·25
3492	$2 As baby	1·25	1·25
3493	$2 As teenager	1·25	1·25
MS3494	120×120 mm. $5 Queen Elizabeth II, c. 1953	2·75	3·00

433 Marilyn Monroe

2006. 80th Birth Anniv of Marilyn Monroe (actress).

3495	**433**	$3 multicoloured	1·50	1·60

434 Trenches dug by Viking 1 Lander on Mars

2006. Space Anniversaries. Multicoloured. (a) 30th Anniv of Viking 1 First Mars Landing.

MS3496	146×96 mm. $2×6 Type **434**; $2 Sunset at Viking 1 Lander site; Chryse Planitia looking north west over Viking 1 Lander; Chryse Planitia (Viking 1 Lander in foreground); Chryse Planitia (Viking 1 Lander in left foreground, dark rocks in background); Chryse Planitia. (b) 40th Anniv of Landing of Luna 9 on Moon	6·00	6·50
MS3497	147×98 mm. $3×4 Luna 9 flight apparatus; Modified SS-6 Sapwood; Luna 9 Soft Lander; Tyuratam (Baikonur Cosmodrome), USSR (all vert). (c) 20th Anniv of Giotto Comet Probe	6·00	6·50
MS3498	147×98 mm. $3×4 Launch of Giotto–Ariane V14 rocket; Giotto spacecraft during the solar simulation test; Halley's Comet develops seven tails; Giotto and Comet Grigg-Skjellerup approach trajectories (all vert)	6·00	6·50
MS3499	Three sheets, each 98×68 mm. (a) $6 Mars Reconnaissance Orbiter. (b) $6 International Space Station. (c) $6 Venus Express Orbiter	8·50	9·00

The three stamps at the foot of No. **MS**3496 form a composite design showing a panorama of Chryse Planitia on Mars taken from First Camera 1.

The two right-hand stamps in No. **MS**3498 form a composite background design.

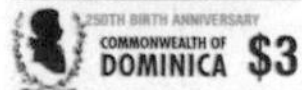

435 Wolfgang Amadeus Mozart

2006. 250th Birth Anniv of Wolfgang Amadeus Mozart (composer). Showing portraits. Multicoloured.

3500	$3 Type **435**	1·90	1·90
3501	$3 Seated at piano	1·90	1·90
3502	$3 Wearing red jacket	1·90	1·90
3503	$3 In profile	1·90	1·90

436 Graceland

2006. 50th Anniv of Purchase of Graceland by Elvis Presley. Sheet 190×127 mm containing T 436 and similar vert designs. Multicoloured.

MS3504	$3×4 Type **436**; Left wing; Right wing; Interior	6·00	6·50

437 John Kennedy on Crutches

2006. John F. Kennedy (US President 1961–3) Commemoration. Multicoloured.

3505	$3 Type **437**	1·50	1·60
3506	$3 In hospital bed (surgery for Addison's disease)	1·50	1·60
3507	$3 Cover of his book "Profiles in Courage"	1·50	1·60
3508	$3 Senator John Kennedy at desk	1·50	1·60
3509	$3 Supporters with placard	1·50	1·60
3510	$3 Kennedy at microphone on campaign	1·50	1·60
3511	$3 Waiting for Concession	1·50	1·60
3512	$3 Addressing the nation	1·50	1·60

Nos. 3505/8 commemorate the 50th anniversary of John F. Kennedy's book "Profiles in Courage" and Nos. 3509/12 the 45th anniversary of his inauguration.

438 *Turbinella angulata*

2006. Shells. Multicoloured.

3513	5c. Type **438**	15	20
3514	10c. *Vasum muricatum*	20	20
3515	15c. *Fusinus closter*	25	20
3516	20c. *Crassispira gibbosa*	25	20
3517	25c. *Terebra strigata*	25	20
3518	50c. *Prunum carneum*	35	30
3519	65c. *Purpura patula*	45	30
3520	90c. *C. chrysostoma*	60	40
3521	$1 *M. nodulosa*	70	50
3522	$2 *Conus regius*	1·10	1·10
3523	$3.50 *Conus hieroglyphus*	1·75	1·90
3524	$5 *Anodontia alba* (vert)	2·50	2·75
3525	$10 *C. cassidiformis*	4·50	4·75
3526	$20 *Strigilla carnaria* (vert)	8·00	9·00

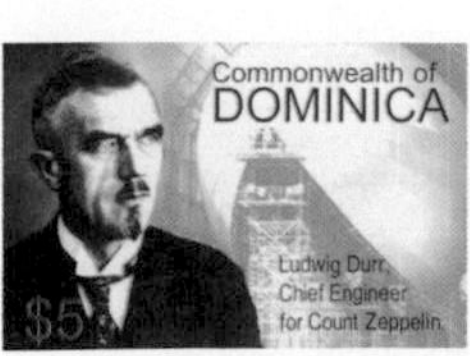

439 Ludwig Durr

2006. 50th Death Anniv of Ludwig Durr (Zeppelin engineer). Sheet 100×70 mm.

MS3527	**439** $5 multicoloured	2·75	3·00

440 Betty Boop

2006. Betty Boop. Multicoloured.

MS3528	178×127 mm. $2×6 Type **440**; Red lips; Head and shoulders portrait, left arm raised; Betty's dog on lead, running; Head and shoulders portrait; Betty's dog, seated	4·25	4·50
MS3529	99×70 mm. $3.50 Close-up portrait; $3.50 Close-up portrait, looking over shoulder	3·50	3·75

The top three stamps within **MS**3528 form a composite design.

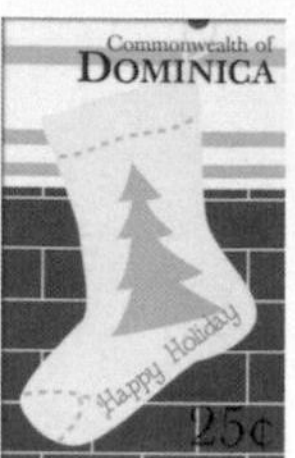

441 Christmas Stocking

2006. Christmas. Christmas stockings with "Happy Holiday" inscription. Multicoloured.

3530	25c. Type **441**	25	15
3531	50c. Green stocking with bell design	40	25
3532	90c. Blue stocking with heart design	65	45
3533	$1 Magenta stocking with snowflake design	75	75
MS3534	150×100 mm. $2×4 As Nos. 3530/4	5·50	6·50

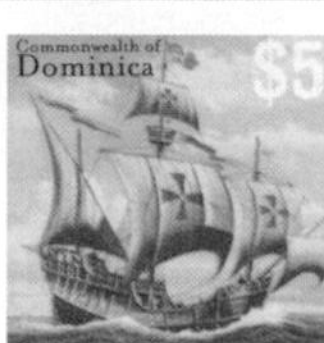

442 *Santa Maria*

2007. 500th Death Anniv (2006) of Christopher Columbus. Sheet 70×100 mm.

MS3535	**442** $5 multicoloured	2·50	2·75

443 Scout Salute

2007. Centenary of World Scouting and 21st World Scout Jamboree, United Kingdom.

3536	**443**	$3.50 multicoloured	1·75	1·90
MS3537	**443**	$5 multicoloured	2·50	2·75

444 Christ

2007. 400th Birth Anniv (2006) of Rembrandt Harmenszoon van Rijn (artist). Details from the painting "Christ Driving the Money-Changers from the Temple". Multicoloured.

3538	$2 Type **444**	1·10	1·10
3539	$2 Man looking upwards	1·10	1·10
3540	$2 Man wearing turban	1·10	1·10
3541	$2 Man with hands shielding his face	1·10	1·10

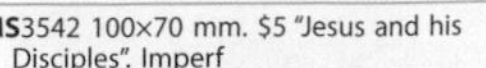

MS3542	100×70 mm. $5 "Jesus and his Disciples". Imperf	2·50	2·75

445 Aircraft 001 F-WTSS

2007. 40th Anniv of Roll-out of the Concorde Prototype. Multicoloured.

3543	$1 Type **445**	70	50
3544	$2 Aircraft 001 F-WTSS (different)	1·10	1·10

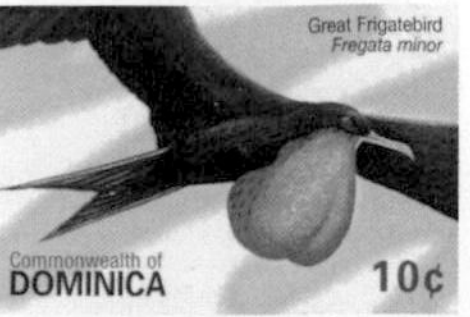

446 Great Frigatebird

2007. Birds of the Caribbean. Multicoloured.

3545	10c. Type **446**	10	10
3546	25c. Peruvian booby	20	25
3547	90c. Black stork (vert)	50	55
3548	$2 Antillean crested hummingbird	1·20	1·20
3549	$2 Rufous-breasted hermit	1·20	1·20
3550	$2 Cuban hummingbird	1·20	1·20
3551	$2 Blue-headed hummingbird	1·20	1·20
3552	$5 Limpkin (vert)	3·00	3·25
MS3553	70×100 mm. $5 Red-capped manakin (vert)	3·00	3·25

447 *Plumeria rubra* (red jasmine)

2007. Flowers of Dominica. Multicoloured.

3554	10c. Type **447**	10	10
3555	25c. *Bougainvillea glabra*	20	25
3556	90c. *Thespesia populnea* (Portia tree)	50	55
3557	$5 *Nerium oleander* (rose bay)	3·00	3·25
MS3558	131×108 mm. $2×4 *Alpinia purpurata* (red ginger); *Adansonia digitata* (baobab); *Petrea kohautiana* (purple wreath); *Thunbergia grandiflora* (all horiz)	4·75	5·00
MS3559	70×100 mm. $5 *Delonix regia* (flamboyant)	3·00	3·25

The stamps and margins of No. **MS**3558 form a composite design.

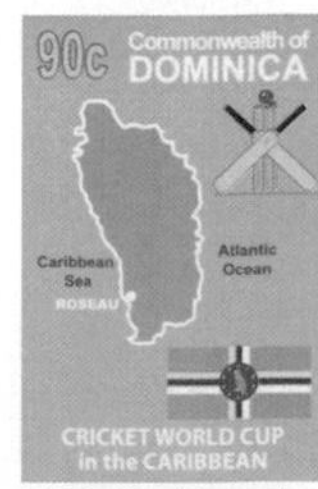

448 Outline Map and Flag of Dominica

2007. World Cup Cricket, West Indies. Multicoloured.

3560	90c. Type **448**	50	55
3561	$1 Billy Doctrove (umpire)	60	65
MS3562	120×93 mm. $5 World Cup Cricket emblem	3·00	3·25

449 *Tolumnia urophylla*

2007. Orchids. Multicoloured.

MS3563 131×109 mm. $1 Type **449**; $1 *Brassavola cucullata*; $2 *Isochilus linearis*; $2 *Spathoglottis plicata* 3·50 3·75

MS3564 70×100 mm. $5 *Oncidium altissumum* 3·00 3·25

The stamps and margins of No. **MS**3563 form a composite design of a river, forest and waterfall.

450 Diana, Princess of Wales

2007. 10th Death Anniv of Diana, Princess of Wales. Multicoloured.

MS3565 150×100 mm. $1 Type **450**; $1 Wearing mauve hat and mauve and white dress; $1 In close-up, wearing white jacket; $2 Wearing white jacket; $2 Wearing grey hat; $2 In close-up, wearing mauve hat 5·00 5·25

MS3566 100×70 mm. $5 Wearing white shirt and grey tank top (37×50 mm) 3·00 3·35

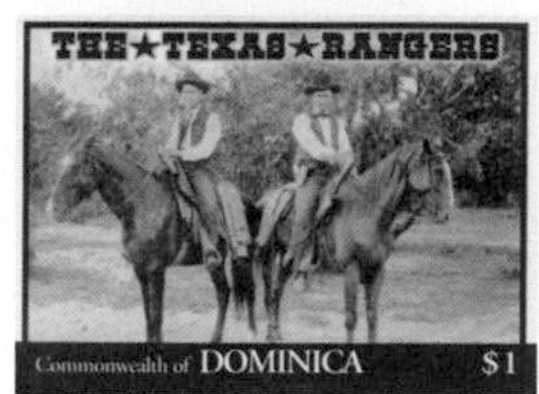

451 Texas Rangers

2007. 150th Anniv of the Remington Revolver. Designs showing 19th-century Texas Rangers. Multicoloured.

3567	$1 Type **451**	60	65
3568	$1 Bill McCawley, Capt. Frank Johnson, Crosky Marsden, Oscar Rountree and three other Rangers	60	65
3569	$1 Texas Rangers with rifles, four kneeling, six standing	60	65
3570	$1 Company of mounted Texas Rangers	60	65
3571	$1 Texas Rangers by barbed wire fence	60	65
3572	$1 Three Rangers outside "Justice of the Peace Law West of the Pecos" building	60	65
3573	$1 Mounted Texas Rangers at tented camp	60	65
3574	$1 Texas Rangers with steam engine	60	65
3575	$1 Five mounted Texas Rangers outside homestead	60	65

MS3576 70×100 mm. $5 Statue of Charles Goodnight (rancher), Canyon, Texas (vert) (150th anniv of him joining the Texas Rangers) 3·00 3·25

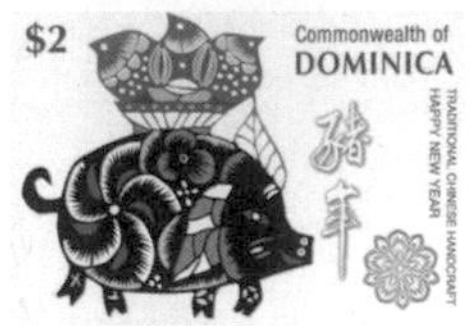

452 Pig

2007. Chinese New Year ('Year of the Pig'). Sheet 110×82 mm.

MS3577 As Type **452** (country name and inscriptions at right in purple, green, blue or plum) 4·00 4·00

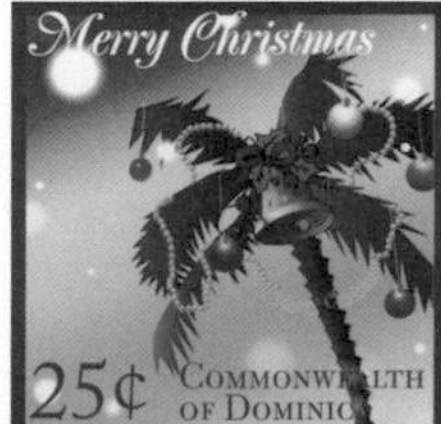

453 Decorated Palm Tree

2007. Christmas. Multicoloured.

3578	25c. Type **453**	20	25
3579	50c. Father Christmas	30	35
3580	90c. Merry Christmas	50	55
3581	$1 Merry Christmas	60	65

454 Rat encircled by the Twelve Chinese Horoscope Animals

2008. Chinese New Year ('Year of the Rat').

3582	**454**	$1 multicoloured	50	55

455 Arms and Dr. Bernard A. Sorhaindo (first Dominican graduate)

2008. 60th Anniv of the University of the West Indies.

3583	**455**	50c. multicoloured	25	30
3584	**455**	65c. multicoloured	35	40
3585	**455**	90c. multicoloured	45	50

MS3586 Three sheets, each 99×70 mm. (a) $5 Arms and scroll. (b) $5 Type **455** (blue background to portrait). (c) $5 Type **455** (black background to portrait) 4·25 4·50

456 Archery

2008. Olympic Games, Beijing. Multicoloured.

3587	$1.40 Type **456**	70	75
3588	$1.40 Gymnastics	70	75
3589	$1.40 Badminton	70	75
3590	$1.40 Boxing	70	75

457 Queen Elizabeth II and Prince Philip

2008. Diamond Wedding of Queen Elizabeth II and Prince Philip (2007). Multicoloured.

3591	$1 Type **457**	50	55
3591	$1 Type 457	50	55
3592	$1 Queen Elizabeth II	50	55
3592	$1 Queen Elizabeth II (inscr in reddish purple)	50	55
3592a	$1 As Type **457** (inscr in black)	50	55
3592b	$1 As No. 3592 (inscr in white)	50	55
3592c	$1 As Type **457** (inscr in reddish purple)	50	55
3592d	$1 As No. 3592 (inscr in black)	50	55

They differ in the colour of the inscriptions 'Commonwealth of DOMINICA' and '$1'.

458 Pope Benedict XVI

2008. First Visit of Pope Benedict XVI to the United States.

3593	**458**	$1.40 multicoloured	70	75

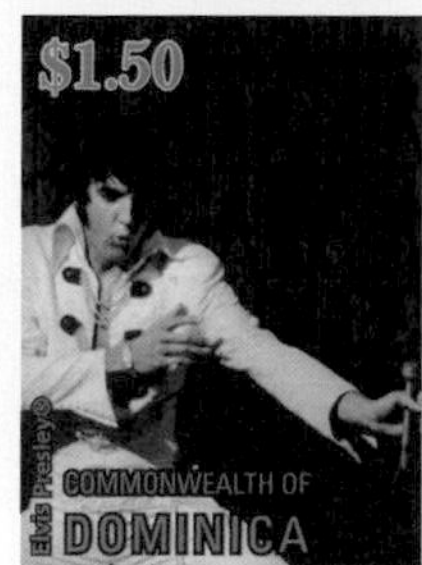

459 Elvis Presley

2008. Elvis Presley Commemoration. Multicoloured.

3594	$1.50 Type **459**	80	85
3595	$1.50 Wearing white jacket with star pattern	80	85
3596	$1.50 Wearing white jacket with embroidery around collar and on front	80	85
3597	$1.50 Wearing white jacket with circle of black embroidery on front	80	85
3598	$1.50 Wearing plain white with necktie	80	85
3599	$1.50 Wearing white jacket with looped braid fastening	80	85

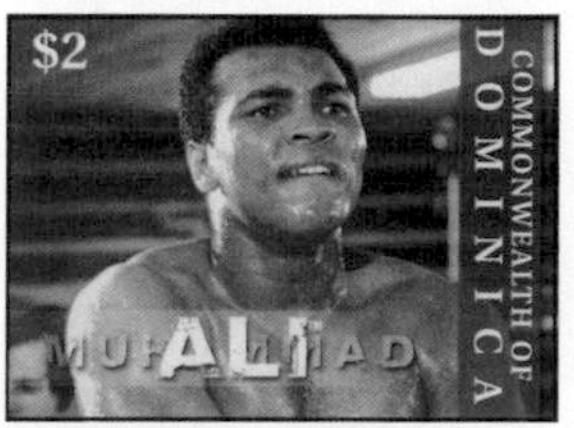

460 Muhammad Ali

2008. Muhammad Ali (world heavyweight boxing champion, 1964, 1974—8). Multicoloured.

3600	$2 Type **460**	1·00	1·10
3601	$2 In close-up	1·00	1·10
3602	$2 Wearing boxing helmet	1·00	1·10
3603	$2 With arms raised in triumph	1·00	1·10
3604	$2 Slumped against ring ropes	1·00	1·10
3605	$2 Shouting into reporter's microphone	1·00	1·10
3606	$2 In close-up (side view)	1·00	1·10
3607	$2 Wearing boxing helmet and gum shield	1·00	1·10

461 Pupils

2008. 150th Anniv of Convent High School.

3608	**461**	50c. multicoloured	25	30
3609	**461**	65c. multicoloured	35	40
3610	**461**	90c. multicoloured	45	50
3611	**461**	$1 multicoloured	50	55

MS3612 100×70 mm. $5 As Type **461** 2·60 2·75

462 Dandie Dinmont Terrier

2008. Dogs of the World. Multicoloured.

3613	25c. Type **462**	15	10
3614	50c. Alaskan malamute	25	30
3615	90c. Welsh springer spaniel	45	50
3616	$1 Pug	50	55
3617	$2 Norfolk terrier	1·00	1·10
3618	$2.50 Akita	1·30	1·40
3619	$2.50 Australian cattle dog	1·30	1·40
3620	$2.50 Border collie	1·30	1·40
3621	$2.50 Staffordshire bull terrier cross	1·30	1·40
3622	$5 Vizsla	2·75	2·75

463 Marilyn Monroe

2008. Marilyn Monroe Commemoration. Multicoloured.

3623	$2 Type **463**	1·00	1·10
3624	$2 Wearing orange, holding mirror	1·00	1·10
3625	$2 Wearing pink, leaning away from wall	1·00	1·10
3626	$2 Wearing orange, holding glass	1·00	1·10

464 Father Christmas

2008. Christmas. Multicoloured.

3627	25c. Type **464**	15	10
3628	50c. Palm tree decorated with bell and baubles	25	30
3629	90c. Christmas stocking	45	50
3630	$1 Poinsettias	50	55

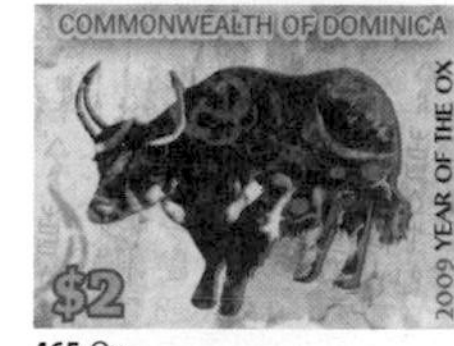

465 Ox

2009. Chinese New Year. Year of the Ox. Sheet 190×78 mm.

MS3631 Type **465**×4 4·00 4·25

466 Pres. Barack Obama (with hand raised)

2009. Inauguration of Pres. Barack Obama.

3632	65c. Type **466**	35	40
3633	90c. Pres. Barack Obama (different)	45	50

MS3634 126×178 mm. $2.25×2 Type **466**; $2.50×2 As No. 3633; Pres Barack Obama (facing left) 4·75 5·00

467 Flags of Dominica and China

2009. 5th Anniv of Diplomatic Relations between Dominica and People's Republic of China.

3635	**467**	50c. multicoloured	25	30
3636	**467**	65c. multicoloured	35	40
3637	**467**	90c. multicoloured	45	50
3638	**467**	$1 multicoloured	50	55

MS3639 100×70 mm. $5 multicoloured 2·75 2·75

468 Peony Flower

2009. China 2009 World Stamp Exhibition, Luoyang. Multicoloured.

3640 75c. Type **468** 35 40

MS3641 100×70 mm. $5 Peony flowers and foliage (44×44 mm) 2·75 2·75

469 Elvis Presley

2009. Elvis Presley Commemoration. Sheet 130×100 mm containing T **469** and similar vert designs. Multicoloured. Litho.

MS3642 Type **469**; Facing left (greenish blue background); Full face (greenish blue background); Eyes looking to left (brown background) 4·75 5·00

470 Franz Josef Haydn

2009. Death Bicentenary of Franz Josef Haydn (composer). Sheet 163×94 mm containing T **470** and similar vert designs. Multicoloured.

MS3643 Type **470**; Haydn's birthplace at Rohrau, Austria; Wolfgang Amadeus Mozart; St. Stephen's Cathedral, Vienna; Nikolaus Esterhazy (sponsor of Haydn); Palace Eszterhazy, Fertod, Hungary 8·25 8·25

471 *Leucopaxillus gracillimus*

2009. Fungi. Multicoloured.

3644 50c. Type **471** 25 30

3645 65c. *Calvatia cyathiformis* 35 40

3646 90c. *Hygrocybe viridiphylla* 45 50

3647 $1 *Boletellus coccineus* 50 55

MS3648 108×143 mm. $2×6 *Hygrocybe acutoconica; Lepiota sulphureocyanescens; Lactariusrubrilacteus; Lactarius ferrugineus; Asterophora lycoperdoides; Amanitapolypyramis* 6·00 6·00

472 Lobed Star Coral (*Montastraea*) and Shark

2009. Coral Reef of Dominica. Multicoloured.

3649 50c. Type **472** 25 30

3650 65c. Orange cup corals (*Tubastraea coccinea*) and fish 35 40

3651 90c. Grooved brain coral (*Diploria labyrinthiformis*) and turtle 45 50

3652 $1 Elkhorn coral (*Acropora palmata*) and fish 50 55

MS3653 134×85 mm. $2×6 Rough star coral (*Isophyllastrea rigida*) and fish; Branched finger coral (*Porites furcata*) and fish; Wire coral (*Cirrhipathes leutkeni*) and manta ray; Great star coral (*Montastrea cavernosa*) and fish; Pillar coral (*Dendrogyra cylindrus*) and angelfish; Rose lace coral (*Stylaster roseus*) and fish 6·00 6·00

473 Banded Orange Heliconian (*Dryadula phaetusa*)

2009. Butterflies of the Caribbean. Multicoloured.

3654 90c. Type **473** 45 50

3655 $1 Gulf fritillary (*Agraulis vanillae*) 50 55

3656 $2 Julia longwing (*Dryas julia*) 1·00 1·10

3657 $5 Zebra longwing (*Heliconius charitonius*) 2·75 2·75

MS3658 100×155 mm. $2.50×4 Cuban cattleheart (*Parides g. gundlachianus*); White peacock (*Anartia jatrophae*); Bahamian swallowtail (*Papilio andraemon tailori*); Tropical buckeye (*Junonia genoveva*) 5·25 5·25

MS3659 70×98 mm. $6 Atala black (*Eumaeus atala*) (51×38 mm) 3·00 3·00

MS3660 70×98 mm. $6 Purple emperor (*Doxocopa thoe*) (51×38 mm) 3·00 3·00

474 *Oliva reticularis*

2009. Seashells. Multicoloured.

3661 50c. Type **474** 25 30

3662 65c. *Vasum muricatum* 35 40

3663 90c. *Olivella nivea* 45 50

3664 $1 *Olivella mutica* 50 55

MS3665 134×85 mm. $2×6 *Hyalina avena; Persicula fluctuata; Agatrix agassizi; Trigonostoma rugosum; Olivella floralia; Marginella eburneola* 6·00 6·00

475 Irrawwady Dolphin (*Orcaella brevirostris*)

2009. Dolphins. Multicoloured.

3666 50c. Type **475** 25 30

3667 65c. Pantropical spotted dolphin (*Stenella attenuata*) 35 40

3668 90c. Atlantic humpback dolphin (*Sousa teuszii*) 45 50

3669 $1 Indian humpback dolphin (*Sousa plumbea*) 50 55

MS3670 150×100 mm. $2×6 Melon-headed whale (*Peponocephala electra*); Striped dolphin (*Stenellacoeruleoalba*); Atlantic spotted dolphin (*Stenella frontalis*); Clymene dolphin (*Stenella clymene*); Pantropical spotted dolphin (*Stenella attenuata graffmani*); Pantropical spotted dolphin (*Stenellaattenuata*) 6·00 6·00

476 Pres. John F. Kennedy

2009. 10th Death Anniv of John Kennedy Jr. Sheet 100×130 mm containing T **476** and similar horiz designs. Multicoloured.

MS3671 $2.50×4 Type **476**; Pres. Kennedy and Mrs. Kennedy with their children Caroline and John Jnr; Pres. Kennedy with Lyndon Johnson; Pres. Kennedy (US flag in background) 9·50 9·50

477 The Bund, Shanghai

2009. World Expo 2010, Shanghai, China. Sheet 101×141 mm containing T **477** and similar horiz designs. Multicoloured.

MS3672 $1.50×4 Type **477**; Shanghai Museum; Yangpu Bridge, Shanghai; Shanghai Theatre 3·25 3·25

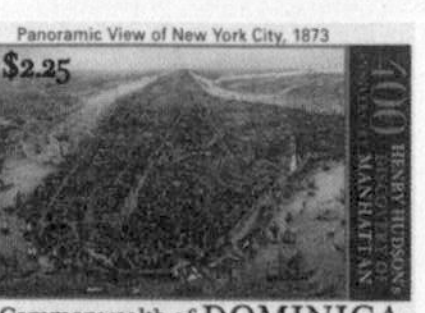

478 Panoramic View of New York City, 1873

2009. 400th Anniv of Henry Hudson's Discovery of Manhattan. Multicoloured.

MS3673 150×110 mm. $2.25×6 Type **478**; *Hudson, the Dreamer* (Jean L. G. Ferris); Portrait of Henry Hudson; *Half Moon* (Hudson's ship); Map of Hudson River, c. 1600s; Henry Hudson Memorial Column, Bronx, New York 8·75 8·75

MS3674 70×100 mm. $6 Aerial view of New York City (vert) 6·00 6·00

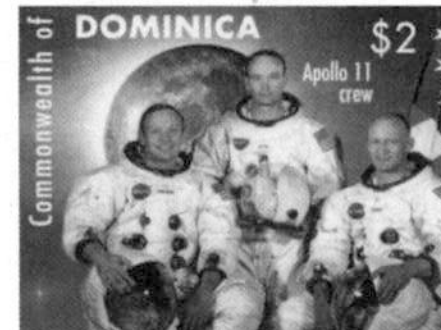

479 Apollo 11 Crew

2009. 40th Anniv of First Manned Moon Landing and International Year of Astronomy. Sheet 150×100 mm containing T **479** and similar horiz designs. Multicoloured.

MS3675 $2×6 Type **479**; Moon landing on television; Final descent of capsule by parachute; Apollo 11, emblem and Earth; Command module in Moon orbit; Project ORION 12·00 12·00

480 Bell

2009. Christmas. Multicoloured.

3676 50c. Type **480** 30 35

3677 65c. Candles and poinsettias 30 35

3678 90c. Gingerbread man 60 55

3679 $1.10 Decorated palm tree 65 70

3680 $2.25 Bell, bauble and Christmas tree with lights 1·50 1·50

3681 $2.75 Women dancing and 'MERRY CHRISTMAS' 1·75 1·75

481 H-5

2009. Centenary of Chinese Aviation. Showing aircraft. Multicoloured.

MS3682 145×95 mm. $2×4 Type **481**; H-6; H-6H; H-6U 4·00 4·00

MS3683 120×79 mm. $6 H-6U aircraft flying in formation with two fighter planes (51×38 mm) 3·00 3·00

481a Dominica Flag and Outline Map

2009. National Stamp

3683a **481a** $3 multicoloured 1·50 1·50

481b 481b

2009. Personalised Stamp

3683b **481b** $3 multicoloured 1·50 1·50

482 People's Republic of China 1986 8f. Year of the Tiger Stamp

2010. Chinese New Year. Year of the Tiger. Sheet 102×72 mm.

MS3684 $5 **482** multicoloured 2·75 2·75

482a People's Republic of China 1986 8f. Year of the Monkey Stamp

2010. Chinese Lunar Calendar. Multicoloured.

MS3684a 60c.×12 Type **482a**; 1981 Year of the Cock 8f. stamp; 1982 Year of the Dog 8f. stamp; 1983 Year of the Pig 8f. stamp; 1984 Year of the Rat 8f. stamp; 1985 Year of the Ox 8f. stamp; 1986 Year of the Tiger 8f. stamp; 1987 Year of the Rabbit 8f. stamp; 1988 Year of the Dragon 8f. stamp; 1989 Year of the Snake 8f. stamp; 1990 Year of the Horse 8f. stamp; 1991 Year of the Sheep 20f. stamp 4·25 4·25

483 Elvis Presley

2010. 75th Birth Anniv of Elvis Presley. Sheet 130×140 mm containing T **483** and similar vert designs showing portraits by Betty Harper. Multicoloured.

MS3685 Type **483**; Looking to left, wearing denim shirt; In profile, facing right; Looking to left, heavier chin 5·25 5·25

484 Pope John Paul II

2010. 5th Death Anniv of Pope John Paul II. Sheet 170×115 mm.

MS3686 Type **484**×4 5·50 5·50

485 Brindle Boxer

2010. 125th Anniv of the American Kennel Club. Multicoloured.

MS3687 100×120 mm. $2.50×4 Type **485**; Tan and white Boxer (shrub in background); Tan and white Boxer (black background); Dark brindle Boxer (white boards background) 5·25 5·25

MS3688 100×120 mm. $2.50×4 Dalmatian (stack of books at right); Dalmatian (stone wall in background); Dalmatian (laying beside swimming pool); Dalmatian (stack of logs in background) 5·25 5·25

486 Denny Hamlin

2010. NASCAR (National Association for Stock Car Auto Racing). Sheet 150×140 mm containing T **486** and similar vert designs. Multicoloured.

MS3689 Type **486**; Kyle Busch; Joey Logano; Car, '11' and Denny Hamlin's signature; Car, '18' and Kyle Busch's signature; Car, '20' and Joey Logano's signature 9·00 9·25

Haiti Earthquake Relief Fund

(487)

2010. Haiti Earthquake Relief Fund

MS3690 150×100 mm. $2×6 Melon-headed whale (*Peponocephala electra*); Striped dolphin (*Stenella coeruleoalba*); Atlantic spotted dolphin (*Stenella frontalis*); Clymene dolphin (*Stenella clymene*); Pantropical spotted dolphin (*Stenella attenuata graffmani*); Pantropical spotted dolphin (*Stenella attenuata* 12·00 12·00

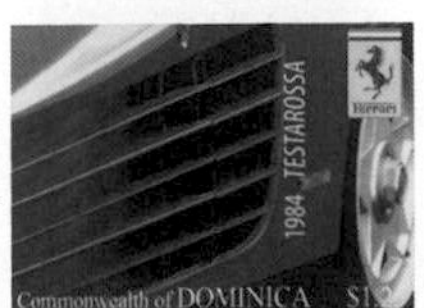

488 Air Intake of Ferrari Testarossa, 1984

2010. Ferrari Cars. Multicoloured.

3691	$1.25 Type **488**	65	70
3692	$1.25 Testarossa, 1984	65	70
3693	$1.25 Engine of 126 C3, 1983	65	70
3694	$1.25 126 C3, 1983	65	70
3695	$1.25 Engine and chassis of 408 4RM, 1987	65	70
3696	$1.25 408 4RM, 1987	65	70
3697	$1.25 Engine of 208 GTB Turbo	65	70
3698	$1.25 208 GTB Turbo	65	70

489 Centenary Emblem and Emergency One Man Carry

2010. Centenary of Boy Scouts of America. Multicoloured.

MS3699 $2.50 Type **489**×2; $2.50 Boy swimming ('Fun with safety')×2 3·00 3·00

MS3700 $2.50 Chopping wood ('Outdoor skills')×2; $2.50 Singing and playing guitar ('Campfire inspirations')×2 3·00 3·00

490 Mother Teresa

2010. Birth Centenary of Mother Teresa. Multicoloured.

MS3701 $2.50 ×4 Type **490**; With rosary beads; Facing camera; Kissing hand of Pope John Paul II 5·25 5·25

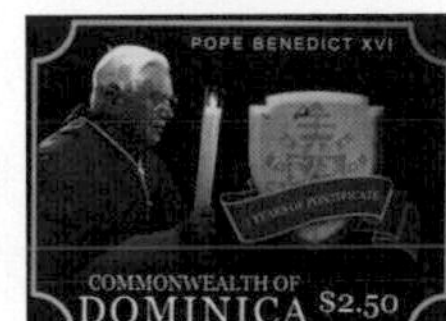

491 Pope Benedict XVI holding Candle

2010. Fifth Anniv of Pontificate of Pope Benedict XVI. Multicoloured.

MS3702 $2.50×4 Type **491**; Wearing gold and white cape ; Wearing red cassock; Wearing white robes 5·25 5·25

492 Mary Magdalene, 1594–6

2010. 400th Death Anniv of Michelangelo Merisi da Caravaggio (artist)

MS3703 172×120 mm. $2.50×4 Type **492**; *Sick Bacchus*, 1593–4; *Bacchus*, 1593–4; *The Inspiration of Saint Matthew*, 1593–4 5·25 5·25

MS3704 100×70 mm. $6 *Saint Gerolamo*, 1605–6 (horiz) 3·00 3·00

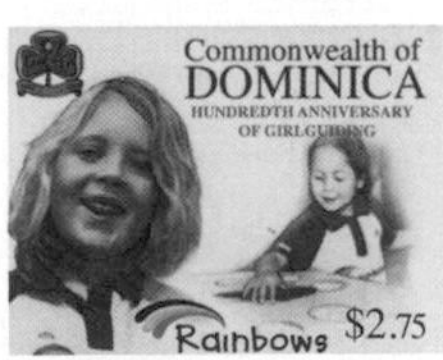

493 Rainbows

2010. Centenary of Girlguiding

MS3705 150×100 mm. $2.75×4 Type **493**; Brownies playing recorders; Guides on bicycles; Senior section guide abseiling 7·00 7·00

MS3706 70×100 mm. $6 Rainbow (vert) 7·00 7·00

494 Elvis Presley

2010. Elvis Presley in Film *Harum Scarum*

MS3707 125x90 mm. $6 Type **494** 3·00 3·00

MS3708 125x90 mm. $6 Film poster for *Harum Scarum* , 1965 3·00 3·00

MS3709 90x125 mm. $6 Wearing jacket and bowtie 3·00 3·00

MS3710 90x125 mm. $6 As Jphnny Tyronne, hanging from rope 3·00 3·00

495 Prince Charles and Princess Diana, c. 1981

2010. Princess Diana Commemoration. Multicoloured.

MS3711 150x104 mm. $2.75×4 Type **495**; Prince Charles and Princess Diana with young Princes William and Harry; Princess Diana (wearing navy and white) shaking hands; Princess Diana (wearing white scarf) 5·00 5·00

MS3712 154×92 mm. $2.75×4 Princess Diana wearing navy, red and white check coat; On wedding day, 1981; Wearing navy blue, receiving bouquet from young girls; Wearing pink dress with white collar and white hat with navy piping 3·00 3·00

The stamps and margins of No. **MS**3712 form composite background designs.

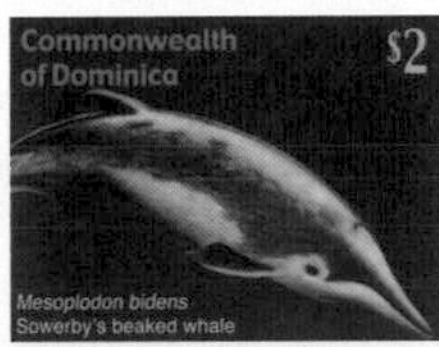

496 Sowerby's Beaked Whale (Mesoplodon bidens)

2010. Whales of the Caribbean. Multicoloured.

MS3713 $2×6 Type **496**; Blainville's beaked whale (*Mesoplodon densirostris*); Short-finned pilot whale (*Globicephala macrorhynchus*); True's beaked whale (*Mesoplodon mirus*); False killer whale (*Pseudorca crassidens*); Dwarf sperm whale (*Kogia simus*) 5·25 5·25

MS3714 101×71 mm. $6 Sperm whale (*Physeter catodon*) 5·50 5·50

497 Abraham Lincoln

2010. Birth Bicentenary (2009) of Abraham Lincoln (US president 1861–5). Multicoloured.

MS3715 $2.50×4 Type **497**; Abraham Lincoln (half-length portrait); With son; Abraham Lincoln (head and shoulders, with beard) 8·75 8·75

MS3716 $2.50×4 Statue, Bascom Hill; Aerial view of Lincoln Memorial; Statue at Lincoln Memorial; Head of Abraham Lincoln at Mount Rushmore 8·75 9·75

APPENDIX

The following stamps have either been issued in excess of postal needs, or have not been made available to the public in reasonable quantities at face value.

1978

History of Aviation. $16×30, each embossed on gold foil.

2003

50th Anniv of Coronation of Queen Elizabeth II. $20 embossed on gold foil.

Pt. 15

DOMINICAN REPUBLIC

The Eastern portion of the island of Hispaniola in the W. Indies finally became independent of Spain in 1865.

1865. 8 reales = 1 peso.
1880. 100 centavos = 1 peso.
1883. 100 centimos = 1 franco.
1885. 100 centavos = 1 peso.

1

1865. Imperf.

1	**1**	½r. black on red	£700	£650
3	**1**	½r. black on green	£550	£475
2	**1**	1r. black on green	£1100	£1000
4	**1**	1r. black on yellow	£1800	£1200

3

1865. Imperf.

5	**3**	½r. black on buff	£200	£160
7	**3**	½r. black on red	60·00	60·00
12	**3**	½r. black on grey	£225	£225
18	**3**	½r. black and blue on red	75·00	50·00
19	**3**	½r. black on yellow	42·00	26·00
9	**3**	1r. black on blue	60·00	38·00
15	**3**	1r. black on flesh	£250	£250
20	**3**	1r. black on green	85·00	70·00
21	**3**	1r. black on lilac	42·00	26·00

4

1879. Perf.

22	**4**	½r. violet	3·00	2·10
24	**4**	1r. red	4·50	2·10

5

1880. Rouletted.

35	**5**	1c. green	95	45
28	**5**	5c. blue	1·50	70
36	**5**	2c. red	95	45
38	**5**	10c. pink	1·60	70
39	**5**	20c. bistre	1·60	95
40	**5**	25c. mauve	1·90	1·10
32	**5**	50c. orange	3·00	1·70
33	**5**	75c. blue	5·75	3·00
34	**5**	1p. gold	7·50	4·25

1883. Surch.

44	5c. on 1c. green	1·50	1·60
73	10c. on 2c. red	2·75	1·80
46	25c. on 5c. blue	6·75	4·00
47	50c. on 10c. pink	27·00	12·50
58	1f. on 20c. bistre	14·50	9·00
51	1f.25 on 25c. mauve	23·00	16·00
52	2f.50 on 50c. orange	16·00	12·00
53	3f.75 on 75c. blue	36·00	31·00
64	5f. on 1p. gold	£180	£180

15

1885. Figures in lower corners only.

77	**15**	1c. green	1·00	50
78	**15**	2c. red	1·00	50
79	**15**	5c. blue	1·40	50
80	**15**	10c. orange	2·20	65
81	**15**	20c. brown	2·20	80
82	**15**	50c. violet	7·50	6·50
83	**15**	1p. red	20·00	13·00
84	**15**	2p. brown	25·00	16·00

1895. As T 15 but figures in four corners.

85	1c. green	1·20	50
86	2c. red	1·20	50
87	5c. blue	1·40	50
88	10c. orange	3·25	1·60

18 Voyage of Mendez from Jamaica to Santo Domingo

19 Sarcophagus of Columbus

1899. Columbus Mausoleum Fund.

98	**19**	¼c. black	75	1·60
99	-	½c. black	75	1·60
89	**18**	1c. purple	7·25	5·25
90	**18**	1c. green	75	65
91	-	2c. red	1·70	65
92	**19**	5c. blue	1·90	60
93	-	10c. orange	5·00	1·60
94	-	20c. brown	10·00	8·25
95	-	50c. green	11·50	9·75
96	-	1p. black on blue	27·00	22·00
97	-	2p. brown on cream	44·00	47·00

DESIGNS—AS TYPE **18**: ½c. (No. 99), 1p. Columbus at Salamanca Assembly; 2c. Enriquillo's Rebellion; 20c. Toscanelli replying to Columbus; 50c. Las Casas defending Indians. As Type **19**: 10c. Hispaniola guarding remains of Columbus; 2p. Columbus Mausoleum, Santo Domingo Cathedral.

20 Island of Hispaniola

1900

100	**20**	¼c. blue	75	40
101	**20**	½c. red	75	40
102	**20**	1c. olive	75	40
103	**20**	2c. green	75	40
104	**20**	5c. brown	75	40
105	**20**	10c. orange	75	40
106	**20**	20c. purple	3·00	2·50
107	**20**	50c. black	2·75	2·50
108	**20**	1p. brown	3·00	2·50

21

1901

109	**21**	½c. lilac and red	70	40
110	**21**	1c. lilac and olive	70	25
111	**21**	2c. lilac and green	80	25
112	**21**	5c. lilac and brown	80	35
113	**21**	10c. lilac and orange	1·40	45
114	**21**	20c. lilac and brown	2·50	95
115	**21**	50c. lilac and black	8·00	5·50
116	**21**	1p. lilac and brown	18·00	10·00

24 Sanchez

25 Fortress of Santo Domingo

1902. 400th Anniv of Santo Domingo.

125	**24**	1c. black & green	35	35
126	**24**	2c. black & red (Duarte)	35	35
127	**24**	5c. blk & blue (Duarte)	35	35
128	**24**	10c. blk & orge (Sanchez)	35	35
129	**24**	12c. blk & violet (Mella)	35	35
130	**24**	20c. black & red (Mella)	60	60
131	**25**	50c. black and brown	95	95

1904. Surch with new value.

132	**21**	2c. on 50c. lilac & black	9·25	7·25
133	**21**	2c. on 1p. lilac & brown	13·50	9·25
134	**21**	5c. on 50c. lilac & black	4·25	2·75
135	**21**	5c. on 1p. lilac and brown	5·25	4·00
136	**21**	10c. on 50c. lilac & black	8·25	6·75
137	**21**	10c. on 1p. lilac & brown	8·75	6·75

1904. Official stamps optd 16 de Agosto 1904 or surch 1 1 also.

138	**O23**	1c. on 20c. blk & yell	4·75	3·00
139	**O23**	2c. black and red	17·00	5·25
140	**O23**	5c. black and blue	5·75	3·00
141	**O23**	10c. black and green	10·50	10·50

1904. Postage Due stamps optd REPUBLICA DOMINICANA CENTAVOS CORREOS or surch 1 also.

142	**D22**	1c. on 2c. sepia	3·50	1·10
143	**D22**	1c. on 4c. sepia	95	70
145	**D22**	2c. sepia	95	60

1905. Surch 1905 and new value.

146	**15**	2c. on 20c. brown	8·75	7·25
147	**15**	5c. on 20c. brown	4·75	2·50
148	**15**	10c. on 20c. brown	8·75	7·25

1905

149	**21**	½c. orange and black	1·80	95
150	**21**	1c. blue and black	1·80	85
151	**21**	2c. mauve and black	2·30	70
152	**21**	5c. red and black	2·50	1·20
153	**21**	10c. green and black	4·25	2·30
154	**21**	20c. olive and black	13·50	8·75
155	**21**	50c. brown and black	47·00	33·00
156	**21**	1p. grey and black	£200	£225

1906. Postage Due stamps surch REPUBLICA DOMINICANA. and new value.

157	**D22**	1c. on 4c. sepia	95	50
158	**D22**	1c. on 10c. sepia	1·10	40
159	**D22**	2c. on 5c. sepia	1·10	40

1907

168	**21**	½c. black and green	85	20
169	**21**	1c. black and red	85	20
170	**21**	2c. black and brown	1·40	20
171	**21**	5c. black and blue	85	20
164	**21**	10c. black and purple	1·40	40
165	**21**	20c. black and olive	7·25	3·25
166	**21**	50c. black and brown	8·75	7·75
167	**21**	1p. black and violet	21·00	13·50

1911. No. O178 optd HABILITADO. 1911.

182	**O23**	2c. black and red	1·60	60

34

1911

183	**34**	½c. black and orange	20	20
184	**34**	1c. black and green	20	10
185	**34**	2c. black and red	20	10
186	**34**	5c. black and blue	70	20
187	**34**	10c. black and purple	1·60	40
188	**34**	20c. black and olive	11·50	11·50
189	**34**	50c. black and brown	3·25	3·25
190	**34**	1p. black and violet	5·75	4·25

For stamps in other colours see Nos. 235/8 and for stamps in similar type see No. 240/6.

35 Jaun Pablo Duarte

1914. Birth Centenary of Duarte. Background in red, white and blue.

195	**35**	½c. black and orange	40	30
196	**35**	1c. black and green	40	30
197	**35**	2c. black and red	40	30
198	**35**	5c. black and grey	40	40
199	**35**	10c. black and mauve	85	70
200	**35**	20c. black and olive	1·80	2·00
201	**35**	50c. black and brown	2·50	2·75
202	**35**	1p. black and lilac	4·75	4·75

1915. Nos. O177/181 optd Habilitado 1915 or surch MEDIO CENTAVO also.

203	**O23**	½c. on 20c. blk & yell	50	30
204	**O23**	1c. black and green	85	20
205	**O23**	2c. black and red	1·20	20
206	**O23**	5c. black and blue	1·00	20
207	**O23**	10c. black and green	2·75	2·50
208	**O23**	20c. black and yellow	9·25	7·25

1915. Optd 1915.

209	**34**	½c. black and mauve	85	20
210	**34**	1c. black and brown	85	10
211	**34**	2c. black and olive	3·25	30
213	**34**	5c. black and red	3·75	30
214	**34**	10c. black and blue	3·75	40
215	**34**	20c. black and red	8·25	1·70
216	**34**	50c. black and green	10·50	4·75
217	**34**	1p. black and orange	21·00	9·25

1916. Optd 1916.

218	½c. black and mauve	2·30	20
219	1c. black and green	3·25	20

1917. Optd 1917.

220	½c. black and mauve	3·50	30
221	1c. black and green	1·60	20
222	2c. black and olive	2·30	20
223	5c. black and red	23·00	85

1919. Optd 1919.

224	2c. black and olive	17·00	20

1920. Optd 1920.

225	½c. black and mauve	60	20
226	1c. black and green	70	20
227	2c. black and olive	70	20
228	5c. black and red	8·75	60
229	10c. black and blue	5·75	20
230	20c. black and red	7·75	60
231	50c. black and green	65·00	21·00

1921. Optd 1921.

233	1c. black and green	5·25	30
234	2c. black and olive	5·75	40

1922

235	½c. black and red	30	20
236	1c. green	3·75	20
237	2c. red	3·75	20
238	5c. blue	5·75	30

41

1924. Straight top to shield.

240	**41**	1c. green	1·60	20
241	**41**	2c. red	85	20
242	**41**	5c. blue	2·30	20
243	**41**	10c. black and blue	31·00	1·80
245	**41**	50c. black and green	60·00	33·00
246	**41**	1p. black and orange	19·00	12·50

43 Exhibition Pavilion

1927. National and West Indian Exn, Santiago.

248	**43**	2c. red	1·10	50
249	**43**	5c. blue	2·10	50

45 Air Mail Routes

1928. Air.

256	**45**	10c. deep blue	5·25	2·75
271	**45**	10c. yellow	3·50	3·50
280	**45**	10c. pale blue	1·80	60
272	**45**	15c. red	6·75	4·75
281	**45**	15c. turquoise	3·25	1·00
273	**45**	20c. green	3·25	85
282	**45**	20c. brown	3·50	85
274	**45**	30c. violet	6·75	5·75
283	**45**	30c. brown	6·25	1·80

46 Ruins of Fortress of Columbus

1928

258	**46**	½c. red	95	40
259	**46**	1c. green	70	20
260	**46**	2c. red	95	20
261	**46**	5c. blue	2·75	40
262	**46**	10c. blue	2·50	30
263	**46**	20c. red	4·75	50

264	46	50c. green	13·50	8·25
265	46	1p. yellow	36·00	27·00

47 Horacio Vasquez

1929. Frontier Agreement with Haiti.

266	47	½c. red	60	30
267	47	1c. green	60	20
268	47	2c. red	70	20
269	47	5c. blue	1·40	40
270	47	10c. blue	2·10	50

48 Jesuit Convent of San Ignacio de Loyola

1930

275	48	½c. brown	70	60
276	48	1c. green	70	20
277	48	2c. red	70	20
278	48	5c. blue	2·10	60
279	48	10c. blue	4·25	1·30

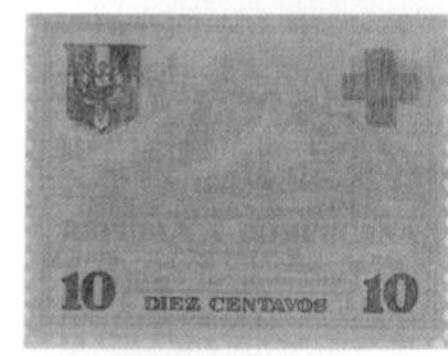

49 After the Hurricane

1930. Hurricane Relief.

284A	-	1c. green and red	20	20
285A	-	2c. red	20	20
286A	49	5c. blue and red	30	20
287A	49	10c. yellow and red	40	30

DESIGN: 1c., 2c. Riverside.

1931. Air. Hurricane Relief. Surch with airplane, HABILITADO PARA CORREO AEREO and premium. Imperf or perf.

288A	5c.+5c. blue and red	6·75	6·75
289A	5c.+5c. black and red	27·00	31·00
290A	10c.+10c. yellow & red	5·25	5·25
291A	10c.+10c. black & red	27·00	31·00

52 Cathedral of Santo Domingo

1931

294	52	1c. green	85	20
295	52	2c. red	60	20
296	52	3c. purple	85	20
297	52	7c. blue	2·50	30
298	52	8c. brown	3·00	95
299	52	10c. blue	5·75	1·20

53 Old Sun Dial, 1754

1931. Air.

300	53	10c. red	3·50	50
301	53	10c. blue	1·70	50
302	53	10c. green	6·25	2·75
303	53	15c. mauve	2·75	50
304	53	20c. blue	6·25	2·30
306	53	30c. green	2·50	30
307	53	50c. brown	6·25	60
308	53	1p. orange	10·50	2·50

54 Fort Ozama

1932

309	54	1c. green	1·70	20
310	54	1c. green	50	20
311	54	3c. violet	1·10	20

No. 310 is inscribed "CORREOS".

1932. Red Cross stamps inscr "CRUZ ROJA DOMINICANA", with cross in red and optd HABILITADO Dic. 20-1932 En. 5-1933 CORREOS or surch also.

312	1c. green	60	40
313	3c. on 2c. violet	85	50
314	5c. blue	2·20	2·00
315	7c. on 10c. blue	6·25	6·75

56 F. A. de Merino

57 Cathedral of Santo Domingo

1933. Birth Centenary of F. A. de Merino.

316	-	½c. violet	40	40
317	56	1c. green	50	30
318	-	2c. red	95	85
319	56	3c. violet	60	30
320	-	5c. blue	70	40
321	-	7c. blue	1·20	50
322	-	8c. green	1·60	1·00
323	56	10c. orange	1·40	60
324	-	20c. red	2·50	1·70
325	57	50c. olive	9·75	7·75
326	57	1p. sepia	26·00	19·00

DESIGNS—VERT: ½c., 5c., 8c. Merino's Tomb; 2c., 7c., 20c. Merino in uniform.

1933. Portraits as T 56.

327	1c. black and green	60	40
328	3c. black and violet	85	40
329	7c. black and blue	2·00	1·00

DESIGNS: 1c., 7c. Pres. Trujillo in uniform; 3c. Pres. Trujillo in evening dress.

1933. Air. Optd CORREO AEREO INTERNO.

330	52	2c. red	50	40

60 Fokker Super Universal over Fort Ozama

1933. Air.

331	60	10c. blue	3·50	50

61 San Rafael Suspension Bridge

1934

332	61	½c. mauve	70	40
333	61	1c. green	1·00	20
334	61	3c. violet	1·70	20

62 Trujillo Bridge

1934. (a) Postage. As T 62 but without airplane and inscr "CORREOS".

335	½c. brown	70	20
336	1c. green	1·00	20
337	3c. violet	1·40	20

(b) Air.

338	62	10c. blue	3·00	50

64 National Palace

1935. For obligatory use on mail addressed to the President.

346	64	25c. orange	3·75	40

1935. Opening of Ramfis Bridge. As T 62 but view of Ramfis Suspension Bridge.

347	1c. green	70	10
348	3c. brown	70	10
349	5c. purple	2·10	1·30
350	10c. pink	4·25	1·90

66 Airplane and Carrier Pigeon

1935. Air.

351	66	10c. light blue and blue	1·60	40

67 President Trujillo

1935. Frontier Agreement.

352	67	3c. brown and yellow	30	20
353	-	5c. brown and orange	40	20
354	-	7c. brown and blue	60	20
355	-	10c. brown and purple	1·00	20

RECTANGULAR DESIGNS: Portrait as Type **67**. Red, white and blue ribbons in side panels on 7c. or diagonally across 5c. and 10c.

69 Post Office, Santiago de los Caballeros

1936

356	69	½c. violet	30	40
357	69	1c. green	30	10

70 Fokker F.10A Super Trimotor

1936. Air.

358	70	10c. blue	2·50	40

71 George Washington Avenue, Ciudad Trujillo

1936. Dedication of George Washington Avenue.

359	71	½c. brown	40	50
360	71	2c. brown and red	40	30
361	71	3c. brown and yellow	70	20
362	71	7c. brown and blue	1·60	1·60

72 Gen. A. Duverge

1936. National Archives and Library Fund. Inscr "PRO ARCHIVO Y BIBLIOTECA NACIONALES".

363	-	½c. lilac	40	20
364	-	1c. green	30	20
365	-	2c. red	30	20
366	-	3c. violet	40	20
367	-	5c. blue	70	30
368	72	7c. blue	1·30	60
369	-	10c. orange	1·30	30
370	-	20c. olive	5·75	3·00
371	-	25c. purple	6·75	8·75
372	-	30c. red	8·25	11·50
373	-	50c. brown	9·75	6·25
374	-	1p. black	26·00	36·00
375	-	2p. brown	80·00	90·00

DESIGNS—As Type **72**: ½c. J. N. de Caceres; 1c. Gen. G. Luperon; 2c. E. Tejera; 3c. Pres. Trujillo; 5c. Jose Reyes; 10c. Felix M. Del Monte; 25c. F. J. Peynado; 30c. Salome Urena; 50c. Gen. Jose Ma. Cabral; 1p. Manuel Js. Galvan; 2p. Gaston F. Deligne. TRIANGULAR: 20c. National Library.

74 "Flight"

1936. Air.

376	74	10c. blue	2·30	30

75 Obelisk in Ciudad Trujillo

1937. 1st Anniv of Naming of Ciudad Trujillo (formerly Santo Domingo).

377	75	1c. green	30	20
378	75	3c. violet	40	20
379	75	7c. blue	1·10	1·10

76 Discus Thrower and National Flag

1937. 1st National Olympic Games, Ciudad Trujillo. Flag blue, white and red.

380	76	1c. green	11·50	1·00
381	76	3c. violet	14·50	1·00
382	76	7c. blue	26·00	5·25

77 "Peace, Labour and Progress"

1937. 8th Year of Trujillo Presidency.

383	77	3c. violet	50	20

78 Martin M-130 Flying Boat and San Pedro de Macoris Airport

1937. Air.

384	78	10c. green	1·00	20

79 Fleet of Columbus

1937. Air. Pan-American Goodwill Flight.

385	79	10c. red	1·70	1·40
386	A	15c. violet	1·40	95
387	B	20c. blue	1·40	1·20
388	A	25c. purple	2·00	1·20

389	B	30c. green	1·70	1·20
390	A	50c. brown	3·50	1·80
391	B	75c. olive	10·50	10·50
392	79	1p. red	6·25	2·50

DESIGNS—A, Junkers F-13 aircraft in Goodwill Flight; B, Junkers F-13 aircraft over Columbus Lighthouse.

83 Father Billini

1938. Birth Centenary of Father Billini.

396	**83**	½c. orange	20	10
397	**83**	5c. violet	60	20

84 Globe and Torch of Liberty

1938. 150th Anniv of U.S. Constitution.

398	**84**	1c. green	50	10
399	**84**	3c. violet	70	10
400	**84**	10c. orange	1·40	20

85 Bastion, Trinitarian Oath and National Flag

1938. Centenary of Trinitarian Rebellion.

401	**85**	1c. green	50	20
402	**85**	3c. violet	60	20
403	**85**	10c. orange	1·20	60

86 Martin M-130 Flying Boat over Obelisk

1938. Air.

404	**86**	10c. green	1·20	20

87 Arms of University

1938. 400th Anniv of Santo Domingo University.

405	**87**	½c. orange	40	30
406	**87**	1c. green	40	20
407	**87**	3c. violet	50	20
408	**87**	7c. blue	1·00	50

89 N.Y. Fair Symbol, Lighthouse, Flag and Cornucopia

1939. New York World's Fair. (a) Postage. Flag in blue, white and red.

418	**89**	½c. orange	50	20
419	**89**	1c. green	50	20
420	**89**	3c. violet	60	20
421	**89**	10c. yellow	1·80	95

(b) Air. Flag, etc, replaced by airplane.

422		10c. green	1·80	85

90 Jose Trujillo Valdez

1939. 4th Death Anniv of Jose Trujillo Valdez. Black borders.

423	**90**	½c. grey	40	20
424	**90**	1c. green	50	20
425	**90**	3c. brown	50	30
426	**90**	7c. blue	1·10	1·20
427	**90**	10c. violet	2·10	50

91

1939. Air.

428	**91**	10c. green	1·60	20

92 Western Hemisphere and Union Flags

1940. 50th Anniv of Pan-American Union. Flags in national colours.

429	**92**	1c. green	40	20
430	**92**	2c. red	40	20
431	**92**	3c. violet	50	10
432	**92**	10c. orange	1·10	20
433	**92**	1p. brown	18·00	13·50

93 Sir Rowland Hill

1940. Centenary of 1st Adhesive Postage Stamps.

434	**93**	3c. mauve	3·25	40
435	**93**	7c. blue	6·75	1·70

94 Julia Molina de Trujillo

1940. Mothers' Day.

436	**94**	1c. green	30	15
437	**94**	2c. red	30	20
438	**94**	3c. orange	40	20
439	**94**	7c. blue	95	50

95 Central America and Arms of Dominican Republic

1940. 2nd Caribbean Conference, Trujillo City.

440	**95**	3c. red	50	20
441	**95**	7c. blue	1·00	20
442	**95**	1p. green	10·50	9·25

96 Lighthouse, Aeroplane and Caravels

1940. Air. Discovery of America and Columbus Memorial Lighthouse. Inscr "PRO FARO DE COLON".

443	**96**	10c. blue	1·10	60
444	-	15c. brown	1·60	1·00
445	-	20c. red	1·60	1·00
446	-	25c. mauve	1·60	50
447	-	50c. green	3·00	1·80

DESIGNS: 15c. Columbus and lighthouse; 20c. Lighthouse; 25c. Columbus; 50c. Caravel and wings.

99 Marion Military Hospital

1940

457	**99**	½c. brown	30	20

100 Post Office, San Cristobal and Douglas DC-4

1941. Air.

458	**100**	10c. mauve	50	20

101 Trujillo Fortress

1941

460	**101**	1c. green	20	10
461	-	2c. red	20	15
462	-	10c. brown	70	20

DESIGN—VERT: 2, 10c. Statue of Columbus, Ciudad Trujillo.

103 Sanchez, Duarte, Mella and Trujillo

1941. Trujillo-Hull Treaty.

463	**103**	3c. mauve	30	15
464	**103**	4c. red	40	30
465	**103**	13c. blue	85	30
466	**103**	15c. brown	2·75	2·10
467	**103**	17c. blue	2·75	2·10
468	**103**	1p. orange	11·50	10·50
469	**103**	2p. grey	25·00	10·50

104 Bastion of 27 February

1941

470	**104**	5c. blue	60	20

105 Rural School, Torch of Knowledge and Pres. Trujillo

1941. Popular Education Campaign.

471	**105**	½c. brown	20	10
472	**105**	1c. green	30	20

106 Globe and Winged Envelope

1941. Air.

473	**106**	10c. brown	50	10
474	**106**	75c. orange	3·25	2·30

107 National Reserve Bank

1942

475	**107**	5c. brown	50	20
476	**107**	17c. blue	1·00	60

108 Symbolic of Communications

1942. 8th Anniv of Postal and Telegraph Services Day.

477	**108**	3c. multicoloured	4·25	70
478	**108**	15c. multicoloured	11·50	5·75

109 Our Lady of Highest Grace

1942. 20th Anniv of Our Lady of Highest Grace.

479	**109**	½c. grey	1·00	20
480	**109**	1c. green	2·10	10
481	**109**	3c. mauve	13·50	10
482	**109**	5c. purple	2·75	20
483	**109**	10c. red	9·75	30
484	**109**	15c. blue	10·50	40

111 Banana Tree

112 Cows

1942

494	**111**	3c. green and brown	60	20
495	**111**	4c. black and red	60	40
496	**112**	5c. brown and blue	60	20
497	**112**	15c. green and purple	1·00	50

113 Party Emblems and Votes

1943. Re-election of Gen. Trujillo to Presidency.

498	**113**	3c. orange	50	10
499	**113**	4c. red	60	30
500	**113**	13c. purple	1·40	30
501	**113**	1p. blue	6·75	2·30

114 Trujillo Market

1943

502	**114**	2c. brown	30	20

115 Douglas DC-3

1943. Air.

503	**115**	10c. mauve	40	20
504	**115**	20c. blue	40	20
505	**115**	25c. olive	5·75	3·25

116 Bastion of 27 February
117 Monument and Dates

1944. Centenary of Independence. (a) Postage. Flag in blue and red.

506	**116**	½c. ochre	20	10
507	**116**	1c. green	20	10
508	**116**	2c. red	20	20
509	**116**	3c. purple	20	20
510	**116**	5c. orange	20	20
511	**116**	7c. blue	30	30
512	**116**	10c. brown	50	40
513	**116**	20c. olive	95	85
514	**116**	50c. blue	2·75	2·50

(b) Air. Flag in grey, blue and red.

515	**117**	10c. multicoloured	50	20
516	**117**	20c. multicoloured	60	20
517	**117**	1p. multicoloured	2·75	2·10

118 Dr. Martos Sanatorium

1944. Tuberculosis Relief Fund.

518	**118**	1c. blue and red	40	30

119 Nurse and Battlefield

1944. 80th Anniv of International Red Cross.

519	**119**	1c. green, red and yellow	20	10
520	**119**	2c. brown, red and yellow	40	20
521	**119**	3c. blue, red and yellow	40	20
522	**119**	10c. red and yellow	85	20

120 Communications Building, Ciudad Trujillo

1944. Air.

523	**120**	9c. blue and green	20	20
524	**120**	13c. red and brown	30	20
525	**120**	25c. red and orange	50	20
526	**120**	30c. blue and black	1·00	95

121 Municipal Building, San Cristobal

1945. Centenary of 1st Constitution of Dominican Republic.

527	**121**	½c. blue	40	20
528	**121**	1c. green	40	20
529	**121**	2c. orange	40	20
530	**121**	3c. brown	40	20
531	**121**	10c. blue	1·30	20

122 Emblem of Communications

1945. Centres in blue and red.

532	**122**	3c. orange (postage)	40	10
533	**122**	20c. green	2·10	20
534	**122**	50c. blue	4·25	70
535	**122**	7c. green (air)	50	30
536	**122**	12c. orange	60	20
537	**122**	13c. blue	85	20
538	**122**	25c. brown	1·60	20

124 Flags and National Anthem

1946. Air. National Anthem.

540	**124**	10c. red	95	40
541	**124**	15c. blue	2·10	85
542	**124**	20c. brown	2·50	85
543	**124**	35c. orange	3·00	95
544	-	1p. green	27·00	10·50

DESIGN: 1p. As Type **124**, but horiz.

125 Law Courts, Ciudad Trujillo

1946

545	**125**	3c. brown and buff	50	10

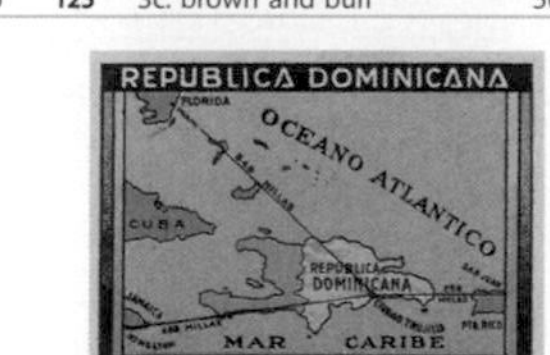

126 Caribbean Air Routes

1946. 450th Anniv of Santo Domingo.

546	**126**	10c. mult (postage)	1·10	20
547	**126**	10c. multicoloured (air)	85	20
548	**126**	13c. multicoloured	1·60	20

127 Jimenoa Waterfall

1947. Centres multicoloured, frame colours given.

549	**127**	1c. green (postage)	20	10
550	**127**	2c. red	20	20
551	**127**	3c. blue	30	10
552	**127**	13c. purple	95	30
553	**127**	20c. brown	2·10	30
554	**127**	50c. yellow	4·00	1·10
555	**127**	18c. blue (air)	1·00	50
556	**127**	23c. red	1·60	60
557	**127**	50c. violet	2·10	60
558	**127**	75c. brown	3·00	1·10

128 Nurse and Child

1947. Obligatory Tax. Tuberculosis Relief Fund.

559	**128**	1c. blue and red	60	30

129 State Building, Ciudad Trujillo

1948

560	**129**	1c. green (postage)	40	10
561	**129**	3c. blue	40	10
562	**129**	37c. brown (air)	2·10	1·00
563	**129**	1p. orange	5·75	2·10

130 Ruins of San Francisco Church, Ciudad Trujillo

1949

564	**130**	1c. green (postage)	40	10
565	**130**	3c. blue	40	10
566	**130**	7c. olive (air)	40	20
567	**130**	10c. brown	40	20
568	**130**	15c. red	1·20	30
569	**130**	20c. green	1·80	60

131 El Santo Socorro Sanatorium

1949. Tuberculosis Relief Fund.

570	**131**	1c. blue and red	50	30

132 General Pedro Santana
133 Monument

1949. Centenary of Battle of Las Carreras.

571	**132**	3c. blue (postage)	40	20
572	**133**	10c. red (air)	60	20

134 Bird and Globe

1949. 75th Anniv of U.P.U.

573	**134**	1c. brown and green	40	20
574	**134**	2c. brown and yellow	40	10
575	**134**	5c. brown and blue	50	10
576	**134**	7c. brown and blue	1·10	20

135 Youth Holding Banner

1950. Tuberculosis Relief Fund.

584	**135**	1c. blue and red	50	30

136 Hotel Jimani

1950. Various Hotels.

585	**136**	½c. brown (postage)	20	10
586	-	1c. green (Hamaca)	20	10
587	-	2c. orange (Hamaca)	20	10
588	-	5c. blue (Montana)	40	20
589	-	15c. orge (San Cristobal)	60	20
590	-	20c. lilac (Maguana)	1·10	20
591	**136**	$1 yellow and brown	4·50	1·90
592	-	12c. bl (Montana) (air)	40	10
593	-	37c. red (San Cristobal)	2·50	2·30

138 Ruins of Church and Hospital of St. Nicholas of Bari

1950. 13th Pan-American Sanitary Congress. Inscr as T 138.

595	**138**	2c. brown & green (postage)	40	10
596	-	5c. brown and blue	50	20
597	-	12c. orange & brn (air)	85	20

DESIGNS—VERT: 5c. Medical school; 12c. Map and aeroplane.

139 "Suffer Little Children to Come Unto Me"
148

148a
148b

1950. Child Welfare. (a) Child at left with light hair.

598	**139**	1c. blue	1·20	30

(b) Child at left with dark hair.

599		1c. blue	6·25	30

(c) Child at left with dark hair.

626	**148**	1c. blue	30	20

(d) Child at left with light hair.

627	**148a**	1c. blue	60	30

(e) Dark hair, smaller figures and square value tablet.

628	**148b**	1c. blue	40	30

There are two versions of No. 628, differing in size. See also Nos. 835 and 907.

140 Isabella the Catholic

1951. 500th Birth Anniv of Isabella the Catholic.

600	**140**	5c. brown and blue	70	20

141 Santiago Tuberculosis Sanatorium

1952. Tuberculosis Relief Fund.

601	**141**	1c. blue and red	50	30

142 Dr. S. B. Gautier Hospital

1952

602	**142**	1c. green (postage)	20	10
603	**142**	2c. red	20	10
604	**142**	5c. blue	50	20
605	**142**	23c. blue (air)	1·10	1·10
606	**142**	29c. red	3·00	2·10

143 Columbus Lighthouse and Flags

1953. 460th Anniv of Columbus's Discovery of Santo Domingo. (a) Postage.

607	**143**	2c. green	30	10
608	**143**	5c. blue	40	10
609	**143**	10c. red	70	30

(b) Air. Similar design inscr "S./S.A.S./XMY", etc.

610	12c. brown	30	20
611	14c. blue	20	20
612	20c. sepia	70	60
613	23c. purple	40	40
614	25c. blue	95	70
615	29c. green	70	60
616	1p. brown	2·00	1·30

MS617 191×130 mm. As Nos. 607/16 but in slightly different colours. Imperf 21·00 21·00

DESIGN: Nos. 610/16, Douglas DC-6 airplane over Columbus Lighthouse.

144

1953. Anti-cancer Fund. No. 619 has "1 c" larger with line through "c" and no stop. No. 620 is as 619 but with smaller "c".

618	**144**	1c. red	70	30
619	**144**	1c. red	60	30
620	**144**	1c. red	60	30

See also Nos. 1029/30, 1066/7, 1171a, 1196a, 1237a, 1270a and 1338a.

145 T.B. Children's Dispensary

1953. Obligatory Tax. Tuberculosis Relief Fund.

621	**145**	1c. blue and red	50	30

There are two versions of this design.

146 Treasury

147 Rio Haina Sugar Factory

1953

622	**146**	½c. brown	10	10
623	**146**	2c. blue	20	10
624	**147**	5c. brown and blue	20	10
625	**146**	15c. orange	1·00	30

149 Jose Marti

1953. Birth Cent of Marti (Cuban revolutionary).

629	**149**	10c. sepia and blue	60	20

150 Monument to Trujillo Peace

1954

630	**150**	2c. green	10	10
631	**150**	7c. blue	30	10
632	**150**	20c. orange	1·10	20

There are two versions of No. 631.

151

1954. Air. Marian Year.

633	**151**	8c. purple	20	20
634	**151**	11c. blue	30	10
635	**151**	33c. orange	1·00	60

152 Rotary Emblem

1955. 50th Anniv of Rotary International.

636	**152**	7c. blue (postage)	70	20
637	**152**	11c. red (air)	50	20

153

1955. Obligatory Tax. Tuberculosis Relief Fund.

638	**153**	1c. black, red & yellow	40	30

154 Pres. R. Trujillo

1955. 25th Year of Trujillo Era.

639	**154**	2c. red (postage)	40	10
640	-	4c. green	40	10
641	-	7c. blue	50	20
642	-	10c. brown	1·10	20
643	-	11c. red, yell & bl (air)	70	10
644	-	25c. purple	1·20	30
645	-	33c. brown	1·80	50

DESIGNS: 4c. Pres. R. Trujillo in civilian clothes; 7c. Equestrian statue; 10c. Allegory of Prosperity; 11c. National flags; 25c. Gen. Hector B. Trujillo in evening clothes; 33c. Gen. Hector B. Trujillo in uniform.

156 Angelita Trujillo

1955. Child Welfare.

654	**156**	1c. violet	85	30

157 Angelita Trujillo **158** Gen. R. Trujillo

1955. Peace and Brotherhood Fair, Ciudad Trujillo.

656	**158**	7c. purple (postage)	40	10
655	**157**	10c. blue and ultramarine	60	20
657	**158**	10c. green	50	20
658	**158**	11c. red (air)	30	20

159 "B.C.G." = "Bacillus" Calmette-Guerin

1956. Obligatory Tax. Tuberculosis Relief Fund.

659	**159**	1c. multicoloured	40	30

160 Punta Caucedo Airport

1956. 3rd Caribbean Region Aerial Navigation Conference.

660	**160**	1c. brown (postage)	20	10
661	**160**	2c. orange	20	10
662	**160**	11c. blue (air)	50	10

161 Cedar Tree

1956. Re-afforestation. Inscr "REPOBLACION FORESTAL".

664	**161**	5c. green, brown and red (postage)	1·60	10
665	-	6c. green and purple	1·90	20
666	-	13c. green & orge (air)	2·30	20

DESIGNS: 6c. Pine tree; 13c. Mahogany tree.

162 Fanny Blankers-Koen and Dutch Flag

1957. Olympic Games (1st issue). Famous Athletes. Flags in national colours.

667	**162**	1c. mult (postage)	20	10
668	-	2c. sepia, purple & blue	20	20
669	-	3c. purple and red	30	20
670	-	5c. orange, pur & blue	40	20
671	-	7c. green and purple	50	30

MS672 169×87 mm. Nos. 667/71 5·75 5·75

673		11c. blue and red (air)	20	20
674		16c. red and green	30	20
675		17c. black and purple	40	20

MS676 169×87 mm. Nos. 673/5 5·75 5·75

DESIGNS—(each with national flag of athlete): 2c. Jesse Owens; 3c. Kee Chung Sohn; 5c. Lord Burghley; 7c. Bob Mathias; 11c. Paavo Nurmi; 16c. Ugo Frigerio; 17c. Mildred Didrickson.

See also Nos. 689/96, 713/21, 748/56 and 784/91.

163 Horse's Head and Globe

1957. 2nd Int Livestock Fair, Ciudad Trujillo.

677	**163**	7c. blue, brown & red	40	20

1957. Hungarian Refugees Fund. Nos. 667/75 surch with red cross in circle surrounded by ASISTENCIA REFUGIADOS HUNGAROS 1957 and +2c.

678	**162**	1c.+2c. (postage)	20	15
679	-	2c.+2c.	20	15
680	-	3c.+2c.	20	20
681	-	5c.+2c.	20	20
682	-	7c.+2c.	30	30

MS683 No. **MS**672+25c. 17·00 17·00

684	11c.+2c. (air)	30	30
685	16c.+2c.	50	50
686	17c.+2c.	50	50

MS687 No. **MS**676+25c. 17·00 17·00

165

1957. Obligatory Tax. Tuberculosis Relief Fund.

688	**165**	1c. multicoloured	40	30

166 Chris Brasher and Union Jack (steeplechase)

1957. Olympic Games (2nd issue). Winning Athletes. Inscr "MELBOURNE 1956". Flags in national colours.

689	-	1c. brown & bl (postage)	20	10
690	-	2c. red and blue	20	10
691	-	3c. blue	20	10
692	-	5c. olive and blue	20	15
693	-	7c. red and blue	30	20
694	-	11c. green & blue (air)	25	25
695	**166**	16c. purple and blue	30	30
696	-	17c. sepia and green	35	35

MS697 140×140 mm. Nos. 689/96 arranged in diamond shape with Olympic Flag in a centre label 8·25 8·25

MS698 As last, but with Olympic Gold Medal replacing Flag in centre label 8·25 8·25

DESIGNS—(each with national flag of athlete): 1c. Lars Hall (Sweden, pentathlon); 2c. Betty Cuthbert (Australia, 100 and 200 m); 3c. Egil Danielson (Norway, javelin-throwing); 5c. Alain Mimoum (France, marathon); 7c. Norman Read (New Zealand, 50 km walk); 11c. Robert Morrow (U.S.A.; 100 and 200 m); 17c. A. Ferreira da Silva (Brazil; hop, step and jump).

1957. 50th Anniv of Boy Scout Movement, and Birth Cent of Lord Baden-Powell. Nos 689/96 surch CENTENARIO LORD BADEN-POWELL, 1857-1957 +2c. surrounding Scout badge.

699	1c.+2c. brn & bl (postage)	15	15
700	2c.+2c. red and blue	40	20
701	3c.+2c. blue	30	30
702	5c.+2c. olive and blue	40	30
703	7c.+2c. red and blue	60	40
704	11c.+2c. grn & blue (air)	60	40

705		16c.+2c. purple and blue	70	70
706		17c.+2c. sepia and green	85	70
MS707		No. **MS**697+40c.	90·00	90·00
MS708		No. **MS**698+40c.	90·00	90·00

168 Mahogany Flower

1957

709	**168**	2c. red and green	10	10
710	**168**	4c. red and mauve	10	10
711	**168**	7c. green and blue	40	15
712	**168**	25c. orange and brown	95	40

169 Gerald Ouellette and Canadian Flag (rifle-shooting) (image scaled to 72% of original size)

1957. Olympic Games (3rd issue). More winning athletes. Flags in national colours.

713	**169**	1c. brown (postage)	10	10
714	-	2c. sepia	10	10
715	-	3c. violet	15	15
716	-	5c. orange	20	15
717	-	7c. slate	25	25
MS718		228×57 mm. Nos. 713/17	4·25	4·25
719		11c. blue (air)	25	20
720		16c. red	40	40
721		17c. purple	40	40
MS722		164×57 mm. Nos. 719/21	3·50	3·50

DESIGNS—(each with national flag of athlete): 2c. Ron Delaney (Ireland, 1500 m); 3c. Tenley Albright (U.S.A., figure-skating); 5c. J. Capilla (Mexico, high-diving); 7c. Ercole Baldini (Italy, cycle-racing); 11c. Hans Winkler (Germany, horse-jumping); 16c. Alfred Oerter (U.S.A., discus-throwing); 17c. Shirley Strickland (Australia, 80 m hurdles).

The designs of Nos. 714, 716 and 720 are arranged with the long side of the triangular format uppermost.

170

1958. Tuberculosis Relief Fund.

723	**170**	1c. red and claret	30	20

See also No. 763.

171 Cervantes, Open Book, Marker and Globe

1958. 4th Latin-American Book Fair.

724	**171**	4c. green	15	10
725	**171**	7c. mauve	20	10
726	**171**	10c. bistre	40	20

1958. U.N. Relief and Works Agency for Palestine Refugees. Nos. 713/21 surch. A. For Jewish Refugees. Star of David and REFUGIADOS.

727		1c.+2c. brown (postage)	20	20
728		2c.+2c. brown	30	30
729		3c.+2c. violet	30	30
730		5c.+2c. orange	40	40
731		7c.+2c. blue	50	50
732		11c.+2c. blue (air)	30	30
733		16c.+2c. red	40	40
734		17c.+2c. purple	50	50

B. For Arab Refugees. Red Crescent and REFUGIADOS.

735		1c.+2c. brown (postage)	20	20
736		2c.+2c. brown	30	30
737		3c.+2c. violet	30	30
738		5c.+2c. orange	40	40
739		7c.+2c. blue	50	50
740		11c.+2c. blue (air)	30	30
741		16c.+2c. red	40	40
742		17c.+2c. purple	50	50

172 Gen. R. Trujillo and Arms of Republic

1958. 25th Anniv of Gen Trujillo's designation as "Benefactor of the Country".

743	**172**	2c. mauve and yellow	10	10
744	**172**	4c. green and yellow	20	10
745	**172**	7c. sepia and yellow	20	15
MS746		152×101 mm. Nos. 743/5. Imperf	1·00	85

173 "Rhadames" (freighter)

1958. Merchant Marine Day.

747	**173**	7c. blue	1·20	30

174 Gillian Sheen and Union Jack (fencing)

1958. Olympic Games (4th issue). More winning athletes. Flags in national colours.

748	**174**	1c. slate, blue and red (postage)	15	10
749	-	2c. brown and blue	15	10
750	-	3c. multicoloured	20	20
751	-	5c. multicoloured	30	25
752	-	7c. multicoloured	30	25
MS753		140×121 mm. Nos. 748/52	3·25	3·25
754		11c. sepia, olive and blue (air)	30	30
755		16c. blue, orge & grn	40	40
756		17c. blue, yell and red	40	40
MS757		140×79 mm. Nos. 754/6	3·25	3·25

DESIGNS (each with national flag of athlete)—VERT: 2c. Milton Campbell (U.S.A., decathlon). HORIZ: 3c. Shozo Sasahara (Japan, featherweight wrestling); 5c. Madeleine Berthod (Switzerland, skiing); 7c. Murray Rose (Australia, 400 m and 1,500 m free-style); 11c. Charles Jenkins and Thomas Courtney (U.S.A., 400 m and 800 m, and 1600 m relay); 16c. Indian team in play (India, hockey); 17c. Swedish dinghies (Sweden, sailing).

175

1958. Inauguration of UNESCO Headquarters Building, Paris.

758	**175**	7c. blue and red	40	20

176 Dominican Republic Pavilion

1958. Brussels International Exhibition.

759	**176**	7c. green (postage)	30	20
760	**176**	9c. grey (air)	30	20
761	**176**	25c. violet	85	40
MS762		137×72 mm. Nos. 759/61	2·30	2·30

1959. Obligatory Tax. Tuberculosis Relief Fund. As T **170** but inscr "1959".

763	**170**	1c. red and lake	30	20

1959. I.G.Y. Nos. 748/56 surch with globe and ANO GEOFISICO INTERNACIONAL 1957-1958 +2c.

764		1c.+2c. (postage)	40	40
765		2c.+2c.	40	40
766		3c.+2c.	50	50
767		5c.+2c.	60	60
768		7c.+2c.	70	70
MS769		No. **MS**753+25c.	25·00	25·00
770		11c.+2c. (air)	70	70
771		16c.+2c.	95	95
772		17c.+2c.	1·40	1·40
MS773		No. **MS**757+15c.	25·00	25·00

178 Leonidas R. Trujillo (Team Captain)

1959. Jamaica–Dominican Republic Polo Match, Trujillo City. Inscr as in T 178.

774	**178**	2c. violet (postage)	15	10
775	-	7c. brown	50	40
776	-	10c. green	60	40
777	-	11c. orange (air)	40	40

DESIGNS—HORIZ: 7c. Jamaican team; 10c. Dominican Republic team's captain on horseback; 11c. Dominican Republic team.

179 Gen. Trujillo before National Shrine

1959. 29th Year of Trujillo Era.

778	**179**	9c. multicoloured	30	20
MS779		141×91 mm. No. 778. Imperf	60	60

180 Gen. Trujillo and Cornucopia

1959. National Census of 1960. Centres in black, red and blue. Frame colours given.

780	**180**	1c. pale blue	20	15
781	**180**	9c. green	40	20
782	**180**	13c. orange	60	30

181 Trujillo Stadium

1959. 3rd Pan-American Games, Chicago.

783	**181**	9c. black and green	50	30

1959. 3rd Pan-American Games, Chicago. Nos. 667/71 and 673/5, surch III JUEGOS DEPORTIVOS PANAMERICANOS + 2 and runner.

784	**162**	1c.+2c. mult (postage)	20	20
785	-	3c.+2c. multicoloured	30	30
786	-	3c.+2c. pur & red	30	30
787	-	5c.+2c. multicoloured	40	40
788	-	7c.+2c. multicoloured	50	50
789	-	11c.+2c. blue, red and orange (air)	60	60
790	-	16c.+2c. red, green and carmine	70	70
791	-	17c.+2c. multicoloured	70	70

182 Emperor Charles V

1959. 4th Death Centenary of Emperor Charles V.

792	**182**	5c. mauve	20	10
793	**182**	9c. blue	30	15

183 Rhadames Bridge

1959. Opening of Rhadames Bridge.

794	-	1c. black and green	15	10
795	**183**	2c. black and blue	20	10
796	-	2c. black and red	20	10
797	**183**	5c. brown and bistre	40	20

DESIGN—Nos. 794, 796, Close-up view of Rhadames Bridge.

184 Douglas DC-4 Airliner, "San Cristobal"

1960. Air. Dominican Civil Aviation.

798	**184**	13c. multicoloured	30	20

185

1960. Obligatory Tax. Tuberculosis Relief Fund.

799	**185**	1c. red, blue and cream	40	30

186 Sosua Refugee Colony

1960. World Refugee Year. Inscr "ANO MUNDIAL DE LOS REFUGIADOS". Centres in black.

800	**186**	5c. green & brn (postage)	15	10
801	**186**	9c. blue, purple & red	20	15
802	**186**	13c. green, brn & orge	30	20
803	-	10c. green, mauve and purple (air)	40	30
804	-	13c. green and grey	50	40

DESIGN: Nos. 802/803, Refugee children.

1960. World Refugee Year Fund. Nos. 800/4 surch +5 with c below.

805	**186**	5c.+5c. green and brown (postage)	20	20
806	**186**	9c.+5c. bl, pur & red	25	25
807	**186**	13c.+5c. green, brown and orange	40	40
808	-	10c.+5c. green, mauve and purple (air)	30	30
809	-	13c.+5c. green & grey	30	30
MS810		140×100 mm. Nos. 805/9	6·25	6·25

188 General Post Office, Ciudad Trujillo

1960

811	**188**	2c. black and blue	20	15

189 Cattle in Street

1960. Agricultural and Industrial Fair, San Juan de la Maguana.

812	**189**	9c. black and red	30	20

190 Gholam Takhti (Iran, lightweight wrestling)

1960. Olympic Games, 1960. More Winning Athletes of Olympic Games, Melbourne, 1956. Flags in national colours.

813	**190**	1c. black, grn & red (postage)	10	10
814	-	2c. brown, turq & orge	10	10
815	-	3c. blue and red	15	15
816	-	5c. brown and blue	20	20
817	-	7c. brn, blue & green	20	20
MS818		158×121 mm. Nos. 813/17	2·50	2·50
819		11c. brown, grey & bl (air)	20	20
820		16c. green, brown & red	30	30
821		17c. ochre, blue & black	40	40
MS822		160×75 mm. Nos. 819/21	2·50	2·50

DESIGNS (each with national flag of athlete): 2c. Mauru Furukawa (Japan, 200 m breast-stroke swimming); 3c. Mildred McDaniel (U.S.A., high jump); 5c. Terence Spinks (spelt "Terrence" on stamp) (Great Britain, featherweight boxing); 7c. Carlo Pavesi (Italy, fencing); 11c. Pat McCormick (U.S.A., high diving); 16c. Mithat Bayrack (Turkey, Greco-Roman welterweight wrestling); 17c. Ursula Happe (Germany, women's 200 m breaststroke swimming).

1961. Surch HABILITADO PARA and value.

823	-	2c. on 1c. black and green (No. 794)	20	10
824	**168**	9c. on 4c. red & mauve	60	15
825	**168**	9c. on 7c. green & blue	60	20
826	**146**	36c. on ½c. brown	1·90	1·70
827	**127**	1p. on 50c. yellow	4·25	3·25

192

1961. Obligatory Tax. Tuberculosis Relief Fund.

828	**192**	1c. red and blue	30	20

See also No. 876.

193 Madame Trujillo and Houses

1961. Welfare Fund.

829	**193**	1c. red	40	30

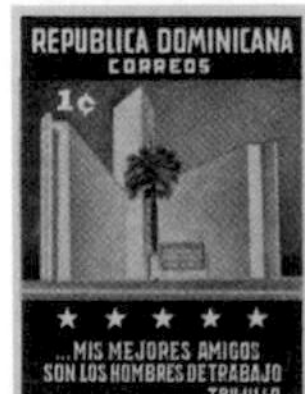

194

1961

830	**194**	1c. brown	10	10
831	**194**	2c. myrtle	15	10
832	**194**	4c. purple	50	40
833	**194**	5c. blue	50	20
834	**194**	9c. orange	50	30

1961. Obligatory Tax. Child Welfare. As Nos. 627/8 but with "ERA DE TRUJILLO" omitted. (a) Size 23½×32 mm.

835	**148a**	1c. blue	40	30

(b) Size 21¾×32 mm.

907	**148b**	1c. blue	40	30

195 Coffee Plant and Cocoa Beans

1961

836	**195**	1c. green (postage)	10	10
837	**195**	2c. brown	10	10
838	**195**	4c. violet	20	15
839	**195**	5c. blue	20	15
840	**195**	9c. grey	40	20
841	**195**	13c. red (air)	30	30
842	**195**	33c. yellow	70	70

1961. 15th Anniv of UNESCO. Nos. 813/21 surch XV ANIVERSARIO DE LA UNESCO +2c.

843	1c.+2c. (postage)	10	10
844	2c.+2c.	10	10
845	3c.+2c.	15	15
846	5c.+2c.	20	20
847	7c.+2c.	20	20
MS848	No. **MS**818+25c.	11·50	11·50
849	11c.+2c. (air)	30	30
850	16c.+2c.	40	40
851	17c.+2c.	40	40
MS852	No. **MS**822+15c.	11·50	11·50

197 Mosquito and Dagger

1962. Malaria Eradication.

853	**197**	10c. mauve (postage)	30	15
854	**197**	10c.+2c. mauve	40	20
855	**197**	20c. sepia	60	30
856	**197**	20c.+2c. sepia	60	30
857	**197**	25c. green	85	40
858	**197**	13c. red (air)	50	30
859	**197**	13c.+2c. red	40	30
860	**197**	33c. orange	95	50
861	**197**	33c.+2c. orange	95	60
MS862		173×103 mm. Nos. 854, 856, 859, 861 and a 25c.+2c. green (postage)	9·25	9·25

198 Plantation

1962. Farming and Industrial Development. Flag in red and blue.

863	**198**	1c. green and blue	10	10
864	**198**	2c. red and blue	10	10
865	**198**	3c. brown and blue	15	10
866	**198**	5c. blue	20	10
867	**198**	15c. orange and blue	40	20

199 Laurel Sprig and Broken Link

1962. 1st Anniv of Assassination of Pres. Trujillo.

868	**199**	1c. mult (postage)	15	10
869	-	9c. red, blue and ochre	40	20
870	-	20c. red, blue & turq	85	40
871	-	1p. red, blue & violet	4·25	2·50
MS872		150×94 mm. Nos. 868/70. Imperf	1·80	1·80
873	**199**	13c. multicoloured (air)	40	30
874	-	50c. red, blue & mauve	1·40	1·00

DESIGNS—VERT: 9c., 1p. "Justice" on map. HORIZ: 20c., 50c. Flag and flaming torch.

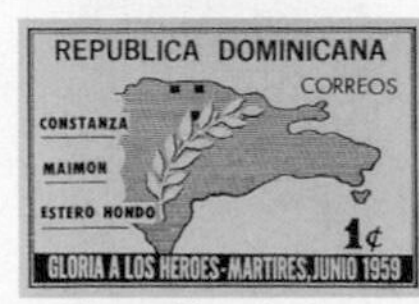

200 Map and Laurel

1962. Martyrs of June 1959 Revolution.

875	**200**	1c. black	40	20

1962. Tuberculosis Relief Fund. As No. 828 but inscr "1962".

876	**192**	1c. red and blue	85	30

201 U.P.A.E. Emblem

1962. 50th Anniv of Postal Union of the Americas and Spain.

877	**201**	2c. red (postage)	15	10
878	**201**	9c. orange	30	15
879	**201**	14c. turquoise	30	20
880	**201**	13c. blue (air)	40	20
881	**201**	22c. brown	50	50

202 Archbishop Nouel

1962. Birth Cent of Archbishop Adolfo Nouel.

882	**202**	2c. myrtle & green (postage)	10	10
883	**202**	9c. brown and orange	30	15
884	**202**	13c. purple and brown	40	20
885	-	12c. blue (air)	40	20
886	-	25c. violet	70	50
MS887		152×91 mm. Nos. 885/6. Imperf	1·20	1·20

DESIGN: Air stamps as Type **202** but different frame.

203 Globe, Riband and Campaign Emblem

1963. Freedom from Hunger. Riband in red and blue.

888	**203**	2c. green	10	10
891	**203**	2c.+1c. green	10	10
889	**203**	5c. mauve	20	10
892	**203**	5c.+2c. mauve	20	20
890	**203**	9c. orange	40	20
893	**203**	9c.+2c. orange	30	30
MS894		169×102 mm. Nos. 891/3. Imperf	2·10	2·10

204 Duarte

1963. 120th Anniv of Separation from Haiti.

895	**204**	2c. blue (postage)	10	10
896	-	7c. green (Sanchez)	20	20
897	-	9c. purple (Mella)	30	20
898	-	15c. salmon (air)	40	30

DESIGN—HORIZ: 15c. Sanchez, Duarte and Mella.

205 Espaillat, de Rojas and Bono

1963. "Centenary of the Restoration".

899	**205**	2c. green	10	10
900	-	4c. red	15	10
901	-	5c. brown	15	10
902	-	9c. blue	20	20
MS903		228×104 mm. Nos. 899/902. Imperf	1·00	1·00

DESIGNS: 4c. Rodriguez, Cabrera and Moncion; 5c. Capotillo Monument; 9c. Polanco, Luperon and Salcedo.

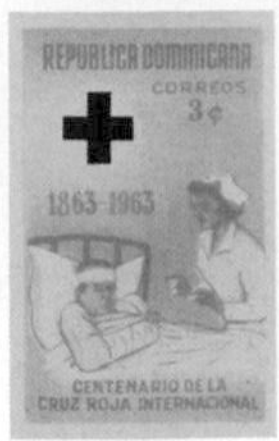

206 Nurse tending Patient

1963. Centenary of Red Cross. Cross in red.

904	**206**	3c. grey (postage)	10	10
905	**206**	6c. green	20	15
906	-	10c. grey (air)	40	30

DESIGN—HORIZ: 10c. Map of continents bordering Atlantic.

207

1963. Obligatory Tax. T.B. Relief Fund.

908	**207**	1c. red and blue	40	30

208 Scales of Justice and Globe

1963. 15th Anniv of Declaration of Human Rights.

911	**208**	6c. red (postage)	20	10
912	**208**	50c. green	85	85
913	**208**	7c. brown (air)	30	20
914	**208**	10c. blue	30	20

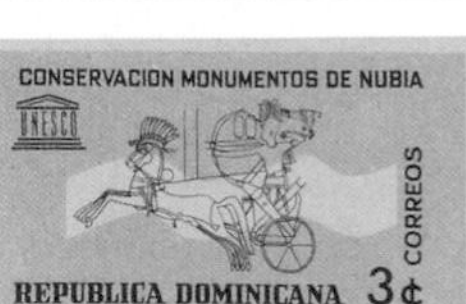

209 Rameses II in War Chariot, Abu Simbel

1964. Nubian Monuments Preservation. Designs as T 209, also surch 2c in circle.

915	**209**	3c. red (postage)	10	10
916	**209**	3c.+2c. red	20	20
917	-	6c. blue	20	15
918	-	6c.+2c. blue	20	20
919	**209**	9c. brown	25	15
920	**209**	9c.+2c. brown	30	30
921	-	10c. violet (air)	30	20
922	-	10c.+2c. violet	20	20
923	-	13c. yellow	30	20
924	-	13c.+2c. yellow	30	30

DESIGNS—HORIZ: 6c. Heads of Rameses II. VERT: 10c., 13c. As Type **209**.

211 M. Gomez (founder)

1964. Bicentenary of Bani Foundation.

925	211	2c. blue & light blue	10	10
926	211	6c. purple and brown	20	15

212 Palm Chat

1964. Dominican Birds. Multicoloured.

927	1c. Narrow-billed tody (postage)	2·50	20
928	2c. Hispaniolan emerald	2·50	20
929	3c. Type **212**	2·50	20
930	6c. Hispaniolan amazon	3·25	20
931	6c. Hispaniolan trogons	4·25	20
932	10c. Hispaniolan woodpecker (air)	5·75	20

The 1c., 2c. and 6c. (No. 931) are smaller (26×37½ mm); the 10c. is horiz (43½×27½ mm).

213 Rocket

1964. "Conquest of Space".

933	-	1c. blue (postage)	10	10
934	213	2c. green	15	10
935	-	3c. blue	20	15
936	213	6c. blue	30	20
937	213	7c. green (air)	30	30
938	-	10c. blue	40	30
MS939		147×81 mm. Nos. 937/8	4·25	4·25

DESIGNS—VERT: 1c. Rocket launching. HORIZ: 3c., 10c. Capsule in orbit.

214 Pres. Kennedy

1964. Air. Pres. Kennedy Commemoration.

940	214	10c. brown and buff	50	30

215 U.P.U. Monument, Berne

1964. 15th U.P.U. Congress, Vienna.

941	215	1c. red (postage)	10	10
942	215	4c. green	20	15
943	215	5c. orange	20	15
944	215	7c. blue (air)	30	20

216 I.C.Y. Emblem

1965. International Co-operation Year.

945	216	2c. blue and light-blue (postage)	10	10
946	216	3c. green and emerald	10	10
947	216	6c. red and pink	20	15
948	216	10c. violet & lilac (air)	40	30

217 Hands and Lily

1965. 4th Mariological and 11th Int Marian Congresses. Multicoloured.

949	2c. Type **217** (postage)	15	10
950	6c. Virgin of the Altagracia	40	30
951	10c. Douglas DC-8 airliner over Basilica of Virgin of Altagracia (39½×31½ mm) (air)	40	20

218 Flags Emblem

1965. 75th Anniv of Organization of American States.

952	218	2c. multicoloured	10	10
953	218	6c. multicoloured	20	15

219 Lincoln

1965. Air. Death Centenary of Abraham Lincoln.

954	219	17c. grey and blue	60	40

220 ½r. Stamp of 1865

1965. Stamp Centenary.

955	220	1c. multicoloured (post)	10	10
956	220	2c. multicoloured	10	10
957	220	6c. multicoloured	20	15
958	-	7c. multicoloured (air)	30	20
959	-	10c. multicoloured	30	30
MS960		100×66 mm. ½r. black on flesh (as No. 1), 1r. black on green (as No. 2) (sold at 50c.)	1·00	1·00

DESIGN: 7c., 10c. As Type **220**, but showing 1r. stamp of 1865.

221 Hibiscus

1966. Obligatory Tax. Tuberculosis Relief Fund.

963	221	1c. red and green	30	20
999	-	1c. mauve, lilac & red	1·00	30
1016	-	1c. multicoloured	30	20
1017	-	1c. multicoloured	60	30
1018	-	1c. multicoloured	1·00	30

DESIGN (21½×30 mm): No. 999, Orchid. (20×28 mm): No. 1016, Dogbane; 1017, Violets; 1018, "Eleanthus capitatus".

222 I.T.U. Emblem and Symbols

1966. Air. Centenary (1965) of I.T.U.

964	222	28c. red and pink	85	85
965	222	45c. green and emerald	1·20	1·20

223 W.H.O. Building

1965. Inaug of W.H.O. Headquarters, Geneva.

966	223	6c. blue	20	10
967	223	10c. purple	30	20

224 Man supporting "Republic"

1966. General Elections.

968	224	2c. black and green	10	10
969	224	6c. black and red	15	10

225 "Ascia monuste"

1966. Butterflies. Multicoloured.

970	1c. Type **225** (postage)	50	20
971	2c. "Heliconius charitonius"	50	20
972	3c. "Phoebis sennae sennae"	50	20
973	6c. "Anteos clorinde clorinde"	70	30
974	8c. "Siderone hemesis"	1·10	60
975	10c. "Eurema gundlachia" (air)	7·25	30
976	50c. "Clothilda pantherata pantherata"	7·75	1·20
977	75c. "Papilio androgeus epidaurus"	7·75	1·60

Nos. 975/7 are larger, 35×24½ mm.

1966. Hurricane Inez Relief. Nos. 970/77 surch PRO DAMNIFICADOS CICLON INES and value.

978	225	1c.+2c. mult (postage)	1·10	30
979	-	2c.+2c. multicoloured	95	20
980	-	3c.+2c. multicoloured	95	20
981	-	6c.+4c. multicoloured	1·10	60
982	-	8c.+4c. multicoloured	1·70	70
983	-	10c.+5c. mult (air)	2·30	85
984	-	50c.+10c. mult	3·50	3·00
985	-	75c.+10c. mult	4·75	3·75

227 National Shrine

1967. (a) Postage.

986	227	1c. blue	10	10
987	227	2c. red	10	10
988	227	3c. green	10	10
989	227	4c. grey	10	10
990	227	5c. yellow	10	10
991	227	6c. orange	15	10

(b) Air. Size 20½×25 mm.

992	7c. olive	20	15
993	10c. lilac	20	20
994	20c. brown	40	30

228 Emblem and Map

1967. Development Year. Emblem and map in black and blue.

996	228	2c. orange and yellow	15	10
997	228	6c. orange	20	10
998	228	10c. green	70	60

229 Rook and Knight

1967. 5th Central American Chess Championship, Santo Domingo.

1000	229	25c. mult (postage)	3·00	50
1001	-	10c. black & grn (air)	1·60	30
MS1002		118×27 mm. Nos. 1000/1. Imperf	12·50	2·50

DESIGN: 10c. Bishop and pawn.

230 Civil Defence Emblem

1967. Obligatory Tax. Civil Defence Fund.

1003	230	1c. multicoloured	30	20

231 Alliance Emblem

1967. 6th Anniv of "Alliance for Progress".

1004	231	1c. green (postage)	10	10
1005	231	8c. grey (air)	40	30
1006	231	10c. blue	50	30

232 Institute Emblem

1967. 25th Anniv of Inter-American Agricultural Institute.

1007	232	3c. green (postage)	15	10
1008	232	6c. pink	20	20
1009	-	12c. mult (air)	60	30

DESIGN: 12c. Emblem and cornucopia.

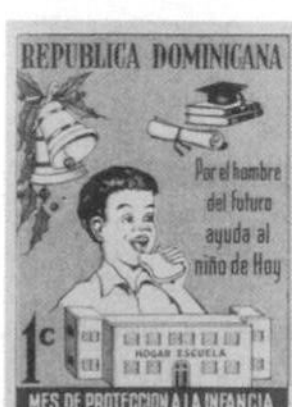

233 Child and Children's Home

1967. Obligatory Tax. Child Welfare.

1010	233	1c. red	50	30
1010a	233	1c. orange	40	30
1011	233	1c. violet	40	30
1011a	233	1c. brown	30	20
1037	233	1c. green	40	30

See also No. 1278a.

234 Hand Holding Invalid

1968. Obligatory Tax. Rehabilitation of the Handicapped.

1012	234	1c. yellow and green	30	20

1013 **234** 1c. blue 30 20
1014 **234** 1c. bright purple 30 20
1015 **234** 1c. brown 85 30

236 W.M.O. Emblem

1968. World Meteorological Day.
1019 **236** 6c. mult (postage) 30 20
1020 **236** 10c. multicoloured (air) 30 20
1021 **236** 15c. multicoloured 40 30

237 Ortiz v. Cruz

1968. World Lightweight Boxing Championship. Designs showing similar scenes of the contest.
1024 **237** 6c. pur & red (postage) 30 20
1025 - 7c. green & yellow (air) 30 20
1026 - 10c. blue and brown 40 20

238 "Lions" Emblem

1968. Lions International.
1027 **238** 6c. mult (postage) 20 15
1028 **238** 10c. multicoloured (air) 30 20

1968. Obligatory Tax. Anti-cancer Fund.
1029 **144** 1c. green 30 20
1030 **144** 1c. orange 30 20

239 Wrestling

1968. Olympic Games, Mexico. Multicoloured.
1031 1c. Type **239** (postage) 20 20
1032 6c. Running 30 20
1033 25c. Boxing 1·00 50
1034 10c. Weightlifting (air) 30 30
1035 33c. Pistol-shooting 1·00 85

240 Map of Americas and House

1969. 7th Inter-American Savings and Loans Congress, Santo Domingo. Multicoloured.
1038 6c. Type **240** (postage) 20 15
1039 10c. Latin-American flags (air) 30 20

241 Carved Stool

1969. Taino Art. Multicoloured.
1040 1c. Type **241** (postage) 10 10
1041 2c. Female idol (vert) 10 10
1042 3c. Three-cornered footstone 15 10
1043 4c. Stone axe (vert) 20 15
1044 5c. Clay pot 20 20
1045 7c. Spatula and carved handles (vert) (air) 20 15
1046 10c. Breast-shaped vessel 30 20
1047 20c. Figured vase (vert) 40 30

242 School Playground and Torch

1969. Obligatory Tax. Education Year.
1048 **242** 1c. blue 30 20

243 Community Emblem

1969. Community Development Day.
1049 **243** 6c. gold and green 30 10

244 C.O.T.A.L. Emblem

1969. 12th C.O.T.A.L. (Confederation of Latin American Tourist Organizations) Congress, Santo Domingo.
1050 **244** 1c. blue, red and light blue (postage) 10 10
1051 - 2c. lt green & green 10 10
1052 - 6c. red 20 15
1053 - 10c. brown (air) 30 20
DESIGNS—VERT: 2c. Boy with flags. HORIZ: (39×31 mm): 6c. C.O.T.A.L. Building and emblem; 10c. "Airport of the Americas", Santo Domingo.

245 I.L.O. Emblem

1969. 50th Anniv of I.L.O.
1054 **245** 6c. blk & turq (postage) 30 20
1055 **245** 10c. black and red (air) 20 20

246 Taking a Catch

1969. World Baseball Championships, Santo Domingo.
1056 **246** 1c. grey and green (postage) 10 10
1057 - 2c. green 10 10
1058 - 3c. brown and violet 20 15
1059 - 7c. orange and purple (air) 45 20
1060 - 10c. red 65 30
1061 - 1p. brown and blue 5·00 3·50
DESIGNS—VERT: 3c. Making for base; 10c. Player making strike. HORIZ: (43×30½ mm): 2c. Cibao Stadium; 7c. Tetelo Vargas Stadium; 1p. Quisqueya Stadium.

247 Las Damas Hydro-electric Scheme

1969. National Electrification Plan.
1062 **247** 2c. mult (postage) 10 10
1063 - 3c. multicoloured 10 10
1064 - 6c. purple 20 10
1065 - 10c. red (air) 45 20
DESIGNS—HORIZ: 3c. Las Damas Dam; 6c. Arroyo Hondo substation; 10c. Haina River power station.

1969. Obligatory Tax. Anti-cancer Fund. T **144** re-drawn in larger format and inscriptions.
1066 **144** 1c. purple 30 20
1067 **144** 1c. green 45 30

248 Tavera Dam

1969. Completion of Dam Projects. Mult.
1068 6c. Type **248** (postage) 20 10
1069 10c. Valdesia Dam (air) 45 20

249 Juan Pablo Duarte

1970. Juan Pablo Duarte (patriot) Commem.
1070 **249** 1c. green (postage) 10 10
1071 **249** 2c. red 10 10
1072 **249** 3c. purple 15 10
1073 **249** 6c. blue 30 20
1074 **249** 10c. brown (air) 65 30

250 Outline Map, Arms of Census Office and Family

1970. National Census.
1075 **250** 5c. blk & grn (postage) 15 10
1076 - 6c. ultram and blue 20 15
1077 - 10c. multicoloured (air) 65 30
DESIGNS: 6c. Arms and quotation; 10c. Arms and buildings.

251 Open Book and Emblem

1970. Obligatory Tax. Int Education Year.
1078 **251** 1c. purple 30 20

252 Abelardo Urdaneta

1970. Birth Cent of A. R. Urdaneta (sculptor).
1079 **252** 3c. blue (postage) 10 10
1080 - 6c. green 20 10
1081 - 10c. blue (air) 45 20
DESIGNS—HORIZ: (39½×27 mm): 6c. "One of Many" (sculpture). VERT: (25×39 mm): 10c. Prisoner (statue).

253 Masonic Symbols

1970. 8th Inter-American Masonic Conference, Santo Domingo.
1082 **253** 6c. green (postage) 20 10
1083 **253** 10c. brown (air) 30 20

254 Telecommunications Satellite

1970. World Telecommunications Day.
1084 **254** 20c. grey & grn (postage) 65 45
1085 **254** 7c. grey and blue (air) 30 20

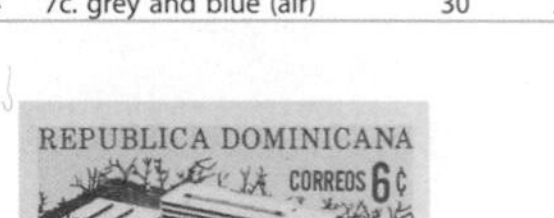

255 New U.P.U. Building

1970. New U.P.U. Headquarters Building, Berne.
1086 **255** 6c. brn & grey (postage) 20 10
1087 **255** 10c. brown & yell (air) 30 20

256 I.E.Y. Emblem

1970. International Education Year.
1088 **256** 4c. purple (postage) 15 10
1089 **256** 15c. mauve (air) 55 30

257 Pedro Alejandrino Pina

1970. 150th Birth Anniv and Death Centenary of Pedro A. Pina (writer).
1090 **257** 6c. black & brown 20 10

258 Children with Book

1970. 1st World Book Exhibition, and Cultural Festival, Santo Domingo.
1091 **258** 5c. green (postage) 15 10
1092 - 7c. multicoloured (air) 30 20
1093 - 10c. multicoloured 45 20
DESIGNS: 7c. Dancers; 10c. U.N. emblem within "wheel".

259 Emblem and Stamp Album

1970. Air. "EXFILICA 70" Inter-American Philatelic Exhibition, Caracas, Venezuela.

1094	**259**	10c. multicoloured	45	30

260 Communications Emblems

1971. Obligatory Tax. Postal and Telecommunications School. (a) Size 18×20½ mm.

1095	**260**	1c. blue and red (white background)	45	30

(b) Size 19×22 mm.

1095a		1c. blue and red (red background)	30	20
1095b		1c. blue, red and green	30	20
1095c		1c. blue, red and yellow	30	20
1095d		1c. blue, red and mauve	30	20
1095e		1c. blue, red and light blue	85	30
1096		1c. blue and red (blue background)	30	20

261 Virgin of Altagracia

1971. Inauguration of Our Lady of Altagracia Basilica. Multicoloured.

1097		3c. Type **261** (postage)	30	20
1098		17c. Basilica (22½×36 mm) (air)	95	55

262 Parcel, Emblem and Map

1971. Air. 25th Anniv of C.A.R.E. (Cooperative for American Relief Everywhere).

1099	**262**	10c. green and blue	30	20

263 Manuel Objio

1971. Death Cent of Manuel Rodriguez Objio (poet).

1100	**263**	6c. blue	20	10

264 Boxing and Canoeing

1971. 2nd National Games.

1101	**264**	2c. brown and orange (postage)	10	10
1102	-	5c. brown and green	15	10
1103	-	7c. purple & grey (air)	30	20

DESIGNS: 5c. Basketball; 7c. Volleyball.

265 Goat and Fruit

1971. 6th National Agricultural Census. Mult.

1104		1c. Type **265** (postage)	10	10
1105		2c. Cow and goose	10	10
1106		3c. Cocoa pods and horse	15	10
1107		6c. Bananas, coffee beans and pig	20	15
1108		25c. Cockerel and grain (air)	65	35

266 Jose Nunez de Caceres

1971. 150th Anniv of 1st Declaration of Independence.

1109	**266**	6c. blue, violet and light blue (postage)	20	10
1110	-	10c. bl, red & yell (air)	30	25

DESIGN: 10c. Flag of the Santo Domingo–Colombia Union.

267 Shepherds and Star

1971. Christmas.

1111	**267**	6c. brn, yell & bl (post)	20	10
1112	-	10c. red, blk & yell (air)	20	15

DESIGN: 10c. Spanish bell of 1493.

268 Child on Beach

1971. 25th Anniv of UNICEF.

1113	**268**	6c. mult (postage)	20	15
1114	**268**	15c. multicoloured (air)	65	45

269 Book Year Emblem

1971. International Book Year.

1115	**269**	1c. green, red and blue (postage)	10	10
1116	**269**	2c. brown, red and blue	15	15
1117	**269**	12c. purple, red and blue (air)	45	30

270 Magnifier on Map

1972. Air. "Exfilima 71" Inter American Philatelic Exhibition, Lima, Peru.

1118	**270**	10c. multicoloured	45	30

271 Orchid

1972. Obligatory Tax. Tuberculosis Relief Fund.

1119	**271**	1c. multicoloured	1·60	45

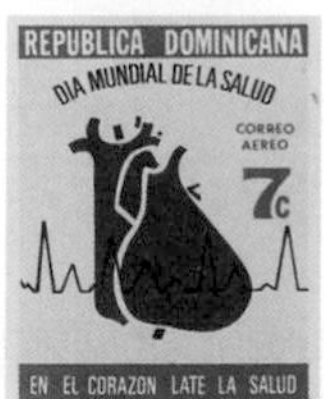

272 Heart Emblem

1972. Air. World Health Day.

1120	**272**	7c. multicoloured	30	20

273 Mask

1972. Taino Arts and Crafts. Multicoloured.

1121		2c. Type **273** (postage)	10	10
1122		4c. Spoon and amulet	15	10
1123		6c. Nasal aspirator (horiz)	15	10
1124		8c. Ritual vase (horiz) (air)	20	15
1125		10c. Atlantic trumpet triton (horiz)	45	20
1126		25c. Ritual spatulas	1·10	65

274 Globe

1972. World Telecommunications Day.

1127	**274**	6c. mult (postage)	20	15
1128	**274**	21c. multicoloured (air)	85	45

275 Map and "Stamps"

1972. 1st National Stamp Exn, Santo Domingo.

1129	**275**	2c. mult (postage)	15	15
1130	**275**	33c. mult (air)	85	55

276 Basketball

1972. Olympic Games, Munich. Mult.

1131		2c. Type **276** (postage)	30	20
1132		33c. Running (air)	1·10	75

277 Club Badge

1972. 50th Anniv of Int Activo 20–30 Club.

1133	**277**	1c. mult (postage)	15	15
1134	**277**	20c. mult (air)	55	30

278 Emilio Morel and Quotation

1972. Morel (poet and journalist). Commem.

1135	**278**	6c. mult (postage)	20	10
1136	**278**	10c. mult (air)	30	20

279 Bank Building

1972. 25th Anniv of Central Bank. Mult.

1137		1c. Type **279**	10	10
1138		5c. One-peso banknote	15	10
1139		25c. 1947 50c. coin and mint	95	65

280 Nativity Scene

1972. Christmas. Multicoloured.

1140		2c. Type **280** (postage)	20	15
1141		6c. Poinsettia (horiz)	30	20
1142		10c. "La Navidad" Fort, 1492 (horiz) (air)	65	20

281 Student and Letter-box

1972. Publicity for Correspondence Schools.

1143	**281**	2c. red and pink	15	10
1144	**281**	6c. blue and light blue	20	15
1145	**281**	10c. green and yellow	45	20

282 View of Dam

1973. Inauguration of Tavera Dam.

1146	**282**	10c. multicoloured	45	20

283 Invalid in Wheel-chair

1973. Obligatory Tax. Rehabilitation of the Handicapped.

1147	**283**	1c. green	30	20

284 Long-jumping, Diving, Running, Cycling and Weightlifting

1973. 12th Central American and Caribbean Games, Santo Domingo. Multicoloured.

1148	2c. Type **284** (postage)	10	10
1149	2c. Boxing, football, wrestling and shooting	10	10
1150	2c. Fencing, tennis, high- jump- ing and sprinting	10	10
1151	2c. Putting the shot, throwing the javelin and show- jumping	10	10
1152	25c. Type **284**	1·30	55
1153	25c. As No. 1149	1·30	55
1154	25c. As No. 1150	1·30	55
1155	25c. As No. 1151	1·30	55
1156	8c. Type **284** (air)	30	20
1157	8c. As No. 1149	30	20
1158	8c. As No. 1150	30	20
1159	8c. As No. 1151	30	20
1160	10c. Type **284**	55	20
1161	10c. As No. 1149	55	20
1162	10c. As No. 1150	55	20
1163	10c. As No. 1151	55	20

285 Hibiscus

1973. Obligatory Tax. Tuberculosis Relief Fund.

1164	**285**	1c. multicoloured	1·10	30

286 Christ carrying the Cross

1973. Easter. Multicoloured.

1165	2c. Type **286** (postage)	15	10
1166	6c. Belfry, Church of Our Lady of Carmen (vert)	20	15
1167	10c. Belfry, Chapel of Our Lady of Succour (vert) (air)	55	20

287 Global Emblem

1973. Air. 70th Anniv of Pan-American Health Organization.

1168	**287**	7c. multicoloured	30	20

288 Weather Zones

1973. Cent of World Meteorological Organization.

1169	**288**	6c. mult (postage)	20	15
1170	**288**	7c. multicoloured (air)	30	20

289 Forensic Scientist

1973. Air. 50th Anniv of International Criminal Police Organization (Interpol).

1171	**289**	10c. blue, green and light blue	45	20

1973. Obligatory Tax. Anti-cancer Fund. As T 144 but dated "1973".

1171a	**144**	1c. olive	45	30

See also Nos. 1270a and 1338a.

290 Maguey Drum

1973. Opening of Museum of Dominican Man, Santo Domingo. Multicoloured.

1172	1c. Type **290** (postage)	10	10
1173	2c. Amber carvings	10	10
1174	4c. Cibao mask (vert)	15	10
1175	6c. Pottery (vert)	20	15
1176	7c. Model ship in mosaic (vert) (air)	20	20
1177	10c. Maracas rattles	45	20

291 Nativity Scene

1973. Christmas. Multicoloured.

1178	2c. Type **291** (postage)	10	10
1179	6c. "Prayer" (stained-glass window) (vert)	15	15
1180	10c. Angels beside crib (air)	30	20

292 Scout Badge

1973. 50th Anniv of Dominican Boy Scouts. Multicoloured.

1181	1c. Type **292** (postage)	10	10
1182	5c. Scouts and flag	15	10
1183	21c. Scouts cooking, and Lord Baden Powell (air)	95	75

No. 1182 is smaller, size 26×36 mm.

293 Stadium and Basketball Players

1974. 12th Central American and Caribbean Games, Santo Domingo. Multicoloured.

1184	2c. Type **293** (postage)	10	10
1185	6c. Arena and cyclist	20	15
1186	10c. Swimming pool and diver (air)	30	20
1187	25c. Stadium, soccer players and discus-thrower	55	45

1974. Obligatory Tax. Rehabilitation of the Handicapped. As T **283** but larger, 22×27 mm.

1187a	**283**	1c. blue	45	30

294 Belfry, Santo Domingo Cathedral

1974. Holy Week.

1188	**294**	2c. mult (postage)	10	10
1189	-	6c. purple, green & ol	20	15
1190	-	10c. multicoloured (air)	45	20

DESIGN—VERT: 6c. "Sorrowful Mother" (D. Bouts). HORIZ: 10c. "The Last Supper" (R. M. Budi).

295 Francisco del Rosario Sanchez Bridge

1974. Dominican Bridges. Multicoloured.

1191	6c. Type **295** (postage)	20	15
1192	10c. Iliguamo Bridge (air)	45	20

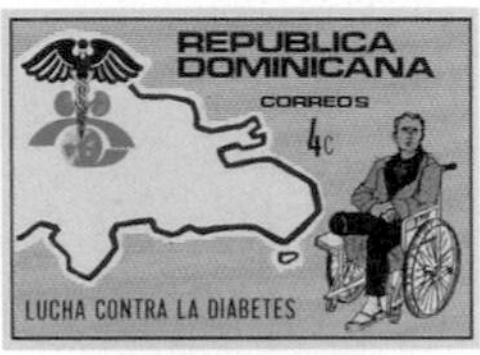

296 Emblem and Patient

1974. Anti-diabetes Campaign. Mult.

1193	4c. Type **296** (postage)	10	10
1194	5c. Emblem and pancreas	10	10
1195	7c. Emblem and Kidney (air)	30	20
1196	33c. Emblem, eye and heart	1·70	1·10

1974. Obligatory Tax. Anti-cancer Fund. As T **144** but dated "1974".

1196a	**144**	1c. orange	45	30

297 Steam Train

1974. Centenary of Universal Postal Union. Mult.

1197	2c. Type **297** (postage)	55	55
1198	6c. Stage-coach	45	30
1199	7c. "Eider" mail steamer (air)	55	45
1200	33c. Boeing 727-200 of Domini- cana Airways	2·10	75
MS1201	120×91 mm. Nos. 1197/1200	6·00	6·00

298 Emblems of World Amateur Golf Council and of Dominican Golf Association

1974. World Amateur Golf Championships.

1202	**298**	2c. black and yellow (postage)	10	10
1203	-	6c. multicoloured	15	15
1204	-	10c. multicoloured (air)	55	30
1205	-	20c. multicoloured	1·10	65

DESIGNS—VERT: 6c. Golfers teeing-off. HORIZ: 10c. Council emblem and golfers; 20c. Dominican Golf Association emblem, golfer and hand with ball and tee.

299 Christmas Decorations

1974. Christmas. Multicoloured.

1206	2c. Type **299** (postage)	10	10
1207	6c. Virgin and Child	15	15
1208	10c. Hand holding dove (horiz) (air)	45	20

300 Tomatoes

1974. 10th Anniv of World Food Programme. Multicoloured.

1209	2c. Type **300** (postage)	95	20
1210	3c. Avocado pears	95	20
1211	5c. Coconuts	95	20
1212	10c. Bee, hive and cask of honey (air)	1·60	20

301 Dr. Defillo

1975. Birth Centenary of Dr. Fernando Defillo (medical scientist).

1213	**301**	1c. brown	10	10
1214	**301**	6c. green	20	20

1975. Obligatory Tax. Rehabilitation of the Handicapped. As T **283** but dated "1975".

1214a	**283**	1c. brown	45	30

302 "I am the Resurrection and the Life"

1975. Holy Week. Multicoloured.

1215	2c. Type **302** (postage)	10	10
1216	6c. Bell tower, Nuestra Senora del Rosario convent	20	15
1217	10c. Catholic emblems (air)	45	20

1975. Obligatory Tax. Tuberculosis Relief Fund. As T 221 but dated "1975".

1217a	**221**	1c. multicoloured	1·40	95

DESIGN: 1c. "Catteeyopsis rosea".

303 Spanish 6c. Stamp of 1850

1975. Air. "Espana 75" International Stamp Exhibition, Madrid.

1218	**303**	12c. black, red & yell	55	30

304 Hands supporting "Agriculture" and Industry

1975. 16th Meeting of Industrial Development Bank Governors, Santo Domingo.

1219	**304**	6c. mult (postage)	20	15
1220	**304**	10c. mult (air)	45	20

305 Earth Station

1975. Opening of Satellite Earth Station. Multicoloured.

1221	5c. Type **305** (postage)	15	10
1222	15c. Hemispheres and satellites (horiz) (air)	65	45

306 "Apollo" Spacecraft with Docking Tunnel

1975. "Apollo–Soyuz" Space Link. Mult.

1223	1c. Type **306** (postage)	10	10
1224	4c. "Soyuz" spacecraft	15	10
1225	2p. Docking manoeuvre (air)	7·50	4·75

The 2p. is larger, 42×28 mm.

307 Father Castellanos

1975. Birth Cent of Father Rafael C. Castellanos.

1226	**307**	6c. brown and buff	20	15

308 Women encircling I.W.Y. Emblem

1975. International Women's Year.

1227	**308**	3c. multicoloured	10	10

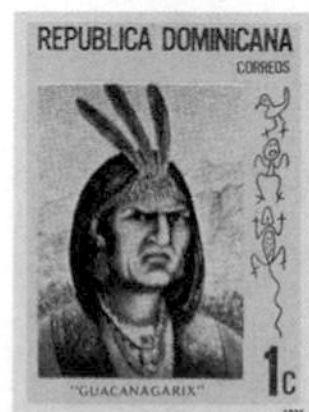

309 Guacanagarix

1975. Indian Chiefs. Multicoloured.

1228	1c. Type **309** (postage)	20	10
1229	2c. Guarionex	20	10
1230	3c. Caonabo	20	10
1231	4c. Bohechio	30	10
1232	5c. Cayacoa	30	15
1233	6c. Anacaona	30	20
1234	9c. Hatuey	45	30
1235	7c. Mayobanex (air)	30	20
1236	8c. Cotubanama with Juan de Esquivel	45	30
1237	10c. Enriquillo and wife, Mencia	55	30

1975. Obligatory Tax. Anti-cancer Fund. As T **144** but dated "1975".

1237a	**144**	1c. violet	45	30

310 Basketball

1975. 7th Pan-American Games, Mexico City. Multicoloured.

1238	2c. Type **310** (postage)	10	10
1239	6c. Baseball	20	15
1240	7c. Volleyball (horiz) (air)	30	20
1241	10c. Weightlifting (horiz)	55	30

311 Carol-singers

1975. Christmas. Multicoloured.

1242	2c. Type **311** (postage)	15	10
1243	6c. "Dominican" Nativity	20	15
1244	10c. Dove and Peace message (air)	30	20

312 Pearl Sergeant Major ("Abudefdul marginatus")

1976. Fishes. Multicoloured.

1245	10c. Type **312**	65	30
1246	10c. Puddingwife ("Halichoeres radiata")	65	30
1247	10c. Squirrelfish ("Holocentrus ascensionis")	65	30
1248	10c. Queen angelfish ("Angelochthys ciliaris")	65	30
1249	10c. Aya snapper ("Lutianus aya")	65	30

313 Valdesia Dam

1976. Air. Inauguration of Valdesia Dam.

1250	**313**	10c. multicoloured	45	20

1976. Obligatory Tax. Rehabilitation of the Disabled. As T **283** but dated "1976".

1250a	**283**	1c. blue	45	30

314 Orchid

1976. Obligatory Tax. Tuberculosis Relief Fund.

1251	**314**	1c. multicoloured	85	30

315 "Magdalene" (E. Godoy)

1976. Holy Week. Multicoloured.

1252	2c. Type **315** (postage)	10	10
1253	6c. "The Ascension" (V. Priego)	25	20
1254	10c. "Mount Calvary" (E. Castillo) (air)	45	30

316 Schooner "Separacion Dominicana"

1976. Navy Day.

1255	**316**	20c. multicoloured	1·20	65

317 National Flower and Maps

1976. Bicentenary of American Revolution, and "Interphil '76" Int Stamp Exn, Philadelphia.

1256	**317**	6c. mult (postage)	20	15
1257	-	9c. multicoloured	30	20
1258	-	10c. multicoloured (air)	45	20
1259	-	75c. black and orange	1·60	1·30

DESIGNS—HORIZ: 9c. Maps within cogwheels; 10c. Maps within hands. VERT: 75c. George Washington and Philadelphia buildings.

318 Flags of Spain and Dominican Republic

1976. Visit of King and Queen of Spain. Multicoloured.

1260	6c. Type **318** (postage)	55	20
1261	21c. King Juan Carlos I and Queen Sophia (air)	1·10	85

319 Various Telephones

1976. Telephone Centenary. Multicoloured.

1262	6c. Type **319** (postage)	20	15
1263	10c. A. Graham Bell (horiz) (air)	45	20

320 "Duarte's Vision" (L. Desangles)

1976. Death Centenary of Juan Duarte (patriot). Multicoloured.

1264	2c. Type **320** (postage)	10	10
1265	6c. "Juan Duarte" (R. Mejia) (vert)	20	15
1266	10c. Text of Duarte's Declaration (vert) (air)	45	20
1267	33c. "Duarte Sailing to Exile" (E. Godoy)	1·60	1·10

321 Fire Hydrant

1976. Dominican Fire Service. Multicoloured.

1268	4c. Type **321** (postage)	15	10
1269	6c. Fire Service emblem	25	20
1270	10c. Fire engine (horiz) (air)	45	30

1976. Obligatory Tax. Anti-cancer Fund. As T **144** but dated "1976".

1270a	**144**	1c. green	45	30

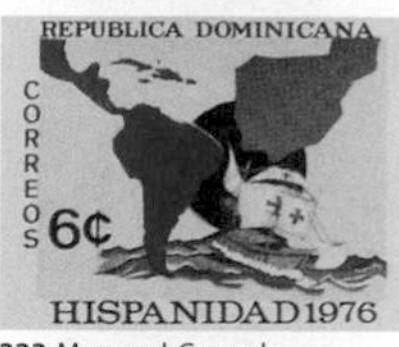

322 Commemorative Text and Emblem

1976. 50th Anniv of Dominican Radio Club.

1271	**322**	6c. black & red (postage)	20	10
1272	**322**	10c. black & blue (air)	45	20

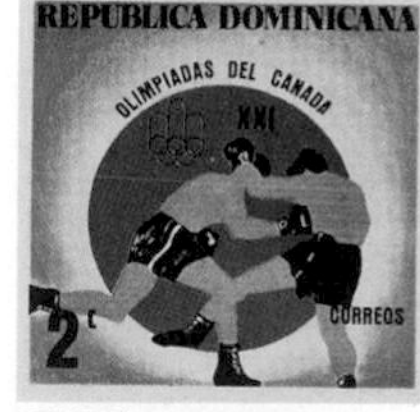

323 Map and Caravel

1976. "Hispanidad 1976". Multicoloured.

1273	6c. Type **323** (postage)	30	20
1274	21c. Heads of Spaniard and Dominicans (air)	70	55

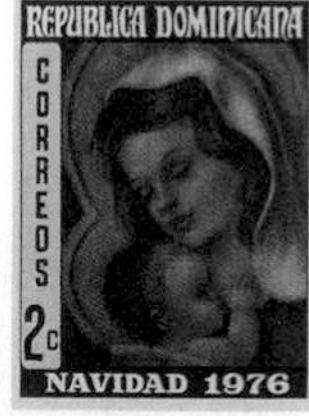

324 Boxing

1976. Olympic Games, Montreal. Mult.

1275	2c. Type **324** (postage)	10	10
1276	3c. Weightlifting	10	10
1277	10c. Running (air)	45	20
1278	25c. Basketball	1·20	75

1976. Obligatory Tax. Child Welfare. As T **233** but dated "1976".

1278a	**233**	1c. mauve	45	30

325 Virgin and Child

1976. Christmas. Multicoloured.

1279	2c. Type **325** (postage)	15	15
1280	6c. The Three Kings (22×32 mm)	20	20
1281	10c. Angel with bells (22×32 mm) (air)	45	30

326 Cable-car and Beach Scenes

1977. Tourism. Multicoloured.

1282	6c. Type **326** (postage)	20	15
1283	10c. Tourist activities (air)	30	20

1284		12c. Fishing and hotel	30	20
1285		25c. Horse-riding and waterfall	75	45

No. 1283 measures 36×36 mm, No. 1284 35×26 mm and No. 1285 26×35 mm.

327 Championships Emblem

1977. 10th Central American and Caribbean Children's Swimming Championships, Santo Domingo.

1286	**327**	3c. mult (postage)	10	10
1287	**327**	5c. multicoloured	15	10
1288	**327**	10c. multicoloured (air)	45	20
1289	**327**	25c. multicoloured	1·20	75

1977. Obligatory Tax. Rehabilitation of the Disabled. As T 283 but dated "1977".

1289a	**283**	1c. blue	45	30

328 Allegory of Holy Week

1977. Holy Week.

1290	**328**	2c. mult (postage)	15	15
1291	-	6c. black and mauve	30	20
1292	-	10c. blk, red & bl (air)	45	20

DESIGNS: 6c. Christ crowned with thorns; 10c. Church and book.

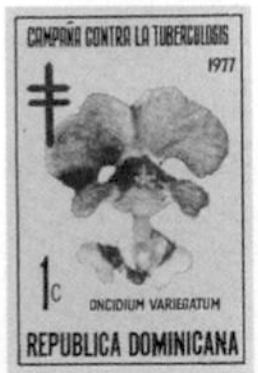

329 "Oncidium variegatum" (orchid)

1977. Obligatory Tax. Tuberculosis Relief Fund.

1293	**329**	1c. multicoloured	1·10	30

330 Gulls in Flight

1977. 12th Annual Lions Clubs Convention, Santo Domingo.

1294	**330**	2c. mult (postage)	15	15
1295	**330**	6c. multicoloured	20	20
1296	**330**	7c. multicoloured (air)	30	20

331 "Battle of Tortuguero" (G. Fernandez)

1977. Navy Day.

1297	**331**	20c. multicoloured	1·20	55

332 "Miss Universe" Emblem

1977. Air. "Miss Universe" Competition.

1298	**332**	10c. multicoloured	45	20

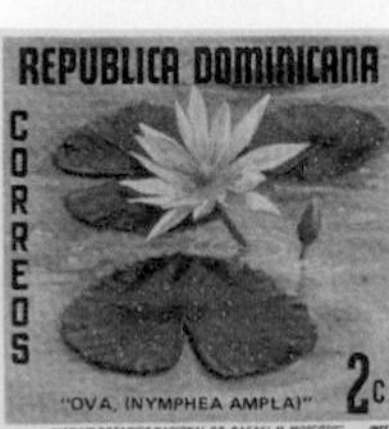

333 "Nymphaea ampla" ("Nymphea" on stamp)

1977. Dominican Flora. Plants in the Dr. Rafael M. Moscoso National Botanical Gardens. Mult.

1299		2c. Type **333** (postage)	20	10
1300		4c. "Broughtonia domingensis"	20	10
1301		6c. "Cordia sebestena"	45	20
1302		7c. "Melocatus lemairei" (cactus) (air)	45	20
1303		33c. "Coccothrinax argentea" (tree)	1·60	1·10

334 Computers and Graph

1977. Seventh Inter-American Statistic Conference. Multicoloured.

1304		6c. Type **334** (postage)	20	15
1305		28c. Factories and graph (27×37 mm) (air)	85	65

335 Haitian Solenodon

1977. 8th Inter-American Veterinary Congress. Multicoloured.

1306		6c. Type **335** (postage)	2·10	30
1307		20c. Iguana	3·75	55
1308		10c. "Red Roman" stud bull (air)	2·50	30
1309		25c. Greater Flamingo (vert)	4·50	55

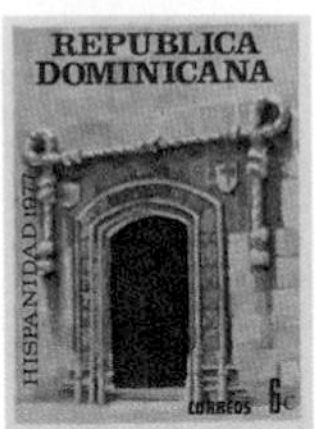

336 Main Gateway of Casa del Cordon

1978. "Hispanidad 1977". Multicoloured.

1310		6c. Type **336** (postage)	20	15
1311		21c. Gothic-style window, Casa del Tostado (28×41 mm) (air)	65	55

337 Tools and Crown of Thorns at Foot of Cross

1978. Holy Week.

1312	**337**	2c. mult (postage)	10	10
1313	-	6c. green	20	15
1314	-	7c. multicoloured (air)	30	20
1315	-	10c. multicoloured	55	30

DESIGNS—(22×33 mm): 6c. Christ wearing Crown of Thorns. (27×37 mm): 7c. Facade of Santo Domingo Cathedral; 10c. Facade of Dominican Convent.

338 Schooner "Duarte"

1978. Air. Navy Day.

1316	**338**	7c. multicoloured	55	20

339 Cardinal Octavio A. Beras Rojas

1978. Consecration of First Cardinal from Dominican Republic.

1317	**339**	6c. mult (postage)	20	15
1318	**339**	10c. multicoloured (air)	45	20

340 Microwave Antenna

1978. Air. 10th World Telecommunications Day.

1319	**340**	25c. multicoloured	75	55

341 First Dominican Airmail Stamp and Map of First Airmail Service

1978. Air. 50th Anniv of First Dominican Airmail Stamp.

1320	**341**	10c. multicoloured	45	20

342 Pres. Manuel de Troncoso

1978. Birth Centenary of President Troncoso.

1321	**342**	2c. brown, mauve & blk	15	15
1322	**342**	6c. brown, grey & black	30	20

343 Globe, Football and Emblem

1978. Air. World Cup Football Championship, Argentina. Multicoloured.

1323		12c. Type **343**	55	45
1324		33c. Emblem and map on football pitch	1·20	95

344 Father Juan N. Zegri y Moreno (founder)

1978. Centenary of Merciful Sisters of Charity. Multicoloured.

1325		6c. Type **344** (postage)	20	15
1326		21c. Symbol of the Order (air)	55	45

345 Boxing

1978. 13th Central American and Caribbean Games, Medellin, Colombia. Multicoloured.

1327		2c. Type **345** (postage)	10	10
1328		6c. Weightlifting	20	15
1329		7c. Baseball (vert) (air)	25	20
1330		10c. Football (vert)	45	20

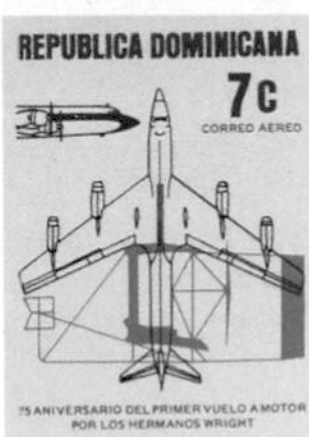

346 Douglas DC-6, Boeing 707 and Wright "Flyer I"

1978. Air. 75th Anniv of First Powered Flight.

1331	**346**	7c. multicoloured	20	20
1332	-	10c. brown, yellow & red	55	20
1333	-	13c. blue & dp blue	75	30
1334	-	45c. multicoloured	2·10	1·40

DESIGNS: 10c. Wright brothers and Wright Glider No. I; 13c. Diagram of airflow over wing; 45c. Wright "Flyer I" and world map.

347 Sun over Landscape

1978. Tourism. Multicoloured.

1335		2c. Type **347** (postage)	20	15
1336		6c. Sun over beach	25	20
1337		7c. Sun and musical instruments (air)	45	20
1338		10c. Sun over Santo Domingo	55	20

1978. Obligatory Tax. Anti-cancer Fund. As T **144** but dated "1977".

1338a	**144**	1c. purple	45	30

348 Galleons

1978. "Hispanidad 1978". Multicoloured.

1339		2c. Type **348** (postage)	15	15
1340		21c. Figures holding hands in front of globe (air)	65	55

349 Flags of Dominican Republic and United Nations

1978. Air. 33rd Anniv of United Nations.

1341 **349** 33c. multicoloured 1·10 80

350 Mother and Child

1978. Obligatory Tax. Child Welfare.

1342 **350** 1c. green 30 20

351 Dove, Lamp and Poinsettia

1978. Christmas. Multicoloured.

1343 2c. Type **351** (postage) 15 10
1344 6c. Dominican family and star 20 15
1345 10c. Statue of the Virgin (vert) (22×33 mm) (air) 45 30

352 Pope John Paul II

1979. Air. Visit of Pope John Paul II.

1346 **352** 10c. multicoloured 3·75 3·20

353 Map of Island, Iguana and Radio Transmitter

1979. Air. 1st Expedition of Radio Amateurs to Beata Island.

1347 **353** 10c. multicoloured 45 20

354 University Seal

1979. Obligatory Tax. 440th Anniv of Santo Domingo University.

1348 **354** 2c. blue 30 20

355 Starving Child

1979. International Year of the Child.

1349 **355** 2c. orge & blk (postage) 10 10
1350 - 7c. multicoloured (air) 20 15
1351 - 10c. multicoloured 45 20
1352 - 33c. multicoloured 1·60 1·10

DESIGNS: 7c. Children reading book; 10c. Head and protective hands; 33c. Hands and vases.

1979. Obligatory Tax. Rehabilitation of the Disabled. As T **283** but dated "1979".

1353 **283** 1c. green 30 20

356 Crucifixion

1979. Holy Week. Multicoloured.

1354 2c. Type **356** (postage) 30 20
1355 3c. Christ carrying cross (horiz) 45 20
1356 10c. Pope John Paul II with Crucifix (air) 1·70 1·30

357 "Turnera ulmifolia"

1978. Obligatory Tax. Tuberculosis Relief Fund. Dated "1978".

1357 **357** 1c. multicoloured 1·10 30

358 Admiral J. Cambiaso

1979. Air. 135th Anniv of Battle of Tortuguero.

1358 **358** 10c. multicoloured 45 20

359 Map, Stamp Album and Philatelic Equipment

1979. Air. "Exfilna" Third National Stamp Exhibition.

1359 **359** 33c. blue, green and black 1·10 80

360 "Stigmaphyllon periplocifolium"

1979. Flowers from National Botanical Gardens.

1360 **360** 50c. grey, yellow and black (postage) 1·40 75
1361 - 7c. multicoloured (air) 45 30
1362 - 10c. multicoloured 55 35
1363 - 13c. blue, mauve & blk 75 65

DESIGNS: 7c. "Passiflora foetida"; 10c. "Isidorea pungens"; 13c. "Calotropis procera".

362 Heart and Section through Artery

1979. Dominican Cardiology Institute.

1364 **362** 3c. mult (postage) 20 20
1365 - 1p. black, red & blue 2·40 1·60
1366 - 10c. multicoloured (air) 30 20

DESIGNS: VERT: 10c. Human figure showing blood circulation. HORIZ: 1p. Cardiology Institute and heart.

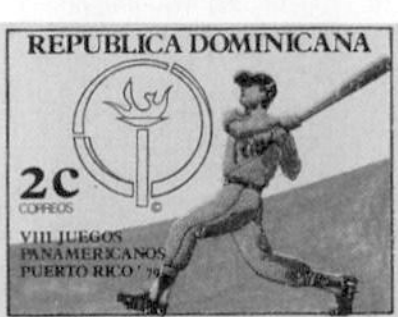

363 Baseball

1979. 8th Pan-American Games, Puerto Rico. Multicoloured.

1367 2c. Type **363** (postage) 15 10
1368 3c. Cycling (vert) 15 10
1369 7c. Running (vert) (air) 45 30

364 Football

1979. 3rd National Games. Multicoloured.

1370 2c. Type **364** (postage) 15 15
1371 25c. Swimming (horiz) 65 45
1372 10c. Tennis (air) 45 30

365 Sir Rowland Hill and First Dominican Republic Stamp

1979. Air. Death Centenary of Sir Rowland Hill.

1373 **365** 2p. multicoloured 4·75 3·25

366 Thomas Edison (inventor)

1979. Centenary of Electric Light-bulb. Mult.

1374 25c. Type **366** (postage) 85 65
1375 10c. "100" forming lightbulb (horiz) (air) 45 30

367 Hand removing Electric Plug

1979. "Save Energy". Multicoloured.

1376 2c. Type **367** 15 15
1377 6c. Car being refuelled 30 20

368 Hispaniolan Conure

1979. Birds. Multicoloured.

1378 2c. Type **368** (postage) 2·10 20
1379 6c. Hispaniolan trogon 2·10 20
1380 7c. Black-crowned palm tanager (air) 2·75 30
1381 10c. Chat-tanager 3·75 30
1382 45c. Black-cowled oriole 9·50 1·60

369 Lions Emblem

1979. 15th Anniv of Dominican Republic Lions Club. Multicoloured.

1383 20c. Type **369** (postage) 65 55
1384 10c. Melvin Jones (founder) (air) 45 20

371 Holy Family

1979. Christmas. Multicoloured.

1386 2c. Type **371** (postage) 15 15
1387 10c. Three Kings (air) 30 25

372 Christ carrying Cross

1980. Holy Week.

1388 **372** 3c. black, red and lilac (postage) 15 10
1389 - 7c. blk, red & yell (air) 20 15
1390 - 10c. black, red & bistre 45 30

DESIGNS: 7c. Crucifixion; 10c. Resurrection.

1980. Obligatory Tax. Rehabilitation of the Disabled. As T **283** but dated "1980".

1391 **283** 1c. olive and green 85 30

374 Navy Crest

1980. Air. Navy Day.

1392 **374** 21c. multicoloured 65 55

375 "Stamp"

1980. Air. 25th Anniv of Dominican Philatelic Society.

1393 **375** 10c. multicoloured 45 30

376 Cocoa Harvest

1980. Agricultural Year. Multicoloured.

1394 1c. Type **376** 25 15
1395 2c. Coffee 25 15
1396 3c. Plantain 30 15
1397 4c. Sugar cane 30 15
1398 5c. Maize 45 20

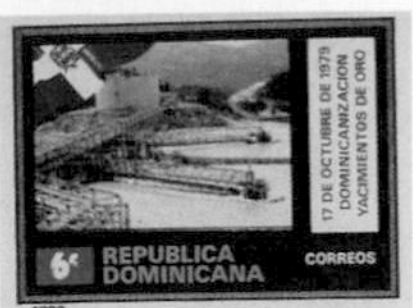

377 Cotuf Gold Mine, Pueblo Viejob

1980. Nationalization of Gold Mines. Mult.

1399 6c. Type **377** (postage) 30 20
1400 10c. Drag line mining (air) 65 30
1401 33c. General view of location of gold mines 1·20 55

378 Blind Man's Buff

1980. Children's Games. Multicoloured.

1402 3c. Type **378** 20 15
1403 4c. Marbles 20 15
1404 5c. Spinning top 30 20
1405 6c. Hopscotch 30 20

379 "Tourism"

1980. Air. World Tourism Conference, Manila, Philippines. Multicoloured.

1406 10c. Type **379** 45 30
1407 33c. Conference emblem 1·60 1·10

380 Cuban Iguana

1980. Animals. Multicoloured.

1408 20c. Type **380** (postage) 2·75 65
1409 7c. American crocodile (air) 2·00 45
1410 10c. Hispaniolan hutia 2·40 45
1411 25c. American manatee 3·75 75
1412 45c. Hawksbill turtle 5·25 1·40

381 "El Merengue" (Jaime Colson)

1980. Paintings. Multicoloured.

1413 3c. Type **381** (postage) 20 15
1414 50c. "The Mirror" (G. H. Ortega) 1·30 95
1415 10c. "Genesis de un Ganga" (Paul Guidicelli) (air) 45 30
1416 17c. "The Countryman" (Yoryi Morel) 75 55

1980. Obligatory Tax. Anti-cancer Fund. As T **144** but dated "1980".

1417 **144** 1c. blue and violet 30 20

383 Map of Catalina Island

1980. Air. Visit of Radio Amateurs to Catalina Island.

1418 **383** 7c. green, blue & black 30 25

384 Rotary Emblem on Globe

1980. Air. 75th Anniv of Rotary International. Multicoloured.

1419 10c. Type **384** 55 45
1420 33c. Rotary emblem in "75" 1·10 85

385 Carrier Pigeons with Letters

1980. Centenary of U.P.U. Membership. Mult.

1421 33c. Type **385** 75 50
1422 45c. Row of stylized pigeons and letter 95 65
1423 50c. Carrier pigeon with letter and letter 1·20 75
MS1424 102×70 mm. 1p.10 Dominican postal services badge and UPU emblem. Imperf 2·40 2·20

1980. Obligatory Tax. Child Welfare. As T **350** but dated "1980".

1425 **350** 1c. blue 30 20

386 The Three Kings

1980. Christmas. Multicoloured.

1426 3c. Type **386** (postage) 15 10
1427 6c. Carol singers 20 15
1428 10c. The Holy Family (air) 45 30

387 Arms of Salcedo

1981. Centenary of Salcedo Province. Mult.

1429 6c. Type **387** (postage) 20 15
1430 10c. Arms and map of Salcedo (air) 30 25

388 Juan Pablo Duarte

1981. Juan Pablo Duarte (patriot). Commemoration.

1431 **388** 2c. brown and ochre 20 15

389 Industrial Symbols

1981. Air. Chemical Engineering Seminar.

1432 **389** 10c. multicoloured 45 30
1433 - 33c. gold and black 75 55

DESIGN: 33c. Emblem of Dominican College of Engineering and Architecture (CODIA).

390 Gymnastics

1981. Fifth National Games (1st issue). Mult.

1434 1c. Type **390** (postage) 20 15
1435 2c. Running 20 15
1436 3c. Pole-vaulting 30 20
1437 6c. Boxing 45 20
1438 10c. Baseball (air) 55 30

See also Nos. 1463/4.

391 Mother Mazzarello

1981. Death Centenary of Mother Mazarello (founder of Daughters of Mary).

1439 **391** 6c. brown and black 20 15

392 Admiral Juan Alejandro Acosta

1981. Air. 137th Anniv of Battle of Tortuguero.

1440 **392** 10c. multicoloured 30 20

1981. Obligatory Tax. Tuberculosis Relief Fund. Dated "1981".

1441 **357** 1c. multicoloured 30 20

393 Radio Waves

1981. Air. World Telecommunications Day.

1442 **393** 10c. multicoloured 30 20

394 Pedro Henriquez Urena

1981. 35th Death Anniv of Pedro Henriquez Urena.

1443 **394** 6c. pale grey and grey 20 10

395 Forest

1981. Forest Conservation. Multicoloured.

1444 2c. Type **395** 10 10
1445 6c. Forest river 30 20

396 Heinrich von Stephan

1981. Air. 150th Birth Anniv of Heinrich von Stephan (founder of U.P.U.).

1446 **396** 33c. brown and yellow 1·10 80

397 "Disabled People"

1981. Air. International Year of Disabled Persons. Multicoloured.

1447 7c. Type **397** 45 30
1448 33c. Cobbler in wheelchair 1·10 85

398 Exhibition Emblem

1981. Air. "Expuridom '81" International Stamp Exhibition, Santo Domingo.

1449 **398** 7c. black, blue and red 30 20

399 Target

1981. Air. 2nd World Air Gun Shooting Championship. Multicoloured.

1450 10c. Type **399** 30 20
1451 15c. Stylized riflemen 45 30
1452 25c. Stylized pistol shooters 75 65

400 Family and House

1981. National Census. Multicoloured.

1453 3c. Type **400** 20 15
1454 6c. Farmer with cow and agricultural produce 30 20

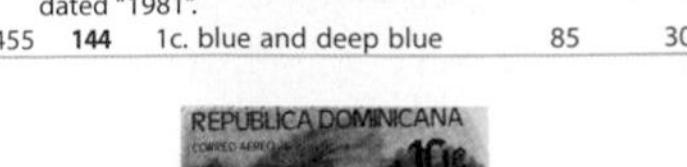

1981. Obligatory Tax. Anti-cancer Fund. As T **144** but dated "1981".

1455 **144** 1c. blue and deep blue 85 30

401 Fruit

1981. Air. World Food Day. Multicoloured.

1456 10c. Type **401** 65 30
1457 50c. Fish, eggs and vegetables 1·60 1·40

402 Gem Stones and Jewellery

1981. Air. Exports. Multicoloured.

1458	7c. Type **402**	45	20
1459	10c. Handicrafts	55	30
1460	11c. Fruit	65	30
1461	17c. Cocoa, coffee, tobacco and sugar	85	55

1981. Obligatory Tax. Child Welfare. As T **350** but dated "1981".

1462	**350**	1c. green	30	20

403 Javelin-throwing

1981. Air. 5th National Games, Barahona (2nd issue). Multicoloured.

1463	10c. Type **403**	45	30
1464	50c. Cycling	2·10	1·80

404 "Encyclia cochleata"

1981. Air. Orchids. Multicoloured.

1465	7c. Type **404**	65	20
1466	10c. "Broughtonia domingensis"	85	30
1467	25c. "Encyclia truncata"	1·30	75
1468	65c. "Elleanthus capitatus"	3·25	2·40

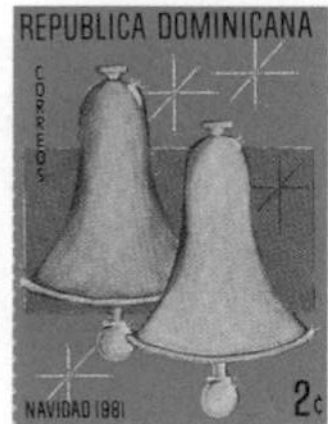

405 Bells

1981. Christmas. Multicoloured.

1469	2c. Type **405** (postage)	15	10
1470	3c. Holly	20	15
1471	10c. Dove and moon (air)	75	45

406 Juan Pablo Duarte

1982. Juan Pablo Duarte (patriot) Commemoration.

1472	**406**	2c. light blue and blue	20	10

407 Citizens arriving at Polling Station

1982. National Elections. Multicoloured.

1473	2c. Type **407**	10	10
1474	3c. Entering polling booth (vert)	15	10

1475	6c. Casting vote	30	20

408 American Air Forces Co-operation Emblem

1982. Air. 22nd American Air Force's Commanders Conference, Buenos Aires.

1476	**408**	10c. multicoloured	45	30

409 Naval Cadet Parade

1982. Air. Battle of Tortuguero Commem.

1477	**409**	10c. multicoloured	45	30

410 Tackling

1982. Air. World Cup Football Championship, Spain. Multicoloured.

1478	10c. Type **410**	45	30
1479	21c. Dribbling	55	45
1480	33c. Heading ball into goal	1·10	85

411 Lord Baden-Powell (statue)

1982. Air. 75th Anniv of Boy Scout Movement. Multicoloured.

1481	10c. Type **411**	30	20
1482	15c. Scouting emblems (horiz)	45	30
1483	25c. Baden-Powell and scout at camp fire	65	45

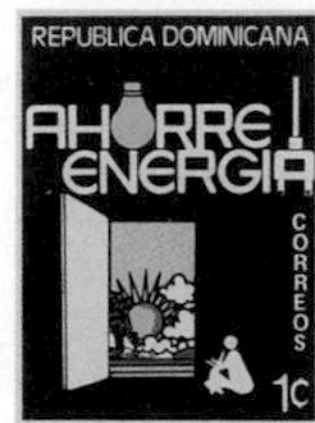

412 "Study of Daylight"

1982. Energy Conservation. Multicoloured.

1484	1c. Type **412**	10	10
1485	2c. "Save rural electricity"	10	10
1486	3c. "Use wind power"	15	10
1487	4c. "Switch off lights"	15	10
1488	5c. "Conserve fuel"	30	20
1489	6c. "Use solar energy"	30	20

413 Cathedral and House

1982. Air. 25th Congress of Latin-American Tourist Organizations Confederation, Santo Domingo. Multicoloured.

1490	7c. Congress emblem	20	15
1491	10c. Type **413**	30	20
1492	33c. Dancers and beach scene	1·20	85

414 Exhibition Emblem

1982. Air. "Espamer '82" Stamp Exhibition, Puerto Rico. Multicoloured.

1493	7c. Stamp bearing map of Puerto Rico (horiz)	20	15
1494	13c. Stylized postage stamps (horiz)	45	30
1495	50c. Type **414**	1·90	1·60

415 Emilio Prud'Homme and Score of Dominican National Anthem

1982. 50th Death Anniv of Emilio Prud'Homme (composer).

1496	**415**	6c. multicoloured	25	10

416 President Guzman

1982. President Antonio Guzman Commemoration.

1497	**416**	6c. multicoloured	25	10

417 Baseball

1982. Central American and Caribbean Games, Cuba. Multicoloured.

1498	3c. Type **417** (postage)	20	15
1499	10c. Basketball (air)	30	20
1500	13c. Boxing	65	30
1501	25c. Gymnastics	75	45

418 "Harbour" (Alejandro Bonilla)

1982. Air. Paintings. Multicoloured.

1502	7c. Type **418**	30	20
1503	10c. "Portrait of a Woman" (Leopoldo Navarro)	45	30
1504	45c. "Portrait of Amelia Francasci" (Luis Desangles)	2·10	1·40
1505	2p. "Portrait" (Abelardo Rodriguez Urdaneta)	9·50	6·00

419 Horse-drawn Carriage

1982. Centenary of San Pedro de Macoris Province. Multicoloured.

1506	1c. Type **419** (postage)	15	15
1507	2c. Stained-glass window, San Pedro Apostle Church (25×34½ mm)	15	15
1508	5c. Centenary emblem	30	25
1509	7c. View of San Pedro de Macoris City (air)	45	30

420 "Santa Maria" and Map of Voyage

1982. Air. 490th Anniv of Discovery of America by Columbus. Multicoloured.

1510	7c. Type **420**	1·10	85
1511	10c. "Santa Maria"	1·60	1·10
1512	21c. Statue of Columbus, Santo Domingo	2·10	1·10

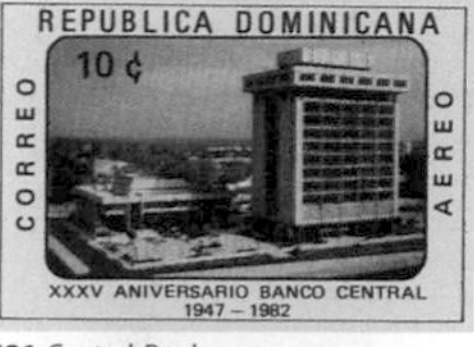

421 Central Bank

1982. 35th Anniv of Central Bank.

1513	**421**	10c. multicoloured	45	30

422 St. Theresa of Avila

1982. 400th Death Anniv of St. Theresa of Avila.

1514	**422**	6c. multicoloured	30	15

423 Christmas Tree Decorations

1982. Christmas. Multicoloured.

1515	6c. Type **423** (postage)	30	20
1516	10c. Tree decorations (different) (air)	55	20

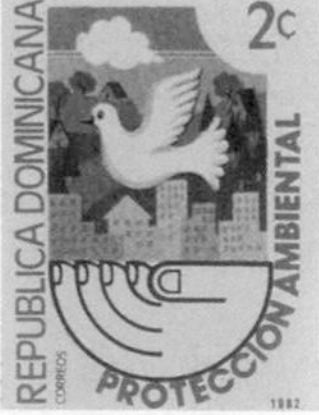

424 Hand holding Rural and Urban Environments

1982. Environmental Protection. Mult.

1517	2c. Type **424**	10	10
1518	3c. Hand holding river in the country	15	10
1519	6c. Hand holding forest	20	15
1520	20c. Hand holding swimming fish	75	55

425 Adults writing

1983. National Literacy Campaign. Mult.

1521		2c. Girl and boy writing on blackboard	10	10
1522		3c. Type **425**	15	10
1523		6c. Children, rainbow and pencil	20	15

426 Clasped Hands and Eiffel Tower

1983. Air. Centenary of French Alliance (French language-teaching association).

1524	426	33c. multicoloured	75	65

427 Arms of Mao City Council

1983. Centenary of Mao City Council. Mult.

1525		1c. Type **427**	15	10
1526		5c. Centenary monument	30	25

428 Frigate "Mella"

1983. Air. Battle of Tortuguero. Commemoration.

1527	428	15c. multicoloured	85	30

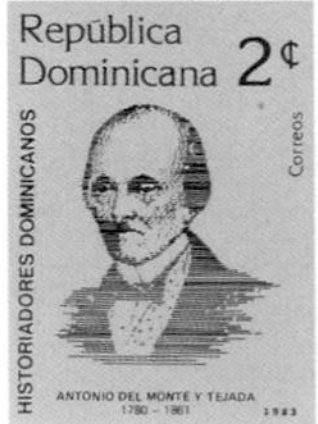

429 Antonio del Monte y Tejada

1983. Dominican Historians.

1528	429	2c. red & brn (postage)	10	10
1529	-	3c. pink and brown	15	10
1530	-	5c. blue and brown	20	15
1531	-	6c. lt brown & brown	20	15
1532	-	7c. pink & brown (air)	30	20
1533	-	10c. grey and brown	45	30

DESIGNS: 3c. Manuel Ubaldo Gomez; 5c. Emiliano Tejera; 6c. Bernardo Pichardo; 7c. Americo Lugo; 10c. Jose Gabriel Garcia.

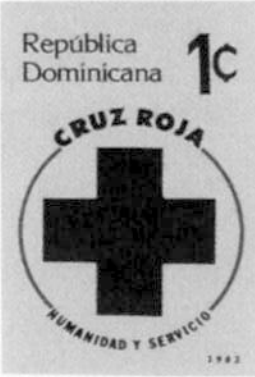

430 Red Cross

1983. Obligatory Tax. Red Cross.

1534	430	1c. red, gold & black	30	20

431 Dish Aerial and W.C.Y. Emblem

1983. Air. World Communications Year.

1535	431	10c. light blue & blue	45	20

432 "Simon Bolivar" (Plutarco Andujar)

1983. Air. Birth Bicentenary of Simon Bolivar.

1536	432	9c. multicoloured	30	20

433 Pictogram of Rehabilitation

1983. Obligatory Tax. Rehabilitation of the Disabled.

1537	433	1c. blue	30	20

434 Basketball and Gymnastics

1983. Air. Pan-American Games, Venezuela. Multicoloured.

1538		7c. Type **434**	55	20
1539		10c. Boxing and pole vaulting	65	20
1540		15c. Baseball, weightlifting and cycling	75	30

435 Emilio Prud'Homme and Jose Reyes (composers)

1983. Cent of Dominican National Anthem.

1541	435	6c. multicoloured	20	15

1983. Obligatory Tax. Anti-cancer Fund. As T **144** but dated "1983".

1542	144	1c. turquoise & green	30	20

436 "Sotavento" (winner of 1982 regatta)

1983. Air. Christopher Columbus Regatta and 500th Anniv (1992) of Discovery of America by Columbus (1st issue).

1543	-	10c. stone, brn & blk	1·10	55
1544	-	21c. multicoloured	1·90	75
1545	436	33c. multicoloured	2·10	85

MS1546 102×102 mm. 50c. blue and olive. Imperf 9·00 9·00

See also Nos. 1583/5, 1617/20, 1649/**MS**1653, 1683/**MS**1687, 1717/**MS**1721, 1754/7, 1777/80, 1791/4 and 1805/8.

437 Arms

1983. 125th Anniv of Dominican Freemasons.

1547	437	4c. multicoloured	20	15

438 Our Lady of Regla Church

1983. 300th Anniv of Our Lady of Regla Church.

1548	438	3c. deep blue & blue	20	10
1549	-	6c. red and deep red	30	20

DESIGN: 6c. Statue of Our Lady of Regla.

439 Clocktower

1983. 450th Anniv of Monte Cristi Province.

1550	439	1c. green and black	15	10
1551	-	2c. multicoloured	15	10
1552	-	5c. grey	25	20
1553	-	7c. grey and blue	30	25

DESIGNS—VERT: 2c. Provincial coat of arms. HORIZ: 5c. Wooden building in which independence of Cuba was signed; 7c. Men digging out salt crystals.

1983. Obligatory Tax. Child Welfare. As T **350** but dated "1983".

1554	350	1c. green	30	20

440 Commission Emblem

1983. Air. 10th Anniv of Latin American Civil Aviation Commission.

1555	440	10c. blue	30	20

441 Baseball, Boxing and Cycling

1983. 6th National Games, San Pedro de Macoris. Multicoloured.

1556		6c. Type **441** (postage)	15	10
1557		10c. Weightlifting, running and swimming (air)	30	20

442 Bells and Christmas Tree Decorations

1983. Air. Christmas.

1558	442	10c. multicoloured	30	20

443 "Portrait of a Girl" (Adriana Billini)

1983. Air. Paintings. Multicoloured.

1559		10c. "The Litter" (Juan Bautista Gomez) (horiz)	20	15
1560		15c. "The Meeting between Maximo Gomez and Jose Marti at Guayubin" (Enrique Garcia Godoy) (horiz)	25	20
1561		21c. "St. Francis" (Angel Perdomo)	45	30
1562		33c. Type **443**	65	30

444 Monument to Heroes of Capotillo

1983. 120th Anniv of Restoration of the Republic.

1563	444	1c. purple and blue	15	10

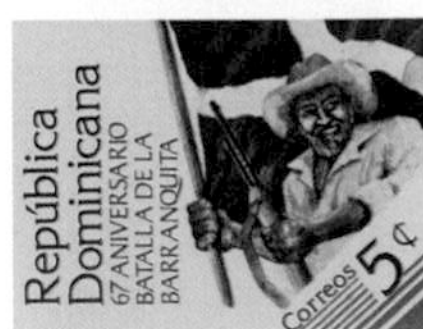

445 Man holding Dominican Flag and Rifle

1983. 67th Anniv of Battle of Barranquita.

1564	445	5c. multicoloured	20	15

446 Matias Ramon Mella and Dominican Flag

1984. 140th Anniv of Independence. Mult.

1565		6c. Type **446**	20	10
1566		25c. Puerta de la Misericordia and Mella's rifle	90	55

447 Dr. Heriberto Pieter

1984. Birth Centenary of Dr. Heriberto Pieter.

1567	447	3c. multicoloured	35	30

448 Jose Maria Imbert, Fernando Valerio, Cannon and National Flag

1984. 140th Anniv of Battle of Santiago.

1568	**448**	7c. multicoloured	35	30

449 Coastguard Patrol Boat

1984. 140th Anniv of Battle of Tortuguero.

1569	**449**	10c. multicoloured	45	20

450 Monument to the Heroes of June 1959

1984. 25th Anniv of Expedition to Constanza, Maimon and Estero Hondo.

1570	**450**	6c. multicoloured	35	30

451 Salome Urena

1984. Birth Centenary of Pedro Henriquez Urena (poet).

1571	**451**	7c. pink and brown	20	10
1572	-	10c. yellow and brown	30	15
1573	-	22c. yellow and brown	35	20

DESIGNS: 10c. Lines from poem "Mi Pedro"; 22c. Pedro H. Urena.

452 Running

1984. Olympic Games, Los Angeles. Each in blue, red and black.

1574		1p. Type **452**	2·10	1·90
1575		1p. Weightlifting	2·10	1·90
1576		1p. Boxing	2·10	1·90
1577		1p. Baseball	2·10	1·90

453 Stygian Owl

1984. Protection of Wildlife. Multicoloured.

1578		10c. Type **453**	3·00	30
1579		15c. Greater flamingo	3·75	35
1580		25c. White-lipped peccary	5·00	50
1581		35c. Haitian solenodon	6·75	70

454 Christopher Columbus landing in Hispaniola

1984. 500th Anniv (1992) of Discovery of America by Columbus (2nd issue).

1582	**454**	10c. multicoloured	20	10
1583	-	35c. multicoloured	65	30
1584	-	65c. brown, yell & blk	1·00	80
1585	-	1p. multicoloured	1·60	1·10

DESIGNS: 35c. Destruction of Fort La Navidad; 65c. First mass in America; 1p. Battle of Santo Cerro.

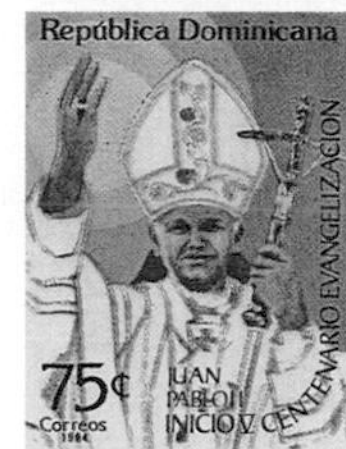

455 Pope John Paul II

1984. Papal Visit to Santo Domingo. 500th Anniv of Christianity in the New World. Multicoloured.

1586		75c. Type **455**	1·90	1·90
1587		75c. Pope in priest's attire and map	1·90	1·90
1588		75c. Globe and Pope in ceremonial attire	1·90	1·90
1589		75c. Bishop's crosier	1·90	1·90

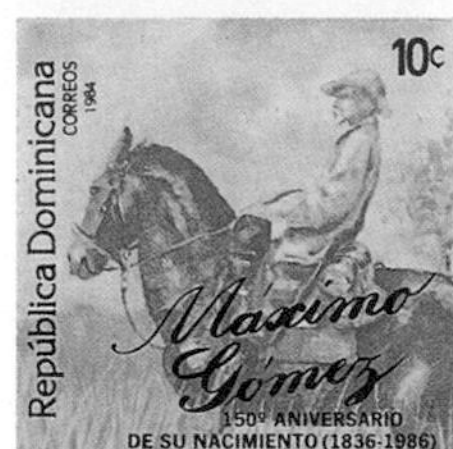

456 Gomez on Horseback

1984. 150th Birth Anniv (1986) of Maximo Gomez (leader of Cuban Revolution). Multicoloured.

1590		10c. Type **456**	20	10
1591		20c. Maximo Gomez	35	20

457 "Navidad 1984"

1984. Christmas.

1592	**457**	5c. mauve, blue and gold	20	10
1593	-	10c. blue, gold & mauve	35	20

DESIGN: 10c. "Navidad 1984" (different).

458 "The Sacrifice of the Kid" (Eligio Pichardo)

1984. Art. Multicoloured.

1594		5c. Type **458**	50	10
1595		10c. "Pumpkin Sellers" (statuette, Gaspar Mario Cruz) (vert)	50	15
1596		25c. "The Market" (Celeste Woss y Gil)	75	45
1597		50c. "Horses in a Storm" (Dario Suro)	1·40	65

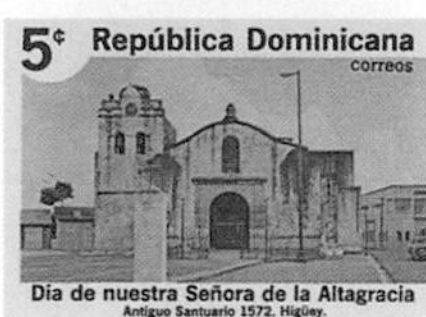

459 Old Church, Higuey

1985. Our Lady of Altagracia's Day. Mult.

1598		5c. Type **459**	20	10
1599		10c. "Our Lady of Altagracia" (1514 painting)	35	15
1600		25c. Basilica of Our Lady of Altagracia, Higuey	55	35

460 Sanchez, Durate and Mella

1985. 141st Anniv of Independence.

1601	**460**	5c. multicoloured	10	10
1602	**460**	10c. multicoloured	20	15
1603	**460**	25c. multicoloured	55	30

461 Gen. Antonia Duverge

1985. 141st Anniv of Azua Battle.

1604	**461**	10c. cream, red & brown	45	15

462 Santo Domingo Lighthouse, 1853

1985. 141st Anniv of Battle of Tortuguero.

1605	**462**	25c. multicoloured	50	25

463 Flags and Emblem

1985. 25th Anniv of American Airforces Co-operation System.

1606	**463**	35c. multicoloured	1·10	45

464 Carlos Maria Rojas (first Governor)

1985. Centenary of Espaillat Province.

1607	**464**	10c. multicoloured	45	20

465 Table Tennis Player

1985. "MOCA 85" (Seventh National Games). Multicoloured.

1608		5c. Type **465**	20	10
1609		10c. Walking race	35	20

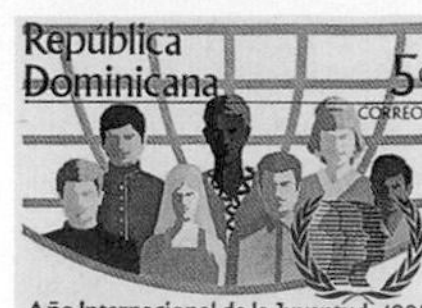

466 Young People of Different Races

1985. International Youth Year. Mult.

1610		5c. Type **466**	35	10
1611		25c. The Haitises	1·10	45
1612		35c. Mt. Duarte summit	1·20	50
1613		2p. Mt. Duarte	7·25	2·75

467 Evangelina Rodriguez (first Dominican woman doctor)

1985. International Decade for Women.

1614	**467**	10c. multicoloured	45	15

468 Emblem

1985. 15th Central American and Caribbean Games, Santiago.

1615	**468**	5c. multicoloured	45	20
1616	**468**	25c. multicoloured	1·20	50

469 Fourth Christopher Columbus Regatta

1985. 500th Anniv (1992) of Discovery of America by Columbus (3rd issue). Multicoloured.

1617		35c. Type **469**	1·40	85
1618		50c. Foundation of Santo Domingo, 1496	1·80	1·20
1619		65c. Chapel of Our Lady of the Rosary, 1496	2·50	1·50
1620		1p. Christopher Columbus's arrival in New World	4·50	2·40

470 Bust of Enriquillo

1985. 450th Death Anniv of Enriquillo (Indian chief). Multicoloured.

1621		5c. Enriquillo in Bahoruco mountains (mural) (46×32 mm)	10	10
1622		10c. Type **470**	45	20

471 Arturo de Merino

1985. Centenary of Ordination of Fernando Arturo de Merino (former President).

1623 **471** 25c. multicoloured 65 45

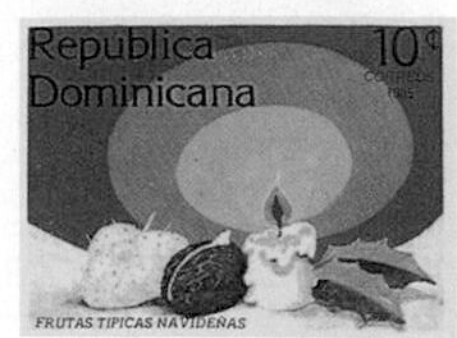

472 Fruit, Candle and Holly

1985. Christmas.

1624 **472** 10c. multicoloured 30 10

1625 **472** 25c. multicoloured 75 45

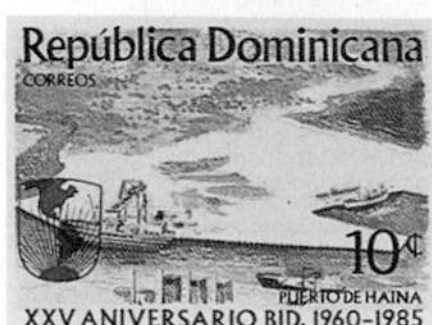

473 Haina Harbour

1985. 25th Anniv of Inter-American Development Bank. Multicoloured.

1626 10c. Type **473** 20 10

1627 25c. Map and ratio diagram of development activities 65 45

1628 1p. Tavera-Bao-Lopez hydro-electric complex 2·50 1·70

474 Mirabal Sisters

1985. 25th Death Anniv of Minerva, Patria and Maria Mirabal.

1629 **474** 10c. multicoloured 35 10

475 Tomb of Duarte, Sanchez and Mella

1986. National Independence Day.

1630 **475** 5c. multicoloured 20 10

1631 **475** 10c. multicoloured 30 15

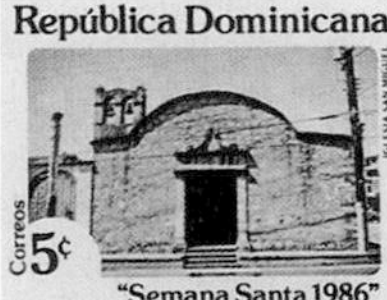

476 St. Michael's Church

1986. Holy Week. Santo Domingo Churches. Multicoloured.

1632 5c. Type **476** 45 20

1633 5c. St. Andrew's Church 45 20

1634 10c. St. Lazarus's Church 50 25

1635 10c. St. Charles's Church 50 25

1636 10c. St. Barbara's Church 50 25

477 "Leonor" (schooner) and Dominican Navy Founders

1986. Navy Day.

1637 **477** 10c. multicoloured 35 20

478 Voters, Ballot Box and Map

1986. National Elections. Multicoloured.

1638 5c. Type **478** 20 10

1639 10c. Hand dropping voting slip into ballot box 35 15

479 Emblem

1986. Creation of "Inposdom" (Dominican Postal Institute).

1640 **479** 10c. blue, red and gold 35 10

1641 **479** 25c. blue, red and silver 90 30

1642 **479** 50c. blue, red and black 1·70 65

480 Weightlifting

1986. 15th Central American and Caribbean Games, Santiago. Multicoloured.

1643 10c. Type **480** 35 20

1644 25c. Gymnast on rings 75 30

1645 35c. Diving 1·10 45

1646 50c. Show-jumping 1·40 70

481 Ercilia Pepin

1986. Writers' Birth Centenaries. Each brown and silver.

1647 5c. Type **481** 20 10

1648 10c. Ramon Emilio Jiminez and Victor Garrido 30 15

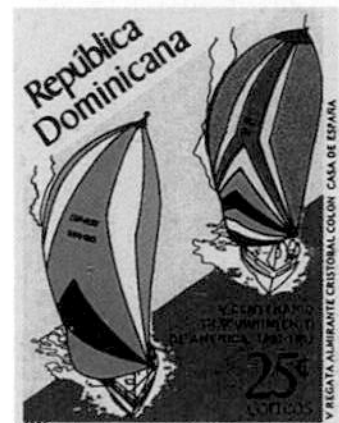

482 Fifth Christopher Columbus Regatta

1986. 500th Anniv (1992) of Discovery of America by Columbus (4th issue). Multicoloured.

1649 25c. Type **482** 65 30

1650 50c. Foundation of Isabela city 1·10 55

1651 65c. Spanish soldiers 1·90 95

1652 1p. Columbus before King of Spain 3·00 1·30

MS1653 86×58 mm. 1p.50 Anniversary emblems. No gum. Imperf 6·25 6·00

483 Goalkeeper saving Ball

1986. World Cup Football Championship, Mexico. Multicoloured.

1654 50c. Type **483** 1·40 65

1655 75c. Footballer and ball 3·00 1·10

484 Maize

1986. 2nd Caribbean Pharmacopoeia Seminar. Medicinal Plants. Multicoloured.

1656 5c. Type **484** 10 10

1657 10c. Arnotto 20 15

1658 25c. "Momordica charantia" 65 20

1659 50c. Custard-apple 1·40 55

485 Town with Christmas Tree

1986. Christmas. Multicoloured.

1660 5c. Type **485** 50 20

1661 25c. Village 1·30 35

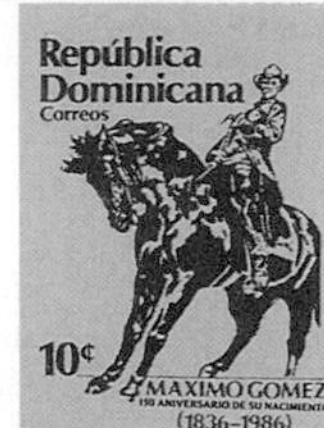

486 Gomez on Horseback

1986. 150th Birth Anniv of Maximo Gomez.

1662 **486** 10c. black and mauve 35 15

1663 - 25c. black and brown 85 35

DESIGN: 25c. Head of Gomez.

488 Emblem

1987. 16th Pan-American Ophthalmology Congress, Santo Domingo.

1676 **488** 50c. red, blue & black 1·40 65

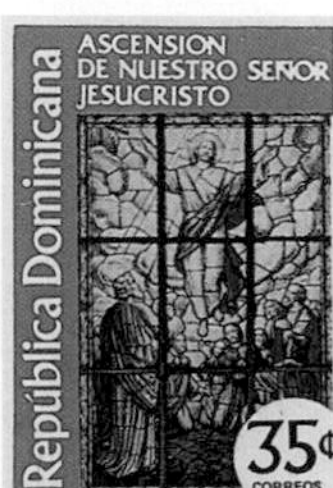

489 "Ascension of Jesus Christ" (stained glass window, St. John Bosco Church)

1987. Ascension Day.

1677 **489** 35c. multicoloured 1·40 50

490 "Sorghum bicolor"

1987. Edible Plants. Multicoloured.

1678 5c. Type **490** 20 10

1679 25c. "Maranta arundinacea" 60 30

1680 65c. "Calathea allouia" 1·90 95

1681 1p. "Voandzeia subterranea" 3·00 1·40

491 Emblem and People on Map

1987. 25th Anniv of Club Activo 20–30 in Dominican Republic.

1682 **491** 35c. multicoloured 1·20 50

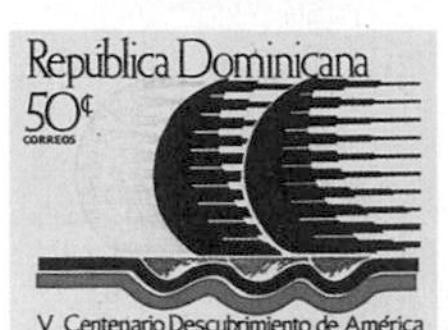

492 Sixth Christopher Columbus Regatta

1987. 500th Anniv (1992) of Discovery of America by Columbus (5th issue). Multicoloured.

1683 50c. Type **492** 1·50 70

1684 75c. Columbus writing diary 2·20 1·00

1685 1p. Foundation of city of Santiago 3·00 1·30

1686 1p.50 Columbus and Bobadilla 4·50 2·00

MS1687 82×70 mm. 2p.50 Centenary of Columbus Monument, Santo Domingo. Imperf 8·50 6·50

493 Games Emblem

1987. 50th Anniv of La Vega Province Games.

1688 **493** 40c. multicoloured 1·10 50

494 Jose Antonio Hungria

1987. Writers' Birth Anniversaries.

1689 **494** 10c. brown & lt brown 20 10

1690 - 25c. dp green & green 75 20

DESIGN: 25c. Joaquin Sergio Inchaustegui.

495 Baseball

1987. 8th National Games, San Cristobal. Multicoloured.

1691 5c. Type **495** 65 20

1692 10c. Boxing 20 10

1693 50c. Karate 1·40 70

496 Statue

1987. 150th Birth Anniv of Fr. Francisco Xavier Billini.

1694	**496**	10c. deep blue and blue	20	10
1695	-	25c. green and olive	60	35
1696	-	75c. brown and pink	2·10	1·10

DESIGNS: 25c. Fr. Billini; 75c. Ana Hernandez de Billini (mother).

497 Maj. Frank Feliz and Curtiss-Wright CW-19

1987. 50th Anniv of Pan-American Flight for Columbus Lighthouse Fund. Multicoloured.

1697 25c. Type **497** 60 30

MS1698 84×106 mm. 2p. Route map and 1937 75c. stamp. Imperf 8·25 6·50

498 Spit-roasting Pig

1987. Christmas. Multicoloured.

1699 10c. Type **498** 55 15

1700 50c. Passengers disembarking from Boeing 727 1·50 60

499 "Bromelia pinguin"

1988. Flowers. Multicoloured.

1701	50c. Type **499**	1·80	70
1702	50c. "Tillandsia compacta" (vert)	1·80	70
1703	50c. "Tillandsia fasciculata"	1·80	70
1704	50c. "Tillandsia hotteana" (vert)	1·80	70

500 St. John Bosco

1988. Death Centenary of St. John Bosco (founder of Salesian Brothers). Multicoloured.

1705	10c. Type **500**	30	10
1706	70c. Stained glass window	2·50	95

501 Rainbow, Doves and Cloud

1988. 25th Anniv of Dominican Rehabilitation Association.

1707 **501** 20c. multicoloured 55 20

502 Perdomo

1988. Birth Centenary of Dr. Manuel Emilio Perdomo.

1708 **502** 20c. brown and flesh 55 20

503 Emblem

1988. 25th Anniv of Dominican College of Engineering and Architecture (CODIA).

1709 **503** 20c. multicoloured 55 20

504 Church and Madonna and Child

1988. Centenary of Parish Church of Our Lady of the Carmelites, Duverge.

1710 **504** 50c. multicoloured 1·20 55

505 Flags and Juan Pablo Duarte (Dominican patriot)

1988. Mexican Independence Day. Mult.

1711	50c. Type **505**	1·30	65
1712	50c. Flags and Miguel Hidalgo (Mexican patriot)	1·30	65

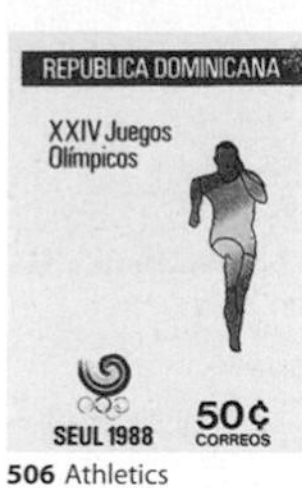

506 Athletics

1988. Olympic Games, Seoul. Multicoloured.

1713	50c. Type **506**	1·10	50
1714	70c. Table tennis	1·60	70
1715	1p. Judo	2·40	95
1716	1p.50 "Ying Yang symbol and Balls" (Tete Marella) (horiz)	3·50	1·60

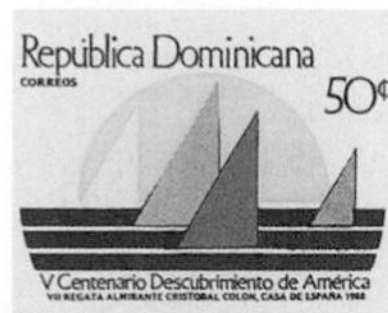

507 Seventh Christopher Columbus Regatta

1988. 500th Anniv of Discovery of America by Columbus (6th issue). Multicoloured.

1717	50c. Type **507**	1·10	65
1718	70c. Building fort at La Vega Real, 1494	1·70	95
1719	1p.50 Bonao Fort	3·50	2·00
1720	2p. Nicolas de Ovando (Governor of Hispaniola)	5·00	2·40

MS1721 77×98 mm. 3p. Columbus's mausoleum, Santo Domingo Cathedral. Imperf 6·25 6·25

508 Duarte, Mella and Sanchez

1988. 150th Anniv of Trinitarian Rebellion.

1722	**508**	10c. silver, red and blue	35	10
1723	-	1p. multicoloured	2·00	85
1724	-	5p. multicoloured	11·50	4·75

DESIGNS: 1p. Plaza La Trinitaria; 5p. Plaza de la Independencia.

509 Parchment, Knife and Pestle and Mortar

1988. 13th Pan-American and 16th Central American Congresses of Pharmacy and Biochemistry.

1725 **509** 1p. multicoloured 1·50 1·30

510 "Doni Tondo" (Michelangelo)

1988. Christmas. Multicoloured.

1726	10c. Type **510**	30	10
1727	20c. Stained glass window	55	30

511 Emblem

1988. 50th Anniv of Dominican Municipal Association.

1728 **511** 20c. multicoloured 55 30

512 Ana Teresa Paradas

1988. 28th Death Anniv of Ana Teresa Paradas (lawyer).

1729 **512** 20c. red 55 30

513 Birds

1989. Bicentenary of French Revolution.

1730 **513** 3p. red, blue and black 3·00 2·75

516 Battle Scene

1989. 145th Anniv of Battle of Tortuguero.

1737 **516** 40c. multicoloured 90 55

517 Drug Addict

1989. Anti-drugs Campaign.

1738	**517**	10c. multicoloured	20	10
1739	**517**	20c. multicoloured	35	15
1740	**517**	50c. multicoloured	55	25
1741	**517**	70c. multicoloured	85	35
1742	**517**	1p. multicoloured	1·20	45
1743	**517**	1p.50 multicoloured	1·70	50
1744	**517**	2p. multicoloured	2·30	70
1745	**517**	5p. multicoloured	5·75	1·50
1746	**517**	10p. multicoloured	11·00	3·75

518 Breast-feeding Baby

1989. Mothers' Day.

1747 **518** 20c. multicoloured 30 10

519 Eugenio Maria de Hostos

1989. 150th Birth Anniversaries. Mult.

1748	20c. Type **519**	50	20
1749	20c. Gen. Gregorio Luperon	50	20

520 Baseball

1989. 50th Anniv of Baseball Minor League.

1750 **520** 1p. multicoloured 1·80 1·00

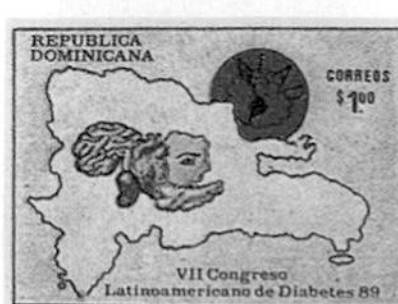

521 Map and Human Organs

1989. 7th Latin American Diabetes Association Congress.

1751 **521** 1p. multicoloured 1·40 70

522 Cohoba Artefact and Ritual Dance

1989. America. Pre-Columbian Culture. Mult.

1752	20c. Type **522**	55	20
1753	1p. Taina vessel, pounding instrument and Indians preparing manioc cake	3·00	1·70

523 Eighth Christopher Columbus Regatta

1989. 500th Anniv (1992) of Discovery of America by Columbus (7th issue). Multicoloured.

1754	50c. Type **523**	60	25
1755	70c. Brother Pedro de Cordoba preaching to Indians (horiz)	75	55
1756	1p. Columbus dividing Indian lands (horiz)	1·60	75
1757	3p. Brother Antonio Montesinos giving sermon (horiz)	3·00	2·20

524 Dead and Living Leaves

1989. National Reafforestation Campaign. Mult.

1758	10c. Type **524**	20	10
1759	20c. Forest	30	15
1760	50c. Forest and lake	90	55
1761	1p. Living tree and avenue of dead trees	1·90	1·20

525 Map and Cyclist

1990. 9th National Games, La Vega. Mult.

1762	10c. Type **525**	20	10
1763	20c. Map and runner	35	15
1764	50c. Map and handball player	1·10	75

526 Mary and Body of Jesus

1990. Holy Week. Multicoloured.

1765	20c. Type **526**	35	20
1766	50c. Jesus carrying cross	1·10	75

527 Cogwheel and Workers

1990. International Labour Day.

1767	**527**	1p. multicoloured	1·50	80

528 Avenida Mexico

1990. Urban Development. Multicoloured.

1768	10c. Type **528**	20	10
1769	20c. Avenida Nunez de Caceres road tunnel	35	15
1770	50c. National Library	70	25
1771	1p. V Centenario Motorway	1·70	80

529 Penny Black

1990. 150th Anniv of the Penny Black. Mult.

1772	1p. Type **529**	2·10	1·50
MS1773	63×81 mm. 3p. Sir Rowland Hill (postal reformer) and Penny Black. Imperf	6·00	6·00

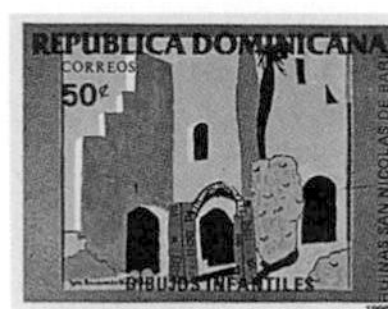

530 "Ruins of St. Nicholas's Church, Bari"

1990. Children's Drawings. Multicoloured.

1774	50c. Type **530**	1·10	75
1775	50c. "House, Tostado"	1·10	75

531 Members' Flags

1990. Centenary of Organization of American States.

1776	**531**	2p. multicoloured	4·50	3·00

532 Yachts (Ninth Christopher Columbus Regatta)

1990. 500th Anniv (1992) of Discovery of America by Columbus (8th issue). Multicoloured.

1777	50c. Type **532**	1·60	70
1778	1p. Confrontation between natives and sailors (horiz)	2·20	1·40
1779	2p. Meeting of Columbus and Guacanagari (horiz)	4·50	3·00
1780	5p. Caonabo imprisoned by Columbus (horiz)	11·00	7·50

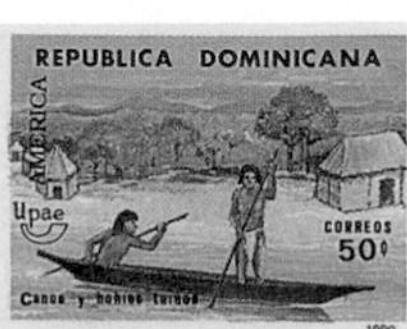

533 Amerindians in Canoe

1990. America. Multicoloured.

1781	50c. Type **533**	1·10	75
1782	3p. Amerindian in hammock	6·25	4·75

534 Perez Rancier

1991. Birth Centenary of Dr. Tomas Eudoro Perez Rancier (physician).

1783	**534**	2p. black and yellow	4·25	1·90

535 First Official Mass in America

1991. Spanish America. Multicoloured.

1784	50c. Type **535**	90	55
1785	1p. Arms (first religious orders)	1·90	1·20
1786	3p. Map of Hispaniola (first European settlement) (horiz)	4·75	2·75
1787	4p. Christopher Columbus (first viceroy and governor)	8·25	5·00

536 Boxing

1991. 11th Pan-American Games, Havana. Multicoloured.

1788	30c. Type **536**	45	20
1789	50c. Cycling	1·10	50
1790	1p. Putting the shot	2·40	1·20

537 Yachts (10th Christopher Columbus Regatta)

1991. 500th Anniv (1992) of Discovery of America by Columbus (9th issue). Multicoloured.

1791	30c. Type **537**	65	20
1792	50c. Meeting of three cultures (horiz)	90	50
1793	3p. Columbus and Doctor Alvarez Chanco (horiz)	5·50	3·00
1794	4p. Enriquillo's war (horiz)	7·50	4·00

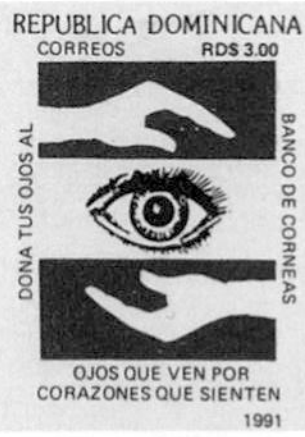

538 Eye and Hands

1991. Cornea Bank.

1795	**538**	3p. black and red	4·25	2·10

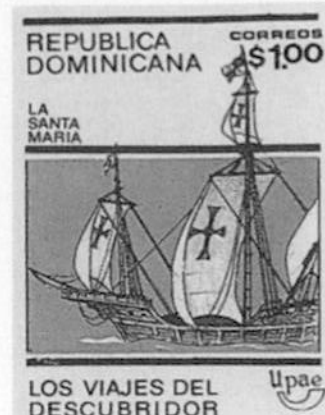

539 "Santa Maria"

1991. America. Voyages of Discovery. Mult.

1796	1p. Type **539**	1·70	80
1797	3p. Columbus and fleet	5·00	3·50

540 Meeting Emblem

1992. 33rd Annual Meeting of Governors of Inter-American Development Bank, Santo Domingo.

1798	**540**	1p. multicoloured	1·80	1·10

541 Valentin Salinero (founder)

1992. Centenary (1991) of Order of the Apostles.

1799	**541**	1p. brown, black & blue	1·80	1·10

542 Flags of Cuba, Dominican Republic and Puerto Rico, and Magnifying Glass

1992. Espanola 92 Stamp Exhibition.

1800	**542**	3p. black, violet & red	5·25	2·75

543 First Monastery in Americas

1992. Ruins. Multicoloured.

1801	50c. Type **543**	75	60
1802	3p. First hospital in Americas	5·50	4·00

544 La Vega Cathedral and Pope

1992. Visit of Pope John Paul II. Mult.

1803	50c. Type **544**	1·20	60
1804	3p. Santo Domingo Cathedral and Pope	4·75	2·40

545 Yacht (11th Christopher Columbus Regatta)

1992. 500th Anniv of Discovery of America by Columbus (10th issue). Multicoloured.

1805	50c. Type **545**	70	30
1806	1p. Amerindian women preparing food and Columbus (horiz)	1·40	75
1807	2p. Amerindians demonstrating use of tobacco to Columbus (horiz)	4·75	2·75
1808	3p. Amerindian woman and Columbus by maize field (horiz)	6·50	3·75

546 Columbus Lighthouse

1992

1809	**546**	30c. multicoloured	90	45
1810	**546**	1p. multicoloured	1·90	70

MS1811 70×133 mm. 3p. multicoloured (Lighthouse at night). Imperf 6·00 6·00

547 Convention Emblem

1992. 23rd Pan-American Round Table Convention, Santo Domingo.

1812	**547**	1p. brown, cream & red	1·70	85

548 First Royal Palace in Americas, Santo Domingo

1992. America. Multicoloured.

1813	50c. Type **548**	65	45
1814	3p. First Vice-regal residence in Americas, Colon	4·00	2·50

See also Nos. 1840 and 1882/3.

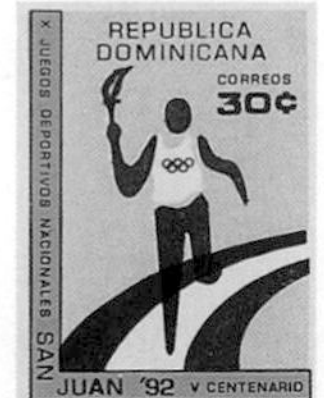

549 Torch Bearer

1992. 10th National Games, San Juan.

1815	**549**	30c. multicoloured	45	20
1816	-	1p. multicoloured	1·50	80
1817	-	4p. black and blue	7·00	3·50

DESIGNS: 1p. Emblem of Secretary of State for Sports Education and Recreation; 4p. Judo.

550 Emblem

1993. 7th Population and Housing Census.

1818	**550**	50c. blue, black & pink	65	40
1819	**550**	1p. blue, black & brown	1·30	80
1820	**550**	3p. blue, black & grey	4·25	2·50
1821	**550**	4p. blue, black & green	5·50	3·25

551 Ema Balaguer

1993. Ema Balaguer (humanitarian worker) Commemoration.

1822	**551**	30c. multicoloured	40	25
1823	**551**	50c. multicoloured	70	45
1824	**551**	1p. multicoloured	1·40	85

552 Emblem and Stylized Figures

1993. 50th Anniv of Santo Domingo Rotary Club. Multicoloured.

1825	30c. Type **552**	40	20
1826	1p. National flags and rotary emblem	1·40	85

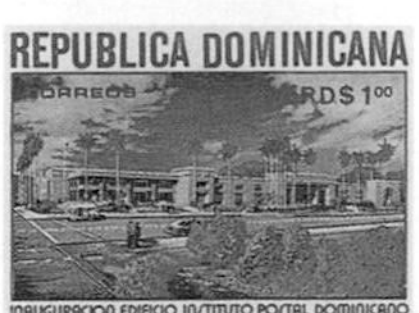

553 Institute

1993. Inauguration of New Dominican Postal Institute Building.

1827	**553**	1p. multicoloured	1·00	80
1828	**553**	3p. multicoloured	3·00	2·40
1829	**553**	4p. multicoloured	3·75	3·00
1830	**553**	5p. multicoloured	4·75	3·75
1831	**553**	10p. multicoloured	9·50	7·50

MS1832 106×96 mm. 5p. As Type **553** but larger (93×85 mm). Imperf 7·50 7·25

554 Palm Chat and Books

1993. Ten Year Education Plan.

1833	**554**	1p.50 multicoloured	1·90	1·20

555 Racketball

1993. 17th Central American and Caribbean Games, Ponce (Puerto Rico). Multicoloured.

1834	50c. Type **555**	60	35
1835	4p. Swimming	5·75	3·00

556 Chest (first university)

1993. American Firsts in Hispaniola (1st series). Multicoloured.

1836	50c. Type **556**	65	40
1837	3p. First arms conferred on American city	4·25	2·30

See also Nos. 1840 and 1882/3.

557 Hispaniolan Conure

1993. America. Endangered Animals. Mult.

1838	1p. Type **557**	1·30	80
1839	3p. Rhinoceros iguana	5·25	2·75

558 Cross and Eucharist (500th anniv of first Mass)

1994. American Firsts in Hispaniola (2nd series).

1840	**558**	2p. multicoloured	2·75	1·60

559 State Flag, 1946 15c. and 1944 3c. Stamps

1994. 5th National Stamp Exhibition.

1841	**559**	3p. multicoloured	4·25	2·40

560 Signing of Independence Treaty (left-hand detail)

1994. 150th Anniv of Independence. Mult.

1842	2p. Type **560**	1·60	1·10
1843	2p. Signing of Independence Treaty (right-hand detail)	1·60	1·10
1844	2p. State flag	1·60	1·10
1845	2p. Soldier with young woman	1·60	1·10
1846	2p. Boy helping woman make flag	1·60	1·10
1847	3p. Revolutionaries (back view of left-hand man)	2·50	1·70
1848	3p. Revolutionaries (window behind men)	2·50	1·70
1849	3p. State arms	2·50	1·70
1850	3p. Revolutionaries (all turned away from door)	2·50	1·70
1851	3p. Revolutionaries with flag	2·50	1·70

MS1852 162×104 mm. 10p. Men before fortress and "Liberty" carrying flag and blunderbuss. Imperf 11·00 10·50

Stamps of the same value were issued together, se-tenant, Nos. 1842/3, 1845/6, 1847/8 and 1850/1 forming composite designs.

561 Solenodon on Dead Wood

1994. The Haitian Solenodon. Multicoloured.

1853	1p. Type **561**	1·70	1·30
1854	1p. Solenodon amongst leaves	1·70	1·30
1855	1p. Solenodon on stony ground	1·70	1·30
1856	1p. Solenodon eating insect	1·70	1·30

562 Fusiliers behind Barricade (19 March)

1994. 150th Anniversaries of Battles of 19 and 30 March. Multicoloured.

1857	2p. Type **562**	2·75	1·60
1858	2p. Battle at fort (30 March)	2·75	1·60

563 Ballot Boxes

1994. National Elections.

1859	**563**	2p. multicoloured	2·75	1·60

564 "Virgin of Amparo"

1994. 150th Anniv of Naval Battle of Puerto Tortuguero.

1860	**564**	3p. multicoloured	3·75	1·90

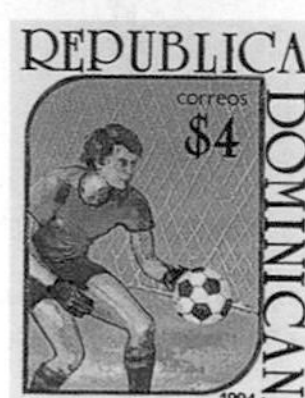

565 Goalkeeper

1994. World Cup Football Championship, U.S.A. Multicoloured.

1861	4p. Type **565**	4·25	2·30
1862	6p. Players contesting possession of ball	6·00	3·25

566 Figures in Houses

1994. Ema Balguer Children's City.

1863	**566**	1p. mauve and brown	1·90	60

567 1866 Medio Real Stamp and Cancellation

1994. Stamp Day.
1864 **567** 5p. red, black & yellow 5·75 3·00

568 Postal Carrier on Horseback

1994. America. Postal Vehicles. Multicoloured.
1865 2p. Type **568** 2·75 1·60
1866 6p. Schooner 8·25 4·75

571 Writing Desk and Constitution

1994. 150th Anniv of First Constitution of Dominican Republic.
1876 **571** 3p. multicoloured 3·75 1·90

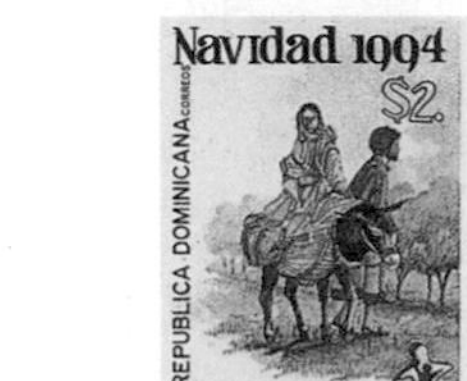

572 Flight into Egypt

1994. Christmas. International Year of the Family. Multicoloured.
1877 2p. Type **572** 3·00 1·60
1878 3p. Family 4·00 2·40

573 Ruins of St. Francis's Monastery

1994. 500th Anniv of Concepcion de la Vega.
1879 **573** 3p. multicoloured 5·00 1·80

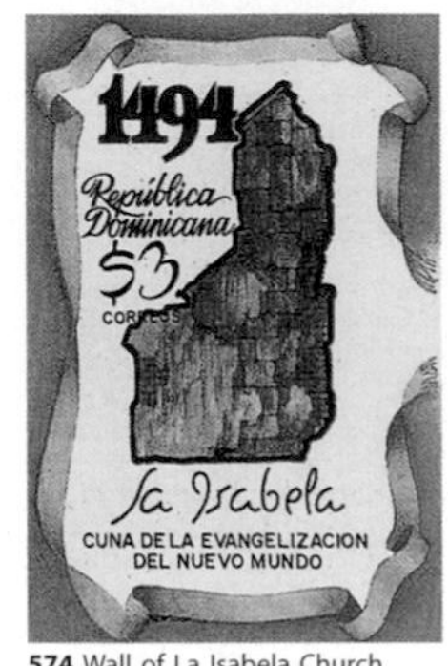

574 Wall of La Isabela Church

1994. 500th Anniv of First Church in Dominican Republic. Multicoloured.
1880 3p. Type **574** 4·25 2·30
1881 3p. Temple of the Americas 4·25 2·30

Nos. 1880/1 were issued together, se-tenant, forming a composite design.

1994. American Firsts in Hispaniola (3rd series). As T 556. Multicoloured.
1882 2p. First coins, 1505 2·75 1·40
1883 5p. Antonio Montesino (first plea for justice (in Advent sermon), 1511) 6·50 3·75

575 "Hypsirhynchus ferox"

1994. National Natural History Museum. Snakes. Multicoloured.
1884 2p. Type **575** 2·75 1·40
1885 2p. "Antillophis parvifrons" 2·75 1·40
1886 2p. "Uromacer catesbyi" 2·75 1·40
1887 2p. Bahama boa ("Epicrates striatus") 2·75 1·40

Nos. 1884/5 and 1886/7 respectively were issued together, se-tenant, each pair forming a composite design of a tree and the snakes.

576 Taekwondo

1995. Pan-American Games, Mar del Plata, Argentine Republic.
1888 **576** 4p. blue, red & black 4·75 3·00
1889 - 13p. green, black & yell 14·50 9·25

DESIGN: 13p. Tennis.

577 Allegory of Dominican Agriculture

1995. 50th Anniv of F.A.O.
1890 **577** 4p. multicoloured 4·00 2·30

578 Jose Marti, Maximo Gomez and Monte Cristi Clock Tower

1995. Centenaries.
1891 **578** 2p. brown, pink & black 1·90 1·10
1892 - 3p. pink, black & blue 2·75 1·60
1893 - 4p. black and pink 3·75 2·10

DESIGNS: 3p. Jose Marti on Cuban national flag (death centenary); 4p. Gomez and Marti signing Monte Cristi manifesto.

579 Emblem

1995. "Centrobasket" Basketball Championship, Santo Domingo.
1894 **579** 3p. blue, red & black 2·75 1·60

580 "Pimenta ozua"

1995. Medicinal Plants. Multicoloured.
1895 2p. Type **580** 1·90 1·10
1896 2p. "Melocactus communis" 1·90 1·10
1897 3p. "Smilax sp." 2·75 1·60
1898 3p. "Zamia sp." 2·75 1·60

581 San Souci Port

1995. Tourism. Multicoloured.
1899 4p. Type **581** 3·00 1·60
1900 5p. Barahona airport 3·75 1·80
1901 6p. G. Luperon airport 4·75 2·10
1902 13p. Las Americas airport 10·00 4·75

582 Ruins of Jacagua Church

1995. 500th Anniv of Santiago de los Caballeros.
1903 **582** 3p. multicoloured 3·75 1·70

583 Sei Whale ("Balaenoptera borealis")

1995. Natural History Museum. Whales. Mult.
1904 3p. Type **583** 2·20 80
1905 3p. Humpback whales ("Megaptera novaeanglide") 2·20 80
1906 3p. Sperm whales ("Physeter macrocephalus") 2·20 80
1907 3p. Cuvier's beaked whales ("Ziphius cavirostris") 2·20 80

584 Rafael Colon

1995. Singers. Multicoloured.
1908 2p. Type **584** 1·70 80
1909 3p. Casandra Damiron 2·20 1·10

585 Cancelled 1880 2c. Stamp

1995. Stamp Day.
1910 **585** 4p. multicoloured 3·25 1·60

586 Player

1995. Centenary of Volleyball. Multicoloured.
1911 6p. Type **586** 4·75 1·90

MS1912 49×79 mm. 5p. Player hitting ball over net. Imperf 4·50 4·25

587 Anniversary Emblem

1995. 50th Anniv of U.N.O.
1913 **587** 2p. blue and gold 1·70 75
1914 - 6p. multicoloured 5·00 1·90

DESIGN—33×55 mm: 6p. Allegorical design.

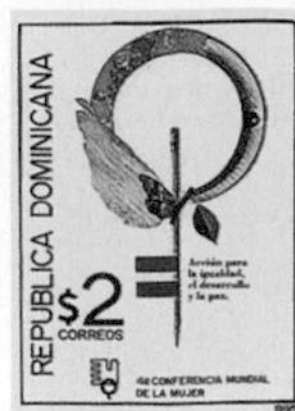

588 Allegory

1995. 4th World Conference on Women, Peking.
1915 **588** 2p. multicoloured 3·75 1·10

589 Columbus Lighthouse

1995
1916 **589** 10p. ultram, blue & blk 7·50 3·75
1994 **589** 10p. green and silver 6·25 3·50
2025 **589** 10p. mauve and silver 6·25 3·50
2089 **589** 10p. yellow and black 6·00 3·00

590 Enriquillo Lake

1995. America. Environmental Protection. Mult.
1917 2p. Type **590** 1·70 65
1918 6p. Mangrove plantation 5·00 1·90

591 Antonio Mesa (tenor)

1995. Singers. Each red and brown.
1919 2p. Type **591** 1·80 80
1920 2p. Susano Polanco (tenor) 1·80 80
1921 2p. Julieta Otero (soprano) 1·80 80

592 Cathedral

1995. Centenary of Santiago Cathedral.
1922 **592** 3p. multicoloured 2·50 1·10

593 Vought 02U Corsair Fighter

1995. 50th Anniv of Dominican Air Force (1st issue). Multicoloured.

1923	2p. Type **593**	1·00	85
1924	2p. Stearman Pt-17 Kaydett bomber	1·00	85
1925	2p. North American T-6 Texan trainer	1·00	85
1926	2p. Consolidated PBY-5A Catalina amphibian	1·00	85
1927	2p. Bristol Type 156 Beaufighter fighter	1·00	85
1928	2p. de Havilland D.H.98 Mosquito bomber	1·00	85
1929	2p. Lockheed P-38 Lightning fighter	1·00	85
1930	2p. North American P-51 Mustang fighter	1·00	85
1931	2p. Boeing B-17 Flying Fortress bomber	1·00	85
1932	2p. Republic P-47 Thunderbolt fighter	1·00	85
1933	2p. de Havilland D.H.100 Vampire FB Mk50	1·00	85
1934	2p. Curtiss C-46 Commando 1	1·00	85
1935	2p. Douglas B-26 Invader	1·00	85
1936	2p. Douglas C-47 Skytrain transport	1·00	85
1937	2p. North America T-28D Trojan	1·00	85
1938	2p. Lockheed T-33A Silverstar	1·00	85
1939	2p. Cessna T-41D	1·00	85
1940	2p. Beech T-34 Mentor	1·00	85
1941	2p. Cessna O-2A Super Skymaster	1·00	85
1942	2p. Cessna A-37B Dragonfly fighter	1·00	85

No. 1934 is wrongly inscr "Commander" and No. 1935 is wrongly inscr "Boeing".

See also Nos. 1958/63, 2026/31 and 2040/4.

594 Brito

1996. 50th Death Anniv of Eduardo Brito (singer).

1943	**594**	1p. multicoloured	60	45
1944	-	2p. multicoloured	1·20	75
1945	-	3p. black and pink	1·90	1·10

DESIGNS—55×35 mm: 2p. Brito playing maracas. As T **594**: 3p. Brito (different).

595 Yachts

1996. Hispaniola Cup Yachting Championship.

1946	**595**	5p. multicoloured	3·25	1·60

596 Children

1996. 50th Anniv of UNICEF.

1947	**596**	2p. black and green	1·40	65
1948	-	4p. black and green	2·75	1·40

DESIGN—4p. As T **596** but motif reversed.

597 Arturo Pallerano, Freddy Gaton and Rafael Herrera

1996. National Journalists' Day.

1949	**597**	5p. multicoloured	3·75	1·60

598 Emblem, Astronaut and Biplane

1996. "Espamer" Spanish–Latin American and "Aviation and Space" Stamp Exhibitions, Seville, Spain.

1950	**598**	15p. multicoloured	8·75	4·25

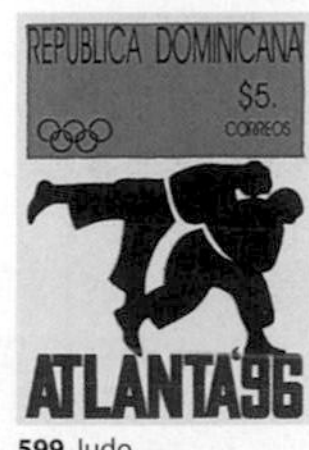

599 Judo

1996. Olympic Games, Atlanta. Each black, blue and red.

1951	5p. Type **599**	3·00	1·40
1952	15p. Torchbearer	9·00	4·25

600 Greek 1896 2l. Olympic Stamp

1996. Centenary of Modern Olympic Games.

1953	**600**	6p. green, red & black	3·75	1·90
1954	-	15p. multicoloured	9·00	4·25

DESIGN: 15p. Dominican Republic 1937 7c. Olympic stamp.

601 "Girl at Postbox"

1996. "The Post is your Friend". Winning Entries in Children's Stamp Design Competition. Mult.

1955	3p. Type **601**	1·90	1·00
1956	3p. Representations of world post	1·90	1·00
1957	3p. Postal carrier on horseback delivering letter (vert)	1·90	1·00

602 Sikorsky S-55

1996. 50th Anniv of Air Force (2nd issue). Helicopters. Multicoloured.

1958	3p. Type **602**	1·70	85
1959	3p. Sud Aviation Alouette II	1·70	85
1960	3p. Sud Aviation Alouette III	1·70	85
1961	3p. OH-6A Cayuse	1·70	85
1962	3p. Bell 205 A-1	1·70	85
1963	3p. Aerospatiale SA.365 Dauphin 2	1·70	85

603 Workers and Children

1996. United Nations Decade against Drug Trafficking.

1964	**603**	15p. multicoloured	8·75	4·75

604 Man

1996. America. Costumes. Multicoloured.

1965	2p. Type **604**	1·40	65
1966	6p. Woman	3·75	1·70

605 Stylized Dinghy

1996. 26th International "Sunfish" Dinghy Sailing Championships. Multicoloured.

1967	6p. Type **605**	3·75	2·00
1968	10p. Sailor in dinghy (horiz)	6·25	3·50

606 1905 1p. Stamp

1996. Stamp Day.

1969	**606**	5p. stone and black	3·25	1·40

607 Ridgway's Hawk ("Buteo ridgwayi")

1996. Birds. Multicoloured.

1970	2p. Type **607**	1·20	1·00
1971	2p. Hispaniolan conure ("Aratinga chloroptera")	1·20	1·00
1972	2p. Hispaniolan amazon ("Amazona ventralis")	1·20	1·00
1973	2p. Rufous-breasted cuckoo ("Hyetornis rufigularis")	1·20	1·00
1974	2p. Hispaniolan lizard cuckoo ("Saurothera longirostris")	1·20	1·00
1975	2p. Least pauraque ("Siphonorhis brewsteri")	1·20	1·00
1976	2p. Hispaniolan emerald ("Chlorostilbon swainsonii")	1·20	1·00
1977	2p. Narrow-billed tody ("Todus angustirostris")	1·20	1·00
1978	2p. Broad-billed tody ("Todus subulatus")	1·20	1·00
1979	2p. Hispaniolan trogon ("Temnotrogon roseigaster")	1·20	1·00
1980	2p. Antillean piculet ("Nesoctites micromegas")	1·20	1·00
1981	2p. Hispaniolan woodpecker ("Melanerpes striatus")	1·20	1·00
1982	2p. La Selle thrush ("Turdus swalesi")	1·20	1·00
1983	2p. Antillean siskin ("Carduelis dominicensis")	1·20	1·00
1984	2p. Palm chat ("Dulus dominicus")	1·20	1·00
1985	2p. Green-tailed ground warbler ("Microligea palustris")	1·20	1·00
1986	2p. Flat-billed vireo ("Vireo nanus")	1·20	1·00
1987	2p. White-winged ground warbler ("Xenoligea montana")	1·20	1·00
1988	2p. La Selle thrush ("Turdus swalesi dodae")	1·20	1·00
1989	2p. Chat-tanager ("Calyptophilus frugivorus tertius")	1·20	1·00
1990	2p. White-necked crow ("Corvus leucognaphalus")	1·20	1·00
1991	2p. Chat-tanager ("Calyptophilus frugivorus neibae")	1·20	1·00

608 Mirabal Sisters

1996. International Day of No Violence against Women.

1992	**608**	5p. multicoloured	3·25	1·60
1993	**608**	10p. multicoloured	6·25	3·25

609 Leatherback Turtles ("Dermochelys coriacea")

1996. Turtles. Multicoloured.

1995	5p. Type **609**	2·75	2·40
1996	5p. Loggerhead turtles ("Caretta caretta")	2·75	2·40
1997	5p. Indian Ocean green turtles ("Chelonia mydas")	2·75	2·40
1998	5p. Hawksbill turtles ("Eretmochelys imbricata")	2·75	2·40

Nos. 1995/8 were issued together, se-tenant, forming a composite design.

610 Youths leaping for Sun

1997. National Youth Day.

1999	**610**	3p. multicoloured	1·90	1·10

611 Flag and Lyrics by Emilio Prudhomne

1997. National Anthem. Each black, blue and red.

2000	2p. Type **611**	1·40	65
2001	3p. Flag and score by Jose Reyes	1·90	95

612 Salome Urena

1997. Death Cent of Salome Urena (educationist).

2002	**612**	3p. multicoloured	1·90	95

613 Comet, Palm Tree and House

1997. Hale-Bopp Comet. Multicoloured.

2003	5p. Type **613**	3·75	1·60

MS2004 76×51 mm. 10p. Comet over sea 7·75 7·50

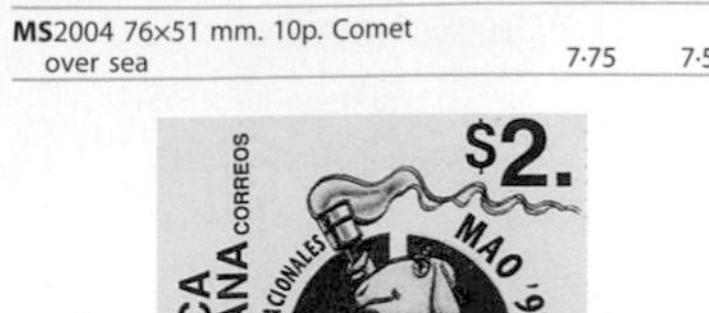

614 Mascot with Torch and Emblem

1997. 11th National Games. Multicoloured.

2005 2p. Type **614** 1·50 65
2006 3p. Mascot with baseball bat (26×36 mm) 2·40 1·00
2007 5p. Athlete breasting tape (36×26 mm) 3·75 1·60

615 Von Stephan

1997. Death Centenary of Heinrich von Stephan (founder of Universal Postal Union). Each violet, black and vermillion.

2008 10p. Type **615** 6·25 3·50

MS2009 51×75 mm. 5p. Portrait of Von Stephan as in Type **615** but with inscription differently arranged. Imperf 3·25 2·75

616 Blood Vessel

1997. 15th International Haemostasis and Thrombosis Congress.

2010 **616** 10p. multicoloured 7·75 3·25

617 Helmet, Flowers and Epaulettes

1997. Death Cent of General Gregorio Luperon.

2011 **617** 3p. multicoloured 1·90 1·00

618 Emblem

1997. 80th Anniv of Spanish House in Santo Domingo.

2012 **618** 5p. multicoloured 3·25 1·60

619 First Minting

1997. Centenary of the Peso.

2013 **619** 2p. multicoloured 1·40 65

620 Icon

1997. 75th Anniv of Coronation of "Our Lady of Altagracia" (icon). Multicoloured.

2014 3p. Type **620** 1·90 85
2015 5p. Icon and church 3·25 1·50

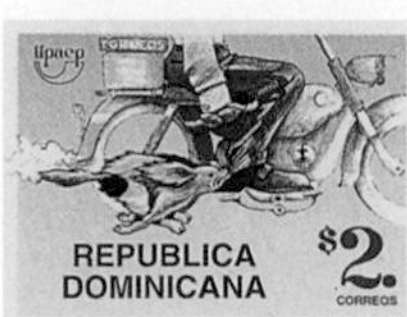

621 Dog attacking Postman on Motor Cycle

1997. America. The Postman. Multicoloured.

2016 2p. Type **621** 1·20 65
2017 6p. Dog attacking postman delivering letter (35½×37 mm) 3·25 1·90

622 Weeping Child, Mother Teresa and Man on Donkey

1997. Int Fight against Poverty Day.

2018 **622** 5p. multicoloured 2·75 1·60

623 1936 and 1899 2p. Stamps

1997. Stamp Day.

2019 **623** 5p. brown and black 2·75 1·60

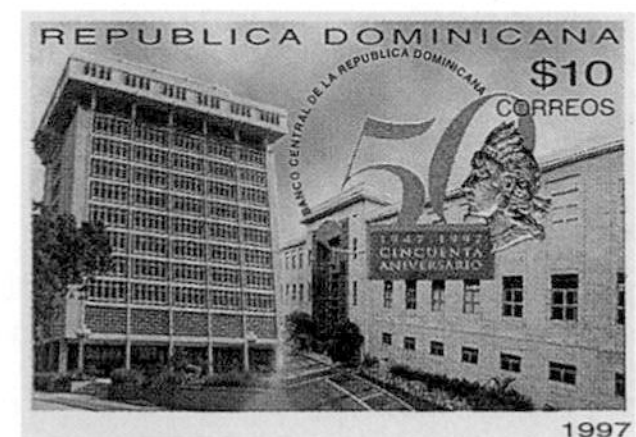

624 Buildings

1997. 50th Anniv of Central Bank.

2020 **624** 10p. multicoloured 5·50 3·25

625 "Erophyllus bombifrons"

1997. Bats. Multicoloured.

2021 5p. Type **625** 2·50 2·50
2022 5p. Cuban fruit-eating bat ("Brachyphylla nana") 2·50 2·50
2023 5p. Kerr's mastiff bat ("Molossus molossus") 2·50 2·50
2024 5p. Red bat ("Lasiurus borealis") 2·50 2·50

626 Air Force Badge

1997. 50th Anniv of Air Force (3rd issue). Division Badges. Multicoloured.

2026 3p. Type **626** 1·80 1·80
2027 3p. Air Command North 1·80 1·80
2028 3p. Air Command 1·80 1·80
2029 3p. Rescue 1·80 1·80
2030 3p. Maintenance Command 1·80 1·80
2031 3p. Combat Squadron 1·80 1·80

627 Facade

1997. 50th Anniv of National Palace.

2032 **627** 10p. multicoloured 6·25 3·50

628 Painting

1998. 1st Regional Symposium on Influence of Pre-Columbian Culture on Contemporary Caribbean Art.

2033 **628** 6p. multicoloured 3·75 1·90

629 Emblem

1998. 75th Anniv of American Chamber of Commerce of Dominican Republic.

2034 **629** 10p. blue, red and gold 6·25 3·25

630 Open Book

1998. 25th Anniv of National Book Fair and First International Book Fair, Santo Domingo.

2035 **630** 3p. blue, red and black 1·90 85
2036 - 5p. blue, red and black 3·25 1·60

DESIGN—40×40 mm: 5p. Book Fair emblem.

631 Emblem

1998. 50th Anniv of Organization of American States. Multicoloured.

2037 5p. Type **631** 3·25 1·60
2038 5p. As Type **631** but inscr for the 50th anniv of signing of the Organization charter 3·25 1·60

632 Olive Branches, Menorah and Star of David

1998. 50th Anniv of State of Israel.

2039 **632** 10p. ultram, bl & mve 6·25 3·25

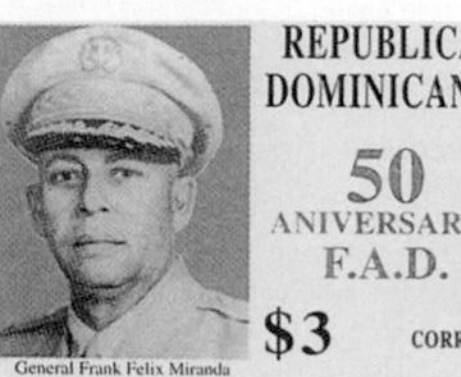

633 General Frank Felix Miranda

1998. 50th Anniv of Air Force (4th issue). Mult.

2040 3p. Type **633** 1·80 1·80
2041 3p. Curtiss-Wright CW 19R 1·80 1·80
2042 3p. Coronel Ernesto Tejeda (portrait at right) 1·80 1·80
2043 3p. As No. 2042, but portrait at left 1·80 1·80
2044 3p. As Type **633**, but portrait at right 1·80 1·80

634 Sundial

1998. 500th Anniv of Santo Domingo. Mult.

2045 2p. Type **634** 1·20 65
2046 3p. St. Lazarus's Church and Hospital (horiz) 1·90 95
2047 4p. First cathedral in the Americas (horiz) 2·50 1·30
2048 5p. Fortress (horiz) 3·25 1·50
2049 6p. Tower of Honour (horiz) 3·75 1·90
2050 10p. St. Nicholas of Bari's Church and Hospital 6·25 3·25

635 Theatre

1998. 25th Anniv of National Theatre.

2051 **635** 10p. multicoloured 6·25 3·00

636 Latin Inscription

1998. 44th Anniv of Latin Union.

2052 **636** 10p. gold, grey & black 6·25 3·00

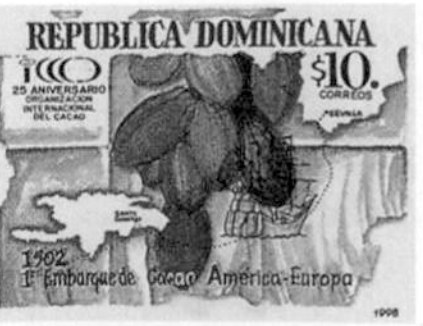

637 Cocoa Beans and Route Map of First American–Europe Shipment, 1502

1998. 25th Anniv of Int Cocoa Organization.

2053 **637** 10p. multicoloured 6·25 3·00

638 Nino Ferrua (stamp designer)

1998. Stamp Day.
2054 **638** 5p. multicoloured 3·25 1·50

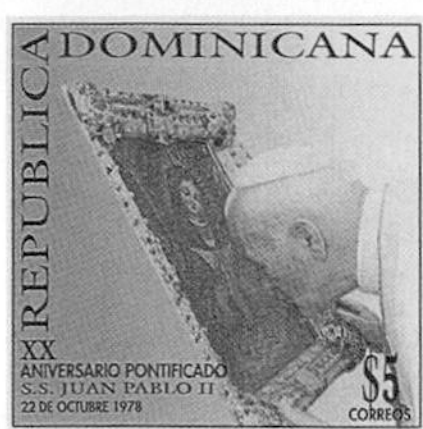

639 Pope John Paul II venerating Portrait of Virgin Mary

1998. 20th Anniv of Pontificate of Pope John Paul II. Multicoloured.
2055 5p. Type **639** 3·25 1·50
2056 10p. Pope John Paul II 6·25 2·10

640 Bay Rum

1998. Medicinal Plants. Multicoloured.
2057 3p. Type **640** 1·80 95
2058 3p. "Pimenta haitiensis" 1·80 95
2059 3p. "Cymbopogon citratus" 1·80 95
2060 3p. Seville orange ("Citrus aurantium") 1·80 95

641 Juana Saltitopa (Independence fighter)

1998. America. Famous Women. Multicoloured.
2061 2p. Type **641** 1·40 65
2062 6p. Anacaona (Indian chief) 3·75 2·00

642 Earth and Emblem

1998. International Year of the Ocean.
2063 **642** 5p. multicoloured 2·75 1·50

643 Statue of Columbus

1998. "Expofila 98" Stamp Exhibition, Santo Domingo. 500th Anniv of Santo Domingo.
2064 **643** 5p. multicoloured 2·75 1·50

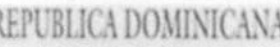

644 Fernando Valerio

1998. Military Heroes. Each brown and green.
2065 3p. Type **644** 1·40 1·30
2066 3p. Benito Moncion 1·40 1·30
2067 3p. Jose Maria Cabral 1·40 1·30
2068 3p. Antonio Duverge 1·40 1·30
2069 3p. Gregorio Luperon 1·40 1·30
2070 3p. Jose Salcedo 1·40 1·30
2071 3p. Fco. Salcedo 1·40 1·30
2072 3p. Gaspar Polanco 1·40 1·30
2073 3p. Santiago Rodriguez 1·40 1·30
2074 3p. Admiral Juan Cambiaso 1·40 1·30
2075 3p. Jose Puello 1·40 1·30
2076 3p. Jose Imbert 1·40 1·30
2077 3p. Admiral Juan Acosta 1·40 1·30
2078 3p. Marcos Adon 1·40 1·30
2079 3p. Matias Mella 1·40 1·30
2080 3p. Francisco Sanchez 1·40 1·30
2081 3p. Juan Pablo Duarte 1·40 1·30
2082 3p. Olegario Tenares 1·40 1·30
2083 3p. General Pedro Santana 1·40 1·30
2084 3p. Juan Sanchez Ramirez 1·40 1·30

645 Banknotes

1998. 150th Anniv of Paper Money.
2085 **645** 10p. multicoloured 4·75 2·10

646 Spit-roasting Pig

1998. Christmas. Multicoloured.
2086 2p. Type **646** 90 55
2087 5p. Three Wise Men on camels 2·20 1·10

647 Couple and Human Rights Emblem

1998. 50th Anniv of Universal Declaration of Human Rights.
2088 **647** 10p. multicoloured 4·50 2·10

648 Vega's Lyria

1998. Shells. Multicoloured.
2090 5p. Type **648** 2·10 1·30
2091 5p. Queen conch ("Strombus gigas") 2·10 1·30
2092 5p. West Indian top shell ("Cittarium pica") 2·10 1·30
2093 5p. Bleeding tooth ("Nerita peloronta") 2·10 1·30

649 Hernandez

1998. Birth Bicentenary of Gaspar Hernandez (priest and Independence fighter).
2094 **649** 3p. multicoloured 1·40 75

650 Earth

1999. 10th National Congress, First International Postgraduate Lectures and 25th Anniv of Dominican Society for Endocrinology and Nutrition.
2095 **650** 10p. multicoloured 4·00 2·10

652 Cigar and Tobacco Leaf

1999. Exports. Multicoloured.
2097 6p. Type **652** 2·40 1·10
2098 10p. Woman sewing (textiles) (vert) 4·00 2·10

653 Magnifying Glass over Map of Dominican Republic

1999. 155th Anniv of Office of Comptroller-General.
2099 **653** 2p. multicoloured 90 45

654 Bosch, "The Seagull" (poem) and Main Tower, Santo Domingo

1999. Contemporary Writers. 90th Birthday of Pres. Juan Bosch (poet). Multicoloured.
2100 2p. Type **654** 65 45
2101 10p. Portrait of Bosch (vert) 3·50 2·10

655 "Pseudophoenix ekmanii"

1999. Flowers and their Fruit. Multicoloured.
2102 5p. Type **655** 2·30 2·20
2103 5p. "Murtigia colabura" 2·30 2·20
2104 5p. "Pouteria dominguensis" 2·30 2·20
2105 5p. "Rubus dominguensis" 2·30 2·20

656 Gen. Juan Pablo Duarte (revolutionary)

1999
2106 **656** 3p. multicoloured 1·10 85

657 Baseball

1999. 13th Pan-American Games, Winnipeg, Canada. Multicoloured.
2107 5p. Type **657** 2·50 1·50
2108 6p. Weightlifting 2·75 1·80

658 Tomas Bobadilla y Briones

1999. Leaders of the Dominican Republic. Mult.
2109 3p. Type **658** 1·10 1·10
2110 3p. Pedro Santana (President, 1844–48, 1853–56 and 1859–61) 1·10 1·10
2111 3p. Manuel Jimenez (President, 1848–49) 1·10 1·10
2112 3p. Buenaventura Baez (President, 1849–53, 1856–58, 1865–66, 1868–74 and 1876–78) 1·10 1·10
2113 3p. Manuel de Regla Motta (President, June–October 1856) 1·10 1·10
2114 3p. Jose Desiderio Valverde (President, 1858–59) 1·10 1·10
2115 3p. Jose Antonio Salcedo 1·10 1·10
2116 3p. Gaspar Polanco 1·10 1·10

659 "St. Christopher"

1999. Jose Vela Zanetti (Spanish artist) Commemoration. Multicoloured.
2117 2p. Type **659** 65 45
2118 3p. "Bride and Groom" 1·10 80
2119 5p. "Burial of Christ" (horiz) 1·80 1·10
2120 6p. "Cock-fighting" 2·10 1·40
2121 10p. "Self-portrait" 3·50 2·10

660 "Strataegus quadrifoveatus"

1999. Insects. Multicoloured.
2122 5p. Type **660** 1·80 1·70
2123 5p. "Anetia jaegeri" (butterfly) 1·80 1·70
2124 5p. "Polyancistroydes tettigonidae" 1·80 1·70

2125 5p. Stick insect ("Phasmidae aploppus") 1·80 1·70

661 Emblem and Cross-section of Skin

1999. 50th Anniv of Dominican Dermatological Society.
2126 **661** 3p. multicoloured 1·10 80

662 Maternity Clinic, Santo Domingo

1999. 900th Anniv of Sovereign Military Order of Malta. Multicoloured.
2127 2p. Type **662** 85 55
2128 10p. Maltese Cross and anniversary emblem (36½×38 mm) 4·50 2·75

663 Children

1999. 50th Anniv of S.O.S. Children's Villages.
2129 **663** 10p. multicoloured 3·50 2·10

664 Man

1999. International Year of the Elderly.
2130 **664** 2p. black and blue 65 45
2131 - 5p. black and red 1·50 1·10
DESIGN: 5p. Woman.

665 Teacher and Students

1999. Teachers' Day.
2132 **665** 5p. multicoloured 1·50 1·10

666 Dove, Skull and Crossbones, Gun, Emblem and Mines

1999. America. A New Millennium without Arms. Multicoloured.
2133 2p. Type **666** 65 45
2134 6p. Atomic cloud and emblem 1·90 1·60

667 Luis F. Thomen (philatelist and author)

1999. Stamp Day.
2135 **667** 5p. drab, black and green 1·50 1·10

668 Globe and Forests

1999. New Millennium. Multicoloured.
2136 3p. Type **668** 90 55
2137 5p. Astronaut, satellite, computer and man 1·50 1·10

669 Map of Caribbean and Whale

1999. 2nd Summit of African, Caribbean and Pacific Heads of State. Multicoloured.
2138 5p. Type **669** 1·50 85
2139 6p. Moai Statues, Easter Island 1·90 1·60
2140 10p. Map of Africa and lion 3·50 2·10

670 Means of Communication

1999. 125th Anniv of Universal Postal Union. Multicoloured.
2141 6p. Type **670** 1·90 1·60
MS2142 50×75 mm. 10p. Airmail envelope on printed circuit. Imperf 3·50 3·50

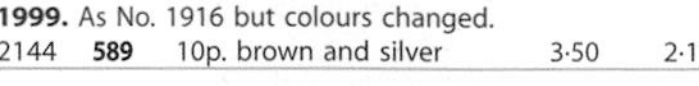

671 Globe and "50"

1999. 50th Anniv of Union of Latin American Universities.
2143 **671** 6p. multicoloured 1·90 1·60

1999. As No. 1916 but colours changed.
2144 **589** 10p. brown and silver 3·50 2·10

672 Juan Garcia (trumpeter)

1999. Classical Musicians.
2145 **672** 5p. blue and black 1·50 85
2146 - 5p. mauve and black 1·50 85
2147 - 5p. green and black 1·50 85
DESIGNS: No. 2146, Manuel Simo (saxophonist); 2147, Jose Ravelo (clarinettist).

673 Santiago and Cotui Banknotes

1999. Centenary of Banknotes. Multicoloured.
2148 2p. Type **673** 65 45
2149 2p. San Francisco de Macoris and La Vega banknotes 65 45
2150 2p. San Cristobal and Samana banknotes 65 45
2151 2p. Santo Domingo and San Pedro de Macoris banknotes (horiz) 65 45
2152 2p. Puerto Plata and Moca banknotes (horiz) 65 45
MS2153 145×125 mm. Nos. 2148/52. Imperf 3·50 3·50

674 Emblem

1999. 75th Anniv of Spanish Chamber of Trade and Industry.
2154 **674** 10p. multicoloured 3·50 2·40

675 Emblem

2000. 25th Anniv of Anti-Drugs Campaign.
2155 **675** 5p. multicoloured 1·80 1·10

676 Institute Facade

2000. Duartiano Institute.
2156 **676** 2p. multicoloured 65 45

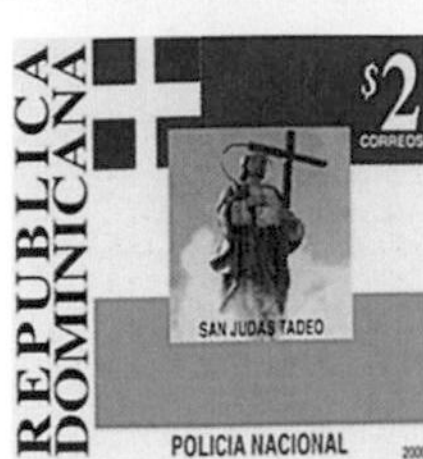

677 Child's Head and Emblem

2000. Prevention of Child Abuse Programme.
2157 **677** 2p. multicoloured 65 45

678 Flag and San Judas Tadeo (statue)

2000. National Police Force. Multicoloured.
2158 2p. Type **678** 65 45
2159 5p. Flag and Police emblem (37×28 mm) 1·80 1·10

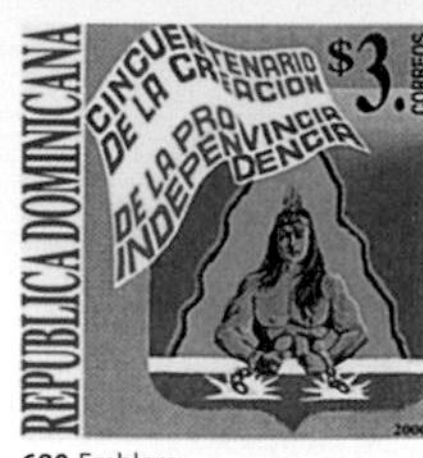

679 Institute Building and Emblem

2000. 25th Anniv of Industry and Technology Institute.
2160 **679** 2p. multicoloured 65 45

680 Emblem

2000. 50th Anniv of Independence.
2161 **680** 3p. multicoloured 1·10 80

681 Baseball Glove and Ball

2000. 12th National Youth Games, La Romana. Multicoloured.
2162 2p. Type **681** 65 45
2163 3p. Boxing gloves 1·10 80
2164 5p. Emblem and mascot (35×36 mm) 1·80 1·10

682 Violinist (Dario Suro)

2000. Art. Multicoloured.
2165 5p. Type **682** 1·80 1·10
2166 10p. Portrait of man (Theodore Chasseriau) 3·50 2·10

683 Building, Scales of Justice and Hand posting Ballot Paper

2000. Presidential Elections.
2167 **683** 2p. multicoloured 65 45

REPUBLICA DOMINICANA
$5
CORREOS
MUSICOS CLASICOS
ENRIQUE DE MARCHENA DUJARRIC (1908-1988)

684 Enrique de Marchena Dujarric (pianist)

2000. Classical Musicians. Each black, orange and brown.

2168	5p. Type **684**	1·80	1·10
2169	5p. Julio Alberto Hernandez Camejo (pianist)	1·80	1·10
2170	5p. Ramon Diaz (flautist)	1·80	1·10

685 Emblem

2000. "EXPO 2000" World's Fair, Hanover. Multicoloured.

2171	5p. Type **685**	1·80	1·10
2172	10p. Emblem	3·50	2·10

686 Santo Cristo de Los Milagros Church, Bayaguana

2000. Holy Year. Multicoloured.

2173	2p. Type **686**	65	45
2174	5p. Cathedral, Santo Domingo (vert)	1·80	1·10
2175	10p. Senora de la Altagracia Basilica, Higuey (vert)	4·50	2·75

2000. Columbus Lighthouse. As T **589**.

2176	10p. ochre, deep brown and silver	4·50	3·50

687 "Prince Arnau"

2000. 25th Death Anniv of Jaime Colson (artist). Multicoloured.

2186	2p. Type **687**	65	45
2187	3p. "Merengue" (dance)	90	55
2188	5p. "Guachupita Fiesta" (horiz)	1·50	85
2189	6p. "Castor and Pollux"	1·90	1·60
2190	10p. "Self-portrait"	3·50	2·10

688 Flags and Chinese Dragon

2000. 60th Anniv of Dominican Republic—China Diplomatic Relations. Multicoloured. Self-adhesive gum.

2191	5p. Type **688**	1·80	1·10
2192	10p. Flags and wooden artefact	4·50	2·75

689 Lizard on Leaf

2000. Environmental Protection. Multicoloured. Self-adhesive gum.

2193	2p. Type **689**	65	45
2194	3p. Trees and hut	90	55
2195	5p. Rapids	1·50	85

690 Sick Child

2000. America. AIDS Awareness Campaign. Multicoloured. Self-adhesive gum.

2196	2p. Type **690**	65	45
2197	6p. Sick child (38×38 mm)	1·90	1·60

691 Emblem and Rose

2000. 50th Anniv of United Nations High Commissioner for Refugees. Self-adhesive gum.

2198	**691**	10p. multicoloured	4·50	2·75

2001. Columbus Lighthouse. As T **589**.

2198a	15p. blue, azure and silver	5·50	4·75

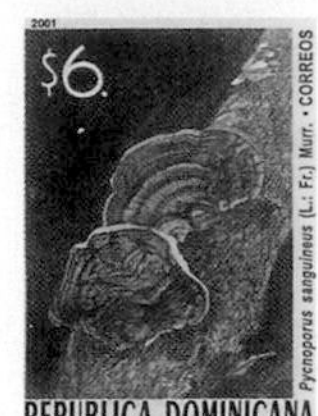

692 *Pycnoporus sanguineus*

2001. Fungi. Multicoloured.

2199	6p. Type **692**	2·30	1·60
2200	6p. *Morchella elata*	2·30	1·60
2201	6p. *Mycena epipterygia*	2·30	1·60
2202	6p. *Coriolopsis polyzona*	2·30	1·60

693 *Isidorea pungens*

2001. 25th Anniv of National Botanic Garden. Multicoloured.

2203	4p. Type **693**	1·40	95
2204	4p. *Pereskia quisqueyana*	1·40	95
2205	4p. *Goetzea ekmanii*	1·40	95
2206	4p. *Cubanola domingensis*	1·40	95

694 Jose Maria Cabral (president, 1866–68)

2001. Leaders of the Dominican Republic. Sheet 129×170 mm containing T 694 and similar vert. Multicoloured.

MS2207 6p.×8, Type **694**; Gregorio Luperon (president, 1879–80); Ignacio Gonzalez (president, 1874–76); Ulises Francisco Espaillet (president, 1876; 1887–99); Pedro Antonio Pimental (president, 1865); Federico de Garcia; Fernando de Merino (president, 1880–84); Ulises Heureaux (president, 1884–85) 11·00 8·50

No. **MS**2207 contains a central label showing the arms of the Dominican Republic.

695 San Felipe Fortress, Puerto Plata

2001. America. UNESCO World Heritage Sites. Each silver and black.

2208	4p. Type **695**	1·40	95
2209	15p. San Nicolás de Bari, Santo Domingo (39×39 mm)	5·75	3·25

696 Dominican Republic 1914 1c. Stamp

2001. Stamp Day.

2210	**696**	5p. multicoloured	1·80	1·10

697 Children encircling Globe

2001. United Nations International Year of Dialogue Among Civilizations.

2211	**697**	12p. multicoloured	3·75	1·90

698 Conception Bona

2001. Death Centenary of Conception Bona (political campaigner).

2212	**698**	10p. multicoloured	4·50	2·75

699 Josemaria Escriva de Balaguer

2002. Birth Centenary of Josemaría Escrivá de Balaguer (founder of Opus Dei (religious organization)).

2213	**699**	10p. multicoloured	3·50	2·10

2002. Columbus Lighthouse. As T **589**.

2213a	15p. multicoloured	3·25	2·75

700 Building and Emblem

2002. 50th Anniv of Polytechnic Institute, Loyola.

2214	**700**	6p. multicoloured	1·90	1·40

701 Flags of Participating Countries surrounding Globe

2002. 12th Spanish American Summit Conference.

2215	**701**	12p. multicoloured	3·75	1·90
2215a	**701**	15p. multicoloured	5·75	3·25

702 Adult and Child Hands Writing

2002. America. Education and Literacy Campaign. Multicoloured.

2216	4p. Type **702**	1·40	95
2217	15p. Child and blackboard	5·00	2·75

703 *Coccothrinax spissa* (palm)

2002

2218	**703**	10p. multicoloured	2·75	1·60

704 Emblem

2003. 14th Pan American Games, Santo Domingo.

2219	**704**	4p. multicoloured	1·10	55
2220	**704**	6p. multicoloured	2·20	95
2221	**704**	12p. multicoloured	3·75	1·90

705 *Hymenaea courbaril*

2003. Medicinal Plants. Trees. Multicoloured.

2222	5p. Type **705**	1·50	85
2223	5p. *Spandias mombin*	1·50	85
2224	5p. *Genipa Americana*	1·50	85
2225	5p. *Guazuma ulmifonia*	1·50	85

Nos. 2222/3 and 2224/5, respectively, were issued together, se-tenant, forming a composite design.

706 Jose Marti with Cuban and Dominican Republic Flags

2003. 150th Birth Anniv of Jose Marti (Cuban writer).

2226	**706**	15p. multicoloured	4·50	2·75

707 Pope John Paul II

2003. 25th Anniv of Pontificate of Pope John Paul II. Multicoloured.

2227 10p. Type **707** 3·25 1·30
2228 15p. Pope John Paul II addressing crowds (horiz) 5·00 2·10
MS2229 57×86 mm. As Nos. 2227/8. Imperf 8·25 7·50

708 Jose Francisco Pena Gomez

2003. 5th Death Anniv of Jose Francisco Pena Gomez (politician).

2230 **708** 10p. multicoloured 3·25 1·30

709 *Aristelliger* (inscr "Aristelliger lar")

2004. America. Flora and Fauna. Multicoloured.

2231 5p. Type **709** 1·50 85
2232 15p. *Copernicia berteroana* (vert) 4·50 2·10

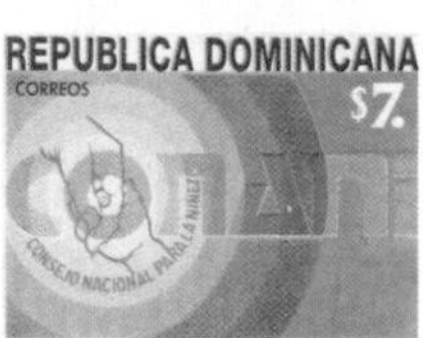

710 Emblem

2004. National Council for Children (CONANI).

2233 **710** 7p. multicoloured 2·40 1·10

711 Flag as Stamp

2004. Exfilna 2004 Stamp Exhibition, Valladolid.

2234 **711** 7p. multicoloured 2·40 1·10

712 Shack

2004. America. Struggle against Poverty. Multicoloured.

2235 10p. Type **712** 3·25 1·90
2236 20p. Girl collecting water 6·50 3·75

713 Flags

2004. 50th Anniv of Dominican Republic—Canada Diplomatic Relations.

2237 **713** 20p. multicoloured 6·50 3·75

714 Flag as Island

2005. Interexpo 05 International Stamp Exhibition, Santo Domingo.

2238 **714** 20p. multicoloured 6·50 3·75

715 Dove carrying Stamp

2005. 50th Anniv of Dominican Philatelic Society. Multicoloured.

2239 7p. Type **715** 2·40 1·10
MS2240 100×69 mm. 10p. As No. 2239. Imperf 2·40 1·10

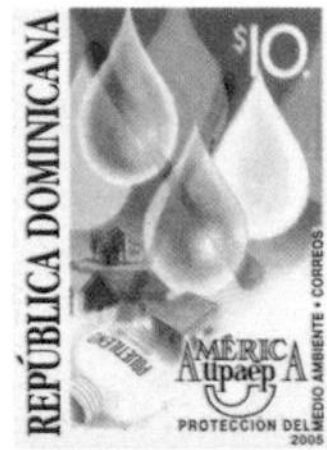

716 Water Droplets

2005. America. Environmental Protection. Multicoloured.

2241 10p. Type **716** 3·25 1·90
2242 20p. Factory 6·50 3·75

717 Juan Ferrua (stamp printer)

2005. Stamp Day.

2243 **717** 10p. multicoloured 3·25 1·90

718 Arms

2005. Twinned Towns–Santa Domingo, Dominican Republic and La Guardia, Spain.

2244 **718** 10p. multicoloured 3·25 1·90

719 Order of Malta, Mother and Baby Clinic

2005

2245 **719** 15p. multicoloured 5·00 2·75

720 Joaquin Balaguer

2006. Joaquin Balaguer Estadista (president 1960–62, 1966–78 and 1986–96) Commemoration. Multicoloured.

2246 7p. Type **720** 2·40 1·10
2247 10p. Holding book 3·25 1·90

721 Art Museum Building

2006. 50th Anniv of Art Museum.

2248 **721** 7p. multicoloured 2·40 1·10

722 Building

2006. 70th Anniv of History Academy.

2249 **722** 10p. multicoloured 3·25 1·90

723 Globe and Gloves

2006. International Boxing Congress, Santo Domingo.

2250 **723** 20p. multicoloured 6·50 3·75

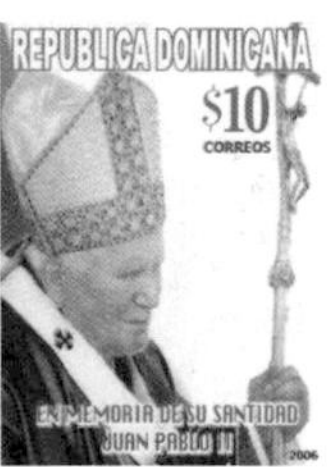

724 Pope John Paul II

2006. Pope John Paul II Commemoration. Multicoloured.

2251 10p. Type **724** 3·25 1·90
2252 20p. With dove (horiz) 6·50 3·75

724a '100'

2006. Centenary of South American Health Organization.

2252a **724a** 20p. multicoloured 6·50 3·75

725 Building Facade

2006. 50th Anniv of Blessing of National Sanctuary of the Sacred Heart of Jesus.

2253 **725** 10p. multicoloured 3·25 1·90

725a *Podilymbus podiceps* (pied billed grebe)

2006

2253a **725a** 20p. multicoloured 6·50 3·75

726 *Gaultheria domingensis*

2007. Latin-American Botanic Conference.

2254 **726** 20p. multicoloured 6·50 3·75

727 Emblem and Tree

2007. Technological Communications Centre. Multicoloured.

2255 10p. Type **727** 3·25 1·90
2256 25p. Emblem and keyboard 8·00 4·50

728 Cardinal Lopez Rodriguez

2007. 25th Anniv of Cardinal Nicolas de Jesus Lopez Rodriguez as Metropolitan Archbishop of Santo Domingo. Multicoloured.

2257 10p. Type **728** 3·25 1·90
2258 15p. With Pope John Paul II 5·00 2·75
2259 25p. Wearing mitre 8·00 4·50

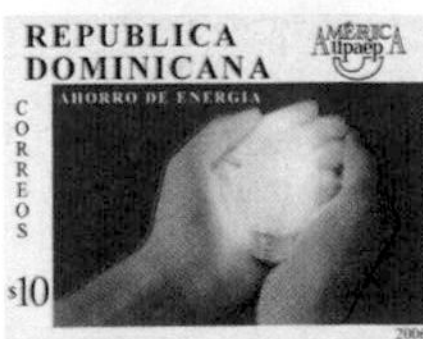

729 Hands enclosing Light-bulb

2007. America. Energy Conservation. Multicoloured.

2260 10p. Type **729** 3·25 1·90
2261 20p. Power lines 6·50 3·75

730 High Jump

2007. Pan American Games, Rio de Janeiro. Multicoloured.

2262 15p. Type **730** 5·00 2·75
2263 20p. Female weightlifter 6·50 3·75

731 Flags

2007. 150th Anniv of Dominican Republic—Netherlands Friendship Treaty.

2264	**731**	25p. multicoloured	9·50	7·00

732 Arms

2007. Centenary of Barahona Province.

2265	**732**	10p. multicoloured	3·75	2·75

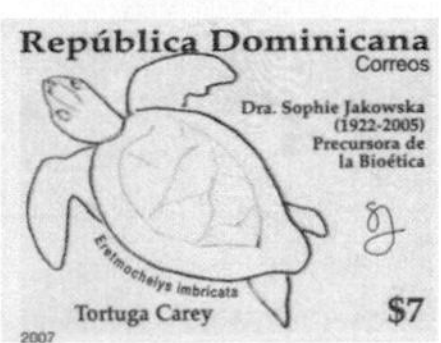
733 *Eretmochelys imbricata* (hawksbill turtle)

2007. 85th Birth Anniv of Sophie Jakowska (Professor of Biology, writer and ecologist). Designs showing illustrations from Los cocodrilos de enrinquillo and Hijos de la Tierra (children's books) (2266/8 and 2270). Multicoloured.

2266	7p. Type **733**	2·60	2·00
2267	7p. *Trichechus manatus* (manati)	2·75	2·75
2268	10p. *Amazona ventralis* (Hispaniolan parrot)	3·75	2·75
2269	10p. Sophie Jakowska	3·75	2·75
2270	15p. *Crocodylus acutus* (American crocodile) (horiz)	5·75	4·25

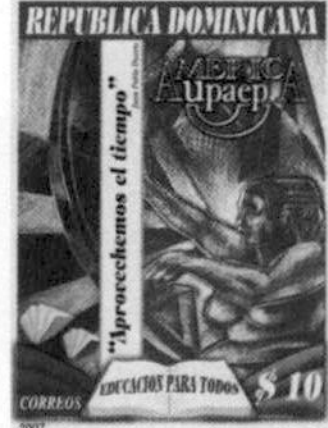
734 Woman, Books and 'Seize the time'

2007. America. Education for All.

2271	**734**	10p. multicoloured	3·75	2·75
2272	**734**	20p. multicoloured	7·50	3·50

735 Building Facade

2007. 50th Anniv of Vice-Regal Palace Museum.

2273	**735**	10p. multicoloured	3·75	2·75

736 *Prunus mume* (ume) and *Swietenia mahagoni* (West Indian mahogany) (inscr 'Swietenia mahaggoni')

2007. Friendship and Cooperation between Dominican Republic and Republic of China. Multicoloured.

2274	10p. Type **736**	3·75	2·75
2275	15p. *Urocissa caerulea* (blue magpie) and *Dulus dominicus* (palm chat)	5·75	4·25
2276	35p. Buildings	13·00	9·75

737 Enrique Alfau

2007. Stamp Day. 110th Birth Anniv of Enrique J. Alfau.

2277	**737**	15p. multicoloured	5·75	4·25

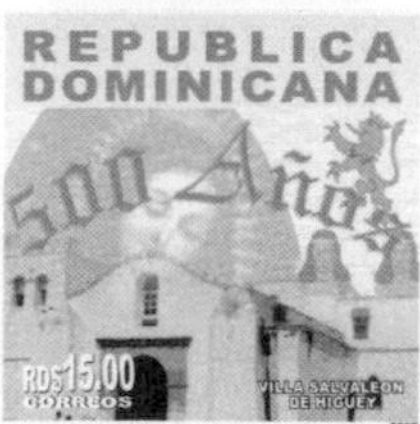
738 Madonna and Iglesia de San Dionisio

2007. 500th Anniv of Salvaleon de Higuey.

2278	**738**	15p. multicoloured	5·75	4·25

739 Juana de la Merced Trinidad

2008. Women for Independence. Multicoloured.

2279	10p. Type **739**	3·75	2·75
2280	10p. Joaquina Filomena Gomez de la Cova	3·75	2·75
2281	10p. Maria Baltasara de los Reyes	3·75	2·75
2282	10p. Rosa Protomartir Duarte y Diez	3·75	2·75
2283	10p. Manuela Diez y Jimenez	3·75	2·75
2284	10p. Petronella Abreu y Delgado	3·75	2·75
2285	10p. Micaela de Rivera de Santana	3·75	2·75
2286	10p. Frollana Febles de Santana	3·75	2·75
2287	10p. Rosa Montas de Duverge	3·75	2·75
2288	10p. Josefa Antonie Perez de la Paz	3·75	2·75
2289	10p. Ana Valverde	3·75	2·75
2290	10p. Maria de la Concepcion Bona y Hernandez	3·75	2·75
2291	10p. Maria de Jesus Pena y Benitez	3·75	2·75
2292	10p. Maria Trinidad Sanchez y Ramona	3·75	2·75

740 Emblem

2008. Emigrants.

2293	**740**	15p. multicoloured	5·75	4·25

741 Scout Badge

2008. Centenary (2007) of Scouting. Multicoloured.

2294	10p. Type **741**	3·75	2·75
2295	15p. Scouts enclosed in rope	5·75	4·25

742 Table Tennis

2008. Olympic Games, Beijing. Multicoloured.

2296	10p. Type **742**	3·75	2·75
2297	10p. Judo	3·75	2·75
2298	10p. Taekwondo	3·75	2·75
2299	10p. Boxing	3·75	2·75

743 Luis Amiama Veloz

2008. Stamp Day. 20th Death Anniv of Luis Amiama Veloz (philatelic writer).

2300	**743**	20p. sepia	7·50	5·75

744 Emblem

2008. 150th Anniv of Freemasonry in Dominican Republic.

2301	**744**	25p. multicoloured	9·50	7·00

745 Children

2008. Stop Child Exploitation Campaign.

2302	**745**	10p. multicoloured	3·75	2·75

746 Emblem

2008. Centenary of International Swimming Federation.

2303	**746**	15p. multicoloured	5·75	4·25

747 Timoteo Orgando

2008. Death Centenary of Timoteo Ogando (nationalist general).

2304	**747**	10p. multicoloured	3·75	2·75

748 Arms

2008. 500th Anniv of Arms of Santiago.

2305	**748**	10p. multicoloured	3·75	2·75

749 Christopher Columbus and *Santa Maria*

2008. Discovery of Quisqueya Island (1492).

2306	**749**	10p. multicoloured	3·75	2·75

750 Freedom Fighters (Trabucazo de la Independencia)

2008. America. Festivals. Multicoloured.

2307	15p. Type **750**	3·75	4·25
2308	25p. Horseman (statue) (Espada de la Retauracion)	9·50	7·00

751 Juan Jose Duatre and Manuela Diez

2009. Duatre Diaz Family. Multicoloured.

2309	10p. Type **751**	3·75	2·75
2310	10p. Vincente and Juan Pablo Duarte Diez	3·75	2·75
2311	10p. Rosa and Manuel	3·75	2·75
2312	10p. Francisca and Filomena	3·75	2·75

Nos. 2309/12 were printed, se-tenant, forming a composite design.

752 Plaza de Confucio (Confucius Plaza)

2009. China Town in Santo Domingo. Multicoloured.

2313	15p. Type **752**	5·75	4·75
2314	20p. Gateway	7·50	5·75

753 '75' and Emblem

2009. 75th Anniv of La Salle School. Multicoloured.

2315	7p. Type **753**	2·60	2·00
2316	10p. Juan Bautista De La Salle (founder) (vert)	3·75	2·75

754 Fighters landing at Constanza

2009. 50th Anniv of Failed Expedition to remove Rafael Trujillo's Dictatorship.

2317	**754**	10p. multicoloured	3·75	2·75

755 Juan Bosch

2009. Birth Centenary of Juan Emilio Bosch Gavino (Juan Bosch) (politician, historian, writer and first freely elected president).

2318	**755**	20p. multicoloured	7·50	3·50

756 *Epilobocera haytensis*

2009. Crabs. Multicoloured.

2319	10p. Type **756**	3·75	2·75
2320	10p. *Gecarcinus ruricola*	3·75	2·75
2321	10p. *Coenobita clypeatus*	3·75	2·75
2322	10p. *Callinectes sapidus*	3·75	2·75

757 Dancers

2009. Christmas. Children's Drawings. Multicoloured.

2323	10p. Type **757**	3·75	2·75
2324	10p. Procession	3·75	2·75
2325	10p. The Nativity	3·75	2·75
2326	10p. Dancers, fire and decorated tree	3·75	2·75

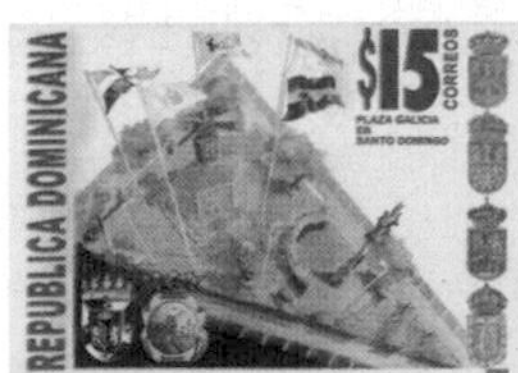

758 Plaza Galicia , Santo Domingo

2009. Plazas. Multicoloured.

2327	15p. Type **758**	5·75	4·25
2328	25p. Plaza Santo Domingo, La Guardia Galicia	8·00	4·50

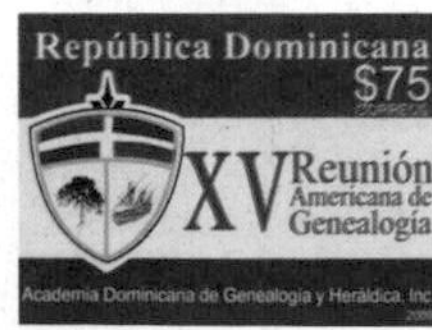

759 Emblem

2009. 15th American Genealogy Reunion.

2329	**759**	75p. multicoloured	23·00	12·00

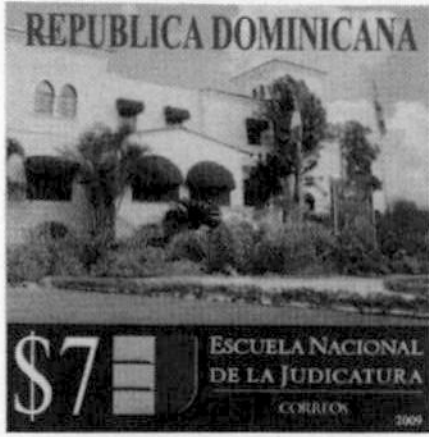

760 Building Facade

2009. National Judiciary School.

2330	**760**	7p. multicoloured	2·60	2·00

761 Fu-Fu

2009. America. Games. Multicoloured.

2331	10p. Type **761**	3·75	2·75
2332	15p. Trucamelo (horiz)	5·75	4·25
MS2333	76×50 mm. 20p. El Panuelo. Imperf	6·50	3·75

762 Benigno Filomeno de Rojas

2009. Presidents of Dominican Republic. Multicoloured.

2334	7p. Type **762**	2·60	2·00
2335	7p. Jacinto B. de Castro	2·60	2·00
2336	7p. Mactos Cabral	2·60	2·00
2337	7p. General Cesareo Guillermo	2·60	2·00
2338	7p. Francisco G. Billini	2·60	2·00
2339	7p. Alejandro Woss y Gil	2·60	2·00
2340	7p. Carlos Felipe Morales Languasco	2·60	2·00
2341	7p. Ramon Caceres	2·60	2·00

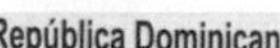

763 Arms

2010. Arms of Dominican Republic

2342	**763**	50p. multicoloured	2·40	2·00

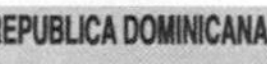

764 Flags of Participants as Globe

2010. 16th Ibero-American Notarial Meeting, Punta Cana

2343	**764**	26p. multicoloured	1·10	70

765 Globe on Ice Cap

2010. Polar Protection Awareness Campaign

2344	**765**	20p. multicoloured	90	60

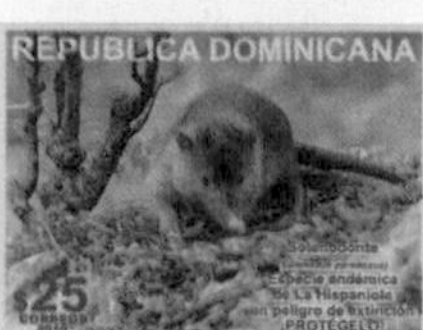

766 Hispaniolan Solenodon

2010. Biodiversity Awareness Campaign

2345	**766**	25p. multicoloured	1·10	70

767 Emblem

2010. 25th Anniv of Philatelic and Numismatic Museum

2346	**767**	33p. black and yellow	1·30	90

768 Juan Pablo Duarte y Díez and his Birthplace

2010. Juan Pablo Duarte y Díez (one of founding fathers of Dominican Republic) Commemoration

2347	**768**	25p. multicoloured	1·10	70

Nos. 2348/9 are vacant.

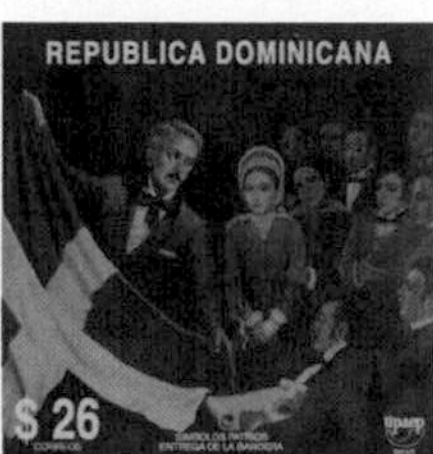

769 Inauguration of National Flag

2010. America. Patriotic Symbols

2350	26p. Type **769**	1·00	70
2351	33p. National pantheon (29×39 mm)	1·30	90

No. 2352, Type **770** are left for Stamp Day, issued on 19 October 2010, not yet received.

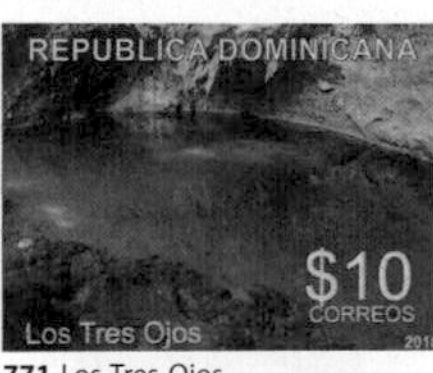

771 Los Tres Ojos

2010. Tourism. Multicoloured.

2353	10p. Type **771**	80	50
2354	10p. Juan Dolio Beach	80	50
2355	10p. Altos de Chavon	80	50
2356	10p. Bayahibe Beach	80	50
2357	10p. Bavaro Beach	80	50
2358	10p. Levantado Key	80	50
2359	10p. Las Terrenas Beach	80	50
2360	10p. Cabarete Beach	80	50
2361	10p. White water rafting, Jarabacoa	80	50
2362	10p. Enriquillo Lake	80	50

772 Lodge Façade

2010. Centenary of Worshipful Lodge Veritas 11

2363	**772**	60p. multicoloured	1·40	90

773 Building Façade

2010. 500th Anniv of Dominican Order in America. Multicoloured.

2364	15p. Type **773**	90	60
2365	26p. Friar and child	1·10	70

EXPRESS DELIVERY STAMPS

E40 Biplane

1920

E232	**E40**	10c. blue	6·75	1·40

E42

1925. Inscr "ENTREGA ESPECIAL".

E247	**E42**	10c. blue	21·00	5·75

1927. Inscr "EXPRESO".

E250	10c. brown	6·75	1·40
E459	10c. green	3·50	4·25

E123

1945

E539	**E123**	10c. blue, red & carm	1·20	20

E137 Shield, Hand and Letter

1950

E594	**E137**	10c. red, grn & blue	60	20

E161

1956

E663	**E161**	25c. green	1·10	30

E228 Pigeon and Letter

1967

E995	**E228**	25c. blue	70	30

E345 Globe, and Pigeon carrying Letter

1978

E1330	**E345**	25c. multicoloured	1·10	45

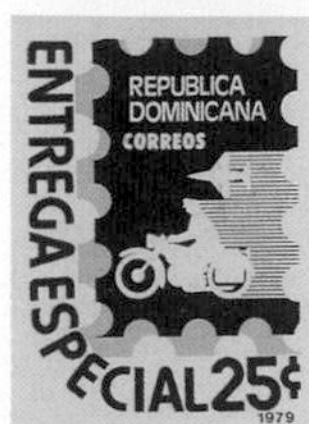
E370 Motorcycle Messenger and Airplane

1979

E1385	**E370**	25c. ultram, bl & red	65	45

E514 Motor Cyclist

1989. Special Delivery.

E1731	**E514**	1p. multicoloured	2·10	95

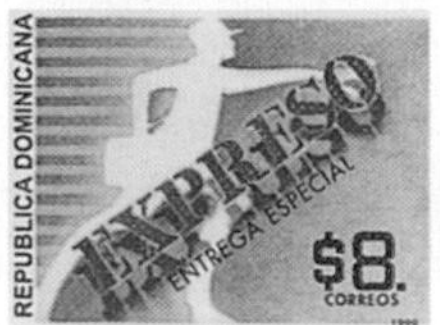
E651 Postman

1999

E2096	**E651**	8p. multicoloured	3·25	1·60

OFFICIAL STAMPS

O23 Bastion of 27 Febuary

1902

O121	**O23**	2c. black and red	65	45
O122	**O23**	5c. black and blue	85	35
O123	**O23**	10c. black and green	1·00	55
O124	**O23**	20c. black and yellow	1·30	55

1910. As Type O 23, but inscr "27 DE FEBRERO 1844" and "10 DE AGOSTO 1865" at sides.

O177	1c. black and green	40	20
O178	2c. black and red	50	20
O179	5c. black and blue	1·00	40
O180	10c. black and green	1·60	95
O181	20c. black and yellow	2·75	2·30

O44 Columbus Lighthouse

1928

O251	**O44**	1c. green	20	20
O252	**O44**	2c. red	20	20
O253	**O44**	5c. blue	30	30
O254	**O44**	10c. blue	40	40
O255	**O44**	20c. yellow	60	60

1931. Air. Optd CORREO AEREO.

O292	10c. blue	16·00	17·00
O293	20c. yellow	16·00	17·00

O82 Columbus Lighthouse

1937. White letters and figures.

O393	**O82**	3c. violet	1·10	20
O394	**O82**	7c. blue	1·20	40
O395	**O82**	10c. yellow	1·30	60

O88 Columbus Lighthouse

1939. Coloured letters and figures.

O409	**O88**	1c. green	50	20
O410	**O88**	2c. red	50	20
O411	**O88**	3c. violet	50	20
O412	**O88**	5c. blue	85	40
O414	**O88**	7c. blue	1·40	20
O415	**O88**	10c. orange	1·40	50
O416	**O88**	20c. brown	4·25	70
O417	**O88**	50c. red	5·00	2·10
O577	**O88**	50c. mauve	8·75	1·70

No. O417 has smaller figures of value than No. O577.

1950. Values inscr "CENTAVOS ORO".

O578	5c. blue	85	20
O581	7c. blue	85	85
O579	10c. yellow	95	40
O582	20c. brown	1·90	1·90
O583	50c. purple	4·75	4·75

POSTAGE DUE STAMPS

D22

1901

D117	**D22**	2c. sepia	90	25
D118	**D22**	4c. sepia	1·10	25
D119	**D22**	5c. sepia	1·90	45
D175	**D22**	6c. sepia	2·75	1·10
D120	**D22**	10c. sepia	3·25	95

1913

D239	1c. olive	70	70
D191	2c. olive	60	30
D192	4c. olive	70	40
D193	6c. olive	1·10	50
D194	10c. olive	1·20	60

D110

1942. Size 20½×25½ mm.

D485	**D110**	1c. red	30	10
D486	**D110**	2c. blue	30	10
D487	**D110**	2c. blue	85	1·20
D488	**D110**	4c. green	30	30
D489	**D110**	6c. brown and buff	40	30
D490	**D110**	8c. orange & yellow	40	40
D491	**D110**	10c. mauve and pink	50	50

1966. Size 21×25½ mm. Inscr larger and in white.

D492	1c. red	85	1·90
D493	2c. blue	85	1·90
D494	4c. green	2·40	2·40

REGISTRATION STAMPS

1935. De Merino stamps of 1933 surch PRIMA VALORES DECLARADOS SERVICIO INTERIOR and value in figures and words.

R339	-	8c. on ½c. (No. 316)	2·75	2·75
R340	-	8c. on 7c. blue	60	20
R342	**56**	15c. on 10c. orange	60	20
R343	-	30c. on 8c. green	2·30	85
R344	-	45c. on 20c. red	3·25	1·10
R345	**57**	70c. on 50c. olive	7·75	1·70

R97 National Coat of Arms

1940

R448	**R97**	8c. black and red	85	30
R449	**R97**	15c. black & orange	1·80	20
R450	**R97**	30c. black and green	2·10	20
R451	**R97**	70c. black & purple	7·25	1·80

R98 National Coat of Arms

1944. Redrawn. Larger figures of value and "c" as in Type R 98.

R452	**R98**	45c. black and blue	2·30	40
R453	**R98**	70c. black and green	2·10	40

1953

R454	8c. black and red	3·25	70
R455	10c. black and red	1·80	30
R456	15c. black & orange	2·10	1·00

R155

1955. Redrawn. Arms and "c" smaller.

R646	**R155**	10c. black and red	40	20
R647	**R155**	10c. black and lilac	1·00	40
R648	**R155**	15c. black & orange	5·25	2·30
R649	**R155**	20c. black & orange	1·20	30
R650	**R155**	20c. black and red	2·50	1·00
R651	**R155**	30c. black and green	2·00	40
R652a	**R155**	40c. black and green	2·10	60
R653	**R155**	45c. black and blue	3·00	2·10
R654	**R155**	60c. black & yellow	2·10	2·10
R655	**R155**	70c. black & brown	6·75	2·30

1963. Redrawn as Type R 97.

R909	10c. black and orange	75	40
R910	20c. black and orange	1·20	50

R221

1965

R961	**R221**	10c. black & lilac	50	20
R962	**R221**	40c. black & yellow	1·90	1·30

R282a

1973

R1335	**R282a**	10c. black & violet	45	20
R1148	**R282a**	20c. black & orge	95	75
R1149	**R282a**	40c. black & green	1·20	55
R1150	**R282a**	70c. black and blue	1·90	1·60

R487

1986. Redrawn with figures of value and "c" smaller. Inscribed "PRIMA DE VALORES DECLARADOS". Arms in black.

R1664	**R487**	20c. mauve	35	10
R1665	**R487**	60c. orange	1·20	85
R1666	**R487**	1p. blue	2·10	1·40
R1667	**R487**	1p.25 pink	2·75	1·80
R1668	**R487**	1p.50 red	3·25	2·50
R1669	**R487**	3p. green	6·25	4·25
R1670	**R487**	3p.50 bistre	7·00	4·50
R1671	**R487**	4p. yellow	8·75	5·50
R1672	**R487**	4p.50 green	9·75	6·25
R1673	**R487**	5p. brown	10·50	7·00
R1674	**R487**	6p. grey	12·50	8·50
R1675	**R487**	6p.50 blue	14·50	9·50

R515

1989. Inscr "PRIMA VALORES DECLARADOS". Arms in black.

R1732	**R515**	20c. purple	35	10
R1733	**R515**	60c. orange	1·00	60

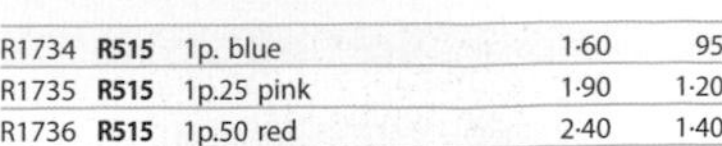

R1734	**R515**	1p. blue	1·60	95
R1735	**R515**	1p.25 pink	1·90	1·20
R1736	**R515**	1p.50 red	2·40	1·40

R569

R570

1994. Arms in black.

R1867	**R569**	50c. mauve	20	10
R1868	**R570**	1p. blue	35	20
R1869	**R570**	1p.50 red	45	30
R1870	**R570**	2p. pink	65	55
R1871	**R570**	3p. blue	90	65
R1872	**R570**	5p. yellow	1·30	95
R1873	**R570**	6p. green	1·80	1·30
R1874	**R570**	8p. green	2·00	1·50
R1875	**R570**	10p. silver	2·75	2·00

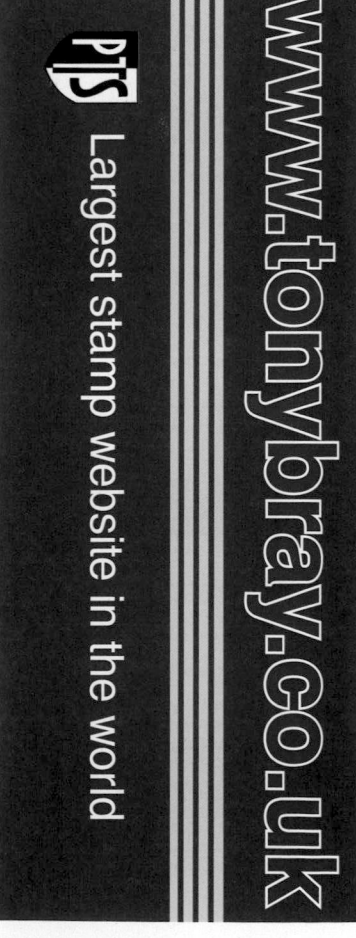

Pt. 19

DUBAI

One of the Trucial States in the Persian Gulf. Formerly used the stamps of Muscat. British control of the postal services ceased in 1963.

On 2 December 1971, Dubai and six other Gulf Sheikhdoms formed the State of the United Arab Emirates. U.A.E. issues commenced in 1973.

1963. 100 naye paise = 1 rupee.
1966. 100 dirhams = 1 riyal.

IMPERF STAMPS. Some of the following issues exist imperf from limited printings.

1 Hermit Crab

2 Shaikh Rashid bin Said

1963

No.	Type	Description	Unused	Used
1	1	1n.p. red & blue (postage)	20	20
2	A	2n.p. brown and blue	20	20
3	B	3n.p. sepia and green	20	20
4	C	4n.p. orange and purple	20	20
5	D	5n.p. black and violet	30	20
6	E	10n.p. black and brown	30	30
7	1	15n.p. red and drab	40	30
8	A	20n.p. orange and red	60	40
18	J	20n.p. blue & brown (air)	2·10	30
9	B	25n.p. brown and green	60	40
19	K	25n.p. purple and yellow	2·30	40
10	C	30n.p. red and grey	60	50
20	J	30n.p. black and red	2·75	50
11	D	35n.p. deep blue and lilac	80	50
21	K	40n.p. purple and brown	3·00	60
12	E	50n.p. sepia and orange	1·30	70
22	J	50n.p. red and green	3·50	70
23	K	60n.p. black and brown	4·00	70
24	J	75n.p. green and violet	6·25	80
13	F	1r. salmon and blue	2·75	1·20
25	K	1r. brown and yellow	7·75	1·00
14	G	2r. brown and bistre	6·25	2·75
15	H	3r. black and red	12·50	6·25
16	1	5r. brown and turquoise	21·00	10·50
17	2	10r. black, turq & purple	46·00	21·00

DESIGNS (Postage)—HORIZ: A, Common cuttlefish; B, Edible snail; C, Crab; D, Turban sea urchin; E, Radish murex; F, Mosque; G, Buildings; H, Ancient wall and tower; I, Dubai view. (Air)—HORIZ: J, Peregrine falcon in flight over bridge. VERT: K, Peregrine falcon.

3 Dhows

1963. Centenary of Red Cross.

No.	Type	Description	Unused	Used
26	3	1n.p. bl, yell & red (postage)	80	40
27	-	2n.p. brown, yellow & red	80	40
28	-	3n.p. brown, orange & red	80	40
29	-	4n.p. brown, red & green	80	40
30	3	20n.p. brn, yell & red (air)	2·10	80
31	-	30n.p. blue, orange & red	2·10	80
32	-	40n.p. black, yellow & red	3·00	90
33	-	50n.p. violet, red & turq	5·25	1·70
MS33b		Four sheets, each 119×99 mm. Block of four of each of Nos. 30/33 in new colour	60·00	60·00

DESIGNS: 2, 30n.p. First aid field post; 3, 40n.p. Camel train; 4, 50n.p. March moth.

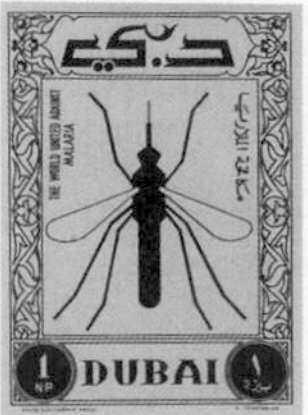

4 Mosquito

1963. Malaria Eradication.

No.	Type	Description	Unused	Used
34	4	1n.p. brown & red (postage)	25	25
35	4	1n.p. brown and green	25	25
36	4	1n.p. red and blue	25	25
37	-	2n.p. blue and red	25	25
38	-	2n.p. red and brown	25	25
39	-	3n.p. blue and brown	25	25
40	4	30n.p. green & purple (air)	40	30
41	-	40n.p. grey and red	60	40
42	-	70n.p. yellow and purple	1·20	80
MS42a		Three sheets, each 100×120 mm. Block of four of each of Nos. 40/42 in new colours. Imperf	25·00	25·00

DESIGNS: 2, 40n.p. Mosquito and snake emblem; 3, 70n.p. Mosquitoes and swamp.

5 Ears of Wheat

1963. Air. Freedom from Hunger.

No.	Type	Description	Unused	Used
43	5	30n.p. brown and violet	50	20
44	-	40n.p. olive and red	80	30
45	-	70n.p. orange and green	1·60	1·50
46	-	1r. blue and brown	2·30	1·50
MS46a		Four sheets, each 100×120 mm. Block of four of each of Nos. 43/6 in new colours surch 5n.p. on 30n.p., 10n.p. on 40n.p., 15n.p. on 70n.p., 20n.p. on 1r. Imperf	41·00	35·00

DESIGNS: 40n.p. Palm and campaign emblem; 70n.p. Emblem within hands; 1r. Woman bearing basket of fruit.

6 U.S. Seal and Pres. Kennedy

1964. Air. Pres. Kennedy Memorial Issue.

No.	Type	Description	Unused	Used
47	6	75n.p. black & green on grn	1·20	70
48	6	1r. black & brown on buff	1·80	80
49	6	1¼r. black & red on grey	2·30	1·10
MS49a		100×60 mm. No. 49 in black and brown. Imperf	9·25	9·25

7 Scout Gymnastics

1964. World Scout Jamboree, Marathon (1963).

No.	Type	Description	Unused	Used
50	7	1n.p. bistre & brown (postage)	20	20
51	-	2n.p. brown and red	20	20
52	-	3n.p. brown and blue	20	20
53	-	4n.p. blue and mauve	20	20
54	-	5n.p. turquoise and blue	40	20
55	7	20n.p. brown & green (air)	50	30
56	-	30n.p. brown and violet	70	40
57	-	40n.p. green and blue	1·00	50
58	-	70n.p. grey and green	1·30	80
59	-	1r. red and blue	2·50	1·30
MS59a		Five sheets each 100×120 mm. Block of four of each of Nos. 55/9 in new colours. Imperf	36·00	36·00

DESIGNS: 2, 30n.p. Bugler; 3, 40n.p. Wolf cubs; 4, 70n.p. Scouts on parade; 5n.p., 1r. Scouts with standard.

1964. Nos. 27/8 surch.

No.	Description	Unused	Used
59b	20n.p. on 2n.p. brown, yellow and red	60·00	
59c	30n.p. on 3n.p. brown, orange and red	60·00	

8 Spacecraft

1964. Air. "Honouring Astronauts". Multicoloured.

No.	Description	Unused	Used
60	1n.p. "Atlas" rocket (vert)	30	30
61	2n.p. "Mercury" capsule (vert)	30	30
62	3n.p. Type **8**	30	30
63	4n.p. Two spacecraft	30	30
64	5n.p. As No. 60	30	30
65	1r. As No. 61	1·30	1·30
66	1½r. Type **8**	2·50	2·50
67	2r. As No. 63	3·00	3·00
MS67a	90×65 mm. No. 67. Imperf	7·75	7·75

9 Globe, New York and Dubai Harbours

1964. New York World's Fair.

No.	Type	Description	Unused	Used
68	9	1n.p. red & blue (postage)	20	20
69	-	2n.p. blue, red and mauve	20	20
70	9	3n.p. green and brown	20	20
71	-	4n.p. red, green & turquoise	20	20
72	9	5n.p. violet, olive & green	20	20
73	-	10n.p. black, brown & red	90	70
74	-	75n.p. black, grn & bl (air)	90	50
75	-	2r. ochre, turquoise & brn	1·50	1·10
76	-	3r. orange, turquoise & green	2·30	1·50
MS76a		110×90 mm. Nos. 75/6 in new colours. Imperf	11·50	10·50

DESIGNS: 2, 4, 10n.p. New York skyline and Dubai hotel; 75n.p., 2, 3r. Statue of Liberty, New York, and "Rigorous" (tug), Dubai.

10 Flame of Freedom and Scales of Justice

1964. Air. 15th Anniv of Human Rights Declaration. Flame in red.

No.	Type	Description	Unused	Used
77	10	35n.p. brown and blue	50	20
78	10	50n.p. green and blue	80	50
79	10	1r. black and turquoise	1·70	80
80	10	3r. ultramarine and blue	4·50	2·30
MS80a		100×60 mm. No. 80 in green and ultramarine. Imperf	8·75	8·75

11 Shaikh Rashid bin Said and View of Dubai

1964

No.	Type	Description	Unused	Used
81	11	10n.p. olive, red & brown (postage)	40	20
82	A	20n.p. brown, red & green	50	20
83	11	30n.p. black, red & blue	60	30
84	A	40n.p. blue, red & cerise	80	40
85	B	1r. olive, red & brn (air)	1·70	80
86	C	2r. brown, red & green	4·00	1·70
87	B	3r. black, red and blue	6·25	3·00
88	C	5r. blue, red and cerise	11·50	5·75

SCENES: A, Waterfront; B, Waterside buildings; C, Harbour.

1964. Air. Winter Olympic Games, Innsbruck. Nos. 55/9 optd with Olympic Rings, Games Emblem and INNSBRUCK 1964.

No.	Type	Description	Unused	Used
89	7	20n.p. brown and green	1·10	55
90	-	30n.p. brown and violet	1·50	75
91	-	40n.p. green and blue	2·10	1·30
92	-	70n.p. grey and green	3·75	2·00
93	-	1r. red and blue	5·25	2·50
MS93a		Five sheets, each 100×120 mm.	65·00	65·00

1964. Air. 48th Birth Anniv of Pres. Kennedy. Optd MAY 29 (late President's birthday).

No.	Type	Description	Unused	Used
94	6	75n.p. blk & grn on grn	3·00	3·00
95	6	1r. black & brown on buff	3·75	3·75
96	6	1¼r. black and red on grey	4·50	4·50
MS97		100×60 mm.	9·00	9·00

1964. Air. Anti-T.B. Campaign. Optd ANTI TUBERCULOSE in English and Arabic, and Cross of Lorraine. Perf or roul.

No.	Type	Description	Unused	Used
101	3	20n.p. brown, yell & red	5·25	5·25
102	-	30n.p. blue, orange & red	5·25	5·25
103	-	40n.p. black, yellow & red	5·25	5·25
104	-	50n.p. violet, red & turq	5·25	5·25
MS104c		Four sheets, each 119×99 mm. Imperf	£170	

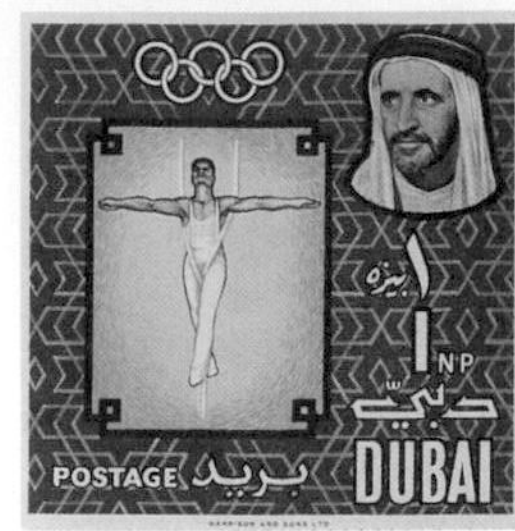

15 Gymnastics

1964. Olympic Games, Tokyo.

No.	Type	Description	Unused	Used
105	15	1n.p. brown and olive	10	10
106	-	2n.p. sepia & turquoise	10	10
107	-	3n.p. blue and brown	10	10
108	-	4n.p. violet and yellow	10	10
109	-	5n.p. ochre and slate	15	15
110	-	10n.p. blue and buff	25	25
111	-	20n.p. olive and red	45	45
112	-	30n.p. blue and yellow	75	75
113	-	40n.p. green and buff	1·60	1·10
114	-	1r. purple and blue	3·75	2·75
MS114a		102×102 mm. No. 114 (larger). Imperf	6·50	6·50

DESIGNS: 2n.p. to 1r. Various gymnastic exercises as Type **15**, each with portrait of Ruler.

1964. Air. 19th Anniv of U.N. Nos. 43/6 optd UNO 19th ANNIVERSARY in English and Arabic.

No.	Type	Description	Unused	Used
115	5	30n.p. brown and violet	1·40	85
116	-	40n.p. olive and red	2·10	1·70
117	-	70n.p. orange and green	3·50	3·25
118	-	1r. blue and brown	4·75	3·75

17 Shaikh Rashid and Shaikh Ahmad of Qatar

1964. "Educational Progress". Portraits in black; torch orange.

No.	Type	Description	Unused	Used
119	17	5n.p. purple (postage)	20	20
120	17	10n.p. red	20	20
121	17	15n.p. blue	30	20
122	-	20n.p. olive	45	20
123	-	30n.p. red (air)	1·60	75
124	-	40n.p. brown	3·75	1·30
125	-	50n.p. blue	4·75	1·60
126	-	1r. green	7·00	2·75
MS126a		100×60 mm. No. 126. Imperf	19·00	10·50

DESIGNS: 20, 30, 40n.p. Shaikh Rashid and Shaikh Abdullah of Kuwait; 50n.p., 1r. Shaikh Rashid and Pres. Nasser of Egypt.

التقدم في الفضاء الخارجي ١٩٦٤

OUTER SPACE ACHIEVEMENTS 1964

(18)

1964. Air. Outer Space Achievements, 1964.

No.	Type	Description	Unused	Used
127	18	1r. multicoloured	4·25	4·25
128	18	1½r. multicoloured	4·25	4·25
129	18	2r. multicoloured	4·25	4·25

(b) Miniature sheet (No. MS67a) optd as Nos. 65/7, but without space capsule and "Ranger 7" which appears larger in sheet margins instead.

No.	Description	Unused	Used
MS129a	90×65 mm	10·50	10·50

19 Globe and Rockets

1964. Space Achievements. Unissued stamps surch as T 19. Multicoloured.

130		10n.p. on 75n.p. "Man on Moon" (25×78 mm)	3·25	3·25
131		20n.p. on 1r.50 Type **19**	3·75	3·75
132		30n.p. on 2r. "Universe" (25×78 mm)	3·75	3·75

1964. Air. 1st Death Anniv of Pres. J. Kennedy. As No. 47 with colours changed, optd 22 NOVEMBER.

133	**6**	75n.p. black and green	13·00	10·50

21 Telephone Handset

1966. Opening of Dubai Automatic Telephone Exchange.

134	**21**	10n.p. brn & grn (postage)	20	15
135	**21**	15n.p. red and plum	30	15
136	**21**	25n.p. green and blue	45	20
137	-	40n.p. blue & grn (air)	65	30
138	-	60n.p. orange and sepia	1·50	65
139	-	75n.p. violet and black	1·70	1·10
140	-	2r. green and red	6·00	3·75
MS141		102×60 mm. No. 14. Imperf	10·50	9·00

DESIGN: Nos. 137/40, As Type **21** but showing telephone dial.

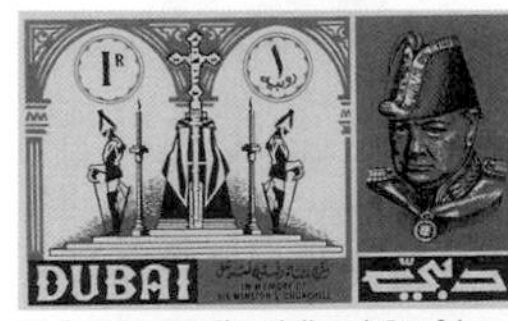

22 Sir Winston Churchill and Catafalque

1966. Churchill Commemoration. (a) Postage.

142	**22**	1r. black and violet	75	55
143	**22**	1r.50 black and olive	1·30	85
144	**22**	3r. black and blue	2·75	2·10
145	**22**	4r. black and red	4·75	3·50
MS146		134×90 mm. Nos. 141/44. Imperf	13·00	13·00

(b) Air. Nos. 142/5 optd AIR MAIL in English and Arabic and with black borders.

147	1r. black and violet	75	55
148	1r.50 black and olive	1·30	85
149	3r. black and blue	2·75	2·10
150	4r. black and red	4·75	3·50
MS151	134×90 mm. Nos. 147/9. Imperf	13·00	13·00

23 Ruler's Palace

24 Bridge

1966

152	**23**	5n.p. brown and blue	30	30
153	**23**	10n.p. black and orange	30	30
154	**23**	15n.p. blue and brown	40	30
155	**A**	20n.p. blue and brown	45	45
156	**A**	25n.p. red and blue	55	55
157	**B**	35n.p. violet and green	75	75
158	**B**	40n.p. turquoise & blue	1·10	75
159	**24**	60n.p. green and red	1·40	1·30
160	**24**	1r. ultramarine and blue	2·10	1·90
161	**C**	1r.25 brown and black	3·00	2·50
162	**D**	1r.50 purple and green	4·75	3·00
163	**D**	3r. brown and violet	9·75	6·00
164	**E**	5r. red	17·00	10·50
165	**E**	10r. blue	36·00	24·00

DESIGNS—HORIZ: (28×21 mm): A, Waterfront, Dubai; B, Bridge and dhow. As Type **24**: C, Minaret (Ruler's portrait on right); D, Fort Dubai. VERT: (32½×42½ mm): E, Shaikh Rashid bin Said.

25 Oil Rig

26 "Tasman" (oil rig)

1966. Air. Oil Exploration. (a) "Land" series as T 25.

166	-	5n.p. black and lilac	45	10
167	-	15n.p. black and bistre	75	30
168	-	25n.p. black and blue	1·10	55
169	-	35n.p. black and red	1·50	65
170	-	50n.p. black and brown	2·10	85
171	**25**	70n.p. black and red	5·25	2·00
MS172		Two sheets, each 60×100 mm. 70n.p. (No. 170) and 1r. black and green. Imperf	16·00	13·00

DESIGNS—HORIZ: 5n.p. Map of Dubai; 15n.p. Surveying; 25n.p. Dubai Petroleum Company building; 35n.p. Oil drilling. VERT: 50n.p. Surveying with level.

(b) "Sea" series as T 26.

173	**26**	10n.p. purple and blue	30	10
174	-	20n.p. mauve and green	55	10
175	**26**	30n.p. brown and green	95	10
176	-	40n.p. lilac and agate	95	20
177	**26**	50n.p. blue and olive	1·60	30
178	-	60n.p. blue and violet	1·80	65
179	**26**	75n.p. green and brown	2·75	85
180	-	1r. green and blue	3·25	1·30
MS181		100×120 mm. Nos. 179/80. Imperf	16·00	13·00

DESIGN: 20, 40, 60n.p. and 1r. Ocean well-head.

27 Rulers of Gulf Arab States (image scaled to 62% of original size)

1966. Gulf Arab States Summit Conference.

182	**27**	35p. multicoloured	2·40	1·10
183	**27**	60p. multicoloured	6·50	2·75
184	**27**	150p. multicoloured	13·00	7·00

28 Jules Rimet Cup

1966. World Cup Football Championship. Multicoloured.

185	40d. Type **28**	75	30
186	60d. Various football scenes	95	55
187	1r. Various football scenes	1·50	75
188	1r.25 Various football scenes	1·90	95
189	3r. Wembley Stadium, London	3·00	2·40
MS190	105×75 mm. 5r. Type **28**	9·75	9·75

1966. England's World Cup Victory. Nos. 185/9 optd ENGLAND WINNERS.

191	**28**	40d. multicoloured	75	30
192	-	60d. multicoloured	95	55
193	-	1r. multicoloured	1·50	75
194	-	1r.25 multicoloured	1·90	95
195	-	3r. multicoloured	3·00	2·40
MS196		105×75 mm. 5r. multicoloured	9·75	9·75

29 Rulers of Dubai and Kuwait, and I.C.Y. Emblem

1966. International Co-operation Year (1965). Currency expressed in rupees.

197	**29**	1r. brown and green	2·10	1·10
198	**A**	1r. green and brown	2·10	1·10
199	**B**	1r. blue and violet	2·10	1·10
200	**C**	1r. blue and violet	2·10	1·10
201	**D**	1r. turquoise and red	2·10	1·10
202	**E**	1r. turquoise and red	2·10	1·10
203	**F**	1r. violet and blue	2·10	1·10
204	**G**	1r. violet and blue	2·10	1·10
205	**H**	1r. red and turquoise	2·10	1·10
206	**I**	1r. red and turquoise	2·10	1·10
MS207		76×101 mm. Nos. 197/8	12·00	12·00

HEADS OF STATE and POLITICAL LEADERS (Ruler of Dubai and): A, Pres. John F. Kennedy. B, Prime Minister Harold Wilson; C, Pres. Helou of the Lebanon; D, Pres. De Gaulle; E, Pres. Nasser; F, Pope Paul VI; G, Ruler of Bahrain; H, Pres. Lyndon Johnson; I, Ruler of Qatar.

30 "Gemini" Capsules manoeuvring

1966. "Gemini" Space Rendezvous. Mult.

208	35d. Type **30**	65	30
209	40d. "Gemini" capsules linked	65	30
210	60d. "Gemini" capsules separating	75	45
211	1r. Schirra and Stafford in "Gemini 6"	1·40	65
212	1r.25 "Gemini" orbits	1·90	1·10
213	3r. Borman and Lovell in "Gemini 7"	3·25	2·10
MS214	130×100 mm. 1r. As 60d. Imperf	9·00	6·50

1967. Nos. 197/206 surch Riyal in English and Arabic and bars.

215	**29**	1r. on 1r.	1·70	1·10
216	**A**	1r. on 1r.	1·70	1·10
217	**B**	1r. on 1r.	1·70	1·10
218	**C**	1r. on 1r.	1·70	1·10
219	**D**	1r. on 1r.	1·70	1·10
220	**E**	1r. on 1r.	1·70	1·10
221	**F**	1r. on 1r.	1·70	1·10
222	**G**	1r. on 1r.	1·70	1·10
223	**H**	1r. on 1r.	1·70	1·10
224	**I**	1r. on 1r.	1·70	1·10
MS225		76×101 mm. Nos. 215/16	13·00	10·50

1967. Gemini Flight Success. Nos. 208/13 optd SUCCESSFUL END OF GEMINI FLIGHT.

226	**30**	35d. multicoloured	65	30
227	-	40d. multicoloured	65	30
228	-	60d. multicoloured	75	45
229	-	1r. multicoloured	1·40	65
230	-	1r.25 multicoloured	1·90	1·10
231	-	3r. multicoloured	3·25	2·10
MS232		130×100 mm. 1r. multicoloured. Imperf	10·00	10·00

1967. Nos. 152/61, 163/5 with currency names changed by overprinting in English and Arabic (except Nos. 244/5 which have the currency name in Arabic only).

233	**23**	5d. on 5n.p.	30	20
234	**23**	10d. on 10n.p.	30	20
235	**23**	15d. on 15n.p.	55	30
236	**A**	20d. on 20n.p.	85	30
237	**A**	25d. on 25n.p.	85	30
238	**B**	35d. on 35n.p.	1·10	30
239	**B**	40d. on 40n.p.	1·50	55
240	**24**	60d. on 60n.p.	2·40	55
241	**24**	1r. on 1r.	3·50	85
242	**C**	1r.25 on 1r.25	6·50	1·70
243	**D**	3r. on 3r.	10·50	4·75
244	**E**	5r. on 5r.	20·00	9·00
245	**E**	10r. on 10r.	32·00	18·00

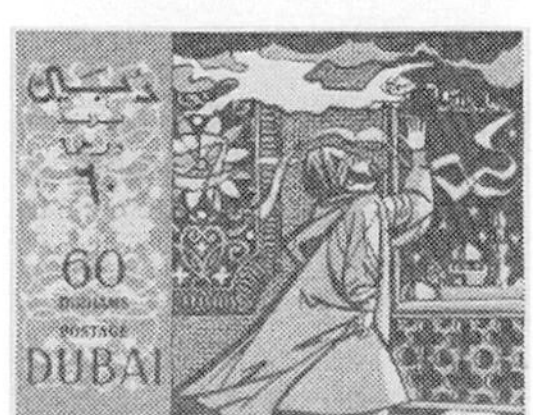

37 "The Moving Finger writes..."

1967. Rubaiyat of Omar Khayyam. Mult.

246	60d. Type **37**	2·75	55
247	60d. "Here with a Loaf of Bread..."	2·75	55
248	60d. "So, while the Vessels..."	2·75	55
249	60d. "Myself when young..."	2·75	55
250	60d. "One Moment in Annihilation's Waste..."	2·75	55
251	60d. "And strange to tell..."	2·75	55
MS252	100×80 mm. 60d. Omar Khayyam (smaller, 43×30 mm). Imperf	6·50	6·50

38 "The Straw Hat" (Rubens)

1967. Paintings. Multicoloured.

253	1r. Type **38**	2·75	55
254	1r. "Thomas, Earl of Arundel" (Rubens)	2·75	55
255	1r. "A peasant boy leaning on a sill" (Murillo)	2·75	55
MS256	105×177 mm. Nos. 253/6 in tete-beche pairs (2×3)	21·00	10·50

See also Nos. 273/5.

39 Ruler and Lanner Falcon

40 "Bayan" (dhow)

1967

257	**39**	5d. red and orange	1·30	45
258	**39**	10d. sepia and green	1·30	45
259	**39**	20d. purple and blue	1·70	45
260	**39**	35d. turquoise & mauve	2·10	45
261	**39**	60d. blue and green	4·50	85
262	**39**	1r. green and purple	6·50	85
263	**40**	1r.25 purple and blue	6·50	1·10
264	**40**	3r. purple and blue	7·50	3·25
265	**40**	5r. violet and green	15·00	6·50
266	**40**	10r. green and mauve	21·00	12·00

41 Globe and Scout Badge

1967. World Scout Jamboree, Idaho. Mult.

267	10d. Type **41**	65	20
268	20d. Dubai scout and dromedaries	1·30	30
269	35d. Bugler	1·70	45
270	60d. Jamboree emblem and U.S. flags	2·75	55
271	1r. Lord Baden-Powell	4·25	1·10
272	1r.25 Idaho on U.S. Map	6·00	2·40

1967. Goya's Paintings in National Gallery, London. As T **38**. Multicoloured.

273	1r. "Dr. Peral"	2·75	55
274	1r. "Dona Isabel Cobos de Porcel"	2·75	55
275	1r. "Duke of Wellington"	2·75	55
MS276	105×178 mm. Nos. 273/5	21·00	10·50

42 Kaiser-i-Hind ("Teinopalpus imperialis")

1968. Butterflies and Moths. Multicoloured.

277	60d. Type **42**	3·00	45
278	60d. "Erasmia pulchella"	3·00	45
279	60d. Gaudy baron ("Euthalia indica")	3·00	45
280	60d. Atlas moth ("Attacus atlas")	3·00	45
281	60d. "Dysphania militaris"	3·00	45
282	60d. "Neochera butleri"	3·00	45
283	60d. African monarch ("Danaus chrysippus")	3·00	45
284	60d. Chestnut tiger ("Danaus tytia")	3·00	45

43 "Madonna and Child" (Ferruzi)

1968. Arab Mothers' Day. Multicoloured.

285 60d. "Games in the Park" (Zandomeneghi)	65	30
286 1r. Type **43**	1·10	55
287 1r.25 "Mrs Cockburn and Children" (Reynolds) (wrongly inscr "Cookburn")	1·30	65
288 3r. "Self-portrait with Daughter" (Vigee-Lebrun)	3·00	1·90

44 "Althea rosea"

1968. Flowers. Multicoloured.

289 60d. Type **44**	2·10	30
290 60d. "Geranium lancastriense"	2·10	30
291 60d. "Catharanthus roseus"	2·10	30
292 60d. "Convolvulus minor"	2·10	30
293 60d. "Opuntia"	2·10	30
294 60d. "Gaillardia aristata"	2·10	30
295 60d. "Heliopsis"	2·10	30
296 60d. "Centaurea moschata"	2·10	30

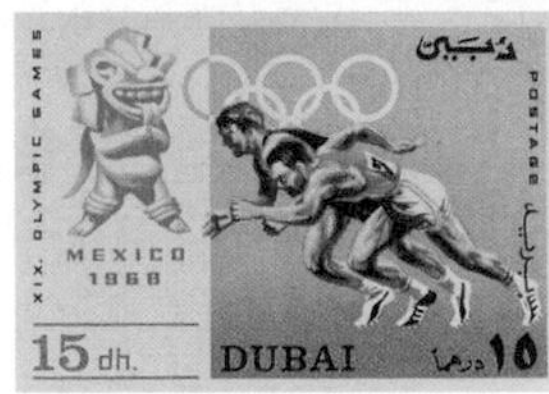

45 Running

1968. Olympic Games, Mexico. Multicoloured.

297 15d. Type **45**	1·30	10
298 20d. Swimming	1·40	10
299 25d. Boxing	2·40	20
300 35d. Water-polo	2·75	30
301 40d. High jump	3·25	30
302 60d. Gymnastics	4·75	55
303 1r. Football	6·50	75
304 1r.25 Fencing	9·00	85
MS305 70×90 mm. No. 303. Imprf	10·50	8·00

46 "Young Girl with Kitten" (Perronneau)

1968. Children's Day. Multicoloured.

306 60d. "Two Boys with Mastiff" (Goya)	65	20
307 1r. Type **46**	85	45
308 1r.25 "Soap Bubbles" (Manet)	1·30	45
309 3r. "The Fluyder Boys" (Lawrence)	3·25	1·30

47 Common Pheasant

1968. Arabian Gulf Birds. Multicoloured.

310 60d. Type **47**	3·25	55
311 60d. Red-collared dove ("Turtle Dove")	3·25	55
312 60d. Western red-footed falcon ("Red-footed flacon")	3·25	55
313 60d. European bee eater ("Bee-eater")	3·25	55
314 60d. Hoopoe	3·25	55
315 60d. Great egret ("Common Egret")	3·25	55
316 60d. Little terns	3·25	55
317 60d. Lesser black-backed gulls	3·25	55

48 "Bamora" (freighter), 1914

1969. 60th Anniv of Dubai Postal Service. Multicoloured.

318 25d. Type **48**	30	30
319 35d. de Havilland D.H.66 Hercules airplane, 1930	55	30
320 60d. "Sirdhana" (liner), 1947	1·10	30
321 1r. Armstrong Whitworth A.W. Atalanta airplane, 1938	1·30	30
322 1r.25 "Chandpara" (freighter), 1949	1·60	30
323 3r. Short Sunderland flying boat, 1943	2·75	55
MS324 117×80 mm. 1r.25 *Bombala* (freighter), 1961, and Vickers Super VC-10 airliner, 1969	11·50	11·50

49 "Madonna and Child" (Bartolome Murillo)

1969. Arab Mothers' Day. Multicoloured.

325 60d. Type **49**	1·10	30
326 1r. "Madonna with Rose" (Francesco Mozzola (Parmigianino))	2·10	30
327 1r.25 "Mother and Children" (Peter Paul Rubens)	2·40	30
328 3r. "Campori Madonna" (Antonio Correggio)	5·25	65

No. 326 wrongly inscribed "Mazzuoli".

50 Porkfish

1969. Fishes. Multicoloured.

329 60d. Type **50**	2·10	45
330 60d. Greasy ("Spotted") grouper	2·10	45
331 60d. Diamond fingerfish ("Moonfish")	2·10	45
332 60d. Striped sweetlips	2·10	45
333 60d. Blue-ringed angelfish ("Blue angel")	2·10	45
334 60d. Roundel ("Texas") skate	2·10	45
335 60d. Black-backed ("Striped") butterflyfish	2·10	45
336 60d. Emperor ("Imperial") angelfish	2·10	45

51 Burton, Doughty, Burckhardt, Thesiger and Map

1969. Explorers of Arabia.

337	**51** 35d. brown and green	1·30	30
338	**51** 60d. blue and brown	2·40	65
339	**51** 1r. green and blue	4·50	85
340	**51** 1r.25 black and red	6·00	2·50

52 Underwater Storage Tank Construction

1969. Oil Industry. Multicoloured.

341 5d. Type **52**	45	20
342 20d. Floating-out storage tank	1·10	20
343 35d. Underwater tank in operation	1·90	20
344 60d. Ruler, oil rig and monument	4·00	20
345 1r. Fateh marine oilfield	5·25	20

53 Astronauts on Moon

1969. 1st Man on the Moon. Multicoloured.

346 60d. Type **53** (postage)	95	40
347 1r. Astronaut and ladder	1·20	40
348 1r.25 Astronauts planting U.S. flag on Moon (horiz) (62×38 mm) (air)	1·70	45

54 "Weather Reporter" launching Radio-Sonde and Handley Page Hastings Weather Reconnaissance Airplane

1970. World Meteorological Day. Mult.

349 60d. Type **54**	55	30
350 1r. Kew-type radio-sonde and dish aerial	1·10	30
351 1r.25 "Tiros" satellite and rocket	1·30	30
352 3r. "Ariel" satellite and rocket	2·50	55

55 New Headquarters Building

1970. New U.P.U. Headquarters Building, Berne. Multicoloured.

353 5d. Type **55**	55	10
354 60d. U.P.U. Monument, Berne	2·10	45

56 Charles Dickens

1970. Death Cent of Charles Dickens. Mult.

355 60d. Type **56**	65	30
356 1r. Signature, quill and London sky-line (horiz)	1·30	30
357 1r.25 Dickens and Victorian street	1·60	1·40
358 3r. Dickens and books (horiz)	3·25	85

57 "The Graham Children" (Hogarth)

1970. Children's Day. Multicoloured.

359 35d. Type **57**	65	30
360 60d. "Caroline Murat and Children" (Gerard) (vert)	1·50	30
361 1r. "Napoleon as Uncle" (Ducis)	2·75	30

58 Shaikh Rashid

1970. Multicoloured.. Multicoloured..

362 5d. Type **58**	20	20
363 10d. Dhow building (horiz)	45	10
364 20d. Al Maktum Bridge (horiz)	75	20
365 35d. Great Mosque	85	10
366 60d. Dubai National Bank (horiz)	1·40	20
367 1r. International airport (horiz)	2·40	45
368 1r.25 Harbour project (horiz)	4·25	1·20
369 3r. Hospital (horiz)	6·00	2·40
370 5r. Trade school (horiz)	8·50	4·75
371 10r. Television and "Intelsat 4"	15·00	8·50

The riyal values are larger, 40×25 or 25×40 mm.

59 Terminal Building and Control Tower

1971. Opening of Dubai International Airport. Multicoloured.

372 1r. Type **59**	3·75	2·10
373 1r.25 Airport entrance	4·75	2·75

60 Telecommunications Map and Satellites

1971. Outer Space Telecommunications Congress, Paris. Multicoloured.

374 60d. Type **60** (postage)	55	30
375 1r. Rocket and "Intelsat 4" (air)	75	55
376 5r. Eiffel Tower and Goonhilly aerial	3·75	3·00

61 Scout Badge, Fan and Map

1971. 13th World Scout Jamboree, Asagiri (Japan). Multicoloured.

377	60d. Type **61**	55	20
378	1r. Canoeing	1·30	55
379	1r.25 Rock-climbing	1·50	65
380	3r. Scouts around camp-fire (horiz)	3·50	1·30

62 Albrecht Durer

1971. Famous People (1st issue). Mult.

381	60d. Type **62** (postage)	1·10	30
382	1r. Sir Isaac Newton (air)	1·30	85
383	1r.25 Avicenna	1·90	1·10
384	3r. Voltaire	5·50	2·50

See also Nos. 388/91.

63 Boy in Meadow

1971. 25th Anniv of UNICEF. Mult.

385	60d. Type **63** (postage)	55	30
386	5r. Children with toys (horiz)	4·75	2·50
387	1r. Mother and children (air)	1·10	45

1972. Famous People (2nd issue). As T 62. Multicoloured.

388	10d. Leonardo da Vinci (postage)	30	30
389	35d. Beethoven	55	30
390	75d. Khalil Gibran (poet) (air)	95	45
391	5r. Charles de Gaulle	6·00	2·75

65 Nurse supervising children

1972. Air. World Health Day. Multicoloured.

392	75d. Type **65**	1·60	65
393	1r.25 Doctor treating baby (horiz)	2·75	1·50

67 Gymnastics

1972. Olympic Games, Munich. Multicoloured.

399	35d. Type **67** (postage)	45	10
400	40d. Fencing	75	10
401	65d. Hockey	1·20	20
402	75d. Water-polo (air)	1·60	20
403	1r. Horse-jumping	1·90	20
404	1r.25 Athletics	2·75	20

POSTAGE DUE STAMPS

1963. Designs as T **1** but inscr "DUE".

D26	**L**	1n.p. red and grey	60	40
D27	**M**	2n.p. blue and bistre	80	50
D28	**N**	3n.p. green and red	1·30	80
D29	**L**	4n.p. red and green	1·70	1·20
D30	**M**	5n.p. black and red	2·00	1·40
D31	**N**	10n.p. violet and olive	2·50	2·00
D32	**L**	15n.p. red and blue	3·50	2·50
D33	**M**	25n.p. green & brown	4·00	2·50
D34	**N**	35n.p. orange and blue	4·75	3·00

DESIGNS—HORIZ: L, Common European cockle; M, Common blue mussel; N, Portuguese oyster.

D66 Shaikh Rashid

1972

D394	**D66**	5d. grey, blue & brn	1·20	1·20
D395	**D66**	10d. brn, ochre & bl	1·70	1·70
D396	**D66**	20d. brn, red and blue	3·25	3·25
D397	**D66**	30d. violet, lilac & blk	4·25	4·25
D398	**D66**	50d. brn, ochre & pur	9·00	9·00

Pt. 1

DUNGARPUR

A state of Rajasthan. Now uses Indian stamps.

12 pies = 1 anna; 16 annas = 1 rupee.

1 State Arms

1933

1	**1**	¼a. yellow		£300
2	**1**	¼a. red	£3750	£900
3	**1**	¼a. brown		£500
4	**1**	1a. blue		£250
5	**1**	1a. red		£3250
6	**1**	1a.3p. mauve		£375
7	**1**	2a. green	£2000	£500
8	**1**	4a. red		£900

2 Maharawal Lakshman Singh

1932. T 2 (various frames).

9	**2**	¼a. orange	£1300	£120
10	**2**	½a. red	£425	85·00
11	**2**	1a. blue	£425	85·00
12	**2**	1a.3p. mauve	£1300	£350
13	**2**	1¼a. violet	£1400	£350
14	**2**	2a. green	£1900	£650
15	**2**	4a. brown	£1400	£300

Pt. 1

DUTTIA (DATIA)

A state of Central India. Now uses Indian stamps.

12 pies = 1 anna; 16 annas = 1 rupee.

2 (2a.) Ganesh

1894. Imperf.

1		½a. black on green	£20000	
2		2a. blue on yellow	£5000	

Nos. 1/2 are as Type **2**, but have rosettes in lower corners.

3 (¼a.) Ganesh

1896. Imperf.

4	**3**	¼a. black on orange	£5500	
5	**3**	½a. black on green	£16000	
6	**3**	2a. black on yellow	£3000	
7	**3**	4a. black on red	£1400	

Stamps of Type **3** come with the circular handstamp as shown on Type **2**. Examples of Nos. 4/5 without handstamp are worth slightly less than the prices quoted.

1896. Imperf.

8b	**2**	½a. black on green	22·00	£375
3	**2**	1a. red	£4250	£7000
9	**2**	1a. black	£140	£425
10	**2**	2a. black on yellow	35·00	£400
11	**2**	4a. black on red	30·00	£250

4 (½a.)

1897. Imperf.

12	**4**	½a. black on green	£130	£700
13	**4**	1a. black	£250	
14	**4**	2a. black on yellow	£140	£700
15	**4**	4a. black on red	£150	£700

5 (¼a.)

1899. Imperf, roul or perf.

16c	**5**	¼a. red	3·75	24·00
37	**5**	¼a. black	5·00	28·00
38	**5**	¼a. blue	2·75	15·00
17	**5**	½a. black on green	2·75	24·00
30	**5**	½a. green	5·50	30·00
35	**5**	½a. blue	3·50	20·00
39	**5**	½a. pink	3·50	16·00
18	**5**	1a. black	3·25	24·00
31	**5**	1a. purple	10·00	35·00
36	**5**	1a. pink	3·50	18·00
19c	**5**	2a. black on yellow	3·25	26·00
32	**5**	2a. brown	15·00	40·00
33	**5**	2a. lilac	7·50	27·00
20	**5**	4a. black on red	4·00	25·00
34	**5**	4a. brown	85·00	

Pt. 5

EAST SILESIA

Special overprints were applied to Czechoslovakian and Polish stamps prior to a plebiscite. The plebiscite was never held, due to disorders, and the area was divided between Czechoslovakia and Poland in 1920.

100 haleru = 1 koruna.
100 fenni = 1 korona.

1920. Stamps of Czechoslovakia optd SO 1920. Imperf or perf.

23	**3**	1h. brown	20	10
2	**2**	3h. mauve	15	10
24	**3**	5h. green	25	30
25	**3**	10h. green	25	30
26	**3**	15h. red	40	15
6	**2**	20h. green	20	10
27	**3**	20h. red	40	30
28	**3**	25h. purple	40	30
9	**2**	30h. olive	20	30
35	**3**	30h. mauve	40	30
10	**2**	40h. orange	25	30
11	**3**	50h. purple	55	45
12	**3**	50h. blue	1·50	1·25
36	**3**	60h. orange	45	45
14	**3**	75h. green	45	45
15	**3**	80h. olive	45	45
16	**2**	100h. brown	80	60
17	**3**	120h. black	1·40	1·25
18	**2**	200h. blue	1·40	1·25
19	**3**	300h. green	6·50	1·90
20	**2**	400h. violet	1·90	1·50
21	**3**	500h. brown	4·25	3·75
22	**3**	1000h. purple	13·00	7·50

1920. Stamps of Poland of 1919 optd S. O. 1920. Perf.

57	**15**	5f. green	10	10
58	**15**	10f. brown	10	10
59	**15**	15f. red	10	10
60	**16**	25f. olive	10	10
61	**16**	50f. green	10	10
62	**17**	1k. green	10	10
63	**17**	1k.50 brown	10	10
64	**17**	2k. blue	10	10
65	**18**	2k.50 purple	10	10
66	**19**	5k. blue	10	10

EXPRESS STAMPS FOR PRINTED MATTER

1920. Express stamps of Czechoslovakia optd S O 1920.

E39	**E4**	2h. purple on yellow	15	10
E40	**E4**	5h. green on yellow	15	10

NEWSPAPER STAMPS

1920. Newspaper stamps of Czechoslovakia optd SO 1920. Imperf.

N41	**N4**	2h. green	20	30
N42	**N4**	6h. red	20	30
N43	**N4**	10h. lilac	35	30
N44	**N4**	20h. blue	50	30
N45	**N4**	30h. brown	50	30

POSTAGE DUE STAMPS

1920. Postage Due stamps of Czechoslovakia optd SO 1920. Imperf.

D46	**D4**	5h. olive	20	15
D47	**D4**	10h. olive	20	10
D48	**D4**	15h. olive	20	15
D49	**D4**	20h. olive	30	30
D50	**D4**	25h. olive	30	30
D51	**D4**	30h. olive	30	30
D52	**D4**	40h. olive	45	45
D53	**D4**	50h. olive	2·10	45
D54	**D4**	100h. brown	2·25	90
D55	**D4**	500h. green	5·75	3·75
D56	**D4**	1000h. violet	9·00	6·75

Pt. 21

EAST TIMOR

Following negotiations between Portugal and Indonesia a referendum was conducted on 30 August 1999 with the majority voting for independence for East Timor. On the 20 September 1999 the first United Nations peace keeping troops arrived in East Timor and the Indonesian troops began to withdraw. By October the United Nations had established the International Force for East Timor (I.N.T.E.R.F.E.T.). On the 19 October 1999 the Indonesian Consultative Assembly confirmed the establishment and on the 25 October 1999 the United Nations voted to replace I.N.T.E.R.F.E.T. with a force to help with the establishment of a United Nations Transitional Administration of East Timor (U.N.T.A.E.T.). The East Timor National Council (E.T.N.C.), which was formed to help with policy recommendations, held its first meeting on 11 December 1999.

100 cents = 1 dollar.

UNITED NATIONS TRANSITIONAL ADMINISTRATION IN EAST TIMOR

1 Man with Arms Raised

2000. (a) Inscr "Dom.".

1	**1**	(21c.) multicoloured	70	70

(b) Inscr "Int.".

2		($1.05) multicoloured	3·50	3·50

No. 1 was for use on Domestic mail and No. 2 was for use on International mail.

INDEPENDENCE

2 Xanana Gusmao (1st president)

2002. Independence. Multicoloured.

3	10c. Type **2**	15	10
4	50c. Island showing Dili	75	65

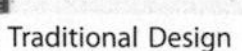

3 Traditional Design

2002. Independence. Multicoloured.

5	25c. Type **3**	50	40
6	50c. Palm frond	75	60
7	$1 Coffee beans	1·50	1·40
8	$2 National flag	2·75	2·75

Pt. 3

EASTERN ROUMELIA AND SOUTH BULGARIA

This area, part of the Turkish Empire, situated south of the Balkan Mts., became semi-autonomous after 1878. In 1885 the population revolted against the Turks, changing the district's name to South Bulgaria. Incorporation into Bulgaria followed in 1886.

40 paras = 1 piastre.

A. EASTERN ROUMELIA

1880. Stamps of Turkey optd R.O.

1	**2**	½pre. on 20pa. green (No. 78)	65·00	55·00
2	**9**	20pa. purple & green (No. 83)	85·00	65·00
3	**9**	2pi. black & orange (No. 85)	£110	95·00
4	**9**	5pi. red and blue (No. 86)	£425	£475

1881. Stamp of Turkey optd R.O and ROUMELIE ORIENTALE.

5	10pa. black and mauve	95·00	90·00

1881. As T **9** of Turkey but inscr "ROUMELIE ORIENTALE" at left.

6	5pa. black and olive	11·00	1·30
11	5pa. lilac	55	55
7	10pa. black and green	19·00	1·30
12	10pa. green	20	55
8	20pa. black and red	1·70	1·10
9	1pi. black and blue	5·50	4·25
10	5pi. red and blue	55·00	80·00

B. SOUTH BULGARIA

1885. As T **9** of Turkey, but inscr "RO " at left and optd with lion.

13	5pa. black and olive	£325	£375
29	5pa. lilac	22·00	55·00
14	10pa. black and green	£850	£800
30	10pa. green	40·00	75·00
15	20pa. black and red	£325	
34	20pa. red	55·00	65·00
18	1pi. black and blue	55·00	£110
26	5pi. red and blue	£550	

1885. As T **9** of Turkey, but inscr "ROUMELIE ORIENTALE" and optd with lion and inscription in frame.

43	5pa. black and olive		
48a	5pa. lilac	22·00	43·00
44	10pa. black and green		
49	10pa. green	55·00	55·00
45	20pa. black and red	25·00	43·00
50	20pa. red	28·00	27·00
46	1pi. black and blue	85·00	£110
47	5pi. red and blue		

Pt. 20

ECUADOR

A Republic on the W. Coast of S. America. Independent since 1830.

1865. 8 reales = 1 peso.
1881. 100 centavos = 1 sucre.
2000. 100c. = 1 dollar (U.S.)

1

2

1865. Imperf.

1b	**1**	½r. blue	34·00	21·00
2d	**1**	1r. yellow	18·00	11·50
3	**1**	1r. green	£275	34·00
4	**2**	4r. red	£375	£140

3

4

1872

10	**3**	½r. blue	20·00	4·50
11	**4**	1r. orange	25·00	6·50
12a	**3**	1p. red	4·75	16·00

5

1881. Various frames.

13	**5**	1c. brown	30	25
14	**5**	2c. lake	30	25
15	**5**	5c. blue	5·50	55
16	**5**	10c. orange	30	30
17	**5**	20c. violet	35	30
18	**5**	50c. green	1·40	3·25

1883. Surch DIEZ CENTAVOS.

19	10c. on 50c. green	32·00	21·00

13

1887. Various frames.

26	**13**	1c. green	25	20
27	**13**	2c. red	55	20
28	**13**	5c. blue	2·00	35
29	**13**	80c. olive	3·75	9·00

19 Pres. Juan Flores

1892

34	**19**	1c. orange	25	40
35	**19**	2c. brown	25	40
36	**19**	5c. red	25	40
37	**19**	10c. green	25	40
38	**19**	20c. brown	25	40
39	**19**	50c. red	25	90
40	**19**	1s. blue	25	1·90
41	**19**	5s. violet	65	3·50

1893. Surch 5 CENTAVOS.

53	5c. on 50c. red	1·10	1·00
49	5c. on 1s. blue	3·75	3·50
50	5c. on 5s. violet	7·00	5·75

20 Pres. Rocafuerte

1894. Dated "1894".

57	**20**	1c. blue	35	30
58	**20**	2c. brown	35	30
59	**20**	5c. green	35	30
60	**20**	10c. red	55	40
61	**20**	20c. black	90	55
62	**20**	50c. orange	4·50	1·40
63	**20**	1s. red	7·00	3·25
64	**20**	5s. blue	9·25	4·25

1895. Dated "1895".

74	1c. blue	65	55
75	2c. brown	65	85
76	5c. green	45	35
77	10c. red	45	35
78	20c. black	55	75
79	50c. orange	2·40	1·40
80	1s. red	17·00	5·50
81	5s. blue	6·00	3·25

These two series were re-issued in 1897 optd "1897–1898".

22

1896. Arms designs, inscr "U.P.U. 1896".

89A	**22**	1c. green	55	40
90A	**22**	2c. red	55	30
91A	**22**	5c. blue	55	30
92A	**22**	10c. brown	45	60
93A	**22**	20c. orange	1·10	1·40
94A	**22**	50c. blue	2·50	2·20
95A	**22**	1s. brown	3·00	3·00
96A	**22**	5s. lilac	11·00	4·25

This series was re-issued in 1897 optd "1897–1898".

F1

1896. Dated "1887 1888". Surch.

112	**F1**	5c. on 10c. orange	15	15
113	**F1**	10c. on 4c. brown	1·40	75

1896. As Type F 1, but dated "1891 1892".

114	**F 1**	10c. on 4c. brown	12·00	9·00

1896. As Type F 1, but dated "1893 1894". Surch.

115	1c. on 1c. red	70	40
116	2c. on 2c. blue	1·40	1·20
117	5c. on 10c. orange	3·50	3·50

34 V. Roca, D. Noboa and J. Olmedo

1896. Triumph of Liberal Party. Dated "1845–1895".

118	**34**	1c. red	55	55
119	-	2c. blue	55	55
120	**34**	5c. green	75	75
121	-	10c. yellow	75	75
122	**34**	20c. red	1·10	3·25
123	-	50c. lilac	1·70	4·75
124	**34**	1s. orange	3·25	8·00

DESIGN: 2c., 10c., 50c. Gen. Elizalde.

This series was re-issued in 1897 optd "1897–1898".

(40)

1896. Surch.

125	**22**	5c. on 20c. orange	28·00	27·00
126	**22**	10c. on 50c. blue	31·00	30·00

1897. 1896 Jubilee issue optd with T 40.

167	**34**	1c. red	3·25	2·75
168	-	2c. blue (No. 119)	3·25	2·75
169	**34**	5c. green	3·25	2·75
170	-	10c. yellow (No. 121)	3·25	2·75

41

1897

173	**41**	1c. green	35	30
174	**41**	2c. red	35	30
175	**41**	5c. lake	35	30
176	**41**	10c. brown	35	30
177	**41**	20c. yellow	45	55
178	**41**	50c. blue	45	95
179	**41**	1s. grey	90	1·20
180	**41**	5s. purple	4·00	5·00

1899. Surch.

191	1c. on 2c. red	2·20	1·20
192	5c. on 10c. brown	1·90	65

45 Louis Varags Torres

1899

193	**45**	1c. black and grey	25	20
205	**45**	1c. black and red	45	10
194	-	2c. black and brown	35	20
206	-	2c. black and green	45	10
195	-	5c. black and red	55	20
207	-	5c. black and lilac	45	10
196	-	10c. black and lilac	55	20
208	-	10c. black and blue	55	30
197	-	20c. black and green	55	20
209	-	20c. black and grey	55	30
198	-	50c. black and red	1·10	30
210	-	50c. black and blue	1·70	95
199	-	1s. black and yellow	5·50	2·75
211	-	1s. black and brown	6·00	2·75
200	-	5s. black and lilac	11·00	7·50
212	-	5s. black and grey	8·75	5·75

PORTRAITS: 2c. A. Calderon. 5c. J. Montalvo. 10c. Mejia. 20c. Espejo. 50c. Carbo. 1s. J. J. Olmendo. 5s. Moncayo.

73 Capt. Abdon Calderon

1904. Birth Centenary of Captain Calderon.

310	**73**	1c. black and red	45	1·10
311	**73**	2c. black and blue	45	1·10
312	**73**	5c. black and yellow	1·90	2·75
313	**73**	10c. black and red	3·75	2·75
314	**73**	20c. black and blue	10·00	8·00
315	**73**	50c. black and yellow	85·00	£120

The 5c. and 50c. are larger (25×30 mm).

76 President Roca

1907. Portraits in black.

323	**76**	1c. red (Roca)	50	20
324	-	2c. blue (Noboa)	1·10	15
325	-	3c. orange (Robles)	1·70	20
326	-	5c. purple (Urvina)	2·10	20
327	-	10c. blue (Garcia Moreno)	4·25	25
328	-	20c. green (Carrion)	5·75	30
329	-	50c. lilac (Espinoza)	12·50	75
330	-	1s. green (Borrero)	17·00	2·10

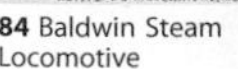
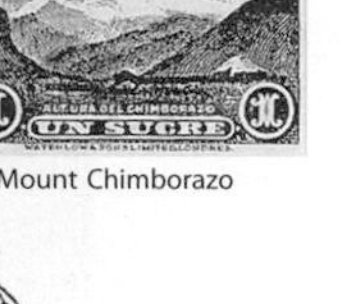

84 Baldwin Steam Locomotive

86 Mount Chimborazo

85 Garcia Moreno

1908. Opening of Guayaquil to Quito Railway.

331	**84**	1c. brown	1·10	2·10
332	**85**	2c. black and blue	1·30	2·30
333	-	5c. black and red	2·75	5·25
334	-	10c. black and yellow	1·70	2·75
335	-	20c. black and green	1·70	3·75
336	-	50c. black and grey	1·70	3·75
337	**86**	1s. black	3·50	8·00

PORTRAITS—As Type **85**: 5c. Gen E. Alfaro. 10c. A. Moncayo. 20c. A. Harman (engineer). 50c. Sivewright.

87 Jose Mejia Vallejo

1909. National Exhibition. Portraits as T 87.

340	**87**	1c. green	35	65
341	-	2c. blue (Espejo)	35	65
342	-	3c. orange (Ascasubi)	35	75
343	-	5c. lake (Salinas)	35	75
344	-	10c. brown (Alegre)	45	75
345	-	20c. grey (Montufar)	45	1·10
346	-	50c. red (Morales)	45	1·10
347	-	1s. olive (Quiroga)	55	1·40
348	**88**	5s. violet	1·20	2·75

88 Exhibition Buildings

1909. Surch CINCO CENTAVOS.

349	5c. on 50c. red (No. 346)	90	75

90 Pres. Roca

91 Pres. Dr. Noboa

92 Robles

93 Pres. Gen. Urvina

94 Pres. Dr. Garcia Moreno

95 Dr. Borrero

98 Valdez

99 Espinoza

1911

354	**90**	1c. black and red	55	30
366	**90**	1c. orange	55	30
355	**91**	2c. black and blue	65	30
367	**91**	2c. green	65	30
356	**92**	3c. black and orange	1·50	30
368	**92**	3c. black	90	30
369	**98**	4c. black and red	35	30
357	**93**	5c. black and red	1·20	30
370	**93**	5c. violet	1·20	30
358	**94**	10c. black and blue	1·50	30
371	**94**	10c. blue	1·50	30
373	**99**	50c. black and violet	3·50	55
359	**95**	1s. black and green	7·75	1·50

See also Nos. 413/6b.

1912. Large Fiscal stamps inscr "TIMBRE CONSULAR" at top. Surch POSTAL and new value.

362	**95**	1c. on 1s. green	65	65
363	**95**	2c. on 2s. red	1·50	1·10
364	**95**	2c. on 5s. blue	1·10	1·10
365	**95**	2c. on 10s. yellow	2·75	2·75

1920. Optd CASA de CORREOS.

374	**90**	1c. orange	90	30

103

1920. Obligatory Tax. Optd CASA de CORREOS or surch also. Dated as shown.

375	**103**	1c. bl & red (no date)	8·25	8·00
376	**103**	1c. bl ("1919–20")	65	30
379	**103**	1c. on 2c. green ("1917–18")	65	30
380	**103**	1c. on 5c. green ("1911–12")	65	30
380a	**103**	1c. on 5c. green ("1913–14")	6·00	85
377	**103**	20c. bl ("1913–14")	1·80	55
378	**103**	20c. ol ("1917–18")	5·50	85

108 Olmedo

109 Monument to "Fathers of the Country"

1920. Centenary of Liberation of Guayaquil. Portraits as T 108.

381	**108**	1c. green	35	30
382	-	2c. red (Ximena)	35	30
383	-	3c. bistre (Roca)	35	30
384	-	4c. green (Vivero)	55	30
385	-	5c. blue (Cordero)	55	30
386	-	6c. orange (Lavayen)	90	45
387	-	7c. brown (Elizalde)	1·20	75
388	-	8c. green (Garcia)	1·20	65
389	-	9c. red (Antepara)	3·50	1·50
390	**109**	10c. blue	1·50	30
391	-	15c. black (Urdaneta)	2·00	55
392	-	20c. purple (Villamil)	2·20	30
393	-	30c. violet (Letamendi)	3·25	1·40
394	-	40c. sepia (Escobedo)	6·00	2·10
395	-	50c. green (Sucre)	4·75	55
396	-	60c. blue (Illingworth)	7·75	2·10
397	-	70c. grey (Roca)	12·00	4·75
398	-	80c. yellow (Rocafuerte)	13·00	4·75
399	-	90c. green (Star and wreath)	14·50	4·75
400	-	1s. blue (Bolivar)	20·00	8·50

112 Post Office, Quito

1920. Obligatory Tax. G.P.O. Rebuilding Fund.

401	**112**	1c. olive	35	30
402	**112**	2c. green	35	30
403	**112**	20c. brown	1·10	30
404	**112**	2s. violet	7·25	5·00
405	**112**	5s. blue	12·00	8·50

1921. Obligatory Tax. Surch Casa de Correos VEINTE CTS. 1921–1922.

405a	**103**	20c. on 1c. blue	44·00	5·00
405b	**103**	20c. on 2c. green	44·00	5·00

1924. Obligatory Tax. Surch DOS CENTAVOS – 2 –.

406	**112**	2c. on 20c. brown	45	25

1924. Oblong Tobacco Tax stamps optd CASA–CORREOS.

407	1c. red (Loco.)	65	15
408	2c. blue (Arms)	65	15

1924. Telegraph stamps as T 103, but inscr "TELEGRAFOS DEL ECUADOR" optd CASA-CORREOS. (a) Inscr "TIMBRE FISCAL".

409	1c. yellow	55	45
410	2c. blue	1·10	55

(b) Inscr "REGION ORIENTAL".

411	1c. yellow	3·50	1·30
412	2c. blue	90	30

1925

413	**90**	1c. blue	35	30
414	**91**	2c. violet	35	30
415	**93**	5c. red	35	30
415a	**93**	5c. brown	65	30
416	**94**	10c. green	45	30
416a	**94**	10c. black	1·20	30
416b	**95**	1s. black and orange	5·50	30

1925. Optd POSTAL over ornament.

417	**112**	20c. brown	2·30	85

1926. Opening of Quito–Esmeraldas Railway. Optd QUITO, railway train and ESMERALDAS 1926.

418	**90**	1c. blue	7·25	6·25
419	**91**	2c. violet	7·25	6·25
420	**92**	3c. black	7·25	6·25
421	-	4c. green (No. 384)	7·25	6·25
422	**93**	5c. red	11·00	6·25
423	**94**	10c. green	11·00	6·25

1927. Optd POSTAL.

424	**112**	1c. olive	25	10
425	**112**	2c. green	25	10
426	**112**	20c. brown	95	10

123 Post Office, Quito

1927. Opening of New Post Office, Quito.

427	**123**	5c. orange	30	10
428	**123**	10c. green	40	20
429	**123**	20c. purple	75	55

1928. Opening of Quito-Cayambe Railway. Stamps of 1920 issue surch Frril. Norte Julio 8 de 1928 Est. Cayambe and value.

431	10c. on 30c. (No. 393)	8·25	8·00
432	50c. on 70c. (No. 397)	10·00	9·75
433	1s. on 80c. (No. 398)	12·00	11·50

1928. National Assembly. Stamps of 1920 surch ASAMBLEA NCNAL. 1928 and value.

434	**108**	1c. on 1c. green (381)	13·00	13·00
435	-	1c. on 2c. red (382)	35	30
436	-	2c. on 3c. bistre (383)	1·90	1·80
437	-	2c. on 4c. green (384)	1·30	1·30
438	-	2c. on 5c. (No. 385)	45	45
440	-	5c. on 6c. (No. 386)	35	30
441	-	10c. on 2c. on 7c. (387)	55	55
442	-	10c. on 7c. (No. 387)	1·10	1·10
443	-	20c. on 8c. (No. 388)	35	30
444	**109**	40c. on 10c. (No. 390)	3·25	3·25
445	-	40c. on 15c. (No. 391)	1·10	1·10
446	-	50c. on 20c. (No. 392)	12·00	11·50
447	-	1s. on 40c. (No. 394)	3·75	3·75
448	-	5s. on 50c. (No. 395)	4·50	4·25
449	-	10s. on 60c. (No. 396)	17·00	16·00

1928. Opening of Railway at Otavalo. Consular Service stamps inscr "TIMBRE-CONSULAR" surch Postal–Frril Norte Est. OTAVALO and value.

450	5c. on 20c. lilac	1·70	1·10
451	10c. on 20c. lilac	1·70	1·10
452	20c. on 1s. green	1·70	1·10
453	50c. on 1s. green	2·10	90
454	1s. on 1s. green	2·75	1·10
455	5s. on 2s. red	8·25	5·75
456	10s. on 2s. red	10·00	7·75

130 Ryan B-5 Brougham over the River Guayas

1929. Air.

458	**130**	2c. black	35	20
459	**130**	5c. red	35	20
460	**130**	10c. brown	35	10
461	**130**	20c. purple	65	10
462	**130**	50c. green	1·20	65
463	**130**	1s. blue	3·75	3·25
467	**130**	1s. red	4·50	65
709	**130**	1s. green	55	30
464	**130**	5s. yellow	15·00	13·00
468	**130**	5s. olive	5·50	5·00
710	**130**	5s. violet	1·20	30
465	**130**	10s. red	85·00	70·00
469	**130**	10s. black	19·00	6·50
711	**130**	10s. blue	2·75	45

1929. As T 103, but inscr "MOVILES" and optd POSTAL.

466	**103**	1c. blue	35	30

1930. Air. Official Air stamps of 1929 optd MENDEZ BOGOTA–QUITO Junio 4 de 1930.

470	**130**	1s. red	28·00	27·00
471	**130**	5s. olive	28·00	27·00
472	**130**	10s. black	28·00	27·00

133 Ploughing

1930. Independence Cent. Dated "1830 1930".

473	**133**	1c. red and yellow	20	10
474	-	2c. green and yellow	20	10
475	-	5c. purple and green	35	10
476	-	6c. red and yellow	45	10
477	-	10c. olive and orange	45	10
478	-	16c. green and red	55	30
479	-	20c. yellow and blue	90	20
480	-	40c. sepia and yellow	75	20
481	-	50c. sepia and yellow	90	55
482	-	1s. black and green	2·00	65
483	-	2s. black and deep blue	5·00	95
484	-	5s. black and purple	9·25	1·90
485	-	10s. black and red	35·00	6·50

DESIGNS—As Type **133**: 1c. Labourer and oxen, ploughing; 2c. Cocoa cultivation; 6c. Tobacco plantation; 10c. Exportation of fruit; 10s. Bolivar's monument (41×37½ mm). LARGER (27×42½ mm): 5c. Cocoa pod; 20c. Sugar plantation; 1s. Olmedo; 2s. Sucre; 5s. Bolivar. (41½×28 mm): 16c. Mountaineer, steam train and airplane; 40, 50c. Views of Quito.

1933. Optd CORREOS.

486	**103**	10c. brown	75	30

1933. Optd CORREOS Emision Junio 1933 Dcto. No 200.

487	10c. brown	45	30

1933. Nos. 476 and 478 surch.

488	5c. on 6c. red and yellow	35	20
489	10c. on 16c. green and red	55	20

1934. Obligatory Tax. Optd CASA de Correos y Telegrafos de Guayaquil. (a) Fiscal stamp as T 103, but inscr "MOVILES" (instead of dates at top).

490	2c. green	20	10

(b) Centenary stamp of 1930 (No. 479).

491	20c. yellow and blue	35	20

(c) Telegraph stamp as T 103, but inscr "TELEGRAFOS DEL ECUADOR" surch 2 ctvos. also.

492	2c. on 10c. brown	45	30

143 Mount Chimborazo

1934

493	**143**	5c. mauve	1·10	55
494	**143**	5c. blue	1·10	55
495	**143**	5c. brown	1·10	55
495a	**143**	5c. grey	1·10	55
496	**143**	10c. red	1·10	55
497	**143**	10c. green	1·10	55
498	**143**	10c. orange	1·10	55
499	**143**	10c. brown	1·10	55
500	**143**	10c. olive	1·10	55

500a	143	10c. black	1·10	55
500b	143	10c. lilac	1·10	55

144 Mount Chimborazo

1934

501	144	1s. red	1·50	55

1934. Optd CASA de Correos y Teleg. de Guayaquil.

502	112	2c. green (No. 425)	45	30

146 Symbol of Telegraphy

1934. G.P.O. Rebuilding Fund.

503	146	2c. green	20	10
504	-	20c. red	35	30

The symbolic design of the 20c. is 38×18½ mm.

1935. Unveiling of Bolivar Monument, Quito. Optd INAUGURACION MONUMENTO A BOLIVAR QUITO, 24 DE JULIO DE 1935 or surch also. (a) Postage. On 1930 Independence Issue.

505	5c. on 6c. red and yellow	55	30
506	10c. on 6c. red and yellow	75	30
507	20c. yellow and blue	1·10	30
508	40c. sepia and yellow	1·40	30
509	50c. sepia and yellow	1·80	45
510	$1 on 5s. black and purple	4·00	1·20
511	$2 on 5s. black and purple	5·25	1·80
512	$5 on 10s. black and red	9·25	5·00

(b) Air. On Official stamps of 1929.

513	130	50c. green	10·50	6·50
514	130	50c. brown	10·50	6·50
515	130	$1 on 5s. olive	10·50	6·50
516	130	$2 on 10s. black	10·50	6·50

1935. Fiscal stamp, but without dates and inscr "TELEGRAFOS DEL ECUADOR", optd POSTAL.

517	103	10c. brown	35	30

1935. Rural Workers Social Insurance Fund. No. 503 surch Seguro Social del Campesino Quito, 16 de Otbre.-1935 and value.

518	146	3c. on 2c. green	20	20

150 Map of Galapagos Islands

1936. Centenary of Darwin's Visit to the Galapagos Islands.

519	150	2c. black	1·00	30
520	-	5c. olive	1·20	30
521	-	10c. brown	2·40	30
522	-	20c. purple	2·75	45
523	-	1s. red	5·00	85
524	-	2s. blue	7·75	1·40

DESIGNS—HORIZ: 10c. Galapagos tortoise. VERT: 5c. Giant lizard; 20c. Charles Darwin and H.M.S. "Beagle"; 1s. Columbus; 2s. View of Galapagos Islands.

1936. Oblong Tobacco Tax Stamps. (a) Charity. Surch Seguro Social del Campesino 3 ctvs.

525	3c. on 1c. red	45	30

(b) Charity. Surch SEGURO SOCIAL DEL CAMPESINO 3 ctvs.

526	3c. on 1c. red	45	30

(c) Optd POSTAL.

527	1c. red	35	30

1936. No. 479 optd Casa de Correos y Telegrafos de Guayaquil.

528	20c. yellow and blue	45	30

160 Ulloa, La Condamine and Juan

1936. Bicentenary of La Condamine Scientific Expedition. (a) Postage.

529	-	2c. blue	45	30
530	160	5c. green	45	30
531	-	10c. orange	45	30
532	160	20c. violet	55	30
533	-	50c. red	1·00	30

(b) Air. Nos. 531/3 optd AEREO.

534		10c. orange	55	30
535	160	20c. violet	55	30
536	-	50c. red	55	30

(c) Air. Inscr "CORREO AEREO".

537	70c. grey	1·10	45

DESIGNS: 2c., 10c., 50c. Godin. La Condamine and Bouguer; 70c. La Condamine, Arms and Maldonado.

162 Woodman

1936. Building and National Defence Funds. Surch 5 Centavos Dect. Junio 13 de 1936.

539	162	5c. on 3c. blue	20	10

1936. Social Insurance.

540	3c. blue	45	30

1936. Oblong Tobacco Tax stamp surch TIMBRE PATRIOTICO DIEZ CENTAVOS.

541	10c. on 1c. red	65	30

165 Independence Monument, Quito

166 Condor and Martin M-130 Flying Boat

1936. 1st International Philatelic Exn, Quito.

541a	165	2c. green (postage)	2·20	1·30
542	165	5c. purple	2·20	1·30
543	165	10c. red	2·20	1·30
543a	165	20c. black	2·20	1·30
544	165	50c. blue	3·25	2·10
545	165	1s. red	75	75
546	166	70c. brown (air)	75	75
547	166	1s. violet	3·50	3·50

1936. Air. Optd AEREA.

547a	165	2c. red	3·50	3·50
547b	165	5c. orange	3·50	3·50
547c	165	10c. brown	3·50	3·50
547d	165	20c. blue	3·50	3·50
547e	165	50c. purple	3·50	3·50
547f	165	1s. green	3·50	3·50

167 Symbolical of Defence

1937. Obligatory Tax. National Defence Fund. (a) Surch POSTAL ADICIONAL and value in figures.

548	167	5c. on 10c. blue	90	30

(b) Without surch.

549	10c. blue	65	30

169

1937. Fiscal stamps inscr "MOVILES" at top optd POSTAL or surch also.

550	169	5c. olive (I)	1·70	30
955a	169	5c. olive (II)	45	30
551	169	10c. blue	1·70	30
819	169	10c. orange	65	30
952	169	20c. on 30c. blue	45	30
953	169	30c. blue	45	30
954	169	40c. on 50c. purple	45	30
955	169	50c. purple	45	30

Nos. 952/3 are smaller (19½×25½ mm). Nos. 550 (I) with imprint. 955a (II) without imprint.

See also No. 685.

171 Andean Landscape

172 Andean Condor over El Altar

1937. (a) Postage.

552	171	2c. green	35	30
553	-	5c. red	35	30
554	-	10c. blue	35	30
555	-	20c. red	90	30
556	-	1s. olive	1·20	45

DESIGNS—VERT: 5c. Atahualpa; 1s. Gold washer. HORIZ: 10c. Straw-hat makers; 20c. Salinas Beach.

(b) Air.

557	172	10c. brown	3·25	20
558	172	20c. olive	4·00	20
558a	172	40c. red	4·00	20
559	172	70c. brown	5·50	30
560	172	1s. slate	8·25	55
561	172	2s. violet	17·00	75

173

1937. Optd TIMBRE PATRIOTICO.

562	173	5c. brown	1·80	45

174 "Liberty" supporting Ecuadorian Flag between American Bald Eagle and Andean Condor

1938. 150th Anniv of U.S. Constitution. Flags in yellow, blue and red.

563	174	2c. blue (postage)	20	10
564	174	5c. violet	35	10
565	174	10c. black	55	10
566	174	20c. purple	65	20
567	174	50c. black	1·10	20
568	174	1s. olive	1·70	30
569	174	2s. brown	3·25	55
570	-	2c. olive (air)	20	10
571	-	5c. black	20	10
572	-	10c. brown	35	10
573	-	20c. blue	55	10
574	-	50c. purple	1·10	20
575	-	1s. black	1·90	30
576	-	2s. violet	4·50	1·10

DESIGN (air): Washington portrait, American bald eagle and flags.

176 Ecuador

1938. Obligatory Tax. Social Insurance Fund for Rural Workers and Guayaquil G.P.O. Rebuilding Funds.

577	176	5c. red	55	20

1938. Obligatory Tax. No. 537 surch CASA DE CORREOS Y TELEGRAFOS DE GUAYAQUIL and 20 in each corner.

578	20c. on 70c. grey	75	20

178 "Road Transport"

1938. National Progress Exn. Inscr "1830 – 1937".

579	178	10c. blue	10	10
580	-	50c. purple	20	10
581	-	1s. red	55	10
582	-	2s. green	90	10

DESIGNS—VERT: 50c. "Railways"; 1s. "Communication". HORIZ: 2s. "Building" (inscr "CONSTRUCCION").

1938. Air. Surch AEREO SEDTA and value.

582a	162	65c. on 3c. blue	35	30

1938. Obligatory Tax. International Anti-cancer Fund. No. 476 surch CAMPANA CONTRA EL CANCER 5 5.

583	5c. on 6c. red and yellow	20	20

181 Running

1939. Ecuadorean Victories at South American Olympic Games, La Paz. Inscr "EN CONMEMORACION DE LA PRIMERA OLIMPIADA BOLIVARIANA DE 1938".

584	-	5c. red (postage)	2·75	55
585	181	10c. blue	3·50	65
586	-	50c. olive	4·50	85
587	-	1s. violet	7·75	85
588	-	2s. green	10·50	95

DESIGNS—HORIZ: 5c. Parade of athletes; 50c. Basketball. VERT: 1s. Wrestling; 2s. Diving.

589	5c. green (air)	90	30
590	10c. orange	1·20	30
591	50c. brown	6·00	30
592	1s. sepia	7·75	55
593	2s. red	10·00	1·30

DESIGNS—HORIZ: 5c. Riding; 1s. Boxing. VERT: 10c. Running; 50c. Tennis; 2s. Olympic flame.

182 Ryan B-5 Brougham over Mt. Chimborazo

1939. Air.

594	182	1s. brown	20	20
595	182	2s. purple	55	20
596	182	5s. black	1·40	20

183 Dolores Mission, San Francisco

184 Golden Gate Bridge and Mountain

1939. San Francisco International Exhibition.

597	183	2c. green (postage)	35	30
598	183	5c. red	35	30
599	183	10c. blue	35	30
600	183	50c. brown	75	30
601	183	1s. slate	1·20	30
602	183	2s. violet	1·70	45
603	184	2c. black (air)	35	30
604	184	5c. red	35	30
605	184	10c. blue	35	30
606	184	50c. purple	35	30
607	184	1s. brown	45	30
608	184	2s. brown	55	30
609	184	5s. green	65	30

185 Symbol of N.Y. World's Fair

186 Empire State Building and Mountain

1939. New York World's Fair.

610	185	2c. olive (postage)	35	30
611	185	5c. orange	35	30
612	185	10c. blue	35	30
613	185	50c. grey	75	30
614	185	1s. red	1·10	30
615	185	2s. brown	1·30	45
616	186	2c. brown (air)	35	30
617	186	5c. red	35	30
618	186	10c. blue	35	30

619	186	50c. olive	35	30
620	186	1s. orange	45	30
621	186	2s. mauve	65	30
622	186	5s. black	1·10	30

1939. Obligatory Tax. Social Insurance Fund for Rural Workers. Oblong Tobacco Tax stamps surch POSTAL ADICIONAL CINCO CENTAVOS.

623	5c. on 1c. pink	55	30

1940. Obligatory Tax. G.P.O. Rebuilding Fund. Oblong Tobacco Tax stamp surch CASAS DE CORREOS Y TELEGRAFOS CINCO CENTAVOS.

624	5c. on 1c. pink	35	15

1940. Obligatory Tax. Guyaquil G.P.O. Rebuilding Fund. No. 567 surch CASA DE CORREOS y TELEGRAFOS DE GUAYAQUIL 20 20.

625	174	20c. on 50c. multicoloured	55	20

1940. Obligatory Tax. National Defence Fund. Oblong Tobacco Tax stamps surch TIMBRE PATRIOTICO VEINTE CENTAVOS.

625b	20c. on 1c. pink	2·10	35

191 Pan-American Union Flags

192 Allegory of Union

1940. 50th Anniv of Pan-American Union.

626	191	5c. black & red (postage)	20	10
627	191	10c. black and blue	20	10
628	191	50c. black and green	45	20
629	191	1s. black and violet	65	30
630	192	10c. blue & orange (air)	20	10
631	192	70c. blue and purple	35	10
632	192	1s. blue and brown	45	20
633	192	10s. blue and black	2·00	95

193 Ploughing

1940. Obligatory Tax. Social Insurance Fund for Rural Workers and Guayaquil G.P.O. Rebuilding Funds.

634	193	5c. red	25	15

194 Symbolic of Communications

1940. Obligatory Tax. G.P.O. Rebuilding Fund.

635	194	5c. brown	25	15
636	194	5c. green	25	15

195 Fighter Aircraft

1941. Obligatory Tax. National Defence Fund.

637	195	20c. blue	40	15

196 Dr. de Santa Cruz y Espejo

1941. 1st National Periodical Exhibition.

638	196	30c. blue (postage)	55	10
639	196	1s. orange	90	30
640	196	3s. red (air)	2·20	20
641	196	10s. orange	4·75	65

197 Francisco de Orellana

198 Early Map of S. America

1942. 400th Anniv of Discovery of R. Amazon.

642	197	10c. brown (postage)	55	30
643	-	40c. red	1·40	30
644	-	1s. violet	2·20	30
645	-	2s. blue	2·75	55
646	198	40c. bistre & black (air)	1·20	30
647	-	70c. olive	1·80	30
648	-	2s. green	2·00	30
649	-	5s. red	2·40	1·10

DESIGNS—VERT: 40c. (No. 643); 70c. Portraits of G. Pizarro and G. Diaz de Pineda; 2s. (No. 645) Quito; 5s. Expedition leaving Quito. HORIZ: 1s. Guayaquil; 2s. (No. 648) Relief map of R. Amazon.

199 R. Crespo Toral

1942

650	199	10c. green (postage)	10	10
651	199	50c. brown	55	20
652	199	10c. violet (air)	55	10

1942. As T 199 but portrait of Pres. A. B. Moreno.

653	10c. green	35	30

201 Mt. Chimborazo

1942

654	201	30c. brown	45	30
654a	201	30c. blue	45	30
654b	201	30c. orange	45	30
654c	201	30c. green	45	30

202 "Defence"

1942. Obligatory Tax. National Defence Fund.

655	202	20c. blue	90	30
655a	202	40c. brown	90	30

1942. Obligatory Tax. National Defence Fund. As T 173 surch.

655b	173	20c. on 5c. pink	50·00	10·50
655c	173	20c. on 1s. brown	50·00	10·50
655d	173	20c. on 2s. green	50·00	10·50

1942. Obligatory Tax. Guayaquil G.P.O. Rebuilding Fund. No. 567 surch CASA DE CORREOS Y TELEGRAFOS DE GUAYAQUIL VEINTE CENTAVOS.

655e	20c. on 50c. mult	90	30

203 Guayaquil Riverside

1943

656	203	20c. red	55	20
656a	203	20c. blue	55	20

1943. Guayaquil G.P.O. Rebuilding Fund. Surch ADICIONAL CINCO CENTAVOS 5 Centavos CASA DE CORREOS DE GQUIL. y.

657	162	5c.+5c. on 3c. blue	90	30

1943. Surch ADICIONAL CINCO CENTAVOS.

658	5c. on 3c. blue	45	30

206 Gen. Alfaro

207 Alfaro's Birthplace

1943. Birth Centenary of Alfaro.

659	206	10c. black & red (postage)	20	10
660	-	20c. brown and olive	20	10
661	-	30c. green and olive	35	10
662	207	1s. red and grey	75	30
663	206	70c. black and red (air)	75	30
664	-	1s. brown and olive	1·30	75
665	-	3s. green and olive	2·00	1·10
666	207	5s. red and grey	2·75	1·30

DESIGNS—HORIZ: 20c., 1s. Devil's Nose Zigzag, Guayaquil-Quito Rly; 30c., 3s. Alfaro Military College.

208 Labourers

1943. Obligatory Tax. Social Insurance Fund for Rural Workers and Guayaquil G.P.O. Rebuilding Funds.

667	208	5c. blue	65	30

1943. Welcome to Henry A. Wallace, Vice-President of U.S.A. Optd BIENVENIDO – WALLACE Abril 15 – 1943.

668	174	50c. mult (postage)	55	55
669	174	1s. multicoloured	1·10	1·10
670	174	2s. multicoloured	1·80	1·70
671	-	50c. multicoloured (No. 574) (air)	1·70	1·10
672	-	1s. multicoloured (No. 575)	1·90	1·20
673	-	2s. multicoloured (No. 576)	2·40	2·10

1943. Obligatory Tax. National Defence Fund. Fiscal stamp optd TIMBRE PATRIOTICO.

674	20c. orange	55·00	2·10

1943. Air. Visits of Presidents of Bolivia, Paraguay and Venezuela to Ecuador. (a) Optd AEREO LOOR A BOLIVIA JUNIO 11 – 1943.

675	50c. purple (No. 580)	35	30
676	1s. red (No. 581)	45	30
677	2s. green (No. 582)	55	30

(b) Optd AEREO LOOR AL PARAGUAY JULIO 5 – 1943.

678	50c. purple (No. 580)	35	30
679	1s. red (No. 581)	45	30
680	2s. green (No. 582)	55	30

(c) Optd AEREO LOOR A VENEZUELA JULIO 23 – 1943.

681	50c. purple (No. 580)	35	30
682	1s. red (No. 581)	75	75
683	2s. green (No. 582)	1·10	1·10

1943. Obligatory Tax National Defence Fund. Fiscal stamp surch TIMBRE PATRIOTICO VEINTE CENTAVOS.

684	20c. on 10c. orange	1·70	30

1943. Fiscal stamp as T 169 surch POSTAL 30 Centavos with or without bars.

685	169	30c. on 50c. brown	55	30

As No. 685 but surch POSTAL 30 Ctvs.

780	30c. on 50c. brown	55	20

213 Arms of Ecuador

1943. Obligatory Tax. National Defence Fund.

686	213	20c. red	55	30

214 Arms of Ecuador and Map of Central America

215 Pres. Arroyo del Rio at Washington

1943. President's Visit to Washington.

687	214	10c. violet (postage)	35	30
698	214	10c. green	35	30
688	214	20c. brown	35	30
699	214	20c. pink	35	30
689	214	30c. orange	35	30
700	214	30c. brown	35	30
690	214	50c. olive	45	45
701	214	50c. purple	35	30
691	214	1s. violet	55	55
702	214	1s. grey	55	55
692	214	10s. brown	5·50	5·00
703	214	10s. orange	6·00	4·50
693	215	50c. brown (air)	55	45
704	215	50c. purple	55	55
694	215	70c. red	75	45
705	215	70c. brown	1·00	55
695	215	3s. blue	90	55
706	215	3s. green	1·00	55
696	215	5s. green	1·90	95
707	215	5s. blue	1·70	1·10
697	215	10s. olive	7·75	3·50
708	215	10s. red	2·20	1·30

1944. Nos. 698/708 surch Hospital Mendez and new value.

711a	214	10c.+10c. grn (postage)	45	45
711b	214	20c.+20c. pink	45	45
711c	214	30c.+20c. brown	45	45
711d	214	50c.+20c. purple	90	85
711e	214	1s.+50c. grey	1·40	1·40
711f	214	10s.+2s. orange	4·50	4·25
711g	215	50c.+50c. pur (air)	4·50	4·25
711h	215	70c.+30c. brown	4·50	4·25
711i	215	3s.+50c. green	4·50	4·25
711j	215	5s.+1s. blue	4·50	4·25
711k	215	10s.+2s. red	4·50	4·25

1944. No. 600. Surch 30 Centavos.

712	183	30c. on 50c. brown	35	20

1944. Obligatory Tax. National Defence Fund. No. 686 surch POSTAL 30 Centavos.

713	213	30c. on 20c. red	55	30

1944. 606 and 619 Surch POSTAL 30 Centavos.

714	184	30c. on 50c. purple	20	10
715	186	30c. on 50c. olive	20	10

218 F. Gonzales Suarez

219 Cathedral, Quito

1944. Birth Cent of F. G. Suarez (Archbishop).

716	218	10c. blue (postage)	10	10
717	218	20c. green	10	10
718	218	30c. purple	35	10
719	218	1s. violet	65	20
720	219	70c. green (air)	75	55
721	219	1s. olive	75	55
722	219	3s. red	1·70	1·10
723	219	5s. red	2·20	1·30

1944. Surch CINCO Centavos.

724	183	5c. on 2c. green	35	20
725	185	5c. on 2c. green	35	20

221 Government Palace, Quito

1944

726	221	10c. green (postage)	20	10
727	221	30c. blue	20	10
728	221	3s. orange (air)	55	30
729	221	5s. brown	1·00	75
730	221	10s. red	2·00	1·10
730a	221	10s. violet	3·75	1·80

222 Red Cross Symbol

1945. 80th Anniv of Int Red Cross. Cross in red.

731	**222**	30c. brown (postage)	1·10	30
732	**222**	1s. brown	1·30	55
733	**222**	5s. green	2·40	1·40
734	**222**	10s. red	6·50	3·75
735	**222**	2s. blue (air)	1·50	1·10
736	**222**	3s. green	1·90	1·30
737	**222**	5s. violet	2·75	1·80
738	**222**	10s. red	8·25	5·75

1945. Air. Surch AEREO 40 Ctvs.

739	**208**	40c. on 5c. blue	35	10

1945. Obligatory Tax. Air. No. 726 surch FOMENTO-AERO-COMUNICACIONES 20 Ctvs.

740	**221**	20c. on 10c. green	55	30

1945. Air. Victory. Optd V SETIEMBRE 5 1945.

742		3s. orange	90	75
743		5s. brown	1·10	95
744		10s. red	2·75	2·10

1945. Visit of Pres. Juan Antonio Rios of Chile. Optd LOOR A CHILE OCTUBRE 2 1945 and five-pointed star. Flags in yellow, blue and red.

745	**174**	50c. black (postage)	65	30
746	**174**	1s. olive	1·00	30
747	**174**	2s. brown	2·10	1·20
748	-	50c. pur (No. 574) (air)	90	45
749	-	1s. black (No. 575)	1·00	85
750	-	2s. violet (No. 576)	1·50	85

227 Marshal Sucre

1945. 150th Birth Anniv of Marshal Sucre.

751	**227**	10c. green (postage)	10	10
752	**227**	20c. brown	10	10
753	**227**	40c. grey	10	10
754	**227**	1s. green	45	30
755	**227**	2s. brown	1·10	55
756	-	30c. blue (air)	35	10
757	-	40c. red	45	20
758	-	1s. violet	90	55
759	-	3s. black	2·00	1·40
760	-	5s. purple	2·75	1·90

DESIGN—Air stamps: Liberty Monument.

1945. Surch c VEINTE CENTAVOS.

761	**221**	20c. on 10c. green	20	10

230 Pan-American Highway

1946. Completion of Pan-American Highway.

762	**230**	20c. brown (postage)	35	30
763	**230**	30c. green	35	30
764	**230**	1s. blue	35	30
765	**230**	5s. purple	1·10	1·10
766	**230**	10s. red	2·40	1·60
767	**230**	1s. red (air)	45	30
768	**230**	2s. violet	55	45
769	**230**	3s. green	90	45
770	**230**	5s. orange	1·10	65
771	**230**	10s. blue	1·70	55

231 Torch of Democracy

232 Popular Suffrage

1946. 2nd Anniv of Revolution.

772	**231**	5c. blue (postage)	10	10
773	**232**	10c. green	10	10
774	-	20c. red	35	10
775	-	30c. brown	65	20
776	**231**	40c. red (air)	10	10
777	**232**	1s. brown	20	10
778	-	2s. blue	90	30
779	-	3s. green	1·40	65

DESIGNS—VERT: 20c., 2s. National flag; 30c., 3s. Pres. J.M. Velasco Ibarra.

1946. Nos. O567/8 optd POSTAL.

781	**172**	10c. brown	20	20
782	**172**	20c. olive	20	20

237 Teacher and Scholar

238 Seal of National Periodicals Union

1946. Adult Instruction.

783	**237**	10c. blue (postage)	20	20
784	**237**	20c. brown	20	20
785	**237**	30c. green	20	20
786	**237**	50c. black	35	30
787	**237**	1s. red	55	55
788	**237**	10s. purple	3·75	95
789	**238**	50c. violet (air)	45	20
790	**238**	70c. green	55	30
791	**238**	3s. red	90	45
792	**238**	5s. blue	1·10	55
793	**238**	10s. brown	1·70	85

239 "Liberty", "Mercury" and Aeroplanes

1946. Obligatory Tax. Air. National Defence Fund.

794	**239**	20c. brown	55	30

240 "Mariana de Jesus Paredes y Flores"

1946. 300th Death Anniv of Blessed Mariana de Jesus Paredes y Flores.

795	**240**	10c. brown (postage)	35	30
796	**240**	20c. green	35	30
797	**240**	30c. violet	35	30
798	-	1s. brown	55	30
799	-	40c. brown (air)	35	30
800	-	60c. blue	45	45
801	-	3s. yellow	90	75
802	-	5s. green	1·90	95

DESIGNS: 40c., 60c. Mariana teaching children; 1s. Urn; 3s., 5s. Cross and lilies.

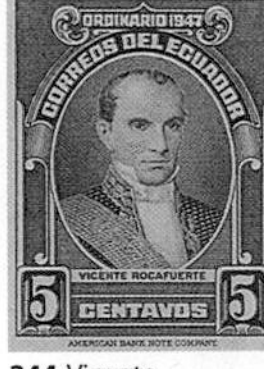

244 Vicente Rocafuerte

245 Jesuit Church, Quito

1947. Vicente Rocafuerte. (a) Postage

803	**244**	5c. brown (postage)	10	10
804	**244**	10c. purple	10	10
805	**244**	15c. black	10	10
806	**245**	20c. lake	20	10
807	**245**	30c. mauve	35	10
808	**245**	40c. blue	45	20
809	-	45c. green	55	20
810	-	50c. grey	55	20
811	-	80c. red	90	20

PORTRAIT: 45c. to 80c. F. J. E. de Santa Cruz y Espejo.

(b) Air

812		60c. green (air)	10	10
813		70c. violet	20	10
814		1s. brown	20	10
815		1s.10 red	20	10
816		1s.30 blue	20	20
817		1s.90 brown	75	20
818		2s. olive	75	20

DESIGNS: 60c. to 1s.10, Father J. de Velasco; 1s.30 to 2s. Riobamba Irrigation Canal.

250 Andres Bello

1948. 83rd Death Anniv of Andres Bello (educationalist).

820	**250**	20c. blue (postage)	35	30
821	**250**	30c. pink	35	30
822	**250**	40c. green	35	30
823	**250**	1s. black	55	30
824	**250**	60c. mauve (air)	35	30
825	**250**	1s.30 green	55	30
826	**250**	1s.90 red	45	30

1948. Economic Conference Optd CONFERENCIA ECONOMICA GRANCOLOMBIANA MAYO 24 DE 1.948.

827	**245**	40c. blue (postage)	45	45
828	-	70c. vio (No. 813) (air)	75	55

252 The "Santa Maria"

253 Christopher Columbus

1948. Completion of Columbus Memorial Lighthouse.

829	**252**	10c. green (postage)	20	10
830	**252**	20c. brown	20	10
831	**252**	30c. violet	55	10
832	**252**	50c. red	75	10
833	**252**	1s. blue	1·10	30
834	**252**	5s. red	3·25	45
835	**253**	50c. green (air)	10	10
836	**253**	70c. red	20	20
837	**253**	3s. blue	75	55
838	**253**	5s. brown	1·20	75
839	**253**	10s. violet	3·75	85

1948. National Fair. Nos. 811 and 816 optd Feria Nacional 1948 ECUADOR de hoy y del MANANA.

840		80c. red (postage)	35	30
841		1s.30c. blue (air)	55	30

255 "Telegrafo I" on First Postal Flight

256 Elia Liut and "Telegrafo I"

1948. 25th Anniv of First Ecuadorian Postal Flight.

842	**255**	30c. orange (postage)	35	30
843	**255**	40c. mauve	35	30
844	**255**	60c. blue	35	30
845	**255**	1s. brown	35	30
846	**255**	3s. brown	1·10	55
847	**255**	5s. black	1·20	55
848	**256**	60c. red (air)	45	30
849	**256**	1s. green	45	45
850	**256**	1s.30 red	45	45
851	**256**	1s.90 violet	45	45
852	**256**	2s. brown	65	45
853	**256**	5s. blue	1·20	75

257 "Reading and Writing"

258 "Education For All"

1948. National Education Campaign.

854	**257**	10c. claret (postage)	10	10
855	**257**	20c. brown	10	10
856	**257**	30c. green	35	10
857	**257**	50c. red	35	10
858	**257**	1s. violet	45	30
859	**257**	10s. blue	4·50	75
860	**258**	50c. violet (air)	55	30
861	**258**	70c. blue	55	30
862	**258**	3s. green	1·00	65
863	**258**	5s. red	1·40	85
864	**258**	10s. brown	2·75	1·10

259 "Freedom from Fear"

260 "Freedom of Religion"

261 "Freedom of Speech and Expression"

262 "Freedom from Want"

1948. Homage to Franklin D. Roosevelt.

865	**259**	10c. red & grey (postage)	35	30
866	**259**	20c. olive and blue	35	30
867	**260**	30c. olive and red	35	30
868	**260**	40c. purple and sepia	45	30
869	**260**	1s. brown and red	55	45
870	**261**	60c. green & brn (air)	10	10
871	**261**	1s. red and black	20	20
872	**262**	1s.50 green & brown	75	55
873	**262**	2s. red and black	1·20	75
874	**262**	5s. blue and black	3·75	85

263 Maldonado at Academy of Sciences, Paris

264 Riobamba Aqueduct

1948. Death Bicentenary of Maldonado (geographer and scientist).

875	**263**	5c. red & black (postage)	35	10
876	**264**	10c. black and red	45	20
877	-	30c. blue and brown	55	20
878	**264**	40c. violet and green	65	20
879	**263**	50c. red and green	75	30
880	-	1s. blue and brown	1·00	45
881	-	60c. red & orange (air)	55	10
882	-	90c. black and red	55	10
883	-	1s.30 orange & mauve	90	30
884	-	2s. green and blue	90	30

DESIGN—VERT: 30c., 60c., 1s.30, Maldonado making road to Esmeraldas; 90c., 1s., 2s. P. Vicente Maldonado.

266 Cervantes, Don Quixote and Windmill

267 Don Quixote and Sheep

1949. 400th Birth Anniv of Cervantes.

885		30c. blue & pur (postage)	55	20
886	**266**	60c. brown & purple	90	45
887	-	1s. red and green	1·50	30
888	**266**	2s. black and red	2·75	45
889	-	5s. green and brown	5·50	1·50
890	-	1s.30 brown & blue (air)	2·75	2·75
891	**267**	1s.90 red and green	75	30
892	-	3s. violet and red	1·10	30
893	**267**	5s. black and red	2·00	30
894	-	10s. purple and green	2·75	20

DESIGNS—HORIZ: 30c., 1s., 5s. (No. 889) Cervantes, Don Quixote and Sancho Panza; 1s.30, 3s., 10s. Don Juan Montalvo and Cervantes.

1949. 2nd Eucharistic Congress. Stamps of 1947 surch II CONGRESO Junio 1949 Eucaristico Ncl. and values. (a) Postage. No. 808 surch.

895	**245**	10c. on 40c. blue	35	10
896	**245**	20c. on 40c. blue	55	20

897	245	30c. on 40c. blue	55	20

(b) Air. No. 815 surch.

898		50c. on 1s.10 red	20	20
899		60c. on 1s.10 red	35	20
900		90c. on 1s.10 red	45	30

269 Equatorial Line Monument

1949

901	269	10c. purple	35	10

274 Lake San Pablo

1949. 75th Anniv of U.P.U. Surch 75 ANIVERSARIO (or Aniversario on air stamps) U.P.U. and value.

902	274	10c. on 50c. grn (postage)	35	30
903	274	20c. on 50c. green	35	30
904	274	30c. on 50c. green	45	30
905	221	60c. on 3s. orge (air)	55	45
906	221	90c. on 3s. orange	55	30
907	221	1s. on 3s. orange	65	45
908	221	2s. on 3s. orange	1·50	45

For unoverprinted stamp Type **274**, see No. 926.

272

1949. Consular Service stamps optd or surch for postal use. I. On T 272. A. Postage. (a) Vert surch POSTAL and value before ct vs.

908a	272	5c. on 10c. red	35	30
909	272	20c. on 25c. brown	20	10
910	272	30c. on 50c. black	35	10

(b) Optd CORREOS diag.

927		10c. red	35	30

(c) Optd POSTAL diag.

929		10c. red	35	30

(d) Vert surch with figs. before and after Ctvs. (i) CORREOS upwards.

928		30c. on 50c. black	45	30

(ii) POSTAL upwards.

930		20c. on 25c. brown	35	30
931		30c. on 50c. black	35	30

(e) Surch POSTAL centavos with figs between.

969		10c. on 20s. blue	35	20
970		20c. on 10s. grey	35	20
971		20c. on 20s. blue	35	20
972		30c. on 10s. grey	35	20
973		30c. on 20s. blue	35	20

B. Air. Surch AEREO and value.

913		60c. on 50c. black	35	20
913a		60c. on 2s. brown	45	30
913b		1s. on 2s. brown (D.)	45	30
913c		1s. on 2s. brown (U.)	35	20
913d		2s. on 2s. brown	65	20
913e		3s. on 5s. violet	90	20

In No. 913b the surch reads down and in No. 913c it reads up.

II. On T 272a. A. Postage. Surch POSTAL and value.

935	272a	30c. on 50c. red	35	30
934	272a	40c. on 25c. blue	45	30
936	272a	50c. on 25c. blue	55	30

B. Air. Surch AEREO and value.

913f		60c. on 1s. green	35	10
913g		60c. on 5s. sepia	45	30
913h		70c. on 5s. sepia	35	20
913i		90c. on 50c. red	35	20
913j		1s. on 1s. green	35	10

1950. Optd POSTAL.

911	194	5c. green	20	10
912	208	5c. blue	20	10

1950. Air. (a) Nos. 816/7 surch 90 ctvs. 90.

914		90c. on 1s.30 blue	35	10
914a		90c. on 1s.90 brown	45	20

(b) No. 816 surch 90 CENTAVOS.

914b		90c. on 1s.30 blue	35	10

1950. Literary Campaign. Optd ALFABETIZACION. Four values also surch with new values and No. 920 also optd POSTAL.

915	269	10c. purple (postage)	35	30
916	264	20c. on 40c. (878)	65	65
917	264	30c. on 40c. (878)	75	75
918	263	50c. red and green	1·20	1·20
919	-	1s. blue & brown (880)	1·50	1·50
920	221	10s. violet	3·75	1·80
921	-	50c. on 1s.10 (815) (air)	45	45
922	-	70c. on 1s.10 (815)	55	45
923	221	3s. orange	90	75
924	221	5s. brown	1·20	65
925	221	10s. violet	1·90	75

1950

926	274	50c. green	35	20

1951. Air. Panagra Airlines' 20,000th Flight across Equator. Optd 20.000 Cruce Linea Ecuatorial PANAGRA 26-Julio-1951.

932	221	3s. orange	1·30	1·30
933	221	5s. brown	2·20	1·90

272a

1951. Adult Education. Surch CAMPANA Alfabetizacion and values. (a) Postage.

937	272a	20c. on 25c. blue	55	20
938	272a	30c. on 25c. blue	55	20

(b) Air.

939	-	60c. on 1s.30 (890)	35	20
940	267	1s. on 1s.90 (891)	35	20

278 Reliquary and St. Peter's, Vatican City

279 St. Mariana de Jesus

1952. Canonization of St. Mariana de Jesus.

941	278	10c. green & lake (postage)	55	30
942	278	20c. blue and violet	55	30
943	278	30c. red and green	55	30
944	279	60c. red & turquoise (air)	65	30
945	279	90c. green and blue	75	30
946	279	1s. red and green	90	30
947	279	2s. blue and mauve	90	30

280 Presidents Plaza and Truman

1952. Visit of President of Ecuador to U.S.A.

948	280	1s. black & red (postage)	45	30
949	-	2s. sepia and blue	1·00	65
950	280	3s. green and lilac (air)	65	45
951	-	5s. olive and brown	1·30	1·30
MS951a		127×61 mm. Nos. 950/1. Imperf	3·25	7·00

DESIGN: 2s., 5s. Pres. Plaza addressing U.S. Congress.

1952. Consular Service stamps surch TIMBRE ESCOLAR 20 ctvs. 20.

957	272	20c. on 1s. red	20	10
958	272	20c. on 2s. brown	20	10
959	272	20c. on 5s. violet	20	10

282 Pres. Urvina, Slave and "Liberty"

1952. Centenary of Abolition of Slavery in Ecuador. Roul.

960	282	20c. green & red (postage)	20	10
961	282	30c. red and blue	35	10
962	282	50c. blue and red	65	10
963	-	60c. red and blue (air)	2·20	55
964	-	90c. lilac and red	2·20	75
965	-	1s. orange and green	2·20	30
966	-	2s. brown and blue	2·20	45

DESIGN—VERT: Nos. 963/6, Pres. Urvina, condor and freed slave.

284 Teacher and Scholars

1952. Obligatory Tax. Literacy Campaign.

967	284	20c. green	40	15

1952. Obligatory Tax. Public Health Fund. Fiscal stamp optd PATRIOTICO y SANITARIO.

968	103	40c. olive	20	15

286 Learning Alphabet

1953. Literacy Campaign. Inscr "UNP LAE".

974	-	5c. blue (postage)	20	10
975	-	10c. red	35	10
976	-	20c. orange	45	10
977	-	30c. purple	65	10
978	-	1s. blue (air)	1·10	20
979	286	2s. red	1·40	20

DESIGNS—VERT: 5c. Teacher and pupils; 10c. Instructor and student; 1s. Hand and torch. HORIZ: 20c. Men and ballot-box; 30c. Teaching the alphabet.

287 Flag-bearer and Health Emblem

1953. Obligatory Tax. Public Health Fund.

980	287	40c. blue	45	15

288

1953. Air. Crossing of Equator by Pan-American Highway.

981	288	60c. yellow	35	30
982	288	90c. blue	45	45
983	288	3s. red	90	65

289 Equatorial Line Monument

1953

984	-	5c. blue and black	35	30
985	289	10c. green and black	35	30
986	-	20c. lilac and black	35	30
987	-	30c. brown and black	35	30
988	-	40c. orange and black	35	30
989	-	50c. red and black	45	30

DESIGNS: 5c. Cuicocha Lagoon; 20c. Quininde landscape; 30c. River Tomebamba; 40c. La Chilintosa rock; 50c. Iliniza Mountains.

290 Cardinal de la Torre

291 Cardinal de la Torre

1954. 1st Anniv of Elevation of De la Torre to Cardinal.

990	290	30c. blk & red (postage)	20	20
991	290	50c. black and purple	20	20
992	291	60c. black & pur (air)	20	20
993	291	90c. black and green	35	20
994	291	3s. black and orange	45	30

292 Isabella the Catholic

293 Isabella the Catholic

1954. 500th Birth Anniv of Isabella the Catholic.

995	292	30c. blk & bl (postage)	55	55
996	292	50c. black and yellow	55	55
997	293	60c. green (air)	35	45
998	293	90c. purple	35	45
999	293	1s. black and pink	35	45
1000	293	2s. black and blue	45	30
1001	293	5s. black and flesh	1·10	30

294 Guayaquil Post Office

1954. Air. Silver Jubilee of Panagra Air Lines. Unissued stamp surch as in T 294.

1002	294	80c. on 20c. red	35	20
1003	294	1s. on 20c. red	35	20

1954. Obligatory Tax. Literacy Campaign. Telegraph stamp (18½×22½ mm) surch ESCOLAR 20 Centavos.

1004		20c. on 30c. brown	35	15

1954. Obligatory Tax. Literacy Campaign. Fiscal stamp as T 103 (19½×25½ mm) optd ESCOLAR.

1004a	103	20c. olive	60	15

1954. Obligatory Tax. Tourist Promotion Fund. (a) Telegraph stamp as No. 1004 but surch Pro-Turismo 1954 10 ctvs. 10.

1005		10c. on 30c. brown	75	15

(b) Judicial stamp as T 103 (19½×25½ mm) optd PRO TURISMO 1954.

1006		10c. red	45	15

(c) Fiscal stamp as T 103 (19½×25½ mm) surch PRO TURISMO 1954 10 ctvs. Diez Centavos.

1006a		10c. on 50c. red	45	15

(d) Consular Service stamp surch PRO TURISMO 1954 10 ctvs.

1007	272a	10c. on 25c. blue	45	15

1954. Consular Service stamp surch 0.20 0.20 ESCOLAR Veinte centavos.

1007a	272	20c. on 10s. grey	60	15

299 "Chasqui" (Inca Message Carrier)

300 Airliner over Building

1954. Postal Employees' Day.

1008	299	30c. sepia (postage)	45	30
1009	300	80c. blue (air)	45	30

301 Bananas

302 Douglas DC-4 over San Pablo Lake

1954

1010	**301**	10c. orange (postage)	10	10
1011	**301**	20c. red	20	10
1012	**301**	30c. mauve	35	10
1013	**301**	40c. myrtle	45	10
1014	**301**	50c. brown	65	10
1015	**302**	60c. orange (air)	35	30
1016	**302**	70c. mauve	35	30
1017	**302**	90c. green	35	30
1018	**302**	1s. myrtle	35	30
1019	**302**	2s. blue	45	30
1020	**302**	3s. brown	75	30

302a

1954. Obligatory Tax. Literacy Fund.

1020a	**302a**	20c. red	40	15

303 Death on Battlefield

1954. Air. 150th Death Anniv of Captain Calderon Garaicoa.

1021	**303**	80c. mauve	55	20
1022	-	90c. blue	55	20

PORTRAIT—VERT: 90c. Capt. Calderon.

304 El Cebollar College

1954. Air. Birth Centenary of F. F. Cordero.

1023	**304**	70c. myrtle	10	10
1024	-	80c. sepia	20	10
1025	-	90c. blue	35	10
1026	-	2s.50 slate	55	20
1027	-	3s. lilac	65	55

DESIGNS—VERT: 80c. Febres Cordero and boys; 90c. Febres Cordero; 2s.50, Tomb. HORIZ: 3s. Monument.

305 "Transport"

1954. Obligatory Tax. Tourist Promotion Fund.

1028	**305**	10c. mauve	55	15

306 Kissing the Flag

1955. Obligatory Tax. National Defence Fund.

1029	**306**	40c. blue	75	15

1955. Air. World Press Exhibition. No. 730a surch E. M. P. 1955 and value.

1030	**221**	1s. on 10s. violet	35	30
1031	**221**	1s.70 on 10s. violet	45	30
1032	**221**	4s.20 on 10s. violet	75	55

308 La Rotonda, Guayaquil

1955. Air. 50th Anniv of Rotary International.

1033	**308**	80c. brown	35	30
1034	-	90c. green	45	45

DESIGN: 90c. Eugenio Espejo Hospital, Quito.

310 Castillo and "Telegrafo 1"

1955. Birth Centenary of Jose Abel Castillo (pioneer aviator).

1035		30c. bistre (postage)	10	10
1036		50c. black	20	10
1037	**310**	60c. brown (air)	75	20
1038	**310**	90c. green	75	20
1039	**310**	1s. mauve	90	20
1040	-	2s. red	1·10	30
1041	-	5s. blue	2·20	85

DESIGNS—VERT: 30c., 50c. Bust of Castillo. HORIZ: 2s., 5s. Castillo and map of Ecuador.

1955. Air. Surch 1 X SUCRE X over ornamental bar.

1042	**130**	1s. on 5s. violet	45	30

312 Palm Trees

1955. Pictorial designs as T 312.

1043	**312**	5c. green (postage)	75	30
1043a	**312**	5c. blue	75	30
1043b	**B**	5c. green	20	20
1044	**C**	10c. blue	75	30
1044a	**C**	10c. brown	75	30
1044b	**B**	10c. brown	20	20
1045	**A**	20c. brown	75	30
1045a	**A**	20c. pink	75	30
1045b	**A**	20c. green	75	30
1045c	**B**	20c. plum	20	20
1046	**D**	30c. black	75	30
1046a	**D**	30c. red	75	30
1046b	**B**	30c. blue	20	20
1046c	**E**	40c. blue	1·10	30
1047	**F**	50c. green	75	30
1047a	**F**	50c. violet	75	30
1048	**E**	70c. olive	55	30
1049	**G**	80c. violet	1·90	30
1049a	**B**	80c. red	20	20
1049b	**G**	90c. blue	1·00	30
1050	**H**	1s. orange	1·00	30
1050a	**H**	1s. sepia	75	30
1050b	**I**	1s. black	75	30
1051	**J**	2s. red	1·90	30
1051a	**J**	2s. brown	1·20	30
1052	**K**	50c. slate (air)	1·20	30
1052a	**K**	50c. green	1·00	30
1053	**L**	1s. blue	1·20	30
1053a	**L**	1s. orange	1·00	30
1054	**M**	1s.30 red	1·80	30
1055	**N**	1s.50 green	1·20	30
1056	**O**	1s.70 brown	75	30
1057	**P**	1s.90 olive	1·30	30
1058	**Q**	2s.40 red	1·50	30
1059	**R**	2s.50 violet	1·50	30
1060	**S**	4s.20 black	1·90	30
1061	**T**	4s.80 yellow	2·75	45

DESIGNS—POSTAGE: A, River Babahoyo; B, "The Virgin of Quito" (after L. y del Arco); C, Manta fisherman; D, Guayaquil; E, Cactus; F, River Pital; G, Orchids; H, Agucate Mission; I, San Pablo; J, Jibaro Indian. AIR: K, Rumichaca Grotto; L, San Pablo; M, "The Virgin of Quito"; N, Cotopaxi Volcano; O, Tungurahua Volcano; P, Guanaco; Q, Selling mats; R, Ingapirca ruins; S, El Carmen, Cuenca; T, Santo Domingo Church.

313 Vazquez in 1883

1956. Air. Birth Centenary of Vazquez.

1062	**313**	1s. green	35	30
1063	-	1s.50 red	35	30
1064	-	1s.70 blue	35	30
1065	-	1s.90 slate	35	30

PORTRAITS OF VAZQUEZ: 1s.50, 1905. 1s.70, 1910. 1s.90, 1931.

314 J. A. Schwarz

315 Title Page of First Book printed in Ecuador

1956. Bicentenary of Printing in Ecuador.

1066	**314**	5c. green (postage)	35	30
1067	**314**	10c. red	35	30
1068	**314**	20c. violet	35	30
1069	**314**	30c. green	35	30
1070	**314**	40c. blue	35	30
1071	**314**	50c. blue	35	30
1072	**314**	70c. orange	35	30
1073	**315**	1s. black (air)	35	30
1074	**315**	1s.70 slate	35	30
1075	**315**	2s. sepia	35	30
1076	**315**	3s. brown	45	30

316 Hands reaching for U.N. Emblem

1956. Air. 10th Anniv of U.N.O.

1077	**316**	1s.70 red	55	30

For stamp as Type **316** see No. 1095.

317 Emblem and Girl with Ball

1956. Air. 6th S. American Women's Basketball Championships.

1078	**317**	1s. mauve	65	30
1079	-	1s.70 green	1·00	30

DESIGN: 1s.70, Map, flags and players.

318 Marquis of Canete

319 Cuenca Cathedral

1957. 400th Anniv of Cuenca.

1082	**318**	5c. blue on flesh (post)	20	10
1083	-	10c. bronze on green	20	10
1084	-	20c. brown on buff	20	10
1085	-	50c. sep on cream (air)	20	10
1086	**319**	80c. red on blue	20	20
1087	-	1s. violet on yellow	20	20

DESIGNS— HORIZ: 10c. Gil Ramirez Davalos and Cuenca landscape; 50c. Early plan of Cuenca; 1s. Municipal Palace. VERT: 20c. Father Vicente Solano.

1957. 2nd National Philatelic Exhibition, Cuenca. Sheet containing two each of Nos. 1082/3 in new colours. Imperf. No gum.

MS1087a 140×120 mm. 5c. black; 20c. brown	65	1·30

1957. Air. 4th Meeting of the Pan-American Geographical and Historical Insitute Commission. Sheet containing four stamps similar to No. 1083. Imperf. No gum.

MS1087b 140×120 mm. 50c. green (four stamps)	1·00	1·60

1957. Air. 3rd Engineers and Architects Conference, Cuenca. Sheet containing Nos. 1085/7 in new colours. Imperf. No gum.

MS1087c 140×120 mm. 50c. red; 80c. brown; 1s. lilac	1·50	2·30

320 Delegates to the 1838 Postal Congress

1957. 7th U.P.A.E. Postal Congress, 1955.

1088	**320**	40c. yellow	20	10
1089	**320**	50c. blue	20	10
1090	**320**	2s. red	75	20

321 Gabriela Mistral (Chilean poet)

1957. Air. Gabriela Mistral Commem.

1091	**321**	2s. grey, black & red	55	20

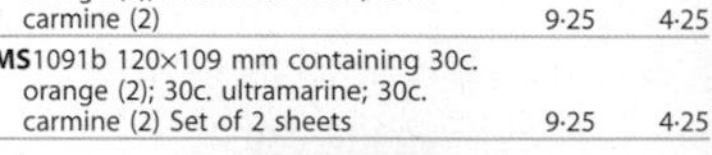

321a Loading Train

1957. Opening of Quito-Ibarra-San Lorenzo Railway. Two sheets each containing five stamps showing various rail-road designs as T 321a.

MS1091a 120×109 mm containing 20c. orange (2); 20c. ultramarine; 20c. carmine (2)	9·25	4·25
MS1091b 120×109 mm containing 30c. orange (2); 30c. ultramarine; 30c. carmine (2) Set of 2 sheets	9·25	4·25

322 Arms of Espejo

1957. Air. Carchi Cantonal Arms. Inscr "PROVINCIA DEL CARCHI". Arms mult.

1092	**322**	1s. red	55	30
1093	-	2s. black (Montufar)	55	30
1094	-	4s.20 blue (Tulcan)	1·10	30

For other Arms as Type **322** see Nos 1124/7, 1147/51, 1155/9, 1197 and 1220/3.

1957. Air. United Nations Day. As T 316 but without dates.

1095	2s. blue	55	45

323 Blue and Yellow Macaw

1958. Tropical Birds. Birds in natural colours. (a) As T 323.

1096	**323**	10c. brown	1·10	20
1097	-	20c. grey and buff	1·10	20
1098	-	30c. green	2·75	20
1099	-	40c. orange	2·75	30

BIRDS: 20c. Red-breasted Toucan. 30c. Andean Condor. 40c. Sword-billed Hummingbird and Black-tailed Trainbearer.

(b) As T 323 but "ECUADOR" at top in black.

1120	20c. turquoise and red	1·20	20
1121	30c. blue and yellow	1·30	20
1122	50c. orange and green	1·90	55
1123	60c. pink & turquoise	3·25	55

BIRDS: 20c. Masked Crimson Tanager. 30c. Andean Cock of the Rock. 50c. Solitary Cacique. 60c. Red-fronted Conures.

324 The Virgin of Sorrows

1958. Air. 50th Anniv of The Miracle of the Virgin of Sorrows of St. Gabriel College, Quito.
1100 **324** 30c. purple on purple 35 20
1101 - 30c. purple on purple 35 20
1102 - 1s. blue on blue 35 20
1103 **324** 1s.70 blue on blue 35 20
DESIGN: Nos. 1101/2, Gateway of St. Gabriel College, Quito.

325 Vice-Pres. Nixon and Flags of Ecuador and the U.S.A.

1958. Visit of Vice-Pres. of the United States. Flags in red, blue and yellow.
1104 **325** 2s. salmon and green 65 20

1958. Visit of Pres. Morales of Honduras. As T 325 but with portrait of Pres. Morales, flags of Ecuador and Honduras, and inscriptions changed. Flags in red, blue and yellow.
1105 2s. brown 65 20

326 Dr. C. Sanz de Santamaria

1958. Visit of Chancellor of Colombia.
1106 **326** 1s.80 multicoloured 65 20

327 Dr. R. M. Arizaga

1958. Air. Birth Cent of Arizaga (diplomat).
1107 **327** 1s. multicoloured 45 30
See also Nos. 1135, 1142 and 1241.

328 Gonzalo Icaza Cornejo Bridge

1958. Air. Inauguration of Gonzalo Icaza Cornejo Bridge.
1108 **328** 1s.30 green 55 20

329 Steam Locomotive

1958. 50th Anniv of Opening of Guayaquil–Quito Railway.
1109 **329** 30c. black 20 10
1110 - 50c. red 35 10
1111 - 5s. brown 1·70 1·10
DESIGNS—HORIZ: 50c. Diesel-electric train; DIAMOND, 5s. State presidents.

330 Basketball Player

1958. Air. South American Basketball Champions' Tournament, Quito.
1112 **330** 1s.30 green & brown 55 45

331 J. C. de Macedo Soares

1958. Visit of Brazilian Chancellor.
1113 **331** 2s.20 multicoloured 65 20

332 Monstrance and Doves

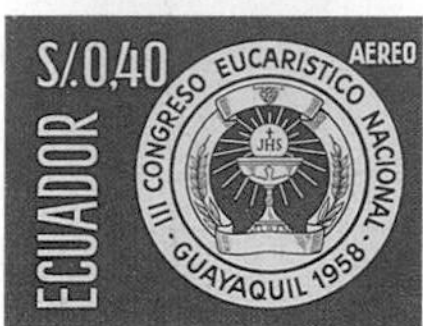

332a Congress Symbol

1958. Air. 3rd National Eucharistic Congress, Guayaquil. Inscr as in T 332.
1114 **332** 10c. violet and yellow 55 30
1115 - 60c. violet and salmon 55 30
1116 **332** 1s. sepia and turquoise 55 30
MS1116a **332a** 115×89 mm. 40c. blue (block of 4) 2·75 2·75
DESIGN: 60c. Guayaquil Cathedral.

333 Stamps of 1865 and 1920

1958. Air. National Stamp Exn, Guayaquil.
1117 **333** 1s.30 red and green 35 30
1118 - 2s. violet and blue 75 45
1119 - 4s.20 sepia 90 55
DESIGNS: 2s. Stamps of 1920 and 1948; 4s.20, Guayaquil Municipal Library and Museum.

1958. Air. Imbabura Cantonal Arms. As T 322. Inscr "PROVINCIA DE IMBABURA". Arms multicoloured.
1124 50c. red and black 55 30
1125 60c. blue, red and black 55 30
1126 80c. yellow and black 55 30
1127 1s.10 red and black 55 30
ARMS: 50c. Cotacachi. 60c. Antonio Ante. 80c. Otavalo. 1s.10, Ibarra.

335 UNESCO Headquarters, Paris

1958. Inauguration of UNESCO Headquarters Building, Paris.
1128 **335** 80c. brown 55 20

336 Emperor Charles V (after Titian)

1958. Air. 400th Death Anniv of Emperor Charles V.
1129 **336** 2s. sepia and red 45 30
1130 **336** 4s.20 brown & black 55 45

337 Globe and Satellites

1958. International Geophysical Year.
1131 **337** 1s.80 blue 1·30 55

338 Paul Rivet (anthropologist)

1958. Air. Rivet Commemoration.
1132 **338** 1s. sepia 45 30
See also No. 1134.

339 Front page of "El Telegrafo"

1959. Air. 75th Anniv of "El Telegrafo" (newspaper).
1133 **339** 1s.30 black and green 35 20

1959. Air. Death Centenary of Alexander von Humboldt (naturalist). Portrait in design as T 338.
1134 2s. grey 35 20

1959. Air. Birth Centenary of Dr. Jose L. Tamayo (statesman). Portrait in design as T 327.
1135 1s.30 multicoloured 45 30

340 House of M. Canizares

1959. Air. 150th Anniv of Independence.
1136 **340** 20c. brown and blue 20 20
1137 - 80c. brown and blue 20 20
1138 - 1s. myrtle and brown 20 20
1139 - 1s.30 orange and blue 20 20
1140 - 2s. brown and blue 20 20
1141 - 4s.20 blue and red 65 45
DESIGNS—HORIZ: 80c. St. Augustine's chapter-house; 1s. The Constitution. VERT: 1s.30, Condor with broken chains; 2s. Royal Palace; 4s.20, "Liberty" (statue).

1959. Air. Birth Centenary of Dr. A. B. Moreno (statesman). Portrait in design as T 327.
1142 1s. multicoloured 45 30

341 Pope Pius XII

1959. Air. Pope Pius XII Commem.
1143 **341** 1s.30 multicoloured 45 30

342 Flags of Argentina, Bolivia, Brazil, Guatemala, Haiti, Mexico and Peru

1959. Air. Organization of American States Commemoration. Flag design inscr "OEA".
1144 **342** 50c. multicoloured 20 10
1145 - 80c. red, blue & yellow 35 20
1146 - 1s.30 multicoloured 55 30
FLAGS: 80c. Chile, Costa Rica, Cuba, Dominican Republic, Panama, Paraguay and U.S.A. 1s.30. Colombia, Ecuador, Honduras, Nicaragua, El Salvador, Uruguay and Venezuela.

1959. Air. Pichincha Cantonal Arms. As T 322. Inscr "PROVINCIA DE PICHINCHA". Arms multicoloured.
1147 10c. red and black 55 30
1148 40c. yellow and black 55 30
1149 1s. brown and black 55 30
1150 1s.30 green and black 55 30
1151 4s.20 yellow and black 55 30
ARMS: 10c. Ruminahui. 40c. Pedro Moncayo. 1s. Mejia. 1s.30, Cayambe. 4s.20, Quito.

343 Arms of Quito and Flags

1960. Air. 11th Inter-American Conference, Quito (1st issue). Centres multicoloured within red circle.
1152 **343** 1s.30 turquoise 20 20
1153 **343** 2s. sepia 20 20

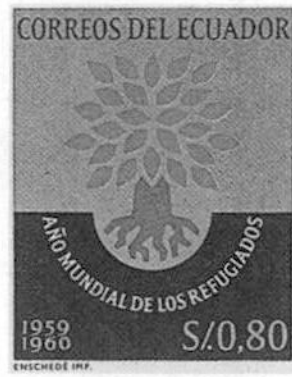

344 "Uprooted Tree"

1960. World Refugee Year.
1154 **344** 80c. green and lake 35 20

1960. Air. Cotopaxi Cantonal Arms. As T 322. Inscr "PROVINCIA DE COTOPAXI". Arms multicoloured.
1155 40c. red and black 35 30
1156 60c. blue and black 35 30
1157 70c. turquoise and black 35 30
1158 1s. red and black 35 30
1159 1s.30 orange and black 45 30
ARMS: 40c. Pangua. 60c. Pujili. 70c. Saquisili. 1s. Salcedo. 1s.30. Latacunga.

345 Giant Ant-eater

1960. 4th Cent of Baeza. Inscr as in T 345.
1160 **345** 20c. black, orge & grn 55 20
1161 - 40c. brown, grn & turq 90 20
1162 - 80c. black, blue & brown 1·30 30
1163 - 1s. orange, blue & purple 2·40 45
DESIGNS: 40c. Mountain tapir; 80c. Spectacled bear; 1s. Puma.

346 Quito Airport

1960. 11th Inter-American Conference, Quito. (2nd issue). Views of Quito. Inscr as in T 346.
1164 **346** 1s. blue and deep blue 20 20
1165 - 1s. violet and black 20 20
1166 - 1s. red and violet 20 20

1167	-	1s. green and blue	20	20
1168	-	1s. blue and violet	20	20
1169	-	1s. brown and blue	20	20
1170	-	1s. brown and violet	20	20
1171	-	1s. red and black	20	20
1172	-	1s. brown and black	20	20

VIEWS: No. 1165, Legislative Palace. No. 1166, Southern approach motorway and flyover. No. 1167, Government Palace. No. 1168, Foreign Ministry. No. 1169, Students' Quarters, Catholic University. No. 1170, Hotel Quito. No. 1171, Students' Quarters, Central University. No. 1172, Social Security Bank.

347 Ambato Railway Bridge

1960. Air. New Bridges.

1173		1s.30 brown	35	10
1174		1s.30 green	35	10
1175	**347**	2s. brown	55	20

DESIGNS—No. 1173, Bridge of the Juntas; No. 1174, Saracay Bridge.

348 "Liberty of Expression"

1960. Five Year Development Plan (1st issue). (a) Postage.

1176	**348**	5c. blue	10	10
1177	-	10c. violet	10	10
1178	-	20c. orange	20	10
1179	-	30c. turquoise	35	20
1180	-	40c. brown and blue	35	20

DESIGNS—VERT: 10c. Mother voting; 20c. People at bus-stop; 30c. Coins. HORIZ: (37×22 mm): 40c. Irrigation project Manabi.

349 Road at Chone Bay

(b) Air.

1181	**349**	1s. 30 black and ochre	35	30
1182	-	4s. 20 lake and green	45	45
1183	-	5s. brown and lemon	65	55
1184	-	10s. indigo and blue	1·50	55

DESIGNS—As Type **349**: 4s.20, Ministry of Works and Communications, Cuenca; 5s. El Coca Airport; 10s. New port of Guayaquil under construction.

See also Nos. 1214/17.

1960. 25th Anniv of the Ecuador Philatelic Association. Sheet containing stamps similar to Nos. 1049 and 1049b.

MS1184a 85×54 mm. 80c. violet on yellow and 90c. green on yellow 3·50 3·50

350 Pres. Camilo Ponce Enriquez and Constitution

1960. Air. 5th Anniv of Constitution.

1185	**350**	2s. black and brown	2·20	30

351 H. Dunant and Red Cross Buildings, Quito

1960. Air. Red Cross Commem.

1186	**351**	2s. purple and red	65	20

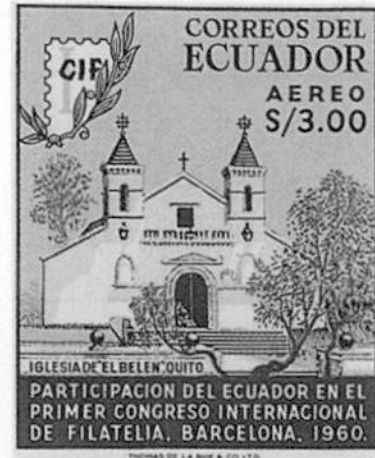

352 "El Belen" Church, Quito

1961. Air. 1st Int Philatelic Congress, Barcelona.

1187	**352**	3s. multicoloured	55	20

353 Map of River Amazon

1961. Air. "Amazon Week". Map in green.

1188	**353**	80c. purple and brown	35	20
1189	**353**	1s.30 blue and grey	55	30
1190	**353**	2s. red and grey	75	30

354 J. Montalvo, J. L. Mera and J. B. Vela

1961. Air. Cent of Tungurahua Province.

1191	**354**	1s.30 black & salmon	55	10

355 1936 Philatelic Exhibition Air Stamp

1961. Air. 3rd International Philatelic Exn, Quito.

1192	**355**	80c. violet and orange	20	20
1193	-	1s.30 multicoloured	45	30
1194	-	2s. black and red	65	30

DESIGNS: 1s.30, San Lorenzo–Belem route map of S. America and 1r. stamp of 1865. (41×33½ mm); 2s., 10s. Independence stamp of 1930 postmarked "QUITO" (41×36 mm).

356 Statue of H. Ortiz Garces

1961. Air. H. Ortiz Garces (national hero). Commemoration. Multicoloured.

1195	1s.30 Type **356**	35	10
1196	1s.30 Portrait	35	10

357 Arms of Los Rios and Great Egret

1961. Air. Centenary of Los Rios Province.

1197	**357**	2s. multicoloured	55	45

358 "Graphium pausianus"

1961. Butterflies.

1198	**358**	20c. yellow, green, black and salmon	55	20
1198a	**358**	20c. yell, grey, blk & grn	75	10
1199	-	30c. yell, black & blue	1·10	30
1200	-	50c. black, grn & yell	1·10	20
1200a	-	50c. blk, grn & salmon	1·30	10
1201	-	80c. pur, yell, blk & grn	2·20	20
1201a	-	80c. turq, yell, blk & brn	2·20	30

BUTTERFLIES: 30c. "Papilio torquatus leptalea". 50c. "Graphium molops molops". 80c. "Battus lycidas".

359 Collared Peccary

1961. 4th Centenary of Tena.

1202	**359**	10c. blue, green & red	65	30
1203	-	20c. brown, violet & blue	1·10	30
1204	-	80c. orange, blk & bistre	2·00	45
1205	-	1s. brown, orge & green	2·75	65

ANIMALS: 20c. Kinkajou. 80c. Jaguar. 1s. Little coatimundi.

360 G. G. Moreno

1961. Air. Centenary of Re-establishment of "National Integrity".

1206	**360**	1s. brown, buff & blue	45	30

1961. Opening of Marine Biology Station on Galapagos Is. and 15th Anniv of UNESCO. Nos. 1/6 of Galapagos Is. optd with UNESCO emblem, obliterating crosses and 1961 Estacion de Biologia Maritima de Galapagos.

1207	**1**	20c. brown (postage)	35	30
1208	-	50c. violet	35	30
1209	-	1s. green	75	30
1210	-	1s. blue (air)	55	30
1211	-	1s.80 purple	75	45
1212	-	4s.20 black	1·10	85

362 R. Crespo Toral

1961. Air. Birth Centenary of Remigio Crespo Toral (writer).

1213	**362**	50c. multicoloured	45	30

362a Soldier and Flag

1961. Obligatory Tax. National Defence Fund.

1213a	**362a**	40c. blue	1·70	20

363 Daniel Enrique Proana School, Quito

1961. Five Year Development Plan.

1214	**363**	50c. black and blue	55	30
1215	-	60c. black and green	55	30
1216	-	80c. black and red	55	30
1217	-	1s. black and purple	55	30

DESIGNS—VERT: 60c. Loja-Zamora Highway. HORIZ: 80c. Aguirre Abad College, Guayaquil; 1s. Epiclachima Barracks, Quito.

364 Pres. C. Arosemena and Duke of Edinburgh

1962. Air. Visit of Duke of Edinburgh.

1218	**364**	1s.30 multicoloured	35	20
1219	**364**	2s. multicoloured	55	20

1962. Air. Tungurahua Cantonal Arms. As T 322. Inscr "PROVINCIA DE TUNGURAHUA". Arms multicoloured.

1220	50c. black (Pillaro)	20	10
1221	1s. black (Pelileo)	35	20
1222	1s.30 black (Banos)	45	20
1223	2s. black (Ambato)	65	30

365 Mountain and Spade in Field

1963. Air. Freedom from Hunger.

1224	**365**	30c. black, grn & yell	35	10
1225	**365**	3s. black, red & orange	75	30
1226	**365**	4s.20 black, blue & yell	1·10	65

366 Mosquito

1963. Air. Malaria Eradication.

1227	**366**	50c. black, yellow & red	10	10
1228	**366**	80c. black, green & red	10	10
1229	**366**	2s. black, pink & purple	45	30

367 Mail Coach and Boeing 707

1963. Air. Centenary of Paris Postal Conf.

1230	**367**	2s. red and orange	45	30
1231	**367**	4s.20 blue and purple	75	55

1963. Air. Unissued Galapagos Is. stamps in designs as Ecuador T 321 surch ECUADOR and value.

1232	**321**	5s. on 2s. mult	1·20	85
1233	**321**	10s. on 2s. mult	2·40	1·70

1963. Air. Red Cross Cent. Optd 1863–1963 Centenario de la Fundacion de la Cruz Roja Internacional.

1234	**351**	2s. purple and red	45	30

370 Pres. Arosemena and Flags of Ecuador

1963. Presidential Goodwill Tour. Mult.

1235	10c. Type **370** (postage)	10	10
1236	20c. Ecuador & Panama flags	20	10
1237	60c. Ecuador & U.S.A. flags	20	10
1238	70c. Type **370** (air)	20	10
1239	2s. Ecuador and Panama flags	55	20
1240	4s. Ecuador & U.S.A. flags	1·30	55

1963. 150th Birth Anniv of Dr. M. Cueva (statesman). Portrait in design as T 327.

1241	2s. multicoloured	55	20

371 "Shield of Security"

1963. 25th Anniv of Social Insurance Scheme. Multicoloured.

1242	10c. Type **371** (postage)	20	10
1243	10s. "Statue of Security" (air)	1·40	1·10

372 Terminal Building

1963. Air. Inauguration of Simon Bolivar Airport, Guayaquil.

1244	**372**	60c. black	10	10
1245	**372**	70c. black and blue	20	10
1246	**372**	5s. purple and black	75	55

373 Nurse and Child

1963. Air. 7th Pan-American Pediatrics Congress, Quito.

1247	**373**	1s.30 blue, black and orange	35	30
1248	**373**	5s. lake, red and grey	65	65

1963. Postal Employees' Day. No. 1049a optd 1961 DIA DEL EMPLEADO POSTAL and posthorn or surch also.

1249	**B**	10c. on 80c. red	10	10
1250	**B**	20c. on 80c. red	10	10
1251	**B**	50c. on 80c. red	20	10
1252	**B**	60c. on 80c. red	20	20
1253	**B**	80c. red	35	20

1964. Nos. 1164, etc, surch.

1254	10c. on 1s. blue and violet	35	20
1255	10c. on 1s. brown & violet	35	20
1256	20c. on 1s. green and blue	35	20
1257	20c. on 1s. brown and blue	35	20
1258	30c. on 1s. red and violet	35	20
1259	40c. on 1s. brown & black	35	20
1260	60c. on 1s. red and black	35	20
1261	80c. on 1s. blue & dp blue	35	20
1262	80c. on 1s. violet & black	35	20

1964. Optd 1961 and ornaments.

1263	**344**	80c. green and lake	2·20	1·50

1964. Air. Optd AEREO. Honduras flag in red, blue and yellow.

1264	**326**	1s.80 violet	75	55
1265	-	2s. brown (No. 1105)	75	55
1266	**331**	2s.20 sepia and green	75	55

1964. "Columbus Lighthouse". (a) Optd FARO DE COLON.

1267	**337**	1s.80 blue (postage)	3·25	2·10

(b) Optd FARO DE COLON AEREO.

1268	1s.80 blue (air)	4·75	2·30

1964. Air. Nos. 1144/6 optd 1961.

1269	**342**	50c. multicoloured	1·00	65
1270	-	80c. red, blue & yellow	1·00	65
1271	-	1s.30 multicoloured	1·00	65

1964. O.E.A. Commemoration. Optd OEA with decorative frame across a block of four stamps.

1272	**344**	80c. green and lake	4·50	4·25

The unused price is for the block of four.

380 "Commerce"

1964. "Alliance for Progress".

1273	-	40c. bistre and violet	20	10
1274	-	50c. red and black	35	10
1275	**380**	80c. blue and brown	55	20

DESIGNS: 40c. "Agriculture"; 50c. "Industry".

1964. Air. 15th Anniv of Declaration of Human Rights. Optd DECLARATION DERECHOS HUMANOS 1964 XV-ANIV.

1276	**316**	1s.70 red	55	30

382 Banana Tree and Map

1964. Banana Conference, Quito.

1277	**382**	50c. olive, brown and grey (postage)	35	30
1278	**382**	80c. olive, blk & orge	35	30
1279	**382**	4s.20 olive, black & ochre (air)	45	30
1280	**382**	10s. olive, blk & red	75	55
MS1280a		120×95 mm. Nos. 1277/80. Imperf	3·25	3·25

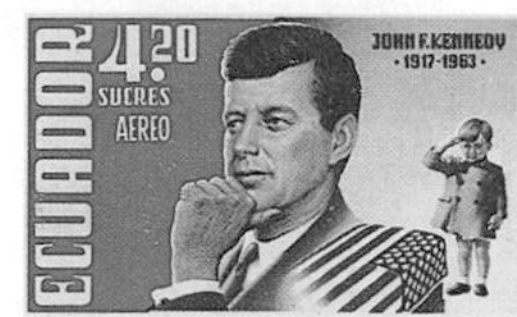

383 Pres. Kennedy and his Son

1964. Air. Pres. Kennedy Commem.

1281	**383**	4s.20 brn, red, bl & grn	1·30	95
1282	**383**	5s. brown, blue & violet	1·70	1·20
1283	**383**	10s. brown, blue & mve	3·00	1·70
MS1283a		115×130 mm. Nos. 1281/3. Imperf	11·00	11·00

384 Old Map of Ecuador and Philip II of Spain

1964. 400th Anniv of Royal High Court, Quito.

1284	**384**	10c. black, buff & red	35	30
1285	-	20c. black, buff & green	35	30
1286	-	30c. black, buff & blue	35	30

DESIGNS: As Type **384** but portrait of Juan de Salinas Loyola (20c.), Hernando de Santillan (30c.).

385 Pole vaulting

1964. Olympic Games, Tokyo. Mult.

1287	80c. Type **385** (postage)	35	20
1288	1s.30 Gymnastics (vert) (air)	35	30
1289	1s.80 Hurdling	35	30
1290	2s. Basketball	35	30
MS1290a	140×107 mm. Nos. 1287/90. Imperf	4·50	4·50

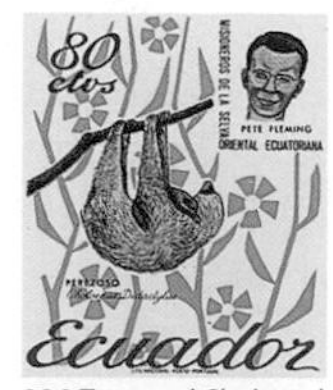

386 Two-toed Sloth and P. Fleming (missionary)

1965. Death of Missionaries in Ecuador's Eastern Forests. Multicoloured.

1291	20c. Nine-banded armadillo and J. Elliot	1·10	30
1292	30c. Eurasian red squirrel and E. McCully	1·10	30
1293	40c. Peruvian guemal and R. Youderian	1·10	30
1294	60c. Piper PA-14 Vagabond airplane over Napo River, and N. Saint	1·10	30
1295	80c. Type **386**	1·10	30

387 Dr. J. B. Vazquez (founder) and College Buildings

1965. Centenary of Benigno Malo College.

1296	**387**	20c. multicoloured	10	10
1297	**387**	60c. multicoloured	10	10
1298	**387**	80c. multicoloured	35	20

388 J. L. Mera (wrongly inscr "MERAN"), A. Neumane and Part of Anthem

1965. Centenary of National Anthem.

1299	**388**	50c. black and red	35	30
1300	**388**	80c. black and green	35	30
1301	**388**	5s. black and ochre	90	55
1302	**388**	10s. black and blue	1·70	1·30

389 "Olympic" Flame and Athletic Events

1965. 5th Bolivar Games, Quito. Flame in gold and black; athletes in black.

1303	**389**	40c. orange (postage)	20	20
1304	-	50c. red	20	20
1305	-	60c. blue	20	20
1306	**389**	80c. green	45	20
1307	-	1s. violet	45	20
1308	-	1s.50 mauve	75	55
1309	-	2s. blue (air)	55	20
1310	-	2s.50 orange	55	20
1311	-	3s. mauve	55	20
1312	-	3s.50 violet	65	55
1313	-	4s. green	65	20
1314	-	5s. red	75	30
MS1314a		215×130 mm. Nos. 1303/4. Imperf	12·00	12·00

DESIGNS: 50c., 1s. Running; 60c., 1s.50, Football; 2s., 3s. Diving, gymnastics, etc; 2s.50, 4s. Cycling; 3s.50, 5s. Pole-vaulting, long-jumping, etc.

390 ½r. and Two 1r. Stamps of 1865

1965. Stamp Centenary.

1315	**390**	80c. multicoloured	35	30
1316	**390**	1s.30 multicoloured	45	30
1317	**390**	2s. multicoloured	55	30
1318	**390**	4s. multicoloured	1·00	30
MS1319		140×125 mm. Nos. 1315/18. Imperf	3·75	3·75

391 Golden-headed Trogon

1966. Birds. Multicoloured.

1320	40c. Type **391** (postage)	1·50	30
1321	50c. Blue-crowned mot-mot	1·50	30
1322	60c. Paradise tanager	1·50	30
1323	80c. Wire-tailed manakin	1·50	30
1324	1s. Yellow bellied grosbeak (air)	1·70	30
1325	1s.30 Black-headed caique	1·70	30
1326	1s.50 Scarlet tanager	1·70	30
1327	2s. Sapphire quail dove	2·75	45
1328	2s.50 Violet-tailed sylph	2·75	45
1329	3s. Lemon-throated barbet	3·75	65
1330	4s. Yellow-tailed oriole	5·00	85
1331	10s. Collared puffbird	7·75	2·10

1967. Various stamps surch. (a) Postage.

1332	30c. on 1s.10 (No. 1127)	45	30
1332a	40c. on 1s.70 (No. 1056)	45	30
1333	40c. on 3s.50 (No. 1312)	45	30
1334	80c. on 1s.50 (No. 1308)	55	30
1335	80c. on 2s.50 (No. 1328)	55	30
1336	1s. on 4s. (No. 1330)	65	30

(b) Air.

1337	80c. on 1s.50 (No. 1326)	55	30
1338	80c. on 2s.50 (No. 1310)	55	30

396 Law Books

1967. Birth Centenary (1964) of Dr. V. M. Penaherrera (law reformer).

1339	**396**	50c. blk & grn (postage)	20	10
1340	-	60c. black and red	20	10
1341	-	80c. black and purple	20	10
1342	-	1s.30 blk & orge (air)	35	20
1343	-	2s. black and blue	35	20

DESIGNS—VERT: 60c. Penaherrera's bust, Central University, Quito; 1s.30, Penaherrera's monument, Avenida Patria, Quito; 2s. Penaherrera's statue, Ibarra. HORIZ: 80c. Open book and laurel.

1967. Nos. 1301/2 surch.

1344	**388**	50c. on 5s. blk & ochre	45	30
1345	**388**	2s. on 10s. black & blue	1·10	30

1968. No. 1057 surch.

1346	**P**	1s.30 on 1s.90 olive	90	65

399 Pres. Arosemena Gomez

1968. 1st Anniv of Dr. Otto Arosemena Gomez as Interim President. Multicoloured.

1347	80c. Type **399** (postage)	20	10
1348	1s. Page from 1967 Constitution	20	10
1349	1s.30 President's inauguration (air)	20	10
1350	2s. Pres. Arosemena Gomez at Punta del Este Conference	35	30

400 Lions Emblem

1968. 50th Anniv (1967) of Lions Int.

1351	**400**	80c. multicoloured	20	20
1352	**400**	1s.30 multicoloured	35	20
1353	**400**	2s. multicoloured	45	20
MS1354		70×105 mm. **400** 5s. multicoloured (39×49)	6·50	6·50

1969. Various stamps surch. (a) "AEREO" obliterated.

1355	**333**	40c. on 1s.30	75	30
1356	**330**	50c. on 1s.30	75	30

(b) Air. Inscr "AEREO".

1357	80c. on 10s. (No. 1331)	75	30
1358	1s. on 10s. (No. 1331)	75	30
1359	2s. on 10s. (No. 1331)	75	30

404 I.L. Arcaya, Foreign Minister of Venezuela

1969. Unissued stamp surch or optd only (No. 1363) RESELLO.

1360	**404**	50c. on 2s. mult	35	30
1361	**404**	80c. on 2s. mult	35	30
1362	**404**	1s. on 2s. mult	35	30

1363	404	2s. multicoloured	35	30

405 Map of Ecuador

1969. Revenue stamp surch.

1364	405	20c. on 30c. mult	45	30
1365	405	40c. on 30c. mult	45	30
1366	405	50c. on 30c. mult	45	30
1367a	405	60c. on 30c. mult	45	30
1368	405	80c. on 30c. mult	45	30
1369	405	1s. on 30c. mult	45	30
1370	405	1s.30 on 30c. mult	65	30
1371	405	1s.50 on 30c. mult	65	30
1372	405	2s. on 30c. mult	90	30
1373	405	3s. on 30c. mult	1·00	30
1374	405	4s. on 30c. mult	1·10	30
1375	405	5s. on 30c. mult	1·30	45

406 John F. Kennedy, Robert Kennedy and Martin Luther King

1969. "Apostles for Peace".

1376	406	4s. multicoloured	65	20
1377	406	4s. blk, green & blue	65	20

407 Handshake Emblem

1969. Air. "Operation Friendship". Multicoloured. Emblem's background colour given.

1378	407	2s. blue	35	20
1379	407	2s. yellow	35	20

408 "Papilio zabreus" (inscr "zagreus" on stamp)

1970. Butterflies. Multicoloured. (a) Coloured backgrounds.

1380	10c. "Thecla coronata" (postage)	2·20	20
1381	20c. Type **408**	2·20	20
1382	30c. "Heliconius erato"	2·20	20
1383	40c. "Eurytides pausanias"	2·20	20
1384	50c. "Pereute leucodrosime"	2·20	20
1385	60c. "Philaethiria dido"	2·20	20
1386	80c. "Morpho cypris"	2·20	20
1387	1s. "Catagramma astarte"	2·20	20
1388	1s.30 "Morpho peleides" (air)	2·20	20
1389	1s.50 "Anartia amathea"	2·20	20

(b) White backgrounds. As Nos. 1380/9.

1390	-	10c. mult (postage)	2·20	45
1391	408	20c. multicoloured	2·20	45
1392	-	30c. multicoloured	2·20	45
1393	-	40c. multicoloured	2·20	20
1394	-	50c. multicoloured	2·20	20
1395	-	60c. multicoloured	2·20	20
1396	-	80c. multicoloured	2·20	20
1397	-	1s. multicoloured	2·20	20
1398	-	1s.30 mult (air)	2·20	20
1399	-	1s.50 multicoloured	2·20	20

1970. Air. No. 1104 surch S/. 5 AEREO.

1400	325	5s. on 2s. mult	2·40	75

1970. Public Works Fiscal Stamps surch POSTAL and value.

1401	1s. on 1s. blue	20	10
1402	1s.30 on 1s. blue	20	10
1403	1s.50 on 1s. blue	35	20
1404	2s. on 1s. blue	45	20
1405	5s. on 1s. blue	1·00	45
1406	10s. on 1s. blue	2·00	75

The basic stamps are inscr "TIMBRE DE LA RECONSTRUCCION".

411 Arms of Zamora Chinchipe

1970. Provincial Arms and Flags. Mult.

1407	50c. Type **411** (postage)	35	20
1408	1s. Esmeraldas	35	20
1409	1s.30 El Oro (air)	35	20
1410	2s. Loja	45	20
1411	3s. Manabi	65	30
1412	5s. Pichincha	90	45
1413	10s. Guayas	1·70	55

412

1971. Revenue stamps surch for postal use.

1414	412	60c. on 1s. violet	35	20
1415	412	80c. on 1s. violet	35	20
1416	412	1s. on 1s. violet	35	20
1417	412	1s.10 on 1s. violet	35	20
1418	412	1s.10 on 2s. green	35	30
1419	412	1s.30 on 1s. violet	35	20
1420	412	1s.30 on 2s. green	35	20
1421	412	1s.50 on 1s. violet	45	20
1422	412	1s.50 on 2s. green	45	20
1423	412	2s. on 1s. violet	45	20
1424	412	2s. on 2s. green	45	20
1425	412	2s.20 on 1s. violet	55	20
1426	412	3s. on 1s. violet	65	20
1427	412	3s. on 5s. blue	65	20
1428	412	3s.40 on 2s. green	65	20
1429	412	5s. on 2s. green	1·00	30
1430	412	5s. on 5s. blue	90	45
1431	412	10s. on 2s. green	1·80	20
1432	412	10s. on 40s. orange	1·70	85
1433	412	20s. on 2s. green	2·75	95
1434	412	50s. on 2s. green	6·50	3·25

413 "Presentation of the Virgin"

1971. Air. Quito Religious Art. Mult.

1435	1s.30 Type **413**	20	10
1436	1s.50 "St. Anne"	35	10
1437	2s. "St. Teresa of Jesus"	35	10
1438	2s.50 Retable, Carmen altar (horiz)	55	20
1439	3s. "Descent from the Cross"	65	20
1440	4s. "Christ of St. Mariana"	90	30
1441	5s. St. Anthony Shrine	90	45
1442	10s. Cross of San Diego	1·90	85

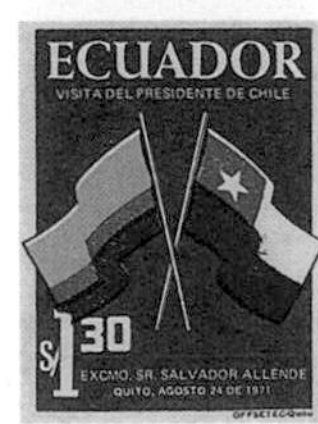
414 Flags of Chile and Ecuador

1971. Visit of Pres. Allende of Chile. Mult.

1443	1s.30 Type **414** (postage)	20	10
1444	2s. Pres. Allende (horiz) (air)	20	10
1445	2s.10 Pres. Ibarra of Ecuador and Pres. Allende (horiz)	20	10

415 Emblem on Globe

1971. Air. Opening of Postal Museum, Quito.

1446	415	5s. blue and black	1·10	55
1447	415	5s.50 purple & black	1·10	55

416 Ismael Paz Pazmino (founder)

1971. 50th Anniv of "El Universo" (newspaper).

1448	416	1s. mult (postage)	20	10
1449	416	1s.50 multicoloured (air)	20	10
1450	416	2s.50 multicoloured	45	15

417 Punch-card and Map

1971. Air. Pan-American Road Conference.

1451	417	5s. multicoloured	1·10	45
1452	-	10s. black and orange	1·80	75
1453	-	20s. black, red & blue	2·75	1·40
1454	-	50s. black, lilac & blue	4·50	2·00

DESIGNS: 10s. Converging roads; 20s. Globe and equator; 50s. Mountain road.

418 C.A.R.E. Parcel

1972. 25th Anniv of C.A.R.E. Organization.

1455	418	30c. purple	10	10
1456	418	40c. green	10	10
1457	418	50c. blue	10	10
1458	418	60c. red	10	10
1459	418	80c. brown	10	10

419 Flags of Ecuador and Argentine Republic

1972. State Visit of President Lanusse of Argentine Republic. Multicoloured.

1460	1s. Type **419** (postage)	10	10
1461	3s. Arms of Ecuador and Argentine Republic (horiz) (air)	35	20
1462	5s. Presidents Velasco Ibarra and Lanusse (horiz)	65	45

420 "Jesus giving Keys to St. Peter" (M. de Santiago)

1972. Religious Paintings of 18th-century Quito School. Multicoloured.

1463	50c. Type **420** (postage)	35	30
1464	1s.10 "Virgin of Mercy" (Quito School)	45	45
1465	2s. "The Immaculate Conception" (M. Samaniego)	75	65
1466	3s. "Virgin of the Flowers" (M. de Santiago) (air)	45	45
1467	10s. "Virgin of the Rosary" (Quito School)	1·50	75
MS1468	Two sheets (a) 129×110 mm. Nos. 1463/5. Imperf; (b) 98×110 mm. Nos. 1466/7	4·75	4·00

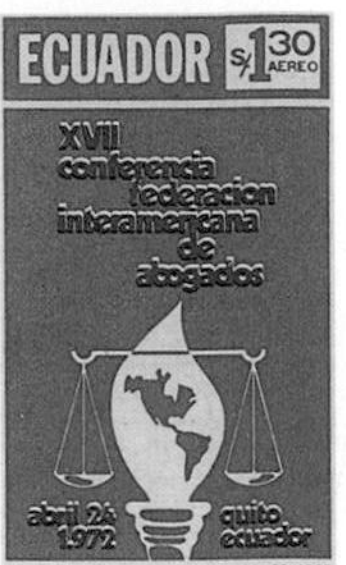
421 Map in Flame, and Scales of Justice

1972. Air. Inter-American Lawyers' Federation Congress, Quito.

1469	421	1s.30 blue and red	45	30

422 "Our Lady of Sorrow" (Caspicara)

1972. 18th-century Ecuador Statues. Mult.

1470	50c. Type **422** (postage)	35	30
1471	1s.10 "Nativity" (Quito School) (horiz)	45	45
1472	2s. "Virgin of Quito" (anon.)	65	65
1473	3s. "St. Dominic" (Quito School) (air)	45	45
1474	10s. "St. Rosa of Lima" (B. de Legarda)	1·40	75
MS1475	Two sheets (a) 129×110 mm. Nos. 1470/2. Imperf; (b) 98×110 mm. Nos. 1473/4	8·00	6·50

423 Juan Ignacio Pareja

1972. 150th Anniv of Battle of Pichincha (1st issue). Multicoloured.

1476	30c. Type **423** (postage)	10	10
1477	40c. Juan Jose Flores	10	10
1478	50c. Leon de Febres Cordero	10	10
1479	60c. Ignacio Torres	10	10

1480	70c. F. de Paula Santander	10	10
1481	1s. Jos M. Cordova	20	10
1482	1s.30 Jose M. Saenz (air)	10	10
1483	3s. Tomas Wright	35	20
1484	4s. Antonio Farfan	45	20
1485	5s. A. Jose de Sucre	75	45
1486	10s. Simon Bolivar	1·40	75
1487	20s. Arms of Ecuador	2·75	1·40

See also Nos. 1508/19.

424 Woman in Poncho

1972. Ecuador Handicrafts and Costumes. Mult.

1488	2s. Type **424** (postage)	35	20
1489	3s. Girl in striped poncho	65	30
1490	5s. Girl in embroidered poncho	90	55
1491	10s. Copper urn	1·90	1·20
1492	2s. Woman in floral poncho (air)	35	20
1493	3s. Girl in banded poncho	65	30
1494	5s. Woman in rose poncho	1·10	55
1495	10s. "Sun" sculpture	1·90	1·20
MS1496	Two sheets each 106×165 mm. (a) Nos. 1488/91. Imperf; (b) Nos. 1492/5	11·00	11·00

425 Epidendrum orchid

1972. Air. Ecuador Flowers. Multicoloured.

1497	4s. Type **425**	1·20	1·20
1498	6s. Canna	2·00	1·90
1499	10s. Jimson weed	2·75	2·75
MS1500	166×106 mm. Nos. 1497/9	20·00	20·00

426 Oil Rigs

1972. Air. Oil Industry.

1501	**426** 1s.30 multicoloured	35	20

427 Arms

1972. Air. Civic and Armed Forces Day.

1502	**427** 2s. multicoloured	35	30
1503	**427** 3s. multicoloured	35	30
1504	**427** 4s. multicoloured	45	30
1505	**427** 4s.50 multicoloured	45	30
1506	**427** 6s.30 multicoloured	1·00	45
1507	**427** 6s.90 multicoloured	1·00	45

428 Statue of Sucre, Santo Domingo

1972. 150th Anniv of Battle of Pichincha (2nd issue). Multicoloured.

1508	1s.20 Type **428** (postage)	20	10
1509	1s.80 San Augustin Monastery	20	10
1510	2s.30 Independence Square	35	20
1511	2s.50 Bolivar's statue, La Alameda	55	20
1512	4s.75 Carved chapel doors	75	30
1513	2s.40 Cloister, San Augustin Monastery (air)	20	20
1514	4s.50 La Merced Monastery	55	30
1515	5s.50 Chapel column	55	45
1516	6s.30 Altar, San Augustin Monastery	75	55
1517	6s.90 Ceiling, San Augustin Monastery	75	55
1518	7s.40 Crucifixion, Cantuna Chapel	1·10	75
1519	7s.90 Ceiling detail, San Augustin Monastery	1·10	75

429 Dish Aerial

1973. Inauguration (1972) of Satellite Earth Station, Chillotal.

1520	**429** 1s. multicoloured	35	10

431 U.N. Emblem

1973. Air. 25th Anniv of U.N. Economic Committee for Latin America (C.E.P.A.L.).

1521	**431** 1s.30 black and blue	35	10

432 O.E.A. Emblem

1973. Air. "Day of the Americas".

1522	**432** 1s.50 multicoloured	45	20

433 Presidents Rodriguez Lara and Caldera

1973. Air. Visit of Pres. Caldera of Venezuela.

1523	**433** 3s. multicoloured	55	30

434 Blue-footed Boobies

1973. Formation of Galapagos Islands Province. Multicoloured.

1524	30c. Type **434** (postage)	55	10
1525	40c. Blue-faced boobies	55	10
1526	50c. Oystercatcher	55	10
1527	60c. Basking Galapagos fur seals	1·10	30
1528	70c. Giant tortoise	1·30	30
1529	1s. Californian sealion	1·90	30
1530	1s.30 Blue-footed boobies (different) (air)	2·75	30
1531	3s. Brown pelican	2·75	30

435 Silver Coin, 1934

1973. Air. Coins. Multicoloured.

1532	5s. Type **435**	75	55
1533	10s. Reverse of silver coin, showing arms	1·30	85
1534	50s. Gold Coin, 1928	6·00	3·50
MS1535	105×77 mm. Nos. 1532/4. Imperf	9·25	9·25

436 Black-chinned Mountain Tanager

1973. Birds. Multicoloured.

1536	1s. Type **436**	55	10
1537	2s. Maniche oriole	55	20
1538	3s. Toucan barbet (vert)	55	30
1539	5s. Masked crimson tanager (vert)	75	65
1540	10s. Blue-necked tanager (vert)	1·70	1·40
MS1541	Two sheets (a) 143×85 mm. Nos. 1536/7. Imperf; (b) 145×87 mm. Nos. 1538/40	22·00	22·00

437 OPEC Emblem

1974. Air. OPEC (Oil exporters) Meeting, Quito.

1542	**437** 2s. multicoloured	45	30

438 Dr. Marco Tulio Varea Quevedo (botanist)

1974. Ecuadorian Personalities (1st series).

1543	**438** 1s. blue	20	10
1544	- 1s. orange	20	10
1545	- 1s. green	20	10
1546	- 1s. brown	20	10

PERSONALITIES: No. 1544, Dr. J. M. Carbo Noboa (medical scientist). No. 1545, Dr. A. J. Valenzuela (physician). No. 1546, Capt. E. Chiriboga (national hero).

See also Nos. 1551/6 and 1565/9.

439 Flag of Ecuador and U.P.U. Emblem

1974. Air. Centenary of U.P.U.

1548	**439** 1s.30 multicoloured	20	15

1974. Personalities (2nd series). As T 438.

1551	60c. red (postage)	35	10
1552	70c. lilac	35	10
1553	1s.20 green	35	10
1554	1s.80 blue	35	10
1555	1s.30 blue and black (air)	20	20
1556	1s.50 grey on pale grey	35	20

PERSONALITIES: 60c. Dr. Pio Jaramillo Alvarado (sociologist). 70c. Prof. Luciano Andrade Marin (naturalist). 1s.20, Dr. Francisco Campos Ruiadaneira (entomologist). 1s.30, Teodore Wolf (geographer). 1s.50, Capt. Edmundo Chiriboga G. (national hero). 1s.80, Luis Vernaza Lazarte (philanthropist).

440 Postman with Letter

1974. Air. 8th Inter-American Postmasters' Congress, Auibo.

1557	**440** 5s. multicoloured	45	30

441 Map of the Americas and F.I.A.F. Emblem

1974. Air. "Exfigua" Stamp Exhibition and Inter-American Philatelic Federation 5th General Assembly, Guayaquil (1973).

1558	**441** 3s. multicoloured	55	20

442 Colonnade

1974. Colonial Monastery, Tilipulo, Cotopaxi Province. Multicoloured.

1559	20c. Type **442**	35	30
1560	30c. Entrance	35	30
1561	40c. Church	35	30
1562	50c. Archway (vert)	35	30
1563	60c. Chapel (vert)	35	30
1564	70c. Cemetery (vert)	35	30

1975. Personalities (3rd series). As T 438.

1565	80c. blue (postage)	20	10
1566	80c. red and pink	20	10
1567	5s. red (air)	65	30
1568	5s. grey	65	30
1569	5s. violet	65	45

PORTRAITS: No. 1565, Dr. Angel Polibio Chaves (statesman). No. 1566, Emilio Estrada Ycaza (archaeologist). No. 1567, Manuel J. Calle (journalist). No. 1568, Leopoldo Benites Vinueza (statesman). No. 1569, Adolfo H. Simmonds G. (journalist).

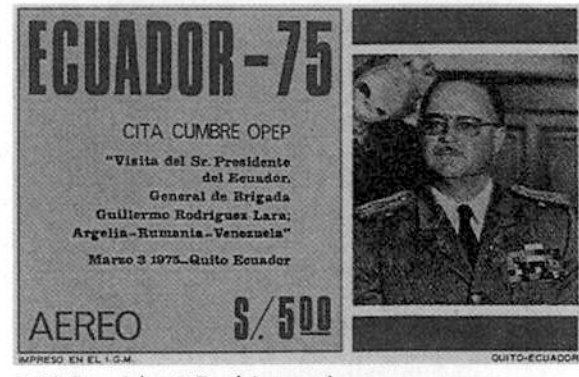

443 President Rodriguez Lara

1975. Air. State Visits of President Rodriguez Lara to Algeria, Rumania and Venezuela.

1570	**443** 5s. black and red	75	45

444 Ministerial Greetings

1975. Meeting of Public Works' Ministers of Ecuador and Colombia, Quito. Multicoloured.

1571	1s. Type **444** (postage)	20	10
1572	1s.50 Ministers at opening ceremony (air)	35	10
1573	2s. Ministers signing treaty	35	10

445 "The Sacred Heart"

1975. Air. 3rd Eucharistic Congress, Quito. Multicoloured.

1574		1s.30 Type **445**	20	10
1575		2s. Golden monstrance	35	10
1576		3s. Quito Cathedral	55	20

446 President Martinez Mera

1975. Air. Birth Centenary of Juan de Dios Martinez Mera (President, 1932–33).

1577	**446**	5s. red and black	65	30

447 Jorge Delgado Panchana (swimming champion)

1975. Air. Jorge Delgado Panchana Commemoration. Multicoloured.

1578		1s.30 Type **447**	20	10
1579		3s. Delgado Panchana in water (horiz)	20	10

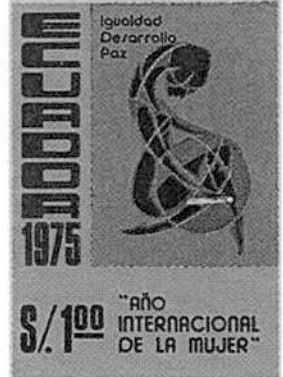

448 "Women of Peace"

1975. International Women's Year. Mult.

1580		1s. Type **448**	35	30
1581		1s. "Women of Action"	45	30

449 "Armed Forces"

1975. 3rd Anniv of 15th February Revolution.

1582	**449**	2s. multicoloured	45	30

450 Hurdling

1975. 3rd Ecuadorian Games, Quito.

1583	**450**	20c. black and orange (postage)	55	30
1584	-	20c. black and yellow	55	30
1585	-	30c. black and mauve	55	30
1586	-	30c. black and buff	55	30
1587	-	40c. black and yellow	55	30
1588	-	40c. black and mauve	55	30
1589	-	50c. black and green	55	30
1590	-	50c. black and red	55	30
1591	-	60c. black and green	55	30
1592	-	60c. black and pink	55	30
1593	-	70c. black and drab	55	30
1594	-	70c. black and grey	55	30
1595	-	80c. black and blue	55	30
1596	-	80c. black and orange	55	30
1597	-	1s. black and olive	55	30
1598	-	1s. black and brown	55	30
1599	-	1s.30 black & orge (air)	55	30
1600	-	2s. black and yellow	55	30
1601	-	2s.80 black and red	65	30
1602	-	3s. black and blue	65	30
1603	-	5s. black and purple	1·10	30

DESIGNS: No. 1584, Chess; No. 1585, Boxing; No. 1586, Basketball; No. 1587, Showjumping; No. 1588, Cycling; No. 1589, Football; No. 1590, Fencing; No. 1591, Golf; No. 1592, Gymnastics; No. 1593, Wrestling; No. 1594, Judo; No. 1595, Swimming; No. 1596, Weightlifting; No. 1597, Handball; No. 1598, Table tennis; No. 1599, Squash; No. 1600, Rifle shooting; No. 1601, Volleyball; No. 1602, Rafting; No. 1603, Inca mask.

451 "Phragmipedum candatum"

1975. Flowers. Multicoloured.

1604		20c. Type **451** (postage)	20	20
1605		30c. "Genciana" (horiz)	20	20
1606		40c. "Bromeliaeae cactaceae"	35	20
1607		50c. "Cachlioda volcanica" (horiz)	35	20
1608		60c. "Odontoglossum hallii (horiz)	45	20
1609		80c. "Cactaceae sp." (horiz)	45	20
1610		1s. "Odontoglossum sp." (horiz)	75	20
1611		1s.30 "Pitcairnia pungens" (horiz) (air)	35	20
1612		2s. "Salvia sp." (horiz)	55	30
1613		3s. "Bomarea" (horiz)	75	45
1614		4s. "Opuntia quitense" (horiz)	1·10	55
1615		5s. "Bomarea" (different) (horiz)	1·70	75

452 Aircraft Tail-fins

1976. Air. 23rd Anniv of TAME Airline. Mult.

1616		1s.30 Type **452**	45	30
1617		3s. Douglas DC-3 and Lockheed L.188 Electra encircling map	55	30

453 Statue of Benalcazar

1976. Air. Sebastian de Benalcazar Commem.

1618	**453**	2s. multicoloured	35	20
1619	**453**	3s. multicoloured	35	20

454 "Venus" (Chorrera Culture)

1976. Archaeological Discoveries. Mult.

1620		20c. Type **454** (postage)	30	25
1621		30c. "Venus" (Valdivia)	35	20
1622		40c. Seated monkey (Chorrera)	35	20
1623		50c. Man wearing poncho (Panzaleo Tardio)	35	20
1624		60c. Mythical figure (Cashaloma)	35	20
1625		80c. Musician (Tolita)	35	20
1626		1s. Chief priest (censer-Mantema)	35	20
1627		1s. Female mask (Tolita)	35	20
1628		1s. Gold and platinum brooch (Tolita)	35	20
1629		1s. "Angry person" mask (Tolita)	35	20
1630		1s.30 Coconut-dealer (Carchi) (air)	35	30
1631		2s. Funerary urn (Tuncahuan)	45	30
1632		3s. Priest (Bahia de Caraquez)	65	45
1633		4s. Seashell (Cuasmal)	1·00	45
1634		5s. Bowl supported by figurines (Guangala)	1·30	45

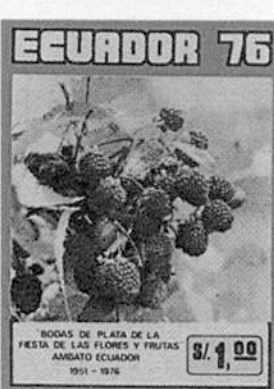

455 Strawberries

1976. Flowers and Fruits Festival, Ambato. Multicoloured.

1635		1s. Type **455** (postage)	20	10
1636		2s. Apples (air)	35	10
1637		5s. Rose	1·10	45

456 S. Cueva Celi

1976. Musical Celebrities. Multicoloured.

1638		1s. Type **456**	35	20
1639		1s. C. Ojeda Davila	35	20
1640		1s. S. Maria Duran	35	20
1641		1s. C. Amable Ortiz	35	20
1642		1s. L. Alberto Valencia	35	20

457 Douglas DC-10 crossing "50" and Dornier Do-JII Wal Flying Boat

1976. Air. 50th Anniv of Lufthansa Airline.

1643	**457**	10s. multicoloured	1·70	75

458 Cerros del Carmen y Santa Ana

1976. Air. 441st Anniv of Guayaquil. Mult.

1644		1s.30 Type **458**	20	10
1645		1s.30 "Pregonero" (vert)	20	10
1646		1s.30 "Estibador" (vert)	20	10
1647		2s. Sebastian de Benalcazar (vert)	35	10
1648		2s. Francisco de Orellana (vert)	35	10
1649		2s. Guayas and Quil (vert)	35	10

459 New Post Office Building

1976. Air. Post Office Building Project.

1650	**459**	5s. multicoloured	45	20

460 Emblem and Wreath

1976. Air. 50th Anniv of Bolivarian Society.

1651	**460**	1s.30 multicoloured	35	30

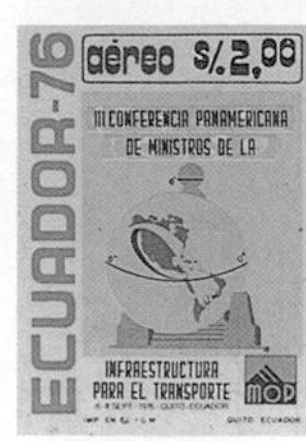

461 The Americas on Globe

1976. Air. 3rd Pan-American Ministers' Conference on Transport Infrastructure, Quito.

1652	**461**	2s. multicoloured	35	10
MS1653		95×115 mm. **461** 5s. multicoloured. Imperf	4·50	4·50

462 Congress Emblem

1976. Air. 10th Inter-American Construction Industry Congress, Quito.

1654	**462**	1s.30 multicoloured	45	30
1655	**462**	3s. multicoloured	55	45
MS1656		90×115 mm. **462** 10s. multicoloured. Imperf	2·40	1·50

463 George Washington

1976. Air. Bicentenary of American Revolution. Multicoloured.

1657		3s. Type **463**	90	45
1658		5s. Battle of Flamborough Head, 1779 (horiz)	1·40	65

464 Dr. H. Noguchi

1976. Air. Birth Centenary of Dr. Hideyo Noguchi (bacteriologist).

1659	**464**	3c. multicoloured	55	20
MS1660		95×114 mm. **464** 10s. multicoloured. Imperf	8·25	7·50

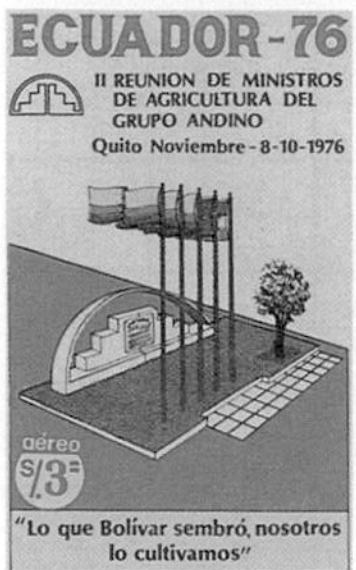

465 Bolivar Memorial

1976. Air. Meeting of Agricultural Ministers of Andean Countries, Quito.

1661	**465**	3s. multicoloured	35	30

MS1662 95×115 mm. **465** 5s. multicoloured. Imperf 2·40 75

466 M. Febres Cordero

1976. Air. Mariuxi Febres Cordero, South American Swimming Champion.

1663	**466**	3s. multicoloured	35	30

467 Dr. Luis Cordero

1976. Air. Pres. Cordero Commemoration.

1664	**467**	2s. multicoloured	35	30

468 Sister Catalina de Jesus Herrera

1977. Air. 260th Birth Anniv of Sister Catalina de Jesus Herrera (religious author).

1665	**468**	1s.30 pink and black	45	30

469 General Assembly Emblem

1977. 11th General Assembly of Technical Committees of the Pan-American Historical and Geographical Institute. Multicoloured.

1666	2s. Type **469** (postage)	35	20
1667	5s. Congress Building, Quito (air)	65	20

MS1668 90×115 mm. 10s. Designs as Nos. 1666/7. Imperf 2·20 2·20

470 Mythological Figure ("La Tolita" ceramic)

1977. Air. 50th Anniv of Foundation of Central Bank of Ecuador. Multicoloured.

1669	7s. Type **470**	1·50	45
1670	9s. "The Holy Shepherdess Spinning" (B. de Legarda)	2·00	55
1671	11s. "The Fruitseller" (B. de Legarda)	2·40	1·20

MS1672 90×115 mm. 20s. gold (embossed) and blue (head of Sun god (pre-Columbian sculpture)). Imperf 10·00 4·75

471 Hands holding Rotary Emblem

1977. 50th Anniv of Guayaquil Rotary Club.

1673	**471**	1s. multicoloured	20	20
1674	**471**	2s. multicoloured	45	20

MS1675 Two sheets each 90×115 mm. **471** 5s. and 10s. multicoloured. Imperf 3·75 3·75

472 President Michelsen of Colombia

1977. Air. Meeting of the Presidents of Colombia and Ecuador. Multicoloured.

1676	2s.60 Type **472**	65	20
1677	5s. Ecuador junta	1·00	30
1678	7s. Ecuador junta (vert)	1·10	55
1679	9s. President Michelsen with Ecuador junta	1·70	85

MS1680 115×90 mm. 10s. As No. 1679. Imperf 1·30 1·10

473 Brother Miguel and St. Peter's, Rome

1977. Air. Beatification of Brother Hermano Miguel.

1681	**473**	2s.60 multicoloured	35	20

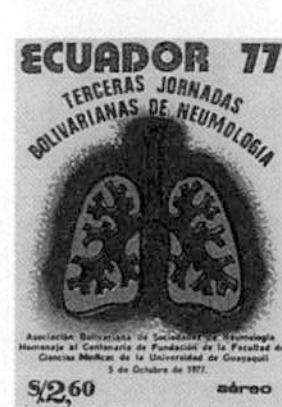

474 Lungs

1977. Air. 3rd Bolivarian Pneumological Seminar.

1682	**474**	2s.60 multicoloured	35	20

475 Jose Peralta

1977. 40th Death Anniv of Jose Peralta (writer).

1683	**475**	1s.80 mult (postage)	20	10
1684	-	2s.40 multicoloured	20	10
1685	-	2s.60 blk, red & yell (air)	55	30

DESIGNS: 2s.40, Statue of Peralta; 2s.60, Titles of Peralta's works, and his "ex libris".

476 Blue-faced Booby

1977. Birds of the Galapagos Islands. Mult.

1686	1s.20 Type **476**	55	10
1687	1s.80 Red-footed booby	75	10
1688	2s.40 Blue-footed boobies	1·30	10
1689	3s.40 Dusky gull	1·90	20
1690	4s.40 Galapagos hawk	2·75	30
1691	5s.40 Map of the islands and finches (vert)	3·50	30

477 Broadcast Tower

1977. Air. World Telecommunications Day.

1692	**477**	5s. multicoloured	55	55

478 Dr. Remigio Romero y Cordero

1978. Air. 10th Death Anniv of Dr. Remigio Romero y Cordero (poet).

1693	**478**	3s. multicoloured	45	30
1694	**478**	10s.60 multicoloured	65	30

MS1695 89×114 mm. 10s. Portrait and poem "A La Dolorosa del Colegio". Imperf 1·70 1·70

479 Children

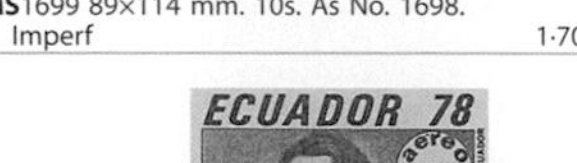

1978. Air. 50th Anniv of Social Insurance Institute. Multicoloured.

1696	7s. Type **479**	90	30
1697	9s. Insurance emblem	1·30	30
1698	11s. Hands reaching for sun	1·70	30

MS1699 89×114 mm. 10s. As No. 1698. Imperf 1·70 1·70

480 General San Martin

1978. Air. Birth Bicent of General San Martin.

1700	**480**	10s.60 multicoloured	2·10	75

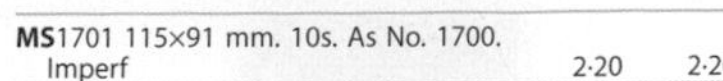

MS1701 115×91 mm. 10s. As No. 1700. Imperf 2·20 2·20

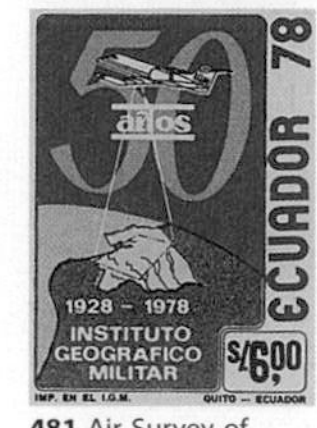

481 Air Survey of Ecuador

1978. 50th Anniv of Military Geographical Institute. Multicoloured.

1702	6s. Type **481** (postage)	90	45
1703	7s.60 Air survey of mountains (air)	1·40	75

MS1704 115×90 mm. 10s. As Nos. 1702/3. Imperf 2·20 2·20

482 Dr. Vicente Corral Moscoso Hospital

1978. Inauguration of Dr. Vicente Corral Moscoso Regional Hospital. Multicoloured.

1705	3s. Type **482** (postage)	35	30
1706	7s.60 Dr. Moscoso (air)	65	30

MS1707 90×115 mm. 5s. Hospital emblem. Imperf 90 90

483 Map of the Americas and Lions Emblem

1978. 7th Meeting of Latin American Lions. Multicoloured.

1708	3s. Type **483** (postage)	75	30
1709	4s.20 Type **483**	1·20	30
1710	5s. As Type **483** but smaller emblem (air)	1·00	30
1711	6s.20 As No. 1710	1·10	55

MS1712 115×90 mm. 10s. Lions emblem. Imperf 1·80 1·30

484 Anniversary Emblem

1978. 70th Anniv of Filanbanco (Philanthropic Bank). Multicoloured.

1713	4s.20 Type **484** (postage)	55	30
1714	5s. Bank emblem (air)	45	30

485 Goal

1978. World Cup Football Championship, Argentina. Multicoloured.

1715	1s.20 Type **485** (postage)	10	10
1716	1s.80 Gauchito and emblem (vert)	20	10
1717	4s.40 Gauchito (vert)	65	30
1718	2s.60 Gauchito, "78" and emblem (air)	35	20
1719	7s. Football	1·10	55
1720	9s. Emblem (vert)	1·40	85

MS1721 Two sheets each 115×90 mm. (a) 5s. Gauchito (postage); (b) 10s. Emblem (air). Imperf 8·25 8·25

486 Old Men of Vilcabamba

1978. Air. Vilcabamba (valley of longevity).

1722	**486**	5s. multicoloured	65	30

487 Bernardo O'Higgins

1978. Air. Birth Bicentenary of General Bernardo O'Higgins (national hero of Chile).

1723	**487**	10s.60 multicoloured	1·00	45
MS1724		115×90 mm. 10s. As No. 1723. Imperf	90	90

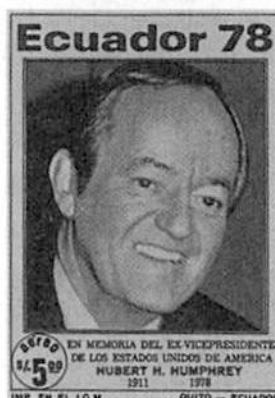

488 Hubert Humphrey (former U.S. Vice-President)

1978. Air. Hubert Humphrey Commem.

1725	**488**	5s. multicoloured	65	30

489 "Virgin and Child"

1978. Air. Christmas. Children's Paintings. Mult.

1726	2s.20 Type **489**	35	10
1727	4s.60 "Holy Family"	65	30
1728	6s.20 "Candle and Children"	1·20	55

490 "Village" (Anibal Villacis)

1978. Air. Ecuadorian Painters. Mult.

1729	5s. Type **490**	75	30
1730	5s. "Mountain Village" (Gilberto Almeida)	75	30
1731	5s. "Bay" (Roura Oxandaberro)	75	30
1732	5s. "Abstract" (Luis Molinari)	75	30
1733	5s. "Statue" (Oswaldo Viteri)	75	30
1734	5s. "Tools" (Enrique Tabara)	75	30

491 Male and Female Symbols

1979. 50th Anniv of Inter-American Women's Commission.

1735	**491**	3s.40 multicoloured	55	20

492 House and Monument

1979. Air. 150th Anniv of Battle of Portete and Tarqui. Multicoloured.

1736	2s.40 Type **492**	35	20
1737	3s.40 Monument (vert)	35	20
MS1738	116×91 mm. 10s. As Nos. 1736/7. Imperf	1·00	95

493 Bank Emblem

1979. 16th Anniv of Ecuadorian Mortgage Bank.

1739	**493**	4s.40 multicoloured	45	30
1740	**493**	5s.40 multicoloured	65	30

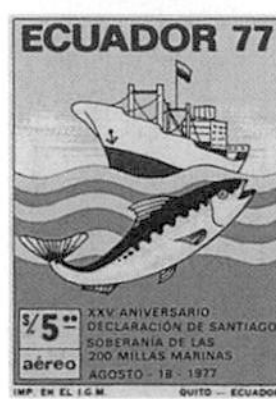

494 Deep Sea Trawler and Fish

1979. Air. 25th Anniv of Extension to 200-mile Offshore Limit. Multicoloured.

1741	5s. Type **494**	75	30
1742	7s. Map of Ecuador and territorial waters (horiz)	1·10	55
1743	9s. Map of South America	1·40	65

495 Street Scene

1979. Galapagos Islands. Multicoloured.

1744	3s.40 Type **495** (postage)	35	30
1745	10s.60 Church bells in tower (horiz) (air)	1·50	75
1746	13s.60 Aerial view of coast	1·80	95
MS1747	115×90 mm. 10s. Nos. 1744/6. Imperf	3·25	95

496 Coat of Arms

1979. Air. 5th Anniv of Ecuador-American Chamber of Commerce.

1748	**496**	7s.60 multicoloured	65	65
1749	**496**	10s.60 multicoloured	1·00	95
MS1750		115×90 mm. 10s. Nos. 1748/9. Imperf	1·00	95

497 Young Girl

1979. Air. International Year of the Child.

1751	**497**	10s. multicoloured	1·10	55

498 Games Emblem

1979. Air. 5th National Games.

1752	**498**	28s. multicoloured	2·40	1·60

499 Rejoicing People with Flags

1979. Air. Restoration of Democracy. Mult.

1753	7s.60 Type **499**	1·30	55
1754	10s.60 President Jamie Roldos Aguilera	1·50	45

500 CIESPAL Building, Quito

1980. Air. Inauguration of CIESPAL (Ecuadorian Institute of Engineers) Building.

1755	**500**	10s.60 multicoloured	1·10	65

501 Jose Joaquin de Olmedo

1980. Birth Bicentenary of Jose Joaquin de Olmedo (physician).

1756	**501**	3s. multicoloured (postage)	35	30
1757	**501**	5s. multicoloured	55	45
1758	**501**	10s. multicoloured (air)	1·20	75

502 Enriquillo (Dominican Republic)

1980. Chiefs of the Indo-American Indian Tribes. Multicoloured.

1759	3s. Type **502** (postage)	75	30
1760	3s.40 Guaycaypuro (Venezuela)	1·00	45
1761	5s. Abayuba (Uruguay)	2·00	65
1762	5s. Atlacati (El Salvador)	2·00	65
1763	7s.60 Cuantemoc (Mexico) (air)	2·00	45
1764	7s.60 Lempira (Honduras)	2·00	45
1765	7s.60 Nicaragua (Nicaragua)	2·00	45
1766	10s. Lambare (Paraguay)	2·40	55
1767	10s. Urraca (Panama)	2·40	55
1768	10s.60 Anacaona (Haiti)	2·40	55
1769	10s.60 Caupolican (Chile)	2·40	55
1770	10s.60 Tecun-Uman (Guatemala)	2·40	55
1771	12s.80 Calarca (Colombia)	3·25	65
1772	12s.80 Garabito (Costa Rica)	3·25	65
1773	12s.80 Hatuey (Cuba)	3·25	65
1774	13s.60 Camarao (Brazil)	3·25	65
1775	13s.60 Tehuelche (Argentina)	3·25	65
1776	13s.60 Tupaj Katari (Bolivia)	3·25	65
1777	17s.80 Sequoyah (U.S.A.)	3·75	85
1778	22s.80 Ruminahui (Ecuador)	4·50	1·60

503 King Juan Carlos and Queen Sophia of Spain

1980. Visit of King and Queen of Spain.

1779	**503**	3s.40 mult (postage)	55	30
1780	**503**	10s.60 mult (air)	1·10	55

504 Provincial Administration Council Building, Pichincha

1980. Air. Pichincha Provincial Council.

1781	**504**	10s.60 multicoloured	1·70	75

505 Cofan Indian (Napo Province)

1980. Equatorial Indians. Multicoloured.

1782	3s. Type **505** (postage)	55	20
1783	3s.40 Zuleta woman (Imbabura)	55	20
1784	5s. Chota negro woman (Imbabura)	90	30
1785	7s.60 Salasaca boy (Tungurahua) (air)	1·30	95
1786	10s. Girl from Amula (Chimborazo)	1·70	1·20
1787	10s.60 Girl from Canar (Canar)	1·90	1·30
1788	13s.60 Colorado Indian (Pichincha)	2·20	1·70

506 U.P.U. Monument

1980. Air. Cent of U.P.U. Membership. Mult.

1789	10s.60 Type **506**	1·70	75
1790	17s.80 Mail box, 1880	2·75	1·20
MS1791	115×90 mm. 25s. As Nos. 1789/90. Imperf	4·50	3·75

507 Our Lady of Mercy Basilica, Quito

1980. Virgin of Mercy, Patron Saint of Ecuadorian Armed Forces. Multicoloured.

1792	3s.40 Type **507** (postage)	55	30
1793	3s.40 Balcony	55	30
1794	3s.40 Tower and cupola	55	30
1795	7s.60 Cupola and cloisters (air)	1·20	75
1796	7s.60 Tower and view of Quito	1·20	75
1797	7s.60 Gold screen	1·20	75
1798	10s.60 Retable	1·70	85
1799	10s.60 Pulpit	1·70	85
1800	13s.60 Cupola	2·20	1·20
1801	13s.60 Statue of Virgin	2·20	1·20
MS1802	Three sheets each 5s. (a) 90×116 mm. As Nos. 1792/3, 1796, 1799; (b) 90×116 mm. As Nos. 1794/5, 1797; (c) 116×90 mm. As Nos. 1798, 1800/1. Imperf	6·50	6·50

508 Olympic Torch

1980. Olympic Games, Moscow. Multicoloured.

1803	5s. Type **508** (postage)	55	45
1804	7s.60 Type **508**	90	55
1805	10s.60 Moscow games emblem (air)	1·10	1·10
1806	13s.60 As No. 1805	1·50	1·50

MS1807 Two sheets each 115×90 mm. Each 30s. containing designs as Nos. 1803 and 1805. (a) Postage, (b) Air. Imperf 17·00 16·00

509 Rotary Anniversary Emblem

1980. Air. 75th Anniv of Rotary International.

1808	**509**	10s. multicoloured	1·70	65

510 "Marshal Sucre" (after Marco Salas)

1980. Air. 150th Death Anniv of Marshal Antonio Jose de Sucre.

1809	**510**	10s.60 multicoloured	1·10	75

511 J. J. Olmeda, Father de Velasco, Government Building and Constitution

1980. 150th Anniv of Constitutional Assembly of Riobamba. Multicoloured.

1810	3s.40 Type **511** (postage)	35	30
1811	5s. Type **511**	90	55
1812	7s.60 Monstrance, Riobamba Cathedral (vert) (air)	90	45
1813	10s.60 As No. 1812	1·20	55

MS1814 Two sheets each 115×90 mm. Each 30s. containing designs as Nos. 1810 and 1812. (a) Postage, (b) Air. Imperf 6·75 6·75

512 The Virgin of the Swans

1980. 50th Anniv of Coronation of the Virgin of the Swans. Multicoloured.

1815	1s.20 Type **512**	20	10
1816	3s.40 The Virgin (different)	65	30

513 Young Indian

1980. 1st Anniv of Return to Democracy. Multicoloured.

1817	1s.20 Type **513** (postage)	20	10
1818	3s.40 Type **513**	65	30
1819	7s.60 President Roldos with Indian (air)	60	65
1820	10s.60 As No. 1819	85	75

MS1821 115×90 mm. 15s. As Nos. 1817 and 1819. Imperf 1·80 1·70

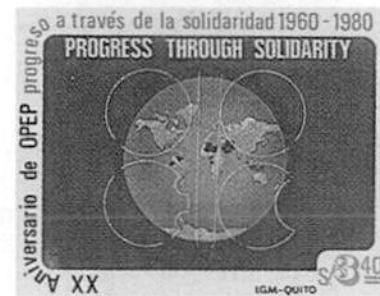

514 O.P.E.C. Emblem and Globe

1980. 20th Anniv of Organization of Petroleum Exporting Countries. Multicoloured.

1822	3s.40 Type **514** (postage)	55	30
1823	7s.60 Figures supporting O.P.E.C. emblem (air)	90	65

515 Dr. Isidro Ayora Cueva

1980. Air. Birth Centenary of Dr. Isidro Ayora Cueva (President, 1926–31).

1824	**515**	18s.20 multicoloured	2·75	1·40

516 Ornamental Hedge, Capitol Gardens

1980. Centenary of Carchi Province. Mult.

1825	3s. Type **516** (postage)	55	20
1826	10s.60 Governor's palace (air)	1·70	75
1827	17s.80 Freedom statue, Zulcan	2·40	1·20

517 "Cattleya maxima"

1980. Orchids. Multicoloured.

1828	1s.20 Type **517** (postage)	90	30
1829	3s. "Comparettia speciosa"	1·20	45
1830	3s.40 "Cattleya iricolor"	1·40	55
1831	7s.60 "Anguloa uniflora" (air)	3·50	85
1832	10s.60 "Scuticaria salesiana"	4·00	55
1833	50s. "Helcia sanguinolenta" (vert)	7·25	1·70
1834	100s. "Anguloa virginalis"	9·25	3·50

MS1835 Three sheets each 115×90 mm, each 20s. (a) Postage. As Nos. 1828/30; (b) Air. As Nos. 1831 and 1833; (c) Air. As Nos. 1832 and 1834. Imperf 14·50 10·00

518 Emblem and Radio Waves

1980. 50th Anniv of Radio Station HCJB.

1836	2s. Type **518** (postage)	55	20
1837	7s.60 Emblem and radio waves (horiz) (air)	1·70	75
1838	10s.60 Anniversary emblem	2·40	1·20

519 Simon Bolivar (after Marco Salas)

1980. Air. 150th Death Anniv of Simon Bolivar.

1839	**519**	13s.60 multicoloured	2·20	1·10

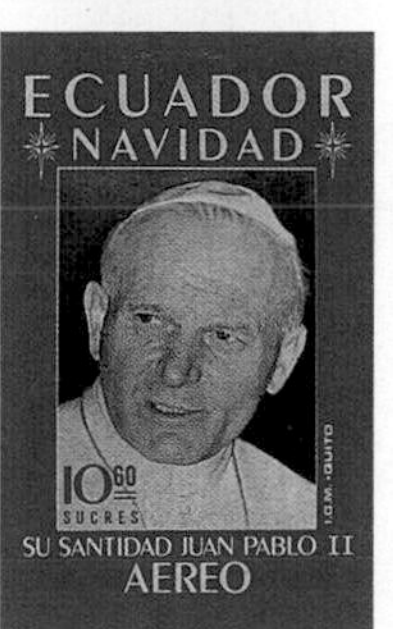

520 Pope John Paul II

1980. Christmas. Multicoloured.

1840	3s.40 Pope John Paul II with children (horiz) (postage)	65	30
1841	7s.60 Pope blessing crowd (air)	1·20	65
1842	10s.60 Type **520**	1·70	85

521 Carlos and Jorge Mantilla Ortega (editors)

1981. 75th Anniv of "El Comercio" (newspaper). Multicoloured.

1843	2s. Type **521**	35	20
1844	3s.40 Cesar and Carlos Mantilla Jacome	55	30

522 Oldest letter-box, Galapagos, 1793

1981. Air. Galapagos Islands.

1845	-	50s. yellow and black	7·75	1·70
1846	**522**	100s. multicoloured	10·00	6·50

DESIGN—HORIZ: 50s. Turtle.

523 Flag, Map and Soldier

1981. National Defence. Multicoloured.

1847	3s.40 Type **523**	35	30
1848	3s.40 Flag, map and Pres. Roldos Aguilera	35	30

524 Theodore E. Gildred and "Ecuador 1"

1981. 50th Anniv of Flight of "Ecuador 1" from San Diego to Quito.

1849	**524**	2s. black and blue	35	20

525 Dr. Octavio Cordero Palacios

1981. 50th Death Anniv (1980) of Dr. Octavio Cordero Palacios.

1850	**525**	2s. multicoloured	45	30

526 Miraculous Painting of the Virgin of Sorrows

1981. 75th Anniv of Miracle of the Virgin blinking at San Gabriel College. Multicoloured.

1851	2s. Type **526**	35	20
1852	2s. San Gabriel College Church	35	20

527 Football Emblem

1981. Air. World Cup Football Championship, Spain (1982). Multicoloured.

1853	7s.60 Type **527**	1·20	65
1854	10s.60 Footballer	1·70	65
1855	13s.60 World Cup trophy	2·00	1·10

MS1856 Two sheets each 115×90 mm. (a) 20s. Type **527**; (b) 20s. As No. 1855 Imperf 7·25 7·00

528 Mendoza Aviles and Bridge

1981. Inauguration of Dr. Rafael Mendoza Aviles Bridge.

1857	**528**	2s. multicoloured	45	30

529 "Still-life"

1981. Air. Birth Centenary of Pablo Picasso (artist). Multicoloured.

1858	7s.60 Type **529**	1·10	55
1859	10s.60 "First Communion" (vert)	1·30	65
1860	13s.60 "Las Meninas" (vert)	1·40	95

MS1861 Two sheets each 114×89 mm. (a) 20s. Type **529**; (b) 20s. As Nos. 1859/60. Imperf 6·50 6·50

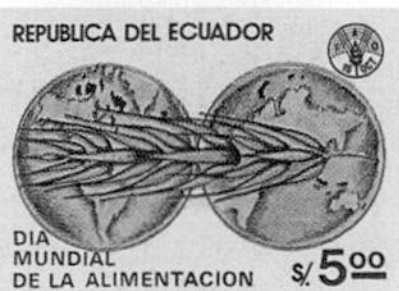

530 Ear of Wheat on World Map

1981. World Food Day. Multicoloured.

1862	5s. Type **530** (postage)	65	30
1863	10s.60 Agricultural products and farmer sowing seed (air)	1·70	75

531 "Isla Salango" (freighter)

1982. 10th Anniv of Transnave Shipping Company.

1864	**531**	3s.50 multicoloured	65	30

532 Person in Wheelchair

1982. International Year of Disabled Persons (1981).

1865	**532**	3s.40 brown, red and black (postage)	45	30
1866	-	7s.60 silver, green and blue (air)	90	45
1867	-	10s.60 brn, blk and red	1·10	55

DESIGNS: 7s.60, I.Y.D.P. emblem; 10s.60, Man breaking crutch.

533 Gateway, Quito

1982. "Quitex '82" National Stamp Exn.

1868	**533**	2s. yellow, brown & blk	35	20
1869	-	3s. yellow, brown & blk	55	20
MS1870		110×90 mm. 6s.×4 (each 51×41 mm), 18th century plan of Quito (composite design)	4·50	4·25

DESIGN: 3s. Old houses, Quito.

534 Flags of Member Countries and Emblem

1982. 22nd American Air Forces' Commanders Conference.

1871	**534**	5s. multicoloured	55	30

535 Juan Montalvo (after C. A. Villacres)

1982. 150th Birth Anniv of Juan Montalvo (writer).

1872	**535**	2s. pink, brown and black (postage)	35	20
1873	-	3s. multicoloured	35	20
1874	-	5s. multicoloured (air)	1·20	65

DESIGNS—VERT: 3s. Mausoleum. HORIZ: 5s. Montalvo's villa.

536 Swimming Pool

1982. World Swimming Championships, Guayaquil. Multicoloured.

1875	1s.80 Type **536** (postage)	35	20
1876	3s.40 Water polo	35	20
1877	10s.20 Games emblem (vert) (air)	1·10	55
1878	14s.20 Diving (vert)	1·40	65

537 Juan Leon Mera (after Victor Mideros)

1982. 150th Birth Anniv of Juan Leon Mera (author).

1879	**537**	5s.40 brn, blk & lt brn	35	30
1880	-	6s. multicoloured	45	30

DESIGN: 6s. Statue of Mera, Ambato.

538 "The Ecstasy of St. Theresa" (detail of sculpture by Bernini)

1983. 400th Death Anniv of St. Theresa of Avila.

1881	**538**	2s. multicoloured	45	30

539 Pres. and Martha Roldos and Independence Monument

1983. Air. 2nd Death Anniv of President and Martha Roldos.

1882	**539**	13s.60 multicoloured	90	55

540 Californian Sealions

1983. 150th Anniv of Ecuadorian Rule over Galapagos Islands and Death Centenary of Charles Darwin (evolutionary biologist). Multicoloured.

1883	3s. Type **540**	1·10	20
1884	5s. James's flamingoes and inset portrait of Darwin	1·70	30

541 Statue of Rocafuerte in Guayaquil

1983. Birth Bicentenary of Vicente Rocafuerte Bejarano (President, 1835–39). Multicoloured.

1885	5s. Type **541**	20	20
1886	20s. Painting of Rocafuerte	1·10	45

542 Bolivar (after Antonio Salguero)

1983. Birth Bicentenary of Simon Bolivar.

1887	**542**	20s. multicoloured	1·10	45

543 Long-distance View of Daniel Palacios Dam

1983. Inauguration of First Stage of Paute Hydro-electric Project. Multicoloured.

1888	5s. Type **543** (postage)	45	30
1889	10s. Close-up of dam	90	65
MS1890	110×89 mm. 20s. Dam (air). Imperf	2·20	2·10

544 W.C.Y. Emblem

1983. World Communications Year.

1891	**544**	2s. multicoloured	45	30

545 Bolivar and Bananas

1983. Centenaries of Provinces of Bolivar and El Oro.

1892	**545**	3s. multicoloured	45	30

546 Atahualpa

1984. 450th Death Anniv (1983) of Atahualpa (last Inca emperor).

1893	**546**	15s. multicoloured	55	45

547 "Holy Family"

1984. Christmas. Multicoloured.

1894	5s. Type **547**	35	20
1895	5s. Jesus and the lawyers	35	20
1896	5s. Marzipan kings	35	20
1897	6s. Marzipan preacher (vert)	35	20

548 Visit to Brazil

1984. President Hurtado's International Policies. Multicoloured.

1898	8s. Type **548**	45	30
1899	9s. Visit to China	55	30
1900	24s. Addressing U.N. General Assembly	1·50	1·10
1901	28s. Meeting President Reagan of U.S.A.	1·90	1·20
1902	29s. Visit to Caracas, Venezuela, for Bolivar's birth bicentenary	2·00	1·30
1903	37s. Opening Latin-American Economic Conference, Quito	2·40	1·70

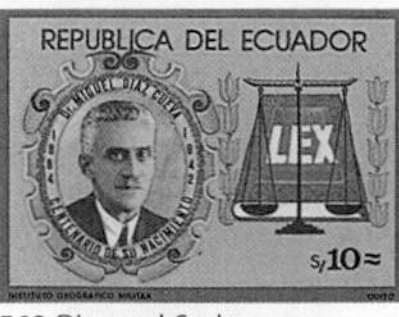

549 Diaz and Scales

1984. Birth Centenary of Miguel Diaz Cueva (lawyer).

1904	**549**	10s. multicoloured	90	30

550 Games Emblem

1984. Winter Olympic Games, Sarajevo. Mult.

1905	2s. Type **550** (postage)	35	30
1906	4s. Ice skating	35	30
1907	6s. Ice skating (different)	35	30
1908	10s. Skiing	65	30
MS1909	90×110 mm. 20s. Ice dancing (air). Imperf	44·00	17·00

551 Montgolfier Balloon

1984. Bicent of Manned Fight (1983). Mult.

1910	3s. Type **551**	20	10
1911	6s. Charles's hydrogen balloon	55	30
MS1912	110×89 mm. 20s. Montgolfier balloon and airship "Graf Zeppelin". Imperf	2·20	1·30

552 La Marimba (dance)

1984. "San Mateo '83" Provincial Stamp Exhibition, Esmeraldas.

1913	**552**	8s. multicoloured	2·20	30
MS1914		89×119 mm. 15s. "La Marimba" (different). Imperf	1·30	1·30

553 Language Academy

1984. Canonization of Brother Miguel. Mult.

1915	9s. Type **553**	45	30
1916	24s. Pope, St. Miguel and St. Peter's, Rome (vert)	1·30	85
MS1917	110×90 mm. 28s. Family home, Cuenca and St. Miguel's parents. Imperf	4·00	2·10

554 Yerovi

1984. 165th Birth Anniv of Jose Maria de Jesus Yerovi, Archbishop of Quito.

1918	**554**	5s. multicoloured	45	30

555 Pope's Arms

1985. Visit of Pope John Paul II. Mult.

1919	1s.60 Type **555**	1·10	30
1920	5s. Pope holding crucifix	1·10	30
1921	9s. Map of papal route	1·10	30
1922	28s. Pope waving	2·75	55
1923	29s. Pope	3·25	65
MS1924 90×110 mm. 30s. Pope in ceremonial dress. Imperf		8·25	8·25

556 Mercedes de Jesus Molina

1985. Beatification of Mercedes de Jesus Molina. Multicoloured.

1925	1s.60 Type **556**	20	10
1926	5s. "Madonna of Czestochowa" (icon)	35	20
1927	9s. "Our Lady of La Alborada" (statue)	55	30
MS1928 89×110 mm. 20s. Mercedes de Jesus Molina reading to children. Imperf		3·25	3·25

557 Hummingbird

1985. Samuel Valarezo Delgado (ornithologist and former Director of Posts).

1929	**557**	2s. red, green & brown	20	20
1930	-	3s. green, yellow and bl	20	20
1931	-	6s. black and brown	45	20

DESIGNS: 3s. Sailfish and tuna; 6s. Valarezo Delgado.

558 Exhibition Emblem

1985. "Espana 84" International Stamp Exhibition, Madrid.

1932	**558**	6s. brn & cinnamon	35	20
1933	-	10s. brn & cinnamon	55	30
MS1934 110×89 mm. 15s. Retiro Park, Madrid. Imperf			1·70	1·70

DESIGN: 10s. Spanish royal family.

559 Dr. Pio Jaramallo Alvarado

1985. Death Centenary (1984) of Dr. Pio Jaramallo Alvarado (historian).

1935	**559**	6s. multicoloured	35	20

560 Sugar Cane and Water Tower

1985. Centenary of Valdez Sugar Refinery. Mult.

1936	50s. Type **560**	1·40	75
1937	100s. Rafael Valdez Cervantes (founder)	3·00	1·40
MS1938 109×89 mm. 30s. Sugar refinery. Imperf		1·90	1·90

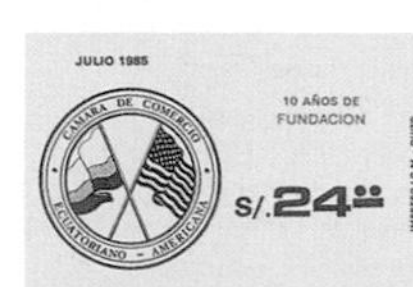

561 Emblem

1985. 10th Anniv of Chamber of Commerce.

1939	**561**	24s. multicoloured	1·00	45
1940	**561**	28s. multicoloured	1·20	65
MS1941 110×90 mm. 50s. black and orange (Independence Monument, Quito and Statue of Liberty, New York). Imperf			2·75	2·75

562 Emblem

1985. 50th Anniv of Ecuador Philatelic Association. Multicoloured.

1942	25s. Type **562**	75	45
1943	30s. Philatelic Exhibition 1s. stamp, 1936 (horiz)	1·20	65

563 Fire Engine, 1882

1985. 150th Anniv of Guayaquil Fire Station. Multicoloured.

1944	6s. Type **563**	35	20
1945	10s. Fire-engine, 1899	55	30
1946	20s. Fire service anniversary emblem	1·10	75

564 Children and Tree

1985. Infant Survival Campaign.

1947	**564**	10s. multicoloured	55	30

565 Israeli Aircraft Industry Kfir-C2

1985. Armed Forces. Multicoloured.

1948	10s. Type **565** (65th anniv of Air Force)	55	30
1949	10s. Seaman and gunboat "Calderon" (centenary of Navy)	55	30
1950	10s. Insignia (30th anniv of Parachute Regiment)	55	30

566 Boxer

1985. Bolivar Games, Cuenca. Each silver, blue and red.

1951	10s. Type **566**	55	30
1952	25s. Gymnast	90	45
1953	30s. Discus thrower	1·10	55

567 "Royal Audience Quarter, Quito" (J. M. Roura)

1985. First National Philatelic Congress and "50th Anniv of Ecuador Philatelic Association" Stamp Exhibition, Quito.

1954	**567**	5s. black, yellow & orge	20	10
1955	-	10s. black, green & red	55	30
1956	-	15s. black, blue and red	75	55
1957	-	20s. black, red and lilac	1·10	75
MS1958 109×90 mm. 4×5s. each black, new blue and vermilion			1·30	1·30

DESIGNS—VERT: 10s. "Riobamba Cathedral" (O. Munoz". HORIZ 15s. House of a Hundred Windows, Guayaquil" (J. M.Roural); 20s. "Rural House, near Cuenca" (J.M. Roura). 47×32 mm-No. **MS**1958, 1779 Riobamba postal marking (first pre-stamp marking); M. Rivadeneira printing press, Quito, 1864; Postman, Cuenca, 1880; First airmail flight, Guayaquil, 1919.

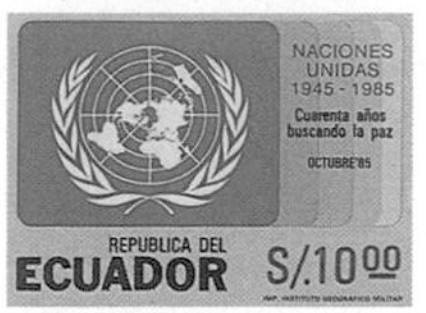

568 U.N. Emblem

1985. 40th Anniv of U.N.O. Multicoloured.

1959	10s. Type **568** (postage)	55	30
1960	20s. State flag	55	30
MS1961 110×90 mm. 50s. U.N. building, New York. (air) Imperf		1·50	1·50

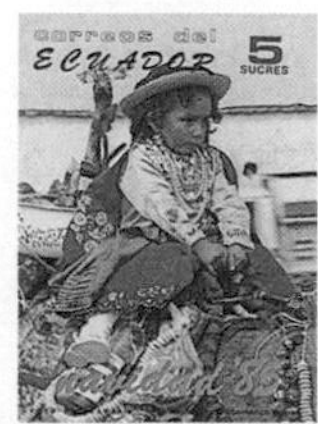

569 Child on Donkey

1985. Christmas. Multicoloured.

1962	5s. Type **569**	20	10
1963	10s. Food display	55	20
1964	15s. Child seated upon display	75	65
MS1965 89×110 mm. 30s. As Type **569** but 69×94 mm. Imperf		1·90	1·60

570 "Embotrium grandiforum"

1986. Flowers. Multicoloured.

1966	24s. Type **570**	1·30	45
1967	28s. Orchid ("Topobea" sp.)	2·10	45
1968	29s. "Befaria resinosa mutis"	2·75	55
MS1969 110×90 mm. 15s. As No. 1966/8. Imperf		8·75	4·75

571 Land Iguana

1986. Galapagos Islands. Multicoloured.

1970	10s. Type **571**	55	30
1971	20s. Californian sealion	1·10	65
1972	30s. Magnificent frigate birds	1·70	1·10
1973	40s. Galapagos penguins	2·20	1·50
1974	50s. Tortoise (25th anniv (1984) of Charles Darwin Foundation)	2·75	1·70
1975	100s. Charles Darwin (150th anniv (1985) of visit)	5·50	3·75
1976	200s. Bishop Tomas de Berlanga and map (450th anniv (1985) of Islands' discovery)	11·00	7·00
MS1977 110×90 mm. 50s.×4 Map of Islands (composite design, each stamp 52×42 mm)		13·00	13·00

572 Antonio Ortiz Mena (President)

1986. 25th Anniv (1985) of Inter-American Development Bank. Multicoloured.

1978	5s. Type **572**	45	30
1979	10s. Felipe Herrera (President, 1960–71)	65	30
1980	50s. Emblem	1·30	65

573 Andres Gomez Santos

1986. 75th Anniv (1985) of Guayaquil Tennis Club. Multicoloured.

1981	10s. Type **573**	55	30
1982	10s. Francisco Segura Cano	55	30
1983	10s. Emblem (horiz)	55	30

574 Prawn

1986. Exports. Seafoods.

1984	**574**	35s. red and blue	1·20	55
1985	-	40s. green and red	1·20	55
1986	-	45s. yellow & mauve	1·40	85
MS1987 110×89 mm. 10s. green, brown and vermilion (as No. 1986 but 49×42 mm); 10s. vermilion, brown and green (as No. 1985 but 49×42 mm); 10s. vermilion and green (as T **574** but 49×36 mm); 10s. green and vermilion (Mask and emblem) (49×36 mm)			2·75	2·75

DESIGNS: 40s. Yellow-finned tuna; 45s. Pacific sardines in tin.

575 Goalkeeper diving for Ball

1986. World Cup Football Championship, Mexico. Multicoloured.

1988	5s. Type **575**	35	20
1989	10s. Player tackling	65	30
MS1990	110×90 mm. 20s. Footballer, flags and football as globe. Imperf	13·00	13·00

576 Betancourt and Cordero

1986. Rumichaca Meeting of Pres. Belisario Betancourt of Colombia and Pres. Leon Febres Cordero of Ecuador. Multicoloured.

1991	20s. Type **576**	55	30
1992	20s. Presidents embracing	55	30

577 Charles-Marie de La Condamine

1986. 250th Anniv of First Geodetic Expedition (to measure Arcs of Meridian).

1993	**577**	10s. green and light green	45	30
1994	-	15s. violet and lilac	55	30
1995	-	20s. green and brown	65	30
MS1996		110×90 mm. 4×10s. each ochre and brown	3·25	3·25

DESIGNS: No. 1994, Maldonado; 1995, Centre of World Monument, Quito; **MS**1996—48×38 mm. Triangulation map, 1736; 48×39 mm. Part of Samuel Fritz's map of Amazon River, 1743—44; 50×39 mm. Expedition base, Plain of Yaruqui, with Caraburo and Oyambaro Hills, Quito (two stamps forming composite design).

578 Emblem of Pichincha Chamber of Trade

1986. 50th Anniversaries of Chambers of Trade.

1997	**578**	10s. black and brown	35	20
1998	-	10s. black and blue	35	20
1999	-	10s. black and green	35	20

DESIGNS: No. 1998, Cuenca; 1999, Guayaquil.

579 National Railways Emblem

1986. 57th Anniv of Ministry of Public Works and Communications. Multicoloured.

2000	5s. Type **579**	20	10
2001	10s. Post Office emblem	35	20
2002	15s. IETEL (telecommunications) emblem	65	30
2003	20s. Ministry of Public Works emblem	75	55

580 Emblem

1987. 50th Anniv of First Zone Chamber of Agriculture.

2004	**580**	5s. multicoloured	45	30

581 Vargas

1988. Death Centenary of Luis Vargas Torres (revolutionary).

2005	**581**	50s. black, gold & grn	1·30	65
2006	-	100s. blue, gold and red	2·75	1·30
MS2007		95×140 mm. 100s.×3, multicoloured	8·25	8·25

DESIGNS: No. 2006, Group of Soldiers; **MS**2007—95×28 mm. Vargas and his mother (top stamp); Arms and group of soldiers (bottom stamp); 95×82 mm. Fragment of letter sent by Vargas to this mother (middle stamp).

582 Las Penas Quarter

1988. 450th Anniv of Guayaquil City. Mult.

2008	15s. Type **582**	35	30
2009	30s. Rafael Mendoza Aviles Bridge of National Unity (horiz)	55	30
2010	40s. Federico de Orellana (founder) (horiz)	65	30

583 Family within Hands

1988. 60th Anniv of Social Security Work. Multicoloured.

2011	50s. Type **583**	90	55
2012	100s. Anniversary emblem	1·90	1·10

584 Yaguarcocha Lake

1988. Death Centenary of Dr. Pedro Moncayo y Esparza (politician). Multicoloured.

2013	10s. Type **584**	20	20
2014	15s. Dr. Moncayo	35	20
2015	20s. Dr. Moncayo's house	35	20
MS2016	90×110 mm. 100s. Dr. Moncayo standing beside table. Imperf	1·70	1·70

585 Junkers F-13 Seaplane

1988. 60th Anniv of Avianca National Airline. Multicoloured.

2017	10s. Type **585**	35	30
2018	20s. Dornier Wal flying boat	35	30
2019	30s. Ford Tri-motor "Tin Goose"	45	30
2020	40s. Boeing 247D	55	30
2021	50s. Boeing 720-059D	65	45
2022	100s. Douglas DC-3	1·50	65
2023	200s. Boeing 727-200	2·75	1·50
2024	300s. Sikorsky S-38 flying boat	4·75	2·10
2025	500s. Anniversary emblem (vert)	7·75	3·75

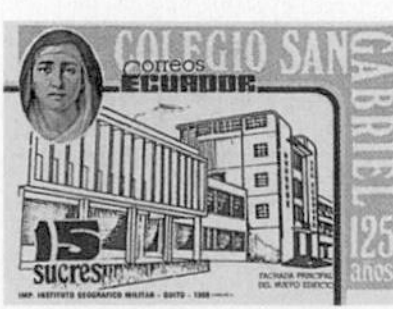

586 New Building

1988. 125th Anniv of San Gabriel College. Multicoloured.

2026	15s. Type **586**	20	20
2027	35s. Door of old building	75	45

587 Institute

1988. 60th Anniv of Military Geographical Institute, Quito. Multicoloured.

2028	25s. Type **587**	55	30
2029	50s. Inside planetarium	1·00	30
2030	60s. Anniversary emblem	1·20	45
2031	500s. Mural by E. Kingman	7·75	3·75
MS2032	109×89 mm. 4×5s. Institute emblem (32×40 mm); Anniversary emblem and top half of Institute emblem (70×40 mm); Inscription "INSTITUTO GEOGRAPHICO MILITAR" (32×39 mm); Bottom half of Institute emblem (70×40 mm)	2·20	2·20

No. 2028 was issued surcharged 800s. on 25 June 1996. Only a few sets were made available to the public at face value, the remainder sold by postal employees at considerably inflated prices.

588 St. John Bosco

1988. Centenary of Salesian Brothers in Ecuador and Death Centenary of St. John Bosco (founder). Multicoloured.

2033	10s. Type **588**	20	20
2034	50s. Group of Brothers	1·00	45
MS2035	109×89 mm. 100s. St. John Bosco and Salesian Monument. Imperf	2·75	1·60

589 Dr. Francisco Campos Coello (founder)

1988. Cent of Guayaquil Welfare Society.

2036	**589**	15s. multicoloured	20	20
2037	-	20s. multicoloured	30	20
2038	-	45s. black, silver & blue	65	30
MS2039		110×90 mm. 10s.×4 multicoloured	1·70	1·70

DESIGNS: 20s. Eduardo M. Arosemena (first Director); 45s. Emblem; **MS**2039, Emblem (composite design).

No. 2038 was issued surcharged 2600s. on 25 June 1996. Only a few sets were made available to the public at face value, the remainder sold by postal employees at considerably inflated prices.

590 Bank

1989. 75th Anniv (1988) of Azuay Bank, Cuenca. Multicoloured.

2040	20s. Type **590**	30	20
2041	40s. Bank (vert)	45	25
MS2042	90×110 mm. 500s. Foundation document. Imperf	11·00	2·75

591 Athletics

1989. Olympic Games, Seoul (1988). Designs showing Hodori the Tiger (mascot).

2043	10s. Type **591**	10	10
2044	20s. Boxing	20	10
2045	30s. Cycling	35	20
2046	40s. Shooting	45	20
2047	100s. Swimming	1·10	65
2048	200s. Weightlifting	2·20	1·40
2049	300s. Taekwondo	3·25	2·10
MS2050	90×110 mm. 200s. Games emblem. Imperf	3·25	3·25

592 "Bird" (sculpture, Joaquin Tinta)

1989. 50th Anniv of Ruminahui State. Mult.

2051	50s. Type **592**	90	30
2052	70s. Sangolqui church (horiz)	1·30	45
MS2053	90×110 mm. 300s. Ruminahui Monument, Sangolqui. Imperf	7·25	2·10

593 Dr. Carrion Mora

1989. Birth Centenary of Dr. Benjamin Carrion Mora (writer). Multicoloured.

2054	50s. Type **593**	45	20
2055	70s. Loja (horiz)	65	30
2056	1000s. Loja university (horiz)	10·50	5·25
MS2057	110×90 mm. 200s. Dr. Carrion Mora (different). Imperf	2·00	2·00

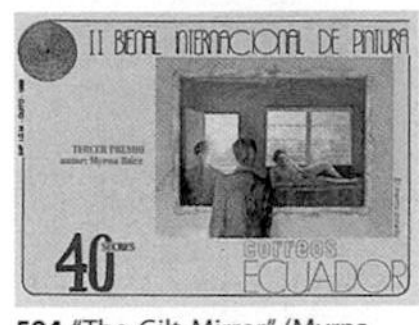

594 "The Gilt Mirror" (Myrna Baez)

1989. 2nd Art Biennale, Cuenca. Mult.

2058	40s. Type **594**	55	30
2059	70s. "Paraguay III" (Carlos Colombino) (vert)	1·10	45
2060	180s. "Modulation 892" (Julio Le Parc) (vert)	2·20	95
MS2061	110×90 mm. 100s. Biennale decree. Imperf	1·80	1·10

595 Ignacio C. Roca Molestina (founding President)

1989. Centenary of Guayaquil Chamber of Commerce. Multicoloured.

2062	50s. Type **595**	45	20
2063	300s. Chamber building (horiz)	2·75	1·60
2064	500s. Trade and progress symbol (horiz)	4·50	2·75
MS2065	110×90 mm. 200s. As No. 2064. Imperf	1·90	1·90

596 Emblems

1989. 60th Anniv of Ministry of Public Works and Communications. Multicoloured.

2066	50s. Type **596**	45	20
2067	100s. IETEL emblem (telecommunications)	90	55
2068	200s. Ministry of Public Works emblem	1·90	1·10
MS2069	90×110 mm. 50s. Ministry of Public Works emblem and road (45×55 mm); 50s. Train and National Railways emblem (45×55 mm); 50s. Post Office emblem and airmail cover (45×54 mm); 50s. Payphone and IETEL emblem (45×54 mm)	1·90	1·90

597 Birds

1989. Bicent of French Revolution. Mult.

2070	20s. Type **597**	20	20
2071	50s. Cathedral fresco (horiz)	55	25
2072	100s. French cock	90	55
MS2073	Two sheets each 90×110 mm. (a) 200s. Emblems of revolution; (b) 12×50s. Various revolutionary and Napoleonic scenes	9·25	9·25

598 Red Cross Worker

1989. 125th Anniv of Red Cross in Ecuador. Multicoloured.

2074	10s. Type **598**	10	10
2075	30s. Emblem (horiz)	25	20
2076	200s. Masked Red Cross workers (horiz)	2·20	1·30

599 Montalvo's Tomb

1989. Death Cent of Juan Montalvo (writer).

2077	50s. Type **599**	45	35
2078	100s. Photograph of Montalvo	1·20	65
2079	200s. Statue of Montalvo	2·10	1·40
MS2080	90×110 mm. 200s. Portrait of Montalvo. Imperf	1·80	1·80

600 Dr. Jaramillo Leon (founder)

1990. 70th Anniv of Cuenca Chamber of Commerce. Multicoloured.

2081	100s. Type **600**	1·10	65
2082	100s. Federico Malo Andrade (first Honorary President)	1·10	65
2083	130s. Roberto Crespo Toral (first President)	1·40	90
2084	200s. Alfonso Jaramillo Leon (founder of savings and credit departments)	2·10	1·30
MS2085	90×110 mm. 100s.×3 Portraits as Nos. 2081/3 (each 85×33 mm)	3·50	3·50

601 Tolita Head-shaped Censer

1990. America. Pre-Columbian Artefacts. Mult.

2086	200s. Type **601**	2·10	1·30
2087	300s. Carchi plate with warrior design (horiz)	3·25	2·00

602 Mercedes de Jesus Molina

1990. Anniversaries. Multicoloured.

2088	100s. Type **602** (centenary of Marianitas)	70	35
2089	200s. Clock tower and roses on open book (centenary of Santa Mariana de Jesus College)	1·40	65

603 Mascot, Quarter Finalists and Ball

1990. World Cup Football Championship, Italy. Multicoloured.

2090	100s. Type **603**	70	35
2091	200s. Finalists' flags and player (vert)	1·40	65
2092	300s. Mascot, map and trophy (vert)	2·40	1·00
MS2093	Two sheets. (a) 110×90 mm. 200s. Player, mascot and flags of Italy and Colombia; (b) 60×90 mm. 300s. Mascot, trophy and Italian colours	5·00	5·00

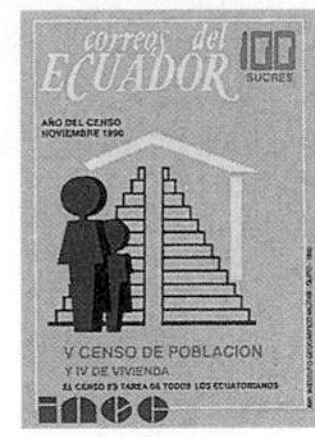

604 Emblem

1990. 5th Population Census and 4th Housing Census. Multicoloured.

2094	100s. Type **604**	60	20
2095	200s. Logo of National Statistics and Census Institute (horiz)	1·30	55
2096	300s. Pencil and population statistics	1·90	75
MS2097	109×89 mm. 3×100s. Motifs similar to Nos. 2094/6 (34×89 mm)	2·00	2·00

605 Iguana (Galapagos)

1990. Tourism. Multicoloured.

2098	100s. Type **605**	85	35
2099	200s. Church of Companionship (Quito) (vert)	1·80	55
2100	300s. Old man of Vilcabamba	2·50	75
MS2101	110×90 mm. 4×100s. Motifs as on Nos. 2098/2100 and railway locomotive (each 22×18 mm)	8·75	3·75

606 Members' Flags

1990. 30th Anniv of Organization of Petroleum Exporting Countries. Multicoloured.

2102	200s. Type **606**	1·30	55
2103	300s. Emblem	1·90	75

607 Anniversary Emblem

1990. 25th Anniv of Organization for Preservation of Traditional Handicrafts. Multicoloured.

2104	200s. Type **607**	1·30	55
2105	300s. Carved and painted parrots	1·90	75
MS2106	90×110 mm. 200s. Carved and painted birds. Imperf	2·10	2·10

608 "Blakea sp."

1990. Flowers. Multicoloured.

2107	100s. Type **608**	1·20	35
2108	100s. "Loasa sp."	1·20	35
2109	100s. "Cattleya sp."	1·20	35
2110	100s. "Sobralia sp." (horiz)	1·20	35

609 Ingapirca

1991. America. World found by the Discoverers. Multicoloured.

2111	100s. Type **609**	70	35
2112	200s. Forest pool	1·70	55

610 Globe and Means of Information

1991. 50th Anniv of National Journalists' Federation. Multicoloured.

2113	200s. Type **610**	1·30	75
2114	300s. Eugenio Espejo	2·00	90
2115	400s. Emblem	2·40	1·20

611 Broadcaster

1991. 50th Anniv of Radio Quito. Mult.

2116	200s. Type **611**	85	45
2117	500s. Family listening to radio (horiz)	2·20	1·00

612 Suarez

1991. Birth Cent of Dr. Pablo Arturo Suarez.

2118	**612**	70s. multicoloured	45	35

613 Columbus's Ships

1991. America. Multicoloured.

2119	200s. Type **613**	1·20	55
2120	500s. Columbus and landing party	2·50	1·20

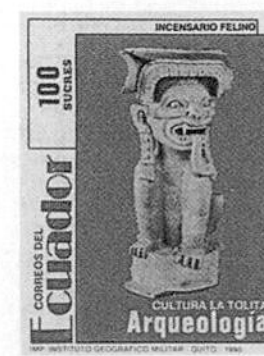

614 Cat-shaped Censer

1991. Archaeology. La Tolita Culture (1st series). Multicoloured.

2121	100s. Type **614**	70	35
2122	200s. Head of old man	1·40	45
2123	300s. Human/animal statuette	2·20	75

See also No. 2144.

615 Hand and Woman's Face

1991. No Violence to Women Day. Mult.

2124	300s. Type **615**	1·40	65
2125	500s. Woman's profile and hand	2·40	1·10

616 Presidents Borja and Paz Zamora

1991. Visit of President Jaime Paz Zamora of Bolivia.

2126	**616**	500s. multicoloured	2·40	1·10

617 Jijon y Caamano

1991. Birth Centenary of Jacinto Jijon y Caamano (historian and geographer).

2127	**617**	200s. multicoloured	95	45
2128	-	300s. blue, blk & mve	1·40	65

DESIGN—HORIZ: 300s. Books and Jijon y Caamano.

618 Pres. Borja

1992. President Rodrigo Borja's Speech to United Nations. Multicoloured.

2129		100s. Type **618**	35	20
2130		1000s. Map and flags of U.N. Security Council members	4·25	2·00

619 "Calderon" (gunboat) and Rafael Moran Valverde

1992. 50th Anniv (1991) of Battle of Jambeli. Multicoloured.

2131		300s. Type **619**	85	55
2132		500s. "Atahualpa" (despatch vessel) and Victor Naranjo Fiallo	1·70	1·00
MS2133		110×90 mm. 500s. Motifs as in Nos. 2131/2. Imperf	3·50	3·00

620 Land Iguana

1992. Galapagos Islands Animals.

2134		100s. Type **620**	95	55
2135		100s. Giant tortoise	95	55
2136		100s. Swallow-tailed gull	95	55
2137		100s. Great frigate bird ("Fregata minor")	95	55
2138		100s. Galapagos penguin (vert)	95	55
2139		100s. Californian sea-lion (vert)	95	55

621 College

1992. 150th Anniv (1991) of Vicente Rocafuerte National College, Guayaquil. Multicoloured.

2140		200s. Type **621**	85	45
2141		400s. Vicente Rocafuerte (Ecuador President 1835–39 and College founder)	1·50	65

622 Alfaro

1992. 150th Birth Anniv of General Eloy Alfaro. Multicoloured.

2142		300s. Type **622**	95	55
2143		700s. Alfaro's house (horiz)	2·40	1·10

623 Ceremonial Mask

1992. Archaeology. La Tolita Culture (2nd series).

2144	**623**	400s. multicoloured	1·90	65

624 "Santa Maria"

1992. America. 500th Anniv of Discovery of America by Columbus. Multicoloured.

2145		200s. Type **624**	95	45
2146		400s. Columbus and map of Americas (vert)	1·90	90

625 Cordova

1992. Birth Centenary of Andres Cordova (President, 1940).

2147	**625**	300s. multicoloured	1·20	60

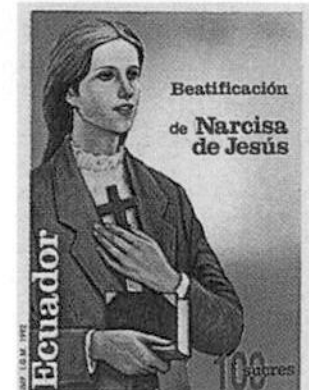

626 Narcisa de Jesus

1992. Beatification of Narcisa de Jesus.

2148	**626**	100s. multicoloured	50	35

627 Infant Jesus

1992. Christmas. Multicoloured.

2149		300s. Type **627**	1·20	60
2150		600s. Children, lamb and baby Jesus	2·40	1·20

628 Velasco (statue)

1992. Death Bicentenary of Juan de Velasco.

2151	**628**	200s. multicoloured	1·00	45

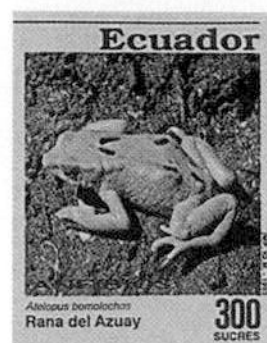

629 "Atelopus bomolochos"

1993. Frogs. Multicoloured.

2152		300s. Type **629**	85	60
2153		300s. Spurrell's tree frog ("Agalychnis spurrelli")	85	60
2154		600s. "Hyla picturata"	2·00	1·20
2155		600s. "Gastrotheca plumbea"	2·00	1·20
2156		900s. Splendid poison-arrow frog ("Dendrobates" sp.)	2·75	1·80
2157		900s. "Sphaenorhynchus lacteus"	2·75	1·80

630 Paez

1993. Birth Centenary of J. Roberto Paez (co-founder of social security system and writer).

2158	**630**	300s. blue	1·10	35

631 1907 3c. Robles Stamp

1993. Death Centenary of Francisco Robles Garcia (President 1856–59).

2159	**631**	500s. multicoloured	1·80	60

632 Arms

1993. National Police.

2160	**632**	300s. multicoloured	1·00	60

633 Velasco

1993. Birth Centenary of Jose Maria Velasco Ibarra (President, 1934–35, 1944–47, 1952–56, 1960–61 and 1968–72).

2161	**633**	500s. multicoloured	1·80	60

634 Lantern Fly

1993. Insects. Multicoloured.

2162		150s. Type **634**	75	35
2163		200s. "Semiotus ligneus"	1·00	40
2164		300s. "Taeniotes pulverulenta"	1·50	45
2165		400s. Orange tiger caterpillar	2·00	60
2166		600s. "Erotylus onagga"	3·00	95
2167		700s. Carpenter bee	3·25	1·10

635 Cevallos Villacreces

1993. Death Centenary of Pedro Fermin Cevallos Villacreces (historian and founder of Language Academy).

2168	**635**	1000s. multicoloured	3·25	1·50

636 Boy releasing Doves

1993. 1st Latin-American Children's Peace Assembly, Quito.

2169	**636**	300s. multicoloured	1·00	45

637 Vela Hervas

1993. 150th Birth Anniv of Juan Benigno Vela Hervas (politician).

2170	**637**	2000s. multicoloured	6·00	3·00

638 "Cinchonia cordifolia"

1993. 250th Anniv of Maldonado and La Condamine's Amazon Expedition. Multicoloured.

2171		150s. Type **638**	35	25
2172		200s. Pedro Maldonado	50	30
2173		1500s. Charles de la Condamine	4·25	2·10

639 Anniversary Emblem

1993. 300th Anniv of Faculty of Medical Sciences, Ecuador Central University.

2174	**639**	300s. multicoloured	1·00	45

640 Bustamante

1993. Birth Centenary of Guillermo Bustamante (writer).

2175	**640**	1500s. multicoloured	5·50	2·40

641 Pacarana

1993. America. Endangered Animals. Mult.

2176		400s. Type **641**	2·00	60
2177		800s. Chestnut-fronted macaw (vert)	3·00	1·20

642 Arroyo del Rio

1993. Birth Centenary of Dr. Carlos Arroyo del Rio (President, 1939–44).

2178	**642**	500s. multicoloured	1·30	60

643 "Nativity" (ivory nut carvings)

1993. Christmas. Multicoloured.

2179		600s. Type **643**	1·70	95
2180		900s. Madonna and Child in landscape (vert)	2·75	1·40

644 Scouts Emblem and Map on Wall

1994. Scouting Movement.

2181	**644**	400s. multicoloured	1·30	60

645 Emblem

1994. International Year of the Family.

2182	**645**	300s. red, green & black	50	45

646 Donoso

1994. Birth Cent of Dr. Julio Tobar Donoso.

2183	**646**	500s. multicoloured	2·20	1·10

647 "Sobralia dichotoma"

1994. 1st Andean Orchid Conservation Convention. Multicoloured.

2184	150s. Type **647**	35	25
2185	150s. "Dracula hirtzii"	35	25
2186	300s. "Encyclia pulcherrima"	85	45
2187	300s. "Lepanthes delhierroi"	85	45
2188	600s. "Masdevallia rosea"	1·80	95
2189	600s. "Telipogon andicola"	1·80	95

648 Cabezas

1994. Death Cent of Dr. Miguel Egas Cabezas.

2190	**648**	100s. multicoloured	50	35

649 Gonzalez Suarez

1994. 150th Birth Anniv of Federico Gonzalez Suarez, Archbishop of Quito.

2191	**649**	200s. multicoloured	60	40

650 Earth as Football

1994. World Cup Football Championship, U.S.A. Multicoloured.

2192	300s. Type **650**	1·20	60
2193	600s. Striker (mascot)	2·40	1·20
2194	900s. Footballer	3·75	1·80
MS2195	108×90 mm. 600s. rosine, ultramarine and black (emblem) (49×24 mm); 600s. "COPA MUNDIAL/ FUTBOL 94" and emblem (49×24 mm); 600s. "COPA/MUNDIAL/USA 94" (48×51 mm); 600s. Striker (mascot) (49×56 mm)	9·75	9·75

651 Cyclists on "Road" of National Colours to Equator Monument

1994. International Junior Cycling Championship, Quito. Multicoloured.

2196	300s. Type **651**	75	45
2197	400s. Stylized cyclist and monument (vert)	1·00	60

652 Espinosa Polit

1994. Birth Centenary of Father Aurelio Espinosa Polit (writer).

2198	**652**	200s. multicoloured	1·00	45

653 Pedro Vicente Maldonado Research Station

1994. Ecuador's Presence in Antarctica. Mult.

2199	600s. Type **653**	2·40	1·20
2200	900s. "Orion" (survey ship)	3·75	1·80

654 Anniversary Emblem

1994. Centenary of National Lottery.

2201	**654**	1000s. multicoloured	5·00	2·40

655 Benjamon Carrion (founder)

1994. 50th Anniv of House of Ecuadorean Culture. Multicoloured.

2202	700s. Type **655**	3·00	1·80
2203	900s. House of Culture (horiz)	4·25	2·10

656 Worker and "75"

1994. 75th Anniv of I.L.O.

2204	**656**	100s. multicoloured	50	35

657 Globe and Postal Emblem

1994. Christmas. Multicoloured.

2205	600s. Type **657**	1·10	70
2206	900s. Nativity (vert)	1·60	1·10

658 Cessna 441 Conquest and Sack of Mail

1994. America. Postal Transport. Mult.

2207	600s. Type **658**	1·10	70
2208	600s. Cessna 441 Conquest, ship and van (horiz)	1·10	70

659 Mera's Country Villa

1994. Death Centenary of Juan Leon Mera (author). Multicoloured.

2209	600s. Type **659**	1·10	70
2210	900s. Mera (after Victor Mideros)	3·00	1·80

660 Sucre

1995. Birth Bicent of Marshal Antonio Jose de Sucre (first Bolivian President). Multicoloured.

2211	1500s. Type **660**	3·75	1·80
2212	2000s. Sucre (looking to left)	5·00	2·40
MS2213	90×110 mm. 3000s. Sucre	5·50	5·50

661 Escriva

1995. 3rd Anniv of Beatification of Josemaria Escriva de Balaguer (founder of Opus Dei).

2214	**661**	900s. multicoloured	1·60	1·10

662 Eloy Alfaro (President 1897–1901 and 1907–11)

1995. Centenary of Alfarist Revolution.

2215	**662**	800s. multicoloured	1·50	95

663 Girl

1995. 50th Anniv of CARE (Co-operative for Assistance and Remittances Overseas).

2216	**663**	400s. black, grn & gold	85	45
2217	-	800s. multicoloured	1·80	95

DESIGN—HORIZ: 800s. People working land.

664 Soldier thinking of Children

1995. "Peace with Dignity". Multicoloured.

2218	200s. Type **664**	50	35
2219	400s. Hand holding Ecuador flag (25×34 mm)	1·00	45
2220	800s. Soldier amongst bamboo	1·80	95

No. 2118 was issued surcharged 200s. on 25 June 1996. Only a few sets were made available to the public at face value, the remainder sold by postal employees at considerably inflated prices.

665 Anniversary Emblem

1995. 25th Anniv of Andean Development Corporation.

2221	**665**	1000s. multicoloured	3·00	1·20

666 "Our Lady of Cisne" (statue, Diego de Robles)

1995

2222	**666**	500s. multicoloured	85	60

667 Anniversary Emblem

1995. 35th Anniv of INNFA (child welfare organization).

2223	**667**	400s. multicoloured	1·00	45

668 Anniversary Emblem

1995. 50th Anniv of U.N.O.

2224	**668**	1000s. blue, gold & blk	2·40	1·20

669 Man with Book (preparation for natural disasters)

1995. International Decade for the Reduction of Natural Disasters. Ecuador Civil Defence Organization. Multicoloured.

2225	1000s. Type **669**	2·40	1·20
2226	1000s. Family hiding beneath table (protection)	2·40	1·20
2227	1000s. Couple escaping from flooded house (maintenance of elevated refugee centres)	2·40	1·20
2228	1000s. Children planting sapling (reforestation)	2·40	1·20
2229	1000s. Family escaping erupting volcano (awareness of warning signs)	2·40	1·20

670 Emblem

1995. 50th Anniv of F.A.O.

2230	**670**	1300s. multicoloured	3·00	1·50

671 Woman, Piano and Book

1995. 50th Anniv of Women's Cultural Club.

2231	**671**	1500s. multicoloured	2·75	1·80

672 Emblem

1995. 39th Annual Assembly of Inter-American Philately Federation.

2232	**672**	1000s. blue and red	1·80	1·20

673 Sepecat Jaguar and Dassault Mirage F1s flying over Mountains

1995. 75th Anniv of Ecuadorean Air Force.

2233	**673**	1000s. multicoloured	2·40	1·40

674 Long-tailed Sylphs ("Aglaiocercus kingi")

1995. Hummingbirds. Multicoloured.

2234	1000s. Type **674**	2·40	1·20
2235	1000s. Collared incas ("Coeligena torquata")	2·40	1·20
2236	1000s. Long-tailed hermits ("Phaethornis superciliosus")	2·40	1·20
2237	1000s. Booted racquet-tails ("Ocreatus underwoodii")	2·40	1·20
2238	1000s. Chimbarazo hillstars ("Oreotrochilus chimborazo")	2·40	1·20
2239	1000s. Violet-tailed sylphs ("Aglaiocercus coelestis")	2·40	1·20

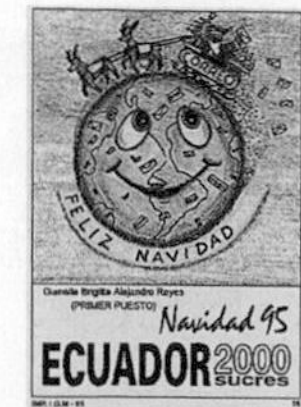
675 "World Post" (Gishella Alejandro Reyes)

1995. Christmas. Children's Painting Competition Winners. Multicoloured.

2240	2000s. Type **675**	5·25	2·40
2241	2600s. "Procession" (Juan Jaramillo Leon)	6·75	3·00

676 Jaramillo

1996. National Music Year. 60th Birth Anniv of Julio Jaramillo (singer and composer). Multicoloured.

2242	2000s. Type **676**	5·00	2·40
MS2243	90×110 mm. 3000s. Jaramillo (different)	5·50	4·25

677 Envelope (postal service)

1996. Modernization of the State. Multicoloured.

2244	1000s. Emblem	2·30	85
2245	1500s. Type **677**	3·25	1·40
2246	2000s. Two-way arrow (customs clearance)	4·50	1·90
2247	2600s. Telecommunications	5·50	2·10
2248	3000s. Ports	6·75	3·00

678 Table Tennis and Boxing

1996. 8th National Games, Esmeraldas. Multicoloured.

2249	400s. Type **678**	85	35
2250	400s. Basketball and football	85	35
2251	600s. Tennis and swimming	1·20	60
2252	800s. Weight-lifting and karate	1·60	70
2253	1000s. Volleyball and gymnastics	2·10	95
2254	1200s. Athletics and judo	2·40	1·20
2255	2000s. Chess and wrestling	4·25	1·90
MS2256	120×100 mm. 2000s. Coquito (mascot). Imperf	4·50	3·50

679 Pitts Special and Emblem

1996. 50th Anniv of Civil Aviation Organization.

2257	**679**	2000s. multicoloured	4·25	2·40

680 Mascot

1996. Olympic Games, Atlanta. Multicoloured.

2258	1000s. Type **680**	2·10	95
2259	2000s. Ecuador Olympic emblem	4·00	1·90
2260	3000s. Jefferson Perez (gold medal, 20km walk) (vert)	5·50	3·00
MS2261	100×120 mm. 2000s. Jefferson Perez wearing medal. Imperf	4·50	3·50

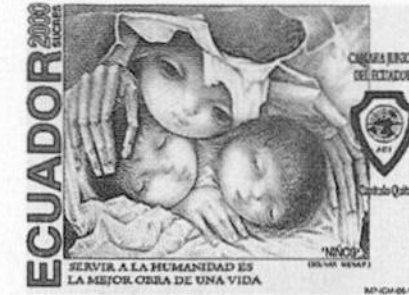
681 Mother and Children

1996. 40th Anniv of International Junior Chambers. Multicoloured.

2262	2000s. Type **681**	5·25	3·50
2263	2600s. "Tree of Life" (relief, Eduardo Vega) (vert)	6·50	4·25

682 University Building (Munoz Marino)

1996. 50th Anniv of Catholic University of Ecuador. Multicoloured.

2264	400s. Type **682**	1·10	70
2265	800s. Window (Munoz Marino) (vert)	2·10	1·40
2266	2000s. University emblem	5·00	3·50

683 Gomez

1996. Birth Centenary (1995) of Eduardo Salzar Gomez (lawyer and politician).

2267	**683**	1000s. multicoloured	2·50	1·70

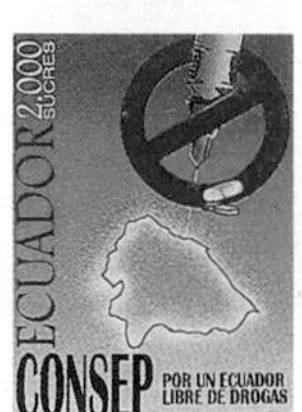
684 Syringe and Outline Map of Ecuador

1996. Anti-drugs Campaign.

2268	**684**	2000s. multicoloured	5·00	3·25

685 Emblem

1996. 25th Anniv of Private Technical University, Loja.

2269	**685**	4700s. multicoloured	12·00	7·75

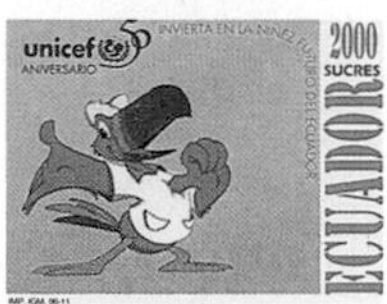
686 Lorito (mascot)

1996. 50th Anniv of United Nations International Children's Emergency Fund.

2270	**686**	2000s. multicoloured	5·00	3·25

687 Headquarters

1996. 75th Anniv of El Universo (newspaper).

2271	**687**	2000s. multicoloured	5·00	3·25

688 Globe and Letters (Maria Belen Canas)

1996. Christmas. Designs showing winning entries in children's painting competition. Multicoloured.

2272	600s. Type **688**	1·50	1·00
2273	800s. Globe and dove (Beatriz Santana)	2·00	1·30
2274	2000s. Child in bed and bird (Oscar Perugachi) (54×34 mm)	5·00	3·25

689 Andean Condor *(Vultur grypus)*

1996. America (1995). Endangered Species. Multicoloured.

2275	1000s. Type **689**	2·50	1·70
2276	1500s. Harpy eagle and chick *(Harpia harpyja)* (vert)	4·00	2·50

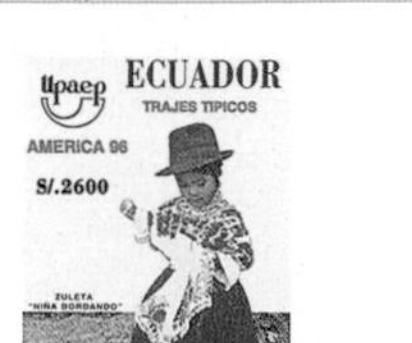
690 Child in Traditional Dress

1996. America. National Costume. Multicoloured.

2277	2600s. Type **690**	7·00	4·75
2278	2600s. Child wearing hat	7·00	4·75

691 Jose Mejia Lequerica and Institute Facade

1997. Centenary of Mejia National Institute.

2279	**691**	1000s. multicoloured	2·50	1·70

692 Emblem

1997. 75th Anniv of Escula Politecnica del Ejercito (military school).

2280	**692**	400s. multicoloured	1·20	80

693 College

1997. 50th Anniv of National Experimental College, Ambato.

2281	**693**	600s. multicoloured	1·50	1·00

694 Rocafuerte

1997. 150th Death Anniv of Vicente Rocafuerte (President 1835–39).

2282	**694**	400s. multicoloured	1·20	80

695 Emblem

1997. 49th International Congress of Americanists, Quito.

2283	**695**	2000s. multicoloured	5·00	3·25

696 *Actinote equatoria*

1997. Butterflies. Multicoloured.

2284	400s. Type **696**	1·20	80
2285	600s. Tiger pierid (*Dismorphia amphione*)	1·50	1·00
2286	800s. *Marpesia corinna*	2·00	1·30
2287	2000s. *Marpesia berania*	5·00	3·25
2288	2600s. *Morpho helenor*	7·00	4·75

697 Emblem

1997. 66th Anniv of Ecuador Flying Club.

2289	**697**	2600s. multicoloured	7·00	4·75

698 *Epidendrum secundum*

1997. Orchids of Mazan Forest. Multicoloured.

2290	400s. Type **698**	1·20	80
2291	600s. *Epidendrum sp.*	1·50	1·00
2292	800s. *Oncidium cultratrum*	2·00	1·30
2293	2000s. *Oncidium sp. mariposa*	5·00	3·25
2294	2600s. *Pleurothalis corrulensis*	7·00	4·75

699 Quartz

1997. International Mining Congress, Cuenca. Minerals. Multicoloured.

2295	400s. Type **699**	1·20	80
2296	600s. Chalcopyrite	1·50	1·00
2297	800s. Gold	2·00	1·30
2298	2000s. Petrified wood	5·00	3·25
2299	2600s. Iron pyrites	7·00	4·75

700 Santa Claus carrying Envelopes (Maria Daniela Delgado)

1997. Christmas. "Design a Stamp" Competition Winners. Multicoloured.

2300	400s. Type **700**	1·20	80
2301	2600s. Star on Christmas tree holding envelopes (Dora Pinargote Tejena)	7·00	4·75
2302	3000s. Child dreaming of Christmas tree of envelopes (Christina Pazmino Montano)	8·25	5·50

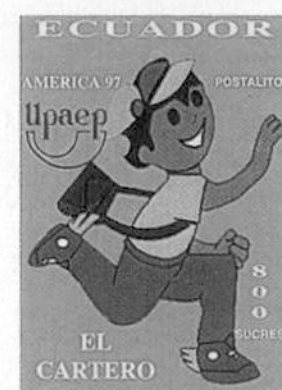

701 Postman with Wings on Heels

1997. America. The Postman. Multicoloured.

2303	800s. Type **701**	2·10	1·40
2304	2000s. Postman on bicycle	5·00	3·25

702 Matilde Hidalgo de Procel (first female politician)

1998. International Women's Day.

2305	**702**	2000s. multicoloured	4·75	3·25

703 Acosta Solis

1998. Misael Acosta Solis (botanist) Commemoration.

2306	**703**	2000s. multicoloured	8·25	5·50

704 Emblem

1998. 50th Anniv of Organization of American States.

2307	**704**	2600s. multicoloured	6·00	4·00

705 Emblem and Trophy

1998. World Cup Football Championship, France. Multicoloured.

2308	2000s. Type **705**	4·75	3·25
2309	2600s. Mascot and trophy (vert)	6·00	4·00
2310	3000s. Players and trophy	7·00	4·75

706 Red Roses and Gypsophila

1998. Flowers. Multicoloured.

2311	600s. Type **706**	1·40	95
2312	800s. *Musa sp.*	1·90	1·30
2313	2000s. Yellow roses	5·00	3·25
2314	2600s. Asters and astilbes	6·00	4·00

707 Cactus (*Jasminocereus thouarsii var. delicatus*)

1998. Galapagos Flora. Multicoloured.

2315	600s. Type **707**	1·40	95
2316	1000s. *Cordia lutea lamarck*	2·40	1·60
2317	2600s. *Montondica charantica*	6·00	4·00

708 San Agustin Church, Quito

1998. Tourism. Multicoloured.

2318	600s. Type **708**	1·40	95
2319	800s. Independence Monument, Guayaquil	1·90	1·30
2320	2000s. Mitad del Mundo Monument, Quito (horiz)	5·00	3·25
2321	2600s. Mojanda Lagoon (horiz)	6·00	4·00

709 Beatriz Cueva de Ayora Institute and Ortega Espinosa (founder)

1998. Birth Centenary of Emiliano Ortega Espinosa (teacher). Multicoloured.

2322	400s. Type **709**	1·20	80
2323	4700s. Ortega	13·00	8·75

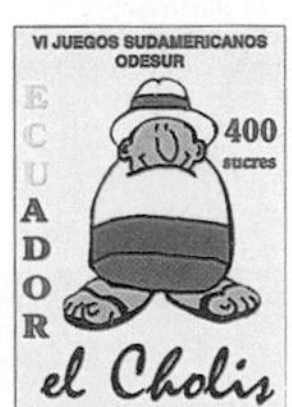

710 Mascot

1998. 6th South American Games, Cuenca. Mult.

2324	400s. Type **710**	1·20	80
2325	1000s. Games emblems and sports pictograms	2·40	1·60
2326	2600s. Mascot and sports pictograms (different)	6·00	4·00

711 Cueva Tamariz

1998. Birth Centenary of Carlos Cueva Tamariz (United Nations ambassador).

2327	**711**	2600s. multicoloured	6·00	4·00

712 Emblem

1998. 75th Anniv of Guayaquil Radio Club.

2328	**712**	600s. multicoloured	1·40	95

713 "Ecuadorian Woman"

1998. 85th Birth Anniv of Eduardo Kigman (artist). Multicoloured.

2329	600s. Type **713**	1·40	95
2330	800s. "World without Answer" (horiz)	1·90	1·30

714 Father Christmas reading Letters

1998. Christmas. Multicoloured.

2331	1000s. Type **714**	2·10	1·40
2332	2600s. Children holding letter (vert)	5·00	3·25
2333	3000s. Father Christmas and letters falling from sack (vert)	6·00	4·00

715 Manuelita Saenz

1999. Manuelita Saenz Commemoration.

2334	**715**	1000s. multicoloured	2·00	1·30

716 Caves

1999. Los Tayos Caves. Multicoloured.

2335	1000s. Type **716**	2·10	1·40
2336	2600s. Caves (horiz)	5·00	3·25

717 Man's Face

1999. 80th Birth Anniv of Oswaldo Guayasamin (artist).

2337	**717**	2000s. multicoloured	4·25	2·75

718 Women

1999. International Campaign to Prevent Violence Against Women.

2338	**718**	4000s. multicoloured	8·25	5·50

719 Building Facade

1999. Centenary of Eloy Alfaro Military College. Multicoloured.

2339	5200s. Type **719**	10·50	7·00
2340	9400s. Soldier and college building	18·00	12·00

720 *Bromelia sp.*

1999. Centenary of Del Puyo Foundation. Mult.

2341	4000s. Type **720**	7·75	5·00
2342	4000s. Scarlet macaws	7·75	5·00

721 Barahona

1999. Death Centenary of Dr. Rafael Barahona.

2343	**721**	5200s. multicoloured	10·50	7·00

722 De Luzarraga

1999. 140th Death Anniv of Gen. Manuel Antonio de Luzarraga.

2344	**722**	2000s. multicoloured	4·25	2·75

No. 2344 is inscribed for the bicentenary of the birth of Gen. Manuel de Luzarraga, who was born in 1776.

723 Wright

1999. Birth Bicentenary of Gen. Tomas Carlos Wright.

2345	**723**	4000s. multicoloured	8·25	5·50

724 Greater Flamingo (*Phoenicopterus ruber*)

1999. Charles Darwin Galapagos Islands Protection Foundation. Multicoloured.

2346	7000s. Type **724**	8·25	5·50
2347	7000s. Galapagos hawk (*Buteo galapagoensis*)	8·25	5·50
2348	7000s. Marine iguana (*Amblyrhynchus cristatus*)	8·25	5·50
2349	7000s. Galapagos land iguana (*Conolophus subcristaus*)	8·25	5·50
2350	7000s. *Opuntia galapagela* (plant)	8·25	5·50
2351	7000s. Vermilion flycatcher (*Pyrocephalus rubinus*)	8·25	5·50
2352	7000s. Blue-footed booby (*Sula nebouxii*)	8·25	5·50
2353	7000s. Blue-faced booby (*Sula dactylatra*)	8·25	5·50
2354	7000s. *Scalesia villosa* (plant)	8·25	5·50
2355	7000s. Galapagos giant tortoise (*G. elephantopus abingdoni*)	8·25	5·50
2356	15000s. *Brachycereus nesioticus* (coral) (horiz)	18·00	12·00
2357	15000s. Yellow warbler (*Dendroica petechia*) (horiz)	18·00	12·00
2358	15000s. Flightless cormorants (*Nannopterum harrisi*) (horiz)	18·00	12·00
2359	15000s. Bottle-nosed dolphin (*Tursiops truncatus*) (horiz)	18·00	12·00
2360	15000s. *Pentaceraster cumingi* (starfish) (horiz)	18·00	12·00
2361	15000s. Galapagos giant tortoise (*G. elephantopus porteri*) (horiz)	18·00	12·00
2362	15000s. Galapagos lava lizards (*Microlophus albemarlensis*) (horiz)	18·00	12·00
2363	15000s. Galapagos fur seal (*Arctocephalus galapagoensis*) (horiz)	18·00	12·00
2364	15000s. Galapagos penguins (*Spheniscus mendiculus*) (horiz)	18·00	12·00
2365	15000s. Cactus ground finch (*Geospiza scandens*) (horiz)	18·00	12·00

725 Emblem

1999. International Year of the Older Person. Multicoloured.

2366	1000s. Type **725**	1·80	1·20
2367	1000s. Child and older person holding hands	1·80	1·20

726 Young Boys

1999. 50th Anniv of S.O.S. Children's Villages. Multicoloured.

2368	2000s. Type **726**	2·50	1·70
2369	2000s. Young girl	2·50	1·70

727 Postman

1999. 125th Anniv of Universal Postal Union. Multicoloured.

2370	1000s. Type **727**	95	65
2371	4000s. Dove carrying letter	4·00	2·75
2372	8000s. Emblem (horiz)	8·00	5·25

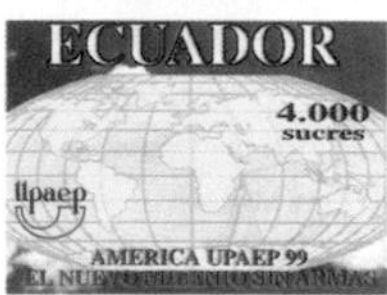

728 World Map

1999. America. Millennium without Arms. Mult.

2373	4000s. Type **728**	6·00	4·00
2374	4000s. Tree, Globe and bird	6·00	4·00

729 Cliff Face

1999. 5th Anniv of South Pacific Commission.

2375	**729**	7000s. multicoloured	8·75	6·00

730 Statue

1999. "Machala, City of Tourism and the Banana". Multicoloured.

2376	3000s. Type **730**	3·75	2·50
2377	3000s. Building facade	3·75	2·50
2378	3000s. View over city (horiz)	3·75	2·50

731 Jorge Bolanos

2000. 70th Anniv of Emelec Football Club (1999). Multicoloured.

2379	1000s. Type **731**	1·50	1·00
2380	1000s. Carlos Raffo	1·50	1·00
2381	2000s. Ivan Kavedes	3·00	2·00
2382	2000s. Team photograph (national championship winners, 1957 (horiz))	3·00	2·00

732 Society Headquarters

2000. 150th Anniv (1999) of Guayas Philanthropic Society. Multicoloured.

2383	1000s. Type **732**	45	30
2384	2000s. Juan Maria Martinez Coello (founder)	85	55
2385	4000s. Emblem	1·70	1·10

733 Statue of Liberty, New York, Equatorial Monument, Quito, Eiffel Tower, Paris and Coliseum, Rome

2000. Ecuadorians living Abroad.

2386	**733**	7000s. multicoloured	2·75	1·90

734 Buildings

2000. World Heritage Sites. Cuenca. Multicoloured.

2387	4000s. Type **734**	1·40	95
2388	4000s. Buildings and church tower (Puente Roto y Barranco del Rio Tomebamba)	1·40	95
2389	4000s. Monastery of the Conception Church	1·40	95
2390	4000s. City view	1·40	95
2391	4000s. San Jose Church	1·40	95

735 Lapenti

2000. Nicolas Lapenti (tennis player).

2392	**735**	8000s. multicoloured	3·00	2·10

736 Masked Flowerpiercer (*Diglossa cyanea*)

2000. Birds of Mazan. Multicoloured.

2393	8000s. Type **736**	2·75	1·90
2394	8000s. Chimborazo hillstar (*Oreotrochilus chimborazo*)	2·75	1·90
2395	8000s. Masked trogon (*Trogon personatus*)	2·75	1·90
2396	8000s. Sparkling violetear (*Colibri coruscans*)	2·75	1·90
2397	8000s. Rufus-naped brush finch (*Atlapetes rufinucha*)	2·75	1·90

737 Riobamba Cathedral

2000. Bicentenary of the Rebuilding of Riobamba. Multicoloured.

2398	8000s. Type **737**	2·75	1·90
2399	8000s. Pedro Vicente Maldonado (statue)	2·75	1·90
2400	8000s. El Chimborazo mountain (horiz)	2·75	1·90

738 General Eloy Alfaro (founder)

2000. Centenary of National Music Conservatory.

2401	**738**	10000s. multicoloured	4·25	2·75

739 *Guayas* (sail training ship) and Armed Forces Emblem

2000. Ships. Multicoloured.

2402	68c. Type **739**	1·70	1·10
MS2403	91×111 mm. $1 As No. 2402 but with country name and emblem in gold. Imperf	7·00	4·75

740 Ivan Ricaurte

2000. 1st Anniv of Ivan Vallejo Ricaurte's Ascent of Everest without Oxygen.

2404	**740**	8000s. multicoloured	4·25	2·75

741 Dolores Sucre Lavayen

2000. 50th Anniv of Dolores Sucre Lavayen College.

2405	**741**	32c. multicoloured	3·50	2·30

742 Commander Rafael Valverde and *Calderon* (battleship)

2000. 59th Anniv of Jambeli Naval Battle. Day of the Armed Forces.

2406	**742**	16c. multicoloured	1·70	1·10

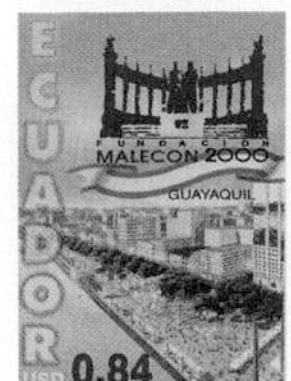

743 Malecon 2000 and Emblem

2000. Opening of Malecon 2000 (waterside development), Guayaquil.

2407	**743**	84c. multicoloured	8·50	5·75

744 Humpback Whale (*Megaptera novaenglike*)

2000. Yaqu pacha (organization for the conservation of South American marine animals). Multicoloured.

2408	84c. Type **744**	8·50	5·75
MS2409	91×111 mm. $1 Humpback whales. Imperf	11·50	9·50

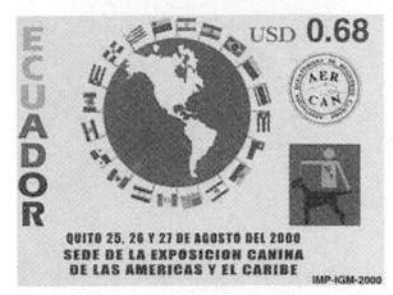

745 Flags encircling Map of Americas and Emblem

2000. Americas and Caribbean Dog Show.

2410	**745**	68c. multicoloured	6·50	4·25

746 Club Emblem

2000. 90th Anniv of Guayaquil Tennis Club.

2411	**746**	84c. multicoloured	7·75	5·25

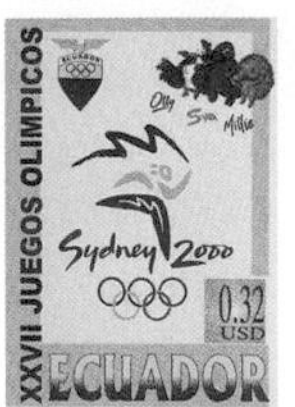

747 Games Emblem

2000. Olympic Games, Sydney. Multicoloured.

2412	32c. Type **747**	3·00	2·10
2413	68c. Jefferson Perez (race walker) (1996 gold medallist)	6·50	4·25
2414	84c. Boris Burov (weightlifter) (gold medallist) (horiz)	7·75	5·25

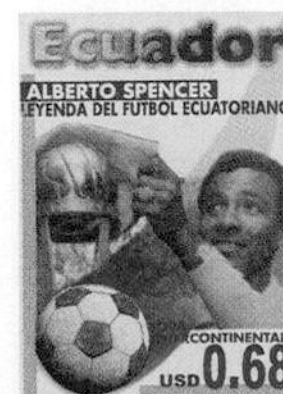

748 Alberto Spencer

2000. Alberto Spencer (footballer). Multicoloured.

2415	68c. Type **748**	6·50	4·25
MS2416	69×100 mm. $1 As No. 2415 but with design enlarged and reversed	10·00	8·50

749 Lighthouse

2000. 60th Anniv of Salinas Yacht Club. Multicoloured.

2417	32c. Type **749**	3·00	2·10
2418	32c. Yacht with "60" on sail	3·00	2·10
2419	68c. Photo montage of yacht, water-skier and coast	6·50	4·25
MS2420	69×100 mm. $1 As No. 2418 but with design enlarged	10·00	8·50

750 Felipe Herrera (1st President) and Salsipuedes Bridge

2000. 40th Anniv of Inter-American Development Bank. Multicoloured.

2421	68c. Type **750**	6·50	4·25
2422	68c. Antonio Ortiz Mena Duale-Peripa dam	6·50	4·25
2423	84c. Enrique Inglesias and Ucubamba water treatment works	7·75	5·25
2424	84c. Bank emblem and Quito History Musuem	7·75	5·25
MS2425	151×91 mm. 25c.×4, As Nos. 2422/4 but with designs enlarged	10·00	8·50

751 Dancer wearing Black Makeup and carrying Doll

2000. La Mama Negra Festival, Latacunga. Multicoloured.

2426	32c. Type **751**	3·00	2·00
2427	32c. Bearded man (Rey Moro (moorish king))	3·00	2·00
MS2428	100×68 mm. $1 Dancer wearing black makeup and doll (different). Imperf	9·25	7·50

752 Emblem

2000. 75th Anniv of Works and Resources Ministry.

2429	**752**	68c. multicoloured	6·00	4·00

753 Emblem

2000. National Union of Journalists.

2430	**753**	16c. multicoloured	1·60	1·00

754 General Eloy Alfaro (president) and Crowd

2000. Centenary of Civil Register. Multicoloured.

2431	68c. Type **754**	6·50	4·25
2432	68c. Fingerprint and family	6·50	4·25

755 Rose

2000. Flower Export Campaign.

2433	**755**	68c. multicoloured	6·50	4·25

756 "50" enclosing Ambato City

2000. 50th International Flower and Fruit Festival (2001). Multicoloured.

2434	32c. Type **756**	3·00	2·10
2435	32c. Volcano	3·00	2·10
2436	84c. Flower	8·00	5·25
2437	84c. Fruit	8·00	5·25
2438	84c. "50", emblem and stem (horiz)	8·00	5·25
MS2439	68×100 mm. $1 Enclosing view of Ambato city. Imperf	9·25	7·50

757 Angel, Stable and Holy Family

2000. Christmas. Children's Paintings. Multicoloured.

2440	68c. Type **757** (Ghiannina Rhor Isaias)	6·50	4·25
2441	68c. Nativity enclosed in tree and farm (Josue Remache Romero)	6·50	4·25
2442	84c. Nativity at night (Maria Cedeno Bazurito)	8·00	5·25
2443	84c. Cattle and Holy Family (Juan Alban Salazar)	8·00	5·25
MS2444	100×69 mm. $1 Holy Family receiving gifts from children (Walther Carvache). Imperf	9·25	7·50

758 Arms

2000. 78th Anniv of Guayas Sports Federation.

2445	**758**	16c. multicoloured	1·70	1·10

759 Museum Building

2000. Oswaldo Guayasamin (artist) "Chapel of Mankind" Museum.

2446	**759**	16c. multicoloured	1·70	1·10

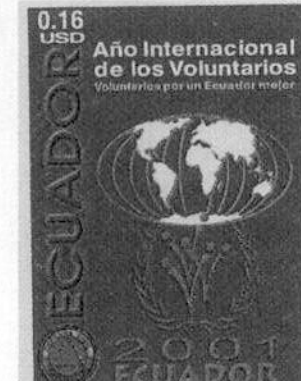

760 Emblem

2000. International Year of Volunteers.

2447	**760**	16c. multicoloured	1·70	1·10

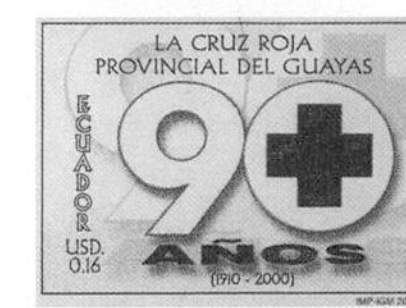

761 "90"

2000. 90th Anniv of Guayas Province Red Cross Society.

2448	**761**	16c. multicoloured	1·70	1·10

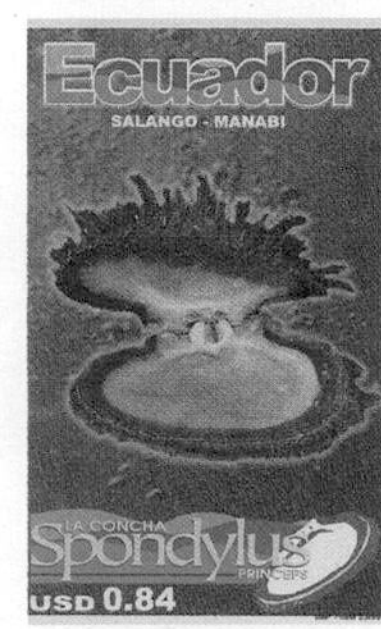

762 Pacific Thorny Oyster (*Spondylus princes*)

2000

2449	**762**	84c. multicoloured	7·75	5·25
MS2450		69×100 mm. **762** $1 multicoloured. Imperf	9·25	7·50

763 Restaurant

2000. Restoration of Bolivar Theatre. Multicoloured.

2451	16c. Type **763**	1·70	1·10
2452	32c. Auditorium (horiz)	3·25	2·20

764 Map and Emblem

2000. 80th Anniv of Spanish Chamber of Trade.

2453	**764**	16c. multicoloured	1·70	1·10

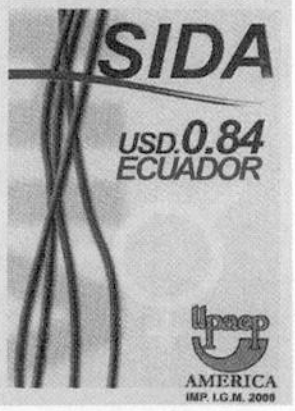

765 Veins, Arteries and Gender Symbols

2000. America. AIDS Awareness Campaign. Multicoloured.

2454	84c. Type **765**	8·50	5·75
2455	84c. Globe described in blood	8·50	5·75

766 Pacific Coast

2001. Tourism. Multicoloured.

2456	16c. Type **766**	1·70	1·10
2457	16c. Andes	1·70	1·10
2458	32c. Emblem	3·50	2·30
2459	68c. Amazon basin	7·00	4·75
2460	84c. Galapagos Islands	8·75	5·75

767 Emblem

2001. 50th Anniv of Merchant Shipping.

2461	**767**	16c. multicoloured	1·60	1·00

768 Rocks, Espanola Island

2001. UNESCO World Heritage Sites. Galapagos Islands. Multicoloured.

2462	16c. Type **768**	1·60	1·00
2463	16c. San Cristobal Island	1·60	1·00
2464	16c. Bartolome Island	1·60	1·00
2465	16c. Inlet, Espanola Island	1·60	1·00
2466	16c. Bartolome and Santiago Island	1·60	1·00
MS2467	100×70 mm $1 Sea spray, Espanola Island. Imperf	10·50	9·00

769 Emblem

2001. 50th Anniv (2000) of Guayas Football Association.

2468	**769**	68c. multicoloured	6·50	4·25

770 Emblem (National Institute for Statistics and Census)

2001. National Census. Multicoloured.

2469	68c. Type **770**	6·50	4·25
2470	68c. Stylized crowd	6·50	4·25

771 Arms and Building Facade

2001. Centenary of Manuela Canizares College.

2471	**771**	84c. multicoloured	8·50	5·75

772 Woman and Child

2001. International Women's Day. Multicoloured.

2472	84c. Type **772**	8·50	5·75
2473	84c. Woman with raised arms	8·50	5·75

773 Raul Huerta

2001. 10th Death Anniv of Raul Clemente Huerta (politician).

2474	**773**	68c. multicoloured	7·00	4·75

774 Antonio Quevedo

2001. Birth Centenary (2000) of Antonio J. Quevedo (politician).

2475	**774**	84c. multicoloured	8·50	5·75

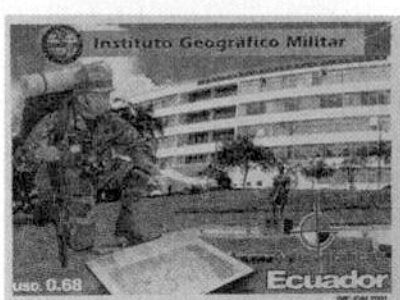

775 Emblem

2001. 15th Anniv of ICAIM (women's education institute).

2476	**775**	84c. multicoloured	8·50	5·75

776 Soldier and Building

2001. 55th Anniv of Military Geographic Institute. Multicoloured.

2477	68c. Type **776**	7·00	4·75
2478	68c. Computers and machinery	7·00	4·75

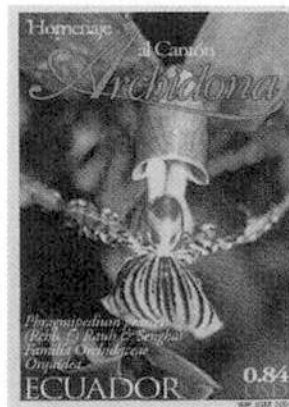

777 University Building

2001. 32nd Anniv of Ambato Technical University. Multicoloured.

2479	32c. Type **777**	3·50	2·40
2480	32c. Tree, couple and building	3·50	2·40

778 *Phragmipedium pearcei*

2001. 20th Anniv of Archidona Canton, Napo Province. Multicoloured.

2481	84c. Type **778**	8·50	5·75
2482	84c. Squirrel monkey (*Saimiri sciureus*)	8·50	5·75
2483	84c. *Brownea macrophylla*	8·50	5·75
2484	84c. Archidona church	8·50	5·75
2485	84c. Native woman and children	8·50	5·75

779 Emblem

2001. 50th Anniv of ANETA (automobile club). Multicoloured.

2486	**780**	84c. multicoloured	8·50	5·75

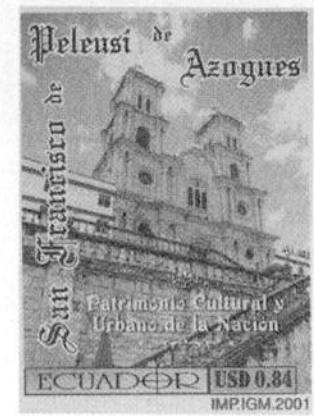

780 Flags forming Map

2001. Signing of Peace Treaty between Ecuador and Peru. Multicoloured.

2487	68c. Type **780**	7·00	4·75
2488	68c. Pioneer brigade emblem	7·00	4·75
2489	68c. Military observers emblem	7·00	4·75
2490	68c. Amazon river	7·00	4·75
2491	68c. Marking the border	7·00	4·75

781 Church of San Francisco de Azogues

2001. Cultural Heritage. San Francisco de Peleusi de Azogues.

2492	**781**	84c. multicoloured	8·50	5·75

782 City Gates

2001. Loja.

2493	**782**	32c. multicoloured	3·50	2·30

783 Alexander von Humboldt

2001. Bicentenary of Alexander von Humboldt's visit to Ecuador.

2494	**783**	84c. multicoloured	7·75	5·25

784 Salvador Bustamante Celi

2001. 125th Birth Anniv of Salvador Bustamante Celi (musician and composer).

2495	**784**	68c. multicoloured	7·00	4·75

785 Orchid Flower

2001. Banos State, Centre for Eco-Tourism. Multicoloured.

2496	86c. Type **785**	7·75	5·25
2497	86c. Nuestra Senora de Banos de Agua Santa basilica	7·75	5·25
2498	86c. Tungurahua volcano	7·75	5·25
2499	86c. Pailon de Diablo waterfalls	7·75	5·25
2500	86c. "Virgin del Rosario de Agua Santa" (statue)	7·75	5·25
MS2501	68×100 mm $1 Pailon de Diablo waterfalls (different). Imperf	10·00	8·50

786 Hand holding Chick and Condor

2001. Endangered Species. Andean Condor. Multicoloured.

2502	86c. Type **786**	7·75	5·25
2503	86c. Condor and FRAPZOO (animal protection organization) emblem	7·75	5·25
MS2504	68×100 mm. $1 Condor in flight. Imperf	10·00	8·50

787 Coastline

2001. Tourism. Esmeralda. Multicoloured.

2505	86c. Type **787**	7·75	5·25
2506	86c. Marimba band and dancers	7·75	5·25

788 Commission Emblem

2001. Atomic Energy Commission.

2507	**788**	70c. multicoloured	7·00	4·75

789 Emblem

2001. 30th Anniv of Guayas Educational Journalists Association.

2508	**789**	16c. multicoloured	1·70	1·10

790 Marcel Laniado de Wind

2001. 3rd Death Anniv of Marcel Laniado de Wind (banker).

2509	**790**	70c. multicoloured	7·00	4·75

791 Emblem

2001. 15th Anniv of Agricultural Development Foundation.

2510	**791**	16c. multicoloured	1·70	1·10

792 Claudia Lars

2001. Latin American Writers. Multicoloured.

2511	86c. Type **792** (poet)	8·50	5·75
2512	86c. Federico Proano (political journalist)	8·50	5·75

793 Union Building

2001. 80th Anniv of Lebanese Union, Guayaquil. Multicoloured.

2513	16c. Type **793**	1·80	1·20
2514	16c. Union emblem	1·80	1·20

794 Virgin del Carmen (statue)

2001. Cultural Heritage. Zaruma. Multicoloured.

2515	68c. Type **794**	6·50	4·25
2516	68c. Orchid flower	6·50	4·25

795 Emblem

2001. Manta Harbour Authority. Multicoloured.

2517	68c. Type **795**	6·50	4·25
2518	68c. Manta port	6·50	4·25

796 Davis Cup Tennis Trophy

2001. Tennis. Multicoloured.

2519	68c. Type **796**	6·50	4·25
2520	68c. Ecuador Davis Cup team, Wimbledon, 2000	6·50	4·25
2521	68c. Francisco Guzman and Miguel Olivera, 1967	6·50	4·25
2522	68c. Francisco "Pancho" Segura Cano (80th birth anniv)	6·50	4·25
2523	68c. Andreas Gomez Santos	6·50	4·25

797 Students

2001. Wilson Popenoe (agricultural and horticultural) Foundation.

2524	**797**	16c. multicoloured	1·70	1·10

798 Emblem

2001. Otonga Foundation (ecology charity). Multicoloured.

2525	16c. Type **798**	1·70	1·10
2526	16c. Weasel (Mustela frenata)	1·70	1·10

799 Couple Planting

2001. 5th Anniv of World Food Summit (No. 2527). World Food Day (2528/9). Multicoloured.

2527	84c. Type **799**	8·50	5·75
2528	84c. Ears of corn	8·50	5·75
2529	84c. Baskets of crops	8·50	5·75

800 Jose Olmedo enclosed in Map and Clouds

2001. Jose Joaquin de Olmedo (writer and politician) Commemoration.

2530	**800**	84c. multicoloured	8·50	5·75

801 Cardinal Echeverria

2001. 1st Death Anniv of Cardinal Bernardino Echeverria.

2531	**801**	84c. multicoloured	8·50	5·75

802 Cupola, San Blas Church

2001. Cultural Heritage. Multicoloured.

2532	25c. Type **802**	2·00	1·30
2533	25c. La Compania de Jesus church, Quito	2·00	1·30

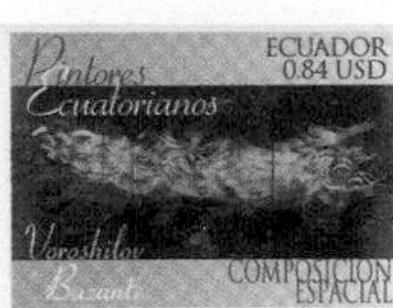

803 "Composicion Espacial"

2001. Voroshilov Bazante (artist) Commemoration. Multicoloured.

2534	64c. Type **803**	8·50	5·75
2535	64c. "Absracto"	8·50	5·75
2536	64c. "Paisaje Urbano"	8·50	5·75
2537	64c. "Abstracto" (different)	8·50	5·75
2538	64c. "Abstracto" (orange)	8·50	5·75

804 Andean Paramo (high altitude grasslands)

2001. La Angel Nature Reserve. Multicoloured.

2539	16c. Type **804**	1·70	1·10
2540	16c. "Frailejones" (Espeletia pycnophylla angelensis)	1·70	1·10

805 Children and Arms

2001. Social Security and Welfare Directorate, Quito.

2541	**805**	68c. multicoloured	6·50	4·25

806 Aerial View of Race Track

2001. "CATI" (motoring club) and Yahuarcocha International Race Circuit, Imbabura. Multicoloured.

2542	68c. Type **806**	6·50	4·25
2543	68c. Aerial view (different)	6·50	4·25

807 International Rotary Emblem

2001. Anniv of Rotary Club (charitable organization) in Ecuador.

2544	**807**	84c. multicoloured	8·50	5·75

808 Pedro Maldonado

2001. Pedro Vincente Maldonado (mathematician and cartographer) Commemoration.

2545	**808**	84c. multicoloured	8·50	5·75

809 Microphone

2001. 70th Anniv of HCJB Radio Broadcasting Station. Multicoloured.

2546	68c. Type **809**	6·50	4·25
2547	68c. Station emblem	6·50	4·25

810 Camilo Ponce Enriquez

2001. Camilo Ponce Enriquez (politician) Commemoration.

2548	**810**	84c. multicoloured	8·50	5·75

811 Emblem

2002. Americas Judicial Summit Meeting (2001), Quito.

2549	**811**	68c. multicoloured	6·50	4·25

812 Nicolas Leoz (president of CSF)

2002. South American Football Association (CSF). Multicoloured.

2550	25c. Type **812**	2·40	1·60
2551	40c. Association emblem	3·75	2·50

813 Club Emblem

2002. Emelec Football Club. Fluorescent security markings.

2552	**813**	70c. blue	6·75	4·50

814 Porpoise, Leaves and Face

2002. World Conservation Union (UICN). Multicoloured.

2553	70c. Type **814**	6·50	4·25
2554	85c. Jaguar and conservation warden (horiz)	7·75	5·25

MS2555 100×70 mm. $1 Booby, giant otter, young women, spectacled bear and children. Imperf 10·00 8·50

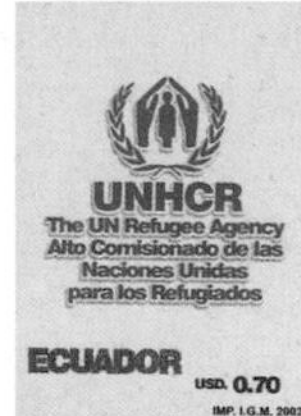

815 Commission Emblem

2002. 50th Anniv of United Nations High Commissioner for Refugees.

2556	**815**	70c. blue and black	6·50	4·25
2557	-	85c. multicoloured	7·75	5·25

MS2558 100×70 mm. $1 multicoloured. Imperf 10·00 8·50

DESIGNS: 85c. Child; $1 Refugees. No. **MS**2558 has the UNHCR emblem foil embossed in top right corner.

816 *Atelopus bomolochos*

2002. Frogs. Multicoloured.

2559	$1.05 Type **816**	7·75	5·25
2560	$1.05 *Atelopus longirostris*	7·75	5·25
2561	$1.05 *Atelopus pachydermus*	7·75	5·25
2562	$1.05 *Atelopus arthuri*	7·75	5·25
2563	$1.05 *Atelopus*	7·75	5·25

MS2564 100×70 mm. $1 *Atelopus ignescens*. Imperf 10·00 8·50

817 Clock Tower

2002. Imbabura Province. Multicoloured.

2565	40c. Type **817**	4·00	2·75
2566	40c. Atahualpa (last Inca ruler) (statue)	4·00	2·75

818 Pacific Beach at Twilight

2002. Tourism. Crucita State. Multicoloured.

2567	40c. Type **818**	4·00	2·75
2568	40c. Paragliding	4·00	2·75

819 "St. Francis" Church" (nave)

2002. Paintings by Wilfrido Martinez. Paintings. Multicoloured.

2569	90c. Type **819**	5·75	3·75
2570	90c. "Guapulo Church"	5·75	3·75
2571	90c. "St. Francis' Church" (apse)	5·75	3·75
2572	90c. "La Compana Church"	5·75	3·75
2573	90c. "El Rosario Church"	5·75	3·75

820 Team Members

2002. Cuenca Football Club. Multicoloured.

2574	25c. Type **820**	2·00	1·30
2575	25c. Club emblem	2·00	1·30

821 Altar Mountain

2002. Tourism. Chimborazo Province. Mult.

2576	90c. Type **821**	5·75	3·75
2577	90c. Rounded peaks, Chimborazo	5·75	3·75
2578	90c. Three peaks, Carihuayrazo	5·75	3·75
2579	90c. Lake, forest and Altar mountain	5·75	3·75
2580	90c. Walker, scree and Cubillin mountain	5·75	3·75

822 Officer and Sniffer Dog

2002. National Narcotics Police Force. Mult.

2581	40c. Type **822**	2·75	1·90
2582	40c. Emblem	2·75	1·90

823 Club Emblem

2002. 233rd Anniv of Club de la Union, Guayaquil.

2583	**823** 90c. blue and vermilion	5·75	3·75

824 Team Emblem

2002. World Cup Football Championships, Japan and South Korea. Multicoloured.

2584	90c. Type **824**	5·75	3·75
2585	$1.05 National team	6·50	4·25
MS2586	100×70 mm. $2 As. No. 2585. Imperf	11·50	9·50

825 Student and Microscope

2002. Institute for Financial Support for Education (IECE). Multicoloured.

2587	25c. Type **825**	2·00	1·30
2588	25c. Emblem	2·00	1·30

826 Blue Abstract

2002. Paintings by Milton Estrella Gavida. Paintings. Multicoloured.

2589	90c. Type **826**	5·75	3·75
2590	90c. Red abstract	5·75	3·75
2591	90c. Green abstract	5·75	3·75
2592	90c. Orange, bottle and vase of flowers	5·75	3·75
2593	90c. Fruit and vase	5·75	3·75

827 Servio Aguirre Villamagua

2002. Aguirre Protective Forest. Multicoloured.

2594	40c. Type **827**	2·50	1·70
2595	40c. Leaf	2·50	1·70

828 Organization Emblem

2002. 50th Anniv of FAO (UN food and agriculture organization).

2596	**828** $1.05 multicoloured	6·50	4·25

829 *Grapsus grapsus* (crab)

2002. Ibero-American Tourism and the Environment Conference. Galapagos Islands Fauna. Multicoloured.

2597	25c. Type **829**	2·10	1·40
2598	25c. Land iguana (*Conolophus subcristatus*)	2·10	1·40
2599	40c. Red-footed booby (*Sula sula*) (vert)	2·50	1·70
2600	40c. Greater flamingo (*Phoenicopterus rubber*) (vert)	2·50	1·70
2601	90c. Californian sea lion and pup (*Zalophus californianus*) (vert)	5·75	3·75
2602	90c. Californian sea lion (vert)	5·75	3·75
2603	90c. Marine iguana (*Amblyrhynchus cristatus*)	5·75	3·75
2604	$1.05 Blue-faced booby (*Sula dactylatra*) (vert)	6·50	4·25
2605	$1.05 Emblem (vert)	6·50	4·25
2606	$1.05 Blue-footed booby (*Sula nebouxxi*)(vert)	6·50	4·25
MS2607	100×70 mm. $2 Frigate bird, tourist and boat. Imperf	12·50	9·50

830 Carved Birds

2002. Directorate General for the Promotion of Exports and Bi-lateral Relations.

2608	**830** 90c. multicoloured	5·75	3·75

831 Emblem and Building Facade

2002. 80th Anniv of Military Polytechnic College (ESPE).

2609	**831** 25c. multicoloured	2·00	1·30

832 Engineering Centre, Quito

2002. Centenary of Military Engineers. Mult.

2610	40c. Type **832**	2·50	1·70
2611	40c. Engineers (vert)	2·50	1·70
MS2612	100×70 mm. $2 Engineers, building and military emblems. Imperf	11·50	9·00

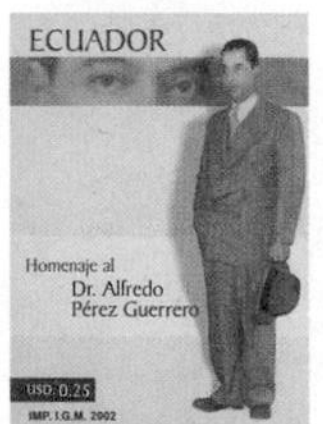
833 Alfredo Perez Guerrero

2002. Alfredo Perez Guerrero (language researcher) Commemoration.

2613	**833** 25c. multicoloured	2·00	1·30

834 Duvan Canga and Jose Cedeno

2002. Duvan Canga and Jose Cedeno-1982 World Tae Kwon-do Championship Silver Medallists.

2614	**834** 40c. multicoloured	2·50	1·70

835 Aboriginal Men

2002. Orellana Province. Multicoloured.

2615	25c. Type **835**	2·00	1·30
2616	25c. Climbing tree	2·00	1·30

836 Children and CARE Emblem

2002. 40th Anniv of CARE (humanitarian organization). Multicoloured.

2617	90c. Type **836**	5·75	3·75
2618	90c. Smiling child	5·75	3·75

837 Emblem

2002. Centenary of Macara Canton.

2619	**837** 40c. multicoloured	2·50	1·70

838 Flag and People

2002. 50th Anniv of International Organization for Migration (IOM).

2620	**838** $1.05 multicoloured	6·50	4·25

839 Orchestra

2002. 50th Anniv of Quito Philharmonic Orchestra.

2621	**839** 25c. multicoloured	2·00	1·30

840 Snow-capped Mountains

2002. 2nd International Mountain Peoples' Meeting. Multicoloured.

2622	90c. Type **840**	5·75	3·75
2623	90c. Indigenous mountain people	5·75	3·75
2624	90c. Village in valley	5·75	3·75
2625	90c. Mountains surrounding town	5·75	3·75
2626	90c. Conference emblem	5·75	3·75

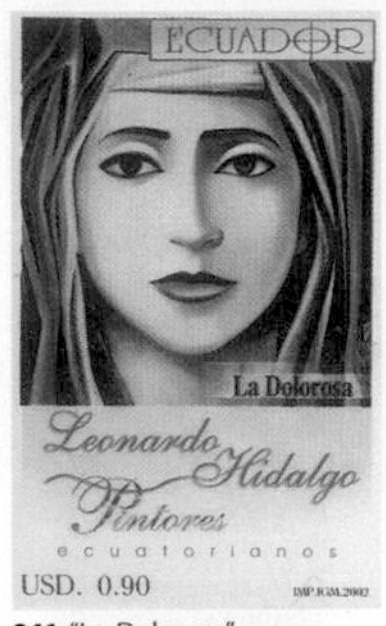

841 "La Dolorosa"

2002. Paintings by Leonardo Hidalgo. Paintings. Multicoloured.
2627 90c. Type **841** 5·75 3·75
2628 90c. "El Hombre Cargano su Fruto" 5·75 3·75
2629 90c. "Frida Kahlo" (inscr "Kalo") 5·75 3·75
2630 90c. "El Hombre Fuerto del Mar" 5·75 3·75
2631 90c. "Jesus" 5·75 3·75

842 Dancer wearing Traditional Costume

2002. Pujili Dances.
2632 **842** $1.05 multicoloured 6·50 4·25

843 Class Room

2002. America. Literacy Campaign. Multicoloured.
2633 25c. Type **843** 2·00 1·30
2634 25c. Toddler and open books 2·00 1·30

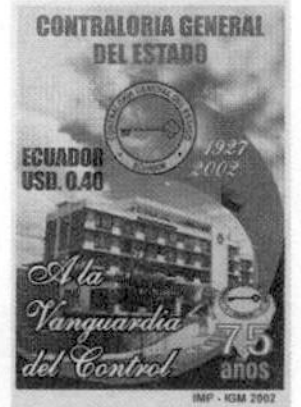

844 Building and Emblem

2002. 75th Anniv of National General Inspectorate.
2635 **844** 40c. multicoloured 2·50 1·70

845 Anniversary Emblem and Map

2002. Centenary of Pan American Health Organization.
2636 **845** $1.05 multicoloured 6·50 4·25

846 Paintings of Pots displayed on Building

2002. Cultural Heritage. Multicoloured.
2637 25c. Type **846** 2·00 1·30
2638 25c. Paintings of flowers on buildings 2·00 1·30

847 University Building

2002. 40th Anniv of Catholic University, Guayaquil.
2639 **847** 40c. multicoloured 2·50 1·70

848 Stars and Emblem

2003. 2nd (2002) South American Presidential Meeting, Guayaquil. Multicoloured.
2640 $1.05 Type **848** 2·00 1·30
2641 $1.05 President and flags 2·00 1·30

849 Pope John Paul II giving Blessing

2003. Papal Benediction of Ecuadorian Emigrants. Multicoloured.
2642 $1.05 Type **849** 6·50 4·25
MS2643 68×100 mm. $2. As No. 2642. Imperf 11·50 9·50

850 Family (Huaita Sisa)

2003. 25th Anniv of World Vision (humanitarian organization).
2644 **850** 40c. multicoloured 2·50 1·70

851 Women in Profile

2003. International Women's Day.
2645 **851** $1.05 multicoloured 6·50 4·25

852 Agustin Cueva Vallejo

2003. 130th Death Anniv of Agustin Cueva Vallejo (politician and journalist).
2646 **852** 40c. multicoloured 2·50 1·70

853 Blasco Moscoso Cuesta (commentator)

2003. 50th Anniv of APDP (association of sports journalists), Pichincha Province.
2647 **853** 25c. multicoloured 2·00 1·30

854 Dome and Cupola (Universidad del Azuay)

2003. Crafts. Multicoloured. Multicoloured.
2648 25c. Type **854** 2·00 1·30
2649 25c. Watering can (horticulture) 2·00 1·30
2650 25c. Pendant (jewellery) 2·00 1·30
2651 25c. Fireworks 2·00 1·30
2652 25c. Saddle (leatherwork) 2·00 1·30
2653 $1.05 Buckle (silverwork) 6·50 4·25
2654 $1.05 Weathervane (metalwork) 6·50 4·25
2655 $1.05 Basket 6·50 4·25
2656 $1.05 Shawl (needlework) 6·50 4·25
2657 $1.05 Pot (ceramics) 6·50 4·25
MS2658 100×68 mm. $2 Crafts. Imperf 11·50 9·50

Nos. 2648/52 and 2653/7, respectively, were issued in horizontal se-tenant strips of five stamps within the sheet.

855 Hands (painting, Eduardo Kingman)

2003. Centenary of Military Geographical Institute. Multicoloured.
2659 40c. Type **855** 2·50 1·70
2660 40c. Emblem (vert) 2·50 1·70
MS2661 100×69 mm. $2 As No. 2659. Imperf 11·50 9·50

856 *Curculionidae*

2003. Flora and Fauna. Multicoloured.
2662 $1.05 Type **856** 6·50 4·25
2663 $1.05 *Lycidae* 6·50 4·25
2664 $1.05 *Acridoidea* 6·50 4·25
2665 $1.05 *Arachnida* (inscr "Arachnidae") 6·50 4·25
2666 $1.05 *Liliaceae* 6·50 4·25

857 ECOCIENCIA (ecological organization) Emblem

2003. Galapagos Marine Reserve. Multicoloured.
2667 40c. Type **857** 2·50 1·70
2668 $1.05 Scalloped hammerhead shark (*Sphyrna lewini*) (horiz) 6·50 4·25
2669 $1.05 *Chelonia mydas agassisi* (horiz) 6·50 4·25
2670 $1.05 Crosshatched triggerfish (*Xanthichthys mento*) (horiz) 6·50 4·25
2671 $1.05 Moorish idol (*Zanclus cornutus*) (horiz) 6·50 4·25
MS2672 100×68 mm. $2 *Tubastrea coccinea*. Imperf 11·50 9·50

858 Spider Monkey

2003. Tourism. Multicoloured.
2673 25c. Type **858** 2·00 1·30
2674 25c. Frigate bird 2·00 1·30
2675 25c. Embroidered cover 2·00 1·30
2676 25c. Cotopaxi volcano 2·00 1·30
2677 25c. Basketwork seller 2·00 1·30

859 Seated Figure

2003. Sierra Norte Pre-Colombian Artefacts. Multicoloured.
2678 25c. Type **859** 2·00 1·30
2679 25c. Three-legged pot 2·00 1·30
2680 25c. Ball-shaped pot with figured handled 2·00 1·30
2681 25c. Tall decorated pot 2·00 1·30

860 Golden Mask (bank emblem)

2003. 75th Anniv of Central Bank. Multicoloured.
2682 25c. Type **860** 2·00 1·30
2683 25c. Window (Guayquil history park) 2·00 1·30
2684 $1.05 Inca figure (Pumapungo (archaeological site) museum, Cuenca) (horiz) 6·50 4·25

861 Envelope with British Consulate Stamp (1879)

2003. 33rd Anniv of Guayaquil Philatelic Club. Multicoloured.
2685 40c. Type **861** 2·50 1·70
2686 40c. Envelope with pre stamp postal mark 2·50 1·70
2687 40c. Envelope with first SCADTA (internal airmail company) postmark (1928) 2·50 1·70
2688 40c. Envelope with French consulate stamp 2·50 1·70
2689 $1.05 Philatelic magazine covers (vert) 6·50 4·25
MS2690 100×69 mm. $2 Ecuador stamps and Guayquil philatelic club emblem. Imperf 11·50 9·50

Nos. 2685/6 and 2687/8, respectively, were issued in se-tenant pairs within the sheets.

862 Santa Ana Lighthouse

2003. Preservation of Guayaquil Old Town. Multicoloured.
2691 90c. Type **862** 5·75 3·75
2692 90c. Colon plaza 5·75 3·75
2693 90c. Malecon gardens 5·75 3·75
2694 90c. Crystal palace 5·75 3·75
2695 90c. San Francisco plaza 5·75 3·75

863 Black-chested Buzzard Eagle (*Geranoaetus melanoleucus*)

2003. International Bird Festival. Multicoloured.

2696	$1.05 Type **863**	6·50	4·25
2697	$1.05 Harpy eagle (Harpia harpyja) (vert)	6·50	4·25

864 Porcupine

2003. 50th Anniv of Zamora Chinchipe Province. Multicoloured.

2698	25c. Type **864**	2·00	1·30
2699	25c. Tayra (*Eira barbata*)	2·00	1·30
2700	25c. Boa constrictor	2·00	1·30
2701	25c. Tapir (*Tapirus terrestris*)	2·00	1·30
2702	25c. Grey-winged trumpeter (*Psophia crepitans*)	2·00	1·30

865 Toucan Barbet (*Semnornis ramphastinus*)

2003. America. Fauna and Flora. Multicoloured.

2703	$1.05 Type **865**	6·50	4·25
2704	$1.05 *Bomarea glaucescens* (flower)	6·50	4·25

866 California Sea Lion (*Zalophus californianus*)

2003. 25th Anniv of Galapagos Islands' UNESCO World Heritage Site Status. Multicoloured.

2705	40c. Type **866**	2·50	1·70
2706	40c. Great frigate bird (*Fregata minor palmerstoni*)	2·50	1·70
2707	40c. Blue footed booby (*Sula nebouxii*) (inscr "nebouxxi excisa")	2·50	1·70
2708	40c. Bartolome island	2·50	1·70
2709	40c. Anniversary emblem	2·50	1·70

867 El Sagrario Church

2003. World Heritage Sites, Quito. Churches. Multicoloured.

2710	40c. Type **867**	2·50	1·70
2711	90c. La Compania de Jesus	5·75	3·75
2712	90c. Santa Barbara	5·75	3·75
2713	$1.05 Convent of St. Francis (vert)	6·50	4·25

868 Tree, Child and Postman (Stephanie Patcheco)

2003. Christmas. Children's Drawings. Multicoloured.

2714	25c. Type **868**	2·00	1·30
2715	25c. Lorry, road and village (Sebastian Tejada)	2·00	1·30
2716	40c. Angel, envelope and people (Maria Claudia Iturralde) (vert)	2·50	1·70
2717	90c. Boy and bear posting letters to Santa (Luis Antonio Ortega)	5·75	3·75
2718	$1.05 Open window, presents and tree (Angel Andres Castro) (vert)	6·50	4·25

869 Open Book (Act of Independence for Guayaquil)

2003. Quayaquil Museum Artefacts. Multicoloured.

2719	40c. Type **869**	2·50	1·70
2720	40c. Punaes ceremonial stone	2·50	1·70
2721	40c. "Proclama Mariano Donoso" (medal struck for the coronation of King Carlos III of Spain)	2·50	1·70
2722	40c. Shrunken heads	2·50	1·70
2723	40c. Huancavilca totem pole	2·50	1·70

870 Aerospatiale SA330 Puma Helicopter

2004. 50th Anniv of Military Aviation. Multicoloured.

2724	40c. Type **870**	2·50	1·70
2725	40c. Soldiers and Aerospatiale SA330 Puma helicopter	2·50	1·70
2726	40c. Emblem (vert)	2·50	1·70
2727	40c. Walker and aircraft (vert)	2·50	1·70

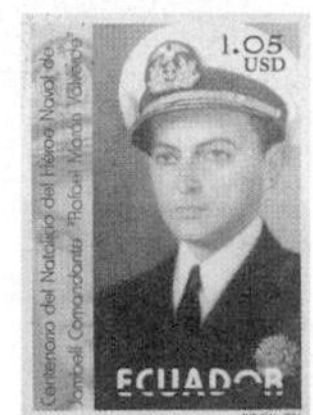

871 Raphael Valverde

2004. Birth Centenary of Raphael Moran Valverde (military hero).

2728	**871**	$1.05 multicoloured	6·50	4·25

872 Documents and Mountains

2004. Military Geographical Institute and National Development.

2729	**872**	$1.05 multicoloured	6·50	4·25

873 Early Stamps

2004. Stamp Day. Multicoloured.

2730	75c. Type **873**	4·00	2·75
2731	75c. Post marks	4·00	2·75
MS2732	100×68 mm. $2 Stamps and magnifying glass. Imperf	11·50	9·50

874 Emblem

2004. National Volleyball Federation.

2733	**874**	75c. multicoloured	4·00	2·75

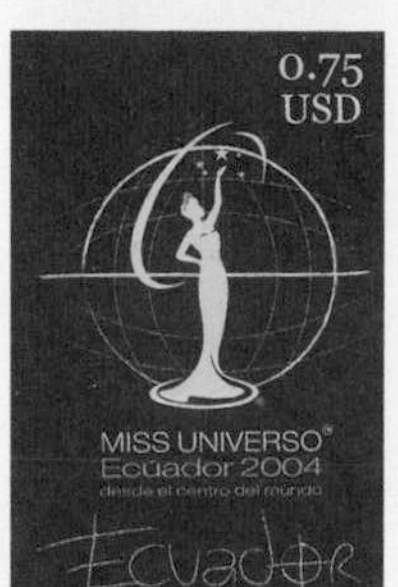

875 Emblem

2004. Miss Universe Pageant, Quito.

2734	**875**	75c. ultramarine	4·00	2·75

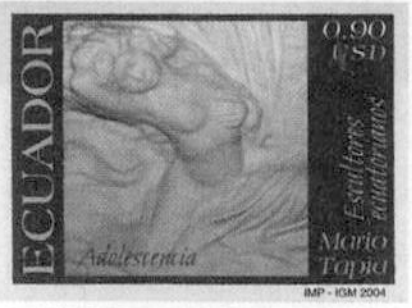

876 "Adolescencia"

2004. Art. Sculptures by Mario Tapia. Mult.

2735	90c. Type **876**	5·75	3·75
2736	90c. "Beato Chaminade"	5·75	3·75
2737	90c. "Delfin de Galapagos"	5·75	3·75
2738	90c. "Pelicano"	5·75	3·75
2739	90c. "Homenaje a Carlo Vidano"	5·75	3·75
MS2740	100×69 mm. $2 "Beato Chaminade". Imperf	11·50	9·50

877 Pedro Maldonado

2004. 300th Birth Anniv Pedro Vicente Maldonado (cartographer).

2741	**877**	90c. multicoloured	5·75	3·75

878 Augustin Tamariz

2004. 25th Death Anniv of Augustin Cueva Tamariz (writer).

2742	**878**	90c. multicoloured	5·75	3·75

879 Emblem

2004. 34th General Assembly of Organization of American States, Quito.

2743	**879**	75c. multicoloured	4·00	2·75

880 Angel Rojas

2004. 95th Birth Anniv of Angel Felicisimo Rojas (writer).

2744	**880**	50c. multicoloured	2·75	1·90

881 Flags

2004. Ecuador—Spain Postal Service.

2745	**881**	$1.05 multicoloured	6·50	4·25

882 Emblems and Mascots

2004. Olympic Games, Athens. Multicoloured.

2746	$1.05 Type **882**	6·50	4·25
2747	$1.05 Alexandra Escobar Guerrero	6·50	4·25

883 *Cattleya maxima*

2004. 30th Anniv of Orchid Association. Mult.

2748	25c. Type **883**	2·00	1·30
2749	$1.05 *Epidendrum bracteolatum*	6·50	4·25

884 Musicians and Stylized Score

2004. Guayaquil Symphony Orchestra.

2750	**884**	90c. multicoloured	5·75	3·75

885 Figure enclosed by Trees

2005. America (2004). Environmental Protection. Multicoloured.

2751	40c. Type **885**	2·50	1·70
2752	$1.05 Female figure enclosing different habitats	6·50	4·25

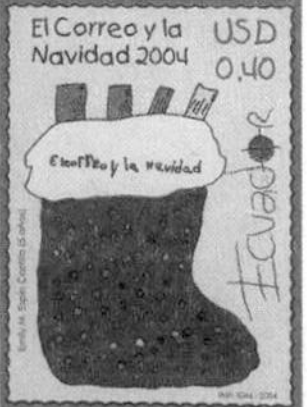

886 Stocking

2005. Christmas (2004). Children's Paintings. Multicoloured.

2753	40c. Type **886**	2·50	1·70
2754	$1.05 Father Christmas and tree (horiz)	6·50	4·25

887 Galapagos Giant Tortoise (*Chelonoidis abingdonii*)

2005. Galapagos Islands. Multicoloured.

No.	Description	Mint	Used
2755	40c. Type **887**	2·50	1·70
2756	90c. Marine iguana (*Amblyrhynchus cristatus*) (vert)	5·75	3·75
2757	$2.15 *Sula granti*	11·50	7·50
2758	$3 Magnificent frigate bird (*Fregata magnificens*) (inscr "magnifiscens")	16·00	10·50
MS2759	68×98 mm. $2 Swallow-tailed gull (*Creagrus furcatus*). Imperf	11·50	9·50

888 Mast Head

2005. "El Murcurio" Newspaper. Multicoloured.

No.	Description	Mint	Used
2760	$1.25 Type **888**	7·00	4·75
2761	$2 Nicanor Merchan Bermeo (founder) (vert)	11·00	7·25
2762	$2.25 Miguel Merchan Ochoa (vert)	11·50	7·75

889 Emblem

2005. Promotion of Tourism.

No.	Type	Description	Mint	Used
2763	**889**	$3.75 multicoloured	18·00	12·50

890 Emblem

2005. 25th Anniv of Chess Federation.

No.	Type	Description	Mint	Used
2764	**890**	$1.25 multicoloured	7·00	4·75

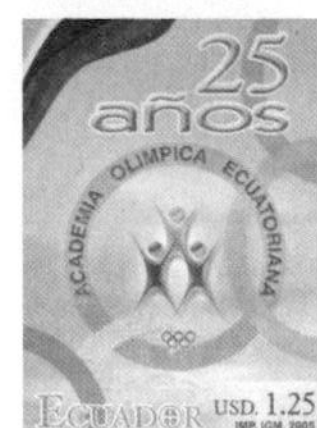

891 Emblem

2005. 25th Anniv of Olympic Academy.

No.	Type	Description	Mint	Used
2765	**891**	$1.25 multicoloured	7·00	4·75
MS2766		69×100 mm. **891** $2 multicoloured. Imperf	11·50	9·50

892 Emblem and Mountaineer on Mt. Chimborazo

2005. Centenary of Rotary International. Multicoloured.

No.	Description	Mint	Used
2767	40c. Type **892**	2·50	1·70
2768	90c. Emblem and crowds on Mt. Cotopaxi	5·75	3·75
2769	125c. Emblem and mountaineer on Mt. Shisha Pangma	7·00	4·75

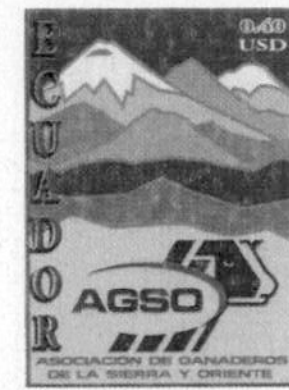

893 Emblem

2005. AGSO (cattle dealers association). Multicoloured.

No.	Description	Mint	Used
2770	40c. Type **893**	2·50	1·70
2771	40c. Cow's head	2·50	1·70

894 Monument and Open Book

2005. International Year of Books and Reading.

No.	Type	Description	Mint	Used
2772	**894**	25c. multicoloured	2·10	1·40

895 Jose de San Martin

2005. 183rd Guayaquil Philatelic Club Conference. Multicoloured.

No.	Description	Mint	Used
2773	90c. Type **895**	5·75	3·75
2774	90c. Simon Boivar	5·75	3·75
MS2775	98×68 mm. $2 Monument. Imperf	11·50	9·50

896 Juan Vargas

2005. Death Centenary (2004) of Juan Isaac Lovato Vargas (writer and jurist).

No.	Type	Description	Mint	Used
2776	**896**	$1.25 multicoloured	7·00	4·75

897 La Casa Blanca Stadium

2005. 75th Anniv of University Sports League, Quito. Multicoloured.

No.	Description	Mint	Used
2777	40c. Type **897**	2·50	1·70
2778	40c. National League champions	2·50	1·70
2779	40c. Emblem	2·50	1·70
2780	40c. Children and league college	2·50	1·70
2781	40c. League club	2·50	1·70

898 Emblem and Mascot

2005. Bolivarian Games.

No.	Description	Mint	Used
2782	25c. multicoloured	2·00	1·30

899 Trophy and South American Championship Winning Team, 1938

2005. National Swimming Federation.

No.	Type	Description	Mint	Used
2783	**899**	25c. multicoloured	2·00	1·30

900 Troops in Esmeralda (1916)

2005. National Army. Multicoloured.

No.	Description	Mint	Used
2784	40c. Type **900**	2·50	1·70
2785	40c. Military school cadets (1928)	2·50	1·70
2786	40c. Cayambe battalion	2·50	1·70
2787	40c. Arms and Gen. Eloy Alfaro's grandsons	2·50	1·70
2788	40c. Imbabura battalion	2·50	1·70
MS2789	98×68 mm. $2 Battle for Guayaquil. Imperf	11·50	9·50

901 Virgin of Cisne

2005

No.	Type	Description	Mint	Used
2790	**901**	$1.25 multicoloured	7·00	4·75

902 Santa Ana, Guayaquil

2005. Tourism. Multicoloured.

No.	Description	Mint	Used
2791	30c. Type **902**	2·30	1·50
2792	30c. Esmeraldas	2·30	1·50
2793	30c. Misahualli	2·30	1·50
2794	30c. Tsunki Shuar, Pastaza	2·30	1·50
2795	40c. Cisne Church, Loja	2·50	1·70
2796	40c. Ingapirca ruins	2·50	1·70
2797	40c. Seal	2·50	1·70
2798	40c. Sea turtle and diver	2·50	1·70

903 Carchi Provincial Arms

2005. Arms. Multicoloured.

No.	Description	Mint	Used
2799	40c. Type **903**	2·50	1·70
2800	40c. Huaca	2·50	1·70
2801	40c. Mira	2·50	1·70
2802	40c. Espejo	2·50	1·70
2803	40c. Montufar	2·50	1·70
2804	40c. Tulcan	2·50	1·70
2805	40c. Bolivar	2·50	1·70

904 Santa Mariana de Jesus Paredes y Flores (sculpture) (Mario Tapia)

2005

No.	Type	Description	Mint	Used
2806	**904**	25c. multicoloured	2·00	1·30

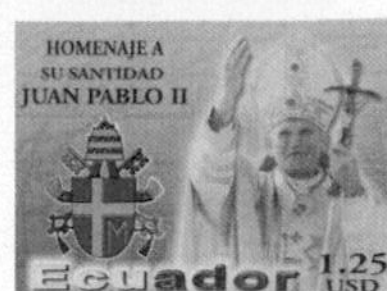

905 Pope John Paul II

2005. Pope John Paul II Commemoration and Enthronement of Pope Benedict XVI. Multicoloured.

No.	Description	Mint	Used
2807	$1.25 Type **905**	1·80	1·20
2808	$2 Pope Benedict XVI	11·50	7·50

906 Mirage FI-JA

2005. 19th Anniv of Cenepa War. Multicoloured.

No.	Description	Mint	Used
2809	$1.25 Type **906**	7·00	4·75
2810	$1.25 Cessna A-37B	7·00	4·75
2811	$1.25 KFIR-C2	7·00	4·75
2812	$1.25 Colonel Carlos Uscateguis	7·00	4·75

907 Jose Abel Castillo (flight manager) and Tail of *Telegrafo I*

2005. 85th Anniv of First Posts and Telegraphs Flight. Multicoloured.

No.	Description	Mint	Used
2813	25c. Type **907**	2·00	1·30
2814	$1 Elia Liut (pilot) and *Telegrafo I*	6·00	4·00

Nos. 2813/14 were issued together, se-tenant, forming a composite design.

908 Female Soldier

2005. United Nations Peace Keeping Mission. Multicoloured.

No.	Description	Mint	Used
2815	75c. Type **908**	4·00	2·75
2816	75c. Two soldiers	4·00	2·75
2817	75c. Parade of soldiers with flags	4·00	2·75
2818	75c. UN flag and cap	4·00	2·75

909 Father Christmas and Tree (Pamela Alejandra Castillo Rocha)

2005. Christmas. Children's Paintings. Multicoloured.

No.	Description	Mint	Used
2819	$1.25 Type **909**	7·00	4·75
2820	$1.25 Nativity (Kira Cadeno)	7·00	4·75
2821	$1.25 Angels (Silvia Moran Burgos)	7·00	4·75
2822	$1.25 Three Wise Men, angel, globe and Bethlehem (Carol Garcia)	7·00	4·75

910 Water Carrier

2005. 19th-century Costumes. Multicoloured.

2823	25c. Type **910**	2·00	1·30
2824	25c. Native governor	2·00	1·30
2825	25c. Dancer, Banos	2·00	1·30
2826	25c. Native woman, Cuenca	2·00	1·30
2827	25c. Municipal Council Juancho	2·00	1·30
2828	25c. Native carrying rockets (voladores)	2·00	1·30
2829	25c. La Mima gigante	2·00	1·30
2830	25c. Butler (mayordomo)	2·00	1·30
2831	25c. Chola pinganilla	2·00	1·30
2832	25c. Street sweeper	2·00	1·30

911 Don Quixote and Windmills

2005. 400th Anniv of "The Ingenious Hidalgo Don Quixote of La Mancha" (novel by Miguel de Cervantes Saavedra). Multicoloured.

2833	$2 Type **911**	11·00	7·25
2834	$2 Don Quixote and tree of books	11·00	7·25

912 Joseph and Jesus

2005. National Institute of Cultural Heritage. Multicoloured.

2835	40c. Type **912**	2·50	1·70
2836	40c. Risen Christ	2·50	1·70
2837	40c. Virgin of Quito	2·50	1·70
2838	40c. St. Augustine	2·50	1·70

913 Liberty and Masthead

2006. Centenary of El Comercio Newspaper. Multicoloured.

2840	40c. Type **913**	2·50	1·70
2843	50c. Emblem (55×34 mm)	2·75	1·90
MS2844	100×69 mm. $2. As No. 2840. Imperf	11·50	9·50

914 Emblem

2006. Cultural Heritage–Quito.

2845	**914**	25c. multicoloured	2·00	1·30

915 Latin American Map and Emblems

2006. Latin America and Caribbean Lions' Forum, Quito. Multicoloured.

2846	90c. Type **915**	5·75	3·75
MS2847	68×99 mm. $2. As No. 2846. Imperf	11·50	9·50

916 Cromacris

2006. Puyo—City of Biodiversity. Multicoloured.

2848	$1 Type **916**	6·00	4·00
2849	$1.20 Desmodus rotundus	7·00	4·75

918 Benito Juarez Garcia

2006. Birth Bicentenary of Benito Juarez Garcia (politician).

2854	**918**	$1.20 multicoloured	7·00	4·75

919 Balsa Mantena

2006

2855	**919**	$1 multicoloured	6·00	4·00

920 Forming Hat

2006. Sombreros of Paja Toquilla. Multicoloured.

2856	40c. Type **920**	2·50	1·70
2857	40c. Woman weaving hat (vert)	2·50	1·70

921 Emblem

2006. National Student Federation (FEUPE). W430b (sideways).

2858	**921**	30c. multicoloured	2·30	1·50

922 Saint Mary of the Sacred Heart

2006. Centenary of Miracle of Dolorosa del Colegio.

2859	**922**	80c. multicoloured	4·50	3·00

923 Founding Fathers

2006. 400th Anniv of Foundation of Ibarra. Multicoloured.

2860	20c. Type **923**	1·80	1·20
MS2861	68×100 mm. $2.50 Cherubs, partially clothed woman and two men. Imperf.	12·00	10·50

924 Baltazara Calderon

2006. Birth Bicentenary of Baltazara Calderon de Rocafuerte (nationalist and philanthropist).

2862	**924**	$1 multicoloured	6·00	4·00

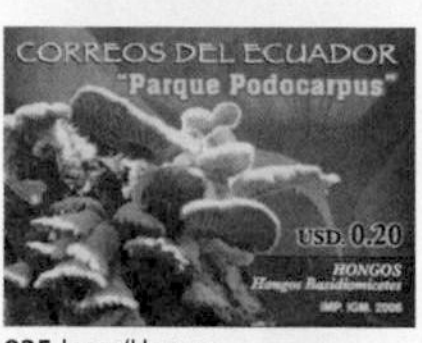

925 Inscr 'Hongos basidiomicetes'

2006. Podocarpus National Park. Multicoloured.

2863	20c. Type **925**	1·80	1·20
2864	25c. *Tremarctos ornatus* (inscr 'Tremarctus ornatus') (spectacled bear)	2·00	1·30
2865	90c. *Harpya harpyja* (harpy eagle)	5·75	3·75

926 Mozart and Casa de la Musica, Quito, Ecuador

2006. 250th Birth Anniv of Wolfgang Amadeus Mozart (composer and musician).

2866	**926**	20c. multicoloured	1·80	1·20

927 Girl (right to national identity)

2006. UNICEF Rights of the Child. Multicoloured.

2867	75c. Type **927**	4·00	2·75
2868	$1 Children and books (right to education)	6·00	4·00

No. 2869 and Type **928** have been left for 'Eloy Alfaro Military School', issued 5 June 2006.

929 Emblem and Original Building

2006. Centenary of Pinchincha Bank. Multicoloured.

2870	40c. Type **929**	2·50	1·70
2871	40c. Building and emblems	2·50	1·70
2872	40c. Banknote	2·50	1·70

Nos. 2870/1 were issued together, *se-tenant*, forming a composite design of the original bank building.

Nos. 2873/80 and Type **930** have been left for 'Football World Cup', issued 9 June 2006.

931 Mothers

2006. Tribute to the Mothers of Plaza de Mayo (association of mothers of disappeared Argentinean children). Multicoloured.

2881	80c. Type **931**	4·50	3·00
MS2882	68×100 mm. $2.50 Mothers (rear view). Imperf	12·50	10·50

932 City at Night

2006. Machala.

2883	**932**	30c. multicoloured	2·30	1·50

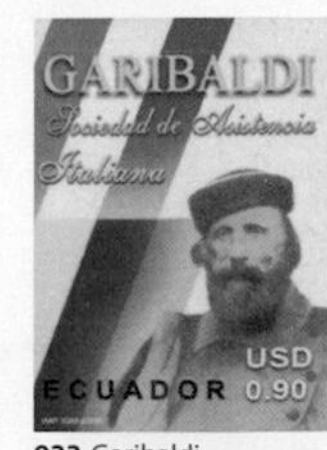

933 Garibaldi

2006. Garibaldi Italian Society.

2884	**933**	90c. multicoloured	5·75	3·75

Nos. 2885/7 and Type **934** have been left for "Railways", issued 22 July 2006.

935 Simon Bolivar

2006. Simon Bolivar College.

2888	20c. Type **935**	1·80	1·20

No. 2889 is left for miniature sheet not yet received.

936 Necklace

2006. National Institute for Cultural Heritage (INPC). Inca Art. Spondylus Artifacts. Multicoloured.

2890	25c. Type **936**	2·00	1·30
2891	$1 Merchant (statue) (vert)	6·00	4·00
2892	$1 Boatmen and boat (vert)	6·00	4·00

Nos. 2891/2 were issued together, se-tenant, forming a composite design.

937 Inca Postman

2006

2893	**937**	25c. multicoloured	2·00	1·30
2894	**937**	30c. multicoloured	2·30	1·50
2895	**937**	40c. multicoloured	2·50	1·70
2896	**937**	60c. multicoloured	3·50	2·40
2897	**937**	80c. multicoloured	4·50	3·00

938 Jorge Icaza

2006. Writers. Multicoloured.

2898	$1 Type **938**	6·00	4·00
2899	$1.20 Pablo Palacio	7·00	4·75

939 Bandera Manabi

2006. Gastronomy. Multicoloured.

2900	$1 Type **939**	6·00	4·00
2901	$1 Viche de Manabi	6·00	4·00

940 *Caucaea olivaceum*

2006. Orchids. Multicoloured.

2902	30c. Type **940**	2·30	1·50
2903	30c. *Cyrtochilum macranthum*	2·30	1·50
2904	30c. *Miltoniopsis vexillaria*	2·30	1·50
2905	30c. *Odontoglossum harryanum*	2·30	1·50
2906	30c. *Cyrtochilum pastasae*	2·30	1·50
2907	30c. *Cyrtochilum loxense*	2·30	1·50
2908	30c. *Cyrtochilum eduardii*	2·30	1·50
2909	30c. *Odontoglossum epidendroides*	2·30	1·50
2910	30c. *Cyrtochilum retusum*	2·30	1·50
2911	30c. *Cyrtochilum geniculatum*	2·30	1·50

941 *En la Ventana*

2006. Art. Works by Giti Neuman. Multicoloured.

2912	30c. Type **941**	2·30	1·50
2913	30c. *Forma en Movimento*	2·30	1·50
2914	30c. *Caminantes*	2·30	1·50
2915	30c. *Caminando* (horiz)	2·30	1·50
2916	30c. *Cabezas Huecas* (horiz)	2·30	1·50

942 Light

2006. America. Energy Conservation.

2917	**942**	$1 multicoloured	5·75	3·75
2918	**942**	$1.20 multicoloured	7·00	4·75

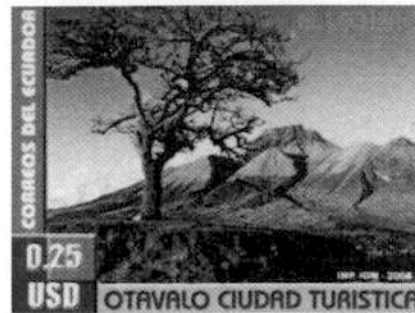

943 El Lechero

2006. Tourism. Otavalo. Multicoloured.

2919	25c. Type **943**	2·00	1·30
2920	30c. El Jordan	2·30	1·50
2921	75c. Nina Otavalena (vert)	4·00	2·75
2922	$1 El Coraza (vert)	5·75	3·75

944 Smoke Cloud

2006. Eruption of Tungurahua Volcano–16 August 2006. Multicoloured.

2923	$1 Type **944**	5·75	3·75
2924	$1 Lava flow	5·75	3·75

945 Municipal Palace

2006. Regeneration of Guayaquil. Multicoloured.

2925	$1 Type **945**	5·75	3·75
2926	$1 Municipal Palace (right)	5·75	3·75
2927	$1 Fragua de Vulcano	5·75	3·75
2928	$1 Jose Joaquin de Olmedo building	5·75	3·75
2929	$1 Metrovia	5·75	3·75

Nos. 2925/9 were issued together, *se-tenant*, forming a composite design of the Municipal Palace.

946 Microphone and Studio

2006. 75th Anniv of HCJB Radio Station.

2930	**946**	$1 multicoloured	5·75	3·75

947 Galo Plaza Lasso

2006. Birth Centenary of Galo Plaza Lasso (president 1948–1952). Multicoloured.

2931	40c. Type **947**	2·50	1·70
2932	80c. Emblem	4·50	3·00

948 Emblems

2006. United Nations Millennium Development Goals.

2933	**948**	$2 multicoloured	11·00	7·25

949 Dog

2006. German Shepherd Dog Breeders Association.

2934	**949**	$1 multicoloured	5·75	3·75

950 Soldiers

2006. 50th Anniv of Parachute Regiment. Multicoloured.

2935	20c. Type **950**	1·80	1·20
2936	40c. Douglas C-47 and soldiers	2·50	1·70
2937	60c. Anniversary emblem, flag and statue (vert)	3·50	2·40
2938	80c. Anniversary emblem, flag and parachutist (vert)	4·25	2·75

Nos. 2939/46 and Type **951** have been left for 'Galapagos Islands', issued 1 Nov 2006.

952 Plaza de Toros, Quito

2006. Bullfighting. Multicoloured.

2947	50c. Type **952**	2·75	1·90
2948	50c. Plaza de Toros, Quito (different)	2·75	1·90
2949	50c. Sebastian Castella (vert)	2·75	1·90
2950	50c. El Juli (vert)	2·75	1·90
2951	50c. Manolo Cadena (vert)	2·75	1·90
MS2952	65×40 mm $3 Christ carrying crucifix. Imperf	14·00	12·50

Nos. 2947/8 forming a composite design of Plaza de Toros, Quito.

No. 2953 and Type **953** have been left for 'Christmas', issued 28 November 2006.

954 Terrier Puppy

2006. Pets. Multicoloured designs.

2954	25c. Type **954**	2·00	1·30
2955	40c. German shepherd puppy (vert)	2·50	1·70
2956	50c. Cream exotic short hair cat (vert)	2·75	1·90
2957	80c. Poodle	4·25	2·75
2958	$1 Persian cat (vert)	5·75	3·75

955 Wearing Vestments

2006. 80th Birth Anniv of Archbishop Emeritus Juan Ignacio Larrea Holguin (archbishop of Guayaquil, first member of the prelature of Opus Dei in Ecuador, lawyer, and author of books about jurisprudence).

2959	40c. Type **955**	2·50	1·70
2960	40c. Wearing cassock	2·50	1·70

956 Regalia

2006. Freemasons in Ecuador. Multicoloured.

2961	25c. Type **956**	2·00	1·30
2962	40c. Emblem	2·50	1·70

Nos. 2963/7 and Type **957** have been left for 'Fauna', issued on 14 December 2006, not yet received.

958 Mother and Baby

2006. Pottery. Erotic Art, Fertility and Life. Multicoloured.

2968	10c. Type **958**	1·70	1·10
2969	20c. Couple	1·80	1·20
2970	$1.20 Pregnant woman	7·00	4·75
2971	$2 Man	11·00	7·25

959 Sailor

2006. Juan Illingworth Naval Museum.

2972	20c. Type **959**	1·80	1·20
2973	25c. Marine guard	2·00	1·30

960 National Flag

2006

2974	**960**	$10 yellow, ultramarine and vermilion	30·00	24·00

961 Postmen and Cycles

2006

2975	**961**	20c. multicoloured	1·80	1·20
2976	**961**	40c. multicoloured	2·50	1·70
2977	**961**	80c. multicoloured	4·25	2·75

962 Exhibition Space

2006. 9th Internationale Biennale of Cuenca.

2978	**962**	5c. multicoloured	1·40	95
2979	**962**	15c. Painting by Ricardo Gonzalez Elias	1·80	1·20

No. 2980 and Type **963** has been left for 'Centenary of Independence Movement', issued on 21 December 2006, not yet received.

964 Guapulo Monastery

2006. International University SEK.

2981	**964**	10c. multicoloured	1·70	1·10

965 Barque and Seals

2006. Pirates of the Galapagos. Multicoloured.

2982	30c. Type **965**	2·30	1·50
2983	30c. Seals and sea battle	2·30	1·50
2984	30c. Sea battle	2·30	1·50
2985	30c. Pirate	2·30	1·50
2986	30c. Skull and crossbones flag	2·30	1·50
2987	40c. Francis Drake (horiz)	2·50	1·70
2988	40c. Barque (horiz)	2·50	1·70
2989	$1 William Dampier (horiz)	5·75	3·75

Nos. 2982/6 were issued together, se-tenant, forming a composite design of sea battle and Galapagos Islands fauna.

Nos. 2987/8 were issued together, se-tenant, forming a composite design showing the sea route of Francis Drake.

966 Emblem

2007. Centenary of Scouting. 23rd InterAmerican Scout Conference (2990). Multicoloured.

2990	25c. Type **966**	2·00	1·30
2991	$2 Scout	11·00	7·25

967 Building Facade

2007. Latin American Festival of Lyrical Poetry .

2992	**967**	10c. multicoloured	1·70	1·10

968 La Casa de los Arcos

2007. 450th Anniv of Cuenca. Multicoloured.

2993	40c. Type **968**	2·50	1·70
2994	75c. Plaza el Vergel	4·00	2·75
2995	80c. Rio Tomebamba Sector el Barranco (horiz)	4·25	2·75
2996	$3 Catedral de la Inmaculada Concepcion	14·00	9·50

969 *Golopha eaucus*

2007. Museum of Natural Sciences (MECN) (1st issue). Giant Beetles. Multicoloured.

2997	40c. Type **969**	2·50	1·70
2998	40c. *Chrysophora chrysochlora*	2·50	1·70
2999	40c. *Dynastes Hercules*	2·50	1·70

970 Megaptera

2007. Museum of Natural Sciences (MECN) (2nd issue). Pre-historic Animals. Multicoloured.

3000	80c. Type **970**	4·25	2·75
3001	80c. Smilodon (horiz)	4·25	2·75

971 Emblem

2007. 80th Anniv of Guayaquil Rotary Club.

3002	**971**	25c. multicoloured	2·00	1·30

972 School Bus

2007. America. Education for All. National Council for Children and Adolescence. Multicoloured.

3003	40c. Type **972**	2·50	1·70
3004	80c. Girl learning to write	4·25	2·75
3005	$1 Children (vert)	5·75	3·75
3006	$1.20 Wheelchair user (vert)	7·00	4·75
MS3007	40×65 mm. $2 Hand prints. Imperf	11·50	9·50

973 Ship and Emperor Penguin

2007. 75th Anniv of Institute of Oceanography (INOCAR). Multicoloured.

3008	10c. Type **973**	1·70	1·10
3009	$3 Survey team and equipment (54×34 mm)	14·00	9·50

974 Building Facade

2007. 80th Anniv of Central Bank.

3010	**974**	$2 multicoloured	11·50	7·50

975 Fire Fighter

2007. Fire Fighters of Guayaquil. Multicoloured.

3011	5c. Type **975**	1·40	95
3012	10c. Fighting flames with water hose	1·70	1·10
3013	15c. Two fire fighters and flames	1·80	1·20
3014	25c. Fire fighter and fire on skyline (horiz)	2·00	1·30
3015	$1 Two fire fighters with backs to flames (horiz)	5·75	3·75

976 Examining Breast

2007. Breast Cancer Awareness Campaign.

3016	**976**	$3 multicoloured	14·00	9·50

977 Las Penas

2007. Tourism. Guayquil. Multicoloured.

3017	5c. Type **977**	1·40	95
3018	10c. Santa Ana lighthouse	1·70	1·10
3019	15c. El Velero bridge	1·80	1·20
3020	25c. South Market (horiz)	2·00	1·30

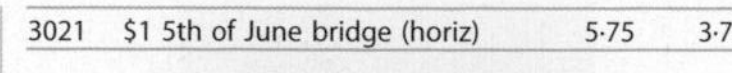

3021	$1 5th of June bridge (horiz)	5·75	3·75

978 Hands holding Seedling

2007. 70th Anniversary of Cuenca Chamber of Commerce.

3022	**978**	1s.20 multicoloured	7·00	4·75

979 Boy

2007. Operation Smile.

3023	**979**	1s. multicoloured	5·75	3·75

980 Covers

2007. 50th Anniv of Vistazo Magazine.

3024	**980**	20c. multicoloured	1·80	1·20

981 Sea Turtle

2007. Galapagos Islands. Multicoloured.

3025	40c. Type **981**	2·50	1·70
3026	80c. Jackass penguin	4·25	2·75
3027	$1 Dolphin	5·75	3·75
3028	$1.20 Tropicbird	7·00	4·75

982 Emblem

2007. 80th Anniv of State Treasury Department.

3029	**982**	20c. multicoloured	1·80	1·20

983 Alexandra Escobar (weightlifter)

2007. Rio 2007–Pan American Games. Showing stylized gold medal winning athletes. Multicoloured.

3030	40c. Type **983**	2·50	1·70
3031	40c. Seledina Nieve (weight-lifter)	2·50	1·70
3032	40c. Jefferson Perez (race walker, 20km.)	2·50	1·70
3033	40c. Xavier Moreno (race walker, 50km.)	2·50	1·70
3034	40c. Under 18 football players	2·50	1·70

Nos. 3030/4 were issued together, se-tenant, forming a composite design of athletes competing.

984 The Annunciation

2007. Christmas. Multicoloured.

3035	20c. Type **984**	1·80	1·20
3036	20c. Three Kings	1·80	1·20
3037	20c. The Nativity	1·80	1·20
3038	20c. Journey into Egypt	1·80	1·20

985 Policeman

2008. 60th Anniv of Guayas Traffic Police.

3039	**985**	1s. multicoloured	5·75	3·75

986 *Pelicanus occidentalis* (eastern brown pelican)

2008. Galapagos Islands. Multicoloured.

3040	40c. Type **986**	2·50	1·70
3041	80c. *Aetobatus narinari* (spotted eagle ray)	4·50	2·75
3042	$1 *Carcharhinus galapagensis* (Galapagos shark)	5·75	3·75
3043	$1.20 Wind farm	7·00	4·75

987 Women

2008. Maternity.

3044	**987**	$1 multicoloured	5·75	3·75

988 Ship

2008. 50th Anniv of Port Authority, Guayaquil.

3045	**988**	20c. multicoloured	1·80	1·20

989 Symbols of Industry

2008. 80th Anniv of Chamber of Industry, Tungurahua.

3046	**989**	$3 multicoloured	14·00	9·50

990 Father Crespi

2008. Father Carlos Crespi Croci (missionary and conservator) Commemoration.

3047 **990** $2 multicoloured 11·00 7·25

991 Santiago de Guayaquil Medallion

2008. Stamp Day.

3048 **991** 30c. multicoloured 2·50 1·50

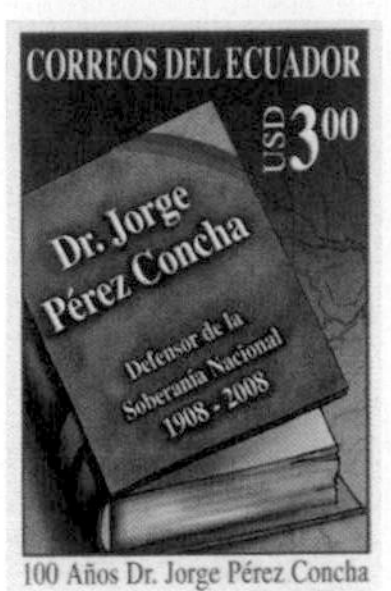

992 Book

2008. Birth Centenary of Jorge Perez Concha (writer).

3049 **992** $3 multicoloured 14·00 9·50

993 Arms

2008. 40th Anniv of Los Pinos High School.

3050 **993** 20c. multicoloured 1·80 1·20

994 Locomotive and 1907 1c. Stamp (Type **84**)

2008. Centenary of Guayaquil—Quito Railway. Multicoloured.

3051 56c. Type **994** 3·00 2·00

MS3052 100×70 mm. $5 1907 1c. Stamp (Type **84**). Imperf 21·00 21·00

995 '50' and Emblem

2008. 50th Anniv of ESPOL (Escuela Superior Politecnica del Litoral).

3053 **995** 32c. multicoloured 2·40 1·60

996 Sun

2008. Ibero-American Youth Year.

3054 **996** 30c. multicoloured 2·30 1·50

997 Fruit and 1930 5c. Stamp (detail) (As Type **134**)

2008. Cocoa (Theobroma cacao). Each including part of 1930 5c. stamp. Multicoloured.

3055 56c. Type **997** 3·00 2·00
3056 56c. Flowers 3·00 2·00
3057 56c. Cultivation 3·00 2·00
3058 56c. Beans and chocolate 3·00 2·00

Nos. 3055/8 were issued together, se-tenant, each sharing part of 1930 5c. stamp, the whole forming a composite design.

998 Masthead and '25'

2008. 25th Anniv of Meridiano Newspaper.

3059 **998** 60c. multicoloured 3·50 2·40

999 World Map and Emblems

2008. Centenary of International Swimming Federation. Multicoloured.

3060 24c. Type **999** 2·00 1·30
3061 24c. Swimmer 2·00 1·30
3062 30c. Swimmer underwater 2·30 1·50

Nos. 3060/1 were issued together-se-tenant forming a composite design.

1000 Emblem

2008. 80th Anniv of PGE.

3063 **1000** 25c. multicoloured 2·00 1·30

1001 Flag

2008. New Constitution. Multicoloured.

3064 32c. Type **1001** 2·30 1·50

MS3065 65×95 mm. $5 Figures and flag. Imperf 21·00 21·00

1002 Buildings

2008. 40th Anniv of Chamber of Construction, Guayaquil.

3066 **1002** $1 multicoloured 5·75 3·75

1002a Museum Building

2008. Centenary of City Museum, Guayaquil. Multicoloured.

3066a 60c. Type **1002a** 4·00 4·00
3066b 60c. Mural 4·00 4·00
3066c $2 Museum building (different) 4·00 4·00

1003 Cotopaxil, Ecuador

2008. 90th Anniv of Ecuador–Japan Relations. Multicoloured.

3067 30c. Type **1003** 2·30 1·50
3068 30c. Mount Fuji, Japan 2·30 1·50

Nos. 3067/8 were issued together, se-tenant, forming a composite design.

1004 Dancers, St. Peter and St. Paul Festival

2008. America. Festivals. Multicoloured.

3069 20c. Type **1004** 1·80 1·20
3070 20c. Guitarist, St Peter and St Paul Festival 1·80 1·20
3071 $1 Dancer wearing red mask, Diablada Pillarena (vert) 5·75 3·75
3072 $1 Dancer wearing black mask, Diablada Pillarena (vert) 5·75 3·75

Nos. 3069/70 and 3071/2 were issued together, se-tenant, forming a composite design.

1005 The Nativity

2008. Christmas. Multicoloured.

3073 30c. Type **1005** 2·30 1·50
3074 80c. The Nativity, Mary with hair in bun 4·25 2·75
3075 80c. The Nativity, Mary wearing hat 4·25 2·75

1007 Performers

2009. Jacchigua Folkloric Ballet. Multicoloured.

3079 $1 Type **1007** 5·75 3·75
3080 $1 Masked dancers 5·75 3·75
3081 $1 Dancing around pole 5·75 3·75
3082 $1 Men in ponchoes 5·75 3·75
3083 $1 Seated woman 5·75 3·75

Nos. 3076/8 and Type **1006** have been left for 60th Anniv of Committee, issued on 7 January 2009, not yet received.

1007a Polar Bear Paws on Melting Ice

2009. Preserve Polar Regions and Glaciers. Multicoloured.

3083a 20c. Type **1007a** 1·80 1·20
3083b 80c. Globe floating in water 1·80 1·20

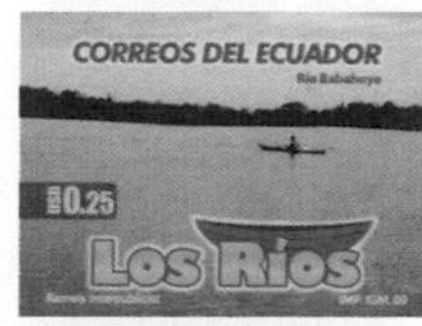

1008 Canoe on Lake (Rio Babahoyo) (Los Rios)

2009. Regions. Multicoloured.

3084 25c. Type **1008** 2·00 1·30
3085 50c. Ruins (Ruinas de Ingapirca) (Canar) 2·75 1·70
3086 75c. Rafting (Rio Quijos) (Napo) 4·00 2·50
3087 $1 Dancers (Grupo de Mrimbo) (Esmeraldas) 5·75 3·75
3088 $1.25 Topiary (Cementerio de Tulcan) (Carchi) 7·00 4·75
3089 $2 Chimborazo 11·00 7·25
3090 $3 *Alcea rosea* (flower) (Morona Santiago) 14·00 8·50
3091 $5 *Acrocinus longimanus* (spider) (Sucumbios) 21·00 13·00

1009 Tweezers, Magnifier and Stamp

2009. Stamp Day.

3092 **1009** 75c. multicoloured 3·75 2·25

1010 Angel (statue)

2009. Artifacts of Santa Clara Monastery. Multicoloured.

3093 $1 Type **1010** 5·75 3·75
3094 $1 Christ 5·75 3·75
3095 $1 Pensive child 5·75 3·75
3096 $1 Virgin Mary (painting) 5·75 3·75
3097 $1 Virgin de Quito (statue) 5·75 3·75

1011 Ambato Cathedral

2009. 50th Anniv of Empresa Electrica (electric company).

3098 **1011** $1 multicoloured 5·75 3·75

1012 Dam

2009. 25th Anniv of Central Paute-Molino Hydro-electric Dam.

3099	**1012**	$2 multicoloured	11·00	7·25

1013 Hands shaping Pot

2009. 45th Anniv of Corporacion Financiera Nacional (National Financial Corporation of Ecuador's development bank).

3100	**1013**	$1.25 multicoloured	7·00	4·25

1014 Front Page

2009. 135th Anniv of El Telegrafico Newspaper.

3101	**1014**	$1.75 multicoloured	9·75	5·75

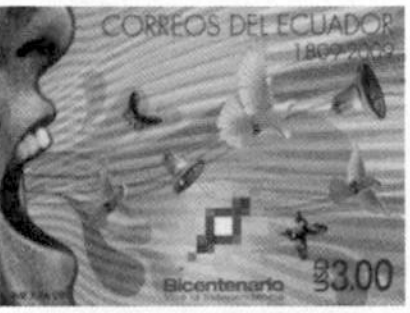

1015 Symbols of Celebration

2009. Bicentenary of Independence (1st issue). Multicoloured.

3102	$3 Type **1015**	14·00	9·50
3103	$3 Doves, bells and Independence Monument, Quito	14·00	9·50
MS3104	100×70 mm. $3×2, As Type **1015**; As No. 3103	26·00	26·00

Nos. 3102/3 were printed, se-tenant, each pair forming a composite design.

The stamps of **MS**3104 are as Nos. 3102/3 but with background changed.

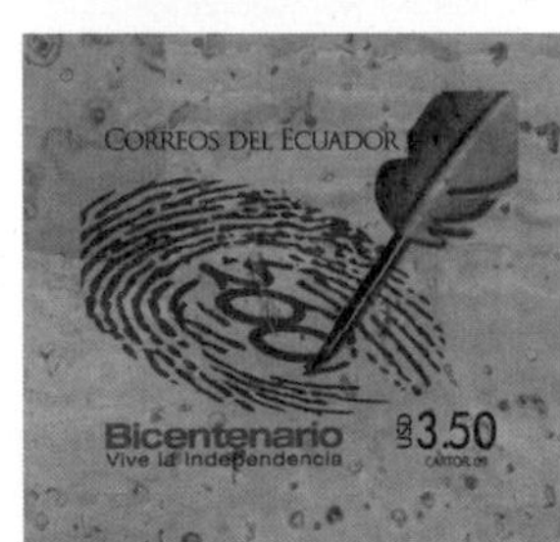

1016 Quill Pen and Fingerprint

2009. Bicentenary of Independence (2nd issue). Cork. Self-adhesive.

3105	**1016**	$3.50 multicoloured	16·00	10·00

No. 3105 is made from finely pressed cork which can be peeled from the backing paper.

1017 Symbols of Ecuador

2009. Centenary of Ecuador–China Diplomatic Relations. Multicoloured.

3106	25c. Type **1017**	2·10	1·30
3107	25c. Symbols of China	2·10	1·30

Nos. 3106/7 were printed, se-tenant, each pair forming a composite design.

1018 Carlos Silva Pareja (musician and composer)

2009. Birth Centenaries. Multicoloured.

3108	25c. Type **1018**	2·10	1·30
3109	25c. Transito Amaguana (indigenous human rights activist)	2·10	1·30
3110	25c. Demetrio Aguilera Malta (writer, filmmaker, painter and diplomat)	2·10	1·30
3111	25c. Carlos Zevallos Menendez (archaeology)	2·10	1·30
3112	25c. Humberto Salvador Guerra (writer)	2·10	1·30

1019 Pichincha

1020 Guayas

1021 Los Rios (As No. 3084)

2009. Tourism. Regions. Multicoloured. Self-adhesive.

3113	25c. Type **1019**	2·10	1·30
3114	25c. Santos Domingo de los Tsachilas	2·10	1·30
3115	25c. Type **1020**	2·10	1·30
3116	25c. Sta. Elena	2·10	1·30
3117	25c. Type **1021**	2·10	1·30
3118	25c. Esmeraldas (As No. 3085)	2·10	1·30
3119	50c. Tungurahua	3·00	2·10
3120	50c. Cotopaxi	3·00	2·00
3121	50c. Mahabi	3·00	2·00
3122	50c. El Oro	3·00	2·00
3123	50c. Carchi (As No. 3086)	3·00	2·00
3124	50c. Canar (As No. 3087)	3·00	2·00
3125	75c. Bolivar	4·00	2·50
3126	75c. Loja	4·00	2·50
3127	75c. Galapagos	4·00	2·50
3128	75c. Imbabura	4·00	2·50
3129	75c. Chimborazo (As No. 3088)	4·00	2·50
3130	75c. Napo (As No. 3089)	4·00	2·50
3131	$1 Azuay	5·75	3·75
3132	$1 Zamora	5·75	3·75
3133	$1 Pastaza	5·75	3·75
3134	$1 Orellana	5·75	3·75
3135	$1 Morona Santiago (As No. 3090)	5·75	3·75
3136	$1 Sucumbios (As No. 3091)	5·75	3·75

1022 Athletes

2009. 50th Anniv of Olympic Committee. Multicoloured.

3137	25c. Type **1022**	2·00	1·30
3138	25c. Athletes and Olympic flame (vert\)	2·00	1·30

1023 Symbols of Technology

2009. Ecuadorian Exports.

3139	**1023**	50c. multicoloured	2·75	1·70

1024 University Buildiing

2009. 150th Anniv of Universidad Nacional de Loja.

3140	**1024**	$2 multicoloured	11·00	7·25

1025 Juan Pio Montufar (key figure in the independence movement)

2009. Bicentenary of Independence (3rd issue). Personalities. Multicoloured.

3141	75c. Type **1025**	4·00	2·00
3142	75c. Jose Mejia Lequerica (journalist)	4·00	2·50
3143	75c. Eugenio Espejo (Francisco Javier Eugenio de Santa Cruz y Espejo) (medical pioneer, writer and lawyer of mestizo origin)	4·00	2·50
3144	75c. Manuela Canizares (key figure in the independence movement)	4·00	2·50
3145	75c. Emblem	4·00	2·50

1026 Charles Darwin, Volcano, Flora and Fauna of Galapagos (image scaled to 54% of original size)

2009. 50th Anniv of Galapagos National Park. Multicoloured.

3146	$5 Type **1026**	21·00	13·00
MS3147	205×165 mm. $1 *Phoenicopterus ruber* (American flamingo); $1 *Ardea herodias* (great blue heron); $1 *Calandrinia galapagosa*; $1 *Conolophus marthae* (pink land iguana); $1 *Geochelone nigra abingdoni* (Lonesome George (Solitario Jorge) last known Pinta Island tortoise) (37×37 mm circular); $1 *Sula granti* (Nazca booby); $1 *Rhincodon typus* (whale shark); $1 *Zalophus wollebaeki* (Galapagos sea lion); $1 *Phalacrocorax harrisi* (flightless cormorant)	45·00	45·00

1027 Children and Baubles

2009. Christmas

3148	**1027**	$1 multicoloured	2·40	1·40

1028 Pelota

2009. America

3149	$1 Type **1028**	2·40	1·40
3150	$1 Go-cart	2·40	1·40

1029 Sta. Elena

2010. Regions. Multicoloured.

3151	25c. Type **1029**	10	10
3152	50c. Bolivar	70	35
3153	$1.25 Tungurahua	1·90	95
3154	$2 Azuay	2·75	1·40

1030 Pilot

2010. First Ecuadorian Unmanned Dirigible

MS3155	$1 Type **1030**; $1 Dirigible over coast; $1 Dirigible over mountains; $3 Dirigible (149×43 mm)	8·50	8·50

EXPRESS LETTER STAMPS

1928. Oblong Tobacco Tax stamp surch "CORREOS EXPRESO" and new value.

E457	2c. on 2c. blue	6·00	7·00
E458	5c. on 2c. blue	5·50	7·00
E459	10c. on 2c. blue	5·50	5·25
E460	20c. on 2c. blue	7·75	7·00
E461	50c. on 2c. blue	9·25	7·00

1945. Surch EXPRESO 20 Ctvs.

E742	**194**	20c. on 5c. green	45	30

LATE FEE STAMP

1945. Surch U. H. 10 Ctvs.

L742	10c. on 5c. green	20	20

OFFICIAL STAMPS

1886. Stamps of 1881 optd OFICIAL.

O20	**5**	1c. brown	1·50	1·50
O21	**5**	2c. red	1·90	1·90
O22	**5**	5c. blue	4·25	5·00
O23	**5**	10c. orange	3·25	1·90
O24	**5**	20c. violet	3·25	3·00
O25	**5**	50c. green	9·00	6·75

1887. Stamps of 1887 optd OFICIAL.

O30	**13**	1c. green	2·00	1·50
O31	**13**	2c. red	2·00	1·70
O32	**13**	5c. blue	3·25	1·50
O33	**13**	80c. green	10·50	5·75

1892. Stamps of 1892 optd FRANQUEO OFICIAL.

O42	**15**	1c. blue	35	30
O43	**15**	2c. blue	35	30
O44	**15**	5c. blue	35	30
O45	**15**	10c. blue	35	40
O46	**15**	20c. blue	35	40
O47	**15**	50c. blue	35	60
O48	**15**	1s. blue	55	70

1894. Stamps of 1894 (dated "1894") optd FRANQUEO OFICIAL.

O65	**20**	1c. grey	35	55
O66	**20**	2c. grey	35	30
O67	**20**	5c. grey	35	30
O68	**20**	10c. grey	25	55
O69	**20**	20c. grey	40	55
O70	**20**	50c. grey	2·00	1·90
O71	**20**	1s. grey	3·00	2·75

This series was re-issued in 1897 optd "1897–1898".

1895. Postal Fiscals as Type F 1 but dated "1891–1892", optd OFICIAL 1894 y 1895.

O72	**F1**	1c. grey	13·00	4·00
O73	**F1**	2c. red	13·50	4·00

1895. Stamps of 1895 (dated "1895") optd FRANQUEO OFICIAL.

O82	**20**	1c. grey	2·75	2·75
O83	**20**	2c. grey	3·75	3·75
O84	**20**	5c. grey	75	75
O85	**20**	10c. grey	4·00	3·75
O86	**20**	20c. grey	5·25	4·75
O87	**20**	50c. grey	40·00	38·00
O88	**20**	1s. grey	1·80	1·70

This series was re-issued in 1897 optd "1897–1898".

1896. Stamps of 1896 optd FRANQUEO OFICIAL in oval.

O97A	**22**	1c. bistre	65	60
O98A	**22**	2c. bistre	65	60
O99A	**22**	5c. bistre	65	60
O100A	**22**	10c. bistre	65	60
O101A	**22**	20c. bistre	65	60
O102A	**22**	50c. bistre	65	60
O103A	**22**	1s. bistre	1·70	1·60
O104A	**22**	5s. bistre	3·25	3·25

F10

O 245 Government Building, Quito

1898. Fiscal stamps as Type F 10, surch CORREOS OFICIAL and value in frame.

O181	**F10**	5c. on 50c. purple	35	35
O184	**F10**	10c. on 20s. orange	70	70
O185	**F10**	20c. on 50c. purple	2·75	2·50
O187	**F10**	20c. on 50s. green	2·75	2·50

1899. Stamps as 1899 optd OFICIAL.

O201	2c. black and orange	55	1·20
O202	10c. black and orange	55	1·20
O203	20c. black and orange	35	1·80
O204	50c. black and orange	35	2·30

1913. Stamps of 1911 (except No. O396) optd OFICIAL.

O374	**90**	1c. black and red	2·75	45
O387	**90**	1c. orange	65	65
O388	**91**	2c. black and blue	1·10	1·10
O424	**91**	2c. green	35	30
O368	**92**	3c. black and orange	1·80	1·70
O390	**92**	3c. black	1·80	1·70
O437	**98**	4c. black and red	35	30
O369	**93**	5c. black and red	3·50	3·50
O393	**93**	5c. violet	1·30	55
O370	**94**	10c. black and blue	3·50	3·50
O395	**94**	10c. blue	65	65
O396	-	20c. blk & grn (No. 328)	3·50	1·30
O429	**95**	1s. black and green	4·50	4·25

1920. Stamps of 1920 (Nos. 381/400) optd OFICIAL.

O401	**108**	1c. green	90	85
O402	-	2c. red	65	65
O403	-	3c. bistre	90	85
O404	-	4c. green	1·30	1·30
O405	-	5c. blue	1·30	1·30
O406	-	6c. orange	1·80	85
O407	-	7c. brown	1·30	1·30
O408	-	8c. green	1·80	1·70
O409	-	9c. red	2·20	2·10
O410	**109**	10c. blue	1·30	1·30
O411	-	15c. black	7·25	7·00
O412	-	20c. purple	9·25	9·00
O413	-	30c. violet	11·00	10·50
O414	-	40c. sepia	13·00	9·00
O415	-	50c. green	9·25	10·50
O416	-	60c. blue	11·00	13·00
O417	-	70c. grey	11·00	9·00
O418	-	80c. yellow	13·00	13·00
O419	-	90c. green	13·00	13·00
O420	-	1s. blue	28·00	27·00

1924. Fiscal stamps of 1919 optd OFICIAL.

O421	**103**	1c. blue	1·40	1·30
O422	**103**	2c. green	8·25	8·00

1924. No. O204 optd Acuerdo No 4.228.

O430	50c. black and orange	1·70	1·60

1925. Stamps of 1925 optd OFICIAL.

O457	**90**	1c. blue	65	65
O439	**93**	5c. red	55	55
O440	**94**	10c. green	35	30

1928. Stamp of 1927 optd OFICIAL.

O463	**123**	20c. purple	7·25	1·70

1929. Official Air stamps. Air stamps of 1929 optd OFICIAL.

O466	**130**	2c. black	75	75
O467	**130**	5c. red	75	75
O468	**130**	10c. brown	75	75
O469	**130**	20c. purple	75	75
O470	**130**	50c. green	2·40	2·30
O474	**130**	50c. brown	2·20	2·10
O471	**130**	1s. blue	2·40	2·30
O475	**130**	1s. red	2·75	2·75
O472	**130**	5s. yellow	11·00	9·00
O476	**130**	5s. olive	6·50	6·50
O473	**130**	10s. red	£130	90·00
O477	**130**	10s. black	13·00	13·00

1936. Stamps of 1936 (Nos. 520/4) optd OFICIAL.

O525	5c. olive	35	30
O526	10c. brown	35	30
O527	20c. purple	55	55
O528	1s. red	90	85
O529	2s. blue	1·30	1·30

1937. Stamps of 1937 optd OFICIAL.

O562	**171**	2c. green (postage)	10	10
O563	-	5c. red	10	10
O564	-	10c. blue	10	10
O565	-	20c. red	20	20
O566	-	1s. olive	35	30
O567	**172**	10c. brown (air)	35	30
O568	**172**	20c. olive	35	30
O569	**172**	70c. brown	45	30
O570	**172**	1s. slate	55	30
O571	**172**	2s. violet	55	55

1941. Air stamp of 1939 optd OFICIAL.

O638	**184**	5s. green	1·30	65

1946. Oblong Tobacco Tax stamp optd CORRESPONDENCIA OFICIAL. Roul.

O803	1c. red	1·30	1·30

1947

O804	**O245**	30c. blue	45	30
O805	**O245**	30c. brown	45	30
O806	**O245**	30c. violet	45	30

1964. Air. Nos. 1269/71 optd Oficial.

O1272	**342**	50c. multicoloured	1·30	1·30
O1273	-	80c. red, blue & yellow	1·30	1·30
O1274	-	1s.30 multicoloured	1·30	1·30

1964. No. 1272 optd oficial on each stamp.

O1275	**344**	80c. green and lake	4·50	4·25

The "OEA" overprint is across four stamps; the "oficial" overprint is on each stamp. The unused price is for a block of four.

POSTAGE DUE STAMPS

D32

1896

D105A	**D32**	1c. green	3·75	4·00
D106A	**D32**	2c. green	3·75	4·00
D107A	**D32**	5c. green	3·75	4·00
D108A	**D32**	10c. green	3·50	8·50
D109A	**D32**	20c. green	3·75	8·75
D110A	**D32**	50c. green	3·75	8·75
D111A	**D32**	100c. green	3·75	9·25

D131

1929

D466	**D131**	5c. blue	10	10
D467	**D131**	10c. yellow	20	20
D468	**D131**	20c. red	45	45

D335

1958

D1128	**D335**	10c. violet	35	30
D1129	**D335**	50c. green	35	30
D1130	**D335**	1s. brown	45	30
D1131	**D335**	2s. red	55	30

APPENDIX

The following stamps have either been listed in excess of postal needs or have not been available to the public in reasonable quantities at face value. Such stamps may later be given full listing if there is evidence of regular postal use.

1966

Cent of I.T.U. Postage 10, 10, 80c.; Air 1s.50, 3, 4s.
Space Achievements. Postage 10c., 1s.; Air 1s.30, 2s., 2s.50, 3s.50.
Dante and Galileo. Postage 10, 80c.; Air 2, 3s.
Pope Paul VI. Postage 10c.; Air 1s.30, 3s.50.
Famous Persons. Postage 10c., 1s.; Air 1s.50, 2s.50, 4s.
Olympic Games. Postage 10, 10, 80c.; Air 1s.30, 3s., 3s.50.
Winter Olympics. Postage 10c., 1s.; Air 1s.50, 2s., 2s.50, 4s.
Franco-American Space Research. Postage 10c.; Air 1s.50, 4s.
Italian Space Research. Postage 10c.; Air 1s.30, 3s.50.
Exploration of the Moon's Surface. Postage 10, 80c., 1s.; Air 2s., 2s.50, 3s.

1967

Olympic Games, Mexico. Postage 10c., 1s.; Air 1s.30, 2s., 2s.50, 3s.50.
Olympic Games, Mexico. Postage 10, 10, 80c.; Air 1s.50, 3, 4s.
Eucharistic Conference. Postage 10, 60, 80c., 1s.; Air 1s.50, 2s.
Paintings of the Madonna. Postage 10, 40, 50c.; Air 1s.30, 2s.50, 3s.
Famous Paintings. Postage 10c., 1s.; Air 1s.50, 2s., 2s.50, 4s.
50th Birth Anniv of J. F. Kennedy. Postage 10, 10, 80c.; Air 1s.30, 3s., 3s.50.
Christmas Postage 10, 10, 40, 50, 60c.; Air 2s.50.

1968

Religious Paintings and Sculptures. Postage 10, 80c., 1s.; Air 1s.30, 1s.50, 2s.
COTAL Tourist Organization Congress. Postage 20, 30, 40, 50, 60, 80c., 1s.; Air 1s.30, 1s.50, 2s.

1969

Visit of Pope Paul VI to Latin America. Postage 40, 40c.; Air 1s.30.
39th Int Eucharistic Congress, Bogota. Postage 1s.; Air 2s.
Paintings of the Virgin Mary. Postage 40, 60c., 1s.; Air 1s.30, 2s.

Pt. 1, Pt. 19

EGYPT

Formerly a kingdom of N.E. Africa. Turkish till 1914, when it became a British Protectorate. Independent from 1922. A republic from 1953.

In 1958 the United Arab Republic was formed, comprising Egypt and Syria, but separate stamps continued to be issued for each territory as they have different currencies. In 1961 Syria became an independent Arab republic and left the U.A.R. but the title was retained by Egypt until a new federation was formed with Libya and Syria in 1971, when the country's name was changed to Arab Republic of Egypt.

1866. 40 paras = 1 piastre.
1888. 1000 milliemes = 1 piastre. 100 piastres = £1 Egyptian.

1

1866. Designs as T 1. Imperf or perf.

1	**1**	5pa. grey	55·00	35·00
2	**1**	10pa. brown	65·00	35·00
3	**1**	20pa. blue	80·00	38·00
4	**1**	1pi. purple	70·00	5·00
5	**1**	2pi. yellow	£100	50·00
6	**1**	5pi. pink	£300	£190
7	**1**	10pi. grey	£350	£300

4

1867

11	**4**	5pa. yellow	40·00	8·00
12b	**4**	10pa. violet	65·00	9·00
13b	**4**	20pa. green	£130	12·00
14	**4**	1pi. red	25·00	1·00
15	**4**	2pi. blue	£140	17·00
16	**4**	5pi. brown	£300	£180

On the piastre values the letters "P" and "E" appear on the upper corners.

7

1872

28	**7**	5pa. brown	8·00	5·00
29	**7**	10pa. mauve	6·00	3·00
37d	**7**	20pa. blue	10·00	2·50
38	**7**	1pi. red	11·00	65
39c	**7**	2pi. yellow	5·50	6·00
40	**7**	2½pi. violet	8·50	6·00
41	**7**	5pi. green	60·00	20·00

1875. As T 7, but "PARA" inscr at left-hand side and figure "5"s inverted.

35	5pa. brown	20·00	3·75

1879. Surch in English and Arabic.

42	**7**	5pa on 2½pi. violet	6·00	6·00
43	**7**	10pa. on 2½pi. violet	11·00	10·00

10

1879. Various frames.

44	**10**	5pa. brown	4·00	1·25
45	**10**	10pa. lilac	55·00	3·00
50	**10**	10pa. purple	55·00	9·50
51	**10**	10pa. grey	17·00	1·75
52	**10**	10pa. green	2·00	1·75
46	**10**	20pa. blue	65·00	1·75
53a	**10**	20pa. red	21·00	50
47	**10**	1pi. pink	38·00	20
54b	**10**	1pi. blue	5·50	20
55b	**10**	2pi. brown	12·00	10
55ba	**10**	2pi. orange	23·00	1·00
49a	**10**	5pi. green	65·00	11·00
56a	**10**	5pi. grey	15·00	50

1884. Surch 20 PARAS in English and Arabic.

57	20pa. on 5pi. green	7·00	1·25

18

1888. Various frames.

58	**18**	1m. brown	3·25	10
59c	**18**	2m. green	1·00	10
60	**18**	3m. purple	6·00	2·00
61c	**18**	3m. yellow	2·75	10
62	**18**	4m. red	4·50	10
63b	**18**	5m. red	5·00	10
64	**18**	10pi. mauve	15·00	80

29 Nile Feluccas **35** Archway of Ptolemy III, Karnak **41** Statue of Rameses II

42 Statue of Rameses II (different inscription)

1914

73	**29**	1m. brown	1·25	40
74	-	2m. green	3·75	20
86	-	2m. red	5·00	2·00
75	-	3m. orange	3·50	35
76	-	4m. red	4·00	65
88	-	4m. green	7·00	6·50
77	-	5m. red	4·00	10
90	-	5m. pink	10·00	20
78	-	10m. blue	6·50	10
92	-	10m. lake	2·50	40
93	**41**	15m. blue	8·50	15
94	**42**	15m. blue	35·00	4·25
79	**35**	20m. olive	6·50	30
96	-	50m. purple	10·00	1·25
81	-	100m. grey	22·00	75
82	-	200m. purple	30·00	3·50

DESIGNS—As Type **29**: 2m. Cleopatra; 3m. Ras-el-Tin Palace, Alexandria; 4m. Pyramids, Giza; 5m. Sphinx; 10m. Colossi of Amenophis III at Thebes. As Type **35**: 50m. Citadel, Cairo; 100m. Rock Temple, Abu Simbel; 200m. Aswan Dam.

1915. Surch 2 Milliemes in English and Arabic.

83	**29**	2m. on 3m. orge (No. 75)	60	2·25

43 "The Kingdom of Egypt, 15 March, 1922"

1922. Stamps of 1914 optd with T 43.

98		1m. brown	1·30	1·10
99	-	2m. red	1·10	65
100	-	3m. orange	1·30	1·10
101	-	4m. green	80	1·00
102	-	5m. pink	2·75	20
103	-	10m. lake	2·75	20
104	**41**	15m. blue	5·25	1·10
105	**42**	15m. blue	4·50	1·10
106	**35**	20m. olive	5·50	65
107	-	50m. purple	6·75	1·10
108	-	100m. grey	27·00	1·30
110	-	200m. purple	25·00	1·60

44 King Fuad I

1923

111	**44**	1m. orange	20	15
112	**44**	2m. black	1·10	20
113	**44**	3m. brown	1·00	65
114	**44**	4m. green	65	25
115	**44**	5m. brown	45	15
116	**44**	10m. pink	2·00	20
117	**44**	15m. blue	3·00	20
118	**44**	20m. green	5·50	20
119	**44**	50m. green	10·00	20
120	**44**	100m. purple	25·00	65
121	**44**	200m. mauve	45·00	2·00
122	-	£E1 violet and blue	£225	27·00

The 20m. to £E1 values are larger (22½×28 mm). The £E1 shows the King in military uniform.

46 Thoth writing name of King Fuad

1925. Int Geographical Congress, Cairo.

123	**46**	5m. brown	11·00	6·75
124	**46**	10m. red	22·00	13·50
125	**46**	15m. blue	22·00	16·00

47 Ploughing with Oxen

1926. 12th Agricultural Exhibition, Cairo.

126	**47**	5m. brown	2·20	2·20
127	**47**	10m. red	1·70	2·20
128	**47**	15m. blue	1·70	3·25
129	**47**	50m. green	14·50	10·00
130	**47**	100m. purple	22·00	17·00
131	**47**	200m. violet	36·00	42·00

49 de Havilland D.H.34 Biplane over Nile

1926. Air.

132	**49**	27m. violet	22·00	27·00
133	**49**	27m. brown	6·75	2·20

50 King Fuad

1926. King's 58th Birthday.

134	**50**	50p. purple	£130	29·00

1926. Surch.

135	**47**	5m. on 50m. green	2·20	2·20
136	**47**	10m. on 100m. purple	2·20	2·20
137	**47**	15m. on 200m. violet	2·20	2·20

52 Ancient Egyptian Ship, Temple of Deir-el-Bahari

1926. International Navigation Congress.

138	**52**	5m. black and brown	2·75	2·20
139	**52**	10m. black and red	3·50	3·25
140	**52**	15m. black and blue	3·50	3·25

1926. Inauguration of Port Fuad. Optd PORT FOUAD.

141		5m. black and brown	£325	£200
142		10m. black and red	£325	£200
143		15m. black and blue	£325	£200
144	**50**	50p. purple	£1700	£1300

55

1927. Int Cotton Congress, Cairo.

145	**55**	5m. green and brown	1·50	1·10
146	**55**	10m. green and red	2·50	1·70
147	**55**	15m. green and blue	2·50	1·70

56

57

58

1927

148	**56**	1m. orange	25	20
149	**56**	2m. black	25	20
150	**56**	3m. brown	25	55
151	**56**	3m. green	45	20
153	**56**	4m. green	1·30	1·10
154	**56**	4m. brown	1·20	55
156	**56**	5m. brown	45	20
157	**56**	10m. red	1·40	20
158	**56**	10m. violet	3·75	20
159	**56**	13m. red	1·40	20
160a	**56**	15m. blue	1·60	20
161	**56**	15m. purple	4·00	20
162	**56**	20m. blue	7·50	20
163a	**57**	20m. olive	3·25	20
164	**57**	20m. blue	9·25	20
165	**57**	40m. brown	4·25	20
166a	**57**	50m. blue	3·00	20
167a	**57**	100m. purple	10·50	35
168a	**57**	200m. mauve	9·25	1·20
171	**58**	500m. blue and brown	£110	8·75
172	-	£E1 brown and green	£110	7·75

DESIGN—VERT: As Type **58**: £E1, King Fuad I.

See also Nos. 233/9.

60 Amenhotep

1927. Statistical Congress, Cairo.

173	**60**	5m. brown	1·30	1·50
174	**60**	10m. red	1·70	1·50
175	**60**	15m. blue	2·40	1·50

61 Imhotep

1928. Medical Congress, Cairo.

176	**61**	5m. brown	1·00	65
177	-	10m. red	1·20	65

DESIGN: 10m. Mohammed Ali Pasha.

63 King Farouk when Crown Prince

1929. Prince's 9th Birthday.

178	**63**	5m. grey and purple	2·20	1·90
179	**63**	10m. grey and red	2·20	1·90
180	**63**	15m. grey and blue	2·20	1·90
181	**63**	20m. grey and turquoise	£130	£110

64 Ancient Agriculture

1931. Agricultural and Industrial Exhibition, Cairo.

182	**64**	5m. brown	80	1·10
183	**64**	10m. red	1·70	2·00
184	**64**	15m. blue	2·20	2·00

49 de Havilland D.H.34 Biplane over Nile

1931. Air. Surch GRAF ZEPPELIN AVRIL 1931 and value in English and Arabic.

185	**49**	50m. on 27m. brown	75·00	75·00
186	**49**	100m. on 27m. brown	75·00	85·00

1932. Surch in English and Arabic.

187	**50**	50m. on 50p. purple	9·25	1·60
188	-	100m. on £E1 violet and blue (No. 122)	£250	£275

67 Locomotive No. 1, 1852

1933. International Railway Congress, Cairo.

189	**67**	5m. black and brown	11·00	7·25
190	-	13m. black and red	22·00	12·00
191	-	15m. black and violet	22·00	12·00
192	-	20m. black and blue	22·00	12·00

DESIGNS: 13m. Locomotive No. 41, 1859; 15m. Locomotive No. 68, 1862; 20m. Locomotive No. 787, 1932.

68 Handley Page H.P.42 over Pyramids

1933. Air.

193	**68**	1m. black and orange	25	65
194	**68**	2m. black and grey	95	2·00
195	**68**	2m. black and orange	3·75	3·25
196	**68**	3m. black and brown	1·00	45
197	**68**	4m. black and green	1·50	1·30
198	**68**	5m. black and brown	1·40	20
199	**68**	6m. black and green	2·10	1·80
200	**68**	7m. black and blue	1·90	1·50
201	**68**	8m. black and violet	1·00	35
202	**68**	9m. black and red	2·30	2·00
203	**68**	10m. brown and violet	80	1·10
204	**68**	20m. brown and green	95	20
205	**68**	30m. brown and blue	2·50	20
206	**68**	40m. brown and red	16·00	90
207	**68**	50m. brown and orange	16·00	20
208	**68**	60m. brown and grey	8·75	1·60
209	**68**	70m. green and blue	4·00	1·50
210	**68**	80m. green and sepia	4·00	1·60
211	**68**	90m. green and orange	5·75	1·60
212	**68**	100m. green and violet	11·00	90
213	**68**	200m. green and red	14·00	2·00

See also Nos. 285/8.

69 Armstrong-Whitworth A.W. 15 Atlanta of Imperial Airways

1933. Int Aviation Congress. Inscr as in T 69.

214	**69**	5m. brown	5·75	3·50
215	**69**	10m. violet	20·00	13·50
216	-	13m. red	23·00	19·00
217	-	15m. purple	23·00	17·00
218	-	20m. blue	29·00	20·00

DESIGNS: 13, 15m. Dornier Do-X flying boat; 20m. Airship "Graf Zeppelin".

72 Khedive Ismail Pasha

73

1934. 10th U.P.U. Congress, Cairo.

219	**72**	1m. orange	60	1·10
220	**72**	2m. black	60	1·10
221	**72**	3m. brown	70	1·20
222	**72**	4m. green	1·30	35
223	**72**	5m. brown	1·40	20
224	**72**	10m. violet	2·50	35
225	**72**	13m. red	4·25	2·20
226	**72**	15m. purple	4·25	1·80
227	**72**	20m. blue	3·00	45
228	**72**	50m. blue	9·25	65
229	**72**	100m. green	21·00	1·30
230	**72**	200m. violet	75·00	7·25
231	**73**	50p. brown	£275	£110
232	**73**	£El blue	£425	£180

1936. As T 56 but inscribed "POSTES".

233	**56**	1m. orange	35	90
234	**56**	2m. black	1·20	20
235	**56**	4m. green	1·40	20
236	**56**	5m. brown	1·20	55
237	**56**	10m. violet	2·30	35
238	**56**	15m. purple	4·75	35
239	**56**	20m. blue	4·75	30

75 Exhibition Entrance

1936. 15th Agricultural and Industrial Exn, Cairo.

240	**75**	5m. brown	1·90	1·50
241	-	10m. violet	2·50	1·70
242	-	13m. red	4·00	4·00
243	-	15m. purple	1·90	1·80
244	-	20m. blue	4·75	4·50

DESIGN—HORIZ: 10m., 13m. Palace of Agriculture; 15m., 20m. Palace of Industry.

77 Nahas Pasha and Treaty Delegates

1936. Anglo-Egyptian Treaty.

245	77	5m. brown	80	1·60
246	77	15m. purple	95	1·70
247	77	20m. blue	1·70	2·00

78 King Farouk

1937. Investiture of King Farouk.

248	78	1m. orange	10	10
249	78	2m. red	10	10
250	78	3m. brown	10	10
251	78	4m. green	10	10
252	78	5m. brown	35	10
253	78	6m. green	95	20
254	78	10m. violet	35	10
255	78	13m. red	35	35
256	78	15m. purple	35	10
257	78	20m. blue	70	35
258	78	20m. violet	1·20	20

79 Medal commemorating Abolition of Capitulations

1937. Abolition of Capitulations at the Montreux Conference.

259	79	5m. brown	70	55
260	79	15m. purple	1·50	1·10
261	79	20m. blue	1·60	1·30

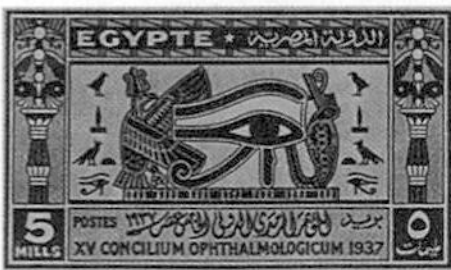

80 Nekhbet, Sacred Eye of Horus and Buto

1937. 15th Ophthalmological Congress, Cairo.

262	80	5m. brown	1·20	1·00
263	80	15m. purple	1·40	1·00
264	80	20m. blue	1·60	1·10

81 King Farouk and Queen Farida

1938. Royal Wedding.

265	81	5m. brown	6·50	5·50

82 Gathering Cotton

1938. 18th International Cotton Congress, Cairo.

266	82	5m. brown	1·70	1·20
267	82	15m. purple	3·00	2·20
268	82	20m. blue	2·30	1·80

83 Pyramids of Giza and Colossus of Thebes

1938. Int Telecommunications Conf, Cairo.

269	83	5m. brown	2·10	1·70
270	83	15m. purple	3·00	1·80
271	83	20m. blue	2·50	1·90

1938. King Farouk's 18th Birthday. Portrait similar to T 81 with inscr "11 FEVRIER 1938" at foot.

272		£E1 brown and green	£190	£200

84 Hydnocarpus

1938. Leprosy Research Congress.

273	84	5m. brown	2·10	1·70
274	84	15m. purple	2·30	1·70
275	84	20m. blue	2·30	1·70

85 King Farouk and Pyramids

86 King Farouk

87

1939

276a	85	30m. grey	60	20
277	85	30m. green	70	20
278	-	40m. brown	1·00	20
279	-	50m. blue	1·60	20
280	-	100m. purple	2·30	20
281	-	200m. violet	8·25	20
282	86	50p. brown and green	10·50	1·10
283	87	£E1 brown and blue	21·00	2·75

DESIGNS (As Type **85**): 40m. Mosque; 50m. Cairo Citadel; 100m. Aswan Dam; 200m. Fuad I University, Giza.

For similar issue with portrait looking to left, see 1947 issue.

88 Princess Ferial (18 months old)

1940. Child Welfare.

284	88	5m.+5m. red	1·20	55

1941. Air.

285	68	5m. brown	45	35
286	68	10m. violet	70	35
287a	68	25m. purple	80	35
288	68	30m. green	80	35

1943. 5th Birthday of Princess Ferial. Optd 1943 in English and Arabic.

289	88	5m.+5m. red	8·75	6·75

90 King Fuad I

1944. 8th Death Anniv of King Fuad.

290	90	10m. purple	35	20

91 King Farouk

1944

291	91	1m. brown	25	20
292	91	2m. red	25	20
293	91	3m. brown	35	45
294	91	4m. green	25	20
295	91	5m. brown	25	20
296	91	10m. violet	70	20
297	91	13m. red	10·50	4·50
298	91	15m. purple	1·30	20
299	91	17m. olive	1·20	20
300	91	20m. violet	1·40	20
301	91	22m. blue	1·40	20

92 King Farouk

1945. 25th Birthday of King Farouk.

302	92	10m. violet	35	30

93 Khedive Ismail Pasha

1945. 50th Death Anniv of Ismail Pasha.

303	93	10m. green	35	30

94 Flags of the Arab Union

1945. Arab Union.

304	94	10m. violet	35	20
305	94	22m. green	45	35

95 Flags of Egypt and Saudi Arabia

1946. Visit of King of Saudi Arabia.

306	95	10m. green	35	20

96 Reproduction of First Egyptian Stamp

1946. 80th Anniv of First Egyptian Postage Stamp.

307	96	1m.+1m. grey	25	20
308	-	10m.+10m. purple	35	20
309	-	17m.+17m. brown	45	40
310	-	22m.+22m. green	70	65
MS311		129×171 mm. Nos. 307/10. Perf	85·00	85·00
MS312		As last but imperf	85·00	85·00

DESIGNS: 10m. Khedive Ismail Pasha; 17m. King Fuad; 22m. King Farouk.

98 King Farouk, Egyptian Flag and Citadel

1946. Evacuation of Cairo Citadel.

313	98	10m. brown and green	35	35

1946. Air. Cairo Aviation Congress. Optd Le Caire 1946 and Arabic characters.

314	68	30m. green (No. 288)	45	35

100 King Farouk and Inshas Palace

1946. Arab League Congress. Portraits.

315	100	1m. green	60	20
316	-	2m. brown	60	20
317	-	3m. blue	60	20
318	-	4m. brown	60	20
319	-	5m. red	60	20
320	-	10m. grey	60	20
321	-	15m. violet	60	20

DESIGNS: 2m. Prince Abdullah of Yemen; 3m. President of Lebanon, Beshara al-Khoury; 4m. King Ibn Saud of Saudi Arabia; 5m. King Faisal II of Iraq; 10m. King Abdullah of Jordan; 15m. Pres of Syria, Shukri Bey al-Quwatli.

101 King Farouk, Delta Barrage and Douglas Dakota Transport

1947. Air.

322	101	2m. red	25	80
323	101	3m. brown	25	90
324	101	5m. red	25	20
325	101	7m. orange	45	20
326	101	8m. green	45	80
327	101	10m. violet	45	20
328	101	20m. blue	70	20
329	101	30m. purple	95	20
330	101	40m. red	1·40	35
331	101	50m. blue	1·70	45
332	101	100m. olive	3·00	65
333	101	200m. grey	6·00	2·75

102 Triad of Mycerinus

1947. International Exhibition of Fine Arts. Inscr "EXPOSITION INTERNATIONALE D'ART CONTEMPORIAN".

334	102	5m.+5m. grey	1·20	90
335	-	15m.+15m. blue	2·10	1·30
336	-	30m.+30m. red	2·50	2·00
337	-	50m.+50m. brown	3·00	2·50

DESIGNS—HORIZ: 15m. Temple of Rameses. VERT: 30m. Queen Nefertiti; 50m. Tutankhamun.

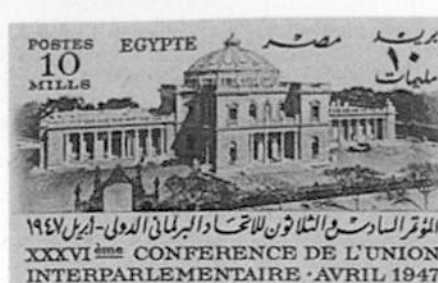

104 Egyptian Parliament Buildings

1947. 36th International Parliamentary Union Conference, Cairo.

338	**104**	10m. green	35	20

105 King Farouk hoisting Flag

1947. Withdrawal of British Troops from Nile Delta.

339	**105**	10m. purple and green	35	30

106 King Farouk and Sultan Hussein Mosque, Cairo **107** King Farouk

1947. Designs as 1939 issue but with portrait altered as T 106 and 107.

340	-	30m. olive	70	10
341	**106**	40m. brown	45	10
342	-	50m. blue	70	10
343	-	100m. purple	5·00	90
344	-	200m. violet	13·00	1·60
345	**107**	50p. brown and green	26·00	10·00
346	-	£El brown and blue	37·00	3·25

DESIGNS—AS Type **106**: 30m. Pyramids; 50m. Cairo Citadel; 100m. Aswan Dam; 200m. Fuad I University, Cairo. As T **107**: £El, King Farouk (different).

109 Cotton Plant

1948. International Cotton Congress.

347	**109**	10m. green	95	65

110 Egyptian Soldiers Entering Palestine

1948. Arrival of Egyptian Troops in Gaza.

348	**110**	10m. green	1·40	1·10

1948. Air. Air Mail Service to Athens and Rome. Surch S.A.I.D.E. 23-8-1948 and value in English and Arabic.

349	**101**	13m. on 100m. olive	80	80
350	**101**	22m. on 200m. grey	1·20	1·10

112 Ibrahim Pasha and Battle of Navarino, 1827

1948. Death Centenary of Ibrahim Pasha (statesman and General).

351	**112**	10m. green and red	45	40

113 Reclining Male Figure symbolising River Nile

114 Protection of Industry and Agriculture by Army

1949. 16th Agricultural and Industrial Exn, Cairo.

352	**113**	1m. green	30	20
353	**113**	10m. violet	55	20
354	**113**	17m. red	55	35
355	**113**	22m. blue	60	45
356	**114**	30m. sepia	95	65
MS357		Two sheets. (a) 172×105 mm. Nos. 352/5 in new colours (b) 108×123 mm. 10m. as Type **114** and No. 356 in new colours. Imperf	11·50	17·00

115 Mohammed Ali and Map

1949. Death Centenary of Mohammed Ali (statesman and General).

358	**115**	10m. green and brown	45	35

116 Globe

1949. 75th Anniv of U.P.U.

359	**116**	10m. red	1·00	55
360	**116**	22m. violet	1·20	1·20
361	**116**	30m. blue	1·40	1·30

117 Scales of Justice

1949. Abolition of Mixed Courts.

362	**117**	10m. green & dp green	35	20

118 Camels by Water-hole

1950. Inaug of Fuad I Desert Institute.

363	**118**	10m. brown and violet	1·00	1·00

119 King Fuad University

1950. 25th Anniv of Fuad I University.

364	**119**	22m. purple and green	1·00	1·00

120 Khedive Ismail and Globe

1950. 75th Anniv of Royal Egyptian Geographical Society.

365	**120**	30m. green and purple	1·20	1·10

121 Girl and Cotton

1951. International Cotton Congress, Cairo.

366	**121**	10m. green	45	40

122 King Farouk and Queen Narriman

1951. Royal Wedding.

367	**122**	10m. brown and green	2·00	1·90
MS368		129×112 mm. No. 367	15·00	25·00

123 Triumphal Arch

1951. 1st Mediterranean Games, Alexandria.

369	**123**	10m. brown	1·40	1·90
370	-	22m. green	1·40	1·90
371	-	30m. blue and green	1·40	1·90
MS372		189×117 mm. Nos. 369/71	14·00	18·00

DESIGNS—VERT: 22m. Badge of Alexandria and map of Mediterranean. HORIZ: 30m. King Farouk and waves.

ملك مصر والسودان
١٦ أكتوبر سنة ١٩٥١

124 "King of Egypt and the Sudan 16th October 1951"

1952. Optd as T 124 (different sizes).

373	**91**	1m. brown (postage)	95	1·10
374	**91**	2m. red	25	20
375	**78**	3m. brown	25	1·90
376	**91**	4m. green	25	20
377	**78**	6m. green	1·40	1·90
378	**91**	10m. violet	45	10
379	**91**	13m. red	1·60	1·90
380	**91**	15m. purple	3·00	2·00
381	**91**	17m. green	2·00	35
382	**91**	20m. violet	1·60	35
383	**91**	22m. blue	3·50	3·25
384	-	30m. green (No. 340)	2·30	1·10
386	**106**	40m. brown	80	20
387	-	50m. blue (No. 342)	1·90	20
388	-	100m. purple (No. 343)	3·00	55
389	-	200m. violet (No. 344)	15·00	2·50
390	**107**	50p. brown and green	20·00	8·25
391	-	£El brn & bl (No. 346)	41·00	9·50
392	**101**	2m. red (air)	25	20
393	**101**	3m. brown	1·30	1·20
394	**101**	5m. red	45	40
395	**101**	7m. brown	60	35
396	**101**	8m. green	2·00	1·70
397	**101**	10m. violet	1·40	1·60
398	**101**	20m. blue	3·50	2·20
399	**101**	30m. purple	1·50	1·50
400	**101**	40m. red	3·00	2·50
401	**101**	50m. blue	3·50	3·25
402	**101**	100m. green	5·25	4·50
403	**101**	200m. grey	11·00	8·25

125 "Egypt"

1952. Abrogation of Anglo-Egyptian Treaty of 1936. Inscr "16 Oct. 1951".

404	**125**	10m. green	70	65
405	-	22m. green and purple	1·20	1·10
406	-	30m. green and brown	1·30	1·20
MS407		134×114 mm. Nos. 404/6	14·00	16·00

DESIGNS: 22m. King Farouk and map of Nile Valley; 30m. King Farouk and flag.

126 Egyptian Flag

1952. Birth of Crown Prince Ahmed Fuad.

408	**126**	10m. green, yellow & blue	45	40
MS409		111×138 mm. No. 408	5·75	9·50

127 "Freedom, Hope and Peace"

1952. Revolution of 23 July 1952. Inscr "23 JUILLET 1952".

410	**127**	4m. orange and green	35	35
411	-	10m. brown and green	35	1·20
412	-	17m. brown and green	1·20	1·30
413	-	22m. green and brown	1·90	1·00

DESIGNS—HORIZ: 10m. Allegory of Egyptian freedom. VERT: 17m. Map of Nile Valley, and Egyptian citizens; 22m. Rejoicing crowd and Egyptian flag.

129 "Agriculture" **130** "Defence" **131** Sultan Hussein Mosque, Cairo

132 Queen Nefertiti

133 Douglas Dakota Transport over Delta Barrage

1953. Inscr "DEFENCE" (A) or "DEFENSE" (B).

414	**129**	1m. brown (postage)	60	20
415	**129**	2m. purple	35	20
416	**129**	3m. blue	60	55
417	**129**	4m. green	35	35
418	**130**	10m. brown (A)	35	55
419	**130**	10m. brown (B)	80	20
420	**130**	15m. grey (B)	60	35
421	**130**	17m. blue (B)	80	35
422	**130**	20m. violet (B)	35	35
423	**131**	30m. green	35	20
424	**131**	32m. blue	95	35
425	**131**	35m. violet	1·20	35
426	**131**	37m. brown	1·90	65
427	**131**	40m. brown	95	35
428	**131**	50m. purple	2·30	20
429	**132**	100m. brown	2·20	35
430	**132**	200m. blue	5·75	80
431	**132**	500m. violet	13·00	1·80
432	**132**	£El red and green	23·00	3·25
433	**133**	5m. brown (air)	60	90
434	**133**	15m. green	1·50	1·20

See also No. 619.

1953. Various issues of King Farouk with portrait obliterated by three horiz bars. (i) Stamps of 1937.

435	**78**	1m. orange	23·00	35·00
436	**78**	3m. brown	70	90
437	**78**	6m. green	35	35

(ii) Stamps of 1944.

438	**91**	1m. brown	35	35
439	**91**	2m. red	35	20
440	**91**	3m. brown	80	90
441	**91**	4m. green	35	20
442	**91**	10m. violet	35	20
443	**91**	13m. red	1·30	1·30
444	**91**	15m. purple	80	20
445	**91**	17m. green	80	35
446	**91**	20m. violet	95	20
447	**91**	22m. blue	1·30	35

(iii) Stamps of 1947.

448	-	30m. green (No. 340)	80	35
449	**106**	40m. brown	60·00	85·00
450	-	50m. blue (No. 342)	1·40	35
451	-	100m. pur (No. 343)	2·00	80
452	-	200m. violet (No. 344)	8·25	1·70
453	**107**	50p. brown and green	19·00	7·25
454	-	£El brn & bl (No. 346)	22·00	4·75

(iv) Air stamps of 1947.

455	**101**	2m. red	3·00	3·00
456	**101**	3m. brown	1·20	2·20
457	**101**	5m. red	1·30	1·90
458	**101**	7m. brown	30	35
459	**101**	8m. green	1·70	2·75
460	**101**	10m. violet	49·00	55·00
461	**101**	20m. blue	2·00	55
462	**101**	30m. purple	3·00	1·30
463	**101**	40m. red	3·00	1·50
464	**101**	50m. blue	5·00	1·70
465	**101**	100m. green	7·50	4·00
466	**101**	200m. grey	80·00	85·00

(v) Stamps of 1952 with "Egypt-Sudan" opt T 124.

467	**91**	1m. brown (postage)	7·75	11·50
468	**91**	2m. red	1·20	2·75
469	**78**	3m. brown	8·75	11·50
470	**91**	4m. green	9·50	11·50
471	**78**	6m. green	27·00	13·50
472	**91**	10m. violet	5·00	6·75
473	**91**	13m. red	1·20	2·20
474	**91**	15m. purple	19·00	23·00
475	**91**	17m. green	19·00	23·00
476	**91**	20m. violet	21·00	23·00
477	**91**	22m. blue	65·00	75·00
477a	-	30m. green (No. 384)	26·00	26·00
478	**106**	40m. brown	3·00	1·30
479	-	200m. violet (No. 389)	6·50	5·00
480	**101**	2m. red (air)	80	45
481	**101**	3m. brown	1·60	1·30
482	**101**	5m. red	35	35
483	**101**	7m. brown	17·00	18·00
484	**101**	8m. green	95	2·20
485	**101**	10m. violet	80	1·70
486	**101**	20m. blue	65·00	80·00
487	**101**	30m. purple	1·70	1·70
488	**101**	40m. red	65·00	80·00
489	**101**	50m. blue	2·75	1·30
490	**101**	100m. green	4·25	4·00
491	**101**	200m. grey	8·25	9·00

135

1953. Electronics Exhibition, Cairo.

492	**135**	10m. blue	80	55

136 "Young Egypt"

1954. 1st Anniv of Republic.

493	**136**	10m. brown	60	35
494	-	30m. blue	80	60

DESIGN: 30m. Marching crowd, Egyptian flag and eagle.

137 "Agriculture"

1954

495	**137**	1m. brown	35	20
496	**137**	2m. purple	35	20
497	**137**	3m. blue	35	35
498	**137**	4m. green	1·40	1·20
499	**137**	5m. red	35	35

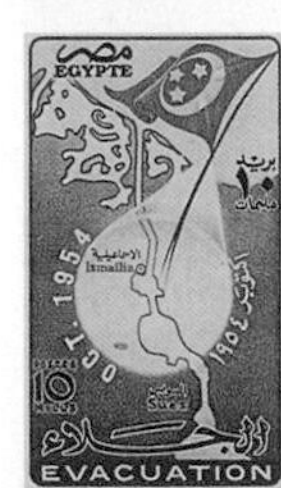

138 Flag and Map showing Area watered by Canal

1954. Evacuation of British Troops from Suez Canal. Inscr "EVACUATION".

500	**138**	10m. purple and green	60	35
501	-	35m. green and red	95	90

DESIGN: 35m. Egyptian army bugler, machine-gunner and map.

1955. Arab Postal Union.

502	**139**	5m. brown	60	35
503	**139**	10m. green	60	55
504	**139**	37m. violet	1·20	1·10

140 P. P. Harris and Rotary Emblem

1955. 50th Anniv of Rotary International.

505	**140**	10m. purple	1·60	45
506	-	35m. blue	2·00	90

DESIGN: 35m. Globe and Rotary emblem.

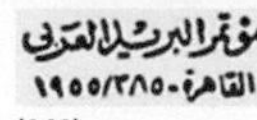

(141)

1955. 2nd Arab Postal Union Conference, Cairo. Optd with T 141.

507	**139**	5m. brown	1·30	1·20
508	**139**	10m. green	1·60	1·60
509	**139**	37m. violet	2·00	1·90

142 Scout Badge

1956. 2nd Arab Scout Jamboree, Aboukir (Alexandria). Inscr "2EME JAMBOREE ARABE", etc.

510	**142**	10m.+10m. green	80	65
511	-	20m.+10m. ultramarine	1·20	90
512	-	35m.+15m. blue	1·50	1·30
MS513		120×160 mm. Nos. 510/2	£1700	£1100
MS514		As last but imperf	£1700	£1100

DESIGNS: 20m. Sea Scout badge; 35m. Air Scout badge.

143 Globes and Laurel Branch

1956. Afro-Asian Festival, Cairo. Inscr "FESTIVAL ASIATICO-AFRICAIN".

515	**143**	10m. green and brown	45	35
516	-	35m. purple and yellow	1·20	80

DESIGN—VERT: 35m. Globe, lamp, dove and ear of corn.

144 Freighter and Map of Suez Canal

1956. Nationalisation of Suez Canal.

517	**144**	10m. blue and buff	70	65

145 Queen Nefertiti

1956. International Museum Week.

518	**145**	10m. green	1·40	1·30

146 Defence of Port Said

1956. "Port Said, Nov. 1956".

519	**146**	10m. purple	1·00	80

1957. Evacuation of British and French Troops from Port Said. Optd EVACUATION 22-12-56 in English and Arabic.

520		10m. purple	80	90

148 Locomotive No. 1, 1852, and Diesel Train

1957. Centenary of Egyptian Railways.

521	**148**	10m. purple and brown	1·40	2·20

149 Mother and Children

1957. Mothers' Day.

522	**149**	10m. red	80	80

150 Battle Scene

1957. 150th Anniv of Victory over British at Rosetta.

523	**150**	10m. blue	35	55

1957. Re-opening of Suez Canal. As T 144 but inscr "REOPENING 1957" in English and Arabic.

524		100m. blue and green	1·70	1·70

151 Al-Azhar University

1957. Millenary of Al-Azhar University, Cairo. Unissued stamps of 1942 as T 151 optd with the present Arabic year (1376).

525	**151**	10m. violet	60	55
526	**151**	15m. purple	95	80
527	**151**	20m. grey	1·40	1·20

152 Map of Gaza

1957. Re-occupation of Gaza Strip.

528	**152**	10m. blue	1·00	80

153 Motor Ambulance

1957. 50th Anniv of Public Aid Society.

529	**153**	10m.+5m. red	80	55

154 Shepheard's Hotel

1957. Re-opening of Shepheard's Hotel, Cairo.

530	**154**	10m. violet	80	55

156 Egyptian Parliament Buildings

1957. Opening of National Assembly.

531	**156**	10m. brown & yellow	80	55

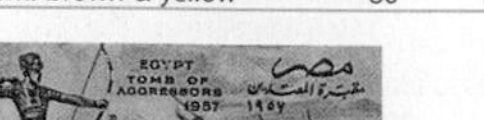

157 Avaris, 1580 B.C.

1957. 5th Anniv of 1952 Revolution.

532	**157**	10m. red	1·90	1·80
533	-	10m. green	1·90	1·80
534	-	10m. purple	1·90	1·80
535	-	10m. blue	1·90	1·80
536	-	10m. brown	1·90	1·80

DESIGNS—HORIZ: No. 533, Saladin at Hattin, A.D. 1187; 534, Ein Galout, A.D. 1260 (Middle East map); 536, Evacuation of Port Said, 1956. VERT: No. 534, Louis IX in chains at Mansourah, A.D. 1250.

159 Ahmed Arabi addressing Revolutionaries

1957. 75th Anniv of Arabi Revolution.

537	**159**	10m. violet	80	55

160 Rameses II

1957

540	-	1m. turquoise	35	35
541	-	5m. sepia	70	45
539	**160**	10m. violet	60	35

DESIGNS: 1m. Country woman and cotton plant; 5m. Factory skyline.

See also Nos. 553/9, 603/19 and 669/72.

162 Ahmed Shawqi

1957. 25th Death Anniv of Ahmed Shawqi and Hafez Ibrahim (poets).

543	**162**	10m. olive	35	35
544	-	10m. brown (Hafez Ibrahim)	35	35

163 Vickers Viscount 700 SU-AIE Airliner and Airline Badge

1957. 25th Anniv of Egyptian Civil Airlines "MISRAIR", and Air Force.

545	**163**	10m. green	80	80
546	-	10m. blue	80	80

DESIGN: No. 546, Ilyushin Il-28 bomber, two Mikoyan Gurevich MiG-17 jet fighters and Air Force emblem.

164 Pyramids, Dove of Peace and Globe

1957. Afro-Asian People's Conference, Cairo.

547	**164**	5m. brown	80	80
548	**164**	10m. green	45	45
549	**164**	15m. violet	60	55

165 Racing Cyclists

1958. 5th Egyptian International Cycle Race.

550	**165**	10m. brown	80	55

166 Mustapha Kamil

1958. 50th Death Anniv of Mustapha Kamil (patriot).

551	**166**	10m. slate	80	35

UNITED ARAB REPUBLIC

For stamps inscribed "U.A.R." but with value in piastres, see under Syria.

167 Congress Emblem

1958. 1st Afro-Asian Ophthalmology Congress.

552	**167**	10m.+5m. orange	1·20	1·10

168 Princess Nofret

1958. Inscr "U A R EGYPT".

553	-	1m. red (as No. 538)	35	35
554	-	2m. blue	25	20
555	**168**	3m. brown	25	20
556	-	4m. green	35	20
557	-	5m. sepia (as No. 541)	35	20
558	**160**	10m. violet	95	20
559	-	35m. blue	5·00	45

DESIGNS—VERT: 2m. Ahmed Ibn Toulon Mosque; 4m. Glass lamp and mosque; 35m. Ship and crate on hoist.

See also Nos. 603/19, 669/72 and 739.

169 Union of Egypt and Syria

1958. Birth of United Arab Republic.

560	**169**	10m. grn & yell (postage)	60	35
561	**169**	15m. brn & blue (air)	65	35

170 Cotton Plant

1958. International Cotton Fair, Cairo.

562	**170**	10m. turquoise	35	20

171 Qasim Amin

1958. 50th Death Anniv of Qasim Amin (reformer).

563	**171**	10m. blue	60	20

172 Dove of Peace

1958. 5th Anniv of Republic.

564	**172**	10m. violet	60	20

173 "Iron and Steel"

173a UAR Flag

1958. 6th Anniv of 1952 Revolution. Egyptian Industries.

565	-	10m. brown	45	20
566	-	10m. green	45	20
567	**173**	10m. red	45	20
568	-	10m. myrtle	45	20
569	-	10m. blue	45	20
MS570 80×75 mm. **173a** green, red and black			16·00	16·00

DESIGNS: Industrial views representing: No. 565, "Cement"; No. 566, "Textiles"; No. 568, "Petroleum"; No. 569, "Electricity and Fertilizers".

174 Sayed Darwich

1958. 35th Death Anniv of Sayed Darwich.

580	**174**	10m. purple	60	20

175 Torch and Broken Chains

1958. Republic of Iraq Commem.

581	**175**	10m. red	60	20

1958. Afro-Asian Economic Conf, Cairo.

582	**176**	10m. blue	60	20

176 Cogwheels, Maps and Emblems of Productivity

1958. Industrial and Agricultural Fair, Cairo. As No. 582 but colour changed, optd INDUSTRIAL & AGRICULTURAL PRODUCTION FAIR in Arabic and English.

583		10m. brown	60	20

178 Dr. Mahmoud Azmy (Egyptian U.N.O. representative)

1958. 10th Anniv of Declaration of Human Rights.

584	**178**	10m. violet	60	20
585	**178**	35m. green	1·30	90

179 "Learning"

1958. 50th Anniv of Cairo University.

586	**179**	10m. green	45	20

180 Egyptian Postal Emblem

1959. Post Day and Postal Employees Social Fund.

587	**180**	10m.+5m. red, black and turquoise	35	35

1959. Surch UAR 55 and equivalent in Arabic.

588	**132**	55m. on 100m. red	2·30	55

182

1959. Afro-Asian Youth Conf, Cairo.

589	182	10m. green	35	20

183 Nile Hilton Hotel

1959. Opening of Nile Hilton Hotel.

590	183	10m. brown	35	20

184 State Emblem

1959. 1st Anniv of United Arab Republic.

591	184	10m. red, black & green	35	20

185 "Telecommunications"

1959. Arab Telecommunications Union Commemoration.

592	185	10m. violet	35	20

186 U.A.R. and Yemeni Flags

1959. 1st Anniv of Proclamation of United Arab States (U.A.R. and Yemen).

593	186	10m. red and green	35	20

187 Oil Derrick and Pipe-lines

1959. 1st Arab Petroleum Congress.

594	187	10m. blue & turquoise	60	20

188 "Railways" (Diesel-electric Train)

1959. 7th Anniv of Revolution and Transport and Communications Commemoration. Frames in slate. Centre colours given.

595	188	10m. lake	1·60	55
596	-	10m. green	1·60	55
597	-	10m. blue	1·60	55
598	-	10m. violet	1·60	55
599	-	10m. plum	1·60	55
600	-	10m. red	1·60	55
MS601		80×75 mm. 50m. green and red	14·00	14·00

DESIGNS: No. 596, "Highways" (bus passing bridge); 597, "Seaways" ("Al Mokattam" (freighter)); 598, "Nile Transport" (motorised river barge); 599, "Telecommunications" (telephone and radio mast); 600, "Postal Services" (Post Office H.Q., Cairo). 57×32 mm—**MS**601, Liner, diesel electric train, airliner and motorcycle mail carrier.

189 "Migration"

1959. 3rd Arab Emigrants' Association Convention, Middle East.

602	189	10m. lake	35	20

1959. As Types 132, 160 and 168, but inscr "UAR" only.

603	-	1m. red (as No. 553)	25	20
604	-	2m. blue (as No. 554)	25	20
605	168	3m. brown	25	20
606	-	4m. green (as No. 556)	25	20
607	-	5m. black (as No. 557)	25	20
608	160	10m. green	35	20
609	-	15m. brown	60	20
610	-	20m. red	1·30	20
611	-	30m. purple	80	20
612	-	35m. blue (as No. 559)	95	20
613	-	40m. brown	1·30	20
614	-	45m. blue	2·75	35
615	-	55m. green	2·20	20
616	-	60m. violet	3·50	20
617	-	100m. green & orange	2·50	35
618	-	200m. brown and blue	5·25	55
619	132	500m. red and blue	16·00	1·90

DESIGNS—VERT: 15m. Omayad Mosque, Damascus; 20m. Tutankhamun's Lamp; 40m. Statue; 55m. Cotton and ears of corn; 60m. Barrage and plant; 100m. Egyptian eagle and hand holding agricultural products. HORIZ: 30m. Stone archway; 45m. Citadel Gate, Aleppo; 200m. Temple ruins.

See also Nos. 669/72 and No. 739.

191 Boeing B-17 Flying Fortress over Pyramids

1959. Air.

620	191	5m. red	35	20
621	-	15m. purple	35	35
622	-	60m. green	95	65
623	-	90m. purple	2·00	1·30

DESIGNS: 15m. Boeing B-17 Flying Fortress bomber over Colossi of Thebes; 60m. Douglas DC-6B airliner over Al-Azhar University; 90m. Airplane over St. Catherine's Monastery, Sinai.

See also Nos. 758/62.

192 "Shield against Aggression"

1959. Army Day.

624	192	10m. red	35	20

193 Children and U.N. Emblem

1959. U.N. Day. UNICEF.

625	193	10m.+5m. purple	60	35
626	193	35m.+10m. blue	95	45

194 Cairo Museum

1959. Centenary of Cairo Museum.

627	194	10m. brown	45	20

195 Rock Temples of Abu Simbel

1959. UNESCO. Campaign for Preservation of Nubian Monuments (1st issue).

628	195	10m. brown	80	35

See also Nos. 650, 676, 728, 754/6, 825/7, 864/6 and 878/9.

196 Mounted Postman

1960. Post Day.

629	196	10m. blue	35	20

197

198 View of projected Aswan High Dam

1960. Laying of Foundation Stone of Aswan High Dam.

630	197	10m. lake	80	80
631	198	35m. lake	1·30	90

199 Aswan Dam Hydro-electric Power Station

1960. Projected Aswan Dam Hydro-electric Power Station.

632	199	10m. black	35	20

200

1960. Industrial and Agricultural Fair.

633	200	10m. green	35	20

1960. No. 432 optd UAR and Arabic equivalent.

634	132	£E1 red and green	20·00	4·25

202 State Emblem with U.A.R. Flag

1960. 2nd Anniv of U.A.R.

635	202	10m. red, black & green	35	20

203 Sculpture and Palette

1960. 3rd Fine Arts Biennale. Alexandria.

636	203	10m. sepia	35	20

204 Arab League Centre, Cairo

1960. Inaug of Arab League Centre, Cairo.

637	204	10m. green and black	35	20

205 Mother and Child pointing to Map of Palestine

1960. World Refugee Year.

638	205	10m. red	70	35
639	205	35m. turquoise	1·20	80

206 Weightlifting

1960. Sports Campaign and Olympic Games.

640	206	5m. grey	70	35
641	-	5m. brown	70	35
642	-	5m. purple	70	35
643	-	10m. red	70	35
644	-	10m. green	70	35
645	-	30m. violet	95	55
646	-	35m. blue	1·20	65
MS647		79×75 mm. 100m. brown and carmine. Imperf	4·00	4·00

DESIGNS—VERT: No. 641, Basketball; 642, Football; 643, Fencing; 644, Rowing. HORIZ: No. 645, Horse-jumping; 646, Swimming. LARGER (57×32 mm.)—**MS**647, Cairo stadium.

207 U.N. Emblem within 15 candles

1960. 15th Anniv of U.N.O.

648		10m. violet	35	20
649	207	35m. red	70	55

DESIGN—VERT: 10m. Dove and U.N. Emblem.

208 Rock Temples of Abu Simbel

1960. UNESCO. Campaign for Preservation of Nubian Monuments (2nd issue).

650	**208**	10m. brown	95	55

209 Modern Post Office

1961. Post Day.

651	**209**	10m. red	60	20

210 State Emblem and Wreath

1961. 3rd Anniv of U.A.R.

652	**210**	10m. purple	35	20

211 Globe, Flags and Wheat

1961. International Agricultural Exn, Cairo.

653	**211**	10m. red	35	20

212 Patrice Lumumba and Map of Africa

1961. 3rd All African Peoples' Conf, Cairo.

654	**212**	10m. black	35	20

213 Hands "reading" Braille

1961. World Health Organization Day.

655	**213**	10m. brown	45	20
656	**213**	35m.+15m. yellow & brn	80	65

214 Tower of Cairo

1961. Inauguration of Tower of Cairo.

657	**214**	10m. blue	35	15

1961. Air. As No. 657, but with aircraft replacing inscr in upper corners and inscr "AIR MAIL" in English and Arabic.

658		50m. blue	1·20	65

215 Refugee Mother and Child, and Map

1961. Palestine Day.

659	**215**	10m. green	45	35

216 "Transport and Communications"

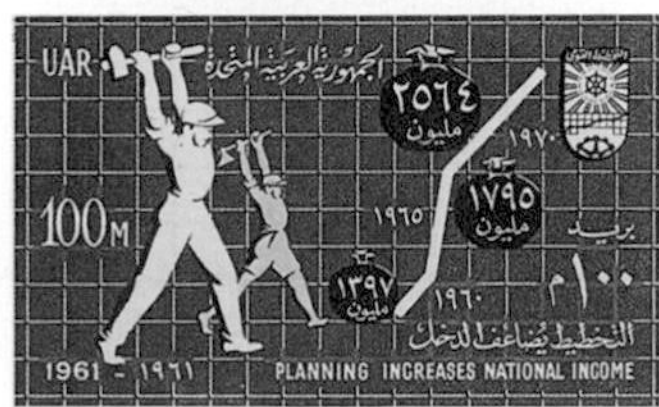

216a Workers and Graph

1961. 9th Anniv of Revolution and Five Year Plan. Inscr "1961".

660	**216**	10m. purple	70	35
661	-	10m. red	70	35
662	-	10m. blue	70	35
663	-	35m. myrtle	95	45
664	-	35m. violet	95	45

MS665 80×75 mm. **216a** 100m. brown. Imperf 4·75 4·50

DESIGNS: No. 661, Worker turning cogwheel and pylons; No. 662, Apartment houses; No. 663, Cotton plant and dam; No. 664, Family moving towards lighted candle.

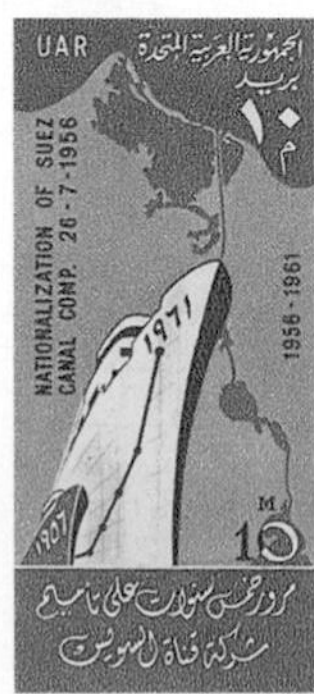

217 Ships and Map of Suez Canal

1961. 5th Anniv of Nationalization of Suez Canal.

666	**217**	10m. olive	60	35

218 Mehalla El Kobra Textile Factories

1961. Misr Bank Organization and 20th Death Anniv of Talaat Harb (founder).

667	**218**	10m. brown	35	15

219 Ship's Wheel and "Al Nasser" (destroyer)

1961. Navy Day.

668	**219**	10m. blue	60	35

1961. As Nos. 553, etc. Inscr "UAR" only (in English). New colours.

669		1m. turquoise (as No. 603)	25	20
670		4m. olive (as No. 606)	25	20
671		10m. violet	35	20
672		35m. slate (as No. 612)	70	20

NEW DESIGN: 10m. Eagle of Saladin.

See also No. 739.

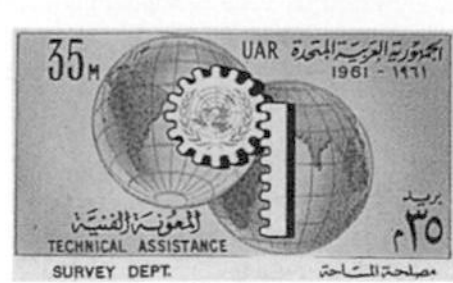

220 "Industrial Worlds"

1961. U.N. Technical Co-operation. Programme and 16th Anniv of U.N.O.

674	-	10m. black and brown	35	20
675	**220**	35m. brown and green	70	45

DESIGN—VERT: 10m. Corncob, wheel and book ("Agriculture, Industry and Education").

221 Philae Temple

1961. 15th Anniv of UNESCO. and Preservation of Nubian Monuments Campaign (3rd issue).

676	**221**	10m. blue	1·00	45

222 "Fine Arts"

1961. 4th Fine Arts Biennale, Alexandria.

677	**222**	10m. brown	35	20

223 "Arts and Sciences"

1961. Education Day.

678	**223**	10m. purple	35	15

224 State Emblem, Torch and Olive Branch

1961. Victory Day.

679	**224**	10m. green and red	35	20

225 Sphinx and Pyramid

1961. "Son et Lumiere" Display.

680	**225**	10m. black	60	35

226 Postal Authority Press Building, El Nasr

1962. Post Day.

681	**226**	10m. brown	45	20

227 King of Morocco and Map

1962. 1st Anniv of African Charter of Casablanca.

682	**227**	10m. blue	35	15

228 Guide and Badge

1962. Silver Jubilee of Egyptian Girl Guides Association.

683	**228**	10m. blue	80	35

229 Gaza Family with Egyptian Flag

1962. 5th Anniv of Egyptian Occupation of Gaza.

684	**229**	10m. myrtle	45	20

230 Mother and Child

1962. Mothers' Day.

694	**230**	10m. purple	35	20

231 League Centre, Cairo, and Emblem

1962. Arab League Week.

695	**231**	10m.+5m. black	60	45

232 W.M.O. Emblem and Weather-vane

1962. World Meteorological Day.

696	**232**	60m. blue and yellow	2·30	1·10

233 Posthorn on North Africa

1962. African Postal Union Commemoration.

697	**233**	10m. brown and red	45	35
698	**233**	50m. brown and blue	1·00	65

234 Cadets on Parade

1962. 150th Anniv of Military Academy.

699	**234**	10m. green	35	15

235 Campaign Emblem

1962. Malaria Eradication.

700	**235**	10m. red and sepia	25	15
701	-	35m. blue and myrtle	70	55

DESIGN: 35m. As Type **235** but with laurel and inscription around emblem.

237 Bilharz and Microscope

1962. Death Centenary of Dr. Theodore Bilharz (discoverer of parasitic disease: bilharzia).

702	**237**	10m. brown	60	20

238 Lumumba

1962. Lumumba Commemoration.

703	**238**	10m. red (postage)	35	20
704	-	35m. multicoloured (air)	60	45

DESIGN: 35m. Lumumba with laurel sprays and flaming torch.

239 "The Charter"

1962. Proclamation of National Charter.

705	**239**	10m. brown and blue	35	15

240 "Birth of the Revolution"

1962. 10th Anniv of 1952 Revolution.

706	**240**	10m. brown and pink	45	35
707	**A**	10m. sepia and blue	45	35
708	**B**	10m. blue and sepia	45	35
709	**C**	10m. blue and olive	45	35
710	**D**	10m. red, black & green	45	35
711	**E**	10m. slate and brown	45	35
712	**F**	10m. purple and brown	45	35
713	**G**	10m. sepia and orange	45	35
MS714		70×80 mm. 100m. emerald, carmine, black and rose. Perf	2·75	2·50
MS715		As last. Imperf	2·75	2·50

DESIGNS: A, Scroll and book; B, Agricultural Scene; C, Globe and dove; D, Flag and eagle emblem; E, Industrial scene and cogwheel; F, Dam construction; G, Eagle, building, cogwheel and ear of corn. **MS**714/15, Eagle emblem, Arab league emblem, United Nations emblems and maps of Africa and Aro-Asia.

241 M. Moukhtar (sculptor) and "La Vestale des Secrets"

1962. Moukhtar Museum Inaug.

716	**241**	10m. olive and blue	45	35

243 Rocket

1962. Launching of U.A.R. Rocket.

718	**243**	10m. red, black & green	45	20

244 Table Tennis Bat, Ball and Net

1962. 1st African Table Tennis Tournament, Alexandria, and 38th World Shooting Championships, Cairo.

719	**244**	5m. red and green	60	60
720	-	5m. red and green	60	60
721	**244**	10m. blue and ochre	70	70
722	-	10m. blue and ochre	70	70
723	**244**	35m. red and blue	1·60	1·60
724	-	35m. red and blue	1·60	1·60

DESIGN: Nos. 720, 722, 724, Rifle and target.

245 Dag Hammarskjold and U.N. Emblem

1962. 17th Anniv of U.N.O. and Dag Hammarskjold (Secretary-General, 1953–61) Commemoration.

725	**245**	5m. blue and violet	70	30
726	**245**	10m. blue and green	80	30
727	**245**	35m. blue & ultramarine	1·20	65

246 Coronation of Queen Nefertari (from small temple of Abu Simbel)

1962. UNESCO. Campaign for Preservation of Nubian Monuments (4th issue).

728	**246**	10m. brown and blue	1·40	45

247 Al Kahira Jet Trainer, College Emblem and de Havilland DH.82 Tiger Moth Biplane

1962. Silver Jubilee of U.A.R. Air Force College.

729	**247**	10m. red and blue	45	20

248 Postal Authority Emblem

1963. Post Day and 1966 International Stamp Exhbition. Inscr "1866 1966".

736	**248**	20m.+10m. red & green	1·30	1·30
737	-	40m.+20m. sepia & brn	2·00	2·00
738	-	40m.+20m. brn & sepia	2·00	2·00

DESIGNS—TRIANGULAR: Egyptian stamps of 1866 – No. 737, 5 paras; No. 738, 10 paras.

1963. As No. 670 but inscr "1963" in English and Arabic and new colours.

739		4m. red, green and sepia	35	20

249 Yemeni Republican Flag and Torch

1963. Proclamation of Yemeni Arab Republic.

740	**249**	10m. red and olive	35	20

250 Maritime Station, Alexandria

1963. Air.

741	**250**	20m. sepia	70	30
742	-	30m. mauve	95	45
743	-	40m. black	1·40	1·10

DESIGNS: 30m. International Airport, Cairo; 40m. Railway Station, Luxor.

251 Tennis-player

1963. 51st Int Lawn Tennis Championships held in U.A.R.

744	**251**	10m. brown and black	80	35

252 Cow and Emblems

1963. Freedom from Hunger.

745	**252**	5m. brown and violet	45	35
746	-	10m. yellow and blue	60	35
747	-	35m. yellow and blue	80	80

DESIGNS—VERT: 10m. Corncob and ear of wheat. HORIZ: 35m. Corncob, ear of wheat, U.N. and F.A.O. emblems.

253 Centenary Emblem within Red Crescent

1963. Centenary of Red Cross.

748	**253**	10m. red, purple & blue	35	15
749	-	35m. red and blue	95	90

DESIGN: 35m. Emblem, Red Crescent, olive branches and Globe.

254 "Arab Socialist Union"

1963. 11th Anniv of Revolution.

750	**254**	10m. mauve and blue	35	20
MS751		70×80 mm. 50m. ultramarine and yellow (Tools, torch and symbol of National Charter)	3·00	3·00
MS752		As last. Imperf	3·00	3·00

255 T.V. Building, Cairo, and Television Receiver

1963. 2nd Int Television Festival, Alexandria.

753	**255**	10m. yellow and blue	35	20

256 Queen Nefertari

1963. UNESCO. Campaign for preservation of Nubian Monuments (5th issue).

754	**256**	5m. yellow and blue	70	40
755	-	10m. orange and black	80	45
756	-	35m. yellow and black	1·90	1·00

DESIGNS—(28×61 mm): 10m. Great Hall of Pillars, Abu Simbel. As Type **256**: 35m. Heads of Colossi, Abu Simbel.

257 Swimmer and Map

1963. Suez Canal Int Long-distance Swimming Race.

757	**257**	10m. red and blue	45	20

1963. Air. As No. 622.

758	50m. brown and blue	2·10	1·10
759	80m. purple and blue	3·75	1·70
761	115m. yellow and brown	4·00	1·60
762	140m. red and violet	4·00	2·20

DESIGNS—VERT: 50m. Cairo Tower and Arch. HORIZ: 80m. As No. 622; 115m. Colossi of Rameses II and Queen Nefertari, Abu Simbel; 140m. Seated colossi of Rameses II (Great Temple, Abu Simbel).

258 Ministry Building

1963. 50th Anniv of Egyptian Ministry of Agriculture.

763	**258**	10m. blue and brown	35	20

259 Map and Blocks of Flats

1963. Afro-Asian Housing Congress.

764	**259**	10m. blue and brown	35	20

259a Globe and Scales of Justice

1963. 15th Anniv of Declaration of Human Rights.

765	**259a**	5m. yellow and green	25	20
766	-	10m. black, brown & bl	35	20
767	-	35m. blk, pink & red	1·00	55

DESIGNS: 10, 35m. As Type **259a** but arranged differently.

259b Statuette, Palette and Arms of Alexandria

1963. 5th Fine Arts Biennale, Alexandria.

768	**259b**	10m. brown and blue	35	20

260 El Mitwalli Gate, Cairo

261 Glass and Enamel Urn

263 King Osircaf

1964

769	-	1m. blue and green	25	20
770	-	2m. bistre and purple	25	20
771	-	3m. blue, orge & salmon	25	20
772	-	4m. brown, black & blue	25	20
773	-	5m. brown, lt brn & blue	25	20
774	-	10m. lt brn, brn & grn	35	20
775	-	15m. yell, ultram & bl	35	20
776	-	20m. brown and blue	95	20
777	**260**	20m. green	1·70	20
778	**261**	30m. brown & yellow	80	20
779	-	35m. brown, bl & orge	95	20
780	-	40m. blue and yellow	2·00	35
781	-	55m. violet	2·30	20
782	-	60m. brown and blue	1·30	55
783	**263**	100m. blue and purple	3·50	80
784	-	200m. brown and blue	8·25	1·10
785	-	500m. orange and blue	17·00	3·25

DESIGNS—As Type **260**. 55m. Kiosk, Sultan Hussein Mosque. As Type **261**—VERT: 1m. 14th-century glass vase; 4m. Minaret and archway; 10m. Eagle emblem and pyramids; 35m. Queen Nefertari; 40m. Nile near Agouza; 60m. Al-Azhar Mosque. HORIZ: 2m. Ancient Egyptian headrest; 3m. Alabaster funerary barge; 5m. Aswan High Dam; 15m. Window, Ahmed ibn Toulon Mosque; 20m. (No. 776), Nile Hilton Hotel and Kasr el Nile Bridge. As Type **263**: 200m. Rameses; 500m. Tutankhamun.

For the 4m. in different colours, and with date "1964" added to design see No. 791.

For stamps as Nos. 777 and 781 but larger and in different colours, see Nos. 1042, 1044, 1134/5 and 1137.

264 Eagle and Pyramids

1964. Post Day.

786	**264**	10m.+5m. green & yell	2·50	1·50
787	**264**	80m.+40m. blk & bl	4·75	2·75
788	**264**	115m.+55m. blk & brn	5·75	3·50

265 Emblems on Map of Africa

1964. 1st Health, Sanitation and Nutrition Commission Conference, Cairo.

789	**265**	10m. yellow and blue	35	20

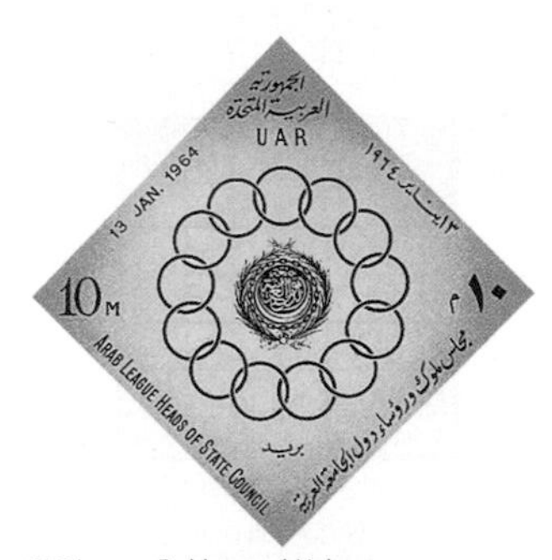

266 League Emblem and Links

1964. Arab League Heads of State Council, Cairo.

790	**266**	10m. black and green	35	20

267 Arch and Minaret

1964. Ramadan Festival.

791	**267**	4m. green, red & black	35	20

268 Map and Old and New Houses

1964. Nubians' Resettlement.

792	**268**	10m. yellow & purple	35	20

269 King Akhnaton and Family (Tutankhamun's tomb)

1964. Mothers' Day.

793	**269**	10m. brown and blue	95	35

270 Diesel Train and Afro-Asian Map

1964. Asian Railways Conference.

794	**270**	10m. yellow and blue	80	35

271 Office Emblem

1964. 10th Anniv of Arab Postal Union's Permanent Office.

795	**271**	10m. blue and brown	35	20

272 W.H.O. Emblem

1964. World Health Day.

796	**272**	10m. blue and red	35	20

273 Statue of Liberty, U.A.R. Pavilion and Pyramids

1964. New York World's Fair.

797	**273**	10m. green, brn & olive	35	20

274 Site of Diversion

1964. Nile High Dam (Diversion of Flow).

798	**274**	10m. black and blue	35	20

275 Map of Africa and Flags

1964. O.A.U. Assembly, Cairo.

799	**275**	10m. black, blue & brn	45	20

276 "Electricity"

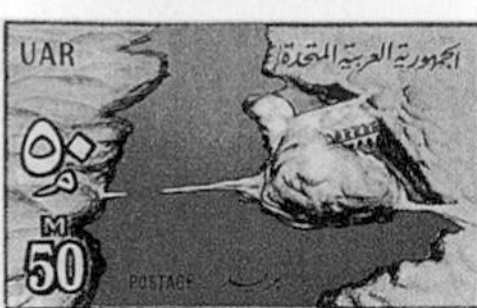

276a Aswan High Dam before Diversion of the Nile

1964. Aswan Dam Projects. (a) as Type 276.

800	276	10m. blue and green	60	35
801	-	10m. green and yellow	60	35

DESIGN: No. 801, "Land Reclamation" (tractor and symbols of land cultivation).

(b) Miniature sheet. Imperf.

MS802	102×82 mm. Two 50m. stamps in black and blue, T **276a** and similar design showing dam after diversion of the Nile. Imperf	4·75	4·75

277 Jamboree Badge

1964. 6th Pan Arab Scout Jamboree, Alexandria.

803	277	10m. green and red	60	35
804	-	10m. red and green	60	35

DESIGN: No. 804, Air Scout badge.

278 Algerian Flag

1964. 2nd Arab League Heads of State Council. Flags in national colours; inscr in green (except Sudan, in blue). Each with country name at foot.

805	10m. Type **278**	80	45
806	10m. Iraq	80	45
807	10m. Jordan	80	45
808	10m. Kuwait	80	45
809	10m. Lebanon	80	45
810	10m. Libya	80	45
811	10m. Morocco	80	45
812	10m. Saudi Arabia	80	45
813	10m. Sudan	80	45
814	10m. Syria	80	45
815	10m. Tunisia	80	45
816	10m. U.A.R.	80	45
817	10m. Yemen	80	45

279 Globe, Dove and Pyramids

1964. Non-aligned Countries Conf, Cairo.

818	279	10m. yellow and blue	35	20

280 Emblem and Map

1964. 1st Afro-Asian Medical Congress.

819	280	10m. violet and yellow	35	20

281 Gymnastics

1964. Olympic Games, Tokyo.

820	-	5m. orange and green	45	20
821	281	10m. ochre and blue	45	20
822	-	35m. ochre and purple	1·40	90
823	-	50m. brown and blue	2·00	1·30

DESIGNS—As Type **281**. HORIZ: 5m. Gymnastics. VERT: 35m. Wrestling. LARGER (61×28 mm): 50m. Charioteer hunting lions.

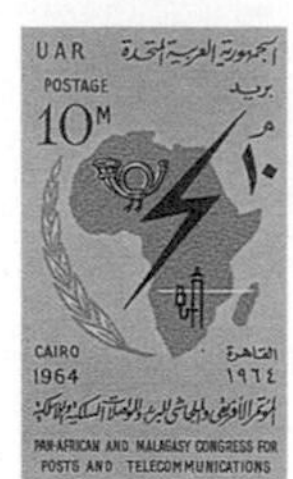

282 Emblems of Posts and Telecommunications and Map

1964. Pan-African and Malagasy Posts and Telecommunications Congress, Cairo.

824	282	10m. sepia and green	35	20

283 Rameses II

1964. UNESCO. Campaign for Preservation of Nubian Monuments (6th issue).

825	-	5m. brown and blue	70	40
826	283	10m. yellow and sepia	1·20	45
827	-	35m. blue and brown	3·00	1·60
MS828		106×63 mm. 50m. green and purple. Imperf	23·00	23·00

DESIGNS—SQUARE (40×40 mm): 5m. Horus and facade of Abu Simbel; 35m. Wall sculpture, Abu Simbel. HORIZ (42×25 mm)—50m. The Goddess Isis.

284 Handicrafts and Weaving

1964. 25th Anniv of Ministry of Social Affairs.

829	284	10m. blue and yellow	35	20

285 U.N. and UNESCO Emblems

1964. UNESCO Day.

830	285	10m. blue and yellow	35	20

286 Emblem and Posthorn

1965. Post Day and 1966 Int Stamp Exn.

831	286	10m.+5m. red, purple and green	1·20	90
832	-	10m.+5m. red, black and blue	1·20	90
833	-	80m.+40m. black, green and red	3·50	3·00

DESIGNS—As Type **286**: No. 832, Posthorn over emblem. As Type **248**: 80m. Bird carrying letter, inscr "STAMP CENTENARY EXHIBITION".

286a Al-Maridani Mosque Minaaret

1965. Ramadan Festival.

834	286a	4m. brown and blue	60	35

287 Police Emblem

1965. Police Day.

835	287	10m. yellow and sepia	1·00	45

288 Oil Derrick

1965. 5th Arab Petroleum Congress and 2nd Petroleum Exhibition.

836	288	10m. sepia and yellow	80	45

289 Emblem and Flags

1965. 20th Anniv of Arab League.

837	289	10m. green and red	95	45
838	-	20m. brown and blue	1·30	65

DESIGN—HORIZ: 20m. Arab League emblem.

290 W.M.O. Emblem and Weather-vane

1965. Air. World Meteorological Day.

839	290	80m. purple and blue	3·75	1·80

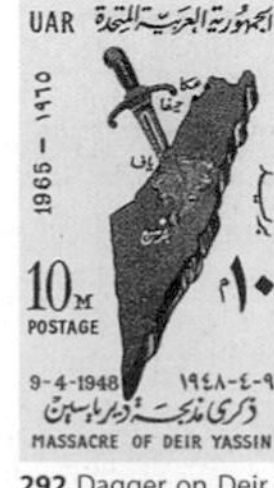

291 W.H.O. Emblem within Red Crescent

1965. World Health Day.

840	291	10m. red and blue	70	45

292 Dagger on Deir Yassin, Palestine

1965. Deir Yassin Massacre.

841	292	10m. red and sepia	1·60	35

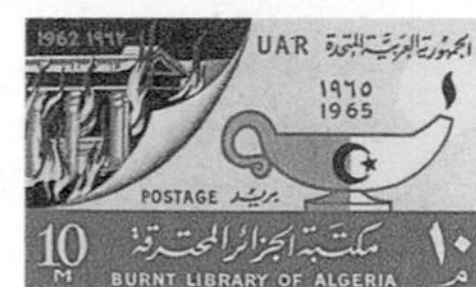

293 I.T.U. Emblem and Symbols

1965. Centenary of I.T.U.

842	293	5m. purple, yell & blk	45	35
843	293	10m. pink, yellow & red	70	35
844	293	35m. blue, yell & dp bl	2·10	1·60

294 Lamp and Burning Library

1965. Reconstitution of Algiers University Library.

845	294	10m. green, red & black	70	20

295 Senet Table of 1350 B.C.

1965. Air. Re-establishment of Egyptian Civil Airlines, "MISRAIR".

846	295	10m. blue and yellow	2·30	45

296 Shaikh Mohamed Abdo

1965. 60th Death Anniv of Shaikh Abdo (mufti).

847	296	10m. brown and blue	35	20

297 "Housing"

1965. 13th Anniv of Revolution.

848	**297**	10m. black and brown	95	55
849	-	10m. brown & yellow	95	55
850	-	10m. indigo and blue	95	55
851	-	100m. black and green	6·50	5·50

DESIGNS—SQUARE: No. 849, "Heavy Industry" (ladle and furnace); 850, "Petroleum and Mining" (refinery and oil rig "Discoverer"). 80×80 mm: No. 851, President Nasser.

298 Stadium, Flag and Torch

1965. 4th Pan-Arab Games, Cairo.

857	**298**	5m. blue & red on blue	45	45
858	-	10m. brown and blue	95	45
859	-	35m. brown and green	1·50	1·30

DESIGNS—As Type **298**: 35m. Horse "Saadoon". DIAMOND (56×56 mm): 10m. Map and emblems of Arab countries.

299 Swimmers Zeitun and Abd el Gelil

1965. Long-distance Swimming Championships, Alexandria.

860	**299**	10m. sepia and blue	70	35

300 Map and Arab League Emblem

1965. 3rd Arab Summit Conf, Casablanca.

861	**300**	10m. sepia and yellow	45	20

301 Land Forces Emblem

1965. Land Forces Day.

862	**301**	10m. black and brown	70	35

302 Flaming Torch on Africa

1965. O.A.U. Assembly, Accra.

863	**302**	10m. purple and red	45	20

303 Rameses II, Abu Simbel

1965. UNESCO. Campaign for Preservation of Nubian Monuments (7th issue).

864	**303**	5m. blue and yellow	1·20	55
865	-	10m. black and blue	2·20	55
866	-	35m. violet and yellow	4·25	2·10
MS867		105×63 mm. 50m. brown and ultramarine. Imperf	5·75	5·50

DESIGNS—As Type **303**: 35m. Colossi, Abu Simbel. VERT: (28×61½ mm): 10m. Hall of Pillars, Abu Simbel. HORIZ (42×25 mm.)—50m. Cartouche of Rameses II and ICY emblem.

304 Al-Maqrizi, Scrolls and Books

1965. 600th Birth Anniv of Al-Maqrizi (historian).

868	**304**	10m. blue and olive	45	20

305 Bust and Flag

1965. 6th Fine Arts Biennale, Alexandria.

869	**305**	10m. multicoloured	45	20

306 Pigeon, Parchment and Horseman

1966. Post Day.

870	**306**	10m. orange, yellow and blue (postage)	95	20
871	-	80m.+40m. purple, yellow and blue (air)	3·75	3·50
872	-	115m.+55m. blue, yellow and purple	5·00	4·75
MS873		106×62 mm. 140m.+60m. black, blue and pink	5·75	5·50

DESIGNS—As T **306**—80m. Pharaonic messengers; 115m. de Havilland DH.34 airplane and 1926 27m. air stamps; **MS**873—5 and 10pi. Stamps of 1866.

307 Glass Lamp

1966. Ramadan Festival.

874	**307**	4m. orange and violet	45	20

308 Exhibition Emblem

1966. Industrial Exhibition, Cairo.

875	**308**	10m. black, blue & lt bl	45	20

309 Arab League Emblem

1966. Arab Publicity Week.

876	**309**	10m. violet and yellow	45	20

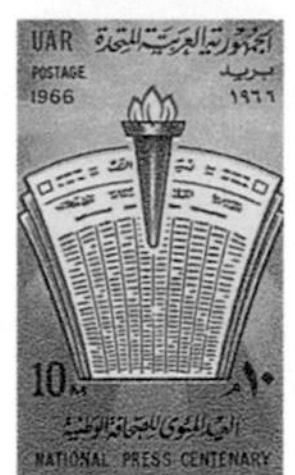

310 Torch and Newspapers

1966. Centenary of Egyptian National Press.

877	**310**	10m. slate and orange	45	20

311 Rock Temples of Abu Simbel

1966. Air. UNESCO. Campaign for Preservation of Nubian Monuments (8th issue).

878	**311**	20m. multicoloured	1·20	65
879	**311**	80m. multicoloured	2·75	2·10

312 Traffic Signals

1966. Traffic Day.

880	**312**	10m. red, emerald & grn	95	35

313 Torch

1966. U.A.R.–Iraq Union Agreement.

881	**313**	10m. red, grn & pur	45	20

314 "Labourers"

1966. 50th Session of I.L.O. Conference.

882	**314**	5m. black & turquoise	35	20
883	**314**	10m. green and purple	35	20
884	**314**	35m. black and orange	1·50	1·10

315 Emblem, People and City

1966. 1st Population Census.

885	**315**	10m. purple and brown	35	20

316 Building "Salah-el-Deen"

317 Arab Dancers

1966. 14th Anniv of Revolution. (a) As T 316.

886	**316**	10m. black, blue & orge	70	35
887	-	10m. purple, yell & grn	70	35
888	-	10m. blue, yellow & blk	70	35
889	-	10m. turq, bl & red	70	35

(b) Miniature sheets. Imperf.

MS890		115×67 mm. **317** 100m. vermilion, blue and brown	7·00	7·00

DESIGNS: No. 886, Type **316** (shipbuilding); 887, Transfer of first stones at Abu Simbel; 888, Map (development of Sinai); 889, El Mahdi hospital, nurse and patient.

318 Suez Canal H.Q., "Southern Cross" (liner), Freighter and Map

1966. 10th Anniv of Suez Canal Nationalization.

891	**318**	10m. red and blue	1·50	55

319 Jamboree Emblem and Camp

1966. Air. 7th Pan-Arab Scout Jamboree, Libya.
892 **319** 20m. red and olive 1·60 55

320 Cotton

1966. Peasants' Day.
893 **320** 5m. violet, yell & blue 35 20
894 - 10m. brn & grn (Rice) 35 20
895 - 35m. orge & bl (Onions) 1·30 1·00

321 W.H.O. Building

1966. U.N. Day.
896 **321** 5m. violet and olive 35 20
897 - 10m. violet and orange 35 20
898 - 35m. violet and blue 1·00 80
DESIGNS: 10m. U.N.R.W.A. (Refugees) emblem; 35m. UNICEF emblem.

322 Globe and Festival Emblem

1966. 5th Int Television Festival.
899 **322** 10m. violet and yellow 60 20

323 St. Catherine's Monastery

1966. Air. 1400th Anniv of St. Catherine's Monastery, Mt. Sinai.
900 **323** 80m. red, yellow & blue 3·50 2·20

324 Eagle and Torch

1966. Victory Day.
901 **324** 10m. red and green 60 20

325 Anubis (God)

1967. Post Day. Designs showing items from Tutankhamun's Tomb.
902 **325** 10m. multicoloured 1·60 45
903 - 35m. brown. pur & bl 3·25 80
904 - 80m.+20m. brown, yellow and blue 4·00 3·25
905 - 115m.+40m. brown, black and blue 6·50 6·25
DESIGNS—As T **325**: 35m. Alabaster head (stopper from canopic urn); 27×60 mm: 80m. Ushabti figure; 115m. Statue of Tutankhamun.

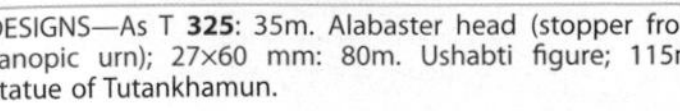

326 Carnations

1967. Ramadan Festival.
906 **326** 4m. violet and olive 45 20

327 Tree-planting

1967. Tree Festival.
907 **327** 10m. lilac and green 45 20

328 Gamal el-Dine el-Afghani and Arab League Emblem

1967. Arab Publicity Week.
908 **328** 10m. brown and green 45 20

329 Workers, Factories and Census Symbol

1967. 1st Industrial Census.
909 **329** 10m. green & orange 45 20

330 Hawker Siddeley Comet 4 Aircraft at Cairo Airport

1967. Air.
910 **330** 20m. blue and brown 1·30 45

331 "Workers" (rock-carving)

1967. Labour Day.
911 **331** 10m. orange and olive 60 35

332 Nefertari and Rameses II

1967. International Tourist Year.
912 **332** 10m. red, yellow and green (postage) 1·20 55
913 - 35m. orange, yell & bl 5·00 1·60
914 - 20m. lilac, black and orange (air) 1·20 35
915 - 80m. brown, yell & bl 2·75 1·90
916 - 115m. orange, bl & brn 6·50 2·75
DESIGNS—As T **332**: 35m. Shooting red-breasted geese; 40×40 mm: 20m. Hotel, El Alamein; 80m. Virgin's Tree; 115m. Hotel and fishes, Red Sea.

333 Pres. Nasser and Map

1967. Arab Solidarity for Palestine Defence.
917 **333** 10m. olive, yell & orge 3·50 1·80

334 "Petroleum" (oil rigs)

335 National Products (image scaled to 36% of original size)

1967. Air. 15th Anniv of Revolution. (a) As Type 334.
930 **334** 50m. black, orange and blue 1·40 90

(b) Miniature sheet. Imperf.
MS931 112×66 mm. **335** 100m. multicoloured (imperf) 4·75 4·75

336 Salama Higazi

1967. 50th Death Anniv of Higazi (lyric stage impresario).
932 **336** 20m. brown and blue 1·20 45

337 Porcelain Dish

1967. U.N. Day. Egyptian Art.
933 20m. blue & red (postage) 1·20 45
934 55m. multicoloured 2·20 90
935 80m. red, yellow & blue (air) 2·50 1·20
DESIGNS: 20m. Type **337**. 55m. "Christ in Glory" (painting); 80m. Tutankhamun and Ankhesenamun (back of throne).

338 Savings Bank "Coffer"

1967. World Savings Day.
936 **338** 20m. blue and pink 70 35

339 Ca d'Oro Palace (Venice) and Santa Maria Cathedral (Florence)

1967. "Save the Monuments of Florence and Venice".
937 **339** 80m.+20m. brown, yellow and green 2·30 2·20
938 - 115m.+30m. bl, yell & ol 3·50 3·25
DESIGN: 115m. Palace of the Doges and Campanile (Venice) and Vecchio Palace (Florence).

340 Rose

1967. Ramadan Festival.
939 **340** 5m. purple and green 60 20

341 Isis

1968. Post Day. Pharaonic Dress.
940 **341** 20m. sepia, green & yell 1·50 45
941 - 55m. brown, yellow & grn 2·50 1·00
942 - 80m. red, blue & blk 4·25 1·50
DESIGNS: 55m. Nefertari; 80m. Isis (different).
See also Nos. 970/3.

342 High Dam and Power Station

1968. Electrification of High Dam.
943 **342** 20m. purple, yellow & bl 60 20

343 Alabaster Vessel (Tutankhamun)

1968. International Museums Festival.
944 **343** 20m. brown, yellow & bl 80 35
945 - 80m. grn, vio & emer 1·70 1·10
DESIGN—39×39 mm: 80m. Capital of Coptic limestone pillar.

344 Head of Woman

1968. 7th Fine Arts Biennale, Alexandria.

946	**344**	20m. black and blue	45	35

345 "The Glorious Koran" (image scaled to 62% of original size)

1968. Air. 1400th Anniv of The Holy Koran.

947	**345**	30m. violet, blue & yell	1·40	1·30
948	**345**	80m. violet, blue & yell	2·50	1·80

346 Tending Cattle

1968. Arab Veterinary Congress.

949	**346**	20m. brown, grn & yell	80	20

347 St. Mark and St. Mark's Cathedral

1968. Air. 1900th Anniv of Martyrdom of St. Mark.

950	**347**	80m. sepia, mauve & grn	2·75	1·30

348 Human Rights Emblem

1968. Human Rights Year.

951	**348**	20m. red, green & olive	60	20
952	**348**	60m. red, green & blue	1·20	1·10

349 Open Book and Symbols

350 Marchers, Cogwheel and open book (image scaled to 53% of original size)

1968. 16th Anniv of Revolution. (a) As T 349.

953	**349**	20m. green and rose	60	20

(b) Miniature sheet. Imperf.

MS954	117×69 mm. **350** 100m. plum, orange and green (imperf)	3·50	3·25

351 W.H.O. Emblem and Imhotep

1968. 20th Anniv of W.H.O.

955	**351**	20m. sepia, yell & blue	1·40	65
956	-	20m. turq, sep & yell	1·40	65

DESIGN: No. 956, W.H.O. emblem and Avicenna.

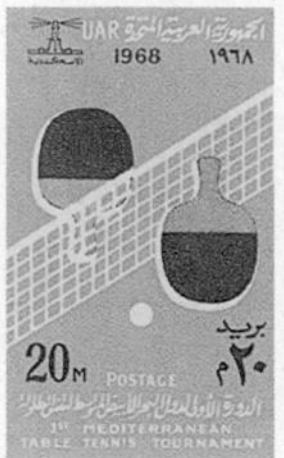

352 Table Tennis Bats, Net and Ball

1968. 1st Mediterranean Table Tennis Tournament.

957	**352**	20m. brown and green	95	35

353 Industrial Skyline

1968. International Industrial Fair, Cairo.

958	**353**	20m. red, indigo and blue	45	20

354 Philae Temple

1968. United Nations Day.

959	-	20m. salmon, vio & blue	1·30	35
960	-	30m. blue, orge & yell	1·90	90
961	**354**	55m. purple, yell & blue	3·25	1·20

DESIGNS (62×29 mm): 20m. Philae Temples (aerial view); (As Type **354**): 30m. Refugee women and children.

355 Scout Badge

1968. 50th Anniv of Egyptian Scout Movement.

962	**355**	10m. blue and orange	80	25

356 Ancient Games

1968. Olympic Games Mexico.

963	**356**	20m. violet, olive & orge	1·00	30
964	-	30m. violet, blue & buff	1·50	80

DESIGN: 30m. Ancient Games (different).

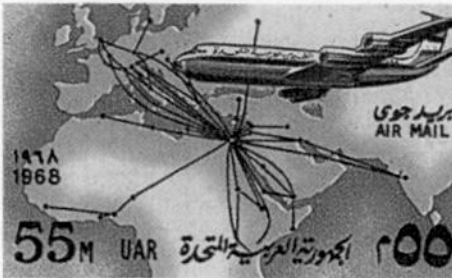

357 Boeing 707 Jetliner and Route Map

1968. Air. 1st United Arab Airlines Boeing Flight, Cairo–London.

965	**357**	55m. red, blue & orange	2·00	1·00

358 Ali Moubarek (educator)

1968. 75th Death Anniv of Ali Moubarek.

966	**358**	20m. lilac, orange & grn	60	20

359 Boy and Girl

1968. World Children's Day.

967	**359**	20m.+10m. red, bl & brn	1·00	1·00
968	-	20m.+10m. bl, brn & grn	1·00	1·00

DESIGN: No. 968, Group of Children.

360 Lotus

1968. Ramadan Festival.

969	**360**	5m. yellow, bl & grn	60	20

1968. Post Day. Pharaonic Dress. As T 341.

970	5m. brown, yellow and blue	80	35
971	20m. yellow, red and blue	1·40	55
972	20m. brown, cinnamon & bl	1·70	65
973	55m. orange, yellow & blue	4·25	1·80

DESIGNS: No. 970, Son of Ramess III; 971, Rameses III; 972, Maiden carrying offerings; 973, Queen Nefertari.

361 H. Nassef (poet and writer)

1969. 50th Death Anniv of Hefni Nassef and Mohamed Farid.

974	**361**	20m. brown and violet	60	55
975	-	20m. brown and green	60	55

DESIGN: No. 975, M. Farid (politician).

362 Ilyushin Il-18 and Route Map

1969. Air. Inauguration of Ilyushin Il-18 Aircraft by United Arab Airlines.

976	**362**	55m. purple, yellow & bl	1·50	1·00

363 Teacher at Blackboard

1969. Arab Teachers' Day.

977	**363**	20m. multicoloured	60	20

364 Flags of Arab Nations

1969. Arab Publicity Week.

978	**364**	20m.+10m. red, bl & grn	70	65

365 I.L.O. Emblem and Factory Stacks

1969. 50th Anniv of I.L.O.

979	**365**	20m. multicoloured	60	20

366 Algerian Flag

1969. African Tourist Year. Flags of African Nations.

980	**366**	10m. red and green	1·20	80
981	-	10m. black, blue & grn	1·20	80
982	-	10m. red and green	1·20	80
983	-	10m. red, yellow & grn	1·20	80
984	-	10m. multicoloured	1·20	80
985	-	10m. yellow, red & blue	1·20	80
986	-	10m. brown, red & grn	1·20	80
987	-	10m. red, yellow & blue	1·20	80
988	-	10m. brown, red & grn	1·20	80
989	-	10m. green, red & black	1·20	80
990	-	10m. multicoloured	1·20	80
991	-	10m. multicoloured	1·20	80
992	-	10m. yellow, grn & bl	1·20	80
993	-	10m. blue, red & green	1·20	80
994	-	10m. multicoloured	1·20	80
995	-	10m. brown, red & grn	1·20	80
996	-	10m. orange & green	1·20	80
997	-	10m. black, red & green	1·20	80
998	-	10m. blue, red & green	1·20	80
999	-	10m. red and blue	1·20	80
1000	-	10m. black, red & green	1·20	80
1001	-	10m. red and green	1·20	80
1002	-	10m. red, black & green	1·20	80
1003	-	10m. brown, red & grn	1·20	80
1004	-	10m. yellow & green	1·20	80
1005	-	10m. multicoloured	1·20	80
1006	-	10m. green and red	1·20	80
1007	-	10m. orange & green	1·20	80
1008	-	10m. green	1·20	80
1009	-	10m. multicoloured	1·20	80
1010	-	10m. green, brown & red	1·20	80
1011	-	10m. blue and green	1·20	80
1012	-	10m. blue and green	1·20	80
1013	-	10m. yellow, green & bl	1·20	80
1014	-	10m. multicoloured	1·20	80
1015	-	10m. multicoloured	1·20	80
1016	-	10m. yellow, grn & red	1·20	80
1017	-	10m. red and green	1·20	80
1018	-	10m. black, yellow & red	1·20	80
1019	-	10m. black, red & green	1·20	80

1020	-	10m. multicoloured	1·20	80

FLAGS: No. 981, Botswana. 982, Burundi. 983, Cameroun. 984, Central African Republic. 985, Chad. 986, Congo-Brazzaville. 987, Congo-Kinshasa. 988, Dahomey. 989, Egypt-U.A.R. 990, Equatorial Guinea. 991, Ethiopia. 992, Gabon. 993, Gambia. 994, Ghana. 995, Guinea. 996, Ivory Coast. 997, Kenya. 998, Lesotho. 999, Liberia. 1000, Libya. 1001, Malagasy Republic. 1002, Malawi. 1003, Mali. 1004, Mauritania. 1005, Mauritius. 1006, Morocco. 1007, Niger. 1008, Nigeria. 1009, Rwanda. 1010, Senegal. 1011, Sierra Leone. 1012, Somalia. 1013, Sudan. 1014, Swaziland. 1015, Tanzania. 1016, Togo. 1017, Tunisia. 1018, Uganda. 1019, Upper Volta. 1020, Zambia.

367 El Fetouh Gate

1969. Cairo Millenary.

1021	**367**	10m. brown, yellow & bl	60	20
1022	-	10m. multicoloured	60	20
1023	-	10m. pink and blue	60	20
1024	-	20m. multicoloured	1·00	45
1025	-	20m. purple, yellow & bl	1·00	45
1026	-	20m. blue, yellow & brn	1·00	45
MS1027		128×70 mm. Four 20m. designs multicoloured	19·00	18·00

DESIGNS—HORIZ (38×22 mm)—No. 1021, T **367**; 1022 Al-Azhar University; 1023 Citadel. (57½×24½ mm)—No. 1024, Two Sculptures from Pharaonic period; 1025 Carved decorations, Coptic era; 1026 Glassware Fatimid dynasty. VERT (31½×21½)—**MS**1027, (a) Coptic dish, (b) Fatimid jewels, (c) Copper vase, Mameluke period, (d) Islamic coins.

368 Development Bank Emblem

1969. 5th Anniv of African Development Bank.

1028	**368**	20m. green, vio & yell	45	20

369 Mahatma Gandhi

1969. Air. Birth Cent of Mahatma Gandhi.

1029	**369**	80m. orange, brn & bl	4·00	1·90

370 "King and Queen" Abu Simbel (UNESCO)

1969. United Nations Day.

1030	**370**	5m. yellow, blue & brn	45	35
1031	-	20m. blue and yellow	1·30	35
1032	-	30m.+10m. mult	1·30	1·10
1033	-	55m. multicoloured	1·70	90

DESIGNS—As T **370**: 20m. Ancient Egyptian Ship (I.M.C.O.); 36×36 mm: 30m.+10m. Arab refugees (U.N.R.W.A.); 55m. Partly submerged temple, Philae (UNESCO).

371 Demonstrators

1969. Anniversaries.

1034	**371**	20m. purple, red & grn	1·20	55
1035	-	20m. brown, yellow & bl	1·70	65
1036	-	20m. multicoloured	1·20	55

DESIGNS AND EVENTS: No. 1034, (50th anniv of 1919 Revolution). LARGER (58×25 mm); No. 1035, Labourers, merchant ships of 1869 and 1969 and map (Suez Canal Centenary); 1036, Performance of "Aida" (Cairo Opera-house Centenary).

372 "Ancient Egyptian Accountants"

1969. International Scientific Accounts Congress, Cairo.

1037	**372**	20m. purple, grn & yell	70	35

373 Poinsettia

1969. Ramadan Festival.

1038	**373**	5m. red, green & yellow	60	20

374 Step Pyramid, Sakkara

375 President Nasser

1969

1039	**374**	1m. brown, ochre & bl	25	20
1040	-	5m. brown, yellow & bl	45	20
1041	-	10m. purple, ochre & bl	45	20
1042	**260**	20m. brown (22×27½ mm)	3·00	35
1043	-	50m. brn, ochre & bl	2·50	55
1044	-	55m. green	4·00	35
1045	**375**	200m. blue & purple	6·00	1·60
1046	**375**	500m. black and blue	13·50	4·00
1047	-	£El green and orange	41·00	9·50

DESIGNS—As Type **374**: 5m. Al-Azhar Mosque, Cairo; 10m. Temple, Luxor; 50m. Qaitbay Fort, Alexandria. 22×27½ mm: 55m. As No. 781. As T **375**: £El, Khafre.

See also Nos. 1131/41.

376a Imam Mohamed El Boukhary

1969. Air. 1100th Death Anniv of Imam El Boukhary (philosopher and writer).

1048	**376a**	30m. brown and olive	70	25

377 Azzahir Beybars Mosque

1969. Air. 700th Anniv of Azzahir Beybars Mosque.

1049	**377**	30m. purple	70	25

378 "Three Veiled Women" (Mahmoud Said)

1970. Post Day.

1050	**378**	100m. multicoloured	4·25	3·25

379 Parliament Building and Emblems

1970. Int Conf on Middle East Crisis, Cairo.

1051	**379**	20m. ultram, brn & bl	80	25

380 Human Rights Emblem and "Three Races"

1970. Racial Equality Day.

1052	**380**	20m.+10m. yellow, brown and green	1·40	1·00

381 Arab League Flag, Arms and Map

1970. 25th Anniv of Arab League.

1053	**381**	20m.+10m. green, brown and blue	1·30	1·10
1054	**381**	30m. grn, plum & orge	70	45

382 Mina House Hotel, Giza, and Sheraton Hotel, Cairo

1970. Centenary of Mina House Hotel and Opening of Sheraton Hotel.

1055	**382**	20m. green, orange & bl	80	35

383 Pharmacists

1970. 30th Anniv of Egyptian Pharmaceutical Industry.

1056	**383**	20m. blue, brown & yell	1·40	35

384 Mermaid

1970. 8th Fine Arts Biennale, Alexandria.

1057	**384**	20m. blk, bl & orge	70	25

385 Lenin

1970. Air. Birth Centenary of Lenin.

1058	**385**	80m. brown and green	2·00	1·50

386 Emblem and Bombed Factory

1970. Air. Attack on Abu Zaabal Factory.

1059	**386**	80m. purple, bl & yell	2·00	1·50

387 Talaat Harb (founder) and Bank

1970. 50th Anniv of Misr Bank.

1060	**387**	20m. brn, ochre & bl	70	25

388 I.T.U. Emblem

1970. World Telecommunications Day.

1061	**388**	20m. blue, yell & brn	85	25

389 New Headquarters Building

1970. New U.P.U. Headquarters Building, Berne.

1062	**389**	20m. purple, green and yellow (postage)	85	35
1063	**389**	80m. black, green and yellow (air)	1·50	1·20

390 Basketball Player, Cup and Map

1970. 5th Africa Men's Basketball Championships.

1064	**390**	20m. blue, brn & yell	1·20	45

391 Emblems of U.P.U., U.N. and African Postal Union

1970. African Postal Union Seminar.

1065	**391**	20m. green, vio & orge	85	25

392 Footballer and Cup

1970. Africa Cup Football Championships.

1066	**392**	20m. brown, yellow & bl	1·10	45

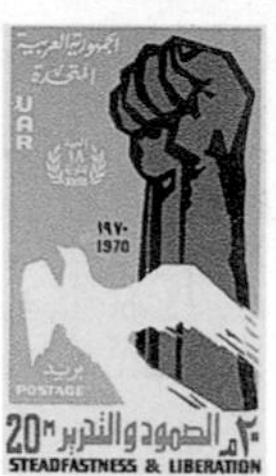

393 Clenched Fists and Dove

1970. 18th Anniv of Revolution.

1067	**393**	20m. orge, blk & grn	95	35
MS1068		111×70 mm. **393** 100m. orange, black and blue. Imperf	6·00	4·50

394 Mosque in Flames

1970. 1st Anniv of Burning of Al Aqsa Mosque, Jerusalem.

1069	**394**	20m. brn, orge & grn	1·40	45
1070	**394**	60m. brown, red & blue	3·25	1·90

395 Globe, Wheat and Cogwheel

1970. World Standards Day.

1071	**395**	20m. brn, blue & grn	85	25

396 "Peace, Justice and Progress" (25th Anniv of U.N.)

1970. United Nations Day.

1072	**396**	5m. blue, lt bl & mve	25	15
1073	-	10m. bl, ochre & brn	25	25
1074	-	20m. multicoloured	70	35
1075	-	20m.+10m. mult	1·10	90
1076	-	55m. brn, bl & ochre	1·50	1·20
1077	-	55m. brn, bl & ochre	1·50	1·20

DESIGNS AND EVENTS—37×37 mm: 10m. U.N. emblem; 55m. (2) Philae Temple (composite design) (UNESCO. Campaign for Preservation of Nubian Monuments); 36×36 mm: 20m. Frightened child and bombed school (Int Education Year); 41×25 mm: 20m.+10m. Palestinian guerrillas and refugees ("Int support for Palestinians").

397 President Nasser

1970. Pres. Gamal Nasser Memorial Issue.

1078	**397**	5m. black and bl (postage)	25	25
1079	-	20m. black and green	70	25
1080	-	30m. black & grn (air)	1·10	45
1081	-	80m. black & brown	3·00	1·50

DESIGN—46×27 mm: 30, 80m. Pres. Nasser and mosque.

398 Medical Association Building

1970. Egyptian Anniversaries.

1082	**398**	20m. brown, yellow and blue	85	55
1083	-	20m. brown, yellow and blue	85	55
1084	-	20m. brown and blue	85	55
1085	-	20m. brown, yellow and blue	85	55
1086	-	20m. brown, yellow and blue	85	55

DESIGNS AND EVENTS: No. 1082, Type **398** (50th anniv of Egyptian Medical Assn); 1083, Old and new library buildings (centenary of National Library); 1084, "The most significant victory..." Pres. Nasser text ("Egyptian Credo"); 1085, Old and new printing works (150th anniv of Govt. Printing Office); 1086, Old and new headquarters (50th anniv of Egyptian Engineering Society).

399 Map of Egypt, Libya and Sudan

1970. Signing of Tripoli Charter.

1087	**399**	20m. green, black & red	85	25

400 Minaret, Qalawun Mosque

1970. Post Day. Mosque Minarets. Each brown, blue and yellow.

1088	5m. Type **400**	85	25
1089	10m. As-Salem Mosque	1·40	35
1090	20m. Isna Mosque	3·00	80
1091	55m. Al-Hakim Mosque	4·25	2·10

See also Nos. 1142/5 and 1189/92.

401 Pres. Gamel Nasser

1971. Inauguration of Aswan High Dam. Sheet 135×80 mm.

MS1092	**401** (a) 100m. black and emerald; (b) 200m. black and blue	17·00	16·00

402 Fair Emblem

1971. Cairo International Fair.

1093	**402**	20m. yellow, blk & pur	70	25

403 Map of Arab States and A.P.U. Emblem

1971. 9th Arab Postal Union Congress, Cairo.

1094	**403**	20m. blue, orange and green (postage)	70	25
1095	**403**	30m. brown, orange and green (air)	1·20	55

404 Globe and Cotton Symbols

1971. Egyptian Cotton Production.

1096	**404**	20m. brown, blue & grn	70	25

405 Army Emblem

1971. Forces' Mail.

1097	**405**	10m. violet	1·80	1·40

The above stamp was issued for civilian use on letters addressed to servicemen and was not valid for any other purpose.

406 Hesy Ra (ancient physician) and Papyrus

1971. World Health Day.

1098	**406**	20m. purple & yellow	1·40	35

407 Pres. Gamal Nasser

1971

1099	**407**	20m. blue and purple	95	25
1100	**407**	55m. plum and blue	3·00	1·00

408 Map and I.T.U. Emblem

1971. African Telecommunications Year.

1101	**408**	20m. multicoloured	70	35

409 El Rifaei and Sultan Hussein Mosques

1971. Air. Multicoloured.

1102	30m. Type **409**	2·30	80
1103	85m. Rameses Square, Cairo	4·75	1·50
1104	110m. Sphinx and Pyramids	6·00	3·25

410 "Industrial Progress"

1971. 19th Anniv of Revolution. Mult.

1105	20m. Type **410**	70	45
1106	20m. Ear of Wheat and Laurel ("Land Reclamation")	70	45
MS1107	130×90 mm. 100m. Candle illuminating map of Africa (40×40 mm). Imperf	7·25	2·30

411 A.P.U. Emblem

1971. 25th Anniv of Founding of Arab Postal Union at Sofar Conference.

1108	**411**	20m. emerald, yellow and green (postage)	70	35
1109	**411**	30m. mult (air)	1·40	70

412 Federal Links

1971. Inaug of Confederation of Arab Republics.

1110	**412**	20m. brown, black and purple (postage)	70	35
1111	**412**	30m. green, black and purple (air)	1·30	70

413 Pres. Gamal Nasser

1971. 1st Death Anniv of President Nasser.

1112	**413**	5m. blue and purple	50	25
1113	**413**	20m. purple and blue	70	25
1114	**413**	30m. blue and brown	1·30	80
1115	**413**	55m. brown and green	2·30	1·20

414 "Princess and Child"

1971. United Nations Day.

1116	**414**	5m. black, brown and cinnamon (postage)	60	30
1117	-	20m. multicoloured	1·20	35
1118	-	55m. multicoloured	2·75	1·50
1119	-	30m. mult (air)	2·40	70

DESIGNS—As Type **414**. VERT: 5m. (UNICEF). HORIZ: 20m. Emblem and four heads (Racial Equality Year); 36×36 mm: 30m. Refugee and Al-Aqsa Mosque (U.N.R.W.A.); 24×58 mm: 55m. Partly submerged pillar, Philae (25th anniv of UNESCO).

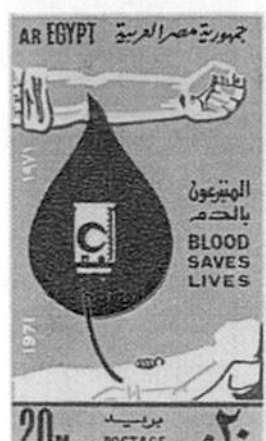

415 "Blood Saves Lives"

1971. Blood Donors.

1120	**415**	20m. red and green	1·20	25

416 New Post Office

1971. Opening of New Head Post Office, Alexandria.

1121	**416**	20m. brown and blue	1·30	35

417 Sunflower

1971. Ramadan Festival.

1122	**417**	5m. multicoloured	50	15

418 Abdallah El Nadim

1971. 75th Death Anniv of Abdallah El Nadim (poet and journalist).

1123	**418**	20m. brown & green	70	25

419 Globe and Earth's Strata

1971. 75th Anniv of Egyptian Geological Survey.

1124	**419**	20m. multicoloured	1·30	25

420 A.P.U. Emblem and Dove with Letter

1971. 10th Anniv of African Postal Union.

1125	**420**	5m. mult (postage)	50	25
1126	**420**	20m. green, orge & blk	95	25
1127	-	55m. black, bl & red	2·30	1·40
1128	-	30m. mult (air)	1·20	70

DESIGN: 30m., 55m. A.P.U. emblem and airmail envelope.

421 "Savings Bank"

1971. 70th Anniv of Post Office Savings Bank.

1129	**421**	20m. multicoloured	95	35

421a Victory Parade (scene from "Aida")

1971. Air. Centenary of First Performance of Verdi's Opera "Aida", in Cairo.

1130	**421a**	110m. yell, grn & brn	7·25	3·50

423 Cairo Citadel

1972. Inscr "A. R. EGYPT".

1131	**374**	1m. blue and brown	25	25
1131a	**374**	1m. brown	35	25
1132	-	5m. blue, yellow & brn (as No. 1040)	50	25
1132a	-	5m. green	50	25
1132b	-	5m. bistre	60	25
1133	-	10m. purple, brown & bl (as No. 1041)	70	25
1133a	-	10m. brown	60	25
1134	**260**	20m. green (22×27½ mm)	1·20	35
1135	**260**	20m. mauve (22×27½ mm)	1·20	35
1136	-	50m. brown, ochre & blue (as No. 1043)	2·50	45
1136a	-	50m. blue	2·50	35
1137	-	55m. mauve (as No. 1044)	4·00	90
1137a	-	55m. green	2·10	35
1138a	**423**	100m. blk, red & bl	3·00	70
1139	-	200m. brown & grn	7·25	1·50
1140	-	500m. brown and blue (as No. 1046)	17·00	4·00
1141	-	£El green & orange (as No. 1047)	33·00	9·50

DESIGNS—As Type **423**: Nos. 1132a/b, Rameses II; 1133a, Head of Seti I; 1136a, Goddess Hathar; 1137a, Sphinx and pyramid. As Type **375**: No. 1139, Head of Userkaf.

1972. Post Day. Mosque Minarets. As T 400. Multicoloured.

1142	5m. Western minaret, An-Nasir Mosque	50	15
1143	20m. Eastern minaret, An-Nasir Mosque	1·30	15
1144	30m. Al-Gawli Mosque	3·00	55
1145	55m. Ahmed Ibn Toulon Mosque	4·25	1·70

424a Police Emblem and Activities

1972. Police Day.

1146	**424a**	20m. yellow, bl & brn	2·40	35

425 Book Year Emblem

1972. International Book Year.

1147	**425**	20m. violet, yellow & grn	1·30	35

426 Globe, Glider, Rocket and Emblem

1972. Air. International Aerospace Education Conference, Cairo.

1148	**426**	30m. brown, blue & yell	2·00	70

427 Monastery Aflame

1972. Air. Burning of St. Catherine's Monastery, Sinai.

1149	**427**	110m. black, brn & red	6·00	4·75

428 "Palette" (Seif Wanli)

1972. 9th Fine Arts Bienniale, Alexandria.

1150	**428**	20m. red, yellow & blk	95	35

429 Fair Emblem

1972. Int Fair, Cairo.

1151	**429**	20m. multicoloured	1·30	35

430 Brig. Abdel Moniem Riad and Battle Scene

1972. 2nd Death Anniv of Brig. Abdel Moniem Riad.

1152	**430**	20m. brown, turq & bl	1·50	35

431 Birds in Tree

1972. Mother's Day.

1153	**431**	20m. multicoloured	1·20	25

432 Head of Tutankhamun (wooden statuette)

1972. 50th Anniv of Discovery of Tutankhamun's Tomb.

1154	**432**	20m. mult (postage)	2·40	70
1155	-	55m. multicoloured	7·25	1·90
1156	-	110m. grn brn & bl (air)	14·50	6·75
1157	-	110m. grn, brn & bl	14·50	6·75
MS1158		95×100 mm. 200m. multi-coloured	48·00	45·00

DESIGNS—Square (As T **436**)—No. 1168, "Science and Faith" emblem. HORIZ: (42×25 mm)—110m. Confederation of Arab Republics flag.

Nos. 1156/7 were issued together, se-tenant, forming a composite design.

433 Nefertiti

1972. 50th Anniv of Society of Friends of Art.

1159	**433**	20m. blk, gold & red	1·30	35

434 Map of Africa

1972. Africa Day.

1160	**434**	20m. brown, bl & vio	85	35

436 Eagle Emblem

1972. 20th Anniv of Revolution.

1167	**436**	20m. gold, blk & grn (postage)	1·20	35
1168	**436**	20m. red, blk & blue	1·20	35
MS1169		70×110 mm. 110m. gold, red and black (air). Imperf	7·25	7·25

437 Al-Azhar Mosque and St. George's Church, Cairo

1972. Air.

1170	**437**	30m. brn, ochre & bl	2·75	55
1171	-	85m. brn, ochre & bl	5·00	2·10

1172 - 110m. brn, ochre & bl 5·75 2·10

DESIGNS: 85m. Temple, Abu Simbel; 110m. Pyramids, Giza.

438 Boxing

1972. Olympic Games, Munich.

1173	**438**	5m. mult (postage)	35	25
1174	-	10m. yellow, blk & red	50	25
1175	-	20m. grn, red & orge	70	35
1176	-	30m. green, buff and red (air)	1·40	55
1177	-	30m. violet, red & turq	1·40	55
1178	-	50m. black, blue & grn	2·30	1·40
1179	-	55m. red, green & blue	2·75	1·60

DESIGNS—HORIZ: 10m. Wrestling; 20m. Basketball, VERT: 30m. (No. 1176), Weightlifting; 30m. (No. 1177), Handball; 50m. Swimming; 55m. Gymnastics.

439 Confederation Flag

1972. 1st Anniv of Confederation of Arab Republics.

1180 **439** 20m. brown, red & blk 95 35

440 J. -F. Champollion and Rosetta Stone

1972. Air. 150th Anniv of Champollion's Translation of Egyptian Heiroglyphics.

1181 **440** 110m. grn, blk & brn 9·00 3·50

441 Heart (World Health Day)

1972. United Nations Day.

1182	-	10m. red, blue & brown	60	35
1183	**441**	20m. black, yell & grn	1·10	45
1184	-	30m. brown, vio & bl	3·25	90
1185	-	55m. gold, brown & bl	3·50	1·10

DESIGNS—22×40 mm: 10m. Emblem of 14th Regional Tuberculosis Conference, Cairo. 47×28 mm: 30m. Refugees (U.N.R.W.A.). 37×37 mm: 55m. Flooded temple, Philae (UNESCO Campaign for Preservation of Nubian Monuments).

442 Hibiscus

1972. Ramadan Festival.

1186 **442** 10m. purple, grn & brn 70 25

443 Work Day Emblem

1972. Social Work Day.

1187 **443** 20m. blue, brown & grn 1·20 25

444 "Rowing Fours" on Nile

1972. 3rd Nile Rowing Festival, Luxor.

1188 **444** 20m. brown and blue 1·70 45

1973. Post Day. Mosque Minarets. As T 400. Each brown, yellow and green.

1189	10m. Al-Maridani Mosque	85	25
1190	20m. Bashtak Mosque	1·40	25
1191	30m. Qusun Mosque	3·00	80
1192	55m. Al-Gashankir Mosque	4·25	2·10

445 Ears of Corn and Globe within Cogwheel

1973. International Fair, Cairo.

1193 **445** 20m. blue, black & grn 70 25

446 Symbolic Family

1973. Family Planning Week.

1194 **446** 20m. black, orge & grn 70 25

447 Telecommunications Map

1973. Air. 5th Int Telecommunications Day.

1195 **447** 30m. blue, black & brn 1·30 35

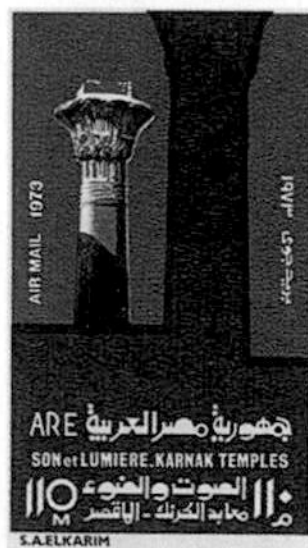

448 Temple Column, Karnak

1973. Air. "Son et Lumiere", Karnak Temples, Luxor.

1196 **448** 110m. black, mve & bl 4·75 3·25

449 Bloody Hand and Boeing 727 Jetliner

1973. Air. Attack on Libyan Airliner over Sinai.

1197 **449** 110m. red, black & bis 7·75 3·25

451 Rifaa el Tahtawi

1973. Death Centenary of Rifaa el Tahtawi (educationist).

1200 **451** 20m. brn, grn & dp grn 95 35

452 Mrs. Hoda Sharawi and Sania Girls Secondary School

1973. Centenary of Egyptian Female Education and 50th Anniv of Women's Union.

1201 **452** 20m. green, brn & bl 85 25

453 Mohamed Korayem

1973. 21st Anniv of Revolution. Leaders of the 1798 Resistance Movement.

1202	**453**	20m. brown, blue & grn	85	35
1203	-	20m. brown, blue & grn	85	35
1204	-	20m. choc, pk & brn	85	35

MS1205 60×60 mm. 110m. gold, black and blue. Imperf 4·25 4·25

DESIGNS—As T **453**: No. 1202, Type **453**; No. 1203, Omar Makram; 1024, Abdel Rahman el Gaberti. (70×92 mm)—**MS**1205, Hands holding weapons and symbols.

454 Refugees and Map of Palestine

1973. Air. Palestinian Refugees.

1206 **454** 30m. purple, brn & bl 3·00 70

455 Rose

1973. Ramadan Festival.

1207 **455** 10m. red, yellow & blue 60 25

456 "Light and Hope"

1973. 25th Anniv of W.H.O.

1208 **456** 20m.+10m. bl & gold 95 90

457 Bank Building

1973. 75th Anniv of National Bank of Egypt.

1209 **457** 20m. blk, grn & orge 85 35

458 Emblem and Weather-vane

1973. Air. Centenary of World Meteorological Organization.

1210 **458** 110m. gold, vio & bl 4·25 2·50

459 Global Emblem

1973. 10th Anniv of World Food Programme.

1211 **459** 10m. blue, grn & brn 70 35

460 Philae Temples

1973. UNESCO. Campaign for the Preservation of Nubian Monuments.

1212 **460** 55m. orge, blue & violet 4·25 1·50

461 Interpol Emblem

1973. Air. 50th Anniv of International Criminal Police Organization (Interpol).

1213 **461** 110m. multicoloured 4·50 2·50

462 Flame Emblem

1973. 25th Anniv of Declaration of Human Rights.

1214 **462** 20m. red, green & blue 85 25

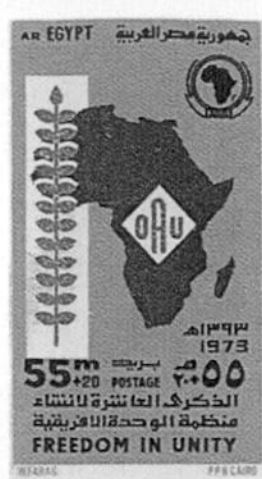

463 Laurel and Map of Africa

1973. 10th Anniv of Organization of African Unity.
1215 **463** 55m.+20m. mult 3·00 3·00

464 "Donation"

1973. Social Work Day.
1216 **464** 20m.+10m. blue, lilac and red 70 55

465 Dr. Taha Hussein (scholar)

1973. Hussein Commemoration.
1217 **465** 20m. brown, blue & grn 70 25

466 Pres. Sadat and Flag

1973. Crossing of the Suez Canal, 6 October 1973.
1218 **466** 20m. black, red & brn 1·40 45
See also No. 1233.

467 Egyptian Postal Services Emblem

1973. Air. Post Day.
1219 **467** 20m. blk, red & grey 60 25
1220 - 30m. vio, orge & blk 85 25
1221 - 55m. mve, grn & blk 1·90 1·20
1222 - 110m. gold, bl & blk 2·50 2·30
DESIGNS—As T **467**: 30m. Arab Postal Union emblem; 55m. African Postal Union emblem; 37×37 mm: 110m. U.P.U. emblem.

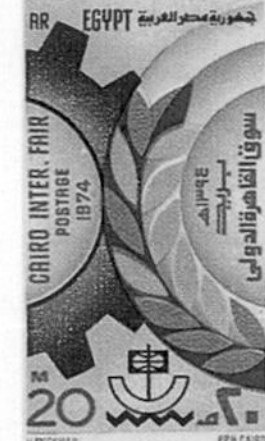

468 Cogwheel, Ear of Corn and Fair Emblem

1974. International Fair, Cairo.
1223 **468** 20m. multicoloured 70 25

469 Madame Sadat with Patient

1974. Society of Faith and Hope (for rehabilitation of the disabled).
1224 **469** 20m.+10m. purple, gold and green 1·30 1·20

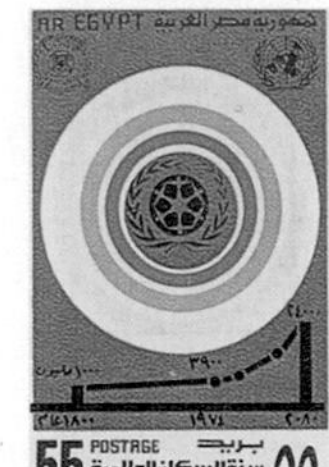

470 Emblem and Graph

1974. World Population Year.
1225 **470** 55m. black, orge & grn 1·40 80

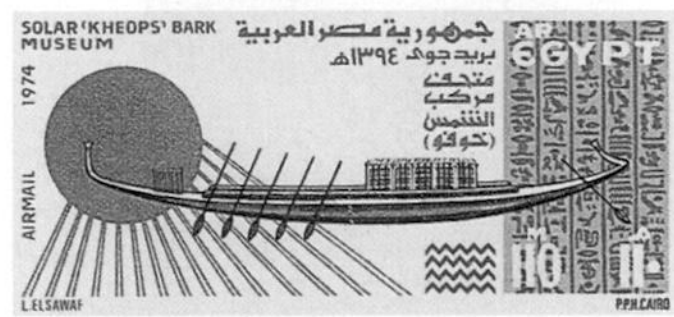

471 Solar Boat of Cheops

1974. Air. Inauguration of Solar Boat Museum.
1226 **471** 110m. brown, gold & bl 4·00 2·75

472 "Ancient Egyptian Workers" (carving from Queen Tee's tomb, Sakara)

1974. Labour Day (1 May).
1227 **472** 20m. black, yellow & bl 95 35

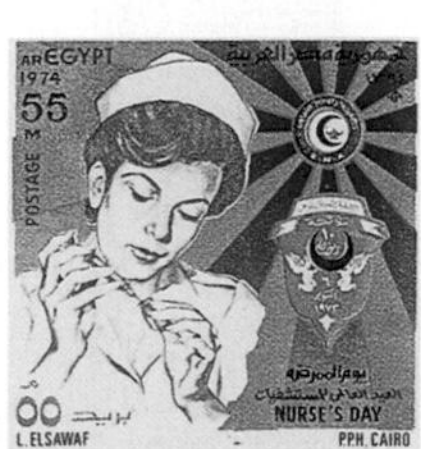

473 Nurse with Syringe

1974. Nurses' Day.
1228 **473** 55m. gold, red & green 2·30 70

474 Troops crossing Barlev Line during October War

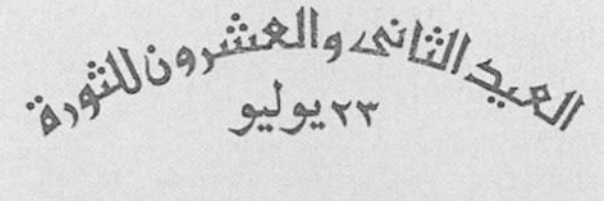

475 Scroll and Emblems (The October Working Paper)

1974. 22nd Anniv of Revolution.
1229 - 20m. gold, black & blue 95 45
1230 - 20m. silver, blk & pur 95 45
1231 **474** 20m. black, orge & bl 95 45
MS1232 72×108 mm. **475** 110m. gold, green and carmine. Imperf 4·75 4·50
DESIGNS—As T **474**: No. 1229, Map of Suez Canal and "Reconstruction". 36×36 mm: No. 1230, Sheet of aluminium.

476 Pres. Sadat and Flag

1974. 1st Anniv of Suez Crossing.
1233 **476** 20m. black, red & yell 1·80 70
See also No. 1218.

477 Teachers' Badge

1974. Teachers' Day.
1234 **477** 20m. brown, blk & bl 85 25

478 Artists' Palette

1974. 6th Plastic Arts Exhibition.
1235 **478** 30m. black, yellow & vio 1·20 45

479 Meridian Hotel

1974. Air. Opening of Meridian Hotel, Cairo.
1236 **479** 110m. multicoloured 2·40 1·40

480 U.P.U. Monument, Brene

1974. Centenary of Universal Postal Union. Sheet 76×101 mm.
MS1237 **480** 110m. multicoloured 7·25 6·75

481 Child and Emblems

1974. Social Work Day.
1238 **481** 30m. green, brown & bl 1·30 45

482 Emblems of Standardization

1974. World Standards Day.
1239 **482** 10m. orange, bl & blk 60 25

483 "Aggression Registers"

1974. Refugees Propaganda.
1240 **483** 20m. blue and red 85 25

484 Philae Temples

1974. UNESCO. Campaign for Preservation of Nubian Monuments.
1241 **484** 55m. brn, stone & bl 3·50 90

485 Arum Lily

1974. Ramadan Festival.

1242	**485**	10m. multicoloured	70	25

486 Pile of Coins

1974. International Savings Day.

1243	**486**	20m. grey, blue & grn	70	25

487 Organization Emblems and Cameos

1974. Health Insurance Organization.

1244	**487**	30m. violet, red & brn	1·10	35

487a Abbas Mahmoud El Akkad (writer)

1974. Famous Egyptians.

1245	**487a**	20m. blue and brown	60	35
1246	-	20m. brown and blue	60	35

DESIGNS: No. 1245, (10th death anniv); No. 1246, Mustafa Lutfy El Manfalouty (journalist).

488 Sacred Ibis

1975. Post Day. Ancient Treasures.

1247	**488**	20m. brown, bl & sil	1·10	35
1248	-	30m. bl, orge & mve	1·40	35
1249	-	55m. brn, gold & grn	2·00	1·10
1250	-	110m. yellow, brn & bl	3·50	2·50

DESIGNS—HORIZ: 30m. Glass "fish" vase. VERT: 55m. Pharaonic gold vase; 110m. Ankh-shaped mirror.

489 Om Kolthoum (Arab singer)

1975. Om Kolthoum Commemoration.

1251	**489**	20m. brown	95	25

490 Crescent and Globe

1975. Mohammed's Birthday.

1252	**490**	20m. violet, silver & bl	95	25

491 Fair Emblem

1975. Cairo International Fair.

1253	**491**	20m. green, blue & red	70	25

492 Kasr El Ainy Hospital

1975. World Health Day.

1254	**492**	20m. brown and blue	95	25

493 Children Reading Book

1975. Science Day.

1255	**493**	20m. blue, red & yell	1·10	45
1256	-	20m. black & brown	1·10	45

DESIGN: No. 1256, Pupils and graph.

494 President Sadat, Ships and Map of Canal

1975. Re-opening of Suez Canal.

1257	**494**	20m. brown, blue and black (postage)	85	35
1258	**494**	30m. turquoise, green and blue (air)	1·90	70
1259	**494**	110m. bl blk & turq	3·00	2·30

495 Belmabgoknis Flower

1975. Festivals.

1260	**495**	10m. blue, grn & lt grn	70	25

496 I.C.I.D. Emblem

1975. Air. 25th Anniv of International Commission on Irrigation and Drainage.

1261	**496**	110m. green, bl & orge	3·00	1·80

497 Spotlight on Village

1975. 23rd Anniv of Revolution.

1262	**497**	20m. blue and brown	85	35
1263	-	20m. orge, blk & grn	85	35
1264	-	110m. multicoloured	8·25	8·00

DESIGNS—38×22 mm: No. 1263, "Tourism" (pyramids and sphinx). 70×79 mm: No. 1264, Tourist map of Egypt.

498 Volleyball

1975. 6th Arab School Sports Tournament. Each blue, orange and green.

1265	20m. Type **498**	1·20	55
1266	20m. Running	1·20	55
1267	20m. Tournament emblem	1·20	55
1268	20m. Basketball	1·20	55
1269	20m. Football	1·20	55

499 Flag and Tanks

1975. 2nd Anniv of Battle of 6 October.

1270	**499**	20m. multicoloured	1·50	45

1975. International Symposium on October War, Cairo University. As T 499 but with additional commemorative inscription at foot and "M" above figures of value.

1271	20m. multicoloured	1·50	45

500 Schistosomiasis Conference Emblem

1975. United Nations Day.

1272	**500**	20m. blue, mauve and brown (postage)	1·20	45
1273	-	55m. purple, yell & bl	2·75	1·40
1274	-	30m. brn, grn & pur (air)	1·50	70
1275	-	110m. blk, orge & grn	4·00	2·75

DESIGNS—27×47 mm: 55m. Wall relief (UNESCO Campaign for Preservation of Nubian Monuments). 48×40 mm: 30m. Refugees and barbed wire (U.N.R.W.A.). 22×40 mm: 110m. Women (International Women's Year).

501 University Emblem

1975. 25th Anniv of Ein Shams University.

1276	**501**	20m. blue, yell & grey	60	10

501a Al-Kanady

1975. Arab Philosophers.

1277	**501a**	20m. brown, grn & bl	1·70	55
1278	-	20m. brown, grn & bl	1·70	55
1279	-	20m. brown, grn & bl	1·70	55

DESIGNS: No. 1278, Al-Farabi, and lute; No. 1279, Al-Biruni, and open book.

502 Ibex

1976. Post Day. Treasures from Tutankhamun's Tomb. Multicoloured.

1280	20m. Type **502**	6·00	2·10
1281	30m. Lioness	9·50	2·75
1282	55m. Sacred Cow	15·00	8·00
1283	110m. Hippopotamus	23·00	16·00

503 High Dam and Industrial Potential

1976. Filling of High Dam Lake.

1284	**503**	20m. multicoloured	1·10	25

504 Fair Emblem

1976. Cairo International Fair.

1285	**504**	20m. violet & orange	50	15

505 Biennale Commemorative Emblem

1976. 11th Fine Arts Biennale, Alexandria.

1286	**505**	20m. yellow, blk & grn	60	15

506 Protective Hands

1976. Society of Faith and Hope.

1287	**506**	20m. yell, grn & dp grn	70	35

507 "Pharaonic Eye" and Emblem

1976. World Health Day.

1288	**507**	20m. brn, yell & grn	95	25

508 Scales of Justice

1976. 5th Anniv of Rectification Movement.

1289	**508**	20m. black, grn & red	60	35

509 Pres. Sadat and Emblem

1976. Centenary of Arbitration Service.

1290	**509**	20m. yellow, grn & ol	60	35

510 Front Page of First Issue

1976. Cent of Newspaper "Al-Ahram".

1291	**510**	20m. brown, blk & red	85	35

511 Pres. Sadat and World Map

1976. 24th Anniv of Revolution.

1292	**511**	20m. yellow, blue & black	85	35
MS1293		86×77 mm. **511** 110m. yellow and brown. Imperf	9·50	9·00

512 Amaryllis

1976. Festivals.

1294	**512**	10m. multicoloured	60	15

513 Map of Red Sea, Pres. Sadat and Abu Redice Oil Refinery

1976. 3rd Anniv of Suez Canal Crossing. Mult.

1295		20m. Type **513**	95	45
1296		20m. Irrigation and reconstruction—map of Suez Canal (48×40 mm)	95	45
1297		110m. Monument to Soldiers of October 6th, 1973 (65×80 mm)	9·50	9·00

514 Animals on Papyrus Leaf ("Literature for Children")

1976. United Nations Day.

1298	**514**	20m. brown, stone & bl	70	25
1299	-	30m. brown, grn & blk	85	35
1300	-	55m. brown and blue	1·80	55
1301	-	110m. red, grn & vio	2·50	1·70

DESIGNS—39×22 mm: 30m. Dome of the Rock (Palestinian Refugees); 110m. UNESCO emblem on figure "30" (30th anniv of UNESCO). 25×59 mm: 55m. Relief showing goddess Isis, Philae Temple (UNESCO Campaign for Preservation of Nubian Monuments).

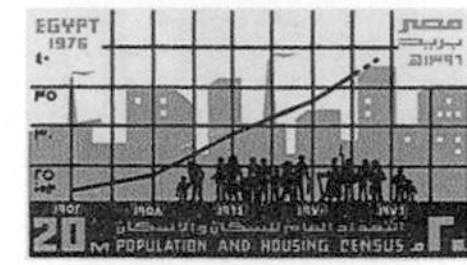

515 Graph, People and Skyline

1976. Population and Housing Census.

1302	**515**	20m. sepia, blue & brn	70	25

516 Society Medal and Map of the Nile

1976. Cent of Egyptian Geographical Society.

1303	**516**	20m. brown, green & bl	70	25

517 King Akhnaton

1977. Post Day.

1304	**517**	20m. brown & black	70	35
1305	-	30m. brown & black	70	35
1306	-	55m. brown & purple	1·30	45
1307	-	110m. brown & purple	5·25	1·40

DESIGNS: 30m. Head of Akhnaton's daughter; 55m. Head of Nefertiti, wife of Akhnaton; 110m. Bust of Akhnaton.

518 Patrolman, Police Car and Map

1977. Police Day.

1308	**518**	20m. red, blue & black	1·30	35

519 Pharaonic Ship

1977. Cairo International Fair.

1309	**519**	20m. green, blk & red	1·10	35

520 O.A.U. and Arab League Emblems on Map

1977. 1st Afro-Arab Summit Conference.

1310	**520**	55m. blue, blk & orge	1·20	55

521 King Faisal

1977. King Faisal of Saudi Arabia Commemoration.

1311	**521**	20m. brown and blue	70	25

522 Healthy Children and Paralysed Child

1977. National Campaign for Prevention of Poliomyelitis.

1312	**522**	20m. dp brn, brn & red	1·10	25

523 A.P.U. Emblem and National Flags

1977. Silver Jubilee of Arab Postal Union.

1313	**523**	20m. multicoloured	50	25
1314	**523**	30m. multicoloured	70	35

524 Children's Village

1977. Inaug of S.O.S. Children's Village, Cairo.

1315	**524**	20m. brown, blue & grn	60	35
1316	**524**	55m. red, blue & green	1·80	80

525 Earth and Satellite

1977. World Telecommunications Day.

1317	**525**	110m. blue, yell & blk	2·40	1·40

526 Loom, Spindle and Factories

1977. 50th Anniv of Egyptian Spinning and Weaving Company, El Mehalla El Kobra.

1318	**526**	20m. green, brn & bis	70	20

527 Egyptian Flag and Symbol of the Revolution

1977. 25th Anniv of Revolution.

1319	**527**	20m. black, red & silver	70	20
MS1320		76×85 mm. 110m. black, red and blue. Imperf	3·50	3·50

DESIGN: 110 mm. Egyptian flag on eagle silhouette.

528 Saad Zaghoul

1977. 50th Death Anniv of Saad Zaghoul (revolutionary).

1321	**528**	20m. brown & green	35	20

529 Archbishop Capucci and Map of Palestine

1977. 3rd Anniv of Arrest of Archbishop Capucci.

1322	**529**	45m. blk, grey & grn	1·40	55

530 Bird of Paradise Flowers

1977. Festivals.

1323	**530**	10m. multicoloured	50	20

531 Title Deeds overshadowing Map of Egypt

1977. 25th Anniv of Agrarian Reform Law.

1324	**531**	20m. black, bl & grn	50	20

532 Soldier, Tanks and 6th October Medal

1977. 4th Anniv of Suez Canal Crossing.

1325	**532**	20m. brn, red & orge	60	25
1326	-	140m. brn, red & gold	9·75	8·00

DESIGN: 46×55 mm: 140m. President Sadat.

533 Diesel Locomotive, Electric Railcar and Steam Locomotive No. 1, 1852

1977. 125th Anniv of Egyptian Railways.

1327	**533**	20m. green, blue & vio	2·00	45

534 Refugees and the Al-Aqsa Mosque (U.N.R.W.A.)

1977. United Nations Day.

1328	**534**	45m. green, red & blk	95	45
1329	-	55m. yellow and blue	1·70	55
1330	-	140m. ochre & brown	3·25	1·80

DESIGNS—36×36 mm: 55m. Relief from Philae showing Horus and goddess Taueret. As T **534** but vert: 140m. Relief from Philae in frame of pharaonic column (UNESCO Campaign for Preservation of Nubian Monuments).

535 Ancient Egyptian Symbol for "Vision" and Film

1977. 50th Anniv of Egyptian Cinema.

1331	**535**	20m. blk, gold & grey	85	25

536 Natural Gas Rig and Factories

1977. National Petroleum Festival.

1332	**536**	20m. blue, blk & grn	1·50	35

537 President Sadat, Olive Branches and Dome of the Rock, Jerusalem

1977. President Sadat's Peace Mission to Israel.

1333	**537**	20m. brown, grn & blk	1·20	35
1334	**537**	140m. blk, grn & brn	4·25	1·80

538 The Three Pyramids at Giza

1978. Air.

1335	**538**	45m. yellow & brown	60	25
1335b	**538**	60m. brown	2·00	1·00
1336	-	115m. brown & blue	1·20	55
1337	-	140m. lilac and blue	1·90	1·00
1337a	-	185m. brown & blue	5·00	2·30

DESIGNS: 115, 185m. Step Pyramid and temple entrance, Sakkara. 140m. Nile feluccas.

539 Statue of Rameses II

1978. Post Day. Multicoloured.

1338	20m. Type **539**	95	45
1339	45m. Relief showing coronation of Queen Nefertari, Abu Simbel	2·00	1·10

540 Irrigation Wheels, Fayoum

1978

1340	**540**	1m. blue	25	15
1341	-	5m. brown	25	15
1342	-	10m. green	25	15
1343	-	20m. brown	35	25
1343b	-	30m. brown	95	70
1344	-	50m. blue	60	25
1345	-	55m. brown	70	45
1346	-	70m. brown	95	35
1346a	-	80m. brown	95	25
1347	-	85m. purple	1·10	55
1348	-	100m. brown	1·50	45
1349	-	200m. indigo & blue	2·75	90
1350	-	500m. brn, bl & yell	8·25	2·75
1351	-	£E1 blue, yell & brn	12·00	5·00

DESIGNS—As T **540**: 5m. Pigeon-loft; 10m. Statue of Horus; 20, 30m. El Rifaei Mosque, Cairo; 50m. Syrian monastery, Wady el Netroon; 55m. Edfu temple; 70, 80m. October Bridge over Suez Canal; 85m. Medom pyramid; 100m. Facade of Abu el Abbas el Morsy Mosque, Alexandria; 200m. El Sawary column and sphinx, Alexandria; 37×45 mm: 500m. Arab horse; £E1, Bird (floor decoration from Akhnaton's palace).

541 Fair Emblem

1978. 11th Cairo International Fair.

1352	**541**	20m. grn, blk & orge	50	15

542 Old Kasr el Ainy Medical School and New Tower

1978. 150th Anniv of Kasr el Ainy Medical School.

1353	**542**	20m. brown, blue & gold	60	25

543 Youssef el Sebai

1978. Youssef el Sebai (assassination victim) and Commando Heroes Commemoration.

1354	-	20m. brown	60	35
1355	**543**	20m. black, brn & yell	60	35

DESIGN: No. 1354, Group of Commandos and emblems.

544 Bienniale Medal and Statue, Port Said

1978. 12th Fine Arts Biennale, Alexandria.

1356	**544**	20m. black, green & bl	60	25

545 Child with Smallpox

1978. World Health Day.

1357	**545**	20m. orge, blk & grn	95	45
1358	-	20m. red, orge & blk	95	45

DESIGN AND EVENT: No. 1357, Type **545** (World Year for the Eradication of Smallpox); 21×38 mm: No. 1358, Heart and downwards pointing arrow (World Hypertension Month).

546 President Sadat

1978. 7th Anniv of Rectification Movement.

1359	**546**	20m. brn, grn & gold	70	35

547 Emblem, Beneficiaries and Olive-branch

1978. 25th Anniv of General Organization of Insurance and Pensions.

1360	**547**	20m. brown and green	35	15

548 Map showing New Cities and Regions suitable for Cultivation (The Green Revolution)

1978. 26th Anniv of Revolution.

1361	**548**	20m. green, yellow & bl	95	35
1362	-	45m. orange, grn & brn	1·90	55

DESIGN: 45m. Map of Egypt and Sudan with ear of wheat (Economic integration of Egypt and Sudan).

549 Wall of Ministerial Emblems

1978. Cent of Egyptian Ministerial System.

1363	**549**	20m. violet, grn & yell	70	35

550 President Sadat, Statue of the Crossing and Factories

1978. 5th Anniv of Suez Canal Crossing.

1364	**550**	20m. yellow, brn & grn	95	35

551 Anti-Apartheid Emblem

1978. United Nations Day.

1365	**551**	20m. orge, blk & grn	50	25
1366	-	45m. yell, brn & grn	95	55
1367	-	55m. orange, brn & bl	1·30	80
1368	-	140m. orge, blk & grn	2·50	1·40

DESIGNS—As T **551**. HORIZ: 55m. Philae temples (UNESCO Campaign for Preservation of Nubian Monuments). VERT: 140m. Dove, flame and olive branch (30th anniv of Declaration of Human Rights); 37×37 mm: 45m. Kobet al-Sakhra Mosque, refugee camp and U.N. emblem (U.N.R.W.A.).

552 Tahtib Folk-dance on Horseback

1978. Festivals.

1369	**552**	10m. orange, brn & bl	50	30
1370	**552**	20m. bistre, brn & bl	60	35

553 Pilgrims at Mount Arafat and Script of Islamic Prayer

1978. Islamic Pilgrimage.
1371 **553** 45m. brown, yell & bl 1·20 45

554 U.N. and Conference Emblems

1978. U.N. Conference on Technical Co-operation amongst Developing Countries.
1372 **554** 20m. black, grn & yell 50 15

555 Oil Pipeline "Sumed", Badge and Map

1978. 1st Anniv of Inauguration of "Sumed" Oil Pipeline.
1373 **555** 20m. brown, orge & bl 70 20

556 Mastheads and Editors

1978. 150th Anniv of "El Wakaea el Massreya" Newspaper.
1374 **556** 20m. black & brown 70 20

557 Ibn Roshd

1978. 800th Death Anniv of Ibn Roshd (philosopher).
1375 **557** 45m. blue, emer & grn 95 35

558 Old and Modern Observatories and Chart of Planet Movements

1978. 75th Anniv of Helwan Observatory.
1376 **558** 20m. blue, brn & yell 1·10 35

559 Wright Brothers' Type A Biplane and I.C.A.O. Emblem

1978. Air. 75th Anniv of First Powered Flight.
1377 **559** 140m. brown, bl & blk 3·50 2·10

560 Daughter of Rameses II

1979. Post Day.
1378 **560** 20m. yellow & brown 70 35
1379 - 140m. yellow, brn & bl 2·75 90
DESIGN—(37½×43 mm). 140m. Small temple and statues of Rameses II, Abu Simbel.

561 Open Book, Globe and Reader

1979. 11th Cairo International Book Fair.
1380 **561** 20m. brown and green 50 15

562 Fair Emblem and Symbols of Industry and Agriculture

1979. Cairo International Fair.
1381 **562** 20m. brown, orge & bl 50 15

563 Poppy and Skull

1979. 50th Anniv of Anti-narcotics General Administration.
1382 **563** 70m. green, red & yell 2·10 70

564 Isis and Horus

1979. Mother's Day.
1383 **564** 140m. yell, brn & blue 3·50 1·20

565 World Map, Koran and Symbols of Arab Accomplishments

1979. The Arabs.
1384 **565** 45m. sep, yell & turq 60 25

566 Doves, President Sadat's Signature and "Peace"

1979. Signing of Egyptian-Israeli Peace Treaty.
1385 **566** 20m. violet & yellow 60 35
1386 **566** 70m. red and green 1·40 55
1387 **566** 140m. red and green 2·40 1·40

567 Honeycomb of Food Projects

1979. Food Security.
1388 **567** 20m. yellow, grn & blk 35 15

568 Examining 1979 Peace Stamp

1979. 50th Anniv of Egyptian Philatelic Society.
1389 **568** 20m. emer, blk & brn 60 25

569 Coins of 1954 and 1979

1979. 25th Anniv of Egyptian Mint.
1390 **569** 20m. grey and yellow 50 15

570 "Sun of Freedom" and Open Book

1979. 27th Anniv of Revolution.
1391 **570** 20m. brown, orge & bl 50 15
MS1392 50×62 mm. 140m. brown and emerald. Imperf 4·75 4·75
DESIGN: 140m. Decorative inscription "23 July 1952".

571 Musicians playing Rabab and Arghoul

1979. Festivals.
1393 **571** 10m. blk, brn & orge 25 15

572 Dove and Map of Sinai

1979. 6th Anniv of Suez Canal Crossing.
1394 **572** 20m. brown and blue 70 35

573 Skeleton of "Arsinotherium zittelli"

1979. 75th Anniv of Egyptian Geological Museum.
1395 **573** 20m. brown, yell & bl 2·50 35

574 Symbols of Engineering

1979. Engineers' Day.
1396 **574** 20m. pur, yell & emer 70 25

575 Human Rights Flame over Globe

1979. United Nations Day.
1397 **575** 45m. orange, bl & grn 70 35
1398 - 140m. brn, yell & red 1·90 1·50
DESIGN: 140m. Child with flower (International Year of the Child).

576 Buildings and Hand placing Coin in Box

1979. International Savings Day.
1399 **576** 70m. multicoloured 1·20 55

577 Championship Emblem

1979. 20th International Military Sports Council Shooting Championship.

1400	**577**	20m. red, blue & yellow	70	35

578 Figure clothed in Palestinian Flag

1979. International Day of Solidarity with Palestinian People.

1401	**578**	45m. multicoloured	95	35

579 Dove, Globe and Rotary Club Emblem

1979. 50th Anniv of Cairo Rotary Club and 75th Anniv (1980) of Rotary International.

1402	**579**	140m. green, blue and yellow	1·90	1·20

580 Cogs and Factories

1979. 25th Anniv of Military Factories.

1403	**580**	20m. green and brown	50	20

581 Ali el Garem (educational writer, 1881–1949)

1979. Writers.

1404	**581**	20m. brown & dp brn	60	35
1405	-	20m. dp brown & brn	60	35

DESIGN: No. 1405, Mahmoud el Baroudy (poet, 1839–1904).

582 Capital of Pharaonic Column

1980. Post Day. Pharaonic Capitals.

1406	**582**	20m. brown and violet	50	35
1407	-	45m. brown and violet	70	70
1408	-	70m. brown and violet	1·20	80
1409	-	140m. brown and violet	3·25	1·80

DESIGNS: 45m. Head capital; 70m. Leaf capital; 140m. Capital with cartouche.

583 Goddess of Writing and Fair Emblem

1980. 12th Cairo International Book Fair.

1410	**583**	20m. brown, blue & yell	1·40	25

584 Exhibition Catalogue and Medal

1980. 13th Fine Arts Bienniale, Alexandria.

1411	**584**	20m. multicoloured	60	35

585 Fair Emblem and Branch

1980. 13th Cairo International Fair.

1412	**585**	20m. blk, grn & orge	60	35

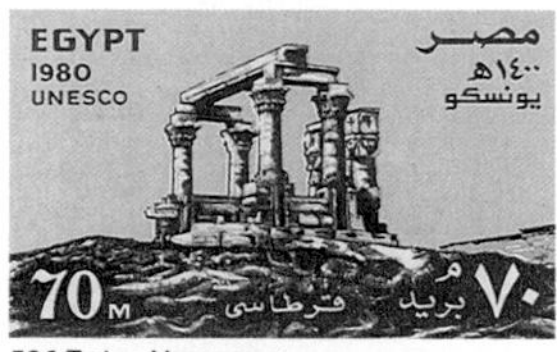

586 Trajan Monument

1980. 20th Anniv of Nubian Monuments Preservation Campaign.

1413	**586**	70m. orange, brn & bl	1·30	90
1414	-	70m. orange, brn & bl	1·30	90
1415	-	70m. orange, brn & bl	1·30	90
1416	-	70m. orange, brn & bl	1·30	90

DESIGNS: No. 1414, Qortasi monument; 1415, Kalabasha monument; 1416, Philae temple.

587 Doctors' Day Medal

1980. Doctors' Day.

1417	**587**	20m. green, blk & brn	60	20

588 President Sadat

1980. 9th Anniv of Rectification Movement.

1418	**588**	20m. green, blk & red	60	20

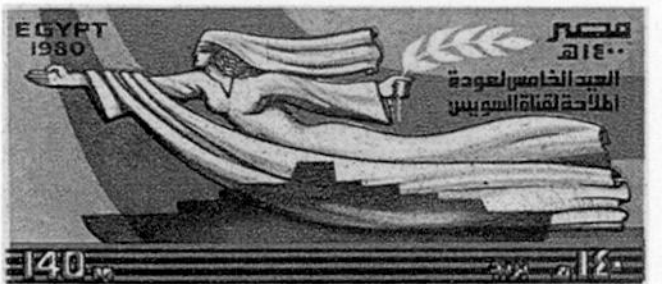

589 Ship and Figure symbolizing Peace and Freedom

1980. 5th Anniv of Re-opening of Suez Canal.

1419	**589**	140m. black, orge & bl	1·30	1·20

590 Pharaonic Cat

1980. Centenary of Society for the Prevention of Cruelty to Animals.

1420	**590**	20m. grey and green	85	25

591 Worker pushing Cogwheel

1980. Industry Day.

1421	**591**	20m. orange, brn & bl	50	20

592 Symbolic Tree

1980. 28th Anniv of Revolution. Social Security Year.

1422	**592**	20m. purple, grn & brn	60	35
MS1423		57×67 mm. 140m. brown, emerald and black. Imperf	4·75	4·50

593 Erksous Seller and Nakrazan Player

1980. Festivals 1980.

1424	**593**	10m. multicoloured	35	15

DESIGN: 140m. Cupped hands holding family.

594 "6 October", Building Construction and Doves

1980. 7th Anniv of Suez Crossing.

1425	**594**	20m. multicoloured	60	25

595 Islamic and Coptic Capitals

1980. United Nations Day.

1426	**595**	70m. yellow and blue	95	70
1427	-	140m. red, grn & brn	1·90	1·50

DESIGN: 140m. I.T.U. emblem (International Telecommunications Day).

596 Spider's Web, Dove and Olive Branch

1980. 1400th Anniv of Hegira.

1428	**596**	45m. yellow, brn & grn	85	35

597 Tankers

1980. Opening of Third Channel of Suez Canal.

1429	**597**	70m. blue, turq & grn	1·20	70

598 Mustafa Sadek el Rafai (writer)

1980. Arab Personalities. Brown and green.

1430	20m. Type **598** (birth cent)	50	35
1431	20m. Dr. Ali Mustafa Moush-arafa (scientist, 30th death anniv)	50	35
1432	20m. Dr. Ali Ibrahim (surgeon, birth centenary)	50	35

599 Scarab from Tutankhamun Collection

1981. Post Day.

1433	**599**	70m. multicoloured	1·30	55
1434	-	70m. yell, brn & grn	1·30	55

DESIGN: No. 1434, Other side of scarab.

600 Heinrich von Stephan

1981. 150th Birth Anniv of Heinrich von Stephan (founder of U.P.U.).

1435	**600**	140m. brown & blue	2·40	1·40

601 Fair Emblem, Globe and Books

1981. 13th Cairo International Book Fair.

1436	**601**	20m. green, yell & brn	60	20

602 Symbols of Agriculture and Industry

1981. 14th Cairo International Fair.

1437	**602**	20m. pink, brown & grn	60	20

603 R.E.A. Emblem, Pylon and Village

1981. 10th Anniv of Rural Electrification Authority.

1438	**603**	20m. yellow, grn & blk	60	20

604 Soldier, Olive Branch and Veteran's Association Emblem

1981. Veteran's Day.

1439	**604**	20m. green, red & brn	60	20

605 Conference Emblem

1981. International Dentistry Conference, Cairo.

1440	**605**	20m. brown and red	60	20

606 Confederation Emblem

1981. 25th Anniv of International Confederation of Arab Trade Unions.

1441	**606**	20m. brown and blue	60	20

607 Nurse

1981. Nurses' Day.

1442	**607**	20m. orange, grn & red	60	20

608 Irrigation Spray

1981. 10th Anniv of Rectification Movement.

1443	**608**	20m. green, brn & yell	60	20

609 Rocket and Military Equipment

1981. Air Defence Day.

1444	**609**	20m. green, blue & red	60	20

610 Map of Afghanistan

1981. Solidarity with Afghan People.

1445	**610**	20m.+10m. brn, red & black (37×36 mm)	95	55
1446	**610**	20m.+10m. brn, red & black (27×22 mm)	6·00	5·75

611 "29" and Social Defence Badge

1981. 29th Anniv of Revolution.

1447	**611**	20m. yellow, grn & brn	50	25
1448	-	20m. blue, black & red	50	25

DESIGN: No. 1448, Map of Suez Canal and ships on graph surrounded by Egyptian flag (25th anniv of Suez Canal nationalization).

612 Water Lilies

1981. Festivals 1981.

1449	**612**	10m. multicoloured	35	15

613 Kemal Ataturk

1981. Birth Centenary of Kemal Ataturk (Turkish statesman).

1450	**613**	140m. brown & green	2·50	1·50

614 Ahmed Arabi

1981. Centenary of Arabi Revolution.

1451	**614**	20m. brown and green	50	20

615 Muscular Athlete, Sphinx and Pyramids

1981. World Muscular Athletics Championship, Cairo.

1452	**615**	45m. yell, blk & brn	95	35

616 Factory on Graph and Atomic Symbol

1981. 25th Anniv of Ministry of Industry.

1453	**616**	45m. yellow, bl & red	60	25

617 Congress Emblem and Imhotep (god of Medicine)

1981. 20th International Medical Industries Congress, Cairo.

1454	**617**	20m. green, blk & orge	60	25

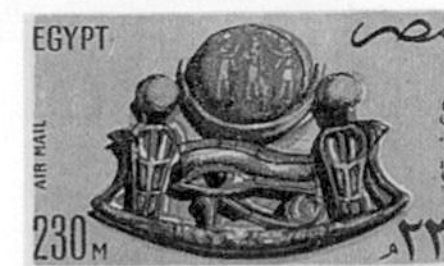

618 Eye

1981. Air.

1455	**618**	230m. bl, orge & brn	3·50	1·50

619 Olive, Dove, Canal and Wheat

1981. 8th Anniv of Suez Crossing.

1456	**619**	20m. green, stone & bl	60	25

620 I.T.U. and W.H.O. Emblems

1981. United Nations Day.

1457	-	10m. yellow, bl & brn	35	15
1458	**620**	20m. blue, orge & blk	35	25
1459	-	45m. purple, grn & blk	55	55
1460	-	230m. orange, grn & blk	4·25	2·50

DESIGNS—HORIZ: 10m. Food and Agriculture Organization Emblem (World Food Day); 230m. Olive branches (Racial Discrimination Day). VERT: 20m. Type **620** (World Telecommunications Day); 45m. International Year of Disabled Persons emblem.

621 President Sadat and Memorial

1981. President Sadat Commemoration.

1461	**621**	30m. brown, grn & red	1·20	80
1462	**621**	230m. brn, grn & red	7·75	6·25

622 Dome of Shura Council, Hands and Candle

1981. 1st Anniv of Shura Council.

1463	**622**	45m. yellow & lilac	60	35

623 Bank Emblem

1981. 50th Anniv of Bank for Development and Agricultural Credit.

1464	**623**	20m. buff, grn & blk	50	10

624 Ali el Gayati

1981. Celebrities.

1465	**624**	30m. brown & green	35	35
1466	-	60m. brown & green	70	70

DESIGNS: Type **624** (journalist, 25th death anniv). 60m. Omar Ebn el Fared (poet, 1181–1234).

625 Dove and Globe forming Figure "20"

1981. 20th Anniv of African Postal Union.

1467	**625**	60m. yellow, bl & red	1·10	45

626 Book and Writing Materials

1982. 14th Cairo International Book Fair.

1468	**626**	3p. brown and yellow	60	15

627 Federation Emblem

1982. 25th Anniv of Egyptian Trade Unions Federation.

1469	**627**	3p. blue and green	35	10

628 Map, "25" and Dome of University

1982. 25th Anniv of Cairo University, Khartoum Branch.

1470	**628**	6p. green and blue	85	55

629 Fair Emblem

1982. 15th Cairo International Fair.

1471	**629**	3p. black, green & orge	35	10

630 Hilton Ramses Hotel

1982. Air. Opening of Hilton Ramses Hotel.

1472	**630**	18½p. brown, yell & bl	2·40	1·40

631 Long-finned Batfish

1982. International Conference on Marine Science and 50th Anniv of Marine Biological Station, El Ghardaka. Multicoloured.

1473		10m. Type **631**	1·10	70
1474		30m. Blue-lined snapper	1·50	80
1475		60m. Yellow boxfish	1·80	1·20
1476		230m. Lined butterflyfish	4·50	2·50

632 Map of Sinai, Olive Branch and Dove

1982. Sinai Restoration.

1477	**632**	3p. brown, stone & grn	60	25

633 de Havilland DH.86B Dragon Express Biplane and Boeing 737 Jetliner

1982. 50th Anniv of Egyptair (state airline).

1478	**633**	23p. blue, mauve & yell	3·75	2·50

634 Minaret

1982. Millenary of El Azhar Mosque.

1479	**634**	6p. yellow, brn & grn	1·10	70
1480	-	6p. yellow, brn & grn	1·10	70
1481	-	6p. yellow, brn & grn	1·10	70
1482	-	6p. yellow, brn & grn	1·10	70

MS1483 60×59 mm. 23p. brown, blue and emerald. Imperf 7·25 6·75

DESIGNS: No. 1479 Type **634**; 1480, Dome and minaret (different); 1481, Minaret with three stages and one ball on top; 1482, Minaret with two balls on top; **MS**1483, General view of mosque.

635 Dove

1982. 30th Anniv of Revolution.

1484	**635**	3p. grn, dp grn & orge	35	25

MS1485 55×73 mm. 23p. black, rosine and emerald. Imperf 4·50 4·25

DESIGN: 23p. Flag arranged to form flower.

636 Hotel, Citadel, Sphinx, Pyramid and St. Catherine's

1982. International Tourism Day.

1486	**636**	23p. blue, orge & brn	4·50	2·75

637 Martyrs' Monument, Egyptian Flag and Map

1982. 9th Anniv of Suez Crossing.

1487	**637**	3p. black, pink & blue	60	25

638 Biennale Emblem and Sailboat

1982. 14th Fine Arts Biennale, Alexandria.

1488	**638**	3p. orange, blue & lilac	60	25

639 Trees and Factory Pollution (World Environment Day)

1982. United Nations Day.

1489	**639**	3p. brown, yell & grn	60	35
1490	-	6p. blue and green	1·20	55
1491	-	6p. blue and brown	1·20	55
1492	-	8p. brown, blue & red	1·40	90

DESIGNS—HORIZ: No. 1490, Olive branch and dove encircling globe (2nd Conference on the Exploration and Peaceful Uses of Outer Space, Vienna); 1492, Dr. Robert Koch and bacillus (centenary of discovery of tubercle bacillus); 36×36 mm: No. 1491, Lord Baden-Powell and scout emblems (125th birth anniv of Lord Baden-Powell (founder) and 75th anniv of boy scout movement).

640 Avro Type 618 Ten and General Dynamics Fighting Falcon

1982. 50th Anniv of Egyptian Air Force.

1493	**640**	3p. blue and black	70	25

641 Ahmed Shawqi and Hafez Ibrahim

1982. 50th Death Annivs of Ahmed Shawqi and Hafez Ibrahim (poets).

1494	**641**	6p. blue and brown	85	55

642 Jubilee Emblem

1982. 25th Anniv of National Research Centre.

1495	**642**	3p. blue and red	95	35

643 Hands holding Flower

1982. Aged People Year.

1496	**643**	23p. green, red & blue	3·75	2·30

644 "Academy" on Open Books

1982. 50th Anniv of Arab League Academy.

1497	**644**	3p. brown, stone & blue	95	55

645 Postal Emblem and Postcoded Letter

1983. Post Day.

1498	**645**	3p. blue, red and blk	50	25

646 Police Emblem

1983. Police Day.

1499	**646**	3p. blue, black & grn	70	25

647 Emblem, Globe and Open Book

1983. 15th Cairo International Book Fair.

1500	**647**	3p. blue and red	85	35

648 Satellite and Map of Africa

1983. 5th U.N. Regional Conference for African Maps, Cairo.

1501 **648** 3p. green and blue 85 35

649 Conference Emblem

1983. 3rd African Ministers of Transport, Communication and Planning Conference, Cairo.

1502 **649** 23p. blue and green 2·00 1·10

650 Emblem, Olive Branch and Cogwheel

1983. 16th Cairo International Fair.

1503 **650** 3p. green, black & red 50 25

651 Footballer heading Ball

1983. Egyptian Football Victories in Africa Cup and African Cup-winners Cup.

1504 **651** 3p. stone, brown & red 50 35

1505 - 3p. stone, brown & red 50 35

DESIGNS: No. 1504, Type **651** (African Cup-winners Cup, Arab Contractors Club); No. 1505, Footballer kicking ball (Africa Cup, National Club).

652 Emblem within Heart

1983. World Health Day. Blood Donation.

1506 **652** 3p. black, red & green 70 35

653 Organization Emblem

1983. 10th Anniv of Trade Union Unity Organization.

1507 **653** 3p. blue and green 70 35

654 Map Dove and Flag

1983. 1st Anniv of Restoration of Sinai.

1508 **654** 3p. green, black & red 70 35

655 Scarab and Microscope

1983. 75th Anniv of Egyptian Entomological Society.

1509 **655** 3p. black and blue 70 35

656 Chrysanthemums

1983. Festivals.

1510 **656** 20m. red and green 35 15

657 Stadium, Player and Championship Emblem

1983. 5th African Handball Championship, Cairo.

1511 **657** 6p. brown and green 70 35

658 Ears of Wheat and "23"

1983. 31st Anniv of Revolution.

1512 **658** 3p. green, yell & brn 50 20

659 Simon Bolivar (statue)

1983. Birth Bicentenary of Simon Bolivar (South American revolutionary leader).

1513 **659** 23p. brown and blue 2·00 1·10

660 Arabi Pasha, Maps of Egypt and Ceylon and House

1983. Centenary of Exile to Ceylon of Arabi Pasha.

1514 **660** 3p. brown, grn & orge 60 25

661 Jar and Museum

1983. Reopening of Islamic Museum.

1515 **661** 3p. lt brown & brown 95 35

662 Monument, Martyrs, Cogwheel, Wheat and Oil Well

1983. 10th Anniv of Suez Crossing.

1516 **662** 3p. green, red & blk 70 25

663 Rally Cars

1983. 2nd International Pharaonic Motor Rally.

1517 **663** 23p. brown, bl & stone 2·50 1·10

664 Radar, Modern Freighter and Pharaonic Ship

1983. United Nations Day.

1518 **664** 3p. blue and black 95 25

1519 - 6p. green and blue 95 70

1520 - 6p. green, orge & blk 95 70

1521 - 23p. blue and brown 3·00 2·10

DESIGNS: No. 1518, Type **664** (25th anniv of International Maritime Organization); 1519, Emblems and concentric circles (World Communications Year); 1520, Ear of wheat and emblems (20th anniv of World Food Programme); 1521, Fishing boat and fish (Fishery Resources).

665 Karate, Pyramids and Sphinx

1983. 4th World Karate Championship, Cairo.

1522 **665** 3p. multicoloured 70 35

666 Dome of the Rock, Jerusalem

1983. International Day of Solidarity with Palestinian People.

1523 **666** 6p. brown, ochre & grn 1·20 35

667 Artist's Palette

1983. 75th Anniv of Faculty of Fine Arts, Helwan University.

1524 **667** 3p. yellow, red & blue 50 20

668 Statue and Cairo University

1983. 75th Anniv of Cairo University.

1525 **668** 3p. lt brn, brn & bl 50 20

669 "Mother and Child" and Emblem

1983. International Egyptian Maternity and Child Care Society.

1526 **669** 2p. blue, black & orge 50 20

670 Emblem and Maps

1983. 20th Anniv of Organization of African Unity.

1527 **670** 3p. green and red 50 20

671 Rameses II, Thebes

1983. 10th Anniv (1982) of World Heritage Convention. Each stone, brown and green.

1528 3p. Type **671** 70 55

1529 3p. Coptic weaving (detail) 70 55

1530 3p. Islamic carved wooden panel 70 55

672 Qaitbay Fort

1984. Post Day. Multicoloured.

1531 6p. Type **672** 95 55

1532 23p. Mohammed Ali Mosque, Saladin's Citadel 2·40 1·50

673 Emblem, Family and Insurance Document

1984. 50th Anniv of Misr Insurance Company.

1533 **673** 3p. ochre, grn & brn 60 30

674 Open Book and Emblem

1984. 16th Cairo International Book Fair.
1534 **674** 3p. pink, green & brn 60 30

675 Fair Emblem within Pyramids

1984. 17th Cairo International Fair.
1535 **675** 3p. orange, brn & grn 60 30

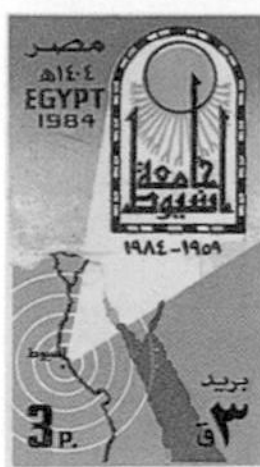

676 University Emblem and Map

1984. 25th Anniv of Assiout University.
1536 **676** 3p. orange, blue and lilac 55 25

677 Emblem

1984. 75th Anniv of Egyptian Co-operatives.
1537 **677** 3p. orange, blue & grn 50 20

678 Curtains, Masks and Globe

1984. World Theatre Day.
1538 **678** 3p. brown, blue and red 50 20

679 Mahmoud Moukhtar and Sculptures

1984. 50th Death Anniv of Mahmoud Moukhtar (sculptor).
1539 **679** 3p. brown and green 50 20

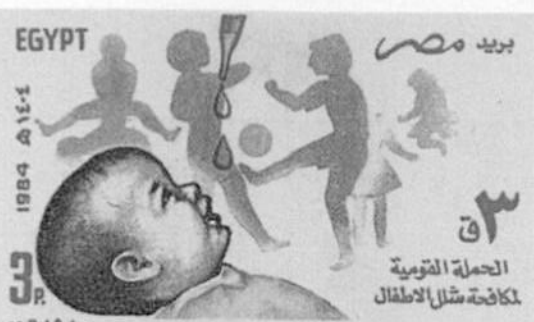

680 Baby receiving Oral Vaccine

1984. World Health Day. Anti-poliomyelitis Campaign.
1540 **680** 3p. yellow, brn & grn 1·20 35

681 Doves over Sinai

1984. 2nd Anniv of Restoration of Sinai.
1541 **681** 3p. stone, green & blue 60 25

682 Map of Africa showing Namibia

1984. Africa Day.
1542 **682** 3p. blue and brown 50 20

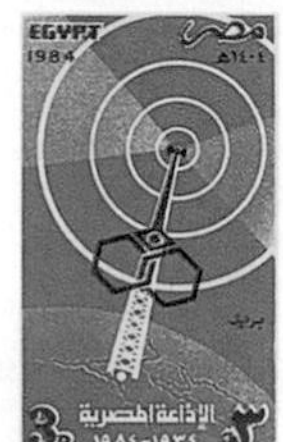

683 Globe and Transmitter

1984. 50th Anniv of Egyptian Broadcasting.
1543 **683** 3p. blue, black and red 50 20

684 Carnation

1984. Festivals.
1544 **684** 2p. red and green 60 35

685 Decorated Mask

1984. 1st Cairo International Biennale.
1545 **685** 3p. multicoloured 50 20

686 Atomic Power

1984. 32nd Anniv of Revolution.
1546 **686** 3p. blue, yellow and red 50 20

687 Boxing

1984. Olympic Games, Los Angeles.
1547 **687** 3p. green, blue and red 50 20
1548 - 3p. green, blue and red 50 20
1549 - 3p. green, blue and red 50 20
1550 - 3p. green, blue and red 50 20
MS1551 130×80 mm. 30p. As Nos. 1547/50 but without values and each 17½×30½ mm. Each green, blue and magenta. Imperf 5·25 5·00
DESIGNS: No. 1548, Basketball; 1549, Volleyball; 1550, Football.

688 Conference Emblem

1984. 2nd Egyptians Abroad Conference, Cairo.
1552 **688** 3p. brn, bl & blk 60 20
1553 **688** 23p. brn, grn & blk 3·00 1·50

689 Couple and Emblem

1984. 30th Anniv of Egyptian Youth Hostels Association.
1554 **689** 3p. green, blk & orge 50 20

690 Emblem and Sphinx

1984. 50th Anniv of Misr Travel Company.
1555 **690** 3p. brown, yellow & bl 55 20

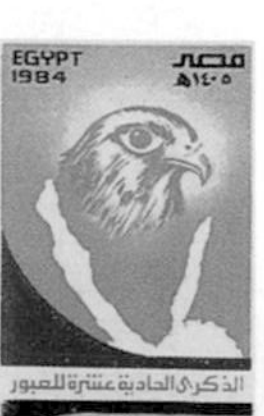

691 Eagle's Head and Map of Sinai

1984. 11th Anniv of Suez Crossing.
1556 **691** 3p. green, red and black 55 20

692 Map of Nile Valley and Integration Badge

1984. 2nd Anniv of Signing of Egypt–Sudan Co-operation Treaty.
1557 **692** 3p. red, black and green 55 20

693 Child's Face within Blossom

1984. United Nations Children's Fund.
1558 **693** 3p. multicoloured 50 20

694 Tank, Anti-aircraft Gun and Emblem

1984. Defence Equipment Exhibition, Cairo.
1559 **694** 3p. yellow, black and red 50 20

695 Kamel Kilany and Books

1984. 25th Death Anniv of Kamel Kilany (children's author and poet).
1560 **695** 3p. brown, yell & bl 50 20

696 Ahmed ibn Toulon Mosque

1984. 1100th Death Anniv of Ahmed ibn Toulon (governor of Egypt).
1561 **696** 3p. lt brn, bl & brn 55 20

697 Congress Emblem

1984. 29th International History of Medicine Congress, Cairo.
1562 **697** 3p. blue, black & red 50 20

698 Emblem and Spotlights

1984. 25th Anniv of Academy of Art.

1563	**698**	3p. multicoloured	50	20

699 Pharaoh receiving Letter (monument) and Postal Museum

1985. Post Day.

1564	**699**	3p. blue, brown & red	55	20

700 Cairo Gate and Tower on Scroll and Emblem

1985. 15th International Union of Architects Conference.

1565	**700**	3p. lilac and blue	50	20

701 Scribe (statue) and Emblem

1985. 17th Cairo International Book Fair.

1566	**701**	3p. blue and orange	70	35

702 Edfu Temple

1985. Air.

1567	**702**	6p. green and blue	1·20	45
1568	**702**	15p. brown and blue	1·90	55
1569	-	18p.50 grn, yell & brn	2·40	1·60
1570	-	23p. brown, yell & bl	3·00	2·00
1571	-	25p. blue, yell & brn	2·30	1·10
1572	-	30p. brown, orge & bl	4·25	1·10

DESIGNS—HORIZ: 23, 30p. Giza Pyramids. VERT: 18p. 50, 25p. Akhnaton.

703 Ear of Wheat, Cogwheels and Emblem

1985. 18th Cairo International Fair.

1573	**703**	3p. multicoloured	60	35

704 Woman holding Heart

1985. 3rd Anniv of Restoration of Sinai.

1574	**704**	5p. multicoloured	1·20	35

705 Priest of god Mout

1985. (a) Size 22×27 mm.

1575	**705**	1p. brown	25	10
1576	-	2p. blue	25	10
1577	-	3p. brown	35	25
1578	-	5p. purple	60	25
1579	-	8p. brown and green	85	45
1580	-	10p. blue and purple	35	25
1581	-	11p. purple	1·10	70
1582	-	15p. brown and ochre	1·70	80
1583	-	20p. green	2·40	70
1584	-	20p. green and yellow	70	35
1585	-	30p. brn & cinnamon	70	25
1586	-	35p. yellow & brown	5·00	1·70
1587	-	50p. lilac and brown	1·20	45

(b) Mosques. Size 22×39 mm.

1588	£E1 brown and orange	3·00	1·00
1589	£E2 brown and yellow	5·75	1·60

DESIGNS: 2, 20p. (1583) Wading birds (relief sculpture); 3, 5p. Statue of Rameses II, Luxor; 8, 15p. Slave kneeling with tray and fruit (wall painting); 10p. Vase; 11p. Carved head; 20p. (1584) Jug; 30p. Flagon; 35p. Capitals of pharaonic columns; 50p. Flask; £E1, Al-Maridani Mosquel; £E2, Al-Azhar Mosque, Cairo.

For designs size 18×22 mm, see Nos. 1772/5.

707 Treble Clef

1985. 50th Anniv of Helwan University Musical Faculty.

1595	**707**	5p. blue and yellow	85	35

708 El Moulid Bride (doll)

1985. Festivals 1985.

1596	**708**	2p. violet, orge & yell	50	10
1597	**708**	5p. red, blue & green	60	35

709 Player and Cup

1985. Egyptian Football Victories. Mult.

1598	5p. Cairo Stadium (left-hand)	85	55
1599	5p. Cairo Stadium (right-hand)	85	55
1600	5p. El Zamalek Club player and Africa Cup (winners, 1984)	85	55
1601	5p. National Club player (red shirt) and African Cup-winners Cup (winners 1984)	85	55
1602	5p. Type **709** (Arab Contractors Club, African Cup-winners Cup winners, 1983)	85	55

Nos. 1598/9 were printed together, se-tenant, forming a composite design.

710 Television Headquarters and Radio Waves

1985. Anniversaries. Multicoloured.

1603	5p. Type **710** (25th anniv of Egyptian television)	85	35
1604	5p. Flag and olive branch entwined. ships and maps of world and Suez Canal (10th anniv of re-opening) (horiz)	85	35
1605	5p. Cars in Ahmed Hamdi Tunnel under Suez Canal (33rd anniv of revolution)	85	35
MS1606	97×79 mm. 30p. Aswan High Dam (25th anniv) (53×50 mm)	4·75	4·50

Nos. 1604 and **MS**1606 also bear 33rd anniv of revolution emblem.

711 Map within Heart and Emblem

1985. 3rd Egyptians Abroad Conference, Cairo.

1607	**711**	15p. multicoloured	1·30	80

712 Akhnaton worshipping Aton and Emblem

1985. 50th Anniv of Tourism Organization.

1608	**712**	5p. multicoloured	60	35

713 Flag and Olive Branch on Map of Sinai

1985. 12th Anniv of Suez Crossing.

1609	**713**	5p. multicoloured	60	35

714 Air Scouts Emblem

1985. 30th Anniv of Air Scouts.

1610	**714**	5p. blue, red & yellow	85	35

715 International Youth Year Emblem

1985. United Nations Day.

1611	**715**	5p. lilac, yellow & grn	60	35
1612	-	5p. multicoloured	60	35
1613	-	15p. blue, yellow and red	1·50	90
1614	-	15p. blue & light blue	1·50	90

DESIGNS: No. 1612, Meteorological map of Egypt (World Meteorology Day); 1613, Dove and U.N. emblem (40th Anniv of United Nations Organization); 1614, International communications development programme emblem.

716 Conference and Association Emblems

1985. 2nd International Conference of Egyptian Association of Dental Surgeons, Cairo.

1615	**716**	5p. blue and brown	70	35

717 Conference Banner and Koran

1985. 4th International Conference of Biography and Sunna (sayings) of Prophet Mohammed.

1616	**717**	5p. blue, yellow & brn	60	35

718 Squash Player

1985. World Squash Championships, Cairo.

1617	**718**	5p. green, yellow & brn	85	35

719 Emblem, Flag and Hand holding Tools

1985. 1st Technical Industrial Education Conference.

1618	**719**	5p. blue, red & black	70	35

720 Emblem and Tomb Paintings

1985. 75th Anniv of Egyptian Olympic Committee.
1619 **720** 5p. multicoloured 85 35

721 Narmer Board

1986. Air. Post Day. Multicoloured.
1620 15p. Type **721** 1·70 1·70
1621 15p. Narmer Board (opposite side) 1·70 1·70

722 Emblem and Relief of Scribe

1986. 18th Cairo International Book Fair.
1622 **722** 5p. brown, yellow & bl 70 35

723 Conference Emblem

1986. 3rd International Conference for Transport in Developing Countries, Cairo.
1623 **723** 5p. blue, green & red 60 35

724 Emblem on Islamic Ornament

1986. 25th Anniv of Central Bank.
1624 **724** 5p. multicoloured 60 35

725 Globe, Sorting Office and Map

1986. Inauguration of Cairo Postal Sorting Centre.
1625 **725** 5p. blue and brown 50 35

726 Tomb Painting, Sakkara

1986. 75th Anniv of Cairo University Commerce Faculty.
1626 **726** 5p. yellow, brown & pur 1·40 35

727 Wheat, Cogwheel, Flags and Emblem

1986. 19th Cairo International Fair.
1627 **727** 5p. multicoloured 60 35

728 Map of Sudan and dead Tree

1986. Relief of Drought Victims in Sudan.
1628 **728** 15p.+5p. bl, brn & yell 2·10 1·50

729 Map of Africa, Boeing 707 and Emblem

1986. 18th Annual General Assembly of African Airlines Association.
1629 **729** 15p. blue, yell & blk 1·40 55

730 Ankh, Red Crescent and Hands

1986. 50th Anniv of Ministry of Health.
1630 **730** 5p. multicoloured 60 35

731 Queen Nefertari and Map of Sinai

1986. 4th Anniv of Restoration of Sinai.
1631 **731** 5p. blue, red & green 85 35

732 Profiles and Map

1986. Census.
1632 **732** 15p. brown, yell & bl 1·30 55

733 Map, Cup and Emblem

1986. Victory in African Nations Cup Football Championship. Multicoloured.
1633 5p. Type **733** 70 45
1634 5p. As No. 1633 but emblem inscr in Arabic 70 45

734 Roses

1986. Festivals 1986.
1635 **734** 5p. purple, green & lilac 60 35

735 Smoke issuing from Factory

1986. World Environment Day.
1636 **735** 15p. black, green & blue 1·40 55

736 Eagle and "23 July"

1986. 34th Anniv of Revolution.
1637 **736** 5p. yellow, green & red 50 35

737 Road on Map of Africa

1986. 6th African Road Conference, Cairo.
1638 **737** 15p. multicoloured 1·30 45

738 Map, Eagle, Olive Branch and Flag

1986. 13th Anniv of Suez Crossing.
1639 **738** 5p. multicoloured 1·20 35

739 Workers holding Books and Tools

1986. 25th Anniv of Workers' Cultural Association.
1640 **739** 5p. orange and lilac 60 25

740 Syndicate Emblem and Engineering Symbols

1986. Engineers' Day. 40th Anniv of Engineers' Syndicate.
1641 **740** 5p. green, brown & blue 50 25

741 Dove and Emblem (International Peace Year)

1986. United Nations Day.
1642 **741** 5p. green, blue & red 35 25
1643 - 15p. yellow, grn & brn 1·40 1·10
1644 - 15p. multicoloured 1·40 1·10

DESIGNS—HORIZ: As T **741**: No. 1643, Harvester and ears of wheat (40th anniv of Food and Agriculture Organization). 46×27 mm: 1644, Emblem, globe and "UNESCO" in Arabic (40th anniv of UNESCO).

742 Map and Old and New Drilling Towers

1986. Centenary of First Egyptian Oilwell, Gemsa.
1645 **742** 5p. green, yellow & blk 60 30

743 Children holding Flower

1986. Children's Day.
1646 **743** 5p. multicoloured 60 30

744 Ahmed Amin

1986. Birth Centenary of Ahmed Amin (literary researcher).
1647 **744** 5p. yellow, brn & grn 50 30

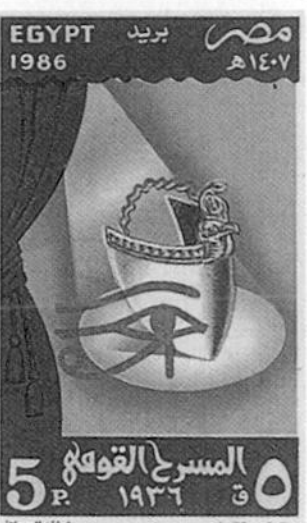

745 Mask and Eye in Spotlight

1986. 50th Anniv of National Theatre.
1648 **745** 5p. multicoloured 60 30

746 Statue of King Zoser and Step Pyramid, Sakkara

1987. Post Day.
1649 **746** 5p. multicoloured 70 30

747 Book and Pencil as "19"

1986. 19th Cairo International Book Fair.
1650 **747** 5p. multicoloured 60 30

748 Emblem

1987. 5th International Conference on Islamic Education.
1651 **748** 5p. multicoloured 50 30

749 Medal

1987. 20th Cairo International Fair.
1652 **749** 5p. black, gold & red 50 30

750 Olive Branch, Profile and National Colours

1987. Veterans' Day.
1653 **750** 5p. red, green & gold 50 30

751 Plants and Emblem

1987. Air. International Garden Festival, Cairo.
1654 **751** 15p. multicoloured 1·30 55

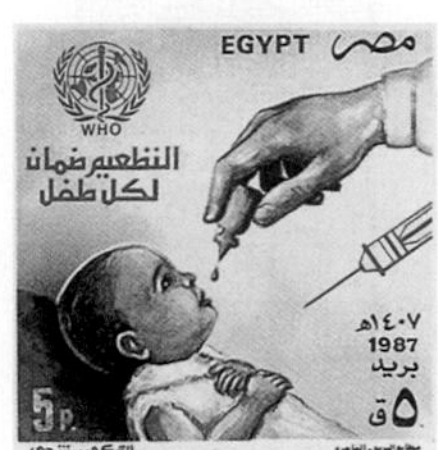

752 Oral Vaccination

1987. International Health Day.
1655 **752** 5p. multicoloured 50 30
1656 - 5p. yellow, grn & blk 50 30
DESIGN: No. 1656, Woman giving baby oral rehydration therapy.

753 Africa Cup

1987. Egyptian Victories in Football Championships. Multicoloured.
1657 5p. Type **753** (El Zamalek team) 60 30
1658 5p. African Nations Cup (national team) 60 30
1659 5p. African Cup Winners Cup (El Ahly team) 60 30
MS1660 115×85 mm. 30p. Flag, Cairo International Stadium and Cups (from left to right). Imperf 4·75 4·25

754 Saladin's Citadel and Map

1987. 5th Anniv of Restoration of Sinai.
1661 **754** 5p. blue and brown 60 30

755 Dahlia

1987. Festivals 1987.
1662 **755** 5p. blue, yellow & mauve 50 20

756 Pyramid and Camel Train

1987. "Saudi Arabia—Yesterday and Today" Exhibition, Cairo.
1663 **756** 15p. multicoloured 1·50 65

757 El Sawary Column and Sphinx and Qaitbay Fort, Alexandria

1987. Tourism. Multicoloured.
1664 15p. Type **757** 1·30 95
1665 15p. St. Catherine's Monastery, Sinai 1·30 95
1666 15p. Colossi of Thebes 1·30 95
1667 15p. Temple, Luxor 1·30 95
MS1668 140×90 mm. 30p. As Nos. 1664/7. Imperf 6·00 5·25
Nos. 1664/7 were printed together, se-tenant, forming a composite design of a map with each illustrated subject pinpointed.

758 Pharaonic Eye on Map

1987. Loyalty Day. 32nd Anniv of General Intelligence Service.
1669 **758** 5p. multicoloured 50 20

759 Ears of Wheat and Emblem

1987. Industrial and Agricultural Exhibition, Alexandria.
1670 **759** 5p. black, grn & orge 60 30

760 Emblems

1987. International Year of Shelter for the Homeless. World Architects' Day.
1671 **760** 5p. yellow, brn & grn 60 30

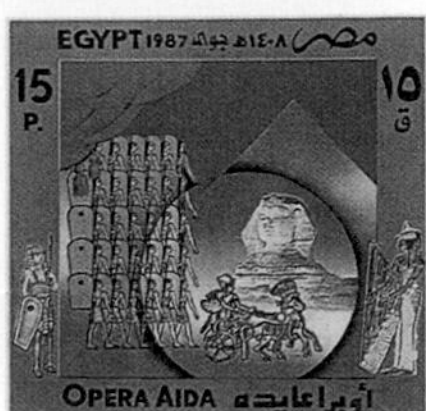

761 Scene from Opera and Sphinx

1987. Performance of Verdi's "Aida" (opera) at the Pyramids. Multicoloured.
1672 15p. Type **761** 1·90 55
MS1673 70×70 mm. 30p. As No. 1672. Imperf 14·50 14·50

762 Train in Station

1987. Inauguration of Cairo Underground Railway.
1674 **762** 5p. multicoloured 1·40 30

763 Head composed of Industrial Symbols

1987. Production Day.
1675 **763** 5p. multicoloured 60 20

764 Horseman and Map

1987. 800th Anniv of Battle of Hattin.
1676 **764** 5p. multicoloured 85 30

765 U.P.U. Emblem

1987. 40th Anniv of Executive Council and 30th Anniv of Consultative Council of U.P.U.
1677 **765** 5p. black, orange & bl 50 20

766 Eye and Art Materials

1987. 16th Fine Arts Biennale. Alexandria.
1678 **766** 5p. multicoloured 35 20

767 Emblem and Ancient Egyptians making Weapons

1987. 2nd International Defence Equipment Exhibition, Cairo.

1679 **767** 5p. multicoloured 60 20

768 Profile and Emblem

1987. 2nd Pan-Arab Anaesthesia and Intensive Care Congress.

1680 **768** 5p. multicoloured 70 30

769 Globe and Emblem on Skeleton

1987. International Orthopaedic and Traumatology Conference, Luxor.

1681 **769** 5p. grey, brown & blue 50 20

770 Selim Hassan (archaeologist) and Hieroglyphics

1987. Birth Centenaries. Multicoloured.

1682 5p. Type **770** 60 20

1683 5p. Abdel Hamid Badawi (politician and International Court of Justice judge) 60 20

771 Mycerinus and Left-hand Pyramid, Giza

1988. Post Day. Multicoloured.

1684 15p. Type **771** 1·30 95

1685 15p. Chefren (with beard) and middle pyramid 1·30 95

1686 15p. Cheops and righthand pyramid 1·30 95

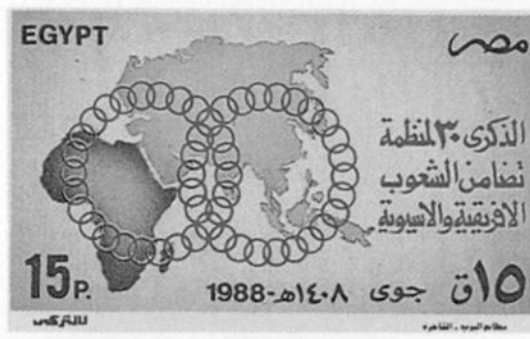

772 Map

1988. 30th Anniv of Asia–Africa Organization.

1687 **772** 15p. multicoloured 1·10 55

773 Emblem, Hieroglyphics and Scribe

1988. 20th Cairo International Book Fair.

1688 **773** 5p. multicoloured 60 20

774 Container Ship

1988. 25th Anniv of Martrans Shipping Line.

1689 **774** 5p. multicoloured 95 20

775 Fair Facade, Globe and Emblem

1988. 21st Cairo International Fair.

1690 **775** 5p. multicoloured 50 20

776 Bowl of Sugar and Emblem

1988. World Health Day. Diabetic Care.

1691 **776** 5p. multicoloured 60 20

777 Prince Ossrite and Fig Tree

1988. Festivals 1988.

1692 **777** 5p. orange, grn & brn 50 20

778 Letters and Emblem

1988. 25th Anniv of African Postal Union.

1693 **778** 15p. blue 1·20 1·10

779 Hands of Different Races reaching for Torch

1988. Anti-racism Campaign.

1694 **779** 5p. multicoloured 35 30

780 Maps of Africa around Emblem

1988. 25th Anniv of Organization of African Unity.

1695 **780** 15p.+10p. mult 1·70 1·50

781 Tawfek el Hakem

1988. 1st Death Anniv of Tawfek el Hakem (dramatist).

1696 **781** 5p. brown and blue 35 20

782 Cubic Art (M. el Razaz)

1988. 50th Anniv of Faculty of Art Education.

1697 **782** 5p. multicoloured 35 20

783 Games Emblem

1988. Air. Olympic Games, Seoul. Multicoloured.

1698 15p. Type **783** 1·20 1·10

MS1699 94×90 mm. 30p. Various sports. Imperf 7·25 6·50

784 Torch, Flag and Palestinians

1988. Air. Palestinian "Intifida" Movement.

1700 **784** 25p. multicoloured 1·70 1·50

785 Soldier and Flag

1988. 15th Anniv of Suez Crossing.

1701 **785** 5p. multicoloured 50 20

786 Model of Opera House

1988. Inauguration of Opera House. Multicoloured.

1702 5p. Type **786** 50 30

MS1703 112×74 mm. 50p. View of Opera House. Imperf 3·50 3·25

787 Red Crescent and Red Cross (125th Anniv of Red Cross)

1988. U.N. Day.

1704 **787** 5p. black, red and green (postage) 35 30

1705 - 20p. yellow, blue and orange 1·70 1·40

1706 - 25p. mult (air) 1·70 1·50

DESIGNS—22×39 mm. 20p. Anniversary emblem (40th anniv of W.H.O.); 47×28 mm. 25p. Globes on scales (40th anniv of Human Rights Declaration).

788 Naguib Mahfouz

1988. Award of Nobel Prize for Literature to Naguib Mahfouz.

1707 **788** 5p. mult (postage) 35 30

1708 **788** 25p. mult (air) 1·70 1·50

789 Tent and "75"

1988. 75th Anniv of Arab Scout Movement.

1709 **789** 25p. multicoloured 1·70 1·50

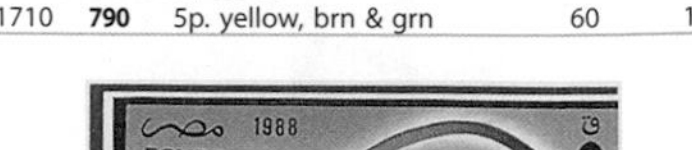

790 Ein Shams University and Association Emblems

1988. Egyptian Orthopaedic Association International Conference, Cairo.

1710 **790** 5p. yellow, brn & grn 60 15

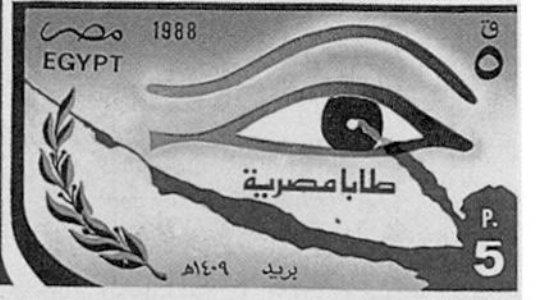

791 Pharaonic Eye and Map

1988. Restoration of Taba.

1711 **791** 5p. multicoloured 35 10

792 "75" in Sun above Plant

1988. 75th Anniv of Ministry of Agriculture.

1712	**792**	5p. blue, yell & orge	35	10

793 Mohamed Hussein Hekal (writer and politician)

1988. Anniversaries. Each brown and green.

1713	5p. Type **793** (birth cent)	35	20
1714	5p. Ahmed Lofty el Sayed (philosopher and politician) (25th death anniv)	35	20

794 Priest (5th dynasty)

1989. Post Day. Statues. Multicoloured.

1715	5p. Type **794**	50	20
1716	25p. Princess Nefert (4th dynasty)	1·90	65
1717	25p. Prince Ra-Hoteb (4th dynasty)	1·90	65

795 Nehru

1989. Birth Centenary of Jawaharlal Nehru (Indian statesman).

1718	**795**	5p. green	35	15

796 Nile Hilton

1989. 30th Anniv of Nile Hilton Hotel.

1719	**796**	5p. multicoloured	35	15

797 Route Map and Train leaving Tunnel

1989. Inauguration of Second Stage of Cairo Underground Railway.

1720	**797**	5p. multicoloured	1·20	20

798 Arms and Map

1989. Restoration of Taba.

1721	**798**	5p. multicoloured	35	15

799 Balcony

1989. Air.

1722	**799**	20p. purple, brn & bl	95	30
1723	-	25p. brn, yell & grn	1·20	45
1724	-	35p. pur, orge & bl	1·40	55
1725	-	45p. yell, blk & red	1·70	65
1725a	-	45p. pur, orge & grn	1·30	20
1726	-	50p. bl, stone & pur	2·10	85
1726a	-	55p. brn, buff & bl	1·90	55
1727	-	60p. pur, stone & bl	2·40	85
1727a	-	65p. pur, brn & grn	1·80	55
1728	**799**	70p. pur, brn & orge	2·30	55
1729	-	85p. yellow, light yellow and brown	2·10	75

DESIGNS: 25, 35, 45p. (1725a) Lantern; 45p. (1725) Carpet; 50, 60, 65p. Dish with gazelle motif; 55, 85p. Dish with fluted edge.

800 Lamp

1989. Festivals 1989.

1730	**800**	5p. multicoloured	35	15

801 Members' Flags

1989. Air. Formation of Arab Co-operation Council. Multicoloured.

1731	25p. Type **801**	1·50	55
MS1732	89×80 mm. 50p. Members' flags (Egypt, Iraq, Jordan, Yemen Arab Republic)	4·75	4·75

802 Olympic Rings, Map and Sports

1989. 1st Arab Olympic Day.

1733	**802**	5p. green, brown & blk	35	15

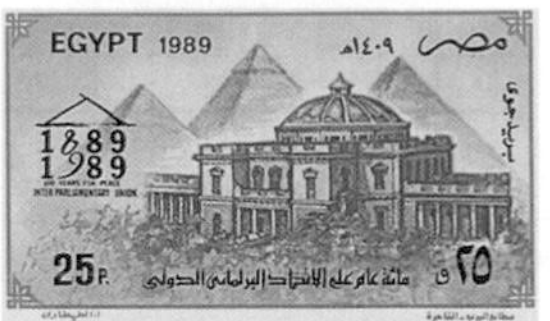

803 Pyramids and Parliament Building

1989. Cent of Interparliamentary Union.

1734	25p. Type **803**	2·00	1·10
MS1735	85×70 mm. 25p. Pyramids, globe and Parliament building	2·40	2·40

804 Egyptian and French Flags

1989. Air. Bicentenary of French Revolution.

1736	**804**	25p. multicoloured	1·90	90

805 Bank Emblem

1989. 25th Anniv of African Development Bank.

1737	**805**	10p. blue, yellow & pur	45	10

806 Conference Centre

1989. Cairo International Conference Centre.

1738	**806**	5p. brown, green & blue	35	10

807 October Panorama

1989. 16th Anniv of Suez Crossing. Mult.

1739	10p. Egyptians in El Qantara (47×28 mm)	35	20
1740	10p. Type **807**	35	20
1741	10p. Crossing the Suez (47×28 mm)	35	20

See also No. 1766.

808 Mohammed Ali Mosque, Saladin's Citadel

1989. Aga Khan Architecture Prize.

1742	**808**	35p. brown, grn & pur	1·40	35

809 Emblem sheltering Family

1989. 25th Anniv of Health Insurance Scheme.

1743	**809**	10p. red, grey & black	35	15

810 Envelopes forming World Map

1989. World Post Day.

1744	**810**	35p. black, blue & yell	1·10	45

811 Colossi of Thebes

1989. International Congress and Convention Association Meeting, Cairo.

1745	**811**	10p. lilac, green & blk	45	20

812 Faculty Emblem

1989. Centenary of Faculty of Agriculture, Cairo University.

1746	**812**	10p. purple, grn & yell	35	15

813 Children at Crossings

1989. 20th Anniv of Egyptian Road Safety Society.

1747	**813**	10p. multicoloured	45	15

814 University Emblem

1989. 50th Anniv of Alexandria University.

1748	**814**	10p. brown and blue	35	15

815 Abdel Kader el Mazni (writer)

1989. Birth Anniversaries.

1749	**815**	10p. ochre and brown	35	20
1750	-	10p. olive and green	35	20
1751	-	10p. multicoloured	35	20

DESIGNS—VERT: No. 1750, Abdel Rahman el Rafei (historian and politician). HORIZ: No. 1751, Ibrahim Pasha and statue in Opera Square, Cairo (son of Mohammed Ali and Viceroy of Egypt, July-November 1848).

816 Statue of Priest Renofr

1990. Post Day. Multicoloured.

1752	30p. Type **816**	1·10	35
1753	30p. Relief of Betah Hoteb from Sakkara	1·10	35

817 Emblem

1990. 1st Anniv of Arab Co-operation Council.

1754	**817**	10p. multicoloured	45	20
1755	**817**	35p. multicoloured	1·10	45

818 Emblem

1990. African Parliamentary Union Conference.

1756	**818**	10p. black, red & green	35	10
MS1757		80×59 mm 30p. multicoloured	1·40	1·20

819 Road Sign and Steering Wheel

1990. International Conference. Road Safety and Accidents in Developing Countries.

1758	**819**	10p. multicoloured	35	10

820 Daisies

1990. Festivals 1990.

1759	**820**	10p. multicoloured	45	10

821 Doves and Map

1990. 8th Anniv of Restoration of Sinai.

1760	**821**	10p. blue, yellow & blk	45	10

822 Trophy and Ball

1990. World Cup Football Championship, Italy. Multicoloured.

1761	10p. Type **822**	45	10
MS1762	80×60 mm. 50p. Trophy	2·50	2·50

823 Pyramid, Sphinx, Mascot and Ball in Basket

1990. World Basketball Championship, Argentina.

1763	**823**	10p. black, blue & orge	45	10

824 Figures forming Pyramid

1990. 5th Anniv of National Population Council.

1764	**824**	10p. brn, lt grn & grn	35	10

825 Battlefield

1990. 17th Anniv of Suez Crossing. Mult.

1765	10p. Type **825**	35	20
1766	10p. As Type **807** but dated "1990"	35	20
1767	10p. Egyptian soldiers with flamethrower	35	20

826 Anniversary Emblem

1990. 125th Anniv of Egyptian Post.

1768	**826**	10p. black, red & blue	35	10

827 Faculty Emblem and Al-Azhar Mosque, Cairo

1990. Centenary of Dar el Eloum Faculty.

1769	**827**	10p. multicoloured	35	10

828 Emblem and Map (40th anniv of U.N. Development Programme)

1990. United Nations Day.

1770	**828**	30p. blue, grn & yell	90	25
1771	-	30p. multicoloured	90	25

DESIGN—VERT: No. 1771, Cables and emblem forming Arabic "125" (125th anniv of I.T.U.).

1990. As previous designs and new design as T 705 but size 18×22 mm.

1772	5p. buff and brown	35	10
1773	10p. blue and lilac	35	10
1774	30p. brown and ochre	55	25
1775	50p. brown and yellow	90	25

DESIGNS: 5p. Jar; 10p. Vase (as No. 1580); 30p. Flagon (as No. 1585); 50p. Flask (as No. 1587).

829 Pictogram, Hand and Disabled Person

1990. Disabled Persons' Day.

1790	**829**	10p. multicoloured	45	10

830 Crown Butterflyfish and Coral

1990. Ras Mohamed National Park. Mult.

1791	10p. Type **830**	55	20
1792	10p. Zebra lionfish	55	20
1793	20p. Two-banded anemonefish and emperor angelfish	60	25
1794	20p. Coral hind	60	25

831 Nabaweya Moussa (educationist)

1990. Birth Centenaries.

1795	**831**	10p. orge, grey & grn	35	20
1796	-	10p. orange, brn & bl	35	20

DESIGN: No. 1796, Dr. Mohamed Fahmy Abdel Meguid (pioneer of free medical care).

832 1866 5pa. Stamp

1991. Post Day. 125th Anniv of First Egyptian Stamps (1st issue).

1797	**832**	5p. grey and black	25	10
1798	-	10p. brown and black	45	20
1799	-	20p. blue and black	50	25

DESIGNS: 10p. 1866 10pa. stamp; 20p. 1866 20pa. stamp.
See also Nos. 1815/17 and 1831, **MS**1832.

833 Birth of Calf

1991. 50th Anniv (1990) of Veterinary Surgeons' Syndicate.

1800	**833**	10p. multicoloured	45	10

834 Newspaper, Quill, Ink and Lens

1991. 50th Anniv of Journalists' Syndicate.

1801	**834**	10p. multicoloured	35	10

835 Narcissi

1991. Festivals 1991.

1802	**835**	10p. multicoloured	35	10

836 "Procession" and Mohamed Nagi

1991. Artists' Anniversaries. Multicoloured.

1803	10p. Type **836** (35th death)	35	15

1804 10p. Mahmoud Mokhtar and sculptures (birth centenary) (horiz) 35 15

837 Riverbank Wildlife (image scaled to 64% of original size)

1991. Centenary of Giza Zoo. Sheet 80×62 mm.
MS1805 **837** 50p. multicoloured 4·00 3·50

838 Saladin's Citadel and Faculty Building

1991. Centenary of Technical Faculty, University of Cairo.
1814 **838** 10p. multicoloured 35 10

1991. 125th Anniv of First Egyptian Stamps (2nd issue) and "Cairo 1991" Stamp Exhibition (1st issue). As T 832.
1815 10p. orange and black 35 20
1816 10p. yellow and black 35 20
1817 10p. purple and black 35 20
MS1818 80×60 mm. 50p. multicoloured. Imperf 1·90 1·70
DESIGNS: No. 1815, 1866 5pi. Stamp; 1816, 1866 2pi. Stamp; 1817, 1866 1pi. Stamp; **MS**1818, Sphinx, pyramid and 1866 10pi. Stamp.

839 Score and Mohamed Abdel el Wahab

1991. Mohamed Abdel el Wahab (composer) Commemoration.
1819 **839** 10p. multicoloured 55 25

840 Session Emblem

1991. 48th Session of International Statistics Institute, Nasr.
1820 **840** 10p. multicoloured 35 10

841 Horus (mascot)

1991. 5th African Games, Cairo. Mult.
1821 10p. Type **841** 35 25
1822 10p. Running, gymnastics and swimming pictograms (horiz) 35 25
1823 10p. Football, basketball and shooting pictograms (horiz) 35 25
1824 10p. Taekwondo, karate and judo pictograms (horiz) 35 25
1825 10p. Table tennis, hockey and tennis pictograms (horiz) 35 25
1826 10p. Boxing, wrestling and weightlifting pictograms (horiz) 35 25
1827 10p. Handball, cycling and volleyball pictrograms (horiz) 35 25
MS1828 80×60 mm. 50p. Mascot, games emblem, torch and running track. Imperf 1·70 1·50

842 New Building

1991. Opening of Dar El Eftaa's New Building.
1829 **842** 10p. multicoloured 35 10

843 Troops in Inflatable Dinghy

1991. 18th Anniv of Suez Crossing.
1830 **843** 10p. multicoloured 55 20

1991. 1st Anniv of Egyptian Stamps (3rd issue) and "Cairo 1991" Stamp Exhibition (2nd issue). As T832.
1831 10p. black and blue 35 10
MS1832 90×59 mm. £E1 multicoloured. Imperf 6·25 5·75
DESIGN: As Type **832**—10p. 188. 10pi stamp. 80×52 mm. £E1 Exhibition emblem, hieroglyphics, pyramids and sphinx.

844 Woman writing

1991. United Nations Day. Multicoloured.
1833 10p. Type **844** (Int Literacy Year) 35 20
1834 10p. Brick "hands" sheltering people (World Shelter for the Homeless Day) (horiz) 35 20
1835 10p. Egyptian and International Standards Organizations emblems (World Standardization Day) (horiz) 35 20

845 Dr. Zaki Mubarak (poet, birth centenary)

1991. Writers' Anniversaries.
1836 **845** 10p. brown 35 20
1837 - 10p. grey 35 20
DESIGN: No. 1837, Abd el Kader Hamza (journalist and historian, 50th death anniv).

846 Scarab Pectoral (from Tutankhamun's tomb)

1992. Post Day. Multicoloured.
1838 10p. Type **846** (postage) 45 35
1839 45p. Eagle pectoral (from Tutankhamun's tomb) (air) 1·60 1·50
1840 70p. Golden saker falcon head (27×47 mm) 2·50 2·20

847 Arabic "40" and Emblem

1992. Police Day.
1841 **847** 10p. multicoloured 35 15

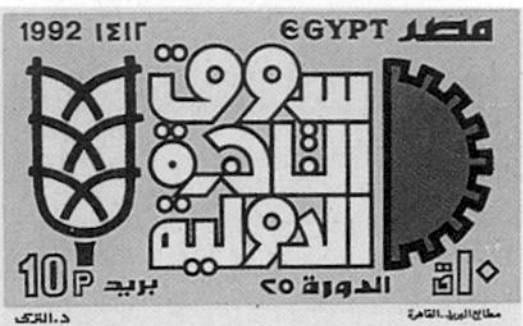

848 Ear of Wheat and Cogwheel

1992. 25th Cairo International Fair.
1842 **848** 10p. multicoloured 35 15

849 Darwish and Opening Bars of "Stand up O Egyptian"

1992. Birth Centenary of Sayed Darwish (composer).
1843 **849** 10p. green and yellow 35 15

850 Hoopoe

1992. Festivals 1992.
1844 **850** 10p. orange, blk & grn 40 15

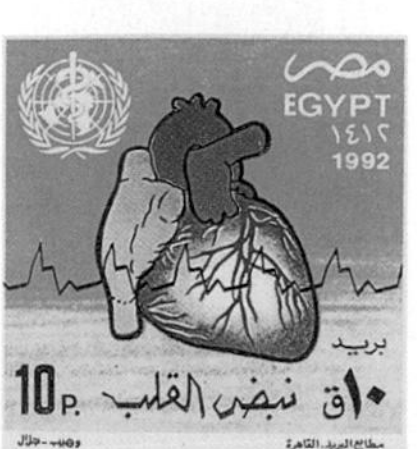

851 Heart and Cardiograph

1992. World Health Day.
1845 **851** 10p. multicoloured 35 15

852 Tent, Emblem and Map

1992. 20th Arab Scout Jamboree.
1846 **852** 10p. multicoloured 35 15

853 Games Emblem, Mascot and Pictograms

1992. Olympic Games, Barcelona. Multicoloured.
1847 10p. Type **853** 35 15
MS1848 80×60 mm. 70p. Games emblem. Imperf 1·80 1·60

854 U.A.R. 1960 60m. Dam Stamp

1992. 90th Anniv of Aswan Dam.
1849 **854** 10p. mauve, yell & blk 35 10

855 "Dar El Helal"

1992. Centenary of "El Helal" (periodical).
1850 **855** 10p. brown, gold & blk 45 20

856 Sphinx and Pyramids

1992. Federation of Travel Companies International Congress, Cairo.
1851 **856** 70p. multicoloured 1·40 1·10

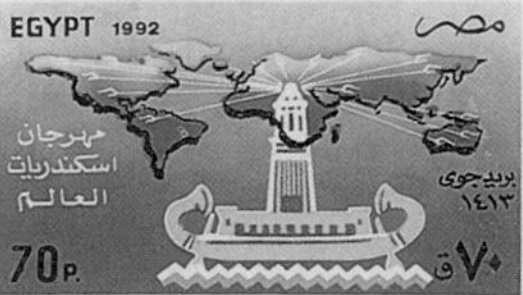

857 World Map, Lighthouse and Pharaonic Ship

1992. Alexandria World Festival.
1852 **857** 70p. multicoloured 1·40 65

858 U.P.U. Emblem

1992. World Post Day.
1853 **858** 10p. bl, blk & ultram 35 10

860 Emblem

1992. 20th Arab Scout Conference, Cairo.
1856 **860** 10p. multicoloured 35 10

859 Girl

1992. United Nations Day. Multicoloured.
1854 10p. Type **859** (Children's Day) 45 20
1855 70p. Wall paintings of agriculture and medicine (International Food, Agriculture and World Health Conference) (36×37 mm) 1·40 1·10

861 Mohamed Taymour

1992. Birth Anniversaries.
1857 **861** 10p. blue, dp blue & bis 35 20
1858 - 10p. blue, dp blue & bis 35 20
1859 - 10p. brown, orge & bl 35 20

DESIGNS: No. 1857, Type **861** (dramatist and theatre critic, centenary); 1851, Ahmed Zaki Abu Shadi (physician and poet, centenary); 1859, Talaat Harb (economist, 125th anniv).

862 Sesostris I

1993. Post Day. Statues of Pharaohs. Mult.
1860 10p. Type **862** 50 20
1861 45p. Amenemhet III 80 65
1862 70p. Hur I 1·30 1·00

863 Book and Statue of Scribe

1993. 25th Cairo International Book Fair.
1863 **863** 15p. multicoloured 45 20

864 Bust

1993. Size 18×22 mm.
1864 **864** 5p. orange and black 60 20
1865 - 15p. brown and ochre 60 20
1866 - 15p. brown and ochre 35 20
1867 - 25p. lt brown & brown 45 20
1868 - 55p. blue and black 1·00 50

DESIGNS—15p. Sphinx*; 25p. Bust of woman; 55p. Bust of Pharaoh.

*On No. 1865 the illustration of the sphinx countinues behind the face value; on No. 1866 the sphinx is cropped so that the value appears on a white background.

For same designs but larger, 21×26 mm, see Nos. 1916/19.

865 Plan and Set Square on Drawing Board

1993. 75th Anniv (1992) of Architects' Association.
1869 **865** 15p. black, orange & bl 45 20

866 Gold Mask of Tutankhamun

1993
1870 - £E1 brown and blue (postage) 2·50 1·30
1871 - £E2 green and brown 7·00 2·20
1872 - £E5 gold and brown 9·25 4·50
1873 **866** 55p. gold and brown (air) 1·90 80
1874 - 80p. gold and brown 3·75 1·10

DESIGNS: 80p. Side view of Tutankhamun's mask; £E1, Bust of woman; £E2, Head of Queen Tiye; £E5, Carved head capital.

867 Old and New Foreign Ministry Buildings and Globe

1993. (a) Egyptian Diplomacy Day.
1875 **867** 15p. multicoloured 45 20

(b) Air. Inauguration of New Foreign Ministry Building. As T **867** but inscr "AIR MAIL MINISTRY OF FOREIGN AFFAIRS".
1876 80p. multicoloured 1·90 1·40

868 Cactus

1993. Festivals 1993.
1877 **868** 15p. multicoloured 45 20

869 First Issue and Emblem

1993. Centenary of "Le Progres Egyptien" (newspaper).
1878 **869** 15p. multicoloured 45 20

870 Dish Aerial, I.T.U. Emblem and Satellite

1993. World Telecommunications Day.
1879 **870** 15p. multicoloured 40 20

871 Globe

1993. U.N. World Conference on Human Rights, Vienna.
1880 **871** 15p. ultram, bl & orge 45 20

872 Emblem, Map of Africa and Stars

1993. 30th Anniv of Organization of African Unity.
1881 **872** 15p. black, silver and green (postage) 45 20
1882 **872** 80p. black, gold and mauve (air) 1·40 1·10

873 Conference Emblem

1993. International Post, Telegraph and Telecommunications Union Conference, Cairo.
1883 **873** 15p. multicoloured 45 20

874 Saladin and Dome of the Rock, Jerusalem

1993. 800th Death Anniv of Saladin.
1884 **874** 55p. multicoloured 1·00 45

875 Soldiers

1993. 20th Anniv of Suez Crossing.
1885 **875** 15p. blk, mve & orge 45 20

876 Pres. Mubarak

1993. Mohammed Hosni Mubarak's 3rd Consecutive Term as President.
1886 **876** 15p. multicoloured 45 20
1887 **876** 55p. multicoloured 1·00 55
1888 **876** 80p. multicoloured 1·50 80
MS1889 90×70 mm. 80p. Portrait and national flag as in Type **876**. Imperf 2·10 2·10

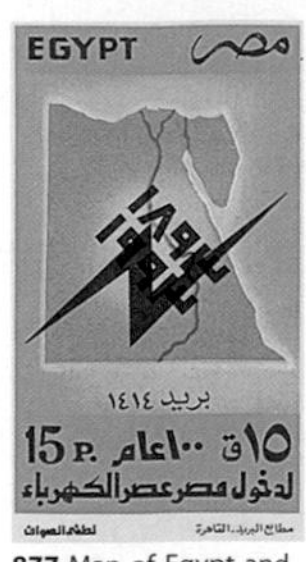

877 Map of Egypt and Electricity Symbol

1993. Centenary of Electricity in Egypt.
1890 **877** 15p. multicoloured 45 20

878 Emblem and Caring Hands

1993. Air. International Decade for Natural Disaster Reduction.
1891 **878** 80p. violet, blue & red 1·50 1·20

879 Pyramids, Sphinx and Dam (congress emblem)

1993. 2nd International Large Dams Congress, Cairo.
1892 **879** 15p. yellow, mve & blk 45 20

880 Trophy and Emblem

1993. Egyptian Victories in International Sports Competitions. Multicoloured.
1893 15p. Type **880** (Junior Men's World Handball Championship) 45 20
1894 15p. Trophy and emblem (World Military Football Championship) 45 20

881 Abdel Aziz al Bishry (50th death)

1993. Writers' Anniversaries.
1895 **881** 15p. blue 45 20
1896 - 15p. turquoise 45 20
1897 - 15p. green 45 20
1898 - 15p. mauve 45 20
DESIGNS: No. 1896, Mohamed Fareed Abu Hadeed (birth centenary); 1897, Ali Moubarak (death centenary); 1898, M. Beram al Tunisy (birth centenary).

882 Amenhotep III

1994. Post Day. Statues of Pharaohs. Multicoloured.
1899 15p. Type **882** 45 20
1900 55p. Queen Hatshepsut 1·20 25
1901 85p. Thutmose III 1·90 35

883 Pyramids

1994. Egyptian Sedimentary Society Congress.
1902 **883** 15p. multicoloured 45 20

884 Firecrests

1994. Festivals 1994. Multicoloured.
1903 15p. Type **884** 45 20
1904 15p. Barn swallows (one perching, one flying) 45 20
1905 15p. Alexandrine parakeets (on tree trunk and branch) 45 20
1906 15p. Eurasian goldfinches (on blossoming branch) 45 20
Nos. 1903/6 were issued together, se-tenant, forming a composite design.

885 Scout Salute and Emblem

1994. 40th Anniv of Arab Scout Movement.
1907 **885** 15p. black, yell & grn 45 20

886 Emblem

1994. 27th Cairo International Fair.
1908 **886** 15p. multicoloured 45 20

887 Radio Waves over Map of Africa

1994. "Africa Telecom 94" Exhibition, Cairo.
1909 **887** 15p. green and brown 45 20

888 Map, Palestine Flag and Olive Branch

1994. Signing in Cairo of Israel-Palestine Agreement on Self-rule for Gaza and Jericho.
1910 **888** 15p. multicoloured 45 20

889 Conference Emblem and Oil Well

1994. 5th Arab Energy Conference, Cairo.
1911 **889** 15p. multicoloured 45 20

890 Emblem

1994. 18th Mediterranean Countries' Biennial Art Exhibition, Alexandria.
1912 **890** 15p. lilac, yellow & blk 45 20

891 Map of Africa and Dove

1994. Africa Day.
1913 **891** 15p. multicoloured 45 20

892 Campaign Emblem Magnfied

1994. Tree Planting Campaign.
1914 **892** 15p. blue, green & black 45 20

893 Library, Family and Open Book

1994. "Reading for All" Summer Festival.
1915 **893** 15p. multicoloured 45 20

1994. As previous designs but size 21×26 mm.
1916 **864** 5p. red and purple 50 20
1917 - 15p. brown and cinnamon (as No. 1866) 50 20
1918 - 25p. orange and brown (as No. 1867) 70 25
1919 - 55p. blue and black (as No. 1868) 95 25

894 Emblem

1994. 75th Anniv of I.L.O.
1925 **894** 15p. grey, blue & black 45 20

895 Conference and United Nations Emblems

1994. U.N. International Conference on Population and Development, Cairo. Multicoloured.
1926 15p. Type **895** (postage) 45 20
1927 80p. Emblems and pharaonic murals (vert) (air) 95 70

896 Player and Trophy

1994. Egyptian Victories in Junior World Squash Championship.
1928 **896** 15p. multicoloured 45 20

897 Anniversary Emblem

1994. Air. 50th Anniv of Signing of Int Civil Aviation Agreement, Chicago.
1929 **897** 80p. blue, yellow & blk 80 45

898 Map on Envelopes

1994. World Post Day.
1930 **898** 15p. multicoloured 45 20

899 Akhenaten and Nefertiti (International Year of the Family)

1994. United Nations Day.
1931 **899** 80p. lilac, red and black (postage) 80 55
1932 - 80p. mult (air) 1·70 90
DESIGN—VERT: No. 1931, Nurses (75th anniv of International Red Crescent/Red Cross Union).

900 Arabic Script over Globes

1994. 50th Anniv of "Akhbar El Yom" (newspaper).
1933 **900** 15p. multicoloured 45 20

901 Emblem, Trophy and Ancient Egyptian Players

1994. African Clubs Hockey Championship.
1934 **901** 15p. multicoloured 45 20

902 Pharaoh and Radames

1994. Performance of Verdi's "Aida" (opera) at Deir al-Bahari temple, Luxor. Multicoloured.
1935 15p. Type **902** (postage) 45 20
MS1936 68×80 mm. 80p. Aida, Great Priest and Pharaoh (air). Imperf 2·30 2·30

903 Centenary Emblem

1994. Cent of Int Olympic Committee.

1937	**903**	15p. multicoloured	45	20

904 Map showing Hostels and Association Emblem

1994. 40th Anniv of Egyptian Youth Hostels Association.

1938	**904**	15p. multicoloured	45	20

905 Player and Globe

1994. 10th Anniv of International Speedball Federation.

1939	**905**	15p. multicoloured	45	20

906 Emblem as Flower

1994. 30th Anniv of African Development Bank.

1940	**906**	15p. multicoloured	45	20

907 Route Maps through Canal and around Africa

1994. 125th Anniv of Suez Canal. Mult.

1941		15p. Type **907**	70	25
1942		80p. Inauguration ceremony, 1869	1·40	70

908 Hassan Fathy (5th death anniv)

1994. Anniversaries.

1943	**908**	15p. brown and flesh	45	20
1944	-	15p. red and pink	45	20

DESIGN: No. 1944, Mahmoud Taimour (birth centenary).

909 Anniversary Emblem

1995. 20th Anniv of World Tourism Organization.

1945	**909**	15p. multicoloured	45	20

910 Akhenaten (statuette)

1995. Post Day. Multicoloured.

1946		15p. Type **910**	50	10
1947		55p. Gold mask of Tutankhamun	1·20	30
1948		80p. Nefertiti (bust)	1·70	45

911 Flowers

1995. Festivals 1995.

1949	**911**	15p. multicoloured	45	20

912 Demonstration, 1919

1995. National Women's Day.

1950	**912**	15p. multicoloured	45	20

913 Emblem and Map

1995. 50th Anniv of Arab League.

1951	**913**	15p. green, bl & gold	45	20
1952	**913**	55p. multicoloured	95	55

914 Hotel

1995. 25th Anniv of Cairo Sheraton Hotel.

1953	**914**	15p. multicoloured	45	20

915 Misr Bank

1995. 75th Anniv of Misr Bank.

1954	**915**	15p. multicoloured	45	20

916 Dish Aerial and Globe

1995. International Telecommunications Day.

1955	**916**	80p. orange, blk & bl	95	55

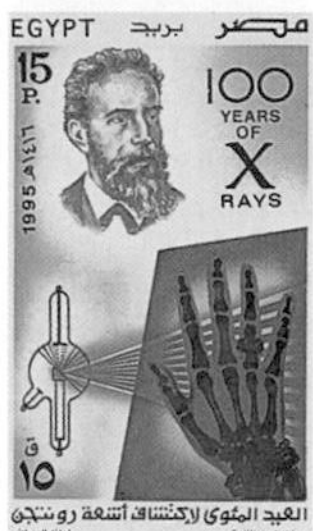

917 Rontgen and X-ray of Hand

1995. Centenary of Discovery of X-rays by Wilhelm Rontgen.

1956	**917**	15p. multicoloured	45	20

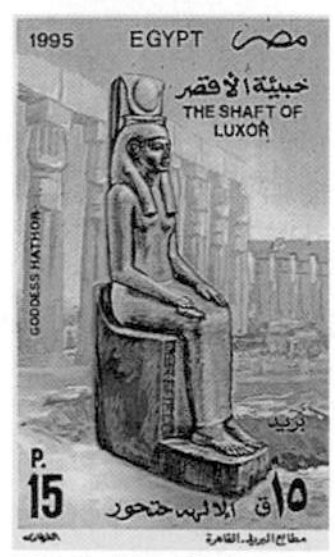

918 Goddess Hathor

1995. 20th Anniv of Membership of World Heritage Committee. Luxor Statues. Multicoloured.

1957		15p. Type **918** (postage)	45	20
1958		15p. God Atoum	45	20
1959		80p. God Amon with Horemheb (air)	1·30	45

Nos. 1957/8 were issued together, se-tenant, forming a composite design.

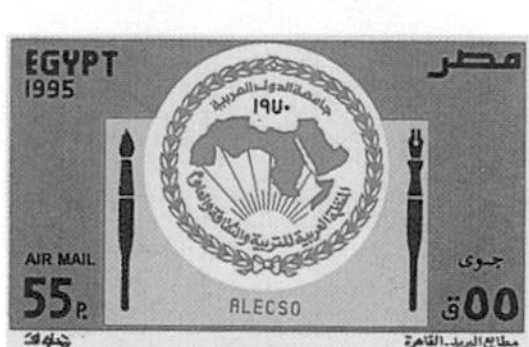

919 Emblem

1995. Air. 25th Anniv of Arab Educational, Scientific and Cultural Organization.

1960	**919**	55p. multicoloured	60	30

920 Children as Flowers

1995. 21st Int Pediatrics Conf, Cairo.

1961	**920**	15p. multicoloured	45	20

921 Ozone Bands over Globe

1995. International Ozone Day.

1962	**921**	15p. multicoloured	45	20
1963	**921**	55p. multicoloured	1·00	40
1964	-	80p. multicoloured	1·50	45

DESIGNS: 80p. As Type **921** but inscribed "The Ozonaction Protection Programme".

See also Nos. 1994/5.

922 Pharaonic Ship and Globe

1995. World Tourism Day.

1965	**922**	15p. multicoloured	1·20	20

923 Emblem and Works, Imbaba

1995. 175th Anniv of Government Printing Offices.

1966	**923**	15p. multicoloured	45	20

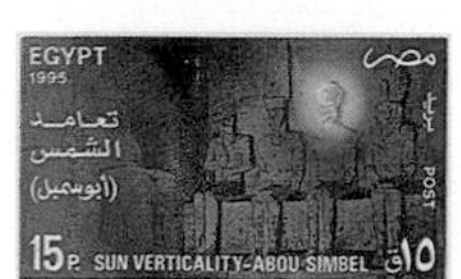

924 Sun illuminating Statue

1995. Overhead Sun Festival, Abu Simbel.

1967	**924**	15p. multicoloured	1·00	30

925 Gold Mask of Tutankhamun

1995. Air. United Nations Day. 50th Anniversaries.

1968	**925**	80p. multicoloured	1·40	85
1969	-	80p. lilac, blue & violet	1·40	85
1970	-	80p. multicoloured	1·40	85

DESIGNS—VERT: No. 1968, Type **925** (UNESCO). HORIZ: No. 1969, Globe, dove, emblem and "50" (U.N.O.); 1970, Farmer and wife working in field (ancient Egyptian mural) (F.A.O.).

926 Dam and Ship

1995. Inauguration of Esna Dam.

1971	**926**	15p. black, blue & grn	70	25

927 Emblem and Pharaonic Mural

1995. 75th Anniv of Egyptian Engineers Society.
1972 **927** 15p. multicoloured 45 20

928 Youssef Wahby

1995. Artists.
1973 **928** 15p. blue and black 45 20
1974 - 15p. green 45 20
1975 - 15p. red and yellow 45 20

DESIGNS: No. 1974, Nagib el Rihany; 1975, Abdel Hallim Hafez.

929 "100"

1995. Centenary of Motion Pictures.
1976 **929** 15p. multicoloured 45 20

930 Pharaonic Mural (left detail)

1996. Post Day. Multicoloured.
1977 55p. Type **930** 1·20 30
1978 80p. Right detail of Pharaonic mural 1·60 45
MS1979 99×81 mm. 100p. Women playing musical instruments and dancing (mural). Imperf 3·75 3·75

Nos. 1977/8 were issued together, se-tenant, forming a composite design.

931 Convolvulus

1996. Festivals 1996. Multicoloured.
1980 15p. Type **931** 45 20
1981 15p. Poppies 45 20

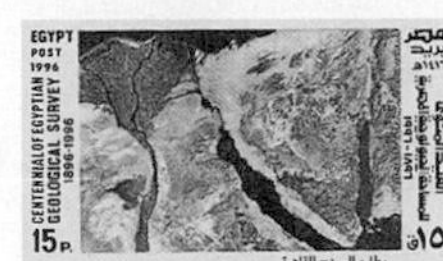

932 Summit Emblem

1996. Middle East Peace Process Summit, Sharm el Shaikh.
1982 **932** 15p. multicoloured 45 20
1983 **932** 80p. multicoloured 1·00 55

933 Geological Map

1996. Centenary of Egyptian Geological Survey Authority.
1984 **933** 15p. multicoloured 45 20

934 Fair Emblem

1996. 29th Cairo International Fair.
1985 **934** 15p. multicoloured 50 20

935 Emblem

1996. Signing of Pelindaba Treaty declaring Africa a Nuclear Weapon-free Zone, Cairo.
1986 **935** 15p. multicoloured 45 20
1987 **935** 80p. multicoloured 1·00 55

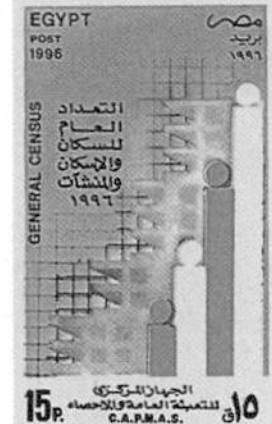

936 Emblem, Calculator, Computer and Abacus

1996. 50th Anniv of Egyptian Society of Accountants and Auditors.
1988 **936** 15p. multicoloured 50 20

937 "People" forming Graph

1996. General Population and Housing Census.
1989 **937** 15p. multicoloured 50 20

938 Emblem

1996. Arab Summit, Cairo.
1990 **938** 55p. multicoloured 80 30

939 Games Emblem

1996. Olympic Games, Atlanta.
1991 **939** 15p. multicoloured 50 20
MS1992 80×116 mm. £E1 Sports pictograms around games emblem 3·25 3·25

940 Emblems

1996. Air. 16th International Congress on Irrigation and Drainage, Cairo.
1993 **940** 80p. multicoloured 95 65

1996. International Ozone Day. As T 921 but inscr "2nd ANNUAL OZONE INTERNATIONAL DAY".
1994 **921** 15p. mult (postage) 35 20
1995 **921** 80p. multicoloured (air) 85 55

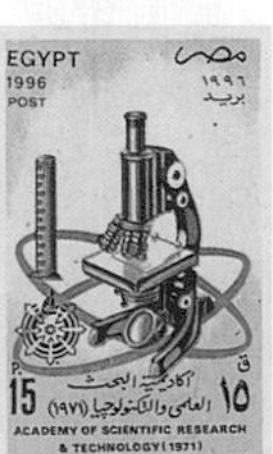

941 Fireworks over City

1996. 2nd Alexandria World Festival.
1996 **941** 80p. multicoloured 80 45

942 Test Tube, Microscope and Atomic Symbol

1996. 25th Anniv of Academy of Scientific Research and Technology.
1997 **942** 15p. multicoloured 40 15

943 Pharaonic Boat (Rowing Festival)

1996. International Tourism Day.
1998 **943** 15p. mult (postage) 70 20
1999 - 55p. grey, black and green (air) 1·00 20
2000 - 80p. multicoloured 1·70 55

DESIGNS: 20×36 mm—55p. Arab horse (Arabian Horse Festival); 47×26 mm—80p. Egyptian figure and hieroglyphs (Tourism Day).

944 Route Map and Train

1996. Inauguration of Second Greater Cairo Metro Line.
2001 **944** 15p. multicoloured 45 20

945 U.P.U. Emblem and Stylized Postal Messengers

1996. Air. World Post Day.
2002 **945** 80p. multicoloured 1·40 45

946 Emblems and Map

1996. Air. Cairo, Cultural Capital of Arab Region.
2003 **946** 55p. blue, orange & blk 60 30

947 Mother and Child (statue)

1996. Air. 50th Anniv of UNICEF.
2004 **947** 80p. multicoloured 1·20 45

948 Council of State Courts

1996. 50th Anniv of Council of State.
2005 **948** 15p. lilac, ultram & bl 45 20

949 Emblem

1996. 25th Conference of International Federation of Training Development Organizations.
2006 **949** 15p. black, blue & yell 45 20

950 Emblem

1996. Economic Summit, Cairo.
2007 **950** 15p. multicoloured. (postage) 45 20
MS2008 80×60 mm. £E1 Emblem, globe, cogwheel, ear of wheat and olive branch 1·70 1·70

951 Emblem and Ear of Wheat

1996. International Nutrition Conf, Rome.
2009 **951** 15p. green, yell & red 45 20

952 Al-Said Ahmed el Badawi Mosque, Tanta

1996. National Day. El Gharbia Governate.
2010 **952** 15p. multicoloured 45 20

953 George Abyad

1996. Artists.
2011 **953** 20p. rose and pink 45 20
2012 - 20p. black and grey 45 20
2013 - 20p. deep brown and brown 45 20
2014 - 20p. black and grey 45 20
DESIGNS: No. 2012, Ali el Kassar; 2013, Mohamed Kareem; 2014, Fatma Roshdi.

954 Tutankhamun and Ankhesenamun (painted ivory plaque)

1996. Post Day. 75th Anniv of Discovery of Tutankaumun's Tomb. Multicoloured.
2015 20p. Type **954** (postage) 50 20
MS2016 60×80 mm. £E1 Tutankhamun and Ankhesenamun (chair back) (air). Imperf 1·80 1·80
See also No. 2056/**MS**2057.

955 Computer, Officers, Emblem and Vehicle

1997. Police Day.
2017 **955** 20p. multicoloured 45 20

956 Pink Asters

1997. Festivals 1997. Multicoloured.
2018 20p. Type **956** 45 20

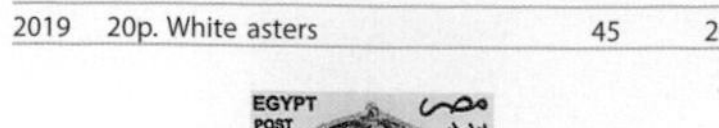
2019 20p. White asters 45 20

957 Queen Tiye

1997
2020 **957** 5p. brown and sepia (postage) 45 20
2020a - 10p. yellow and mauve 25 10
2021 - 20p. brown, ochre and grey 30 20
2022 - 20p. black and grey 35 20
2023 - 25p. yellow and green 35 20
2023a - 30p. yellow, brown and blue 35 20
2024 - 75p. black and orange 95 85
2025 - £E1 multicoloured 1·20 85
2026 - £E2 multicoloured 2·30 1·60
2027 - £E5 green, lilac and black 5·75 4·25
2029 - 25p. blue, buff and brown (air) 45 20
2030 - 75p. black, grey and blue 95 85
2031 - £E1 brown, yellow and black 1·40 85
2032 - 125p. brown, yellow and green 1·70 1·10
DESIGNS—POSTAGE—21×26 mm: No. 2020a, 2023, 2023a, Goddess Silakht. 23×27 mm: No. 2021, Queen Nofret. 21×26 mm: No. 2022, Horemheb; 75p. Amenhotep III. 21×38 mm: £E1 Queen Nefertari; £E5 Thutmose V ("Thotmes IV"). 22×38 mm: £E2 Mummiform coffin of Tutankhamun. AIR—22×40 mm: 25p. Akhnaton. 21×39 mm: 75p. Thutmose III ("Thotmes III"); £E1 Gilded wooden statue of Tutankhamun; 125p Wooden statue of Tutankhamun.

958 Globe and Emblem

1997. World Civil Defence Day.
2035 **958** 20p. multicoloured 45 20

959 Emblem and Colours

1997. 30th Cairo International Fair.
2036 **959** 20p. multicoloured 45 20

960 Compass Rose and Wind Vane

1997. Air. World Meteorological Day.
2037 **960** £E1 multicoloured 2·10 85

961 Said

1997. Birth Centenary of Mahmoud Said (artist). Multicoloured.
2038 20p. Type **961** (postage) 45 20
MS2039 80×60 mm. £E1 "The City" (air). Imperf 1·40 1·40

962 Stephan and U.P.U. Monument, Berne

1997. Death Cent of Heinrich von Stephan (founder of Universal Postal Union).
2040 **962** £E1 multicoloured 1·90 1·10

963 Emblem

1997. 50th Anniv of Institute of African Research and Studies.
2041 **963** 75p. multicoloured 70 65

964 Emblem, Building and Satellite

1997. Inauguration of State Information Service's New Headquarters.
2042 **964** 20p. multicoloured 45 20

965 Emblem, Mascot and Trophy

1997. Under-17 Football World Championship, Egypt.
2043 **965** 20p. mult (postage) 45 20
2044 **965** 75p. mult (air) 70 65
MS2045 81×60 mm. £E1 multicoloured (air). Imperf 1·40 1·40
DESIGN: £E1 Mascot, pitch and emblems.

966 Mascot with Torch and Gold Medal

1997. Air. Egypt's Winning Medal Tally at Eighth Pan-Arab Games, Beirut.
2046 **966** 75p. multicoloured (wrongly inscr "Ban Arab Games") 70 65

967 Emblem

1997. Air. 98th Interparliamentary Union Conference, Cairo.
2047 **967** £E1 multicoloured 1·00 85

968 Emblem

1997. 10th Anniv of Montreal Protocol (on reduction of use of chlorofluorocarbons).
2048 **968** 20p. mult (postage) 70 30
2049 **968** £E1 mult (air) 2·10 95

969 Train

1997. Inauguration of Second Stage of Underground Railway.
2050 **969** 20p. multicoloured 60 30

970 Sarabas

1997. Air. "Fayoum's Portraits" Exhibition.
2051 **970** £E1 multicoloured 1·90 85

971 Pharaonic Musician and Queen Hatshepsut's Temple

1997. 125th Anniv of First Performance of "Aida" (opera by Verdi), at Old Opera House, Cairo.
2052 **971** 20p. multicoloured 60 20
MS2053 80×74 mm. **971** £E1 multicoloured (54×54 mm) (air). Imperf 5·25 5·25

972 Open Book showing Emblem

1997. Air. World Book and Copyright Day.
2054 **972** £E1 green, black & blue 1·60 85

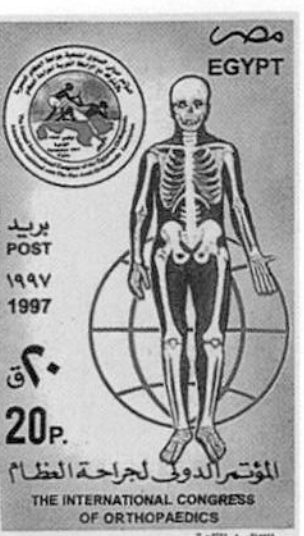

973 Skeleton and Globe

1997. Int Orthopaedics Congress, Cairo.
2055 **973** 20p. multicoloured 45 20

974 Goddess Serket (statuette protecting canopic chest)

1997. 75th Anniv of Discovery of Tutankhamun's Tomb (2nd issue). Multicoloured.

2056	20p. Type **974** (postage)	50	20
MS2057	80×70 mm. £E1 Decoration with scarab in centre (air). Imperf	1·50	1·50

975 Conference Emblem

1997. Air. 11th African Transport and Communications Ministers' Conference, Cairo.

2058	**975**	75p. multicoloured	80	65

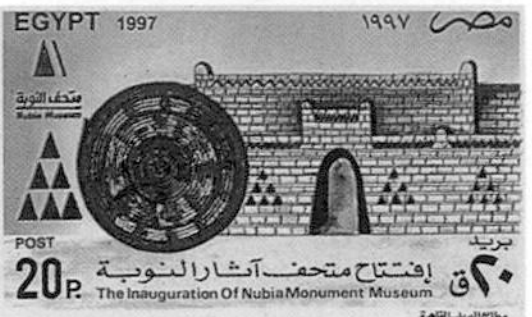
976 Museum

1997. Inauguration of Nubia Monuments Museum.

2059	**976**	20p. multicoloured	1·00	20

977 Emblem and Scout Bugler

1997. Air. 85th Anniv of Arab Scout Movement.

2060	**977**	75p. multicoloured	80	65

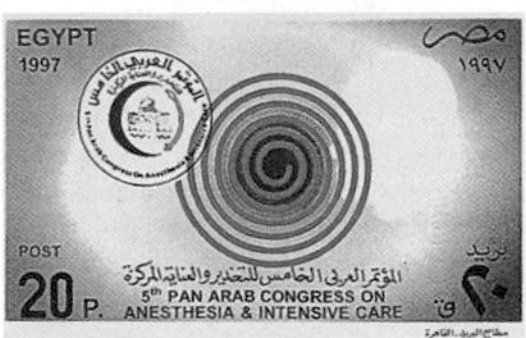
978 Emblem

1997. 5th Pan-Arab Anaesthesia and Intensive Care Congress.

2061	**978**	20p. multicoloured	45	20

979 Emblem

1997. 50th Anniv of Arab Land Bank.

2062	**979**	20p. multicoloured	45	20

980 "Egypt is the Cradle of Arts throughout the Ages"

1997. Dramatic Arts.

2063	**980**	20p. blue	45	20
2064	-	20p. black	45	20
2065	-	20p. black	45	20
2066	-	20p. black	45	20
2067	-	20p. black	45	20

DESIGNS: No. 2064, Zaky Tolaimat (founder and director of Institute of Drama); 2065, Ismael Yassen (actor); 2066, Zaky Roustom (actor); 2067, Soliman Naguib (actor and director of Opera House).

981 Map showing Canal

1997. 15th Anniv of Restoration of Sinai. Inaug of El Salaam ("Peace") Canal.

2068	**981**	20p. multicoloured	45	20

982 Guard to Tutankhamun (statue)

1998. Post Day. Multicoloured.

2069	20p. Type **982**	50	20
2070	75p. "Coronation of Rameses III" (sculpture)	1·30	65
2071	£E1 Mummiform coffin of Tutankhamun (29×49 mm)	1·60	85

983 Flowers

1998. Festivals 1998. Multicoloured.

2072	20p. Type **983**	45	20
2073	20p. Pale pink flowers	45	20

984 Emblem

1998. Cairo International Fair.

2074	**984**	20p. multicoloured	45	20

985 New and Old Headquarters

1998. Centenary of National Bank of Egypt.

2075	**985**	20p. multicoloured	45	20

986 Ancient Egyptians supporting Trophy

1998. Victory of Egypt in 21st African Nations Cup Football Championship. Multicoloured.

2076	20p. Type **986** (postage)	50	20
2077	75p. mult (air)	1·30	65
MS2078	80×60 mm. £E1 Map of Africa, flags of competing nations, mascot and trophy (air).Imperf	1·60	1·60

987 Emblem

1998. Air. 8th Summit Meeting of G-15 Countries, Cairo.

2079	**987**	£El multicoloured	1·20	85

988 Lighthouse of Alexandria and Bust of Alexander the Great

1998. Air.

2080	**988**	£El multicoloured	1·70	85

989 Satellite over Earth

1998. Egyptian "Nile Sat" Satellite.

2081	**989**	20p. multicoloured	45	20

990 Emblem of Environment Agency within Pharaonic Eye

1998. World Environment Day. Multicoloured.

2082	20p. Type **990** (postage)	70	20
MS2083	49×70 mm. £E1 Endangered flora and fauna (air)	4·25	4·25

991 Zewail

1998. Receipt of Franklin Institute Award by Dr. Ahmed Zewail.

2084	20p. Type **991** (postage)	45	20
2085	£E1 black & yell (air)	1·20	85

992 Mohamed el Shaarawi

1998. Imam Sheikh Mohamed Metwalli el-Shaarawi (preacher) Commemoration.

2086	**992**	20p. brown, ochre and black (postage)	45	20
2087	**992**	£El brown, green and black (air)	1·20	85

993 Ornament

1998. Air. Arab Post Day.

2088	**993**	£El multicoloured	1·20	85

994 Pharaonic Mermaid

1998. Nile Flood Day.

2089	**994**	20p. multicoloured	45	20

995 Emblem and Scientific Equipment

1998. Cent of Chemistry Administration.

2090 **995** 20p. multicoloured 45 20

996 Anniversary Emblem

1998. 25th Anniv of Suez Crossing. Multicoloured.

2091 20p. Type **996** (postage) 45 20

MS2092 50×70 mm. £E2 Motif as in Type **969** (air) 3·25 3·25

997 Globe in Envelope

1998. Air. World Post Day.

2093 **997** 125p. multicoloured 1·50 1·20

998 Pharaonic Survey

1998. Centenary of Egyptian Survey Authority.

2094 **998** 20p. multicoloured 50 25

999 Emblems in Handcuffs

1998. Air. 67th Interpol Meeting, Cairo.

2095 **999** 125p. multicoloured 1·50 1·20

1000 Anniversary Emblem

1998. Air. 50th Anniv of Universal Declaration of Human Rights.

2096 **1000** 125p. multicoloured 1·50 1·20

1001 Woman and University

1998. 90th Anniv of Cairo University.

2097 **1001** 20p. multicoloured 50 25

1002 Emblem and Pharaonic Workers

1998. Centenary of Trade Union Movement.

2098 **1002** 20p. multicoloured 50 25

1003 Pharaonic Mural (19th Dynasty)

1999. Post Day. Multicoloured.

2099 20p. Type **1003** 50 25

MS2100 50×70 mm. 125p. Wall carving 2·10 2·10

1004 Flowers

1999. Festivals 1999. Multicoloured.

2101 20p. Type **1004** 50 25

2102 20p. Gladioli 50 25

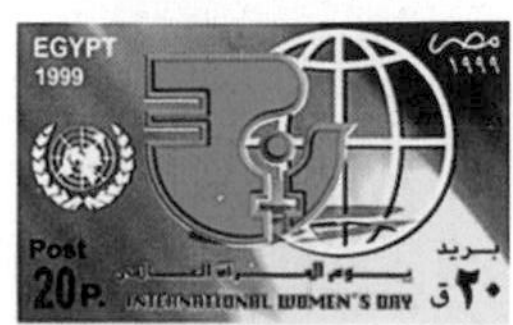

1005 Emblem and Globe

1999. International Women's Day.

2103 **1005** 20p. multicoloured 50 25

1006 Emblem and Colour Spectrum

1999. Cairo International Fair.

2104 **1006** 20p. multicoloured 50 25

1007 Train passing under Nile

1999. Inauguration of El Tahrir–Cairo University Section of Underground Railway.

2105 **1007** 20p. multicoloured 50 25

1008 U.P.U. Emblem and Messenger

1999. 125th Anniv of Universal Postal Union. Multicoloured.

2106 20p. Type **1008** (postage) 50 25

2107 £E1 Type **1008** (air) 1·50 95

2108 125p. Messenger delivering letter (painting) (vert) 1·90 1·20

MS2109 50×70 mm. 125p. Painting as in No. 2108 and U.P.U. emblem 2·30 2·30

1009 Hands supporting Pyramid and Egyptian Red Crescent Emblem

1999. 50th Anniv of Geneva Conventions.

2110 **1009** 20p. multicoloured (postage) 50 25

2111 **1009** 125p. multicoloured (air) 1·50 1·20

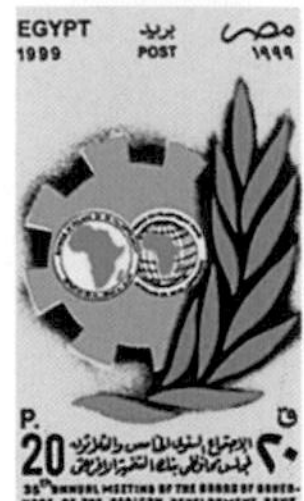

1010 Emblems

1999. 35th Annual Board of Governors Meeting of African Development Bank.

2112 **1010** 20p. multicoloured (postage) 50 25

2113 **1010** £E1 multicoloured (air) 1·00 95

1011 Player and Pyramids

1999. 16th World Men's Handball Championship. Multicoloured.

2114 20p. Type **1011** (postage) 50 25

2115 £E1 Games mascot and pyramids (air) 1·00 95

2116 125p. Mascot and goalkeeper 1·30 1·20

1012 Emblem

1999. 50th Anniv of S.O.S. Children's Villages.

2117 **1012** 20p. blue, green and black (postage) 50 25

2118 **1012** 125p. blue, stone and black (air) 1·30 1·20

1013 Sameera Moussa

1999. Personalities. Multicoloured.

2119 20p. Type **1013** 50 25

2120 20p. Aisha Abdel Rahman 50 25

1014 Touny

1999. 2nd Death Anniv of Ahmed Eldemerdash Touny.

2121 **1014** 20p. multicoloured 50 25

1015 President Mubarak

1999. Re-election of Mohammed Hosni Mubarak to Fourth Consecutive Term as President. Multicoloured.

2122 20p. Type **1015** (postage) 50 25

2123 £E1 As T **1015** but with coloured border instead of frame line (air) 1·00 95

2124 125p. As No. 2123 1·30 1·20

MS2125 70×50 mm. 125p. Portrait of Mubarak as in Type **1015**. 2·30 2·10

1016 Harpist and Sphinx

1999. Air. Performance of Verdi's Opera "Aida" at the Pyramids.

2126 **1016** 125p. multicoloured 2·30 1·70

1017 Rosetta Stone and Jean Champollion (decipherer of hieroglyphics)

1999. Air. Bicentenary of the Discovery of Rosetta Stone.

2127 **1017** 125p. black, brown and cream 2·30 1·70

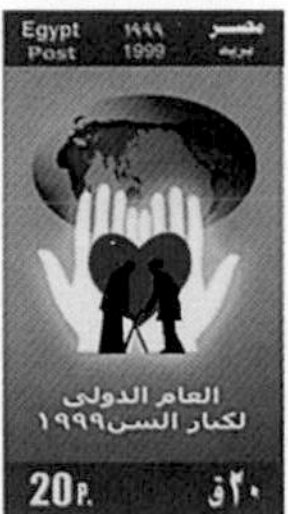

1018 Globe, Elderly Couple, Open Hands and Heart

1999. International Year of the Elderly. Mult.

2128 20p. Type **1018** (postage) 50 25

2129 £E1 As T **1018**, but inscription below motif in English (air) 1·00 95

2130 125p. As No. 2129 1·30 1·20

1019 Children and Jigsaw Pieces

1999. Children's Day.

2131 **1019** 20p. multicoloured 50 25

1020 Zewail and Pyramids

1999. Air. Ahmed Zewail, Winner of 1999 Nobel Prize for Chemistry. Sheet 70×50 mm. Imperf.

MS2132 125p. multicoloured 2·30 1·70

1021 Assia Dagher (film producer)

1999. Personalities. Each black, grey and blue.

2133 20p. Type **1021** 50 25

2134 20p. Anwar Wagdi (actor) 50 25

2135 20p. Farid el Attrash (musician) 50 25

2136 20p. Laila Mourad (singer and actress) 50 25

1022 Corner of Paper Revealing "2000"

2000. New Millennium. Multicoloured.

2137 20p. Type **1022** (postage) 50 25

2138 125p. Year dates culminating in "2000" (air) 1·30 1·20

MS2139 70×50 mm. £E2 "The Virgin Tree in Mataria" (painting). Imperf 4·50 4·50

1023 King and Prince on Thrones

2000. Post Day. 19th Dynasty Murals. Multicoloured.

2140 20p. Type **1023** 50 25

2141 20p. Woman making offering to Queen 50 25

MS2142 70×51 mm. 125p. Rameses II in war chariot. Imperf 3·75 3·75

1024 Emblem and Main Building

2000. 50th Anniv of Ain Shams University, Cairo.

2143 **1024** 20p. multicoloured 50 25

1025 Flower

2000. Festivals 2000. Multicoloured.

2144 20p. Type **1025** 50 25

2145 20p. Roses 50 25

Nos. 2144/5 were issued together, se-tenant, forming a composite design.

1026 Emblem

2000. 25th Anniv of Islamic Development Bank.

2146 **1026** 20p. multicoloured 50 25

1027 Emblem and Pyramids

2000. 1st Common Market for Eastern and Southern Africa Regional Economic Conference.

2147 **1027** 125p. multicoloured 1·30 1·20

1028 Thoum

2000. 25th Death Anniv of Omkol Thoum.

2148 **1028** 20p. black and green 50 25

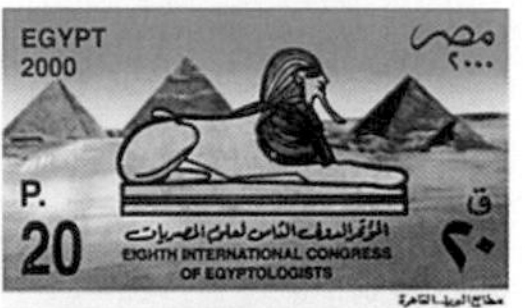

1029 Congress Emblem and Pyramids

2000. 8th International Congress of Egyptologists, Cairo.

2149 **1029** 20p. multicoloured 50 25

1030 Emblem

2000. Europe—Africa Summit, Cairo.

2150 **1030** 125p. multicoloured 1·30 1·20

1031 Emblem and Pyramids

2000. 10th Group 15 Summit, Cairo.

2151 **1031** 125p. multicoloured 1·30 1·20

1032 Skull and Syringe

2000. International Day Against Drug Abuse.

2152 **1032** 20p. multicoloured 50 25

See also No. 2202.

1033 Emblem and Arabic Inscription

2000. Centenary of the National Insurance Company. Multicoloured.

2153 20p. Type **1033** 50 25

MS2154 91×70 mm. 125p. Emblem and different Arabic inscriptions. Imperf 2·30 2·30

1034 Emblem

2000. Olympic Games, Sydney. Multicoloured.

2155 20p. Type **1034** (postage) 50 25

2156 15p. As No. 2155 (air) 1·30 1·20

There are some minor differences in the designs of Nos. 2155/6.

1035 Pottery

2000. 25th Anniv of Co-operative Production Union.

2157 **1035** 20p. multicoloured 50 25

1036 Emblem

2000. Air. World Tourism Day.

2158 **1036** 125p. multicoloured 1·50 1·20

1037 Train and Pyramids

2000. Inaug of Fourth Stage of Second Metro Line.

2159 **1037** 20p. multicoloured 50 25

1038 Emblem and Olive Branch

2000. World Post Day.

2160 **1038** 125p. green, mauve and black 1·50 1·20

1039 Flag and Dome of the Rock

2000. Solidarity.

2161	**1039**	20p. mult (postage)	50	25
2162	**1039**	125p. mult (horiz)	1·50	1·20
2163	**1039**	125p. mult (air)	1·50	1·20

1040 Map and Train on Bridge

2000. Inauguration of El Ferdan Bridge.

2164	**1040**	20p. multicoloured	50	25

1041 Disabled Sign and Olympic Medal

2000. Disabled Persons' Day.

2165	**1041**	20p. multicoloured	50	25

1042 Emblem

2000. Air. 50th Anniv of United Nations High Commission for Refugees.

2166	**1042**	125p. multicoloured	1·50	1·20

1043 Building

2000. Inauguration of New Al Azhar Professoriate Building.

2167	**1043**	20p. multicoloured	50	25

1044 Red and Yellow Flowers

2000. Festivals 2001. Multicoloured.

2168	20p. Type **1044**	50	25
2169	20p. Mauve flowers	50	25

1045 Karem Mahmoud

2000. Artists.

2170	**1045**	20p. black and ochre	50	25
2171	-	20p. black and green	50	25
2172	-	20p. black and pink	50	25
2173	-	20p. black and lilac	50	25
2174	-	20p. black and blue	50	25

DESIGNS: No. 2171, Mahmoud el Miligi; 2172, Mohamed Fawzi; 2173, Hussein Riyad; 2174, Abdel Wares Asser.

1046 Buildings (image scaled to 64% of original size)

2001. Jerusalem. Sheet 80×80 mm. Imperf.

MS2175 **1046**	£E2 multicoloured	1·50	1·50

1047 Mural

2001. Post Day. Multicoloured.

2176	20p. Type **1047** (postage)	65	25
MS2177	79×61 mm. 125p. Mural depicting charioteers. Imperf	1·90	1·90
2178	125p. Mural including pair of scales (air)	1·30	1·20

1048 Emblem

2001. Arab Labour Organization.

2179	**1048**	20p. multicoloured	50	25

1049 Pass Book

2001. Centenary of Postal Savings Bank.

2180	**1049**	20p. multicoloured	50	25

1050 Emblem

2001. 1st Anniv of National Council of Women.

2181	**1050**	30p. mult (postage)	50	25
2182	**1050**	125p. mult (air)	1·40	1·20

1051 Emblem

2001. Cairo International Fair.

2183	**1051**	30p. multicoloured	50	25

1052 Emblem

2001. 25th Anniv of Helwan University.

2195	**1052**	30p. multicoloured	50	25

1053 New Library Building

2001. Ancient Library of Alexandria Project.

2196	**1053**	12p. multicoloured	1·30	1·20

1054 Emblem

2001. Pan-African Conference on Future of Children, Cairo. Multicoloured.

2197	30p. Type **1054** (postage)	50	25
2198	125p. As Type **1054** but with English inscr (air)	1·40	1·20

1055 Globe on Sunflower

2001. World Environment Day.

2199	**1055**	125p. multicoloured	1·40	1·20

1056 Mascot

2001. World Military Football Championship, Cairo. Multicoloured.

2200	30p. Type **1056**	50	25
2201	125p. Mascot and emblem	1·40	1·20

2001. International Day against Drug Abuse.

2202	**1032**	30p. multicoloured	50	25

1057 Trophy and Emblem (image scaled to 69% of original size)

2001. Egyptian Victory in 39th World Military Football Championship, Cairo.

MS2203 **1057**	125p. multicoloured	1·50	1·30

1058 Steam Locomotive

2001. 150th Anniv of Egyptian Railways.

2204	**1058**	30p. multicoloured	65	35

1059 Aziz Abaza Pasha (28th anniv)

2001. Poets' Death Anniversaries.

2205	**1059**	30p. black and blue	50	25
2206	-	30p. black and pink	50	25

DESIGN: No. 2206, Ahmed Rami (20th anniv).

1060 Emblem

2001. International Year of Volunteers.

2207	**1060**	125p. yellow and blue	1·40	1·20

1061 Couple dancing

2001. Ismaelia Folklore Festival.
2208 **1061** 30p. multicoloured 50 25

1062 Building and Satellite Dish

2001. 25th Anniv of First Telecommunications Ground Station.
2209 **1062** 30p. multicoloured 50 25

1063 Bridge spanning Suez Canal

2001. Inauguration of Suez Canal Road Bridge. Multicoloured.
2210 30p. Type **1063** 50 25
2211 125p. Bridge spanning road 1·40 1·20
MS2212 81×60 mm. 125p. Bridge spanning Suez Canal. Imperf 1·90 2·00

Nos. 2110/11 were issued together, se-tenant, forming a composite design.

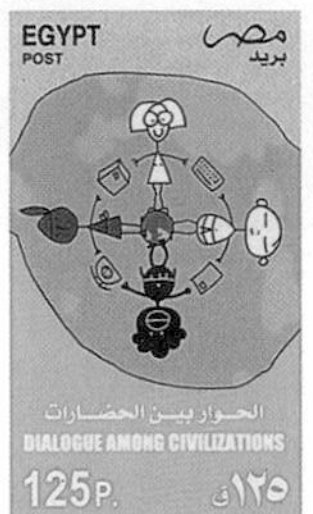

1064 Children encircling Globe

2001. United Nations Year of Dialogue Among Civilizations. Multicoloured.
2213 125p. Type **1064** 1·40 1·20
2214 125p. Globe and symbols of Egypt (horiz) 1·40 1·20

1065 Mask of San Xing Dui

2001. Egypt–China Joint Issue. Golden Masks. Multicoloured.
2215 30p. Type **1065** 50 25
2216 30p. Mask of Tutankhamun 50 25

1066 Cars leaving Tunnel

2001. Inauguration of Al Azhar Road Tunnel, Cairo.
2217 **1066** 30p. multicoloured 50 25

1067 Emblem

2001. 25th Anniv of El Menoufia University.
2218 **1067** 30p. multicoloured 50 25

1068 Zakareya Ahmed

2001. Composers' Death Anniversaries. Each black and lilac.
2219 30p. Type **1068** (40th anniv) 50 25
2220 30p. Riyadh el Sonbati (20th anniv) 50 25
2221 30p. Mahmoud el Sherif (11th anniv) 50 25
2222 30p. Mohamed el Kasabgi (35th anniv) 50 25

1069 Bird

2001. Festivals 2002. Birds. Multicoloured.
2223 30p. Type **1069** 50 25
2224 30p. Gulls 50 25
2225 30p. Parrot 50 25
2226 30p. Blue bird 50 25

1070 Tomb of Anhur Khawi (mural, 20th dynasty)

2002. Post Day. Multicoloured.
2227 30p. Type **1070** 50 25
MS2228 80×59 mm. 125p. Tomb of Irinefer (mural). Imperf 2·30 2·30

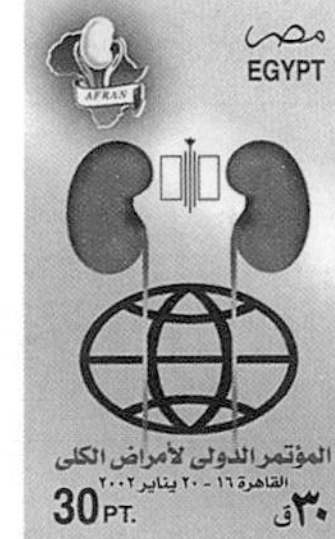

1071 Emblems and Kidneys

2002. International Nephrology Congress.
2229 **1071** 30p. multicoloured 50 25

1072 Emblem

2002. 50th Anniv of Police Day.
2230 **1072** 30p. multicoloured 50 25
MS2231 79×50 mm. **1072** 30p. multicoloured. Imperf 1·60 1·60

1073 Wind-surfers and Diver

2002. 20th Anniv of Return of Sinai to Egypt.
2232 **1073** 30p. multicoloured 25 25

1074 Facade

2002. 50th Anniv of Cairo Bank.
2233 **1074** 30p. multicoloured 25 25

1075 Man wearing Animal Skin and Couple Enthroned (20th Dynasty wall painting)

2002. Multicoloured.. Multicoloured..
2234 **1075** 10p. multicoloured 20 10
2235 - 25p. yellow, mauve and black 25 15
2236 - 30p. yellow, mauve and blue 40 20
2237 - 50p. multicoloured 65 35
2238 - 110p. yellow, brown and violet 1·30 95
2239 - 125p. multicoloured 1·40 1·00
2240 - 150p. multicoloured 1·80 1·40
2241 - 225p. multicoloured 2·75 2·30
2242 - £E1 ochre, blue and brown 35 15
2243 - £E5 multicoloured 6·00 5·25

DESIGNS: As Type **1075**—25p. Sesostris (statue); 30p. Merit Aton (bust); HORIZ:50p. Royal couple, children and musicians (20th Dynasty wall painting); £E1 Snefru's pyramid, Dahshur. 24×41 mm:110p. Wife of Ka-Aper ("Sheikh el Balad") (bust); 125p. Psusennes I (bust); 150p. Tutankhamun holding spear (statue); 225p. Ramses II obelisk, Luxor; £E5 Karnak Temple ruins.

1076 Ibrahim Shams (1948)

2002. Olympic Gold Medal Weightlifters. Multicoloured.
2244 30p. Type **1076** 50 25
2245 30p. Khidre El Tourney (1936) 50 25

1077 Building and World Map

2002. 50th Anniv of Al Akhba (newspaper).
2246 **1077** 30p. multicoloured 50 25

1078 Stamps of 1952 (image scaled to 61% of original size)

2002. 50th Anniv of Revolution of 23 July 1952. Sheet 80×95 mm. Imperf.
MS2247 **1078** 125p. multicoloured 1·30 1·20

1079 Aswan Dam

2002. Centenary of Aswan Dam. Multicoloured.
2248 30p. Type **1079** 50 25
2249 30p. Part of dam and shoreline 50 25

Nos. 2248/9 were issued together, se-tenant, forming a composite design.

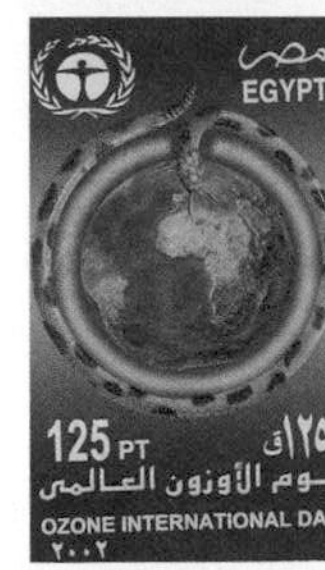

1080 Globe encircled by Snake

2002. International Ozone Day.
2250 **1080** 125p. multicoloured 1·50 1·30

1081 Man with Bandaged Head and Traffic Lights

2002. International Road Safety Conference.
2251 **1081** 30p. multicoloured 50 25

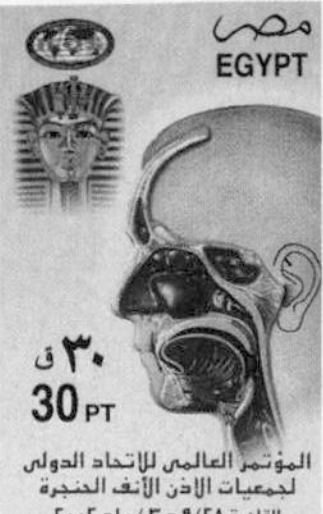

1082 Cross Section of Head showing Cavities

2002. 17th Oto-Rhino Laryngological Societies (IFOS) Congress, Cairo.

2252 **1082** 30p. multicoloured 50 25

1083 UPU Emblem

2002. World Post Day. 125th Anniv of Universal Postal Union.

2253 **1083** 125p. multicoloured 1·30 1·20

1084 Library Building

2002. Inauguration of Bibliotheca Alexandrina (library), Alexandria. Multicoloured.

2254 30p. Type **1084** 50 25
2255 125p. Inscribed column and sunset (vert) 1·30 1·20
MS2256 60×81 mm. 125p. Interior of ancient Alexandria library. Imperf 1·40 1·40

1085 Hassan Faek

2002. Actors. Each pink and grey.

2257 30p. Type **1085** 50 25
2258 30p. Aziza Amir 50 25
2259 30p. Farid Shawki 50 25
2260 30p. Mary Mounib 50 25

1086 Bee-eater

2002. Festivals 2003. Multicoloured.

2261 30p. Type **1086** 50 25
2262 30p. Swallow 50 25
2263 30p. Red-throated bee-eater 50 25
2264 30p. Roller 50 25

Nos. 2261/4 were issued together, se-tenant, forming a composite design.

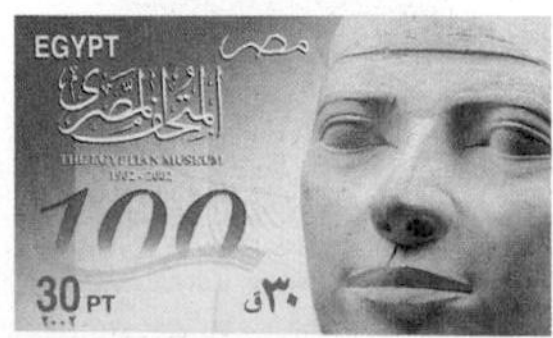

1087 Face (sculpture)

2002. Centenary of Egyptian Museum, Cairo. Multicoloured.

2265 30p. Type **1087** 50 25
MS2266 80×60 mm. 125p. Building facade and statue. Imperf 1·40 1·40

1088 Bridge

2002. Inauguration of Aswan Suspension Bridge. Multicoloured.

2267 30p. Type **1088** 50 25
2268 30p. Bridge right 50 25

Nos. 2267/8 were issued together, se-tenant, forming a composite design of the bridge.

1089 University Emblem

2002. 25th Anniv of Suez Canal University, Ismailia.

2269 **1089** 30p. multicoloured 50 25

1090 Pumping Station

2002. Inauguration of Toshka Irrigation Project.

2270 **1090** 30p. multicoloured 50 25

1091 Pharaonic Tomb Mural

2003. Post Day. Multicoloured.

2271 30p. Type **1091** 50 25
2272 30p. Mural showing wings 50 25
2273 125p. Mural showing pharaoh and goddess 1·30 1·20

1092 Emblem

2003. International Communications and Information Technology Fair, Cairo.

2274 **1092** 30p. multicoloured 50 25

1093 Festival Emblem

2003. 4th International Nile Children's Song Festival.

2275 **1093** 30p. multicoloured 50 25
2276 **1093** 125p. multicoloured 1·30 1·20

1094 Association Emblem, Bat and Ball

2003. Egypt International Open Table Tennis Championship, Cairo.

2277 **1094** 30p. multicoloured 50 25
2278 **1094** 125p. multicoloured 1·30 1·20

1095 Exhibition Emblem and Construction Workers

2003. 10th International Building and Construction Conference.

2279 **1095** 30p. multicoloured 50 25
2280 **1095** 125p. multicoloured 1·30 1·20

1096 Emblem

2003. 80th Anniv of Arab Lawyers Union.

2281 **1096** 30p. multicoloured 50 25
2282 **1096** 125p. multicoloured 1·30 1·20

1097 Smart Village Emblem and Building

2003. Smart Village (technology business park), Cairo. Multicoloured.

2283 30p. Type **1097** 50 25
2284 125p. No. 2283 1·30 1·20
MS2285 80×59 mm. 100p. Smart Village and environs. Imperf 1·40 1·40

1098 Ihsan Abdul Qudous

2003. Writers. Multicoloured.

2286 30p. Type **1098** 50 25
2287 30p. Youssef Idris 50 25

1099 Hand, Ball and Net

2003. Men's African Nations Basketball Championship.

2288 **1099** 30p. multicoloured 50 25
2289 **1099** 125p. multicoloured 1·30 1·20

1100 Planets and Emblem

2003. Centenary of National Institute for Astrological and Geophysical Research.

2290 **1100** 30p. multicoloured 50 25

1101 Emblem

2003. Egypt's Bid to Host 2010 World Cup Football Championship. Multicoloured.

2291 30p. Type **1101** 50 25
2292 125p. Emblem and Tutankhamen (vert) 1·30 1·20

1102 Tent Maker and Market

2003. World Tourism Day.

2293 **1102** 30p. multicoloured 50 25
2294 **1102** 125p. multicoloured 1·30 1·20

1103 Soldier

2003. 30th Anniv of October War.

2295 **1103** 30p. multicoloured 1·00 25

1104 UPU Emblem and Computer

2003. World Post Day.

2296 **1104** 125p. multicoloured 1·30 1·20

1105 Emblem

2003. 91st Anniv of Bar Association.
2297 **1105** 30p. multicoloured 1·00 25

1106 Alstromeria

2003. Festivals 2004. Multicoloured.
2298 30p. Type **1106** 50 25
2299 30p. White rose 50 25
2300 30p. Red rose 50 25
2301 30p. Sunflower 50 25
Nos. 2298/2301 were issued together, se-tenant, forming a composite design.

1107 Salah Abou Seif

2003. Cinema Directors. Each black and azure.
2302 30p. Type **1107** 50 25
2303 30p. Kamal Selim 50 25
2304 30p. Henri Bakarat 50 25
2305 30p. Hassan el Emam 50 25

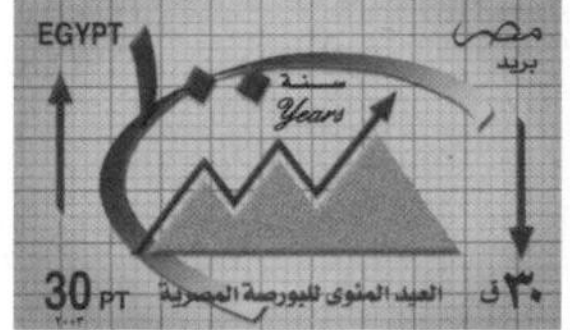

1108 Emblem

2003. Centenary of Cairo Bourse (stock exchange).
2306 **1108** 30p. multicoloured 1·00 25

1109 Emblem and Building

2003. 50th Anniv of El Gomhoreya Newspaper.
2307 **1109** 30p. multicoloured 1·00 25

1110 Mrs. Suzanne Mubarak

2003. 5th E-9 Ministerial Meeting.
2308 **1110** 30p. multicoloured 50 25
2309 **1110** 125p. multicoloured 1·30 1·20
MS2310 80×60 mm. **1110** £E2 multi-coloured. Imperf 1·90 1·70

1111 Emblems

2004. 25th Anniv of Delta International Bank.
2311 **1111** 30p. multicoloured 50 25
2312 **1111** 125p. multicoloured 1·30 1·20
MS2313 81×60 mm. **1111** £E2 multi-coloured (horiz) Imperf 1·90 1·70

1112 Post Emblem

2004. World Post Day.
2314 **1112** 30p. multicoloured 50 25
2315 **1112** 125p. multicoloured 1·30 1·20

1113 Conference Emblem

2004. International Communication and Information Technology Fair, Cairo (1st series).
2316 **1113** 30p. multicoloured 1·00 25
See also No. 2392.

1114 First President

2004. 98th Anniv of National Bar Association.
2317 **1114** 30p. blue and black 50 25
2318 - 30p. blue and black 50 25
2319 - 30p. blue and black 50 25
2320 - 30p. blue and black 50 25
2321 - 30p. blue and black 50 25
2322 - 30p. rose and black 50 25
2323 - 30p. rose and black 50 25
2324 - 30p. rose and black 50 25
2325 - 30p. rose and black 50 25
2326 - 30p. rose and black 50 25
2327 - 30p. salmon and black 50 25
2328 - 30p. salmon and black 50 25
2329 - 30p. salmon and black 50 25
2330 - 30p. salmon and black 50 25
2331 - 30p. salmon and black 50 25
2332 - 30p. green, vermilion and black 50 25
2333 - 30p. green and black 50 25
2334 - 30p. green and black 50 25
2335 - 30p. green and black 50 25
2336 - 30p. green and black 50 25
2337 - 30p. blue, vermilion and black 50 25
2338 - 30p. blue and black 50 25
2339 - 30p. blue and black 50 25
2340 - 30p. blue and black 50 25
2341 - 30p. blue and black 50 25
DESIGNS: Nos. 2317/31 Presidents of association; No. 2332 Emblem; Nos. 2333/6 Presidents of association; No. 2337 Emblem; Nos. 2338/41 Presidents of association.

1115 Anniversary Emblem

2004. 50th Anniv of IBM (computer company) in Egypt.
2342 **1115** 30p. multicoloured 1·00 25

1116 Club and Anniversary Emblems

2004. 75th Anniv of Cairo Rotary Club.
2343 **1116** 30p. multicoloured 1·00 25

1117 Trophy, Globe and Computers

2004. Egypt, Winners of Regional Information Technology Competition.
2344 **1117** 30p. multicoloured 1·00 25

1118 Council Emblem

2004. 4th National Council for Women Conference, Alexandria.
2345 **1118** 30p. multicoloured 50 25
2346 **1118** 125p. multicoloured 1·30 1·20

1119 Poppy Head and Emblem

2004. 75th Anniv of Anti-Narcotic Administration.
2347 **1119** 30p. multicoloured 1·00 25
MS2348 80×60 mm. **1119** 125p. multicoloured. Imperf 1·40 1·40

1120 Flower and Boy

2004. Orphans' Day.
2349 **1120** 30p. multicoloured 1·00 25
See also No. 2397.

1121 Map of Africa, Conference Emblem and Satellite

2004. Telecom Africa Fair and Conference, Cairo.
2350 **1121** 30p. multicoloured 1·00 25

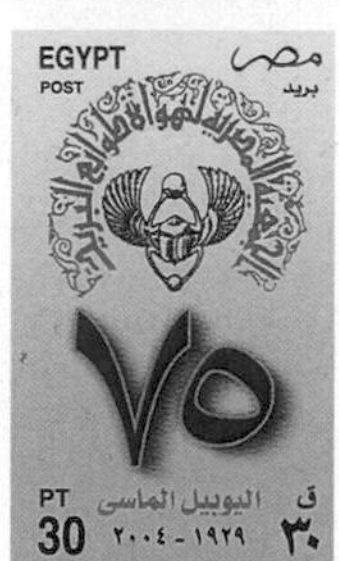

1122 Society Emblem

2004. 75th Anniv of Egyptian Philatelic Society. Multicoloured.
2351 30p. Type **1122** 1·00 25
MS2352 80×60 mm. 125p. Magnifying glass, stamp and emblem (horiz) Imperf 1·30 1·20

1123 Information Service Building

2004. 50th Anniv of State Information Service.
2353 **1123** 30p. multicoloured 1·00 25

1124 President Mubarak

2004. Arab Regional Conference. Multicoloured.
2354 30p. Type **1124** 50 25
2355 125p. Type **1124** 1·00 95
2356 125p. Sunrise and stylized couple (vert) 1·00 95
MS2357 80×60 mm. £E2 As Type **1124** but with design enlarged. Imperf 1·40 1·40

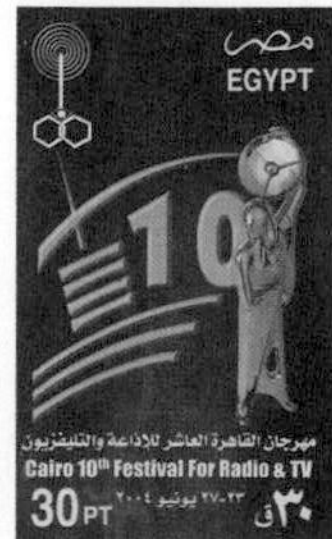

1125 Anniversary Emblem

2004. 10th Television Festival. Multicoloured.
2358 30p. Type **1125** 50 25

2359	£E1 Type **1125**	1·00	95
2360	125p. Sphinx, emblem and film (horiz)	1·30	1·20

MS2361 80×60 mm. £E2 As No. 2360 but with design enlarged. Imperf 1·40 1·40

1126 Bank and Anniversary Emblems

2004. 25th Anniv of Housing and Construction Bank.

2362 **1126** 30p. multicoloured 1·00 25

1127 Olympic Emblems

2004. Olympic Games, Athens 2004.

2363	**1127**	30p. multicoloured	50	25
2364	**1127**	125p. multicoloured	1·30	1·20

1128 Scout Emblem

2004. 90th Anniv of Egyptian Scouting Movement.

2365 **1128** 30p. multicoloured 1·00 25

1129 Festival Emblem

2004. 14th Ismaelia Folklore Festival.

2366 **1129** 30p. multicoloured 1·00 25

1130 Blind Justice and Anniversary Emblem

2004. 50th Anniv of Administrative Attorney Establishment.

2367 **1130** 30p. multicoloured 1·00 25

MS2368 60×80 mm. **1130** £E1 multi-coloured. Imperf 1·40 1·40

1131 Tugra (Imperial Ottoman monogram)

2004. 175th Anniv of Egyptian Archive. 50th Anniv of National Archive.

2369 **1131** 30p. multicoloured 1·00 25

1132 Emblems as Spectacles

2004. 50th Anniv of Light and Hope Society (charitable organization).

2370 **1132** 30p. multicoloured 1·00 25

1133 Pen Nib enclosing Union Emblem

2004. 10th General Arab Journalists Union Conference.

2371 **1133** 125p. multicoloured 1·30 60

1133a Emblem

2004. 150th Anniv of First Telegraph Cable between Cairo and Alexandria.

2371a **1133a** 30p. multicoloured 1·00 45

No. 2371a was withdrawn from sale a few days later as it shows the incorrect anniversary emblem.

1134 Chariot

2004. 50th Anniv of Military Production Day.

2372 **1134** 30p. multicoloured 1·00 25

1135 Post Horn and UPU Emblem

2004. World Post Day.

2373 **1135** 150p. multicoloured 1·60 80

1136 Association Emblem

2004. 50th Anniv of Egypt Youth Hostel Association.

2374 **1136** 30p. multicoloured 1·00 25

1137 Rose

2004. Festivals 2005. Multicoloured.

2375	30p. Type **1137**	50	35
2376	30p. Songbird (horiz)	50	35

1138 Scouts

2004. 24th Arab Scouting Conference.

2377 **1138** 30p. multicoloured 50 35

1139 Anniversary Emblems

2004. 50th Anniv of Arab Scouting Association.

2378 **1139** 30p. multicoloured 50 35

1140 Decorated Pot

2004. Centenary of Islamic Art Foundation.

2379 **1140** 30p. multicoloured 50 35

1141 Anniversary Emblems

2004. Centenary of FIFA (Federation Internationale de Football Association).

2380 **1141** 150p. multicoloured 1·60 80

1142 Abd El Rahman El Sharquawi

2004. Personalities. Multicoloured.

2381	30p. Type **1142** (writer)	50	35
2382	30p. Fekri Abaza (journalist)	50	35

1143 Emblems

2004. 150th Anniv of First Telegraph Cable between Cairo and Alexandria.

2383	**1143**	30p. vermillion and black	50	35
2384	**1143**	125p. vermillion and black	1·30	1·20

1144 Pipeline

2005. Inauguration of Gas Pipeline from Egypt to Jordan.

2385 **1144** 30p. multicoloured 1·00 35

1145 Post Box

2005. Post Day.

2386 **1145** 30p. multicoloured 1·00 35

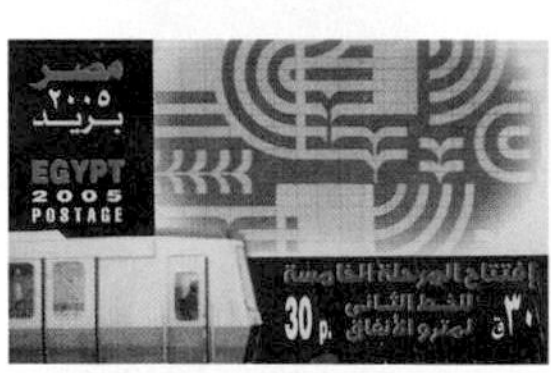

1146 Metro Line and Train

2005. Inauguration of Fifth Phase of Metro Underground Rail Line.

2387 **1146** 30p. multicoloured 1·00 35

MS2388 80×60 mm. **1146** 150p. multicoloured. Imperf 1·60 1·60

1147 President Mubarak

2005. Police Day.

2389 **1147** 30p. multicoloured 1·00 35

MS2390 80×60 mm. **1147** £E1 multi-coloured. Imperf 1·30 1·20

1148 Emblem

2005. 25th Anniv of El Mohandes Insurance Company.

2391 **1148** 30p. multicoloured 1·00 35

1149 Emblem

2005. International Communications and Information Technology Fair, Cairo (2nd series).
2392 **1149** 30p. multicoloured 1·00 35

1150 Emblem

2005. University Youth Week.
2393 **1150** 30p. multicoloured 1·00 35

1151 Emblem

2005. Centenary of Rotary International.
2394 **1151** 30p. multicoloured 1·00 35

1152 Emblems

2005. Cairo International Fair.
2395 **1152** 30p. multicoloured 1·00 35

1153 Map and Emblem

2005. 60th Anniv of Arab League.
2396 **1153** 30p. multicoloured 1·00 35

2005. Orphans' Day. As T 1120.
2397 **1120** 30p. multicoloured 1·00 35

1154 Foundation Headquarters

2005. Centenary of Heliopolis Foundation.
2398 **1154** 30p. multicoloured 1·00 35

1155 Anniversary Emblem

2005. 50th Anniv of National Centre for Social and Criminological Research.
2399 **1155** 30p. multicoloured 1·00 35

1156 Egyptian Flag and European Stars

2005. 10th Anniv of Barcelona Declaration. First Anniv of Egyptian European Association Agreement.
2400 **1156** 30p. multicoloured 1·00 35

1157 Buildings, Water and Emblem

2005. World Environment Day.
2401 **1157** 30p. multicoloured 1·00 35

1158 Emblem

2005. World Information Society Summit, Tunis.
2402 **1158** 150p. multicoloured 1·60 1·60

1159 Emblem

2005. 50th Anniv of Ministry of Youth.
2403 **1159** 30p. multicoloured 50 35
2404 **1159** 125p. multicoloured 1·30 1·20

1160 Ballot Box

2005. Presidential Election.
2405 **1160** 30p. multicoloured 1·00 35

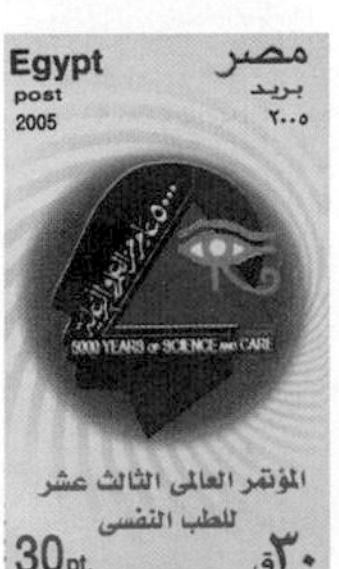

1161 Profile and Emblem

2005. World Psychiatry Congress. Multicoloured.
2406 30p. Type **1161** 1·00 25
MS2407 80×61 mm. 150p. Emblem. Imperf 1·60 1·60

1162 Blackboard, Reader and Emblem

2005. World Illiteracy Eradication Day.
2408 **1162** 30p. multicoloured 1·00 35

1163 Sphinx

2005. Presidential Elections.
2409 **1163** 30p. multicoloured 1·00 35

1164 Mohamed El-Baradei

2005. Mohamed El-Baradei—2005 Nobel Peace Price Winner.
2410 **1164** 30p. multicoloured 50 35
2411 **1164** 150p. multicoloured 1·60 1·20

1165 UPU Emblem

2005. World Post Day.
2412 **1165** 30p. multicoloured 50 35
2413 **1165** 150p. multicoloured 1·60 1·20

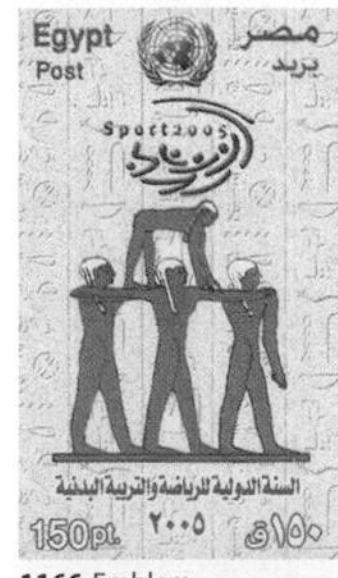

1166 Emblem

2005. International Year of Sport and Physical Education.
2414 **1166** 150p. multicoloured 1·60 1·20

1167 Emblem and Buildings

2005. 60th Anniv of United Nations.
2415 **1167** 150p. multicoloured 1·60 1·20

1168 Flowers

2005. Festivals (2006).
2416 **1168** 30p. multicoloured 1·00 45

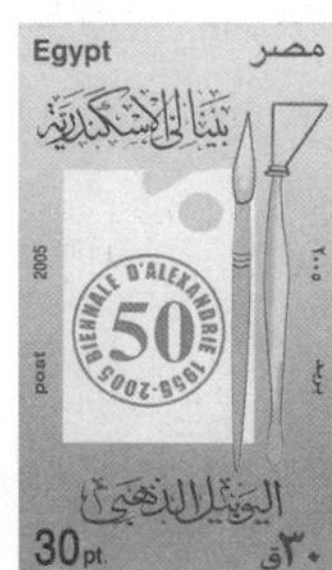

1169 Anniversary Emblem

2005. 50th Anniv of Alexandria Biennale (cultural and scientific event).
2417 **1169** 30p. multicoloured 1·00 45

1170 Nanchang k-8 and Sphinx

2005. Aircraft Training Programme.
2418 30p. Type **1170** 50 35
2419 150p. Karakorum 8 1·60 1·20

1171 Sayed Mekkawy

2005. Personalities. Multicoloured.

2420 30p. Type **1171** 50 35
2421 30p. Kamal el Taweel 50 35
2422 30p. Mohamed El Mogy 50 35
2423 30p. Ali Ismail 50 35
2424 30p. Mohamed Roshdi 50 35

1172 Emblem

2006. Post Day.

2425 **1172** 30p. multicoloured 1·00 45

1173 Games Mascot

2006. African Nations Cup, Egypt.

2426 **1173** 30p. multicoloured 1·00 45

1174 Emblem

2006. Arab Universities Week.

2427 **1174** 30p. multicoloured 1·00 45

1175 Emblem

2006. 10th International Communications and Information Technology Fair, Cairo.

2428 **1175** 30p. multicoloured 1·00 45

1176 President Mubarak holding Trophy

2006. Egypt—African Nations Cup Football Champions—2006. Multicoloured.

2429 30p. Type **1176** 1·00 45
MS2430 80×60 mm. 150p. As No. 2429. Imperf 1·80 1·70

1177 Emblem

2006. 20th Anniv of Information Support Centre.

2431 **1177** 30p. multicoloured 1·00 45

1178 Rocks and Eclipse

2006. Solar Eclipse—2006. Multicoloured.

2432 30p. Type **1178** 1·00 45
MS2433 81×60 mm. 150p. As No. 2432. Imperf 1·90 1·90

1179 Flower and Boy

2006. Orphans' Day.

2434 **1179** 30p. multicoloured 1·00 45

1180 Gamal Hemdan

2006. Gamal Hemdan (geographical historian) Commemoration.

2435 **1180** 30p. multicoloured 1·00 45

1181 Ibn Khaldoun

2006. 600th Death Anniv of Abd El-Rahman Ibn Khaldoun (philosopher).

2436 **1181** 30p. multicoloured 1·00 45

1182 White Desert

2006. World Environment Day. Multicoloured.

2437 30p. Type **1182** 50 25
2438 150p. Tree in desert 1·80 1·20

1183 Abu Simble Temple, Egypt

2006. 50th Anniv of Egypt-China Diplomatic Relations. Multicoloured.

2439 150p. Type **1183** 1·80 1·20
2440 150p. South Gate Pavilion, China 1·80 1·20

No. 2439 is incorrectly described as 'ABU SIMPLE'.

1183a Emblems

2006. 50th Anniv of Military Academy New Headquarters.

2441 **1183a** 30p. multicoloured 1·00 45

1184 Emblems

2006. 50th Anniv of Suez Canal Nationalization.

2442 **1184** 30p. multicoloured 1·00 45

1185 Emblems

2006. World Post Day.

2443 **1185** 30p. multicoloured 50 25
2444 **1185** 150p. multicoloured 1·80 1·20

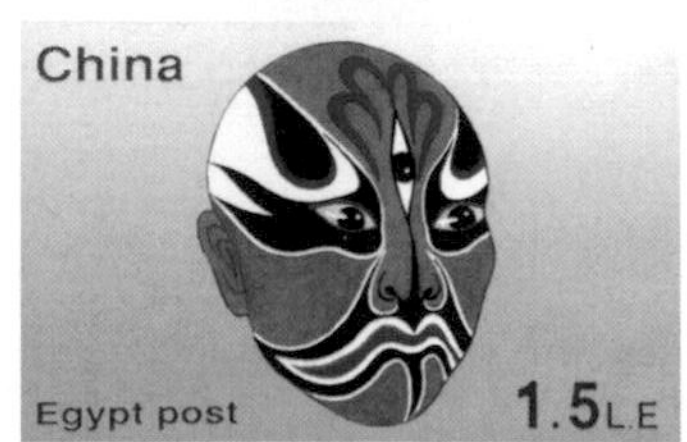

1186 Chinese Mask

2006. China—Africa Forum. Multicoloured.

2445 £1.50 Type **1186** 1·80 1·20
2446 £1.50 African masks 1·80 1·20

1187 Emblem

2006. Census.

2447 **1187** 30p. multicoloured 1·00 45

1188 Building

2006. 130th First Edition of "Al-Ahram" (English language weekly). Multicoloured.

2448 30p. Type **1188** 50 35
2449 30p. Symbols of Egypt 50 35
MS2450 81×60 mm. 150p. Building and symbols. Imperf 1·90 1·90

1189 Emblem

2006. National Mother and Child Council.

2451 **1189** £1.50 multicoloured 1·80 1·20

1190 Musicians

2006. Festivals 2007.

2452 **1190** 30p. multicoloured 1·00 45

1191 Emblem

2007. Post Day.

2453 **1191** 30p. multicoloured 1·00 45

1192 Early Car and Emblems

2007. Automobile and Touring Club of Egypt. Multicoloured.

2454 30p. Type **1192** 1·00 45
MS2455 80×60 mm. 150p. As No. 2454. Imperf 1·90 1·90

1193 Figure

2007. 50th Death Anniv of Ali el Kasser (artist).

2456 **1193** 30p. multicoloured 1·00 45

1194 President Mubarak, Flag and Emblem

2007. Police Day. Multicoloured.

2457 30p. Type **1194** 1·00 45

MS2458 80×60 mm. 150p. As No. 2457. Imperf 1·90 1·90

1195 Sunset, Archway and Book

2007. 60th Anniv of Academy of Arabic Language.

2459 **1195** 30p. multicoloured 1·00 45

1196 Emblems

2007. World Health Day.

2460 **1196** 30p. multicoloured 1·00 45

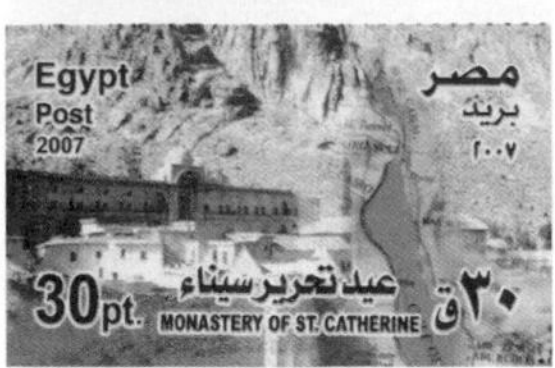

1196a St. Catherine Monastery

2007. Tourism. Multicoloured.

2461 30p. Type **1196a** 50 25

2462 30p. Salah el Din Castle 50 25

2463 30p. Diving, Sharm el-Sheikh 50 25

2464 30p. Nabq Oasis 50 25

Nos. 2461/4 were issued together, se-tenant, forming a composite design.

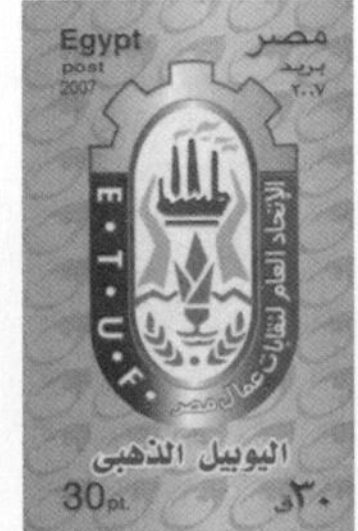

1197 Emblem

2007. 50th Anniv of National Trade Union Federation.

2465 **1197** 30p. multicoloured 1·00 45

1198 Anniversary Emblem and Early Airliner

2007. 75th Anniv of EgyptAir Airlines. Multicoloured.

2466 30p. Type **1198** 50 25

2467 150p. Emblem, modern and early airliners 1·80 1·20

1199 Rumi

2007. 800th Birth Anniv of Mawlana Jalal ad-Din Muhammed Rumi.

2468 **1199** 150p. multicoloured 1·80 1·20

1200 Sinai Baton Blue

2007. World Environment Day. Multicoloured.

2469 30p. Type **1200** 50 25

2470 150p. Melting ice (horiz) 1·80 1·20

1201 '100'

2007. Centenary of Scouting.

2471 **1201** 150p. multicoloured 1·80 1·20

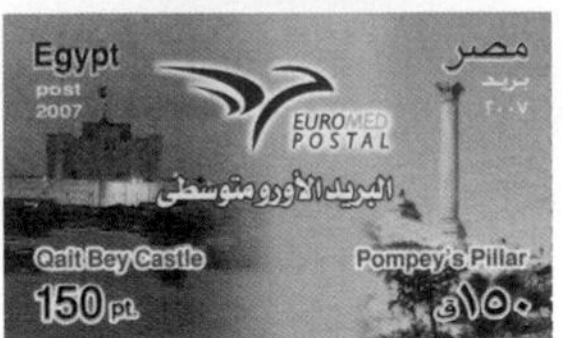

1202 Qait Bey Castle and Pompey's Pillar

2007. EuroMed Postal.

2472 **1202** 150p. multicoloured 1·80 1·20

1203 Statuettes

2007. 50th Anniv of Egypt—Nepal Diplomatic Relations.

2473 **1203** 150p. multicoloured 1·80 1·20

1204 Lockheed Martin F-16 Fighting Falcon and de Havilland DH.82 Tiger Moth

2007. 75th Anniv of National Air Force.

2474 **1204** 30p. multicoloured 1·00 45

1205 Cat

2007. Arab Games–2007, Egypt. Multicoloured.

2475 150p. Type **1205** 1·80 1·20

MS2476 95×75 mm. 150p. Map and emblem. Imperf 1·90 1·90

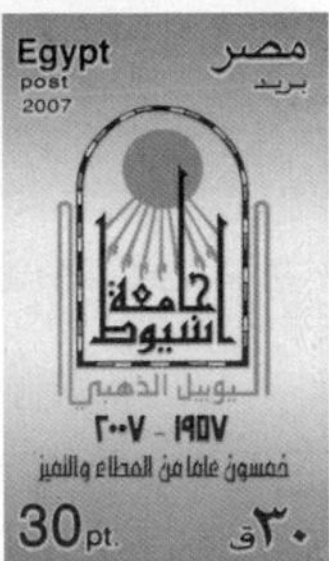

1206 Emblem

2007. 50th Anniv of Assiut University.

2477 **1206** 30p. multicoloured 1·00 45

1207 Hafez Ibrahim

2007. Poets' 75th Death Anniversaries. Multicoloured.

2478 30p. Type **1207** 1·00 45

2479 30p. Ahmed Shawqi 1·00 45

1208 Emblem

2007. 50th Anniv of National Handball Federation.

2480 **1208** 30p. multicoloured 1·00 45

1211 Trophy

2008. Egypt–Winner of 2008 Africa Cup of Nations, Ghana.

2483a **1211** 30p. multicoloured 1·00 45

No. 2481 and Type **1209** have been left for 'Festival', issued on 1 January 2008, not yet received.

No. 2482 and Type **1210** have been left for 'Post Day', issued on 7 February 2008, not yet received.

1213 Emblem

2008. Centenary of Cairo University.

2486 **1213** 30p. multicoloured 1·00 45

No. 2484/5 and Type **1212** have been left for 'World Environment Day', issued on 10 February 2008, not yet received.

1214 Mine and Hand

2008. Removal of World War II Landmines Campaign. Multicoloured.

2487 150p. Type **1214** 1·50 95

2488 150p. One-legged boy and mine-field (horiz) 1·50 95

1215 Emblem

2008. Telecom Africa 2008, International Convention and Exhibition Centre, Cairo.

2489 **1215** 30p. multicoloured 1·00 45

1216 Stylized Lungs, Emblems and Factory

2008. World Environment Day.

2490 **1216** 30p. multicoloured 50 25

2491 **1216** 150p. multicoloured 1·50 95

1217 Script

2008. Centenary of Fine Arts Faculty.

2492 **1217** 30p. multicoloured 50 25

2493 **1217** 150p. multicoloured 1·50 95

1218 Emblem

2008. PAPU Conference.

2494	**1218**	150p. multicoloured	1·50	95

1219 Airliner

2008. EgyptAir Airlines.

2495	**1219**	150p. multicoloured	1·50	95

1220 Emblem

2008. Alexandria–Islamic Capital of Culture.

2496	**1220**	150p. multicoloured	1·50	95

1221 Pigeon (image scaled to 66% of original size)

2008. Arab Post Day. Multicoloured.

2497	150p. Type **1221**	1·30	80
2498	150p. Camels	1·30	80

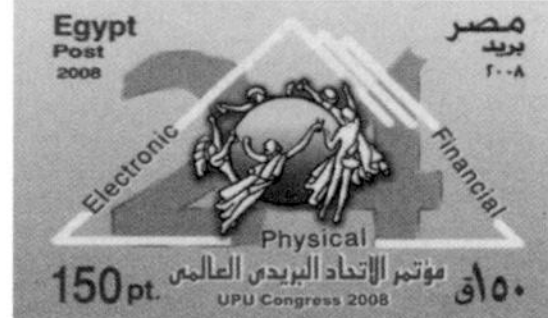
1221a Emblem

2008. UPU Congress, Cairo.

2498a	**1221a**	150p. multicoloured	1·50	95

1222 Emblem

2008. 50th Anniv of Sport's Education for Men.

2499	**1222**	30p. multicoloured	1·00	45

1223 Ancient Egyptian holding Emblem

2008. International Postal Technology Conference (POSTECH), Sharm el-Sheikh. Multicoloured.

2500	30p. Type **1223**	50	25
2501	150p. Statue and hand holding emblem	1·50	95

1224 Emblem

2008. Centenary of Egyptian Co-operative Movement.

2502	**1224**	30p. multicoloured	1·00	45

1225 Building Facade

2008. 25th Anniv of National Telecommunications Institute (NTI).

2503	**1225**	30p. multicoloured	1·00	45

1226 Runner and Emblem

2009. National Sports.

2504	**1226**	150p. multicoloured	1·50	95

1227 Flower and Boy

2009. Orphans' Day.

2505	**1227**	150p. multicoloured	1·50	95

1228 Emblem

2009. 90th Anniv of International Labour Organization.

2506	**1228**	150p. multicoloured	1·50	95

1228a Suzanne Mubarak and Library Facade

2009. Mubarak Public Library, Damanhour.

2506a	**1228a**	150p. multicoloured	1·50	95

1228b

2009. 1st Egypt Post Creative Forum.

2506b	**1228b**	150p. multicoloured	1·50	95

1229 Globe

2009. Suzanne Mubarak Women's International Peace Movement. Cyber Peace Initiative.

2507	**1229**	150p. multicoloured	1·50	95

1229a Ahmed Zewail

2009. PAPU Conference, Cairo. Sheet 298×199 mm containing T **1229a** and similar horiz designs. Multicoloured.

MS2507a 150p.×16, Type **1229a**; Desmond Tutu; Wangari Mathai; Muhammad Anwar Al Sadat; Naguib Mahfouz; Alan Cormack; Nelson Mandela; Wole Soyinka; Sydney Brenner; Frederik Willem de Klerk; Nadine Gordimer; Max Theiler; Mohamed Mostafa El Baradei; Albert Luthuli; Kofi Annan; John Maxwell Coetzee — 24·00 24·00

1230 Emblem

2009. 15th Non-Aligned Movement Summit.

2508	**1230**	150p. multicoloured	1·50	95

1231 Emblem

2009. al-Quds—2009 Capital of Arab Culture.

2509	**1231**	150p. multicoloured	1·50	95

1231a Championship Emblem and Paraguay Flag

2009. FIFA U-20 Football World Cup Championship, Egypt.

MS2509a 150p.×16, Type **1231a**; Brazil; Uruguay; Germany; Nigeria; South Korea; Venezuela; Ghana; United Arab Emirates; South Africa; Egypt; Spain; Italy; Hungary; Czech Republic; Costa Rica — 24·00 24·00

1232 Symbols of China and Africa

2009. Fourth Ministerial Conference of the China-Africa Cooperation Forum (FOCAC), Sharm El Sheikh.

2510	**1232**	150p. multicoloured	1·50	95

1233 Symbols of Internet

2009. Internet Governance Forum, Sharm El Sheikh.

2511	**1233**	150p. multicoloured	1·50	95

1233a Masks

2009. Luxor

2511a	**1233a**	250p. multicoloured	2·30	1·30

1234 Emblems

2009. Centenary of Egyptian Society of Political, Economy, Statistics and Legislation.

2512	**1234**	150p. multicoloured	1·50	95

1235 '30' and Emblem

2010. 30th Anniv of PAPU (Pan African Postal Union)

2513	**1235**	150p. multicoloured	1·50	95

1236 '10' and Emblem

2010. Tenth Anniv of National Council for Women

2514	**1236**	30p. multicoloured	1·00	45

1237 Emblem and 1960 10m. Stamp (Type **204**)

2010. 50th Anniv of Arab League

2515	**1237**	200p. multicoloured	2·00	1·20

1238 Flower and Boy

2010. Orphan's Day

2516	**1238**	30p. multicoloured	1·00	45

EXPRESS LETTER STAMPS

E52 Postman on Motor-cycle

1926

E138	**E52**	20m. green	26·00	9·50
E139	**E52**	20m. black and red	5·50	1·70

1943. As Type E 52, but inscr "POSTES".

E289	26m. black and red	5·75	6·75
E290	40m. black and brown	5·25	5·50

1952. No. E290 optd as T 124.

E404	40m. black & brown	2·30	1·90

OFFICIAL STAMPS

O25

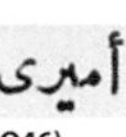

(O46)

1893

O64	**O25**	(–) brown	3·50	10

1907. Stamps of 1879 and 1888 optd O.H.H.S. and Arabic equivalent.

O73	**18**	1m. brown	1·75	30
O74	**18**	2m. green	4·00	10
O75	**18**	3m. yellow	4·25	1·25
O86	**18**	4m. red	6·50	4·50
O76	**18**	5m. red	7·00	10
O77	**10**	1p. blue	3·00	20
O78	**10**	5p. grey	16·00	6·50

1913. No. 63 optd in English only. (a) Optd "O.H.H.S." (with inverted commas).

O79	5m. pink		£325

(b) Optd O.H.H.S. (without inverted commas).

O80	5m. pink	9·00	60

1915. Stamps of 1914 optd O.H.H.S. and Arabic equivalent.

O83	**29**	1m. sepia	2·25	4·75
O99	-	2m. red	9·00	22·00
O85	-	3m. orange	3·50	5·50
O87	-	5m. lake	4·00	2·50
O101	-	5m. pink	18·00	5·50

1922. Stamps of 1914 optd O.H.E.M.S. and Arabic equivalent.

O111	**29**	1m. brown	1·60	3·25
O112	**29**	2m. red	2·10	4·50
O113	**29**	3m. orange	3·25	5·00
O114	**29**	4m. green	7·25	9·00
O115	**29**	5m. pink	4·00	1·10
O116	**29**	10m. blue	7·25	9·00
O117	**29**	10m. red	10·00	4·00
O118	**41**	15m. blue	8·25	7·25
O119	**42**	15m. blue	£170	£170
O120	-	50m. purple	20·00	19·00

1923. Stamps of 1923 optd with Type O 46.

O123	**44**	1m. orange	1·70	2·10
O124	**44**	2m. black	2·20	3·00
O125	**44**	3m. brown	5·50	5·50
O126	**44**	4m. green	6·75	6·75
O127	**44**	5m. brown	1·70	85
O128	**44**	10m. red	4·50	3·25
O129	**44**	15m. blue	7·75	5·50
O130	-	50m. green	20·00	11·00

O52

1926

O138	**O52**	1m. orange	85	45
O139	**O52**	2m. black	55	35
O140	**O52**	3m. brown	1·60	1·10
O141	**O52**	4m. green	1·40	1·20
O142	**O52**	5m. brown	1·70	45
O143	**O52**	10m. lake	4·25	45
O144	**O52**	10m. violet	2·50	50
O145	**O52**	15m. blue	4·25	1·00
O146	**O52**	15m. purple	4·25	90
O147	**O52**	20m. blue	4·50	1·30
O148	**O52**	20m. olive	6·00	2·20
O149	**O52**	50m. green	8·00	1·60

Nos. O148/9 are larger, 22½×27½ mm.

O85

1938

O276	**O85**	1m. orange	35	90
O277	**O85**	2m. red	35	35
O278	**O85**	3m. brown	1·30	1·60
O279	**O85**	4m. green	85	1·30
O280	**O85**	5m. brown	40	45
O281	**O85**	10m. mauve	50	65
O282	**O85**	15m. purple	1·20	1·10
O283	**O85**	20m. blue	1·20	1·10
O284	**O85**	50m. green	2·30	1·70

1952. Optd as T 124.

O404	1m. orange	1·60	1·50
O405	2m. red	1·60	1·50
O406	3m. brown	1·80	1·70
O407	4m. green	1·80	1·70
O408	5m. brown	1·80	1·70
O409	10m. mauve	1·80	1·70
O410	15m. purple	2·20	2·10
O411	20m. blue	2·75	2·50
O412	50m. green	5·75	5·50

O174

1958

O685	**O174**	1m. orange	35	45
O686	**O174**	4m. green	60	65
O687	**O174**	5m. brown	60	15
O571	**O174**	10m. purple	70	20
O688	**O174**	10m. brown	60	20
O572	**O174**	35m. blue	1·60	35
O689	**O174**	35m. violet	2·30	45
O690	**O174**	50m. green	3·75	55
O691	**O174**	100m. lilac	7·50	1·70
O692	**O174**	200m. red	15·00	8·25
O693	**O174**	500m. black	23·00	14·50

O334 Eagle

1967

O918	**O334**	1m. blue	20	35
O919	**O334**	4m. brown	25	35
O920	**O334**	5m. olive	25	10
O921	**O334**	10m. brown	95	65
O922	**O334**	10m. purple	1·00	45
O923	**O334**	20m. purple	60	20
O924	**O334**	35m. violet	95	35
O925	**O334**	50m. orange	1·00	45
O926	**O334**	55m. violet	1·30	45
O927	**O334**	100m. red and green	2·30	80
O928	**O334**	200m. red and blue	4·75	2·00
O929	**O334**	500m. red and olive	9·50	9·50

O435 Eagle

1972

O1161a	**O435**	1m. blue & black	30	25
O1162a	**O435**	10m. red & black	35	25
O1163	**O435**	20m. green & blk	1·10	35
O1165	**O435**	20m. brown & vio	95	10
O1166	**O435**	30m. brown & lilac	60	35
O1169	**O435**	60m. orange & blk	70	35
O1170	**O435**	70m. green & blk	85	45
O1171	**O435**	80m. green & blk	95	35
O1294	**O435**	50m. orange & blk	60	55
O1295	**O435**	55m. lilac & black	2·40	80

O706 Eagle

1985. Size 20×25 mm.

O1589	**O706**	1p. red	25	20
O1590	**O706**	2p. brown	25	10
O1591	**O706**	3p. brown	25	20
O1592a	**O706**	5p. orange	35	35
O1593	**O706**	8p. green	70	35
O1594	**O706**	10p. brown	25	20
O1595	**O706**	15p. lilac	1·50	70
O1596	**O706**	20p. blue	85	80
O1597	**O706**	25p. red	1·70	1·00
O1598	**O706**	30p. purple	95	70
O1599	**O706**	50p. green	2·10	2·00
O1600	**O706**	60p. green	2·00	1·40

1991. As Nos. O1589/1600 but smaller, 17×22 mm.

O1806	5p. orange	15	10
O1807	10p. brown	25	15
O1808	15p. brown	25	10
O1808a	20p. blue	35	15
O1808b	20p. violet	15	10
O1809	25p. lilac	45	20
O1810	30p. lilac	50	25
O1811	50p. green	80	65
O1812	55p. red	70	55
O1812a	75p. brown	75	55
O1813	£E1 blue	1·00	80
O1814	£E2 green	2·10	1·60

POSTAGE DUE STAMPS

D16

1884

D57	**D16**	10pa. red	55·00	9·00
D58	**D16**	20pa. red	£120	35·00
D64	**D16**	1pi. red	35·00	9·50
D65	**D16**	2pi. red	35·00	4·00
D61	**D16**	5pi. red	15·00	48·00

1888. As Type D 16, but values in "Milliemes" and "Piastres".

D66	2m. green	22·00	26·00
D67	5m. red	42·00	26·00
D68	1p. blue	£140	35·00
D69	2p. orange	£150	16·00
D70	5p. grey	£225	£200

D24

1889. Inscr "A PERCEVOIR POSTES EGYPTIENNES".

D71	**D24**	2m. green	8·00	50
D72	**D24**	4m. purple	2·75	50
D73	**D24**	1p. blue	5·50	50
D74bw	**D24**	2p. orange	5·00	70

1898. Surch 3 Milliemes in English and Arabic.

D75	3m. on 2p. orange	2·00	6·00

1921. As Type D 24, but inscr "POSTAGE DUE EGYPT POSTAGE".

D98	**D23**	2m. green	2·75	6·00
D99	**D23**	2m. red	1·50	2·75

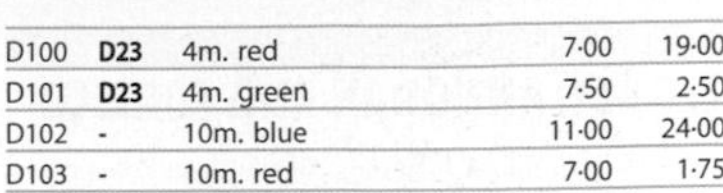

D100	**D23**	4m. red	7·00	19·00
D101	**D23**	4m. green	7·50	2·50
D102	-	10m. blue	11·00	24·00
D103	-	10m. red	7·00	1·75

The 10m. values have "MILLIEMES" in a bar across the figure of value.

1922. Optd with T 43 inverted.

D111	**D24**	2m. red (No. D99)	90	3·25
D112	**D24**	4m. green (No. D101)	1·30	3·25
D113	**D24**	10m. red (No. D103)	2·20	1·60
D114	**D24**	2p. orge (No. D74)	6·25	9·00

D59

1927

D173	**D59**	2m. black	70	35
D730	**D59**	2m. orange	60	1·00
D175a	**D59**	4m. green	70	35
D176	**D59**	4m. sepia	6·50	4·00
D177	**D59**	5m. brown	3·50	1·00
D575	**D59**	6m. green	2·30	1·80
D179	**D59**	8m. purple	1·30	55
D180a	**D59**	10m. lake	95	20
D732	**D59**	10m. brown	2·30	1·10
D181	**D59**	12m. red	1·50	4·00
D182	**D59**	20m. brown	1·70	2·50
D183	**D59**	30m. violet	3·75	3·25

The 30m. is larger, 22×27½ mm.

1952. Optd as T 124.

D404	2m. orange	1·20	1·40
D405	4m. green	1·20	1·50
D406	6m. green	1·40	2·10
D407	8m. purple	1·80	1·70
D408	10m. lake	2·75	1·50
D410	12m. red	1·80	1·70
D411	30m. violet	2·75	2·40

D298

1965

D852	**D298**	2m. violet on orange	1·20	1·10
D853	**D298**	8m. blue on lt blue	1·60	1·50
D854	**D298**	10m. green on yell	2·30	1·60
D855	**D298**	20m. violet on lt bl	2·75	2·20
D856	**D298**	40m. green on orge	5·25	4·50

Pt. 9

ELOBEY, ANNOBAN AND CORISCO

A group of Spanish islands off the west coast of Africa in the Gulf of Guinea. In 1909 became part of Spanish Guinea. In 1959 Annobon became part of Fernando Poo, and Elobey and Corisco part of Rio Muni.

100 centimos = 1 peseta.

1903. "Curly Head" key-type inscr "ELOBEY, ANNOBON Y CORISCO". Dated "1903".

1	Z	¼c. red	85	60
2	Z	½c. purple	85	60
3	Z	1c. black	85	60
4	Z	2c. red	85	60
5	Z	3c. green	85	60
6	Z	4c. green	85	60
7	Z	5c. lilac	85	60
8	Z	10c. red	1·80	1·60
9	Z	15c. orange	5·75	2·75
10	Z	25c. blue	10·00	7·25
11	Z	50c. brown	12·00	12·50
12	Z	75c. brown	12·00	16·00
13	Z	1p. red	19·00	24·00
14	Z	2p. brown	50·00	70·00
15	Z	3p. green	80·00	85·00
16	Z	4p. purple	£180	£120
17	Z	5p. green	£200	£120
18	Z	10p. blue	£400	£225

1905. "Curly Head" key-type inscr "ELOBEY, ANNOBON Y CORISCO" and dated "1905".

19	1c. pink	1·60	85
20	2c. purple	7·00	85
21	3c. black	1·60	85
22	4c. red	1·60	85
23	5c. green	1·60	85
24	10c. green	5·75	1·10
25	15c. lilac	7·00	6·00
26	25c. red	7·00	6·00
27	50c. orange	12·00	9·50
28	75c. blue	12·00	9·50
29	1p. brown	24·00	21·00
30	2p. brown	27·00	29·00
31	3p. red	27·00	29·00
32	4p. brown	£200	£110
33	5p. green	£200	£110
34	10p. red	£550	£350

1906. Preceding issue surch 1906 and value, with or without ornamental frame.

35d	10c. on 1c. pink	16·00	7·50
36	15c. on 2c. purple	12·50	10·00
38	25c. on 3c. black	12·50	10·00
40	50c. on 4c. red	12·50	10·00

3 King Alfonso XIII

1907

41	3	1c. purple	50	50
42	3	2c. black	50	50
43	3	3c. red	50	50
44	3	4c. green	50	50
45	3	5c. green	50	50
46	3	10c. lilac	6·25	6·75
47	3	15c. pink	2·10	2·20
48	3	25c. buff	2·10	2·20
49	3	50c. blue	2·10	2·20
50	3	75c. brown	7·00	3·00
51	3	1p. brown	11·00	5·50
52	3	2p. red	15·00	19·00
53	3	3p. brown	15·00	19·00
54	3	4p. green	18·00	19·00
55	3	5p. red	25·00	19·00
56	3	10p. pink	55·00	39·00

1908. Surch HABILITADO PARA 05 CTMS.

57	05c. on 1c. purple	3·75	2·50
58	05c. on 2c. black	3·75	2·50
59	05c. on 3c. red	4·00	2·50
60	05c. on 4c. green	4·00	2·50
61	05c. on 10c. lilac	9·75	9·25
62	25c. on 10c. lilac	37·00	21·00

1909. Fiscal stamps inscr "POSESIONES ESPANOLES DE AFRICA OCCIDENTAL", surch 1909 CORREOS 10 cen de peseta.

63	10c. on 50c. green	27·00	18·00
64	10c. on 1p.25 lilac	41·00	22·00
65	10c. on 2p. brown	£160	£120
66	10c. on 2p.50 blue	£160	£120
67	10c. on 10p. brown	£170	£120
68	10c. on 15p. grey	£160	£120
69	10c. on 25p. brown	£160	£120

For later issues see **SPANISH GUINEA**.

Pt. 15

EL SALVADOR

A republic of C. America, independent since 1838.

1867. 8 reales = 100 centavos = 1 peso.
1912. 100 centavos = 1 colon.

1 San Miguel Volcano

1867

1	1	½r. blue	75	90
2	1	1r. red	75	75
3	1	2r. green	2·75	3·25
4	1	4r. brown	5·75	4·50

1874. Optd CONTRA SELLO 1874 and arms in circle.

5B	½r. blue.	8·25	4·50
6B	1r. red	8·25	4·50
7B	2r. green	9·00	4·50
8B	4r. brown	26·00	23·00

4

1879

9	4	1c. green	2·50	1·30
15	4	2c. red	3·50	3·50
16	4	5c. blue	5·75	4·50
12	4	10c. black	11·50	4·50
13	4	20c. purple	20·00	13·00

8 9 10

1887

18	8	3c. brown (perf)	65	40
19	9	5c. blue (roul)	65	40
20	10	10c. orange (perf)	3·75	1·30

1889. Surch 1 centavo.

21	8	1c. on 3c. brown	90	65

A number of postage stamps listed above are found overprinted **1889**.

1889. As T 8, but with bar at top. Perf.

22	1c. green	40	25

14

1890

30	14	1c. green	40	40
31	14	2c. brown	40	40
32	14	3c. yellow	40	40
33	14	5c. blue	40	40
34	14	10c. violet	40	40
35	14	20c. orange	40	40
36	14	25c. red	65	1·30
37	14	50c. purple	40	90
38	14	1p. red	50	1·90

15

1891

39	15	1c. red	40	40
40	15	2c. green	40	40
41	15	3c. violet	40	40
42	15	5c. red	1·30	2·50
43	15	10c. blue	40	40
44	15	11c. violet	40	40
45	15	20c. green	40	40
46	15	25c. brown	40	50
47	15	50c. blue	40	1·10
48	15	1p. brown	40	1·90

1891. Surch 1 centavo.

49	1c. on 2c. green	2·75	2·30

1891. Surch UN CENTAVO.

50	1c. on 2c. green	2·00	1·90

1891. Surch 5 CENTAVOS.

51	5c. on 3c. violet	5·00	4·50

19 Landing of Columbus

1892

52	19	1c. green	50	40
53	19	2c. brown	50	40
54	19	3c. blue	50	40
55	19	5c. grey	50	40
56	19	10c. red	50	40
57	19	11c. brown	50	50
58	19	20c. orange	50	50
59	19	25c. purple	50	75
60	19	50c. yellow	50	1·40
61	19	1p. red	50	2·50

1892. Surch.

62a	1c. on 5c. grey	1·00	65
64	1c. on 20c. orange	1·70	1·00
66	1c. on 25c. purple	1·90	1·70

23 Gen. Ezeta

24 Founding the City of Isabella

1893. Dated "1893".

67	23	1c. blue	40	40
68	23	2c. red	40	40
69	23	3c. violet	40	40
70	23	5c. brown	40	40
71	23	10c. brown	40	40
72	23	11c. red	40	40
73	23	20c. green	40	50
74	23	25c. black	40	65
75	23	50c. orange	40	75
76	23	1p. black	40	1·00
77	24	2p. green	1·00	
78	-	5p. violet	1·00	
79	-	10p. red	1·00	

DESIGNS—VERT: 5p. Columbus Statue, Genoa; 10p. Departure from Palos.

1893. Surch UN CENTAVO.

80	23	1c. on 2c. red	65	50

28 Liberty

29 Columbus before the Council

1894. Dated "1894".

81	28	1c. brown	40	50
82	28	2c. blue	40	50
83	28	3c. purple	40	50
84	28	5c. brown	40	75
85	28	10c. violet	40	75
86	28	11c. red	40	1·50
87	28	20c. blue	40	2·00
88	28	25c. orange	40	2·50
89	28	50c. black	40	3·50
90	28	1p. blue	40	4·75
91	29	2p. blue	1·00	
92	-	5p. red	1·30	
93	-	10p. brown	1·30	

DESIGNS—HORIZ: 5p. Columbus protecting hostages; 10p. Columbus received by King and Queen.

1894. Surch 1 Centavo.

94	28	1c. on 11c. red	1·90	1·00

31

1895. Optd with Arms obliterating portrait. Various frames.

95	31	1c. olive	40
96	31	2c. green	40
97	31	3c. brown	40
98	31	5c. blue	40
99	31	10c. orange	40
100	31	12c. red	40
101	31	15c. red	40
102	31	20c. yellow	40
103	31	24c. violet	40
104	31	30c. blue	40
105	31	50c. red	40
106	31	1p. black	40

34

1895. Various frames.

115	34	1c. olive	75	65
116	34	2c. green	40	40
117	34	3c. brown	40	40
118	34	5c. blue	40	40
119	34	10c. orange	90	50
120	34	12c. red	90	50
121	34	15c. red	40	50
122	34	20c. green	40	65
123	34	24c. lilac	40	65
124	34	30c. blue	40	65
125	34	50c. red	1·70	1·70
126	34	1p. brown	2·00	2·30

1895. Surch.

132	1c. on 12c. red	1·30	1·30
133	1c. on 24c. lilac	1·30	1·30
134	1c. on 30c. blue	1·30	1·30
135	2c. on 20c. green	1·30	1·30
136	3c. on 30c. blue	1·70	1·40

37 Peace

1896

137	37	1c. blue	40	40
138	37	2c. brown	40	40
139	37	3c. green	40	40
140	37	5c. olive	40	40
141	37	10c. yellow	40	40
142	37	12c. blue	1·00	1·10
143	37	15c. violet	40	40
144	37	20c. red	90	65
145	37	24c. red	40	40
146	37	30c. orange	40	50
147	37	50c. black	40	65
148	37	1p. red	40	1·10

38 Arms

39 Government Building

1896. Dated "1896".

158A	38	1c. green	40	40
159A	39	2c. lake	40	40
160A	-	3c. orange	25	35
161A	-	5c. blue	40	40
162A	-	10c. brown	40	40
163A	-	12c. grey	40	40
164A	-	15c. green	40	40
165A	-	20c. red	40	50
166A	-	24c. violet	40	50
167A	-	30c. green	40	50
168A	-	50c. orange	40	50
169A	-	100c. blue	40	1·10

DESIGNS: 3c. Locomotive; 5c. Mt. San Miguel; 10, 12c. Steamship; 15c. Post Office; 20c. Lake Ilopango; 24c. Magra Falls; 30, 50c. Arms; 100c. Columbus.

1896. No. 166 surch Quince centavos.

218B	15c. on 24c. violet	5·00	3·75

1897. As Nos. 158/69. New colours.

220A	1c. red	40	40
221A	2c. green	40	40
222A	3c. brown	40	40
223A	5c. orange	40	40
224B	10c. green	1·00	65
225A	12c. blue	50	40
226B	15c. black	2·50	2·50
227A	20c. slate	40	40
228A	24c. yellow	40	40
229A	30c. red	40	40
230A	50c. violet	40	65
231A	100c. lake	3·25	2·50

55

1897. Federation of Central America.

270	55	1c. multicoloured	65	1·90
271	55	5c. multicoloured	65	1·90

1897. Nos. 228/31 surch TRECE centavos.

272A	13c. on 24c. yellow	3·25	3·25
273A	13c. on 30c. red	3·25	3·25
274A	13c. on 50c. violet	3·25	3·25
275A	13c. on 100c. lake	3·25	3·25

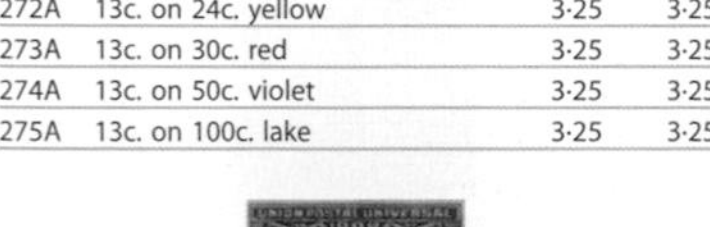

57 Union of Central America

1898

276	57	1c. red	40	40
277	57	2c. red	40	40
278	57	3c. green	40	40
279	57	5c. green	40	40
280	57	10c. blue	40	40
281	57	12c. violet	40	40
282	57	13c. lake	40	40
283	57	20c. blue	40	50
284	57	24c. blue	40	50
285	57	26c. brown	40	65
286	57	50c. orange	40	75
287	57	1p. yellow	3·25	2·50

Some values of the above set exist optd with a wheel as Type **58**.

(58)

59 Ceres

1899. Optd with T **58**.

318	59	1c. brown	65	25
319	59	2c. green	1·00	25
320	59	3c. blue	1·00	40
321	59	5c. orange	50	25
322	59	10c. brown	65	40
323	59	12c. green	1·70	65
324	59	13c. red	1·40	90
325	59	24c. blue	17·00	13·00
326	59	26c. red	4·50	2·50
327	59	50c. red	4·50	3·50
328	59	100c. violet	4·50	4·50

1899. Optd 1900.

398	57	1c. red	3·00	2·50

1900. Stamps of 1898 surch 1900 and new value, with or without wheel opt. T **58**.

400	1c. on 10c. blue	9·50	9·00
401	1c. on 13c. lake	£350	
403	2c. on 13c. lake	3·00	2·00
414	2c. on 12c. violet	3·50	3·50
404	2c. on 20c. blue	3·00	3·00
406b	3c. on 12c. violet	60·00	60·00
407	3c. on 50c. orange	33·00	33·00
419	5c. on 12c. violet	38·00	38·00
409	5c. on 24c. blue	30·00	30·00
410a	5c. on 26c. brown	60·00	60·00
411	5c. on 1p. yellow	38·00	38·00

On Nos. 406b and 410a the surcharge is inverted.

1900. Stamps of 1899 surch 1900 and new value, with or without wheel optd as T **58**.

424	59	1c. on 2c. green	50	30
420	59	1c. on 13c. red	1·00	1·00
426	59	2c. on 12c. green	2·30	1·70
422	59	2c. on 13c. red	2·50	2·20
423	59	3c. on 12c. green	2·50	2·20
429	59	5c. on 24c. blue	3·75	1·90
430	59	5c. on 26c. red	1·60	1·30

(66)

1900. T 59 with date altered to "1900" and optd as T **66**.

438	1c. green	25	20
468	2c. red	25	20
469	3c. black	25	20
470	5c. blue	25	20
471	10c. blue	45	25
472	12c. green	45	30
473	13c. brown	25	20
474	24c. black	50	45
475	26c. brown	65	50
447	50c. red	2·30	2·20

1902. Nos. 468, 469 and 472 surch 1 centavo.

483	1c. on 2c. red	3·50	3·50
484	1c. on 3c. black	2·50	1·80
485	1c. on 5c. blue	1·70	1·30

70 Columbus Monument

1903

486	70	1c. green	50	25
487	70	2c. red	50	40
488	70	3c. orange	1·00	65
489	70	5c. blue	50	40
490	70	10c. purple	50	40
491	70	12c. grey	50	40
492	70	13c. brown	50	50
493	70	24c. red	3·25	1·70
494	70	26c. brown	3·25	1·70
495	70	50c. yellow	1·70	1·00
496	70	100c. blue	4·75	3·25

1905. Surch in words or figures and words.

514	1c. on 2c. red	75	40
517	5c. on 12c. grey	2·50	2·30

1905. Surch in figures only and two black circles.

515	1c. on 13c. brown	1·90	1·30
516	3c. on 13c. brown	65	50

1905. Surch in figures twice.

527	5c. on 12c. grey	2·75	1·90

1905. Surcharged in figures repeated four times.

529	5c. on 12c. grey	2·50	1·50

1905. Surch 1 1 at top of stamp and 1 CENTAVO 1 at foot.

523	1c. on 2c. red	40	40
524	1c. on 10c. purple	40	40
525	1c. on 12c. grey	1·30	65
526	1c. on 13c. brown	5·00	4·50
530	6c. on 12c. grey	2·50	2·30
531	6c. on 13c. brown	1·30	65

1905. Stamps dated "1900", with or without opt T **66**, and optd 1905 or 01905.

552	59	1c. green	7·75	4·50
546	59	2c. red	75	65
543	59	3c. black	9·00	4·25
547	59	5c. blue	2·20	95
548	59	10c. blue	1·10	95

1906. Stamps dated "1900", with or without opt T **66**, and optd 1906 or surch also.

560	2c. on 26c. brown	65	50
562	3c. on 26c. brown	4·50	3·75
564	10c. blue	2·50	2·50

89 President Pedro Jose Escalon

1906

570	89	1c. black and green	25	15
571	89	2c. black and red	25	15
572	89	3c. black and yellow	25	15
573	89	5c. black and blue	25	15
574	89	6c. black and red	25	15
575	89	10c. black and violet	25	15
576	89	12c. black and violet	25	15
577	89	13c. black and brown	25	15
578	89	24c. black and red	50	50
579	89	26c. black and brown	50	50
580	89	50c. black and yellow	50	65
581	89	100c. black and blue	3·75	3·75

1907. Nos. 570/2 optd as T **66**.

592	1c. black and green	40	25
593	2c. black and red	40	25
594	3c. black and yellow	40	25

1907. Surch with new value and black circles and optd with shield, T **66**.

595	1c. on 5c. black & blue	25	15
596	1c. on 6c. black and red	40	25
597	2c. on 6c. black and red	2·50	1·30
598	10c. on 6c. black & red	65	50

91 President's Palace

1907. Optd with shield, T **66**.

599	91	1c. black and green	25	15
600	91	2c. black and red	25	15
601	91	3c. black and yellow	25	15
602	91	5c. black and blue	25	15
603b	91	6c. black and red	25	15
604	91	10c. black and violet	25	15
605	91	12c. black and violet	25	15
606	91	13c. black and sepia	25	15
607	91	24c. black and red	25	15
608	91	26c. black and brown	40	25
609	91	50c. black and yellow	65	50
610	91	100c. black and blue	1·30	65

1908. Surch UN CENTAVO and one black circle.

621	1c. on 2c. black and red	50	40

1909. Optd 1821 15 septiembre 1909.

633	1c. black and green	2·75	1·40

1909. Surch with new value and 1909.

634	2c. on 13c. black & brown	1·90	1·50
635	3c. on 26c. black & brown	2·30	1·80

99 Gen. Figueroa

1910

642	99	1c. black and brown	25	15
643	99	2c. black and green	25	25
644	99	3c. black and orange	25	25
645	99	4c. black and red	25	25
646	99	5c. black and violet	25	25
647	99	6c. black and red	25	25
648	99	10c. black and violet	40	25
649	99	12c. black and blue	40	25
650	99	17c. black and green	40	25
651	99	19c. black and brown	40	25
652	99	29c. black and brown	40	25
653	99	50c. black and yellow	25	25
654	99	100c. black and blue	40	25

100 M. J. Arce

1911. Centenary of Insurrection of 1811.

655B	-	5c. brown and blue	15	15
656B	100	6c. brown and orange	15	15
657B	-	12c. black and mauve	15	15

DESIGNS: 5c. Portrait of J. M. Delgado; 12c. Centenary Monument.

1911. T 91 without shield optd as T **66**.

658	91	1c. red	10	10
659	91	2c. brown	30	30
660	91	13c. green	20	20
661	91	24c. yellow	30	30
662	91	50c. brown	30	30

101 Jose Matias Delgado

107 Independence Monument

108 National Palace

110 National Arms

1912

663	101	1c. black and blue	40	15
664	-	2c. black and brown	40	25
665	-	5c. black and red	40	25
666	-	6c. black and green	40	25
667	-	12c. black and olive	1·30	25
668	-	17c. grey and purple	75	25
669	107	19c. grey and red	1·50	40
670	108	29c. grey and orange	2·00	40
671	-	50c. grey and blue	2·30	65
672	110	1col. grey and black	3·25	1·30

DESIGNS—As Type **101**: 2c. M. J. Arce; 5c. F. Morazan; 6c. R. Campo; 12c. T. Cabanas; 17c. Barrios Monument. As Type **108**: 50c. Rosales Hospital.

111 J. M. Rodriguez

1914

673	111	10c. brown and orange	3·25	1·00
674	-	25c. brown and violet	3·50	1·00

PORTRAIT: 25c. Dr. M. E. Araujo.

1915. Re-issue of T **91**. No shield. Optd 1915.

675	91	1c. grey	20	15
676	91	2c. red	20	15
677	91	5c. blue	20	15
678	91	6c. blue	20	15
679	91	10c. yellow	75	40
680	91	12c. brown	65	25
681	91	50c. purple	40	40
682	91	100c. brown	1·60	1·80

113 National Theatre

114 Pres. Carlos Melendez

1916. Various frames.

683	113	1c. green	15	10
684	113	2c. red	25	25
685	113	5c. blue	25	25
686	113	6c. violet	40	10
687	113	10c. brown	40	10
688	113	12c. purple	3·25	65
689	113	17c. orange	50	40
690	113	25c. brown	1·00	40
691	113	29c. black	6·50	1·00
692	113	50c. grey	3·25	1·90
693	114	1col. black and blue	75	75

1917. Official stamps of 1915, with word "OFICIAL" cancelled with five bars.

694	91	2c. red (No. O686)	65	65
695	91	5c. blue (No. O687)	65	50

1918. Official stamps of 1915 optd CORRIENTE and bar.

696	1c. grey (No. O685)	2·30	1·70
697	2c. red	2·30	1·70
698	5c. blue	11·50	7·75
699	6c. blue	90	65
700	10c. yellow	1·30	65
701	12c. brown	1·10	90
702	50c. purple	90	65

1918. Official stamps of 1916 optd CORRIENTE and bar or surch also.

704	113	1c. on 6c. violet (No. O696)	2·30	1·30
705	113	5c. blue	1·90	1·30
706	113	6c. violet	10·00	10·00

1919. Surch with new value and square or circles or bars.

710	1c. on 6c. violet	1·90	1·00
711	1c. on 12c. purple	40	40
712	1c. on 17c. orange	40	40
713	2c. on 10c. brown	40	40
714	5c. on 50c. grey	50	25
715	6c. on 25c. brown	50	25
716	15c. on 29c. black	1·30	1·00
717	26c. on 29c. black	1·30	65
719	35c. on 50c. grey	1·30	75
720	60c. on 1col. blk & bl	40	40

1919. No. O699 surch 1 CENTAVO 1.

721	1c. on 12c. purple	1·30	1·30

1920. Municipal stamps (Arms) surch Correos Un centavo 1919.

722	1c. olive	10	10
723	1c. on 5c. yellow	10	10
724	1c. on 10c. blue	20	10
725	1c. on 25c. green	10	10
726	1c. on 50c. olive	20	20
727	1c. on 1p. black	30	30

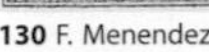

130 F. Menendez

131 Confederation Coin

132 Delgado Speaking

133 Arms of the Confederation

135 Independence Monument

1921. Portraits are as T **130**.

728	130	1c. green	30	10
729	-	2c. black (M. J. Arce)	30	10
730	131	5c. orange	1·10	30
731	132	6c. red	55	10
732	133	10c. blue	55	10
733	-	25c. grn (F. Morazan)	2·75	20
734	135	60c. violet	6·25	50
735	-	1col. sepia (Columbus)	11·50	1·00

1921. Centenary of Independence. Nos. 728/31 optd CENTENARIO.

735a	130	1c. green	5·25	4·00
735b	-	2c. black	5·25	4·00
735c	131	5c. orange	5·25	4·00
735d	132	6c. red	5·25	4·00

1923. As last, surch.

745	131	1c. on 5c. orange	40	25
741	-	1c. on 25c. green	30	20
746	131	2c. on 5c. orange	40	40
737		5c. on 6c. red	30	20
747	133	6c. on 10c. blue	40	25
742	-	6c. on 25c. green	20	20
738	-	10c. on 2c. black	55	20
739	132	20c. on 6c. red	40	30
743	-	20c. on 25c. green	55	30
744	-	20c. on 1col. sepia	75	40

139 J. S. Canas

1923. Centenary of Abolition of Slavery.

740	139	5c. blue	55	30

1924. U.P.U. Commemoration. Surch 15 Sept. 1874 – 1924 5 5 U.P.U. CINCO CENTAVOS.

749	135	5c. on 60c. violet	5·50	4·50

141 Daniel Hernandez

146 Central America

150

1924

750	141	1c. purple	15	10
751	-	2c. red	35	10
752	-	3c. brown	25	10
753	-	5c. black	25	10
754	-	6c. blue	35	10
755	146	10c. orange	75	25
756	-	20c. green	1·30	35
757	-	35c. green and red	3·25	45
758	-	50c. brown	2·50	35
759	150	1col. blue and green	3·75	45

DESIGNS—VERT: 2c. National Gymnasium; 3c. Atlacatl; 20c. Balsam tree; 35c. Senora T. S. Morazan. HORIZ: 5c. Conspiracy of 1811; 6c. Bridge over R. Lempa; 50c. Columbus at La Rabida.

1925. 400th Anniv of San Salvador. Surch 1525 2 2 1925 Dos centavos.

760	135	2c. on 60c. violet	1·40	1·30

152 View of San Salvador

1925. 400th Anniv of San Salvador.

761	152	1c. blue	1·00	90
762	152	2c. green	1·00	90
763	152	3c. red	1·00	90

1928. Santa Ana Industrial Exn. Type **146** surch Exposicion Santaneca Julio de 1928 and value in figures.

764	3c. on 10c. orange	1·10	65

1928. No. 753 surch.

765	1c. on 5c. black	40	25

155 Dr. P. R. Bosque and Gen. L. Chacon

1930. Inauguration of Railway Link between Salvador and Guatemala.

766	155	1c. purple and mauve	55	40
767	155	3c. purple and brown	55	40
768	155	5c. purple and green	55	40
769	155	10c. purple and orange	55	40

1930. Air. Nos. 755/759 optd Servicio Aereo or surch also.

770B	146	15c. on 10c. orange	65	65
771B	-	20c. green	95	90
772B	-	25c. on 35c. grn & red	80	80
773A	-	40c. on 50c. brown	75	50
774B	150	50c. on 1col. bl & grn	1·90	1·80

158 Curtiss "Jenny" over San Salvador

1930. Air.

775	158	15c. red	35	15
776	158	20c. green	35	15
777	158	25c. purple	35	15
778	158	40c. blue	55	15

158a Tomb of F. Menendez

1930. Birth Centenary of Menendez.

779	158a	1c. violet	4·25	3·25
780	158a	3c. brown	4·25	3·25
781	158a	5c. green	4·25	3·25
782	158a	10c. orange	4·25	3·25

158b Simon Bolivar

1930. Air. Death Centenary of Bolivar.

783	158b	15c. red	5·75	4·50
784	158b	20c. green	5·75	4·50
785	158b	25c. purple	5·75	4·50
786	158b	40c. blue	5·75	4·50

1931. Air. Optd with Curtiss "Jenny" Biplane.

787	150	1col. blue and green	4·25	2·75

1931. New G.P.O. Building Fund. Nos. 756 and 758 surch EDIFICIOS POSTALES and value.

790	1c. on 20c. green	40	25
788	1c. on 50c. brown	40	25
789	2c. on 20c. green	40	25
791	2c. on 50c. brown	40	25

162 Church of Mercy, San Salvador

1931. Air. 120th Anniv of Independence.

792	162	15c. red	4·25	3·00
793	162	20c. green	4·25	3·00
794	162	25c. purple	4·25	3·00
795	162	40c. blue	4·25	3·00

1932. Issues of 1924–26 optd 1932.

796	141	1c. purple	25	15
797	-	2c. red	25	25
798	-	3c. brown	40	15
799	-	5c. black	40	15
800	-	6c. blue	55	15
801	146	10c. orange	1·50	25
802	-	20c. green	2·20	65
803	-	35c. green and red	3·00	1·00
804	-	50c. brown	4·25	1·30
805	150	1col. blue and green	7·00	3·00

164 Jose Matias Delgado

1932. Air. Death Centenary of J. M. Delgado.

806	164	15c. red and violet	1·10	1·00
807	164	20c. green and blue	1·50	1·30
808	164	25c. violet and red	1·50	1·30
809	164	40c. blue and green	1·70	1·60

166 Ford "Tin Goose" over Columbus's Fleet

1933. Air. 441st Anniv of Departure of Columbus from Palos.

810	166	15c. orange	1·90	1·70
811	166	20c. green	2·75	2·40
812	166	25c. mauve	2·75	2·40
813	166	40c. blue	2·75	2·40
814	166	1col. bronze	2·75	2·40

1934. Issues of 1924 and 1926 surch.

815	-	2 on 5c. blk (No. 753)	25	15
816	-	2 on 50c. brn (No. 758)	40	25
817	146	3 on 10c. orange	40	15
818	150	8 on 1col. blue & green	25	25
819	-	15 on 35c. green and red (No. 757)	40	50

169 Police Headquarters

1934

820	169	2c. brown	20	10
821	169	5c. red	20	10
822	169	8c. blue	20	10

1934. Air. Inscr "SERVICIO AEREO".

823	25c. violet	55	25
824	30c. brown	85	40
825	1col. black	2·20	90

171 Discus Thrower

172 Runner breasting the Tape

1935. 3rd Central American Athletic Games.

826	171	5c. red (postage)	2·75	2·20
827	171	8c. blue	3·00	2·50
828	171	10c. yellow	4·00	2·75
829	171	15c. brown	4·25	3·00
830	171	37c. green	5·75	4·25
831	172	15c. red (air)	4·25	4·00
832	172	25c. violet	4·25	4·00
833	172	30c. brown	4·00	3·00
834	172	55c. blue	23·00	15·00
835	172	1col. black	15·00	14·00

1935. Nos. 826/35 optd HABILITADO.

836	171	5c. red (postage)	4·75	2·75
837	171	8c. blue	6·75	2·75
838	171	10c. yellow	6·75	3·25
839	171	15c. brown	6·75	3·25
840	171	37c. green	11·00	5·25
841	172	15c. red (air)	4·25	2·40
842	172	25c. violet	4·25	2·40
843	172	30c. brown	4·25	2·40
844	172	55c. blue	31·00	24·00
845	172	1col. black	14·00	10·00

174 National Flag

1935

846	**174**	1c. blue (postage)	25	10
847	**174**	2c. grey	25	10
848	**174**	3c. purple	25	10
849	**174**	5c. red	40	10
850	**174**	8c. blue	40	15
851	**174**	15c. brown	55	40
852	**174**	30c. black (air)	75	40

175 The Settlers' Oak

1935. Tercentenary of San Vicente. Value in black.

853	**175**	2c. grn & brn (postage)	75	40
854	**175**	3c. green	75	40
855	**175**	5c. green and red	75	40
856	**175**	8c. green and blue	75	50
857	**175**	15c. green and brown	75	65
858	**175**	10c. green & yell (air)	1·10	90
859	**175**	15c. green and brown	1·10	90
860	**175**	20c. green	1·10	90
861	**175**	25c. green and violet	1·10	90
862	**175**	30c. green and brown	1·10	90

178 Cutuco Harbour

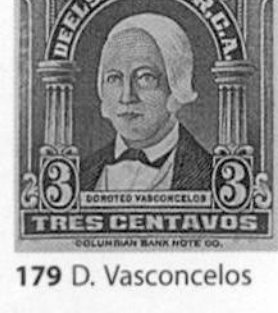

179 D. Vasconcelos

181 Sugar Refinery

182 Coffee Cargo

1935

863	-	1c. violet	20	20
864	**178**	2c. brown	20	20
865	**179**	3c. green	20	20
866	-	5c. red	55	20
867	-	8c. blue	25	20
868	**181**	10c. yellow	55	20
869	**182**	15c. bistre	55	20
870	-	50c. blue	2·75	1·60
871	-	1col. black	7·00	4·00

DESIGNS—As Type **178**: 1c. Mt. Izalco; 5c. Campo de Marte playing-fields. As Type **179**: 8c. T. G. Palomo. As Type **181**: 1col. Dr. M. Araujo; 50c. Balsam tree.

1937. Air. Optd AEREO in frame.

872	**182**	15c. bistre	55	40

1937. Air. No. 844 surch 30 in frame.

873	**172**	30 on 55c. blue	2·75	1·00

186 Douglas DC-3 over Panchimalco Church

1937. Air.

874	**186**	15c. orange	30	20
875	**186**	20c. green	30	20
876	**186**	25c. violet	30	20
877	**186**	30c. brown	25	10
878	**186**	40c. blue	30	40
879	**186**	1col. black	1·30	40
880	**186**	5col. red	4·25	3·00

1938. Surch.

881	**178**	1c. on 2c. brown	20	10
882	-	1c. on 5c. red (No. 866)	20	10
883	**181**	3c. on 10c. yellow	20	10
884	**182**	8c. on 15c. bistre	30	20

1938. Death Cent of J. Simeon Canas. Surch 3.

885	**139**	3 on 5c. blue	30	20

190 Flags and Book of Constitution

1938. 150th Anniv of U.S. Constitution. (a) Postage (without airliner).

886	**190**	8c. red, yellow and blue	85	65

(b) Air.

887		30c. multicoloured	85	65

191 J. S. Canas

1938. Air. Death Centenary of J. S. Canas.

888	**191**	15c. orange	1·30	1·20
889	**191**	20c. green	1·60	1·20
890	**191**	30c. brown	1·70	1·20
891	**191**	1col. black	5·50	4·00

192 Native Women at Washing Pool

1938

892	-	1c. violet	20	10
893	**192**	2c. green	20	10
894	-	3c. brown	30	10
895	-	5c. red	30	10
896	-	8c. blue	1·90	25
897	-	10c. orange	2·75	25
898	-	20c. brown	2·50	25
899	-	50c. violet	3·00	65
900	-	1col. black	2·75	1·00

DESIGNS: 1c. Native sugar-mill; 3c. Girl at spring; 5c. Native ploughing; 8c. Yucca plant; 10c. Champion cow; 20c. Extraction of Peruvian balsam; 50c. Maquilishuat tree in flower; 1col. G.P.O., San Salvador.

195 Golden Gate Bridge

1939. Air. Golden Gate Int Exn, San Francisco.

901	**195**	15c. black and yellow	40	25
902	**195**	30c. black and brown	40	25
903	**195**	40c. black and blue	55	40

1939. Centenary of Battle of San Pedro Perulapan. Surch 25 Sept 1839 1939 BATALLA SAN PEDRO PERULAPAN and value.

904	-	8c. on 50c. bl (No. 870)	40	25
905	-	10c. on 1col. black (No. 871)	75	25
906	**150**	50c. on 1col. bl & grn	4·00	3·00

197 Sir Rowland Hill

1940. Cent of 1st Adhesive Postage Stamps.

907	**197**	8c. black & blue (postage)	5·75	1·80
908	**197**	30c. black & brown (air)	7·75	2·40
909	**197**	80c. black and red	20·00	16·00

198 Western Hemisphere and "Peace"

1940. Air. 50th Anniv of Pan-American Union.

910	**198**	30c. blue and brown	40	25
911	**198**	80c. black and red	75	50

199 Coffee Tree in Bloom

1940. Air.

912	**199**	15c. orange	1·50	40
913	**199**	20c. green	2·00	40
914	**199**	25c. violet	2·30	50
915	-	30c. brown	2·75	25
916	-	1col. black	8·50	65

DESIGN: 30c., 1col. Coffee tree in fruit.

200 Dr. Lindo, Gen. Mallespin and New National University of El Salvador

1941. Air. Cent of El Salvador University.

917	**200**	20c. red and green	1·10	65
918	-	40c. orange and blue	1·10	65
919	-	60c. brown and violet	1·30	65
920	-	80c. green and red	2·75	1·80
921	-	1col. orange and black	2·75	1·80
922	**200**	2col. purple and orange	2·75	1·80
MS922a		178×183 mm. Nos. 917/922	14·00	14·00

PORTRAITS: 40c., 80c. Dr. N. Monterey and A. J. Canas; 60c., 1col. Dr. I. Menendez and Dr. C. Salazar.

201 Map of El Salvador

1942. 1st National Eucharistic Congress. Inscr "NOVIEMBRE 1942".

923	-	8c. blue (postage)	75	25
924	**201**	30c. orange (air)	75	40
MS924a		124×122 mm. Nos. 923/4 (two of each). Imperf. No gum	22·00	21·00

DESIGN 8c. Patron Saint and Cathedral of San Salvador, in medallions.

1943. Air. Surch in large figures.

925	**195**	15 on 15c. black & yellow	40	25
926	**195**	20 on 30c. black & brown	55	40
927	**195**	25 on 40c. black & blue	1·00	65

1944. Air. Surch in small figures.

928		15 on 15c. black & yell	40	25
929		20 on 30c. black & brn	55	40
930		25 on 40c. black & blue	1·10	40

205 Cuscatlan Bridge

1944. Optd with small shield.

931	**205**	8c. black & blue (postage)	35	20
932	**205**	30c. black & red (air)	40	25

206 Presidential Palace

1944. Air.

933	**206**	15c. mauve	20	15
934	-	20c. green	40	15
935	-	25c. purple	40	15
936	-	30c. red	40	15
937	-	40c. blue	40	40
938	-	1col. black	1·30	40

DESIGNS: 20c. National Theatre; 25c. National Palace; 30c. Mayan Pyramid; 40c. Public Gardens; 1col. Aeronautics School.

207 Gen. J. J. Canas

1945. Gen. J. J. Canas (author of National Anthem).

939	**207**	8c. blue	55	15

1945. No. 893 surch 1.

940		1c. on 2c. green	25	15

1945. Air. Optd Aereo.

942		1col. black (No. 900)	85	25

210 Juan Ramon Uriarte

1945. Air. J. R. Uriarte, former Director General of Posts.

943	**210**	12c. blue	40	25
944	**210**	14c. orange	40	15

211 Alberto Masferrer

1945. Air. Alberto Masferrer (writer).

945	**211**	12c. red	40	20
946	**211**	14c. green	40	15

212 Lake Ilopango

1946

947	**212**	1c. blue	35	20
948	-	2c. green	40	20
949	-	5c. red	35	20

DESIGNS: 2c. Ceiba tree; 5c. Water carriers (larger).

1946. 4th Centenary of San Salvador's City Charter. Sheet 118×162 mm containing various vert designs.

MS949a		40c. brown (Charles I of Spain); 60c. red (Juan Manuel Rodriguez); 1col. green (Arms of San Salvador); 2col. blue (Salvador flag)	4·25	4·25

215 Isidro Menendez

1947

950	**215**	1c. red	10	10
951	-	2c. yellow (Salazar)	10	10
952	-	3c. violet (Bertis)	10	10
953	-	5c. grey (Duenas)	10	10
954	-	8c. blue (Belloso)	10	10
955	-	10c. bistre (Trigueros)	20	10
956	-	20c. green (Gonzalez)	40	20
957	-	50c. black (Castaneda)	1·00	35

958	-	1col. red (Castro)	2·00	45

217 Alfredo Espino

1947. Air.

959		12c. brown (F. Soto)	25	20
960	**217**	14c. blue	25	20

218 M. J. Arce

1948. Death Centenary of M. J. Arce.

961	**218**	8c. blue (postage)	40	25
962	**218**	12c. green (air)	25	15
963	**218**	14c. red	40	15
964	**218**	1col. purple	3·00	1·80

219 Mackenzie King, Roosevelt and Churchill

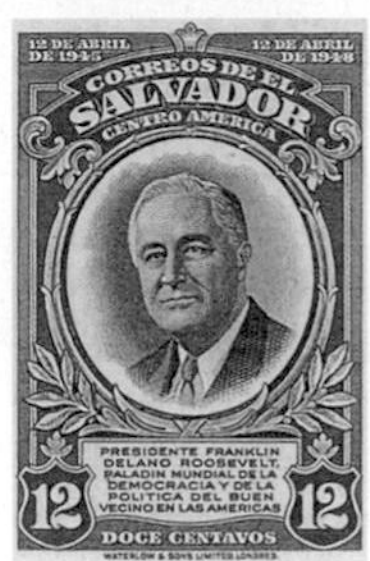

220 Franklin D. Roosevelt

1948. 3rd Death Anniv of Franklin D. Roosevelt.

965	-	5c. black & bl (postage)	25	15
966	-	8c. black and green	25	15
967	**220**	12c. black and violet	25	25
968	**219**	15c. black and red	40	25
969	-	20c. black and lake	40	25
970	-	50c. black and grey	1·00	65

MS970a 111×85 mm. 1col. sepia and olive (T **219**) 3·75 2·00

971	**220**	12c. black & grn (air)	55	40
972	-	14c. black and olive	55	40
973	-	20c. black and brown	55	40
974	-	25c. black and red	55	40
975	**219**	1col. black and purple	2·00	1·00
976	-	2col. black and lilac	3·00	1·70

MS976a 111×85 mm. 4col. sepia and slate (as 25c.) 5·00 3·50

DESIGNS—HORIZ: 5c., 14c. Pres. Roosevelt bestowing decorations; 8c., 25c. Pres. and Mrs. Roosevelt; 20c. (2) Pres. Roosevelt and Secretary Hull; 50c., 2col. Pres. Roosevelt's funeral.

1948. Air. Optd Aereo.

977	5c. grey (No. 953)	15	15
978	10c. bistre (No. 955)	25	15
979	1col. red (No. 958)	1·70	65

1949. Air. No. 936 surch 10.

980	10c. on 30c. red	25	15

222 Torch and Wings

1949. 75th Anniv of U.P.U.

981	**222**	8c. blue (postage)	1·00	50
982	**222**	5c. brown (air)	55	15
983	**222**	10c. black	75	15
984	**222**	1col. violet	22·00	16·00

223 Civilian and Soldier

224 Flag and Arms

1949. 1st Anniv of Revolution. (a) Postage.

985	**223**	8c. blue	40	40

(b) Air. Centres in blue and yellow.

986	**224**	5c. brown	25	15
987	**224**	10c. green	25	15
988	**224**	15c. violet	40	15
989	**224**	1col. red	85	50
990	**224**	5col. purple	7·00	5·25

225 Isabella the Catholic

1951. Air. 500th Birth Anniv of Isabella the Catholic. Backgrounds in blue, red and yellow.

991	**225**	10c. green	35	10
992	**225**	20c. violet	35	20
993	**225**	40c. red	50	20
994	**225**	1col. brown	1·60	60

226

227

1952. 1948 Revolution and 1950 Constitution. (a) Postage. Wreath in green.

995	**226**	1c. green	15	10
996	**226**	2c. purple	15	10
997	**226**	5c. brown	15	10
998	**226**	10c. yellow	15	15
999	**226**	20c. green	25	25
1000	**226**	1col. red	1·30	95

(b) Air. Flag in blue.

1001	**227**	10c. blue	15	10
1002	**227**	15c. brown	25	15
1003	**227**	20c. blue	25	15
1004	**227**	25c. grey	25	15
1005	**227**	40c. violet	35	25
1006	**227**	1col. orange	1·00	50
1007	**227**	2col. brown	3·00	2·40
1008	**227**	5col. blue	3·00	1·30

1952. Surch in figures and words (No. 1009) or in figures only (remainder). (a) Postage.

1009	-	2c. on 3c. violet (952)	15	10
1010	-	2c. on 8c. blue (954)	20	10
1011	-	2c. on 12c. brn (959)	20	10
1012	**217**	2c. on 14c. blue	20	10
1013	-	3c. on 8c. blue (954)	20	10
1014	-	5c. on 8c. blue (954)	20	15
1015	-	5c. on 12c. brn (959)	20	15
1016	-	7c. on 8c. blue (954)	20	15
1017	**217**	10c. on 14c. blue	20	20
1018	-	10c. on 50c. blk (957)	25	20

(b) Air.

1019	20c. on 25c. pur (935)	30	25

230 Jose Marti

1953. Birth Centenary of Marti.

1020	**230**	1c. red (postage)	15	10
1021	**230**	2c. green	20	10
1022	**230**	10c. blue	30	15
1023	**230**	10c. violet (air)	30	20
1024	**230**	20c. brown	40	20
1025	**230**	1col. orange	1·40	50

1953. 4th Pan-American Social Medicine Congress. Nos. 952 and 953 optd "IV Congreso Medico Social Panamericano 16/19 Abril, 1953".

1026	3c. violet (postage)	20	15
1027	25c. purple (air)	50	25

232 Signing Act of Independence

233 Campanile of Our Saviour

1953. Independence.

1028	**232**	1c. red (postage)	10	10
1029	**232**	2c. turquoise	10	10
1030	**232**	3c. violet	10	10
1031	**232**	5c. blue	15	15
1032	**232**	7c. brown	15	15
1033	**232**	10c. ochre	25	15
1034	**232**	20c. orange	65	25
1035	**232**	50c. green	85	30
1036	**232**	1col. grey	1·70	1·10
1037	**233**	5c. red (air)	15	15
1038	**233**	10c. turquoise	25	15
1039	**233**	20c. blue	30	30
1040	**233**	1col. violet	1·10	60

234 General Barrios

1953. Optd C de C.

1041	**234**	1c. green	10	10
1042	**234**	2c. blue	10	10
1043	-	3c. green	10	10
1044	**234**	5c. red	10	10
1045	-	7c. blue	20	15
1046	-	10c. red	30	15
1047	**234**	20c. violet	35	25
1048	-	22c. violet	50	25

PORTRAIT: 3c., 7c., 10c., 22c. Gen. Morazan.

235

236

237 General Barrios Square

238 Balboa Park

1954

1049	**A**	1c. red & olive (postage)	15	10
1050	**237**	1c. violet	15	10
1051	**B**	1c. olive and green	15	10
1052	**235**	2c. red	20	15
1053	**236**	2c. red	20	15
1054	**237**	2c. green and blue	20	15
1055	**F**	3c. slate and blue	20	15
1056	**C**	3c. green and blue	20	15
1057	**I**	3c. lake	20	15
1058	**F**	5c. violet and blue	20	15
1059	**I**	5c. green	20	15
1060	**C**	7c. brown and buff	20	15
1061	**B**	7c. green and blue	20	15
1062	**238**	7c. red and brown	20	15
1063	**G**	10c. blue, brown & red	20	15
1064	**236**	10c. turquoise	20	15
1065	**D**	10c. lake and pink	20	15
1066	**H**	20c. orange and buff	25	20
1067	**E**	22c. blue	25	35
1068	**J**	50c. black and drab	85	35
1069	**G**	1col. blue, brn & chest	1·40	80
1070	**E**	1col. blue	1·40	80
1071	**235**	5c. red (air)	25	10
1072	**B**	5c. brown and buff	25	10
1073	**G**	10c. blue, green & emer	35	10
1074	**237**	10c. olive and grey	35	10
1075	**E**	10c. red	35	15
1076	**238**	10c. violet and brown	35	10
1077	**I**	10c. blue	35	10
1078	**D**	15c. slate and blue	50	20
1079	**A**	20c. violet and slate	50	20
1080	**E**	25c. green and blue	55	20
1081	**H**	30c. red and pink	55	20
1082	**J**	40c. chestnut & brown	75	35
1083	**236**	80c. lake	1·70	1·20
1084	**C**	1col. red and pink	1·90	1·20
1085	**236**	2col. orange	3·75	1·20

DESIGNS—32½×22½ mm: A, Litoral Bridge; B, Fishing boats; C, Izalco Volcano and Atecosol Baths; D, Lake Ilopango and Apulo Baths; E, "Fle-Ja-Lis" (coastguard cutter). 37½×22½ mm: F, Guayabo Dam; G, Six Prime Ministers and flag of O.D.E.C.A.; H, Workers' houses. 22½×32½ mm: I, Gen. Arce. 21×35½ mm: J, Sonsonate–Puerto Acajutla Highway.

239 Captain General Barrios

1956

1086	**239**	1c. red (postage)	15	15
1087	**239**	2c. green	35	30
1088	**239**	3c. blue	35	30
1089	**239**	20c. violet	45	30
1090	**239**	20c. brown (air)	35	30
1091	**239**	30c. lake	35	35

240 Gathering Coffee Beans

1956. Centenary of Santa Ana.

1092	**240**	3c. brown (postage)	15	10
1093	**240**	5c. orange	25	10
1094	**240**	10c. blue	25	20
1095	**240**	2col. red	1·70	1·20
1096	**240**	5c. brown (air)	10	10
1097	**240**	10c. green	10	10
1098	**240**	40c. purple	30	25
1099	**240**	80c. green	85	50
1100	**240**	5col. slate	4·25	2·40

241

1956. Centenary of Chalatenango Province.

1101	**241**	2c. blue (postage)	20	10
1102	**241**	7c. red	40	30
1103	**241**	50c. brown	65	40
1104	**241**	10c. red (air)	10	10
1105	**241**	15c. orange	20	10
1106	**241**	20c. olive	20	15
1107	**241**	25c. lilac	40	25
1108	**241**	50c. brown	65	40
1109	**241**	1col. blue	95	80

242 Arms of Nueva San Salvador

1957. Centenary of Nueva San Salvador City.

1110	**242**	1c. red (postage)	10	10
1111	**242**	2c. green	10	10
1112	**242**	3c. violet	15	10

1113	**242**	7c. orange	40	25
1114	**242**	10c. blue	20	10
1115	**242**	50c. brown	50	25
1116	**242**	1col. red	75	70
1117	**242**	10c. salmon (air)	20	15
1118	**242**	20c. red	25	15
1119	**242**	50c. red	35	25
1120	**242**	1col. green	85	45
1121	**242**	2col. red	2·30	1·20

1957. Surch.

1121a		1c. on 2c. green	15	15
1121b		5c. on 7c. orange	30	20
1122	**C**	6c. on 7c. brown and buff (No. 1060)	30	25
1123	**B**	6c. on 7c. green and blue (No. 1061)	30	25
1124	**241**	6c. on 7c. red	25	20
1125	**242**	6c. on 7c. orange	30	25

244 Salvador Hotel

1958. Salvador Hotel Commem. Centre mult, frame colour below.

1126	**244**	3c. brown	10	10
1127	**244**	6c. red	10	10
1128	**244**	10c. blue	15	10
1129	**244**	15c. green	20	15
1130	**244**	20c. violet	30	20
1131	**244**	30c. green	40	30

245 Presidents Eisenhower and Lemus

1959. Visit of Pres. Lemus to U.S. Flags in red and blue. Portraits in brown.

1132	**245**	3c. pink & blue (postage)	20	10
1133	**245**	6c. green and blue	20	10
1134	**245**	10c. red and blue	30	15
1135	**245**	15c. orge & blue (air)	25	20
1136	**245**	20c. green and blue	30	20
1137	**245**	30c. red and blue	30	25

1960. 20th Anniv of Salvador Philatelic Society. Optd 5 Enero 1960 XX Aniversario Fundacion Sociedad Filatelica de El Salvador.

1138	**242**	2c. green	15	15

1960. Air. World Refugee Year. Optd ANO MUNDIAL DE LOS REFUGIADOS 1959-1960.

1139	**240**	10c. green	30	25

248 Block of Flats

1960. "I.V.U." Building Project. Centres multicoloured.

1140	**248**	10c. red	15	10
1141	**248**	15c. purple	20	15
1142	**248**	25c. green	30	20
1143	**248**	30c. turquoise	35	20
1144	**248**	40c. olive	50	35
1145	**248**	80c. blue	85	80

249 Poinsettias

1960. Christmas. Flowers in yellow, red and green. Background colours given.

1146	**249**	3c. yellow (postage)	15	15
1147	**249**	6c. orange	20	15
1148	**249**	10c. blue	30	15
1149	**249**	15c. blue	30	20
MS1149a		100×75 mm. **249** 40c. silver	1·30	1·30
1150		20c. mauve (air)	35	20
1151		30c. grey	40	35
1152		40c. grey	55	25
1153		50c. salmon	85	40
MS1153a		100×75 mm. **249** 60c. gold. Imperf	1·70	1·60

250 Fathers Nicolas, Vincent and Manuel Aguilar

1961. 150th Anniv of Revolution against Spain.

1154	**250**	1c. sepia and grey	10	10
1155	**250**	2c. brown and pink	10	10
1156	-	5c. green and brown	20	10
1157	-	6c. sepia and mauve	20	15
1158	-	10c. sepia and blue	20	10
1159	-	20c. sepia and violet	30	15
1160	-	30c. mauve and blue	40	20
1161	-	40c. sepia and brown	55	30
1162	-	50c. sepia & turquoise	85	45
1163	-	80c. blue and grey	1·40	80

DESIGNS: 5c., 6c. Manuel Arce, Jose Delgado and Juan Rodriguez; 10c., 20c. Pedro Castillo, Domingo de Lara and Santiago Celis; 30c., 40c. Parochial Church of San Salvador, 1808; 50c., 80c. Monument, Plaza Libertad.

1962. 3rd Central American Industrial Exn. Nos. 1048, 1069, 1116 and 1121 optd "III Exposicion Industrial Centroamericana Diciembre de 1962". Nos. 1166/7 additionally optd AEREO.

1165		22c. violet (postage)	40	25
1166	**G**	1col. blue, brown and chestnut (air)	1·50	1·00
1167	**242**	1col. red	75	50
1168	**242**	2col. red	1·50	90

1962. Nos. 1161/2, 1141 and 1070 surch.

1169	-	6c. on 40c. sep & brn	30	10
1170	-	6c. on 50c. sep & turq	30	10
1164	**248**	10c. on 15c. purple	30	10
1171	**E**	10c. on 1col. blue	30	15

1963. Surch in figures.

1172	**248**	6c. on 15c. purple (postage)	30	15
1176	**249**	10c. on 30c. grey	30	15
1173	-	10c. on 50c. sepia and turquoise (No. 1162)	30	15
1174	-	10c. on 80c. blue and grey (No. 1163) (air)	30	15
1175	**242**	10c. on 1col. green	1·40	30
1177	**242**	10c. on 1col. red (No. 1167)	30	20
1178	**242**	10c. on 2col. red (No. 1168)	1·40	30

1963. Freedom from Hunger. No. 1161 optd CAMPANA MUNDIAL CONTRA EL HAMBRE and Campaign emblem.

1179		40c. sepia and brown	85	45

259 Coyote

1963. Fauna. Multicoloured.

1180		1c. Type **259** (postage)	25	20
1181		2c. Black spider monkey (vert)	25	20
1182		3c. Common racoon	25	20
1183		5c. King vulture (vert)	25	20
1184		6c. Northern coati	25	20
1185		10c. Kinkajou	25	20
1186		5c. As No. 1183 (vert) (air)	25	20
1187		6c. Yellow-headed amazon (vert)	25	20
1188		10c. Spotted-breasted oriole	30	25
1189		20c. Turquoise-browed motmot	45	30
1190		30c. Great-tailed grackle	60	30
1191		40c. Great curassow (vert)	70	35
1192		50c. White-throated magpie-jay	90	40
1193		80c. Golden-fronted wood-pecker (vert)	1·30	70

260 Statue of Christ on Globe

1964. 2nd National Eucharistic Congress, San Salvador.

1194	**260**	6c. bl & brn (postage)	15	10
1195	**260**	10c. blue and bistre	15	10
MS1195a		75×100 mm **260** 60c. blue and violet. Imperf	1·10	1·00
1196		10c. slate & blue (air)	15	10
1197		25c. blue and red	25	20
MS1197a		75×100 mm. **260** 80c. blue and green. Imperf	1·10	1·00

261 President Kennedy

1964. Pres. Kennedy Commem.

1198	**261**	6c. blk & stone (postage)	15	10
1199	**261**	10c. black and drab	20	10
1200	**261**	50c. black and pink	65	35
MS1200a		100×75 mm. **261** 70c. black and green. Imperf	1·10	1·00
1201		15c. black & grey (air)	25	20
1202		20c. black and green	30	20
1203		40c. black and yellow	50	30
MS1203a		100×75 mm. **261** 80c. black and blue. Imperf	1·50	1·50

262 Water-lily

1965. Flora. Multicoloured.

1204		3c. Type **262** (postage)	10	10
1205		5c. "Maquilishuat"	10	10
1206		6c. "Cinco Negritos"	10	10
1207		30c. Hydrangea	25	20
1208		50c. "Maguey"	75	25
1209		60c. Geranium	85	25
1210		10c. Rose (air)	15	15
1211		15c. "Platanillo"	20	15
1212		25c. "San Jose"	25	20
1213		40c. Hibiscus	35	25
1214		45c. Bougainvillea	50	25
1215		70c. "Flor de Fuego"	75	45

1965. Centenary of La Libertad Province. Sheet Nos. MS1195a and MS1197a optd CREACION DEPARTAMENTO DE LA LIBERTAD... etc.

MS1215a	Two sheets each 75×100 mm. 60c. and 80c	3·25	3·25

263 I.C.Y. Emblem

1965. International Co-operation Year. Laurel in gold.

1216	**263**	5c. brn & yell (postage)	10	10
1217	**263**	6c. brown and red	10	10
1218	**263**	10c. brown and grey	15	10
1219	**263**	15c. brn & blue (air)	15	15
1220	**263**	30c. brown and violet	25	20
1221	**263**	50c. brown and orange	40	30

1965. Centenary of La Union Province. Sheet Nos. MS1195a and MS1197a optd CREACION DEPARTAMENTO DE LA UNION... etc.

MS1221a	Two sheets each 75×100 mm. 60c. and 80c	3·25	3·25

1965. Centenary of Usulutan Province. Sheet Nos. MS1195a and MS1197a optd CREACION DEPARTMENTO DE USULUTAN... etc.

MS1221b	Two sheets each 75×100 mm. 60c. and 80c	3·25	3·25

1965. Death Centenary of Captain General Barrios. No. 1163 optd 1er. Centenario Muerte Cap. Gral. Gerardo Barrios 1865 29 de Agosto 1965.

1222	80c. blue and grey	85	60

265 F. A. Gavidia (philosopher)

1965. Gavidia Commemoration.

1223	**265**	2c. mult (postage)	20	15
1224	**265**	3c. multicoloured	20	15
1225	**265**	6c. multicoloured	20	15
1226	**265**	10c. multicoloured (air)	20	15
1227	**265**	20c. multicoloured	35	25
1228	**265**	1col. multicoloured	1·60	65

1965. Birth Centenary of Dr. M. E. Araujo. Optd 1865 12 de Octubre 1965 Dr. Manuel Enrique Araujo. Laurel in gold.

1229	**263**	10c. brn & grey (postage)	15	10
1230	**263**	50c. brown & orge (air)	65	45

267 Fair Emblem

1965. International Fair, El Salvador.

1231	**267**	6c. mult (postage)	15	10
1232	**267**	10c. multicoloured	15	10
1233	**267**	20c. multicoloured	25	20
1234	**267**	20c. multicoloured (air)	35	15
1235	**267**	80c. multicoloured	85	70
1236	**267**	5col. multicoloured	4·25	3·25

268 W.H.O. Building

1966. Inaug of W.H.O. Headquarters, Geneva.

1237	**268**	15c. mult (postage)	20	15
1238	**268**	50c. multicoloured (air)	50	30

1966. Air. 150th Birth Anniv of St. Juan Bosco. No. 1197 optd 1816 1966 150 anos Nacimiento San Juan Bosco.

1239	**260**	25c. blue and red	50	35

1966. Civic Commem of Independence Month. No. 1163 optd Mes de Conmemoracion Civica de la Independencia Centroamericana 15 Sept. 1821 1966.

1240	80c. ultramarine and grey	65	60

271 UNESCO Emblem

1966. 20th Anniv of UNESCO.

1241	**271**	20c. blue, grey and black (postage)	30	20
1242	**271**	1col. blue, green & blk	1·10	50
1243	**271**	30c. blue, brown and black (air)	30	20
1244	**271**	2col. blue, green & blk	2·00	1·30

272 Map, Cogwheels and Flags

1966. 2nd International Fair, El Salvador.

1245	**272**	6c. mult (postage)	15	10
1246	**272**	10c. multicoloured	15	10
1247	**272**	15c. multicoloured (air)	20	15
1248	**272**	20c. multicoloured	25	20
1249	**272**	60c. multicoloured	65	45

1967. Air. 9th International Catholic Education Congress. No. 1197 optd IX-Congreso Interamericano de Educacion Catolica 4 Enero 1967.

1250	**260**	25c. blue and red	40	30

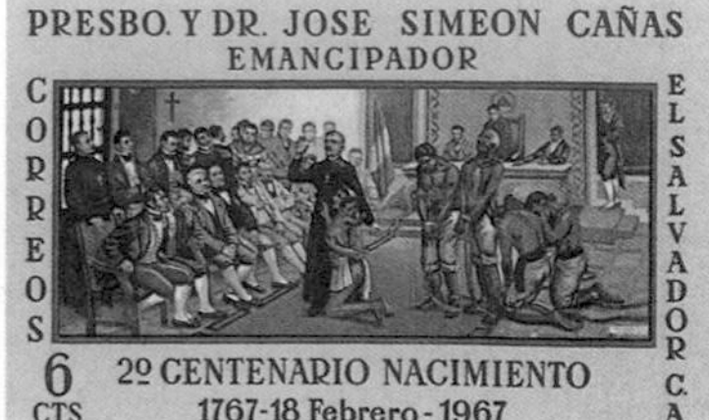

274 Father Canas pleading for Slaves

1967. Birth Centenary of Father J. S. Canas y Villacorta (slavery emancipator).

1251	**274**	6c. mult (postage)	20	15
1252	**274**	10c. multicoloured	20	15
1253	**274**	5c. mult (air)	20	15
1254	**274**	45c. multicoloured	85	50

1967. 15th Lions Convention, El Salvador. No. 1161 optd "XV Convencion de Clubes de Leones, etc.

1255	40c. sepia and brown	65	35

276 Central Design of First El Salvador Stamp

1967. Stamp Centenary.

1256	**276**	70c. brn & mve (postage)	1·30	70
1257	**276**	50c. brn & olive (air)	65	35

1967. 8th Central-American Pharmaceutical and Biochemical Congress. Nos. 1237/8 optd VIII CONGRESO CENTROAMERICANO, etc.

1258	**268**	15c. mult (postage)	35	10
1259	**268**	50c. mult (air)	25	25

1967. 1st Central American and Caribbean Basket-ball Games, San Salvador. Nos. 1204 and 1212 optd 1 Juegos Centroamericanos, etc.

1260	**262**	3c. mult (postage)	15	10
1261	-	25c. mult (air)	35	25

1968. Human Rights Year. Nos. 1216 and 1220 optd 1968 ANO INTERNACIONAL DE LOS DERECHOS HUMANOS.

1262	**263**	5c. mult (postage)	15	10
1263	**263**	30c. mult (air)	45	30

280 Weather Map, Satellite and W.M.O. Emblem

1968. World Meteorological Day.

1264	**280**	1c. multicoloured	15	10
1265	**280**	30c. multicoloured	35	20

1968. 20th Anniv of W.H.O. Nos. 1237/8 optd 1968 XX ANIVERSARIO DE LA ORGANIZACION MUNDIAL DE LA SALUD.

1266	**268**	15c. mult (postage)	25	20
1267	**268**	50c. mult (air)	65	50

1968. Rural Credit Year. Nos. 1231 and 1235 optd 1968 Ano del Sistema de Credito Rural.

1268	**267**	6c. mult (postage)	15	10
1269	**267**	80c. mult (air)	85	50

283 A. Masferrer (philosopher)

1968. Birth Centenary of Alberto Masferrer.

1270	**283**	2c. mult (postage)	10	10
1271	**283**	6c. multicoloured	15	10
1272	**283**	25c. multicoloured	35	20
1273	**283**	5c. multicoloured (air)	15	10
1274	**283**	15c. multicoloured	20	15

284 Building Construction ("Service to the Community")

1968. 7th Inter-American Scout Conference, San Salvador.

1275	**284**	25c. mult (postage)	35	25
1276	-	10c. multicoloured (air)	15	10

DESIGN—HORIZ: 10c. Scouts and Conference emblem.

285 Map, Presidents and Flags

1968. Meeting of Pres. Lyndon B. Johnson (U.S.A.) with Central American Presidents, San Salvador.

1277	**285**	10c. mult (postage)	15	10
1278	**285**	15c. multicoloured	25	15
1279	**285**	20c. mult (air)	25	15
1280	**285**	1col. multicoloured	1·00	60

286 "Heliconius charithonius"

1969. Butterflies. Multicoloured.

1281	5c. Type **286** (postage)	30	20
1282	10c. "Diaethria astala"	30	20
1283	30c. "Heliconius hortense"	50	30
1284	50c. "Pyrrhogyra arge"	65	35
1285	20c. "Ageronia amphinome" (air)	35	20
1286	1col. "Smyrna karkwinskii"	85	55
1287	2col. "Papilio photinus"	2·00	1·20
1288	10col. "Papilio consus"	10·00	6·00

287 Red Cross Activities

1969. 50th Anniv of League of Red Cross Societies. Multicoloured.

1289	10c. Type **287** (postage)	15	10
1290	20c. Type **287**	15	15
1291	40c. Type **287**	30	20
1292	30c. Red Cross emblems (air)	30	20
1293	1col. As No. 1292	1·10	50
1294	4col. As No. 1292	3·75	2·50

Nos. 1292/4 are smaller, size 34×25 mm.

1969. 1st Man on the Moon. Nos. 1200 and 1203 (Kennedy) optd Alunizaje Apolo - 11 21 Julio 1969.

1295	**261**	50c. blk & pink (postage)	85	45
MS1296		100×75 mm. **261** 70c. black and green. Imperf	1·90	1·80
1297		40c. blk & yellow (air)	65	35
MS1298		100×75 mm. **261** 80c. black and blue. Imperf	1·90	1·80

289 Social Security Hospital

1969. Salvador Hospitals. Multicoloured.

1299	6c. Type **289** (postage)	10	10
1300	10c. Type **289**	15	10
1301	30c. Type **289**	35	20
1302	1col. Benjamin Bloom Children's Hospital, San Salvador (air)	1·30	60
1303	2col. As No. 1302	2·20	1·20
1304	5col. As No. 1302	5·25	3·00

290 I.L.O. Emblem

1969. 50th Anniv of I.L.O.

1305	**290**	10c. mult (postage)	15	10
1306	**290**	50c. multicoloured (air)	50	30

291 Los Chorros Baths

1969. Tourism. Multicoloured.

1307	10c. Type **291** (postage)	15	15
1308	40c. Jaltepeque estuary	40	30
1309	80c. Fountains, Amapulapa	85	60
1310	20c. Devil's Gate (air)	20	15
1311	35c. Gardens, Ichanmichen	35	25
1312	60c. Port of Acajutla	65	45

292 "Euchroma gigantea" (image scaled to 74% of original size)

1970. Insects. Multicoloured.

1313	5c. Type **292** (postage)	10	10
1314	25c. "Pterophylla" sp.	25	20
1315	30c. "Chlorion cyaneum"	35	25
1316	2col. "Eulema dimidiata" (air)	2·00	1·10
1317	3col. "Elaterida"	3·25	1·60
1318	4col. "Tenodora sinensis"	4·25	2·30

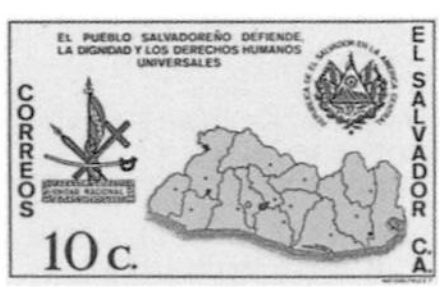

293 Map, Emblem and Arms

1970. "Human Rights".

1319	**293**	10c. mult (postage)	15	10
1320	**293**	40c. multicoloured	65	25
1321	-	20c. multicoloured (air)	25	15
1322	-	80c. multicoloured	1·00	45

DESIGN—VERT: Nos. 1321/2 are similar to Type **293**.

294 Infantry with National Flag

1970. Army Day. Multicoloured.

1323	10c. Type **294** (postage)	15	10
1324	30c. Anti-aircraft gun position	35	20
1325	20c. Republic P-47 Thunderbolt Fighter aircraft (air)	25	15
1326	40c. Artillery gun and crew	50	25
1327	50c. "Nohaba" (coastguard patrol boat)	65	25

295 Brazilian Team

1970. Air. World Cup Football Championship, Mexico. National Teams. Multicoloured.

1328	1col. Belgium	1·50	95
1329	1col. Type **295**	1·50	95
1330	1col. Bulgaria	1·50	95
1331	1col. Czechoslovakia	1·50	95
1332	1col. El Salvador	1·50	95
1333	1col. England	1·50	95
1334	1col. West Germany	1·50	95
1335	1col. Israel	1·50	95
1336	1col. Italy	1·50	95
1337	1col. Mexico	1·50	95
1338	1col. Morocco	1·50	95
1339	1col. Peru	1·50	95
1340	1col. Rumania	1·50	95
1341	1col. Russia	1·50	95
1342	1col. Sweden	1·50	95
1343	1col. Uruguay	1·50	95

296 Lottery Building

1970. Centenary of National Lottery.

1344	**296**	20c. mult (postage)	25	15
1345	**296**	80c. multicoloured (air)	85	40

297 Education Year and U.N. Emblems

1970. International Education Year.

1346	**297**	50c. mult (postage)	50	30
1347	**297**	1col. multicoloured	1·10	60
1348	**297**	20c. multicoloured (air)	30	20
1349	**297**	2col. multicoloured	2·00	1·20

298 Globe and Fair Symbols

1970. 4th International Fair, El Salvador.

1350	**298**	5c. mult (postage)	10	10
1351	**298**	10c. multicoloured	20	10
1352	**298**	20c. multicoloured (air)	30	15
1353	**298**	30c. multicoloured	40	20

1970. Cent of National Library. Nos. 1212/3 optd Ano del Centenario de la Biblioteca Nacional 1970.

1354	**283**	25c. mult (postage)	35	25
1355	**283**	5c. mult (air)	10	10

300 Beethoven and Music

1971. 2nd Int Music Festival, San Salvador.

1356	**300**	50c. brown, yellow and green (postage)	65	25
1357	-	40c. multicoloured (air)	50	25

DESIGN: 40c. Bach, manuscript and harp.

301 Maria Elena Sol

1971. Maria Elena Sol's Election as "World Tourism Queen", Punta del Este, Uruguay.

1358	**301**	10c. mult (postage)	15	10
1359	**301**	30c. multicoloured	35	25
1360	**301**	20c. mult (air)	25	15
1361	**301**	60c. multicoloured	65	35

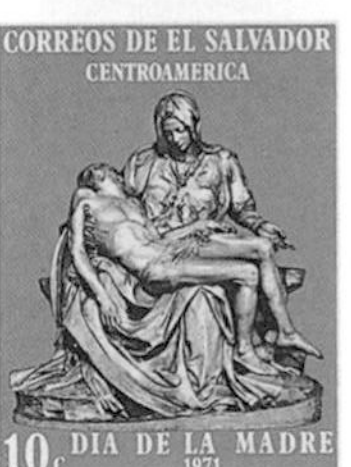

302 Michelangelo's "Pieta"

1971. Mothers' Day.

1362	**302**	10c. pur & pink (post)	15	10
1363	**302**	40c. pur & grn (air)	35	25

1971. 104th Anniv of National Police Force. Nos. 1320/1 optd 1867 CIV Aniversario Fundacion de la Policia Nacional 6-Julio 1971.

1364	**293**	40c. mult (postage)	50	25
1365	-	20c. mult (air)	25	35

304 Tiger Shark

1971. Fishes. Multicoloured.

1366	10c. Type **304** (postage)	30	10
1367	40c. Swordfish	35	20
1368	30c. Small-toothed sawfish (air)	25	30
1369	1col. Sailfish	85	60

305 Izalco Church

1971. Churches. Multicoloured.

1370	20c. Type **305** (postage)	25	15
1371	30c. Sonsonate Church	35	20
1372	15c. Metapan Church (air)	20	15
1373	70c. Panchimalco Church	1·00	30

1971. Air. 20th Anniv of El Salvador Navy. No. 1327 optd 1951-12 Octubre-1971 XX Aniversario MARINA NACIONAL.

1374	50c. multicoloured	50	30

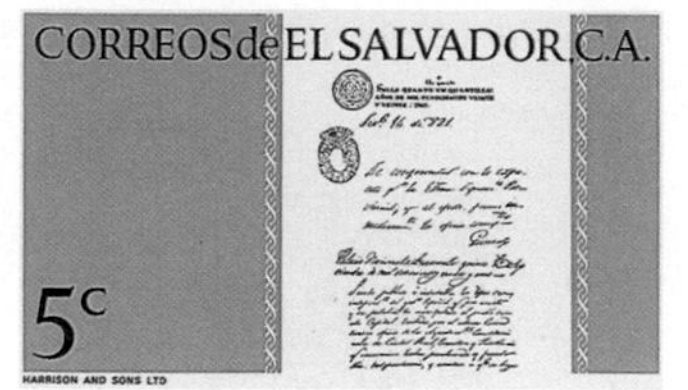

307 Declaration of Independence

1971. 150th Anniv of Central American Independence.

1375	**307**	5c. blk & grn (postage)	10	10
1376	-	10c. black and purple	15	10
1377	-	15c. black and red	15	10
1378	-	20c. black and mauve	20	15
1379	-	30c. black & blue (air)	30	20
1380	-	40c. black and brown	35	25
1381	-	50c. black and yellow	50	30
1382	-	60c. black and grey	65	40
MS1383 173×192 mm. Nos. 1375/82. Imperf			2·40	2·20

DESIGNS: Nos. 1376/82 as Type **307**, but showing different manuscripts.

1972. Air. 5th Int Fair, El Salvador. No. 1235 optd V Feria Internacional 3-20 Noviembre de 1972.

1384	**267**	80c. multicoloured	1·30	50

1972. American Tourist Year. No. 1359 optd 1972 Ano del Turismo de las Americas.

1385	**301**	30c. multicoloured	30	10

1972. Air. 30th Anniv of Inter-American Agricultural Science Institute. No. 1221 optd 1972 - XXX Aniversario Creacion Instituto Interamericano de Ciencias Agricolas.

1386	**263**	50c. multicoloured	50	30

1973. 3rd Int Music Festival. Nos. 1356/7 optd III Festival Internacional de Musica 9 - 25 Febrero - 1973.

1387	**300**	50c. brown, yellow and green (postage)	35	20
1388	-	40c. multicoloured (air)	40	20

312 Lions Emblem

1973. 31st Convention of Lions International District D.

1389	**312**	10c. mult (postage)	10	10
1390	**312**	25c. multicoloured	15	15
1391	-	20c. mult (air)	20	15
1392	-	40c. multicoloured	40	20

DESIGN: 20c., 40c. Map of Central America.

1973. 50th Anniv of El Salvador Air Force. No. 1324 optd 1923 1973 50 ANOS FUNDACION FUERZA AEREA.

1393	30c. multicoloured	25	20

314 Hurdling

1973. Olympic Games, Munich (1972). Mult.

1394	5c. Type **314** (postage)	30	10
1395	10c. High-jumping	30	10
1396	25c. Running	30	15
1397	60c. Pole-vaulting	30	30
1398	20c. Throwing the javelin (air)	35	15
1399	80c. Throwing the discus	1·00	45
1400	1col. Throwing the hammer	1·20	65
1401	2col. Putting the shot	2·40	1·10

1973. Nos. 1256/7 surch.

1402	**276**	10c. on 70c. brown and mauve (postage)	10	10
1403	**276**	25c. on 50c. brown and olive (air)	20	15

1973. 150th Anniv of Slaves' Liberation in Central America. Nos. 1251 and 1254 surch 1823 – 1973 150 Aniversario Liberacion Esclavos en Centroamerica and value.

1404	**274**	5c. on 6c. multicoloured	10	10
1405	**274**	10c. on 45c. mult	10	10

No. 1405 has the word "AEREO" obliterated.

1974. Centenary of Santiago de Maria. No. MS1883 optd Centenario Ciudad Santiago de Maria 1874 1974.

MS1406 173×192 mm	1·60	1·50

1974. Nos. 1198 and 1238 surch.

1407	**261**	5c. on 6c. black and stone (postage)	15	10
1408	**268**	25c. on 50c. mult (air)	20	15

318 Institute Emblem

1974. 10th Anniv of Institute for the Rehabilitation of Invalids.

1409	**318**	10c. mult (postage)	10	10
1410	**318**	25c. multicoloured (air)	30	15

1974. Air. No. 1235 surch.

1411	**267**	10c. on 80c. mult	10	10

1974. Air. West Germany's Victory in World Cup Football Championship. Nos. 1328/43 optd ALEMANIA 1974.

1412	1col. Belgium	1·20	65
1413	1col. Type **158**	1·20	65
1414	1col. Bulgaria	1·20	65
1415	1col. Czechoslovakia	1·20	65
1416	1col. El Salvador	1·20	65
1417	1col. England	1·20	65
1418	1col. West Germany	1·20	65
1419	1col. Israel	1·20	65
1420	1col. Italy	1·20	65
1421	1col. Mexico	1·20	65
1422	1col. Morocco	1·20	65
1423	1col. Peru	1·20	65
1424	1col. Rumania	1·20	65
1425	1col. Russia	1·20	65
1426	1col. Sweden	1·20	65
1427	1col. Uruguay	1·20	65

1974. No. 1271 surch.

1428	**283**	5c. on 6c. multicoloured	10	10

322 Interpol Headquarters, Paris

1974. 50th Anniv of International Criminal Police Organization (Interpol).

1429	**322**	10c. mult (postage)	20	20
1430	**322**	25c. multicoloured (air)	30	30

323 F.A.O. and W.F.P. Emblems

1974. 10th Anniv of World Food Programme.

1431	**323**	10c. gold, turquoise and blue (postage)	20	20
1432	**323**	25c. gold, turquoise and blue (air)	25	20

271 UNESCO Emblem

276 Central Design of First El Salvador Stamp

1974. Surch.

1432a	**271**	25c. on 1col. blue, green & black (postage)	25	20
1433	**276**	10c. on 50c. brown and olive (air)	10	10
1434	**271**	25c. on 2col. blue, green and black	45	25

1974. 12th Central American and Caribbean Chess Tournament. Surch XII Serie Ajedrez de Centro America y del Caribe Oct. 1974.

1435	**265**	5c. on 6c. mult	10	10

1974. Surch.

1436	**289**	5c. on 6c. mult (postage)	10	10
1437	**265**	10c. on 3c. mult	10	10
1438	-	10c. on 45c. mult (No. 1214) (air)	15	10
1439	-	10c. on 70c. mult (No. 1215)	15	10
1441	-	25c. on 1col. mult (No. 1293)	25	20
1440	-	25c. on 2col. mult (No. 1287)	25	15
1442	-	25c. on 4col. mult (No. 1294)	25	20
1443	-	25c. on 5col. mult (No. 1304)	25	20

1974. Inter-American Social Security Conference. No. MS1383 optd X ASAMBLEA GENERAL DE LA CONFERENCIA INTERAMERICANA DE SEGURIDAD SOCIAL Y XX REUNION DEL COMITE PERMANENTE INTER-AMERICANO DE SEGURIDAD SOCIAL, 24–30 NOVIEMBRE 1974.

MS1444 173×192 mm	2·50	2·40

327 25-cent Silver Coin, 1914

1974. El Salvador Coins. Multicoloured.

1445	10c. Type **327** (postage)	10	10
1446	15c. 50-cent silver coin, 1953	15	10
1447	25c. 25-cent silver coin, 1943	20	10
1448	30c. 1-centavo copper coin, 1892	20	10
1449	20c. 1-peso silver coin, 1892 (air)	15	15
1450	40c. 20-cent silver coin, 1828	30	20
1451	50c. 20-peso gold coin, 1892	55	30
1452	60c. 20-col. gold coin, 1925	65	40

328 U.P.U. Emblem

1975. Centenary of U.P.U.

1453	**328**	10c. mult (postage)	15	15
1454	**328**	60c. multicoloured	35	30
1455	**328**	25c. mult (air)	20	15
1456	**328**	30c. multicoloured	30	20

329 Acajutla Harbour

1975. Opening of Acajutla Port.

1457	**329**	10c. mult (postage)	10	10
1458	**329**	15c. mult (air)	15	10

331 Central Post Office, San Salvador

1975

1459	**331**	10c. mult (postage)	10	10
1460	**331**	25c. mult (air)	25	20

332 Map of El Salvador and the Americas

1975. "Miss Universe" Contest.

1461	**332**	10c. mult (postage)	15	10
1462	**332**	40c. multicoloured	35	30
1463	**332**	25c. mult (air)	25	20
1464	**332**	60c. multicoloured	55	40

333 Claudia Lars (poet)

1975. International Women's Year.

1465	**333**	10c. blue & yellow (post)	10	10
1466	**333**	15c. blue & lt blue (air)	15	10
1467	-	25c. blue & green	25	15

DESIGN: 25c. I.W.Y. emblem.

334 Nurses with Patient

1975. Honouring Nursing Profession.

1468	**334**	10c. mult (postage)	10	10
1469	**334**	25c. mult (air)	30	20

335 Conference Emblem

1975. 15th Conference of Inter-American Security Printers Federation, San Salvador.

1470	**335**	10c. mult (postage)	10	10
1471	**335**	30c. mult (air)	25	25

1975. 16th Central American Medical Congress, San Salvador. Optd XVI CONGRESO MEDICO CENTROAMERICANO SAN SALVADOR, EL SALVADOR DIC. 10-13, 1975.

1472	**268**	15c. multicoloured	20	15

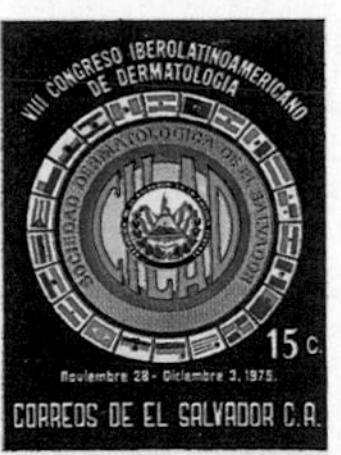

337 Congress Emblem and Flags

1975. 8th Iberian and Latin-American Dermatological Congress, El Salvador.

1473	**337**	15c. mult (postage)	15	15
1474	**337**	50c. multicoloured	30	20
1475	**337**	20c. mult (air)	20	15
1476	**337**	30c. multicoloured	30	20

338 Congress Emblem

1975. 7th Latin-American Charity Congress, San Salvador.

1477	**338**	10c. brn & red (postage)	10	10
1478	**338**	20c. lt blue & blue (air)	20	15

339 UNICEF Emblem

1975. Air. 25th Anniv (1971) of UNICEF.

1479	**339**	15c. silver and green	15	15
1480	**339**	20c. silver and red	15	15

1976. Air. Nos. 1316/18 surch.

1481	25c. on 2col. multicoloured	25	20
1482	25c. on 3col. multicoloured	25	20
1483	25c. on 4col. multicoloured	25	20

341 "Caularthron bilamellatum"

1976. Air. Orchids. Multicoloured.

1484	25c. Type **341**	30	20
1485	25c. "Oncidium oliganthum"	30	20
1486	25c. "Epidendrum radicans"	30	20
1487	25c. "Cyrtopodium punctatum"	30	20
1488	25c. "Epidendrum vitellinum"	30	20
1489	25c. "Pleurothallis schiedei"	30	20
1490	25c. "Lycaste cruenta"	30	20
1491	25c. "Spiranthes speciosa"	30	20

1976. "Cencamex '76" 3rd Nurses' Congress. Surch III CONGRESO ENFERMERIA CENCAMEX 76.

1492	**334**	10c. multicoloured	10	10

343 Map of El Salvador

1976. 10th Anniv of Central Inter-American Tax-collectors Association.

1493	**343**	10c. mult (postage)	10	10
1494	**343**	50c. mult (air)	40	20

344 Torch and Flags of El Salvador and U.S.A.

1976. Bicent of American Revolution. Mult.

1495	10c. Type **344** (postage)	10	10
1496	40c. "Spirit of '76" (A. M. Willard) (vert)	25	25
1497	25c. Type **344** (air)	30	20
1498	5col. As 40c.	4·00	2·50

345 "Crocodylus acutus"

1976. Reptiles. Multicoloured.

1499	10c. Type **345** (postage)	20	10
1500	20c. "Iguana iguana rhinolopha"	25	15
1501	30c. "Ctenosaura similis"	30	25
1502	15c. "Sceloporus malachiticus" (air)	20	10
1503	25c. "Basiliscus vittatus"	20	15
1504	60c. "Anolis sp."	50	45

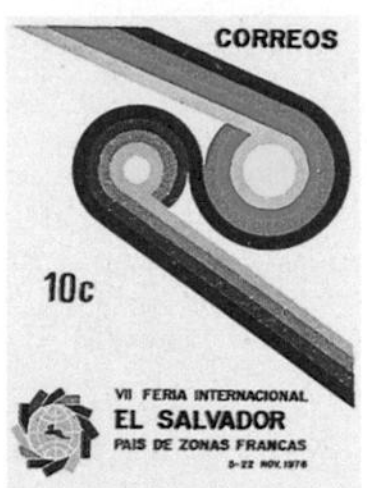

346 Fair Emblem

1976. 7th International Fair.

1505	**346**	10c. mult (postage)	15	10
1506	**346**	30c. multicoloured	25	20
1507	**346**	25c. multicoloured (air)	20	20
1508	**346**	70c. multicoloured	55	40

347 Post-classical Lead Vase (San Salvador)

1976. Pre-Columbian Art. Multicoloured.

1509	10c. Type **347** (postage)	15	10
1510	15c. Brazier with classical effigy (Tazumal)	20	10
1511	40c. Vase with classical effigy (Tazumal)	25	20
1512	25c. Brazier with pre-classical effigy (El Trapiche) (air)	20	15
1513	50c. Kettle with pre-classical effigy (Atiquizaya)	40	30
1514	70c. Classical whistling vase (Tazumal)	55	40

348 Child beside Christmas Tree

1976. Christmas.

1515	**348**	10c. mult (post)	15	10
1516	**348**	15c. multicoloured	20	10
1517	**348**	30c. multicoloured	25	20
1518	**348**	40c. multicoloured	30	25
1519	**348**	25c. multicoloured (air)	20	20
1520	**348**	50c. multicoloured	40	30
1521	**348**	60c. multicoloured	50	30
1522	**348**	75c. multicoloured	55	40

349 Rotary Emblem on Map of El Salvador

1977. 50th Anniv of San Salvador Rotary Club.

1523	**349**	10c. gold, bl & blk (post)	15	10
1524	**349**	15c. multicoloured	15	10
1525	**349**	25c. mult (air)	20	20
1526	**349**	1col. multicoloured	85	50

350 Hydro-electric Station, Cerron Grande

1977. Industrial Development. Multicoloured.

1527	10c. Type **350** (postage)	10	10
1528	10c. Sugar refinery, Jiboa	10	10
1529	15c. As No. 1528	15	20
1530	30c. Radar station, Izalco (vert)	25	15
1531	25c. As No. 1530 (air)	25	15
1532	50c. As No. 1528	40	20
1533	75c. Type **192**	60	40

1977. Surch.

1534	**283**	15c. on 2c. mult (postage)	15	10
1535	**274**	25c. on 6c. mult	25	15
1536	-	25c. on 80c. mult (No. 1322) (air)	30	20
1537	**274**	30c. on 5c. mult	25	20
1538	**274**	40c. on 5c. mult	30	20
1539	**274**	50c. on 5c. mult	35	25

352 Microphone and A.S.D.E.R. Emblem

1977. 50th Anniv of Broadcasting in El Salvador.

1540	**352**	10c. mult (postage)	15	10
1541	**352**	15c. multicoloured	15	10
1542	**352**	20c. multicoloured (air)	20	15
1543	**352**	25c. multicoloured	25	20

353 King, Pawn and Championship Emblem

1977. Air. El Salvador's Victory in Arab Chess Olympiad, Tripoli.

1544	**353**	25c. multicoloured	25	20
1545	**353**	50c. multicoloured	40	30

354 Basketball

1977. Air. 2nd Central American Games, San Salvador. Multicoloured.

1546	10c. Type **354**	10	10
1547	10c. Football	10	10
1548	15c. Javelin throwing	15	10
1549	15c. Weightlifting	15	10
1550	20c. Boxing (horiz)	15	15
1551	20c. Volleyball	15	15
1552	25c. Baseball	20	15
1553	25c. Softball (horiz)	20	15
1554	30c. Swimming (horiz)	35	20
1555	30c. Fencing (horiz)	35	20
1556	40c. Cycle-racing (horiz)	45	30
1557	50c. Rifle-shooting (horiz)	55	30
1558	50c. Tennis (horiz)	55	30
1559	60c. Judo	65	35
1560	75c. Wrestling (horiz)	70	45
1561	1col. Gymnastics (horiz)	90	55
1562	1col. Horse-jumping (horiz)	90	55
1563	2col. Table-tennis (horiz)	1·30	90
MS1564	100×119 mm. 5col. Games poster. Imperf	4·75	4·25

1978. Air. Centenary of Chalchuapa City. No. 1514 optd CENTENARIO CIUDAD DE CHALCHUAPA 1878-1978.

1565	70c. Classical whistling vase (Tazumal)	55	50

356 Map of South America and Emblem

1978. Air. World Cup Football Championship, Argentina.

1566	**356**	25c. multicoloured	30	20
1567	**356**	60c. multicoloured	50	35
1568	**356**	5col. multicoloured	4·25	3·00

357 Wooden Drum

1978. Musical Instruments. Multicoloured.

1569	5c. Type **357** (postage)	10	10
1570	10c. Flutes	10	10
1571	25c. Drum (vert) (air)	20	15
1572	50c. Rattles	40	20
1573	80c. Xylophone	60	40

358 "Man and Engineering"

1978. 4th Nat Engineers' Congress, San Salvador.

1574	**358**	10c. mult (postage)	10	10
1575	**358**	25c. multicoloured (air)	15	15

359 Dish Aerials

1978. Inauguration of Izalco Satellite Earth Station.

1576	**359**	10c. mult (postage)	10	10
1577	**359**	75c. multicoloured (air)	60	40

360 Softball, Bat and Hemispheres

1978. Air. 4th Women's Softball Championships, San Salvador.

1578	**360**	25c. multicoloured	25	20
1579	**360**	1col. multicoloured	85	50

361 Henri Dunant

1978. 150th Birth Anniv of Henri Dunant (founder of Red Cross).

No.	Type	Description	Mint	Used
1580	**361**	10c. yellow, black and red (postage)	15	10
1581	**361**	25c. turquiose, black and red (air)	25	20

362 Fair Poster

1978. 8th International Fair.

No.	Type	Description	Mint	Used
1582	**362**	10c. mult (postage)	15	10
1583	**362**	20c. multicoloured	20	15
1584	**362**	15c. multicoloured (air)	15	10
1585	**362**	25c. multicoloured	20	15

363 Globe as Cotton Boll

1978. 37th Plenary Session of Cotton Growers' Association, San Salvador.

No.	Type	Description	Mint	Used
1586	**363**	15c. mult (postage)	20	10
1587	**363**	40c. multicoloured (air)	30	20

364 "Nativity with Angel" (stained glass window)

1978. Christmas.

No.	Type	Description	Mint	Used
1588	**364**	10c. mult (postage)	20	10
1589	**364**	15c. multicoloured	15	10
1590	**364**	25c. multicoloured (air)	25	20
1591	**364**	1col. multicoloured	75	50

365 Arms of Salvador Athenium

1978. Millenary of Castilian Language.

No.	Type	Description	Mint	Used
1592	**365**	5c. mult (postage)	15	10
1593	**365**	25c. mult (air)	25	20

366 Four Candles

1979. Four Year Plan "Welfare for All".

No.	Type	Description	Mint	Used
1594	**366**	10c. mult (postage)	10	10
1595	**366**	15c. multicoloured	15	20
1596	**366**	25c. multicoloured (air)	25	20
1597	**366**	1col. multicoloured	75	50

367 Torch and Letter beside U.P.U. Statue

1979. Centenary of U.P.U. Membership.

No.	Type	Description	Mint	Used
1598	**367**	10c. mult (postage)	15	10
1599	**367**	75c. multicoloured (air)	60	40

368 Emblem and "75"

1979. 75th Anniv of Pan-American Health Organization.

No.	Type	Description	Mint	Used
1600	**368**	10c. turq & yell (postage)	15	10
1601	**368**	25c. turq & rose (air)	25	20

369 I.S.S.S. Emblem

1979. Air. 25th Anniv of Social Insurance Institute (I.S.S.S.).

No.	Type	Description	Mint	Used
1602	**369**	25c. blue and black	25	20
1603	**369**	60c. mauve and black	55	35

370 Pope John Paul II and Map of Americas

1979. Pope John Paul II. Multicoloured.

No.	Type	Description	Mint	Used
1604		10c. Type **370** (postage)	10	10
1605		20c. Type **370**	15	15
1606		60c. Pope John Paul II and Aztec pyramid (air)	50	30
1607		5col. As 60c.	4·25	2·50

371 Games Emblem

1979. Air. 8th Pan-American Games, Puerto Rico.

No.	Type	Description	Mint	Used
1608	**371**	25c. multicoloured	20	15
1609	**371**	40c. multicoloured	30	25
1610	**371**	70c. multicoloured	50	40

372 Mastodon

1979. Prehistoric Animals. Multicoloured.

No.	Type	Description	Mint	Used
1611		10c. Type **372** (postage)	10	10
1612		20c. Sabre-toothed tiger	15	15
1613		30c. Toxodon	25	20
1614		15c. Mammoth (air)	15	15
1615		25c. Giant sloth (vert)	25	20
1616		2col. Hyenas	1·70	95

373 J. Cauas (lyric writer) and Chorus of Anthem

1979. Centenary of National Anthem.

No.	Type	Description	Mint	Used
1617		10c. Type **373** (postage)	15	10
1618		40c. J. Aberle (composer) and score (air)	30	20

374 Cogwheel encircling Central America

1979. 8th Mechanical, Electrical and Allied Trade Engineers' Congress, San Salvador.

No.	Type	Description	Mint	Used
1619	**374**	10c. mult (postage)	15	10
1620	**374**	50c. multicoloured (air)	40	30

375 Children of Different Races

1979. International Year of the Child.

No.	Type	Description	Mint	Used
1621	**375**	10c. mult (postage)	10	10
1622	-	15c. multicoloured	15	10
1623	-	25c. yell, red & blk (air)	20	20
1624	-	30c. blue and black	25	20

DESIGNS—HORIZ: 30c. S.O.S. Children's Village emblem. VERT: 15c. Children with nurses; 25c. Children dancing in circle.

376 Map of Central and South America

1979. 5th Latin-American Clinical Biochemistry Congress, San Salvador.

No.	Type	Description	Mint	Used
1625	**376**	10c. orange, red and black (postage)	15	10
1626	**376**	25c. yellow, red and black (air)	25	20

377 Coffee Bushes in Bloom

1979. 50th Anniv of Salvador Coffee Association. Multicoloured.

No.	Type	Description	Mint	Used
1627		10c. Type **377** (postage)	15	10
1628		30c. Planting coffee bushes (vert)	25	20
1629		40c. Coffee beans	30	20
1630		50c. Picking coffee beans (air)	40	30
1631		75c. Drying coffee beans (vert)	60	40
1632		1col. Coffee exports	75	60

378 Dove, Star and Children holding Candles

1979. Christmas.

No.	Type	Description	Mint	Used
1633	**378**	10c. multicoloured	10	10

379 Diseased Animal

1980. Campaign against Foot and Mouth Disease.

No.	Type	Description	Mint	Used
1634	**379**	10c. mult (postage)	10	10
1635	**379**	60c. multicoloured (air)	50	30

380 Grand Ark

1980. Shells. Multicoloured.

No.	Type	Description	Mint	Used
1636		10c. Type **380** (postage)	15	10
1637		30c. "Ostrea iridescens"	25	20
1638		40c. White-mouthed turritella	30	25
1639		15c. Regal murex (air)	15	10
1640		25c. Spiral moon	20	15
1641		75c. Jenner's cowrie	50	40
1642		1col. Prostitute venus	85	60

381 Resplendent Quetzal

1980. Birds. Multicoloured.

No.	Type	Description	Mint	Used
1643		10c. Type **381** (postage)	20	15
1644		20c. Highland guan	25	20
1645		25c. Emerald toucanet (air)	25	20
1646		50c. Fulvous owl	40	30
1647		75c. Slate-coloured solitaire	60	40

382 "Porthidium godmani"

1980. Snakes. Multicoloured.

No.	Type	Description	Mint	Used
1648		10c. Type **382** (postage)	10	10
1649		20c. "Agkistrodon bilineatus"	15	15
1650		25c. "Crotalus durissus" (air)	20	15
1651		50c. "Micrurus nigrocinctus"	40	30

383 Corporation Emblem

1980. 50th Anniv of Corporation of Auditors.

No.	Type	Description	Mint	Used
1652	**383**	15c. mult (postage)	15	10
1653	**383**	20c. multicoloured	20	15

1654	383	50c. multicoloured (air)	40	25
1655	383	75c. multicoloured	60	40

384 Hands releasing Dove (cartoon by "Nando")

1980. "Man and Peace" Caricature Contest Winner.

1656	384	5c. bl, blk & brn (post)	10	10
1657	384	10c. blue, black & yellow	10	10
1658	384	25c. bl, blk & grn (air)	20	15
1659	384	60c. blue, black & orge	50	30

385 Decade Emblem

1981. Air. International Decade for Women.

1660	385	25c. black and green	25	20
1661	385	1col. black & orange	85	50

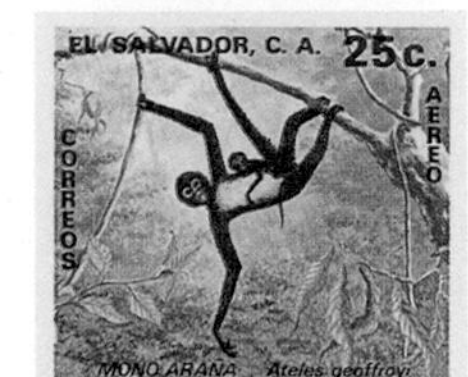

386 Black-handed Spider Monkey

1981. Air. Protected Animals. Multicoloured.

1662		25c. Type **386**	20	15
1663		40c. Tropical gar	30	25
1664		50c. Common iguana	40	30
1665		60c. Hawskbill turtle	50	35
1666		75c. Ornate hawk eagle	60	40

387 Heinrich von Stephan

1981. Air. 150th Birth Anniv of Heinrich von Stephan (founder of U.P.U.).

1667	387	15c. pink and black	15	10
1668	387	2col. blue and black	1·70	95

1981. Air. Nos. 1573 and 1610 surch.

1669	-	50c. on 80c. mult	40	30
1670	371	1col. on 70c. mult	85	60

389 Dental Association Emblems

1981. 50th Anniv of El Salvador Dental Society, and 25th Anniv of Odontological Federation of South America and Panama.

1671	389	15c. grn & blk (postage)	15	10
1672	389	5col. blue & blk (air)	5·00	3·00

390 Eye, Hands and Braille Book

1981. International Year of Disabled People.

1673	390	10c. mult (postage)	15	10
1674	390	25c. multicoloured (air)	20	15
1675	-	50c. green and blue	40	30
1676	390	75c. multicoloured	60	40
1677	-	1col. black and blue	85	60

DESIGN: 50c., 1col. I.Y.D.P. emblem.

391 Los Proceres Auditorium

1981. 25th Anniv of Roberto Quinonez National Agricultural College.

1678	391	10c. mult (postage)	15	10
1679	391	50c. multicoloured (air)	40	30

392 Map of El Salvador and Hand holding Maize

1981. World Food Day.

1680	392	10c. mult (postage)	15	10
1681	392	25c. multicoloured (air)	25	20

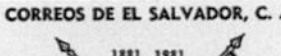

393 Open Book and El Salvador Flags of 1881 and 1981

1981. Air. Centenary of Land Registry Office.

1682	393	1col. black, bl & red	85	60

394 Boeing 737

1981. Air. 50th Anniv of "TACA" National Airline.

1683	394	15c. multicoloured	15	10
1684	394	25c. multicoloured	25	15
1685	394	75c. multicoloured	60	40

395 Goalkeeper

1981. World Cup Football Preliminary Round, Honduras. Multicoloured.

1686		10c. Type **395** (postage)	15	10
1687		40c. World Cup, football and flags of competing countries	35	25
1688		25c. Type **395** (air)	25	15
1689		75c. As No. 1687	60	40

396 Salvador Lyceum

1981. Centenary of Salvador Lyceum.

1690	396	10c. mult (postage)	15	10
1691	396	25c. multicoloured (air)	20	15

397 Ceremonial Axe

1982. Pre-Columbian Stone Sculptures. Mult.

1692		10c. Type **397** (postage)	15	10
1693		20c. Sun disc	20	15
1694		40c. Stela of Tazumal	30	25
1695		25c. Ehecatl (god of the winds) (air)	20	15
1696		30c. Rock mask of jaguar	25	20
1697		80c. Flint sculpture	70	50

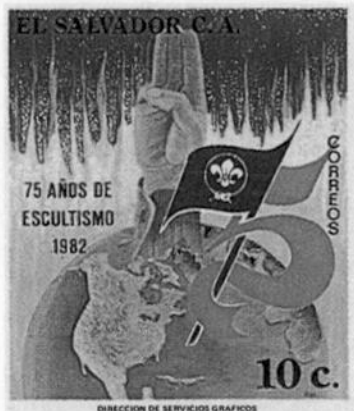

398 Scout Salute, Flag and Globe

1982. Boy Scout and Girl Guide Movements. Multicoloured.

1698		10c. Type **398** (Scout Movement, 75th anniv) (postage)	15	10
1699		30c. Girl guide helping old lady	25	20
1700		25c. Scout and Lord Baden-Powell (125th birth anniv) (air)	20	15
1701		50c. Girl Guide with emblem and national flag	40	30

399 Dr. Robert Koch

1982. Air. Cent of Discovery of Tubercle Bacillus.

1702	399	50c. multicoloured	40	30

400 Emblem and Soldier

1982. Armed Forces.

1703	400	10c. black, green and brown (postage)	15	10
1704	400	25c. multicoloured (air)	20	15

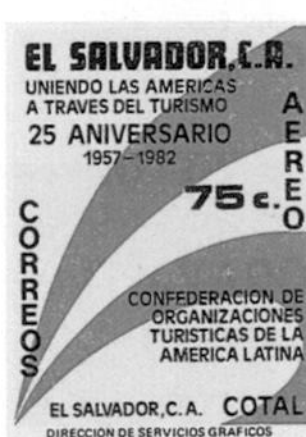

401 Converging Lines

1982. Air. 25th Anniv of Confederation of Latin American Tourist Organizations.

1705	401	75c. yellow, grn & blk	60	40

402 Hexagonal Pattern

1982. Air. World Telecommunications Day.

1706	402	15c. multicoloured	15	10
1707	402	2col. multicoloured	1·70	95

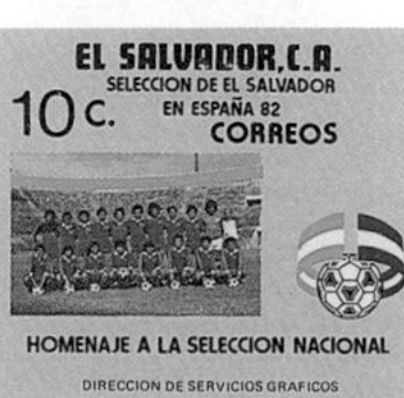

403 Salvador Football Team

1982. World Cup Football Championship, Spain (1st issue). Multicoloured.

1708		10c. Type **403** (postage)	15	10
1709		25c. As 10c. but different logo (air)	25	20
1710		60c. Trophy and map of El Salvador	50	30
1711		2col. National team and results of qualifying rounds (66×45 mm)	1·70	95

404 Flag of Italy

1982. Air. World Cup Football Championship, Spain (2nd issue). Multicoloured. (a) Flags.

1712		15c. Type **404**	15	10
1713		15c. West Germany	15	10
1714		15c. Argentine Republic	15	10
1715		15c. England	15	10
1716		15c. Spain	15	10
1717		15c. Brazil	15	10
1718		15c. Poland	15	10
1719		15c. Algeria	15	10
1720		15c. Belgium	15	10
1721		15c. France	15	10
1722		15c. Honduras	15	10
1723		15c. Russia	15	10
1724		15c. Peru	15	10
1725		15c. Chile	15	10
1726		15c. Hungary	15	10
1727		15c. Czechoslovakia	15	10
1728		15c. Yugoslavia	15	10
1729		15c. Scotland	15	10
1730		15c. Cameroun	15	10
1731		15c. Austria	15	10
1732		15c. El Salvador	15	10
1733		15c. Kuwait	15	10
1734		15c. Northern Ireland	15	10
1735		15c. New Zealand	15	10

(b) Coat of Arms.

1736		25c. Italy	25	20
1737		25c. Poland	25	20
1738		25c. West Germany	25	20
1739		25c. Algeria	25	20
1740		25c. Argentine Republic	25	20
1741		25c. Belgium	25	20
1742		25c. Peru	25	20
1743		25c. Cameroun	25	20
1744		25c. Chile	25	20
1745		25c. Austria	25	20
1746		25c. Hungary	25	20
1747		25c. El Salvador	25	20
1748		25c. England	25	20
1749		25c. France	25	20
1750		25c. Spain	25	20
1751		25c. Honduras	25	20
1752		25c. Brazil	25	20
1753		25c. Russia	25	20
1754		25c. Czechoslovakia	25	20
1755		25c. Kuwait	25	20
1756		25c. Yugoslavia	25	20
1757		25c. Northern Ireland	25	20
1758		25c. Scotland	25	20
1759		25c. New Zealand	25	20

(c) 89×67 mm.

1760		5col. El Salvador team, World Cup and flags of competing countries	4·25	2·50

405 Fair Poster

1982. 10th International Fair. Multicoloured.

1761		10c. Type **405** (postage)	15	10
1762		15c. Fair emblem (air)	15	10

406 Hand supporting Family

1983. Air. World Food Day.

1763	**406**	25c. multicoloured	20	15

407 St. Francis with Wolf

1982. Air. 800th Birth Anniv of St. Francis of Assisi.

1764	**407**	1col. multicoloured	85	60

408 Campaign Emblem

1982. Air. National Labour Campaign.

1765	**408**	50c. multicoloured	40	30

409 Christmas Retable

1982. Christmas. Multicoloured.

1766	5c. Type **409** (postage)	15	10
1767	25c. Christmas triptych (air)	20	15

410 Dance

1983. Pre-Columbian Ceramics. Mult.

1768	10c. Type **410** (postage)	10	10
1769	20c. The sower	15	15
1770	25c. Flying man	15	15
1771	60c. Archer hunting (left) (air)	50	45
1772	60c. Archer hunting (right)	50	45
1773	1col. Procession (left)	85	75
1774	1col. Procession (right)	85	75

Nos. 1771/2 and 1773/4 were issued together, each pair forming a composite design.

411 Papal Arms and Maria Auxiliadora Church

1983. Papal Visit. Multicoloured.

1775	25c. Type **411**	20	15
1776	60c. Pope John Paul II and Christ on Globe monument	50	40

412 Ricardo Aberle

1983. 50th Anniv of Air Force. Mult.

1777	10c. Type **412**	15	10
1778	10c. Air Force emblem	15	10
1779	10c. Enrico Massi	15	10
1780	10c. Juan Ramon Munes	15	10
1781	10c. American Airforces Co-operation emblem	15	10
1782	10c. Belisario Salazar	15	10

413 "Papilio torquatus" (male)

1983. Butterflies. Multicoloured.

1783	5c. Type **413**	15	10
1784	5c. "Metamorpha steneles"	15	10
1785	10c. "Papilio torquatus" (female)	15	10
1786	10c. "Anaea marthesia"	15	10
1787	15c. "Prepona brooksiana"	15	15
1788	15c. "Caligo atreus"	15	15
1789	25c. "Emperor"	25	25
1790	25c. "Dismorphia praxinoe"	30	25
1791	50c. "Morpho polyphemus"	35	30
1792	50c. "Metamorpha epaphus"	35	30

414 Simon Bolivar

1983. Birth Bicentenary of Simon Bolivar.

1793	**414**	75c. multicoloured	60	50

415 Dr. Jose Mendoza (founder)

1983. 40th Anniv of Medical College.

1794	**415**	10c. pink, black & grn	15	10

416 "Rural School" (L. A. Caceres Madrid)

1983. Air. Paintings. Multicoloured.

1795	25c. "Potters of Paleca" (M. Ortiz Villacorta)	20	15
1796	25c. Type **416**	20	15
1797	75c. "To the Wash" (Julia Diaz) (vert)	60	45
1798	75c. "La Pancha" (Mejia Vides) (vert)	60	45
1799	1col. "Meanguera del Golfo" (Elas Reyes) (vert)	85	60
1800	1col. "The Muleteers" (Noe Canjura) (vert)	85	60

417 David J. Guzman (founder)

1983. Centenary of David J. Guzman National Museum. Multicoloured.

1801	10c. Type **417** (postage)	15	10
1802	50c. Guzman and Museum (air)	40	30

418 Gen. Juan Jose Canas and Dr. Francisco Duenas

1983. World Communications Year. Mult.

1803	10c. Type **418** (postage)	15	10
1804	25c. Postman delivering letter (vert) (air)	20	15
1805	50c. Central sorting office	40	30

419 Dove and Globe

1983. Christmas. Multicoloured.

1806	10c. Type **419** (postage)	15	10
1807	25c. Christmas crib (air)	20	15

420 Bus emitting Exhaust Fumes

1983. Environmental Protection. Mult.

1808	10c. Type **420** (postage)	10	10
1809	15c. Fig tree (air)	15	10
1810	25c. Paca	20	15

421 Fisherman with Catch

1983. Air. Fishery Resources. Multicoloured.

1811	25c. Type **421**	20	15
1812	75c. Fish farming	70	40

422 Tweezers holding First Stamp of El Salvador

1984. Philatelists' Day.

1813	**422**	10c. blue, blk & orge	10	10

423 Maize

1984. Agricultural Products. Multicoloured.

1814	10c. Type **423**	10	10
1815	15c. Cotton	10	10
1816	25c. Coffee	15	10
1817	50c. Sugar	20	15
1817a	55c. Cotton	25	20
1817b	70c. Type **423**	30	20
1818	75c. Kidney bean	35	25
1818a	90c. Sugar cane	40	30
1819	1col. Agave	45	35
1819a	2col. Beans	95	60
1820	5col. Balsam	2·10	1·40
1820a	10col. Agave	4·25	3·00

424 Caluco Church

1984. Colonial Churches. Multicoloured.

1821	5c. Type **424** (postage)	10	10
1822	10c. Salcoatitan	10	10
1823	15c. Huizucar (air)	15	10
1824	25c. Santo Domingo	20	15
1825	50c. Pilar	25	20
1826	75c. Nahuizalco	35	25

425 Banknote

1984. 50th Anniv of General Reserve Bank. Multicoloured.

1827	10c. Type **425** (postage)	10	10
1828	25c. Bank Building (air)	20	15

426 Running

1984. Olympic Games, Los Angeles. Multicoloured.

1829	10c. Boxing (horiz) (postage)	10	10
1830	25c. Type **426** (air)	20	15
1831	40c. Cycling (horiz)	30	20
1832	50c. Swimming (horiz)	40	30
1833	75c. Judo	50	40
1834	1col. Pierre de Coubertin (horiz)	60	50

427 New Building

1984. New Servicios Graficos (Government printer) Building.

1835	**427**	10c. multicoloured	15	10

428 "5th November" Hydro-electric Plant

1984. National Energy Resources. Mult.
1836 20c. Type **428** (postage) 20 10
1837 55c. "Cerron Grande" hydro-electric plant 30 20
1838 70c. Ahuachapan geothermal plant (air) 40 30
1839 90c. Mural, Guajoyo hydro-electric plant 50 40
1840 2col. "15th September" hydro-electric plant 1·00 60

429 Playing Marbles

1984. Children's Games. Multicoloured.
1841 55c. Type **429** 30 20
1842 70c. Spinning a top 45 30
1843 90c. Flying a kite 55 40
1844 2col. "Capirucho" 1·10 60

430 Fair Emblem

1984. 11th International Fair, El Salvador. Mult.
1845 25c. Type **430** (postage) 20 15
1846 70c. Fair building and flags (air) 55 40

431 Los Chorros Tourist Centre

1984. Tourism. Multicoloured.
1847 15c. Type **431** 20 15
1848 25c. The Americas Square 30 20
1849 70c. El Salvador International Airport 55 30
1850 90c. El Tunco beach 45 30
1851 2col. Sihuatehucan Tourist Centre 1·10 60

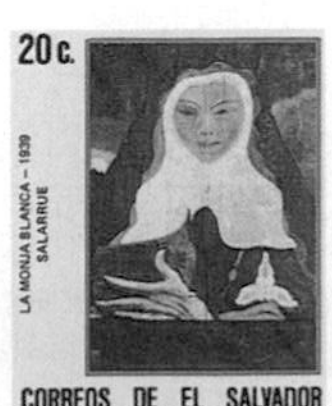

432 "The White Nun" (Salarrue)

1984. Paintings. Multicoloured.
1852 20c. Type **432** (postage) 10 10
1853 55c. "The Paper of Papers" (Roberto Antonio Galicia) (horiz) (air) 30 20
1854 70c. "Supreme Elegy to Masferrer" (Antonio Garcia Ponce) (wrongly inscr "Figuras en Palco") 16·00 15·00
1854a 70c. "Supreme Elegy to Masferrer" (correct inscription) 45 30
1855 90c. "Transmutation" (Armando Solis) (horiz) 55 40
1856 2col. "Figures in Theatre Box" (Carlos Canas) (wrongly inscr "Suprema Elegia a Masferrer") 21·00 20·00
1856a 2col. "Figures in Theatre Box" (correct inscription) 1·10 60

Nos. 1854a and 1856a are overprinted with the correct inscription.

433 Christmas Tree Decoration

1984. Christmas. Multicoloured.
1857 25c. Type **433** (postage) 15 10
1858 70c. Christmas tree decorations and dove (air) 45 30

434 Spot-crowned Woodcreeper

1984. Birds. Multicoloured.
1859 15c. Type **434** (postage) 45 15
1860 25c. Slaty finch 65 20
1861 55c. Purple-breasted ground dove (air) 85 60
1862 70c. Tody-motmot 1·10 80
1863 90c. Belted flycatcher 1·30 1·00
1864 1col. Red-faced warbler 1·50 1·00

435 Emblem and Share Certificate

1985. Centenary of El Salvador Bank.
1865 **435** 25c. multicoloured 20 10

436 Share Certificate and Emblem

1985. 50th Anniv of El Salvador Mortgage Bank.
1866 **436** 25c. multicoloured 20 10

437 I.Y.Y. Emblem

1985. International Youth Year.
1867 **437** 25c. blk & grn (postage) 30 20
1868 - 55c. mult (air) 45 30
1869 - 70c. multicoloured 55 40
1870 - 1col.50 multicoloured 80 50

DESIGNS: 55c. Woodwork class; 70c. Boys raising tray of equipment by pulley; 1col.50, Parade.

438 Pre-classic seated Figurine

1985. Archaeological Finds. Multicoloured.
1871 15c. Type **438** (postage) 15 10
1872 20c. Late classic engraved vase 20 15
1873 25c. Post-classic lead animal pot 30 20
1874 55c. Post-classic figurine (air) 45 30
1875 70c. Late post-classic figurine of Xipe Totec 55 40
1876 1col. Late post-classic clay animal on wheels 65 50
MS1877 100×75 mm. 2col. Tazumal ruins (horiz) 1·30 1·00

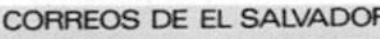

439 Red Cross and Hand holding "100"

1985. Cent of El Salvador Red Cross. Mult.
1878 25c. Type **439** (postage) 20 10
1879 55c. Red Cross workers and inflatable inshore lifeboat (horiz) (air) 30 20
1880 70c. Blood donor and Red Cross workers (horiz) 45 30
1881 90c. Tending injured man 55 40

440 Hand holding Pin Figures and Houses

1985. Child Welfare. Multicoloured.
1882 25col. Type **440** (postage) 20 10
1883 55c. Children outside house (air) 30 20
1884 70c. Children dancing 45 30
1885 80c. Oral vaccination 55 40

441 Child and Soldiers on Map

1985. El Salvador Army. Multicoloured.
1886 25c. Type **441** (postage) 20 10
1887 70c. Armed soldier and flag (air) 45 30

442 Flag, Open Book and Laurel

1985. Election of President Duarte.
1888 **442** 25c. multicoloured 20 10
1889 - 70c. black & yellow 45 30

DESIGN: 70c. Extract from constitution.

443 Hydro-electric Station and Emblem

1985. 25th Anniv of Inter-American Development Bank. Multicoloured.
1890 25c. Type **443** (postage) 20 10
1891 70c. Emblem and map (air) 45 30
1892 1col. Emblem and arms 55 40

1985. Air. No. 1829 surch.
1893 1col. on 10c. mult 85 50

445 Three-spotted Cichlid

1985. Fresh Water Fishes. Multicoloured.
1894 25c. Type **445** (postage) 30 20
1895 55c. Guatemalan long-whiskered catfish (air) 50 30
1896 70c. Black molly 55 35
1897 90c. Convict cichlid 65 40
1898 1col. Banded astyanax 80 45
1899 1col.50 Pacific fat sleeper 95 60

446 Food spilling from Basket

1985. 40th Anniv of Food and Agriculture Organization. Multicoloured.
1900 20c. Type **446** 15 10
1901 40c. Centeotl, Nahuat god of maize 25 20

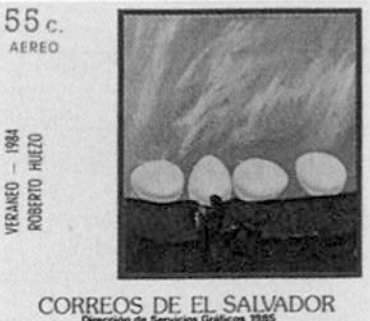

447 "Cordulegaster godmani mclachlan"

1985. Dragonflies. Multicoloured.
1902 25c. Type **447** (postage) 30 20
1903 55c. "Libellula herculea karsch" (air) 40 30
1904 70c. "Cora marina selys" 55 40
1905 90c. "Aeshna cornigera braver" 60 50
1906 1col. "Mecistogaster ornata rambur" 70 55
1907 1col.50 "Hetaerina smaragdalis de marmels" 95 70

449 St. Vicente Tower

448 "Summer Holiday" (Roberto Huezo)

1985. Paintings. Multicoloured.
1908 25c. "Profiles" (Rosa Mena Valenzuela) (vert) (postage) 30 20
1909 55c. Type **448** (air) 35 30
1910 70c. "La Entrega" (Fernando Llort) 40 35
1911 90c. "For Decorating Pots" (Pedro Acosta Garcia) 55 40
1912 1col. "Still Life" (Miguel Angel Orellana) (vert) 70 55

1985. 350th Anniv of City of St. Vicente de Austria y Lorenzana. Multicoloured.
1913 15c. Type **449** 15 15
1914 20c. St. Vicente Cathedral 20 20

450

1986. International Peace Year. Mult.

1915	15c. Type **450** (postage)	15	10
1916	70c. People reaching towards peace dove (air)	70	55

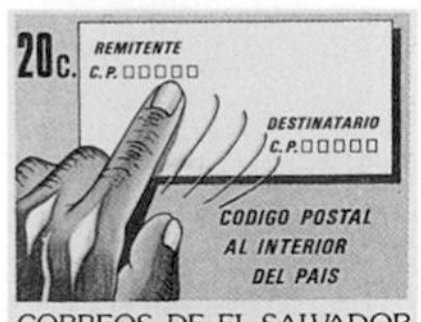

451 Hand and Interior Mail Envelope

1986. Introduction of Post Codes. Mult.

1917	20c. Type **451**	15	10
1918	25c. Hand and airmail envelope	20	10

452 Microphone

1986. 60th Anniv of Radio El Salvador. Multicoloured.

1919	25c. Type **452** (postage)	15	10
1920	70c. "60", map and radio waves (air)	70	55

453 Margay

1986. Mammals. Multicoloured.

1921	15c. Type **453** (postage)	15	10
1922	20c. Tamandua	25	15
1923	1col. Nine-banded armadillo (air)	1·00	70
1924	2col. Collared peccary	2·00	1·60

454 Flags and Mascot

1986. World Cup Football Championship, Mexico. Multicoloured.

1925	70c. Type **454**	70	45
1926	1col. Footballers and Trophy (vert)	95	70
1927	2col. Footballer (vert)	1·90	1·50
1928	5col. Goal and emblem	4·75	3·50

455 Dr. Dario Gonzalez (medicine)

1986. Teachers (1st series). Multicoloured.

1929	20c. Type **455** (postage)	20	10
1930	20c. Valero Lecha (art)	20	10
1931	40c. Prof. Marcelino Garcia Flamenco	35	25
1932	40c. Camilo Campos	35	25
1933	70c. Prof. Saul Flores (educationist) (air)	50	35
1934	70c. Prof. Jorge Larde (law)	50	35
1935	1col. Prof. Francisco Moran	60	45
1936	1col. Mercedes Maiti de Luarca	60	45

See also Nos. 1973/80.

456 Tlaloc Seal

1986

1937	**456**	25c. mult (postage)	25	10
1938	**456**	55c. mult (air)	35	25
1939	**456**	70c. multicoloured	50	35
1940	**456**	90c. multicoloured	55	40
1941	**456**	1col. multicoloured	60	45
1942	**456**	1col.50 multicoloured	85	60

457 Open Book on "100" as Stand

1986. Air. Centenary of Constitution.

1943	**457**	1col. multicoloured	60	45

458 "Spathiphyllum phryniifolium"

1986. Flowers. Multicoloured.

1944	20c. Type **458** (postage)	15	10
1945	25c. "Asclepias curassavica" (horiz)	20	15
1946	70c. "Tagetes tenuifolia" (horiz) (air)	50	35
1947	1col. "Ipomoea lilacea"	60	45

459 Unloading Fishing Boat

1986. World Food Day.

1948	**459**	20c. multicoloured	25	10

460 Hugo Lindo

1986. Air. 1st Death Anniv of Hugo Lindo (writer and poet).

1949	**460**	1col. multicoloured	60	45

461 Emblem

1986. Air. 25th Anniv of Central American Economic Integration Bank.

1950	**461**	1col.50 blk, bl & mve	85	60

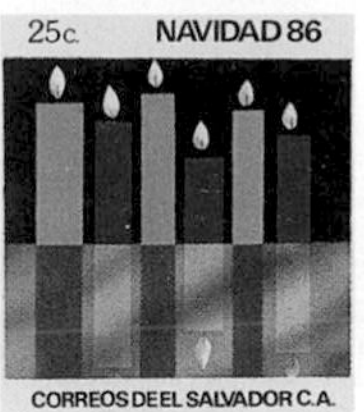

462 Candles

1986. Christmas. Multicoloured.

1951	25c. Type **462** (postage)	25	25
1952	70c. Birds flying towards light (air)	70	35

463 Baskets

1986. Traditional Crafts. Multicoloured.

1953	25c. Type **463**	25	10
1954	55c. Pottery	35	25
1955	70c. Guitars (vert)	50	35
1956	1col. Eastern reed baskets	60	45

464 "Church" (Mario Araujo Rajo)

1986. Paintings. Multicoloured.

1957	25c. Type **464** (postage)	25	10
1958	70c. "Landscape" (Francisco Reyes) (air)	50	35

465 Emblem

1987. Air. 12th International Fair, El Salvador.

1959	**465**	70c. multicoloured	50	35

466 Stamps

1987. Philately.

1960	**466**	25c. multicoloured	25	10

467 Maps, Globe and Foodstuffs

1987. International Solidarity.

1961	**467**	15c. multicoloured	25	10
1962	**467**	70c. multicoloured	50	35
1963	**467**	1col.50 mult	85	60
1964	**467**	5col. multicoloured	3·00	2·10

468 "Maxillaria tenuifolia"

1987. Orchids. Multicoloured.

1965	20c. Type **468** (postage)	25	10
1966	20c. "Ponthieva maculata"	25	10
1967	25c. "Meiracyllium trinasutum" (horiz)	35	25
1968	25c. "Encyclia vagans" (horiz)	35	25
1969	70c. "Encyclia cochleata" (horiz) (air)	50	35
1970	70c. "Maxillaria atrata" (horiz)	50	35
1971	1col.50 "Sobrialia xantholeuca" (horiz)	85	60
1972	1col.50 "Encyclia microcharis" (horiz)	85	60

469 C. de Jesus Alas (music)

1987. Teachers (2nd series).

1973	**469**	15c. black & bl (postage)	25	10
1974	-	15c. black and blue	25	10
1975	-	20c. black and brown	30	15
1976	-	20c. black and brown	30	15
1977	-	70c. black & orange (air)	50	35
1978	-	70c. black and orange	50	35
1979	-	1col.50 black & green	85	60
1980	-	1col.50 black & green	85	60

DESIGNS: No. 1974, Dr. Luis Edmundo Vasquez (medicine); 1975, Dr. David Rosales (law); 1976, Dr. Guillermo Trigueros (medicine); 1977, Manuel Farfan Castro; 1978, Iri Sol (singing); 1979, Carlos Arturo Imendia (primary education); 1980, Dr. Benjamin Orozco (chemistry).

470 Man on Roof above Houses

1987. Air. Int Year of Shelter for the Homeless.

1981	**470**	70col. multicoloured	50	35
1982	-	1col. blue	60	45

DESIGN: 1p. Emblem.

471 Emblem

1987. 10th Pan-American Games, Indianapolis, U.S.A. Multicoloured.

1983	20c. Type **471** (postage)	25	10

1984 20c. Table tennis 25 10
1985 25c. Wrestling (horiz) 30 15
1986 25c. Fencing (horiz) 30 15
1987 70c. Softball (horiz) (air) 50 35
1988 70c. Showjumping (horiz) 50 35
1989 5col. Weightlifting 3·00 2·10
1990 5col. Hurdling 3·00 2·10

472 Nicolas Aguilar

1987. Independence Leaders. Multicoloured.
1991 15c. Type **472** (postage) 25 10
1992 20c. Domingo Antonio de Lara 30 15
1993 70c. Juan Manuel Rodriguez (air) 50 35
1994 1col.50 Pedro Pablo Castillo 85 60

473 Man tending Crops

1987. World Food Day.
1995 **473** 50c. multicoloured 35 25

474 The Three Kings (crochet)

1987. Christmas. Multicoloured.
1996 25c. Stained glass window from Church of Virgin of the Everlasting Succour (postage) 15 10
1997 70c. Type **474** (air) 50 35

475 "Self-portrait"

1987. Salvador Salazar Arrue (writer and painter). Multicoloured.
1998 25c. Type **475** (postage) 15 10
1999 70c. "Lake" (air) 50 35

476 Man with Ceramic Drum

1987. Pre-Columbian Musical Instruments. Mult.
2000 20c. Type **476** (postage) 25 10
2001 70c. Parade of musicians from Saluan ceramic vase (left) (air) 50 35
2002 70c. Parade of musicians from Saluan ceramic vase (right) 50 35
2003 1col.50 Conch shell trumpet 85 45

Nos. 2001/2 are each 31×30 mm.

477 King Ferdinand of Spain

1987. 500th Anniv (1992) of Discovery of America by Columbus (1st issue). Multicoloured.
2004 1col. Type **477** 60 45
2005 1col. Queen Isabella of Spain 60 45
2006 1col. Banner and North America 60 45
2007 1col. Islands, coat of arms and ships 60 45
2008 1col. Caribbean 60 45
2009 1col. Ships and South America 60 45
2010 1col. Native figure and South America 60 45
2011 1col. South America and compass rose 60 45
2012 1col. Anniversary logo 60 45
2013 1col. Columbus 60 45

Nos. 2004/13 were printed together in se-tenant sheetlets, Nos. 2006/11 forming a composite design of a contemporary map.

See also Nos. 2040/9, 2065/70, 2116/21, 2166/71 and 2206/9.

478 Words and Stamps

1988. Philately.
2014 **478** 25c. multicoloured 25 15

479 Crowd and Emblem

1988. Empesarios Juveniles (youth education programme).
2015 **479** 25c. multicoloured 25 15

480 Bosco (after N. Musio)

1988. Death Centenary of St. John Bosco (founder of Salesian Brothers).
2016 **480** 20c. multicoloured 20 10

481 Felling of Trees and Children Planting Saplings

1983. Environmental Protection. Mult.
2017 20c. Type **481** (postage) 20 10
2018 70c. Rubbish in river and monkey in forest (air) 50 35

482 High Jumping

1988. Olympic Games, Seoul (1988) and Barcelona (1992). Multicoloured.
2019 1col. Type **482** 60 45
2020 1col. Throwing the javelin 60 45
2021 1col. Pistol shooting 60 45
2022 1col. Wrestling 60 45
2023 1col. Basketball 60 45
MS2024 115×75 mm. 2col. Olympic torch 2·40 1·80

483 Rural Youth

1988. World Food Day.
2025 **483** 20c. multicoloured 20 10

484 Fair Emblem

1988. 13th International Fair, El Salvador.
2026 **484** 70c. multicoloured 50 35

1988. "Prenfil '88" International Philatelic Literature and Press Exhibition, Buenos Aires. No. 1905 surch C5.00 PRENFIL '88 EXPOSICION MUNDIAL DE LITERATURA Y PRENSA FILATELICA BUENOS AIRES ARGENTINA DEL 25 DE NOVIEMBRE AL 2 DE DICEMBRE and emblem.
2027 5col. on 90c. multicoloured 3·00 2·10

486 Father and Son flying Heart-shaped Kite

1988. Infant Protection Campaign. Mult.
2028 15c. Type **486** 25 10
2029 20c. Happy child hugging adult's leg 30 15

487 "Virgin and Child with St. John and St. Anthony"

1988. Christmas. 500th Birth Anniv of Titian (painter). Multicoloured.
2030 25c. Type **487** (postage) 25 10
2031 70c. "Virgin and Child in Glory with St. Francis and St. Alvise" (vert) (air) 50 35

488 Emblems

1988. Air. 18th Organization of American States General Assembly.
2032 **488** 70c. multicoloured 50 35

489 Hands holding Scroll

1988. "Return to Moral Values".
2033 **489** 25c. multicoloured 25 15

490 "Esperanza de los Soles" (Victor Rodriguez Preza)

1988. Paintings. Multicoloured.
2034 40c. Type **490** (postage) 35 15
2035 1col. "Pastoral" (Luis Angel Salinas) (horiz) (air) 60 45
2036 2col. "Children" (Julio Hernandez Aleman) (horiz) 1·20 95
2037 5col. "El Nino de las Alcancias" (Camilo Minero) 3·00 2·30

491 Emblem within Laurel Wreath, People and Map

1988. 40th Anniv of Declaration of Human Rights. Multicoloured.
2038 25c. Type **491** (postage) 25 15
2039 70c. U.N. and Human Rights emblems and map (air) (horiz) 50 35

492 El Tazumal

1988. 500th Anniv (1992) of Discovery of America by Columbus (2nd issue). Multicoloured.
2040 1col. Type **492** 60 45
2041 1col. Earthenware bowl 60 45
2042 1col. San Andres 60 45
2043 1col. Dish for burning aromatic substances 60 45
2044 1col. Sihuatan 60 45
2045 1col. Effigy of rain god 60 45
2046 1col. Cara Sucia 60 45
2047 1col. Monkey-shaped pot 60 45
2048 1col. San Lorenzo 60 45
2049 1col. Round pot with monkey-head spout 60 45
MS2050 100×75 mm. 2col. scarlet and black (Christopher Columbus) 1·40 1·20

493 Margay

1989. Endangered Animals. Multicoloured.
2051 25c. Type **493** 35 25
2052 25c. Margay (different) 35 25
2053 55c. Ocelot in tree 50 35
2054 55c. Ocelot resting 50 35

494 Flag, Map and Compass Rose

1989. Centenary of El Salvador Meteorological Services. Multicoloured.

2055	15c. Type **494**	10	10
2056	20c. Sea, land and measuring equipment	20	15

495 El Salvador Philatelic Society Emblem

1989. Philately.

2057	**495**	25c. grey, black & bl	20	15

496 Basketball

1989. Olympic Games, Barcelona (1992). Mult.

2058	20c. Type **496** (postage)	10	10
2059	25c. Boxing	20	15
2060	25c. Athletics	20	15
2061	40c. Showjumping	25	25
2062	55c. Badminton (horiz) (air)	35	30
2063	55c. Handball (horiz)	35	30
MS2064	Two sheets each 83×109 mm. (a) 1col. Throwing the hammer; (b) 1col. Cycling	3·00	2·30

497 Fire Engine

1989. 106th Anniv of Fire Service. Mult.

2065	25c. Type **497**	20	10
2066	70c. Firemen fighting fire	50	35

498 Birds

1989. Bicent of French Revolution. Mult.

2067	90c. Type **498**	60	45
2068	1col. Storming the Bastille	65	55

499 1893 10p. Columbus Stamp

1989. 500th Anniv (1992) of Discovery of America by Columbus (3rd issue). El Salvador Stamps featuring Columbus.

2069	**499**	50c. orange	35	25
2070	-	50c. blue	35	25
2071	-	50c. green	35	25
2072	-	50c. red	35	25
2073	-	50c. violet	35	25
2074	-	50c. brown	35	25
MS2075		100×75 mm. 2col. mult	1·80	1·80

DESIGNS: No. 2070, 1894 2p. stamp; 2071, 1893, 2p. stamp; 2072, 1894 5p. stamp; 2073, 1893 5p. stamp; 2074, 1894 10p. stamp; **MS**2075, Statue of Queen Isabela and Christopher Columbus.

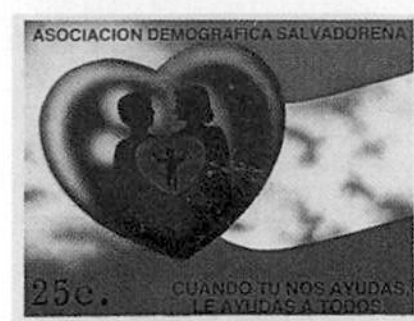

500 People within Heart

1989. 27th Anniv of El Salvador Demographic Association.

2076	**500**	25c. multicoloured	20	10

501 "Signing the Act of Independence" (Luis Vergara Ahumada)

1989. 168th Anniv of Independence. Mult.

2077	25c. Type **501** (postage)	20	10
2078	70c. Flag, independence leaders and arms (air)	50	35

502 Flags of El Salvador and United States

1989. World Cup Football Championship, Italy (1990) (1st issue). Preliminary Rounds. Multicoloured.

2079	20c. Type **502**	20	10
2080	20c. Flags of El Salvador and Guatemala	20	10
2081	25c. Flags of El Salvador and Costa Rica	25	15
2082	25c. Flags of El Salvador and Trinidad and Tobago	25	15
2083	55c. Flags and ball	35	25
2084	1col. Ball and Cuscatlan Stadium	60	45

See also Nos. 2109/15.

503 Marcelino Champagnat and Arms of Order

1989. Birth Bicent of Jose Benito Marcelino Champagnat (founder of Maristas Brothers).

2085	**503**	20c. multicoloured	20	10

504 "The Farmer" (bowl decoration)

1989. America. Multicoloured.

2086	25c. Type **504**	20	10
2087	70c. Pre-Columbian pottery production	50	35

505 Man tending Crops

1989. World Food Day. "One Land, One Community, One Future". Multicoloured.

2088	15c. Type **505**	15	10
2089	55c. Food production activities in chain links	35	20

506 Children under Umbrella

1989. Children's Rights.

2090	**506**	25c. multicoloured	15	10

507 Holy Family in Stable

1989. Christmas. Multicoloured.

2091	25c. Type **507**	15	10
2092	70c. Holy Family	35	25

508 King Vulture

1989. Birds. Multicoloured.

2093	70c. Type **508**	50	35
2094	1col. Common caracara (horiz)	70	45
2095	2col. Sharp-shinned hawk	1·20	95
2096	10col. Ferruginous pygmy owl (horiz)	6·00	4·75

509 Treasury, Map and "50"

1990. 50th Anniv of Treasury.

2097	**509**	50c. blue, gold & black	35	15

510 Baden-Powell

1990. 133rd Birth Anniv of Lord Baden-Powell (founder of Boy Scouts Movement).

2098	**510**	25c. multicoloured	20	10

511 Young Girl

1990. International Women's Day.

2099	**511**	25c. multicoloured	20	10

512 Hourglass

1990. 50th Anniv of El Salvador Philatelic Society.

2100	**512**	25c. mult (postage)	15	10
2101	**512**	55c. mult (air)	30	15
MS2102		100×70 mm. 2col. grey, black and blue	1·40	1·20

DESIGNS: 34×38 mm. 2col. Society emblem.

513 "No to Alcoholic Drinks"

1990. Problems of Addiction. Multicoloured.

2103	20c. Type **513** (postage)	10	10
2104	25c. "No to Tobacco"	25	15
2105	1col.50 "No to Drugs" (air)	85	60

514 Player

1990. Air. Victory by El Salvador at Fourth International Football Championship for Amputees (1989).

2106	**514**	70c. multicoloured	50	35

515 First Page and Map

1990. 75th Anniv of "La Prensa Grafica" (newspaper). Multicoloured.

2107	15c. Type **515**	15	10
2108	25c. Newspaper as diamond and "75"	20	10

516 Group A

1990. World Cup Football Championship, Italy (2nd issue). Multicoloured.

2109	55c. Type **516**	35	25
2110	55c. Group B	35	25
2111	70c. Group C	50	35
2112	70c. Group D	50	35
2113	1col. Group E	60	45
2114	1col. Group F	60	45
2115	1col.50 Winner's medal (vert)	95	70

517 Ferdinand the Catholic

1990. 500th Anniv (1992) of Discovery of America by Columbus (4th issue). Multicoloured.

2116	1col. Type **517**	60	45
2117	1col. Isabella the Catholic	60	45
2118	1col. Arms and topsail	60	45
2119	1col. Anniversary emblem	60	45
2120	1col. "Santa Maria"	60	45
2121	1col. "Pinta" and "Nina"	60	45
MS2122	100×75 mm. 2col. Columbus and map	1·80	1·80

1990. Germany, World Cup Football Championship Winner. No. 2112 surch 90c. ALEMANIA CAMPEON.

2123	90c. on 70c. multicoloured	60	45

519 Globe and Figures

1990. World Summit on Children, New York.

2124	**519**	5col. blue, bis & blk	3·50	2·30

520 Sir Rowland Hill (instigator of first postage stamps)

1990. 150th Anniv of the Penny Black.

2125	**520**	2col. multicoloured	1·20	95
2126	-	2col. multicoloured	1·20	95
2127	-	2col. multicoloured	1·20	95
2128	-	2col. multicoloured	1·20	95
2129	-	2col. multicoloured	1·20	95
2130	-	2col. multicoloured	1·20	95

DESIGNS: No. 2126, 1d. Black; 2127, El Salvador 1889 1c. stamp; 2128, Post Headquarters; 2129, United Kingdom and El Salvador flags; 2130, El Salvador 1949 1col. U.P.U. stamp.

521 Chichontepec Volcano

1990. America. Natural World. Multicoloured.

2131	25c. Type **521**	25	15
2132	70c. Coatepeque Lake	50	35

522 "Food for the Future"

1990. World Food Day.

2133	**522**	5col. multicoloured	3·00	2·30

523 Light Bulb

1990. Centenary of San Salvador Electric Light Company. Multicoloured.

2134	20c. Type **523**	15	10
2135	90c. Maintenance of overhead power lines	60	45

524 Road Signs

1990. 8th Anniv of National Commission for Education and Road Safety. Multicoloured.

2136	25c. Type **524**	20	10
2137	40c. Family at road junction (horiz)	30	15

525 Anniversary Emblem

1990. 75th Anniv of Chamber of Trade and Commerce.

2138	**525**	1col. blue, gold & black	60	45

526 "Papilio garamas amerias"

1990. Butterflies. Multicoloured.

2139	15c. "Eurytides calliste"	60	35
2140	20c. Type **526**	70	45
2141	25c. "Papilio garamas"	70	45
2142	55c. "Hypanartia godmani" (vert)	95	70
2143	70c. "Anaea (Consul) excellens" (vert)	1·20	95
2144	1col. "Papilio pilumnus" (vert)	1·40	1·20
MS2145	100×75 mm. 2col. "Anaea" (Memphis) "proserpina"	3·50	3·50

527 Children

1990. Christmas. Multicoloured.

2146	25c. Type **527**	15	10
2147	70c. Nativity (vert)	50	35

528 Elderly Couple

1991. Month of the Third Age.

2148	**528**	15c. black and violet	15	10

529 University Emblem

1991. 150th Anniv of El Salvador University.

2149	**529**	25c. black and silver	20	10
2150	-	70c. multicoloured	50	35
2151	-	1col.50 multicoloured	95	80

DESIGNS: 70c. Footsteps leading to light; 1col.50, Pencil, pen and dove on globe.

530 Auditorium

1991. Restoration of Santa Ana Theatre. Mult.

2152	20c. Type **530**	25	10
2153	70c. Facade	50	35

531 Mexican Tree Frog

1991. Frogs. Multicoloured.

2154	25c. Type **531**	35	25
2155	70c. Robber frog	60	45
2156	1col. "Plectrohyla guatemalensis"	85	70
2157	1col.50 Morelet's frog	1·20	95

532 National Colours, Map and Child

1991. S.O.S. Children's Villages. Mult.

2158	20c. Type **532**	20	10
2159	90c. Children playing in village	60	45

533 Family building Map

1991. Family Unity Month.

2160	**533**	50c. multicoloured	35	25

534 Blue and White Mockingbird

1991. Birds. Multicoloured.

2161	20c. Type **534**	30	20
2162	25c. Red-winged blackbird	35	25
2163	70c. Rufous-naped wren	60	45
2164	1col. Bushy-crested jay	70	60
2165	5col. Long-tailed manakin	3·50	2·30

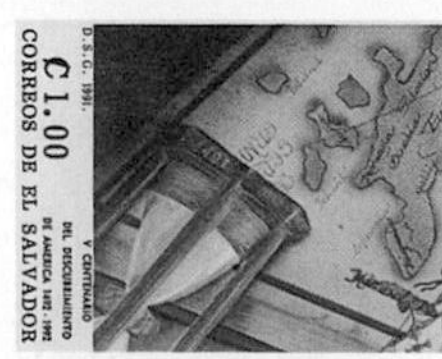

535 Hourglass and Atlas

1991. 500th Anniv (1992) of Discovery of America by Columbus (5th issue). Multicoloured.

2166	1col. Type **535**	60	45
2167	1col. "Santa Maria's" sails and atlas	60	45
2168	1col. Map and caravel	60	45
2169	1col. Caravels and edge of atlas	60	45
2170	1col. Compass rose and map	60	45
2171	1col. Map and anniversary emblem	60	45
MS2172	100×75 mm. 2col. Portion of sail and Mexican pyramid	1·80	1·80

Nos. 2166/71 were issued together, se-tenant, forming a composite design.

536 Battle of Acaxual

1991. America. Voyages of Discovery. Mult.

2173	25c. Type **536**	20	10
2174	70c. First Mass in Cuzcatlan	50	35

537 Tree-globe and Plant and Animal Life

1991. World Food Day. "The Tree, Fountain of Life for the World".

2175	**537**	50c. multicoloured	35	25

538 Manuscript and Mozart

1991. Death Bicentenary of Wolfgang Amadeus Mozart (composer).

2176	**538**	1col. multicoloured	70	45

539 Nativity

1991. Christmas. Multicoloured.

2177	25c. Type **539**	15	10
2178	70c. Carol singers (horiz)	50	35

540 Moon and Left Half of Eclipse

1991. Total Eclipse of the Sun. Mult.

2179	70c. Type **540**	50	35
2180	70c. Right half of eclipse and Moon	50	35

Nos. 2179/80 were issued together, se-tenant, forming a composite design.

541 Lifeguards with rescued Swimmer

1992. Red Cross Lifeguards. Multicoloured.

2181	3col. Type **541**	1·80	1·30
2182	4col.50 Lifeguards in sea	3·00	2·10

542 St. Vincent de Paul and Sick Man

1992. Centenary of St. Vincent de Paul Society of Sisters of Charity.

2183	**542**	80c. multicoloured	60	45

543 Anniversary Emblem

1992. 50th Anniv of Lions International in El Salvador.

2184	**543**	90c. multicoloured	60	45

544 Cyclist ("Non- polluting Transport")

1992. Ecology. Multicoloured.

2185	60c. Type **544**	35	25
2186	80c. Children and butterfly ("Fauna, ecology and education")	50	35
2187	1col.60 Man working on allotment ("Harmony with nature")	1·10	70
2188	2col.20 Animals beside clean river ("Do not pollute rivers")	1·40	1·10
2189	3col. Fruits ("Eat natural foods")	1·90	1·30
2190	5col. Recycling bins ("Energy without contamination")	3·25	2·30
2191	10col. Landscape ("Conserve nature")	6·00	4·50
2192	25col. Wild animals ("Do not destroy fauna")	16·00	11·50

545 Roberto Orellana Valdes (gynaecologist)

1992. Doctors. Multicoloured.

2193	80c. Type **545**	60	45
2194	1col. Carlos Gonzalez Bonilla (surgeon)	70	60
2195	1col.60 Andres Gonzalez Funes (paediatrician)	95	70
2196	2col.20 Joaquin Coto (anaesthetist)	1·30	1·10

546 Mascot and Census Document

1992. 5th Population and Fourth Housing Census. Multicoloured.

2197	60c. Type **546**	50	35
2198	80c. Graph and globe	60	45

548 Simon Bolivar

1992

2205	**548**	2col.20 multicoloured	1·60	80

549 Carvings

1992. 500th Anniv of Discovery of America by Columbus (6th series). Multicoloured.

2206	1col. Type **549**	90	35
2207	1col. Caravel reflected in human eye	90	35
2208	1col. Caravel and Mexican pyramids	90	35
2209	1col. "500", caravel and satellite	90	35
MS2210	100×75 mm. 3col. Pyramid	3·00	3·00

550 Footprints on Globe

1992. Emigration. Multicoloured.

2211	2col.20 Type **550**	1·40	80
2212	2col.20 Happy cloud and footprints	1·40	80

551 Morazan

1992. Birth Bicent of General Francisco Morazan.

2213	**551**	1col. multicoloured	85	35

552 Radio Waves on Map

1992. Salvadoran and Int Broadcasting Day.

2214	**552**	2col.20 multicoloured	1·40	80

553 Cross, Pyramid, Church and Carving

1992. America. 500th Anniv of Discovery of America by Columbus. Multicoloured.

2215	80c. Type **553**	60	35
2216	2col.20 Map and stern of caravel	1·60	80

554 Map and Sails

1992. "Exfilna '92" National Stamp Exn.

2217	**554**	5col. multicoloured	4·25	1·80

555 Sun and Stylized Dove

1992. Peace.

2218	**555**	50c. blue, yellow & blk	50	25

556 Christmas Tree and Children

1992. Christmas. Multicoloured.

2219	80c. Type **556**	80	35
2220	2col.20 Holy Family (vert)	1·80	80

557 Baird's Tapir

1993. Mammals. Multicoloured.

2221	50c. Type **557**	55	25
2222	70c. Water opossum	65	35
2223	1col. Tayra	1·40	45
2224	3col. Jaguarundi	2·75	1·10
2225	4col.50 White-tailed deer	4·00	1·80

558 Head

1993. "Third Age" Month.

2226	**558**	80c. black	60	35
2227	-	2col.20 multicoloured	1·60	80

DESIGN: 2col.20, Young boy beside elderly man holding tree.

559 Church of the Divine Providence

1993. AGAPE (social organization). Mult.

2228	1col. Type **559**	60	35
2229	1col. Family and AGAPE emblem	60	35

560 Secretary

1993. Secretary's Day. 25th Anniv of Salvadoran Association of Executive Secretaries.

2230	**560**	1col. multicoloured	65	35

561 Hospital

1993. Inauguration of Reconstructed Benjamin Bloom Children's Hospital.

2231	**561**	5col. multicoloured	3·00	1·30

562 Flags, Clasped Hands and Chapultepec Castle

1993. State Visit of Pres. Carlos Salinas de Gortari of Mexico.

2232	**562**	2col.20 multicoloured	1·40	80

563 White Ibis

1993. Birds. Multicoloured.

2233	80c. Type **563**	50	25
2234	1col. American wood ibis	65	35
2235	2col.20 Great blue heron	1·40	80
2236	5col. Roseate spoonbill	3·00	1·20

564 Anniversary Emblem

1993. Centenary of Pharmaceutical Industry Standards Council.

2237	**564**	80c. mauve, blk & yell	55	25

565 Agouti

1993. America. Endangered Animals. Mult.

2238	80c. Type **565**	50	35
2239	2col.20 Common racoon	1·40	60

566 Pulgarcito (mascot)

1993. 5th Central American Games, El Salvador (1994). Multicoloured.

2240	50c. Type **566**	50	25
2241	1col.60 Games emblem, flags and Olympic rings	1·00	60
2242	2col.20 Mascot and map of Central America (horiz)	1·40	95
2243	4col.50 Mascot and map of El Salvador (horiz)	2·75	1·20

567 Holy Family

1993. Christmas. Multicoloured.

2244		80c. Type **567**	35	25
2245		2col.20 Nativity scene and Christmas tree	1·10	70

568 Masferrer

1993. 125th Birth Anniv of Alberto Masferrer (sociologist).

2246	**568**	2col.20 multicoloured	1·40	1·10

569 "Solanum mammosum"

1993. Medicinal Plants. Multicoloured.

2247		1col. Type **569**	60	45
2248		1col. "Hamelia patens"	60	45
2249		1col. "Tridax procumbens"	60	45
2250		1col. "Calea urticifolia"	60	45
2251		1col. "Ageratum conyzoides"	60	45
2252		1col. "Pluchea odorata"	60	45

570 I.Y.F. and United Nations Emblems

1994. International Year of the Family.

2253	**570**	2col.20 multicoloured	1·60	1·10

571 Hospital

1994. Centenary of Military Hospital. Mult.

2254		1col. Type **571**	70	45
2255		1col. Medical corps soldier treating wounded	70	45

572 Santa Ana Arms

1994. Centenary of Uprising of the 44 at Santa Ana. Multicoloured.

2256		60c. Type **572**	50	35
2257		80c. Commemorative inscription, laurel wreath and ribbon	60	45

573 Goalkeeper and Flags of U.S.A., Switzerland, Colombia and Rumania

1994. World Cup Football Championship, U.S.A. Various footballing scenes and flags of participating countries. Multicoloured.

2258		60c. Type **573**	35	25
2259		80c. Brazil, Russia, Cameroun and Sweden	50	35
2260		1col. Germany, Bolivia, South Korea and Spain	70	45
2261		2col.20 Argentina, Greece, Nigeria and Bulgaria	1·40	95
2262		4col.50 Italy, Ireland, Norway and Mexico	2·75	1·80
2263		5col. Belgium, Morocco, Holland and Saudi Arabia	3·00	2·10

574 Order of Malta Square, Santa Elena, Cuscatlan

1994. Work of Sovereign Military Order of Malta in El Salvador.

2264	**574**	2col.20 multicoloured	1·40	95

575 Tiger and the Stag (San Juan Nonualco)

1994. Traditional Dances. Multicoloured.

2265		1col. Type **575**	70	45
2266		2col.20 The Speckled Bull (Santa Cruz Analquito and Estanzuelas)	1·40	1·20

576 Sweet Pepper

1994. Edible Plants. Multicoloured.

2267		70c. Type **576**	50	25
2268		80c. Cacao	60	35
2269		1col. Sweet potato	70	45
2270		5col. Pacaya	3·00	1·50

577 Mail Van

1994. America. Postal Vehicles. Mult.

2271		80c. Type **577**	50	25
2272		2col.20 Steam mail train	1·40	80

578 Cyclists

1994. 22nd Tour of El Salvador Cycling Championship.

2273	**578**	80c. multicoloured	50	35

579 National Colours and Globe as Crate

1994. 16th International Fair.

2274	**579**	5col. multicoloured	3·00	1·90

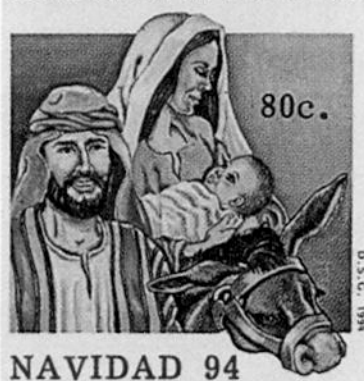

580 Holy Family and Donkey

1994. Christmas. Multicoloured.

2275		80c. Type **580**	50	35
2276		2col.20 Wise men and baby Jesus	1·40	75

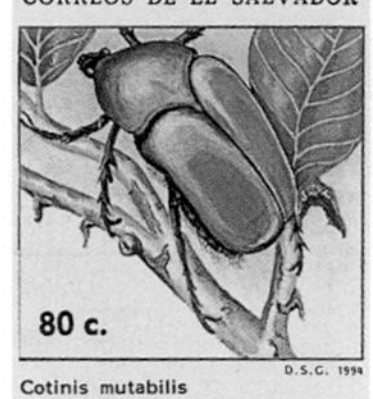

581 "Cotinis mutabilis"

1994. Beetles. Multicoloured.

2277		80c. Type **581**	50	35
2278		1col. "Phyllophaga sp."	60	45
2279		2col.20 "Galofa sp."	1·40	60
2280		5col. Longhorn beetle	3·00	1·10

582 Books

1995. 40th Anniv of Cultural Centre. Anniversary emblems. Multicoloured.

2281		70c. Type **582**	50	35
2282		1col. "40" and arrows	70	45

583 Vase

1995. World Heritage Site. Joya de Ceren. Multicoloured.

2283		60c. Type **583**	35	20
2284		70c. Three-footed dish	50	30
2285		80c. Two-handled pot	60	40
2286		2col.20 Jug	1·60	75
2287		4col.50 Building No. 3	3·50	1·50
2288		5col. Building No. 4	3·75	1·60

584 Menendez

1995. Birth Bicent of Isidro Menendez (politician).

2289	**584**	80c. multicoloured	70	35

585 Anniversary Emblem

1995. 80th Anniv of La Centro Americana, S.A. (welfare organization). Multicoloured.

2290		80c. Type **585** (safeguarding the future of the child)	50	30
2291		2col.20 "Child in Fancy Dress" (Jorge Driottez) (first "Expresiones" painting competition)	1·40	90

586 College and Map of Founding Sisters' Voyage

1995. Cent of College of the Sacred Heart.

2292	**586**	80c. multicoloured	60	30

587 Emblem

1995. 50th Anniv of F.A.O.

2293	**587**	2col.20 multicoloured	1·60	90

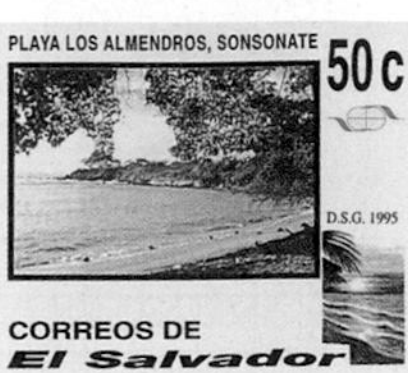

588 Los Almendros Beach, Sonsonate

1995. 20th Anniv of World Tourism Organization. Multicoloured.

2294		50c. Type **588**	35	15
2295		60c. Apaneca Lake	40	30
2296		2col.20 Guerrero Beach, La Union	1·40	80
2297		5col. Usulutan Volcano	3·25	1·60

589 National Arms and Symbols of Development

1995. 174th Anniv of Central American Independence. Multicoloured.

2298		80c. Type **589**	55	30
2299		25col. El Salvador exports (sustained economic development)	17·00	10·50

590 "Lemboglossum stellatum"

1995. Orchids. Multicoloured.

2300	60c. "Pleurothallis glandulosa"	50	25
2301	60c. "Pleurothallis grobyi"	50	25
2302	70c. Type **590**	55	30
2303	70c. "Pleurothallis fuegii"	55	30
2304	1col. "Pleurothallis hirsuta"	85	40
2305	1col. "Lepanthes inaequalis"	85	40
2306	3col. "Hexadesmia micrantha"	2·75	1·30
2307	3col. "Pleurothallis segoviense"	2·75	1·30
2308	4col.50 "Stelis aprica"	4·00	2·20
2309	4col.50 "Platystele stenostachya"	4·00	2·20
2310	5col. "Stelis barbata"	4·75	2·50
2311	5col. "Pleurothallis schiedeii"	4·75	2·50

591 Pygmy Kingfisher

1995. America. Conservation. Multicoloured.

2312	80c. Type **591**	65	35
2313	2col. Green kingfisher	1·80	80

592 Anniversary Emblem

1995. 50th Anniv of U.N.O. Multicoloured.

2314	80c. Type **592**	65	35
2315	2col.20 Hands supporting emblem	1·80	80

593 Children with Sparklers

1995. Christmas. Multicoloured.

2316	80c. Type **593**	65	35
2317	2col.20 Family celebrating at midnight	1·80	80

594 Great Horned Owl ("Bubo virginianus")

1995. Wildlife of Montecristo. Multicoloured.

2318	80c. Type **594**	60	45
2319	80c. Kinkajou ("Potos flavus")	60	45
2320	80c. "Porthidium godmani" (snake)	60	45
2321	80c. Ocelot ("Felis pardalis")	60	45
2322	80c. "Deliathis bifurcata" (long-horn beetle)	60	45
2323	80c. Puma ("Felis concolor")	60	45
2324	80c. Red brocket ("Mazama americana")	60	45
2325	80c. "Leptophobia aripa" (butterfly)	60	45
2326	80c. Salamander ("Bolitoglossa salvinii")	60	45
2327	80c. Rivoli's hummingbird ("Eugenes fulgens")	60	45

Nos. 2318/27 were issued together, se-tenant, forming a composite design of a forest.

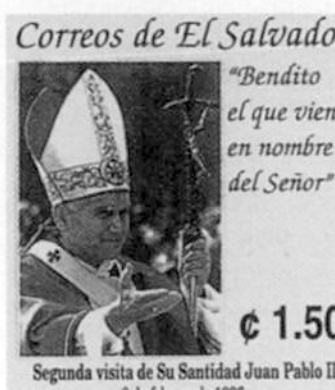

595 Pope John Paul II in Mitre

1996. 2nd Papal Visit. Multicoloured.

2328	1col.50 Type **595**	1·20	70
2329	5col.40 Pope and Metropolitan Cathedral	4·75	2·40

596 Arrival of Spaniards

1996. 450th Anniv of Grant of City Status to San Salvador. Multicoloured.

2330	2col.50 Type **596**	1·90	1·20
2331	2col.70 Diego de Holguin (first governor) and chapel	2·20	1·30
2332	3col.30 Former National Palace, 1889	2·50	1·70
2333	4col. Boulevard de los Heroes	3·00	1·90

597 ANTEL Emblem incorporating Globes

1996. Telecommunications Workers' Day. Mult.

2334	1col.50 Dish aerial and hand holding optic fibres (horiz)	95	65
2335	5col. Type **597**	3·25	1·90

598 Rey Avila (El Chele) (singer)

1996. Entertainers' Death Anniversaries. Mult.

2336	1col. Type **598** (1st death)	80	55
2337	1col.50 Maria Moreira (Dona Teresfora) (singer, 1st death)	1·10	80
2338	2col.70 Francisco Lara (Pancho Lara) (musician and composer, 7th death)	1·80	1·20
2339	4col. Carlos Pineda (Aniceto Porsisoca) (singer, 3rd death)	2·75	1·80

599 Anniversary Emblem

1996. 40th Anniv of YSKL Radio Station.

2340	**599**	1col.40 multicoloured	1·20	70

600 Throwing the Discus

1996. Centenary of Modern Olympic Games and Olympic Games, Atlanta. Ancient Greek athletes. Multicoloured.

2341	1col.50 Type **600**	1·20	75
2342	3col. Hurdling	2·30	1·40
2343	4col. Wrestling	3·00	1·80
2344	5col. Throwing the javelin	3·50	2·20

601 Northern Oriole ("Icterus galbula")

1996. Migratory Birds. Multicoloured.

2345	1col.50 Type **601**	1·20	75
2346	1col.50 American kestrel ("Falco sparverius")	1·20	75
2347	1col.50 Yellow warbler ("Dendroica petechia")	1·20	75
2348	1col.50 Kingbird ("Tyrannus forficatus")	1·20	75
2349	1col.50 Rose-breasted grosbeak ("Pheucticus ludovicianus")	1·20	75

602 Printed Hand releasing Letters

1996. 60th Anniv of "El Diario de Hoy" (newspaper).

2350	**602**	5col.20 multicoloured	4·00	2·75

603 Station Emblem

1996. 30th Anniv of Channel 2 (television station).

2351	**603**	10col. multicoloured	7·50	5·25

604 Child and Anniversary Emblem

1996. 50th Anniv of UNICEF.

2352	**604**	1col. multicoloured	80	55

605 Nahuizalco Woman

1996. America. Costumes. Multicoloured.

2353	1col.50 Type **605**	1·40	75
2354	4col. Panchimalco woman	3·25	1·80

606 Christmas Eve Mass (Doris Landaverde)

1996. Christmas. Children's Paintings. Mult.

2355	2col.50 Type **606**	1·80	1·20
2356	4col. Christmas morning (Isabel Perez)	3·00	1·80

607 Jerusalem

1996. 3000th Anniv of Jerusalem.

2357	**607**	1col. multicoloured	80	55

608 White-nosed Sharks ("Nasolamia velox")

1996. Marine Life. Multicoloured.

2358	1col. Type **608**	95	70
2359	1col. Pacific sierra ("Scomberomorus sierra")	95	70
2360	1col. Common dolphins ("Delphinus delphis")	95	70
2361	1col. Hawksbill turtle ("Eretmochelys imbricata")	95	70
2362	1col. Starry grouper ("Epinephelus labriformis")	95	70
2363	1col. Cortez angelfish ("Pomacanthus zonipectus")	95	70
2364	1col. Mexican parrotfish ("Scarus perrico")	95	70
2365	1col. Pacific seahorse ("Hippocampus ingens")	95	70

Nos. 2358/65 were issued together, se-tenant, forming a composite design.

609 Gong and 1983 Constitution

1996. Constitution Day.

2366	**609**	1col. multicoloured	80	55

610 Newspapers and Computer

1997. 30th Anniv of "El Mundo" (newspaper).

2367	**610**	10col. multicoloured	7·50	5·25

611 Steam Locomotive No. 58441, 1925

1997. "Exfilna 97" National Stamp Exhibition, San Salvador.
2368 **611** 4col. multicoloured 2·75 1·90

612 Church and Mother Clara

1997. 80th Anniv of Foundation of Carmelite Order of St. Joseph.
2369 **612** 1col. multicoloured 80 55

613 Anniversary Emblem

1997. 50th Anniv of American School.
2370 **613** 25col. multicoloured 19·00 11·50

614 Custard Apple ("Annona diversifolia")

1997. Tropical Fruits. Multicoloured.
2371 1col.50 Type **614** 1·30 95
2372 1col.50 Cashew ("Anacardium occidentale") 1·30 95
2373 1col.50 Melon ("Cucumis melo") 1·30 95
2374 1col.50 Sapodilla ("Pouteria mammosa") 1·30 95
MS2375 110×85 mm. 4col. Papaya ("Carica papaya") 3·00 2·75

615 Anniversary Emblem

1997. 55th Anniv of Lions International in El Salvador.
2376 **615** 4col. multicoloured 3·00 1·80

616 Hand protecting Ecosystem

1997. Int Ozone Layer Day (2377) and Int-American Water Day (2378). Multicoloured.
2377 1col.50 Type **616** 1·20 75
2378 4col. Boy drinking clean water 3·00 1·80

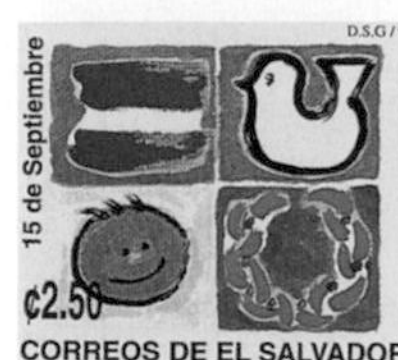

617 Flag, Duck, Face and Wreath

1997. 176th Anniv of Independence. Mult.
2379 2col.50 Type **617** 1·80 1·20
2380 5col.20 National flag, celebrating crowd and peace dove 3·25 2·30

618 Cervantes, Book and Don Quixote and Sancho

1997. 450th Birth Anniv of Miguel de Cervantes (writer).
2381 **618** 4col. multicoloured 3·00 1·80

619 Emblem

1997. 75th Anniv of Scout Movement in El Salvador.
2382 **619** 1col.50 multicoloured 1·60 90

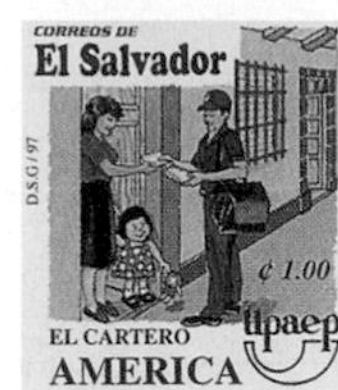

620 Postman handing Letter to Woman

1997. America. The Postman. Multicoloured.
2383 1col. Type **620** 85 55
2384 4col. Dog chasing postman on scooter 3·00 1·90

621 Motor Car

1997. 26th Anniv of El Salvador Automobile Club.
2385 **621** 10col. multicoloured 7·50 5·25

622 Open-air Feast

1997. Christmas. Children's paintings. Mult.
2386 1col.50 Type **622** 1·60 90
2387 1col.50 Family gathering 1·60 90

623 Map and St. John Bosco (founder)

1997. Centenary of Salesian Brothers in El Salvador. Multicoloured.
2388 1col.50 Type **623** 70 60
2389 1col.50 St. Cecilia College, Santa Tecla 70 60
2390 1col.50 St. Joseph College, Santa Ana 70 60
2391 1col.50 Ricaldone Technical College 70 60
2392 1col.50 Maria Auxiliadora Church and statue 70 60
2393 1col.50 Don Bosco Citadel, Soyapango, and electronics class 70 60

624 Standard, 1946

1997. Motor Cars. Multicoloured.
2394 2col.50 Type **624** 95 60
2395 2col.50 Chrysler, 1936 95 60
2396 2col.50 Jaguar, 1954 95 60
2397 2col.50 Ford, 1930 95 60
2398 2col.50 Mercedes Benz, 1953 95 60
2399 2col.50 Porsche, 1956 95 60

625 St. Joseph's Church, Ahuachapan

1998. 125th Anniv of St. Joseph's Order. Mult.
2400 1col. Type **625** 40 25
2401 4col. Jose Vilaseca and Cesarea Esparza (founders) 1·80 1·10

626 Air Traffic Control Tower

1998. Modernisation of El Salvador International Airport.
2402 **626** 10col. multicoloured 4·50 3·00

627 Player with Ball and Sacre Coeur, Paris

1998. World Cup Football Championship, France. Multicoloured.
2403 1col.50 Type **627** 80 60
2404 1col.50 Player and Eiffel Tower, Paris 80 60
2405 1col.50 Player and the Louvre, Paris 80 60
2406 1col.50 Goalkeeper and Notre Dame Cathedral, Paris 80 60
MS2407 110×85 mm. 4col. Football 2·50 2·50

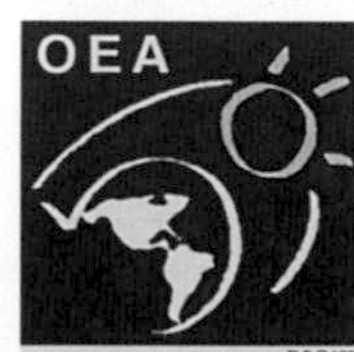

628 Sun around Map of Americas

1998. 50th Anniv of Organization of American States.
2408 **628** 4col. multicoloured 1·70 1·10

629 Swimming, Tennis and Water Polo Medals

1999. El Salvador, Champion of Sixth Central American Games. Multicoloured.
2409 1col.50 Type **629** 60 35
2410 1col.50 Body-building, judo and shooting medals 60 35
2411 1col.50 Gymnastics, weightlifting and karate medals 60 35
2412 1col.50 Discus, volleyball and netball medals 60 35

630 Guerrero

1998. 40th Death Anniv of Dr. Jose Gustano Guerrero (former President of Tribunal of Justice, The Hague).
2413 **630** 1col. multicoloured 35 25

631 Maps on Cubes

1998. 18th International Fair.
2414 **631** 4col. multicoloured 1·70 1·10

632 Arce's Deathbed

1998. 150th Death Anniv of Manuel Jose Arce (President of United Provinces of Central America, 1825–29).
2415 **632** 4col. multicoloured 1·70 1·10

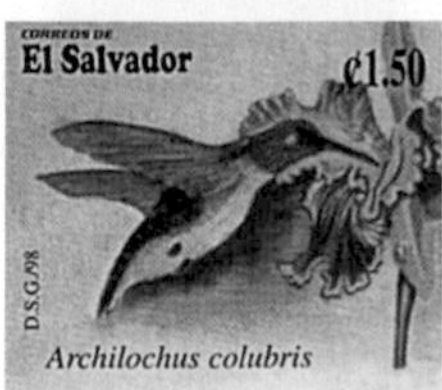

633 Ruby-throated Hummingbird

1998. Hummingbirds. Multicoloured.
2416 1col.50 Type **633** 80 60
2417 1col.50 Cinnamon hummingbird ("Amazilia rutila") 80 60
2418 1col.50 Blue-throated hummingbird ("Hylocharis eliciae") 80 60
2419 1col.50 Green violetear ("Colibri thalassinus") 80 60
2420 1col.50 Violet sabrewing ("Campylopterus hemileucurus") 80 60
2421 1col.50 Amethyst-throated hummingbird ("Lampornis amethystinus") 80 60

634 House and Figure

1998. 25th Anniv of Housing Social Fund.
2422 **634** 10col. multicoloured 4·50 3·00

635 Scroll

1998. 50th Anniv of National Archives.
2423 **635** 1col.50 multicoloured 65 45

636 Alice Larde de Venturino (writer)

1998. America. Famous Women. Multicoloured.
2424 1col. Type **636** 40 30
2425 4col. Maria de Baratta (composer) 1·80 1·10

637 Nativity

1998. Christmas. Children's Paintings. Mult.
2426 1col. Type **637** 40 30
2427 4col. Angels and shepherds going to church 1·80 1·10

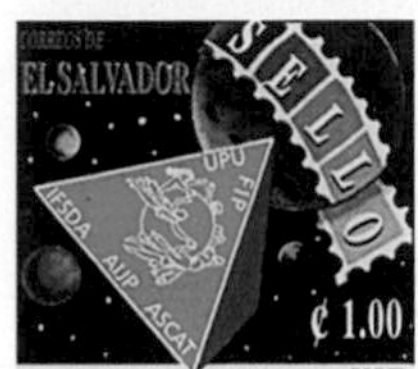

638 Planets and Philatelic Emblems on Pyramid

1998. World Post Day.
2428 **638** 1col. multicoloured 55 35

639 Douglas C-47T Transport and Badge

1998. 75th Anniv of El Salvador Air Force. Mult.
2429 1col.50 Type **639** 70 55
2430 1col.50 TH-300 training helicopter and badge 70 55
2431 1col.50 Bell UH-1H utility helicopter and badge 70 55
2432 1col.50 Cessna A-37B Dragonfly bomber and badge 70 55

640 Papaw and Palm Leaf Salad

1998. Traditional Dishes. Multicoloured.
2433 1col.50 Type **640** 70 55
2434 1col.50 Black pudding soup ("Sopa de Mondongo") 70 55
2435 1col.50 Alhuaiste prawns 70 55
2436 1col.50 Panela honey fritters 70 55
2437 1col.50 Chilled salad ("Refresco de Ensalada") 70 55
2438 1col.50 Avocado salad ("Ensalada de Aguacate") 70 55
2439 1col.50 Water rice and cabbage soup ("Sopa de Arroz ...") 70 55
2440 1col.50 Typical El Salvador dish 70 55
2441 1col.50 Banana rissoles ("Empanadas de Platano") 70 55
2442 1col.50 Barley water ("Horchata") 70 55

641 Roberto d'Aubuisson signing Constitution

1998. 15th Anniv of Constitution.
2443 **641** 25col. black and blue 9·25 5·75

642 "Salvador" (steamship)

1999. 1st National Thematic Stamps Exhibition, San Salvador.
2444 **642** 2col.50 multicoloured 1·20 80

643 Anniversary Emblem

1999. 40th Anniv of National Television.
2445 **643** 4col. multicoloured 1·20 90

644 Moorhen

1999. Water Birds. Multicoloured.
2446 1col. Type **644** 50 35
2447 1col. American purple gallinule ("Porphyrula martinica") 50 35
2448 1col. Spotted rail ("Pardirallus maculatus") 50 35
2449 1col. Blue-winged teal ("Anas discors") 50 35
2450 1col. Red-billed whistling duck ("Dendrocygna autumnalis") 50 35
2451 1col. American coot ("Fulica americana") 50 35
2452 1col. Northern jacana ("Jacana spinosa") 50 35
2453 1col. Sora crake ("Porzana carolina") 50 35
2454 1col. Limpkin ("Aramus guarauna") 50 35
2455 1col. Masked duck ("Oxyura dominica") 50 35
MS2456 99×75 mm. 4col. Lesser scaup ("Aythya affinia") (40×35 mm) 1·80 1·80

645 E.U. and El Salvador Flags

1999. Co-operation between European Union and El Salvador. Multicoloured.
2457 5col.20 Type **645** 2·00 1·30
2458 10col. Handshake, El Salvador arms and E.U. emblem 3·75 2·75

646 Flags and Arms of El Salvador and U.S.A.

1999. Visit of U.S. President William Clinton to El Salvador. Multicoloured.
2459 5col. Type **646** 2·00 1·30
2460 5col. Presidents Armando Calderon Sol and Clinton 2·00 1·30

Nos. 2459/60 were issued together, se-tenant, forming a composite design.

647 Stylized People and Globe

1999. 5th Anniv of Salvadoran Institute for Professional Development.
2461 **647** 5col.40 multicoloured 2·20 1·40

648 Common Long-tongued Bat

1999. Bats. Multicoloured.
2462 1col.50 Type **648** 80 60
2463 1col.50 Common vampire bat ("Desmodus rotundus") 80 60
2464 1col.50 Mexican bulldog bat (Noctilio leporinus) 80 60
2465 1col.50 False vampire bat ("Vampyrum spectrum") 80 60
2466 1col.50 Honduran white bat ("Ectophylla alba") 80 60
2467 1col.50 Black-whiskered bat ("Myotis nigricans") 80 60

649 Drilling Tower, Ahuachapan

1999. Energy in the 21st Century. Geothermal Technology. Multicoloured.
2468 1col. Type **649** 35 25
2469 4col. Geothermal power station, Berlin, Usulutan 1·70 1·10

650 Globe and Items for Export

1999. 24th Anniv of Corporation of Exporters.
2470 **650** 4col. multicoloured 1·70 1·10

651 Dove, Typewriter and Map

1999. National Journalists' Day.
2471 **651** 1col.50 multicoloured 65 40

652 "Cattleya skinneri var. alba"

1999. Orchids. Multicoloured.
2472 1col.50 Type **652** 80 60
2473 1col.50 "Cattleya skinneri var. coerulea" 80 60
2474 1col.50 "Cattleya skinneri" 80 60
2475 1col.50 "Cattleya guatemalensis" 80 60
2476 1col.50 "Cattleya aurantiaca var. flava" 80 60
2477 1col.50 "Cattleya aurantiaca" 80 60

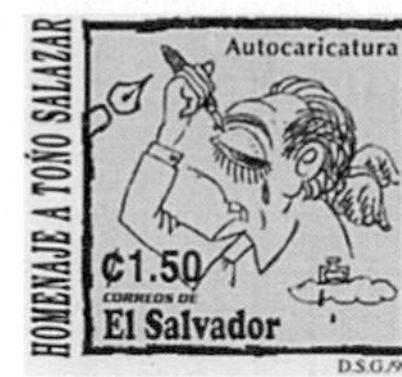

653 Self-portrait

1999. 120th Birth Anniv of Tono Salazar (caricaturist). Each blue and black.
2478 1col.50 Type **653** 80 60
2479 1col.50 Salarrue 80 60
2480 1col.50 Claudia Lars 80 60
2481 1col.50 Francisco Gavidia 80 60
2482 1col.50 Miguel Angel Asturias 80 60

654 Flask, Computer and Children eating

1999. Central American Institute of Nutrition, Panama. Multicoloured.
2483 5col.20 Type **654** 1·90 1·30
2484 5col.40 Foodstuffs 2·00 1·30

655 Gen. Manuel Jose Arce and Capt. Gen. Gerardo Barrios

1999. 175th Anniv of the Army. Multicoloured.
2485 1col. Type **655** 40 30
2486 1col.50 Soldier and flag 65 40

656 Emblem

1999. International Year of the Elderly.
2487 **656** 10col. multicoloured 3·25 2·30

657 Dove, Globe and Children

1999. America. A New Millennium without Arms. Multicoloured.
2488 1col. Type **657** 40 30
2489 4col. Globe and sign crossing out gun 1·60 1·10

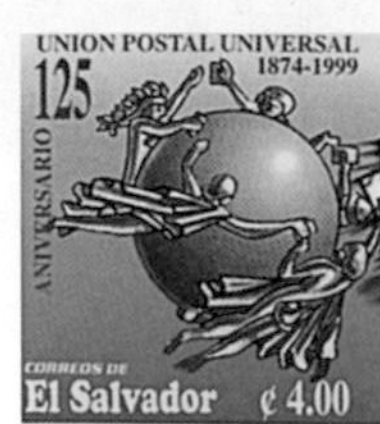

658 Emblem

1999. 125th Anniv of Universal Postal Union. Mult.
2490 4col. Type **658** 2·00 1·50
2491 4col. Mail and modes of transport 2·00 1·50

Nos. 2490/1 were issued together, se-tenant, forming a composite design.

659 Star and Temples (Delmy Guandique)

1999. Christmas. Paintings. Multicoloured.
2492 1col.50 Type **659** 60 40
2493 1col.50 Woman holding poinsettias (Margarita Orellana) 60 40
2494 4col. The Holy Family (Lolly Sandoval) 1·70 1·10
2495 4col. The Nativity (Jose Francisco Guadron) 1·70 1·10

660 Emblem

1999. 40th Anniv of International Development Bank.
2496 **660** 25col. multicoloured 9·75 6·50

661 Golden-fronted Woodpecker

1999. Woodpeckers. Multicoloured.
2497 1col.50 Type **661** 80 60
2498 1col.50 Golden-olive woodpecker (*Piculus rubiginosus*) 80 60
2499 1col.50 Yellow-bellied sapsucker (*Sphyrapicus varius*) 80 60
2500 1col.50 Lineated woodpecker (*Dryocopus lineatus*) 80 60
2501 1col.50 Acorn woodpecker (*Melanerpes formicivorus*) 80 60

662 Emblem

1999. 70th Anniv of Coffee Farmers' Association.
2502 **662** 10col. multicoloured 4·25 2·75

663 Emblem

2000. New Year.
2503 **663** 1col.50 multicoloured 80 45

664 Fireman rescuing Child

2000. 25th Anniv of National Fire Service. Mult.
2504 2col.50 Type **664** 1·10 70
2505 25col. Fire service emblem 9·00 5·50

665 Children, Books and Map of El Salvador

2000. 30th Anniv of Educational Work.
2506 **665** 1col. multicoloured 60 35

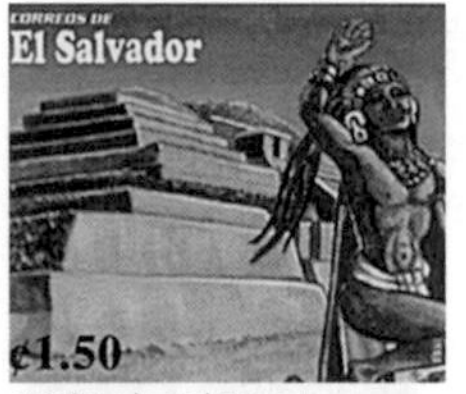

666 Temple and Dancer

2000. New Millennium (1st series). Multicoloured.
2507 1col.50 Type **666** 80 60
2508 1col.50 *Santa Maria* and Columbus (discovery of America by Columbus) 80 60
2509 1col.50 Soldier and native 80 60
2510 1col.50 Court room (Declaration of Independence, 1841) 80 60

See also Nos. 2533/6.

667 Acceso Gate

2000. El Imposible National Park, Ahuachapan. Multicoloured.
2511 1col. Type **667** 35 30
2512 1col. Ocelot cub 35 30
2513 1col. Paca 35 30
2514 1col. Venado River falls 35 30
2515 1col. Great curassow 35 30
2516 1col. Tree with yellow leaves 35 30
2517 1col. Orchid 35 30
2518 1col. Blue-crowned motmot 35 30
2519 1col. Painted bunting 35 30
2520 1col. Plant 35 30
2521 1col. Information centre 35 30
2522 1col. White-eared ground sparrow 35 30
2523 1col. Green frog 35 30
2524 1col. Fungi growing on branch 35 30
2525 1col. Flower (Guaco de Tierra) 35 30
2526 1col. Emerald toucanet 35 30
2527 1col. View over park 35 30
2528 1col. Brazilian agouti 35 30
2529 1col. Tamandua 35 30

2530 1col. El Imposible River falls 35 30

668 Ink Pen, Text and Emblem

2000. 85th Anniv of La Prensa Grafica (bilingual newspaper).
2531 **668** 5col. multicoloured 2·40 1·80

669 Champagnat

2000. Canonization (1999) of Marcelino Champagnat (Catholic priest).
2532 **669** 10col. multicoloured 4·00 2·50

670 Casa Blanca, San Salvador, 1890

2000. New Millennium (2nd series). Each black and brown.
2533 1col.50 Type **670** 70 45
2534 1col.50 Market, 1920 70 45
2535 1col.50 Tram outside Nuevo Mundo Hotel, 1924 70 45
2536 1col.50 Motor cars, 2a South Avenue, 1924 70 45

671 Athletics

2000. Olympic Games, Sydney. Multicoloured.
2537 1col. Type **671** 55 35
2538 1col. Gymnastics 55 35
2539 1col. High-jumping 55 35
2540 1col. Weightlifting 55 35
2541 1col. Fencing 55 35
2542 1col. Cycling 55 35
2543 1col. Swimming 55 35
2544 1col. Shooting 55 35
2545 1col. Archery 55 35
2546 1col. Judo 55 35

672 Baldwin Steam Locomotive

2000. Trains. Multicoloured.
2547 1col.50 Type **672** 70 45
2548 1col.50 General Electric Corporation locomotive 70 45
2549 1col.50 Open-sided carriage 70 45
2550 1col.50 Presidential carriage 70 45

673 Globe, Envelope and Computer

2000. World Post Day.
2551 **673** 5col. multicoloured 2·40 1·80

674 Snowman

2000. Christmas. Multicoloured.
2552 1col. Type **674** 60 35
2553 1col. Bells 60 35
2554 1col. Baubles 60 35
2555 1col. Candy stick 60 35
2556 1col. Candles 60 35
2557 1col. Sleigh 60 35
2558 1col. Presents 60 35
2559 1col. Father Christmas 60 35
2560 1col. Christmas hat 60 35
2561 1col. Boot 60 35

675 "The Traveller" (Roberto Mejia Ruiz)

2000. Paintings. Multicoloured.
2562 4col. Type **675** 3·00 2·30
2563 4col. Man kneeling (Alex Cuchilla) 3·00 2·30
2564 4col. Woman wearing hat (Nicolas Fredy Shi Quan) 3·00 2·30
2565 4col. Swallows (Jose Bernardo Pacheco) 3·00 2·30
2566 4col. Man on Globe (Oscar Soles) 3·00 2·30

US Dollars were introduced as dual currency in 2001. As stamps were designated in both currencies they have been continued to be listed in colons.

676 West Highland White Terriers

2001. Pets. Multicoloured.
2567 1col.50 Type **676** 1·10 60
2568 1col.50 West highland white terrier and cat 1·10 60
2569 2col.50 Budgerigars 1·80 1·20
2570 2col.50 Rough-coated terrier and English toy terrier 1·80 1·20

677 Children's Playground

2001. 25th Anniv of Saburo Hirao Park, San Salvador. Multicoloured.
2571 5col. Type **677** 2·40 1·80
2572 25col. Japanese garden 18·00 11·50

678 Claudia Lars and Federico Proano

2001. Latin American Writers.

2573	**678**	10col. multicoloured	5·25	4·00

679 Building, Nun and Children

2001. 125th Anniv of Hogar del Nino San Vicente de Paul (children's home), Quito, Ecuador.

2574	**679**	4col. multicoloured	2·20	1·60

680 Indigo Milky (*Lactarius indigo*)

2001. Fungi. Multicoloured.

2575	1col.50 Type **680** (inscr Lactaius)	1·40	95
2576	1col.50 Oyster mushroom (*Pleurotus ostreatus*)	1·40	95
2577	1col.50 *Ramaria sp.*	1·40	95
2578	1col.50 White worm coral fungus (*Clavaria vermicularis*)	1·40	95
2579	4col. Fly agaric (*Amanita muscaria*)	3·75	2·30
2580	4col. *Phillipsia sp.*	3·75	2·30
2581	4col. Emetic russula (*Russula*)	3·75	2·30
2582	4col. Collared earthstar (*Geastrum triplex*)	3·75	2·30

681 Josemaria Escriva de Balaguer

2002. Birth Centenary of Josemaria Escriva de Balaguer (founder of Opus Dei (religious organization)). Multicoloured.

2583	1col. Type **681**	70	45
2584	5col. Facing left	4·25	3·50

682 Clasped Hands

2002. 10th Anniv of Peace Accord. Multicoloured.

2585	2col.50 Type **682**	1·80	1·20
2586	2col.50 Sun and dove	1·80	1·20
MS2587	150×120 mm. 2col.50×2, Dove holding olive branch; Dove as flag	4·50	4·50

683 Weightlifter, Archer and Show Jumper

2002. 19th Central America and Caribbean Games. Multicoloured.

2588	1col. Type **683**	95	70
2589	1col. Cyclists	95	70
2590	1col. Blocks containing stylized sportsmen	95	70
2591	1col. Young gymnast	95	70
MS2592	120×90 mm. 4col. Stylized birds	3·75	3·75

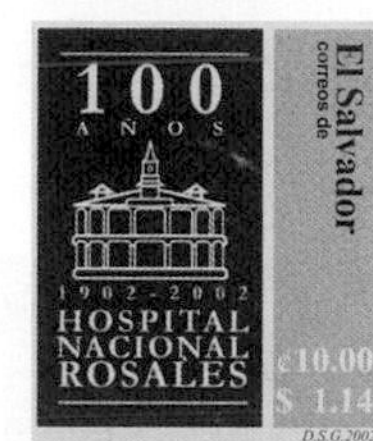

684 Anniversary Emblem

2002. Rosales Hospital Centenary.

2593	**684**	10col. ultramarine and black	9·25	7·00

685 Seoul Stadium

2002. World Cup Football Championships, Japan and South Korea. Designs showing stadia. Multicoloured.

2594	1col. Type **685**	95	60
2595	1col. Busan	95	60
2596	1col. Incheon	95	60
2597	1col. Suwon	95	60
2598	1col.50 Niigata	1·40	95
2599	1col.50 Saitama	1·40	95
2600	1col.50 Miyagi	1·40	95
2601	1col.50 Osaka	1·40	95
MS2602	110×85 mm. 4col. Brazilian flag	3·75	3·75

686 Lions Club Emblem

2002. 50th Anniv (2001) of San Miguel Lions Club (charitable organization).

2603	**686**	5col. multicoloured	4·50	3·50

687 Academy Emblem

2002. 10th Anniv of National Public Security Academy.

2604	**687**	1col. multicoloured	95	70

688 Parliamentary Emblem

2002. 10th Anniv (2001) of Central American Parliament.

2605	**688**	25col. blue and black	24·00	18·00

689 Organization Building

2002. Centenary of Pan American Health Organization. Multicoloured.

2606	2col.70 Type **689**	2·75	1·80
2607	2col.70 Anniversary emblem	2·75	1·80

690 Stylized Child standing on Open Book

2002. America. Literacy Campaign. Multicoloured.

2608	1col. Type **690**	95	70
2609	1col.50 Classroom	1·10	60

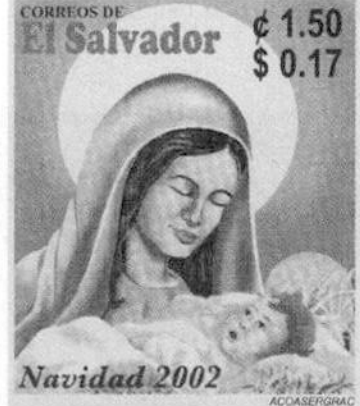

691 Mary and Jesus

2002. Christmas. Multicoloured.

2610	1col.50 Type **691**	1·10	60
2611	2col.50 Joseph and Jesus	2·20	1·80

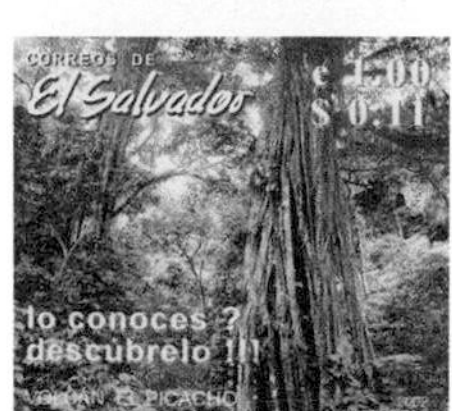

692 El Picacho, San Salvador Volcano

2002. Tourism. Multicoloured.

2612	1col. Type **692**	95	70
2613	1col. Jiquilisco Bay	95	70
2614	4col. Joya de Ceren archaeological site	3·00	2·30
2615	4col. Juayua, Sonsonate	3·00	2·30

693 Emblem and Scouts

2002. 80th Anniv of El Salvador Scouting Movement.

2616	**693**	25col. multicoloured	2·75	1·90

694 Women seated at Desks

2003. Centenary of Daughters of Mary (religious organization). Multicoloured.

2617	70c. Type **694**	35	25
2618	1col.50 Mary and Jesus (statue)	70	45

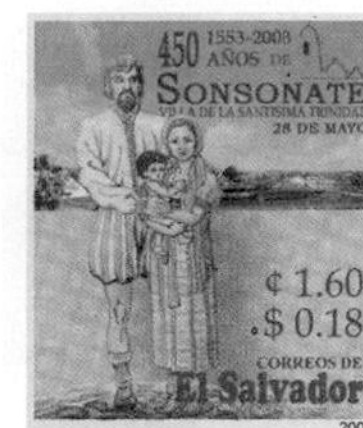

695 Early Family

2003. 450th Anniv of Sonsonate City.

2619	**695**	1col.60 multicoloured	1·60	1·20

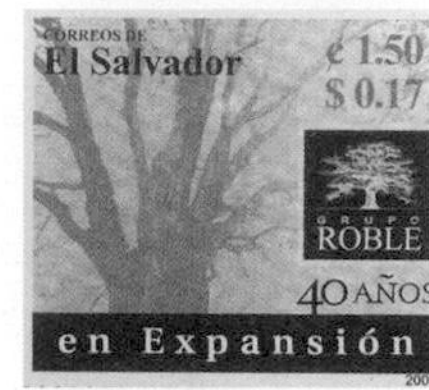

696 Leafless Tree

2003. 40th Anniv of Grupo Roble (entrepreneurial group). Multicoloured.

2620	1col.50 Type **696**	1·40	70
2621	1col.50 Fruiting tree	1·40	70
MS2622	75×100 mm. 40col. Bird on nest	3·75	3·75

697 Anniversary Emblem

2003. 50th Anniv of Regional Organization for Farming Health (OIRSA).

2623	**697**	25col. multicoloured	24·00	18·00

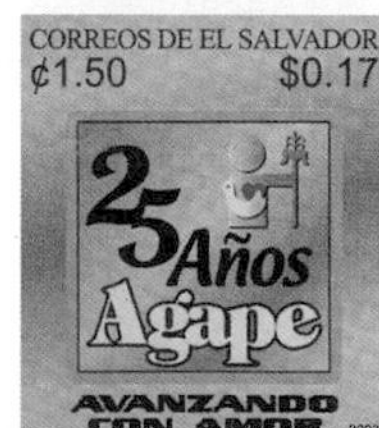

698 Emblem

2003. 25th Anniv of AGAPE (Catholic social organization).

2624	**698**	1col.50 multicoloured	1·40	1·10

699 Maria Felipe Aranzamendi

2003. Women of the Independence Movement. Multicoloured.

2625	2col.50 Type **699**	2·20	1·80
2626	2col.70 Manuela Arce de Lara	2·75	1·90
MS2627	75×100 mm. 4col. Celebration	3·75	3·75

700 Children, Farmers and Produce

2003. 25th Anniv of United Nations Food and Agriculture Organization in El Salvador. Multicoloured.

2628 1col.50 Type **700** 1·40 1·10

MS2629 100×75 mm. 4col. Girl behind tree and food workers 3·75 3·75

701 Bee (inscr "Abejorro")

2003. Flora and Fauna (1st issue). Multicoloured.

2630 1col.50 Type **701** 1·40 90
2631 1col.50 *Chrysina quetzalcoatli* 1·40 90
2632 1col.50 *Anartia Fatima* 1·40 90
2633 1col.50 *Manduca* 1·40 90
2634 1col.50 *Manduca sexta* 1·40 90
2635 1col.50 *Tabebuia chrysantha* 1·40 90
2636 1col.50 *Alpina purpurata* 1·40 90
2637 1col.50 *Tecoma stans* 1·40 90
2638 1col.50 *Tabebuia rosea* 1·40 90
2639 1col.50 *Passiflora edulis* 1·40 90

MS2640 100×75 mm. 4col. *Tabebuia rosea* and Anartia Fatima (vert) 3·75 3·75

See also Nos. 2653/4.

702 Mary and Jesus

2003. Christmas. Multicoloured.

2641 1col.50 Type **702** 1·40 70
2642 4col. Holy Family 3·25 2·30

703 Church of the Immaculate Conception, Citalia

2003. Churches. Multicoloured.

2643 4col. Type **703** 3·00 1·50
2644 4col. St. James Apostle, Chalchuapa 3·00 1·50
2645 4col. St. Peter Apostle, Metapan 3·00 1·50
2646 4col. Our Lady Santa Ana, Chapeltique 3·00 1·50
2647 4col. St. James Apostle, Conchagua 3·00 1·50

MS2648 75×100 mm. 5col. El Cavario, San Salvador (vert) 3·50 3·50

704 Procession of Brotherhood of Panchimalco

2003. Tourism. Multicoloured.

2649 1col.50 Type **704** 1·40 70
2650 1col.50 Church cupola, Juayua 1·40 70
2651 1col.50 Shalpa beach, La Libertad 1·40 70
2652 1col.50 Maya ruins, Tazumal 1·40 70

705 *Fernaldia pandurata*

2003. Flora and Fauna (2nd issue). Multicoloured.

2653 1col.50 Type **705** 1·40 70
2654 4col. *Lepidophyma smithii* 3·25 2·30

706 Panama and El Salvador Flags

2004. Centenary of Panama Independence. Centenary of Panama—El Salvador Diplomatic Relations. Multicoloured.

2655 10col. Type **706** 5·50 3·00
2656 25col. Ship in canal 18·00 11·50

707 Stars

2004. Europe Day (2657). Enlargement of European Union (2658). Multicoloured.

2657 2col.70 Type **707** 2·75 1·90
2658 5col. Stars and map of Europe 3·50 2·30

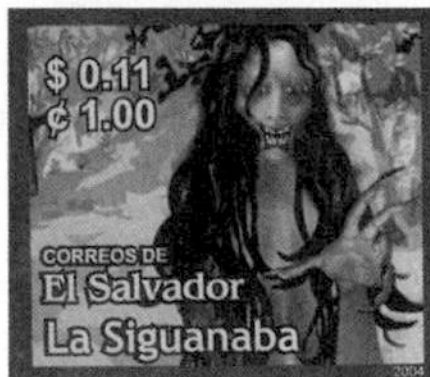

708 "La Siguanaba"

2004. Legends. Multicoloured.

2659 1col. Type **708** 95 70
2660 1col. "La Carreta Chillona" 95 70
2661 1col.60 "El Cipitio" 1·60 1·20
2662 1col.60 "Justo Juez de la Noche" 1·60 1·20

709 Flasks

2004. Centenary of Pharmaceutical College. Litho.

2663 **709** 10col. multicoloured 4·00 2·50

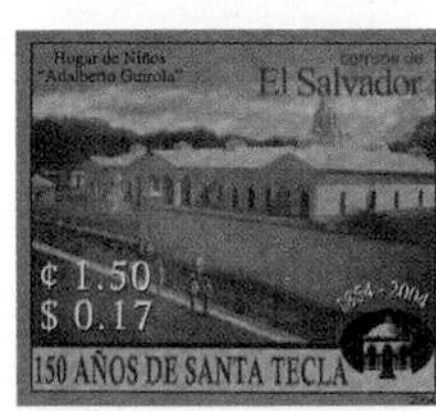

710 Adalberto Guirola Children's Home

2004. 150th Anniv of Santa Tecla (town). Multicoloured.

2664 1col.50 Type **710** 70 45
2664a 4col. Second Avenue 2·20 1·60

711 Wilbur and Orville Wright

2004. Centenary of Powered Flight (2003). Aviation pioneers. Multicoloured.

2665 1col.50 Type **711** 70 45
2666 1col.50 Alberto Santos Dumont 70 45
2667 1col.50 Louis Bleriot 70 45
2668 1col.50 Glenn Curtiss 70 45
2669 1col.50 Hugo Junkers 70 45
2670 4col. Charles Lindbergh 2·20 1·60
2671 4col. Amelia Earhart 2·20 1·60
2672 4col. Chuck Yeagar 2·20 1·60
2673 4col. Robert With 2·20 1·60
2674 4col. Richard Rutan and Jeana Yeagar 2·20 1·60

MS2675 70×93 mm. 4col. Wilbur and Orville Wright (34×40 mm) 3·00 3·00

712 The Nativity

2004. Christmas. Multicoloured.

2676 1col.50 Type **712** 70 45
2677 2col.50 Shepherd and star 1·80 1·20
2678 4col. Three Wise Men 2·20 1·60
2679 5col. Flight into Egypt 2·40 1·80

713 *Akko rossi*

2004. America. Fauna. Multicoloured.

2680 1col.40 Type **713** 65 40
2681 2col.20 *Chromodoris sphoni* 1·60 1·20

714 Masthead

2005. 90th Anniv of *La Prensa* Newspaper.

2682 **714** 25col. multicoloured 24·00 18·00

715 Metropolitan Cathedral, San Salvador

2005. 25th Death Anniv of Oscar Arnulfo Romero (Archbishop of San Salvador). Multicoloured.

2683 2col.50 Type **715** 2·20 1·80
2684 5col. Archbishop Romero 3·00 2·30

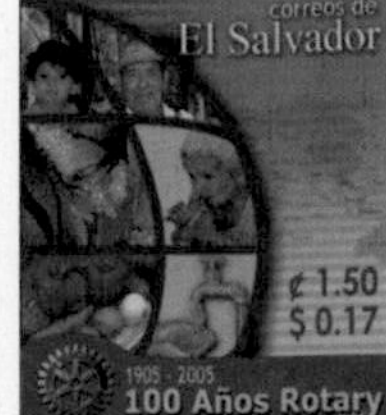

716 Globe enclosing People, Crops and Water Pipe

2005. Centenary of Rotary International. Multicoloured.

2685 1col.50 Type **716** 70 45

MS2686 92×69 mm. 4col. Children 3·00 2·75

717 La Union Port

2005. 150th Anniv of Puerto de San Carlos de La Union. Multicoloured.

2687 10col. Type **717** 5·50 4·50

MS2688 94×69 mm. 4col. Isla Pirigallo 2·20 1·60

718 Wrestling

2005. Central American Games, El Salvador. Multicoloured.

2689 1col.60 Type **718** 1·60 1·20
2690 2col.20 High jump 2·10 1·60
2691 2col.70 Karate 2·75 1·90
2692 4col. Speed skating 3·00 2·30

MS2693 94×70 mm. 4col. Karate, high jump and wrestling 3·00 2·75

719 Agustin Lara (Mexico)

2005. Latin American Musicians Commemorations. Multicoloured.

2694 1col.50 Type **719** 70 45
2695 1col.50 Pedro Infante (Mexico) 70 45
2696 1col.50 Libertad Lamarque (Argentina) 70 45
2697 1col.50 Carlos Gardel (Argentina) 70 45
2698 1col.50 Celia Cruz (Cuba) 70 45
2699 1col.50 Damaso Perez Prado (Cuba) 70 45
2700 1col.50 Daniel Santos (Puerto Rico) 70 45
2701 1col.50 Pedro Vargas (Mexico) 70 45
2702 1col.50 Beny More (Cuba) 70 45
2703 1col.50 Jorge Negrete (Mexico) 70 45

MS2704 94×69 mm. 4col. Guitar 3·00 2·75

720 Lilian Serpas

2005. Writers Commemorations. Multicoloured.

2705 1col. Type **720** 55 35
2706 1col. Oswaldo Escobar Velado 55 35
2707 4col. Alvaro Menendez Leal 2·20 1·60
2708 4col. Roque Daltomn 2·20 1·60

2709	5col. Italo Lopez Vallecillos	2·40	2·00
2710	5col. Pedro Geoffroy Rivas	2·40	2·00

721 Man holding Bread

2005. America. Struggle against Poverty. 60th Anniv of United Nations. Multicoloured.

2711	1col.50 Type **721**	70	45
2712	4col. Shanty town dwellings	2·20	1·60

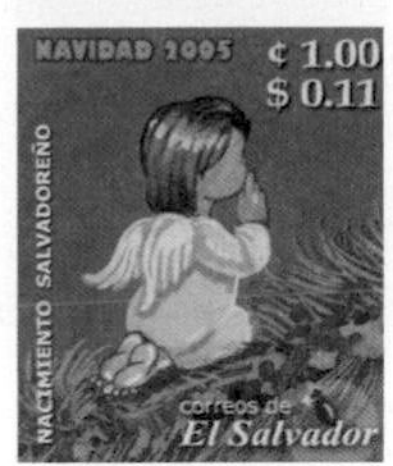

722 Girl Angel

2005. Christmas. Multicoloured.

2713	1col. Type **722**	55	35
2714	1col. Hen	55	35
2715	1col. Rooster	55	35
2716	1col. Boy Angel	55	35
2717	1col. Donkey	55	35
2718	1col. Mary and Jesus	55	35
2719	1col. Joseph	55	35
2720	1col. Cow	55	35
2721	1col. Camel and Wise Man	55	35
2722	1col. Camel and kneeling Wise Man	55	35
2723	1col. Wise Man wearing blue and camel	55	35
2724	1col. Shepherd	55	35
2725	1col. Woman and cooking pot	55	35
2726	1col. Carter	55	35
2727	1col. Musicians	55	35
2728	1col. Wedding	55	35
2729	1col. Kneeling woman and dog	55	35
2730	1col. Shepherd carrying lamb	55	35
2731	1col. Two women carrying pots	55	35
2732	1col. Water birds	55	35

Nos. 2713/32 were issued together, se-tenant, forming a composite design of the Nativity.

722a Linked Hands

2005. 70th Anniv of Diplomatic Relations with Japan. Multicoloured.

2732a	2col.50 Type **722a**	2·20	1·80
2732b	9col. Symbols of progress	4·00	3·50

723 Jose Mariano Calderon y San Martin

2006. Elections 2006. Multicoloured.

2733	10col. Type **723**	4·50	4·25
2734	25col. Miguel Jose de Castro y Lara	10·00	10·00

724 Stinson SM-1 Aircraft

2006. 75th Anniv of TACA Airlines. Multicoloured.

2735	5col. Type **724**	2·30	2·10
2736	5col. Airbus A-319	2·30	2·10

725 Statues

2006. Centenary of Santa Ana Cathedral. Multicoloured.

2737	1col.50 Type **725**	60	45
2738	5col. Cathedral façade	2·30	2·10

726 *Pteroglossus torquatus*

2006. Fauna and Flora. Multicoloured.

2739	1col. Type **726**	45	40
2740	1col. *Smyrna blomfildia* (inscr "blonfildia")	45	40
2741	1col. *Hypanartia dione*	45	40
2742	1col. *Sciurus variegatoides*	45	40
2743	1col. *Ceiba pentandra*	45	40
2744	1col. *Ramphastos sulfuratus*	45	40
2745	1col. *Eunica tatila*	45	40
2746	1col. *Catanephele numilia*	45	40
2747	1col. *Mephitis macroura*	45	40
2748	1col. *Enterolobium cyclocarpum*	45	40

727 Argentina '78

2006. World Cup Football Championship, Germany. Designs showing symbols of the country named. Multicoloured.

2749	2col.20 Type **727**	1·10	90
2750	2col.20 Spain '82	1·10	90
2751	2col.20 Mexico '86	1·10	90
2752	2col.20 Italy '90	1·10	90
2753	2col.20 USA '94	1·10	90
2754	2col.20 France '98	1·10	90
2755	2col.20 South Korea—Japan 2002	1·10	90
2756	2col.20 Germany 2006	1·10	90
MS2757	93×70 mm. 4col. Football (horiz)	2·00	2·00

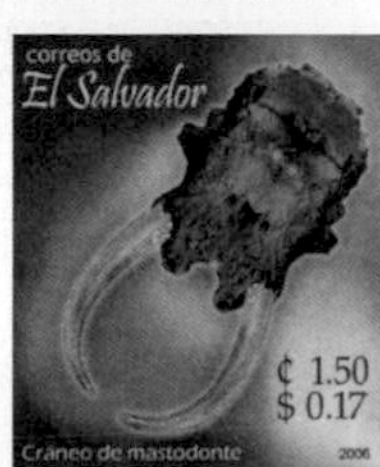

728 Mastodon Tusks

2006. Fossils. Multicoloured.

2758	1col.50 Type **728**	60	45
2759	1col.60 Giant sloth vertebra	65	50
2760	5col. Giant sloth jaw bone	2·30	2·10
2761	10col. Giant sloth foot bones	4·50	4·25

729 Volcano

2006. International Year of Deserts and Desertification. Multicoloured.

2762	1col.50 Type **729**	60	45

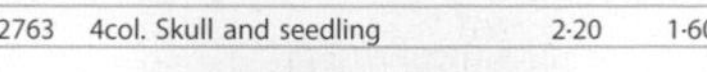

2763	4col. Skull and seedling	2·20	1·60

730 Woman in Kitchen

2006. America. Energy Conservation. Mult.

2764	1col.50 Type **730**	60	45
2765	4col. Light bulb jumping from socket	2·20	1·60

731 Taipei 101 Tower

2006. National Celebration of the Chinese Republic in Taiwan. Multicoloured.

2766	9col. Type **731**	4·00	3·50
2767	10col. Residential area	4·50	4·25

732 Building

2006. Centenary of La Constancia Industries.

2768	**732** 25col. multicoloured	10·00	10·00

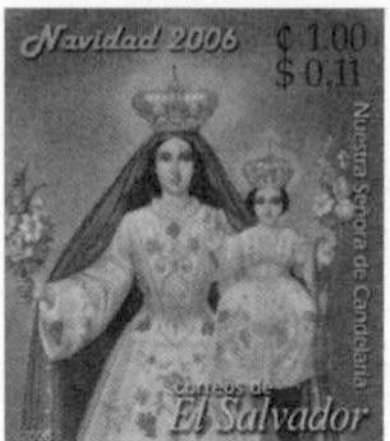

733 Nuestra Senora de Candelaria

2006. Christmas. Designs showing Madonna and Child. Multicoloured.

2769	1col. Type **733**	45	40
2770	1col.50 Nuestra Senora del Carmen	60	45
2771	5col. Maria Auxiliadora	2·30	2·10
2772	10col. Nuestra Senora de la Paz	4·50	4·25

Stamps are now designated in Dollars only and are listed as such.

734 Owl with Clipboard

2007. Census 2007.

2773	**734** 1c. multicoloured	10	10

735 Hand and Dove enclosing People

2007. Year of Social Peace.

2774	**735** $10 multicoloured	4·50	4·25

736 Robert Baden Powell (founder)

2007. Centenary of Scouting. Multicoloured.

2775	10c. Type **736**	10	10
2776	10c. Scouts	10	10

737 Juan Lindo (1841–1842)

2007. Early Presidents. Multicoloured.

2777	5c. Type **737**	10	10
2778	5c. Jose Escolastico Marin (1842)	10	10
2779	5c. Dionisio Villacorta (1842)	10	10
2780	5c. Juan Jose Guzman (1842–1844)	10	10
2781	5c. Fermin Palacios (1844, 1845, 1846)	10	10
2782	5c. Francisco Malespin (1844)	10	10
2783	5c. Joaquin Eufrasio Guzman (1844–1845; 1845–1846; 1859)	10	10
2784	5c. Eugenio Aguilar (1846–1848)	10	10
2785	5c. Tomas Medina (1848)	10	10
2786	5c. Jose Felix Quiroz (1848, 1851)	10	10

738 *Apogon dovii*

2007. Coral Reef Fauna. Sheet 227×100 mm containing T 738 and similar horiz designs. Multicoloured.

MS2787	10c.×10, Type **738**; *Cirrhitus rivulatus*; *Holacanthus passer*; *Acanthurus xanthopterus*; *Thalassoma lucasanum*; *Diodon holocantus*; *Stegastes flavilatus*; *Amphiaster insignis*; *Hypselodoris agassizi* (inscr 'agassizzi'); *Cypraecassis coarctata*	1·10	1·10

The stamps and margins of **MS**2787 form a composite design of a coral reef.

739 Printing Press

2007. 40th Anniv of El Mundo Newspaper.

2788	**739** $5 multicoloured	2·20	1·60

740 Terracota Figure, Chalchuapa

2007. Archaeology. Multicoloured.

2789	25c. Type **740**	15	10
2790	25c. Sacrificial stone (Tazamul), Chalchuapa	15	10
2791	25c. Mayan village under the ash of a volcano, Joya de Ceren	15	10

2792 25c. San Andres Acropolis, La Libertad 15 10

741 Don Quixote and Sancho Panza

2007. America. Education for All. Novels. Multicoloured.
2793 $1 Type **741** (*El Ingenioso Hidalgo Don Quijote de la Mancha* by Miguel de Cervantes Saavedra) 45 40
2794 $1 Crucified Christ (*El Cristo Negro* by Salvador Efrain Salazar Arrue (Salarrue)) 45 40

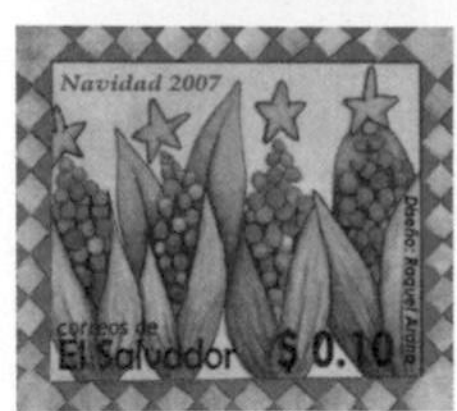

742 Star topped Plants

2007. Christmas.
2795 10c. Type **742** 10 10
2796 10c. Presents, teddy and tree 10 10
2797 10c. Candles 10 10
2798 10c. Decorating the tree 10 10

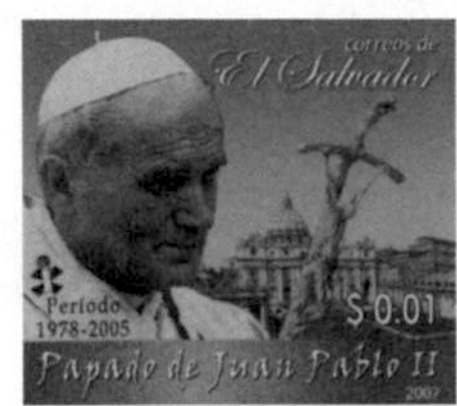

743 Pope John Paul II

2007. Popes John Paul II and Benedict XVI. Multicoloured.
2799 1c. Type **743** 10 10
2800 10c. Pope Benedict XVI 10 10

744 *Bombycilla cedrorum* (cedar waxwing)

2007. Birds. Multicoloured.
2801 10c. Type **744** 20 10
2802 10c. *Colaptes auratus* (northern flicker) 20 10
2803 10c. *Anas clypeata* (northern shoveler) 20 10
2804 10c. *Falco peregrinus* (peregrine falcon) 20 10
MS2805 93×70 mm. 50c. *Passerina ciris* 1·00 1·00

745 Fire Fighters

2008. 125th Anniv of Fire Fighters. Multicoloured.
2806 15c. Type **745** 25 15
2807 15c. Modern fire appliance 25 15
2808 15c. Early fire appliance 25 15
2809 15c. Rescue vehicle 25 15

746 Emblems

2008. Lions' Forum.
2810 **746** 1c. multicoloured 10 10

2008. Presidents. As T **737**. Multicoloured.
2811 10c. Francisco Duenas 20 10
2812 10c. Jose Maria San Martin 20 10
2813 10c. Rafael Campo 20 10
2814 10c. Gerardo Barrios
2815 10c. Rafael Zaldivar 20 10
2816 10c. Fernando Figueroa 20 10
2817 10c. Francisco Menendez 20 10
2818 10c. Carlos Ezeta 20 10
2819 10c. Rafael Antonio Gurierrez 20 10
2820 10c. Tomas Regalado 20 10
2821 10c. Pedro Jose Escalon 20 10
2822 10c. Manuel Enrique Araujo 20 10
2823 10c. Carlos Melendez 20 10
2824 10c. Alfonso Quinonez Molina 20 10
2825 10c. Jorge Melendez 20 10
2826 10c. Pio Romero Bosque 20 10
2827 10c. Arturo Araujo 20 10
2828 10c. Maximliano Hernandez Martinez 20 10
2829 10c. Salvador Castaneda Castro 20 10
2830 10c. Oscar Osorio 20 10

747 Symbols of Israel

2008. 60th Anniv of El Salvador—Israel Diplomatic Relations.
2831 **747** 10c. multicoloured 20 10

747a Weight Lifting

2008. Olympic Games, Beijing. Multicoloured.
2832 20c. Type **747a** 40 20
2833 20c. Athletics 40 20
2834 20c. Cycling 40 20
2835 20c. Tennis 40 20
MS2836 93×70 mm. 50c. Judo and wrestling 1·00 1·00

748 Studio and Equipment

2008. 82nd Anniv of Radio. Multicoloured.
2837 25c. Type **748** 50 30
2838 65c. Modern mixing desk 1·20 70

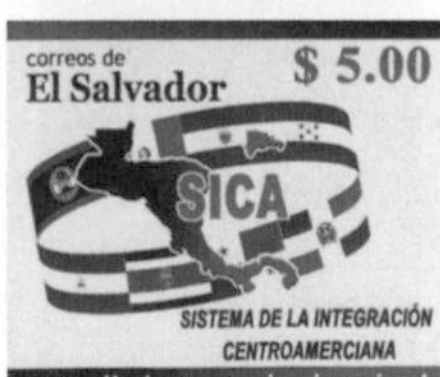

749 Emblem

2008. SICA–Central American Integration.
2839 **749** $5 multicoloured 2·40 1·70

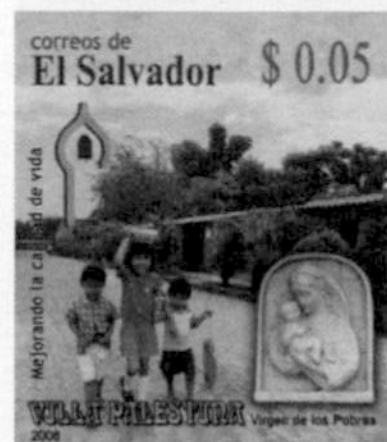

750 Children and *Virgen de los Pobres*

2008. Villa Palestina (housing development)–Improving Quality of Life.
2840 **750** 5c. multicoloured 15 10

751 House and Figure

2008. Fernando Llort (artist). Sheet 218×88 mm containing T **751** and similar horiz designs. Multicoloured.
MS2841 20c.×10, Type **751**; Pyramid shape, figure and llama; Trees and house; Trees, mother and child; Pyramid shape and turkey; Road and bird; Horse rider; Women; Seated figure and houses; Trees, water pump, woman and houses 1·80 1·80

The stamps of **MS**2841 form a composite design of the painting.

752 Emblem

2008. 25th Anniv of FUSADES (Economic and Social Development Foundation).
2842 **752** $1 multicoloured 1·30 75

753 Figure and 'JUVENTUD'

2008. Ibero-American Summit. Youth Development.
2843 **753** $1 multicoloured 1·30 75

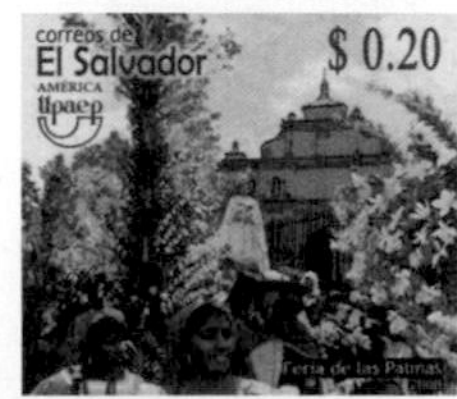

754 Fiesta de las Palmas

2008. America. Festivals. Multicoloured.
2844 20c. Type **754** 45 20
2845 75c. Fiestas del Divino Salvador del Mundo 1·20 70

755 '150' and Emblem

2009. 150th Anniv of Ministry of Foreign Affairs.
2846 **755** 10c. multicoloured 30 20

756 Ballot Box

2009. Supreme Court and Presidential Elections.
2847 **756** 10c. multicoloured 30 20

757 Galileo Galilei

2009. International Year of Astronomy. Multicoloured.
2848 25c. Type **757** 50 30
2849 25c. Galilean moons 50 30
2850 25c. Observatory, San Juan 50 30
2851 25c. Meade 10 inch Schmidt–Cassegrain telescope 50 30

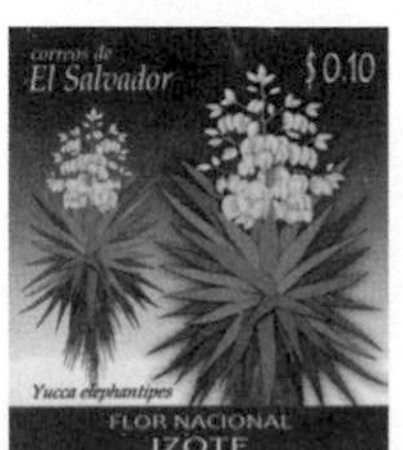

758 *Yucca elephantipes* (Izote)

2009. Arms, Flora and Fauna. Two sheets, each 160×99 mm containing T **758** and similar vert designs. Multicoloured.
MS2852 10c.×8, Type **758**; Arms, La Paz; Arms, Cabanas; Arms, San Vicente; Arms, Usulutan; Arms, San Miguel; Arms, Morazan; Arms, La Union 2·50 2·50
MS2853 10c.×8, *Eumomota superciliosa* (Torogoz); Arms, Ahuachapan; Arms, Santa Ana; Arms, Sonsonate; Arms, La Libertad; Arms, Chalatenango; Arms, San Salvador; Arms, Cuscatlan 2·50 2·50

759 Izalco, Sonsonate

2009. Tourism. Multicoloured.
2854 5c. Type **759** 20 10
2855 5c. Rio Sapo, Arambala 20 10
2856 5c. Caracol cascade, Arambala 20 10
2857 5c. Playitas, la Union 20 10
2858 5c. Ilobasco, Cabanas 20 10
2859 5c. Jaltepeque estuary, Costa del sol 20 10
2860 5c. Church, Guatajigua, Morazan 20 10
2861 5c. San Vicente volcano 20 10

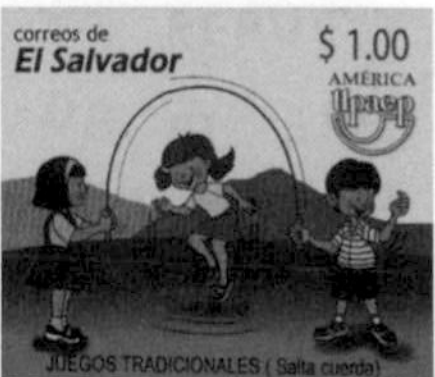

760 Skipping

2009. America. Games. Multicoloured.
2862 1col. Type **760** 1·30 75
2863 1col. Hopscotch 1·30 75

761 Bible and Candles

2009. Christmas. Multicoloured.

2864	10c. Type **761**	40	20
2865	10c. Mary and Jesus	40	20
2866	10c. Joseph	40	20
2867	10c. Three Wise Men	40	20

Nos. 2864/7 were printed, se-tenant, each strip forming a composite design.

ACKNOWLEDGEMENT OF RECEIPT STAMP

AR53

1897

AR264	**AR53**	5c. green	40	

EXPRESS LETTER

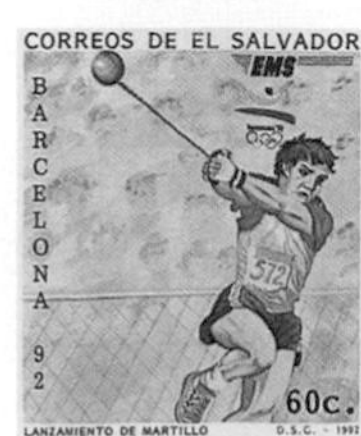

E547 Throwing the Hammer

1992. Olympic Games, Barcelona. Mult.

E2199	60c. Type E **547**	55	35
E2200	80c. Volleyball	65	45
E2201	90c. Putting the shot (decathlon)	1·10	70
E2202	2col.20 Long jumping	1·80	80
E2203	3col. Gymnastics (vaulting)	2·75	1·10
E2204	5col. Gymnastics (floor exercise)	4·25	1·80

OFFICIAL STAMPS

1896. Stamps of 1896 (first issue) optd FRANQUEO OFICIAL in oval.

O170	**37**	1c. blue	25	
O171	**37**	2c. brown	25	
O172	**37**	3c. green	1·80	
O173	**37**	5c. olive	25	
O174	**37**	10c. yellow	25	
O175	**37**	12c. blue	50	
O176	**37**	15c. violet	25	
O177	**37**	20c. red	1·80	
O178	**37**	24c. red	25	
O179	**37**	30c. orange	1·80	
O180	**37**	50c. black	75	
O181	**37**	1p. red	50	

1896. Stamps of 1896 (second issue) optd FRANQUEO OFICIAL in oval.

O182	**38**	1c. green	25	
O183	**39**	2c. lake	25	
O184	**39**	3c. orange	25	
O185	**39**	5c. blue	25	
O186	**39**	10c. brown	25	
O187	**39**	12c. grey	40	
O188	**39**	15c. green	40	
O189	**39**	20c. red	40	
O190	**39**	24c. violet	40	
O191	**39**	30c. green	40	
O192	**39**	50c. orange	40	
O193	**39**	100c. blue	50	

1896. Stamps of 1895 (first issue) optd CORREOS DE EL SALVADOR DE OFICIO in circle and band.

O194	**37**	1c. blue	19·00	
O195	**37**	2c. brown	19·00	
O196	**37**	3c. green	19·00	
O197	**37**	5c. olive	19·00	
O198	**37**	10c. yellow	22·00	
O199	**37**	12c. blue	28·00	
O200	**37**	15c. violet	28·00	
O201	**37**	20c. red	28·00	
O202	**37**	24c. red	28·00	
O203	**37**	30c. orange	28·00	
O204	**37**	50c. black	38·00	
O205	**37**	1p. red	38·00	

1896. Stamps of 1896 (second issue) optd CORREOS DE EL SALVADOR DE OFICIO in circle and band.

O206	**38**	1c. green	15·00	
O207	**39**	2c. lake	15·00	
O208	**39**	3c. orange	15·00	
O209	**39**	5c. blue	15·00	
O210	**39**	10c. brown	15·00	
O211	**39**	12c. grey	28·00	
O212	**39**	15c. green	28·00	
O219	**39**	15c. on 24c. violet (No. 218)	15·00	
O213	**39**	20c. red	28·00	
O214	**39**	24c. violet	28·00	
O215	**39**	30c. green	28·00	
O216	**39**	50c. orange	28·00	
O217	**39**	100c. blue	28·00	

1897. Stamps of 1897 optd FRANQUEO OFICIAL in oval.

O232	1c. red	25	25
O233	2c. green	2·75	2·75
O234	3c. brown	2·30	2·00
O235	5c. orange	25	25
O236	10c. green	25	
O237	12c. blue	50	
O238	15c. black	50	1·30
O239	20c. grey	40	
O240	24c. yellow	40	
O241	30c. red	1·00	
O242	50c. violet	2·75	2·30
O243	100c. lake	3·75	

1897. Stamps of 1897 optd CORREOS DE EL SALVADOR DE OFICIO in circle and band.

O244	1c. red	15·00	15·00
O245	2c. green	15·00	15·00
O246	3c. brown	15·00	15·00
O247	5c. orange	15·00	15·00
O248	10c. green	18·00	18·00
O249	12c. blue		
O250	15c. black		
O251	20c. grey	30·00	
O252	24c. yellow	35·00	
O253	30c. red		
O254	50c. violet		
O255	100c. lake		

1898. Stamps of 1898 optd FRANQUEO OFICIAL in oval.

O288	**57**	1c. red	25	
O289	**57**	2c. red	25	
O290	**57**	3c. green	3·00	
O291	**57**	5c. green	25	
O292	**57**	10c. blue	25	
O293	**57**	12c. violet	3·00	
O294	**57**	13c. lake	40	
O295	**57**	20c. blue	25	
O296	**57**	24c. blue	25	
O297	**57**	26c. brown	40	
O298	**57**	50c. orange	25	
O299	**57**	1p. yellow	40	

1899. Stamps of 1899, with wheel opt as T 58 optd FRANQUEO OFICIAL in curved type.

O329	**59**	1c. brown	1·00	1·00
O330	**59**	2c. green	1·90	1·90
O331	**59**	3c. blue	1·00	1·00
O332	**59**	5c. orange	1·00	1·00
O333	**59**	10c. brown	1·30	1·30
O334	**59**	12c. green		
O335	**59**	13c. red	2·50	2·50
O336	**59**	24c. blue	50·00	50·00
O337	**59**	26c. red	1·30	1·30
O338	**59**	50c. red	2·50	2·50
O339	**59**	100c. violet	2·50	2·50

1900. Federation issue of 1897 optd CORREOS DE EL SALVADOR DE OFICIO in circle and band.

O355	**55**	1c. multicoloured	38·00	38·00
O356	**55**	5c. multicoloured	38·00	38·00

1900. Stamps of 1900, dated "1900", optd FRANQUEO OFICIAL in oval, and with or without shield opt T 66.

O448	**59**	1c. green (No. 438)	70	70
O449	**59**	2c. red	75	70
O450	**59**	3c. black	45	45
O451	**59**	5c. blue	45	45
O452	**59**	10c. blue	1·30	1·30
O453	**59**	12c. green	1·30	1·30
O454	**59**	13c. brown	1·30	1·30
O455	**59**	24c. black	90	1·30
O461	**59**	26c. brown	1·00	1·00
O462	**59**	50c. red	1·30	1·10

1903. As T 70, but inscr "FRANQUEO OFICIAL" across statue.

O497	1c. green	55	35
O498	2c. red	55	25
O499	3c. orange	1·80	1·40
O500	5c. blue	55	25
O501	10c. purple	90	55
O502	13c. brown	90	55
O503	15c. brown	6·25	3·00
O504	24c. red	55	55
O505	50c. brown	90	35
O506	100c. blue	90	1·40

1905. Nos. O500/502 surch with new value and two black circles.

O518	2c. on 5c. blue	7·00	5·75
O519	3c. on 5c. blue		
O520	3c. on 10c. purple	11·50	7·75
O521	3c. on 13c. brown	1·70	1·40

1905. No. O450 optd 1905.

O558	3c. black	3·75	3·25

1906. Nos. O449/50 optd 1906.

O567	2c. red	22·00	20·00
O568	3c. black	3·00	2·50

1906. As T 89, but inscr "FRANQUEO OFICIAL" at foot of portrait.

O582	1c. black and green	25	15
O583	2c. black and red	25	15
O584	3c. black and yellow	25	15
O585	5c. black and blue	25	1·30
O586	10c. black and violet	25	15
O587	13c. black and brown	25	15
O588	15c. black and red	40	15
O589	24c. black and red	50	65
O590	50c. black and orange	50	2·50
O591	100c. black and blue	65	7·75

1908. As T 91, but inscr "FRANQUEO OFICIAL" below building.

O611	1c. black and green	15	15
O612	2c. black and red	15	15
O613	3c. black and yellow	15	15
O614	5c. black and blue	15	15
O615	10c. black and violet	40	40
O616	13c. black and violet	40	40
O617	15c. black and sepia	40	40
O618	24c. black and red	40	40
O619	50c. black and yellow	40	40
O620	100c. black and blue	65	40

These stamps also exist optd with shield, Type **66**.

1910. As T 99, but inscr "OFICIAL" below portrait.

O655	2c. black and green	25	25
O656	3c. black and orange	25	25
O657	4c. black and red	25	25
O658	5c. black and violet	25	25
O659	6c. black and red	25	25
O660	10c. black and violet	25	25
O661	12c. black and blue	25	25
O662	17c. black and green	25	25
O663	19c. black and brown	25	25
O664	29c. black and brown	25	25
O665	50c. black and yellow	25	25
O666	100c. black and blue	25	25

1911. Stamps of 1900, dated "1900", optd OFICIAL and black circles or surch also.

O667	1c. green	20	20
O668	3c. on 13c. brown	20	20
O669	5c. on 10c. green	20	20
O670	10c. green	20	20
O671	12c. green	20	20
O672	13c. brown	20	20
O673	50c. on 10c. green	20	20
O674	1col. on 13c. brown	20	20

O112

1914. Words of background in green, shield and word "PROVISIONAL" in black.

O675	**O112**	2c. brown	20	20
O676	**O112**	3c. yellow	20	20
O677	**O112**	5c. blue	20	20
O678	**O112**	10c. red	20	20
O679	**O112**	12c. green	20	20
O680	**O112**	17c. violet	20	20
O681	**O112**	50c. brown	20	20
O682	**O112**	100c. brown	20	20

O113

1915

O683	**O113**	2c. green	20	20
O684	**O113**	3c. orange	20	20

1915. Stamps of 1915, with opt 1915 optd OFICIAL.

O685	**91**	1c. grey (No. 675)	50	40
O686	**91**	2c. red	50	40
O687	**91**	5c. blue	50	50
O688	**91**	6c. blue	80	60
O689	**91**	10c. yellow	50	40
O690	**91**	12c. brown	1·10	1·00
O691	**91**	50c. purple	1·20	1·00
O692	**91**	100c. brown	2·50	2·20

1916. Stamps of 1916 optd OFICIAL.

O694	**113**	1c. green	55	1·10
O695	**113**	2c. red	2·50	2·50
O696	**113**	5c. blue	1·90	2·50
O697	**113**	6c. violet	70	1·10
O698	**113**	10c. brown	70	1·10
O699	**113**	12c. purple	3·00	4·25
O700	**113**	17c. orange	70	1·10
O701	**113**	25c. brown	70	1·10
O702	**113**	29c. black	70	1·10
O703	**113**	50c. grey	70	1·10

1922. Stamps of 1921 optd OFICIAL.

O736	**130**	1c. green	20	10
O737	-	2c. black	20	10
O738	**131**	5c. orange	30	20
O739	**132**	6c. red	20	10
O740	**133**	10c. blue	40	30
O741	-	25c. green	1·10	50
O742	**135**	60c. sepia	1·40	80
O743	-	1col. sepia	1·50	90

1925. Stamps of 1924 optd OFICIAL.

O768	**141**	1c. purple	30	10
O769	-	2c. red	65	10
O770	-	5c. black	65	20
O765		6c. blue	7·50	6·25
O766	**146**	10c. orange	1·20	50
O767	**150**	1col. blue and green	3·25	1·80

1947. Stamps of 1947 optd OFICIAL.

O959	**215**	1c. red	80·00	40·00
O960	-	2c. yellow	80·00	40·00
O961	-	5c. grey	80·00	40·00
O962	-	10c. yellow	80·00	40·00
O963	-	20c. green	80·00	40·00
O964	-	50c. black	80·00	40·00

1964. No. O963 further surch 1 CTS. X X.

O1198	1c. on 20c. green		

OFFICIAL REGISTRATION STAMP

1897. Registration stamp optd FRANQUEO OFICIAL in oval.

OR268	**R54**	10c. blue	40	

PARCEL POST STAMPS

P35 Hermes

1895

P127	**P35**	5c. orange	75	1·30
P128	**P35**	10c. blue	75	1·30
P129	**P35**	15c. red	75	1·90
P130	**P35**	20c. orange	75	1·90
P131	**P35**	50c. green	75	1·90

POSTAGE DUE STAMPS

D33

1895

D107	**D33**	1c. green	25	25
D108	**D33**	2c. green	25	25
D109	**D33**	3c. green	25	25
D110	**D33**	5c. green	25	25
D111	**D33**	10c. green	25	25
D112	**D33**	15c. green	25	65
D113	**D33**	25c. green	25	75
D114	**D33**	50c. green	75	1·30

1896

D150	1c. red	25	40
D151	2c. red	25	40
D152	3c. red	50	50
D153	5c. red	65	65
D154	10c. red	65	65
D155	15c. red	75	25
D156	25c. red	75	25
D157	50c. red	75	25

1897

D256	1c. blue	25	25
D257	2c. blue	25	25
D258	3c. blue	25	40
D259	5c. blue	25	40
D260	10c. blue	40	65
D261	15c. blue	40	65
D262	25c. blue	25	75
D263	50c. blue	25	90

1898

D302	1c. violet	25	25
D303	2c. violet	25	25
D304	3c. violet	25	40
D305	5c. violet	25	40
D306	10c. violet	40	65
D307	15c. violet	40	65
D308	25c. violet	25	75
D309	50c. violet	25	90

1899. Optd with T 35.

D347	1c. orange	1·00	1·00
D348	2c. orange	1·00	1·00
D349	3c. orange	1·00	1·00
D350	5c. orange	1·40	1·40
D351	10c. orange	2·20	2·20
D352	15c. orange	2·20	2·20
D353	25c. orange	2·50	2·50
D354	50c. orange	3·25	3·25

D72 Columbus Monument

1903

D507	**D72**	1c. green	2·50	2·20
D508	**D72**	2c. red	4·25	3·00
D509	**D72**	3c. orange	4·25	3·00
D510	**D72**	5c. blue	4·25	3·00
D511	**D72**	10c. purple	4·25	3·00
D512	**D72**	25c. green	4·25	3·00

1908. Stamps of 1907 optd Deficiencia de franqueo.

D623	**91**	1c. black and green	75	65
D624	**91**	2c. black and red	65	50
D625	**91**	3c. black & yellow	75	75
D626	**91**	5c. black & blue	1·50	1·00
D627	**91**	10c. black & violet	2·30	2·00

1908. Stamps of 1907 optd DEFICIENCIA DE FRANQUEO.

D628		1c. black and green	50	50
D629		2c. black and red	65	65
D632	-	3c. blk & yell (No. O613)	1·50	1·30
D630		5c. black and blue	1·00	95
D631		10c. black & mauve	2·00	1·90

1910. As T 99, but inscr "FRANQUEO DEFICIENTE" below portrait.

D655	1c. black and brown	25	25
D656	2c. black and green	25	25
D657	3c. black and yellow	25	25
D658	4c. black and red	25	25
D659	5c. black and violet	25	25
D660	12c. black and blue	25	25
D661	24c. black and red	25	25

REGISTRATION STAMP

R54 Gen. R. A. Gutierrez

1897

R266	**R54**	10c. lake	40	40

Pt. 12

EQUATORIAL GUINEA

The former Spanish Overseas Provinces of Fernando Poo and Rio Mundi united on 12 October 1968, to become the Republic of Equatorial Guinea.

1968. 100 centimos = 1 peseta.
1973. 100 centimos = 1 ekuele (plural:bipkwele).
1985. 100 centimos = 1 franc (CFA).

1 Clasped Hands

1968. Independence.

1	**1**	1p. sepia, gold and blue	10	10
2	**1**	1p.50 sepia, gold & green	20	10
3	**1**	6p. sepia, gold and red	35	15

2 President Macias Nguema

1970. 1st Anniv (12.10.69) of Independence.

4	**2**	50c. red, purple & orange	10	10
5	**2**	1p. purple, green & mauve	10	10
6	**2**	1p.50 green and purple	15	10
7	**2**	2p. green and buff	20	10
8	**2**	2p.50 blue and green	20	15
9	**2**	10p. purple, blue & brown	1·00	25
10	**2**	25p. brown, black & grey	2·30	35

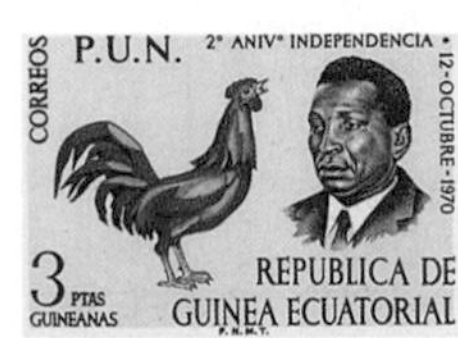

3 Pres. Macias Nguema and Cockerel

1971. 2nd Anniv of Independence.

11	**3**	3p. multicoloured	20	10
12	**3**	5p. multicoloured	30	15
13	**3**	10p. multicoloured	65	20
14	**3**	25p. multicoloured	1·60	45

5 Flaming Torch

1972. 3rd Year of Independence.

17	**5**	50p. multicoloured	1·50	50

Issues of 1972–79. These are listed at the end of Equatorial Guinea in the Appendix.

6 Pres. Macias Nguema, Hands and Fruit

1979. 4th Anniv of Independence (1972). Mult.

18	1p.50 Type **6**	10	10
19	2p. Classroom	10	10
20	3p. Soldiers and sailors on parade	40	25
21	4p. As No. 19	45	30
22	5p. As No. 20	80	40

7 Party Emblem

1979. United National Workers' Party.

23	**7**	1p. multicoloured	10	10
24	**7**	1p.50 multicoloured	10	10
25	**7**	2p. multicoloured	20	15
26	**7**	4p. multicoloured	25	20
27	**7**	5p. multicoloured	45	25

8 Ekuele Coin

1979. 5th Anniv of Independence (1973) (1st issue).

28	**8**	1e. multicoloured	1·30	50

9 State Palace

1979. Independence (1973) (2nd issue). National Enterprises. Multicoloured.

29	1e. Bata harbour	50	25
30	1e.50 Type **9**	20	15
31	2e. Bata Central Bank	30	20
32	2e.50 Nguema Biyogo bridge	35	25
33	3e. Pres. Nguema and scenes as on Nos. 29/32	40	30

10 Pres. Macias Nguema

1979. 3rd Congress of United National Workers' Party.

34	**10**	1e.50 multicoloured	50	25

11 Salvador Ndongo Ekang

1979. Martyrs of Independence. Mult.

35	1e. Enrique Nvo	10	10
36	1e.50 Type **11**	15	10
37	2e. Acacio Mane	20	10

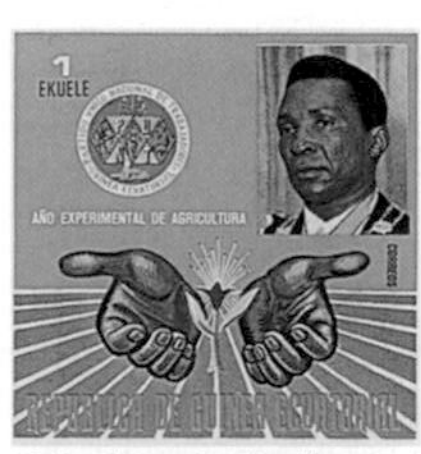

12 Hands cupping Seedling

1979. Experimental Agriculture Year.

38	**12**	1e. multicoloured	65	30
39	**12**	1e.50 multicoloured	1·10	50

12a Boy and Bells

1980. Christmas.

39b	**12a**	25b. multicoloured	3·50	1·00

13 Obiang Esono Nguema

1981. National Heroes.

40	**13**	5b. blue, yellow & black	15	10
41	-	15b. purple, brown & blk	20	10
42	-	25b. red, grey and black	50	10
43	-	35b. green, pink & black	75	25
44	-	50b. blue, green & black	1·00	40
45	-	100b. multicoloured	2·00	75

DESIGNS: 15b. Fernando Nvara Engonga; 25b. Ela Edjodjomo Mangue; 35b. Lt.-Col. Obiang Nguema Mbasogo; 50b. Hipolito Micha Eworo; 100b. National coat of arms.

14 King Juan Carlos and Pres. Obiang Nguema

1981. Visit of King and Queen of Spain. Mult.

46	50b. Royal couple and President at reception	1·20	20
47	100b. Official welcoming ceremony at airport	2·75	55
48	150b. Type **14**	3·00	75

15 Choristers

1981. Christmas.

49	**15**	100b. multicoloured	1·20	80
50	-	150b. brown, blue & yellow	1·80	1·20

DESIGN: 150b. Three Kings on camels and head of African.

16 Pope John Paul II

1982. Papal Visit. Multicoloured.

51	100b. Arms of Pope and Equatorial Guinea	1·30	50
52	200b. President Obiang Nguema greeting Pope	3·25	1·40
53	300b. Type **16**	4·75	2·30

17 Footballer and Emblem

1982. World Cup Football Championship, Spain. Multicoloured.

54 40b. Type **17** 60 25
55 60b. Footballer and championship mascot 1·00 40
56 100b. World Cup and footballer 1·80 75
57 200b. Footballers 3·50 1·40

18 Stars

1982. Christmas. Multicoloured.

58 100b. Type **18** 1·00 40
59 200b. King offering gift 2·20 75

19 Gorilla

1982. Protected Animals. Multicoloured.

60 40b. Type **19** 80 20
61 60b. Hippopotamus 1·50 45
62 80b. African brush-tailed porcupine 1·90 60
63 120b. Leopard 2·75 90

20 Postal Runner

1983. World Communications Year. Mult.

64 150b. Type **20** 1·60 80
65 200b. Drummer and microwave station 2·20 1·50

21 Tropical Flowers

1983. Multicoloured

66 300b. Type **21** 3·00 1·20
67 400b. Forest 4·00 1·70

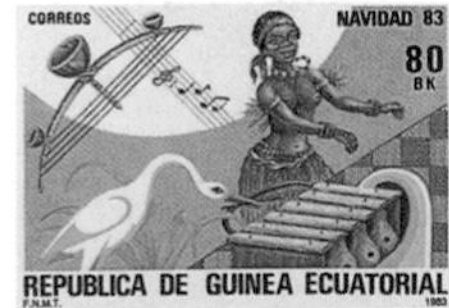

22 Great Egret, Dancer and Musical Instruments

1983. Christmas. Multicoloured.

68 80b. Type **22** 1·20 40
69 100b. Holy Family 1·40 50

23 Annobon and Bioko

1984. Constitution of State Powers. Multicoloured.

70 50b. Type **23** 1·30 65
71 100b. Mainland regions 2·30 1·10

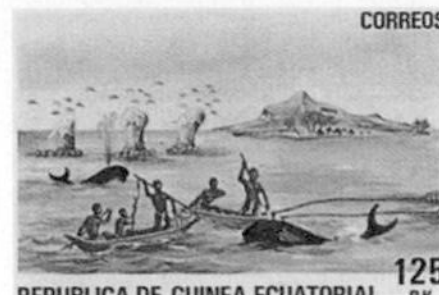

24 Hunting Sperm Whales

1984. Marine Resources. Multicoloured.

72 125b. Type **24** 4·50 1·70
73 150b. Capturing a turtle 4·00 1·10

25 Pawpaw

1984. World Food Day. Multicoloured.

74 60b. Type **25** 2·00 75
75 80b. Malanga 2·60 1·10

26 Mother and Child

1984. Christmas. Multicoloured.

76 60b. Type **26** 1·00 45
77 100b. Musical instruments 1·90 1·00

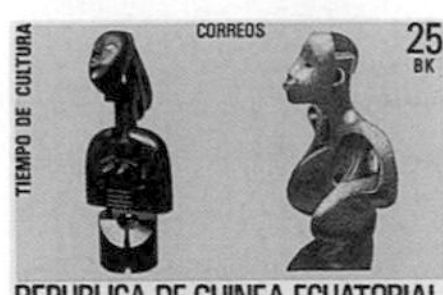

27 "Black Gazelle" and "Anxiety" (wood carvings)

1985. Art.

78 **27** 25b. multicoloured 30 20
79 - 30b. multicoloured 40 25
80 - 60b. multicoloured 1·00 45
81 - 75b. black, red & yellow 1·40 65
82 - 100b. multicoloured 1·90 85
83 - 150b. multicoloured 3·00 1·20

DESIGNS—HORIZ: 30b. "Black Gazelle" (different) and "Woman" (wood carvings); 150b. "Man and Woman" and "Bust of Woman" (wood carvings). VERT: 60b. "Man and Woman" (different); 75b. Poster; 100b. "Mother and Child" (wood carving).

28 Mission Emblem

1985. Immaculate Conception Mission. Centenary. Multicoloured.

84 50f. Type **28** 50 15
85 60f. Nun teaching children in African village 75 25
86 80f. First Guinean nuns 1·10 35
87 125f. Nuns landing on Bata beach 1·70 75

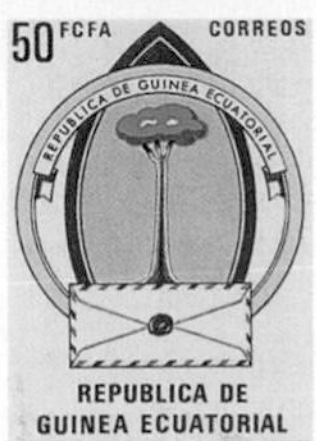

29 Postal Emblem

1985. Postal Service. Multicoloured.

88 50f. Type **29** 1·10 35
89 80f. Jose Mavule Ndjong, first Guinean postman 1·80 60

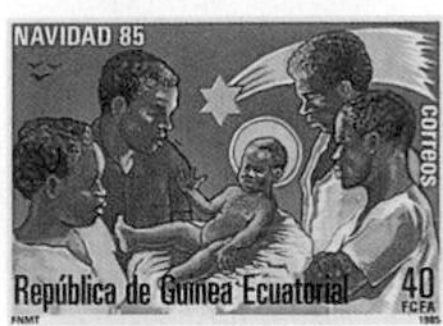

30 Nativity

1985. Christmas. Multicoloured.

90 40f. Type **30** 70 35
91 70f. Musicians, dancer and woman with baby 1·70 65

31 Crab and Snail

1986. Nature Protection. Multicoloured.

92 15f. Type **31** 1·00 25
93 35f. Butterflies, bees, chaffinch and grey-headed kingfisher 4·50 1·30
94 45f. Plants 2·50 1·00
95 65f. Men working on cacao crop 3·50 1·00

32 Mekuyo Dancers

1986. Folk Customs. Multicoloured.

96 10f. Type **32** 25 10
97 50f. Kokom dancers 75 30
98 65f. Bisila girl 1·10 35
99 80f. Ndong-Mba man 1·40 60

33 Footballers and Emblem

1986. World Cup Football Championship, Mexico. Designs showing various footballing scenes.

100 **33** 50f. multicoloured 30 20
101 - 100f. multicoloured 70 30
102 - 150f. mult (vert) 1·00 50
103 - 200f. mult (vert) 1·40 60

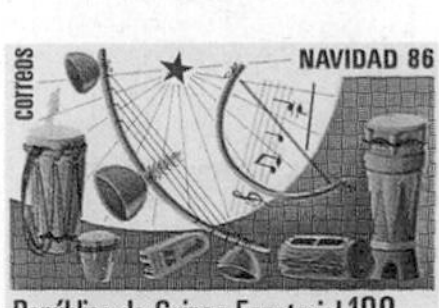

34 Musical Instruments

1986. Christmas. Multicoloured.

104 100f. Type **34** 1·40 45
105 150f. Mother breast-feeding baby 1·60 75

35 Map and Member Countries' Flag

1986. Union of Central African States Conference. Multicoloured.

106 80f. Type **35** 1·20 40
107 100f. Maps 1·40 55

36 Coins and Hen with Chick

1987. Campaign against Hunger.

108 **36** 60f. purple, orange & blk 50 20
109 - 80f. blue, orange & black 1·10 45
110 - 100f. brown, orange & blk 1·40 55

DESIGNS: 80f. Coins and fish in net; 100f. Coins and ear of wheat.

37 Dove and Open Door

1987. International Peace Year. Mult.

111 100f. Type **37** 80 40
112 200f. Hands holding dove 1·70 80

38 Night Sky and Envelope

1987. World Stamp Day. Multicoloured.

113 150f. Type **38** 1·20 50
114 300f. Banner of national colours and envelope 2·30 1·00

39 Mother and Child

1987. Christmas. Wood Sculptures. Mult.

115 80f. Type **39** 1·20 45
116 100f. Mother and child (different) 1·60 65

40 Man climbing Palm Tree

1988. International Labour Day. Mult.

117 50f. Type **40** 60 30
118 75f. Woman with catch of fish 85 45
119 150f. Chopping down tree 1·80 90

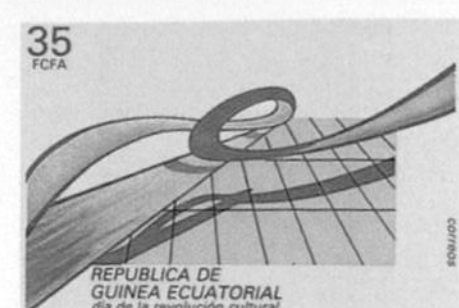

41 Ribbons

1988. Cultural Revolution Day. Mult.

120	35f. Type **41**	25	15
121	50f. Cubes and sphere	40	25
122	100f. Stylized dove	80	40

42 Party Badge

1988. 1st Anniv of Democratic Party of Equatorial Guinea. Multicoloured.

123	40f. Type **42**	30	20
124	75f. Torch and concentric circles (horiz)	55	35
125	100f. Torch (horiz)	80	40

43 Musician

1988. Christmas. Multicoloured.

126	50f. Type **43**	45	25
127	100f. Mother, child and stars	90	45

44 Lorry loaded with Logs

1989. 20th Anniv of Independence. Mult.

128	10f. Type **44**	50	20
129	35f. Traditional folk gathering	15	40
130	45f. President at official function	1·20	55

45 Bathers at Ilachi Waterfall

1989. Water. Multicoloured.

131	15f. Type **45**	40	20
132	25f. La Selva waterfall	65	30
133	60f. Boy drinking from green coconut and youths in water	1·30	70

46 Palace of Congresses

1989. 1st Democratic Party Congress. Mult.

134	25f. Type **46**	30	10
135	35f. Torch (party emblem) (vert)	50	20
136	40f. Pres. Obiang Nguema Mbasogo (vert)	55	20

47 Stringed Instrument

1989. Christmas. Multicoloured.

137	150f. Type **47**	1·60	65
138	300f. Mother with child and drummer (horiz)	3·00	1·40

48 Sir Robert Baden-Powell (founder)

1990. Boy Scout Movement. Multicoloured.

139	100f. Type **48**	1·30	55
140	250f. Scout saluting	3·25	1·50
141	350f. Scout with bugle	4·50	2·00

49 Player and Map of Italy

1990. World Cup Football Championship, Italy. Multicoloured.

142	100f. Type **49**	60	30
143	250f. Goalkeeper and ball in net	1·50	80
144	350f. Trophy and globe	1·90	1·00

50 Drums and Horn (Ndowe tribe)

1990. Musical Instruments. Multicoloured.

145	100f. Type **50**	1·00	40
146	250f. Drums, horn, pipes and stringed instruments (Fang)	2·30	1·00
147	350f. Flute and cup, bell and horn (Bubi)	3·25	1·50

51 Arrival in America of Columbus

1990. 500th Anniv (1992) of Discovery of America by Columbus (1st issue). Multicoloured.

148	170f. Type **51**	2·50	80
149	300f. "Santa Maria", "Pinta" and "Nina"	4·50	1·50

See also Nos. 165/7.

52 Mother and Child

1990. Christmas. Multicoloured.

150	170f. Type **52**	1·10	50
151	300f. Bubi man ringing handbell	2·75	1·10

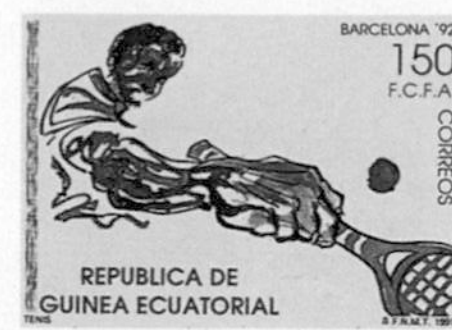

53 Tennis

1991. Olympic Games, Barcelona (1992) (1st issue). Multicoloured.

152	150f. Type **53**	2·75	1·10
153	250f. Cycling	5·25	2·40
MS154	120×80 mm. 500f. Equestrian events	10·50	5·00

See also No. 168/**MS**170.

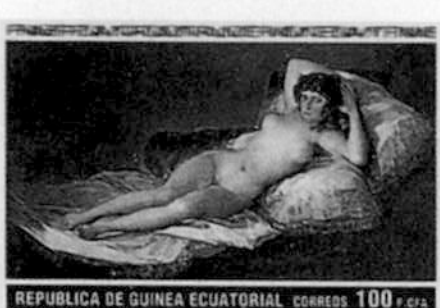

54 "The Naked Maja" (Francisco de Goya)

1991. Paintings. Multicoloured.

155	100f. Type **54**	1·40	70
156	250f. "Eve" (Albrecht Durer) (vert)	2·60	90
157	350f. "The Three Graces" (Peter Paul Rubens) (vert)	3·50	1·30

55 Mandrill

1991. The Mandrill. Multicoloured.

158	25f. Type **55**	1·80	85
159	25f. Close-up of face	1·80	85
160	25f. On all fours (horiz)	1·80	85
161	25f. With foreleg raised	1·80	85

56 Class EF53 Electric Locomotive, 1932, Japan

1991. Railway Locomotives. Multicoloured.

162	150f. Type **56**	1·80	75
163	250f. Steam locomotive, 1873, U.S.A.	3·50	80
MS164	105×78 mm. 500f. German locomotive, 1841	7·00	2·20

57 Vicente Pinzon and "Nina"

1991. 500th Anniv (1992) of Discovery of America by Columbus (2nd issue). Multicoloured.

165	150f. Type **57**	1·80	75
166	250f. Martin Pinzon and "Pinta"	3·25	1·40
167	350f. Christopher Columbus and "Santa Maria"	4·25	1·90

58 Basketball

1992. Olympic Games, Barcelona (2nd issue). Multicoloured.

168	200f. Type **58**	1·75	75
169	300f. Swimming	2·50	1·30
MS170	82×106 mm. 400f. Baseball	14·00	6·00

59 "Columbus Departing from Palos"

1992. 500th Anniv of Discovery of America by Columbus (3rd issue). Sheet 105×83 mm containing T 59 and similar horiz designs. Multicoloured.

MS171	300f. Type **59**; 500f. "Columbus's Landing on Guanahani" (D. T. da la Puebla)	14·00	6·00

60 Blue-breasted Kingfisher and Black-winged Stilt

1992. Nature Protection. Multicoloured.

172	150f. Type **60**	4·50	2·00
173	250f. Great blue turaco and grey parrot	7·50	2·50
MS174	79×104 mm. 500f. Butterfly (Nymphalidae) (horiz)	9·00	4·00

61 Scene from "Casablanca"

1992. Centenary of Motion Pictures.

175	**61**	100f. blue and black	2·00	1·00
176	-	250f. green and black	3·00	1·50
177	-	350f. brown and black	5·00	2·00

DESIGNS: 250f. Scene from "Viridiana"; 350f. Scene from "A Couple of Gypsies".

62 "Termitomyces globulus"

1992. Fungi. Multicoloured.

178	75f. Type **62**	1·00	30
179	125f. "Termitomyces letestui"	1·60	65
180	150f. "Termitomyces robustus"	2·00	85

63 "Virgin and Child amongst the Saints" (Claudio Coello)

1993. Painters' Anniversaries. Multicoloured.

181	200f. Type **63** (300th death anniv)	1·80	60
182	300f. "Apollo, Conqueror of Marsyas" (Jacob Jordaens) (400th birth anniv)	2·75	1·00
MS183	105×78 mm, 400f. "Meleager and Atalanta" (Jordaens)	8·00	4·00

64 Scene from "Romeo and Juliet" and Pyotr Ilyich Tchaikovsky

1993. Composers' Death Centenaries. Mult.

184	100f. Type **64**	1·30	60

185	200f. Scene from "Faust" (opera) and Charles Gounod	2·75	90

65 Quincy Watts (400 m)

1993. Gold Medal Winners at Olympic Games, Barcelona, and Winter Olympic Games, Albertville. Multicoloured.

186	100f. Type **65**	1·00	40
187	250f. Martin Lopez Zubero (200 m backstroke)	2·75	85
188	350f. Petra Kronbreger (slalom and combined)	4·00	1·30
189	400f. "Flying Dutchman" class yacht (Luis Doreste and Domingo Manrique)	4·75	1·50

66 Ford's First Motor Car

1993. 130th Birth Anniv of Henry Ford (motor car manufacturer).

190	**66**	200f. multicoloured	2·50	80
191	-	300f. multicoloured	3·75	1·20
192	-	400f. black and red	5·25	1·40

DESIGNS—HORIZ: 300f. Model "T" motor car. VERT: 400f. Henry Ford.

67 Pres. Obiang Nguema Mbasogo

1993. 25th Anniv of Independence. Mult.

193	150f. Type **67**	90	35
194	250f. Oil refinery, ship, map and radio mast (horiz)	1·80	65
195	300f. Hydro-electric station, Riaba, and waterfall (horiz)	2·20	75
196	350f. Woman, bridge and man (horiz)	2·60	85

68 Lunar Module "Eagle"

1994. 25th Anniv of First Manned Moon Landing. Multicoloured.

197	500f. Type **68**	4·00	2·00
198	700f. Buzz Aldrin, Michael Collins and Neil Armstrong (astronauts)	5·75	2·75
199	900f. Footprint on Moon and module reflected in astronaut's visor	7·40	3·75

69 German Team (1990 champions)

1994. World Cup Football Championship, U.S.A. Multicoloured.

200	200f. Type **69**	1·50	40
201	300f. Rose Bowl Stadium, Los Angeles	2·30	90
202	500f. Player dribbling ball (vert)	3·50	1·50

70 "Chasmosauraus belli"

1994. Prehistoric Animals. Multicoloured.

203	300f. Type **70**	1·50	55
204	500f. "Tyrannosaurus rex"	2·75	60
205	700f. "Triceratops horridus"	5·75	85
MS206	105×78 mm. 800f. "Sttyracosaurus albertensis"	10·00	5·00

71 Gold Calcite

1994. Minerals. Multicoloured.

207	300f. Type **71**	2·50	95
208	400f. Pyromorphite	3·50	1·30
209	600f. Fluorite	5·00	1·90
210	700f. Halite	6·00	2·20

72 Poster for "Elena y los Hombres" and Jean Renoir (film director)

1994. Anniversaries. Multicoloured.

211	300f. Type **72** (birth cent)	2·20	75
212	500f. Map and Ferdinand Marie de Lesseps (director of Suez Canal development, death centenary)	3·75	1·40
213	600f. Illustration from "The Little Prince" and Antoine de Saint-Exupery (pilot and writer, 50th death anniv)	4·50	1·50
214	700f. Bauhaus (75th anniv) and Walter Gropius (architect)	5·00	1·90

73 Kitten

1995. Domestic Animals. Multicoloured.

215	500f. Type **73**	3·00	80
216	500f. Pekingese	3·00	80
217	500f. Pig	3·00	80

74 Blue Diadem ("Hypolimnas salmacis")

1995. Butterflies. Multicoloured.

218	400f. Type **74**	3·25	1·30
219	400f. Fig-tree blue ("Myrina silenus")	3·25	1·30
220	400f. "Palla ussheri"	3·25	1·30
221	400f. Boisduval's false acraea ("Pseudacraea boisduvali")	3·25	1·30

75 Steam Locomotive, Great Britain

1995. Railways. Multicoloured.

222	500f. Type **75**	3·75	1·50
223	500f. Diesel locomotive, Germany	3·75	1·50
224	500f. "Hikari" express train, Japan	3·75	1·50
MS225	105×78 mm. 800f. Rack railcar, Switzerland	9·00	5·00

76 Signing of Japanese Surrender Document

1995. Anniversaries. Multicoloured.

226	350f. Type **76** (50th anniv of end of Second World War)	3·75	1·30
227	450f. Palais des Nations, Geneva (50th anniv of U.N.O.)	4·00	1·50
228	600f. Basel 1845 2½r. stamp and Sir Rowland Hill (birth bicentenary)	5·00	2·00

77 J. Manuel Fangio (1951 and 1954–7)

1996. Formula 1 Racing Champions. Mult.

229	400f. Type **77**	3·50	1·40
230	400f. Ayrton Senna (1988, 1990, 1991)	3·00	1·40
231	400f. Jim Clark (1963, 1965)	3·00	1·40
232	400f. Jochen Rindt (1970)	3·00	1·40

78 Alfred Nobel (chemist)

1996. Anniversaries. Multicoloured.

233	500f. Type **78** (death centenary)	4·50	1·80
234	500f. Anton Bruckner (composer, death centenary)	4·50	1·80
235	500f. "Abraham and the Three Angels" (Giovanni Tiepolo), (painter, birth tercentenary)	4·50	1·80
MS236	106×78 mm. 800f. "Charles IV and Family" (Francisco de Goya), (painter), 250th birth anniv)	7·50	3·50

79 Marilyn Monroe (actress)

1996. Personalities. Multicoloured.

237	350f. Type **79**	2·00	75
238	350f. Elvis Presley (entertainer)	2·00	75
239	350f. James Dean (actor)	2·00	75
240	350f. Vittorio de Sica (actor and film director)	2·00	75

80 Illustration from *Book of Chess, Dice and Tablings* by King Alfonso X of Castile and Leon

1996. Chess Competitions. Multicoloured.

241	400f. Type **80** (32nd Chess Olympiad, Yerevan, Armenia)	3·50	1·50
242	400f. Girl playing chess (World Junior Chess Championship, Minorca, Spain)	3·50	1·50
243	400f. Chess pieces (Women's World Chess Championship, Jaen, Spain)	3·50	1·50
244	400f. Anatoly Yevgenievich Karpov (World Chess Championship title match, Elisa, Russian Federation)	3·50	1·50

81 19th-century Sail/Steam Warship

1996. Ships. Multicoloured.

245	500f. Type **81**	4·00	1·30
246	500f. *Galatea* (cadet ship)	4·00	1·30
247	500f. Modern ferry	4·00	1·30

82 Olympic Stadium, Athens, 1896

1996. Olympic Games, Atlanta. Centenary of Modern Olympic Games. Multicoloured.

248	400f. Type **82**	2·50	75·00
249	400f. Cycling	2·50	75
250	400f. Tennis	2·50	75
251	400f. Show jumping	2·50	75

83 False Blusher

1997. Fungi. Multicoloured.

252	400f. Type **83**	2·60	80
253	400f. Common morel (*Morchella esculenta*)	2·60	80
254	400f. Orange peel fungus (*Aleuria aurantia*)	2·60	80
255	400f. *Sparassis laminosa*	2·60	80

84 Franz Schubert and Score

1997. Anniversaries and Events. Multicoloured.

256	500f. Type **84** (composer, birth bicentenary)	3·50	1·50
257	500f. Head of ox (Chinese New Year—Year of the Ox)	3·50	1·50
258	500f. Johannes Brahms and score (composer, death centenary)	3·50	1·50
MS259	106×78 mm. 880f. Miguel de Cervantes (writer, 450th birth anniv)	5·00	2·50

85 Players

1997. World Cup Football Championship, France.

260	300f. Type **85**	2·50	95
261	300f. Stadium	2·50	95
262	300f. Players wearing yellow and blue shirts	2·50	95

86 Snake

1998. Fauna. Multicoloured.

263	400f. Type **86**	2·75	85
264	400f. Snail	2·75	85

265	400f. Turtle	2·75	85
266	400f. Lizard	2·75	85

87 French Infantry, Alsace Regiment, 1767

1998. Military Uniforms. Multicoloured.

267	400f. Type **87**	2·75	85
268	400f. 18th-century British Admiral	2·75	85
269	400f. 18th-century Georgian Hussars, Russia	2·75	85
270	400f. 19th-century Prussian field artillery	2·75	85

88 "The Crucifixion" (Velazquez)

1999. Birth Bimillenary (2000) of Jesus Christ.

271	500f. Type **88**	3·25	1·00
272	500f. "Adoration of the Magi" (Peter Paul Rubens)	3·25	1·00
273	500f. "The Holy Family" (Miguel Angel Buonarroti)	3·25	1·00

89 *Cattleya leopoldii*

1999. Orchids. Multicoloured.

274	400f. Type **89**	4·00	1·70
275	400f. *Angraecum eburneum*	4·00	1·70
276	400f. *Paphiopedilum insigne*	4·00	1·70
277	400f. *Ansellia africana*	4·00	1·70

90 "The Coronation of Thorns" (Anthony van Dyck)

1999. Anniversaries. Multicoloured.

278	100f. Type **90** (artist, 400th birth anniv)	65	30
279	250f. Johann Wolfgang Goethe (writer, 250th birth anniv)	1·60	70
280	500f. Bust of Jacques-Etienne Montgolfier (balloonist, death bicentenary)	3·25	1·50
281	750f. Frederic Chopin (composer, 150th death anniv)	6·00	2·00

91 Golden Conure

1999. Birds. Multicoloured.

282	500f. Type **91**	3·75	1·00
283	500f. Buffon's macaw (*Ara ambigua*)	3·75	1·00
284	500f. Hyacinth macaw (*Anodorhynchus hyacinthinus*)	3·75	1·00
MS285	105×79 mm. 800f. Amboina king parrot	7·00	4·50

92 Purple Emperor (*Apatura iris*)

1999. Butterflies. Multicoloured.

286	400f. Type **92**	4·00	1·70
287	400f. Peacock (*Inachis io*)	4·00	1·70
288	400f. Purple-edged copper (*Palaeochrysophanus hippothoe*)	4·00	1·70
289	400f. Niobe fritillary (*Fabriciana niobe*)	4·00	1·70

93 Swiss Electric Locomotive, Linares–Almeria Line, Spain

1999. Railway Locomotives. Multicoloured.

290	500f. Type **93**	3·75	1·00
291	500f. German diesel locomotive	3·75	1·00
292	500f. Japanese series 269 electric locomotive	3·75	1·00
MS293	82×106 mm. 800f. A.V.E. (Spanish high-speed train)	7·00	4·50

94 Anniversary Emblem

2000. 125th Anniv of UPU.

294	**94**	40f. multicoloured	1·50	1·50

95 Carnotaurus

2001. Prehistoric Fauna. Multicoloured.

295	500f. Type **95**	2·75	70
296	500f. Iberomesornis	2·75	7·00
297	500f. Troodon	2·75	70
MS298	107×78 mm. 800f. Diplodocus	5·50	3·00

96 Indigo Boletus (*Gyroporus cyanescens*)

2001. Fungi. Multicoloured.

299	400f. Type **96**	2·75	85
300	400f. *Terfezia arenaria*	2·75	85
301	400f. *Battarrea stevenii*	2·75	85
302	400f. Fly agaric (*Amanita muscaria*)	2·75	85

97 Merryweather Fire Appliance (1915)

2001. Fire Engines. Multicoloured.

303	400f. Type **97**	3·00	1·40
304	400f. De Dion Bouton appliance TE-450 (1943)	3·00	1·40
305	400f. Magirus appliance E-2 (1966)	3·00	1·40
306	400f. Merryweather appliance (1888)	3·00	1·40

98 Infantry Officer, 1700

2001. Military Uniforms. Multicoloured.

307	400f. Type **98**	3·00	1·40
308	400f. Arquebusier, 1534	3·00	1·40
309	400f. 17th-centuary musketeer	3·00	1·40
310	400f. Fusilier, 1815	3·00	1·40

EXPRESS LETTER STAMPS

E4 Guinea Archer

1971. 3rd Anniv of Independence.

E15	**E4**	4p. multicoloured	5·00	25
E16	**E4**	8p. multicoloured	11·00	40

APPENDIX

The following stamps have either been issued in excess of postal needs or have not been available to the public in reasonable quantities at face value. Such stamps may later be given full listing if there is evidence of regular postal use.

1972

Space Flight of "Apollo 15". Postage 1, 3, 5, 8, 10p.; Air 15, 25p.
Winter Olympic Games, Sapporo, Japan. Postage 1, 2, 3, 5, 8p.; Air 15, 50p.
Christmas 1971. Paintings. Postage 1, 3, 5, 8, 10p.; Air 15, 25p.
Easter. Postage 1, 3, 5, 8, 10p.; Air 15, 25p.
Olympic Games, Munich 1972. Augsburg Events. Postage 1, 2, 3, 5, 8p.; Air 15, 50p.
Winter Olympic Games, Sapporo, Japan. Gold medal winners. Postage 1, 2, 3, 5, 8p.; Air 15, 50p.
Olympic Games, Munich 1972. Buildings and previous medal winners. Postage 1, 2, 3, 5, 8p.; Air 15, 50p.
Olympic Games. Sailing and rowing, Kiel. Postage 1, 2, 3, 5, 8p.; Air 15, 50p.
Olympic Games Munich. Modern sports. Postage 1, 2, 3, 5, 8p.; Air 15, 50p.
Olympic Games, Munich. Equestrian events. Postage 1, 2, 3, 5, 8p.; Air 15, 50p.
Centenary of Japanese Railway. Various steam locomotives. Postage 1, 3, 5, 8, 10p.; Air 15, 25p.
Olympic Games, Munich. Gold medal winners. Postage 1, 2, 3, 5, 8p.; Air 15, 50p.
Christmas 1972. Paintings by Cranach. Postage 1, 3, 5, 8, 10p.; Air 15, 25p.
Cosmonauts Memorial. Designs with black borders. Postage 1, 3, 5, 8, 10p.; Air 15, 25p.

1973

Transatlantic Yacht Race 1972. Postage 1, 2, 3, 5, 8p.; Air 15, 50p.
Renoir Paintings. Postage 1, 2, 3, 5, 8p.; Air 15, 50p.
Conquest of Venus. Postage 1, 3, 5, 8, 10p.; Air 15, 25p.
Easter. Religious Paintings by Old Masters. Postage 1, 3, 5, 8, 10p.; Air 15, 25p.
"Tour de France" Cycle Race. Postage 1, 2, 3, 5, 8p.; Air 15, 50p.
Paintings by European Old Masters. Postage 1, 2, 3, 5, 8p.; Air 15, 50p.
World Football Cup Championship, West Germany (1974) (1st issue). Previous Finals. Postage 5, 10, 15, 20, 25, 55, 60c.; Air 5, 70p.
Paintings by Rubens. Postage 1, 2, 3, 5, 8p.; Air 15, 50p.
Christmas. Religious Paintings. Postage 1, 3, 5, 8, 10p.; Air 15, 25p.
World Cup Football Championship, West Germany (1974) (2nd issue). Famous players. Postage 30, 35, 40, 45, 50, 65, 70c.; Air 8, 60p.
Paintings by Picasso. Postage 30, 35, 40, 45, 50c.; Air 8, 60e.

1974

500th Birth Anniv of Nicolas Copernicus (astronomer). Postage 5, 10, 15, 20c.; Air 4, 10, 70e.
World Cup Football Championship, West Germany (3rd issue). Venues of Qualifying Matches. Postage 75, 80, 85, 90, 95c., 1e., 1e.25; Air 10, 50e.
Easter. Postage 1, 3, 5, 8, 10p.; Air 15, 25p.
Holy Year. Postage 5, 10, 15, 20c., 3e.50; Air 10, 70e.
World Cup Football Championship, West Germany (4th issue). Famous Players. Postage 1e.50, 1e.75, 2e., 2e.25, 2e.50, 3e., 3e.50; Air 10, 60e.
Centenary of U.P.U. (1st issue). Postage 60, 70, 80c., 1e.50; Air 30, 50e.
First Death Anniv of Picasso. Postage 55, 60, 65, 70, 75c.; Air 10, 50e.
"The Wild West". Postage 30, 35, 40, 45, 50c.; Air 8, 60p.
Protected Flowers. Postage 5, 10, 15, 20, 25c., 1, 3, 5, 8, 10p.; Air 5, 15, 25, 70p.
Christmas. Postage 60, 70, 80c., 1e., 1e.50; Air 30, 50e.
75th Anniv of FC Barcelona. Postage 1, 3, 5, 8, 10e.; Air 15, 60e.
Centenary of U.P.U. (2nd issue) and "Espana '75" International Stamp Exhibition, Madrid. Postage 1e.25, 1e.50, 1e.75, 2e., 2e.25; Air 35, 60e.
Nature Protection (1st series). Australian Animals. Postage 80, 85, 90, 95c., 1e.; Air 15, 40e.
Nature Protection (2nd series). African Animals. Postage 50, 60, 65, 70, 75c.; Air 10, 70e.
Nature Protection (3rd series). South American and Australian Birds. Postage 1p.25, 1p.50, 1p.75, 2p., 2p.25, 2p.50, 2p.75, 3p., 3p.50, 4p.; Air 20, 25, 30, 35p.
Nature Protection (4th series). Endangered Species. Postage 10, 15, 20, 25, 30, 35, 40, 45, 50, 55, 60c., 1e.; Air 2, 10, 70e.

1975

Paintings by Picasso. Postage 5, 10, 15, 20, 25c.; Air 5, 70e.
Easter. Postage 60, 70, 80c., 1e., 1e.50; Air 30, 50e.
Winter Olympic Games, Innsbruck (1976). 5, 10, 15, 20, 25, 30, 35, 40, 45c., 25, 70e.
Paintings of Don Quixote. Postage 30, 35, 40, 45, 50c.; Air 25, 60e.
Bicent of American Revolution (1st issue). Postage 5, 20, 40, 75c., 2, 5, 8e.; Air 25, 30e.
Bullfighting. Postage 80, 85, 90c., 8e.; Air 35, 40e.
"Apollo–Soyuz" Space Test Project. Postage 1, 2, 3, 5e., 5e.50, 7e., 7e.50, 9, 15e.; Air 20, 30e.
Bicent of American Revolution (2nd issue). Postage 10, 30, 50c., 1, 3, 6, 10e.; Air 12, 40e.
Nude Paintings. Postage 5, 10, 15, 20, 25, 30, 35, 40, 45, 50, 55, 60c., 1, 2e.; Air 10, 70e.
Ships. Postage 30, 35, 40, 45, 50, 55, 60, 65, 70, 75c.; Air 8, 10, 50, 60e.
Christmas. Postage 60, 70, 80c., 1e., 1e.50; Air 30, 50e.
Olympic Games, Montreal (1st issue). Postage 50, 60, 70, 80, 90, c.; Air 35, 60e.
Bicent of American Revolution (3rd issue). Presidents. Postage 5, 10, 20, 30, 40, 50, 75c., 1, 2, 3, 5, 6, 8, 10e.; Air 12, 25, 30, 40e.
Monkeys. Postage 5, 10, 15, 20, 25, 30, 35, 40, 45, 50, 55, 60c., 1, 2e.; Air 10, 70e.
Butterflies (1st series). Postage 5, 10, 15, 20, 25, 30, 35, 40, 45, 50, 55, 60c., 1, 2e.; Air 10, 70e.
Fish (1st series). Postage 5, 10, 15, 20, 25, 30, 35, 40, 45, 50, 55, 60c., 1, 2e.; Air 10, 70e.
Cats (1st series). Postage 5, 10, 15, 20, 25, 30, 35, 40, 45, 50, 55, 60c., 1, 2e.; Air 10, 70e.
Pres. Francisco Macias Nguema. Postage 1e.50, 3e.50, 7e.; Air 300e.
Arms. Postage 3e.; Air 100e.
Government House. 5e.
International Women's Year. 10e.

1976

Winter Olympic Games, Innsbruck (1st issue). Postage 50, 55, 60, 65, 70, 75, 80, 85, 90c.; Air 35, 60e.
Winter Olympic Games, Innsbruck (2nd issue). Postage 3, 5, 50e.; Air 200e.
Bicent of American Revolution (4th issue). Flora and Fauna. Postage 1e.50, 3, 5, 7, 25, 100e.; Air 200e.
Apollo–Soyuz Project. Optd on Arms issue. Air 100e.
Concorde's First Commercial Flight. Optd on Arms issue. Air 100e.
Nude Paintings. 7, 10, 25e.
Easter. Air 200e.
Olympic Games, Montreal (2nd issue). Postage 7, 10, 25e.; Air 200e.
Apollo–Soyuz Project, Concorde, and Telephone Centenary. Postage 3, 5, 50e.; Air 200e.
Bicent of American Revolution (5th issue). Fauna. Postage 1e.50, 3, 5, 7, 25, 100e.; Air 200e.
Cavalry Officers. Postage 5, 10, 15, 20, 25c.; Air 5, 70p.
Paintings by El Greco. Postage 1, 3, 5, 8, 10p.; Air 15, 25p.
Olympic Games, Montreal (3rd issue). Rowing and Sailing events. Postage 50, 60, 70, 80, 90c.; Air 30, 60e.
Olympic Games, Montreal (4th issue). Postage 50, 55, 60, 65, 70, 75, 80, 85, 90c.; Air 35, 60e.
Veteran Cars. Postage 1, 3, 5, 8, 10p.; Air 15, 25p.
Nature Protection (5th series). European animals. Postage 5, 10, 15, 20, 25c.; Air 5, 70p.
Racing Motorcyclists. 1, 2, 3, 4, 5, 10, 30, 40e.
Nature Protection (6th series). Flowers of South America and Oceania. Postage 30, 35, 40, 45, 50, 80, 85, 90, 95c., 1p.; Air 8, 15, 40, 60p.
Nature Protection (7th series). Asian animals and birds. Postage 30, 35, 40, 45, 55, 60, 65, 70, 75c., 8p.; Air 50c., 10, 50, 60p.
Chess Pieces. 1, 3, 5, 8, 15, 30, 60, 100e.
Nature Protection (8th series). African birds and flowers. Postage 30, 35, 40, 45, 50, 55, 60, 65, 70, 75c.; Air 8, 10, 50, 60p.
Steamships. Postage 80, 85, 90, 95c., 1p.; Air 15, 40p.
Nature Protection (9th series). European birds. Postage 5, 10, 15, 20, 25c.; Air 5, 70p.
Paintings of Ships. Postage 5, 10, 15, 20, 25, 30e.; Air 50, 60, 65, 70e.

1977

Nature Protection (10th series). Birds of North America. Postage 80, 85, 90, 95c., 1p.; Air 15, 40p.
Cats (2nd series). Postage 5, 10, 15, 20, 25c.; Air 15, 70e.
Silver Jubilee of Queen Elizabeth II. Postage 2, 4, 5, 8, 10, 15e.; Air 20, 35e.
Nude Drawings. Postage 5, 10, 50, 50e.; Air 15, 200e.
Dogs (1st series). Postage 5, 10, 15, 20, 25, 30, 35, 40, 45, 50, 55, 60c., 1, 2e.; Air 10, 70e.
World War Air Aces. Postage 5, 10, 15, 20, 25, 30, 35, 40, 45, 50, 55, 60c.; Air 10, 70e.
Football. Postage 2, 4, 5, 8, 10, 15e.; Air 20, 35e.
Butterflies (2nd series). Postage 80, 85, 90, 95c., 8e.; Air 35, 40e.
Cars. Postage 5, 10, 15, 20, 25, 30, 35, 40, 45, 50, 55, 60c., 1, 2e.; Air 10, 70e.
Chinese Art. Postage 60, 70, 80c., 1e., 1e.50; Air 30, 50e.
African Masks. Postage 5, 10, 15, 20, 25c.; Air 5, 70e.
Nature Protection (11th series). Animals of North America. Postage 1e.25, 1e.50, 1e.75, 2e., 2e.25; Air 20, 50e.
Napoleon. Scenes from his life. Postage 5, 10, 15, 20, 25, 30, 35, 40, 45, 50, 55, 60c., 1, 2e.; Air 10, 70e.
Napoleon. Military uniforms. Postage 5, 10, 15, 20, 25, 30, 35, 40, 45, 50, 55, 60c., 1, 2e.; Air 10, 70e.
Nature Protection (12th series). Animals of South America. Postage 2e.50, 2e.75, 3e., 3e.50, 4e.; Air 25, 35e.
Nature Protection (13th series). European flowers. Postage 2e.50, 2e.75, 3e.50, 4e.; Air 25, 30e.

1978

25th Anniv of Queen Elizabeth II's Coronation. Members of Royal Family. Postage 2, 5, 8, 10, 12, 15e.; Air 30, 50, 150e.
Knights. Postage 5, 10, 15, 20, 25c.; Air 15, 70e.

Cats (3rd series). 1, 3, 5, 8, 15, 30, 60, 100e.
American Astronauts. 1, 3, 5, 8, 15, 30, 60, 100e.
25th Anniv of Queen Elizabeth II's Coronation. Medals. 1, 3, 5, 8, 25, 50, 75, 200e.
Queen Elizabeth II's Coronation. 25th Anniv Scenes from previous coronations. Air 1, 3, 5, 8, 15, 30, 60, 100e.
Dogs (2nd series). 1, 3, 5, 8, 15, 30, 60, 100e.
World Famous Paintings. 1, 3, 5, 8, 25, 50, 75, 200e.
Butterflies (3rd series). 1, 3, 5, 8, 15, 30, 60, 100e.
Nature Protection (14th series). Asian flowers. Postage 1e.25, 1e.50, 1e.75, 2e., 2e.25; Air 20, 50e.
Flowers. 1, 3, 5, 8, 15, 30, 60, 100e.
Water Birds. 1, 3, 5, 8, 15, 30, 60, 100e.
World Cup Football Championship. Air 150e.
Belgrade Conference. Air 250e.
"Eurphila 78" Exhibition. Air 250e.
Winter Olympic Games, Lake Placid (1980). Postage 5, 10, 20, 25e.; Air 70e.
150th Death Anniv of Goya. Air 150e.
Christmas. Painting by Titian. Air 150e.
Prehistoric Animals. Postage 30, 35, 40, 45, 50c.; Air 25, 60e.
Cats (4th series). Postage 2e.50, 2e.75, 3e., 3e.50, 4e.; Air 25, 40e.

1979

Death Centenary of Sir Rowland Hill (1st series). 3, 5, 8, 15, 30, 75, 220e.
Wright Brothers, 1, 3, 5, 8, 15, 30, 60, 100e.
Death Bicentenary of Capt. James Cook. Air 100e.
Fish (2nd series). Postage 5, 10, 20, 25c., 1e.50; Air 15, 70e.
Death Centenary of Sir Rowland Hill (2nd series). Stamps. Postage 8, 15, 20, 20, 30e.; Air 50e.
International Year of the Child (1st series). Postage 5, 7, 11, 24e.; Air 75e.
Death Anniversaries of Schubert, Voltaire, Rousseau and Cranach. Air 100, 100, 100, 100e.
10th Anniv (1972) of "Apollo XI" Space Flight. "Apollo 15" stamps each surch 50e. and inscription. Postage 50e. on 1, 3, 5, 8, 10p.; Air 50e. on 15, 25p.
European Space Agency Satellite. 200e.
Fairy Tales. Postage 2, 3, 5, 10, 15, 18e.; Air 24, 35e.
Automobiles. Air 35, 50e.
Fish (3rd series). 5, 10, 15, 20, 25, 30, 35, 40, 45, 50, 55, 60, 70c., 1, 2, 10e.
International Year of the Child (2nd series). Various 1978 stamps optd with I.Y.C. emblem. On Cats (3rd series). 1, 3, 5, 8, 15, 30, 60, 100e. On Dogs. 1, 3, 5, 8, 15, 30, 60, 100e. On Butterflies. 1, 3, 5, 8, 15, 30, 60, 100e. On Water Birds. 1, 3, 5, 8, 15, 30, 60, 100e.
"London 1980" Stamp Exhibition. Rowland Hill (1st series) stamps optd 1, 3, 5, 8, 15, 30, 75, 200e.
Olympic Games, Moscow (1st series). Postage 2, 3, 5, 8, 10, 15e.; Air 30, 50e.
Olympic Games, Moscow (2nd series). Water sports. Postage 5, 10, 20, 25e.; Air 70e.

Pt. 8

ERITREA

A former Italian colony on the Red Sea, north-east Africa. Under British Administration from 1942 to September 1952, when Eritrea was federated with Ethiopia. Eritrea was declared an independent state in May 1993.

1893. 100 centesimi = 1 lira.
1991. 100 cents = 1 birr.
1997. Nakfa.

ITALIAN COLONY

1893. Stamps of Italy optd Colonia Eritrea (1 to 5c.) or COLONIA ERITREA (others).

1	4	1c. green	12·00	6·50
2	5	2c. brown	4·25	4·25
3	23	5c. green	£150	8·50
4	12	10c. red	£150	9·50
5	12	20c. orange	£350	9·50
6	12	25c. blue	£1200	37·00
7	14	40c. brown	16·00	19·00
8	14	45c. green	16·00	26·00
9	14	60c. mauve	16·00	43·00
10	14	1l. brown and orange	48·00	48·00
11	29	5l. red and blue	£700	£375

1895. Stamps of Italy optd Colonia Eritrea (1 to 5c.) or COLONIA ERITREA (others).

12	21	1c. brown	19·00	10·00
13	22	2c. brown	3·25	2·00
14	24	5c. green	3·25	2·00
15	25	10c. lake	4·75	85
16	26	20c. orange	5·25	3·00
17	27	25c. blue	5·25	4·00
18	27	45c. olive	35·00	35·00

1903. Stamps of Italy optd Colonia Eritrea.

19	30	1c. brown	1·10	1·20
20	31	2c. brown	1·10	85
21	31	5c. green	55·00	85
22	33	10c. red	85·00	85
30	33	15c. on 20c. orange	48·00	13·00
23	33	20c. orange	5·25	1·40
24	33	25c. blue	£475	20·00
25	33	40c. brown	£650	30·00
26	33	45c. olive	6·50	10·50
27	33	50c. violet	£160	32·00
28	34	1l. brown and green	7·50	1·90
29	34	5l. blue and red	37·00	55·00

1908. Stamps of Italy optd ERITREA (20c.) or Colonia Eritrea (others).

31	37	5c. green	2·10	1·30
32	37	10c. red	2·10	1·30
41	37	15c. grey	25·00	16·00
42	41	20c. orange	6·50	16·00
33	39	25c. blue	8·50	3·25
43	39	40c. brown	55·00	37·00
44	39	50c. violet	19·00	5·25
45	39	60c. red	35·00	29·00
46	34	10l. green and red	£450	£600

3 Ploughing

1910

34	3	5c. green	1·60	2·10
35	3	10c. red	7·50	5·25
40	-	15c. grey	55·00	65·00
37	-	25c. blue	9·50	16·00

DESIGN: 15, 25c. Government Palace, Massawa.

1916. Red Cross Society stamps of Italy optd ERITREA.

47	53	10c.+5c. red	5·25	16·00
48	54	15c.+5c. grey	21·00	32·00
50	54	20c.+5c. orange	5·25	37·00
49	54	20c. on 15c.+5c. grey	21·00	37·00

1916. No. 40 surch with new value and bars or crosses.

51	5c. on 15c. grey	15·00	19·00
52	20c. on 15c. grey	4·25	4·25

1922. Victory stamps of Italy optd ERITREA.

53	62	5c. green	2·75	8·50
54	62	10c. red	2·75	4·25
55	62	15c. grey	2·75	6·50
56	62	25c. blue	2·75	6·50

1922. Stamps of Somalia optd ERITREA and bars.

57	1	2c. on 1b. brown	8·00	19·00
58	1	5c. on 2b. green	8·00	16·00
59	2	10c. on 1a. red	8·00	4·25
60	2	15c. on 2a. brown	8·00	4·25
61	2	25c. on 2½a. blue	8·00	4·25
62	2	50c. on 5a. orange	25·00	15·00
63	2	1l. on 10a. lilac	27·00	28·00

1923. Propagation of the Faith stamps of Italy optd ERITREA.

64	66	20c. orange and green	8·00	37·00
65	66	30c. orange and red	8·00	37·00
66	66	50c. orange and violet	5·25	43·00
67	66	1l. orange and blue	5·25	60·00

1923. Fascist March on Rome stamps of Italy optd ERITREA.

68	73	10c. green	8·00	16·00
69	73	30c. violet	8·00	16·00
70	73	50c. red	8·00	16·00
71	74	1l. blue	8·00	43·00
72	74	2l. brown	8·00	55·00
73	75	5l. black and blue	8·00	75·00

1924. Manzoni stamps of Italy optd ERITREA.

74	77	10c. black and purple	8·00	37·00
75	-	15c. black and green	8·00	37·00
76	-	30c. black	8·00	37·00
77	-	50c. black and brown	8·00	37·00
78	-	1l. black and blue	65·00	£275
79	-	5l. black and purple	£750	£2500

1924. Stamps of Italy optd ERITREA.

80	30	1c. brown	13·50	14·00
81	31	2c. orange	5·25	10·50
82	37	5c. green	13·50	12·00

1925. Holy Year stamps of Italy optd ERITREA.

90	-	20c.+10c. brown & green	4·25	27·00
91	81	30c.+15c. brown & dp brn	4·25	27·00
92	-	50c.+25c. brown & violet	4·25	27·00
93	-	60c.+30c. brown & red	4·25	32·00
94	-	1l.+50c. purple and blue	5·25	37·00
95	-	5l.+2l.50 purple & red	5·25	55·00

1925. Stamps of Italy optd Colonia Eritrea.

123	92	7½c. brown	27·00	80·00
96	39	20c. green	21·00	16·00
124	39	20c. purple	8·50	6·50
97	39	30c. grey	21·00	21·00
125	92	50c. mauve	85·00	55·00
126	39	60c. orange	£120	£160
127	34	75c. red and carmine	95·00	10·50
128	34	1l.25 blue & ultramarine	55·00	6·50
98	34	2l. green and orange	80·00	85·00
129	34	2l.50 green and orange	£200	70·00

1925. Royal Jubilee stamps of Italy optd ERITREA.

99B	82	60c. red	2·75	7·50
100B	82	1l. blue	2·75	13·00
101A	82	1l.25 blue	5·25	27·00

1926. St. Francis of Assisi stamps of Italy optd ERITREA (20 to 60c.) or Eritrea (others).

102	83	20c. green	3·25	16·00
103	-	40c. violet	3·25	16·00
104	-	60c. red	3·25	21·00
105	-	1l.25 blue	3·25	32·00
106	-	5l.+2l.50 brown	7·50	65·00

1926. Colonial Propaganda stamps Nos. 30/5 of Cyrenaica, but inscr "ERITREA".

107	5c.+5c. brown	1·10	7·50
108	10c.+5c. olive	1·10	7·50
109	20c.+5c. green	1·10	7·50
110	40c.+5c. red	1·10	7·50
111	60c.+5c. orange	1·10	7·50
112	1l.+5c. blue	1·10	7·50

1926. Portrait stamps of Italy optd ERITREA.

113	34	75c. red and carmine	85·00	21·00
114	34	1l.25 blue & ultramarine	55·00	21·00
115	34	2l.50 green and orange	£160	48·00

1927. 1st National Defence issue of Italy optd ERITREA.

116	89	40c.+20c. black & brn	3·25	32·00
117	89	60c.+30c. brown & red	3·25	32·00
118	89	1l.25+60c. black and blue	3·25	55·00
119	89	5l.+2l.50 blk & grn	6·50	75·00

1927. Centenary of Volta issue of Italy optd Eritrea.

120	90	20c. violet	8·50	32·00
121	90	50c. orange	12·00	21·00
122	90	1l.25 blue	19·00	55·00

1928. Portrait stamps of Italy optd Eritrea (130) or ERITREA (others).

130	91	50c. grey and brown	22·00	8·50
131	92	50c. mauve	70·00	48·00
132	91	1l.75 brown	£110	37·00

1928. 45th Anniv of the Italian-African Society. As Nos. 43/6 of Cyrenaica but inscr "ERITREA".

133	20c.+5c. green	3·25	10·50
134	30c.+5c. red	3·25	10·50
135	50c.+10c. violet	3·25	16·00
136	1l.25+20c. blue	3·25	21·00

1929. 2nd National Defence issue of Italy (colours changed) optd ERITREA.

137	89	30c.+10c. black & red	5·25	21·00
138	89	50c.+20c. grey & lilac	5·25	21·00
139	89	1l.25+50c. blue & brn	8·00	43·00
140	89	5l.+2l. black and green	8·00	65·00

1929. Montecassino stamps of Italy (colours changed) optd Eritrea (10l.) or ERITREA (others).

141	104	20c. green	7·50	17·00
142	-	25c. red	7·50	17·00
143	-	50c.+10c. red	7·50	21·00
144	-	75c.+15c. brown	7·50	21·00
145	104	1l.25+25c. purple	15·00	37·00
146	-	5l.+1l. blue	15·00	43·00
147	-	10l.+2l. brown	15·00	65·00

1930. Royal Wedding stamps of Italy (colours changed) optd ERITREA.

148	109	20c. green	2·10	5·25
149	109	50c.+10c. red	1·60	8·50
150	109	1l.25+25c. red	1·60	19·00

21 Telegraph Linesman

1930

151	-	2c. black and blue	3·25	10·50
152	-	5c. black and violet	4·25	3·25
153	-	10c. black and brown	4·25	3·25
154	21	15c. black and green	4·25	3·25
155	-	25c. black and green	4·25	2·10
156	-	35c. black and red	12·00	21·00
157	-	1l. black and blue	4·25	2·10
158	-	2l. black and brown	12·00	24·00
159	-	5l. black and green	16·00	37·00
160	-	10l. black and blue	30·00	65·00

DESIGNS—VERT: 2, 35c. Lancer; 5, 10c. Postman; 25c. Rifleman. HORIZ: 1l. Massawa; 2l. Railway Bridge; 5l. Asmara Deghe Selam; 10l. Camel transport.

1930. Ferrucci issue of Italy (colours changed) optd ERITREA.

161	114	20c. violet	3·75	4·25
162	-	25c. green (283)	3·75	4·25
163	-	50c. black (284)	3·75	10·50
164	-	1l.25 blue (285)	3·75	16·00
165	-	5l.+2l. red (286)	12·00	30·00

1930. 3rd National Defence issue of Italy (colours changed) optd ERITREA.

166	89	30c.+10c. grn & dp grn	27·00	32·00
167	89	50c.+10c. purple & grn	27·00	48·00
168	89	1l.25+30c. lt brn & brn	27·00	65·00
169	89	5l.+1l.50 green & blue	85·00	£150

22

1930. 25th Anniv of Italian Colonial Agricultural Institute.

170	22	50c.+20c. brown	3·75	19·00
171	22	1l.25+20c. blue	3·75	19·00
172	22	1l.75+20c. green	3·75	21·00
173	22	2l.55+50c. violet	6·00	37·00
174	22	5l.+1l. red	8·00	55·00

1930. Bimillenary of Virgil issue of Italy (colours changed) optd ERITREA.

175	15c. grey	1·10	6·50
176	20c. brown	1·10	3·25
177	25c. green	1·10	3·25
178	30c. brown	1·10	3·25
179	50c. purple	1·10	3·25
180	75c. red	1·10	4·25
181	1l.25 blue	1·10	8·50
182	5l.+1l.50 purple	7·50	43·00
183	10l.+2l.50 brown	7·50	75·00

1931. St. Antony of Padua issue of Italy (colours changed) optd ERITREA.

184	121	20c. brown	2·75	15·00
185	-	25c. green	2·75	6·50
186	-	30c. brown	2·75	6·50
187	-	50c. purple	2·75	6·50
188	-	75c. grey	2·75	17·00
189	-	1l.25 blue	2·75	34·00
190	-	5l.+2l.50 brown	8·00	75·00

24 King Victor Emmanuel III

1931

191	24	7½c. brown	1·60	4·25
192	24	20c. red and blue	1·60	10
193	24	30c. purple and olive	1·60	10
194	24	40c. green and blue	2·10	60
195	24	50c. olive and brown	1·10	10
196	24	75c. red	5·25	10
197	24	1l.25 blue and purple	6·50	3·25
198	24	2l.50 green	6·50	10·50

25 Dromedary

1933

199	25	2c. blue	1·60	4·25
200	-	5c. black	3·25	60
201	25	10c. brown	3·25	60
202	-	15c. brown	4·25	2·10
203	-	25c. green	3·25	60
204	-	35c. violet	8·50	12·00
205	-	1l. blue	1·10	10
206	-	2l. olive	29·00	4·25
207	-	5l. red	16·00	6·50
208	-	10l. orange	21·00	30·00

DESIGNS—HORIZ: 5c., 15c. Fish wharf; 25c. Baobab tree; 35c. Native village; 2l. African Elephant. VERT: 1l. Ruins at Cholloe; 5l. Eritrean man; 10l. Eritrean woman.

1934. Honouring the Duke of the Abruzzi. Designs as Nos. 201/2 and 204/8 optd ONORANZE AL DUCA DEGLI ABRUZZI.

209	25	10c. blue	13·00	21·00
210	-	15c. blue	13·00	21·00
211	-	35c. green	10·50	21·00
212	-	1l. red	10·50	21·00
213	-	2l. red	18·00	21·00
214	-	5l. violet	16·00	43·00
215	-	10l. green	16·00	48·00

30 Grant's Gazelle

1934. 2nd International Colonial Exn, Naples.

216	**30**	5c. brown & grn (postage)	6·50	17·00
217	**30**	10c. black and brown	6·50	17·00
218	**30**	20c. slate and red	6·50	17·00
219	**30**	50c. brown and violet	6·50	17·00
220	**30**	60c. blue and brown	6·50	24·00
221	**30**	1l.25 green and blue	6·50	35·00
222	-	25c. orange & blue (air)	6·50	17·00
223	-	50c. blue and green	6·50	17·00
224	-	75c. orange and brown	6·50	17·00
225	-	80c. green and brown	6·50	17·00
226	-	1l. green and red	6·50	24·00
227	-	2l. brown and blue	6·50	35·00

DESIGNS—36×43 mm: Nos. 222/4, Caproni Ca 101 airplane over landscape; 225/7, Savoia Marchetti S-66 flying boat over globe.

31 King Victor Emmanuel III and Caproni Ca 101 Airplane

1934. Air. Rome–Mogadiscio Flight.

228	**31**	25c.+10c. green	6·50	13·00
229	**31**	50c.+10c. brown	6·50	13·00
230	**31**	75c.+15c. red	6·50	13·00
231	**31**	80c.+15c. black	6·50	13·00
232	**31**	1l.+20c. brown	6·50	13·00
233	**31**	2l.+20c. blue	6·50	13·00
234	**31**	3l.+25c. violet	32·00	80·00
235	**31**	5l.+25c. red	32·00	80·00
236	**31**	10l.+30c. purple	32·00	80·00
237	**31**	25l.+2l. green	32·00	80·00

33 Macchi Castoldi MC-94 Flying Boat over Zebu-drawn Plough

1936. Air.

238	**33**	25c. green	2·75	5·25
239	-	50c. brown	2·10	65
240	-	60c. orange	4·25	10·50
241	-	75c. brown	3·25	2·10
242	-	1l. blue	55	65
243	**33**	1l.50 violet	3·25	85
244	-	2l. blue	3·25	4·25
245	-	3l. lake	29·00	19·00
246	-	5l. green	16·00	10·50
247	-	10l. red	37·00	27·00

DESIGNS: 50c., 2l. Caproni Ca 101 airplane over Massawa–Asmara Railway; 60c., 5l. Savoia Marchetti S-74 airplane over Dom palm trees; 75c., 10l. Savoia Marchetti S-73 airplane over roadway through cactus trees; 1, 3l. Caproni Ca 101 airplane over bridge.

INDEPENDENT STATE

35 Soldier with Flag and Scales of Justice

1991. 30th Anniv of Liberation Struggle. (a) As T 35. Size 26×36 mm.

250	5c. black, orange and blue	5·00
251	15c. black, orange & green	5·00
252	20c. black, orange & yellow	5·00

(b) As T 35, but redrawn with dates added either side of "30". Size 24×33 mm.

253	3b. black, orange & silver	30·00
254	5b. black, orange and gold	50·00

36 Map on Ballot Box

1993. Independence Referendum.

255	**36**	15c. multicoloured	40	25
256	-	60c. red, violet & green	1·00	85
257	-	75c. black, red and blue	1·30	1·20
258	-	1b. multicoloured	1·50	1·60
259	-	2b. blue, black & green	3·25	3·00

DESIGNS: 60c. Arrows; 75c. "YES" and "NO" signpost; 1b. Candle; 2b. Dove, posthorn and map.

38 Eritrean Flag

1993. Multicoloured, colour of frame given.

260	**38**	5c. brown	3·00	1·50
261	**38**	5c. blue	6·00	3·00
262	**38**	15c. red	3·00	1·50
263	**38**	20c. gold	15·00	10·00
264	**38**	20c. blue		
265	**38**	25c. blue	3·50	1·50
266	**38**	35c. blue	8·00	4·00
267	**38**	40c. blue	17·00	8·00
268	**38**	50c. blue	6·00	4·00
269	**38**	60c. yellow	4·50	3·00
270	**38**	70c. mauve	4·50	3·00
271	**38**	70c. blue	6·00	4·00
272	**38**	80c. blue	6·00	4·00
273	**38**	3b. green	10·00	6·00
274	**38**	5b. silver	15·00	9·00

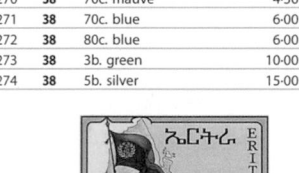

39 National Flag and Map

1994. Multicoloured, colour of frame given.

275	**39**	5c. yellow	40	30
276	**39**	10c. green	45	30
277	**39**	20c. orange	60	35
278	**39**	25c. red	65	35
279	**39**	40c. mauve	70	50
280	**39**	60c. turquoise	90	65
281	**39**	70c. green	1·00	80
282	**39**	1b. orange	1·30	80
283	**39**	2b. orange	2·00	1·80
284	**39**	3b. blue	3·75	2·75
285	**39**	5b. mauve	6·00	3·75
286	**39**	10b. lilac	11·00	7·50

40 Fishermen

1995. 20th Anniv of World Tourism Organization. Multicoloured.

287	10c. Type **40**	50	40
288	35c. Monument (vert)	1·00	60
289	85c. Mountain road	2·50	1·50
290	2b. Archaeological site (vert)	5·00	4·00

41 Red Sea Bannerfish

1995. Marine Life. Multicoloured.

291	30c. Type **41**	50	45
292	55c. Hooded butterflyfish	90	65
293	70c. Shrimp and lobster	1·10	80
294	1b. Blue-lined snapper	1·50	1·10

42 Mountain and broken Manacles

1995. Independence Day. Multicoloured.

295	25c. Type **42**	20	20
296	40c. Planting national flag on mountain top (vert)	30	25
297	70c. Men with national flag and scimitar (vert)	50	35
298	3b. National flag and fireworks (vert)	2·00	1·00

43 Construction Works

1995. "Towards the Bright Future".

299	**43**	60c. black, orange & red	50	30
300	-	80c. multicoloured	70	40
301	-	90c. black, orange & red	75	50
302	-	1b. brown, orange & red	80	60

DESIGNS: 80c. Tree; 90c. Village; 1b. Camels.

44 Dove flying around Map

1995. Council for Mutual Economic Assistance in Africa. Multicoloured.

303	40c. Type **44**	70	35
304	50c. Tree with member countries' names on leaves	80	55
305	60c. Emblem and handshake	90	65
306	3b. Emblem and flags of member countries (horiz)	1·00	1·90

45 Headquarters, New York, and Anniversary Emblem

1995. 50th Anniv of U.N.O. Multicoloured.

307	40c. Type **45**	50	35
308	60c. U.N. Emblem forming tree	70	50
309	70c. Anniversary emblem and peace dove	80	75
310	2b. Type **45**	2·50	1·90

46 Bowl and Spoon

1995. 50th Anniv of F.A.O. Multicoloured.

311	5c. Type **46**	20	15
312	25c. Agriculture	30	20
313	80c. Bird feeding young	90	60
314	3b. Cornucopia of crops	2·75	2·00

47 Eritreans raising Flag

1996. Martyrs' Day. Multicoloured.

315	40c. Type **47**	40	20
316	60c. Man laying wreath on grave	70	40
317	70c. Breast-feeding	80	50
318	80c. Planting seedlings	1·10	60

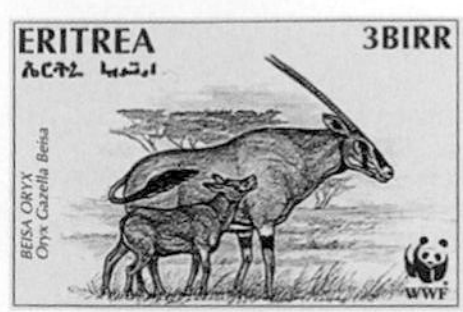

48 Adult and Young

1996. Endangered Animals. Multicoloured. (a) Gemsbok.

319	3b. Type **48**	2·50	1·50
320	3b. Adult eating	2·00	1·50
321	3b. Encounter between two males	2·00	1·50
322	3b. Gemsbok	2·00	1·50

(b) Mammals.

323	3b. Savanna (inscr "Green") monkey	2·00	1·50
324	3b. Aardwolf	2·00	1·50
325	3b. Dugong	2·00	1·50
326	3b. Maned rat	2·00	1·50

(c) White-eyed Gull.

327	3b. Preening	3·00	2·00
328	3b. Flying	3·00	2·00
329	3b. Pair of gulls on rock	3·00	2·00
330	3b. Gull on rock	3·00	2·00

49 Emblem and Mother and Child

1996. 50th Anniv of UNICEF. Designs showing Fund emblem. Multicoloured.

331	40c. Type **49**	50	30
332	55c. Nurse and child	75	35
333	60c. Weighing baby	85	40
334	95c. Amputee beside bed	1·40	70

50 Taking Oath of Allegiance

1996. National Service. Multicoloured.

335	40c. Type **50**	55	30
336	55c. National rebuilding programmes	70	45
337	60c. Road-building (horiz)	95	55
338	95c. Man with club (horiz)	1·30	70

51 Track-laying

1997. Revival of Eritrean Railways. Mult.

339	40c. Type **51**	50	35
340	55c. Steam locomotive on seafront line	1·40	80
341	60c. Seafront tourist diesel locomotive	1·80	1·00
342	95c. Railway tunnel through mountain	2·40	1·40

52 Volleyball

1997. Olympic Games, Atlanta (1996). Mult.

343	2b. Type **52**	90	60
344	2b. Laurel wreath and stars	90	60
345	2b. Basketball (three players reaching for ball)	90	60
346	2b. Torch (with flame to right)	90	60
347	2b. Cycling (facing forward)	90	60
348	2b. Torch (with flame to left)	90	60
349	2b. Cycling (facing right)	90	60
350	2b. Gold medal	90	60
351	2b. Football	90	60
352	3b. Football match (horiz)	1·40	1·00
353	3b. Cycling road race (horiz)	1·80	1·00
354	3b. Volleyball match	1·40	1·00
355	3b. Basketball match	1·40	1·00
MS356	Two sheets each 76×106 mm. (a) 10b. Cycling. (b) 10b. Football	8·00	5·00

53 "Heliconius melpomerie cytherea"

1997. Butterflies and Moths. Multicoloured.

357	1b. Mustard white	40	35
358	2b. Type **53**	80	60
359	3b. "Papilio polymnestor"	1·20	80
360	3b. Paradise birdwing ("Ornithoptera paradisea")	1·20	80
361	3b. "Graphium marcellus"	1·20	80
362	3b. Jersey tiger moth ("Panaxia quadripunctaria")	1·20	80
363	3b. "Cardui japonica"	1·20	80
364	3b. "Papilio childrence"	1·20	80
365	3b. "Philosamea cynthis"	1·20	80
366	3b. Luna moth ("Actias luna")	1·20	80
367	3b. "Heticopis acit"	1·20	80
368	3b. "Psaphis eusehemoides" (vert)	1·20	80
369	3b. "Papilio brookiana" (vert)	1·20	80
370	3b. "Parnassius cynthis" (vert)	1·20	80
371	3b. Blue morpho ("Morpho cypris") (vert)	1·20	80
372	3b. Monarch ("Danaus plexippus") (vert)	1·20	80
373	3b. Gaudy commodore ("Precis octavia") (vert)	1·20	80
374	3b. Kaiser-i-hind ("Teinopalpus imperialis") (vert)	1·20	80
375	3b. "Samia gloreri" (moth) (vert)	1·20	80
376	3b. "Automeris nyctimene" (vert)	1·20	80
377	4b. "Ornithoptera goliath"	1·70	1·10
378	8b. "Heliconius astraea rondonia"	3·00	2·10
MS379	Two sheets, each 84×66 mm. (a) 10b. Small apollo("Parnassius phoebus"); (b). 10b. Tiger swallowtail ("Papilio glaucus") Set of 2 sheets	10·00	7·00

Nos. 359/67 and 368/76 respectively were issued together, se-tenant, the backgrounds forming composite designs.

There are some errors in the Latin inscriptions.

54 Agricultural Land

1997. Environmental Conservation. Mult.

380	60c. Type **54**	1·50	70
381	90c. Hillside tree plantation	2·50	1·00
382	95c. Terraced hillside	2·75	1·20

55 Local Meeting

1997. Adoption of National Constitution. Mult.

383	10c. Type **55**	1·00	40
384	40c. Dove holding open book	1·60	65
385	85c. Open book in hands	1·70	75

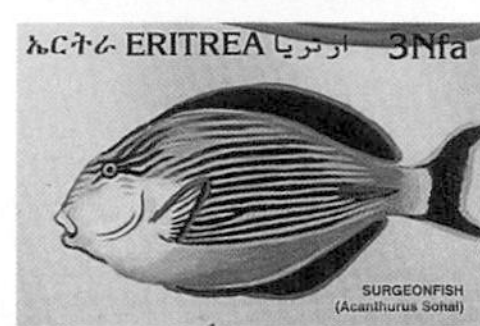

56 Red Sea Surgeonfish

1997. Marine Life. Multicoloured.

386	3n. Sergeant major and white-tipped reef shark	1·10	80
387	3n. Hawksbill turtle and manta ("Devil") ray	1·10	80
388	3n. Type **56**	1·10	80
389	3n. Needlefish ("Red Sea Houndfish") and humpback whale	1·10	80
390	3n. Manta ("Devil") ray	1·10	80
391	3n. Manta ("Devil") ray and two-banded anemonefishes ("Clownfishes")	1·10	80
392	3n. Forceps ("Long-nosed") butterflyfish	1·10	80
393	3n. Needlefish ("Red Sea Houndfish") and yellow sweetlips	1·10	80
394	3n. White moray eel	1·10	80
395	3n. Blue-cheeked ("Masked") butterflyfishes	1·10	80
396	3n. Shark sucker ("Suckerfish") and whale shark	1·10	80
397	3n. Sunrise dottyback and bluefin trevally	1·10	80
398	3n. Moon wrasse, purple moon angel and yellow-tailed ("Two-banded") anemonefish	1·10	80
399	3n. Lionfish	1·10	80
400	3n. White-tipped reef shark and Niki's sanddiver	1·10	80
401	3n. Golden trevallys ("Golden Jacks") and yellow-edged lyretail ("Lunar tailed grouper")	1·10	80
402	3n. Narrow-banded batfishes	1·10	80
403	3n. Red-toothed ("Black") triggerfish	1·10	80
MS404	Two sheets, each 106×76 mm. (a) 10n. Twin spot wrasse (wrongly inscr "Coris angulata"; (b) 10n. Powder-blue surgeonfish ("Acanthurus leucosternon") Set of 2 sheets	9·00	6·00

Nos. 386/94 and 395/403 respectively were issued together, se-tenant, forming a composite design.

57 Village Weaver

1998. Birds. Multicoloured.

405	3n. Type **57** (inscr "Black Headed Weaver")	1·30	80
406	3n. Abyssinian roller	1·30	80
407	3n. Abyssinian ground hornbills	1·30	80
408	3n. Lichtenstein's sandgrouse	1·30	80
409	3n. Erckel's francolin	1·30	80
410	3n. Arabian bustard	1·30	80
411	3n. Chestnut-backed sparrow-lark ("Chestnut-backed Finchlark")	1·30	80
412	3n. Desert lark	1·30	80
413	3n. Hoopoe lark ("Bifasciated Lark")	1·30	80
414	3n. African darter	1·30	80
415	3n. White-headed vulture	1·30	80
416	3n. Egyptian vultures	1·30	80
417	3n. Yellow-billed hornbill	1·30	80
418	3n. Helmet guineafowl	1·30	80
419	3n. Secretary bird	1·30	80
420	3n. Martial eagle	1·30	80

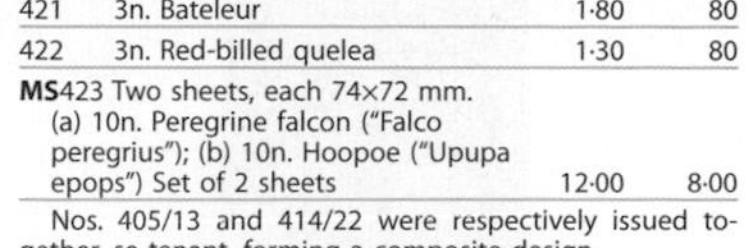

421	3n. Bateleur	1·80	80
422	3n. Red-billed quelea	1·30	80
MS423	Two sheets, each 74×72 mm. (a) 10n. Peregrine falcon ("Falco peregrius"); (b) 10n. Hoopoe ("Upupa epops") Set of 2 sheets	12·00	8·00

Nos. 405/13 and 414/22 were respectively issued together, se-tenant, forming a composite design.

58 Highland Dwelling

1998. Traditional Houses. Multicoloured.

424	50c. Type **58**	90	50
425	60c. Lowland dwelling	1·10	60
426	85c. Danakil dwelling	1·50	90

59 Cunama Hair Style

1998. Traditional Hair Styles. Multicoloured.

427	10c. Type **59**	20	10
428	50c. Tigrinya	1·10	40
429	85c. Bilen	1·70	80
430	95c. Tigre	1·90	1·00

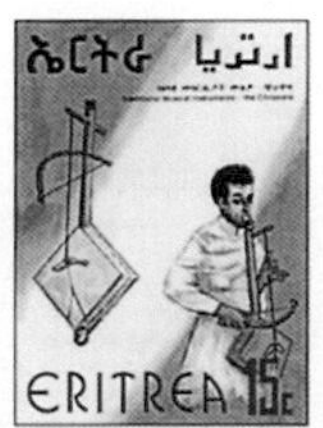

60 Chirawata

1998. Traditional Musical Instruments. Mult.

431	15c. Type **60**	40	25
432	60c. Imbilta, malaket and shambeko (wind instruments)	1·80	90
433	75c. Kobero (drum)	2·20	1·10
434	85c. K'rar (stringed instrument)	2·60	1·30

61 Planting Flag

1999. 8th Anniv of Independence.

435	**61**	60c. multicoloured	50	35
436	**61**	1n. multicoloured	1·00	65
437	**61**	3n. multicoloured	3·00	2·00

62 1 Nafka Banknote

1999. 2nd Anniv of Currency Reform. Multicoloured.

438	10c. Type **62**	25	20
439	60c. 5 nafka banknote	50	40
440	80c. 10 nafka banknote	1·70	90
441	1n. 20 nafka banknote	1·10	70
442	2n. 50 nafka banknote	3·00	1·50
443	3n. 100 nafka banknote	3·00	2·30

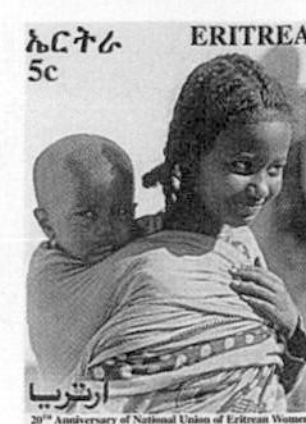

63 Girl carrying Baby

1999. 20th Anniv of National Union of Eritrean Women. Multicoloured.

444	5c. Type **63**	20	10
445	10c. Women reading (horiz)	25	15
446	25c. Crowd (horiz)	35	20
447	1n. Soldier using binoculars (horiz)	1·00	80

64 Flag and Man

2000. Millennium. Designs showing the Eritrean Flag and a local scene. Multicoloured.

448	5c. Type **64**	25	25
449	10c. *Denden Assab* (freighter)	50	40
450	25c. Procession in stadium	20	20
451	60c. Soldiers and camp	30	20
452	1n. Raised hand and names of indigenous language groups	50	30
453	2n. Crowd sitting beneath tree	1·00	50
454	3n. Hand posting ballot paper	1·60	90
455	5n. Military equipment	4·25	1·00
456	7n. State emblem	4·00	2·00
457	10n. Eritrean 10n. banknote	6·00	3·00

65 Black-tipped Grouper (*Epinephelus fasciata*)

2000. Marine Life. Multicoloured.

458	3n. Type **65**	1·10	95
459	3n. Regal angelfish (*Pygoplites diacanthus*)	1·10	95
460	3n. Coral hind (*Cephalopholis miniata*)	1·10	95
461	3n. Eibl's angelfish (*Centropyge eibli*)	1·10	95
462	3n. Yellow boxfish (*Ostracion cubicus*)	1·10	95
463	3n. Pennant coralfish (*Heniochus acuminatus*)	1·10	95
464	3n. *Chilomycterus spilostylus*	1·10	95
465	3n. Gray humbug (*Dascyllus marginatus*)	1·10	95
466	3n. Undulate triggerfish (*Balistapus undulatus*)	1·10	95
467	3n. Semicircle angelfish (*Pomacanthus semicirculatus*)	1·10	95
468	3n. Picasso triggerfish (*Rhinecanthus assasi*)	1·10	95
469	3n. Millepora (coral)	1·10	95
470	3n. Coachwhip ray	1·10	95
471	3n. Sulfur damselfish	1·10	95
472	3n. Grey moray	1·10	95
473	3n. Sabre squirrelfish	1·10	95
474	3n. Rusty parrotfish	1·10	95
475	3n. Striped eel catfish	1·10	95
476	3n. Spangled emperor	1·10	95
477	3n. Devil scorpionfish	1·10	95
478	3n. Crown squirrelfish	1·10	95
479	3n. Vanikoro sweeper	1·10	95
480	3n. Sergeant major	1·10	95
481	3n. Giant manta	1·10	95
MS482	Four sheets, each 92×73 mm. (a) 10n. Sea goldis ("Anthias squamipinnis"); (b) 10n. Lemon-peel angelfish ("Centropyge flavissimus"); (c) 10n. Fourline wrasse ("Larabicus quadrillineatus"); (d) 15n. Yellow-banded angelfish ("Pomacathus maculossus")	17·00	13·00

66 Women talking

2001. 10th Anniv of Independence. Multicoloured.

483	20c. Type **66**	20	15
484	60c. Flag and doves (vert)	55	40
485	1n. Emblem (vert)	1·30	70
486	3n. Celebrating (vert)	3·50	2·00
MS487	200×115 mm. Nos. 483/6	7·00	

67 Adult lying down

2001. Aardwolf (Proteles cristatus). Multicoloured.

488	3n. Type **67**	1·00	70
489	3n. Cubs	1·00	70
490	3n. Adult walking	1·00	70
491	3n. Adult head	1·00	70

68 Aardvark

2001. Wild Animals. Two sheets, each 149×83 mm, containing T 68 and similar horiz designs. Multicoloured.

MS492 (a) 3n. Type **68**; 3n. Black-backed jackal; 3n. Striped hyaena; 3n. Spotted hyaena; 3n. Leopard; 3n. African elephant; (b) 3n. Salts dik-dik (inscr "Dick Dick"); 3n. Klipspringer; 3n. Greater kudu (inscr "Tragelophus"); 3n. Soemmerring's gazelle (inscr "soemmering"); 3n. Dorcas gazelle; 3n. African ass (inscr "Equu") Set of 2 sheets 7·50 5·00

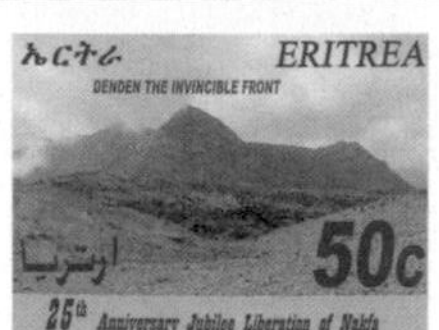

69 Denden

2002. 25th Anniv of Nakfa. Multicoloured.

493	50c. Type **69**	25	20
494	1n. "Nafka 1977" (79×27 mm)	55	30
495	3n. First congress (79×27 mm)	1·60	70

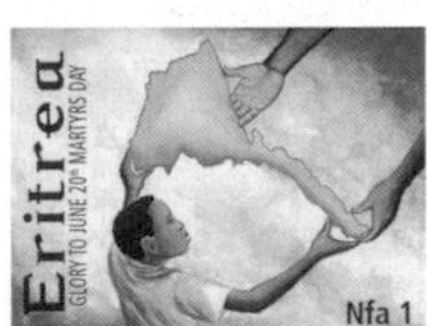

70 Child receiving Map

2002. Martyrs' Day. Multicoloured.

496	1n. Type **70**	30	20
497	2n. Flag	60	35
498	3n. Ship and flag	1·00	55
499	5n. Dove (53×27 mm) (triangular)	1·60	90

71 Flag and Meeting under Tree

2002. National Flag. Multicoloured.

500	30c. Type **71**	2·00	1·50
501	45c. Warrior holding sword	2·00	1·50
502	50c. Celebrations	2·00	1·50
503	60c. Soldiers	2·00	1·50
504	75c. *Denden* (ship)		
505	3n. Ballot box	3·00	2·00

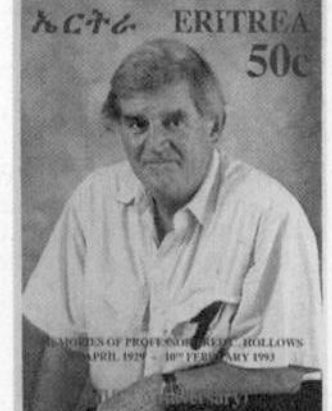

72 Fred Hollows

2003. 10th Death Anniv of Fred Hollows (ophthalmologist and health worker). Multicoloured.

506	50c. Type **72**	30	20
507	1n. Wearing examination equipment	60	40
508	2n. With patient	1·20	80

73 Flags and Clasped Hands

2003. 10th Anniv of Eritrea—China Diplomatic Relations.

509	**73**	4n.50 multicoloured	1·30	1·00

74 Celebrations

2003. National Symbols. Multicoloured.

510	50n. Type **74**	5·50	3·50
511	75n. Massawa (horiz)	7·50	5·00
512	100n. Railway workers (As T **75**) (horiz)	12·00	6·50

75 Railway Workers

2004. Railways.

513	**75**	5c. multicoloured	10	10
514	**75**	10c. multicoloured	10	10
515	**75**	15c. multicoloured	10	10
516	**75**	35c. multicoloured	10	10
517	**75**	50c. multicoloured	25	10
518	**75**	90c. multicoloured	50	20
519	**75**	1n. multicoloured	60	20
520	**75**	2n. multicoloured	1·00	50
521	**75**	10n. multicoloured	3·00	2·00

76 Tanks

2004. 14th Anniv of Operation Fenkil. Mult.

522	40c. Type **76**	1·00	75
523	50c. Gunboat	1·30	1·00

MS524 100×120 mm. Size 80×30 mm. 3n. Type **76**; 3n. Crashed aircraft, people and water; 4n. Three women and water 5·00 3·75

77 "A Long Way but Hopeful"

2004. Paintings by Ghide Ghebremicael. Mult.

525	20c. Type **77**	10	10
526	25c. As Type **77**	10	10
527	40c. As Type **77**	15	10
528	50c. "Young and Promising" (horiz)	15	20
529	55c. "Young and Promising" (horiz)	20	20
530	60c. "Young and Promising" (horiz)	30	25
531	80c. "Highland Woman"	40	35
532	1n. "Highland Woman"	60	45
533	4n.50 "Highland Woman"	2·00	1·60

CONCESSIONAL LETTER POST

1939. No. CL267 of Italy optd ERITREA.

CL248	**CL 109**	10c. brown	29·00	37·00

EXPRESS LETTER STAMPS

1907. Express Letter stamps of Italy optd Colonia Eritrea.

E31	**E35**	25c. red	32·00	24·00
E34	**E 41**	30c. blue and red	£160	£180
E53	**E 35**	50c. red	8·00	25·00

E13

1924

E83	**E13**	60c. brown and red	8·50	30·00
E84	**E13**	2l. pink and blue	27·00	36·00

1926. Surch.

E113	**E 13**	70 on 60c. brn & red	8·50	21·00
E116	**E 13**	1l.25 on 60c. brown and red	16·00	5·25
E114	**E 13**	2l.50 on 2l. pink and blue	27·00	37·00

OFFICIAL AIR STAMP

1934. Optd SERVIZIO DI STATO and Crown.

O238	**31**	25l.+2l. red		£3250

PARCEL POST STAMPS

PRICES: Unused prices are for complete stamps, used prices for a half stamp.

1916. Parcel Post stamps of Italy optd ERITREA on each half of stamp.

P61	**P53**	5c. brown	3·25	7·50
P62	**P53**	10c. blue	3·25	7·50
P63	**P53**	20c. black	3·25	7·50
P64	**P53**	25c. red	3·25	7·50
P65	**P53**	50c. orange	6·50	13·00
P66	**P53**	1l. violet	6·50	13·00
P67	**P53**	2l. green	6·50	13·00
P68	**P53**	3l. yellow	6·50	13·00
P69	**P53**	4l. grey	6·50	16·00
P70	**P53**	10l. purple	70·00	£130
P71	**P53**	12l. brown	£160	£325
P72	**P53**	15l. green	£160	£325
P73	**P53**	20l. purple	£160	£325

1927. Parcel Post stamps of Italy optd ERITREA on each half of stamp.

P123	**P92**	10c. blue	£4250	£700
P124	**P92**	25c. red	£300	55·00
P125	**P92**	30c. blue	3·25	17·00
P126	**P92**	50c. orange	£375	30·00
P127	**P92**	60c. red	5·25	17·00
P128	**P92**	1l. violet	£300	37·00
P129	**P92**	2l. green	£250	37·00
P130	**P92**	3l. yellow	8·00	37·00
P131	**P92**	4l. grey	8·00	37·00
P132	**P92**	10l. mauve	£450	£600
P133	**P92**	20l. purple	£450	£600

POSTAGE DUE STAMPS

1903. Postage Due stamps of Italy optd Colonia Eritrea.

D53	**D12**	5c. mauve & orange	4·25	16·00
D54	**D12**	10c. mauve & orge	6·50	16·00
D32	**D12**	20c. mauve & orge	13·50	27·00
D33	**D12**	30c. mauve & orge	19·00	35·00
D57	**D12**	40c. mauve & orge	37·00	37·00
D58	**D12**	50c. mauve & orge	27·00	32·00
D59	**D12**	60c. mauve & orge	27·00	37·00
D116	**D12**	60c. brown & orge	£100	£150
D37	**D12**	1l. mauve and blue	16·00	65·00
D38	**D12**	2l. mauve and blue	£160	£160
D39	**D12**	5l. mauve and blue	£250	£275
D63	**D12**	10l. mauve and blue	43·00	85·00
D41	**D 13**	50l. yellow	£650	£275
D42	**D 13**	100l. blue	£400	£160

1934. Postage Due stamps of Italy optd ERITREA.

D216	**D141**	5c. brown	1·10	8·50
D217	**D141**	10c. blue	1·10	2·10
D218	**D141**	20c. red	3·75	3·25
D219	**D141**	25c. green	3·75	3·25
D220	**D141**	30c. orange	3·75	8·50
D221	**D141**	40c. brown	3·75	8·50
D222	**D141**	50c. violet	3·75	1·10
D223	**D141**	60c. blue	8·00	16·00
D224	**D 142**	1l. orange	5·25	2·10
D225	**D 142**	2l. green	27·00	43·00
D226	**D 142**	5l. violet	40·00	55·00
D227	**D 142**	10l. blue	48·00	60·00
D228	**D 142**	20l. red	60·00	75·00

For British Administration see **BRITISH OCCUPATION OF ITALIAN COLONIES.**

Pt. 10

ESTONIA

A former province of the Russian Empire on the S. Coast of the Gulf of Finalnd. Under Russian rule until 1918 when it became an independent republic. The area was incorporated into the Soviet Union from 1940; for issueds made during 1941 see GERMAN OCCUPATION OF ESTONIA.

Estonia once again became independent in 1991.

Note: An asterisk * after the date indicates that the stamps have a network background in colour.

1918. 100 kopeks = 1 rouble.
1919. 100 penni = 1 Estonian mark.
1928. 100 senti = 1 kroon.
1991. 100 kopeks = 1 rouble.
1992. 100 senti = 1 kroon
2011. 100 cents = 1 Euro

2

1918. Imperf.

1	**2**	5k. pink	80	70
2	**2**	15k. blue	80	70
3	**2**	35p. brown	85	85
4	**2**	70p. olive	1·70	2·10

4 Seagulls

1919. Imperf.

5	**4**	5p. yellow	2·00	2·75

5 **6** **7**

9 Viking Longship

1919. Imperf (10p., 15m. and 25m. also perf).

6	**5**	5p. orange	10	15
7	**5**	10p. green	20	20
8	**6**	15p. red	10	25
9	**7**	35p. blue	15	25
10	**7**	70p. lilac	20	25
11a	**9**	1m. blue and brown	1·10	55
12a	**9**	5m. yellow and black	2·00	80
33	**9**	15m. green and violet	8·00	60
34	**9**	25m. blue and brown	11·50	2·10

10 L.V.G. Schneider Biplane

1920. Air. Imperf.

15	**10**	5m. black, blue & yellow	5·00	6·00

11 Tallinn

1920. Imperf.

16	**11**	25p. green	30	30
17	**11**	25p. yellow	50	50
18	**11**	35p. red	50	30
19	**11**	50p. green	50	15
20	**11**	1m. red	1·30	40
21	**11**	2m. blue	1·30	40
23	**11**	2m.50 blue	1·30	40

12 Wounded Soldier **13**

1920. War Victims' Fund. Imperf.

24	**12**	35+10p. grey and red	85	1·70
25	**13**	70+15p. bistre and blue	85	1·70

1920. Surch.

26	**6**	1m. on 15p. red	1·00	40
27	**11**	1m. on 35p. red	1·50	85
29	**12**	1m. on 35+10p. grey and red	40	30
28	**7**	2m. on 70p. lilac	1·70	85
30	**13**	2m. on 70+15p. bistre and blue	40	30

17

1921. Red Cross. Imperf or perf.

31A	**17**	2½–3½m. brn, red & orge	2·40	4·00
32A	**17**	5–7m. brn, red & blue	2·40	4·00

18 Weaver **19** Blacksmith

1922. Imperf or perf.

35B	**18**	½m. orange	1·30	50
36B	**18**	1m. brown	2·40	50
37B	**18**	2m. green	2·50	30
38B	**18**	2½m. red	4·75	50
39B	**18**	3m. green	2·50	30
40B	**19**	5m. red	3·75	30
41B	**19**	9m. red	5·25	1·70
42B	**19**	10m. blue	6·25	30
72B	**19**	10m. grey	4·00	6·00
42Ba	**19**	12m. red	7·50	2·10
42Bb	**19**	15m. purple	7·50	85
42Bc	**19**	20m. blue	22·00	50

20 Map of Estonia

1923

43	**20**	100m. blue and olive	23·00	2·75
43a	**20**	300m. blue and brown	85·00	13·50

1923. Air. No. 15 optd 1923 or surch 15 Marka 1923.

44	**10**	5m. black, blue & yellow	10·50	34·00
45	**10**	15m. on 5m. blk, bl & yell	16·00	30·00

1923. Air. Pairs of No. 15 surch 1923 and new value.

46	10m. on 5m.	13·00	38·00
47	20m. on 5m.	25·00	37·00
48	45m. on 5m.	90·00	£200

1923. Red Cross stamps optd Aita hadalist. Imperf or perf.

49A	**17**	2½–3½m. brn, red & orge	65·00	95·00
50A	**17**	5–7m. brown, red & blue	70·00	95·00

24 Junkers F-13 with Floats

1924. Air. Various aircraft. Imperf or perf.

51B	-	5m. black and yellow	1·40	4·25
52B	-	10m. black and blue	1·40	4·25
53B	**24**	15m. black and red	1·40	8·50
54B	-	20m. black and green	1·40	4·25
55B	-	45m. black and violet	1·40	17·00

DESIGNS: 5m. Sabaltnig PIII; 10m. Sabaltnig PIII with floats; 20m. Junkers F-13 with wheels; 45m. Junkers F-13 with skis.

25 National Theatre

1924. Perf.

57	**25**	30m. black and violet	14·00	4·25
58	-	40m. sepia and blue	11·50	2·75
59	**25**	70m. black and red	20·00	5·75

DESIGN: 40m. Vanemuine Theatre, Tartu.

1926. Red Cross stamps surch in figures only. Perf.

60	**17**	5–6 on 2½–3½ brown, red and orange	4·25	8·50
61	**17**	10–12 on 5–7m. brown, red and blue	5·00	8·50

28 Kuressaare Castle **30** Tallinn

1927. Liberation War Commemoration Fund.

62	**28**	5m.+5m. brown & green	95	3·75
63	-	10m.+10m. brown & blue	95	3·75
64	-	12m.+12m. green & red	95	4·00
65	-	20m.+20m. purple & blue	95	6·75
66	**30**	40m.+40m. grey & brown	95	6·75

DESIGNS—As Type **28**: 10m. Tartu Cathedral; 12m. Parliament House, Tallinn. As Type **30**: 20m. Narva Fortress.

1928. 10th Anniv of Independence. Surch 1918 24/11 1928 S. S. Perf.

67	**18**	2s. on 2m. green	1·80	1·30
68	**19**	5s. on 5m. red	1·80	1·30
69	**19**	10s. on 10m. blue	3·25	1·30
70	**19**	15s. on 15m. purple	6·00	1·30
71	**19**	20s. on 20m. blue	5·25	1·30

32 Arms of Estonia

1928

73	**32**	1s. grey	50	10
74	**32**	2s. green	55	10
75	**32**	4s. green	1·30	15
76	**32**	5s. red	1·70	10
77	**32**	8s. purple	3·25	15
78	**32**	10s. blue	1·70	10
79	**32**	12s. red	2·40	15
80	**32**	15s. yellow	3·25	10
80a	**32**	15s. red	25·00	1·50
81	**32**	20s. blue	4·75	10
82	**32**	25s. mauve	7·50	15
83	**32**	25s. blue	21·00	1·50
84	**32**	40s. orange	12·00	60
86	**32**	60s. grey	21·00	60
87	**32**	80s. sepia	25·00	1·10

1930. Surch in KROON.

88	**25**	1k. on 70m. black & red	13·00	6·75
89	**20**	2k. on 300m. blue & brown	32·00	11·50
90	**20**	3k. on 300m. blue & brown	65·00	34·00

35 "Succour"

1931. Red Cross Fund.

91	**35**	2s.+3s. green and red	10·50	8·50
92	-	5s.+3s. rose and red	10·50	8·50
93	-	10s.+3s. blue and red	10·50	8·50
94	**35**	20s.+3s. blue and red	15·00	21·00

DESIGN: 5s., 10s. "The Light of Hope".

37 Tartu Observatory

1932. 300th Anniv of Tartu University.

95	**37**	5s. red	8·00	60
96	-	10s. blue	3·75	60
97	**37**	12s. red	13·00	3·00
98	-	20s. blue	8·25	1·20

DESIGN: 10s., 20s. Tartu University.

39 Narva Falls

1933

99	**39**	1k. black	8·50	3·50
99a	**39**	1k. green	1·70	12·50

40 Ancient Bard

1933. 10th All-Estonian Choral Festival.

100	**40**	2s. green	2·20	25
101	**40**	5s. red	3·50	25
102	**40**	10s. blue	4·50	15

41 Invalid and Nurse

1933. Anti-tuberculosis Fund.

103	**41**	5s.+3s. red	7·75	8·50
104	-	10s.+3s. blue	7·75	8·50
105	-	12s.+3s. red	10·00	12·50
106	-	20s.+3s. blue	13·00	17·00

DESIGNS—HORIZ: 10s., 20s. Taagepera Sanatorium. VERT: 12s. Cross of Lorraine.

43 Harvesting

1935

107	**43**	3k. brown	1·70	5·00

44 Arms of Narva

1936. Charity. Social Relief Fund.

108	**44**	10s.+10s. blue & green	3·75	8·50
109	-	15s.+15s. blue and red	4·50	12·50
110	-	25s.+25s. orange & blue	5·25	17·00
111	-	50s.+50s. yellow & blk	21·00	42·00

DESIGNS—Arms of Parnu (15s.), Tartu (25s.) and Tallinn (50s.).

45 Pres. Konstantin Pats

1936

112	**45**	1s. brown	95	25
113	**45**	2s. green	95	25
113a	**45**	3s. orange	11·50	8·50
114	**45**	4s. purple	1·90	85
115	**45**	5s. green	2·40	25

116	**45**	6s. red	2·00	25
117	**45**	6s. green	34·00	38·00
118	**45**	10s. blue	2·40	25
119	**45**	15s. red	3·00	40
119a	**45**	15s. blue	5·50	3·50
120	**45**	18s. red	27·00	6·00
121	**45**	20s. mauve	4·75	25
122	**45**	25s. blue	12·50	1·70
123	**45**	30s. yellow	20·00	1·70
123a	**45**	30s. blue	25·00	6·75
124	**45**	50s. brown	11·50	1·30
125	**45**	60s. mauve	25·00	6·00

46 Restored Portal

1936. 500th Anniv of St. Brigitte Abbey.

126	**46**	5s. green	55	50
127	-	10s. blue	60	50
128	-	15s. red	2·50	4·25
129	-	25s. blue	3·50	6·00

DESIGNS: 10s. Ruins of the Abbey; 15s. Ruined facade; 25s. Old seal.

47 Paide

1937. Social Relief Fund. Inscr "CARITAS 1937".

130	**47**	10s.+10s. green	2·50	4·25
131	-	15s.+15s. red	2·50	5·00
132	-	25s.+25s. blue	4·75	8·50
133	-	50s.+50s. purple	8·50	19·00

DESIGNS—Arms of: Rakvere (15s.); Valga (25s.); Viljandi (50s.).

48 Paldiski (Port Baltic)

1938. Social Relief Fund. Inscr "CARITAS 1938".

134	**48**	10s.+10s. brown	3·50	8·50
135	-	15s.+15s. grn & red	3·50	7·50
136	-	25s.+25s. red & blue	6·75	21·00
137	-	50s.+50s. yell & blue	17·00	42·00
MS138 106×150 mm. Nos. 134/7			46·00	85·00

DESIGNS: Arms of: Voru (15s.); Haapsalu (25s.); Kuresaare (50s.).

49 Cargo Liner "Aegna" in Tallinn Harbour

1938

139	**49**	2k. blue	1·70	7·50

50 Dr. F. R. Faehlmann

1938. Centenary of Estonian Literary Society. Designs showing Society founders.

140	**50**	5s. green	65	60
141	-	10s. brown	65	60
142	-	15s. red	1·20	6·00
143	**50**	25s. blue	2·50	7·50
MS143a 90×40 mm. Nos. 140/3			14·00	85·00

DESIGN: 10s., 15s. Dr. F. R. Kreutzwald.

51 Arms of Viljandi

1939. Social Relief Fund. Inscr "CARITAS 1939".

144	**51**	10s.+10s. green	4·25	5·75
145	-	15s.+15s. red (Parnu)	4·25	5·75
146	-	25s.+25s. blue (Tartu)	8·50	13·00
147	-	50s.+50s. pur (Harju)	18·00	35·00
MS147a 90×137 mm. Nos. 144/7			55·00	£110

52 Sanatorium, Parnu

1939. Centenary of Parnu.

148	**52**	5s. green	1·90	95
149	-	10s. violet	1·00	95
150	**52**	18s. red	2·50	6·00
151	-	30s. blue	3·50	7·50
MS151a 137×90 mm. Nos. 148/51			30·00	95·00

DESIGN—10s., 30s. Beach Hotel, Parnu.

53 Laanemaa

1940. Social Relief Fund. Arms. Inscr "CARITAS 1940".

152		10s.+10s. green and blue (Vorumaa)	4·25	8·50
153		15s.+15s. red and blue (Jarvemaa)	4·25	12·50
154	**53**	25s.+25s. blue and red	6·25	25·00
155	-	50s.+50s. orange and blue (Saaremaa)	9·75	34·00

54 Carrier Pigeon and Airplane

1940. Cent of 1st Adhesive Postage Stamps.

156	**54**	3s. orange	25	25
157	**54**	10s. violet	25	15
158	**54**	15s. brown	35	15
159	**54**	30s. blue	3·50	1·30

55 State Arms

1991

161	**55**	5k. red and orange	35	35
162	**55**	10k. green & emerald	25	25
163	**55**	15k. blue and light blue	35	35
164	**55**	30k. black and grey	50	50
165	**55**	50k. brown and orange	70	70
166	**55**	70k. purple and mauve	85	85
167	**55**	90k. magenta & mauve	1·00	1·00
168	**55**	1r. brown (21×27 mm)	1·30	1·30
169	**55**	2r. blue (21×27 mm)	2·50	2·50

See also Nos. 194/205.

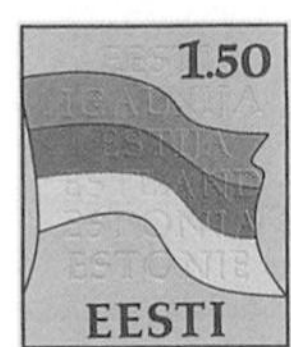

56 Flag

1991

170	**56**	1r.50 multicoloured	2·10	2·10
171	-	2r.50 black, grey & green	3·00	3·00

DESIGN—HORIZ: 2r.50, Map of Europe showing Estonia.

57 State Arms

1992. Value expressed by letter.

172	**57**	E (1r.) green and yellow	25	25
173	**57**	R (10r.) red and pink	85	85
174	**57**	I (20r.) green & blue	1·40	1·40
175	**57**	A (40r.) blue & lt blue	3·00	3·00

See also Nos. 179/81, 182/4 and 189/91.

58 Olympic Rings and Pattern

1992. Olympic Games, Barcelona.

176	**58**	1k.+50s. red	15	35
177	-	3k.+1k.50 green	50	95
178	-	5k.+2k.50 black & blue	60	1·30

DESIGNS: 3k. Olympic rings and pattern (different); 5k. Estonian flag, rings and pattern.

1992. As Nos. 172 and 174/5 but colours changed.

179	**57**	E (10s.) orange & yellow	25	25
180	**57**	I (1k.) green	60	60
181	**57**	A (2k.) blue	1·70	1·70

1992. Value expressed by letter. Size 21×27 mm.

182	X (10s.) brown	25	25
183	X (10s.) green	25	25
184	X (10s.) black	25	25

59 Osprey ("Pandion haliaetus")

1992. Birds of the Baltic.

185	**59**	1k. black and red	70	70
186	-	1k. brown, black & red	70	70
187	-	1k. sepia, brown & red	70	70
188	-	1k. brown, black & red	70	70

DESIGNS: No. 186, Black-tailed godwit ("Limosa limosa"); 187, Goosander ("Mergus merganser"); 188, Common shelducks ("Tadorna tadorna").

1992. Value expressed by letter. Size 21×27 mm.

189	**57**	Z (30s.) mauve	25	25
190	**57**	Z (30s.) red	25	25
191	**57**	Z (30s.) black	25	25

60 Decorated Christmas Tree

1992. Christmas.

192	**60**	30s. multicoloured	15	15
193	**60**	2k. multicoloured	50	50

1993. As Nos. 161/9 but face values in senti.

194	**55**	10s. grey and blue (18×21 mm)	10	10
194a	**55**	10s. brown and blue (18×21 mm)	10	10
195	**55**	20s. black and green (21×27 mm)	10	10
196	**55**	30s. purple and grey (21×27 mm)	10	10
197	**55**	50s. blue and brown (18×21 mm)	10	10
198	**55**	60s. green and purple (18×21 mm)	10	10
199	**55**	80s. blue and mauve (21×27 mm)	10	10
200	**55**	2k.50 turquoise and green (18×21 mm)	40	40
201	**55**	3k.10 red and violet	40	40
202	**55**	3k.30 lilac and violet (18×21 mm)	50	50
203	**55**	3k.60 blue & cobalt	50	50
203a	**55**	3k.60 violet and blue (18×21 mm)	50	50
204	**55**	4k.50 brown & lt brn	50	50
205	**55**	5k. mauve and brown (23×28 mm)	70	70
205a	**55**	5k. mauve and yellow (23×28 mm)	85	85
206	**55**	10k. green and blue (23×28 mm)	1·10	1·10
207	**55**	20k. green and lilac (23×28 mm)	2·10	2·10
209	**55**	60s. brn (21×27 mm)	10	10

61 Birds, Flowers and Envelope within Heart

1993. Friendship.

210	**61**	1k. multicoloured	15	15

62 Anniversary Emblem

1993. 75th Anniv of Republic.

211	**62**	60s. multicoloured	10	10
212	**62**	1k. multicoloured	15	15
213	**62**	2k. multicoloured	40	40

1993. No. 163 surch 0.60.

214	**55**	60s. on 15k. blue & lt blue	15	15

64 Wrestling

1993. Baltic Sea Games. Multicoloured.

215	60s. Type **64**	15	15
216	1k.+25s. Ship with map of Baltic on sail and colours of participating countries as shields	15	15
217	2k. Athlete putting the rock and sports pictograms	35	35

65 Toompea Castle, Tallinn

1993

218	-	1k. black and brown	25	25
219	**65**	2k. brown & lt brown	25	25
219a	-	2k.50 deep lilac and lilac	40	40
219b	-	2k.50 grey	40	40
220	-	2k.70 blue and cobalt	40	40
221	-	2k.90 dp green & green	40	40
222	-	3k. brown and pink	40	40
222a	-	3k.20 dp green & green	40	40
223	-	4k. violet and lilac	50	50
224	-	4k.80 brown and pink	60	60

DESIGNS—HORIZ: 1k. Toolse Castle; 2k.70, Hermann's Castle, Narva; 2k.90, Haapsalu Castle; 3k.20, Rakvere Castle; 4k. Kuressaare Castle; 4k.80, Viljandi Castle. VERT: 2k.50 (219a), Paide Castle; 2k.50 (219b), Purtse Castle; 3k. Kiiu Castle.

66 1918 5k. Stamp and Anniversary Emblem

1993. 75th Anniv of First Estonian Stamps.

225	**66**	1k. multicoloured	15	15
MS226 74×91 mm. 4k. Type **66** against enlarged background of posthorn blower (sold at 5k.)			3·00	3·00

1993. "Mare Balticum" Stamp Exhibition. No. MS226 optd FILATEELIANAITUS MARE BALTICUM '93 24. – 28. NOVEMBER 1993.

MS227	**66**	4k. multicoloured	17·00	17·00

68 Haapsalu Church

1993. Christmas.

228	**68**	80s. red	15	15
229	-	2k. blue	25	25

DESIGN—VERT: 2k. Tallinn church.

69 Lydia Koidula

1993. 150th Birth Anniv of Lydia Koidula (writer).

230	**69**	1k. multicoloured	15	15

70 Ski Jumping

1994. Winter Olympic Games, Lillehammer, Norway. Multicoloured.

231	1k.+25s. Type **70**	15	15
232	2k. Speed skating	25	25

71 Tartu 1869 Emblem

1994. 125th Song Festival. Multicoloured.

233	**71**	1k.+25s. yell, brn & grn	15	15
234	-	2k. brown and blue	25	25
235	-	3k. bistre, brown and stone	40	40
MS236		120×95 mm. 15k. multicoloured	2·50	2·50

DESIGNS: 2k. Tallinn 1923 emblem; 3k. Tallinn 1969 emblem; 15k. 1994 emblem.

72 Squirrel

1994. The Siberian Flying Squirrel. Mult.

237	1k. Type **72**	15	15
238	2k. Squirrel on broad-leafed branch	25	25
239	3k. Squirrel on pine branch	35	35
240	4k. Squirrel with young	50	50

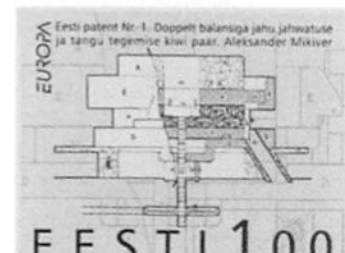

73 Mill (Patent No. 1. Aleksander Mikiver)

1994. Europa. Inventions. Multicoloured.

241	1k. Type **73**	40	40
242	2k.70 "Minox" mini camera (Patent No. 2628, Walter Zapp)	85	85

74 Mustjala Woman

1994. Costumes (1st series). Multicoloured.

243	1k. Type **74**	25	25
244	1k. Jamaja couple	25	25

See also Nos. 254/5, 274/5, 298/9, 316/17, 340/1, 377/8 and 411/12.

75 Kadriorg Palace

1994. 75th Anniv of Estonian Art Museum, Tallinn.

245	**75**	1k.70 multicoloured	25	25

76 "The Holy Family" (Lichtenstein Master)

1994. International Year of the Family.

246	**76**	1k.70 multicoloured	25	25

77 Ruhnu Church

1994. Christmas.

247	**77**	1k.20 brown	15	15
248	-	2k.50 green	35	35

DESIGN—HORIZ: 2k.50, Urvaste Church.

1994. Victims of the "Estonia" Ferry Disaster Fund. No. 248 surch +20 kr 28. 09. 1994 59°23POHJALAIUST 21°42IDAPIKKUST "ESTONIA" laevahuku ohvrite fondi.

249	2k.50+20k. green	7·25	7·25

79 Gustav II Adolphus

1994. 400th Birth Anniv of King Gustav II Adolphus of Sweden.

250	**79**	2k.50 purple	40	40

80 Barnacle Geese

1995. Matsalu Wetland Reserve. Mult.

251	1k.70 Type **80**	35	35
252	3k.20 Greylag geese	50	50

81 "Labourer's Family at Table" (Efraim Allsalu)

1995. 50th Anniv of F.A.O.

253	**81**	2k.70 multicoloured	40	40

1995. Costumes (2nd series). As T 74. Mult.

254	1k.70 Muhu couple	35	35
255	1k.70 Muhu women	35	35

82 Beach Hotel, Parnu (Estonia)

1995. Via Baltica Motorway Project. Multicoloured.

256	1k.70 Type **82**	25	25
MS257	99×109 mm. 3k.20 Type **82**; 3k.20 Bauska Castle (Latvia); 3k.20 Kaunas (Lithuania)	3·00	3·00

83 Broken Barbed Wire

1995. Europa. Peace and Freedom.

258	**83**	2k.70 brown and mauve	85	85

84 U.N. Emblem and Landscape

1995. 50th Anniv of U.N.O.

259	**84**	4k. multicoloured	50	50

85 Lighthouse and Chart

1995. Pakri Lighthouse.

260	**85**	1k.70 multicoloured	25	25

86 Vanemuine Theatre

1995. 125th Anniv of Vanemuine Theatre.

261	**86**	1k.70 orange, black & grn	25	25

87 White-tailed Sea Eagle

1995. "Keep the Estonian Sea Clean".

262	**87**	2k.+25s. black and blue	40	40

88 Pasteur and Bacteria

1995. Death Cent of Louis Pasteur (chemist).

263	**88**	2k.70 multicoloured	40	40

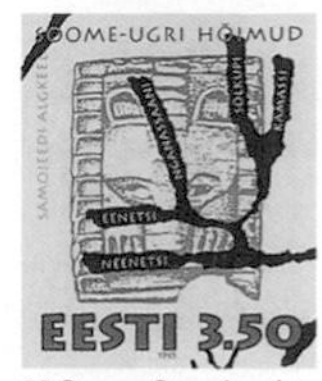

89 Bronze Bear Amulet (Samoyedic group)

1995. Finno-Ugric Peoples. Multicoloured.

264	2k.50 Shaman's drum (Saami group)	40	40
265	2k.50 Karelian writing (Baltic-Finnic group)	40	40
266	3k.50 Duck brooch of Kama area (Volga group)	60	60
267	3k.50 Type **89**	60	60
268	4k.50 Duck-feet pendant (Permic group)	85	85
269	4k.50 Khanty band ornament (Ugric group)	85	85

90 Kunileid and Music

1995. 150th Birth Anniv of Aleksandr Kunileid (composer).

270	**90**	2k. blue	40	40

91 St. Martin's Church, Turi

1995. Christmas.

271	**91**	2k. yellow	35	35
272	-	3k.50 red	50	50

DESIGN: 3k.50, Charles's Church, Tallinn.

92 "Lembit" (submarine)

1996. 60th Anniv of "Lembit".

273	**92**	2k.50 multicoloured	40	40

1996. Costumes (3rd series). As T 74. Mult.

274	2k.50 Emmaste mother and bride	40	40
275	2k.50 Reigi women	40	40

93 1896 Gold Medal

1996. Centenary of Modern Olympic Games and Olympic Games, Atlanta. Sheet 110×66 mm containing T 93 and similar vert designs. Mult.

MS276	2k.50 Type **93**; 3k.50 Alfred Neuland (weightlifter and first Estonian gold medal winner, 1920); 4k. Cycling	1·50	1·50

94 Marie Under (poet)

1996. Europa. Famous Women.

277	**94**	2k.50 multicoloured	85	85

95 Marconi and Wireless Telegraph

1996. Centenary of Guglielmo Marconi's Patented Wireless Telegraph.

278	**95**	3k.50 multicoloured	60	60

96 "Suur Toll"

1996. 82nd Anniv of "Suur Toll" (ice-breaker).

279	**96**	2k.50 multicoloured	50	50

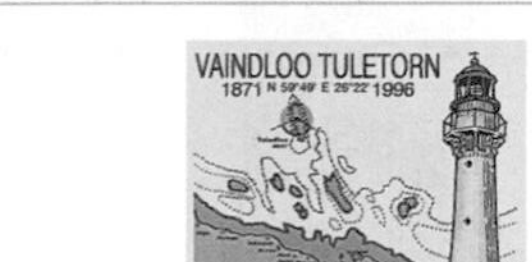
97 Lighthouse and Chart

1996. 125th Anniv of Vaindloo Lighthouse.

280	**97**	2k.50 multicoloured	40	40

98 Class Gk Steam Locomotive

1996. Cent of Narrow-gauge Railway. Mult.

281	3k.20 Type **98**	50	50
282	3k.50 Class DeM diesel railcar	50	50
283	4k.50 Class Sk steam locomotive	70	70

99 Elf and Mother and Child

1996. Christmas (1st issue).

284	**99**	2k.50 multicoloured	40	40

100 Harju-Madise Church

1996. Christmas (2nd issue).

285	**100**	3k.30 blue	50	50
286	-	4k.50 purple	60	60

DESIGNS: 4k.50, Church of the Holy Spirit, Tallinn.

101 Map and Lighthouse

1997. 120th Anniv of Ruhnu Lighthouse.

287	**101**	3k.30 multicoloured	40	40

102 Steller's Sea Eagle

1997. Captive Breeding Programmes at Tallinn Zoo. Multicoloured.

288	3k.30 Type **102**	40	40
289	3k.30 European mink	40	40
290	3k.30 Cinereous vulture	40	40
291	3k.30 Amur leopard	40	40
292	3k.30 Black rhinoceros	40	40
293	3k.30 East Caucasian tur	40	40

103 Von Stephan (after Anton Weber)

1997. Death Cent of Heinrich von Stephan (founder of Universal Postal Union).

294	**103**	7k. gold and black	85	85

104 Goldspinner

1997. Europa. Tales and Legends. "The Goldspinners".

295	**104**	4k.80 multicoloured	1·30	1·30

105 Maasilinn Ship

1997. Baltic Sailing Ships.

296	**105**	3k.30 multicoloured	50	50

1997. Costumes (4th series). Folk Costumes of Swedish Communities in Estonia. As T 74. Multicoloured.

298	3k.30 Couple, Ruhnu Island	40	40
299	3k.30 Family, Vormsi Island	40	40

106 1 Kroon Coin

1997

299a	**106**	10k. silver, black & red	1·10	1·10
300	**106**	25k. silver, black & grn	3·50	3·50
301	**106**	50k. silver, black & grn	8·50	8·50
302	**106**	100k. gold, black & blue	12·00	12·00

107 "Tormilind"

1997. 75th Anniv of Completion of "Tormilind" (barquentine).

305	**107**	5k.50 multicoloured	70	70

108 "Stone Bridge, Tartu" (Tiina Tarve)

1997

306	**108**	3k.30 multicoloured	40	40

109 Title Page

1997. 311th Anniv of Publication of "Wastne Testament" (first translation, by Andreas Verginius, into South Estonian dialect of New Testament).

307	**109**	3k.50 black, ochre & bl	40	40

110 St. Anne's Church, Halliste

1997

308	**110**	3k.30 brown	40	40

111 Dwarves

1997. Christmas.

309	**111**	2k.90 multicoloured	40	40

112 Cross-country Skier

1998. Winter Olympic Games, Nagano, Japan.

310	**112**	3k.60 multicoloured	50	50

113 Arms

1998. 80th Anniv of 1918 Declaration of Independence. Sheet 68×58 mm. Imperf.

MS311	**113** 7k. multicoloured	1·00	95

114 "Porgu", 1932

1998. Birth Centenary of Eduard Wiiralt (artist). Sheet 79×94 mm containing T 114 and similar vert designs. Each black.

MS312	3k.60 Type **114**; 3k.60 "Porgu", 1930; 5k.50 "Enfer", 1932	3·00	2·75

115 Chart and Lighthouse

1998. 99th Anniv of Kunda Lighthouse.

313	**115**	3k.60 multicoloured	50	50

116 Players

1998. World Cup Football Championship, France.

314	**116**	7k. black, red and violet	1·00	95

117 St. John's Eve Bonfire

1998. Europa. National Festivals.

315	**117**	5k.20 multicoloured	1·30	1·20

118 Tallinn Codex, 1282

1998. 750th Anniv of Adoption by Tallinn of Lubeck Law in Charter by King Erik IV of Denmark.

316	**118**	4k.80 multicoloured	85	80

119 Barn Swallow over House

1998. Beautiful Homes Year.

317	**119**	3k.60 multicoloured	50	50

120 Yacht

1998. World 470 Class Junior Yachting Championships, Tallinn Bay.

318	**120**	5k.50 dp blue, bl & red	85	80

1998. Costumes (5th series). As T 74. Mult.

319	3k.60 Couple, Kihnu Island	50	50
320	3k.60 Family, Kihnu Island	50	50

121 "The Bottle Genie" (illustrated by Eduard Jarv)

1998. 50th Death Anniv of Juhan Jaik (children's writer).

321	**121**	3k.60 yellow, blue & blk	50	50

122 Siberian Tiger

1998. Tallinn Zoo.

322	**122**	3k.60 multicoloured	50	50

123 1923 9m. Stamp

1998. 80th Anniv of Estonian Post.
323 **123** 3k.60 red, orange & blk 50 50

124 Freedom Cross

1998. Estonian–Finnish Friendship.
324 **124** 4k.50 multicoloured 50 50

125 Father Christmas and Boy

1998. Christmas. Multicoloured.
325 3k.10 Type **125** 35 30
326 5k. Angels and Christmas tree 70 65

126 Faehlmann

1998. Birth Bicentenary of Friedrich Robert Faehlmann (writer and founder of Learned Estonian Society).
327 **126** 3k.60 multicoloured 50 50

127 Chart and Lighthouse

1999. 190th Anniv of Vilsandi Lighthouse.
328 **127** 3k.60 multicoloured 50 50

128 Snow Leopards

1999. Tallinn Zoo.
329 **128** 3k.60 multicoloured 50 50

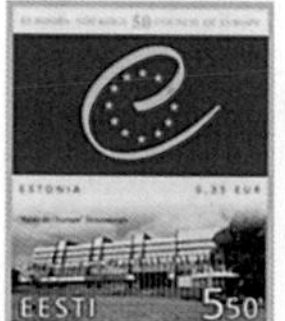

129 Emblem and Palais de l'Europe, Strasbourg

1999. 50th Anniv of Council of Europe.
330 **129** 5k.50 multicoloured 1·30 1·20

130 Meri

1999. 70th Birth Anniv of President Lennart Meri.
331 **130** 3k.60 multicoloured 50 50

131 Tolkuse Bog, Parnu

1999. Europa. Parks and Gardens.
332 **131** 5k.50 multicoloured 85 80

132 Emblem and Bank Headquarters, Tallinn

1999. 80th Anniv of Bank of Estonia.
333 **132** 5k. multicoloured 70 65

133 Olustvere Hall

1999
334 **133** 3k.60 multicoloured 50 50

134 Band and Score

1999. 130th Anniv of National Anthem.
335 **134** 3k.60 multicoloured 40 40

135 Observation Tower

1999. 60th Anniv of Observation Tower on Suur Munamagi (highest point in Baltics).
336 **135** 5k.20 multicoloured 85 80

136 Family and State Flag

1999. 10th Anniv of Baltic Chain (human chain uniting the Capitals of Estonia, Latvia and Lithuania). Multicoloured.
337 3k.60 Type **136** 50 50
MS338 110×72 mm. 5k.50 Type **136** (28×38 mm); 5k.50 Family and Latvian flag (28×38 mm); 5k.50 Family and Lithuanian flag (28×38 mm) 2·50 2·40

137 U.P.U. Emblem

1999. 125th Anniv of Universal Postal Union.
339 **137** 7k. multicoloured 95 90

1999. Costumes (6th series). Setu Costumes of South-east Estonia. As T 74. Multicoloured.
340 3k.60 Bride and bridegroom 60 55
341 5k. Two young men 70 65

138 State Arms

1999
342 **138** 10s. red and pink 10 10
343 **138** 20s. brown and grey 10 10
344 **138** 30s. light blue and blue 10 10
346 **138** 1k. brown and pink 10 10
348 **138** 2k. black 20 20
352 **138** 3k.60 blue and turquoise 50 50
354 **138** 4k.40 deep green and green 60 55
355 **138** 5k. green and light green 85 80
355a **138** 5k. deep green and green 85 80
355b **138** 5k. 50 deep green and green 70 65
356 **138** 6k. brown and yellow 1·00 95
357 **138** 6k.50 brown and yellow 1·10 1·10
359 **138** 8k. brown and pink 1·30 1·20

139 Santa's Helpers

1999. Christmas. Multicoloured.
360 3k.10 Type **139** 40 40
361 7k. Christmas tree (558th anniv of first public Christmas tree in Tallinn) (vert) 1·00 95

1999. New Year Lottery. As No. 360 but with additional premium and lottery numbers.
362 **139** 3k.10+1k.90 mult 85 80

140 Hands of Clock

1999. Year 2000.
363 **140** 5k.50 multicoloured 85 80

141 Faces

2000. Population and Housing Census.
364 **141** 3k.60 multicoloured 50 50

142 Signatures on Treaty

2000. 80th Anniv of Tartu Peace Treaty (between Estonia and Russia).
365 **142** 3k.60 multicoloured 50 50

143 Ristna Lighthouse and Chart

2000. Lighthouses on Kopu Peninsula. Mult.
366 3k.60 Type **143** 50 50
367 3k.60 Kopu lighthouse and chart 50 50

Nos. 366/7 were issued together, se-tenant, forming a composite design.

144 State Arms and Emblem

2000. 10th Anniv of Estonian Congress.
368 **144** 3k.60 multicoloured 50 50

145 Cornflower

2000. National Flower.
369 **145** 4k.80 multicoloured 85 80

146 "E" and Text

2000. National Book Year. 475th Anniv of Publication of Lutheran Catechism (oldest known publication in Estonian).
370 **146** 3k.60 multicoloured 50 50

147 Building Europe

2000. Europa.
371 **147** 4k.80 multicoloured 1·70 1·60

148 Palmse Hall

2000
372 **148** 3k.60 multicoloured 50 50

149 Amur Long-tailed Goral

2000. Tallinn Zoo (1st series).
373 **149** 3k.60 multicoloured 50 50
See also No. 409.

150 Locomotive

2000. Centenary of Viljandi–Tallinn Narrow Gauge Railway.
374 **150** 4k.50 multicoloured 70 65

IX Rahvusvaheline Fennougristika Kongress
EESTI 5.00
151 Hand-woven Girdle

2000. 9th Finno-Ugric Congress, Tartu.
375 **151** 5k. multicoloured 85 80

152 Discus thrower

2000. Olympic Games, Sydney.
376 **152** 8k. multicoloured 1·30 1·20

2000. Costumes (7th series). As T 74. Mult.
377 4k.40 Family, Hargla 70 65
378 8k. Women, Polva 1·20 1·10

153 Malk

2000. Birth Centenary of August Malk (author).
379 **153** 4k.40 multicoloured 85 80

154 European Smelt (*Osmerus eperlanus spirinchus*) and Vendace (*Coregonus albula*)

2000. Fish from Lake Peipsi. Multicoloured.
380 6k.50 Type **154** 1·00 95
381 6k.50 Zander (*Stizostedion lucioperca*) and whitefish (*Coregonus lavaretus maenoides*) 1·00 95

155 Illustration and Emblem

2000. Centenary of National Bookplate. Sheet 80×58 mm containing T 155 and similar vert design. Multicoloured.
MS382 6k. Type **155**; 6k. Man ploughing and emblem 1·90 1·90

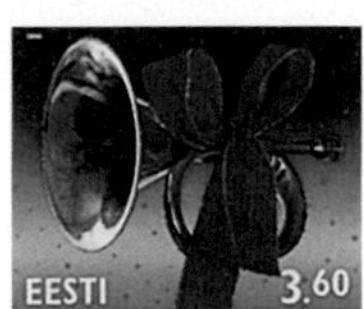

156 Horn with Ribbon

2000. Christmas. Multicoloured.
383 3k.60 Type **156** 60 55
384 6k. Tree decorations 85 80

157 Nool celebrating

2001. Olympic Games, Sydney. Erki Nool (decathlete, gold medallist).
385 **157** 4k.40 multicoloured 85 80

158 Mohni Lighthouse, Lahemaa National Park, Cape Purekkari

2001
386 **158** 4k.40 multicoloured 60 55

159 Couple kissing

2001. St. Valentines Day.
387 **159** 4k.40 yellow, blue & red 60 55

160 Facade

2001. Inauguration (2000) of Stenbock House as Seat of Government and State Chancellery.
388 **160** 6k.50 multicoloured 1·00 95

161 "Girl at the Spring" (detail)

2001. 175th Birth Anniv of Johann Koler (artist). Sheet 58×83 mm containing T 161 and similar horiz design. Multicoloured.
MS389 4k.40 Type **161**; 4k.40 "Eve of the Pomegranate" (detail) 1·30 1·30

162 Text and Emblem

2001. European Year of Languages.
390 **162** 4k.40 multicoloured 85 80

163 Northern Lapwing

2001. Northern Lapwing (Vanellus vanellus).
391 **163** 4k.40 multicoloured 70 65

164 Laupa Hall

2001
392 **164** 4k.40 multicoloured 60 55

165 Sluice, Lake Soodla

2001. Europa. Water Resources.
393 **165** 6k.50 multicoloured 1·30 1·20

166 Emblem

2001. Cent of Kalev (Estonian Sports Association).
394 **166** 6k.50 multicoloured 1·00 95

167 Mud Baths Main Building

2001. 750th Anniv of Parnu.
395 **167** 4k.40 multicoloured 85 80

168 Pockus beside Lake

2001. Pokuland (children's book by Edgar Valter). Multicoloured.
396 3k.60 Type **168** 50 50
397 3k.60 Pocku and owl 50 50
398 3k.60 Pocku and stork 50 50
399 3k.60 Pocku on branch and bird in nest 50 50
400 4k.40 Two Pockus on fence 70 65
401 4k.40 Pocku smelling flower 70 65
402 4k.40 Pocku hugging dog 70 65
403 4k.40 Pocku watching moon 70 65

169 Barn Swallow

2001. 10th Anniv of Independence.
404 **169** 4k.40 multicoloured 85 80

170 Virgin and Child (wooden altarpiece)

2001. 800th Anniv of St. Mary's Land (conversion to Christianity of Estonia, Livonia and Courland).
405 **170** 6k.50 multicoloured 1·00 95

171 1991 5k. State Arms Stamp

2001. 10th Anniv of Re-adoption of Estonian Stamps.
406 **171** 4k.40 multicoloured 85 80

172 Rocky Coastline, Lahemaa, Estonia

2001. Baltic Sea Coast. Multicoloured.
407 4k.40 Type **172** 85 80
MS408 125×60 mm. 6k. As Type **172** (36×30 mm); 6k. Beach, Vidzeme, Latvia (36×30 mm); 6k. Sand dunes, Palanga, Lithuania (36×30 mm) 3·00 2·75

Stamps in similar designs were issued by Latvia and Lithuania.

173 Chinese Alligator (*Alligator sinenesis*)

2001. Tallinn Zoo (2nd series).
409 **173** 4k.40 multicoloured 85 80

174 Estonia 26-9 Racing Car

2001
410 **174** 6k. multicoloured 1·00 95

2001. Costumes (8th series). As T 74. Multicoloured.
411 4k.40 Woman, Paistu 85 80
412 7k.50 Man, Tarvastu 1·20 1·10

175 Snowflake

2001. Christmas. Multicoloured.
413 3k.60 Type **175** 60 55
414 6k.50 Dove (horiz) 1·10 1·10

176 First Radio Station Building and Felix Moor (presenter)

2001. 75th Anniv of National Radio Broadcasting.
415 **176** 4k.40 multicoloured 85 80

177 Skier

2002. Winter Olympic Games, Salt Lake City.
416 **177** 8k. multicoloured 1·10 1·10

178 Sangaste Hall

2002
417 **178** 4k.40 multicoloured 60 55

179 Laidunina Lighthouse, Saaremaa Island, Gulf of Riga

2002
418 **179** 4k.40 multicoloured 60 55

180 Eurasian Tree Sparrow (*Passer montanus*) and House Sparrow(*Passer domesticus*)

2002
419 **180** 4k.40 multicoloured 60 55

181 Apple Blossom

2002
420 **181** 4k.40 multicoloured 60 55

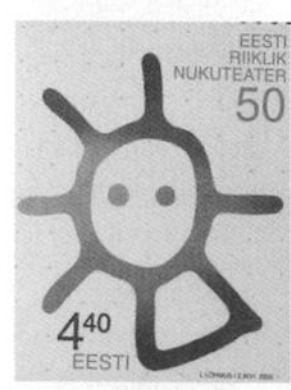

182 Theatre Emblem (E. Kivi)

2002. 50th Anniv Estonian Puppet Theatre, Tallinn.
421 **182** 4k.40 multicoloured 60 55

183 Oppelennuk PTO-4 Training Aircraft

2002
422 **183** 6k. multicoloured 85 80

184 Andrus Veerpalu

2002. Andrus Veerpalu Nordic Skiing Olympic Gold Medallist.
423 **184** 4k.40 multicoloured 60 55

185 University Building

2002. 370th Anniv of Tartu University. Bicentenary of Re-opening. Multicoloured.
424 4k.40 Type **185** 60 55
425 4k.40 Library building 60 55

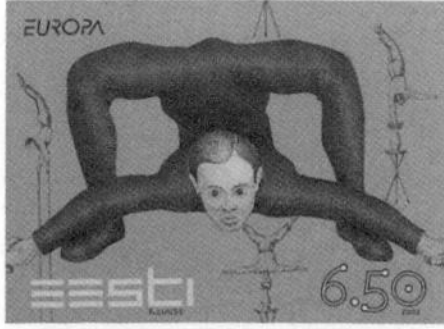

186 Acrobat

2002. Europa. Circus.
426 **186** 6k.50 multicoloured 1·30 1·20

187 Emblem

2002. 10th Anniv of New Constitution.
427 **187** 4k.40 ultramarine and blue 60 55

188 Ancient Coin and Modern Arms

2002. 700th Anniv of Granting of Lubek Charter to Rakvere.
428 **188** 4k.40 multicoloured 60 55

189 Lydia Koidula (poet)

2002. 10th Anniv of Re-introduction of the Kroon (currency). Sheet 53×76 mm containing T 189 and similar horiz design. Multicoloured.
MS429 4k.40 Type **189**; 4k.40 Carl Robert Jackson (writer) 1·20 1·10

190 Top Left Quarter of Decorated Plate

2002. Birth Centenary of Adamson-Eric (artist). Sheet 86×75 mm containing T 190 and similar horiz designs. Multicoloured.
MS430 4k.40 Type **190**; 4k.40 Top right; 4k.40 Bottom left; 4k.40 Bottom right 2·40 2·30

The stamps in No. **MS**430 form a composite design of a decorated plate.

191 Wild Boar (*Sus scofa*)

2002
431 **191** 4k.40 multicoloured 60 55

192 Limestone Cliff, Cape Pakri

2002. Limestone (National Stone).
432 **192** 4k.40 multicoloured 60 55

193 Women, Kolga-Jaani Region

2002. Folk Costumes. Multicoloured.
433 4k.40 Type **193** 60 55
434 5k.50 Couple dancing, Suure-Janni region 75 75

See also Nos. 501/2.

194 Lamb wearing Ribbon

2002. Christmas. Multicoloured.
435 3k.60 Type **194** 40 40
436 6k.50 Tree covered in snow (vert) 85 80

195 Keri Lighthouse, Prangli Island, Gulf of Riga

2003
437 **195** 4k.40 multicoloured 60 55

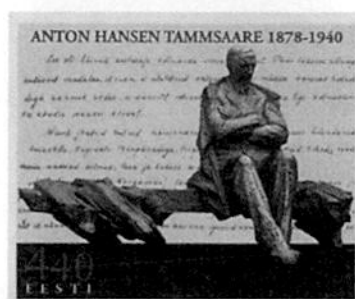

196 Anton Tammsaare (sculpture, Jaak Soans and Rein Luup)

2003. 125th Birth Anniv of Anton Hansen Tammsaare (writer).
438 **196** 4k.40 multicoloured 60 55

197 Magpie (*Pica pica*)

2003
439 **197** 4k.40 multicoloured 60 55

198 Tulips (*Tulipa*)

2003. Flowers. Sheet 130×67 mm containing T 198 and similar vert designs. Multicoloured.
MS440 4k.40×4, Type **198**; Hellebore (*Helleborus purpurascens*); Pheasant's eye daffodil (*Narcissus poeticus*) (inscr "Nartcissus"); Crocus (*Crocus vernus*) 2·50 2·40

199 Alatskivi Hall

2003
441 **199** 4k.40 multicoloured 60 55

200 President Ruutel

2003. 75th Birth Anniv of Arnold Ruutel, President of Estonia.
442 **200** 4k.40 multicoloured 60 55

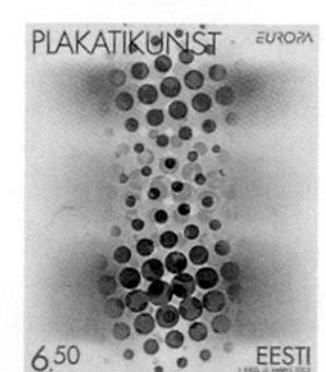

201 Multicoloured Printing Raster

2003. Europa. Poster Art.
443 **201** 6k.50 multicoloured 1·30 1·20

202 Globe Flower (*Trollius ledebourii*)

2003. Bicentenary of Tartu University Botanic Garden.
444 **202** 4k.40 multicoloured 60 55

203 Championship Emblem

2003. 14th World Under 21 Orienteering Championship, Polva.
445 **203** 7k.50 multicoloured 1·00 95

204 Adam von Krusenstern and *Neva* and *Nadezhda*

2003. Bicentenary of Adam Johann von Krusenstern's Circumnavigation of the World.
446 **204** 8k. multicoloured 1·10 1·10

205 Ringed Seal (*Phoca hispida*)

2003
447 **205** 4k.40 multicoloured 60 55

206 *Vostok* and Fabian von Bellingshausen

2003. 225th Birth Anniv of Fabian Gottlieb von Bellingshausen (explorer).
448 **206** 8k. blue, sepia and ochre 1·10 1·10

207 Danish Coin and "Arrival of Scandinavian Seamen" (detail)

2003. Ancient Trade Route along Gulf of Finland and Dnieper River, Ukraine. Multicoloured.

449	6k.50 Type **207**	85	80
450	6k.50 11th-century silver coin and Viking ship	85	80

2003. Folk Costumes. As T 193. Multicoloured.

451	4k.40 Aksi women, Tartu	60	55
452	5k.50 Family, Otepää region	85	80

208 Great Tit holding Rose

2003. Christmas. Multicoloured.

453	3k.60 Type **208**	40	40
454	6k. Mary and Jesus (stained glass)	75	75

209 "Voyage to the End of the World" (book illustration, Kristjan Raud)

2003. Birth Bicentenary of Friedrich Reinhold Kreutzwald (writer). Sheet 100×73 mm containing T 209 and similar vert design.

MS455	4k.40 blue and black; 6k.50 multicoloured	1·40	1·40

DESIGNS: Type **209**; 6k.50 Friedrich Reinhold Kreutzwald.

210 Lighthouse, Sorgu Island, Gulf of Riga

2004. Centenary of Sorgu Lighthouse.

456	**210**	4k.40 multicoloured	60	50

211 Wolf (*Canis lupus*)

2004

457	**211**	4k.40 multicoloured	70	55

212 Map and Wheel

2004. 150th Anniv of Hioma (Estonian barque) Voyage around Cape Horn.

458	**212**	8k. multicoloured	1·70	1·60

213 Violet (*Viola riviniana*)

2004. Flowers. Sheet 130×66 mm containing T 213 and similar vert designs. Multicoloured.

MS459	4k.40×4, Type **213**; Wood anemone (*Anemone nemorosa*); Hepatica nobilis; Globeflower (*Trollius europaeus*)	4·25	4·00

214 Adult and Chicks

2004. Endangered Species. White Stork (Ciconia ciconia).

460	**214**	4k.40 multicoloured	1·00	80

215 NATO Emblem

2004. Accession to NATO (North Atlantic Treaty Organization).

461	**215**	6k. blue, ultramarine and orange	85	65

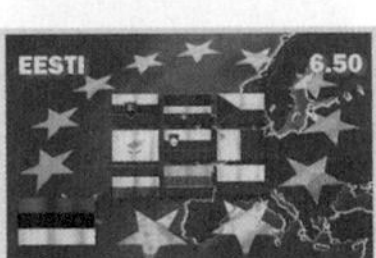

216 New Member Flags and EU Emblem

2004. Accession to European Union.

462	**216**	6k.50 multicoloured	1·40	1·40

217 Sailing (image scaled to 69% of original size)

2004. Europa. Holidays.

463	**217**	6k.50 multicoloured	1·40	1·40

218 Town Hall

2004. 600th Anniv of Tallinn Town Hall.

464	**218**	4k.40 multicoloured	60	50

219 Otepaa Church and Flag

2004. 120th Anniv of National Flag.

465	**219**	4k.40 multicoloured	85	65

220 Vasalemma Hall

2004

466	**220**	4k.40 multicoloured	85	65

221 Runner carrying Torch

2004. Olympic Games, Athens 2004.

467	**221**	8k. multicoloured	2·00	1·60

222 Dragon ClassYacht

2004. 75th Dragon Class European Championship, Tallin, Estonia.

468	**222**	6k. multicoloured	1·50	1·20

223 Dandelion

2004. Self-adhesive gum.

469	**223**	30s. multicoloured	10	10

224 Harjumaa

2004. Town Arms (1st series). Each emerald, scarlet and black. Self-adhesive gum.

470	4k.40 Type **224**	85	65
471	4k.40 Hiiumaa	85	65

See also Nos. 481/2, 494/5, 509/10, 513, 530; 540 and 552.

2004. Folk Costumes. As T 193. Multicoloured.

472	4k.40 Couple, Viru-Jaagupi	95	75
473	7k.50 Johvi women	1·60	1·20

225 Candle and Fir Twigs

2004. Christmas. Multicoloured.

474	4k.40 Type **225**	95	75
475	6k.50 Poinsettia (horiz)	1·40	1·20

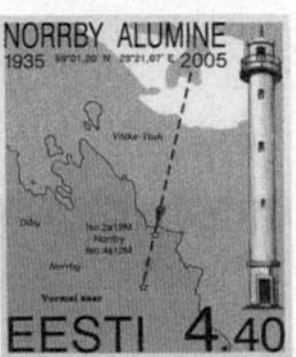

226 Norrby Alumine Lighthouse

2005. 70th Anniv of Norrby Lighthouses, Vormsi Islands. Multicoloured.

476	4k.40 Type **226**	1·20	90
477	4k.40 Norrby Ulemine	1·20	90

227 Beaver (*Castor fiber*)

2005

478	**227**	4k.40 multicoloured	1·20	90

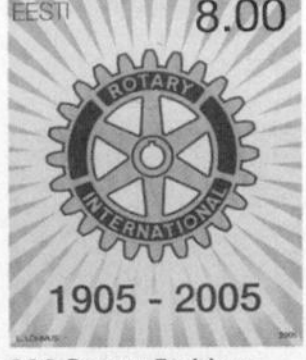

228 Rotary Emblem

2005. Centenary of Rotary International (charitable organisation).

479	**228**	8k. multicoloured	2·00	1·50

229 National Flag flying from Pikk Herman Tower

2005

480	**229**	5k. multicoloured	1·20	90

2005. Town Arms (2nd series). As T 224. Multicoloured. Self-adhesive gum.

481	4k.40 Ida-Virumaa	1·20	90
482	4k.40 Jarvamaa	1·20	90

230 Two Swans

2005. Spring. Sheet 89×69 mm containing T 230 and similar horiz designs. Multicoloured.

MS483	4k.40×4, Type **230**; Swan and bulrushes; Swan and pondweed: Two swans (different)	3·75	3·75

231 Goshawk (*Accipiter gentiles*)

2005

484	**231**	4k.40 multicoloured	1·20	90

232 Hands exchanging Flower

2005. Mothers' Day.

485	**232**	4k.40 multicoloured	1·20	90

233 Vegetable Cornucopia

2005. Europa. Gastronomy. Multicoloured.

486	6k. Type **233**	1·50	1·10
487	6k.50 Vegetables as rainbow	1·70	1·30

234 Eduard Tubin

2005. Birth Centenary of Eduard Turbin (composer).
488 **234** 6k. multicoloured 1·50 1·10

235 Swallows

2005. International Children's Day. Multicoloured.
489 4k.40 Type **235** 1·10 80
490 4k.40 Butterflies 1·10 80

236 *Epipactis palustris*

2005. Flowers. Multicoloured.
491 4k.40 Type **236** 1·10 80
492 8k. *Epipogium aphyllum* 1·90 1·70

237 St. John's Church

2005. 975th Anniv of Tartu (city).
493 **237** 4k.40 multicoloured 1·10 80

2005. Arms (3rd series). As T 224. Multicoloured. Self-adhesive.
494 4k.40 Jogeva county 1·10 80
495 4k.40 Laane county 1·10 80

238 Kiltsi Hall

2005
496 **238** 4k.40 multicoloured 1·10 80

239 Church Facade

2005. St. Catherine's Karja Church.
497 **239** 4k.40 multicoloured 1·10 90

240 "Igavesti voidutsev armastus"

2005. 150th Birth Anniv of Amandus Adamson (artist). Sheet 116×50 mm containing T 240 and similar vert designs. Multicoloured.
MS498 6k.50×4, Type **240**; "Luuriline muusika"; "Memento mori"; "Koit ja Hamarik" 6·25 6·25

241 Kazak Tazi (hound)

2005. Hunting Dogs. Multicoloured.
499 6k.50 Type **241** 1·50 1·20
500 6k.50 Estonia hound 1·50 1·20

Stamps of similar design were issued by Kazakhstan.

2005. Folk Costumes. As T 193. Multicoloured.
501 4k.40 Family, Ambla 1·10 90
502 8k. Turi women 2·00 1·60

242 New Year Goat

2005. Christmas and New Year. Multicoloured.
503 **242** 4k.40 multicoloured 1·10 90
504 - 8k. bright crimson 2·00 1·60

DESIGNS: 4k.40 Type **242**; 8k. Magi (15th-century woodcut).

As from No. 505 stamps are denominated in both Euros and Kroon.

243 Emblem

2006. 50th Anniv of Europa Stamps. Multicoloured.
505 6k. Type **243** 1·40 1·10
MS506 73×68 mm. 6k.50 "1956–2006" 1·50 1·50

2006. National Flag flying from Pikk Herman Tower. Self-adhesive.
507 **229** 11k. multicoloured 2·30 2·20

244 Skiers

2006. Winter Olympic Games, Turin.
508 **244** 8k. multicoloured 1·90 1·50

2006. Arms (4th series). As T 224. Multicoloured. Self-adhesive.
509 4k.40 Laane-Viru county 1·10 90
510 4k.40 Polva county 1·10 90

245 Elk (*Alces alces*)

2006
511 **245** 4k.40 multicoloured 1·10 90

247 Museum Building

2006. Opening of Kumu, National Art Museum.
512 **247** 4k.40 multicoloured 1·10 90

2006. Arms (5th series). As T 224. Multicoloured. Self-adhesive.
513 4k.40 Parnumaa 1·10 90

249 Costume Designs for *Vikerlased* (opera by Evald Aav)

2006. Centenary of National Opera. Sheet 130×68 mm containing T 249 and similar vert design. Multicoloured.
MS514 6k.50×2, Type **249**; Helmi Puur (ballerina) *(Swan Lake* by Tchaikovsky) 3·25 3·25

250 Kristina Smigun (image scaled to 71% of original size)

2006. Kristina Smigun—Olympic Gold Medallist—Turin, 2006 (514). Kristina Smigun and Andrus Veerpalu—Double Gold Medallists (MS516). Multicoloured.
515 4k.40 Type **250** 1·10 90
MS516 96×42 mm. Size 33×29 mm. 8k.×2, Andrus Veerpalu; Kristina Smigun 4·25 4·25

251 Yellow Wagtail (*Motacilla flava*)

2006
517 **251** 4k.40 multicoloured 1·10 90

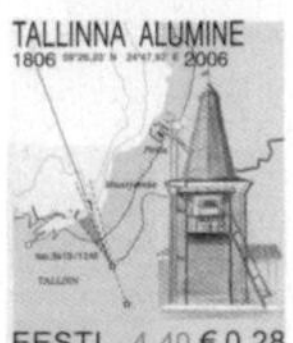

252 Tallinna Alumine Lighthouse

2006. Bicentenary of Tallinn Lighthouses. Mult.
518 4k.40 Type **252** 1·10 90
519 6k.50 Tallinna Ulemine 1·10 90

253 Trophy and Emblem

2006. 75th Anniv of Sport Shooting Association.
520 **253** 4k.40 red and silver 1·60 1·30

254 Faces

2006. Europa. Integration.
521 **254** 6k.50 multicoloured 1·10 90

255 Chocolates

2006. Bicentenary of Confectionary Industry.
522 **255** 4k.40 multicoloured 1·70 1·40

256 Bands of Grey

2006. My Stamp. Self-adhesive.
523 **256** 4k.40 multicoloured 1·10 90

257 *Hepatica nobilis*

2006. Self-adhesive.
524 **257** 30s. multicoloured 1·10 90

258 Duck Family

2006. 60th Anniv of UNICEF.
525 **258** 4k.40+1k. multicoloured 10 10

259 Chestnut with Blaze

2006. 150th Anniv of Tori Stud Farm. Sheet 52×75 mm containing T 259 and similar horiz design. Multicoloured.
MS526 4k.40×2, Type **259**; Bright bay, mares and foal 2·25 2·25

260 Naval Arms

2006. Victory Day.
527 **260** 4k.40 multicoloured 1·10 90

261 Organ Pipes

2006. 20th International Organ Music Festival, Tallinn.
528 **261** 4k.40 multicoloured 1·10 90

262 Taagepera Hall

2006
529 **262** 4k.40 multicoloured 1·10 90

2006. Arms. As T 224. Self-adhesive.
530 4k.40 Raplama 1·10 90

263 St Lawrence's Church, Noo

2006. Churches.
531 **263** 4k.40 multicoloured 1·10 90

264 Betti Alver

2006. Birth Centenary of Betti Alver (poet).
532 **264** 4k.40 multicoloured 1·10 90

265 *Balaenoptera acutorostrata*

2006. Antarctica. Multicoloured.
533 8k. Type **265** 1·90 1·60
534 8k. *Aptenodytes forsteri* 1·90 1·60

266 Santa on Skis

2006. Christmas. Multicoloured.
535 4k.40 Type **266** 1·20 95
536 6k. Lantern 1·20 95

267 Lotte

2007. Lotte from Gadgetville (cartoon character).
537 **267** 4k.40 multicoloured 1·20 95

2007. National Flag flying from Pikk Herman Tower. Self-adhesive.
538 **229** 5k. multicoloured 1·30 1·10

268 *Leucanthemum vulgare*

2007. Self-adhesive.
539 **268** 30s. multicoloured 1·00 80

2007. Arms. As T 224. Self-adhesive.
540 4k.40 Saaremaa 1·20 95

269 Sagadi Hall

2007
541 **269** 5k.50 multicoloured 1·40 1·10

270 Bands of Blue

2007. My Stamp. Self-adhesive.
542 **270** 5k.50 multicoloured 1·40 1·10

271 Juminda Lighthouse

2007. 70th Anniv of Juminda Lighthouse.
543 **271** 6k. multicoloured 1·40 1·20

272 Badger (*Meles meles*)

2007
544 **272** 4k.40 multicoloured 1·20 95

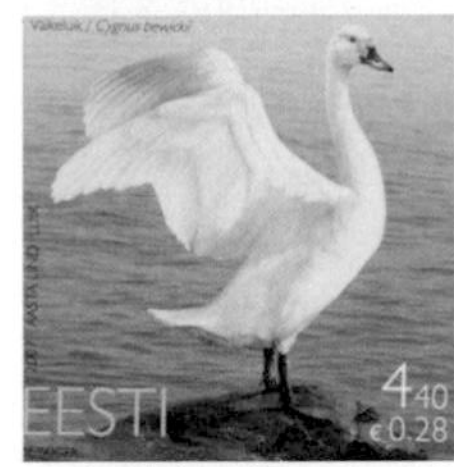

273 Bewick Swan (*Cygnus bewickii*)

2007
545 **273** 4k.40 multicoloured 1·20 95

274 *Paeonia officinalis*

2007. Flowers. Sheet 130×68 mm containing T 274 and similar vert designs. Multicoloured.
MS546 4k.40×4, Type **274**; *Lilium lancifolium*; *Rosa ecae*; *Iris latifolia* 4·50 4·25

275 Robert Baden-Powell and Scouts

2007. Europa. Centenary of Scouting.
547 **275** 20k.50 multicoloured 5·25 5·00

276 Balloons

2007. International Children's Day.
548 **276** 10k. multicoloured 2·50 2·30

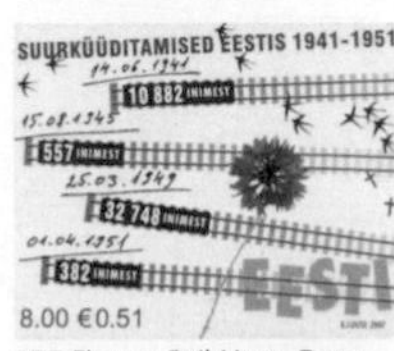

277 Flower, Rail Lines, Dates and Numbers of Deported

2007. Deportation of Estonians. Sheet 71×58 mm.
MS549 8k. multicoloured 2·10 1·90

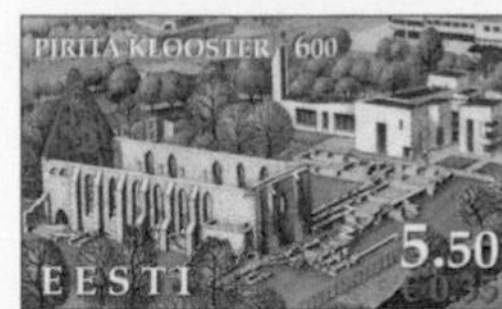

278 Old and New Convent Buildings

2007. 600th Anniv of Pirita Convent.
550 **278** 5k.50 multicoloured 1·40 1·20

279 *Centaurea phrygia* (knapweed)

2007. Self-adhesive.
551 **279** 1k.10 multicoloured 1·00 90

2007. Arms (8th series). As T 224. Multicoloured. Self-adhesive.
552 5k.50 Tartumaa 1·40 20

2007. Flag on Tower.
553 **229** 10k. multicoloured 2·50 2·30

280 Hellenurme Water Mill

2007
554 **280** 5k.50 multicoloured 1·40 1·20

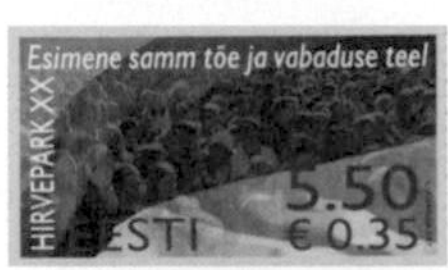

281 Demonstrators

2007. 20th Anniv of Independence Demonstration, Hirvepark.
555 **281** 5k.50 multicoloured 1·40 1·20

282 Woman and Trees

2007. 150th Birth Anniv of Mathias Johann Eisen (folklore collector). Sheet 51×66 mm. Imperf.
MS556 10k. multicoloured 2·50 2·30

283 Ragnar Nurkse

2007. Birth Centenary of Ragnar Nurkse (economist).
557 **283** 10k. multicoloured 2·50 2·30

284 St John's Church, Kanepi

2007. Churches.
558 **284** 5k.50 multicoloured 1·40 1·20

285 Arms

2007. Viljandi City.
559 **285** 5k.50 multicoloured 1·40 1·20

286 Star enclosing Children

2007. Christmas. Multicoloured. Self-adhesive.
560 5k.50 Type **286** 1·50 1·30
561 8k. Snow scene viewed through window (horiz) 2·00 2·80

287 Posthorn

2008. Self-adhesive.
562 **287** 5k.50 orange 1·50 1·30

288 Gustav Ernesaks

2008. Birth Centenary of Gustav Ernesaks (composer and conductor).
563 **288** 5k.50 multicoloured 1·50 1·30

289 Mehikoorma Lighthouse

2008. 70th Anniv of Mehikoorma Lighthouse.
564 **289** 5k.50 multicoloured 1·50 1·30

290 Arms

2008. Valga County. Self-adhesive.
565 **290** 5k.50 multicoloured 1·50 1·30

291 *Plecotus auritus* (brown long-eared bat)

2008. Fauna.
566 **291** 5k.50 multicoloured 1·50 1·30

292 Oak Tree

2008. 90th Anniv of Estonia Republic.
567 **292** 5k.50 multicoloured 1·50 1·30

2008. Post Horn. Self-adhesive.
568 **287** 6k.50 green 1·70 1·50

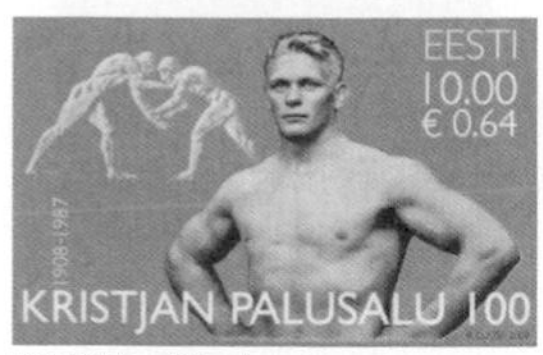

293 Kristjan Palusalu

2008. Birth Centenary of Kristjan Palusalu (Olympic wrestling gold medalist–1936).
569 **293** 10k. multicoloured 2·75 2·50

294 Order of National Coat of Arms (Estonia)

2008. Baltic State's Orders. Multicoloured.
570 5k.50 Type **294** 1·50 1·20
MS571 116×51 mm. Size 10k.×3, As Type **571**; Order of Three Stars (Latvia); Order of Vytautas the Great with Golden Chain (Lithuania) 2·50 2·50

Stamps of similar design were issued by Latvia and Lithuania.

295 Arms

2008. Viljandi County.
572 **295** 5k.50 multicoloured 1·50 1·20

2008. Post Horn. Self-adhesive.
573 **287** 9k. blue 2·20 1·70

296 Black Grouse (*Tetrao tetrix*)

2008
574 **296** 5k.50 multicoloured 1·50 1·20

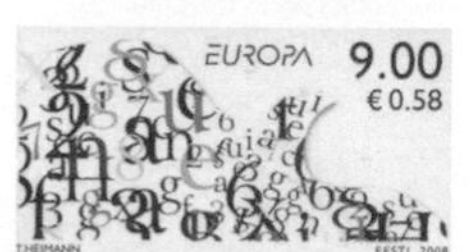

297 Letters

2008. Europa. The Letter.
575 **297** 9k. multicoloured 2·20 1·70

298 Otto Strandman

2008. Heads of State. August (Otto) Strandman (prime minister May–November 1919, State Elder 1929–31).
576 **298** 5k.50 multicoloured 1·50 1·20

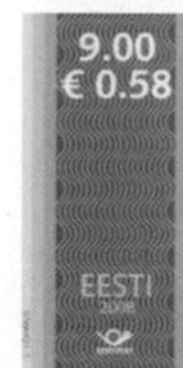

299 Bands of Blue

2008. My Stamp. Self-adhesive.
577 **299** 9k. multicoloured 2·20 1·70

2008. Post Horn. Self-adhesive.
578 **287** 50s. grey 1·00 80

300 Peasants

2008. 150th Anniv of Peasant Uprising at Mahtra.
579 **300** 5k.50 multicoloured 1·50 1·20

301 Discobolus of Myron

2008. Olympic Games, Beijing.
580 **301** 9k. multicoloured 9·00 6·25

302 Polma Windmill

2008
581 **302** 5k.50 multicoloured 1·50 1·20

303 Kalvi Hall

2008
582 **303** 5k.50 multicoloured 1·50 1·20

304 Gerd Kanter

2008. Gerd Kanter, Olympic Games, Beijing Discus Gold Medallist.
583 **304** 5k.50 multicoloured 1·50 1·20

305 Church of the Holy Cross, Audru

2008. Churches.
584 **305** 5k.50 multicoloured 1·50 1·20

306 Arms

2008. Voru County.
585 **306** 5k.50 multicoloured 1·50 1·20

307 '90'

2008. 90th Anniv of Estonian Post.
586 **307** 5k.50 multicoloured 1·50 1·20

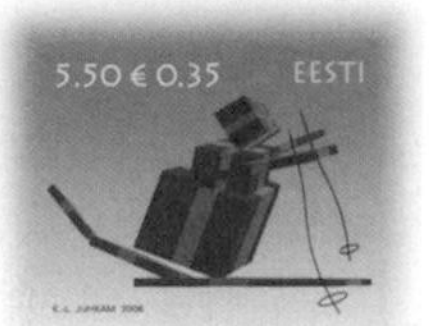

308 Presents as Skier

2008. Christmas. Multicoloured. Self-adhesive.
587 5k.50 Type **308** 1·50 1·20
588 9k. Snowman and present 2·50 1·75

309 Antarctic Glacier

2009. International Polar Year. Sheet 120×78 mm containing T 309 and similar square design. Multicoloured.
MS589 15k.×2, Type **309**; Glacier (different) 8·00 8·00

310 Julius Kuperjanov (nationalist leader) and Partisans

2009. 90th Anniv of Puju Battle.
590 **310** 5k.50 multicoloured 1·50 1·20

311 Johan Laidoner

2009. 125th Birth Anniv of Johan Laidoner (Commander in Chief of Armed Forces).
591 **311** 5k.50 multicoloured 1·50 1·20

312 Ants Pip

2009. Heads of State. Ants Pip (Minister of War 1920—21, Foreign Minister 1921—22, 1925—26, 1933 and 1939—40).
592 **312** 5k.50 claret and red 1·50 1·20

316 Cell Structure of Universe (discovered by Jan Einasto)

2009. Europa. Astronomy. Multicoloured.
596 9k. Type **316** 2·20 1·70
597 9k. Universe 2·20 1·70

Nos. 596/7 were printed together, se-tenant, forming a composite design.

317 Emblem

2009. 275th Anniv of Rapina Papermill.
598 **317** 5k.50 multicoloured 1·50 1·20

318 Flag

2009. 125th Anniv of National Flag. Self-adhesive.
599 **318** 9k. multicoloured 2·50 2·00

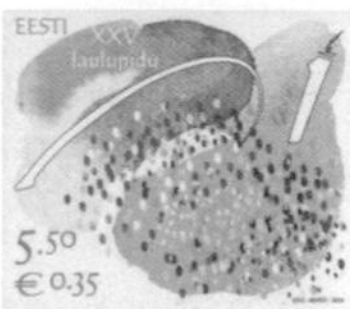

319 Crowd

2009. 25th Song Festival.
600 **319** 5k.50 multicoloured 1·50 1·20

320 Church

2009. 125th Anniv of Alexander Church, Narva.
601 **320** 5k.50 multicoloured 1·50 1·20

321 *Ursus arctos* (brown bear)

2009. Fauna.
602 **321** 5k.50 multicoloured 5·25 4·25

322 Stylized Athlete

2009. Centenary of Estonian Athletics.

603	**322**	5k.50 multicoloured	5·25	4·25

323 Hara

2009. Lighthouses.

604	**323**	5k.50 multicoloured	5·25	4·25

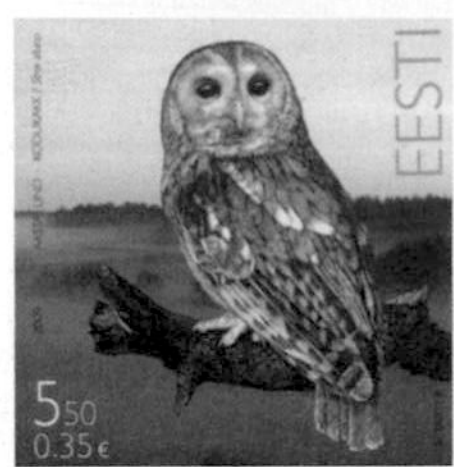

324 *Strix aluco* (Eurasian tawny owl)

2009

605	**324**	5k.50 multicoloured	1·50	1·20

325 Angla Windmill

2009

606	**325**	5k.50 mutlicoloured	1·50	1·20

326 Saku Hall

2009

607	**326**	5k.50 multicoloured	1·50	1·20

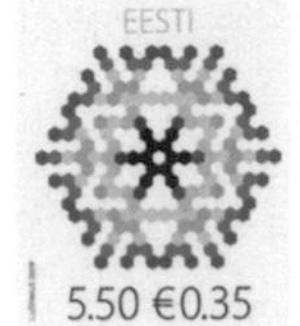

327 Multicoloured Snowflake

2009. Christmas. Multicoloured. Self-adhesive.

608		5k.50 Type **327**	1·50	1·20
609		9k. Red bells, ribbon bow and fir twigs (horiz)	2·50	2·00

328 Textile

2010. Textile

610	**328**	50k. multicoloured	14·00	11·00

329 Juri Jaakson

2010. Heads of State. Juri Jaakson (member of State Council 1938–40).

611	**329**	5k.50 yellow-olive and pale yellow-olive	1·50	1·20

330 Emblem

2010. European Figure Skating Championships, Tallinn.

612	**330**	9k. multicoloured	2·50	2·00

331 Bullets as Candles

2010. 90th Anniv of Tartu Peace Treaty (confirming Estonian independence).

613	**331**	5k.50 multicoloured	1·50	1·20

332 Skier

2010. Winter Olympic Games, Vancouver.

614	**332**	9k. multicoloured	2·50	2·00

2010. Post Horn

615	**287**	9k. bright new blue	2·50	2·00

333 Butterfly Orchid (*Platanthera bifolia*)

2010. Flora.

616	**333**	5k.50 multicoloured	2·50	2·00

334 Flags and Building

2010. Expo 2010, Shanghai.

617	**334**	9k. multicoloured	2·50	2·00

2010. Post Horn

617a	**287**	5k.50 magenta	1·60	1·30

334a St Catherine's Church, Parnu

2010. Cultural Heritage

617b	**334a**	6k.50 multicoloured	1·50	2·00

334b Juhan Kukk

2010. Heads of State. Juhan (Johann) Kukk (finance minister 1918–20, author of Manifesto for Independence)

617c	**334b**	5k.50 bistre	1·50	1·20

334c Wooden Lighthouse, Suurupi

2010. Lighthouses. Multicoloured.

617d		6k.50 Type **334c**	1·60	1·30
617e		8k. Stone lighthouse, Suurupi	2·20	1·80

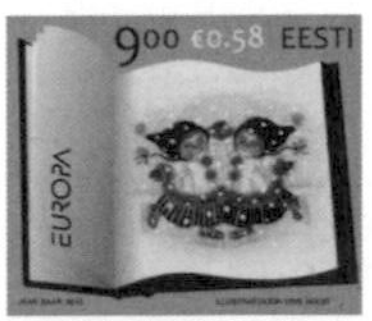

335 Girls skating (book illustration by Viive Noor)

2010. Europa. Children's Books. Multicoloured.

618		9k. Type **335**	2·50	2·00
619		9k. Mouse family (book illustration by Juri Mildeberg)	2·50	2·00

336 Shrike (*Lanius collurio*)

2010. Shrike

620	**336**	5k.50 multicoloured	1·50	1·20

2010. Textile (shades of green)

621	**328**	26k. multicoloured (green)	6·50	5·75

337 Child and Flowers (Helina Madar)

2010. International Children's Day

622	**337**	5k.50 multicoloured	1·50	1·20

339 Figures and Heart (Lost in Tallinn)

2010. Tallinn–European Capital of Culture, 2011

626	**339**	5k.50 multicoloured	1·50	1·20

340 Dormouse

2010. Endangered Species

627	**340**	5k.50 multicoloured	1·50	1·20

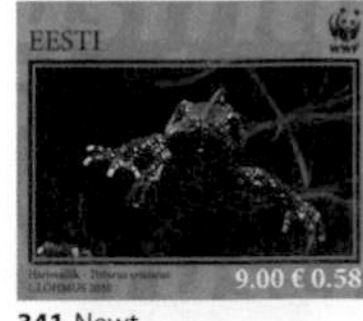

341 Newt

2010. Protected Species. Multicoloured.

628		9k. Type **341**	2·50	2·00
629		9k. Facing down with legs splayed and raised tail	2·50	2·00
630		9k. On land against rock	2·50	2·00
631		9k. Juvenile swimming	2·50	2·00

342 Lennuk (Nikolai Triik)

2010. Art

632	**342**	9k. multicoloured	2·50	2·00

343 Angel

2010. Christmas. Multicoloured.

633		5k.50 Type **343**	1·50	1·20
634		9k. Santa's helper	2·50	2·00

344 Euro Coin

2011. Estonia's Accession to the Euro

635	**344**	€1 multicoloured	20	1·80

2011. Posthorn

636		1c. bright orange-yellow	20	15
637		5c. bright salmon-pink	50	30
638		10c. pale bright reddish lilac	90	60
639		10c. pale bright blue	2·30	1·90
640		65c. bright green	2·50	2·10

338 Suuremoisa Manor

2010. Architecture

623	**338**	5k.50 multicoloured	1·50	1·20

2010. Posthorn

624	**287**	9k. chrome yellow	2·50	2·00

2010. Textile (shades of purple)

625	**328**	26k. multicoloured (purple)	6·50	5·75

345 Rabbit

2011. Chinese New Year

641	**345**	58c. multicoloured	1·10	90

346 Friedebert Tuglas

2011. 40th Death Anniv of Friedebert Tuglas (writer)

642	**346**	58c. dull yellow-green, black and silver	1·10	1·10

347 Villem Reiman

2011. 150th Birth Anniv of Villem Reiman (historian and journalist)

643	**347**	35c. multicoloured	1·00	80

Pt. 12

ETHIOPIA

Formerly called Abyssinia. An ancient empire on the E. coast of Africa. From 1936 to 1941, part of Italian East Africa. Federated with Ethiopia from 1952 to 1993. In 1974 Emperor Haile Selassie was deposed and a republic proclaimed.

1894. and 1907. 16 guerche = 1 Maria Theresa-Thaler.
1905. 100 centimes = 1 franc.
1908. 16 piastres = 1 thaler.
1928. 16 mehaleks = 1 thaler.
1936. 100 centimes = 1 thaler.
1936. 100 centesimi = 1 lira.
1946. 100 cents = 1 Ethiopian dollar.
1976. 100 cents = 1 birr.

INDEPENDENT EMPIRE

1 Menelik II

2 Lion of the Tribe of Judah

1894

1	**1**	¼g. green	8·00	10·00
2	**1**	½g. red	4·00	5·00
3	**1**	1g. blue	4·00	5·00
4	**1**	2g. brown	4·00	8·00
5	**2**	4g. red	4·00	8·00
6	**2**	8g. mauve	4·00	8·00
7	**2**	16g. black	6·00	8·00

1901. Optd Ethiopie.

15	**1**	¼g. green	21·00	21·00
16	**1**	½g. red	21·00	21·00
17	**1**	1g. blue	23·00	23·00
18	**1**	2g. brown	23·00	23·00
19	**2**	4g. red	23·00	23·00
20	**2**	8g. mauve	32·00	32·00
21	**2**	16g. black	42·00	42·00

በስጣ::

(4)

1902. Optd with T 4.

22	**1**	¼g. green	9·00	9·00
23	**1**	½g. red	9·00	9·00
24	**1**	1g. blue	12·00	12·00
25	**1**	2g. brown	12·00	12·00
26	**2**	4g. red	19·00	19·00
27	**2**	8g. mauve	24·00	24·00
28	**2**	16g. black	50·00	50·00

መልክት::

(5)

1903. Optd with T 5.

29	**1**	¼g. green	8·50	8·50
30	**1**	½g. red	8·50	8·50
31	**1**	1g. blue	13·00	13·00
32	**1**	2g. brown	15·00	15·00
33	**2**	4g. red	15·00	15·00
34	**2**	8g. mauve	35·00	35·00
35	**2**	16g. black	55·00	55·00

ምልክት

(6)

1904. Optd with T 6.

36	**1**	¼g. green	8·25	8·25
37	**1**	½g. red	10·00	10·00
38	**1**	1g. blue	13·50	13·50
39	**1**	2g. brown	15·00	15·00
40	**2**	4g. red	17·00	17·00
41	**2**	8g. mauve	32·00	32·00
42	**2**	16g. black	50·00	50·00

1905. Surch in figures.

43	**1**	05 on ¼g. green	10·00	11·00
44	**1**	10 on ½g. red	10·00	11·00
45	**1**	20 on 1g. blue	10·00	11·00
46	**1**	40 on 2g. brown	13·00	15·00
47	**2**	80 on 4g. red	22·00	24·00
48	**2**	1.60 on 8g. mauve	20·00	28·00
49	**2**	3.20 on 16g. black	40·00	30·00

The above surcharge was also applied to some stamps optd with **Ethiopie** and Types **4**, **5** and **6**.

1905. Surch in figures and words.

90	5c. on 16g. blk (No. 28)	£125	£150

1905. No. 2 divided diagonally and surch 5c/m.

86	**1**	5c. on half of ½g. red	6·00	7·00

1905. Surch 5c/m.

71	5c. on ¼g. grn (No. 22)	14·00	17·00

ምኒልክ

(10)

1906. Optd with T 10 and surch in figures.

94		05 on ¼g. green	7·00	7·00
95		10 on ½g. red	9·50	9·50
96		20 on 1g. blue	9·50	9·50
97		40 on 2g. brown	9·50	9·50
98	**2**	80 on 4g. red	11·50	11·50
99	**2**	1.60 on 8g. mauve	16·00	16·00
100	**2**	3.20 on 16g. black	42·00	42·00

1906. Surch with figures and Amharic characters.

101	**1**	05 on ¼g. green	9·00	9·00
102	**1**	10 on ½g. red	15·00	15·00
103	**1**	20 on 1g. blue	15·00	15·00
104	**1**	40 on 2g. brown	15·00	15·00
105	**2**	80 on 4g. red	21·00	21·00
106	**2**	1.60 on 8g. mauve	21·00	21·00
107	**2**	3.20 on 16g. black	50·00	50·00

ዳግማዊ::

(13)

1907. Optd with T 13 and surch in figures between stars.

115	**1**	¼ on ¼g. green	9·00	9·00
116	**1**	½ on ½g. red	9·00	9·00
117	**1**	1 on 1g. blue	11·00	11·00
118	**1**	2 on 2g. brown	14·00	14·00
119	**2**	4 on 4g. red	14·00	14·00
120	**2**	8 on 8g. mauve	18·00	18·00
121	**2**	16 on 16g. black	36·00	36·00

1908. Entry into U.P.U. Nos. 1/7 surch in figures and words.

133	**1**	¼pi. on ¼g. green	4·50	4·50
134	**1**	½pi. on ½g. red	4·50	4·50
129	**1**	1pi. on ½g. red	15·00	15·00
135	**1**	1pi. on 1g. blue	6·00	6·00
136	**1**	2pi. on 2g. brown	10·00	10·00
137	**2**	4pi. on 4g. red	14·00	14·00
138	**2**	8pi on 8g. mauve	26·00	26·00
139	**2**	16pi. on 16g. black	35·00	35·00

19 Throne of Solomon

20 Emperor Menelik

1909

147	**19**	¼g. green	1·50	2·20
148	**19**	½g. red	1·50	1·30
149	**19**	1g. orange and green	5·00	4·50
150	**20**	2g. blue	5·50	4·50
151	**20**	4g. red and green	8·50	7·00
152	-	8g. grey and red	14·50	9·50
153	-	16g. red	22·00	15·00

DESIGN: 8g., 16g. Another portrait.

1911. T 1 and 2 optd AFF EXCEP FAUTE TIMB and surch in manuscript.

154	**1**	¼g. on ¼g. green	£110	60·00
155	**1**	½g. on ½g. red	£110	60·00
156	**1**	1g. on 1g. blue	£110	60·00
157	**1**	2g. on 2g. brown	£110	60·00
158	**2**	4g. on 4g. red	£110	60·00
159	**2**	8g. on 8g. mauve	£110	60·00
160	**2**	16g. on 16g. black	£110	60·00

(22)

1917. Coronation. Optd with T 22 (and similar type).

161	**19**	¼g. green	7·50	8·50
162	**19**	½g. red	7·50	8·50
163	**20**	2g. blue	10·00	10·50
164	**20**	4g. red and green	15·00	15·00
165	-	8g. grey and red (No. 152)	25·00	27·00
166	-	16g. red (No. 153)	40·00	45·00

ተፈሪ::
11/2/1917.

(24)

1917. Optd with T 24 (and similar type).

168	**19**	¼g. green	60	60
169	**19**	½g. red	60	60
170	**19**	1g. orange and green	4·25	4·25
171	**20**	2g. blue	1·40	1·40
174	**20**	4g. red and green	2·75	2·75
175	-	8g. grey & red (No. 152)	2·30	2·30
176	-	16g. red (No. 153)	4·00	4·00

1917. Nos. 175/6 surch with large figure.

177	¼ on 8g. grey and red	5·00	5·00
178	½ on 8g. grey and red	5·00	5·00
179	1 on 16g. red	11·50	11·50
180	2 on 16g. red	11·50	11·50

28 Gerenuk

29 Ras Tafari, later Emperor Haile Selassie

30 African Buffalo

1919

181	**28**	⅛g. brown and violet	25	45
182	-	¼g. grey and green	25	25
183	-	½g. green and red	25	25
184	-	1g. black and purple	25	40
185	**29**	2g. brown and blue	25	50
186	-	4g. orange and blue	50	65
187	-	6g. orange and blue	55	70
188	-	8g. black and olive	70	80
189	-	12g. grey and purple	2·50	2·50
190	-	$1 black and red	5·00	5·00
191	**30**	$2 brown and black	7·00	7·00
192	-	$3 red and green	13·00	12·00
193	-	$4 pink and brown	13·50	13·50
194	-	$5 grey and red	16·00	14·00
195	-	$10 yellow and olive	25·00	22·00

DESIGNS—VERT: As Type **28**: ¼g. Giraffes; ½g. Leopard. As Type **29**: 1g., 4g. Ras Tafari (different portraits); $4, $5, $10, Empress Zauditu (different portraits). HORIZ: As Type **30**: 6g. St. George's Cathedral, Addis Ababa; 8g. Black rhinoceros; 12g. Ostriches; $1, African elephant; $3, Lions.

1919. Stamps of 1919 variously surch.

197	**28**	½g. on ⅛g. brn & violet	1·50	1·50
207	-	½g. on 8g. blk & olive	2·90	2·50
202	-	½g. on $1 black and red	1·50	1·50
203	-	½g. on $5 grey and red	2·90	2·90
198	-	1g. on ¼g. grey & green	4·25	4·25
204	-	1g. on 6g. orge & blue	2·50	2·50
208	-	1g. on 12g. grey & pur	4·75	4·75
205	-	1g. on $3 red and green	10·00	7·00
206	-	1g. on $10 yell & olive	2·80	2·80
198c	-	2g. on 1g. black & pur	1·15	1·15
199	-	2g. on $4 pink & brown	35·00	35·00
200	-	2½g. on ½g. grn & red	1·90	1·90
201	**29**	4g. on 2g. brn & blue	1·90	1·90
196	-	4g. on $4 pink & brown	3·50	3·50

39 Ras Tafari, later Emperor Haile Selassie

40 Empress Zauditu

፲፱፻፳

ፖ: ቴ: ቴ:
የተመረቀበት:
ቀን: መታሰቢያ:

(41)

1928. Opening of P.O. at Addis Ababa. Optd with T 41.

213	**39**	⅛m. blue and orange	2·75	3·75
214	**40**	¼m. red and blue	2·75	3·75
215	**39**	½m. black and green	2·75	3·75
216	**40**	1m. black and red	2·75	3·75
217	**39**	2m. black and blue	2·75	3·75
218	**40**	4m. olive and yellow	2·75	3·75
219	**39**	8m. olive and mauve	2·75	3·75
220	**40**	1t. mauve and brown	3·75	4·50
221	**39**	2t. brown and green	5·00	6·50
222	**40**	3t. green and purple	5·00	6·50

1928

223	**39**	⅛m. blue and orange	2·00	2·25
224	**40**	¼m. red and blue	1·25	2·00
225	**39**	½m. black and green	2·20	2·40
226	**40**	1m. black and red	1·10	1·25
227	**39**	2m. black and blue	1·10	1·25
228	**40**	4m. olive and yellow	1·10	1·25
229	**39**	8m. olive and mauve	3·25	4·00
230	**40**	1t. mauve and brown	6·00	6·00
231	**39**	2t. brown and green	2·50	2·75
232	**40**	3t. green and purple	7·75	9·75

1928. Elevation of Ras Tafari to Negus. Optd with crown, Amharic characters and NEGOUS TEFERI.

233	**39**	⅛m. blue and orange	6·00	9·50
234	**39**	½m. black and green	6·00	9·50
235	**39**	2m. black and blue	6·00	12·00
236	**39**	8m. olive and mauve	6·00	12·00
237	**39**	2t. brown and green	6·00	12·00

1929. Air. Arrival of First Airplane of the Ethiopian Government. Optd with airplane and Amharic text (= "16 Aug 1929. Ethiopian Government Air Mail").

238	-	⅛m. blue and orange	3·00	3·50
239	**40**	¼m. red and blue	3·00	3·50
240	**39**	½m. black and green	3·25	3·75
241	**40**	1m. black and red	3·25	3·75
242	**39**	2m. black and blue	3·25	3·75
243	**40**	4m. olive and yellow	3·25	3·75
244	**39**	8m. olive and mauve	3·25	3·75
245	**40**	1t. mauve and brown	4·25	5·75

246	39	2t. brown and green	7·00	7·50
247	40	3t. green and purple	7·00	7·50

1930. Accession of Ras Taffari as Emperor Haile Selassie. Optd HAYLE (or HAILE) SELASSIE 1er 3 Avril 1930 and Amharic text.

248	39	⅛m. blue and orange	1·40	1·40
249	40	¼m. red and blue	1·40	1·40
250	39	½m. black and green	1·40	1·40
261	40	1m. black and red	1·10	1·10
262	39	2m. black and blue	1·10	1·10
263	40	4m. olive and yellow	2·10	2·10
264	39	8m. olive and mauve	3·00	3·00
265	40	1t. mauve and brown	5·00	5·00
266	39	2t. brown and green	6·00	6·00
267	40	3t. green and purple	9·00	9·00

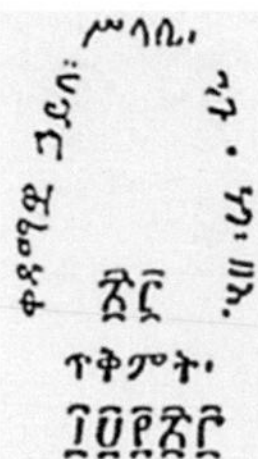

46 "The Emperor of the Kings of Ethiopia, 2 Nov., 1930, Haile Selassie"

1930. Coronation of Emperor Haile Selassie (1st issue). Optd with T 46.

268	39	⅛m. blue and orange	1·10	1·30
269	40	¼m. red and blue	1·10	1·30
270	39	½m. black and green	1·10	1·30
271	40	1m. black and red	1·10	1·30
272	39	2m. black and blue	1·10	1·30
273	40	4m. olive and yellow	1·10	1·30
274	39	8m. olive and mauve	1·90	1·90
275	40	1t. mauve and brown	3·00	3·00
276	39	2t. brown and green	4·50	4·50
277	40	3t. green and purple	7·00	7·00

47 The Ethiopian Lion and Symbols

1930. Coronation of Emperor Haile Selassie (2nd issue).

278	47	1g. orange	1·00	1·00
279	47	2g. blue	1·00	1·00
280	47	4g. purple	1·00	1·75
281	47	8g. green	1·00	2·25
282	47	1t. brown	1·25	1·50
283	47	3t. green	3·25	4·00
284	47	5t. brown	5·00	5·00

1931. Issue of 1928 surch in mehaleks.

285	40	⅛m. on 1m. black & red	80	1·20
286	39	⅛m. on 2m. black & blue	80	1·20
287	40	⅛m. on 4m. green & yell	80	1·20
288	40	¼m. on 1m. black & red	80	1·20
289	39	¼m. on 2m. black & blue	1·50	1·90
290	40	¼m. on 4m. green & yell	1·50	1·90
291	40	½m. on 1m. black & red	1·50	1·90
292	39	½m. on 2m. black & blue	1·50	1·90
293	40	½m. on 4m. green & yell	1·50	1·90
294	40	½m. on 3t. green & purple	12·00	16·00
295	39	1m. on 2m. black & blue	3·00	3·25

49 Potez 25A2 over Map of Ethiopia

1931. Air.

296	49	1g. red	65	1·20
297	49	2g. blue	65	1·20
298	49	4g. mauve	1·00	1·50
299	49	8g. green	2·25	2·50
300	49	1t. brown	3·50	4·00
301	49	2t. red	9·00	11·00
302	49	3t. green	13·00	16·00

50 Ras Makonnen

1931

303	50	⅛g. red	40	1·00
304	-	¼g. olive	2·25	1·50
305	50	½g. purple	1·10	1·25
306	-	1g. orange	1·10	1·25
307	-	2g. blue	1·10	1·25
308	-	4g. lilac	2·25	2·50
309	-	8g. green	4·75	5·25
310	-	1t. brown	14·00	14·00
311	-	3t. green	15·00	16·00
312	-	5t. brown	20·00	20·00

DESIGNS—HORIZ: ¼g. Railway Bridge over R. Awash. VERT: 1g. Empress Menen (profile); 2g., 8g. Haile Selassie (profile); 4g., 1t. Statue of Menelik II; 3t. Empress Menen (full face); 5t. Haile Selassie (full face).

1936. Red Cross. As T 50 optd with red cross.

313	1g. green	1·90	1·90
314	2g. pink	1·90	1·90
315	4g. blue	1·90	1·90
316	8g. brown	2·40	2·40
317	1t. violet	2·40	2·40

1936. As T 50 surch with value and Amharic text.

318	50	1c. on⅛g. red	3·50	2·00
319	-	2c. on ¼g. green	3·50	1·50
320	50	3c. on ½g. purple	3·50	2·00
321	-	5c. on 1g. orange	3·00	2·00
322	-	10c. on 2g. blue	3·00	1·50

ITALIAN COLONY

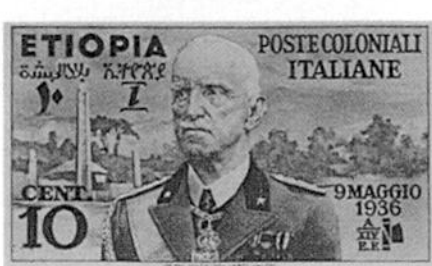

54 King Victor Emmanuel III

1936. Annexation of Ethiopia.

322a	54	10c. brown	18·00	10·50
322b	-	20c. violet	16·00	4·25
322c	-	25c. green	10·50	1·10
322d	-	30c. brown	10·50	2·10
322e	-	50c. red	5·25	1·10
322f	-	75c. orange	40·00	10·50
322g	-	1l.25 blue	40·00	17·00

DESIGNS—VERT: 25c., 30c., 50c. Victor Emmanuel III. HORIZ: Victor Emmanuel III and: 20c. Mountain scenery; 75c. Gonder Castle; 1l.25, Tomb of Scec Hussen and Dordola Hills.

INDEPENDENCE RESTORED

56 Haile Selassie I in Coronation Robes

1942. 1st issue. "Centimes" with capital initial and small letters.

323	56	4c. black and green	1·40	1·25
324	56	10c. black and red	2·75	1·25
325	56	20c. black and blue	4·00	2·25

1942. 2nd issue. "CENTIMES" in block capital letters.

326	4c. black and green	85	35
327	8c. black and orange	90	40
328	10c. black and red	1·25	50
329	12c. black and violet	1·25	75
330	20c. black and blue	1·60	1·00
331	25c. black and green	2·40	1·50
332	50c. black and brown	4·00	3·00
333	60c. black and mauve	5·25	3·50

1943. Restoration of Obelisk and 13th Anniv of Coronation of Haile Selassie. Stamps of 1942 inscr "CENTIMES" surch OBELISK 3 NOV. 1943 and value.

334	5c. on 4c. black & grn	75·00	75·00
335	10c. on 8c. black & orge	75·00	75·00
336	15c. on 10c. black & red	75·00	75·00
337	20c. on 12c. black & vio	75·00	75·00
338	30c. on 20c. black & bl	75·00	75·00

In No. 338 the figure "3" is surcharged on the "2" of "20" to make "30" and this value is confirmed by the Amharic characters.

58 Royal Palace, Addis Ababa

59 Menelik II

1944. Birth Cent of Emperor Menelik II.

339	58	5c. green	1·60	1·75
340	59	10c. red	2·50	1·75
341	-	20c. blue	4·75	1·75
342	-	50c. violet	5·25	3·75
343	-	65c. orange	9·25	5·00

DESIGNS—VERT: 20c. Equestrian statue of Menelik II; 65c. Menelik in royal robes. HORIZ: 50c. Menelik's mausoleum.

60 Patient and Nurse (Amharic characters = "Victory")

1945. Victory. Optd V in red.

344		5c. green	3·25	3·00
345		10c. red	4·00	3·50
346	60	25c. blue	5·00	4·50
347	-	50c. brown	6·75	6·00
348	-	1t. violet	8·25	11·50

DESIGNS: 5c. Nurse and baby; 10c. Native soldier; 50c. Nurse and child; 1t. "Supplication".

The above stamps without the "V" were not issued for postal purposes.

1946. Air. Resumption of National Air Mail Services. (a) Surch at sides and top in Amharic, with 20-4-39 and value below.

349	56	12c. on 4c. blk & grn	75·00	75·00

(b) Surch REPRISE POSTE AERIENNE ETHIOPIENNE at sides and top, with 29.12.46 and values below.

350	0.50 on 25c. black & green	75·00	75·00
351	$2 on 60c. black & mauve	95·00	95·00

63 Lion of the Tribe of Judah

64 Postal Transport by Mule and by Bus

1947. 50th Anniv of Postal Service.

352	63	10c. yellow	5·00	2·25
353	-	20c. blue	7·00	2·75
354	64	30c. brown	16·00	5·00
355	-	50c. green	23·00	17·00
356	-	70c. mauve	33·00	11·00

DESIGNS—VERT: 20c. Menelik II (as in Type **1**). HORIZ: 50c. G.P.O., Addis Ababa; 70c. Menelik and Haile Selassie.

65 Negus Sahle Selassie

1947. 150th Anniv of Selassie Dynasty.

357	65	20c. blue	4·00	2·50
358	-	30c. purple	4·00	3·50
359	-	$1 green	18·00	12·00

DESIGNS—HORIZ: 30c. View of Ancober. VERT: $1, Negus Sahle Selassie.

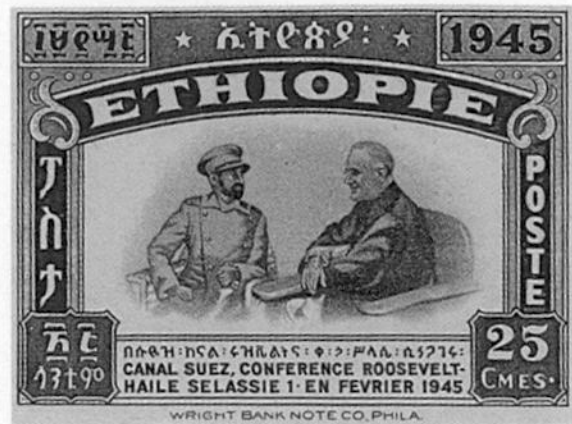

67 Emperor Haile Selassie and Pres. Roosevelt

1947. 2nd Death Anniv of Pres. Roosevelt.

360	67	12c. green & red (postage)	2·00	1·55
361	67	25c. red and blue	2·25	3·25
362	-	65c. blue, red and black	3·25	6·25
363	-	$1 brown & purple (air)	8·00	16·00
364	-	$2 blue and red	12·00	25·00

DESIGNS—HORIZ: 65c. Pres. Roosevelt and U.S. flags. VERT: $1, Pres. Roosevelt; $2, Haile Selassie.

1947. Surch 12 centimes in French and Amharic with six bars.

365	56	12c. on 25c. black & grn	80·00	90·00

69 Lake Tana

70 Douglas DC-3 over Zoquala Volcano

1947. Views with medallion portrait of Haile Selassie inset. (a) Postage.

366	-	1c. purple	30	25
367	-	2c. violet	30	25
368	-	4c. green	30	25
369	-	5c. green	40	25
370	69	8c. orange	60	30
371	-	12c. red	80	40
371a	-	15c. olive	75	50
372	-	20c. blue	1·25	60
373	-	30c. brown	2·00	1·00
373a	-	60c. red	2·00	60
374	-	70c. mauve	4·00	80
375	-	$1 red	5·50	2·75
376	-	$3 blue	16·00	7·00
377	-	$5 olive	22·00	12·00

DESIGNS: 1c. Amba Alagi; 2c. Trinity Church, Addis Ababa; 4c. Debra Sina; 5c. Mecan mountain pathway, near Ashangi; 12c., 15c. Parliament Building, Addis Ababa; 20c. Aiba mountain scenery, near Mai Chio; 30c. Nile Bridge; 60c., 70c. Canoe on Lake Tana; $1, Omo Falls; $3, Mt. Alamata; $5, Ras Dashan Mountains.

(b) Air.

378		8c. purple	1·25	35
379	70	10c. green	2·00	45
379a	-	25c. purple	1·50	1·00
380	-	30c. orange	3·00	1·50
380a	-	35c. blue	2·50	1·00
380b	-	65c. purple	2·50	1·00
381	-	70c. red	5·00	2·50
382	-	$1 blue	6·00	3·25
383	-	$3 mauve	14·00	6·00
384	-	$5 brown	24·00	9·00
385	-	$10 violet	42·00	22·00

DESIGNS: 8c. Ploughing with oxen; 30c., 35c. Tehis Isat Falls, Blue Nile; 65c., 70c. Amba Alagi; $1, Sacala source of River Nile; $3, Gorgora and Dembia on Lake Tana; $5, Magdala Fort; $10, Ras Dasnan Mountains and Lake.

72 Emperor, Empress, Lion and Map

1949. 8th Anniv of Liberation.

386		20c. blue	3·50	1·50
387	72	30c. orange	4·50	2·50
388	-	50c. violet	8·00	4·50
389	-	80c. green	12·00	7·50
390	-	$1 red	14·00	8·50

DESIGNS: 20c. Emperor and Empress with sceptres and orb; 50c. Coat of arms; 80c. Shield and spears; $1, Star of Solomon.

1949. Industrial and Agricultural Exn. Nos. 370/1 and 373/5 surch EXPOSITION 1949, and new value and two lines of Amharic characters.

391	8c.+8c. orange	8·00	8·00
392	12c.+5c. red	11·00	11·00
393	30c.+15c. brown	16·00	16·00
394	70c.+70c. mauve	30·00	30·00
395	$1+80c. red	35·00	35·00

74 Emperor and U.P.U. Monument, Berne

1950. Air. 75th Anniv of U.P.U.

396	74	5c. red and green	90	70
397	74	15c. red and blue	1·10	70
398	74	25c. green and yellow	1·75	90
399	74	50c. blue and red	3·00	2·10

1950. Red Cross Fund. As Nos. 344/8 but without V opt and surch + 10 ct. below a cross.

399a	5c.+10c. green	2·50	2·50
399b	10c.+10c. red	3·75	3·75
399c	25c.+10c. blue	6·50	5·25
399d	50c.+10c. brown	10·00	9·00
399e	$1+10c. violet	20·00	24·00

75 Lion of the Tribe of Judah

1950. 20th Anniv of Coronation.

400	-	5c. violet	1·60	1·00
401	-	10c. mauve	3·00	1·25
402	-	20c. red	6·50	2·75
403	75	30c. green	9·50	4·50
404	-	50c. blue	16·00	7·50

DESIGNS—HORIZ: 5c. Dejach Balcha Hospital; 50c. Emperor, Empress and palace. VERT: 10c. Abuna Petros; 20c. Emperor hoisting flag.

76 Emperor and Abbaye Bridge

1951. Opening of Abbaye Bridge.

405	76	5c. brown and green	3·25	1·00
406	76	10c. black and orange	6·25	2·00
407	76	15c. brown and blue	9·50	2·50
408	76	30c. mauve and olive	19·00	4·50
409	76	60c. blue and brown	37·00	9·00
410	76	80c. green and violet	50·00	12·50

1951. 55th Anniv of Battle of Adwa. As T 76, but Emperor and Tomb of Ras Makonnen.

411	5c. black and green	2·25	1·25
412	10c. black and blue	2·50	1·75
413	15c. black and blue	4·25	2·50
414	30c. black and red	8·50	5·00
415	80c. black and red	22·00	13·00
416	$1 black and brown	27·00	16·00

1951. Industrial and Agricultural Exhibition. Nos. 391/5 further optd 1951 with Amharic characters above.

417	8c.+8c. orange	2·25	2·25
418	12c.+5c. red	2·50	2·50
419	30c.+15c. brown	5·25	5·25
420	70c.+70c. mauve	20·00	20·00
421	$1+80c. red	25·00	25·00

79 "Tree of Health"

1951. Anti-tuberculosis Fund. Cross and inscr in red.

422	79	5c.+2c. green	1·50	1·25
423	79	10c.+3c. orange	1·50	1·25
424	79	15c.+3c. blue	2·50	2·50
425	79	30c.+5c. red	4·00	4·50
426	79	50c.+7c. brown	6·00	6·00
427	79	$1+10c. purple	12·00	12·00

80 Haile Selassie I

1952. Emperor Haile Selassie's 60th Birthday.

428	80	5c. green	60	30
429	80	10c. orange	1·25	50
430	80	15c. black	1·50	90
431	80	25c. blue	3·50	1·25
432	80	30c. violet	4·00	1·60
433	80	50c. red	6·00	2·50
434	80	65c. sepia	8·50	3·50

81 Ethiopian Flag over the Sea

1952. Celebration of Federation of Eritrea with Ethiopia.

435	-	15c. lake	1·50	95
436	-	25c. brown	1·50	1·25
437	-	30c. brown	3·00	1·60
438	-	50c. purple	4·00	1·75
439	-	65c. black	8·00	2·75
440	-	80c. green	6·00	3·25
441	-	$1 red	11·00	4·50
442	81	$2 blue	20·00	7·50
443	-	$3 mauve	45·00	11·00

DESIGNS: 15c., 30c. Port Assab; 25c., 50c. Port Massawa; 65c. Map; 80c. Allegory of Federation; $1, Emperor raising flag; $3, Emperor in 1936.

82 Emperor and Massawa Harbour

1953. 1st Anniv of Federation of Ethiopia and Eritrea.

444	82	10c. brown and red	4·75	2·00
445	-	15c. green and blue	4·25	2·50
446	82	25c. brown and orange	13·00	7·50
447	-	30c. green and brown	8·00	5·50
448	82	50c. brown and purple	14·00	8·50

DESIGN—HORIZ: 15c., 30c. Emperor aboard freighter at sea.

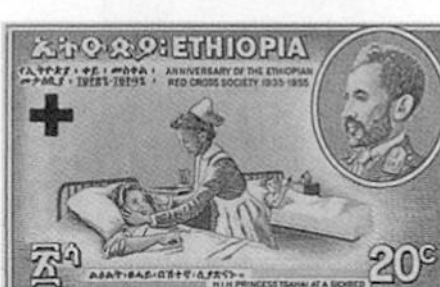

83 Princess Tsahai tending sick Child

1953. 20th Anniv of Ethiopian Red Cross Society. Cross in red.

449	83	15c. blue and brown	3·50	1·50
450	83	20c. orange and green	2·50	1·00
451	83	30c. green and blue	5·25	2·25

84 Promulgating the Constitution

1955. Silver Jubilee of Emperor. Inscr "1930–1955".

452	84	5c. brown and green	75	35
453	-	20c. green and red	3·50	55
454	-	25c. black and mauve	4·50	70
455	-	35c. red and brown	6·25	2·40
456	-	50c. blue and brown	9·00	3·00
457	-	65c. red and lilac	12·00	4·25

DESIGNS—HORIZ: 20c. Bishop's consecration; 25c. Emperor presenting standard to troops; 50c. Emperor, Empress and symbols of progress; 65c. Emperor and Empress in coronation robes. VERT: 35c. Allegory of re-union of Ethiopia and Eritrea.

85 Emperor Haile Selassie

1955. Silver Jubilee Fair, Addis Ababa.

458	85	5c. olive and green	75	30
459	85	10c. blue and red	1·25	45
460	85	15c. green and black	2·00	75
461	85	50c. lake and mauve	5·00	2·50

86 Convair CV 240 Airliner

1955. Air. 10th Anniv of Ethiopian Airlines.

462	86	10c. multicoloured	1·25	80
463	86	15c. multicoloured	1·75	90
464	86	20c. multicoloured	2·50	1·25

87 Promulgating the Constitution

1956. Air. 25th Anniv of Constitution.

465	87	10c. blue and brown	65	35
466	87	15c. green and red	90	45
467	87	20c. orange and blue	1·25	60
468	87	25c. green and lilac	1·60	75
469	87	30c. brown and green	2·10	85

88 Aksum

1957. Air. Ancient Capitals of Ethiopia. Centres in green.

470	88	5c. brown	75	35
471	-	10c. red (Lalibela)	85	45
472	-	15c. orange (Gondar)	2·10	1·40
473	-	20c. blue (Makalle)	2·75	1·80
474	-	25c. mauve (Ankober)	3·50	3·50

89 Amharic "A"

1957. Air. 70th Anniv of Addis Ababa. Amharic characters in red and miniature views of buildings as in T 89.

475	89	5c. blue on salmon	80	35
476	-	10c. green on flesh	70	45
477	-	15c. purple on buff	1·10	90
478	-	20c. green on buff	1·50	1·25
479	-	25c. mauve on lavender	2·20	1·60
480	-	30c. brown on green	2·50	2·00

AMHARIC CHARACTERS: 10c. "DD1"; 15c. "S"; 20c. "A"; 25c. "BE"; 30c. "BA".

The set spells out "Addis Ababa" in Amharic.

90 Emperor Haile Selassie, Map of Africa, Building and Monument

1958. Air. Conference of Independent African States, Accra.

481	90	10c. green	40	30
482	90	20c. red	1·00	85
483	90	30c. blue	1·50	1·40

1958. Anti-tuberculosis Fund. As Nos. 422/7 but new values.

483a	79	20c.+3c. purple & red	70	1·25
483b	79	25c.+4c. green & red	80	1·25
483c	79	35c.+5c. purple & red	3·25	2·75
483d	79	60c.+7c. blue and red	5·50	4·75
483e	79	65c.+7c. violet & red	6·75	6·00
483f	79	80c.+9c. carmine & red	8·50	8·25

91 Emperor Haile Selassie, Map of Africa and U.N. Emblem

1958. Air. 1st Session of U.N. Economic Conference for Africa, Addis Ababa.

484	91	5c. green	25	30
485	91	20c. red	75	60
486	91	25c. blue	90	70
487	91	50c. purple	1·90	1·40

1959. Red Cross Commem. Surch RED CROSS CENTENARY 1859-1959 in English and Amharic and premium. Colours changed. Cross in red.

488	83	15c.+2c. red & brown	1·75	1·60
489	83	20c.+3c. green & violet	3·00	2·75
490	83	30c.+5c. blue and red	2·00	2·00

1959. Air. 30th Anniv of Air Mail Service in Ethiopia. Nos. 378/81 optd 30th Airmail Ann. 1929-1959.

491	8c. purple	50	30
492	10c. green	60	50
493	25c. purple	1·40	95
494	30c. orange	1·75	1·25
495	35c. blue	2·25	1·50
496	65c. violet	4·00	2·75
497	70c. red	4·50	3·00

1960. World Refugee Year. Optd World Refugee Year 1959-1960 in English and Amharic.

498	20c. blue (No. 372)	1·50	1·25
499	60c. red (No. 373a)	3·00	2·75

1960. Ethiopian Red Cross Society's Silver Jubilee. As Nos. 344/8 but without V opt surch Silver Jubilee 1960 in English and Amharic and premium.

500	5c.+1c. green	50	40
501	10c.+2c. red	65	70
502	25c.+3c. blue	2·75	2·40
503	50c.+4c. brown	5·00	4·50
504	$1+5c. violet	9·25	8·50

96 Woman with Torch

1960. 2nd Independent African States Conf, Addis Ababa.

505	**96**	20c. green and red	1·00	1·25
506	**96**	80c. violet and red	3·50	3·00
507	**96**	$1 lake and red	4·50	4·00

97 Emperor Haile Selassie

1960. 30th Anniv of Emperor's Coronation.

508	**97**	10c. brown and blue	75	65
509	**97**	25c. violet and green	1·50	1·10
510	**97**	50c. blue and buff	3·75	3·50
511	**97**	65c. green and salmon	4·75	4·50
512	**97**	$1 blue and purple	7·00	6·75

98 Africa Hall, Addis Ababa

1961. Africa Day.

513	**98**	80c. blue	3·75	3·50

99 Emperor Haile Selassie and Map of Ethiopia

1961. 20th Anniv of Liberation.

514	**99**	20c. green	60	55
515	**99**	30c. blue	85	70
516	**99**	$1 brown	3·25	2·50

100 African Ass

1961. Ethiopian Fauna.

517	**100**	5c. black and green	50	25
518	-	15c. brown and green	75	25
519	-	25c. sepia and green	1·50	40
520	-	35c. brown and green	2·75	1·00
521	-	50c. red and green	4·00	1·60
522	-	$1 brown and green	8·25	2·50

DESIGNS: 15c. Eland; 25c. African elephant; 35c. Giraffe; 50c. Gemsbok; $1, Lion and lioness.

See also Nos. 641/5.

101 Emperor Haile Selassie I and Empress Menen

1961. Golden Wedding of Emperor and Empress.

523	**101**	10c. green	60	50
524	**101**	50c. blue	2·40	1·50
525	**101**	$1 red	5·25	2·75

102 Guks (jousting)

1962. Sports.

526	**102**	10c. red and green	70	45
527	-	15c. brown and red	1·20	75
528	-	20c. black and red	1·60	1·25
529	-	30c. purple and blue	2·50	1·75
530	-	50c. green and buff	4·00	2·75

DESIGNS: 15c. Ganna (Ethiopian hockey); 20c. Cycling; 30c. Football (3rd Africa Cup game); 50c. Abbebe Bikila (Marathon winner, Olympic Games Rome, 1960).

103 Mosquito on World Map

1962. Malaria Eradication.

531	**103**	15c. black	50	35
532	**103**	30c. purple	2·00	90
533	**103**	60c. brown	3·00	1·75

104 Abyssinian Ground Hornbill

1962. Ethiopian Birds (1st series). Mult.

534		5c. Type **104** (postage)	1·20	40
535		15c. Abyssinian roller	2·25	80
536		30c. Bateleur (vert)	4·50	1·50
537		50c. Double-toothed barbet (vert)	8·00	2·50
538		$1 Didric cuckoo	15·00	5·00
539		10c. Dark-headed oriole (air)	2·00	35
540		15c. Broad-tailed paradise whydah (vert)	2·50	65
541		20c. Lammergeier (vert)	3·00	1·00
542		50c. White-cheeked turaco	7·00	2·25
543		80c. Village indigobird	11·50	3·50

See also Nos 633/7 and 673/7.

105 "Collective Security"

1962. Air. 2nd Anniv of Ethiopian U.N. Forces in Congo and 70th Birthday of Emperor.

544	**105**	15c. multicoloured	25	20
545	**105**	50c. multicoloured	60	35
546	**105**	60c. multicoloured	1·10	45

106 Assab Hospital

1962. 10th Anniv of Federation of Ethiopia and Eritrea.

547	**106**	3c. purple	10	10
548	-	15c. blue	25	20
549	-	20c. green	40	30
550	-	50c. brown	1·50	70
551	-	60c. red	1·60	95

DESIGNS: 15c. Assab school; 20c. Massawa church; 50c. Massawa mosque; 60c. Assab port.

107 Bazan, "The Nativity" and Bethlehem

1962. Ethiopian Rulers (1st issue). Mult.

552		10c. Type **107**	30	15
553		15c. Ezana and monuments, Aksum	40	20
554		20c. Kaleb and fleet in Adulis port	55	30
555		50c. Lalibela, Christian figures from Lalibela churches (vert)	1·40	70
556		60c. Yekuno Amlak and Abuna Tekle Haimanot preaching in Ankober	1·60	85
557		75c. Zara Yacob and ceremonial pyre	2·00	1·00
558		$1 Lebna Bengel and battle against Mohammed Gragn	2·75	1·40

108 Telephone and Communications Map

1963. 10th Anniv of Ethiopian Imperial Telecommunications Board.

559	**108**	10c. red	50	30
560	-	50c. blue	2·25	90
561	-	60c. brown	2·75	1·75

DESIGNS: 50c. Radio aerial; 60c. Telegraph pole.

109 Campaign Emblem

1963. Freedom from Hunger.

562	**109**	5c. red	20	10
563	**109**	10c. mauve	30	15
564	**109**	15c. violet	70	25
565	**109**	30c. green	1·25	70

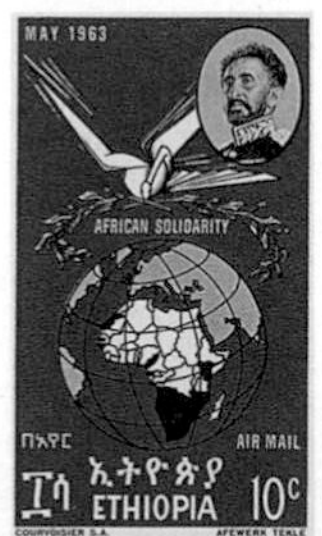

110 "African Solidarity"

1963. Air. Conference of African Heads of States, Addis Ababa.

566	**110**	10c. black and purple	50	25
567	**110**	40c. black and green	2·75	1·20
568	**110**	60c. black and blue	3·50	1·25

111 Disabled Boy

1963. "Aid for the Disabled" Fund.

569	**111**	10c.+2c. blue	75	75
570	**111**	15c.+3c. red	1·00	1·00
571	**111**	50c.+5c. green	3·00	3·00
572	**111**	60c.+5c. purple	3·25	3·25

112 Bishop Abuna Salama

1964. Ethiopian Spiritual Leaders.

573	**112**	10c. blue	35	30
574	-	15c. green (Abuna Aregawi)	1·00	75
575	-	30c. lake (Abuna Tekle Haimanot)	1·90	1·50
576	-	40c. blue (Yared)	2·50	1·90
577	-	60c. brn (Zara Yacob)	3·75	2·75

113 Queen Sheba

1964. Ethiopian Empresses. Multicoloured.

578		10c. Type **113**	80	40
579		15c. Helen	1·20	70
580		50c. Seble Wongel	4·25	2·40
581		60c. Mentiwab	5·00	3·00
582		80c. Taitu	6·50	3·50

114 Priest teaching Alphabet

1964. "Education".

583	**114**	5c. brown	20	15
584	-	10c. green	25	20
585	-	15c. purple	40	30
586	-	40c. blue	1·10	45
587	-	60c. purple	1·60	75

DESIGNS—HORIZ: 10c. Pupils in classroom. VERT: 15c. Teacher with pupil; 40c. Students in laboratory; 60c. Graduates in procession.

115 Swimming

1964. Air. Olympic Games, Tokyo. Mult.

588		5c. Type **115**	40	15
589		10c. Basketball (vert)	75	20
590		15c. Throwing the javelin	1·10	40
591		80c. Football at Addis Ababa stadium	4·50	1·80

116 Eleanor Roosevelt

1964. Eleanor Roosevelt Commem.

592	**116**	10c. blue and bistre	25	20
593	**116**	60c. blue and brown	2·10	1·30
594	**116**	80c. blue, gold and green	3·00	1·80

1964. Ethiopian Rulers (2nd issue). As T 107. Multicoloured.

595		5c. Serse Dengel and view of Gondar, 1563	25	15
596		10c. Fasiladas and Gondar, 1632	65	35
597		20c. Yassu the Great and Gondar, 1682	1·40	90

598		25c. Theodore II and map of Ethiopia	1·80	1·10
599		60c. John IV and Battle of Gura, 1876	3·75	2·50
600		80c. Menelik II and Battle of Adwa, 1896	4·75	3·50

118 Queen Elizabeth II and Emperor Haile Selassie

1965. Air. Visit of Queen Elizabeth II.

601	**118**	5c. multicoloured	30	15
602	**118**	35c. multicoloured	1·70	1·30
603	**118**	60c. multicoloured	3·00	2·00

119 Abyssinian Rose

1965. Ethiopian Flowers. Multicoloured.

604		5c. Type **119**	25	20
605		10c. Kosso tree	75	65
606		25c. St. John's wort	1·80	1·20
607		35c. Parrot tree	2·50	1·70
608		60c. Maskal daisy	2·00	2·75

120 I.T.U. Emblem and Symbols

1965. Centenary of I.T.U.

609	**120**	5c. yellow, indigo & blue	20	20
610	**120**	10c. orange, dp blue & bl	40	30
611	**120**	60c. mauve, dp blue & bl	2·30	1·30

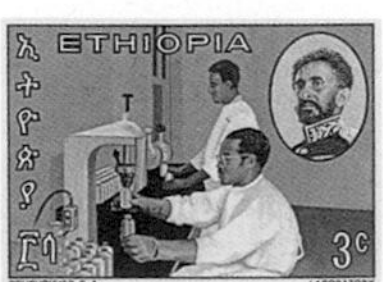

121 Laboratory Technicians

1965. Multicoloured.. Multicoloured..

612		3c. Type **121** (postage)	15	10
613		5c. Textile mill	20	10
614		10c. Sugar factory	60	20
615		20c. Mountain highway	1·30	35
616		25c. Motor coach	1·50	45
617		30c. Diesel locomotive	3·00	2·00
618		35c. Railway Station, Addis Ababa	2·30	75
619		15c. Sisal (inscr "SUGAR CANES") (air)	55	20
620		40c. Koka Dam	1·00	30
621		50c. Blue Nile Bridge	1·20	45
622		60c. Gondar castles	1·50	65
623		80c. Coffee tree	2·50	40
624		$1 Cattle	3·25	1·00
625		$3 Camels	9·00	3·75
626		$5 Boeing 720B airliner	18·00	7·00

122 I.C.Y. Emblem

1965. I.C.Y.

627	**122**	10c. red and turquoise	40	35
628	**122**	50c. red and blue	1·60	1·20
629	**122**	80c. red and blue	2·50	1·80

123 Commercial Bank's Seal

1965. Ethiopian National and Commercial Banks.

630	**123**	10c. black, blue and red	30	25
631	-	30c. black, blue & ultram	90	70
632	-	60c. yellow, blue & black	1·60	1·30

DESIGNS: 30c. National Bank's Seal; 60c. Banking halls and main building.

1966. Air. Ethiopian Birds (2nd series). As T 104. Multicoloured.

633		10c. White-collared kingfisher	2·50	40
634		15c. Blue-breasted bee eater	2·50	40
635		25c. African paradise fly-catcher	2·50	60
636		40c. Village weaver	4·50	1·60
637		60c. White-collared pigeon	7·00	2·20

124 Press Building

1966. Inauguration of "Light and Peace" Printing Press, Addis Ababa.

638	**124**	5c. black and red	20	15
639	**124**	15c. black and green	50	40
640	**124**	30c. black and yellow	1·10	85

125 Black Rhinoceros

1966. Air. Animals.

641	**125**	5c. black, grey & green	2·00	50
642	-	10c. brown, black & grn	2·00	50
643	-	20c. black, green & ol	2·00	90
644	-	30c. ochre, black & green	2·50	1·50
645	-	60c. brown, black & grn	3·00	2·60

ANIMALS: 10c. Leopard; 20c. Eastern black and white colobus; 30c. Mountain nyala; 60c. Ibex.

126 Kebero Drum

1966. Musical Instruments.

646	**126**	5c. black and green	25	10
647	-	10c. black and blue	50	10
648	-	35c. black and orange	1·80	1·10
649	-	50c. black and yellow	2·50	1·70
650	-	60c. black and red	3·00	2·00

INSTRUMENTS: 10c. Begena harp; 35c. Mesenko stringed instrument; 50c. Krar lyre; 60c. Washent flutes.

127 Emperor Haile Selassie

1966. "Fifty Years of Leadership".

651	**127**	10c. multicoloured	40	25
652	**127**	15c. multicoloured	85	45
653	**127**	40c. black, grey & gold	2·00	1·20

128 UNESCO Emblem and Map of Africa

1966. 20th Anniv of UNESCO.

654	**128**	15c. red, black and blue	60	45
655	**128**	60c. blue, brown & green	2·50	1·80

129 W.H.O. Building

1966. Inaug of W.H.O. Headquarters, Geneva.

656	**129**	5c. green, sepia & blue	70	50
657	**129**	40c. sepia, green & violet	2·75	2·00

130 Ethiopian Pavilion

1967. World Fair, Montreal.

658	**130**	30c. multicoloured	80	50
659	**130**	45c. multicoloured	90	65
660	**130**	80c. multicoloured	1·60	1·10

131 Diesel Train and Route-Map

1967. 50th Anniv of Completion of Djibouti–Addis Ababa Railway.

661	**131**	15c. multicoloured	1·30	75
662	**131**	30c. multicoloured	2·50	1·80
663	**131**	50c. multicoloured	4·25	2·00

132 "Papilio aethiops" (inscr "Papilionidae")

1967. Butterflies (1st series). Multicoloured.

664		5c. Type **132**	1·00	35
665		10c. "Charaxes epijasius"	1·50	40
666		20c. "Charaxes varans"	3·00	1·50
667		35c. "Euphaedra neophron"	5·50	3·25
668		40c. "Salamis aethiops"	7·00	4·00

See also Nos. 915/19.

133 Haile Selassie I

1967. Emperor Haile Selassie's 75th Birthday.

669	**133**	10c. multicoloured	25	25
670	**133**	15c. multicoloured	40	40
671	**133**	$1 multicoloured	2·75	2·10
MS672		120×75 mm. No. 671 with colours changed (sold at $1.50)	17·00	22·00

1967. Air. Birds (3rd series). As T 104. Mult.

673		10c. Blue-winged goose (vert)	2·00	1·00
674		15c. African yellow-bill	2·00	1·00
675		20c. Wattled ibis	2·00	60
676		25c. Lesser striped swallow	3·00	80
677		40c. Black-winged lovebird (vert)	5·00	2·00

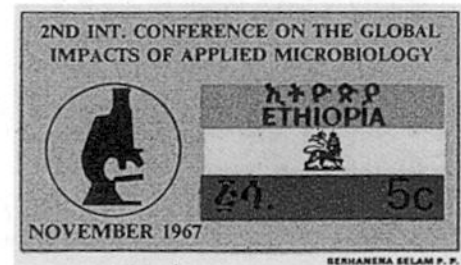

134 Microscope and Flag

1967. 2nd International Conference on Global Impacts of Applied Microbiology, Addis Ababa.

678	**134**	5c. multicoloured	25	15
679	**134**	30c. multicoloured	1·00	85
680	**134**	$1 multicoloured	2·75	2·00

135 Wall Painting, Gondar

1967. International Tourist Year. Multicoloured.

681		15c. Type **135**	2·30	1·50
682		25c. Ancient votive stone and statuary, Atsbe Dera (vert)	2·50	1·60
683		35c. Cave paintings of animals, Harrar Province	4·25	2·40
684		50c. Prehistoric stone tools, Melke Kontoure (vert)	5·25	3·50

136 Cross of Biet-Maryam (bronze)

1967. Crosses of Lalibela (1st series). Crosses in black and silver.

685	**136**	5c. black and lemon	40	30
686	-	10c. black and orange	55	35
687	-	15c. black and violet	80	55
688	-	20c. black and red	1·00	90
689	-	50c. black and yellow	2·50	1·90

CROSSES: 10c. "Zagwe King's" cross; 15c. Copper, Biet-Maryam; 20c. Typical cross of Lalibela region; 50c. Copper, Medhani Alem.

See also Nos. 737/40.

137 Emperor Theodore II with Lions

1968. Death Cent of Emperor Theodore II.

690		10c. brown, lilac & yellow	60	40
691	**137**	20c. lilac, brown & mauve	1·20	50
692	-	50c. red, orange & green	2·75	2·50

DESIGNS—VERT: 10c. Emperor Theodore; 50c. Imperial crown.

138 Human Rights Emblem

1968. Human Rights Year.

693	**138**	15c. black and red	55	25
694	**138**	$1 black and blue	2·40	1·80

139 Shah of Iran and Haile Selassie I

1968. State Visit of Shah of Iran.

695	**139**	5c. multicoloured	20	10
696	**139**	15c. multicoloured	35	20
697	**139**	30c. multicoloured	1·00	75

140 Haile Selassie I and Addressing League of Nations, 1936

1968. "Ethiopia's Struggle for Peace".

No.	Type	Description	Mint	Used
698	**140**	15c. multicoloured	35	25
699	-	35c. multicoloured	75	50
700	-	$1 multicoloured	2·50	2·50

HAILE SELASSIE and: 35c. Africa Hall; $1, World map ("International Relations").

141 W.H.O. Emblem

1968. 20th Anniv of W.H.O.

No.	Type	Description	Mint	Used
701	**141**	15c. black and green	40	25
702	**141**	60c. black and purple	2·00	1·20

142 Running

1968. Olympic Games, Mexico. Multicoloured.

No.	Type	Description	Mint	Used
703		10c. Type **142**	30	10
704		15c. Football	50	15
705		20c. Boxing	80	25
706		40c. Basketball	1·50	1·30
707		50c. Cycling	1·90	1·50

143 Arrussi Costume

1968. Ethiopian Costumes (1st series). Mult.

No.	Type	Description	Mint	Used
708		5c. Type **143**	25	25
709		15c. Gemu Gofa	50	25
710		20c. Godjam	80	25
711		30c. Kaffa	1·20	25
712		35c. Harar	1·40	65
713		50c. Illubabor	2·00	1·00
714		60c. Eritrea	2·40	1·20

See also Nos. 768/74.

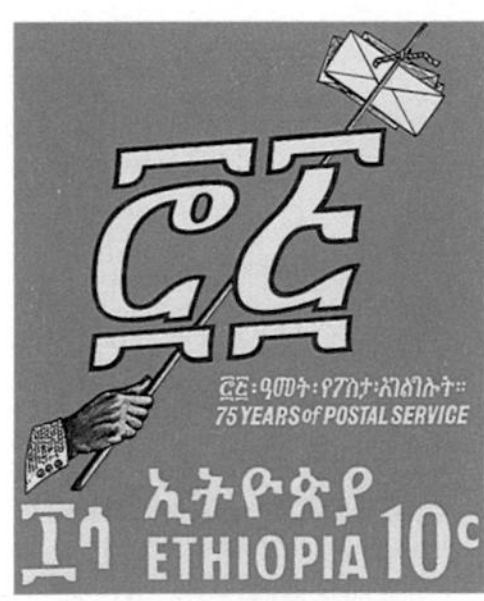

144 Postal Service Emblem and Initials

1969. 75th Anniv of Ethiopian Postal Service.

No.	Type	Description	Mint	Used
715	**144**	10c. black, brown & green	45	25
716	**144**	15c. black, brown & yell	70	70
717	**144**	35c. black, brown & red	1·60	1·60

145 I.L.O. Emblem

1969. 50th Anniv of I.L.O.

No.	Type	Description	Mint	Used
718	**145**	15c. orange and black	70	60
719	**145**	60c. green and black	1·80	1·70

146 Red Cross Emblems

1969. 50th Anniv of League of Red Cross Societies.

No.	Type	Description	Mint	Used
720	**146**	5c. red, black and blue	25	20
721	**146**	15c. red, green & blue	60	50
722	**146**	30c. red, ultram & blue	1·20	1·10

147 Silver Coin of Endybis (3rd cent)

1969. Ancient Ethiopian Coins.

No.	Type	Description	Mint	Used
723	**147**	5c. silver, black & blue	25	20
724	-	10c. gold, black & red	50	40
725	-	15c. gold, black & brown	70	60
726	-	30c. bronze, black & red	1·40	1·20
727	-	40c. bronze, black & grn	1·70	1·40
728	-	50c. silver, black & violet	2·20	1·70

COINS: 10c. Gold coin of Ezana (4th century); 15c. Gold coin of Kalob (6th century); 30c. Bronze coin of Armah (7th century); 40c. Bronze coin of Wazena (7th century); 50c. Silver coin of Gersem (8th century).

148 "Hunting"

1969. African Tourist Year. Multicoloured.

No.	Type	Description	Mint	Used
729		5c. Type **148**	35	25
730		10c. "Camping"	1·10	1·00
731		15c. "Fishing"	1·20	1·00
732		20c. "Watersports"	1·90	1·50
733		25c. "Mountaineering" (vert)	2·25	1·75

149 Dove of Peace

1969. 25th Anniv of U.N. Multicoloured.

No.	Type	Description	Mint	Used
734		10c. Type **149**	30	20
735		30c. Stylized flowers (vert)	1·00	1·00
736		60c. Peace dove and emblem	1·70	1·80

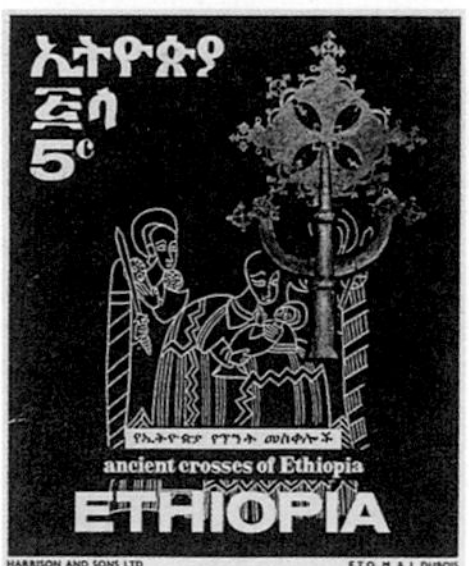

150 Ancient Cross and "Holy Family"

1969. Ancient Ethiopian Crosses (2nd series).

No.	Type	Description	Mint	Used
737	**150**	5c. black, yellow & green	30	40
738	-	10c. black and yellow	30	50
739	-	25c. black, green & yell	1·20	1·60
740	-	60c. black and yellow	2·75	3·25

DESIGNS—VERT: 10c., 25c. and 60c. show different crosses and drawings similar to Type **150**.

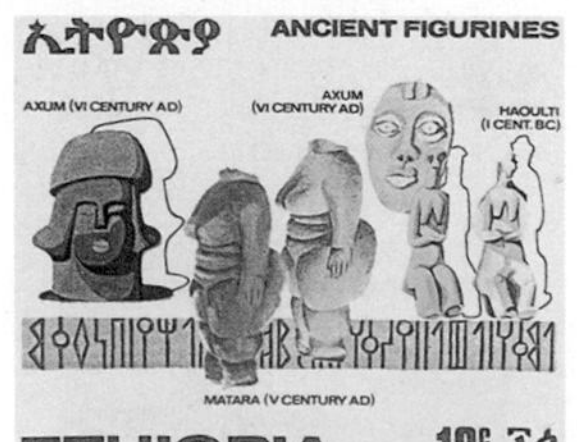

151 Ancient Figurines

1970. Ancient Ethiopian Pottery. Mult.

No.	Type	Description	Mint	Used
741		10c. Type **151**	25	20
742		20c. Decorated jar, Yeha	50	50
743		25c. Axum Pottery	1·20	1·40
744		35c. "Bird" jug, Matara	1·80	2·10
745		60c. Christian pottery, Adulis	3·00	3·50

152 Medhane Alem Church

1970. Rock Churches of Lalibela. Mult.

No.	Type	Description	Mint	Used
746		5c. Type **152**	10	10
747		10c. Bieta Amanuel	10	10
748		15c. Four churches	20	35
749		20c. Bieta Mariam	55	55
750		50c. Bieta Giorgis	1·40	1·40

153 Sail-finned Tang

1970. Fishes. Multicoloured.

No.	Type	Description	Mint	Used
751		5c. Type **153**	40	50
752		10c. Undulate triggerfish	80	50
753		15c. Blue-cheeked butterflyfish	1·20	1·10
754		25c. Hooded butterflyfish	2·10	1·90
755		50c. Emperor angelfish	4·00	3·50

154 I.E.Y. Emblem

1970. International Education Year.

No.	Type	Description	Mint	Used
756	**154**	10c. multicoloured	30	25
757	**154**	20c. multicoloured	50	40
758	**154**	50c. multicoloured	1·40	1·30

155 O.A.U. Emblem

1970. Organization of African Unity. Mult.

No.	Type	Description	Mint	Used
759		20c. Type **155**	55	45
760		30c. O.A.U. flag	70	65
761		40c. O.A.U. Headquarters, Addis Ababa	1·00	90

156 Haile Selassie I

1970. 40th Anniv of Haile Selassie's Coronation.

No.	Type	Description	Mint	Used
762	**156**	15c. multicoloured	40	40
763	**156**	50c. multicoloured	1·40	1·40
764	**156**	60c. multicoloured	1·70	1·50

157 Ministry Buildings

1970. Inauguration of New Posts and Telecommunications Buildings, Addis Ababa.

No.	Type	Description	Mint	Used
765	**157**	10c. multicoloured	30	30
766	**157**	50c. multicoloured	1·20	1·20
767	**157**	80c. multicoloured	2·00	1·80

1971. Ethiopian Costumes (2nd series). As T 143. Multicoloured.

No.	Type	Description	Mint	Used
768		5c. Begemedir and Semain Costume	40	40
769		10c. Bale	50	45
770		15c. Wolega	75	55
771		20c. Showa	1·00	65
772		25c. Sidamo	1·20	80
773		40c. Tigre	1·90	1·40
774		50c. Wello	2·30	1·80

159 Tail of Boeing 707

1971. Air. 25th Anniv of Ethiopian Airlines. Multicoloured.

No.	Type	Description	Mint	Used
775		5c. Type **159**	40	40
776		10c. "Ethiopian Life"	50	50
777		20c. Nose of Boeing 707 and control tower	1·10	80
778		60c. Airliner's flight deck and jet engine	3·00	2·75
779		80c. Route map	4·00	3·50

160 "Fountain of Life" (15th-cent Gospel)

1971. Ethiopian Paintings. Multicoloured.

No.	Type	Description	Mint	Used
780		5c. Type **160**	20	40
781		10c. "King David" (15th-cent manuscript)	40	40
782		25c. "St. George" (17th-cent canvas)	90	70
783		50c. "King Kaleb" (18th-cent triptych, Lalibela)	1·70	1·70
784		60c. "Yared singing to King Kaleb" (18th-cent mural, Axum)	2·00	2·00

161 Black and White Heads

1971. Racial Equality Year.

No.	Type	Description	Mint	Used
785	**161**	10c. black, red & orange	50	40
786	-	60c. multicoloured	1·40	1·10
787	-	80c. multicoloured	1·70	1·50

DESIGN: 60c. Black and white hands holding Globe; 80c. Heads of four races.

162 Emperor Menelik II and Proclamation

1971. 75th Anniv of Victory of Adwa. Mult.

No.	Type	Description	Mint	Used
788		10c. Type **162**	50	60
789		30c. Ethiopian army on the march	1·10	1·20
790		50c. Battle of Adwa	1·90	2·30
791		60c. Ethiopian soldiers	2·20	2·70

163 Emperor Menelik II, Ras Makonnen and Early Telephones

1971. 75th Anniv of Ethiopian Telecommunications. Multicoloured.

792		5c. Type **163**	35	40
793		10c. Emperor Haile Selassie and radio masts	45	50
794		30c. T.V. set and Ethiopians	1·20	1·20
795		40c. Microwave equipment	1·50	1·40
796		60c. Telephone dial and part of Globe	2·50	2·10

164 Mother and Child

1971. 25th Anniv of UNICEF. Mult.

797		5c. Type **164**	35	30
798		10c. Refugee children	45	40
799		15c. Man embracing child	75	60
800		30c. Children with toys	1·50	1·20
801		50c. Students	2·00	2·00

165 Lion's Head

1971. Tourism. Embossed on gold foil.

802	**165**	$15 gold	20·00	
803	-	$15 gold	20·00	

DESIGN: No. 803, Visit of Queen of Sheba to King Solomon.

1972. 1st U.N. Security Council Meeting in Africa (1st issue). Nos. 615/8 Optd U.N. SECURITY COUNCIL FIRST MEETING IN AFRICA 1972 in English and Amharic.

804		20c. multicoloured	1·30	1·00
805		25c. multicoloured	1·30	1·00
806		30c. multicoloured	3·25	2·00
807		35c. multicoloured	3·25	1·75

See also Nos. 832/4.

167 Reed Raft, Lake Haik

1972. Ethiopian River Craft. Multicoloured.

808		10c. Type **167**	55	50
809		20c. Canoes, Lake Abaya	95	75
810		30c. Punts, Lake Tana	1·50	1·50
811		60c. Dugout canoes, Baro River	2·75	2·75

168 Cuneiform Proclamation of Cyrus the Great

1972. 2500th Anniv of Persian Empire.

812	**168**	10c. multicoloured	30	30
813	**168**	60c. multicoloured	2·20	2·20
814	**168**	80c. multicoloured	3·00	3·00

169 "Beehive" Hut, Sidamo Province

1972. Architecture of Ethiopian Provinces.

815	**169**	5c. multicoloured	25	30
816	-	10c. black, grey & brown	30	30
817	-	20c. multicoloured	60	65
818	-	40c. multicoloured	1·20	1·10
819	-	80c. multicoloured	2·40	2·30

DESIGNS: 10c. Two-storey houses, Tigre Province; 20c. House with veranda, Eritrea Province; 40c. Town house, Addis Ababa; 80c. Thatched huts, Shoa Province.

170 "Development" within Cupped Hands

1972. Emperor Haile Selassie's 80th Birthday. Multicoloured.

820		5c. Type **170**	25	30
821		10c. Ethiopians within cupped hands	35	35
822		25c. Map, hands and O.A.U. emblem	60	65
823		50c. Handclasp and U.N. emblem	1·20	1·10
824		60c. Peace dove within hands	1·60	1·50

171 Running

1972. Olympic Games, Munich. Mult.

825		10c. Type **171**	40	40
826		30c. Football	1·30	1·20
827		50c. Cycling	2·10	2·00
828		60c. Boxing	2·30	2·30

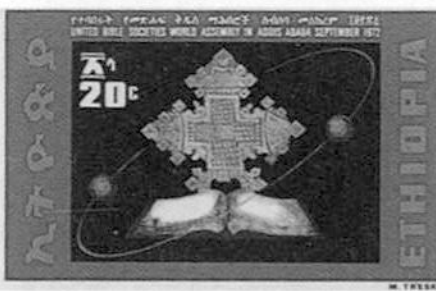

172 Cross and Open Bible

1972. World Assembly of United Bible Societies, Addis Ababa. Multicoloured.

829		20c. Type **172**	65	50
830		50c. First office of B.F.B.S., and new H.Q. (vert)	2·10	1·80
831		80c. Amharic Bible	2·75	2·75

173 Council in Session

1972. 1st U.N. Security Council Meeting in Africa (2nd issue). Multicoloured.

832		10c. Type **173**	30	30
833		60c. Africa Hall, Addis Ababa	2·10	2·00
834		80c. Map of Africa and flags	3·00	2·75

174 "Polluted Waters"

1973. World Campaign against Sea Pollution. Multicoloured.

835		20c. Type **174**	80	40
836		30c. Fishing in polluted sea	1·20	1·10
837		80c. Beach pollution	1·10	2·75

175 Interpol and Ethiopian Police Badges

1973. 50th Anniv of International Criminal Police Organization (Interpol).

838	**175**	40c. black and orange	1·25	1·25
839	-	50c. black, brown & bl	1·75	1·50
840	-	60c. black and red	2·00	1·75

DESIGNS: 50c. Interpol badge and Headquarters, Paris; 60c. Interpol badge.

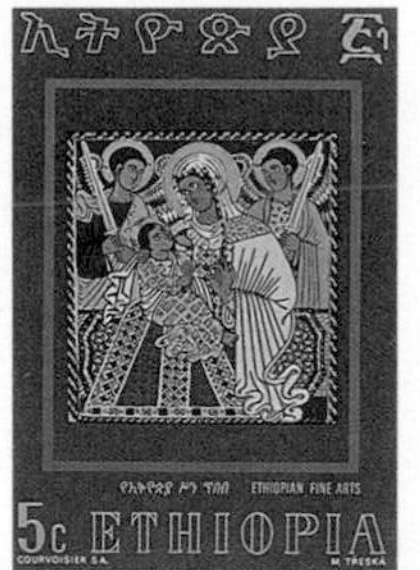

176 "The Virgin and Child" (Fere Seyoum Zana Yacob period)

1973. Ethiopian Fine Arts. Multicoloured.

841		5c. Type **176**	20	30
842		15c. "The Crucifixion" (Zara Yacob period)	50	35
843		30c. "St. Mary" (Entoto Mariam church painting)	1·25	55
844		40c. "Saint" mosaic (Addis Ababa Art School)	1·80	1·60
845		80c. Sculptured relief (Addis Ababa Art School)	3·25	3·25

177 African Colonial Maps, 1963 and 1973

1973. 10th Anniv of Organization of African Unity. Multicoloured.

846		5c. Type **177**	20	20
847		10c. Map, Headquarters and flags	30	35
848		20c. Map and emblems	60	45
849		40c. Map and "population" ranks	1·20	1·20
850		80c. Map on globe, O.A.U. and U.N. emblems	2·20	2·20

178 Ethiopian Scout Flags

1973. 40th Anniv of Scouting in Ethiopia. Mult.

851		5c. Type **178**	20	30
852		15c. "Scout" sign on highway	55	30
853		30c. Guide teaching old man to read	1·40	1·40
854		40c. "First Aid"	1·90	1·80
855		60c. Ethiopian scout	3·50	3·50

179 W.M.O. Emblem

1973. Cent of World Meteorological Organization.

856	**179**	40c. black, blue & lt blue	1·40	1·30
857	-	50c. black and blue	1·70	1·70
858	-	60c. multicoloured	2·00	2·00

DESIGNS: 50c. Wind gauge and emblem; 60c. Weather satellite.

180 Old Wall, Harar

1973. Inauguration of Prince Makonnen Memorial Hospital. Multicoloured.

859		5c. Type **180**	20	30
860		10c. Prince Makonnen, equipment and patients	30	40
861		20c. Operating theatre	3·00	1·30
862		40c. Scouts giving first-aid	4·00	3·00
863		80c. Prince Makonnen	1·50	4·00

181 Haile Selassie I

1973

864	**181**	5c. multicoloured	10	25
865	**181**	10c. multicoloured	20	25
866	**181**	15c. multicoloured	20	25
867	**181**	20c. multicoloured	15	10
868	**181**	25c. multicoloured	25	25
869	**181**	30c. multicoloured	50	45
870	**181**	35c. multicoloured	50	45
871	**181**	40c. multicoloured	70	50
872	**181**	45c. multicoloured	80	60
873	**181**	50c. multicoloured	1·00	60
874	**181**	55c. multicoloured	1·20	70
875	**181**	60c. multicoloured	1·40	80
876	**181**	70c. multicoloured	2·50	90
877	**181**	90c. multicoloured	3·00	1·20
878	**181**	$1 multicoloured	3·50	1·30
879	**181**	$2 multicoloured	5·00	2·40
880	**181**	$3 multicoloured	8·00	3·50
881	**181**	$5 multicoloured	12·00	6·00

182 Flame Emblem

1973. 25th Anniv of Declaration of Human Rights.

882	**182**	40c. gold, green & yell	75	60
883	**182**	50c. gold, grn & emerald	90	75
884	**182**	60c. gold, grn & orge	1·10	1·10

183 Wicker Furniture

1974. Ethiopian Wickerwork. Various Wicker handicrafts.

885	**183**	5c. multicoloured	20	20
886	-	10c. multicoloured	30	35
887	-	30c. multicoloured	90	85
888	-	50c. multicoloured	1·40	1·40
889	-	60c. multicoloured	1·70	1·60

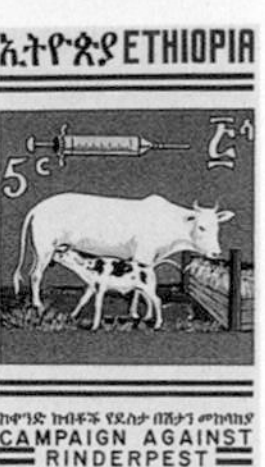

184 Cow, Calf and Syringe

1974. Campaign Against Rinderpest. Mult.

890	5c. Type **184**	20	25
891	15c. Inoculation	30	35
892	20c. Bullock and syringe	90	85
893	50c. Laboratory technician	1·40	1·40
894	60c. Symbolic map	1·70	1·60

185 Umbrella Manufacture

1974. 20th Anniv of Haile Selassie I Foundation. Multicoloured.

895	10c. Type **185**	25	30
896	30c. Weaving	55	50
897	50c. Children with books and toys	1·20	1·20
898	60c. Foundation building	1·30	1·30

186 Bitwoded Robe

1974. Traditional Ceremonial Robes. Mult.

899	15c. Type **186**	45	45
900	25c. Wagseyoum	90	90
901	35c. Ras	1·30	1·30
902	40c. Leol Ras	1·50	1·50
903	60c. Negusenegest	2·30	2·30

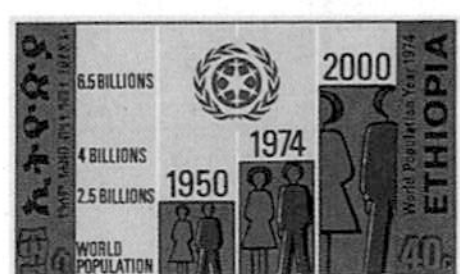

187 "Population Growth"

1974. World Population Year. Multicoloured.

904	40c. Type **187**	85	85
905	50c. Diagram with large family	1·10	1·10
906	60c. "Rising Population"	1·30	1·30

188 U.P.U. and Ethiopian P.T.T. Emblems

1974. Centenary of Universal Postal Union. Multicoloured.

907	15c. Type **188**	25	30
908	50c. Emblem and letters	1·10	1·20
909	60c. U.P.U. emblem	1·40	1·40
910	70c. U.P.U. emblem and H.Q., Berne	1·60	1·50

189 Landscape

1974. Meskel Festival.

911	**189**	5c. multicoloured	20	30
912	-	10c. multicoloured	30	30
913	-	20c. multicoloured	60	65
914	-	80c. multicoloured	2·40	2·00

DESIGNS: Nos. 912/4, Various festive scenes similar to Type **189**.

190 "Nymphalidae precis clelia CR"

1975. Butterflies (2nd series). Multicoloured.

915	10c. Type **190**	15	15
916	25c. "Nymphalidae charaxes achaemenes F."	30	30
917	45c. "Papilionidae P. dardanus"	80	80
918	50c. "Nymphalidae charaxes druceanus B."	1·10	1·10
919	60c. "Papilionidae P. demodocus"	1·30	1·30

191 "The Magi"

1975. Religious Paintings in Ethiopian Churches. Multicoloured.

920	5c. Type **191**	20	20
921	10c. "The Entombment"	30	30
922	15c. "Christ with the Apostles"	40	40
923	30c. "The Miracle of the Blind"	80	70
924	40c. "The Crucifixion"	1·10	1·00
925	80c. "Christ in Majesty"	2·30	1·90

192 Warthog

1975. Animals. Multicoloured.

926	5c. Type **192**	20	30
927	10c. Aardvark	30	35
928	20c. Simien jackal	85	90
929	40c. Gelada	1·90	1·60
930	80c. African civet	3·75	3·25

193 Dove crossing Globe

1975. International Women's Year. Mult.

931	40c. Type **193**	60	40
932	50c. I.W.Y. emblem and symbols	75	70
933	90c. "Equality"	1·50	1·40

194 Reception Desk

1975. Opening of National Postal Museum.

934	**194**	10c. multicoloured	25	20
935	-	30c. multicoloured	65	45
936	-	60c. multicoloured	1·20	85
937	-	70c. multicoloured	1·40	1·20

DESIGNS: 30c. to 70c. Views of museum display area.

195 Map Emblem

1975. 1st Anniv of Socialist Government.

938	**195**	5c. multicoloured	10	10
939	**195**	10c. multicoloured	10	10
940	**195**	25c. multicoloured	40	20
941	**195**	50c. multicoloured	1·00	80
942	**195**	90c. multicoloured	1·40	90

196 U.N. Emblem

1975. 30th Anniv of United Nations.

943	**196**	40c. multicoloured	55	55
944	**196**	50c. multicoloured	75	70
945	**196**	90c. multicoloured	1·50	1·30

197 Illubabor

1975. Regional Hairstyles (1st series). Mult.

946	5c. Type **197**	20	30
947	15c. Arussi	35	30
948	20c. Eritrea	45	35
949	30c. Bale	75	55
950	35c. Kaffa	95	75
951	50c. Begemder	1·40	1·00
952	60c. Shoa	1·70	1·30

See also Nos. 1027/33.

198 "Delphinium wellbyi"

1975. Ethiopian Flowers. Multicoloured.

953	5c. Type **198**	30	25
954	10c. "Plectocephalus varians"	40	30
955	20c. "Brachystelma asmarensis" (horiz)	75	60
956	40c. "Ceropegia inflata"	1·30	1·10
957	80c. "Erythrina brucei"	2·30	2·30

199 Goalkeeper diving

1976. 10th African Football "Cup of Nations" Championship. Multicoloured.

958	5c. Type **199**	20	20
959	10c. Footballers in tackle	35	30
960	25c. Player shooting at goal	80	85
961	50c. Defender clearing ball	1·50	85
962	90c. Ball and Ethiopian flag	3·00	2·40

200 Early and Modern Telephones

1976. Telephone Centenary. Multicoloured.

963	30c. Type **200**	90	70
964	60c. A. Graham Bell	1·80	1·70
965	90c. Aerial complex	2·74	2·40

201 Amulets

1976. Ethiopian Jewellery.

966	**201**	5c. multicoloured	20	25
967	-	10c. multicoloured	30	25
968	-	20c. multicoloured	65	50
969	-	40c. multicoloured	1·40	1·30
970	-	80c. multicoloured	2·75	2·25

Nos. 967/70 are similar to Type **201** showing models with jewellery.

202 Boxing

1976. Olympic Games, Montreal. Mult.

971	10c. Type **202**	35	25
972	80c. Shot-putting	2·00	2·00
973	90c. Cycling	2·75	2·30

203 Campaign Emblem

1976. "Development Through Co-operation" Campaign.

974	**203**	5c. multicoloured	20	2·00
975	**203**	10c. multicoloured	25	20
976	**203**	25c. multicoloured	40	35
977	**203**	50c. multicoloured	95	75
978	**203**	90c. multicoloured	1·50	1·30

204 Map Emblem

1976. 2nd Anniv of Republic.

979	**204**	5c. multicoloured	20	20
980	**204**	10c. multicoloured	25	20
981	**204**	25c. multicoloured	40	35
982	**204**	50c. multicoloured	90	75
983	**204**	90c. multicoloured	1·50	1·30

205 Crest with Sunburst

1976

984	**205**	5c. gold, green & black	10	25
985	**205**	10c. gold, orange & blk	10	25
986	**205**	15c. gold, blue & black	10	10
987	**205**	20c. gold, lilac & black	15	10
988	**205**	25c. gold, green & blk	15	10
989	**205**	30c. gold, red & black	20	15
990	**205**	35c. gold, yellow & blk	25	15
991	**205**	40c. gold, green & blk	55	20
992	**205**	45c. gold, green & blk	65	50
993	**205**	50c. gold, mauve & blk	75	55
994	**205**	55c. gold, blue & black	85	65
995	**205**	60c. gold, brown & blk	1·00	65
996	**205**	70c. gold, pink & black	1·20	70
997	**205**	90c. gold, blue & black	1·50	75
998	**205**	$1 gold, green & black	2·00	1·30
999	**205**	$2 gold, grey & black	5·00	2·50
1000	**205**	$3 gold, purple & black	8·50	4·00
1001	**205**	$5 gold, blue & black	12·00	6·00

See also Nos. 1263a/c.

206 Donkey Boy and Aircraft

1976. 30th Anniv of Ethiopian Airlines. Multicoloured.

1002	5c. Type **206**	15	25
1003	10c. Crescent on globe	30	40
1004	25c. "Star" of crew and passengers	75	60
1005	50c. Propeller and jet engines	1·50	1·40
1006	90c. Aircraft converging on map	2·60	2·40

207 Tortoise

1976. Reptiles. Multicoloured.

1007	10c. Type **207**	20	30
1008	20c. Chameleon	80	60
1009	30c. Python	1·20	1·00
1010	40c. Monitor (lizard)	1·50	1·30
1011	80c. Crocodile	2·75	2·60

208 Cessna 170A dropping Supplies

1976. Relief and Rehabilitation. Mult.

1012	5c. Type **208**	10	10
1013	10c. Carved hand with hammer	20	10
1014	45c. Child supported by banknote	1·20	80
1015	60c. Map of Ogaden region and desert tracks	1·80	1·20
1016	80c. Waif within broken egg-shell, camera & film	2·30	1·80

209 Dengour Ruins and Elephant Figurine

1977. Ethiopian Archaeology. Multicoloured.

1017	5c. Type **209**	20	20
1018	10c. Yeha temple and bronze ibex	30	35
1019	25c. Sourre Kabanawa dolmen and ancient pot	80	60
1020	50c. Melka Kontoure site and stone axe	1·60	1·10
1021	80c. Omo Valley, skull and jawbone	2·50	1·90

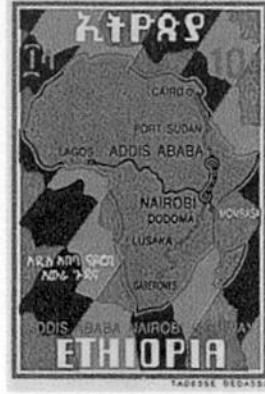

210 Route Map

1977. Inauguration of Trans-East African Highway.

1022	**210**	10c. multicoloured	30	25
1023	**210**	20c. multicoloured	60	40
1024	**210**	40c. multicoloured	1·30	80
1025	**210**	50c. multicoloured	1·50	1·25
1026	**210**	60c. multicoloured	1·90	1·50

1977. Regional Hairstyles (2nd series). As T 197. Multicoloured.

1027	5c. Wollega	15	20
1028	10c. Godjam	20	20
1029	15c. Tigre	45	30
1030	20c. Harrar	60	40
1031	25c. Gemu Gofa	75	55
1032	40c. Sidamo	1·25	90
1033	50c. Wollo	1·50	1·25

211 Addis Ababa

1977. Ethiopian Towns. Multicoloured.

1034	5c. Type **211**	15	20
1035	10c. Asmara	30	20
1036	25c. Harrar	50	40
1037	50c. Jimma	1·50	1·25
1038	90c. Dessie	2·50	1·90

212 "Terebratula abyssinica"

1977. Fossil Shells. Multicoloured.

1039	5c. Type **212**	15	20
1040	10c. "Terebratula subalata"	40	30
1041	25c. "Cuculloea lefeburiaua"	1·20	70
1042	50c. "Ostrea (gryphea) plicatissima"	2·25	1·80
1043	90c. "Trigonia cousobrina"	4·00	3·50

213 Shattered Imperial Crown

1977. 3rd Anniv of Republic. Mult.

1044	5c. Type **213**	15	20
1045	10c. Emblem of revolutionary regime	20	20
1046	25c. Warriors with hammer and sickle	50	35
1047	60c. Soldiers and map	1·00	90
1048	80c. Crest of revolutionary regime	1·50	1·25

214 "Cicindela petitii"

1977. Insects. Multicoloured.

1049	5c. Type **214**	15	20
1050	10c. "Heliocopris dillonii"	40	25
1051	25c. "Poekilocerus vignaudii"	95	85
1052	50c. "Pepsis heros"	2·00	1·70
1053	90c. "Pepsis dedjaz"	3·75	3·25

215 Lenin, Globe and Map of Ethiopia

1977. 60th Anniv of Russian Revolution.

1054	**215**	5c. multicoloured	15	20
1055	**215**	10c. multicoloured	20	20
1056	**215**	25c. multicoloured	50	35
1057	**215**	50c. multicoloured	1·00	90
1058	**215**	90c. multicoloured	1·40	1·20

216 Moon Wrasse

1978. Fishes. Multicoloured.

1059	5c. Type **216**	15	20
1060	10c. Yellow boxfish	40	25
1061	25c. Summan grouper	95	85
1062	50c. Sea perch	2·00	1·70
1063	90c. Northern pufferfish	3·75	3·25

217 Cattle

1978. Domestic Animals. Multicoloured.

1064	5c. Type **217**	15	20
1065	10c. Donkeys	30	20
1066	25c. Sheep	50	40
1067	50c. Camels	1·50	1·20
1068	90c. Horses	2·50	1·90

218 Emblem and Weapons

1978. "Call of the Motherland". Mult.

1069	5c. Type **218**	15	20
1070	10c. Armed workers	20	20
1071	25c. Map of Africa	45	40
1072	60c. Soldiers	1·70	1·20
1073	80c. Nurse and blood donor	2·50	2·00

219 Ibex

1978. Ancient Bronzes. Multicoloured.

1074	5c. Type **219**	15	20
1075	10c. Lion (horiz)	40	25
1076	25c. Lamp	95	85
1077	50c. Goat (horiz)	2·00	1·70
1078	90c. Axe, chisel and sickle	3·75	3·25

220 Globe and Emblem

1978. World Cup Football Championship, Argentina. Multicoloured.

1079	5c. Type **220**	10	15
1080	20c. Player kicking ball	20	15
1081	30c. Ball in net	50	40
1082	55c. F.I.F.A. emblem and ball	1·20	1·00
1083	70c. World Cup emblem and pitch (vert)	1·75	1·25

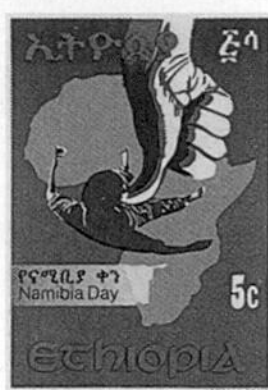

221 Man under Thumb

1978. Namibia Day. Multicoloured.

1084	5c. Type **221**	10	15
1085	10c. Man with pistol	15	15
1086	25c. Soldier	40	35
1087	60c. Bound figure	1·20	1·00
1088	80c. Head of African	1·80	1·30

222 Armed Forces

1978. 4th Anniv of Revolution. Mult.

1089	80c. Type **222**	90	90
1090	1b. Revolutionaries	1·10	1·10

223 Open Globe filled with Tools

1978. U.N. Conference on Technical Co-operation among Developing Countries. Multicoloured.

1091	10c. Type **223**	10	20
1092	15c. Symbols	20	20
1093	25c. World map and gear wheels	40	25
1094	60c. Hands passing spanner over globe	80	75
1095	70c. Geese and tortoise over world map	95	1·00

224 Human Rights Emblem

1978. 30th Anniv of Human Rights Declaration.

1096	**224**	5c. multicoloured	10	20

1097 **224** 15c. multicoloured 10 20
1098 **224** 25c. multicoloured 40 25
1099 **224** 35c. multicoloured 50 45
1100 **224** 1b. multicoloured 1·40 1·30

225 Manacled Hands and Anti-Apartheid Emblem

1978. International Anti-Apartheid Year.
1101 **225** 5c. multicoloured 10 20
1102 **225** 20c. multicoloured 15 20
1103 **225** 30c. multicoloured 45 20
1104 **225** 55c. multicoloured 80 80
1105 **225** 70c. multicoloured 1·00 1·00

226 Stone Monument at Osole

1979. Ancient Carved Stones from Soddo. Mult.
1106 5c. Type **226** 15 20
1107 10c. Garashino 25 20
1108 25c. Wado 70 40
1109 60c. Ambeut 1·80 1·30
1110 80c. Detail of decoration, Tiya 2·30 1·80

227 Cotton Plant

1979. Cotton Industry. Multicoloured.
1111 5c. Type **227** 15 20
1112 10c. Women spinning cotton 20 20
1113 20c. Reeling cotton onto poles 2·20 1·60
1114 65c. Weaving 2·75 1·60
1115 80c. Shemma work 2·75 2·00

228 Grar

1979. Trees. Multicoloured.
1116 5c. Type **228** 15 10
1117 10c. Weira 30 15
1118 25c. Tidh 75 65
1119 50c. Shola 1·30 1·20
1120 90c. Zigba 2·50 2·40

229 Plough and Sickle (agriculture)

1979. National Revolutionary Development Campaign. Multicoloured.
1121 10c. Type **229** 15 10
1122 15c. Industry 20 20
1123 25c. Transport and communications 1·20 65
1124 60c. Education and Health 1·40 1·20
1125 70c. Commerce 1·60 1·30

230 Family holding Hands

1979. International Year of the Child. Mult.
1126 10c. I.Y.C. Emblem 15 10
1127 15c. Type **230** 20 20
1128 25c. Helping a crippled child 50 45
1129 60c. Circle of children 1·40 1·20
1130 70c. Black and white children embracing 1·60 1·30

231 Revolutionaries and Emblem

1979. 5th Anniv of Revolution. Mult.
1131 10c. Type **231** 25 20
1132 15c. Soldiers and agriculture 40 25
1133 25c. Emblem of revolution 55 40
1134 60c. Students with torch 1·30 1·10
1135 70c. Citizens and emblems 1·50 1·30

232 "Communications"

1979. 3rd World Telecommunications Exhibition, Geneva.
1136 **232** 5c. blue, mauve & blk 40 20
1137 - 30c. multicoloured 1·60 95
1138 - 35c. multicoloured 2·50 1·10
1139 - 45c. multicoloured 2·75 1·40
1140 - 65c. multicoloured 3·75 2·00
DESIGN: 30c. Telephone handset; 35c. Communications satellite; 45c. Ground receiving aerial; 65c. Television camera.

233 Incense Container

1979. Wickerwork. Multicoloured.
1141 5c. Type **233** 20 15
1142 10c. Flower vase 50 30
1143 25c. Earthenware cover 1·30 65
1144 60c. Milk container 3·25 1·70
1145 80c. Storage container 3·75 2·20

234 Dish

1980. Woodwork. Multicoloured.
1146 5c. Type **234** 20 15
1147 30c. Table and chair 85 65
1148 35c. Pestles and mortars 1·00 75
1149 45c. Stools 1·20 95
1150 65c. Pots 1·70 1·50

235 Lappet-faced Vulture

1980. Birds of Prey. Multicoloured.
1151 10c. Type **235** 75 50
1152 15c. Long-crested eagle 1·00 75
1153 25c. Secretary bird 1·75 1·25
1154 60c. Abyssinian long-eared owl 5·00 4·00
1155 70c. Lanner falcon 5·00 4·00

236 W.H.D. Emblem and Cigarette

1980. Anti-smoking Campaign. Multicoloured.
1156 20c. Skull superimposed on cigarette packet 60 40
1157 60c. Type **236** 1·80 1·60
1158 1b. Pipe, cigarette and infected lungs 3·25 2·75

237 Lenin in Hiding at Rasliv

1980. 110th Birth Anniv of Lenin. Mult.
1159 5c. Lenin's House, Pskov 15 15
1160 15c. Type **237** 20 20
1161 20c. Lenin as student 60 40
1162 40c. Lenin returns to Russia 1·20 80
1163 1b. Lenin speaking on the Goerlo plan 2·75 2·25

238 Grevy's Zebra

1980. Endangered Animals. Multicoloured.
1164 10c. Type **238** 20 15
1165 15c. Dibatag 25 20
1166 25c. Hunting dog 1·30 80
1167 60c. Hartebeest 2·50 1·60
1168 70c. Cheetahs 6·25 3·75

239 Running

1980. Olympic Games, Moscow. Multicoloured.
1169 30c. Type **239** 75 50
1170 70c. Cycling 2·00 1·50
1171 80c. Boxing 2·25 1·75

240 Man cutting Blindfold

1980. 6th Anniv of Revolution. Mult.
1172 30c. Type **240** 75 50
1173 40c. Crowd 1·00 85
1174 50c. Woman cutting chain 1·30 1·10
1175 70c. Crowd and flags 1·90 1·40

241 Meal Basket

1980. Bamboo Folk Craft. Multicoloured.
1176 5c. Type **241** 20 10
1177 15c. Hand basket 25 20
1178 25c. Stool 40 30
1179 35c. Fruit compote 65 40
1180 1b. Lamp shade 2·75 2·25

242 Mekotkocha (weeding tool)

1980. Traditional Cultivating and Harvesting Tools. Multicoloured.
1181 10c. Type **242** 20 15
1182 15c. Layda 25 20
1183 40c. Mensh 2·00 1·10
1184 45c. Medekdekia 2·30 1·60
1185 70c. Mofer and kenber 3·25 2·40

243 Baro River

1981. Baro River Bridge. Multicoloured.
1186 15c. Type **243** 50 25
1187 65c. Bridge under construction 2·75 2·00
1188 1b. Bridge 4·75 3·00

244 Wawel Castle, Poland

1981. World Heritage (1st series). Mult.
1189 5c. Type **244** 25 20
1190 15c. Quito Cathedral, Ecuador 70 45
1191 20c. Island of Goree, Senegal 90 65
1192 30c. Messa Verde, U.S.A. 1·40 1·10
1193 80c. Simien National Park, Ethiopia 3·50 2·40
1194 1b. L'Anse aux Meadows, Canada 4·50 3·25
See also Nos. 1200/1205.

245 Drinking Vessel

1981. Ancient Pottery. Multicoloured.
1195 20c. Type **245** 60 30
1196 25c. Spice container 1·00 70
1197 35c. Jug 1·30 1·10
1198 40c. Cooking apparatus 1·50 1·20
1199 60c. Animal figurine 2·25 1·70

246 Biet Medhani Alem Church, Ethiopia

1981. World Heritage (2nd series). Mult.

No.	Description	Unused	Used
1200	10c. Type **246**	25	35
1201	15c. Nehanni National Park, Canada	50	40
1202	20c. Lower Falls of the Yellowstone River, U.S.A.	1·00	80
1203	30c. Aachen Cathedral, West Germany	1·70	1·20
1204	80c. Kicker Rock, San Cristobel Island, Ecuador	4·50	3·25
1205	1b. Holy Cross Chapel, Poland (vert)	5·50	4·00

247 Disabled Child learning to write

1981. International Year of Disabled Persons. Multicoloured.

No.	Description	Unused	Used
1206	5c. Disabled, artificial limbs and crutch	50	20
1207	15c. Type **247**	50	40
1208	20c. Artificial limbs	75	55
1209	40c. Disabled hands learning to knit	1·50	1·10
1210	1b. Disabled people learning to weave	3·75	2·75

248 Children at Work and Play

1981. 7th Anniv of Revolution. Mult.

No.	Description	Unused	Used
1211	20c. Type **248**	35	25
1212	60c. Disabled revolutionaries	1·40	1·25
1213	1b. Printing and distributing "Serto Ader Gazette"	2·25	2·00

249 Ploughing by Oxen, Tilling and Harvesting by hand

1981. World Food Day. Multicoloured.

No.	Description	Unused	Used
1214	5c. Air-drop of food and starving Ethiopians	20	20
1215	15c. Type **249**	40	30
1216	20c. Desert and agricultural scenes	1·00	65
1217	40c. Agricultural lecture and farmlands	1·60	1·20
1218	1b. Cattle and corn	4·00	3·00

250 Animal-shaped Pitcher

1981. Ancient Bronze Implements.

No.	Type	Description	Unused	Used
1219	**250**	15c. multicoloured	30	20
1220	-	45c. silver, black & brn	1·00	75
1221	-	50c. multicoloured	1·20	1·20
1222	-	70c. multicoloured	1·90	1·60

DESIGNS: 45c. Tsenatsil; 50c. Pitcher; 70c. Pot.

251 Cup

1981. Horn Work. Multicoloured.

No.	Description	Unused	Used
1223	10c. Tobacco container	20	20
1224	15c. Type **251**	30	20
1225	40c. Tej container	1·00	50
1226	45c. Goblet	1·20	1·10
1227	70c. Spoon	1·80	1·50

252 Coffee Plantation

1982. Ethiopian Coffee. Multicoloured.

No.	Description	Unused	Used
1228	5c. Type **252**	20	15
1229	15c. Coffee bush	75	40
1230	25c. Mature plantation	1·30	1·10
1231	35c. Picking coffee	2·20	1·60
1232	1b. Pouring and drinking coffee	5·00	4·25

253 Players and Football

1982. World Cup Football Championship, Spain. Multicoloured.

No.	Description	Unused	Used
1233	5c. Type **253**	20	15
1234	15c. Player with ball	30	25
1235	20c. Goalkeeper saving ball	60	35
1236	40c. Player kicking ball	1·00	90
1237	1b. Ball, clasped hands and shirts	2·50	2·25

254 Cattle

1982. Centenary of Discovery of Tubercle Bacillus. Multicoloured.

No.	Description	Unused	Used
1238	15c. Type **254**	20	15
1239	20c. Magnifying glass and bacillus	60	40
1240	30c. Koch with microscope	1·00	85
1241	35c. Dr. Robert Koch	1·20	1·00
1242	80c. T.B. patient and Dr. Koch	2·50	2·40

255 Preventing Theft

1982. 8th Anniv of Revolution. Mult.

No.	Description	Unused	Used
1243	80c. Type **255**	1·50	1·20
1244	1b. Voting	1·90	1·70

256 Primitive Measurements of Length

1982. World Standards Day. Multicoloured.

No.	Description	Unused	Used
1245	5c. Type **256**	20	15
1246	15c. Primitive balance	30	20
1247	20c. Metric measurement	60	35
1248	40c. Weights and scales	1·40	1·10
1249	1b. Ethiopian standards emblem	3·00	2·75

257 Wildlife Conservation

1982. 10th Anniv of U.N. Environment Programme. Multicoloured.

No.	Description	Unused	Used
1250	5c. Type **257**	20	15
1251	15c. Village (Environmental health and settlement)	60	20
1252	20c. Forest protection	95	35
1253	40c. National literacy campaign	2·00	1·30
1254	1b. Soil and water conservation	4·75	3·00

258 Grand Gallery

1983. Sof Omar Caves. Multicoloured.

No.	Description	Unused	Used
1255	5c. Type **258**	20	15
1256	10c. Chamber of Columns	25	20
1257	15c. Route through cave	30	45
1258	70c. Map of caves	3·00	2·40
1259	80c. Entrance to cave	3·00	2·75

259 "25" on Emblem

1983. 25th Anniv of Economic Commission for Africa.

No.	Type	Description	Unused	Used
1260	**259**	80c. multicoloured	1·30	1·20
1261	**259**	1b. multicoloured	1·90	1·70

260 I.M.O. Emblem and Waves

1983. 25th Anniv of International Maritime Organization. Multicoloured.

No.	Description	Unused	Used
1262	85c. Type **260**	3·75	2·75
1263	1b. Lighthouse and liner	5·25	3·75

1983. As Nos. 998/1000 but with value expressed in "BIRR".

No.	Type	Description	Unused	Used
1263a	**205**	1b. grn, gold & blk	3·50	2·00
1263b	**205**	2b. grey, gold & blk	11·50	5·75
1263c	**205**	3b. pur, gold & blk	7·00	3·00

261 U.P.U. Monument, Berne

1983. World Communications Year. Mult.

No.	Description	Unused	Used
1264	25c. Type **261**	50	40
1265	55c. Antenna, satellite and drum	2·20	2·10
1266	1b. River bridge and railway tunnel	5·00	3·50

262 Peace Dove on Globe

1983. 9th Anniv of Revolution. Mult.

No.	Description	Unused	Used
1267	25c. Type **262**	40	25
1268	55c. Red star	1·10	65
1269	1b. Crest	1·90	1·80

263 Hura and Shepherd

1983. Musical Instruments. Multicoloured.

No.	Description	Unused	Used
1270	5c. Type **263**	20	15
1271	15c. Dinke and funeral	30	20
1272	20c. Meleket and announcing royal proclamation	70	45
1273	40c. Embilta and royal procession	1·30	1·20
1274	1b. Tom and dancers	2·90	2·75

264 "Charaxes galawadiwosi"

1983. Butterflies. Multicoloured.

No.	Description	Unused	Used
1275	10c. Type **264**	30	20
1276	15c. "Epiphora elianae"	45	30
1277	55c. "Batiama rougeoti"	4·25	3·50
1278	1b. "Achaea saboeaereginae"	7·75	6·00

265 I.A.A.Y. Emblem

1984. International Anti-Apartheid Year.

No.	Type	Description	Unused	Used
1279	**265**	5c. multicoloured	20	15
1280	**265**	15c. multicoloured	25	20
1281	**265**	20c. multicoloured	35	30
1282	**265**	40c. multicoloured	95	80
1283	**265**	1b. multicoloured	2·50	1·90

266 "Protea gaguedi"

1984. Flowers. Multicoloured.

No.	Description	Unused	Used
1284	5c. Type **266**	20	15
1285	25c. "Sedum epidendrum"	1·30	80
1286	50c. "Echinops amplexicaulis"	2·50	1·80
1287	1b. "Canarina eminii"	5·00	3·25

267 Konso House

1984. Ethiopian House Architecture. Mult.

No.	Description	Unused	Used
1288	15c. Type **267**	30	20
1289	65c. Dorze house	2·40	1·80
1290	1b. Harer houses	3·75	3·25

268 Torch on Map and Crowd of Workers

1984. 10th Anniv of Revolution. Mult.

No.	Description	Unused	Used
1291	5c. Type **268**	20	10
1292	10c. Countrywoman and ploughing with oxen	30	15
1293	15c. Crowd with flag	50	20
1294	20c. Pres. Mengistu, flag, map and crowd	75	30
1295	25c. Soldiers ploughing with oxen	1·00	45
1296	40c. Workers writing	1·40	65
1297	45c. Pres. Mengistu addressing Party conference	1·70	80
1298	50c. Schoolchildren	1·80	1·20
1299	70c. Pres. Mengistu and statue	2·50	1·70
1300	1b. Pres. Mengistu addressing Organization of African Unity meeting	3·75	2·50

269 "Gugs"

1984. Traditional Games. Multicoloured.

1301	5c. Type **269**	20	15
1302	25c. Tigil (wrestling)	1·00	75
1303	50c. Gerna (hockey)	2·50	1·60
1304	1b. Gebeta (board game)	4·75	3·00

270 Harwood's Francolin

1985. Birds. Multicoloured.

1305	5c. Type **270**	35	35
1306	15c. Rouget's rail	90	65
1307	80c. Little bee eater	5·00	4·00
1308	85c. Red-headed weaver	5·25	4·25

271 Hippopotamuses

1985. Mammals. Multicoloured.

1309	20c. Type **271**	30	20
1310	25c. Gerenuk	1·00	55
1311	40c. Common duiker	1·90	1·50
1312	1b. Gunther's dik-dik	5·25	3·75

272 Degen's Barb

1985. Freshwater Fish. Multicoloured.

1313	10c. Type **272**	20	20
1314	20c. Cylinder labeo	55	30
1315	55c. Toothed tetra	3·75	2·50
1316	1b. African lungfish	6·00	4·00

273 "Securidaca longepedunculata"

1985. Medicinal Plants. Multicoloured.

1317	10c. Type **273**	20	15
1318	20c. "Plumbago zeylanicum"	30	25
1319	55c. "Brucea antidysenteric"	3·00	2·00
1320	1b. "Dorstenia barminiana"	5·50	4·00

274 "50" and First Aid

1985. 50th Anniv of Ethiopian Red Cross. Multicoloured.

1321	35c. Type **274**	70	60
1322	55c. Community aid scenes	2·75	1·50
1323	1b. Nursing scenes	4·50	3·25

275 Kombolcha Textile Mills

1985. 11th Anniv of Revolution. Mult.

1324	10c. Type **275**	20	15
1325	80c. Mugher cement factory	1·90	1·60
1326	1b. Views of famine and drought and resettlement of victims	2·40	2·20

276 U.N. Emblem

1985. 40th Anniv of U.N.O.

1327	**276**	25c. multicoloured	40	25
1328	**276**	55c. multicoloured	1·60	1·40
1329	**276**	1b. multicoloured	2·75	2·50

277 Man with Caliper, Boy, Microscope and Crutch

1986. Anti-polio Campaign. Multicoloured.

1330	5c. Type **277**	20	15
1331	10c. Child on crutches	60	50
1332	20c. Doctor fitting child with caliper	90	80
1333	55c. Man with caliper working sewing machine	2·75	2·00
1334	1b. Doctor vaccinating baby	4·75	3·25

278 "Millettia ferruginea"

1986. Trees. Multicoloured.

1335	10c. Type **278**	25	15
1336	30c. "Syzyigum guineense"	1·20	80
1337	50c. "Cordia africana"	2·25	1·80
1338	1b. "Hagenia abyssinica"	4·50	3·50

279 Ginger

1986. Spices and Herbs. Multicoloured.

1339	10c. Type **279**	35	20
1340	15c. Basil	65	45
1341	55c. Mustard	3·00	2·10
1342	1b. Cumin	5·25	3·75

280 One Cent Coin

1986. Coins. Multicoloured.

1343	5c. Type **280**	20	15
1344	10c. 25 cents	1·50	1·10
1345	35c. 5 cents	50	50
1346	50c. 50 cents	2·00	1·75
1347	1b. 10 cents	4·25	3·25

281 Globe, Map and Skeleton

1986. 12th Anniv of Discovery of Oldest Known Hominid Skeleton.

1348	**281**	2b. multicoloured	11·00	10·00

282 Military Training

1986. 12th Anniv of Revolution. Mult.

1349	20c. Type **282**	50	30
1350	30c. Tiglachin Monument, Addis Ababa	50	35
1351	55c. Emblem of Delachin Historical Exhibition	2·25	1·60
1352	85c. Merti food-processing plant	3·50	2·50

283 Boeing 767

1986. 40th Anniv of Ethiopian Airlines. Mult.

1353	10c. Type **283**	75	50
1354	20c. Douglas DC-3	1·30	85
1355	30c. Emblem on tail-fin of airplane and crew	2·40	1·60
1356	40c. Mechanic working on engine	3·75	2·75
1357	1b. Map and Boeing 727 airliner	4·25	3·50

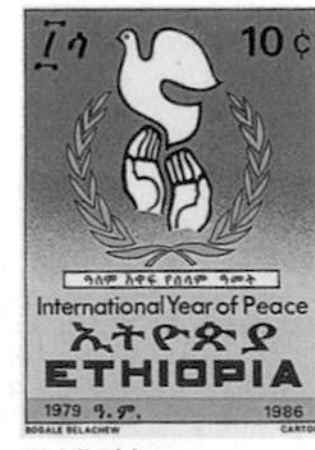

284 Emblem

1986. International Peace Year.

1358	**284**	10c. multicoloured	20	15
1359	**284**	80c. multicoloured	1·80	1·40
1360	**284**	1b. multicoloured	3·50	3·00

285 Mother breastfeeding Baby

1986. UNICEF. Child Survival Campaign. Multicoloured.

1361	10c. Type **285**	30	25
1362	35c. Doctor vaccinating child and vaccination chart	1·80	1·20
1363	50c. Fly on feeding bottle and oral rehydration therapy formula	2·50	2·00
1364	1b. Baby on scales and growth chart	5·25	3·75

286 Auxum, Tigray

1987. Traditional Umbrellas. Multicoloured.

1365	35c. Type **286**	1·20	75
1366	55c. Negele-Borena, Sidamo	1·90	1·50
1367	1b. Jimma, Kafa	3·50	2·75

287 "Affar"

1987. "Defender of his Country". Paintings by Afewerk Tekle. Multicoloured.

1368	50c. Type **287**	1·70	1·20
1369	2b. "Adwa"	6·25	4·50

288 People behind Man holding Torch

1987. "The Struggle of the African People" (stained glass windows) by Afewerk Tekle. Multicoloured.

1370	50c. Type **288**	7·50	6·00
1371	80c. Robed skeleton, dragon and men covering their faces (23×36 mm)	12·00	9·50
1372	1b. Robed skeleton, man killing dragon and people on map of Africa (23×36 mm)	15·00	12·00

289 Simien Fox

1987

1373	**289**	5c. multicoloured	20	35
1374	**289**	10c. multicoloured	40	35
1375	**289**	15c. multicoloured	60	45
1376	**289**	20c. multicoloured	1·20	60
1377	**289**	25c. multicoloured	1·60	80
1378	**289**	45c. multicoloured	3·00	1·40
1379	**289**	55c. multicoloured	3·75	1·80

For similar stamps dated "1991" see Nos. 1564/1573 and dated "1993" see Nos. 1596/1615.

290 Finfine, Empress Taitu and Emperor Menelik II in "100"

1987. Centenary of Addis Ababa. Mult.

1380	5c. Type **290**	20	15
1381	10c. Traditional housing	30	25
1382	80c. Central Addis Ababa	3·25	2·25
1383	1b. Aerial view of city	3·75	2·75

291 Newspaper and People on Map

1987. 13th Anniv of Revolution. Mult.

1384	5c. Type **291**	20	15
1385	10c. People queuing by ballot box and open book	30	25

1386	80c. Ballot paper and map	3·00	2·10
1387	1b. Boeing 727 airliner on runway at Bahir Dar airport	10·00	7·25

292 Spoon fron Hurso, Harerge

1987. Wooden Spoons. Multicoloured.

1388	85c. Type **292**	3·75	2·50
1389	1b. Spoon from Borena, Sidamo	4·25	3·25

293 Village Programme

1988. International Year of Shelter for the Homeless (1987). Multicoloured.

1390	10c. Type **293**	30	25
1391	35c. Airdrop to devastated area and resettlement programme	2·75	1·50
1392	50c. Urban improvement programme	2·00	1·50
1393	1b. Co-operative and Government housing	4·00	3·50

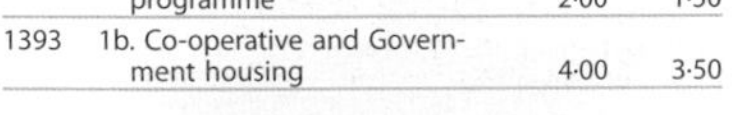

294 Lenin and Delegates

1988. 70th Anniv of Russian Revolution.

1394	**294**	1b. multicoloured	2·50	1·70

295 Bow and Arrows

1988. Traditional Hunting Weapons. Mult.

1395	85c. Type **295**	3·25	2·50
1396	1b. Double-pronged spear	3·75	3·00

296 Anniversary Emblem

1988. 125th Anniv of Red Cross.

1397	**296**	85c. multicoloured	2·75	2·50
1398	**296**	1b. multicoloured	3·75	2·75

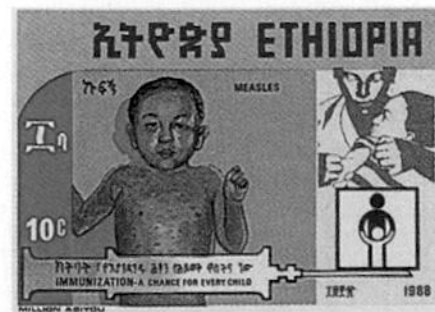
297 Measles

1988. UNICEF. Child Vaccination Campaign. Multicoloured.

1399	10c. Type **297**	25	20
1400	35c. Tetanus	1·60	1·30
1401	50c. Whooping cough	2·25	1·90
1402	1b. Diphtheria	4·75	3·75

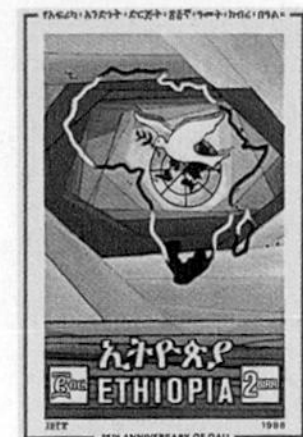
298 "Let there be Peace in Africa and the World" (detail, Afewerk Tekle)

1988. 25th Anniv of Organization of African Unity.

1403	**298**	2b. multicoloured	3·75	2·50

299 Mikoyan Gurevich MiG-23 above Simien Mountains and Farmland

1988. "The Victory of Ethiopia" (triptych) by Afewerk Tekle. Details of the mural in Heroes' Centre, Debre Zeit. Multicoloured.

1404	10c. Type **299**	50	40
1405	20c. Coffee plantation, rural homelife and farmers going to work	50	40
1406	35c. New Ethiopia rising above flags and people	1·00	80
1407	55c. Mikoyan Gurevich MiG-21 over port of Assab (horiz)	1·90	1·40
1408	80c. Worker in foundry (horiz)	2·20	1·80
1409	1b. Villagers engaged in cottage industries (horiz)	3·00	2·30

300 Sidamo Bracelet

1988. Bracelets. Multicoloured.

1410	15c. Type **300**	35	25
1411	85c. Arsi bracelet	1·90	1·30
1412	1b. Harerge bracelet	2·30	1·50

301 Dollars on Map

1988. International Agricultural Development Fund. Multicoloured.

1413	15c. Type **301**	40	30
1414	85c. Agricultural activities	1·90	1·20
1415	1b. Farmer and produce	2·20	1·50

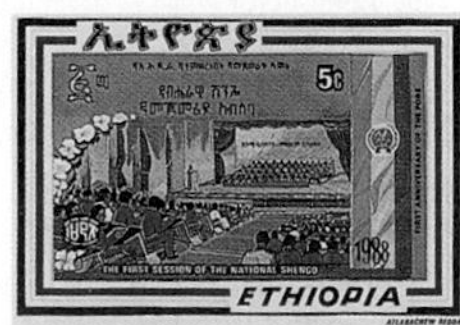
302 First Session of National Shengo (assembly)

1988. 1st Anniv of People's Democratic Republic of Ethiopia. Multicoloured.

1416	5c. Type **302**	10	20
1417	10c. President Lt.-Col. Mengistu Haile Mariam	20	30
1418	80c. State emblem and flag	1·70	1·10
1419	1b. State Council building	2·20	1·50

303 One Birr Note

1988. Banknotes. Multicoloured.

1420	5c. Type **303**	25	25
1421	10c. Five birr note	45	35
1422	20c. Ten birr note	80	50
1423	75c. 50 birr note	3·00	1·90
1424	85c. 100 birr note	3·00	2·30

1988. World Aids Day. Nos. 1376/9 optd WORLD AIDS DAY.

1425	**289**	20c. multicoloured	3·00	3·00
1426	**289**	25c. multicoloured	3·00	3·00
1427	**289**	45c. multicoloured	3·00	3·00
1428	**289**	55c. multicoloured	3·00	3·00

305 Emblem within "40"

1988. 40th Anniv of W.H.O.

1429	**305**	50c. multicoloured	1·40	85
1430	**305**	65c. multicoloured	1·90	1·10
1431	**305**	85c. multicoloured	2·50	1·60

306 Gambella Gere (leg rattle)

1989. Musical Instruments. Multicoloured.

1432	30c. Type **306**	1·00	60
1433	40c. Konos fanfa (pipes)	1·40	90
1434	50c. Konso chancha (waist rattle)	1·80	1·20
1435	85c. Gendeberet negareet (drum)	3·00	1·90

307 "Abyot" (container ship)

1989. 25th Anniv of Ethiopian Shipping Lines. Multicoloured.

1436	15c. Type **307**	60	55
1437	30c. "Wolwol" (container ship)	1·40	1·20
1438	55c. "Queen of Sheba" (freighter)	2·70	2·00
1439	1b. "Abbay Wonz" under construction	5·00	3·75

308 Yellow-faced Parrot

1989. Birds. Multicoloured.

1440	10c. Type **308**	1·10	75
1441	35c. White-winged chiffchat	1·90	1·00
1442	50c. Yellow-rumped seedeater	3·50	2·30
1443	1b. Dark-headed oriole	6·00	4·00

309 Making Vellum

1989. Ethiopian Manuscripts. Multicoloured.

1444	5c. Type **309**	25	20
1445	10c. Making inks, ink horns and pens	35	30
1446	20c. Preparing writing materials and scribe	70	50
1447	75c. Binding books	2·50	1·80
1448	85c. Finished books	2·75	2·00

310 Greater Kudu

1989. Wildlife. Multicoloured.

1449	30c. Type **310**	85	55
1450	40c. Lesser kudu	1·20	85
1451	50c. Roan antelope	1·50	1·20
1452	85c. Nile lechwe	2·50	1·90

311 Melka Wakana Hydro-electric Power Station

1989. 2nd Anniv of People's Democratic Republic of Ethiopia. Multicoloured.

1453	15c. Type **311**	40	30
1454	75c. Adea Berga Dairy Farm	1·60	1·50
1455	1b. Pawe Hospital	3·00	2·20

312 Bank Emblem

1989. 25th Anniv of African Development Bank.

1456	**312**	20c. multicoloured	50	40
1457	**312**	80c. multicoloured	2·20	1·80
1458	**312**	1b. multicoloured	2·75	2·10

313 Emblem

1990. 10th Anniv of Pan-African Postal Union.

1459	**313**	50c. multicoloured	1·30	1·00
1460	**313**	70c. multicoloured	1·80	1·40
1461	**313**	80c. multicoloured	2·00	1·60

314 Unhappy Man with Newspaper Upside Down

1990. International Literacy Year. Mult.

1462	15c. Type **314**	60	35
1463	85c. Adults learning to read	2·00	1·80
1464	1b. Happy man reading newspaper	2·75	2·30

315 Marathon Race

1990. Abebe Bikila (marathon runner). Mult.

1465	5c. Type **315**	35	20
1466	10c. Bikila carrying national flag during Olympic opening ceremony	55	35
1467	20c. Bikila running in number 11 vest	95	65
1468	75c. Bikila running in number 69 vest	3·25	2·30
1469	85c. Bikila with medals and cups (vert)	3·50	2·50

316 Revolutionary Flag

1990

1470	**316**	5c. multicoloured	15	30
1471	**316**	10c. multicoloured	20	30
1472	**316**	15c. multicoloured	25	30
1473	**316**	20c. multicoloured	30	30
1474	**316**	25c. multicoloured	40	30
1475	**316**	30c. multicoloured	60	30
1476	**316**	35c. multicoloured	80	40
1477	**316**	40c. multicoloured	1·00	50
1478	**316**	45c. multicoloured	1·70	1·10
1479	**316**	50c. multicoloured	1·40	90
1480	**316**	55c. multicoloured	1·50	1·00
1481	**316**	60c. multicoloured	1·70	1·10
1482	**316**	70c. multicoloured	2·00	1·20
1483	**316**	80c. multicoloured	2·40	1·30
1484	**316**	85c. multicoloured	2·50	1·40
1485	**316**	90c. multicoloured	2·75	1·60
1486	**316**	1b. multicoloured	3·00	1·80
1487	**316**	2b. multicoloured	6·00	3·50
1488	**316**	3b. multicoloured	9·00	5·00

317 Ploughing and Sowing

1990. Teff. Multicoloured.

1489	5c. Type **317**	10	30
1490	10c. Harvesting	30	30
1491	20c. Oxen threshing grain underfoot	55	40
1492	75c. Grinding teff flour and making starter batter	2·00	1·50
1493	85c. Family eating baked injera	2·30	1·80

318 Male and Female Ibexes

1990. Walia Ibex. Multicoloured.

1494	5c. Type **318**	60	50
1495	15c. Male ibex	60	50
1496	20c. Male ibex (different)	50	50
1497	1b. Male ibexes fighting (horiz)	6·00	5·00

319 Deterioration in Victim's Health

1991. World Aids Day. Multicoloured.

1498	15c. Type **319**	75	50
1499	85c. Aids education	3·00	2·00
1500	1b. Preventive measures and family sheltered by umbrella	3·25	2·50

320 Volcano

1991. International Decade for Natural Disaster Reduction. Multicoloured.

1501	5c. Type **320**	40	35
1502	10c. Earthquake	40	25
1503	15c. Drought	60	45
1504	30c. Flood	1·40	1·20
1505	50c. W.H.O. hygiene instruction	3·25	2·00
1506	1b. Red Cross workers helping disaster victims	5·50	3·50

321 Constructing Cannon

1991. Emperor Theodor's Cannon "Sevastopol". Multicoloured.

1507	15c. Type **321**	50	30
1508	85c. Completed cannon on carriage	2·50	1·70
1509	1b. Hauling cannon uphill	2·75	2·30

322 Diadem Squirrelfish

1991. Fishes. Multicoloured.

1510	5c. Type **322**	25	25
1511	15c. Blue-cheeked butterflyfish	75	50
1512	80c. Regal angelfish	3·00	2·00
1513	1b. Grey reef shark	4·00	2·50

323 Balambaras

1992. Traditional Ceremonial Robes (military group). Multicoloured.

1514	5c. Type **323**	25	25
1515	15c. Kegnazmatch	60	40
1516	80c. Fitawurari (Army Commander)	2·30	1·70
1517	1b. Dedjazmatch	3·00	2·20

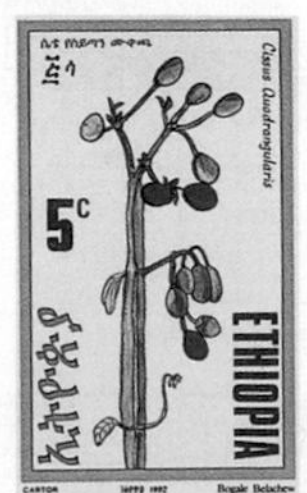

324 Devil's Mortar

1992. Flowers. Multicoloured.

1518	5c. Type **324**	25	25
1519	15c. "Delphinium dasycaulon"	65	45
1520	80c. Cow's salt	1·20	80
1521	1b. Red hot poker	3·50	2·30

325 Afar House

1992. Ethiopian Houses. Multicoloured.

1522	15c. Type **325**	50	25
1523	35c. Anuak house	1·20	80
1524	50c. Gimira house	1·80	1·30
1525	1b. Oromo house	3·50	2·30

326 Plate

1992. Pottery from Sixth Tomb, Yeha. Mult.

1526	15c. Type **326**	50	50
1527	85c. Milk jar	3·75	2·25
1528	1b. Wine vessel	4·50	3·00

327 Campaign Emblem

1992. Pan-African Rinderpest Campaign.

1529	**327**	20c. gold, green & black	55	35
1530	**327**	80c. multicoloured	2·20	1·70
1531	**327**	1b. multicoloured	3·00	2·20

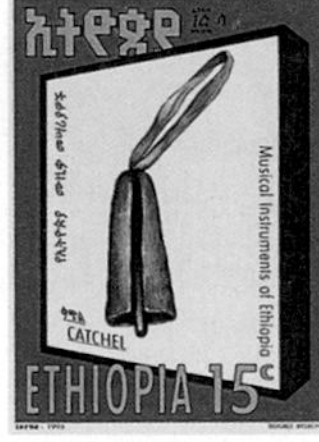

328 Catchel (hand rattle)

1993. Traditional Musical Instruments. Mult.

1532	15c. Type **328**	40	30
1533	35c. Huldudwa (wind instrument)	1·00	75
1534	50c. Dita (stringed instrument)	1·40	1·20
1535	1b. Atamo (drum)	2·75	2·30

329 Banded Barbets

1993. Birds. Multicoloured.

1536	15c. Type **329**	60	45
1537	35c. Ruppell's chats	1·60	1·20
1538	50c. Abyssinian catbirds	2·30	1·60
1539	1b. White-billed starling	4·50	3·00

330 Honey Badger

1993. Mammals. Multicoloured.

1540	15c. Type **330**	30	25
1541	35c. Spotted-necked otter	80	60
1542	50c. Rock hyrax	1·30	85
1543	1b. White-tailed mongoose	2·30	1·80

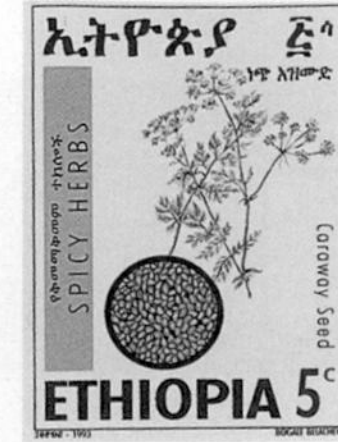

331 Caraway Seed

1993. Spicy Herbs. Multicoloured.

1544	5c. Type **331**	15	10
1545	15c. Garlic	40	25
1546	80c. Turmeric	2·40	1·70
1547	1b. Capsicum peppers	2·75	2·00

332 Southern White-banded Papilio

1993. Butterflies. Multicoloured.

1548	20c. Type **332**	55	30
1549	30c. King swallowtail	1·20	80
1550	50c. Small striped swallowtail	2·00	1·40
1551	1b. Veined swallowtail	4·00	2·70

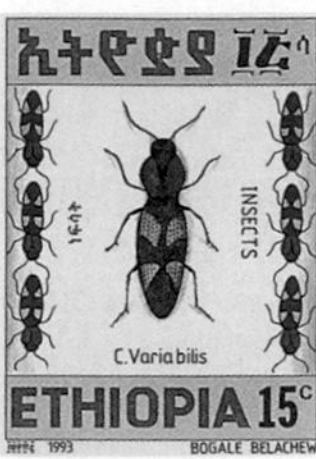

333 "C. variabilis"

1993. Beetles. Multicoloured.

1552	15c. Type **333**	30	20
1553	35c. "Lycus trabeatus"	70	45
1554	50c. "Malachius bifasciatus"	1·10	85
1555	1b. "Homoeogryllus xanthographus"	2·40	1·90

334 "Euphorbia amliphylla"

1993. Trees. Multicoloured.

1556	15c. Type **334**	30	25
1557	35c. "Erythrina brucei"	80	60
1558	50c. "Draceana steudneri"	1·30	85
1559	1b. "Allophylus abbyssinicus"	2·30	1·80

335 Lake Wonchi

1993. Lakes. Multicoloured.

1560	15c. Type **335**	30	25
1561	35c. Lake Zuquala	80	60
1562	50c. Lake Ashengi	1·30	85
1563	1b. Lake Tana	2·30	1·80

336 Simien Fox

1994. Dated "1991". Mult, frame colours given.

1564	**336**	5c. lilac		
1565	**336**	10c. brown		
1566	**336**	15c. yellow		
1567	**336**	20c. pink		
1568	**336**	40c. pink		
1569	**336**	55c. green		
1570	**336**	60c. blue		
1571	**336**	80c. blue		
1572	**336**	85c. green		
1573	**336**	1b. green		

337 Flag and Fighter

1994. 3rd Anniv of Ethiopian People's Revolutionary Democratic Front Transitional Government. Multicoloured.

1574	15c. Type **337** (control of Addis Ababa, May 1991)	25	20
1575	35c. Peaceful and Democratic Transition Conference, Addis Ababa, July 1991	40	25
1576	50c. Elections, June 1994	75	40
1577	1b. Flag and Government arms	1·40	90

338 Emblem

1994. International Year of the Family.

1578	**338**	15c. multicoloured	20	15
1579	**338**	85c. multicoloured	1·00	90
1580	**338**	1b. multicoloured	1·30	1·20

339 Postal Messengers

1994. Centenary of Postal Services in Ethiopia. Multicoloured.

1581	60c. Postal workers, magnifying glass over 1st Ethiopian stamp and early postal messenger	1·30	50
1582	75c. Type **339**	1·50	80
1583	80c. Old post office and early mechanized post transport	1·90	1·40
1584	85c. Rural service	2·40	1·60
1585	1b. Express Mail Service	3·00	2·00

340 Plant

1994. The Enset Plant. Multicoloured.

1587	10c. Type **340**	25	15
1588	15c. Enset growing beside house	30	20
1589	25c. Gathering and preparation	40	30
1590	50c. Plantation	85	60
1591	1b. Prepared food	1·70	1·50

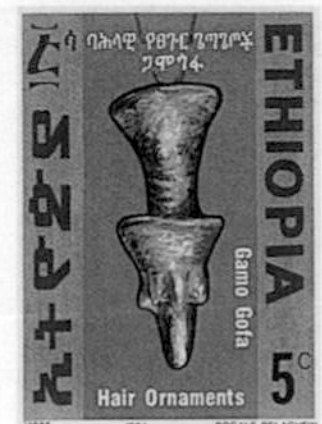

341 Iron Ornament, Gamo Gofa

1994. Hair Ornaments. Multicoloured.

1592	5c. Type **341**	15	10
1593	15c. Aluminium beads, Sidamo	25	20
1594	80c. Metal ornament, Gamo Gofa (different)	1·20	1·00
1595	1b. Silver hairpin, Wello	1·40	1·20

342 Simien Fox

1994. Dated "1993". Mult, frame colours given.

1596	**342**	5c. lilac		
1597	**342**	10c. brown		
1598	**342**	15c. yellow		
1599	**342**	20c. pink		
1600	**342**	25c. yellow		
1601	**342**	30c. yellow		
1602	**342**	35c. orange		
1603	**342**	40c. pink		
1604	**342**	45c. orange		
1605	**342**	50c. mauve		
1606	**342**	55c. green		
1607	**342**	60c. blue		
1608	**342**	65c. lilac		
1609	**342**	70c. green		
1610	**342**	75c. green		
1611	**342**	80c. blue		
1612	**342**	85c. green		
1614	**342**	1b. green		
1615	**342**	2b. brown		

344 Anniversary Emblem

1994. 50th Anniv of I.C.A.O.

1620	**344**	20c. blue, yell & mve	20	15
1621	**344**	80c. blue and yellow	1·00	90
1622	**344**	1b. bl, yell & ultram	1·30	1·20

1994. 30th Anniv of African Development Bank. Nos. 1608/10 and 1612 optd with map of Africa and 30TH ANNIVERSARY OF BANQUE AFRICAINE DE DEVELOPPEMENT AFRICAN DEVELOPMENT BANK.

1623	**342**	65c. multicoloured		
1624	**342**	70c. multicoloured		
1625	**342**	75c. multicoloured		
1626	**342**	95c. multicoloured		

346 Erbo (dish)

1995. Traditional Food Serving Utensils. Multicoloured.

1627	30c. Type **346**	25	20
1628	70c. Sedieka (round table)	85	70
1629	1b. Tirar (rectangular table)	1·30	1·20

347 Kuncho (young boys and girls)

1995. Traditional Hairstyles. Multicoloured.

1630	25c. Type **347**	20	15
1631	75c. Gamme (unmarried women)	95	70
1632	1b. Sadulla (married women until birth of first child)	1·30	1·00

348 Anniversary Emblem

1995. 50th Anniv of F.A.O.

1633	**348**	20c. multicoloured	15	15
1634	**348**	80c. multicoloured	95	70
1635	**348**	1b. multicoloured	1·30	1·00

349 Dangora (digging tool)

1995. Traditional Agricultural Tools. Mult.

1636	15c. Type **349**	10	10
1637	35c. Gheso (hoe)	40	30
1638	50c. Akafa (hoe)	60	40
1639	1b. Ankasse (digging tool)	1·30	1·10

350 Anniversary Emblem

1995. 50th Anniv of U.N.O.

1640	**350**	20c. multicoloured	20	15
1641	**350**	80c. multicoloured	95	70
1642	**350**	1b. multicoloured	1·20	90

351 Reforestation

1995. 10th Anniv of Intergovernmental Authority on Drought and Development. Multicoloured.

1643	15c. Type **351**	20	15
1644	35c. People moving from drought area	55	40
1645	50c. Boy picking fruit	75	70
1646	1b. Member countries' flags and map of East Africa	1·50	1·50

352 Map of Battle Site

1996. Cent of Victory at Battle of Adwa. Mult.

1647	40c. Type **352**	60	25
1648	50c. Map of Africa and emblem	80	40
1649	60c. Ship and Italian soldiers	1·00	60
1650	70c. Battle scenes	1·20	80
1651	80c. Soldiers surrendering and frontline	1·40	1·00
1652	1b. Emperor Menelik II and Empress Zauditu	1·80	1·20
MS1653	175×85 mm. Nos. 1647/52	7·00	7·00

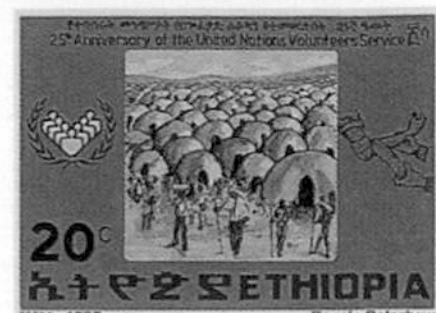

353 Village

1996. 25th Anniv of United Nations Volunteers' Service. Multicoloured.

1654	20c. Type **353**	20	15
1655	30c. Planting	35	25
1656	50c. Teacher and pupils	55	50
1657	1b. Parents and child	1·40	1·10

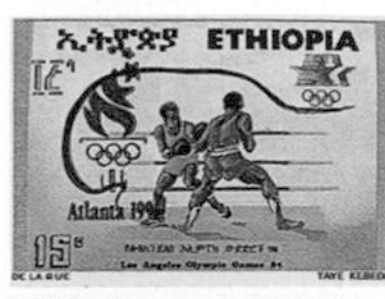

354 Boxing

1996. Olympic Games, Atlanta. Unissued stamps (for 1984 Olympics) optd with Atlanta Olympics emblem as in T 354. Multicoloured.

1658	15c. Type **354**	20	15
1659	20c. Swimming	40	30
1660	40c. Cycling	1·30	60
1661	85c. Running	1·90	1·40
1662	1b. Football	2·30	1·80

355 Child Vaccination

1996. 50th Anniv of UNICEF. Mult.

1663	10c. Anniversary emblem	15	10
1664	15c. Type **355**	30	15
1665	25c. Girl carrying water bottle and boy drinking from tap	40	30
1666	50c. School children writing	75	65
1667	1b. Mother breastfeeding	1·50	1·40

356 Discussion of Constitution

1996. Establishment of Federal Democratic Republic (August 1995). Multicoloured.

1668	10c. Type **356**	25	20
1669	20c. Ballot papers and boxes	45	35
1670	30c. Voting methods and Parliament building	65	45
1671	40c. Parliament building, ballot paper and meeting of legislature	90	65
1672	1b. New national flag, President and Prime Minister, Parliament Building and legislature	2·30	1·80

357 Baskets from Jimma

1997. Basketwork (1st series). Multicoloured.

1673	5c. Type **357**	20	30
1674	15c. Containers from Wello	60	35
1675	80c. Baskets from Welega	2·75	2·10
1676	1b. Bags from Shewa	3·25	2·50

See also Nos. 1677/9 and 1718/20.

1997. Basketwork (2nd series). As T 357. Mult.

1677	35c. Baskets from Arssi (vert)	1·30	1·00
1678	65c. Baskets from Gojam (vert)	2·30	1·80

1679		1b. Baskets from Harer (vert)	3·25	2·50

358 Emblem

1997. United Nations Decade against Drug Abuse and Trafficking.

1680	**358**	20c. multicoloured	20	15
1681	**358**	80c. multicoloured	1·10	80
1682	**358**	1b. multicoloured	1·40	1·10

359 Bitweded Haile Giorgis's House

1997. Historic Buildings of Addis Ababa (1st series). Multicoloured.

1683		45c. Type **359**	50	35
1684		55c. Alfred Elg's house (vert)	75	65
1685		3b. Menelik's elfign	3·75	3·00

360 Ras Biru W/Gabriel's House

1997. Historic Buildings of Addis Ababa (2nd series). Multicoloured.

1686		60c. Type **360**	65	55
1687		75c. Sheh Hojele Alhassen's house	95	75
1688		80c. Fitawrari H/Giorgis Dinegde's house	1·00	80
1689		85c. Etege Taitu Hotel	1·10	90
1690		1b. Dejazmach Wube Atnaf-seged's house	1·30	1·10

361 Golden-mantled Woodpecker ("Golden-backed Woodpecker")

1998. Multicoloured, colour of panel at right given. (21×28 mm).

1691	**361**	5c. blue	10	30
1692	**361**	10c. yellow	20	30
1693	**361**	15c. blue	20	30
1694	**361**	20c. orange	1·00	35
1695	**361**	25c. violet	20	20
1696	**361**	30c. blue	20	20
1697	**361**	35c. red	25	20
1698	**361**	40c. mauve	25	20
1699	**361**	45c. green	25	20
1700	**361**	50c. pink	25	20
1701	**361**	55c. blue	25	20
1702	**361**	60c. red	25	20
1703	**361**	65c. violet	30	20
1704	**361**	70c. yellow	40	20
1705	**361**	75c. lilac	60	40
1706	**361**	80c. green	75	35
1707	**361**	85c. grey	85	35
1708	**361**	90c. orange	1·10	60
1709	**361**	1b. green	1·30	65
1710	**361**	2b. pink	3·00	1·20
1711	**361**	3b. mauve	4·00	1·80
1712	**361**	5b. yellow	6·00	2·75
1713	**361**	10b. yellow	12·00	5·00

362 Emblem and Bushbuck

1998. 18th Anniv of Pan-African Postal Union. Multicoloured.

1714		45c. Type **362** (inscr "Deculla Bushback")	55	40
1715		55c. Soemmerring's gazelle	70	50
1716		1b. Defassa waterbuck	1·30	85
1717		2b. African ("Black") buffalo	2·00	1·70

1998. Basketwork (3rd series). As T 357. Mult.

1718		45c. Baskets from Gonder	1·00	55
1719		55c. Baskets from Harere	1·30	70
1720		3b. Baskets from Tigray	4·75	3·75

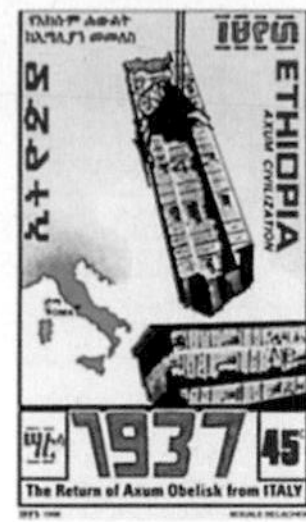

363 Map of Italy and Removal of Obelisk

1998. Project to Return the Axum Obelisk from Rome to Ethiopia. Multicoloured.

1721		45c. Type **363**	1·00	55
1722		55c. Axum obelisk in Rome	1·30	70
1723		3b. Map of Ethiopia, obelisk and Axum	4·75	3·75

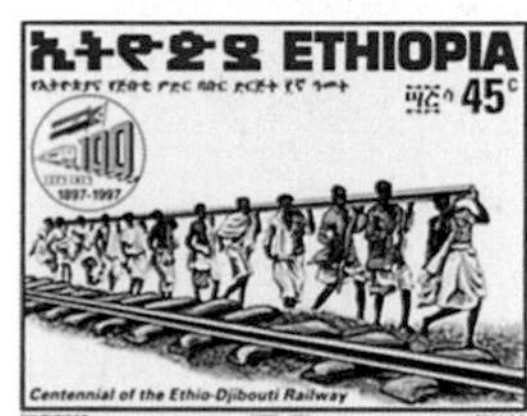

364 Workers carrying Rail

1998. Centenary (1997) of Addis Ababa–Djibouti Railway. Multicoloured.

1724		45c. Type **364**	1·00	55
1725		55c. Steam locomotive No. 404	1·50	70
1726		1b. Railway station, Addis Ababa	2·00	1·50
1727		2b. Diesel locomotive	5·00	2·30

365 Anniversary Emblem and Globe of People

1998. 50th Anniv of Universal Declaration of Human Rights.

1728	**365**	45c. multicoloured	40	30
1729	**365**	55c. multicoloured	60	50
1730	**365**	1b. multicoloured	1·10	85
1731	**365**	2b. multicoloured	2·40	1·80

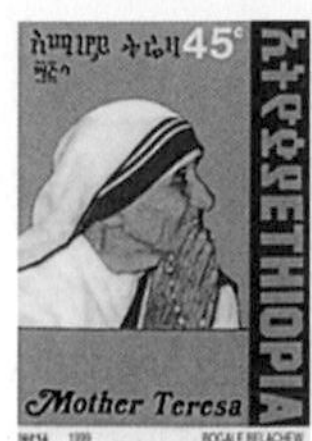

366 Mother Teresa

1999. Mother Teresa (founder of Missionaries of Charity) Commemoration. Multicoloured.

1732		45c. Type **366**	90	55
1733		55c. Praying	1·10	75
1734		1b. Carrying child	2·00	1·50
1735		2b. Smiling	4·00	2·75

367 Head of Fish

1999. International Year of the Ocean.

1736	**367**	45c. multicoloured	90	55
1737	**367**	55c. multicoloured	1·10	75
1738	**367**	1b. multicoloured	2·00	1·50
1739	**367**	2b. multicoloured	4·00	2·75

368 Emblem and Globe

1999. World Environment Day.

1740	**368**	45c. multicoloured	50	40
1741	**368**	55c. multicoloured	60	45
1742	**368**	1b. multicoloured	1·10	85
1743	**368**	2b. multicoloured	2·10	1·50

369 Abijata-Shalla Lakes National Park

1999. National Parks (1st series). Multicoloured.

1744		45c. Type **369**	70	40
1745		70c. Nechisar National Park	1·20	80
1746		85c. Bale Mountains National Park	1·40	1·00
1747		2b. Awash National Park (horiz)	3·50	2·30

See also Nos 1752/5.

370 "125" and Emblem

1999. 125th Anniv of Universal Postal Union.

1748	**370**	20c. multicoloured	25	20
1749	**370**	80c. multicoloured	95	65
1750	**370**	1b. multicoloured	1·10	85
1751	**370**	2b. multicoloured	2·00	1·80

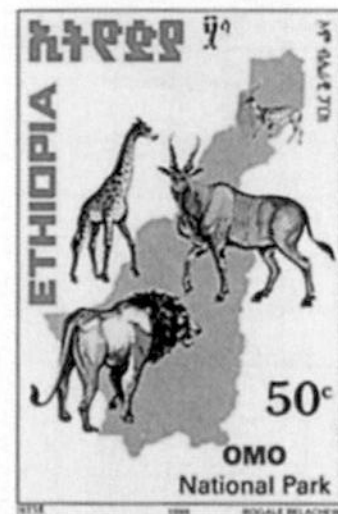

371 Omo National Park

1999. National Parks (2nd series). Multicoloured.

1752		50c. Type **371**	95	60
1753		70c. Mago National Park	1·40	90
1754		80c. Yangudi-Rassa National Park	1·70	1·00
1755		2b. Gambella National Park (horiz)	4·00	2·50

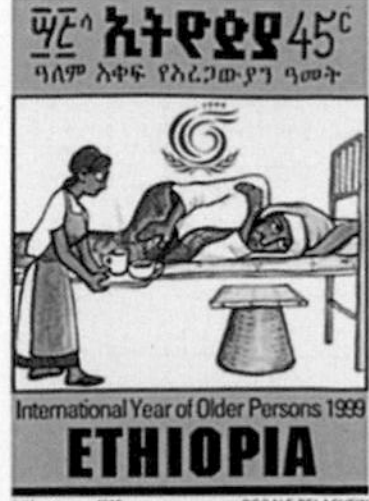

372 Woman nursing Elderly Man

1999. International Year of the Elderly. Mult.

1756		45c. Type **372**	60	40
1757		70c. Elderly couple gardening	95	70
1758		85c. Elderly man with three youths	1·20	90
1759		2b. Elderly man with two youths	2·75	2·00

373 Aleksandr Pushkin

2000. Birth Bicentenary of Aleksandr Pushkin (Russian writer). Multicoloured.

1760		45c. Type **373**	50	20
1761		70c. With folded arms	65	20
1762		85c. Wearing hat	85	55
1763		2b. Facing right	1·00	1·10

374 Afro Ayigeba

2000. The Cross of Lalibela (Afro Ayigeba).

1764	**374**	4b. multicoloured	3·50	2·00

376 Meeting

2000. "Operation Sunset". Multicoloured.

1789		45c. Type **376**	50	50
1790		55c. Soldiers	60	40
1791		1b. Families returning home	1·10	70
1792		2b. Farmer ploughing and villagers	2·30	1·40

377 "50" enclosing Emblem

2000. 50th Anniv of World Meteorological Organization.

1793	**377**	40c. multicoloured	40	30
1794	**377**	75c. multicoloured	75	45
1795	**377**	85c. multicoloured	85	55
1796	**377**	2b. multicoloured	1·00	1·20

378 Harari

2000. Flags of Ethiopia. Multicoloured.

1797	25c. Type **378**	20	20
1798	30c. Oromia	30	20
1799	50c. Amhara	50	20
1800	60c. Tigrai	60	25
1801	70c. Benishangul Gumuz	80	50
1802	80c. Somale	10	10
1803	90c. Southern Nation Nationalities	95	55
1804	95c. Gambella	1·10	60
1805	1b. Afar	1·20	70
1806	2b. Federal Democratic Republic of Ethiopia	2·40	1·20

379 Haile Gebreselassie

2000. Haile Gebreselassie (athlete and Olympic Gold Medal winner). Designs showing Haile Gebreselassie running. Multicoloured.

1807	50c. Type **379**	45	30
1808	60c. With left arm raised	60	40
1809	90c. With right arm raised	1·00	65
1810	2b. Winning pose and flag	2·20	1·40

380 Anniversary Emblem

2000. 50th Anniv of Addis Ababa University.

1811	**380**	4b. multicoloured	3·00	2·00

381 Anniversary Emblem and "We thank you for your support"

2000. 50th Anniv of United Nations High Commissioner for Refugees.

1812	**381**	40c. chestnut and gold	40	30
1813	**381**	75c. emerald and gold	75	50
1814	**381**	85c. new blue and gold	85	55
1815	**381**	2b. gold and black	2·30	1·40

Nos. 1813/15 were printed without the inscription "We thank you for your support".

382 Grazing Zebra

2001. Endangered Species. Grevy's Zebra. Multicoloured.

1816	45c. Type **382**	40	10
1817	55c. Galloping	50	40
1818	1b. Lying down	95	60
1819	3b. Head	3·00	1·70

383 Sharp-toothed Catfish (*Clarius gariepinus*)

2001. Freshwater Fish. Multicoloured.

1820	45c. Type **383**	65	35
1821	55c. Nile mouthbrooder (inscr "Tilapia") (*Oreochromis niloticus*)	85	45
1822	3b. Nile perch (*Lates niloticus*)	3·50	2·40

384 Rider and Cart

2001. Traditional Transport. Multicoloured.

1823	40c. Type **384**	55	30
1824	60c. Camels	90	50
1825	1b. Rider and laden mule	1·30	85
1826	2b. Mules carrying hay	2·40	1·50

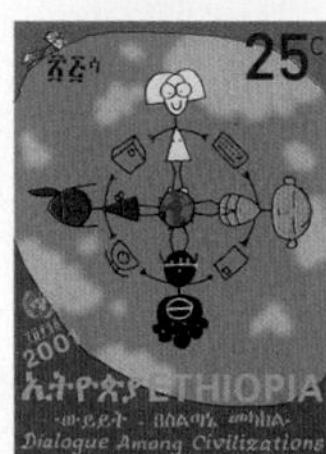
385 Children encircling Globe

2001. United Nations Year of Dialogue Among Civilizations.

1827	**385**	25c. multicoloured	20	15
1828	**385**	75c. multicoloured	45	30
1829	**385**	1b. multicoloured	1·20	65
1830	**385**	2b. multicoloured	2·20	1·30

386 Inscr "White-tailed Swallow"

2001. Birds. Multicoloured.

1831	50c. Type **386**	85	55
1832	60c. Inscr "Spot-breasted plover"	1·00	40
1833	90c. Inscr "Abyssinian long claw"	1·70	95
1834	2b. Inscr "Prince Ruspoli's Turaco"	3·50	2·20

387 Beehives

2002. Traditional Beehives (1st issue). Multicoloured.

1835	40c. Type **387**	45	30
1836	70c. Straw covered hives	85	55
1837	90c. Barrel-shaped hive	1·20	75
1838	2b. Conical hive in tree	2·50	1·60

See also Nos. 1851/4.

388 Storage Jar

2002. Traditional Grain Storage. Multicoloured.

1839	30c. Type **388**	40	25
1840	70c. Raised hut	85	55
1841	1b. Conical hut	1·30	80
1842	2b. Hut supported by branches	2·50	1·60

389 Lions International Emblem

2002. Lions Club International (charitable organization). Multicoloured.

1843	45c. Type **389**	75	40
1844	55c. Solar-powered water pump	90	65
1845	1b. Medical symbols	1·60	1·20
1846	2b. Wheelchair user	3·25	2·30

390 *Acacia abyssinica*

2002. Trees. Multicoloured.

1847	50c. Type **390**	80	45
1848	60c. *Boswellia papyrifera* (vert)	90	70
1849	90c. *Aningeria adolfi-friederici* (vert)	1·30	95
1850	2b. *Prunus africanus* (vert)	3·00	2·40

391 Cone-shaped Hive

2002. Traditional Beehives (2nd issue). Multicoloured.

1851	45c. Type **391**	60	40
1852	55c. Narrow log hive	75	60
1853	1b. Woven straw hive	1·30	95
1854	2b. Large log hive	2·50	1·60

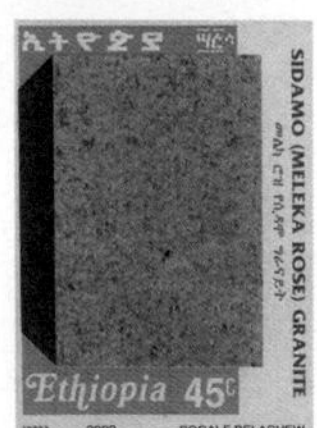
392 Sidamo Granite

2002. Granite. Multicoloured.

1855	45c. Type **392**	60	45
1856	55c. Harrar	75	55
1857	1b. Tigray	1·60	1·00
1858	2b. Wollega	2·75	2·00

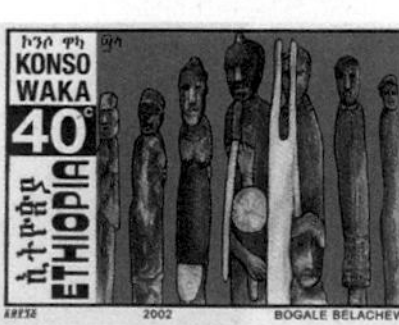
393 Men, Women and Warrior

2002. Konso Waka (memorial wood carvings). Multicoloured, background colour given.

1859	40c. Type **393**	55	30
1860	60c. Carvings (blue)	90	50
1861	1b. Carvings (yellow)	1·30	85
1862	2b. Carvings (red)	2·20	1·50

DESIGNS: 60c. to 2b. Different carvings.

394 Menelik's Bushbuck

2002. Menelik's Bushbuck (2nd series).

1863	**394**	5c. multicoloured	10	50
1864	**394**	10c. multicoloured	10	50
1865	**394**	15c. multicoloured	10	10
1866	**394**	20c. multicoloured	10	50
1867	**394**	25c. multicoloured	10	10
1868	**394**	30c. multicoloured	10	10
1869	**394**	35c. multicoloured	10	10
1870	**394**	40c. multicoloured	10	10
1871	**394**	45c. multicoloured	10	10
1872	**394**	50c. multicoloured	10	10
1873	**394**	55c. multicoloured	10	10
1873a	**394**	60c. multicoloured	20	15
1874	**394**	65c. multicoloured	20	15
1875	**394**	70c. multicoloured	20	15
1876	**394**	75c. multicoloured	25	15
1877	**394**	80c. multicoloured	25	15
1878	**394**	85c. multicoloured	30	15
1879	**394**	90c. multicoloured	35	15
1880	**394**	95c. multicoloured	1·50	50
1881	**394**	1b. multicoloured	50	25
1882	**394**	2b. multicoloured	1·40	30
1883	**394**	3b. multicoloured	2·00	5·00
1884	**394**	5b. multicoloured	3·50	2·00
1885	**394**	10b. multicoloured	7·00	4·00
1886	**394**	20b. multicoloured	14·00	8·00

395 Abyssinian Mustard (*Brassica carinata*)

2002. Oil Producing Seeds. Multicoloured.

1887	40c. Type **395**	35	25
1888	60c. Linseed (*Linum usitatissimum*)	55	35
1889	3b. Niger (*Guizotia abyssinica*)	2·60	1·90

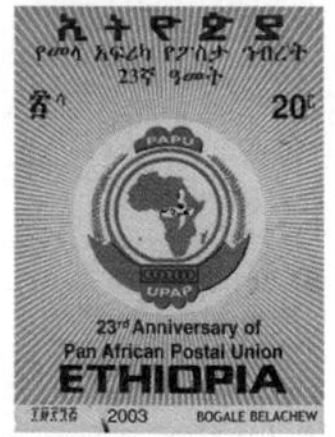
396 Emblem

2003. 23rd Anniv of Pan African Postal Union.

1890	**396**	20c. multicoloured	25	20
1891	**396**	80c. multicoloured	65	40
1892	**396**	1b. multicoloured	85	60
1893	**396**	2b. multicoloured	1·80	1·20

397 Milk Opal

2003. Opals. Multicoloured.

1894	45c. Type **397**	65	30
1895	60c. Brown	95	70
1896	95c. Fire	1·50	1·10
1897	2b. Yellow	3·00	2·30

398 Amulet

2003. 1st Anniv of Return of Emperor Tewodro's (Ethiopian ruler) Amulet. Multicoloured.

1898	40c. Type **398**	50	30
1899	60c. Leather pouch	75	60
1900	3b. Amulet and pouch	3·25	1·90

399 *Kniphofia isoetfolia*

2003. Plants. Multicoloured.

1901	45c. Type **399**	55	30
1902	55c. *Kniphofia insignis*	65	55
1903	1b. *Crinum bambusetum*	1·10	75
1904	2b. *Crinum abyssinicum* (horiz)	2·20	1·40

400 Village, Terraces and Produce

2003. Konso Terracing System. Multicoloured.

1905	40c. Type **400**	50	30
1906	60c. Field of crop and couple	75	60
1907	1b. Terraces	1·30	70
1908	2b. Men hoeing	2·50	1·40

401 Amaranth Grains

2004. Amaranth. Multicoloured.

1909	20c. Type **401**	20	20
1910	80c. Grain on plant	90	70
1911	1b. Flowers	1·30	70
1912	2b. Grinding equipment	2·60	1·40

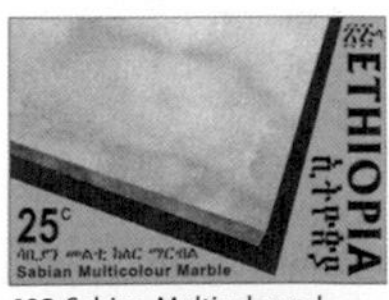

402 Sabian Multicoloured Marble

2004. Marble. Multicoloured.

1913	25c. Type **402**	25·00	25
1914	75c. Eshet blue	1·20	95
1915	1b. Sabian rose green	1·60	1·30
1916	2b. Sabian purple	3·00	2·50

403 "100" and Anniversary Emblem

2004. Centenary of Federation Internationale de Football Association (FIFA). Multicoloured.

1917	5c. Type **403**	10	10
1918	9c. "100" and white ball	15	10
1919	1b. "100" and boots	1·00	70
1920	2b. "100" and black and white ball	2·30	1·60

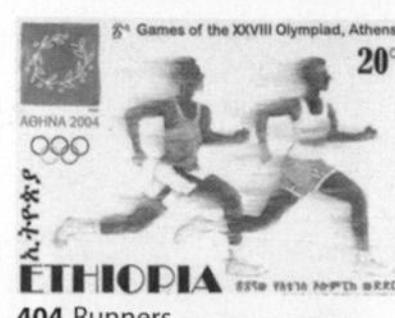

404 Runners

2004. Olympic Games, Athens. Multicoloured.

1921	20c. Type **404**	20	15
1922	35c. Hammer throwing	35	25
1923	45c. Boxing	55	30
1924	3b. Cycling	4·00	2·40

405 Chipped

2004. Rhamnaceae. Multicoloured.

1925	40c. Type **405**	20	15
1926	60c. Branches (horiz)	35	25
1927	1b. Logs	55	30
1928	2b. Fruiting twig	4·00	2·40

406 Black Rhinoceros (*Diceros bicornis*)

2005

1929	**406**	4c. multicoloured	10	25
1930	**406**	5c. multicoloured	15	25
1931	**406**	10c. multicoloured	20	25
1932	**406**	15c. multicoloured	40	25
1933	**406**	20c. multicoloured	65	25
1934	**406**	25c. multicoloured	80	30
1935	**406**	30c. multicoloured	1·00	35
1936	**406**	35c. multicoloured	1·20	40
1937	**406**	40c. multicoloured	1·50	65
1938	**406**	45c. multicoloured	2·00	75

408 Woman

2005. Women's Hairstyles. Multicoloured.

1943	15c. Type **408**	20	15
1944	40c. Woman facing left	35	25
1945	45c. Five heads	45	30
1946	3b. Woman facing right	4·00	2·30

409 *Chlorophytum neghellense*

2006. Endemic Plants. Multicoloured.

1947	45c. Type **409**	70	40
1948	55c. *Aloe bertemariae* (vert)	80	50
1949	3b. *Aloe schelpei* (vert)	4·25	2·60

410 Douglas C-47A Dakota III, 1946

2006. 60th Anniv of Ethiopian Airlines. Multicoloured.

1950	15c. Type **410**	50	35
1951	40c. Douglas DC-6B Super Cloudmaster, 1958	10	10
1952	45c. Boeing 720-060B, 1962	65	40
1953	1b. Boeing 767-300ER, 2003	1·40	80
1954	2b. Inscr 'Boeing 787 Dream-liner, 2008'	3·00	1·80

411 Emblems

2006. International Year of Deserts and Desertification. Multicoloured.

1955	15c. Type **411**	25	20
1956	40c. Map of Ethiopia showing vulnerable areas, 1998	55	30
1957	45c. Map of Africa showing vulnerable areas, 1992	75	35
1958	1b. World Map showing vulnerable areas, 1992	1·30	90

412 Emblem

2007. Ethiopian Millennium (2000).

1959	**412**	40c. multicoloured	55	35
1960	**412**	60c. multicoloured	80	50
1961	**412**	3b. multicoloured	4·00	2·40

413 Gypsum

2007. Industrial Minerals. Multicoloured.

1962	40c. Type **413**	55	35
1963	60c. Quartz	80	50
1964	1b. Inscr 'Ambo Sandstone'	1·40	85
1965	2b. Feldspar	2·75	1·70

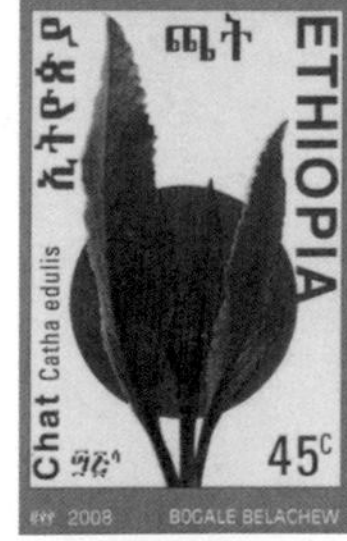

413a *Catha edulis*

2008. Khat (*Catha edulis*)

1966	45c. Type **413a**	60	40
1967	55c. Picking leaves	80	60
1968	3b. Stems and leaves	4·25	3·25

414 '60' enclosing Flowers

2008. 60th Anniv of Ethiopia–India Diplomatic Relations. Multicoloured.

1969	30c. Type **414**	40	25
1970	70c. 60	95	60
1971	3b. 60	4·00	2·40

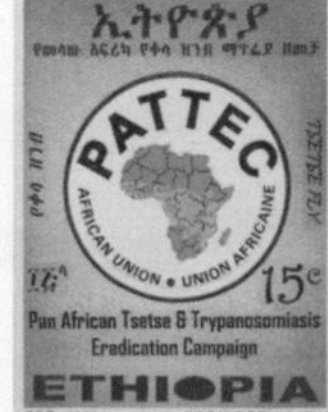

415 Emblem

2009. Pan-African Tsetse and Trypanosomiasis Eradication Campaign. Multicoloured.

1972	15c. Type **415**	20	15
1973	40c. Tsetse fly from above	55	35
1974	45c. Tsetse fly facing right (horiz)	55	35
1975	3b. Infected animal, area affected by disease and figure with infection (horiz)	4·00	2·40

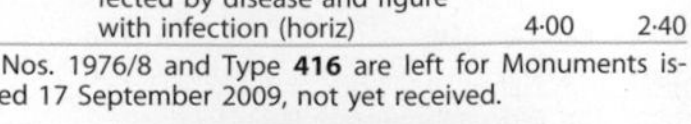
Nos. 1976/8 and Type **416** are left for Monuments issued 17 September 2009, not yet received.

417 Laboratory

2009. Ethiopia free of Rinderpest (disease of bovines). Multicoloured.

1979	15c. Type **417**	20	15
1980	40c. Certificate of eradication	50	25
1981	45c. Dead animals	55	40
1982	3b. Engueda Johannes and Alemework Beyene (pioneers)	3·25	1·70

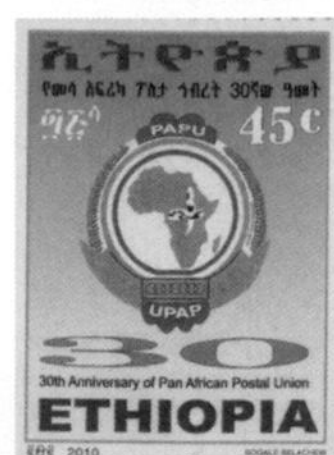

418 PAPU Emblem and '30'

2010. Pan African Postal Union

1983	**418**	45c. multicoloured	60	35
1984	**418**	55c. multicoloured	80	50
1985	**418**	3b. multicoloured	4·25	2·75

EXPRESS LETTER STAMPS

E65 Motor-cycle Messenger

1947. Inscr "EXPRESS".

E357	**E65**	30c. brown	4·00	3·00
E358	-	50c. blue	3·50	2·50

DESIGN: 50c. G.P.O., Addis Ababa.

POSTAGE DUE STAMPS

(D3)

1896. Optd with Type D 3.

D8	1	¼g. green	2·50
D9	1	½g. red	2·50
D10	1	1g. blue	2·50
D11	1	2g. brown	2·50
D12	1	4g. red	1·40
D13	1	8g. mauve	1·40
D14	1	16g. black	1·40

1905. Optd TAXE a PERCEVOIR T.

D108		¼g. green	16·00	16·00
D109		½g. red	16·00	16·00
D110		1g. blue	16·00	16·00
D111		2g. brown	16·00	16·00
D112	2	4g. red	16·00	16·00
D113	2	8g. mauve	22·00	22·00
D114	2	16g. black	48·00	48·00

1907. As above further optd with value in figures between stars.

D122	1	¼g. green	17·00	17·00
D123	1	½g. red	17·00	17·00
D124	1	1g. blue	17·00	17·00
D125	1	2g. brown	17·00	17·00
D126	2	4g. red	17·00	17·00
D127	2	8g. mauve	17·00	17·00
D128	2	16g. black	25·00	25·00

1908. Optd with Amharic inscription and large T in triangle.

D140	1	¼g. green	1·60	1·60
D141	1	½g. red	1·60	1·60
D142	1	1g. blue	1·60	1·60
D143	1	2g. brown	2·75	2·75
D144	2	4g. red	5·50	5·50
D145	2	8g. mauve	10·00	10·00
D146	2	16g. black	25·00	25·00

1913. Stamps of 1909 and the 1g. of 1919 optd with Amharic inscription and large T in triangle.

D161	19	¼g. green	2·00	1·50
D162	19	½g. red	2·00	2·00
D163	19	1g. orange and green	5·00	4·00
D210	-	1g. black & pur (No. 184)	15·00	15·00
D164	20	2g. blue	8·00	6·00
D165	20	4g. red and green	13·00	10·00
D166	-	8g. grey & red (No. 152)	16·00	12·00
D167	-	16g. red (No. 153)	40·00	25·00

D77

1951

D417	D77	1c. green	40	1·00
D418	D77	5c. red	50	1·00
D419	D77	10c. violet	85	1·50
D420	D77	20c. brown	1·75	2·50
D421	D77	50c. blue	4·50	6·00
D422	D77	$1 purple	9·00	12·00

Pt. 1

FALKLAND ISLANDS

A British colony in the South Atlantic.

1878. 12 pence = 1 shilling; 20 shillings = 1 pound.
1971. 100 (new) pence = 1 pound.

3

6

1878

17b	3	½d. green	2·00	3·25
23	3	1d. red to brown	8·50	2·75
26	3	2d. purple	6·00	11·00
30	3	2½d. blue	48·00	13·00
32	3	4d. black	13·00	21·00
3	3	6d. green	£100	75·00
34	3	6d. yellow	50·00	48·00
35	3	9d. orange	50·00	55·00
38	3	1s. brown	70·00	48·00
41	-	2s.6d. blue	£275	£275
42	6	5s. red	£250	£250

DESIGN: 2s.6d. As Type **6**, but different frame.

1891. No. 23 bisected diagonally and each half surch ½d.

13	3	½d. on half of 1d. brown	£600	£300

7

8

1904

43	7	½d. green	5·50	1·50
44b	7	1d. red	1·25	3·75
45	7	2d. purple	23·00	23·00
46	7	2½d. blue	29·00	7·50
47	7	6d. orange	42·00	48·00
48	7	1s. brown	42·00	32·00
49b	8	3s. green	£140	£120
50	8	5s. red	£225	£150

1912. As T 7/8 but portrait of King George V.

60	½d. green	2·75	3·50
74	1d. red	5·00	2·00
75	2d. purple	21·00	8·00
76b	2½d. blue	13·00	16·00
77	2½d. purple on yellow	4·50	38·00
64	6d. orange	15·00	20·00
65	1s. brown	32·00	30·00
66	3s. green	90·00	90·00
67	5s. red	£110	£110
67b	5s. purple	£110	£120
68	10s. red on green	£170	£250
69	£1 black on red	£450	£550

1918. As 1912, optd WAR STAMP.

70b	½d. green	50	6·50
71c	1d. red	50	3·75
72a	1s. brown	4·00	50·00

1928. No. 75 surch 2½D.

115	2½d. on 2d. purple	£1200	£1300

13 Fin Whale and Gentoo Penguins

1929

116	13	½d. green	1·25	3·00
117	13	1d. red	3·75	80
118	13	2d. grey	3·75	3·00
119	13	2½d. blue	4·25	2·25
120	13	4d. orange	22·00	13·00
121	13	6d. purple	22·00	14·00
122	13	1s. black on green	24·00	35·00
123	13	2s.6d. red on blue	65·00	65·00
124	13	5s. green on yellow	£100	£110
125	13	10s. red on green	£200	£250
126	13	£1 black on red	£300	£375

15 Romney Marsh Ram

1933. Centenary of British Administration. Inscr "1833–1933".

127	15	½d. black and green	3·50	9·00
128	-	1d. black and red	3·50	2·25
129	-	1½d. black and blue	19·00	21·00
130	-	2d. black and brown	14·00	24·00
131	-	3d. black and violet	21·00	27·00
132	-	4d. black and orange	22·00	24·00
133	-	6d. black and grey	60·00	80·00
134	-	1s. black and olive	60·00	90·00
135	-	2s.6d. black and violet	£190	£325
136	-	5s. black and yellow	£800	£1200
137	-	10s. black and brown	£750	£1300
138	-	£1 black and red	£2100	£2900

DESIGNS—HORIZ: 1d. Iceberg; 1½d. Whale-catcher; 2d. Port Louis; 3d. Map of Falkland Islands; 4d. South Georgia; 6d. Fin whale; 1s. Government House, Stanley. VERT: 2s.6d. Battle Memorial; 5s. King penguin; 10s. Arms; £1 King George V.

1935. Silver Jubilee. As T 10a of Gambia.

139	1d. blue and red	3·25	40
140	2½d. brown and blue	12·00	1·75
141	4d. green and blue	18·00	6·50
142	1s. grey and purple	14·00	3·75

1937. Coronation. As T 10b of Gambia.

143	½d. green	30	10
144	1d. red	1·00	50
145	2½d. blue	1·50	1·40

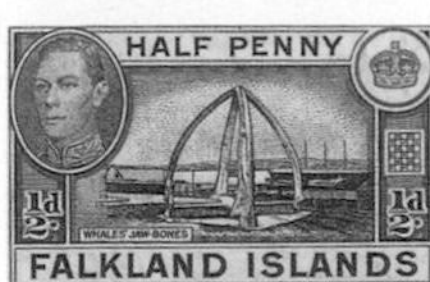

27 Whales' Jaw Bones

1938

146	27	½d. black and green	30	75
147a	A	1d. black and red	3·75	85
148	B	1d. black and violet	2·50	1·75
149	B	2d. black and violet	1·25	50
150	A	2d. black and red	2·00	3·75
151	C	2½d. black and blue	1·25	30
152	D	2½d. black and blue	6·50	8·00
153	C	3d. black and blue	7·00	5·00
154	D	4d. black and purple	3·25	1·50
155	E	6d. black and brown	10·00	2·50
156	E	6d. black	6·50	4·25
157	F	9d. black and blue	26·00	4·00
158a	G	1s. blue	55·00	4·50
159	H	1s.3d. black and red	2·50	1·40
160	I	2s.6d. black	55·00	19·00
161	J	5s. blue and brown	£140	85·00
162	K	10s. black and orange	£160	60·00
163	L	£1 black and violet	£130	60·00

DESIGNS—HORIZ: A, Black-necked swan; B, Battle memorial; C, Flock of sheep; D, Magellan goose; E, "Discovery II" (polar supply vessel); F, "William Scoresby" (research ship); G, Mount Sugar Top; H, Turkey vultures; I, Gentoo penguins; J, Southern sealion; K, Deception Is.; L, Arms of Falkland Islands.

1946. Victory. As T 11a of Gambia.

164	1d. violet	30	75
165	3d. blue	45	50

1948. Silver Wedding. As T 11b/c of Gambia.

166	2½d. blue	2·00	1·00
167	£1 mauve	90·00	60·00

1949. U.P.U. As T 11d/g of Gambia.

168	1d. violet	1·75	1·00
169	3d. blue	5·00	3·75
170	1s.3d. green	3·25	2·25
171	2s. blue	3·00	8·00

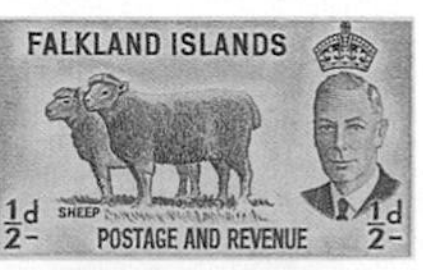

39 Sheep

1952

172	39	½d. green	1·25	70
173	-	1d. red	2·50	40
174	-	2d. violet	4·50	2·50
175	-	2½d. black and blue	2·00	50
176	-	3d. blue	2·25	1·00
177	-	4d. purple	12·00	1·50
178	-	6d. brown	12·00	1·00
179	-	9d. yellow	9·00	2·00
180	-	1s. black	24·00	80
181	-	1s.3d. orange	18·00	5·00
182	-	2s.6d. olive	21·00	11·00
183	-	5s. purple	19·00	9·50
184	-	10s. grey	29·00	15·00
185	-	£1 black	35·00	24·00

DESIGNS—HORIZ: 1d. "Fitzroy" (supply ship); 2d. Magellan goose; 2½d. Map; 4d. Auster Autocrat aircraft; 6d. "John Biscoe I" (research ship); 9d. View of the Two Sisters; 1s.3d. Kelp goose and gander; 10s. Southern sealion and South American fur seal; £1 Hulk of "Great Britain". VERT: 3d. Arms; 1s. Gentoo penguins; 2s.6d. Sheep shearing; 5s. Battle Memorial.

1953. Coronation. As T 11h of Gambia.

186	1d. black and red	80	1·50

1955. As 1952 issue but with portrait of Queen Elizabeth II.

187	½d. green	1·00	1·25
188	1d. red	1·25	1·25
189	2d. violet	3·25	4·50
190	6d. brown	8·50	60
191	9d. yellow	10·00	17·00
192	1s. black	10·00	1·50

54 Austral Thrush

1960. Birds.

227	54	½d. black and green	30	40
194	-	1d. black and red	3·25	1·75
195	-	2d. black and blue	4·50	1·25
196	-	2½d. black and bistre	2·50	1·00
197	-	3d. black and olive	1·25	50
198	-	4d. black and red	1·50	1·25
199	-	5½d. black and violet	3·25	2·50
200	-	6d. black and sepia	3·50	30
201	-	9d. black and orange	2·50	1·25
202	-	1s. black and purple	1·25	40
203	-	1s.3d. black and blue	12·00	13·00
204	-	2s. black and brown	32·00	2·50
205	-	5s. black and turquoise	28·00	11·00
206	-	10s. black and purple	48·00	20·00
207	-	£1 black and yellow	48·00	27·00

BIRDS: 1d. Southern black-backed gull; 2d. Gentoo penguins; 2½d. Long-tailed meadow lark; 3d. Magellan goose; 4d. Falkland Island flightless steamer ducks; 5½d. Rock-hopper penguins; 6d. Black-browed albatross; 9d. Silver grebe; 1s. Magellanic oystercatcher; 1s.3d. Chilean teal; 2s. Kelp geese; 5s. King cormorants; 10s. Common caracara; £1 Black-necked swan.

69 Morse Key

1962. 50th Anniv of Establishment of Radio Communications.

208	69	6d. red and orange	75	40
209	-	1s. green and olive	80	40
210	-	2s. violet and blue	90	1·75

DESIGNS: 1s. One-valve receiver; 2s. Rotary spark transmitter.

1963. Freedom from Hunger. As T 21a of Gambia.

211	1s. blue	10·00	1·50

1963. Centenary of Red Cross. As T 21b of Gambia.

212	1d. red and black	3·00	75
213	1s. red and blue	13·00	4·75

1964. 400th Birth Anniv of Shakespeare. As 35a of Gambia.

214	6d. black	1·50	50

72 H.M.S. "Glasgow"

1964. 50th Anniv of Battle of the Falkland Islands.

215	72	2½d. black and red	12·00	3·75
216	-	6d. black and blue	50	25
217	-	1s. black and red	50	1·00
218	-	2s. black and blue	35	75

DESIGNS—HORIZ: 6d. H.M.S. "Kent"; 1s. H.M.S. "Invincible". VERT: 2s. Battle Memorial.

1965. Centenary of I.T.U. As T 45 of Gibraltar.

219	1d. light blue and deep blue	50	30
220	2s. lilac and yellow	3·50	1·75

1965. I.C.Y. As T 46 of Gibraltar.

221	1d. purple and turquoise	1·50	40
222	1s. green and lavender	4·00	1·10

1966. Churchill Commemoration. As T 47 of Gibraltar.

223	½d. blue	65	2·25
224	1d. green	1·75	20
225	1s. brown	6·00	3·00
226	2s. violet	4·00	3·50

76 Globe and Human Rights Emblem

1968. Human Rights Year.

228	76	2d. multicoloured	40	20
229	76	6d. multicoloured	40	20
230	76	1s. multicoloured	50	20
231	76	2s. multicoloured	65	30

77 Dusty Miller

1968. Flowers. Multicoloured.

232	½d. Type **77**	15	1·75
233	1½d. Pig vine	40	15
234	2d. Pale maiden	50	15
235	3d. Dog orchid	6·00	1·00
236	3½d. Sea cabbage	30	1·00
237	4½d. Vanilla daisy	1·50	2·00
238	5½d. yellow, brown and green (Arrowleaf marigold)	1·50	2·00
239	6d. red, black and green (Diddle dee)	75	20
240	1s. Scurvy grass	1·00	1·50
241	1s.6d. Prickly burr	5·50	14·00
242	2s. Fachine	5·50	6·50
243	3s. Lavender	8·00	8·00

244	5s. Felton's flower	30·00	13·00
245	£1 Yellow orchid	13·00	3·25

Nos. 233, 236, 238/40 and 244 are horiz.

91 de Havilland Canada DHC-2 Beaver Seaplane

1969. 21st Anniv of Government Air Services. Multicoloured.

246	2d. Type **91**	50	30
247	6d. Noorduyn Norseman V	50	35
248	1s. Auster Autocrat	50	35
249	2s. Arms of the Falkland Islands	1·00	2·00

92 Holy Trinity Church, 1869

1969. Centenary of Bishop Stirling's Consecration.

250	**92**	2d. black, grey and green	40	60
251	-	6d. black, grey and red	40	60
252	-	1s. black, grey and lilac	40	60
253	-	2s. multicoloured	50	75

DESIGNS: 6d. Christ Church Cathedral, 1969; 1s. Bishop Stirling; 2s. Bishop's Mitre.

96 Mounted Volunteer

1970. Golden Jubilee of Defence Force. Mult.

254	2d. Type **96**	1·50	70
255	6d. Defence Post (horiz)	1·50	70
256	1s. Corporal in No. 1 Dress uniform	1·50	70
257	2s. Badge (horiz)	1·50	75

97 S.S. "Great Britain" (1843)

1970. S.S. "Great Britain" Restoration. Stamps show S.S. "Great Britain" in year given. Multicoloured.

258	2d. Type **97**	80	40
259	4d. 1845	80	75
260	9d. 1876	80	75
261	1s. 1886	80	75
262	2s. 1970	1·10	75

1971. Decimal Currency. Nos. 232/44 surch.

263	½p. on ½d. multicoloured	25	20
264	1p. on 1½d. multicoloured	30	15
265	1½p. on 2d. multicoloured	30	15
266	2p. on 3d. multicoloured	50	20
267	2½p. on 3½d. multicoloured	30	20
268	3p. on 4½d. multicoloured	30	20
269	4p. on 5½d. yellow, brn & grn	30	20
270	5p. on 6d. red, black and green	30	20
271	6p. on 1s. multicoloured	7·00	7·00
272	7½p. on 1s.6d. multicoloured	6·00	7·50
273	10p. on 2s. multicoloured	6·50	3·00
274	15p. on 3s. multicoloured	3·00	2·75
275	25p. on 5s. multicoloured	2·50	3·25

1972. Decimal Currency. Nos. 232/44 inscr in decimal currency.

276	½p. multicoloured	35	4·75
277	1p. multicoloured	30	40
278	1½p. multicoloured	30	4·50
279	2p. multicoloured	12·00	1·25
280	2½p. multicoloured	35	4·50
281	3p. multicoloured	35	1·25
282	4p. yellow, brown and green	40	1·00
283	5p. red, black and green	40	55
285	7½p. multicoloured	1·25	3·50
286	10p. multicoloured	8·00	3·75
287	15p. multicoloured	2·25	4·00
288	25p. multicoloured	2·25	4·75
295	6p. multicoloured	1·50	2·25

1972. Royal Silver Wedding. As T 98 of Gibraltar but with Romney Marsh Sheep and Giant Sea Lions in background.

289	1p. green	40	40
290	10p. blue	60	85

1973. Royal Wedding. As T 101a of Gibraltar. Background colour given. Multicoloured.

291	5p. mauve	25	10
292	15p. brown	35	20

101 South American Fur Seal

1974. Tourism. Multicoloured.

296	2p. Type **101**	1·75	1·90
297	4p. Trout-fishing	2·25	1·50
298	5p. Rockhopper penguins	8·00	2·50
299	15p. Long-tailed meadow lark ("Military Starling")	10·00	5·00

102 19th-century Mail-coach

1974. U.P.U. Multicoloured.

300	2p. Type **102**	20	25
301	5p. Packet ship, 1841	25	45
302	8p. First U.K. aerial post, 1911	30	55
303	16p. Ship's catapult mail, 1920s	35	75

103 Churchill and Houses of Parliament

1974. Birth Centenary of Sir Winston Churchill. Multicoloured.

304	16p. Type **103**	80	1·25
305	20p. Churchill with H.M.S. "Inflexible" and H.M.S. "Invincible", 1914	80	1·25
MS306	108×83 mm. Nos. 304/5	9·00	8·50

104 H.M.S. "Exeter"

1974. 35th Anniv of Battle of the River Plate. Multicoloured.

307	2p. Type **104**	2·25	1·60
308	6p. H.M.N.Z. "Achilles"	3·25	3·50
309	8p. "Admiral Graf Spee"	4·00	4·50
310	16p. H.M.S. "Ajax"	7·00	15·00

105 Seal and Flag Badge

1975. 50th Anniv of Heraldic Arms. Multicoloured.

311	2p. Type **105**	80	35
312	7½p. Coat of arms, 1925	1·25	1·40
313	10p. Coat of arms, 1948	1·40	1·60
314	16p. Arms of the Dependencies, 1952	2·00	3·25

106 ½p. Coin and Brown Trout

1975. New Coinage. Multicoloured.

316	2p. Type **106**	1·00	50
317	5½p. 1p. coin and Gentoo penguin	2·00	1·50
318	8p. 2p. coin and Magellan goose	2·50	1·75
319	10p. 5p. coin and Black-browed albatross	2·50	2·00
320	16p. 10p. coin and Southern sealion	2·75	3·00

107 Gathering Sheep

1976. Sheep Farming Industry. Multicoloured.

321	2p. Type **107**	60	50
322	7½p. Shearing	85	1·60
323	10p. Dipping	1·10	1·75
324	20p. Shipping	1·60	3·50

108 The Queen awaiting Anointment

1977. Silver Jubilee. Multicoloured.

325	6p. Visit of Prince Philip, 1957	1·50	1·00
326	11p. The Queen, ampulla and anointing spoon	20	60
327	33p. Type **108**	30	75

109 Map of Falkland Islands

1977. Telecommunications. Multicoloured.

328	3p. Type **109**	75	15
329	11p. Ship to shore communications	1·00	40
330	40p. Telex and telephone service	1·75	1·75

110 "A.E.S.", 1957–74

1978. Mail Ships. Multicoloured.

331A	1p. Type **110**	20	30
332A	2p. "Darwin", 1957–73	50	30
333A	3p. "Merak-N", 1951–52	25	1·50
334A	4p. "Fitzroy", 1936–57	30	1·50
335A	5p. "Lafonia", 1936–41	30	30
336A	6p. "Fleurus", 1924–33	30	50
337A	7p. "Falkland", 1914–34	30	2·75
338A	8p. "Oravia", 1900–12	35	1·25
339A	9p. "Memphis", 1890–97	35	1·00
340A	10p. "Black Hawk", 1873–80	35	50
341B	20p. "Foam", 1863–72	1·00	3·00
342B	25p. "Fairy", 1857–61	1·00	3·00
343B	50p. "Amelia", 1852–54	1·25	3·75
344B	£1 "Nautilus", 1846–48	1·40	4·50
345B	£3 "Hebe", 1842–46	3·50	9·50

Nos. 331/45 come with and without date imprint.

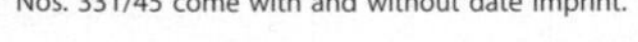

111 Short Hythe at Stanley

1978. 26th Anniv of First Direct Flight, Southampton–Port Stanley. Multicoloured.

346	11p. Type **111**	3·25	2·50
347	33p. Route map and Short Hythe flying boat	3·75	3·00

112 Red Dragon of Wales

1978. 25th Anniv of Coronation. Multicoloured.

348	**112**	25p. brown, blue and silver	60	1·00
349	-	25p. multicoloured	60	1·00
350	-	25p. brown, blue and silver	60	1·00

DESIGNS: No. 349, Queen Elizabeth II; 350, Hornless ram.

113 First Fox Bay P.O. and 1d. Stamp of 1878

1978. Centenary of First Falkland Islands Postage Stamp. Multicoloured.

351	3p. Type **113**	25	20
352	11p. Second Stanley P.O. and 4d. stamp of 1878	30	50
353	15p. New Island P.O. and 6d. stamp of 1878	40	60
354	22p. First Stanley P.O. and 1s. stamp of 1878	60	1·00

114 "Macrocystis pyrifera"

1979. Kelp and Seaweed. Multicoloured.

355	3p. Type **114**	25	25
356	7p. "Durvillea sp."	30	40
357	11p. "Lessonia sp." (horiz)	35	45
358	15p. "Callophyllis sp." (horiz)	45	60
359	25p. "Iradaea sp."	55	1·10

115 Britten Norman BN-2 Islander over Falkland Islands

1979. Opening of Stanley Airport. Multicoloured.

360	3p. Type **115**	40	20
361	11p. Fokker F.27 Friendship over South Atlantic	70	60
362	15p. Fokker F.28 Fellowship over Airport	75	60
363	25p. Cessna 172 Skyhawk, Britten Norman BN-2 Islander, Fokker F.27 Friendship and Fokker F.28 Fellowship over runway	1·25	80

116 Sir Rowland Hill and 1953 Coronation 1d. Commemorative

1979. Death Centenary of Sir Rowland Hill.

364	3p. Type **116**	25	25
365	11p. 1878 1d. stamp (vert)	40	70
366	25p. Penny Black	60	85
MS367	137×98 mm. 33p. 1916 5s. stamp (vert)	85	1·50

117 Mail Drop by de Havilland Canada Beaver Aircraft

1979. Centenary of U.P.U. Membership. Multicoloured.

368	3p. Type **117**	20	20
369	11p. Mail by horseback	40	55
370	25p. Mail by schooner "Gwendolin"	50	1·00

118 Peale's Porpoise

1980. Dolphins and Porpoises. Multicoloured.

371	3p. Type **118**	30	45
372	6p. Commerson's dolphin (horiz)	35	55
373	7p. Hour-glass dolphin (horiz)	35	55
374	11p. Spectacled porpoise	40	70
375	15p. Dusky dolphin (horiz)	40	80
376	25p. Killer whale (horiz)	55	1·40

119 1878 Falkland Islands Postmark

1980. "London 1980" International Stamp Exhibition.

377	**119**	11p. black, gold and blue	20	30
378	-	11p. black, gold and yellow	20	30
379	-	11p. black, gold and green	20	30
380	-	11p. black, gold and purple	20	30
381	-	11p. black, gold and red	20	30
382	-	11p. black, gold and flesh	20	30

POSTMARKS: No. 378, 1915 New Island; 379, 1901 Falkland Islands; 380, 1935 Port Stanley; 381, 1952 Port Stanley first overseas airmail; 382, 1934 Fox Bay.

120 Queen Elizabeth the Queen Mother at Ascot, 1971

1980. 80th Birthday of Queen Mother.

383	**120**	11p. multicoloured	40	30

121 Forster's Caracara

1980. Birds of Prey. Multicoloured.

384	3p. Type **121**	50	25
385	11p. Red-backed buzzard	60	45
386	15p. Common caracara	70	55
387	25p. Peregrine falcon	75	75

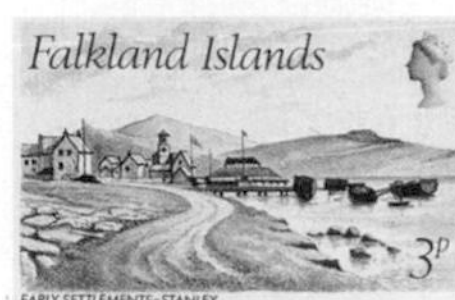

122 Stanley

1981. Early Settlements. Multicoloured.

388	3p. Type **122**	15	15
389	11p. Port Egmont	20	35
390	25p. Port Louis	45	65
391	33p. Mission House, Keppel Island	50	80

123 Sheep

1981. Farm Animals. Multicoloured.

392	3p. Type **123**	15	30
393	11p. Cattle	20	55
394	25p. Horse	40	1·00
395	33p. Dogs	50	1·25

124 Bowles and Carver, 1779

1981. Early Maps.

396	**124**	3p. multicoloured	20	25
397	-	10p. multicoloured	30	35
398	-	13p. multicoloured	30	35
399	-	15p. multicoloured	30	35
400	-	25p. multicoloured	35	40
401	-	26p. black, pink and stone	35	40

MAPS: 10p. J. Hawkesworth, 1773; 13p. Eman Bowen, 1747; 15p. T. Boutflower, 1768; 25p. Philippe de Pretot, 1771; 26p. Bellin "Petite Atlas Maritime", Paris, 1764.

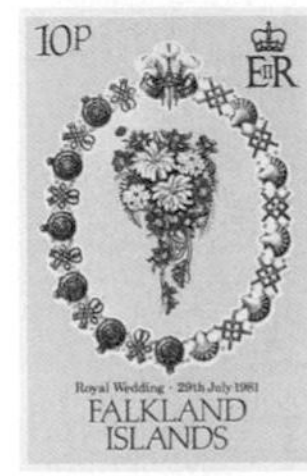

125 Wedding Bouquet from Falkland Islands

1981. Royal Wedding. Multicoloured.

402	10p. Type **125**	25	30
403	13p. Prince Charles riding	30	35
404	52p. Prince Charles and Lady Diana Spencer	70	1·00

126 "Handicrafts"

1981. 25th Anniv of Duke of Edinburgh Award Scheme. Multicoloured.

405	10p. Type **126**	15	20
406	13p. "Camping"	20	30
407	15p. "Canoeing"	30	40
408	52p. Duke of Edinburgh	35	60

127 "The Adoration of the Holy Child" (16th-century Dutch Artist)

1981. Christmas. Paintings. Multicoloured.

409	3p. Type **127**	20	20
410	13p. "The Holy Family in an Italian Landscape" (17th-century Genoan artist)	35	45
411	26p. "The Holy Virgin" (Reni)	55	75

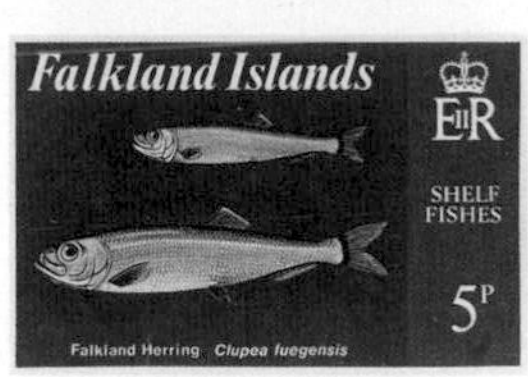

128 Patagonian Sprat

1981. Shelf Fishes. Multicoloured.

412	5p. Type **128**	15	20
413	13p. Gunther's rockcod (vert)	20	35
414	15p. Argentine hake	20	40
415	25p. Southern blue whiting	35	75
416	26p. Grey-tailed skate (vert)	35	75

129 "Lady Elizabeth", 1913

1982. Shipwrecks. Multicoloured.

417	5p. Type **129**	20	35
418	13p. "Capricorn", 1882	25	40
419	15p. "Jhelum", 1870	30	50
420	25p. "Snowsquall", 1864	40	60
421	26p. "St. Mary", 1890	40	60

130 Charles Darwin

1982. 150th Anniv of Charles Darwin's Voyage. Multicoloured.

422	5p. Type **130**	30	25
423	17p. Darwin's microscope	35	60
424	25p. Falkland Islands wolf	55	80
425	34p. H.M.S. "Beagle"	75	1·10

131 Falkland Islands Coat of Arms

1982. 21st Birthday of Princess of Wales. Multicoloured.

426	5p. Type **131**	15	20
427	17p. Princess at Royal Opera House, Covent Garden, November, 1981	30	40
428	37p. Bride and groom in doorway of St. Paul's	50	70
429	50p. Formal portrait	65	90

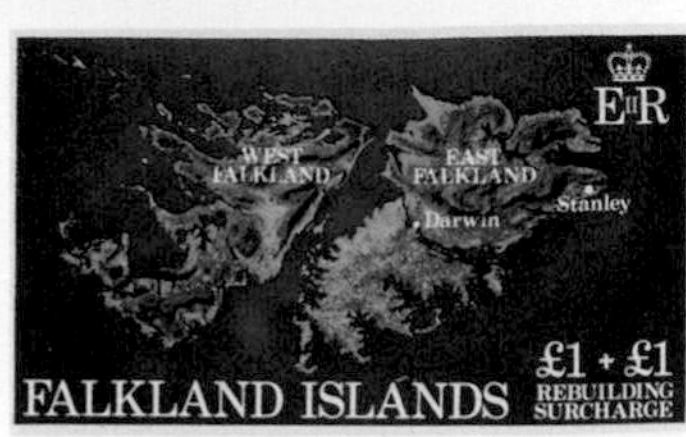

132 Map of Falkland Islands

1982. Rebuilding Fund.

430	**132**	£1+£1 multicoloured	1·50	3·00

1982. Commonwealth Games, Brisbane. Nos. 335 and 342 optd 1st PARTICIPATION COMMONWEALTH GAMES 1982.

431	5p. "Lafonia", 1936–41	15	30
432	25p. "Fairy", 1857–61	35	1·10

134 Blackish Cinclodes ("Tussock Bird")

1982. Birds of the Passerine Family. Multicoloured.

433	5p. Type **134**	25	35
434	10p. Black-chinned siskin	30	35
435	13p. Sedge wren ("Grass Wren")	30	35
436	17p. Black-throated finch	30	35
437	25p. Correndera pipit ("Falkland-Correndera Pipit")	35	50
438	34p. Dark-faced ground-tyrant	40	65

135 Raising Flag, Port Louis, 1833

1983. 150th Anniv of British Administration. Multicoloured.

439	1p. Type **135**	20	30
440	2p. Chelsea pensioners and barracks, 1849 (horiz)	25	40
441	5p. Development of wool trade, 1874	25	40
442	10p. Ship-repairing trade, 1850–1890 (horiz)	35	70
443	15p. Government House, early 20th century (horiz)	35	80
444	20p. Battle of Falkland Islands, 1914	45	1·25
445	25p. Whalebone Arch (horiz)	45	1·25
446	40p. Contribution to War effort, 1939–45	50	1·25
447	50p. Duke of Edinburgh's visit, 1957 (horiz)	60	1·25
448	£1 Royal Marine uniforms	75	1·75
449	£2 Queen Elizabeth II	1·50	2·25

136 1933 British Administration Centenary 3d. Commemorative

1983. Commonwealth Day. Multicoloured.

450	5p. Type **136**	15	15
451	17p. 1933 British Administration Centenary ½d. commemorative	20	35
452	34p. 1933 British Administration Centenary 10s. commemorative (vert)	40	80
453	50p. 1983 British Administration 150th anniv £2 commemorative (vert)	60	1·00

137 British Army advancing across East Falkland

1983. 1st Anniv of Liberation. Multicoloured.

454	5p. Type **137**	20	30
455	13p. S.S. "Canberra" and M.V. "Norland" at San Carlos	30	60
456	17p. R.A.F. Hawker Siddeley Harrier fighter	35	70
457	50p. H.M.S. "Hermes" (aircraft carrier)	75	1·40
MS458	169×130 mm. Nos. 454/7	1·50	2·50

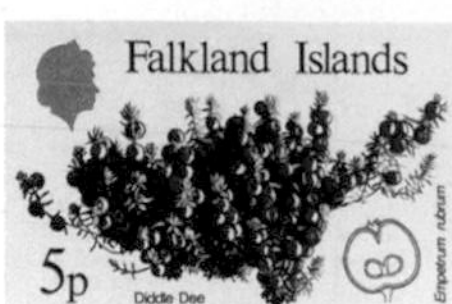

138 Diddle Dee

1983. Native Fruits. Multicoloured.

459	5p. Type **138**	15	20
460	17p. Tea berry	25	35
461	25p. Mountain berry	35	50
462	34p. Native strawberry	45	70

139 Britten Norman BN-2 Islander

1983. Bicentenary of Manned Flight. Mult.

463	5p. Type **139**	15	20
464	13p. de Havilland Canada DHC-2 Beaver	25	35
465	17p. Noorduyn Norseman V	30	40
466	50p. Auster Autocrat	70	1·00

1984. Nos. 443 and 445 surch.

467	17p. on 15p. Government House, early 20th century	60	60
468	22p. on 25p. Whalebone Arch, 1933	65	65

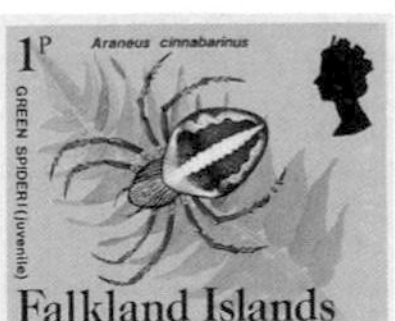

141 "Araneus cinnabarinus" (juvenile spider)

1984. Insects and Spiders. Multicoloured.

469A	1p. Type **141**	20	80
470A	2p. "Alopophion occidentalis" (fly)	2·00	2·00
471A	3p. "Pareuxoina falklandica (moth)	40	80
472A	4p. "Lissopterus quadrinotatus" (beetle)	30	80
473A	5p. "Issoria cytheris" (butterfly)	30	80
474A	6p. "Araneus cinnabarinus" (adult spider)	30	80
475A	7p. "Trachysphyrus penai" (fly)	30	65
476A	8p. "Caphornia ochricraspia" (moth)	30	65
477A	9p. "Caneorhinus biangulatus" (weevil)	30	65
478A	10p. "Syrphus octomaculatus" (fly)	30	65
479A	20p. "Malvinius compressiventris" (weevil)	2·00	75
480A	25p. "Metius blandus" (beetle)	50	90
481A	50p. "Parudenus falklandicus" (cricket)	80	1·50
482A	£1 "Emmenomma beauchenieus" (spider)	1·00	2·25
483A	£3 "Cynthia carye" (butterfly)	2·75	6·00

No. 470 comes with or without imprint date.

142 "Wavertree" (sail merchantman)

1984. 250th Anniv of "Lloyd's List" (newspaper). Multicoloured.

484	6p. Type **142**	45	40
485	17p. "Bjerk" (whale catcher) at Port Stanley	65	50
486	22p. "Oravia" (liner) stranded	65	55
487	52p. "Cunard Countess" (liner)	90	1·75

143 Ship, Lockheed C-130 Hercules Aircraft and U.P.U. Logo

1984. Universal Postal Union Congress, Hamburg.

488	**143** 22p. multicoloured	55	75

144 Great Grebe

1984. Grebes. Multicoloured.

489	17p. Type **144**	80	1·00
490	22p. Silvery grebe ("Silver Grebe")	1·00	1·10
491	52p. White-tufted grebe ("Rolland's Grebe")	1·50	3·25

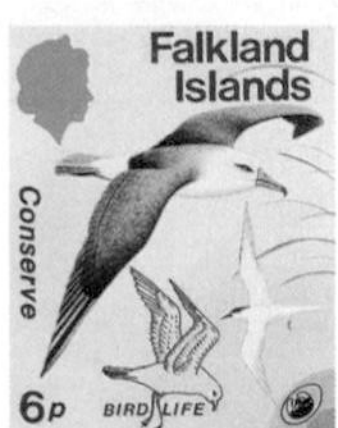

145 Black-browed Albatross, Wilson's Storm Petrel and South American Tern

1984. Nature Conservation. Multicoloured.

492	6p. Type **145**	1·00	60
493	17p. Tussock grass	65	70
494	22p. Dusky dolphin and Southern sea lion	70	80
495	52p. Rockcod (fish) and krill	1·00	2·25
MS496	130×90 mm. Nos. 492/5	4·00	7·00

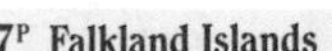

146 Technical Drawing of Class "Wren" Locomotive

1985. 70th Anniv of Camber Railway. Each black, brown and light brown.

497	7p. Type **146**	30	30
498	22p. Sail-propelled trolley	50	70
499	27p. Class "Wren" locomotive at work	55	90
500	54p. "Falkland Islands Express" passenger train (76×25 mm)	85	1·75

147 Construction Workers' Camp

1985. Opening of Mount Pleasant Airport. Multicoloured.

501	7p. Type **147**	45	40
502	22p. Building construction	60	75
503	27p. Completed airport	75	80
504	54p. Lockheed L-1011 TriStar 500 airliner over runway	1·00	1·75

148 The Queen Mother on 84th Birthday

1985. Life and Times of Queen Elizabeth the Queen Mother. Multicoloured.

505	7p. Attending reception at Lancaster House	25	20
506	22p. With Prince Charles, Mark Phillips and Princess Anne at Falklands Memorial Service	60	50
507	27p. Type **148**	70	60
508	54p. With Prince Henry at his christening (from photo by Lord Snowdon)	1·25	1·25
MS509	91×73 mm. £1 With Princess Diana at Trooping the Colour	3·25	2·25

149 Captain J. McBride and H.M.S. "Jason", 1765

1985. Early Cartographers. Multicoloured.

510	7p. Type **149**	60	40
511	22p. Commodore J. Byron and H.M.S. "Dolphin" and "Tamar", 1765	1·00	80
512	27p. Vice-Admiral R. FitzRoy and H.M.S. "Beagle", 1831	1·10	85
513	54p. Admiral Sir B. J. Sullivan and H.M.S. "Philomel", 1842	1·75	1·75

149a Philibert Commerson and Commerson's Dolphin

1985. Early Naturalists. Multicoloured.

514	7p. Type **149a**	60	40
515	22p. Rene Primevere Lesson and "Lessonia sp." (kelp)	75	85
516	27p. Joseph Paul Gaimard and Common diving petrel ("Diving Petrel")	1·40	1·50
517	54p. Charles Darwin and "Calceolaria darwinii"	1·50	2·50

150 Painted Keyhole Limpet

1986. Seashells. Multicoloured.

518	7p. Type **150**	75	60
519	22p. "Provocator palliata"	1·25	1·10
520	27p. Patagonian or Falkland scallop	1·40	1·60
521	54p. Rough thorn drupe	2·25	3·00

1986. 60th Birthday of Queen Elizabeth II. As T 120a of Hong Kong. Multicoloured.

522	10p. With Princess Margaret at St. Paul's, Walden Bury, Welwyn, 1932	15	25
523	24p. Queen making Christmas television broadcast, 1958	25	50
524	29p. In robes of Order of the Thistle, St. Giles Cathedral, Edinburgh, 1962	25	60
525	45p. Aboard Royal Yacht "Britannia", U.S.A., 1976	1·00	1·25
526	58p. At Crown Agents Head Office, London, 1983	60	1·50

151 S.S. "Great Britain" crossing Atlantic, 1845

1986. "Ameripex '86" International Stamp Exhibition, Chicago. Centenary of Arrival of S.S. "Great Britain" in Falkland Islands. Multicoloured.

527	10p. Type **151**	25	60
528	24p. Beached at Sparrow Cove, 1937	30	80
529	29p. Refloated on pontoon, 1970	35	90
530	58p. Undergoing restoration, Bristol, 1986	50	2·25
MS531	109×100 mm. Nos. 527/30	1·10	2·75

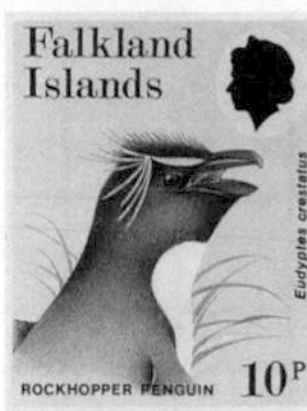

152 Head of Rockhopper Penguin

1986. Rockhopper Penguins. Multicoloured.

532	10p. Type **152**	80	70
533	24p. Rockhopper penguins at sea	1·40	1·50
534	29p. Courtship display	1·50	1·75
535	58p. Adult with chick	2·00	4·00

153 Prince Andrew and Miss Sarah Ferguson presenting Polo Trophy, Windsor

1986. Royal Wedding. Multicoloured.

536	17p. Type **153**	1·00	60
537	22p. Prince Andrew and Duchess of York on wedding day	1·10	75
538	29p. Prince Andrew in battledress at opening of Fox Bay Mill	1·40	1·10

154 Survey Party, Sapper Hill

1987. Bicentenary of Royal Engineers' Royal Warrant. Multicoloured.

539	10p. Type **154**	1·25	80
540	24p. Mine clearance by robot	1·75	1·50
541	29p. Boxer Bridge, Stanley	2·00	2·50
542	58p. Unloading mail, Mount Pleasant Airport	2·75	4·00

155 Southern Sea Lion

1987. Seals. Multicoloured.

543	10p. Type **155**	85	65
544	24p. Falkland fur seal	1·50	90
545	29p. Southern elephant seal	1·60	1·50
546	58p. Leopard seal	2·25	4·00

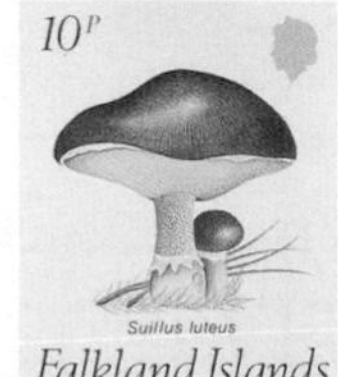

156 "Suillus luteus"

1987. Fungi. Multicoloured.

547	10p. Type **156**	1·75	85
548	24p. "Mycena sp."	2·75	2·00
549	29p. "Hygrophorus adonis" ("Camarophyllus adonis")	3·00	3·00
550	58p. "Gerronema schusteri"	4·50	5·00

157 Victoria Cottage Home, c. 1912

1987. Local Hospitals. Multicoloured.

551	10p. Type **157**	50	25
552	24p. King Edward VII Memorial Hospital, c. 1914	85	55
553	29p. Churchill Wing, King Edward VII Memorial Hospital, c. 1953	95	60
554	58p. Prince Andrew Wing, New Hospital, 1987	1·50	1·25

158 Morris Truck, Fitzroy, 1940

1988. Early Vehicles. Multicoloured.

555	10p. Type **158**	50	25
556	24p. Citroen "Kegresse" half-track, San Carlos, 1929	85	55
557	29p. Ford one ton truck, Port Stanley, 1933	95	60
558	58p. Ford "Model T" car, Darwin, 1935	1·50	1·25

159 Kelp Goose

1988. Falkland Islands Geese. Multicoloured.

559	10p. Type **159**	2·00	55
560	24p. Magellan ("Upland") goose	2·75	70
561	29p. Ruddy-headed goose	3·00	90
562	58p. Ashy-headed goose	4·50	2·00

159a Silver from Lloyd's Nelson Collection

1988. 300th Anniv of Lloyd's of London. Mult.

563	10p. Type **159a**	40	30
564	24p. Falkland Islands hydroponic market garden (horiz)	75	65
565	29p. "A.E.S." (mail ship) (horiz)	1·50	75
566	58p. "Charles Cooper" (full-rigged ship), 1866	2·00	1·25

160 "Padua" (barque)

1989. Cape Horn Sailing Ships. Multicoloured.

567	1p. Type **160**	1·75	80
613	2p. "Priwall" (barque) (vert)	1·25	1·00
614	3p. "Passat" (barque)	1·25	1·00
570	4p. "Archibald Russell" (barque) (vert)	2·50	80
571	5p. "Pamir" (barque) (vert)	2·50	80
617	6p. "Mozart" (barquentine)	1·75	1·25
573	7p. "Pommern" (barque)	2·50	1·00
574	8p. "Preussen" (full-rigged ship)	2·50	1·00
620	9p. "Fennia" (barque)	1·75	1·40
576	10p. "Cassard" (barque)	2·50	1·00
577	20p. "Lawhill" (barque)	4·00	2·00
578	25p. "Garthpool" (barque)	4·00	2·00
579	50p. "Grace Harwar" (full-rigged ship)	5·00	3·00
625	£1 "Criccieth Castle" (full-rigged ship)	3·75	3·75
581	£3 "Cutty Sark" (full-rigged ship) (vert)	14·00	8·50
582	£5 "Flying Cloud" (full-rigged ship)	22·00	9·00

161 Southern Right Whale

1989. Baleen Whales. Multicoloured.

583	10p. Type **161**	1·25	40
584	24p. Minke whale	2·00	85
585	29p. Humpback whale	2·25	1·25
586	58p. Blue whale	3·50	2·50

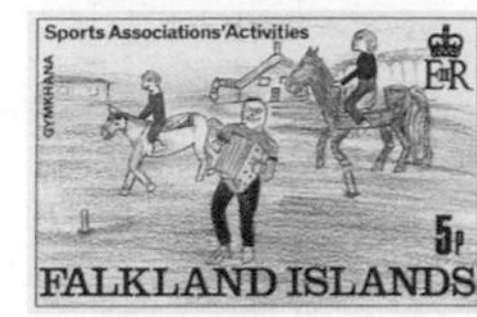

162 "Gymkhana" (Sarah Gilding)

1989. Sports Associations' Activities. Children's Drawings. Multicoloured.

587	5p. Type **162**	20	20
588	10p. "Steer Riding" (Karen Steen)	30	30
589	17p. "Sheep Shearing" (Colin Shepherd)	45	45
590	24p. "Sheepdog Trials" (Rebecca Edwards)	60	70
591	29p. "Horse Racing" (Dilys Blackley)	70	80
592	45p. "Sack Race" (Donna Newell)	1·00	1·10

163 Vice-Admiral Sturdee and H.M.S. "Invincible" (battle cruiser)

1989. 75th Anniv of the Battle of the Falkland Islands and 50th Anniv of Battle of the River Plate. Mult.

593	10p. Type **163**	1·00	30
594	24p. Vice-Admiral Graf von Spee and "Scharnhorst" (German cruiser)	1·75	75
595	29p. Commodore Harwood and H.M.S. "Ajax" (cruiser)	1·90	85
596	58p. Captain Langsdorff and "Admiral Graf Spee" (German pocket battleship)	2·50	2·00

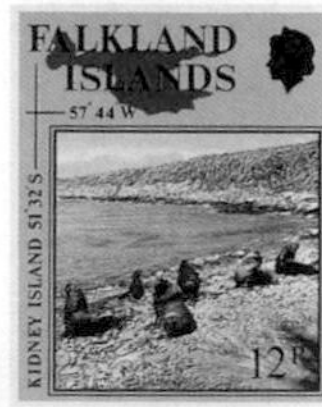

164 Southern Sea Lions on Kidney Island

1990. Nature Reserves and Sanctuaries. Mult.

597	12p. Type **164**	60	35
598	26p. Black-browed albatrosses on Beauchene Island	1·40	70
599	31p. Penguin colony on Bird Island	1·40	90
600	62p. Tussock grass on Elephant Jason Island	1·50	1·75

165 Supermarine Spitfire Mk I "Falkland Islands I"

1990. "Stamp World London 90" International Stamp Exhibition, London. Presentation Spitfires. Multicoloured.

601	12p. Type **165**	65	45
602	26p. Supermarine Spitfire Mk I "Falkland Islands VII"	1·25	80
603	31p. Cockpit and wing of "Falkland Islands I"	1·25	1·10
604	62p. Squadron scramble, 1940	1·75	2·50
MS605	114×100 mm. £1 Supermarine Spitfire Mk I in action, 1940	4·00	2·50

For No. **MS**605 with additional inscription see No. **MS**628.

165a Queen Mother in Dover

1990. 90th Birthday of Queen Elizabeth the Queen Mother.

606	**165a** 26p. multicoloured	1·00	65
607	- £1 black and red	2·75	2·75

DESIGN: £1 On bridge of liner "Queen Elizabeth", 1946 (29×33 mm).

166 Black-browed Albatrosses

1990. Black-browed Albatrosses. Multicoloured.

608	12p. Type **166**	75	50
609	26p. Female with egg	1·40	1·00
610	31p. Adult and chick	1·60	1·25
611	62p. Black-browed albatrosses in flight	2·75	3·00

1991. 2nd Visit of H.R.H. The Duke of Edinburgh. As No. MS605, but with Exhibition emblem replaced by "SECOND VISIT OF HRH THE DUKE OF EDINBURGH".

MS628	144×100 mm. £1 Spitfire Mk. I in action	7·50	9·00

The margin of No. **MS**628 also shows the exhibition emblem omitted and has the same commemorative inscription added.

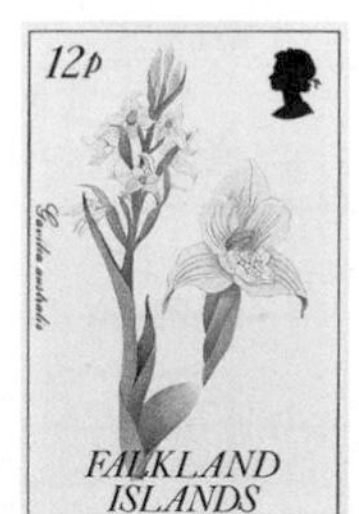

167 "Gavilea australis"

1991. Orchids. Multicoloured.

629	12p. Type **167**	75	70
630	26p. Dog orchid	1·25	1·00
631	31p. "Chlorea gaudichaudii"	1·40	1·50
632	62p. Yellow orchid	2·50	3·75

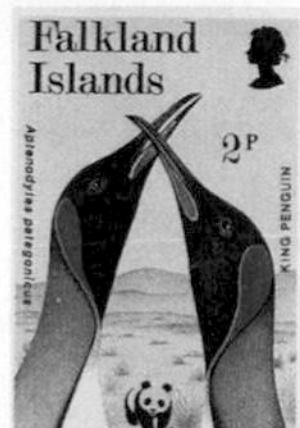

168 Heads of Two King Penguins

1991. Endangered Species. King Penguin. Mult.

633	2p. Type **168**	70	70
634	6p. Female incubating egg	90	90
635	12p. Female with two chicks	1·25	1·00
636	20p. Penguin underwater	1·50	1·25
637	31p. Parents feeding their chick	1·60	1·90
638	62p. Courtship dance	2·25	2·75

Nos. 637/8 do not include the W.W.F. panda emblem.

169 ½d. and 2½d. Stamps of September, 1891

1991. Cent of Bisected Surcharges. Mult.

639	12p. Type **169**	60	50
640	26p. Cover of March, 1891 franked with strip of five ½d. bisects	1·00	1·00
641	31p. Unsevered pair of ½d. surcharge	1·25	1·50
642	62p. "Isis" (mail ship)	2·00	3·25

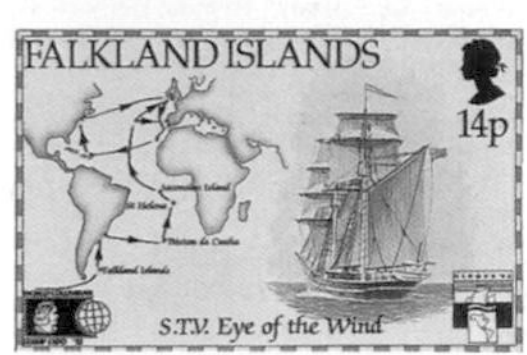

169a Map of Re-enactment Voyages and "Eye of the Wind" (cadet brig)

1991. 500th Anniv of Discovery of America by Columbus. Re-enactment Voyages. Multicoloured.

643	14p. Type **169a**	60	60
644	29p. Compass rose and "Soren Larsen" (cadet brigantine)	1·25	1·40
645	34p. "Santa Maria", "Pinta" and "Nina"	1·50	1·75
646	68p. Columbus and "Santa Maria"	2·50	4·00

1992. 40th Anniv of Queen Elizabeth II's Accession. As T 179a of Gibraltar. Multicoloured.

647	7p. "Stanley through the Narrows" (A. Asprey)	45	35
648	14p. "Hill Cove" (A. Asprey)	70	60
649	29p. "San Carlos Water" (A. Asprey)	1·10	95
650	34p. Three portraits of Queen Elizabeth	1·25	1·25
651	68p. Queen Elizabeth II	1·75	2·00

170 Laying Foundation Stone, 1890

1992. Centenary of Christ Church Cathedral, Stanley. Multicoloured.

652	14p. Type **170**	75	55
653	29p. Interior of Cathedral, 1920	1·40	1·00
654	34p. Bishop's chair	1·60	1·25
655	68p. Cathedral in 1900 (horiz)	2·00	1·90

170a San Carlos Cemetery

1992. 10th Anniv of Liberation. Multicoloured.

656	14p.+6p. Type **170a**	75	1·60
657	29p.+11p. War Memorial, Port Stanley	1·25	2·25
658	34p.+16p. South Atlantic medal	1·25	2·25
659	68p.+32p. Government House, Port Stanley	2·00	3·25
MS660	115×115 mm. Nos. 656/9	5·00	7·00

The premiums on Nos. 656/9 were for the S.S.A.F.A.

171 Captain John Davis and Backstaff

1992. 400th Anniv of First Sighting of the Falkland Islands. Multicoloured.

661	22p. Type **171**	1·25	90
662	29p. Captain John Davis	1·50	1·25
663	34p. Queen Elizabeth I and Queen Elizabeth II	1·75	1·75
664	68p. "Desire" sighting Falkland Islands	2·75	5·00

172 Private, Falkland Islands Volunteers, 1892

1992. Centenary of Falkland Islands Defence Force and 50th Anniv of Affiliation to West Yorkshire Regiment. Multicoloured.

665	7p. Type **172**	50	60
666	14p. Officer, Falkland Islands Defence Corps, 1914	75	75
667	22p. Officer, Falkland Islands Defence Force, 1920	1·00	80
668	29p. Private, Falkland Islands Defence Force, 1939–45	1·25	1·25
669	34p. Officer, West Yorkshire Regiment, 1942	1·50	1·60
670	68p. Private, West Yorkshire Regiment, 1942	2·50	3·75

173 South American Tern

1993. Gulls and Terns. Multicoloured.

671	15p. Type **173**	1·00	75
672	31p. Brown-hooded gull ("Pink-breasted Gull")	1·25	1·25
673	36p. Magellan gull ("Dolphin Gull")	1·75	1·75
674	72p. Southern black-backed gull ("Dominican Gull")	2·75	5·75

174 "Queen Elizabeth 2"

1993. Visit of "Queen Elizabeth 2". Cruise liner. Sheet 60×42 mm.

MS675	£2 multicoloured	7·50	8·50

174a Avro Vulcan B.1A

1993. 75th Anniv of Royal Air Force. Multicoloured.

676	15p. Type **174a**	75	1·00
677	15p. Lockheed C-130k Hercules	75	1·00
678	15p. Boeing-Vertol CH-47 Chinook	75	1·00
679	15p. Lockheed L-1011 TriStar 500	75	1·00
MS680	110×77 mm. 36p. Hawker Siddeley Andover CC.2; 36p. Westland Wessex HC-2 helicopter; 36p. Panavia Tornado F Mk 3; 36p. McDonnell Douglas F-4M Phantom II	3·75	4·75

175 Short-finned Squid

1993. Fisheries. Multicoloured.

681	15p. Type **175**	60	60
682	31p. Catch of whip-tailed hake	1·25	1·50
683	36p. "Falklands Protector" (fisheries patrol vessel)	1·50	1·75
684	72p. Britten Norman BN-2 Islander patrol aircraft and "Pomorze" (fish factory ship)	2·25	5·00

176 "Great Britain" in Dry Dock, Bristol

1993. 150th Anniv of Launch of "Great Britain" (liner). Multicoloured.

685	8p. Type **176**	75	50
686	£1 "Great Britain" at sea	2·75	5·50

177 "Explorer" (liner)

1993. Tourism. Multicoloured.

687	16p. Type **177**	1·25	70
688	34p. Rockhopper penguins	2·00	1·50
689	39p. "World Discoverer" (liner)	2·25	2·00
690	78p. "Columbus Caravelle" (liner)	2·75	6·00

178 Pony

1993. Pets. Multicoloured.

691	8p. Type **178**	60	60
692	16p. Lamb	75	75
693	34p. Puppy and cat	1·75	1·75
694	39p. Kitten (vert)	2·00	2·00
695	78p. Collie dog (vert)	2·75	5·50

1994. "Hong Kong '94" International Stamp Exhibition. Nos. 691/5 optd HONG KONG '94 and emblem.

696	8p. Type **178**	80	1·00
697	16p. Lamb	1·00	1·25
698	34p. Puppy and cat	2·25	2·75
699	39p. Kitten (vert)	2·50	3·00
700	78p. Collie dog (vert)	3·25	6·00

179 Goose Barnacles

1994. Inshore Marine Life. Multicoloured.

701	1p. Type **179**	75	50
702	2p. Painted shrimp (horiz)	1·50	50
703	8p. Patagonian copper limpet (horiz)	1·75	75
704	9p. Eleginops ("Mullet") (horiz)	1·75	75
705	10p. Sea anemones (horiz)	1·75	60
706	20p. Flathead eelpout (horiz)	2·50	1·00
707	25p. Spider crab (horiz)	2·50	1·00
708	50p. Lobster krill	2·50	2·00
709	80p. Falkland skate (horiz)	2·50	2·50
710	£1 Centollon crab (horiz)	2·50	2·50
711	£3 Wilton's notothen ("Rock Cod") (horiz)	8·00	7·00
712	£5 Octopus	15·00	12·00

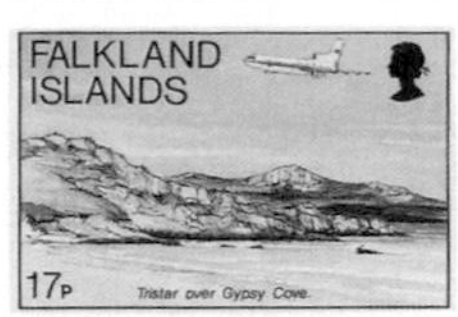

180 Dockyard Blacksmith's Shop and Sir James Clark Ross (explorer)

1994. 150th Anniv of Founding of Stanley. Multicoloured.

713	9p. Type **180**	60	50
714	17p. 21 Fitzroy Road (home of Chaplain James Moody)	85	60
715	30p. Stanley Cottage (built by Dr. Henry Hamblin)	1·40	1·25
716	35p. Pioneer Row and Sgt.-Maj. Henry Felton	1·60	1·75
717	40p. Government House (designed by Governor R. Moody)	1·75	1·90
718	65p. View of Stanley and Edward Stanley, Earl of Derby (Secretary of State for Colonies)	2·50	3·00

181 Lockheed L-1011 TriStar over Gypsy Cove

1994. Falkland Beaches. Multicoloured.

719	17p. Type **181**	85	70
720	35p. "Explorer" (liner) off Sea Lion Island	1·60	1·40
721	40p. Pilatus Britten Norman BN-2 Islander aircraft at Pebble Island	2·00	2·00
722	65p. Landrover at Volunteer Beach	2·25	3·50

182 Mission House, Keppel Island

1994. 150th Anniv of South American Missionary Society. Multicoloured.

723	5p. Type **182**	35	40
724	17p. Thomas Bridges (compiler of Yahgan dictionary)	65	65
725	40p. Fuegian Indians	1·40	1·75
726	65p. Capt. Allen Gardiner and "Allen Gardiner" (schooner)	2·25	2·50

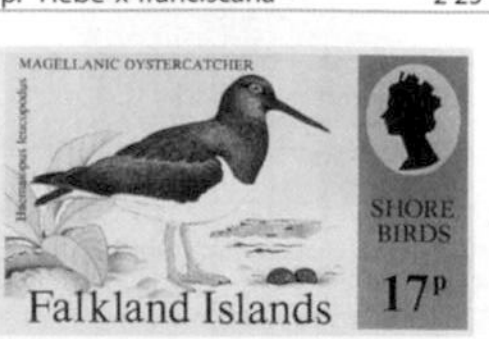

183 "Lupinus arboreus"

1995. Flowering Shrubs. Multicoloured.

727	9p. Type **183**	60	50
728	17p. "Hebe elliptica"	80	70
729	30p. "Fuschia magellanica"	1·10	95
730	35p. "Berberis ilicifolia"	1·25	1·10
731	40p. "Ulex europaeus"	1·40	1·25
732	65p. "Hebe x franciscana"	2·25	2·75

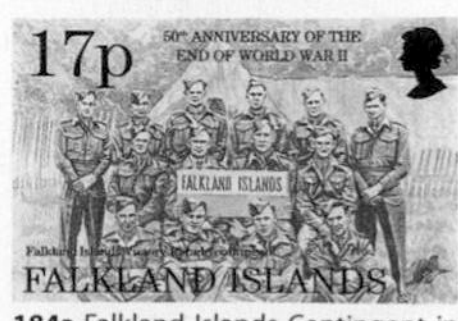

184 Magellanic Oystercatcher

1995. Shore Birds. Multicoloured.

733	17p. Type **184**	1·25	85
734	35p. Rufous-chested dotterel	1·75	1·50
735	40p. Blackish oystercatcher	1·90	1·90
736	65p. Two-banded plover	3·50	6·50

184a Falkland Islands Contingent in Victory Parade

1995. 50th Anniv of End of Second World War. Multicoloured.

737	17p. Type **184a**	1·10	75
738	35p. Governor Sir Alan Cardinall on Bren gun-carrier	1·75	1·40
739	40p. H.M.A.S. "Esperance Bay" (troopship)	1·90	1·75
740	65p. H.M.S. "Exeter" (cruiser)	3·50	3·75
MS741	75×85 mm. £1 Reverse of 1939–45 War Medal (vert)	3·00	3·75

185 Ox and Cart

1995. Transporting Peat. Multicoloured.

742	17p. Type **185**	60	60
743	35p. Horse and cart	1·10	1·10
744	40p. Caterpillar tractor pulling sleigh	1·25	1·25
745	65p. Lorry	2·25	3·50

186 Kelp Geese

1995. Wildlife. Multicoloured.

746	35p. Type **186**	2·25	1·50
747	35p. Black-browed albatross	2·25	1·50
748	35p. Blue-eyed cormorants	2·25	1·50
749	35p. Magellanic penguins	2·25	1·50
750	35p. Fur seals	2·25	1·50
751	35p. Rockhopper penguins	2·25	1·50

Nos. 746/51 were printed together, se-tenant, forming a composite design.

187 Cottontail Rabbit

1995. Introduced Wild Animals. Multicoloured.

752	9p. Type **187**	75	65
753	17p. Brown hare	1·10	75
754	35p. Guanacos	1·75	1·40
755	40p. Fox	1·90	1·60
756	65p. Otter	2·75	3·00

188 Princess Anne and Government House

1996. Royal Visit. Multicoloured.

757	9p. Type **188**	70	45
758	19p. Falklands War Memorial, San Carlos Cemetery	80	65
759	30p. Christ Church Cathedral	1·10	1·10
760	73p. Westland Sea King helicopter over Goose Green	4·00	5·50

188a Steeple Jason

1996. 70th Birthday of Queen Elizabeth II. Each incorporating a different photograph of the Queen. Multicoloured.

761	17p. Type **188a**	70	50
762	40p. "Tamar" (container ship)	1·75	1·25
763	45p. New Island	1·75	1·40
764	65p. Falkland Islands Community School	1·90	1·60
MS765	64×66 mm. £1 Queen Elizabeth II	2·75	3·25

189 Mounted Postman, c. 1890

1996. "CAPEX '96" International Stamp Exhibition. Mail Transport. Multicoloured.

766	9p. Type **189**	75	60
767	40p. Noorduyn Norseman V seaplane	1·75	1·50
768	45p. "Forrest" (freighter) at San Carlos	1·75	1·60
769	76p. de Havilland DHC.2 Beaver seaplane	2·75	2·75
MS770	110×80 mm. £1 L.M.S. Class "Jubilee" steam locomotive No. 5606 "Falkland Islands" (47×31 mm)	2·40	3·50

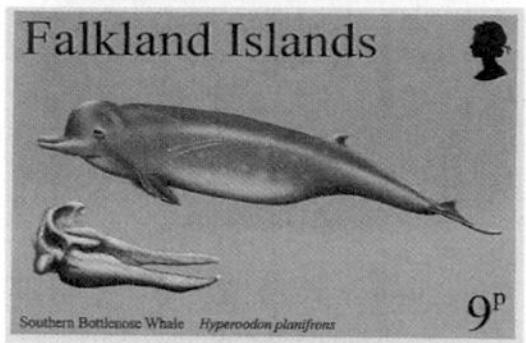

190 Southern Bottlenose Whale

1996. Beaked Whales. Multicoloured.

771	9p. Type **190**	55	45
772	30p. Cuvier's beaked whale	1·10	1·10
773	35p. Straptoothed beaked whale	1·25	1·25
774	75p. Gray's beaked whale	2·40	2·40

191 Magellanic Penguins performing Courtship Dance

1997. Magellanic Penguins. Multicoloured.

775	17p. Type **191**	1·25	55
776	35p. Penguins in burrow	2·00	1·00
777	40p. Adult and chick	2·00	1·25
778	65p. Group of Penguins swimming	2·75	2·25

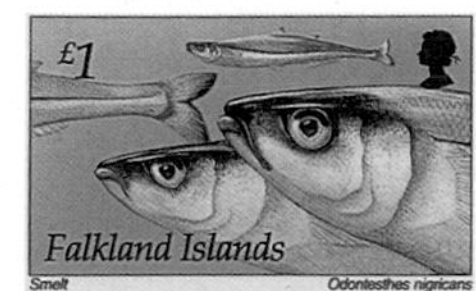

192 Black Pejerry

1997. "HONG KONG '97" International Stamp Exhibition. Sheet 130×90 mm.

MS779	**192** £1 multicoloured	3·00	2·50

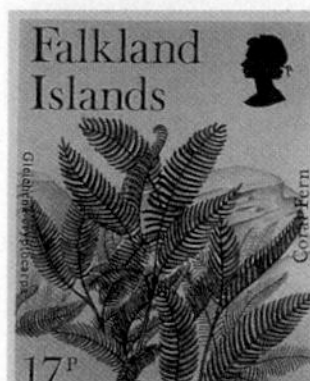

193 Coral Fern

1997. Ferns. Multicoloured.

780	17p. Type **193**	1·25	45
781	35p. Adder's tongue fern	1·75	1·00
782	40p. Fuegian tall fern	1·75	1·10
783	65p. Small fern	2·50	2·25

1997. Return of Hong Kong to China. Sheet 130×90 mm, containing design as No. 710.

MS784	£1 Centollón crab	2·50	2·50

193a Queen Elizabeth II

1997. Golden Wedding of Queen Elizabeth II and Prince Philip. Multicoloured.

785	9p. Type **193a**	1·00	60
786	9p. Prince Philip and horse, 1995	1·00	60
787	17p. Queen Elizabeth in phaeton at Trooping the Colour, 1996	1·25	80
788	17p. Prince Philip in R.A.F. uniform	1·25	80
789	40p. Queen Elizabeth wearing red coat, 1986	1·60	1·10
790	40p. Prince William and Princess Beatrice on horseback	1·60	1·10
MS791	110×71 mm. £1.50, Queen Elizabeth and Prince Philip in landau (horiz)	7·00	3·75

Nos. 785/6, 787/8 and 789/90 respectively were printed together, se-tenant, with the backgrounds forming composite designs.

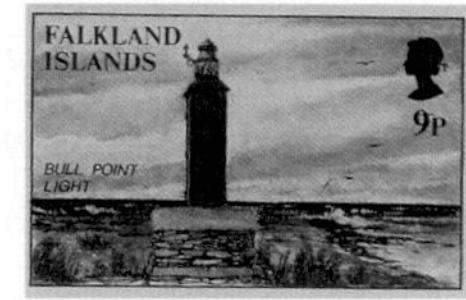

194 Bull Point Lighthouse

1997. Lighthouses. Multicoloured.

792	9p. Type **194**	1·75	65
793	30p. Cape Pembroke Lighthouse	2·50	1·25
794	£1 Cape Meredith Lighthouse	5·75	3·75

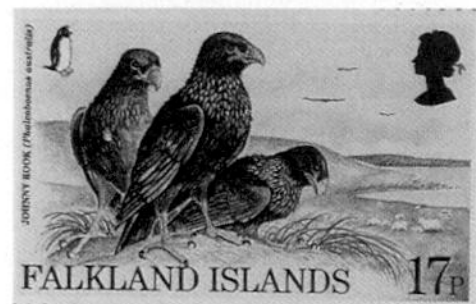

195 Forster's Caracara ("Johnny Rock")

1997. Endangered Species. Multicoloured.

795	17p. Type **195**	2·75	1·50
796	19p. Southern sealion	1·50	1·50
797	40p. Felton's flower	2·50	2·25
798	73p. Trout	4·25	6·50

196 Merryweather and Son Greenwich Gem Fire Engine

1998. Centenary of Falkland Islands Fire Service. Multicoloured.

799	9p. Type **196**	1·75	90
800	17p. Merryweather's Hatfield trailer pump	2·25	90
801	40p. Coventry Climax Godiva trailer pump	3·50	2·50
802	65p. Carmichael Bedford "Type B" water tender	4·00	6·50

196a Wearing Black Jacket, 1990

1998. Diana, Princess of Wales Commemoration.

MS803	145×70 mm. 30p. Type **196a**, 30p. Wearing red dress, 1988; 30p. Resting head on hand, 1991; 30p. Wearing landmine protection clothing, Angola (sold at £1.20 + 20p. charity premium)	3·25	3·25

197 Tawny-throated Dotterel

1998. Rare Visiting Birds. Multicoloured. (a) Designs 39½×23½ mm.

804	1p. Type **197**	75	1·50
805	2p. Hudsonian godwit	75	1·50
806	5p. Eared dove	1·00	1·50
807	9p. Great grebe	1·50	1·00
808	10p. Southern lapwing	1·50	1·00
809	16p. Buff-necked ibis	1·90	2·00
810	30p. Ashy-headed goose	2·00	1·75
811	65p. Red-legged cormorant ("Red-legged Shag")	3·00	2·50
812	88p. Argentine shoveler ("Red Shoveler")	3·50	4·25
813	£1 Red-fronted coot	4·00	4·50
814	£3 Chilian flamingo	9·00	11·00
815	£5 Fork-tailed flycatcher	12·00	16·00

(b) Designs 35×22 mm.

816	9p. Roseate spoonbill	4·00	4·50
817	17p. Austral conure ("Austral Parakeet")	1·00	1·50
818	35p. American kestrel	2·50	2·75

198 "Penelope" (auxillary ketch)

1998. Local Vessels. Multicoloured.

819	17p. Type **198**	1·50	75
820	35p. "Ilen" (auxillary ketch)	2·25	1·60
821	40p. "Weddell" (schooner)	2·50	1·60
822	65p. "Lively" (tug) (31×22 mm)	3·25	4·50

199 Auster J-5 Autocar First Medivac Air Ambulance Service, 1948

1998. 50th Anniv of Falkland Islands Government Air Service. Multicoloured.

823	17p. Type **199**	3·00	60
824	£1 F.I.G.A.S. Beaver and Islander aircraft over map	6·50	8·00

200 Marine at Port Egmont, Saunders Island, 1766

1998. Royal Marine Uniforms. Multicoloured.

825	17p. Type **200**	1·75	75
826	30p. Officer at Port Louis, East Falklands, 1833	2·50	2·00

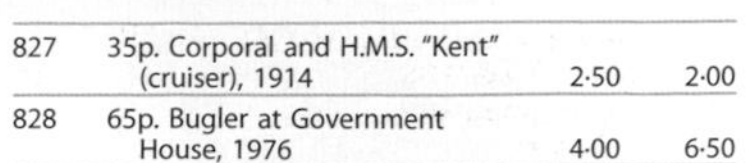

827	35p. Corporal and H.M.S. "Kent" (cruiser), 1914	2·50	2·00
828	65p. Bugler at Government House, 1976	4·00	6·50

201 Altar, St. Mary's Church

1999. Centenary of St. Mary's Roman Catholic Church, Stanley. Multicoloured.

829	17p. Type **201**	1·75	70
830	40p. St. Mary's Church	2·75	2·50
831	75p. Laying of foundation stone, 1899	5·00	7·00

202 H.M.S. "Beagle" (Darwin)

1999. "Australia '99" World Stamp Exhibition, Melbourne. Maritime History. Multicoloured.

832	25p. Type **202**	2·25	1·75
833	35p. H.M.A.S. "Australia" (battle cruiser)	2·50	1·75
834	40p. "Canberra" (liner)	2·75	2·00
835	50p. "Great Britain" (steam/sail)	3·50	4·50
836	50p. All-England Cricket Team, 1861–62	3·50	4·50

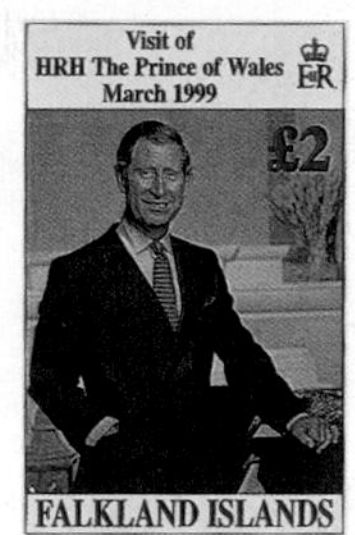

203 Prince of Wales (from photo by Clive Arrowsmith)

1999. Royal Visit.

837	**203** £2 multicoloured	9·00	9·00

203a Prince Edward and Miss Sophie Rhys-Jones

1999. Royal Wedding. Multicoloured.

838	80p. Type **203a**	4·25	4·00
839	£1.20 Engagement photograph	5·50	6·00

204 "Jeanne d'Arc" (French cruiser)

1999. "PHILEXFRANCE '99", International Stamp Exhibition, Paris. First Flight over Falkland Islands, 1931. Multicoloured.

840	35p. Type **204**	2·75	3·00
841	40p. CAMS 37 (flying boat) taking off	2·75	3·00
MS842	115×63 mm. £1 CAMS 37 over Port Stanley (47×31 mm)	9·00	9·00

204a On Board Ship, Port of London, 1939

1999. "Queen Elizabeth the Queen Mother's Century". Multicoloured.

843	9p. Type **204a**	1·25	75
844	20p. With Queen Elizabeth II, 1996	2·00	1·25
845	30p. With Prince Charles and his sons, 1995	2·25	1·40
846	67p. Presenting colours to Queen's Royal Hussars	4·00	6·50
MS847	145×70 mm. £1.40, Duchess of York, 1936, and Shackleton, Scott and Wilson in the Antarctic, 1902	11·00	10·00

205 Chiloe Wigeon

1999. Waterfowl. Multicoloured.

848	9p. Type **205**	1·75	1·25
849	17p. Crested duck	2·00	1·25
850	30p. Georgian teal ("Brown Pintail")	2·75	2·50
851	35p. Versicolor teal ("Silver Teal")	2·75	2·50
852	40p. Chilean teal ("Yellow-billed Teal")	2·75	2·50
853	65p. Falkland Islands flightless steamer duck	4·50	6·50

206 Hulk of "Vicar of Bray", 1999

1999. 150th Anniv of California Goldrush. Mult.

854	9p. Type **206**	2·00	1·25
855	35p. Panning for gold, 1849	3·25	2·50
856	40p. Gold rocking cradle, 1849	3·25	2·50
857	80p. "Vicar of Bray" (barque) at sea, 1849	6·00	8·00
MS858	105×63 mm. £1 "Vicar of Bray" in San Francisco (47×31 mm)	9·50	11·00

207 Magellan Goose ("Upland Goose") on Nest

1999. New Millennium. Multicoloured.

859	9p. Type **207**	2·00	2·00
860	9p. Southern black-backed gull ("Kelp Gull") at sunrise	2·00	2·00
861	9p. Christ Church Cathedral, Stanley	2·00	2·00
862	30p. Black-crowned night heron ("Night Heron") at sunset	3·25	3·25
863	30p. Family and Christmas tree	3·25	3·25
864	30p. King penguins	3·25	3·25

208 Princess Alexandra and Meadow

2000. Visit of Princess Alexandra. Multicoloured.

865	9p. Type **208**	1·50	75
866	£1 Princess Alexandra and plantation of saplings	6·00	7·50

208a "Endurance" off Caird Coast

2000. Shackleton's Trans-Antarctic Expedition, 1914–1917, Commemoration.

867	**208a**	17p. multicoloured	3·25	1·25
868	-	45p. blue and black	5·00	3·25
869	-	75p. multicoloured	7·50	9·00

DESIGNS: 45p. "Endurance" beset in the Weddell Sea pack-ice; 75p. Sir Ernest Shackleton and "Yelcho" (Chilean resone tug).

208b Queen Elizabeth I

2000. "Stamp Show 2000" International Stamp Exhibition, London. Kings and Queens of England. Multicoloured.

870	40p. Type **208b**	2·25	2·25
871	40p. King James II	2·25	2·25
872	40p. King George I	2·25	2·25
873	40p. King William IV	2·25	2·25
874	40p. King Edward VIII	2·25	2·25
875	40p. Queen Elizabeth II	2·25	2·25

208c Wearing Fireman's helmet, 1988

2000. 18th Birthday of Prince William. Mult.

876	10p. Type **208c**	1·25	75
877	20p. At Eton, 1995	1·50	1·00
878	37p. Prince William in Cardiff, 2000 (horiz)	2·25	2·25
879	43p. Prince William in 1998 (horiz)	2·25	2·50
MS880	175×95 mm. 50p. With golden retriever, 1997 (horiz) and Nos. 876/9	9·50	10·00

2000. Queen Elizabeth the Queen Mother's 100th Birthday. No. MS847 optd 100 birthday.

MS881	145×70 mm. £1.40, Duchess of York, 1936, and Shackleton, Scott and Wilson in the Antarctic, 1902	11·00	11·00

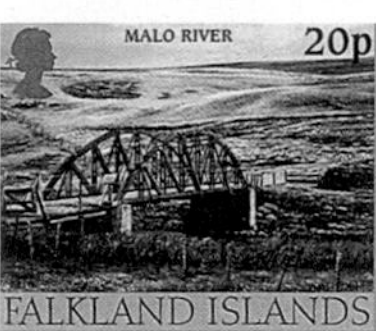

210 Malo River Bridge

2000. Bridges. Multicoloured.

882	20p. Type **210**	3·00	2·00
883	37p. Bodie Creek Bridge	4·50	4·00
884	43p. Fitzroy River Bridge	4·75	4·25

211 Shepherd with Lamb

2000. Christmas. Multicoloured.

885	10p. Type **211**	1·25	75
886	20p. Angel with Shepherds	1·90	85
887	33p. The Nativity	2·25	1·00
888	43p. Angel with Wise Men	2·50	1·25
889	78p. Camel	4·25	7·00
MS890	160×75 mm. Nos. 885/9	12·00	12·00

212 Sunset over Islands

2001. Sunrise and Sunsets. Multicoloured.

891	10p. Type **212**	1·00	1·00
892	20p. Sunset over Stanley	1·75	1·75
893	37p. Sunset over Stanley Harbour	2·50	2·50
894	43p. Sunrise over islands	2·75	3·00

213 Forster's Caracara ("Striated caracara")

2001. "HONG KONG 2001" Stamp Exhibition. Sheet 150×90 mm, containing T 213 and similar horiz design showing bird of prey. Multicoloured.

MS895	37p. Type **213**; 37p. Hodgsons hawk eagle ("Mountain hawk")	6·50	7·00

214 1878 1d. Claret Stamp

2001. Death Centenary of Queen Victoria. Multicoloured.

896	3p. Type **214**	90	1·00
897	10p. *Great Britain* (steam/sail) (horiz)	2·00	90
898	20p. Stanley Harbour, 1888 (horiz)	2·25	1·10
899	43p. Cape Pembroke Lighthouse and first telephone line, 1897	4·00	2·00
900	93p. Royal Marines, 1900	4·50	5·50
901	£1.50 "Queen Victoria, 1859" (Franz Winterhalter)	5·00	7·00
MS902	105×80 mm. £1 Queen Victoria's funeral cortege in the streets of Windsor	7·00	7·50

215 *Welfare* (first British landing on Falkland Islands, 1690)

2001. Royal Navy Connections with the Falkland Islands. Multicoloured.

903	10p. Type **215**	1·75	1·00
904	17p. H.M.S. *Invincible* (battle cruiser), 1914	2·50	1·00
905	20p. H.M.S. *Exeter* (cruiser), 1939	2·50	1·50
906	37p. SR N6 hovercraft, 1967	3·00	1·75
907	43p. H.M.S. *Protector* (ice patrol ship)	3·00	2·25
908	68p. *Desire* (Cavendish and Davis), 1592	4·25	7·00

216 Blackish Cinclodes ("Tussac Bird")

2001. Off-shore Islands (1st series). Carcass Island. Multicoloured.

909	37p. Type **216**	2·50	2·75
910	37p. Yellow violet	2·50	2·75
911	43p. Black-crowned night heron	2·75	3·00
912	43p. Carcass Island settlement	2·75	3·00

See also Nos. 941/4, 972/5, 993/6, 1025/8, 1050/3 and 1083/6.

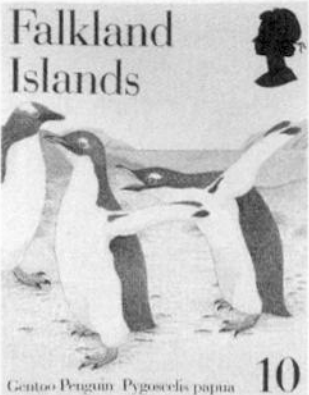

217 Young Gentoo Penguins

2001. Gentoo Penguins. Multicoloured.

913	10p. Type **217**	1·00	1·00
914	33p. Adult feeding chick	1·60	1·50
915	37p. Adult on eggs	1·75	1·75
916	43p. Group of penguins	2·00	2·25

218 Rounding-up Wild Cattle

2002. 150th Anniv of Falkland Islands Company. Multicoloured.

917	10p. Type **218**	1·00	75
918	20p. *Amelia*, (postal schooner), 1852	2·00	1·25
919	43p. F. E. Cobb (Colonial Manager), 1867	2·50	1·75
920	£1 W. W. Bertrand, (sheep farmer) and sheep dipping	4·50	6·50

219 Princess Elizabeth reading, 1945

2002. Golden Jubilee.

921	**219**	20p. agate, violet and gold	1·40	1·00
922	-	37p. multicoloured	1·90	1·25
923	-	43p. brown, violet and gold	2·00	1·50
924	-	50p. multicoloured	2·50	3·00
MS925		162×95 mm. Nos. 921/4 and 50p. multicoloured	7·00	8·00

DESIGNS—HORIZ: 37p. Queen Elizabeth, New Zealand, 1977; 43p. Princess Elizabeth with Prince Charles at his christening, 1949; 50p. Queen Elizabeth in Garter robes, Windsor, 1994. VERT (38×51 mm)—50p. Queen Elizabeth after Annigoni.

Designs as Nos. 921/4 in No. **MS**925 omit the gold frame around each stamp and the "Golden Jubilee 1952–2002" inscription.

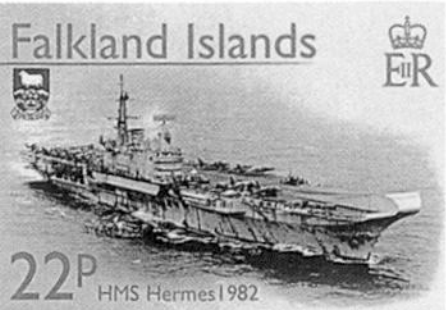

220 H.M.S. *Hermes* (aircraft carrier), 1982

2002. 20th Anniv of Liberation. Multicoloured.

926	22p. Type **220**	1·75	2·00
927	22p. *Dorada* (fishery patrol vessel), 2002	1·75	2·00
928	40p. Troops landing, 1982	2·25	2·50
929	40p. Mine clearing, 2002	2·25	2·50
930	45p. Harrier jet on H.M.S. *Hermes*, 1982	2·25	2·50
931	45p. R.A.F. Tristar, 2002	2·25	2·50

221 Queen Elizabeth visiting Royal Farms, Windsor, 1946

2002. Queen Elizabeth the Queen Mother Commemoration.

932	**221**	22p. brown, gold and purple	1·25	1·00
933	-	25p. multicoloured	1·25	1·00
934	-	95p. black, gold and purple	3·50	3·75

935	- £1.20 multicoloured	4·00	4·50
MS936	145×70 mm. Nos. 934/5	10·00	11·00

DESIGNS: 25p. Queen Mother at Guildhall lunch for Queen's Golden Wedding, 1997; 95p. Queen Elizabeth at a garden party, 1947; £1.20, Queen Mother at Scrabster, 1986.

Designs as Nos. 934/5 in No. **MS**936 omit the "1900–2002" inscription and the coloured frame.

222 Rockhopper Penguin

2002. Endangered Species. Penguins. Multicoloured.

937	36p. Type **222**	2·00	1·50
938	40p. Magellanic penguin	2·00	1·50
939	45p. Gentoo penguin	2·00	1·60
940	70p. Macaroni penguin	2·75	5·00

2002. Off-shore Islands (2nd series). West Point Island. As T 216, but horiz. Multicoloured.

941	40p. *Calandrinia feltonii* (plant)	2·25	2·50
942	40p. Black-browed albatross	2·25	2·50
943	45p. Rockhopper penguin	2·25	2·50
944	45p. West Point Island settlement	2·25	2·50

223 Prince Andrew as Naval Helicopter Pilot, 1982

2002. Visit of Duke of York to Falkland Islands.

945	**223**	22p. black and blue	2·50	2·00
946	-	£1.52 multicoloured	6·00	7·50

DESIGN: £1.52, Duke of York and San Carlos Cemetery.

224 Gun Hill Shanty, Little Chartres

2003. Shepherds' Houses. Multicoloured.

947	10p. Type **224**	80	75
948	22p. Paragon House, Lafonia	1·50	90
949	45p. Dos Lomas, Lafonia	2·00	1·50
950	£1 The Old House, Shallow Bay Farm	4·00	6·00

225 Queen Elizabeth II

2003

951	**225**	£2 black, orange and brown	6·00	6·00

226 Prince William at Queen Mother's 101st Birthday and at Eton College

2003. 21st Birthday of Prince William of Wales. Multicoloured.

952	95p. Type **226**	3·75	3·75
953	95p. With Prince Harry at polo match and at Sighthill Community Education Centre	3·75	3·75

227 Chiloe Wigeon

2003. Birds. Multicoloured.

954	1p. Type **227**	50	85
955	2p. Dolphin gull (vert)	60	1·00
956	5p. Falkland Islands flightless steamer duck	75	1·25
957	10p. Black-throated finch (vert)	1·00	1·00
958	22p. White-tufted grebe	1·50	1·00
959	25p. Rufous-chested dotterel (vert)	1·50	1·00
960	45p. Magellan goose ("Upland Goose")	2·25	1·50
961	50p. Dark-faced ground tyrant (vert)	2·25	2·25
962	95p. Black-crowned night heron	3·25	3·50
963	£1 Red-backed buzzard ("Red-backed Hawk") (vert)	3·50	3·50
964	£3 Black-necked swan	8·50	9·00
965	£5 Short-eared owl (vert)	15·00	17·00

(b) Self-adhesive.

966	(–) Rockhopper penguins	1·40	1·60

No. 966 was inscribed "Airmail Postcard".

228 Albatross on Nest

2003. Bird Life International. Black-browed Albatross. Multicoloured.

967	22p. Type **228**	1·40	1·40
968	22p. Nestling	1·40	1·40
969	40p. Adults displaying (vert)	2·50	2·00
970	£1 Immature bird (grey beak) on nest (vert)	4·75	6·50
MS971	175×80 mm. 16p. Albatrosses in flight and Nos. 967/70	12·00	13·00

2003. Off-shore Islands (3rd series). New Island. Multicoloured. As T 216, but horiz.

972	40p. Forster's caracara ("Striated Caracara")	3·25	3·25
973	40p. Lady's slipper orchids	3·25	3·25
974	45p. The Stone Cottage	3·25	3·25
975	45p. King penguin	3·25	3·25

229 Pale Maiden Flowers

2003. Christmas. National Flower. Pale Maiden (Olysnium filifolium). Multicoloured.

976	16p. Type **229**	1·50	65
977	30p. Bouquet of Pale Maiden flowers	2·50	1·10
978	40p. Pale Maiden plant	2·75	1·50
979	95p. Pale Maiden plant growing on moorland	5·00	8·00

230 Hand Shearing

2004. History of Sheep Farming in the Falklands. Multicoloured.

980	19p. Type **230**	1·75	80
981	22p. Driving flock of sheep	1·75	85
982	45p. The "Big House", Hill Cove	2·50	1·40
983	70p. Woman in Victorian-style dress	3·50	4·00
984	£1 *Fitzroy* (supply ship) collecting wool	6·50	7·50

231 Volunteer planting Tussac

2004. 25 Years of Wildlife Conservation in Falklands. Multicoloured.

985	20p. Type **231**	1·00	75
986	24p. Conservation watch group clearing debris from beach	1·00	85
987	50p. Satellite tracking of rock-hopper penguins	3·50	3·50
988	£1 Weighing black-browed albatross chick	6·00	7·00

232 Sir Rowland Hill and 1898 Falkland Islands Stamp

2004. 125th Death of Sir Rowland Hill (postal reformer). Showing Sir Rowland Hill and early Falkland Islands stamps. Multicoloured.

989	24p. Type **232**	1·75	70
990	50p.5s. King penguin (No. 136)	3·00	2·50
991	75p.5s. Southern sealion (No. 161)	4·25	4·50
992	£1 6d. HMS *Glasgow* (No. 216 error)	5·00	6·50

2004. Off-shore Islands (4th series). Sea Lion Island. As T 216 but horiz. Multicoloured.

993	42p. King cormorant	3·25	3·25
994	42p. Dog orchid	3·25	3·25
995	50p. Magellanic penguin	3·25	3·25
996	50p. Sea Lion Lodge	3·25	3·25

233 Short-eared Owl

2004. Owls. Multicoloured.

997	18p. Type **233**	1·25	80
998	45p. Short-eared owl on rock	2·00	1·40
999	50p. Barn owl in flight	3·00	2·00
1000	£1.50 Barn owl on fence	5·00	7·00
MS1001	74×54 mm. £2 Barn owl flying	9·00	9·50

234 HMS *Kent*, HMS *Inflexible* and HMS *Carnarvon*

2004. 90th Anniv of the Battle of the Falkland Islands. Multicoloured.

1002	24p. Type **234**	1·90	2·25
1003	24p. HMS *Cornwall*, HMS *Glasgow* and HMS *Invincible*	1·90	2·25
1004	24p. HMS *Invincible* and two medals	1·90	2·25
1005	50p. SMS *Scharnhorst* and two coins	3·25	3·50
1006	50p. SBS *Scharnhorst*, SMS *Leipzig* and SMS *Dresden*	3·25	3·50
1007	50p. SMS *Nurnberg* and SMS *Gneisenau*	3·25	3·50

Nos. 1002/4 and 1005/7 were each printed together, se-tenant, with the backgrounds forming composite designs.

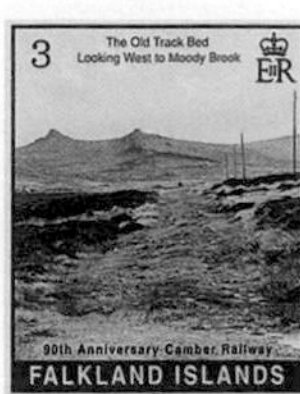

235 The Old Track Bed

2005. 90th Anniv of the Camber Railway. Multicoloured.

1008	3p. Type **235**	30	40
1009	24p. Kerr Stuart "Wren" Class locomotive at Camber depot (horiz)	1·25	65
1010	50p. Falkland Islands Express (horiz)	2·00	1·50
1011	£2 Camber Sailing Wagon	7·50	9·50

236 Prince Charles and Mrs. Camilla Parker-Bowles

2005. Royal Wedding. Multicoloured.

1012	24p. Type **236**	1·25	75
1013	50p. Prince Charles and Mrs. Camilla Parker-Bowles at evening reception (vert)	1·75	2·00
MS1014	120×65 mm. £2 Prince Charles and Mrs. Camilla Parker-Bowles and Windsor Castle	6·50	7·00

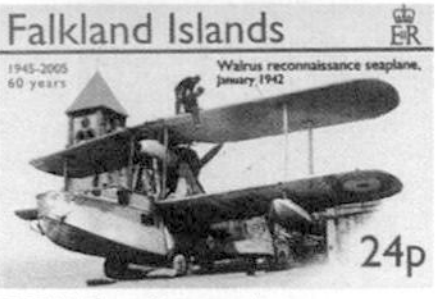

237 Walrus Reconnaissance Seaplane, 1942

2005. 60th Anniv of End of Second World War. Multicoloured.

1015	24p. Type **237**	1·75	2·00
1016	24p. Supermarine Spitfire X4616, presented to No. 92 Squadron, 1940	1·75	2·00
1017	80p. HMS *Exeter* at Port Stanley for repairs after Battle of the River Plate, 1939	3·50	3·75
1018	80p. The Governor, Rear Admiral Harwood, Captain Bell and hospital staff, 1939	3·50	3·75
1019	£1 *Fitzroy* in Antarctic, Operation Tabarin I, 1943–44	4·25	4·50
1020	£1 HMS *William Scoresby*, Operation Tabarin I, 1943–44	4·25	4·50

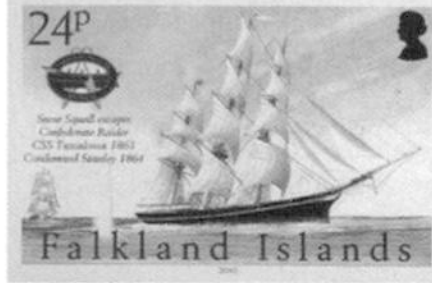

238 *Snow Squall* (clipper) pursued by CSS *Tuscaloosa*, 1863

2005. Maritime Heritage (1st series). Multicoloured.

1021	24p. Type **238**	1·25	75
1022	55p. *Charles Cooper* (North Atlantic packet)	2·25	2·50
1023	55p. *Jhelum* (barque)	2·25	2·50
1024	£1.20 *Imo* and *Mont Blanc* after collision, Halifax, Canada, 1917	3·75	4·75

2005. Off-shore Islands (5th series). Pebble Island. As T 216. Multicoloured.

1025	45p. Falkland lavender (*Perezia recurvata*)	2·50	2·50
1026	45p. Gentoo penguin	2·50	2·50
1027	55p. Black-necked swan	2·50	2·50
1028	55p. Pebble Island Lodge	2·50	2·50

239 *The Little Mermaid*

2005. Birth Bicentenary of Hans Christian Andersen (writer). Multicoloured.

1029	18p. Type **239**	1·00	70
1030	30p. *The Snowman*	1·50	1·00
1031	45p. *The Ugly Duckling*	1·75	1·50
1032	£1 *Thumbelina*	3·75	5·00

240 Wounded Nelson on Deck of HMS *Victory*

2005. Bicentenary of the Battle of Trafalgar. Sheet 110×75 mm.

MS1033	**240** £2 multicoloured	7·50	7·50

241 Black-crowned Night Heron

2006. Black-crowned Night Heron (Nycticorax cyanocephalus). Multicoloured.

1034	24p. Type **241**	1·25	90
1035	55p. Heron on seashore	2·00	2·00
1036	80p. Juvenile heron	2·25	2·75
1037	£1 Head of juvenile heron	3·25	3·75

242 Queen Elizabeth II, London, 2001

2006. 80th Birthday of Queen Elizabeth II. Multicoloured.

1038	24p. Type **242**	1·00	90
1039	55p. At Macmillan Centre, Queen Elizabeth Hospital, 2002	2·00	2·00
1040	80p. Opening Norfolk Constabulary Operations and Communications Centre, 2002	2·25	2·50
1041	£1 At Essex University, 2004	3·25	3·75
MS1042	94×64 mm. £2 Queen in 1953 and 2004 (horiz)	6·50	7·00

243 Bow of *Great Britain*

2006. Brunel's Steamship SS Great Britain. Multicoloured.

1043	24p. Type **243**	1·50	90
1044	55p. Stern of *Great Britain*	2·25	1·75
1045	£1.50 *Great Britain* in dry dock at Bristol	5·00	7·00

Nos. 1043/5 were issued on the Birth Bicentenary of Isambard Kingdom Brunel (engineer).

244 Gentoo Penguin Chicks

2006. Tourism. Seabirds. Multicoloured.

1046	25p. Type **244**	1·25	1·25
1047	25p. King cormorant landing	1·25	1·25
1048	60p. King penguin stretching	2·25	2·50
1049	60p. Wandering albatross landing on sea	2·25	2·50

2006. Off-shore Islands (6th series). Bleaker Island. As T 216. Multicoloured.

1050	50p. Head of macaroni penguin	2·25	2·50
1051	50p. Woolly Falkland ragwort	2·25	2·50
1052	60p. Long-tailed meadowlark	2·50	2·75
1053	60p. "The Outlook" (house)	2·50	2·75

245 Lt. Colonel H. Jones VC

2006. 150th Anniv of the Victoria Cross. Multicoloured.

1054	60p. Type **245**	2·00	2·25
1055	60p. Sergeant Ian McKay VC	2·00	2·25
MS1056	120×60 mm. Nos. 1054/5; £1 Victoria Cross	3·50	4·00

Stamps from No. **MS**1056 do not have white borders.

2006. As Nos. 959 and 965, and new value.

1057	20p. Black-browed albatross (vert)	1·50	1·00
1058	25p. Rufous-chested dotterel (vert)	1·50	1·00
1059	£5 Short-eared owl (vert)	16·00	18·00

246 Adult and Juvenile

2006. Endangered Species. Striated Caracara (Phalcoboenus australis). Multicoloured.

1062	25p. Type **246**	1·25	90
1063	50p. In flight	2·25	1·75
1064	60p. On ground by tussock grass clump	2·50	2·75
1065	85p. Perched on heap of shells	2·75	3·50

247 Fishermen and Fisheries Protection Ship *Dorada*

2007. 20th Anniv of Falkland Islands Fisheries. Multicoloured.

1066	3p. Type **247**	40	50
1067	11p. Night work on board ship	70	75
1068	25p. Fishermen at end of shift	1·25	1·00
1069	30p. Japanese jigger (squid fishing vessel)	1·25	1·10
1070	60p. *Dorada* on patrol	2·50	3·00
1071	£1.05 Trawler transferring catch to reefer (freezer container ship)	3·50	4·25

248 HMS *Plymouth* joins Task Force, April 1982

2007. Maritime Heritage. HMS Plymouth (Rothesay class, type 12, anti-submarine frigate, launched 1959). Multicoloured.

1072	25p. Type **248**	1·40	95
1073	40p. HMS *Plymouth* supports SBS, 26 May 1982	2·00	1·75
1074	60p. HMS *Plymouth* under attack, 8 June 1982	2·50	2·75
1075	£1.05 HMS *Plymouth* at Port Stanley, 17 June 1982	3·50	4·50

249 Vulcan Prototype VX770, 1952

2007. 25th Anniv of the Liberation of the Falkland Islands (1st issue). Vulcan Bomber. Multicoloured.

MS1076	183×89 mm. 60p.×4; Type **249**; Vulcan XM597 on "Black Buck" raids; Vulcan XM607 "Black Buck 1"; Avro Vulcan XH558 (Vulcan to the Sky Project)	9·00	10·00

250

2007. 25th Anniv of the Liberation of the Falkland Islands (2nd issue). "Lest We Forget". Multicoloured.

MS1077	Two sheets, each 210×150 mm. (a) 25p.×8 listing the fallen. (b) 60p.×8 listing the fallen	23·00	25·00

The stamps within **MS**1077a/b each show a list of 16 different names of those that fell during the Falklands conflict. Both miniature sheets have composite background designs showing Falkland Islands landscapes and sky.

251 Sea Scouts on *Discovery*, 1937

2007. 70th Anniv of the Transfer of Capt. Scott's Polar Research Ship Discovery to the Boy Scouts Association and Centenary of Scouting. Multicoloured.

1078	10p. Type **251**	70	70
1079	20p. Duke of Kent (Commodore of the Sea Scouts) and Lord Baden-Powell on board	1·10	80
1080	25p. Duke of Kent and Lord Baden-Powell inspecting sea scouts	1·25	85
1081	£2 *Discovery* moored at The Embankment, London, October 1937	6·50	8·00

252 Princess Diana walking in Minefield, Angola

2007. 10th Death Anniv of Diana, Princess of Wales.

1082	**252** 60p. multicoloured	1·90	2·25

2007. Off-shore Islands (7th series). Saunders Island. As T 216 but horiz. Multicoloured.

1083	50p. Rockhopper penguin	2·75	2·75
1084	50p. Dusty Miller (*Primula magellanica*)	2·75	2·75
1085	55p. Crested caracara	2·75	2·75
1086	55p. Ruins of earliest British settlement, Port Egmont	2·75	2·75

253 Profiles of Queen Elizabeth II and Duke of Edinburgh

2007. Diamond Wedding of Queen Elizabeth II and Duke of Edinburgh.

1087	**253** £1 grey-blue and grey	6·00	6·00

254 James Weddell and *Jane*, 1822–23

2008. International Polar Year 2007–2009. Polar Explorers. Multicoloured.

1088	4p. Type **254**	60	75
1089	25p. James Clark Ross and HMS *Erebus*, 1839–41	1·50	1·00
1090	85p. William Spiers Bruce and *Scotia*, 1902–4	4·00	4·00
1091	£1.61 James Marr and *Discovery II*	6·50	7·50

255 Elephant Seal Pup

2008. Southern Elephant Seals (Mirounga leonina). Multicoloured.

1092	27p. Type **255**	1·25	90
1093	55p. Bull seal and female	1·90	1·75
1094	65p. Young bull seals play fighting	2·50	2·50
1095	£1.10 Tussock bird searching for food in nose of young male	3·50	4·00

256 Taylorcraft Auster Mk5

2008. Aircraft. Multicoloured.

1096	1p. Type **256**	20	30
1097	2p. Boeing 747-300	20	30
1098	5p. de Havilland Canada DHC-6 Twin Otter	35	50
1099	10p. Lockheed C-130 Hercules	50	50
1100	27p. De Havilland Canada DHC-2 Beaver	1·25	75
1101	55p. Airbus A320	2·00	1·50
1102	65p. Lockheed L-1011-385-3 Tristar C2	2·50	2·50
1103	90p. Avro Vulcan B2	3·25	3·25
1104	£1 Britten-Norman BN-2 Islander	3·25	3·25
1105	£2 Panavia Tornado F.3	6·00	6·50
1106	£3 de Havilland Canada DHC-7-110 Dash 7	8·50	8·50
1107	£5 BAE Sea Harrier	14·00	14·00

2008. 90th Anniv of the Royal Air Force. Sheet 101×75 mm containing stamps as Nos. 1099, 1102/3 and 1105 but with RAF anniversary emblem at bottom left.

MS1108	10p. Lockheed C-130 Hercules; 65p. Lockheed L-1011-385-3 Tristar C2; 90p. Avro Vulcan B2; £2 Panavia Tornado F.3	14·00	15·00

257 Sailor from HMS *Clio* raising Union Flag, Port Louis, 1833

2008. 175th Anniv of Port Louis (first permanent British settlement in Falkland Islands). Multicoloured.

1109	27p. Type **257**	1·25	1·00
1110	65p. Three Royal Marines, 1833	2·00	2·25
MS1111	100×63 mm. £2 Captain Onslow overseeing flag raising ceremony, 1833	7·00	7·00

258 The Slipper

2008. Islands, Stacks and Bluffs (1st series). Multicoloured.

1112	22p. Type **258**	80	65
1113	40p. Kidney Island	1·50	1·40
1114	60p. Stephens Bluff and Castle Rock	2·25	2·50
1115	£1 The Colliers	3·50	4·00

259 *Queen Elizabeth 2*

2008. Farewell Voyage of Queen Elizabeth 2. Multicoloured.

1116	23p. Type **259**	1·25	1·00
1117	27p. *Queen Elizabeth 2* and RAF Tornado F3, Falkland Islands, 2007	1·40	1·00
1118	65p. Upper decks and funnel of *QE2* and aerial view of The Palm Jumeirah, Dubai	2·50	2·50
1119	£2 *Queen Elizabeth 2* (70×35 mm)	6·00	7·00

260 King Penguin

2008. Breeding Penguins. Multicoloured.

1120	(55p.) Type **260**	2·25	2·25
1121	(55p.) Macaroni penguin	2·25	2·25
1122	(55p.) Magellanic penguin	2·25	2·25
1123	(55p.) Rockhopper penguin	2·25	2·25
1124	(55p.) Gentoo penguin	2·25	2·25
1125	(55p.) Albino rockhopper penguin	2·25	2·25
MS1126	145×105 mm. Nos. 1120/5	12·00	12·00

Nos. 1120/5 were inscribed 'Airmail Postcard' and sold for 55p.

261 Charles Darwin

2009. Birth Bicentenary of Charles Darwin (naturalist and evolutionary theorist). Multicoloured.

1127	4p. Type **261**	50	60
1128	27p. Warrah (extinct native Falklands fox)	1·40	1·00
1129	65p. HMS *Beagle*, Berkeley Sound, 1834	2·50	2·50
1130	£1.10 Darwin encounters a Magellan penguin	3·00	3·50

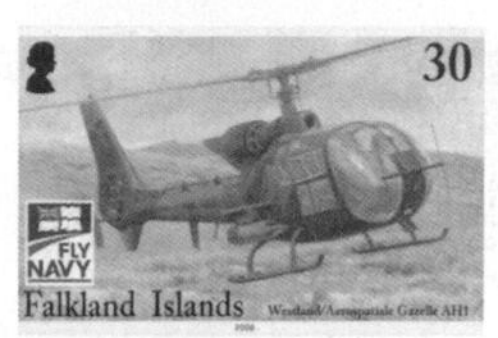

262 Westland/Aerospatiale Gazelle AH1, 1982

2009. Centenary of Naval Aviation. Multicoloured.

1131	30p. Type **262**	1·50	1·00
1132	50p. Westland Lynx HAS2 helicopter, 1982	2·50	2·25
1133	65p. Westland Wessex HU5 helicopter, 1982	3·25	3·00
1134	£1.10 Westland Sea King HAS5 helicopter, 1982	4·50	5·50
MS1135	85×62 mm. £2 BAe Sea Harrier FRS1 taking off from HMS *Hermes*, 1982	7·50	7·50

2009. Islands, Stacks and Bluffs (2nd series). As T 258. Multicoloured.

1136	27p. Seal Rocks	80	65
1137	40p. Beauchene Island	1·10	1·25
1138	65p. Jason East Cay and Steeple Jason	2·50	2·50
1139	£1.50 Horse Block	3·25	3·50

263 Black-browed Albatross

2009. Albatrosses. Multicoloured.

1140	22p. Type **263**	90	65
1141	27p. Grey-headed albatross	1·25	1·00
1142	60p. Light-mantled sooty albatross	2·50	2·50
1143	90p. Wandering albatross	3·25	3·50

264 Cobb's Wren

2009. Endangered Species. Cobb's Wren *(Troglodytes cobbi)*. Multicoloured.

1144	27p. Type **264**	80	65
1145	65p. Adult and juveniles in rock cavity nest	1·75	1·90
1146	90p. Adult singing from top of boulder	2·75	3·00
1147	£1.10 Two juveniles	3·00	3·25
MS1148	113×100 mm. As Nos. 1144/7 but with Falklands Conservation penguin emblem instead of WWF emblem	7·50	7·50

Nos. 1144/7 were also printed without a white border.

265 HMS *Exeter* (York class heavy cruiser, 1931–42)

2009. HMS Exeter. Multicoloured.

1149	4p. Type **265**	20	20
1150	20p. HMS *Exeter* (1931–42) and biplane	65	65
1151	30p. HMS *Exeter* (Type 42 destroyer, 1980–2009) (side view)	95	95
1152	£1.66 HMS *Exeter* (1980–2009) (bow view)	4·00	4·00

266 Early Morning Mist, Carcass Island (Spring)

2010. Atmospheres: Four Seasons. Multicoloured.

1153	27p. Type **266**	80	65
1154	55p. View from beach on New Island, West Falkland (Summer)	1·75	1·90
1155	65p. Rainbow over Stanley (Autumn)	2·00	1·75
1156	£1.10 Coastal scene (Winter)	3·25	3·50

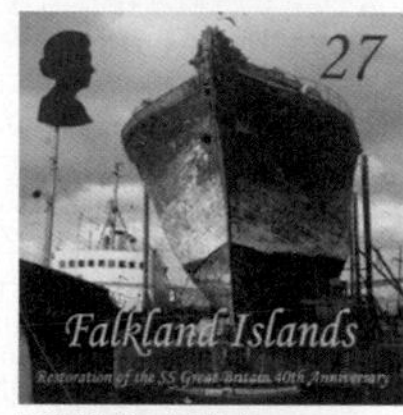

267 SS *Great Britain* on Pontoon, Stanley, 1970

2010. Restoration of the SS Great Britain. Multicoloured.

1157	27p. Type **267**	80	65
1158	50p. Beached at Sparrow Cove, Falkland Islands, 1937–70	1·50	1·25
1159	65p. Bow section	2·00	1·75
1160	£1.10 Mast and remains of rigging	3·25	3·50

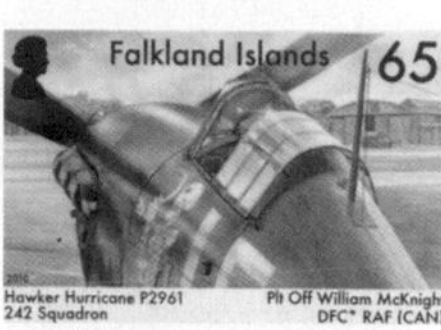

268 Hawker Hurricane P2961, 242 Squadron

2010. London 2010 Festival of Stamps. Multicoloured.

1161	65p. Type **268**	1·75	1·90
1162	65p. Supermarine Spitfire P9398, 54 Squadron	1·75	1·90
1163	65p. Hawker Hurricane P3854, 11 Group	1·75	1·90
1164	65p. Supermarine Spitfire P7350, 603 Squadron	1·75	1·90
1165	65p. Hawker Hurricane V6665, 303 Squadron	1·75	1·90
1166	65p. Supermarine Spitfire L1035, 64 Squadron	1·75	1·90
1167	65p. Hawker Hurricane P3576, 249 Squadron	1·75	1·90
1168	65p. Supermarine Spitfire X4620, 611 Squadron	1·75	1·90

Nos. 1161/8 were printed together, *se-tenant*, in sheetlets of eight, with Nos. 1167/8 forming a composite background design.

269 Sooty Shearwater

2010. Petrels and Shearwaters. Multicoloured.

1169	27p. Type **269**	80	85
1170	70p. White-chinned petrel	1·75	1·90
1171	95p. Southern giant petrel	2·75	3·00
1172	£1.15 Greater shearwater	3·25	3·50
MS1173	110x84 mm. As Nos. 1169/72	8·00	8·00

Stamps from **MS**1173 do not have white borders, the stamps and margins forming a composite design of seabirds and islands.

270 King Penguin

2010. Breeding Penguins (2nd series). Multicoloured.

1174	(60p.) Type **270**	2·00	2·10
1175	(60p.) Macaroni penguin	2·00	2·10
1176	(60p.) Rockhopper penguin	2·00	2·10
1177	(60p.) Albino rockhopper penguin	2·00	2·10
1178	(60p.) Magellanic penguin	2·00	2·10
1179	(60p.) Gentoo penguin	2·00	2·10
MS1180	150×150 mm. Nos. 1174/9	12·00	12·00

Nos. 1174/9 were inscribed 'Airmail Letter' and sold for 60p. each.

271 Fuchsia magellanica

2010. Flowering Shrubs of the Falkland Islands. Multicoloured.

1181	27p. Type **271**	80	85
1182	70p. Boxwood (*Hebe elliptica*)	1·50	1·60
1183	95p. Gorse (*Ilex europeus*)	2·50	2·75
1184	£1.15 Honeysuckle (*Lonicera periclymenum*)	3·25	3·50

272 RAF Rescue Helicopter at Mount Pleasant Airfield

2011. 70th Anniv of Royal Air Force Search and Rescue. Multicoloured.

1185	27p. Type **272**	80·00	85
1186	70p. RAF Sea King Mk 3 helicopter in flight	1·50	1·75
1187	95p. Crew in cockpit	2·50	2·75
1188	£1.15 Helicopter in flight with winchman on rope	3·25	3·50

2011. Islands, Stacks and Bluffs (3rd series). Multicoloured.

1189	3p. Bird Island	15	20
1190	27p. Eddystone Rock	80	85
1191	70p. Round Island and Sail Rock	1·75	1·90
1192	£1.71 Direction Island	4·75	5·00

273 Prince William, Miss Catherine Middleton and Westminster Abbey

2011. Royal Wedding

1193	**273**	£2 multicoloured	5·25	5·50

POSTAGE DUE STAMPS

D1 King Penguin

1991

D1	**D1**	1p. red and mauve	10	50
D2	**D1**	2p. orange and light orange	10	50
D3	**D1**	3p. ochre and yellow	15	50
D4	**D1**	4p. green and light green	20	50
D5	**D1**	5p. blue and light blue	20	50
D6	**D1**	10p. deep blue and blue	30	60
D7	**D1**	20p. violet and lilac	70	1·25
D8	**D1**	50p. green and light green	1·40	2·25

D2 Magellanic Penguins

2005. Penguins. Multicoloured.

D9	1p. Type D **2**	20	40
D10	3p. Close up of Gentoo penguin	20	40
D11	5p. King penguins	35	50
D12	10p. Rockhopper penguins on rocky beach	50	60
D13	20p. Rockhopper penguins at water's edge	1·00	1·00
D14	50p. Rockhopper penguins on rocks	1·75	1·75
D15	£1 Gentoo penguins walking on beach	3·25	3·25
D16	£2 Rockhopper penguins looking out to sea	6·00	6·50
D17	£3 Gentoo penguin coming ashore	8·50	9·00
D18	£5 Gentoo penguin in sea	14·00	15·00

Pt. 1

FALKLAND ISLANDS DEPENDENCIES

Four groups of Islands situated between the Falkland Is. and the South Pole. In 1946 the four groups ceased issuing separate issues which were replaced by a single general issue. From 1963 the stamps of British Antarctic Territory were used in all these islands except South Georgia and South Sandwich for which separate stamps were issued inscribed "SOUTH GEORGIA" from 1963 until 1980.

Under the new constitution effective on 3 October 1985, South Georgia and South Sandwich Islands ceased to be dependencies of the Falkland Islands.

1944. 12 pence = 1 shilling; 20 shillings = 1 pound.
1971. 100 (new) pence = 1 pound.

GRAHAM LAND

1944. Stamps of Falkland Islands of 1938 optd GRAHAM LAND DEPENDENCY OF.

A1	**27**	½d. black and green	30	2·00
A2	-	1d. black and violet	30	1·00
A3	-	2d. black and red	50	1·00
A4	-	3d. black and blue	50	1·00
A5	-	4d. black and purple	2·00	1·75
A6	-	6d. black and brown	21·00	2·25
A7	-	9d. black and blue	1·25	1·50
A8	-	1s. blue	1·25	1·50

SOUTH GEORGIA

1944. Stamps of Falkland Islands of 1938 optd SOUTH GEORGIA DEPENDENCY OF.

B1	**27**	½d. black and green	30	2·00
B2	-	1d. black and violet	30	1·00
B3	-	2d. black and red	50	1·00
B4	-	3d. black and blue	50	1·00
B5	-	4d. black and purple	2·00	1·75
B6	-	6d. black and brown	21·00	2·25
B7	-	9d. black and blue	1·25	1·50
B8	-	1s. blue	1·25	1·50

SOUTH ORKNEYS

1944. Stamps of Falkland Islands of 1938 optd SOUTH ORKNEYS DEPENDENCY OF.

C1	**27**	½d. black and green	30	2·00
C2	-	1d. black and violet	30	1·00
C3	-	2d. black and red	50	1·00
C4	-	3d. black and blue	50	1·00
C5	-	4d. black and purple	2·00	1·75
C6	-	6d. black and brown	21·00	2·25
C7	-	9d. black and blue	1·25	1·50
C8	-	1s. blue	1·25	1·50

SOUTH SHETLANDS

1944. Stamps of Falkland Islands of 1938 optd SOUTH SHETLAND DEPENDENCY OF.

D1	**27**	½d. black and green	30	2·00
D2	-	1d. black and violet	30	1·00
D3	-	2d. black and red	50	1·00
D4	-	3d. black and blue	50	1·00
D5	-	4d. black and purple	2·00	1·75
D6	-	6d. black and brown	21·00	2·25

D7	-	9d. black and blue	1·25	1·50
D8	-	1s. blue	1·25	1·50

GENERAL ISSUES

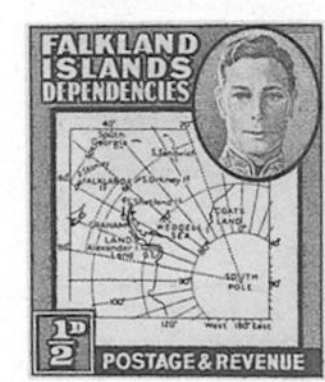

G1

1946

G1	G1	½d. black and green	1·00	3·50
G2	G1	1d. black and violet	1·25	1·75
G3	G1	2d. black and red	1·25	2·50
G11b	G1	2½d. black and blue	6·50	4·00
G4	G1	3d. black and blue	1·25	5·00
G5	G1	4d. black and red	2·25	4·75
G6	G1	6d. black and orange	3·50	5·00
G7	G1	9d. black and brown	2·00	3·75
G8	G1	1s. black and purple	2·00	4·25

1946. Victory. As T 11a of Gambia.

G17	1d. violet	50	50
G18	3d. blue	75	50

1949. Silver Wedding. As T 11b/c of Gambia.

G19	2½d. blue	1·75	3·00
G20	1s. blue	1·75	2·50

1949. U.P.U. As T 11d/g of Gambia.

G21	1d. violet	1·00	3·50
G22	2d. red	5·00	3·75
G23	3d. blue	3·50	1·25
G24	6d. orange	4·00	3·00

1953. Coronation. As T 11h of Gambia.

G25	1d. black and violet	1·10	1·25

G3 "Trepassey", 1945–47

1954. Ships.

G26	-	½d. black and green	30	4·00
G27	G3	1d. black and sepia	1·75	3·00
G28	-	1½d. black and olive	2·50	4·00
G29	-	2d. black and red	3·00	3·50
G30	-	2½d. black and yellow	1·25	35
G31	-	3d. black and blue	1·75	35
G32	-	4d. black and purple	6·00	3·25
G33	-	6d. black and lilac	7·00	3·25
G34	-	9d. black	6·50	4·00
G35	-	1s. black and brown	4·75	3·25
G36	-	2s. black and red	19·00	14·00
G37	-	2s.6d. black and turquoise	24·00	12·00
G38	-	5s. black and violet	42·00	14·00
G39	-	10s. black and blue	60·00	28·00
G40	-	£1 black	85·00	48·00

SHIPS—VERT: 1½d. "John Biscoe"; 6d. "Discovery"; 9d. "Endurance"; 2s.6d. "Francais"; 5s. "Scotia"; £1 "Belgica". HORIZ: 1½d. "Wyatt Earp"; 2d. "Eagle"; 2½d. "Penola"; 3d. "Discovery II"; 4d. "William Scoresby"; 1s. "Deutschland"; 2s. "Pourquoi pas?"; 10s. "Antarctic".

1956. Trans-Antarctic Expedition. Nos. G27, G30/1 and G33 optd TRANS-ANTARCTIC EXPEDITION 1955-1958.

G41	G3	1d. black and sepia	10	35
G42	-	2½d. black and yellow	50	60
G43	-	3d. black and blue	50	30
G44	-	6d. black and lilac	50	30

For later issues see **BRITISH ANTARCTIC TERRITORIES** and **SOUTH GEORGIA**.

ISSUES FOR SOUTH GEORGIA AND SOUTH SANDWICH ISLANDS

In 1980 stamps were again inscribed "FALKLAND ISLANDS DEPENDENCIES" for use in the above area.

28 Map of Falkland Islands Dependencies

1980. Multicoloured.. Multicoloured..

74A	1p. Type **28**	30	30
75A	2p. Shag Rocks	30	30
76A	3p. Bird and Willis Islands	30	30
77A	4p. Gulbrandsen Lake	30	30
78A	5p. King Edward Point	30	30
79A	6p. Sir Ernest Shackleton's memorial cross, Hope Point	40	30
80A	7p. Sir Ernest Shackleton's grave, Grytviken	40	40
81A	8p. Grytviken Church	30	40
82A	9p. Coaling Hulk "Louise" at Grytviken	30	45
83A	10p. Clerke Rocks	30	45
84B	20p. Candlemas Island	1·50	1·50
85B	25p. Twitcher Rock and Cook Island, Southern Thule	1·50	2·50
86A	50p. R.R.S. "John Biscoe II" in Cumberland Bay	70	1·50
87A	£1 R.R.S. "Bransfield" in Cumberland Bay	75	2·25
88A	£3 H.M.S. "Endurance" in Cumberland Bay	2·00	4·50

These stamps come with or without date imprint.

29 Magellanic Clubmoss

1981. Plants. Multicoloured.

89	3p. Type **29**	10	25
90	6p. Alphine cat's-tail	10	30
91	7p. Greater burnet	10	30
92	11p. Antarctic bedstraw	15	30
93	15p. Brown rush	15	35
94	25p. Antarctic hair grass	25	50

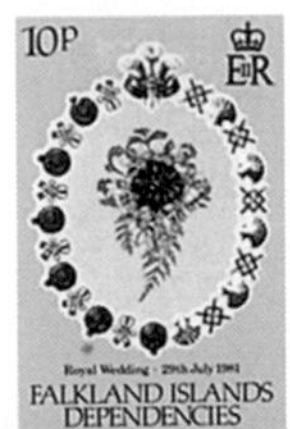

30 Wedding Bouquet from Falkland Islands Dependencies

1981. Royal Wedding. Multicoloured.

95	10p. Type **30**	15	30
96	13p. Prince Charles dressed for skiing	20	35
97	52p. Prince Charles and Lady Diana Spencer	65	85

31 Introduced Reindeer during Calving, Spring

1982. Reindeer. Multicoloured.

98	5p. Type **31**	20	65
99	13p. Bull at rut, Autumn	20	85
100	25p. Reindeer and mountains, Winter	30	1·10
101	26p. Reindeer feeding on tussock, late Winter	30	1·10

32 "Gamasellus racovitzai" (tick)

1982. Insects. Multicoloured.

102	5p. Type **32**	10	25
103	10p. "Alaskozetes antarcticus" (mite)	15	35
104	13p. "Cryptopygus antarcticus" (spring-tail)	15	40
105	15p. "Notiomaso australis" (spider)	15	40
106	25p. "Hydromedion sparsutum" (beetle)	25	50
107	26p. "Parochlus steinenii" (midge)	25	50

33 Lady Diana Spencer at Tidworth, Hampshire, July 1981

1982. 21st Birthday of Princess of Wales. Multicoloured.

108	5p. Falkland Islands Dependencies coat of arms	10	15
109	17p. Type **33**	30	35
110	37p. Bride and groom on steps of St. Paul's	35	55
111	50p. Formal portrait	75	85

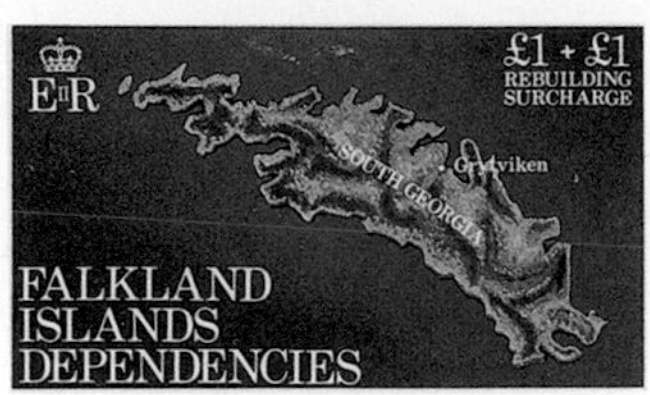

34 Map of South Georgia

1982. Rebuilding Fund.

112	34	£1+£1 multicoloured	1·50	2·75

35 Westland Whirlwind

1983. Bicentenary of Manned Flight. Multicoloured.

113	5p. Type **35**	25	35
114	13p. Westland AS-1 Wasp helicopter	35	60
115	17p. Vickers Supermarine Walrus II	35	60
116	50p. Auster Autocrat	70	1·25

36 "Euphausia superba"

1983. Crustacea. Multicoloured.

117	5p. Type **36**	40	20
118	17p. "Glyptonotus antarcticus"	50	50
119	25p. "Epimeria monodon"	60	60
120	34p. "Serolis pagenstecheri"	70	80

37 Zavodovski Island

1984. Volcanoes of South Sandwich Islands. Mult.

121	6p. Type **37**	55	80
122	17p. Mt. Michael, Saunders Island	1·25	1·40
123	22p. Bellingshausen Island	1·25	1·50
124	52p. Bristol Island	1·50	3·00

38 Grey-headed Albatross

1985. Albatrosses. Multicoloured.

125	7p. Type **38**	1·00	85
126	22p. Black-browed albatross	1·25	1·40
127	27p. Wandering albatross	1·50	1·60
128	54p. Light-mantled sooty albatross	1·75	2·50

39 The Queen Mother

1985. Life and Times of Queen Elizabeth the Queen Mother. Multicoloured.

129	7p. At Windsor Castle on Princess Elizabeth's 14th Birthday, 1940	30	30
130	22p. With Princess Anne, Lady Sarah Armstrong-Jones and Prince Edward at Trooping the Colour	60	70
131	27p. Type **39**	70	80
132	54p. With Prince Henry at his christening (from photo by Lord Snowdon)	1·25	1·40
MS133	91×73 mm. £1 Disembarking from Royal Yacht *Britannia*	2·75	2·75

1985. Early Naturalists. As T 149a of Falkland Islands. Multicoloured.

134	7p. Dumont d'Urville and "Durvillea antarctica" (kelp)	65	80
135	22p. Johann Reinhold Forster and king penguin	1·25	1·50
136	27p. Johann Georg Adam Forster and tussock grass	1·25	1·75
137	54p. Sir Joseph Banks and dove prion	1·75	2·75

For later issues see **SOUTH GEORGIA AND THE SOUTH SANDWICH ISLANDS**.

Pt. 1

FARIDKOT

A state of the Punjab, India. Now uses Indian stamps.

1879. 1 folus = 1 paisa = 1/4 anna.
1886. 2 pies = 1 anna; 16 annas = 1 rupee.

N1 (1 folus) **N2** (1 paisa)

1879. Imperf.

N5	N1	1f. blue	2·75	4·25
N6	N2	1p. blue	5·00	14·00

1887. Stamps of India (Queen Victoria) optd FARIDKOT STATE.

1	23	½a. turquoise	2·50	2·00
3	-	1a. purple	2·25	3·25
4	-	2a. blue	3·25	8·50
7	-	3a. orange	4·25	7·50
8	-	4a. green (No. 96)	10·00	20·00
11	-	6a. brown (No. 80)	2·25	21·00
12	-	8a. mauve	20·00	55·00
14	-	12a. purple on red	55·00	£500
15	-	1r. grey	45·00	£400
16	37	1r. green and red	48·00	£130
17	40	3p. red	1·75	55·00

OFFICIAL STAMPS

1886. Stamps of India (Queen Victoria) optd SERVICE FARIDKOT STATE.

O1	23	½a. turquoise	75	1·00
O2	-	1a. purple	1·00	2·75
O4	-	2a. blue	2·00	14·00
O6	-	3a. orange	7·50	14·00
O8	-	4a. green (No. 96)	5·00	38·00
O11	-	6a. brown (No. 80)	30·00	35·00
O12	-	8a. mauve	16·00	38·00
O14	-	1r. grey	60·00	£350
O15	37	1r. green and red	95·00	£850

Pt. 11

FAROE ISLANDS

A Danish possession in the North Atlantic Ocean. Under British Administration during the German Occupation of Denmark, 1940/5.

100 ore = 1 krone.

1940. Stamps of Denmark surch with new value (twice on Type 43).

2	**43**	20ore on 1ore green	45·00	65·00
3	**43**	20ore on 5ore purple	45·00	27·00
1	**40**	20ore on 15ore red	70·00	15·00
4	**43**	50ore on 5ore purple	£350	65·00
5	**43**	60ore on 6ore orange	£140	£200

2 1673 Map of the Faroe Islands **3** "Vidoy and Svinoy" (E. Nohr)

1975

6	**2**	5ore brown	25	20
7	-	10ore blue and green	25	20
8	**2**	50ore blue	25	20
9	-	60ore brown and blue	1·10	95
10	-	70ore black and blue	1·10	95
11	-	80ore brown and blue	55	55
12	**2**	90ore red	1·00	85
13	-	120ore blue and deep blue	90	45
14	-	200ore black and blue	90	85
15	-	250ore green, brown & blue	90	75
16	-	300ore green, brown & blue	5·75	2·20
17	**3**	350ore multicoloured	1·10	95
18	-	450ore multicoloured	1·10	1·10
19	-	500ore multicoloured	1·10	1·10

DESIGNS—As Type **2** but HORIZ: 10, 60, 80, 120ore Northern map (A. Ortelius); 70, 200ore West Sandoy; 250, 300ore Streymoy and Vagar. As Type **3**: 450ore "Nes" (R. Smith); 500ore "Hvitanes and Skalafjordur" (S. Joensen-Mikines).

4 Rowing Boat

1976. Inauguration of Faroese Post Office.

20	**4**	125ore red	2·00	1·40
21	-	160ore multicoloured	70	45
22	-	800ore green	2·30	1·20

DESIGNS—24×34 mm: 160ore Faroese flag. 24×31 mm: 800ore Faroese postman.

5 Motor Fishing Boat

1977. Faroese Fishing Vessels.

23	**5**	100ore black, lt green & green	5·75	4·50
24	-	125ore black, rose and red	80	75
25	-	160ore black, lt blue & blue	1·20	1·10
26	-	600ore black, ochre & brown	1·70	1·20

DESIGNS: 125ore "Niels Pauli" (inshore fishing cutter); 160ore "Krunborg" (seine fishing boat); 600ore "Polarfisk" (deep-sea trawler).

6 Common Snipe

1977. Birds. Multicoloured.

27	70ore Type **6**	35	30
28	180ore Oystercatcher	50	50
29	250ore Whimbrel	75	70

7 Atlantic Puffins over North Coast

1978. Views of Mykines Island. Multicoloured.

30	100ore Type **7**	25	25
31	130ore Mykines village (horiz)	35	35
32	140ore Cultivated fields (horiz)	55	50
33	150ore Aerial view of Mykines	45	45
34	180ore Map of Mykines (37×26 mm)	45	45

8 Northern Gannet

1978. Sea Birds. Multicoloured.

35	140ore Type **8**	75	60
36	180ore Atlantic puffin	95	90
37	400ore Common guillemot	1·20	1·10

9 Old Library Building

1978. 150th Anniv of National Library.

38	**9**	140ore olive and blue	55	55
39	-	180ore brown and flesh	70	70

DESIGN: 180ore New National Library building.

10 Guide, Tent and Campfire

1978. 50th Anniv of Girl Guides.

40	**10**	140ore multicoloured	65	60

11 Ram

1979. Sheep-rearing.

41	**11**	25k. multicoloured	6·25	3·75

12 Bisect of Denmark 4ore Blue, 1919

1979. Europa. Multicoloured.

42	**12**	140ore bl & yell on stone	60	55
43	-	180ore ol & mve on stone	70	70

DESIGN: 180ore Denmark 1919 2ore surcharge on 5ore.

13 Girl in Festive Costume

1979. International Year of the Child. Multicoloured designs showing childrens' drawings.

44	110ore Type **13**	50	45
45	150ore Man fishing from boat	50	45
46	200ore Two friends	55	50

14 Sea Plantain

1980. Flowers. Multicoloured.

47	90ore Type **14**	30	25
48	110ore Glacier buttercup	35	35
49	150ore Purple saxifrage	50	45
50	200ore Starry saxifrage	60	45
51	400ore Faroese lady's mantle	1·00	90

15 Jakob Jakobsen (linguist and folklorist)

1980. Europa.

52	**15**	150ore green	40	40
53	-	200ore brown	45	45

DESIGN: 200ore Vensel Ulrich Hammershaimb (theologian and linguist).

16 Virgin and Child

1980. Pews of Kirkjubour Church (1st series).

54	**16**	110ore multicoloured	45	35
55	-	140ore multicoloured	45	35
56	-	150ore multicoloured	45	35
57	-	200ore black and buff	50	45

DESIGNS: 140ore St. John the Baptist; 150ore St. Peter; 200ore St. Paul.

See also Nos. 90/3.

17 Timber Houses, Torshavn

1981. Old Torshavn. Designs show different views.

58	**17**	110ore green	45	35
59	-	140ore black	45	35
60	-	150ore brown	45	35
61	-	200ore blue	50	45

18 Garter Dance

1981. Europa.

62	**18**	150ore green and brown	40	40
63	-	200ore brown and green	50	45

DESIGN: 200ore Ring dance.

19 Rune Stone

1981. Historic Writings of the Faroes.

64	**19**	10ore blue, black and grey	25	15
65	-	1k. lt brown, black & brn	35	25
66	-	3k. grey, black and red	1·10	55
67	-	6k. red, black and grey	2·20	1·10
68	-	10k. stone, brown and black	2·75	2·00

DESIGNS: 1k. Score of folksong, 1846; 3k. Manuscript of Sheep Farming Law, 1298; 6k. Seal showing heraldic ram, 1533; 10k. Title page of "Faeroae et Faeroa Reserata" and library.

20 Map of Viking Voyages in North Atlantic

1982. Europa.

69	**20**	1k.50 blue	50	45
70	-	2k. black	75	70

DESIGN: 2k. Archaeological excavations at Kvivik village.

21 Gjogv

1982. Villages.

71	**21**	180ore black and blue	50	45
72	-	220ore black and brown	1·10	70
73	-	250ore black and brown	75	70

DESIGNS: 220ore Hvalvik; 250ore Kvivik.

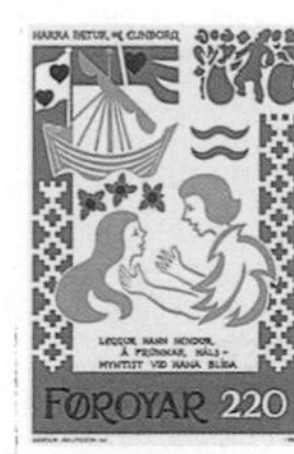

22 Elinborg's Promise to remain Faithful

1982. The Ballad of Harra Paetur and Elinborg. Multicoloured.

74	220ore Type **22**	75	55
75	250ore Elinborg longing for Paetur	75	55
76	350ore Paetur in disguise greets Elinborg	1·00	85
77	450ore Elinborg and Paetur sail away	1·30	1·10

23 "Arcturus"

1983. Old Cargo Liners on the Faroes Run. Multicoloured.

78	220ore Type **23**	65	60
79	250ore "Laura"	75	65
80	700ore "Thyra"	2·30	1·90

24 King

1983. 19th-century Chess Pieces by Pol i Bud from Nolsoy.

81	**24**	250ore brown and black	1·90	1·70
82	-	250ore blue and black	1·90	1·70

DESIGN: No. 82, Queen.

25 Niels R. Finsen (founder of phototherapy)

1983. Europa.

83	**25**	250ore blue	85	80
84	-	400ore purple	1·50	1·40

DESIGN: 400ore Sir Alexander Fleming (discoverer of penicillin).

26 Torsk

1983. Fishes. Multicoloured.

85	250ore Type **26**	75	70
86	280ore Haddock	95	90
87	500ore Atlantic halibut	1·50	1·40
88	900ore Atlantic wolffish	2·75	2·50

27 Greenland, Halsingland (Sweden) and Iceland Costumes

1983. Inauguration of Nordic House (cultural centre), Torshavn. Sheet 120×67 mm containing T 27 and similar horiz designs.

MS89	250ore Type **27**; 250ore Finnmark (Norway), Funen (Denmark) and Aland costumes; 250ore Telemark (Norway), Faroes and Ostra Nyland (Finland) costumes	11·50	12·50

1984. Pews of Kirkjubour Church (2nd series). As T 16.

90	250ore multicoloured	75	60
91	300ore lt brown, black & brn	1·30	95
92	350ore brown, grey & black	1·10	1·00
93	400ore multicoloured	1·50	1·30

DESIGNS: 250ore St. John; 300ore St. Jacob; 350ore St. Thomas; 400ore Judas Taddeus.

28 Bridge

1984. Europa. 25th Anniv of European Post and Telecommunications Conference.

94	**28**	250ore red	75	70
95	**28**	500ore blue	1·80	1·70

29 Sverri Patursson

1984. Writers.

96	**29**	200ore green	60	55
97	-	250ore red	90	80
98	-	300ore blue	95	90
99	-	450ore violet	1·50	1·40

DESIGNS: 250ore Joannes Patursson; 300ore Janus Djurhuus; 450ore Hans Andrias Djurhuus.

30 Fisherman

1984. Fishing Industry.

100		280ore blue	80	75
101		300ore brown	95	90
102	**30**	12k. green	4·00	3·75

DESIGNS—HORIZ: 280ore Fishing ketch "Westward Ho". VERT: 300ore Fishermen on deck.

31 "Beauty of the Veils"

1984. Fairy Tales. Designs showing woodcuts by Elinborg Lutzen.

103	**31**	140ore blue, green & brn	5·50	5·00
104	-	280ore green and brown	5·50	5·00
105	-	280ore dp green, grn & brn	5·50	5·00
106	-	280ore brown and green	5·50	5·00
107	-	280ore dp green, grn & brn	5·50	5·00
108	-	280ore brn, grn & dp brn	5·50	5·00

DESIGNS: No. 104, "Beauty of the Veils" (different); 105, "The Shy Prince"; 106, "The Glass Sword"; 107, "Little Elin"; 108, "The Boy and the Ox".

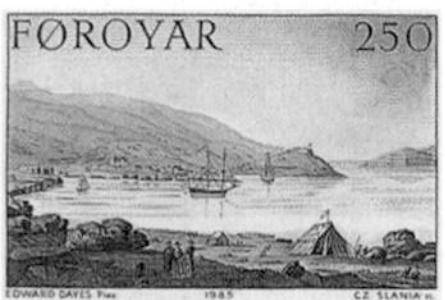

32 Torshavn

1985. J. T. Stanley's Expedition to the Faroes, 1789. Paintings by Edward Dayes.

109	**32**	250ore brown and blue	80	70
110	-	280ore brown, green & bl	95	90
111	-	550ore green, brown & bl	1·70	1·80
112	-	800ore brown, green & bl	2·75	2·50

DESIGNS: 280ore Mount Skaeling; 550ore Hoyvik; 800ore The Rocking Stones, Eysturoy.

33 Cellist, Pianist and Flautist

1985. Europa. Music Year. Multicoloured.

113	280ore Type **33**	1·20	1·10
114	550ore Drummer, guitarist and saxophonist	2·20	2·10

34 "Self-portrait" (Ruth Smith)

1985. Paintings. Multicoloured.

115	280ore "The Garden, Hoyvik" (Tummas Arge) (horiz)	1·40	1·30
116	450ore Type **34**	2·00	1·90
117	550ore "Winter's Day in Nolsoy" (Steffan Danielsen) (horiz)	2·75	2·50

35 Nolsoy Lighthouse

1985. Lighthouses. Multicoloured.

118	270ore Type **35**	1·60	1·50
119	320ore Torshavn	1·90	1·80
120	350ore Mykines	2·00	1·90
121	470ore Map of the Faroes showing lighthouse sites	2·50	2·30

36 Douglas DC-3, Faroe Airways

1985. Aircraft. Multicoloured.

122	300ore Type **36**	2·75	2·50
123	300ore Fokker F.27 Friendship, Flugfelag Islands	2·75	2·50
124	300ore Boeing 737 Special, Maersk Air	2·75	2·50
125	300ore Beech 50 Twin Bonanza, Bjorum Fly	2·75	2·50
126	300ore Bell 212 helicopter, Snipan	2·75	2·50

37 Peasant in Forest

1986. Skrimsla (dancing ballad). Mult.

127	300ore Type **37**	1·10	1·00
128	420ore Giant challenges peasant to chess game	1·80	1·60
129	550ore Peasant beats giant	2·00	1·90
130	650ore Peasant and castle	2·40	2·10

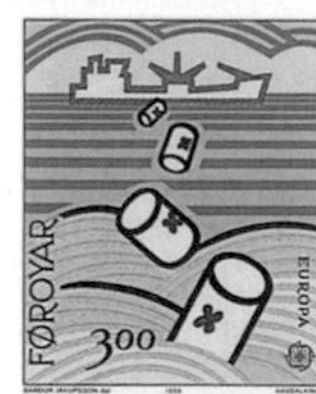

38 Ship dumping Dangerous Canisters at Sea

1986. Europa. Multicoloured.

131	3k. Type **38**	1·30	1·50
132	5k.50 Contents of damaged canister escaping into sea	2·40	2·40

39 Birds escaping from Cage

1986. 25th Anniv of Amnesty International. Multicoloured.

133	3k. Type **39**	1·50	1·40
134	4k.70 Faces (horiz)	1·80	1·70
135	5k.50 Man behind bars and woman with children	2·30	2·20

40 Ship at Anchor in Bay

1986. "Hafnia 87" International Stamp Exhibition, Copenhagen (1st issue). Sheet 108×76 mm containing T 40 and similar vert designs showing "Torshavn East Bay" (watercolour) by Christian Rosenmeyer. Multicoloured.

MS136	3k. Type **40**; 4k.70 Rowing boat in bay; 6k.50 Houses (sold at 20k.)	13·50	12·50

See also No. **MS**154.

41 Glyvrar Bridge, Eysturoy

1986. Bridges.

137	**41**	2k.70 brown	2·40	2·20
138	-	3k. blue	2·30	2·20
139	-	13k. green	5·75	5·25

DESIGNS—VERT: 3k. Leypanagjogv, Vagar. HORIZ: 13k. Skaelingur, Streymoy.

42 Farmhouse, Depli

1987. Farm Buildings.

140	**42**	300ore dp blue & blue	1·40	1·30
141	-	420ore brown & lt brown	2·75	2·50
142	-	470ore green & lt green	2·75	2·50
143	-	650ore black & grey	3·25	3·00

DESIGNS: 420ore Barn, Depli; 470ore Cowshed and blacksmith's, Frammi vid Gjonna; 650ore Farmhouse, Frammi vid Gjonna.

43 Windows

1987. Europa. Architecture. Details of Nordic House, Torshavn (by O. Steen and K. Ragnarsdottir).

144	**43**	300ore blue	1·30	1·20
145	-	550ore brown	2·40	2·30

DESIGN: 550ore Entrance.

44 "Joannes Patursson"

1987. Trawlers. Multicoloured.

146	300ore Type **44**	1·30	1·20
147	550ore "Magnus Heinason" (side trawler)	2·50	2·30
148	800ore "Sjurdarberg" (stern trawler)	4·75	4·00

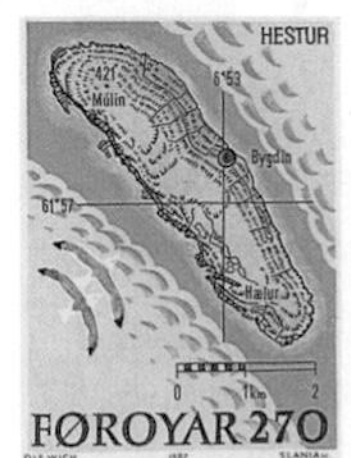

45 Map

1987. Hestur Island. Multicoloured.

149	270ore Type **45**	1·20	1·10
150	300ore Harbour (horiz)	1·10	1·00
151	420ore Alvastakkur needle	1·90	1·80
152	470ore Fagradalsvatn Lake (horiz)	2·00	1·80
153	550ore Bygdin village	2·20	2·10

46 Ships in Bay

1987. "Hafnia 87" International Stamp Exhibition, Copenhagen (2nd issue). Sheet 75×54 mm showing "Torshavn West Bay" (watercolour) by Christian Rosenmeyer.

MS154	46	3k. multicoloured (sold at 4k.)	3·75	3·50

47 "West Bay"

1987. Torshavn Views. Collages by Zacharias Heinesen. Multicoloured.

155	4k.70 "East Bay"	2·20	2·00
156	6k.50 Type **47**	3·00	2·75

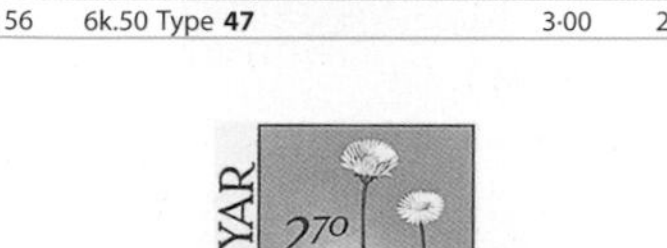

48 Daisy

1988. Flowers. Multicoloured.

157	2k.70 Type **48**	1·40	1·30
158	3k. Heath spotted orchid	1·20	1·10
159	4k.70 Tormentil	2·20	2·00
160	9k. Common butterwort	3·75	3·25

49 Container Ship and Dockside Scene

1988. Europa. Transport and Communications. Multicoloured.

161	3k. Dish aerial and satellite	1·20	1·10
162	5k.50 Type **49**	2·40	2·30

50 Jorgen-Frantz Jacobsen

1988. Writers.

163	**50**	270ore green	1·70	1·50
164	-	300ore red	1·10	1·00
165	-	470ore blue	1·90	1·80
166	-	650ore brown	3·00	2·75

DESIGNS: 300ore Christian Matras; 470ore William Heinesen; 650ore Hedin Bru.

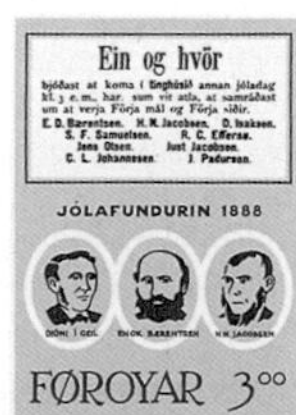

51 Notice of Christmas Meeting and Conveners

1988. Centenary of Christmas Meeting to Establish National Movement. Multicoloured.

167	3k. Type **51**	1·10	1·00
168	3k.20 Drawing by William Heinesen of a People's Meeting, 1908, and conveners	1·60	1·50
169	12k. Opening words of Joannes Patursson's poem "Now the Hour has Come", conveners and oystercatcher	5·25	5·00

52 Exterior View of Cathedral

1988. Kirkjubour Cathedral Ruins.

170	**52**	270ore green	2·40	2·20
171	-	300ore blue	1·40	1·30
172	-	470ore brown	2·40	2·10
173	-	550ore purple	2·75	2·20

DESIGNS—VERT: 300ore Window; 470ore Crucifixion (relief). HORIZ: 550ore Nave.

53 Church

1989. Bicentenary of Torshavn Church.

174	**53**	350ore green	1·40	1·30
175	-	500ore brown	2·30	2·20
176	-	15k. blue	6·00	5·25

DESIGNS—VERT: 500ore "The Last Supper" (altarpiece); 15k. Bell from "Norske Love" (shipwreck).

54 Wooden Toy Boat

1989. Europa. Children's Toys. Multicoloured.

177	3k.50 Type **54**	1·30	1·40
178	6k. Wooden horse	2·40	2·30

55 Sjostuka Man

1989. Nordic Countries' Postal Co-operation. Traditional Costumes. Multicoloured.

179	350ore Type **55**	1·30	1·40
180	600ore Stakkur woman	2·20	2·30

56 Rowing

1989. Sports. Multicoloured.

181	200ore Type **56**	1·10	1·00
182	350ore Handball	1·50	1·40
183	600ore Football	2·50	2·30
184	700ore Swimming	3·00	2·75

57 Tvoran

1989. Bird Cliffs of Suduroy. Each brown, green and blue.

185	320ore Type **57**	1·20	1·10
186	350ore Skuvanes	1·50	1·30
187	500ore Beinisvord	1·90	1·80
188	600ore Asmundarstakkur	2·75	2·50

58 Unloading Boxes of Fish from Trawler

1990. Fish Processing Industry. Mult.

189	3k.50 Type **58**	1·20	1·10
190	3k.70 Cleaning Atlantic cod	1·50	1·30
191	5k. Filleting fish	2·40	2·00
192	7k. Packed processed fish	2·75	2·50

59 Old Post Office, Gjogv

1990. Europa. Post Office Buildings. Mult.

193	3k.50 Type **59**	1·90	1·80
194	6k. Klaksvik post office	2·75	2·50

60 Faroese Flag

1990. 50th Anniv of Official Recognition of Faroese Flag. Sheet 116×75 mm containing T 60 and similar vert designs. Multicoloured.

MS195	3k.50 Type **60**; 3k.50 "Nyggjaberg" (trawler); 3k.50 "Sanna" (schooner)	5·50	5·00

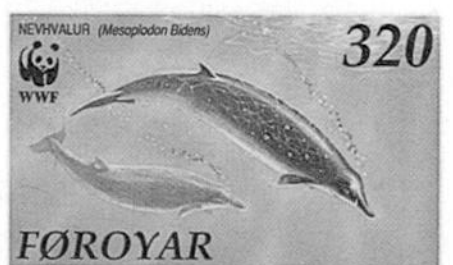

61 Sowerby's Beaked Whale

1990. Whales. Multicoloured.

196	320ore Type **61**	1·60	1·50
197	350ore Bowhead whale	1·80	1·60
198	600ore Black right whale	2·75	2·20
199	700ore Northern bottle-nosed whale	3·50	3·00

62 Nolsoy from Hilltop

1990. Nolsoy. Paintings by Steffan Danielsen. Multicoloured.

200	50ore Type **62**	20	25
201	350ore Church	1·20	1·00
202	500ore Village	2·20	2·00
203	1000ore Cliffs by moonlight	4·25	3·75

63 Ribwort Plantain

1991. Anthropochora. Multicoloured.

204	3k.70 Type **63**	1·80	1·50
205	4k. Northern dock	2·40	1·90
206	4k.50 Black beetle	3·25	2·20
207	6k.50 Earthworm	3·50	3·00

64 Town Hall

1991. 125th Anniv of Torshavn as Capital. Multicoloured.

208	3k.70 Type **64**	1·60	1·70
209	3k.70 Eastern Tinganes (old part of Torshavn)	1·60	1·70

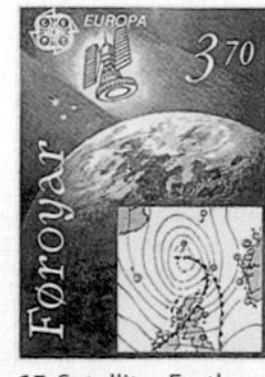

65 Satellite, Earth and Weather Map

1991. Europa. Europe in Space. Mult.

210	3k.70 Type **65**	1·60	1·40
211	5k.50 Chart of Plough constellation and Pole Star, and sailors navigating by stars	2·50	2·50

66 Arctic Terns

1991. Birds. Multicoloured.

212	3k.70 Type **66**	1·80	1·40
213	3k.70 Black-legged kittiwakes	1·80	1·40

67 Saksun

1991. Nordic Countries' Postal Co-operation. Tourism. Multicoloured.

214	370ore Type **67**	1·30	1·20
215	650ore Vestmanna cliffs	2·50	2·30

68 "Handanagardur"

1991. 85th Birth Anniv of Samal Joensen-Mikines (painter). Multicoloured.

216	340ore "Funeral Procession"	1·70	1·40
217	370ore "The Farewell"	1·60	1·30
218	550ore Type **68**	2·10	1·70
219	1300ore "Winter Morning"	5·75	4·25

69 "Ruth"

1991. Mail Ships. Multicoloured.

220	200ore Type **69**	1·10	1·00
221	370ore "Ritan"	1·60	1·10
222	550ore "Sigmundur"	2·40	1·50
223	800ore "Masin"	3·25	2·50

70 Map and Viking Ship (Leif Eriksson)

1992. Europa. 500th Anniv of Discovery of America by Columbus. Multicoloured.

224	3k.70 Type **70**	2·50	2·00
225	6k.50 Map and "Santa Maria"	3·00	2·50

MS226		85×67 mm. Nos. 224/5	5·50	4·50

71 Grey Seal ("Halichoerus grypus")

1992. Seals. Multicoloured.

227		3k.70 Type **71**	1·60	1·30
228		3k.70 Common seal ("Phoca vitulina")	1·60	1·30

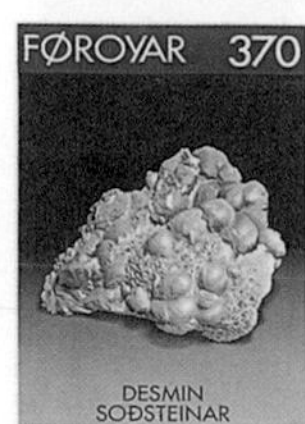

72 Desmine

1992. Minerals. Multicoloured.

229		370ore Type **72**	1·60	1·40
230		650ore Mesolite	2·40	2·30

73 Glyvra Hanus's House

1992. Old Houses in Nordragota, Eysturoy. Multicoloured.

231		3k.40 Type **73**	1·40	1·20
232		3k.70 Village and church	1·70	1·40
233		6k.50 Blasastova	3·00	2·30
234		8k. Jakupsstova	3·25	2·50

74 Musicians at Jazz, Folk and Blues Festival

1993. 10th Anniv of Nordic House, Torshavn. Multicoloured.

235		400ore "The Lost Musicians" (William Heinesen)	1·60	1·30
236		400ore Joannes Andreassen (pianist)	1·60	1·30
237		400ore Type **74**	1·60	1·30
MS238		140×80 mm. Nos. 235/7	6·00	5·75

75 Landscape

1993. Nordic Countries' Postal Co-operation. Gjogv. Multicoloured.

239		4k. Type **75**	1·50	1·40
240		4k. Village	1·50	1·40

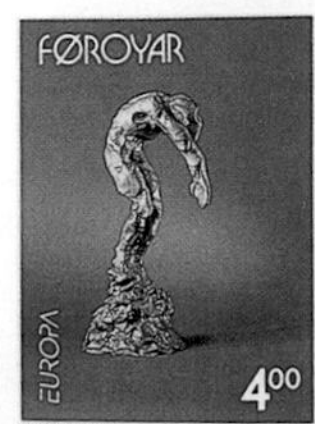

76 "Reflection"

1993. Europa. Contemporary Art. Bronzes by Hans Pauli Olsen. Multicoloured.

241		4k. Type **76**	1·70	1·30
242		7k. "Movement"	2·40	2·30

77 Horse's Head

1993. Horses.

243	**77**	400ore brown	1·40	1·30
244	-	20k. lilac	7·00	6·00

DESIGN—HORIZ: 20k. Mare and foal.

78 "Apamea zeta"

1993. Butterflies and Moths. Multicoloured.

245		350ore Type **78**	1·60	1·20
246		400ore "Hepialus humuli"	1·60	1·50
247		700ore Red admiral	3·00	2·30
248		900ore "Perizoma albulata"	3·75	2·75

79 Three-spined Stickleback

1994. Fishes. Multicoloured.

249		10ore Type **79**	20	15
250		4k. False boarfish	1·80	1·40
251		7k. Brown trout	2·40	2·00
252		10k. Orange roughy	5·00	3·25

80 St. Brendan discovering Faroe Islands

1994. Europa. St. Brendan's Voyages. Mult.

253		4k. Type **80**	1·60	1·30
254		7k. St. Brendan visiting Iceland	2·40	2·00
MS255		81×76 mm. Nos. 253/4	8·00	5·75

81 Sailing Ship and Sailor using Sextant

1994. Centenary (1993) of Faroese Nautical School, Torshavn. Multicoloured.

256		3k.50 Type **81**	1·90	1·50
257		7k. Modern ship and sailor using modern equipment	2·40	2·10

82 Dog and Sheep

1994. Sheepdogs. Multicoloured.

258		4k. Type **82**	1·60	1·50
259		4k. Dog's head (18×25 mm)	1·60	1·50

83 Viking Ship

1994. "Brusajokil's Lay" (traditional song). Multicoloured.

260		1k. Type **83**	35	30
261		4k. Asbjorn at entrance to Brusajokil's cave	1·60	1·30
262		6k. Trolls appearing after Ormar had killed cat	2·10	1·90
263		7k. Ormar pulling off Brusajokil's beard	2·75	2·50

84 First to Tenth Days

1994. Christmas. Designs illustrating "On the First Day of Christmas St. Martin gave to Me". Multicoloured.

264		400ore Type **84**	1·50	1·40
265		400ore 11th to 15th days	1·50	1·40

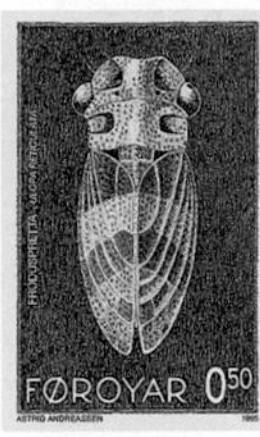

85 "Ulopa reticulata"

1995. Leafhoppers. Multicoloured.

266		50ore Type **85**	25	25
267		4k. "Streptanus sordidus"	1·40	1·30
268		5k. "Anoscopus flavostriatus"	1·60	1·50
269		13k. "Macrosteles alpinus"	5·00	4·25

86 Vatnsdalur

1995. Nordic Countries' Postal Co-operation. Tourism. Multicoloured.

270		400ore Type **86**	1·60	1·30
271		400ore Fomjin	1·60	1·30

87 Vidar, Vali and Baldur

1995. Europa. Peace and Freedom. Mult.

272		4k. Type **87**	1·50	1·40
273		7k. Liv and Livtrasir	2·75	2·50

88 Museum of Art, Torshavn

1995. 50th Anniv of Nordic Artists Association. Multicoloured.

274		2k. Type **88**	80	70
275		4k. "Woman" (Frimod Joensen) (vert)	1·50	1·40
276		5k.50 Self-portrait (Joensen) (vert)	2·20	2·00

89 Common Raven

1995. The Raven. Multicoloured.

277		400ore Type **89**	1·50	1·30
278		400ore White speckled raven	1·50	1·30

90 St. Olaf

1995. Birth Millenary of St. Olaf.

279	**90**	4k. multicoloured	1·50	1·30

91 Dairy Maids

1995. Rural Life.

280	**91**	4k. green	1·50	1·30
281	-	6k. brown	2·50	1·90
282	-	15k. blue	5·00	4·75

DESIGNS—VERT: 6k. Sheep shearing; 15k. Fishermen.

92 St. Mary's Catholic Church

1995. Christmas. Multicoloured.

283		400ore Type **92**	1·60	1·50
284		400ore Stained glass window, St. Mary's Church	1·60	1·50

93 Risin and Kellingin (rocks)

1996

285	**93**	450ore multicoloured	1·50	1·40

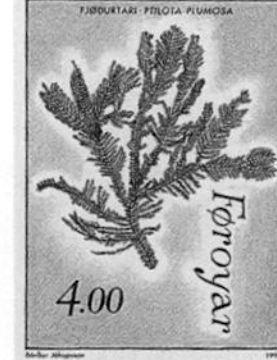

94 "Ptilota plumosa"

1996. Seaweed. Multicoloured.

286		4k. Type **94**	1·50	1·20
287		5k.50 Flat wrack	2·20	1·60
288		6k. Knotted wrack	2·40	2·00
289		9k. Forest kelp	3·00	2·40

95 "Young Girl"

1996. Europa. Famous Women. Paintings by Samal Joensen-Mikines. Multicoloured.

290		4k.50 Type **95**	1·60	1·40
291		7k.50 "Old Woman" (vert)	2·75	2·20

96 Bohemian Waxwing

1996. Birds (1st series). Multicoloured.

292	4k.50 Type **96**	1·50	1·40
293	4k.50 Red crossbill ("Loxia curvirostra")	1·50	1·40

See also Nos. 321/2, 336/7 and 355/6.

97 Faroe Islands and Compass Rose

1996. Maps.

301	**97**	10k. multicoloured	2·40	2·40
302	**97**	11k. multicoloured	2·75	2·50
303	**97**	14k. multicoloured	3·50	3·50
304	**97**	15k. multicoloured	3·75	3·50
305	**97**	16k. multicoloured	4·25	4·25
306	**97**	18k. multicoloured	4·25	4·50
309	**97**	22k. multicoloured	5·25	5·00

98 Boy Playing with Hoop (Bugvi)

1996. "Nordatlantex 96" Stamp Exhibition, Torshavn. Children's Drawings. Sheet 98×61 mm containing T 98 and similar vert designs. Mult.

MS314	4k.50 Type **98**; 4k.50 Girls and traffic lights (Gudrid); 4k.50 Street and child on bicycle (Herborg)	4·75	4·50

99 "Flock of Sheep"

1996. Paintings by Janus Kamban. Mult.

315	4k.50 Type **99**	1·50	1·40
316	6k.50 "Fishermen on way Home"	2·00	1·80
317	7k.50 "View from Torshavn's Old Quarter"	2·40	2·30

100 Klaksvik Church

1996. Christmas. Multicoloured.

318	4k.50 Type **100**	1·50	1·30
319	4k.50 Altarpiece depicting biblical scenes (21×38 mm)	1·50	1·30

101 Queen Margrethe in Faroese National Costume

1997. Silver Jubilee of Queen Margrethe. Sheet 81×61 mm.

MS320	**101** 450ore multicoloured	3·00	2·75

1997. Birds (2nd series). As T 96. Mult.

321	4k.50 Redpolls ("Carduelis flammea")	1·30	1·20
322	4k.50 Northern bullfinches ("Pyrrhula pyrrhula")	1·30	1·20

102 "Hygrocybe helobia"

1997. Fungi. Multicoloured.

323	4k.50 Type **102**	1·50	1·30
324	6k. "Hygrocybe chlorophana"	2·20	1·60
325	6k.50 Snowy wax cap	2·30	2·00
326	7k.50 Parrot wax cap	2·50	2·20

103 Seal

1997. 600th Anniv of Kalmar Union (of Denmark, Norway and Sweden).

327	**103**	4k.50 violet	1·30	1·20

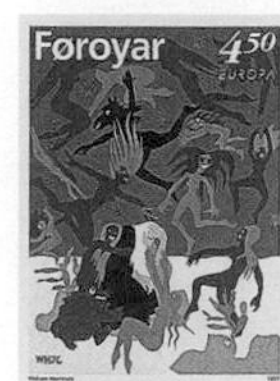

104 "Temptations of Saint Anthony"

1997. Europa. Tales and Legends. Illustrations by William Heinesen. Multicoloured.

328	4k.50 Type **104**	1·60	1·30
329	7k.50 "The Merman" (eating fish bait)	2·75	2·20

105 Hvalvik Church

1997. Christmas. Multicoloured.

330	4k.50 Type **105**	1·30	1·20
331	4k.50 Church interior	1·30	1·20

106 Arrival of Poul Aggerso

1997. "Barbara" (film from novel by Jorgen-Frantz Jacobsen). Scenes from the film. Multicoloured.

332	4k.50 Type **106**	1·30	1·20
333	6k.50 Annike van der Lippe and Lars Simonsen as Barbara and Aggerso	1·90	1·80
334	7k.50 Barbara and men in boat	2·40	2·00
335	9k. Barbara in rowing boat	2·75	2·50

107 Blackbird

1998. Birds (3rd series). Multicoloured.

336	4k.50 Type **107**	1·30	1·20
337	4k.50 Common starling ("Sturnus vulgaris")	1·30	1·20

108 Wall of Fire around King Budle and Brynhild

1998. "Brynhild's Ballad" (traditional poem). Multicoloured.

338	450ore Type **108**	1·30	1·20
339	650ore Sigurd on his horse Grane jumps through the flames	1·80	1·60
340	750ore Golden rings around Sigurd and Brynhild	2·10	2·00
341	1000ore Gudrun (Sigurd's widow) leading Grane	3·00	2·75

109 Atlantic White-sided Dolphin

1998. International Year of the Ocean. Whales and Dolphins. Multicoloured.

342	4k. Type **109**	1·20	1·10
343	4k.50 Killer whale	1·30	1·20
344	7k. Bottle-nosed dolphin	2·40	1·90
345	9k. White whale	2·75	2·50

110 Procession with Flags

1998. Europa. National Festivals. St. Olav's Day. Multicoloured.

346	4k.50 Type **110**	1·30	1·20
347	7k.50 Members of Parliament and clergy processing through the streets	2·30	2·10

111 Hands cradling Family

1998. 50th Anniv of Universal Declaration of Human Rights.

348	**111**	750ore multicoloured	2·10	2·00

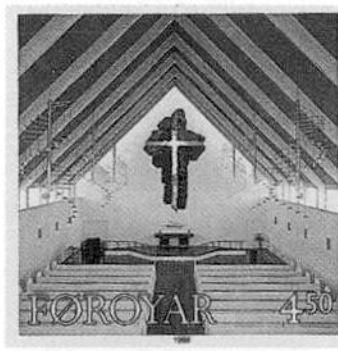

112 Interior of Frederik's Church, Nes

1998. Christmas. Multicoloured.

349	4k.50 Type **112**	1·30	1·20
350	4k.50 Exterior of church	1·30	1·20

113 "Hagamynd"

1998. Paintings by Hans Hansen. Mult.

351	4k.50 Type **113**	1·30	1·20
352	5k.50 "Bygdarmynd"	1·80	1·50
353	6k.50 "Portrait of a Man"	1·90	1·70
354	8k. "Self-portrait"	2·75	2·10

114 Winter Wren

1999. Birds (4th series). Multicoloured.

355	4k.50 Type **114**	1·20	1·10
356	4k.50 House sparrow ("Passer domesticus")	1·20	1·10

115 "Smiril" (ferry), 1896

1999. Suduroy–Torshavn Passenger Ferries. Mult.

357	4k.50 Type **115**	1·10	1·00
358	5k. "Smiril", 1932	1·30	1·30
359	8k. "Smyril", 1967	2·20	2·00
360	13k. "Smyril" (car ferry), 1975	3·50	3·50

116 Kalsoy

1999. Islands of the Faroes. Multicoloured.

361	50ore Type **116**	25	20
362	100ore Vidoy	25	25
363	200ore Skuvoy	60	60
365	400ore Svinoy	1·20	1·10
366	450ore 50 Fugloy	1·60	1·30
367	500ore Bour	1·60	1·30
368	500ore Gasadalur	1·60	1·30
368a	550ore Stora Dimun	1·70	1·30
369	600ore Kunoy	1·60	1·50
370	650ore Hestoy	2·00	1·40
370a	700ore Litla Dimun	1·90	1·60
371	750ore Koltur	2·30	1·70
372	800ore Bardoy	2·30	2·20
375	1000ore Nolsoy	3·25	2·30

117 Svartifossur, Hoydalar

1999. Europa. Waterfalls. Multicoloured.

379	6k. Type **117**	1·80	1·60
380	8k. Foldarafossur, Hov	2·10	2·10

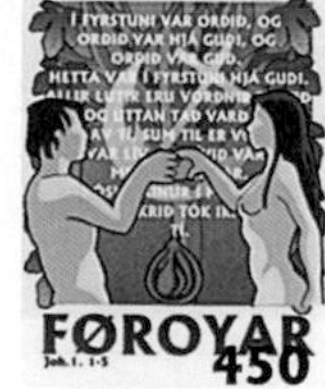

118 Adam and Eve

1999. Christmas. Multicoloured.

381	450ore Type **118**	1·30	1·20
382	600ore The Annunciation	1·70	1·60

119 "Bygd"

1999. Paintings by Ingalvur av Renyi. Mult.

383	4k.50 Type **119**	1·20	1·10
384	6k. "Husavik"	1·70	1·40
385	8k. "Reytt regn" (vert)	1·90	1·90
386	20k. "Genta" (vert)	4·50	4·50

120 Rasmus Rasmussen and Simun av Skardi (founders)

2000. Centenary (1999) of Folk High School, Torshavn. Multicoloured.

387	4k.50 Type **120**	1·30	1·10
388	4k.50 Sanna av Skardi and Anna Suffia Rasmussen (housekeepers and teachers)	1·30	1·10

121 Arrival of Sigmundur

2000. One Thousand Years of Christianity on the Faroe Islands. Multicoloured.

389	4k.50 Type **121**	1·20	1·10
390	5k.50 Killing of bishop by rebels	1·30	1·20
391	8k. People with flags of Denmark and Faroe Islands	1·90	1·80
392	16k. Children on shore and sun rising	4·25	3·75

122 "Building Europe"

2000. Europa.

393	**122**	8k. multicoloured	2·10	1·90

123 Girl unlocking Door by Remote Control and House (Katrin Mortensen)

2000. "Stampin' the Future". Winning Entries in Children's International Painting Competition Multicoloured.

394	4k. Type **123**	1·00	95
395	4k.50 Boy dreaming of future (Sigga Andreassen)	1·20	1·10
396	6k. Offshore oil rig (Steingrimur Joensen)	1·50	1·40
397	8k. Spaceman and television (Dion Dam Frandsen)	2·10	1·80

124 Mary and Joseph

2000. Christmas. Multicoloured.

398	4k.50 Type **124**	1·20	1·10
399	6k. Mary holding Jesus	1·50	1·40

125 Apostle holding Cross

2001. Pew Gables, St. Olav's Church, Kirkjubour.

400	**125**	450ore buff, black & grey	1·40	1·40
401	-	650ore buff, black & cinn	1·70	1·60
402	-	800ore buff, black & grn	3·00	2·75
403	-	18k. buff, black and brown	6·50	6·00

DESIGNS: 650ore Apostle holding knife; 800ore Apostle holding book in right hand; 18k. Apostle holding book in left hand.

126 Elderly Woman

2001. 75th Anniv of Faroese Red Cross. Multicoloured.

404	4k.50 Type **126**	1·10	1·00
405	6k. Red Cross volunteers carrying patient on stretcher	1·40	1·30

127 Skjuts (early postal service) Boat

2001. 25th Anniv of Faroese Postal Administration. Sheet 138×101 mm containing T **127** and similar vert designs. Each buff, black and silver.

MS406	4k.50 Type **127**; 4k.50 First Post Office, Torshavn; 4k50 Postman	4·25	4·00

128 Hognis and Tidrik Tattneson ("Hognis Ballad")

2001. Nordic Myths and Legends. Multicoloured.

407	6k. Type **128**	1·50	1·40
408	6k. Tree and birds nests ("The Tree of the Year")	1·50	1·40
409	6k. Woman beside river ("The Harp")	1·50	1·40
410	6k. Sigurd the Dragonslayer's horse Grane and sword Gram	1·50	1·40
411	6k. Sigurd fighting dragon ("Ballad of Nornagest")	1·50	1·40
412	6k. Hogni Jukeson and brothers on ship ("Hognis Ballad")	1·50	1·40

129 Hydro-electric Power Station, Fossaverkio, Vestmanna

2001. Europa. Water Resources. Multicoloured.

413	6k. Type **129**	1·80	1·60
414	8k. Hydro-electric power station, Eidisverkio, Eysturoy	2·30	2·20

130 "The Artist's Mother"

2001. Paintings by Zacharias Heinesen. Multicoloured.

415	4k. Type **130**	1·00	95
416	4k.50 "Uti a Reyni"	1·20	1·10
417	10k. "Ur Vagunum"	2·75	2·50
418	15k. "Sunrise"	4·00	3·75

131 Sperm Whale (*Physeter macrocephalusi*)

2001. Whales. Multicoloured.

419	4k.50 Type **131**	1·20	1·10
420	6k.50 Fin whales (*Balaenoptera physalus*)	1·80	1·70
421	9k. Blue whales (*Balaenoptera musculus*)	2·30	2·20
422	20k. Sei whales (*Balaenoptera borealis*)	5·25	4·75

132 Simeon and Mary

2001. Christmas. Multicoloured.

423	5k. Type **132**	1·30	1·20
424	6k.50 Flight into Egypt	1·70	1·60

133 Atlantic Bob-tailed Squid (*Sepiola atlantica*)

2002. Molluscs. Multicoloured.

425	5k. Type **133**	1·30	1·20
426	7k. Horse mussel (*Modiolus modiolus*)	1·70	1·60
427	7k.50 Sea slug (*Polycera faeroensis*)	1·80	1·70
428	18k. Common northern whelk (*Buccinum undatum*)	4·25	4·00

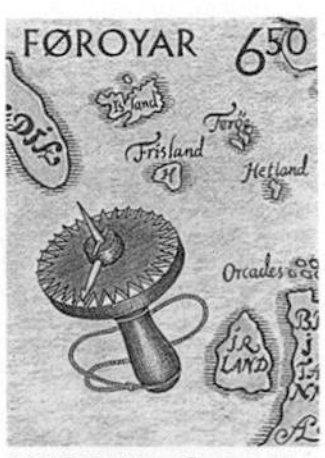

134 Primitive Compass

2002. Viking Voyages. Sheet 160×70 mm containing T **134** and similar vert designs. Multicoloured.

MS429	6k.50 Type **134**; 6k.50 Viking sailor using compass; 6k.50 Viking ship	6·00	5·75

135 "Depths of the Ocean"

2002. Nordic Countries' Postal Co-operation. Art by Trondur Patursson. Multicoloured.

430	5k. Type **135**	1·30	1·20
431	6k.50 "Cosmic Space"	1·60	1·50

136 Clowns (Anna Katrina Olsen)

2002. Europa. Circus. Showing winning designs in children's painting competition. Multicoloured.

432	6k.50 Type **136**	1·70	1·50
433	8k. Animals in Circus Tent (Sara Zachariasardottir)	2·00	1·80

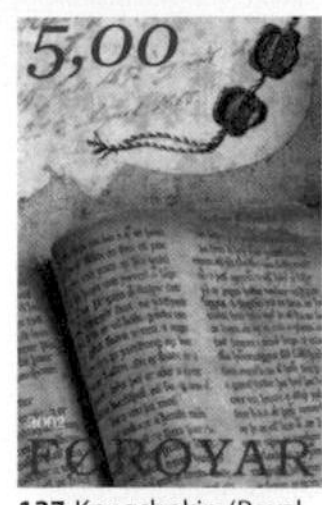

137 Kongsbokin (Royal Book)

2002. 150th Anniv of Foroya Logting (Faroese Representative Council). Sheet 100×70 mm containing T **137** and similar vert design. Multicoloured.

MS434	5k. Type **137**; 6k.50, Introduction of the 1852 Logting protocol	3·75	3·50

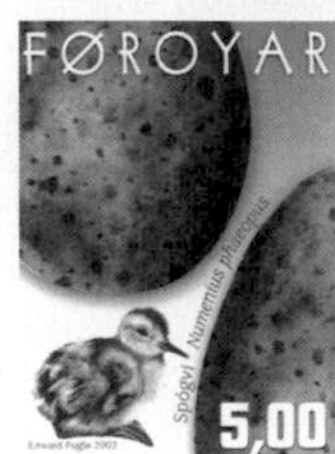

138 Whimbrel (*Numenius phaeopus*)

2002. Birds. Showing chicks and eggs. Multicoloured.

435	5k. Type **138**	1·30	1·20
436	7k.50 Common snipe (*Gallinago gallinago*)	1·80	1·70
437	12k. Oystercatcher (*Haematopus ostralegus*)	3·00	2·75
438	20k. Golden plover (*Pluvialis apricaria*)	5·25	4·75

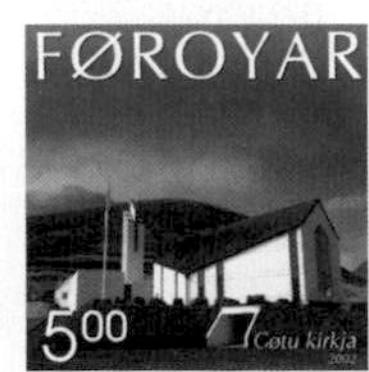

139 Church

2002. Gøta Church. Multicoloured.

439	5k. Type **139**	1·40	1·30
440	6k.50 Church interior	1·80	1·70

140 Cliffs and Blue Whiting (*Micromesistius poutassou*)

2002. Centenary of International Council for the Exploration of the Sea. Sheet 186×61 mm, containing T 140 and similar vert design. Multicoloured.

MS441 8k. Type **140**; 8k. *Magnus Heinason* (trawler) and blue whiting 4·75 4·50

Stamps of a similar design were issued by Denmark and Greenland.

141 Male Merlin (*Falco columbarius subaesalon*)

2002

442 **141** 30k. multicoloured 8·00 7·50

142 Engine Drilling

2003. Completion of Vagatunnilin (tunnel under Vestmannasund). Multicoloured.

443 5k. Type **142** 1·40 1·30
444 5k. Miners and equipment 1·40 1·30

143 Heid

2003. Norse Myths and Legends. Voluspa. Multicoloured.

445 6k.50 Type **143** 1·50 1·40
446 6k.50 Creation of the universe 1·50 1·40
447 6k.50 Creation of humans 1·50 1·40
448 6k.50 Norns (deities of fate) and Yggdrasil (world tree) 1·50 1·40
449 6k.50 Thor with raised hammer 1·50 1·40
450 6k.50 Odin hurling spear 1·50 1·40
451 6k.50 Baldur dying and his infant brother Hodlyn 1·50 1·40
452 6k.50 Ship and Nidhog (giant serpent) 1·50 1·40
453 6k.50 Hodlyn killing serpent 1·50 1·40
454 6k.50 Hodur and Baldur 1·50 1·40

144 "Omma Ludvik"

2003. Children's Songs. Sheet 166×80 mm containing T 144 and similar vert designs. Multicoloured.

MS455 5k.×10, Type **144** and nine different designs depicting children's songs 12·50 11·50

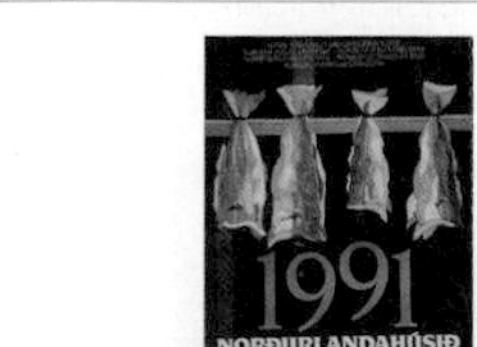

145 "Fish Tree" (tapestry) (Astrid Andreasen)

2003. Europa. Poster Art. Multicoloured.

456 6k.50 Type **145** 1·70 1·50
457 8k. "Chrysalis", "Reclining Form" and "Jazz III" (ceramics) (Gudrid Poulsen) 2·00 1·80

146 Fuglafjordur

2003. Island Post Office Centenaries. Sheet 170×120 mm containing T 146 and similar horiz designs. Each black and grey.

MS458 5k. Type **146**; 5k. Strendur; 5k. Sandur; 5k. Eidi; 5k. Vestmanna; 5k. Vagur; 5k. Midvagur; 5k. Hvalba 9·75 9·00

147 Jesper Rasmussen Brochmand

2003. Theologians. Multicoloured.

459 5k. Type **147** 1·20 1·20
460 6k.50 Thomas Kingo 1·70 1·60

148 "Dance in Main Room" (Emil Krause)

2003. Czeslaw Slania's 100th Stamp for Faroese Posts. Sheet 88×72 mm.

MS461 **148** 25k. multicoloured 6·25 5·75

149 Sandvok

2004. Settlements on Suduroy Island. Sheet 135×204 mm containing T 149 and similar horiz designs. Multicoloured.

MS462 5k.×10, Type **149**; Hvalba; Frodba; Oravok; Fámjin; Hov; Porkeri; Akrar; Sumba; Akraberg 20·00 17·00

150 Thor (god) and the Midgard Serpent

2004. Nordic Mythology. Sheet 105×70 mm containing T 150 and similar vert design. Multicoloured.

MS463 6k.50×2, Type **150**; Ran (sea goddess) 5·25 4·25

Stamps of a similar theme were issued by Aland Islands, Denmark, Finland, Greenland, Iceland, Norway and Sweden.

151 Gasholmur and Tindholmur

2004. 150th Anniv of Journal of Cruise of Maria (yacht) by Samuel Rathbone and E. H. Greig. Sheet 176×140 mm containing T 151 and similar horiz designs showing illustrations from the journal. Multicoloured.

MS464 6k.50×8, Type **151**; *Diamantunum* (yacht); Houses; Mylingur; Mylingur (different); Kalsoyggin; Yacht and rowing boats; Kunoynni 20·00 17·00

152 Prince Frederik and Mary Donaldson

2004. Marriage of Crown Prince Frederik and Mary Elizabeth Donaldson. Multicoloured.

MS465 130×65 mm. 5k. Type **152**; 6k.50 As 5k. but with design reversed 4·75 3·75

Stamps of same design were issued by Denmark and Greenland.

153 Club Emblems and Players

2004. Football Centenaries. Multicoloured.

466 5k. Type **153** (KI) (Klasvik) and HB (Torshavn) football clubs 1·40 1·20
467 6k.50 Tackling for ball (FIFA) 2·00 1·80

154 Cliffs and Yacht, Hestur

2004. Europa. Holidays. Multicoloured.

468 6k.50 Type **154** 2·00 1·80
469 8k. Walking on foreshore, Stora Dimun 3·75 2·50

155 Vagur Church

2004. Christmas. Churches. Multicoloured.

470 5k.50 Type **155** 1·80 1·50
471 7k.50 Tvoroyri church 3·50 2·00

156 Sea, Woman and Columns

2004. Poems by Jens Hendrik Oliver (Janus) Djurhuus. Sheet 158×126 mm containing T 156 and similar vert designs. Multicoloured.

MS472 7k.50×10, Type **156** ("Atlantis"); Woman, children, man and ship ("Grimur Kamban"); Face in storm ("Gandkvædi Trondar"); Seated man ("Til Faroya I-II"); Woman and sea ("Min sorg"); Snake, woman and man ("Loki"); Birds, wren and crows ("I buri og Slatur"); Giantess and ship at sea ("Heimferd Nolsyar Pals"); Moses and stone tablets ("Moses a Sinai fjalli"); Cello and man wearing raincoat and hat ("Cello") 30·00 25·00

157 Vikar

2005. Settlements on Vagar Island. Sheet 135×206 mm containing T 157 and similar horiz designs. Multicoloured.

MS473 5k.50×10, Type **157**; Gasadalur; Bour; Slaettanes; Kvigandalsa; Sorvagur; Sandavagur; Vatnsoyrar; Fjallavatn; Miovagur 22·00 19·00

158 Farmers and Sheep

2005. Everyday Life in Viking Age. Sheet 161×70 mm containing T 158 and similar vert designs. Multicoloured.

MS474 7k.50×3, Type **158**; Making hay; Woman milking cow 9·00 7·75

The stamps and margin of **MS**474 form a composite design of a Viking community.

159 White Snow Hare

2005. Faroese Snow Hare (Lepus timidus). Multicoloured.

475 5k.50 Type **159** 2·20 1·80
476 5k.50 Dark (blue) hare 2·20 1·80

160 Lambs' Heads, Stew, Bread and Fish (image scaled to 68% of original size)

2005. Europa. Gastronomy. Multicoloured.

477 7k.50 Type **160** 3·00 2·00
478 10k. Fish heads, rhubarb and stuffed puffins 3·50 2·75

161 Leach's Storm Petrel (*Oceanodroma leucorhoa*)

2005. Petrels. Multicoloured.

479 8k.50 Type **161** 4·00 2·75
480 9k. British storm petrel (*Hydrobates pelagicus*) 4·25 3·00
481 12k. Leach's storm petrel 6·00 4·25
482 20k. British storm petrel 8·00 5·75

162 "Christmas Song"

2005. Christmas. Religious Songs. Multicoloured.

483 5k.50 Type **162** 1·80 1·50
484 7k.50 "The Rudis Ballad" 3·50 2·00

163 Soldiers

2005. British Occupation during World War II, 1940–45.

485	**163**	5k.50 black and azure	1·80	1·50
486	-	9k. black and stone	4·25	3·00

DESIGN: 9k. Soldiers with children.

164 Landscape

2005. Art. Paintings by Jogvan Waagstein. Multicoloured.

487	7k.50 Type **164**	2·75	2·00
488	7k.50 Houses and sea	2·75	2·00
489	7k.50 Inlet	2·75	2·00
490	7k.50 Road through hills	2·75	2·00
491	7k.50 Large pool and sea	2·75	2·00
492	7k.50 Coastline	2·75	2·00
493	7k.50 Road and rocks	2·75	2·00
494	7k.50 Sea, houses and road	2·75	2·00
495	7k.50 Church	2·75	2·00

165 *Himantolophus groenlandicus*

2006. Deepwater Fish. Multicoloured.

496	5k.50 Type **165**	1·80	1·50
497	5k.50 *Gonostoma elongatum*	1·80	1·50
498	5k.50 *Sebastes mentella*	1·80	1·50
499	5k.50 *Neoraja caerulea*	1·80	1·50
500	5k.50 *Rhinochimaera atlantica*	1·80	1·50
501	5k.50 *Linophryne Lucifer*	1·80	1·50
502	5k.50 *Ceratias holboelli*	1·80	1·50
503	5k.50 *Lampris guttatus*	1·80	1·50
504	5k.50 *Argyropelecus olfersi*	1·80	1·50
505	5k.50 *Lophius piscatorius*	1·80	1·50

166 Syorugota

2006. Villages. Multicoloured.

506	7k. Type **166**	2·75	2·00
507	12k. Fuglafjorour	5·50	4·25
508	20k. Lerivik	7·75	6·75

167 Shipbuilding

2006. Ormurin Langi (ballad of "The Long Serpent"). Multicoloured.

509/18 5k. 50×10, Type **167**; Launch; King Olaf on throne; Fleet at sea; Ships watched by enemies ashore; Long Serpent with Ulf the Red at the helm; King Olaf and Erik the Archer on the quarterdeck; Battle scene; Boarding and capture; Battle over 20·00 13·50

168 Nornur (fate)

2006. Nordic Mythology. Multicoloured.

MS519 105×70 mm. 7k.50×2, Type **168**; Sjodreygil (sea ghost) 6·00 4·75

Stamps of a similar theme were issued by Aland Islands, Denmark, Greenland, Finland, Iceland, Norway and Sweden.

169 Tunnel, Road and Fish

2006. Nordoyatunnilin (tunnel between Eystruroy and Bordoy). Multicoloured.

520	5k.50 Type **169**	2·20	1·20
521	5k.50 Tunnel, road and boat	2·20	1·20

170 Clasped Hands

2006. Europa. Integration. Multicoloured.

522	7k.50 Type **170**	3·00	2·50
523	10k. Downward clasped hands	3·75	3·00

171 Weathervane

2006. Sandur—Oldest Faroese Church. Mult.

524	5k.50 Type **171**	2·00	1·20
525	7k.50 Door, window and pews	3·25	2·50

172 Sunnan fyri Skopun

2006. Settlements on Sandoy Island. Sheet 180×121 mm containing T 172 and similar horiz designs. Multicoloured.

MS526 7k.50×8, Type **172**; Dalur; Soltuvik; Skalavik; Skopun; Sandur; Skarvanes; Husavik 19·00 17·00

173 Man watching Seal

2007. Myths and Legends. Kopakonan (seal woman). Multicoloured.

527	5k.50 Type **173**	1·80	1·20
528	5k.50 Seal women dancing	1·80	1·20
529	5k.50 Stealing seal woman's skin	1·80	1·20
530	5k.50 Seal woman and farmer	1·80	1·20
531	5k.50 Seal woman and mate	1·80	1·20
532	5k.50 Seal woman and small children	1·80	1·20
533	5k.50 Seal woman and children	1·80	1·20
534	5k.50 Seal woman and man	1·80	1·20
535	5k.50 Farmer killing seal woman's mate and cubs	1·80	1·20
536	5k.50 Seal woman as she-troll	1·80	1·20

174 *Le Recherche*

2007. Lithographs by Barthelemy Lauvergne. Multicoloured.

537	5k.50 Type **174**	2·00	1·40
538	7k.50 Skaelingsfjall	3·25	2·50

175 Wave

2007. 10th Anniv of West Nordic Council. Tidal Energy.

539	**175**	7k.50 multicoloured	3·25	2·50

176 Scout

2007. Europa. Centenary of Scouting. Multicoloured.

540	5k.50 Type **176**	2·20	1·40
541	10k. Tent	4·25	3·50

177 Ketil killing Whale

2007. "Feogar a fero" (Old Man and his Sons) novel by Heoin Bru. Multicoloured.

542	7k.50 Type **177**	2·25	1·80
543	7k.50 Klavus with broken leg	2·25	1·80
544	7k.50 Kalvur and Klavusardottir	2·25	1·80
545	7k.50 Ketil and Klavur fishing	2·25	1·80
546	7k.50 Ketil's wife arguing with her daughter-in-law	2·25	1·80
547	7k.50 Ketil catching fulmars	2·25	1·80
548	7k.50 Kalvur	2·25	1·80
549	7k.50 Ketil and Kalvur with cow	2·25	1·80

178 Jakup Dahl

2007. Faroese Bible Translators. Sheet 110×70 mm containing T 178 and similar vert designs. Multicoloured.

MS550 5k.50×3, Type **178**; Kristian O. Videro; Victor Danielsen 7·00 6·50

The stamps of **MS**550 form a composite design.

179 Chickens

2007. Domestic Fowl. Multicoloured.

551	9k. Type **179**	3·50	2·75
552	20k. Ducks	7·00	5·75
553	25k. Geese	9·00	8·25

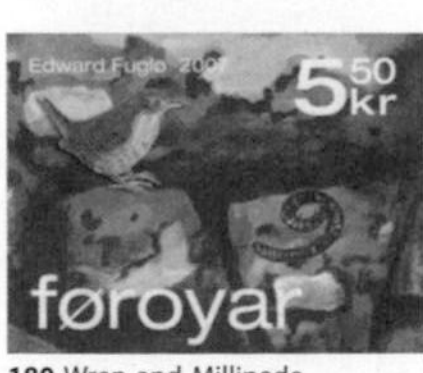

180 Wren and Millipede

2007. Wildlife of Stone Fences. Sheet 170×100 mm containing T 180 and similar horiz designs. Multicoloured.

MS554 5k.50×8, Type **180**; Beetles; Mouse; Crane fly; Storm petrel and hawkbit; Wheatear and buttercup; Earwigs; Starling and eggs 17·00 16·00

The stamps and margins of **MS**554 form a composite design.

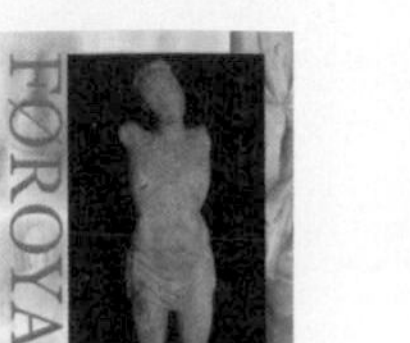

181 Christ Figurine

2007. Statues from Small White Church. Multicoloured.

555	5k.50 Type **181**	2·00	1·80
556	7k.50 Madonna of Kirkjubour	3·50	3·00

182 Coastline, Hoyvik

2007. SEPAC (small European mail services).

557	**182**	7k.50 multicoloured	3·25	2·75

183 Symbols of Klaksvik

2008. Centenary of Klaksvik.

558	**183**	5k.50 multicoloured	2·75	2·50

184 Patients and Sanatorium

2008. Centenary of Tuberculosis Sanatorium, Hoydalar. Multicoloured.

559	5k.50 Type **184**	2·75	2·50
560	9k. Dr. Vilhelm Magnussen (pioneer specialist) X-raying patient and child being vaccinated	4·00	3·75

185 Mountain and Houses

2008. Illustrations by Elinborg Eutzens. Sheet 130×83 mm containing T 185 and similar multicoloured designs.

MS561 10k.×6, Type **185**; Milkmaids (30×30 mm); Houses; Underwater reef; Cockerel (30×30 mm); Wharf 22·00 21·00

186 Buildings (rebuilt after fire in 1673)

2008. Tinganes (ancient parliament).

562	**186**	14k. multicoloured	6·50	6·25

187 Alvheyggur

2008. Norse Mythology. Mythical Places. Sheet 101×70 mm containing T 187 and similar horiz designs. Multicoloured.

MS563	7k.50×2, Type **187**; Klovin-gasteinur	7·25	6·25

188 Niels Winther

2008. Cultural Personlities. Sheet 96×102 mm containing T 188 and similar vert designs. Multicoloured.

MS564	5k.50×6, Type **188** (politician); Susanna Patursson (writer); Rasmus Effersoe (writer and nationalist); Jorgvan Poulsen (writer); Friorikur Petersen (writer); Andreas Evensen (writer, educationalist and politician)	14·50	13·50

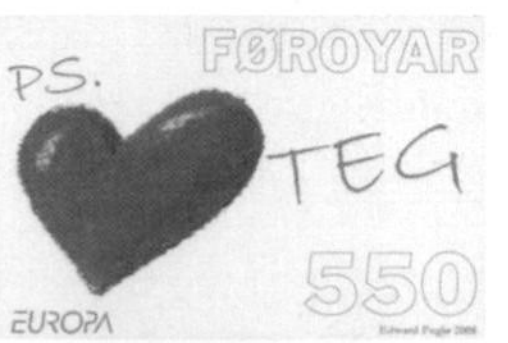
189 Heart, 'PS' and 'TEG'

2008. Europa. The Letter. Multicoloured.

565	5k.50 Type **189**	2·75	2·50
566	7k. 50 @	3·25	2·75

190 *Caltha palustris*

2008. Marsh Marigold—National Flower.

567	**190**	30k. multicoloured	14·00	13·00

191 Processional Cross, Kirkjubour

2008. Ancient Crosses. Multicoloured.

568	6k. Type **191**	3·00	2·30
569	10k. Wooden Cross, Leirvík	5·25	4·75

192 *Gymnocarpium dryopteris*

2008. Ferns. Multicoloured.

570	8k. Type **192**	4·00	3·50
571	8k. *Polypodium vulgare*	4·00	3·25
572	8k. *Dryopteris dilatata*	4·00	3·25
573	8k. *Asplenium adiantum nigrum*	4·00	3·25
574	8k. *Athyrium felix femina*	4·00	3·25
575	8k. *Dryopteris felix mas*	4·00	3·25
576	8k. *Cystopteris fragilis*	4·00	3·25
577	8k. *Phegopteris connectilis*	4·00	3·25
578	8k. *Polystichum lonchitis*	4·00	3·25
579	8k. *Asplenium trichomanes*	4·00	3·25

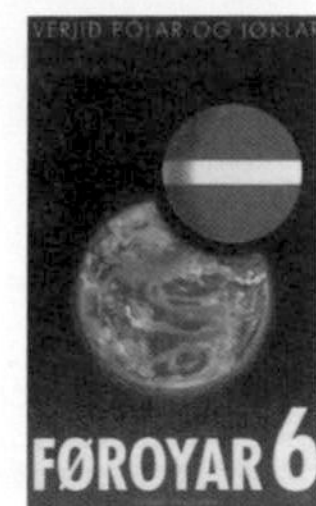
193 Globe and Stop Sign

2009. Global Warming Awareness Campaign. Multicoloured.

580	6k. Type **193**	3·00	2·30
581	8k. Globe as water droplet	4·00	3·25
MS582	120×80 mm. Nos. 580/1	7·00	5·50

194 Father, Brothers and Aeolian Harp

2009. The Lost Musicians (De Fortabte Spilemaend) by William Heinesen. Designs showing scenes from the book. Multicoloured.

583	8k. Type **194**	4·00	3·25
584	8k. Dancers	4·00	3·25
585	8k. The brothers	4·00	3·25
586	8k. Moritz and Eliana	4·00	3·25
587	8k. Playing the cello	4·00	3·25
588	8k. Playing to the old men	4·00	3·25
589	8k. Orpheus listening	4·00	3·25
590	8k. Orpheus leaving to study	4·00	3·25

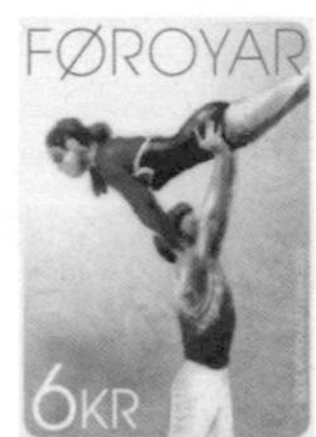
195 Pair of Gymnasts

2009. Centenary of Faroese Gymnastics. Multicoloured. (a) Ordinary gum.

591	6k. Type **195**	3·00	2·30
592	10k. Handstand	5·25	4·75
593	26k. Using rings	10·00	9·25

(b) Self-adhesive.

594	6k. As Type **195**	3·00	2·30
595	10k. As No. 592	5·25	4·75

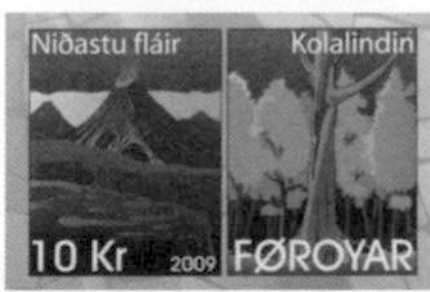
196 Volcano, Lava and Trees

2009. Origins of Faroe Islands. Sheet 119×94 mm containing T 196 and similar horiz designs. Multicoloured.

MS596	10k.×6, Type **196**; Volcano and ash; 60 million years ago; 15 million years ago; Mid Atlantic ridge; Ice age and rock erosion	22·00	21·00

The stamps of **MS**596 share a common background design.

197 Saturn

2009. Europa. Astronomy. Multicoloured.

597	10k. Type **197**	5·25	4·75
598	12k. Jupiter	6·00	4·50

198 Altarpiece, Vestmanna

2009. Christmas. Altarpieces. Multicoloured.

599	6k. Type **198**	3·00	2·30
600	10k. Altarpiece (Oggi Lamhauge), Hattarvik (41×20 mm)	5·25	4·75

199 Sheep grazing, Leynar

2009. SEPAC (small European mail services).

601	**199**	10k. multicoloured	5·25	4·75

200 Two Pigeons

2009. Rock Pigeon (Columba livia). Multicoloured.

602	14k. Type **200**	6·50	6·25
603	36k. Pigeon and two in flight	19·00	16·00

201 Seaweeds

2010. Marine Life. Multicoloured.

604	1k. Type **201**	50	45
605	6k. Seaweeds, with red extrusion, at left	3·00	2·30
606	8k. Seaweeds, tall and brightly coloured	4·00	3·25
607	12k. Seaweeds, tall, with crab, at centre	4·50	1·80

202 *Inachis io*

2010. Butterflies and Moths. Multicoloured.

608	6k. Type **202**	3·00	2·30
609	8k. *Vanessa cardui*	4·00	3·25
610	14k. *Agrius convolvuli*	3·00	2·20
611	16k. *Acherontia atropos*	7·75	6·50

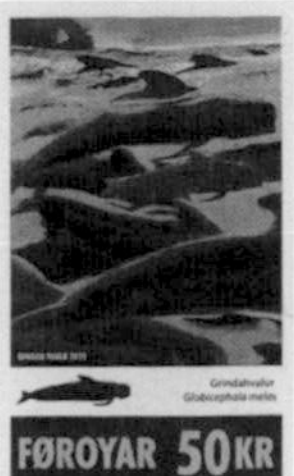
203 *Globicephala melas*

2010. Long-finned Pilot Whale.

612	**203**	50k. black and silver	26·00	23·00

204 Salmon

2010. Life at the Coast. Aquaculture. Sheet 105×70 mm containing T 204 and similar vert design. Multicoloured.

MS613	10k.×2, Type **204**; Aquaculture operative	10·50	10·50

The stamps and margins of **MS**613 form a composite design.

Stamps of a similar theme were issued by Denmark, Greenland, Aland Islands, Finland, Iceland, Norway and Sweden.

205 *A Dog, a Cat and a Mouse* (Barour Oskarsson)

2010. Europa. Children's Books. Multicoloured. (a) Ordinary gum.

614	10k. Type **205**	5·25	4·75
615	12k. *Moss Mollis' Journey* (Janus á Husagaroi)	6·00	4·50

(b) Self-adhesive.

616	10k. As Type **205**	5·25	4·75
617	12k. As No. 615	6·00	4·50

206 Valley

2010. Art. Landscape Paintings by Eli Smith using Pigments found on Faroes Islands. Multicoloured.

618	18k. Type **206**	9·50	8·00
619	24k. Flower, coastline and figure	12·00	9·00

207 Potato

2010. Root Vegetables. Multicoloured.

620	6k. Type **207**	3·25	2·50
621	8k. Turnip	4·50	3·50

208 Litla fitta nissa mín (Alexander Kristinsen)

2010. Christmas. Multicoloured.

622	6k. Type **208**	3·25	2·50
623	10k. *Á barnaárum ungu* (Hans Andreas Djurhuus)	5·75	5·00

209 Jens Christian Svabo

2010. Jens Christian Svabo (writer and ballad collector) Commemoration. Multicoloured.

624	6k. pale grey-blue and black	3·00	2·50
625	12k. pale orange-brown and black	6·50	5·75
626	14k. pale grey-blue and black	8·00	6·25
627	22k. pale orange-brown and black	11·50	9·75

Designs:- 6k. Type **209**; 12k. Writing at his desk; 14k. Writing whilst standing; 22k. As older man with pile of papers and inkwell

210 Black and White Cat

2011. Domestic Cats. Multicoloured.

628	6k. Type **210**	3·25	2·50
629	10k. Ginger and white	5·75	5·00

Nos. 630/1 are left for self-adhesive stamps not yet received.

211 Nursing

2011. Traditional Female Professions. Multicoloured.

632	6k. Type **211**	3·25	2·50
633	16k. Midwifery	9·00	7·50

212 Symbols of Womanhood

2011. Centenary of International Women's Day

634	**212**	10k. multicoloured	5·75	5·00

213 Annika i Dimun

2011. Annika i Dimun. Multicoloured.

MS635	10k.×3, Type **213**; Seated with two guards; Bound and entering the sea	17·00	17·00

214 *Sterjut strond*

2011. Art. Multicoloured.

636	2k. Type **214**	1·00	80
637	24k. *Ur Nólsay*	11·50	9·25

215 *Urtagarður*

2011. Art. Multicoloured.

638	6k. Type **215**	3·00	2·30
639	26k. *Kona*	12·00	9·50

216 Hurricane Damaged Trees, Tórshavn

2011. Europa. Multicoloured.

640	10k. Type **216**	5·25	4·75
641	12k.641 New plantation, Kunoy (vert)	6·00	4·50

217 *Silene dioica* (campion)

2011. Flora. Multicoloured.

642	14k. Type **217**	6·50	4·50
643	20k. *Geranium sylvaticum*	9·50	7·75

Pt. 1

FEDERATED MALAY STATES

A British protectorate in South East Asia, comprising the States of Negri Sembilan (with Sungei Ujong), Pahang, Perak and Selangor.

Separate issues for each of these states appeared in 1936.

100 cents = $1 (Straits).

1900. Stamps of Negri Sembilan optd FEDERATED MALAY STATES and bar.

1	**3**	1c. purple and green	3·00	9·00
2	**3**	2c. purple and brown	29·00	65·00
3	**3**	3c. purple and black	2·75	5·00
4	**3**	5c. purple and yellow	70·00	£180
5	**3**	10c. purple and orange	13·00	40·00
6	**3**	20c. green and olive	90·00	£120
7	**3**	25c. green and red	£250	£400
8	**3**	50c. green and black	£100	£160

1900. Stamps of Perak optd FEDERATED MALAY STATES and bar.

9	**31**	5c. purple and yellow	25·00	70·00
10	**31**	10c. purple and orange	80·00	65·00
11	**32**	$1 green	£180	£250
12	**32**	$2 green and red	£170	£300
13	**32**	$5 green and blue	£500	£750
14	**32**	$25 green and orange	£11000	

3

4

1900

15a	**3**	1c. black and green	4·00	1·00
29	**3**	1c. green	10·00	20
30	**3**	1c. brown	2·25	90
53	**3**	1c. black	75	20
31	**3**	2c. green	2·50	30
54	**3**	2c. brown	7·50	9·50
16a	**3**	3c. black and brown	6·00	35
34	**3**	3c. red	4·50	10
35	**3**	3c. grey	2·50	20
57	**3**	3c. green	1·25	1·50
58	**3**	3c. brown	3·75	50
36d	**3**	4c. black and red	6·50	80
38	**3**	4c. red	1·75	15
60	**3**	4c. orange	1·50	10
18	**3**	5c. green and red on yellow	2·50	3·00
61	**3**	5c. mauve on yellow	1·00	20
62	**3**	5c. brown	3·50	10
63	**3**	6c. orange	1·00	45
64	**3**	6c. red	1·50	10
41bb	**3**	8c. black and blue	9·00	4·75
42	**3**	8c. blue	13·00	1·00
43b	**3**	10c. black and mauve	35·00	65
44a	**3**	10c. blue	6·50	1·00
66	**3**	10c. black and blue	2·00	75
67	**3**	10c. purple and yellow	3·75	40
68	**3**	12c. blue	1·25	10
69	**3**	20c. mauve and black	4·00	1·75
70	**3**	25c. purple and mauve	2·75	2·25
71	**3**	30c. purple and orange	3·25	4·25
46	**3**	35c. red on yellow	5·50	12·00
73	**3**	35c. red and purple	13·00	14·00
74	**3**	50c. black and orange	13·00	15·00
75	**3**	50c. black on green	4·00	2·50
76a	**4**	$1 green	23·00	55·00
77	**3**	$1 black and red on blue	12·00	4·50
78	**4**	$2 green and red	35·00	90·00
79	**3**	$2 green and red on yellow	50·00	45·00
80	**4**	$5 green and blue	£160	£225
81	**3**	$5 green and red on green	£250	£250
82	**4**	$25 green and orange	£1300	£1500

POSTAGE DUE STAMPS

D1

1924

D1	**D1**	1c. violet	4·75	42·00
D2w	**D1**	2c. black	4·00	3·25
D3	**D1**	4c. green	2·25	5·00
D4w	**D1**	8c. red	15·00	18·00
D5	**D1**	10c. orange	9·00	17·00
D6w	**D1**	12c. blue	15·00	12·00

Pt. 9

FERNANDO POO

A Spanish island off the west coast of Africa, in the Gulf of Guinea. Became part of Spanish Guinea in 1909. In 1959 Fernando Poo became an overseas province of Spain, comprising the island and Annobon. On 12 October 1968 became independent and joined Rio Muni to form Equatorial Guinea.

1868. Currencies stated below issue.
1894. 1000 milesimas = 100 centavos = 1 peso.
1901. 100 centimos = 1 peseta.

1 Isabella II

1868

1	**1**	20c. brown	£800	£190

The face value of No. 1 is expressed in centimos de escudo. It was in use until Dec 1868. Stamps of Cuba were then used until 1879.

1879. "Alfonso XII" key-type inscr "FERNANDO POO".

5	**X**	1c. green	13·00	7·75
6	**X**	2c. red	19·00	13·50
2	**X**	5c. green	70·00	18·00
7	**X**	5c. lilac	60·00	18·00
3	**X**	10c. red	34·00	18·00
8	**X**	10c. brown	90·00	9·75
4	**X**	50c. blue	£120	18·00

Nos. 2, 3 and 4 have face values expressed in centimos de peseta and the remainder are in centavos de peso.

1884. Nos. 5, 6 and 7 surch as T 3.

9A	50c. on 1c. green	£150	34·00
10A	50c. on 2c. red	41·00	10·50
11A	50c. on 5c. lilac	£190	55·00

(3)

1893. On plain paper.

12A	**3**	50c. on blue	19·00	19·00

1894. "Baby" key-type inscr "FERNANDO POO".

13	**Y**	⅛c. grey	33·00	5·50
14	**Y**	2c. red	23·00	4·25
15	**Y**	5c. green	23·00	4·25
16	**Y**	6c. purple	20·00	5·50
18	**Y**	10c. red	70·00	17·00
19	**Y**	10c. brown	16·00	4·25
20	**Y**	12½c. brown	17·00	5·00
21	**Y**	20c. blue	17·00	5·00
22	**Y**	25c. red	33·00	5·00

1896. Nos. 13/22 surch HABILITADO 5 C. DE PESO in circle.

23	5c. on⅛c. grey	£130	43·00
24	5c. on 2c. red	65·00	26·00
25	5c. on 6c. purple	£190	70·00
26a	5c. on 10c. brown	85·00	70·00
28	5c. on 12½c. brown	47·00	21·00
29	5c. on 20c. blue	£190	70·00
30	5c. on 25c. red	£190	55·00

7

1896. Fiscal stamps optd HABILITADO PARA CORREOS (Nos. 60/1) or surch CORREOS 5 CENTAVOS (59).

31b	**7**	5c. on 10c. red	25·00	14·00
32	**7**	10c. red	40·00	17·00
61a	**7**	15c. on 10c. green	35·00	25·00

1897. Nos. 13 etc surch 5 Cen. in circle.

33	**Y**	5c. on⅛c. grey	37·00	19·00
34a	**Y**	5c. on 2c. red	18·00	16·00
35a	**Y**	5c. on 5c. green	£100	22·00
36a	**Y**	5c. on 6c. purple	25·00	18·00
37a	**Y**	5c. on 10c. brown	£120	25·00
38	**Y**	5c. on 10c. red	£400	£425
40a	**Y**	5c. on 12½c. brown	48·00	8·00
41a	**Y**	5c. on 20c. blue	30·00	10·00
42	**Y**	5c. on 25c. red	45·00	31·00

1898. Nos. 13 etc surch as T 3.

43	50c. on⅛c. grey	£350	£130
44a	50c. on 2c. red	55·00	20·00
45	50c. on 5c. green	£250	90·00
46a	50c. on 10c. brown	£120	28·00
47a	50c. on 10c. red	£120	28·00
49a	50c. on 12½c. brown	£110	28·00
50	50c. on 25c. red	£225	80·00

10

1899. Fiscal stamps variously optd. (a) Surch Fernando Poo 1899 Habilitado para Corrreos and new value.

62	**10**	10c. on 25c. green	£130	80·00
63	**10**	15c. on 25c. green	£200	£140

(b) Optd or surch CORREOS.

65	15c. on 25c. green	£3250	£2250
64	25c. green	£475	£225

1899. "Curly Head" key-type inscr "FERNANDO POO 1899".

66	**Z**	1m. brown	2·75	1·00
67	**Z**	2m. brown	2·75	1·00
68	**Z**	3m. brown	2·75	1·00
69	**Z**	4m. brown	2·75	1·00
70	**Z**	5m. brown	2·75	1·00

71	Z	1c. purple	2·75	1·00
72	Z	2c. green	2·75	1·00
73	Z	3c. brown	2·75	1·00
74	Z	4c. orange	18·00	2·50
75	Z	5c. red	2·75	1·00
76	Z	6c. blue	2·75	1·00
77	Z	8c. brown	10·50	1·00
78	Z	10c. red	7·25	1·00
79	Z	15c. grey	7·25	1·00
80	Z	20c. purple	20·00	2·50
81	Z	40c. lilac	£140	44·00
82	Z	60c. black	£140	44·00
83	Z	80c. brown	£140	44·00
84	Z	1p. green	£450	£200
85	Z	2p. blue	£450	£200

1900. No. 80 surch HABILITADO 5 C. DE PESO.

86	5c. on 20c. purple	£375	26·00

1900. No. 80 surch 5 Cen. in circle.

87	5c. on 20c. purple	13·00	6·75

1900. No. 80 surch with T 3.

88	50c. on 20c. purple	16·00	6·75

1900. "Curly Head" key-type inscr "FERNANDO POO 1900".

91	1m. black	4·25	1·00
92	2m. black	4·25	1·00
93	3m. black	4·25	1·00
94	4m. black	4·25	1·00
95	5m. black	4·25	1·00
96	1c. green	4·25	1·00
97	2c. lilac	4·25	1·00
98	3c. pink	4·25	1·00
99	4c. brown	4·25	1·00
100	5c. blue	4·25	1·00
101	6c. orange	4·25	4·25
102	8c. green	4·25	4·25
103	10c. red	4·25	1·00
104	15c. purple	4·25	1·00
105	20c. brown	4·25	1·00
106	40c. brown	10·00	4·50
107	60c. green	24·00	4·50
108	80c. blue	24·00	7·50
109	1p. brown	£130	60·00
110	2p. orange	£225	£130

1900. Fiscal stamps as T 7 but dated 1900 optd or surch.
(a) CORREOS and 5 Cen. in circle.

111	7	5c. on 10c. blue	85·00	35·00

(b) CORREOS CORREOS and 5 Cen. in circle.

113	5c. on 10c. blue	£140	85·00

(c) CORREOS.

114a	10c. blue	32·00	8·25

1900. Fiscal stamp as T 7 but dated 1900 surch CORREOS 5 CENTAVOS.

115	5c. on 10c. blue	£650	£500

1900. Nos. 74 and 105 surch with T 3.

116a	Z	50c. on 4c. orange	12·00	6·50
117	Z	50c. on 20c. brown	28·00	8·25

14a

1900. Fiscal stamp surch. (a) CORREOS and 5 Cen. in circle.

118a	14a	5c. on 25c. brown	£650	£375

(b) CORREOS HABILITADO 5 C. DE PESO.

119	5c. on 25c. brown	£650	£350

1901. "Curly Head" key-type inscr "FERNANDO POO 1901".

124	Z	1c. black	2·75	1·70
125	Z	2c. brown	2·75	1·70
126	Z	3c. purple	2·75	1·70
127	Z	4c. lilac	2·75	1·70
128	Z	5c. red	1·80	1·70
129	Z	10c. brown	1·80	1·70
130	Z	25c. blue	1·80	1·70
131	Z	50c. purple	2·75	1·70
132	Z	75c. brown	2·20	1·70
133	Z	1p. green	65·00	15·00
134	Z	2p. brown	41·00	22·00
135	Z	3p. green	41·00	30·00
136	Z	4p. red	41·00	30·00
137	Z	5p. green	50·00	30·00
138	Z	10p. orange	£110	90·00

1902. "Curly Head" key-type inscr "FERNANDO POO 1902". With control figures on back.

140	5c. green	2·75	50
141	10c. grey	2·75	50
142	25c. red	6·75	1·40
143	50c. brown	17·00	5·00
144	75c. lilac	17·00	5·00
145	1p. red	21·00	8·25
146	2p. green	43·00	21·00
147	5p. red	65·00	48·00

1903. "Curly Head" key-type inscr "FERNANDO POO PARA 1903". With control figures on back.

154	¼c. purple	40	40
155	½c. black	40	40
156	1c. red	40	40
157	2c. green	40	40
158	3c. green	40	40
159	4c. lilac	40	40
160	5c. red	55	40
161	10c. orange	70	55
162	15c. green	3·00	1·90
163	25c. brown	3·00	3·00
164	50c. brown	5·00	5·00
165	75c. red	20·00	9·75
166	1p. brown	26·00	18·00
167	2p. green	39·00	25·00
168	3p. purple	39·00	25·00
169	4p. blue	47·00	43·00
170	5p. blue	70·00	50·00
171	10p. orange	£150	80·00

1905. "Curly Head" key-type inscr "FERNANDO POO PARA 1905". With control figures on back.

172	1c. purple	50	50
173	2c. black	50	50
174	3c. red	50	50
175	4c. green	50	50
176	5c. green	55	50
177	10c. lilac	2·00	95
178	15c. red	2·00	95
179	25c. orange	18·00	3·00
180	50c. green	11·00	5·00
181	75c. brown	16·00	16·00
182	1p. brown	18·00	16·00
183	2p. red	31·00	23·00
184	3p. brown	48·00	27·00
185	4p. green	55·00	35·00
186	5p. red	90·00	55·00
187	10p. blue	£140	80·00

17 King Alfonso XIII

1907. With control figures on back.

188	17	1c. black	20	20
189	17	2c. pink	20	20
190	17	3c. purple	20	20
191	17	4c. black	20	20
192	17	5c. buff	20	20
193	17	10c. purple	1·70	90
194	17	15c. black	40	40
195	17	25c. brown	41·00	22·00
196	17	50c. green	20	20
197	17	75c. red	35	20
198	17	1p. blue	2·75	95
199	17	2p. brown	11·00	8·75
200	17	3p. pink	11·00	8·75
201	17	4p. lilac	11·00	8·75
202	17	5p. brown	11·00	8·75
203	17	10p. brown	11·00	8·75

1908. Surch HABILITADO PARA 05 CTMS.

204	5c. on 10c. purple	5·00	4·25

1929. Seville and Barcelona Exhibition stamps of Spain (Nos. 504, etc) optd FERNANDO POO.

209	5c. red	35	35
210	10c. green	35	35
211	15c. blue	35	35
212	20c. violet	35	35
213	25c. red	35	35
214	30c. brown	35	35
215	40c. blue	95	95
216	50c. orange	2·10	2·10
217	1p. grey	8·25	8·25
218	4p. red	40·00	40·00
219	10p. brown	50·00	50·00

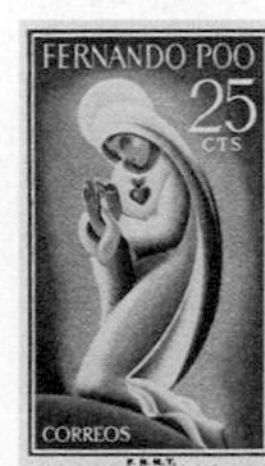

24 Woman at Prayer

1960

220	24	25c. grey	35	20
221	24	50c. drab	35	20
222	24	75c. brown	35	20
223	24	1p. red	35	20
224	24	1p.50 turquoise	35	20
225	24	2p. purple	35	20
226	24	3p. blue	3·25	1·00
227	24	5p. brown	40	20
228	24	10p. olive	50	25

25 De Falla (composer)

1960. Child Welfare.

229	25	10c.+5c. purple	60	60
230	-	15c.+5c. brown	60	60
231	-	35c. green	60	60
232	25	80c. green	60	60

DESIGNS—VERT: (De Falla's ballets): 15c. Spanish dancer ("Love, the Magician"); 35c. Tricorne, stick and windmill ("Three-cornered Hat").

26 Sperm Whale

1960. Stamp Day.

233	26	10c.+5c. red	60	60
234	-	20c.+5c. green	60	60
235	26	30c.+10c. brown	60	60
236	-	50c.+20c. brown	60	60

DESIGN: 20, 50c. Natives harpooning humpback whale.

27 "The Blessing"

1961. Child Welfare. Inscr "PRO-INFANCIA 1961".

237	27	10c.+5c. lake	65	65
238	-	25c.+10c. violet	65	65
239	27	80c.+20c. green	70	70

DESIGN: 25c. African kneeling before Cross.

28

1961. 25th Anniv of Gen. Franco as Head of State.

240	-	25c. grey	60	60
241	28	50c. brown	60	60
242	-	70c. green	60	60
243	28	1p. orange	60	60

DESIGNS—VERT: 25c. Map; 70c. St. Isabel Cathedral.

29 Great Turtle

1961. Stamp Day. Inscr "DIA DEL SELLO 1961".

244	29	10c.+5c. red	60	60
245	-	25c.+10c. plum	60	60
246	29	30c.+10c. purple	60	60
247	-	1p.+10c. orange	60	60

DESIGN: 25c., 1p. Native porters, palm trees and shore.

30 Spanish Freighter "Okume"

1962. Child Welfare. Inscr "PRO-INFANCIA 1962".

248	30	25c. violet	65	65
249	-	50c. olive	65	65
250	30	1p. brown	70	70

DESIGN: 50c. Spanish freighter "San Francisco".

31 Postman

1962. Stamp Day. Inscr "DIA DEL SELLO 1962".

251	31	15c. green	65	65
252	-	35c. mauve	65	65
253	31	1p. brown	70	70

DESIGN—HORIZ: 35c. Mail transport.

32 Native Shrine

1963. Seville Flood Relief.

254	32	50c. brown	75	75
255	32	1p. purple	75	75

33 Sister and Child

1963. Child Welfare.

256	-	25c. purple	65	65
257	33	50c. green	65	65
258	-	1p. red	70	70

DESIGN—HORIZ: 25c., 1p. Two sisters.

34 Child and Arms

1963. "For Barcelona".

259	34	50c. brown	75	75
260	34	1p. red	75	75

35 Governor Chacon

1964. Stamp Day.

261	35	25c. violet	65	65
262	-	50c. brown	65	65
263	35	1p. red	70	70

DESIGN—VERT: 50c. Orange blossom.

36 Canoe

1964. Child Welfare. Inscr "PRO INFANCIA 1964".

264	36	25c. violet	65	65
265	-	50c. olive (Pineapple)	65	65
266	36	1p. purple	70	70

37 Ring-necked Francolin

1964. Birds.

267	37	15c. brown	35	25
268	-	25c. violet	35	25
269	-	50c. green	35	25
270	37	70c. green	35	25
271	-	1p. brown	35	25
272	-	1p.50 blue	35	25
273	37	3p. blue	50	25
274	-	5p. purple	1·50	25
275	-	10p. green	2·75	1·00

DESIGNS: 25c., 1, 5p. Mallard; 50c., 1p.50, 10p. Great blue turaco.

38 "The Three Kings"

1964. Stamp Day.

276		50c. green	60	60
277	38	1p. red	60	60
278	-	1p.50 green	60	60
279	38	3p. blue	1·70	1·70

DESIGN—VERT: 50c., 1p.50, King presenting gift to Infant Jesus.

39 Native

1965. 25th Anniv of End of Spanish Civil War.

280	39	50c. blue	65	65
281	-	1p. red	65	65
282	-	1p.50 turquoise	70	70

DESIGNS: 1p. "Agriculture" (fruit farming); 1p.50, "Education" (child writing).

40 "Metopodontus savagei" (stag beetle)

1965. Child Welfare. Insects.

283		50c. green	65	65
284	40	1p. red	65	65
285	-	1p.50 blue	70	70

DESIGN—VERT: 50c., 1p.50, "Plectrocnemia cruciata" (squashbug).

41 Pole Vaulting

1965. Stamp Day.

286	41	50c. green	65	65
287	-	1p. brown	65	65
288	41	1p.50 blue	70	70

DESIGN—VERT: 1p. Arms of Fernando Poo.

42 European and African Women

1966. Child Welfare.

289	42	50c. green	65	65
290	42	1p. red	65	65
291	-	1p.50 blue	70	70

DESIGN—VERT: 1p.50, St. Isabel of Hungary.

43 Greater White-nosed Monkey

1966. Stamp Day.

292	43	10c. blue and yellow	60	60
293	-	40c. blue and brown	60	60
294	43	1p.50 olive and brown	60	60
295	-	4p. brown and green	70	70

DESIGN—VERT: 40c., 4. p. Moustached monkey.

44 Flowers

1967. Child Welfare and similar floral design.

296	44	10c. red and green	60	60
297	-	40c. brown and orange	60	60
298	44	1p.50 purple & brown	60	60
299	-	4p. blue and green	70	70

45 African Linsang

1967. Stamp Day.

300	45	1p. black and bistre	65	65
301	-	1p.50 brown and olive	65	65
302	-	3p.50 purple and green	95	95

DESIGNS—VERT: 1p.50, Western needle-clawed bush-baby. HORIZ: 3p.50, Lord Derby's flying squirrel.

46 Arms of San Carlos and Stamp of 1868

1968. Stamp Centenary.

303	46	1p. brown and purple	65	65
304	-	1p.50 brown and blue	65	65
305	-	2p.50 chestnut & brown	95	95

DESIGNS—Each with stamp of 1868: 1p.50, Arms of Santa Isabel; 2p.50, Arms of Fernando Poo.

47 Libra (scales)

1968. Child Welfare. Signs of the Zodiac.

306	47	1p. mauve on yellow	65	65
307	-	1p.50 brown on pink	65	65
308	-	2p.50 violet on yellow	95	95

DESIGNS: 1p.50, Lion (Leo); 2p.50, Water carrier (Aquarius).

For later issues see **EQUATORIAL GUINEA**.

Pt. 6

FEZZAN

A desert territory in N. Africa taken from Turkey by Italy and captured by French forces in 1943. Algerian stamps used from April 1944, until 1946, and then under French control until the end of 1951 when it was incorporated in the independent kingdom of Libya.

100 centimes = 1 franc.

(a) Issues For Fezzan And Ghadames

1943. Optd FEZZAN Occupation Francaise or surch in addition. (a) Postage. No. 247 of Italy optd.

1	103	50c. violet	75·00	80·00

Stamps of Libya surch.

2	4	0f.50 on 5c. green & black	£140	£140
3	5	1f. on 10c. pink and black	£170	£170
4	6	2f. on 30c. brown & black	£350	£350
5	9	3f. on 20c. green	£110	90·00
6	5	3f.50 on 25c. blue & dp blue	£130	£110
7	6	5f. on 50c. green & black	46·00	46·00
8	6	10f. on 1l.25 blue and indigo	£1500	£1300
9	9	20f. on 1l.75 orange	£5500	£5500
10	7	50f. on 75c. red & purple	£6500	£6500

(b) Air. No. 271 of Italy optd.

11	10	50c. brown	£110	£110

(c) Air. No. 72 of Libya surch.

12	18	7f.50 on 50c. red	£130	£130

1943. Handstamped locally. (a) Postage. No. 247 of Italy handstamped R.F. 0,50 FEZZAN around circle and within dotted circle.

13	103	0f.50 on 50c. violet	£5000	£375

(b) Postage. No. 27 of Libya handstamped R.F. 1 Fr FEZZAN in two lines.

14	5	1f. on 25c. blue & dp blue	£5500	£350

(c) Air. No. 271 of Italy handstamped as No. 13.

15	110	0f.50 on 50c. brown	£6500	£1100

1943. Parcel Post stamps of Libya handstamped across each half as No. 14.

16	P53	1f. on 5c. brown	£800	£350
17	P92	1f. on 10c. blue	£800	£350
18	P92	1f. on 50c. orange	£800	£350
19	P92	1f. on 1l. violet	£800	£350
20	P92	1f. on 2l. green	£5500	£1500
21	P92	1f. on 3l. bistre	£6500	£2250
22	P92	1f. on 4l. black	£5500	£1500

The prices are for each half of the parcel post stamps.

4 Fort of Sebha

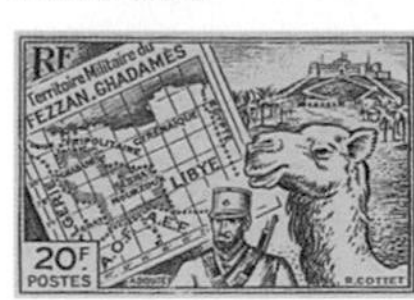

6 Map and Fort of Sebha

1946

23	4	10c. black	60	6·25
24	4	50c. red	1·10	7·00
25	4	1f. brown	90	7·25
26	4	1f.50 green	1·40	7·00
27	4	2f. blue	90	7·50
28	-	2f.50 violet	2·00	7·50
29	-	3f. red	1·90	8·00
30	-	5f. brown	1·90	9·00
31	-	6f. green	2·30	9·00
32	-	10f. blue	2·20	8·25
33	6	15f. violet	3·00	9·25
34	6	20f. red	3·00	11·00
35	6	25f. brown	2·75	11·00
36	6	40f. green	3·00	12·00
37	6	50f. blue	2·50	12·00

DESIGN—36×21½ mm: 2f.50 to 10f. Turkish fort and mosque at Murzuk.

(b) Issues For Fezzan Only

7 Douglas C-47B Skytrain at Fezzan Airfield

1948. Air.

38	7	100f. red	7·00	33·00
39	-	200f. blue	11·00	39·00

DESIGN—VERT: 200f. Airplane over Fezzan.

9 Djerma

10 Well at Gorda

1949

40	9	1f. black	1·70	8·75
41	9	2f. pink	1·70	8·75
42	-	4f. brown	2·00	11·50
43	-	5f. green	3·50	11·00
44	10	8f. blue	3·75	11·00
45	10	10f. brown	4·00	14·00
46	10	12f. green	4·25	23·00
47	-	15f. red	4·75	27·00
48	-	20f. black	3·25	15·00
49	-	25f. blue	3·00	18·00
50	-	50f. red	5·25	27·00

DESIGNS—HORIZ: 4f., 5f. Beni Khettab tombs; 15f., 20f. Col. Colonna d'Ornano and fort; 25f., 50f. Gen. Leclerc and map of Europe and N. Africa.

11 "Charity"

12 Mother and Child

1950. Charity.

51	11	15f.+5f. lake	5·50	13·00
52	12	25f.+5f. blue	7·25	13·50

14 Camel Breeding

15 Ahmed Bey

1951

59	14	30c. brown (postage)	4·00	9·50
60	14	1f. blue	5·25	9·50
61	14	2f. red	5·25	9·50
62	-	4f. red	6·25	9·50
63	-	5f. green	6·25	10·00
64	-	8f. blue	6·00	10·00
65	-	10f. brown	10·50	20·00
66	-	12f. green	11·00	21·00
67	-	15f. red	12·00	25·00
68	15	20f. brown	2·40	25·00
69	15	25f. blue and deep blue	5·25	31·00
70	15	50f. brown and blue	4·75	31·00
71	-	100f. blue (air)	17·00	45·00
72	-	200f. red	21·00	50·00

DESIGNS—HORIZ: 4f. to 8f. Arab hoeing; 100f. Brak Oasis; 200f. Sebha Fort. VERT: 10f. to 15f. Artesian well.

POSTAGE DUE STAMPS

1943. Postage Due stamps of Libya optd FEZZAN Occupation Francaise or surch in addition with bars obliterating old inscr and values.

D13	D141	0f.50 on 5c. brown	£1300	£1000
D14	D141	1f. on 10c. blue	£1300	£1000
D15	D141	2f. on 25c. green	£1300	£1000
D16	D141	3f. on 50c. violet	£1300	£1000
D17	D142	5f. on 1l. orange	£13000	£13000

D13 Brak Oasis

1950

D53	D13	1f. black	3·00	9·25
D54	D13	2f. green	3·00	9·25
D55	D13	3f. lake	3·00	9·75
D56	D13	5f. violet	4·25	10·50
D57	D13	10f. red	5·75	16·00
D58	D13	20f. blue	6·00	24·00

Pt. 1

FIJI

A British colony in the South Pacific, which became independent within the Commonwealth during October 1970. Following a military coup on 25 September 1987 Fiji was declared a republic on 7 October. The Governor-General resigned on 15 October 1987 and Fiji's Commonwealth membership lapsed until 1 October 1997 when the country was readmitted following further constitutional changes.

1870. 12 pence = 1 shilling; 20 shillings = 1 pound.
1969. 100 cents = 1 dollar.

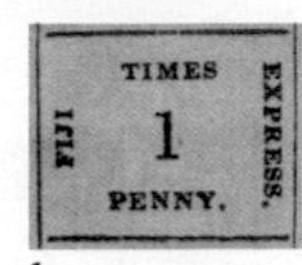

1

1870

5	1	1d. black on pink	£1000	£2000
6	1	3d. black on pink	£1700	£3250
7	1	6d. black on pink	£1400	£2000
8	1	9d. black on pink	£3000	£3500
9	1	1s. black on pink	£1700	£1800

2

1871

10	2	1d. blue	55·00	£120
11	2	3d. green	£110	£350
12	2	6d. red	£150	£300

1872. Surch in words.

13a	2c. on 1d. blue	50·00	55·00
14	6c. on 3d. green	80·00	80·00
15	12c. on 6d. red	£110	80·00

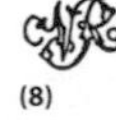

(5)

1874. Optd as T 5.

16	2c. on 1d. blue	£1000	£250
17	6c. on 3d. green	£1800	£700
18	12c. on 6d. red	£800	£200

1875. Nos. 17 and 18 surch 2d.

22	2d. on 6c. on 3d. green	£650	£200
26	2d. on 12c. on 6d. red	£2500	£850

(8)

1876. Optd with T 8, and the 3d. surch in words also.

31	1d. blue	25·00	42·00
29a	2d. on 3d. green	55·00	60·00
34	4d. on 3d. mauve	95·00	25·00
33	6d. red	55·00	35·00

10

12

1878. Surch on Nos. 36 and 41/2 in words.

35	10	1d. blue	14·00	14·00
40	10	2d. green	28·00	1·00
36	10	2d. on 3d. green	10·00	30·00
54	10	4d. mauve	17·00	22·00
41	10	4d. on 1d. mauve	65·00	55·00
42	10	4d. on 2d. mauve	85·00	14·00
59a	10	6d. red	12·00	3·75
67	12	1s. brown	50·00	12·00
69	12	5s. red and black	65·00	30·00

1891. Surch in figures or words.

72a	10	½d. on 1d. blue	55·00	75·00
70	10	2½d. on 2d. green	50·00	50·00
73	10	5d. on 4d. mauve	55·00	75·00
74a	10	5d. on 6d. red	60·00	65·00

20

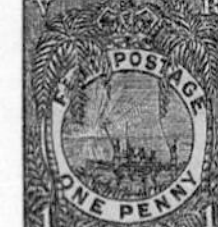

21 Native Canoe

1891

99	20	½d. grey	1·00	4·25
87	21	1d. black	12·00	7·00
101	21	1d. mauve	9·50	1·00
89	21	2d. green	8·50	80
103a	10	2½d. brown	5·50	5·00
85	21	5d. blue	18·00	7·50

23

1903

104	23	½d. green	2·25	2·00
105	23	1d. purple and black on red	14·00	55
119	23	1d. red	15·00	10
106	23	2d. purple and orange	3·75	1·25
107	23	2½d. purple and blue on blue	14·00	1·50
120	23	2½d. blue	6·50	7·50
108	23	3d. purple	1·50	2·75
109	23	4d. purple and black	1·50	2·50
110	23	5d. purple and green	1·50	2·00
111	23	6d. purple and red	1·50	1·75
121	23	6d. purple	21·00	35·00
112	23	1s. green and red	13·00	75·00
122	23	1s. black on green	7·50	10·00
113	23	5s. green and black	75·00	£160
123	23	5s. green and red on yellow	70·00	95·00
114	23	£1 black and blue	£350	£450
124	23	£1 purple and black on red	£300	£275

1912. As T 23, but portrait of King George V.

125a	¼d. brown	1·50	40
126b	½d. green	1·75	50
127	1d. red	2·00	10
231	1d. violet	1·25	10
232	1½d. red	4·00	1·00
233	2d. grey	1·25	10
129	2½d. blue	3·00	3·50
130	3d. purple on yellow	4·25	8·00
234	3d. blue	2·75	1·00
235	4d. black and red on yellow	10·00	7·00
236	5d. purple and olive	1·50	1·50
237	6d. purple	2·00	1·25
134a	1s. black on green	1·00	14·00
239	2s. purple and blue on blue	25·00	70·00
240	2s.6d. black and red on blue	11·00	32·00
136	5s. green and red on yellow	32·00	40·00
137a	£1 purple and black on red	£250	£275

1916. Nos. 126/7 optd WAR STAMP.

138b	½d. green	1·50	4·00
139a	1d. red	3·00	75

1935. Silver Jubilee. As T 10a of Gambia.

242	1½d. blue and red	1·00	9·00
243	2d. blue and grey	1·50	35
244	3d. brown and blue	2·75	4·00
245	1s. grey and purple	11·00	13·00

1937. Coronation. As T 10b of Gambia.

246	1d. violet	60	1·25
247	2d. grey	60	2·25
248	3d. blue	60	2·25

28 Native Sailing Canoe

29 Native Village

32 Government Offices

1938

249	28	½d. green	20	75
250	29	1d. brown and blue	50	20
252c	-	1½d. red	2·25	1·25
254	-	2d. brown and green	20·00	16·00
255	32	2d. green and mauve	40	60
256b	-	2½d. brown and green	1·00	80
257	-	3d. blue	1·25	30
258	-	5d. blue and red	42·00	12·00
259	-	5d. green and red	20	30
261b	-	6d. black	2·50	1·50
261c	-	8d. red	2·25	3·25
262	-	1s. black and yellow	1·50	70
263	-	1s.5d. black and red	20	10
263a	-	1s.6d. blue	3·50	2·75
264	-	2s. violet and orange	2·50	40
265	-	2s.6d. green and brown	4·50	1·50
266	-	5s. green and purple	4·50	1·75
266a	-	10s. orange and green	38·00	45·00
266b	-	£1 blue and red	50·00	55·00

DESIGNS—HORIZ (As Type **32**): 1½d. Camakua (canoe); 2d. (No. 254), 2½d., 6d. Map of Fiji Is. HORIZ (As Type **29**): 3d. Canoe and arms; 8d., 1s.5d., 1s.6d. Arms; 2s. Suva Harbour; 2s.6d. River scene; 5s. Chief's hut. VERT (As Type **29**): 5d. (Nos. 258/9), Sugar cane; 1s. Spearing fish; 10s. Paw-paw tree; £1 Police bugler.

1941. No. 254 surch 2½d.

267	2½d. on 2d. brown and green	2·50	1·00

1946. Victory. As T 11a of Gambia.

268	2½d. green	10	1·50
269	3d. blue	10	10

1948. Silver Wedding. As T 11b/c of Gambia.

270	2½d. green	40	1·75
271	5s. blue	14·00	8·00

1949. U.P.U. As T 11d/g of Gambia.

272	2d. purple	30	75
273	3d. blue	2·00	5·50
274	8d. red	30	4·25
275	1s.6d. blue	35	2·75

43 Children Bathing

1951. Health stamps. Inscr "HEALTH".

276	43	1d.+1d. brown	10	1·25
277	-	2d.+1d. green	50	1·00

DESIGNS—VERT: 2d. Rugby footballer.

1953. Coronation. As T 11h of Gambia.

278	2½d. black and green	2·00	50

1953. Royal Visit. As No. 261c, but with portrait of Queen Elizabeth II and inscr "ROYAL VISIT 1953".

279	8d. red	30	15

46 Queen Elizabeth II (after Annigoni)

48 Loading Copra

1954. Queen Elizabeth II. (I) inscr "FIJI". (II) Inscribed "Fiji".

280	28	½d. green	1·00	1·50
298	46	½d. green	15	2·50
281	46	1d. turquoise (I)	1·75	10
299	46	1d. blue (II)	3·50	2·50
282	46	1½d. sepia (I)	2·75	65
300	46	1½d. sepia (II)	3·50	2·50
283	32	2d. green and mauve	1·25	40
312	46	2d. red (I)	50	10
284	46	2½d. violet (I)	3·00	10
302	46	2½d. brown (I)	1·50	4·25
285	48	3d. brown and purple	4·75	20
287	-	6d. black (As No. 261)	2·50	85
303	A	6d. red and black	1·50	10
288	-	8d. red (As No. 261d)	8·00	1·50
316	B	10d. brown and red	60	50
289	-	1s. black and yellow (As No. 262)	2·50	10
306	C	1s. blue	1·50	10
290	D	1s.6d. blue and green	16·00	1·00
291	E	2s. black and red	4·75	60
292a	-	2s.6d. green and brown (As No. 265)	1·25	10
320	F	2s.6d. black and purple	2·75	1·00
293	G	5s. ochre and blue	8·00	1·25
294	-	10s. orange and green (As No. 266a)	7·00	18·00
309	H	10s. green and sepia	3·00	1·25
295	-	£1 bl & red (As No. 266b)	32·00	14·00
310	I	£1 black and orange	6·50	3·25

DESIGNS—HORIZ (As Type **48**): A, Fijian beating lali; B, Yaqona ceremony; C, Location map; D, Sugar cane train; E, Preparing bananas for export; F, Nadi Airport; G, Gold industry; H, Cutting sugar-cane; I, Arms of Fiji.

52 River Scene

1954. Health stamps.

296	52	1½d.+½d. brown and green	15	1·00
297	-	2½d.+½d. orange and black	15	20

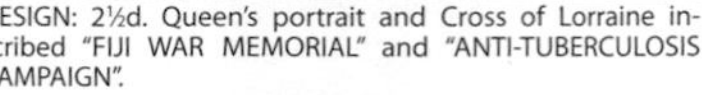
DESIGN: 2½d. Queen's portrait and Cross of Lorraine inscribed "FIJI WAR MEMORIAL" and "ANTI-TUBERCULOSIS CAMPAIGN".

56 Hibiscus

1959

313	-	3d. multicoloured	25	10
304	56	8d. multicoloured	50	25
315	56	9d. multicoloured	90	65
318	-	1s.6d. multicoloured	1·50	90
319	-	2s. yellow, green and copper	10·00	3·50
308	-	4s. multicoloured	1·75	1·25
323	-	5s. red, yellow and grey	10·00	35

DESIGNS—HORIZ: 1s.6d. International date line; 4s. Kandavu shining parrot ("Kandavu Parrot"); 5s. Orange dove. VERT: 2s. White orchid. 23×28 mm: 3d. Queen Elizabeth II.

1963. Royal Visit. Optd ROYAL VISIT 1963.

326		3d. mult (No. 313)	40	20
327	C	1s. blue (No. 306)	60	20

1963. Freedom from Hunger. As T 21a of Gambia.

328	2s. blue	1·00	1·50

69 Running

1963. 1st South Pacific Games, Suva. Inscr as in T 69.

329	69	3d. brown, yellow and black	25	10
330	-	9d. brown, violet and black	25	1·50
331	-	1s. brown, green and black	25	10
332	-	2s.6d. brown, blue and black	60	60

DESIGNS—VERT: 9d. Throwing the discus; 1s. Hockey. HORIZ: 2s.6d. High-jumping.

1963. Centenary of Red Cross. As T 21b of Gambia.

333	2d. red and black	35	10
334	2s. red and blue	75	2·50

1963. Opening of COMPAC (Trans-Pacific Telephone Cable). No. 306 optd COMPAC CABLE IN SERVICE DECEMBER 1963 and ship.

335	C	1s. blue	55	10

74 Jamborette Emblem

1964. 50th Anniv of Fijian Scout Movement.

336	74	3d. multicoloured	15	25
337	-	1s. violet and brown	15	30

DESIGN: 1s. Scouts of three races.

76 Flying-boat "Aotearoa"

1964. 25th Anniv of 1st Fiji–Tonga Airmail Service.

338	76	3d. black and red	50	10

339	-	6d. red and blue	80	1·00
340	-	1s. black and turquoise	80	1·00

DESIGNS—VERT: 6d. de Havilland DH.114 Heron 2. HORIZ (37½×25 mm): 1s. "Aotearoa" and map.

1965. Centenary of I.T.U. As T 45 of Gibraltar.

341	3d. blue and red	20	10
342	2s. yellow and bistre	50	25

1965. I.C.Y. As T 46 of Gibraltar.

343	2d. purple and turquoise	20	10
344	2s.6d. green and lavender	80	25

1966. Churchill Commemoration. As T 47 of Gibraltar.

345	3d. blue	70	10
346	9d. green	90	85
347	1s. brown	90	10
348	2s.6d. violet	1·00	85

1966. World Cup Football Championships. As T 48 of Gibraltar.

349	2d. multicoloured	25	10
350	2s. multicoloured	75	20

79 H.M.S. "Pandora" approaching Split Island, Rotuma

1966. 175th Anniv of Discovery of Rotuma. Mult.

351	3d. Type **79**	30	10
352	10d. Rotuma chiefs	30	10
353	1s.6d. Rotumans welcoming H.M.S. "Pandora"	50	30

1966. Inauguration of W.H.O. Headquarters, Geneva. As T 54 of Gibraltar.

354	6d. black, green and blue	1·25	25
355	2s.6d. black, purple and ochre	2·75	2·50

82 Running

1966. 2nd South Pacific Games.

356	**82**	3d. black, brown and green	10	10
357	-	9d. black, brown and blue	15	15
358	-	1s. multicoloured	15	15

DESIGNS—VERT: 9d. Putting the shot. HORIZ: 1s. Diving.

85 Military Forces Band

1967. International Tourist Year. Multicoloured.

360	3d. Type **85**	40	10
361	9d. Reef diving	15	10
362	1s. Beqa fire walkers	15	10
363	2s. "Oriana" (cruise liner) at Suva	40	15

89 Bligh (bust), H.M.S. "Providence" and Chart

1967. 150th Death Anniv of Admiral Bligh.

364	**89**	4d. multicoloured	10	10
365	-	1s. multicoloured	20	10
366	-	2s.6d. multicoloured	20	15

DESIGNS (As Type **89**): 2s.6d. Bligh's tomb. (54×20 mm): 1s. "Bounty's longboat being chased in Fiji waters".

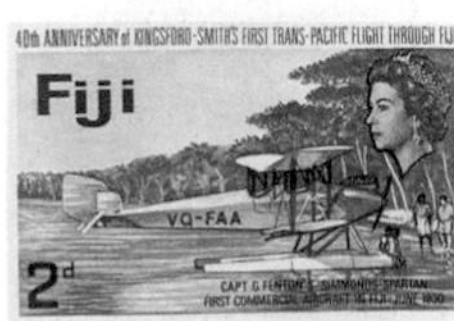

92 Simmonds Spartan Seaplane

1968. 40th Anniv of Kingsford Smith's Pacific Flight via Fiji.

367	**92**	2d. black and green	15	10
368	-	6d. blue, black and lake	15	10
369	-	1s. violet and green	20	10
370	-	2s. brown and blue	30	15

DESIGNS: 6d. Hawker Siddeley H.S.748 and airline insignias; 1s. "Southern Cross" and crew; 2s. "Lady Southern Cross".

96 Bure Huts

1968

371	**96**	½d. multicoloured	10	10
372	-	1d. blue, red and yellow	10	10
373	-	2d. blue, brown and ochre	10	10
374	-	3d. green, blue and ochre	35	10
375	-	4d. multicoloured	80	2·00
376	-	6d. multicoloured	25	10
377	-	9d. multicoloured	15	2·00
378	-	10d. blue, orange and brown	1·25	20
379	-	1s. blue and red	20	10
380	-	1s.6d. multicoloured	3·00	4·50
381	-	2s. turquoise, black and red	75	2·00
382	-	2s.6d. multicoloured	75	30
383	-	3s. multicoloured	1·50	6·00
384	-	4s. ochre, black and olive	4·50	2·75
385	-	5s. multicoloured	2·50	1·50
386	-	10s. brown, black and ochre	1·00	3·00
387	-	£1 multicoloured	1·25	3·00

DESIGNS—As T **96**: 1d. Passion flowers; 2d. Chambered or pearly nautilus; 4d. "Psilogramma jordana" (moth); 6d. Pennant coralfish; 9d. Bamboo raft; 10d. "Asota woodfordi" (moth); 3s. Golden cowrie shell. 33×22 mm: 2s. Sea snake; 2s.6d. Outrigger canoes; 5s. Bamboo orchids; £1 Queen Elizabeth and Arms of Fiji. 23×33 mm: 3d. Reef heron; 1s. Black marlin; 1s.6d. Orange-breasted honeyeaters ("Sun Birds"); 4s. Mining industry; 10s. Ceremonial whale's tooth.

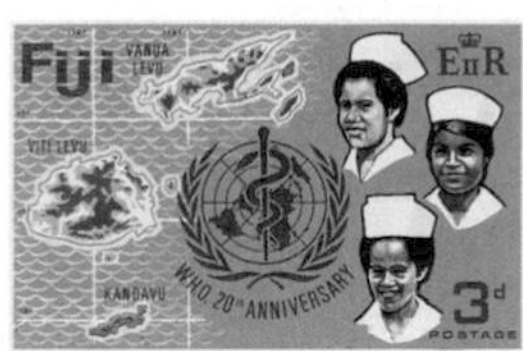

113 Map of Fiji, W.H.O. Emblem and Nurses

1968. 20th Anniv of W.H.O. Multicoloured.

388	3d. Type **113**	15	10
389	9d. Transferring patient to medical ship "Vuniwai"	20	15
390	3s. Recreation	25	30

116 Passion Flowers

1969. Decimal Currency. Designs as T 96 etc, but with values inscr in decimal currency as in T 116.

391	**116**	1c. blue, red and yellow	10	10
392	-	2c. blue, brown and ochre (As 373)	10	10
393	-	3c. green, blue and ochre (As 374)	1·25	1·50
394	-	4c. multicoloured (As 375)	1·50	1·50
395	-	5c. multicoloured (As 376)	20	10
396	**96**	6c. multicoloured	10	10
397	-	8c. multicoloured (As 377)	10	10
398	-	9c. blue, orange and brown (As 378)	1·50	2·75
399	-	10c. blue and red (As 379)	20	10
400	-	15c. multicoloured (As 380)	6·00	5·00
401	-	20c. turquoise, black and red (As 381)	1·25	80
402	-	25c. multicoloured (As 382)	1·00	20
403	-	30c. multicoloured (As 383)	4·50	1·50
404	-	40c. ochre, black and olive (As 384)	7·50	4·00
405	-	50c. multicoloured (As 385)	3·00	20
406	-	$1 brown, black and ochre (As 386)	1·50	40
407	-	$2 multicoloured (As 387)	2·00	1·50

117 Fijian Soldiers overlooking the Solomon Islands

1969. 25th Anniv of Fijian Military Forces' Solomons Campaign.

408	**117**	3c. multicoloured	20	10
409	-	10c. multicoloured	25	10
410	-	25c. multicoloured	35	20

DESIGNS: 10c. Regimental flags and soldiers in full dress and battledress; 25c. Sefanaia Sukanai-valu and Victoria Cross.

120 Javelin Throwing

1969. 3rd South Pacific Games, Port Moresby.

411	**120**	4c. black, brown and red	10	10
412	-	8c. black, grey and blue	10	10
413	-	20c. multicoloured	20	20

DESIGNS: 8c. Sailing dinghy; 20c. Games medal and winner's rostrum.

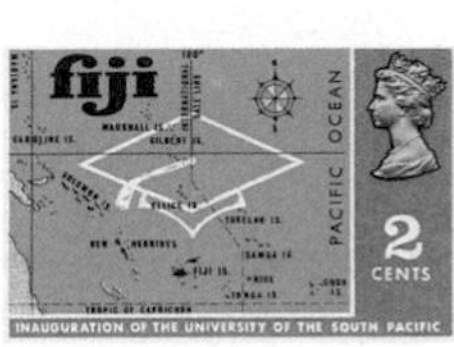

123 Map of South Pacific and "Mortar-board"

1969. Inauguration of University of the South Pacific. Multicoloured.

414	2c. Type **123**	10	15
415	8c. R.N.Z.A.F. Badge and Short S25 Sunderland flying boat over Laucala Bay (site of University)	15	10
416	25c. Science students at work	25	15

1970. Royal Visit. Nos. 392, 399 and 402 optd ROYAL VISIT 1970.

417	2c. blue, brown and ochre	10	20
418	10c. blue and red	10	10
419	25c. multicoloured	20	10

127 Chaulmugra Tree, Makogai

1970. Closing of Leprosy Hospital, Makogai.

420	**127**	2c. multicoloured	10	50
421	-	10c. green and black (vert)	40	65
422	-	10c. blue, black and mauve (vert)	40	65
423	-	30c. multicoloured	70	50

DESIGNS: 10c. (No. 421) "Cascade" (Semisi Maya); 10c. (No. 422) "Sea Urchins" (Semisi Maya); 30c. Makogai Hospital.

131 Abel Tasman and Log, 1643

1970. Explorers and Discoverers.

424	**131**	2c. black, brown & turq	30	25
425	-	3c. multicoloured	60	25
426	-	8c. multicoloured	60	15
427	-	25c. multicoloured	30	15

DESIGNS: 3c. Captain Cook and H.M.S. "Endeavour", 1774; 8c. Captain Bligh and long-boat, 1789; 25c. Fijian and ocean-going Canoe.

135 King Cakobau and Cession Stone

1970. Independence. Multicoloured.

428	2c. Type **135**	10	10
429	3c. Children of the world	10	10
430	10c. Prime Minister and Fijian flag	70	10
431	25c. Dancers in costume	25	20

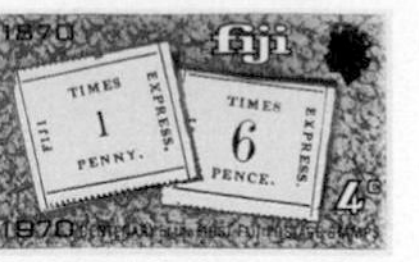

139 1d. and 6d. Stamps of 1870

1970. Stamp Centenary. Multicoloured.

432	4c. Type **139**	15	10
433	15c. Fijian stamps of all reigns (61×21 mm)	40	15
434	20c. "Fiji Times" office and modern G.P.O.	40	15

140 Grey-backed White-eye

1971. Birds and Flowers. Multicoloured.

435	1c. "Cirrhopetalum umbellatum"	15	30
436	2c. Cardinal honeyeater	30	10
437	3c. "Calanthe furcata"	85	20
438	4c. "Bulbophyllum sp. nov."	75	2·00
439	5c. Type **140**	35	10
510	6c. "Phaius tancarvilliae"	2·75	20
441	8c. Blue-headed flycatcher ("Blue-crested Broadbill")	35	10
442	10c. "Acanthephippium vitiense"	40	10
513	15c. "Dendrobium tokai"	2·50	40
444	20c. Slaty flycatcher	1·50	30
468	25c. Yellow-faced honeyeater ("Kandavu Honeyeater")	2·00	90
516	30c. "Dendrobium gordonii"	5·00	1·00
517	40c. Masked shining parrot ("Yellow-breasted Musk Parrot")	4·50	60
448	50c. White-throated pigeon	3·50	50
449	$1 Collared lory	4·00	1·00
520	$2 "Dendrobium platygastrium"	1·25	1·25

The 25c. to $2 are larger, 22½×35½ mm.

142 Women's Basketball

1971. 4th South Pacific Games, Tahiti.

451	**142**	8c. multicoloured	10	10
452	-	10c. blue, black and brown	10	10
453	-	25c. green, black and brown	30	25

DESIGNS: 10c. Running; 25c. Weightlifting.

143 Community Education

1972. 25th Anniv of South Pacific Commission. Multicoloured.

454	2c. Type **143**	10	25
455	4c. Public health	10	10

456 50c. Economic growth 70 80

144 "Native Canoe"

1972. South Pacific Festival of Arts, Suva.
457 **144** 10c. black, orange and blue 10 10

145 Flowers, Conch and Ceremonial Whale's Tooth

1972. Royal Silver Wedding. Multicoloured. Background colour given.
474 **145** 10c. green 30 25
475 **145** 25c. purple 40 25

1972. Hurricane Relief. Nos. 400 and 403 surch HURRICANE RELIEF + and premium.
476 15c.+5c. multicoloured 15 25
477 30c.+10c. multicoloured 15 25

147 Line Out

1973. Diamond Jubilee of Rugby Union. Mult.
478 2c. Type **147** 45 3·00
479 8c. Body tackle 85 10
480 25c. Conversion 1·50 40

148 Forestry Development

1973. Development Projects. Multicoloured.
481 5c. Type **148** 10 35
482 8c. Rice irrigation scheme 10 10
483 10c. Low income housing 10 10
484 25c. Highway construction 20 30

149 Christmas

1973. Festivals of Joy. Multicoloured.
485 3c. Type **149** 10 10
486 10c. Diwali 10 10
487 20c. Id-Ul-Fitar 15 25
488 25c. Chinese New Year 15 25

150 Athletics

1974. Commonwealth Games, Christchurch, New Zealand. Multicoloured.
489 3c. Type **150** 15 10
490 8c. Boxing 15 10
491 50c. Bowling 50 75

151 Bowler

1974. Centenary of Cricket. Multicoloured.
492 3c. Type **151** 50 15
493 25c. Batsman and wicket-keeper 80 15
494 40c. Fielder (horiz) 90 1·40

152 Fiji Postman

1974. Centenary of U.P.U. Multicoloured.
495 3c. Type **152** 10 10
496 8c. Loading mail onto "Fijian Princess" 10 10
497 30c. Fijian post office and mailbus 20 40
498 50c. B.A.C. One Eleven 200/400 modern aircraft 35 2·75

153 Cubs lighting Fire

1974. 1st National Scout Jamboree, Lautoka. Multicoloured.
499 3c. Type **153** 15 10
500 10c. Scouts reading map 20 10
501 40c. Scouts and Fijian flag (vert) 65 3·25

154 Cakobau Club and Flag

1974. Centenary of Deed of Cession and 4th Anniv of Independence. Multicoloured.
502 3c. Type **154** 10 10
503 8c. King Cakobau and Queen Victoria 10 10
504 50c. Raising the Royal Standard at Nasova Ovalau 30 2·00

155 "Diwali" (Hindu Festival)

1975. "Festivals of Joy". Multicoloured.
521 3c. Type **155** 10 10
522 15c. "Id-Ul-Fitar" (Muslim Festival) 10 10
523 25c. Chinese New Year 15 15
524 30c. Christmas 20 1·90
MS525 121×101 mm. Nos. 521/4 1·00 6·00

156 Steam Locomotive No. 21

1976. Sugar Trains. Multicoloured.
526 4c. Type **156** 25 20
527 15c. Diesel loco No. 8 45 40
528 20c. Diesel loco No. 1 50 1·00
529 30c. Free passenger train 60 3·00

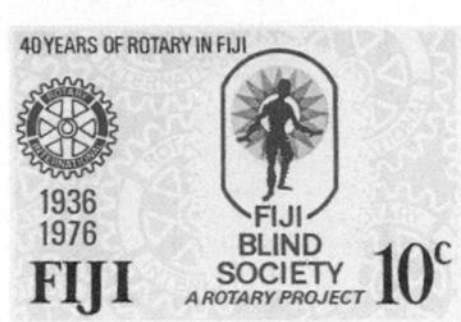

157 Fiji Blind Society and Rotary Symbols

1976. 40th Anniv of Rotary in Fiji.
530 **157** 10c. blue, green and black 15 25
531 - 25c. multicoloured 40 75
DESIGN: 25c. Ambulance and Rotary Symbol.

158 de Havilland Australia DHA.3 Drover 1

1976. 25th Anniv of Air Services. Multicoloured.
532 4c. Type **158** 40 20
533 15c. B.A.C. One Eleven 200/400 75 1·50
534 25c. Hawker Siddeley H.S.748 80 1·50
535 30c. Britten Norman BN-2A Mk III "long nose" Trislander 90 3·50

159 The Queen's Visit to Fiji, 1970

1977. Silver Jubilee. Multicoloured.
536 10c. Type **159** 10 10
537 25c. King Edward's Chair 15 10
538 30c. The Queen wearing cloth of gold supertunica 25 15

160 Map of the World

1977. E.E.C./A.C.P.* Council of Ministers Conference. Multicoloured.
539 4c. Type **160** 10 10
540 30c. Map of Fiji group 30 1·75
*A.C.P. = African, Caribbean, Pacific Group.

161 "Hibiscus rosa-sinensis"

1977. 21st Anniv of Fiji Hibiscus Festival.
541 **161** 4c. multicoloured 10 10
542 - 15c. multicoloured 15 15
543 - 30c. multicoloured 25 30
544 - 35c. multicoloured 40 1·25
Nos. 542/44 show different varieties of "Hibiscus rosa-sinensis".

162 Drua

1977. Canoes. Multicoloured.
545 4c. Type **162** 15 10
546 15c. Tabilai 25 20
547 25c. Takai 30 25
548 40c. Camakua 40 80

163 White Hart of Richard II

1978. 25th Anniv of Coronation. Multicoloured.
549 **163** 25c. brown, green and silver 15 20
550 - 25c. multicoloured 15 20
551 - 25c. brown, green and silver 15 20
DESIGNS: No. 550, Queen Elizabeth II; No. 551, Banded iguana.

164 Defence Force surrounding "Southern Cross", Suva

1978. Aviation Anniversaries. Multicoloured.
552 4c. Type **164** 30 10
553 15c. "Southern Cross" prior to leaving Naselai Beach 50 30
554 25c. Wright "Flyer I" 60 60
555 30c. Bristol F2B "Brisfit" 60 1·25
The 25c. value commemorates the 75th anniv of Powered Flight, the 30c. the 60th anniv of R.A.F. and the other values the 50th anniv of First Trans-Pacific Flight by Kingsford-Smith.

165 Shallow Wooden Oil Dish in Shape of Human Figure

1978. Fijian Artifacts. Multicoloured.
556 4c. Type **165** 10 10
557 15c. Necklace of cachalot teeth (horiz) 10 10
558 25c. Double water bottle (horiz) 15 10
559 30c. Finely carved Ula or throwing club 15 15

166 Advent Crown with Candles (Christmas)

1978. Festivals. Multicoloured.

560	4c. Type **166**	10	10
561	15c. Lamps (Diwali)	15	10
562	25c. Coffee pot, cups and fruit (Id-Ul-Fitr)	20	10
563	40c. Lion (Chinese New Year)	35	40

167 Banded Iguana

1979. Endangered Wildlife. Multicoloured.

564	4c. Type **167**	60	10
565	15c. Tree frog	1·10	15
566	25c. Long-legged warbler	4·25	40
567	30c. Pink-billed parrot finch	4·25	2·40

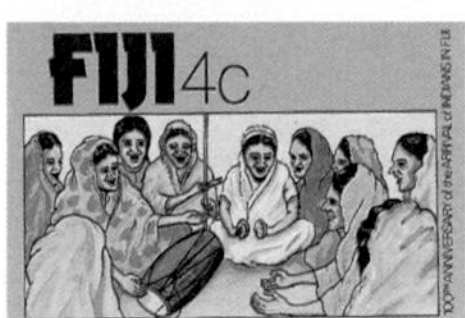

168 Women with Dholak

1979. Centenary of Arrival of Indians. Multicoloured.

568	4c. Type **168**	10	10
569	15c. Men sitting around tanoa	10	10
570	30c. Farmer and sugar cane plantation	15	10
571	40c. Sailing ship "Leonidas"	40	25

169 Soccer

1979. 6th South Pacific Games. Multicoloured.

572	4c. Type **169**	30	10
573	15c. Rugby Union	70	20
574	30c. Lawn tennis	80	80
575	40c. Weightlifting	80	1·40

170 Indian Child and Map of Fiji

1979. International Year of the Child. Multicoloured.

576	4c.+1c. Type **170**	10	10
577	15c.+2c. European child	15	15
578	30c.+3c. Chinese child	15	15
579	40c.+4c. Fijian child	15	20

171 Old Town Hall, Suva

1979. Architecture. Multicoloured.

580A	1c. Type **171**	15	60
581Bc	2c. Dudley Church, Suva	30	20
582A	3c. Fiji International Telecommunications Building, Suva	35	80
722	4c. Lautoka Mosque	30	30
583A	5c. As 4c.	15	10
584B	6c. General Post Office, Suva	15	10
724	8c. Public School, Levuka	2·75	2·25
585A	10c. Fiji Visitors Bureau, Suva	20	10
586A	12c. As 8c.	20	2·75
726	15c. Colonial War Memorial Hospital, Suva	30	20
588A	18c. Labasa sugar mill	20	30
589A	20c. Rewa Bridge, Nausori	55	30
590A	30c. Sacred Heart Cathedral, Suva (vert)	65	50
591A	35c. Grand Pacific Hotel, Suva	30	1·50
592A	45c. Shiva Temple, Suva	30	45
593A	50c. Serua Island Village	30	40
594A	$1 Solo Rock Lighthouse (30×46 mm)	75	2·50
595A	$2 Baker Memorial Hall, Nausori (46×30 mm)	75	1·60
595cA	$5 Government House (46×30 mm)	1·00	2·75

Most values come with or without date imprint.

172 "Southern Cross", 1873

1980. "London 1980" Int Stamp Exhibition. Mult.

596	6c. Type **172**	25	10
597	20c. "Levuka", 1910	35	10
598	45c. "Matua", 1936	40	50
599	50c. "Oronsay", 1951	40	1·00

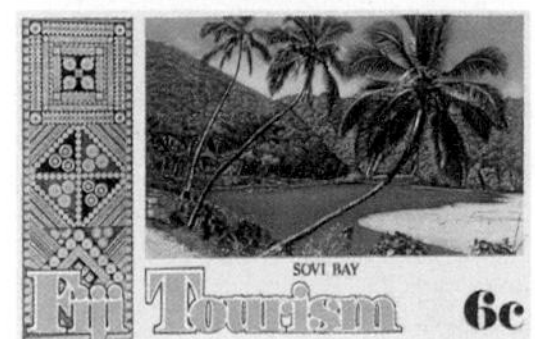

173 Sovi Bay

1980. Tourism. Multicoloured.

600	6c. Type **173**	10	10
601	20c. Evening scene, Yanuca Island	15	15
602	45c. Dravuni Beach	20	40
603	50c. Wakaya Island	20	45

174 Official Opening of Parliament, 1979

1980. 10th Anniv of Independence. Multicoloured.

604	6c. Type **174**	10	10
605	20c. Fiji coat of arms (vert)	15	10
606	45c. Fiji flag	20	30
607	50c. Queen Elizabeth II (vert)	25	60

175 "Coastal Scene" (painting, Semisi Maya)

1981. Int Year for Disabled Persons. Mult.

608	6c. Type **175**	10	10
609	35c. "Underwater Scene" (Semisi Maya)	35	30
610	50c. Semisi Maya (disabled artist) at work (vert)	40	40
611	60c. "Peacock" (Semisi Maya) (vert)	45	45

176 Prince Charles Sailing

1981. Royal Wedding. Multicoloured.

612	6c. Wedding bouquet from Fiji	10	10
613	45c. Type **176**	30	15
614	$1 Prince Charles and Lady Diana Spencer	50	60

177 Operator Assistance Centre

1981. Telecommunications. Multicoloured.

615	6c. Type **177**	10	10
616	35c. Microwave station	35	50
617	50c. Satellite earth station	40	75
618	60c. Cable ship "Retriever"	55	90

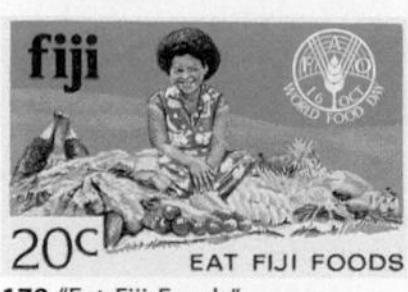

178 "Eat Fiji Foods"

1981. World Food Day.

619	**178** 20c. multicoloured	30	10

179 Ratu Sir Lala Sukuna (first Speaker, Legislative Council)

1981. Commonwealth Parliamentary Association Conference, Suva.

620	**179** 6c. black, buff and brown	10	10
621	- 35c. multicoloured	20	30
622	- 50c. multicoloured	30	45
MS623	73×53 mm. 60c. mult	70	1·00

DESIGNS: 35c. Mace of the House of Representatives; 50c. Suva Civic Centre; 60c. Flags of C.P.A. countries.

180 Bell P-39 Airacobra

1981. World War II Aircraft. Multicoloured.

624	6c. Type **180**	1·10	10
625	18c. Consolidated PBY-5 Catalina	1·90	40
626	35c. Curtiss P-40E Warhawk	2·50	95
627	60c. Short Singapore III	3·00	6·00

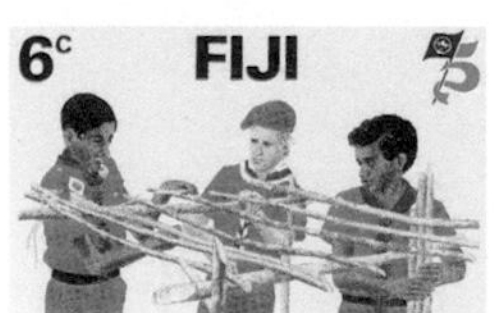

181 Scouts constructing Shelter

1982. 75th Anniv of Boy Scout Movement. Mult.

628	6c. Type **181**	15	10
629	20c. Scouts sailing (vert)	35	30
630	45c. Scouts by campfire	40	50
631	60c. Lord Baden-Powell (vert)	50	1·00

182 Fiji Soldiers at U.N. Checkpoint

1982. Disciplined Forces. Multicoloured.

632	12c. Type **182**	50	10
633	30c. Soldiers engaged on rural development	60	45
634	40c. Police patrol	1·75	1·25
635	70c. "Kiro" (minesweeper)	1·75	5·50

183 Footballers and Fiji Football Association Logo

1982. World Cup Football Championship, Spain.

636	**183** 6c. red, black and yellow	10	10
637	- 18c. multicoloured	25	20
638	- 50c. multicoloured	70	70
639	- 90c. multicoloured	1·10	2·00

DESIGNS: 18c. Footballers and World Cup emblem; 50c. Football and Bernabeu Stadium; 90c. Footballers and Naranjito (mascot).

184 Bride and Groom leaving St. Paul's

1982. 21st Birthday of Princess of Wales. Mult.

640	20c. Fiji coat of arms	20	15
641	35c. Lady Diana Spencer at Broadlands, May 1981	35	25
642	45c. Type **184**	40	40
643	$1 Formal portrait	1·25	2·25

185 Prince Philip

1982. Royal Visit. Multicoloured.

644	6c. Type **185**	75	25
645	45c. Queen Elizabeth II	1·25	3·00
MS646	128×88 mm. Nos. 644/5 and $1 Royal Yacht "Britannia" (horiz)	2·00	3·50

186 Baby Jesus with Mary and Joseph

1982. Christmas. Multicoloured.

647	6c. Type **186**	10	10
648	20c. Three Wise Men presenting gifts	30	20
649	35c. Carol-singing	45	35
MS650	94×42 mm. $1 "Faith" (from the "Three Virtues" by Raphael)	1·25	1·50

187 Red-throated Lorikeet ("Red-throated Lory")

1983. Parrots. Multicoloured.

651	20c. Type **187**	1·25	20
652	40c. Blue-crowned lory	1·50	50
653	55c. Masked shining parrot ("Sulphur-breasted Musk Parrot")	1·75	1·50
654	70c. Kandavu shining parrot ("Red-breasted Musk Parrot")	2·25	4·75

188 Bure in Traditional Village

1983. Commonwealth Day. Multicoloured.

655	8c. Type **188**	10	10
656	25c. Barefoot firewalkers	20	15
657	50c. Sugar industry	30	35
658	80c. Kava "Yagona" ceremony	55	70

189 First Manned Balloon Flight, 1783

1983. Bicentenary of Manned Flight. Multicoloured.
659 8c. Type **189** 25 10
660 20c. Wright brothers' "Flyer I" 35 30
661 25c. Douglas Super DC-3 40 40
662 40c. de Havilland DH.160 Comet 1 60 60
663 50c. Boeing 747 70 70
664 58c. Space shuttle 80 80

190 Nawanawa

1983. Flowers (1st series). Multicoloured.
665 8c. Type **190** 10 10
666 25c. Rosawa 25 30
667 40c. Warerega 30 50
668 $1 Saburo 50 1·40
See also Nos. 680/3.

191 Fijian beating Lali and Earth Satellite Station

1983. World Communications Year.
669 **191** 50c. multicoloured 50 1·25

192 "Dacryopinax spathularia"

1984. Fungi. Multicoloured.
670 8c. Type **192** 85 15
671 15c. "Podoscypha involuta" 1·00 25
672 40c. "Lentinus squarrosulus" 1·75 1·00
673 50c. "Scleroderma cepa" ("Scleroderma flavidum") (horiz) 1·75 1·25
674 $1 "Phillipsia domingensis" (horiz) 2·25 3·50

193 "Tui Lau" (freighter) on Reef

1984. 250th Anniv of "Lloyd's List" (newspaper). Multicoloured.
675 8c. Type **193** 70 10
676 40c. "Tofua" (cargo liner) 1·50 80
677 55c. "Canberra" (liner) 1·50 1·50
678 60c. "Nedlloyd Madras" (freighter) at Suva wharf 1·50 1·75

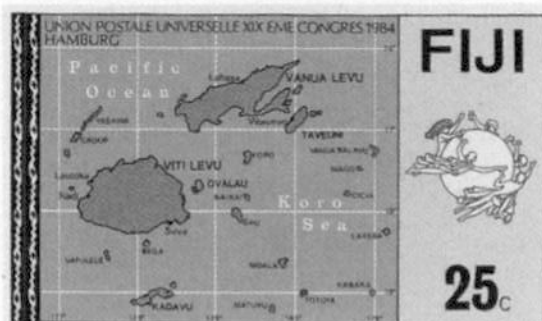

194 Map of Fijian Islands

1984. Universal Postal Union Congress, Hamburg. Sheet 77×65 mm.
MS679 **194** 25c. multicoloured 2·75 2·25

1984. Flowers (2nd series). As T 190. Multicoloured.
680 15c. Drividrivi 25 25
681 20c. Vesida 30 40
682 50c. Vuga 40 90
683 70c. Qaiqi 45 1·40

195 Prize Bull, Yalavou Cattle Scheme

1984. "Ausipex" International Stamp Exhibition, Melbourne. Multicoloured.
684 8c. Type **195** 15 10
685 25c. Wailoa Power Station (vert) 30 40
686 40c. Air Pacific Boeing 737 airliner 1·75 1·25
687 $1 Container ship "Fua Kavenga" 1·10 4·00

196 The Stable at Bethlehem

1984. Christmas. Children's Paintings. Mult.
688 8c. Type **196** 10 10
689 20c. Outrigger canoe 30 20
690 25c. Father Christmas and Christmas tree 30 25
691 40c. Going to church 30 70
692 $1 Decorating Christmas tree (vert) 45 1·75

197 "Danaus plexippus"

1985. Butterflies. Multicoloured.
693 8c. Type **197** 1·50 15
694 25c. "Hypolimnas bolina" 2·50 60
695 40c. "Lampides boeticus" (vert) 3·25 2·25
696 $1 "Precis villida" (vert) 4·50 7·00

198 Outrigger Canoe off Toberua Island

1985. "Expo '85" World Fair, Japan. Multicoloured.
697 20c. Type **198** 55 30
698 25c. Wainivula Falls 1·00 40
699 50c. Mana Island 1·10 1·10
700 $1 Sawa-I-Lau Caves 1·40 2·50

199 With Prince Charles at Garter Ceremony

1985. Life and Times of Queen Elizabeth the Queen Mother. Multicoloured.
701 8c. With Prince Andrew on her 60th Birthday 20 10
702 25c. Type **199** 50 40
703 40c. The Queen Mother at Epsom Races 1·25 80
704 50c. With Prince Henry at his christening (from photo by Lord Snowdon) 1·25 1·25
MS705 91×73 mm. $1 With Prince Andrew at Royal Wedding, 1981 3·50 2·00

200 Horned Squirrelfish

1985. Shallow Water Marine Fishes. Multicoloured.
706 40c. Type **200** 1·00 55
707 50c. Yellow-banded goatfish 1·25 1·10
708 55c. Yellow-edged lyretail ("Fairy cod") 1·25 1·75
709 $1 Peacock hind 1·75 5·00

201 Collared Petrel

1985. Seabirds. Multicoloured.
710 15c. Type **201** 2·00 50
711 20c. Lesser frigate bird 2·00 50
712 50c. Brown booby 3·75 3·75
713 $1 Crested tern 5·50 8·00

1986. 60th Birthday of Queen Elizabeth II. As T 120a of Hong Kong. Multicoloured.
714 20c. With Duke of York at Royal Tournament, 1936 20 25
715 25c. Royal Family on Palace balcony after Princess Margaret's wedding, 1960 20 25
716 40c. Queen inspecting guard of honour, Suva, 1982 25 45
717 50c. In Luxembourg, 1976 30 60
718 $1 At Crown Agents Head Office, London, 1983 45 1·60

202 Children and "Peace for Fiji and the World" Slogan

1986. International Peace Year. Multicoloured.
736 8c. Type **202** 40 25
737 40c. Peace dove and houses 1·00 1·00

203 Halley's Comet in Centaurus Constellation and Newton's Reflector

1986. Appearance of Halley's Comet. Multicoloured.
738 25c. Type **203** 2·25 40
739 40c. Halley's Comet over Lomaiviti 2·50 85
740 $1 "Giotto" spacecraft photographing comet nucleus 3·50 8·00

204 Ground Frog

1986. Reptiles and Amphibians. Multicoloured.
741 8c. Type **204** 65 10
742 20c. Burrowing snake 1·10 30
743 25c. Spotted gecko 1·25 35
744 40c. Crested iguana 1·40 90
745 50c. Blotched skink 1·50 3·25
746 $1 Speckled skink 1·90 6·50

205 Gatawaka

1986. Ancient War Clubs. Multicoloured.
747 25c. Type **205** 90 35
748 40c. Siriti 1·25 60
749 50c. Bulibuli 1·40 1·60
750 $1 Culacula 2·50 3·00

206 Weasel Cone

1987. Cone Shells of Fiji. Multicoloured.
751 15c. Type **206** 70 30
752 20c. Pertusus cone 70 40
753 25c. Admiral cone 75 40
754 40c. Leaden cone 80 1·40
755 50c. Imperial cone 90 2·75
756 $1 Geography cone 1·10 5·00

207 Tagimoucia Flower

1987. Tagimoucia Flower. Sheet 72×55 mm.
MS757 **207** $1 multicoloured 2·75 2·00

1987. "Capex '87" International Stamp Exhibition, Toronto. No. MS757 optd CAPEX '87.
MS758 72×55 mm. $1 Type **207** 11·00 11·00
Stamps from Nos. **MS**757 and **MS**758 are identical as the overprint on **MS**758 appears on the margin of the sheet.

209 Traditional Fijian House

1987. Int Year of Shelter for the Homeless. Mult.

759	55c. Type **209**	45	50
760	70c. Modern bungalows	55	60

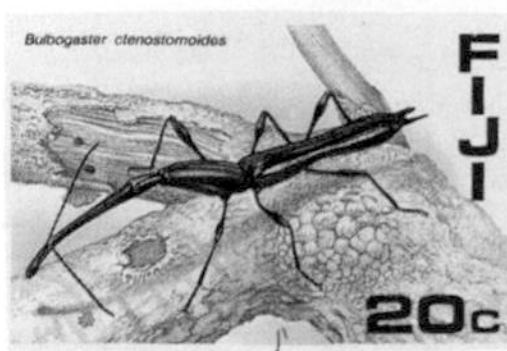

210 "Bulbogaster ctenostomoides" (stick insect)

1987. Fijian Insects. Multicoloured.

761	20c. Type **210**	2·50	50
762	25c. "Paracupta flaviventris" (beetle)	2·50	50
763	40c. "Cerambyrhynchus schoenherri" (beetle)	3·25	1·75
764	50c. "Rhinoscapha lagopyga" (weevil)	3·25	3·75
765	$1 "Xixuthrus heros" (beetle)	4·25	10·00

211 The Nativity

1987. Christmas. Multicoloured.

766	8c. Type **211**	1·00	10
767	40c. The Shepherds (horiz)	2·50	40
768	50c. The Three Kings (horiz)	3·00	1·50
769	$1 The Three Kings presenting gifts	3·75	5·00

212 Windsurfer and Beach

1988. "Expo '88" World Fair, Brisbane.

770	**212**	30c. multicoloured	1·50	1·40

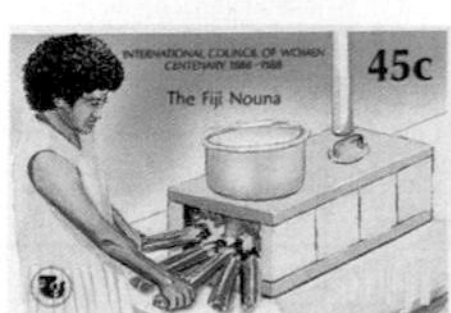

213 Woman using Fiji "Nouna" (stove)

1988. Centenary of International Council of Women.

771	**213**	45c. multicoloured	1·00	1·50

214 Pottery Bowl

1988. Ancient Fijian Pottery. Multicoloured.

772	9c. Type **214**	15	10
773	23c. Cooking pot	25	25
774	58c. Priest's drinking vessel	50	1·25
775	63c. Drinking vessel	55	1·60
776	69c. Earthenware oil lamp	60	1·75
777	75c. Cooking pot with relief pattern (vert)	70	1·75

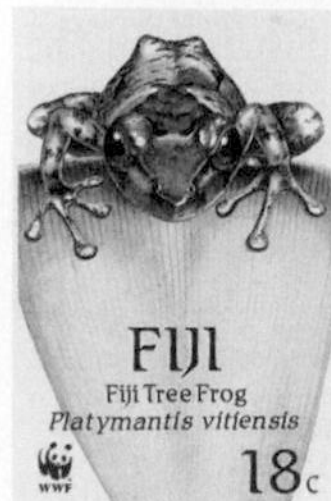

215 Fiji Tree Frog

1988. Fiji Tree Frog. Multicoloured.

778	18c. Type **215**	2·75	1·50
779	23c. Frog climbing grass stalks	3·00	1·50
780	30c. On leaf	3·50	3·50
781	45c. Moving from one leaf to another	4·00	5·00

216 "Dendrobium mohlianum"

1988. Native Flowers. Multicoloured.

782	9c. Type **216**	65	15
783	30c. "Dendrobium cattilare"	90	45
784	45c. "Degeneria vitiensis"	90	70
785	$1 "Degeneria roseiflora"	1·60	2·75

217 Battle of Solferino, 1859

1989. 125th Anniv of International Red Cross.

786	**217**	58c. multicoloured	1·10	80
787	-	63c. multicoloured	1·10	1·00
788	-	69c. multicoloured	1·40	1·25
789	-	$1 black and red	1·50	1·50

DESIGNS—VERT: 63c. Henri Dunant (founder); $1 Anniversary logo. HORIZ: 69c. Fijian Red Cross worker with blood donor.

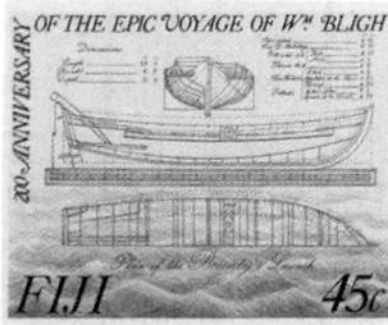

218 Plan of "Bounty's" Launch

1989. Bicent of Capt. Bligh's Boat Voyage. Mult.

790	45c. Type **218**	1·75	50
791	58c. Cup, bowl and Bligh's journal	1·90	1·25
792	80c. Bligh and extract from journal	3·00	2·75
793	$1 "Bounty's" launch and map of Fiji	4·00	3·00

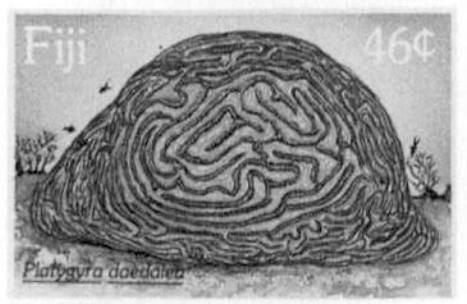

219 "Platygyra daedalea"

1989. Corals. Multicoloured.

794	46c. Type **219**	1·50	75
795	60c. "Caulastrea furcata"	1·75	1·75
796	75c. "Acropora echinata" (vert)	2·00	2·25
797	90c. "Acropora humilis" (vert)	2·25	2·75

220 Goalkeeper

1989. World Cup Football Championship, Italy (1990). Multicoloured.

798	35c. Type **220**	1·25	40
799	63c. Goalkeeper catching ball	2·00	2·25
800	70c. Player with ball	2·25	2·50
801	85c. Tackling	2·25	3·00

221 Congregation in Church

1989. Christmas. Multicoloured.

802	9c. Type **221**	25	10
803	45c. "Delonix regia" (Christmas tree)	75	35
804	$1 The Nativity	1·50	2·00
805	$1.40 Fijian children under tree	1·75	4·50

222 River Snapper

1990. Freshwater Fishes. Multicoloured.

806	50c. Type **222**	1·75	70
807	70c. Kner's grunter ("Orange-spotted Therapon")	2·25	3·00
808	85c. Spotted scat	2·50	3·50
809	$1 Rock flagtail	2·75	4·00

223 1968 3d. Reef Heron Definitive

1990. "Stamp World London 90" International Stamp Exhibition, London. Sheet 120x70 mm, containing T 223 and similar vert design. Multicoloured.

MS810	$1 Type **223**; $2 1968 1s.6d. Orange-breasted honeyeaters definitive	8·50	9·00

224 Vertiver Grass Contours

1990. Soil Conservation. Multicoloured.

811	50c. Type **224**	1·50	50
812	70c. Mulching	1·75	1·75
813	90c. Hillside contour cultivation	1·90	2·25
814	$1 Land use rotation (vert)	2·00	2·50

225 "Dacrydium nidulum"

1990. Timber Trees. Multicoloured.

815	25c. Type **225**	75	20
816	35c. "Decussocarpus vitiensis"	85	30
817	$1 "Agathis vitiensis"	2·50	3·00
818	$1.55 "Santalum yasy"	3·50	5·50

226 "Hark the Herald Angels sing"

1990. Christmas. Carols. Multicoloured.

819	10c. Type **226**	30	10
820	35c. "Still the Night, Holy the Night"	75	30
821	65c. "Joy to the World!"	1·25	1·75
822	$1 "The Race that long in Darkness pined"	2·00	2·75

227 Sigatoka Sand Dunes

1991. Environmental Protection. Multicoloured.

823	35c. Type **227**	1·00	30
824	50c. Monu and Monuriki Islands	1·75	1·00
825	65c. Ravilevu Nature Reserve, Taveuni	2·00	2·75
826	$1 Colo-I-Suva Forest Park	3·00	4·25

228 H.M.S. "Pandora" (frigate)

1991. Bicentenary of Discovery of Rotuma Island. Multicoloured.

827	54c. Type **228**	2·25	1·00
828	70c. Map of Rotuma	2·50	2·75
829	75c. Natives welcoming H.M.S. "Pandora"	2·50	2·75
830	$1 Mount Soloroa and Uea Island	3·75	4·50

229 "Scylla serrata"

1991. Mangrove Crabs. Multicoloured.

831	38c. Type **229**	90	35
832	54c. "Metopograpsus messor"	1·25	85
833	96c. "Parasesarma erythrodactyla"	2·25	3·00
834	$1.65 "Cardisoma carnifex"	3·25	5·50

230 Mary and Joseph travelling to Bethlehem

1991. Christmas. Multicoloured.

835	11c. Type **230**	40	10
836	75c. Manger scene	1·50	1·25
837	96c. Presentation in the Temple	1·75	3·00
838	$1 Infant Jesus with symbols	1·75	3·00

231 de Havilland D.H.89 Dragon Rapide of Fiji Airways

1991. 40th Anniv of Air Pacific. Multicoloured.

839	54c. Type **231**	1·75	1·00
840	75c. Douglas DC-3	2·25	2·25
841	96c. Aerospatial/Aeritalia ATR42	2·50	3·25

842	$1.40 Boeing 767	3·50	5·00

232 Ethnic Dancers

1992. "Expo 92" World's Fair, Seville, Spain. Multicoloured.

843	27c. Type **232**	65	45
844	75c. Peoples of Fiji	1·60	1·75
845	96c. Gold bars and sugar cane train	8·00	5·50
846	$1.40 "Queen Elizabeth 2" (cruise liner) at Suva	8·50	8·00

233 "Tabusoro"

1992. Inter-Islands Shipping. Multicoloured.

847	38c. Type **233**	2·25	55
848	54c. "Degei II"	2·75	1·40
849	$1.40 "Dausoko"	4·75	4·25
850	$1.65 "Nivanga"	4·75	4·25

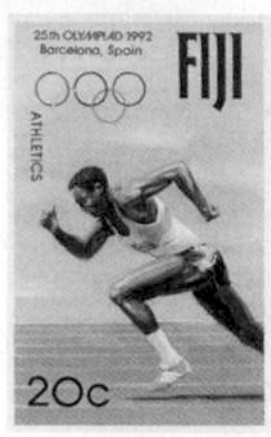

234 Running

1992. Olympic Games, Barcelona. Multicoloured.

851	20c. Type **234**	1·00	20
852	86c. Dinghy sailing	3·00	2·50
853	$1.34 Swimming	3·50	4·00
854	$1.50 Judo	3·50	4·00

235 European War Memorial, Levuka

1992. Historic Levuka (former capital). Mult.

855	30c. Type **235**	30	30
856	42c. Map of Fiji	45	55
857	59c. Beach Street	65	1·00
858	77c. Sacred Heart Church (vert)	80	1·50
859	$2 Deed of Cession site (vert)	1·75	3·75

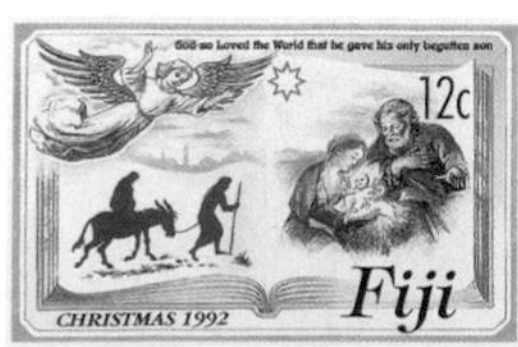

236 The Nativity

1992. Christmas. Multicoloured.

860	12c. Type **236**	75	10
861	77c. Shepherds and family giving presents	2·25	1·60
862	83c. Shepherds at manger and giving presents to pensioners	2·25	1·75
863	$2 Wise Men and collecting Fiji produce	3·75	6·00

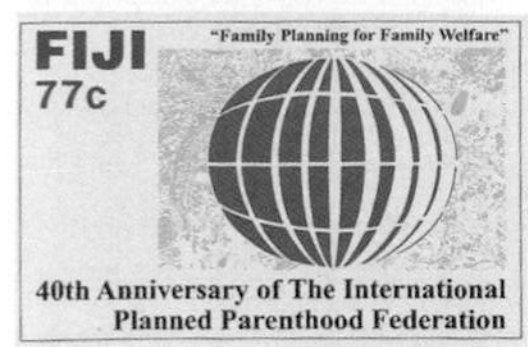

237 International Planned Parenthood Federation Logo

1992. 40th Anniv of International Planned Parenthood Federation. Multicoloured.

864	77c. Type **237**	1·00	85
865	$2 Man weeping and pregnant mother with children	2·75	3·50

238 Dove and Peace Corps Emblem

1993. 25th Anniv of Peace Corps in Fiji. Mult.

866	59c. Type **238**	1·10	75
867	77c. Handshake	1·40	1·40
868	$1 Educational symbols	1·75	1·75
869	$2 Symbols of home businesses scheme	3·00	5·00

239 Fijian Players performing Cibi (traditional dance)

1993. Hong Kong Rugby Sevens Competition. Multicoloured.

870	77c. Type **239**	2·00	1·40
871	$1.06 Players and map of Pacific	3·75	3·00
872	$2 Scrum and stadium	4·50	6·00

1993. 75th Anniv of Royal Air Force. As T 174a of Falkland Islands. Multicoloured.

873	59c. Gloster Gauntlet II	1·60	75
874	77c. Armstrong Whitworth Whitley Mk V	1·75	1·40
875	83c. Bristol F2B "Brisfit"	1·90	1·60
876	$2 Hawker Tempest Mk V	3·25	4·50
MS877	110×77 mm. $1 Vickers Vildebeest III; $1 Handley Page Hampden; $1 Vickers FB-27 Vimy; $1 British Aerospace Hawk T.1	6·50	6·50

240 "Chromodoris fidelis"

1993. Nudibranchs. Multicoloured.

878	12c. Type **240**	65	10
879	42c. "Halgerda carlsoni"	1·40	55
880	53c. "Chromodoris lochi"	1·50	1·25
881	83c. Blue sea lizard	2·25	2·25
882	$1 "Phyllidia bourguini"	2·50	2·50
883	$2 Spanish dancer	3·75	6·00

241 Mango

1993. Tropical Fruits. Multicoloured.

884	30c. Type **241**	1·90	45
885	42c. Guava	2·00	80
886	$1 Lemon	3·75	2·75
887	$2 Soursop	7·00	8·00

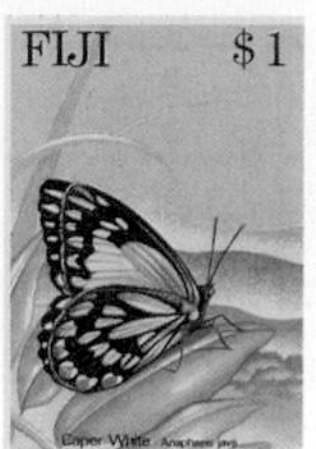

242 "Anaphaesis java"

1994. "Hong Kong '94" International Stamp Exhibition. (a) No. MS877 optd HONG KONG '94 and emblem on each stamp.

MS888	110×77 mm. $1 Vickers Vildebeest III; $1 Handley Page Hampden; $1 Vickers FB-27 Vimy; $1 British Aerospace Hawk T.1	5·00	7·50

(b) Sheet 122×85 mm containing T 242 and similar vert designs showing butterflies. Multicoloured.

MS889	$1 Type **242**; $1 *Euploea leucostictos*; $1 *Vagrans egista*; $1 *Acraea andromache*	4·50	6·00

243 The Last Supper

1994. Easter. Multicoloured.

890	59c. Type **243**	1·25	60
891	77c. The Crucifixion (vert)	1·50	1·25
892	$1 The Resurrection	2·00	2·25
893	$2 Examining Christ's wounds (vert)	3·50	6·50

244 Sagati

1994. Edible Seaweeds. Multicoloured.

894	42c. Type **244**	90	45
895	83c. Nama	1·75	2·00
896	$1 Lumicevata	2·00	2·50
897	$2 Lumiwawa	3·50	6·50

245 White-collared Kingfisher on Branch

1994. White-collared Kingfisher. Sheet 98×84 mm, containing T 245 and similar vert design. Multicoloured.

MS898	$1.50, Type **245**; $1.50, Kingfisher with crab in beak	8·50	10·00

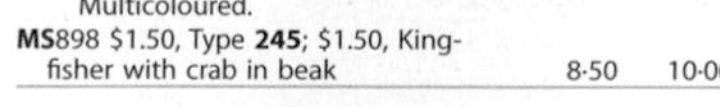

246 "Neoveitchia storckii"

1994. "Singpex '94" International Stamp Exhibition. Endemic Palm. Sheet 97×69 mm, containing T 246 and similar vert design. Multicoloured.

MS899	$1.50, Type **246**; $1.50, Palm flowers	8·00	10·00

247 Father Ioane Batita

1994. 150th Anniv of Arrival of Catholic Missionaries in Fiji. Multicoloured.

900	23c. Type **247**	35	25
901	31c. Local catechist	45	30
902	44c. Sacred Heart Cathedral, Suva	60	70
903	63c. Lomary Church	80	1·10
904	81c. Pope Gregory XVI	1·50	1·75
905	$2 Pope John Paul II	3·00	4·50

248 Waterfall and Banded Iguana

1995. Eco-Tourism in Fiji. Sheet 140×80 mm, containing T 248 and similar square designs. Multicoloured.

MS906	81c. Type **248**; 81c. Mountain trekkers and Fiji Tree Frog; 81c. Bilibili River trip and White-collared kingfisher ("Kingfisher"); 81c. Historic sites and Flying Fox	4·75	7·00

1995. 50th Anniv of End of Second World War. As T 184a of Falkland Islands. Multicoloured.

907	13c. Fijian soldiers guarding crashed Japanese Mitsubishi A6M Zero-Sen aircraft	60	20
908	63c. Aeronica L-3 Grasshopper American spotter plane landing on Kameli Airstrip, Solomon Islands	1·75	1·50
909	87c. Corporal Sukanaivalu and Victoria Cross	2·00	2·50
910	$1.12 H.M.S. "Fiji" (cruiser)	2·50	2·75
MS911	75×85 mm. $2 Reverse of 1939–45 War Medal (vert)	2·25	2·75

249 Red-headed Parrot Finch

1995. Birds. Multicoloured.

912	1c. Type **249**	75	1·00
913	2c. Golden whistler	75	1·00
914	3c. Ogea flycatcher	75	1·00
915	4c. Peale's pigeon	75	1·00
916	6c. Blue-headed flycatcher ("Blue-crested Broadbill")	75	1·00
917	13c. Island thrush	55	20
918	23c. Many-coloured fruit dove	55	30
919	31c. Green-backed heron ("Mangrove heron")	55	35
920	44c. Purple swamphen	70	40
921	63c. Fiji goshawk	1·00	50
922	81c. Kandavu fantail ("Kadavu Fantail")	1·25	65
923	87c. Collard lory	1·75	75
924	$1 Scarlet robin	2·00	85
925	$2 Peregrine falcon	2·50	1·75
926	$3 Barn owl	3·50	3·25
927	$5 Masked shining parrot ("Yellow-breasted musk parrot")	4·50	4·50

1995. "JAKARTA '95" Stamp Exhibition, Indonesia. No. MS898 optd "JAKARTA '95" and emblem on sheet margin.

MS928	$1.50, Type **245**; $1.50, White-collared kingfisher with crab in beak	8·50	10·00

250 "Arundina graminifolia"

1995. Orchids. Sheet 100×80 mm, containing T 250 and similar vert design.

MS929	$1 Type **250**; $1 "Phaius tankervilliae"	4·50	6·00

No. **MS**929 also includes "Singapore '95" and emblem on the sheet margin.

251 Pres. Ratu Sir Kamisese Mara, Parliament Building and National Flag

1995. 25th Anniv of Independence. Multicoloured.

930	81c. Type **251**	1·25	1·00
931	87c. Young citizens of Fiji	1·00	1·10
932	$1.06 Rugby players	1·75	2·25
933	$2 Boeing 747 "Island of Viti Levu"	3·25	5·00

252 "Praying Madonna with the Crown of Stars" (workshop of Correggio)

1995. Christmas. Multicoloured.

934	10c. Type **252**	25	10
935	63c. "Madonna and Child with Crowns" (on porcelain)	90	80
936	87c. "The Holy Virgin with Holy Child and St. John" (after Titian)	1·25	1·25
937	$2 "The Holy Family and St. John" (workshop of Rubens)	2·75	5·50

253 Trolling Lure

1996. 50th Anniv of Resettlement of Banabans (inhabitans of Ocean Island) in Fiji. Multicoloured.

938	81c. Type **253**	1·00	1·10
939	87c. Banaban fishing canoes	1·25	1·25
940	$1.12 Banaban warrior (vert)	1·40	2·00
941	$2 Great frigate bird (vert)	6·00	6·50

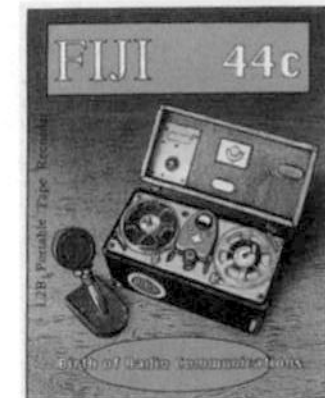

254 L2B Portable Tape Recorder

1996. Centenary of Radio. Multicoloured.

942	44c. Type **254**	70	45
943	63c. Broadcasting House, Fiji	90	70
944	81c. Communications satellite	1·40	1·25
945	$3 Guglielmo Marconi	4·00	6·50

255 Winged Monster and Ring (bronze), c. 450 B.C.

1996. "CHINA '96" 9th Asian International Stamp Exhibition, Peking. Multicoloured.

946	63c. Type **255**	85	65
947	81c. Archer (terracotta sculpture), 210 B.C	1·10	1·10
948	$1 Dragon plate, 1426–35	1·40	1·50
949	$2 Central Asian horseman (sculpture), 706	2·75	5·00
MS950	81×127 mm. 30c. "Yan Deng Mountains" (painting) (48½×76 mm)	2·25	3·00

256 Hurdling

1996. Cent of Modern Olympic Games. Mult.

951	31c. Type **256**	65	30
952	63c. Judo	1·25	80
953	87c. Sailboarding	1·40	1·75
954	$1.12 Swimming	1·60	2·50
MS955	59×99 mm. $2 Winning athlete, 1896	2·50	3·25

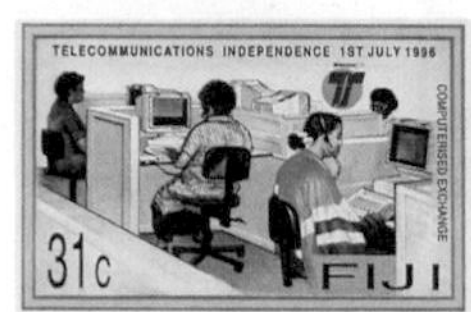

257 Computerized Telephone Exchange

1996. Inauguration of Independent Postal and Telecommunications Companies. Multicoloured.

956	31c. Type **257**	40	30
957	44c. Unloading mail from aircraft	80	65
958	81c. Manual telephone exchange (vert)	1·00	1·50
959	$1 Postman on motorbike (vert)	1·75	2·00
MS960	120×77 mm. $1.50, Fiji 1938 ½d. Sailing canoe stamp (vert); $1.50, Fiji 1985 20c. "Expo '85" stamp (vert)	11·00	12·00

258 "Our Children Our Future"

1996. 50th Anniv of UNICEF. Children's Paintings. Multicoloured.

961	81c. Type **258**	1·50	1·25
962	87c. "Village Scene"	1·50	1·25
963	$1 "Living in Harmony the World over"	1·60	1·60
964	$2 "Their Future"	2·50	5·50

259 First Seaplane in Fiji, 1921

1996. 50th Anniv of Nadi International Airport. Multicoloured.

965	31c. Type **259**	65	30
966	44c. Nadi Airport in 1946	80	50
967	63c. Arrival of Boeing 707, first jet airliner, 1959	1·25	1·00
968	87c. Airport entrance	1·40	1·50
969	$1 Control tower	1·60	1·75
970	$2 Diagram of Global Positioning System	2·75	5·00

260 The Annunciation and Fijian beating Lali (drum)

1996. Christmas. Multicoloured.

971	13c. Type **260**	40	15
972	81c. Shepherds with sheep, and canoe	1·40	85
973	$1 Wise men on camels, and people on cross	1·60	1·40
974	$3 The Nativity, and Fijian blowing conch	4·75	7·00

261 Brahman

1997. "HONG KONG '97" International Stamp Exhibition. Cattle. Sheet 130×92 mm, containing T 261 and similar horiz designs. Multicoloured.

MS975	$1 Type **261**; $1 Friesian (Holstein); $1 Hereford; $1 Fiji draught bullock	5·00	6·50

No. **MS**975 is inscribed "FREISIAN" in error.

262 Black-throated Shrikebill

1997. "SINGPEX '97" Stamp Exhibition, Singapore. Sheet 92×78 mm.

MS976	**262** $2 multicoloured	2·75	3·75

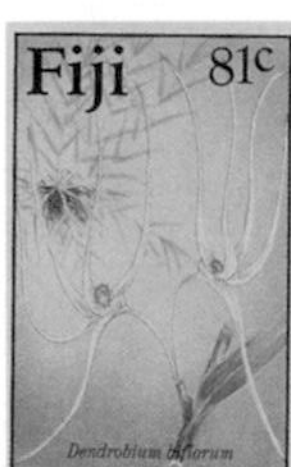

263 "Dendrobium biflorum"

1997. Orchids. Multicoloured.

977	81c. Type **263**	1·50	1·25
978	87c. "Dendrobium dactylodes"	1·50	1·25
979	$1.06 "Spathoglottis pacifica"	1·75	2·00
980	$2 "Dendrobium macropus"	3·00	4·50

264 Hawksbill Turtle laying Eggs

1997. Life Cycle of Hawksbill Turtle. Sheet 140×85 mm, containing T 264 and similar horiz designs. Multicoloured.

MS981	63c. Type **264**; 81c. Turtles hatching; $1.06, Young turtles swimming; $2 Adult turtle	7·50	9·00

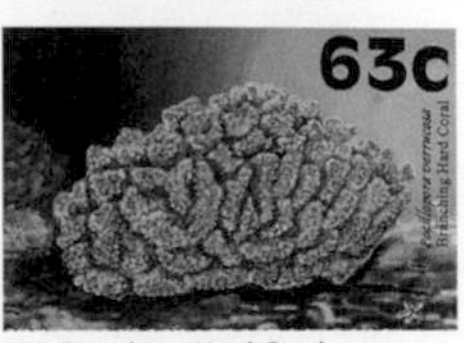

265 Branching Hard Coral

1997. Year of the Coral Reef. Multicoloured.

982	63c. Type **265**	1·00	55
983	87c. Massive hard coral	1·40	1·25
984	$1 White soft coral	1·60	1·60
985	$3 Pink soft coral	4·25	7·00

266 Fijian Monkey-faced Bat

1997. Endangered Species. Fijian Monkey-faced Bat.

986	**266** 44c. multicoloured	70	40
987	- 63c. multicoloured	90	60
988	- 81c. multicoloured	1·25	1·10
989	- $2 multicoloured	2·50	4·50
MS990	157×106 mm. Nos. 986/9×2	8·00	10·00

DESIGNS: 63c. to $2 Showing different bats.

267 Waisale Serevi (Captain)

1997. Fiji Rugby Club's Victory in Hong Kong Rugby Sevens Competition. Multicoloured.

991	50c. Type **267**	65	85
992	50c. Taniela Qauqau	65	85
993	50c. Jope Tuikabe	65	85
994	50c. Leveni Duvuduvukula	65	85
995	50c. Inoke Maraiwai	65	85
996	50c. Aminiasi Naituyaga	65	85
997	50c. Lemki Koroi	65	85
998	50c. Marika Vunibaka	65	85
999	50c. Luke Erenavula	65	85
1000	50c. Manasa Bari	65	85
1001	$1 Fijian rugby team (56×42 mm)	80	1·00

268 Shepherd and Angel

1997. Christmas. Multicoloured.

1002	13c. Type **268**	25	10
1003	31c. Mary, Joseph and baby Jesus	50	30
1004	87c. The Three Kings	1·25	90
1005	$3 Mary and baby Jesus	3·50	6·50

269 Chief in War Dress

1998. Traditional Chiefs' Costumes. Multicoloured.

1006	81c. Type **269**	85	75
1007	87c. Formal dress	95	90
1008	$1.12 Presentation dress	1·40	1·75
1009	$2 War dress of Highland chief	2·00	3·50

270 Man in Wheelchair using Computer

1998. Asian and Pacific Decade of Disabled People. Multicoloured.

1010	63c. Type **270**	1·50	60
1011	87c. Woman with child	1·60	80
1012	$1 Man at desk	1·90	1·40
1013	$2 Wheelchair race	2·75	4·25

270a Diana, Princess of Wales, 1990

1998. Diana, Princess of Wales Commemoration.

1014	**270a** 81c. multicoloured	1·00	1·00
MS1015	145×70 mm. 81c. As No. 1014; 81c. Wearing blue jacket, 1991; 81c. Wearing high-necked blouse, 1990; 81c. Carrying bouquet. Sold at $3.24 + 50c. charity premium	2·25	3·25

270b R-34 Airship

1998. 80th Anniv of Royal Air Force. Multicoloured.

1016	44c. Type **270b**	70	30
1017	63c. Handley Page H.P.50 Heyford	1·00	60
1018	87c. Supermarine Swift FR.5	1·40	1·00
1019	$2 Westland Whirlwind	2·25	3·00
MS1020	110×77 mm. $1 Sopwith Dolphin; $1 Avro 504K; $1 Vickers Warwick V; $1 Shorts Belfast	3·75	4·50

271 Pod of Sperm Whales Underwater

1998. Sperm Whales. Multicoloured.

1021	63c. Type **271**	1·25	55
1022	81c. Female and calf	1·40	90
1023	87c. Pod on surface	1·60	1·00
1024	$2 Ceremonial whale tooth	2·25	3·50
MS1025	90×68 mm. No. 1024	3·00	4·00

272 Athletics

1998. 16th Commonwealth Games, Kuala Lumpur. Multicoloured.

1026	44c. Type **272**	85	30
1027	63c. Lawn bowls	1·10	45
1028	81c. Throwing the javelin	1·50	1·10
1029	$1.12 Weightlifting	1·75	2·50
MS1030	63×77 mm. $2 Waisale Serevi (Fiji rugby captain)	2·50	3·25

273 Takia (traditional raft)

1998. Maritime Past and Present (1st series). Multicoloured.

1031	13c. Type **273**	25	10
1032	44c. Camakau (outrigger canoe)	50	30
1033	87c. Drua (outrigger canoe)	1·00	90
1034	$3 "Pioneer" (inter-island ship)	4·25	6·50
MS1035	105×75 mm. $1.50, Camakau (outrigger canoe)	2·25	3·50

See also Nos. 1044/48.

274 "Jesus in a Manger" (Grace Lee)

1998. Christmas. Children's Paintings. Multicoloured.

1036	13c. Type **274**	40	10
1037	50c. "A Time with Family and Friends" (Brian Guevara)	90	35
1038	$1 "What Christmas Means to Me" (Naomi Tupou) (vert)	1·50	1·00
1039	$2 "The Joy of Christmas" (Lauretta Ah Sam) (vert)	2·00	4·00

275 Women's Sitting Dance

1999. Traditional Fijian Dances. Multicoloured.

1040	13c. Type **275**	75	15
1041	81c. Club dance	2·00	1·25
1042	87c. Women's fan dance	2·00	1·25
1043	$3 Kava-serving dance	5·00	7·00

1999. Maritime Past and Present (2nd series). As T 273. Multicoloured.

1044	63c. "Tofua I" (cargo liner)	1·50	55
1045	81c. "Adi Beti" (government launch)	1·60	75
1046	$1 "Niagara" (liner)	1·75	1·50
1047	$2 "Royal Viking Sun" (liner)	3·00	4·00
MS1048	105×75 mm. $1.50, "Makatea" (inter-island freighter)	2·75	3·50

276 Wandering Whistling Duck

1999. "iBRA '99" International Stamp Exhibition, Nuremberg. Sheet 100×95 mm, containing T 276 and similar vert design. Multicoloured.

MS1049	$2 Type **276**; $2 Pacific black duck	4·00	4·25

277 "Calanthe ventilabrum"

1999. Orchids. Multicoloured.

1050	44c. Type **277**	85	35
1051	63c. "Dendrobium prasinum"	1·10	45
1052	81c. "Dendrobium macrophyllum"	1·40	70
1053	$3 "Dendrobium tokai"	3·00	5·00

277a Astronaut preparing to enter Module

1999. 30th Anniv of First Manned Landing on Moon. Multicoloured.

1054	13c. Type **277a**	35	10
1055	87c. Third stage rockets firing near Moon	1·00	70
1056	$1 Buzz Aldrin on Moon's surface	1·10	1·00
1057	$2 Command module returning to Earth	1·75	2·50
MS1058	90×80 mm. $2 Earth as seen from Moon (circular, 40 mm diam)	2·00	2·50

1999. "Queen Elizabeth the Queen Mother's Century." As T 204a of Falkland Islands. Mult.

1059	13c. Inspecting bomb damage, Hull, 1940	50	10
1060	63c. With Prince Charles, 1950	1·00	55
1061	81c. Meeting soldiers from the Light Infantry	1·50	85
1062	$3 Saying goodbye to Prince Charles, 1986	2·75	4·25
MS1063	145×70 mm. $2 Lady Elizabeth Bowes-Lyon, 1923 and Armistice Day celebrations, 1918	2·75	3·25

278 Sugar Mills Diesel Locomotive

1999. 125th Anniv of U.P.U. Sugar Mill Locomotives.

1064	50c. Type **278**	65	35
1065	87c. Steam locomotive	1·00	75
1066	$1 Diesel locomotive "Hunsley"	1·10	90
1067	$2 Free passenger service	2·00	3·50

279 Exchanging Gifts

1999. Christmas. Multicoloured.

1068	13c. Type **279**	20	15
1069	31c. Two angels over Earth	40	30
1070	63c. Open Bible	70	45
1071	87c. Joseph and Mary on donkey (vert)	85	70
1072	$1 The Nativity (vert)	95	80
1073	$2 Children and Father Christmas (vert)	1·60	3·25

280 Sun rising over Islands and Hands holding Ceremonial Objects

2000. New Millennium. Multicoloured.

1074	$5 Type **280**	5·00	6·00
1075	$5 Traditional sailing canoe and globe (vert)	5·00	6·00
1076	$5 Fijian warrior beating drum, palm trees and hut	5·00	6·00
1077	$5 Fijian flag and map of islands (vert)	5·00	6·00
MS1078	133×93 mm. $10 Macgillivary's petrel; $10 Crested iguana; $10 Prawns; $10 Indigenous flowers	38·00	42·00

281 *Paracupta sulcata* (beetle)

2000. Beetles. Multicoloured.

1079	15c. Type **281**	35	10
1080	87c. *Agrilus* sp.	1·00	65
1081	$1.06 *Cyphogastra abdominalis*	1·25	1·50
1082	$2 *Paracupta* sp.	2·00	3·00

282 Big Bird

2000. Sesame Street (children's T.V. programme). Multicoloured.

1083	50c. Type **282**	70	85
1084	50c. Oscar the Grouch in dustbin	70	85
1085	50c. Cookie Monster eating cookie	70	85
1086	50c. Grover (turquoise background)	70	85
1087	50c. Elmo (blue background)	70	85
1088	50c. Ernie (yellow background)	70	85
1089	50c. Zoe (pink background)	70	85
1090	50c. The Count (blue background)	70	85
1091	50c. Bert (green background)	70	85
MS1092	Two sheets, each 139×86 mm. (a) $2 Bert and birthday cake (horiz). (b) $2 Big Bird, Elmo and Ernie in tree house (horiz) Set of 2 sheets	4·00	5·00

283 President Ratu Sir Kamisese Mara and Forestry Plantation

2000. 80th Birthday of President Ratu Sir Kamisese Mara. Multicoloured.

1093	15c. Type **283**	25	15
1094	81c. Pres. Mara and Fijians	70	55
1095	$1 Pres. Mara and harvesting sugar	80	65
1096	$3 Wearing naval uniform and patrol boats	3·25	5·00

2000. 18th Birthday of Prince William. As T 208c of Falkland Islands. Multicoloured.

1097	$1 Prince William wearing fireman's helmet	1·25	1·25
1098	$1 At Clarence House, 1995	1·25	1·25
1099	$1 Prince William waving (horiz)	1·25	1·25
1100	$1 At Christmas service, 1998 (horiz)	1·25	1·25
MS1101	175×95 mm. $1 Wearing Parachute Regiment uniform and Nos. 1097/1100	7·50	7·50

284 Swimming

2000. Olympic Games, Sydney. Multicoloured.

1102	44c. Type **284**	60	35
1103	87c. Judo	95	60
1104	$1 Running (horiz)	1·10	1·10
1105	$2 Windsurfing (horiz)	2·00	3·50

285 Top Left Leaf Fronds of *Alsmithia longpipes*

2000. Alsmithia longpipes (Endemic Palm of Fiji). Sheet 121×85 mm, containing T 285 and similar horiz designs forming a complete palm.

MS1106	$1 Type **285**; $1 Top right leaf fronds; $1 Flower and stem of palm; $1 Stem of palm and berries	3·75	4·50

286 Pottery Fragment and Site on Yanuca Island, Nadroga

2000. Lapita Pottery. Showing excavation sites and pottery fragments. Multicoloured.

1107	44c. Type **286**	55	35
1108	63c. Vutua, Mago Island	75	55
1109	$1 Ugaga Island, Beqa	1·10	1·25
1110	$2 Sigatoka Sand Dunes	1·75	2·75

287 Three Kings in Jungle

2000. Christmas. Journey of the Three Kings in Fijian Setting. Multicoloured.

1111	15c. Type **287**	30	10
1112	81c. Three Kings on precipice	95	55
1113	87c. Three Kings by lagoon	1·00	60
1114	$3 Three Kings on canoe	2·75	4·75

288 Orange Dove

2001. Taveuni Rainforest. Sheet 122×86 mm, containing T 288 and similar vert design. Multicoloured.

MS1115	$2 Type **288**; $2 *Xisuthrus heyrovskyi* (beetle)	4·75	6·00

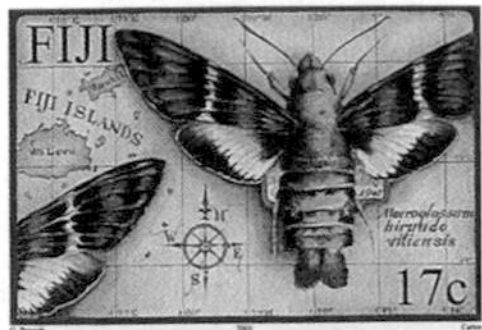

289 *Macroglossum hirundo vitiensis* (moth)

2001. Hawk Moths of Fiji. Multicoloured.

1116	17c. Type **289**	30	10
1117	48c. *Hippotion celerio*	55	40
1118	69c. *Gnatholhlibus erotus eras*	75	65
1119	89c. *Theretra pinastrina intersecta*	85	95
1120	$1.17 *Deilephila placida torenia*	95	1·40
1121	$2 *Psilogramma jordana*	1·50	2·75

290 Red Junglefowl Hen

2001. Jungle Fowl of Fiji. Sheet 122×86 mm, containing T 290 and similar horiz dseign. Multicoloured.

MS1122	$2 Type **290**; $2 Red junglefowl cock	5·50	6·50

291 Girl with "Mile-a-Minute" (cat)

2001. Fijian Society for the Prevention of Cruelty to Animals. Multicoloured.

1123	34c. Type **291**	40	30
1124	96c. Boy with two puppies	90	90
1125	$1.23 Girl with "Twistie" (cat)	1·00	1·25
1126	$2 Boy with "Rani" (dog)	1·50	2·50

292 White-throated Pigeon

2001. Pigeons. Multicoloured.

1127	69c. Type **292**	1·00	75
1128	89c. Pacific pigeon (vert)	1·40	1·00
1129	$1.23 Peale's pigeon (vert)	1·75	1·60
1130	$2 Rock pigeon	2·25	3·50

No. 1129 is inscribed "PEAL'S PIGEON" in error.

293 Bank of New South Wales (1901)

2001. Centenary of the Westpac Bank. Multicoloured.

1131	48c. Type **293**	50	40
1132	96c. Bank of New South Wales (1916)	90	85
1133	$1 Bank of New South Wales (1934)	90	85
1134	$2 Westpac Bank (2001)	1·60	2·50

294 Yellow-finned Tuna

2001. Game Fish (1st series). Multicoloured.

1135	50c. Type **294**	70	55
1136	96c. Wahoo	90	75
1137	$1.17 Dolphin fish	1·00	1·25
1138	$2 Blue marlin	1·75	2·75

See also Nos. 1282/5.

295 Angel appearing to Mary on Beach

2001. Christmas. The Nativity Story in a Fijian setting. Multicoloured.

1139	17c. Type **295**	45	10
1140	34c. Birth of Jesus in stable	60	15
1141	48c. Local shepherds visiting the baby	75	45
1142	69c. Fijian wise men bringing gifts	1·10	70
1143	89c. Holy family boarding canoe	1·40	75
1144	$2 Jesus with purple-capped fruit dove	3·00	4·00

296 Colonial Building

2001. 125th Anniv of Colonial Mutual Life Assurance Ltd in Fiji. Multicoloured.

1145	17c. Type **296**	50	10
1146	48c. Women at Colonial cash point	90	45
1147	$1 Private hospital, Suva	1·75	1·10
1148	$3 Deed of Cession ceremony, 1874	3·25	5·00

297 Fiji Airways de Havilland Australia DHA-3 Drover Aircraft (1950s)

2001. 50th Anniv of Air Pacific. Multicoloured.

1149	89c. Type **297**	1·60	1·75
1150	96c. Hawker Siddeley 748 (1967)	1·75	2·00
1151	$1 Douglas DC-10 (1980s)	1·75	2·00
1152	$2 Boeing 747-200 (1985)	2·25	2·50

Nos. 1149/52 were printed together, se-tenant, with the backgrounds forming a composite design.

298 Pepper

2002. Spices. Multicoloured.

1153	69c. Type **298**	80	55
1154	89c. Nutmeg	1·00	70
1155	$1 Vanilla	1·40	1·60
1156	$2 Cinnamon	1·75	3·25

299 Balaka Palm Tree with Bird and Butterfly

2002. Seemann's Balaka Palm. Sheet 97×107 mm, containing T 299 and similar vert design. Multicoloured.

MS1157	$2 Type **299**; $2 Balaka palm in fruit with lizard on trunk	5·50	6·00

300 *Redigobius sp.*

2002. Freshwater Fish. Multicoloured.

1158	48c. Type **300**	65	35
1159	96c. Spotted flagtail	1·25	1·00
1160	$1.23 Silver-stripe mudskipper	1·40	1·60
1161	$2 Snakehead gudgeon	1·75	3·00

301 Breadfruit

2002. Tropical Fruit. Multicoloured.

1162	25c. Type **301**	40	20
1163	34c. Wi fruit	50	25
1164	$1 Jakfruit	1·25	1·00
1165	$3 Avocado	2·75	4·75

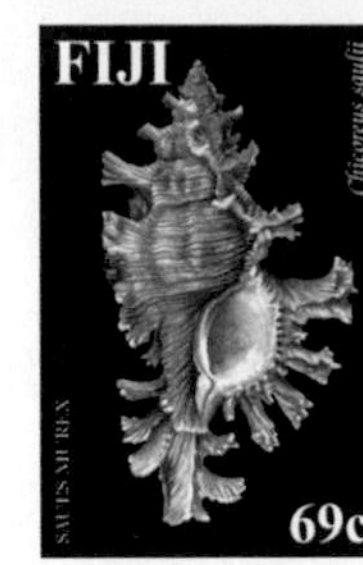

302 Saul's Murex Shell

2002. Murex Shells. Multicoloured.

1166	69c. Type **302**	1·00	55
1167	96c. Caltrop murex	1·75	1·25
1168	$1 Purple Pacific drupe	1·75	1·25
1169	$2 Ramose murex	2·50	3·50

303 Adult Fiji Goshawk and Eggs

2002. Fiji Goshawk. Multicoloured.

1170	48c. Type **303**	1·00	50
1171	89c. Chicks in nest	1·60	85
1172	$1 Juvenile Fiji goshawk on branch	1·75	1·25
1173	$3 Adult Fiji goshawk	3·50	5·00

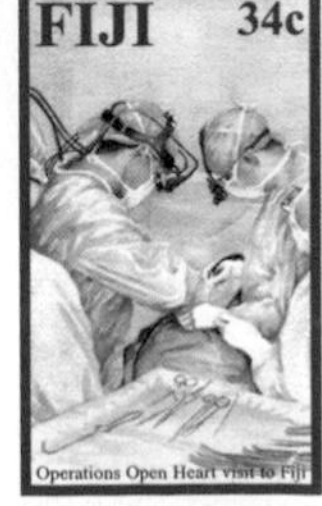

304 Drs. Nicholson and Menzie operating on Patient

2002. "Operation Open Heart" (Work of Australian cardiac team in Fiji). Multicoloured.

1174	34c. Type **304**	80	25
1175	69c. Dr. Gale listening to boy's heart (horiz)	1·50	60
1176	$1.17 Beverly Jacobsen (ultrasound technician) using echocardiograph (horiz)	2·00	1·75
1177	$2 Dr. Baines (anaesthetist) and Nurse Scarfe preparing patient	3·00	3·75

305 Bottle of Fiji Natura Artesian Water

2002. Fiji Natural Water Industry. Multicoloured.

1178	25c. Type **305**	60	20
1179	48c. Bottling plant, Viti Levu (horiz)	85	35
1180	$1 Local delivery van (horiz)	2·00	1·25
1181	$3 Fijian children with bottled water	3·50	4·75

306 Methodist Church, Wakaya Island

2002. Christmas. Religious Buildings. Mult.

1182	17c. Type **306**	40	15
1183	89c. Mosque, Yaqara	1·25	70
1184	$1 Hindu temple, Suva	1·40	85
1185	$3 Methodist church, Suva	3·50	4·75

307 General Post Office, Suva

2003. Opening of New Mail Centre. Multicoloured.

1186	48c. Type **307**	75	35
1187	96c. Mail Centre	1·40	1·25
1188	$1 Postal Logistics Centre	1·40	1·25
1189	$2 Smart Mail installation	2·25	3·25

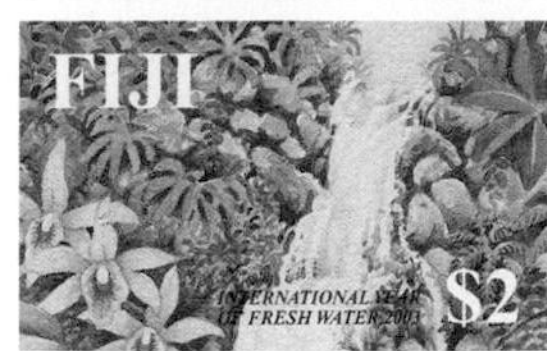

308 Orchids and Waterfall

2003. International Year of Fresh Water. Sheet 86×104 mm containing T 308 and similar horiz design. Multicoloured.

MS1190 $2 Type **308**; $2 Butterfly on vegetation and waterfall plunging into pool 5·50 6·00

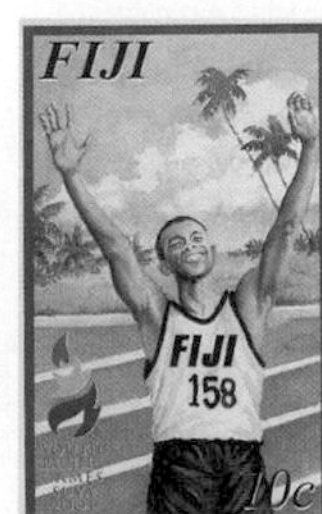

309 Athlete

2003. South Pacific Games, Fiji (1st issue). Multicoloured.

1191	10c. Type **309**	30	15
1192	14c. Baseball	35	15
1193	20c. Netball	40	25
1194	$5 Shot put	5·00	6·00

310 Netball Players, National Stadium and Multi-Purpose Sports Complex (image scaled to 40% of original size)

2003. South Pacific Games, Fiji (2nd issue). Sheet 120×85 mm. Imperf.

MS1195 **310** $5 multicoloured 5·50 6·50

311 Uspi Rabbitfish

2003. Uspi Rabbitfish. Multicoloured.

1196	58c. Type **311**	85	40
1197	83c. Two rabbitfish	1·25	75
1198	$1.15 Rabbitfish, coral and moorish idols	1·60	1·40
1199	$3 Rabbitfish feeding on algae	4·00	5·25

312 Long-legged Warbler

2003. Bird Life International. Fiji's Rarest Land Birds. Multicoloured.

1200	41c. Type **312**	1·40	75
1201	60c. Silktail	1·90	95
1202	$1.07 Red-throated lorikeet	2·50	1·75
1203	$3 Pink-billed parrot finch	5·50	6·50

313 Pacific Slender-toed Gecko

2003. Geckos. Multicoloured.

1204	83c. Type **313**	1·75	85
1205	$1.07 Indopacific tree gecko	2·00	1·60
1206	$1.15 Mann's gecko	2·00	1·60
1207	$2 Voracious gecko	3·25	4·25

314 Christmas Tree and Children (Shalini Amrita Nand)

2003. Christmas. Showing winning entries from Christmas "United Fiji for all" stamp design competition. Multicoloured.

1208	18c. Type **314**	25	15
1209	41c. Children with Fiji flag (Kelerayani Gavidi)	55	40
1210	58c. Santa and children in reindeer-drawn sleighs (Ronald Patrick) (vert)	70	60
1211	83c. Christmas presents and Santa on chimney (Cadillac Graphics) (vert)	1·25	1·00
1212	$1.07 Children with candles and Christmas tree (Shuetal Shamlee) (vert)	1·40	1·75
1213	$1.15 Santa with children (Roselyn Roshika) (vert)	1·50	1·90

MS1214 100×75 mm. $1.41 Handshake and cross (Viliame Vosabeci) 1·75 2·00

315 Tagimoucia (The Flower of Fiji)

2003. Fiji's First Personalised Stamps. Sheet 296×210 mm.

MS1215 50c. multicoloured 1·50 1·75

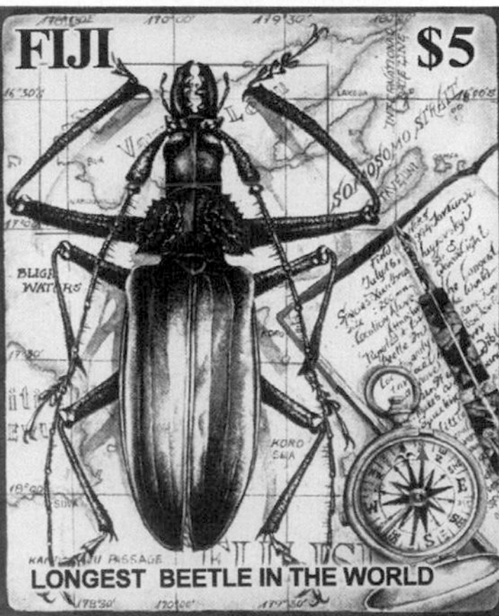

316 Longhorn Beetle (image scaled to 62% of original size)

2004. Longest Beetle in the World. Sheet 80×95 mm. Imperf.

MS1216 $5 multicoloured 6·50 7·00

317 Skipjack Tuna

2004. Endangered Species. Tuna. Sheet 130×90 mm containing T 317 and similar horiz designs. Multicoloured.

MS1217 58c. Type **317**; 83c. Albacore tuna; $1.07 Yellowfin tuna; $3 Bigeye tuna 6·00 7·00

318 *Malleated Placostyle*

2004. Land Snails. Multicoloured.

1218	18c. Type **318**	40	15
1219	41c. *Kandavu Placostyle*	80	35
1220	$1.15 *Fragile Orpiella*	1·50	1·25
1221	$3 Thin Fijian Placostyle	3·00	4·50

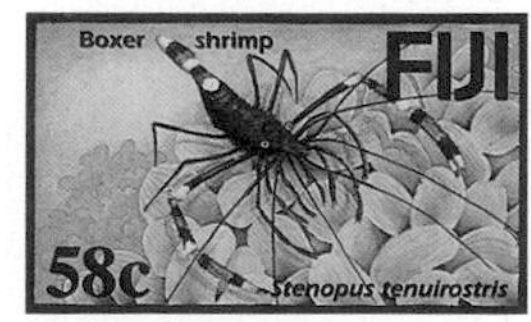

319 Boxer Shrimp

2004. Coral Reef Shrimps. Multicoloured.

1222	58c. Type **319**	80	40
1223	83c. Bumblebee shrimp	1·25	70
1224	$1.07 Mantis shrimp	1·40	1·10
1225	$3 Anemone shrimp	3·00	4·50

2004. As No. 917 but with new value.

1226	18c. Island Thrush	50	15

320 Wandering Tattler

2004. Migrating Shorebirds. Multicoloured.

1229	41c. Type **320**	1·10	45
1230	58c. Whimbrel ("Wimbrel")	1·40	70
1231	$1.15 Pacific golden plover	2·50	1·40
1232	$3 Bristle-thighed curlew	5·00	6·00

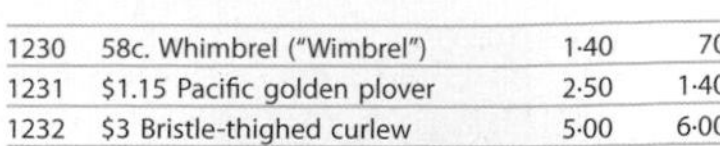

321 Swimming

2004. Olympic Games, Athens. Multicoloured.

1233	41c. Type **321**	70	40
1234	58c. Judo (vert)	80	50
1235	$1.41 Weight lifting (vert)	1·40	1·25
1236	$2 Sprinting	2·75	3·75

322 Yachts Racing

2004. 25th Anniv of the Musket Cove—Port Vila Yacht Race. Multicoloured.

1237	83c. Type **322**	1·00	65
1238	$1.07 Two catamarans (vert)	1·40	1·50
1239	$1.15 Two yachts with white sails	1·60	1·75
1240	$2 One yacht (vert)	2·50	3·25
MS1241	100×70 mm. $2 As No. 1240	2·50	3·25

Stamps of a similar design were issued by Vanuatu.

323 Coconut Crab

2004. Coconut Crab. Sheet 74×89 mm.

MS1242 **323** $5 multicoloured 6·00 7·00

324 New Adult Swallowtail Butterfly

2004. Swallowtail Butterflies. Multicoloured.

1243	58c. Type **324**	80	55
1244	83c. Larva (horiz)	1·25	75
1245	$1.41 Adult feeding on nectar (horiz)	1·75	1·75
1246	$3 Pupa	3·75	5·00

325 Mary and Archangel Gabriel

2004. Christmas. Multicoloured.

1247	18c. Type **325**	45	10
1248	58c. Baby Jesus	1·00	40
1249	$1.07 Mary and Jesus	1·50	1·00
1250	$3 The Shepherds with Mary and Jesus	4·00	6·00

326 Green-backed Heron

2005. Herons and Egrets.Multicoloured.

1251	$1 Type **326**	2·00	2·25
1252	$1 Great egret ("Great White Egret")	2·00	2·25
1253	$1 White-faced egret ("White-faced Heron")	2·00	2·25
1254	$1 Reef heron ("Pacific Reef Heron")	2·00	2·25

Nos. 1251/4 were printed together, se-tenant, forming a composite background design.

327 *Cananga odorata*

2005. Perfumed Flowers of Fiji. Multicoloured.

1255	58c. Type **327**	80	40
1256	$1.15 *Euodia hortensis*	1·40	1·10
1257	$1.41 *Pandannus tecorius*	1·60	1·50
1258	$2 *Santalum yasi*	2·75	4·25

328 Peregrine Falcon

2005. Fiji Peregrine Falcon. Multicoloured.

1259	41c. Type **328**	1·25	55
1260	83c. Peregrine falcon with eggs	1·75	1·00
1261	$1.07 Two chicks	2·00	1·40
1262	$3 Peregrine falcon perched on rock	4·50	6·00

329 Picasso Triggerfish ("Whitebanded Triggerfish")

2005. Triggerfish. Multicoloured.

1263	58c. Type **329**	85	50
1264	83c. Jigsaw triggerfish ("Yellow Spotted Triggerfish")	1·25	70
1265	$1.15 Undulate triggerfish ("Orange-lined Triggerfish")	1·50	1·25
1266	$2 Clown triggerfish	2·50	3·50

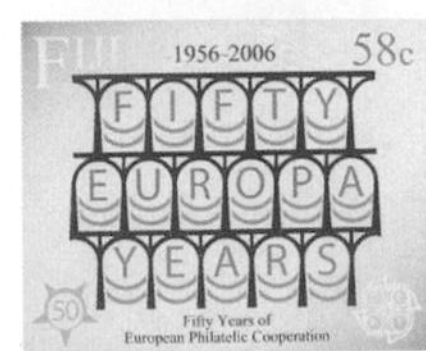

330 "FIFTY EUROPA YEARS"

2005. 50th Anniv of First Europa Stamp.

1267	**330**	58c. multicoloured	70	55
1268	**330**	83c. multicoloured	1·10	80
1269	**330**	$1.41 multicoloured	1·60	1·50
1270	**330**	$4 multicoloured	4·50	6·50
MS1271		106×81 mm. Nos. 1267/70	7·00	9·00

331 HMNZS *Achilles*

2005. 60th Anniv of the End of World War II. "Route to Victory". Multicoloured.

1272	83c. Type **331**	1·10	1·25
1273	83c. Japanese Yokosuka E14Y "Glen" aircraft over Suva Harbour	1·10	1·25
1274	83c. Fijian "South Pacific Scouts" troops in Solomon Islands	1·10	1·25
1275	83c. USS *Chicago*	1·10	1·25
1276	83c. Patrol vessel HMS *Viti*	1·10	1·25
1277	83c. Prime Minister Winston Churchill	1·10	1·25
1278	83c. HMS *Hood* (battle cruiser)	1·10	1·25
1279	83c. Avro Type 683 Lancaster bomber on "Dambusters" raid, May 1943	1·10	1·25
1280	83c. German King Tiger tank in Ardennes, December 1944	1·10	1·25
1281	83c. US General Dwight Eisenhower	1·10	1·25

332 Great Barracuda

2005. Game Fish (2nd series). Multicoloured.

1282	41c. Type **332**	80	35
1283	58c. Narrow-barred spanish mackerel	95	60
1284	$1.07 Giant trevally	1·60	1·25
1285	$3 Indo-Pacific sailfish	3·50	4·50

333 Pope John Paul II

2005. Pope John Paul II Commemoration.

1286	**333**	$1 multicoloured	2·25	2·25

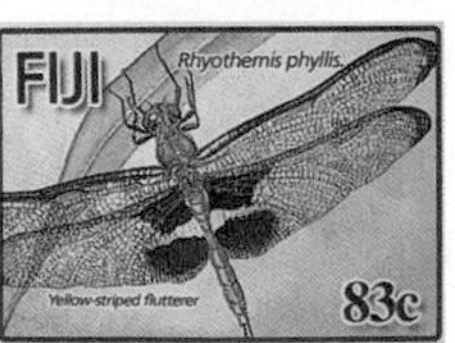

334 *Rhyothemis Phyllis*

2005. Dragonflies. Multicoloured.

1287	83c. Type **334**	1·00	60
1288	$1.07 *Agrionoptera insignis*	1·40	1·40
1289	$1.15 *Orthetrum serapia*	1·50	1·50
1290	$2 *Diplacodes bipunctata*	2·50	3·25

335 Albert Einstein as Boy

2005. 50th Death Anniv of Albert Einstein (physicist). Multicoloured.

1291	83c. Type **335**	1·25	60
1292	$1.07 In library, 1905	1·60	1·40
1293	$1.15 Albert Einstein and equations	1·75	1·60
1294	$2 As old man	3·00	3·75

336 *Manihot utilissima* (cassava)

2005. Staple Root Crops of Fiji. Multicoloured.

1295	41c. Type **336**	65	40
1296	83c. *Ipomoea satatas* (sweet potato)	1·00	70
1297	$1.41 *Colocasia esculenta* (taro)	1·75	1·75
1298	$2 *Dioscorea sativa* (yams)	2·50	3·50

337 *Eliza* (brig)

2005. Tall Ships in Fiji's Past. Multicoloured.

1299	83c. Type **337**	1·50	80
1300	$1.15 *Elbe*	2·00	1·75
1301	$1.41 HMS *Rosario*	2·25	2·00
1302	$2 *L'Astrolabe* (D'Urville)	3·00	3·75

No. 1299 *Eliza of Providence* is wrongly inscribed "Eliza of Province".

338 Barn Owl on Nest

2006. Barn Owl (Tyto alba). Multicoloured.

1303	18c. Type **338**	75	40
1304	$1.15 Fledgeling	2·25	1·75
1305	$1.41 Owl flying with prey	2·50	2·25
1306	$2 Owl perched on post	3·25	3·75

339 Fiji Ground Frog

2006. Fiji Ground Frog (Platymantis vitianus). Multicoloured.

1307	50c. Type **339**	80	40
1308	83c. Frog at base of tree	1·50	80
1309	$1.15 Frog on ground	1·75	1·75
1310	$2 Frog in leaf litter	2·75	3·75

340 Pygmy Snake-eyed Skink

2006. Skinks of Fiji. Multicoloured.

1311	18c. Type **340**	35	20
1312	58c. Brown-tailed copper-striped skink	75	55
1313	$1.15 Pacific black skink	1·60	1·60
1314	$3 Pacific blue-tailed skink	3·50	4·50

341 Princess Elizabeth

2006. 80th Birthday of Queen Elizabeth II. Multicoloured.

1315	50c. Type **341**	70	35
1316	65c. Queen wearing tiara	80	45
1317	90c. Wearing pale blue hat and pearls	1·25	75
1318	$3 Wearing blue hat	3·75	4·50
MS1319	143×75 mm. $2 As No. 1316; $2 As No. 1317	5·00	6·00

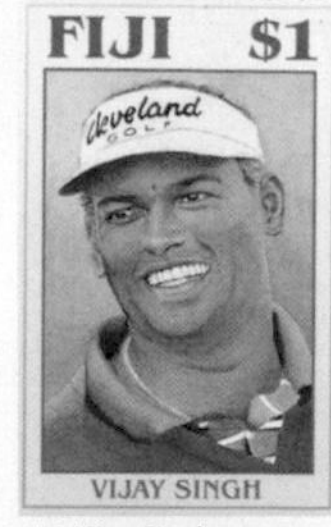

342 Vijay Singh

2006. Vijay Singh's Golf Victories. Sheet 150×180 mm containing T 342 and similar vert designs. Multicoloured.

MS1320	$1 Type **342**; $1 With arm raised in triumph; $1 Holding trophy (59×87 mm); $1 Standing on golf course; $1 Driving golf ball	5·50	6·50

343 Tackling

2006. World Cup Football Championship, Germany. Multicoloured.

1321	65c. Type **343**	70	45
1322	90c. Players competing for ball	1·00	65
1323	$1.20 Two players in white	1·50	1·75
1324	$2 Goalkeeper	2·50	3·25

344 Purple Swamphen

2006. Purple Swamphen (Porphyrio porphyrio). Sheet 88×77 mm containing T 344 and similar horiz design. Multicoloured.

MS1325	$2 Type **344**; $2 Purple swamphen on nest	4·50	4·75

The stamps within **MS**1325 are incorrectly inscribed "*Prophyrio prophyrio*".

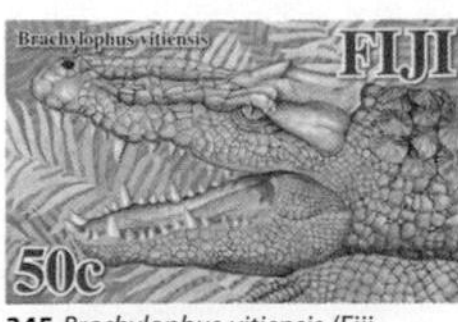

345 *Brachylophus vitiensis* (Fiji crocodile)

2006. Fiji's Extinct Megafauna. Multicoloured.

1326	50c. Type **345**	65	30
1327	$1.10 *Natunaornis gigoura* (Viti-levu giant pigeon) (vert)	1·40	1·25
1328	$1.20 *Vitirallus watlingi* (flight-less rail) (vert)	1·50	1·40
1329	$1.50 *Platymantis megabotonivi-ti* (giant Fiji ground frog)	1·60	1·75

346 *Hermarchus apollonius* (giant stick insect)

2006. Fiji's Phasmids. Multicoloured.

1330	10c. Type **346**	20	20
1331	$1.10 *Cotylosoma dipneusticum* (Fijian stick insect)	1·40	1·25
1332	$1.20 *Chitoniscus feejeeanus* (leaf insect)	1·50	1·40
1333	$2 *Graeffea crouanii* (coconut stick insect)	2·75	3·25

347 Queen Bee and Workers

2006. Honey Production in Fiji. Multicoloured.

1334	18c. Type **347**	40	30
1335	40c. Beekeeper removing honeycomb (horiz)	80	55
1336	$1 Beehives (horiz)	1·60	1·60
1337	$3 Boy with bottle of Fiji honey	3·00	3·50

348 *Premnas biaculeatus* (spine-cheek anemonefish)

2006. Anemonefish. Multicoloured.

1338	18c. Type **348**	40	30
1339	60c. *Amphiprion perideraion* (pink anemonefish) (vert)	1·00	60
1340	90c. *Amphiprion chrysopterus* (orange-fin anemonefish) (vert)	1·40	80
1341	$3 *Amphiprion melanopus* (dusky anemonefish) (orange colour form)	3·25	3·75

349 *Decaspermum vitiense* (Fiji Christmas bush)

2006. Christmas. Flowers. Multicoloured.

1342	18c. Type **349**	40	20
1343	65c. *Quisqualis indica* (sinu-kakala)	1·00	55
1344	90c. *Mussaenda raiateensis* (vobo)	1·40	70
1345	$3 *Delonix regia* (flamboy-ant tree)	3·25	4·50

2007. Nos. 912 and 916 surch.

1310a	1c. on 6c. Blue-headed flycatcher ('Blue-crested Broadbill')	50	60
1310b	1c. on 6 c. Blue-headed flycatcher	3·00	4·00
1310e	1c. on 23c. Many-coloured fruit dove	1·25	1·50
1310f	2c. on 1c. Type **249**	2·00	2·00
1310j	2c. on 6c. Blue-headed flycatcher ('Blue-crested Broadbill')	50	50
1310l	3c. on 1c. Type **249**	50	60
1310m	4c. on 1c. Type **249**	50	70
1310n	4c. on 6c. Blue-headed flycatcher ('Blue-crested Broadbill')	50	50
1310r	18c. on 6c. Blue-headed flycatcher ("Blue-crested Broadbill")	10·00	15·00
1310s	20c. on 6c. Blue-headed flycatcher ('Blue-crested Broadbill'	2·00	1·40

354 Mangrove Lobster

2007. Mangrove Lobster (Thalassina anomala). Sheet 96×73 mm.

MS1350	**354** $4 multicoloured	3·75	4·25

355 Coastal Dwelling House, Navuso, Naitasiri

2007. Traditional Fijian Houses. Multicoloured.

1351	20c. Type **355**	45	35
1352	65c. Houses of western Vitilevu and coast of western Fiji	85	55
1353	$1.10 Navatanitawake Temple, Bau	1·40	1·00
1354	$3 Lauan style house	3·00	4·00

356 *Sicyopterus lagocephalus*

2007. Freshwater Gobies. Multicoloured.

1355	20c. Type **356**	45	35
1356	$1.10 *Stiphodon rutilaureus*	1·40	1·00
1357	$1.20 *Sicyopus zosterophorum*	1·50	1·10
1358	$2 *Stiphodon* sp.	2·00	2·75

357 Red-vented Bulbul

2007. Exotic Birds. Multicoloured.

1359	50c. Type **357**	70	35
1360	65c. Spotted dove (horiz)	1·00	65
1361	$1.50 Australian magpie (horiz)	2·00	2·00
1362	$2 Java sparrow	2·25	3·00

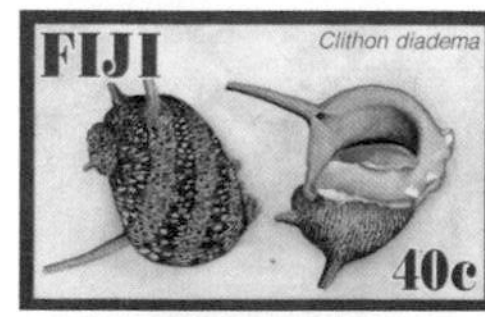

358 *Clithon diadema*

2007. Freshwater Snails. Multicoloured.

1363	40c. Type **358**	60	30
1364	90c. *Neritina variegate*	1·25	75
1365	$1.20 *Fijidoma maculate*	1·40	1·10
1366	$2 *Neritina squamaepicta*	2·00	2·75

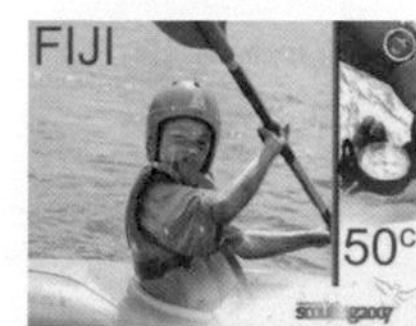

359 Scout Kayaking

2007. Centenary of Scouting. Multicoloured.

1367	50c. Type **359**	60	30
1368	90c. Three scouts	1·25	75
1369	$1.50 Scout in adventure playground	2·00	2·00
1370	$2 Scout on expedition	2·25	3·00
MS1371	90×65 mm. $1.50 Scout badge (*vert*); $1.50 Lord Baden-Powell (*vert*)	3·25	3·75

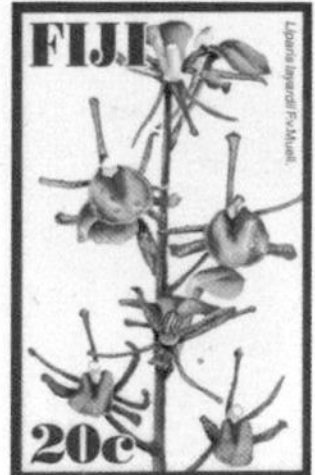

360 *Liparis layardii*

2007. Indigenous Orchids. Multicoloured.

1372	20c. Type **360**	45	30
1373	65c. *Dendrobium catillare* (horiz)	1·00	70
1374	$1.10 *Dendrobium mohlianum* (horiz)	1·40	1·10
1375	$3 *Glomera Montana*	3·25	4·00

361 *Variola louti* (Coronation trout)

2007. Coral Trout. Multicoloured.

1376	50c. Type **361**	70	30
1377	90c. *Plectropomus pessuliferus* (roving coral trout)	1·40	80
1378	$1.50 *Plectropomus areolatus* (squaretail coral trout)	2·00	2·00
1379	$2 *Plectropomus laevis* (Chinese footballer)	2·25	3·00

362 *Polyura caphontis*

2007. Butterflies. Multicoloured.

1380	20c. Type **362**	45	30
1381	$1.10 *Hypolimnas bolina* (horiz)	1·50	1·25
1382	$1.20 *Doleschallia bisaltide* (horiz)	1·60	1·40
1383	$2 *Danaus hamata*	2·40	3·25

363 Barred-winged Rail

2007. Barred-winged Rail (Nesoclopeus poecilopterus). Sheet 96×83 mm containing T 363 and similar horiz design.

MS1384	$2 Type **363**; $2 Chicks	4·25	4·75

364 Medal of the Order of Fiji

2008. The Order of Fiji. Multicoloured.

1385	50c. Type **364**	60	45
1386	65c. Member of the Order of Fiji	1·00	70
1387	$1.20 Officer of the Order of Fiji	1·60	1·25
1388	$2 Order of Fiji (Companion)	2·00	2·75

365 *Prosopeia tabuensis koroensis*

2008. Red-breasted Musk Parrots (Prosopeia tabuensis). Multicoloured.

1389	65c. Type **365**	1·10	70
1390	90c. *Prosopeia tabuensis atrogularis* (horiz)	1·50	80
1391	$1.50 *Prosopeia tabuensis tavienensis* (horiz)	2·25	2·00
1392	$2 *Prosopeia tabuensis splendens*	2·50	3·00

20c xxx
(366)

2008. No. 918 surch with 20c..

1393	20c. on 23c. Many-coloured fruit dove	1·00	70

367 Painted Lobster (*Panulirus versicolor*)

2008. Fiji's Spiny Lobster. Sheet 90×75 mm.

MS1394	multicoloured	4·25	4·50

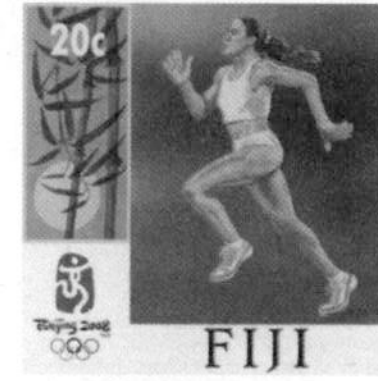

368 Athletics

2008. Olympic Games, Beijing. Multticoloured.

1395	20c. Type **368**	50	35
1396	65c. Judo	1·00	65
1397	90c. Shooting	1·50	1·25
1398	$1.50 Swimming	2·25	3·00

369 Fokker FVII b-3 Monoplane *Southern Cross* approaching Suva

2008. 80th Anniv of the First Flight across the Pacific Ocean.Multicoloured.

1399	20c. Type **369**	45	35
1400	90c. *Southern Cross* after landing at Albert Park, Suva	1·40	80
1401	$1.50 *Southern Cross* guarded by Fiji policemen at Albert Park	2·00	2·00
1402	$2 James Warner (wireless operator), Charles Kingsford-Smith (pilot), Charles Ulm (co-pilot) and Harry Lyon (navigator)	2·25	2·75

370 Two Humpback Whales

2008. Humpback Whale (Megaptera novaeangliae). Multicoloured.

1403	20c. Type **370**	20	20
1404	50c. Whale about to breach (leap from water)	55	55
1405	$1.10 Re-entering water after breaching	1·25	1·25
1406	$3 Tail of humpback whale	3·25	3·25

371 *Musa sapientum*

2008. Fiji's Bananas. Multicoloured.

1407	65c. Type **371**	70	70
1408	$1.10 *Musa velutina*	1·25	1·25
1409	$1.20 'Lady-fingers'	1·40	1·40
1410	$2 'Cooking bananas'	2·25	2·25

372 *Anguilla obscura*

2008. Freshwater Eels. Multicoloured.

1411	50c. Type **372**	55	55
1412	90c. *Anguilla marmorata*	1·50	1·50
1413	$1.50 *Anguilla obscura* (different)	1·75	1·75
1414	$2 *Gymnothorax potyuranodon*	2·25	2·25

373 Choir

2008. Christmas. 'A Celebration in Song'. Multicoloured.

1415	20c. Type **373**	25	25
1416	50c. Women's choir wearing turquoise and white	60	60
1417	65c. Choir wearing white	95	95
1418	$3 Conductor and choir	3·50	3·50

374 Many-coloured Fruit Dove (*Ptilinopus perousii*)

2009. Fijian Fruit Doves. Multicoloured.

1419	50c. Type **374**	50	50
1420	65c. Crimson-crowned fruit dove (*Ptilinopus porphyraceous*)	70	70
1421	90c. Whistling dove (*Ptilinopus layardi*)	1·50	1·50
1422	$3 Orange dove (*Ptilinopus victor*)	3·25	3·25

375 Chinese Wedding

2009. Weddings in Fiji. Multicoloured.

1423	20c. Type **375**	25	25
1424	40c. Muslim wedding	60	60
1425	$1.50 Indian wedding	95	95
1426	$3 Fijian wedding (vert)	3·25	3·25

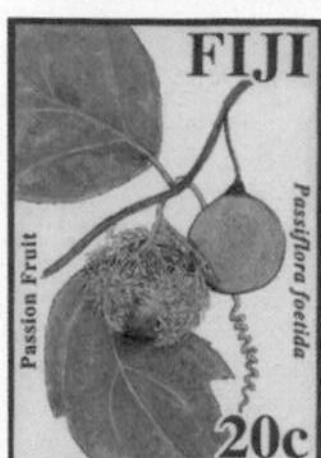

376 *Passiflora foetida*

2009. Passion Fruit. Multicoloured.

1427	20c. Type **376**	25	25
1428	65c. *Passiflora edulis* (yellow fruit)	55	55
1429	$1.20 *Passiflora maliformis*	1·50	1·50
1430	$2 *Passiflora edulis* (purple fruit)	2·00	2·00

377 Giant Panda

2009. 60th Anniv of the People's Republic of China

MS1431 **377**	$5 multicoloured	6·00	6·00

378 Cyathea lunulata

2010. Ferns of Fiji. Multicoloured.

1432	20c. Type **378**	25	25
1433	40c. *Asplenium australasicum*	50	50
1434	$1.50 *Diplazium proliferum*	2·00	2·00
1435	$3 *Nephrolepsis biserrata*	3·50	3·50

379 Yellow-bellied Sea Snake (*Pelamis platurus*)

2010. Snakes of Fiji. Multicoloured.

1436	20c. Type **379**	25	25
1437	90c. Fiji burrowing snake (*Ogmodon vitianus*)	90	90
1438	$1.10 Banded sea krait (*Laticauda colubrina*)	1·25	1·25
1439	$2 Pacific boa (*Candoia bibroni*)	1·90	1·90

379a Pink Peony

2010. China World Stamp Exhibition and Peony Festival, Luoyang. Multicoloured.

1439a	20c. Type **379a**	45	45
1439b	40c. Red peony	1·00	1·00

380 Newly Emerged Cicada

2010. Cicada (*Raiateana knowlesi*) (The Nanai). Multicoloured.

1440	20c. Type **380**	25	25
1441	$1.50 Mature cicada	2·00	2·00

381 Crested Iguana

2010. Endangered Species. Crested Iguana (*Brachylophus vitiensis*). Multicoloured.

MS1442	$2 Type **381**×2; $2 Climbing through foliage, facing left×2; Facing right, close up of head and upper body×2; On branch, facing left×2	18·00	18·00

The stamps and margins of **MS**1442 form a composite design.

382 *Citrus maxima* (pomelo)

2010. Fruits of Fiji. Multicoloured.

1443	20c. Type **382**	25	25
1444	40c. *Barringtonia edulis*(inscr '*Barringtinia*') (cutnut)	45	45
1445	65c. *Pometia pinnata* (Fijian longan)	75	75
1446	$1.20 Inscr '*Musa troglogytarum*'and 'Fei banana'	1·40	1·40
1447	$10 *Syzygium malaccensis* (inscr '*malacensis*') (Malay apple)	10·50	10·50

POSTAGE DUE STAMPS

D1

1917

D5a	**D1**	½d. black	£475	£300
D2	**D1**	1d. black	£450	£140
D3	**D1**	2d. black	£300	80·00
D4	**D1**	3d. black	£450	£125
D5	**D1**	4d. black	£1100	£550

D3

1918

D6	**D3**	½d. black	3·00	27·00
D7	**D3**	1d. black	3·50	5·00
D8	**D3**	2d. black	3·25	7·50
D9	**D3**	3d. black	3·25	50·00
D10	**D3**	4d. black	6·00	28·00

D4

1940

D11	**D4**	1d. green	8·50	70·00
D12	**D4**	2d. green	14·00	70·00
D13	**D4**	3d. green	17·00	75·00
D14	**D4**	4d. green	18·00	80·00
D15	**D4**	5d. green	21·00	85·00
D16	**D4**	6d. green	23·00	85·00
D17	**D4**	1s. red	23·00	£110
D18	**D4**	1s.6d. red	23·00	£160

Pt. 11

FINLAND

A country to the east of Scandinavia. A Russian Grand-Duchy until 1917, then a Republic.

1856. 100 kopeks = 1 rouble.
1865. 100 pennia = 1 markka.
2002. 100 cents = 1 euro.

1

1856. Imperf.

1	**1**	5k. blue	£5500	£1100
2	**1**	10k. pink	£6500	£300

Used prices are for stamps with penmark cancellation only. Stamps with postmark as well are worth more.

2

1860. Values in "KOP". Roul.

10	**2**	5k. blue on blue	£800	£160
13	**2**	10k. pink on pink	£600	50·00

1866. As T 2, but values in "PEN" and "MARK". Roul.

19	5p. brown on grey	£300	£140
46	8p. black on green	£275	£140
31	10p. black on buff	£700	£225
36	20p. blue on blue	£600	55·00
40	40p. pink on lilac	£550	70·00
49	1m. brown	£1800	£850

5

1875. Perf.

81	**5**	2p. grey	12·50	11·00
82	**5**	5p. yellow	45·00	5·25
83	**5**	5p. red	60·00	6·00
97	**5**	5p. green	18·00	55
71	**5**	8p. green	£180	50·00
85	**5**	10p. brown	95·00	17·00
99	**5**	10p. pink	25·00	2·20
87	**5**	20p. blue	45·00	1·70
102	**5**	20p. orange	27·00	50
89	**5**	25p. red	45·00	7·25
103	**5**	25p. blue	55·00	2·20
79	**5**	32p. red	£300	32·00
90	**5**	1m. mauve	£325	34·00
105	**5**	1m. grey and pink	37·00	15·00
106	**5**	5m. green and pink	£550	£275
107	**5**	10m. brown and pink	£700	£450

6

1889

108	**6**	2p. grey	1·10	1·00
148	**6**	5p. green	85	30
149	**6**	10p. red	1·10	30
150	**6**	20p. yellow	1·10	30
151	**6**	25p. blue	1·10	50
119	**6**	1m. grey and pink	5·50	3·00
120a	**6**	5m. green and red	29·00	44·00
122	**6**	10m. brown and red	44·00	70·00

7

8

9

10 11

1891. Similar to Russian types, but with circles added in designs.

133	**7**	1k. yellow	5·25	7·00
134	**7**	2k. green	6·50	6·75
135	**7**	3k. pink	11·50	12·00
136	**8**	4k. pink	11·00	11·50
137	**7**	7k. blue	7·50	2·00
138	**8**	10k. blue	15·00	11·50
139	**9**	14k. red and blue	21·00	17·00
140	**8**	20k. red and blue	16·00	13·50
141	**9**	35k. green and purple	24·00	32·00
142	**8**	50k. green and purple	30·00	26·00
143	**10**	1r. orange and brown	80·00	60·00
144	**11**	3½r. grey and black	£275	£275
145	**11**	7r. yellow and black	£225	£190

12 13 14

15

1901. Similar to Russian types, but value in Finnish currency.

161	**12**	2p. orange	65	90
162b	**12**	5p. green	1·80	40
169a	**13**	10p. red	45	25
170	**12**	20p. blue	55	25
165a	**14**	1m. green and purple	90	40
166	**15**	10m. grey and black	£140	38·00

16 17 18

1911

176	**16**	2p. orange	30	30
177	**16**	5p. green	30	15
180	**17**	10p. red	65	40
181	**16**	20p. blue	30	15
182	**18**	40p. blue and purple	30	20

19

1917

187a	**19**	5p. green	25	20
188	**19**	5p. grey	25	20
189	**19**	10p. red	25	20
190	**19**	10p. green	2·20	65
191a	**19**	10p. blue	35	25
192	**19**	20p. orange	25	20
193	**19**	20p. red	65	25
194	**19**	20p. brown	1·10	50
195	**19**	25p. blue	45	25
196	**19**	25p. brown	25	20
234	**19**	30p. green	55	40
198a	**19**	40p. purple	25	20
246	**19**	40p. green	45	85
200	**19**	50p. brown	60	40
201	**19**	50p. blue	4·25	50
247	**19**	50p. green	35	45
237	**19**	60p. purple	45	35
204	**19**	75p. yellow	25	40
205	**19**	1m. black and pink	13·50	25
248	**19**	1m. orange	30	35
207	**19**	1½m. purple and green	30	35
208a	**19**	2m. black and green	4·50	50
250	**19**	2m. blue	30	35
251	**19**	3m. black and blue	35	40
242	**19**	5m. black and purple	90	40
212	**19**	10m. black and bistre	1·10	90
213	**19**	25m. orange and red	1·30	21·00

20

1918. With white circle round figure of value.

214	**20**	5p. green	30	65
215	**20**	10p. pink	30	65
216	**20**	30p. grey	90	1·70
217	**20**	40p. lilac	30	65
218	**20**	50p. brown	60	1·70
219	**20**	70p. brown	2·20	10·50
220	**20**	1m. black and red	60	1·00
221	**20**	5m. black and lilac	49·00	65·00

1919. Surch with new figure of value three times.

222	**19**	10 on 5p. green	25	30
223	**19**	20 on 10p. red	35	30
224	**19**	50 on 25p. blue	1·30	35
225	**19**	75 on 20p. orange	25	30

1921. Surch with value, P and bars.

226	**19**	30p. on 10p. green	90	25
227	**19**	60p. on 40p. purple	3·50	65
228	**19**	90p. on 20p. red	40	35
229	**19**	1½m. on 50p. blue	2·20	25

23

1922. Red Cross.

230	**23**	1m.+50p. red and grey	1·30	8·50

26

1927. 10th Anniv of Independence.

255	**26**	1½m. mauve	25	35
256	**26**	2m. blue	35	1·30

1928. Philatelic Exhibition. Optd Postim. näytt. 1928 Frim. utställn.

258	**19**	1m. orange	10·50	13·00
259	**19**	1½m. purple and green	10·50	13·00

28 Freighter "Bore" leaving Turku (Abo)

1929. 700th Anniv of Abo.

260	**28**	1m. olive	2·75	3·75
261	-	1½m. brown	6·25	3·00
262	-	2m. grey	1·30	3·75

DESIGNS—VERT: 1½m. Cathedral. HORIZ: 2m. Castle.

31 **32** Olavinlinna

1930

263	**31**	5p. brown	25	25
264	**31**	10p. lilac	25	25
265	**31**	20p. green	55	35
266	**31**	25p. brown	25	20
267	**31**	40p. green	3·00	40
268	**31**	50p. yellow	90	35
268a	**31**	50p. green	30	20
269	**31**	60p. grey	55	40
371	**31**	75p. orange	35	35
270	**31**	1m. orange	90	35
372	**31**	1m. green	30	20
271	**31**	1m.20 red	45	55
271a	**31**	1m.25 yellow	35	30
272	**31**	1½m. mauve	4·50	25
272a	**31**	1½m. red	45	25
272b	**31**	1½m. grey	30	15
272c	**31**	1m.75 yellow	90	40
273	**31**	2m. blue	45	25
273a	**31**	2m. mauve	9·00	25
273b	**31**	2m. red	45	20
373	**31**	2m. orange	45	25
373a	**31**	2m. green	70	25
273c	**31**	2½m. blue	4·50	30
374	**31**	2½m. red	30	20
425	**31**	2½m. green	60	20
273d	**31**	2m.75 purple	25	15
375	**31**	3m. red	45	20
375a	**31**	3m. yellow	60	40
426	**31**	3m. grey	60	40
274a	**31**	3½m. blue	13·50	40
427	**31**	3m. green	3·75	35
376	**31**	3½m. green	30	20
377	**31**	4m. green	50	15
378	**31**	4½m. blue	25	20
275	**32**	5m. blue	45	25
379	**31**	5m. blue	90	20
379a	**31**	5m. violet	1·00	30
379b	**31**	5m. yellow	2·20	20
379c	**31**	6m. red	90	25
429	**31**	6m. green	1·10	40
430	**31**	7m. red	1·20	1·20
379d	**31**	8m. violet	50	15
431	**31**	8m. green	2·75	1·90
432	**31**	9m. red	90	25
433	**31**	9m. orange	1·30	30
276b	-	10m. lilac	1·10	25
379e	**31**	10m. blue	2·20	25
434	**31**	10m. violet	2·75	20
435	**31**	10m. brown	8·25	20
436	**31**	10m. green	3·50	20
437	**31**	12m. blue	3·00	20
438	**31**	12m. red	1·60	20
410	**32**	15m. purple	2·20	25
439	**31**	15m. blue	4·75	20
440	**31**	15m. purple	18·00	20
441	**31**	15m. red	3·00	20
442	**31**	20m. blue	8·00	20
443	**31**	24m. purple	2·00	40
277	-	25m. brown	2·75	35
444	**31**	25m. blue	3·50	20
445	**32**	35m. violet	7·00	25
445a	-	40m. brown	3·50	25

DESIGNS—As Type **32**: 10m. Lake Saimaa; 25, 40m. Wood-cutter.

35

1930. Red Cross Fund.

278	**35**	1m.+10p. red & orange	2·75	9·25
279	-	1½m.+15p. red & green	2·00	8·75
280	-	2m.+20p. red and blue	4·00	35·00

DESIGNS: 1½m. Drapery; 2m. Viking longship.

1930. Air. No. 276b optd ZEPPELIN 1930.

281		10m. lilac	£150	£190

39 Church at Hattula

1931. Red Cross Fund.

282	**39**	1m.+10p. green & red	3·00	9·25
283	-	1½m.+15p. brown & red	22·00	13·00
284	-	2m.+20p. blue & red	2·20	17·00

DESIGNS: 1½m. Hameen Castle; 2m. Viipuri Castle.

40 Elias Lonnrot

1931. Finnish Literary Society's Centenary.

285	**40**	1m. brown	4·50	3·75
286	-	1½m. blue	28·00	3·75

DESIGN—HORIZ: 1½m. Society's seal with inscr as T **40**.

42

1931. 75th Anniv of First Finnish Postage Stamps.

287	**42**	1½m. red	3·75	5·25
288	**42**	2m. blue	3·75	5·25

43

1931. Granberg Collection Fund.

289	**43**	1m.+4m. black	17·00	35·00

1931. Surch.

290	**31**	50PEN. on 40p. green	1·80	40
291	**31**	1,25 MK. on 50p. yellow	6·25	1·40

45

1931. President Svinhufvud's 70th Birthday.

292	**45**	2m. black and blue	3·00	2·10

47 St. Nicholas Cathedral

1932. Red Cross Fund.

293	-	1¼m.+10p. bistre & red	2·75	11·50
294	**47**	2m.+20p. purple & red	1·10	6·00
295	-	2½m.+25p. blue & red	1·30	20·00

DESIGNS—HORIZ: 1¼m. University Library, Helsinki; 2½m. Houses of Parliament.

48 Magnus Tawast

1933. Red Cross Fund.

296	**48**	1¼m.+10p. brown & red	6·25	8·00
297	-	2m.+20p. purple & red	90	2·10
298	-	2½m.+25p. blue & red	1·20	4·50

DESIGNS: 2m. Michael Agricola; 2½m. Isacus Rothovius.

51 Evert Horn

1934. Red Cross Fund.

299	**51**	1¼m.+10p. brown & red	90	2·30
300	-	2m.+20p. mauve & red	3·25	4·50
301	-	2½m.+25p. blue & red	1·30	3·25

DESIGNS: 2m. Torsten Stalhandske; 2½m. Jacob de la Gardie ("Lazy Jack").

52 Aleksis Kivi, after medallion by V. Aaltonen

1934. Birth Centenary of Kivi (poet).

302	**52**	2m. purple	3·50	3·25

53 Calonius

1935. Red Cross Fund. Cross in red.

303	**53**	1¼m.+15p. brown	90	2·00
304	-	2m.+20p. mauve	3·50	4·75
305	-	2½m.+25p. blue	1·30	1·80

PORTRAITS: 2m. H. G. Porthan. 2½m. A. Chydenius.

54 Finnish Bards

1935. Centenary of Publication of "Kalevala" (Finnish National Poems).

306	**54**	1¼m. red	1·80	1·50
307	-	2m. brown	5·25	1·20
308	-	2½m. blue	4·50	1·50

DESIGNS: 2m. Louhi's failure to recover the "Sampo"; 2½m. Kullervo's departure to war.

57 R. H. Rehbinder

1936. Red Cross Fund. Cross in red.

309	**57**	1¼m.+15p. brown	90	2·20
310	-	2m.+20p. purple	5·25	5·00
311	-	2½m.+25p. blue	90	2·20

PORTRAITS: 2m. G. M. Armfeldt. 2½m. Arvid Horn.

58 "Lodbrok", 1771

1937. Red Cross Fund. Warships. Cross in red.

312		1¼m.+15p. brown	1·30	2·40
313	**58**	2m.+20p. red	22·00	8·25
314	-	3½m.+35p. blue	1·60	3·75

DESIGNS—HORIZ: 1¼m. "Thorborg" (inscr "Uusiman"); 3½m. "Styrbjorn" (inscr "Hameenmaa").

1937. Surch 2 MARKKAA.

315	**31**	2m. on 1½m. red	8·00	90

60 Marshal Mannerheim

1937. Marshal Mannerheim's 70th Birthday.

316	**60**	2m. blue	90	80

61 A. Makipeska

1938. Red Cross Fund. Cross in red.

317	**61**	50p.+5p. green	60	1·30
318	-	1¼m.+15p. brown	90	2·00
319	-	2m.+20p. red	8·00	6·75
320	-	3½m.+35p. blue	90	2·50

PORTRAITS: 1¼m. R. I. Orn. 2m. E. Bergenheim, 3½m. J. M. Nordenstam.

62 Cross-country Skiing

1938. International Skiing Contest, Lahti.

321	**62**	1m.25+75p. black	4·50	8·00
322	-	2m.+1m. red	4·50	8·00
323	-	3m.50+1m.50 blue and light blue	4·50	8·00

DESIGNS: 2m. Ski jumping; 3m.50, Downhill skiing contest.

63 War Veteran

1938. Disabled Soldiers' Relief Fund. 20th Anniv of Independence.

324	**63**	2m.+½m. blue	3·00	3·50

64 Colonizers felling Trees

1938. Tercentenary of Scandinavian Settlement in America.

325	**64**	3½m. brown	1·80	2·10

65 Ahvenkoski P.O., 1787

1938. Tercentenary of Finnish Postal Service.

326	**65**	50p. green	45	65
327	-	1¼m. blue	1·80	2·10
328	-	2m. red	1·80	90
329	-	3½m. grey	7·00	5·75

DESIGNS: 1¼m. Sledge-boat; 2m. Junkers Ju 52/3m mail plane; 3½m. G.P.O., Helsinki.

66 Battlefield of Solferino

1939. Red Cross Fund and 75th Anniv of International Red Cross. Cross in red.

330	**66**	50p.+5p. green	1·30	1·70
331	**66**	1¼m.+15p. brown	1·60	2·50
332	**66**	2m.+20p. red	18·00	10·50
333	**66**	3½m.+35p. blue	1·30	2·50

67 G.P.O., Helsinki

1939

334	**67**	4m. brown	45	25

See also Nos. 382/4.

68 Crossbowman

1940. Red Cross Fund. Cross in red.

335	**68**	50p.+5p. green	1·30	1·60
336	-	1¼m.+15p. brown	1·30	2·40
337	-	2m.+20p. red	1·80	2·50
338	-	3½m.+35p. blue	1·80	4·50

DESIGNS: 1¼m. Mounted cavalrymen; 2m. Unmounted cavalrymen; 3½m. Officer and infantryman.

69 Lion of Finland

1940. National Defence Fund.

339	**69**	2m.+2m. blue	45	1·30

70 Helsinki University

1940. 300th Anniv of Founding of Helsinki University.

340	**70**	2m. deep blue and blue	45	1·10

1940. Surch.

341	**31**	1m.75 on 1m.25 yellow	1·30	2·00
342	**31**	2m.75 on 2m. red	6·75	60

72 Builder

1941. Red Cross Fund. Cross in red.

343	**72**	50p.+5p. green	45	75
344	-	1m.75+15p. sepia	90	1·70
345	-	2m.75+25p. brown	6·25	9·00
346	-	3m.50+35p. blue	1·30	2·20

DESIGNS: 1m.75, Farmer; 2m.75, Mother and child; 3m.50, Flag.

See also Nos. 405/8.

73 Farewell Review

1941. President Kallio Memorial.

347	**73**	2m.75 black	45	80

74 Knight

1941. "Brothers-in-Arms" Welfare Fund.

348	**74**	2m.75+25p. blue	45	1·10

75 Viipuri Castle

1941. Reconquest of Viipuri.

349	**75**	1m.75 orange	35	1·00
350	**75**	2m.75 purple	30	65
351	**75**	3m.50 blue	90	1·50

76 Pres. Risto Ryti

77 Marshal Mannerheim

1941. (a) President Ryti.

352	**76**	50p. green	70	1·10
353	**76**	1m.75 brown	80	1·10
354	**76**	2m. red	70	1·10
355	**76**	2m.75 violet	90	1·10
356	**76**	3m.50 blue	75	1·10
357	**76**	5m. grey	75	1·10

(b) Marshal Mannerheim.

358	**77**	50p. green	70	1·30
359	**77**	1m.75 brown	70	1·30
360	**77**	2m. red	70	1·30
361	**77**	2m.75 violet	90	1·30
362	**77**	3m.50 blue	90	1·30
363	**77**	5m. grey	90	1·30

79 Aland

1942. Red Cross Fund. Cross in red.

364	**79**	50p.+5p. green	90	1·50
365	-	1m.75+15p. brown	1·30	2·75
366	-	2m.75+25p. red	1·60	2·75
367	-	3m.50+35p. blue	1·30	3·00
368	-	4m.75+45p. grey	1·20	2·75

ARMS: 1m.75, Uusimaa (Nyland); 2m.75, Finland Proper; 3m.50, Karelia; 4m.75, Satakunta.

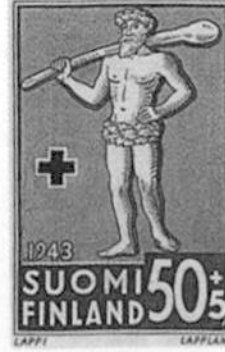

80 Tampere

1942

369	**80**	50m. brown	2·75	40
370	-	100m. blue	3·00	40

DESIGN: 100m. Helsinki Harbour.

For 100m. in green without "mk" see No. 557b.

81 New Testament

82 Mediaeval Press

1942. Tercentenary of Introduction of Printing into Finland.

380	**81**	2m.75 brown	45	80
381	**82**	3m.50 blue	65	1·50

1942

382	**67**	7m. brown	90	25
383	**67**	9m. mauve	60	25
384	**67**	20m. brown	1·60	25

83 Lapland

1943. Red Cross Fund. Cross in red.

385	**83**	50p.+5p. green	45	80
386	-	2m.+20p. brown	70	1·90
387	-	3m.50+35p. red	70	1·90
388	-	4m.50+45p. blue	1·80	8·50

ARMS: 2m. Hame (Tavastland); 3m.50, Pohjanmaa (Osterbotten); 4m.50, Savo (Savolaks).

1943. Surch 3½mk.

389	**31**	3½m. on 2m.75 purple	25	25

85 Military Tokens

1943. National Relief Fund.

390	**85**	2m.+50p. brown	45	75
391	-	3m.50+1m. purple	45	75

DESIGN—VERT: 3m.50, Widow and Orphans.

87 Red Cross Train

1944. Red Cross Fund. Inscr "1944". Cross in red.

392	**87**	50p.+25p. green	25	40
393	-	2m.+50p. violet	35	80
394	-	3m.50+75p. red	35	80
395	-	4m.50+1m. blue	65	3·50

DESIGNS: 2m. Ambulance; 3m.50, Hospital, Helsinki; 4m.50, Airplane.

88 Minna Canth

1944. Birth Cent of Minna Canth (authoress).

396	**88**	3m.50 green	45	75

89 Douglas DC-2 Mail Plane

1944. Air. 20th Anniv of Air Mail Service.

397	**89**	3m.50 brown	45	90

90 Pres. Svinhufvud

1944. Mourning for Pres. P. E. Svinhufvud.

398	**90**	3½m. black	45	75

91

1944. National Relief Fund.

399	**91**	3m.50+1m.50 brown	45	90

92 Wrestling

1945. Sports Fund.

400	**92**	1m.+50p. green	25	65
401	-	2m.+1m. red	25	65
402	-	3m.50+1m.75 violet	25	65
403	-	4m.50+2m.25 blue	25	65
404	-	7m.+3m.50 brown	70	1·90

DESIGNS: 2m. Vaulting; 3m.50, Running; 4m.50, Skiing; 7m. Throwing the javelin.

1945. Red Cross Fund. As Nos. 343/6, but dated "1945". Cross in red.

405	1m.+25p. green	25	50
406	2m.+50p. brown	25	65
407	3m.50+75p. brown	25	65
408	4m.50+1m. blue	60	1·30

DESIGNS: 1m. Builder; 2m. Farmer; 3m.50, Mother and child; 4m.50, Flag.

93 Pres. Stahlberg

1945. 80th Birth Anniv of Pres. K. J. Stahlberg.

409	**93**	3m.50 violet	35	55

94 Sibelius

1945. 80th Birthday of Sibelius (composer).

411	**94**	5m. green	1·00	35

95 Fishermen

1946. Red Cross Fund. Cross in red.

412	**95**	1m.+25p. green	25	40
413	-	3m.+75p. purple	30	40
414	-	5m.+1m.25 red	30	40
415	-	10m.+2m.50 blue	45	65

DESIGNS: 3m. Butter-making; 5m. Harvesting; 10m. Logging.

1946. Surch with bold figures and bars.

416	**31**	8m. on 5m. violet	35	25
416a	**31**	12m. on 10m. violet	90	25

97 Athletes

1946. National Games.

417	**97**	8m. purple	45	50

98 Nurse and Children

1946. Anti-tuberculosis Fund.

418	**98**	5m.+1m. green	30	60
419	-	8m.+2m. purple	30	60

DESIGN: 8m. Lady doctor examining child.

99 Uto Lighthouse, and Sailing Ship

1946. 250th Anniv of Foundation of Pilotage Institution.

420	**99**	8m. violet	45	50

100 Postal Motor Coach

1946

421	**100**	16m. black	70	75
421a	**100**	30m. black	1·60	25

101 Town Hall

1946. 600th Anniv of Founding of Porvoo (Borga).

422	**101**	5m. black	30	40
423	-	8m. purple	30	40

DESIGN—VERT: 8m. Bridge and church.

103 Tammisaari

1946. 400th Anniv of Tammisaari (Ekenas).

424	**103**	8m. green	35	40

104 Pres. Paasikivi

1947

446	**104**	10m. black	35	40

1947. Anti-tuberculosis Fund. Nos. 418/19 surch.

447	**98**	6+1 on 5m.+1m. grn	35	90
448	-	10+2 on 8m.+2m. pur	35	90

106 Bank Emblem

1947. 60th Anniv of Finnish Postal Savings Bank.

449	**106**	10m. purple	40	50

107 Athletes

1947. National Sports Festival.

450	**107**	10m. blue	40	50

108 Ilmarinen Ploughing

1947. Conclusion of Peace Treaty.

451	**108**	10m. black	40	50

109 Emblem of Savings Bank Association

1947. 125th Anniv of Savings Bank Assn.

452	**109**	10m. brown	40	50

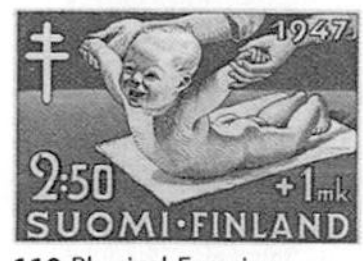

110 Physical Exercise

1947. Anti-tuberculosis Fund.

453	**110**	2m.50+1m. green	40	1·00
454	-	6m.+1m.50 red	45	1·10
455	-	10m.+2m.50 brown	45	1·10
456	-	12m.+3m. blue	60	1·60
457	-	20m.+5m. mauve	70	2·20

DESIGNS—VERT: 6, 10, 20m. Various infant exercises. HORIZ: 12m. Mme. Paasikivi and child.

111 Sower

1947. 150th Anniv of Central League of Agricultural Societies.

458	**111**	10m. grey	35	40

112 Heights of Koli

1947. 60th Anniv of Tourist Society.

459	**112**	10m. blue	35	40

113 Z. Topelius

1948. Red Cross Fund. Dated "1948". Cross in red.

460	**113**	3m.+1m. green	45	75
461	-	7m.+2m. red	55	1·10
462	-	12m.+3m. blue	55	1·10
463	-	20m.+5m. violet	60	1·50

PORTRAITS: 7m. Fr. Pacius; 12m. J. L. Runeberg; 20m. F. R. Cygnaeus.

1948. Anti-tuberculosis Fund. Nos. 454/5 and 457 surch.

464	7m.+2m. on 6m.+1m.50 red	1·20	2·20
465	15m.+3m. on 10m.+2m.50 brown	1·30	2·20
466	24m.+6m. on 20m.+5m. mauve	1·80	3·50

115 Michael Agricola (after sculpture by C. Sjostrand)

1948. 400th Anniv of Translation of New Testament into Finnish by Michael Agricola.

467	**115**	7m. purple	90	1·30
468	-	12m. blue	90	1·40

DESIGN: 12m. Agricola translating New Testament (after painting by A. Edelfelt).

116 King's Gate, Suomenlinna

1948. Bicentenary of Suomenlinna (Sveaborg).

469	**116**	12m. green	1·90	1·70

117 Finnish Mail-carrier's Badge

1948. Helsinki Philatelic Exhibition.

470	**117**	12m. green	8·00	14·50

Sold only at the Exhibition, at 62m. (including 50m. entrance fee).

118 Girl Bundling Twigs

1949. Red Cross Fund. Inscr "SAUNA BASTU 1949". Cross in red.

471	**118**	5m.+2m. green	45	65
472	-	9m.+3m. red	45	90
473	-	15m.+5m. blue	55	75
474	-	30m.+10m. brown	90	2·75

DESIGNS: 9m. Bathing scene; 15m. Heating sauna in winter; 30m. Bathers leaving sauna for plunge in lake.

119 Anemone

1949. Tuberculosis Relief Fund.

475	**119**	5m.+2m. green	50	65
476	-	9m.+3m. red	50	90
477	-	15m.+5m. brown	70	90

DESIGNS: 9m. Rose; 15m. Coltsfoot.

120 Trees and Papermill

1949. 3rd World Forestry Congress. Inscr "IIIE CONGRES FORESTIER MONDIAL 1949".

478	**120**	9m. brown	2·20	2·50
479	-	15m. green (Tree and Globe)	2·20	2·50

121 Girl with Torch

1949. 50th Anniv of Labour Movement.

480	**121**	5m. green	4·50	8·50
481	-	15m. red (Man with mallet)	4·50	8·50

122 Kristiinankaupunki

1949. Tercent of Kristiinankaupunki (Kristinestad).

482	**122**	15m. blue	1·50	2·20

123 "Salmetar" (lake steamer), Lappeenranta

1949. Tercent of Lappeenranta (Villmanstrand).

483	**123**	5m. green	90	75

124 Church, Raahe

1949. Tercentenary of Raahe (Brahestad).

484	**124**	9m. purple	90	1·00

125 Seal of Technical High School

1949. Cent of Technical High School, Helsinki.

485	**125**	15m. blue	90	90

126 Hannes Gebhard (founder)

1949. 50th Anniv of Finnish Co-operative Movement.

486	**126**	15m. green	90	90

127

1949. 75th Anniv of U.P.U.

487	**127**	15m. blue	90	1·10

128 Douglas DC-6

1950. Air.

488	**128**	300m. blue	11·00	5·50

For 300m. stamp without "mk" see No. 585 and for 3m. stamp see No. 679.

129 White Water-lily

1950. Tuberculosis Relief Fund.

489	**129**	5m.+2m. green	1·30	1·50
490	-	9m.+3m. mauve	1·00	1·50
491	-	15m.+5m. blue	1·00	1·50

DESIGNS: 9m. Pasque flower; 15m. Clustered bellflower.

130 Plan of Helsinki, 1550

1950. 400th Anniv of Helsinki.

492	**130**	5m. green	45	65
493	-	9m. brown	60	1·30
494	-	15m. blue	60	75

DESIGNS: 9m. J. A. Ehrenstrom and C. L. Engel; 15m. Town Hall and Cathedral.

131 President Paasikivi

1950. President's 80th Birthday.

495	**131**	20m. blue	60	45

132 Hospital, Helsinki

1951. Red Cross Fund. Cross in red.

496	**132**	7m.+2m. brown	90	90
497	-	12m.+3m. violet	90	90
498	-	20m.+5m. red	1·10	1·90

DESIGNS: 12m. Blood donor and nurse; 20m. Blood donor's badge.

133 Town Hall

1951. 300th Anniv of Kajaani (Kajana).

499	**133**	20m. brown	60	65

134 Western Capercaillie

1951. Tuberculosis Relief Fund.

500	**134**	7m.+2m. green	2·20	2·50
501	-	12m.+3m. lake	2·20	2·50
502	-	20m.+5m. blue	2·20	2·50

DESIGNS: 12m. Common Cranes; 20m. Caspian Terns.

135 Diving

1951. 15th Olympic Games, Helsinki.

503	**135**	12m.+2m. red	1·20	1·40
504	-	15m.+2m. green	1·20	1·40
505	-	20m.+3m. blue	1·20	1·50
506	-	25m.+4m. brown	1·60	1·60

DESIGNS—HORIZ: 15m. Football; 25m. Running. VERT: 20m. Olympic stadium.

138 Marshal Mannerheim

1952. Red Cross Fund. Cross in red.

507	**138**	10m.+2m. black	1·10	1·50
508	**138**	15m.+3m. purple	1·10	1·90
509	**138**	25m.+5m. blue	1·10	1·50

139 Arms of Pietarsaari

1952. 300th Anniv of Founding of Pietarsaari (Jakobstad).

510	**139**	25m. blue	60	80

140 Vaasa

1952. Centenary of Fire of Vaasa (Vasa).

511	**140**	25m. brown	60	90

141 Knight, Rook and Chessboard

1952. 10th Chess Olympiad, Helsinki.

512	**141**	25m. black	1·60	2·20

142 Great Tit

1952. Tuberculosis Relief Fund. Birds.

513	**142**	10m.+2m. green	1·80	2·10
514	-	15m.+3m. red	1·80	2·10
515	-	25m.+5m. blue	1·80	2·10

BIRDS: 15m. Spotted Flycatchers; 25m. Eurasian Swifts.

143 "Flame of Temperance"

1953. Cent of Finnish Temperance Movement.

516	**143**	25m. blue	90	90

144 Aerial view of Hamina

1953. 300th Anniv of Hamina (Fredrikshamn).

517	**144**	25m. slate	60	80

145 Eurasian Red Squirrel

1953. Tuberculosis Relief Fund.

518	**145**	10m.+2m. brown	2·20	2·50
519	-	15m.+3m. violet	2·20	2·50
520	-	25m.+5m. green	2·20	2·50

DESIGNS: 15m. Brown bear; 25m. Elk.

146 Wilskman

1954. Birth Centenary of Ivar Wilskman (gymnast).

521	**146**	25m. blue	70	80

147 Mother and Children

1954. Red Cross Fund. Cross in red.

522	**147**	10m.+2m. green	70	1·20
523	-	15m.+3m. blue	90	1·10
524	-	25m.+5m. brown	90	1·10

DESIGNS: 15m. Old lady knitting; 25m. Blind man and dog.

148

1954

525	**148**	1m. brown	45	40
526	**148**	2m. green	45	25
527	**148**	3m. orange	35	25
527a	**148**	4m. grey	45	35
528	**148**	5m. blue	60	25
529	**148**	10m. green	90	35
530	**148**	15m. red	2·75	25
530a	**148**	15m. orange	7·00	25
531	**148**	20m. purple	8·50	40
531a	**148**	20m. red	1·80	25
532	**148**	25m. blue	2·75	25
532a	**148**	25m. purple	11·00	25
532b	**148**	30m. blue	2·00	25

See also Nos. 647, etc.

149 "In the Outer Archipelago" (after Edelfelt)

1954. Birth Centenary of A. Edelfelt (painter).

533	**149**	25m. black	60	80

150 White-tailed Bumble Bees collecting Pollen

1954. Tuberculosis Relief Fund. Cross in red.

534	**150**	10m.+2m. brown	1·30	1·30
535	-	15m.+3m. red	1·80	1·60
536	-	25m.+5m. blue	1·80	1·60

DESIGNS: 15m. Apollo (butterfly) and wild rose; 25m. "Aeshna juncea" (dragonfly).

151 J. J. Nervander

1955. 150th Birth Anniv of Nervander (astronomer and poet).

537	**151**	25m. blue	70	90

152 Parliament Building

1955. National Philatelic Exhibition, Helsinki.

538	**152**	25m. black	6·75	12·50

153 St. Henry

1955. 800th Anniv of Establishment of Christianity in Finland.

539	**153**	15m. purple	65	75
540	-	25m. green	65	75

DESIGN: 25m. Arrival of Christian preachers in 1155.

154 Conference in Session

1955. Interparliamentary Conference, Helsinki.

541	**154**	25m. green	1·10	1·30

155 Barque "Ilma" and Cargo

1955. 350th Anniv of Oulu (Uleaborg).

542	**155**	25m. brown	1·10	1·30

156 Eurasian Perch

1955. Tuberculosis Relief Fund. Cross in red.

543	**156**	10m.+2m. green	1·30	1·30
544	-	15m.+3m. brown (Northern pike)	1·80	1·50
545	-	25m.+5m. blue (Atlantic salmon)	1·80	1·50

157 Town Hall, Lahti

1955. 50th Anniv of Lahti.

546	**157**	25m. blue	90	1·50

158 J. Z. Duncker

1955. Red Cross. Cross in red.

547	-	10m.+2m. blue	70	1·10
548	**158**	15m.+3m. brown	80	1·30
549	-	25m.+5m. green	80	1·30

DESIGNS: 10m. Von Dobeln on horseback; 25m. Young soldier.

159 "Telegraphs"

1955. Centenary of Telegraphs in Finland. Inscr "1855–1955 Telegrafen".

550	**159**	10m. green	1·10	1·10
551	-	15m. violet	1·10	1·00
552	-	25m. blue	1·30	1·50

DESIGNS: 15m. Otto Nyberg; 25m. Telegraph pole.

160 Lighthouse at Porkkala

1956. Return of Porkkala to Finland.

553	**160**	25m. blue	60	75

161 Lammi Church

1956. Value expressed as "5" etc.

553a	-	5m. green	35	20
554	**161**	30m. green	70	35
555	-	40m. lilac	2·20	25
556	**161**	50m. green	5·25	25
557	-	60m. purple	9·75	25
557a	-	75m. black	3·50	25
557b	-	100m. green	20·00	25
557c	-	125m. green	19·00	50

DESIGNS: 5m. View of lake, Keuru; 40m. Houses of Parliament; 60m. Olavinlinna; 75m. Pyhakoski Dam; 100m. Helsinki Harbour; 125m. Turku Castle.

No. 557b differs from No. 370 in that "FINLAND" is without the scroll, the figures "100" are upright and "mk" is omitted.

See also Nos. 660, etc.

162 J. V. Snellman (after sculpture by E. Wikstrom)

1956. 150th Birth Anniv of Snellman (statesman).

558	**162**	25m. brown	90	75

163 Athletes

1956. Finnish Games.

559	**163**	30m. blue	90	80

164

1956. Centenary of First Finnish Postage Stamp and International Philatelic Exhibition, Helsinki. Roul.

560	**164**	30m. blue	3·75	4·50

165 Bohemian Waxwing

1956. Tuberculosis Relief Fund. Cross in red.

561	**165**	10m.+2m. brown	1·30	95
562	-	20m.+3m. green	1·80	1·60
563	-	30m.+5m. blue	1·80	1·60

DESIGNS: 20m. Eagle Owl; 30m. Mute Swan.

166 Vaasa Town Hall

1956. 350th Anniv of Vaasa.

564	**166**	30m. blue	90	90

1956. Northern Countries' Day. As T 100 of Denmark.

565		20m. red	2·20	1·20
566		30m. blue	6·75	1·20

167 P. Aulin

1956. Red Cross. Inscr "1956". Cross in red.

567	**167**	5m.+1m. green	90	80
568	-	10m.+2m. brown	1·10	1·10
569	-	20m.+3m. red	1·60	2·00
570	-	30m.+5m. blue	1·60	1·60

PORTRAITS: 10m. L. von Pfaler; 20m. G. Johansson; 30m. V. M. von Born.

168 University Hospital, Helsinki

1956. Bicentenary of National Health Service.

571	**168**	30m. green	1·60	90

169 Scout Badge and Saluting Hand

1957. 50th Anniv of Boy Scout Movement.

572	**169**	30m. blue	1·60	1·00

171 "In Honour of Work"

1957. 50th Anniv of Finnish Trade Union Movement.

573	**171**	30m. red	70	80

172 "Lex" (sculpture by W. Runeberg)

1957. 50th Anniv of Finnish Parliament.

574	**172**	30m. olive	1·00	80

173 Wolverine

1957. Tuberculosis Relief Fund. Inscr "1957". Cross in red.

575	**173**	10m.+2m. purple	1·30	1·10
576	-	20m.+3m. sepia	1·50	1·40
577	-	30m.+5m. blue	1·80	1·40

DESIGNS: 20m. Lynx; 30m. Reindeer.
See also Nos. 642/4.

174 Factories within Cogwheel

1957. 50th Anniv of Central Federation of Finnish Employers.

578	**174**	20m. blue	70	75

175 Red Cross Flag

1957. Red Cross Fund and 80th Anniv of Finnish Red Cross. Cross in red.

579	**175**	10m.+2m. green	1·40	1·90
580	**175**	20m.+3m. lake	1·40	1·90
581	**175**	30m.+5m. blue	1·40	1·90

176 Ida Aalberg (after Edelfelt)

1957. Birth Cent of Ida Aalberg (actress).

582	**176**	30m. maroon & purple	70	75

177 Arms of Finland

1957. 40th Anniv of Independence.

583	**177**	30m. blue	90	80

178 Bust of Sibelius (Waino Aaltonen)

1957. Death of Sibelius (composer).

584	**178**	30m. black	1·10	1·00

1958. Air. As No. 488 but with "mk" omitted.

585	**128**	300m. blue	33·00	1·10

See also No. 679.

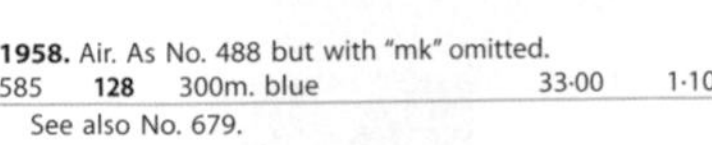

179 Ski Jumping

1958. World Ski Championships.

586	**179**	20m. green	90	1·30
587	-	30m. blue	90	1·30

DESIGN—VERT: 30m. Cross-country skiing.

180 "March of the Bjorneborgienses" (after Edelfelt)

1958. 400th Anniv of Founding of Pori (Bjorneborg).

588	**180**	30m. purple	1·10	75

181 Lily of the Valley

1958. Tuberculosis Relief Fund. Cross in red.

589	**181**	10m.+2m. green	1·10	1·10
590	-	20m.+3m. red	1·80	1·60
591	-	30m.+5m. blue	1·80	1·60

DESIGNS: 20m. Red clover; 30m. Anemone.

182 Lyceum Seal

1958. Centenary of Jyvaskyla Lyceum (secondary school).

592	**182**	30m. red	1·10	95

183 Convair CV 340 OH-LRD over Lakes

1958. Air.

593	**183**	34m. blue	90	80
594	**183**	45m. blue	1·80	1·70

See also Nos. 678/a.

184 Cloudberry

1958. Red Cross Fund. Cross in red.

595	**184**	10m.+2m. orange	90	1·10
596	-	20m.+3m. red	1·60	1·50
597	-	30m.+5m. blue	1·60	1·50

DESIGNS: 20m. Cowberry; 30m. Blueberry.

185 Missionary Emblem and Globe

1959. Centenary of Finnish Missionary Society.

598	**185**	30m. purple	70	55

186 Opening of Diet, 1809

1959. 150th Anniv of Re-convening of Finnish Diet at Porvoo.

599	**186**	30m. blue	70	55

1959. Air. No. 593 surch 45.

600		45m. on 34m. blue	1·80	3·75

188 Multiple Saws

1959. Centenaries of Kestila Sawmill (10m.) and Finnish Forestry Department (30m.).

601	**188**	10m. brown	45	55
602	-	30m. grn (Forest firs)	45	60

1959. Tuberculosis Relief Fund. As T 181 but inscr "1959". Cross in red.

603	10m.+2m. green	1·80	1·50
604	20m.+3m. brown	2·20	2·10
605	30m.+5m. blue	2·20	2·10

DESIGNS: 10m. Marguerite; 20m. Cowslip; 30m. Cornflower.

189 Gymnast

1959. Birth Centenary of Elin Oihonna Kallio (Women's Gymnastics pioneer).

606	**189**	30m. purple	70	65

190 Oil Lamp

1959. Cent of Trade Freedom in Finland.

607	**190**	30m. blue	60	65

191 Arms of the Towns

1960. Extra Privileges for Finnish Towns–Hyvinkaa, Kouvola, Riihimaki, Rovaniemi, Salo and Seinajoki.

608	**191**	30m. violet	1·00	75

192 5k. "Serpentine Roulette" Stamp of 1860

1960. Stamp Exhibition, Helsinki, and Centenary of "Serpentine Roulette" stamps. Roul.

609	**192**	30m. blue and grey	6·25	7·50

193 Refugees and Symbol

1960. World Refugee Year.

610	**193**	30m. red	45	50
611	**193**	40m. blue	45	50

194 J. Gadolin

1960. Birth Bicent of Johan Gadolin (chemist).

612	**194**	30m. brown	70	65

195 H. Nortamo

1960. Birth Cent of H. Nortamo (writer).

613	**195**	30m. green	70	65

196 European Cuckoo

1960. Karelian National Festival, Helsinki.

614	**196**	30m. red	80	75

197 "Geodesy" (Geodetic instrument)

1960. 12th International Geodesy and Geophysics Union Assembly, Helsinki.

615	**197**	10m. sepia and blue	45	50
616	-	30m. brn, red & verm	45	65

DESIGN: 30m. "Geophysics" (representation of Northern Lights).

198 Pres. Kekkonen

1960. President Kekkonen's 60th Birthday.

617	**198**	30m. blue	80	50

1960. Europa. As T 373 of Belgium but size 31×20½ mm.

618	30m. blue and ultramarine	70	65
619	40m. purple and sepia	70	65

199 Pastor Cygnaeus

1960. 150th Birth Anniv of Pastor Uno Cygnaeus (founder of elementary schools).

620	**199**	30m. purple	90	65

200 Reindeer

1960. Red Cross Fund. Cross in red.

621	**200**	10m.+2m. purple	1·10	1·30
622	-	20m.+3m. violet	1·80	1·70
623	-	30m.+5m. purple	1·60	1·70

DESIGNS: 20m. Hunter with lasso; 30m. Mountain and lake.

201 "Pommern" (barque)

1961. Cent of Marianhamina (Mariehamn).

624	**201**	30m. blue	2·20	2·10

202 Savings Bank's New Emblem

1961. 75th Anniv of Finnish Postal Savings Bank.

625	**202**	30m. blue	90	50

203 Symbol of Standardization

1961. General Assembly of Int. Organization for Standardization, Helsinki.

626	**203**	30m. green & orange	70	65

1961. Tuberculosis Relief Fund. As T 173. Cross in red.

627	10m.+2m. purple	1·10	1·30
628	20m.+3m. blue	1·80	1·50
629	30m.+5m. green	1·80	1·80

ANIMALS: 10m. Muskrat; 20m. European otter; 30m. Ringed seal.

204 J. Aho

1961. Birth Centenary of Aho (writer).

630	**204**	30m. brown	80	65

205 Helsinki Cathedral

1961. 150th Anniv of Finnish Central Building Board.

631	**205**	30m. black	80	65

206 A. Jarnefelt

1961. Birth Centenary of Arvid Jarnefelt (writer).

632	**206**	30m. purple	80	65

207 Bank Facade

1961. 150th Anniv of Bank of Finland.

633	**207**	30m. purple	80	65

208 First locomotive, "Ilmarinen"

1962. Centenary of Finnish Railways.

634	**208**	10m. green	1·30	65
635	-	30m. blue	1·30	65
636	-	40m. purple	3·00	65

LOCOMOTIVES: 30m. Class Hr-1 steam locomotive and Type Hk wagon; 40m. Class Hr-12 diesel locomotive and passenger carriages.

209 Mora Stone

1962. 600th Anniv of Finnish People's Political Rights.

637	**209**	30m. purple	80	65

210 Senate Place, Helsinki

1962. 150th Anniv of Proclamation of Helsinki as Finnish Capital.

638	**210**	30m. brown	80	65

211 Customs Board Crest

1962. 150th Anniv of Finnish Customs Board.

639	**211**	30m. red	1·00	65

212 Emblem of Commerce

1962. Cent of 1st Finnish Commercial Bank.

640	**212**	30m. green	1·00	65

213 S. Alkio

1962. Birth Cent of Santeri Alkio (writer and founder of Young People's Societies' Movement).

641	**213**	30m. purple	1·00	65

1962. Tuberculosis Relief Fund. As T 173. Cross in red.

642	10m.+2m. black	1·40	1·30
643	20m.+3m. purple	1·80	1·60
644	30m.+5m. blue	1·80	1·60

DESIGNS: 10m. Brown hare; 20m. Pine marten; 30m. Stoat.

214 Finnish Labour Emblem on Conveyor Belt

1962. Home Production.

645	**214**	30m. purple	80	40

215 Hunting Pembroke making Aerial Survey

1962. 150th Anniv of Finnish Land Survey Board.

646	**215**	30m. green	90	75

216

1963. (a) Lion Type.

647	**216**	1p. brown	20	25
648	**216**	2p. green	20	15
649	**216**	4p. grey	55	40
650	**216**	5p. blue	45	20
651	**216**	10p. green	60	40
652	**216**	15p. orange	1·30	35
653a	**216**	20p. red	90	20
654a	**216**	25p. purple	90	40
656	**216**	30p. blue	1·30	40
657	**216**	35p. blue	1·20	20
657a	**216**	35p. yellow	70	30
658	**216**	40p. blue	1·30	40
658b	**216**	40p. orange	90	40
659	**216**	50p. blue	2·50	25
659a	**216**	50p. purple	70	25
659b	**216**	60p. blue	60	25

(b) Views. Values expressed as "0,05" (pennia values) or "1,00" (mark values).

660	-	5p. green (As No. 553a) (postage)	55	25
661	-	25p. multicoloured	45	25
662	-	30p. multicoloured	1·30	25
663	-	40p. lilac (As No. 555)	5·25	25
664	**161**	50p. green	4·50	25
665	-	60p. purple (As No. 557)	10·50	25
666	-	65p. purple (As No. 557)	1·30	30
667	-	75p. black (As No. 557a)	1·80	25
668	-	80p. multicoloured	4·75	35
669	-	90p. multicoloured	1·20	45
670	-	1m. green (As No. 557b)	3·00	25
671	-	1m.25 green (As No. 557c)	1·80	35
672	-	1m.30 multicoloured	90	40
673	-	1m.50 green	3·50	25
674	-	1m.75 blue	1·20	25
675	-	2m. green	13·50	25
676	-	2m.50 blue & yellow	5·50	40
677	-	5m. green	18·00	35
678	**183**	45p. blue (air)	1·30	35
678a	**183**	57p. blue	2·00	1·00
679	-	3m. blue (585)	18·00	55

NEW DESIGNS: As Type **161**—VERT: 30p. Nasinneula Tower, Tampere; 80p. Keuruu church; 1m.30, Helsinki Railway Station. HORIZ: 25p. Country mail bus; 90p. Hameen Bridge, Tampere; 1m.50, Loggers afloat; 1m.75, Parainen Bridge; 2m. Country house by lake; 2m.50, Aerial view of Punkaharju; 5m. Ristikallio Gorge.

No. 679 is as No. 585, but with a comma after "3".

217 Mother and Child

1963. Freedom from Hunger.

680	**217**	40p. brown	70	50

218 Hands reaching for Red Cross

1963. Centenary of Red Cross.

681	**218**	10p.+2p. brn & red	60	75
682	**218**	20p.+3p. violet & red	90	1·40
683	**218**	30p.+5p. green & red	90	1·60

219 Crown of Thorns

1963. Lutheran World Federation Assembly, Helsinki.

684	**219**	10p. lake	45	35
685	-	30p. green	60	65

DESIGN: 30p. Head of Christ.

220 "Co-operation"

1963. Europa.

686	**220**	40p. purple	2·40	75

221 House of Estates, Helsinki

1963. Cent of Finnish Representative Assembly.

687	**221**	30p. purple	60	55

222 Convair CV 440 Metropolitan Airliner

1963. 40 Years of Finnish Civil Aviation.

688	**222**	35p. green	70	65
689	-	40p. blue	70	50

DESIGN: 40p. Sud-Aviation SE 210 Caravelle in flight.

223 M. A. Castren (after E. J. Lofgren)

1963. 150th Birth Anniv of M. A. Castren (explorer and scholar).

690	**223**	35p. blue	80	50

224 Soapstone Elk's Head

1964. "For Art" (centenary of Finnish Artists' Society).

691	**224**	35p. green and buff	90	40

225 E. N. Setala

1964. Birth Centenary of Emil Setala (philologist and statesman).

692	**225**	35p. brown	90	55

226 Doctor tending Patient on Sledge

1964. Red Cross Fund. Cross in red.

693	**226**	15p.+3p. blue	90	80
694	-	25p.+4p. green	1·20	1·00
695	-	35p.+5p. purple	1·20	1·00
696	-	40p.+7p. green	1·30	1·00

DESIGNS: 25p. Red Cross hospital ship; 35p. Military sick parade; 40p. Distribution of Red Cross parcels.

227 Emblem of Medicine

1964. 18th General Assembly of World Medical Association.

697	**227**	40p. green	90	55

228 Ice Hockey Players

1965. World Ice Hockey Championships.

698	**228**	35p. blue	90	55

229 Centenary Medal

1965. Cent of Finnish Communal Self-Government.
699 **229** 35p. green 90 55

230 K. J. Stahlberg and Runeberg's sculpture, "Lex"

1965. Birth Cent of K. J. Stahlberg (statesman).
700 **230** 35p. brown 90 55

231 I.C.Y. Emblem

1965. International Co-operation Year.
701 **231** 40p. multicoloured 80 55

232 "The Fratricide"

1965. Birth Centenary of A. Gallen-Kallela (artist). Multicoloured.
702 25p. Type **232** 1·20 75
703 35p. "Head of a Young Girl" 1·20 75

233 Spitz

1965. Tuberculosis Relief Fund. Dogs.
704 **233** 15p.+3p. brn & red 1·20 1·10
705 - 25p.+4p. blk & red 1·80 1·60
706 - 35p.+5p. sep & red 1·80 1·60
FINNISH DOGS: 25p. Karelian bear dog. 35p. Finnish stovare.

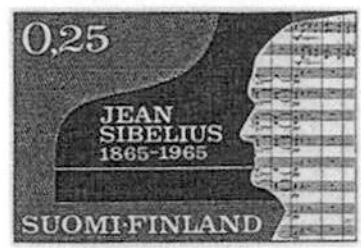

234 Piano, Profile and Score of "Finlandia"

1965. Birth Centenary of Sibelius (composer).
707 **234** 25p. violet 70 50
708 - 35p. green 70 75
DESIGN: 35p. Part of score of "Finlandia" and dove.

235 Dish Aerial

1965. Centenary of I.T.U.
709 **235** 35p. blue 75 65

236 "Winter Day" (after P. Halonen)

1965. Birth Cent of Pekka Halonen (painter).
710 **236** 35p. multicoloured 75 50

237 Europa "Sprig"

1965. Europa.
711 **237** 40p. multicoloured 2·00 50

238 "Kiss of Life"

1966. Red Cross Fund. Multicoloured.
712 15p.+3p. Type **238** 70 1·10
713 25p.+4p. Diver and submerged car 70 1·10
714 35p.+5p. Sud-Aviation SE 3130 Alouette II Red Cross helicopter 70 1·10

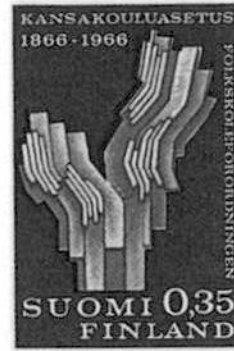

239 "Growing Up"

1966. Cent of Finnish Elementary School Decree.
715 **239** 35p. bl & ultramarine 65 50

240 Old Post Office

1966. "Nordia 1966" Stamp Exn., Helsinki, and Centenary of 1st Postage Stamps in Finnish Currency.
716 **240** 35p. blue, brown & yell 4·50 5·75

241 Globe and UNESCO Emblem

1966. 20th Anniv of UNESCO.
717 **241** 40p. multicoloured 80 55

242 Police Emblem

1966. 150th Anniv of Finnish Police Force.
718 **242** 35p. silver, black & blue 90 55

243 Anniversary Medal (after K. Kallio)

1966. 150th Anniv of Finnish Insurance.
719 **243** 35p. olive and lake 80 55

244 U.N.I.C.E.F Emblem

1966. 20th Anniv of UNICEF.
720 **244** 15p. violet, green & blue 75 35

245 FINEFTA Symbol

1967. Abolition of Industrial Customs Tariffs by European Free Trade Association.
721 **245** 40p. blue 80 50

246 Windmill

1967. 350th Anniv of Uusikaupunki (Nystad).
722 **246** 40p. multicoloured 85 40

247 Birch Tree and Foliage

1967. Tuberculosis Relief Fund. Mult.
723 20p.+3p. Type **247** 90 90
724 25p.+4p. Pine and foliage 1·00 1·10
725 40p.+7p. Spruce and foliage 1·00 1·10
See also Nos. 753/5.

248 Mannerheim Statue (A. Tukiainen)

1967. Birth Cent of Marshal Mannerheim.
726 **248** 40p. multicoloured 70 40

249 "Solidarity"

1967. Finnish Settlers in Sweden.
727 **249** 40p. multicoloured 70 40

250 Watermark of Thomasbole Factory

1967. 300th Anniv of Finnish Paper Industry.
728 **250** 40p. blue and bistre 70 40

251 Martin Luther (from painting by Lucas Cranach the Elder)

1967. 450th Anniv of the Reformation.
729 **251** 40p. multicoloured 70 40

252 Horse-drawn Ambulance

1967. Red Cross Fund. Multicoloured.
730 20p.+3p. Type **252** 60 1·00
731 25p.+4p. Modern ambulance 80 1·00
732 40p.+7p. Red Cross emblem 80 1·00

253 Northern Lights

1967. 50th Anniv of Independence.
733 **253** 20p. green and blue 60 40
734 - 25p. blue & light blue 60 35
735 - 40p. mauve and blue 60 35
DESIGNS: 25p. Flying swan; 40p. Ear of wheat.

254 Z. Topelius and "Bluebird"

1968. 150th Anniv of Zacharias Topelius (writer).
736 **254** 25p. multicoloured 55 50

255 Skiing

1968. Winter Tourism.
737 **255** 25p. multicoloured 55 75

256 "Paper- making" (from wood relief by H. Autere)

1968. 150th Anniv of Tervakoski Paper Factory.
738 **256** 45p. brown, buff & red 45 40

257 W.H.O. Emblem

1968. 20th Anniv of W.H.O.
739 **257** 40p. multicoloured 55 35

258 "Infantryman" (statue by L. Leppanen, Vaasa)

1968. 50th Anniv of Finnish Army. Mult.
740 20p. Type **258** 70 50
741 25p. Memorial (V. Aaltonen), Hietaniemi cemetery 70 50
742 40p. Modern soldier 70 50

259 Holiday Camp

1968. Tourism.
743 **259** 25p. multicoloured 75 1·00

260 Pulp Bale (with outline of tree in centre) and Paper Reel

1968. Finnish Wood-processing Industry.
744 **260** 40p. multicoloured 55 40

261 O. Merikanto

1968. Birth Cent of Oskar Merikanto (composer).
745 **261** 40p. multicoloured 55 40

262 Mustola Lock

1968. Opening of Saima Canal.
746 **262** 40p. multicoloured 55 40

263 Dock Cranes, "Ivalo" (container ship) and Chamber of Commerce Emblem

1968. "Finnish Economic Life". 50th Anniv of Finnish Central Chamber of Commerce.
747 **263** 40p. multicoloured 55 40

264 Welding

1968. Finnish Metal Industry.
748 **264** 40p. multicoloured 55 30

265 Lyre Emblem

1968. Finnish Student Unions.
749 **265** 40p. brn, bl & ultram 55 40

1969. 50th Anniv of Northern Countries' Union. As T 159 of Denmark.
750 40p. blue 1·20 50

266 City Hall and Arms, Kemi

1969. Centenary of Kemi (Kemin).
751 **266** 40p. multicoloured 55 40

267 Colonnade

1969. Europa.
752 **267** 40p. multicoloured 6·50 70

1969. Tuberculosis Relief Fund. As T 247, but inscr "1969". Multicoloured.
753 20p.+3p. Juniper and berries 65 90
754 25p.+4p. Aspen and catkins 80 1·00
755 40p.+7p. Wild cherry and flowers 80 1·00

268 I.L.O. Emblem

1969. 50th Anniv of I.L.O.
756 **268** 40p. blue, lt blue & red 55 35

269 A. Jarnefelt (after V. Sjostrom)

1969. Birth Cent of Armas Jarnefelt (composer).
757 **269** 40p. multicoloured 55 35

270 Fairs Symbol

1969. Finnish National and Int. Fairs.
758 **270** 40p. multicoloured 55 35

271 J. Linnankoski

1969. Birth Centenary of Johannes Linnankoski (writer).
759 **271** 40p. multicoloured 55 40

272 Board Emblems

1969. Centenary of Central Schools Board.
760 **272** 40p. violet, green & grey 55 40

273 Douglas DC-8-62F over Helsinki Airport

1969. Aviation.
761 **273** 25p. multicoloured 90 90

274 Golden Eagle and Eyrie

1970. Nature Conservation Year.
762 **274** 30p. multicoloured 2·20 1·00

275 "Fabric" Factories

1970. Finnish Textile Industry.
763 **275** 50p. multicoloured 55 40

276 "Molecular Structure" and Factories, Nysta

1970. Finnish Chemical Industry.
764 **276** 50p. multicoloured 55 40

277 UNESCO Emblem and Lenin

1970. Finnish Co-operation with United Nations.
765 **277** 30p. multicoloured 55 40
766 - 30p. multicoloured 55 40
767 - 50p. gold, ultram & bl 55 40

DESIGNS—VERT: 30p. (No. 765), Type **277** (Lenin Symposium of UNESCO, Tampere); 30p. (No. 766), "Nuclear data" (Int. Atomic Energy Agency Conference, Otaniemi). HORIZ: 50p. U. N. emblem and globe (United Nations 25th Anniv).

278 "The Seven Brothers"

1970. Red Cross Fund. Multicoloured.
768 25p.+5p. Type **278** 60 90
769 30p.+6p. "Juhani on top of Impivaara" (vert) 60 90
770 50p.+10p. "The Pale Maiden" 60 90

279 Invalid playing Handball

1970. 30th Anniv of Finnish Invalids League.
771 **279** 50p. black, red & orange 55 40

280 "Aurora Society Meeting" (E. Jarnefelt)

1970. Bicentenary of Aurora Society.
772 **280** 50p. multicoloured 55 35

281 City Hall and Old Schoolhouse, Uusikaarlepyy

1970. 350th Anniv of Uusikaarlepyy (Nykarleby) and Kokkola (Gamlakarleby) (towns). Mult.
773 50p. Type **281** 55 40
774 50p. Kokkola and arms 55 40

282 Pres. Kekkonen (from medal by A. Tukiainen)

1970. President Urho Kekkonen's 70th Birthday.
775 **282** 50p. silver and blue 55 40

283 "S.A.L.T." and Globe

1970. Strategic Arms Limitation Talks, Helsinki.
776 **283** 50p. multicoloured 55 40

284 Pres. Paasikivi (after sculpture by E. Renvall)

1970. Birth Centenary of President Paasikivi.
777 **284** 50p. black, blue & gold 55 35

285 Cogwheels

1971. Finnish Industry.
778 **285** 50p. multicoloured 55 40

286 Felling Trees

1971. Tuberculosis Relief Fund. Timber Industry. Multicoloured.
779 25p.+5p. Type **286** 45 90
780 30p.+6p. Tug and log raft 55 1·00
781 50p.+10p. Sorting logs 55 1·10

287 Europa Chain

1971. Europa.
782 **287** 50p. yellow, pink & blk 4·50 90

288 Tornio Church

1971. 350th Anniv of Tornio (Torneaa).
783 **288** 50p. multicoloured 75 40

289 "Front-page News" (in Swedish, Finnish and French)

1971. Bicentenary of Finnish Press.
784 **289** 50p. multicoloured 70 40

290 Hurdling, High-jumping and Discus-throwing

1971. European Athletic Championships, Helsinki. Multicoloured.
785 30p. Type **290** 1·10 65
786 50p. Throwing the javelin and running 1·70 65

These two designs form a composite picture when placed side by side.

291 "Lightning" Dinghies

1971. Int "Lightning" Class Sailing Championships, Helsinki.

787	**291**	50p. multicoloured	90	50

292 Silver Pot, Seal and Tools

1971. 60th Anniv of Jewellery and Precious-metal Crafts.

788	**292**	50p. multicoloured	70	30

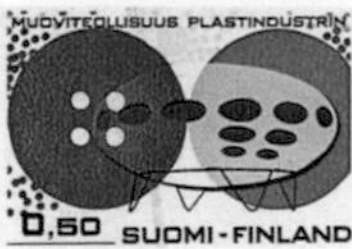

293 Plastic Buttons

1971. Finnish Plastics Industry.

789	**293**	50p. multicoloured	80	40

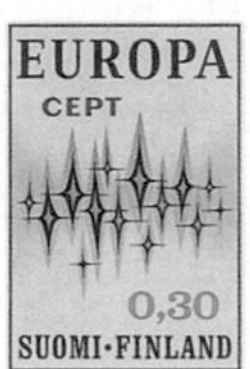

294 "Communications"

1972. Europa.

790	**294**	30p. multicoloured	2·75	50
791	**294**	50p. multicoloured	4·50	50

295 National Theatre Building

1972. Centenary of Finnish National Theatre.

792	**295**	50p. multicoloured	75	50

296 Globe

1972. Conclusion of the Strategic Arms Limitation Talks, Helsinki.

793	**296**	50p. multicoloured	90	35

297 Map and Arms

1972. 50th Anniv of Local Self-government for the Aland Islands.

794	**297**	50p. multicoloured	2·40	75

298 Cadet Ship "Suomen Joutsen"

1972. Start of the Tall Ships' Race, Helsinki.

795	**298**	50p. multicoloured	90	40

299 Post Office, Tampere

1972. Multicoloured.. Multicoloured..

797	40p. Type **299**	70	20
798	60p. National Museum (28×40 mm)	75	40
799	70p. Market Place, Helsinki (39×27 mm)	80	20
800	80p. As 70p.	70	25

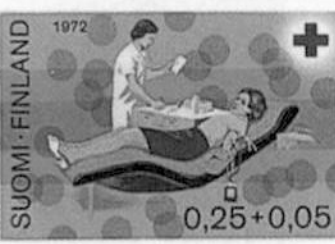

301 Blood Donation

1972. Red Cross Fund. Blood Service. Mult.

820	25p.+5p. Type **301**	65	1·00
821	30p.+6p. Laboratory research (vert)	65	1·00
822	50p.+10p. Blood transfusion	90	1·10

302 Voyri Man

1972. Ancient and National Costumes. Multicoloured.

823	50p. Pernio woman	1·80	40
824	50p. Married couple, Tenala	1·80	40
825	50p. Nastola girl	1·80	40
826	50p. Type **302**	1·80	40
827	50p. Lapp winter costumes	1·80	40
828	60p. Kaukola girl	3·00	35
829	60p. Jaaski woman	3·00	35
830	60p. Koivisto couple	3·00	35
831	60p. Mother and son, Sakyla	3·00	35
832	60p. Heinavesi girl	3·00	35

303 "European Co-operation"

1972. European Security and Co-operation Conf, Helsinki (1st issue).

833	**303**	50p. multicoloured	2·40	50

See also No. 839.

304 "Treaty" and National Colours

1973. 25th Anniv of Friendship Treaty with Russia.

834	**304**	60p. multicoloured	75	50

305 Pres. K. Kallio

1973. Birth Cent of Pres. Kyosti Kallio.

835	**305**	60p. multicoloured	75	30

306 Europa "Posthorn"

1973. Europa.

836	**306**	60p. green, turq & blue	1·60	50

1973. Nordic Countries' Postal Co-operation. As T 201 of Denmark.

837	60p. multicoloured	90	35
838	70p. multicoloured	90	35

307 "EUROPA" on Map

1973. European Security and Co-operation Conf, Helsinki (2nd issue).

839	**307**	70p. multicoloured	90	50

308 Canoe Paddle

1973. World Canoeing Championships, Tampere.

840	**308**	60p. multicoloured	75	40

309 Radiosonde Balloon

1973. Cent of World Meteorological Organization.

841	**309**	60p. multicoloured	75	40

310 E. Saarinen

1973. Birth Cent of Eliel Saarinen (architect).

842	**310**	60p. multicoloured	75	50

311 "Young Girl with Lamb" (H. Simberg)

1973. Tuberculosis Relief Fund. Artists' Birth Centenaries. Multicoloured.

843	30p.+5p. Type **311**	90	90
844	40p.+10p. "Summer Evening" (W. Sjostrom)	1·20	1·30
845	60p.+15p. "At a Mountain Spring" (J. Rissanen)	1·20	1·30

312 Douglas DC-10-30

1973. 50th Annivs. of Finnair (airline) and Regular Air Services in Finland.

846	**312**	60p. multicoloured	90	40

313 Santa Claus

1973. Christmas.

847	**313**	30p. multicoloured	90	35

314 Scene from "The Barber of Seville"

1973. Centenary of Finnish State Opera Company.

848	**314**	60p. multicoloured	75	40

315 Porcelain Products

1973. Finnish Porcelain Industry.

849	**315**	60p. green, blk & bl	80	40

316 "Paavo Nurmi" (Statue by W. Aaltonen)

1973. Paavo Nurmi (Olympic athlete) Commem.

850	**316**	60p. multicoloured	90	40

317 Hanko Casino, Harbour and Map

1974. Centenary of Hanko (Hango).

851	**317**	60p. multicoloured	75	40

318 Arms of Finland, 1581

1974

852	**318**	10m. multicoloured	3·00	35
852a	-	20m. multicoloured	7·00	50

DESIGN: 20m. Arms as in T **318** but different border.

319 Ice Hockey Players

1974. World and European Ice Hockey Championships.

853	**319**	60p. multicoloured	90	35

320 Herring Gulls

1974. Baltic Area Marine Environmental Conference, Helsinki.

854	**320**	60p. multicoloured	80	35

321 "Goddess of Victory bestowing Wreath on Youth" (W. Aaltonen)

1974. Europa.

855	**321**	70p. multicoloured	3·75	50

322 Ilmari Kianto

1974. Birth Centenary of Ilmari Kianto ("Iki Kianto") (writer).

856	**322**	60p. multicoloured	75	40

323 Society Emblem

1974. Finnish Society for Popular Education.

857	**323**	60p. multicoloured	75	40

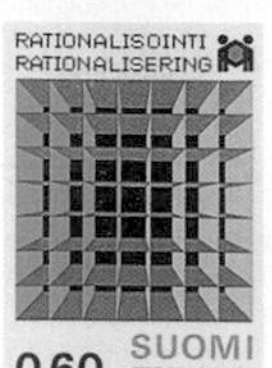

324 "Rationalization"

1974. Finnish Rationalization in Social Development.

858	**324**	60p. multicoloured	75	40

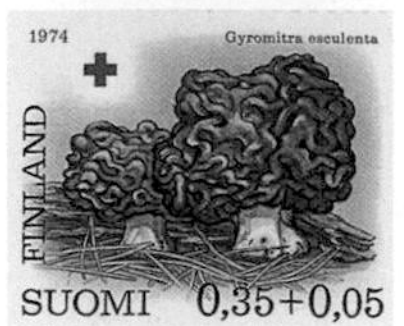

325 Beefsteak Morel

1974. Red Cross Fund. Mushrooms (1st series). Multicoloured.

859	35p.+5p. Type **325**	1·10	80
860	50p.+10p. Chanterelle	1·60	1·70
861	60p.+15p. Cep	1·60	1·70

See also Nos. 937/9 and 967/9.

326 U.P.U. Emblem

1974. Centenary of Universal Postal Union.

862	**326**	60p. multicoloured	65	30
863	**326**	70p. multicoloured	65	30

327 Christmas Gnomes

1974. Christmas.

864	**327**	35p. multicoloured	1·10	50

328 Aunessilta Granite Bridge and Modern Reinforced Concrete Bridge

1974. 175th Anniv of Finnish Road and Waterways Board.

865	**328**	60p. multicoloured	75	35

329 National Arms

1975

865a	**329**	10p. purple	20	15
865c	**329**	20p. yellow	20	15
865d	**329**	30p. red	25	15
866	**329**	40p. orange	30	15
867	**329**	50p. green	30	15
868	**329**	60p. blue	35	15
869	**329**	70p. brown	40	15
870	**329**	80p. red and green	45	15
871	**329**	90p. violet	45	15
872	**329**	1m. brown	40	20
873	**329**	1m.10 yellow	50	15
874	**329**	1m.20 blue	50	15
875	**329**	1m.30 green	50	25
875a	**329**	1m.40 violet	60	15
875b	**329**	1m.50 blue	60	15
875c	**329**	1m.60 red	60	15
875d	**329**	1m.70 grey	60	15
875e	**329**	1m.80 green	75	15
875f	**329**	1m.90 orange	65	15
1161	**329**	2m. green	1·60	65

330 Finnish 32p. Stamp of 1875

1975. "Nordia 1975" Stamp Exhibition.

876	**330**	70p. brown, black & buff	3·00	3·25

331 "A Girl Combing Her Hair" (M. Enckell)

1975. Europa. Multicoloured.

877	70p. Type **331**	2·20	45
878	90p. "Washerwomen" (T. Sallinen)	2·20	45

332 Office Seal

1975. 150th Anniv of State Economy Controllers' Office.

879	**332**	70p. multicoloured	65	35

333 "Niilo Saarinen" (lifeboat) and Sinking Ship

1975. 12th International Salvage Conference, Helsinki.

880	**333**	70p. multicoloured	75	35

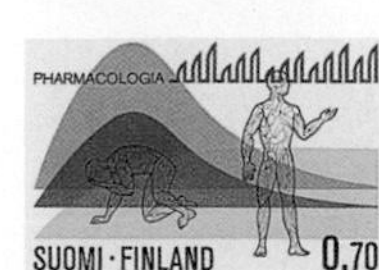

334 "Pharmacology"

1975. 6th International Pharmacological Congress, Helsinki.

881	**334**	70p. multicoloured	75	35

335 Olavinlinna Castle

1975. 500th Anniv of Olavinlinna Castle.

882	**335**	70p. multicoloured	75	35

336 Finlandia Hall (Conference Headquarters) and Barn Swallow

1975. European Security and Co-operation Conference, Helsinki.

883	**336**	90p. multicoloured	90	35

337 "Echo" (E. Thesleff)

1975. Tuberculosis Relief Fund. Paintings by female artists. Multicoloured.

884	40p.+10p. Type **337**	65	90
885	60p.+15p. "Portrait of Hilda Wiik" (Maria Wiik)	90	1·10
886	70p.+20p. "At Home" (Helene Schjerfbeck)	90	1·10

338 Men and Women supporting Globe

1975. International Women's Year.

887	**338**	70p. multicoloured	75	40

339 Graphic Quarter- circle

1975. Centenary of Finnish Society of Industrial Art.

888	**339**	70p. multicoloured	75	35

340 Nativity Play

1975. Christmas.

889	**340**	40p. multicoloured	75	35

341 State Debenture

1975. Cent. of Finnish State Treasury.

890	**341**	80p. multicoloured	70	30

342 Finnish Glider

1976. 15th World Gliding Championships, Rayskala.

891	**342**	80p. multicoloured	80	35

343 Disabled Ex-servicemen's Association Emblem

1976. Finnish War Invalids Fund.

892	**343**	70p.+30p. mult	90	65

344 Cheese Frames

1976. Traditional Finnish Arts.

893	-	1m.50 multicoloured	75	40
893a	-	2m. multicoloured	1·20	25
893b	-	2m.20 multicoloured	80	30
894	**344**	2m.50 multicoloured	90	40
895	-	3m. multicoloured	1·10	40
896	-	4m.50 multicoloured	1·60	40
896b	-	4m.80 multicoloured	1·50	65
897	-	5m. multicoloured	1·80	40
898	-	6m. multicoloured	1·80	25
899	-	7m. multicoloured	2·75	35
899a	-	8m. brown and black	2·75	35
899b	-	9m. black and blue	3·00	65
899c	-	12m. ochre, drab & brn	4·00	75

DESIGNS—VERT: 1m.50, Rusko drinking bowl, 1542; 4m.50, Spinning distaffs; 5m. Weathercock, Kirvu (metalwork); 6m. Kaspaikka (Karelian towel); 7m. Bridal rug, 1815; 8m. Arsenal door, Hollola church (iron forging). HORIZ: 2m., 4m.80, Old-style sauna; 2m.20, Kerimaki Church and belfry (peasant architecture); 3m. Shuttle and raanu (patterned cover); 9m. Four-pronged fish spear, c. 1000; 12m. Damask with tulip pattern.

345 Heikki Klemetti

1976. Birth Centenary of Professor Heikki Klemetti (composer).

900	**345**	80p. multicoloured	75	30

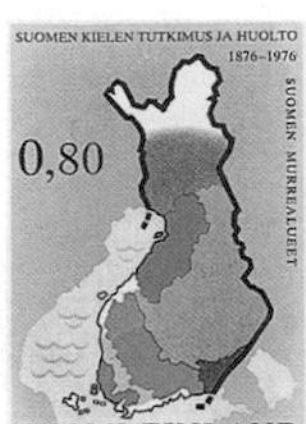

346 Map of Finnish Dialect Regions

1976. Centenary of Finnish Language Society.

901	**346**	80p. multicoloured	75	30

347 "Aino Ackte in Paris" (A. Edelfelt)

1976. Birth Cent of Aino Ackte (opera singer).

902	**347**	70p. multicoloured	75	35

348 Ancient Knives and Belts

1976. Europa.
903 **348** 80p. multicoloured 5·50 45

349 "Radio Broadcasting"

1976. 50th Anniv of Radio Broadcasting in Finland.
904 **349** 80p. multicoloured 70 30

350 Wedding Dance

1976. Tuberculosis Relief Fund. Traditional Wedding Customs. Multicoloured.
905 50p.+10p. Wedding procession (horiz) 65 65
906 70p.+15p. Type **350** 65 90
907 80p.+20p. Wedding breakfast (horiz) 90 90

351 Sleigh arriving at Church

1976. Christmas.
908 **351** 50p. multicoloured 75 30

352 Medieval Seal and Text

1976. 700th Anniv of Cathedral Chapter, Turku.
909 **352** 80p. multicoloured 70 30

353 Hugo Alvar Aalto and Finlandia Hall, Helsinki

1976. Hugo Alvar Aalto (architect) Commem.
910 **353** 80p. multicoloured 70 40

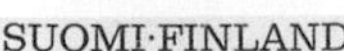

354 "Disaster Relief"

1977. Red Cross Fund. Centenary of Finnish Red Cross. Multicoloured.
911 50p.+10p. Type **354** 65 90
912 80p.+15p. "Community Work" 65 90
913 90p.+20p. "Blood Transfusion Service" 90 90

355 Figure Skating

1977. European Figure Skating Championships, Helsinki.
914 **355** 90p. multicoloured 75 30

1977. Northern Countries' Co-operation in Nature Conservation and Environment Protection. As T 229 of Denmark.
915 90p. multicoloured 80 35
916 1m. multicoloured 80 35

356 "Urho" (ice-breaker) and Freighter

1977. Centenary of Winter Navigation between Finland and Sweden.
917 **356** 90p. multicoloured 70 30

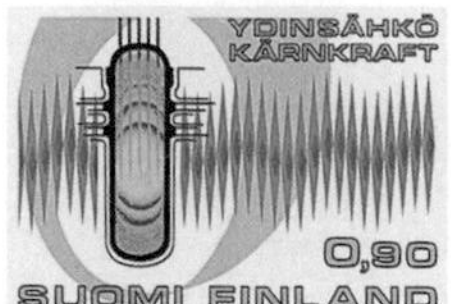

357 "Nuclear Reactor"

1977. Inauguration of Hastholm Island Nuclear Power Station.
918 **357** 90p. multicoloured 70 30

358 Autumn Landscape

1977. Europa.
919 **358** 90p. multicoloured 3·50 45

359 Tree with Nest

1977. 75th Anniv of Co-operative Banks.
920 **359** 90p. multicoloured 70 30

360 New Church of Valamo Cloister, Heinavesi

1977. 800th Anniv of Finnish Orthodoxy and Inauguration of Valamo Cloister.
921 **360** 90p. multicoloured 65 30

361 Paavo Ruotsalainen

1977. Birth Centenary of Paavo Ruotsalaninen (leader of Pietistic Movement).
922 **361** 90p. multicoloured 70 30

362 "Defence and Protection"

1977. Civil Defence.
923 **362** 90p. multicoloured 65 30

363 Volleyball

1977. European Volleyball Championships.
924 **363** 90p. multicoloured 65 30

364 Women's Relay Skiing

1977. World Ski Championships, Lahti. Mult.
925 80p.+40p. Type **364** 1·80 1·90
926 1m.+50p. Ski jumper 1·80 1·70

365 Children taking Water to the Sauna

1977. Christmas.
927 **365** 50p. multicoloured 70 30

366 Finnish Flag

1977. 60th Anniv of Independence.
928 **366** 80p. multicoloured 60 30
929 **366** 1m. multicoloured (37×25½ mm) 90 30

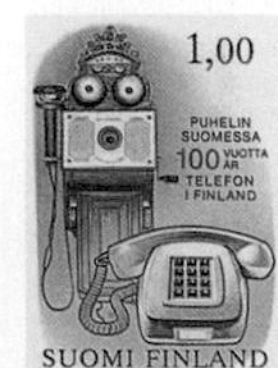

367 Early and Modern Telephones

1977. Centenary of Finnish Telephone.
930 **367** 1m. multicoloured 55 30

368 Kotka Harbour

1978. Centenary of Kotka.
931 **368** 1m. multicoloured 75 30

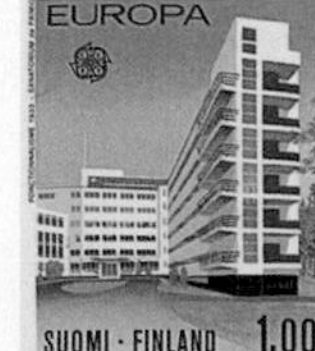

369 Sanatorium, Paimio

1978. Europa. Multicoloured.
932 1m. Type **369** 5·00 1·50
933 1m.20 Studio House, Hvittrask (37×25½ mm) 9·75 7·25

370 Buses

1978. Provincial Bus Service.
934 **370** 1m. multicoloured 60 30

371 Eino Leino

1978. Birth Cent of Eino Leino (poet).
935 **371** 1m. multicoloured 75 30

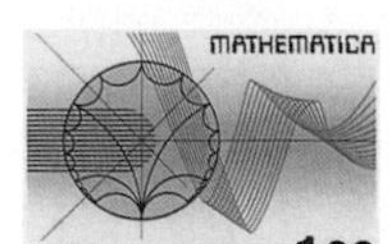

372 Function Theory Diagram

1978. International Congress of Mathematicians, Finland.
936 **372** 1m. multicoloured 75 30

1978. Red Cross Fund. Mushrooms (2nd series). As T 325. Multicoloured.
937 50p.+10p. "Lactarius deterrimus" 90 75
938 80p.+15p. Parasol mushroom (vert) 1·10 1·10
939 1m.+20p. The gypsy 1·20 1·10

373 Girl feeding Corn to Great Tits

1978. Christmas.
940 **373** 50p. multicoloured 75 30

374 Child, Hearts and Flowers

1979. International Year of the Child.
941 **374** 1m.10 multicoloured 1·50 35

375 Orienteer

1979. 8th World Orienteering Championships.
942 **375** 1m.10 multicoloured 80 30

376 Old Training College, Hamina, and Academy Flag

1979. Bicentenary of Officer Training.
943 **376** 1m.10 multicoloured 75 30

377 Turku Buildings

1979. 750th Anniv of Turku (Abo).
944 **377** 1m.10 multicoloured 75 30

378 Tram in City Street

1979. Helsinki Tram Service.
945 **378** 1m.10 multicoloured 75 30

379 "Tammerkoski Waterfall" (lithograph, P. Gaimard)

1979. Bicent of Tampere (Tammerfors) (1st issue).
946 **379** 90p. brown, buff & black 60 30
See also No. 953.

380 Letter establishing Finnish Postal Service, 1638

1979. Europa.
947 **380** 1m.10 blk, brn and ochre 2·75 35
948 - 1m.30 blk, brn and grey 5·75 1·00
DESIGN—HORIZ: 1m.30, A. E. Edelcrantz's optical telegraph, 1796.

381 Pehr Kalm and Title Page

1979. Tuberculosis Relief Fund. Finnish Scientists. Multicoloured.
949 60p.+10p. Type **381** 65 90
950 90p.+15p. Wheat and title page of Pehr Gadd's "Svenska Landt-skot-selen" (vert) 65 1·00
951 1m.10+20p. Petter Forsskaal and title page 90 1·00

382 Town Street with Trade-signs

1979. Centenary of Business and Industry Law.
952 **382** 1m.10 multicoloured 75 30

383 Stylized View of Tampere

1979. Bicentenary of Tampere (2nd issue).
953 **383** 1m.10 multicoloured 75 30

384 Early and Modern Cars at Pedestrian Crossing

1979. The Private Car.
954 **384** 1m.10 multicoloured 65 30

385 House of Korppi, Lapinjarvi, Uusimaa

1979. Peasant Architecture. Mult.
955 1m.10 Type **385** 65 50
956 1m.10 House of Syrjala, Tammela, Hame (left-hand part) 65 50
957 1m.10 House of Syrjala (right-hand part) 65 50
958 1m.10 House of Murtovaarsa, Valtimo, North Karelia 65 50
959 1m.10 House of Antila, Lapua, Pohjanmaa 65 50
960 1m.10 Gable loft of Luukila, Haukipudas and loft of Keskikangas, Yliharma, Pohjanmaa 65 50
961 1m.10 Gate, house of Kanajarvi, Kalvola, Hame 65 50
962 1m.10 Porch, house of Havusel-ka, Kauhajoki, Pohjanmaa 65 50
963 1m.10 Dinner bell and House of Maki-Rasinpera, Kuortane, Pohjanmaa 65 50
964 1m.10 Gable and eaves of granary of Rasula, Kuortane, Pohjanmaa 65 50
See also Nos. 1024/33.

386 "Brownies" feeding Horse

1979. Christmas.
965 **386** 60p. multicoloured 75 30

387 Maria Jotuni

1980. Birth Centenary of Maria Jotuni (writer).
966 **387** 1m.10 multicoloured 75 30

1980. Finnish Red Cross Fund. Mushrooms (3rd series). As T 325. Multicoloured.
967 60p.+10p. Woolly milk cap 65 75
968 90p.+15p. Red cap 80 1·10
969 1m.10+20p. "Russula paludosa" 1·10 1·10

388 Frans Eemil Sillanpaa

1980. Europa. Finnish Nobel Prize Winners. Multicoloured.
970 1m.10 Type **388** (Literature, 1939) 1·60 50
971 1m.30 Artturi Ilmari Virtanen (Chemistry, 1945) (vert) 3·00 1·00

389 Pres. Kekkonen

1980. President Urho Kekkonen's 80th Birthday.
973 **389** 1m.10 multicoloured 70 30

390 Back-piece Harness

1980. Nordic Countries' Postal Co-operation. Multicoloured.
974 1m.10 Type **390** 65 35
975 1m.30 Collar harness (vert) 65 35

391 Biathlon

1980. Biathlon World Championship, Lahti.
976 **391** 1m.10 multicoloured 70 30

392 Trials of Strength

1980. Christmas. Multicoloured.
977 60p. Type **392** 60 30
978 1m.10 "To put out the shoe maker's eye" (children's game) 85 30

393 Kauhaneva Swamps, Kauhajoki

1981. National Parks.
979 **393** 70p. pink, brown & grn 45 40
980 - 1m.60 multicoloured 65 40
981 - 1m.80 multicoloured 75 40
982 - 2m.40 multicoloured 90 35
983 - 4m.30 multicoloured 1·30 85
DESIGNS—VERT: 1m.60, Forest of Multiharju, Seitseminen National Park. HORIZ: 1m.80, Razorbills, Eastern Gulf National Park; 2m.40, Urho Kekkonen National Park; 4m.30, Archipelago National Park.

394 Boxing

1981. European Boxing Championships, Tampere.
990 **394** 1m.10 multicoloured 70 40

395 Glass-blowing and 19th-century Bottle

1981. 300th Anniv of Finnish Glass Industry.
991 **395** 1m.10 multicoloured 80 40

396 "Furst Menschikoff" (paddle-steamer)

1981. "Nordia 1981" Stamp Exhibition, Helsinki.
992 **396** 1m.10 brown & stone 2·75 3·25

397 Rowing to Church

1981. Europa. Multicoloured.
993 1m.10 Type **397** 1·10 35
994 1m.50 Midsummer Eve celebrations 2·00 65

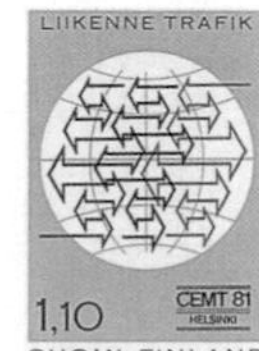

398 "International Traffic Movement"

1981. Council Session of European Conference of Ministers of Transport, Finland.
995 **398** 1m.10 multicoloured 70 30

399 Children on Winged Horse

1981. Centenary of Finnish Youth Associations.
996 **399** 1m. multicoloured 70 40

400 Fuchsia

1981. Tuberculosis Relief Fund. Potted Plants. Multicoloured.
997 70p.+10p. Type **400** 65 75
998 1m.+15p. African violet ("Saintpaulia ionantha") 75 75
999 1m.10+20p. Pelargonium 90 75

401 Face on Graph

1981. International Year of Disabled Persons.
1000 **401** 1m.10 multicoloured 70 40

402 Children bringing Home Christmas Tree

1981. Christmas. Multicoloured.
1001 70p. Type **402** 65 30
1002 1m.10 Decorating the Christmas tree (vert) 70 30

404 Hame Castle

1982

1007	**404**	90p. brown	45	35
1008	-	1m. brown and blue	65	40

DESIGN—VERT: 1m. Windmill, Harrstrom.

405 First Issue of "Om konsten att ratt Behaga" and Modern Periodical

1982. Bicentenary of Finnish Periodicals.

1015	**405**	1m.20 multicoloured	70	30

406 Kuopio Cathedral and Puijo Tower

1982. Bicentenary of Kuopio.

1016	**406**	1m.20 multicoloured	70	30

407 Neck of Stringed Instrument and Staves of Music

1982. Music Jubilee.

1017	**407**	1m.20 multicoloured	70	30

408 Flats, Factories and Houses

1982. Centenary of Electricity in Finland.

1018	**408**	1m.20 multicoloured	70	30

409 Vegetable and Fruit Garden

1982. Cent of First Finnish Horticultural Society.

1019	**409**	1m.10 multicoloured	70	30

410 Cover of "Abckiria" and sculpture of M. Agricola by O. Jauhiainen

1982. Europa. Multicoloured.

1020		1m.20 Type **410**	2·00	45
1021		1m.50 "Turku Academy Inaugural Procession in 1640" (fresco copied by Johannes Gebhard from painting by Albert Edelfelt) (47×31 mm)	3·00	65

411 Emblems and Symbolic Design

1982. International Monetary Fund and World Bank Committees' Meetings, Helsinki.

1022	**411**	1m.60 multicoloured	70	30

412 Interior of Parliament and "Future" (sculpture by W. Aaltonen)

1982. 75th Anniv of Single Chamber Parliament.

1023	**412**	2m.40 blue, dp bl & blk	1·00	65

1982. Manor Houses. As T 385. Mult.

1024	1m.20 Kuitia, 1490s	70	50
1025	1m.20 Louhisaari, 1655	70	50
1026	1m.20 Frugard, 1780	70	50
1027	1m.20 Jokioinen, 1798	70	50
1028	1m.20 Moisio, 1820	70	50
1029	1m.20 Sjundby, 1560s	70	50
1030	1m.20 Fagervik, 1773	70	50
1031	1m.20 Mustio, 1792	70	50
1032	1m.20 Fiskars, 1818	70	50
1033	1m.20 Kotkaniemi, 1836	70	50

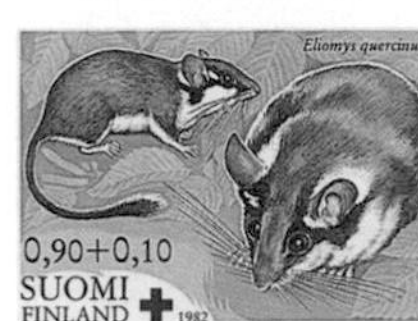

413 Garden Dormouse

1982. Red Cross Fund. Endangered Mammals. Multicoloured.

1034	90p.+10p. Type **413**	60	90
1035	1m.10+15p. Siberian flying squirrel (vert)	90	1·00
1036	1m.20+20p. European mink	1·00	1·00

414 Brownie Children feeding Forest Animals

1982. Christmas. Multicoloured.

1037	90p. Type **414**	65	30
1038	1m.20 Brownie children eating porridge	65	30

415 Gold Prospector

1983. Nordic Countries' Postal Co-operation. "Visit the North". Multicoloured.

1039	1m.20 Type **415**	65	30
1040	1m.30 Descending the Kitajoki river rapids	65	30

416 Postman, Letters and Computer

1983. World Communications Year. Mult.

1041	1m.30 Type **416**	60	30
1042	1m.70 Modulated wave, pulse stream and optical cables	80	40

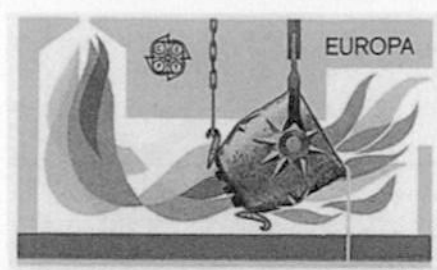

418 Flash Smelting

1983. Europa. Multicoloured.

1044	1m.30 Type **418**	4·00	35
1045	1m.70 Interior of Temppeliaukio Church (Timo and Tuomo Suomalainen)	9·25	1·10

419 President Relander

1983. Birth Centenary of Lauri Kristian Relander (President, 1925–1931).

1046	**419**	1m.30 multicoloured	70	30

420 Throwing the Javelin

1983. World Athletics Championships, Helsinki. Multicoloured.

1047	1m.20 Type **420**	65	35
1048	1m.30 Running (vert)	70	30

421 Kuula and Ostrobothnia

1983. Birth Cent of Toivo Kuula (composer).

1049	**421**	1m.30 multicoloured	70	30

422 Chickweed Wintergreen

1983. Tuberculosis Relief Fund. Wild Flowers. Multicoloured.

1050	1m.+20p. Type **422**	60	80
1051	1m.20+25p. Marsh Violet	65	80
1052	1m.30+30p. Marsh Marigold	1·10	85

423 "Santa Claus" (Eija Myllyviita)

1983. Christmas. Children's Drawings.

1053	**423**	1m. blue & deep blue	65	30
1054	-	1m.30 multicoloured	70	35

DESIGN—VERT: 1m.30, "Two Candles" (Camilla Lindberg).

424 Koivisto

1983. President Mauno Henrik Koivisto's 60th Birthday.

1055	**424**	1m.30 bl, blk & dp bl	65	30

425 Second Class Letters

1984. Re-classification of Postal Items.

1056	**425**	1m.10 green	45	20
1057	-	1m.40 orange & red	45	20

DESIGN—VERT: 1m.40, First class letter.

426 Hydraulic Turbine Manufacture

1984. "Work and Skill" Centenary of Workers' Associations.

1058	**426**	1m.40 multicoloured	70	30

427 Crossbow, Pot and Chalice

1984. Museum Activities.

1059	**427**	1m.40 multicoloured	70	30

428 Bridge

1984. Europa. 25th Anniv of European Post and Telecommunications Conference.

1060	**428**	1m.40 orange, deep orange and black	3·75	45
1061	**428**	2m. blue, violet and black	6·75	1·00

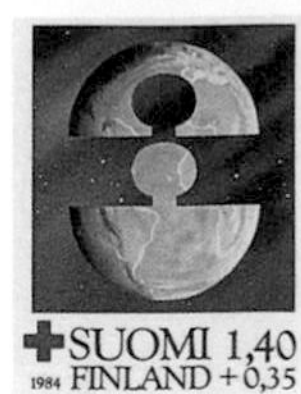

429 Globe as Jigsaw Puzzle

1984. Finnish Red Cross Fund. Multicoloured.

1062	1m.40+35p. Type **429**	80	90
1063	2m.+40p. Spheres around globe	90	1·20

430 Teeth and Dentist treating Patient

1984. International Dental Federation Congress, Helsinki.

1064	**430**	1m.40 multicoloured	90	30

431 Observatory, Planets and Sun

1984. Cent of University of Helsinki Observatory.

1065	**431**	1m.10 multicoloured	70	30

432 Statute Book and Title Page

1984. 250th Anniv of 1734 Common Law.
1066 **432** 2m. multicoloured 85 50

433 "Mother and Child" (Waino Aaltonen) and Lines from "Song of my Heart"

1984. 150th Birth Anniv of Aleksis Kivi (writer).
1067 **433** 1m.40 grey and black 70 30

434 Father Christmas and Brownie

1984. Christmas.
1068 **434** 1m.10 multicoloured 65 30

435 Symbolic Representation of International Trade

1985. 25th Anniversary of European Free Trade Association.
1069 **435** 1m.20 multicoloured 70 40

436 Medal of Johan Ludwig Runeberg (by Walter Runeberg) and Emblem

1985. Centenary of Society of Swedish Literature in Finland.
1070 **436** 1m.50 multicoloured 65 30

437 "Saints Sergei and Herman" (icon, Petros Sasaki)

1985. Centenary of Saint Sergei and Saint Herman Order (home missionary organization of Finnish Orthodox Church).
1071 **437** 1m.50 multicoloured 70 30

438 Pedri Semeikka (rune singer)

1985. 150th Anniv of "Kalevala" (Karelian poems collected by Elias Lonnrot). Multicoloured.
1072 1m.50 Type **438** 65 40
1073 2m.10 Larin Paraske (legend teller) (after Albert Edelfelt) 1·10 65

439 "Mermaid" (Ville Vallgren)

1985. "Nordia 1985" International Stamp Exhibition, Helsinki.
1074 **439** 1m.50 black, grey and blue 3·50 4·50

440 1886 5m. Banknote

1985. Centenary of Finnish Banknote Printing. Multicoloured.
1075 1m.50 Type **440** 90 50
1076 1m.50 1909 50m. banknote showing sailing ship (horiz) 90 50
1077 1m.50 50m. banknote showing waterfall 90 50
1078 1m.50 1000m. banknote showing lake (left side) 90 50
1079 1m.50 1000m. banknote showing lake (right side) 90 50
1080 1m.50 500m. banknote showing harvesters 90 50
1081 1m.50 1000m. banknote showing arms and tree, and part of 50m. banknote (horiz) 90 50
1082 1m.50 1955 5000m. banknote showing J. V. Snellman 90 50

441 Children playing Recorders

1985. Europa. Music Year. Multicoloured.
1083 1m.50 Type **441** 3·50 35
1084 2m.10 Cathedral columns and score of "Ramus Virens Olivarum" 12·00 1·40

442 Finlandia Hall and Barn Swallow

1985. 10th Anniv of European Security and Co-operation Conference, Helsinki.
1085 **442** 2m.10 multicoloured 1·00 75

443 Provincial Arms and Seal of Per Brahe

1985. 350th Anniv of Provincial Administration.
1086 **443** 1m.50 multicoloured 70 30

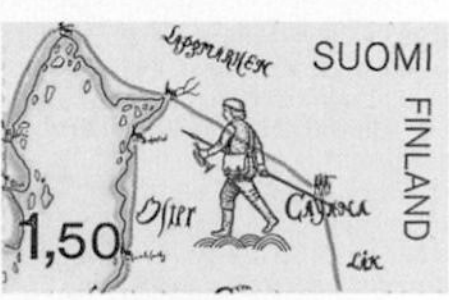

444 Foot Messenger

1985. "Finlandia 88" International Stamp Exhibition, Helsinki (1st issue). Sheet 135×90 mm containing T 444 and similar multicoloured designs forming a composite design of 1698 postal map of Sweden and Finland.
MS1087 1m.50 Type **444**; 1m.50 Raft; 1m.50 Mounted messanger (vert); 1m.50 Iceboat (sold at 8m.) 9·00 8·75
See also Nos. **MS**1107, **MS**1122, 1149 and **MS**1152.

445 I.Y.Y. Emblem

1985. International Youth Year.
1088 **445** 1m.50 multicoloured 70 30

446 Bird Decoration and Tulips

1985. Christmas. Multicoloured.
1089 1m.20 Type **446** 65 30
1090 1m.20 St. Thomas's cross and hyacinths 65 30

447 Orbicular Granite

1986. Centenary of Geological Society. Mult.
1091 1m.30 Type **447** 60 40
1092 1m.60 Rapakivi (granite) 60 30
1093 2m.10 Veined gneiss 85 40

448 Saimaa Ringed Seal

1986. Europa. Multicoloured.
1094 1m.60 Type **448** 4·50 55
1095 2m.20 Landscape seen through window 8·00 1·10

449 Baghdad Conference Palace (Kaija and Heikki Siren)

1986. Modern Architecture. Multicoloured.
1096 1m.60 Type **449** 80 50
1097 1m.60 Lahti Theatre (Pekka Salminen and Esko Koivisto) (value in blue) 80 50
1098 1m.60 Kuusamo Municipal Offices (Marja and Keijo Petaja) (value in red) 80 50
1099 1m.60 Hamina police and court building (Timo and Tuomo Suomalainen) and Greek church (value in green) 80 50
1100 1m.60 Finnish Embassy, New Delhi (Raili and Reima Pietila) (value in green) 80 50
1101 1m.60 Day care centre, Western Sakyla (Kari Jarvinen and Timo Airas) (value in red) 80 50

450 Orange-tip

1986. Finnish Red Cross Fund. Butterflies. Multicoloured.
1102 1m.60+40p. Type **450** 90 90
1103 2m.10+45p. Camberwell beauty 1·10 1·60
1104 5m.+50p. Apollo 2·20 2·50

451 Auditorium, Joensuu

1986. Nordic Countries' Postal Co-operation. Twinned Towns. Multicoloured.
1105 1m.60 Type **451** 80 35
1106 2m.20 Emblem of University of Jyvaskyla 1·00 1·30

452 Paddle-steamer "Aura"

1986. "Finlandia 88" International Stamp Exhibition, Helsinki (2nd issue). Sheet 135×90 mm containing T 452 and similar designs, each deep brown and buff.
MS1107 1m.60 Type **452**; 1m.60 Steamship "Alexander"; 2m.20 Steamship "Nicolai"; 2m.20 Ice-breaker "Express II" (vert) (sold at 10m.) 9·00 8·75

453 Maupertuis, Globe, Quadrant and Sledge

1986. 250th Anniv of Measurement of Arcs of Meridian.
1108 **453** 1m.60 bl, ultram & blk 1·00 30

454 Kekkonen

1986. Urho Kekkonen (President, 1956–81). Commemoration.
1109 **454** 5m. black 1·80 95

455 Cloud, Rainbow and Emblem

1986. International Peace Year.
1110 **455** 1m.60 multicoloured 75 30

456 Angels and Garland

1986. Christmas. Multicoloured.
1111 1m.30 Type **456** 75 30
1112 1m.30 Angels and garland (different) 75 30
1113 1m.60 Brownies and garland 85 30

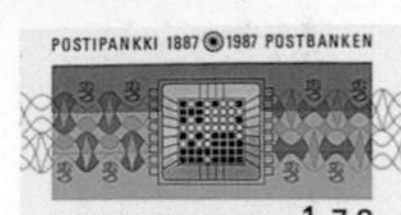

457 Microchip

1987. Centenary of Postal Savings Bank.

1114 **457** 1m.70 multicoloured 75 30

458 Prototype Metre Measuring Bar as Parcel

1987. Centenary of Metric System in Finland.

1115 **458** 1m.40 multicoloured 70 50

459 "Borea" (liner), Diesel Train, Snow Scene and Skier

1987. Tourism. Multicoloured.

1116 1m.70 Type **459** 60 35

1117 2m.30 Douglas DC-10 airplane, bus, yachts on lake and hiker 85 75

460 Wrestlers

1987. European Wrestling Championships, Helsinki.

1118 **460** 1m.70 multicoloured 85 30

461 Madetoja and Score of Cradlesong

1987. Birth Centenary of Leevi Madetoja (composer).

1119 **461** 2m.10 multicoloured 90 30

462 Balls and Pins

1987. 11th World Ten Pin Bowling Championships.

1120 **462** 1m.70 multicoloured 85 30

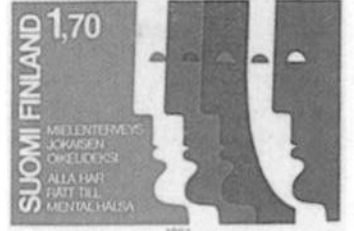

463 Profiles

1987. 90th Anniv of Finnish Association for Mental Health.

1121 **463** 1m.70 multicoloured 85 30

464 Locomotive "Lemminkainen", 1862

1987. "Finlandia 88" International Stamp Exhibition, Helsinki (3rd issue). Sheet 135×90 mm containing T 464 and similar horiz designs, depicting trains on the Helsinki–Hameenlinna and Riihimaki–St. Petersburg routes.

MS1122 1m.70 green, orange and blue (Type **464**); 1m.70 multicoloured (Mail van No. 9935, 1871); 1m.70 multicoloured (Mail van No. 9991, 1899); 2m.30 green and blue (Locomotive No. 57, 1874) (sold at 10m.) 9·00 8·75

465 "Strawberry Girl" (Nils Schillmark)

1987. Centenary of Ateneum Art Museum. Paintings. Multicoloured.

1123 1m.70 Type **465** 1·40 65

1124 1m.70 "Still Life on a Lady's Work-table" (Ferdinand von Wright) 1·40 65

1125 1m.70 "Old Woman with Basket" (Albert Edelfelt) 1·40 65

1126 1m.70 "Boy and Crow" (Akseli Gallen-Kallela) 1·40 65

1127 1m.70 "Late Winter" (Tyko Sallinen) 1·40 65

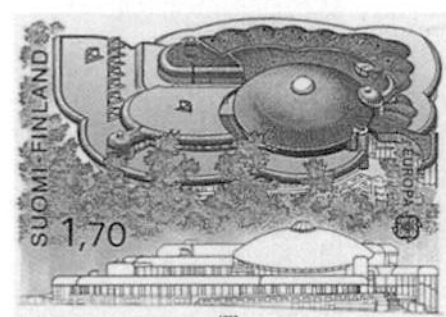

466 Tampere Main Library (Railia and Reima Pietila)

1987. Europa. Art and Architecture. Mult.

1128 1m.70 Type **466** 5·25 35

1129 2m.30 "Stoa" (Hannu Siren) 13·00 1·30

467 Arrows

1987. 7th European Physics Society General Conference.

1130 **467** 1m.70 multicoloured 70 30

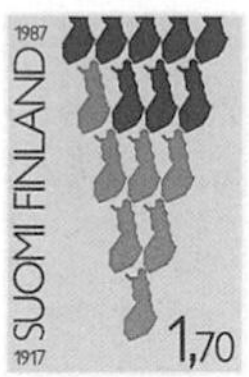

468 Outline Maps of Finland

1987. 70th Anniv of Independence.

1131 **468** 1m.70 silver, grey & bl 85 30

1132 **468** 10m. silver, blue and azure (26×37 mm) 4·00 1·30

469 Baby with Ball and Prof. Ylppo

1987. 100th Birthday of Arvo Ylppo (paediatrician).

1133 **469** 1m.70 multicoloured 75 30

470 Father Christmas and Brownies

1987. Christmas. Multicoloured.

1134 1m.40 Type **470** 55 30

1135 1m.70 Mother Christmas and brownie (vert) 90 30

471 Birds flying from Globe to Finland

1987. Centenary of Finnish News Agency.

1136 **471** 2m.30 multicoloured 85 90

472 Pihkala

1988. Birth Centenary of Lauri Pihkala ("Tahko") (writer and sport organizer).

1137 **472** 1m.80 deep blue, blue and black 85 30

473 Telephone and Mail Boxes

1988. 350th Anniv of Posts and Telecommunications Services (1st issue). Multicoloured.

1138 1m.80 Type **473** 70 30

1139 1m.80 Airplane and lorry 70 30

1140 1m.80 Fork-lift truck carrying parcels 70 30

1141 1m.80 Postman 70 30

1142 1m.80 Woman receiving letter 70 30

Nos. 1138/42 were printed together, se-tenant, Nos. 1141/2 forming a composite design.

See also Nos. 1165/70.

474 Conifer Branches (Christmas)

1988. Finnish Red Cross Fund. Festivals. Multicoloured.

1143 1m.40+40p. Type **474** 80 1·10

1144 1m.80+45p. Narcissi (Easter) 1·20 75

1145 2m.40+50p. Rose (Midsummer) 1·30 2·00

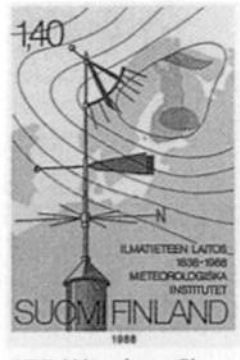

475 Weather Chart and Measuring Equipment

1988. 150th Anniv of Meteorological Institute.

1146 **475** 1m.40 multicoloured 70 45

476 Map, Settlers, Indians, "Calmare Nyckel" and "Fagel Grip"

1988. 350th Anniv of Founding of New Sweden (Finnish and Swedish settlement in North America).

1147 **476** 3m. multicoloured 1·90 1·00

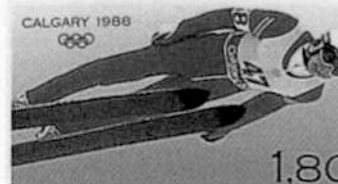

477 Matti Nykanen (triple gold medal winner)

1988. Finnish Success at Winter Olympic Games, Calgary.

1148 **477** 1m.80 multicoloured 85 35

478 Agathon Faberge (philatelist)

1988. "Finlandia 88" International Stamp Exhibition, Helsinki.

1149 **478** 5m. multicoloured 13·50 13·50

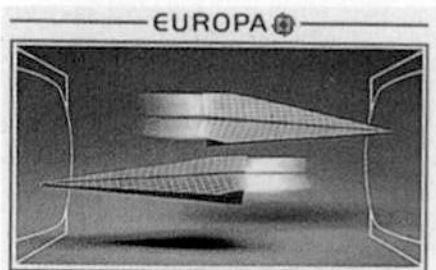

479 Paper Airplanes between VDUs

1988. Europa. Transport and Communications. Multicoloured.

1150 1m.80 Type **479** 4·00 45

1151 2m.40 Horse tram, 1890 8·50 1·30

480 Breguet 14 Biplane with Skis

1988. "Finlandia 88" International Stamp Exhibition, Helsinki (5th issue). Sheet 135×90 mm containing T 480 and similar horiz designs.

MS1152 1m.80 blue and red (Type **480**); 1m.80 blue and mauve (Junkers F-13); 1m.80 blue and orange (Douglas DC-3); 2m.40 ultramarine and blue (Douglas DC-10-30) (sold at 11m.) 10·50 10·00

481 Steam-driven Fire Pump, Turku Fire Brigade

1988. 150th Anniv of Fire Brigades in Finland.

1163 **481** 2m.20 multicoloured 85 50

482 "Missale Aboense" and Illuminated Page

1988. 500th Anniv of Publishing of "Missale Aboense" (first printed book for Finland).

1164 **482** 1m.80 multicoloured 85 30

483 1638 Postal Tariffs

1988. 350th Anniv of Posts and Telecommunications Services (2nd issue). Multicoloured.

1165 1m.80 Type **483** 1·00 50

1166 1m.80 Rural postman, 1860s 1·00 50

1167 1m.80 Postman delivering from mail van 1·00 50

1168 1m.80 Malmi Post Office 1·00 50

1169 1m.80 Skiers using mobile telephone 1·00 50

1170 1m.80 Communications satellite 1·00 50

484 Teacher with Children

1988. Church Playgroups.

1171 **484** 1m.80 multicoloured 75 30

485 Decorations

1988. Christmas.

1172 **485** 1m.40 multicoloured 80 30

1173 **485** 1m.80 multicoloured 90 30

486 Market Place, Town Plan and Arms

1989. 350th Anniv of Hameenlinna Town Charter.

1174 **486** 1m.90 multicoloured 85 30

487 Skier

1989. World Skiing Championships, Lahti.

1175 **487** 1m.90 multicoloured 85 30

488 Photographer with Box Camera on Tripod

1989. 150th Anniv of Photography.

1176 **488** 1m.50 multicoloured 75 40

489 Christmas Collection

1989. Cent of Salvation Army in Finland.

1177 **489** 1m.90 multicoloured 85 30

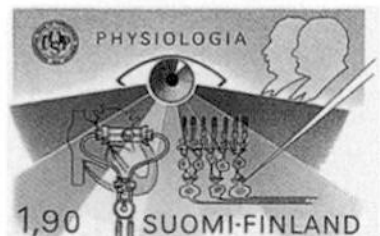

490 Professors Tigerstedt and Granit and Research Fields

1989. 31st International Physiological Sciences Congress, Helsinki.

1178 **490** 1m.90 multicoloured 90 30

491 Skiing

1989. Sport. Multicoloured.

1179 1m.90 Type **491** 85 60

1180 1m.90 Jogging 85 60

1181 1m.90 Cycling 85 60

1182 1m.90 Canoeing 85 60

492 Lapponian Herder

1989. Centenary of Finnish Kennel Club. Sheet 114×90 mm containing T 492 and similar horiz designs. Multicoloured.

MS1183 1m.90 Type **492**; 1m.90 Finnish spitz; 1m.90 Karelian bear dog; 1m.90 Finnish hound 3·50 3·25

493 Hopscotch

1989. Europa. Children's Activities. Mult.

1184 1m.90 Type **493** 3·00 45

1185 2m.50 Sledging 5·75 1·00

494 Man from Sakyla

1989. Nordic Countries' Postal Co-operation. Traditional Costumes. Multicoloured.

1186 1m.90 Type **494** 85 30

1187 2m.50 Woman from Veteli 1·20 80

495 Foxglove and Pharmaceutical Equipment

1989. 300th Anniv of Pharmacies in Finland.

1188 **495** 1m.90 multicoloured 95 30

496 Snow Leopard

1989. Cent of Helsinki Zoo. Multicoloured.

1189 1m.90 Type **496** 85 30

1190 2m.50 Markhor goat 1·30 80

497 Savonlinna

1989. 350th Anniv of Savonlinna.

1191 **497** 1m.90 multicoloured 85 30

498 Brown Bear

1989

1192 **498** 50m. multicoloured 18·00 10·50

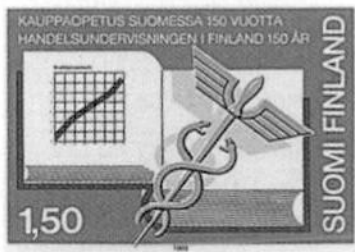

499 Open Book and Mercury's Staff

1989. 150th Anniv of Commercial Studies in Finland.

1193 **499** 1m.50 multicoloured 80 40

500 Emblem and Columns in Finland's Parliament

1989. Cent of Interparliamentary Union.

1194 **500** 1m.90 multicoloured 90 30

501 Bridges

1989. Accession of Finland to, and 40th Anniv of Council of Europe.

1195 **501** 2m.50 multicoloured 1·20 80

502 Kolehmainen winning 5000 m, Olympic Games, 1912

1989. Birth Cent of Hannes Kolehmainen (runner).

1196 **502** 1m.90 multicoloured 90 30

503 Students, Open Book and Keyboard

1989. Centenary of Folk High Schools.

1197 **503** 1m.90 multicoloured 85 40

504 Decorated Street

1989. Christmas. Multicoloured.

1198 1m.50 Type **504** 80 25

1199 1m.90 Sodankyla Church, Lapland 90 25

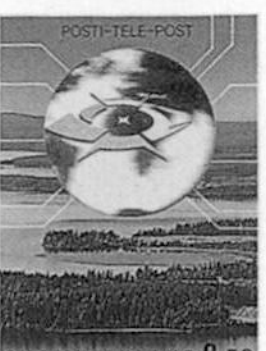

505 Emblem and Lake Paijanne

1990. Formation of Posts and Telecommunications into State Commercial Company.

1200 **505** 1m.90 multicoloured 1·00 80

1201 **505** 2m.50 multicoloured 1·00 1·30

506 Wood Anemone (Uusimaa province)

1990. Provincial Plants. Multicoloured.

1205 2m. Type **506** 70 25

1206 2m.10 Rowan (Northern Savo) 65 60

1207 2m.70 Heather (Kainuu) 90 35

1208 2m.90 Shrub sea buck-thorn (Satakunta) 1·00 35

1209 3m.50 Oak (Varsinais Suomi) 1·20 50

No. 1206 also comes self-adhesive and imperforate.

See also Nos. 1273/4, 1303, 1309, 1327 and 1354.

507 Erik Ferling (first orchestra leader) conducting

1990. Bicentenary of Foundation of Turku Musical Society (first Finnish orchestra).

1220 **507** 1m.90 multicoloured 90 30

508 Snowflake

1990. 50th Anniv of End of Russo–Finnish Winter War.

1221 **508** 2m. blue & ultramarine 90 25

509 Disabled Ex-serviceman

1990. 50th Anniv of Disabled Ex-servicemen's Association.

1222 **509** 2m. multicoloured 85 25

510 Nuvvus Postal Agency

1990. Europa. Post Office Buildings. Mult.

1223 2m. Type **510** 4·50 45

1224 2m.70 Turku Postal Centre 8·00 90

511 Queen Christina

1990. 350th Anniv of Grant of Charter to Turku Academy (later Helsinki University). Mult.

1225 2m. Type **511** 85 30

1226 3m.20 Main building of Helsinki University 1·20 1·00

512 Scarce Copper on Goldrod

1990. Finnish Red Cross Fund. Butterflies. Multicoloured.

1227 1m.50+40p. Type **512** 80 80
1228 2m.+50p. Amanda's blue on meadow vetchling 80 1·00
1229 2m.70+60p. Peacock on tufted vetch 1·20 1·30

See also Nos. 1279/81.

513 Postman at Larsmo, 1890, and Modern Address Sign

1990. Compilation of Address Register and Centenary of Rural Postal Service.

1230 **513** 2m. multicoloured 85 25

514 "Ali Baba and the Forty Thieves"

1990. Birth Centenary of Rudolf Koivu (artist). Designs showing Koivu's illustrations of fairy tales. Multicoloured.

1231 2m. Type **514** 1·00 50
1232 2m. "The Great Musician" (Raul Roine) 1·00 50
1233 2m. "The Giants, the Witches and the Daughter of the Sun" (Koivu) 1·00 50
1234 2m. "The Golden Bird, the Golden Horse and the Princess" (Grimm Brothers) 1·00 50
1235 2m. "Lamb Brother" (Koivu) 1·00 50
1236 2m. "The Snow Queen" (Hans Christian Andersen) 1·00 50

515 Youth feeding Horse

1990. Youth Hobbies. Horse Riding. Sheet 118×63 mm containing T 515 and similar vert designs. Multicoloured.

MS1237 2m. Type **515**; 2m. Two riders; 2m. Girl saddling pony; 2m. Girl grooming horse 4·50 4·50

516 Brownies dealing with Father Christmas's Mail

1990. Christmas. Multicoloured.

1238 1m.70 Type **516** 85 30
1239 2m. Father Christmas and reindeer 90 30

517 Player and Turku Castle

1991. World Ice Hockey Championship, Turku, Tampere and Helsinki.

1246 **517** 2m.10 multicoloured 85 30

518 Teacher and Pupils preparing Meal

1991. Cent of Domestic Science Teacher Training.

1247 **518** 2m.10 multicoloured 85 25

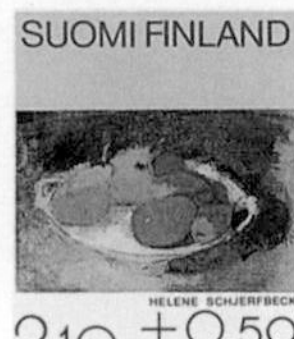

519 "Green Still Life"

1991. Pro Filatelia. Paintings by Helene Schjerfbeck. Multicoloured.

1248 2m.10+50p. Type **519** 1·60 1·80
1249 2m.10+50p. "The Little Convalescent" 1·60 1·80

520 Great Tit

1991. Birds (1st series). Multicoloured.

1250 10p. Type **520** 45 30
1251 60p. Pair of chaffinches 90 55
1252 2m.10 Northern bullfinch 65 45

See also Nos. 1282/4 and 1322/4.

521 Fly-fishing for RainbowTrout

1991. Centenary of Central Fishery Organization. Multicoloured.

1253 2m.10 Type **521** 75 50
1254 2m.10 Stylized Eurasian perch and float 75 50
1255 2m.10 Stylized fish and crayfish 75 50
1256 2m.10 Trawling for Baltic herring 75 50
1257 2m.10 Restocking with whitefish from lorry 75 50

522 Seurasaari Island

1991. Nordic Countries' Postal Co-operation. Multicoloured.

1258 2m.10 Type **522** 85 35
1259 2m.90 Saimaa ferry 1·20 90

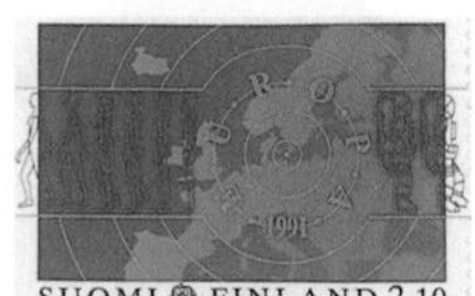

523 Map of Europe and Human Figures

1991. Europa. Europe in Space. Mult.

1260 2m.10 Type **523** 4·50 55
1261 2m.90 Map of Europe, satellites and dish aerials 11·00 1·20

524 Iris Vase

1991. 61st Death Anniv of Alfred Finch (painter and ceramic artist). Multicoloured.

1262 2m.10 Type **524** 75 30
1263 2m.90 "The English Coast at Dover" 1·60 95

525 Kittens and "Kiss-Kiss" Sweet

1991. Centenary of Opening of Karl Fazer's Confectionery (beginning of Finnish Sweet Industry).

1264 **525** 2m.10 multicoloured 90 25

526 "Sun" (Kaisa Niemi)

1991. Children's Stamp Design Competition Winners. Sheet 100×60 mm containing T 526 and similar horiz design. Multicoloured.

MS1265 2m.10 Type **526**; 2m.10 "Rainbow" (Elina Aro); 2m.10 "Cows grazing" (Noora Kaunisto) 2·75 2·75

527 Leisure Skiing

1991. Youth Hobbies. Skiing. Sheet 118×64 mm containing T 527 and similar vert designs. Mult.

MS1266 2m.10 Type **527**; 2m.10 Skiboarding; 2m.10 Freestyle skiing; 2m.10 Speed skating 3·50 3·25

528 Iisalmi

1991. Centenary of Granting of Town Rights to Iisalmi.

1267 **528** 2m.10 multicoloured 85 40

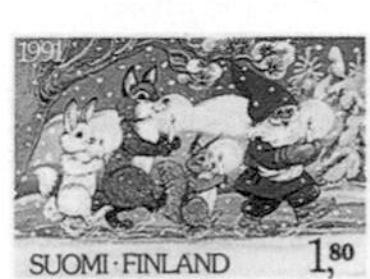

529 Forest Animals and Elf

1991. Christmas. Multicoloured.

1268 1m.80 Type **529** 85 25
1269 2m.10 Father Christmas in sleigh over new Arctic Circle post office (vert) 85 25

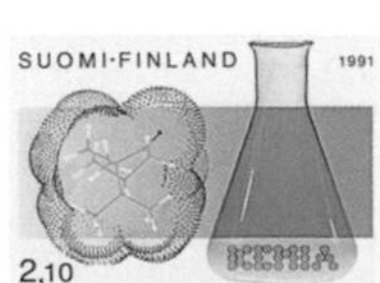

530 Camphor Molecule and Erlenmeyer Flask

1991. Cent of Organized Chemistry in Finland.

1270 **530** 2m.10 multicoloured 90 30

No. 1270 covers either of two stamps which were issued together as a horizontal gutter pair, the stamps differing very slightly in the diagram of the molecule. The gutter pair is stated to produce a three-dimensional image without use of a special viewer.

531 Skiing

1992. Winter Olympic Games, Albertville (1271) and Summer Games, Barcelona (1272). Multicoloured.

1271 2m.10 Type **531** 85 35
1272 2m.90 Swimming 1·10 60

532 Globe Flower (Lapland)

1992. Provincial Plants. With service indicator. Multicoloured.

1273 2KLASS (1m.60) Type **532** 85 25
1274 1KLASS (2m.10) Hepatica (Hame) 1·20 30

See also Nos. 1303, 1309, 1327 and 1354.

533 Finnish Exhibition Emblem

1992. "Expo '92" World's Fair, Seville.

1275 **533** 3m.40 multicoloured 1·40 90

534 Map of Europe

1992. 3rd Meeting of Council of Foreign Ministers of European Security and Co-operation Conference, Helsinki.

1276 **534** 16m. multicoloured 5·75 3·75

535 Church of the Holy Cross, Town Hall and Brigantine

1992. 550th Anniv of Rauma Town Charter.

1277 **535** 2m.10 multicoloured 85 25

536 Thoughts within Head

1992. Healthy Brains Campaign.

1278 **536** 3m.50 multicoloured 1·60 1·30

1992. Finnish Red Cross Fund. Centenary of Training of Visually Handicapped. Moths. As T 512. Multicoloured.

1279 1m.60+40p. Taiga dart 85 90
1280 2m.10+50p. Fjeld tiger 1·00 1·10
1281 5m.+60p. Baneberry looper moth 1·80 2·30

537 Pied Wagtail

1992. Birds (2nd series). Multicoloured.

1282 10p. Type **537** 45 50
1283 60p. European robin 90 1·10
1284 2m.10 Three Bohemian waxwings 65 50

538 "Santa Maria" and Route Map

1992. Europa. 500th Anniv of Discovery of America by Columbus. Multicoloured.

1285	2m.10 Type **538**	1·80	45
1286	2m.10 Route map and Columbus	1·80	45

Nos. 1285/6 were issued together, se-tenant, forming a composite design.

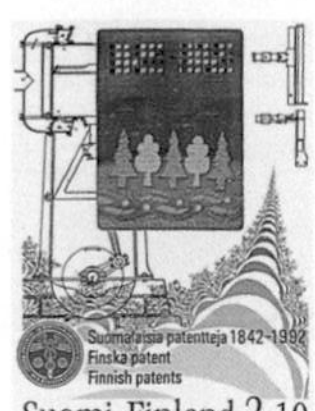

539 Blowing Machine (first Finnish patent, 150th anniv)

1992. Technology. Multicoloured.

1287	2m.10 Type **539** (50th anniv of National Board of Patents and Registration of Trademarks)	1·00	85
1288	2m.90 Triangles and circuits (Finnish chairmanship of EUREKA (European technology development scheme))	1·10	1·00
1289	3m.40 Inverted triangles (50th anniv of Government Technology Research Centre)	1·40	90

540 Currant Harvesting

1992. Cent of National Board of Agriculture.

1290	**540**	2m.10 multicoloured	85	25

541 Aurora Karamzin

1992. Notable Finnish Women. Mult.

1291	2m.10 Type **541** (founder of Helsinki Deaconesses' Institution)	90	65
1292	2m.10 Sophie Mannerheim (nursing pioneer)	90	65
1293	2m.10 Laimi Leidenius (Professor of Obstetrics and Gynaecology, Helsinki University)	90	65
1294	2m.10 Miina Sillanpaa (first woman Cabinet Minister)	90	65
1295	2m.10 Edith Sodergran (poet)	90	65
1296	2m.10 Kreetta Haapasalo (folk singer)	90	65

542 Flag in Garden (Niina Pennanen)

1992. 75th Anniv of Independence.

1297	**542** 2m.10 multicoloured	85	25
MS1298	116×53 mm. 2m.10 Birds and birch grove (29×36 mm)	1·10	95

543 Moomin looking into River ("Moominland Midwinter")

1992. "Nordia 1993" International Stamp Exhibition. Stamp Day. Designs showing illustrations from her stories by Tove Jansson. Multicoloured.

1299	2m.10 Type **543**	1·80	65
1300	2m.10 Moomin and trolls ("Moominland Midwinter")	1·80	65
1301	2m.10 Theatre performance on water ("Moomin Summer Madness")	1·80	65
1302	2m.10 Moomin and inhabitants ("Tales from Moomin Valley")	1·80	65

544 Rosebay Willowherb (Etela-Pohjanmaa)

1992. Provincial Plants. With service indicator. Self-adhesive. Imperf.

1303	**544**	1KLASS (2m.10) mult	1·20	70

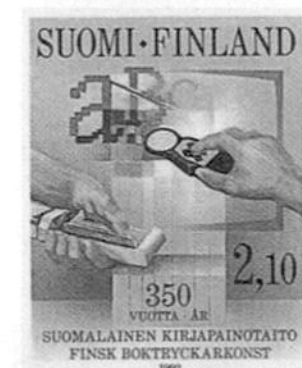

545 Computerized and Hot Metal Typesetting

1992. 350th Anniv of Printing in Finland.

1304	**545**	2m.10 multicoloured	85	55

546 St. Lawrence's Church, Vantaa

1992. Christmas. Multicoloured.

1305	1m.80 Type **546**	70	25
1306	2m.10 Stained glass window, Karkkila Church (vert)	85	25

547 Couple

1993. 75th Anniv of Central Chamber of Commerce.

1307	**547**	1m.60 multicoloured	70	50

548 Birds, Flowers and Envelope within Heart

1993. Friendship.

1308	**548**	1KLASS (2m.10) mult	1·10	50

549 Iris (Kymenlaakso)

1993. Provincial Plants. With service indicator. Self-adhesive. Imperf.

1309	**549**	2KLASS (1m.90) mult	1·10	55

550 Fox in Winter Coat

1993. Endangered Species. The Arctic Fox. Multicoloured.

1310	2m.30 Type **550**	1·20	65
1311	2m.30 Two foxes in winter coat	1·20	65
1312	2m.30 Mother with young in summer coat	1·20	65
1313	2m.30 Two foxes in summer coat	1·20	65

551 "Autumn Landscape of Lake Pielisjarvi" (left half)

1993. Pro Filatelia. 130th Birth Anniv of Eero Jarnefelt (painter). Multicoloured.

1314	2m.30+70p. Type **551**	1·20	1·30
1315	2m.30+70p. "Autumn Landscape of Lake Pielisjarvi" (right half)	1·20	1·30

Nos. 1314/15 were issued together, se-tenant, forming a composite design of the entire painting.

552 "Rumba" (Martti Aiha)

1993. Europa Contemporary Art. Sculptures. Multicoloured.

1316	2m. Type **552**	1·20	35
1317	2m.90 "Complete Works" (Kari Caven)	2·10	90

553 Burnet Rose

1993. Centenary of Helsinki Philatelic Association.

1318	**553**	2m.30 multicoloured	1·30	60

554 Castle and Courier Route Map

1993. 700th Anniv of Vyborg Castle.

1319	**554**	2m.30 multicoloured	1·10	50

555 Naantali

1993. Nordic Countries' Postal Co-operation. Tourism. Multicoloured.

1320	2m.30 Type **555**	1·00	45
1321	2m.90 Imatra	1·10	65

556 Tengmalm's Owl

1993. Birds (3rd series). Multicoloured.

1322	10p. Type **556**	55	75
1323	20p. Common redstart	60	75
1324	2m.30 White-backed woodpecker	1·10	75

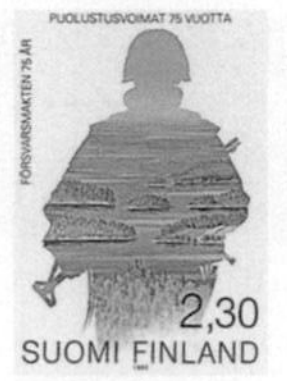

557 Finnish Landscape in Soldier's Silhouette

1993. 75th Anniv of Military Forces. Mult.

1325	2m.30 Type **557**	80	25
1326	3m.40 Checkpoint of Finnish soldiers serving with U.N. peacekeeping force	1·20	75

558 Labrador Tea (Northern Ostrobothnia)

1993. Provincial Plants. With service indicator. Self-adhesive. Imperf.

1327	**558**	1KLASS (2m.30) mult	1·20	30

559 Child skiing (cover illustration from "Kotiliesi")

1993. Birth Centenary of Martta Wendelin (artist). Multicoloured.

1328	2m.30 Type **559**	1·10	60
1329	2m.30 Mother and daughter knitting (illustration from "First Book of the Home and School")	1·10	60
1330	2m.30 Children making snowman (illustration from "First Book of the Home and School")	1·10	60
1331	2m.30 Rural scene (postcard)	1·10	60
1332	2m.30 Young girl and lamb (cover illustration from "Kotiliesi")	1·10	60

560 Flock of Black-throated Divers

1993. Water Birds. Multicoloured.

1333	2m.30 Type **560**	1·30	1·00
1334	2m.30 Pair of black-throated divers ("Gavia arctica") (53x28 mm)	1·30	1·00
1335	2m.30 Goosander ("Mergus merganser") (26x39 mm)	1·30	1·00
1336	2m.30 Mallards ("Anas platy rhynchos") (26x39 mm)	1·30	1·00
1337	2m.30 Red-breasted merganser ("Mergus serrator") (26x39 mm)	1·30	1·00

561 Gymnastics and Football

1993. 150th Anniv of Compulsory Physical Education in Schools.

1338	**561**	2m.30 multicoloured	85	25

562 "Ostobothnians" (Leevi Madetoja)

1993. Inauguration of New National Opera House. Sheet 120×80 mm containing T 562 and similar horiz designs showing scenes from operas and ballets. Multicoloured.

MS1339 2m.30 Type **562**; 2m.30 "The Faun" (Claude Debussy, choreographed by Jorma Uotinen); 2m.90 "The Magic Flute" (Mozart); 3m.40 "Giselle" (Adolphe Adam) 5·00 4·50

563 Brownies and Christmas Tree (Anna Kymalainen)

1993. Christmas. Children's Drawings. Mult.

1340	1m.80 Type **563**	70	25
1341	2m.30 Three angels and star (Taina Tuomola)	80	25

564 Koivisto

1993. 70th Birthday of President Mauno Koivisto.

1342	**564**	2m.30 multicoloured	80	25

565 "Moominland Winter"

1994. Moomin. With service indicator. Illustrations from her stories by Tove Jansson. Multicoloured.

1343	1klass (2m.30) Type **565**	1·30	30
1344	1klass (2m.30) "Moominland Storm"	1·30	30

566 Marja-Liisa Kirvesniemi and Marjo Matikainen

1994. "Finlandia 95" International Stamp Exhibition, Helsinki (1st issue) and Centenary of International Olympic Committee. Sheet 120×80 mm containing T 566 and similar vert designs showing Finnish Winter Olympic Games Competitors. Multicoloured.

MS1345 4m.20 Type **566**; 4m.20 Clas Thunberg; 4m.20 Veikko Kankkonen; 4m.20 Veikko Hakulinen 6·25 6·25

567 "Peace"

1994. Birth Centenary of Waino Aaltonen (sculptor). Multicoloured.

1346	2m. Type **567**	75	25
1347	2m. "Muse"	75	25

568 Postal Clerk and Customer

1994. Centenary of Postal Service Civil Servants Federation.

1348	**568**	2m.30 multicoloured	90	25

569 Ploughing

1994. Finnish Red Cross Fund. Horses. Multicoloured.

1349	2m. Type **569**	1·10	90
1350	2m.30 Marinka (trotting horse)	1·30	1·10
1351	4m.20 Cavalry horses (vert)	1·80	2·00

570 Paper Roll, Nitrogen-fixing Technique, Padlock and "Fennica" (ice-breaker)

1994. Europa. Discoveries and Inventions. Multicoloured.

1352	2m.30 Type **570**	1·40	65
1353	4m.20 Balloon, radiosonde, mobile telephone, fishing lure and lake oxygenation equipment	2·10	1·50

571 Rose (North Karelia)

1994. Provincial Plants. With service indicator. Self-adhesive. Imperf.

1354	**571**	1KLASS (2m.30) mult	1·20	30

572 Riitta Salin and Pirjo Haggman (runners)

1994. "Finlandia 95" International Stamp Exhibition (2nd issue) and European Athletics Championships, Helsinki. Sheet 120×80 mm containing T 572 and similar vert designs showing Finnish athletes. Multicoloured.

MS1355 4m.20 Type **572**; 4m.20 Lasse Viren (runner); 4m.20 Tiina Lillak (javelin thrower); 4m.20 Pentti Nikula (pole vaulter) 6·25 6·25

573 Seven-spotted Ladybirds

1994. "Finlandia 95" International Stamp Exhibition, Helsinki.

1356	**573**	16m. multicoloured	6·25	6·25

See also No. 1393.

574 Perforate St. John's Wort ("Hypericum perforatum")

1994. Flowers. With service indicator. Mult.

1357	1klass (2m.30) Type **574**	1·30	45
1358	1klass (2m.30) Sticky catchfly ("Lychnis viscaria")	1·30	45
1359	1klass (2m.30) Harebell ("Campanula rotundifolia")	1·30	45
1360	1klass (2m.30) Clustered bellflower ("Campanula glomerata")	1·30	45
1361	1klass (2m.30) Bloody cranesbill ("Geranium sanguineum")	1·30	45
1362	1klass (2m.30) Wild strawberry ("Fragaria vesca")	1·30	45
1363	1klass (2m.30) Germander speedwell ("Veronica chamaedrys")	1·30	45
1364	1klass (2m.30) Meadow saxifrage ("Saxifraga granulata")	1·30	45
1365	1klass (2m.30) Wild pansy ("Viola tricolor")	1·30	45
1366	1klass (2m.30) Silver-weed ("Potentilla anserina")	1·30	45

575 Patrik Sjoberg (high jump)

1994. Sweden–Finland Athletics Meeting, Stockholm. Multicoloured.

1367	2m.40 Sepo Raty (javelin)	1·10	35
1368	2m.40 Type **575**	1·10	35

576 Crowd on Registration List

1994. 450th Anniv of Population Registers.

1369	**576**	2m.40 multicoloured	85	25

577 Emblem

1994. International Year of the Family.

1370	**577**	3m.40 multicoloured	1·20	65

578 Postman greeting Woman

1994. Stamp Day. Dog Hill Kids (cartoon characters) at the Post Office. Sheet 112×88 mm containing T 578 and similar horiz designs. Mult.

MS1371 2m.80 Type **578**; 2m.80 Postmaster handing letter to postman; 2m.80 Messenger playing bugle; 2m.80 Couple posting letters 6·25 6·25

579 Northern Bullfinches on Reindeer's Antlers

1994. Christmas. Multicoloured.

1372	2m.10 Type **579**	75	25
1373	2m.80 Father and son selecting Christmas tree (vert)	90	35

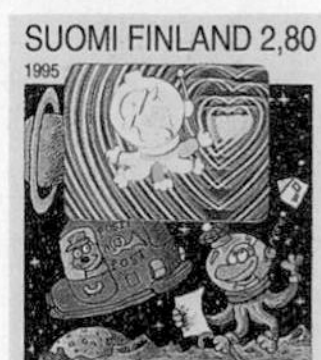

580 Postman delivering Letter to Alien

1995. Greetings stamps. Multicoloured.

1374	2m.80 Type **580**	1·30	65
1375	2m.80 Cat writing letter	1·30	65
1376	2m.80 Postman delivering letter to elderly dog	1·30	65
1377	2m.80 Teenage dog writing letter	1·30	65
1378	2m.80 Dog receiving postcard	1·30	65
1379	2m.80 Dog on train reading letter	1·30	65
1380	2m.80 Guitarist dog with Valentine greeting	1·30	65
1381	2m.80 Baby dog	1·30	65

581 Paivi Ikola (Pesapallo)

1995. "Finlandia 95" International Stamp Exhibition, Helsinki (4th issue). Team Sports. Sheet containing T 581 and similar vert designs. Multicoloured.

MS1382 3m.40 Type **581**; 3m.40 Jari Kurri (ice hockey); 3m.40 Jari Litmanen (football); 3m.40 Lea Hakala (basketball) 5·00 5·00

582 Shooting Star and Stars

1995. Admission of Finland to European Union.

1383	**582**	3m.50 blue, yell & blk	1·20	90

583 "Boys playing on the Shore"

1995. Pro Filatelia. Paintings by Albert Edelfelt. Multicoloured.

1384	2m.40+60p. Type **583**	1·30	1·00
1385	2m.40+60p. "Queen Blanche" (21×30½ mm)	1·30	1·00

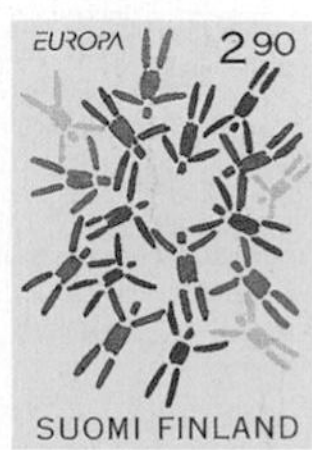

584 Figures forming Parachute

1995. Europa. Peace and Freedom.

1386	**584**	2m.90 multicoloured	2·00	50

585 Lynx

1995. Endangered Animals. Multicoloured.

1387	2m.90 Type **585**	1·10	1·00

1388	2m.90 Landscape	1·10	1·00
1389	2m.90 Shoreline	1·10	1·00
1390	2m.90 Ringed seal	1·10	1·00

586 Daisy (Keski-Suomi)

1995. Provincial Plants. With service indicator. Self-adhesive. Imperf.

1391	**586**	1KLASS (2m.80) mult	1·20	30

587 Mini

1995. "Finlandia 95" International Stamp Exhibition, Helsinki (5th issue). Motor Sports. Sheet 120×80 mm containing T 587 and similar vert designs. Multicoloured.

MS1392	3m.50 Type **587** (Timo Makinen, rally driver); 3m.50 Rally car (Juha Kankkunen, rally driver); 3m.50 Tommi Ahvala on motor cycle (trials); 3m.50 Heikki Mikkola on motor cycle (motocross)	6·25	5·75

588 Dung Beetle

1995. "Finlandia 95" International Stamp Exhibition, Helsinki.

1393	**588**	19m. multicoloured	7·50	7·00

589 Linnanmaki Amusement Park, Helsinki

1995. Nordic Countries' Postal Co-operation. Tourism. Multicoloured.

1394	2m.80 Type **589**	90	40
1395	2m.90 Mantyharju church (400th anniv of parish)	1·00	80

590 Loviisa Market and Church

1995. 250th Anniv of Loviisa.

1396	**590**	3m.20 multicoloured	1·20	75

591 Silver Birch (incorrectly inscr "Betula pendula")

1995. 20th International Union of Forestry Research Organizations World Congress, Tampere. Leaves and flowers of trees. Multicoloured.

1397	2m.80 Type **591**	2·00	60
1398	2m.80 Scots pine ("Pinus sylvestris")	2·00	60
1399	2m.80 Norway spruce ("Picea abies")	2·00	60
1400	2m.80 Propagating tree from needle	2·00	60

592 Rontgen Tube and X-Ray Theory

1995. Centenary of Discovery of X-Rays by Wilhelm Rontgen.

1401	**592**	4m.30 multicoloured	1·60	1·00

593 Somali

1995. Cats. Multicoloured.

1402	2m.80 Type **593**	1·10	60
1403	2m.80 Siamese	1·10	60
1404	2m.80 Domestic cat in grass (58×35 mm)	1·10	60
1405	2m.80 Norwegian forest cat	1·10	60
1406	2m.80 Colourpoint Persian	1·10	60
1407	2m.80 Kittens playing in grass (58×35 mm)	1·10	60

Nos. 1404 and 1407 form a composite design.

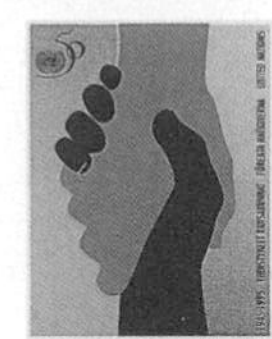

594 Handshake

1995. 50th Anniv of U.N.O.

1408	**594**	3m.40 multicoloured	1·30	75

595 Father Christmas on Skates

1995. Christmas. Multicoloured.

1409	2m. Type **595**	1·30	25
1410	2m.80 Poinsettias in snow (horiz)	90	40

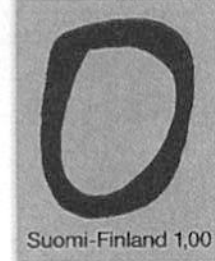

596 "O"

1996. Greeting Stamps. Letters of the Alphabet.

1411	**596**	1m. vio, grn & blk ("M")	50	40
1412	**596**	1m. bl, mauve and black (Type **596**)	50	40
1413	**596**	1m. red, yell & blk ("I")	50	40
1414	**596**	1m. bl, red & blk ("H")	50	40
1415	**596**	1m. red, grn & blk ("E")	50	40
1416	**596**	1m. yell, bl & blk ("J")	50	40
1417	**596**	1m. grn, red & blk ("A")	50	40
1418	**596**	1m. yellow, mauve and black ("N")	50	40
1419	**596**	1m. yell, grn & blk ("T")	50	40
1420	**596**	1m. red, bl & blk ("P")	50	40
1421	**596**	1m. lt bl, bl & blk ("U")	50	40
1422	**596**	1m. yell, mve & blk ("S")	50	40

Nos. 1411/22 were intended to be arranged on envelopes to spell out a desired message.

597 "Smile" (Mauno Paavola)

1996. 50th Anniv of UNICEF.

1423	**597**	2m.80 multicoloured	1·10	35

598 Hoop Exercise

1996. Centenary of Women's Gymnastics Associations in Finland.

1424	**598**	2m.80 multicoloured	1·10	35

599 Mother and Children at Polling Station

1996. Europa. 90th Anniv of Women's Suffrage in Finland.

1425	**599**	3m.20 multicoloured	4·25	75

600 Chicks

1996. Finnish Red Cross Fund. Chickens. Multicoloured.

1426	2m.80+60p. Type **600**	1·20	1·30
1427	3m.20+70p. Hens	1·60	1·50
1428	3m.40+70p. Cock (vert)	1·80	1·70

601 J. Gronroos (circus director) at Film Projector

1996. Centenary of Motion Pictures. Mult.

1429	2m.80 Valle Saikko and Irma Seikkula in "Juha"	1·20	65
1430	2m.80 Alli Riks and Theodor Tugai in "Wide Road" ("Den Breda Vagen")	1·20	65
1431	2m.80 Ake Lindman in "The Unknown Soldier" ("Okana Soldat")	1·20	65
1432	2m.80 Type **601**	1·20	65
1433	2m.80 Antti Litja in "Year of the Hare" ("Harens Ar")	1·20	65
1434	2m.80 Mirjami Kuosmanen in "The White Forest" ("Den Vita Renen")	1·20	65
1435	2m.80 Ansa Ikonen and Tauno Palo in "Complete Love" ("Alla Alskar")	1·20	65
1436	2m.80 Matti Pellonpaa in "Shadow in Paradise" ("Skuggor i Paradiset")	1·20	65

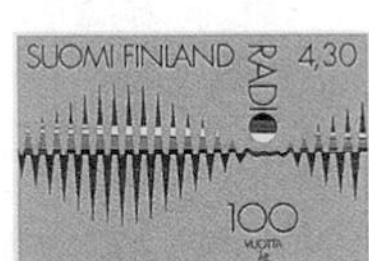

602 Radio Waves

1996. Centenary (1995) of First Radio Transmission.

1437	**602**	4m.30 multicoloured	1·50	1·40

603 Canoeing

1996. Centenary of Modern Olympic Games. Watersports. Multicoloured.

1438	3m.40 Type **603**	1·40	1·10
1439	3m.40 Sailing	1·40	1·10
1440	3m.40 Rowing	1·40	1·10
1441	3m.40 Swimming	1·40	1·10

604 White Water Lily (Southern Savonia)

1996. Provincial Plants. With service indicator. Self-adhesive. Imperf.

1442	**604**	1KLASS (2m.80) mult	1·20	30

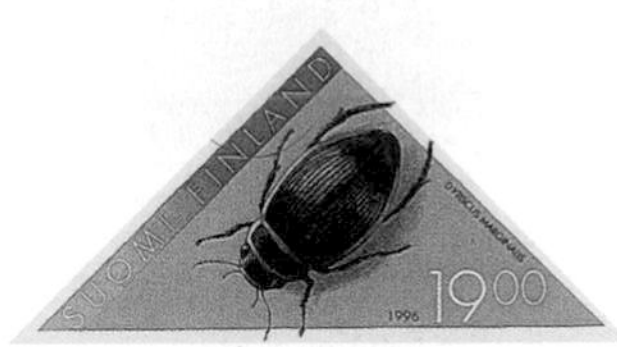

605 Great Diving Beetle

1996

1443	**605**	19m. multicoloured	7·00	7·50

606 Common Snipe ("Gallinago gallinago")

1996. Stamp Day. Wading Birds. Sheet 121× 72 mm containing T 606 and similar vert designs. Multicoloured.

MS1444	2m.80 Curlew ("Numenius arquata") (29×53 mm); 2m.80 Type **606**; 2m.80 Oystercatcher ("Haematopus ostralegus"); 2m.80 Woodcock ("Scolopax rusticola"); 2m.80 Lapwing ("Vanellus vanellus")	5·75	5·50

607 Professor Itikaisen (Ilmari Vainio)

1996. Centenary of Comic Strips. Each red and black.

1445	2m.80 Type **607**	1·10	65
1446	2m.80 Pekka Puupaa (Peter Blockhead) receiving letter from booth (Ola Fogelberg)	1·10	65
1447	2m.80 Joonas resting chin on hand (Veikko Savolainen)	1·10	65
1448	2m.80 Posti-Aune from "Mammila" in motor cycle helmet (Tarmo Koivisto)	1·10	65
1449	2m.80 Rymy-Eetu smoking pipe (Erkki Tanttu)	1·10	65
1450	2m.80 Kieku (duck) writing letter (Asmo Alho)	1·10	65
1451	2m.80 Pikku Risunen from "Hyvissa naimisissa" (Well-married) in headdress with big ears (Riitta Uusitalo)	1·10	65
1452	2m.80 Kiti from "Vihrea Rapsodia" (Green Rhapsody) holding pencil (Kati Kovacs)	1·10	65

608 Father Christmas and Musicians

1996. Christmas. Multicoloured.

1453	2m. Type **608**	75	30
1454	2m.80 Reindeer and hare	90	30
1455	3m.20 Father Christmas reading letters (vert)	1·20	65

609 Player

1997. World Ice Hockey Championship, Helsinki, Turku and Tampere.

1456	**609**	2m.80 multicoloured	1·10	25

610 Parcel

1997. Cent of Mail Order Sales in Finland.

1457	**610**	2m.80 multicoloured	1·10	65

611 Angels

1997. Greetings Stamps. With service indicator. Old Scrapbook Illustrations. Multicoloured.

1458	1klass (2m.80) Type **611**	1·30	60
1459	1klass (2m.80) Basket of mixed flowers	1·30	60
1460	1klass (2m.80) Barn swallow on hand extended through wreath of roses	1·30	60
1461	1klass (2m.80) Children playing	1·30	60
1462	1klass (2m.80) Child and four-leaf clovers in envelope	1·30	60
1463	1klass (2m.80) Man's and woman's hands extended through heart-shaped wreaths of roses	1·30	60
1464	1klass (2m.80) Roses	1·30	60
1465	1klass (2m.80) Angel	1·30	60

612 Arctic Hares

1997. Easter.

1466	**612**	2m.80 multicoloured	90	30

613 Golden Merganser casting Reflection of Girl

1997. Europa. Tales and Legends. "The Girl who turned into a Golden Merganser" (folktale). Illustrations by Mika Launis. Multicoloured.

1467	3m.20 Type **613**	1·60	65
1468	3m.40 Girl falling into water	2·00	1·00

614 Bird Cherry (Birkaland)

1997. Provincial Plants. With service indicator. Self-adhesive. Imperf.

1469	**614**	1KLASS (2m.80) mult	1·20	35

615 Nurmi running 3000 m (Olympic Games, Paris, 1924)

1997. Birth Cent of Paavo Nurmi (runner).

1470	**615**	3m.40 multicoloured	1·00	75

616 Couple dancing in Meadow

1997. The Tango. With service indicator.

1471	**616**	1klass (2m.80) black and pink	1·20	45

617 "Astrid" (galeasse)

1997. Centenary of Finnish Lifeboat Society. Sailing Ships. Multicoloured.

1472	2m.80 Type **617**	1·30	65
1473	2m.80 "Jacobstads Wapen" (replica of schooner)	1·30	65
1474	2m.80 "Suomen Joutsen" (cadet ship) (48×25 mm)	1·30	65
1475	2m.80 "Tradewind" (brigantine)	1·30	65
1476	2m.80 "Merikokko" (lifeboat)	1·30	65
1477	2m.80 "Sigyn" (barque) (48×25 mm)	1·30	65

618 Globe and Ahtisaari

1997. 60th Birthday of President Martii Ahtisaari.

1478	**618**	2m.80 multicoloured	1·00	30

619 Clouds (Summer)

1997. 80th Anniv of Independence. The Four Seasons. Multicoloured.

1479	2m.80 Lily of the valley (Spring)	1·30	65
1480	2m.80 Type **619**	1·30	65
1481	2m.80 Leaves (Autumn)	1·30	65
1482	2m.80 Snowflakes (Winter)	1·30	65

620 Crane with Chick

1997. The Common Crane (Grus grus). Sheet 120×80 mm containing T 620 and similar multicoloured designs.

MS1483	2m.80 Type **620**; 2m.80 Adults, one with frog in beak; 2m.80 Courting dance; 2m.80 Adults in flight (31×34 mm)	5·00	5·00

621 Vainamoinen proposing to Aino

1997. Pro Filatelia. "Aino" (triptych) by Akseli Gallen-Kallela. Multicoloured.

1484	2m.80+60p. Type **621**	1·40	1·20
1485	2m.80+60p. Aino in water escaping from Vainamoinen (33×47 mm)	1·40	1·20
1486	2m.80+60p. Mermaids luring Aino into water	1·40	1·20

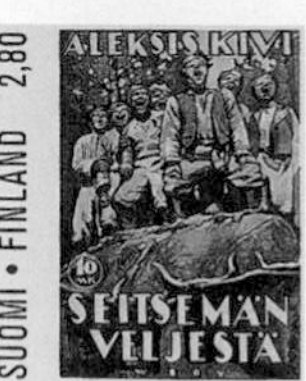

622 "Seven Brothers" (Aleksis Kivi)

1997. Centenary of Finnish Writers' Association. Book Covers. Multicoloured.

1487	2m.80 Type **622**	1·20	65
1488	2m.80 "Sinuhe the Eyptian" (Mika Waltari)	1·20	65
1489	2m.80 "Under the North Star" (Vaino Linna)	1·20	65
1490	2m.80 "Farewell River Iijoki" (Kalle Paatalo)	1·20	65
1491	2m.80 "Eagle, My Beloved" (Kaari Utrio)	1·20	65
1492	2m.80 "Midsummer Dance" (Hannu Salama)	1·20	65
1493	2m.80 "Manilla Rope" (Veijo Meri)	1·20	65
1494	2m.80 "Uppo-Nalle ja Kumma" (Elina Karjalainen)	1·20	65

623 Church and Houses

1997. Christmas. Multicoloured.

1495	2m. Type **623**	60	35
1496	2m.80 Candelabra, Petajavesi Church (vert)	90	50
1497	3m.20 St. John's Church, Eira, Helsinki (35×24 mm)	1·20	65

624 Zander

1998. Provincial Birds and Fish (1st series). Uusimaa. With service indicator. Mult. Self-adhesive.

1498	2klass (2m.40) Type **624**	1·10	65
1499	1KLASS (2m.80) Blackbird	1·30	30

625 Moominpappa writing Play

1998. Moomin. Illustrations from her stories by Tove Jansson. With service indicator. Multicoloured.

1500	1klass (2m.80) Type **625**	1·40	50
1501	1klass (2m.80) Moomin-mamma making jam	1·40	50
1502	1klass (2m.80) Too-ticky playing barrel organ and Littly My dancing	1·40	50
1503	1klass (2m.80) Moomintroll dancing with the Snork Maiden	1·40	50

626 Nurses of 1898 and 1998

1998. Cent of Finnish Federation of Nurses.

1504	**626**	2m.80 multicoloured	1·00	25

627 Gold Heart and Musical Notes

1998. St. Valentine's Day. With service indicator. Multicoloured.

1505	1klass (2m.80) Type **627**	1·20	75
1506	1klass (2m.80) Gold heart and elephant	1·20	75
1507	1klass (2m.80) Gold heart and puppy on blanket	1·20	75
1508	1klass (2m.80) Gold heart and kittens	1·20	75
1509	1klass (2m.80) Gold heart and dog	1·20	75
1510	1klass (2m.80) Gold heart and flowers	1·20	75

The gold hearts could be scratched off to reveal a complete design.

628 Harebell (Central Ostrobothnia)

1998. Provincial Plants. With service indicator. Self-adhesive. Imperf.

1511	**628**	1KLASS (2m.80) mult	1·20	30

629 Sow and Litter

1998. Finnish Red Cross Fund. Pigs. Mult.

1512	2m.80+60p. Type **629**	1·20	1·30
1513	3m.20+70p. Three piglets	1·50	1·50
1514	3m.40+70p. Boar	1·80	1·60

630 Coltsfoot

1998. Spring.

1515	**630**	2m.80 multicoloured	1·10	30

631 Students with Balloons (Labour Day)

1998. Europa. National Festivals. Mult.

1516	3m.20 Type **631**	1·60	50
1517	3m.40 Couple by lake (Midsummer)	2·00	1·30

632 "Aranda" (research vessel)

1998. Nordic Countries' Postal Co-operation. Shipping. Multicoloured.

1518	2m.80 Type **632** (80th anniv of Finnish Marine Research Institute)	1·00	40
1519	3m.20 "Vega" (120th anniv of Nils Nordenskjold's navigation of the North-east Passage)	1·30	90

633 Flag and Score

1998. 150th Anniv of First Performance of "Our Country" (national anthem).

1520	**633** 5m. multicoloured	1·80	1·00

634 Bernese Mountain Dog

1998. World Dog Show, Helsinki. With service indicator. Multicoloured.

1521	1klass (2m.80) Type **634**	1·20	65
1522	1klass (2m.80) Pumis	1·20	65
1523	1klass (2m.80) Boxers	1·20	65
1524	1klass (2m.80) Bichon frises	1·20	65
1525	1klass (2m.80) Finnish lap-phounds	1·20	65
1526	1klass (2m.80) Dachshunds	1·20	65
1527	1klass (2m.80) Cairn terriers	1·20	65
1528	1klass (2m.80) Labrador retrievers	1·20	65

635 Downhill Competitor and 19th-century Cyclist

1998. Centenary of Cycling Union of Finland.

1529	**635** 3m. multicoloured	90	60

636 Eagle Owl "Bubo bubo"

1998. Stamp Day. Owls. Sheet 120×80 mm containing T 636 and similar multicoloured designs.

MS1530	3m. Type **636**; 3m. Wing-tip of eagle owl (25×49 mm); 3m. Tengmalm's owl ("Aegolius funereus") (23×42 mm); 3m. Great grey owl ("Stris nebulosa") (24×42 mm); 3m. Snowy owl ("Nyctea scandiaca") (29×42 mm)	5·50	4·50

637 Kilta Tableware (Kaj Franck)

1998. Finnish Industrial Design. Mult.

1531	3m. Savoy Vase (Alvar Aalto)	1·30	85
1532	3m. Karuselli 412 chair (Yrjo Kukkapuro) (29×34 mm)	1·30	85
1533	3m. Tasaraita T-shirts (Annika Rimala) (29×34 mm)	1·30	85
1534	3m. Type **637**	1·30	85
1535	3m. Cast-iron cooking pot (Timo Sarpaneva) (29×34 mm)	1·30	85
1536	3m. Carelia cutlery (Bertel Gardberg) (29×34 mm)	1·30	85

638 Children and Christmas Tree

1998. Christmas. Multicoloured.

1537	2m. Type **638**	60	30
1538	3m. Children tobogganing (horiz)	90	40
1539	3m.20 Snow-bound cottage on island (horiz)	90	50

639 Hakkinen and Racing Car

1999. Mika Hakkinen, Formula 1 World Champion 1998. Sheet 115×70 mm.

MS1540	**639** 3m. multicoloured	1·50	1·30

640 Atlantic Salmon

1999. Provincial Birds and Fish (2nd series). Lapland. With service indicator. Multicoloured. Self-adhesive.

1541	2klass (2m.40) Type **640**	80	50
1542	1KLASS (3m.) Bluethroat (vert)	1·00	40

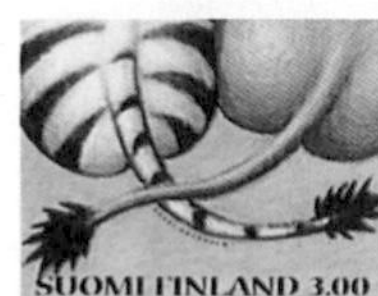

641 Zebra and Lion Tails

1999. Friendship. Multicoloured. Self-adhesive.

1543	3m. Type **641**	1·10	90
1544	3m. Cat and dog tails	1·10	90

642 Monument to Eetu Salin (founder) (Aimo Tukiainen)

1999. Centenary of Founding of Finnish Labour Party (predecessor of Social Democrat Party).

1545	**642** 4m.50 multicoloured	1·30	1·20

643 Horse Brooch

1999. 150th Anniv of New Kalevala (Karelian poems collected by Elias Lonnrot). Sheet 120×74 mm containing T 643 and similar vert designs. Multicoloured.

MS1546	3m. Type **643**; 3m. Kuhmoinen Cocks brooch; 3m. Virusmaki brooch	3·25	3·25

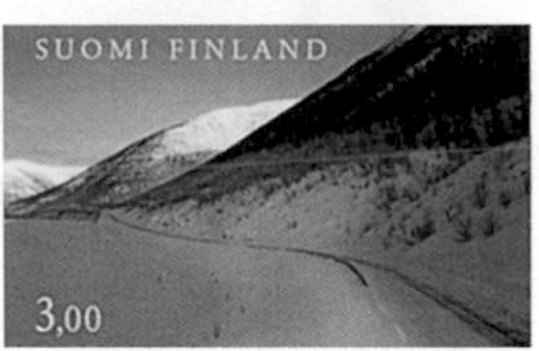

644 Road by River Tenojoki, Utsjoki

1999. Bicentenary of National Road Administration. Multicoloured.

1547	3m. Type **644**	1·50	65
1548	3m. Motorway intersection, Jyvaskyla	1·50	65
1549	3m. Raippaluoto bridge, Vaasa	1·50	65
1550	3m. North Karelian forest road, Kitee	1·50	65

645 Esplanade, Helsinki

1999. Europa. Parks and Gardens. Multicoloured.

1551	2m.70 Type **645**	1·50	75
1552	3m.20 Ruissalo island, Turku	2·00	90

646 Martha Circle

1999. Centenary of Martha Organization (for education and development of women).

1553	**646** 3m. multicoloured	90	35

647 Crocuses

1999. Easter.

1554	**647** 3m. multicoloured	1·20	40

648 Cowslip (Aland Islands)

1999. Provincial Plants. With service indicator. Self-adhesive. Imperf.

1555	**648** 1KLASS (3m.) mult	1·20	35

649 Nightingale ("Luscinia luscinia")

1999. Nocturnal Summer Birds. Sheet 120×80 mm containing T 649 and similar multicoloured designs.

MS1556	3m. Type **649**; 3m. European cuckoo ("Cuculus canorus) (24×39½ mm); 3m. Eurasian bittern ("Botaurus stellaris") (44×29 mm); 3m. European nightjar ("Caprimulgus europaeus") (24½×36 mm); 3m. Corncrake ("Crex crex") (24½×37 mm)	6·75	5·00

650 Figure reaching for E.U. Stars

1999. Finland's Presidency of European Union.

1557	**650** 3m.50 multicoloured	1·10	60

651 Harmony Sisters

1999. Entertainers. Multicoloured.

1558	3m.50 Type **651**	1·30	75
1559	3m.50 Olavi Virta (tango and jazz singer) (29×34 mm)	1·30	75
1560	3m.50 Georg Malmsten (composer and band leader) (29×34 mm)	1·30	75
1561	3m.50 Topi Karki (composer) and Reino Helismaa (lyricist)	1·30	75
1562	3m.50 Tapio Rautavaara (composer and folk singer) (29×34 mm)	1·30	75
1563	3m.50 Esa Pakarinen (folk artist and actor) (29×34 mm)	1·30	75

652 "Garden of Death"

1999. Pro Filatelia. Paintings by Hugo Simberg. Multicoloured.

1564	3m.50+50p. Type **652**	1·30	1·20
1565	3m.50+50p. "Wounded Angel"	1·30	1·20

653 Fiskars Secateurs and Pruning Shears Designed by Olavi Linden

1999. Finnish Industrial Design. Multicoloured.

1566	3m.50 Type **653**	1·30	85
1567	3m.50 Zoel Versoul guitar (Kari Nieminen) (29×34½ mm)	1·30	85
1568	3m.50 Ergo II Silenta hearing protectors (Jyrki Jarvinen) (29×34½ mm)	1·30	85
1569	3m.50 Ponsse Cobra HS10 harvester (Pentti Hukkanen, Jorma Hyvonen, Jouko Kelppe and Heikki Koivurova)	1·30	85
1570	3m.50 Suunto sailing compass (Heikki Metsa-Ketela and Erikki Vainio) (29×34½ mm)	1·30	85
1571	3m.50 Exel Avanti QLS ski stick (Pasi Jarvinen, Matti Lyly and Mika Vesalainen) (29×34½ mm)	1·30	85

654 Santa Claus

1999. Christmas. Multicoloured.

1572	2m.50 Type **654**	80	40
1573	3m. "Nativity" (Giorgio de Chirico) (horiz)	1·10	60
1574	3m.50 Two hares (horiz)	1·20	50

655 Earth, Sun and Moon

2000. Friendship. Multicoloured.

1575	3m.50 Type **655**	1·30	75
1576	3m.50 Painting a smile on Jupiter	1·30	75
1577	3m.50 Birds using Neptune as balloon	1·30	75
1578	3m.50 Martian using magnet to rescue traveller from Mars	1·30	75
1579	3m.50 People on Saturn's rings	1·30	75
1580	3m.50 Pluto as igloo and polar bear	1·30	75

656 Herring Market

2000. 450th Anniv of Helsinki (European City of Culture, 2000). Multicoloured.

1581	3m.50 Type **656**	1·10	90
1582	3m.50 Museum of Contemporary Art, Kiasma (24×48 mm)	1·60	1·60
1583	3m.50 Statue and Cathedral, Senate Square (42×24 mm)	1·60	1·60
1584	3m.50 Finlandia Hall (42×24 mm)	1·60	1·60
1585	3m.50 Glass Palace Film and Media Centre (24×48 mm)	1·60	1·60
1586	3m.50 "Looking for the Lost Crown" (children's tour), Suomenlin Sea Fortress (24×48 mm)	1·60	1·60
1587	3m.50 Type **656**	1·60	1·60
1588	3m.50 "Forces of Light" celebration (42×24 mm)	1·60	1·60
1589	3m.50 Open-air concert, Kaivopuisto Park (24×48 mm)	1·60	1·60

657 Fortifications at Sveaborg

2000. Sveaborg Fortress.

1590	**657**	7m.20 multicoloured	2·50	1·80

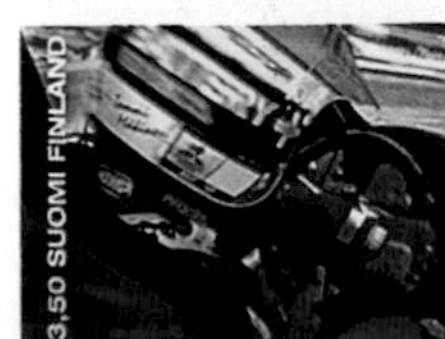

658 Makinen at Wheel of Rally Car

2000. Tommi Makinen, Rally World Champion (1999). Sheet 109×80 mm containing T 658 and similar horiz design. Multicoloured.

MS1591	3m.50 Type **658**; 3m.50 Mitsubishi Lancer rally car	2·75	2·75

659 Marsh Marigold

2000. Spring.

1592	**659**	3m.50 multicoloured	1·20	40

660 Interior of Turku Cathedral

2000. Holy Year 2000. 700th Anniv of Turku Cathedral. Multicoloured.

1593	3m.50 Type **660**	1·40	1·00
1594	3m.50 Woman lighting candle	1·40	1·00
1595	3m.50 "Transfiguration of Christ" (altarpiece)	1·40	1·00
1596	3m.50 Christening	1·40	1·00

661 Emma the Theatre Rat and Moomins at Table

2000. Moomin. Illustrations from her stories by Tove Jansson. With service indicator. Multicoloured.

1597	1klass (3m.50) Type **661**	1·20	65
1598	1klass (3m.50) Park keeper and Hattifatteners growing from the grass	1·20	65
1599	1klass (3m.50) Snufkin walking through forest	1·20	65
1600	1klass (3m.50) Snufkin surrounded by forest children	1·20	65

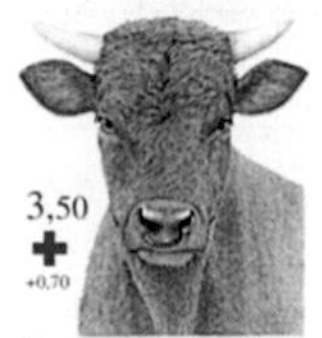

662 Bull

2000. Finnish Red Cross Fund. Cattle. Mult.

1601	3m.50+70p. Type **662**	1·30	1·20
1602	4m.80+80p. Cow and calf (horiz)	1·90	1·80

663 "Building Europe"

2000. Europa.

1603	**663**	3m.50 multicoloured	1·70	95

665 Girls in Laboratory

664 Spring Anemone (South Karelia)

2000. Provincial Plants. With service indicator. Self-adhesive. Imperf.

1604	**664**	1KLASS (3m.50) mult	1·20	30

2000. Heureka Science Centre. Sheet 120×80 mm containing T 665 and similar multicoloured designs.

MS1605	3m.50 Type **665**; 3m.50 DNA double helix and man's face (parallelogram, 20×20 mm); 3m.50 Man's face and Sierinski Triangle aerial (27×27 mm)	3·75	3·50

666 Common Whitefish

2000. Provincial Birds and Fish (3rd series). Southern Lapland. With service indicator. Multicoloured. Self-adhesive.

1606	2klass (2m.70) Type **666**	90	40
1607	1KLASS (3m.30) Willow grouse	1·10	65

667 "Flame" Rug (Akseli Gallen-Kallela)

2000. Finnish Industrial Design. Multicoloured.

1608	3m.50 Type **667**	1·30	85
1609	3m.50 Pearl Bird (Birger Kaipiainen) (29×34 mm)	1·30	85
1610	3m.50 Pot (Kyllikki Salmenhaara) (29×34 mm)	1·30	85
1611	3m.50 "Leaf" platter (Tapio Wirkkala)	1·30	85
1612	3m.50 "Lichen" (furnishing fabric pattern, Dora Jung) (29×34 mm)	1·30	85
1613	3m.50 Glass vase (Valter Jung) (29×34 mm)	1·30	85

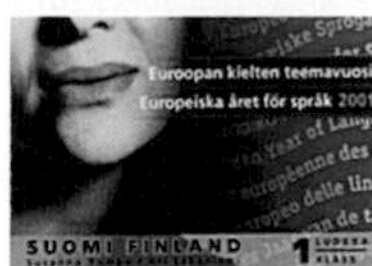

668 Three Wise Men and Star

2000. Christmas. Multicoloured. Self-adhesive.

1614	2m.50 Type **668**	80	35
1615	3m.50 Northern bullfinch sitting on wreath (vert)	1·00	60

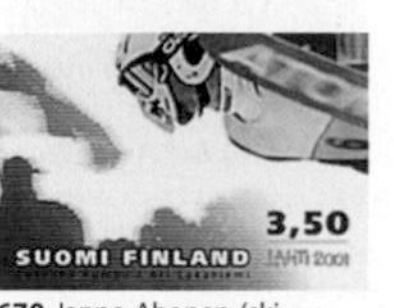

669 Woman's Head

2001. European Year of Languages. With service indicator.

1616	**669**	1KLASS (3m.50) mult	1·20	35

670 Janne Ahonen (ski jumper)

2001. Nordic World Skiing Championships, Lahti. Multicoloured.

1617	3m.50 Type **670**	1·10	40
1618	3m.50 Mika Myllyla	1·10	40

671 Garland of Flowers

2001. Greetings Stamps. Flowers. Multicoloured. Self-adhesive.

1619	1KLASS (3m.50) Type **671**	1·20	65
1620	1KLASS (3m.50) Basket of flowers	1·20	65
1621	1KLASS (3m.50) Heart-shaped garland	1·20	65
1622	1KLASS (3m.50) Bouquet	1·20	65
1623	1KLASS (3m.50) Flowers, cake and cups	1·20	65
1624	1KLASS (3m.50) Flowers and heart-shaped cake	1·20	65

672 Cover of First Magazine published in Finland, 1951

2001. 50th Anniv of The Donald Duck Magazine in Finland. Sheet 130×80 mm containing T 672 and similar vert designs. Multicoloured.

MS1625	1klass Type **672**; 1klass Silhouette of boy and page from magazine; 1klass Toy carrying flag and Chip and Dale (24×30 mm); 1klass Silhouette of Donald Duck and Vainamoinen; 1klass Donald Duck and Helsinki Cathedral	6·00	5·75

673 Father Christmas in Sleigh

2001. Santa Claus. With service indicator. Self-adhesive.

1630	**673**	1klass (3m.50) multicoloured	1·10	1·00

674 Face of Chick

2001. Easter. Multicoloured.

1631	3m.60 Type **674**	2·10	70
1632	3m.60 Easter egg	2·10	70

675 Roof of Mill and Trees

2001. Verla Groundwood and Board Mill Museum, Jaala. Sheet 80×120 mm containing T 676 and similar vert designs. Multicoloured.

MS1633	3m.60 Type **675**; 3m.60 Mill manager's house, mill building and river; 3m.60 Main mill building and trees; 3m.60 Mill building and river	5·25	5·00

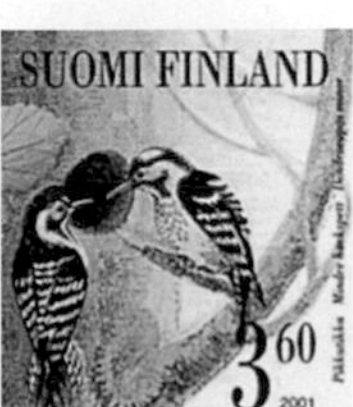

676 Lesser Spotted Woodpecker (*Dendrocopos minor*)

2001. Woodpeckers. Sheet 79×119 mm containing T 677 and similar vert designs. Mult.

MS1634	3m.60 Type **676**; 3m.60 Three-toed woodpecker (*Picoides tridactylus*) (28×35 mm); 3m.60 White-backed woodpecker (*Dendrocopos leucotos*) (32×41 mm); 3m.60 Great spotted woodpecker (*Dendrocopos major*) (28×41 mm); 3m.60 Grey-headed green woodpecker (*Picus canus*) (32×41 mm); 3m.60 Black woodpecker (*Dryocopus martius*) (28×41 mm)	6·75	6·75

677 Haapavitja Rapids, Runna

2001. Europa. Water Resources.

1635	**674** 5m.40 multicoloured	3·00	1·70

678 Compass and Emblem

2001. Orienteering World Championship, Tampere.

1636	**678** 3m.60 multicoloured	1·00	40

679 Cornflower (Pajat-Hame)

2001. Provincial Flowers. With service indicator. Self-adhesive.

1637	1KLASS (3m.50) Type **679**	1·20	40
1638	1KLASS (3m.50) Pasque flower (Kanta-Hame)	1·20	40

680 Lampern (*Lampetra fluviatilis*) (Satakunta)

2001. Provincial Fish. With service indicator. Multicoloured. Self-adhesive.

1639	2klass (2m.70) Type **680**	1·00	60
1640	2klass (2m.70) Asp (*Aspius aspius*) (Pirkanmaa)	1·00	60
1641	2klass (2m.70) Vendace (*Coregonus albula*) (Savonia)	1·00	60

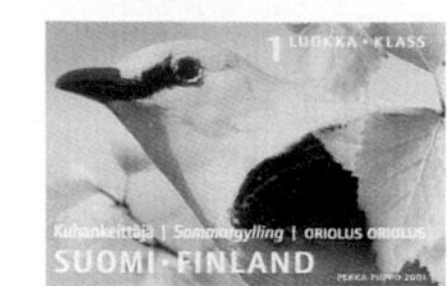

681 Golden Oriole (*Oriolus oriolus*) (Satakunta)

2001. Provincial Birds. With service indicator. Multicoloured. Self-adhesive.

1642	1KLASS (3m.60) Type **681**	1·10	60
1643	1KLASS (3m.60) Blue tit (*Parus caeruleus*) (Pirkanmaa)	1·10	60
1644	1KLASS (3m.60) Pied wagtail (*Motacilla alba*) (South Savonia)	1·10	60

682 18th-century Captain's Quarters, Merchant Ship

2001. Gulf of Finland (1st series). Multicoloured.

1645	1KLASS (3m.60) Type **682**	1·20	65
1646	1KLASS (3m.60) Uto Lighthouse (32×27 mm)	1·20	65
1647	1KLASS (3m.60) *Sankt Mikael* (Dutch sailing ship) (33×27 mm)	1·20	65
1648	1KLASS (3m.60) Diver on *Sankt Mikael* and treasure (33×27 mm)	1·20	65
1649	1KLASS (3m.60) Opossum shrimp, isopod and bladder wrack (33×27 mm)	1·20	65

See also Nos. 1675/9 and 1753/7.

683 Elf Girl reading

2001. Christmas. Multicoloured. Self-adhesive.

1650	2m.50 Type **683**	80	35
1651	3m.60 Elf boy sledding (horiz)	1·00	40

684 Water Forget-me-not (*Myosotis scorpoides*)

2002. Flowers. Showing water forget-me-nots (5c.) or lily-of-the-valley (10c.). Multicoloured. Self-adhesive.

1652	5c. Type **684**	15	15
1653	5c. Four flowers	15	15
1654	5c. One open flower and four buds	15	15
1655	5c. Spray of flowers	15	15
1656	5c. Five flower heads	15	15
1657	10c. Spray of five lily-of-the-valley flowers (*Convallaria majallis*)	25	25
1658	10c. Spray of eight flowers between two leaves	25	25
1659	10c. Two flowers	25	25
1660	10c. Spray of six flowers against leaf	25	25
1661	10c. Lily-of-the-valley growing through grass	25	25

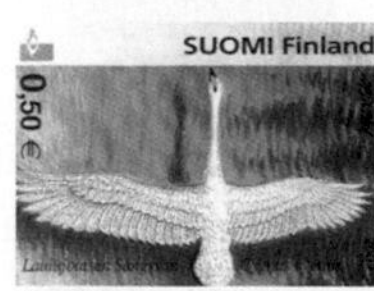

685 Whooper Swan (*Cygnus cygnus*)

2002. Self-adhesive.

1662	**685** 50c. multicoloured	95	40

686 Birch (*Betula pendula*)

2002. Trees. Self-adhesive.

1663	60c. Type **686**	1·20	60
1664	€2.50 Norway spruce (*Picea abies*)	4·50	2·50
1665	€3.50 Scots pine (*Pinus sylvestris*)	6·25	3·75

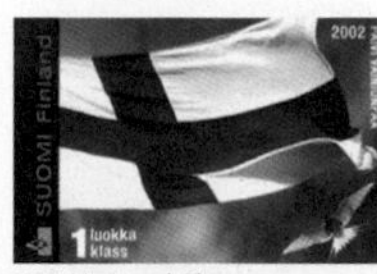

687 National Flag .

2002. With service indicator. Self-adhesive.

1666	**687** 1klass (60c.) mult	1·20	1·00

No. 1666 was for use on domestic first class mail.

688 "Kymintehtaalta" (Victor Westerholm)

2002. Finnish Landscapes. Self-adhesive. Multicoloured.

1667	90c. Type **688**	1·70	1·50
1668	€1.30 Granite substrata	2·30	1·30

689 Heraldic Lion

2002. Winning entry in Stamp Design Competition. Multicoloured. Self- adhesive.

1669	€1 Type **689**	1·80	1·00
1670	€5 No. 1668	9·00	7·50

690 Witch riding Broomstick

2002. Easter. Self-adhesive.

1671	**690** 60c. multicoloured	1·20	50

691 Plantain

2002. Birth Bicentenary of Elias Lonnrot (linguist, botanist and physician). Sheet 120×80 mm, containing T 691 and similar vert designs. Multicoloured.

MS1672	60c. Type **691**; 60c. Tip of feather and text; 60c. Base of feather and text; 60c. Elias Lonnrot	4·75	4·25

692 Houses

2002. UNESCO World Heritage Site. 560th Anniv of Rauma. Sheet 82×122 mm, containing T 692 and similar vert designs. Multicoloured.

MS1673	60c. Type **692**; 60c. Church of the Holy Cross; 60c. Left side of Rauma museum (face value at left); 60c. Right side of museum (face value at right)	4·75	4·25

693 Circus Performers

2002. Europa. Circus.

1674	**693** 60c. multicoloured	3·00	65

694 Fishing Boat and Net

2002. Gulf of Finland (2nd series). Multicoloured.

1675	1KLASS (60c.) Type **694**	1·20	1·00
1676	1KLASS (60c.) Arctic terns, island and perch (fish) (32×27 mm)	1·20	1·00
1677	1KLASS (60c.) Island, dinghy and buoy (32×27 mm)	1·20	1·00
1678	1KLASS (60c.) Flounder (32×27 mm)	1·20	1·00
1679	1KLASS (60c.) Zooplankton, herring and cod (32×27 mm)	1·20	1·00

Nos. 1675/9 were issued together, se-tenant, forming a composite design.

695 "Passio Muscicae" (Sibelius Monument) (sculpture, Eila Hiltunen)

2002. Nordic Countries' Postal Co-operation. Modern Art.

1680	**695** 60c. multicoloured	1·10	40

696 Juniper (*Juniperus communis*)

2002. Self-adhesive.

1681	**696** 60c. multicoloured	1·20	40

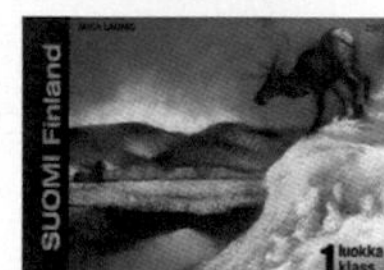

697 Reindeer, Lapland

2002. Self-adhesive.

1682	**697** 60c. multicoloured	1·20	50

698 Horse-drawn Sleigh

2002. Christmas. Multicoloured. Self-adhesive.

1683	45c. Type **698**	90	75
1684	60c. Angel (vert)	1·30	1·00

699 Northern Pike (*Esox lucius*)

2003. Provincial Fish. With service indicator. Multicoloured. Self-adhesive.

1685	2KLASS (50c.) Type **699**	1·00	90
1686	2KLASS (50c.) Bream (*Abramis brama*)	1·00	90
1687	2KLASS (50c.) Lake trout (*Salmo trutta lacustris*)	1·00	90

700 European Cuckoo (*Cuculus canorus*)

2003. Provincial Birds. With service indicator. Multicoloured. Self-adhesive.

1688	1KLASS (60c.) Type **700**	1·20	1·00
1689	1KLASS (60c.) Eurasian sky lark (*Alauda arvensis*)	1·20	1·00
1690	1KLASS (60c.) Siberian jay (*Perisoreus infaustus*)	1·20	1·00

701 Viivi and Wagner

2003. Friendship. With service indicator. Showing Viivi and Wagner (cartoon characters). Multicoloured. Self-adhesive.

1691	1KLASS (60c.) Type **701**	1·20	1·00
1692	1KLASS (60c.) Dancing	1·20	1·00
1693	1KLASS (60c.) Viivi writing letter	1·20	1·00
1694	1KLASS (60c.) In bed	1·20	1·00
1695	1KLASS (60c.) Kissing	1·20	1·00
1696	1KLASS (60c.) Wagner receiving letter	1·20	1·00

702 Games Mascot

2003. World Ice Hockey Championships, Helsinki, Tampere and Turku.

1697	**702**	65c. multicoloured	1·40	1·10

703 Pansy (*Viola wittrockiana*)

2003. Self-adhesive.

1698	**703**	65c. multicoloured	1·40	1·10

704 St. Birgitta (Bridget) (detail, altar screen, Naantali Convent Church)

2003. 700th Birth Anniv of St. Birgitta.

1699	**704**	65c. multicoloured	1·40	1·10

705 Aerospatvale Super Caravelle

2003. Centenary of First Powered Flight. 80th Anniv of Finnair. Multicoloured.

1700	65c. Type **705**	1·20	90
1701	65c. Airbus Industries Airbus 320	1·20	90
1702	65c. Junkers Ju 52/3m	1·20	90
1703	65c. Douglas DC-3	1·20	90

706 "The Fighting Capercailles" (Ferdinand von Wright)

2003. Self-adhesive.

1704	**706**	90c. multicoloured	2·30	1·60

707 Heart (Lasse Hietala)

2003. Europa. Poster Art. Design showing "Someone is waiting for your letter" posters by Lasse Hietala. Multicoloured.

1705	65c. Type **707**	1·80	1·10
1706	65c. Mother	1·80	1·10

708 Butterfly

2003. Summer. T 708 and similar multicoloured designs.

MS1707 65c. Type **708**; 65c. Dragonfly (45×35 mm); 65c. Flowers and caterpillar; 65c. Frog (45×36 mm); 65c. Magpie (36×46 mm) (vert); 65c. Hedgehogs (45×29 mm)	8·50	7·00

709 Moomin Family

2003. Moomins. With service indicator. Illustrations from Moominland Midwinter by Tove Jansson. Multicoloured. Self-adhesive.

1708	1klass (65c.) Type **709**	1·20	1·10
1709	1klass (65c.) Tooticky, Little My and Moomintroll sitting by stove	1·20	1·10
1710	1klass (65c.) Moomintroll performing handstand and Little My	1·20	1·10
1711	1klass (65c.) Moonmintroll and squirrel	1·20	1·10
1712	1klass (65c.) Tooticky, Moominmamma and Little My in snow	1·20	1·10
1713	1klass (65c.) Snufkin walking through forest	1·20	1·10

710 Ligonberry (*Vaccinium vitis-idaea*)

2003. Self-adhesive.

1714	**710**	65c. multicoloured	1·50	1·10

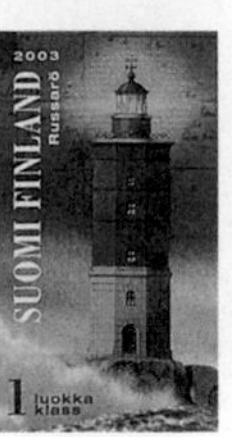

711 Russaro Lighthouse

2003. Lighthouses. With service indicator. Sheet 120×80 mm containing T 711 and similar vert designs. Multicoloured.

MS1715 1klass (65c.) Bengtskar (29×40 mm); 1klass (65c.) Type **711**; 1klass (65c.) Ronnskar; 1klass (65c.) Harmaja Grahara; 1klass (65c.) Soderskar	7·25	6·25

712 Maria and Juho Lallukka

2003. Scientific and Cultural Patrons. Multicoloured.

1716	65c. Type **712**	1·20	1·10
1717	65c. Emil Aaltonen (vert)	1·20	1·10
1718	65c. Heikki Huhtamaki (vert)	1·20	1·10
1719	65c. Jenny and Antti Wihuri	1·20	1·10
1720	65c. Alfred Kordelin (vert)	1·20	1·10
1721	65c. Amos Andersson (vert)	1·20	1·10

713 Elf Boy posting Letters

2003. Christmas. Multicoloured. Self-adhesive.

1722	45c. Type **713**	85	90
1723	65c. Elf girl holding ginger bread on tray (vert)	1·20	1·10

714 President Halonen

2003. 60th Birth Anniv of Tarja Halonen, President of Finland.

1724	**714**	65c. multicoloured	2·00	1·50

715 *Linnaea borealis*

2004. Self-adhesive.

1725	**715**	30c. multicoloured	1·10	90

716 Jean Sibelius' Hands playing Piano

2004. Ainola Museum (Jean Sibelius (composer)'s house). Multicoloured. Self-adhesive.

1726	2klass (55c.) Type **716**	1·80	1·40
1727	2klass (55c.) Swans and score	1·80	1·40
1728	2klass (55c.) *En Saga Jean Sibelius* (painting, Akseli Gallen-Kalhla)	1·80	1·40
1729	1klass (65c.) *Voices Intimae* score (detail)	2·00	1·60
1730	1klass (65c.) Drawing of Ainola	2·00	1·60
1731	1klass (65c.) *Aino Sibelius* (Eero Järnfelt) and *Jean Sibelius* (Albert Edelfelt)	2·00	1·60

717 Silhouette of Johan Runeberg

2004. Birth Bicentenary of Johan Ludvig Runeberg (writer). Sheet 118×80 mm containing T 717 and similar vert designs. Each stone, black and red.

MS1732 65c.×4, Type **717**; Sven Dufa at the Battle of Koljonvirta (Albert Edelfelt) Landscape (Albert Edelfelt) and Värt Land (national anthem); Johan Runeberg (statue, Walter Runeberg)	7·50	7·00

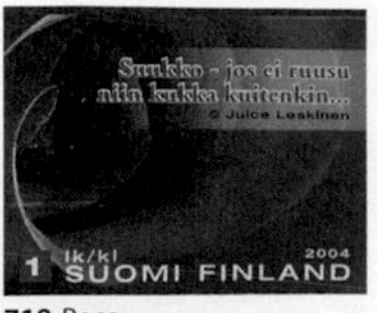

718 Rose

2004. Greetings Stamps. Each black and red. Self-adhesive.

1733	1klass (65c.) Type **718**	2·00	1·60
1734	1klass (65c.) Pursed lips	2·00	1·60
1735	1klass (65c.) Eye	2·00	1·60
1736	1klass (65c.) Man and woman	2·00	1·60
1737	1klass (65c.) Elderly woman	2·00	1·60
1738	1klass (65c.) Hand and flower	2·00	1·60

719 Bear Cub

2004. Self-adhesive.

1739	**719**	2klass (55c.) mult	1·80	1·40

720 Rose

2004. Self-adhesive.

1740	**720**	1klass (65c.). mult	2·00	1·60

721 Daffodils, Narcissi and Grape Hyacinths

2004. Easter. Self-adhesive.

1741	**721**	65c. multicoloured	2·00	1·60

2004. As T 689. Self-adhesive.

1742	**689**	€3 multicoloured	8·50	8·00

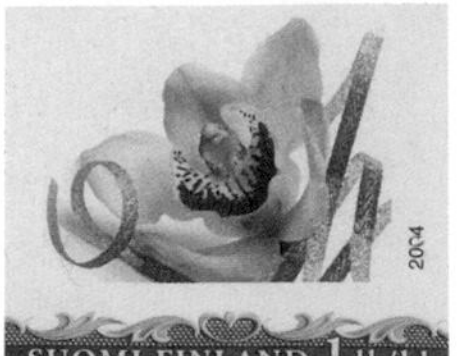

722 Orchid

2004. Greetings Stamps. Multicoloured. Self-adhesive gum.

1743	1 klass (65c.) Type **722**	2·00	1·60
1744	1 klass (65c.) Swallow and martins	2·00	1·60

723 "Luonnotar" (detail) (Akseli Gallen-Kallela)

2004. Nordic Mythology. Sheet 105×70 mm containing T 723 and similar multicoloured design.

MS1745 65c.×2, Type **723**; "Luonnotar" (different) (22×42 mm)	3·75	3·50

Stamps of a similar theme were issued by Aland Islands, Denmark, Faroe Islands, Greenland, Iceland, Norway and Sweden.

724 Wild Strawberry

2004. Self-adhesive.
1746 **724** 65c. multicoloured 2·00 1·60

725 "From the Luxembourg Gardens" (Albert Edelfelt)

2004. Self-adhesive.
1747 **725** 1 klass (65c.) mult 2·00 1·60

726 Fire on Beach

2004. Europa. Holidays. Multicoloured.
1748 65c. Type **726** 1·80 1·50
1749 65c. Rowers 1·80 1·50

727 Red Squirrel

2004. Fauna. Sheet 80×120 mm containing T 727 and similar multicoloured designs.
MS1750 65c.×6, Type **727**; Crow (40×31 mm); Rabbit; Weasels; Lizard; Fox (40×40 mm) 11·00 10·50

728 Snufkin and Moomin Troll

2004. 90th Birth Anniv of Tove Jansson (artist and writer). 50th Anniv of Moomins (cartoon strip by Tove Jansson).
1751 **728** 1 klass (65c.) mult 2·00 1·60

729 Trees and Stone Wall

2004. UNESCO World Heritage Sites. Sammallahdenmäki Bronze Age Ruins. Sheet 120×80 mm containing T 729 and similar square design. Multicoloured.
MS1752 65c.×2, Type **729**; Lichen covered stones 4·00 3·75

730 Jug (*Egelskar*)

2004. Gulf of Finland (3rd series). Showing artefacts from ships. Multicoloured.
1753 1 klass (65c.) Type **730** 2·00 1·60
1754 1 klass (65c.) Seal (*Vrouw Maria*) 2·00 1·60
1755 1 klass (65c.) Gold watch (*St. Michael*) 2·00 1·60
1756 1 klass (65c.) Figurehead (*St. Nikolai*) (24×40 mm) 2·00 1·60
1757 1 klass (65c.) Powder box (*Mulan*) 2·00 1·60

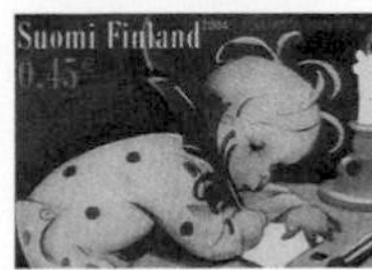

731 Child writing Letter (Martta Wendelin)

2004. Christmas. Drawings by Martta Wendelin. Self-adhesive.
1758 45c. Type **731** 1·60 1·40
1759 65c. Tree decorations (vert) 2·00 1·60

732 Two Girls

2004. 25th Anniv of United Nations Convention on Rights of the Child. Multicoloured.
1760 65c. Type **732** 2·00 1·60
1761 65c. Boy painting 2·00 1·60

733 World Map of Rotary Emblems

2005. Centenary of Rotary International (charitable organization).
1762 **733** 65c. ultramarine and gold 2·30 2·00

734 Child with Bucket and Spade

2005. 400th Anniv of Oulu City. Multicoloured.
1763 65c. Type **734** 2·00 1·60
1764 65c. Cyclist 2·00 1·60
Nos. 1763/4 were issued together, se-tenant, pairs forming a composite design.

735 Sibelius Concert Hall

2005. Centenary of Lahti City. Multicoloured.
1765 65c. Type **735** 2·00 1·60
1766 65c. Radio masts 2·00 1·60

736 Lion and Tiger

2005. Toys. Multicoloured. Self-adhesive.
1767 1 klass (65c.) Type **736** 2·00 1·60
1768 1 klass (65c.) Elephant and dog 2·00 1·60
1769 1 klass (65c.) Airplane, car and train 2·00 1·60
1770 1 klass (65c.) Teddy bear and rabbit 2·00 1·60

737 Earth and Moon (waxing moon)

2005. 300th Anniv of First Finnish Almanac. Self-adhesive.
1771 **737** 65c. multicoloured 2·00 1·60

738 Door Decoration

2005. Hvittrask (Art Nouveau house), Kirkkonummi. Multicoloured. Self-adhesive.
1772 2 klass (55c.) Type **738** (Eliel Saarinen and Santtu Hartman) 1·90 1·60
1773 2 klass (55c.) Copper stove door 1·90 1·60
1774 2 klass (55c.) Chair (detail) 1·90 1·60
1775 1 klass (65c.) Stained glass window (Olga Gummerus-Ehrstrom) 2·10 1·80
1776 1 klass (65c.) Living room 2·10 1·80
1777 1 klass (65c.) Facade 2·10 1·80

739 Woman Auxiliary feeding Soldier and Veteran Organization Emblems

2005. 65th Anniv of End of 105-day Winter War.
1778 **739** 65c. multicoloured 2·30 2·00

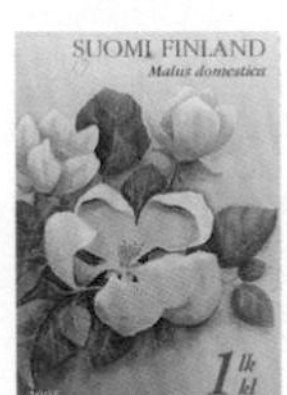

740 Apple Blossom

2005. Self-adhesive.
1779 **740** 1 klass (65c.) mult 2·30 2·00

741 Easter Witch carrying Bouquet

2005. Easter. Self-adhesive.
1780 **741** 65c. multicoloured 2·30 2·00

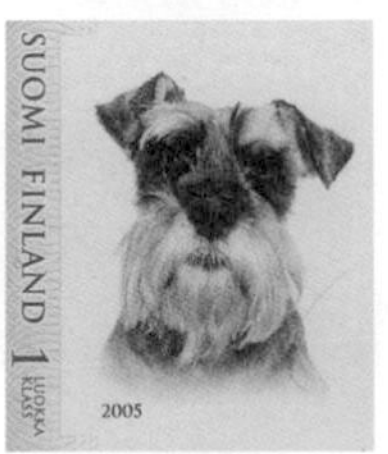

742 Zeus (miniature Schnauzer)

2005. Greetings Stamps. Self-adhesive.
1781 **742** 1 klass (65c.) mult 2·00 1·60

743 Coach (1940)

2005. Centenary of Buses in Finland. Self-adhesive.
1782 **743** 65c. black 2·00 1·60

744 Runners

2005. 10th IAAF World Athletics Championships, Helsinki. Self-adhesive.
1783 **744** 65c. multicoloured 2·00 1·60

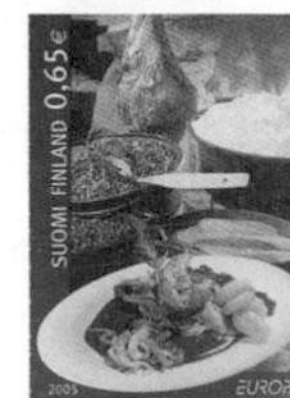

745 Reindeer Meat

2005. Europa. Gastronomy. Multicoloured.
1784 65c. Type **745** 2·00 1·60
1785 65c. Fish and beetroot tartare 2·00 1·60

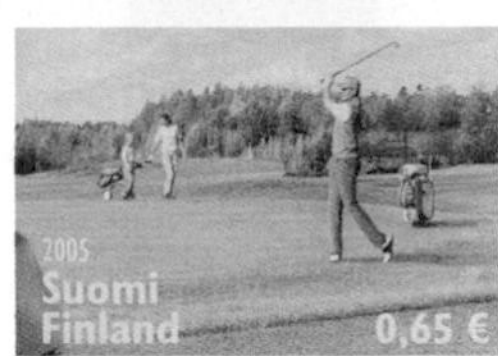

746 Golfer

2005. Golf. Sheet 121×81 mm containing T 746 and similar multicoloured designs.
MS1786 65c.×4, Type **746**; Girl holding flag (vert); Boy putting (vert); Putter and ball 7·75 7·25
The stamps and margins of **MS**1786 were issued together, se-tenant, forming a composite design.

747 Icelandic Pony

2005. Ponies. Self-adhesive. Multicoloured.
1787 1 klass (65c.) Type **747** 1·90 1·50
1788 1 klass (65c.) Welsh pony 1·90 1·50
1789 1 klass (65c.) New Forest pony 1·90 1·50
1790 1 klass (65c.) Shetland pony 1·90 1·50

748 Cloudberry (*Rubus chamaemorus*)

2005. Self-adhesive.
1791 **748** 1 klass (65c.) mult 2·10 1·70

749 *Urho*

2005. Icebreakers (ships). Multicoloured.
1792 1 klass (65c.) Type **749** 1·90 1·50
1793 1 klass (65c.) *Otso* 1·90 1·50
1794 1 klass (65c.) *Fennica* 1·90 1·50
1795 1 klass (65c.) *Botnica* 1·90 1·50

750 Bell Tower

2005. Petajavesi Church. Sheet 80×120 mm containing T 750 and similar vert designs. Multicoloured.
MS1796 65c.×4, Type **750**; Church building (34×40 mm.); Angel (26×38 mm.); Chandelier (26×38 mm.) 7·75 7·25

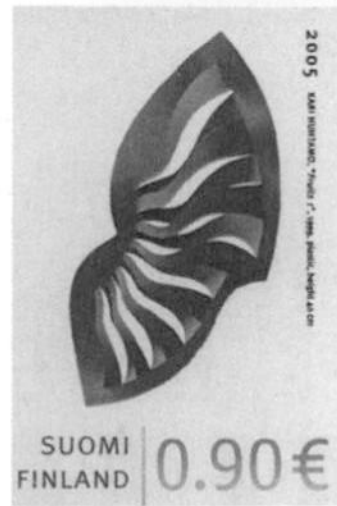
751 "Fruits" (Kari Huhtamo)

2005. Greetings Stamps. Self-adhesive.

1797	**751**	90c. multicoloured	3·00	2·75

752 Father Christmas reading Letters

2005. Christmas. Drawings by Mauri Kunnas. Multicoloured. Self-adhesive.

1798	50c. Type **752**	1·50	1·20
1799	1 klass (65c.) Father and Mrs Christmas dancing (horiz)	2·00	1·60

753 Wood Anemones

2005. 150th Anniv of First Finnish Stamp (1st issue). Sheet 160×97 mm containing T 753 and similar horiz design showing Winter Egg designed by Alma Pihl-Klee and made by Carl Faberge.
MS1800 €3.50×2, Type **753**; Surface of egg 21·00 20·00

754 Early and Modern Postman

2006. Centenary of Postal Union (PAU).

1801	**754**	65c. multicoloured	2·10	1·70

755 Heart

2006. St. Valentine's Day. Self-adhesive.

1802	**755**	65c. pink	2·10	1·70

756 Winter Landscape

2006. Self-adhesive.

1803	**756**	1 klass (65c.) mult	2·10	1·70

757 Atrium

2006. Inauguration of National Library. Self-adhesive.

1804	**757**	1 klass (65c.) mult	2·10	1·70

758 Oldsmobile (1906)

2006. Centenary of Taxis. Each sepia and yellow. Self-adhesive.

1805	65c. Type **758**	1·90	1·50
1806	65c. Chevrolet (1929)	1·90	1·50
1807	65c. Pobeda (1957)	1·90	1·50
1808	65c. Modern Mercedes-Benz	1·90	1·50

759 J. V. Snellman (drawing)

2006. Birth Bicentenary of Johan Vilhelm Snellman (philosopher and journalist). Sheet 140×90 mm containing T 759 and similar horiz designs. Multicoloured.
MS1809 65c.×4, Type **759**; J. V. Snellman on banknote; J. V. Snellman and railway map; Locomotive Ilmarinen 7·75 7·25

760 Emblem

2006. Centenary of Finnish Parliament. Self-adhesive.

1810	**760**	1 klass (65c.) gold, black and lemon	2·10	1·70

761 Bil-Bol (car advertisement) (1907)

2006. Posters by Akseli Gallen-Kallela. Self-adhesive Coil Stamps. Multicoloured.

1811	2 klass (55c.) Type **761**	1·90	1·50
1812	2 klass (55c.) Eroittaja 2 (Helsinki art exhibition) (1906)	1·90	1·50
1813	2 klass (55c.) Concert Finnois (Finnish concert, World Fair, Paris) (1900)	1·90	1·50

762 Flag

2006. 150th Anniv of Finnish Stamps (1st issue). National Flag.

1814	**762**	1 klass (65c.) mult	2·10	1·70

763 Lilac

2006. Self-adhesive.

1815	**763**	1 klass (65c.) mult	2·30	1·90

764 Chick

2006. Easter. Self-adhesive.

1816	**764**	65c. multicoloured	2·10	1·70

765 "Madonna"

2006. Tarvaspaa, Gallen-Kallela Museum. 140th Birth Anniv of Akseli Gallen-Kallela (artist). Self-adhesive. Multicoloured.

1817	1 klass (65c.) Type **765**	2·20	1·80
1818	1 klass (65c.) "Self-portrait"	2·20	1·80
1819	1 klass (65c.) Tarvaspaa building	2·20	1·80

766 "Fortune Teller" (Helene Schjerfbeck)

2006. Self-adhesive.

1820	**766**	95c. multicoloured	3·00	2·50

767 Fairy

2006. Nordic Mythology. Book Illustrations by Rudolf Koivu. Sheet 105×70 mm containing T 767 and similar multicoloured design.
MS1821 65c.×2, Type **767**; Fairy and elf (vert) 4·00 3·75

Stamps of a similar theme were issued by Aland Islands, Denmark, Faroe Islands, Greenland, Iceland, Norway and Sweden.

768 Tandem

2006. Europa. Integration.

1822	**768**	65c. multicoloured	2·10	1·70

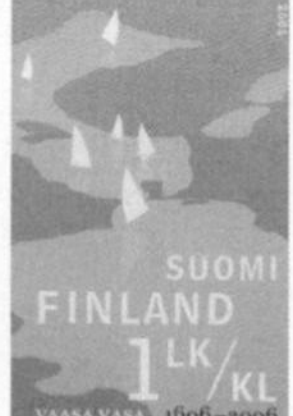
769 Waterway and Sailboats

2006. 400th Anniv of Vaasa.

1823	**769**	1klass (65c.) mult	2·10	1·70

770 Postman's Badge

2006. Personalized Stamp. Self-adhesive.

1824	**770**	1klass (65c.) multicoloured	2·10	1·70

771 King's Port and Pojama Class Frigate

2006. Sveaborg Fortress, Suomenlinna—World Heritage Site. Multicoloured.

1825	1klass Type **771**	2·10	1·70
1826	1klass Von Fersen's Tenaille and Turkoma class frigate	2·10	1·70
1827	1klass Hjarne Bastion and Udema class frigate	2·10	1·70

Stamps of the same design were issued by Sweden.

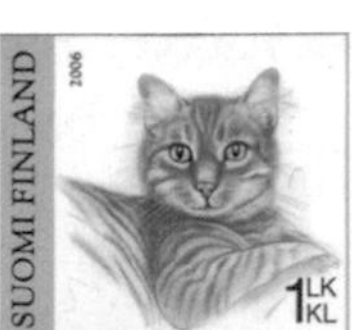
772 Ginger Shorthair

2006. Cats. Self-adhesive. Multicoloured.

1828	1klass (65c.) Type **772**	2·10	1·70
1829	1klass (65c.) British blue shorthair	2·10	1·70
1830	1klass (65c.) Ragdoll	2·10	1·70
1831	1klass (65c.) Persian	2·10	1·70

773 Fishing

2006. Summer. Self-adhesive. Multicoloured.

1832	1klass (65c.) Type **773**	2·10	1·70
1833	1klass (65c.) Children making daisy chains	2·10	1·70
1834	1klass (65c.) Man seated by lake	2·10	1·70
1835	1klass (65c.) Woman picking flowers	2·10	1·70

774 Blueberry (*Vaccinium myrtillus*)

2006. Self-adhesive.

1836	**774**	1klass (70c.) mult	2·30	2·00

775 Family watching Television

2006. Family Life. Self-adhesive.

1837	1 klass (70c.) Type **775**	2·30	2·00
1838	1 klass (70c.) Wife writing letter to husband	2·30	2·00

776 Newspaper Banner and Text

2006. Newspaper Journalism. Self-adhesive.

1839	**776**	70c. black and vermilion	2·30	2·00

777 "Points" (Ritva Puotila)

2006. Personal Stamp. Textile Art. Self-adhesive.

1840	**777**	1klass (70c.) mult	2·30	2·00

778 *Dryas octopetala*

2006. Self-adhesive.

1841	**778**	1klass (70c.) mult	2·30	2·00

779 Horse (Steve Brice, Charles Dash, Carl Eady and Michael Gresham)

2006. Snow Art (ice sculpture). Self-adhesive. Multicoloured.

1842	1klass (70c.) Type **779**	2·30	2·00
1843	1klass (70c.) Snow Castle, Kemi	2·30	2·00
1844	1klass (70c.) Wall (Kimmo Frosti)	2·30	2·00
1845	1klass (70c.) Lantern of snow balls	2·30	2·00

780 Boy and Great Tit

2006. Christmas. Multicoloured. Self-adhesive.

1846	50c. Type **780**	1·80	1·40
1847	1klass (70c.) Waxwing (vert)	2·00	1·60

781 1930 Heraldic Lion (from stamp drawn by Signe Hammarsten-Jansson)

2006. 150th Anniv of First Stamp. Sheet 120×74 mm containing T 781 and similar vert designs.

MS1848 70c. ultramarine and vermilion; 95c. red, ultramarine and vermilion; €1.40 gold, ultramarine, vermilion and red	9·00	8·50

DESIGNS: 70c. Type **781**; 95c. 1856 10k. oval stamp (detail); €1.40 1975 coat of arms (from stamp drawn by Pirkko Vahtero) (detail).

782 Cameraman

2007. 50th Anniv of Television. Self-adhesive.

1849	**782**	70c. multicoloured	2·30	2·00

783 Winter Landscape, Haminalahti (Ferdinand von Wright)

2007. Self-adhesive.

1850	**783**	1 klass (70c.) multicoloured	2·30	2·00

784 Faces (Aino-Maija Metsola)

2007. St. Valentine's Day. Self-adhesive.

1851	**784**	70c. multicoloured	2·30	2·00

785 Polar Landscape and Snow Crystal (image scaled to 46% of original size)

2007. International Polar Year. Sheet 105×70 mm as T 785.

MS1852 70c.×2, Landscape; Snow crystal	4·25	3·75

The stamps of **MS**1852 overlap and share a central area containing hologram of a snow crystal.

786 Logging Truck in Snow (image scaled to 58% of original size)

2007. Centenary of Truck Transport. Self-adhesive. Multicoloured.

1853	70c. Type **786**	2·00	1·60
1854	70c. Milk truck	2·00	1·60
1855	70c. Tipper truck	2·00	1·60
1856	70c. Truck and trailer	2·00	1·60

787 "Sunset" (Aino-Maija Metsola)

2007. Self-adhesive.

1857	**787**	€1.40 multicoloured	2·30	2·00

788 Rabbit with Basket of Eggs

2007. Easter. Self-adhesive.

1858	**788**	1klass (70c.) multicoloured	2·30	2·00

789 Lily "Enchantment"

2007. Self-adhesive.

1859	**789**	1klass (70c.) multicoloured	2·30	2·00

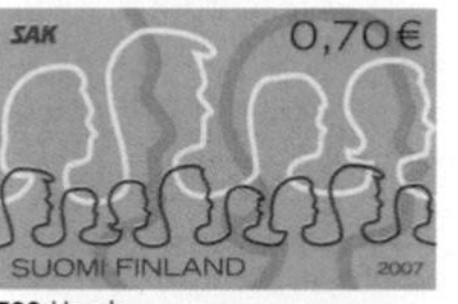

790 Heads

2007. Centenary of Central Organization of Finnish Trade Unions.

1860	**790**	70c. multicoloured	2·30	2·00

791 Young Players

2007. Centenary of Finnish Football Association. Self-adhesive.

1861	**791**	70c. multicoloured	2·30	2·00

No. 1861 has a brief description of Finnish football history on the backing paper.

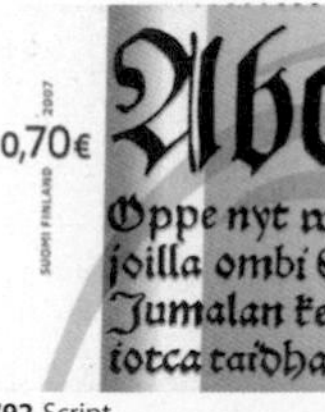

792 Script

2007. 450th Birth Anniv of Mikael Agricola (church reformer and founder of written Finnish). Sheet 140×80 mm containing T 792 and similar vert design. Multicoloured.

MS1862 70c.×2, Type **792**; Preacher	4·25	3·75

793 "Eurovision"

2007. Eurovision Song Contest, Helsinki. Sheet 63×130 mm containing T 793 and similar multicoloured designs. Self-adhesive.

MS1863 70c.×4, Type **793**; Laila Kinunen, Marion Rung, Kirka Babitzin and Katri Helena (49×29 mm); Lordi (band) (49×23 mm); Mr Lordi (Tomi Putaansu) (singer) (35×29 mm)	8·50	8·00

794 Sea Scouts

2007. Europa. Centenary of Scouting. Multicoloured.

1864	70c. Type **794**	2·10	1·70
1865	70c. Girl scouts and campfire	2·10	1·70

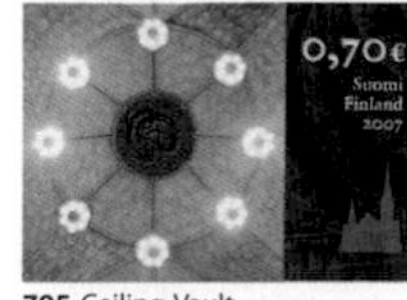

795 Ceiling Vault

2007. Centenary of Tampere Cathedral.

1866	**795**	70c. multicoloured	2·30	2·00

796 Commuter Train

2007. Public Transport. Multicoloured. Self-adhesive. Multicoloured.

1867	1 klass (70c.) Type **796**	2·10	1·70
1868	1 klass (70c.) City tram	2·10	1·70
1869	1 klass (70c.) Metro train	2·10	1·70
1870	1 klass (70c.) Kamppi Bus Terminal	2·10	1·70

797 Little My

2007. Moomins. Multicoloured. Self-adhesive.

1871	1 klass (70c.) Type **797**	2·10	1·70
1872	1 klass (70c.) Moomintroll	2·10	1·70
1873	1 klass (70c.) Moominpappa	2·10	1·70
1874	1 klass (70c.) Snork Maiden	2·10	1·70
1875	1 klass (70c.) Moomin-momma	2·10	1·70
1876	1 klass (70c.) Snufkin	2·10	1·70

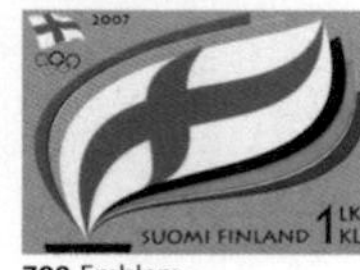

798 Emblem

2007. Centenary of National Olympic Committee. Self-adhesive.

1877	**798**	1 klass (70c.) mult	2·30	2·00

799 Raspberry (*Rubus idaeus*)

2007. Self-adhesive.

1878	**799**	1 klass (70c.) mult	2·30	2·00

800 Wall and Skylight, St John's Church, Mannisto (designed by Juha Leiviska)

2007. Personal Stamp. Architecture. Self-adhesive.

1879	**800**	1 klass (70c.) mult	2·30	2·00

801 'Porvoo Garland' Wallpaper (Biedermeier)

2007. Antiques. Multicoloured. Self-adhesive.

1880	1 klass (70c.) Type **801**	2·30	2·00
1881	1 klass (70c.) '2+3' wallpaper (Ilmari and Annikki Tapiovaara) and 20th-century Paimio chair (Alvar Aalto)	2·30	2·00

802 *Apatura iris* and 19th-century Empire-style Chair

2007. Butterflies. Multicoloured. Self-adhesive.

1882	1 klass (70c.) Type **802**	2·40	2·00
1883	1 klass (70c.) *Scolitantides orion*	2·40	2·00
1884	1 klass (70c.) *Colias palaeno*	2·40	2·00

803 Hauling Wood

2007. Memories of Finland. 90th Anniv of Finnish Independence. Winning Designs in Photography Competition. Sheet 160×104 mm containing T 803 and similar horiz designs. Multicoloured.

MS1885 70c.×8, Type **803** (c.1930); Bonfire (1999); Toddler blowing birch horn (1943); Boy ski jumping (1999); Two pairs of twins on skis (c.1950); Boy leaping into lake (2005); Making coffee outdoors (1958); Ice fisher (2005) 16·00 4·50

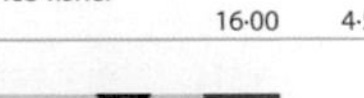
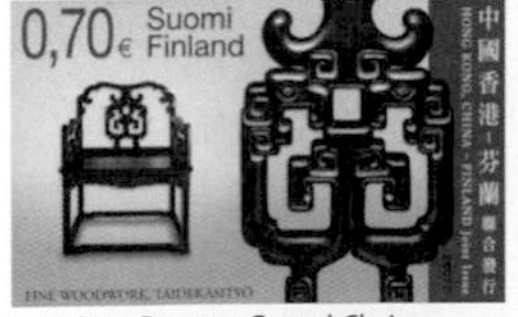

804 Qing Dynasty Carved Chair

2007. Woodcraft. Sheet 106×70 mm containing T 804 and similar horiz design. Multicoloured.

MS1886 106×70 mm. 70c.×2, Type **804**; Wooden bowls 4·75 4·00

Stamps of a similar design were issued by Hong Kong.

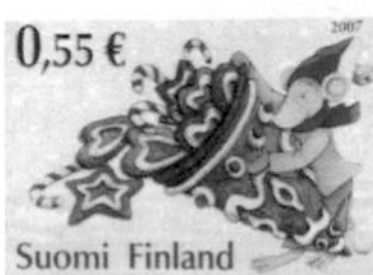

805 Mouse with Gingerbread Cornucopia

2007. Christmas. Multicoloured. Self-adhesive.

1887	55c. Type **805**	1·75	1·50
1888	1 klass (70c.) Mouse and Christmas straw goat (vert)	2·50	2·30

806 Water

807 Water

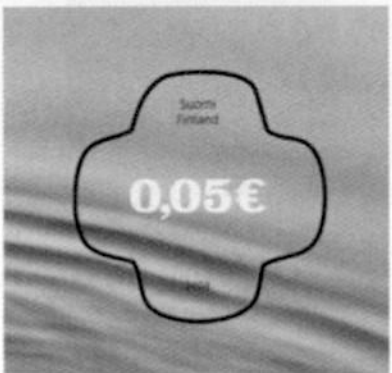

808 Water

809 Archipelago

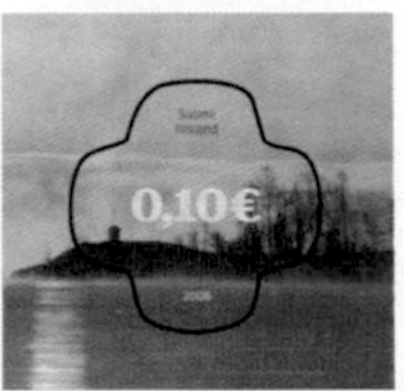

810 Archipelago

811 Archipelago

2008. Landscapes. Water and Archipelago.

1889	**806**	5c. multicoloured	40	20
1890	**807**	5c. multicoloured	40	20
1891	**808**	5c. multicoloured	40	20
1892	**809**	10c. multicoloured	40	20
1893	**810**	10c. multicoloured	40	20
1894	**811**	10c. multicoloured	40	20

Nos. 1889/91 form a composite design of rippling water and 1892/4 form a composite design of an archipelago.

812 Robot

2008. Centenary of University of Technology, Helsinki. Sheet 130×80 mm containing T 812 and similar horiz design.

MS1895 1 Klass (70c.)×2, Type **812**; University building, Otaniemi 5·00 4·50

The stamps and margins of **MS**1895 form a composite design.

813 Matti Raty (free-skier)

2008. Alpine Sports. Sheet containing T 813 and similar multicoloured designs.

MS1896 1 Klass (70c.)×4, Type **813**; Antti Autti (snow-boarder) (*horiz*); Tapio (Arska) Saarimaki (downhill skiing); Tanja Poutianen (slalom) 9·50 9·00

The stamps and margins of **MS**1896 form a composite design.

814 Airplane towing Heart

2008. Greetings Stamps. Sheet 90×130 mm containing T 814 and similar multicoloured designs.

MS1897 1 Klass (70c.)×5, Type **814**; Bird carrying envelope; Heart shaped clouds; Heart shaped air balloon; Hearts in a bottle afloat 12·00 11·00

The stamps and margins of **MS**1897 form a composite design.

815 Icon and Candlestick

2008. Easter. Self-adhesive.

1898	**815**	1 Klass (70c.) mult	2·75	2·50

816 *Master Carl Gustaf Swann at his Desk* (Eero Jarnfelt), *Reading Girls* (Helene Schjerfbeck) and Pixel Mosaic of Children Reading

2008. 150th Anniv of Finnish Book Publishers Association. Self-adhesive.

1899	**816**	1 Klass (70c.) mult	2·75	2·50

817 Sweet Pea Flowers and Braille Letters

2008. 80th Anniv of Finnish Federation of Visually Impaired. Self-adhesive.

1900	**817**	1 Klass (70c.) mult	2·75	2·50

818 Red Fin on Perch (dry weather)

2008. Folklore Weather Forecasting. Multicoloured. Self-adhesive.

1901	1 Klass (70c.) Type **818**	2·75	2·50
1902	1 Klass (70c.) Sheep gambolling (wet weather)	2·75	2·50
1903	1 Klass (70c.) Frogs taking long hops (dry weather)	2·75	2·50
1904	1 Klass (70c.) Low flying swallows (wet weather)	2·75	2·50
1905	1 Klass (70c.) Snail with feelers extended (dry weather)	2·75	2·50

819 Desk, Porcelain Clock (Arabia) and Lamp

2008. Antiques. Art Nouveau. Self-adhesive.

1906	**819**	€1.05 multicoloured	4·00	4·00

820 Rock God of Astuvansalmi

2008. Norse Mythology. Mythical Places. Sheet 105×70 mm containing T 820 and similar vert design.

MS1907 70c.×2, Type **820**; Amber head (found at Astuvansalmi) 5·50 5·25

Stamps of a similar theme were issued by Aland Islands, Denmark, Faroe Islands, Greenland, Iceland, Norway and Sweden.

821 Script and Pekka Halonen

2008. Europa. The Letter. Letters between Pekka Halonen and his Wife, Maija. Multicoloured.

1908	70c. Type **821**	2·75	2·50
1909	70c. Script and Maija Halonen	2·75	2·50

822 *Deilephila elpenor*

2008. Moths. Multicoloured. Self-adhesive.

1910	1 Klass (70c.) Type **822**	2·75	2·50
1911	1 Klass (70c.) *Aglia tau*	2·75	2·50
1912	1 Klass (70c.) *Arctia caja*	2·75	2·50

Nos. 1910/12 each include a clear varnish overprint showing the wing of the relevant insect.

823 Melting Cake

2008. Greetings Stamps. Multicoloured. Self-adhesive.

1913	1 Klass (70c.) Type **823**	2·75	2·50
1914	1 Klass (70c.) Guitars	2·75	2·50
1915	1 Klass (70c.) Winged face	2·75	2·50
1916	1 Klass (70c.) High-heeled boots	2·75	2·50
1917	1 Klass (70c.) Balloons	2·75	2·50
1918	1 Klass (70c.) Stilt walkers	2·75	2·50
1918	1 Klass (70c.) Stilt walkers	2·75	2·50

No. 1913/18 form a composite design.

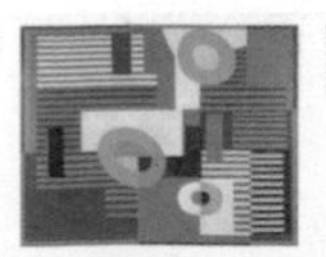

824 *Sinista ja punaista/Blatt och vitt* (Sam Vanni)

2008. Art. Multicoloured. Self-adhesive.

1919	1 Klass (70c.) Type **824**	2·75	2·50
1920	1 Klass (70c.) *Merirosvol-aiva/Sjorovarfartyg* (Kimmo Kaivanto)	2·75	2·50
1921	1 Klass (70c.) *Hiljaisuuden ku-untelija/Lyssnar till tystnaden* (Juhani Linnovaara)	2·75	2·50
1922	1 Klass (70c.) *Odotan kevaan tuloa/Jag väntar pa varen* (Goran Auguston)	2·75	2·50
1923	1 Klass (70c.) *Minaa/Jag* (Caro-lus Enckell)	2·75	2·50
1924	1 Klass (70c.) *Poyta, Bord* (Reino Heitanen)	2·75	2·50

825 Rising Island and Scale

2008. Kvarken Archipelago—UNESCO World Heritage Site. Self-adhesive.

1925	**825**	€1.50 black and vermilion	5·50	5·25

826 Fireworks

2008. Personal Stamp.

1925a	**826**	1klass (80c.) indigo	3·25	3·00

827 Mika Waltari

2008. Birth Centenary of Mika Waltari (writer). Sheet 100×80 mm containing T 827 and similar vert design. Multicoloured.

MS1926 80c.×2, Type **827**; Cover of *Komisario Palmun Erehdys* (novel) (drawn by Eeeli Jaatinen) 6·25 6·25

828 Kimi Raikkonen

2008. Kimi Raikkonen—2007 Formula One World Champion. Sheet 132×70 mm containing T 828 and similar vert design. Multicoloured.

MS1927 1klass (80c.)×2, Type **828**; Ferrari race car (74×31 mm) 6·25 6·25

829 Finnish Spitz

2008. Dogs. Self-adhesive gum. Multicoloured.

1928	1 Klass (80c.) Type **829**	3·25	3·00
1929	1 Klass (80c.) Collie	3·25	3·00
1930	1 Klass (80c.) Boxer	3·25	3·00
1931	1 Klass (80c.) Finnish hound	3·25	3·00
1932	1 Klass (80c.) King Charles spaniel	3·25	3·00
1933	1 Klass (80c.) Jack Russell terrier	3·25	3·00

830 Adolf Nordenskiold

2008. 140th Anniv of Adolf Erik Nordenskiold's Arctic Expedition to Svalbard. Sheet 165×60 mm containing T 830 and similar multicoloured design.

MS1934 1klass (80c.)×2, Type **830**; *Sofia* (expedition ship), 1883 (date of voyage to Greenland) (58×33 mm) 6·00 6·00

831 Bear's and their Christmas Tree

2008. Christmas. Multicoloured.

1935	60c. Type **831**	2·75	2·50
1936	1klass (80c.) Animals encircling Christmas tree (horiz)	3·50	3·25

832 Snowflake

2008. Frosty Night. Transparent plastic.

1937	**832**	1klass (80c.) multicoloured	3·50	3·25

833 Martti Ahtisaari

2008. Martti Ahtisaari–Nobel Peace Prize Winner, 2008.

1938	**833**	80c. blue	3·75	3·50

834 Nurses

2009. In Praise of Hospital Workers.

1939	**834**	80c. multicoloured	3·50	3·25

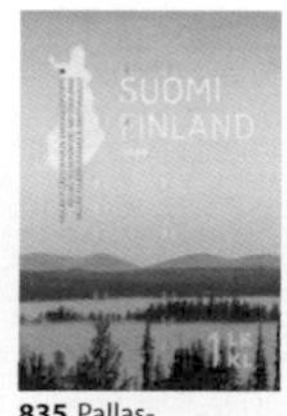

835 Pallas-Yllastunturi, Lapland

2009. National Parks. Self-adhesive.

1940	**835**	1 klass (80c.) multicoloured	3·00	2·75

836 Tsar Alexander I of Russia

2009. Bicentenary of Nationhood. Sheet 147×105 mm containing T 836 and similar vert designs. Multicoloured.

MS1941 80c.×4, Type **836**; George Magnus Sprengtporten; Carl Erik Mannerheim; Gustaf Mauritz Armfelt 13·00 13·00

837 Boy as Policeman

2009. Multicultural Finland.Showing children. Multicoloured. Self-adhesive.

1942	1 klass (80c.) Type **837**	3·25	3·00
1943	1 klass (80c.) As doctor	3·25	3·00
1944	1 klass (80c.) As fire crew	3·00	3·25
1945	1 klass (80c.) As skier	3·25	3·00
1946	1 klass (80c.) As construction worker	3·25	3·00

838 Dressing Up

2009. Greetings Stamps. Sheet 103×100 mm containing T 838 and similar droplet shaped designs. Multicoloured. Self-adhesive.

MS1947 1 klass (80c.) ×5, Type **838**; Cupid; Temple; Bear holding heart; Two swans with necks entwined 16·00 16·00

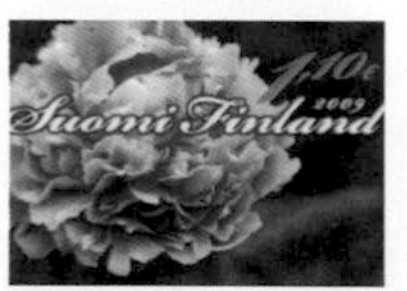

839 Peony

2009. Self-adhesive.

1948	**839**	€1.10 multicoloured	1·00	1·00

840 Roast Lamb, Potatoes and Chocolate Mousse

2009. Easter. Self-adhesive.

1949	**840**	1 Klass (80c.) multicoloured	3·25	3·00

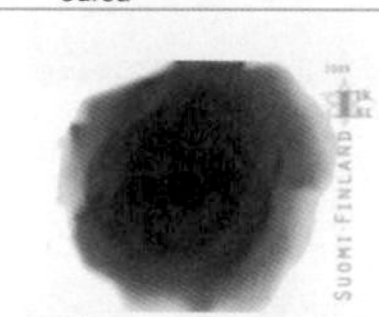
841 Rose

2009. Self-adhesive.

1950	**841**	1 Klass (80c.) multicoloured	3·25	3·00

842 Emblem and Sky

2009. Preserve Polar Regions and Glaciers. Sheet 80×120 mm containing T 842 and similar circular design. Multicoloured.

MS1951 1 Klass (80c.)×2, Type **842**; Emblem and polar sea 6·50 6·50

843 Parcel and Tulips

2009. Greetings Stamps. Multicoloured.

1952	1 Klass (80c.) Type **843**	3·25	3·00
1953	1 Klass (80c.) Strawberries and cake	3·25	3·00
1954	1 Klass (80c.) Dahlias	3·25	3·00
1955	1 Klass (80c.) Cup of coffee	3·25	3·00
1956	1 Klass (80c.) Dove	3·25	3·00

844 Moon, Celestial Phenomena and Lake

2009. Europa. Astronomy. Multicoloured.

1957	80c. Type **844**	3·50	3·25
1958	80c. Celestial phenomena, lake, Saturn and planets	3·50	3·25

Nos. 1957/8 were printed, se-tenant, in horizontal pairs within the sheet, each pair forming a composite design.

845 Dress (Anna and Tuomas Laiten)

2009. Fashion. Sheet 160×110 mm containing T 845 and similar multicoloured designs. Self-adhesive.

MS1959 1 Klass (80c.)×5, Type **845**; Handbag (Lumi (Sanna Kantola)) (29×34 mm); Dress (Jasmin Santanen); Red shoes (Minna Parikka) (29×25 mm); Grey shoes (Finsk by Julia Lundsten) (29×31 mm) 16·00 16·00

846 Moominmama

2009. Moomins (cartoon strip by Tove Jansson). Each lemon and black, colour of face value given. Self-adhesive.

1960	1 Klass (80c.) Type **846**	3·50	3·25
1961	1 Klass (80c.) Moominpappa (bright yellow-green)	3·50	3·25
1962	1 Klass (80c.) Little My (new blue)	3·50	3·25
1963	1 Klass (80c.) Snork Maiden (magenta)	3·50	3·25
1964	1 Klass (80c.) Moomintroll and Snufkins (bright yellow-green)	3·50	3·25
1965	1 Klass (80c.) Moominpappa trips (bright orange)	3·50	3·25

847 Towels, Bucket and Birch Twigs

2009. Sauna. Multicoloured. Self-adhesive.

1966	1 Klass (80c.) Type **843**	3·50	3·25
1967	1 Klass (80c.) Men in sauna	3·50	3·25
1968	1 Klass (80c.) Lake and sauna building	3·50	3·25
1969	1 Klass (80c.) Birch twigs (vert)	3·50	3·25
1970	1 Klass (80c.) Bowls (vert)	3·50	3·25

849 Desk, Porcelain Clock (Arabia) and Lamp

2009. Antiques. Gustavian. Self-adhesive.

1971	**849**	1 Klass (80c.) multicoloured	3·50	3·25

No. 1971 has a brief description of the stamp on the backing paper.

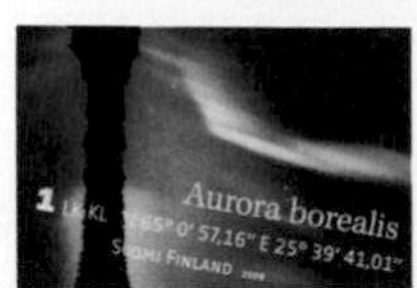

850 Aurora borealis

2009. Aurora borealis. Multicoloured. Self-adhesive.

1972	1 Klass (80c.) Type **850**	3·50	3·25
1973	1 Klass (80c.) Aurora borealis, blue, central burst	3·50	3·25
1974	1 Klass (80c.) Aurora borealis, green, conifers at left	3·50	3·25

851 *Leijonankitoja* (Helene Schjerfbeck)

2009. Art. Multicoloured. Self-adhesive.

1975	1 Klass (80c.) Type **851**	3·50	3·25
1976	1 Klass (80c.) Irises (*Kukkivat lirikset* (Waino Aaltonen))	3·50	3·25
1977	1 Klass (80c.) Peonies (*Juhannusruusuja* (Eero Jarnefelt))	3·50	3·25
1978	1 Klass (80c.) Arum (*Yksinainen kalla* (Ester Helenius))	3·50	3·25
1979	1 Klass (80c.) Amaryllis blooms in vase (*Amaryllisasetelma* (Birger Carlstedt))	3·50	3·25
1980	1 Klass (80c.) Carnation (*Neilikka-asetelma* (Tuomas von Boehm))	3·50	3·25

852 Wreath

2009. Christmas is Near (Finnish carol). Multicoloured. Self-adhesive.

1981	60c. Type **852**	2·75	2·50
1982	60c. Girl with apples	2·75	2·50

853 Amaryllis

2009. Christmas. Self-adhesive.

1983	**853**	1st Klass (80c.) multicoloured	3·50	3·25

854 Reindeer

2009. Personal Stamp. Winter Magic. Self-adhesive.

1984	**854**	1st Klass (80c.) multicoloured	3·50	3·25

855 *Antennaria dioica*

2010. Flora. Self-adhesive.

1985	**855**	1st Klass (80c.) multicoloured	3·50	3·25

856 Seated Flower Fairy

2010. St Valentine's Day. Fairies. Sheet 110×130 mm containing T 856 and similar vert designs. Multicoloured. Self-adhesive.

MS1986 1k.×5, Type **856**; Fairy carrying red heart; Fairy on swing; Fairy playing violin; Fairy with string of stars	18·00	18·00

Several techniques were used to print **MS**1986 giving an effect of varnish and glitter, the whole forming a composite design.

857 Eppu Normaali

2010. Rock and Pop Musicians. Multicoloured. Self-adhesive.

1987	1k. Type **857**	3·50	3·25
1988	1k. Yo	3·50	3·25
1989	1k. Maarit	3·50	3·25
1990	1k. Dingo	3·50	3·25
1991	1k. Popeda	3·50	3·25
1992	1k. Mamba	3·50	3·25

858 Rings (designed by Kirsti Doukas)

2010. My Easter. Self-adhesive.

1993	**858**	1k. multicoloured	3·50	3·25

859 Rabbit Twins

2010. Easter. Self-adhesive.

1994	**859**	1k. multicoloured	3·50	3·25

860 Tomato

2010. Funny Vegetables. Multicoloured. Self-adhesive.

1995	1k. Type **860**	3·50	3·25
1996	1k. Two onions	3·50	3·25
1997	1k. Pumpkin	3·50	3·25
1998	1k. Marrow	3·50	3·25
1999	1k. Aubergine	3·50	3·25
2000	1k. Carrot	3·50	3·25
2001	1k. Broccoli	3·50	3·25
2002	1k. Potato	3·50	3·25

861 Children with Fish

2010. Romance of the Countryside. Each brownish black and gold.

2003	1k. Type **861**	2·75	2·50
2004	1k. Barn, pony, girls and wild strawberries	2·75	2·50
2005	1k. Old style tractor	2·75	2·50
2006	1k. Hay stooks, milk churns and woman milking by hand	2·75	2·50
2007	1k. Musicians and dancers	2·75	3·50

862 Rita-Liisa Pohjalinen (jewelry, clothing and art designer)

2010. Famous Finnish Women. Multicoloured.

2008	1k. Type **862**	2·75	2·50
2009	1k. Elina Haavio-Mannila (sociologist)	2·75	2·50
2010	1k. Aira Samulin (dance instructor and entrepreneur)	2·75	2·50
2011	1k. Maria-Liisa Nevala (literary scholar and National Theatre director)	2·75	2·50
2012	1k. Laila Hirvisaari (writer)	2·75	2·50
2013	1k. Leena Palotie (geneticist)	2·75	2·50

863 Trawler

2010. Life at the Coast. Norden by the Sea. Multicoloured.

MS2014 105x70 mm. 1k. x 2, Type **863**; Yacht (vert)	5·25	5·25

The stamps and margins of **MS**2008 form a composite design.

Stamps of a similar theme were issued by Aland, Denmark, Greenland, Faröe Islands, Iceland, Norway and Sweden.

864 Butterfly

2010. Personal Stamp

2015	**864**	1k. multicoloured	3·00	3·00

865 Children, Book Cover as Door and Characters

2010. Europa. Multicoloured.

2016	80c. Type **865**	2·75	2·50
2017	80c. Boy and characters reading	2·75	2·50

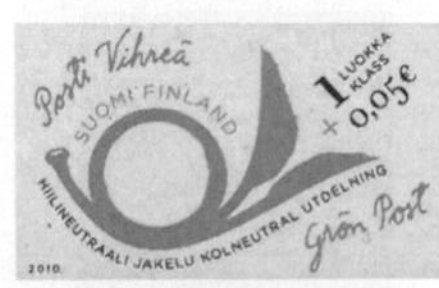

866 Posthorn as Leaves

2010. Carbon Neutral Stamp

2018	**866**	1klass (80c.)+5c. apple green and black	3·00	2·75

The premium was for funding of Solar Power Plant.

867 Kirnu, Aerial View

2010. Expo 2010, Shanghai. Kirnu (giant's kettle) (Finnish pavillion). Multicoloured.

MS2019 130x70 mm. 1k.x2, Type **867**; Kirnu, external view	5·50	5·50

868 Male Figure

2010. Greetings Stamps. Multicoloured, figure colour given.

MS2020 195x95 mm. 1k.x5, Type **868**; Female figure (magenta); Female (yellow); Male (new blue); Female (bright blue-green)	13·50	13·50

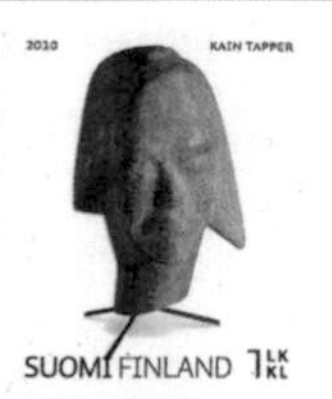

869 Hymy (Kain Tapper)

2010. Finnish Sculpture. Multicoloured.

2021	1k. Type **869**	2·75	2·50
2022	1k. *Hefaistos* (Laila Pullinen)	2·75	2·50
2023	1k. *Polkupyöräilija* (Pekko Aarnio)	2·75	2·50
2024	1k. *Konstructio* (Kari Huhtamo)	2·75	2·50
2025	1k. *Salvos* (Mauno Hartman) (55×21 mm)	2·75	2·50
2026	1k. *Joy* (Miina Äkkijrkka) (55×21 mm)	2·75	2·50

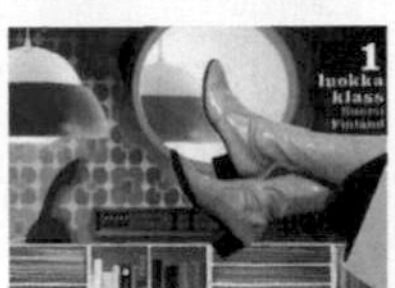
870 Iconic Designs of 1960's

2010. 1960's Pop Antiques

2027	**870**	1k. multicoloured	2·75	2·50

871 Tree and Moorland

2010. Torronsuo National Park

2028	**871**	1k. multicoloured	2·75	2·50

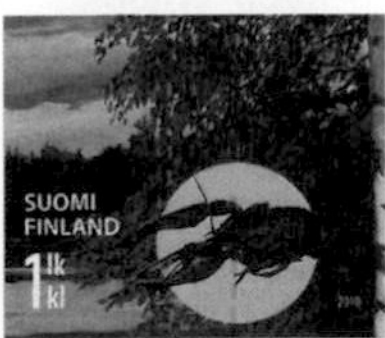

872 Freshwater Crayfish

2010. Autumn. Multicoloured.

MS2029 130x70 mm. 1k.x3, Type **872**; Mallard; Elk	7·75	7·75

No. **MS**2029 was embossed with the stamp values and country name in Braille.

873 Santa Claus

2010. Finland–Japan Winter Stamps. Multicoloured.
MS2030 187x68 mm. 55c.x5, Type **873**; Poinsettias with bell and ribbon; Santa's sleigh flying over church (horiz); Heart-shaped wreath; Reindeer 9·50 9·50

Stamps of the same design were issued by Japan.

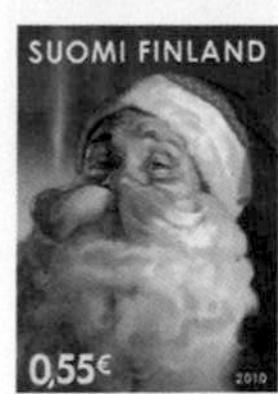

874 Santa Claus

2010. Christmas. Multicoloured.

2031		55c. Type **874**	90	80
2032		55c. Santa's reindeer	90	80
2033		1 Klass (80c.) Santa's sleigh flying over Finnish landscape (horiz)	2·20	2·00

Stamps of a similar design were issued by Japan.

875 Bud

2011. Birch. Multicoloured.

2034		20c. Type **875**	1·00	90
2035		30c. Leaves and catkins	1·20	1·10

876 Bird perching

2011. Spring Stamps. Multicoloured.

2036		2k. Type **876**	2·50	2·40
2037		2k. Bird in flight, facing left	2·50	2·40
2038		2k. Flowers	2·50	2·40
2039		2k. Bird perching, singing, facing left	2·50	2·40
2040		2k. Bird in flight, facing right	2·50	2·40

877 Scene from The Red Line (Aulis Sallinen)

2011. Centenary of Finnish National Opera
MS2041 80x120 mm. 2k.x4, Type **877**; Couple running towards each other (*Der Rosenkavalier* (Richard Strauss)) (horiz); Couple embracing (*Der Rosenkavalier*) (horiz); Woman wearing red (*The Last Temptations* (Joonas Kokkonen)) 10·00 10·00

878 Bird

879 Friendship (image scaled to 40% of original size)

2011. Friendship Day (St. Valetine's Day). T **878** forming overall design T **879**. Multicoloured.
MS2042 120x120 mm. 2k.x5, Type **878**; Magenta bird, blue background with yellow baubles; Green bird, orange background with green baubles; Large green bird, yellow background with purple baubles; Blue bird, magenta background with blue baubles 12·50 12·50

880 Mailbox

2011. Mailboxes. Multicoloured.

2043		2k. Type **880**	2·50	2·40
2044		2k. Snow-covered, house-shaped mailbox	2·50	2·40
2045		2k. Boy collecting mail from green mailbox	2·50	2·40
2046		2k. Shelter and mailbox inscribed '012'	2·50	2·40
2047		2k. Top opening metal mailbox inscribed '4' and 'POSTI'	2·50	2·40

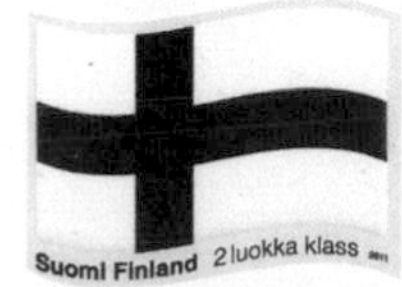

881 Siniristilippu ('Blue Cross Flag')

2011. National Flag

2048	**881**	2k. ultramarine	2·75	2·50

MILITARY FIELD POST

M76

1941. No value indicated. Imperf.

M352	**M76**	(-) black on red	30	60

M86

1943. No value indicated.

M392	**M86**	(-) green	30	35
M393	**M86**	(-) purple	30	40

1943. Optd KENTTA-POSTI FALTPOST.

M394	**31**	2m. orange	30	65
M395	**31**	3½m. blue	30	50

1944. As Type M 86, but smaller (20x16 mm) and inscr "1944".

M396		(-) violet	25	25
M397		(-) green	25	30

M222

1963. No value indicated.

M688	**M222**	(-) violet	£120	£130

1983. No. M688 optd 1983.

M1043		(-) violet	£150	£110

PARCEL POST STAMPS

P118

1949. Printed in black on coloured backgrounds. Roul.

P471	**P118**	1m. green	2·20	3·25
P472	**P118**	5m. red	16·00	16·00
P473	**P118**	20m. orange	29·00	27·00
P474	**P118**	50m. blue	14·00	12·50
P475	**P118**	100m. brown	14·00	12·50

P137

1952

P507	**P137**	5m. red	3·50	3·75
P508	**P137**	20m. orange	8·00	4·75
P509	**P137**	50m. blue	18·00	10·00
P510	**P137**	100m. brown	24·00	16·00

P216

1963. Figures of value in black.

P647	**P216**	5p. mauve	2·40	2·00
P648	**P216**	20p. orange	2·75	3·25
P649	**P216**	50p. blue	3·00	3·00
P650	**P216**	1m. brown	2·20	4·25

P403 "SISU" Bus

1981. Figures of values in black.

P1003	**P403**	50p. blue	90	3·75
P1004	**P403**	1m. brown	1·30	4·00
P1005	**P403**	5m. green	3·50	8·50
P1006	**P403**	10m. purple	4·50	17·00

Pt. 10

FINNISH OCCUPATION OF AUNUS

The Russian town of Olonets was occupied by Finnish troops from April 1919 to May 1919.

1919. Arms of Finland optd Aunus.

1	**19**	5p. green	6·50	10·50
2	**19**	10p. pink	6·50	10·50
3	**19**	20p. orange	6·50	10·50
4	**19**	40p. violet	6·50	10·50
5	**19**	50p. brown	70·00	£110
6	**19**	1m. black and pink	80·00	£130
7	**19**	5m. black and lilac	£300	£475
8	**19**	10m. black and brown	£800	£1300

Pt. 10

FINNISH OCCUPATION OF EASTERN KARELIA

Part of Russia, extending East to Lake Onega, occupied by Finland from 1941 to 1944.

100 penni = 1 markka

1941. Types of Finland in unissued colours optd ITA-KARJALA Sot.hallinto. (a) Arms and pictorial issue.

1A	**31**	50p. green	40	1·10
2A	**31**	1m.75 grey	1·60	1·10
10	**31**	2m. orange	50	1·30
11	**31**	2m.75 orange	30	70
12	**31**	3½m. blue	50	1·30
13	**32**	5m. purple	1·10	3·00
14	-	10m. brown (as No. 276b)	1·90	5·25
15	-	25m. green (as No. 277)	2·10	6·00

(b) President Ryti.

16	**76**	50p. green	30	1·10
17	**76**	1m.75 slate	30	1·10
18	**76**	2m. red	30	1·10
19	**76**	2m.75 brown	45	1·10
20	**76**	3m.50 blue	45	1·10
21	**76**	5m. purple	45	1·10

(c) Marshal Mannerheim.

22	**77**	50p. green	45	1·10
23	**77**	1m.75 slate	45	1·10
24	**77**	2m. red	45	1·10
25	**77**	2m.75 brown	30	1·10
26	**77**	3m.50 blue	30	1·10
27	**77**	5m. purple	30	1·10

4 Arms of E. Karelia

1943. National Relief Fund.

28	**4**	3m.50+1m.50 olive	40	1·90

Pt. 8

FIUME

A seaport and territory on the Adriatic Sea formerly belonging to Hungary and occupied by the Allies in 1918/19. Between 1919 and 1924 the territory was a Free State, controlled by D'Annunzio and his legionaries, until annexation to Italy in 1924. For later issues see Fiume and Kupa Zone; Venezia Giulia. Ceded to Yugoslavia in 1947 and now known as Rijeka.

1918. 100 filler = 1 krone.
1919. 100 centesimi = 1 corona.
1920. 100 centesimi = 1 lira.

1918. Various issues of Hungary optd FIUME. On "Harvesters" and "Parliament" issue of 1916.

1	**18**	2f. brown	5·25	2·75
2	**18**	3f. red	5·25	2·75
3	**18**	5f. green	5·25	2·75
4	**18**	6f. green	5·25	2·75
5	**18**	10f. red (No. 250)	55·00	32·00
6	**18**	10f. red (No. 243)	55·00	32·00
7	**18**	15f. violet (No. 251)	5·25	2·75
8	**18**	15f. violet (No. 244)	37·00	19·00
9	**18**	20f. brown	5·25	2·75
10	**18**	25f. blue	9·50	3·25
11	**18**	35f. brown	10·50	5·25
12	**18**	40f. olive	90·00	32·00
13	**19**	50f. purple	6·50	4·25
14	**19**	75f. blue	13·00	5·25
15	**19**	80f. green	13·00	4·25
16	**19**	1k. lake	35·00	9·50
17	**19**	2k. brown	10·50	5·25
18	**19**	3k. grey and violet	48·00	19·00
19	**19**	5k. brown	90·00	27·00
20	**19**	10k. lilac and brown	£325	£225

On "Charles" and "Zita" issue of 1918.

21	**27**	10f. red	4·25	4·25
22	**27**	20f. brown	3·25	3·25
23	**28**	40f. olive	27·00	10·50

On War charity issue of 1916.

24	**20**	10+2f. red	6·50	4·25
25	-	15+2f. violet	6·50	4·25
26	**22**	40+2f. lake	8·50	4·25

On Newspaper issue of 1900.

27	**N9**	(2f.) orange	4·25	2·10

On Express Letter stamp of 1916.

28	**E18**	2f. olive and red	4·25	3·25

On Saving Bank stamp and surch FRANCO and value.

29	**B17**	15 on 10f. purple	17·00	15·00

On Postage Due stamps of 1915 with figures in red and surch FRANCO and value.

30	**D9**	45 on 6f. green	10·50	13·00
31	**D9**	45 on 20f. green	27·00	13·00

2 Liberty

3 Clock Tower over Market in Fiume

4

5 Port of Fiume

1919. Inscr "FIUME".

32	**2**	2c. blue	1·10	1·10
33	**2**	3c. brown	1·10	1·10
35	**2**	5c. green	1·10	1·10
36	**3**	10c. red	27·00	10·50
57	**3**	15c. violet	1·10	1·10

39	3	20c. green	2·10	1·60
59	4	25c. blue	2·10	1·10
60	5	30c. violet	3·25	2·10
43	4	40c. brown	2·10	2·10
62	4	45c. orange	2·10	1·60
63	5	50c. green	2·10	1·10
46	5	60c. lake	2·10	1·10
65	5	1cor. brown	4·25	1·60
48	5	2cor. blue	4·25	2·10
49	5	3cor. red	5·25	2·10
50	5	5cor. brown	27·00	27·00
51	5	10cor. olive	24·00	65·00

6 Statue of Romulus, Remus and Wolf

1919. Students' Education Fund. 200th Day of Peace.

71	6	5c.+5l. green	16·00	10·50
72	6	10c.+5l. red	16·00	10·50
73	6	15c.+5l. grey	16·00	10·50
74	6	20c.+5l. orange	16·00	10·50
75	-	45c.+5l. olive	16·00	10·50
76	-	60c.+5l. red	16·00	10·50
77	-	80c.+5l. violet	16·00	10·50
78	-	1cor.+5l. grey	16·00	10·50
79	-	2cor.+5l. red	16·00	10·50
80	-	3cor.+5l. brown	16·00	10·50
81	-	5cor.+5l. brown	16·00	10·50
82	-	10cor.+5l. violet	16·00	10·50

DESIGNS—HORIZ: 45, 60, 80c., 1cor. 13th-century Venetian war galley; 2, 3, 5, 10cor. Piazza of St. Mark, Venice.

1919. As T 2 to 5, but inscr "POSTA FIUME".

83	2	5c. green	1·10	1·10
84	3	10c. red	2·10	1·10
85	5	30c. violet	5·25	3·25
86	4	40c. brown	2·10	3·25
87	4	45c. orange	3·25	2·10
88	5	50c. green	7·50	5·25
89	5	60c. lake	7·50	5·25
90	5	10cor. olive	7·50	13·00

9 Dr. Grossich

1919. Dr. Grossich Foundation.

91	9	25c. (+2cor.) blue	3·25	4·25

1919. Stamps of 1919 surch FRANCO and value. (a) Inscr "FIUME".

92	3	5 on 20c. green	1·10	1·10
93	4	10 on 45c. orange	1·10	1·10
94	5	25 on 50c. green	16·00	29·00
95	5	55 on 1cor. brown	43·00	27·00
96	5	55 on 2cor. blue	5·25	8·50
97	5	55 on 3cor. red	5·25	8·50
98	5	55 on 5cor. brown	5·25	8·50

(b) Inscr "POSTA FIUME".

99	4	5 on 25c. blue	1·10	1·10
100	5	15 on 30c. violet	1·10	1·10
101	4	15 on 45c. orange	1·10	1·10
102	5	15 on 60c. lake	1·10	1·10
103	5	25 on 50c. green	1·10	1·10
104	5	55 on 10cor. olive	27·00	32·00

1919. Nos. 71/82 and 91 surch Valore globale and value.

105	6	5c. on 5c. green		2·10
106	6	10c. on 10c. red		2·10
107	6	15c. on 15c. grey		2·10
108	6	20c. on 20c. orange		2·10
109	-	45c. on 45c. green		2·10
110	-	60c. on 60c. red		2·10
111	-	80c. on 80c. violet		1·10
112	-	1cor. on 1cor. grey		1·10
113	-	2cor. on 2cor. brown		3·25
114	-	3cor. on 3cor. brown		6·50
115	-	5cor. on 5cor. brown		7·50
122	9	25c. on 25c. blue		1·10
130	-	10cor. on 10cor. violet		2·10

16 Gabriele d'Annunzio

1920. Background in ochre

131	16	5c. green		1·10
132	16	10c. red		1·10
133	16	15c. grey		1·10
134	16	20c. orange		1·10
135	16	25c. blue		2·10
136	16	30c. brown		2·10
137	16	45c. olive		3·25
138	16	50c. lilac		3·25
139	16	55c. yellow		3·25
140	16	1l. black		19·00
141	16	2l. red		19·00
142	16	3l. green		19·00
143	16	5l. brown		43·00
144	16	10l. lilac		24·00

1920. Nos. M145/8 optd Reggenza Italiana del Carnaro or surch also.

146	M17	1 on 5c. green		1·10
147	-	2 on 25c. blue		1·10
148	M17	5c. green		2·10
149	-	10c. red		2·10
150	-	15 on 10c. red		2·10
151	-	15 on 20c. brown		2·10
152	-	15 on 25c. blue		2·10
153	-	20c. brown		2·10
154	-	25c. blue	2·10	2·10
155	-	25 on 10c. red		2·10
156	-	55 on 20c. brown		3·25
157	M17	55 on 5c. green		4·25
158	-	1l. on 10c. red		24·00
159	-	1l. on 25c. blue		95·00
160	M17	2l. on 5c. green		32·00
161	-	5l. on 10c. red		£160
162	-	10l. onn 20c. brown		£550

1921. Issue of d'Annunzio optd Governo Provvisorio or also surch LIRE UNA (No. 173).

163	16	5c. green	1·10	1·10
164	16	10c. red	1·10	1·10
165	16	15c. grey	1·10	1·10
166	16	20c. orange	2·10	2·10
167	16	25c. blue	2·10	2·10
168	16	30c. brown	2·10	2·10
169	16	45c. olive	2·10	2·10
170	16	50c. lilac	3·25	2·10
171	16	55c. yellow	2·10	2·10
172	16	1l. black	£160	£140
173	16	1l. on 30c. brown	1·10	3·25
174	16	2l. red	32·00	32·00
175	16	3l. green	32·00	32·00
176	16	5l. brown	32·00	32·00
177	16	10l. lilac	32·00	32·00

1921. Charity Stamps of 1919 optd 24 - IV - 1921 Costituente Fiumana (and L over "Cor." in high values).

178	5c. green	2·10	3·25
179	10c. red	2·10	3·25
180	15c. grey	2·10	3·25
181	20c. orange	2·10	3·25
182	45c. green	7·50	8·50
183	60c. red	7·50	8·50
184	80c. violet	10·50	10·50
185	1l. on 1cor. grey	13·00	15·00
186	1l. on 2cor. brown	65·00	2·10
187	3l. on 3cor. brown	65·00	75·00
188	5l. on 5cor. brown	65·00	4·25
189	10l. on 10cor. violet	85·00	85·00

1922. Charity Stamps of 1919 optd 24 - IV - 1921 Costituente Fiumana 1922 (and L over "Cor." in high values).

190	5c. green	3·25	3·25
191	10c. red	1·10	1·10
192	15c. grey	18·00	8·50
193	20c. orange	2·10	2·10
194	45c. green	13·00	10·50
195	60c. red	1·10	3·25
196	80c. violet	1·10	3·25
197	1l. on 1cor. grey	2·10	3·25
198	2l. on 2cor. brown	19·00	13·00
199	3l. on 3cor. brown	2·10	3·25
200	5l. on 5cor. brown	2·10	3·25

21 Medieval Ship

1923

201	21	5c. green	1·10	1·10
202	21	10c. mauve	1·10	1·10
203	21	15c. brown	1·10	1·10
204	-	20c. red	1·10	1·10
205	-	25c. grey	1·10	1·10
206	-	30c. green	1·10	1·10
207	-	50c. blue	1·10	1·10
208	-	60c. red	1·10	2·10
209	-	1l. blue	2·10	2·10
210	-	2l. brown	60·00	14·00
211	-	3l. olive	43·00	34·00
212	-	5l. brown	43·00	43·00

DESIGNS: 20, 25, 30c. Roman Arch; 50, 60c., 1l. St. Vitus; 2, 3, 5l. Tarsatic Column.

1924. Issue of 1923 optd REGNO D'ITALIA in frame.

213	21	5c. green	1·10	4·25
214	21	10c. mauve	1·10	4·25
215	21	15c. brown	1·10	4·25
216	-	20c. red	1·10	4·25
217	-	25c. grey	1·10	4·25
218	-	30c. green	1·10	4·25
219	-	50c. blue	1·10	4·25
220	-	60c. red	1·10	4·25
221	-	1l. blue	1·10	4·25
222	-	2l. brown	3·25	14·00
223	-	3l. olive	7·50	18·00
224	-	5l. brown	7·50	18·00

1924. Issue of 1923 optd ANNESSIONE ALL'ITALIA in frame with 22 Febb 1924 below.

225	21	5c. green	1·10	2·10
226	21	10c. mauve	1·10	2·10
227	21	15c. brown	1·10	2·10
228	-	20c. red	1·10	2·10
229	-	25c. grey	1·10	2·10
230	-	30c. green	1·10	2·10
231	-	50c. blue	1·10	2·10
232	-	60c. red	1·10	2·10
233	-	1l. blue	1·10	2·10
234	-	2l. brown	2·10	6·50
235	-	3l. olive	3·25	7·50
236	-	5l. brown	3·25	7·50

EXPRESS LETTER STAMPS

E17

1920

E145	E17	30c. green	32·00	27·00
E146	E17	50c. red	32·00	27·00

1920. Nos. M147 and M145 surch Reggenza Italiana del Carnaro ESPRESSO and new value.

E163	30c. on 20c. bistre	55·00	75·00
E164	50c. on 5c. green	£110	65·00

1921. Optd Governo Provvisorio.

E178	30c. blue	13·00	16·00
E179	50c. red	19·00	16·00

E25 Fiume in 16th Century

1923

E213	E25	60c. red	21·00	16·00
E214	E25	2l. blue	21·00	16·00

1924. Optd REGNO D'ITALIA in frame with arms between the two words.

E225	60c. red	2·75	8·50
E226	2l. blue	2·75	8·50

1924. Optd ANNESSIONE ALL'ITALIA in frame with 22 Febbraio 1924 below.

E237	60c. red	2·75	6·50
E238	2l. blue	2·75	6·50

MILITARY POST STAMPS

M17 Severing the Gordian Knot

1920. 1st Anniv of Capture of Fiume by D'Annunzio's "Legionaries".

M145	M17	5c. green	65·00	37·00
M146	-	10c. red	32·00	27·00
M147	-	20c. bistre	65·00	27·00
M148	-	25c. blue	32·00	60·00

DESIGNS: 10c. Arms of Fiume; 20c. "Crown of Thorns"; 25c. Daggers raised in clenched fists.

NEWSPAPER STAMPS

N9

1919

N91	N9	2c. brown	8·50	13·00

N17 Mail Steamer

1920

N145	N17	1c. green	3·25	3·25

POSTAGE DUE STAMPS

1918. Postage Due stamps of Hungary of 1903 (figures in black), optd FIUME.

D29	D9	6f. green (D21)	£180	95·00
D30	D9	12f. green (D31)	£180	55·00
D31	D9	50f. green (D33)	65·00	27·00

1918. Postage Due stamps of Hungary of 1915 (figures in red), optd FIUME.

D32	1f. green	32·00	19·00
D33	2f. green	3·25	2·10
D34	5f. green	32·00	32·00
D35	6f. green	3·25	3·25
D36	10f. green	43·00	6·50
D37	12f. green	3·25	3·25
D38	15f. green	27·00	27·00
D39	20f. green	3·25	3·25
D40	30f. green	32·00	27·00

D9

1919

D91	2c. brown	2·10	2·10
D92	5c. brown	2·10	2·10

1921. Nos. 105/30 surch Segnatasse, new value and device obliterating old surch.

D191	6	2c. on 15c. grey	2·10	2·10
D192	6	4c. on 10c. red	2·10	2·10
D193	9	5c. on 25c. blue	2·10	2·10
D194	6	6c. on 20c. orange	2·10	2·10
D195	6	10c. on 20c. orange	2·10	2·10
D188	-	20c. on 45c. green	2·10	4·25
D183	-	30c. on 1cor. grey	2·10	4·25
D184	-	40c. on 80c. violet	2·10	2·10
D185	-	50c. on 60c. red	2·10	2·10
D189	-	60c. on 45c. green	2·10	4·25
D190	-	80c. on 45c. green	2·10	4·25
D187	-	1l. on 2cor. brown	4·25	4·25

For stamps of Italy surch **3-V-1945 FIUME RIJEKE** and new value, see Venezia Giulia and Istria, Nos. 18/24.

Pt. 3

FIUME AND KUPA ZONE

The zone comprised Fiume (Rijeka), Susak and the Kupa River area.

100 pares = 1 dinar.

1941. Nos 414, etc. of Yugoslavia optd ZONA OCCUPATA FIUMANO KUPA.

1	**99**	25p. black	5·25	3·25
2	**99**	50p. orange	2·50	1·60
3	**99**	1d. green	2·50	1·60
4	**99**	1d.50 red	2·50	1·60
5	**99**	3d. brown	3·25	2·10
6	**99**	4d. blue	6·25	4·25
7	**99**	5d. blue	12·50	7·75
8	**99**	5d.50 violet	12·50	7·75
9	**99**	6d. blue	47·00	26·00
10	**99**	8d. brown	33·00	18·00
11	**99**	12d. violet	£800	£450
12	**99**	16d. purple	£225	£120
13	**99**	20d. blue	£2000	£1300
14	**99**	30d. pink	£11000	£9000

1941. Maternity and Child Welfare Fund. Nos 2/4 further optd O.N.M.I.

15		50p. orange	5·25	6·25
16		1d. green	5·25	6·25
17		1d.50 red	5·25	6·25

1941. Italian Naval Exploit at Buccari (Bakar), 1918. No. 415 of Yugoslavia surch MEMENTO AVDERE SEMPER L1 BVCCARI.

18		1l. on 50p. orange	31·00	37·00

1942. Maternity and Child Welfare. Nos 15/17 further optd Pro Maternita e Infanzia.

19		50p. orange	12·50	16·00
20		1d. green	12·50	16·00
21		1d.50 red	12·50	16·00

Nos. 1/21 were valid until 26 June 1942 after which un-overprinted Italian stamps were used until the Italian Occupation ended.

Pt. 6

FRANCE

A republic in the W. of Europe.

1849. 100 centimes = 1 franc.
2002. 100 cents = 1 euro.

NOTE. Stamps in types of France up to the 1877 issue were also issued for the French Colonies and where the values and colours are the same they can only be distinguished by their shade or postmark or other minor differences which are outside the scope of this Catalogue. They are priced here by whichever is the lower of the quotations under France or French Colonies in the Stanley Gibbons Catalogue, Part 6 (France). Numbers with asterisks are French Colonies numbers.

1 Ceres

1849. Imperf.

157	**1**	5c. green	£300	£200
15*	**1**	10c. bistre	£325	£130
4	**1**	15c. green	£2750	£1100
6	**1**	20c. black	£550	65·00
17*	**1**	20c. blue	£450	£120
18*	**1**	25c. blue	£140	7·25
22*	**1**	30c. brown	£120	22·00
19*	**1**	40c. orange	£225	14·50
23*	**1**	80c. red	£450	£130
17	**1**	1f. orange	£26000	£3000
19	**1**	1f. red	£15000	£1000

For 10c. brown on pink and 15c. bistre, imperf, see French Colonies Nos. 16 and 20.

2 Louis Napoleon, President

1852. Imperf.

37a	**2**	10c. yellow	£45000	£750
39	**2**	25c. blue	£3750	44·00

3 Napoleon III, Emperor of the French

1853. Imperf.

42	**3**	1c. olive	£275	£110
45	**3**	5c. green	£1100	£110
50	**3**	10c. yellow	£500	13·00
51	**3**	20c. blue	£325	2·20
63	**3**	25c. blue	£3000	£325
64	**3**	40c. orange	£3000	20·00
70	**3**	80c. red	£2750	60·00
72	**3**	1f. red	£8500	£3500

1862. Perf.

87		1c. green	£225	50·00
89		5c. green	£300	13·00
91		10c. bistre	£2000	3·25
95		20c. blue	£475	2·20
97		40c. orange	£1800	6·50
98		80c. pink	£1800	44·00

4 Head with Laurel Wreath

5 Head with Laurel Wreath

1863. Perf.

102	**4**	1c. green	32·00	17·00
104	**4**	2c. brown	£100	33·00
109	**4**	4c. grey	£325	65·00
113a	**5**	10c. bistre	£325	7·75
115a	**5**	20c. blue	£275	2·20
116	**5**	30c. brown	£950	22·00
120	**5**	40c. orange	£1000	14·50
122	**5**	80c. pink	£1200	30·00

For imperforate stamps in these designs see French Colonies.

6

1869

131	**6**	5f. lilac	£7000	£1100

7 Ceres

1870. Imperf.

148	**7**	1c. green	£180	£190
152	**7**	2c. brown	£300	£275
156	**7**	4c. grey	£425	£350

For 1c. green on blue, 2c. brown on yellow and 5c. green as Type **7** and imperf, see French Colonies.

1870. Perf.

185	**7**	1c. green	95·00	22·00
187	**7**	2c. brown	£180	20·00
189	**7**	4c. grey	£425	55·00
192	**7**	5c. green	£300	13·00
136	**1**	10c. bistre	£800	95·00
194	**1**	10c. bistre on pink	£400	15·00
204	**1**	15c. bistre	£550	6·50
137	**1**	20c. blue	£350	8·75
198	**1**	25c. blue	£160	2·20
205	**1**	30c. brown	£850	8·75
140	**1**	40c. orange	£700	8·75
142	**1**	40c. red	£750	11·00
208	**1**	80c. red	£900	17·00

10 Peace and Commerce

1876

212	**10**	1c. green	£200	£100
245	**10**	1c. black on blue	10·50	1·10
225	**10**	2c. green	£170	22·00
248	**10**	2c. brown on buff	12·50	2·20
249	**10**	3c. brown on yellow	£325	55·00
251	**10**	3c. grey	9·50	2·20
214	**10**	4c. green	£225	75·00
252	**10**	4c. brown on grey	12·50	2·20
254	**10**	4c. purple on blue	18·00	4·50
282	**10**	5c. green	32·00	2·20
216	**10**	10c. green	£1300	22·00
284	**10**	10c. black on lilac	42·00	3·25
232	**10**	15c. lilac	£900	2·75
279	**10**	15c. blue	13·50	55
219	**10**	20c. brown on yellow	£850	19·00
260	**10**	20c. red on green	65·00	5·50
234	**10**	25c. blue	£650	1·10
262	**10**	25c. black on red	£1600	28·00
263	**10**	25c. bistre on yellow	£425	5·50
267	**10**	25c. black on pink	£130	1·10
237	**10**	30c. brown	£140	1·70
268	**10**	35c. brown on yellow	£800	39·00
269	**10**	40c. red on yellow	£170	2·20
273	**10**	50c. red	£325	3·50
223	**10**	75c. red	£1500	8·75
274	**10**	75c. brown on orange	£350	50·00
240	**10**	1f. green	£200	7·75
287	**10**	2f. brown on blue	£200	44·00
277	**10**	5f. mauve on lilac	£650	£100

For imperforate stamps in this design see French Colonies.

For 5f. red, perf, see No. 412.

11 "Blanc" type

12 "Mouchon" type

13 "Olivier Merson" type

1900

288	**11**	1c. grey	85	55
289	**11**	2c. purple	1·10	35
290	**11**	3c. red	1·10	70
292a	**11**	4c. brown	3·75	2·20
295	**11**	5c. green	£110	33·00
300	**12**	10c. red	35·00	2·20
301	**12**	15c. orange	9·50	55
297	**12**	20c. brown	65·00	11·00
302	**12**	25c. blue	£160	2·40
299	**12**	30c. mauve	95·00	6·50
303	**13**	40c. red and blue	17·00	90
304	**13**	45c. green and blue	37·00	2·75
305	**13**	50c. brown and lilac	£120	1·80
306	**13**	1f. red and green	33·00	90
369	**13**	1f. red and yellow	60·00	1·50
307	**13**	2f. lilac and buff	£1000	£100
308	**13**	5f. blue and buff	£110	5·50

For further values in these designs, see 1920 issues (following No. 379).

14 "Mouchon" type redrawn

1902

309	**14**	10c. red	55·00	1·40
310	**14**	15c. red	12·50	55
311	**14**	20c. brown	£100	18·00
312	**14**	25c. blue	£110	2·50
313	**14**	30c. mauve	£300	19·00

15 Sower

1903

314	**15**	10c. red	15·00	35
316c	**15**	15c. green	5·25	35
317	**15**	20c. purple	£130	2·20
318	**15**	25c. blue	£150	1·70
319	**15**	30c. lilac	£350	7·25

16 Ground below Feet

1906

325	**16**	10c. red	3·25	2·20

18 No Ground

1906

331	**18**	5c. green	2·10	15
333	**18**	10c. red	2·10	15
337	**18**	20c. brown	6·25	70
339	**18**	25c. blue	3·25	15
343	**18**	30c. orange	21·00	1·70
345	**18**	35c. violet	11·50	1·10

See also Nos. 497 etc. and 454/a.

1914. Red Cross Fund. Surch with red cross and 5c.

351		10c.+5c. red	6·25	6·50

20

1914. Red Cross Fund.

352	**20**	10c.+5c. red	42·00	4·50

21 War Widow

23 Woman replaces Man

26 Spirit of War

1917. War Orphans' Fund.

370	**21**	2c.+3c. red	5·25	5·50
371	-	5c.+5c. green	26·00	13·00
372	**23**	15c.+10c. green	37·00	31·00
373	**23**	25c.+15c. blue	95·00	70·00
374	-	35c.+25c. violet and grey	£180	£150
375	-	50c.+50c. brown	£300	£225
376	**26**	1f.+1f. red	£500	£475
377	**26**	5f.+5f. blue and black	£2000	£2000

DESIGNS—As Type **21**: 5c. Orphans. As Type **26**: 35c. Front line trench; 50c. Lion of Belfort.

See also Nos. 450/3.

27 Sinking of "Charles Roux" Hospital Ship, and Bombed Hospital

1918. Red Cross Fund.

378	**27**	15c.+5c. red & green	£150	75·00

1919. Surch ½ centime.

379	**11**	½c. on 1c. grey	30	35

1920

497	**18**	1c. bistre	15	35
497a	**18**	1c. brown	15	35
498	**18**	2c. green	15	35
499	**18**	3c. red	15	35
380	**18**	5c. orange	1·50	35
500	**18**	5c. mauve	15	35
413	**11**	7½c. mauve*	1·10	1·10
381	**18**	10c. green	70	55
413a	**11**	10c. lilac	4·75	55
501	**18**	10c. blue	2·00	35
414	**18**	15c. brown	55	15
415	**18**	20c. mauve	30	20
415b	**18**	25c. brown	55	20
382a	**18**	30c. mauve	1·40	90

416	18	30c. blue	4·75	55
503	18	30c. red	55	35
505	18	35c. green	85	70
417	18	40c. green	1·60	55
418	18	40c. red	3·25	55
418a	18	40c. violet	2·40	1·10
418b	18	40c. blue	1·60	55
419	15	45c. violet	7·50	2·40
420	15	50c. green	8·00	1·40
421	15	50c. red	1·20	35
592	15	50c. blue	1·90	55
384	13	60c. violet and blue	1·10	55
385	15	60c. violet	7·25	2·00
385a	15	65c. red	3·25	1·70
422	15	65c. green	8·50	2·50
423	15	75c. mauve	6·50	70
424	15	80c. red	32·00	10·00
386	15	85c. red	16·00	2·75
425	15	1f. blue	7·50	90
426	18	1f.05 red	10·50	5·75
427	18	1f.10 mauve	13·00	2·75
428	18	1f.40 mauve	22·00	25·00
387	13	2f. orange and green	60·00	55
428a	18	2f. green	17·00	1·80
429	13	3f. violet and blue	32·00	8·75
430	13	3f. mauve and red	65·00	2·50
431	13	10f. green and red	£150	19·00
432	13	20f. mauve and green	£250	44·00

***PRECANCEL.** No. 413 was issued only pre-cancelled. The "unused" price is for stamp with full gum and the used price for stamp without gum.

1922. War Orphans' Fund. Nos. 370/7 surch with new value, cross and bars.

388	21	1c. on 2c.+3c. red	55	55
389	-	2½c. on 5c.+5c. green	85	85
390	23	5c. on 15c.+10c. green	1·50	1·50
391	23	5c. on 25c.+15c. blue	3·00	3·00
392	-	5c. on 35c.+25c. violet and grey	17·00	17·00
393	-	10c. on 50c.+50c. brn	28·00	28·00
394	26	25c. on 1f.+1f. red	38·00	38·00
395	26	1f. on 5f.+5f. blue and black	£180	£180

30 Pasteur

1923

396	30	10c. green	85	35
396a	30	15c. green	2·00	35
396b	30	20c. green	3·50	1·10
397	30	30c. red	1·10	2·00
397a	30	30c. green	85	55
398	30	45c. red	2·75	2·50
399	30	50c. blue	5·50	55
400	30	75c. blue	4·75	1·40
400a	30	90c. red	13·50	4·50
400b	30	1f. blue	26·00	55
400c	30	1f.25 blue	33·00	11·00
400d	30	1f.50 blue	6·50	35

1923. Optd CONGRES PHILATELIQUE DE BORDEAUX 1923.

400e	13	1f. red and green	£600	£700

31 Stadium and Arc de Triomphe

1924. Olympic Games.

401	31	10c. green & light green	2·75	1·20
402	-	25c. deep red and red	3·75	1·00
403	-	30c. red and black	10·50	14·50
404	-	50c. ultramarine & blue	31·00	5·50

DESIGNS—HORIZ: 25c. Notre Dame and Pont Neuf. VERT: 30c. Milan de Crotone (statue); 50c. The victor.

35 Ronsard

1924. 400th Birth Anniv of Ronsard.

405	35	75c. blue	2·40	2·00

36

1924. International Exhibition of Modern Decorative Arts. Dated "1925".

406	36	10c. yellow and green	85	1·10
407	-	15c. green & deep green	85	1·20
408	-	25c. red and purple	85	55
409	-	25c. mauve and blue	1·80	1·10
410	-	75c. blue and grey	4·00	3·00
411	36	75c. blue and deep blue	21·00	8·50

DESIGNS—HORIZ: 25c. (No. 408); 75c. (No. 410) Potter and vase; 25c. (No. 409), Chateau and steps. VERT: 15c. Stylized vase.

1925. Paris Int Philatelic Exhibition.

412	10	5f. red	£170	£170
MS412a 140×220 mm. No. 412 in block of four			£1600	£1600

1926. Surch with new value and bars.

433	18	25c. on 30c. blue	30	55
434	18	25c. on 35c. violet	30	55
436	15	50c. on 60c. violet	1·50	1·40
437	15	50c. on 65c. red	85	65
438	30	50c. on 75c. blue	4·00	2·20
439	15	50c. on 80c. red	1·50	1·40
440	15	50c. on 85c. red	2·40	1·20
441	18	50c. on 1f.05 red	1·50	90
442	30	50c. on 1f.25 blue	3·25	2·75
443	15	55c. on 60c. violet*	£180	75·00
444	18	90c. on 1f.05 red	3·00	3·50
445	18	1f.10 on 1f.40 red	1·20	1·10

***PRECANCEL.** No. 443 was issued only precancelled. The "unused" price is for stamp with full gum and the used price for stamp without gum.

1926. War Orphans' Fund.

450	21	2c.+1c. purple	2·10	1·70
451	-	50c.+10c. brn (as No. 375)	26·00	17·00
452	26	1f.+25c. red	65·00	55·00
453	26	5f.+1f. blue and black	£130	£120

1927. Strasbourg Philatelic Exhibition.

454	18	5f. blue	£325	£325
454a	18	10f. red	£325	£325
MS454b 110×140 mm. 5f.+10f. and label inscr "STRASBOURG 1927"			£1400	£1400

1927. Air. 1st International Display of Aviation and Navigation, Marseilles. Optd with Bleriot XI airplane and Poste Aerienne.

455	13	2f. red and green	£275	£275
456	13	5f. blue and yellow	£275	£275

44 Marcelin Berthelot

1927. Birth Centenary of Berthelot.

457	44	90c. red	2·40	70

45 Lafayette, Washington, "Paris" (liner) and Lindbergh's Ryan NYP "Spirit of St. Louis"

1927. Visit of American Legion.

458	45	90c. red	2·00	1·50
459	45	1f.50 blue	4·75	2·50

1927. Sinking Fund. Surch Caisse d'Amortissement or C A and premium.

460	18	40c.+10c. blue	6·25	6·50
461	15	50c.+25c. green	9·50	10·00
462	30	1f.50+50c. orange	19·00	17·00

See also Nos. 466/8, 476/8, 485/7 and 494/6.

48

1928. Sinking Fund.

463	48	1f.50+8f.50 blue	£190	£200

1928. Air ("Ile de France"). Surch 10 FR. and bars.

464	44	10f. on 90c. red	£3250	£3250
465	30	10f. on 1f.50 blue	£14000	£14000

1928. Sinking Fund. Surch as Nos. 460/2.

466	18	40c.+10c. violet	12·50	11·00
467	15	50c.+25c. red	37·00	33·00
468	30	1f.50+50c. mauve	65·00	50·00

50 Joan of Arc

1929. 500th Anniv of Relief of Orleans.

469	50	50c. blue	2·40	35

1929. Optd EXPOSITION LE HAVRE 1929 PHILATELIQUE.

470	13	2f. red and green	£900	£900

52 Reims Cathedral 53 Mont St. Michel

1929. Views.

470a	-	90c. mauve	4·25	1·20
471	-	2f. red	44·00	1·10
472	52	3f. blue	80·00	3·25
473a	53	5f. brown	26·00	90
474b	-	10f. blue	£130	20·00
475b	-	20f. brown	£350	46·00

DESIGNS—HORIZ: 90c. Le Puy-en-Velay; 2f. Arc de Triomphe; 10f. Port de la Rochelle; 20f. Pont du Gard.

1929. Sinking Fund. Surch as Nos. 460/2.

476	18	40c.+10c. green	21·00	19·00
477	15	50c.+25c. mauve	37·00	33·00
478	30	1f.50+50c. brown	70·00	70·00

54 Bay of Algiers

1930. Centenary of French Conquest of Algeria.

479	54	50c. red and blue	3·25	55

55 "Le Sourire de Reims"

1930. Sinking Fund.

480	55	1f.50+3f.50 purple	£110	£110

1930. I.L.O. Session, Paris. Optd CONGRES DU B.I.T. 1930.

481	15	50c. red	3·00	2·50
482	30	1f.50 blue	22·00	17·00

57 Farman F.190 over Notre Dame de la Garde, Marseilles

1930. Air.

483	57	1f.50 red	27·00	5·00
484	57	1f.50 blue	27·00	2·50

1930. Sinking Fund. Surch as Nos. 460/2.

485	18	40c.+10c. red	26·00	26·00
486	15	50c.+25c. brown	47·00	44·00
487	18	1f.50+50c. violet	85·00	85·00

58 Woman of the Fachi tribe 59 "French Colonies"

1930. International Colonial Exhibition.

488	58	15c. black	1·50	55
489	58	40c. brown	2·75	55
490	58	50c. red	1·10	15
491	58	1f.50 blue	11·50	70
492	59	1f.50 blue	55·00	2·40

60 "French Provinces"

1931. Sinking Fund.

493	60	1f.50+3f.50 green	£180	£190

1931. Sinking Fund. Surch as Nos. 460/2.

494	18	40c.+10c. green	65·00	44·00
495	15	50c.+25c. violet	£150	£120
496	18	1f.50+50c. red	£130	£120

61 Peace

1932

502	61	30c. green	1·10	70
506	61	40c. mauve	30	35
507	61	45c. brown	2·10	1·40
508	61	50c. red	20	15
508d	61	55c. violet	85	35
508e	61	60c. bistre	30	55
509	61	65c. purple	55	45
509a	61	65c. blue	30	15
510	61	75c. green	20	35
510a	61	80c. orange	20	35
511	61	90c. red	44·00	2·50
511a	61	90c. green	20	15
511b	61	90c. blue	1·10	15
512	61	1f. orange	3·75	35
512a	61	1f. pink	4·75	55
513	61	1f.25 olive	90·00	6·00
513a	61	1f.25 red	2·75	2·20
513b	61	1f.40 mauve	7·50	6·50
514	61	1f.50 blue	30	20
515	61	1f.75 mauve	5·25	55

1933. Surch ½ centime.

515a	18	½c. on 1c. bistre	30	55
515b	18	½c. on 1c. brown	1·10	1·70

62 Briand

1933. Portraits.

516	62	30c. green	32·00	10·00
517	-	75c. mauve (Doumer)	32·00	1·70
518	-	1f.25 red (Victor Hugo)	7·50	2·50

65 Dove of Peace

1934

519	65	1f.50 blue	65·00	19·00

66 J. M. Jacquard

1934. Death Centenary of Jacquard.

520	66	40c. blue	4·25	1·10

67 Jacques Cartier, "Grande Hermine" and "Petite Hermine"

1934. 4th Cent of Cartier's Discovery of Canada.

521	67	75c. mauve	32·00	2·50
522	67	1f.50 blue	55·00	5·00

68 Bleriot XI

1934. Air. 25th Anniv of Channel Flight.
523 **68** 2f.25 violet 26·00 7·75

1934. Surch in figures and bars.
524 **61** 50c. on 1f.25 olive 4·75 70
524a **61** 80c. on 1f. orange 55 70

69 Breton River Scene

1935
525 **69** 2f. green 42·00 1·10

70 "Normandie"

1935. Maiden Trip of Liner "Normandie".
526 **70** 1f.50 blue 16·00 2·50

71 St. Trophime, Arles

1935
527 **71** 3f.50 brown 34·00 5·00

72 B. Delessert

1935. Opening of Int Savings Bank Congress.
528 **72** 75c. green 23·00 1·70

73 Victor Hugo

1935. 50th Death Anniv of Victor Hugo.
529 **73** 1f.25 purple 5·75 2·50

74 Cardinal Richelieu

1935. Tercentenary of French Academy by Richelieu.
530 **74** 1f.50 red 26·00 1·70

75 Jacques Callot

1935. Death Tercentenary of Callot (engraver).
531 **75** 75c. red 12·50 70

77 Symbolic of Art

1935. Unemployed Intellectuals' Relief Fund. Inscr "POUR L'ART ET LA PENSEE".
532 - 50c.+10c. blue 3·25 3·25
533 **77** 50c.+2f. red 70·00 60·00
DESIGN—HORIZ: No. 532, Help for intellectuals (inscr "POUR LES CHOMEURS INTELLECTUELS").

78 Caudron C-635 Simoun over Paris

1936. Air.
534 **78** 85c. green 3·25 2·75
535 **78** 1f.50 blue 13·50 6·50
536 **78** 2f.25 violet 25·00 8·25
537 **78** 2f.50 red 32·00 10·00
538 **78** 3f. blue 26·00 2·50
539 **78** 3f.50 brown 80·00 30·00
540 **78** 50f. green £1200 £450

79 Caudron C-635 Simoun over Paris

1936. Air.
541 **79** 50f. blue and pink £950 £450

80 Statue of Liberty

1936. Nansen (Refugee) Fund.
541a **80** 50c.+25c. blue 4·75 5·00
542 **80** 75c.+50c. violet 13·00 12·00

81 Andre-Marie Ampere

1936. Death Centenary of Ampere.
543 **81** 75c. brown 24·00 2·50

82 Daudet's Mill, Fontvieille

1936
544 **82** 2f. blue 5·25 55

83 Children of the Unemployed

1936. Children of the Unemployed Fund.
545 **83** 50c.+10c. red 6·50 5·50

84 Pilatre de Rozier and Montgoldier Balloon

1936. 150th Death Anniv of Pilatre de Rozier.
546 **84** 75c. blue 24·00 3·25

85 Rouget de Lisle

1936. Death Centenary of Rouget de Lisle, Composer of the "Marseillaise".
547 **85** 20c. green 4·50 2·50
548 - 40c. brown 7·25 4·25
DESIGN—HORIZ: 40c. Female figure inscr "LA MARSEILLAISE".

87 Canadian War Memorial, Vimy

1936. Unveiling of Canadian War Memorial, Vimy Ridge.
549 **87** 75c. red 12·00 2·50
550 **87** 1f.50 blue 21·00 11·00

88 Jean Jaures as an Orator

1936. Jaures Commemoration.
551 **88** 40c. brown 4·75 1·80
552 - 1f.50 blue 18·00 4·50
The 1f.50 has a head and shoulders portrait of Jaures.

91 Latecoere 300 Flying Boat

1936. 100th Flight between France and S. America.
553 1f.50 blue 24·00 6·00
554 **91** 10f. green £450 £170
DESIGN—VERT: 1f.50, Airplane and old-time sailing ship.

92 Herald **93** "World Exhibition"

1936. Paris International Exhibition.
555 **92** 20c. mauve 60 70
556 **92** 30c. green 3·50 2·00
557 **92** 40c. blue 1·90 90
558 **92** 50c. orange 1·70 45
559 **93** 90c. red 16·00 9·50
560 **93** 1f.50 blue 44·00 5·00

94 "Vision of Peace"

1936. Universal Peace Propaganda.
561 **94** 1f.50 blue 20·00 5·00

1936. Unemployed Intellectuals' Fund. No. 533 surch + 20c.
562 **77** 20c. on 50c.+2f. red 4·75 4·75

96 Jacques Callot

1936. Unemployed Intellectuals' Fund. Inscr as in T 96.
563 **96** 20c.+10c. lake 3·50 3·25
564 - 40c.+10c. green 3·50 4·50
565 - 50c.+10c. red 6·00 4·50
566 - 1f.50+50c. blue 27·00 24·00
DESIGNS: 40c. Hector Berlioz; 50c. Victor Hugo; 1f.50, Louis Pasteur.
See also Nos. 603/5 and 607.

97 Ski Jumper

1937. Chamonix-Mont Blanc Skiing Week.
567 **97** 1f.50 blue 9·00 2·00

98 Pierre Corneille (author)

1937. 300th Anniv of First Performance of "Le Cid" (play).
568 **98** 75c. red 2·75 1·80

99 France and Minerva

1937. Paris International Exhibition.
569 **99** 1f.50 blue 3·25 1·40

100 Mermoz **101** Jean Mermoz Memorial

1937. Mermoz Commemoration.
570 **100** 30c. green 60 90
571 **101** 3f. violet 8·25 4·50

102 Paris–Orleans Midi Electric Train

1937. 13th International Railway Congress, Paris.
572 **102** 30c. green 1·20 1·80
573 - 1f.50 blue 10·00 9·25
DESIGN: 1f.50, Nord streamlined steam locomotive.

103 Rene Descartes

1937. 300th Anniv of Publication of "Discours". (a) Wrongly inscr "DISCOURS SUR LA METHODE".
574 **103** 90c. red 2·75 1·80

(b) Corrected to "DISCOURS DE LA METHODE".
575 90c. red 8·25 2·20

104 Anatole France

1937. Unemployed Intellectuals' Relief Fund.

576	**104**	30c.+10c. green	2·75	3·25
577	-	90c.+10c. red	8·25	7·75

DESIGN—HORIZ: 90c. Auguste Rodin.
See also Nos. 602 and 606.

107 Ramblers

1937. Postal Workers' Sports Fund.

578		20c.+10c. brown	2·20	2·50
579		40c.+10c. lake	2·20	2·50
580	**107**	50c.+10c. purple	2·20	2·50

DESIGNS—HORIZ: 20c. Tug-of-War; 40c. Runners and discus thrower.

1937. Inter Philatelic Ex, Paris. As T **1**, printed in miniature sheets of four (578×858ins.) inscr "PEXIP PARIS 1937" between stamps.

MS581 5c. brown and blue; 15c. carmine and red; 30c. red and blue; 50c. brown and red £550 £450

108 Pierre Loti and Constantinople

1937. Pierre Loti Memorial Fund.

585	**108**	50c.+20c. red	5·50	4·50

109 "Victory" of Samothrace

1937. National Museums.

586	**109**	30c. green	£100	55·00
587	**109**	55c. red	£100	55·00

110 "France" and Child

1937. Public Health Fund.

588	**110**	65c.+25c. purple	4·50	3·25
588a	**110**	90c.+30c. blue	3·00	3·25

111 France congratulating U.S.A.

1937. 150th Anniv of U.S. Constitution.

589	**111**	1f.75 blue	3·50	2·50

112 Iseran Pass

1937. Opening of Col de l'Iseran Road.

590	**112**	90c. green	2·75	35

113 Ceres

1938

591	**113**	1f.75 blue	95	65
591a	**113**	2f. red	35	20
591b	**113**	2f.25 blue	12·00	1·10
591c	**113**	2f.50 green	2·00	90
591d	**113**	2f.50 blue	80	90
591e	**113**	3f. mauve	80	55

1938. Shipwrecked Mariners Society. As T **104** but portrait of Jean Charcot.

593		65c.+35c. green	1·90	3·25
593a		90c.+35c. purple	16·00	14·50

113a Gambetta

1938. Birth Centenary of Leon Gambetta (politician).

594	**113a**	55c. lilac	60	70

113b Champagne Girl

1938

594a	-	90c. red on blue	1·20	1·40
595	**113b**	1f.75 blue	5·50	4·50
596	-	2f. brown	1·20	75
597	-	2f.15 purple	6·00	1·10
598	-	3f. red	18·00	5·00
599	-	5f. blue	95	55
600	-	10f. purple on blue	2·40	2·20
601	-	20f. green	60·00	23·00

DESIGNS—VERT: 2f.15, Coal miners; 10f. Vincennes. HORIZ: 90c. Chateau de Pau; 2f. Arc de Triomphe at Orange; 3f. Papal Palace, Avignon; 5f. Carcassonne; 20f. St. Malo.

1938. Unemployed Intellectuals' Relief Fund. As Nos. 563/6 and 576/7, inscr "POUR LES CHOMEURS INTELLECTUELS".

602	30c.+10c. red	2·40	2·40
603	35c.+10c. green	3·50	3·50
604	55c.+10c. violet	8·25	5·00
605	65c.+10c. blue	8·25	5·00
606	1f.+10c. red	7·25	6·50
607	1f.75+25c. blue	24·00	22·00

PORTRAITS—As Type **96**: 35c. Callot; 55c. Berlioz; 65c. Victor Hugo; 1f.75, Louis Pasteur. As No. 577: 1f. Auguste Rodin. As Type **104**: 30c. Anatole France.

114 Palais de Versailles

1938. French National Music Festivals.

608	**114**	1f.75+75c. blue	27·00	24·00

115 Soldier in Trench

1938. Infantry Monument Fund.

609	**115**	55c.+70c. purple	6·50	6·00
610	**115**	65c.+1f.10 blue	6·50	6·00

116 Medical Corps Monument at Lyons

1938. Military Medical Corps' Monument Fund.

611	**116**	55c.+45c. red	16·00	14·50

117 Saving a Goal

1938. World Football Cup.

612	**117**	1f.75 blue	18·00	17·00

117a Clement Ader and 'Avion III'

1938. Clement Ader (air pioneer).

612a	**117a**	50f. blue	£130	90·00

118 Jean de La Fontaine

1938. La Fontaine (writer of fables).

613	**118**	55c. green	80	1·40

1938. Reims Cathedral Restoration Fund. As T 52, but inscr "REIMS 10.VII.1938".

614	65c.+35c. blue	12·00	14·00

119 Houses of Parliament, "Friendship" and Arc de Triompe

1938. Visit of King George VI and Queen Elizabeth to France.

615	**119**	1f.75 blue	80	1·40

120 "France" welcoming Frenchmen repatriated from Spain

1938. French Refugees' Fund.

616	**120**	65c.+60c. red	5·25	6·50

121 Pierre and Marie Curie

1938. International Anti-cancer Fund. 40th Anniv of Discovery of Radium.

617	**121**	1f.75+50c. blue	12·00	14·00

122 Arc de Triomphe and Allied Soldiers

1938. 20th Anniv of 1918 Armistice.

618	**122**	65c.+35c. red	4·50	5·00

123 Mercury

1938. Inscr "REPUBLIQUE FRANCAISE".

618a	**123**	1c. brown	25	20
619	**123**	2c. green	25	20
620	**123**	5c. red	20	15
621	**123**	10c. blue	20	15
622	**123**	15c. orange	20	35
622a	**123**	15c. brown	90	90
623	**123**	20c. mauve	20	15
624	**123**	25c. green	20	15
625	**123**	30c. red	20	15
626	**123**	40c. violet	20	15
627	**123**	45c. green	60	90
627b	**123**	50c. green	60	70
627c	**123**	50c. blue	25	20
628	**123**	60c. orange	20	35
629	**123**	70c. mauve	25	35
629a	**123**	75c. brown	5·50	3·00

For similar stamps inscr "POSTES FRANCAISES", see Nos. 750/3.

124 Nurse and Patient

1938. Students' Fund.

630	**124**	65c.+60c. blue	11·00	10·00

125 Blind Radio Listener

1938. "Radio for the Blind" Fund.

631	**125**	90c.+25c. purple	10·50	11·00

126 Monument to Civilian War Victims, Lille

1939. War Victims' Monument Fund.

632	**126**	90c.+35c. brown	12·00	12·00

127 Paul Cezanne

1939. Birth Cent of Paul Cezanne (painter).

633	**127**	2f.25 blue	4·75	4·50

128 Red Cross Nurse

1939. 75th Anniv of Red Cross Society. Cross in red.

634	**128**	90c.+35c. blue & black	9·50	9·25

129 Military Engineer

1939. To the Glory of French Military Engineers.

635	**129**	70c.+50c. red	8·25	8·50

130 Ministry of Posts, Telegraphs and Telephones

1939. P.T.T. Orphans' Fund.

636	**130**	90c.+35c. blue	27·00	25·00

131 "Dunkerque" Class Battleship

1939. Laying down Keel of Battleship "Clemenceau".

637	**131**	90c. blue	80	90

132 French Pavilion, New York Exhibition

1939. New York World's Fair.

638	**132**	2f.25 blue	10·50	7·75
638a	**132**	2f.50 blue	13·00	12·00

133 Mother and Child

1939. Children of the Unemployed Fund.

639	**133**	90c.+35c. red	3·25	3·00

134 Niepce and Daguerre

1939. Photographic Centenary.

640	**134**	2f.25 blue	9·50	7·75

135 Eiffel Tower

1939. 50th Anniv of Erection of Eiffel Tower.

641	**135**	90c.+50c. purple	11·00	10·00

136 Iris

1939

642	**136**	80c. brown	25	35
643	**136**	1f. green	95	35
643a	**136**	1f. red	35	35
643b	**136**	1f.30 blue	20	35
643c	**136**	1f.50 orange	20	35

See also Nos. 861/8.

137 Marly Water Works

1939. International Water Exhibition, Liege.

644	**137**	2f.25 blue	16·00	6·00

138 Balzac

1939. Unemployed Intellectuals' Fund.

645	-	40c.+10c. red	1·50	1·00
646	-	70c.+10c. purple	5·50	3·00
647	**138**	90c.+10c. mauve	4·75	3·25
648	-	2f.25+25c. blue	20·00	14·50

PORTRAITS—VERT: 40c. Puvis de Chavannes. HORIZ: 70c. Claude Debussy; 2f.25, Claude Bernard.

See also Nos 667b/d.

139 St. Gregory of Tours

1939. 1400th Birth Anniv of St. Gregory of Tours.

649	**139**	90c. red	60	90

140 Mother and Children

1939. Birth-rate Development Fund.

650	-	70c.+80c. vio, bl & grn	4·50	5·00
651	**140**	90c.+60c. brn, pur & sep	6·25	6·50

DESIGN: 70c. Mother and children admiring infant in cot.

141 Oath of the Tennis Court

1939. 150th Anniv of French Revolution.

652	**141**	90c. green	2·50	2·40

142 Strasbourg Cathedral

1939. 5th Centenary of Completion of Strasbourg Cathedral Spire.

653	**142**	70c. red	1·20	1·70

143 Porte Chaussee, Verdun

1939. 23rd Anniv of Battle of Verdun.

654	**143**	90c. grey	80	1·20

144 "The Letter"

1939. Postal Museum Fund.

655	**144**	40c.+60c. brown	3·25	4·25

145 Statue to Sailors lost at Sea

1939. Boulogne Monument Fund.

656	**145**	70c.+30c. plum	17·00	15·00

146 Languedoc

1939

657	**146**	70c. black on blue	60	70

147 Lyons

1939

658	**147**	90c. purple	80	1·10

148 French Soldier and Strasbourg Cathedral

1940. Soldiers' Comforts Fund.

659	**148**	40c.+60c. purple	2·75	3·25
660	-	1f.+50c. blue	2·75	3·25

DESIGN: 1f. Veteran French colonial soldier and African village.

149 French Colonial Empire

1940. Overseas Propaganda Fund.

661	**149**	1f.+25c. red	2·40	3·00

See also Nos. 708 and 953.

150 Marshal Joffre

1940. War Charities. Inscr as in T **150**.

662	**150**	80c.+45c. brown	6·00	7·75
663	-	1f.+50c. violet	10·00	7·75
664	-	1f.50+50c. red	5·25	5·00
665	-	2f.50+50c. blue	10·50	14·00

DESIGNS—HORIZ: 1f.50, General Gallieni; 2f.50, Ploughing. VERT: 1f. Marshal Foch.

151 Nurse and Wounded Soldier

1940. Red Cross. Cross in red.

666		80c.+1f. green	6·50	7·75
667	**151**	1f.+2f. brown	8·25	7·75

DESIGN: 80c. Doctor, nurse, soldier and family.

152 G. Guynemer (pilot)

1940

667a	**152**	50f. blue	12·00	11·00

1940. Unemployed Intellectuals' Fund. As T **138**. Inscr "POUR LES CHOMEURS INTELLECTUELS".

667b	80c.+10c. brown	6·50	10·00
667c	1f.+10c. purple	6·50	10·00
667d	2f.50+25c. blue	6·50	10·00

PORTRAITS: 80c. Debussy; 1f. Balzac.; 2f.50, Bernard.

153 Nurse, wounded Soldier and Family

1940. War Victim's Fund.

667e	**153**	1f.+2f. violet	1·30	1·40

154 Harvesting

1940. National Relief Fund. Inscr "SECOURS NATIONAL".

668	**154**	80c.+2f. sepia	2·20	2·75
669	-	1f.+2f. brown	2·20	2·75
670	-	1f.50+2f. violet	2·40	2·75
671	-	2f.50+2f. green	3·25	2·75

DESIGNS: 1f. Sowing; 1f.50, Gathering grapes; 2f.50, Cattle.

1940. Surch with new value and with bars on all except T 113.

672	18	30c. on 35c. green	20	40
673	61	50c. on 55c. violet	20	40
674	61	50c. on 65c. blue	20	15
675	61	50c. on 75c. green	20	40
676	123	50c. on 75c. brown	20	40
677	61	50c. on 80c. orange	20	40
678	61	50c. on 90c. blue	20	15
679	61	1f. on 1f.25 red	20	40
680	61	1f. on 1f.40 mauve	20	55
681	61	1f. on 1f.50 blue	1·20	1·50
682	113	1f. on 1f.75 blue	25	40
683	-	1f. on 2f.15 purple (No. 597)	40	55
684	113	1f. on 2f.25 blue	25	40
685	113	1f. on 2f.50 green	1·20	1·90
686	-	2f.50 on 5f. blue (No. 599)	40	55
687	-	5f. on 10f. purple on blue (No. 600)	1·70	2·50
688	-	10f. on 20f. green (No. 601)	1·30	2·20
689	117a	20f. on 50f. blue	48·00	50·00

155 Marshal Petain

1940

690	155	40c. brown	35	55
691	155	80c. green	35	70
692	155	1f. red	25	35
693	155	2f.50 blue	1·30	1·50

See also Nos. 774/5.

156 Prisoners of War

1941. Prisoners of War Fund.

696	156	80c.+5f. green	1·30	2·10
697	-	1f.+5f. red	1·50	2·20

DESIGN: 1f. Group of soldiers.

157 Frederic Mistral

1941. Frederic Mistral (poet).

698	157	1f. red	20	35

158 Science against Cancer

1941. Anti-cancer Fund.

699	158	2f.50+50c. blk and brn	1·30	1·90

159 Beaune Hospital, 1443

1941. Views.

700	159	5f. brown	35	35
701	-	10f. violet	60	70
702	159	15f. red	50	70
703	-	20f. brown	95	1·40

DESIGNS: 10f. Angers; 20f. Ramparts of St. Louis, Aigues-Mortes.

1941. National Relief Fund. Surch + 10c.

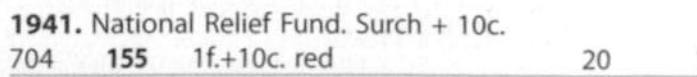

704	155	1f.+10c. red	20	15

160

1941. Winter Relief Fund. Inscr as in T 160.

705	160	1f.+2f. purple	2·20	1·80
706	-	2f.50+7f.50 blue	7·00	3·25

DESIGN: 2f.50, "Charity" helping a pauper.

162 Liner "Pasteur"

1941. Seamen's Dependants Relief Fund. Surch.

707	162	1f.+1f. on 70c. green	35	55

1941. As No. 661, but without "R.F." and dated "1941".

708	149	1f.+1f. multicoloured	60	70

163

164 Marshal Petain

165

1941. Frame in T 164 is 17×20½ mm.

709	163	20c. purple	20	15
710	163	30c. red	20	15
711	163	40c. blue	20	15
712	164	50c. green	20	15
713	164	60c. violet	20	15
714	164	70c. blue	20	15
715	164	70c. orange	20	15
716	164	80c. brown	20	20
717	164	80c. green	20	15
718	164	1f. red	20	15
719	164	1f.20 brown	20	15
720	165	1f.50 pink	20	15
721	165	1f.50 brown	20	15
722	165	2f. green	20	15
723	165	2f.40 red	20	35
724	165	2f.50 blue	35	1·10
725	165	3f. orange	20	15
725a	164	4f. blue	20	35
725b	164	4f.50 green	60	90

See also Nos. 740/1.

166 Fisherman

1941. National Seamen's Relief Fund.

726	166	1f.+9f. green	80	1·20

167 Arms of Nancy

1942. National Relief Fund.

727	167	20c.+30c. black	2·40	3·25
728	-	40c.+60c. brown	2·40	3·25
729	-	50c.+70c. blue	2·40	3·25
730	-	70c.+80c. red	2·40	3·25
731	-	80c.+1f. red	2·40	3·25
732	-	1f.+1f. black	2·40	3·25
733	-	1f.50+2f. blue	2·40	3·25
734	-	2f.+2f. violet	2·40	3·75
735	-	2f.50+3f. green	2·40	3·75
736	-	3f.+5f. brown	2·40	3·75
737	-	5f.+6f. blue	2·40	3·75
738	-	10f.+10f. red	2·40	3·75

DESIGNS—As Type **167**. Nos. 728/38 show respectively the Arms of Lille, Rouen, Bordeaux, Toulouse, Clermont-Ferrand, Marseilles, Lyons, Rennes, Reims, Montpellier and Paris.

See also Nos. 757/68.

168 Jean-Francois de La Perouse, "L'Astrolabe" and "La Boussole"

1942. Birth Bicentenary of La Perouse (navigator and explorer) and National Relief Fund.

739	168	2f.50+7f.50 blue	1·30	2·00

1942. Frame 18×21½ mm.

740	164	4f. blue	25	35
741	164	4f.50 green	25	35

169 Potez 63-11 Bombers

1942. Air Force Dependants Relief Fund.

742	169	1f.50+3f.50 violet	2·20	3·25

170 Alexis Emmanuel Chabrier

1942. Birth Centenary of Chabrier (composer) and Musicians' Mutual Assistance Fund.

743	170	2f.+3f. brown	95	1·80

171 Symbolical of French Colonial Empire

1942. Empire Fortnight and National Relief Fund.

744	171	1f.50+8f.50 black	95	1·50

172 Marshal Petain

173 Marshal Petain

1942

745	172	5f. green	25	35
746	173	50f. black	3·75	5·50

See also Nos. 772/3.

174 Jean de Vienne

1942. 600th Birth Anniv of Jean de Vienne (admiral) and Seamen's Relief Fund.

748	174	1f.50+8f.50 brown	95	1·80

175 Jules Massenet

1942. Birth Centenary of Massenet (composer).

749	175	4f. green	25	35

1942. As T 123, but inscr "POSTES FRANCAISES".

750		10c. blue	15	15
751		30c. red	15	15
752		40c. violet	15	35
753		50c. blue	15	15

1942. National Relief Fund. Surch + 50 S N.

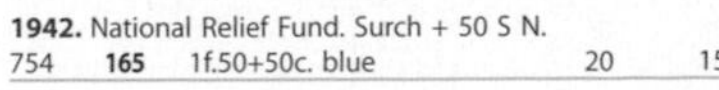

754	165	1f.50+50c. blue	20	15

177 Stendhal (Marie Henri Beyle)

1942. Death Centenary of Stendhal (novelist).

755	177	4f. brown and red	60	70

178 Andre Blondel

1942. Andre Blondel (physicist).

756	178	4f. blue	60	70

1942. National Relief Fund. Arms of French towns as T **167**.

757		50c.+60c. black	3·50	5·00
758		60c.+70c. green	2·75	4·25
759		80c.+1f. red	2·75	4·25
760		1f.+1f.30 green	2·75	4·25
761		1f.20+1f.50 red	2·75	4·50
762		1f.50+1f.80 blue	2·75	4·75
763		2f.+2f.30 red	2·75	4·75
764		2f.40+2f.80 green	3·00	4·75
765		3f.+3f.50 violet	3·00	4·75
766		4f.+5f. blue	3·50	4·75
767		4f.50+6f. red	3·50	4·75
768		5f.+7f. lilac	3·50	5·00

DESIGNS: Nos. 757/68 respectively show the Arms of Chambery, La Rochelle, Poitiers, Orleans, Grenoble, Angers, Dijon, Limoges, Le Havre, Nantes, Nice and St. Etienne.

179 Legionary and Grenadiers

1942. Tricolor Legion.

769	179	1f.20+8f.80 blue	8·25	14·00
770	179	1f.20+8f.80 red	8·25	14·00

180 Belfry, Arras Town Hall

1942

771	180	10f. green	20	35

1943. National Relief Fund.

772	173	1f.+10f. blue	1·90	3·25
773	173	1f.+10f. red	1·90	3·25
774	155	2f.+12f. blue	1·90	3·25
775	155	2f.+12f. red	1·90	3·25

182 Arms of Lyonnais

1943. Provincial Coats of Arms.

776	182	5f. red, blue & yellow	35	55
777	-	10f. black and brown	60	70
778	-	15f. yellow, blue & red	1·70	1·90
779	-	20f. yellow, blue & brn	1·20	2·10

ARMS: 10f. "Bretagne"; 15f. "Provence"; 20f. "Ile-de-France".

For other provinces in this series, see Nos. 814/7, 971/4, 1049/53, 1121/5, 1178/83, 1225/31, 1270/3.

For arms of French towns, see Nos. 1403/10, etc.

183 "Work"

184 Marshal Petain

1943. National Relief Fund.

780		1f.20+1f.40 purple	14·50	20·00
781	**183**	1f.50+2f.50 red	14·50	20·00
782	-	2f.40+7f. brown	14·50	20·00
783	-	4f.+10f. violet	14·50	20·00
784	**184**	5f.+15f. brown	14·50	20·00

DESIGNS: 1f.20, Marshal Petain bareheaded; 2f.40, "Family"; 4f. "Country".

185 Lavoisier

1943. Birth Bicentenary of Lavoisier (chemist).

785	**185**	4f. blue	25	35

186 Lake Lerie and the Meije Peak

1943

786	**186**	20f. green	95	1·20

187 Nicholas Rolin and Guisone de Salins

1943. 500th Anniv of Beaune Hospital.

787	**187**	4f. blue	20	35

188 Victims of Bombed Towns

1943. National Relief Fund.

788	**188**	1f.50+3f.50 black	60	70

189 Prisoners' Families' Relief Work

1943. Prisoners' Families Relief Fund. Inscr as in T 189.

789	-	1f.50+8f.50 brown	95	1·20
790	**189**	2f.40+7f.60 green	95	1·20

DESIGN—VERT: 1f.50, Prisoner's family.

190 Chevalier de Bayard

1943. National Relief Fund.

791	-	60c.+80c. green	1·70	2·75
792	-	1f.20+1f.50 black	1·70	2·75
793	-	1f.50+3f. blue	1·70	2·75
794	**190**	2f.40+4f. red	1·70	2·75
795	-	4f.+6f. brown	1·70	3·00
796	-	5f.+10f. green	1·90	3·00

PORTRAITS: 60c. Michel de Montaigne (essayist); 1f.20, Francois Clouet (painter); 1f.50, Ambroise Pare (surgeon); 4f. Duc de Sully (King Henri IV's finance minister); 5f. King Henri IV.

191 Picardy

1943. National Relief Fund. Provincial costumes.

797	**191**	60c.+1f.30 brown	2·10	2·75
798	-	1f.20+2f. violet	2·10	2·75
799	-	1f.50+4f. blue	2·10	2·75
800	-	2f.40+5f. red	2·10	2·75
801	-	4f.+6f. blue	2·40	4·00
802	-	5f.+7f. red	2·40	4·00

DESIGNS: 1f.20, "Bretagne"; 1f.50, "Ile de France"; 2f.40, "Bourgogne"; 4f. "Auvergne"; 5f. "Provence".

196 Admiral de Tourville

1944. 300th Birth Anniv of Admiral de Tourville.

810	**196**	4f.+6f. red	80	1·10

197 Branly

1944. Birth Centenary of Branly (physicist).

811	**197**	4f. blue	25	35

198 Gounod

1944. 50th Death Anniv of Gounod (composer).

812	**198**	1f.50+3f.50 brown	80	1·10

200 Flanders

1944. Provincial Coats of Arms.

814	**200**	5f. black, orange & red	20	35
815	-	10f. yellow, red & brown	20	35
816	-	15f. yellow, blue & brown	85	1·10
817	-	20f. yellow, red & blue	1·20	1·40

ARMS: 10f. "Languedoc"; 15f. "Orleanais"; 20f. "Normandie".

201 Marshal Petain

202 Petain gives France Workers' Charter

1944. Petain's 88th Birthday.

818	**201**	1f.50+3f.50 brown	3·25	5·00
819	-	2f.+3f. blue	60	90
820	**202**	4f.+6f. red	60	90

DESIGN—As Type **202**: 2f. inscr "Le Marechal institua la Corporation Paysanne" (Trans. "The Marshal set up the Peasant Corporation").

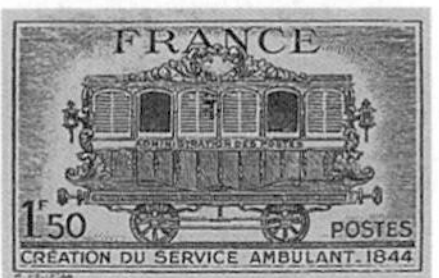

203 Paris–Rouen Travelling Post Office Van, 1844

1944. Centenary of Mobile Post Office.

821	**203**	1f.50 green	60	90

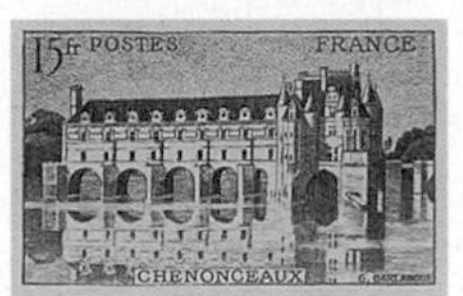

204 Chateau of Chenonceaux

1944

822	**204**	15f. brown	35	70
823	**204**	25f. black	60	90

The 15f. is inscr "FRANCE".

205 Louis XIV

1944. National Relief Fund.

824	-	50c.+1f.50 red	1·90	2·75
825	-	80c.+2f.20 green	1·30	2·10
826	-	1f.20+2f.80 black	1·30	2·10
827	-	1f.50+3f.50 blue	1·30	2·10
828	-	2f.+4f. brown	1·30	2·10
829	**205**	4f.+6f. orange	1·30	2·10

DESIGNS: 50c. Moliere (dramatist); 80c. Jean Hardouin-Manzart (scholar); 1f.20, Blaise Pascal (mathematician); 1f.50, Louis, Prince de Conde; 2f. Jean-Baptiste Colbert (King Louis XIV's chief minister).

206 Old and Modern Locomotives

1944. National Relief Fund. Centenary of Paris–Orleans and Paris–Rouen Railways.

830	**206**	4f.+6f. black	1·90	2·50

207 Claude Chappe

1944. 150th Anniv of Invention of Semaphore Telegraph.

831	**207**	4f. blue	20	35

208 Gallic Cock

209 "Marianne"

1944

832	**208**	10c. green	25	20
833	**208**	30c. lilac	35	55
834	**208**	40c. blue	25	20
835	**208**	50c. red	25	20
836	**209**	60c. brown	25	20
837	**209**	70c. mauve	25	20
838	**209**	80c. green	95	1·50
839	**209**	1f. violet	25	35
840	**209**	1f.20 red	25	35
841	**209**	1f.50 blue	25	20
842	**208**	2f. blue	25	20
843	**209**	2f.40 red	1·30	2·00
844	**209**	3f. green	25	35
845	**209**	4f. blue	25	35
846	**209**	4f.50 black	25	20
847	**209**	5f. blue	4·00	6·00
848	**208**	10f. violet	4·50	6·50
849	**208**	15f. brown	4·75	6·50
850	**208**	20f. green	4·00	6·00

210 Arc de Triomphe, Paris

1944

851	**210**	5c. purple	20	15
852	**210**	10c. grey	20	15
853	**210**	25c. brown	20	15
854	**210**	50c. green	20	15
855	**210**	1f. green	20	15
856	**210**	1f.50 pink	20	15
857	**210**	2f.50 violet	20	15
858	**210**	4f. blue	20	15
859	**210**	5f. black	35	35
860	**210**	10f. orange	26·00	30·00

See also Nos. 936/45.

1944. New colours and values.

861	**136**	80c. green	20	35
862	**136**	1f. blue	20	15
863	**136**	1f.20 violet	20	15
864	**136**	1f.50 brown	20	15
865	**136**	2f. brown	20	15
866	**136**	2f.40 red	20	35
867	**136**	3f. orange	20	15
868	**136**	4f. blue	20	35

211 "Marianne"

1944

869	**211**	10c. blue	25	15
870	**211**	30c. brown	25	15
871	**211**	40c. blue	25	15
872	**211**	50c. orange	25	15
873	**211**	60c. blue	25	15
874	**211**	70c. brown	25	15
875	**211**	80c. green	25	15
876	**211**	1f. lilac	25	15
877	**211**	1f.20 green	25	15
878	**211**	1f.50 red	25	15
879	**211**	2f. brown	25	15
880	**211**	2f.40 red	25	15
881	**211**	3f. olive	25	15
882	**211**	4f. blue	25	35
883	**211**	4f.50 grey	25	35
884	**211**	5f. orange	25	35
885	**211**	10f. green	25	35
886	**211**	15f. red	25	35
887	**211**	20f. orange	1·30	2·00
888	**211**	50f. violet	2·75	3·25

212 St. Denis Basilica

1944. 8th Centenary of St. Denis Basilica.

889	**212**	2f.40 brown	35	55

213 Marshal Bugeaud

1944. Centenary of Battle of Isly.

890	**213**	4f. green	25	35

214 Angouleme Cathedral

1944. Cathedrals of France (1st issue).

891	**214**	50c.+1f.50 black	80	1·10
892	-	80c.+2f.20 purple	80	1·10
893	-	1f.20+2f.80 red	80	1·10
894	-	1f.50+3f.50 blue	80	1·10
895	-	4f.+6f. red	80	1·10

DESIGNS: 80c. Chartres; 1f.20, Amiens; 1f.50, Beauvais; 4f. Albi.

1944. Nos. 750/3 optd RF.

896		10c. blue	20	15
897		30c. red	20	15
898		40c. violet	20	15
899		50c. blue	20	15

215 Arms of De Villayer

1944. Stamp Day.

900	**215**	1f.50+3f.50 brown	20	35

216 "France" exhorting Resistance Forces

1945. Liberation.

901	**216**	4f. blue	60	55

217 Shield and Broken Chains **218** Ceres **219** Marianne

220 Marianne

1945

902	**217**	10c. brown	20	15
903	**217**	30c. green	20	15
904	**217**	40c. mauve	20	15
905	**217**	50c. blue	20	15
906	**218**	60c. blue	20	15
907	**218**	80c. green	20	15
908	**218**	90c. green*	95	70
909	**218**	1f. red	20	15
910	**218**	1f.20 black	20	15
997	**218**	1f.30 blue	20	20
911	**218**	1f.50 purple	20	15
912	**219**	1f.50 red	20	15
913	**219**	2f. green	20	15
914	**218**	2f. green	20	15
915	**219**	2f.40 red	60	55
916	**218**	2f.50 brown	20	15
997a	**219**	2f.50 brown*	3·50	1·90
917	**219**	3f. brown	20	15
918	**219**	3f. red	20	15
998	**219**	3f. green	3·00	60
999	**219**	3f. mauve	40	35
1000	**219**	3f.50 brown and red	1·30	80
919	**219**	4f. blue	20	15
920	**219**	4f. violet	20	15
1001	**219**	4f. green	40	35
1001a	**219**	4f. orange	5·00	1·40
1002	**219**	4f.50 blue	40	20
921	**219**	5f. green	35	15
1003	**219**	5f. red	20	20
1004	**219**	5f. blue	40	35
1004b	**219**	5f. violet	80	20
922	**219**	6f. blue	35	35
1005	**219**	6f. red	40	20
1005a	**219**	6f. green	10·50	85
1006	**219**	8f. blue	65	35
924	**219**	10f. orange	95	70
928	**219**	10f. blue	1·90	70
1007	**219**	10f. violet	40	20
1007a	**219**	12f. blue	5·00	60
1007b	**219**	12f. orange	1·30	35
926	**219**	15f. purple	4·75	2·50
1007c	**219**	15f. red	1·60	25
1007d	**219**	15f. blue	55	20
1007e	**219**	18f. red	27·00	2·10
930	**219**	20f. green	1·90	70
932	**220**	20f. green	1·90	1·50
931	**219**	25f. red	13·00	2·00
933	**220**	25f. violet	2·40	1·80
934	**220**	50f. brown	2·75	2·75
935	**220**	100f. red	18·00	8·50

***PRECANCELS.** See note below No. 432.

1945

936	**210**	30c. black and orange	20	15
937	**210**	40c. black and grey	20	15
938	**210**	50c. black and green	20	15
939	**210**	60c. black and violet	20	15
940	**210**	80c. black and green	20	15
941	**210**	1f.20 black and brown	20	15
942	**210**	1f.50 black and red	20	15
943	**210**	2f. black and yellow	20	15
944	**210**	2f.40 black and red	20	15
945	**210**	3f. black and purple	20	15

221 Arms of Strasbourg

1945. Liberation of Metz and Strasbourg.

946	-	2f.40 blue	40	35
947	**221**	4f. brown	40	35

DESIGN: 2f.40, Arms of Metz.

222 Patient in Deck Chair

1945. Anti-tuberculosis Fund.

948	**222**	2f.+1f. orange	40	35

223 Refugee Employee and Family

1945. Postal Employees War Victims' Fund.

949	**223**	4f.+6f. brown	40	35

224 Sarah Bernhardt

1945. Birth Cent of Sarah Bernhardt (actress).

950	**224**	4f.+1f. brown	65	60

225 Alsatian and Lorrainer in Native Dress

1945. Liberation of Alsace-Lorraine.

951	**225**	4f. brown	40	35

226 Children in Country

1945. Fresh Air Crusade.

952	**226**	4f.+2f. green	40	35

1945. As No. 661 but incorporating Cross of Lorraine and inscr "1945".

953	**149**	2f. blue	40	35

227 Destruction of Oradour

1945. Destruction of Oradour-sur-Glane.

954	**227**	4f.+2f. brown	40	35

228 Louis XI

1945. Stamp Day.

955	**228**	2f.+3f. blue	85	80

229 Dunkirk

1945. Devastated Towns.

956	**229**	1f.50+1f.50 red	85	80
957	-	2f.+2f. violet	85	80
958	-	2f.40+2f.60 blue	85	80
959	-	4f.+4f. black	85	80

DESIGNS: 2f. Rouen; 2f.40c. Caen; 4f. St. Malo.

230 Alfred Fournier

1946. Prophylaxis Fund.

960	**230**	2f.+3f. red	65	60
961	**230**	2f.+3f. blue	65	60

231 Henri Becquerel

1946

962	**231**	2f.+3f. violet	65	60

1946. Surcharged 3F.

963	**222**	3f. on 2f.+1f. orange	40	35

233 "Les Invalides"

1946. War Invalids' Relief Fund.

964	**233**	4f.+6f. brown	65	60

234 "Emile Bertin" (cruiser) and "Lorraine" (battleship)

1946. Naval Charities.

965	**234**	2f.+3f. black	1·30	1·20

235 "The Letter"

1946. Postal Museum Fund.

966	**235**	2f.+3f. red	85	80

236 Iris **237** Jupiter carrying off Egine

1946. Air.

967	-	40f. green	1·30	60
968	**236**	50f. pink	1·30	60
969	**237**	100f. blue	11·50	1·60
970	-	200f. red	9·00	2·40

DESIGNS—VERT: 40f. Centaur. HORIZ: 200f. Apollo and chariot.

239 Arms of Corsica

1946. Provincial Coats of arms.

971	**239**	10c. black and blue	20	20
972	-	30c. black, red and yellow	20	20
973	-	50c. brown, yellow & red	20	20
974	-	60c. red, blue & black	20	20

DESIGNS: 30c. Alsace; 50c. Lorraine; 60c. Nice.

241 Fouquet de la Varane

1946. Stamp Day.

975	**241**	3f.+2f. brown	1·10	1·00

244 Luxembourg Palace

245 Roc-Amadour

1946. Views.

976	-	5f. mauve	40	35
977	-	6f. red	2·50	1·00
978	**244**	10f. blue	40	35
979	**244**	12f. red	5·00	1·00
980	**245**	15f. purple	7·00	80
980a	**244**	15f. red	1·30	1·20
981	-	20f. blue	2·10	35
982	-	25f. brown	7·00	60
982a	-	25f. blue	19·00	2·00

DESIGNS—HORIZ: 5f. Vezelay; 6f. Cannes; 20f. Pointe du Raz; 25f. (both) Stanislas Place, Nancy.

248 "Peace"

1946. Peace Conference.

983	**248**	3f. green	40	35
984	-	10f. blue	40	35

DESIGN: 10f. Woman releasing dove.

250 Francois Villon

1946. National Relief Fund. 15th-century Figures.

985	**250**	2f.+1f. blue	2·50	2·40
986	-	3f.+1f. blue	2·50	2·40
987	-	4f.+3f. red	2·50	2·40
988	-	5f.+4f. blue	2·75	2·50
989	-	6f.+5f. brown	2·75	2·50
990	-	10f.+6f. orange	2·75	2·50

DESIGNS: 3f. Jean Fouquet; 4f. Philippe de Commynes; 5f. Joan of Arc; 6f. Jean Gerson; 10f. Charles VII.

251

1946. UNESCO Conference, Paris.

991	**251**	10f. blue	40	35

252 St. Julien Cathedral, Le Mans

1947. National Relief Fund. Cathedrals of France (2nd issue). As T 214 and 252.

992	-	1f.+1f. red	1·70	1·60
993	-	3f.+2f. black	5·00	4·50
994	-	4f.+3f. red	2·50	2·40
995	**252**	6f.+4f. blue	2·50	2·40
996	-	10f.+6f. green	5·00	4·50

DESIGNS—VERT: 1f. St. Sernin, Toulouse; 3f. Notre-Dame du Port, Clermont-Ferrand; 10f. Notre-Dame, Paris. HORIZ: 4f. St. Front, Perigueux.

253 Louvois

1947. Stamp Day.

1008	**253**	4f.50+5f.50 red	2·50	2·30

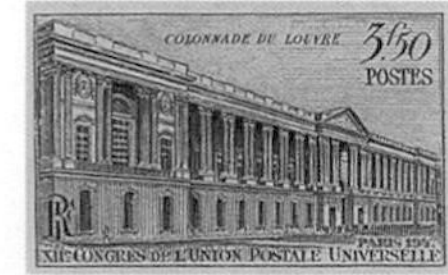
254 The Louvre Colonnade

255 Herring Gull over Ile de la Cite

1947. 12th U.P.U. Congress.

1009	**254**	3f.50 purple (postage)	65	60
1010	-	4f.50 grey	95	60
1011	-	6f. red	1·90	1·50
1012	-	10f. blue	1·90	1·50
1013	**255**	500f. green (air)	85·00	65·00

DESIGNS—As Type **254**: 4f.50, La Conciergerie; 6f. La Cite; 10f. Place de la Concorde.

256 Auguste Pavie

1947. Birth Cent of Auguste Pavie (explorer).

1014	**256**	4f.50 purple	65	60

257 Fenelon

1947. Fenelon, Archbishop of Cambrai.

1015	**257**	4f.50 brown	65	60

258 St. Nazaire Monument

1947. 5th Anniv of British Commando Raid on St. Nazaire.

1016	**258**	6f.+4f. blue	1·10	1·00

259

1947. Boy Scouts' Jamboree.

1017	**259**	5f. brown	65	60

260 Milestone on Road of Liberty

1947. Road Maintenance Fund.

1018	**260**	6f.+4f. green	1·70	1·50

261 "Resistance"

1947. Resistance Movement.

1019	**261**	5f. purple	1·10	1·00

1947. No. 997 surch 1F.

1020	**218**	1f. on 1f.30 blue	25	25

263 Conques Abbey

1947

1021	**263**	15f. red	7·00	1·50
1022	**263**	18f. blue	7·00	60

No. 1022 is inscribed "FRANCE".

264 Louis Braille

1948. Louis Braille (inventor of system of writing and printing for the blind).

1023	**264**	6f.+4f. violet	65	60

265 A. de Saint-Exupery (pilot and writer) and Douglas DB-7

1948. Air. Famous Airmen.

1024	**265**	50f.+30f. purple	5·25	4·75
1025	-	100f.+70f. blue	6·75	5·75
1026	-	40f.+10f. blue	2·75	2·30

DESIGNS: 40f. "Avion III" and Douglas DB-7 (Clement Ader); 100f. Jean Dagnaux. Douglas DB-7.

267 Etienne Arago

1948. Stamp Day and Centenary of First French Adhesive Postage Stamps.

1027	**267**	6f.+4f. violet	1·10	1·00

268 Lamartine

1948. National Relief Fund and Cent of 1848 Revolution. Dated "1848 1948".

1028	**268**	1f.+1f. green	2·10	2·00
1029	-	3f.+2f. red	2·10	2·00
1030	-	4f.+3f. purple	2·10	2·00
1031	-	5f.+4f. blue	5·25	5·00
1032	-	6f.+5f. blue	4·00	3·75
1033	-	10f.+6f. red	4·00	3·75
1034	-	15f.+7f. blue	5·25	5·00
1035	-	20f.+8f. violet	5·25	5·00

PORTRAITS: 3f. Alexandre-Auguste Ledru-Rollin; 4f. Louis Blanc; 5f. A. M. Albert; 6f. Pierre Joseph Proudhon; 10f. Louis-Auguste Blanqui; 15f. Armand Barbes; 20f. Denis-Auguste Affre.

269 Dr. Calmette

1948. 1st International B.C.G. (Vaccine) Congress.

1036	**269**	6f.+4f. slate	1·30	1·00

270 Gen. Leclerc

1948. Gen. Leclerc Memorial.

1037	**270**	6f. black	65	60

See also Nos. 1171/a.

271 Chateaubriand

1948. Death Centenary of Chateaubriand.

1038	**271**	18f. blue	65	60

272 Genissiat Barrage

1948. Inauguration of Genissiat Barrage.

1039	**272**	12f. red	1·30	1·20

273 Aerial View of Chaillot Palace

1948. U.N. Assembly, Paris.

1040	-	12f. red	85	80
1041	**273**	18f. blue	85	80

DESIGN: 12f. Ground level view of Chaillot Palace.

274 Paul Langevin

1948. Transfer of Ashes of Paul Langevin and Jean Perrin to the Pantheon.

1042	**274**	5f. brown	65	35
1043	-	8f. green (Perrin)	65	35

1949. Surch 5F.

1044	**219**	5f. on 6f. red	40	35

276 Ploughing

1949. Workers.

1045	**276**	3f.+1f. purple	1·60	1·00
1046	-	5f.+3f. blue	1·60	1·20
1047	-	8f.+4f. blue	1·60	1·20
1048	-	10f.+6f. red	1·90	1·50

DESIGNS: 5f. Fisherman; 8f. Miner; 10f. Industrial worker.

277 Arms of Burgundy

1949. Provincial Coats of Arms.

1049	**277**	10c. red, yellow & blue	20	20
1050	-	50c. yellow, red & blue	20	20
1051	-	1f. red and brown	85	60
1052	-	2f. red, yellow & green	85	35
1053	-	4f. blue, yellow & red	65	60

ARMS: 50c. "Guyenne"; 1f. "Savoie"; 2f. "Auvergne"; 4f. "Anjou".

See also Nos. 1121/5, 1178/83, 1225/31 and 1270/3.

278 Due de Choiseul

1949. Stamp Day.

1054	**278**	15f.+5f. green	1·90	1·70

279 Lille

279a Paris

1949. Air. Views.

1055	**279**	100f. purple	1·90	60
1056	-	200f. green	22·00	1·20
1057	-	300f. violet	26·00	16·00
1058	-	500f. red	£100	8·25
1059	**279a**	1000f. purple & black	£200	36·00

DESIGNS—As Type **279**: 200f. Bordeaux; 300f. Lyons; 500f. Marseilles.

280 Polar Scene

1949. Polar Expeditions.

1060	**280**	15f. blue	65	60

1949. French Stamp Centenary. (a) Imperf.

1061	**1**	15f. red	5·25	4·75
1062	**1**	25f. blue	5·25	4·75

(b) Perf.

1063	**219**	15f. red	5·25	4·75
1064	**219**	25f. blue	5·25	4·75

281 Collegiate Church of St. Bernard, Romans

1949. 600th Anniv of Cession of Dauphiny to King of France.

1065	**281**	12f. brown	65	60

282 Emblems of U.S.A. and France

1949. Franco-American Amity.

1066	**282**	25f. blue and red	1·00	95

284 St. Wandrille Abbey

1949. Views.

1067	-	20f. red	40	35
1068	**284**	25f. blue	65	35
1068a	**284**	30f. blue	7·75	6·00
1068b	-	30f. blue	1·60	35
1069	-	40f. green	24·00	60
1070	-	50f. purple	3·75	35

DESIGNS: 20f. St. Bertrand de Comminges; 30f. (1068b) Arbois (Jura); 40f. Valley of the Meuse (Ardennes); 50f. Mt. Gerbier-de-Jone, Vivarais.

285 Jean Racine

1949. 250th Death Anniv of Racine (dramatist).

1071	**285**	12f. purple	65	60

1949. French Stamp Centenary ("CITEX"). T **1** with dates "1849 1949" below, repeated ten times (2×5) with "1849–1949" centred above.

MS1071a 280×155 mm. 10f. (+100f.) orange-red.	85·00	65·00

286 Claude Chappe

287 Alexander III Bridge and "Petit Palais"

1949. International Telephone and Telegraph Congress, Paris.

1072	**286**	10f. red (postage)	1·40	1·30
1073	-	15f. violet	1·60	1·50
1074	-	25f. red	3·75	3·25
1075	-	50f. blue	7·25	5·75
1076	**287**	100f. red (air)	11·50	8·25

PORTRAITS—As Type **286**: 15f. Arago and Ampere; 25f. Emile Baudot; 50f. Gen. Ferrie.

288 Allegory of Commerce

1949. French Chambers of Commerce.

1077	**288**	15f. red	40	35

289 Allegory

1949. 75th Anniv of U.P.U.

1078	**289**	5f. green	40	35
1079	**289**	15f. red	65	35
1080	**289**	25f. blue	2·10	1·30

290 Montesquieu

1949. National Relief Fund.

1081	**290**	5f.+1f. green	5·25	4·75
1082	-	8f.+2f. blue	5·25	4·75
1083	-	10f.+3f. brown	6·00	5·50
1084	-	12f.+4f. violet	6·00	5·50
1085	-	15f.+5f. red	7·75	7·25
1086	-	25f.+10f. blue	10·00	9·25

PORTRAITS: 8f. Voltaire; 10f. Watteau; 12f. Buffon; 15f. Dupleix; 25f. Turgot.

291 "Spring"

1949. National Relief Fund. Seasons.

1087	**291**	5f.+1f. green	2·75	2·50
1088	-	8f.+2f. yellow	3·50	3·25
1089	-	12f.+3f. violet	3·75	3·25
1090	-	15f.+4f. blue	6·50	5·50

DESIGNS: 8f. "Summer"; 12f. "Autumn"; 15f. "Winter".

292 Postman

1950. Stamp Day.

1091	**292**	12f.+3f. blue	5·50	4·00

293 Raymond Poincare

1950. Honouring Poincare.

1092	**293**	15f. blue	60	55

294 Charles Peguy

1950. Honouring Charles Peguy (writer).

1093	**294**	12f. purple	60	55

295 Francois Rabelais

1950. Honouring Francois Rabelais (writer).

1094	**295**	12f. lake	1·20	1·10

296 Andre Chenier

1950. National Relief Fund (revolutionaary celebrities). Frames in blue.

1095	**296**	5f.+2f. purple	16·00	15·00
1096	-	8f.+3f. sepia	16·00	15·00
1097	-	10f.+4f. red	17·00	16·00
1098	-	12f.+5f. brown	19·00	18·00
1099	-	15f.+6f. green	20·00	20·00
1100	-	20f.+10f. blue	20·00	20·00

PORTRAITS: 8f. Louis David; 10f. Lazare Carnot; 12f. Danton; 15f. Robespierre; 20f. Hoche.

297 Chateaudun

1950

1101	**297**	8f. brown & lt brown	1·20	80
1102	-	12f. brown	1·60	1·10

DESIGN: 12f. Palace of Fontainebleau.

298 Madame Recamier

1950

1103	**298**	12f. green	95	80
1104	-	15f. blue	95	80

PORTRAIT: 15f. Madame de Sevigne.

299 "L'Amour" (after Falconet)

1950. Red Cross. Cross in red.

1105		8f.+2f. blue	3·25	3·25
1106	**299**	15f.+3f. purple	4·00	3·50

DESIGN: 8f. Bust of Alexandre Brongniart (after Houdon).

300 T.P.O. Sorting Van

1951. Stamp Day.

1107	**300**	12f.+3f. violet	5·50	5·25

301 J. Ferry (statesman)

1951

1108	**301**	15f. red	80	75

302 Shuttle

1951. Textile Industry.

1109	**302**	25f. blue	1·50	90

303 De La Salle

1951. Birth Tercentenary of Jean Baptiste de la Salle (educational reformer).

1110	**303**	15f. brown	95	75

304 Anchor and Map

1951. 50th Anniv of Formation of Colonial Troops.

1111	**304**	15f. blue	1·20	80

305 Vincent D'Indy

1951. Birth Centenary of Vincent D'Indy (composer).

1112	**305**	25f. green	2·75	2·75

306 A. de Musset

1951. National Relief Fund. Frames in sepia.

1113	**306**	5f.+1f. green	9·50	9·25
1114	-	8f.+2f. purple	11·50	11·00
1115	-	10f.+3f. green	9·50	9·25
1116	-	12f.+4f. brown	11·50	11·00
1117	-	15f.+5f. red	11·50	11·00
1118	-	30f.+10f. blue	18·00	18·00

PORTRAITS: 8f. Delacroix; 10f. Gay-Lussac; 12f. Surcouf; 15f. Talleyrand; 30f. Napoleon.

307 Nocard, Bouley and Chauveau

1951. French Veterinary Research.

1119	**307**	12f. mauve	85	75

308 Picque, Roussin and Villemin

1951. Military Health Service.

1120	**308**	15f. purple	85	75

1951. Provincial Coats of Arms as T 277.

1121	10c. yellow, blue and red	20	15
1122	50c. black, red and green	20	15
1123	1f. red, yellow and blue	35	35
1124	2f. yellow, blue and red	1·30	55
1125	3f. yellow, blue and red	1·20	55

ARMS: 10c. "Artois"; 50c. "Limousin"; 1f. "Bearn"; 2f. "Touraine"; 3f. "Franche-Comte".

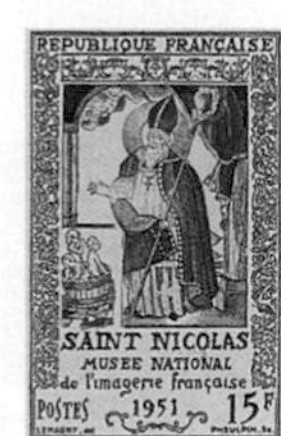

309 St. Nicholas

1951. Popular Pictorial Art Exhibition, Epinal. Multicoloured centre.

1126	**309**	15f. blue	2·00	1·50

310 Seal of Mercantile Guild

1951. Bimillenary of Paris.

1127	**310**	15f. brown, blue & red	95	55

311 M. Nogues

1951. M. Nogues (aviator).

1128	**311**	12f. indigo and blue	1·30	1·10

312 C. Baudelaire

1951. Famous French Poets.

1129	**312**	8f. violet	1·20	1·00
1130	-	12f. grey	1·20	1·00
1131	-	15f. green	1·20	1·00

DESIGNS: 12f. Paul Verlaine; 15f. Arthur Rimbaud.

313 Eiffel Tower and Chaillot Palace

1951. U.N.O. General Assembly.

1132	**313**	18f. red	1·70	1·10
1133	**313**	30f. blue	3·00	1·60

314 L. G. Clemenceau (statesman)

1951. 110th Birth Anniv of Clemenceau and 33rd Anniv of Armistice.

1134	**314**	15f. sepia	80	75

315 Chateau Clos-Vougeot

1951. 400th Anniv of Chateau Clos-Vougeot.

1135	**315**	30f. dp brown & brown	9·00	3·50

316 15th-century Child

1951. Red Cross. Cross in red.

1136	**316**	12f.+3f. brown	4·50	4·50
1137	-	15f.+5f. blue	5·50	5·25

DESIGN: 15f. 18th-century child (De La Tour).

317 Observatory, Pic du Midi de Bigorre

1951

1138	**317**	40f. violet	8·25	35
1139	-	50f. brown	7·25	35

VIEW—VERT: 50f. Church of St. Etienne, Caen.

319 19th-cent Mail Coach

1952. Stamp Day.

1140	**319**	12f.+3f. green	6·50	6·25

320 Marshal de Lattre de Tassigny

1952

1140a	**320**	12f. indigo and blue	2·75	1·80
1141	**320**	15f. brown	1·50	90

321 Gate of France, Vaucouleurs

1952

1142	**321**	12f. brown	1·90	1·40

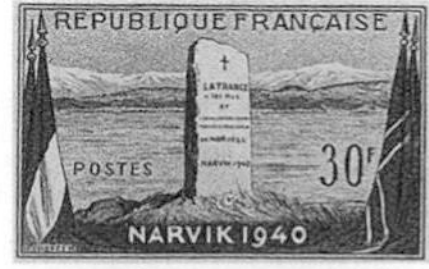

322 French Monument, Narvik

1952. Battle of Narvik.

1143	**322**	30f. blue	4·75	3·25

323 Chambord Chateau

1952

1144	**323**	20f. violet	80	35

324 Council of Europe Building, Strasbourg

1952. Council of Europe Assembly.

1145	**324**	30f. green	11·50	8·00

325 Bir Hakeim Monument

1952. 10th Anniv of Battle of Bir Hakeim.

1146	**325**	30f. lake	5·25	2·75

326 Abbey of the Holy Cross, Poitiers

1952. 1400th Anniv of Abbey of the Holy Cross, Poitiers.

1147	**326**	15f. red	80	75

327 Medaille Militaire, in 1852 and 1952

1952. Centenary of Medaille Militaire.

1148	**327**	15f. brown, yell & grn	95	80

328 Garabit Railway Viaduct

1952

1149	**328**	15f. blue	95	75

329 Leonardo, Amboise Chateau and Town of Vinci

1952. 500th Birth Anniv of Leonardo da Vinci.

1150	**329**	30f. blue	12·00	9·75

330 Flaubert (after E. Giraud)

1952. National Relief Fund. Frames in sepia.

1151	**330**	8f.+2f. blue	10·00	9·75
1152	-	12f.+3f. blue	10·00	9·75
1153	-	15f.+4f. green	10·00	9·75
1154	-	18f.+5f. sepia	13·50	13·00
1155	-	20f.+6f. red	13·50	13·00
1156	-	30f.+7f. violet	13·50	13·00

PORTRAITS: 12f. Manet; 15f. Saint-Saens; 18f. H. Poincare; 20f. Haussmann (after Yvon); 20f. Thiers.

331 R. Laennec (physician)

1952

1157	**331**	12f. green	1·20	85

332 "Cherub" (bas-relief)

1952. Red Cross Fund. Sculptures from Basin of Diana, Versailles. Cross in red.

1158	**332**	12f.+3f. green	7·25	7·00
1159	-	15f.+5f. blue	7·25	7·00

DESIGN: 15f. "Cherub" (facing left).

333 Versailles Gateway

1952

1160	**333**	18f. purple	4·25	2·75
1160a	**333**	18f. indigo, blue & brn	13·00	8·75

334 Count D'Argenson

1953. Stamp Day.

1161	**334**	12f.+3f. blue	4·75	4·50

335 "Gargantua" (Rabelais)

337 Mannequin and Place Vendome, Paris

1953. Literary Figures and National Industries.

1162	**335**	6f. lake and red	50	35
1163	-	8f. blue and indigo	50	35
1164	-	12f. green and brown	50	35
1165	-	18f. sepia and purple	90	55
1166	-	25f. sepia, red & brown	20·00	75
1166a	-	25f. blue and black	1·50	35
1167	**337**	30f. violet and blue	1·40	55
1167a	-	30f. blue & turquoise	3·50	35
1168	-	40f. brown & chocolate	6·00	55
1169	-	50f. brn, turq & blue	3·50	35
1170	-	75f. lake and red	20·00	1·60

DESIGNS—As Types **335/337**: 8f. "Celimene" (Moliere); 12f. "Figaro" (Beaumarchais); 18f. "Hernani" (Victor Hugo); 25f. (No. 1166) Tapestry; 25f. (No. 1166a) Mannequin modelling gloves; 30f. (No. 1167a) Rare books and book-binding; 40f. Porcelain and cut-glass; 50f. Gold plate and jewellery; 75f. Flowers and perfumes.

1953. General Leclerc. As T **270** but inscr "GENERAL LECLERC MARECHAL DE FRANCE".

1171	**270**	8f. brown	1·50	1·30
1171a	**270**	12f. turquoise & green	4·50	2·75

338 Olivier de Serres

1953. National Relief Fund.

1172	-	8f.+2f. blue	9·50	9·25
1173	**338**	12f.+3f. green	9·50	9·25
1174	-	15f.+4f. lake	16·00	15·00
1175	-	18f.+5f. blue	16·00	15·00
1176	-	20f.+6f. violet	16·00	15·00
1177	-	30f.+7f. brown	17·00	16·00

PORTRAITS: 8f. St. Bernard; 15f. Rameau; 18f. Monge; 20f. Michelet; 30f. Marshal Lyautey.

1953. Provincial Coats of Arms as T **277**.

1178	50c. yellow, red and blue	35	35
1179	70c. yellow, blue and red	35	35
1180	80c. yellow, red and blue	35	35
1181	1f. yellow, red and black	35	35
1182	2f. yellow, blue and brown	70	55
1183	3f. yellow, blue and red	95	55

ARMS: 50c. "Picardie"; 70c. "Gascogne"; 80c. "Berri"; 1f. "Poitou"; 2f. "Champagne"; 3f. "Dauphine".

339 Cyclists and Map

1953. 50th Anniv of "Tour de France" Cycle Race.

1184	**339**	12f. black, blue & red	3·25	1·80

340 Swimming

1953. Sports.

1185	**340**	20f. brown and red	3·50	35
1186	-	25f. brown and green	19·00	80
1187	-	30f. brown and blue	3·50	55
1188	-	40f. indigo and brown	17·00	80
1189	-	50f. brown and green	12·00	35
1190	-	75f. lake and orange	50·00	18·00

SPORTS: 25f. Running; 30f. Fencing; 40f. Canoeing; 50f. Rowing; 75f. Horse-jumping.
See also Nos. 1297/1300.

341 Mme. Vigee-Lebrun and Daughter (self- portrait)

1953. Red Cross Fund. Cross in red.

1191	**341**	12f.+3f. brown	12·00	9·75
1192	-	15f.+5f. blue	16·00	14·00

DESIGN: 15f. "The Return from the Baptism" (L. Le Nain).

1953. Surch 15F.

1193	**219**	15f. on 18f. red	80	75

343 Fouga Magister CM-170

1954. Air.

1194	-	100f. brown and blue	4·25	35
1195	-	200f. purple and blue	13·50	55
1196	**343**	500f. red and orange	£300	18·00
1197	-	1000f. blue, pur & turq	£160	23·00

AIRCRAFT: 100f. Dassault Mystere IVA; 200f. Nord 2501 Noratlas; 1000f. Breguet Br 763 Provence.
See also No. 1457.

344 Harvester

345 Gallic Cock

1954. (a) Precancelled*.

1198	**344**	4f. blue	35	25
1198a	**345**	5f. brown	60	30
1199	**344**	6f. red	8·25	1·70
1199a	**345**	8f. violet	95	35
1199b	**345**	10f. blue	3·00	55
1200	**345**	12f. mauve	5·50	1·10
1200b	**345**	15f. purple	3·75	1·10
1200c	**345**	20f. green	2·75	1·40
1201	**345**	24f. green	29·00	7·00
1201a	**345**	30f. red	17·00	4·50
1201b	**345**	40f. red	6·50	3·50
1201c	**345**	45f. green	32·00	20·00
1201d	**345**	55f. green	27·00	16·00

(b) Without precancel.

1201e	**344**	6f. brown	20	15
1201f	**344**	10f. green	1·20	15
1201g	**344**	12f. purple	35	35

***PRECANCELS.** See note below No. 432. See also Nos. 1470/3.

346 Lavallette

1954. Stamp Day.

1202	**346**	12f.+3f. green & brown	6·50	5·25

347 Exhibition Buildings

1954. 50th Anniv of Paris Fair.

1203	**347**	15f. lake and blue	60	55

348 "D-Day"

1954. 10th Anniv of Liberation.

1204	**348**	15f. red and blue	3·00	2·00

349 Lourdes

1954. Views.

1205	**349**	6f. indigo, blue & grn	70	55
1206	-	8f. green and blue	50	35
1207	-	10f. brown and blue	50	15
1208	-	12f. lilac and violet	70	15
1209	-	12f. brown & chocolate	2·40	2·10
1210	-	18f. indigo, blue & grn	4·75	1·30
1211	-	20f. brn, chestnut & bl	4·25	35
1211a	**349**	20f. brown and blue	60	35

VIEWS—HORIZ: 8f. Seine Valley at Andelys; 10f. Royan; 12f. (No. 1209), Limoges; 18f. Cheverny Chateau; 20f. (No. 1211), Ajaccio Bay. VERT: 12f. (No. 1208), Quimper.

350 Jumieges Abbey

1954. 13th Centenary of Jumieges Abbey.

1212	**350**	12f. indigo, blue & grn	2·40	1·70

351 Abbey Church of St. Philibert, Tournus

1954. 1st Conference of Romanesque Studies, Tournus.

1213	**351**	30f. blue and indigo	7·25	6·25

352 Stenay

1954. Tercent of Return of Stenay to France.

1214	**352**	15f. brown and sepia	1·20	90

353 St. Louis

1954. National Relief Fund.

1215	**353**	12f.+4f. blue	31·00	30·00
1216	-	15f.+5f. violet	31·00	30·00
1217	-	18f.+6f. sepia	31·00	30·00
1218	-	20f.+7f. red	43·00	41·00
1219	-	25f.+8f. blue	43·00	41·00
1220	-	30f.+10f. purple	43·00	41·00

PORTRAITS: 15f. Bossuet; 18f. Sadi Carnot; 20f. A. Bourdelle; 25f. Dr. E. Roux; 30f. Paul Valery.

354 Villandry Chateau

1954. Four Centuries of Renaissance Gardens.

1221	**354**	18f. green and blue	7·25	5·75

355 Cadet and Flag

1954. 150th Anniv of St. Cyr Military Academy.

1222	**355**	15f. indigo, blue & red	1·90	1·80

356 Napoleon Conferring Decorations

1954. 150th Anniv of First Legion of Honour Presentation.

1223	**356**	12f. red	2·40	1·70

357 "Basis of Metric System"

1954. 150th Anniv of Metric System.

1224	**357**	30f. sepia and blue	7·25	6·25

1954. Provincial Coats of Arms as T **277**.

1225	50c. yellow, blue and black	35	35
1226	70c. yellow, red and green	35	35
1227	80c. yellow, blue and red	35	35
1228	1f. yellow, blue and red	20	15
1229	2f. yellow, red and black	20	15
1230	3f. yellow, red and brown	20	15
1231	5f. yellow and blue	20	15

ARMS: 50c. "Maine"; 70c. "Navarre"; 80c. "Nivernais"; 1f. "Bourbonnais"; 2f. "Angoumois"; 3f. "Aunis"; 5f. "Saintonge".

359 "Young Girl with Doves" (J.-B. Greuze)

1954. Red Cross Fund. Cross in red.

1232	-	12f.+3f. indigo & blue	17·00	14·50
1233	**359**	15f.+5f. brn & dp brn	19·00	16·00

DESIGN: 12f. "The Sick Child" (E. Carriere).

360 Saint-Simon

1955. Death Bicentenary of Saint-Simon (writer).

1234	**360**	12f. purple & brown	95	90

361 "Industry", "Agriculture" and Rotary Emblem

1955. 50th Anniv of Rotary International.

1235	**361**	30f. orange, blue and deep blue	4·00	2·30

362 "France"

1955

1236	**362**	6f. brown	4·25	2·75
1237	**362**	12f. green	4·75	1·80
1238	**362**	15f. red	35	15
1238a	**362**	18f. green	1·80	1·10
1238b	**362**	20f. blue	70	15
1238c	**362**	25f. red	2·10	15

363 Thimonnier and Sewing-machines

1955. French Inventors (1st series).

1239	-	5f. blue & light blue	1·10	1·00
1240	**363**	10f. brown & chestnut	1·30	1·30
1241	-	12f. green	1·80	1·70
1242	-	18f. blue and grey	4·25	4·00
1243	-	25f. violet and plum	4·75	3·50
1244	-	30f. vermilion & red	4·75	3·50

DESIGNS: 5f. Le Bon (gaslight); 12f. Appert (food canning); 18f. Sainte-Claire Deville (aluminium); 25f. Martin (steel); 30f. Chardonnet (artificial silk).

See also Nos. 1324/7.

364 Mail Balloon "Armand Barbes", 1870

1955. Stamp Day.

1245	**364**	12f.+3f. brown, green and blue	7·25	6·25

365 Florian and Pastoral scene

1955. Birth Bicent of Florian (fabulist).

1246	**365**	12f. turquoise	1·20	90

366 Eiffel Tower and Television Aerials

1955. Television Development.

1247	**366**	15f. blue & deep blue	1·50	1·30

367 Observation Tower and Fence

1955. 10th Anniv of Liberation of Concentration Camps.

1248	**367**	12f. black and grey	1·50	1·30

368 Electric Locomotive

1955. Electrification of Valenciennes–Thionville Railway Line.

1249	**368**	12f. brown and grey	3·00	1·80

369 The "Jacquemart" (campanile), Moulins

1955

1250	**369**	12f. brown	2·20	1·80

370 Jules Verne and Capt. Nemo on the "Nautilus"

1955. 50th Death Anniv of Jules Verne (author).

1251	**370**	30f. blue	10·50	7·00

371 Maryse Bastie (airwoman) and Caudron C-635 Simoun F-ANXH

1955. Air. Maryse Bastie Commemoration.

1252	**371**	50f. claret and red	9·50	5·75

372 Vauban

1955. National Relief Fund.

1253	-	12f.+5f. violet	24·00	22·00
1254	-	15f.+6f. blue	24·00	22·00
1255	**372**	18f.+7f. green	26·00	24·00
1256	-	25f.+8f. slate	36·00	30·00
1257	-	30f.+9f. lake	38·00	34·00
1258	-	50f.+15f. turquoise	43·00	40·00

PORTRAITS: 12f. King Philippe-Auguste; 15f. Malherbe; 25f. Vergennes; 30f. Laplace; 50f. Renoir.

373 A. and L. Lumiere

1955. 60th Anniv of French Cinema Industry.

1259	**373**	30f. brown	9·00	6·25

374 Jacques Coeur (merchant prince)

1955

1260	**374**	12f. violet	3·25	2·20

375 "La Capricieuse"

1955. Centenary of Voyage of "La Capricieuse" (sail warship).

1261	**375**	30f. blue & turquoise	7·25	6·25

376 Marseilles

1955. Views.

1262	-	6f. red	50	35
1263	**376**	8f. blue	95	35
1264	-	10f. blue	50	35
1265	-	12f. brown and grey	50	35
1265a	-	15f. indigo and blue	85	75
1266	-	18f. blue and green	1·20	35
1267	-	20f. violet & dp violet	4·75	35
1268	-	25f. brown & chestnut	1·80	35
1268a	-	35f. turquoise & green	5·50	1·30
1268b	-	70f. black and green	29·00	2·75

DESIGNS—HORIZ: 6f., 35f. Bordeaux; 10f. Nice; 12f., 70f. Valentre Bridge, Cahors; 18f. Uzerche; 20f. Mount Pele, Martinique; 25f. Ramparts of Brouage. VERT: 15f. Douai Belfry.

377 Gerard de Nerval

1955. Death Centenary of De Nerval (writer).

1269	**377**	12f. sepia and red	60	55

1955. Provincial Coats of Arms as T **277**.

1270	50c. multicoloured	25	25
1271	70c. yellow, blue and red	25	25
1272	80c. yellow, red & brown	25	25
1273	1f. yellow, red and blue	25	25

ARMS: 50c. "Comte de Foix"; 70c. "Marche"; 80c. "Roussillon"; 1f. "Comtat Venaissin".

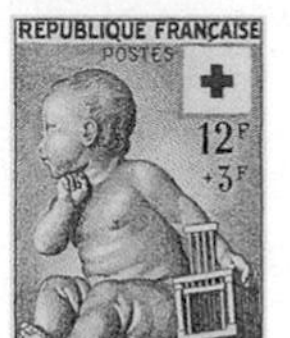

379 "Child and Cage" (after Pigalle)

1955. Red Cross Fund. Cross in red.

1274	**379**	12f.+3f. lake	12·00	11·50
1275	-	15f.+5f. blue	7·75	7·50

DESIGN: 15f. "Child and goose" (Greek sculpture).

380

1956. National Deportation Memorial.

1276	**380**	15f. sepia and brown	95	75

381 Colonel Driant

1956. Birth Centenary of Col. Driant.

1277	**381**	15f. blue	65	55

382 Trench Warfare

1956. 40th Anniv of Battle of Verdun.

1278	**382**	30f. blue and brown	2·75	2·10

383 Francis of Taxis

1956. Stamp Day.

1279	**383**	12f.+3f. brn, grn & bl	4·25	4·00

384 J. H. Fabre (entomologist)

1956. French Scientists.

1280	**384**	12f. dp brown & brn	1·50	90
1281	-	15f. black and grey	1·50	90
1282	-	18f. blue	2·75	2·30
1283	-	30f. green & dp green	6·75	4·00

DESIGNS: 15f. C. Tellier (refrigeration engineer); 18f. C. Flammarion (astronomer); 30f. P. Sabatier (chemist).

385 Grand Trianon, Versailles

1956

1284	**385**	12f. brown, green & blk	2·30	1·40

386 "Latin America" and "France"

1956. Franco-Latin American Friendship.

1285	**386**	30f. brown and sepia	3·00	2·30

387 "Reims" and "Florence"

1956. Reims-Florence Friendship.

1286	**387**	12f. green and black	1·20	1·10

388 Order of Malta and Leper Colony

1956. Order of Malta Leprosy Relief.

1287	**388**	12f. red, brown & sepia	85	75

389 St. Yves de Treguier

1956. St. Yves de Treguier Commemoration.

1288	**389**	15f. black and grey	65	55

390 Marshal Franchet d'Esperey

1956. Birth Centenary of Marshal d'Esperey.

1289	**390**	30f. purple	4·00	2·75

391 Monument

1956. Centenary of Montceau-les-Mines.

1290	**391**	12f. sepia	85	75

392 Bude

1956. National Relief Fund.

1291	**392**	12f.+3f. blue	8·25	8·00
1292	-	12f.+3f. grey	8·25	8·00
1293	-	12f.+3f. red	8·25	8·00
1294	-	15f.+5f. green	12·00	11·50
1295	-	15f.+5f. brown	12·00	11·50
1296	-	15f.+5f. violet	12·00	11·50

PORTRAITS: No. 1292, Goujon; No. 1293, Champlain; No. 1294, Chardin; No. 1295, Barres; No. 1296, Ravel.

393 Pelota

1956. Sports.

1297		30f. black and grey	2·10	35
1298	**393**	40f. purple and brown	8·50	55
1299	-	50f. violet and purple	3·00	35
1300	-	75f. grn, black & blue	17·00	3·25

DESIGNS: 30f. Basketball; 50f. Rugby; 75f. Alpine climbing.

394

1956. Europa.

1301	**394**	15f. red and pink	1·50	35
1302	**394**	30f. ultramarine and blue	8·50	1·40

395 Donzere-Mondragon Barrage

1956. Technical Achievements.

1303	**395**	12f. grey and brown	2·40	1·60
1304	-	18f. blue	4·75	3·25
1305	-	30f. blue and indigo	20·00	8·75

DESIGNS—VERT: 18f. Aiguille du Midi cable railway. HORIZ: 30f. Port of Strasbourg.

396 A. A. Parmentier (agronomist)

1956. Parmentier Commemoration.

1306	**396**	12f. brown and sepia	1·30	90

397 Petrarch

1956. Famous Men.

1307	**397**	8f. green	1·20	90
1308	-	12f. purple (Lully)	1·20	90
1309	-	15f. red (Rousseau)	1·80	90
1310	-	18f. blue (Franklin)	4·00	3·25
1311	-	20f. violet (Chopin)	5·50	2·50
1312	-	30f. turq (Van Gogh)	8·25	4·25

398 Pierre de Coubertin (reviver of Olympic Games)

1956. Coubertin Commemoration.

1313	**398**	30f. purple and grey	3·00	2·10

399 "Jeune Paysan" (after Le Nain)

1956. Red Cross Fund. Cross in red.

1314	**399**	12f.+3f. olive	4·25	4·00
1315	**399**	15f.+5f. lake	4·25	4·25

DESIGN: 15f. "Gilles" (after Watteau).

400 Pigeon and Loft

1957. Pigeon-fanciers' Commemoration.

1316	**400**	15f. blue, indigo & pur	65	55

401 Sud Aviation SE 212 Caravelle

1957. Air.

1318	-	300f. olive & turquoise	9·50	4·50
1319	**401**	500f. black and blue	42·00	5·25
1320	-	1000f. black, vio & sep	90·00	31·00

AIRCRAFT: 300f. Morane Saulnier MS-760 Paris I airplane; 1000f. Sud Aviation SE3130 Alouette II helicopter.

See also Nos. 1458/60.

402 Victor Schoelcher (slavery abolitionist)

1957. Schoelcher Commem.

1321	**402**	18f. mauve	95	90

403 18th-century Felucca

1957. Stamp Day.

1322	**403**	12f.+3f. black & grey	2·75	2·20

404 "La Baigneuse" (after Falconet) and Sevres Porcelain

1957. Bicentenary of National Porcelain Industry at Sevres.

1323	**404**	30f. blue and light blue	1·20	90

405 Plante and Accumulators

1957. French Inventors (2nd series).

1324	**405**	8f. purple and sepia	70	70
1325	-	12f. black, blue & green	85	80
1326	-	18f. lake and red	2·00	2·00
1327	-	30f. myrtle and green	3·50	3·50

DESIGNS: 12f. Beclere (radiology); 18f. Terrillon (antiseptics); 30f. Oehmichen (helicopter).

406 Uzes Chateau

1957

1328	**406**	12f. black, brown & bl	60	55
1334	-	8f. green	20	15
1335	-	15f. black and green	20	15

DESIGNS—VERT: 8f., 15f. Le Quesnoy.

407 Jean Moulin

1957. Heroes of the Resistance (1st issue). Inscr as in T **407**.

1329	**407**	8f. chocolate & brown	1·60	75
1330	-	10f. blue and black	1·60	75
1331	-	12f. green and brown	1·60	1·30
1332	-	18f. black and violet	2·75	2·10
1333	-	20f. blue & turquoise	2·40	1·40

PORTRAITS: 10f. H. d'Estienne d'Orves; 12f. R. Keller; 18f. P. Brossolette; 20f. J.-B. Lebas.

See also Nos. 1381/4, 1418/22, 1478/82 and 1519/22.

409 Emblems of Auditing

1957. 150th Anniv of Court of Accounts.

1336	**409**	12f. blue and green	35	35

410 Joinville

1957. National Relief Fund.

1337	**410**	12f.+3f. olive & sage	4·00	3·75
1338	-	12f.+3f. black & turq	4·00	3·75
1339	-	15f.+5f. red & verm	5·25	5·25
1340	-	15f.+5f. bl & ultram	5·25	5·00
1341	-	18f.+7f. black & grn	6·25	6·00
1342	-	18f.+7f. choc & brn	6·25	6·00

PORTRAITS: No. 1338, Bernard Palissy; No. 1339, Quentin de la Tour; No. 1340, Lamennais; No. 1341, George Sand; No. 1342, Jules Guesde.

See also Nos. 1390/5.

411 "Public Works"

1957. French Public Works.

1343	**411**	30f. brn, dp brn & grn	3·00	1·80

412 Port of Brest

1957

1344	**412**	12f. green and brown	1·70	1·60

413 Leo Lagrange (founder) and Stadium

1957. Universities World Games.

1345	**413**	18f. black and grey	80	75

414 Auguste Comte

1957. Death Centenary of Auguste Comte (philosopher).

1346	**414**	35f. sepia and brown	60	55

415 "Agriculture and Industry"

1957. Europa.

1347	**415**	20f. green and brown	90	40
1348	**415**	35f. blue and sepia	1·70	1·30

416 Roman Theatre, Lyons

1957. Bimillenary of Lyons.

1349	**416**	20f. purple & brown	60	55

417 Sens River, Guadeloupe

1957. Tourist Publicity Series.

1350	**417**	8f. brown and green	25	15
1351	-	10f. chocolate & brown	25	15
1351a	-	15f. multicoloured	60	55
1352	-	18f. brown and blue	40	35
1353	-	25f. brown and grey	1·00	35
1353a	-	30f. green	3·75	35
1354	-	35f. mauve and red	40	15
1355	-	50f. brown & green	85	15
1356	-	65f. blue and indigo	1·00	55
1356a	-	85f. purple	5·50	55
1356b	**417**	100f. violet	45·00	55

DESIGNS—HORIZ: 10f., 30f., Palais de l'Elysee, Paris; 15f. Chateau de Foix; 25f. Chateau de Valencay; 50f. Les Antiques, Saint Remy; 65f., 85f. Evian-les-Bains. VERT: 18f. Beynac-Cazenac (Dordogne); 35f. Rouen Cathedral.

418 Copernicus

1957. Famous Men.

1357	**418**	8f. brown	1·30	90
1358	-	10f. green	1·30	90
1359	-	12f. violet	1·30	1·10
1360	-	15f. brown & dp brown	1·70	1·30
1361	-	18f. blue	2·40	1·50
1362	-	25f. purple and lilac	2·40	1·50
1363	-	35f. blue	2·75	2·00

PORTRAITS: 10f. Michelangelo; 12f. Cervantes; 15f. Rembrandt; 18f. Newton; 25f. Mozart; 35f. Goethe.

See also Nos. 1367/74.

419 L.-J. Thenard

1957. Death Centenary of Thenard (chemist).

1364	**419**	15f. green and bistre	60	55

420 "The Blind Man and the Beggar" (after J. Callot)

1957. Red Cross Fund. Cross in red.

1365	**420**	15f.+7f. blue	6·00	5·75
1366	-	20f.+8f. brown	7·75	7·50

DESIGN: 20f. "The Beggar and the One-eyed Woman" (after J. Callot).

1958. French Doctors. As T **418**.

1367	8f. brown	1·30	90
1368	12f. violet	1·30	90
1369	15f. blue	2·00	1·10
1370	35f. black	2·50	1·60

PORTRAITS: 8f. Dr. Pinel; 12f. Dr. Widal; 15f. Dr. C. Nicolle; 35f. Dr. R. Leriche.

1958. French Scientists. As T **418**.

1371	8f. violet and blue	1·30	90
1372	12f. grey and brown	1·60	90
1373	15f. green and deep green	2·50	1·30
1374	35f. red and lake	3·50	1·80

PORTRAITS: 8f. Lagrange (mathematician); 12f. Le Verrier (astronomer); 15f. Foucault (physicist); 35f. Berthollet (chemist).

421 Rural Postal Services

1958. Stamp Day.

1375	**421**	15f.+5f. deep green, green and brown	2·50	1·80

422 Le Havre

1958. Municipal Reconstruction.

1376	**422**	12f. red and olive	95	75
1377	-	15f. brown and violet	95	75
1378	-	18f. indigo and blue	1·60	1·10
1379	-	25f. brown, turq & blue	1·90	1·10

DESIGNS—VERT: 15f. Maubeuge; 18f. Saint-Die. HORIZ: 25f. Sete.

423 French Pavilion

1958. Brussels International Exhibition.

1380	**423**	35f. green, blue & brn	35	35

1958. Heroes of the Resistance (2nd issue). Portraits inscr as in T **407**.

1381	8f. black and violet	1·10	1·00
1382	12f. green and blue	1·10	1·00
1383	15f. grey and sepia	2·75	1·40
1384	20f. blue and brown	2·10	1·60

PORTRAITS: 8f. Jean Cavailles; 12f. Fred Scamaroni; 15f. Simone Michel-Levy; 20f. Jacques Bingen.

424 Boules

1958. French Traditional Games.

1385	**424**	12f. brown and red	1·50	1·30
1386	-	15f. dp grn, grn & bl	1·90	1·40
1387	-	18f. brown and green	3·50	1·80
1388	-	25f. blue and brown	5·00	2·75

DESIGNS—HORIZ: 15f. Nautical jousting. VERT: 18f. Archery; 25f. Breton wrestling.

425 Senlis Cathedral

1958. Senlis Cathedral Commemoration.

1389	**425**	15f. blue and indigo	60	55

1958. Red Cross Fund. French Celebrities as T **410**.

1390	12f.+4f. green	2·50	2·50
1391	12f.+4f. blue	2·50	2·50
1392	15f.+5f. purple	2·75	2·75
1393	15f.+5f. blue	3·00	2·75
1394	20f.+8f. red	3·00	2·75
1395	35f.+15f. green	3·75	3·75

PORTRAITS: No. 1390, J. du Bellay; No. 1391, Jean Bart; No. 1392, D. Diderot; No. 1393, G. Courbet; No. 1394, J. B. Carpeaux; No. 1395, Toulouse-Lautrec.

426 Fragment of the Bayeux Tapestry

1958

1396	**426**	15f. red and blue	65	65

1958. Europa. As T 345 of Belgium. Size 22×36 mm.

1397	20f. red	60	45
1398	35f. blue	1·80	1·30

427 Town Halls of Paris and Rome

1958. Paris–Rome Friendship.

1399	**427**	35f. grey, blue & red	60	55

428 UNESCO Headquarters, Paris

1958. Inauguration of UNESCO Building.

1400	**428**	20f. bistre and turq	25	25
1401	-	35f. red and myrtle	35	35

DESIGN: 35f. Different view of building.

429 Flanders Grave

1958. 40th Anniv of First World War Armistice.

1402	**429**	15f. blue and green	85	55

430 Arms of Marseilles

1958. Arms of French Towns.

1403	**430**	50c. blue & deep blue	20	15
1404	-	70c. multicoloured	20	15
1405	-	80c. red, yellow & bl	20	15
1406	-	1f. red, yellow & blue	20	15
1407	-	2f. red, green & blue	20	15
1408	-	3f. multicoloured	20	15
1409	-	5f. red and brown	20	15
1410	-	15f. multicoloured	35	15

ARMS: 70c. "Lyon"; 80c. "Toulouse"; 1f. "Bordeaux"; 2f. "Nice"; 3f. "Nantes"; 5f. "Lille"; 15f. "Alger".

See also Nos. 1452, 1454, 1498a/99f, 1700/1 and 1735.

431 St. Vincent de Paul

1958. Red Cross Fund. Cross in red.

1411	**431**	15f.+7f. green	1·90	1·80
1412	-	20f.+8f. violet	1·90	1·80

PORTRAIT: 20f. J. H. Dunant (founder).

432 Arc du Carrousel and Flowers

1959. Paris Flower Festival.

1413	**432**	15f. multicoloured	80	55

433 Symbols of Learning and "Academic Palms"

1959. 150th Anniv of "Academic Palms".

1414	**433**	20f. black, vio & lake	35	35

434 Father Charles de Foucauld (missionary)

1959. Charles de Foucauld Commem.

1415	**434**	50f. multicoloured	80	75

435 Douglas DC-3 Mail Plane making Night-landing

1959. Stamp Day.

1416	**435**	20f.+5f. mult	95	90

See also No. 1644.

436 Miner's Lamp, Picks and School Building

1959. 175th Anniv of School of Mines.

1417	**436**	20f. turq, blk & red	35	35

437 "Five Martyrs"

1959. Heroes of the Resistance (3rd series).

1418	**437**	15f. black and violet	65	35
1419	-	15f. violet and purple	65	65
1420	-	20f. brown & chestnut	65	65
1421	-	20f. turquoise & green	90	85
1422	-	30f. violet and purple	1·10	90

PORTRAITS—As T **407**: No. 1419, Yvonne Le Roux; No. 1420, Martin Bret; No. 1421, Mederic-Vedy; No. 1422, Moutardier.

438 Foum el Gherza Dam

1959. French Technical Achievements.

1423	**438**	15f. turq and brown	60	35
1424	-	20f. purple, red & brn	85	80
1425	-	30f. brn, turq & blue	85	80
1426	-	50f. blue and green	1·30	90

DESIGNS—VERT: 20f. Marcoule Atomic Power Station; 30f. Oil derrick and pipe-line at Hassi-Messaoud, Sahara. HORIZ: 50f. National Centre of Industry and Technology, Paris.

439 C. Goujon and C. Rozanoff (test pilots)

1959. Goujon and Rozanoff Commem.

1427	**439**	20f. brown, red & blue	80	75

440 Villehardouin (chronicler)

1959. Red Cross Fund.

1428	**440**	15f.+5f. blue	1·90	1·80
1429	-	15f.+5f. myrtle	1·90	1·80
1430	-	20f.+10f. bistre	1·90	1·80
1431	-	20f.+10f. grey	2·10	2·10
1432	-	30f.+10f. lake	2·10	2·10
1433	-	30f.+10f. brown	2·40	2·10

PORTRAITS: No. 1429, Le Notre (Royal gardener); No. 1430, D'Alembert (philosopher); No. 1431, D'Angers (sculptor); No. 1432, Bichat (physiologist); No. 1433, Bartholdi (sculptor).

441 M. Desbordes-Valmore

1959. Death Centenary of Marceline Desbordes-Valmore (poetess).

1434	**441**	30f. brown, blue & grn	35	35

442 "Marianne" in Ship of State

1959

1437	**442**	25f. red and black	60	15

See also No. 1456.

443 Tancarville Bridge

1959. Inauguration of Tancarville Bridge.

1438	**443**	30f. green, brown & blue	60	55

444 Jean Jaures

1959. Birth Centenary of Jean Jaures (socialist leader).

1439	**444**	50f. brown	60	55

1959. Europa. As T **360** of Belgium but size 22×36 mm.

1440		25f. green	60	25
1441		50f. violet	2·40	1·60

445 "Giving Blood"

1959. Blood Donors.

1442	**445**	20f. grey and red	35	35

446 Clasped Hands of Friendship

1959. Tercent of Treaty of the Pyrenees.

1443	**446**	50f. red, blue & mauve	80	55

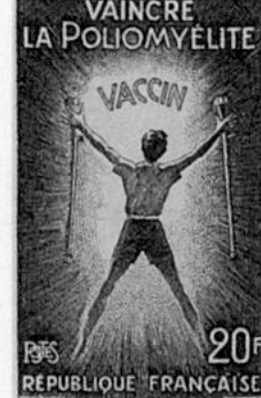

447 Youth throwing away Crutches

1959. Infantile Paralysis Relief Campaign.

1444	**447**	20f. blue	35	35

448 Henri Bergson

1959. Birth Centenary of Bergson (philosopher).

1445	**448**	50f. brown	60	55

449 Avesnes-sur-Helpe

1959

1446	**449**	20f. blue, brown & blk	60	35
1447	-	30f. brown, purple & bl	60	55

DESIGN: 30f. Perpignan Castle.

450 Abbe C. M. de l'Epee (teacher of deaf mutes)

1959. Red Cross Fund. Cross in red.

1448	**450**	20f.+10f. purple & blk	3·00	3·00
1449	-	25f.+10f. black & blue	3·50	3·50

PORTRAIT: 25f. V. Hauy (teacher of the blind).

451 N.A.T.O. Headquarters, Paris

1959. 10th Anniv of N.A.T.O.

1450	**451**	50f. brown, green & bl	80	75

1959. Frejus Disaster Fund. Surch FREJUS + 5f.

1451	**442**	25f.+5f. red & black	35	35

453 Sower

1960. T **453** and previous designs but new currency.

1452	-	5c. red & brn (as 1409)	7·25	25
1453	**344**	10c. green	80	15
1454	-	15c. mult (as 1410)	1·20	25
1455	**453**	20c. red & turquoise	35	15
1456	**442**	25c. blue and red	3·25	15
1456a	**453**	30c. blue and indigo	2·40	55

1960. Air. As previous designs but new currency and new design (No. 1457b).

1457	-	2f. pur & blk (as 1195)	2·40	35
1457b	-	2f. indigo and blue	1·40	35
1458	-	3f. brn & bl (as 1318)	2·40	25
1459	**401**	5f. black and blue	4·75	1·10
1460	-	10f. black, violet and brown (as 1320)	19·00	2·75

DESIGN: No. 1457b, Dassault Berguet Mystere Falcon.

454 Laon Cathedral

1960. Tourist Publicity.

1461	**454**	15c. indigo and blue	60	35
1462	-	30c. pur, grn & blue	3·75	45
1463	-	45c. vio, pur & sepia	1·20	35
1464	-	50c. purple and green	2·50	15
1465	-	65c. brn, grn & blue	1·90	35
1466	-	85c. sepia, grn & blue	3·75	35
1467	-	1f. violet, grn & turq	3·75	30

DESIGNS—HORIZ: 30c. Fougeres Chateau; 65c. Valley of the Sioule; 85c. Chaumont Railway Viaduct. VERT: 45c. Kerrata Gorges, Algeria; 50c. Tlemcen Mosque, Algeria; 1f. Cilaos Church and Great Bernard Mountains, Reunion.

See also Nos. 1485/7.

455 Pierre de Nolhac

1960. Birth Centenary (1959) of Pierre de Nolhac (historian).

1468	**455**	20c. black	80	55

456 St. Etienne Museum

1960. Museum of Art and Industry, St. Etienne.

1469	**456**	30c. brown, red & blue	80	55

1960. As T **345** but with values in new currency.

1470	**345**	8c. violet	1·20	25
1471	**345**	20c. green	3·75	80
1472	**345**	40c. red	13·50	3·00
1473	**345**	55c. green	43·00	23·00

Nos. 1470/3 were only issued precancelled (see note below No. 432).

457 Assembly Emblem and View of Cannes

1960. 5th Meeting of European Mayors Assembly.

1474	**457**	50c. brown and green	1·20	90

458 "Ampere" (cable-laying ship)

1960. Stamp Day.

1475	**458**	20c.+5c. blue & turq	2·30	1·70

459 Girl of Savoy

1960. Centenary of Attachment of Savoy and Nice to France.

1476	**459**	30c. green	1·00	80
1477	-	50c. brown, red and yellow (Girl of Nice)	1·00	55

1960. Heroes of the Resistance (4th series). Portraits as T **407**.

1478	20c. black and brown	2·50	1·70
1479	20c. lake and red	2·50	1·70
1480	30c. violet & deep violet	3·75	2·30
1481	30c. blue and indigo	3·75	2·30
1482	50c. brown and green	5·00	3·50

PORTRAITS: No. 1478, E. Debeaumarche; No. 1479, P. Masse; No. 1480, M. Ripoche; No. 1481, L. Vieljeux; No. 1482, Abbe Rene Bonpain.

460 Child Refugee

1960. World Refugee Year.

1483	460	25c.+10c. bl, brn & grn	60	55

461 "The Road to Learning"

1960. 150th Anniv of Strasbourg Teachers' Training College.

1484	461	20c. violet, pur & blk	35	35

1960. Views as T **454**.

1485	15c. sepia, grey and blue	60	55
1485a	20c. blue, green and buff	35	35
1486	30c. sepia, green and blue	1·20	90
1487	50c. brown, green & red	1·00	90

DESIGNS: 15c. Lisieux Basilica; 20c. Bagnoles de l'Orne; 30c. Chateau de Blois; 50c. La Bourboule.

462 L'Hospital (statesman)

1960. Red Cross Fund.

1488	462	10c.+5c. violet & red	2·50	2·30
1489	-	20c.+10c. turq & grn	3·75	3·50
1490	-	20c.+10c. green & brn	3·75	3·50
1491	-	30c.+10c. blue & vio	5·00	4·50
1492	-	30c.+10c. crim & red	5·00	4·50
1493	-	50c.+15c. blue and slate	6·25	5·75

DESIGNS: No. 1489, Boileau (poet); No. 1490, Turenne (military leader); No. 1491, Bizet (composer); No. 1492, Charcot (neurologist); No. 1493, Degas (painter).

463 "Marianne"

1960

1494	463	25c. grey and red	35	15

464 Cross of Lorraine

1960. 20th Anniv of De Gaulle's Appeal.

1495	464	20c. brown, grn & sep	1·00	55

465 Jean Bouin and Olympic Stadium

1960. Olympic Games.

1496	465	20c. brown, red & blue	60	55

1960. Europa. As T **373** of Belgium, but size 36×22½ mm.

1497	25c. turquoise and green	35	25
1498	50c. purple and red	1·00	55

1960. Arms. As T **430**.

1498a	1c. blue and yellow	20	15
1498b	2c. yellow, green and blue	20	15
1499	5c. multicoloured	20	15
1499a	5c. red, yellow and blue	20	15
1499b	10c. blue, yellow and red	20	15
1499c	12c. red, yellow and black	20	15
1499d	15c. yellow, blue and red	20	15
1499e	18c. multicoloured	60	55
1499f	30c. red and blue	75	15

ARMS: 1c. "Niort"; 2c. "Gueret"; 5c. (No. 1499) "Oran"; 5c. (No. 1499a) "Amiens"; 10c. "Troyes"; 12c. "Agen"; 15c. "Nevers"; 18c. "Saint-Denis (Reunion)"; 30c. "Paris".

466 Madame de Stael (after Gerard)

1960. Madame de Stael (writer).

1500	466	30c. olive and purple	60	55

467 Gen. Estienne, Morane Saulnier Type L Airplane and Tank

1960. Birth Centenary of Gen. Estienne.

1501	467	15c. sepia and lilac	60	55

468 Sangnier

1960. 10th Death Anniv of Marc Sangnier (patriot).

1502	468	20c. black, violet & blue	35	35

469 Order of the Liberation

1960. 20th Anniv of Order of the Liberation.

1503	469	20c. green and black	60	55

470 Atlantic Puffins at Les Sept Iles

1960. Nature Protection.

1504	470	30c. multicoloured	35	35
1505	-	50c. multicoloured	1·20	55

DESIGN: 50c. European bee eaters, Camargue.

471 A. Honnorat

1960. 10th Death Anniv of Andre Honnorat (philanthropist).

1506	471	30c. black, green & blue	35	35

472 Mace of St. Martin's Brotherhood

1960. Red Cross Fund. Cross in red.

1507	472	20c.+10c. lake	5·00	4·50
1508	-	25c.+10c. blue	5·00	4·50

DESIGN: 25c. St. Martin (after 16th-cent. wood-carving).

473 St. Barbe and College

1960. 500th Anniv of St. Barbe College.

1509	473	30c. multicoloured	60	55

474 Northern Lapwings

1960. Study of Bird Migration. Inscr "ETUDE DES MIGRATIONS".

1510	474	20c. multicoloured	35	35
1511	-	45c. multicoloured	1·00	1·10

DESIGN: 45c. Green-winged teal.

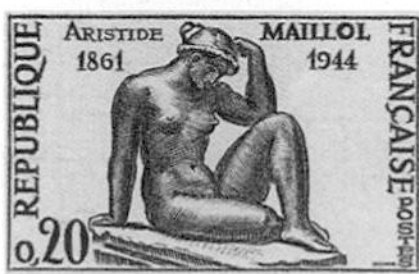

475 "Mediterranean" (after Maillol)

1961. Birth Cent of Aristide Maillol (sculptor).

1512	475	20c. blue and red	35	35

476 "Marianne"

1961

1513	476	20c. red and blue	35	15

477 Orly Airport

1961. Opening of New Installations at Orly Airport.

1514	477	50c. turq, blue & blk	80	55

478 Georges Melies

1961. Birth Centenary of Georges Melies (cinematograph pioneer).

1515	478	50c. blue, brown & vio	1·20	90

479 Postman of Paris "Little Post" 1760

1961. Stamp Day and Red Cross Fund.

1516	479	20c.+5c. grn, red & brn	1·20	90

480 Jan Nicquet and Tobacco Flowers and Leaves

1961. 400th Anniv of Introduction of Tobacco into France.

1517	480	30c. red, brown & grn	35	35

The portrait on No. 1517 is of Jan Nicquet, a Flemish merchant, and not Jean Nicot as inscribed.

481 Father Lacordaire (after Chasseriau)

1961. Death Centenary of Father Lacordaire (theologian).

1518	481	30c. black and brown	60	55

1961. Heroes of the Resistance (5th issue). Portrait inscr as in T **407**.

1519	20c. violet and blue	1·50	90
1520	20c. blue and green	1·50	90
1521	30c. black and brown	2·50	1·30
1522	30c. black and blue	2·00	1·50

PORTRAITS: No. 1519, J. Renouvin; No. 1520, L. Dubray; No. 1521, P. Gateaud; No. 1522, Mother Elisabeth.

482 Dove, Globe and Olive Branch

1961. World Federation of Old Soldiers Meeting, Paris.

1523	482	50c. red, blue & green	60	55

483 Deauville, 1861

1961. Centenary of Deauville.

1524	483	50c. lake	2·75	2·00

484 Du Guesclin (Constable of France)

1961. Red Cross Fund.

1525	484	15c.+5c. black & pur	2·50	2·30
1526	-	20c.+10c. green & blue	3·75	3·50
1527	-	20c.+10c. crimson & red	3·75	3·50
1528	-	30c.+10c. black & brn	3·75	3·50
1529	-	45c.+10c. brown & grn	5·00	4·50
1530	-	50c.+15c. violet & red	5·00	4·50

PORTRAITS: No. 1526, Puget (sculptor); No. 1527, Coulomb (physicist); No. 1528, General Drouot; No. 1529, Daumier (caricaturist); No. 1530, Apollinaire (writer).

485 Champmesle ("Roxane")

1961. French Actors and Actresses. Frames in red.

1531	485	20c. brown and green	1·50	55
1532	-	30c. brown and red	1·50	75
1533	-	30c. myrtle and green	1·50	75
1534	-	50c. brown & turquoise	2·10	1·10
1535	-	50c. brown and olive	2·00	90

PORTRAITS: No. 1532, Talma ("Oreste"); No. 1533, Rachel ("Phedre"); No. 1534, Raimu ("Cesar"); No. 1535, Gerard Philipe ("Le Cid").

486 Mont Dore, Snow Crystal and Cable Rly

1961. Mont Dore.

1536	**486**	20c. purple and orange	35	35

487 Thann

1961. 800th Anniv of Thann.

1537	**487**	20c. violet, brn & grn	1·00	75

488 Pierre Fauchard

1961. Birth Bicentenary of Pierre Fauchard (dentist).

1538	**488**	50c. black and green	80	75

489 Doves

1961. Europa.

1539	**489**	25c. red	35	25
1540	**489**	50c. blue	1·00	55

490 Sully-sur-Loire

1961. Tourist Publicity.

1541	-	15c. slate, pur & turq	20	15
1542	-	20c. brown and green	35	35
1543	-	30c. blue, grn & sepia	35	35
1544	-	30c. black, grey & grn	1·90	1·10
1545	**490**	45c. brown, green & blue	35	15
1546	-	50c. myrt, turq & grn	2·00	35
1547	-	65c. blue, brown & myrt	60	35
1548	-	85c. blue, brown & myrt	80	55
1549	-	1f. brown, blue & myrt	6·25	55
1550	-	1f. brown, green & blue	80	15

VIEWS—HORIZ: 15c. Saint-Paul; 30c. (No. 1543), Arcachon; 30c. (No. 1544), Law Courts, Rennes; 50c. Cognac; 65c. Dinan; 85c. Calais; 1f. (No. 1549), Medea, Algeria; 1f. (No. 1550), Le Touquet-Paris-Plage, golf-bag and Handley Page H.P.R.7 Dart Herald airplane. VERT: 20c. Laval, Mayenne.

See also Nos. 1619/23, 1654/7, 1684/8, 1755/61, 1794, 1814/18, 1883/5, 1929/33, 1958/61, 2005/8, 2042/4, 2062/4, 2115/20, 2187/97, 2258/64, 2310/15, 2360/5, 2403/10, 2503/8, 2566/70, 2630/4, 2652/6, 2710/14, 2762/6, 2834/6, 2883/6, 2973/6, 3024/6, 3077/80, 3124/9, 3180/3, 3240/3, 3330/3, 3375/9, 3487/91, 3580/3, 3642/5, 3720/3, 3800/1, 3908/11, 3946/9 and 4084/7.

491 "14th July" (R. de la Fresnaye)

1961. Modern French Art.

1551		50c. multicoloured	5·00	2·30
1552		65c. blue, green & violet	7·50	3·50
1553		85c. red, bistre and blue	3·75	2·30
1554	**491**	1f. multicoloured	6·25	3·50

PAINTINGS: 50c. "The Messenger" (Braque); 65c. "Blue Nudes" (Matisse); 85c. "The Cardplayers" (Cezanne).

See also Nos. 1590/2, 1603/6, 1637/9, 1671/4, 1710/4, 1742/5, 1786/9, 1819/22, 1877/80, 1908/10, 1944/7, 1985/8, 2033/6, 2108/13, 2159/60, 2243, 2290/2, 2338/41, 2398/9, 2531/4, 2580/2, 2608/12, 2672/6, 2721/5, 2773/6, 2850/3, 2858/60, 2966/8, 3008/9, 3085, 3245/7, 3306/7, 3368/9, 3483/6, 3561/3, 3638/4, 3702/5, 3899, 3990, 3902, 3951/4 and 4074/7.

493 "It is so sweet to love" (Wood-carving from Rouault's "Miserere")

1961. Red Cross Fund. Cross in red.

1555	**493**	20c.+10c. black & pur	3·50	3·25
1556	-	25c.+10c. black & pur	4·25	4·00

DESIGN: 25c. "The blind leading the blind" (from Rouault's "Miserere").

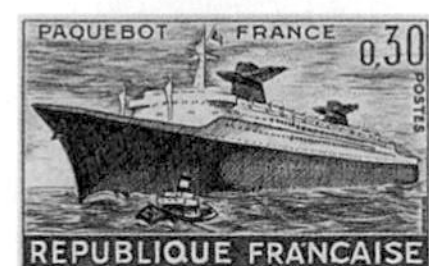

494 Liner "France"

1962. Maiden Voyage of Liner "France".

1557	**494**	30c. black, red & blue	1·20	75

495 Skier at Speed

1962. World Ski Championships, Chamonix.

1558	**495**	30c. violet and blue	35	35
1559	-	50c. green, blue & vio	80	55

DESIGN: 50c. Slalom-racer.

496 M. Bourdet

1962. 60th Birth Anniv of Maurice Bourdet (journalist and radio commentator).

1560	**496**	30c. grey	35	35

497 Dr. P.-F. Bretonneau

1962. Death Centenary of Dr. Pierre-Fidele Bretonneau (medical scientist).

1561	**497**	50c. violet and blue	60	55

498 Gallic Cock

1962

1562	**498**	25c. red, blue & brown	35	15
1562a	**498**	30c. red, green & brn	1·20	15

499 Royal Messenger of late Middle Ages

1962. Stamp Day.

1563	**499**	20c.+5c. brn, bl & red	1·20	1·10

500 Vannes

1962

1564	**500**	30c. blue	1·20	1·10

501 Globe and Stage Set

1962. World Theatre Day.

1565	**501**	50c. lake, grn & ochre	80	55

502 Harbour Installations

1962. 300th Anniv of Cession of Dunkirk to France.

1566	**502**	95c. purple, brown & green	1·90	90

503 Mount Valerien Memorial

1962. Resistance Fighters' Memorials (1st issue).

1567	**503**	20c. myrtle and drab	1·20	90
1568	-	30c. blue	1·20	90
1569	-	50c. indigo and blue	1·50	1·10

MEMORIALS—VERT: 30c. Vercors; 50c. Ile de Sein.

See also Nos. 1609/10.

504 Emblem and Swamp

1962. Malaria Eradication.

1570	**504**	50c. red, blue & green	60	45

505 Nurses and Child

1962. National Hospitals Week.

1571	**505**	30c. brown, grey & grn	35	35

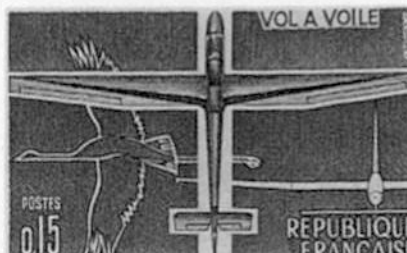

506 Gliders and Stork

1962. Civil and Sports Aviation.

1572	**506**	15c. brown and chest	80	55
1573	-	20c. red and purple	80	55

DESIGN: 20c. Jodel Ambassadeur and early aircraft.

507 Emblem and School of Horology

1962. Cent of School of Horology, Besancon.

1574	**507**	50c. vio, brown & red	80	55

508 "Selecting a Tapestry"

1962. Tercentenary of Manufacture of Gobelin Tapestries.

1575	**508**	50c. turq, red & grn	80	55

509 Pascal

1962. Death Tercent of Pascal (philosopher).

1576	**509**	50c. red and green	80	55

510 Denis Papin (inventor)

1962. Red Cross Fund.

1577		15c.+5c. sepia & turquoise	2·50	2·30
1578		20c.+10c. brown and red	3·75	3·50
1579		20c.+10c. blue and grey	3·75	3·50
1580		30c.+10c. indigo and blue	3·75	3·50
1581		45c.+15c. pur and brown	3·75	3·50
1582		50c.+20c. black and blue	3·75	3·50

DESIGNS: No. 1577, Type **510**; 1578, Edme Bouchardon (sculptor); 1579, Joseph Lakanal (politician); 1580, Gustave Charpentier (composer); 1581, Edouard Estauni (writer); 1582, Hyacinthe Vincent (scientist).

511 "Modern" Rose

1962. Rose Culture.

1583	**511**	20c. red, green & olive	1·00	55
1584	-	30c. red, myrt & olive	1·00	75

DESIGN: 30c. "Old fashioned" rose.

512 Europa "Tree"

1962. Europa.

1585	**512**	25c. violet	35	25

1586	**512**	50c. brown	1·00	55

513 Telecommunications Centre, Pleumeur-Bodou

1962. 1st Trans-Atlantic Telecommunications Satellite Link.

1587	**513**	25c. buff, green & grey	35	35
1588	-	50c. bl, grn & indigo	80	55
1589	-	50c. brown and blue	80	55

DESIGNS: 50c. (No. 1588), "Telstar" satellite, globe and television receiver; 50c. (No. 1589), Radio telescope, Nancay (Cher).

1962. French Art. As T **491**.

1590	50c. multicoloured	5·00	2·30
1591	65c. multicoloured	5·00	2·30
1592	1f. multicoloured	7·50	3·50

PAINTINGS—HORIZ: 50c. "Bonjour, Monsieur Courbet" (Courbet); 65c. "Madame Manet on a Blue Sofa" (Manet). VERT: 1f. "Officer of the Imperial Horse Guards" (Gericault).

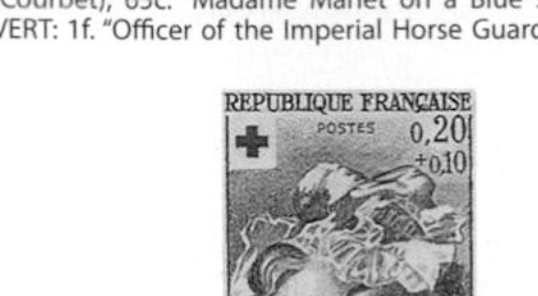

514 "Rosalie Fragonard" (after Fragonard)

1962. Red Cross Fund. Cross in red.

1593	**514**	20c.+10c. brown	1·90	1·70
1594	-	25c.+10c. green	3·00	2·75

PORTRAIT: 25c. "Child as Pierrot" (after Fragonard).

515 Bathyscaphe "Archimede"

1963. Record Undersea Dive.

1595	**515**	30c. black and blue	35	35

516 Flowers and Nantes Chateau

1963. Nantes Flower Show.

1596	**516**	30c. blue, red & green	35	35

517 Jacques Amyot (Bishop of Auxerre)

1963. Red Cross Fund.

1597	**517**	20c.+10c. purple, violet and grey	1·50	1·40
1598	-	20c.+10c. deep brown, brown and blue	1·90	1·70
1599	-	30c.+10c. grn & pur	1·50	1·40
1600	-	30c.+10c. black, green and brown	1·90	1·70
1601	-	50c.+20c. grn, brn & bl	1·90	1·70
1602	-	50c.+20c. blk, bl & brn	2·50	2·30

DESIGNS: No. 1598, Etienne Mehul (composer); No. 1599 Pierre de Marivaux (dramatist); No. 1600, N.-L. Vauquelin (chemist); No. 1601, Jacques Daviel (oculist); No. 1602, Alfred de Vigny (poet).

1963. French Art. As T **491**.

1603	50c. multicoloured	5·00	3·50
1604	85c. multicoloured	2·75	1·80
1605	95c. multicoloured	1·00	90
1606	1f. multicoloured	6·25	4·50

DESIGNS—VERT: 50c. "Jacob's Struggle with the Angel" (Delacroix); 85c. "The Married Couple of the Eiffel Tower" (Chagall); 95c. "The Fur Merchants" (stained glass window, Chartres Cathedral); 1f. "St. Peter and the Miracle of the Fishes" (stained glass window, Church of St. Foy de Conches).

518 Roman Post Chariot

1963. Stamp Day.

1607	**518**	20c.+5c. purple & brn	35	35

519 Woman reaching for Campaign Emblem

1963. Freedom from Hunger.

1608	**519**	50c. brown & myrtle	60	55

520 Glieres Memorial

1963. Resistance Fighters' Memorials (2nd issue).

1609	**520**	30c. olive and brown	80	75
1610	-	50c. black	80	75

DESIGN: 50c. Deportees Memorial, Ile de la Cite (Paris).

521 Beethoven (West Germany)

1963. Celebrities of European Economic Community Countries.

1611	**521**	20c. blue, brown & grn	60	55
1612	-	20c. black, violet & red	60	55
1613	-	20c. blue, pur & olive	60	55
1614	-	20c. brown, pur & brn	60	55
1615	-	30c. sepia, violet & brn	60	55

PORTRAITS AND VIEWS: No. 1611, Birthplace and modern Bonn; No. 1612, Emile Verhaeren (Belgium: Family grave and residence, Roisin); No. 1613, Giuseppe Mazzini (Italy: Marcus Aurelius statue and Appian Way, Rome); No. 1614, Emile Mayrisch (Luxembourg: Colpach Chateau and Steel Plant, Esch); No. 1615, Hugo de Groot (Netherlands: Palace of Peace, The Hague, and St. Agatha's Church, Delft).

522 Hotel des Postes, Paris

1963. Centenary of Paris Postal Conference.

1616	**522**	50c. sepia	60	55

523 College Building

1963. 400th Anniv of Louis the Great College, Paris.

1617	**523**	30c. myrtle	35	35

524 St. Peter's Church and Castle Keep, Caen

1963. 36th French Philatelic Societies Federation Congress, Caen.

1618	**524**	30c. brown and blue	35	35

1963. Tourist Publicity. As T **490**. Inscr "1963".

1619	30c. ochre, blue & green	60	25
1620	50c. red, blue & turquoise	60	25
1621	60c. red, turquoise & blue	1·00	45
1622	85c. purple, turquoise & grn	2·10	45
1623	95c. black	1·20	35

DESIGNS—HORIZ: 30c. Amboise Chateau; 50c. Cote d'Azur, Var; 85c. Vittel. VERT: 60c. Saint-Flour; 95c. Church and cloisters, Moissac.

525 Water-skiing

1963. World Water-skiing Championships, Vichy.

1624	**525**	30c. black, red & turq	35	35

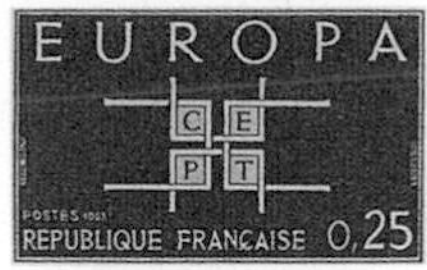

526 "Co-operation"

1963. Europa.

1625	**526**	25c. brown	50	35
1626	**526**	50c. green	75	55

527 "Child with Grapes" (Angers)

1963. Red Cross Fund. Cross in red.

1627	**527**	20c.+10c. black	1·20	1·10
1628	-	25c.+10c. green	1·20	1·10

DESIGN: 25c. "The Piper" (Manet).

528 "Philately"

1963. "PHILATEC 1964" International Stamp Exhibition, Paris (1st issue).

1629	**528**	25c. red, green & grey	35	35

See also Nos. 1640/3 and 1651.

529 Radio-T.V. Centre

1963. Opening of Radio-T.V. Centre, Paris.

1630	**529**	20c. slate, ol & brn	35	35

530 Emblems of C.P. Services

1964. Civil Protection.

1631	**530**	30c. blue, red & orange	60	55

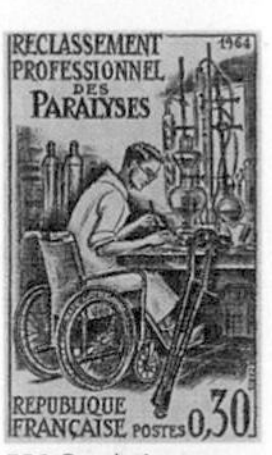

531 Paralytic at Work in Invalid Chair

1964. Professional Rehabilitation of Paralytics.

1632	**531**	30c. brn, chestnut & grn	35	35

532 18th-century Courier

1964. Stamp Day.

1633	**532**	20c.+5c. myrtle	35	35

533 "Deportation"

1964. 20th Anniv of Liberation (1st issue).

1634	**533**	20c.+5c. slate	1·00	90
1635	-	50c.+5c. green	1·20	1·10

DESIGN: 50c. "Resistance" (memorial).

See also Nos. 1652/3 and 1658.

534 Pres. Rene Coty

1964. Pres. Coty Commemoration.

1636	**534**	30c.+10c. brown & red	60	55

1964. French Art. As T **491**.

1637	1f. multicoloured	2·50	1·80
1638	1f. multicoloured	1·90	1·40
1639	1f. multicoloured	1·00	90

DESIGNS—VERT: No. 1637, Jean le Bon (attributed to Girard of Orleans); No. 1638, Tomb plaque of Geoffrey IV (12th-century "champleve" (grooved) enamel from Limousin); No. 1639, "The Lady with the Unicorn" (15th-century tapestry).

535 "Blanc" 2c. Stamp of 1900

1964. "PHILATEC 1964" International Stamp Exhibition, Paris (2nd issue).

1641	**535**	25c. purple and bistre	60	55
1642	-	25c. blue and bistre	60	55
1640	-	30c. blue, black & brn	60	55
1643	-	30c. red, black & blue	60	55

DESIGNS: No. 1640, "Postal Mechanization" (letter-sorting equipment and parcel conveyor); No. 1642, "Mouchon" 25c. stamp of 1900; No. 1643, "Telecommunications" (telephone dial, teleprinter and T.V. tower).

1964. 25th Anniv of Night Airmail Service. As T **435** but additionally inscr "25E ANNIVERSAIRE" and colours changed.

1644	**435**	25c. multicoloured	35	35

536 Stained Glass Window

1964. 800th Anniv of Notre Dame, Paris.

1645	**536**	60c. multicoloured	80	75

537 Calvin

1964. 400th Death Anniv of Calvin (reformer).

1646	**537**	30c.+10c. brown, sepia and turquoise	60	55

538 Gallic Coin

1964. Pre-cancels.

1647	**538**	10c. brown and green	60	35
1647a	**538**	15c. brown & orange	35	35
1647b	**538**	22c. violet and green	85	55
1647c	**538**	25c. brown and violet	60	75
1647d	**538**	26c. brown & purple	1·00	35
1647e	**538**	30c. brn & lt brown	1·00	90
1647f	**538**	35c. blue and red	1·90	90
1648	**538**	45c. brown and green	2·50	1·10
1648a	**538**	50c. brown and blue	1·20	1·30
1648b	**538**	70c. brown and blue	8·00	4·50
1649	**538**	90c. brown and red	3·00	1·80

See note below No. 432 (1920).

For stamps as Type **538** but inscribed "FRANCE", see Nos. 2065a/1.

539 Pope Sylvester II

1964. Pope Sylvester II Commemoration.

1650	**539**	30c.+10c. pur & grey	60	55

540 Rocket and Horseman

1964. "PHILATEC 1964" International Stamp Exhibition, Paris (3rd issue).

1651	**540**	1f. blue, red & brown	37·00	29·00
MS1651a		145×285 mm. No. 1651 ×8 plus labels bearing "PHILATEC" emblem	£375	£275

Sold at 4f. incl. entrance fee to Exhibition.

541 Landings in Normandy and Provence

1964. 20th Anniv of Liberation (2nd issue).

1652	**541**	30c.+5c. sep, brn & bl	1·20	1·10
1653	-	30c.+5c. red, sep & brn	1·20	1·10

DESIGN: No. 1653, Taking prisoners in Paris, and tank in Strasbourg.

1964. Tourist Publicity. As T **490**. Inscr "1964".

1654	40c. brown, green & chest	50	35
1655	70c. purple, turquoise & blue	60	15
1656	1f.25 green, blue & bistre	1·20	45
1657	1f.30 chestnut, choc & brn	2·20	55

DESIGNS—HORIZ: 40c., 1f.25, Notre-Dame Chapel, Haut-Ronchamp (Haute-Saone). VERT: 70c. Caesar's Tower, Provins; 1f.30, Joux Chateau (Doubs).

542 De Gaulle's Appeal of 18th June, 1940

1964. 20th Anniv of Liberation (3rd issue).

1658	**542**	25c.+5c. blk, red & bl	1·50	1·40

543 Judo

1964. Olympic Games, Tokyo.

1659	**543**	50c. purple and blue	60	55

544 G. Mandel

1964. 20th Death Anniv of Georges Mandel (statesman).

1660	**544**	30c. purple	35	35

545 Soldiers departing for the Marne by Taxi-cab

1964. 50th Anniv of Victory of the Marne.

1661	**545**	30c. black, red & blue	35	35

546 Europa "Flower"

1964. Europa.

1662	**546**	25c. red, brown & grn	35	25
1663	**546**	50c. red, green & vio	1·00	35

547 Co-operation

1964. French, Africa and Malagasy Co-operation.

1664	**547**	25c. choc, blue & brn	35	35

548 J. N. Corvisart (physician)

1964. Red Cross Fund.

1665	**548**	20c.+10c. black and red	60	55
1666	-	25c.+10c. black and red	60	55

DESIGN: 25c. D. Larrey (military surgeon).

549 La Rochefoucauld

1965. Red Cross Fund. Inscr "1965".

1667	**549**	30c.+10c. blue & brn	60	55
1668	-	30c.+10c. brown & red	80	75
1669	-	40c.+10c. slate and brown	80	75
1670	-	40c.+10c. brown, blue and chestnut	80	75

PORTRAITS: No. 1668, Nicolas Poussin (painter); No. 1669, Paul Dukas (composer); No. 1670, Charles d'Orleans.

1965. French Art. As T **491**.

1671	1f. multicoloured	75	55
1672	1f. multicoloured	60	55
1673	1f. multicoloured	60	55
1674	1f. black, rose and red	60	55

DESIGNS—VERT: No. 1671, "L'Anglaise du `Star' au Havre" (Toulouse-Lautrec); No. 1673, "The Apocalypse" (14th-century tapestry). HORIZ: No. 1672, "Hunting with Falcons" (miniature from manuscript "Les Tres Riches Heures du Duc de Berry", by the Limbourg brothers); No. 1674, "The Red Violin" (R. Dufy).

550 "La Guienne" (steam packet)

1965. Stamp Day.

1675	**550**	25c.+10c. blk, grn & bl	1·20	1·10

551 Deportees

1965. 20th Anniv of Return of Deportees.

1676	**551**	40c. green	80	55

552 Youth Club

1965. 20th Anniv of Youth Clubs ("Maisons des Jeunes et de la Culture").

1677	**552**	25c. blue, brn & grn	35	35

553 Girl with Bouquet

1965. "Welcome and Friendship" Campaign.

1678	**553**	60c. red, orge & grn	60	55

555 I.T.U. Emblem, "Syncom", Morse Key and Pleumeur-Bodou Centre

554 Allied Flags and Broken Swastika

1965. 20th Anniv of Victory in World War II.

1679	**554**	40c. red, blue & black	60	35

1965. Centenary of I.T.U.

1680	**555**	60c. brown, black & bl	80	75

556 Croix de Guerre

1965. 50th Anniv of Croix de Guerre.

1681	**556**	40c. brown, red & green	80	75

557 Bourges Cathedral

1965. National Congress of Philatelic Societies, Bourges.

1682	**557**	40c. brown and blue	60	55

558 Stained Glass Window

1965. 800th Anniv of Sens Cathedral.

1683	**558**	1f. multicoloured	75	55

1965. Tourist Publicity. As T **490**. Inscr "1965".

1684	50c. blue, green and bistre	60	25
1685	60c. brown and blue	1·20	40
1686	75c. brown, green & blue	2·00	1·40
1687	95c. brown, green & blue	6·25	1·40
1688	1f. grey, green and brown	2·20	30

DESIGNS—HORIZ: 50c. Moustiers Ste. Marie (Basses-Alpes); 95c. Landscape, Vendee; 1f. Monoliths, Carnac. VERT: 60c. Yachting, Aix-les-Bains; 75c. Tarn gorges.

559 Mont Blanc from Chamonix

1965. Opening of Mont Blanc Road Tunnel.

1689	**559**	30c. violet, blue & plum	35	35

560 Europa "Sprig"

1965. Europa.

1690	**560**	30c. red	1·00	35
1691	**560**	60c. grey	1·60	90

561 Etienne Regnault and "Le Taureau"

1965. Tercent of Colonisation of Reunion.

1692	**561**	30c. blue and red	35	35

562 "One Million Hectares"

1965. Reafforestation.

1693	**562**	25c. brown, yellow & grn	35	35

563 Atomic Reactor and Emblems

1965. 20th Anniv of Atomic Energy Commission.

1694	**563**	60c. black and blue	80	75

564 Aviation School, Salon-de-Provence

1965. 30th Anniv of Aviation School.

1695	**564**	25c. green, indigo & blue	60	35

565 Rocket "Diamant"

1965. Launching of 1st French Satellite.

1696	**565**	30c. blue, turq & ind	35	35
1697	-	60c. blue, turq & ind	60	35

DESIGN: 60c. Satellite "A1".

566 "Le Bebe a la Cuiller"

1965. Red Cross Fund. Paintings by Renoir.

1698	**566**	25c.+10c. blue and red	35	35
1699	-	30c.+10c. brown & red	60	55

DESIGN: 30c. "Coco ecrivant" (portrait of Renoir's small son writing).

1966. Arms. As T **430**.

1700		5c. red and blue	20	15
1701		25c. blue and brown	1·40	35

DESIGNS: 5c. "Auch"; 25c. "Mont-de-Marsan".

568 St. Pierre Fourier and Basilica, Mattaincourt (Vosges)

1966. Red Cross Fund.

1702	**568**	30c.+10c. brown & grn	60	55
1703	-	30c.+10c. purple & grn	60	55
1704	-	30c.+10c. bl, brn & grn	60	55
1705	-	30c.+10c. blue & brn	60	55
1706	-	30c.+10c. brown & grn	60	55
1707	-	30c.+10c. black & brn	60	55

DESIGNS: No. 1703, F. Mansart (architect) and Carnavalet House, Paris; No. 1704, M. Proust (writer) and St. Hilaire Bridge, Illiers (Eure-et-Loir); No. 1705, G. Faure (composer), statuary and music; No. 1706, Hippolyte Taine (philosopher) and birthplace; No. 1707, Elie Metchnikoff (scientist), microscope and Pasteur Institute.

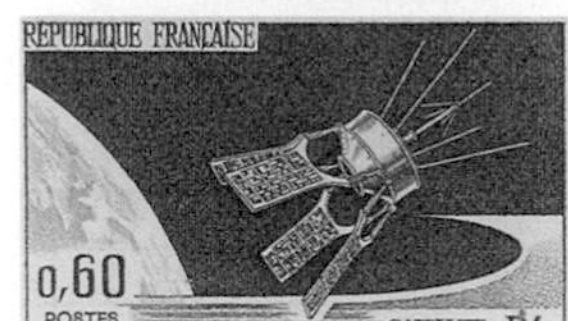

569 Satellite "D1"

1966. Launching of Satellite "D1".

1708	**569**	60c. red, blue & green	35	35

570 Engraving a die

1966. Stamp Day.

1709	**570**	25c.+10c. deep brown, grey and brown	35	35

1966. French Art. As T **491**.

1710		1f. bronze, green & purple	60	55
1711		1f. multicoloured	60	55
1712		1f. multicoloured	60	55
1713		1f. multicoloured	60	55
1714		1f. multicoloured	60	55

DESIGNS—HORIZ: No. 1710, Detail of Vix Crater (wine-bowl); No. 1711, "The New-born Child" (G. de la Tour); No. 1712, "Baptism of Judas" (stained glass window, Sainte Chapelle, Paris); No. 1714, "Crispin and Scapin" (after H. Daumier). VERT: No. 1713, "The Moon and the Bull" (Lurcat tapestry).

571 Knight and Chessboard

1966. International Chess Festival, Le Havre.

1715	**571**	60c. grey, brown & vio	1·00	90

572 Pont St. Esprit Bridge

1966. 700th Anniv of Pont St. Esprit.

1716	**572**	25c. black and blue	35	35

573 St. Michel

1966. Millenary of Mont St. Michel.

1717	**573**	25c. multicoloured	35	35

574 King Stanislas, Arms and Palace

1966. Bicentenary of Reunion of Lorraine and Barrois with France.

1718	**574**	25c. brown, grn & blue	35	35

575 Niort

1966. National Congress of Philatelic Societies, Niort.

1719	**575**	40c. slate, green & blue	60	35

576 "Angel of Verdun"

1966. 50th Anniv of Verdun Victory.

1720	**576**	30c.+5c. slate, bl & grn	35	35

577 Fontenelle

1966. Tercentenary of Academy of Sciences.

1721	**577**	60c. brown and lake	60	55

578 William the Conqueror, Castle and Landings

1966. 900th Anniv of Battle of Hastings.

1722	**578**	60c. brown and blue	80	55

579 Globe and Railway Track

1966. 19th International Railway Congress, Paris.

1723	**579**	60c. brown, blue & lake	1·20	90

580 Oleron Bridge

1966. Opening of Oleron Bridge.

1724	**580**	25c. brown, green & bl	35	35

581 Europa "Ship"

1966. Europa.

1725	**581**	30c. blue	60	35
1726	**581**	60c. red	1·20	55

582 Vercingetorix

1966. History of France (1st series). Inscr "1966".

1727	**582**	40c. brown, blue & grn	60	55
1728	-	40c. brown and black	60	55
1729	-	60c. red, brown & violet	80	55

DESIGNS—VERT: 40c. (No. 1728), Clovis. 60c. Charlemagne.

See also Nos. 1769/71, 1809/11, 1850/2, 1896/8, 1922/4, 1975/7 and 2017/19.

583 Route Map

1966. Centenary of Paris Pneumatic Post.

1730	**583**	1f.60 blue, lake & brn	1·20	90

584 Chateau de Val

1966. Chateau de Val.

1731	**584**	2f.30 brown, grn & bl	2·50	55

585 Rance Barrage

1966. Inauguration of Rance River Tidal Power Station.

1732	**585**	60c. slate, grn & brn	80	75

586 Nurse tending wounded soldier (1859)

1966. Red Cross Fund. Cross in red.

1733	**586**	25c.+10c. green	80	75
1734	-	30c.+10c. blue	80	75

DESIGN: 30c. Nurse tending young girl (1966).

1966. Arms. As T **430**. Multicoloured.

1735		20c. "Saint-Lo"	20	15

588 Beaumarchais (playwright)

1967. Red Cross Fund.

1736	**588**	30c.+10c. violet & red	60	55
1737	-	30c.+10c. blue & indigo	60	55
1738	-	30c.+10c. purple & brn	60	55
1739	-	30c.+10c. violet & bl	60	55

PORTRAITS: No. 1737, Emile Zola (writer); No. 1738, A. Camus (writer); No. 1739, St. Francois de Sales (reformer).

589 Congress Emblem

1967. 3rd International Congress of European Broadcasting Union (U.E.R.).

1740	**589**	40c. red and blue	35	35

590 Postman of the Second Empire

1967. Stamp Day.

1741	**590**	25c.+10c. grn, red & bl	35	35

1967. French Art. As T **491**.

1742	1f. multicoloured	60	55
1743	1f. multicoloured	60	55
1744	1f. brown, blue and black	60	55
1745	1f. multicoloured	60	55

DESIGNS—HORIZ: No. 1742, "Old Juniet's Trap" (after H. Rousseau); No. 1745, "The Window-makers" (stained glass window, St. Madeleine's Church, Troyes). VERT: No. 1743, "Francois I" (after Jean Clouet); No. 1744, "The Bather" (Ingres).

591 Winter Olympics Emblem

1967. Publicity for Winter Olympic Games, Grenoble (1968).

1746	**591**	60c. red, lt blue & bl	60	55

592 French Pavilion

1967. World Fair, Montreal.

1747	**592**	60c. green and blue	60	55

593 Cogwheels

1967. Europa.

1748	**593**	30c. blue and grey	60	35
1749	**593**	60c. brown and blue	1·60	90

594 Nungesser, Coli Lavasseur PL-8 and "L'Oiseau Blanc"

1967. 40th Anniv of Trans-Atlantic Flight Attempt by Nungesser and Coli.

1750	**594**	40c. blue, brown & pur	80	55

595 Great Bridge, Bordeaux

1967. Inauguration of Great Bridge, Bordeaux.

1751	**595**	25c. black, olive & brn	35	35

596 Gouin Mansion, Tours

1967. National Congress of Philatelic Societies, Tours.

1752	**596**	40c. brown, blue & red	80	75

597 Gaston Ramon (vaccine pioneer) and College Gates

1967. Bicentenary of Alfort Veterinary School.

1753	**597**	25c. brown, green & bl	35	35

598 Esnault-Pelterie, Rocket and Satellite

1967. 10th Death Anniv of Robert Esnault-Pelterie (rocket pioneer).

1754	**598**	60c. indigo and blue	80	75

1967. Tourist Publicity. As T **490**. Inscr "1967".

1755	50c. brown, dp blue & blue	60	35
1756	60c. brown, dp blue & blue	85	80
1757	70c. brown, blue and red	60	15
1758	75c. blue, red and brown	1·90	1·30
1759	95c. violet, green & blue	1·90	1·80
1760	1f. blue	1·00	15
1761	1f.50 red, blue and green	1·90	55

DESIGNS—VERT: 50c. Town Hall, St. Quentin (Aisne); 60c. Clock-tower and gateway, Vire (Calvados); 1f. Rodez Cathedral; 1f.50, Morlaix–views and carved buttress. HORIZ: 70c. St. Germain-en-Laye Chateau; 75c. La Baule; 95c. Boulogne-sur-Mer.

599 Orchids

1967. Orleans Flower Show.

1762	**599**	40c. red, purple & violet	1·20	90

600 Scales of Justice

1967. 9th Int Accountancy Congress, Paris.

1763	**600**	60c. brown, blue & pur	1·00	90

601 Servicemen and Cross of Lorraine

1967. 25th Anniv of Battle of Bir-Hakeim.

1764	**601**	25c. ultramarine, bl & brn	35	35

602 Marie Curie and Pitchblende

1967. Birth Centenary of Marie Curie.

1765	**602**	60c. ultramarine & blue	60	55

603 Lions Emblem

1967. 50th Anniv of Lions International.

1766	**603**	40c. violet and lake	1·20	75

604 "Republique"

1967

1767	**604**	25c. blue	60	55
1768	**604**	30c. purple	60	25
1768b	**604**	40c. red	60	25
1843	**604**	30c. green	35	25

See also No. 1882.

1967. History of France (2nd series). As T **582**, but inscr "1967".

1769	40c. ultramarine, grey & bl	60	55
1770	40c. black and slate	60	55
1771	60c. green and brown	80	55

DESIGNS—HORIZ: No. 1769, Hugues Capet elected King of France. VERT: No. 1770, Philippe-Auguste at Bouvines; 1771, Saint-Louis receiving poor.

605 "Flautist"

1967. Red Cross Fund. Ivories in Dieppe Museum. Cross in red.

1772	**605**	25c.+10c. brown & vio	80	75
1773	-	30c.+10c. brown & grn	80	75

DESIGNS: 30c. "Violinist".

606 Anniversary Medal

1968. 50th Anniv of Postal Cheques Service.

1774	**606**	40c. bistre and green	35	35

607 Cross-country Skiing and Ski Jumping

1968. Winter Olympic Games, Grenoble.

1775	30c.+10c. brown, grey & red	60	55
1776	40c.+10c. pur, bis & dp pur	60	55
1777	60c.+20c. red, purple & grn	80	75
1778	75c.+25c. brown, grn & pur	80	75
1779	95c.+35c. brown, mve & bl	85	80

DESIGNS: 30c. Type **607**; 40c. Ice hockey; 60c. Olympic flame; 75c. Figure skating; 95c. Slalom.

608 Road Signs

1968. Road Safety.

1780	**608**	25c. red, blue and purple	35	35

609 Rural Postman of 1830

1968. Stamp Day.

1781	**609**	25c.+10c. indigo, blue and red	35	35

610 F. Couperin (composer) and Concert Instruments

1968. Red Cross Fund. Inscr "1968".

1782	**610**	30c.+10c. lilac & vio	35	35
1783	-	30c.+10c. brown & grn	35	35
1784	-	30c.+10c. red & brown	35	35
1785	-	30c.+10c. purple & lil	35	35

DESIGNS: No. 1783, General Desaix, and death scene at Marengo; No. 1784, Saint Pol-Roux (poet) and "Evocation of Golgotha"; No. 1785, Paul Claudel (poet) and "Joan of Arc".

1968. French Art. As T **491**.

1786	1f. multicoloured	80	75
1787	1f. multicoloured	1·00	75
1788	1f. olive and red	1·00	55
1789	1f. multicoloured	1·20	75

DESIGNS—HORIZ: No. 1786, Wall painting, Lascaux; No. 1787, "Arearea" (Gauguin). VERT: No. 1788, "La Danse" (relief by Bourdelle in Champs-Elysees Theatre, Paris); No. 1789, "Portrait of a Model" (Renoir).

611 Congress Palace, Royan

1968. World Co-operation Languages Conf, Royan.

1790	**611**	40c. blue, brown & grn	60	55

612 Europa "Key"

1968. Europa.

1791	**612**	30c. brown and purple	60	25

1792 **612** 60c. red and brown 1·60 90

613 Alain R. Le Sage

1968. 300th Birth Anniv of Le Sage (writer).
1793 **613** 40c. purple and blue 35 35

1968. Tourist Publicity. As T **490**, but inscr "1968".
1794 60c. blue, purple & green 95 75
DESIGN—HORIZ: 60c. Langeais Chateau.

614 Pierre Larousse (encyclopedist)

1968. Larousse Commem.
1795 **614** 40c. brown & violet 60 55

615 Forest Trees

1968. Link of Black and Rambouillet Forests.
1796 **615** 25c. brown, green & blue 60 55

616 Presentation of the Keys, and Map

1968. 650th Anniv of Papal Enclave, Valreas.
1797 **616** 60c. violet, bistre & brn 80 75

617 Louis XIV, and Arms of Flanders and France

1968. 300th Anniv of (First) Treaty of Aix-la-Chapelle.
1798 **617** 40c. lake, bistre & grey 35 35

618 Martrou Bridge, Rochefort

1968. Inauguration of Martrou Bridge.
1799 **618** 25c. black, brown & blue 35 35

619 Letord 4 Lorraine Bomber and Route Map

1968. 50th Anniv of 1st Regular Internal Airmail Service.
1800 **619** 25c. indigo, blue & red 80 55

620 Tower of Constance, Aigues-Mortes

1968. Bicent. of Release of Huguenot Prisoners.
1801 **620** 25c. purple, brown & bl 35 35

621 Cathedral and Old Bridge, Beziers

1968. National Congress of Philatelic Societies, Beziers.
1802 **621** 40c. ochre, green & blue 1·20 75

622 "Victory" and White Tower, Salonika

1968. 50th Anniv of Armistice on Salonika Front.
1803 **622** 40c. purple & lt purple 35 35

623 Louis XV and Arms of Corsica and France

1968. Bicent of Union of Corsica and France.
1804 **623** 25c. blue, green & blk 35 35

624 Relay-racing

1968. Olympic Games, Mexico.
1805 **624** 40c. blue, green & brn 80 75

625 Polar Landscape

1968. French Polar Exploration.
1806 **625** 40c. turq, red & blue 60 55

626 "Ball of the Little White Beds" (opera) and Bailby

1968. 50th Anniv of "Little White Beds" Children's Hospital Charity.
1807 **626** 40c. red, orge & brn 35 35

627 "Angel of Victory" over Arc de Triomphe

1968. 50th Anniv of Armistice on Western Front.
1808 **627** 25c. blue and red 35 35

1968. History of France (3rd series). Designs as T **582**, but inscr "1968".
1809 40c. green, grey and red 60 55
1810 40c. blue, green & brown 60 55
1811 60c. brown, blue & ultram 1·00 75
DESIGNS—HORIZ: No. 1809, Philip the Good presiding over States-General. VERT: No. 1810, Death of Du Guesclin; No. 1811, Joan of Arc.

628 "Spring"

1968. Red Cross Fund. Cross in red.
1812 **628** 25c.+10c. blue & vio 60 55
1813 - 30c.+10c. red & brown 60 55
DESIGN: 30c. "Autumn".
See also Nos. 1853/4.

1969. Tourist Publicity. Similar to T **490** but inscr "1969".
1814 45c. green, brown and blue 35 25
1815 70c. brown, indigo and blue 60 55
1816 80c. brown, purple & bistre 60 20
1817 85c. grey, blue and green 1·20 1·00
1818 1f.15 lt brown, brown & blue 1·20 95
DESIGNS—HORIZ: 45c. Brou Church, Bourg-en-Bresse (Ain); 70c. Hautefort Chateau; 80f. Vouglans Dam, Jura; 85f. Chantilly Chateau; 1f.15, La Trinite-sur-Mer, Morbihan.

1969. French Art. As T **491**.
1819 1f. brown and black 1·00 75
1820 1f. multicoloured 1·00 75
1821 1f. multicoloured 1·00 75
1822 1f. multicoloured 1·00 75
DESIGNS—VERT: No. 1819, "February" (bas-relief, Amiens Cathedral); No. 1820, "Philippe le Bon" (Rogier de la Pasture, called Van der Weyden); No. 1822, "The Circus" (Georges Seurat). HORIZ: No. 1821, "Savin and Cyprien appearing before Ladicius" (Romanesque painting, Church of St. Savin, Vienne).

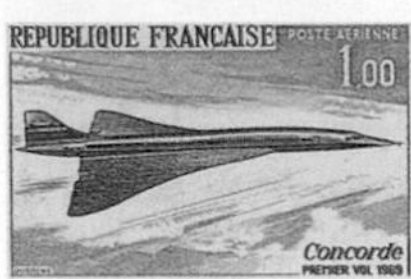

629 Concorde in Flight

1969. Air. 1st Flight of Concorde.
1823 **629** 1f. indigo and blue 1·40 85

630 Postal Horse-bus of 1890

1969. Stamp Day.
1824 **630** 30c.+10c. green, brown and black 35 35

631 A. Roussel (composer)

1969. Red Cross Fund. Celebrities.
1825 **631** 50c.+10c. blue 60 55
1826 - 50c.+10c. red 60 55
1827 - 50c.+10c. grey 60 55

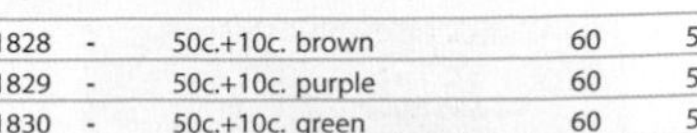
1828 - 50c.+10c. brown 60 55
1829 - 50c.+10c. purple 60 55
1830 - 50c.+10c. green 60 55
PORTRAITS: No. 1826, General Marceau; No. 1827, C. A. Sainte-Beuve (writer); No. 1828, Marshal Lannes; No. 1829, G. Cuvier (anatomist and naturalist); No. 1830, A. Gide (writer).

632 Irises

1969. International Flower Show, Paris.
1831 **632** 45c. multicoloured 60 55

633 Colonnade

1969. Europa.
1832 **633** 40c. mauve 60 25
1833 **633** 70c. blue 1·00 55

634 Battle of the Garigliano (Italy)

1969. 25th Anniv of "Resistance and Liberation".
1834 **634** 45c. black and violet 80 75
1835 - 45c. ultram, bl & grey 1·90 75
1836 - 45c. grey, blue & green 1·20 90
1837 - 45c. brown and grey 1·50 90
1838 - 45c. indigo, blue & red 1·20 1·10
1839 - 45c.+10c. green & grey 1·50 1·40
1840 - 70c.+10c. grn, pur & brn 3·75 3·50
DESIGNS—VERT: No. 1835, Parachutists and Commandos ("D-Day Landings"); 1836, Memorial and Resistance fighters (Battle of Mont Mouchet). HORIZ: No. 1837, Troops storming beach (Provence Landings); 1838, French pilot, Soviet mechanic and Yakovlev Yak-9 fighter aircraft (Normandy-Niemen Squadron); 1839, General Leclerc, troops and Les Invalides (Liberation of Paris); 1840, As No. 1839 but showing Strasbourg Cathedral (Liberation of Strasbourg).

635 "Miners" (I.L.O. Monument, Geneva) and Albert Thomas (founder)

1969. 50th Anniv of I.L.O.
1841 **635** 70c. brn, bl & dp brn 60 55

636 Chalons-sur-Marne

1969. National Congress of Philatelic Societies, Chalons-sur-Marne.
1842 **636** 45c. ochre, blue & grn 60 55

637 Canoeing

1969. World Kayak-Canoeing Championships, Bourg-St. Maurice.
1844 **637** 70c. brown, green & blue 60 55

638 Napoleon as Young Officer, and Birthplace

1969. Birth Bicent of Napoleon Bonaparte.

1845 **638** 70c. grn, violet & blue 60 55

639 "Diamond Crystal" in Rain Drop

1969. European Water Charter.

1846 **639** 70c. black, green & bl 60 55

640 Mouflon

1969. Nature Conservation.

1847 **640** 45c. black, brn & grn 1·00 75

641 Aerial View of College

1969. College of Arts and Manufactures, Chatenay-Malabry.

1848 **641** 70c. grn, orge & dp grn 60 55

642 "Le Redoutable"

1969. 1st French Nuclear Submarine "Le Redoutable".

1849 **642** 70c. green, emer & bl 60 55

1969. History of France (4th series). As T **582** but inscr "1969".

1850 80c. bistre, brown & green 80 55

1851 80c. brown, blk & lt brn 80 55

1852 80c. blue, black and violet 80 55

DESIGNS—HORIZ: No. 1850, Louis XI and Charles the Bold; 1852, Henry IV and Edict of Nantes, VERT: No. 1851, Bayard at the Battle of Brescia.

1969. Red Cross Fund. Paintings by N. Mignard. As T **628**. Cross in red.

1853 40c.+15c. brown & choc 80 75

1854 40c.+15c. blue & violet 80 75

DESIGNS: No. 1853, "Summer"; 1854, "Winter".

643 Gerbault aboard "Firecrest"

1970. Alain Gerbault's World Voyage, 1923–29.

1855 **643** 70c. indigo, grey & blue 1·00 75

644 Gendarmerie Badge and Activities

1970. National Gendarmerie.

1856 **644** 45c. blue, green & brown 1·50 75

645 L. Le Vau (architect)

1970. Red Cross Fund.

1857 **645** 40c.+10c. lake 60 55

1858 - 40c.+10c. blue 60 55

1859 - 40c.+10c. green 60 55

1860 - 40c.+10c. brown 60 55

1861 - 40c.+10c. slate 60 55

1862 - 40c.+10c. blue 60 55

DESIGNS: No. 1858, Prosper Merimee (writer); 1859, Philbert de l'Orme (architect); 1860, Edouard Branly (scientist); 1861, Maurice de Broglie (physicist); 1862, Alexandre Dumas (pere) (writer).

646 Handball Player

1970. 7th World Handball Championship.

1863 **646** 80c. green 80 55

647 Marshal Alphonse Juin and Les Invalides, Paris

1970. Marshal Juin Commem.

1864 **647** 45c. brown and blue 60 35

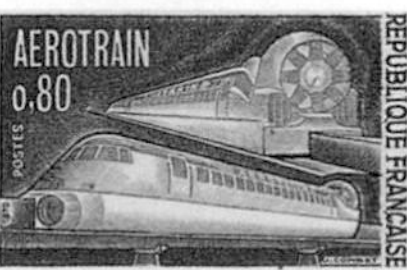

648 Gas-turbine Monorail Aerotrain "Orleans 1-80"

1970. 1st Aerotrain in Service.

1865 **648** 80c. drab and violet 1·00 70

649 Postman of 1830 and Paris Scene

1970. Stamp Day.

1866 **649** 40c.+10c. black, blue and red 60 55

650 P.-J. Pelletier and J. B. Caventou with Formula

1970. 150th Anniv of Discovery of Quinine.

1870 **650** 50c. green, mauve & bl 60 55

651 Greater Flamingo

1970. Nature Conservation Year.

1871 **651** 45c. mauve, grey & grn 60 35

652 Rocket and Dish Aerial

1970. Launching of "Diamant B" Rocket from Guyana.

1872 **652** 45c. green 1·00 75

653 "Health and Sickness"

1970. W.H.O. "Fight Cancer" Day (7th April).

1873 **653** 40c.+10c. mauve, brown and blue 35 35

654 "Flaming Sun"

1970. Europa.

1874 **654** 40c. red 60 35

1875 **654** 80c. blue 1·00 80

655 Marshal de Lattre de Tassigny and Armistice Meeting

1970. 25th Anniv of Berlin Armistice.

1876 **655** 40c.+10c. blue & turq 1·00 90

1970. French Art. As T **491**.

1877 1f. multicoloured 80 75

1878 1f. chestnut 80 75

1879 1f. multicoloured 1·20 90

1880 1f. multicoloured 1·20 90

DESIGNS—VERT: No. 1877, 15-cent. Savoy Primitive painting on wood; No. 1880, "The Ballet-dancer" (Degas). HORIZ: No. 1878, "The Triumph of Flora" (sculpture by J. B. Carpeaux); No. 1879, "Diana's Return from the Hunt" (F. Boucher).

656 Arms of Lens, Miner's Lamp and Pithead

1970. 43rd French Federation of Philatelic Societies Congress, Lens.

1881 **656** 40c. red 35 35

657 "Republique" and Perigueux

1970. Transfer of French Govt Printing Works to Perigueux.

1882 **657** 40c. red 60 35

The above stamp and label which together comprise No. 1882 were issued together se-tenant in sheets for which special printing plates were laid down. The stamp is virtually indistinguishable from the normal 40c. definitive, No. 1768b.

1970. Tourist Publicity. As T **490**, but inscr "1970".

1883 50c. purple, blue & green 60 15

1884 95c. brown, red and olive 1·50 1·10

1885 1f. green, blue and red 1·00 20

DESIGNS: 50c. Diamond Rock, Martinique; 95c. Chancelade Abbey (Dordogne); 1f. Gosier Island, Guadeloupe.

658 Javelin-thrower in Wheelchair

1970. World Games for the Physically Handicapped, St.-Etienne.

1886 **658** 45c. red, green & blue 70 55

659 Hand and Broken Chain

1970. 25th Anniv of Liberation from Concentration Camps.

1887 **659** 45c. brown, ultram & bl 80 55

660 Observatory and Nebula

1970. Haute-Provence Observatory.

1888 **660** 1f.30 violet, blue & grn 2·50 1·40

661 Pole Vaulting

1970. 1st European Junior Athletic Championships, Paris.

1889 **661** 45c. indigo, blue & purple 75 55

662 Didier Daurat, Raymond Vanier and Douglas DC-4

1970. Air. Pioneer Aviators.

1890 **662** 5f. brown, green & blue 3·75 35

1891 - 10f. grey, violet & red 7·50 55

1892 - 15f. grey, mauve & brn 11·00 90

1893 - 20f. indigo and blue 15·00 1·00

DESIGNS: 10f. Helene Boucher, Maryse Hilsz and de Havilland Gipsy Moth and Caudron monoplane; 15f. Henri Guillaumet, Paul Codos, "Lieutenant de Vaisseau Paris" (flying boat) and wreck of Potez 25A2 airplane; 20f. Jean Mermoz, Antoine de Saint-Exupery and Concorde.

663 Bath-House, Arc-et-Senans (Doubs)

1970. Royal Salt Springs, Chaux (founded by N. Ledoux).

1895 **663** 80c. brown, grn & bl 85 70

1970. History of France (5th series). As T **582**, but inscr "1970".

1896 45c. mauve, grey & black 1·00 75
1897 45c. brown, green & yellow 1·00 75
1898 45c. grey, brown & orange 1·00 90

DESIGNS: No. 1896, Richelieu and siege of La Rochelle, 1628; 1897, King Louis XIV; 1898, King Louis XV at Battle of Fontenoy (after painting by H. Vernet).

664 U.N. Emblem, New York Headquarters and Palais des Nations, Geneva

1970. 25th Anniv of United Nations.

1899 **664** 80c. violet, green & blue 80 55

665 Bordeaux and "Ceres" Stamp

1970. Centenary of Bordeaux "Ceres" Stamp Issue.

1900 **665** 80c. violet and blue 80 55

666 Col. Denfert-Rochereau and "Lion of Belfort" (after Bartholdi)

1970. Centenary of Belfort Siege.

1901 **666** 45c. blue, brown & grn 60 55

667 "Lord and Lady" (c. 1500)

1970. Red Cross Fund. Frescoes from Dissay Chapel, Vienne. Cross in red.

1902 **667** 40c.+15c. green 1·00 90
1903 - 40c.+15c. red 1·00 90

DESIGN: No. 1903, "Angel with instruments of mortification".

668 "Marianne"

1971

1904 **668** 45c. blue 60 20
1904ap **668** 60c. green 1·00 20
1904b **668** 80c. green 1·00 20
1905 **668** 50c. red 60 20
1905bp **668** 80c. red 1·00 20
1905d **668** 1f. red 80 20

669 Balloon "Ville d'Orleans" leaving Paris

1971. Air. Centenary of Paris Balloon Post.

1907 **669** 95c. multicoloured 1·20 90

1971. French Art. As T 491.

1908 1f. brown 1·20 90
1909 1f. multicoloured 1·00 75
1910 1f. multicoloured 1·00 75

DESIGNS: No. 1908, "St. Matthew" (sculpture, Strasbourg Cathedral); No. 1909, "The Winnower" (Millet); No. 1910, "Songe Creux" (G. Rouault).

670 Ice Skaters

1971. World Ice Skating Championships, Lyon.

1911 **670** 80c. ultramarine, blue and indigo 80 75

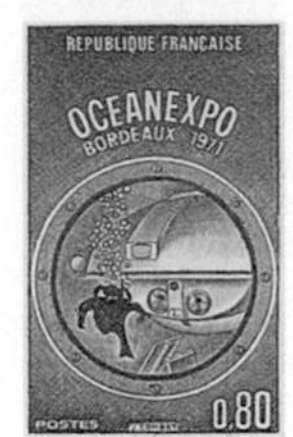

671 Diver and Bathysphere

1971. "Oceanexpo" Exhibition, Bordeaux.

1912 **671** 80c. turquoise & blue 80 55

672 General D. Brosset and Fourviere Basilica, Lyon

1971. Red Cross Fund. Celebrities.

1913 **672** 50c.+10c. brown & grn 85 80
1914 - 50c.+10c. brn & choc 85 80
1915 - 50c.+10c. brown & red 85 80
1916 - 50c.+10c. lilac & blue 85 80
1917 - 50c.+10c. pur & plum 85 80
1918 - 50c.+10c. bl & indigo 85 80

DESIGNS: No. 1914, Esprit Auber (composer) and manuscript of "Fra Diavolo"; 1915, Victor Grignard (chemist) and Nobel Prize for Chemistry; 1916, Henri Farman (aviation pioneer) and Farman Voisin No. 1 bis (airplane); 1917, General C. Delestraint (Resistance leader) and "Secret Army" proclamation; 1918, J. Robert-Houdin (magician) and levitation act.

673 Field Post Office, World War I

1971. Stamp Day.

1919 **673** 50c.+10c. blue, brown and bistre 80 55

674 Barque "Antoinette"

1971. French Sailing Ships.

1920 **674** 80c. violet, indigo & bl 1·50 90

See also Nos. 1967, 2011 and 2100.

675 Chamois

1971. Inaug of Western Pyrenees National Park.

1921 **675** 65c. brown, bl & choc 85 75

1971. History of France (6th series). As T 582 but inscr "1971".

1922 45c. purple, blue & red 80 55
1923 45c. red, brown & blue 1·00 70
1924 65c. brown, purple & blue 1·20 90

DESIGNS: No. 1922, Cardinal, noble and commoner (Opening of the States-General, 1789); No. 1923, Battle of Valmy, 1792; No. 1924, Fall of the Bastille, 1789.

676 Basilica of Santa Maria, Venice

1971. Europa.

1925 **676** 50c. brown and blue 95 55
1926 - 80c. purple 1·20 80

DESIGN: 80c. Europa chain.

677 View of Grenoble

1971. 44th French Federation of Philatelic Societies Congress, Grenoble.

1927 **677** 50c. red, pink & brown 60 35

678 A.F.R. Emblem and Town

1971. 25th Anniv (1970) of Rural Family Aid.

1928 **678** 40c. blue, violet & green 60 35

1971. Tourist Publicity. As T 490, but inscr "1971".

1929 60c. black, blue and green 75 35
1930 65c. black, violet & brown 1·00 35
1931 90c. brown, green & ochre 1·00 35
1932 1f.10 brown, blue & green 1·00 90
1933 1f.40 purple, blue & green 1·20 35

DESIGNS—VERT: 60c. Sainte Chapelle, Riom; 65c. Church and fountain, Dole; 90c. Gate-tower and houses, Riquewihr; 1f.40, Ardeche gorges. HORIZ: 1f.10, Fortress, Sedan.

679 Bourbon Palace, Paris

1971. 59th Interparliamentary Union Conference, Paris.

1934 **679** 90c. blue 1·00 90

680 Embroidery and Instrument-making

1971. 40th Anniv of 1st Meeting of Crafts Guilds Association.

1935 **680** 90c. purple and red 1·00 55

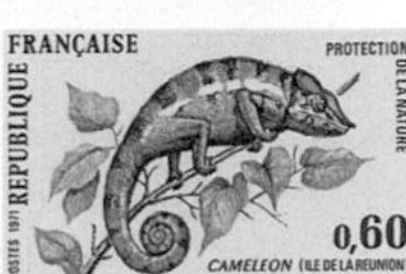

681 Reunion Chameleon

1971. Nature Conservation.

1936 **681** 60c. green, brn & yell 1·20 90

682 De Gaulle in Uniform (June 1940)

1971. 1st Death Anniv of General Charles de Gaulle.

1937 **682** 50c. black 1·20 1·10
1938 - 50c. blue 1·20 1·10
1939 - 50c. red 1·20 1·10
1940 - 50c. black 1·20 1·10

DESIGNS: No. 1938, De Gaulle at Brazzaville, 1944; No. 1939, Liberation of Paris, 1944; No. 1940, De Gaulle as President of the French Republic, 1970.

683 Baron Portal (1st President) and First Assembly

1971. 150th Anniv of National Academy of Medicine.

1941 **683** 45c. plum and purple 60 55

684 "Young Girl with Little Dog"

1971. Red Cross Fund. Paintings by J.-B. Greuze. Cross in red.

1942 **684** 30c.+10c. blue 1·00 90
1943 - 50c.+10c. red 1·00 90

DESIGN: No. 1943. "The Dead Bird".

1972. French Art. As T 491. Multicoloured.

1944 1f. "L'Etude" (portrait of a young girl) (Fragonard) (vert) 1·20 90
1945 1f. "Women in a Garden" (Monet) (vert) 2·00 1·00
1946 2f. "St. Peter presenting Pierre de Bourbon" (Master of Moulins) (vert) 2·50 1·70
1947 2f. "The Barges" (A. Derain) 3·75 2·50

685 King Penguin, Map and "Le Mascarin" (Dufresne)

1972. Bicentenary of Discovery of Crozet Islands and Kerguelen (French Southern and Antarctic Territories).

1948 **685** 90c. black, blue & orge 1·00 75

686 Skier and Emblem

1972. Winter Olympic Games, Sapporo, Japan.

1949	**686**	90c. red and green	80	55

687 Aristide Berges (hydro-electric engineer)

1972. Red Cross Fund. Celebrities.

1950	**687**	50c.+10c. black, emerald and green	1·00	80
1951	-	50c.+10c. black, blue and ultramarine	1·00	80
1952	-	50c.+10c. black, purple and plum	1·00	80
1953	-	50c.+10c. black, red and crimson	1·00	80
1954	-	50c.+10c. black, chestnut and brown	1·00	80
1955	-	50c.+10c. black, orange and red	1·00	80

DESIGNS: No. 1951, Paul de Chomedey, Maisonneuve (founder of Montreal); No. 1952, Edouard Belin (communications scientist); No. 1953, Louis Bleriot (pioneer airman) and Bleriot XI., No. 1954, Theophile Gautier (writer); No. 1955, Admiral Francois de Grasse.

688 Rural Postman of 1894

1972. Stamp Day.

1956	**688**	50c.+10c. blue, drab and yellow	1·20	90

689 Heart and W.H.O. Emblems

1972. World Heart Month.

1957	**689**	45c. red, orange & grey	60	55

1972. Tourist Publicity. As Type 490, but inscr "1972".

1958	1f. brown and yellow	95	35
1959	1f.20 blue and brown	1·00	45
1960	2f. purple and green	1·60	55
1961	3f.50 brown, red and blue	2·50	90

DESIGNS—VERT: 1f. Red deer stag and forest, Sologne Nature Reserve. HORIZ: 1f.20, Charlieu Abbey; 2f. Bazoches-du-Morvand Chateau; 3f.50, St. Just Cathedral, Narbonne.

690 Eagle Owl

1972. Nature Conservation.

1962	-	60c. black, green & bl	3·00	1·70
1963	**690**	65c. brown, bis & grey	1·20	90

DESIGN—HORIZ: 60c. Atlantic salmon.

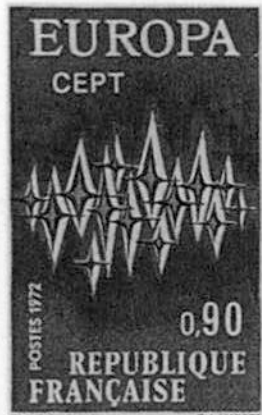

691 "Communications"

1972. Europa.

1964	-	50c. purple, yellow & brn	1·00	45
1965	**691**	90c. multicoloured	1·20	80

DESIGN: 50c. Aix-la-Chapelle Cathedral.

692 "Tree of Hearts"

1972. 20th Anniv of Post Office Employees' Blood-donors Association.

1966	**692**	40c. red	35	35

693 "Cote d'Emeraude" Grand Banks Fishing barquentine

1972. French Sailing Ships.

1967	**693**	90c. blue, green & orge	1·20	90

694 St.-Brieuc Cathedral (from lithograph of 1840)

1972. 45th French Federation of Philatelic Societies Congress, St.-Brieuc.

1968	**694**	50c. red	35	35

695 Hand and Code Emblems

1972. Postal Code Campaign.

1969	**695**	30c. red, black & green	25	15
1970	**695**	50c. yellow, black & red	60	35

696 Old and New Communications

1972. 21st World Congress of Post Office Trade Union Federation (I.P.T.T.), Paris.

1971	**696**	45c. blue and grey	60	35

697 Hurdling

1972. Olympic Games, Munich.

1972	**697**	1f. green	80	55

698 Hikers on Road

1972. "Walking Tourism Year".

1973	**698**	40c. multicoloured	1·60	90

699 Cycling

1972. World Cycling Championships.

1974	**699**	1f. brown, purple & grey	1·90	1·30

1972. History of France (7th series). The Directory. As T 582 but dated "1972".

1975	45c. purple, olive & green	60	55
1976	60c. blue, red and black	1·20	75
1977	65c. purple, brown & blue	1·40	90

DESIGNS—VERT: 45c. "Incroyables et Merveilleuses" (fashionable Parisians), 1794; 60c. Napoleon Bonaparte at the Bridge of Arcole, 1796; 65c. Discovery of antiquities, Egyptian Expedition, 1798.

700 J.-F. Champollion and Hieroglyphics

1972. 150th Anniv of Champollion's Translation of Egyptian Hieroglyphics.

1978	**700**	90c. brown, blue & blk	80	55

701 Nicholas Desgenettes (military physician)

1972. Red Cross Fund. Doctors of the 1st Empire. Cross in red.

1979	**701**	30c.+10c. green and bronze	1·00	90
1980	-	50c.+10c. red & brown	1·00	90

DESIGN: No. 1980, Francois Broussais (pathologist).

702 St. Theresa and Porch of Notre Dame, Alencon

1973. Birth Centenary of St. Theresa of Lisieux.

1981	**702**	1f. indigo & turquoise	1·20	75

703 Anthurium

1973. Martinique Flower Cultivation.

1982	**703**	50c. multicoloured	60	55

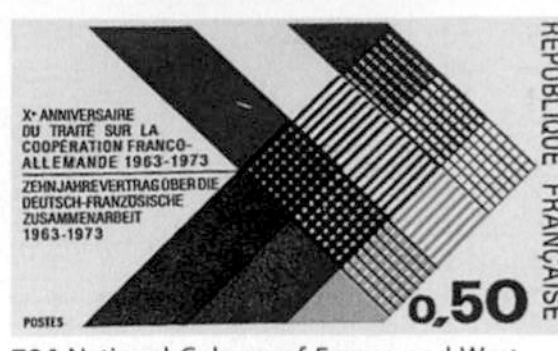

704 National Colours of France and West Germany

1973. 10th Anniv of Franco-German Co-operation Treaty.

1983	**704**	50c. multicoloured	60	55

705 Polish Immigrants

1973. 50th Anniv of Polish Immigration.

1984	**705**	40c. red, green & brown	35	35

1973. French Art. As T 491.

1985	2f. multicoloured	1·90	1·40
1986	2f. red and yellow	1·90	1·40
1987	2f. maroon and brown	1·90	1·40
1988	2f. multicoloured	1·90	1·40

DESIGNS: No. 1985, "The Last Supper" (carved capital, St. Austremoine Church, Issoire); No. 1986, "Study of a Kneeling Woman" (Charles le Brun); No. 1987, Wood-carving, Moutier d'Ahun; No. 1988, "La Finette" (girl with lute) (Watteau).

706 Admiral G. de Coligny (Protestant leader)

1973. Red Cross Fund. Celebrities' Annivs.

1989	**706**	50c.+10c. blue, brown and purple	1·00	90
1990	-	50c.+10c. mauve, grey and orange	1·00	90
1991	-	50c.+10c. green, purple and yellow	1·00	90
1992	-	50c.+10c. red, purple and bistre	1·00	90
1993	-	50c.+10c. grey, purple and brown	1·00	90
1994	-	50c.+10c. brown, lilac and blue	1·00	90
1995	-	50c.+10c. blue, purple and brown	1·00	90

DESIGNS: No. 1989, 400th death anniv (1972); 1990, Ernest Renan (philologist and writer, 150th birth anniv); 1991, Santos-Dumont (pioneer aviator, birth centenary); and "Balloon No. 6", "Balloon No.14" and biplane 14bis; 1992, Colette (writer, birth centenary); 1993, Duguay-Trouin (naval hero, 300th birth anniv); 1994, Louis Pasteur (scientist, 150th birth anniv 1972); 1995, Tony Garnier (architect, 25th death anniv).

707 Mail Coach, c. 1835

1973. Stamp Day.

1996	**707**	50c.+10c. blue	60	55

708 Tuileries Palace and New Telephone Exchange

1973. French Technical Achievements.

1997	**708**	45c. blue, grey & green	35	35
1998	-	90c. black, blue & pur	85	75
1999	-	3f. black, blue & grn	2·50	1·80

DESIGNS: 90c. Francois I Lock, Le Havre; 3f. Airbus Industrie A300B2-100 airplane.

709 Town Hall, Brussels

1973. Europa.

2000	**709**	50c. brown and red	95	55
2001	-	90c. multicoloured	2·20	1·30

DESIGN—HORIZ: 90c. Europa "Posthorn".

710 Guadeloupe Racoon

1973. Nature Conservation.

2002	**710**	40c. mauve, grn & pur	60	35
2003	-	60c. black, red & blue	85	75

DESIGN: 60c. White storks.

711 Masonic Emblem

1973. Bicentenary of Masonic Grand Orient Lodge of France.

2004	**711**	90c. blue and purple	80	55

1973. Tourist Publicity. As T 490, but inscr "1973".

2005	60c. blue, green and light blue	60	35
2006	65c. violet and red	60	35
2007	90c. brown, dp blue & bl	80	35
2008	1f. green, brown and blue	80	35

DESIGNS—VERT: 60c. Waterfall, Doubs; 1f. Clos-Luce Palace, Amboise; HORIZ: 65c. Palace of the Dukes of Burgundy, Dijon; 90c. Gien Chateau.

712 Globe and "Heart"

1973. 50th Anniv of Academy of Overseas Sciences.

2009	**712**	1f. green, brown & pur	80	55

713 Racing-car at Speed

1973. 50th Anniv of Le Mans 24-hour Endurance Race.

2010	**713**	60c. blue and brown	1·00	75

714 Five-masted Barque "France II"

1973. French Sailing Ships.

2011	**714**	90c. lt blue, indigo & bl	1·50	90

715 Bell-tower, Toulouse

1973. 46th French Federation of Philatelic Societies Congress, Toulouse.

2012	**715**	50c. brown and violet	60	35

716 Dr. G. Hansen

1973. Centenary of Hansen's Identification of Leprosy Bacillus.

2013	**716**	45c. brown, olive & grn	60	35

717 Eugene Ducretet (radio pioneer)

1973. 75th Anniv of Eiffel Tower–Pantheon Experimental Radio Link.

2014	**717**	1f. green and red	80	75

718 Moliere as "Sganarelle"

1973. 300th Death Anniv of Moliere (playwright).

2015	**718**	1f. brown and red	80	55

719 Pierre Bourgoin (parachutist) and Philippe Kieffer (Marine Commando)

1973. Heroes of World War II.

2016	**719**	1f. claret, blue & red	80	55

1973. History of France (8th series). As Type 582, but inscr "1973".

2017	45c. purple, grey and blue	80	55
2018	60c. brown, bistre & green	80	75
2019	1f. red, brown and green	1·00	75

DESIGNS—HORIZ: 45c. Napoleon and Portalis (Preparation of Civil Code, 1800–1804); 60c. Paris Industrial Exhibition, Les Invalides, 1806. VERT: 1f. "The Coronation of Napoleon, 1804" (David).

720 Eternal Flame, Arc de Triomphe

1973. 50th Anniv of Tomb of the Unknown Soldier, Arc de Triomphe.

2020	**720**	40c. red, blue and lilac	60	35

721 "Mary Magdalene"

1973. Red Cross Fund. Tomb Figures, Tonnerre.

2021	**721**	30c.+10c. grn & red	80	75
2022	-	50c.+10c. blk & red	80	75

DESIGN: 50c. Female saint.

722 Weathervane

1973. 50th Anniv of French Chambers of Agriculture.

2023	**722**	65c. black, blue & green	60	55

723 Figure and Human Rights Emblem

1973. 25th Anniv of Declaration of Human Rights.

2024	**723**	45c. brown, orge & red	60	35

724 Facade of Museum

1973. Opening of New Postal Museum Building.

2025	**724**	50c. lt brown, pur & brn	60	25

725 Exhibition Emblem

1974. "ARPHILA 75" International Stamp Exhibition, Paris.

2026	**725**	50c. brown, blue & pur	35	35

726 St. Louis-Marie Grignion de Montfort

1974. Red Cross Fund. Celebrities.

2027	**726**	50c.+10c. brown, green and red	75	70
2028	-	50c.+10c. red, purple and blue	75	70
2029	-	80c.+15c. purple, deep purple & blue	80	75
2030	-	80c.+15c. blue, black and purple	80	75

DESIGNS: No. 2028, Francis Poulenc (composer); No. 2029, Jean Giraudoux (writer); No. 2030, Jules Barbey d'Aurevilly (writer).

727 Automatic Letter-sorting

1974. Stamp Day.

2031	**727**	50c.+10c. brn, red & grn	60	55

728 Concorde over Airport

1974. Opening of Charles de Gaulle Airport, Roissy.

2032	**728**	60c. violet and brown	60	55

1974. "Arphila 1975" Stamp Exhibition. French Art. As Type 491. Multicoloured.

2033	2f. "Cardinal Richelieu" (P. de Champaigne)	1·90	1·40
2034	2f. "Abstract after Original Work" (J. Miro)	1·90	1·40
2035	2f. "Loing Canal" (A. Sisley)	1·90	1·60
2036	2f. "Homage to Nicolas Fouquet" (E. de Mathieu)	1·90	1·60

729 French Alps and Gentian

1974. Centenary of French Alpine Club.

2037	**729**	65c. vio, grn & blue	60	55

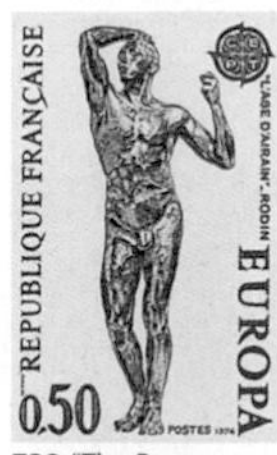

730 "The Brazen Age" (Rodin)

1974. Europa. Sculptures.

2038	**730**	50c. black and purple	95	55
2039	-	90c. brown and bistre	1·50	80

DESIGN—HORIZ: 90c. "The Expression" (reclining woman) (A. Maillol).

731 Shipwreck and "Pierre Loti" (lifeboat)

1974. French Lifeboat Service.

2040	**731**	90c. blue, red & brown	80	55

732 Council Headquarters, Strasbourg

1974. 25th Anniv of Council of Europe.

2041	**732**	45c. blue, lt blue & brn	60	55

733 "Cornucopia of St. Florent" (Corsica)

1974. Tourist Publicity.

2042	-	65c. brown and green	60	55
2043	-	1f.10 brown & green	80	55
2044	-	2f. purple and blue	1·50	55
2045	**733**	3f. blue, red & green	2·00	90

DESIGNS—As Type **490**. HORIZ: 65c. Salers; 1f.10, Lot Valley; VERT: 2f. Basilica of St. Nicolas-de-Port.

734 European Bison

1974. Nature Conservation.

2046	**734**	40c. purple, bl & brn	60	35
2047	-	65c. grey, green & blk	60	55

DESIGN: 65c. Giant Armadillo of Guiana.

735 Normandy Landings

1974. 30th Anniv of Liberation.

2048	**735**	45c. blue, red & green	1·20	90
2049	-	1f. red, brown & violet	80	55
2050	-	1f. brown, blk & red	1·00	75
2051	-	1f.+10c. brn, grn & blk	1·00	90

DESIGNS—HORIZ: No. 2050, Resistance medal and torch; 2051, Order of Liberation and honoured towns. VERT: No. 2049, General Koenig and liberation monuments.

736 Colmar

1974. 47th Congress of French Philatelic Societies.

2052	**736**	50c. red, purple & brn	35	35

737 Board and Chess Pieces

1974. 21st Chess Olympiad, Nice.

2053	**737**	1f. red, brown & blue	1·00	55

738 Commemorative Medallion

1974. 300th Anniv of "Hotel des Invalides".

2054	**738**	40c. black, brn & bl	35	35

739 French Turbotrain TGV 001

1974. Completion of Turbotrain TGV 001 Project.

2055	**739**	60c. red, black & blue	1·40	90

740 "Nuclear Power"

1974. Completion of Phenix Nuclear Generator.

2056	**740**	65c. brown, mve & red	60	55

741 Peacocks with Letter

1974. Centenary of Universal Postal Union.

2057	**741**	1f.20 red, green & blue	80	55

742 Copernicus and Heliocentric System

1974. 500th Birth Anniv (1973) of Nicolas Copernicus (astronomer).

2058	**742**	1f.20 mauve, brn & blk	80	55

743 Children playing on Beach

1974. Red Cross Fund. Seasons. Cross in red.

2059	**743**	60c.+15c. red, brown and blue	80	75
2060	-	80c.+15c. red, brown and blue	1·00	90

DESIGN: 80c. Child in garden looking through window.
See also 2098/9.

744 Dr. Albert Schweitzer

1975. Birth Centenary of Dr. Albert Schweitzer.

2061	**744**	80c.+20c. brown, red and green	85	80

1975. Tourist Publicity. As Type 490 but inscr "1975".

2062	85c. blue and brown	80	35
2063	1f.20 brown, dp brn & bl	80	35
2064	1f.40 blue, brown & green	1·00	55

DESIGNS—HORIZ: 85c. Law Courts, Rouen; 1f.40, Chateau de Rochechouart. VERT: 1f.20, St. Pol-de-Leon.

745 Little Egrets

1975. Nature Conservation.

2065	**745**	70c. brown and blue	70	55

1975. Precancels. As T 538, but inscribed "France".

2065a	42c. red and orange	2·30	90
2065b	48c. red and turquoise	1·90	1·70
2065c	50c. brown & turquoise	1·90	1·10
2065d	52c. brown and red	60	90
2065e	60c. brown and mauve	2·50	2·00
2065f	62c. brown & mauve	1·90	1·70
2065g	70c. red and mauve	3·75	2·10
2065h	90c. brown and pink	3·75	2·50
2065i	95c. brown and sepia	1·90	1·70
2065j	1f.35 red and green	4·00	2·30
2065k	1f.60 brown and violet	6·25	4·00
2065l	1f.70 brown and blue	5·00	3·50

See note below No. 432 (1920).

746 Edmond Michelet (politician)

1975. Red Cross Fund. Celebrities.

2066	**746**	80c.+20c. ind & bl	80	75
2067	-	80c.+20c. blk & bl	1·20	1·10
2068	-	80c.+20c. blk & bl	80	75
2069	-	80c.+20c. blk, turq & bl	80	75

DESIGNS—VERT: No. 2067, Robert Schuman (statesman); No. 2068, Eugene Thomas (former Telecommunications Minister). HORIZ: No, 2069, Andre Siegfried (geographer and humanist).

747 Eye

1975. "Arphila 75" International Stamp Exhibition, Paris.

2070	**747**	1f. orange, vio & red	60	55
2071	-	2f. black, red & green	1·20	90
2072	-	3f. green, grey & brown	1·90	1·30
2073	-	4f. green, red & orange	2·50	1·80
MS2074		152×143 mm. 2f. blue and red (Type **747**); 3f. deep blue, red and blue (as No. 2071); 4f. blue, deep blue and red (as No. 2072); 6f. deep blue, blue and red (as No. 2073)	12·50	11·50

DESIGNS: 2f. Capital; 3f. "Arphila 75 Paris"; 4f. Head of Ceres.

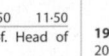

748 Postman's Badge

1975. Stamp Day.

2075	**748**	80c.+20c. blk, yell & bl	80	75

749 Pres. G. Pompidou

1975. Pres. Georges Pompidou Commem.

2076	**749**	80c. black and blue	60	35

750 "Paul as Harlequin" (Picasso)

1975. Europa. Multicoloured.

2077	80c. Type **750**	95	55
2078	1f.20 "In the Square" or "Woman leaning on Balcony" (Van Dongen) (horiz)	1·40	1·00

751 Machine Tools and Emblem

1975. 1st World Machine-Tools Exhibition, Paris.

2079	**751**	1f.20 black, red & blue	1·50	55

752 First Assembly at Luxembourg Palace

1975. Centenary of French Senate.

2080	**752**	1f.20 bistre, brn & red	1·00	75

753 Seals, Signatures and Symbols

1975. Centenary of Metre Convention.

2081	**753**	1f. purple, mve & brn	80	55

754 Sud Aviation SA 341 Gazelle Helicopter

1975. Development of Gazelle Helicopter.

2082	**754**	1f.30 green and blue	1·00	80

755 Youth and Health Symbols

1975. Students' Health Foundation.
2083 **755** 70c. black, purple & red 60 55

756 Underground Train

1975. Opening of Metro Regional Express Service.
2084 **756** 1f. deep blue and blue 1·20 80

757 Bussang Theatre and M. Pottecher (founder)

1975. 80th Anniv of People's Theatre, Bussang.
2085 **757** 85c. lilac, brown & blue 60 55

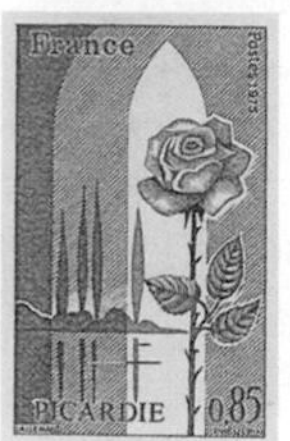

758 Picardy Rose

1975. Regions of France.
2086 **758** 85c. orange, turq & blue 1·00 55
2087 - 1f. lake, red & yellow 1·00 55
2088 - 1f.15 green, bl & ochre 1·00 55
2089 - 1f.30 black, red & blue 1·20 75
2090 - 1f.90 blue, bistre & blk 1·50 80
2091 - 2f.80 blue, red, & black 2·10 1·40

DESIGNS—VERT: 1f. Bourgogne agriculture emblems; 1f.15, Loire scene; 1f.30, Auvergne (bouquet of carnations); 1f.90, Allegory, Poitou-Charentes. HORIZ: 2f.80, "Nord-Pas-de-Calais".

See also Nos. 2102/6, 2150/7, 2246/8, 2329, 2508, 2555 and 2613.

759 Concentration Camp Victims

1975. 30th Anniv of Liberation of Concentration Camps.
2092 **759** 1f. green, blue and red 80 55

760 "Ballon d'Alsace" (Mine-clearers Monument)

1975. 30th Anniv of Mine Clearance Service.
2093 **760** 70c. green, bistre & blue 60 35

761 "Urban Development"

1975. New Towns.
2094 **761** 1f.70 blue, grn & brn 1·20 90

762 St. Nazaire Bridge

1975. Opening of St. Nazaire Bridge.
2095 **762** 1f.40 black, bl & grn 1·00 55

763 Rainbow over Women's Faces

1975. International Women's Year.
2096 **763** 1f.20 multicoloured 80 55

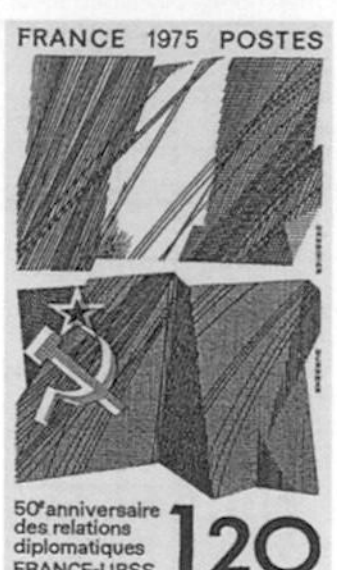

764 French and Russian Flags

1975. 50th Anniv of Franco-Soviet Diplomatic Relations.
2097 **764** 1f.20 yellow, red & blue 80 55

1975. Red Cross Fund. "The Seasons". As T 743.
2098 60c.+15c. red and green 80 75
2099 80c.+20c. brn, orge & red 1·00 90

DESIGNS: 60c. Child on swing; 80c. Rabbits under umbrella.

765 Cadet Ship "La Melpomene"

1975. French Sailing Ships.
2100 **765** 90c. blue, orge & red 1·40 70

766 Concorde

1976. Air. Concorde's First Commercial Flight, Paris–Rio de Janeiro.
2101 **766** 1f.70 black, blue & red 1·20 75

1976. Regions of France. As T 758.
2102 25c. green and blue 35 35
2103 60c. green, blue & purple 35 35
2104 70c. blue, green, & black 85 55
2105 1f.25 blue, brown & green 1·00 90
2106 2f.20 multicoloured 1·70 1·40

DESIGNS—HORIZ: 25c. Industrial complex in the Central region; 60c. Aquitaine; 2f.20, Pyrenees. VERT: 70c. Limousin; 1f.25, Guiana.

1976. French Art. As T 491.
2108 2f. grey and blue 1·70 1·40
2109 2f. yellow and brown 1·50 1·30
2110 2f. multicoloured 1·70 1·40
2111 2f. multicoloured 1·50 1·10
2112 2f. multicoloured 1·50 1·10
2113 2f. multicoloured 1·50 1·10

DESIGNS—VERT: No. 2108, "The Two Saints", St.-Genis-des-Fontaines (wood-carving); No. 2109, "Venus of Brassempouy" (ivory sculpture); No. 2110, "La Joie de Vivre" (Robert Delaunay). HORIZ: No. 2111, Rameses II in war-chariot (wall-carving); No. 2112, Painting by Carzou; No. 2113, "Still Life with Fruit" Maurice de Vlaminck).

767 French Stamp Design of 1876

1976. International Stamp Day.
2114 **767** 80c.+20c. lilac & blk 60 55

1976. Tourist Publicity. As T 490, but dated "1976".
2115 1f. brown, green and red 60 35
2116 1f.10 blue 80 55
2117 1f.40 blue, green & brown 1·00 35
2118 1f.70 purple, green & blue 1·20 35
2119 2f. mauve, red and brown 1·40 35
2120 3f. brown, blue and green 1·70 55

DESIGNS—HORIZ: 1f. Chateau Bonaguil; 1f.40, Basque coast, Biarritz. 3f. Chateau de Malmaison. VERT: 1f.10, Lodeve Cathedral; 1f.70, Thiers. 2f. Ussel.

768 Old Rouen

1976. 49th Congress of French Philatelic Societies.
2121 **768** 80c. green and brown 60 35

769 "Duguay Trouin VIII" (cruiser), "Duguay Trouin IX" (destroyer) and Naval Emblem

1976. 50th Anniv of Central Marine Officers' Reserve Association.
2122 **769** 1f. yellow, blue & red 85 55

770 Youth

1976. "Juvarouen 76" Youth Stamp Exhibition, Rouen.
2123 **770** 60c. indigo, blue & red 60 35

771 Strasbourg Jug

1976. Europa. Multicoloured.
2124 80c. Type **771** 95 45
2125 1f.20 Sevres plate 1·50 85

772 Vergennes and Franklin

1976. Bicentenary of American Revolution.
2126 **772** 1f.20 black, red & blue 80 55

773 Marshal Moncey

1976. Red Cross. Celebrities.
2127 **773** 80c.+20c. purple, black and brown 80 75
2128 - 80c.+20c. grn & brn 80 75
2129 - 80c.+20c. mve & grn 80 75
2130 - 1f.+20c. black, light blue and blue 85 80
2131 - 1f.+20c. blue, mauve and purple 85 80
2132 - 1f.+20c. grey & red 85 80

DESIGNS: No. 2128, Max Jacob (poet); 2129, Mounet-Sully (tragedian); 2130, General Daumesnil; 2131, Eugene Fromentin (writer and painter); 2132, Anna de Noailles.

774 People talking

1976. "Communication".
2133 **774** 1f.20 black, red & yell 80 75

775 Verdun Memorial

1976. 60th Anniv of Verdun Offensive.
2134 **775** 1f. red, brown & green 80 55

776 Troncais Forest

1976. Nature Conservation.
2135 **776** 70c. brown, green & blue 60 35

777 Cross of Lorraine Emblem

1976. 30th Anniv of Free French Association.
2136 **777** 1f. red, dp blue & blue 1·00 55

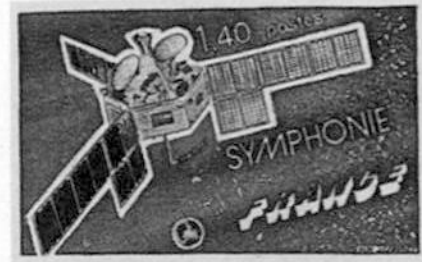

778 Satellite "Symphonie"

1976. Launch of "Symphonie No. 1" Satellite.

2137	**778**	1f.40 brn, choc & vio	1·00	75

779 Carnival Figures

1976. "La Fete" (Summer Festivals Exhibition, Tuileries, Paris).

2138	**779**	1f. red, green & blue	80	55

780 Yachting

1976. Olympic Games, Montreal.

2139	**780**	1f.20 ind, ultram & bl	1·00	55

781 Officers in Military and Civilian Dress

1976. Centenary of Reserve Officers Corps.

2140	**781**	1f. grey, red & blue	80	35

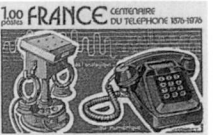

782 Early and Modern Telephones

1976. Telephone Centenary.

2141	**782**	1f. grey, brown & blue	80	35

783 Bronze Statue and Emblem

1976. 10th Anniv of International Tourist Film Association.

2142	**783**	1f.40 brown, red & grn	1·00	75

784 Police and Emblems

1976. 10th Anniv of National Police Force.

2143	**784**	1f.10 green, red & blue	80	55

785 Symbol of Nuclear Science

1976. European Research into Nuclear Science.

2144	**785**	1f.40 multicoloured	1·20	90

786 Fair Emblem

1976. 50th Anniv of French Fairs and Exhibitions Federation.

2145	**786**	1f.50 blue, green & brn	1·20	75

787 St. Barbara

1976. Red Cross Fund. Statuettes in Brou Church.

2146	**787**	80c.+20c. vio & red	80	75
2147	-	1f.+25c. brn & red	1·20	1·10

DESIGN: 1f. Cumaean Sybil.

788 "Douane" Symbol

1976. French Customs Service.

2148	**788**	1f.10 multicoloured	80	75

789 Museum and "Duchesse Anne" (cadet ship)

1976. Atlantic Museum, Port Louis.

2149	**789**	1f.45 brown, blue & blk	1·00	75

1977. Regions of France. As T 758.

2150	1f.45 mauve and green	1·00	55
2151	1f.50 multicoloured	1·00	75
2152	2f.10 yellow, blue & green	1·50	1·10
2153	2f.40 brown, green & blue	1·70	55
2154	2f.50 multicoloured	1·70	1·10
2155	2f.75 green	2·20	1·10
2156	3f.20 brown, green & blue	2·50	1·30
2157	3f.90 red, brown and blue	3·25	2·00

DESIGNS—HORIZ: 1f.45, Birds and flowers (Reunion); 2f.40, Coastline (Bretagne); 2f.75, Mountains (Rhone-Alpes). VERT: 1f.50, Banana tree (Martinique); 2f.10, Arms and transport (Franche-Comte); 2f.50, Fruit and yachts (Languedoc-Roussillon); 3f.20, Champagne and scenery (Champagne-Ardenne); 3f.90, Village church (Alsace).

790 Centre Building

1977. Opening of Georges Pompidou National Centre of Arts and Culture, Paris.

2158	**790**	1f. red, blue & green	60	35

1977. French Art. As T 491.

2159	2f. multicoloured	1·50	1·10
2160	2f. multicoloured	1·90	1·10

DESIGNS—HORIZ: No. 2159, "Mantes Bridge" (Corot). VERT: No. 2160, "Virgin and Child" (Rubens).

791 Dunkirk Harbour

1977. Dunkirk Port Extensions.

2161	**791**	50c. blue, indigo & brn	35	35

792 Torch and Dagger Emblem

1977. 90th Anniv of "Le Souvenir Francais" (French War Graves Organization).

2162	**792**	80c. brown, red & blue	80	55

793 Marckolsheim Post Relay Sign

1977. Stamp Day.

2163	**793**	1f.+20c. grey & blue	80	75

794 "Pisces"

1977. Precancels. Signs of the Zodiac.

2164	**794**	54c. violet	1·00	55
2165	-	58c. green	1·20	55
2166	-	61c. blue	80	55
2167	-	68c. brown	1·00	75
2168	-	73c. red	1·90	1·10
2169	-	78c. orange	1·20	75
2170	-	1f.05 mauve	2·10	1·80
2171	-	1f.15 orange	3·00	2·30
2172	-	1f.25 green	1·50	1·40
2173	-	1f.85 green	4·50	2·30
2174	-	2f. turquoise	3·75	3·50
2175	-	2f.10 mauve	2·30	1·80

DESIGNS: 58c. Cancer; 61c. Sagittarius; 68c. Taurus; 73c. Aries; 78c. Libra; 1f.05, Scorpio; 1f.15, Capricorn; 1f.25, Leo; 1f.85, Aquarius; 2f. Virgo; 2f.10, Gemini.

See note below No. 432 (1920).

795 "Geometric Design" (Victor Vasarely)

1977. Philatelic Creations. Works of Art by Modern Artists.

2176	**795**	3f. green and lilac	2·30	1·10
2177	-	3f. black and red	2·50	1·80
2178	-	3f. multicoloured	2·50	1·80

DESIGNS—VERT: No. 2177, Profile heads of man and hawk (Pierre-Yves Tremois). HORIZ: No. 2178, Abstract in Blue (R. Excoffon).

See also Nos. 2249, 2331/2, 2346/8, 2434/5, 2547 and 2578/9.

796 Flowers and Ornamental Garden

1977. 50th Anniv of National Horticultural Society.

2179	**796**	1f.70 red, brown & grn	1·20	75

797 Provencal Village

1977. Europa.

2180	**797**	1f. red, brown & blue	95	45
2181	-	1f.40 blk, brn & grn	1·50	55

DESIGN: 1f.40, Breton port.

798 Stylized Plant

1977. International Flower Show, Nantes.

2182	**798**	1f.40 mve, yell & bl	1·20	90

799 Battle of Cambrai

1977. 300th Anniv of Reunification of Cambrai with France.

2183	**799**	80c. mauve, brown & bl	60	55

800 Church, School and Map

1977. Centenary of French Catholic Institutes.

2184	**800**	1f.10 brown, bl & choc	80	75

801 Modern Constructions

1977. Meeting of European Civil Engineering Federation, Paris.

2185	**801**	1f.10 red, bistre & blue	80	55

802 Annecy

1977. 50th Congress of French Philatelic Societies.

2186	**802**	1f. brown, grn & olive	80	55

1977. Tourist Publicity. As T 490.

2187		1f.25 grey, brown & red	80	55
2188		1f.40 blue, purple & pink	1·00	55
2189		1f.45 sepia, brown & blue	1·00	55
2190		1f.50 olive, red & brown	1·00	55
2191		1f.90 yellow and black	1·40	65
2192		2f.40 bistre, green & black	1·50	55

DESIGNS—HORIZ: 1f.25, Premontres Abbey, Pont-a-Mousson; 1f.50, Statue and cloisters, Fontenay Abbey, Cote d'Or; 2f.40, Chateau de Vitre. VERT: 1f.40, Abbey tower of St. Amand-les-Eaux, Nord; 1f.45, Le Dorat Church, Haute-Vienne; 1f.90, Bayeux Cathedral.

803 School Building

1977. Polytechnic School, Palaiseau.

2193	**803**	1f.70 green, red & blue	1·20	55

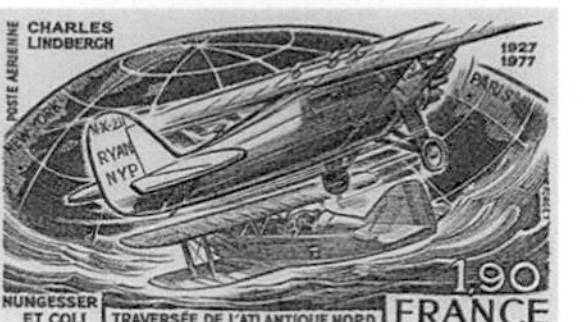

804 "Spirit of St. Louis" and "L'Oiseau Blanc"

1977. Air. 50th Anniv of North Atlantic Flights.

2194	**804**	1f.90 indigo, blue & grn	1·20	90

805 French Football Cup and Players

1977. 60th Anniv of French Football Cup.

2195	**805**	80c. bistre, blue & red	1·20	80

806 De Gaulle Memorial

1977. 5th Anniv of General de Gaulle Memorial.

2196	**806**	1f. multicoloured	1·20	90

807 "Map of France"

1977. 25th Anniv of Junior Chambers of Commerce.

2197	**807**	1f.10 blue and red	80	55

808 Battle of Nancy

1977. 500th Anniv of Battle of Nancy.

2198	**808**	1f.10 slate and blue	1·40	90

809 Seal of Burgundy

1977. 500th Anniv of Union of Burgundy with France.

2199	**809**	1f.25 green and olive	80	55

810 Compass on Globe

1977. 10th Anniv of International Association of French Language Parliaments.

2200	**810**	1f.40 red and blue	1·00	55

811 Red Cicada

1977. Nature Protection.

2201	**811**	80c. multicoloured	80	55

812 Hand and Examples of Craftsmanship

1977. French Craftsmanship.

2202	**812**	1f.40 brown and olive	1·20	75

813 Edouard Herriot (statesman)

1977. Red Cross Fund. Celebrities.

2203	**813**	1f.+20c. black	95	85
2204	-	1f.+20c. brn & grn	95	85
2205	-	1f.+20c. brn, bis & grn	95	85
2206	-	1f.+20c. bl, lt bl & red	95	85

DESIGNS: No. 2204, Abbe Breuil (archaeologist); 2205, Guillaume de Machault (poet); 2206, Charles Cros (poet).

814 "Agriculture and Industry"

1977. 30th Anniv of Economic and Social Council.

2207	**814**	80c. bistre, green & brn	60	35

815 "Old Man"

1977. Red Cross Fund. Carved Christmas Crib Figures from Provence.

2208	**815**	80c.+20c. black & red	80	75
2209	-	1f.+25c. green & red	1·00	90

DESIGN: 1f. "Old Woman".

816 "Sabine" (after Louis David)

1977. Inscr "FRANCE".

2210	**816**	1c. black	20	20
2211	**816**	2c. blue	20	20
2212	**816**	5c. green	20	15
2213	**816**	10c. red	20	15
2214	**816**	15c. blue	60	55
2215	**816**	20c. green	20	15
2216	**816**	30c. orange	20	15
2216a	**816**	40c. brown	35	35
2217	**816**	50c. violet	35	15
2217a	**816**	60c. red	35	35
2218	**816**	70c. blue	35	35
2219	**816**	80c. green	1·20	35
2220	**816**	80c. yellow	35	35
2221	**816**	90c. mauve	60	55
2222	**816**	1f. red	1·20	15
2223	**816**	1f. emerald	1·00	15
2224	**816**	1f. olive	60	15
2225	**816**	1f.10 green	1·00	35
2226	**816**	1f.20 red	1·00	15
2226a	**816**	1f.20 green	80	15
2227	**816**	1f.30 red	1·00	15
2228	**816**	1f.40 blue	2·20	90
2228a	**816**	1f.40 red	1·00	15
2229	**816**	1f.60 violet	1·50	55
2230	**816**	1f.70 blue	1·40	75
2230a	**816**	1f.80 brown	1·40	90
2231	**816**	2f. green	1·20	15
2232	**816**	2f.10 purple	1·40	35
2233	**816**	3f. brown	1·70	55
2233a	**816**	3f.50 green	2·10	90
2234	**816**	4f. red	2·75	80
2234a	**816**	5f. blue	50·00	35

For values inscr "REPUBLIQUE FRANCAISE" see Nos. 2423/5.

817 Table Tennis

1977. 50th Anniv of French Table Tennis Federation.

2240	**817**	1f.10 grn, pur & orge	3·50	1·70

818 Percheron

1978. Nature Conservation.

2241	**818**	1f.70 multicoloured	1·50	1·10
2242	-	1f.80 brn, olive & grn	1·40	75

DESIGN—VERT: (23×37 mm) 1f.80, Osprey.

1978. French Art. As T 491.

2243		2f. black	3·00	1·70

DESIGN: 2f. Tournament under Louis XIV, Les Tuileries, 1662.

819 Flags of France and Sweden of 1878

1978. Centenary of Return of St. Barthelemy Island to France.

2244	**819**	1f.10 brn, red & mve	80	55

820 College Building

1978. Centenary of National Telecommunications College.

2245	**820**	80c. blue	60	45

1978. Regions of France. As T 758.

2246		1f. red, blue and black	80	35
2247		1f.40 blue, orange & green	1·20	75
2248		1f.70 gold, red and black	1·70	90

DESIGNS—VERT: 1f. Symbol of Ile de France. HORIZ: 1f.40, Flower and port (Haute-Normandie); 1f.70, Ancient Norman ship (Basse-Normandie).

1978. "Philatelic Creations". As T 795.

2249		3f. multicoloured	3·00	1·80
2250		3f. multicoloured	2·50	1·60

DESIGNS—HORIZ: No. 2249 "Institut de France and Pont des Arts, Paris" (B. Buffet); 2250, "Camargue Horses" (Yves Brayer).

821 Marie Noel (poet)

1978. Red Cross Fund. Celebrities.

2251	**821**	1f.+20c. indigo & bl	95	85
2252	-	1f.+20c. green, brown and blue	95	85
2253	-	1f.+20c. mve & vio	95	85
2254	-	1f.+20c. green & brn	95	85
2255	-	1f.+20c. mve & red	95	85
2256	-	1f.+20c. black, brown and red	95	85

DESIGNS: No. 2252, Georges Bernanos (writer); 2253, Leconte de Lisle (poet); 2254, Leo Tolstoy (novelist); 2255, Voltaire and J.-J. Rousseau; 2256, Claude Bernard (physician).

822 Jigsaw Map of France

1978. 15th Anniv of Regional Planning Boards.

2257	**822**	1f.10 green & violet	80	45

1978. Tourist Publicity. As T 490.

2258		50c. green, blue & dp green	35	35
2259		80c. dp green, blue & grn	60	35
2260		1f. black	60	35
2261		1f.10 violet, brown & grn	1·00	55
2262		1f.10 brown, blue & green	1·00	55
2263		1f.25 brown and red	1·20	55
2264		1f.70 black and brown	1·50	90

DESIGNS—VERT: 50c. Verdon Gorge; 1f. Church of St. Saturnin, Puy de Dome. HORIZ: 80c. Pont-Neuf, Paris; 1f.10 (No. 2261), Notre-Dame du Bec-Hellouin Abbey; 1f.10 (No. 2262), Chateau d'Esquelbecq; 1f.25, Abbey Church of Aubazine; 1f.70, Fontevraud Abbey.

823 Head of Girl

1978. "Juvexniort" Youth Philately Exhibition, Niort.
2265 **823** 80c. brn, choc & mve 60 35

824 Postman emptying Pillar Box, 1900

1978. Stamp Day.
2266 **824** 1f.+20c. grn & blue 80 75

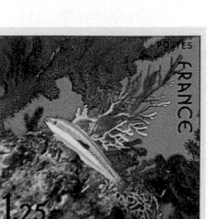

825 Underwater Scene and Rainbow Wrasse

1978. Port Cros National Park.
2267 **825** 1f.25 multicoloured 1·50 1·40

826 Floral Arch and Garden

1978. "Make France Bloom".
2268 **826** 1f.70 red, blue & green 1·90 75

827 Hands encircling Sun

1978. Energy Conservation.
2269 **827** 1f. yellow, brn & bistre 80 55

828 War Memorial, Notre Dame de Lorette

1978. Hill of Notre Dame de Lorette (War Cemetery).
2270 **828** 2f. brown and bistre 1·50 70

829 Fontaine des Innocents, Paris

1978. Europa. Fountains.
2271 **829** 1f. blk, bistre & blue 1·20 40
2272 - 1f.40 brn, grn & blue 1·50 70
DESIGN: 1f.40, Fontaine du Parc Floral, Paris.

830 Hotel de Mauroy, Troyes

1978. 51st Congress of French Philatelic Societies.
2273 **830** 1f. black, red & blue 80 55

831 Tennis Player and Stadium

1978. 50th Anniv of Roland Garros Tennis Stadium.
2274 **831** 1f. grey, brown & blue 3·00 70

832 Open Hand

1978. Handicrafts.
2275 **832** 1f.30 brown, grn & red 80 55

833 Citadel and Church

1978. 300th Anniv of Reunification of Franche-Comte with France.
2276 **833** 1f.20 grey, blue & grn 80 45

834 Emblem

1978. State Printing Office.
2277 **834** 1f. green, black & blue 60 45

835 Valenciennes and Maubeuge

1978. 300th Anniv of Return of Valenciennes and Maubeuge to France.
2278 **835** 1f.20 brown, vio & grey 80 55

836 Sower

1978. 50th Anniv of Academie de Philatelie.
2279 **836** 1f. blue, purple & violet 80 55

837 Morane-Saulnier Type H and Route

1978. Air. 65th Anniv of First Airmail Flight Villacoublay–Pauillac.
2280 **837** 1f.50 brown, blue & grn 1·20 80

838 Gymnasts, White Stork and Strasbourg Cathedral

1978. 19th World Gymnastics Championships, Strasbourg.
2281 **838** 1f. red, sepia & brown 85 55

839 Sporting Activities

1978. Sport for All.
2282 **839** 1f. violet, mauve & blue 1·20 90

840 "Freedom holding Dying Warrior" (A. Greck)

1978. Polish Fighters' War Memorial.
2283 **840** 1f.70 lake, red & green 1·20 90

841 Railway Carriage, Rethondes, and Armistice Monument

1978. 60th Anniv of Armistice.
2284 **841** 1f.20 black 1·20 55

842 Symbols of Readaptation

1978. Help for Convalescents.
2285 **842** 1f. red, brown & orge 80 55

843 "The Hare and the Tortoise"

1978. Red Cross Fund. Fables of La Fontaine.
2286 **843** 1f.+25c. brown, red and green 1·00 90
2287 - 1f.20+30c. green, red and brown 1·20 1·10
DESIGN: 1f.20, "The Town and the Country Mouse".

844 Human Figures balanced on Globe

1978. 30th Anniv of Human Rights.
2288 **844** 1f.70 blue and brown 1·20 55

845 Seated Child

1979. International Year of the Child.
2289 **845** 1f.70 red, vio & brn 4·25 2·30

1979. French Art. As T 491.
2290 2f. multicoloured 1·90 1·10
2291 2f. brown, black & dp brn 1·90 1·40
2292 2f. multicoloured 4·00 1·70
DESIGNS—HORIZ: No. 2290, "Music" (15th century miniature by Robinet Testart). VERT: No. 2291, "Diana in her Bath" (mantelpiece originally from Chalons-sur-Marne, now in Chateau d'Ecouen); 2292, "Auvers-sur-Oise Church" (Vincent van Gogh).

846 Marshal de Bercheny (Cavalry leader)

1979. Red Cross Fund. Celebrities.
2293 **846** 1f.20+30c. brown, blue and deep blue 1·20 1·10
2294 - 1f.20+30c. black and yellow 1·20 1·10
2295 - 1f.20+30c. deep brown, red & brown 1·20 1·10
2296 - 1f.20+30c. blue, mauve and red 1·20 1·10

2297	-	1f.30+30c. red and brown	1·20	1·10
2298	-	1f.30+30c. blue and ultramarine	1·20	1·10

DESIGNS: No. 2294, Leon Jouhaux (Nobel Peace Prize winner); 2295, Abelard and Heloise; 2296, Georges Courteline (playwright); 2297, Simone Weil (social philosopher); 2298, Andre Malraux (writer and politician).

847 "Amanita caesarea"

1979. Precancelled. Mushrooms.

2299	**847**	64c. red	80	35
2300	-	83c. brown	80	55
2301	-	1f.30 yellow	1·40	90
2302	-	2f.25 lilac	2·00	1·60

DESIGNS: 83c. "Craterellus comucopioides"; 1f.30, "Omphalotus olearius"; 2f.20, "Ramaria botrytis".

See note below No. 432 (1920).

848 Segalen, Pirogue, Pagoda and "Durance"

1979. 60th Death Anniv of Victor Segalen (writer and explorer).

2303	**848**	1f.50 turq, brn & red	1·00	55

849 Hibiscus Flower

1979. International Flower Show, Martinique.

2304	**849**	35c. lilac, mve & grn	35	35

850 Seated Buddha

1979. Borobudur Temple Preservation.

2305	**850**	1f.80 turquoise & green	1·40	55

851 Head Post Office, Paris

1979. Stamp Day.

2306	**851**	1f.20+30c. blue, red and brown	1·00	75

852 Street Urchin

1979. Birth Centenary of Francisque Poulbot (artist).

2307	**852**	1f.30 multicoloured	1·00	55

853 "Apis mellifera"

1979. Nature Conservation.

2308	**853**	1f. green, brown & orge	1·20	55

854 St.-Germain-des-Pres Abbey

1979. St.-Germain-des-Pres Abbey Restoration.

2309	**854**	1f.40 red, grey and blue	1·00	55

1979. Tourist Publicity. As T 490.

2310	45c. violet, blue & ultram	35	35
2311	1f. green, dp grn & lt grn	60	55
2312	1f. sepia, brown and lilac	60	55
2313	1f.20 brown, blue and green	80	55
2314	1f.50 sepia, red & brown	1·00	55
2315	1f.70 blue and brown	1·00	90

DESIGNS—VERT: No. 2311, Interiors of Abbeys of Bernay and St. Pierre-sur-Dives, Normandy; 2312, Auray; 2313, Windmill at Steenvoorde, Dunkirk (after Pierre Spas). HORIZ: No. 2310, Chateau de Maisons-Laffitte; 2314, Niaux Grotto; 2315, Palace of Kings of Majorca, Perpignan.

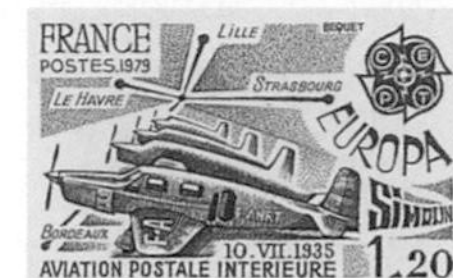

855 Caudron C.635 Monoplanes

1979. Europa.

2316	**855**	1f.20 blue, grn & turq	1·20	35
2317	-	1f.70 green, turq & red	2·50	80

DESIGN: 1f.70, Boule de Moulins (floating container used to carry letters during the Siege of Paris).

856 Sailing Ship at Nantes

1979. Federation of French Philatelic Societies Congress, Nantes.

2318	**856**	1f.20 blue, vio & grey	80	55

857 "Camille Desmoulins addressing Crowd" (engraving by Huyot)

1979. 190th Anniv of Palais Royal, Paris.

2319	**857**	1f. red and violet	60	35

858 Flags of Member Countries and Strasbourg Cathedral

1979. First Direct Elections to European Assembly.

2320	**858**	1f.20 multicoloured	80	35

859 Joan of Arc Monument, Rouen

1979. National Monument.

2321	**859**	1f.70 mauve	1·20	75

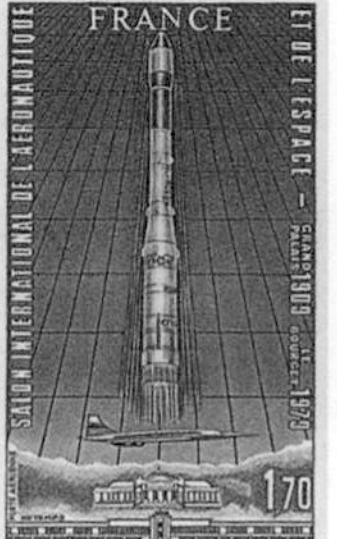

860 "Ariane" Rocket and Concorde over Grand Palais, Paris and Le Bourget Airport

1979. Air. International Aeronautics and Space Exhibition, Le Bourget.

2322	**860**	1f.70 bl, orge & brn	1·70	1·30

861 Felix Guyon (urologist)

1979. 18th Congress of International Society of Urologists, Paris.

2323	**861**	1f.80 blue and brown	1·20	55

862 Lantern Tower, La Rochelle

1979. Pre-cancelled. Historic Monuments (1st series).

2324	**862**	68c. lilac	60	55
2325	-	88c. blue	60	75
2326	-	1f.40 green	1·20	90
2327	-	2f.35 brown	1·90	1·40

DESIGNS: 88c. Cathedral towers, Chartres; 1f.40, Cathedral towers, Bourges; 2f.35, Cathedral towers, Amiens.

See note below No. 432 (1920).

See also Nos. 2342/5, 2383/6 and 2509/12.

863 "Telecom 79"

1979. Third World Telecommunications Exhibition, Geneva.

2328	**863**	1f.10 brn, turq & grn	80	35

1979. Regions of France. As T 758.

2329	2f.30 black, yellow & red	1·50	55

DESIGN: 2f.30, Thistle, Lorraine.

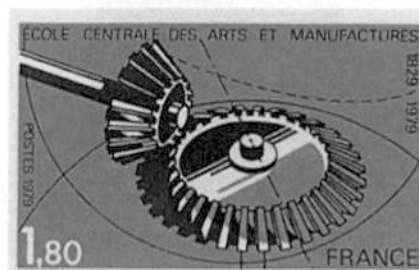

864 Gear-wheels

1979. 150th Anniv of Central Technical School, Paris.

2330	**864**	1f.80 yellow, blk & grn	1·20	90

1979. "Philatelic Creations". As T 795.

2331	3f. multicoloured	2·20	1·40
2332	3f. brown and green	2·30	1·40

DESIGNS: No. 2331, "Marianne" (Salvador Dali); 2332, "Fire Dancer from 'The Magic Flute'" (Chapelain-Midy).

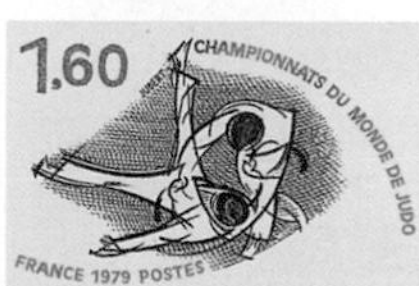

865 Judo

1979. World Judo Championships, Paris.

2333	**865**	1f.60 blk, lt grn & grn	1·00	55

866 Woman's Head

1979. Red Cross Fund. Stained Glass Windows, Church of St. Joan of Arc, Rouen.

2334	**866**	1f.10+30c. brown, green and red	80	75
2335	-	1f.30+30c. brown, green and red	1·20	90

DESIGN: 1f.30, Simon the Magician.

The windows came originally from the Church of St. Vincent, Rouen, destroyed during the Second World War.

867 Violins

1979. Handicrafts. Violin Manufacture.

2336	**867**	1f.30 blk, red & lake	1·00	55

868 Eurovision Satellite

1980. 25th Anniv of Eurovision (European Broadcasting Union).

2337	**868**	1f.80 bl, dp bl & blk	1·40	1·10

1980. French Art. Design similar to T 491.

2338	3f. brown, ochre & green	2·30	1·40
2339	3f. multicoloured	2·50	1·50
2340	3f. multicoloured	2·50	1·50
2341	4f. multicoloured	3·00	1·60

DESIGNS—VERT: No. 2338, "Woman with Fan" (sculpture by Ossip Zadkine); 2340, "The Peasant Family" (Louis le Nain); 2341, "Woman with Blue Eyes" (Modigliani). HORIZ: No. 2339, "Homage to J. S. Bach" (tapestry by Jean Picart Le Doux).

1980. Pre-cancelled. Historic Monuments (2nd series). Designs as T 862.

2342	76c. turquoise	60	35
2343	99c. green	60	55
2344	1f.60 red	1·20	1·10
2345	2f.65 brown	1·90	1·40

DESIGNS: 76c. Chateau d'Angers; 99c. Chateau de Kerjean; 1f.60, Chateau de Pierrefonds; 2f.65, Chateau de Tarascon.

See note below No. 432 (1920).

1980. Philatelic Creations. Design similar to T 795.

2346	3f. blue, black and brown	2·30	1·40
2347	4f. multicoloured	3·00	1·70
2348	4f. black and blue	3·00	1·70

DESIGNS—As T **795**: HORIZ: No. 2346, Abstract (Raoul Ubac). VERT: No. 2348, Abstract (Hans Hartung). 43×49 mm: No. 2347, "Message of Peace" (Yaacov Agam).

869 Processional Figures and Carnival Crowd

1980. "Giants of the North" Festival.

2349	**869**	1f.60 red, grn & blue	1·00	55

870 Viollet-le-Duc (architect and writer)

1980. Red Cross Fund. Celebrities.

2350	**870**	1f.30+30c. black and grey	1·20	90
2351	-	1f.30+30c. brown and green	2·00	1·80
2352	-	1f.40+30c. deep blue and blue	1·20	90
2353	-	1f.40+30c. black	1·20	90
2354	-	1f.40+30c. grey and black	1·20	90
2355	-	1f.40+30c. turquoise and green	1·20	90

DESIGN—VERT: No. 2351, Jean Monnet (statesman); 2352, Jean-Marie de la Mennais (Christian educationalist) (portrait after Paulin-Guerin); 2353, Frederic Mistral (poet); 2355, Saint-John Perse (poet and diplomat). HORIZ: No. 2354, Pierre Paul de Riquet (constructor of Canal du Midi).

871 French Cuisine

1980. French Gastronomical Exn, Paris.

2356	**871**	90c. brown and red	1·20	90

872 "The Letter to Melie" (Mario Avati)

1980. Stamp Day.

2357	**872**	1f.30+30c. mult	1·00	90

873 "Woman Embroidering" (Toffoli)

1980. Handicrafts. Embroidery.

2358	**873**	1f.10 blue, yell & brn	80	55

874 Smoker and Non-smoker (poster)

1980. Anti-smoking Campaign.

2359	**874**	1f.30 blue, red & black	80	45

1980. Tourist Publicity. Designs as T 490.

2360	1f.50 orange, brown & blue	1·00	35
2361	2f. black and red	1·20	55
2362	2f.20 brown, blue & green	1·40	55
2363	2f.30 green, brown & blue	1·50	55
2364	2f.50 blue, violet and mauve	1·50	35
2365	3f.20 brown and blue	2·10	80

DESIGNS—VERT: 1f.50, Cordes; 2f.30, Montauban; 2f.50, Praying nun and St. Peter's Abbey, Solesmes; 3f.20, Puy Cathedral. HORIZ: 2f. Chateau de Maintenon; 2f.20, Chateau de Rambouillet.

875 Aristide Briand (statesman)

1980. Europa.

2366	**875**	1f.30 multicoloured	1·20	45
2367	-	1f.80 red and brown	1·90	85

DESIGN: 1f.80, St. Benedict (illuminated letter from manuscript).

876 La Rouchefoucauld-Liancourt (founder) and Map

1980. Bicentenary of National Technical High School.

2368	**876**	2f. green and violet	1·20	70

877 Town Hall and Cranes, Dunkirk

1980. Federation of French Philatelic Societies Congress, Dunkirk.

2369	**877**	1f.30 bl, red & ultram	80	35

878 Isabel

1980. Nature Conservation.

2370	**878**	1f.10 multicoloured	1·20	75

879 Albert Durer (self portrait)

1980. "Philexfrance 82" International Stamp Exhibition, Paris (1st issue).

2371	**879**	2f. multicoloured	2·10	2·00

See also Nos. 2415/16, 2520/1 and **MS**2539.

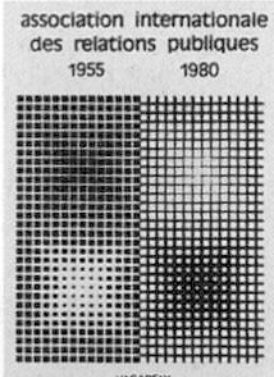

880 Symbolic Design

1980. 25th Anniv of International Public Relations Association.

2372	**880**	1f.30 blue and red	1·00	55

881 "Marianne" and Architecture

1980. Heritage Year.

2373	**881**	1f.50 blue and black	1·00	55

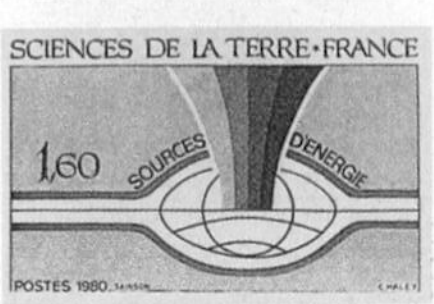

882 Sources of Energy

1980. 26th International Geological Congress, Paris.

2374	**882**	1f.60 red, brown & ol	1·20	75

883 Rochambeau landing at Newport

1980. Bicentenary of Rochambeau's arrival at Newport, Rhode Island.

2375	**883**	2f.50 mve, red & grey	1·90	1·10

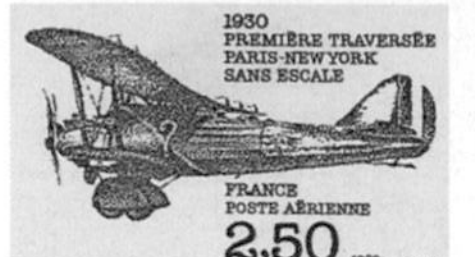

884 Breguet 19 Super TR "Point d'Interrogation"

1980. Air. 50th Anniv of First Non-stop Paris–New York Flight.

2376	**884**	2f.50 purple and blue	1·70	55

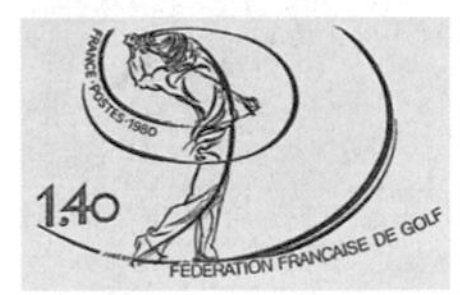

885 Golf

1980. French Golf Federation.

2377	**885**	1f.40 brown & green	1·00	55

886 Comedie-Francaise

1980. 300th Anniv of Comedie-Francaise.

2378	**886**	2f. blue, red and grey	1·40	75

887 Abstract based on Lorraine Cross and French Flag

1980. 40th Anniv of Appeal by, and 10th Death Anniv of, General de Gaulle.

2379	**887**	1f.40 multicoloured	1·70	75

888 Guardsman

1980. Centenary of Reorganization and Naming of Republican Guard.

2380	**888**	1f.70 blue and red	1·40	75

889 "Filling the Granaries"

1980. Red Cross Fund. Stall Carvings from Amiens Cathedral.

2381	**889**	1f.20+30c. brown and red	1·00	90
2382	-	1f.40+30c. brown and red	1·20	1·10

DESIGN: 1f.40, "Grapes from the Promised Land".

1981. Pre-cancelled. Historic Monuments (3rd series). Horiz designs as T 862.

2383	88c. mauve	60	35
2384	1f.14 blue	60	55
2385	1f.84 green	1·20	1·10
2386	3f.05 brown	1·90	1·50

DESIGNS: 88c. Imperial Chapel, Ajaccio; 1f.14, Astronomical Clock, Besancon; 1f.84, Castle ruins, Coucy-le-Chateau; 3f.05, Cave paintings, Font-de Gaume, Les Eyzies-de Tayac.

See note below No. 432 (1920).

890 Micro-electronics

1981. Technology.

2387	**890**	1f.20 multicoloured	80	55
2388	-	1f.20 multicoloured	80	55
2389	-	1f.40 multicoloured	1·00	55
2390	-	1f.80 dp bl, bl & yell	1·20	90
2391	-	2f. blue, red and black	1·50	1·10

DESIGNS: No. 2388, Biology; 2389, New energy sources; 2390, Sea bed exploitation; 2391, Telematics.

891 Louis Armand (engineer and Academician)

1981. Red Cross Fund. Celebrities.

2392	**891**	1f.20+30c. green and brown	1·00	90
2393	-	1f.20+30c. mult	1·00	90
2394	-	1f.40+30c. deep green and green	1·20	1·10
2395	-	1f.40+30c. blue and black	1·20	1·10
2396	-	1f.40+30c. blue and violet	1·40	1·30
2397	-	1f.40+30c. brown and bistre	1·50	1·40

DESIGNS—VERT: No. 2393, Louis Jouvet (theatre and film director and actor); 2396, R. P. Pierre Teilhard de Chardin (palaeontologist and philosopher). HORIZ: No. 2394, Anne-Marie Javouhey (missionary); 2395, Jacques Offenbach (composer); 2397, Pastor Marc Boegner.

1981. French Art. As T 491. Multicoloured.

2398	2f. "The Footpath" (Camille Pissarro) (horiz)	1·50	1·30
2399	4f. "Composition 1920/23" (Albert Gleizes) (vert)	2·75	1·30

892 "The Love Letter" (Goya)

1981. Stamp Day.

2400	**892**	1f.40+30c. mult	1·20	1·10

893 Angel pouring Water on France

1981. Water.

2401	**893**	1f.40 red, blue & blk	1·00	55

1981. Tourist Publicity. Designs similar to T 490.

2403	1f.40 brown and red	1·00	35
2404	1f.70 brown, green & blue	1·40	75

2405	2f. black and red	1·50	75
2406	2f.20 black and blue	1·50	75
2407	2f.20 sepia and brown	1·50	75
2408	2f.50 brown, blue & green	1·50	55
2409	2f.60 red and green	1·70	55
2410	2f.90 green	2·00	35

DESIGNS—VERT: 1f.40, St. John's Cathedral, Lyon; 1f.70, Maison Carree, Nimes; 2f.20 (2406), St. Anne's Church, Auray; 2f.90, Crest. HORIZ: 2f. Interior, Notre Dame Abbey, Vaucelles; 2f.20 (2407), Notre Dame Church, Louviers; 2f.50, Chateau de Sully, Rosny-sur-Seine; 2f.60, Saint-Emilion.

894 Bookbinding Press

1981. Handicrafts. Bookbinding.

2411	**894**	1f.50 olive and red	1·20	75

895 Bourree Croisee dance

1981. Europa.

2412	**895**	1f.40 brown, blk & grn	1·20	35
2413	-	2f. black, brn & blue	1·90	90

DESIGN: 2f. Sardane (Catalan dance).

896 Military and Sporting Scenes

1981. Cent of Saint-Maixent Military Academy.

2414	**896**	2f.50 mauve, blue & vio	1·50	55

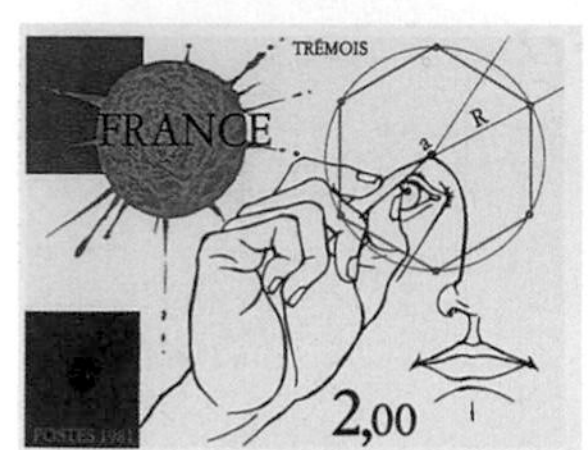

897 "France"

1981. "Philexfrance 82" International Stamp Exhibition, Paris (2nd issue). Multicoloured.

2415	2f. Type **897**	1·70	1·30
2416	2f. "Paris"	1·70	1·30

898 Theophraste Renaudot and Emile de Girardin

1981. 350th Anniv of First French Newspaper "La Gazette", Death Centenary of Emile de Girardin (founder of newspaper "La Presse") and Cent of Law on Freedom of the Press.

2417	**898**	2f.20 black and red	1·50	90

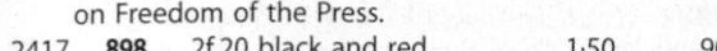

899 Thermal Waters of Vichy

1981. Federation of French Philatelic Societies Congress, Vichy.

2418	**899**	1f.40 brown, bl & grn	1·00	55

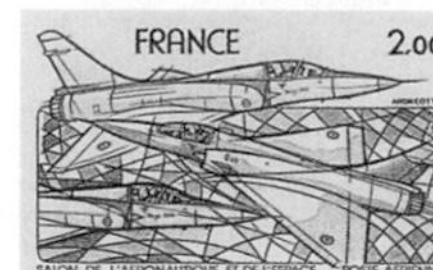

900 Dassault Mirage 2000 Aircraft

1981. Air. 34th International Aeronautics and Space Exhibition.

2419	**900**	2f. mauve, blue & violet	2·50	90

901 "HEC"

1981. Centenary of Paris Commercial College.

2420	**901**	1f.40 blue, green & red	1·00	55

902 Grey Heron and La Palissade, Camargue

1981. Conservation of Littoral Regions.

2421	**902**	1f.60 green, brn & red	1·40	90

903 Fencing

1981. World Fencing Championships, Clermont-Ferrand.

2422	**903**	1f.80 black & brown	1·40	90

1981. Vert designs as T 816 but inscr "REPUBLIQUE FRANCAISE".

2423	1f.40 green	1·00	20
2424	1f.60 red	1·00	20
2425	2f.30 blue	2·75	1·30

904 Car colliding with Glass

1981. Campaign against Drinking and Driving.

2428	**904**	1f.60 brown, red & olive	1·40	55

905 Costes, Le Brix and Breguet 19 Super TR "Nungesser et Coli"

1981. Air. Dieudonne Costes and Joseph Le Brix (pilots of first non-stop South Atlantic flight) Commemoration.

2429	**905**	10f. black, brn & red	6·25	90

906 Bird

1981. 45th International Congress of P.E.N. Club, Lyon and Paris.

2430	**906**	2f. black, violet & grn	1·40	55

907 Stylized Bird

1981. Centenary of National Savings Bank.

2431	**907**	1f.40 green, bl & red	1·00	35
2432	**907**	1f.60 carmine, blue & red	1·20	45

908 Jules Ferry (education reformer)

1981. Cent of National Education System.

2433	**908**	1f.60 vio, brn & blk	1·20	55

1981. Philatelic Creations. As T 795. Mult.

2434	4f. "The Divers" (Edouard Pignon) (horiz)	2·75	1·30
2435	4f. "Alleluia" (Alfred Manessier)	2·75	1·30

909 "Borda" (warship) and Naval School, Lanveoc-Poulmic

1981. 150th Anniv of Naval School.

2436	**909**	1f.40 brown, blue & red	1·20	55

910 "Vision of St. Hubert" (15th-cent sculpture)

1981. Hunting and Nature Museum, Hotel de Guenegaud, Paris.

2437	**910**	1f.60 brown & stone	1·40	55

911 J. Moulin, J. Jaures, V. Schoelcher and Pantheon

1981. Pantheon.

2438	**911**	1f.60 purple and blue	1·20	45

912 Disabled Draughtsman

1981. International Year of Disabled Persons.

2439	**912**	1f.60 black, bl & red	1·00	55

913 Pastoral Scene (2nd-century mosaic)

1981. 2000th Death Anniv of Virgil (poet).

2440	**913**	2f. multicoloured	1·90	1·30

914 "Scourges of the Passion"

1981. Red Cross Fund. Stained Glass Windows by Fernand Leger from the Church of the Sacred Heart, Audincort. Multicoloured.

2441	1f.40+30c. Type **914**	1·20	1·10
2442	1f.60+30c. "Peace"	1·40	1·10

915 Memorial (Antoine Rohal)

1981. Martyrs of Chateaubriant (Second World War victims).

2443	**915**	1f.40 black, purple & bl	1·00	55

916 "Liberty" (from "Liberty guiding the People" by Delacroix)

1982

2444	**916**	5c. green	35	35
2445	**916**	10c. brown	20	15
2446	**916**	15c. purple	60	55
2447	**916**	20c. green	20	15
2448	**916**	30c. orange	20	15
2449	**916**	40c. brown	35	35
2450	**916**	50c. mauve	35	15
2451	**916**	60c. brown	35	15
2452	**916**	70c. blue	60	35
2453	**916**	80c. green	60	15
2454	**916**	90c. mauve	60	35
2455	**916**	1f. green	60	35
2456	**916**	1f.40 green	1·20	15
2457	**916**	1f.60 red	1·00	15
2458	**916**	1f.60 green	1·20	20
2460	**916**	1f.80 red	1·20	20
2461	**916**	1f.80 green	1·20	20
2464	**916**	2f. red	1·20	20
2465	**916**	2f. green	1·20	20
2466	**916**	2f.10 red	1·20	20
2467	**916**	2f.20 red	1·20	20
2468	**916**	2f.30 blue	2·75	1·60
2469	**916**	2f.60 blue	2·50	1·40
2470	**916**	2f.80 blue	2·50	1·30
2471	**916**	3f. brown	1·90	35
2472	**916**	3f. blue	2·50	90
2473	**916**	3f.20 blue	3·75	1·10
2474	**916**	3f.40 blue	2·50	1·10
2475	**916**	3f.60 blue	1·90	75
2476	**916**	3f.70 purple	1·90	55

2477	**916**	4f. red	2·20	35
2478	**916**	5f. blue	3·25	20
2479	**916**	10f. violet	5·00	20
2484	**916**	1f.70 green	1·20	75
2487	**916**	1f.90 green	1·90	55

1982. Tourist Publicity. As T 490.

2503	1f.60 blue, green and black	1·20	35
2504	2f. red and mauve	1·20	55
2505	2f.90 green, dp brn & brn	1·90	1·10
2506	3f. deep blue and blue	1·70	75
2507	3f. red, yellow and blue	1·70	55

DESIGNS—VERT: No. 2503, Fishing boats and map of St. Pierre et Miquelon. HORIZ: No. 2504, Aix-en-Provence; 2505, Chateau de Ripaille, Haute-Savoie; 2506, Chateau Henri IV, Pau; 2507, Collonges-la-Rouge.

1982. Regions of France. As T 758.

2508	1f.90 blue and red	1·20	55

DESIGN: 1f.90, Map of Corsica, containing sun and sea, superimposed on mountain.

1982. Pre-cancelled. Historic Monuments (4th series). As T 862.

2509	97c. green	60	35
2510	1f.25 red	60	55
2511	2f.03 brown	1·20	1·10
2512	3f.36 blue	1·90	1·40

DESIGNS: 97c. Chateau de Tanlay; 1f.25, Salses Fort; 2f.03, Montlhery Tower; 3f.36, Chateau d'If.
See note below No. 432 (1920).

918 Guillaume Postel (scholar)

1982. Red Cross Fund. Celebrities.

2513	**918**	1f.40+30c. black and brown	1·40	1·30
2514	-	1f.40+30c. brown and grey	1·40	1·30
2515	-	1f.60+30c. lilac, violet and purple	1·40	1·30
2516	-	1f.60+40c. blue and brown	1·40	1·30
2517	-	1f.60+40c. blue	1·50	1·40
2518	-	1f.80+40c. brown	1·70	1·60

DESIGNS: No. 2514, Henri Mondor (doctor and writer); 2515, Andre Chantemesse (doctor and bacteriologist); 2516, Louis Pergaud (writer); 2517, Robert Debre (professor of medicine); 2518, Gustave Eiffel (engineer).

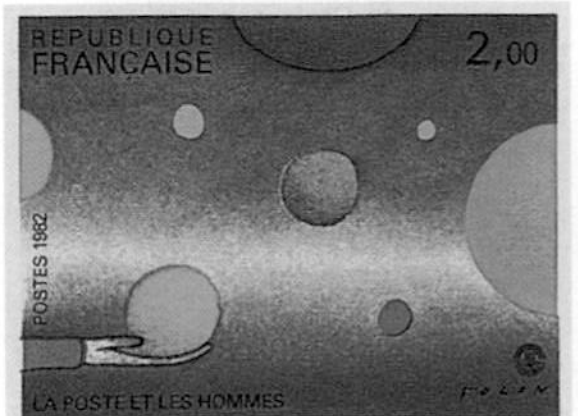

919 St. Francis of Assisi

1982. 800th Birth Anniv of St. Francis of Assisi.

2519	**919**	2f. black and blue	1·40	75

920 "The Post and Man"

1982. "Philexfrance 82" International Stamp Exhibition, Paris (3rd issue). Multicoloured.

2520	2f. Type **920**	3·75	2·75
2521	2f. Cogwheels ("The Post and Technology")	3·75	2·75

921 Lord Baden-Powell and Scouts

1982. 75th Anniv of Boy Scout Movement and 125th Birth Anniv of Lord Baden-Powell (founder).

2522	**921**	2f.30 black & green	1·40	55

922 "Marianne" on Map of France

1982. Population Census.

2523	**922**	1f.60 multicoloured	1·00	45

923 Basel-Mulhouse Airport

1982

2524	**923**	1f.90 blue, brn & red	1·50	75

924 Clasped Wrists

1982. Anti-racism Campaign.

2525	**924**	2f.30 orange & brown	1·50	75

925 "Woman Reading" (Picasso)

1982. Stamp Day.

2526	**925**	1f.60+40c. mult	1·40	90

926 "Blacksmith" (Toffoli)

1982. Handicrafts. Iron Work.

2527	**926**	1f.40 yellow, red & blk	1·00	75

927 Map of Europe and Seal (Treaty of Rome)

1982. Europa.

2528	**927**	1f.60 blue	1·50	75
2529	-	2f.30 brn, blk & grn	1·90	75

DESIGN: 2f.30, Seal of Charles the Bald (Treaty of Verdun, 843).

928 Goalkeeper and Stadium

1982. World Cup Football Championship, Spain.

2530	**928**	1f.80 green, red & bl	2·30	55

1982. Art. Designs as T 491.

2531	4f. yellow, blue and brown	2·75	1·30
2532	4f. multicoloured	2·75	1·30
2533	4f. multicoloured	2·75	1·40
2534	4f. pink and grey	2·75	1·40

DESIGNS—VERT: No. 2531, "Ephebus of Agde" (ancient Greek bronze sculpture); 2533, "The Lacemaker" (Vermeer); 2534, "The Family" (sculpture, Marc Boyan). HORIZ: 2532, "Embarkation of St. Paul at Ostia" (Claude Gellee (Le Lorrain)).

929 Festival Poster (Federico Fellini)

1982. 35th International Film Festival, Cannes.

2535	**929**	2f.30 multicoloured	1·50	1·10

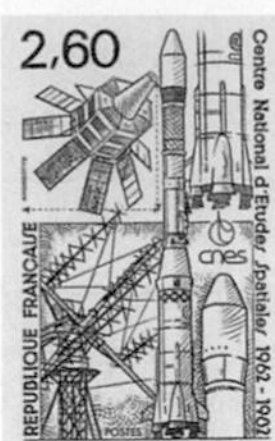

930 "Eole" Satellite, "Ariane" Rocket and Antenna

1982. 20th Anniv of National Space Studies Centre.

2536	**930**	2f.60 dp blue, bl & red	1·50	90

931 Interlocking Lines

1982. Industrialized Countries Summit, Versailles.

2537	**931**	2f.60 multicoloured	1·50	90

932 Valles

1982. 150th Birth Anniv of Jules Valles (journalist).

2538	**932**	1f.60 dp green & green	1·20	45

933 "Marianne"

1982. "Philexfrance 82" International Stamp Exhibition, Paris (4th issue). Sheet 100×71 mm.

MS2539 **933**	4f. blue and red; 6f. red and blue	19·00	19·00

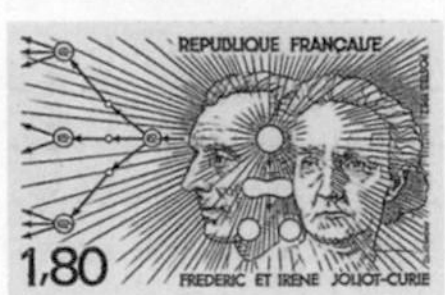

934 The Joliot-Curies

1982. Frederic and Irene Joliot-Curie (nuclear physicists) Commemoration.

2540	**934**	1f.80 pur, mve & vio	1·20	55

935 Grenoble Street Scene

1982. Centenary of Electric Street Lighting.

2541	**935**	1f.80 purple, bl & vio	1·20	35

936 Firemen

1982. Cent of National Federation of Fire Fighters.

2542	**936**	3f.30 brown and red	2·30	80

937 Marionnettes

1982

2543	**937**	1f.80 red, blue & lilac	1·20	55

938 Rugby

1982

2544	**938**	1f.60 blue, grn & red	2·50	90

939 Lecture Room

1982. Teacher Training Colleges.

2545	**939**	1f.80 grey & brown	1·20	55

940 Lille

1982

2546	**940**	1f.80 red and green	1·20	55

1982. Philatelic Creations. As T 795. Mult.

2547	4f. "The Turkish Room" (Balthus)	2·75	1·40

941 Dr. Robert Koch, Microscope and Bacillus

1982. Cent of Discovery of Tubercle Bacillus.

2548	**941**	2f.60 black and red	1·50	75

942 "Five Weeks in a Balloon"

1982. Red Cross Fund. Works by Jules Verne.

2549	**942**	1f.60+30c. brown & red	1·40	90
2550	-	1f.80+40c. green & red	1·40	90

DESIGN: 1f.80, "20,000 Leagues Under the Sea".

943 St. Theresa of Avila

1982. 400th Death Anniv of St. Theresa of Avila.

2551	**943**	2f.10 brn, blk & grn	1·40	75

944 Latecoere 300 Flying Boat F-AKGF "Croix du Sud"

1982. Air. 46th Anniv of Disappearance of "Croix du Sud".

2552	**944**	1f.60 lilac and blue	1·20	1·10

945 Cavelier de la Salle and Map of Louisiana

1982. 300th Anniv of Discovery of Louisiana.

2553	**945**	3f.25 brn, red & grn	1·90	80

946 Leon Blum

1982. 110th Birth Anniv of Leon Blum (politician).

2554	**946**	1f.80 brown & lt brn	1·20	45

1983. Regions of France. As T 758.

2555		1f. multicoloured	80	35

DESIGN—HORIZ: 1f. Map and coastline, Provence, Alpes, Cote d'Azur.

947 Andre Messager (composer)

1983. Red Cross Fund. Celebrities.

2556	**947**	1f.60+30c. blk & bl	1·40	1·30
2557	-	1f.60+30c. blk & yell	1·40	1·30
2558	-	1f.80+40c. blk & vio	1·50	1·40
2559	-	1f.80+40c. blk & red	1·50	1·40
2560	-	2f.+40c. blk & grn	1·60	1·50
2561	-	2f.+40c. black & bl	1·60	1·50

DESIGNS: No. 2557, Jacques-Ange Gabriel (architect); 2558, Hector Berlioz (composer); 2559, Max-Pol Fouchet (writer); 2560, Rene Cassin (diplomat); 2561, Stendhal (writer).

948 Budding Plant (spring)

1983. Pre-cancelled. The Four Seasons.

2562	**948**	1f.05 green	60	55
2563	-	1f.35 red	60	55
2564	-	2f.19 brown	1·20	1·10
2565	-	3f.63 violet	1·90	1·40

DESIGNS: 1f.35, Wheat (summer); 2f.19, Berries (autumn); 3f.63, Tree in snow (winter).

See note below No. 432 (1920).

949 Charleville Mezieres (image scaled to 61% of original size)

1983. Tourist Publicity.

2566		1f.80 brown, grn & bl	1·20	35
2567		2f. brown and black	1·20	55
2568		3f. brown and blue	1·70	90
2569	**949**	3f.10 brown and red	2·00	1·10
2570	-	3f.60 black, brn & bl	2·30	55

DESIGNS—As T **490**: 1f.80, Brantome, Perigord; 2f. Jarnac; 3f. Concarneau; 3f.60, Noirlac Abbey.

See also Nos. 2838 and 3642/5.

950 Martin Luther

1983. 500th Birth Anniv of Martin Luther (Protestant reformer).

2571	**950**	3f.30 brown & stone	2·10	80

951 Woman reading and Globe

1983. Centenary of French Alliance (language-teaching and cultural institute).

2572	**951**	1f.80 blue, red & brn	1·20	55

952 "Man dictating Letter" (Rembrandt)

1983. Stamp Day.

2573	**952**	1f.80+40c. stone and black	1·50	1·10

953 Danielle Casanova (resistance leader)

1983. International Women's Day.

2574	**953**	3f. brown and black	1·70	70

954 Figure within Globe releasing Dove

1983. World Communications Year.

2575	**954**	2f.60 multicoloured	1·50	1·10

955 Montgolfier Brothers' Hot-air Balloon

1983. Bicentenary of Manned Flight. Mult.

2576	2f. Type **955** (first manned flight by Pilatre de Rozier and Marquis d'Arlandes, Nov 1783)	1·50	90
2577	3f. Hydrogen balloon over Tuileries, Paris (flight by J. Charles and M. N. Robert, Dec 1783)	1·90	1·10

1983. Philatelic Creations. As T 795. Mult.

2578	4f. "Aurora-Set" (Dewasne) (horiz)	2·75	1·40
2579	4f. "Marianne" licking envelope (Jean Effel) (vert)	2·75	1·40

1983. Art. As T 491.

2580	4f. brown and buff	2·75	1·40
2581	4f. black and red	2·75	1·40
2582	4f. multicoloured	2·75	1·40

DESIGNS—VERT: No. 2580, "Venus and Psyche" (preparatory sketch for fresco, Raphael); 2581, "Blue-beard giving Keys to his wife" from Perrault's "Tales" (engraving by Gustave Dore). HORIZ: 2582, "The agile Rabbit Inn" (Utrillo).

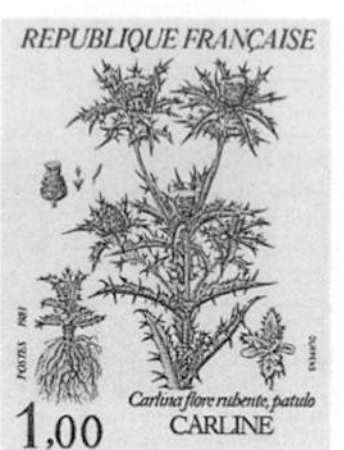

956 Thistle

1983. Flowers. Engravings from Paris Natural History Museum Library. Multicoloured.

2583	1f. Type **956**	60	35
2584	2f. Turk's cap lily (after Nicolas Robert)	1·40	45
2585	3f. Aster (after Nicolas Robert)	2·00	80
2586	4f. Aconite	2·75	80

957 Camera Diaphragm (photography)

1983. Europa. Each brown and deep brown.

2587	1f.80 Type **957**	2·20	55
2588	2f.60 Light rays entering eye and film (cinema)	2·50	1·10

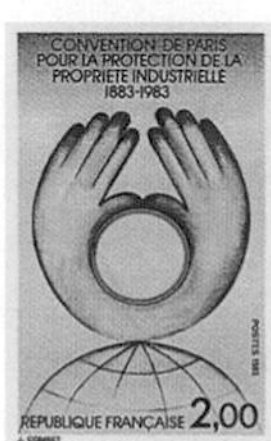

958 Hands on Globe

1983. Centenary of Paris Convention for the Protection of Industrial Property.

2589	**958**	2f. multicoloured	1·20	45

959 Marseille

1983. Federation of French Philatelic Societies Congress, Marseille.

2590	**959**	1f.80 red and blue	1·20	55

960 Air France Colours and Emblem

1983. 50th Anniv of Air France.

2591	**960**	3f.45 blue, red & black	2·30	1·30

961 "France defending U.S.A. from England" (medal by Augustin Dupre)

1983. Bicentenary of Treaties of Versailles and Paris.

2592	**961**	2f.80 brown & black	1·70	90

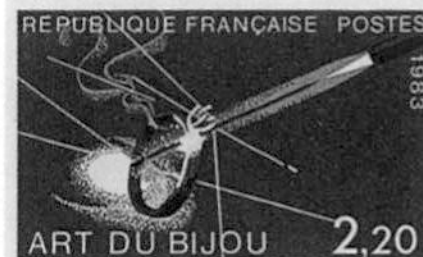

962 Forging a Ring

1983. Handicrafts. Jewellery.

2593	**962**	2f.20 multicoloured	1·20	55

963 Customs Museum, Bordeaux

1983. 30th Anniv of Customs Co-operation Council.

2594	**963**	2f.30 blk, dp grn & grn	1·20	75

964 Pierre and Ernest Michaux's Bicycle

1983. The Bicycle.

2595	**964**	1f.60 black, blue & red	1·90	55

965 Globe and Weather-Satellite and Map

1983. National Meteorology.

2596	**965**	1f.50 dp blue, brn & bl	1·00	45

966 Renee Levy

1983. Heroines of the Resistance.

2597	**966**	1f.60 brown & blue	1·00	55
2598	-	1f.60 brown and green	1·00	55

DESIGN: No. 2598, Berthie Albrecht.

967 Virgin and Child, Baillon

1983. Red Cross Fund. Wood Sculptures.

2599	**967**	1f.60+40c. brn & red	1·20	90
2600	-	2f.+40c. blue & red	1·40	90

DESIGN: 2f. Virgin and Child, Genainville.

968 Pierre Mendes France

1983. 1st Death Anniv of Pierre Mendes France (statesman).

2601	**968**	2f. black and red	1·20	45

969 Emile Littre (lexicographer and writer)

1984. Red Cross Fund. Celebrities.

2602	**969**	1f.60+40c. purple and black	1·20	1·10
2603	-	1f.60+40c. green and black	1·20	1·10
2604	-	1f.70+40c. violet and black	1·40	1·30
2605	-	2f.+40c. grey and black	1·40	1·30
2606	-	2f.10+40c. brown and black	1·40	1·30
2607	-	2f.10+40c. blue and black	1·40	1·30

DESIGNS: No. 2603, Jean Zay (politician); 2604, Pierre Corneille (dramatist); 2605, Gaston Bachelard (philosopher and poet); 2606, Jean Paulhan (writer); 2607, Evariste Galois (mathematician).

1984. Art. As T 491. Multicoloured.

2608	4f. "Cesar" film award (Cesar Baldaccini) (vert)	2·75	1·30
2609	4f. "The Four Corners of Heaven" (Jean Messagier) (horiz)	2·75	1·40
2610	4f. "Corner of Dining Room at Cannet" (Pierre Bonnard) (horiz)	2·75	1·40
2611	5f. "Pythia" (Andre Masson) (vert)	3·75	1·40
2612	5f. "The Painter trampled by his Model" (Jean Helion) (vert)	3·75	1·40

1984. Regions of France. As T 758.

2613	2f.30 violet, purple & red	1·20	55

DESIGN—HORIZ: 2f.30, Map and dancers, Guadeloupe.

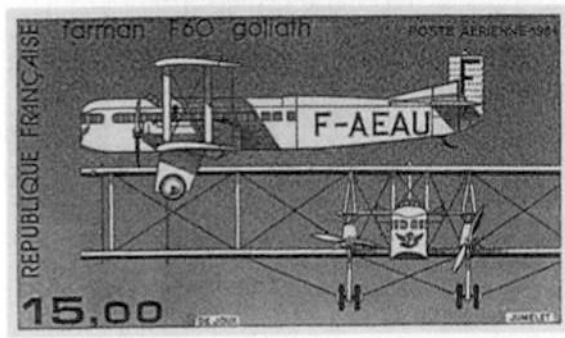

970 Farman F60 Goliath

1984. Air.

2614b	-	20f. red	10·00	90
2641	**970**	15f. blue	7·50	90
2614c	-	30f. violet	15·00	2·30
2614d	-	50f. green	20·00	7·00

DESIGNS: 20f. CAMS 53 flying boat; 30f. Wibault 283 trimotor; 50f. Dewoitine D-338 trimotor.

971 Flora Tristan

1984. International Women's Day.

2615	**971**	2f.80 purple and black	1·70	75

972 "Diderot" (L. M. van Loo)

1984. Stamp Day.

2616	**972**	2f.+40c. blue & blk	1·50	1·30

973 Pierre Waldeck-Rousseau (politician)

1984. Centenary of Trade Union Legislation.

2617	**973**	3f.60 black and blue	2·10	55

974 Emblem

1984. 2nd Direct Elections to European Parliament.

2618	**974**	2f. orange, yell & bl	1·20	45

975 Hearts

1984. Precancels. Playing Cards.

2619	**975**	1f.14 violet and red	60	55
2620	-	1f.47 blue and black	1·00	70
2621	-	2f.38 brown and red	1·50	1·10
2622	-	3f.95 green and black	1·90	1·60

DESIGNS: 1f.47, Spades; 2f.38, Diamonds; 3f.95, Clubs.
See note below No. 432 (1920).

976 Jacques Cartier and "Grande Hermine"

1984. 450th Anniv of Jacques Cartier's Voyage to Canada.

2623	**976**	2f. multicoloured	1·20	35

977 Children and "Sower" Stamp

1984. "Philex-Jeunes 84" Stamp Exhibition, Dunkirk.

2624	**977**	1f.60 brn, red & vio	1·00	55

978 Bridge

1984. Europa. 25th Anniv of European Post and Telecommunications Conference.

2625	**978**	2f. red	1·90	70
2626	**978**	2f.80 blue	2·50	1·00

979 Legionnaires at Camerone, Mexico, 1863

1984. Foreign Legion.

2627	**979**	3f.10 red, grn & blk	1·90	80

980 Resistance Fighter

1984. 40th Anniv of Liberation.

2628	**980**	2f. red, brown and black	1·20	80
2629	-	3f. red, brown and black	2·00	90

DESIGN: 3f. Soldiers disembarking.

1984. Tourist Publicity. As T 490.

2630	1f.70 blue and red	1·20	45
2631	2f.10 brown, green & red	1·40	45
2632	2f.50 brown, green & blue	1·50	55
2633	3f.50 purple and black	2·75	55
2634	3f.70 purple, violet & red	2·10	55

DESIGNS—HORIZ: 1f.70, Monastery of Grande, Chartreuse; 2f.10, Cheval's Ideal Palace, Hauterives; 2f.50, Vauban's Citadel, Belle-Ile-en-Mer, Brittany; 3f.70, Chateau de Montsegur. VERT: 3f.50, Cordouan lighthouse, Gironde.

981 Olympic Sports (image scaled to 61% of original size)

1984. Olympic Games, Los Angeles, and 90th Anniv of International Olympic Committee.

2635	**981**	4f. lilac, blue & green	2·50	1·40

982 Engraver

1984. Handicrafts. Engraving.

2636	**982**	2f. brown, blk & grn	1·20	40

983 Bordeaux

1984. Federation of French Philatelic Societies Congress, Bordeaux.

2637	**983**	2f. red	1·20	40

984 Anniversary Emblem

1984. 40th Anniv of National Centre for Telecommunications Studies.

2638	**984**	3f. blue and deep blue	1·70	65

985 Contour Map of Alps (image scaled to 61% of original size)

1984. 25th International Geography Congress, Paris.

2639	**985**	3f. blue, black & orge	1·70	85

986 "Telecom 1"

1984. "Telecom 1" Communications Satellite.

2640	**986**	3f.20 multicoloured	2·10	85

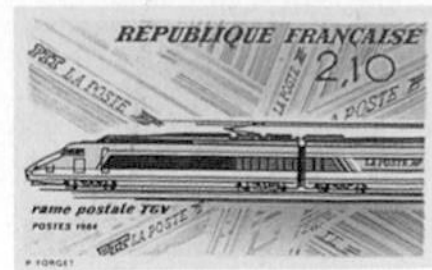

987 TGV Mail Train

1984. Inauguration of TGV High-speed Paris–Lyon Mail Service.

2641	**987**	2f.10 multicoloured	1·90	45

988 Marx Dormoy

1984. Marx Dormoy (politician) Commemoration.

2642	**988**	2f.40 black and blue	1·50	65

989 Lammergeier

1984. Birds of Prey. Multicoloured.

2643	1f. Type **989**	60	40
2644	2f. Short-toed eagle	1·50	65
2645	3f. Northern sparrowhawk	2·10	1·30
2646	5f. Peregrine falcon	3·50	90

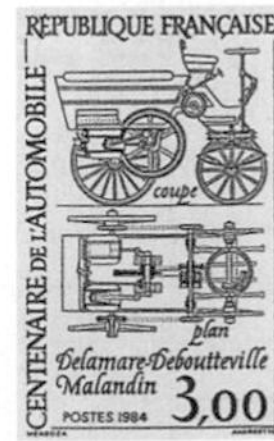

990 Delmare-Debouteville Malandin Automobile

1984. Centenary of Motor Car.

2647	**990**	3f. brown, blue & red	2·30	65

991 Vincent Auriol

1984. Birth Centenary of Vincent Auriol (President, 1947–54).

2648	**991**	2f.10 brown & green	1·20	40

992 "The Pink Basket" (Caly)

1984. Red Cross Fund.

2649	**992**	2f.10+50c. mult	1·50	1·40

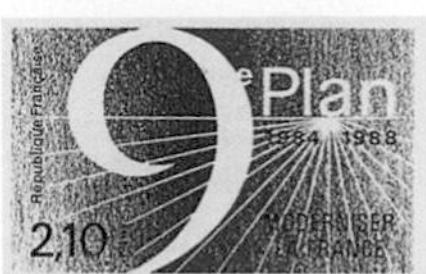

993 Emblem

1984. 9th Five-year Plan.

2650	**993**	2f.10 blue, red and black	1·40	50

994 Four Heads

1985. Promotion of French Language.

2651	**994**	3f. deep blue & blue	1·70	65

1985. Tourist Publicity. As T 490.

2652	1f.70 green, olive & brown	1·20	40
2653	2f.10 brown and orange	1·40	65
2654	2f.20 multicoloured	1·40	40
2655	3f. brown, red and blue	1·70	95
2656	3f.90 brown, red and blue	2·50	65

DESIGNS—HORIZ: 1f.70, Vienne, Isere; 2f.10, Montpellier Cathedral; 3f. Talmont Church; 3f.90, Solutre. VERT: 2f.20, St. Michael of Cuxa Abbey.

995 Coloured Dots

1985. 50th Anniv of French Television.

2657	**995**	2f.50 multicoloured	1·50	85

996 Snowflake (January)

1985. Precancels. Months of the Year (1st series).

2658	**996**	1f.22 violet and lilac	1·20	65
2659	-	1f.57 grey and blue	1·50	1·30
2660	-	2f.55 brown & green	1·90	2·00
2661	-	4f.23 green & orange	3·50	2·75

DESIGNS: 1f.57, Bare branch and bird (February); 2f.55, Rain-drops and sun-rays (March); 4f.23, Flowers (April).

See note below No. 432 (1920).

See also Nos. 2699/2702 and 2750/3.

997 Couple, Heart-shaped Letter-box and Cherubs

1985. St. Valentine's Day.

2662	**997**	2f.10 multicoloured	1·40	40

998 Jean-Paul Sartre

1985. Red Cross Fund. Writers.

2663	**998**	1f.70+40c. violet and purple	3·50	3·25
2664	-	1f.70+40c. purple and violet	3·50	3·25
2665	-	1f.70+40c. violet and deep violet	3·50	3·25
2666	-	2f.10+50c. deep violet and violet	3·50	3·25
2667	-	2f.10+50c. violet and purple	3·50	3·25
2668	-	2f.10+50c. purple and violet	3·50	3·25

DESIGNS: No. 2664, Romain Rolland; 2665, Jules Romains; 2666, Francois Mauriac; 2667, Victor Hugo; 2668, Roland Dorgeles.

1000 Pauline Kergomard

1985. International Women's Day. 60th Death Anniv of Pauline Kergomard (reformer of infant schools).

2670	**1000**	1f.70 blue and brown	1·20	55

1001 Daguin Cancelling Machine

1985. Stamp Day.

2671	**1001**	2f.10+50c. brown, grey and black	1·50	1·50

1985. Art. As T 491.

2672	5f. multicoloured	3·75	1·70
2673	5f. multicoloured	3·75	1·70
2674	5f. multicoloured	3·75	1·70
2675	5f. red, green and black	3·75	1·70
2676	5f. black and yellow	3·75	1·70

DESIGNS—VERT: No. 2672, "Judgement of Solomon" (stained glass window, Strasbourg Cathedral); 2675, Painting by Pierre Alechinsky. HORIZ: No. 2673, "Still Life with Candlestick" (Nicholas de Stael); 2674, Painting by Dubuffet; 2676, "The Dog" (sculpture by Alberto Giacometti).

1002 Landevennec Abbey

1985. 1500th Anniv of Landevennec Abbey.

2677	**1002**	1f.70 green & purple	1·20	55

1003 Modern Housing, Givors (Jean Renaudie)

1985. Contemporary Architecture.

2678	**1003**	2f.40 blk, grn & orge	1·50	85

1004 Adam de la Halle (composer)

1985. Europa. Music Year.

2679	**1004**	2f.10 dp bl, bl & blk	1·60	85
2680	-	3f. black, bl & dp bl	2·50	1·30

DESIGN: 3f. Darius Milhaud (composer).

1005 Soldier with Rifle

1985. 40th Anniv of V.E. (Victory in Europe) Day.

2681	**1005**	2f. black, red & blue	1·20	85
2682	-	3f. black, red & blue	1·70	1·10

DESIGN: 3f. Prisoners of war.

1006 Tours Cathedral

1985. Federation of French Philatelic Societies Congress, Tours.

2683	**1006**	2f.10 indigo and blue	1·40	65

1007 Vaccinating Patient (after Le Riverend)

1985. Centenary of Anti-rabies Vaccination.

2684	**1007**	1f.50 brn, grn & red	1·00	40

1008 Mystere/Falcon

1985. 36th International Aeronautics and Space Exhibition, Le Bourget.

2685	**1008**	10f. blue	5·75	3·00

1009 Capsized Boat and Lifeboat

1985. Centenary of Lake Geneva International Life-Saving Society.

2686	**1009**	2f.50 black, red & bl	1·50	85

1010 U.N. Emblem

1985. 40th Anniv of U.N.O.

2687	**1010**	3f. blue, grey & dp bl	1·70	65

1011 Huguenot Cross

1985. French Huguenots (300th Anniv of Revocation of Edict of Nantes).

2688	**1011**	2f.50 brown, red & bl	1·50	85

1012 Beech

1985. Trees.

2689	**1012**	1f. black, green & blue	80	40
2690	-	2f. black, green & red	1·50	45
2691	-	3f. black, green & violet	2·00	1·10
2692	-	5f. black, green & brn	3·00	1·30

DESIGNS: 2f. Scotch elm; 3f. Pedunculate oak; 5f. Norwegian spruce.

1013 "Marianne"

1985. National Memorial Day.

2693	**1013**	1f.80 pur, orge & blk	1·20	40

1014 Dullin and Theatre

1985. Birth Centenary of Charles Dullin (actor).

2694	**1014**	3f.20 black & blue	1·90	85

1015 World Map on Open Book and Keyboard

1985. 40th Anniv of French Information Service.

2695	**1015**	2f.20 black and red	1·20	40

1016 "Concert of Angels" (M. Grunewald) (detail, Isenheim Altarpiece)

1985. Red Cross Fund.

2696	**1016**	2f.20+50c. mult	1·50	1·30

1017 Siamese Envoys before King Louis XIV

1986. 300th Anniv of Diplomatic Relations with Thailand.

2697	**1017**	3f.20 purple & black	2·10	1·10

1018 "Leisure Activities" (Fernand Leger)

1986. 50th Anniv of Popular Front.

2698	**1018**	2f.20 multicoloured	1·20	40

1986. Precancels. Months of the Year (2nd series). As T 996.

2699	1f.28 pink and green	1·20	65
2700	1f.65 green & turquoise	1·20	1·30
2701	2f.67 blue and red	1·90	2·00
2702	4f.44 orange and brown	3·75	2·75

DESIGNS: 1f.28, Butterflies (May); 1f.65, Flowers (June); 2f.67, Phrygian cap (July); 4f.44, Sun (August).

See note below No. 432 (1920).

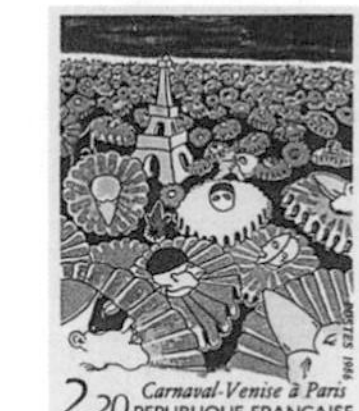

1019 Masked Revellers

1986. Venetian Carnival in Paris.

2703	**1019**	2f.20 multicoloured	1·20	40

1020 Francois Arago (physicist and politician)

1986. Red Cross Fund. Celebrities.

2704	**1020**	1f.80+40c. black, blue & turquoise	1·20	1·10
2705	-	1f.80+40c. black, blue & turquoise	1·20	1·10
2706	-	1f.80+40c. black, blue & turquoise	1·20	1·10
2707	-	2f.20+50c. black, turquoise & blue	1·60	1·30
2708	-	2f.20+50c. black, turquoise & blue	1·60	1·30
2709	-	2f.20+50c. brown	1·90	2·00

DESIGNS: No. 2705, Henri Moissan (chemist); 2706, Henri Fabre (engineer) and seaplane "Hydravion"; 2707, Marc Seguin (locomotive engineer); 2708, Paul Heroult (chemist); 2709, Pierre Cot (politician).

1986. Tourist Publicity. As T 490 and 949.

2710	1f.80 multicoloured	1·20	40
2711	2f. blue and black	1·40	95
2712	2f.20 brown, blue & green	1·40	65
2713	2f.50 dp brown & brown	1·70	65
2714	3f.90 orange and black	3·00	1·30

DESIGNS: As T **490**—HORIZ: 1f.80, Filitosa, Corsica; 2f. Chateau de Loches; 2f.20, Manor of St. Germain de Livet, Calvados. VERT: 2f.50, Cloisters, Notre Dame en Vaux, Marne. As T **949**: 3f.90, Monpazier, Dordogne.

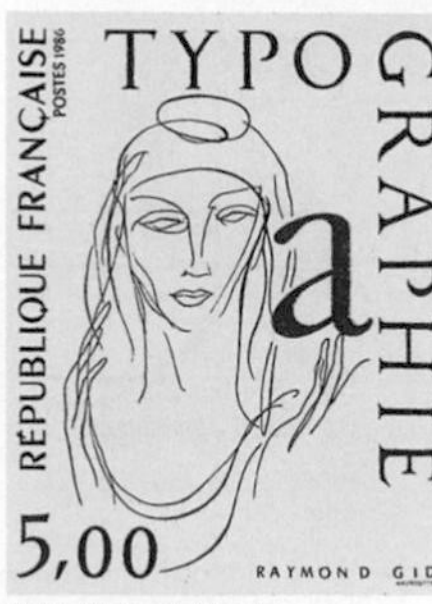

1021 Woman's Head

1986. Typography.

2715	**1021**	5f. black and red	3·75	1·70

1022 Louise Michel (writer)

1986. International Women's Day.

2716	**1022**	1f.80 black and red	1·20	40

1023 La Villette

1986. Science and Industry City, La Villette.

2717	**1023**	3f.90 multicoloured	2·50	85

1024 Britska Mail Coach

1986. Stamp Day.

2718	**1024**	2f.20+60c. pink and brown	1·70	1·70
2719	**1024**	2f.20+60c. yellow and black	1·90	1·90

1025 Map and Latitude Lines

1986. 50th Anniv of African and Asian Studies Centre.

2720	**1025**	3f.20 multicoloured	1·90	65

1986. Art. As T 491.

2721	5f. multicoloured	3·75	1·90
2722	5f. multicoloured	3·75	1·90
2723	5f. multicoloured	3·75	1·90
2724	5f. multicoloured	3·75	1·90
2725	5f. grey, black & violet	3·75	1·90

DESIGNS—HORIZ: No. 2721, "Skibet" (Maurice Esteve); 2722, "Virginia" (Alberto Magnelli); 2725, Abstract by Pierre Soulages. VERT: 2723, "The Dancer" (Hans Arp); 2724, "Isabelle d'Este" (Leonardo da Vinci).

1026 Genet

1986. Europa.

2726	**1026**	2f.20 black and red	1·90	55
2727	-	3f.20 black and red	2·50	1·10

DESIGN: 3f.20, Lesser horseshoe bat.

1027 Victor Basch

1986. International Peace Year.

2728	**1027**	2f.50 black & green	1·50	65

1028 Vianney

1986. Birth Bicentenary of Saint J. M. B. Vianney, Cure d'Ars.

2729	**1028**	1f.80 brown, deep brown and orange	1·20	40

1029 City Gate

1986. Federation of French Philatelic Societies Congress, Nancy.

2730	**1029**	2f. blue and green	1·20	45

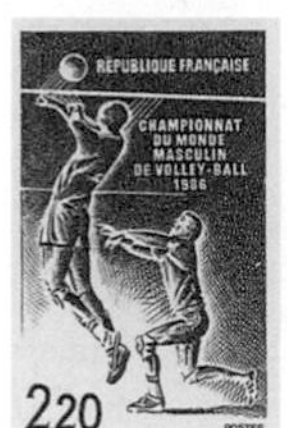

1030 Players

1986. Men's World Volleyball Championships.

2731	**1030**	2f.20 purple, vio & red	1·20	65

1031 Head of Statue

1986. Centenary of Statue of Liberty.

2732	**1031**	2f.20 blue and red	1·20	40

1032 "Liberty" (after Delacroix)

1986. No value expressed.

2733	**1032**	(1f.90) green	1·20	40

See also Nos. 2784 and 2949/50.

1033 Mont Blanc, J. Balmat and M. G. Paccard

1986. Bicentenary of First Ascent of Mont Blanc.

2734	**1033**	2f. blue, dp bl & brn	1·20	85

1034 Maupertuis and La Condamine

1986. 250th Anniv of Measurement of Arcs of Meridian.

2735	**1034**	3f. black, lt bl & bl	1·90	85

1035 Marcasite

1986. Minerals.

2736	**1035**	2f. multicoloured	1·40	40
2737	-	3f. multicoloured	1·70	55
2738	-	4f. blue, brown & mve	2·50	1·30
2739	-	5f. turq, mve & bl	3·00	1·10

DESIGNS: 3f. Quartz; 4f. Calcite; 5f. Fluorite.

1036 Musidora in "The Vampires" (dir. Louis Feuillade)

1986. 50th Anniv of French Film Institute. Sheet 143×179 mm containing T 1036 and similar horiz designs, each black, deep grey and deep grey-brown.

MS2740	2f.20 Type **1036**; 2f.20 Max Linder; 2f.20 Sacha Guitry in "Story of a Cheat" (dir. Guitry); 2f.20 Pierre Fresnay and Eric von Stroheim in "The Great Illusion" (dir. Jean Renoir); 2f.20 Raimu and Ginette Leclerc in "The Baker's Wife" (dir. Marcel Pagnol); 2f.20 Rene Ferte in "The Triple Mirror" (dir. Jean Epstein); 2f.20 Gerard Philipe and Martine Carol in "Beauties in the Night" (dir. Rene Clair); 2f.20 Jean Gabin and Mireille Balin in "Face of Love" (dir. Jean Gremillon); 2f.20 Simone Signoret in "Casque d'Or" (Golden Marie) (dir. Jacques Becker); 2f.20 Francois Truffaut and Jean-Pierre Cargol in "The Wild Child" (dir. Truffaut)	19·00	17·00

1037 Woman's Head, Printed Circuit and Drawing Instruments

1986. Centenary of Technical Education.

2741	**1037**	1f.90 blue & mauve	1·20	40

1038 Scene from "Le Grand Meaulnes"

1986. Birth Centenary of Henri Alain-Fournier (writer).

2742	**1038**	2f.20 brown & red	1·20	65

1039 Emblem

1986. World Energy Conference, Cannes.
2743 **1039** 3f.40 blue, mve & red 2·10 1·10

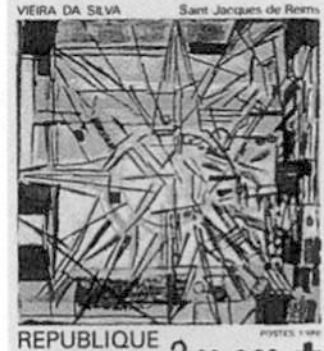

1041 Detail of Window by Vieira da Silva, St. John's Church, Rheims

1986. Red Cross Fund.
2745 **1041** 2f.20+60c. mult 1·70 1·50

1042 Car, Steam Locomotive and Carpet

1986. Mulhouse Technical Museums.
2746 **1042** 2f.20 red, black & blue 1·90 1·10

1043 Museum Facade

1986. Quai d'Orsay Museum.
2747 **1043** 3f.70 dp blue & blue 2·10 1·10

1044 Underground Train in Tunnel

1987. 50th Death Anniv (1986) of Fulgence Bienvenue (designer of Paris Metro).
2748 **1044** 2f.50 pur, grn & brn 1·90 1·10

1045 Raoul Follereau

1987. 10th Death Anniv of Raoul Follereau (leprosy pioneer).
2749 **1045** 1f.90 dp grn & grn 1·30 1·00

1987. Precancels. Months of the Year (3rd series). As T 996.
2750 1f.31 brown and orange 1·30 1·00
2751 1f.69 orange and purple 1·60 1·30
2752 2f.74 grey and blue 2·20 1·80
2753 4f.56 green and mauve 3·75 3·00
DESIGNS: 1f.31, Grapes (September); 1f.69, Posthorn (October); 2f.74, Falling leaves (November); 4f.56, Christmas tree (December).
See note below No. 432 (1920).

1046 Charles Richet (physiologist)

1987. Red Cross Fund. Medical Celebrities.
2754 **1046** 1f.90+50c. blue 1·30 1·00
2755 - 1f.90+50c. lilac 1·30 1·00
2756 - 1f.90+50c. grey 1·30 1·00
2757 - 2f.20+50c. grey 1·40 1·10
2758 - 2f.20+50c. blue 1·40 1·10
2759 - 2f.20+50c. lilac 1·40 1·10
DESIGNS: No. 2755, Eugene Jamot (sleeping sickness pioneer); 2756, Bernard Halpern (immunologist); 2757, Alexandre Yersin (bacteriologist, discoverer of plague bacillus); 2758, Jean Rostand (geneticist); 2759, Jacques Monod (molecular biologist).

1047 Grinding Blades

1987. Handicrafts. Thiers Cutlery.
2760 **1047** 1f.90 black and red 1·30 90

1048 "Liberty" and "Philexfrance 89"

1987. "Philexfrance 89" International Stamp Exhibition, Paris (1st issue).
2761 **1048** 2f.20 red 1·30 90
The stamp and label which together comprise No. 2761 were printed together se-tenant. For stamp without label, see No. 2466.
See also No. 2821.

1987. Tourist Publicity. As T 490 and 949.
2762 2f.20 green, grey & mauve 1·30 90
2763 2f.20 multicoloured 1·30 90
2764 2f.50 green and blue 1·80 1·30
2765 2f.50 black, red and blue 1·80 1·30
2766 3f. brown and violet 2·10 1·50
2767 3f.70 blue, lilac & brown 2·50 1·80
DESIGNS—As T **490**: No. 2762, Redon Abbey; 2763, Etretat (after Eugene Delacroix); 2764, Azay-le-Rideau Chateau; 2765, Montbenoit le Saugeais; 2766, Les Baux-de-Provence. As T **949**: No. 2767, Cotes de Meuse.

1049 Berlin

1987. Stamp Day.
2768 **1049** 2f.20+60c. brown and yellow 1·80 1·30
2769 **1049** 2f.20+60c. deep blue and blue 1·90 1·40

1050 "Divine Proportion"

1987. Birth Centenary of Charles-Edouard Jeanneret "Le Corbusier" (architect).
2770 **1050** 3f.70 multicoloured 1·90 1·40

1051 "57 Metal", Boulogne-Billancourt (Claude Vasconi)

1987. Europa. Architecture.
2771 **1051** 2f.20 blue and green 1·90 1·40
2772 - 3f.40 brown & green 2·50 1·80
DESIGN: 3f.40, Rue Mallet-Stevens, Paris (Robert Mallet-Stevens).

1987. Art. As T 491.
2773 5f. multicoloured 3·75 2·75
2774 5f. multicoloured 3·75 2·75
2775 5f. multicoloured 3·75 2·75
2776 5f. brn, lt brn & blk 3·75 2·75
DESIGNS—HORIZ: No. 2773, "Abstract" (Bram van Velde); 2774, "Woman with Parasol" (Eugene Boudin); 2776, "World" (sculpture, Antoine Pevsner). VERT: No. 2775, "Pre-Cambrian" (Camille Bryen).

1052 Gaspard of the Mountains

1987. Birth Centenary of Henri Pourrat (writer).
2777 **1052** 1f.90 brown and green 1·30 90

1053 Lens

1987. Federation of French Philatelic Societies Congress, Lens.
2778 **1053** 2f.20 red & brown 1·30 90

1054 Gen. Pershing, Soldiers and U.S. Flag

1987. 70th Anniv of Entry of U.S. Troops into First World War.
2779 **1054** 3f.40 red, blue & green 2·20 1·40

1055 Cable Cars

1987. 6th International Cable Transport Congress, Grenoble.
2780 **1055** 2f. black, bl & grn 1·40 90

1056 Noyon Cathedral and Symbol

1987. Millenary of Election of Hugues Capet as King of France.
2781 **1056** 1f.90 black and blue 1·30 75

1057 Prytanee

1987. Prytanee National Military School (for French Soldiers' Children), La Fleche.
2782 **1057** 2f.20 black, grn & red 1·30 90

1058 Black Footprints on Map of France

1987. "25 Years After" World Assembly of Repatriated French-Algerians, Nice.
2783 **1058** 1f.90 multicoloured 1·30 75

1987. No value expressed. As T 1032 but inscr "B".
2784 (2f.) green 1·30 55

1059 Globe and Wrestlers

1987. World Wrestling Championship, Clermont-Ferrand.
2785 **1059** 3f. brown, grey & vio 1·50 90

1060 "Gyroporus cyanescens"

1987. Fungi.
2786 **1060** 2f. multicoloured 1·40 65
2787 - 3f. multicoloured 1·80 1·20
2788 - 4f. black, bistre & brn 2·50 1·40
2789 - 5f. multicoloured 3·25 1·80
DESIGNS: 3f. "Gomphus clavatus"; 4f. "Morchella conica"; 5f. "Russula virescens".

1061 Bayeux Tapestry (detail)

1987. 900th Death Anniv of William the Conqueror.
2790 **1061** 2f. multicoloured 1·30 90

1062 Institute

1987. Centenary of Pasteur Institute.
2791 **1062** 2f.20 red and blue 1·30 90

1063 Cendrars (after Modigliani)

1987. Birth Centenary of Blaise Cendrars (writer).

2792	**1063**	2f. buff, black and green	1·30	90

1064 "Flight into Egypt" (Melchior Broederlam) (detail, Champmol Charterhouse retable)

1987. Red Cross Fund.

2793	**1064**	2f.20+60c. mult	1·60	90

1065 Leclerc, Oasis, Tank, Pantheon and Strasbourg Cathedral

1987. 40th Death Anniv of Marshal Leclerc.

2794	**1065**	2f.20 blk, brn & dp brn	1·60	90

1066 Treaty Document, Brunehaut, Childebert II and King Guntram of Burgundy

1987. 1400th Anniv of Treaty of Andelot.

2795	**1066**	3f.70 blk, dp bl & bl	2·40	1·10

1067 Dr. Konrad Adenauer (West German Chancellor) and Charles de Gaulle (French President)

1988. 25th Anniv of Franco-German Co-operation Treaty.

2796	**1067**	2f.20 purple & black	1·90	90

1068 Dassault and Aircraft

1988. 2nd Death Anniv of Marcel Dassault (aircraft engineer).

2797	**1068**	3f.60 brown, red & bl	2·50	1·40

1069 People on Airplane flying around Globe (Rene Pellos)

1988. Communications. Designs by comic strip artists. Multicoloured.

2798		2f.20 Type **1069**	1·30	90
2799		2f.20 Monkey writing in light from table lamp (Jean-Marc Reiser)	1·30	90
2800		2f.20 Sitting Bull and smoke signals (Marijac (Jacques Dumas))	1·30	90
2801		2f.20 Couple with love letter (Fred (Othon Aristides))	1·30	90
2802		2f.20 Man watching levitating letter (Moebius (Jean Giraud))	1·30	90
2803		2f.20 Globe and astronaut (Paul Gillon)	1·30	90
2804		2f.20 Man playing letter and pen "guitar" (Claire Bretecher)	1·30	90
2805		2f.20 Hand posting letter in talking letter-box (Jean-Claude Forest)	1·30	90
2806		2f.20 Rocket behind astronaut reading letter (Jean-Claude Mezieres)	1·30	90
2807		2f.20 Woman with mystery letter (Jacques Tardi)	1·30	90
2808		2f.20 Baby reading letter in pram with attached letter-box (Jacques Lob)	1·30	90
2809		2f.20 Woman pilot with letters (Enki Bilal)	1·30	90

1070 Bird flying (Air)

1988. Precancels. The Elements.

2810	**1070**	1f.36 blue and black	1·30	90
2811	-	1f.75 blue and black	1·60	1·10
2812	-	2f.83 red and black	2·20	1·60
2813	-	4f.75 green & black	3·75	2·75

DESIGNS: 1f.70, Splash of water (Water); 2f.83, Flames (Fire); 4f.75, Tree (Earth).

See note below No. 432 (1920).

1071 Dove and Interior

1988. Rue Victoire Synagogue, Paris.

2814	**1071**	2f. black and gold	1·30	90

1072 Abraham Duquesne and Map

1988. Red Cross Fund. Explorers. Each blue, brown and black.

2815		2f.+50c. Type **1072**	1·30	90
2816		2f.+50c. Pierre Andre de Suffren Saint Tropez	1·30	90
2817		2f.+50c. Jean Francois de Galaup, Comte de La Perouse	1·30	90
2818		2f.+50c. Bertrand Francois Mahe de La Bourdonnais	1·30	90
2819		2f.20+50c. Louis Antoine de Bougainville	1·30	90
2820		2f.20+50c. Jules Dumont d'Urville	1·30	90

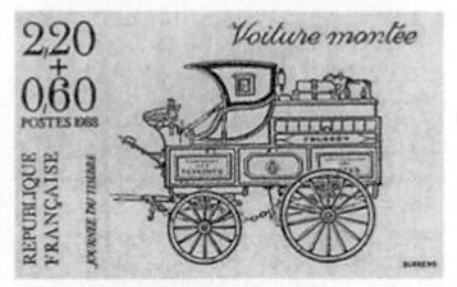

1073 "Liberty" and Emblem

1988. "Philexfrance 89" International Stamp Exhibition, Paris (2nd issue).

2821	**1073**	2f.20 red, black & bl	1·30	55

1074 Mail Coach

1988. Stamp Day.

2822	**1074**	2f.20+60c. purple and mauve	1·80	1·10
2823	**1074**	2f.20+60c. brown and flesh	1·80	1·10

1075 Emblem

1988. Centenary of Post Office National College.

2824	**1075**	3f.60 bl, grn & red	2·20	1·00

1076 "Stamps"

1988. "Philex-Jeunes 88" Stamp Exhibition, Nevers.

2825	**1076**	2f. blue, violet & mve	1·30	75

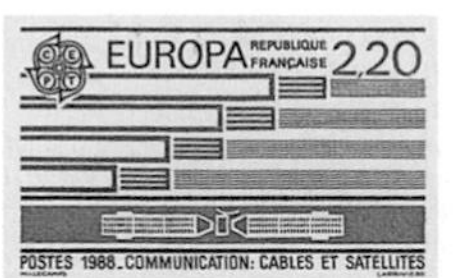

1077 Blood Drop

1988. Blood Donation Service.

2826	**1077**	2f.50 red, blk & yell	1·60	90

1988. No. 2467 surch ECU 0,31.

2827	**916**	0.31ECU on 2f.20 red	1·90	90

ECU stands for European Currency Unit.

1079 Cable and Satellite Communications

1988. Europa. Transport and Communications.

2828	**1079**	2f.20 grey, black & bl	1·90	1·40
2829	-	3f.60 pur, blk & lt pur	2·50	1·80

DESIGN: 3f.60, Two-car electric train.

1080 Monnet

1988. Birth Centenary of Jean Monnet (statesman).

2830	**1080**	2f.20 blue and brown	1·60	90

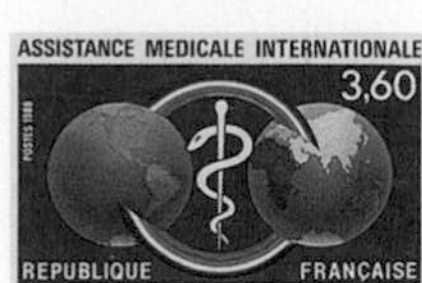

1081 Town Hall and Roman Carved Stone Heads

1988. Federation of French Philatelic Societies Congress, Valence.

2831	**1081**	2f.20 orge, dp bl & bl	1·30	90

1082 Rod of Aesculapius, Globes and Rainbows

1988. International Medical Assistance.

2832	**1082**	3f.60 multicoloured	2·20	90

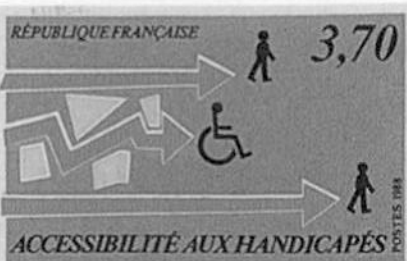

1083 Typical Access Routes

1988. Easy Access for the Handicapped.

2833	**1083**	3f.70 multicoloured	2·20	90

1988. Tourist Publicity.

2834	2f. multicoloured	1·30	75
2835	2f.20 brown, bl & turq	1·30	90
2836	2f.20 blue, turq & grn	1·30	90
2837	3f. violet, green and brown	1·80	90
2838	3f.70 black, blue and red	2·10	1·50

DESIGNS—As T **490**. HORIZ: No. 2834, Ship Museum, Douarnenez; 2836, Perouges; 2837, Cirque de Gavarnie (rock formation). VERT: No. 2835, Sedieres Chateau, Correze. As T **949**: No. 2838, "Double-headed Hermes of Frejus" (Roman sculpture).

1084 Otters

1988. Animals. Illustrations from "Natural History" by Comte de Buffon.

2839	**1084**	2f. black and green	1·30	45
2840	-	3f. black and red	1·80	90
2841	-	4f. black and mauve	2·40	1·40
2842	-	5f. black and blue	3·00	1·80

DESIGNS: 3f. Stag; 4f. Fox; 5f. Badger.

1085 "Assembly of the Three Estates, Vizille" (Alexandre Debelle)

1988. Bicentenary of French Revolution (1st issue). Each black, blue and red.

2843	3f. Type **1085**	1·80	1·10
2844	4f. "Day of the Tiles, Grenoble" (Alexandre Debelle)	2·20	1·30

See also Nos. 2857, 2863/8, 2871/3, **MS**2889, **MS**2890, **MS**3005 and **MS**3083.

1086 Soldiers of 1888 and 1988

1988. Centenary of Alpine Troops.

2845	**1086**	2f.50 dp bl, bl & red	1·90	1·40

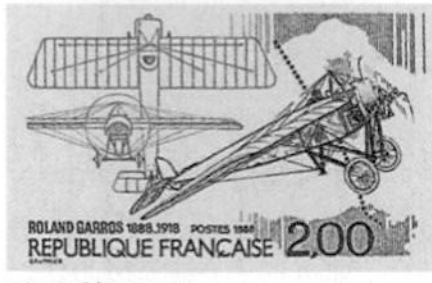

1087 Bleriot XI

1988. Birth Centenary of Roland Garros (aviator).

2846	**1087**	2f. green, olive and blue	1·60	90

1088 Soldiers

1988. 70th Anniv of Armistice.

2847	**1088**	2f.20 multicoloured	1·60	90

1089 "Tribute to Leon Degand" (Robert Jacobsen)

1988. French–Danish Cultural Year.
2848 **1089** 5f. red & black on grey 3·75 1·70

1090 City Arms

1988. 2000th Anniv of Strasbourg.
2849 **1090** 2f.20 multicoloured 1·40 90

1988. Art. As T 491.
2850 5f. brown 3·75 1·70
2851 5f. multicoloured 3·75 1·70
2852 5f. multicoloured 3·75 1·70
2853 5f. multicoloured 3·75 1·70
DESIGNS—48×38 mm: No. 2850, St. Mihiel's Sepulchre (Ligier Richier); 2851, "Composition" (Serge Poliakoff); 2852, "Meta" (Tinguely). 48×43 mm: No. 2853, "Pieta de Villeneuve-les-Avignon" (Enguerrand Quarton).

1091 Activities at Spas

1988. Thermal Spas.
2854 **1091** 2f.20 red, blue & grn 1·30 90

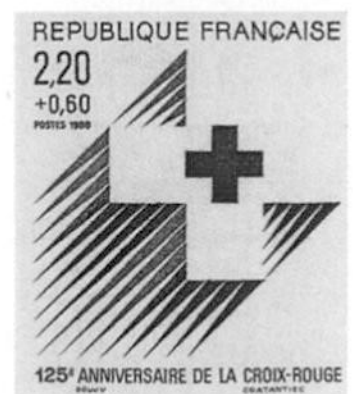

1092 Cross

1988. Red Cross Fund.
2855 **1092** 2f.20+60c. red, blue and black 1·60 90

1093 Earth

1988. 40th Anniv of Universal Declaration of Human Rights.
2856 **1093** 2f.20 dp blue & blue 1·90 1·10

1094 Birds

1989. Bicentenary of French Revolution (2nd issue).
2857 **1094** 2f.20 blue, red & blk 1·30 90

1989. Art. As T 491. Multicoloured.
2858 5f. "Anthropometry of the Blue Era" (Yves Klein) 3·50 1·50
2859 5f. "Oath of the Tennis Court" (sketch, David) 3·50 1·50
2860 5f. "Regetta with Wind Astern" (Lapicque) (vert) 3·50 1·50

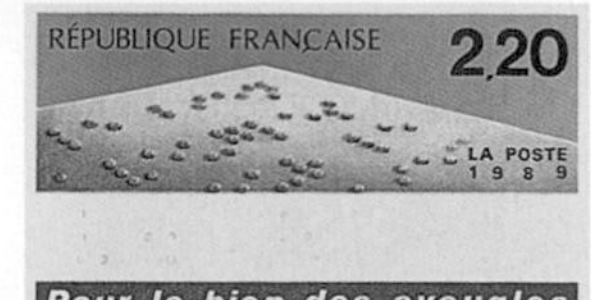

1095 Page of Braille

1989. The Blind.
2861 **1095** 2f.20 bl, orge & mve 1·30 90

1096 "E"

1989. Centenary of Estienne School.
2862 **1096** 2f.20 blk, grey & red 1·30 90

1097 Comte de Sieyes

1989. Red Cross Fund. Bicentenary of French Revolution (3rd issue). Personalities. Mult.
2863 2f.20+50c. Type **1097** 1·40 1·10
2864 2f.20+50c. Comte de Mirabeau 1·40 1·10
2865 2f.20+50c. Vicomte de Noailles 1·40 1·10
2866 2f.20+50c. Marquis de Lafayette 1·40 1·10
2867 2f.20+50c. Antoine Barnave 1·40 1·10
2868 2f.20+50c. Jean Baptiste Drouet 1·40 1·10

1098 Emblem on Spectrum

1989. Direct Elections to European Parliament.
2869 **1098** 2f.20 multicoloured 1·30 90

1099 Flags, Astronauts and Satellite

1989. French–Soviet Space Flight.
2870 **1099** 3f.60 multicoloured 2·50 1·40

1100 "Liberty"

1989. Bicentenary of French Revolution (4th issue) and Declaration of Rights of Man (1st issue). Paintings by Roger Druet. Multicoloured.
2871 2f.20 Type **1100** 1·30 90
2872 2f.20 "Equality" 1·30 90
2873 2f.20 "Fraternity" 1·30 90

1101 Paris–Lyon Stage Coach

1989. Stamp Day.
2874 **1101** 2f.20+60c. deep blue and blue 1·50 1·00
2875 **1101** 2f.20+60c. lilac and mauve 1·80 1·10

1102 Arche de la Defense

1989. Paris Panorama. Multicoloured.
2876 2f.20 Type **1102** 1·60 90
2877 2f.20 Eiffel Tower 1·60 90
2878 2f.20 Pyramid, Louvre 1·60 90
2879 2f.20 Notre Dame Cathedral 1·60 90
2880 2f.20 Bastille Opera House 1·60 90

1103 Hopscotch

1989. Europa. Children's Games. Mult.
2881 2f.20 Type **1103** 2·50 45
2882 3f.60 Ball game 3·75 1·60

1989. Tourist Publicity. As T 490 and 949.
2883 2f.20 green, brown & orge 1·40 75
2884 3f.70 red, blue and black 2·40 90
2885 3f.70 black and brown 2·40 1·30
2886 4f. blue 2·50 1·40
DESIGNS—As T **490**. HORIZ: No. 2883, Fontainebleau forest. VERT: No. 2884, Malestroit. As T **949**: No. 2885, Chateau of Vaux-le-Vicomte; 2886, La Brenne.

1104 Emblems and Buildings

1989. International Telecommunications Union Plenipotentiaries Conference, Nice.
2887 **1104** 3f.70 red, blue & orge 2·20 1·10

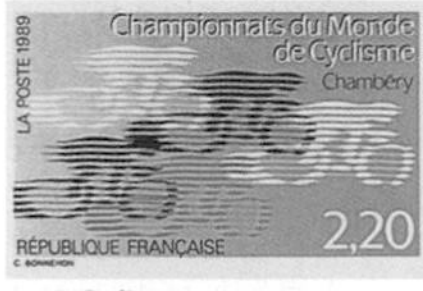

1105 Cyclists

1989. International Cycling Championships, Chambery.
2888 **1105** 2f.20 multicoloured 1·80 90

1106 Madame Roland

1989. Bicentenary of French Revolution (5th issue). Personalities. Sheet 78×105 mm containing T 1106 and similar vert designs. Multicoloured.
MS2889 2f.20 Type **1106**; 2f.20 Camille Desmoulins; 2f.20 Marquis de Condorcet; 2f.20 Major-Gen. Francois Kellerman 5·75 5·50

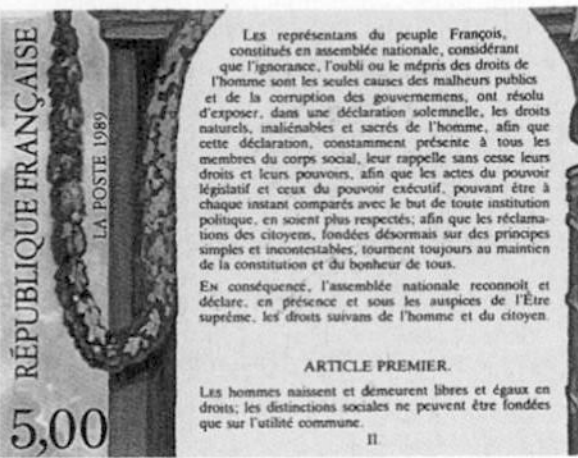

1107 "LES repesentans du people Francois,..."

1989. Bicentenary of French Revolution (6th issue) and Declaration of Rights of Man (2nd issue). Sheet 130×143 mm containing T 1107 and similar horiz designs. Multicoloured.
MS2890 5f. Type **1107**; 5f. "NUL home ne peut etre accuse..."; 5f. "LE but de toute association politique..."; 5f. "LA garantie des droits de l'homme..." (sold at 50f.) 26·00 26·00

1108 Arche de la Defense

1989. Summit Conference of Industrialised Countries, Paris.
2891 **1108** 2f.20 multicoloured 1·30 90

1109 Preamble

1989. Bicentenary of Declaration of Rights of Man (3rd issue). Multicoloured.
2892 2f.50 Type **1109** 1·40 90
2893 2f.50 Articles II to VI 1·40 90
2894 2f.50 Articles VII to XI 1·40 90
2895 2f.50 Articles XII to XVII 1·40 90

1110 Harp

1989. Precancels. Musical Instruments (1st series).
2896 **1110** 1f.39 lt blue & blue 1·30 65
2897 - 1f.79 brn & lt brn 1·50 90
2898 - 2f.90 orange & brn 2·50 1·40
2899 - 4f.84 orange & brn 3·75 2·75
DESIGNS: 1f.79, Piano; 2f.90, Trumpet; 4f.84, Violin.
See note below No. 432 (1920).
See also Nos. 2993/9, 3052/62, 3095/8 and 3145/8.

1111 Train

1989. TGV "Atlantique" Express Train.
2900 **1111** 2f.50 blue, silver & red 2·50 1·20

1112 Tram

1989. Cent of Clermont-Ferrand Electric Tramway.
2901 **1112** 3f.70 black & brown 2·50 1·10

1113 King Francois I

1989. 450th Anniv of Villers-Cotterets Ordinance.

2902	**1113**	2f.20 red and black	1·30	90

1114 Cauchy, Graphs and Formula

1989. Birth Bicentenary of Augustin Louis Cauchy (mathematician).

2903	**1114**	3f.60 blue, blk & red	2·20	1·10

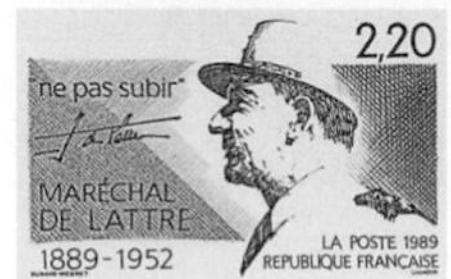

1115 Marshal Lattre de Tassigny

1989. Birth Centenary of Marshal Jean de Lattre de Tassigny.

2904	**1115**	2f.20 black, blue & red	1·60	90

1116 Bird feeding Chicks (18th-century silk painting)

1989. Red Cross Fund.

2905	**1116**	2f.20+60c. mult	1·60	1·00

1117 Harkis

1989. Harkis (French North African troops).

2906	**1117**	2f.20 multicoloured	1·60	90

1118 "Marianne"

1989. Imperf (2943), perf or imperf (2910, 2915, 2916), perf (others).

2907	**1118**	10c. brown	25	20
2908	**1118**	20c. green	25	20
2909	**1118**	50c. violet	25	20
2943b	**1118**	70c. brown	14·00	5·50
2910	**1118**	1f. orange	65	45
2911	**1118**	2f. green	1·30	45
2912	**1118**	2f. blue	1·30	45
2913	**1118**	2f.10 green	1·30	45
2914	**1118**	2f.20 green	1·90	60
2916	**1118**	2f.30 red	1·30	75
2917	**1118**	2f.40 green	1·60	45
2918	**1118**	2f.50 red	1·90	90
2919	**1118**	2f.70 green	1·80	65
2920	**1118**	3f.20 blue	2·20	90
2921	**1118**	3f.40 blue	2·10	90
2922	**1118**	3f.50 green	2·20	45
2923	**1118**	3f.80 mauve	2·40	90
2924	**1118**	3f.80 blue	2·20	90
2925	**1118**	4f. mauve	3·00	90
2926	**1118**	4f.20 mauve	2·50	90
2927	**1118**	4f.40 blue	2·50	90
2928	**1118**	4f.50 mauve	2·50	1·20
2929	**1118**	5f. blue	2·75	90
2930	**1118**	10f. violet	5·50	90

The imperforate stamps are self-adhesive.

For designs as T **1118** but inscr "D" for face value, see Nos. 3036/7, and with no value at all see No. 3122.

1990. No value expressed. As T 1032 but inscr "C".

2949	(2f.10) green	1·30	45
2950	(2f.30) red	1·30	45

1119 Lace

1990

2951	**1119**	2f.50 white and red	1·60	90

1120 Games Emblem

1990. Winter Olympic Games, Albertville (1992) (1st issue).

2952	**1120**	2f.50 multicoloured	1·60	90

See also Nos. 2953/62 and 3048.

1121 Emblem and Ice Skaters

1990. Winter Olympic Games, Albertville (1992) (2nd issue). Each black, blue and red.

2953	2f.30+20c. Type **1121**	1·60	90
2954	2f.30+20c. Ski jumping	1·60	90
2955	2f.30+20c. Speed skiiing	1·60	90
2956	2f.30+20c. Slalom	1·60	90
2957	2f.30+20c. Cross-country skiing	1·60	90
2958	2f.30+20c. Ice hockey	1·60	90
2959	2f.50+20c. Luge	1·60	90
2960	2f.50+20c. Curling	1·60	90
2961	2f.50+20c. Artistic skiing	1·60	90
2962	2f.50+20c. Downhill skiing	1·60	90
MS2963	143×126 mm. 10 ×2f.50+20c. As Nos. 2953/62	19·00	19·00

1122 Cross of Lorraine and De Gaulle

1990. Birth Centenary of Charles de Gaulle (President, 1959–69).

2964	**1122**	2f.30 blue, black & vio	1·90	1·20

1123 Aircraft and Hymans

1990. 90th Birth Anniv of Max Hymans (civil aviation pioneer).

2965	**1123**	2f.30 green, violet & bl	1·30	90

1990. Art. As T 491.

2966	5f. multicoloured	3·50	1·40
2967	5f. blue, brown and ochre	3·50	1·40
2968	5f. multicoloured	3·50	1·40
2969	5f. multicoloured	3·50	1·40

DESIGNS—VERT: No. 2966, "Woman's Profile" (Odilon Redon); 2967, "Seated Cambodian Woman" (Auguste Rodin); 2968, "Head of Christ of Wissembourg"; 2969, "Yellow and Grey" (Roger Bissiere).

1124 Eyes and Keyboard

1990. Stamp Day.

2970	**1124**	2f.30+60c. blue, ultramarine and yellow	1·90	1·20
2971	**1124**	2f.30+60c. deep green, green, blue and yellow	1·90	1·40

1125 Guehenno

1990. Birth Cent of Jean Guehenno (writer).

2972	**1125**	3f.20 brown & lt brn	1·90	1·10

1990. Tourist Publicity. As T 490.

2973	2f.30 orange, blue & black	1·50	90
2974	2f.30 black, blue & green	1·50	90
2975	3f.80 brown and green	2·50	1·20
2976	3f.80 purple, brown & blue	2·50	1·20

DESIGNS: No. 2973, Cluny; 2974, Aqueduct, Briare Canal; 2975, Flaran-Gers Abbey; 2976, Cap Canaille Cassis.

1126 Macon Post Office

1990. Europa. Post Office Buildings.

2978	**1126**	2f.30 black, ochre and blue	1·90	85
2979	-	3f.20 multicoloured	2·50	1·30

DESIGN: 3f.20, Cerizay post office.

1127 Crowd

1990. Centenary of Labour Day.

2980	**1127**	2f.30 multicoloured	1·30	90

1128 Quimper Faience Plate

1990. Red Cross Fund.

2981	**1128**	2f.30+60c. mult	1·80	1·00

1129 Institute Building

1990. Arab World Institute.

2982	**1129**	3f.80 dp blue, bl & red	2·40	1·10

1130 Detail of Stonework, Notre Dame des Marais

1990. Federation of French Philatelic Societies Congress, Villefranche-sur-Saone.

2983	**1130**	2f.30 black, grn & red	1·30	90

1131 "La Poste"

1990. Round the World Yacht Race.

2984	**1131**	2f.30 multicoloured	1·30	90

1132 Georges Brassens

1990. Red Cross Fund. French Singers. Mult.

2985	2f.30+50c. Aristide Bruant	1·60	1·20
2986	2f.30+50c. Maurice Chevalier	1·60	1·20
2987	2f.30+50c. Tino Rossi	1·60	1·20
2988	2f.30+50c. Edith Piaf	1·60	1·20
2989	2f.30+50c. Jacques Brel	1·60	1·20
2990	2f.30+50c. Type **1132**	1·60	1·20

1133 Cross of Lorraine and Marianne

1990. 50th Anniv of De Gaulle's Call to Resist.

2991	**1133**	2f.30 red, blue & blk	1·60	90

1134 Aerial View of House

1990. 5th Anniv of France–Brazil House, Rio de Janeiro.

2992	**1134**	3f.20 multicoloured	2·10	1·10

1990. Precancels. Musical Instruments (2nd series). As T **1110**.

2993	1f.46 emerald and green	1·60	90
2994	1f.80 brown and orange	1·90	90
2995	1f.93 green & deep green	1·60	90
2996	2f.39 mauve and purple	1·90	1·30
2997	2f.74 violet and blue	3·00	1·70
2998	3f.06 blue and deep blue	2·50	1·80
2999	5f.10 violet and purple	4·25	2·75

DESIGNS: 1 f 46, Accordion; 1f.89, Breton bagpipe; 1f.93, Harp; 2f.39, Piano; 2f.74, Violin; 3f.06, Provencal drum; 5f.10, Hurdy-gurdy.

See note below No. 432 (1920).

1135 Relief Map of France

1990. 50th Anniv of National Geographical Institute.

3000	**1135**	2f.30 multicoloured	1·60	90

1136 Roach

1990. Freshwater Fishes. Multicoloured.

3001	2f. Type **1136**	1·30	65
3002	3f. Eurasian perch	1·80	1·00
3003	4f. Atlantic salmon	2·50	1·40
3004	5f. Northern pike	3·00	1·70

1137 Gaspard Monge (Navy Minister)

1990. Bicentenary of French Revolution (7th issue). Sheet 79×106 mm containing T 1137 and similar vert designs.

MS3005 2f.50 Type **1137**; 2f.50 Abbe Henri Gregorie; 2f.50 Creation of national flag; 2f.50 Creation of departments 6·50 6·50

1138 Genevoix

1990. Birth Centenary of Maurice Genevoix (writer).

3006	**1138**	2f.30 green & black	1·30	90

1139 World Map

1990. 30th Anniv of Organization for Economic Co-operation and Development.

3007	**1139**	3f.20 blue & ultram	1·90	1·10

1991. Art. As T 491.

3008	5f. multicoloured	3·50	1·70
3009	5f. black and stone	3·50	1·70
3010	5f. black	3·50	1·70
3011	5f. multicoloured	3·50	1·70

DESIGNS—VERT: No. 3008, "The Swing" (Auguste Renoir); 3009, "The Black Knot" (Georges Seurat); 3010, "Volta faccia" (Francois Rouan). HORIZ: No. 3011, "Oh Black Painting" (Roberto Matta).

1140 Paul Eluard (after Pablo Picasso)

1991. Red Cross Fund. French Poets. Each grey, black and blue.

3013	2f.50+50c. Type **1140**	1·80	1·30
3014	2f.50+50c. Andre Breton (after Man Ray)	1·80	1·30
3015	2f.50+50c. Louis Aragon (after Henri Matisse)	1·80	1·30
3016	2f.50+50c. Francis Ponge (after Stella Mertens)	1·80	1·30
3017	2f.50+50c. Jacques Prevert (after Picasso)	1·80	1·30
3018	2f.50+50c. Rene Char (after Valentine Hugo)	1·80	1·30

1141 Mail Sorting by Hand and by Machine

1991. Stamp Day. Multicoloured, colour of machine given.

3019	**1141**	2f.50+60c. blue	1·80	1·10
3020	**1141**	2f.50+60c. violet	1·90	1·40

1142 Children, Bicycle and Dove

1991. "Philexjeunes 91" Youth Stamp Exhibition, Cholet.

3021	**1142**	2f.50 multicoloured	1·60	90

1143 Mozart and Globe

1991. Death Bicentenary of Wolfgang Amadeus Mozart (composer).

3022	**1143**	2f.50 black, blue & red	1·60	90

1144 Eyes and Forms of Writing

1991. 350th Anniv of State Printing Office.

3023	**1144**	4f. multicoloured	2·40	1·30

1991. Tourist Publicity. As T 490.

3024	2f.50 multicoloured	1·60	90
3025	2f.50 multicoloured	1·60	90
3026	4f. lilac	2·40	1·10

DESIGNS—VERT: No. 3024, Chevire Bridge, Nantes. HORIZ: No. 3025, Carennac; 3026, Munster Valley.

1145 Poster

1991. 90th Anniv of Concours Lepine (French Association of Small Manufacturers and Inventors).

3028	**1145**	4f. multicoloured	2·40	1·30

1146 "Ariane" Rocket and Map of French Guiana

1991. Europa. Europe in Space. Each blue, red and green.

3029	2f.50 Type **1146**	1·90	90
3030	3f.50 "TDF-1" broadcasting satellite, eyes and globe	3·75	1·80

1147 Perpignan

1991. Federation of French Philatelic Societies Congress, Perpignan.

3031	**1147**	2f.50 red, grey & blue	1·60	90

1148 Painting by Joan Miro

1991. Centenary of French Open Tennis Championships.

3032	**1148**	3f.50 multicoloured	2·40	1·30

1149 La Tour d'Auvergne ("First Grenadier of France")

1991. Bicentenary of French Revolution (8th issue). Sheet 105×80 mm containing T 1149 and similar horiz designs. Multicoloured.

MS3033 2f.50 Type **1149**; 2f.50 Tree of Liberty; 2f.50 Mounted gendarme; 2f.50 Louis Saint-Just 6·50 6·50

1150 Organ Pipes

1991. Organ of St. Nicholas's, Wasquehal.

3034	**1150**	4f. buff and brown	2·50	1·20

1151 Illustration from Gaston's "Book of Hunting"

1991. 600th Death Anniv of Gaston III Phoebus, Count of Foix.

3035	**1151**	2f.50 multicoloured	1·60	90

1991. No value expressed. As T 1118 but inscr "D". Imperf (self-adhesive) or perf (3037), perf (3036).

3036	(2f.20) green	1·60	45
3037	(2f.50) red	1·60	45

1152 Brown Bear

1991. Nature. Multicoloured.

3039	2f. Type **1152**	1·40	90
3040	3f. Hermann's tortoise	1·80	90
3041	4f. Eurasian beaver	2·50	1·40
3042	5f. River kingfisher	3·25	1·40

1153 Forest

1991. 10th World Forestry Congress, Paris.

3043	**1153**	2f.50 green, bl & blk	1·60	90

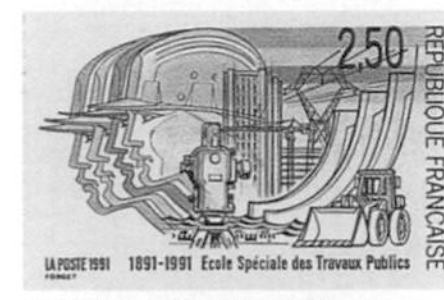

1154 Aspects of Public Works

1991. Centenary of School of Public Works.

3044	**1154**	2f.50 multicoloured	1·60	90

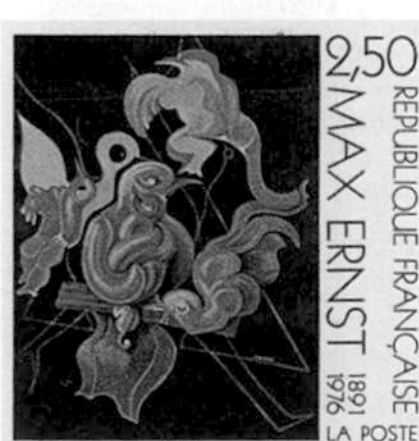

1155 "Bird Monument" (detail)

1991. Birth Centenary of Max Ernst (painter).

3045	**1155**	2f.50 multicoloured	1·90	1·10

1156 Cerdan

1991. 75th Birth Anniv of Marcel Cerdan (boxer).

3046	**1156**	2f.50 black and red	1·60	90

1157 "Amnesty International"

1991. 30th Anniv of Amnesty International.

3047	**1157**	3f.40 bl, mve & blk	2·20	1·10

1158 Stylized Flame

1991. Winter Olympic Games, Albertville (1992) (3rd issue).

3048	**1158**	2f.50 blue, blk & red	1·60	1·00

1159 "Toulon" (Francois Nardi)

1991. Red Cross Fund.
3049 **1159** 2f.50+60c. mult 1·80 1·10

1160 Bird

1991. 5th Paralympic Games, Tignes (1992).
3050 **1160** 2f.50 blue 1·60 90

1161 Shore

1991. 150th Anniv of Voluntary Adhesion of Mayotte to France.
3051 **1161** 2f.50 multicoloured 1·60 90

1992. Precancels. Musical Instruments (3rd series). As T 1110.

3052a	1f.60 brown and orange	7·75	5·50
3053	1f.98 bistre and ochre	6·00	3·00
3054	2f.08 orange and yellow	3·00	1·80
3055	2f.46 violet	3·00	1·80
3056	2f.98 lilac and mauve	3·00	1·80
3057	3f.08 purple and red	8·75	4·50
3058	3f.14 green and turquoise	3·75	2·30
3059	3f.19 grey and black	10·50	4·50
3060	5f.28 green and lt green	6·50	4·50
3061	5f.30 ultramarine & blue	5·00	3·50
3062	5f.32 brown & dp brown	5·00	3·50

DESIGNS: 1f.60, Guitar; 1f.98, Accordion; 2f.08, Saxophone; 2f.46, Breton bagpipe; 2f.98, Banjo; 3f.08, Provencal drum; 3f.14, Hurdy-gurdy; 3f.19, Harp; 5f.28, Xylophone; 5f.30, Piano; 5f.32, Violin.

See note below No. 432 (1920).

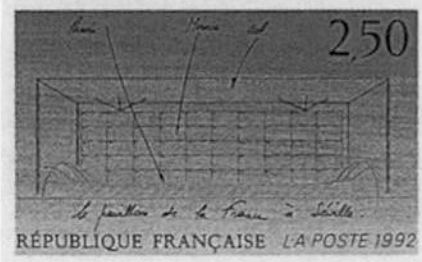

1162 Plan of French Pavilion

1992. "Expo '92" World's Fair, Seville.
3063 **1162** 2f.50 blue, blk & grn 1·60 90

1163 Post Office, Reception Area and Postal Self-service Machines

1992. Stamp Day.

3064	**1163**	2f.50+60c. black, blue and yellow	1·80	1·00
3065	**1163**	2f.50+60c. red, blue, black & yell	1·90	1·20

1164 Runner

1992. Olympic Games, Barcelona.
3066 **1164** 2f.50 multicoloured 1·90 90

1165 Cesar Franck

1992. Red Cross Fund. Composers. Mult.

3067	2f.50+50c. Type **1165**	1·80	1·30
3068	2f.50+50c. Erik Satie	1·80	1·30
3069	2f.50+50c. Florent Schmitt	1·80	1·30
3070	2f.50+50c. Arthur Honegger	1·80	1·30
3071	2f.50+50c. Georges Auric	1·80	1·30
3072	2f.50+50c. Germaine Tailleferre	1·80	1·30

1166 Marguerite d'Angouleme (after Clouet)

1992. 500th Birth Anniv of Marguerite d'Angouleme, Queen of Navarre.
3073 **1166** 3f.40 multicoloured 2·20 1·10

1167 "Madonna, Child and Angel" (Botticelli)

1992. 500th Anniv of Ajaccio.
3074 **1167** 4f. multicoloured 2·40 1·30

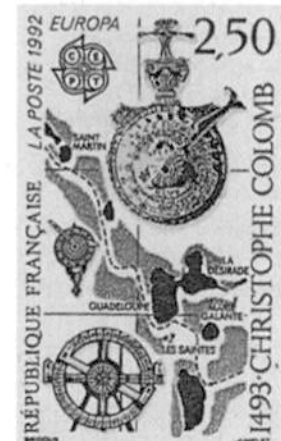

1168 Navigational Instruments and Map

1992. Europa. 500th Anniv of Discovery of America by Columbus. Multicoloured.

3075	2f.50 Type **1168**	1·90	90
3076	3f.40 Caravel, map and compass rose	3·75	1·80

1992. Tourist Publicity. As T 490.

3077	2f.50 brown, blue & green	1·60	90
3078	3f.40 brown, green & blue	2·20	1·20
3079	4f. blue, black and green	2·40	1·10
3080	4f. green, lt green & brown	2·40	1·30

DESIGNS—VERT: No. 3077, Chateau de Biron, Dordogne; 3078, Mont Aiguille, Isere (500th anniv of first ascent). HORIZ: No. 3079, 4f. L'Ourcq Canal; 3080, Lorient.

1169 Wheat, Poppies and Loaves

1992. International Bread and Cereals Congress.
3081 **1169** 3f.40 multicoloured 2·20 1·30

1170 Couple leaping through Stamp

1992. Federation of French Philatelic Societies Congress, Niort.
3082 **1170** 2f.50 multicoloured 1·90 90

1171 Olympic Rings

1992. Winter Olympic Games, Albertville, and Summer Games, Barcelona.
3083 **1171** 2f.50 multicoloured 1·90 90

1172 Tautavel Man

1992
3084 **1172** 3f.40 multicoloured 2·20 1·20

1992. Art. As T 491.
3085 5f. black and stone 3·50 1·70
DESIGN—VERT: 5f. "Portrait of Claude Deruet" (Jacques Callot).

1173 Sand Lily

1992. Flowers. Multicoloured.

3086	2f. Type **1173**	1·30	45
3087	3f. Sundew	1·80	90
3088	4f. "Orchis palustris"	2·30	1·40
3089	5f. Yellow water lily	3·00	1·80

1174 Marianne and National Colours

1992. Bicentenary of Year One of First Republic.
3090 **1174** 2f.50 multicoloured 1·60 90

1175 Marianne

1992. Bicentenary of Declaration of First Republic. Each red.

3091	2f.50 Type **1175**	1·60	90
3092	2f.50 Tree of Liberty	1·60	90
3093	2f.50 Marianne as cockerel	1·60	90
3094	2f.50 "Republique Francaise"	1·60	90

1992. Precancels. Musical Instruments (4th series). As T 1110.

3095	1f.73 deep green & green	1·30	60
3096	2f.25 red and orange	1·60	90
3097	3f.51 ultramarine & blue	3·25	1·40
3098	5f.40 red and mauve	3·75	2·10

DESIGNS: 1f.73, Guitar; 2f.25, Saxophone; 3f.51, Banjo; 5f.40, Xylophone.

See note below No. 432 (1920).

1176 Symbol of Market

1992. European Single Market.
3099 **1176** 2f.50 multicoloured 1·60 90

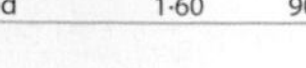

1177 Farman HF16 and Boeing 737-500

1992. 80th Anniv of Nancy–Luneville Air Mail Service.
3100 **1177** 2f.50 multicoloured 1·60 90

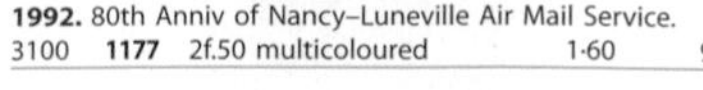

1178 Paul and Electricity Pylon

1992. 10th Death Anniv of Marcel Paul (politician).
3101 **1178** 4f.20 blue & purple 3·00 1·20

1179 "Woman at Window" (Paul Delvaux)

1992. Contemporary Art.

3102	**1179**	5f. multicoloured	3·00	1·40
3103	-	5f. multicoloured	3·00	1·40
3104	-	5f. black, mauve & yell	3·00	1·40
3105	-	5f. black and yellow	3·00	1·40

DESIGNS: No. 3103, "Portrait of Man" (Francis Bacon); 3104, Abstract (Alberto Burri); 3105, Abstract (Antoni Tapies).

See also Nos. 3154, 3176, 3285 and 3301/2.

1180 Birds holding Strings (T. Ungerer)

1992. Red Cross Fund. Mutual Aid Meeting, Strasbourg.
3106 **1180** 2f.50+60c. mult 1·80 1·00

1181 Horse, Guitar and Dancer

1992. Gypsies.
3107 **1181** 2f.50 multicoloured 1·60 90

1182 Smew Pair

1993. Ducks. Multicoloured.
3108 2f. Type **1182** 1·30 65
3109 3f. Ferruginous duck and drake 1·90 1·10
3110 4f. Common sheldrake pair 2·50 1·50
3111 5f. Red-breasted merganser pair 3·25 1·80

1183 "La Poste" (yacht) and Globe

1993. "Postmen around the World". Post Office Team Participation in Around the World Yacht Race.
3112 **1183** 2f.50 yell, ultram & bl 2·10 1·10
3113 **1183** 2f.80 yell, ultram & bl 2·50 1·10

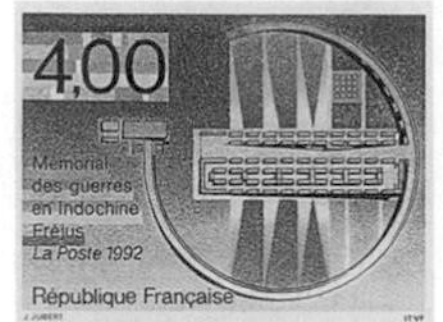

1184 Memorial

1993. Indo-China Wars Memorial, Frejus.
3114 **1184** 4f. multicoloured 2·40 1·50

1185 Postman with Bicycle

1993. Stamp Day.
3115 **1185** 2f.50 multicoloured 1·90 90
3116 **1185** 2f.50+60c. mult 1·80 1·20

1186 Yacht and Runner

1993. Mediterranean Games, Agde and Roussillon (Languedoc).
3117 **1186** 2f.50 multicoloured 1·60 1·10

1187 Maria Deraismes and Georges Martin (founders)

1993. Centenary of Le Droit Humain (International Mixed Freemasons Order).
3118 **1187** 3f.40 black and blue 2·20 1·30

1188 "Red Rhythm Blue" (Olivier Debre)

1993. Europa. Contemporary Art. Mult.
3119 2f.50 Type **1188** 1·90 1·30
3120 3f.40 "Le Griffu" (bronze, Germaine Richier) (vert) 2·50 2·00

1993. As T 1118 but no value expressed. Imperf (self-adhesive) or perf.
3122 **1118** (-) red 1·30 55
No. 3122 was sold at the current inland rate (at time of issue 2f.50).

1993. Tourist Publicity. As T 490 and 949.
3124 2f.80 green, brown and blue 1·90 1·10
3125 3f.40 red, green and blue 2·40 1·30
3126 4f.20 dp green, green & brn 2·50 1·70
3127 4f.20 brown and green 2·50 1·70
3128 4f.40 black, green and red 2·50 1·80
3129 4f.40 multicoloured 2·50 1·80
DESIGNS—As T **490**. HORIZ: No. 3124, La Chaise-Dieu Abbey, Haute-Loire; 3128, Montbeliard-Doubs. VERT: No. 3125, Artouste train, Laruns; 3126, Minerve-Herault; 3129, Le Jacquemard, Lambesc. As T **949**: No. 3127, Chinon.

1189 Guy de Maupassant

1993. Red Cross Fund. Writers. Mult.
3131 2f.50+50c. Type **1189** 1·80 1·50
3132 2f.50+50c. Alain 1·80 1·50
3133 2f.50+50c. Jean Cocteau 1·80 1·50
3134 2f.50+50c. Marcel Pagnol 1·80 1·50
3135 2f.50+50c. Andre Chamson 1·80 1·50
3136 2f.50+50c. Marguerite Yourcenar 1·80 1·50

1190 Map of Europe and Liberty

1993. 9th European Constitutional Court Conference on Human Rights.
3137 **1190** 2f.50 multicoloured 1·60 1·10

1191 Reinhardt

1993. 40th Death Anniv of Django Reinhardt (guitarist).
3138 **1191** 4f.20 multicoloured 2·50 1·70

1192 Weiss

1993. Birth Centenary of Louise Weiss (women's rights campaigner).
3139 **1192** 2f.50 blk, orge & red 1·90 1·10

1193 TGV and Eurostar Trains at Lille

1993. Federation of French Philatelic Societies Congress, Lille.
3140 **1193** 2f.50 lt bl, bl & mve 1·60 1·10

1194 Emblem

1993. Bicentenary of National Natural History Museum, Paris.
3141 **1194** 2f.50 multicoloured 1·60 1·10

1195 Bas-relief (Georges Jeanclos) (left half)

1993. Martyrs and Heroes of the Resistance. Multicoloured.
3142 2f.50 Type **1195** 1·80 90
3143 4f.20 Right half of bas-relief 2·50 1·40
Nos. 3142/3 were issued together, se-tenant, forming a composite design.

1196 Central Telegraph Tower, Paris

1993. Bicentenary of Chappe's Optical Telegraph.
3144 **1196** 2f.50 black, stone and blue 1·60 1·10

1993. Precancels. Musical Instruments (5th series). As T 1110.
3145 1f.82 grey and black 1·30 70
3146 2f.34 brown and orange 1·60 1·10
3147 3f.86 red and pink 3·25 1·70
3148 5f.93 violet and mauve 3·75 2·50
DESIGNS: 1f.82, Trumpet; 2f.34, Drum; 3f.86, Hurdy-gurdy; 5f.93, Xylophone.

1197 Map of Corsica and "Casabianca" (submarine)

1993. 50th Anniv of Liberation of Corsica.
3149 **1197** 2f.80 black, red & bl 1·90 1·10

1993. Art. As T 491. Multicoloured.
3150 5f. "Saint Thomas" (Georges de la Tour) (vert) 3·50 1·90
3151 5f. "The Muses" (Maurice Denis) (vert) 3·25 1·80

1198 Le Val-de-Grace, Paris

1993. Bicentenary of Conversion of Monastery of Le Val-de-Grace to Military Hospital (now museum).
3152 **1198** 3f.70 black, grn & brn 2·20 1·30

1199 Clowns

1993. National Centre for Circus Arts, Chalons-sur-Marne.
3153 **1199** 2f.80 multicoloured 1·90 1·10

1993. Contemporary Art. As T 1179.
3154 5f. red and black 3·00 1·70
3155 5f. multicoloured 3·00 1·70
DESIGNS: No. 3154, Abstract (Takis); 3155, "Enhanced Engraving" (Maria Elena Vieira da Silva).

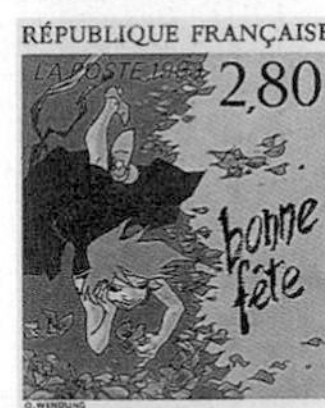

1200 Girl studying Flower ("Happy Holiday") (C. Wendling)

1993. Greetings Stamps. "The Pleasure of Writing". Designs by comic strip artists. Multicoloured.
3156A 2f.80 Type **1200** 1·70 1·40
3157A 2f.80 Clowns ("Happy Holiday") (B. Olivie) 1·70 1·40
3158A 2f.80 Cat on birthday cake ("Happy Birthday") (S. Colman) 1·70 1·40
3159A 2f.80 Girl with cake ("Happy Birthday") (G. Sorel) 1·70 1·40
3160A 2f.80 Man courting woman on balcony ("With Passion") (J. M. Thiriet) 1·70 1·40
3161A 2f.80 Man playing large fountain pen ("Pleasure of Writing") (E. Davodeau) 1·70 1·40
3162A 2f.80 Pig with letter ("Greetings") (J. de Moor) 1·70 1·40
3163A 2f.80 Jester in horseshoe ("Good Luck") (Mezzo) 1·70 1·40
3164A 2f.80 Clowns running ("Best Wishes") (N. de Crecy) 1·70 1·40
3165A 2f.80 Girl and cat watching tree fairy ("Best Wishes") (F. Magnin) 1·70 1·40
3166A 2f.80 Cards tumbling from Santa Claus's sack ("Happy Christmas") (T. Robin) 1·70 1·40
3167A 2f.80 Mouse dressed as Santa Claus ("Happy Christmas") (P. Prugne) 1·70 1·40

1201 Rhododendron

1993. 1st European Stamp Salon, Flower Gardens, Paris (1994) (1st issue). Sheet 106×78 mm containing T 1201 and similar horiz design. Multicoloured.
MS3168 2f.40 Type **1201**; 2f.40 View of Gardens (sold at 15f.) 19·00 18·00

1202 Louvre, 1793

1993. Bicentenary of Louvre Museum. Mult.
3169 2f.80 Type **1202** 2·20 1·90
3170 4f.40 Louvre, 1993 2·50 2·00
Nos. 3169/70 were issued together, se-tenant, forming a composite design.

1203 "St. Nicholas"

1993. Red Cross Fund. Metz Engravings.
3171 **1203** 2f.80+60c. mult 2·20 1·70

1204 Cast-iron Sign at Metro Entrance, Paris (detail, Hector Guimard)

1994. Art Nouveau. Multicoloured.
3172 2f.80 Type **1204** 1·60 1·10
3173 2f.80 "Roses of France Cup" (vase, Emile Galle) 1·60 1·10
3174 4f.40 Drawing-room table with bronze water-lily decoration (Louis Majorelle) 2·20 1·70
3175 4f.40 Stoneware teapot (Pierre-Adrien Dalpayrat) 2·20 1·70

1994. Contemporary Art. As T 1179. Mult.
3176 6f.70 Abstract (Sean Scully) 3·75 2·40
3177 6f.70 "Couple" (Georg Baselitz) 3·75 2·40

1205 "Death of St. Stephen"

1994. 12th-century Stained Glass Window, Le Mans Cathedral.
3179 **1205** 6f.70 multicoloured 3·75 2·40

1994. Tourist Publicity. As T 490.
3180 2f.80 multicoloured 1·70 1·10
3181 2f.80 blue 1·70 1·10
3182 3f.70 brown, dp green & grn 2·50 1·40
3183 4f.40 brown and blue 2·40 1·70
3184 4f.40 brown and red 2·40 1·70
DESIGNS—HORIZ: No. 3180, "Mount Sainte Victoire" (Paul Cezanne); 3181, Bridge at Rupt aux Nonains, Saulx Region, Meuse; 3184, Argentat. VERT: No. 3182, La Grand Cascade, Saint-Cloud Park; 3183, Old port and St. John the Baptist Church, Bastia.

1206 European Union Flag

1994. European Parliament Elections.
3185 **1206** 2f.80 blue, yell & grey 1·90 1·10

1207 Mourguet and Guignol

1994. 150th Death Anniv of Laurent Mourguet (creator of Guignol (puppet)).
3186 **1207** 2f.80 multicoloured 1·60 1·10

1208 Emblem

1994. Bicent of Polytechnic Institute, Paris.
3187 **1208** 2f.80 multicoloured 1·60 1·10

1209 "Marianne"

1994. Stamp Day. 50th Anniv of Edmond Dulac's "Marianne" Design.
3188 **1209** 2f.80 red and blue 1·80 1·50
3190 **1209** 2f.80+60c. red & bl 1·90 1·80

1210 "The Vikings" (detail, Bayeux Tapestry)

1994. Franco-Swedish Cultural Relations. Mult.
3191 2f.80 Type **1210** 3·75 3·25
3192 2f.80 Viking longships (different detail) 3·75 3·25
3193 2f.80 Costume design for sailor by Fernand Leger in Swedish Ballet production of "Skating Rink" 3·75 3·25
3194 2f.80 Costume design for gentleman in "Skating Rink" 3·75 3·25
3195 3f.70 "Banquet for Gustav III at the Trianon, 1784" (Niclas Lafrensen the younger) 5·25 4·50
3196 3f.70 Swedish and French flags 5·25 4·50
Nos. 3195/6 are larger, 49×37 mm.

1211 Mountain Ambush

1994. 50th Anniv of Liberation. The Maquis (resistance movement).
3197 **1211** 2f.80 multicoloured 1·60 1·10

1212 Pompidou

1994. 20th Death Anniv of Georges Pompidou (Prime Minister 1962–68, President 1969–74).
3198 **1212** 2f.80 brown 1·60 1·10

1213 Boy netting Stamps

1994. "Philex Jeunes 94" Youth Stamp Exhibition, Grenoble.
3199 **1213** 2f.80 multicoloured 1·60 1·10

1214 AIDS Virus

1994. Europa. Discoveries. Multicoloured.
3200 2f.80 Type **1214** (11th anniv of discovery) 1·90 1·10
3201 3f.70 Wavelength formula (70th anniv of Louis de Broglie's proof of undulatory theory of matter) 3·25 1·70

1215 Bank Emblem

1994. 27th Assembly of Asian Development Bank, Nice.
3202 **1215** 2f.80 multicoloured 1·60 1·10

1216 British Lion and French Cockerel over Tunnel

1994. Opening of Channel Tunnel. Mult.
3203 2f.80 Type **1216** 1·60 1·10
3204 2f.80 Symbolic hands over Eurostar express train 1·60 1·10
3205 4f.30 Type **1216** 2·50 1·70
3206 4f.30 As No. 3204 2·50 1·70

1217 Martigues inside Fish

1994. Federation of French Philatelic Societies Congress, Martigues.
3207 **1217** 2f.80 violet, bl & grn 1·60 1·10

1218 Court Building, Ile de la Cite, Paris

1994. Court of Cassation.
3208 **1218** 2f.80 multicoloured 1·60 1·10

1219 Landing Forces and Beach Defences

1994. 50th Anniv of Normandy Landings.
3209 **1219** 4f.30 red, ind & bl 2·50 1·70

1220 Allied Forces

1994. 50th Anniv of Liberation.
3210 **1220** 4f.30 multicoloured 2·50 1·70

1221 Sorbonne University and Pierre de Coubertin (founder)

1994. Centenary of International Olympic Committee.
3211 **1221** 2f.80 multicoloured 2·40 1·10

1222 Organ Pipes

1994. Poitiers Cathedral Organ.
3212 **1222** 4f.40 multicoloured 2·50 1·70

1223 Flag, Map and Soldier

1994. 50th Anniv of Allied Landings in Southern France.
3213 **1223** 2f.80 multicoloured 1·90 1·30

1224 Oak

1994. Precancels. Leaves.

3321	-	1f.87 brown & green	1·40	65
3214	**1224**	1f.91 olive & green	1·30	75
3322	-	2f.18 red and lake	1·80	90
3215	-	2f.46 green & lt green	1·90	1·00
3216	-	4f.24 red and orange	2·75	1·50
3323	-	4f.66 yellow & green	3·25	1·80
3217	-	6f.51 turquoise & blue	4·25	2·75
3324	-	7f.11 turquoise & blue	4·50	2·75

DESIGNS: 1f.87, Ash; 2f.18, Beech; 2f.46, Plane; 4f.24, Chestnut; 4f.66, Walnut; 6f.51, Holly; 7f.11, Elm.

1225 "Moses and the Daughters of Jethro" (drawing) (image scaled to 61% of original size)

1994. 400th Birth Anniv of Nicolas Poussin (artist).
3218 **1225** 4f.40 brown & black 2·50 1·70

1226 Yvonne Printemps (singer and actress)

1994. Entertainers. Multicoloured.
3219 2f.80+60c. Type **1226** 1·90 1·70
3220 2f.80+60c. Fernandel (Fernand Contandin) (actor) 1·90 1·70
3221 2f.80+60c. Josephine Baker (music hall performer) 1·90 1·70
3222 2f.80+60c. Bourvil (Andre Raimbourg) (actor) 1·90 1·70
3223 2f.80+60c. Yves Montand (singer and actor) 1·90 1·70
3224 2f.80+60c. Coluche (Michel Colucci) (comedian) 1·90 1·70

1227 Map and Foucault's Pendulum

1994. Bicentenary of National Conservatory of Arts and Craft.
3225 **1227** 2f.80 pur, bl & red 1·60 1·10

1228 Doorway

1994. Bicent of Ecole Normale Superieure.
3226 **1228** 2f.80 blue and red 1·60 1·10

1229 Simenon and Quai des Orfevres, Paris

1994. 5th Death Anniv of Georges Simenon (novelist).
3227 **1229** 2f.80 multicoloured 1·90 1·10

1230 Headless Drug Addict (after Vladimir Velickovic)

1994. National Drug Addiction Prevention Day.
3228 **1230** 2f.80 multicoloured 1·60 1·10

1231 Gardens

1994. 1st European Stamp Salon, Flower Gardens, Paris (2nd issue). Sheet 106×78 mm containing T 1231 and similar multicoloured designs.
MS3229 2f.80 Type **1231**; 2f.80 Dahlias (25×39 mm) (sold at 16f.) 20·00 18·00

1232 Lodge Emblem and Symbols of Freemasonry

1994. Centenary of Grand Lodge of France.
3230 **1232** 2f.80 brown, red & bl 1·60 1·10

1233 Stormy Sea and Colas

1994. 16th Death Anniv of Alain Colas (yachtsman).
3231 **1233** 3f.70 blk, grn & emer 2·40 1·70

1234 St. Vaast

1994. Red Cross Fund. 15th-century Arras Tapestry.
3232 **1234** 2f.80+60c. mult 2·20 1·70

1235 AIDS Virus (image scaled to 61% of original size)

1994. AIDS Day.
3233 **1235** 2f.80 multicoloured 2·50 2·20
The stamp and se-tenant label, as illustrated, comprise No. 3233. For stamp without attached label, see No. 3200.

1236 Slogan

1994. 50th Anniv of National Press Federation.
3234 **1236** 2f.80 purple & yellow 1·60 1·10

1237 Champs Elysees (image scaled to 61% of original size)

1994. New Year.
3235 **1237** 4f.40 multicoloured 3·00 1·10

1238 Projector and Scene from Film

1995. Centenary of Motion Pictures. Sheet 105×78 mm containing T 1238 and similar horiz designs. Multicoloured.
MS3236 2f.80 Type **1238**; 2f.80 Projector and head of man in cap; 2f.80 Projector and monster's head; 2f.80 Reel of films and Indian's head 7·75 6·50

1239 Normandy Bridge (image scaled to 61% of original size)

1995. Inauguration of Normandy Bridge (over Seine between Le Havre and Honfleur).
3237 **1239** 4f.40 multicoloured 3·00 1·70

1240 Emblem

1995. European Public Notaries.
3238 **1240** 2f.80 multicoloured 1·60 1·10

1241 Pasteur

1995. Death Centenary of Louis Pasteur (chemist).
3239 **1241** 3f.70 multicoloured 2·50 1·30

1995. Tourist Publicity. As T 490.
3240 2f.80 green and olive 1·70 1·00
3241 2f.80 green, brown & blue 1·70 1·00
3242 4f.40 multicoloured 2·50 1·40
3243 4f.40 black, lilac & green 2·50 1·40
DESIGNS—HORIZ: No. 3240, Malt works, Stenay; 3241, Remiremont, Vosges; 3242, Nyons Bridge, Drome. VERT: No. 3243, Margot gate and St. Martial's Church, Correze.

1995. Art. As T 491.
3245 6f.70 black, yellow & red 3·75 2·40
3246 6f.70 black, blue & dp blue 3·75 2·40
3247 6f.70 multicoloured 3·75 2·40
3248 6f.70 multicoloured 3·75 2·40
DESIGNS—VERT: No. 3245, Reliquary of St. Taurin, Evereux; 3248, "The Cradle" (Berthe Morisot). HORIZ: No. 3246, Study for "The Dream of Happiness" (Pierre Prud'hon); 3247, Seascape (Zao Wou-Ki).

1242 Band-tailed Pigeons

1995. Bird Paintings by John James Audubon (ornithologist). Multicoloured.
3249 2f.80 Type **1242** 1·60 1·10
3250 2f.80 Snowy egret 1·60 1·10
3251 4f.30 Common tern 2·20 1·70
3252 4f.40 Rough-legged buzzards 2·20 1·70
MS3253 113×120 mm. Nos. 2149/52 9·00 8·25

1243 "Marianne"

1995. Stamp Day. 50th Anniv of Pierre Gandon's "Marianne" Design.
3255 **1243** 2f.80 green, bl & red 5·25 4·50
3256 **1243** 2f.80+60c. green, ultramarine & red 2·50 2·20

1244 Hour Glass

1995. 50th Anniv of Works Councils.
3257 **1244** 2f.80 brown, lt bl & bl 1·60 1·10

1245 Means of Communications

1995. Centenary (1994) of Advanced Institute of Electricity.
3258 **1245** 3f.70 lt blue, bl & red 2·20 1·40

1246 Forms of Writing

1995. Bicentenary of School of Oriental Languages.
3259 **1246** 2f.80 multicoloured 1·60 1·10

1247 Giono

1995. Birth Centenary of Jean Giono (writer).
3260 **1247** 3f.70 blk, blue & red 2·50 1·40

1248 "Ariane" Rocket and Map of French Guiana

1995. French Space Centre in French Guiana.
3261 **1248** 2f.80 blue, grn & red 2·10 1·10

1249 Steel and Worker

1995. Lorraine's Iron and Steel Industry.
3262 **1249** 2f.80 multicoloured 1·60 1·10

1250 "Freedom"

1995. Europa. Peace and Freedom. Mult.
3263 2f.80 Type **1250** 1·90 1·10
3264 3f.70 "Peace" 3·25 2·20

1251 Lumberjack

1995. Forestry in the Ardennes.
3265 **1251** 4f.40 brn, blk & grn 2·50 1·70

1252 Paris Landmarks and Charles de Gaulle

1995. 50th Anniv of End of Second World War.
3266 **1252** 2f.80 multicoloured 2·20 1·10

1253 Marianne in Assembly Building

1995. National Assembly.
3267 **1253** 2f.80 multicoloured 1·70 1·00

1254 "King Louis XIII on Horseback" (Saumur tapestry)

1995. Red Cross Fund.
3268 **1254** 2f.80+60c. mult 2·20 1·70

1255 Winged Hand

1995. 50th Anniv of French People's Relief Association (welfare organization).

3270 **1255** 2f.80 multicoloured 1·70 1·00

1256 Brittany

1995. Landscapes.

3271 **1256** 2f.40 green 1·30 90
3272 - 2f.40 green 1·30 90
3273 - 2f.80 red 1·60 1·00
3274 - 2f.80 red 1·60 1·00

DESIGNS: No. 3272, Vosges; 3273, Auvergne; 3274, Camargue.

1257 Orleans

1995. Federation of French Philatelic Societies Congress, Orleans.

3275 **1257** 2f.80 multicoloured 1·60 1·10

1258 "The Grasshopper and The Ant"

1995. 300th Death Anniv of Jean de la Fontaine (writer of fables). Multicoloured.

3276 2f.80 Type **1258** 2·10 1·40
3277 2f.80 "The Fat Frog and the Ox" 2·10 1·40
3278 2f.80 "The Wolf and the Lamb" 2·10 1·40
3279 2f.80 "The Raven and the Fox" 2·10 1·40
3280 2f.80 "The Cat, the Weasel and the Little Rabbit" 2·10 1·40
3281 2f.80 "The Hare and the Tortoise" 2·10 1·40

1259 Flower, Star and Wire

1995. 53rd Anniv of Internment of Jews in Velodrome d'Hiver, Paris.

3282 **1259** 2f.80 multicoloured 1·60 1·10

1260 Maginot and Roof

1995. 63rd Death Anniv of Andre Maginot (politician and instigator of Maginot Line (fortifications on French–German border)).

3283 **1260** 2f.80 brown, grn & red 1·60 1·10

1261 Lodge Emblem

1995. 50th Anniv of Women's Grand Masonic Lodge of France.

3284 **1261** 2f.80 multicoloured 1·60 1·10

1995. Contemporary Art. As T 1179. Mult.

3285 6f.70 Abstract (Kirkeby) 3·75 2·20

1262 Apothecary and Molecules

1995. 500th Anniv of Hospital Pharmacies.

3286 **1262** 2f.80 multicoloured 1·60 1·10

1263 "Thatched Cottages in Barbizon" (Narcisse Diaz de a Pena)

1995. 170th Anniv of Barbizon School (artists' settlement).

3287 **1263** 4f.40 multicoloured 2·50 1·70

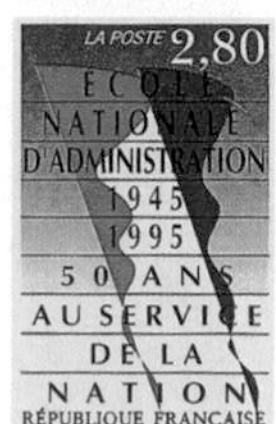

1264 Institute Emblem

1995. 50th Anniv of National Civil Servants' Training Institute, Paris.

3288 **1264** 2f.80 multicoloured 1·60 1·10

1265 Institute Building

1995. Bicentenary of French Institute, Paris.

3289 **1265** 2f.80 black, red & grn 1·60 1·10

1266 New and Old Motor Vehicles and Headquarters

1995. Centenary of French Automobile Club.

3290 **1266** 4f.40 black, bl & red 2·50 1·70

1267 Dove, Blue Helmet and Anniversary Emblem

1995. 50th Anniv of U.N.O.

3291 **1267** 4f.30 multicoloured 2·50 1·70

1268 Shepherd

1995. Red Cross Fund. Crib Figures from Provence. Multicoloured.

3292 2f.80+60c. Type **1268** 1·90 1·70
3293 2f.80+60c. Miller 1·90 1·70
3294 2f.80+60c. Simpleton and tambourine player 1·90 1·70
3295 2f.80+60c. Fishmonger 1·90 1·70
3296 2f.80+60c. Knife grinder 1·90 1·70
3297 2f.80+60c. Elderly couple 1·90 1·70

1269 Jammes

1995. 127th Birth Anniv of Francis Jammes (poet).

3298 **1269** 3f.70 black and blue 2·20 1·40

1270 Architect's Plans

1995. Completion of Evry Cathedral.

3299 **1270** 2f.80 multicoloured 1·80 1·10

1271 Pitch and Balls

1995. World Cup Football Championship, France (1998).

3300 **1271** 2f.80 multicoloured 1·60 1·10

1996. Contemporary Art. As T 1179.

3301 6f.70 black, red and blue 3·75 2·20
3302 6f.70 multicoloured 3·75 2·20

DESIGNS: No. 3301, "Sculpture" (Lucien Wercollier); 3302, "Horizon" (Jan Dibbets).

1272 Pottery Dog

1996. Completion of Archaeological Excavations in Saint-Martin Island, Guadeloupe.

3305 **1272** 2f.80 multicoloured 1·60 1·10

1996. Art. As T 491.

3306 6f.70 multicoloured 3·75 2·20
3307 6f.70 multicoloured 3·75 2·20
3308 6f.70 gold, copper & blk 3·75 2·20

DESIGNS—HORIZ: No. 3306, "Narni Bridge" (Camille Corot); 3308, "Cellos" (Arman). VERT: No. 3307, Bronze horse (found at Neuvy-en-Sullias).

1273 "St. Patrick" (stained glass window, Evie Hone)

1996. "L'imaginaire Irlandais" Festival of Contemporary Irish Arts, France.

3311 **1273** 2f.80 multicoloured 1·60 1·10

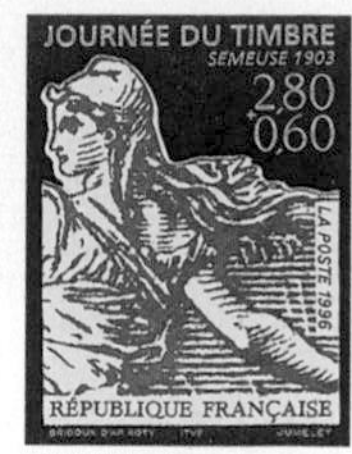

1274 "The Sower"

1996. Stamp Day. 93rd Anniv of Louis-Oscar Roty's "The Sower" design.

3313 **1274** 2f.80 mauve & violet 5·00 4·50
3314 **1274** 2f.80+60c. mauve and violet 2·50 1·90

1275 Rueff and New 1 Franc Coin of 1960

1996. Birth Centenary of Jacques Rueff (economist).

3315 **1275** 2f.80 black, bl & brn 1·60 1·10

1276 Descartes (after Frans Hals)

1996. 400th Birth Anniv of Rene Descartes (philosopher and scientist).

3316 **1276** 4f.40 red 2·50 1·70

1277 Lightbulb and Flame

1996. 50th Anniv of Electricite de France and Gaz de France.

3317 **1277** 3f. multicoloured 1·90 1·10

1278 Eurasian Beaver and Columbine, Cevennes

1996. National Parks. Multicoloured.

3318 3f. Type **1278** 1·80 1·00
3319 4f.40 Lammergeier and saxifrage, Mercantour 2·75 1·40
3320 4f.40 Ibex and gentian, Vanoise 2·75 1·40

See also Nos. 3380/3.

1280 Mme. de Sevigne (writer)

1996. Europa. Famous Women.
3325 **1280** 3f. multicoloured 1·80 1·30

1281 Test Tubes and Flower held with Tweezers

1996. 50th Anniv of National Institute for Agronomic Research.
3326 **1281** 3f.80 multicoloured 2·50 1·40

1282 Joan of Arc's Cottage, Domremy la Pucelle, Vosges

1996. 75th Anniv (1995) of Canonization of Joan of Arc.
3327 **1282** 4f.50 multicoloured 2·75 1·70

1283 Fishes, Sea and Coastline

1996. 20th Anniv of Ramoge Agreement on Environmental Protection of the Mediterranean.
3328 **1283** 3f. multicoloured 2·50 1·10

1284 Notre-Dame de Clermont and the Jacquemart (Cathedral clock)

1996. Federation of French Philatelic Societies Congress, Clermont-Ferrand.
3329 **1284** 3f. green, brown & red 1·90 1·10

1996. Tourist Publicity. As T 490.
3330 3f. multicoloured 1·90 1·10
3331 3f. multicoloured 1·90 1·10
3332 3f.80 brown and mauve 2·10 1·30
3333 4f.50 multicoloured 2·40 1·70

DESIGN—HORIZ: 3f. (No. 3330), Bitche Castle, Moselle; 3f. (No. 3331), Sanguinaries Islands, Corsica; 3f.80, Cloisters, Thoronet Abbey, Var; 4f.50, Detail of trompe l'oeil by Casimir Vicario, Chambery Cathedral.

1285 Lens

1996. World Cup Football Championship, France (1998) (1st issue). Host Cities. Multicoloured.
3335 3f. Type **1285** 1·80 1·30
3336 3f. Montpellier 1·80 1·30
3337 3f. Saint-Etienne 1·80 1·30
3338 3f. Toulouse 1·80 1·30

See also Nos. 3401/4, 3464/5 and 3472.

1286 Throwing the Discus

1996. Centenary of Modern Olympic Games.
3339 **1286** 3f. multicoloured 1·90 1·10

1287 Marette

1996. 12th Death Anniv of Jacques Marette (journalist and politician).
3340 **1287** 4f.40 lilac 2·50 1·80

1288 Diesel Railcar Set

1996. Centenary of Ajaccio–Vizzavona Railway, Corsica.
3341 **1288** 3f. multicoloured 1·90 1·10

1289 Basilica

1996. Centenary of Our Lady of Fourviere Basilica, Lyon.
3342 **1289** 3f. black and yellow 1·90 1·10

1290 Baptism of Clovis (illus from "Grandes Chroniques de France")

1996. Inauguration of Committee for Commemoration of Origins: from Gaul to France. 1500th Anniv of Baptism of Clovis.
3343 **1290** 3f. multicoloured 1·90 1·10

1291 Arsene Lupin (Maurice Leblanc)

1996. Red Cross Fund. Heroes of Crime Novels. Multicoloured.
3344 3f.+60c. Rocambole (Pierre Ponson du Terrail) 2·10 1·80
3345 3f.+60c. Type **1291** 2·10 1·80
3346 3f.+60c. Joseph Rouletabille (Gaston Leroux) 2·10 1·80
3347 3f.+60c. Fantomas (Pierre Souvestre and Marcel Allain) 2·10 1·80
3348 3f.+60c. Commissioner Maigret (Georges Simenon) 2·10 1·80

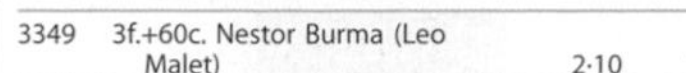
3349 3f.+60c. Nestor Burma (Leo Malet) 2·10 1·80

1292 School Building

1996. Bicentenary of Henri IV School, Paris.
3350 **1292** 4f.50 blue, brn & grn 2·50 1·70

1293 Children of Different Nations

1996. 50th Anniv of UNICEF.
3351 **1293** 4f.50 multicoloured 2·50 1·70

1294 Iena Palace (headquarters)

1996. 50th Anniv of Economic and Social Council.
3352 **1294** 3f. black, red & blue 1·90 1·10

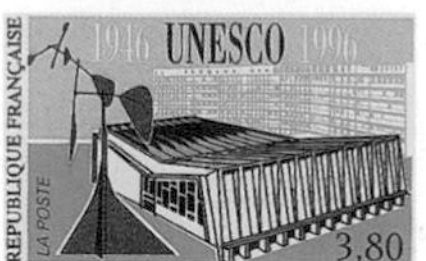

1295 Headquarters, Paris

1996. 50th Anniv of UNESCO.
3353 **1295** 3f.80 multicoloured 2·20 1·30

1296 Magnifying Glass over Eiffel Tower

1996. 50th Anniv of Autumn Stamp Show, Paris.
3354 **1296** 3f. multicoloured 1·90 1·10

1297 "Woman"

1996. 50th Anniv of Creation of French Overseas Departments of Martinique, Guadeloupe, Guiana and La Reunion.
3355 **1297** 3f. multicoloured 1·90 1·10

1298 Snowman and Polar Bear in Hot-air Balloon

1996. Red Cross Fund. Christmas.
3356 **1298** 3f.+60c. mult 2·20 1·70

1299 Temple, Delphi

1996. 150th Anniv of French School in Athens.
3357 **1299** 3f. multicoloured 1·90 1·10

1300 Malraux

1996. 20th Death Anniv of Andre Malraux (writer and politician).
3358 **1300** 3f. blue 1·90 1·10

1301 Clapperboard, Camera and Golden Palm

1996. 50th Int Film Festival, Cannes.
3359 **1301** 3f. multicoloured 1·90 1·10

1302 New Building

1996. Inauguration of New National Library Building, Paris.
3360 **1302** 3f. yellow, blue & red 1·90 1·10

1303 Mitterrand

1997. Francois Mitterrand (President, 1981–95) Commemoration.
3361 **1303** 3f. multicoloured 1·90 1·10

1304 Wire Figures

1997. "Participatory Innovation" (suggestions schemes).
3362 **1304** 3f. multicoloured 1·90 1·10

1305 Detail of Building

1997. 20th Anniv of Georges Pompidou National Centre of Art and Culture.

3363 **1305** 3f. multicoloured 1·90 1·10

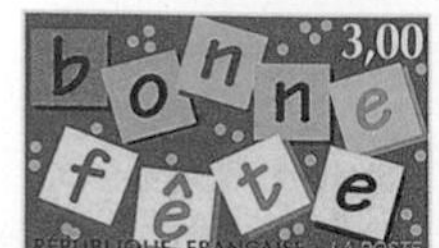

1306 "bonne fete" (Happy Holiday)

1997. Greetings stamps. Multicoloured.

3364 3f. Type **1306** 1·90 1·10

3365 3f. "joyeux anniversaire" (Happy Birthday) 1·90 1·10

1307 New Building, Marne-la-Vallee

1997. 250th Anniv of National School of Bridges and Highways.

3366 **1307** 3f. multicoloured 1·90 1·10

1308 Gateway and Buildings

1997. National Historic Landmark Status of Former Penal Colony, Saint-Laurent-du-Maroni, French Guiana.

3367 **1308** 3f. multicoloured 1·90 1·10

1997. Art. As T **491**.

3368 6f.70 Fresco (detail), St. Nicholas's Church, Tavant (Indre et Loire) (vert) 3·75 2·20

3369 6f.70 Abstract (Bernard Moninot) 3·75 2·20

3370 6f.70 "The Thumb" (sculpture, Cesar Baldaccini) (vert) 3·75 2·20

3371 6f.70 "Grapes and Pomegranates" (Jean Baptiste Chardin) 3·75 2·20

1309 "Mouchon" type

1997. Stamp Day. 97th Anniv of Louis-Eugene Mouchon's Design.

3372 **1309** 3f.+60c. blue, mauve and silver 2·20 1·40

3373 **1309** 3f. blue, mauve & silver 3·75 2·75

1997. Tourist Publicity. As T **490**.

3375 3f. emerald, dp green & grn 1·90 1·10

3376 3f. green, red and orange 1·90 1·10

3377 3f. brown, blue and green 1·90 1·10

3378 3f. brown, choc & green 1·90 1·10

3379 3f. green, blue and brown 1·90 1·10

DESIGN—VERT: No. 3375, Millau, Aveyron; 3376, Buttress of "Calvary" and church, Guimiliau. HORIZ: No. 3377, Sable-sur-Sarthe; 3378, St. Maurice's Cathedral, Epinal; 3379, Sceaux estate.

1997. National Parks. As T **1278**. Mult.

3380 3f. Golden eagle and blue thistle, Ecrins 1·80 1·10

3381 3f. Racoon and La Soufriere (volcano), Guadeloupe 1·80 1·10

3382 4f.50 Manx shearwater and coves, Port-Cros 2·40 1·40

3383 4f.50 Chamois and mountain, Pyrenees 2·40 1·40

1310 "Puss in Boots" (engraving by Gustav Dore)

1997. Europa. Tales and Legends.

3384 **1310** 3f. blue 1·90 1·70

1311 Teenager "flying" Stamp

1997. "Philexjeunes 97" Youth Stamp Exhibition, Nantes.

3385 **1311** 3f. multicoloured 1·90 1·10

1312 Envelope writing Letter

1997. The Journey of a Letter. Multicoloured. Ordinary or self-adhesive gum.

3392 3f. Type **1312** 2·20 1·90

3393 3f. Smiling letter climbing up to post box 2·20 1·90

3394 3f. Letter as van 2·20 1·90

3395 3f. Letters holding hands and postman carrying letter 2·20 1·90

3396 3f. Girl kissing letter 2·20 1·90

3397 3f. Girl reading long letter 2·20 1·90

1313 Soldier and Map

1997. French Army Operations in North Africa, 1952–62.

3398 **1313** 3f. multicoloured 1·90 1·10

1314 Palace of Versailles (image scaled to 62% of original size)

1997. 70th Federation of French Philatelic Societies Congress, Versailles.

3399 **1314** 3f. multicoloured 1·90 1·70

1315 Chateau du Plessis-Bourre

1997

3400 **1315** 4f.40 multicoloured 2·40 1·70

1997. World Cup Football Championship, France (1998) (2nd issue). Host Cities. As T 1285. Multicoloured.

3401 3f. Lyon 1·80 1·10

3402 3f. Marseille 1·80 1·10

3403 3f. Nantes 1·80 1·10

3404 3f. Paris 1·80 1·10

1316 Detail of Fresco

1997. Restoration of Frescoes in St. Eutrope's Church, Les Salles-Lavauguyon.

3405 **1316** 4f.50 multicoloured 2·40 1·70

1317 St. Martin (from Tours Missal)

1997. 1600th Death Anniv of St. Martin, Bishop of Tours.

3406 **1317** 4f.50 multicoloured 2·50 1·70

1318 "Marianne of 14 July"

1997. No value expressed.

3407 **1318** (3f.) red 1·50 1·10

1997

3415 **1318** 10c. brown 25 20

3416 **1318** 20c. green 25 20

3417 **1318** 50c. violet 25 20

3418 **1318** 1f. orange 50 45

3419 **1318** 2f. blue 90 75

3420 **1318** 2f.70 green 1·40 1·20

3423 **1318** 3f.50 green 1·50 1·30

3425 **1318** 3f.80 blue 1·70 1·40

3427 **1318** 4f.20 red 1·80 1·50

3428 **1318** 4f.40 blue 1·90 1·70

3429 **1318** 4f.50 mauve 2·10 1·80

3430 **1318** 5f. blue 2·50 2·20

3431 **1318** 6f.70 green 3·25 2·75

3432 **1318** 10f. violet 4·50 3·75

MS3439 (a) Nos. 3415/19, 3430 and 3432; (b) Nos. 3407, 3420/9 and 3431 26·00 22·00

1319 Rowers

1997. World Rowing Championships, Lake Aiguebelette, Savoie.

3440 **1319** 3f. mauve, bl & red 1·90 1·10

1320 Sailors and Privateer Ship

1997. Basque Corsairs.

3441 **1320** 3f. multicoloured 1·90 1·10

1321 Horse-drawn Fish Cart

1997. Fresh Fish Merchants from Boulogne.

3442 **1321** 3f. green, violet & blue 1·90 1·10

1322 Kudara Kannon (statue from Horyu Temple, Nara) and Japanese Cultural Centre, Paris

1997. Japan Year.

3443 **1322** 4f.90 blue, orge & blk 2·75 1·70

1323 Contest

1997. World Judo Championships, Paris.

3444 **1323** 3f. multicoloured 1·90 1·10

1324 Emblem

1997. Sar-Lor-Lux (Saarland–Lorraine–Luxembourg) European Region.

3445 **1324** 3f. multicoloured 1·90 1·10

1325 College and King Francois I (founder)

1997. Le College de France.

3446 **1325** 4f.40 green, brn & blk 2·40 1·70

1326 Team with Coloured Ribbons

1997. French Movement for Quality.

3447 **1326** 4f.50 multicoloured 1·90 1·70

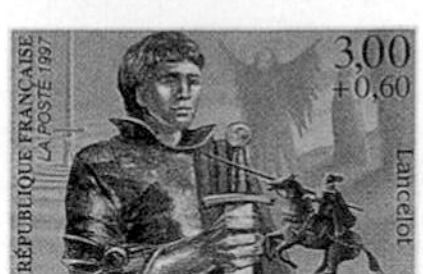

1327 Lancelot (Chretien de Troyes)

1997. Red Cross Fund. Literary Heroes. Multicoloured.

3448 3f.+60c. Type **1327** 2·10 1·80

3449 3f.+60c. Pardaillan (Michel Zevaco) 2·10 1·80

3450 3f.+60c. D'Artagnan ("The Three Musketeers" by Alexandre Dumas) 2·10 1·80

3451 3f.+60c. Cyrano de Bergerac (Edmond Rostand) 2·10 1·80

3452 3f.+60c. Captain Fracasse (Theophile Gautier) 2·10 1·80

3453 3f.+60c. Lagardere as Le Bossu (Paul Feval) 2·10 1·80

1328 Teddy Bear with Gifts in Spaceship

1997. Red Cross Fund. Christmas.

3454 **1328** 3f.+60c. mult 2·20 1·70

1329 Mouse giving Gift to Cat

1997. "Best Wishes".

3455 **1329** 3f. multicoloured 1·90 1·10

1330 Breguet 14 Biplane

1997. Air.

3456 **1330** 20f. multicoloured 7·75 3·25

1331 Teddy Bear holding Toy Windmill

1997. Protection of Abused Children Campaign.

3457 **1331** 3f. multicoloured 1·90 1·10

1332 Flying Postman

1997. "Best Wishes".

3458 **1332** 3f. multicoloured 1·90 1·10

1333 Cross of Lorraine on Map of France and Leclerc

1997. 50th Death Anniv of Marshal Leclerc.

3459 **1333** 3f. multicoloured 1·90 1·10

1334 "Marianne of 14 July" and Emblem

1997. "Philexfrance 99" International Stamp Exhibition, Paris.

3460 **1334** 3f. red and blue 1·90 1·10

1335 Carving and Buildings

1997. Millenary of Foundation of Moutier D'Ahun Monastery, Creuse.

3461 **1335** 4f.40 multicoloured 2·50 1·70

1336 Debre

1998. 2nd Death Anniv of Michel Debre (Prime Minister, 1958–62).

3462 **1336** 3f. black, blue & red 1·90 1·10

1337 Anniversary Emblem

1998. Bicentenary of National Assembly.

3463 **1337** 3f. red and blue 1·90 1·10

1998. World Cup Football Championship, France (3rd issue). Host Cities. As T 1285. Multicoloured.

3464 3f. Bordeaux 1·90 1·10

3465 3f. Saint-Denis, Paris 1·90 1·10

MS3466 148×140 mm. Nos. 3335/8, 3401/4 and 3464/5 13·00 11·00

1338 Cherub with Letter and Flowers

1998. St. Valentine's Day.

3467 **1338** 3f. multicoloured 1·90 1·10

1339 Mediator and People

1998. 25th Anniv of Mediator of the Republic (ombudsman).

3468 **1339** 3f. multicoloured 1·90 1·10

1340 "Blanc" Type

1998. Stamp Day. 98th Anniv of Joseph Blanc's Design.

3469 **1340** 3f.+60c. red, green and silver 2·20 1·40

3470 **1340** 3f. red, grn & silver 4·75 2·75

1341 Football

1998. World Cup Football Championship, France (4th issue). Ordinary or self-adhesive gum.

3472 **1341** 3f. multicoloured 1·90 1·10

MS3474 No. 3472 plus 7 labels showing the World Cup mascot demonstrating various shots 10·50 10·00

1342 Stock

1998. 50th Death Anniv of Father Franz Stock (wartime prison chaplain).

3475 **1342** 4f.50 blue 2·40 1·70

1343 "Happy Birthday"

1998. Greeting Stamp.

3476 **1343** 3f. multicoloured 1·90 1·10

1344 Citeaux Abbey

1998. 900th Anniv of Founding of Citeaux Abbey.

3477 **1344** 3f. multicoloured 1·90 1·10

1345 Mulhouse, 1798

1998. Bicentenary of Union of Mulhouse with France.

3478 **1345** 3f. multicoloured 1·90 1·10

1346 Sub-prefect's Residence, Saint-Pierre

1998. Reunion's Architectural Heritage.

3479 **1346** 3f. multicoloured 1·90 1·10

1347 "The Return"

1998. Birth Centenary of Rene-Ghislain Magritte (painter).

3480 **1347** 3f. multicoloured 1·90 1·10

1348 King Henri IV

1998. 400th Anniv of Edict of Nantes.

3481 **1348** 4f.50 multicoloured 2·50 1·70

1349 Slave wearing Cap of Liberty

1998. 150th Anniv of Abolition of Slavery by France.

3482 **1349** 3f. multicoloured 1·90 1·10

1998. Art. As T **491**. Multicoloured.

3483 6f.70 "The Crusaders' Arrival in Constantinople" (detail, Eugene Delacroix) (vert) 3·75 2·20

3484 6f.70 "Spring" (Pablo Picasso) 3·75 2·20

3485 6f.70 "Nine Idiot Bachelors" (Marcel Duchamp) 3·75 2·20

3486 6f.70 "Vision after the Sermon" (Paul Gaugin) 3·75 2·20

1998. Tourist Publicity. As T **490**.

3487 3f. multicoloured 1·90 1·10

3488 3f. multicoloured 1·90 1·10

3489 3f. green, blue and cream 1·90 1·10

3490 3f. multicoloured 1·90 1·10

3491 4f.40 multicoloured 2·50 1·70

DESIGNS—As Type **490**: No. 3487, Le Gois Causeway, Noirmoutiers Island; 3489, Crussol Chateau, Ardeche; 3490, Liberty Tower, Saint-Die, Vosges. 26×38 mm: No. 3488, Bay of Somme. 26×36 mm: No. 3491, Mantes-la-Jolie collegiate church, Yvelines.

1350 Dove Carrying Letter to Noah's Ark

1998. History of the Letter. Multicoloured. Ordinary or self-adhesive gum.

3492 3f. Type **1350** 1·90 1·10

3493 3f. Egyptian carving tablet 1·90 1·10

3494 3f. Ancient Greek carrying letter from Marathon to Athens 1·90 1·10

3495 3f. Knight on horseback carrying letter and pen 1·90 1·10

3496 3f. Man writing with quill 1·90 1·10

3497 3f. Spaceman posting letter 1·90 1·10

1351 Figure with Butterfly Wings

1998. Cent of League of Human Rights.

3504 **1351** 4f.40 multicoloured 2·40 1·70

1352 Collet

1998. 47th Death Anniv of Henri Collet (composer).

3505 **1352** 4f.50 black & stone 2·40 1·70

1353 Statue of Jean Bart, Cathedral and "Sandettie II" (light-ship)

1998. Federation of French Philatelic Societies Congress, Dunkirk.

3506 **1353** 3f. red, orange & blue 1·90 1·10

1354 Mont Saint Michel

1998

3507 **1354** 3f. multicoloured 1·90 1·10

1355 Pan playing Flute (Festival of Music)

1998. Europa. National Festivals.

3508 **1355** 3f. multicoloured 1·90 1·10

1998. France, World Cup Football Champion. As No. 3472 but additionally inscribed "Champion du Monde FRANCE".

3509 3f. multicoloured 1·90 1·10

1356 Potez 25 Biplane

1998. Air.

3510 **1356** 30f. multicoloured 13·00 8·75

1357 Convolvulus

1998. Precancels. Flowers. Multicoloured.

3511	1f.87 Type **1357**	1·40	55
3512	2f.18 Poppy	1·80	90
3513	4f.66 Violet	3·25	1·80
3514	7f.11 Buttercup	4·50	2·75

1358 Mallarme

1998. Death Centenary of Stephane Mallarme (poet).

3515	**1358**	4f.40 multicoloured	2·40	1·70

1359 Balloon and Early Airplane

1998. Centenary of Aero Club of France.

3516	**1359**	3f. multicoloured	1·90	1·10

1360 The Little Prince

1998. "Philexfrance 99" International Stamp Exhibition, Paris (1st issue). "The Little Prince" (novel) by Antoine de Saint-Exupery. Multicoloured.

3517	3f. Type **1360**	1·90	1·10
3518	3f. On wall watching snake (vert)	1·90	1·10
3519	3f. On planet (vert)	1·90	1·10
3520	3f. Watering flower (vert)	1·90	1·10
3521	3f. On hillside with fox	1·90	1·10
MS3522	111×157 mm. Nos. 3517/21 (sold at 25f.)	11·00	10·00

See also No. **MS**3576.

1361 Hall of Supreme Harmony, Forbidden City, Peking, China

1998. Cultural Heritage. Multicoloured.

3523	3f. Type **1361**	1·90	1·10
3524	4f.90 Louvre Palace, Paris	2·50	1·70

1362 Violin and Ballet Dancer

1998. National Opera House, Paris.

3525	**1362**	4f.50 multicoloured	2·50	1·70

1363 Camargue

1998. Horses. Multicoloured.

3526	2f.70 Type **1363**	1·80	1·00
3527	3f. French trotter	1·90	1·10
3528	3f. Pottok	1·90	1·10
3529	4f.50 Ardennais	2·50	1·70

1364 Dion-Bouton and Racing Cars

1998. Centenary of Paris Motor Show.

3530	**1364**	3f. multicoloured	1·90	1·10

1365 Marianne and Flag

1998. 40th Anniv of Constitution of Fifth Republic.

3531	**1365**	3f. multicoloured	1·90	1·10

1366 Romy Schneider

1998. Film Stars. Multicoloured.

3532	3f.+60c. Type **1366**	2·10	1·80
3533	3f.+60c. Simone Signoret	2·10	1·80
3534	3f.+60c. Jean Gabin	2·10	1·80
3535	3f.+60c. Louis de Funes	2·10	1·80
3536	3f.+60c. Bernard Blier	2·10	1·80
3537	3f.+60c. Lino Ventura	2·10	1·80

1367 State Flags

1998. 80th Anniv of Signing of First World War Armistice.

3538	**1367**	3f. multicoloured	1·90	1·10

1368 Flora and Fauna, Child and Emblem

1998. 50th Anniv of International Union for the Conservation of Nature and Natural Resources.

3539	**1368**	3f. multicoloured	1·90	1·10

1369 Elf on Christmas Bauble

1998. Red Cross Fund. Christmas.

3540	**1369**	3f.+60c. mult	2·10	1·20

1370 Father Christmas Snowboarding

1998. Christmas and New Year. Multicoloured.

3541	3f. Type **1370** (violet background)	1·90	1·10
3542	3f. Decorated house (daytime)	1·90	1·10
3543	3f. Type **1370** (bright yellow background)	1·90	1·10
3544	3f. Decorated house (night-time)	1·90	1·10
3545	3f. Type **1370** (green background)	1·90	1·10

1371 Child expressing Ambition and People of Different Nations

1998. Medecins sans Frontieres (volunteer medical and relief organization).

3546	**1371**	3f. multicoloured	1·90	1·10

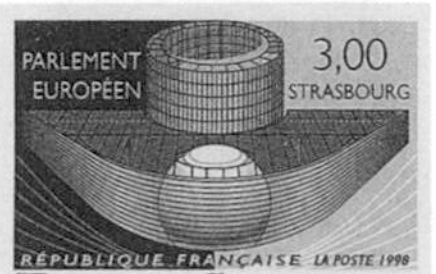

1372 Architectural Drawing

1998. Construction of New European Parliament Building, Strasbourg (designed by Architecture Studio Europe).

3547	**1372**	3f. multicoloured	1·90	1·10

1373 Rene Cassin, Eleanor Roosevelt and Palais de Chaillot

1998. 50th Anniv of Universal Declaration of Human Rights. Multicoloured.

3548	3f. Type **1373**	1·90	1·10
3549	3f. Globe and people of different races	1·90	1·10

1374 Radium

1998. Centenary of Discovery of Radium by Marie and Pierre Curie and 50th Anniv of ZOE Reactor, Chatillon.

3550	**1374**	3f. multicoloured	1·90	1·10

1375 1849 Ceres Design

1999. 150th Anniv of First French Postage Stamp (1st issue).

3551	**1375**	3f. black and red	6·50	5·50
3552	-	3f. black and red	1·90	1·10

DESIGN: No. 3552, As Type **1375** but with stamp and text transposed.

See also No. 3596.

1376 Euro Symbol

1999. Introduction of the Euro (European currency). Ordinary or self-adhesive gum.

3553	**1376**	3f. red and blue	2·20	1·30

No. 3553 is denominated both in French francs and in euros.

1377 Open Hands

1999. 150th Anniv of Public Welfare Hospitals of Paris (administration of Paris health services).

3555	**1377**	3f. blue, mve & grn	1·90	1·10

1378 Flags of France and Israel

1999. 50th Anniv of Diplomatic Relations between France and Israel.

3556	**1378**	4f.40 multicoloured	2·50	1·70

1379 Heart

1999. St. Valentine's Day. Multicoloured. Ordinary and self-adhesive gum.

3557	3f. Type **1379**	1·90	1·10
3558	3f. Heart-shaped rose	1·90	1·10

1999. Art. As T **491**.

3561	6f.70 brown and orange	3·50	2·40
3562	6f.70 multicoloured	3·50	2·40
3563	6f.70 multicoloured	3·50	2·40
3564	6f.70 multicoloured	3·50	2·40

DESIGNS—VERT: No. 3561, "St. Luke the Evangelist" (sculpture, Jean Goujon); 3562, Stained glass window (Arnaud de Moles), Chapelle de la Compassion, Auch Cathedral; 3564, "Charles I, King of England" (Anton van Dyck). HORIZ: No. 3563, "Water Lilies, Effect of Evening" (Claude Monet).

1380 Flowers on Map of France

1999. 33rd Population Census.

3565	**1380**	3f. multicoloured	1·90	1·10

1381 "The Capture of Europa" (mosaic from Byblos)

1999. Cultural Heritage of Lebanon.
3566 **1381** 4f.40 multicoloured 2·40 1·70

1382 Asterix

1999. Stamp Day. Asterix the Gaul (cartoon character) by Albert Uderzo and Rene Goscinny.

3567	**1382**	3f. multicoloured	1·90	1·10
3569	**1382**	3f.+60c. mult	3·25	2·75
MS3570		102×77 mm. No. 3569	3·75	3·75

1383 Council Emblem on World Map

1999. 50th Anniv of Council of Europe.
3571 **1383** 3f. multicoloured 1·90 1·10

1384 Two Doves and Hearts (wedding)

1999. Greetings Stamps. Multicoloured.

3572	3f. Type **1384**	1·90	1·10
3573	3f. "Thank you" in different languages	1·90	1·10
3574	3f. Stork carrying blue bundle ("It's a boy")	1·90	1·10
3575	3f. Stork carrying pink bundle ("It's a girl")	1·90	1·10

1385 "Venus de Milo" (statue)

1999. "Philexfrance 99" International Stamp Exhibition, Paris (2nd issue). Art. Sheet 159×111 mm containing T 1385 and similar designs.
MS3576 5f. sepia (Type **1385**); 5f. multicoloured ("Mona Lisa" (Leonardo da Vinci)) (37×49 mm); 10f. multicoloured ("Liberty guiding the People" (Eugene Delacroix)) (36×37 mm) (sold at 50f.) 50·00 55·00

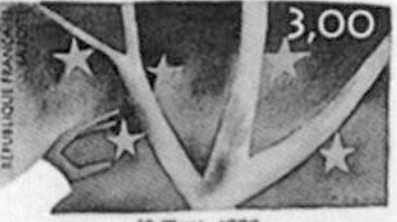

1386 Branches and Hand reaching for Star

1999. European Parliament Elections.
3577 **1386** 3f. multicoloured 1·90 1·10

1387 Richard the Lion Heart (from "Historia Anglorum")

1999. 800th Death Anniv of King Richard I of England.
3578 **1387** 3f. multicoloured 1·90 1·10

1388 Airbus A300-B4

1999. Air.
3579 **1388** 15f. multicoloured 9·00 7·75

1389 Dieppe Castle

1999. Tourist Publicity.

3580	**1389**	3f. multicoloured	1·90	1·10
3581	-	3f. multicoloured	1·90	1·10
3582	-	3f. multicoloured	1·90	1·10
3583	-	3f. multicoloured	1·90	1·10

DESIGNS—As T **949**: No. 3581, Haut-Koenigsbourg Castle, Lower Rhine. As T **490**: No. 3582, Place des Ecritures, Figeac; 3583, Arnac-Pompadour Chateau.
No. 3583 is denominated in both francs and euros.

1390 The Camargue

1999. Europa. Parks and Gardens.
3584 **1390** 3f. multicoloured 1·90 1·10

1391 Cake and Music Notes ("Happy Birthday")

1999. Greetings Stamps. Multicoloured.

3585	3f. Type **1391**	1·90	1·10
3586	3f. Seagull and sun wearing sunglasses ("Have a nice holiday")	1·90	1·10
3587	3f. Float on water ("Long live holidays") (vert)	1·90	1·10

1392 St. Pierre and Mt. Pelee

1999. Heritage of Martinique.
3588 **1392** 3f. multicoloured 1·90 1·10

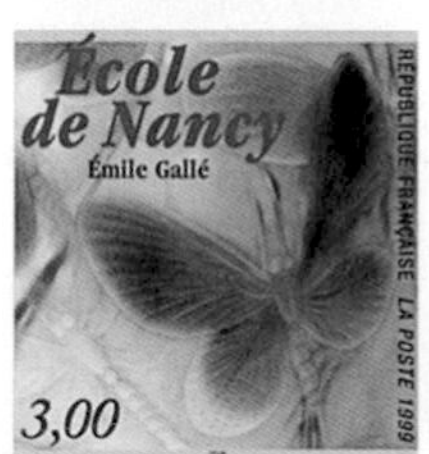

1393 "Noctuelles" Dish (detail, Emile Galle)

1999. Nancy School (art movement).
3589 **1393** 3f. multicoloured 1·90 1·10

1394 "Mme. Alfred Carriere"

1999. Old Roses. Sheet 111×160 mm containing T **1394** and similar vert designs. Multicoloured.
MS3590 3f. Type **1394**; 4f.50 "Mme. Caroline Testout"; 4f.50 "La France" 11·50 11·00

1395 Ruins, Grape Vines and Seal

1999. 800th Anniv of Granting of City Rights to Saint-Emilion and 50th Anniv of Re-institution of the Jurade (controllers of St.-Emilion wine appellation).
3591 **1395** 3f.80 multicoloured 2·20 1·40

1396 The Mint, Paris

1999
3592 **1396** 4f.50 red, blue & black 2·50 1·70

1397 Model Girls

1999. Birth Bicentenary of Countess de Segur (children's writer).
3593 **1397** 3f. multicoloured 1·90 1·10

1398 Sun and Doves in Mosaic

1999. Post Office "Pleasure to Welcome" Customer Campaign.
3594 **1398** 3f. multicoloured 1·90 1·10

1399 Caillie

1999. Birth Bicentenary of Rene Caillie (explorer).
3595 **1399** 4f.50 violet, yellow and orange 2·50 1·70

1400 1849 Ceres Design

1999. 150th Anniv of First French Postage Stamp (2nd issue).
3596 **1400** 6f.70 multicoloured 4·50 2·40

DENOMINATION. From No. 3597 to 3769 French stamps were denominated both in francs and in euros. As no cash for the latter was in circulation, the catalogue refers to the franc value.

1401 Spinning Globe

1999. Year 2000.
3597 **1401** 3f. multicoloured 1·90 1·10

1402 Winning Entry by Morgane Toulouse

1999. "Design a Stamp for Year 2000" Children's Drawing Contest.
3598 **1402** 3f. multicoloured 1·90 1·10

1403 Total Eclipse

1999. Solar Eclipse (11 August).
3599 **1403** 3f. multicoloured 1·90 1·10

1404 "Simon Bolivar" (Venezuelan cadet barque)

1999. "Armada of the Century", Rouen. Sailing Ships. Multicoloured.

3600	1f. Type **1404**	65	55
3601	1f. "Iskra" (Polish cadet ship)	65	55
3602	1f. "Statsraad Lehmkuhl" (barque)	65	55
3603	1f. "Asgard II" (cadet brigantine)	65	55
3604	1f. "Belle Poule" (sail frigate)	65	55
3605	1f. "Belem" (barque)	65	55
3606	1f. "Amerigo Vespucci" (cadet ship)	65	55
3607	1f. "Sagres" (cadet barque)	65	55
3608	1f. "Europa" (barque)	65	55
3609	1f. "Cuauhtemoc" (barque)	65	55

1405 "School, 1956" (Robert Doisneau)

1999. French Photographers. Multicoloured.

3610	3f.+60c. Type **1405**	2·20	1·90
3611	3f.+60c. "St. James's Tower, View of Notre Dame, 1936" (Gilberte Brassai)	2·20	1·90
3612	3f.+60c. "Renee on the way to Paris, Aix-les-Bains" (Jacques Henri Lartigue)	2·20	1·90
3613	3f.+60c. "Hyeres, France, 1932" (Henri Cartier-Bresson)	2·20	1·90
3614	3f.+60c. "Travelling Salesman" (Eugene Atget)	2·20	1·90
3615	3f.+60c. "Debureau at the Camera" (Nadar)	2·20	1·90

1406 Players

1999. 4th World Cup Rugby Championship, Great Britain, Ireland and France.
3616 **1406** 3f. multicoloured 1·70 1·00

1407 Ozanam (after Louis Janmot)

1999. 146th Death Anniv of Frederic Ozanam (historian and social campaigner).

3617	**1407**	4f.50 deep green, brown and red	2·30	1·50

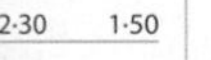

1408 People holding Hands

1999. 50th Anniv of Emmaus Movement (welfare organization).

3618	**1408**	3f. multicoloured	1·70	1·00

1409 Chartreuse Cat

1999. Domestic Pets. Multicoloured.

3619	2f.70 Type **1409**	1·40	1·00
3620	3f. European tabby cat	1·40	1·00
3621	3f. Pyrenean mountain dog	1·40	1·00
3622	4f.50 Brittany spaniel	2·30	2·00

1410 Chopin (after George Sand)

1999. 150th Death Anniv of Frederic Chopin (composer).

3623	**1410**	3f.80 blue, deep violet and orange	1·40	1·20

1411 Star playing Drum with Clock Face

1999. Red Cross Fund. New Year.

3624	**1411**	3f.+60c. mult	1·80	1·30

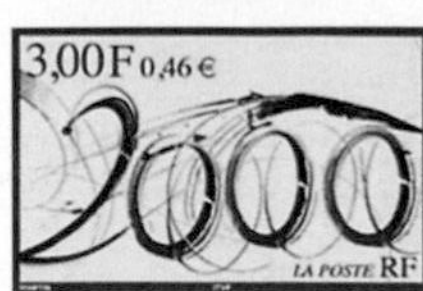

1412 "2000"

1999. Year 2000. Multicoloured.

3625	3f. Type **1412**	1·50	1·00
3626	3f. Half-unwrapped parcel (vert)	1·50	1·00

1413 Metro Signs

1999. Centenary of Paris Metro.

3627	**1413**	3f. multicoloured	1·50	1·00

1414 Column and Pediment

1999. Bicentenary of Council of State.

3628	**1414**	3f. blue and grey	1·50	1·00

1415 San Juan de Salvamento and La Rochelle Lighthouses

2000. Reconstruction of San Juan de Salvamento Lighthouse, Staten Island.

3629	**1415**	3f. multicoloured	1·50	1·00

1416 Snakes forming Heart

2000. Yves St. Laurent (couturier). Multicoloured. Ordinary or self-adhesive gum.

3630	3f. Type **1416**	1·50	1·00
3631	3f. Woman's face	1·50	1·00
MS3632	95×150 mm. Nos. 3630 ×3 and No. 3631 ×2	6·75	6·50

1417 Bank Entrance

2000. Bicentenary of Bank of France.

3635	**1417**	3f. multicoloured	1·10	1·00

1418 Couzinet 70 *Arc en Ciel*

2000. Air.

3636	**1418**	50f. multicoloured	22·00	19·00

1419 Emblem

2000. Bicentenary of Prefectorial Corps.

3637	**1419**	3f. multicoloured	1·10	1·00

2000. Art. As T **491**.

3638	6f.70 multicoloured (vert)	3·25	2·00
3639	6f.70 multicoloured (vert)	3·25	2·00
3640	6f.70 multicoloured (vert)	3·25	2·00

DESIGNS: No. 3638, Detail of "Venus and the Graces offering Gifts to a Young Girl" (Sandro Botticelli); 3639, "The Waltz" (sculpture, Camille Claudel); 3640, "Visage Rouge" (Gaston Chaissac).

2000. Tourist Publicity. As T **949**.

3642	3f. multicoloured	1·10	1·00
3643	3f. multicoloured	1·10	1·00
3644	3f. multicoloured	1·10	1·00
3645	3f. multicoloured	1·10	1·00

DESIGNS: No. 3642, Carcassonne. As Type **490**: 37×27 mm—No. 3643, Saint Guilhem le Desert, Herault; 3644, Valley of the Lakes, Gerardmer. 36×23 mm—No. 3645, Ottmarsheim Abbey church.

1420 Tintin and Snowy

2000. Tintin (cartoon character) by Georges Renu (Herge).

3646	**1420**	3f. multicoloured	1·60	1·00
3648	**1420**	3f.+60c. mult	2·75	2·00
MS3649		101×76 mm. No. 3648	3·50	3·00

1421 Parliament Building

2000. Restoration of Breton Regional Parliament, Rennes.

3650	**1421**	3f. multicoloured	1·10	1·00

1422 Periwinkle

2000

3651	**1422**	4f.50 multicoloured	1·70	1·50

1423 "Congratulations"

2000. Greetings Stamp. Multicoloured.

3652	3f. Type **1423**	1·10	1·00
3653	3f. "bonnes vacances"	1·10	1·00

1424 Football World Cup Trophy (France, World Champions, 1998)

2000. The Twentieth Century (1st series). Sporting Achievements. Sheet 185×245 mm containing five different 3f. designs as T **1424**, each ×2. Multicoloured.

MS3654	3f. Type **1424**; 3f. Marcel Cerdan (World Middleweight Champion, 1948); 3f. Carl Lewis (Olympic Gold medallist 100m, 200m, 100m relay and long jump, 1984) (vert); 3f. Charles Lindbergh and *Spirit of St. Louis* (first solo Atlantic crossing,1927); 3f. Jean-Claude Killy (Winter Olympic Gold medallist downhill, giant slalom and special slalom, 1968) (vert)	14·00	13·00

See also No. **MS**3687, **MS**3710, **MS**3756, **MS**3814 and **MS**3861.

1425 Bugatti 35

2000. "Philexjeunes 2000" International Youth Stamp Exhibition, Annely. Vintage Cars. Multicoloured.

3655	1f. Type **1425**	45	40
3656	1f. Citroen Traction	45	40
3657	1f. Renault 4CV	45	40
3658	1f. Simca Chamord	45	40
3659	1f. Hispano Suiza K6	45	40
3660	2f. Volkswagen Beetle	90	80
3661	2f. Cadillac 62	90	80
3662	2f. Peugeot 203	90	80
3663	2f. Citroen DS19	90	80
3664	2f. Ferrari 250 GTO	90	80

1426 "Building Europe"

2000. Europa.

3665	**1426**	3f. multicoloured	2·30	2·00

1427 Du Monceau

2000. 300th Birth Anniv of Henry-Louis Duhamel du Monceau (technologist and natural scientist).

3666	**1427**	4f.50 multicoloured	1·70	1·50

1428 Porte du Croux and Earthenware Jug

2000. 73rd French Philatelic Federation Congress, Nevers.

3667	**1428**	3f. multicoloured	1·10	1·00

1429 Mountaineers

2000. 50th Anniv of French Ascent of Mt. Annapurna, Himalayas.

3668	**1429**	3f. multicoloured	1·10	1·00

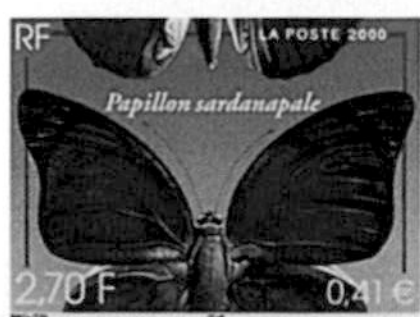

1430 *Agrias sardanapalus*

2000. National Museum of Natural History. Mult.

3669	2f.70 Type **1430**	1·10	1·00
3670	3f. Giraffe (vert)	1·10	1·00
3671	3f. Allosaurus	1·10	1·00
3672	4f.50 *Tulipa lutea* (vert)	1·70	1·50
MS3673	110×160 mm. Nos. 3669/72	5·75	5·75

1431 Saint-Exupery and Caudron C.690

2000. Birth Centenary of Antoine de Saint-Exupery (aviator and writer).

3674	**1431**	3f. multicoloured	1·10	1·00

1432 Train

2000. Centenary of the Yellow Train (Villefranch de Conflent–Latourde Card service), Cerdagne.

3675	**1432**	3f. multicoloured	1·10	1·00

1433 "Folklores" and Characters

2000

3676	**1433**	4f.50 multicoloured	1·70	1·50

1434 Cycling, Fencing and Relay

2000. Olympic Games, Sydney. Multicoloured.

3677	3f. Type **1434**	1·40	1·00
3678	3f. Relay, judo and diving	1·40	1·00
MS3679	210×143 mm. Nos. 3677/8, each ×5 plus label	15·00	15·00

Nos. 3677/8 were issued together, se-tenant, forming a composite design.

1435 Eric Tabarly (yachtsman)

2000. French Adventurers. Multicoloured.

3680	3f.+60c. Type **1435**	2·00	1·70
3681	3f.+60c. Alexandra David-Neel (explorer)	2·00	1·70
3682	3f.+60c. Haroun Tazieff (geologist and vulcanologist)	2·00	1·70
3683	3f.+60c. Paul-Emile Victor (polar explorer)	2·00	1·70
3684	3f.+60c. Jacques-Yves Cousteau (underwater explorer)	2·00	1·70
3685	3f.+60c. Norbert Casteret (archeologist and speleologist)	2·00	1·70

1436 Stanke

2000. 25th Death Anniv of Brother Alfred Stanke (German wartime prison hospital Chaplain who helped French prisoners).

3686	**1436**	4f.40 brown, ultramarine and blue	1·70	1·50

1437 Edwin E. Aldrin on Moon (first manned Moon landing, 1969)

2000. The Twentieth Century (2nd series). Sheet 185×245 mm containing five different 3f. designs as T **1437**, each ×2. Multicoloured.

MS3687 VERT: 3f. Type **1437**. HORIZ: 3f. Family paddling in sea (entitlement to paid holiday, 1936); 3f. Modern washing machine (invention of washing machine, 1901); 3f. Women posting voting slips (women given right to vote, 1944); 3f. Graffiti (Declaration of Human Rights, 1948) 14·00 14·00

1438 Man telephoning Helpline

2000. 40th Anniv of S.O.S. Amitie (telephone support service).

3688	**1438**	3f. multicoloured	1·10	1·00

1439 Globe and Methods of Communication

2000. New Millennium.

3689	**1439**	3f. multicoloured	1·10	1·00

1440 Detail of Mosaic

2000. Germigny-des-Pres Mosaic, Loire Valley.

3690	**1440**	6f.70 multicoloured	2·75	2·00

1441 Young Couple and Bandstand (R. Peynet)

2000

3691	**1441**	3f. multicoloured	2·30	1·00

1442 Brown Kiwi (New Zealand)

2000. Endangered Species. Multicoloured.

3692	3f. Type **1442**	1·40	1·00
3693	5f.20 Lesser kestrel (France)	2·30	2·00

1443 Toy Aeroplane and Gifts

2000. Red Cross Fund. New Year.

3694	**1443**	3f.+60c. mult	1·50	1·30

1444 World Map in Envelope

2000. Third Millennium.

3695	**1444**	3f. multicoloured	1·40	1·10

1445 "Bonne annee" and Snowflakes

2000. Christmas and New Year. Multicoloured.

3696	3f. Type **1445**	1·10	1·00
3697	3f. "Meilleurs voeux", Globe and gifts	1·10	1·00

1446 Eiffel Tower and Space Rocket

2000. Centenary of Union of Metallurgy and Mining Industries.

3698	**1446**	4f.50 multicoloured	1·80	1·50

1447 Emblem

2001. World Handball Championship, France.

3699	**1447**	3f. multicoloured	1·10	1·00

1448 Stone covered Heart

2001. St. Valentine's Day.

3700	**1448**	3f. multicoloured	1·10	1·00
MS3701		136×143 mm. No. 3700 ×5	7·00	7·00

2001. Art. As T **491**.

3702	6f.70 multicoloured	2·75	2·00
3703	6f.70 multicoloured	2·75	2·00
3704	6f.70 multicoloured	2·75	2·00
3705	6f.70 multicoloured	2·75	2·00

DESIGNS—Horiz: No. 3702, "The Peasant Dance" (Pieter Brugel the Elder); 3703, St. James of Compostela and Angel (mural, hospital of Order of St. John of Jerusalem, Toulouse), 3705, "Honfleur at Low Tide" (Johan Barthold Jongkind). VERT: 3704, "Yvette Guilbert singing Linger, Longer Loo" (Henri Toulouse-Lautrec).

1449 Gaston Lagaffe

2001. Gaston Lagaffe (cartoon character) by Andre Franquin.

3706	**1449**	3f. multicoloured	1·10	1·00
3708	**1449**	3f.+60c. multicoloured	2·75	1·50
MS3709		101×75 mm. No. 3708	3·50	3·50

1450 Nounours, Pimprenelle and Nicolas from "Bonne Nuit les Petits" (chilren's televison programme, 1965)

2001. The Twentieth Century (3rd series). Forms of Communication. Sheet 186×245 mm containing five different 3f. designs as T 1450, each ×2. Multicoloured.

MS3710 3f. Type **1450**; 3f. Hand holding compact disc (development of analogue technology); 3f. The Little Miner and road sign (cinema advertising character created by Jean Mineur, 1950); 3f. Couple dancing and early radio (*Salut les Copians* (first broadcast by popular radio programme, 1959)); 3f. Baby, mobile phone and globe (development of digital mobile phone technology, 1991) 14·00 14·00

1451 Flower ("merci")

2001. Greetings Stamps. Multicoloured.

3711	3f. Type **1451**	1·20	1·00
3712	3f. Teddy bear wearing bow tie ("c'est un garcon")	1·20	1·00
3713	3f. Teddy bear wearing yellow ribbon ("c'est une fille")	1·20	1·00
3714	4f.50 Two hearts ("oui")	1·80	1·50

1452 Eurasian Red Squirrel

2001. Animals. Multicoloured.

3715	2f.70 Type **1452**	1·20	1·00
3716	3f. Roe deer (horiz)	1·20	1·00
3717	3f. West European hedgehog (horiz)	1·20	1·00
3718	4f.50 Stoat	1·80	1·50
MS3719	161×111 mm. Nos. 3715/18	6·00	6·00

2001. Tourist Publicity. As T 490. Multicoloured.

3720	3f. Nogent-le-Rotrou (vert)	1·20	1·00
3721	3f. Besancon, Doubs	1·20	1·00
3722	3f. Calais	1·20	1·00
3723	3f. Chateau de Grignan, Drome	1·20	1·00

1453 Water Droplet and Globe

2001. Europa. Water Resources.

3724	**1453**	3f. multicoloured	1·80	1·50

1454 Gardens (image scaled to 64% of original size)

2001. Versailles Palace Gardens.

3725	**1454**	4f.40 multicoloured	1·80	1·50

1455 Lyon

2001

3726	**1455**	3f. multicoloured	1·20	1·00

1456 Claude Francois

2001. Singers. Multicoloured.

3727	3f. Type **1456**	1·20	1·00
3728	3f. Leo Ferre	1·20	1·00
3729	3f. Serge Gainsbourg	1·20	1·00
3730	3f. Dalida	1·20	1·00
3731	3f. Michel Berger	1·20	1·00
3732	3f. Barbara	1·20	1·00
MS3733	135×143 mm. Nos. 3727/32 (sold at 28f.)	14·50	14·50

1457 Craftsman, Wilson Bridge and St. Gatien Cathedral

2001. 74th French Philatelic Federation Congress, Tours.

3734	**1457**	3f. multicoloured	1·20	1·00

1458 Vilar

2001. 30th Death Anniv of Jean Vilar (theatre director).

3735	**1458**	3f. multicoloured	1·20	1·00

1459 Footprint in Sand

2001. Greetings Stamps. Holidays. Ordinary or self-adhesive gum.

3736	**1459**	3f. multicoloured	1·20	1·00

1460 1 Euro Coin

2001. The European Currency.

3738	**1460**	3f. multicoloured	1·80	1·00

1461 Caquot, Airship and Bridge

2001. 120th Birth Anniv of Albert Caquot (civil engineer).

3739	**1461**	4f.50 multicoloured	1·80	1·50

1462 Jigsaw Pieces

2001. Centenary of Freedom of Association Law.

3740	**1462**	3f. multicoloured	1·20	1·00

1463 Eurostar Express Train

2001. Locomotives. Multicoloured.

3741	1f.50 Type **1463**	70	60
3742	1f.50 American 220 steam locomotive	70	60
3743	1f.50 Ae 6/8 "Crocodile" locomotive	70	60
3744	1f.50 Crampton steam locomotive	70	60
3745	1f.50 Garratt type 59 steam locomotive	70	60
3746	1f.50 Pacific Chapelon steam locomotive	70	60
3747	1f.50 LNER Class A4 steam locomotive No. 4468 *Mallard*, 1938, Great Britain	70	60
3748	1f.50 Capitole electric locomotive	70	60
3749	1f.50 Autorail	70	60
3750	1f.50 230 Class P8 type 230 steam locomotive	70	60

1464 Emblem

2001. 50th Anniv of United Nations High Commissioner for Refugees.

3751	**1464**	4f.50 green, magenta and blue	1·80	1·50

2001. No value expressed. As T **1318** but with "RF" in lower left corner and "LA POSTE" in upper right corner.

3752	(3f.) red	1·20	50

1465 Fermat and Mathematical Equations

2001. 400th Birth Anniv of Pierre de Fermat (mathematician).

3755	**1465**	4f.50 multicoloured	1·80	1·50

1466 Yuri Gagarin and Vostok 1 (first man in space, 1961)

2001. The Twentieth Century (4th issue). Science. Sheet 185×244 mm containing five different 3f. designs as T 1466, each×2. Multicoloured.

MS3756	3f. Type **1466**; 3f. Human body and DNA double helix (identification of DNA molecule, 1953); 3f. Hand holding credit card (development of chip card) (horiz); 3f. Laser treatment for correcting eye sight (development of laser technology); 3f. Bacteriologist and penicillin culture (discovery of penicillin, 1928) (horiz)	14·50	14·50

1467 Astrolabe (sculpture, Alain Le Boucher)

2001. 25th Anniv of Val-de-Reuil.

3757	**1467**	3f. multicoloured	1·20	1·00

1468 Pumpkin

2001. Halloween.

3758	**1468**	3f. multcoloured	1·20	1·00
MS3759		135×144 mm. No. 3759 ×5	6·00	6·00

1469 Father Christmas

2001. Red Cross Fund. Christmas.

3760	**1469**	3f.+60c. multicoloured	1·40	1·20

1470 Pierre-Bloch

2001. 2nd Death Anniv of Jean Pierre-Bloch (politician).

3761	**1470**	4f.50 blue, ultramarine and deep blue	1·80	1·50

1471 Eiffel Tower and Arc de Triomphe dancing

2001. Birth Centenary of Albert Decaris (artist and engraver).

3762	**1471**	3f. violet, brown and blue	1·50	1·00

1472 Children and Snowman

2001. New Year. Multicoloured. Self-adhesive or ordinary gum.

3763	3f. Type **1472**	1·20	1·00
3764	3f. Children and wheelbarrow	1·20	1·00

1473 Chaban-Delmas

2001. Jaques Chaban-Delmas (politician) Commemoration.

3767	**1473**	3f. multicoloured	1·30	1·00

1474 Nejjarine Fountain, Fez, Morocco

2001. French–Moroccan Cultural Heritage. Fountains. Multicoloured.

3768	3f. Type **1474**	1·30	1·00
3769	3f.80 Wallace Fountain, Paris	2·50	1·50

After the adoption by France of the euro currency on 1 January 2002, No. 3752 were sold at 46c.

2002. As T 1318 but with "RF" in lower left corner, "LAPOSTE" in upper right corner and values expressed in euros. (a) Sheet stamps.

3770	1c. yellow	20	15
3771	2c. brown	20	15
3772	5c. green	20	15
3773	10c. violet	40	15
3774	20c. orange	65	20
3775	41c. green	1·60	40
3776	50c. blue	1·90	50
3777	53c. green	1·90	80
3778	58c. blue	1·90	1·30
3778a	58c. green	1·90	50
3779	64c. orange	2·50	1·00
3780	67c. blue	2·50	1·30
3781	69c. mauve	2·50	1·00
3782	70c. green	2·50	70
3783	75c. blue	2·50	70
3784	90c. blue	3·25	1·50
3785	€1 turquoise	3·75	1·00
3786	€1.02 green	3·75	1·00
3787	€1.11 purple	3·75	1·10
3788	€1.90 purple	6·50	2·00
3789	€2 violet	6·50	2·00

(b) Coil stamp. (i) With face value.

3790	(41c.) green	2·50	1·00
3792	(46c.) red	1·50	1·00

(ii) No value expressed.

3791	41c. green	2·50	1·00

(c) Miniature sheets. Two sheets, each 145×143 mm.

MS3794	(a) Nos. 3770/4, 3776, 3785 and 3789; (b) Nos. 3775, 3752, 3777/8, 3779/81 and 3789	50·00	50·00

1475 *Orchis insularis*

2002. Orchids. Multicoloured.

3795	29c. Type **1475**	1·50	1·20
3796	33c. *Orphrys fuciflora*	1·70	1·30

Nos. 3795/6 were only issued precancelled.

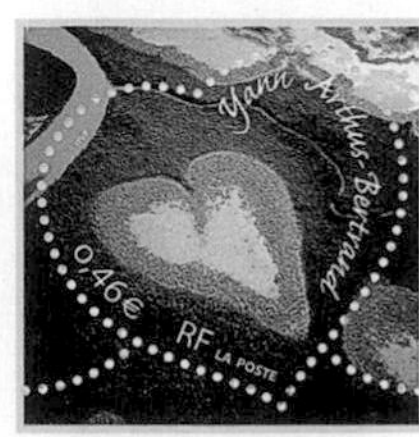

1476 Heart Shape in Landscape, New Caledonia

2002. St. Valentine's Day.

3797	**1476**	46c. multicoloured	1·30	1·00
MS3798		135×142 mm. No. 3797×5	6·50	6·50

1477 Snowboarder

2002. Winter Olympic Games, Salt Lake City, U.S.A.

3799	**1477**	46c. multicoloured	1·30	1·00

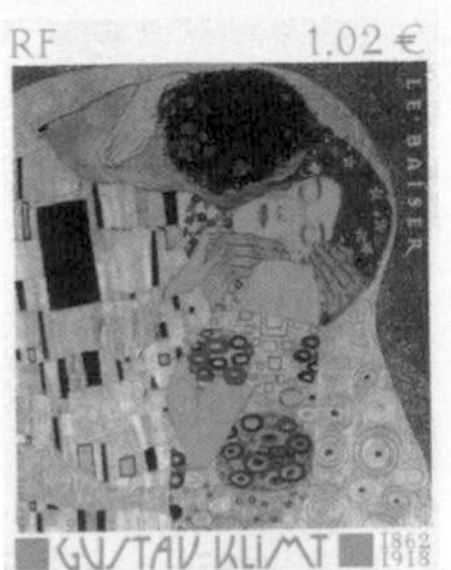

1478 The Kiss (Gustav Klimt)

2002. Art. Designs as T 1478. Multicoloured.
3800 €1.02 "The Kiss" (Gustav Klimt) 3·25 2·00
3801 €1.02 "The Dancers" (painting, Fernando Botero) 3·25 2·00

1479 Bosquet

2002. 4th Death Anniv of Alain Bosquet (Anatole Bisk) (writer).
3804 **1478** 58c. brown, orange and blue 1·70 1·30

1480 Bee wearing Crown ("c'est une fille")

2002. Greetings Stamps. Multicoloured.
3805 46c. Type **1479** 1·30 1·00
3806 46c. Bee wearing cap ("c'est un garcon") 1·30 1·00
3807 69c. "Oui" in flowers 1·90 1·50

1481 Elephant, Performers and Horse

2002. Europa. Circus.
3808 **1481** 46c. multicoloured 1·90 1·50

1482 Boule, Bill and Birds

2002. Boule and Bill (cartoon characters) by Jean Roba. Multicoloured.
3809 46c. Type **1482** 1·30 1·00
3811 46c. + 9c. Boule, Bill and ball 2·50 2·00
MS3812 100×75 mm. As No. 3811 3·25 3·25

1483 Amphitheatre, Nimes

2002
3813 **1483** 46c. multicoloured 1·30 1·00

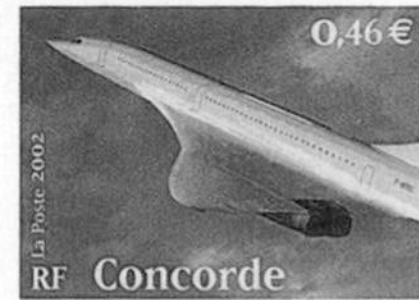

1484 Concorde (first flight, 1969)

2002. The Twentieth Century (5th series).Transport. Sheet 185×245 mm, containing five different 46c. designs as T 1484, each×2. Multicoloured.
MS3814 46c. Type **1484**; 46c. TGV train (high speed passenger train); 46c. "La Mobylette" (motorcycle) (vert); 46c. *France* (transatlantic passenger liner) (vert); 46c. 2CV (motor car) (vert) 19·00 19·00

1485 Matthew Flinders, Map of Australia and H.M.S. *Investigator* (ship of the line)

2002. France—Australia Joint Issue. Bicentenary of Nicolas Baudin–Matthew Flinders Meeting at Encounter Bay, Australia. Multicoloured.
3815 46c. Type **1485** 1·30 1·00
3816 79c. *Geographie* (corvette), map of Australia and Nicolas Baudin 2·50 1·60

1486 La Charite-sur-Loire Church, Nievre

2002. UNESCO. World Heritage Site.
3817 **1486** 46c. multicoloured 1·40 1·00

1487 Butterflies and Gift ("Anniversaire")

2002. Greetings Stamps. Multicoloured.
3818 46c. Type **1487** 1·40 1·00
3819 46c. Bird and envelopes ("Invitation") 1·40 1·00

1488 Cyclists

2002. 100th Paris–Roubaix Cycle Race.
3820 **1488** 46c. multicoloured 1·40 1·00

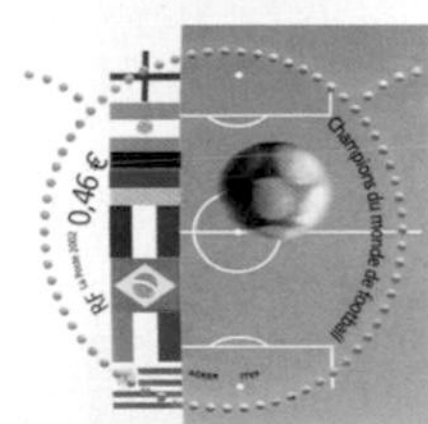

1489 Winners' Flags and Football

2002. World Cup Football Championship, Japan and South Korea. Multicoloured.
3821 46c. Type **1489** 1·40 1·00
3822 46c. Footballer 1·40 1·00
MS3823 143×210 mm. Nos. 3821/2, each ×5 17·00 17·00

No. **MS**3823 was inscribed on the back, with the groups around the edge and with facilities for recording the results between the stamps, over the gum.

1490 Leatherback Turtle

2002. Animals. Multicoloured.
3824 41c. Type **1490** 1·40 1·00
3825 46c. Killer whale (horiz) 1·40 1·00
3826 46c. Bottle-nosed dolphin (horiz) 1·40 1·00
3827 69c. Common seal 2·75 2·00
MS3828 109×160 mm. Nos. 3824/7 4·50 4·50

1491 Old Port, Marseille (image scaled to 63% of original size)

2002. 75th French Federation of Philatelic Societies Congress, Marseille.
3829 **1491** 46c. multicoloured 1·40 1·00

1492 Medal

2002. Bicentenary of Legion d'Honneur (medal).
3830 **1492** 46c. multicoloured 1·40 1·00

1493 Rocamadour, Lot

2002
3831 **1493** 46c. multicoloured 1·40 1·00

1494 Delgres

2002. Death Bicentenary of Louis Delgres (soldier and anti-slavery campaigner).
3832 **1494** 46c. multicoloured 1·40 1·00

1495 Woman in Hammock

2002. Holidays. Ordinary or self-adhesive gum.
3833 **1495** 46c. multicoloured 1·40 1·00

1496 Wheelchair Racers

2002. World Disabled Athletics Championship, Lille-Villeneuve-d'Ascq.
3835 **1496** 46c. multicoloured 1·40 1·00

1497 Collioure Lighthouse (painting, Andre Derain)

2002. Collioure, Pyrenees.
3836 **1497** 46c. multicoloured 1·40 1·00

1498 Chapel

2002. Saint-Ser Chapel, Puyloubier, Bouches-du-Rhone.
3837 **1498** 46c. multicoloured 1·40 1·00

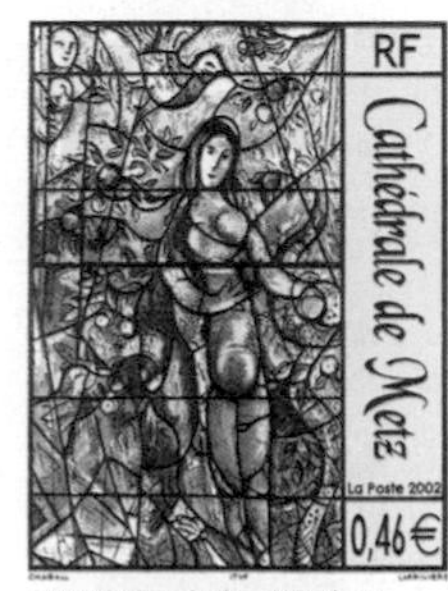

1499 Stained Glass Window (Mark Chagall)

2002. Metz Cathedral.
3838 **1499** 46c. multicoloured 1·70 1·00

2002. Tourist Publicity. As Type 490. Multicoloured.
3839 46c. Lacronan, Finistere (vert) 1·40 1·00
3840 46c. Neufchateau, Vosges 1·40 1·00

1500 Louis Armstrong

2002. Jazz. Multicoloured.
3841 46c. Type **1500** 1·40 1·00
3842 46c. Ella Fitzgerald 1·40 1·00
3843 46c. Duke Ellington 1·40 1·00
3844 46c. Stephane Grappelli 1·40 1·00
3845 46c. Michel Petrucciani (horiz) 1·40 1·00
3846 46c. Sidney Bechet (horiz) 1·40 1·00
MS3847 135×143 mm. Nos. 3841/6 (sold at €4.36) 17·00 17·00

No. **MS**3847 was sold with a premium of €1.60 for the benefit of the Red Cross.

1501 Building Facade

2002. 150th Anniv of Notre-Dame de la Salette, Isere.
3848 **1501** 46c. multicoloured 1·40 1·00

1502 Hands (image scaled to 63% of original size)

2002. Choreography.
3849 **1502** 53c. multicoloured 2·10 1·10

1503 Honda CB 750 Four

2002. Motorcycles. Multicoloured.

3850	16c. Type **1503**	55	40
3851	16c. Terrot 500 RGST	55	40
3852	16c. Majestic 350	55	40
3853	16c. Norton Commando 750	55	40
3854	16c. Voxon 1000 Cafe Racer	55	40
3855	30c. BMW R 90 S	1·10	60
3856	30c. Harley Davidson FL Hydra-Glide	1·10	60
3857	30c. Triumph T120 Bonneville 650	1·10	60
3858	30c. Ducati 916	1·10	60
3859	30c. Yamaha 500 XT	1·10	60

1504 Perec

2002. 20th Death Anniv of Georges Perec (writer).

3860	**1504**	46c. multicoloured	1·40	1·00

1505 Family on Motor Scooter

2002. The Twentieth Century (6th series). Everyday Life. Sheet 185×243 mm, containing five different 46c. designs as T 1505, each× 2. Multicoloured.

MS3861	46c. Type **1505**; 46c. Man with horse and cart (horiz); 46c. Woman ironing (horiz); 46c. Boy at water pump; 46c. Girl at school desk	17·00	17·00

1506 Zola

2002. Death Centenary of Emile Zola (writer).

3862	**1506**	46c. multicoloured	1·40	1·00

1507 Self-portrait (Uffizi museum, Florence)

2002. 160th Death Anniv of Elisabeth Vigee-Lebrun (artist).

3863	**1507**	€1.02 multicoloured	3·50	2·00

1508 Airbus

2002. 30th Anniv of First Flight of Airbus A300-B1.

3864	**1508**	€3 multicoloured	9·75	6·00

1509 "Sleeping Jesus" (Giovanni Battista Salvi)

2002. Red Cross Fund. Christmas.

3865a	**1509**	46c.+9c. multicoloured	1·70	80

1510 Trevi Fountain

2002. European Capitals. Rome. Sheet 144×36 mm containing T 1510 and similar multicoloured designs.

MS3866	46c. Type **1510**; 46c. Coliseum (horiz); 46c. Trinita dei Monti church; 46c. St. Peter's Basilica (horiz)	8·25	8·25

1511 World embedded in Computer Circuit

2002. Enterprise.

3867	**1511**	46c. multicoloured	1·40	1·00

1512 Snow-covered House

2002. New Year. Ordinary or Self-adhesive gum.

3868	**1512**	46c. multicoloured	1·40	1·00

1513 "Sphere Concorde" (Jesus Rafael)

2002

3870	**1513**	75c. multicoloured	2·75	1·50

1514 Dumas

2002. Birth Bicentenary of Alexandre Dumas (writer).

3871	**1514**	46c. multicoloured	1·40	1·00

1515 Senghor

2002. 1st Death Anniv of Leopold Sedar Senghor (writer and linguist).

3872	**1515**	46c. multicoloured	1·40	1·00

1516 Baby and "naissance"

2003. Greetings Stamps. Multicoloured.

3873	46c. Type **1516**	1·40	1·00
3874	46c. "MERCI" and oak leaf	1·40	1·00

1517 Heart

2003. St. Valentine's Day. Multicoloured.

3875	46c. Type **1517**	1·40	1·00
3876	69c. Heart and roses	2·10	1·50
MS3877	136×144 mm. As No. 3875×5	7·00	7·00

1518 Face

2003. 40th Anniv of French–German Co-operation Treaty.

3878	**1518**	46c. multicoloured	2·75	2·00

1519 Map

2003. 40th Anniv of Delegation for Land Use Planning and Regional Action (DATAR).

3879	**1519**	46c. multicoloured	1·40	1·00

1520 Genevieve De Gaulle Anthioniz

2003. 1st Death Anniv of Genevieve De Gaulle Anthioniz (resistance fighter and writer).

3880	**1520**	46c. multicoloured	1·40	1·00

1521 Eiffel Tower

2003. Bicentenary of Chamber of Commerce and Industry.

3881	**1521**	46c. multicoloured	1·40	1·00

1522 Lucky Luke

2003. Lucky Luke (cartoon character) by Morris. Multicoloured.

3882	46c. Type **1522**	1·40	1·00
3884	46c.+9c. Lucky Luke and Rantanplan (dog)	2·10	1·10
MS3885	101×75 mm. 46c. As No. 3882	3·50	3·50

1523 Blue-headed Hummingbird

2003. Birds. Multicoloured.

3886	41c. Type **1523**	1·10	80
3887	46c. Toucan	1·40	1·00
3888	46c. Purple-throated carib	1·40	1·00
3889	69c. Mascarene paradise fly-catcher	2·10	1·50
MS3890	110×160 mm. Nos. 3886/9	7·00	7·00

1524 Tram and Nantes Town Hall

2003. Nantes City.

3891	**1524**	46c. multicoloured	1·40	1·00

1525 Pierre Beregovoy

2003. 10th Death Anniv of Pierre Beregovoy (resistance fighter and politician).

3892	**1525**	46c. multicoloured	1·40	1·00

1526 Milan Stefanik

2003. Milan Rastislav Stefanik Commemoration (founder of Czechoslovakia).

3893	**1526**	50c. multicoloured	1·40	1·00

1527 Monsavon Cow and Dubonnet Man (Raymond Savignac)

2003. Europa. Poster Art.

3894	**1527**	50c. multicoloured	2·10	1·50

1528 *Charles de Gaulle* (aircraft carrier) and Dassault Rafale M

2003

3895	**1528**	50c. multicoloured	2·10	1·50

1529 Figure with Winged Shadow

2003. European Union Charter of Fundamental Rights.
3896 **1529** 50c. multicoloured 2·10 1·50

1530 Beach Huts

2003. Regions (1st issue). Sheet 286×110 mm containing T 1530 and similar multicoloured designs.
MS3897 50c. Type **1530**; 50c. Fishing hut; 50c. Vinyards; 50c. Camembert cheese (vert); 50c. Foie gras; 50c. Petanque; 50c. "Guignol" (puppet) (vert); 50c. Crepes (vert); 50c. Cassoulet (casserole); 50c. Porcelain 17·00 17·00

See also Nos. **MS**4083, **MS**4121, **MS**4169, **MS**4209, **MS**4269, **MS**4329, **MS**4379, **MS**4493.

2003. Art. Design as T 491. Multicoloured.
3898 75c. "La Boulee Rouge" (Paul Signac) 2·75 1·50
3899 75c. "The Dying Slave" and "The Rebel Slave" (sculptures, Michelangelo) 2·75 1·50
3900 €1.11 "Untitled" (Vassily Kandinsky) 3·50 2·20

1531 Marsupilami (cartoon character) (Andre Franquin)

2003. Greetings Stamp. Birthday.
3902 **1531** 50c. multicoloured 1·40 1·00

2003. Orchids. As T 1475. Multicoloured.
3903 30c. *Platanthera chlorantha* 1·70 60
3904 35c. *Dactylorhiza savogiensis* 1·80 70

1532 Mulhouse Museums Building and Bugatti Car

2003. 76th French Federation of Philatelic Associations Congress.
3905 **1532** 50c. multicoloured 1·40 1·00

1533 Woman and Children Sunbathing

2003. Holidays. Ordinary or self-adhesive gum.
3906 **1533** 50c. multicoloured 1·80 1·00

2003. Tourist Publicity. As T 490.
3908 50c. multicoloured 1·50 1·00
3909 50c. lilac, orange and green 1·50 1·00
3910 50c. multicoloured 1·50 1·00
3911 50c. multicoloured 1·50 1·00

DESIGNS: No. 3908, Tulle (35×26 mm); No. 3909, Notre-Dame de l'Epine (vert). 50c. Arras (80×24 mm). 50c. Pontarlier (25×39 mm).

1534 Jacqueline Auriol and Dassault Mirage III Fighter

2003. Air. 3rd Death Anniv of Jaqueline Auriol (aviation pioneer).
3912 **1534** €4 multicoloured 12·00 8·00

1535 Square and Compass

2003. 1275th Anniv of French Freemasonry.
3913 **1535** 50c. blue, orange and red 1·50 1·00

1536 Maurice Garin (1903 race winner)

2003. Centenary of Tour de France Cycle Race. Multicoloured.
3914 50c. Type **1536** 1·50 1·00
3915 50c. Modern competitor 1·50 1·00

1537 Saint-Pere-sous-Vezelay Church, Yonne

2003
3916 **1537** 50c. multicoloured 1·50 1·00

1538 Athletes (image scaled to 64% of original size)

2003. 9th IAAF World Athletics Championships, Paris and Saint Denis.
3917 **1538** 50c. multicoloured 1·50 1·00

1539 Eugene-Francois Vidocq (undercover police officer and writer)

2003. Literature. Multicoloured.
3918 50c. Type **1539** 1·50 1·00
3919 50c. Esmeralda (character from *The Hunchback of Notre Dame*, Victor Hugo) 1·50 1·00
3920 50c. Claudine (character from Claudine novels, *Colette*) 1·50 1·00
3921 50c. Nana (character from *Nana*, Emile Zola) 1·50 1·00
3922 50c. Edmond Dantes (character from *The Count of Monte-Cristo*, Alexandre Dumas) 1·50 1·00
3923 50c. Gavroche (character from Les *Miserables*, Victor Hugo) 1·50 1·00
MS3924 135×144 mm. 50c. ×6 Nos. 3918/23 15·00 15·00

No. **MS**3924 was sold with a premium of €1.60 for the benefit of the Red Cross.

1540 Ahmad Massoud

2003. 50th Birth Anniv of Ahmad Shah Massoud (Afghan resistance fighter).
3925 **1540** 50c. multicoloured 1·50 1·00

2003. Regions (2nd issue). Sheet 286×110 mm containing multicoloured designs as T 1530.
MS3926 50c. Chenonceau Chateau; 50c. Alsatian house; 50c. Dormer windows, Hospices de Beaune; 50c. Genoese tower, Cap Corse (vert); 50c. Arc de Triomphe, Paris (vert); 50c. Mas (country house), Provence; 50c. Pointe de Raz (vert); 50c. Mont Blanc (vert); 50c. Basque house; 50c. Pont du Gard (Roman bridge) 18·00 18·00

1541 Buttes-Chaumont Park, Paris

2003. French Gardens. Sheet 286×109 mm containing T 1541 and similar design. Multicoloured.
MS3927 €1.90 Type **1541**; €1.90 Luxembourg Gardens 12·00 12·00

See also No. **MS**3978.

1542 Isobloc Type 648 DP 102 Coach (1954)

2003. Philexjeunes 2003 International Stamp Exhibition, Annely. Utility Vehicles. Sheet 108×183 mm containing T 1542 and similar horiz designs. Multicoloured.
MS3928 20c.×5 Type **1542**; SVF Type 302 tractor (1950); Delahaye Fire appliance with ladder (1938); Renault Kangoo postal van; Renault Type TN6 coach (1932); 30c.×5 Berliet 22 HP Type M delivery truck (1910); Berliet T 100 (1957); Citroen Police van (1960); Heuliez and Citroen DS ambulance; Hotchkiss Type PL 50 rescue truck (1964) 9·00 9·00

1543 "Meilleurs Voeux"

2003. New Year. Ordinary or self-adhesive gum.
3929 **1543** 50c. multicoloured 1·50 1·00

No. 3929 was intended for use by corporate customers.

1544 Robin

2003. New Year. Ordinary or Self-adhesive gum.
3930 **1544** 50c. multicoloured 3·75 2·00

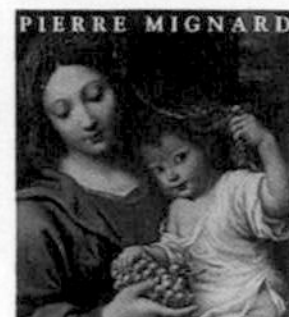

1545 "The Virgin of the Grapes" (Pierre Mignard)

2003. Red Cross Fund. Christmas.
3932 **1545** 50c. multicoloured 2·30 1·30

1546 "The Sower"

2003. Centenary of "The Sower" (sculpture, O. Roty). Self-adhesive.
3933 **1546** 50c. red 3·00 2·00

1547 Notre-Dame Cathedral

2003. European Capitals. Luxembourg. Sheet 144×136 mm containing T 1547 and similar multicoloured designs.
MS3934 50c.×4, Type **1547**; Saint Esprit plateau (vert); Grand Ducal Palace; Adolphe Bridge (vert) 7·50 7·50

1548 "Marilyn"

2003. 16th Death Anniv of Andy Warhol (artist).
3935 **1548** €1.11 multicoloured 3·75 2·20

1549 Cockerel amongst Foliage

2003. 15th-century Illuminations. Multicoloured.
3936 50c. Type **1549** 1·50 1·00
3937 90c. Peacock 3·00 2·00

Stamps of a similar design were issued by India.

1550 *Queen Mary 2*

2003. Launch of Queen Mary 2 (ocean liner).
3938 **1550** 50c. multicoloured 2·30 1·00

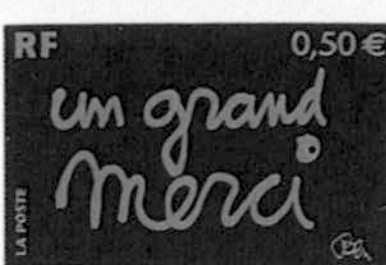

1551 "ceci est une invitation"

2004. Greetings Stamps. Multicoloured.
3939 50c. Type **1551** 2·00 1·00
3940 50c. "un grand merci" 2·00 1·00
See also Nos. 4072/3.

1552 Baby wearing Bee Costume ("c'est une fille")

2004. Greetings Stamps. Multicoloured. Self-adhesive.
3941 50c. Type **1552** 2·00 1·00
3942 50c. Baby wearing butterfly costume ("c'est un garcon") 2·00 1·00

1553 Perfume Bottle

2004. St. Valentine's Day. Multicoloured.
3943 50c. Type **1553** 1·80 1·00
3944 75c. Eiffel tower and woman 3·00 1·50
MS3945 135×143 mm. No. 3944×5 8·25 8·25

2004. Tourist Publicity. As T 490. Multicoloured.
3946 50c. Lille (European capital of culture, 2004) 2·00 1·00
3947 50c. Bridge and tram, Gironde, Bordeaux (79×25 mm) 2·00 1·00
3948 50c. Vaux sur Mer, Charente–Maritime 2·00 1·00
3949 50c. Lucon cathedral, Vendee (vert) 2·00 1·00

2004. Art. As T 491.
3951 75c. multicoloured 2·75 1·50
3952 90c. green, red and gold 3·00 2·00
3953 € 1.11 multicoloured 3·75 2·20
3954 €1.11 multicoloured 3·75 2·20
DESIGN: No. 3951, "La Meridienne d'apres Millet" (Vincent van Gogh); 3952, " The statue of Liberty" (sculpture, Auguste Barthodli) (horiz); 3953, €1.11 "Cock Fight" (Jean-Leon Gerome); 3954 "Galatee aux Spheres" (Salvador Dali).

1554 Eleanor of Aquitaine

2004. 600th Death Anniv of Eleanor of Aquitaine (wife of King Henry II of England).
3955 **1554** 50c. multicoloured 1·70 1·00

1555 Mickey Mouse

2004. 75th Anniv of Mickey Mouse (cartoon character). Multicoloured.
3956 45c. Donald Duck 4·25 2·00
3957 50c. Type **1555** 1·70 1·00
3958 75c. Minnie Mouse 2·50 1·50

1556 Emblem

2004. Bicentenary of Civil Code.
3959 **1556** 50c. blue, black and red 1·70 1·00

1557 George Sand

2004. Birth Bicentenary of George Sand (Aurore Dupin) (writer).
3960 **1557** 50c. multicoloured 1·70 1·00

1558 Vercingetorix (Gaullist leader) (statue) (Auguste Bartholdi)

2004. Clermont-Ferrand, Puy-de-Dome, Auvergne.
3961 **1558** 50c. multicoloured 1·70 1·00

2004. Regions (3rd issue). Sheet 286×110 mm containing multicoloured designs as T 1530.
MS3962 50c.×10 Cutlery; Vegetables of Provence (vert); Grapes, Beaujolais (vert); Bread; Madras cotton Creole headdress (vert); Oyster (vert); Quiche Lorraine; Course Landes, Aquitaine; Clafoutis (fruit flan); Pipe band 20·00 20·00

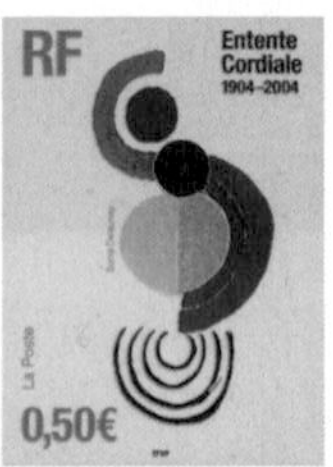

1559 "Coccinelle" (Sonia Delaunay)

2004. Centenary of the Entente Cordiale. Contemporary Paintings.
3963 **1559** 50c. grey, black and rose 1·70 1·00
3964 - 75c. multicoloured 2·50 1·50
DESIGN: 75c. "Lace 1 (trial proof) 1968" (Sir Terry Frost).
Stamps of similar designs were issued by Great Britain.

1560 Heart-shaped Seat Belt Buckle and Body as Map

2004. Road Safety. Two phosphor bands.
3965 **1560** 50c. multicoloured 1·70 1·00

1561 Rabbit

2004. Farm Animals. Multicoloured.
3966 45c. Type **1561** 1·50 90
3967 50c. Hen and chicks 1·70 1·00
3968 50c. Cow (vert) 1·70 1·00
3969 75c. Donkey (vert) 3·00 1·50
MS3970 160×110 mm. Nos. 3966/9 8·25 8·25

1562 Map of EU as Flags

2004. Enlargement of European Union.
3971 **1562** 50c. multicoloured 1·70 1·00

1563 Soldiers and Douglas C-47 Skytrain

2004. 50th Anniv of Battle of Dien Bieen Phu.
3972 **1563** 50c. multicoloured 1·70 1·00

1564 Yachts (painting) (Raoul Dufy)

2004. Europa. Holidays. Ordinary or self-adhesive gum.
3973 **1564** 50c. multicoloured 1·70 1·00

1565 Emblem as Graffiti and Blake and Mortimer

2004. Birth Centenary of Edgar Pierre Jacobs (creator of Blake and Mortimer (comic strip)). Multicoloured.
3975 50c. Type **1565** 1·70 1·00
3976 €1 Blake and Mortimer (horiz) 3·25 2·00
Stamps of a similar design were issued by Belgium.

1566 FIFA Emblem

2004. Centenary of FIFA (Federation Internationale de Football Association).
3977 **1566** 50c. multicoloured 1·70 1·00

2004. French Gardens. Sheet 286×109 mm containing designs as T 1541. Multicoloured.
MS3978 €1.90 Jardin des Tuileries; €1.90 Parc Floral de Paris 13·00 13·00

1567 Woman throwing Flowers to Soldiers

2004. 60th Anniv of Liberation of France.
3979 **1567** 50c. multicoloured 1·70 1·00

1568 Smiling Hand and Organs

2004. Organ Donation Campaign.
3980 **1568** 50c. multicoloured 1·70 1·00

1569 Mounted Rifleman

2004. Napoleon I's Imperial Guard. Multicoloured.
3981 50c. Type **1569** 1·70 1·00
3982 50c. Gunner (horiz) 1·70 1·00
3983 50c. Dragoon 1·70 1·00
3984 50c. Mameluk 1·70 1·00
3985 50c. Napoleon I 1·70 1·00
3986 50c. Bombardier 1·70 1·00
MS3987 135×143 mm. Nos. 3981/6 17·00 17·00
No. **MS**3987 was sold at €4.60, the premium for the benefit of the Red Cross.

1570 Pierre Dugua de Mons (founder of Arcadia)

2004. 400th Anniv of French Landing in Maine, USA and Nova Scotia.
3988 **1570** 90c. blue and ochre 3·25 2·00

1571 Eiffel Tower holding Postcard

2004. 77th French Federation of Philatelic Associations Congress.
3989 **1571** 50c. multicoloured 1·80 1·00

1572 Canoeist, Tennis Player and Show Jumper

2004. Olympic Games Athens 2004. Sheet 183×108 mm containing T 1572 and similar horiz designs. Multicoloured.
MS3990 50c.×10, Type **1572**×5; Early Greek athletes×5 18·00 18·00

2004. French Gardens. Salon du Timber. Sheet 210×143 mm Containing design as T 1541. Multicoloured.
MS3990a As Nos. **MS**3927 and **MS**3978 27·00 27·00

1573 Marie Marvingt and Bleriot XI

2004. 40th Death Anniv (2003) of Marie Marvingt (aviation pioneer).
3991 **1573** €5 multicoloured 20·00 11·00

1574 Waiter carrying Candlelit Cake

2004. Greetings Stamp.
3992 **1574** 50c. multicoloured 1·80 1·00
MS3993 135×143 mm. No. 3992×5 9·00 9·00

1575 Marianne and Emblem

2004. Campaign to Combat AIDS, Tuberculosis and Malaria.
3994 **1575** (50c.) bright scarlet 1·80 1·00

1576 Skateboarding

2004. Sport. Multicoloured.
MS3995 108×184 mm. 20c.×5, Type **1576**; Parachuting; Windsurfing; Surfing; Tobogganing; 30c.×5, BMX cycling; Paragliding; Jet skiing; Snowboarding; Roller skating 9·00 9·00

2004. Regions (4th issue). Sheet 286×110 mm containing multicoloured designs as T 1530.
MS3996 50c.×10 Thatched house, Normandy; Chateau, Chambord; Gorge, Tarn (vert); Notre Dame cathedral, Paris (vert); Northern windmill (vert); Troglodyte houses; Stream, Cassis (vert); Lighthouse, Cap Ferrat (vert); Cathar chateau; Alpine chalet 20·00 20·00

1577 Pumpkin and Witch

2004. Halloween.
3997 **1577** 50c. multicoloured 1·80 1·00

1578 Felix Eboue

2004. 120th Birth Anniv of Felix Eboue (politician).
3998 **1578** 50c. multicoloured 1·80 1·00

1579 Lighthouse, Ouistreham

2004
3999 **1579** 50c. multicoloured 1·80 1·00

1580 Virgin and Child (15th-century Cretan school)

2004. Red Cross Fund. Christmas.
4000 **1580** 50c. multicoloured 2·75 1·50

2004. 60th Anniv of "Marianne d'Alger". Two phosphor bands. Self-adhesive.
4001 **209** 50c. scarlet 2·50 2·00

1581 Academy

2004. European Capitals. Athens. Sheet 144×134 mm containing T 1581 and similar multicoloured designs.
MS4002 50c.×4, Type **1581**; Parthenon; Odeon of Herode Atticus; Church of the Holy Apostles (vert) 9·00 9·00

1582 "Meilleurs Voeux"

2004. Christmas and New Year.
4003 **1582** 50c. multicoloured 1·80 1·00

1583 "Meilleurs Voeux" and Bird

2004. Christmas and New Year. Multicoloured. Ordinary gum or self-adhesive gum.
4004 50c. Type **1583** 3·50 1·60
4005 50c. Baubles hanging from branch 3·50 1·60
4006 50c. Stars holding snowballs 3·50 1·60
4007 50c. Star holding flower 3·50 1·60
4008 50c. Stars 3·50 1·60

1584 Henri Wallon

2004. Death Centenary of Henri Wallon (politician).
4014 **1584** 50c. multicoloured 1·80 1·00

1585 Millau Viaduct (image scaled to 63% of original size)

2004
4015 **1585** 50c. multicoloured 2·75 1·00

1586 "Marianne de Francais"

2005. (i) With face value.

4016	**1586**	1c. yellow	35	15
4017	**1586**	5c. agate	35	15
4018	**1586**	10c. black	55	15
4019	**1586**	10c. violet	55	15
4025	**1586**	55c. ultramarine	2·75	50
4027	**1586**	58c. yellow	2·75	85
4028	**1586**	60c. ultramarine	2·30	30
4030	**1586**	64c. green	2·75	60
4031a	**1586**	70c. green	2·75	40
4031b	**1586**	72c. green	2·75	40
4032	**1586**	75c. blue	2·75	75
4034	**1586**	82c. rose	3·50	80
4034a	**1586**	85c. violet	3·50	80
4034b	**1586**	86c. rose	3·50	80
4034c	**1586**	88c. rose	3·50	80
4035	**1586**	90c. indigo	3·50	1·50
4036	**1586**	€1 orange	5·25	1·00
4040	**1586**	€1.11 purple	6·25	2·00
4040a	**1586**	€1.15 blue	4·00	50
4041	**1586**	€1.22 purple	5·25	1·30
4041a	**1586**	€1.25 cobalt	4·50	55
4042	**1586**	€1.30 purple	4·50	65
4042a	**1586**	€1.33 purple	5·25	60
4045	**1586**	€1.90 brown	6·75	1·80
4046	**1586**	€1.98 purple	8·50	1·80
4048	**1586**	€2.11 claret	7·50	1·00
4048a	**1586**	€2.18 chocolate	8·00	85

(ii) Without face value.
4050 (45c.) emerald 1·80 15
4051 (50c.) scarlet 2·10 20
4052 (65c.) blue 3·50 60

(iii) Self-adhesive.
4057 (50c.+20c.) scarlet 2·20 20
4058 (65c.) blue 3·50 1·00

1587 "Solidarite Asie"

2005. Red Cross Fund. For Victims of the Tsunami Disaster.
4060 **1587** (50c.)+20c. scarlet 2·50 1·40

1588 Rashi

2005. 900th Death Anniv of Rabbi Solomon bar Isaac (Rashi) of Troyes (Biblical and Talmudic scholar).
4061 **1588** 50c. ultramarine, green and brown 1·80 1·00

1589 Rooster

2005. New Year. "Year of the Rooster".
4062 **1589** (50c.) multicoloured 1·80 1·00

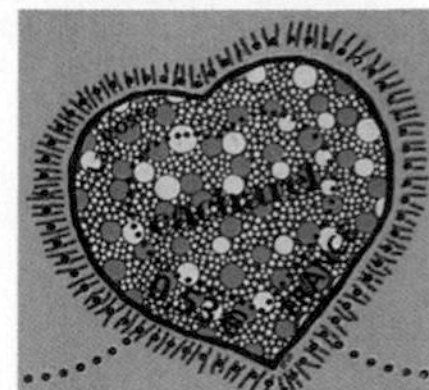
1590 Heart

2005. St. Valentine's Day. Multicoloured.
4063 53c. Type **1590** 2·00 1·10
4064 82c. Heart containing bird 3·00 1·70
MS4065 136×144 mm. 53c.×5, As No. 4063×5 9·75 9·75

2005. Orchids. Aas T 1475.
4066 **1475** 39c. multicoloured 1·80 1·00
No. 4066 was only issued pre-cancelled in black.

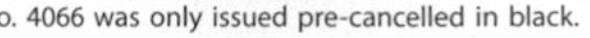

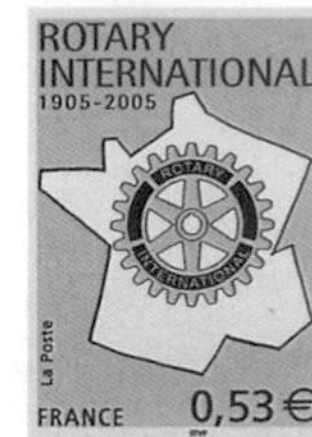

1591 Emblem

2005. Centenary of Rotary International (charitable organization). Ordinary or self-adhesive gum.
4067 **1591** 53c. lemon, ultramarine and vermilion 1·80 1·10

1592 Manu

2005. Titeuf (cartoon created by Philippe Chappuis (Zep). Multicoloured.
4069 (45c.) Type **1592** 3·25 2·00
4068 (50c.) Titeuf 1·60 1·00
4071 (90c.) Nadia 3·00 1·80

2005. Greetings Stamps. As T 1551. Multicoloured.
4072 (53c.) As No. 3939 1·80 1·10
4073 (53c.) As No. 3940 1·80 1·10
Nos. 4072/3 were for use on mail within France weighing 20 grams or less.

2005. Art Design. As T 491.
4074 82c. multicoloured 2·75 1·70
4075 90c. multicoloured 3·00 1·80
4076 €1.22 multicoloured 4·00 2·50
4077 €1.22 multicoloured 4·00 2·50
DESIGNS: No. 4074, 82c. "Le guitariste" (Jean-Baptiste Greuze) (36×48 mm); 4075, "Ours Blanc" (sculpture, Francois Pompon) (48×38 mm); 4706, "Sicile" (painting, Nicolas de Stael) (48×38 mm); 4077, €1.22 Les Halles Centrales (Victor Baltard) (architect) (birth bicentenary)) (48×38 mm).

1593 *Paphiopedilum* "Mabel Saunders"

2005. Orchids. Multicoloured.
4078 53c. Type **1593** 1·80 1·10
4079 53c. *Cypripedium calceolus* 1·80 1·10
4080 55c. *Oncidium papilio* 1·80 1·10
4081 82c. *Paphinia cristata* (horiz) 2·75 1·70
MS4082 110×160 mm. Nos. 4078/81 8·00 8·00

2005. Regions (5th issue). Sheet 286×110 mm containing multicoloured designs as T 1530.
MS4083 53c.×10 Nautical jousting; Clocks (vert); Cantal cheese (vert); Accordion player; Bouillabaisse (soup); Le P'tit Quinquin (statue), Lille (vert); Les rillettes (pig meat); La choucroute (fermented cabbage, sausages, pork and potatoes); Pelote player (vert); Sugar cane (vert) 18·00 18·00

2005. Tourist Publicity. As T 490. Multicoloured.

4084	53c. Aix-en-Provence	1·80	1·10
4085	53c. Golfe du Mobihan (75×23 mm)	1·80	1·10
4086	53c. Villefranche-sur-Mer	1·80	1·10
4087	53c. La Roque-Gageac	1·80	1·10

1594 Becassine (character created by Caumery and Pinchon)

2005. Greetings Stamp. Birthday.

4088	**1594**	(53c.) multicoloured	1·80	1·10

1595 Albert Einstein

2005. 50th Death Anniv of Albert Einstein (physicist). International Year of Physics.

4089	**1595**	53c. multicoloured	1·80	1·10

1596 Alexis de Tocqueville

2005. Birth Bicentenary of Alexis de Tocqueville (sociologist).

4090	**1596**	90c. multicoloured	3·00	1·80

1597 Prisoner supported by American and Russian Soldiers

2005. 60th Anniv of Liberation of Concentration Camps.

4091	**1597**	53c. multicoloured	1·80	1·10

1598 Napoleon I

2005. Bicentenary of the Battle of Austerlitz.

4092	**1598**	55c. multicoloured	1·80	1·10

A stamp of the same design was issued by Czech Republic.

1599 Stanislas Place, Nancy (image scaled to 62% of original size)

2005. Federation of French Philatelic Association Congress, Nancy.

4093	**1599**	53c. multicoloured	1·80	1·10

1600 Chef and Table

2005. Europa. Gastronomy.

4094	**1600**	53c. multicoloured	1·80	1·10

1601 Jardin de la Fontaine, Nimes

2005. French Gardens. Sheet 285×110 mm containing T 1601 and similar design. Mult.

MS4095	€1.98×2, Type **1601**; Cherubs and vase	13·00	13·00

1602 Woman and Beach Huts

2005. Holidays. Self-adhesive. No value expressed.

4096	**1602**	(53c.) multicoloured	1·80	1·10

No. 4096 was for use on letters up 20g.

1603 Octopus (*20,000 Leagues under the Sea*)

2005. Death Centenary of Jules Verne (writer). Multicoloured.

4097	53c. Type **1603**	1·80	1·10
4098	53c. *Five Weeks in a Balloon*	1·80	1·10
4099	53c. *Around the World in Eighty Days*	1·80	1·10
4100	53c. *From the Earth to the Moon*	1·80	1·10
4101	53c. *Michael Strogoff* (horiz)	1·80	1·10
4102	53c. *Voyage to the Centre of the Earth* (horiz)	1·80	1·10
MS4103	135×144 Nos. 4097/4102 (sold at €4.80)	16·00	16·00

No. **MS**4103 was sold with a premium of €1.62 for the benefit of the Red Cross.

1604 Formula 1 Race Car

2005. Centenary of First French Gordon Bennett Cup Race. Multicoloured.

4104	53c. Type **1604**	1·80	1·10
4105	53c. Van in sand (Paris—Dakar race)	1·80	1·10
4106	53c. Two rally cars (horiz)	1·80	1·10
4107	53c. Race car (Endurance race) (horiz)	1·80	1·10
4108	53c. Early race car facing right (horiz)	1·80	1·10
4109	53c. Early race car facing left (horiz)	1·80	1·10

1605 Hands, Swallow and Mountain (image scaled to 61% of original size)

2005. Environmental Charter.

4110	**1605**	53c. multicoloured	1·80	1·10

1606 Hand holding Figure

2005. February 11th Law (equal rights for the disabled).

4111	**1606**	53c. multicoloured	1·80	1·10

1607 Baby asleep in Flower ("c'est une fille")

2005. Greetings Stamps. No value expressed. Self-adhesive. Multicoloured.

4112	(53c.) Type **1607**	1·80	1·10
4113	(53c.) Baby facing right ("c'est un garcon")	1·80	1·10

Nos. 4112/13 were for use on letters up to 20g.

2005. Valentine's Day. As T 1553 and T 1590. Self-adhesive.

4114	50c. As Type No. 1553	1·60	1·00
4115	53c. As Type **1590**	1·80	1·10
4116	75c. As No. 3944	2·40	1·50
4117	82c. As No. 4064	2·75	1·70

1608 Horse's Head and Building Facade

2005. Le Haras du Pin (Royal stud and stables).

4118	**1608**	53c. multicoloured	1·80	1·10

1609 Brandenburg Gate

2005. European Capitals. Berlin. Sheet 144×134 mm containing T 1609 and similar multicoloured designs.

MS4119	53c.×4, Type **1609**; Kaiser Wilhelm Memorial Church (vert); Philharmonie; Reichstag	7·00	7·00

2005. Orchids. As T 1475.

4120	**1475**	39c. multicoloured	1·50	95

2005. Regions (6th issue). Sheet 286×110 mm containing multicoloured designs as T 1530.

MS4121	53c.×10 D'Annecy Lake; Les falaises d'Etretat (vert); Pigeon loft (vert); Pool Lavoir; Banks of Seine; Megaliths, Carnac, Solognote house; Dunes, Pilat; Old lighthouse, Stiff (vert); Borie (dry stone hut) (vert)	18·00	18·00

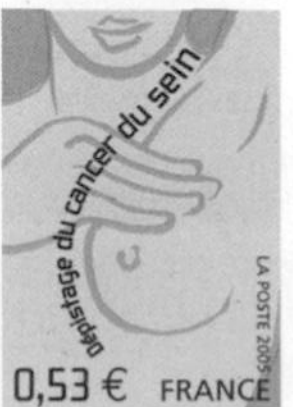

1610 Self-Examination

2005. Breast Cancer Awareness Campaign.

4122	**1610**	53c. multicoloured	1·80	1·10

1611 Cat holding Stamp

2005. "Sourires". Designs showing "Cat" (cartoon character created by Philippe Geluck). Multicoloured. Self-adhesive.

4123	(53c.) Type **1611**	1·80	1·10
4124	(53c.) Seated at typewriter	1·80	1·10
4125	(53c.) With female cat	1·80	1·10
4126	(53c.) With diagram of human	1·80	1·10
4127	(53c.) Wearing satchel containing envelopes	1·80	1·10
4128	(53c.) Holding letter	1·80	1·10
4129	(53c.) Writing letter	1·80	1·10
4130	(53c.) With folded arms/paws	1·80	1·10
4131	(53c.) On stage	1·80	1·10
4132	(53c.) Holding stamps (different)	1·80	1·10

Nos. 4123/32 were issued in booklets of ten stamps for use on mail within France weighing 20 grams or less.

1612 Raymond Aron

2005. Birth Centenary of Raymond Aron (philosopher).

4133	**1612**	53c. blue, indigo and black	1·80	1·10

1613 Adrienne Bolland, Andes and Caudron G3

2005. 30th Death Anniv of Adrienne Bolland (1st woman to fly over the Andes).

4134	**1613**	€2 multicoloured	6·50	4·00

1614 Link

2005. Video Game Characters. Sheet 109×184 mm containing T 1614 and similar horiz designs. Multicoloured.

MS4135	20c.×5, Type **1614**; Pac-Man; Prince of Persia; Spyro; Donkey Kong. 33c.×5, Mario; Adibou; Rayman; Lara Croft; Les Sims	9·75	9·75

1615 "Marianne Dulac"

2005. 60th Anniv of "Marianne Dulac" (stamp designed by Edmond Dulac). Self-adhesive. 60th Anniv of "Marianna Dula" (stamp designed by Edmond Dulac).

4136	**1615**	53c. scarlet	1·80	1·10

1616 Virgin and Child (Hans Memling)

2005. Red Cross Fund. Christmas.

4137	**1616**	53c. multicoloured	2·20	1·40

1617 "The Annunciation"

2005. Art. "The Annunciation" by Raffello Sanzio (Raphael). Sheet 131×86 mm containing T 1617 and similar horiz design.
MS4138 53c. Type **1617**; 55c. "The Annunciation" (different) 3·50 3·50

Stamps of a similar design were issued by Vatican City.

1618 Avicenne

2005. 1025th Birth Anniv of Avicenne (Ibn Sina) (doctor and philosopher).
4139 **1618** 53c. multicoloured 1·80 1·10

1619 Bear and Penguin pulling Sledge

2005. Christmas and New Year. No Value expressed. Self-adhesive . Multicoloured.

4140	(53c.) Type **1619**	1·80	1·10
4141	(53c.) Penguins, deer and snowman	1·80	1·10
4142	(53c.) Penguins and deer on sledge	1·80	1·10
4143	(53c.) Penguins holding snowballs	1·80	1·10
4144	(53c.) Bear and penguins on sledge	1·80	1·10

Nos. 4140/4 were for use on letters weighing up to 20 grams.

1620 Jacob Kaplan

2005. 110th Birth Anniv of Jacob Kaplan (chief Rabbi).
4145 **1620** 53c. multicoloured 1·80 1·10

1621 Church Tower and Document

2005. Centenary of Law separating Church and State.
4146 **1621** 53c. multicoloured 1·80 1·10

1622 Heart containing Hearts

2006. St. Valentine's Day. No value expressed. Multicoloured.

4147	(53c.) Type **1622**	1·80	1·10
4148	(82c.) Heart containing jewelled heart	2·75	1·70
MS4148a	136×144 mm. 53c.×5, As No. 4147×5	9·25	9·25

No. 4147/8 also come self-adhesive.

No. 4147 was for use on letters up to 20 grams and Nos. 4148 and 4150 for letters up to 50 grams.

1623 Dog

2006. New Year. Year of the Dog. No value expressed.
4151 **1623** (53c.) multicoloured 1·80 1·10

No. 4151 was for use on letters up to 20 grams.

1624 "Portraits a la Campagne" (Gustave Caillebotte)

2006. Impressionist Paintings. Multicoloured. Self-adhesive.

4152	(53c.) Type **1624**	1·80	1·10
4153	(53c.) "La Chasse aux Papillons" (Berthe Morisot)	1·80	1·10
4154	(53c.) "Mere et Enfant" (Mary Cassat)	1·80	1·10
4155	(53c.) "Jeunes Filles au Piano" (Auguste Renoir)	1·80	1·10
4156	(53c.) "La Beregere" (Camille Pissarro)	1·80	1·10
4157	(53c.) "Mademoiselle Gachet dans son Jardin" (Vincent van Gogh)	1·80	1·10
4158	(53c.) "L'air du Soir" (Henri-Edmond Cross)	1·80	1·10
4159	(53c.) "Danseuses" (Edgar Degas)	1·80	1·10
4160	(53c.) "Le Dejeuner sur L'Herbe (Eduard Manet)	1·80	1·10
4161	(53c.) "Femmes de Tahiti" (Paul Gauguin)	1·80	1·10

Nos. 4152/61 were for use on letters up to 20 grams.

1625 Biathlon

2006. Winter Olympic Games, Turin.
4162 **1625** 53c. multicoloured 1·80 1·10

1626 Spirou

2006. 70th Anniv of Spirou (cartoon character drawn by Jose Luis Munuera). Multicoloured.

4164	(48c.) Spirou and Fantasio	1·40	90
4163	(53c.) Type **1626**	1·80	1·10
4165	(90c.) Fantasio	2·75	1·80

No. 4163 was for use on second class, No. 4164 was for use on first class and No. 4165 was for use on international mail up to 20 grams.

1627 Miner

2006. Centenary of Courrieres Mine Disaster.
4166 **1627** 53c. multicoloured 1·80 1·10

1628 Graves and Cloister

2006. Douaumont Ossuary (war grave).
4167 **1628** 53c. green, blue and brown 1·80 1·10

1629 Village from Lake

2006. 700th Anniv of Yvoire, Haute-Savoie.
4168 **1629** 53c. multicoloured 1·80 1·10

2006. Regions (7th issue). Sheet 286×110 mm containing multicoloured designs as T 1530.
MS4169 53c.×10, Fruit (La mirabelle); Les marais salant; Butter (le beurre); Roquefort cheese (vert); Olive oil (vert); Child in headdress (Le carnaval) (vert), Grapes (Les vendanges) (vert); Waiter (vert); Crops and punt (Les hortillomages) 18·00 18·00

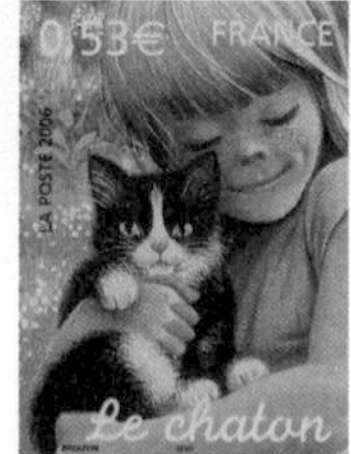

1630 Well of Moses (Claus Sluter) and St. Benigne Church

2006. Dijon, Cote-d'Or.
4170 **1630** 53c. multicoloured 1·80 1·10

1631 "The Bathers"

2006. Death Centenary of Paul Cezanne (artist).
4171 **1631** 82c. multicoloured 2·75 1·70

1632 Girl holding Kitten

2006. Young Domestic Animals. Multicoloured.

4172	53c. Type **1632**	1·90	1·10
4173	53c. Puppy	1·90	1·10
4174	55c. Foal (horiz)	1·90	1·10
4175	82c. Lamb (horiz)	2·75	1·70
MS4176	110×161 mm. Nos. 4173/5	8·00	8·00

The stamps and margins of **MS**4176 form a composite design of children and young animals.

1633 Parc de la Valle aux Loups

2006. French Gardens. Sheet 285×110 mm containing T 1633 and similar design. Multicoloured.
MS4177 €1.98×2, Type **1633**; Bridge, Albert Kahn gardens 13·50 13·50

1634 Faces and Stars

2006. Europa. Integration.
4178 **1634** 53c. multicoloured 1·90 1·10

1635 Pierre Bayle

2006. 300th Death Anniv of Pierre Bayle (philosopher).
4179 **1635** 53c. green, blue and brown 1·90 1·10

1636 Figure connected to Broken Chain

2006. Abolition of Slavery Day.
4180 **1636** 53c. multicoloured 1·90 1·10

1637 Animals

2006. 50th Anniv of Discovery of Rouffignac Caves, Dordogne.
4181 **1637** 55c. multicoloured 2·00 1·20

1638 Substitutes

2006. World Cup Football Championship, Germany. Sheet 211×143 mm containing T 1639 and similar multicoloured designs.
MS4182 53c.×10, Type **1638**; Supporters; Ball at chest (Controle) (circular) (32×32 mm); Centre (circular) (32×32 mm); Throw in (Degagement) (circular) (32×32 mm); Kicking from horizontal (Retourne) (circular) (32×32 mm); Tackling (Feitne de corps) (circular) (32×32 mm); Referee (vert); Trainers; Journalists 17·00 17·00

1639 Woman in Hammock

2006. Holidays. Self Adhesive.
4183 **1639** (53c.) multicoloured 1·90 1·10

No. 4182 was issued for use on internal mail weighing up to 20 grams.

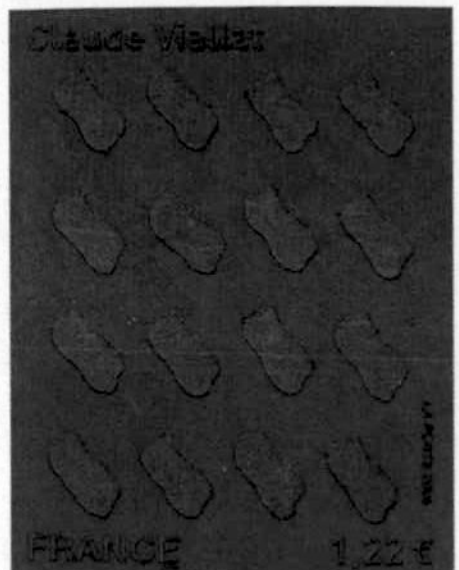

1640 Untitled

2006. 70th Birth Anniv of Claude Viallat (artist).

4184 **1640** €1.22 magenta and green 4·00 2·50

1641 "The Abduction from the Seraglio" (Varona)

2006. Operas by Wolfgang Amadeus Mozart. Costume Designs. Multicoloured.

4185 53c. Type **1641** 1·90 1·10
4186 53c. "Cosi fan Tutte" (Erte) 1·90 1·10
4187 53c. "The Magic Flute" (Chapelin-Midy) 1·90 1·10
4188 53c. "Don Giovanni" (Marillier) 1·90 1·10
4189 53c. "The Marriage of Figaro" (Enzio Frigerio) 1·90 1·10
4190 53c. "The Clemency of Titus" (Graf) 1·90 1·10
MS4191 136×143 mm. Nos. 4185/90 14·50 14·50

1642 Provins

2006. World Heritage Sites. Multicoloured.

4192 53c. Type **1642** 1·90 1·10
4193 90c. Mont Saint Michel 3·00 1·80

Stamps of a similar design were issued by United Nations.

2006. Salon de Timbre (European Stamp Salon). Sheet 212×143 mm containing vert designs as T 1601. Multicoloured.

MS4194 €1.98×4, Jardin de la Fontaine, Nimes (T **1601**) (**MS**4095); Cherubs and vase (**MS**4095); Parc de la Vallee aux Loups; Bridge (**MS**4177); Albert Kahn gardens (**MS**4177) 19·00 19·00

1643 Building Facade

2006. Opera Garnier. 79th French Philatelic Association Congress.

4195 **1643** 53c. olive, blue and lemon 1·90 1·10

1644 Babar

2006. Greetings Stamp. Birthdays.

4196 **1644** (53c.) multicoloured 1·90 1·10

No. 4196 was for use on letters up to 20g.

1645 Chrysaliniotissa Church

2006. European Capitals. Nicosia. Sheet 144×134 mm containing T 1645 and similar horiz designs. Multicoloured.

MS4197 53c.×4, Type **1645**; Archaeological Museum; Famagouste Gate; Archbishop's Palace 7·50 7·50

1646 Dancers

2006. Tango. Multicoloured.

4198 53c. Type **1646** 1·90 1·10
4199 90c. Musician 3·00 1·80

Stamps of a similar design were issued by Argentina.

1647 "@"

2006. 10th Anniv of La Poste's Business Foundation.

4200 **1647** (53c.) orange, rosine and black 1·90 1·10

No. 4200 was for use on letters up to 20g.

1648 Airbus A380

2006. Air.

4201 **1648** €3 multicoloured 10·00 6·00

1649 Golfers

2006. France Open Golf Tournament.

4202 **1649** 53c. blue and rosine 1·90 1·10

1649a Arms and Football

2006. Thank you "Les Bleus" (celebration of French team reaching semi-final of World Cup Football Championship).

4203 **1649a** 53c. multicoloured 1·90 1·90

1650 Statue and Building (image scaled to 61% of original size)

2006. Opening of Quai Branley Museum (designed by Jean Nouvel).

4204 **1650** 53c. multicoloured 1·90 1·10

1651 Receiving Legion d'Honneur

2006. Centenary of Rehabilitation of Captain Richard Dreyfus.

4205 **1651** 53c. multicoloured 1·90 1·10

1652 Rouget de Lisle

2006. 170th Death Anniv of Rouget de Lisle (writer of "Marsailles" (national anthem)).

4205 **1652** 53c. multicoloured 1·90 1·10

1653 Town and Walls

2006. Antibes Juan-les-Pins.

4207 **1653** 53c. multicoloured 1·90 1·10

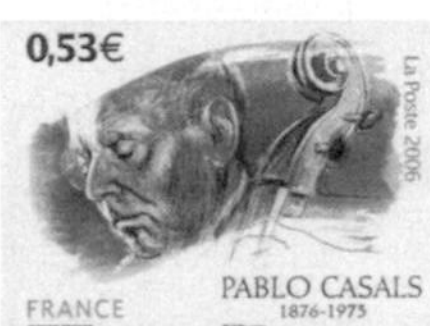

1654 Pablo Casals

2006. 130th Birth Anniv of Pablo Casals (cellist).

4208 **1654** 53c. multicoloured 1·90 1·10

2006. Regions (8th issue). Sheet 251×110 mm containing multicoloured designs as T 1530.

MS4209 54c.×10, Castle on rocks (Tours catalanes); Beach (La Croisette); Grave (La foret de Broceliande); Tree-covered crater (Les volcans d'Auvergne) (vert); Building at night (Les Invalides) (vert); Le chateau de Chaumont-sur-Loire, Rock bridge (Les gorges de l'Ardeche) (vert); Le moulin de Valmy (vert); La grotte de Lourdes; Cliffs (Calanche de Piana) 16·00 16·00

1657 Thionville, Moselle

2006

4210 **1657** 54c. multicoloured 1·90 1·10

1658 Cubitus as Stamp on Letter to Senechal

2006. "Sourires". Designs showing "Cubitus" (cartoon character created by Dupa (Luc Dupanloup)). Multicoloured. Self-adhesive.

4211 (54c.) Type **1658** 1·90 1·10
4212 (54c.) With stamp stuck on nose 1·90 1·10
4213 (54c.) With puppy 1·90 1·10
4214 (54c.) With Senechal, Semaphore and puppy 1·90 1·10
4215 (54c.) Holding envelopes by open letterbox 1·90 1·10
4216 (54c.) Dressed as Marianne 1·90 1·10
4217 (54c.) Holding letter with hearts 1·90 1·10
4218 (54c.) With Semaphore 1·90 1·10
4219 (54c.) With snail 1·90 1·10
4220 (54c.) Hand stroking Cubitus 1·90 1·10

Nos. 4211/20 were for use on mail within France weighing 20 grams or less.

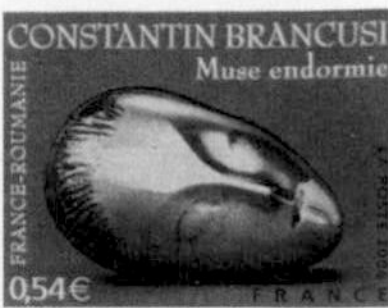

1659 "Muse endormie"

2006. 130th Birth Anniv of Constantin Brancusi (sculptor). Multicoloured.

4221 54c. Type **1659** 1·90 1·10
4222 85c. "Le sommeil" 2·75 1·70

Stamps of a similar design were issued by Romania.

1660 Cessna 208 Caravan, Child and Aid Box

2006. Aviation Sans Frontieres (humanitarian organization).

4223 **1660** 54c. multicoloured 1·90 1·10

1661 Henri Moisson

2006. Death Centenary (2007) of Henri Moissan (winner of Nobel Prize for Chemistry—1906).

4224 **1661** 54c. multicoloured 1·90 1·10

1662 "Memoire Partagee" (shared memory)

2006. UNESCO First International Conference—"Memory of the World".

4225 **1662** 54c. multicoloured 1·90 1·10

1663 Marianne

2006. 60th Anniv of Marianne de Gandon (stamp designed by P. Gandon). Multicoloured. Self-adhesive.

4226 54c. Type **1663** 1·90 1·10
4227 (54c.) As No. 4051 1·90 1·10

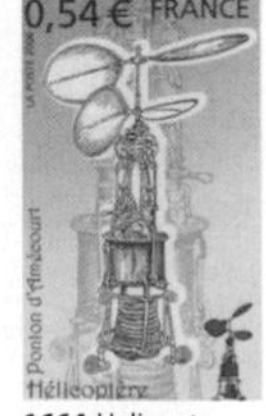

1664 Helicopter (helicoptere) (Gustave de Ponton d'Amecourt) (1863)

2006. Flying Machines. Multicoloured.

4228 54c. Type **1664** 1·90 1·10
4229 54c. *Demoiselle* (Alberto Santos-Dumont) (1908) (horiz) 1·90 1·10
4230 54c. Flying boat (barque ailee) (Jean-Marie le Bris) (1856) (horiz) 1·90 1·10
4231 54c. *Avion III* (Clement Ader) (1897) (horiz) 1·90 1·10
4232 54c. Hydravion (hydravion) (Henri Fabre) (1910) (horiz) 1·90 1·10
4233 54c. Balloon with oars (ballon a rames) (Jean-Pierre Blanchard) (1784) 1·90 1·10

1665 "Three Beggars at the Door of a House" (etching)

2006. 400th Birth Anniv of Rembrandt Harmenszoon van Rijn (artist).

4234 **1665** €1.30 sepia, brown and red 4·50 2·50

1666 Engine

2006. Tram-Train (from Aulnay-sous-Bois to Bondy) (1st issue).

4235 **1666** 54c. multicoloured 1·90 1·10

1667 "Fleur" (Yacine Lorafy)

2006. Red Cross Fund. Christmas. Children's Paintings. Multicoloured.

4236 (54c.) Type **1667** 1·90 1·10
4237 (54c). "Petite fleur" (Margot Deram) 1·90 1·10

Nos. 4236/7 were for use on letters weighing up to 20 grams.

1668 Penguins pulling Sledge carrying Reindeer

2006. Christmas and New Year. No Value expressed. Multicoloured. Self-adhesive.

4238 (54c.) Type **1668** 1·90 1·10
4239 (54c.) Reindeer and penguins fishing 1·90 1·10
4240 (54c.) Reindeer and penguins dressing tree 1·90 1·10
4241 (54c.) Reindeer skating 1·90 1·10
4242 (54c.) Reindeer, penguins and parcels 1·90 1·10

Nos. 4238/42 were for use on letters weighing up to 20 grams.

1669 Square and Compass

2006. National Grand Lodge of Masons.

4243 **1669** 54c. ultramarine and grey 1·90 1·10

1670 Alain Poher

2006. 10th Death Anniv of Alain Poher (politician and twice interim president).

4244 **1670** 54c. multicoloured 1·90 1·10

1671 Tram

2006. Paris Tramway (return of trams to southern Paris).

4245 **1671** 54c. multicoloured 1·90 1·10

2007. Orchids. As T 1475. Multicoloured.

4246 31c. As No. 3903 1·10 65
4247 36c. As No. 3904 1·30 75
4248 43c. As Type **1475** 1·60 95

Nos. 3246/8 were only issued pre-cancelled in black.

1672 Decorated Heart

2007. St. Valentine's Day. No value expressed. Multicoloured. Ordinary gum.

4249 **1672** (54c.) scarlet and black 1·90 1·10
4250 **1672** (86c.) black and vermilion 2·75 1·70
MS4251 136×144 mm. (54c.)×5, As No. 4249×5 9·25 9·25

(b) Self-adhesive

4252 (54c.) scarlet and black 1·90 1·10
4253 (86c.) black and vermillion 2·75 1·70

No. 4249 and 4251 were for use on letters up to 20 grams and No. 4250 and 4252 for letters up to 50 grams.

1673 Pig

2007. New Year. Year of the Pig. No value expressed.

4254 **1673** (54c.) multicoloured 1·90 1·10

No. 4254 was for use on letters up to 20 grams.

1674 Hippopotamus (Egypt)

2007. Antiquities. No Value expressed. Multicoloured. Self-adhesive.

4255 (54c.) Type **1674** 1·90 1·10
4256 (54c.) Aphrodite (Greece) 1·90 1·10
4257 (54c.) Victory of Samothrace (Greece) 1·90 1·10
4258 (54c.) Fresco from Pompeii (Rome) 1·90 1·10
4259 (54c.) Amenemhat III (Egypt) 1·90 1·10
4260 (54c.) Juno (Rome) 1·90 1·10
4261 (54c.) Harpist (Egypt) 1·90 1·10
4262 (54c.) Etruscan sarcophagus 1·90 1·10
4263 (54c.) Scribe (Egypt) 1·90 1·10
4264 (54c.) Pericles (Greece) 1·90 1·10

Nos. 4255/64 were for use on letters weighing up to 20 grams.

1675 Watteau Fountain

2007. Valenciennes.

4265 **1675** 54c. blue and vermilion 1·90 1·10

1676 Pantheon, Paris

2007. Justes de France.

4266 **1676** 54c. blue and black 1·90 1·10

1677 Illuminated Letter

2007. Humanist Library, Selestat.

4267 **1677** 60c. multicoloured 2·00 1·20

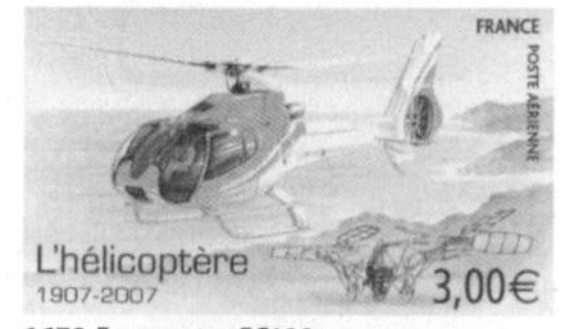

1678 Eurocopter EC130

2007. Centenary of the Helicopter.

4268 **1678** €3 multicoloured 10·00 7·00

2007. Regions (9th issue). Sheet 251×110 mm containing multicoloured designs as T 1530.

MS4269 54c.×10, Hill town (Les Baux-de-Provence); Beach (Bords de Loire); Mountains (Le massif de la Grande-Chartreuse); Harbour (Saint Tropez); Waterfall (Cascade Doubs) (vert); Rocks and trees (Le foret de Fontainebleau) (vert); Chateau reflected in water (Le chateau de Chantilly); Seawall (Saint-Malo); Flowers (Le ballon d'Alsace) (vert); Towpath (Le canal du Midi) (vert) 17·00 17·00

1679 Harry Potter (Daniel Radcliffe)

2007. Fete du Timbres. "Harry Potter" (character created by J. K. Rowling). No Value expressed. Multicoloured.

4270 (54c.) Type **1679** 1·90 1·10
4271 (54c.) Hermione Granger (Emma Watson) 1·90 1·10
4272 (54c.) Ron Weasley (Rupert Grint) 1·90 1·10

1680 Albert Londres

2007. Albert Londres (journalist) Commemoration.

4273 **1680** 54c. blue, green and sepia 1·90 1·10

1681 Building Facade

2007. Bicentenary of Court of Auditors. Ordinary or self-adhesive gum.

4274 **1681** 54c. blue and vermilion 1·90 1·10

1682 Haute-Vienne, Limoges

2007

4275 **1682** 54c. multicoloured 1·90 1·10

1683 Cut-out Figures

2007. 50th Anniv of Treaty of Rome.

4276 **1683** 54c. multicoloured 1·90 1·10

1684 Vauban

2007. 300th Death Anniv of Sebastian le Preste, Marquis de Vauban (Marshall of France, military strategist and engineer).

4277 **1684** 54c. claret, green and orange 1·90 1·10

1685 Players

2007. Rugby. "Allez les Petits" (catchphrase of Roger Coudrec (sports commentator)).

4278 **1685** 54c. multicoloured 1·90 1·10

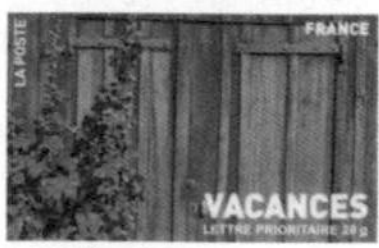

1686 Blue Doors

2007. Holidays. No value expressed. Multicoloured. Self-adhesive.

4279 (54c.) Type **1686** 1·90 1·10
4280 (54c.) Angelfish 1·90 1·10
4281 (54c.) Gentians 1·90 1·10
4282 (54c.) Blueberries 1·90 1·10
4283 (54c.) Boats 1·90 1·10
4284 (54c.) Drying wool 1·90 1·10
4285 (54c.) Snow peaks 1·90 1·10
4286 (54c.) Palm tree 1·90 1·10
4287 (54c.) Beach umbrellas 1·90 1·10
4288 (54c.) Colour pigment boxes 1·90 1·10

Nos. 4279/88 were for use on letters weighing up to 20 grams.

1687 Racoon

2007. Endangered Species of Overseas Departments. Multicoloured.

4289 54c. Type **1687** 1·90 1·10
4290 54c. Iguana (*vert*) 1·90 1·10
4291 60c. Jaguar 2·00 1·20
4292 86c. Barau's petrel 2·75 1·70
MS4293 110×161 mm. Nos. 4289/92 8·50 8·50

1688 Flowers and Pergola

2007. Salon du Timbres et de l'Ecrit 2008. French Gardens. Parc de la Tete d'Or. Sheet 285×110 mm containing T 1688 and similar design. Multicoloured.

MS4294 €2.11×2, Type **1688**; Path and glass house	14·00	14·00

No. **MS**4294 was divided into five parts by four lines of rouletting, the whole forming a composite design.

1689 Scouts

2007. Europa. Centenary of Scouting.

4295	1689	60c. multicoloured	2·00	1·20

1690 Yachts (image scaled to 58% of original size)

2007. Centenary of International Sailing Federation.

4296	1690	85c. multicoloured	2·75	1·70

1691 Tintin and Snowy

2007. Birth Centenary of Georges Remi (Herge) (creator of Tintin). Showing characters from Tintin graphic novels. Multicoloured.

4297	54c. Type **1691**	1·90	1·10
4298	54c. Bianca Castafiore	1·90	1·10
4299	54c. Captain Haddock	1·90	1·10
4300	54c. Thompson and Thompson	1·90	1·10
4301	54c. Professor Calculus	1·90	1·10
4302	54c. Chang	1·90	1·10
MS4303	136×142 mm. Nos. 4297/302	15·00	15·00

No. **MS**4303 was sold for €5, the premium for the benefit of the Red Cross.

1692 Arcachon, Gironde

2007

4304	1692	54c. multicoloured	1·90	1·10

1693 The Nativity (15th-century miniature)

2007. Year of Armenia in France. Multicoloured.

4305	54c. Type **1693**	1·90	1·10
4306	85c. 'L'Ange au sourire' (the angel with a smile), Rheims Cathedral	2·75	1·70

1694 Boar

2007. Gallic Boar (military ensign), Art and Archaeology Museum, Soulac-sur-Mer.

4307	**1694**	€1.30 multicoloured	4·50	2·50

1695 TGV

2007. TGV Europe.

4308	**1695**	54c. multicoloured	1·90	1·10

1696 Notre Dame la Grande

2007. 80th French Federation of Philatelic Associations Conference, Poitiers.

4309	**1696**	54c. brown and yellow	1·90	1·10

1697 Scrum, Player and Ball (melee)

2007. Rugby World Cup Championship (1st issue). Sheet 210×143 mm containing T 1697 and similar multicoloured designs.

MS4310 54c.×10, Type **1697**; Two players (attaque); One player prone (essai); Players reaching for ball (touche) (elliptical); Player kicking conversion (transformation) (elliptical); Passing the ball (passe); Player defending the ball (raffut); New Zealand team (haka); Tackle (plaquage); Fans (supporteurs)	17·00	17·00

See also No. 4315.

1698 Maison du Roi

2007. European Capitals. Brussels. Sheet 144×134 mm containing T 1698 and similar horiz designs. Multicoloured.

MS4311 54c.×4, Type **1698**; Hotel de Ville (vert); Manneken Pis (vert); Atomium	7·50	7·50

1699 Marianne

2007. Centenary of the Association of Mayors.

4312	**1699**	54c. multicoloured	1·90	1·10

1700 Pierre Pflimlin

2007. Birth Centenary of Pierre Pflimlin (mayor of Strasbourg 1959–83 and president of European Union 1984–7).

4313	**1700**	60c. multicoloured	2·00	1·20

1701 Garden

2007. Castres, Tarn.

4314	**1701**	54c. green, deep green and violet	1·90	1·10

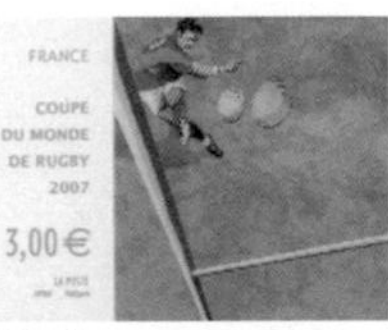
1702 Player

2007. Rugby World Cup, France (2nd issue).

4315	**1702**	€3 multicoloured	6·75	5·00

2007. Greetings Stamps. Sheet 90×220 mm. As T 1704. Multicoloured.

MS4315a (54c.)×5, As Type **1704**; As No. 4319; As No. 4318; As No. 4321; As No. 4320	9·50	4·75

1703 Sylvain, Sylvette and Cake (cartoon characters created by Maurice Cuvillier)

2007. Greetings Stamp. 'Happy Birthday'.

4316	**1703**	(54c.) multicoloured	1·90	1·10

No. 4316 was for use on letters weighing up to 20 grams.

1704 Box and Butterflies

2007. Greetings Stamps. No value expressed. Multicoloured. Self-adhesive.

4317	(54c.) Type **1704**	1·90	1·10
4318	(54c.) Box and hearts	1·90	1·10
4319	(54c.) Box and flowers	1·90	1·10
4320	(54c.) Box and bubbles	1·90	1·10
4321	(54c.) Box and musical notes	1·90	1·10

Nos. 4317/21 were for use on letters weighing up to 20 grams. Firminy, Loire.

2007. Greeting Stamps. Sheet 90×220 mm. Vert stamps as T 1704 Multicoloured.

MS4321a (54c.)×5 As Type **1704**; As No. 4319; As No. 4318; As No. 4321; As No. 4320	9·25	9·25

No. **MS**4294 was divided into five parts by four lines of rouletting, the whole forming a composite design.

1705 St. Peter's Church, Firminy, Loire (Le Corbusier)

2007

4322	**1705**	54c. blue, black and green	1·90	1·10

1706 Sully Prudhomme Firminy, Loire

2007. Death Centenary of Sully Prudhomme (poet) (winner of Nobel Prize for Literature, 1901).

4323	**1706**	€1.30 ultramarine, blue and green	4·50	2·50

1707 Cow licking Stamps

2007. "Sourires". No value expressed. Multicoloured. Self-adhesive.

4324	(54c.) Type **1707**	1·90	1·10
4325	(54c.) Cow covered in stamps	1·90	1·10
4326	(54c.) Cow posting milk bottle with stamp	1·90	1·10
4327	(54c.) Cow date stamped	1·90	1·10
4328	(54c.) Cow singing	1·90	1·10

Nos. 4324/8 were issued for use on mail within France weighing 20 grams or less.

2007. Regions (10th issue). Sheet 251×110 mm containing multicoloured designs as T 1530.

MS4329 54c.×10, Sevres porcelain; Parfum de Grasse (perfume); Christmas market; Marseille soap; Les geants (giants), (vert); Basque beret (vert); Aubusson tapestry; Le bouchon Lyonnais (restaurant); Les charentaises (slippers) (vert); Melon (vert)	16·00	16·00

1708 Satellites

2007. 50th Anniv of Space Exploration.

4330	**1708**	85c. multicoloured	3·00	1·70

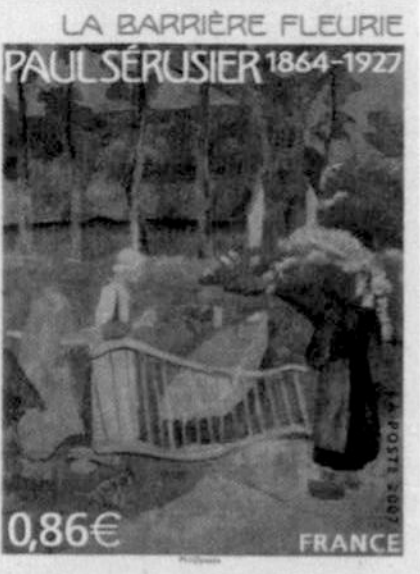
1709 *La Barriere Fleurie*

2007. 70th Death Anniv of Paul Serusier (artist).

4331	**1709**	86c. multicoloured	3·00	1·70

1710 Researcher

2007. 60th Anniv of Medical Research Foundation.
4332 **1710** 54c. multicoloured 1·90 1·10

1711 Guy Moquet

2007. Guy Moquet (17 year old communist resister, executed, 1941) Commemoration.
4333 **1711** 54c. violet and buff 2·00 1·10

1712 Dole, Jura (Louis Pasteur's birthplace)

2007
4334 **1712** 54c. multicoloured 2·00 1·10

1713 Marianne de Cheffer

2007. 40th Anniv of Marianne de Cheffer (stamp drawn by Henry Cheffer). Each scarlet. Self-adhesive.
4335 54c. Type **1713** 2·00 1·10
4336 (54c.) As No. 4057 2·00 1·10

1714 Jean-Baptiste Charcot

2007. Jean-Baptiste Charcot (arctic explorer) Commemoration. Multicoloured.
4337 **1714** 54c. blue, ultramarine and brown 2·00 1·10
4338 - 60c. multicoloured 2·10 1·20
DESIGNS: 54c. Type **1714**; 60c. *Pourquoi-Pas?*(55×33 mm).

1715 Cap Frehel Lighthouse

2007. Lighthouses. Sheet 143×105 mm containing T 1715 and similar multicoloured designs showing lighthouses.
MS4339 54c.×6, Type **1715**; L'Espiguette; D'Ar-Men; Grand-LEon; Porquerolles (horiz); Chassiron (horiz) 11·50 11·50

1716 Players

2007. Women's World Handball Championship, France.
4340 **1716** 54c. multicoloured 2·00 1·10

1717 Galerie de Glaces (mirror gallery) (designed by Jules Hardoui-Mansart), Chateau de Versailles

2007. Ordinary or self-adhesive gum.
4341 **1717** 85c. multicoloured 3·00 1·70

1718 'LES ENFANTS=AMOUR'

2007. Red Cross. No value expressed. Multicoloured. Self-adhesive.
4342 (54c.) Type **1718** 2·10 1·20
4343 (54c.) QUE TOUS LES ENFANTS DU MONDE SOIENT HEUREUX 2·10 1·20
Nos. 4342/3 were for use on letters weighing up to 20 grams.

1719 Squirrel

2007. Christmas and New Year. No value expressed. Multicoloured. Self-adhesive.
4344 (54c.) Type **1719** 2·00 1·10
4345 (54c.) Bird 2·00 1·10
4346 (54c.) Hedgehog 2·00 1·10
4347 (54c.) Puppy 2·00 1·10
4348 (54c.) Deer 2·00 1·10
Nos. 4344/8 were issued for use on letters weighing up to 20 grams.

1720 Heart containing Faces

2008. St. Valentine's Day. No value expressed. Multicoloured.

(a) Ordinary gum.
4349 (54c.) Type **1720** 2·00 1·10
4350 (83c.) Heart containing hearts as plant 3·00 1·70
MS4351 136×144 mm. 53c.×5, As No. 4349×5 10·00 10·00

(b) Self-adhesive.
4351a (54c.) As No. 4349 2·00 1·10
Nos. 4349 was for use on letters up to 20 grams and No. 4350 for letters up to 50 grams.

1721 Rat and Grapes

2008. New Year. 'Year of the Rat'.
4352 **1721** (54c.) multicoloured 2·00 1·10

1722 *Scenes from the life of Saint Francis* (Giotto di Bondone)

2008. Art. Multicoloured. Self-adhesive.
4353 (54c.) Type **1722** 2·00 1·10
4354 (54c.) *Sea Port at Sunset* (La Lorrain) 2·00 1·10
4355 (54c.) *Girl with a Pearl Earring* (Johannes Vermeer) (vert) 2·00 1·10
4356 (54c.) *La Joconde* (Leonardo de Vinci) (vert) 2·00 1·10
4357 (54c.) *The Money Lender and his Wife* (Quentin Metsys) (vert) 2·00 1·10
4358 (54c.) *The Birth of Venus* (Sandro Botticelli) 2·00 1·10
4359 (54c.) *Bonaparte* (Jacques Louis David) 2·00 1·10
4360 (54c.) *La Belle Jardiniere* (Madonna and Child with Saint John the Baptist) (Raphael) (vert) 2·00 1·10
4361 (54c.) *L'Ete* (summer) (Guiseppe Arcimboldo) (vert) 2·00 1·10
4362 (54c.) *L'Infante Marie Marguerite* (Diego Velasquez) (vert) 2·00 1·10

1723 Stadium

2008. 10th Anniv of Stade de France Stadium, Saint-Denis.
4363 **1723** 54c. multicoloured 2·10 1·20

1724 Loir-et-Cher, Vendome

2008
4364 **1724** 54c. multicoloured 2·10 1·20

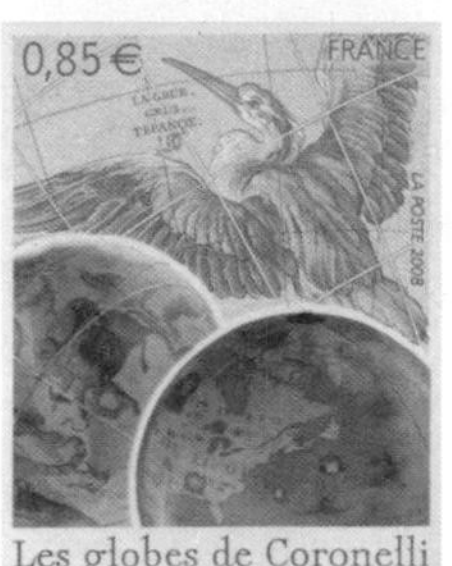

1725 Globes and Detail

2008. Coronelli Globes (Marly globes).
4365 **1725** 85c. multicoloured 3·25 1·80
DESIGN: Two globes, terrestial globe, showing the world as it was known in the late 17th century and celestial globe, shows stars and their constellations, made by Vincenzo Coronelli in 1681 and 1683 for Louis XIV.

1726 Abd el-Kader

2008. Birth Bicentenary of Abd al-Qadir al-Jaza'iri (Abd el-Kader) (Algerian Islamic scholar, Sufi, political and military leader).
4366 **1726** 54c. multicoloured 2·10 1·20

1727 *Aquilegia*

2008. Flowers. Multicoloured.
4367 37c. Type **1727** 1·60 90
4368 38c. *Tulipa* 1·60 90
4369 44c. *Bellis perennis* 1·90 1·10
4370 45c. *Primula veris* 1·90 1·10
No. 4367/70 were only issued pre-cancelled in black.

1728 Droopy

2008. Stamp Day. Birth Centenary of Tex Avery (cartoonist and animator). Designs showing Droopy and characters from Red Hot Riding Hood. Multicolourd. (a) Ordinary gum.
4371 55c. Type **1728** 2·10 1·20
4372 55c. The Girl (Red) 2·10 1·20
4373 55c. The Wolf (Wolfie) 2·10 1·20
MS4374 105×72 mm. €2.18 Droopy (40×30 mm) 8·25 8·25

(b) Self adhesive.
4375 (55c.) As Type **1728** 2·40 1·40
4376 (55c.) As No. 4373 2·40 1·40
4377 (55c.) As No. 4372 2·40 1·40
The stamp of **MS**4374 contains an area, which when rubbed, shows a message in English.

1729 Book, CD and Ear

2008. 35th (2007) Anniv of Audio Book Readers Association.
4378 **1729** 55c. multicoloured 2·10 1·20

2008. Regions (11th issue). Sheet 251×110 mm containing multicoloured designs as T 1530.
MS4379 55c.×10, Le chateau d'Usse; Vezelay; Le Marais, Paris; Le Marais, Poitevin (boats); Le moulin de Cugarel (windmill); La cote de granit rose (shoreline); Honfleur (harbour); La Petite France (waterfront); Sarlat-la-Caneda; Le cirque de Mafate, La Reunion 19·00 19·00

1730 Saint-George Bridge, Lyon, Rhone

2008
4380 **1730** 55c. multicoloured 2·10 1·20

1731 Saint-Nicolas Tower, Old Port and La Chaine Tower, La Rochelle (image scaled to 62% of original size)

2008
4381 **1731** 55c. multicoloured 2·10 1·20

1732 Water Garden, Parc Longchamp, Marseille

2008. Salon du Timbre et de l'Ecrit 2008. French Gardens. Sheet 285×110 mm containing T 1732 and similar design. Multicoloured.
MS4382 €2.18×2, Type **1732**; Pagoda, Parc Borely, Marseille 15·00 15·00

1733 Smilodon

2008. Prehistoric Animals.

4383	55c. Type **1733**	2·10	1·20
4384	55c. Phorusrhacos	2·10	1·20
4385	65c. Megaloceros	2·50	1·50
4386	88c. Mammoth	3·25	1·80
MS4387	110×160 mm. Nos. 4383/6	9·75	9·75

1734 Bandaged Heart

2008. 40th Anniv of First Heart Transplant in Europe.
4388 **1734** 55c. multicoloured 2·10 1·20

1735 Bridge

2008. 700th Anniv of Pont Valentre de Cahors.
4389 **1735** 55c. multicoloured 2·10 1·20

1736 Quill

2008. Europa. The Letter. Ordindary or self-adhesive gum.
4390 **1736** 55c. multicoloured 2·30 1·30

1737 Samuel de Champlain's Ship, Native Canoe and New Settlement of Quebec, 1608

2008. 400th Anniv of City of Quebec.
4391 **1737** 85c. multicoloured 3·50 2·00

A stamp in a similar design was issued by Canada.

1738 Noddy (character created by Enid Blyton)

2008. Greetings Stamp. Happy Birthday.
4392 **1738** (55c.) multicoloured 2·30 1·30

No. 4392 was inscribed 'Lettre prioritaire 20g' and was for use on domestic mail up to 20 grams.

1739 Teddy

2008. Congratulations. Multicoloured. Self-adhesive gum.

4393	(55c.) Type **1739**	2·30	1·30
4394	(55c.) Duck	2·30	1·30

Nos. 4393/4 was inscribed 'Lettre prioritaire 20g' and was for use on domestic mail up to 20 grams.

Nos. 4393/4 includes an area which when rubbed reveals the child is a boy.

1740 Ferns

2008. Holidays. No value expressed. Multicoloured. Self-adhesive.

4395	(55c.) Type **1740**	2·30	1·30
4396	(55c.) Butterfly	2·30	1·30
4397	(55c.) Leaves	2·30	1·30
4398	(55c.) Coconut tree	2·30	1·30
4399	(55c.) Park	2·30	1·30
4400	(55c.) Golf putt	2·30	1·30
4401	(55c.) Water lily	2·30	1·30
4402	(55c.) Watering cans	2·30	1·30
4403	(55c.) Kiwi fruit slices	2·30	1·30
4404	(55c.) Peas	2·30	1·30

No. 4395/404 were inscribed 'Lettre prioritaire 20g' and was for use on domestic mail up to 20 grams.

1741 Beffroi d'Evreux (Evreux belfry)

2008
4405 **1741** 55c. multicoloured 2·30 1·30

1742 Grand Palais

2008
4406 **1742** 55c. indigo, brown and orange 2·30 1·30

1743 Marianne of Europe

2008. (a) Ordinary gum. (i) With face value.

4407	1c. yellow	40	15
4408	5c. agate	40	15
4409	10c. black	60	15
4410	72c. green	3·00	1·70
4410a	73c. green	3·00	1·60
4410b	75c. olive-green (1 band) (12.6.10)	3·00	1·60
4411	85c. violet	3·50	2·00
4411b	87c. bright violet (2 bands) (12.6.10)	3·50	1·75
4412	88c. rose	3·75	2·10
4412a	90c. rose	3·50	1·75
4412b	95c. brown-rose (2 bands)	3·75	2·00
4413	€1 orange	4·25	2·30
4414	€1.25 blue	4·50	2·50
4414a	€1.35 purple	5·00	2·50
4414b	€1.35 new blue (2 bands)	5·25	2·75
4415	€1.33 purple	5·25	2·75
4415b	€1.40 bright purple (2 bands)	2·25	2·75
4416	€2.18 claret	7·75	4·25
4416a	€2.22 claret	8·00	4·00
4416b	€2.30 deep claret (2 bands)	8·25	4·25

(ii) Without face value.

4417	(50c.) emerald	2·10	1·10
4418	(55c.) scarlet	2·30	1·30
4419	(65c.) ultramarine	2·75	1·50

(b) Coil stamps.

4420	(50c.) emerald	3·00	1·60
4421	(55c.) scarlet	3·00	1·70
4422	(65c.) ultramarine	3·75	2·10

(c) Self-adhesive.

4440	(55c.) scarlet	2·30	1·30
4441	(65c.) ultramarine	2·75	1·50
4442	73c. green	4·25	2·30
4442a	75c. olive-green (1 band)	4·25	2·30
4443	90c. rose	5·25	2·75
4443a	87c. bright violet (2 bands)	5·25	2·75
4444b	95c. brown-rose (2 bands)	7·25	4·00
4444a	€1.30 blue	7·25	4·00
4445a	€1.35 purple	7·50	4·25
4445b	€1.35 new blue (2 bands)	7·50	4·25
4446a	€1.40 bright purple (2 bands)	11·00	6·50
4446b	€2.22 claret	10·50	5·75
4447	€2.30 deep claret (2 bands)	12·00	8·00

Nos. 4447/57 are left vacant for possible additions to this series.

1744 Tree (paperless office)

2008. Environmental Protection. Sustainability. Multicoloured. Self-adhesive.

4459	(55c.) Type **1744**	2·30	1·30
4460	(55c.) Bicycle (transport)	2·30	1·30
4461	(55c.) Map (green tourism)	2·30	1·30
4462	(55c.) VDU and keyboard (electronics recycling)	2·30	1·30
4463	(55c.) Water droplets (water conservation)	2·30	1·30
4464	(55c.) Sun (renewable energy)	2·30	1·30
4465	(55c.) Detergent bottles (cleaning)	2·30	1·30
4466	(55c.) Plastic bottles (plastics recycling)	2·30	1·30
4467	(55c.) Apple core (sustainable food production)	2·30	1·30
4468	(55c.) Strawberry (food security)	2·30	1·30

1745 Hand holding Tree

2008. Marianne, Democracy and Environment. Self-adhesive.

4469	55c. scarlet	2·30	1·30
4470	55c. scarlet	2·30	1·30
4471	55c. scarlet	2·30	1·30
4472	65c. ultramarine	2·75	1·50
4473	65c. ultramarine	2·75	1·50
4474	65c. ultramarine	2·75	1·50

DESIGNS: 4470, Type **1745**; 4471, Dove and olive branch; 4472, Hand and ballot box; 4473, As Type **1745**; 4474, As No. 4471; 4475, As No. 4472.

2008. Salon du Timbres et de l'Ecrit 2008. French Gardens. Planete Timbre. Sheet 210×143 mm containing T 1688 and similar design. Multicoloured.
MS4475 €2.11×2, Type **1688**; Glass house and path (as **MS**4294); €2.18×2, Type **1732**; Pagoda Parc Borely (as **MS**4382) 31·00 31·00

1746 Trapeze Artiste

2008. Circus. Multicoloured.

4476	55c. Type **1746**	2·30	1·30
4477	55c. Bareback rider (vert)	2·30	1·30
4478	55c. L'Auguste (clown) (vert)	2·30	1·30
4479	55c. Lion tamer (vert)	2·30	1·30
4480	55c. Le clown blanc (white faced clown) (vert)	2·30	1·30
4481	55c. Juggler (vert)	2·30	1·30
MS4482	135×143 mm. Nos. 4476/81	19·00	19·00

No. **MS**4482 was on sale for €5.10, the premium was for the benefit of French Red Cross Society.

1747 Show Jumping and Cycling

2008. Olympic Games, Beijing. Sheet 210×143 mm containing T 1747 and similar multicoloured designs.
MS4483 55c.×10, Type **1747**×2; Swimming and rowing×3 (horiz); Judo and fencing×3 (horiz); Tennis and athletics×2 20·00 20·00

1748 Charles de Gaulle Memorial, Colomby-les-Deux-Eglises

2008
4484 **1748** 55c. indigo, green and brown 2·30 1·30

1749 '€' and €1 Coin (Euro)

2008. European Projects. Sheet 143×105 mm containing T 1749 and similar multicoloured designs.
MS4485 55c.×4, Type **1749**; Flag (French presidency of EU) (horiz); Satellite (Galileo) (horiz); Young people and flags (Erasmus) 9·25 9·25

1750 Untitled (Gerard Garouste)

2008. Art.
4486 **1750** €1.33 multicoloured 5·50 3·00

1751 *Grande Hermine* (Jacques Cartier)

2008. Famous Ships. Sheet 143×105 mm containing T 1751 and similar multicoloured designs.
MS4487 55c.×6, Type **1751**; *Boudeuse* (Louis Antoine de Bougainville); *La Confiance* (Robert Surcouf) (vert); *La Boussole* (Jean-Francois de Galaup de La Perouse) (vert); *Astrolabe*; *Hermione* (Marquis de La Fayette); 14·00 14·00

The stamps and margins of **MS**4487 form a composite design.

1752 Amazon Rain Forest

2008. Landscapes. Multicoloured.

4488	55c. Type **1752**	2·30	1·30
4489	85c. Mer de Glace	3·50	2·00

Nos. 4488/9 were issued in se-tenant forming a composite design.

Stamps of a similar design were issued by Brazil.

1753 Port

2008. Toulon, Var.

4490 **1753** 55c. multicoloured 2·30 1·30

1754 Gate and Cardinal Richelieu (statue)

2008. Richelieu, Indre-et-Loire.

4491 **1754** 55c. multicoloured 2·30 1·30

1755 Olive Tree

2008. Mediterranean Union Summit, Paris.

4492 **1755** 55c. multicoloured 2·30 1·30

2008. Regions (12th issue). Living France. Sheet 251×110 mm containing multicoloured designs as T 1530.

MS4493 55c.×10, Les espadrille; Le pot au feu; La Chataigne (chestnuts); Le Feux d'artifice (fireworks); L'image d'Epinal; La lentille (lentils); Le reblochon (cheese); Le calisson (biscuits); Les echasses (stilt walker); La moutade (mustard) 21·00 21·00

1756 Town Hall

2008. Le Havre.

4494 **1756** 55c. multicoloured 2·30 1·30

1757 Fly Past

2008. Air. La Patrouille de France (precision aerobatic demonstration team of the French Air Force).

4495 **1757** €3 multicoloured 12·50 8·00

1758 Garfield and Letterbox

2008. "Sourires". Garfield (character created by Jim Davis). No Value Expressed. Designs showing Garfield. Multicoloured. Self-adhesive.

4496 (55c.) Type **1758** 2·30 1·30
4497 (55c.) Wearing glasses 2·30 1·30
4498 (55c.) Eating pizza 2·30 1·30
4499 (55c.) Odie licking Garfield 2·30 1·30
4500 (55c.) Eating envelope 2·30 1·30
4501 (55c.) Taking envelope from letterbox 2·30 1·30
4502 (55c.) Kicking Odie 2·30 1·30
4503 (55c.) With Arlene holding envelope 2·30 1·30
4504 (55c.) Holding extra large pencil 2·30 1·30
4505 (55c.) Lying in letterbox 2·30 1·30

1759 Castle

2008. Josselin, Morbihan.

4506 **1759** 55c. multicoloured 2·30 1·30

1760 Charles de Gaulle, Constitution and Coin

2008. 50th Anniv of Fifth Republic.

4507 **1760** 55c. multicoloured 2·30 1·30

1761 'Je Suis Sport'

2008. Sport.

4508 **1761** 55c. multicoloured 2·30 1·30

1762 Baie d'Along, Vietnam

2008. France–Vietnam Relations. Multicoloured.

4509 55c. Type **1762** 2·30 1·30
4510 85c. Strait of Bonifacio, France 3·50 2·00

Stamps of a similar design were issued by Vietnam.

1763 *Jeune Fille se Chauffant les Mains a un Grand Poele* (Jean-Jaques Henner)

2008. Art.

4511 **1763** 88c. multicoloured 3·75 2·10

1764 Marianne in Ship of State (Andre Reganon) (1959) (As Type **442**)

2008. Marianne–Symbol of the Republic. Designs showing Marianne. Self-adhesive.

4512 55c. multicoloured 2·30 1·30
4513 55c. multicoloured 2·30 1·30
4514 55c. multicoloured 2·30 1·30
4515 55c. multicoloured 2·30 1·30
4516 55c. multicoloured 2·30 1·30
4517 55c. multicoloured 2·30 1·30
4518 55c. scarlet 2·30 1·30
4519 55c. scarlet 2·30 1·30
4520 55c. vermilion 2·30 1·30
4521 55c. vermilion 2·30 1·30
4522 55c. vermilion 2·30 1·30
4523 55c. vermilion 2·30 1·30

DESIGNS: 4512 Type **1764**; 4513 Marianne (Albert Ducaris) (1960) (As Type **463**); 4514 Marianne (Jean Cocteau) (1961) (As Type **476**); 4515 Gallic cock (Albert Ducaris) (1962) (As Type **498**); 4516 'Republique' (Henri Cheffer) (1967) (As Type **604**); 4517 Marianne (Pierre Bequet) (1971) (As Type **668**); 4518 'Sabine' (after Louis David) (Pierre Gandon) (1977) (As Type **816**); 4519 'Liberty' (from *Liberty guiding the People* by Delacroix) (Pierre Gandon) (1982) (As Type **916**); 4520 Marianne (Louis Briat) (1989) (As Type **1118**); 4521 'Marianne of 14 July' (Eve Luquet) (1997) (As Type **1318**); 4522 'Marianne de Francais' (Thierry Lamouche) (2004) (As Type **1586**); 4523 Marianne of Europe (Yves Beaujard) (2008) (As Type **1743**).

1765 Air France DC3, Envelope and Haifa

2008. 60th Anniv of France–Israel Relations. 60th Anniv of First Flight from Israel to France. Multicoloured.

4524 55c. Type **1765** 2·30 1·30
4525 85c. Paris, envelope and aircraft 3·50 2·00

Stamps of a similar design were issued by Israel.

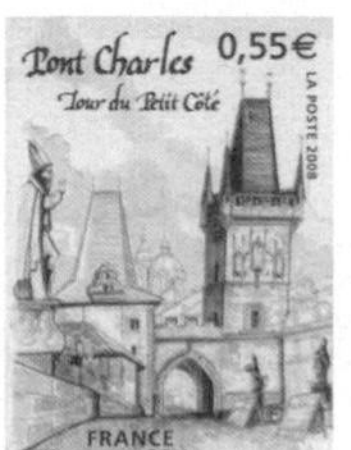

1766 Charles Bridge Tower

2008. European Capitals. Prague. Sheet 143×135 mm containing T 1766 and similar multicolured designs.

MS4526 55c.×4, Type **1766**; Old Town Hall Tower and astronomical clock; Church of Our Lady before Tyn; Prague Castle 9·00 9·00

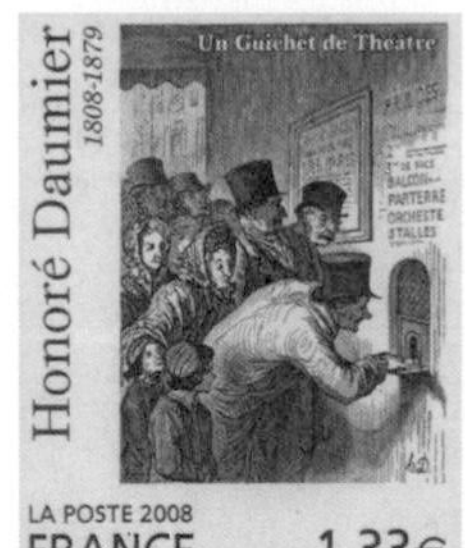

1767 *Un Guichet de Theatre*

2008. Birth Bicentenary of Honore Daumier (artist).

4527 **1767** €1.33 indigo and maroon 5·50 3·00

1768 Stylized Figure

1769 Dancing Feet

2008. Greetings Stamps. Winning Designs in Students Design-a-Stamp Competition. No Value Expressed. Multicoloured. Self-adhesive.

4528 (55c.) Type **1768** (20×26 mm) 2·30 1·30
4529 (55c.) Smile (20×26 mm) 2·30 1·30
4530 (55c.) Stars (20×26 mm) 2·30 1·30
4531 (55c.) Type **1769** (37×23 mm) 2·30 1·30
4532 (55c.) Hearts and flowers (37×23 mm) 2·30 1·30
4533 (55c.) Female figure with lizard's head (37×23 mm) 2·30 1·30
4534 (55c.) Balloons (37×23 mm) 2·30 1·30
4535 (55c.) Stylized planets (20×26 mm) 2·30 1·30
4536 (55c.) String figure jumping (20×26 mm) 2·30 1·30
4537 (55c.) Heart containing symbols of celebration (20×26 mm) 2·30 1·30
4538 (55c.) Figure swinging from moon (37×23 mm) 2·30 1·30
4539 (55c.) Bonnes Fetes 2·30 1·30
4540 (55c.) Bonnes Fetes 2·30 1·30
4541 (55c.) Family (37×23 mm) 2·30 1·30

Nos. 4528/41 were issued for use on mail within France weighing 20 grams or less.

1770 Globe, Animals, Rainbow and Butterflies

2008. Red Cross. Winning Designs in Childrens Design-a-Stamp Competition. No value expressed. Multicoloured. Self-adhesive.

4542 (55c.) Type **1770** 3·00 1·60
4543 (55c.) Globe showing northern and southern hemishperes 3·00 1·60

Nos. 4542/3 were for use on letters weighing up to 20 grams.

1771 Soldiers and Families

2008. 90th Anniv of End of First World War.

4544 **1771** 55c. blue, black and brown 2·40 1·40

1772 *Helianthus annuus*

2008. Flowers. Multicoloured.

4545 31c. Type **1772** 1·30 75
4546 38c. *Magnolia* 1·50 85

No. 4545/6 were only issued pre-cancelled in black.

1773 Oak, Map of Mediterranean and Cedar Tree

2008. France–Lebanon Relations.

4547 **1773** 85c. multicoloured 3·75 2·10

A stamp of a similar design was issued by Lebanon.

1774 Louis Braille

2009. Birth Bicentenary of Louis Braille (inventor of Braille writing for the blind).

4548 **1774** 55c. black and violet 2·40 1·40

1775 Ox

2009. Chinese New Year. Year of the Ox. No value expressed.

4549 **1775** (55c.) multicoloured 2·40 1·40

No. 4549 was for use on letters weighing up to 20 grams and was originally on sale for 55c.

1776 Glasswork

2009. Artistic Trades. No value expressed. Multicoloured. Self-adhesive.

4550	(55c.) Type **1776**	2·40	1·40
4551	(55c.) Horology	2·40	1·40
4552	(55c.) Marquetry	2·40	1·40
4553	(55c.) Faience (tin-glazed pottery)	2·40	1·40
4554	(55c.) Fresco	2·40	1·40
4555	(55c.) Tapestry	2·40	1·40
4556	(55c.) Stained glass	2·40	1·40
4557	(55c.) Fine woodwork	2·40	1·40
4558	(55c.) Ironwork	2·40	1·40
4559	(55c.) Mosaic	2·40	1·40
4560	(55c.) Jewellery	2·40	1·40
4561	(55c.) Crystal	2·40	1·40

Nos. 4550/61 were for use on letters weighing up to 20 grams and were originally on sale for 55c.

1777 Rene of Anjou

2009. 600th Birth Anniv of Rene of Anjou (Duke of Anjou and King of Naples (1438–1442)).

4562	**1777**	55c. multicoloured	2·50	1·50

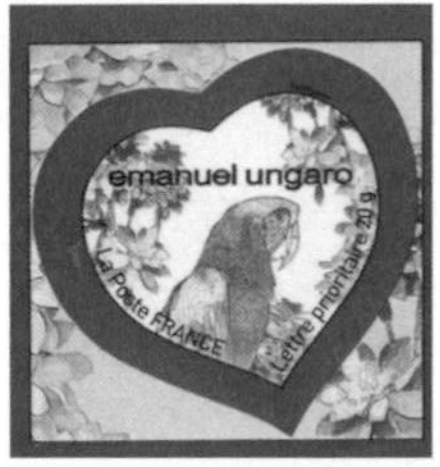

1778 Heart enclosing Parrot

2009. St. Valentine's Day. No value expressed. Multicoloured. (a) Ordinary gum.

4563	(55c.) Type **1778**	2·40	1·40
4564	(85c.) Heart enclosing two parrots	4·00	2·20
MS4565	143×136 mm. (55c.)×5, As No. 4563×5	12·50	12·50

(b) Self-adhesive gum.

4566	(85c.) As No. 4563	4·00	2·20

No. 4563 was for use on letters up to 20 grams and Nos. 4564/5 for letters up to 50 grams.

1779 Les Sables d'Olonne, Vendee

2009

4567	**1779**	55c. multicoloured	2·50	1·50

1780 Combined

2009. Alpine Skiing World Championship, Val d' Isere. Sheet 143×105 containing T 1780 and similar horiz designs. Multicoloured.

MS4568 55c.×5, Type **1780**; Slalom; Downhill; Giant Slalom; Competitors 12·00 12·00

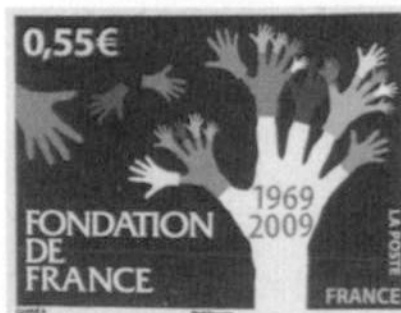

1781 Tree of Hands

2009. 40th Anniv of Fondation de France (charity).

4569	**1781**	55c. multicoloured	2·50	1·40

1782 Cherub

2009. Cathedrale Sainte-Cecile, Albi. Ordinary or self-adhesive gum.

4570	85c. multicoloured	3·75	2·10

1783 Menton, Alpes-Maritimes

2009

4572	**1783**	56c. multicoloured	2·50	1·40

1784 Coyote and Road Runner

2009. Stamp Day. Designs showing characters from Looney Tunes (cartoon series by Warner Brothers). Multicoloured. (a) Ordinary gum.

4573	56c. Type **1784**	2·50	1·40
4574	56c. Sylvester and Tweetie Pie	2·50	1·40
4575	56c. Bugs Bunny	2·50	1·40
MS4576	105×72 mm. €1 Looney Tunes characters (80×26 mm)	4·50	2·50

(b) No value expressed. Self-adhesive.

4577	(56c.) As Type **1784**	2·50	1·40
4578	(56c.) As No. 4574	2·50	1·40
4579	(56c.) As No. 4575	2·50	1·40

1785 Emblem

2009. 50th Anniv (2008) of Constitutional Council (Conseil Constitutionnel). Ordinary of self-adhesive gum.

4580	**1785**	56c. multicoloured	2·50	1·40

1786 Palais de Papes, Avignon

2009

4581	**1786**	70c. multicoloured	3·00	1·70

1787 Helena (USA)

2009. Women of the World. No Value Expressed. Designs showing women. Multicoloured. Self-adhesive.

4582	(56c.) Type **1787**	2·50	1·40
4583	(56c.) Dayu (Indonesia)	2·50	1·40
4584	(56c.) Deborah (France)	2·50	1·40
4585	(56c.) Kabari (Bangladesh)	2·50	1·40
4586	(56c.) Mei Mei (China)	2·50	1·40
4587	(56c.) Malika (Morocco)	2·50	1·40
4588	(56c.) Dayan (Colombia)	2·50	1·40
4589	(56c.) Francine (Rwanda)	2·50	1·40
4590	(56c.) Blessing (Nigeria)	2·50	1·40
4591	(56c.) Nandita (India)	2·50	1·40
4592	(56c.) Elmas (Turkey)	2·50	1·40
4593	(56c.) Nadia (Brazil)	2·50	1·40

1788 Macon, Saone-et-Loire

2009

4594	**1788**	56c. multicoloured	2·50	1·40

1789 Polar Landscape

2009. Preserve Polar Regions and Glaciers. Sheet 143×105 mm containing T 1789 and similar multicoloured design.

MS4595 56c.×2, Type **1789**; Emperor penguins (horiz) 6·25 6·25

1790 Aime Cesaire

2009. Aime Cesaire (writer and politician) Commemoration.

4596	**1790**	56c. multicoloured	2·50	1·40

1791 Quetsche Plum, Alsace

2009. Regional Flora. No Value Expressed. Multicoloured. Self-adhesive.

4597	(56c.) Type **1791**	2·50	1·40
4598	(56c.) Mirabelle plum, Lorraine	2·50	1·40
4599	(56c.) Birch trees, Centre	2·50	1·40
4600	(56c.) Bee orchid, Champagne–Ardenne	2·50	1·40
4601	(56c.) Lily, Paris	2·50	1·40
4602	(56c.) Blue bells, Ile de France	2·50	1·40
4603	(56c.) Gorse, Bretagne	2·50	1·40
4604	(56c.) Lily of the Valley, Pays de la Loire	2·50	1·40
4605	(56c.) Apples, Basse Normandie	2·50	1·40
4606	(56c.) Beech leaves, Haute Normandie	2·50	1·40
4607	(56c.) Rose, Picardie	2·50	1·40
4608	(56c.) Potatoes, Pas le Calais	2·50	1·40
4609	(56c.) Olives and lavender field, Provence–Alpes–Cote d'Azur	2·50	1·40
4610	(56c.) Chestnut, Corse	2·50	1·40
4611	(56c.) Thyme, Languedoc–Roussillon	2·50	1·40
4612	(56c.) Yellow gentian, Auvergne	2·50	1·40
4613	(56c.) Fungi, Limousin	2·50	1·40
4614	(56c.) Salicorne Salicornia, Poitou–Charentes	2·50	1·40
4615	(56c.) Maritime pine, Aquitaine	2·50	1·40
4616	(56c.) Spruce, Franche–Covete	2·50	1·40
4617	(56c.) Cordyline, Guyane	2·50	1·40
4618	(56c.) Violet, Midi-Pyrenees	2·50	1·40
4619	(56c.) Myrtle berries, Rhone–Alpes	2·50	1·40
4620	(56c.) Blackcurrant, Baugogne	2·50	1·40

Nos. 4597/620 were for use on mail within France weighing 20 grams or less.

1792 Saturn

2009. Europa. Astronomy. Sheet 143×105 mm containing T **1792** and similar vert design. Multicoloured.

MS4621 70c.×2, Type **1792**; Exoplanet 6·25 6·25

1793 Director's Chair

1794 Cockerel

2009. Holidays. No Value Expressed. Multicoloured. Self-adhesive.

4622	(56c.) Type **1793** (20×26 mm)	2·50	1·40
4623	(56c.) Ladybird (20×26 mm)	2·50	1·40
4624	(56c.) Tomatoes (20×26 mm)	2·50	1·40
4625	(56c.) Type **1794** (37×23 mm)	2·50	1·40
4626	(56c.) Poppy (37×23 mm)	2·50	1·40
4627	(56c.) Bonaire, Netherlands Antilles vehicle number plate (37×23 mm)	2·50	1·40
4628	(56c.) Butterfly (37×23 mm)	2·50	1·40
4629	(56c.) Tennis ball and court (20×26 mm)	2·50	1·40
4630	(56c.) Turban (20×26 mm)	2·50	1·40
4631	(56c.) Air bed (20×26 mm)	2·50	1·40
4632	(56c.) Raspberries (37×23 mm)	2·50	1·40
4633	(56c.) Door knocker (37×23 mm)	2·50	1·40
4634	(56c.) 11	2·50	1·40
4635	(56c.) Mooring rope (37×23 mm)	2·50	1·40

1795 Timber-framed House, Alsace

2009. France on Stamps. No Value Expressed. Multicoloured. Self-adhesive.

4636	(68c.) Type 1795	3·00	1·70
4637	(68c.) Chateau, Azay-le-Rideau	3·00	1·70
4638	(68c.) Notre Dame Cathedral, Paris	3·00	1·70
4639	(68c.) Vineyards, Bordeaux	3·00	1·70
4640	(68c.) Promenade des Anglais, Nice	3·00	1·70
4641	(68c.) Mont Saint Michel	3·00	1·70
4642	(68c.) Eiffel Tower, Paris	3·00	1·70
4643	(68c.) Saint-Paul-de-Vence, Provence	3·00	1·70

Nos. 4636/43 were issued for use on International mail weighing 20 grams or less.

1796 'CHAUMONT'

2009. Chaumont, Haute-Marne. 20th International Poster and Graphic Arts Festival.

4644	**1796**	56c. multicoloured	2·50	1·40

1799 John Calvin

2009. 500th Birth Anniv of Jean Calvin (religious reformer).

4647	**1799**	56c. multicoloured	2·50	1·40

1800 Cocoa Fruit

2009. 400th Anniv of Arrival of Chocolate in France. Sheet 160×110 mm containing T **1800** and similar vert designs. Multicoloured.

MS4648 56c.×10, Type **1800**; Quetzacoatl; Hernan Cortes; Alhambra de Granada, Spain; Map and 'BAYONNE 1609'; Anne of Austria and Louis XIII of France; Chocolate factory; Chocolate block; Pot of hot chocolate and cup; Eating bar of chocolate 23·00 23·00

The stamps and margins of No. **MS**4648 form a composite design of a chocolate bar and produce the scent of chocolate when rubbed.

1801 Chateau de la Batie d'Urfe, Loire

2009

4649 **1801** 56c. multicoloured 2·50 1·40

1802 Tarbes

2009

4650 **1802** 56c. multicoloured 2·50 1·40

1803 *Le Pont Neuf Wrapped*, 1985 (Christo and Jeanne-Claude)

2009. Art. Self-adhesive or ordinary gum.

4651 **1803** €1.35 multicoloured 5·75 3·25

1804 Place Royale (now Place de la Bourse) (image scaled to 63% of original size)

2009. Bordeaux, Gironde

4652 **1804** 56c. multicoloured 2·50 1·40

1805 Jean Moulin

2009. Jean Moulin (member of the French Resistance) Commemoration. Self-adhesive or ordinary gum.

4653 **1805** 56c. multicoloured 2·50 1·40

1805a Giant Panda

2009. Endangered Species. Multicoloured.

4654	56c. Type **1805a**	2·50	1·40
4655	56c. Rhinocerus	2·50	1·40
4656	70c. Auroch (horiz)	3·00	1·60
4657	90c. Californian condor (horiz)	10·50	5·75
MS4658	160×110 mm. Nos. 4654/7	11·00	11·00

1805b Early Aircraft

2009. Centenary of Coupe Aeronautique Gordon-Bennett.

4659 **1805b** 56c. deep brown and black 2·50 1·40

1806 Etienne Dolet

2009. 500th Birth Anniv of Etienne Dolet (scholar, translator and printer).

4660 **1806** 56c. deep brownish grey, dull orange and dull vermilion 2·50 1·40

1807 Louis Bleriot and *Bleriot XI*

2009. Centenary of Bleriot's Cross Channel Flight.

4661 **1807** €2 multicoloured 8·00 5·00

1808 Chair-O-Plane ('Les Chaise Volante')

2009. The Funfair. Sheet 143×135 mm containing T 1808 and similar vert designs. Multicoloured.

MS4662 56c.×6, Type **1808**; Big Wheel ('La Grande Roue'); Roller Coaster ('Les Montagnes Russes'); Carousel ('Le Manege'); Toffee apple ('La Pomme D'Amour'); Fishing for ducks ('La Peche aux Canards') 14·50 14·50

1809 Woman wearing Green Dress

1810 Woman wearing Trousers

2009. Greetings Stamps. No Value Expressed. Multicoloured. Self-adhesive.

4663	(56c.) Type **1809** (20×26 mm)	2·50	1·40
4664	(56c.) Rear view of seated girl holding balloons (20×26 mm)	2·00	1·40
4665	(56c.) Cakes (20×26 mm)	2·50	1·50
4666	(56c.) Type **1810** (37×23 mm)	2·50	1·40
4667	(56c.) Figure with arms and legs raised (37×23 mm)	2·50	1·40
4668	(56c.) Woman holding letter facing left (37×23 mm)	2·50	1·40
4669	(56c.) Clown (37×23 mm)	2·50	1·40
4670	(56c.) Woman wearing tiered dress holding letters (20×26 mm)	2·50	1·40
4671	(56c.) Bird (20×26 mm)	2·50	1·40
4672	(56c.) Acrobat (20×26 mm)	2·50	1·40
4673	(56c.) Figure wearing blue tiered trousers facing left (37×23 mm)	2·50	1·40
4674	(56c.) Cake, cake slice and heart (37×23 mm)	2·50	1·40
4675	(56c.) Cow holding flowers (37×23 mm)	2·50	1·40
4676	(56c.) Grey haired woman (37×23 mm)	2·50	1·40

Nos. 4663/76 were issued for use on mail within France weighing 20 grams or less.

1811 'Geoffroy' **1812** 'Chouette, des nouvelles'

2009. Sourires

4677	(56c.) Type **1811** (20×26 mm)	2·50	1·40
4678	(56c.) Nicolas	2·50	1·40
4679	(56c.) Joachim	2·50	1·40
4680	(56c.) Type **1812** (37×23 mm)	2·50	1·40
4681	(56c.) Vous me ferez cent lignes!	2·50	1·40
4682	(56c.) J	2·50	1·40
4683	(56c.) C	2·50	1·40
4684	(56c.) Nicolas	2·50	1·40
4685	(56c.) Eudes	2·50	1·40
4686	(56c.) Nicolas	2·50	1·40
4687	(56c.) Nicolas writing on typewriter (37×23 mm)	2·50	1·40
4688	(56c.) Chere Maman	2·50	1·40
4689	(56c.) C	2·50	1·40
4690	(56c.) moi, je vieux pas grand chose reellement	2·50	1·40

Nos. 4677/90 were issued for use on mail within France weighing 20 grams or less.

1813 Eugene Vaille

2009. 50th Death Anniv of Eugene Vaille (first curator of the Postal Museum of France, the forerunner of the Museum of La Poste). Self-adhesive.

4692 **1813** 56c. brown, black and orange-brown 2·50 1·40

1814 Henry Dunant

2009. Red Cross. 150th Anniv of Battle of Solferino (witnessed by Henry Dunant who instigated campaign resulting in establishment of Geneva Conventions and Red Cross). Sheet 160×110 mm containing T 1814 and similar designs. Each black, ultramarine and scarlet-vermilion.

MS4693 56c.×5, Type **1814**; Wounded, Battle of Solferino; *Pelias Et Nelee* (Georges Braque) (horiz); Committee members, Geneva Convention; Globe (International Federation of Red Cross and Red Crescent) 21·00 21·00

1815 Bandstand

2009. Salon de Timbre. Gardens of France. Jardin des Plantes, Paris. Sheet 95×110 mm containing T 1815 and similar vert design. Multicoloured.

MS4694 €2.22×2, Type **1815**; Mexican Hothouse, built by Rohault de Fleury 19·00 19·00

1816 Abbaye de Royaumont, Val d'Oise

2009

4695 **1816** 56c. multicoloured 2·50 1·40

1817 Rene de Saint-Marceaux (sculptor and creator of statue used as emblem of Universal Postal Union) and UPU Monument

2009. Centenary of UPU Monument. Rene de Saint-Marceaux (sculptor and creator of statue used as emblem of Universal Postal Union) Commemoration.

4696 **1817** 70c. multicoloured 3·00 1·70

1818 Porcelain Doll

2009. Dolls

MS4697 144x105 mm. 56c.×6, Type **1818**; Inscr 'Poupée GéGé' (horiz); Rag doll (horiz); Bella doll (horiz); Inscr 'Baigneur petitcollin' (horiz); Bisque doll 17·00 17·00

1819 *Le Promenade* (Jean-Jaques Waltz (Hansi))

2009. Art. Ordinary or self-adhesive gum.

4698 **1819** 90c. multicoloured 4·00 2·20

1820 Telegraph Machine and Juliette Dodu

2009. Birth Centenary of Juliette Dodu (spy and heroine of 1870 war). Ordinary or self-adhesive gum.

4700 **1820** 56c. multicoloured 2·50 1·40

1821 Jeronimos Monastery

2009. European Capitals. Lisbon. Sheet 143×135 mm containing T 1821 and similar multicoloured designs.

MS4702	56c.×4, Type **1821**; Bario Alto quarter (vert); Belem Tower; Discoveries Monument	10·00	10·00

2009. Marianne of Europe. The Colours of Marianne. Sheet 141×139 containing vert designs as T 1743.

MS4703	1c. chrome yellow; 5c. agate; 10c. agate; (51c.) emerald; (56c.) scarlet; (70c.) dull ultramarine; 73c. olive-green; 85c. bright violet; 90c. brown-rose; €1 bright orange; €1.30 new blue; €1.35 bright purple; €2.22 deep claret	44·00	44·00

1822 *Monsieur et Madame Bernheim de Villers*

2009. Art. Paintings by Auguste Renoir. Sheet 143×105 mm containing T 1822 and similar vert design. Multicoloured.

MS4704	85c. Type **1822**; €1.35 *Gabrielle a la Rose*	9·50	9·50

1823 Francisco Miranda

2009. Sebastian Francisco de Miranda y Rodriguez (Francisco Miranda) (Venezuelan revolutionary) Commemoration.

4705	**1823** 85c. multicoloured	3·75	2·10

A stamp of a similar design was issued by Venezuela.

1824 Map of Mediterranean and Emblem

2009. Euromed Postal Conference, Egypt.

4706	**1824** 56c. multicoloured	2·50	1·40

1825 Flowers and Window

2009. Christmas and New Year. No Value Expressed. Multicoloured. Self-adhesive.

4707	(56c.) Type **1825**	2·50	1·40
4708	(56c.) Ladder, woman's face and lantern	2·50	1·40
4709	(56c.) Faces and baubles	2·50	1·40
4710	(56c.) Blonde woman wearing orange dress	2·50	1·40
4711	(56c.) Sprite riding blue lion	2·50	1·40
4712	(56c.) Two older women exchanging presents	2·50	1·40
4713	(56c.) Santa releasing doves holding envelopes	2·50	1·40
4714	(56c.) Flowers and stylized dove	2·50	1·40
4715	(56c.) Guitarist	2·50	1·40
4716	(56c.) Bouquet and tiny women on arm	2·50	1·40
4717	(56c.) Blonde woman kneeling	2·50	1·40
4718	(56c.) Figure in air balloon basket throwing symbols of good luck	2·50	1·40
4719	(56c.) Figure in Zeppelin basket throwing symbols of good luck	2·50	1·40
4720	(56c.) Woman catching gifts in box	2·50	1·40

Nos. 4707/20 were issued for use on mail within France weighing 20 grams or less.

1826 *Jeanne d'Arc*

2009. *Jeanne d'Arc* (French Navyhelicopter cruiser). Multicoloured.

4721	56c. Type **1826**	2·50	1·40
4722	56c. Crew members (29×35 mm)	2·50	1·40

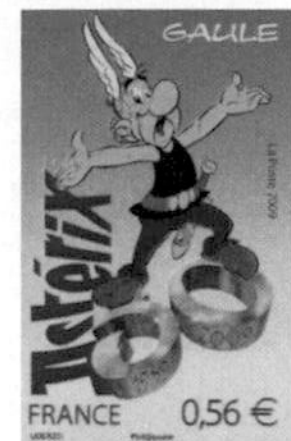

1827 Asterix

2009. 50th Anniv of Asterix (character created by writer Rene Goscinny and illustrated by Albert Uderzo). Red Cross (MS4724). Multicoloured.

4723	56c. Type **1827**	2·50	1·40
MS4724	205×95 mm. 56c.×6, Cacofonix bound, hanging from tree (40×30 mm); As Type **1827**; Villagers queuing for potion from Getafix (80×26 mm); Panacea (30×40 mm); Dogmatix and bone (22×18 mm); Obelix carrying menhir (49×100 mm)	15·00	15·00

No. **MS**4724 was sold for €5.20, the premium being for the benefit of the Red Cross.

1828 Woman reading

2010. St. Valentine's Day. Multicoloured.

4725	56c. Type **1828**	2·50	1·40
4726	90c. Woman with arms raised	4·00	2·20
MS4727	143×136 mm. 56c.×5, As Type **1828**	12·50	12·50

Nos. 4728/9 are left for stamps not yet received.

1829 Tiger

2010. Chinese New Year. Year of the Tiger.

4730	**1829** 56c. multicoloured	2·50	1·40

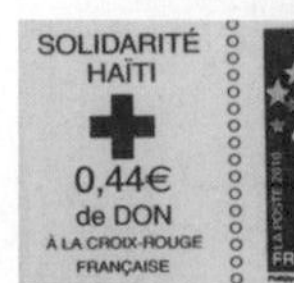

1830 'Solidarite Haiti'

2010. Red Cross Fund. For Victims of Haiti Earthquake. (a) Ordinary gum

4731	**1830** (56c.) + 44c. scarlet	4·00	2·25

(b) Self-adhesive gum

4732	(56c.) + 44c. scarlet	4·00	2·25

1831 Abbe Pierre

2010. Abbe Pierre (Henri Marie Joseph Groues) (member of WWII resistance and founder of Emmaus movement, helping the poor, homeless and refugees) Commemoration. Ordinary or self-adhesive gum.

4733	**1831** 56c. dull aquamarine, greenish blue and deep reddish purple	2·50	1·40

1832 Angel playing Harp (Gustav Moreau)

2010. Music . Multicoloured.

4735	(56c.) Type **1832**	2·50	1·40
4736	(56c.) Woman playing concert harp (Francois Andre Vincent)	2·50	1·40
4737	(56c.) Woman and man playing cello (Karl Gustav Klingstedt)	2·50	1·40
4738	(56c.) Woman playing guitar (Camille Roqueplan)	2·50	1·40
4739	(56c.) Horn players (Daniel Rabel)	2·50	1·40
4740	(56c.) Man playing saxaphone (Marthe and Juliette Vesque)	2·50	1·40
4741	(56c.) Ornate pipe organ (Francois Garas)	2·50	1·40
4742	(56c.) Soldier holding cornet (Auguste Mayer)	2·50	1·40
4743	(56c.) Man playing violin and woman playing harpsichord (Carmontelle)	2·50	1·40
4744	(56c.) Woman playing piano (Pierre-Desire Lamy)	2·50	1·40
4745	(56c.) Woman playing tambourine (Theodore Chasseriau)	2·50	1·40
4746	(56c.) Horse mounted drums (Jaques-Antoine Delaistre)	2·50	1·40

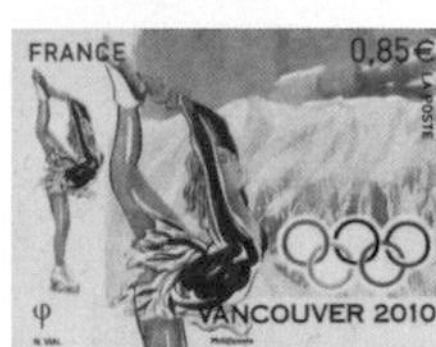

1833 Figure Skater

2010. Winter Olympic Games, Vancouver. Multicoloured.

4747	85c. Type **1833**	3·75	2·10
4748	85c. Alpine skier	3·75	2·10

Nos. 4747/8 were printed, se-tenant, each pair forming a composite design.

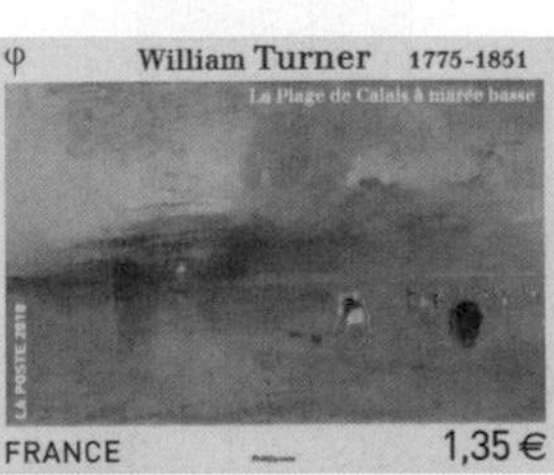

1834 *Calais Beach at Low Tide*

2010. Joseph Mallord William Turner (artist) Commemoration. Ordinary or self-adhesive gum.

4749	**1834** €1.35 multicoloured	5·75	3·25

No. 4751 and Type **1835** are left for Stamp Day (1st issue) issued on 27 February 2010, not yet received.

1836 Dolphins (sea mammals)

2010. Stamp Day (2nd issue). Water. Multicoloured. Self-adhesive.

4752	(56c.) Type **1836**	2·50	1·40
4753	(56c.) Oil covered sea bird (black seas)	2·50	1·40
4754	(56c.) 5 M	2·50	1·40
4755	(56c.) Waterfalls (water sources)	2·50	1·40
4756	(56c.) Electricity pylon (hydro-electric power)	2·50	1·40
4757	(56c.) Hot springs (geo-thermal power)	2·50	1·40
4758	(56c.) Paddy fields (irrigation)	2·50	1·40
4759	(56c.) Surf and African children	2·50	1·40
4760	(56c.) Sewage pipe (algae growth)	2·50	1·40
4761	(56c.) Cracked soil and watering can (drought)	2·50	1·40
4762	(56c.) Factory chimney and denuded forest (acid rain)	2·50	1·40
4763	(56c.) Polar bear (melting glaciers)	2·50	1·40

1837 Horse

2010. Stamp Day (3rd issue). Apollo Fountain, Palace of Versailles. Sheet 105×72 mm.

MS4764	multicoloured	8·00	5·00

1838 Conifer, Alpine Meadow, Mountain and Treaty

2010. 150th Anniv of Treaty of Turin (formalizing attachment of Duchy of Savoy to France). (a) Ordinary gum

4765	**1838** 56c. multicoloured	2·50	1·40

(b) Self-adhesive gum

4766	56c. multicoloured	2·50	1·40

1839 Henri Fabre and *Le Canard*

2010. Air. Centenary of First Seaplane (invented, manufactured and piloted by Henri Fabre) to take off from Water under its Own Power.

4767	**1839** €3 multicoloured	12·00	7·50

1840 Fort Saint Andre

2010. Villeneuve-lez-Avignon.

(a) Ordinary gum

4768	**1840** 56c. multicoloured	2·50	1·40

(b) Self-adhesive

4769	**1840** 56c. multicoloured	2·50	1·40

1841 Women

2010. International Year of Violence against Women Awareness Campaign

4770	(56c.) Type **1841**	2·50	1·40
4771	(56c.) Woman at microphone with raised arms	2·50	1·40

4772 Woman standing with hand over face (vert) 2·50 1·40
4773 (56c.) Woman standing with arms folded (vert) 2·50 1·40
4774 (56c.) Girl wearing black head-covering (vert) 2·50 1·40
4775 (56c.) Woman wearing neck-laces and headcovering with central safety pin (vert) 2·50 1·40
4776 (56c.) School girls wearing blue and yellow uniforms 2·50 1·40
4777 (56c.) School girls wearing red t-shirts 2·50 1·40
4778 (56c.) Woman with braided hair facing left (vert) 2·50 1·40
4779 (56c.) Older woman with very short hair (vert) 2·50 1·40
4780 (56c.) Girl wearing multicol-oured woven poncho (vert) 2·50 1·40
4781 (56c.) Older woman wearing sari (vert) 2·50 1·40

1842 Little Venice and La Maison des Têtes Hotel

2010. Colmar Haut-Rhin

(a) Ordinary gum
4782 **1842** 56c. multicoloured 2·50 1·40

(b) Self-adhesive
4783 **1842** 56c. multicoloured 2·50 1·40

1843 Merino Ram and Buildings

2010. Bergerie, Rambouillet (national centre for agricultural education, sustainable agriculture, local development and rural tourism)
4784 **1843** 90c. multicoloured 3·75 2·10

1844 Girl reading and Characters from Children's Literature

2010. Europa
4785 **1844** 70c. multicoloured 3·25 1·90

1845 Building Façade

2010. Orcival Basilica, Puy-de-Dôme
4786 **1845** 56c. multicoloured 2·50 1·40

1846 Franklin Delano Roosevelt

2010. 150th Anniv of Bourse aux Timbres (stamp show). Each black, ochre and red-brown.
MS4787 56c.×5, Type **1846**; Lucien Berthelot; Louis Yvert (horiz); Arthur Mauray (horiz); Alberto Bolaffi 13·00 13·00

1847 '2010' and Beach

2010. 150th Anniv of Deauville
4788 **1847** 85c. multicoloured 3·50 2·00

1848 Pool and Exhibits

2010. Museum of Art and Industry (The Pool), Roubaix

(a) Ordinary gum
4789 **1848** 85c. multicoloured 1·80 1·00

(b) Self-adhesive
4790 **1848** 85c. multicoloured 1·80 1·00

1849 Castle and Old Port

2010. Pornic, Loire-Atlantique
4791 **1849** 56c. multicoloured 2·50 1·40

1850 Mother Teresa

2010. Birth Centenary of Agnes Gonxha Bojaxhiu (Mother Teresa) (founder of Missionaries of Charity)

(a) Ordinary gum
4792 **1850** 85c. blue, brown-purple and black 1·80 1·00

(b) Self-adhesive
4793 **1850** 85c. blue, brown-purple and black 1·80 1·00

1851 Abbe Breuil, Prince Albert I, Institute Building and Grimaldi Caves

2010. Institute of Human Paleontology, Paris
4794 **1851** 56c. multicoloured 2·50 1·40

1852 Players

2010. Football
4795 €5 silver 20·00 17·00

1853 Nice

2010. 150th Anniv of Affiliation of Nice to France

(a) Ordinary gum
4796 **1853** 56c. multicoloured 2·40 1·40

(b) Self-adhesive
4797 **1853** 56c. multicoloured 2·50 1·40

1854 Eclade

2010. Flavours of France. Multicoloured.

4798	(56c.) Type **1854**		2·50	1·40
4799	(56c.) Baeckaoffe		2·50	1·40
4800	(56c.) Tomme des Pyrénées		2·50	1·40
4801	(56c.) Tarte aux mirabelles		2·50	1·40
4802	(56c.) Potage au cresson		2·50	1·40
4803	(56c.) Flamiche		2·50	1·40
4804	(56c.) Pont l'Evêque		2·50	1·40
4805	(56c.) Blanc-manger		2·50	1·40
4806	(56c.) Caviar		2·50	1·40
4807	(56c.) Chapon		2·50	1·40
4808	(56c.) Fourme d'Ambert		2·50	1·40
4809	(56c.) Tarte Tatin		2·50	1·40
4810	(56c.) Quenelles		2·50	1·40
4811	(56c.) Escalope normande		2·50	1·40
4812	(56c.) Maroilles		2·50	1·40
4813	(56c.) Clafoutis		2·50	1·40
4814	(56c.) Gougères		2·50	1·40
4815	(56c.) Tian		2·50	1·40
4816	(56c.) Brocciu		2·50	1·40
4817	(56c.) Abricots rouge au miel		2·50	1·40
4818	(56c.) Homard breton		2·50	1·40
4819	(56c.) Brochet au beurre blanc		2·50	1·40
4820	(56c.) Chaource		2·50	1·40
4821	(56c.) Paris-Brest		2·50	1·40

1855 Launch Pad

2010. Launch of Soyuz Spacecraft from Sinnamary, Guyana

(a) Ordinary gum
4823 **1855** 85c. multicoloured 3·50 2·75

(b) Self-adhesive
4824 **1855** 85c. multicoloured 3·50 2·75

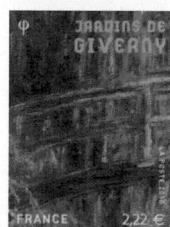

1856 Bridge at Giverny (detail)

2010. Gardens of Giverny . Multicoloured.
MS4825 €2.22×2, Type **1856**; Pond at Giverny (detail) 17·00 17·00

2010. Salon de Timbres, Gardens of France. Jardin des Plantes, Paris and Gardens of Giverny. Multicoloured.
MS4826 €2.22×4, As Type **1815**; Mexican Hothouse, built by Rohault de Fleury; As Type **1856**; Pond at Giverny (detail, *Le Bassin aux nymphéas* by Claude Monet) 35·00 35·00
No. **MS**4826 contains the stamps of **MS** and **MS**4825.

1857 'tu y crois?' (do you believe?)
1858 a fond!' ('flat out!')

2010. World Cup Football Championships, South Africa (1st issue)
4827 **1857** 56c. multicoloured 2·50 1·40
4828 **1858** 56c. multicoloured 2·50 1·40

1859 Players Legs and Ball

2010. World Cup Football Championships, South Africa (2nd issue)
MS4829 85c.×4, Type **1859**; Players, rear view (vert); Parliament Building, Pretoria (vert); Cape Town, South Africa 11·50 11·50

1860 Bas-relief, Tournus

2010. Romanesque Art. Multicoloured.

(a) Booklet stamps
4830 (56c.) Type **1860** 2·50 1·40
4831 (56c.) Arched nave, Léoncel 2·50 1·40
4832 (56c.) Beatus (Apocalypse) (detail), St.-Sever 2·50 1·40
4833 (56c.) Serrabone Abbey, Boule d'Amont 2·50 1·40
4834 (56c.) Carved stone birds, L'Île-Bouchard 2·50 1·40
4835 (56c.) Illuminated letter from Book of Job, Citeaux Abbey 2·50 1·40
4836 (56c.) Fresco, St. Martin's Church, Nohant-Vic 2·50 1·40
4837 (56c.) Bas-relief, Clermont-Ferrand Cathedral 2·50 1·40
4838 (56c.) Fresco, St. Jacques des Guérets church 2·50 1·40
4839 (56c.) Stone carving, Angoulême Cathedral 2·50 1·40
4840 (56c.) Illuminated manuscript, Cluny Abbey 2·50 1·40
4841 (56c.) Carved tympanum, Conques church 2·50 1·40

(b) Sheet stamps
4842 (56c.) As No. 4831 2·50 1·40
4843 (56c.) As No. 4834 2·50 1·40

1861 Montbrun-Lauragais

2010. Windmills
MS4844 56c.×6, Type **1861**; Cassel; Aigremonts Bléré (horiz); Daudet Fontveille (horiz) ; Villeneuve-d'Ascq; Birlot Île-de-Bréhat (horiz) 14·00 14·00

1862 Young People and Singapore Skyline

2010. Youth Olympic Games, Singapore
4845 **1862** 85c. multicoloured 3·00 1·70

1863 Maman

2010. Louise Joséphine Bourgeois (artist and sculptor) Commemoration

(a) Ordinary gum

4846	**1863**	€1.35 multicoloured	6·00	3·25

(b) Self-adhesive

4847	**1863**	€1.35 multiocoloured	6·00	3·25

1864 General de Gaulle and Microphone

2010. 70th Anniv of Appeal of 18 June 1940 by Charles de Gaulle, leader of Free French Forces (origin of French Resistance)

MS4848	multicoloured	10·00	10·00

1865 La Conciergerie

2010. Fédération Françaises des Associations Philatélique (FFAP) Congress, Paris.

4849	**1865**	56c. multicoloured	2·50	1·40

No. 4849 has a half stamp size illustrated label attached at right.

1866 French Pavilion

2010. Expo 2010, Shanghai

4850	**1866**	85c. multicoloured	3·50	2·75

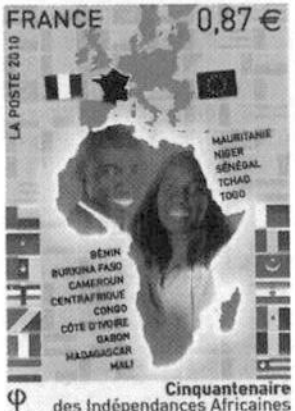
1867 Couple enclosed in Map of Africa

2010. 50th Anniv of French African Colonies Independence

(a) Ordinary gum

4851	**1867**	87c. multicoloured	2·50	1·40

(b) Self-adhesive

4852	**1867**	87c. multicoloured	2·50	1·40

1868 *Morpho menelaus* (blue morpho)

2010. Butterflies

4853	58c. Type **1868**	2·50	1·40
MS4854	110×160 mm. 58c. As Type **1868**; 58c.*Cerura vinula* (caterpillar)75c. *Thersamolycaena dispar* (vert); 95c. *Callophrys rubi*	10·00	10·00

1869 Children writing in Hebrew and French

2010. 150th Anniv of France–Israel Alliance

4855	**1869**	58c. multicoloured	2·50	1·40

1870 Arcueil and Cachan Aqueduct

2010. Arcueil and Cachan Aqueduct, Val-de-Marne

4856	**1870**	58c. multicoloured	2·50	1·40

1871 Figure riding Paper Airplane

2010. Sourire (humour). Multicoloured.

4857	(58c.) Type **1871**	2·50	1·40
4858	(58c.) Female figure with paper hat and scarf	2·50	1·40
4859	(58c.) Male figure wearing glasses and riding paper horse	2·50	1·40
4860	(58c.) Male figure on paper island	2·50	1·40
4861	(58c.) Couple in paper house	2·50	1·40
4862	(58c.) Male figure with telescope in paper boat	2·50	1·40
4863	(58c.) Couple joined by paper heart	2·50	1·40
4864	(58c.) Male figure in paper vehicle	2·50	1·40
4865	(58c.) Two figures and paper speech bubble	2·50	1·40
4866	(58c.) Boy wearing paper hat and carrying sword	2·50	1·40
4867	(58c.) Hands picking petals from paper flower	2·50	1·40
4868	(58c.) Male figure declaiming from paper stage	2·50	1·40

1872 Elise Deroche (first woman to receive pilot's licence) and Caudron G-3

2010. Pioneers of Aviation. Multicoloured.

(a) Ordinary gum

4869	58c. Type **1872**	2·75	1·70
MS4870	135×143 mm. 58c.×6, Hubert Latham (first attempt to cross English Channel) and *Antoinette* monoplane; As Type **1872**; Orville and Wilbur Wright (first manned flight) and *Wright Flyer*; Henry Farman (first cross-country flight) and Voisin biplane; Jules Vedrines (first flight over 100 mph, 1912) and Deperdussin racing monoplane; Léon Delagrange (first flight with passenger) and Voisin biplane	32·00	32·00

(b) Self-adhesive

4871	58c. As Type **1872**	2·75	1·70

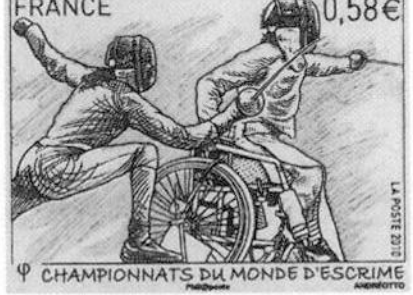
1873 Able-bodied and Wheelchair Competitors

2010. World Fencing Championships, Grand Palais, Paris. Multicoloured.

4872	58c. Type **1873**	2·75	1·70
4873	87c. Two competitors attacking	4·00	2·20

1874 Eiffel Tower and 'Barreau de Paris'

2010. Bicentenary of Barreau de Paris (Paris bar)

(a) Ordinary gum

4874	**1874**	58c. multicoloured	2·75	1·70

(b) Self-adhesive

4875	**1874**	58c. black and new blue	2·75	1·70

1875 Bridge, Villeneuve-sur-Lot

2010. Villeneuve-sur-Lot, Lot-et-Garonne

4876	**1875**	58c. multicoloured	2·50	1·40

1876 Stars and Cherub

2010. Greetings. Multicoloured.

4877	(58c.) Type **1876**	2·50	1·40
4878	(58c.) Santa Claus and children	2·50	1·40
4879	(58c.) Christmas tree bauble and flowers	2·50	1·40
4880	(58c.) Couple, baubles, flowers and striped ribbon	2·50	1·40
4881	(58c.) Parcel outline, Santa Claus decorations and baubles	2·50	1·40
4882	(58c.) Reindeer, tree and rose	2·50	1·40
4883	(58c.) Swallow carrying flowers and silver coloured heart	2·50	1·40
4884	(58c.) Flying fish, tag and flower outlines	2·50	1·40
4885	(58c.) Champagne bottle and star-shaped baubles	2·40	1·50
4886	(58c.) Green and red buttonhole decoration and tag inscribed 'DREAM'	2·40	1·50
4887	(58c.) Inscribed outline heart and multicoloured swallow	2·50	1·40
4888	(58c.) Outline yule log, mother and daughter	2·50	1·40
4889	(58c.) Christmas tree and outline trumpe	2·50	1·40
4890	(58c.) Gerbera flower, candles, lily-of-the-valley and horse shoe	2·50	1·40

1877 Emergency Phone-call

2010. French Red Cross. Multicoloured (except Red Cross emblem).

MS4891	58c.×5, Type **1877**; Recovery position; Red Cross emblem (bright vermilion and ultramarine) (horiz); Heimlich manoeuvre; Giving CPR (Cardiopulmonary resuscitation)	20·00	20·00

1878 Arc de Triomphe

2010. European Capitals

MS4892	58c.×4, Type **1878**; Notre Dame Cathedral; Palais Garnier Opera House; Eiffel Tower (vert)	9·75	9·75

1879 Spring (detail)

2010. 500th Death Anniv of Sandro Botticelli (1st issue). Multicoloured.

MS4893	87c. Type **1879**; €1.40 Three dancers (*Spring* (detail))	9·50	9·50

1880 Virgin and Child (Caen)

2010. Flemish Primitive Art in French and Belgian Collections. Multicoloured.

MS4894	€1.80×2, Type **1880**; *Portrait of Laurent Froimont* (Brussels)	15·00	15·00

1881 Tax Stamp

2010. 150th Anniv of First Tax Stamp

4895	**1881**	(58c.) chocolate	2·50	1·40

2010. 500th Death Anniv of Sandro Botticelli (2nd issue). Multicoloured.

4896	87c. *Spring* (detail) (As Type **1879**)	3·75	2·10
4897	€1.40 Three dancers (*Spring* (detail))	6·00	3·75

1882 Map of Central and South America and Libertarian Authors' Names on Book Covers

2010. Bicentenary of Latin American Freedom from Colonialism

4898	**1882**	87c. multicoloured	3·75	2·20

1883 Rabbit

2011. Chinese New Year

4899	**1883**	58c. multicoloured	2·50	1·40

1884 Heart

2011. St. Valentine's Day. Multicoloured.

(a) Self-adhesive gum

4900	58c. Type **1884**	2·50	1·40
4901	95c. Red heart	4·25	2·50

(b) Minature sheet. Ordinary gum

MS4902 135×142 mm. (55c.)×5, As No. 4900×5	15·00	15·00

1885 France

2011. World Fabrics. Multicoloured.

4903	(55c.) Type **1885**	2·50	1·40
4904	(55c.) Ivory Coast	2·50	1·40
4905	(55c.) Polynesia	2·50	1·40
4906	(55c.) Italy	2·50	1·40
4907	(55c.) Iran	2·50	1·40
4908	(55c.) Egypt	2·50	1·40
4909	(55c.) India	2·50	1·40
4910	(55c.) China	2·50	1·40
4911	(55c.) Japan	2·50	1·40
4912	(55c.) Japan	2·50	1·40
4913	(55c.) Morocco	2·50	1·40
4914	(55c.) France (different)	2·50	1·40

FRANK STAMP

1939. Optd F.

F652	**61**	90c. blue	2·75	3·25

MILITARY FRANK STAMPS

1901. Optd F. M.

M309	**12**	15c. orange	90·00	8·75

1903. Optd F. M.

M314	**14**	15c. red	90·00	8·75

1904. Optd F. M.

M323	**15**	10c. red	47·00	10·00
M324	**15**	15c. green	85·00	10·00

1907. Optd F. M.

M348	**18**	10c. red	2·10	1·10

1929. Optd F. M.

M471	**15**	50c. red	6·25	1·10

1933. Optd F. M.

M516	**61**	50c. red	4·25	90
M517	**61**	65c. blue	55	55
M518	**61**	90c. blue	70	70

M 236

1946. No value indicated.

M967	**M 236**	green	2·40	1·90
M968	**M 236**	red	65	35

M545 Flag

1964. No value indicated.

M1661	**M 545**	multicoloured	60	55

NEWSPAPER STAMPS

J6

1868. With or without gum. (a) Imperf.

J131	**J6**	2c. mauve	£375	95·00
J132	**J6**	2c. blue	£750	£375

(b) Perf.

J133	**J 6**	2c. mauve	65·00	28·00
J134	**J 6**	2c. blue	95·00	44·00
J135	**J 6**	2c. pink	£325	£130
J136	**J 6**	5c. mauve	£1600	£800

POSTAGE DUE STAMPS

D4

1859

D87	**D4**	10c. black	47·00	22·50
D88	**D4**	15c. black	55·00	17·00
D212	**D4**	25c. black	£200	70·00
D213	**D4**	30c. black	£325	£180
D214	**D4**	40c. blue	£550	£650
D216	**D4**	60c. yellow	£650	£1700
D217	**D4**	60c. blue	£110	£170

D11

1882

D279	**D11**	1c. black	3·25	2·75
D280	**D11**	2c. black	55·00	33·00
D281	**D11**	3c. black	75·00	31·00
D282	**D11**	4c. black	95·00	50·00
D283	**D11**	5c. black	£190	39·00
D297	**D11**	5c. blue	30	50
D284	**D11**	10c. black	£225	2·75
D298	**D11**	10c. brown	30	50
D285	**D11**	15c. black	£130	13·00
D317	**D11**	15c. green	37·00	1·90
D286	**D11**	20c. black	£550	£170
D300	**D11**	20c. green	8·00	85
D301	**D11**	25c. red	8·00	5·00
D287	**D11**	30c. black	£325	2·75
D302	**D11**	30c. red	30	35
D288	**D11**	40c. black	£225	75·00
D304	**D11**	40c. red	16·00	5·50
D305	**D11**	45c. green	10·50	6·00
D289	**D11**	50c. black	£950	£275
D306	**D11**	50c. purple	55	55
D290	**D11**	60c. black	£950	70·00
D307	**D11**	60c. green	1·10	55
D291	**D11**	1f. black	£1200	£500
D308	**D11**	1f. pink on yellow	£800	£500
D309	**D11**	1f. brown on yellow	11·50	55
D310	**D11**	1f. brown	1·40	55
D293	**D11**	2f. black	£2000	£1000
D294	**D11**	2f. brown	£300	£190
D311	**D11**	2f. red	£375	85·00
D312	**D11**	2f. mauve	85	1·30
D313	**D11**	3f. mauve	85	1·20
D295	**D11**	5f. black	£4250	£22500
D296	**D11**	5f. brown	£700	£450
D314	**D11**	5f. orange	3·75	3·00

D19

1908

D348	**D19**	1c. olive	1·20	1·70
D349	**D19**	10c. violet	1·50	55
D350	**D19**	20c. bistre	55·00	1·70
D351	**D19**	30c. bistre	15·00	55
D352	**D19**	50c. red	£450	75·00
D353	**D19**	60c. red	3·25	5·50

1917. Surch.

D378	20c. on 30c. bistre	42·00	5·00
D379	40c. on 50c. red	12·50	5·00
D433	50c. on 10c. violet	4·25	5·00
D434	60c. on 1c. olive	7·50	6·00
D435	1f. on 60c. red	24·00	17·00
D436	2f. on 60c. red	24·00	17·00

D43

1927

D454	**D43**	1c. green	1·60	1·80
D455	**D43**	10c. red	2·40	2·75
D456	**D43**	30c. bistre	6·25	55
D457	**D43**	60c. red	6·25	55
D458	**D43**	1f. purple	18·00	4·00
D459	**D43**	1f. green	21·00	1·00
D460	**D43**	2f. blue	£110	55·00
D461	**D43**	2f. brown	£190	34·00

1929. Surch.

D471	1f.20 on 2f. blue	55·00	18·00
D472	5f. on 1f. purple	75·00	19·00

1931. Surch UN FRANC.

D494	1f. on 60c. red	37·00	2·20

D187 Wheat Sheaves

1943. Inscr "CHIFFRE-TAXE".

D787	**D187**	10c. brown	20	20
D788	**D187**	30c. purple	20	20
D789	**D187**	50c. green	20	20
D790	**D187**	1f. blue	20	20
D791	**D187**	1f.50 red	20	35
D792	**D187**	2f. blue	20	35
D793	**D187**	3f. red	20	35
D794	**D187**	4f. violet	4·50	3·75
D795	**D187**	5f. pink	50	45
D796	**D187**	10f. orange	3·00	2·50
D797	**D187**	20f. bistre	9·00	3·75

1946. As Type D 187 but inscr "TIMBRE TAXE".

D985	10c. brown	1·80	1·70
D986	30c. purple	1·80	1·70
D987	50c. green	37·00	13·50
D988	1f. blue	40	35
D989	2f. blue	40	35
D990	3f. red	40	35
D991	4f. violet	40	35
D992	5f. pink	40	35
D993	10f. red	40	35
D994	20f. brown	2·75	60
D995	50f. green	38·00	2·00
D996	100f. green	£120	9·50

D457

1960. New Currency.

D1474	**D457**	5c. mauve	5·00	90
D1475	**D457**	10c. red	7·50	80
D1476	**D457**	20c. brown	6·25	35
D1477	**D457**	50c. green	19·00	1·60
D1478	**D457**	1f. green	75·00	2·75

D539 Poppies

1964

D1650	-	5c. red. grn & pur	20	15
D1651	-	10c. bl, grn & pur	20	15
D1652	**D 539**	15c. red, green & brown	35	35
D1653	-	20c. pur, grn & turq	20	15
D1654	-	30c. bl, grn & brn	20	15
D1655	-	40c. yell, red & turq	35	35
D1656	-	50c. red, grn & bl	35	35
D1657	-	1f. vio, grn & bl	1·00	35

DESIGNS: 5c. Knapweed; 10c. Gentian; 20c. Little periwinkle; 30c. Forget-me-not; 40 c Columbine; 50c. Clover; 1f. Soldanella.

D917 "Ampedus cinnabarinus"

1982. Beetles.

D2493	**D917**	10c. brown & black	20	15
D2494	-	20c. black	20	15
D2495	-	30c. red, brn & blk	35	35
D2496	-	40c. bl, brn & blk	60	35
D2497	-	50c. red and black	35	35
D2498	-	1f. black	60	55
D2499	-	2f. yellow and black	1·20	90
D2500	-	3f. black and red	1·90	55
D2501	-	4f. brown and black	2·75	90
D2502	-	5f. bl, red & blk	2·75	55

DESIGNS: 20c. "Dorcadion fuliginator"; 30c. "Leptura cordigera"; 40c. "Paederus littoralis"; 50c. "Pyrochroa coccinea"; 1f. "Scarites laevigatus"; 2f. "Trichius gallicus"; 3f. "Adalia alpina"; 4f. "Apoderus coryli"; 5f. "Trichodes alvearius".

COUNCIL OF EUROPE STAMPS

Until March 25th, 1960, these stamps could only be used by delegates and permanent officials of the Council of Europe on official correspondence at Strasbourg. From that date they could be used on all correspondence posted within the Council of Europe building.

1950. No. 1354 optd CONSEIL DE L'EUROPE.

C1	35f. mauve and red	1·70	3·25

C2 Council Flag

1958

C2	**C2**	8f. blue, orange & pur	35	35
C3	**C2**	20f. blue, yellow & brn	35	35
C4	**C2**	25f. blue, pur & myrtle	70	70
C5	**C2**	35f. blue and red	55	55
C6	**C2**	50f. blue and purple	1·40	1·40

1963

C7	20c. blue, yellow & brn	1·40	1·40
C8	25c. blue, pur & myrt	2·75	2·00
C9	25c. multicoloured	1·40	1·10
C10	30c. blue, yellow & red	1·10	1·10
C11	40c. multicoloured	1·70	1·50
C12	50c. blue and purple	3·25	2·75
C13	50c. multicoloured	3·25	2·20
C14	60c. multicoloured	1·70	1·70
C15	70c. multicoloured	5·50	4·00

1975. As Type C 2, but inscr "FRANCE".

C16	60c. multicoloured	1·70	1·50
C17	80c. yellow, blue and red	2·20	1·90
C18	1f. multicoloured	4·50	4·50
C19	1f.20 multicoloured	6·50	5·00

C3 New Council of Europe Building, Strasbourg

1977

C20	**C3**	80c. red, lt brn & brn	1·10	1·10
C21	**C3**	1f. brown, blue & grn	55	55
C22	**C3**	1f.40 grey, grn & brn	2·50	2·50
C23	**C3**	1f.40 green	1·10	1·10
C24	**C3**	2f. blue	1·40	1·40

1978. 25th Anniv of European Convention on Human Rights. As Type C 3 with the addition of the Human Rights emblem.

C25	1f.20 black, purple & grn	70	70
C26	1f.70 turquoise, blue & grn	1·10	1·10

C5 Exterior and Interior of New Council Building, Strasbourg

1981

C27	**C5**	1f.40 violet, blue & pur	90	90
C28	**C5**	1f.60 green & brown	90	90
C29	**C5**	1f.70 green	1·10	1·10
C30	**C5**	1f.80 red, green & pur	1·20	1·20
C31	**C5**	2f. red, green & blue	1·10	1·10
C32	**C5**	2f.10 red	1·20	1·20
C33	**C5**	2f.30 green, turq & bl	1·10	1·10
C34	**C5**	2f.60 purple, bl & grey	1·40	1·40
C35	**C5**	2f.80 brown, dp bl & bl	1·40	1·40
C36	**C5**	3f. blue	1·70	1·70

C6 Foot Breaking through Shell

1985

C37	**C6**	1f.80 green	1·10	1·10
C38	**C6**	2f.20 red	1·40	1·40
C39	**C6**	3f.20 blue	1·70	1·70

C7 Council of Europe Building, Strasbourg

1986

C40	**C7**	1f.90 green	1·40	1·40
C41	**C7**	2f. green	1·40	1·40
C42	**C7**	2f.20 red	1·50	1·50
C43	**C7**	3f.40 blue	2·20	2·20
C44	**C7**	3f.60 blue	2·20	2·20

C8 Stars, Doves and Girl

1989. 40th Anniv of Council of Europe.

C45	**C8**	2f.20 multicoloured	1·70	1·70
C46	**C8**	3f.60 multicoloured	2·20	2·20

C9 Map of Europe

1990

C47	**C9**	2f.30 multicoloured	1·70	1·70
C48	**C9**	2f.50 multicoloured	1·70	1·70
C49	**C9**	3f.20 multicoloured	2·20	2·20
C50	**C9**	3f.40 multicoloured	2·20	2·20

C10 "36 Heads" (Friedensreich Hundertwasser)

1994

C51	**C10**	2f.80 multicoloured	2·40	2·00
C52	**C10**	3f.70 multicoloured	3·00	2·40

C11 Palace of Human Rights, Strasbourg

1996

C53	**C11**	3f. multicoloured	2·75	2·75
C54	**C11**	3f.80 multicoloured	3·25	3·25

C12 "Charioteer of Delphi" (replica of ancient Greek statue)

1999. Sculptures presented by Member states.

C55	3f. Type **C12**	3·00	3·00
C56	3f.80 "Nike" (Petras Mazuras)	3·50	3·50

C13 "I am black, I am white, I am black and white" (drawing, Tom Ungerer)

2001

C57	**C13**	3f. multicoloured	3·25	3·25
C58	**C13**	3f.80 multicoloured	3·75	3·75

C14 "Walking on Stars" (drawing, Tom Ungerer)

2003

C59	**C14**	50c. multicoloured	2·75	3·75
C60	**C14**	75c. multicoloured	3·25	3·25

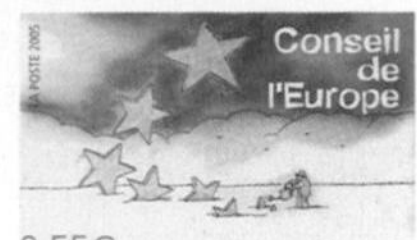

C15 "Conseil de l'Europe, semeur d'espoirs" (drawing, Tom Ungerer)

2005. Two phosphor bands. Multicoloured.

C61	55c. Type **C15**	2·75	2·75
C62	75c. Clouds in flag (Rafal Olbinski)	3·25	3·25

C16 Emblem and Globe

2007. Multicoloured.. Multicoloured..

C63	60c. Type **C16**	2·20	2·20
C64	85c. Statues (Mariano Gonzalez Beltran)	2·75	2·75

C17 '60'

2009. 60th Anniv of Council of Europe. Multicoloured.

C65	56c. Type **C17**	2·50	2·50
C66	70c. Court Building (50th Anniv of European Court of Human Rights)	2·75	2·75

C18 Tree and Roots (institutional communications emblem)

2010. 60th Anniv of European Convention on Human Rights. Multicoloured.

C67	75c. Type **C18**	3·50	3·50
C68	87c. Broken chain as '60' (anniversary emblem)	4·00	4·00

UNESCO STAMPS

For use on correspondence posted within the UNESCO headquarters building.

U1 Buddha and Hermes

1961

U1	**U1**	20c. bistre, blue & brown	55	55
U2	**U1**	25c. purple, green & blk	55	55
U3	**U1**	30c. brown & dp brown	1·40	1·10
U4	**U1**	50c. red, violet & black	1·40	1·40
U5	**U1**	60c. brown, mauve & bl	2·00	1·70

U2 Open Book and Globe

1966

U6	**U2**	25c. brown	55	55
U7	**U2**	30c. red	85	85
U8	**U2**	60c. green	1·40	1·40

U3 "Human Rights"

1969

U9	**U3**	30c. red, green & brown	90	90
U10	**U3**	40c. red, mauve & brn	1·10	90
U11	**U3**	50c. red, blue & brown	2·00	1·80
U12	**U3**	70c. red, violet & blue	3·00	2·75

1975. As Type **U3**, but inscribed "France".

U13	60c. red, green and brown	1·70	1·40
U14	80c. red, brown and lake	2·20	1·70
U15	1f.20 red, blue and purple	4·50	4·50

U4 "Leaf"

1976

U16	**U4**	80c. blue, brown & pur	1·10	1·10
U17	**U4**	1f. orange, green & blue	55	55
U18	**U4**	1f.20 blue, red & green	70	70
U19	**U4**	1f.40 brn, mve & orge	2·50	2·50
U20	**U4**	1f.70 red, green & brn	1·10	90

U5 Old Slave Dungeons, Goree, Senegal

1980. Sites in Need of Protection.

U21	**U5**	1f.20 blue, green & red	85	85
U22	-	1f.40 mauve, blue & grn	1·10	1·10
U23	-	2f. violet, green & red	1·40	1·40

DESIGNS: 1f.40, Moenjodaro, Pakistan; 2f. Palace of Sans-Souci, Haiti.

U6 Gateway, Fez, Morocco

1981. Sites in Need of Preservation.

U24	**U6**	1f.40 brown, blue & red	90	90
U25	-	1f.60 blue, red & grn	90	90
U26	-	1f.80 violet, pur & bl	1·20	1·20
U27	-	2f.30 brown, grn & bl	1·10	1·10
U28	-	2f.60 black, bl & red	1·40	1·40

DESIGNS—VERT: 1f.60, Seated Buddha Sukhotai, Thailand; 1f.80, Hue, Vietnam; 2f.60, Sao Miguel Cathedral, Brazil. HORIZ: 2f.30, Fort St. Elmo, Malta.

U7 Chinguetti Mosque, Mauritania

1983. Sites in Need of Preservation.

U29		1f.70 brown and green	1·10	1·10
U30	**U 7**	2f. brown, blue & blk	1·10	1·10
U31	-	2f.10 brown, bl & turq	1·20	1·20
U32	-	2f.80 black, bl & brn	1·40	1·40
U33	-	3f. orange, brn & grn	1·70	1·70

DESIGNS: 1f.70, Lalibela Church, Ethiopia; 2f.10, Sana'a, Yemen Arab Republic; 2f.80, City walls, Istanbul, Turkey; 3f. St. Mary's Church, Kotor, Yugoslavia.

U8 Amphitheatre, Carthage

1985. Protected Sites. Each grey, green and blue.

U34	1f.80 Type **U8**	1·60	1·40
U35	2f.20 Old Square, Havana, Cuba	1·60	1·40
U36	3f.20 Temple of Anuradhapura, Sri Lanka	2·75	2·75

U9 Temple of Tikal, Guatemala

1986. Protected Sites. Each grey, brown and green.

U37	1f.90 Type **U9**	1·70	1·70
U38	3f.40 Bagerhat Mosque, Bangladesh	3·00	3·00

U10 Acropolis, Athens

1987. Protected Sites. Each brown, chestnut and blue.

U39	2f. Type **U10**	1·90	1·90
U40	3f.60 Philae Temple, Egypt	3·00	3·00

U11 St. Francis's Monastery, Lima, Peru

1990. Protected Sites.

U41	**U11**	2f.30 brn, grn & blk	2·00	2·00
U42	-	3f.20 brn, orge & bl	2·75	2·75

DESIGN—HORIZ: 3f.20 Shibam, People's Democratic Republic of Yemen.

U12 Temple of Bagdaon, Nepal

1991. Protected Sites.

U43	**U12**	2f.50 brown and red	2·00	2·00
U44	-	3f.40 brown & green	3·00	3·00

DESIGN—HORIZ: 3f.40, Herat Fort, Afghanistan.

U13 Angkor, Cambodia

1993. Protected Sites. Multicoloured.

U45	2f.80 Type **U13**	2·00	2·00
U46	3f.70 Cave paintings, Tassili n'Ajjer National Park, Algeria (horiz)	2·75	2·75

U14 Ayers Rock, Uluru, Australia

1996. Protected Sites. National Parks. Mult.

U47	3f. Type **U14**	2·75	2·75
U48	3f.80 Glacier, Los Glaciares, Argentine Republic	3·25	3·25

U15 Detail of Fresco from Villa of Mysteries, Pompeii

1998. Protected Sites. Multicoloured.

U49	3f. Type **U15**	3·00	3·00
U50	3f.80 Statues, Easter Island (horiz)	3·50	3·50

U16 Sphinx and Pyramids, Giza, Egypt

2001. Protected Sites. Multicoloured.

U51	3f. Type **U16**	3·25	3·25
U52	3f.80 Komodo National Park, Indonesia	3·75	3·75

U 17 Reindeer, Lapland

2003. Protected Sites. Multicoloured.

U53	50c. Type **U17**	2·75	2·75
U54	75c. Church of the Resurrection, St. Petersburg (300th anniv) (vert)	3·25	3·25

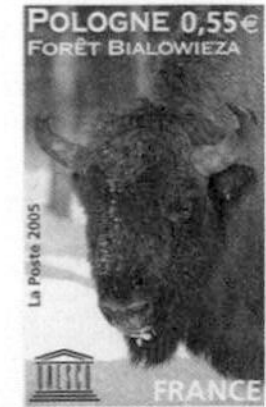

U18 Bison, Bialowieza Forest

2005. Protected Sites. Multicoloured.

U55	55c. Type **U18**	2·75	2·75
U56	90c. Rock building, Jordan (horiz)	3·25	3·25

U19 Tiger, Siberia

2006. Protected Sites. Multicoloured.

U57	60c. Type **U19**	2·20	2·20
U58	85c. Luang Prabang, Laos (horiz)	2·75	2·75

U20 Ksar of Ait-Ben-Haddou, Morocco

2007. Protected Sites. Multicoloured.

U59	60c. Type **U20**	2·20	2·20
U60	85c. Koala bear, Austalia (vert)	2·75	2·75

U21 Mountain Gorilla, Virunga National Park

2008. Protected Sites. Multicoloured.

U61	65c. Type **U21**	2·20	2·20
U62	85c. Machu Picchu, Peru	2·75	2·75

U22 Alhambra, Granada, Spain

2010. Cultural and Natural Heritage. Multicoloured.

U63	75c. Type **U22**	3·50	3·50
U64	87c. Alpaca	3·50	3·50

Pt. 6, Pt. 19

FREE FRENCH FORCES IN THE LEVANT

After British and Free French troops had occupied Syria and Lebanon in June 1941 the following stamps were issued for the use of Free French forces in those areas.

100 centimes = 1 franc.

1942. Surch with Lorraine Crosses, FORCES FRANCAISES LIBRES LEVANT and value. (i) On No. 252 of Syria.

1		50c. on 4p. orange	8·00	22·00

(ii) On Nos. 251 and 212 of Lebanon.

2	**16a**	1f. on 5p. blue	4·00	21·00
3	**22**	2f.50 on 12½p. blue	5·00	20·00

1942. Air. Nos. 269/70 of Syria surch with Lorraine Crosses, LIGNES AERIENNES F.A.F.L. and value.

4	4f. on 50p. black	6·00	18·00
5	6f.50 on 50p. black	6·00	13·50
6	8f. on 50p. black	5·50	13·50
7	10f. on 100p. mauve	5·75	21·00

3 Camelry and Ruins at Palmyra

4 Wings bearing Lorraine Crosses

1942. Buff background.

8	**3**	1f. red (postage)	1·80	3·50
9	**3**	1f.50 violet	1·40	5·25
10	**3**	2f. orange	1·30	5·50
11	**3**	2f.50 brown	1·30	6·75
12	**3**	3f. blue	1·30	7·50
13	**3**	4f. green	1·20	7·00
14	**3**	5f. purple	95	6·25
15	**4**	6f.50 red (air)	1·00	7·00
16	**4**	10f. purple and blue	60	7·25
MS16a		106×16 mm. Nos. 15/16. No gum	32·00	65·00

1942. Air. No. 15 surch 4 and bars.

17	4f. on 6f.50 red	2·00	9·25

1943. Surch RESISTANCE and premium.

18	**3**	1f.+9f. red (postage)	6·75	7·75
19	**3**	5f.+20f. purple	6·75	7·75
20	**4**	6f.50+48f.50 red (air)	50·00	75·00
21	**4**	10f.+100f. pur & bl	55·00	75·00

1943. Air. No. 12 surch 4F, bars and airplane.

22	**3**	4f. on 3f. blue and buff	2·00	4·25

Pt. 6

FRENCH COLONIES

General issues for use in French Colonies which had no special stamps.

100 centimes = 1 franc.

NOTE. For other stamps issued for French Colones see the note at the beginning of France.

A Eagle

1859. Imperf.

1	**A**	1c. green	16·00	18·00
2	**A**	5c. green	21·00	9·25
3	**A**	10c. brown	18·00	6·00
4	**A**	20c. blue	19·00	14·00
5	**A**	40c. orange	12·00	5·00
6	**A**	80c. red	85·00	28·00

B Laureated

D Laureated

1871. Imperf.

7	**B**	1c. green	85·00	70·00
9	**D**	30c. brown	£140	65·00
10	**D**	80c. red	£900	£120

E Ceres

F Ceres

1871. Imperf.

11	**E**	1c. green on blue	20·00	7·75
12	**E**	2c. brown on buff	£450	£650
14	**E**	5c. green	27·00	4·50
16	**F**	15c. bistre	£275	14·00
20	**F**	10c. brown on pink	£170	16·00

H Peace and Commerce

1877. Imperf.

24	**H**	1c. green	40·00	65·00
25	**H**	2c. green	15·00	14·00
26	**H**	4c. green	20·00	12·00
27	**H**	5c. green	30·00	3·00
28	**H**	10c. green	£100	9·00
29	**H**	15c. grey	£200	75·00
30	**H**	20c. brown on yellow	50·00	2·00
31a	**H**	25c. blue	55·00	5·00
32	**H**	30c. brown	60·00	60·00
33	**H**	35c. black on yellow	55·00	23·00
34	**H**	40c. red on yellow	23·00	13·00
35a	**H**	75c. red	70·00	70·00
36	**H**	1f. green	60·00	20·00

1878. Imperf.

37	1c. black on blue	22·00	10·00
38	2c. brown on buff	20·00	14·00
39	4c. brown on grey	25·00	18·00
40	10c. black on lilac	£110	25·00
41	15c. blue on blue	33·00	6·00
42	20c. red on green	85·00	10·00
43	25c. black on red	£500	£250
44	25c. brown on yellow	£600	22·00

J Commerce

1881. Perf.

45	**J**	1c. black on blue	2·50	2·30
46	**J**	2c. brown on buff	8·75	3·00
47	**J**	4c. brown on grey	5·00	3·25
48	**J**	5c. green on green	15·00	1·50
49	**J**	10c. black on lilac	18·00	2·50
50	**J**	15c. blue on blue	23·00	1·20
51	**J**	20c. red on green	65·00	7·00
52	**J**	25c. brown on yellow	17·00	2·00
53	**J**	25c. black on pink	15·00	1·00
54	**J**	30c. brown on drab	16·00	18·00
55	**J**	35c. black on orange	60·00	35·00
56	**J**	40c. red on yellow	38·00	20·00
57	**J**	75c. red on pink	85·00	70·00
58	**J**	1f. green	80·00	26·00

K Map of France

L Colonies offering France Aid

1943. Aid to Resistance Movement.

82	**K**	50c.+4f.50 green	2·00	5·25
83	**K**	1f.50+8f.50 red	2·00	5·25
84	**K**	3f.+12f. blue	2·00	5·50
85	**K**	5f.+15f. grey	2·00	5·25
86	**L**	9f.+41f. purple	4·00	6·25

M Resisters

1943. Aid to Resistance Movement. Roul.

87	**M**	1f.50+98f.50 bl & grey	30·00	65·00

N

1943. French Solidarity Fund.

88	**N**	10f.+40f. blue	5·00	8·00

O

1944. Air. Aviation Fund.

89	O	10f.+40f. green	6·00	10·50

POSTAGE DUE STAMPS

U

1884. Imperf.

D59	U	1c. black	70	2·30
D60	U	2c. black	1·30	2·50
D61	U	3c. black	1·00	3·00
D62	U	4c. black	1·40	3·00
D63	U	5c. black	3·50	2·00
D64	U	10c. black	8·00	3·00
D65	U	15c. black	6·25	5·50
D66	U	20c. black	9·00	6·50
D67	U	30c. black	15·00	3·00
D68	U	40c. black	25·00	10·00
D69	U	60c. black	45·00	20·00
D70	U	1f. brown	55·00	40·00
D71	U	2f. brown	25·00	21·00
D72	U	5f. brown	£120	80·00

1893. Imperf.

D73	5c. blue	1·00	85
D74	10c. brown	25	10
D75	15c. green	70	1·20
D76	20c. olive	60	4·00
D77	30c. red	1·70	1·80
D78	50c. red	2·75	2·10
D79	60c. brown on yellow	4·50	3·75
D81	1f. red on yellow	11·00	13·00

V

1945. Perf.

D90	V	10c. blue	20	7·00
D91	V	15c. green	1·80	7·00
D92	V	25c. orange	1·70	6·75
D93	V	50c. black	3·50	7·25
D94	V	60c. brown	5·00	7·25
D95	V	1f. red	5·00	7·75
D96	V	2f. red	5·50	7·75
D97	V	4f. grey	9·25	11·50
D98	V	5f. blue	10·50	12·00
D99	V	10f. violet	38·00	33·00
D100	V	20f. brown	11·00	13·00
D101	V	50f. green	19·00	21·00

Pt. 6

FRENCH CONGO

A French colony in central Africa, in 1903 divided into Gabon, Middle Congo, Ubangi-Shari and Chad.

100 centimes = 1 franc.

1891. Stamps of French Colonies, "Commerce" type, surch Congo francais and value in figures.

2	J	5c. on 1c. black on blue	£180	£120
3	J	5c. on 15c. blue	£350	£180
4	J	5c. on 25c. black on red	£130	60·00
11	J	10c. on 25c. black on red	£325	£150
12	J	15c. on 25c. black on red	£450	£200

1892. Stamps of French Colonies. "Commerce" type, surch COngo Francais and value in figures.

5	5c. on 20c. red on green	£1200	£550
6	5c. on 25c. black on red	£225	£100
7	10c. on 25c. black on red	£250	80·00
8	10c. on 40c. red on yellow	£2750	£425
9	15c. on 25c. black on red	£250	65·00

1892. Postage Due stamps of French Colonies surch Congo francais Timbre poste and value in figures.

13	U	5c. on 5c. black	£190	£170
14	U	5c. on 20c. black	£190	£160
15	U	5c. on 30c. black	£250	£190
16	U	10c. on 1f. brown	£200	£160

1892. "Tablet" key-type inscr "CONGO FRANCAIS" in red (1, 5, 15, 25, 50 (No. 31), 75c. and 1f.) or blue (others).

17	D	1c. black on blue	1·00	1·90
18	D	2c. brown on buff	3·00	3·25
19	D	4c. brown on grey	2·50	3·75
20	D	5c. green on light green	6·00	7·50
21	D	10c. black on lilac	24·00	21·00
22	D	10c. red	3·00	2·30
23	D	15c. blue	65·00	21·00
24	D	15c. grey	10·00	12·50
25	D	20c. red on green	20·00	25·00
26	D	25c. black on pink	28·00	21·00
27	D	25c. blue	13·00	17·00
28	D	30c. brown on drab	20·00	23·00
29	D	40c. red on yellow	45·00	38·00
30	D	50c. red on pink	50·00	36·00
31	D	50c. brown on blue	13·00	13·50
32	D	75c. brown on orange	45·00	36·00
33	D	1f. green	65·00	37·00

6 Leopard in Ambush

8 Woman of the Bakalois Tribe

1900

36c	6	1c. brown and grey	1·30	1·80
37	6	2c. brown and yellow	1·10	95
38	6	4c. red and grey	2·30	1·50
39	6	5c. green and light green	2·75	1·50
40	6	10c. red and light red	8·00	3·50
41	6	15c. violet and green	3·00	1·60
42	8	20c. green and red	3·50	3·25
43	8	25c. blue and light blue	3·75	2·50
44	8	30c. red and yellow	5·00	2·75
45	8	40c. brown and green	5·50	3·25
46	8	50c. violet and lilac	7·00	6·25
47	8	75c. red and orange	16·00	10·50
48	-	1f. grey and green	21·00	20·00
49	-	2f. red and brown	38·00	24·00
50	-	5f. orange and black	90·00	95·00

DESIGN—28×40 mm: 1, 2, 5f. Coconut palms, Libreville.

1903. Surch in figures.

51	8	5c. on 30c. red & yellow	£325	£180
52	-	0,10 on 2f. red & brn (No. 49)	£400	£180

PARCEL POST STAMPS

P3

1891

P13	P3	10c. black on blue	£300	£225

1893. Receipt stamp of France optd Congo Francais COLIS POSTAUX.

P34	10c. grey	£225	£200

Pt. 6

FRENCH EQUATORIAL AFRICA

In 1910 Gabon, Middle Congo and Ubangi-Shari-Chad were federated to form French Equatorial Africa: each colony continued to issue its own stamps until 1936.

In 1958 the four constituent colonies became autonomous republics as Gabon, Congo Republic, Central African Republic (formerly Ubangi-Shari) and Chad.

100 centimes = 1 franc.

1936. Middle Congo stamps of 1933 optd AFRIQUE EQUATORIALE FRANCAISE.

1	15	1c. brown	45	5·75
2	15	2c. blue	35	6·25
3	15	4c. green	2·10	6·75
4	15	5c. purple	1·30	7·00
5	15	10c. green	4·25	7·25
6	15	15c. purple	4·75	5·75
7	15	20c. red on pink	4·00	7·75
8	15	25c. orange	7·00	9·00
9	-	40c. brown	5·25	8·75
10	-	50c. purple	5·25	3·50
11	-	75c. black on pink	5·75	6·00
12	-	90c. red	6·25	8·75
13	-	1f.50 blue	4·50	4·25
14	-	5f. blue	70·00	45·00
15	-	10f. black	41·00	32·00
16	-	20f. brown	46·00	40·00

1936. Gabon Stamps of 1933 optd AFRIQUE EQUATORIALE FRANCAISE.

17	21	1c. red	35	6·00
18	21	2c. black on pink	70	5·25
19	21	4c. green	1·60	8·00
20	21	5c. blue	1·70	7·00
21	21	10c. red on yellow	2·75	4·00
22	22	40c. purple	4·25	7·00
23	22	50c. brown	4·00	3·00
24	22	1f. green on blue	34·00	16·00
25	22	1f.50 blue	9·25	5·25
26	22	2f. red	20·00	13·50

1937. International Exhibition, Paris. As T 58a of Guadeloupe.

27	20c. violet	3·00	7·00
28	30c. green	3·00	5·00
29	40c. red	3·00	5·00
30	50c. brown and blue	2·50	4·25
31	90c. red	3·25	4·00
32	1f.50 blue	3·25	6·75
MS33	120×100 mm. 3f. red. Imperf	14·00	40·00

8 Logging near Mayumba

9 Chad Family

10 Count Savorgnan de Brazza

12 Savoia Marchetti S-73 over Stanley Pool

1937

34	8	1c. brown & yell (postage)	35	6·25
35	8	2c. violet and green	35	5·00
36	8	3c. blue and yellow	70	7·00
37	8	4c. mauve and blue	45	6·25
38	8	5c. deep green & green	55	5·25
39	9	10c. mauve and blue	45	3·00
40	9	15c. blue and pink	35	1·00
41	9	20c. brown and yellow	1·00	1·30
42	9	25c. red and blue	2·30	1·60
44	10	30c. deep green & green	2·30	4·25
45	10	30c. blue and pink	80	6·75
46	9	35c. green & light green	2·20	2·75
47	10	40c. red and blue	45	55
48	10	45c. blue and green	5·25	7·25
49	10	45c. green & light green	1·60	7·25
50	10	50c. brown and yellow	45	40
51	10	55c. violet and blue	2·20	2·75
52	10	60c. purple and blue	1·30	6·25
53	A	65c. blue and green	1·50	95
54	A	70c. violet and orange	1·70	6·75
55	A	75c. black and yellow	7·25	6·00
56	A	80c. brown and yellow	1·00	2·40
57	A	90c. red and orange	90	1·70
58	A	1f. violet and green	3·50	1·60
59	10	1f. red and orange	2·75	2·30
60	A	1f. green and blue	1·30	4·25
61	B	1f.25 red and orange	2·75	3·50
62	B	1f.40 brown and green	1·60	4·50
63	B	1f.50 blue and light blue	3·00	4·00
64	B	1f.60 violet and orange	1·40	4·25
65	B	1f.75 brown and yellow	2·30	2·75
66	A	1f.75 blue and light blue	1·30	4·25
67	B	2f. green and light green	1·40	80
68	C	2f.15 violet and yellow	2·30	4·75
69	C	2f.25 blue and light blue	2·75	7·75
70	C	2f.50 purple and orange	1·60	2·75
71	C	3f. blue and pink	90	55
72	C	5f. green and light green	2·00	1·50
73	C	10f. violet and blue	3·50	3·75
74	C	20f. black and yellow	4·25	4·75
75	D	1f.50 black & yellow (air)	85	6·25
76	D	2f. mauve and blue	2·75	6·50
77	D	2f.50 green and pink	1·40	85
78	D	3f.75 brown and green	2·50	3·50
79	12	4f.50 red and blue	2·50	3·25
80	12	6f.50 blue and green	3·25	6·50
81	12	8f.50 red and orange	3·25	7·00
82	12	10f.75 violet and green	3·00	8·00

DESIGNS: A, Emile Gentil; B, Paul Crampel; C, Victor Liotard; D, Latecoere 300 flying boat over Pointe Noire.

1938. Anti-cancer Fund. As T 58b of Guadeloupe.

94	1f.75+50c. blue	11·50	60·00

1938. Social Welfare. Surch with premium in figures.

95	A	65c.+35c. (No. 53)	2·30	8·00
96	A	1f.75+50c. (No. 66)	2·75	9·75

16 Bouet-Willaumez and "La Malouine"

1938. Centenary of Landing of Bouet-Willaumez in Gabon.

97	16	65c. brown	2·00	4·00
98	16	1f. red	1·70	2·75
99	16	1f.75 blue	2·10	5·75
100	16	2f. violet	2·75	3·00

1939. New York World's Fair. As T 58c of Guadeloupe.

101	1f.25 red	2·00	6·75
102	2f.25 blue	2·50	7·00

1939. 150th Anniv of French Revolution. As T 58d of Guadeloupe.

103	45c.+25c. green and black (postage)	15·00	37·00
104	70c.+30c. brown & black	15·00	37·00
105	90c.+35c. orange & black	15·00	37·00
106	1f.25+1f. red and black	15·00	37·00
107	2f.25+2f. blue and black	15·00	37·00
108	4f.50+4f. blk & orge (air)	40·00	65·00

1940. Adherence to General de Gaulle. A. Postage stamps of 1936 and 1937. (a) Optd AFRIQUE FRANCAISE LIBRE.

109	8	1c. brown and yellow	2·20	8·00
110	8	2c. violet and green	2·20	8·00
111	8	3c. blue and yellow	2·20	8·00
112	8	5c. green & light green	2·20	8·00
113	9	10c. mauve and blue	2·75	6·50
114	9	15c. blue and pink	2·75	6·25
115	9	20c. brown and yellow	2·75	5·75
116	9	25c. red and blue	9·25	17·00
117	9	35c. green & lt green	2·75	5·00

(b) Optd LIBRE.

118	-	4c. green (No. 3)	22·00	21·00
119a	10	30c. dp green & green	7·00	4·50
120a	10	30c. blue and pink	17·00	25·00
121	10	40c. red and blue	2·10	2·30
122	10	45c. green & lt green	1·70	5·25
123	10	50c. brown and yellow	6·50	11·50
124	10	55c. violet and blue	1·70	3·00
125	10	60c. purple and blue	1·30	2·50
126	A	65c. blue and green	1·30	2·75
127	A	70c. violet and orange	1·50	5·00
128	A	75c. black and yellow	85·00	95·00
129	A	80c. brown and yellow	75	4·00
130	A	90c. red and orange	1·30	2·10
131	10	1f. red and orange	1·90	3·00
132	A	1f. green and blue	9·00	20·00
133	B	1f.40 brown and green	1·30	2·75
134	B	1f.50 blue & light blue	1·00	1·80
135	B	1f.60 violet & orange	1·00	5·00
136	B	1f.75 brown & yellow	1·00	3·75
137	C	2f.15 violet and yellow	1·30	5·00
138	C	2f.25 blue & light blue	1·30	3·75
139	C	2f.50 purple & orange	1·20	1·30
140	C	3f. blue and pink	1·90	4·50
141	C	5f. green & light green	4·50	4·50
142	C	10f. violet and blue	3·75	3·75
143	C	20f. black and yellow	1·90	3·00

(c) Surch LIBRE and value in figures.

144	10	75c. on 50c. brn & yell	1·00	1·30
145	A	1f. on 65c. blue & green	75	75

(d) Optd Afrique Francaise Libre.

146	8	1c. brown and yellow	3·25	1·80
147	8	2c. violet and green	3·50	2·75
148	8	3c. blue and yellow	3·75	3·00
149	8	5c. blue and green	3·25	4·00
150	9	10c. mauve and blue	2·50	1·50
151	9	15c. blue and pink	2·30	2·75
152	9	20c. brown and yellow	2·30	2·20
153	9	25c. red and blue	7·75	8·75
154	9	35c. green & light green	3·25	2·75

B. Air stamps of 1937 optd Afrique Francaise Libre or surch also.

155	D	1f.50 black and yellow	£250	£275
156	D	2f.50 green and pink	2·50	3·00
157	D	3f.75 brown and green	£250	£275
158	12	4f.50 red and blue	2·50	3·00
159	12	6f.50 blue and green	3·75	7·25

160	12	8f.50 red and orange	3·00	6·25
161	D	10f. on 2f.50 grn & pk	£140	£160
162	12	50f. on 10f.75 vio & grn	6·50	19·00

C. No. 71 of Middle Congo optd AFRIQUE FRANCAISE LIBRE.

163	15	4c. green	90·00	90·00

22 Phoenix

1941. Free French Issue. (a) Postage.

164	22	5c. brown	25	3·50
165	22	10c. blue	25	2·50
166	22	25c. green	25	2·75
167	22	30c. orange	25	2·75
168	22	40c. green	40	2·30
169	22	80c. purple	40	5·00
170	22	1f. mauve	95	65
171	22	1f.50 red	1·20	75
172	22	2f. black	1·20	90
173	22	2f.50 blue	1·50	1·80
174	22	4f. violet	75	35
175	22	5f. yellow	1·00	45
176	22	10f. brown	1·30	75
177	22	20f. green	1·40	1·50

(b) Air. As T 63a of Guadeloupe.

178	1f. orange	85	4·75
179	1f.50 red	1·30	6·00
180	5f. purple	1·60	6·00
181	10f. black	2·50	3·00
182	25f. blue	2·30	7·00
183	50f. green	2·30	4·75
184	100f. red	2·00	3·25

24 Count Savorgnan de Brazza and Stanley Pool

1941. De Brazza Memorial Fund.

185	24	1f.+2f. brown and red	1·90	5·75

1942. Commemorating the Arrival of Gen. de Gaulle at Brazzaville in 1940. Optd LIBRE 24-10-40.

186	A	80c. brown and yellow	24·00	17·00
187	10	1f. red and orange	27·00	18·00
188	A	1f. green and blue	25·00	21·00
189	B	1f.50 blue and pale blue	23·00	17·00

1943. Free French Funds. Nos. 69, 73 and 82 surch Afrique Francaise Combattante, cross and value.

190	2f.25+50f. bl & lt bl (postage)	15·00	35·00
191	10f.+100f. violet and blue	60·00	75·00
192	10f.75+200f. vio & grn (air)	£225	£225

1944. French Aid Fund. Various stamps surch RESISTANCE and value.

195	22	5c.+10f. brn (No. 164)	13·50	23·00
196	22	10c.+10f. blue (No. 165)	13·50	23·00
197	22	25c.+10f. grn (No. 166)	10·00	23·00
198	22	30c.+10f. orge (No. 167)	10·50	23·00
199	22	40c.+10f. grn (No. 168)	12·50	23·00
193	A	80c.+10f. brown and yellow (No. 169)	33·00	60·00
200	22	1f.+10f. mve (No. 170)	11·50	23·00
194	B	1f.50+15f. blue and light blue (No. 171)	43·00	60·00
201	22	2f.+20f. black (No. 172)	12·50	23·00
202	22	2f.50+25f. bl (No. 173)	13·00	23·00
203	22	4f.+40f. violet (No. 174)	12·00	23·00
204	22	5f.+50f. yellow (No. 175)	12·50	15·00
205	22	10f.+100f. brn (No. 176)	13·50	27·00
206	22	20f.+200f. grn (No. 177)	13·50	27·00

1944. French Aid Fund. Nos. 164/8, 170, 172/3, 186 and 189 surch LIBERATION and value.

209	22	5c.+10f. brown	12·00	27·00
210	22	10c.+10f. blue	12·00	27·00
211	22	25c.+10f. green	13·50	27·00
212	22	30c.+10f. orange	12·00	27·00
213	22	40c.+10f. green	10·50	27·00
207	A	80c.+10f. brown & yell	55·00	60·00
214	22	1f.+10f. mauve	12·00	27·00
208	B	1f.50+15f. bl & lt blue	50·00	60·00
215	22	2f.+20f. black	10·50	27·00
216	22	2f.50+25f. blue	10·50	27·00

1944. Mutual Aid and Red Cross Funds. As T 58e of Guadeloupe.

217	5f.+20f. blue	95	7·50

1945. Surch with new values and bars.

218	50c. on 5c. brown	1·30	8·25
219	60c. on 5c. brown	1·30	8·25
220	70c. on 5c. brown	1·30	8·25
221	1f.20 on 5c. brown	1·60	8·25
222	2f.40 on 25c. green	1·50	8·25
223	3f. on 25c. green	1·60	8·25
224	4f.50 on 25c. green	2·00	8·25
225	15f. on 2f.50 blue	2·00	8·25

1945. Eboue. As T 58f of Guadeloupe.

226	2f. black	40	45
227	25f. green	1·10	8·25

1946. Air. Victory. As T 63b of Guadeloupe.

228	8f. red	65	1·20

1946. Air. From Chad to the Rhine. As Nos. 226/31 of Cameroun.

229	5f. purple	2·40	8·25
230	10f. green	1·60	8·25
231	15f. blue	2·00	9·50
232	20f. red	3·00	10·00
233	25f. black	2·75	10·00
234	50f. red	3·75	9·50

34 Black Rhinoceros **36** Boatman

37 Caudron Goeland over Beach

1947

235	34	10c. blue (postage)	25	6·50
236	34	30c. violet	25	6·50
237	34	40c. orange	55	5·75
238	-	50c. blue	80	5·25
239	-	60c. red	55	5·75
240	-	80c. green	80	7·25
241	-	1f. orange	1·30	45
242	-	1f.20 red	1·70	5·00
243	-	1f.50 green	2·50	4·50
244	-	2f. brown	2·75	45
245	-	3f. red	2·50	60
246	-	3f.60 brown	4·50	10·00
247	-	4f. blue	2·30	45
248	36	5f. purple	2·75	45
249	36	6f. blue	2·50	60
250	36	10f. black	2·30	45
251	-	15f. brown	2·00	15
252	-	20f. red	2·50	15
253	-	25f. black	1·60	15
254	-	50f. brown (air)	4·75	2·30
255	37	100f. green	8·00	3·00
256	-	200f. blue	11·50	5·00

DESIGNS—As Type **36**: 50c. to 80c. Palms and cataract; 1f. to 1f.50, River view; 2f. to 4f. Tropical forest; 15f. to 25f. Bakongo girl. As Type **37**: 50f. Savoia Marchetti S.M.75 airplane over village; 200f. Savoia Marchetti S.M.75 over column of porters.

39 People of Five Races, Aircraft and Globe

1949. Air. 75th Anniv of U.P.U.

267	39	25f. green	8·00	34·00

40 Doctor and Patient

1950. Colonial Welfare Fund.

268	40	10f.+2f. purple & green	6·75	19·00

42 De Brazza and Landscape

1951. Birth Cent of Count Savorgnan de Brazza.

269	-	10f. green & blue (postage)	1·30	30
270	42	15f. red, blue & brn (air)	4·00	1·50

DESIGN—22×31½ mm: 10f. De Brazza.

43 Monseigneur Augouard

1952. Air. Birth Centenary of Mgr. Augouard (First Bishop of the Congo).

271	43	15f. sepia, purple & olive	4·75	5·25

44

1952. Centenary of Military Medal.

272	44	15f. multicoloured	6·75	12·50

45 Sailing Canoe

1953. Air.

273	-	50f. brown, green & blue	4·25	90
274	45	100f. grn, turq & sepia	8·00	1·10
275	-	200f. red and lake	6·75	2·30
276	-	500f. blue, black & grn	47·00	11·50

DESIGNS: 50f. Logs in river; 200f. Native driver and docks; 500f. African darters.

46 Normandy Landings, 1944

1954. Air. 10th Anniv of Liberation.

277	46	15f. brown and violet	8·00	5·25

47 Lieut.-Governor Cureau

1954

278	47	15f. brown and green	1·50	45

48 Felix Eboue

1955. Air. Governor-General Eboue Commem.

279	48	15f. sepia, brown & blue	3·00	2·10

49 Lizard

1955. Nature Protection.

280	49	8f. green and purple	2·75	1·80

50 Boali Waterfall and Power Station

1956. Economic and Social Development Fund.

281	50	5f. purple and sepia	95	15
282	-	10f. green and black	1·50	15
283	-	15f. grey and blue	1·30	30
284	-	20f. vermilion and red	1·50	30

DESIGNS: 10f. Cotton production, Chad; 15f. Brazzaville Hospital, Middle Congo; 20f. Libreville harbour, Gabon.

51 Coffee

1956. Coffee.

285	51	10f. violet and lilac	1·90	1·00

52 Riverside Hospital

1957. Order of Malta Leprosy Relief.

286	52	15f. turquoise, grn & red	1·50	70

53 Gen. Faidherbe and African Trooper

1957. Air. Centenary of African Troops.

287	53	15f. brown & chestnut	4·25	7·00

54 Lion and Lioness

1957

288	-	1f. brown and green	1·00	2·75
289	54	2f. olive and green	1·30	3·25
290	-	3f. black, blue & green	1·50	2·50
291	-	4f. brown and grey	1·60	2·50

DESIGNS—HORIZ: 1f. Giant eland. VERT: 3f. African elephant; 4f. Greater kudu.

55 Regional Bureau, Brazzaville

1958. 10th Anniv of W.H.O.

292	55	20f. brown and green	1·10	75

56 "Euadania"

1958. Tropical Flora.

293	**56**	10f. yellow, grn & violet	80	40
294	-	25f. red, yellow & green	95	45

DESIGN: 25f. "Spathodea".

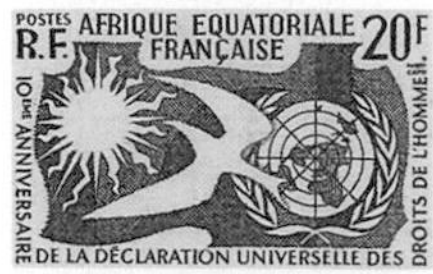

57 "Human Rights"

1958. 10th Anniv of Declaration of Human Rights.

295	**57**	20f. turquoise and blue	65	60

POSTAGE DUE STAMPS

D13

1937

D83	**D13**	5c. blue and purple	80	7·25
D84	**D13**	10c. pink and red	25	6·75
D85	**D13**	20c. lt green & green	35	6·25
D86	**D13**	25c. pink and brown	35	7·25
D87	**D13**	30c. blue and red	55	7·00
D88	**D13**	45c. green & mauve	90	7·50
D89	**D13**	50c. pink and green	1·00	7·50
D90	**D13**	60c. yellow & purple	1·30	8·00
D91	**D13**	1f. yellow and brown	1·50	7·75
D92	**D13**	2f. pink and blue	1·80	7·00
D93	**D13**	3f. blue and brown	2·10	6·75

D38

1947

D257	**D38**	10c. red	15	6·75
D258	**D38**	30c. orange	15	7·25
D259	**D38**	50c. black	40	7·25
D260	**D38**	1f. red	45	7·25
D261	**D38**	2f. green	1·50	7·25
D262	**D38**	3f. mauve	1·70	7·50
D263	**D38**	4f. blue	2·30	8·00
D264	**D38**	5f. brown	2·30	6·25
D265	**D38**	10f. blue	5·00	6·50
D266	**D38**	20f. brown	4·00	6·25

Pt. 6

FRENCH GUIANA

Formerly a French colony on the N.E. coast of S. America, now an overseas department using the stamps of France.

100 centimes = 1 franc.

1886. "Peace and Commerce" and "Commerce" types surch Dec. 1886. GUY. FRANC. 0f 05.

2	**H**	0f.05 on 2c. green	£475	£475
4	**J**	0f.05 on 2c. brown on buff	£475	£450

1887. "Ceres" and "Peace and Commerce" types surch Avril 1887. GUY. FRANC. and value.

6	**H**	0f.05 on 2c. green	£130	£130
7b	**H**	0f.20 on 35c. blk on yell	65·00	70·00
8	**F**	0f.25 on 30c. brown	55·00	65·00

No. 7b has the "Av" of "Avril" inverted; stamps with these letters normal are worth more.

1887. "Ceres" and "Peace and Commerce" types surch DEC. 1887. GUY. FRANC. 5c.

9		5c. on 30c. brown	£130	£130
10	**H**	5c. on 30c. brown	£1000	£1000

1888. "Ceres" and "Peace and Commerce" types surch Fevrier 1888 GUY. FRANC. and value.

11	**F**	5 on 30c. brown	£120	£130
12	**H**	10 on 75c. red	£225	£225

1892. Optd GUYANE. (a) On "Ceres" type.

14	**F**	30c. brown	£130	£130

(b) On "Peace and Commerce" type.

15	**H**	2c. green	£650	£650
16	**H**	35c. black on orange	£2250	£2500
17	**H**	40c. red on yellow	£130	£130
18	**H**	75c. red	£140	£140
19	**H**	1f. green	£130	£130

(c) On "Commerce" type.

20	**J**	1c. black on blue	50·00	60·00
21	**J**	2c. brown on buff	33·00	55·00
22	**J**	4c. brown on grey	37·00	65·00
23	**J**	5c. green on light green	55·00	39·00
24	**J**	10c. black on lilac	55·00	60·00
25	**J**	15c. blue on light blue	60·00	55·00
26	**J**	20c. red on green	37·00	14·50
27	**J**	25c. black on pink	65·00	20·00
28	**J**	30c. brown on drab	21·00	55·00
29	**J**	35c. black on orange	£180	£190
30	**J**	40c. red on yellow	£130	£130
31	**J**	75c. red on pink	£130	£130
32	**J**	1f. green	£190	£190

1892. "Tablet" key-type inscr "GUYANE" in red (1, 5, 15, 25, 50 (No. 56), 75c., 1, 2f.) or blue (others).

38	**D**	1c. black on blue	1·10	1·40
39	**D**	2c. brown on buff	1·30	75
40	**D**	4c. brown on grey	1·90	3·00
52	**D**	5c. green	80	1·30
42	**D**	10c. black on lilac	11·00	8·75
53	**D**	10c. red	2·75	75
43	**D**	15c. blue	46·00	4·50
54	**D**	15c. grey	£100	£120
44	**D**	20c. red on green	20·00	14·50
45	**D**	25c. black on red	13·00	6·50
55	**D**	25c. blue	18·00	44·00
46	**D**	30c. brown on drab	18·00	28·00
47	**D**	40c. red on yellow	25·00	15·00
48	**D**	50c. red on pink	26·00	15·00
56	**D**	50c. brown on blue	50·00	46·00
49	**D**	75c. brown on yellow	37·00	50·00
50	**D**	1f. green	15·00	14·50
57	**D**	2f. violet on pink	£150	6·50

1892. "Commerce" type surch DEC. 92. 0f05 GUYANE.

51	**J**	0.05 on 15c. blue on blue	50·00	55·00

8 Giant Anteater

9 Gold-washer

10 Plantation of Coconut Palms, Cayenne

1904

58	**8**	1c. black	20	35
59	**8**	2c. blue	35	40
60	**8**	4c. brown	35	1·40
61	**8**	5c. green	1·70	1·10
83	**8**	5c. orange	55	3·25
62	**8**	10c. red	1·80	35
84	**8**	10c. green	65	2·00
104	**8**	10c. red on blue	60	1·40
63	**8**	15c. violet	85	55
64	**9**	20c. brown	55	2·30
65	**9**	25c. blue	3·50	95
85	**9**	25c. violet	65	55
66	**9**	30c. black	90	90
86	**9**	30c. red	40	1·40
105	**9**	30c. orange	35	2·00
106	**9**	30c. green	2·30	3·75
66a	**9**	35c. black on yellow	1·50	1·00
67	**9**	40c. red	55	1·70
87	**9**	40c. black	3·00	2·75
68	**9**	45c. brown	3·00	3·00
69	**9**	50c. lilac	5·00	2·75
88	**9**	50c. blue	35	2·50
107	**9**	50c. grey	2·00	1·00
108	**9**	60c. mauve on pink	1·40	3·00
109	**9**	65c. green	2·40	5·50
70	**9**	75c. green	2·75	2·75
110	**9**	85c. purple	50	3·50
71	**10**	1f. red	2·50	1·40
111	**10**	1f. blue on light blue	1·70	4·00
112	**10**	1f. blue on green	2·50	8·25
113	**10**	1f.10 pink	3·00	5·50
72	**10**	2f. blue	2·75	2·30
114	**10**	2f. red on yellow	3·00	8·75
73	**10**	5f. black	10·00	8·25
115	**10**	10f. green on yellow	12·00	39·00
116	**10**	20f. red	17·00	55·00

1912. "Tablet" key-type surch in figures.

74A	**D**	05 on 2c. brown on buff	2·30	5·00
75A	**D**	05 on 4c. brown on grey	55	3·00
76A	**D**	05 on 20c. red on green	1·40	4·50
77A	**D**	05 on 25c. black on pink	4·50	12·00
78A	**D**	05 on 30c. brown on drab	1·30	5·00
79A	**D**	10 on 40c. red on yellow	1·80	7·25
80A	**D**	10 on 50c. red	4·00	10·50

1915. Red Cross. Surch with red cross and 5.

81	**8**	10c.+5c. red	20·00	20·00

1915. Red Cross. Surch 5c and red cross.

82		10c.+5c. red	85	3·50

1922. Surch in figures with bars.

89		0,01 on 15c. violet	35	2·75
90		0,02 on 15c. violet	35	2·00
91		0,04 on 15c. violet	35	2·50
92		0,05 on 15c. violet	75	5·00
95		25c. on 15c. violet	1·70	3·75
96	**10**	25c. on 2f. blue	1·50	6·50
97	**9**	65 on 45c. brown	1·80	6·00
98	**9**	85 on 45c. brown	2·40	7·75
99	**9**	90 on 75c. red	2·40	4·00
100	**10**	1f.05 on 2f. brown	2·40	4·75
101	**10**	1f.25 on 1f. blue on blue	1·10	4·50
102	**10**	1f.50 on 1f. blue	2·75	2·50
103	**10**	3f. on 5f. violet	75	1·80

1924. Surch in words.

93		10f. on 1f. green on yellow	17·00	50·00
94		20f. on 5f. mauve on red	12·00	50·00

20 Carib Archer

21 Shooting the Rapids, R. Maroni

22 Government Building, Cayenne

1929

117	**20**	1c. blue and lilac	10	5·25
118	**20**	2c. green and red	10	2·50
119	**20**	3c. green and violet	10	6·50
120	**20**	4c. mauve and brown	20	4·25
121	**20**	5c. red and blue	35	3·75
122	**20**	10c. brown and mauve	10	2·00
123	**20**	15c. red and brown	85	3·00
124	**20**	20c. green and blue	35	3·50
125	**20**	25c. brown and red	1·60	2·75
126	**21**	30c. lt green & green	1·10	5·50
127	**21**	30c. brown and green	35	5·25
128	**21**	35c. green and blue	3·75	7·00
129	**21**	40c. drab and brown	35	3·50
130	**21**	45c. brown and green	2·50	6·00
131	**21**	45c. green and olive	1·70	6·25
132	**21**	50c. brown and blue	35	35
133	**21**	55c. red and blue	2·50	7·75
134	**21**	60c. green and red	1·20	6·25
135	**21**	65c. green and red	1·50	3·50
136	**21**	70c. green and blue	1·70	8·00
137	**21**	75c. light blue and blue	3·50	5·00
138	**21**	80c. blue and black	3·25	6·50
139	**21**	90c. red and carmine	2·75	6·00
140	**21**	90c. brown and mauve	2·40	8·00
141	**21**	1f. brown and mauve	65	3·75
142	**21**	1f. red and carmine	4·25	5·00
143	**21**	1f. blue and black	1·10	4·25
144	**22**	1f.05 green and red	6·50	14·00
145	**22**	1f.10 mauve and brown	3·75	12·00
146	**22**	1f.25 green and brown	2·75	6·50
147	**22**	1f.25 red and carmine	1·70	6·50
148	**22**	1f.40 mauve and brown	2·00	7·50
149	**22**	1f.50 light blue & blue	1·30	2·50
150	**22**	1f.60 green and brown	1·80	6·50
151	**22**	1f.75 brown and red	4·25	3·75
152	**22**	1f.75 ultramarine & bl	3·25	6·00
153	**22**	2f. red and green	1·30	1·40
154	**22**	2f.25 ultramarine & bl	1·40	5·00
155	**22**	2f.50 brown and red	1·70	3·50
156	**22**	3f. mauve and brown	1·70	3·25
157	**22**	5f. green and violet	1·30	2·75
158	**22**	10f. blue and brown	2·00	3·00
159	**22**	20f. red and blue	2·50	5·25

1931. "Colonial Exhibition" key-types inscr "GUYANE FRANCAISE".

160	**E**	40c. black and green	4·00	11·00
161	**F**	50c. black and mauve	4·25	9·75
162	**G**	90c. black and red	4·00	14·50
163	**H**	1f.50 black and blue	8·25	13·00

25 Cayenne

1933. Air.

164	**25**	50c. brown	1·70	1·40
165	**25**	1f. green	35	90
166	**25**	1f.50 blue	30	95
167	**25**	2f. orange	50	55
168	**25**	3f. black	1·20	3·25
169	**25**	5f. violet	70	1·40
170	**25**	10f. olive	65	2·30
171	**25**	20f. red	90	1·30

26 Cayenne recaptured by D'Estrees, 1676

27 Local Products

1935. West Indies Tercentenary.

172	**26**	40c. brown	9·50	12·50
173	**26**	50c. red	24·00	18·00
174	**26**	1f.50 blue	10·00	11·50
175	**27**	1f.75 red	13·00	21·00
176	**27**	5f. brown	10·00	11·00
177	**27**	10f. green	11·00	22·00

1937. International Exhibition, Paris. As 58a of Guadeloupe.

178		20c. violet	1·10	4·75
179		30c. green	90	4·00
180		40c. red	75	3·25
181		50c. brown and agate	75	3·00
182		90c. red	85	5·25
183		1f.50 blue	90	5·50
MS183a		120×100 mm. 3f. violet. Imperf	12·00	31·00

1938. International Anti-cancer Fund. As T 58b of Guadeloupe.

184		1f.75+50c. blue	9·25	32·00

1939. New York World's Fair. As T 58c of Guadeloupe.

185		1f.25 red	1·00	6·50
186		2f.25 blue	1·20	4·75

1939. 150th Anniv of French Revolution. As T 58d of Guadeloupe.

187		45c.+25c. grn & blk (post)	10·00	22·00
188		70c.+30c. brown & black	10·00	22·00
189		90c.+35c. orange & black	10·00	22·00
190		1f.25+1f. red & black	10·00	22·00
191		2f.25+2f. blue & black	10·00	22·00
192		5f.+4f. black & orange (air)	20·00	42·00

28 View of Cayenne and Marshal Petain

1941. Marshal Petain Issue.

192a	**28**	1f. purple	85	6·25
192b	**28**	2f.50 blue	75	5·25

1944. Mutual Aid and Red Cross Funds. As T 58e of Guadeloupe.

193		5f.+20f. purple	50	5·50

1945. Felix Eboue. As T 58f of Guadeloupe.

194		2f. black	20	4·00
195		25f. green	35	4·75

28a Arms of French Guiana

1945

196	**28a**	10c. blue	85	6·75
197	**28a**	30c. brown	50	5·50
198	**28a**	40c. blue	75	7·25
199	**28a**	50c. purple	75	6·00
200	**28a**	60c. yellow	60	6·50
201	**28a**	70c. brown	60	7·25
202	**28a**	80c. green	65	7·25
203	**28a**	1f. blue	65	4·25
204	**28a**	1f.20 lilac	1·00	7·25
205	**28a**	1f.50 orange	1·00	6·75
206	**28a**	2f. black	1·10	6·75
207	**28a**	2f.40 red	1·30	7·50
208	**28a**	3f. pink	1·00	4·00
209	**28a**	4f. blue	1·20	4·00
210	**28a**	4f.50 green	75	4·50
211	**28a**	5f. brown	75	4·75
212	**28a**	10f. violet	75	3·75
213	**28a**	15f. red	1·00	3·25
214	**28a**	20f. olive	1·40	7·25

1945. Air. As T 63a of Guadeloupe.

215		50f. green	90	3·75
216		100f. red	1·30	6·25

1946. Air. Victory. As T 63b of Guadeloupe.

217		8f. black	55	5·25

1946. Air. From Chad to the Rhine. As T 63c of Guadeloupe.

218		5f. blue	90	7·25
219		10f. red	90	7·25
220		15f. purple	90	7·25
221		20f. green	1·10	7·50
222		25f. purple	1·10	7·50
223		50f. mauve	1·80	8·00

29 Hammock

33 Red-billed Toucans

35 Yellow-throated Caracara

1947

224	**29**	10c. green (postage)	35	4·50
225	**29**	30c. red	10	5·00
226	**29**	50c. purple	10	5·50
227	-	60c. grey	45	4·50
228	-	1f. brown	75	4·00
229	-	1f.50 brown	1·40	6·50
230	-	2f. green	1·70	7·00
231	-	2f.50 blue	2·20	6·25
232	-	3f. brown	2·50	7·25
233	-	4f. brown	3·75	6·75
234	-	5f. blue	3·50	4·50
235	-	6f. brown	3·75	7·75
236	**33**	10f. blue	7·25	10·00
237	**33**	15f. brown	7·25	6·75
238	**33**	20f. brown	8·00	15·00
239	-	25f. green	8·75	9·25
240	-	40f. brown	9·25	18·00
241	**35**	50f. green (air)	20·00	33·00
242	-	100f. lake	20·00	50·00
243	-	200f. blue	42·00	65·00

DESIGNS—As Types **29** and **33**—HORIZ: 60c. to 1f.50, Riverside village; 2f. to 3f. Pirogue; 25f., 40f. Blue and yellow macaw, military macaw and white-eyed conure. VERT: 4f. to 6f. Girl. As Type **35**—VERT: 100f. Airplane over peccary and palms. HORIZ: 200f. Sud Ouest Corse II airplane, channel-billed toucan, red-billed toucan and black-necked aracari.

POSTAGE DUE STAMPS

1925. Postage Due stamps of France optd GUYANE FRANCAISE or surch also centimes a percevoir and value in figures.

D117	**D11**	5c. blue	35	6·75
D118	**D11**	10c. brown	55	3·75
D119	**D11**	15c. on 20c. olive	35	4·25
D120	**D11**	20c. olive	1·30	7·00
D121	**D11**	25c. on 5c. blue	1·80	7·25
D122	**D11**	30c. on 20c. olive	1·20	6·50
D123	**D11**	45c. on 10c. brown	1·50	4·25
D124	**D11**	50c. red	1·40	5·75
D125	**D11**	60c. on 5c. blue	1·50	4·50
D126	**D11**	1f. on 20c. olive	1·70	4·75
D127	**D11**	2f. on 50c. red	1·50	9·25
D128	**D11**	3f. mauve	8·00	33·00

D23 Palm Trees

1929

D160	**D23**	5c. blue & dp blue	40	4·00
D161	**D23**	10c. blue & brown	35	4·00
D162	**D23**	20c. red and green	35	4·00
D163	**D23**	30c. red and brown	40	5·50
D164	**D23**	50c. brown & mauve	1·40	4·50
D165	**D23**	60c. brown and red	1·40	4·50
D166	-	1f. red and blue	1·50	7·25
D167	-	2f. green and red	2·00	9·25
D168	-	3f. grey and mauve	2·50	10·00

DESIGN: 1f. to 3f. Creole girl.

D36

1947

D244	**D36**	10c. red	10	6·50
D245	**D36**	30c. green	20	6·50
D246	**D36**	50c. black	20	6·50
D247	**D36**	1f. blue	35	7·50
D248	**D36**	2f. lake	40	7·50
D249	**D36**	3f. violet	50	7·50
D250	**D36**	4f. red	85	8·25
D251	**D36**	5f. purple	90	8·75
D252	**D36**	10f. green	1·20	10·00
D253	**D36**	20f. purple	1·90	11·50

Pt. 6

FRENCH GUINEA

A French colony on the W. coast of Africa incorporated in French West Africa in 1944. Became completely independent in 1958 (see Guinea).

100 centimes = 1 franc.

1892. "Tablet" key-type inscr "GUINEE FRANCAISE" in red (1, 5, 15, 50 (No. 17), 75c., 1f.) or blue (others).

1	**D**	1c. black on blue	2·75	3·25
2	**D**	2c. brown on buff	1·70	2·50
3	**D**	4c. brown on grey	3·00	2·75
4	**D**	5c. green on light green	6·25	5·00
5	**D**	10c. black on lilac	12·50	11·00
14	**D**	10c. red	33·00	65·00
6	**D**	15c. blue	12·00	3·75
15	**D**	15c. grey	85·00	£120
7	**D**	20c. red on green	28·00	28·00
8	**D**	25c. black on pink	9·75	4·25
16	**D**	25c. blue	14·50	31·00
9	**D**	30c. brown on drab	35·00	39·00
10	**D**	40c. red on yellow	50·00	40·00
11	**D**	50c. red on pink	50·00	55·00
17	**D**	50c. brown on blue	31·00	44·00
12	**D**	75c. brown on yellow	75·00	65·00
13	**D**	1f. green	60·00	60·00

1 Fulas Shepherd

1904

18	**1**	1c. black on green	55	45
19	**1**	2c. brown on yellow	55	55
20	**1**	4c. red on blue	1·30	1·30
21	**1**	5c. green on light green	1·50	65
22	**1**	10c. red	3·25	1·10
23	**1**	15c. lilac on pink	5·50	3·25
24	**1**	20c. red on green	10·00	20·00
25	**1**	25c. blue	14·50	10·50
26	**1**	30c. brown	17·00	20·00
27	**1**	40c. red on yellow	28·00	29·00
28	**1**	50c. brown on green	22·00	25·00
29	**1**	75c. blue on yellow	25·00	55·00
30	**1**	1f. green	55·00	65·00
31	**1**	2f. red on orange	£110	£120
32	**1**	5f. blue on green	£120	£130

1906. "Faidherbe", "Palms" and "Balay" key-types inscr "GUINEE" in blue (10c., 5f.) or red (others).

33	**I**	1c. slate	45	55
34	**I**	2c. brown	1·40	1·20
35	**I**	4c. brown on blue	65	90
36	**I**	5c. green	3·75	1·70
37	**I**	10c. red	28·00	1·50
38	**J**	20c. black on blue	2·50	4·75
39	**J**	25c. blue	4·25	5·00
40	**J**	30c. brown on pink	4·50	8·75
41	**J**	35c. black on yellow	1·50	1·70
43	**J**	45c. brown on green	2·50	8·75
44	**J**	50c. violet	9·25	11·00
45	**J**	75c. green on orange	4·75	6·00
46	**K**	1f. black on blue	13·00	39·00
47	**K**	2f. blue on pink	36·00	70·00
48	**K**	5f. red on yellow	39·00	90·00

1912. Surch in figures.

49A	**D**	05 on 2c. brown on buff	1·00	3·00
50A	**D**	05 on 4c. brown on grey	1·30	2·75
51A	**D**	05 on 15c. blue	50	50
52A	**D**	05 on 20c. red on green	3·00	7·75
53A	**D**	05 on 30c. brown on drab	3·50	11·00
54A	**D**	10 on 40c. red on yellow	75	2·75
55A	**D**	10 on 75c. brown on yellow	5·00	14·50

1912. Surch in figures.

56A	**1**	05 on 2c. brown on yellow	75	1·50
57A	**1**	05 on 4c. red on blue	30	60
58A	**1**	05 on 15c. lilac on pink	35	1·20
59A	**1**	05 on 20c. red on green	35	1·20
60A	**1**	05 on 25c. blue	60	1·00
61A	**1**	05 on 30c. brown	1·30	1·90
62A	**1**	10 on 40c. red on yellow	45	2·30
63A	**1**	10 on 50c. brown on green	2·00	5·25

3 Ford at Kitim

1913

64	**3**	1c. blue and violet	10	20
65	**3**	2c. chocolate and brown	10	35
66	**3**	4c. black and grey	20	1·20
67	**3**	5c. green and light green	1·00	60
83	**3**	5c. green and purple	20	2·30
68	**3**	10c. pink and red	1·80	1·20
84	**3**	10c. green & light green	1·30	3·25
85	**3**	10c. red and lilac	35	65
69	**3**	15c. red and purple	1·10	1·70
86	**3**	15c. green & light green	30	3·25
87	**3**	15c. mauve and purple	1·00	1·80
70	**3**	20c. violet and brown	35	1·70
88	**3**	20c. green	55	4·25
89	**3**	20c. brown and red	1·10	1·10
71	**3**	25c. blue & ultramarine	3·00	2·50
90	**3**	25c. violet and black	1·40	55
72	**3**	30c. green and purple	3·00	6·50
91	**3**	30c. pink and red	1·90	6·25
92	**3**	30c. green and red	65	2·50
93	**3**	30c. green and olive	2·75	2·20
73	**3**	35c. pink and blue	1·80	3·50
74	**3**	40c. grey and green	2·30	1·40
75	**3**	45c. red and brown	2·00	2·50
76	**3**	50c. black and blue	7·25	7·75
94	**3**	50c. blue & ultramarine	1·80	3·25
95	**3**	50c. green and brown	1·70	35
96	**3**	60c. violet on pink	75	6·50
97	**3**	65c. blue and brown	2·30	5·25
77	**3**	75c. blue and pink	2·00	4·50
98	**3**	75c. light blue and blue	75	5·00
99	**3**	75c. green and mauve	2·30	2·30
100	**3**	85c. purple and green	1·20	8·00
101	**3**	90c. mauve and red	5·00	8·00
78	**3**	1f. black and violet	2·30	1·70
102	**3**	1f.10 brown and violet	5·25	20·00
103	**3**	1f.25 brown and violet	3·25	4·75
104	**3**	1f.50 light blue and blue	5·50	4·00
105	**3**	1f.75 mauve and brown	2·00	2·75
79	**3**	2f. brown and orange	3·00	2·20
106	**3**	3f. mauve on pink	10·00	6·50
80	**3**	5f. violet and black	14·50	39·00
107	**3**	5f. black and blue	2·20	3·25

1915. Surch 5c and red cross.

81		10c.+5c. pink and red	2·00	2·75

1922. Surch in figures and bars.

108		25c. on 2f. brown & orange	1·00	6·75
109		25c. on 5f. black & blue	1·00	6·75
110		60 on 75c. violet on pink	1·70	6·50
111		65 on 75c. blue and pink	1·40	9·25
112		85 on 75c. blue and pink	2·00	9·50
113		90c. on 75c. mve & red	1·30	8·75
114		1f.25 on 1f. ultram & bl	1·20	4·00
115		1f.50 on 1f. lt blue & blue	1·50	2·50
116		3f. on 5f. grey & mauve	3·75	10·00
117		10f. on 5f. green & blue	8·25	13·00
118		20f. on 5f. brown and mauve on pink	19·00	55·00

1931. "Colonial Exhibition" key-types inscr "GUINEE FRANCAISE".

119	**E**	40c. black and green	4·50	5·50
120	**F**	50c. black and purple	4·50	6·00
121	**G**	90c. black and red	6·00	9·25
122	**H**	1f.50 black and blue	4·50	5·50

1937. International Exhibition, Paris. As T 58a of Guadeloupe.

123		20c. violet	1·30	4·50
124		30c. green	1·40	4·75
125		40c. red	1·30	4·50
126		50c. brown and agate	1·10	2·75
127		90c. red	1·10	2·75
128		1f.50 blue	1·10	1·40

MS128a 120×100 mm. 3f. green and deep green. Imperf 8·25 33·00

4 Native Village

1938

129	**4**	2c. red	15	1·30
130	**4**	3c. blue	15	2·75
131	**4**	4c. green	30	2·50
132	**4**	5c. red	10	1·50
133	**4**	10c. blue	85	1·10
134	**4**	15c. purple	15	2·20
135	-	20c. red	35	1·10
136	-	25c. blue	1·00	1·50
137	-	30c. blue	45	1·00
138	-	35c. green	2·20	2·75
139	-	40c. brown	85	6·00
140	-	45c. green	2·50	6·75
141	-	50c. red	65	2·20
142	-	55c. blue	1·50	3·50
143	-	60c. blue	2·00	4·75
144	-	65c. green	1·20	1·00
145	-	70c. green	3·00	7·50
146	-	80c. purple	1·50	4·25
147	-	90c. purple	1·80	6·25
148	-	1f. red	3·50	2·50
149	-	1f. brown	1·00	2·50
150	-	1f.25 red	2·75	7·00
151	-	1f.40 brown	2·50	4·00
152	-	1f.50 brown	1·70	4·25
153	-	1f.60 red	3·50	5·00
154	-	1f.75 blue	1·50	1·70
155	-	2f. mauve	1·80	1·80
156	-	2f.25 blue	2·50	5·25
157	-	2f.50 brown	2·75	2·50
158	-	3f. blue	1·50	70
159	-	5f. purple	1·20	1·00
160	-	10f. green	1·40	2·20
161	-	20f. brown	2·75	3·00

DESIGNS—HORIZ: 20c. to 50c. Wooden pot makers; 55c. to 1f.50, Waterfall. VERT: 1f.60 to 20f. Native women.

1938. International Anti-cancer Fund. As T 58b of Guadeloupe.

162		1f.75+50c. blue	5·50	33·00

1939. Death Centenary of R. Caillie. As T 21 of French Sudan.

163		90c. orange	75	3·50
164		2f. violet	75	1·70
165		2f.25 blue	1·00	5·50

1939. New York World's Fair. As T 58c of Guadeloupe.

166		1f.25 red	2·20	6·00
167		2f.25 blue	1·80	4·50

1939. 150th Anniv of French Revolution. As T 58d of Guadeloupe.

168		45c.+25c. green & black	7·25	17·00
169		70c.+30c. brown & black	7·25	17·00
170		90c.+35c. orange & black	7·25	17·00

171		1f.25+1f. red and black	7·25	17·00
172		2f.25+2f. blue and black	7·25	17·00

6a Airplane over Jungle

1940. Air.

173	**6a**	1f.90 blue	1·00	4·00
174	**6a**	2f.90 red	65	3·75
175	**6a**	4f.50 green	90	7·25
176	**6a**	4f.90 olive	1·00	8·00
177	**6a**	6f.90 orange	1·40	7·75

1941. National Defence Fund. Surch SECOURS NATIONAL and value.

178		+1f. on 50c. (No. 141)	1·40	5·75
179		+2f. on 80c. (No. 146)	10·00	11·50
180		+2f. on 1f.50 (No. 152)	6·50	14·50
181		+3f. on 2f. (No. 155)	13·00	14·50

7 Ford at Kitim and Marshal Petain

1941

182	**7**	1f. green	65	3·25
183	**7**	2f.50 blue	95	6·50

8 Dakar Maternity Hospital

1942. Air. Colonial Child Welfare.

184	**8**	1f.50+3f.50 green	1·80	8·00
185	**8**	2f.+6f. brown	1·90	8·00
186	**8**	3f.+9f. red	90	8·00

9a "Vocation"

1942. Air.

187	**9a**	50f. olive and green	1·50	10·50

POSTAGE DUE STAMPS

D2 Woman of Futa Jallon

1905

D33	**D2**	5c. blue	1·90	1·70
D34	**D2**	10c. brown	2·75	1·70
D35	**D2**	15c. green	3·50	4·00
D36	**D2**	30c. red	4·00	5·25
D37	**D2**	50c. black	6·50	9·50
D38	**D2**	60c. orange	13·50	14·50
D39	**D2**	1f. lilac	50·00	60·00

1906. "Natives" key-type inscr "GUINEE".

D49	**L**	5c. green	8·25	7·25
D50	**L**	10c. purple	3·25	4·50
D51	**L**	15c. blue on blue	2·75	8·75
D52	**L**	20c. black on yellow	2·75	6·25
D53	**L**	30c. red on cream	14·50	65·00
D54	**L**	50c. violet	8·75	65·00
D55	**L**	60c. black on buff	8·25	60·00
D56	**L**	1f. black on pink	3·75	41·00

1914. "Figure" key-type inscr "GUINEE".

D81	**M**	5c. green	20	4·00
D82	**M**	10c. red	65	5·25
D83	**M**	15c. grey	1·10	5·75
D84	**M**	20c. brown	90	5·25
D85	**M**	30c. blue	1·00	6·50
D86	**M**	50c. black	1·00	7·75
D87	**M**	60c. orange	2·20	8·75
D88	**M**	1f. violet	2·00	7·00

1927. Surch in figures.

D119		2F. on 1f. mauve	4·50	21·00
D120		3F. on 1f. brown	3·75	29·00

D7 Native Idol

1938

D162	**D7**	5c. violet	10	6·50
D163	**D7**	10c. red	10	6·50
D164	**D7**	15c. green	10	6·50
D165	**D7**	20c. brown	10	6·50
D166	**D7**	30c. purple	35	6·75
D167	**D7**	50c. brown	55	7·25
D168	**D7**	60c. blue	70	8·00
D169	**D7**	1f. red	70	8·00
D170	**D7**	2f. blue	1·20	8·75
D171	**D7**	3f. black	1·30	9·25

For later issues see **GUINEA**.

Pt. 6

FRENCH INDIAN SETTLEMENTS

A group of five small French settlements in India. The inhabitants voted to join India in 1954.

1892. 100 centimes = 1 franc.
1923. 24 caches = 1 fanon; 8 fanons = 1 rupee.

1892. "Tablet" key-type inscr "ETABLISSEMENTS DE L'INDE" in red (1, 5, 15, 25, 35, 45, 50 (No. 19), 75c., 1f.) or blue (others).

1	**D**	1c. black on blue	1·00	80
2	**D**	2c. brown on buff	1·70	1·20
3	**D**	4c. brown on grey	3·50	3·25
4	**D**	5c. green on light green	5·50	4·25
5	**D**	10c. black on lilac	10·00	3·75
14	**D**	10c. red	3·00	2·30
6	**D**	15c. blue	5·50	5·75
15	**D**	15c. grey	18·00	37·00
7	**D**	20c. red on green	5·75	8·75
8	**D**	25c. black on pink	3·50	3·75
16	**D**	25c. blue	13·00	32·00
9	**D**	30c. brown on drab	55·00	60·00
17	**D**	35c. black on yellow	8·50	9·00
10	**D**	40c. red on yellow	4·75	12·50
18	**D**	45c. black on green	4·25	8·25
11	**D**	50c. red on pink	5·25	15·00
19	**D**	50c. brown on blue	11·00	31·00
12	**D**	75c. brown on yellow	7·25	27·00
13	**D**	1f. green	5·50	20·00

1903. Surch in figures.

20		0,05 on 25c. blk on pink	£250	£200
21		0,10 on 25c. blk on pink	£300	£225
22		0,15 on 25c. blk on pink	90·00	£110
23		0,40 on 50c. red on pink	£450	£350

1903. Fiscal stamp bisected and each half surch Inde Fcaise POSTES 0,05.

24		0.05 black and blue	22·00	23·00

3 Brahma

4 Temple near Pondicherry

1914

26	**3**	1c. black and grey	40	30
27	**3**	2c. black and purple	35	1·00
52	**3**	2c. purple and green	40	6·75
28	**3**	3c. black and brown	35	1·50
29	**3**	4c. black and orange	1·50	2·00
30	**3**	5c. black and green	1·20	2·30
53	**3**	5c. black and purple	2·00	7·25
31	**3**	10c. black and red	2·50	2·50
54	**3**	10c. black and green	2·10	7·25
32	**3**	15c. black and violet	3·00	3·00
33	**3**	20c. black and red	3·25	6·75
34	**3**	25c. black and blue	4·25	4·00
55	**3**	25c. red and blue	2·75	3·75
35	**3**	30c. black and blue	3·75	7·75
56	**3**	30c. black and red	3·00	7·50
36	**4**	35c. black and brown	4·00	6·75
37	**4**	40c. black and red	4·25	4·25
38	**4**	45c. black and green	4·25	8·00
39	**4**	50c. black and red	3·00	6·75
57	**4**	50c. blue and ultramarine	3·25	7·75
40	**4**	75c. black and blue	3·75	9·00
41	**4**	1f. black and yellow	4·25	8·00
42	**4**	2f. black and violet	7·75	17·00
43	**4**	5f. black and blue	5·25	10·00
58	**4**	5f. black and red	6·50	11·00

See also Nos. 88/107.

1915. Red Cross surch with plain cross and premium.

44	**3**	10c.+5c. black and red	1·40	6·00

1916. Surch 5 and Maltese cross.

48		10c.+5c. black and red	5·00	50·00

1916. Surch with Maltese cross and 5 C.

49		10c.+5c. black and red	1·00	7·25

1922. Surch in figures and bars.

59		0.01 on 15c. black & violet	70	7·50
60		0.02 on 15c. black & violet	50	7·00
61		0.05 on 15c. black & violet	50	7·00

1923. Surch in new currency (caches, fanons and rupees) in figures and words.

62		1ca. on 1c. black and grey	35	4·00
63		2ca. on 5c. black & purple	40	2·00
64		3ca. on 3c. black & brown	65	3·50
65		4ca. on 4c. black & orange	55	2·40
66		6ca. on 10c. black & green	1·60	2·20
67	**4**	6ca. on 45c. black & green	55	6·00
68	**3**	10ca. on 20c. green & red	3·75	9·50
69	**3**	12ca. on 15c. black & violet	1·70	2·75
70	**3**	15ca. on 20c. black & red	1·00	4·00
71	**4**	16ca. on 35c. brown & blue	3·75	8·25
72	**3**	18ca. on 30c. black & red	1·90	1·10
73	**4**	20ca. on 45c. pink & green	3·50	4·25
74	**3**	1fa. on 25c. red and green	3·00	10·50
75	**4**	1fa.3ca. on 35c. blk & brn	2·00	2·75
76	**4**	1fa.6ca. on 40c. black & red	2·75	2·10
77	**4**	1fa.12ca. on 50c. blue and ultramarine	3·00	3·50
78	**4**	1fa.12ca. on 75c. black & bl	60	8·00
79	**4**	1fa.16ca. on 75c. grn & red	4·00	6·75
80	**3**	2fa.9ca. on 25c. red & blue	1·70	6·00
81	**4**	2fa.12ca. on 1f. brn & mve	5·25	7·50
82	**4**	3fa.3ca. on 1f. black & yell	2·20	8·00
83	**4**	6fa.6ca. on 2f. black & vio	5·25	15·00
84	**4**	1r. on 1f. blue and green	9·75	19·00
85	**4**	2r. on 5f. black and red	7·50	19·00
86	**4**	3r. on 2f. violet and grey	12·00	39·00
87	**4**	5r. on 5f. blk & pink on green	28·00	55·00

1929. As T 3 and 4 but with value in caches, fanons or rupees.

88	**3**	1ca. black and brown	35	4·25
89	**3**	2ca. black and purple	35	5·25
90	**3**	3ca. black and brown	15	3·00
91	**3**	4ca. black and orange	30	7·25
92	**3**	6ca. green and deep green	50	1·80
93	**3**	10ca. green and red	1·00	2·75
94	**4**	12ca. green & deep green	40	4·50
95	**3**	16ca. black and blue	80	4·25
96	**3**	18ca. red and carmine	1·20	8·00
97	**3**	20ca. green & bl on azure	45	45
98	**4**	1fa. red and green	70	2·75
99	**4**	1fa.6ca. black and orange	1·20	7·50
100	**4**	1fa.12ca. blue and dp blue	1·20	5·50
101	**4**	1fa.16ca. green and red	1·90	7·50
102	**4**	2fa.12ca. brown and mauve	60	2·20
103	**4**	6fa.6ca. black and violet	1·30	8·50
104	**4**	1r. blue and green	1·30	4·25
105	**4**	2r. black and red	1·30	2·50
106	**4**	3r. lilac and black	2·75	5·25
107	**4**	5r. black & red on green	3·00	5·50

1931. "Colonial Exhibition" key-types inscr "ETS FRANCAIS DANS L'INDE".

108	**E**	10ca. green	4·00	8·50
109	**F**	12ca. mauve	4·00	8·50
110	**G**	18ca. red	5·00	8·50
111	**H**	1fa.12 blue	4·00	8·50

1937. International Exhibition, Paris. As T 58a of Guadeloupe.

112		8ca. violet	1·50	6·00
113		12ca. green	2·50	5·25
114		16ca. red	1·50	5·25
115		20ca. brown	1·50	5·25
116		1fa.12 red	1·50	5·25
117		2fa.12 blue	1·50	6·00
MS117a		120×100 mm. 5fa. purple. Imperf	11·00	36·00

1938. International Anti-cancer Fund. As T 58b of Guadeloupe.

118		2fa.12ca.+20ca. blue	10·50	38·00

1939. New York World's Fair. As T 58c of Guadeloupe.

119		1fa.12 red	2·20	8·25
120		2fa.12 blue	2·50	9·75

1939. 150th Anniv of French Revolution. As T 58d of Guadeloupe.

121		18ca.+10ca. green & black	7·50	21·00
122		1fa.6ca.+12ca. brn & blk	7·50	21·00
123		1fa.12ca.+16ca. orge & blk	7·50	21·00
124		1fa.16ca.+1fa.16ca. red & blk	7·50	21·00
125		2fa.12ca.+3fa. blue & blk	7·50	21·00

1941. Optd FRANCE LIBRE. (a) Stamps of 1923.

126	**3**	15ca. on 20ca. black & red	80·00	£120
127	**3**	18ca. on 30ca. black & red	4·25	10·50
128a	**4**	1fa.3 on 35ca. black & brn	90·00	£100
132	**3**	2fa.9 on 25ca. red & blue	£1200	£1000

(b) Stamps of 1929.

133		2ca. black and purple	7·75	13·00
134		3ca. black and brown	1·60	9·25
135		4ca. black and orange	6·00	18·00
136		6ca. green and deep green	2·00	8·50
137		10ca. green and red	3·75	10·00
139	**4**	12ca. green & deep green	2·30	10·00
140	**3**	16ca. black and blue	2·30	9·25
141	**3**	18ca. red and carmine	£700	£700
142	**3**	20ca. green & bl on azure	2·75	9·00
143	**4**	1fa. red and green	1·90	8·50
144	**4**	1fa.6 black and red	2·20	9·50
145	**4**	1fa.12 blue and deep blue	3·50	13·50
146	**4**	1fa.16 green and red	2·30	8·25
147	**4**	2fa.12 brown and mauve	2·40	1·90
148	**4**	6fa.6 black and violet	2·50	10·00
149	**4**	1r. blue and green	3·00	9·75
150	**4**	2r. black and red	3·00	10·00
151	**4**	3r. lilac and black	3·00	9·75
152	**4**	5r. black & red on green	8·00	26·00

(c) Paris Exhibition stamps of 1937.

154		8ca. violet	5·00	24·00
157		12ca. green	3·25	13·50
158		16ca. red	3·25	13·50
159		1fa.12 red	3·25	13·50
160		2fa.12 blue	3·25	13·50
MS160b		5fa. bright purple (**MS**117a)	£800	£700

(d) New York World's Fair stamps of 1939.

161		1fa.12 red	2·50	11·50
162		2fa.12 blue	3·25	12·00

1941. Various issues optd FRANCE TOUJOURS and Cross of Lorraine. (a) On Nos. 70, 72 and 75.

162a	**3**	15ca. on 20c. black & red	£1000	£300
162b	**3**	18ca. on 30c. black & red	£1500	£750
162c	**4**	1fa.3 on 35c. black & brn	£1000	£300

(b) On Nos. 89/90, 92 and 94/107.

162d	**3**	2ca. black and purple	£950	£275
162e	**3**	3ca. black and brown	£950	£250
162f	**3**	6ca. green and deep green	£950	£250
162g	**4**	12ca. green and deep green	£950	£250
162h	**3**	16ca. black and blue	£950	£250
162i	**3**	18ca. red and carmine	£1600	£950
162j	**3**	20ca. green & bl on azure	£950	£250
162k	**4**	1fa. red and green	£950	£250
162l	**4**	1fa.6 black and orange	£950	£250
162m	**4**	1fa.12 blue and deep blue	£950	£250

162n	4	1fa.16 green and red	£950	£250
162o	4	2fa.12 brown and mauve	£950	£250
162p	4	6fa.6 black and violet	£950	£250
162q	4	1r. blue and green	£950	£250
162r	4	2r. black and red	£950	£250
162s	4	3r. lilac and black	£950	£250
162t	4	5r. black and red on green	£950	£250

(c) On Nos. 112/14 and 116/17.

162u	8ca. violet	£950	£275
162v	12ca. green	£950	£275
162w	16ca. red	£950	£275
162x	1fa.12 red	£950	£275
162y	2fa.12 blue	£950	£275

(d) On Nos. 119/20.

162z	1fa.12 red	£950	£275
162za	2fa.12 blue	£950	£275

1942. Optd FRANCE LIBRE and Cross of Lorraine. (a) Nos. 72 and 88/107.

163	3	18ca. on 30c. black and red (No. 72)	£300	£225
164	3	2ca. black and purple	2·30	7·25
165	3	3ca. black and brown	50	6·25
166b	3	6ca. green and deep green	3·00	£160
167	4	12ca. green & deep green	5·75	9·25
168	3	16ca. black and blue	3·00	7·50
169	3	18ca. red and carmine	30	6·25
170	3	20ca. green & bl on azure	50	7·50
171	4	1fa. red and green	30	4·00
172a	4	1fa.6 black and red	3·50	5·25
173	4	1fa.12 blue and deep blue	3·75	5·50
174	4	1fa.16 green and red	50	65
175	4	2fa.12 brown and mauve	2·50	2·10
176	4	6fa.6 black and violet	3·25	11·50
177	4	1r. blue and green	6·25	20·00
178	4	2r. black and red	5·00	19·00
179a	4	3r. lilac and black	5·00	21·00
180	4	5r. black & red on green	5·00	23·00

(b) Paris Exhibition stamps of 1937.

189	8ca. violet	13·00	22·00
190	12ca. green	8·00	23·00
191	16ca. red	£1000	£1000
192	1fa.12 red	2·75	8·50
193	2fa.12 blue	3·75	12·00

(c) New York World's Fair stamps of 1939.

194	1fa.12 red	4·00	10·00
195	2fa.12 blue	6·50	12·00

1942. No. 103 surch with value only.

203	1ca. on 6fa.6 black and violet	50·00	40·00
204	4ca. on 6fa.6 black and violet	55·00	46·00
205	10ca. on 6fa.6 black & violet	25·00	20·00
207	1fa.3 on 6fa.6 black & violet	44·00	44·00
208	2fa.9 on 6fa.6 black & violet	22·00	46·00
209	3fa.3 on 6fa.6 black & violet	26·00	25·00
206	15fa. on 6fa.6 black & violet	25·00	20·00

1942. Stamps of 1929 surch FRANCE LIBRE, Cross of Lorraine and new value.

196	3	1ca. on 16ca. black & blue	75·00	70·00
210	4	1ca. on 6fa.6 black & violet	2·00	12·00
211	4	1ca. on 1r. blue and green	1·50	13·50
212	4	2ca. on 1r. blue and green	60	5·00
197	3	4ca. on 16ca. black & blue	85·00	70·00
213	4	4ca. on 6fa.6 black & violet	3·00	22·00
214	4	4ca. on 1r. blue and green	50	7·25
215	4	6ca. on 2r. black and red	70	6·25
198	3	10ca. on 16ca. black & blue	55·00	30·00
216	3	10ca. on 6fa.6 black & vio	1·80	10·00
217	3	10ca. on 2r. black and red	60	7·00
218	3	12ca. on 2r. black and red	50	6·75
199	3	15ca. on 16ca. black & blue	65·00	50·00
219	4	15ca. on 6f.6 black & violet	2·00	7·50
220	4	15ca. on 3r. lilac and black	80	8·50
221	4	16ca. on 3r. lilac and black	60	8·50
200	3	1fa.3ca. on 16ca. black and blue	85·00	75·00
222	4	1fa.3 on 6fa.6 black & vio	3·00	13·50
223	4	1fa.3 on 3r. lilac and black	60	8·75
224	4	1fa.6 on 5r. black and red on green	70	9·25
225	4	1fa.12 on 5r. black and red on green	65	9·25
226	4	1fa.16 on 5r. black and red on green	75	8·50
201	3	2fa.9ca. on 16ca. black and blue	70·00	70·00
227	4	2fa.9 on 6fa.6 black & vio	3·00	16·00
202	3	3fa.3ca. on 16ca. black and blue	60·00	60·00
228	3	3fa.3 on 6fa.6 black & vio	4·50	21·00

20 Lotus Flowers

1942. Free French issue. (a) Postage.

229	20	2ca. brown	40	5·00
230	20	3ca. blue	40	2·50
231	20	4ca. green	40	3·25
232	20	6ca. orange	40	2·50
233	20	12ca. green	1·00	2·50
234	20	16ca. purple	2·20	4·25
235	20	20ca. purple	2·00	3·00
236	20	1fa. red	1·40	1·60
237	20	1fa.18 black	1·40	1·90
238	20	6fa.6 blue	1·40	6·75
239	20	1r. violet	2·00	4·25
240	20	2r. bistre	2·50	8·25
241	20	3r. brown	2·50	8·75
242	20	5r. green	2·50	9·50

(b) Air. As T 63a of Guadeloupe.

243	4fa. orange	1·40	4·25
244	1r. red	1·20	6·75
245	2r. purple	1·40	6·50
246	5r. black	1·40	6·50
247	8r. blue	2·50	8·25
248	10r. green	2·75	10·00

1944. Mutual Aid and Red Cross Funds. As T 58e of Guadeloupe.

249	3fa.+1r.4fa. bistre	70	8·75

1945. Eboue. As T 58f of Guadeloupe.

250	3fa.8 black	20	5·00
251	5r.1fa.16 green	55	9·00

1946. Air. Victory. As T 63b of Guadeloupe.

252	4fa. green	60	9·00

1946. Air. From Chad to the Rhine. As Nos. 226/31 of Cameroun.

253	2fa.12 brown	70	8·50
254	5fa. blue	70	8·50
255	7fa.12 violet	60	9·00
256	1r.2fa. green	1·10	9·00
257	1r.4fa.12 red	1·20	9·75
258	3r.1fa. purple	1·20	9·75

22 Apsara

1948

259	22	1ca. olive	10	3·50
260	22	2ca. brown	10	4·50
261	22	4ca. violet on cream	10	2·75
262	A	6ca. orange	50	1·90
263	A	8ca. slate	70	3·25
264	A	10ca. green on green	80	3·50
265	B	12ca. purple	1·30	1·70
266	B	15ca. blue	1·30	3·50
267	C	18ca. lake	5·50	8·25
268	B	1fa. violet on red	1·50	1·70
269	D	1fa.6 red	1·30	4·00
270	C	1fa.15 violet	5·75	9·00
271	D	2fa. green	1·50	95
272	D	2fa.2 blue on cream	1·20	6·25
273	E	2fa.12 brown	1·70	4·75
274	E	3fa. red	2·00	1·30
275	C	4fa. olive	6·25	6·50
276	E	5fa. purple on red	2·00	3·00
277	F	7fa.12 brown	2·10	8·75
278	F	1r.2fa. black	3·25	14·00
279	F	1r.4fa.12c. green	2·20	19·00

DESIGNS—As Type **22**: A, Dvarabalagar standing erect; B, Vishnu; C, Brahmin idol; D, Dvarabalagar with leg raised; E, Temple Guardian; F, One of the Tigoupalagar.

25 Douglas DC-4 and Bas-relief

1949. Air.

281	25	1r. red and yellow	5·75	13·00
282	-	2r. deep green & green	6·50	17·00
283	-	5r. purple and blue	17·00	42·00

DESIGNS—VERT: 2r. Wing and temple; 5r. Short-toed eagle and palm trees.

1949. Air. 75th Anniv of U.P.U. As T 39 of French Equatorial Africa.

284	6fa. red	5·00	27·00

1950. Colonial Welfare Fund. As T 40 of French Equatorial Africa.

285	1fa.+10ca. blue & grey	3·00	9·00

1952. Centenary of Military Medal. As T 44 of French Equatorial Africa.

286	1fa. brown, yellow & green	3·50	10·00

1954. Air. 10th Anniv of Liberation. As T 46 of French Equatorial Africa.

287	1fa. purple and sepia	13·50	21·00

POSTAGE DUE STAMPS

1923. Postage Due stamps of France surch in figures and letters.

D88	D11	4ca. on 20c. violet	80	8·50
D89	D11	6ca. on 10c. brown	1·10	8·50
D90	D11	12ca. on 25c. red	1·20	8·50
D91	D11	15ca. on 20c. olive	1·00	9·00
D92	D11	1fa. on 30c. orange	2·50	9·50
D93	D11	1fa.6 on 30c. red	3·50	32·00
D94	D11	1fa.12 on 50c. purple	2·00	10·00
D95	D11	1fa.15 on 5c. blue	1·50	10·50
D96	D11	1fa.16 on 5c. black	2·20	9·00
D97	D11	3fa. on 1f. green	2·50	11·50
D98	D11	3fa.3 on 1f. brn on yell	1·00	11·00

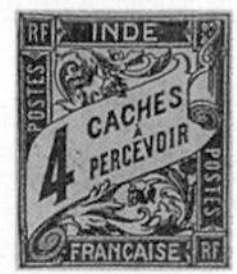

D14

1929

D108	D14	4ca. red	40	8·00
D109	D14	6ca. blue	50	8·00
D110	D14	12ca. green	60	8·00
D111	D14	1fa. brown	70	8·50
D112	D14	1fa.12 violet	1·60	8·50
D113	D14	1fa.16 brown	1·90	8·50
D114	D14	3fa. mauve	2·50	10·00

D24

1948

D280	D24	1ca. violet	20	7·25
D281	D24	2ca. brown	30	7·25
D282	D24	6ca. green	30	7·50
D283	D24	12ca. red	60	7·50
D284	D24	1fa. mauve	70	7·50
D285	D24	1fa.12 brown	1·80	8·00
D286	D24	2fa. blue	1·90	8·75
D287	D24	2fa.12 lake	1·30	9·00
D288	D24	5fa. green	2·00	10·50
D289	D24	1r. violet	2·50	12·50

For later issues see GUINEA.

Pt. 6

FRENCH MOROCCO

Part of the Sultanate of Morocco, which was a French protectorate from 1912 until independence was granted on 2 March 1956. For issues before 1912 see French Post Offices in Morocco, and for stamps used in the International Zone see French Post Offices in Tangier.

100 centimes = 1 franc

1914. Surcharged "Blanc", "Mouchon" and "Merson" key-types of French Post Offices in Morocco optd PROTECTORAT FRANCAIS.

40	A	1c. on 1c. grey	70	1·10
41	A	2c. on 2c. red	20	1·00
42	A	3c. on 3c. orange	90	2·00
43	A	5c. on 5c. green	1·10	55
44	B	10c. on 10c. red	75	35
45	B	15c. on 15c. orange	80	35
46	B	20c. on 20c. red	3·25	3·25
47	B	25c. on 25c. blue	1·10	65
48	B	25c. on 25c. brown	1·50	10
49	B	30c. on 30c. brown	13·50	14·50
50	B	35c. on 35c. lilac	2·50	1·30
51	C	40c. on 40c. red and blue	8·50	6·50
52	C	45c. on 45c. green & blue	50·00	65·00
53	C	50c. on 50c. brn & lilac	1·30	20
54	C	1p. on 1f. red and green	1·50	35
55	C	2p. on 2f. lilac and yellow	2·30	1·00
56	C	5p. on 5f. blue & yellow	10·00	18·00

1914. Surch 5c and red cross. (a) No. 32 of French Post Offices in Morocco.

65	5	10c.+5c. on 10c. red	2·10	7·75

(b) As No. 43 but without previous surcharge.

62	4	5c.+5c. green	1·10	2·00

(c) No. 44.

59	5	10c.+5c. on 10c. red	2·50	6·00

1915. No. 352 of France optd MAROC and in Arabic.

63	20	10c.+5c. red	4·00	12·00

13

1915. Optd PROTECTORAT FRANCAIS.

64	13	10c.+5c. red	2·30	2·00

15 Tower of Hassan, Rabat

16 Fez

1917

76	15	1c. black	65	2·20
123	15	1c. green	1·00	1·10
124	15	2c. purple	40	45
125	15	3c. brown	35	75
79	16	5c. green	1·00	70
126	16	5c. yellow	40	40
80	16	10c. red	1·10	65
127	16	10c. green	55	60
128	16	15c. grey	1·00	60
129	A	20c. purple	1·70	1·30
131	A	25c. blue	85	20
84	A	30c. lilac	4·75	5·00
132	A	30c. red	40	45
133	A	30c. blue	95	45
85	B	35c. orange	4·00	8·00
134	B	35c. purple	80	1·40
86	B	40c. blue	1·90	1·30
135	B	40c. orange	65	35
136	B	45c. green	45	60
88	C	50c. brown	6·50	2·75
137	C	50c. blue	1·30	90
138	B	50c. green	1·70	20
139	C	60c. mauve	1·10	1·00
140a	C	75c. purple	1·10	35
89	C	1f. grey	8·00	10·00
141	C	1f. brown	70	85
142	C	1f.05 brown	1·90	5·00
143	C	1f.40 pink	1·10	85
144	C	1f.50 blue	1·20	35
145	D	2f. brown	1·30	95
146	D	3f. red	2·00	65
147	D	5f. green	2·20	1·90
148	D	10f. brown	5·00	7·75

DESIGNS—VERT: A, Chella; B, Marrakesh. Horiz: C, Meknes; D, Volubilis.

22 Breguet 14T Biplane over Casablanca

1922. Air.

112	22	5c. orange	60	2·20

113	22	25c. blue	1·40	2·00
114	22	50c. blue	1·60	45
115	22	75c. blue	85·00	12·00
116	22	75c. green	2·00	70
117	22	80c. brown	1·10	75
118	22	1f. red	1·60	40
119	22	1f.40 red	1·40	3·25
120	22	1f.90 blue	2·50	9·25
121	22	2f. violet	2·50	2·50
122	22	3f. black	1·90	2·75

23 Ploughing with Camel and Donkey

1928. Air. Flood Relief.

149	-	5c. blue	4·25	15·00
150	23	25c. orange	4·00	15·00
151	-	50c. red	3·75	15·00
152	-	75c. brown	3·75	17·00
153	-	80c. green	3·75	15·00
154	-	1f. orange	3·75	15·00
155	-	1f.50 blue	3·75	17·00
156	-	2f. brown	3·75	15·00
157	-	3f. purple	8·50	18·00
158	-	5f. black	3·75	15·00

DESIGNS: 5c. Moorish tribesmen; 50c. Caravan nearing Safi; 75c. Walls of Marrakesh; 80c. Sheep grazing at Azrou; 1f. Gateway at Fez; 1f.50, Aerial view of Tangier; 2f. Aerial view of Casablanca; 3f. White storks at Rabat; 5f. "La Hedia", a Moorish entertainment.

1930. Stamps of 1917 surch.

163	B	15c. on 40c. orange	1·10	1·40
164	A	25c. on 30c. blue	2·75	3·75
165	C	50c. on 60c. mauve	95	35
166	C	1f. on 1f.40 pink	2·50	1·50

1931. Air. Surch.

167	22	1f. on 1f.40 red	1·90	1·10
168	22	1f.50 on 1f.90 blue	2·75	4·25

27 Sultan's Palace, Tangier

28 Saadian Tombs, Marrakesh

1933

169	27	1c. black	40	1·70
170	27	2c. mauve	35	2·50
171	-	3c. brown	35	2·50
172	-	5c. lake	60	60
173	-	10c. green	55	55
174	-	15c. black	75	1·20
175	-	20c. purple	1·70	35
176	-	25c. blue	1·60	45
177	-	30c. green	1·90	50
178	-	40c. sepia	90	65
179	-	45c. purple	1·20	1·20
180	-	50c. green	2·20	20
181	-	65c. red	65	50
182	-	75c. purple	85	40
183	-	90c. red	1·40	50
184	-	1f. brown	1·90	20
185	-	1f.25 black	1·90	1·70
186	-	1f.50 blue	1·70	20
187	-	1f.75 green	1·40	35
188	-	2f. brown	2·75	20
189	-	3f. red	35·00	5·00
190	28	5f. lake	2·50	1·10
191	28	10f. black	4·50	7·25
192	28	20f. grey	5·25	17·00

DESIGNS—HORIZ: 3c., 5c. Agadir Bay; 10c. to 20c. G.P.O., Casablanca; 25c. to 40c. Moulay Idriss; 45c. to 65c. Rabat; 1f.50 to 3f. Quarzazat. VERT: 75c. to 1f.25, Attarine College, Fez.

29 Hassan Tower, Rabat

1933. Air.

193	29	50c. blue	2·75	2·50
194	29	80c. brown	1·60	75
195	29	1f.50 lake	1·80	45
196	-	2f.50 red	3·00	1·10
197	-	5f. violet	3·50	1·90
198	-	10f. green	3·25	4·00

DESIGN: 2f.50 to 10f. Casablanca.

30 Marshal Lyautey

1935. Lyautey Memorial Fund.

199	30	50c.+50c. red (postage)	8·00	19·00
200	30	1f.+1f. green	8·00	19·00
201	30	5f.+5f. brown	36·00	90·00
202	-	1f.50+1f.50 blue (air)	22·00	55·00

DESIGN—HORIZ: 1f.50, Lyautey in profile.

1938. Child Welfare Fund. Stamps of 1933 surch O.S.E. and premium.

203	27	2c.+2c. mauve (postage)	2·75	19·00
204	-	3c.+3c. brown	2·75	19·00
205	-	20c.+20c. purple	2·75	19·00
206	-	40c.+40c. sepia	2·75	19·00
207	-	65c.+65c. red	2·75	25·00
208	-	1f.25+1f.25 black	2·75	19·00
209	-	2f.+2f. brown	2·75	19·00
210	28	5f.+5f. lake	2·75	19·00
211	29	50c.+50c. blue (air)	5·00	17·00
212	-	10f.+10f. green	5·00	18·00

1939. No. 180 surch 40c.

213	40c. on 50c. green	2·75	55

34 Mosque at Sale

36 Shepherd and Arganier Trees

42 Dewoitine D-338 Trimotor over Morocco

1939

214	34	1c. mauve (postage)	35	2·75
215	A	2c. green	70	3·00
216	A	3c. blue	45	2·75
217	34	5c. green	45	2·00
218	A	10c. purple	45	65
219	B	15c. green	1·10	2·75
220	B	20c. brown	75	1·20
221	36	30c. blue	35	1·80
222	36	40c. brown	35	1·20
223	36	45c. green	75	7·25
224	E	50c. red	3·25	5·50
293	E	50c. green	35	35
226	E	60c. blue	2·50	3·00
227	E	60c. brown	55	1·30
228	C	70c. violet	60	1·10
229	F	75c. green	1·00	3·25
230	F	80c. blue	35	55
231	F	80c. green	65	1·70
232	E	90c. blue	75	1·00
233	B	1f. brown	65	35
234	F	1f.20 mauve	90	3·25
295	F	1f.20 brown	45	1·30
235	F	1f.25 red	75	3·75
296	A	1f.30 blue	55	5·50
236	F	1f.40 purple	65	4·50
238	E	1f.50 pink	1·50	75
297	E	1f.50 red	35	1·80
239	D	2f. green	50	35
240	D	2f.25 blue	70	2·20
241	34	2f.40 red	40	1·40
242	34	2f.50 red	85	1·20
243	34	2f.50 blue	65	1·40
299	D	3f. brown	20	20
300	36	3f.50 red	55	85
245	34	4f. blue	1·00	1·10
246	F	4f.50 green	55	1·10
301	C	4f.50 mauve	40	1·50
302	C	5f. blue	45	2·75
303	F	6f. blue	20	35
248	C	10f. red	1·10	1·90
305	C	15f. green	1·20	2·00
306	C	20f. purple	1·40	8·75
307	C	25f. brown	1·60	1·90

DESIGNS—VERT: A, Mosque at Sefrou; B,Horseman and Cedar tree; C, Scimitar oryxes; D, Fez. HORIZ: E, Ramparts at Sale; F, Draa Valley.

251	G	80c. green (air)	35	1·30
252	G	1f. brown	35	75
253	42	1f.90 blue	35	3·00
254	42	2f. purple	35	1·50
255	42	3f. brown	40	70
256	G	5f. violet	1·10	3·00
257	42	10f. blue	90	2·20

DESIGN—VERT: G, Storks and Mosque at Chella.

1940. No. 181 surch 35c.

258a	35c. on 65c. red	2·75	7·00

1942. French Child Refugees in Morocco Fund. Types of 1939 surch Enfants de France au Maroc and premium.

259	36	45c.+2f. green	4·00	18·00
260	E	90c.+4f. blue	5·25	18·00
261	F	1f.25+6f. red	3·75	18·00
262	34	2f.50+8f. red	3·75	18·00

45 "La Marseillaise"

1943

263	45	1f.50 blue	1·10	5·00

46 Tower of Hassan

1943

264	46	10c. lilac	30	55
265	46	30c. blue	30	2·30
266	46	40c. red	30	45
267	46	50c. green	30	35
268	46	60c. brown	30	1·10
269	46	70c. lilac	30	35
270	46	80c. green	30	35
271	46	1f. red	30	35
272	46	1f.20 violet	30	60
273	46	1f.50 red	30	35
274	46	2f. green	40	2·00
275	46	2f.40 red	30	1·50
276	46	3f. brown	30	1·30
277	46	4f. blue	30	20
278	46	4f.50 black	40	1·20
279	46	5f. blue	45	35
280	46	10f. brown	60	1·20
281	46	15f. green	85	45
282	46	20f. purple	1·10	1·50

47 Sud Est SE 161 Languedoc over Desert

1944. Air.

283	47	50c. green	65	1·10
284	47	2f. blue	55	90
285	47	5f. red	85	75
286	47	10f. violet	95	75
287	47	50f. black	95	4·50
288	47	100f. blue and red	3·50	31·00

1944. Air. Mutual Aid Fund. Surch ENTR'AIDE FRANCAISE +98F 50.

289	1f.50+98f.50 red & bl	1·60	9·75

49 Potez 56 over Minarets

1945. Air.

290	49	50f. brown	2·20	5·25

1945. Anti-tuberculosis Fund. No. 239 surch AIDEZ LES TUBERCULEUX + 1f.

308	D	2f.+1f. green	30	4·00

51 Mausoleum

1945. Solidarity Fund. Marshal Lyautey's Mausoleum.

309a	51	2f.+3f. blue	1·60	3·25

1946. No. 308 surch 3f and bars.

310	D	3f. on 2f.+1f. green	20	2·75

1946. Air. 6th Anniv of Gen. De Gaulle's Call to Arms. Surch + 5 F 18 Juin 1940 18 Juin 1946.

311	47	5f.+5f. red	1·20	6·00

54 Marshal Lyautey Statue, Casablanca

1946. Solidarity Fund.

312	54	2f.+10f. black (postage)	85	8·75
313	54	3f.+15f. red	85	8·75
314	54	10f.+20f. blue	1·10	10·00
315	54	10f.+30f. green (air)	1·30	10·00

1947. Stamp Day. No. 301 surch JOURNEE DU TIMBRE 1947 +5F50.

316	C	4f.50+5f.50 mauve	1·60	8·25

56 Coastline and Symbols of Prosperity

1947. 25th Anniv of Sherifian Phosphates Office.

317	56	3f.50+5f.50 green	2·00	8·50

57 The Terraces

58 Coastal Fortress

59 Barracks on the Mountains

65 La Medina Barracks

1947. (a) Postage.

318	57	10c. brown	20	3·75
319	57	30c. red	20	6·50
320	57	30c. violet	20	7·00
321	57	50c. blue	20	55
322	57	60c. purple	20	3·25
323	58	1f. black	20	35
324	58	1f.50 blue	20	90
325	59	2f. green	80	1·20
325a	58	2f. purple	85	1·20
326	59	3f. lake	70	35
327	-	4f. violet	55	85
328	-	4f. green	55	2·50
329	-	5f. green	60	1·80

329a	-	5f. green	75	1·30
330	-	6f. red	30	20
330a	-	8f. orange	85	2·75
331	-	10f. blue	55	60
332a	-	10f. red	55	90
333	**58**	12f. red	65	90
334	-	15f. green	75	2·40
334a	-	15f. red	75	20
335	-	18f. blue	80	1·50
336	-	20f. red	30	35
337	-	25f. violet	95	2·50
337a	-	25f. blue	65	45
337b	-	25f. violet	1·50	3·75
337c	-	30f. blue	60	65
337d	-	35f. brown	80	55
337e	-	50f. slate	1·10	20

DESIGNS—HORIZ: 4f., 6f. Marrakesh; 5f. (No. 329), 8f., 10f. blue, The Gardens, Fez; 5f. (No. 329a) Fortified oasis; 15f. red, 25f. (Nos. 337a/b), Walled city; 30f., 35f., 50f. Todra Valley. VERT: 10f. red, 15f. green, 18f., 20f., 25f. (No. 337) Barracks in oasis.

(b) Air.

338		9f. red	1·20	65
339		40f. blue	1·40	45
340		50f. purple	1·40	1·20
341	**65**	100f. blue	2·10	1·40
342	**65**	200f. red	2·50	2·50
342a	-	300f. violet	15·00	13·00

DESIGNS—VERT: 9, 40, 50f. Sud Est SE 161 Languedoc airplane over Moulay Idriss. HORIZ: 300f. Oudayas Kasbah, Rabat.

67 "Energy"

1947. Solidarity Fund. Inscr "SOLIDARITE 1947".

343	**67**	6f.+9f. red (postage)	1·20	8·50
344	-	10f.+20f. blue	1·20	9·00
345	-	9f.+16f. green (air)	3·00	9·25
346	-	20f.+35f. brown	1·90	8·50

DESIGNS—VERT: 10f. Red Cross unit ("Health"). HORIZ: 9f. Freighter at quayside and Sud Est SE 161 Languedoc airplane ("Supplies"); 20f. Sud Est SE 161 Languedoc airplane over landscape ("Agriculture").

1948. Stamp Day. View of Meknes (as No. 88) inscr "JOURNEE DU TIMBRE 1948" below central vignette.

347		6f.+4f. brown	90	7·75

68 Marshal Lyautey's Mausoleum

1948. Air. Lyautey Exhibition, Paris.

348	**68**	10f.+25f. green	1·70	6·25

69 P.T.T. Clubhouse, Ifrane

1948. Air. P.T.T. Employees' Holiday Camp Fund.

349	**69**	6f.+34f. green	1·80	9·25
350	**69**	9f.+51f. red	2·00	8·50

70 "Dunkerque" (battleship) and Coastline

1948. Naval Charities.

351	**70**	6f.+9f. violet	1·90	9·00

1948. Stamp of 1939 surch 8f.

352	**C**	8f. on 20f. purple (No. 306)	30	2·30

72 Wheat and View of Meknes

1949. Solidarity Fund. Inscr "SOLIDARITE 1948".

353	**72**	1f.+2f. orange (postage)	1·30	7·75
354	-	2f.+5f. red	1·30	7·75
355	-	3f.+7f. blue	1·30	7·75
356	-	5f.+10f. purple	1·30	7·75
MS356a		120×96 mm. Nos. 353/6	20·00	60·00

357	5f.+5f. green (air)	1·60	8·75
358	6f.+9f. red	1·60	8·75
359	9f.+16f. brown	1·60	8·75
360	15f.+25f. slate	1·60	8·75
MS360a	96×120 mm. Nos. 357/60	20·00	60·00

DESIGNS—HORIZ: (postage): 2f. Olive grove and Taroudant; 3f. Trawling; 5f. Plums and Aguedal Gardens, Marrakesh. VERT: (air): Airplane over— 5f. Agadir; 6f. Fez; 9f. Atlas Mountains; 15f. Draa Valley.

74 Gazelle Hunter

1949. Stamp Day and 50th Anniv of Mazagan-Marrakesh Local Postage Stamp.

361	**74**	10f.+5f. red and purple	1·60	8·00

75 Soldiers with Flag

1949. Army Welfare Fund.

362	**75**	10f.+10f. red	1·30	9·00

76 Oudayas Gate, Rabat **77** Nejjarine Fountain, Fez **78** Gardens at Meknes

1949

363	**76**	10c. black	35	3·75
364	**76**	50c. lake	35	3·75
365	**76**	1f. violet	40	45
366	**77**	2f. red	35	35
367	**77**	3f. blue	35	65
368	**77**	5f. green	70	35
369	**78**	8f. green	55	35
370	**78**	10f. red	75	35

79 Post Office, Meknes

1949. 75th Anniv of U.P.U.

371	**79**	5f. green	1·60	3·75
372	**79**	15f. red	1·70	6·00
373	**79**	25f. blue	1·80	6·25

80 Breguet 14T Biplane over Globe

1950. Air. Stamp Day and 25th Anniv of First Mail Flight from Casablanca to Dakar.

374	**80**	15f.+10f. blue, grn & red	1·80	9·00

81 Carpets

1950. Solidarity Fund. Inscr "SOLIDARITE 1949".

375	**81**	1f.+2f. red (postage)	1·10	8·25
376	-	2f.+5f. blue	1·10	8·25
377	-	3f.+7f. violet	1·10	8·25
378	-	5f.+10f. brown	1·10	8·25
MS378a		96×120 mm. Nos. 375/8	26·00	65·00

379	5f.+5f. blue (air)	95	8·00
380	6f.+9f. green	95	8·00
381	9f.+16f. brown	95	8·00
382	15f.+25f. brown	95	8·00
MS382a	120×96 mm. Nos. 379/82	26·00	65·00

DESIGNS—VERT: Postage: 2f. Pottery; 3f. Books; 5f. Copperware. HORIZ: Air—(Maps of Morocco): 5f. N.W.; 6f. N.E.; 9f. S.W.; 15f. S.E.

83 Ruins of Sala-Colonia (Chella)

1950. Army Welfare Fund. Inscr "OUVRES SOCIALES DE L'ARMEE".

383	**83**	10f.+10f. red (postage)	1·10	7·50
384	**83**	15f.+15f. slate	1·10	7·50
385	-	10f.+10f. sepia (air)	1·50	8·75
386	-	15f.+15f. green	1·50	8·75

DESIGN: 10f., 15f. Triumphal Arch of Caracalla, Volubilis.

1950. Stamps of 1939 and 1947 surch.

387	**F**	1f. on 1f.20 brn (No. 295)	10	2·20
388	**A**	1f. on 1f.30 blue (No. 296)	20	45
389	-	5f. on 6f. red (No. 330)	25	35

84 General Leclerc

1951. Gen. Leclerc Monument, Casablanca.

390	**84**	10f. green (postage)	1·60	6·50
391	**84**	15f. red	1·70	7·00
392	**84**	25f. blue	1·80	7·00
393	**84**	50f. violet (air)	2·10	11·00

85 New Hospital, Meknes

1951. Solidarity Fund. Inscr "SOLIDARITE 1950".

394	-	10f. violet & blue (postage)	1·30	6·50
395	**85**	15f. brown and green	1·60	6·50
396	-	25f. blue and brown	1·70	4·50
397	-	50f. green & violet (air)	1·80	5·50

DESIGNS: 10f. Loustau Hospital, Oujda; 25f. New Hospital, Rabat; 50f. Sanatorium, Ben Smine.

86 Fountain and Doves **87** Karaouine Mosque, Fez **88** Old Moroccan Courtyard

1951

398	**86**	5f. purple (A)	35	20
434	**86**	5f. purple (B)	4·25	5·50
399	**87**	6f. green	1·90	1·70
400	**86**	8f. brown	95	35
401	**87**	10f. red	2·20	35

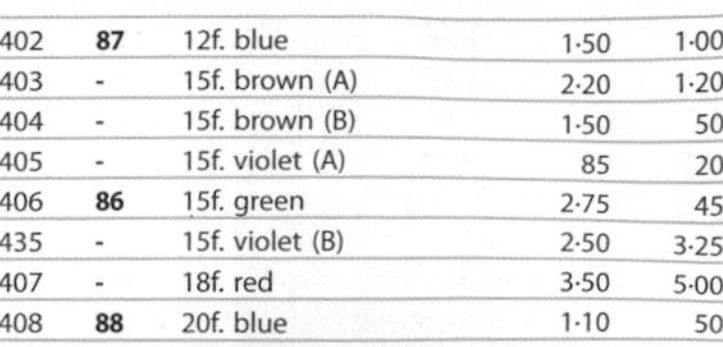

402	**87**	12f. blue	1·50	1·00
403	-	15f. brown (A)	2·20	1·20
404	-	15f. brown (B)	1·50	50
405	-	15f. violet (A)	85	20
406	**86**	15f. green	2·75	45
435	-	15f. violet (B)	2·50	3·25
407	-	18f. red	3·50	5·00
408	**88**	20f. blue	1·10	50

DESIGNS—As Type **86/7**: 15f. brown (2) Oudayas Courtyard; 15f. violet (2), 18f. Oudayas Point, Rabat.

Two types each of: 5f. (A) 18×22 mm, (B) 17×21½ mm: 15f. brown (A) "MAROC" not in tablet, (B) "MAROC" in white tablet; 15f. violet (A) 18×22½ mm, (B) 16½×21½ mm.

89 Casablanca P.O. and Reproduction of Type **22**

1952. Air. Stamp Day and 30th Anniv of First Moroccan Air Stamps.

409	**89**	15f.+5f. blue & brown	3·75	15·00

90 Saadian Capital

1952. Solidarity Fund. Inscr "SOLIDARITE 1951". Column capitals as T 90.

410	-	15f. blue (Omeiyad)	1·60	8·00
411	-	20f. red (Almohad)	1·60	6·50
412	-	25f. violet (Merinid)	1·60	5·50
413	**90**	50f. green	1·60	4·50

91 Ramparts of Chella, Rabat

1952. Air.

414	**91**	10f. green	2·10	1·50
415	-	40f. red	1·80	45
416	-	100f. brown	3·25	45
417	-	200f. violet	5·50	3·50

DESIGN: Lockheed Constellation over—HORIZ: 40f. Marrakesh. VERT: 100f. Fort in Anti-Atlas Mts.; 200f. Fez.

92 War Memorial, Casablanca

1952. Centenary of Military Medal.

418	**92**	15f. brown, yellow & green	1·10	7·75

93 Jewellery from Fez

1953. Solidarity Fund. Inscr "SOLIDARITE 1952".

419	-	15f. red (postage)	1·60	8·75
420	**93**	20f. brown	1·60	3·75
421	-	25f. blue	1·60	3·75
422	-	50f. green (air)	1·90	8·75

DESIGNS: 15f. Daggers from S. Morocco; 25f. Jewellery from Anti-Atlas; 50f. Jewellery from N. Morocco.

94 Arab Courier and Scribe

1953. Stamp Day.

423	**94**	15f. purple	1·10	9·75

95 Bine el Ouidane Barrage

1953. Inauguration of Barrage.

424	**95**	15f. blue	1·30	7·50
424a	**95**	15f. blue and brown	65	90

96 Mogador Battlements

1953. Army Welfare Fund.

425	**96**	15f. green	1·30	5·50
426	-	30f. brown	85	4·00

DESIGN: 30f. Moorish horsemen.

1954. Nos. 324 and 335 surch.

427	**58**	1f. on 1f.50 blue	75	85
428	-	15f. on 18f. blue	2·20	3·25

98 Meknes

1954. Air. Solidarity Fund. Inscr "1953".

429	**98**	10f. olive	2·00	3·75
430	-	20f. violet (Rabat)	2·00	8·75
431	-	40f. brn (Casablanca)	2·00	7·25
432	-	50f. green (Fedala)	2·00	3·50

99 Mail Van and Postmen

1954. Stamp Day.

433	**99**	15f. green	1·20	8·00

100 Schooner and Destroyer

1954. Air. Naval Welfare Fund.

436	**100**	15f. green	2·75	7·00
437	**100**	30f. blue	2·50	8·50

101 Marshal Lyautey at Khenifra

1954. Birth Centenary of Marshal Lyautey.

438	-	5f. blue	2·10	10·50
439	**101**	15f. green	2·10	11·00
440	-	30f. lake	2·10	11·00
441	-	50f. brown	2·10	7·75

DESIGNS—HORIZ: 5f. Lyautey receiving Moroccan notables at Rabat. VERT: 30f. Lyautey in dockyards; 50f. Portrait of Lyautey (after Laszlo).

102 Moroccan Scholar

1955. Solidarity Fund.

442		5f. blue	1·30	5·00
443	**102**	15f. red	85	5·50
444	-	30f. brown	95	4·75
445	-	50f. green	90	5·00

DESIGNS—HORIZ: 5f. French and Moroccan schoolchildren; 30f. Muslim School, Camp-Boulhaut. VERT: 50f. Moulay Idriss College, Fez.

103 Mazagan P.O.

1955. Day of the Stamp.

446	**103**	15f. red	85	6·50

104 Map of Morocco

1955. 50th Anniv of Rotary International.

447	**104**	15f. blue and brown	65	7·50

105 Bab el Mrissa, Sale

106 Mahakma, Casablanca

1955

448	**105**	50c. purple	35	3·00
449	**105**	1f. blue	35	65
450	**105**	2f. purple	70	90
451	**105**	3f. blue	90	70
452	-	5f. red	1·00	70
453	-	6f. green	1·00	1·20
454	-	8f. brown	2·50	7·25
455	-	10f. purple	1·10	35
456	-	12f. turquoise	80	70
457	-	15f. lake	1·10	35
458	**106**	18f. myrtle	1·30	1·50
459	**106**	20f. lake	95	20
460	-	25f. blue	2·00	1·40
461	-	30f. green	2·00	45
462	-	40f. red	1·00	35
463	-	50f. sepia	2·10	35
464	-	75f. turquoise	1·70	1·10

DESIGNS—As Type **105**: 5f., 6f., 8f. Bab Chorfa, Fez; 10f., 12f., 15f. Chella Minaret, Rabat. As Type **106**—HORIZ: 25f. Coastal castle, Safi; 30f. Menara, Marrakesh; 40f. Tafraout; 50f. Portuguese cistern, Mazagan. VERT: 75f. Oudaya gardens, Rabat.

107 Bou Regreg Estuary

1955. Air.

465		100f. violet	2·50	45
466	**107**	200f. red	5·50	75
467	-	500f. blue	6·25	4·00

DESIGNS—VERT: 100f. Village in the Anti-Atlas. HORIZ: 500f. Ksar es Souk.

PARCEL POST STAMPS

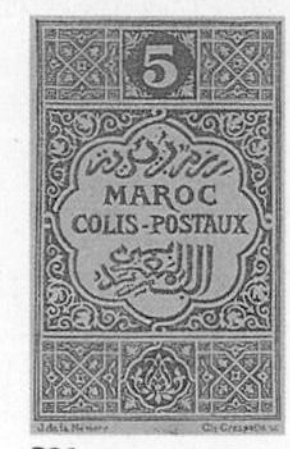
P21

1917

P101	**P21**	5c. green	75	2·50
P102	**P21**	10c. red	1·40	2·50
P103	**P21**	20c. brown	2·50	2·75
P104	**P21**	25c. blue	1·90	2·30
P105	**P21**	40c. brown	2·50	3·00
P106	**P21**	50c. red	3·50	2·30
P107	**P21**	75c. grey	5·25	4·50
P108	**P21**	1f. blue	5·75	1·50
P109	**P21**	2f. grey	5·25	1·40
P110	**P21**	5f. violet	8·50	90
P111	**P21**	10f. black	15·00	1·20

POSTAGE DUE STAMPS

1915. Postage Due stamps of France surch with figure and Arabic word, and further optd PROTECTORAT FRANCAIS.

D66	**D11**	1c. on 1c. black	85	5·50
D67	**D11**	5c. on 5c. blue	1·30	6·00
D68	**D11**	10c. on 10c. brown	2·10	5·25
D69	**D11**	20c. on 20c. green	2·10	5·25
D70	**D11**	30c. on 30c. red	2·75	11·50
D71	**D11**	50c. on 50c. purple	3·25	4·50

1915. Postage Due stamps of France with surch and optd as above.

D72	**D19**	1c. on 1c. olive	1·10	6·50
D73	**D19**	10c. on 10c. violet	3·50	6·25
D74	**D19**	30c. on 30c. bistre	2·30	10·00
D75	**D19**	50c. on 50c. red	3·25	9·50

D21

1917

D93	**D21**	1c. black	30	1·50
D94	**D21**	5c. blue	30	1·70
D95	**D21**	10c. brown	40	95
D96	**D21**	20c. green	75	1·30
D97	**D21**	30c. red	35	60
D98	**D21**	50c. brown	35	15
D99	**D21**	1f. purple on yellow	75	70
D308	**D21**	1f. red	1·60	7·00
D100	**D21**	2f. violet	1·10	1·30
D310	**D21**	3f. blue	75	2·20
D311	**D21**	4f. orange	1·80	4·00
D312	**D21**	5f. green	85	90
D313	**D21**	10f. bistre	1·70	35
D314	**D21**	20f. red	4·50	2·30
D315	**D21**	30f. brown	2·75	8·25

1944. Surch.

D289	50c. on 30c. red	6·25	19·00
D290	1f. on 10c. brown	7·00	19·00
D291	3f. on 10c. brown	15·00	44·00

For later issues see **MOROCCO**.

Pt. 2

FRENCH OCCUPATION OF HUNGARY

Arad later became part of Rumania.

100 filler = 1 korona.

ARAD

1919. Stamps of Hungary Optd Occupation francaise or surch also. (a) War Charity stamps of 1916.

1	**20**	11f. (+2f.) red	32·00	32·00
2	-	15f. (+2f.) lilac	2·20	2·20
3	**22**	40f. (+2f.) red	3·25	3·25

(b) Harvesters and Parliament Types.

4	**18**	2f. brown	55	55
5	**18**	3f. red	20	20
6	**18**	5f. green	5·50	5·50
7	**18**	6f. blue	55	55
8	**18**	10f. red	1·10	1·10
9	**18**	15f. purple	1·10	1·10
10	**18**	15f. violet (No. 244)	55·00	55·00
11	**18**	20f. brown	13·00	13·00
12	**18**	35f. brown	22·00	22·00
13	**18**	40f. green	11·00	11·00
14	**18**	45 on 2f. brown	2·75	2·75
15a	**18**	45 on 3f. red	37·00	
16	**18**	50 on 3f. red	2·75	2·75
18	**19**	50f. purple	1·60	1·60
19	**19**	75f. blue	55	55
20	**19**	80f. green	1·10	1·10
21	**19**	1k. red	6·50	6·50
22	**19**	2k. brown	1·10	1·10
23	**19**	3k. grey and violet	6·50	6·50
24	**19**	5k. brown	7·50	7·50
25	**19**	10k. mauve and brown	55·00	55·00

(c) Charles and Zita stamps.

26	**27**	10f. red	19·00	19·00
27	**27**	20f. brown	20	20
28	**27**	25f. blue	55	55
29	**28**	40f. green	1·10	1·10

(d) Harvester stamps inscr "MAGYAR POSTA".

30	**18**	5f. green	27·00	27·00
31	**18**	10f. red	1·60	1·60
32	**18**	20f. brown	16·00	16·00

(e) Stamps of 1919 optd KOZTARSASAG. (i) Harvesters and Parliament Types.

33		2f. brown	55	55
34		3f. red	3·25	3·25
35		4f. grey	55	55
36		5f. green	20	20
37		6f. blue	3·75	3·25
38		10f. red	32·00	32·00
39		20f. brown	4·25	4·25
40		40f. green	55	55
41	**19**	1k. red	75	75
42	**19**	3k. grey and violet	3·50	3·50
43	**19**	10(k)on 1k. red	3·50	3·50

(ii) Charles and Zita stamps.

44	**27**	25f. blue	1·10	1·10
45	**28**	40f. green	22·00	22·00
46	**28**	50f. violet	2·20	2·20

EXPRESS LETTER STAMP

1919. No. E245 optd Occupation francaise.

E48	**E18**	2f. green and red	20	20

NEWSPAPER STAMP

1919. No. N136 optd Occupation francaise.

N47	**N9**	(2f.) orange	30	30

POSTAGE DUE STAMPS

1919. (a) No. D191 of Hungary optd Occupation francaise.

D49	**D 9**	2f. red and green	1·60	1·60
D50	**D 9**	10f. red and green	1·10	1·10
D51	**D 9**	12f. red and green	11·00	11·00
D52	**D 9**	15f. red and green	11·00	11·00
D53	**D 9**	20f. red and green	11·00	11·00

(b) No. N47 of Arad surch Porto and new value.

D54	**N 9**	12 on (2f.) orange	3·25	3·25
D55	**N 9**	15 on (2f.) orange	3·25	3·25
D56	**N 9**	30 on (2f.) orange	3·25	3·25
D57	**N 9**	50 on (2f.) orange	3·25	3·25
D58	**N 9**	100 on (2f.) orange	3·25	3·25

Pt. 6

FRENCH POLYNESIA

The French Settlements in the South Pacific, formerly called Oceanic Settlements.

100 centimes = 1 franc.

1 Girl playing Guitar

2 Polynesian

3 "The Women of Tahiti" (after Gauguin)

1958

1	**1**	10c. brn, grn & turq (postage)	40	5·75
2	**1**	25c. purple, red and green	30	6·75
3	**1**	1f. sepia, red and blue	1·80	2·00
4	**1**	2f. violet, choc & brown	2·75	3·25
5	**2**	4f. myrtle, green & yellow	2·75	3·00
6	-	5f. brown, violet & green	4·75	4·00
7	**2**	7f. brown, green & orange	4·00	4·25
8	**2**	9f. purple, green & orange	4·75	4·00
9	-	10f. red, blue and brown	5·25	3·75
10	-	16f. multicoloured	6·75	6·50
11	-	17f. brown, blue & turquoise	10·00	3·75
12	-	20f. brown, violet & pink	10·00	4·00
13	-	13f. brn, grn & drab (air)	10·00	6·25
14	**3**	50f. multicoloured	9·50	9·25
15	-	100f. multicoloured	11·50	16·00
16	-	200f. slate and lilac	34·00	50·00

DESIGNS: As Types **1/2**—VERT: 5f. Spearfishing; 10f., 20f. Polynesian girl on beach. HORIZ: 16f. Post Office, Papeete; 17f. Tahitian dancers. As Type **3**—VERT: 13f. Mother-of-pearl engraver; 100f. "The White Horse" (after Gauguin). HORIZ: 200f. Night-fishing off Moorea.

1958. 10th Anniv of Declaration of Human Rights. As T 57 of French Equatorial Africa.

17		7f. grey and blue	5·25	14·50

1959. Tropical Flora. As T 56 of French Equatorial Africa. Multicoloured.

18		4f. "Artocarpus"	2·75	6·00

7 Douglas DC-8 over Papeete Airport

1960. Air. Inauguration of Papeete Airport.

19	**7**	13f. violet, purple & green	4·00	3·00

8 "Saraca indica"

1962. Flowers.

20		15f. Type **8**	9·00	12·50
21		25f. Hibiscus	9·50	40·00

9 Pacific Map and Palms

1962. 5th South Pacific Conference, Pago-Pago.

22	**9**	20f. multicoloured	8·00	13·00

10 "Telstar" Satellite

1962. Air. 1st Trans-Atlantic T.V. Satellite Link.

23	**10**	50f. blue, brown and purple	6·25	15·00

11 Spined Squirrelfish

1962. Fishes. Multicoloured.

24		5f. Type **11**	3·50	5·75
25		10f. Teardrop butterflyfish	3·50	3·75
26		30f. Radial lionfish	6·00	7·50
27		40f. Long-horned cowfish	9·50	13·00

12 Football

1962. 1st South Pacific Games, Suva, Fiji.

28	**12**	20f. brown and blue	8·50	29·00
29	-	50f. blue and red	8·50	15·00

DESIGN: 50f. Throwing the javelin.

13 Centenary Emblem

1963. Centenary of Red Cross.

30	**13**	15f. red, grey and purple	7·50	34·00

14 Globe and Scales of Justice

1963. 15th Anniv of Declaration of Human Rights.

31	**14**	7f. violet and green	8·50	10·00

1964. "PHILATEC 1964" International Stamp Exhibition, Paris. As T 528 of France.

32		25f. red, black and green	8·00	32·00

16 Dancer

1964. Tahitian Dancers.

33	**16**	1f. multicoloured (postage)	85	70
34	**16**	3f. orange, sepia & purple	1·10	1·20
35	-	15f. multicoloured (air)	3·00	2·75

DESIGN—VERT: (27×46½ mm): 15f. Dancer in full costume.

17 Tahitian Volunteers

1964. Polynesia's War Effort in Second World War. Multicoloured.

36		5f. Type **17** (postage)	6·75	11·50
37		16f. Badges and map of Tahiti (48×27 mm) (air)	10·00	26·00

18 Tuamotu Lagoon (after J. D. Lajoux)

1964. Landscapes. Multicoloured.

38		2f. Type **18** (postage)	2·20	2·00
39		4f. Bora-Bora (after Lajoux)	2·50	1·90
40		7f. Papeete (after A. Sylvain)	3·25	2·20
41		8f. Marquesas (Gauguin's grave)	2·10	2·30
42		20f. Gambier (after Mazellier)	4·50	2·75
43		23f. Moorea (after Sylvain) (48×27 mm) (air)	7·25	5·25

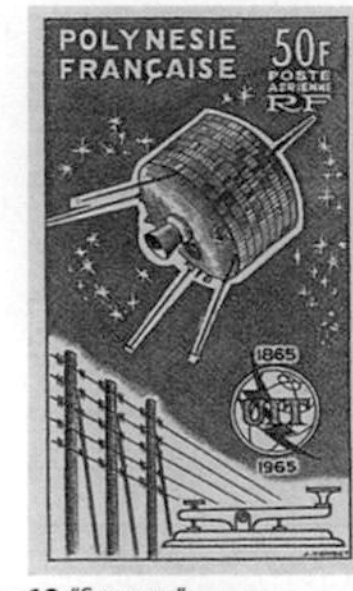

19 "Syncom" Communications Satellite, Telegraph Poles and Morse Key

1965. Air. Centenary of I.T.U.

44	**19**	50f. brown, blue & violet	50·00	65·00

20 Museum Buildings

1965. Air. Gauguin Museum.

45	**20**	25f. green	6·00	11·00
46	-	40f. turquoise	10·00	25·00
47	-	75f. brown	15·00	26·00

DESIGNS: 40f. Statues and hut; 75f. Gauguin.

21 Skin-diver with Harpoon

1965. Air. World Under-water Swimming Championships, Tuamoto.

48	**21**	50f. blue, brown & green	60·00	£120

22 Tropical Foliage

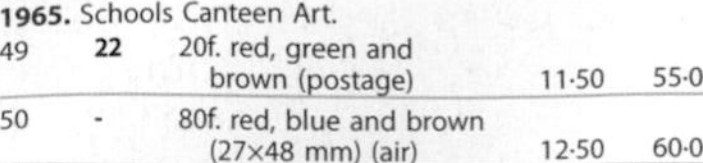

1965. Schools Canteen Art.

49	**22**	20f. red, green and brown (postage)	11·50	55·00
50	-	80f. red, blue and brown (27×48 mm) (air)	12·50	60·00

DESIGN: 80f. Totem, and garland in harbour.

23 Aerial, Globe and Palm

1965. Air. 50th Anniv of 1st Radio Link with France.

51	**23**	60f. brown, green & orge	11·50	46·00

1966. Air. Launching of 1st French Satellite. As Nos. 1696/7 (plus se-tenant label) of France.

52	7f. brown, purple & green	3·50	18·00
53	10f. brown, purple & green	4·50	21·00

1966. Air. Launching of Satellite "D1". As T 569 of France.

54	20f. red, brown and green	4·75	16·00

26 Papeete Port

1966. Air.

55	**26**	50f. multicoloured	9·50	50·00

27 Pirogue

1966. Polynesian Boats.

56	**27**	10f. red, green and blue	3·25	3·00
57	-	11f. red, green and blue	3·50	3·50
58	-	12f. purple, green & blue	4·50	4·75
59	-	14f. brown, blue & green	6·00	3·75
60	-	19f. green, red and blue	6·75	5·25
61	-	22f. green, blue & purple	9·50	6·00

DESIGNS—VERT: 11f. Schooner; 19f. Early schooner. HORIZ: 12f. Fishing launch; 14f. Pirogues; 22f. Coaster "Oiseau des Iles II".

28 Tahitian Dancer and Band

1966. Air. "Vive, Tahiti!" (tourist publicity).

62	**28**	13f. multicoloured	7·50	17·00

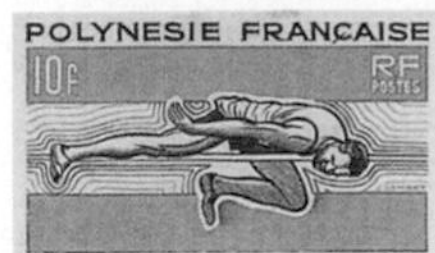

29 High-jumping

1966. 2nd South Pacific Games, Noumea.

63	**29**	10f. bistre and red	2·75	7·50
64	-	20f. green and blue	4·25	4·25
65	-	40f. purple and green	7·00	6·50
66	-	60f. blue and brown	8·50	34·00

DESIGNS—VERT: 20f. Pole-vaulting; 40f. Basketball. HORIZ: 60f. Hurdling.

30 Stone Pestle

1967. 50th Anniv of Oceanic Studies Society.

67	**30**	50f. blue and orange	8·50	14·00

31 Spring Dance

1967. July Festival.

68	**31**	5f. blue, purple and drab	2·30	2·00
69	-	13f. purple, violet & green	3·00	2·30
70	-	15f. brown, purple & green	2·75	2·50
71	-	16f. purple, green & blue	3·25	3·50
72	-	21f. brown, green & blue	5·00	11·00

DESIGNS—VERT: 13f. Javelin-throwing; 16f. Fruit-porters' race. HORIZ: 15f. Horse-racing; 21f. Pirogue-racing.

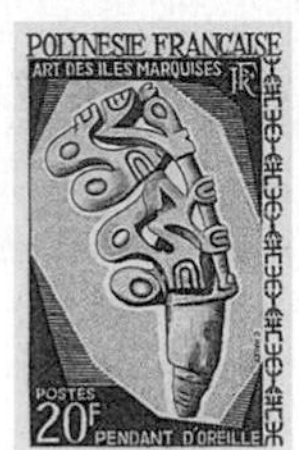

32 Earring

1967. Ancient Art of the Marquesas Islands.

73		10f. blue, red & purple	3·25	3·50
74		15f. black and green	3·50	7·00
75	**32**	20f. brown, green & lake	2·75	6·50
76	-	23f. brown and ochre	4·25	8·50
77	-	25f. brown, purple & blue	4·50	5·25
78	-	30f. brown and purple	5·50	12·00
79	-	35f. blue and brown	7·50	28·00
80	-	50f. brown, blue & green	6·75	28·00

DESIGNS: 10f. Sculpture on mother-of-pearl; 15f. Paddle-blade; 23f. Receptacle for anointing oil; 25f. Hunting stirrups; 30f. Fan handles; 35f. Tattooed man; 50f. "Tikis".

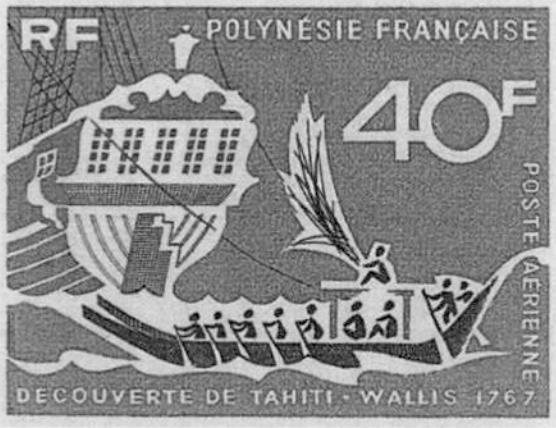

33 Ship's Stern and Canoe ("Wallis, 1767")

1968. Air. Bicentenary of Discovery of Tahiti.

81	**33**	40f. brown, blue & green	12·50	13·00
82	-	60f. orange, black & blue	12·50	21·00
83	-	80f. salmon, lake & purple	11·50	14·00
MS84		180×100 mm. Nos. 81/3	£160	£190

DESIGNS—HORIZ: 60f. Ship and witch-doctor ("Cook, 1769"). VERT: 80f. "Bougainville, 1768" (portrait).

34 Bouquet, Sun and W.H.O. Emblem

1968. 20th Anniv of World Health Organization.

85	**34**	15f. violet, red and green	5·25	16·00
86	**34**	16f. green, purple & orange	5·25	34·00

35 "The Meal" (Gauguin)

1968. Air.

87	**35**	200f. multicoloured	22·00	60·00

36 Human Rights Emblem

1968. Human Rights Year.

88	**36**	15f. red, blue and brown	5·00	10·50
89	**36**	16f. blue, brown & purple	5·75	9·75

37 Putting the Shot

1968. Air. Olympic Games, Mexico.

90	**37**	35f. green, purple & red	11·50	28·00

38 Tiare Apetahi

1969. Flowers. Multicoloured.

91	9f. Type **38**	3·75	3·25
92	17f. Tiare Tahiti	10·00	7·50

39 Concorde in Flight

1969. Air. 1st Flight of Concorde.

93	**39**	40f. brown and red	65·00	70·00

40 Polynesian with Guitar

1969. Air. Pacific Area Travel Association (P.A.T.A.) Congress, Tahiti (1970) (1st issue).

94	**40**	25f. multicoloured	17·00	23·00

See also Nos. 109/11.

41 Diver and Fish

1969. Air. World Underwater Hunting Championships.

95	**41**	48f. black, purple & turq	20·00	46·00
96	-	52f. black, red and blue	30·00	65·00

DESIGN—VERT: 52f. "Flag" Fish.

42 Boxing

1969. 3rd South Pacific Games, Port Moresby, New Guinea.

97	**42**	9f. brown and violet	3·75	7·00
98	-	17f. brown and red	4·25	4·50
99	-	18f. brown and blue	5·50	12·50
100	-	22f. purple and green	7·50	9·50

DESIGNS—VERT: 17f. High jumping; 18f. Running; 22f. Long jumping.

43 "Bonaparte as Commander-in-Chief, Italy" (Rouillard)

1969. Air. Birth Bicentenary of Napoleon Bonaparte.

101	**43**	100f. multicoloured	60·00	£120

44 I.L.O. Building, Geneva

1969. 50th Anniv of International Labour Organization.

102	**44**	17f. drab, green & orange	6·25	16·00
103	**44**	18f. blue, brown & orange	6·50	17·00

45 Territorial Assembly Building

1969. Polynesian Buildings. Multicoloured.

104	13f. Type **45**	3·50	4·50
105	14f. Governor's residence	4·50	4·25
106	17f. Tourist offices	6·25	10·50
107	18f. Maeva Hotel	8·75	5·25
108	24f. Taharaa Hotel	10·50	7·50

46 Tiki holding P.A.T.A. Emblem

1970. P.A.T.A. Congress (2nd issue).

109	**46**	20f. blue, brown & purple	8·50	11·50
110	-	40f. blue, purple & green	12·50	20·00
111	-	60f. dp brown, blue & brn	13·50	34·00

DESIGNS—HORIZ: 40f. Globe, airliner and "tourists". VERT: 60f. Polynesian holding globe.

47 New U.P.U. Building, Berne

1970. New U.P.U. Headquarters Building.

112	**47**	18f. lt brown, violet & brn	10·50	11·50
113	**47**	20f. blue, brown & purple	10·00	10·50

48 Tower of the Sun and Mt. Fuji

1970. Air. "EXPO 70" World Fair, Osaka, Japan. Multicoloured.

114	30f. Type **48**	10·00	25·00
115	50f. Eiffel Tower and Torii Gate (vert)	20·00	41·00

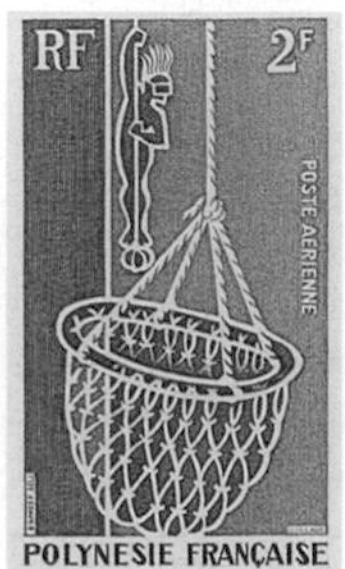

49 Diver and Basket

1970. Air. Pearl-diving.

116	**49**	2f. brown, indigo & blue	2·75	4·00
117	-	5f. ultramarine, orge & bl	3·25	2·00
118	-	18f. grey, orange & purple	4·75	3·50
119	-	27f. lilac, brown & purple	8·50	7·00
120	-	50c. orange, grey & brown	13·50	17·00

DESIGNS—VERT: 5f. Diver gathering black-lipped pearl oysters; 27f. Pearl in opened oyster; 50f. Woman with pearl jewellery. HORIZ: 18f. Opening oyster-shell.

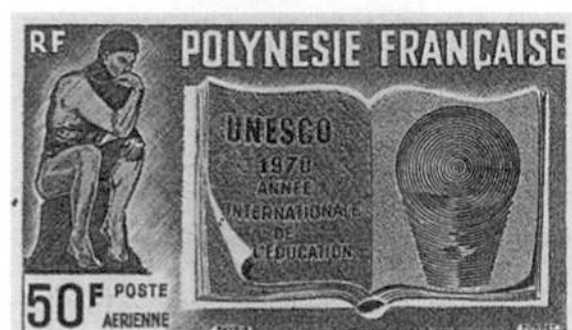

50 I.E.Y. Emblem, Open Book and "The Thinker" (statue)

1970. Air. International Education Year.

121	**50**	50f. blue, brown & lt blue	13·50	28·00

51 "Polynesian Woman" (Y. de St. Front)

1970. Air. Paintings by Polynesian Artists (1st series). Multicoloured.

122	20f. Type **51**	10·50	16·00
123	40f. "Harbour Scene" (F. Fay)	11·50	24·00
124	60f. "Niu" (abstract, J. Guillois)	13·50	20·00
125	80f. "Beach Hut" (J. Masson)	15·00	36·00
126	100f. "Polynesian Girl" (J. C. Bouloc) (vert)	36·00	55·00

See also Nos. 147/51, 160/4, 172/6, 189/93 and 205/9.

52 Games Emblem

1971. Air. 4th South Pacific Games, Tahiti (1st issue).

127	**52**	20f. multicoloured	6·75	14·00

53 Flame of Remembrance

1971. Air. Erection of General de Gaulle Monument.

128	**53**	5f. multicoloured	8·00	15·00

54 Volunteer, Crest and Tricolour

1971. Air. 30th Anniv of Departure of Tahitian "Free French" Volunteers.

129	**54**	25f. multicoloured	11·00	20·00

55 Marara Fisherman

1971. Water Sports. Multicoloured.

130	10f. Type **55** (postage)	8·50	18·00
131	15f. Surfing (vert) (air)	5·25	14·00
132	16f. Skin-diving (vert)	6·25	18·00
133	20f. Paragliding	9·00	9·75

56 Red Flower

1971. "Day of the 1,000 Flowers". Mult.

134	8f. Type **56**	2·75	2·00
135	12f. Hibiscus (horiz)	2·75	2·10
136	22f. Porcelain rose	5·25	3·75

57 Yachting

1971. Air. 4th South Pacific Games, Tahiti (2nd issue). Multicoloured.

137	15f. Type **57**	12·50	9·25
138	18f. Golf	12·50	8·50
139	27f. Archery	11·00	14·00
140	53f. Tennis	16·00	25·00
MS141	138×170 mm. Nos. 137/40	£200	£225

58 Water-skiing

1971. 1st World Water-ski Championships, Papeete.

142	**58**	10f. red, green & brown	11·00	7·25
143	-	20f. red, brown & green	10·50	9·25
144	-	40f. purple, brown & grn	20·00	34·00

DESIGNS—VERT: 20f. Ski-jumping. HORIZ: 40f. Acrobatics on one ski.

1971. 1st Death Anniv of General de Gaulle. As Nos. 1937 and 1940 of France.

145	30f. black and purple	12·50	16·00
146	50f. black and purple	13·50	22·00

1971. Air. Paintings by Polynesian Artists (2nd series). As T 51. Multicoloured.

147	20f. "Polynesian Village" (I. Wolf)	8·00	16·00
148	40f. "Lagoon" (A. Dobrowolski)	11·00	28·00
149	60f. "Polynesian Woman" (F. Seli) (vert)	13·50	28·00
150	80f. "The Holy Family" (P. Heymann) (vert)	20·00	29·00
151	100f. "Faces in a Crowd" (N. Michoutouchkine)	26·00	70·00

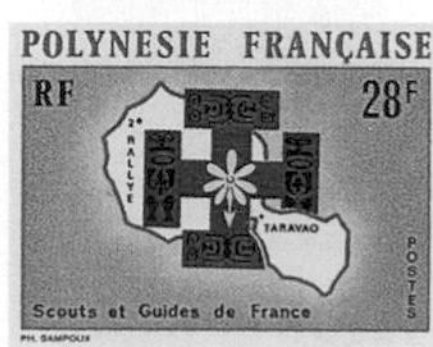

60 Cross Emblem

1971. 2nd French Pacific Scouts and Guides Rally, Taravao.

152	**60**	28f. multicoloured	9·50	32·00

61 Harbour, Papeete

1972. Air. 10th Anniv of Autonomous Port of Papeete.

153	**61**	28f. multicoloured	18·00	28·00

62 Figure-skating

1972. Air. Winter Olympic Games, Sapporo, Japan.

154	**62**	20f. red, green & violet	13·00	16·00

63 Commission H.Q., Noumea, New Caledonia

1972. Air. 25th Anniv of South Pacific Commission.

155	**63**	21f. multicoloured	13·00	20·00

64 Alcoholic behind Bars

1972. Campaign Against Alcoholism.

156	**64**	20f. multicoloured	8·50	8·50

65 Floral Emblem

1972. Air. South Pacific Arts Festival, Fiji.

157	**65**	36f. orange, green & blue	8·50	10·00

66 Raft "Kon-Tiki" and Route-map

1972. Air. 25th Anniv of Arrival of "Kon-Tiki" Expedition in French Polynesia.

158	**66**	16f. multicoloured	7·50	8·00

67 De Gaulle and Monument

1972. Air. Completion of De Gaulle Monument.

159	**67**	100f. grey	55·00	90·00

1972. Air. Paintings by Polynesian Artists (3rd series). As Type 51. Multicoloured.

160	20f. "Horses" (G. Bovy)	10·50	5·75
161	40f. "Harbour" (R. Juventin) (vert)	16·00	14·00
162	60f. "Landscape" (A. Brooke)	30·00	16·00
163	80f. "Polynesians" (D. Adam) (vert)	28·00	34·00
164	100f. "Dancers" (A. Pilioko) (vert)	23·00	70·00

68 St. Theresa and Lisieux Basilica

1973. Air. Birth Centenary of St. Theresa of Lisieux.

165	**68**	85f. multicoloured	28·00	50·00

69 Copernicus and Planetary System

1973. Air. 500th Birth Anniv of Nicolas Copernicus (astronomer).

166	**69**	100f. violet, brown & pur	15·00	70·00

70 Aeroplane and Flying Fish

1973. Air. Inauguration of "Air France" Round-the-World Service via Tahiti.

167	**70**	80f. multicoloured	30·00	46·00

71 Douglas DC-10 over Papeete Airport

1973. Air. Inauguration of "DC-10" Service.

168	**71**	20f. blue, green & lt blue	26·00	14·00

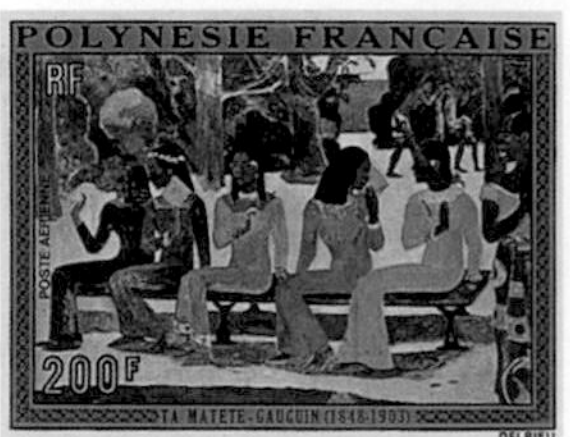

72 "Ta Matete" (Gauguin)

1973. Air. 125th Birth Anniv of Gauguin.

169	**72**	200f. multicoloured	25·00	65·00

73 Loti, Fishermen and Polynesian Girl

1973. Air. 50th Death Anniv of Pierre Loti (writer).

170	**73**	60f. multicoloured	60·00	50·00

74 Polynesian Mother and Child

1973. Opening of Tahitian Women's Union Creche.

171	**74**	28f. multicoloured	12·50	10·50

1973. Air. Paintings by Polynesian Artists (4th series). As Type 51. Multicoloured.

172	20f. "Sun God" (J.-F. Favre) (vert)	7·50	7·00
173	40f. "Polynesian Girl" (E. de Gennes) (vert)	16·00	20·00
174	60f. "Abstract" (A. Sidet) (vert)	18·00	21·00
175	80f. "Bus Passengers" (F. Ravello) (vert)	50·00	60·00
176	100f. "Boats" (J. Bourdin)	32·00	65·00

75 "Teeing Off"

1974. Atimaono Golf Course, Tahiti. Mult.

177	16f. Type **75**	8·50	4·00
178	24f. View of golf course	9·75	4·50

76 "A Helping Hand"

1974. Polynesian Animal Protection Society.

179	**76**	21f. multicoloured	14·00	8·00

77 Mountains and Lagoon

1974. Polynesian Landscapes. Multicoloured.

180	2f. Type **77**	3·75	2·30
181	5f. Beach games	5·25	2·75
182	6f. Canoe fishing	3·50	3·00
183	10f. Mountain peak (vert)	5·50	3·00
184	15f. "Regina Maris" (schooner) in sunset scene	10·50	4·00
185	20f. Island and lagoon	6·25	3·00

78 Bird, Stylized Angelfish, Leaf and Flower

1974. Air. Protection of Nature.

186	**78**	12f. multicoloured	10·50	10·00

79 Catamarans

1974. Air. 2nd World Catamaran Sailing Championships, Papeete.

187	**79**	100f. multicoloured	15·00	60·00

80 Polynesian Woman

1974. Centenary of Universal Postal Union.

188	**80**	65f. multicoloured	6·25	26·00

1974. Air. Paintings by Polynesian Artists (5th series). As Type 51. Multicoloured.

189	20f. "Flower arrangement" (R. Temarui-Masson) (vert)	10·50	10·00
190	40f. "Palms on Beach" (M. Chardon) (vert)	22·00	11·00
191	60f. "Portrait of Man" (M. F. Avril) (vert)	32·00	21·00
192	80f. "Polynesian Girl" (H. Robin) (vert)	60·00	23·00
193	100f. "Lagoon at Night" (D. Farsi)	75·00	55·00

81 "The Travelling Gods"

1975. Air. "50 Years of Tahitian Aviation".

194	**81**	50f. violet, red & brown	9·50	10·00
195	-	75f. blue, red & green	30·00	36·00
196	-	100f. brown, mve & grn	27·00	48·00

DESIGNS: 75f. Tourville's flying boat; 100f. Boeing 707 airliner.

82 Polynesian Girl and French "Ceres" Stamp of 1870

1975. Air. "Arphila 75" International Stamp Exhibition, Paris.

197	**82**	32f. red, brown & black	10·00	8·00

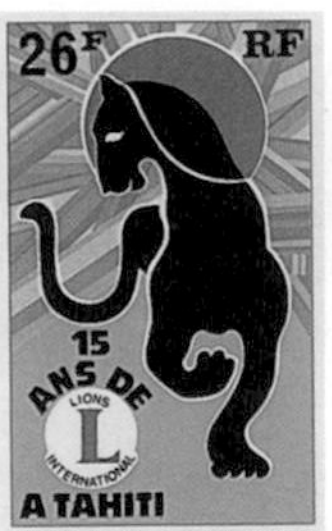

83 Tahiti Lions' Emblem

1975. 15th Anniv of Tahiti Lions' Club.

198	**83**	26f. multicoloured	25·00	12·00

84 "Protect Nature"

1975. Nature Protection.

199	**84**	19f. blue and green	6·25	10·00

85 Putting the Shot

1975. Air. 5th South Pacific Games, Guam. Mult.

200	25f. Type **85**	7·75	16·00
201	30f. Volleyball	7·50	7·75
202	40f. Swimming	12·50	23·00

86 Athlete and View of Montreal

1975. Air. Olympic Games, Montreal (1976).

203	**86**	44f. black, blue and red	12·50	14·00

87 Boeing 737 Airliner and Letters

1975. Air. World U.P.U. Day.

204	**87**	100f. blue, olive & brn	20·00	44·00

1975. Air. Paintings by Polynesian Artists (6th series). As T 51. Multicoloured.

205	20f. "Beach Scene" (R. Marcel-Marius)	8·00	6·75
206	40f. "Rooftop Aerials" (M. Anglade)	8·50	9·75
207	60f. "Street Scene" (J. Day)	12·50	10·50
208	80f. "Tropical Waters" (J. Steimetz) (vert)	35·00	30·00
209	100f. "Portrait of a Woman" (A. van der Heyde) (vert)	36·00	32·00

88 Concorde

1976. Air. Concorde's First Commercial Flight.

210	**88**	100f. dp blue, blue & mve	55·00	55·00

89 President Pompidou

1976. 2nd Death Anniv of Georges Pompidou (President of France, 1969–74).

211	**89**	49f. grey and blue	13·50	18·00

90 Battle of the Saints

1976. Air. Bicentenary of American Revolution.

212	**90**	24f. blue, brown & black	10·00	10·50
213	-	31f. purple, red & brown	10·50	11·00

DESIGN: 31f. Sea battle of The Chesapeake.

91 King Pomare 1

1976. Air. Pomare Dynasty. Multicoloured.

214	18f. Type **91**	5·00	3·25
215	21f. King Pomare II	3·50	2·75
216	26f. Queen Pomare IV	3·75	4·00
217	30f. King Pomare V	3·50	4·25

See also Nos. 234/7.

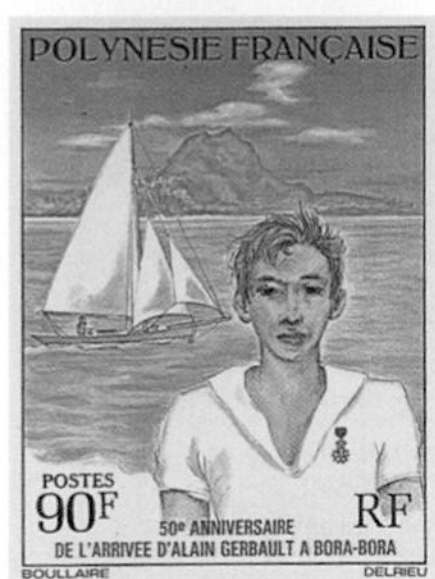

92 Gerbault and "Firecrest"

1976. 50th Anniv of Alain Gerbault's Arrival at Bora-Bora.

218	**92**	90f. multicoloured	16·00	26·00

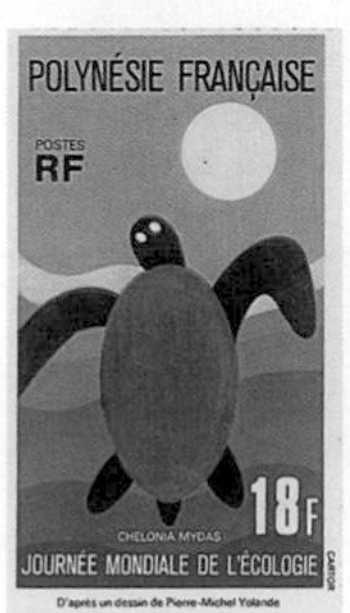

93 Turtle

1976. World Ecology Day. Multicoloured.

219	18f. Type **93**	10·50	13·00
220	42f. Doves in hand	11·50	23·00

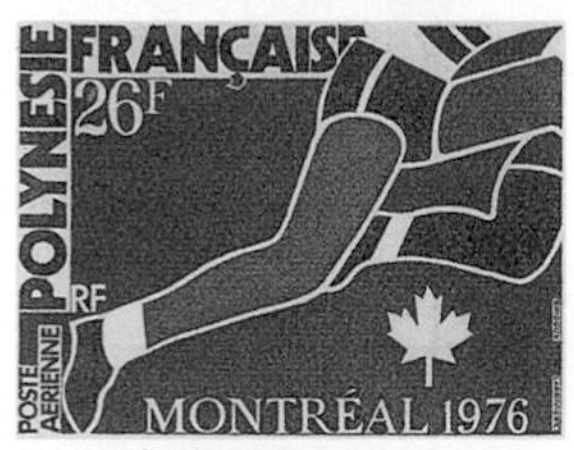

94 Legs of Runner

1976. Air. Olympic Games, Montreal.

221	**94**	26f. brown, purple & blue	5·00	5·50
222	-	34f. purple, brown & blue	6·00	7·00
223	-	50f. brown, blue & purple	10·50	13·00
MS224		181×101 mm. Nos. 222/24	95·00	£130

DESIGNS—VERT: 34f. Runners. HORIZ: 50f. Olympic Flame and flowers.

95 A. Graham Bell, early Telephone and Dish Aerial

1976. Telephone Centenary.

225	**95**	37f. red, blue & brown	19·00	9·00

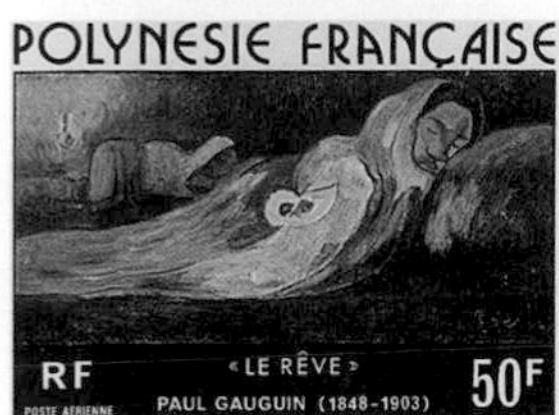

96 "The Dream" (Gauguin)

1976. Air.

226	**96**	50f. multicoloured	22·00	25·00

97 Marquesas Pirogue

1976. Ancient Pirogues. Multicoloured.

227	25f. Type **97**	5·25	7·25
228	30f. Raiatea pirogue	5·50	5·50
229	75f. Tahiti pirogue	11·50	16·00
230	100f. Tuamotu pirogue	13·50	21·00

98 Marquesas Cone

1977. Air. Sea Shells (1st series). Mult.

231	25f. Maurus murex	3·25	4·50
232	27f. Gaugin's cone	4·25	3·25
233	35f. Type **98**	5·75	3·75

See also Nos. 268/70 and 307/9.

1977. Air. "Sovereigns of Archipelago". As T 91. Multicoloured.

234	19f. Maputeoa (Mangareva)	3·75	4·25
235	33f. Tamatoa V (Raiatea)	2·75	2·75
236	39f. Vaekehu (Marquesas)	3·50	8·75
237	43f. Teuruarii III (Rurutu)	3·25	3·50

99 "Acropora"

1977. Air. 3rd Coral Reefs Symposium, Miami.

238	25f. Type **99**	5·25	3·50
239	33f. "Pocillopora" (vert)	5·50	9·50

1977. Air. 5th Anniv of General de Gaulle Memorial. As T 806 of France.

255	40f. multicoloured	7·25	9·00

101 Dancer

1977. Air. Polynesian Dancer.

256	**101**	27f. multicoloured	9·00	4·50

102 Lindbergh and "Spirit of St. Louis"

1977. Air. 50th Anniv of Lindbergh's Transatlantic Flight.

257	**102**	28f. multicoloured	19·00	14·00

103 "Hibiscus tiliaceus"

1977. Air. Polynesian Flowers (1st series). Multicoloured.

258	8f. Type **103**	1·80	3·00
259	12f. "Plumeria acuminata"	3·00	4·25

See also Nos. 276/7 and 288/9.

104 Palm Tree

1977. Air. Forest Conservation.

260	**104**	32f. multicoloured	12·00	9·75

105 "Portrait of Rubens' Son, Albert"

1977. Air. 400th Birth Anniv of Peter Paul Rubens.

261	**105**	100f. red and blue	12·50	24·00

106 Cutter

1977. Sailing Ships. Multicoloured.

262	20f. Type **106**	3·75	5·00
263	50f. "Tiare Taporo" (schooner)	4·75	5·75
264	85f. Barque	6·50	10·50
265	120f. Full-rigged ship	9·75	10·50

107 Captain Cook and H.M.S. "Discovery"

1978. Air. Bicent of Discovery of Hawaii.

266	**107**	33f. mauve, red and blue	8·00	10·50
267	-	39f. green, blue & mauve	8·75	11·00

DESIGN: 39f. Captain Cook and H.M.S. "Resolution".

1978. Air. Sea Shells (2nd series). As T 98. Multicoloured.

268	22f. Walled cowrie	3·50	3·50
269	24f. Ventral cowrie	3·50	3·50
270	31f. False scorpion conch	4·50	7·00

108 "Tahitian Woman and Boy" (Gauguin)

1978. Air. 75th Death Anniv of Paul Gauguin.

271	**108**	50f. multicoloured	16·00	26·00

109 Microwave Antenna

1978. Air. World Telecommunications Day.

272	**109**	80f. multicoloured	8·50	11·50

110 Match Scene

1978. Air. World Cup Football Championship, Argentina.

273	**110**	28f. multicoloured	3·75	6·50

111 Fungia

1978. Air. Coral (1st series). Multicoloured.

274	26f. Type **111**	3·00	4·25
275	34f. Millepora (vert)	3·25	5·25

See also Nos. 292/3.

112 "Hibiscus aros sinensis"

1978. Flowers (2nd series). Multicoloured.

276	13f. Type **112**	3·25	5·00
277	16f. "Fagraea berteriana"	4·25	5·50

113 Polynesian Girl and Aerial

1978. Air. Papenoo Ground Receiving Station.

278	**113**	50f. black and blue	6·50	5·00

114 Bird and Rainbow over Tropical Island

1978. Air. Nature Protection.

279	**114**	23f. multicoloured	4·25	9·00

115 Polynesian Girl on Beach

1978. 20th Anniv of First French Polynesian Stamps.

280	**115**	20f. brown, violet & red	6·50	6·50
281	-	28f. brown, green & yell	6·75	7·75
282	-	36f. brown, red and blue	9·75	8·00
MS283		130×100 mm. Nos. 280/82 in different colours	28·00	60·00

DESIGNS: 28f. Polynesian (as T **2**); 36f. Girl playing guitar (as T **1**).

116 "Tahiti" (inter-island ship)

1978. Ships. Multicoloured.

284		15f. Type **116**	3·75	4·00
285		30f. "Monowai" (liner)	4·00	4·25
286		75f. "Tahitien" (inter-island ship)	4·50	4·50
287		100f. "Mariposa" (cargo liner)	5·50	5·75

1979. Flowers (3rd series). As T 112. Mult.

288		10f. "Vanda sp."	3·50	4·00
289		22f. "Gardenia tahitensis" (vert)	3·75	3·25

1979. Air. Death Bicentenary of Captain James Cook (explorer). Nos. 266/7 optd "1779-1979" BICENTENAIRE DE LA MORT DE.

290	**107**	33f. mauve, red & blue	5·00	8·00
291	-	39f. green, blue & mauve	5·25	8·25

1979. Coral (2nd series). As T 111. Mult.

292		32f. Porytes	2·75	7·50
293		37f. Montipora and white-tailed damselfish	3·50	7·75

118 Raiatea

1979. Landscapes.

294		1f. Bora Bora	1·40	1·40
469		2f. Ua Pou	1·10	2·50
470		3f. Motu Tapu	1·60	3·25
470a		4f. Type **118**	4·00	4·25
471		5f. Motu	2·10	2·50
472		6f. Case au Taumotu	85	3·00

119 Children and Toys

1979. Air. International Year of the Child.

300	**119**	150f. mauve, blue & turq	6·25	15·00

120 "You are waiting for a Letter?" (Gauguin)

1979. Air.

301	**120**	200f. multicoloured	19·00	18·00

121 Conch and Stone Head of a Tiki

1979. Air. Tahiti and the Islands Museum.

302	**121**	44f. brown, red & lake	5·25	8·50

122 Fetia

1979. Traditional Dancing Costumes. Multicoloured.

303		45f. Type **122**	2·30	6·75
304		51f. Teanuanua	2·75	4·00
305		74f. Temaeva	5·00	5·75

123 Sir Rowland Hill, British and Polynesian Stamps

1979. Death Centenary of Sir Rowland Hill.

306	**123**	100f. mauve, violet & grn	5·00	6·00

1979. Sea Shells (3rd series). As T 98. Mult.

307		20f. Strigate auger	1·20	2·75
308		28f. Snake mitre	1·80	2·10
309		35f. Wavy-edge spindle	2·50	8·75

124 Arrows converging on Tahiti

1979. Air. 19th South Pacific Conference, Tahiti.

310	**124**	23f. multicoloured	2·10	6·75

125 Carving and Rotary Emblem

1979. 20th Anniv of Papeete Rotary Club.

311	**125**	47f. multicoloured	4·75	4·75

126 Short Sandringham 7 Bermuda Flying Boat

1979. Air. Aircraft (1st series). Multicoloured.

312		24f. Type **126**	4·75	3·00
313		40f. Douglas DC-4	7·00	5·75
314		60f. Britten Norman BN-2 Islander	7·75	6·25
315		80f. Fokker/Fairchild Friendship F.27A	10·00	5·25
316		120f. Douglas DC-8	12·00	6·25

See also Nos. 335/8.

127 Emperor Angelfish

1980. Fishes (1st series). Multicoloured.

317		7f. Big-eyed soldierfish	1·50	6·50
318		8f. Hump-headed wrasse	1·40	6·75
319		12f. Type **127**	2·30	3·50

See also Nos. 339/41, 360/2 and 386/8.

128 "Window in Tahiti"

1980. Air. 50th Anniv of Henri Matisse's Visit to Tahiti.

320	**128**	150f. multicoloured	11·00	9·50

1980. 75th Anniv of Rotary International. No. 311 surch 75eme ANNIVERSAIRE 1905-1980 77F.

321	**125**	77f. on 47f. mult	6·25	5·75

130 National Centre for Exploitation of Oceans

1980. Aquaculture (1st series). Multicoloured.

322		15f. Type **130**	1·20	3·50
323		22f. Sea-water shrimp	1·40	4·25

See also Nos. 343/4.

131 General Post Office, Papeete

1980. Opening of New General Post Office.

324	**131**	50f. multicoloured	3·00	3·00

132 Tiki Statuette, Marquesas Islands

1980. 3rd South Pacific Arts Festival, Papua New Guinea.

325		34f. Type **132**	2·30	3·00
326		39f. Pahu (drum), Marquesas Islands	2·50	7·50
327		49f. Adze, Society Islands	2·30	8·75
MS328		136×100 mm. Nos. 325/7	18·00	47·00

133 "Tehamana's Ancestors" (Gauguin)

1980. Air.

329	**133**	500f. multicoloured	26·00	50·00

134 Sydney Town Hall and 1955 Oceanic Settlements 9f. stamp

1980. Air. "Sydpex 80" Stamp Exhibition, Sydney.

330	**134**	70f. multicoloured	5·25	23·00

135 White Tern

1980. Birds (1st series). Multicoloured.

331		25f. Type **135**	4·00	4·75
332		35f. Tahitian lory (vert)	3·75	7·50
333		45f. Great frigate bird	3·50	8·00

See also Nos. 350/52 and 379/81.

136 Charles de Gaulle

1980. 10th Death Anniv of Charles de Gaulle (French statesman).

334	**136**	100f. multicoloured	3·75	4·75

1980. Air. Aircraft (2nd series). As T 126. Mult.

335		15f. Consolidated PBY-5A Catalina amphibian	3·50	6·00
336		26f. de Havilland Canada DH-6 Twin Otter	3·75	3·25
337		30f. CAMS 55 flying boat	3·50	3·50
338		50f. Douglas DC-6	7·75	6·25

1981. Fishes (2nd series). As T 127. Mult.

339	13f. Zebra unicornfish	2·75	5·75
340	16f. Black-tailed snapper	3·75	5·75
341	24f. Purple-spotted grouper	4·00	2·75

137 "And the Gold of their Bodies" (Gauguin)

1981. Air.

342	**137**	100f. multicoloured	13·00	11·00

1981. Aquaculture (2nd series). As T 130. Mult.

343	23f. Shrimp hatching room, National Centre for Exploitation of Oceans	1·70	6·50
344	41f. Green mussels	2·10	5·75

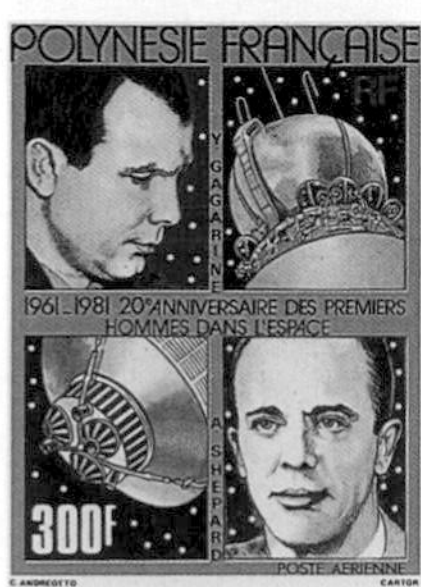

138 Yuri Gagarin and Alan Shepard

1981. Air. 20th Anniv of First Men in Space.

345	**138**	300f. multicoloured	8·00	23·00

139 Dancers

1981. Folklore. Multicoloured.

346	26f. Type **139**	2·50	1·60
347	28f. Drummer	1·90	2·50
348	44f. Two dancers (vert)	3·50	4·75

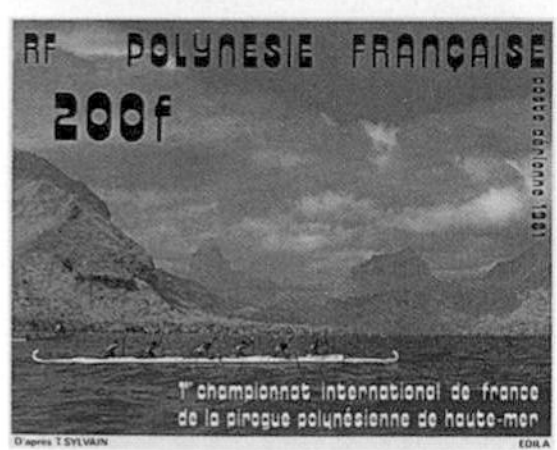

140 Racing Pirogue

1981. Air. 1st International Pirogue Championship, Polynesia.

349	**140**	200f. multicoloured	10·00	8·00

141 Common Waxbill

1981. Birds (2nd series). Multicoloured.

350	47f. Crested terns	2·10	6·75
351	53f. Grey-green fruit dove	2·30	7·00
352	65f. Type **141**	2·75	8·25

142 Huahine

1981. French Polynesian Islands (1st series). Multicoloured.

353	34f. Type **142**	2·75	5·75
354	134f. Maupiti	5·00	7·00
355	136f. Bora Bora	5·00	7·00

See also Nos. 376/8.

143 "Matavai Bay" (William Hodges)

1981. Air. 18th-century Paintings. Mult.

356	40f. Type **143**	5·50	6·25
357	60f. "Poedea" (John Webber) (wrongly inscr "Weber") (vert)	3·25	6·50
358	80f. "Omai" (Sir Joshua Reynolds) (vert)	4·50	7·00
359	120f. "Point Venus" (Georges Tobin)	10·50	11·00

1982. Fishes (3rd series). As T 127. Mult.

360	30f. Indo-Pacific hump-headed parrotfish	1·60	2·30
361	31f. Regal angelfish	1·70	3·25
362	45f. Greasy grouper	2·10	6·50

144 Family, Bacillus and Dr Robert Koch

1982. Air. Centenary of Discovery of Tubercle Bacillus.

363	**144**	200f. blue, grey & brown	7·00	9·50

145 Oyster Farm

1982. Pearl Industry. Multicoloured.

364	7f. Type **145**	90	5·50
365	8f. Grafting oysters	95	4·50
366	10f. Pearls	1·70	4·50

146 Girl and Tahiti 25c. stamp

1982. "Philexfrance 82" International Stamp Exhibition, Paris.

367	**146**	15f. brown, green & blue	5·25	15·00

MS368 122×95 mm. **146** 150f. rose, green and blue 23·00 50·00

147 Footballers

1982. Air. World Cup Football Championship, Spain.

369	**147**	250f. multicoloured	4·75	22·00

148 Priest

1982. Polynesian Folklore. King's Enthroning. Multicoloured.

370	12f. Type **148**	1·30	1·30
371	13f. Enthroning ceremony	1·40	1·70
372	17f. Priest and King	1·50	4·75

149 "Hobie Cat 16" Class Catamaran

1982. 4th World "Hobie Cat" Championship, Tahiti.

373	**149**	90f. multicoloured	2·75	8·00

150 Island Scene

1982. Air. Overseas Week.

374	**150**	110f. brown, blue & grn	4·50	8·25

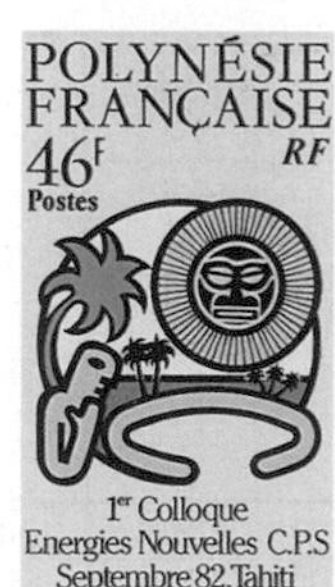

151 Sun, Man and Pacific Scene

1982. 1st South Pacific Commission Conference on New Energy Sources, Tahiti.

375	**151**	46f. multicoloured	2·00	7·00

1982. French Polynesian Islands (2nd series). As T 142. Multicoloured.

376	20f. Motu	1·60	4·00
377	33f. Tupai Atoll	2·00	1·10
378	35f. Gambier	1·70	5·75

1982. Birds (3rd series). As T 141. Mult.

379	37f. Reef heron (horiz)	2·75	1·40
380	39f. Pacific golden plover	2·75	7·75
381	42f. Chestnut-breasted mannikins	3·25	5·25

152 "Tahitian Girl" (Maximilien Radiguet)

1982. Air. 19th-century Paintings. Mult.

382	50f. Type **152**	4·75	6·50
383	70f. "Tahiti Souvenir" (Charles Giraud) (horiz)	2·50	7·00
384	100f. "Pounding Material" (Jules Louis Le Jeune) (horiz)	2·75	8·00
385	160f. "Papeete Harbour" (Constance Gordon Cumming) (horiz)	8·00	14·00

1983. Fishes (4th series). As T 127. Mult.

386	8f. Clown surgeonfish	1·70	4·00
387	10f. Blue-finned trevally	2·10	3·00
388	12f. Black-finned reef shark	1·40	6·00

153 "The Way of the Cross"

1983. Religious Sculptures by Damien Haturau. Multicoloured.

389	7f. Type **153**	85	3·25
390	21f. "The Virgin and the Infant Jesus"	1·60	4·50
391	23f. "Christ"	1·80	4·50

154 "The Axeman"

1983. Air. 80th Death Anniv of Gauguin (painter).

392	**154**	600f. multicoloured	17·00	38·00

155 Acacia and Pandanus Hat

1983. Polynesian Hats (1st series). Mult.

393	11f. Type **155**	1·30	2·75
394	13f. High-crowned hat made from coconut leaves	1·10	3·75
395	25f. Coffee-coloured openwork hat	1·60	5·25
396	35f. Bamboo hat	1·70	5·50

See also Nos. 423/6.

156 Bligh, Route Map and Breadfruit

1983. Air. Re-enactment of Captain William Bligh's Open-boat Voyage after the "Bounty" Mutiny.

397	**156**	200f. multicoloured	10·50	16·00

157 Chief of St. Christine

1983. Costumes (1st series). Multicoloured.

398	15f. Type **157**	1·30	3·00
399	15f. St. Christine man	1·40	3·50
400	28f. St. Christine woman	1·60	5·25

See also Nos. 427/9 and 454/6.

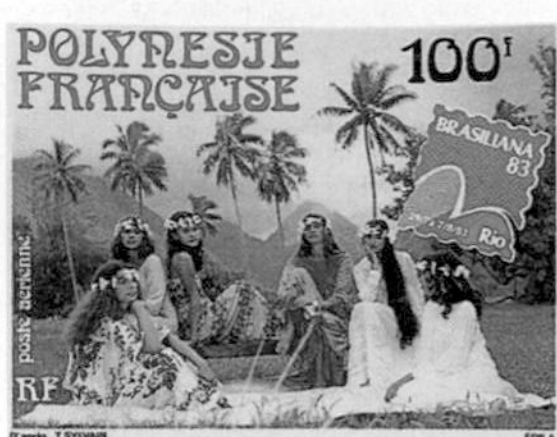

158 Polynesian Girls

1983. Air. "Brasiliana 83" International Stamp Exhibition, Rio de Janeiro.
401 **158** 100f. multicoloured 3·25 7·50
MS402 131×92 mm. No. 401 6·00 16·00

159 Polynesian and Thai Girls

1983. Air. "Bangkok 1983" International Stamp Exhibition.
403 **159** 110f. multicoloured 3·75 10·50
MS404 92×131 mm. No. 403 13·00 17·00

160 Fragrant Fern Headdress

1983. Floral Headdresses (1st series). Multicoloured.
405 41f. Type **160** 3·00 6·25
406 44f. Gardenias 3·25 6·50
407 45f. Mixed flowers 3·50 6·75
See also Nos. 433/5.

161 Luther and Church

1983. 500th Birth Anniv of Martin Luther (Protestant reformer).
408 **161** 90f. black, blue & brown 3·00 8·00

162 "Arrival of Escort Ship" (Nicolas Mordvinoff)

1983. Air. 20th-century Paintings. Mult.
409 40f. "View of Moorea" (William MacDonald) (horiz) 3·25 6·25
410 60f. "Fei Porter" (Adrian Herman Gouwe) 2·30 5·75
411 80f. Type **162** 4·00 7·50
412 100f. "Women on the Veranda" (Charles Lemoine) (horiz) 2·75 7·00

163 Me'ae of Peke, Nuku-Hiva

1984. Marquesian Tikis. Multicoloured.
413 14f. Type **163** 90 3·25
414 16f. Me'ae of Paeke (different) 1·00 1·70
415 19f. Me'ae Oipona, Hiva-Oa 1·10 4·00

165 Island Canoeists

1984. Air. "Espana 84" International Stamp Exhibition, Madrid.
420 **165** 80f. red and blue 2·75 6·50
MS421 144×100 mm. **165** 200f. blue 9·50 30·00

166 "Woman with Mango" (Gauguin)

1984. Air.
422 **166** 400f. multicoloured 25·00 28·00

1984. Polynesian Hats (2nd series). As T 155. Multicoloured.
423 20f. Reed hat 1·10 90
424 24f. Pandanus leaves hat 1·50 3·50
425 26f. Fei and bamboo hat 1·60 3·50
426 33f. Pandanus hat decorated with toetoe flowers 1·90 3·50

1984. Costumes (2nd series). As T 157. Mult.
427 34f. Tahitian boy playing nose flute 1·80 6·00
428 35f. Priest from Oei-Eitia 2·50 4·50
429 39f. Tahitian woman and her son 2·75 2·30

167 "Human Sacrifice" (detail, John Webber)

1984. Air. "Ausipex 84" International Stamp Exhibition, Melbourne. Multicoloured.
430 120f. Type **167** 5·00 16·00
431 120f. Different detail of "Human Sacrifice" 5·00 16·00
MS432 127×93 mm. 200f. Type **167** 25·00 50·00

1984. Floral Headdresses (2nd series). As T 160. Multicoloured.
433 46f. Ylang ylang 1·60 3·50
434 47f. Garden vine 1·60 6·25
435 53f. Bougainvillea 1·70 3·75

168 Tiki and Native

1984. 4th South Pacific Arts Festival, Noumea, New Caledonia.
436 **168** 150f. multicoloured 3·50 7·75
See also No. 453.

169 "Tahitian Girls on the Beach" (Pierre Heyman)

1984. 20th-century Paintings. Multicoloured.
437 50f. "After Church" (Jacques Boulaire) (vert) 2·50 6·00
438 65f. "Anaa Countryside" (Jean Masson) 2·75 5·75
439 75f. "Festival" (Robert Tatin) 2·75 5·50
440 85f. Type **169** 3·25 8·75

170 Pair of Tikis

1985. Wooden Tikis. Multicoloured.
441 30f. Type **170** 1·40 3·50
442 36f. Joined tikis 1·50 1·50
443 40f. Tiki 1·70 1·70

171 Girl wearing Lei

1985. Polynesian Faces (1st series). Multicoloured.
444 22f. Type **171** 1·10 3·00
445 39f. Girl's profile 1·80 3·50
446 44f. Girl wearing shell necklace 2·00 4·75
See also Nos. 473/5 and 498/500.

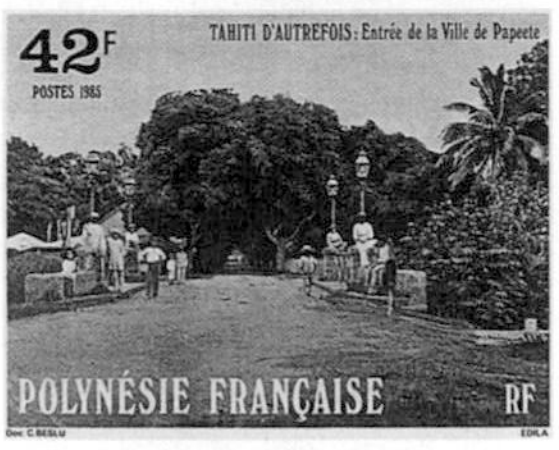

172 "Where Have We come From? What are We? Where are We Going?" (Gauguin) (image scaled to 66% of original size)

1985. Air.
447 **172** 550f. multicoloured 16·00 36·00

173 East Bridge, Papeete

1985. Tahiti in Olden Days (1st series). Mult.
448 42f. Type **173** 2·30 5·00
449 45f. Inhabitants of Papeete (vert) 1·20 5·00
450 48f. Papeete market 1·70 5·50
See also Nos. 477/9, 528/30, 703/5 and 742/4.

174 Coral Reef

1985. 5th International Coral Reefs Congress, Tahiti.
451 **174** 140f. multicoloured 6·75 9·00

175 National Flag

1985
452 **175** 9f. multicoloured 1·70 3·25

1985. 4th Pacific Arts Festival, Papeete. As T 168 but with "Sud Noumea" omitted, different emblem, inscr "29 juin au 15 juillet" and dated "1985".
453 200f. multicoloured 6·75 8·00
The Festival was originally to be held in New Caledonia in 1984 but was cancelled and subsequently held in Tahiti in 1985.

1985. Costumes (3rd series). As T 157. Mult.
454 38f. Tahitian dancer 2·50 4·75
455 55f. Tahitian couple 2·75 5·25
456 70f. Tahitian king 3·00 2·30

176 Couple holding Blue-faced Booby

1985. Air. International Youth Year.
457 **176** 250f. multicoloured 12·00 14·00

177 19th-century French Warship in Papeete Harbour

1985. Air. "Italia '85" International Stamp Exhibition, Rome.
458 **177** 130f. green 8·00 7·25
MS459 143×100 mm. **177** 240f. blue 10·50 29·00

178 Traditional Foods

1985. Tahitian Oven Pit. Multicoloured.
460 25f. Type **178** 2·20 4·75
461 35f. Man tending oven 2·30 2·75

179 St. Michael's Cathedral, Rikitea (Gambier Island)

1985. Catholic Churches. Multicoloured.
462 90f. St Anne's Church, Otepipi (Anaa) 4·50 6·50
463 100f. Interior of St. Michael's Cathedral, Rikitea (Gambier Island) 4·00 6·50
464 120f. Type **179** 6·00 8·00

180 Fiddler Crab

1986. Crabs. Multicoloured.

465	18f. Type **180**	1·20	3·00
466	29f. Hermit land crab	1·50	4·75
467	31f. Coconut crab	1·60	5·00

181 Youth with Pufferfish

1986. Polynesian Faces (2nd series). Multicoloured.

473	43f. Type **181**	2·00	5·00
474	49f. Boy holding coral	2·10	5·00
475	51f. Youth and turtle (vert)	2·20	5·25

182 Marlin and Emblem

1986. Air. 1st International Marlin Fishing Contest.

476	**182**	300f. multicoloured	5·25	10·00

1986. Tahiti in Olden Days (2nd series). As T 173. Multicoloured.

477	52f. Papeete	1·80	5·25
478	56f. Harpoon fishing	1·90	5·25
479	57f. King's Palace, Papeete	2·00	5·25

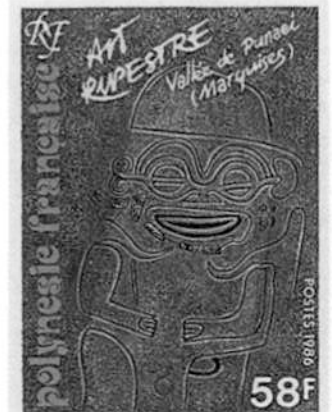

183 Tiki, Punaei Valley

1986. Rock Carvings (1st series). Mult.

480	58f. Type **183**	1·90	5·25
481	59f. Human figure, Hane Valley	2·40	5·25

See also Nos. 507/8.

184 Fish in Coconut Milk

1986. Polynesian Food Dishes (1st series). Multicoloured.

482	80f. Type **184**	3·75	5·00
483	110f. Fafaru	4·75	8·50

See also Nos. 504/5 and 524/5.

185 Arrival of Sailing Ships, 1880

1986. Air.

484	**185**	400f. blue	10·50	18·00

186 "Tifaifai" (sewn collage)

1986. Polynesian Folklore. Traditional Crafts. Multicoloured.

485	8f. Type **186**	75	3·25
486	10f. Wickerwork	85	3·25
487	12f. Making "mores" (dance skirts)	1·40	3·25

187 Map of Tahiti, Daniel Carl Solander and Anders Sparrmann

1986. Air. "Stockholmia 86" International Stamp Exhibition.

488	**187**	150f. grn, dp bl & bl	5·50	7·25

MS489	143×105 mm. **187** 210f. green, turquoise and blue	7·50	21·00

188 Building a Pirogue

1986. Pirogue Construction. Multicoloured.

490	46f. Type **188**	95	5·00
491	50f. Constructing the hull	1·30	5·25

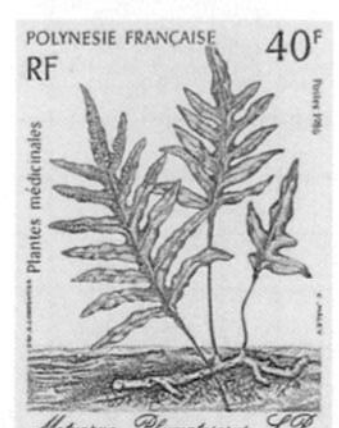

189 Metuapua

1986. Medicinal Plants (1st series). Designs showing illustrations by Gilles Cordonnier.

492	**189**	40f. green	3·25	2·75
493	-	41f. green	3·25	2·75
494	-	60f. green	3·75	5·50

DESIGNS: 41f. Hotu; 60f. Miri.

See also Nos. 514/16 and 545/7.

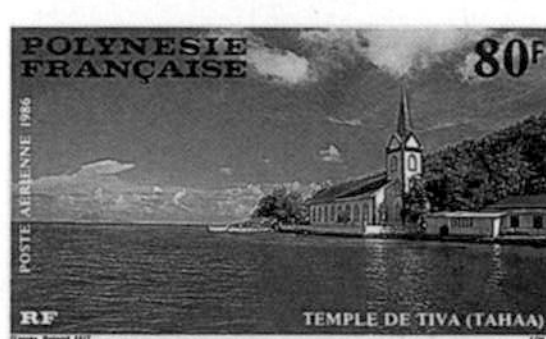

190 Tiva Church

1986. Air. Protestant Churches. Mult.

495	80f. Type **190**	4·50	6·00
496	200f. Avera church	6·75	7·25
497	300f. Papetoai church	10·00	12·50

191 Old Man

1987. Polynesian Faces (3rd series). Mult.

498	28f. Type **191**	1·70	3·00
499	30f. Girl holding baby	1·80	4·75
500	37f. Elderly woman	2·30	4·50

192 Reef Crab

1987. Crustaceans. Multicoloured.

501	34f. Type **192**	2·30	4·00
502	35f. "Parribacus antarcticus"	2·50	5·00
503	39f. "Justitia longimana"	2·75	5·25

1987. Polynesian Food Dishes (2nd series). As T 184. Multicoloured.

504	33f. Papaya po'e	1·30	3·75
505	65f. Chicken fafa	2·30	4·25

193 Broche Barracks

1987. Air. Centenary of Broche Army Barracks.

506	**193**	350f. multicoloured	10·50	21·00

1987. Rock Carvings (2nd series). As T 183. Multicoloured.

507	13f. Double-headed figure, Tipaerui	85	3·25
508	21f. Turtle, Raiatea	1·20	2·30

194 George Vancouver, Map of Rapa Island and Quotation

1987. Air. "Capex '87" International Stamp Exhibition, Toronto.

509	**194**	130f. brown and red	8·00	8·00

MS510	143×100 mm. 260f. brown, blue and deep blue. Imperf	8·50	21·00

DESIGN: 260f. Motifs as T **194**, Polynesian, Red Indian, and Polynesian and Canadian scenes.

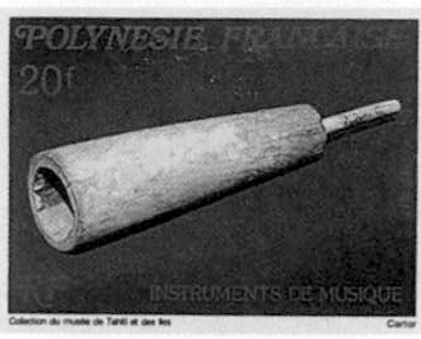

195 Marquesas Islands Miro Wood and Bamboo Horn

1987. Musical Instruments. Multicoloured.

511	20f. Type **195**	1·00	3·50
512	26f. Trumpet triton horn with coconut fibre cord	1·40	4·75
513	33f. Bamboo flutes	1·50	5·00

1987. Medicinal Plants (2nd series). As T 189, showing illustrations by Gilles Cordonnier.

514	46f. green	2·10	5·00
515	53f. mauve	2·40	5·25
516	54f. black	2·50	5·25

DESIGNS: 46f. Miro; 53f. Tiapito; 54f. Taataahiara.

197 "Soyez Mysterieuses" (wood sculpture, Paul Gauguin) (image scaled to 62% of original size)

1987. Air.

520	**197**	600f. multicoloured	16·00	24·00

198 Mgr. Rene Dordillon, Bishop of Marquesas Islands

1987. Catholic Missionaries. Multicoloured.

521	95f. Type **198**	3·00	6·50
522	105f. Mgr. Tepano Jaussen	3·25	6·75
523	115f. Mgr. Paul Maze, Archbishop of Papeete	5·75	7·75

1988. Polynesian Food Dishes (3rd series). As T 184. Multicoloured.

524	40f. Crayfish (vert)	1·70	3·50
525	75f. Bananas in coconut milk (vert)	3·00	4·25

199 James Norman Hall

1988. Birth Centenaries (1987) of Nordhoff and Hall (writers).

526	**199**	62f. black, cream & sil	2·75	5·50
527	-	85f. black, grey and silver	3·25	6·50

DESIGN: 85f. Charles Bernard Nordhoff.

200 Lighthouse and Anchor

1988. 120th Anniv of Venus Point Lighthouse.

531	**200**	400f. multicoloured	23·00	17·00

1988. Tahiti in Olden Days (3rd series). As T 173. Multicoloured.

528	11f. Taranpoo house raft, Raiatea	3·75	4·25
529	15f. Small Tahitian huts	3·00	4·25
530	17f. Large Tahitian hut	3·00	4·25

201 "River Scene"

1988. Tapa (cloth made from beaten bark) Paintings by Paul Engdahl. Multicoloured.

532	52f. Type **201**	3·75	5·50
533	54f. "River scene" (different)	4·50	4·00
534	64f. "Jungle"	4·75	6·50

196 Penu, War Club, Adze and Nose Flute

1987. Tools and Weapons. Designs showing plates from "The Voyages of Captain Cook".

517	**196**	25f. black and green	2·50	3·50
518	-	27f. blue & turquoise	2·50	4·75
519	-	32f. dp brn & brn	3·50	4·75

DESIGNS: 27f. War club, tattooing comb, paddle and chisels; 32f. Head bands, head and chest ornaments and adze.

202 Dish Aerial, Papenoo, Tahiti

1988. Polysat Satellite Communications Network.

535	**202**	300f. multicoloured	10·00	14·00

203 Doll in More Skirt

1988. Polynesian Folklore. Tahitian Dolls. Mult.

536	42f. Type **203**	2·50	3·50
537	45f. Doll in city clothing	1·80	5·00
538	48f. Doll in city clothing (different)	2·00	5·50

204 Carved Figures (detail)

1988. "Sydpex 88" International Stamp Exhibition, Australia. Engraving by J. and E. Verreaux from Atlas by Baron von Krusenstern (explorer).

539	**204**	68f. brown	6·50	5·25
MS540		142×100 mm. 145f. red, green and ochre. Imperf	9·50	17·00

DESIGN: 145f. Russian officer in marae (cemetery) at Nuku Hiva.

205 Route Map

1988. 30th Death Anniv of Eric de Bisschop (leader of "Tahiti Nui" expedition).

541	**205**	350f. blue, black & brown	19·00	20·00

206 "Kermia barnardi"

1988. Sea Shells (1st series). Multicoloured.

542	24f. Type **206**	1·60	4·75
543	35f. "Vexillum suavis"	1·80	5·00
544	44f. "Berthelinia" sp.	1·90	5·25

See also Nos. 573/5.

1988. Medicinal Plants (3rd series). As T 189, showing illustrations by Gilles Cordonnier.

545	23f. red	2·50	4·25
546	36f. brown	3·00	4·75
547	49f. blue	3·50	5·25

DESIGNS: 23f. Tiatiamona; 36f. Patoa purahi; 49f. Haehaa.

207 Henry Nott and "Duff"

1988. Protestant Missionaries. Multicoloured.

548	80f. Type **207**	7·25	6·25
549	90f. Papeiha	8·25	6·50
550	100f. Samuel Raapoto	8·50	7·25

208 Papeete Post Office, 1875

1989. Taihitian Postal History.

551	**208**	30f. brown, green & blue	2·75	2·30
552	-	40f. brown, green & blue	3·25	2·30

DESIGN: 40f. Papeete Post Office, 1915.

209 Bowl with Wooden Cover, Marquesas Islands

1989. 8th Anniv of Arts and Crafts Centre. Multicoloured.

553	29f. Type **209**	2·75	4·75
554	31f. Mother-of-pearl pendant, Marquesas Islands	3·00	5·00

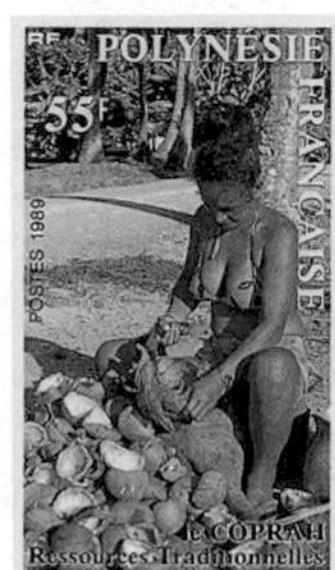

210 Woman splitting Coconuts

1989. Copra Production. Multicoloured.

555	55f. Type **210**	£110	£120
556	70f. Drying copra (horiz)	4·00	6·25

211 Wooden Statue with Tapa Covering

1989. Tapa (bark of paper-mulberry tree) Decorations. Multicoloured.

557	43f. Type **211**	2·75	3·75
558	51f. Fern leaf decoration, Society Islands (horiz)	3·25	5·25
559	56f. Concentric circles decoration, Austral Islands (horiz)	3·50	5·50

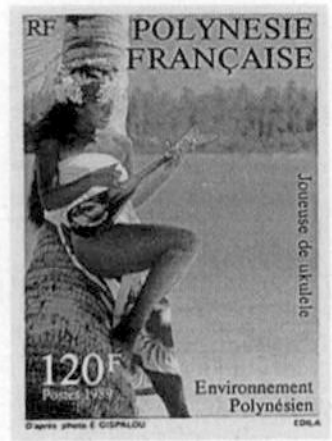

212 Woman playing Ukulele

1989. Polynesian Environment. Mult.

560	120f. Type **212**	5·00	8·75
561	140f. Diver collecting marlin-spike auger shells	7·50	9·75

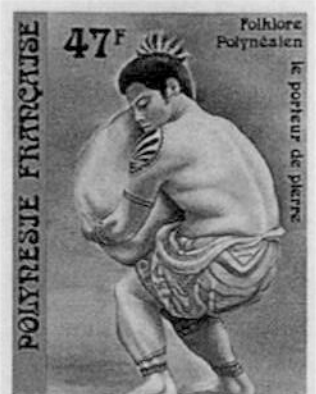

213 Lifting Stone

1989. Polynesian Folklore. July Festivals. Mult.

562	47f. Type **213**	3·75	5·00
563	61f. Dancer	4·00	5·50
564	67f. Group of singers (horiz)	4·25	6·25

214 "Mutineers casting Bligh adrift" (detail, Robert Dodd)

1989. Bicentenaries of French Revolution and Mutiny on the "Bounty".

565	**214**	100f. dp blue, blue & grn	7·00	7·25
MS566		140×100 mm. 200f. brown, green and black. Imperf	10·00	22·00

DESIGN: 200f. Complete painting by Dodd and French Colonies 1939 150th Anniv of Revolution omnibus issue.

215 Fr. O'Reilly

1989. 1st Death Anniv of Father Patrick O'Reilly (founder of Gauguin Museum).

567	**215**	52f. green and brown	2·75	5·00

216 "Get Well Soon"

1989. Greetings Stamps. Multicoloured.

568	42f. Type **216**	3·75	6·50
569	42f. Horseshoe ("Good Luck")	3·75	6·50
570	42f. Cake ("Happy Anniversary")	3·75	6·50
571	42f. Letters and telephone ("In Touch")	3·75	6·50
572	42f. Presents ("Congratulations")	3·75	6·50

1989. Sea Shells (2nd series). As T 206. Mult.

573	60f. "Triphoridae"	2·75	3·75
574	69f. "Favartia"	2·50	4·75
575	73f. Checkerboard engina and grape drupe	2·75	5·75

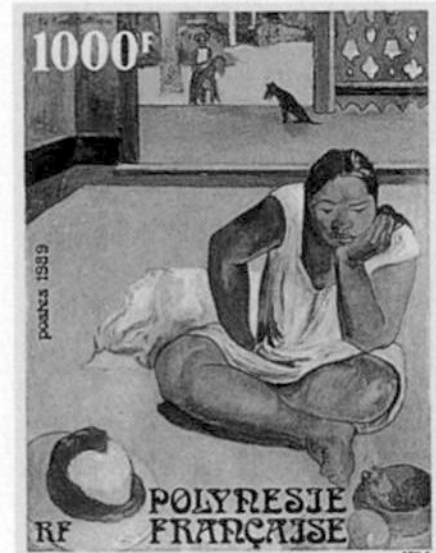

217 "Te Faaturuma" (Paul Gauguin)

1989

576	**217**	1000f. multicoloured	23·00	60·00

218 "Legend of Maui: Birth of the Islands"

1989. Polynesian Legends (1st series). Mult.

577	66f. Type **218**	2·75	4·00
578	82f. "Legend of the Pierced Mountain" (horiz)	5·25	6·00
579	88f. "Legend of Hina, the Eel from Lake Vaihiria"	3·25	6·25

See also Nos. 599/601.

219 Flower

1990. Traditional Resources. Vanilla. Mult.

580	34f. Type **219**	2·50	1·80
581	35f. Pods	2·75	3·25

220 Spotted Flagtail

1990. Fresh Water Animals. Multicoloured.

582	40f. Type **220**	3·50	3·50
583	50f. Shrimp	3·75	2·75

221 Sandwich Islands Man and Hawaiian Islands

1990. Maori World (1st series).

584	**221**	58f. black	5·75	5·25
585	-	59f. blue	50·00	50·00
586	-	63f. green	4·50	5·25
587	-	71f. blue	5·00	5·50

DESIGNS: 59f. Easter Island man and map; 63f. New Zealand man and map; 71f. Octopus and Tahiti.

See also Nos. 610/12 and 644/6.

222 Old Town Hall

1990. Centenary of Township of Papeete. Mult.

588	150f. Type **222**	7·75	6·50
589	250f. New Town Hall	12·50	10·50

223 Sooty Crake

1990. Birds. Multicoloured.

590	13f. Type **223**	2·50	4·00
591	20f. Ultramarine lory	2·75	4·00

224 Young People reading

1990. 30th Anniv of Papeete Lions Club.

592	**224**	39f. multicoloured	3·25	3·50

225 New Zealand Man and Map

1990. "New Zealand 1990" International Stamp Exhibition, Auckland.

593	**225**	125f. blue, green & purple	6·75	6·25
MS594		100×76 mm. **225** 230f. purple, olive and green. Imperf	12·00	26·00

226 De Gaulle and Globe

1990. Birth Centenary of Charles de Gaulle (French statesman).

595	**226**	200f. blue, brown & red	5·50	14·00

227 Girls in Pareos

1990. World Tourism Day.

596	**227**	8f. multicoloured	3·50	3·00
597	-	10f. multicoloured	3·50	3·00
598	-	12f. multicoloured	3·50	3·00

DESIGNS: 10, 12f. Girls in pareos (different).

1990. Polynesian Legends (2nd series). As T 218. Multicoloured.

599	170f. "Legend of Uru" (horiz)	4·75	11·50
600	290f. "Legend of Pipiri-Ma"	12·50	15·00
601	375f. "Legend of Hiro, God of Thieves"	10·50	14·00

228 Girl wearing Tiare Headdress

1990. Tiare Flower. Multicoloured.

602	28f. Type **228**	2·00	2·50
603	30f. Tiare bush	2·10	2·50
604	37f. Girl wearing flower over ear and lei	2·20	2·50

229 Pineapple Plants

1991. Traditional Resources. The Pineapple. Multicoloured. Self-adhesive. Backing paper perf.

605	42f. Type **229**	2·00	3·50
606	44f. Plantation	2·00	3·50

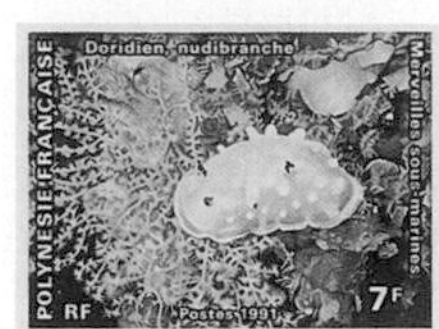

230 Doridian Nudibranch

1991. Undersea Wonders. Multicoloured.

607	7f. Type **230**	75	1·40
608	9f. "Galaxaura tenera" (red alga)	75	3·00
609	11f. Cuming's cowrie	1·50	3·00

1991. Maori World (2nd series). As T 221 showing 18th-century engravings.

610	68f. green	65·00	65·00
611	84f. black	6·00	6·25
612	94f. brown	9·50	5·75

DESIGNS—VERT: 68f. Woman, child and statues, Easter Island. HORIZ: 84f. Sandwich Islands pirogue race; 94f. Maori village, New Zealand.

231 Basketball Players

1991. Centenary of Basketball.

613	**231**	80f. multicoloured	3·25	5·75

232 Tuamotu Kingfisher

1991. Protected Birds. Multicoloured.

614	17f. Type **232**	2·50	2·50
615	21f. Kuhl's lory	2·40	2·75

233 "Oranges of Tahiti" (Gauguin)

1991. Centenary of Paul Gauguin's Arrival in Tahiti.

616	**233**	700f. multicoloured	34·00	32·00

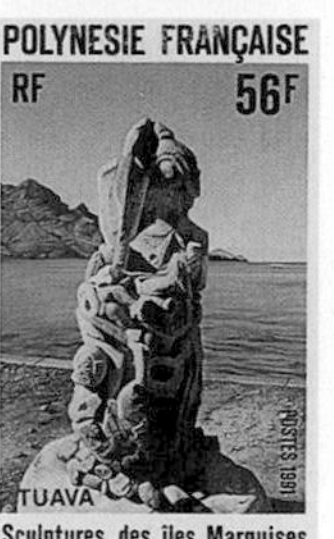

234 "Tuava"

1991. Marquesas Islands Sculptures. Mult.

617	56f. Type **234**	2·75	2·75
618	102f. "Te Hina o Motu Haka"	3·00	4·50
619	110f. "Kooka" (horiz)	3·25	4·75

235 Pianist's Hands, Conductor and Orchestra

1991. Death Bicentenary of Wolfgang Amadeus Mozart (composer).

620	**235**	100f. multicoloured	7·25	4·75

236 Fishing Canoes

1991. Stone Fishing. Multicoloured.

621	25f. Type **236**	3·25	3·25
622	57f. Fisherman swinging stone (used to beat the water)	2·10	4·75
623	62f. Fish in entrapment area (horiz)	5·00	5·25

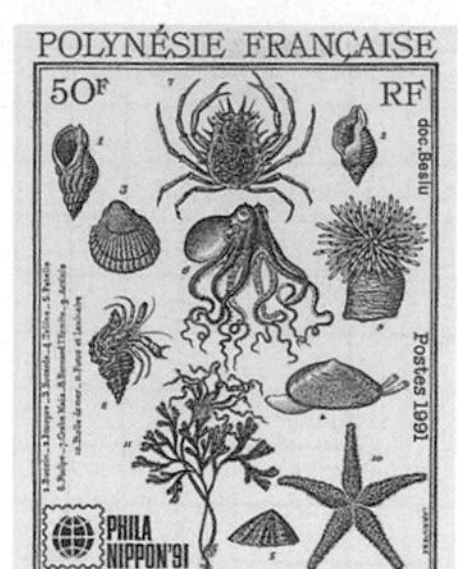

237 Sketches of Shells and Marine Life by Rene Lesson

1991. "Phila Nippon '91" International Stamp Exhibition, Tokyo.

624	**237**	50f. brown, red & violet	3·00	4·75
625	-	70f. blue, red & green	5·25	5·00
MS626		100×75 mm. 250f. scarlet, indigo and black (motifs as Nos. 624/5). Imperf	11·00	25·00

DESIGN—HORIZ: 70f. "View of Venus Point at Matavae, Tahiti".

238 Financed Projects

1991. 50th Anniv of Central Economic Co-operation Bank.

627	**238**	307f. multicoloured	12·50	10·50

239 Father Christmas

1991. "Christmas under the Sea". Mult.

628	55f. Type **239**	4·25	4·75
629	83f. Corals decorated with baubles	5·50	6·25
630	86f. Crib among corals (vert)	5·75	6·25

240 Setting Nets along Shore

1992. Tourist Activities. Multicoloured.

631	1f. Type **240**	3·75	3·00
632	2f. Horse riding along beach	3·75	3·00
633	3f. Woman holding sailfish	3·75	3·00
634	4f. Exploring waterfall (vert)	3·75	3·00
635	5f. Yachting	4·00	3·25
636	6f. Sikorsky S-61N helicopter flight to waterfall (vert)	4·00	3·25

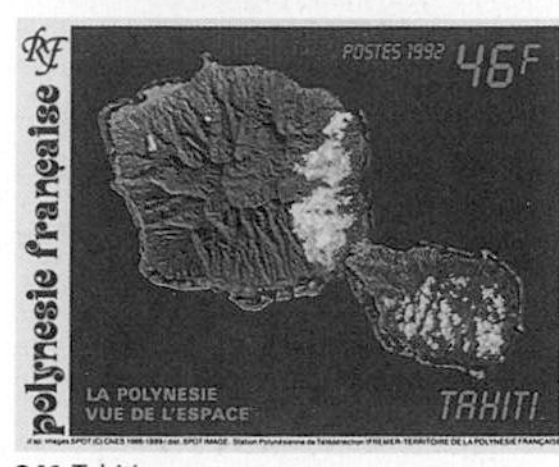

241 Tahiti

1992. "SPOT" Satellite Pictures of French Polynesia. Multicoloured.

637	46f. Type **241**	4·25	4·00
638	72f. Mataiva	6·00	5·25
639	76f. Bora-Bora	6·25	5·50
MS640	130×100 mm. 230f. Satellite highlighting Polynesian Islands. Imperf	11·00	18·00

242 "Orange Carriers" (L. Taerea)

1992. World Health Day. "Health in Rhythm with the Heart".

641	**242**	136f. multicoloured	10·00	5·75

243 Sailor asking for Directions

1992. "World Columbian Stamp Expo '92" Exhibition, Chicago.

642	**243**	130f. multicoloured	11·50	8·75
MS643		140×100 mm. 250f. Scene incorporating Type **243**. Imperf	15·00	20·00

244 Dancers, Tahiti

1992. Maori World (3rd series). Traditional Dances.

644	**244**	95f. brown	7·25	6·25
645	-	105f. brown	7·75	6·50

646	-	115f. green, brn & choc	8·25	7·00

DESIGNS: 105f. Hawaiian dancers; 115f. Night Dance by Tongan women.

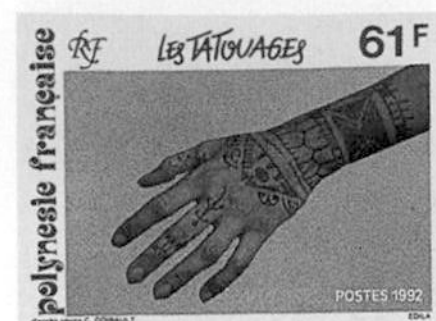

245 Tattooed Hand

1992. Tattoos. Multicoloured.

647		61f. Type **245**	4·25	5·25
648		64f. Tattooed man (vert)	4·25	5·50

246 Sailing Model Outrigger Canoes

1992. Children's Pastimes. Multicoloured.

649		22f. Type **246**	4·25	4·25
650		31f. String game	4·50	4·50
651		45f. Stilt walking (vert)	4·75	5·00

247 Melville and Books

1992. Writers of the South Seas. 150th Anniv of Arrival in Polynesia of Herman Melville (novelist).

652	**247**	78f. multicoloured	8·75	6·25

248 Raft, Gambier Islands

1992. 6th Pacific Arts Festival, Rarotonga, Cook Islands.

653	**248**	40f. red	5·25	3·50
654	-	65f. blue	6·50	4·50

DESIGN: 65f. Pirogues off Taihiti.

249 Arrival of Mail at Cercle Bougainville Post Office, Papeete

1992. Centenary of First French Oceanic Settlements Stamp.

655	**249**	200f. multicoloured	15·00	7·25

250 "Fare Tamarii" (Erhard Lux)

1992. Artists in Polynesia. Multicoloured.

656		55f. Type **250**	3·50	5·00
657		60f. "Symphonie de Monettes" (Uschi)	3·50	5·25
658		75f. "Spear Fisherman" (Pierre Kienlen)	4·25	5·50
659		85f. "Maternity" (Octave Morillot)	4·50	6·00

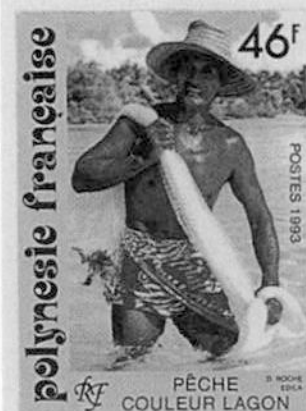

252 Cast-net Fisherman

1993. Fishing in Couleur Lagoon. Self-adhesive. Imperf.

(a) Size 26×36 mm.

670	**252**	46f. multicoloured	3·50	4·25

(b) Size 17×23 mm.

671		46f. multicoloured	3·00	3·50

253 Hanging Skipjack Tuna on Rack

1993. Bonito Fishing. Multicoloured.

672		68f. Bone hook and line	5·50	4·75
673		84f. Fishing launch (horiz)	6·25	5·00
674		86f. Type **253**	6·75	5·25

254 U.S. Flag, Pilot Lookheed P-38 Lighting and Airstrip

1993. 50th Anniv of Bora-Bora Airfield.

675	**254**	120f. multicoloured	7·00	5·50

255 "Pahi Moorea"

1993. Birth Centenary of Jacques Boullaire (artist).

676	**255**	32f. brown	3·00	4·00
677	-	36f. orange	3·75	4·00
678	-	39f. violet	2·75	3·25
679	-	51f. brown	3·00	3·50

DESIGNS: 36f. "Pahi Tuamoto"; 39f. "Pahi Rurutu"; 51f. "Pahi Nuku-hiva".

256 Sportsman

1993. Sports Festival.

680	**256**	30f. multicoloured	4·25	2·75

257 Contestant

1993. 15th Anniv of Australian Mathematics Competition.

681	**257**	70f. multicoloured	4·25	3·50

258 Pele, Goddess of Volcanoes

1993. International Symposium on Intra-plate Volcanism, Punaauia (Tahiti).

682	**258**	140f. pink, brown & blk	5·25	5·50

259 Red Junglefowl crowing

1993. "Taipei 93" International Stamp Exhibition, Taipeh.

683	**259**	46f. multicoloured	3·25	2·75

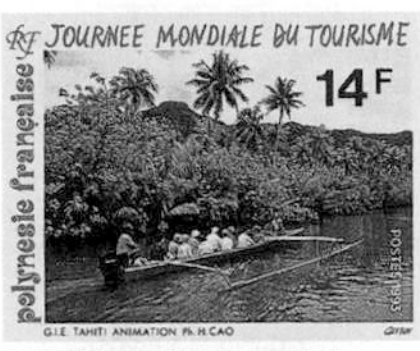

260 Sight-seeing Canoe Trip

1993. International Tourism Day. Mult.

684		14f. Type **260**	2·75	2·50
685		20f. Tahitian women decorating tourist (vert)	2·50	2·30
686		29f. Beach picnic	2·75	2·50

261 Municipal Guard of 1843 and Modern Gendarme

1993. 150th Anniv of Arrival of First Gendarme in Tahiti.

687	**261**	100f. multicoloured	5·25	3·25

262 Gerbault and "Firecrest"

1993. Birth Centenary of Alain Gerbault (round the world sailor).

688	**262**	150f. blue, red & green	7·00	5·75

263 Woman Dancing to Guitar Music (Vaea Sylvain)

1993. Artists in Polynesia. Multicoloured.

689		40f. Type **263**	2·50	3·00
690		70f. Portrait of Polynesian woman (Andre Marere) (vert)	3·50	3·25
691		80f. Four generations of women (Jean Shelsher)	3·75	3·50

692		90f. Woman in hat (Paul-Emile Victor) (vert)	5·00	3·75

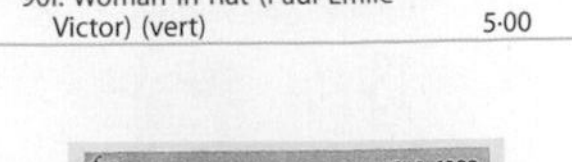

264 Relief (Vahineroo Terupe)

1993. 30th Anniv of French Pacific School.

693	**264**	200f. multicoloured	7·50	5·25

265 Spinner Dolphins

1994. Marine Mammals. Multicoloured.

694		25f. Spinner dolphin	2·75	2·30
695		68f. Type **265**	4·50	3·50
696		72f. Humpback whales (vert)	4·75	3·50

266 Spaniel

1994. "Hong Kong '94" Int Stamp Exhibition.

697	**266**	51f. multicoloured	3·75	2·30

267 Sister Germaine Bruel and Child

1994. 150th Anniv of Arrival of Sisters of St. Joseph of Cluny Congregation.

698	**267**	180f. multicoloured	6·00	6·50

268 Tahiti Temple

1994. 150th Anniv of Arrival in Polynesia of Church of Jesus Christ of Latter Day Saints.

699	**268**	154f. multicoloured	7·50	4·50

269 Father Gregoire (founder) and Polynesians

1994. Bicentenary of National Conservatory of Arts and Crafts, Paris, and 15th Anniv of Papeete Regional Associated Centre.

700	**269**	316f. multicoloured	15·00	7·00

270 Emblem and Polynesians

1994. 10th Anniv of Internal Autonomy.

701	**270**	500f. multicoloured	17·00	12·50

271 "Fare Vana'a"

1994. 20th Anniv of Tahiti Academy.

702	**271**	136f. black, red & blue	5·25	3·75

272 Papara

1994. Tahiti in Olden Days (4th series). Mult.

703	22f. Type **272**	3·00	3·00
704	26f. Mataiea coast	3·25	3·00
705	51f. Bamboo forest, Taravao (vert)	3·50	3·25

273 "Faaturuma" (Paul Gauguin)

1994

706	**273**	1000f. multicoloured	36·00	28·00

274 "Epiphyllum oxipetalum"

1994. Beauty of the Night (cactus).

707	**274**	51f. multicoloured	3·75	1·80

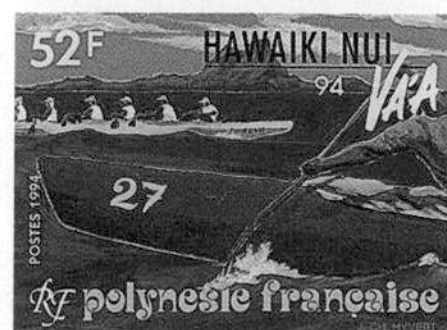

275 Bow of Pirogue No. 27

1994. "Hawaiki Nui Va'a 94" Pirogue Race. Multicoloured.

708	52f. Type **275**	3·75	2·30
709	76f. Pirogue (detail)	4·25	2·50
710	80f. Pirogue (different detail)	4·50	2·75
711	94f. Stern of pirogue and pirogue No. 60	4·75	4·00

Nos. 708/11 were issued together, se-tenant, forming a composite design.

276 Portrait by Michelle Villemin

1994. Artists in Polynesia. Paintings by artists named. Multicoloured.

712	62f. Type **276**	2·50	3·25
713	78f. Michele Dallet	4·00	3·50
714	102f. Johel Blanchard	3·25	3·75
715	110f. P. Lacouture (horiz)	5·25	3·75

277 Don Domingo de Boenechea and Frigate

1995. 220th Anniv of Spanish Expeditions to Tautira.

716	**277**	92f. multicoloured	4·50	2·75

278 "Women on the Sea Shore" (Paul Gauguin)

1995. South Pacific Tourism Year.

717	**278**	92f. multicoloured	4·25	3·75

279 Pigs

1995. Chinese New Year. Year of the Pig.

718	**279**	51f. multicoloured	3·50	2·30

280 Emblem

1995. Pacific University Teachers' Training Institute.

719	**280**	59f. multicoloured	3·75	3·00

281 Head of Green Turtle

1995. Protected Species. Multicoloured.

720	22f. Type **281**	3·00	2·75
721	29f. Green turtle	3·25	2·75
722	91f. Black coral	4·75	3·75

282 Pasteur

1995. Death Centenary of Louis Pasteur (chemist).

723	**282**	290f. blue and lt blue	12·00	6·50

283 Scene from Novel

1995. 113th Anniv of Publication of "Le Mariage de Loti" by Pierre Loti.

724	**283**	66f. multicoloured	3·75	3·25

284 Woman with Bowl of Monoi

1995. Tahiti Monoi (blend of coconut oil and tiare flower).

725	**284**	150f. multicoloured	4·50	3·50

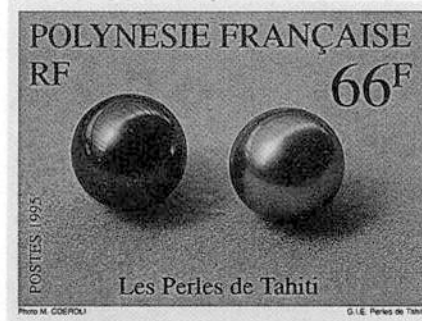

285 Rapa Island Fruit Dove

1995. "Unique Birds of the World". Mult.

726	22f. Type **285**	2·75	2·00
727	44f. Marquesas pigeon	3·50	2·30

286 Black Pearls

1995. Tahitian Pearls. Multicoloured.

728	66f. Type **286**	3·00	3·00
729	84f. Coloured pearls	3·50	3·50

287 Alvaro de Mendana de Neira and "Todos los Santos" (galleon)

1995. 400th Anniv of Discovery of Marquesas Islands. Multicoloured.

730	161f. Type **287**	5·25	4·75
731	195f. Pedro Fernandez de Quiros and map of islands	6·00	5·75

288 Games Mascot

1995. 10th South Pacific Games, Tahiti.

732	**288**	83f. multicoloured	3·25	3·50

289 Pandanus Tree

1995. "Singapore'95" International Stamp Exhibition. Multicoloured.

733	91f. Type **289**	4·25	3·75
734	91f. Pandanus (flower)	4·25	3·75
735	91f. Pandanus (fruit)	4·25	3·75
736	91f. Plaiting leaves	4·25	3·75

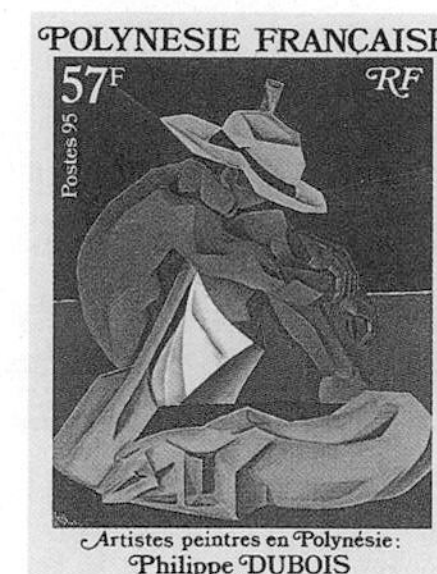

290 Man and Woman wearing Headdresses and Emblem

1995. 50th Anniv of U.N.O.

737	**290**	420f. multicoloured	13·50	7·50

291 "Paddler with Yellow Dog" (Philippe Dubois)

1996. Artists in Polynesia. Multicoloured.

738	57f. Type **291**	2·75	3·00
739	76f. "Afternoon in Vaitape" (Maui Seaman)	3·50	3·25
740	79f. "Woman with White Hat" (Simone Testeguide) (horiz)	3·75	3·25
741	100f. "Kellum House in Moorea" (Christian Deloffre) (horiz)	4·00	3·50

1996. Tahiti in Olden Days (5th series). As T 272. Multicoloured.

742	18f. La Fautaua	1·60	2·50
743	30f. Punaauia Grove	1·80	2·30
744	35f. Coconut palm forest, Tautira	1·90	2·75

292 Rats

1996. Chinese New Year. Year of the Rat.

745	**292**	51f. multicoloured	2·30	2·00

293 Queen Pomare

1996. No value expressed. (a) Size 26×36 mm.

746	**293**	(51f.) multicoloured	2·10	2·00

(b) Size 17×23 mm. Self-adhesive.

747	(51f.) multicoloured	2·30	3·00

294 Victor and Hemispheres

1996. Paul-Emile Victor (polar explorer) Commemoration.

748	**294**	500f. multicoloured	15·00	8·75

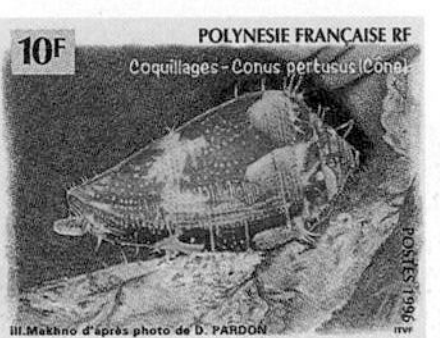
295 Pertusus Cone

1996. Sea Shells. Multicoloured.

749	10f. Type **295**	1·60	2·10
750	15f. "Cypraea alisonae" (cowrie)	1·80	2·30
751	25f. "Vexillum roseotinctum" (ribbed mitre)	2·20	2·50

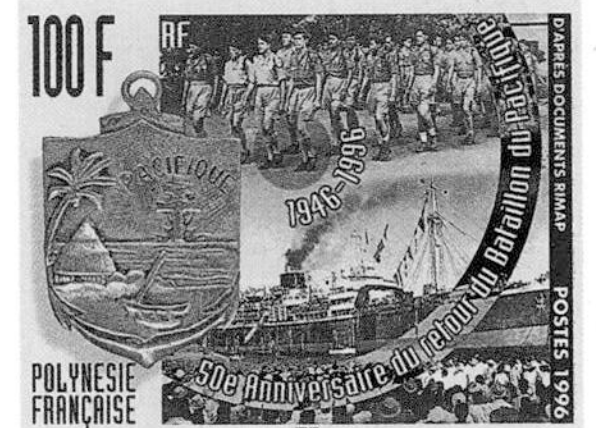
296 Badge, Soldiers and "Sagittaire" (troopship)

1996. 50th Anniv of Return of Pacific Battalion from Second World War.

752	**296**	100f. multicoloured	3·75	3·50

297 Dancers

1996. "China'96" Int Stamp Exn, Peking.

753	**297**	50f. multicoloured	2·50	1·60
MS754		100×76 mm. 200f. Staff and pupils of Chinese school, Tahiti, 1940. Inmperf	6·75	10·00

298 Red-footed Booby

1996. Marine Birds. Multicoloured.

755	66f. Type **298**	2·50	2·75
756	79f. Great frigate bird	3·00	3·00
757	84f. Common noddy	3·25	3·25

299 Pahu, Ukulele and Toere

1996. Musical Instruments. Multicoloured.

758	5f. Type **299**	1·80	90
759	9f. Toere	1·90	1·60
760	14f. Pu and vivo (wind instruments)	2·00	2·00

300 Polynesian Cicada

1996

761	**300**	66f. multicoloured	2·75	2·30

301 Ruahatu, God of the Ocean

1996. 7th Pacific Arts Festival.

762	**301**	70f. black and blue	3·00	2·50

302 Lemasson's 1913 Tahitian Girl Stamp Design

1996. Stamp Day. 40th Death Anniv of Henri Lemasson (photographer and stamp designer).

763	**302**	92f. multicoloured	4·00	3·50

303 Assembly Building

1996. 50th Anniversaries of Territorial Assembly and Autumn Stamp Salon.

764	**303**	85f. multicoloured	2·75	3·50

304 "Woman sitting on Shore" (T. Becaud)

1996. Artists in Polynesia. Multicoloured.

765	70f. Type **304**	3·25	3·00
766	85f. "Woman with leaf head-dress" (M. Noguier) (vert)	3·50	3·25
767	92f. "Woman with yellow head-dress" (C. de Dinechin) (vert)	3·75	3·50
768	96f. "Two women" (A. Lang) (vert)	4·00	3·75

305 Hand writing

1997. 80th Anniv of Society for Oceanic Studies.

769	**305**	55f. brown	1·80	2·00

306 Oxen

1997. Chinese New Year. Year of the Ox.

770	**306**	13f. multicoloured	2·50	2·75

307 Arrival of "Duff" (full-rigged missionary ship)

1997. Bicentenary of Evangelical Church of French Polynesia. Multicoloured.

771	43f. Type **307**	2·00	2·30
772	43f. Missionaries at Matavai	2·00	2·30

308 Uru Leaves

1997. Tifaifai. Multicoloured.

773	1f. Type **308**	2·00	2·30
774	5f. Tiare flower	2·00	2·30
775	70f. Hibiscus flowers	2·50	2·75

309 "Papeete-Zelee" (schooner)

1997. "Pacific '97" International Stamp Exhibition, San Francisco. Maritime Link between San Francisco and Papeete. Mult.

790	92f. Type **309**	3·75	3·75
791	92f. "Tropic Bird" (barquentine)	3·75	3·75
MS792	100×75 mm. Nos. 790/1 (sold at 400f.)	26·00	29·00

310 Tiare Flower

1997. Tourism. Multicoloured.

793	85f. Type **310**	3·75	3·75
794	85f. Canoeing	3·75	3·75
795	85f. Spearman	3·75	3·75
796	85f. Tahiti	3·75	3·75
797	85f. Barrier reef anemone-fish	3·75	3·75
798	85f. Women on shore	3·75	3·75
799	85f. Shell	3·75	3·75
800	85f. Outrigger canoe at sunset	3·75	3·75
801	85f. Snorkelling	3·75	3·75
802	85f. Pineapples and bananas	3·75	3·75
803	85f. Palm tree on beach	3·75	3·75
804	85f. Dancers	3·75	3·75

311 Male Dancer

1997. Dance Costumes. Multicoloured.

805	4f. Type **311**	2·20	2·50
806	9f. Female dancer	2·50	2·75
807	11f. Couple	2·50	2·75

312 "Kon Tiki" (after Christian Faugerat)

1997. 50th Anniv of Thor Heyerdahl's "Kon Tiki" (replica of balsa raft) Expedition from Peru to Tuamoto Island, South Pacific.

808	**312**	88f. multicoloured	3·25	3·50

313 Man carrying Fruits on Yoke (Monique Garnier-Bissol)

1997. Artists in Polynesia. Multicoloured.

809	85f. Type **313**	2·75	3·25
810	96f. Mother-of-pearl mermaid and turtles (Camelia Maraea)	3·00	3·50
811	110f. Pot (Peter Owen) (vert)	3·25	3·50
812	126f. Coconut halves in water (Elisabeth Stefanovitch)	3·50	4·00

314 "Te arii vahine" (Paul Gauguin)

1997. Autumn Salon, Paris.

813	**314**	600f. multicoloured	16·00	14·00

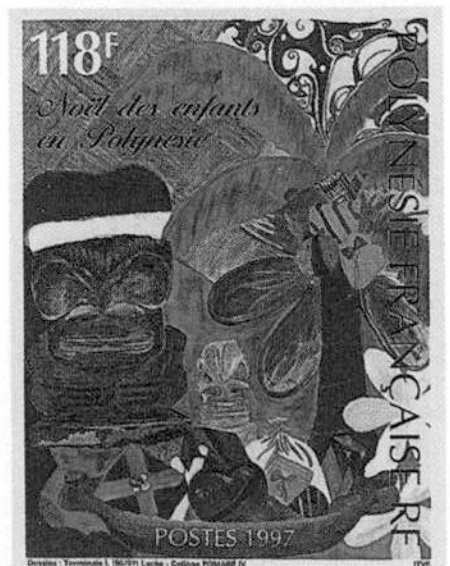
315 Santa Claus Hat on Statue, Candy-striped Palm Tree and Dish of Gifts

1997. Christmas.

814	**315**	118f. multicoloured	3·25	3·75

316 Adult and Cub

1998. Chinese New Year. Year of the Tiger.
815 **316** 96f. multicoloured 4·00 3·50

317 Grumman Widgeon

1998. Aviation. Multicoloured.
816 70f. Type **317** 3·50 3·25
817 70f. Fairchild Hiller FH-227 3·50 3·25
818 85f. de Havilland Canada DHC-6 Twin Otter 3·75 3·50
819 85f. Aerospatiale ATR 42-500 3·75 3·50
No. 816 is wrongly inscribed "Grumann".

318 "Dendrobium" "Royal King"

1998. Orchids. Multicoloured.
820 5f. Type **318** 2·20 1·70
821 20f. "Oncidium" "Ramsey" (vert) 2·50 2·30
822 50f. "Ascocenda" "Laksi" (vert) 2·75 2·75
823 100f. "Cattleya" hybrid 3·25 3·50

319 "The Lovers"

1998. 150th Birth Anniv of Paul Gauguin (artist).
824 **319** 1000f. multicoloured 22·00 20·00

320 Boy in Football Strip

1998. World Cup Football Championship, France.
825 **320** 85f. multicoloured 2·50 2·00

321 Woman wearing Shell Necklaces

1998. Necklaces and Headdresses. Mult.
826 55f. Type **321** 2·75 2·20
827 65f. Woman wearing shell necklaces and bracelet 3·00 3·00
828 70f. Woman in floral headdress 2·75 2·20
829 80f. Woman with floral head-dress and garland 3·00 3·00

322 Painting by Stanley Haumani

1998. Undersea Life.
830 **322** 200f. multicoloured 5·00 4·00

323 "Papeete Bay"

1998. Autumn Stamp Salon, Paris. Paintings by R. Gillotin. Multicoloured.
831 250f. Type **323** 6·00 5·00
832 250f. "Papeete Bay" (different) 6·00 5·00
MS833 142×105 mm. Nos. 831/2. Imperf 12·50 16·00

1998. French Victory in World Cup Football Championship. As No. 825 but additionally inscr "FRANCE championne du monde" on boy's shirt and with colours of French flag forming frame around design.
834 **320** 85f. multicoloured 3·00 2·75

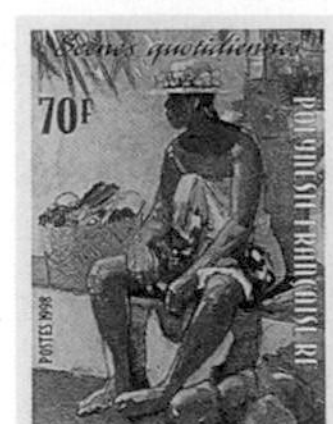

324 "Return from the Market" (A. Deymonaz)

1998. Daily Life. Paintings by Andre Deymonaz. Multicoloured.
835 70f. Type **324** 3·00 2·00
836 100f. "Sellers of Skipjack Tuna" 3·25 3·25
837 102f. "Fishermen Departing" (horiz) 3·25 3·25
838 110f. "Women in Sunday Best" (horiz) 3·50 3·50

325 Hares

1999. Chinese New Year. Year of the Hare.
839 **325** 118f. multicoloured 4·25 3·50

326 Couple

1999. St. Valentine's Day.
840 **326** 96f. multicoloured 3·00 3·25

327 Thorny Seahorse

1999. Marine Life. Multicoloured.
841 70f. Lionfish 3·00 2·30
842 85f. Type **327** 3·25 2·75
843 90f. Painted angler 3·50 2·75
844 120f. Three-spined scorpionfish 3·75 3·50

328 Tattooed Man

1999. Tattooes. Multicoloured.
845 90f. Type **328** 3·50 3·25
846 120f. Tattooed man with cloak 4·25 3·50

329 Children

1999. Mothers' Day. Multicoloured.
847 85f. Type **329** 3·25 2·00
848 120f. Two children with heart of blossoms (horiz) 3·50 2·75

330 Papaya

1999. Fruits of Fenua (Tahiti) (1st series). Multicoloured.
849 85f. Type **330** 3·25 3·25
850 85f. Guava ("La goyave") 3·25 3·25
851 85f. Red mombin 3·25 3·25
852 85f. Rambutan 3·25 3·25
853 85f. Star-apple ("La pomme-etoile") 3·25 3·25
854 85f. Gooseberry tree ("La seurette") 3·25 3·25
855 85f. Rose apple ("La pomme-rose") 3·25 3·25
856 85f. Five fingers ("La carambole") 3·25 3·25
857 85f. Spanish lime 3·25 3·25
858 85f. Sugar-apple ("La pomme-cannelle") 3·25 3·25
859 85f. Cashew ("La pomme de cajou") 3·25 3·25
860 85f. Passion fruit 3·25 3·25
See also Nos. 864/5.

331 Cancellation, 1997 9f. Stamp and Islanders

1999. 150th Anniv of First French Stamp.
861 **331** 180f. multicoloured 4·25 4·25
MS862 101×70 mm. No. 861 14·00 16·00

332 Chopin and Score

1999. 150th Death Anniv of Frederic Chopin (composer).
863 **332** 250f. multicoloured 6·50 5·00

333 Breadfruit

1999. Fruit of Fenua (2nd series). Multicoloured.
864 85f. Type **333** 3·25 2·20
865 120f. Coconut (horiz) 3·75 3·50

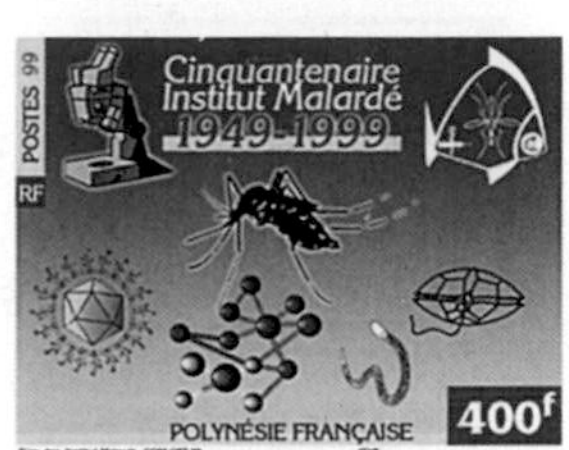

334 Microscope, Disease Carriers and Atomic Model

1999. 50th Anniv of Louis Malarde Institute (for research into public health).
866 **334** 400f. multicoloured 8·75 7·00

335 Nude by J. Sorgniard

1999. Painters and the Nude in Tahiti. Showing paintings by artists named. Multicoloured.
867 85f. Type **335** 3·50 2·75
868 120f. J. Dubrusk 3·75 3·50
869 180f. C. Deloffre 4·75 4·00
870 250f. J. Gandouin 6·50 5·00

336 Woman blowing Conch

1999. Year 2000.
871 **336** 85f. multicoloured 2·75 3·00

337 Emblem

1999. 5th Marquesas Islands' Art Festival.

872	**337**	90f. multicoloured	3·00	3·00

338 Adult holding Baby's Hand

2000. New Millennium. Multicoloured.

873	85f. Type **338**	3·00	2·20
874	120f. Part of child's face (horiz)	3·25	2·50

339 Dragons

2000. Chinese New Year. Year of the Dragon.

875	**339**	180f. multicoloured	3·00	4·00

340 Stamps and Postal Emblem

2000. Philately.

876	**340**	90f. multicoloured	2·50	3·25

341 Tattooed Hand

2000. 1st International Tattooing Festival, Raiatea. Multicoloured.

877	85f. Type **341**	2·75	2·20
878	120f. Woman with tattooed hand and ear	3·25	3·25
879	130f. Man with tattooed hands	3·25	3·25
880	160f. Man holding tattooed hand in front of eye	3·50	3·50

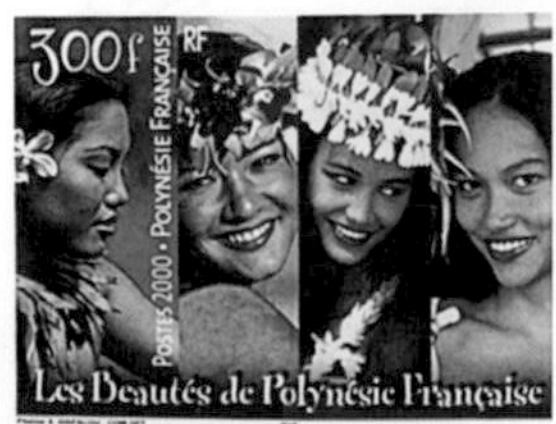

342 Polynesian Women

2000. Polynesian Women.

881	**342**	300f. multicoloured	8·25	6·00
MS882		106×80 mm. No. 881 (sold at 500f.)	14·00	10·00

343 White Dress

2000. Traditional Costumes. Showing women wearing different traditional dresses. Multicoloured.

883	85f. Type **343**	2·75	2·20
884	120f. Green and white floral dress with hat	3·25	3·25
885	160f. White lace tunic and long cap skirt	3·50	3·50
886	250f. Embroidered red dress	6·00	5·25

344 Mt. Aorai and Mt. Orohena

2000. Mountains over 2000 Metres on Tahiti. Mult.

887	90f. Type **344**	3·25	2·20
888	180f. Mt. Aorai and Mt. Orohena (different)	4·75	3·25

345 Fruit Carriers' Race

2000. Traditional Sports. Multicoloured.

889	120f. Type **345**	3·75	3·25
890	250f. Stone lifting (vert)	7·00	5·50

346 Woven Fans

2000. Traditional Crafts. Multicoloured.

891	85f. Type **346**	3·25	2·10
892	85f. Woven hat	3·25	2·10

347 Stylized Couple

2000. National Tahitian Language Year.

893	**347**	120f. yellow, red & blk	3·75	3·25

348 Flower and Satellite

2000. New Millennium.

894	**348**	85f. multicoloured	3·25	2·00

349 Main Gateway

2001. Centenary of Ecole Centrale. Multicoloured.

895	85f. Type **349**	3·25	2·00
896	85f. Present day main building	3·25	2·00

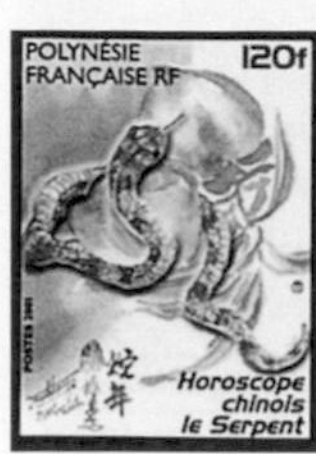

350 Snake and Flower

2001. Chinese New Year. Year of the Snake.

897	**350**	120f. multicoloured	3·75	3·25

351 Vaiharuru Waterfall, Papenoo, Tahiti

2001. Polynesian Nature. Multicoloured.

898	35f. Type **351**	1·40	1·20
899	50f. Lake Vaihiria, Tahiti (horiz)	1·90	1·60
900	90f. Hakaui Valley, Nuku Hiva, Marquesas Islands	2·50	2·10

352 Children

2001. Year of the Polynesian Child.

901	**352**	55f. multicoloured	1·70	1·70

353 Eddie Lund (pianist and songwriter)

2001. Entertainers. Multicoloured.

902	85f. Type **353**	1·90	1·90
903	120f. Charley Mauu (musician)	2·50	2·20
904	130f. Bimbo Moetrauri (musician)	2·75	2·40
905	180f. Marie Mariteragi (singer and dancer) and Emma Terangi (singer) (horiz)	3·25	3·00

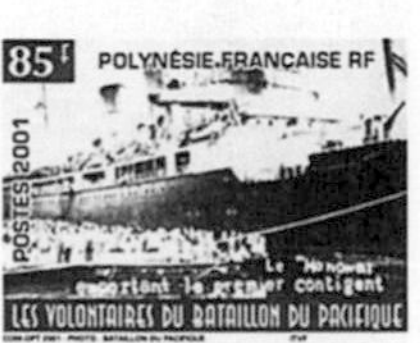

354 *Monovai* (liner)

2001. 60th Anniv of Departure of Pacific Battalion Volunteers.

906	**354**	85f. multicoloured	2·40	1·80

355 Wave

2001. Teahupoo Wave.

907	**355**	120f. multicoloured	6·50	4·00

356 Emblem

2001. 17th Anniv of Internal Autonomy.

908	**356**	250f. multicoloured	4·75	3·25
MS909		142×105 mm. No. 908	14·00	14·00

357 Men racing

2001. "Heiva 2001" Traditional Arts and Sports Festival. Canoe Racing. Multicoloured.

910	85f. Type **357**	1·90	1·80
911	120f. Women racing	3·00	2·50
MS912	140×105 mm. Nos. 910/11. Imperf (sold at 250f.)	8·00	8·00

358 Tou

2001. Native Hardwood Trees. Multicoloured.

913	90f. Type **358**	1·60	1·50
914	130f. Ati	2·75	2·20
915	180f. Miro	3·75	2·75

359 Couple and Emblem

2001. A.I.D.S. Awareness Campaign.

916	**359**	55f. multicoloured	1·60	1·40

360 "Building Europe"

2001. U.N. Year of Dialogue among Civilizations.

917	**360**	500f. multicoloured	9·00	6·50

361 Tiare (*Gardenia tahitensis*)

2001. Native Flowers. Multicoloured.

918	35f. Type **361**	1·50	1·40
919	50f. Pua (*Fagraea berteriana*)	1·80	1·60
920	85f. Taina (*Gardenia jasminoides*)	2·10	1·80

362 Polynesian Crib

2001

921	**362**	120f. multicoloured	2·50	2·20

363 Parcel and Flowers ("Joyeuses fetes")

2002. Greetings Stamps. Multicoloured.

922		55c. Type **363**	1·80	1·50
923		55c. Pink hibiscus ("Felicitations")	1·80	1·50
924		85c. As No. 922 but with blue background	2·20	1·80
925		85c. Red hibiscus ("Felicitations")	2·20	1·80

364 Horses

2002. Chinese New Year. Year of the Horse.

926	**364**	130f. multicoloured	3·25	2·30

365 Canoeist and Emblem

2002. 10th World Outrigger Canoe Championship. Multicoloured.

927		120f. Type **365**	2·75	2·20
928		120f. Masked canoeist and emblem	3·50	2·75

366 Urchin (*Echinometra sp.*)

2002. Sea Urchins. Multicoloured.

929		35f. Type **366**	1·60	1·40
930		50f. *Heterocentrotus trigonarius*	1·80	1·70
931		90f. Banded urchin (*Echinothrix calamaris*)	2·30	1·90
932		120f. *Toxopneustes sp.*	2·75	2·20

367 Couple holding Droplet of Blood

2002. Blood Donation.

933	**367**	130f. multicoloured	2·50	2·20

368 Children holding Football

2002. World Cup Football Championship, Japan and South Korea.

934	**368**	85f. multicoloured	2·30	1·70

369 Coconut Pulp Peeling

2002. "Heiva 2002" Traditional Arts and Sports Festival. Multicoloured.

935		85f. Type **369**	2·40	1·70
936		120f. Fruit carrying races	2·75	3·00
937		250f. Javelin throwing	5·75	4·25

370 James Norman Hall and House

2002. Inauguration of James Norman Hall House (museum).

938	**370**	90f. multicoloured	2·75	2·00

The museum commemorates the writer James Norman Hall.

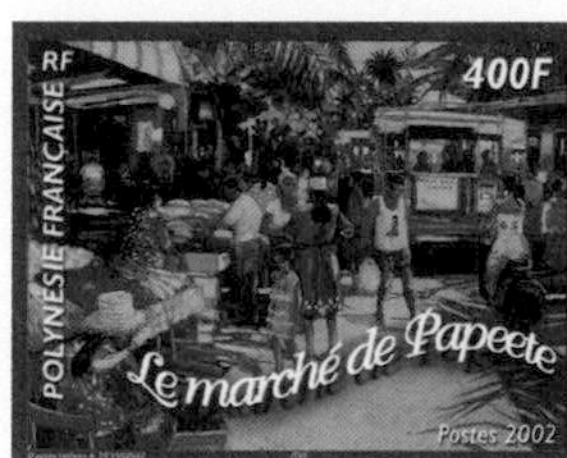

371 Market Place, Papeete (A. Deymonaz)

2002

939	**371**	400f. multicoloured	7·25	6·50
MS940		142×105 mm. No. 939	14·00	14·00

No. **MS**940 is inscribed for "Amphilex 2002" International Stamp Exhibition, Amsterdam in the margin.

372 Lagoon, Fish, Crustaceans and Bottles

2002. French Research Institute for Marine Exploitation. Multicoloured.

941		55f. Type **372**	1·80	1·40
942		90f. Aerial view of centre	2·30	1·90

373 Surfer

2002. "Taapuna Master 2002" Surfing Competition, Tahiti.

943	**373**	120f. multicoloured	3·00	2·50

374 *Hibiscus tiliaceus*

2002. Seaside Flowers. Multicoloured.

944		85f. Type **374**	2·75	2·30
945		130f. *Scaveola sericea*	3·50	3·00
946		180f. *Guettarda speciosa*	4·50	3·75

375 Bus and Dancers

2002. Festivals. Multicoloured.

947		55f. Type **375**	1·90	1·70
948		120f. Musicians (vert)	3·25	2·75

376 Goats

2003. New Year. Year of the Goat.

949	**376**	120f. multicoloured	3·25	2·75

377 Two Women

2003. Polynesian Women.

950	**377**	55f. multicoloured	1·90	1·70

378 Waterfall, Trees and Lake

2003. Polynesian Waterfalls.

951	**378**	330f. multicoloured	8·50	7·25

379 Building with Balcony

2003. Papeete in Old Photographs. Multicoloured.

952		55f. Type **379**	1·90	1·70
953		85f. Sailing ship (horiz)	2·75	2·30
954		90f. Men with bicycles (52×32 mm)	2·75	2·30
955		120f. Tree-lined street (52×32 mm)	3·50	3·00
MS956		148×106 mm. Nos. 952/5	14·00	14·00

380 Fish

2003. Polynesian Marine Life.

957	**380**	460f. multicoloured	12·00	11·00

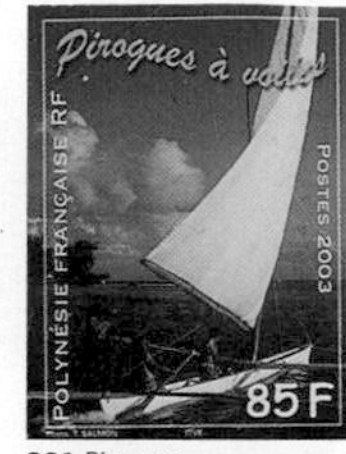

381 Pirogue

2003. Pirogues (sailing canoes). Multicoloured.

958		85f. Type **381**	2·75	2·30
959		85f. Boy seated on sail beam	2·75	2·30
960		85f. Twin-sailed craft with hills behind (horiz)	2·75	2·30
961		85f. Craft with three crew members (horiz)	2·75	2·30

382 Fire Walkers

2003

962	**382**	130f. multicoloured	3·50	3·00

383 Bi-valve

2003. Shellfish.

963	**383**	420f. multicoloured	11·00	10·00

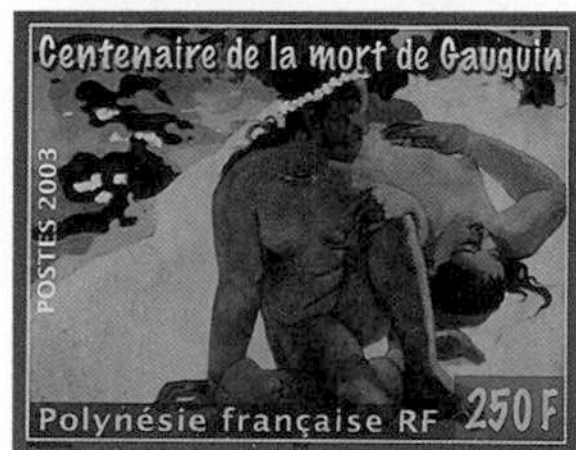

384 "Ahaoe Feii ou Quoi?" (Are you jealous?)

2003. Death Centenary of Paul Gauguin (artist).

964	**384**	250f. multicoloured	6·50	6·00

385 Flag

2003

965	**385**	(60f.) multicoloured	2·00	1·70

386 Orchid

2003. Flowers. Multicoloured.

966		90f. Type **386**	2·75	2·20
967		130f. Rose	4·00	3·25

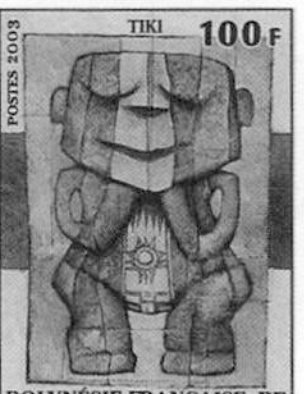

387 Figure

2003. Tiki (1st issue).
968 **387** 100f. multicoloured 3·25 2·75
See also No. 971.

388 Island and Trees

2003. Bora Bora. Multicoloured.
969 60f. Type **388** 2·00 1·70
970 60f. Aerial view of island 2·00 1·70

389 Face

2003. Tiki (2nd issue).
971 **389** 190f. multicoloured 6·00 5·00

390 Landscape

2003
972 **390** 90f. multicoloured 3·00 2·50

391 Monkeys

2004. Year of the Monkey.
973 **391** 130f. multicoloured 4·00 3·25

392 Women ironing Cloth

2004. Scenes from Daily Life. Multicoloured.
974 60f. Type **392** 2·00 1·70
975 90f. Street scene (vert) 3·00 2·50

393 Woman seated in Cane Chair

2004. Polynesian Women.
976 **393** 55f. multicoloured 3·00 2·50

394 Ceremonial Dance

2004
977 **394** 500f. multicoloured 14·50 12·50

395 Airplanes, Boules and Palm Trees

2004. Economic Development.
978 **395** 500f. multicoloured 14·50 12·50

396 Vanilla

2004
979 **396** 90f. multicoloured 3·00 2·50

397 Mobile Cafe

2004
980 **397** 300f. multicoloured 9·00 7·50

398 Plaiting (Society Islands)

2004. Handicrafts. Multicoloured.
981 60f. Type **398** 2·00 1·70
982 60f. Carved shell (Tuamoto Islands) 2·00 1·70
983 90f. Plaited hat (Australs Islands) 3·00 2·50
984 90f. Wood carving(Marquesas Islands) 3·00 2·50

399 Emblem

2004. 20th Anniv of Autonomy.
985 **399** 60f. multicoloured 2·00 1·70

400 Globe and Island Sunset

2004. Expansion of South Pacific Post and Telecommunication Service. Multicoloured.
986 100f. Type **400** 3·50 3·00
987 130f. Satellite dish and resort 4·00 3·25

401 Satellite and Receiver

2004. Information Technology. Multicoloured.
988 190f. Type **401** 6·00 5·00
989 190f. "@" and keyboard 6·00 5·00

402 Omai (first Polynesian to visit London)

2004
990 **402** 250f. multicoloured 8·00 6·50

403 Women with Buckets

2004. Tourism.
991 **403** 60f. multicoloured 2·00 1·70

404 Figure wearing Crown

2004. Christmas. Children's Drawings.
992 **404** 60f. multicoloured 2·00 1·70

405 Bamboo

2005
993 **405** 130f. multicoloured 4·25 3·50

406 Shopping

2005. Scenes from Daily Life.
994 **406** 90f. multicoloured 3·00 2·50

407 Woman

2005. Polynesian Women. Multicoloured.
995 60f. Type **407** 2·00 1·70
996 90f. Seated woman 3·00 2·50

408 Flowers

2005. Le Tifaifai (patchwork).
997 **408** 5f. multicoloured 1·00 85

409 Weaving

2005. Tapa (bark cloth).
998 **409** 250f. multicoloured 8·00 6·50

410 *Centropyge bispinosa*

2005. Angelfish. Multicoloured.
999 90f. Type **410** 3·00 2·50
1000 90f. *Centropyge loricula* 3·00 2·50
1001 130f. *Centropyge heraldi* 4·25 3·50
1002 130f. *Centropyge flavissima* 4·25 3·50
MS1003 106×145 mm. Nos. 999/1002 14·00 14·00

411 TAI DC8 (first jet airplane in Tahiti) (1961)

2005. Aviation. Multicoloured.
1004 60f. Type **411** 2·00 1·70
1005 60f. Pan Am Boeing 707 (first foreign flight) (1963) 2·00 1·70
1006 100f. Air Tahiti Nui Airbus A 340-300 (first Tahitian airline) (2000) 3·50 3·00
1007 100f. Air France Boeing 707 (first flight by Air France) (1973) 3·50 3·00

412 Wooden Pipes

2005. Musical Instruments. Multicoloured.
1008 130f. Type **412** 4·25 3·50
1009 130f. Drum (vert) 4·25 3·50

413 Mountains and Lagoon

2005. Tourism.

1010	**413**	300f. multicoloured	8·75	7·25

414 Pineapple

2005. Pineapple. Multicoloured.

1011	90f. Type **414**	3·00	2·50
1012	130f. Fruit and leaves	4·00	3·25

Nos. 1011/12 were impregnated with the scent of pineapple which was released when rubbed.

415 Marae, Windward Island

2005. Cultural Heritage. Multicoloured.

1013	500f. Type **415**	14·00	11·50
1014	500f. Marquesan Tohua	14·00	11·50

416 Landscape

2005

1015	**416**	100f. multicoloured	3·25	2·75

417 Reindeer and Sleeping Santa

2005. Christmas.

1016	**417**	90f. multicoloured	3·00	2·50

418 Lotus Flower

2006

1017	**418**	130f. multicoloured	4·25	3·50

419 Heart

2006. St. Valentine's Day.

1018	**419**	60f. multicoloured	2·00	1·70
1019	-	90f. magenta and cinnamon	3·00	2·50

DESIGNS: 60f. Type **418**; 90f. Pink heart.

420 Woman

2006. Polynesian Women. Multicoloured.

1020	60f. Type **420**	2·00	1·70
1021	90f. Woman with head in hand	3·00	2·50

421 Maupiti

2006

1022	**421**	500f. multicoloured	14·00	11·50

422 Early Inhabitants

2006. Marquesas (Washington Isles). Multicoloured.

1023	60f. Type **422**	2·00	1·70
1024	130f. Sail ship	4·25	3·50
MS1025	91×130 mm. Nos. 1023/4	6·50	6·50

423 Women and Musicians

2006. Scenes from Daily Life.

1026	**423**	300f. multicoloured	9·00	7·50

424 *Prosobonia cancellata*

2006. Polynesian Birds. Multicoloured.

1027	250f. Type **424**	7·50	6·25
1028	250f. *Gallicolumba erythroptera*	7·50	6·25

425 Canoeists

2006. Heiva (festival). Multicoloured.

1029	90f. Type **425**	3·00	2·50
1030	130f. Tattooed man	4·25	3·50
1031	190f. Woman in costume	6·00	5·00

426 Frangipani Flowers

2006

1032	**426**	90f. multicoloured	3·00	2·50

No. 1032 was impregnated with scent which was released when the stamp was rubbed.

427 Stone Carvings

2006. World Tourism Day. Multicoloured.

1033	40f. Type **427**	1·70	1·40
1034	90f. Woman, child and waterfall	3·00	2·50
1035	130f. Traditional clothes	4·25	3·50

428 "Javelin Throwing" (Monique Garnier Bissol (Mono))

2006. Paintings. Multicoloured.

1036	60f. Type **428**	2·00	1·70
1037	90f. "Market Life" (Albert Luzuy) (horiz)	3·00	2·50
1038	100f. "Island Quay" (Gilbert Chaussoy) (horiz)	3·50	3·00
1039	190f. "Vahine" (Olivier Louze)	6·00	5·00

429 Women

2006. Paul Gauguin Engravings. Multicoloured.

1040	60f. Type **429**	2·00	1·70
1041	130f. Cow and man with yoke	4·25	3·50

430 Woman

2006. Children's Drawings.

1042	**430**	90f. multicoloured	3·00	2·50

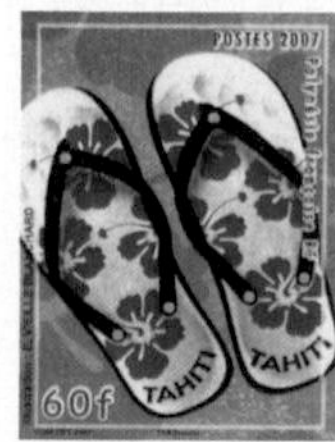

431 Flip-flops

2007. Tourism. Multicoloured. Self-adhesive.

1043	60f. Type **431**	2·00	1·70
1044	90f. Surf board	3·00	2·50

432 Pig and Piglets

2007. New Year. Year of the Pig.

1045	**432**	130f. multicoloured	4·25	3·50

433 Woman (Mathius)

2007. Polynesian Women. Multicoloured.

1046	60f. Type **433**	2·00	1·70
1047	90f. Woman (art photograph by John Stember) (horiz)	3·00	2·50

434 Building Facade

2007. Bicentenary of Court of Auditors.

1048	**434**	90f. blue and vermilion	3·00	2·50

435 *Lambis crocata pilsbryi*

2007. Shells. Multicoloured.

1049	10f. Type **435**	1·00	85
1050	60f. *Cypraea Thomasi*	2·00	1·70
1051	90f. *Cyrtulus serotinus*	3·00	2·50
1052	130f. *Chicoreus laqueatus*	4·25	3·50
MS1053	90×130 mm 10f. As Type **435**; 60f. As No. 1050; 90f. As No. 1051; 130f. As No. 1052	12·00	12·00

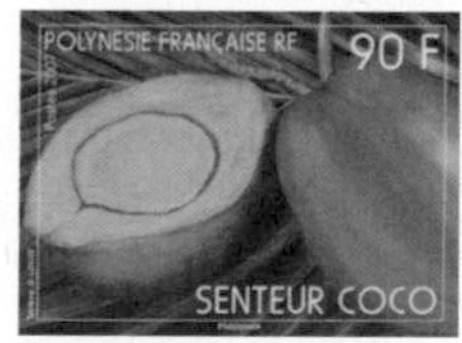

436 Coconut

2007. The Scent of Coconut.

1054	**436**	90f. multicoloured	3·00	2·50

437 *La Zelee*

2007. Famous Ships. Multicoloured.

1055	250f. Type **437**	7·50	6·25
1056	250f. *Le Sagittaire*	7·50	6·25

438 Dancer

2007. Heiva (festival). Multicoloured.

1057	65f. Type **438**	2·40	2·00
1058	100f. Dancer with fan	3·75	3·25
1059	140f. Masked dancer	4·75	4·25

439 Mask and 'EXPEDITION KON-TIKI'

2007. 60th Anniv of Kon-Tiki Expedition by Thor Heyerdahl.

1060	**439**	300f. olive and black	9·75	8·25

440 Ship entering Harbour

2007. Scenes from Daily Life.

1061	**440**	190f. multicoloured	6·50	5·50

441 Rue Gauguin, 2007

2007. Papeete Past and Present. Multicoloured.

1062	65f. Type **441**	2·40	2·00
1063	100f. Rue de la Pologne, 1907	3·75	3·25

442 2 franc Note, c. 1919

2007. Early Currency.

1064	**442**	65f. chocolate and bistre	2·40	2·00
1065	-	140f. blue and bistre	4·75	4·25
1066	-	500f. orange, chocolate and bistre	15·00	13·50

DESIGNS: 65f. Type **442**; 140f. 2 franc note, c. 1942; 500f. 50 cent note, c. 1943.

443 Hibiscus

2007. Flowers. Multicoloured.

1067	100f. Type **443**	3·75	3·25
1068	140f. Bird of Paradise	4·75	4·25

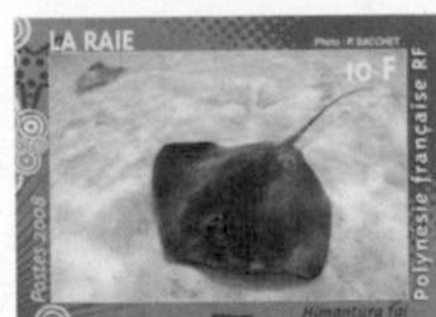

444 Santa on the Beach

2007. Christmas. Children's Drawings.

1069	**444**	100f. multicoloured	3·75	3·25

446 Rat

2008. New Year. Year of the Rat.

1074	**446**	140f. multicoloured	5·75	5·00

447 Woman

2008. Polynesian Women. Multicoloured.

1075	65f. Type **447**	2·75	2·40
1076	100f. Two women	4·50	3·75

448 Man (Raymond Vigor)

2008. Polynesian Artists. Multicoloured.

1077	100f. Type **448**	4·50	3·75
1078	100f. Still life (Teurarea Prokop) (horiz)	4·50	3·75
1079	100f. Cliffs, yacht and lagoon (Torea Chan)	4·50	3·75

449 Pouvanaa

2008. Pouvanaa a Oopa (nationalist politician) Commemoration.

1080	**449**	500f. multicoloured	20·00	18·00

450 Family on Scooter

2008. Tour d'Ile. Multicoloured. Self-adhesive.

1081	65f. Type **450**	2·75	2·40
1082	100f. Bus (horiz)	4·50	3·75

451 Woman

2008. Heiva 2008 Traditional Arts and Sports Festival. Multicoloured.

1083	65f. Type **451**	3·00	2·40
1084	140f. Male dancer	6·00	5·00
1085	190f. Woman dancer	8·00	6·50

452 Weightlifter

2008. Sports. Multicoloured.

1086	140f. Type **452**	6·00	5·00
1087	140f. Table tennis	6·00	5·00

453 Eric de Bisschop

2008. 50th Death Anniv of Eric de Bisschop (navigator and transoceanic traveller) and End of Tahiti Nui II Expedition (unsuccessful voyage from South America to Polynesia).

1088	**453**	190f. multicoloured	8·50	7·00

454 Tiare Tahiti (*Gardenia taitensis*)

2008. National Flower.

1089	**454**	100f. multicoloured	4·75	4·00

No. 1089 wasimpregnated with scent which was released when rubbed.

455 Anniversary Emblem

2008. 10th Anniv of Air Tahiti (1104) or 50th Anniv of Paris—Tahiti Flights by TAI (French airline) (1105). Multicoloured.

1104	250f. Type **455**	11·00	9·25
1105	250f. Douglas DC6B and Tahitians	11·00	9·25

Nos. 1090/102 have been left for booklet stamps, issued on 17 September, not yet received.

456 1958 2f. Stamp (As Type **1**)

2008. 50th Anniv of First Stamp.

1106	65f. green, sepia and violet	3·00	2·50
1107	100f. sepia and green	4·75	4·00
1108	140f. multicoloured	6·25	5·25
MS1108a	150×110 mm. As Nos. 1106/8	14·00	14·00

DESIGNS: Type **456**; 100f. 1958 13f. Air stamp (As No. 13); 140f. 1958 3f. Postage Due stamp (As No. D18).

457 Youth and Sport (Manuhiti Marama)

2008. Children's Drawing.

1109	**457**	100f. multicoloured	4·75	4·00

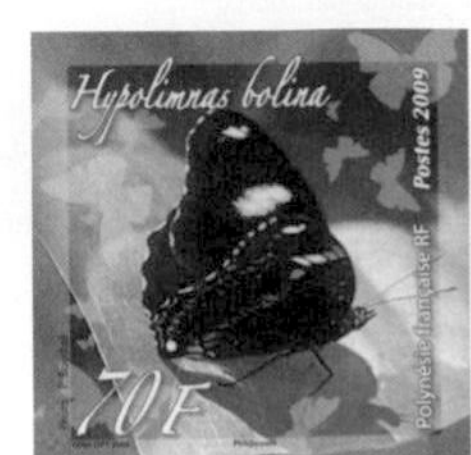

458 *Hypolimnas bolina*

2009

1110	**458**	70f. multicoloured	3·25	2·75

459 Firefighter

2009. Firefighters. Multicoloured.

1111	70f. Type **459**	3·25	2·75
1112	140f. Fire tender	6·25	5·25

460 Woman

2009. Polynesian Women. Multicoloured.

1113	70f. Type **460**	3·00	2·75
1114	100f. Woman with guitar	6·25	5·75

461 Jacques Brel

2009. 80th Birth Anniv of Jacques Romain Georges Brel (singer, songwriter, actor and director).

1115	**461**	70f. ultramarine	3·00	2·75
1116	**461**	100f. deep rose-red	4·50	3·75

462 Pareo

2009. Pareo (or pareu) (light cotton fabric featuring bright colours and usually flower motifs). Self-adhesive.

1117	**462**	(70f.) blue	3·50	3·00
1118	**462**	(100f.) scarlet-vermilion	5·00	4·25
1119	**462**	(140f.) emerald	13·00	11·50

No. 1117 was for use on mail within Polynesia, No. 1118 was for use on mail to France and No. 1119 was for mail to the rest of the world.

463 Dancers

2009. Heiva (festivals) of the Past. Multicoloured designs, inscription colour given.

1120	70f. Type **463** (green)	3·50	3·00
1121	100f. Dancers in line (yellow) (horiz)	5·00	5·25
1122	140f. Dancers (blue) (horiz)	6·50	5·50

464 Surfer on the Moon

2009. 40th Anniv of Moon Landing.

1123	**464**	140f. multicoloured	6·50	5·50

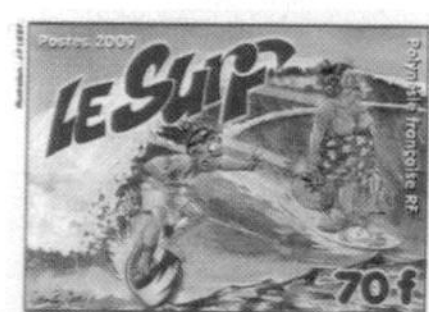

465 Surfer

2009. Surfing versus Canoeing. Multicoloured. Self-adhesive.

1124	70f. Type **465**	3·25	2·75
1125	100f. Pirogue canoe	6·50	5·50

466 Passion Fruit

2009. Scents.

1126	**466**	100f. multicoloured	6·50	5·50

No. 1126 is impregnated with the scent of passion fruit which is released when the stamp is rubbed.

467 *Chaetodon lunula*

2009. Fish. Multicoloured. Self-adhesive.

1127	70f. Type **467**	3·25	2·75
1128	70f. *Chaetodon trichrous*	3·25	2·75
1129	70f. *Chaetodon ornatissimus*	3·25	2·75
1130	70f. *Chaetodon pelewensis*	3·25	2·75
1131	100f. *Pterois antennata*	4·50	3·75
1132	100f. *Myripristis berndti*	4·50	3·75
1133	100f. *Priacanthus hamrur*	4·50	3·75
1134	100f. *Epinephelus polyphekadion*	4·50	3·75
1135	140f. *Thalassoma lutescens*	4·50	3·75
1136	140f. *Thalassoma hardwicke*	4·50	3·75
1137	140f. *Pygoplites diacanthus*	4·50	3·75
1138	140f. *Coris gaimard*	4·50	3·75

468 Diver

2009. Marine Life. Multicoloured.

1139	70f. Type **468**	3·25	2·75
1140	100f. *Chelonia mydas* (green turtle) (horiz)	4·50	3·75
1141	140f. *Megaptera novaeangliae* (humpback whale) (horiz)	4·50	3·75
MS1142	105×150 mm. 70f. Type **468**; 100f. *Chelonia mydas* (green turtle) (horiz); 140f. *Megaptera novaeangliae* (humpback whale) (horiz)	13·50	12·00

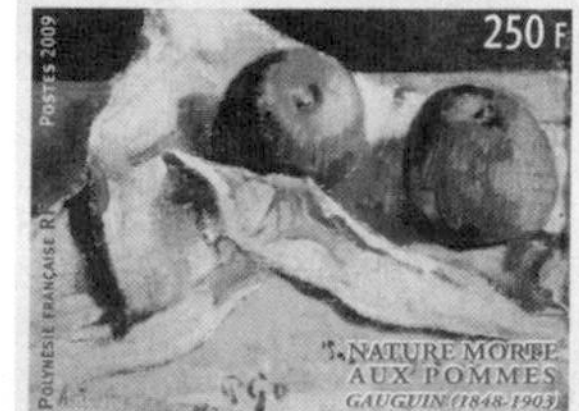

469 *Still Life with Apples*

2009. Art. Paintings by Paul Gauguin. Multicoloured.

1143	250f. Type **469**	11·50	9·50
1144	250f. *Still Life with Statuette* (vert)	11·50	9·50

470 1955 9f. Stamp

2009. Young Girl of Bora Bora.

1145	**470**	500f. ultramarine, agate and vermilion	22·00	19·00

OFFICIAL STAMPS

O100 Uru

1977. Native Fruits.

O240	**O100**	1f. multicoloured	3·75	4·25
O241	**O100**	2f. multicoloured	2·75	3·25
O242	**O100**	3f. multicoloured	4·50	5·25
O243	**O100**	5f. multicoloured	2·50	3·25
O244	-	7f. multicoloured	5·00	5·50
O245	-	8f. multicoloured	2·75	5·25
O246	-	10f. multicoloured	2·75	4·50
O247	-	15f. multicoloured	6·25	4·75
O248	-	19f. multicoloured	6·00	4·75
O249	-	20f. multicoloured	5·00	5·00
O250	-	25f. multicoloured	8·50	6·00
O251	-	35f. multicoloured	9·50	5·75
O252	-	50f. multicoloured	8·25	11·50
O253	-	100f. multicoloured	10·50	11·50
O254	-	200f. multicoloured	34·00	26·00

DESIGNS: 7f., 8f., 10f., 15f. Vi Tahiti; 19f., 20f., 25f., 35f. Avocat; 50f., 100f., 200f. Vi Popaa.

O251 1840 French Colonies 40c. Stamps

1993

O660	**O251**	1f. red, brown & blk	2·75	2·50
O777	-	2f. multicoloured	2·75	2·75
O662	-	3f. black, red & yell	2·75	2·50
O779	-	5f. black, red & yell	2·75	2·75
O780	-	9f. multicoloured	2·75	2·75
O781	-	10f. multicoloured	2·75	3·25
O782	-	20f. multicoloured	3·25	3·25
O666	-	46f. multicoloured	4·00	3·50
O666a	-	51f. multicoloured	4·00	4·00
O785	-	70f. multicoloured	3·50	3·75
O786	-	85f. multicoloured	3·50	4·00
O787	-	100f. multicoloured	4·00	4·00
O788	-	200f. multicoloured	5·25	5·25

DESIGNS—HORIZ: 2f. French Colonies 1877 Peace and Commerce 40c. and 1872 Ceres 25c. stamps; 3f. French Colonies Peace and Commerce stamp with Papeete 1884 postmark; 5f. 1884 Papeete postmark; 9f. Pair of Oceanic Settlements 1948 15f. stamps with Papeete postmark; 10f. Oceanic Settlements 1892 5c. stamp and 1894 postmark; 20f. Oceanic Settlements 1892 10 and 15c. stamps with Tahiti postmark; 46f. Oceanic Settlements 1930 90c. Kanakas stamps; 51f. Oceanic Settlements 1942 5 and 10f. Free French stamps with Vaitepaua postmark; 70f. "Visit Tahiti" postmark; 100f. Oceanic Settlements 1956 3f. Dry dock stamp; 200f. Oceanic Settlements 1953 14f. Gauguin stamps. VERT: 85f. Oceanic Settlements 1921 25 on 15c. stamp.

POSTAEG DUE STAMPS

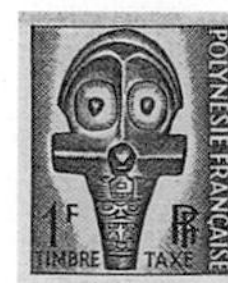

D4 Polynesian Mask

1958

D17	**D4**	1f. green and brown	1·20	11·00
D18	**D4**	3f. red and indigo	1·30	11·00
D19	**D4**	5f. blue and brown	1·40	12·50

D164 Mother of Pearl Fish-hook

1984. Multicoloured.. Multicoloured..

D416	1f. Type D **164**	1·10	5·25
D417	3f. Tahitian bowl (horiz)	1·50	5·25
D418	5f. Marquesian fan (horiz)	95	5·25
D419	10f. Lamp stand	1·60	5·25
D420	20f. Wooden head-rest (horiz)	2·00	5·50
D421	50f. Scoop (horiz)	2·75	5·75

Pt. 6

FRENCH POST OFFICES IN CHINA

General issues for the French post offices in China, which were closed in 1922.

1894. 100 centimes = 1 franc.
1907. 100 cents = 1 piastre.

Stamps of Indo-China optd **CHINE** are listed under Indo-Chinese Post Offices in China.

1894. Stamps of France optd Chine.

2	**10**	5c. green	3·50	1·30
4	**10**	10c. black on lilac	6·50	3·00
6	**10**	15c. blue	11·00	2·75
8	**10**	20c. red on green	3·75	2·50
9	**10**	25c. black on pink	12·00	1·30
10	**10**	30c. brown	6·75	7·00
11	**10**	40c. red on yellow	8·75	5·75
12	**10**	50c. red	28·00	5·00
14	**10**	75c. brown on orange	£100	70·00
15	**10**	1f. green	15·00	3·25
16	**10**	2f. brown on blue	47·00	35·00
17	**10**	5f. mauve on lilac	£120	75·00

1900. No. 15 surch 25.

18	**10**	25 on 1f. green	£100	70·00

1901. No. 9 surch.

19	**10**	2c. on 25c. black on pink	£900	£250
20	**10**	4c. on 25c. black on pink	£850	£250
21	**10**	6c. on 25c. black on pink	£900	£325
22	**10**	16c. on 25c. black on pink	£275	£170

1902. "Blanc", "Mouchon" and "Merson" key-types inscr "CHINE".

37a	**A**	5c. green	7·25	1·10
38	**B**	10c. red	3·25	1·70
39	**B**	15c. red	3·50	2·10
40	**B**	20c. brown	5·75	6·25
41	**B**	25c. blue	6·25	1·40
42	**B**	30c. mauve	9·25	11·50
43	**C**	40c. red and blue	17·00	23·00
44	**C**	50c. brown and lilac	11·00	10·00
45	**C**	1f. red and green	32·00	13·50
46	**C**	2f. lilac and buff	55·00	60·00
47	**C**	5f. blue and buff	90·00	65·00

1903. No. 39 surch 5.

48	**B**	5 on 15c. red	21·00	12·00

1907. Stamps of 1902 surch with new value in French and Chinese.

92	**A**	1c. on 5c. orange	5·25	8·50
84	**A**	2c. on 5c. green	3·00	1·00
93	**B**	2c. on 10c. green	8·25	12·50
94	**B**	3c. on 15c. orange	14·50	21·00
77	**B**	4c. on 10c. red	4·75	75
95	**B**	4c. on 20c. brown	21·00	24·00
96	**B**	5c. on 25c. purple	9·00	10·50
78	**B**	6c. on 15c. red	2·50	1·00
97	**B**	6c. on 30c. red	18·00	29·00
87	**B**	8c. on 20c. brown	2·75	1·40
80	**B**	10c. on 25c. blue	2·30	50
98	**B**	10c. on 50c. blue	22·00	29·00
81	**C**	20c. on 50c. brown & lilac	5·00	1·50
89	**B**	20c. on 50c. blue	70·00	70·00
99	**C**	20c. on 1f. red and green	55·00	60·00
90	**C**	40c. on 1f. red and green	9·00	4·00
100	**C**	40c. on 2f. red and green	60·00	60·00
101	**C**	1pi. on 5f. blue and buff	£150	£150
83	**C**	2pi. on 5f. blue and buff	29·00	15·00
91	**C**	$2 on 5f. blue and buff	£140	£140

POSTAGE DUE STAMPS

1901. Postage Due stamps of France optd Chine.

D23	**D11**	5c. blue	5·00	2·30
D24	**D11**	10c. brown	11·50	11·00
D25	**D11**	15c. green	17·00	7·75
D26	**D11**	20c. olive	9·00	17·00
D27	**D11**	30c. red	22·00	10·00
D28	**D11**	50c. red	27·00	11·50

1903. Stamps of 1894 and 1902 optd A PERCEVOIR.

D62A	**A**	5c. green	£1100	£600
D62B	**10**	5c. green	£1100	£600
D51B	**10**	10c. black on lilac	£7500	£6500
D63A	**B**	10c. red	£300	60·00
D60A	**10**	15c. blue	£1000	90·00
D64A	**B**	15c. red	£650	70·00
D61B	**10**	30c. brown	£500	85·00

1911. Postage Due stamps of France surch with new value in French and Chinese.

D102	**D11**	1c. on 5c. blue	95·00	95·00
D92	**D11**	2c. on 5c. blue	1·60	2·75
D103	**D11**	2c. on 10c. brown	£110	£110
D93	**D11**	4c. on 10c. brown	2·30	2·30
D104	**D11**	4c. on 20c. olive	£110	£110
D94	**D11**	8c. on 20c. olive	4·25	3·50
D105	**D11**	10c. on 50c. red	£110	£110
D95	**D11**	20c. on 50c. red	3·50	2·30

Pt. 6

FRENCH POST OFFICES IN CRETE

These offices were closed in 1914.

100 centimes = 1 franc.
25 centimes = 1 piastre.

1902. "Blanc", "Mouchon" and "Merson" key-types inscr "CRETE".

1	**A**	1c. grey	2·75	1·20
2	**A**	2c. red	55	90
3	**A**	3c. red	1·50	1·80
4	**A**	4c. brown	2·75	3·75
5	**A**	5c. green	2·30	1·80
6	**B**	10c. red	3·25	2·50
7	**B**	15c. orange	3·25	4·75
8	**B**	20c. red	2·75	5·25
9	**B**	25c. blue	5·25	2·75
10	**B**	30c. mauve	7·50	16·00
11	**C**	40c. red and blue	17·00	24·00

12	C	50c. brown and lavender	12·00	24·00
13	C	1f. red and green	18·00	23·00
14	C	2f. lilac and buff	50·00	60·00
15	C	5f. blue and buff	50·00	50·00

1903. Surch in figures and words.

16	B	1pi. on 25c. blue	55·00	50·00
17	C	2pi. on 50c. brown & lav	65·00	80·00
18	C	4pi. on 1f. red and green	£100	£120
19	C	8pi. on 2f. lilac and buff	£110	£120
20	C	20pi. on 5f. blue and buff	£130	£130

Pt. 6

FRENCH POST OFFICES IN ETHIOPIA

100 centimes = 1 franc.

1906. Perf or imperf.

25	A	25c. blue	25·00	80·00
26	B	50c. brown and lavender	£170	£170
27	B	1f. red and green	£400	£400

Pt. 6

FRENCH POST OFFICES IN MOROCCO

French Post Offices were first established in Morocco in 1862, using the stamps of France. For stamps used by French Post Offices in Tangier after 1912 see under that heading.

100 centimos = 1 peseta.

1891. Stamps of France surch in Spanish currency (centimos on equivalent centime values).

1	10	5c. on 5c. green	10·50	2·20
5	10	10c. on 10c. blk on lilac	48·00	1·90
6	10	20c. on 20c. red on grn	26·00	18·00
7	10	25c. on 25c. blk on pink	23·00	2·20
8a	10	50c. on 50c. red	80·00	22·00
10	10	1p. on 1f. green	75·00	80·00
11	10	2p. on 2f. brown on blue	£150	£200

1893. Postage Due stamps of France optd TIMBRE POSTE and bar.

12	D11	5c. black	£1900	£750
13	D11	10c. black	£1700	£550

1902. "Blanc", "Mouchon" and "Merson" key types inscr "MAROC" and surch in Spanish currency in figures and words.

14	A	1c. on 1c. grey	55	40
15	A	2c. on 2c. red	80	40
16	A	3c. on 3c. red	1·30	1·10
17	A	4c. on 4c. brown	5·75	5·00
18a	A	5c. on 5c. green	8·50	55
19	B	10c. on 10c. red	5·75	35
20	B	20c. on 20c. red	12·50	2·20
21	B	25c. on 25c. blue	42·00	75
22	B	35c. on 35c. lilac	11·50	10·00
23	C	50c. on 50c. brown & lilac	25·00	3·25
24	C	1p. on 1f. red and green	65·00	50·00
25	C	2p. on 2f. lilac and yellow	90·00	70·00

1903. Postage Due stamps of 1896 optd P.P. in box.

26	D11	5c. on 5c. blue	£1200	
27	D11	10c. on 10c. brown	£2250	

1911. Key-types surch with figure of value and Arabic word.

28	A	1c. on 1c. grey	70	75
29	A	2c. on 2c. red	25	50
30	A	3c. on 3c. orange	70	1·10
31	A	5c. on 5c. green	1·80	35
32	B	10c. on 10c. red	85	15
33	B	15c. on 15c. orange	2·20	2·50
34	B	20c. on 20c. red	2·10	2·50
35	B	25c. on 25c. blue	2·50	1·00
36	B	35c. on 35c. lilac	3·50	1·10
37	C	40c. on 40c. red and blue	8·50	17·00
38	C	50c. on 50c. brown & lilac	12·00	5·50
39	C	1p. on 1f. red and green	8·00	20·00

POSTAGE DUE STAMPS

1896. Postage Due stamps of France surch in Spanish currency in figures and words.

D14	D11	5c. on 5c. blue	10·50	3·25
D15	D11	10c. on 10c. brown	15·00	3·50
D16	D11	30c. on 30c. red	30·00	15·00
D17	D11	50c. on 50c. red	19·00	17·00
D18	D11	1p. on 1f. brown	£275	£250

1909. Postage Due stamps of France surch in Spanish currency.

D28	D19	1c. on 1c. olive	1·50	2·30
D29	D19	10c. on 10c. violet	21·00	60·00
D30	D19	30c. on 30c. bistre	26·00	60·00
D31	D19	50c. on 50c. red	65·00	80·00

1911. Postage Due stamps of France surch with figure and Arabic word.

D40	D11	5c. on 5c. blue	3·00	9·50
D41	D11	10c. on 10c. brown	3·50	15·00
D42	D11	50c. on 50c. purple	6·50	50·00

1911. Postage Due stamps of France surch in figures and Arabic.

D43	D19	1c. on 1c. olive	1·10	1·20
D44	D19	10c. on 10c. violet	2·10	10·50
D45	D19	30c. on 30c. bistre	3·50	15·00
D46	D19	50c. on 50c. red	6·75	44·00

For later issues see **FRENCH MOROCCO**.

Pt. 6

FRENCH POST OFFICES IN TANGIERS

By Franco-Spanish Treaty of 27 November 1912, Tangier was given a special status outside the protectorates. After the Tangier Convention of 1924 the zone was administered by an international commission. Tangier was occupied by Spain in 1940 and the French P.O.'s closed in 1942.

100 centimes = 1 franc.

1918. "Blanc", "Mouchon" and "Merson" key-types of French Post Offices in Morocco optd TANGER.

1a	A	1c. grey	35	3·50
2	A	2c. red	75	4·00
3	A	3c. orange	55	3·00
4	A	5c. green	1·00	1·40
5	A	5c. orange	2·30	3·25
6	B	10c. red	1·00	75
7	B	10c. green	2·30	6·00
8	B	15c. orange	1·20	1·60
9	B	20c. red	1·80	2·30
10	B	25c. blue	1·70	90
11	B	30c. red	3·75	11·00
12	B	35c. lilac	2·40	5·50
13	C	40c. red and blue	3·00	6·75
14	C	50c. brown and lilac	11·00	11·00
15	B	50c. blue	14·00	11·00
16	C	1f. red and green	4·50	8·75
17	C	2f. red and green	60·00	£120
18	C	5f. blue and yellow	55·00	£110

1928. Air. Nos. 149/58 of French Morocco optd Tanger.

30	5c. blue	2·75	18·00
31	25c. orange	2·50	14·50
32	50c. red	2·00	17·00
33	75c. brown	2·00	17·00
34	80c. green	2·00	17·00
35	1f. orange	2·00	17·00
36	1f.50 blue	2·00	17·00
37	2f. brown	1·80	18·00
38	3f. purple	6·25	18·00
39	5f. black	2·00	17·00

POSTAGE DUE STAMPS

1918. Postage Due stamps of France optd TANGER.

D19	D11	1c. black	30	2·75
D20	D11	5c. blue	1·00	7·50
D21	D11	10c. brown	1·40	7·00
D22	D11	15c. green	3·00	12·00
D23	D11	20c. olive	3·25	14·00
D24	D11	30c. red	6·50	40·00
D25	D11	50c. purple	8·25	46·00

1918. Postage Due stamps of France optd TANGER.

D26	D19	1c. olive	55	6·50
D27	D19	10c. violet	2·75	8·25
D28	D19	20c. bistre	7·25	24·00
D29	D19	40c. red	12·00	50·00

Pt. 6

FRENCH POST OFFICES IN THE TURKISH EMPIRE

General issues for the French Post Offices in the Turkish Empire.

1885. 25 centimes = 1 piastre.
1921. 40 paras = 1 piastre.

1885. Stamps of France surch in figures and words.

1	10	1pi. on 25c. bistre on yellow	£400	4·50
2	10	3pi. on 75c. red	65·00	11·00
3	10	4pi. on 1f. green	60·00	5·50
4	10	1pi. on 25c. black on pink	6·50	65
5	10	2pi. on 50c. pink	42·00	90
7	10	8pi. on 2f. brown on blue	42·00	22·00
8	10	20pi. on 5f. mauve	£120	55·00

1902. "Blanc", "Mouchon" and "Merson" key-types inscr "LEVANT".

9	A	1c. grey	20	35
10	A	2c. purple	45	75
11	A	3c. red	45	1·50
12	A	4c. brown	3·50	1·70
13a	A	5c. green	3·00	20
14	B	10c. red	3·50	10
15	B	15c. red	2·50	30
16	B	20c. brown	3·75	2·30
17	B	30c. lilac	6·50	4·00
18	C	40c. red and blue	8·25	5·00

1902. Surch in figures and words.

19	B	1pi. on 25c. blue	3·25	10
20	C	2pi. on 50c. brown & lav	5·25	90
21	C	4pi. on 1f. red & green	5·00	3·00
22	C	8pi. on 2f. lilac & yellow	40·00	16·00
23	C	20pi. on 5f. blue & yellow	8·75	8·00

1905. Surch 1 Piastre Beyrouth.

24	B	1pi. on 15c. orange	£1500	£375

1921. Stamps of France surch in figures and words.

28	18	30pa. on 5c. green	1·40	3·50
29	18	30pa. on 5c. orange	4·25	3·75
30	18	1pi.20 on 10c. red	1·80	1·90
31	18	1pi.20 on 10c. green	2·00	1·40
39	18	3pi.30 on 15c. green	32·00	55·00
32	18	3pi.30 on 25c. blue	1·50	65
33	18	4pi.20 on 30c. orange	1·30	1·30
40	18	7pi.20 on 35c. violet	36·00	55·00
34	15	7pi.20 on 50c. blue	75	75
35	13	15pi. on 1f. red & green	3·00	1·70
36	13	30pi. on 2f. red & green	13·00	17·00
37	13	75pi. on 5f. blue & yellow	11·50	8·25

For stamps issued by the Free French forces during 1942/3 see under **FREE FRENCH FORCES IN THE LEVANT**.

Pt. 6

FRENCH POST OFFICES IN ZANZIBAR

The French post office in Zanzibar operated from 1889 to 1904.

16 annas = 1 rupee.

Stamps of France surcharged

1894. Surch in figures and words.

1a	10	½a. on 5c. green	13·00	9·25
3	10	1a. on 10c. black on lilac	23·00	23·00
4a	10	1½a. on 15c. blue	50·00	41·00
6	10	2a. on 20c. red on green	18·00	28·00
7	10	2½a. on 25c. black on red	17·00	13·00
8	10	3a. on 30c. brown	44·00	36·00
9	10	4a. on 40c. red on yellow	32·00	40·00
10	10	5a. on 50c. red	60·00	33·00
11	10	7½a. on 75c. brn on orge	£350	£300
12a	10	10a. on 1f. olive	£100	80·00
14	10	50a. on 5f. mve on lilac	£225	£225

1894. Surch ZANZIBAR and value in Indian currency (in figures and words) and in corresponding French currency (in figures only on Nos. 15/18).

15	10	½a. and 5 on 1c. black on blue	£170	£190
16	10	1a. and 10 on 3c. grey	£160	£170
17	10	2½a. and 25 on 4c. lilac on grey	£200	£225
18	10	5a. and 50 on 20c. red on green	£200	£225
19	10	10a. and 1f. on 40c. red on yellow	£400	£400

1896. Surch ZANZIBAR and new value in Indian currency only.

22	10	½a. on 5c. green	8·75	7·25
24	10	1a. on 10c. black on lilac	9·25	6·50
26	10	1½a. on 15c. blue	13·00	12·00
28	10	2a. on 20c. red on green	6·75	7·75
29	10	2½a. on 25c. black on red	13·00	7·75
30	10	3a. on 30c. brown	8·75	6·75
31	10	4a. on 40c. red on yellow	7·75	7·25
32	10	5a. on 50c. red	14·50	11·00
35a	10	10a. on 1f. olive	16·00	30·00
37	10	20a. on 2f. brown on blue	23·00	50·00
38	10	50a. on 5f. mve on lilac	60·00	60·00

1897. Nos. 1-4 and 8-9 further surch with new figures of value in French and Indian currency and optd ZANZIBAR vert.

42	10	2½ and 25 on ½a. on 5c.	£1100	£160
43	10	2½ and 25 on 1a. on 10c.	£2000	£750
44	10	2½ and 25 on 1½a. on 15c.	£2000	£750
45	10	5 and 50 on 3a. on 30c.	£2000	£750
46	10	5 and 50 on 4a. on 40c.	£1800	£750

PosteFrance 5 Annas 50c ZANZIBAR

(4)

1897

47	4	2½a. and 25c. black on green and white		£1000
48	4	2½a. and 25c. black on lilac and white		£2750
49	4	2½a. and 25c. black on blue and white		£2250
50	4	5a. and 50c. black on buff and white		£2000
51	4	5a. and 50c. black on yellow and white		£2750
52	4	5a. and 50c. on white		£2750

1902. "Blanc", "Mouchon" and "Merson" key-types inscr "ZANZIBAR" and surch in figures and words.

53	A	½a. on 5c. green	6·50	11·50
54	B	1a. on 10c. red	10·00	19·00
55	B	1½a. on 15c. orange	25·00	38·00
56	B	2a. on 20c. red	24·00	34·00
57	B	2½a. on 25c. blue	30·00	18·00
58	B	3a. on 30c. mauve	10·00	25·00
59	C	4a. on 40c. red and blue	50·00	60·00
60	C	5a. on 50c. brown & lav	32·00	37·00
61	C	10a. on 1f. red and green	60·00	30·00
62	C	20a. on 2f. lilac & yellow	70·00	75·00
63	C	50a. on 5f. blue & yellow	90·00	£120

1904. Nos. 30/31 further surch with both currencies in figures on either side of bars.

65	10	"25 c 2½" on 4a. on 40c.		£850
66	10	"50 5" on 3a. on 30c.		£950
67	10	"50 5" on 4a. on 40c.		£950
68	10	"1fr 10" on 3a. on 30c.		£1500
69	10	"1fr 10" on 4a. on 40c.		£1500

1904. "Blanc" key-type surch with both currencies in large figures.

70	A	"2 25" on ½a. on 5c. green (No. 53)		£110

1904. "Mouchon" key-type surch with both currencies in figures or in figures and words.

71	B	"25c 2½" on 1a. on 10c. red (No. 54)		£130
72	B	"25c 2½" on 3a. on 30c. mauve (No. 58)		£2000
73	B	"50 c cinq" on 3a. on 30c. mauve (No. 58)		£950
74	B	"1 fr dix" on 3a. on 30c. mauve (No. 58)		£1300

1904. Postage Due stamps optd. (a) Timbre.

75	D11	½a. on 5c. blue		£375

(b) Affrancht.

76	D11	1a. on 10c. brown		£375

(c) With red line at top and bottom obliterating words "CHIFFRE" and "TAXE".

77	D11	1½a. on 15c. green		£850

POSTAGE DUE STAMPS

1897. Postage Due stamps of France surch ZANZIBAR and value in figures and words.

D39	D11	½a. on 5c. blue	46·00	4·50
D40	D11	1a. on 10c. brown	42·00	9·25
D41	D11	1½a. on 15c. green	60·00	10·00
D42	D11	3a. on 30c. red	46·00	16·00
D43	D11	5a. on 50c. purple	65·00	12·00

Pt. 6

FRENCH SOMALI COAST

A French colony on the Gulf of Aden, E. coast of Africa. Renamed French Territory of the Afars and the Issas in 1967.

100 centimes = 1 franc.

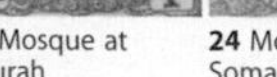

23 Mosque at Tajurah　24 Mounted Somalis　25 Somali Warriors

1902

121	**23**	1c. orange and purple	2·00	80
137	**23**	1c. black and brown	75	1·20
122	**23**	2c. green and brown	1·60	75
138	**23**	2c. black and brown	1·40	1·00
123	**23**	4c. red and blue	2·50	2·75
139	**23**	4c. black and red	4·00	2·00
124	**23**	5c. green & deep green	3·25	1·30
140a	**23**	5c. black and green	6·50	3·75
125	**23**	10c. orange and red	7·25	6·50
141a	**23**	10c. black and red	18·00	2·75
126	**23**	15c. blue and orange	5·50	5·00
142	**23**	15c. black and brown	30·00	18·00
127	**24**	20c. green and lilac	17·00	23·00
143	**24**	20c. black and lilac	23·00	50·00
128	**24**	25c. blue	16·00	12·00
129	**24**	25c. blue and indigo	32·00	8·25
144	**24**	25c. black and blue	10·00	5·00
130	**24**	30c. black and red	11·00	10·00
131	**24**	40c. blue and yellow	35·00	35·00
145	**24**	40c. black and orange	16·00	14·50
132	**24**	50c. red and green	60·00	70·00
146	**24**	50c. black and green	30·00	12·00
133	**24**	75c. mauve and orange	16·00	14·50
147	**24**	75c. black and brown	11·00	10·50
134	**25**	1f. purple and red	27·00	28·00
148	**25**	1f. black and red	22·00	30·00
135	**25**	2f. red and green	50·00	65·00
149	**25**	2f. black and green	13·00	12·00
136	**25**	5f. blue and orange	34·00	38·00
150	**25**	5f. black and orange	23·00	50·00

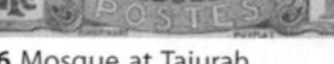

26 Mosque at Tajurah

27 Mounted Somalis

1909

151	**26**	1c. brown and purple	45	65
152	**26**	2c. green and violet	55	50
153	**26**	4c. blue and brown	90	75
154	**26**	5c. olive and green	4·25	1·40
155	**26**	10c. orange and red	6·50	1·70
156	**26**	20c. brown and black	5·00	10·00
157	**27**	25c. blue and deep blue	8·00	2·75
158	**27**	30c. red and brown	6·50	17·00
159	**27**	35c. green and violet	10·00	6·25
160	**27**	40c. violet and pink	10·50	16·00
161	**27**	45c. green and brown	16·00	9·50
162	**27**	50c. brown and purple	10·00	8·75
163	**27**	75c. green and red	17·00	38·00
164	**25**	1f. brown and violet	29·00	50·00
165	**25**	2f. pink and brown	50·00	65·00
166	**25**	5f. green and brown	75·00	90·00

28 Drummer

29 Somali Woman

30 Railway Bridge at Holl-Holli

1915. No. 172 surch 5c and red cross.

167	**29**	10c.+5c. red & carmine	6·50	8·50

1915

168	**28**	1c. brown and violet	10	30
169	**28**	2c. blue and bistre	10	30
170a	**28**	4c. red and brown	1·00	1·50
171	**28**	5c. green & light green	1·30	75
195	**28**	5c. red and orange	20	1·00
172	**29**	10c. red and carmine	2·50	2·50
196	**29**	10c. green & light green	1·60	4·50
214	**29**	10c. green and red	90	1·10
173	**29**	15c. pink and lilac	1·30	1·50
174	**29**	20c. brown and orange	70	1·60
215	**29**	20c. light green & green	1·00	2·20
216	**29**	20c. red and green	60	1·40
175	**29**	25c. blue & ultramarine	2·00	2·50
197	**29**	25c. green and black	45	30
176	**29**	30c. green and black	5·25	7·50
198	**29**	30c. brown and red	2·75	4·50
217	**29**	30c. green and violet	45	1·10
218	**29**	30c. olive and green	90	1·70
177	**29**	35c. pink and green	2·20	3·50
178	**29**	40c. lilac and blue	2·50	2·30
179	**29**	45c. blue and brown	2·50	3·00
180	**29**	50c. black and pink	30·00	17·00
199	**29**	50c. blue & ultramarine	2·50	7·00
219	**29**	50c. purple and brown	30	20
220	**29**	60c. purple and green	80	5·00
221	**29**	65c. green and red	65	1·80
181	**29**	75c. brown and lilac	2·00	2·75
222	**29**	75c. blue and deep blue	60	90
223	**29**	75c. brown and mauve	3·25	7·25
224	**29**	85c. green and purple	90	7·75
225	**29**	90c. carmine and red	5·50	5·50
182	**30**	1f. red and brown	2·50	1·00
226	**30**	1f.10 blue and brown	6·50	14·50
227	**30**	1f.25 brown and blue	15·00	27·00
228	**30**	1f.50 blue & light blue	1·10	65
229	**30**	1f.75 red and green	10·00	4·50
183	**30**	2f. black and violet	6·50	2·00
230	**30**	3f. mauve on pink	16·00	8·75
184	**30**	5f. black and red	11·00	2·75

1922. Surch 1922 and value in figures in frame.

193	**28**	10 on 5c. green & lt grn	1·10	1·60
194	**29**	50 on 25c. bl & ultram	1·70	2·40

1922. Surch in figures.

200		0.01 on 15c. pink and lilac	55	5·50
201		0.02 on 15c. pink and lilac	1·20	5·50
202		0.04 on 15c. pink and lilac	55	5·50
203		0.05 on 15c. pink and lilac	55	4·25
204	**30**	25c. on 5f. black & red	3·00	8·00
205	**29**	60 on 75c. violet & green	45	2·50
206	**29**	65 on 15c. pink and lilac	1·80	6·50
207	**29**	85 on 40c. lilac and blue	1·80	8·25
208	**29**	90 on 75c. red	3·25	4·50
209	**30**	1f.25 on 1f. ultram & bl	1·90	3·25
210	**30**	1f.50 on 1f. bl & lt bl	2·50	1·60
211	**30**	3f. on 5f. mauve & red	5·75	3·75
212	**30**	10f. on 5f. brown & red	12·50	15·00
213	**30**	20f. on 5f. pink & green	22·00	13·00

1931. "Colonial Exhibition" key-types inscr "COTE FR. DES SOMALIS".

233	**E**	40c. green and black	3·75	5·50
234	**F**	50c. mauve and black	3·75	5·50
235	**G**	90c. red and black	3·75	12·00
236	**H**	1f.50 blue and black	4·50	7·00

1937. Int Exn, Paris. As T 58a of Guadeloupe.

237	20c. violet	2·00	3·25
238	30c. green	1·50	3·25
239	40c. red	1·10	4·50
240	50c. brown and blue	90	2·50
241	90c. red	1·00	3·00
242	1f.50 blue	1·00	4·25

1938. International Anti-cancer Fund. As T 58b of Guadeloupe.

244	1f.75+50c. blue	2·75	19·00

34 Mosque at Djibouti

35 Somali Warriors

37 Djibouti

1938

245	**34**	2c. purple	10	1·80
246	**34**	3c. green	10	1·60
247	**34**	4c. brown	10	3·50
248	**34**	5c. red	10	3·75
249	**34**	10c. blue	10	1·90
250	**34**	15c. black	10	4·25
251	**34**	20c. red	35	3·75
252	**35**	25c. brown	55	2·50
253	**35**	30c. blue	45	3·75
254	**35**	35c. green	65	6·25
255	**34**	40c. brown	1·50	7·50
256	**34**	45c. green	1·10	6·75
257	**35**	50c. red	45	2·75
258	**35**	55c. purple	90	6·75
259	**35**	60c. black	55	6·25
260	**35**	65c. brown	80	4·25
261	**35**	70c. violet	1·20	10·00
262	-	80c. black	1·40	8·00
263	**35**	90c. mauve	1·70	9·00
264	-	1f. red	1·80	2·50
265	-	1f. black	75	3·25
266	-	1f.25 red	1·60	9·25
267	-	1f.40 blue	2·20	9·50
268	-	1f.50 green	65	2·75
269	-	1f.60 red	2·50	9·50
270	-	1f.75 blue	1·10	3·25
271	-	2f. red	85	1·00
272	-	2f.25 blue	1·80	7·50
273	-	2f.50 brown	2·20	10·00
274	-	3f. purple	90	1·80
275	**37**	5f. brown & deep brown	1·40	2·75
276	**37**	10f. light blue and blue	1·20	3·25
277	**37**	20f. blue and red	1·60	3·75

DESIGN—VERT: 80c. and 1f. to 3f. Governor L. Lagarde.

1939. New York World's Fair. As T 58c of Guadeloupe.

288	1f.25 red	75	6·25
289	2f.25 blue	3·75	3·25

1939. 150th Anniv of French Revolution. As T 58d of Guadeloupe.

290	45c.+25c. green & black	9·50	20·00
291	70c.+30c. brown & black	9·50	20·00
292	90c.+35c. orange & black	9·50	20·00
293	1f.25+1f. red and black	9·50	20·00
294	2f.25+2f. blue and black	9·50	20·00

1941. Air. Free French Issue. As T 63a of Guadeloupe, but inscr "DJIBOUTI".

295	**32**	1f. orange	65	75
296	**32**	1f.50 red	1·20	2·75
297	**32**	5f. purple	1·00	1·40
298	**32**	10f. black	1·60	2·75
299	**32**	25f. blue	1·70	8·25
300	**32**	50f. green	1·40	4·50
301	**32**	100f. red	1·80	2·75

1942. Optd or surch also FRANCE LIBRE or France Libre.

302	**28**	1c. brown and violet	2·75	8·75
303	**28**	2c. blue and bistre	3·25	9·50
304	**34**	2c. purple	1·60	6·50
305	**34**	3c. green	2·50	7·75
306	**28**	4c. red and brown	32·00	65·00
307	**34**	4c. brown	3·25	7·00
308	**28**	5c. red and orange	1·70	7·50
309	**34**	5c. red	2·50	5·50
310	**34**	10c. blue	75	6·00
311	**29**	15c. pink and lilac	7·00	27·00
312	**34**	15c. black	1·90	6·00
313	**29**	20c. red and green	1·70	8·25
314	**34**	20c. red	2·00	4·75
315	**35**	25c. brown	3·25	6·50
316	**29**	30c. olive and green	1·50	9·75
317	**35**	30c. blue	55	4·00
318	**35**	35c. green	3·25	6·75
319	**34**	40c. brown	35	3·75
320	**34**	45c. green	3·75	6·25
321	**29**	50c. purple and brown	1·30	6·50
322	**35**	50c. on 65c. brown	30	90
323	**35**	55c. purple	2·30	6·25
324	**35**	60c. black	20	3·00
325	**29**	65c. green and red	1·00	7·75
326	**35**	70c. violet	30	3·50
327	-	80c. black (No. 262)	20	3·50
328	**35**	90c. mauve	35	2·30
329	-	1f.25 red (No. 266)	2·20	6·75
330	-	1f.40 blue (No. 267)	55	4·50
331	**30**	1f.50 blue & light blue	1·40	6·50
332	-	1f.50 green (No. 268)	2·00	3·75
333	-	1f.60 red (No. 269)	1·40	5·25
334	**30**	1f.75 red and green	14·00	29·00
335	-	1f.75 blue (No. 270)	8·25	26·00
336	-	2f. red (No. 271)	20	2·00
337	-	2f.25 blue (No. 272)	1·00	6·25
338	-	2f.50 brown (No. 273)	1·20	2·75
339	-	3f. purple (No. 274)	1·50	3·75
340	**37**	5f. brown & deep brown	9·25	33·00
341	**37**	10f. light blue and blue	£160	£170
342	**37**	20f. blue and red	8·25	16·00

41 Symbolical of Djibouti

1943. Free French issue.

361	**41**	5c. blue	10	5·50
362	**41**	10c. red	10	5·00
363	**41**	25c. green	30	6·50
364	**41**	30c. black	35	6·25
365	**41**	40c. violet	45	6·50
366	**41**	80c. purple	70	6·75
367	**41**	1f. blue	1·00	90
368	**41**	1f.50 red	1·30	1·80
369	**41**	2f. bistre	1·00	85
370	**41**	2f.50 blue	1·20	1·30
371	**41**	4f. orange	1·10	2·50
372	**41**	5f. mauve	1·30	3·25
373	**41**	10f. blue	1·90	2·00
374	**41**	20f. green	1·50	2·00

1944. Mutual Aid and Red Cross Funds. As T 58e of Guadeloupe.

375	5f.+20f. green	1·10	9·75

1945. Eboue. As T 58f of Guadeloupe.

376	2f. black	55	5·00
377	25f. green	65	8·25

1945. Surch.

378	50c. on 5c. blue	90	5·75
379	60c. on 5c. blue	85	6·25
380	70c. on 5c. blue	85	6·50
381	1f.20 on 5c. blue	2·00	7·25
382	2f.40 on 25c. green	1·90	7·00
383	3f. on 25c. green	1·30	4·75
384	4f.50 on 25c. green	2·00	5·25
385	15f. on 2f.50 blue	2·00	6·50

1946. Air. Victory. As T 63b of Guadeloupe.

386	8f. blue	55	3·50

1946. Air. From Chad to the Rhine. As T 63c of Guadeloupe.

387	5f. black	2·50	10·50
388	10f. red	1·80	5·50
389	15f. brown	1·50	6·25
390	20f. mauve	2·50	7·75
391	25f. green	1·50	9·50
392	50f. blue	1·30	5·50

43 Danakil Tent

44 Outpost at Khor-Angar

45 Somali

46 Government Palace, Djibouti

1947

393	**43**	10c. orge & vio (postage)	10	3·75
394	**43**	30c. orange and green	10	5·25
395	**43**	40c. orange and purple	10	5·25
396	**44**	50c. orange and green	35	3·00
397	**44**	60c. yellow and brown	30	4·25
398	**44**	80c. orange and violet	55	5·00
399	-	1f. brown and blue	35	85
400	-	1f.20 green and grey	1·00	7·75
401	-	1f.50 blue and orange	90	5·25
402	-	2f. mauve and grey	55	20
403	-	3f. blue and brown	90	65
404	-	3f.60 brown and red	2·20	7·75
405	-	4f. brown and grey	75	45
406	-	5f. orange and brown	1·00	35
407	-	6f. blue and grey	75	55
408	-	10f. purple and blue	1·00	35
409	-	15f. brown, blue & buff	2·00	30
410	-	20f. blue, orange & blue	2·00	1·10
411	-	25f. red, blue & purple	1·70	55

412	**45**	50f. brown & blue (air)	1·40	65
413	-	100f. yellow and green	1·50	1·70
414	**46**	200f. green, yell & blue	2·75	2·30

DESIGNS—HORIZ: As Type **44**: 1f. to 1f.50, Obock Tajurah road; 2f. to 4f. Woman carrying dish; 5f. to 10f. Somali village; 15f. to 25f. Mosque. Djibouti. As Type **46**: 100f. Frontier post, Loyada.

1949. Air. 75th Anniv of U.P.U. As T 39 of French Equatorial Africa.

425	30f. multicoloured	2·30	38·00

1950. Colonial Welfare Fund. As T 40 of French Equatorial Africa.

426	10f.+2f. red and brown	2·50	20·00

1952. Centenary of Medaille Militaire. As T 44 of French Equatorial Africa.

427	15f. violet, yellow and green	3·00	6·50

1954. Air. 10th Anniv of Liberation. As T 46 of French Equatorial Africa.

428	15f. violet and blue	7·00	24·00

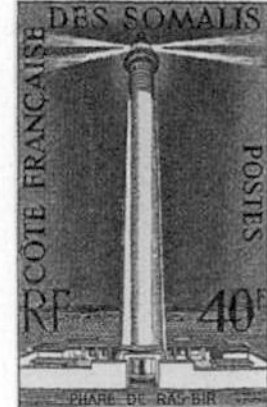

48 Ras-Bir Lighthouse

49 Aerial Map of Djibouti

1956

429	**48**	40f. blue & dp bl (postage)	2·75	90
430	**49**	500f. purple & vio (air)	37·00	70·00

50 Freighter at Wharf, Djibouti

1956. Economic and Social Development Fund.

431	**50**	15f. violet	2·75	65

51 Warthog

1958. Animals, Fishes and Birds.

432	**51**	30c. brown & red (postage)	45	4·75
433	-	40c. brown and bistre	65	5·25
434	-	50c. purple, grey & green	55	4·75
435	-	1f. orge, blue & brown	50	40
436	-	2f. multicoloured	1·40	2·20
437	-	3f. brown and violet	1·00	55
438	-	4f. brn, orange & blue	1·60	2·30
439	-	5f. black and blue	2·00	1·00
440	-	10f. red, brown & green	6·00	3·50
441	-	15f. yellow, green & mve	5·50	3·00
442	-	20f. purple, red and blue	3·00	1·30
443	-	25f. blue, red and green	3·25	2·50
444	-	30f. black, red and blue	10·50	7·50
445	-	60f. green and blue	6·50	2·75
446	-	75f. yellow, brown & grn	18·00	25·00
447	-	100f. brown, grn & bl (air)	7·00	5·00
448	-	200f. brown, blk & orge	19·00	14·00
449	-	500f. multicoloured	28·00	50·00

DESIGNS—HORIZ: As Type **51**: 40c. Cheetah; 1f. Blue-barred orange parrotfish; 3f. Blue marlin; 4f. Blue spotted boxfish; 5f. African eagle ray; 15f. Little bee eater; 20f. Undulate triggerfish; 25f. Yellow-wedged triggerfish; 30f. Sacred ibis; 60f. Smooth hammerhead; 48×27 mm: 100f. Bohar reedbucks and airplane; 200f. Great bustard; 500f. Salt caravan, Lake Assal. VERT: As Type **51**: 50c. Gerenuks; 2f. Pennant coralfish; 10f. Greater flamingo; 75f. Pink-backed pelican.

1958. Tropical Flora. As T 56 of French Equatorial Africa.

450	10f. red, green and yellow	1·00	1·40

DESIGN—HORIZ: 10f. "Haemanthus".

1958. 10th Anniv of Declaration of Human Rights. As T 57 of French Equatorial Africa.

451	20f. violet and blue	55	1·50

53 Governor Bernard

1960. Air. 25th Death Anniv of Governor Bernard.

452	**53**	55f. brown, blue & red	1·60	1·70

54 "Forbin", Obock, 1862

1962. Air. Centenary of Obock.

453	**54**	100f. brown and blue	4·00	3·25

55 Dragon Tree

1962. Fauna and Flora.

454	**55**	2f. multicoloured	3·25	4·00
455	-	4f. brown and ochre	2·75	2·75
456	-	6f. multicoloured	3·75	5·50
457	-	25f. bistre, green and red	5·50	7·50
458	-	40f. brown, black & blue	13·00	5·50
459	-	50f. brown, purple & blue	11·00	12·00

DESIGNS—HORIZ: 4f. Large-toothed rock hyrax; 6f. Giant trevally (fish); 25f. Fennec foxes; 40f. Griffon vulture. VERT: 50f. Klipspringer.

55a Campaign Emblem

1962. Malaria Eradication.

460	**55a**	25f.+5f. blue	4·25	20·00

56 Black-lip Pearl Oyster

1962. Shells of the Red Sea. Multicoloured. (a) Postage. As T 56.

461	8f. Type **56**	1·50	2·50
462	10f. Fluted giant clam (horiz)	1·50	1·60
463	25f. Three knobbed conch (horiz)	2·50	2·75
464	30f. Knobbed top	2·50	2·40

(b) Air. 50×28 mm.

465	60f. Arabian tibia	3·00	4·50
466	100f. Giant spider conch	4·25	3·00

1962. Air. 1st Trans-Atlantic TV Satellite Link. As T 10 of French Polynesia.

467	20f. purple and green	45	90

1963. Red Cross Centenary. As T 13 of French Polynesia.

468	50f. red, grey and brown	3·25	7·75

57 Large Star Coral

1963. Corals. Multicoloured. (a) Postage. As T 57.

469	5f. Type **57**	1·40	4·25
470	6f. Organ-pipe coral	1·50	1·50

(b) Air. Horiz (48×27 mm).

471	40f. Stinging coral	1·80	1·70
472	55f. Brain coral	3·25	5·50
473	200f. Branched coral	6·50	16·00

1963. 15th Anniv of Declaration of Human Rights. As T 14 of French Polynesia.

474	70f. blue and brown	6·00	12·00

1964. "PHILATEC 1964" International Stamp Exhibition, Paris. As T 528 of France.

475	80f. brown, green & purple	4·25	22·00

58 Houri

1964. Local Dhows. Multicoloured. (a) Postage. As T 58.

476	15f. Type **58**	2·50	3·50
477	25f. Sambuk	2·75	3·25

(b) Air. Size 48×27 mm.

478	50f. Building sambuk	3·25	3·25
479	85f. Zaruk	2·75	8·75
480	300f. Ziema	14·50	16·00

59 Rameses II and Nefertari Temple, Philae

1964. Air. Nubian Monuments Preservation.

481	**59**	25f.+5f. brown, green and red	4·25	28·00

60 "The Discus Thrower" (Ancient Greece)

1964. Air. Olympic Games, Tokyo.

482	**60**	90f. purple, red & black	8·75	30·00

1965. Air. Centenary of I.T.U. As T 19 of French Polynesia.

483	95f. blue, brown & purple	12·00	32·00

61 Ghoubet Kharab

1965. Landscapes.

484	-	6f. brn, bl & grn (postage)	3·50	4·50
485	-	20f. green, blue & brown	2·20	2·50
486	-	45f. brn, bl & dp bl (air)	3·25	9·75
487	**61**	65f. brown, ochre & blue	3·75	6·75

VIEWS—26×22 mm: 6f. Dadwayya; 20f. Tajurah. As Type **61**: 45f. Lake Abbe.

62 "Life and Death"

1965. Anti-tuberculosis Campaign.

488	**62**	25f.+5f. brn, grn & turq	2·30	7·75

1966. Air. Launching of 1st French Satellite. As Nos. 1696/7 of France.

489	25f. brown, bistre and red	3·75	6·50
490	30f. brown, bistre and red	4·50	10·00

63 Senna

1966. Flowers.

491	**63**	5f. orange, green and brown (postage)	2·20	2·30
492	-	8f. orange, green & brown	3·50	5·00
493	-	25f. red, blue and green	2·30	3·75
494	-	55f. lake, green and myrtle (air)	3·75	8·00

FLOWERS—VERT: 8f. Poinciana; 25f. Aloes. HORIZ: (48½×27 mm); 55f. Stapelia.

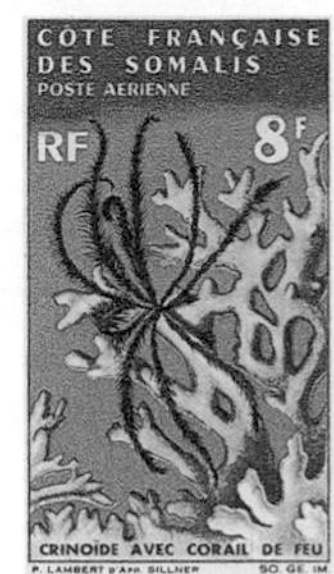

64 Feather Star and Flame Coral

1966. Air. Marine Life. Multicoloured.

495	8f. Type **64**	3·50	6·75
496	25f. Regal angelfish	3·75	6·00
497	40f. Yellow-banded angelfish	5·00	17·00
498	50f. Saddle anemonefish	6·50	22·00
499	70f. Spined squirrelfish	14·00	37·00
500	80f. Red Sea surgeonfish	10·00	40·00
501	100f. Lunulate lionfish	13·00	36·00

1966. Air. Launching of Satellite "D1". As T 569 of France.

502	48f. green, brown and blue	2·00	8·25

65 Grey Monitor

1967. Somali Fauna.

503	**65**	20f. purple, chest & brn	6·00	9·00

POSTAGE DUE STAMPS

D31 Somali Spears

1915

D278	**D31**	5c. blue	10	5·50
D279	**D31**	10c. red	10	5·50
D187	**D31**	15c. black	85	4·00
D281	**D31**	20c. violet	35	7·00
D282	**D31**	30c. yellow	65	5·75
D190	**D31**	50c. red	2·30	5·50
D283	**D31**	50c. brown	45	5·75
D284	**D31**	60c. green	55	8·50
D285	**D31**	1f. blue	65	11·50
D286	**D31**	2f. red	65	9·00
D287	**D31**	3f. sepia	1·00	8·50

1927. Surch in figures.

D231	2f. on 1f. red	4·25	26·00

D232		3f. on 1f. mve	3·50	17·00

1942. (a) Optd FRANCE LIBRE.

D343		5c. blue	90	9·75
D344		10c. red	90	9·75
D345		15c. black	90	9·75
D346		20c. violet	90	9·75
D347		30c. yellow	90	9·75
D348		50c. red	1·10	9·75
D349		60c. green	1·40	9·75
D350		1f. blue	3·75	25·00

(b) Optd France Libre.

D351		5c. blue	1·00	10·00
D352		10c. red	90	10·00
D353		15c. black	75	10·00
D354		20c. violet	45	10·00
D355		30c. yellow	45	10·00
D356		50c. brown	45	10·00
D357		60c. green	55	10·00
D358		1f. blue	90	10·00
D359		2f. red	2·50	10·00
D360		3f. sepia	1·80	10·00

D47

1947

D415	**D47**	10c. mauve	10	5·00
D416	**D47**	30c. brown	10	6·25
D417	**D47**	50c. green	10	6·75
D418	**D47**	1f. brown	10	7·00
D419	**D47**	2f. red	35	7·00
D420	**D47**	3f. brown	65	7·25
D421	**D47**	4f. blue	90	5·50
D422	**D47**	5f. red	1·00	7·50
D423	**D47**	10f. green	1·00	8·75
D424	**D47**	20f. blue	1·10	9·25

For later issues see **FRENCH TERRITORY OF THE AFARS AND THE ISSAS**.

Pt. 6

FRENCH SOUTHERN & ANTARCTIC TERRITORIES

Stamps issued for use in the French settlements in the southern Indian Ocean and in the Antarctic.

100 centimes = 1 franc.

1955. No. 324 of Madagascar optd TERRES AUSTRALES ET ANTARCTIQUES FRANCAISES.

1	**39**	15f. blue and green	30·00	70·00

2 Rockhopper Penguins

4 Emperor Penguins, Snowy Petrel and South Pole

1956

2	-	30c. brn, grn & bl (postage)	55	2·10
3	-	40c. blk, purple and blue	55	2·75
4	**2**	50c. blue, ochre & brown	50	3·75
5	**2**	1f. blue, orange and grey	1·40	4·50
6	-	2f. black, brown and blue	7·00	12·00
7	-	4f. brown, green and blue	20·00	55·00
8	-	5f. blue and light blue	4·25	13·50
9	-	8f. brown and grey	14·00	60·00
10	-	10f. blue	4·25	32·00
11	-	12f. black and blue	17·00	60·00
12	-	15f. purple and blue	7·00	34·00
13	-	20f. blue, yellow & lt blue	21·00	60·00
14	-	25f. black, brown & green	95·00	£130
15	-	85f. orange, blue and black	28·00	60·00
16	**4**	50f. green and olive (air)	46·00	65·00
17	**4**	100f. indigo and blue	50·00	70·00
18	-	200f. black, blue & purple	65·00	80·00

DESIGNS—VERT: As Type **2**: 30c. Light-mantled sooty albatross; 2f. Black-faced sheathbills; 12f. Kerguelen cormorants; 20f. Territorial arms; 85f. King penguin. HORIZ: (36×22 mm). 40c. Antarctic skuas; 4f. Leopard seal; 5f., 8f. Kerguelen fur seal and settlement; 10f., 15f. Southern elephant-seal; 25f. Kerguelen fur seal. As Type **4**: 200f. Wandering albatross.

See also Nos. 26/34.

5 Polar Camp and Meteorologist

1957. International Geophysical Year.

19	**5**	5f. black and violet	5·50	16·00
20	**5**	10f. red	7·25	18·00
21	**5**	15f. blue	7·75	25·00

1959. Tropical Flora. As T 56 of French Equatorial Africa.

22		10f. multicoloured	7·75	30·00

DESIGN—HORIZ: 10f. "Pringlea".

6 Yves-Joseph Kerguelen-Tremarec and "Dauphine"

1960. Kerguelen Archipelago Discovery Commem.

23	**6**	25f. brown, chestnut & blue	28·00	60·00

7 Jean Charcot, Compass and "Pourquoi Pas?"

1962. 25th Anniv of Disappearance of Jean Charcot.

24	**7**	25f. brown, red and green	18·00	55·00

1962. Air. 1st Trans-Atlantic T.V. Satellite Link. As T 10 of French Polynesia.

25		50f. green, olive and blue	17·00	60·00

1963. Designs as T 2 and 4.

26		5f. violet and blue (postage)	22·00	12·50
27		8f. indigo, purple and blue	12·00	41·00
28		10f. black, blue and brown	50·00	65·00
29		12f. green, blue and brn	15·00	39·00
30		15f. blue, black and brown	12·00	16·00
31		20f. grey, orange and green	£325	£275
32		45f. green, brown and blue	12·50	21·00
33		25f. purple, brown & bl (air)	19·00	16·00
34		50f. black, purple and blue	44·00	£110
35		5f. brown, black and blue	55·00	80·00

DESIGNS—HORIZ: As Type **2**: 5f. (No. 26) Blue whale; 5f. (No. 35) Crozet Archipelago; 8f. Southern elephant-seals in combat; 12f. Phylica (tree), New Amsterdam island; 15f. Killer whale, Crozet islands. As Type **4**: 50f. Adelie penguins. VERT: As Type **2**: 10f. Pintado petrel; 20f. Black-browed albatross; 45f. Kerguelen cabbage. As Type **4**: 25f. Ionospheric research pylon, Adelie Land.

9 Observation Station

1963. "International Year of the Quiet Sun".

36	**9**	20f. slate, brown and violet (postage)	55·00	70·00
37	-	100f. red, blue & black (air)	90·00	£110

DESIGN—VERT: (27×48 mm); 100f. Pylons and Adelie penguins.

10 Landfall of Dumont d'Urville

1965. Air. Discovery of Adelie Land, 1840.

38	**10**	50f. indigo and blue	90·00	£100

1965. Air. Centenary of I.T.U. As T 19 of French Polynesia.

39		30f. brown, mauve and blue	£140	£150

1966. Air. Launching of 1st French Satellite. As Nos. 1696/7 of France.

40		25f. blue, green and brown	8·75	32·00
41		30f. blue, green and brown	9·00	33·00

1966. Air. Launching of Satellite "D1". As T 569 of France.

42		50f. violet, purple & orange	33·00	15·00

11 Space Probe

1967. Launching of 1st Space Probe, Adelie Land.

43	**11**	20f. black, purple & blue	14·50	11·50

12 Dumont D'Urville, "L'Astrolabe" and "Zelee"

1968. Dumont D'Urville Commem.

44	**12**	30f. brown, dp blue & lt bl	£110	£120

13 Port-aux-Francais

1968. Air.

45	-	40f. slate and blue	44·00	60·00
46	**13**	50f. black, green & blue	£140	£110

DESIGN: 40f. Aerial View of St. Paul Island.

14 Kerguelen and Rocket

1968. Air. Launching of "Dragon" Space Rockets.

47	**14**	25f. brown, green & blue	22·00	8·00
48	-	30f. blue, brown & green	23·00	8·50

DESIGN: 30f. Adelie Land and rocket.

1968. 20th Anniv of W.H.O. As T 34 of French Polynesia.

49		30f. blue, yellow and red	50·00	29·00

1968. Human Rights Year. As T 36 of French Polynesia.

50		30f. red, blue and brown	44·00	26·00

15 Eiffel Tower and Badge of Paris, and Ship in Antarctica

1969. Air. 5th Antarctic Treaty Consultative Meeting, Paris.

51	**15**	50f. blue	30·00	60·00

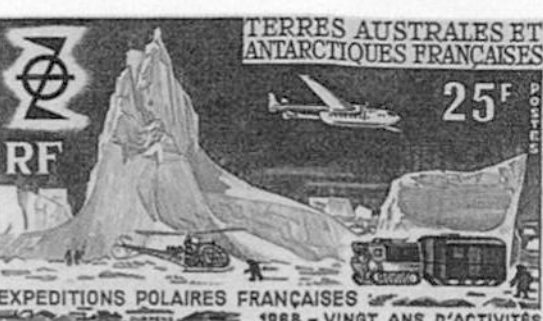

16 Antarctic Scene

1969. French Polar Exploration.

52	**16**	25f. blue, red & turquoise	23·00	50·00

1969. Air. 1st Flight of Concorde. As T 39 of French Polynesia.

53		85f. turquoise and blue	60·00	65·00

17 Possession Island, Crozet Archipelago

1969. Air.

54	**17**	50f. green, red and blue	14·00	7·75
55	-	100f. black, grey and blue	75·00	£100
56	-	200f. brown, green & blue	80·00	90·00
57	-	500f. blue	12·50	37·00

DESIGNS—HORIZ: 100f. Relief Map of Kerguelen. VERT: 200f. Cape Geology Archipelago map; 500f. Territorial arms.

1970. 50th Anniv of International Labour Organization. As T 44 of French Polynesia.

58		20f. purple, blue and red	13·00	14·00

18 Relief Map of New Amsterdam Island

1970. Air. 20th Anniv of Meteorological Station, New Amsterdam Island.

59	**18**	30f. brown	17·00	11·00

1970. New U.P.U. Headquarters Building, Berne. As T 47 of French Polynesia.

60		50f. brown, purple and blue	40·00	12·00

19 Long-nosed Icefish

1971. Fishes.

61	**19**	5f. blue, yellow and green	5·50	2·50
62	-	10f. brown, violet and blue	7·50	5·25
63	-	20f. green, orange & purple	7·75	3·50
64	-	22f. red, violet and brown	15·00	25·00
65	-	25f. blue, yellow and green	6·50	3·50
66	-	30f. grey, blue and brown	10·00	8·50
67	-	35f. multicoloured	10·50	8·75
68	-	135f. red, brown and blue	13·50	29·00

DESIGNS: 10f. Marbled rockcod; 20f. Antarctic rockcod; 22f. Hanson's rockcod; 25f. Orange-throated rockcod; 30f. Blue-gilled rockcod; 35f. Bemacchi's rockcod; 135f. Spiny pigfish.

20 Port-aux-Francais, 1950

1971. Air. 20th Anniv of Port-aux-Francais, Kerguelen.

69	**20**	40f. brown, green & blue	24·00	32·00
70	-	50f. green, blue & brown	25·00	33·00

DESIGN: 50f. Port-aux-Francais, 1970.

21 Treaty Emblem

1971. 10th Anniv of Antarctic Treaty.

71	**21**	75f. red	18·00	9·25

22 "Christiansenia dreuxi"

1972. Insects.

72	**22**	15f. brown, purple and red	7·25	3·50
73	-	22f. yellow, blue and green	8·25	12·00
74	-	25f. violet, purple & green	10·50	23·00
75	-	30f. multicoloured	12·50	14·50
76	-	40f. black, brown & choc	7·75	11·50
77	-	140f. brown, green & blue	8·00	34·00

DESIGNS: 22f. "Phtirocoris antarcticus"; 25f. "Microzetia mirabilis" (midge); 30f. "Antarctophytosus atriceps" (rove beetle); 40f. "Paractora dreuxi"; 140f. "Pringleophaga kerguelenensis" (scavenger moth).

23 Landing on Crozet Islands

1972. Air. Bicentenary of Discovery of Crozet Islands and Kerguelen.

78	**23**	100f. black	26·00	14·00
79	-	250f. black and brown	£110	95·00

DESIGN: 250f. Hoisting the flag on Kerguelen.

1972. 1st Death Anniv of General De Gaulle. As Nos. 1937 and 1940 of France.

80	50f. black and green	10·00	5·75
81	100f. black and green	12·00	6·50

24 "Gallieni"

1973. Air. Antarctic Voyages of the "Gallieni" (supply ship).

82	**24**	100f. black and blue	17·00	9·00

25 "Azorella selago"

1973. Plants.

83	**25**	61f. green, grey & brown	7·50	12·50
84	-	87f. green, blue and red	8·00	14·50

DESIGN: 87f. "Acaena ascendens".

26 "Mascarin", 1772

1973. Air. Antarctic Ships.

85	**26**	120f. brown	8·00	10·00
86	-	145f. blue	8·50	13·50
87	-	150f. blue	10·00	10·50
88	-	185f. brown	13·00	19·00

DESIGNS: 145f. "L'Astrolabe", 1840; 150f. "Le Roland", 1774; 185f. "Vitoria", 1522.

See also Nos. 93/4.

27 Part of Alfred Faure Base

1974. 10th Anniv of Alfred Faure Base, Crozet Archipelago.

89	**27**	75f. brown, blue & ultram	12·00	8·25
90	-	110f. brown, blue & ultram	16·00	10·50
91	-	150f. brown, blue & ultram	20·00	17·00

Nos. 89/91 were issued together se-tenant within the sheet, making a composite picture of the base.

28 Emperor Penguin, Globe and Letters

1974. Air. Centenary of Universal Postal Union.

92	**28**	150f. brown, black & blue	11·50	9·50

1974. Air. Charcot's Antarctic Voyages. As T 26.

93	100f. blue	5·50	12·00
94	200f. red	7·25	16·00

DESIGN: 100f. "Francais" (1903–05 voyage); 200f. "Pourquoi Pas?" (1908–10 voyage).

29 Mail Ship "Sapmer"

1974. 25th Anniv of Postal Service.

95	**29**	75f. black, blue & mauve	7·00	6·75

30 Rockets over Kerguelen Islands

1975. Air. "ARAKS" Franco-Soviet Magnetosphere Research Project.

96	**30**	45f. red, blue and lilac	6·00	6·00
97	-	90f. red, lilac and blue	9·00	9·00

DESIGN: 90f. Map of North Coast of U.S.S.R.

31 Antarctic Tern

32 "La Curieuse" (topsail schooner)

1976

98	**31**	40c. black, blue and orange (postage)	8·00	15·00
99	-	50c. brown, lt blue & blue	9·50	13·50
100	-	90c. brown and blue	11·00	18·00
101	-	1f. brown, blue & violet	14·00	33·00
102	-	1f.20 green, blue & brown	20·00	45·00
103	-	1f.40 blue, green & orange	22·00	20·00
104	**32**	1f.90 bl, ultram & brn (air)	8·00	12·00
105	-	2f.70 brown, bl & ultram	9·00	21·00
106	-	4f. blue and red	10·00	20·00

DESIGNS—As T **31**. HORIZ: 50c. Antarctic petrel; 90c. Kerguelen fur seal; 1f. Weddell seal. VERT: 1f.20, Kerguelen cormorant; 1f.40, Gentoo penguin. As T **32**: 2f.70, "Commandant Charcot" (ice patrol ship); 4f. "Marion Dufresne" (Antarctic supply ship).

33 Dumont d'Urville Base, 1956

1976. Air. 20th Anniv of Dumont d'Urville Base, Adelie Land.

107	**33**	1f.20 brown, orge & blue	10·00	9·00
108	-	4f. orange, blue & brown	16·00	11·50

DESIGNS: 4f. Dumont d'Urville Base, 1976.

34 Kerguelen Island

1976. Air. Bicent of Cook's Passage to Kerguelen.

109	**34**	3f.50 slate and blue	10·00	23·00

35 Captain Cook

1976. Cook Commemoration.

110	**35**	70c. blue, brown & yellow	11·00	17·00

36 First Ascent of Mt. Ross (5 Jan 1975)

1976. Ross Commemoration.

111	**36**	30c. red, brown and blue	6·00	6·50
112	-	3f. violet, brown and blue	7·00	7·25

DESIGN: 3f. Sir James Clark Ross.

37 Blue Whale

1977. Marine Mammals.

113	**37**	1f.10 deep blue & blue	11·00	20·00
114	-	1f.50 indigo, blue & brown	11·00	20·00

DESIGN: 1f.50, Commerson's dolphin.

38 Seaweed, "Macrocystis"

1977

115	**38**	40c. brown and bistre	3·50	6·50
116	-	70c. green, brown & black	3·00	7·25
117	-	1f. grey	2·75	4·50
118	-	1f.20 red, green and blue	4·50	6·00
119	-	1f.40 red, blue and grey	4·75	14·50

DESIGNS—HORIZ: 70c. Seaweed, "Durvillea"; 1f.20, "Magga Dan" (Antarctic supply ship); 1f.40, "Thala Dan" (Antarctic supply ship). VERT: 1f. Oceanology.

39 Kerguelen Satellite

1977. Air. Satellites.

120	**39**	2f.70 multicoloured	6·75	13·00
121	-	3f. blue and light blue	7·75	18·00

DESIGN: 3f. Adelie Land satellite.

See also No. 143.

40 Polar Explorer with Flags

1977. 30th Anniv of French Polar Expeditions.

122	**40**	1f.90 orange, red & blue	9·00	5·25

41 Atlantic Salmon and Breeding Tanks

1977. Antarctic Fauna.

123	**41**	50c. violet & blue (postage)	4·00	6·00
124	-	90c. brown, blue & green	4·00	8·25
125	-	10f. brown, blue & red (air)	17·00	50·00

DESIGNS—As T **41**: 90c. Head of light-mantled sooty albatross. 36×48 mm: 10f. Kerguelen fur seal and cub.

42 R. Rallier du Baty

1979. R. Rallier du Baty Commemoration.

126	**42**	1f.20 blue and bistre	3·75	6·25

43 Memorial and Names of French Navigators

1979. French Navigators' Memorial, Hobart.

127	**43**	1f. brown, turq & blue	3·25	5·75

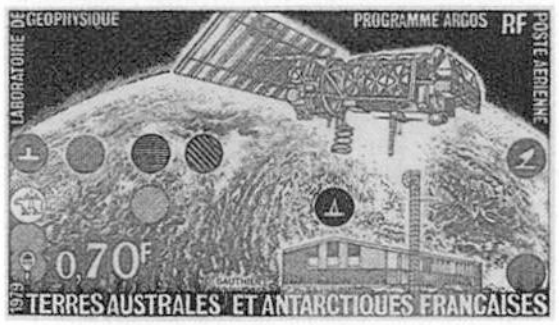

44 "Argos" Satellite and Geophysical Laboratory

1979. Air. Satellite Research.

128	**44**	70c. turquiose, vio & grn	3·50	6·00
129	-	1f.90 black, brown & mve	4·25	6·00

DESIGN: 1f.90, Satellite and Kerguelen Receiving Station.

45 Kerguelen Cormorant

1979. Antarctic Fauna.

130	**45**	1f.40 green, blue and sepia (postage)	3·00	8·25
131	-	4f. ultramarine, blue and green (air)	4·00	9·50
132	-	10f. brown, green & blk	7·00	26·00

DESIGNS—VERT: (36×48 mm): 4f. As No. 125, (27×48 mm): 10f. Southern elephant-seal.

See also Nos. 138/9.

46 Destroyer "Forbin"

1979. Ships.

133	**46**	40c. black, turquoise & grn	5·25	5·50
134	-	50c. black, turquoise & grn	5·25	5·50

DESIGN: 50c. Helicopter carrier "Jeanne d'Arc".

See also Nos. 136/7.

47 H.M.S. "Challenger" in the Antarctic (from engraving in "Illustrated London News")

1979. Air. Expedition of the "Challenger", 1872–6.

135	**47**	2f.70 black and blue	6·00	8·25

1980. Frigates. As T 46.

136	1f.10 blue, ultram & vio	1·70	5·25
137	1f.50 black, blue & dp bl	2·00	6·50

DESIGNS—VERT: 1f.10, "Doudart de Lagree". HORIZ: 1f.50, "Commandant Bourdais".

1980. Antarctic Fauna. As T 45.

138	70c. black, red and blue	2·00	7·50
139	1f. brown and blue	2·20	7·75

DESIGNS—VERT: 70c. Royal penguins. HORIZ: 1f. Head of soft-plumaged petrel.

50 Admiral d'Entrecasteaux

1980. Admiral d'Entrecasteaux Commemoration.

140	**50**	1f.20 black, violet & blue	2·00	2·50

51 El Cano

1980. Sebastian de El Cano (discoverer of Amsterdam Island) Commemoration.

141	**51**	1f.40 grey, orange & red	2·30	5·50
142	-	4f. multicoloured	3·00	7·75

DESIGN: 4f. El Cano's ship "Vitoria".

1980. Air. Kerguelen Satellite.

143	**39**	50c. grey, blue & brown	2·00	7·50

52 Lion Rock

1980. Air. Dumont d'Urville Base.

144	**52**	90c. multicoloured	1·00	2·75

53 "La Recherche" and "L'Esperance" (after Roux)

1980. Air. Arrival at Amsterdam Island of D'Entrecasteaux and De Kermadec Commemoration.

145	**53**	1f.90 blue	3·25	4·50

54 H.M.S. "Terror" (bomb ketch) at Arched Rock, Kerguelen (after Williams)

1980. Air.

146	**54**	2f.70 black, green & brn	2·75	9·00

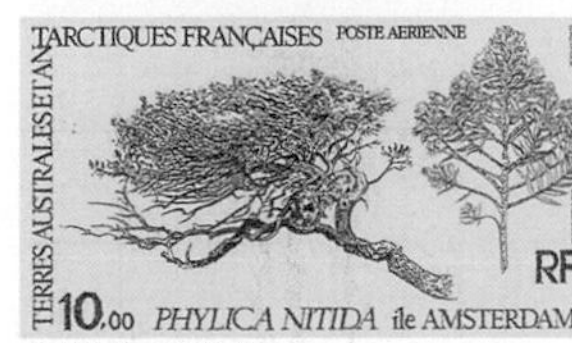

55 "Phylica nitida"

1980. Air.

147	**55**	10f. black, green & brown	3·00	25·00

56 Charles de Gaulle

1980. Air. 10th Death Anniv of Charles de Gaulle.

148	**56**	5f.40 purple, blue & red	8·75	50·00

57 Adelie Penguins

1981. Antarctic Fauna.

149	**57**	50c. lilac	3·00	5·25
150	-	60c. blue, green & turq	1·70	5·50
151	**57**	1f.20 black, blue & violet	3·00	3·75
152	-	1f.30 black, brown & blue	2·75	4·50
153	-	1f.80 brown, green & bis	2·75	4·50

DESIGNS—HORIZ: 1f.30; 1f.80, Leopard seal. (48×28 mm) 60c. Head of Adelie penguin.

58 "HB 40 Castor"

1981. Air. Antarctic Transport.

154	**58**	2f.40 blue, orange & violet	2·00	7·00

59 "Saint Marcouf"

1981. Air. Antarctic Supply Ships.

155	**59**	3f.50 grey, blue & red	1·90	5·75
156	-	7f.30 blue, turq & lilac	2·50	10·50

DESIGN: 7f.30, "Norsel".

60 Map of Antarctica

1981. 20th Anniv of Antarctic Treaty.

157	**60**	1f.80 blue, dp blue & brn	4·75	18·00

61 Sud Aviation SE 3130 Alouette II Helicopter

1981

158	**61**	55c. blue, turq & brown	2·00	6·25
159	**61**	65c. turquoise, green & bl	2·00	6·25

62 Compacted Ice, Dumont d'Urville

1981. Air.

160	**62**	1f.30 dp blue, blue & grey	1·80	6·25

63 Loranchet

1981. Jean Loranchet Commemoration.

161	**63**	1f.40 dp green, green & ol	1·20	6·25

64 Black-faced Sheathbill

1981. Air.

162	**64**	1f.50 black	2·75	7·00

65 "Adele Dumont d'Urville" (Michele Garreau)

1981. Air.

163	**65**	2f. brown and black	1·60	2·50

66 "Arcad III" Satellite over Antarctic

1981. Air.

164	**66**	3f.85 green, bl & dp bl	3·25	11·50

67 Charcot Station

1981. Air. 25th Anniv of Charcot Antarctic Station.

165	**67**	5f. red, blue and violet	3·00	10·50

68 "Antares" (dispatch vessel)

1981. Air.
166 **68** 8f.40 purple, grey & blue 3·00 11·50

69 Rockhopper, Gentoo and King Penguins

1982. Air. "Philexfrance 82" International Stamp Exhibition, Paris.
167 **69** 8f. brown, blue & black 7·25 21·00

70 "Commandant Charcot" (ice patrol ship)

1982. Air. Overseas Week.
168 **70** 5f. blue and green 5·00 11·50

71 Lighter "Le Gros Ventre"

1983
169 **71** 55c. dp brown, green & bl 2·50 6·25

72 Apostles Islands

1983. Air.
170 **72** 65c. dp blue, brown & bl 1·50 7·00

73 Church and Statue of Virgin and Child

1983. Church of Our Lady of the Winds, Kerguelen.
171 **73** 1f.40 blue, brown & green 1·20 3·75

74 Pintails

1983
172 **74** 1f.50 dp brown, brn & bl 1·20 7·00
173 **74** 1f.80 brown and green 1·20 7·00

75 Vivies

1983. Paul Martin de Vivies Commemoration.
174 **75** 1f.60 blue 1·10 5·50

76 Trawler "Austral"

1983
175 **76** 2f.30 brown, blue & pur 3·00 6·50

77 Dog Sledge

1983. Air.
176 **77** 4f.55 blue 6·25 11·50

78 "Sputnik I" Satellite

1983. Air. Anniversaries. Each black, blue and brown.
177 1f.50 Type **78** (25th anniv of International Geophysical Year) 60 3·50
178 3f.30 Orange Bay, Cape Horn (cent of first Polar Year) (49×36 mm) 1·00 3·75
179 5f.20 Scoresby Sound, Greenland (50th anniv of second Polar Year) (49×36 mm) 2·10 4·50

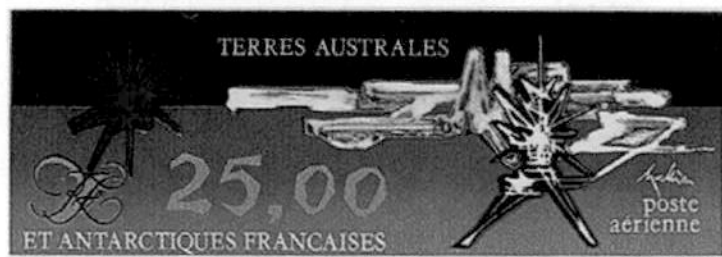

79 "Antarctica" (Georges Mathieu) (image scaled to 62% of original size)

1983. Air.
180 **79** 25f. blue, black and red 8·25 46·00

80 "Lady Franklin" (Antarctic supply ship)

1983
181 **80** 5f. blue, dp blue & black 5·75 18·00

81 Drilling for Samples

1984. Glaciology.
182 **81** 15c. brown, orange & bl 2·10 5·00
183 **81** 1f.70 blue, orange & red 2·50 4·50

82 Crabeater Seal

1984. Antarctic Wildlife.
184 **82** 60c. green, grey & brown 2·10 4·50
185 - 70c. blue, dp blue & brown 2·50 4·50
186 - 2f. green, blue and brown 3·00 5·25
187 **82** 5f.90 black, blue and red 4·25 7·00
DESIGNS: 70 c, 2f. Rockhopper penguins.

83 Faure

1984. Alfred Faure Commemoration.
188 **83** 1f.80 black, brown & red 1·60 3·50

84 H.M.S. "Erebus" (bomb ketch) in Antarctic (after Davis)

1984. Air.
189 **84** 2f.60 deep blue & blue 2·10 8·00

85 Balloons and Airships

1984. Air. Bicentenary of Manned Flight.
190 **85** 3f.50 red, brown & blue 2·75 8·00
191 - 7f.80 brown, blue & violet 3·75 11·50
DESIGN: 7f.80, Montgolfier balloon, Renard and Krebs' airship "La France", balloon "Zodiac" and other balloons and airships.

86 Polar Aurora

1984. Air.
192 **86** 3f.50 multicoloured 3·75 9·25

87 Port Jeanne d'Arc, Kerguelen, 1930

1984. Air.
193 **87** 4f.70 turquoise, bl & dp bl 2·50 14·00

88 "Albatros"

1984. Air. Commissioning of Patrol Boat "Albatros".
194 **88** 11f.30 dp blue, red & bl 4·25 18·00

89 Survey Barquentine "Gauss"

1984. Air. "Nordposta" International Stamp Exhibition, Hamburg.
195 **89** 9f. mauve and blue 7·25 21·00

90 Mouflons

1985. Antarctic Wildlife.
196 - 1f.70 black, brown and orange (postage) 4·25 6·50
197 - 2f.80 turquoise, blk & bl 4·00 5·00
198 **90** 70c. brown, bl & mve (air) 3·00 5·25
199 - 3f.90 brown, grey & orge 4·25 9·75
DESIGNS—HORIZ: 1f.70, Emperor penguins; 2f.80, Snow petrel. VERT: 3f.90, Amsterdam albatross.

91 Emblem, Humpback Whales, Krill and Research Vessel

1985. Biomass.
200 **91** 1f.80 dp blue, mve & bl 3·75 5·00
201 **91** 5f.20 blue, lt bl & red 4·25 5·25

92 Liotard

1985. Andre-Frank Liotard (explorer) Commem.
202 **92** 2f. purple and violet 1·80 3·50

93 Port Martin Base, Adelie Land

1985

203	**93**	2f.20 blue, brn & dp bl	2·50	2·30

94 "La Novara" (frigate) at Saint Paul (after J. Noel)

1985. Air.

204	**94**	12f.80 black and orange	7·25	11·50

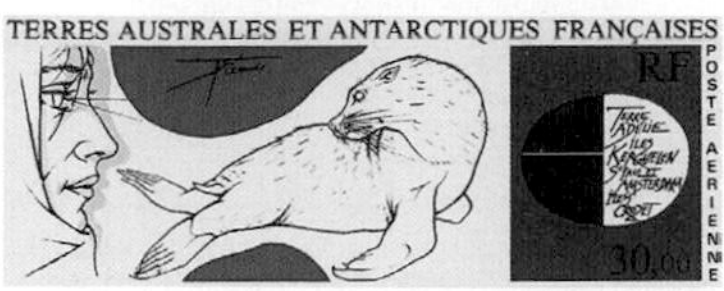

95 "Explorer and Fur Seal" (image scaled to 62% of original size)

1985. Air.

205	**95**	30f. multicoloured	10·50	28·00

96 Various Motifs, Rope and Kerguelen's Ships

1985. Air. 30th Anniv of French Southern and Antarctic Territories. Each blue, brown-olive and black.

206	2f. Type **96**	1·00	4·25
207	12f.80 Motifs, rope and ships (different)	3·00	6·50

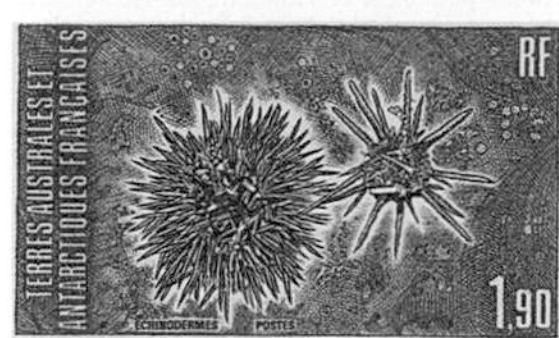

97 Southern Fulmars

1986. Birds.

208	**97**	1f. blue & black (postage)	2·30	2·75
209	-	1f.70 black, grn & brn	2·75	4·75
210	-	4f.60 brn, yell & red (air)	2·50	7·00

DESIGNS: 1f.70, Giant petrels; 4f.60. Southern black-backed gull.

98 Echinoderms

1986

211	**98**	1f.90 brown and blue	2·10	2·75

99 "Polarbjorn" (Antarctic supply ship)

1986. Ships.

212	-	2f.10 deep blue and blue	2·50	4·50
213	**99**	3f. red, light blue and blue	3·25	5·00

DESIGN: 2f.10, B.C.A. "Var A 608" (patrol boat).

100 Charcot and "Pourquoi Pas?" leaving Harbour

1986. Air. 50th Death Anniv of Jean Charcot (explorer). Each brown, blue and red.

214	2f.10 Type **100**	1·60	3·50
215	14f. Charcot and "Pourquoi Pas?" in heavy seas	5·25	18·00

101 "Cotula plumosa"

1986. Plants.

216	**101**	2f.30 green, yell & blk	1·60	5·00
217	-	6f.20 green and red	3·00	5·75

DESIGN: 6f.20, "Lycopodium saururus".

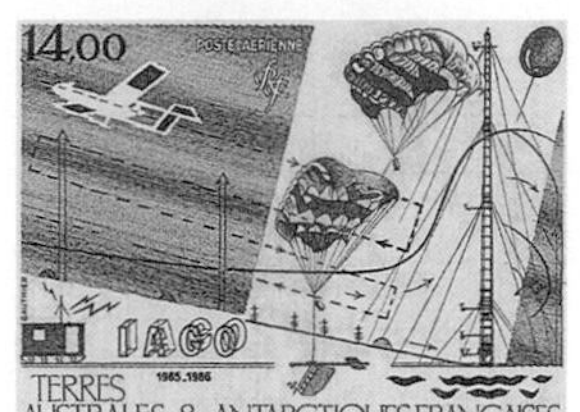

102 IAI Aravo, Parachutes and Aerial

1986. Scientific Research.

218	**102**	14f. red, black & orange	5·25	21·00

103 Satellite over Antarctic

1986. Air. "SPOT" Surveillance Satellite.

219	**103**	8f. brown, green & blue	3·00	14·00

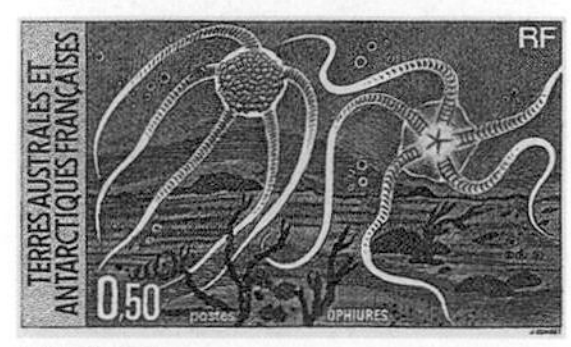

104 Starfish

1987

220	**104**	50c. blue, orange & green	2·50	3·50

105 "Poa cookii"

1987. Plants.

221	**105**	1f.80 green and blue	1·20	4·50
222	-	6f.50 green, red and blue	3·00	7·25

DESIGN: 6f.50, Lichen.

106 Marret Base, Adéelie Land

1987

223	**106**	2f. brown, blue & purple	3·75	5·00

107 Admiral Mouchez

1987

224	**107**	2f.20 blue, black & brown	2·50	5·25

108 Reindeer

1987. Antarctic Wildlife.

225	**108**	2f.50 black	4·25	5·00
226	-	4f.80 multicoloured	6·25	7·25

DESIGN: 4f.80, Macaroni penguins.

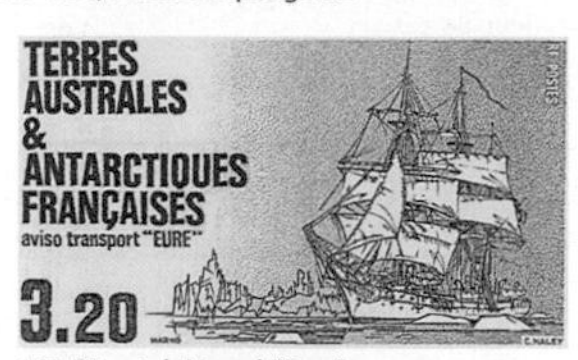

109 Dispatch Vessel "Eure"

1987

227	**109**	3f.20 turquoise, bl & grn	3·75	5·75

110 "J. B. Charcot" (schooner)

1987. Air.

228	**110**	14f.60 purple, bl & brn	5·75	16·00

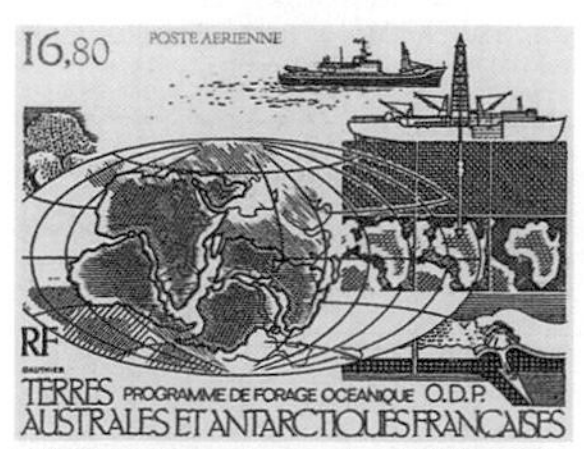

111 Globe, Research Vessel and Drilling Ship

1987. Air. Scientific Research.

229	**111**	16f.80 dp blue, bl & brn	4·25	18·00

112 "Inmarsat" Satellite

1987. Air.

230	**112**	16f.80 brown and black	6·25	23·00

113 Darrieus Wind Generator

1988

231	**113**	1f. blue, indigo & lt bl	2·10	4·50

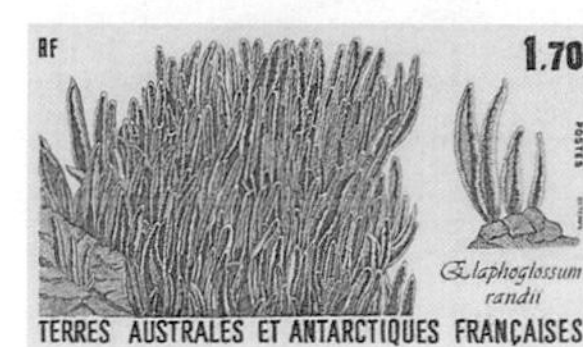

114 Elephant Grass

1988

232	**114**	1f.70 green, bis & dp grn	2·10	4·50

115 Globe and Father Lejay

1988

233	**115**	2f.20 black and violet	2·10	4·75

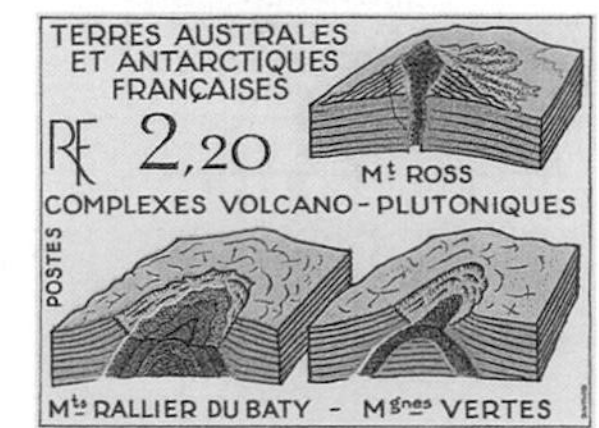

116 Geological Sections of Volcanoes

1988. Antarctic Geology. Multicoloured.

234	2f.20 Type **116**	1·60	3·50
235	15f.10 Geological map of Kerguelen Islands	5·25	16·00

117 Gessain

1988. 2nd Death Anniv of Robert Gessain (explorer).

236	**117**	3f.40 red, grey and green	2·10	4·25

118 "Le Gros Ventre" (frigate)

1988. Ships.

237	**118**	3f.50 brown, grn & bl	2·10	4·50
238	-	4f.90 blue and black	3·75	5·75
239	-	5f. blue and black	3·00	5·75

DESIGNS—HORIZ: 4f.90, Mermaid with anvil and "Jules Verne" (Antarctic supply ship). VERT: 5f. "La Fortune" (sail warship).

119 Penguin Island

1988. Air. Penguin Island.

240	**119**	3f.90 brown and blue	2·50	5·75
241	-	15f.10 blue, brown & grn	6·00	11·50

DESIGN: 15f.10, Views of island from sea and air.

120 Wilson's Storm Petrels

1988

242	**120**	6f.80 blue, black & brn	4·25	8·00

121 Igloos

1988. Air. 40th Anniv of French Polar Expeditions.

243	**121**	20f. green, purple and red	7·75	21·00

122 Crab

1989. Flora and Fauna.

244	**122**	1f.10 lt brown, bl & brn	2·10	3·50
245	-	2f. black, brn & grn	2·50	4·50
246	-	2f.80 green, red & brn	2·75	4·75
247	-	3f.60 blue, dp bl & blk	3·25	5·00

DESIGNS: 2f. Kerguelen sheep; 2f.80, "Blechnum penna marina"; 3f.60, Blue petrel.

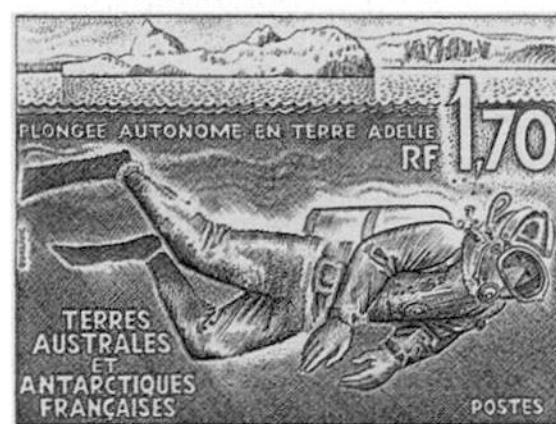

123 Diver

1989. Diving off Adelie Land.

248	**123**	1f.70 brown, green & bl	2·10	4·50

124 Henry and Rene Bossiere

1989. Kerguelen Islands Pioneers.

249	**124**	2f.20 brown, green & bl	2·10	4·50

125 "La Curieuse" (topsail schooner), 1913

1989. Air. Ships. Each blue, black and red.

250	2f.20 Type **125**	1·60	4·50
251	15f.50 "La Curieuse" (supply ship), 1989	4·75	10·50

126 Mesotype

1989. Crystals.

252	**126**	5f.10 turquoise, blk & bl	2·50	4·75
253	-	7f.30 mauve, grn & grey	3·25	5·75

DESIGN: 7f.30, Analcime.

127 Map

1989. Air. Apostles Islands.

254	**127**	8f.40 blue, grey & green	4·75	5·25

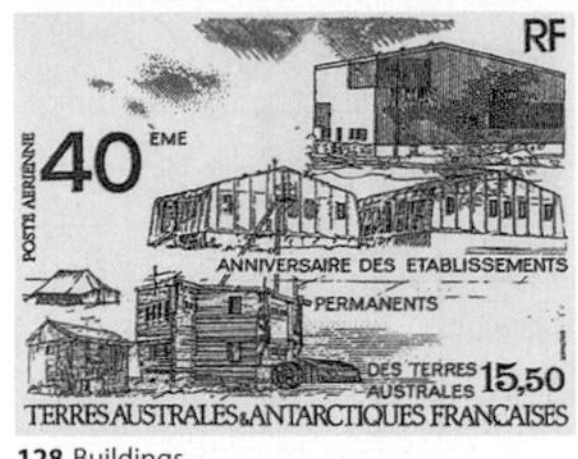

128 Buildings

1989. Air. 40th Anniv of Establishment of Permanent Antarctic Bases.

255	**128**	15f.50 brown	5·75	13·00

129 Allegory

1989. Air. Bicentenary of French Revolution.

256	**129**	5f. blue, green & mauve	7·25	7·50

MS257	150×120 mm. **129** 5f. ×4 blue, red and light blue	12·50	33·00

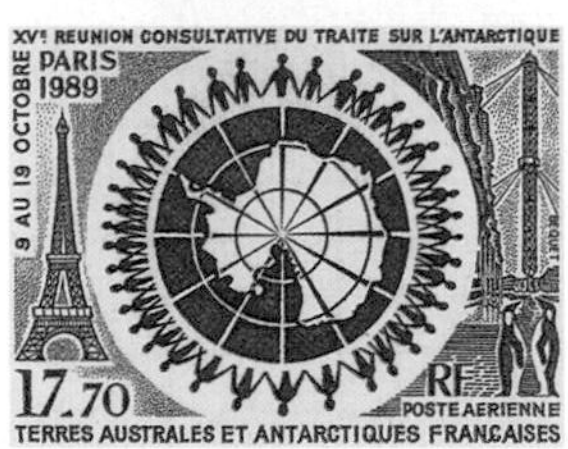

130 Figures around Map

1989. Air. 15th Antarctic Treaty Consultative Meeting, Paris.

258	**130**	17f.70 red, purple & blue	8·25	17·00

131 "Chonotriches", "Copepodes" and Map of Kerguelen

1990. Protistology.

259	**131**	1f.10 blue, brown & black	1·60	4·25

132 Cattle

1990. Restoration of Amsterdam Island.

260	**132**	1f.70 brown, green & blue	1·80	4·50

133 Quoy and Decollate Planaxis (shell)

1990. Birth Bicentenary of Jean Rene C. Quoy (doctor and naturalist).

261	**133**	2f.20 blue, dp brn & brn	2·40	5·00

134 Yellow-nosed Albatrosses

1990

262	**134**	2f.80 multicoloured	2·50	5·25

135 Dumont d'Urville

1990. Birth Bicentenary of Jules Dumont d'Urville (explorer).

263	**135**	3f.60 brown and blue	2·75	5·75

136 Aragonite

1990. Minerals.

264	**136**	5f.10 brown and blue	3·00	5·00

137 Pigs Island

1990. Air.

265	**137**	7f.30 green, brown & blue	3·50	6·50

138 "Ranunculus pseudo trullifolius"

1990

266	**138**	8f.40 green, blue & orge	4·25	7·50

139 "L'Astrolabe"

1990. Air. 150th Anniv of Discovery of Adelie Land by Dumont d'Urville.

267	**139**	15f.50 brown and red	6·25	11·50

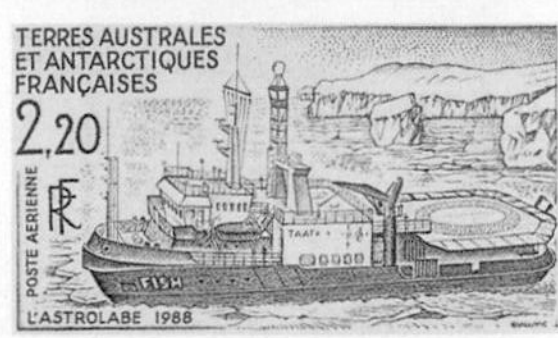

140 "L'Astrolabe" (fishery control vessel), 1988

1990. Air. Ships. Each blue, green and red.

268	2f.20 Type **140**	2·10	3·25
269	15f.50 "L'Astrolabe" (Dumont d'Urville's ship), 1840	8·25	13·00

141 Bird (image scaled to 62% of original size)

1990. Air.

270	**141**	30f. multicoloured	14·50	17·00

142 Map, Emperor Penguin and Envelopes

1991. 30th Anniv of Postal Service to Crozet.

271	**142**	50c. blue, ultram & blk	2·50	3·25

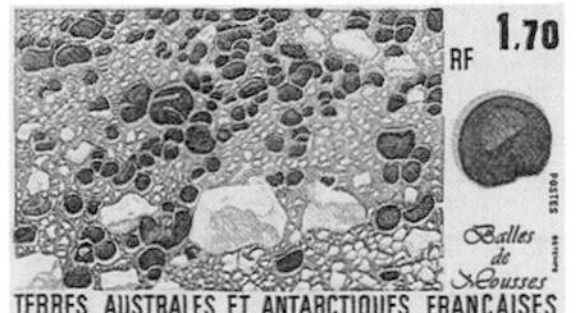

143 Moss Balls in Shingle

1991

272	**143**	1f.70 grey, brown & blk	3·00	4·25

144 Wandering Albatrosses and "Argos" Satellite

1991. Air.

273	**144**	2f.10 brown, blue & red	2·75	3·75

145 Douguet and Flag

1991. Admiral Max Douguet Commemoration.

274	**145**	2f.30 blue, black & orge	2·40	3·25

146 "L'Aventure" (landing craft)

1991

275	**146**	3f.20 brown, blue & grn	3·00	5·00

147 Fur Seals

1991

276	**147**	3f.60 brown and blue	3·25	4·25

148 Infra-red Image and Measuring Equipment (study of ozone layer)

1991. Air. Climatic Research. Each green, violet and orange.

277		3f.60 Type **148**	3·00	4·00
278		20f. Research vessel and rock samples (palaeoclimatology)	10·50	15·00

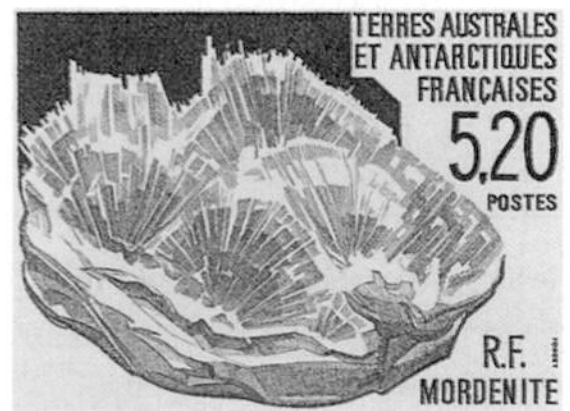

149 Mordenite

1991

279	**149**	5f.20 blue, green & black	3·75	4·25

150 Mackerel Icefish

1991

280	**150**	7f.80 green and blue	5·25	6·50

151 Map

1991. 30th Anniv of Antarctic Treaty.

281	**151**	9f.30 grn, dp grn & red	3·25	5·00

152 De Gaulle and Map

1991. Air. Birth Centenary of Charles de Gaulle (French statesman).

282	**152**	18f.80 black, blue & red	10·50	12·50

153 Research Worker greeting Penguin (Antarctic)

1991. Air. French Institute for Polar Research and Technology. Multicoloured.

283		15f. Type **153**	10·00	13·00
284		15f. Research worker greeting polar bear (Arctic)	10·00	13·00

Nos. 283/4 were printed together, se-tenant, forming a composite design.

154 Arms

1992

285	**154**	10c. black	55	1·70
286	**154**	20c. blue	70	1·70
287	**154**	30c. red	90	1·70
288	**154**	40c. green	1·60	1·70
289	**154**	50c. orange	1·70	2·00

155 "Colobanthus kerguelensis"

1992

295	**155**	1f. brown, green & blue	1·80	2·50

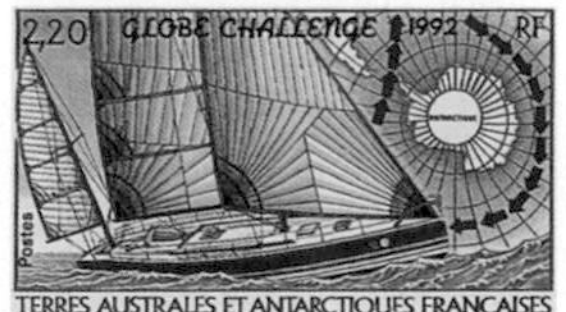

156 "Groupe Safap-Helvim" (yacht) and Antarctic Route

1992. "Globe Challenge" Round the World Sailing Race.

296	**156**	2f.20 multicoloured	3·00	4·50

157 Blenny Rockcod

1992

297	**157**	2f.30 green, blue & brn	3·25	3·25

158 Paul Tchernia (scientist)

1992

298	**158**	2f.50 grn, brn & dp brn	2·75	3·25

159 Pintado Petrels

1992. Air.

299	**159**	3f.40 brown, blk & grn	4·50	5·00

160 Marion-Dufresne (after Meryon)

1992. 220th Death Anniv of Marion-Dufresne (explorer).

300	**160**	3f.70 black, red & blue	4·00	3·25

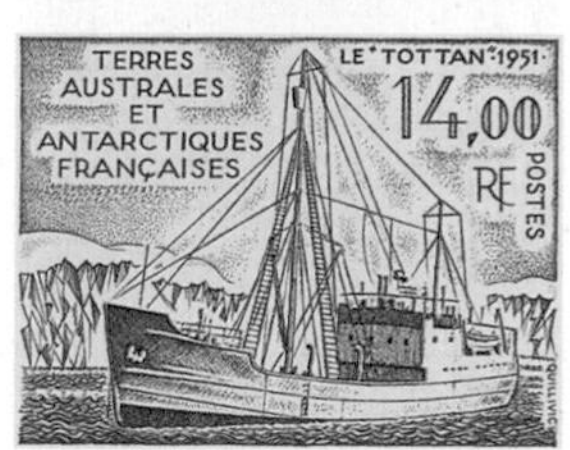

161 "Tottan" (supply ship)

1992

301	**161**	14f. brown, turq & blue	9·25	13·00

162 Columbus's Fleet, Montgolfier Balloon and Columbus

1992. Air. 500th Anniv of Discovery of America by Columbus.

302	**162**	22f. brown, pur & dp brn	16·00	23·00

163 Satellite in Orbit

1992. Air. "Topex Poseidon" Satellite.

303	**163**	24f.50 red, black & blue	16·00	13·00

164 Ocean Currents, Research Vessel and Pipes

1992. WOCE Research Programme.

304	**164**	25f.40 brown, orge & bl	17·00	26·00

165 Adelie and Emperor Penguins on Landing Strip (image scaled to 62% of original size)

1992. Air. Completion of Landing Strip at Dumont D'Urville Research Station, Adelie Land.

305	**165**	25f.70 multicoloured	18·00	18·00

166 Violet-tinted Garnet

1993

306	**166**	1f. purple, green & black	1·20	1·80

167 Radio Equipment, Handshake and Globe

1993. Air. Amateur Radio Enthusiasts.

307	**167**	2f. black, red & mauve	1·80	2·75

168 "Marion Dufresne"

1993. 20th Anniv of the "Marion Dufresne" (Antarctic supply ship).

308	**168**	2f.20 mauve, black & bl	2·00	3·25

169 "Lyallia kerguelensis"

1993

309	**169**	2f.30 blue, green & yell	1·80	3·25

170 Killer Whale

1993

310	**170**	2f.50 black and purple	2·40	3·25

171 Antarctic Skuas

1993
311 **171** 2f.50 black 2·40 3·25

172 Andre Prud'homme (meteorologist)

1993. 43rd Anniv of Meteo France (weather service) in the Antarctic. Each black, blue and red.
312 2f.50 Type **172** 2·40 3·25
313 22f. Meteorologists recording wind speed on Adelie Land (35×37 mm) 12·00 13·00

173 Red-banded Snipefish

1993
314 **173** 3f.40 red, brown & blue 3·50 3·75

174 "Italo Marsano"

1993. 43rd Anniv of Chartering of the "Italo Marsano" (freighter).
315 **174** 3f.70 purple, brown & bl 3·00 3·25

175 King Penguins on Television and Platform

1993. ECOPHY Research Programme.
316 **175** 14f. brown, blue & black 7·25 5·00

176 "L'Astrolabe" and Route Map

1993. Voyage of "L'Astrolabe" (fishery control ship) through North-East Passage.
317 **176** 22f. red and blue 10·00 8·25

177 Scientists examining Arctic Tern and using Microscope

1993. Air. Animal Biology Laboratory, Adelie Land.
318 **177** 25f.40 brn, grn & dp grn 11·00 8·50

178 Camp, Snow Vehicles and Map

1993. Air. Antarctic Expedition Base D 10.
319 **178** 25f.70 brown, red & blue 11·50 8·50

179 Lockheed C-130 Hercules over Adelie Land

1993. Air. Inauguration of Air Strip, Adelie Land.
320 **179** 30f. black, blue & green 16·00 9·00

180 Cordierite

1994
321 **180** 1f. blue, green & black 2·75 2·30

181 Domestic Cat

1994
322 **181** 2f. black, green & emer 3·00 3·00

182 Lowering Probe into Sea

1994. 1000th Sea-bed Sample.
323 **182** 2f.40 black and blue 3·50 3·00

183 Pommier and Dog

1994. 75th Birth Anniv of Robert Pommier (explorer).
324 **183** 2f.80 blue, pur & orge 3·75 3·00

184 Salvin's Prion

1994
325 **184** 2f.80 blue 3·75 3·00

185 C. A. Vincendon Dumoulin (hydrographic engineer)

1994. Navy Hydrographic and Oceanographic Service. Each black and blue.
326 2f.80 Type **185** 3·75 3·00
327 23f. Measuring magnetic force (35×36 mm) 13·00 12·50

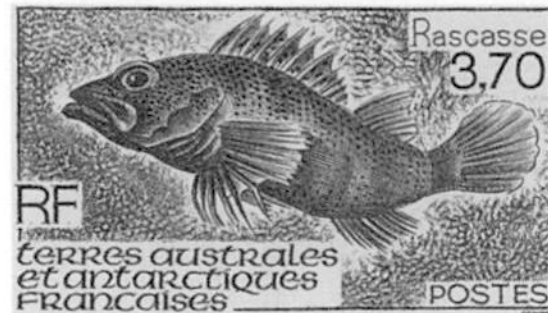

186 Rascasse Scorpionfish

1994
328 **186** 3f.70 orange and green 3·25 3·50

187 "Kerguelen de Tremarec" (trawler)

1994
329 **187** 4f.30 lilac, red & green 3·50 4·00

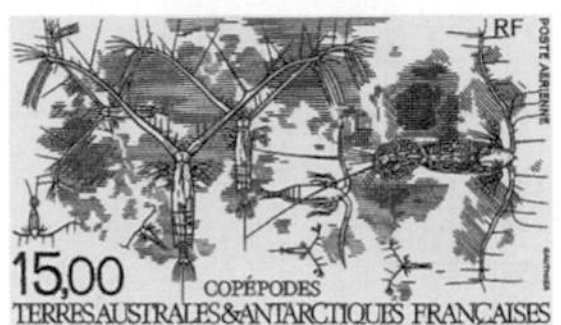

188 "Copepoda"

1994. Air.
330 **188** 15f. black 9·50 7·25

189 Trawler and Chart of Fishing Sectors around Kerguelen Islands

1994. Air. Scientific Management of Fishing Industry.
331 **189** 23f. purple, blue & red 14·50 12·50

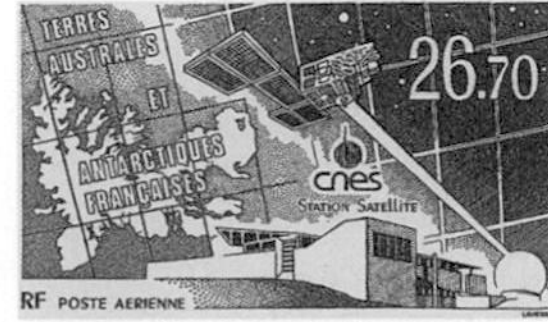

190 Map of Antarctic, Satellite and Earth Station

1994. Air. National Centre for Space Study Satellite Station, Kerguelen.
332 **190** 26f.70 lilac, bl & ultram 16·00 13·50

191 Lidar Station and Map

1994. Air. Lidar Research Station, Adelie Land.
333 **191** 27f.30 blue, green & mve 17·00 14·50

192 Penguins (image scaled to 64% of original size)

1994. Air. Migration of Emperor Penguins.
334 **192** 28f. black and blue 20·00 16·00

193 Olivine

1995
335 **193** 1f. olive, green and lilac 3·50 2·75

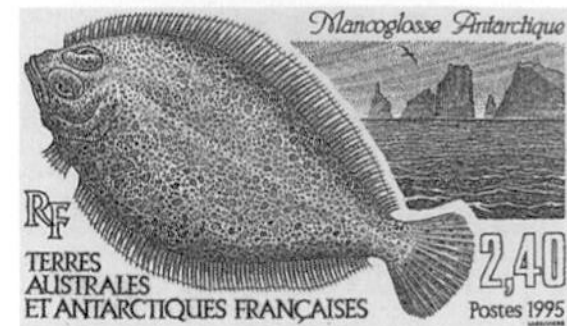

194 Southern Flounder

1995
336 **194** 2f.40 brown, blue & mve 3·75 3·00

195 Andree and Edgar Aubert de la Rue (naturalists)

1995
337 **195** 2f.80 brown, blue & mve 4·00 3·00

196 SODAR Station (wind study centre)

1995
338 **196** 2f.80 mauve, red & violet 4·00 3·00

197 Mont d'Alsace, Kerguelen

1995
339 **197** 3f.70 brown, violet & bl 4·50 3·25

198 "Antarctica" (research vessel)

1995. Air. Mt. Erebus Expedition.
340 **198** 4f.30 blue, green & mve 4·75 3·50

199 Waving Farewell

1995. Air. Departure of Winter Residents from Charcot Station.
341 **199** 15f. multicoloured 8·50 7·25

200 Minke Whale

1995
342 **200** 23f. dp blue, blue & pur 17·00 10·50

201 "Tamaris" and Tagged Grey-headed Albatross

1995. Voyage of "Tamaris" (full-rigged ship).
343 **201** 25f.80 brn, turq & bl 18·00 13·50

202 "Heroine" (full-rigged ship)

1995. Expedition of "Heroine" to Crozet Islands in 1837.
344 **202** 27f.30 blue 18·00 14·00

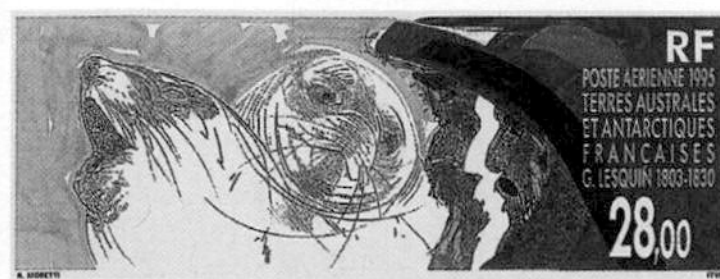

203 Seals (image scaled to 62% of original size)

1995. 165th Death Anniv of G. Lesquin.
345 **203** 28f. multicoloured 19·00 14·50

1995. 40th Anniv of French Southern and Antarctic Territories. Sheet 143×84 mm, containing reproductions of 1956 issue. Multicoloured. Imperf.
MS346 50c. Type **2**; 8f. Kerguelen fur seal and settlement; 10f. Southern Elephant seal 22·00 22·00

204 Amazonite

1996
347 **204** 1f. blue, green and black 3·25 2·75

205 White-chinned Petrel

1996
348 **205** 2f.40 blue 3·50 3·25

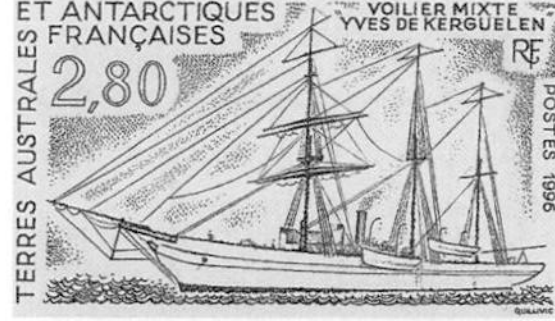

206 "Yves de Kerguelen" (expedition ship)

1996
349 **206** 2f.80 brown, blue & pur 3·75 3·50

207 Station

1996. Benedict Point Scientific Research Station, Amsterdam Island.
350 **207** 2f.80 brn, dp grn & grn 3·75 3·50

208 Victor crossing Greenland, 1936

1996. Paul-Emile Victor Commemoration. Each black, blue and red.
351 2f.80 Type **208** 3·75 3·50
352 23f. Victor, emperor penguins and Dumont d'Urville Base, Terre Adelie 16·00 16·00

209 Jacquinot

1996. Birth Bicentenary of Admiral Jacquinot.
353 **209** 3f.70 ultramarine & blue 3·50 3·25

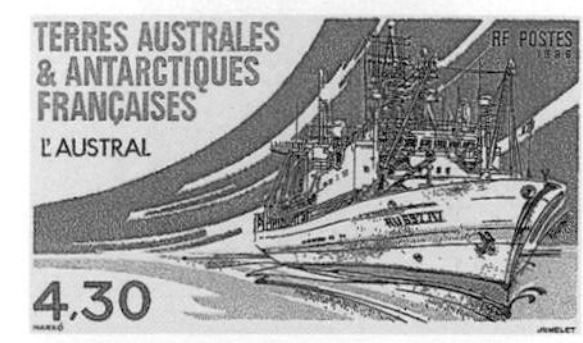

210 "Austral" (trawler)

1996
354 **210** 4f.30 black, blue & grn 3·75 3·50

211 "Lycopodium magellanicum"

1996
355 **211** 7f.70 green and purple 6·25 4·00

212 Drilling and Micrometeorite

1996. Micrometeorites of Cape Prudhomme.
356 **212** 15f. black, violet & blue 12·50 9·00

213 East Island

1996. Air.
357 **213** 20f. brown, blue & lt brn 15·00 11·00

214 Tractor and Camp

1996. Air. Raid Dome/C.
358 **214** 23f. blue 16·00 13·00

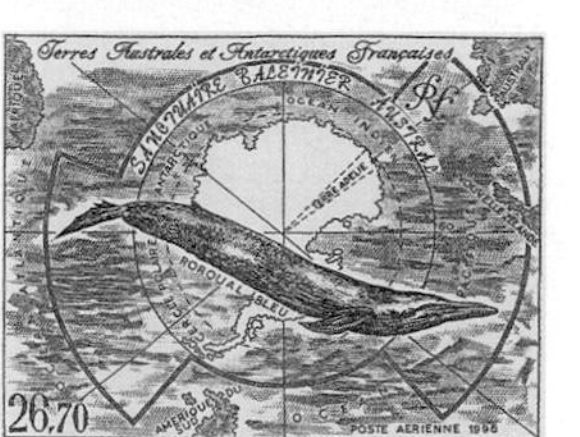

215 Blue Rorqual and Map of Sanctuary Area

1996. Air. Southern Whale Sanctuary.
359 **215** 26f.70 purple, bl & orge 18·00 13·50

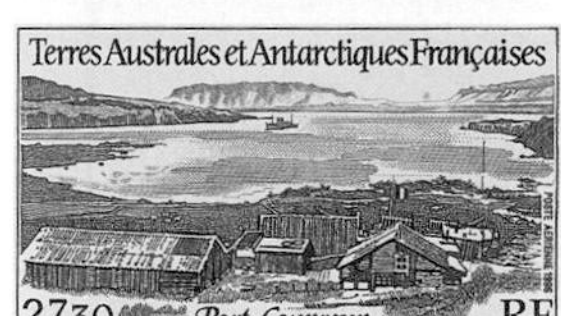

216 Port-Couvreux

1996. Air.
360 **216** 27f.30 blue, green & brn 18·00 13·50

217 Amethyst

1997
361 **217** 1f. mauve, grey & blue 3·25 2·75

218 Grey-backed Stormy Petrels

1997
362 **218** 2f.70 grey, blue & green 3·75 3·25

219 Ships (image scaled to 47% of original size)

1997. Refit of "Marion Dufresne" (Antarctic supply ship).
363 **219** 3f. multicoloured 4·00 3·50

220 Garcia

1997. 2nd Death Anniv of Rene Garcia (explorer).
364 **220** 3f. black, blue & brown 4·00 3·50

221 Turquet

1997. 130th Birth Anniv of Jean Turquet.
365 **221** 4f. brown and black 4·25 3·75

222 Spiny Lobster

1997. Air.
366 **222** 5f.20 multicoloured 4·75 4·00

223 Antarctic Terns, Bell Tower and Church

1997. Church of Our Lady of the Birds, Crozet.
367 **223** 5f.20 brown, blue & red 4·75 4·00

224 Service Emblem and Operation

1997. Forces Health Service.
368 **224** 8f. red, brown & purple 6·50 4·75

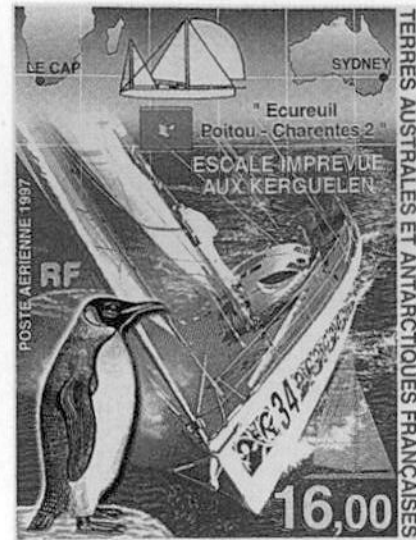

225 Map, "Ecureuil Poitou-Charantes 2" and King Penguin

1997. Air. Unscheduled Stop at Kerguelen by Contestant in BOC Challenge Yacht Race.

369	**225**	16f. multicoloured	11·50	8·00

226 Nunn at Hope Cottage, Point Charlotte

1997. Air. John Nunn (shipwreck survivor).

370	**226**	20f. red, purple & brown	12·50	9·00

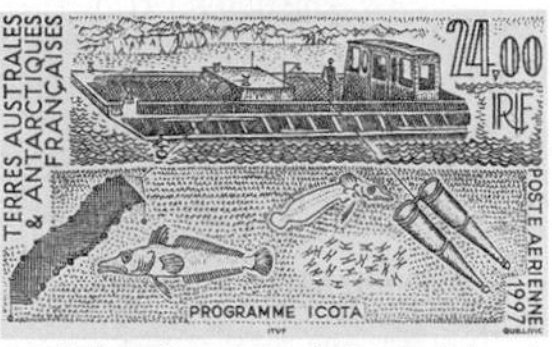

227 Lighter, Nets, Antarctic Dragonfish and Crocodile Icefish

1997. Air. Icota Programme (fish research project).

371	**227**	24f. green, blue and red	15·00	13·50

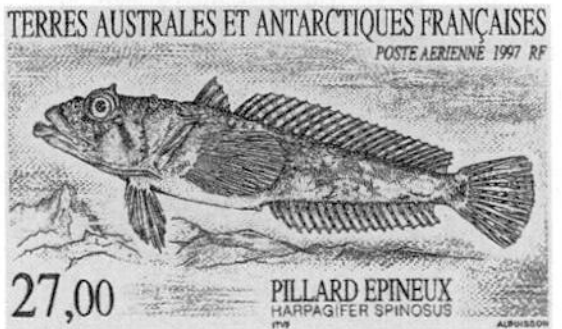

228 Spiny Plunderfish

1997. Air.

372	**228**	27f. black, purple & blue	16·00	15·00

229 "Poa kerguelensis"

1997

373	**229**	29f.20 brown, grn & mve	17·00	16·00

230 Snow Tractors, Greenland

1997. 50th Anniv of First French Polar Expedition. Multicoloured.

374		1f. Type **230**	1·50	1·70
375		1f. Port Martin and Marret Bases, Adelie Land	1·50	1·70
376		1f. Dumont d'Urville Base in 1956 and 1997 and Charcot Station	1·50	1·70

Nos. 374/6 were issued together, se-tenant, forming a composite design.

231 Kerguelen-Tremarec

1997. Bicentenary of Disappearance of Admiral Yves Kerguelen-Tremarec (discoverer of Kerguelen Land). Each black, green and red.

377		3f. Type **231**	3·00	3·00
378		24f. Christmas Harbour (from "Atlas of Cook's Voyages") (37×38 mm)	14·00	12·00

232 Rock-crystal

1998

379	**232**	1f. blue, violet & black	3·50	2·75

233 Launch approaching Trawlers

1998. Fisheries Control.

380	**233**	2f.60 blue, black & brn	2·75	2·30
381	-	2f.60 blue, black & red	2·75	2·30

DESIGN: No. 381, Inspectors measuring fish and checking records.

234 Grey-headed Albatrosses

1998

382	**234**	2f.70 multicoloured	3·75	2·75

235 Broad-billed Prion and Helicopter over Saint Paul Island

1998. Ecological Rehabilitation of Saint Paul Island (rat and rabbit eradication).

383	**235**	3f. blue, green & brown	4·25	3·25

236 Peau

1998. Etienne Peau (Antarctic researcher) Commemoration.

384	**236**	3f. blue, mauve & black	4·25	3·25

237 Laclavere

1998. 4th Death Anniv of Georges Laclavere (geographer and head of French National Antarctic Research Committee).

385	**237**	4f. brown, orange & blk	4·25	3·50

238 Preparation for Deep Boring and Map

1998. Air. Epica Dome C Programme.

386	**238**	5f.20 brown and mauve	5·00	4·00

239 Station Buildings

1998. Air. 1st Meteorological Radio Station, Port-aux-Francais.

387	**239**	8f. black, blue and red	6·00	6·00

240 "Argos" Satellite and King Penguins with Radio Transmitters

1998. Air. Penguin Research.

388	**240**	16f. multicoloured	11·50	8·50

241 "Ranunculus moseleyi"

1998

389	**241**	24f. green, lt green & yell	15·00	12·50

242 Porbeagle Shark pursuing Fish

1998

390	**242**	27f. grey, blue and green	17·00	14·50

243 "Le Cancalais" (schooner)

1998

391	**243**	29f.20 sepia, blue & brn	22·00	16·00

244 Antarctic Base (image scaled to 50% of original size)

1998. 40th Anniv of International Geophysical Year.

392	**244**	5f.20 blue, red and black	4·75	3·50

245 Epidote

1999

393	**245**	1f. emerald, green & blk	2·50	2·75

246 Bearded Penguins

1999

394	**246**	2f.70 indigo, blue & brn	3·25	3·00

247 King Penguins (image scaled to 62% of original size)

1999. Crozet Penguin Colony.

395	**247**	3f. multicoloured	4·00	3·25

248 Sicaud

1999. Death Commemoration (1998) of Pierre Sicaud (scientist).

396	**248**	3f. green and black	4·00	3·25

249 Martin

1999. 50th Death Anniv of Jacques-Andre Martin (scientist).

397	**249**	4f. ultramarine, blk & bl	4·50	3·50

250 Ray

1999

398	**250**	5f.20 brown, blue & pur	5·00	3·75

251 "Floreal" (frigate)

1999

399	**251**	5f.20 multicoloured	5·00	3·75

252 Cats, Scientists and Map

1999. Cat Research Programme, Kerguelen Islands.

400	**252**	8f. green, blue and red	6·50	4·25

253 Amsterdam Island Albatrosses and Ornithologist

1999. Artificial Nests, Amsterdam Island.

401	**253**	16f. green, black and olive	10·00	8·00

254 "Festuca contracta"

1999

402	**254**	24f. blue, green & dp grn	16·00	12·50

255 Geologist, Fishery Control Vessel and Map

1999. Geoleta Programme, Adelie Land.

403	**255**	29f.20 blue, black and red	19·00	14·50

256 Research Base, Amsterdam Island

1999. 50th Anniv of Research Bases on Kerguelen and Amsterdam Islands. Each red, blue and green.

404	3f. Type **256**	2·50	2·50
405	24f. Research base, Kerguelen	13·00	12·50

257 Loading Ship at La Reunion

1999. Tourism. Booklet Stamps. No value expressed. Multicoloured.

406	(5f.20) Type **257**	7·75	5·25
407	(5f.20) Diners on board the "Marion Dufresne" (Antarctic supply ship)	7·75	5·25
408	(5f.20) King penguin colony	7·75	5·25
409	(5f.20) Handstamping letters, Crozet (vert)	7·75	5·25
410	(5f.20) Research station, Port-aux-Francais, Kerguelen	7·75	5·25
411	(5f.20) Port Couvreux, Kerguelen	7·75	5·25
412	(5f.20) Unloading ships, Port-aux-Francais, Kerguelen	7·75	5·25
413	(5f.20) Port Jeanne d'Arc, Kerguelen	7·75	5·25
414	(5f.20) St. Paul Island	7·75	5·25
415	(5f.20) Remains of crayfish canning industry, St. Paul Island	7·75	5·25
416	(5f.20) Martin de Vivies base, Amsterdam Island	7·75	5·25
417	(5f.20) Unloading ships, Amsterdam Island	7·75	5·25

258 Madagascar 1946 5f. Stamp and Kerguelen Islands Handstamp

1999. "Philexfrance 99" International Stamp Exhibition, Paris. Sheet 148×81 mm containing T 258 and similar multicoloured designs.

MS418	5f.20 Type **258**; 5f.20 French Southern and Antarctic Territories 1961 25f. stamp and Crozet Islands handstamp; 5f.20 Madagascar 1946 10f. stamp and Amsterdam Island handstamp (39×51 mm); 5f.20 Madagascar 1948 100f. overprinted stamp and Adelie Land handstamp (39×51 mm) (sold at 25f.)	17·00	16·00

259 Mica

2000

419	**259**	1f. black, green and blue	2·75	1·80

260 Pale-footed Shearwaters

2000

420	**260**	2f.70 multicoloured	3·50	2·40

261 Beauge

2000. 3rd Death Anniv of Andre Beauge (scientist).

421	**261**	3f. black, brn & dp brn	3·75	2·75

262 Penguins (Crozet Island)

2000. "Third Millennium on French Southern and Antarctic Territories". Sheet 138×190 mm containing T 262 and similar vert designs.

MS422	3f. Type **262**; 3f. Walruses (Kerguelen Island); 3f. Lobster (St. Paul and Amsterdam Islands); 3f. Exploration vehicle (Adelie Land)	9·75	8·25

263 Yves Joseph Kerguelen-Tremarec

2000. Explorers. Multicoloured.

423	3f. Type **263**	2·50	2·10
424	3f. Dumont D'Urville	2·50	2·10
425	3f. Raymond Rallier du Baty	2·50	2·10
426	3f. E. Aubert de la Rue	2·50	2·10
427	3f. Paul-Emile Victor	2·50	2·10

264 Abby Jane Morrell

2000

428	**264**	4f. black, yellow & brn	3·75	3·25

265 Seal and Maps

2000. Oceanographic Survey (seal tracking).

429	**265**	4f.40 multicoloured	4·25	3·50

266 Hobbs (sledge dog)

2000

430	**266**	5f.20 black, blue & orge	4·50	3·75

267 Yellow-nosed Albatross

2000. Demographic Database of Birds. Mult.

431	5f.20 Type **267**	2·50	2·75
432	8f. Wandering albatross and graph (Crozet Island) (50×28 mm)	4·00	4·50
433	16f. Emperor penguins and graph (Adélie Land) (50×28 mm)	8·00	5·75

Nos. 431/3 were issued together, se-tenant, forming a composite design.

268 Map of Antarctica and Computer Images (image scaled to 63% of original size)

2000. Sleep Research.

434	**268**	8f. multicoloured	3·75	3·75

269 *La Perouse* (supply frigate)

2000

435	**269**	16f. deep blue, blue & grn	7·25	5·25

270 Lantern Fishes

2000

436	**270**	24f. black, blue & purple	11·00	7·75

271 Penguins

2000. Larose Bay Penguin Colony.

437	**271**	27f. multicoloured	12·00	8·25

272 Old and New Headquarters

2000. Relocation of Administrative Headquarters.

438	**272**	27f. multicoloured	12·00	8·25

273 Magnetite

2001

439	**273**	1f. grey, green & turquoise	2·50	2·30

274 Common Diving Petrels

2001

440 **274** 2f.70 blue, violet & black 3·00 2·50

275 Richert

2001. 9th Death Anniv of Xavier-Charles Richert.

441 **275** 3f. black, blue and indigo 3·25 2·75

276 Man pulling Sledge

2001. Armee de Terre's Expedition to Adelie Land.

442 **276** 3f. multicoloured 3·25 2·75

277 L'Arche des Kerguelen, Christmas Harbour

2001

443 **277** 3f. black 3·25 2·75

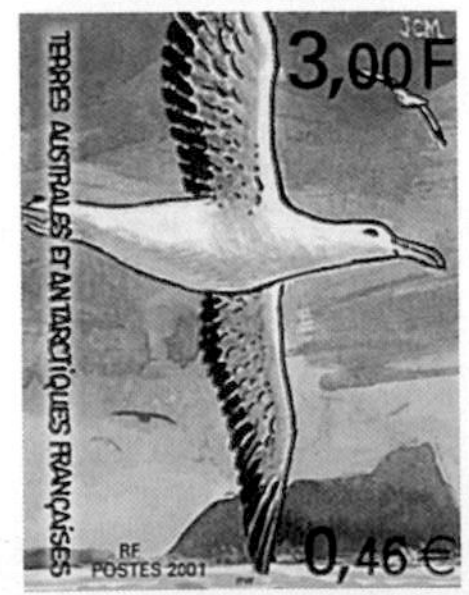

278 Albatrosses (Kerguelen Island)

2001. Wildlife on French Southern and Antarctic Territories. Sheet 138×190 mm containing T 278 and similar multicoloured designs.

MS444 3f. Type **278**; 3f. Emperor penguins (Adelie Land) (horiz); 3f. Eared seals (St. Paul and Amsterdam Islands) (horiz); 3f. Killer whale (Crozet Island) 7·25 7·25

279 Jean Coulomb

2001

445 **279** 4f. multicoloured 3·75 3·00

280 *Carmen* (brigantine)

2001. Ships. Sheet 143×102 mm containing T 280 and similar horiz designs.

MS446 5f.20 azure, blue and brown (Type **280**); 5f.20 chestnut, ochre and blue (*Austral* (supply ship)); 5f.20 ochre, chestnut and blue (*Ramuntcho* (ketch)); 5f.20 azure, blue and brown (*Sapmer 1* (supply ship)) 9·25 9·25

281 Memorial Plaque

2001. 127th Anniv of French Astronomers' Visit to St. Paul Island to Observe Transit of Venus across the Sun.

447 **281** 8f. brown and black 4·50 2·75

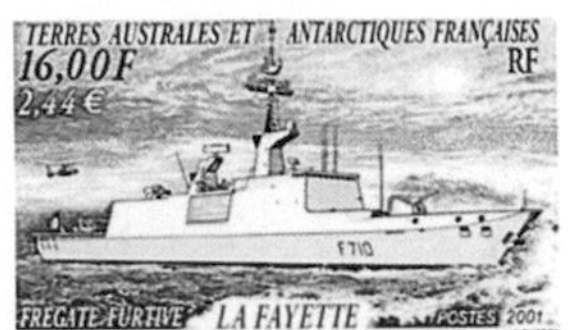

282 *La Fayette* (frigate)

2001

448 **282** 16f. multicoloured 7·25 4·50

283 Squid

2001

449 **283** 24f. multicoloured 11·00 6·50

284 "Mir", Earth and Computer

2001. Amateur Radio Link between "Mir" Space Station and Crozet Island.

450 **284** 27f. multicoloured 13·00 7·25

285 *Bryum laevigatum*

2001

451 **285** 29f.20 multicoloured 14·00 8·25

286 Map of Antarctica and Compass

2001. 40th Anniv of Antarctic Treaty.

452 **286** 5f.20 blue and indigo 3·75 1·80

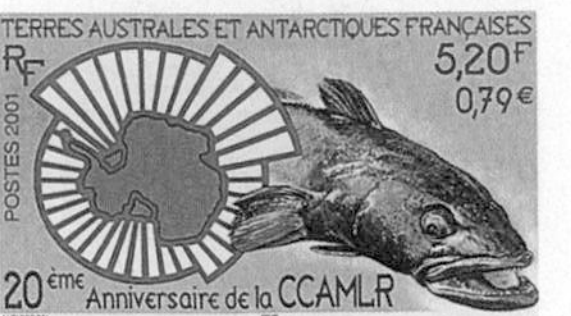

287 Map of Antarctica and Fish

2001. 20th Anniv of Commission for the Conservation of Antarctic Marine Living Resources.

453 **287** 5f.20 multicoloured 3·75 1·80

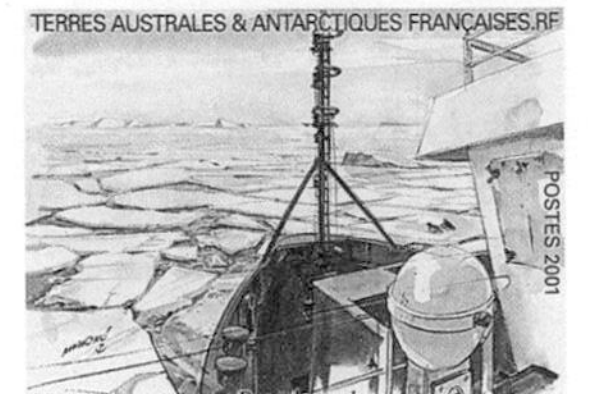

288 Ship in Pack Ice

2001. Adelie Land. No value expressed. Multicoloured.

454 (5f.20) Type **288** 5·00 3·75
455 (5f.20) Statue of Dumont d'Urville (explorer), Dumont d'Urville Base 5·00 3·75
456 (5f.20) Adelie penguin colony 5·00 3·75
457 (5f.20) Astrolabe glacier 5·00 3·75
458 (5f.20) Geology Point Archipelago 5·00 3·75
459 (5f.20) Releasing weather balloon 5·00 3·75
460 (5f.20) Convoy of equipment 5·00 3·75
461 (5f.20) Helicopter delivering supplies 5·00 3·75
462 (5f.20) Emperor penguins 5·00 3·75
463 (5f.20) Radio communications centre 5·00 3·75
464 (5f.20) Statue of Paul Emile Victor (explorer) 5·00 3·75
465 (5f.20) Cap Prud'homme 5·00 3·75
466 (5f.20) *Astrolabe* (fishery control vessel) and penguins 5·00 3·75
467 (5f.20) Men leaving by helicopter 5·00 3·75

2002. As T 154 but with face values expressed in euros.

468 1c. black 60 30
469 2c. blue 60 30
470 5c. red 60 30
471 10c. green 85 45
472 20c. orange 1·20 65

289 Nepheline

2002

480 **289** 15c. multicoloured 1·20 65

290 Albatross

2002

481 **290** 41c. black, yellow and blue 2·20 1·30

291 *Marion Dufresne* (Antarctic supply ship)

2002

482 **291** 46c. blue, red and black 2·50 1·40

292 Shed and Pylon

2002. Cable Cars on Crozet Island (1963–1983).

483 **292** 46c. multicoloured 2·50 1·40

293 Albatrosses and Rock (Kerguelen Islands)

2002. "The French Southern Antarctic Olympic Games". Sheet 139×191 mm containing T 293 and similar multicoloured designs.

MS484 46c. Type **293**; 46c. Lobsters diving (St. Paul and Amsterdam Islands); 46c. Emperor penguins sliding (Adelie Land) (vert); 46c. Killer whales leaping (Crozet Island) (vert) 7·50 7·75

294 Geological Diagram

2002. 11th Anniv (2001) of Cartoker Geological Survey of Kerguelen Islands. Multicoloured.

485 46c. Type **294** 2·50 1·30
486 €3.66 Map of Kerguelen Islands 8·75 6·50

295 Dubois and Scientific Equipment

2002. 2nd Death Anniv of Jacques Dubois (Antarctic researcher).

487 **295** 61c. multicoloured 2·50 1·30

296 Engraved Rock, St. Paul Island

2002

488 **296** 79c. sepia, blue and green 3·25 1·90

297 Emperor Penguin and Chicks

2002. Antarctic Animals and their Young. Sheet 104×143 mm, containing T 297 and similar vert designs. Multicoloured.

MS489 79c. Type **297**; 79c. Grey seal and pup; 79c. Abatross and chick; 79c. Elephant seal and pups 10·00 10·50

298 Kerguelen Cabbage

2002

490	**298**	€1.22 multicoloured	3·25	1·70

299 Ship

2002. Centenary of Visit of Guass (survey barquentine) to Kerguelen Islands.

491	**299**	€2.44 multicoloured	5·50	3·00

300 Crab

2002

492	**300**	€3.66 multicoloured	8·25	5·50

301 Diatoms and Pack Ice

2002. Diatoms (microscopic algae) of the Antarctic Pack Ice.

493	**301**	€4.12 multicoloured	11·00	6·00

302 Door and Facade

2002. 181st Anniv of French Geographical Society.

494	**302**	€4.45 multicoloured	11·50	6·50

303 Penguins incubating "€"

2002. Introduction of the Euro.

495	**303**	46c. black and blue	2·20	1·20

304 Apatite

2003

496	**304**	15c. mauve, blue and black	1·10	50

305 Factory, St. Paul Island

2003

497	**305**	41c. black, green and blue	2·20	1·00

306 Emperor Penguins

2003

498	**306**	46c. multicoloured	2·75	1·20

307 Glaciers

2003. Luc Marie Bayle (artist) Commemoration.

499	**307**	46c. multicoloured	2·75	1·20

308 Louis XV and Penguins wearing Neckties on Crozet Island

2003. 18th-century French Personalities transposed to Southern Antarctic Territories. Sheet 139×191 mm containing T 308 and similar vert designs. Multicoloured.

MS500 Type **308**; 46c. "Triumph of Venus" on St. Paul and Amsterdam Islands; 46c. Dumont and Adele D'urville on Adelie Land; 46c. Le Chavalier Yves de Kerguelen on Kerguelen Island — 8·25 — 7·50

309 Map, Satellite and Hydrophone

2003. Research Station, Crozet Island.

501	**309**	61c. green and blue	3·00	1·40

310 Damaged and Restored Buildings

2003. Restoration of Port Jeanne d'Arc.

502	**310**	79c. multicoloured	3·25	1·50

311 Man wearing Furs, 1898

2003. Polar Clothing. Multicoloured.

503	79c. Type **311**	3·25	1·50
504	79c. Man wearing brown hat, 1912	3·25	1·50
505	79c. Penguins and man wearing yellow parka, 2002	3·25	1·50
506	79c. Dogs and man wearing blue jacket, 1980	3·25	1·50
507	79c. Snowmobiles and man wearing red all-in-one suit, 1996	3·25	1·50

312 Phylica (tree), Amsterdam Island

2003

508	**312**	€1.22 multicoloured	3·75	1·80

313 *Bougainville* (research ship)

2003

509	**313**	€2.44 multicoloured	7·25	4·50

314 Penguin Island

2003

510	**314**	€3.66 black	8·25	5·50

315 Cabot

2003

511	**315**	€3.66 multicoloured	8·25	5·50

316 Super Dual Auroral Radar Network (Super DARN) (image scaled to 63% of original size)

2003

512	**316**	€4.12 multicoloured	9·75	7·00

317 Jean-Baptiste Charcot (scientist and expedition leader)

2003. Centenary of Expedition to Antarctic Territories.

513	**317**	79c. brown, blue and violet	2·75	1·40
514	-	€1.22 brown, blue and pink (48×27 mm)	3·75	1·80
515	-	€2.44 violet, blue and orange (48×27 mm)	6·50	3·75

DESIGNS: 79c. Type **317**; €1.22, *Le Francais* at anchor; €2.44, *Le Francais* in port.

317a Fish

2003. Antarctic Voyages. No value expressed. Multicoloured.

515a	(90c.) Type **317a**	3·75	2·50
515b	(90c.) Sheep	3·75	2·50
515c	(90c.) Mint		
515d	(90c.) Salmon and waterfall	3·75	2·50
515e	(90c.) Leaping fish	3·75	2·50
515f	(90c.) Bighorn sheep	3·75	2·50
515g	(90c.) Cattle	3·75	2·50
515h	(90c.) Penguins and rabbits	3·75	2·50
515i	(90c.) Reindeer	3·75	2·50
515j	(90c.) Mussels	3·75	2·50
515k	(90c.) Lobster	3·75	2·50
515l	(90c.) Ice cream	3·75	2·50

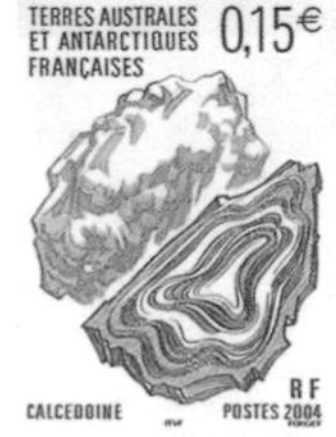

318 Calcedone

2004

516	**318**	15c. purple, ochre and blue	1·30	65

319 Mario Marret

2004. Mario Marret (Antarctic explorer and writer) Commemoration.

517	**319**	41c. blue, red and green	2·00	1·30

320 Base Camp Buildings (image scaled to 57% of original size)

2004. 40th Anniv of Alfred-Faure Base, Crozet Island.
518 **320** 50c. multicoloured 2·75 1·60

321 Robert Genty

2004. Colonel Robert Genty (pilot) Commemoration.
519 **321** 50c. black, red and green 2·75 1·60

322 Whaling Museum, Jeanne d'Arc Port, Kerguelen Island

2004. Fantasy Tourist Attractions in Southern Antarctic Territories. Sheet 139×191 mm containing T 322 and similar horiz designs. Multicoloured.
MS520 50c.×4, Type **322**; Showgirls and sea lions on St. Paul and Amsterdam Islands; Couple with ice creams (Ice palace on Adelie Land); Girl sunbathing amongst penguins (Hotel Marina on Crozet Island) 9·25 9·25

323 Southern Right-whale Dolphin

2004
521 **323** 75c. multicoloured 3·25 2·00

324 de Havilland Twin Canada DHC-7 Otter Airplane and Map of Antarctica

2004
522 **324** 90c. multicoloured 3·50 2·40

325 Amsterdam Island Postal Buildings

2004. Antarctic Postal Buildings. Sheet 162×114 mm containing T 325 and similar horiz designs. Multicoloured.
MS523 90c.×4, Type **325**; Crozet Island; Kerguelen Island; Adelie Island 13·50 13·50

326 Iceberg

2004
524 **326** €1.30 blue and lilac 4·75 2·75

327 Cairn and Cross

2004. Volage (British sail training ship) Sailor's Grave.
525 **327** €2.50 blue, indigo and red 9·25 4·75

328 Krill (*Euphausia superba*)

2004
526 **328** €4 blue, orange and brown 14·50 7·25

329 *Dives*

2004
527 **329** €4.50 multicoloured 16·00 10·50

330 Scientists taking Readings from Sea Bed

2004. Hydrographic Surveys in Adelie Land. Sheet 107×81 mm.
MS528 **330** €4.90 multicoloured 19·00 19·00

331 Penguin holding Sea-lion Mask

2004
529 **331** €4.50 multicoloured 16·00 10·50

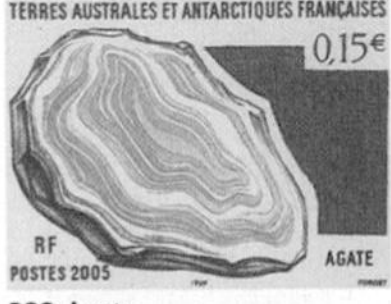

332 Agate

2005
530 **332** 15c. green, blue and black 1·30 65

333 Albert Bauer

2005. Albert Bauer (explorer) Commemoration.
531 **333** 45c. brown and blue 2·10 1·50

334 Roger Barberot

2005. 90th Birth Anniv of Roger Barberot (administrator).
532 **334** 50c. black, brown and blue 2·30 1·60

335 *Cap Horn*

2005
533 **335** 50c. multicoloured 2·30 1·60

336 Cauldron

2005
534 **336** 50c. multicoloured 2·30 1·60

337 MacGillivray's Prion (Prion de MacGillivray)

2005
535 **337** 75c. black, yellow and blue 3·25 2·00

338 Studer Valley

2005
536 **338** 90c. multicoloured 3·75 2·50

339 "Peigne de Neriedes"

2005
537 **339** €2.50 multicoloured 9·25 4·75

340 *Harpovoluta charcoti*

2005
538 **340** €4 multicoloured 15·00 7·50

341 Murray's Skate ("Raie de Murray")

2005
539 **341** €4.50 multicoloured 16·00 9·00

342 Elephant Seal and Oceanographic Chart (image scaled to 63% of original size)

2005
540 **342** €4.90 multicoloured 18·00 9·75

343 Concordia, French—Italian Base (image scaled to 63% of original size)

2005
541 **343** 50c. multicoloured 2·10 1·40

344 Jean-Baptiste Charcot and Penguins

2005. Centenary of the Return of Le Francais (exploration ship).
542 **344** €4.50 multicoloured 16·00 9·00

345 Paul-Emile Victor

2005. 10th Death Anniv of Paul-Emile Victor (polar explorer and writer).
543 **345** 50c. multicoloured 2·10 1·40

346 Arms

2005. 50th Anniv of French Southern and Antarctic Territories (1st issue). No value expressed.
544 **346** (90c.) black, blue and yellow 3·75 2·10

See also Nos. 557 and **MS**558.

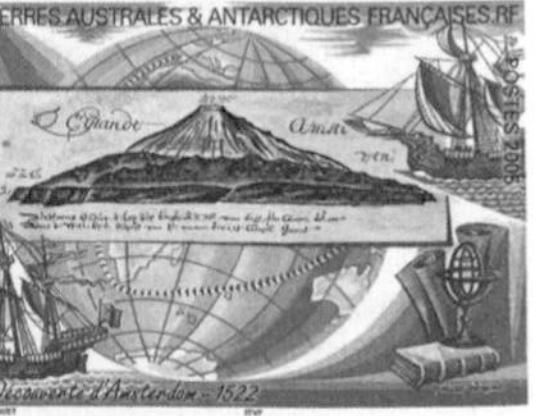

347 Volcano (discovery of Amsterdam Island, 1522)

2005. Antarctic Voyages. No value expressed. Multicoloured.

545 (90c.) Type **347** 3·75 2·10
546 (90c.) Marie-Joseph Marion Dufresne (discovery of Crozet, 1772) 3·75 2·10
547 (90c.) Ship (discovery of Kerguelen, 1772) (vert) 3·75 2·10
548 (90c.) Sailors landing (discovery of Adelieland, 1840) 3·75 2·10
549 (90c.) Huts (watching the transit of Venus across sun from Ilse Saint Paul, 1874) (vert) 3·75 2·10
550 (90c.) Wreck of *Strathmore*, 1875 3·75 2·10
551 (90c.) Jeanne d'Arc Port, 1908 3·75 2·10
552 (90c.) Farm, Port Couvreux, 1925 3·75 2·10
553 (90c.) Port-Martin base, 1950 3·75 2·10
554 (90c.) Map (Antarctic treaty, 1959) 3·75 2·10
555 (90c.) Buildings (permanent base, 1963/4) 3·75 2·10
556 (90c.) As No. 544 (vert) 3·75 2·10

348 15f. Stamp of Madagascar optd with French Southern and Antarctic Territories (1st stamp) and Penguins

2005. 50th Anniv of French Southern and Antarctic Territories (2nd issue).

557 **348** 90c. multicoloured 3·75 2·10

349 Crozet Archipelago

2005. 50th Anniv of French Southern and Antarctic Territories (3rd issue). Sheet 160×115 mm containing T 349 and similar horiz designs.

MS558 50c.×4, Type **349**; Amsterdam and Saint Paul Islands; Kerguelen; Adelieland 7·50 7·50

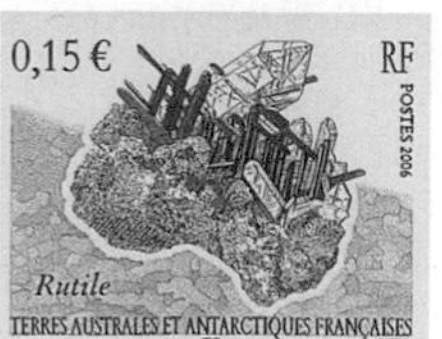

350 Rutile

2006. Minerals.

559 **350** 15c. sepia and green 1·40 70

351 Charles Velain

2006. 160th Birth Anniv of Charles Velan (geologist).

560 **351** 48c. lilac and vermilion 2·10 95

352 Albert Seyrolle

2006. Albert Seyrolle (sailor) Commemoration.

561 **352** 53c. black and blue 2·30 1·40

353 "Jardin d'Amsterdam"

2006

562 **353** 53c. multicoloured 2·30 1·40

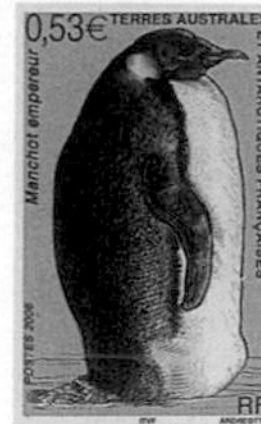

354 Emperor Penguin

2006. Penguins. Sheet 125×195 mm containing T 354 and similar vert designs.

MS563 53c.×6, Type **354**; King; Gentoo; Adelie; Macaroni; Rockhopper 11·00 11·00

355 Dumont D'Urville Base (image scaled to 61% of original size)

2006. 50th Anniv of Dumont D'Urville Base.

564 **355** 90c. multicoloured 3·50 1·80

356 *Osiris*

2006

565 **356** 90c. multicoloured 3·50 1·80

357 "La Vierge des Phoquiers"

2006

566 **357** €2.50 chestnut, blue and ultramarine 9·25 5·00

358 *Lagenorhynchus cruciger*

2006. Dolphin.

567 **358** €4 black, azure and ultramarine 16·00 7·50

359 Colin de Kerguelen (*Notothenia rossii*)

2006

568 **359** €4.53 multicoloured 17·00 8·75

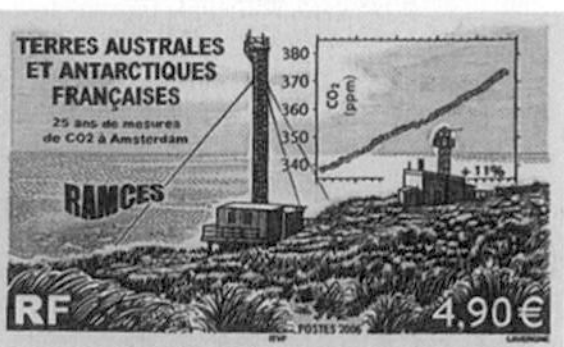

360 Tower and Buildings

2006. 25th Anniv of CO2 Measurements on Amsterdam Island.

569 **360** €4.90 multicoloured 17·00 10·00

361 Albatross on Nest

2006. Salon de Timbre et de l'Ecrit. Sheet 150×110 mm.

MS570 **361** €4.53 multicoloured 17·00 16·00

2007. Albatross. Sheet 143×104 mm. As No. MS570 but colours changed.

MS570a 90c. multicoloured 3·50 1·80

362 Corundum

2007

571 **362** 15c. multicoloured 1·30 60

363 Louis Aleno Saint Aloüarn

2007. Louis Francois Marie Aleno de Saint Alouarn (explorer) Commemoration.

572 **363** 49c. brown, orange and ultramarine 2·00 95

364 Marthe Emmanuel

2007. Marthe Emmanuel (writer) Commemoration.

573 **364** 54c. black, brown, and blue 2·10 1·00

365 Bull and Island

2007. Amsterdam Island Cattle.

574 **365** 54c. ultramarine, brown and yellow 2·10 1·00

366 Amsterdam Albatross

2007. Albatrosses. Sheet 190×140 mm containing T 366 and similar horiz designs. Multicoloured.

MS575 54c.×5, Type **366**; Great albatross; Albatross with dark eye; Albatross with yellow beak; Albatross fuliginous 10·50 10·50

367 Polar Expeditions' Building

2007. 60th Anniv of French Polar Expedition. Multicoloured.

576 54c. Type **367** 2·00 1·20
577 €4.41 Avenue du Marechal Fayolle, Paris 14·50 6·75

368 Ile de la Baleine

2007

578 **368** 90c. multicoloured 3·50 1·70

369 Tonkinois

2007

579 **369** 90c. violet, blue and black 3·50 1·70

370 Taking Measurements

2007. Archaeology on Saint Paul Island.

580 **370** €2.50 multicoloured 9·25 4·25

371 *Lampris immaculatus*

2007

581 **371** €4 multicoloured 14·50 6·75

372 Equipment

2007. Astronomy at Concordia.

582 **372** €4.90 multicoloured 16·00 7·50

373 Penguin

2007. International Polar Year. 50th Anniv of International Geophysical Year. Multicoloured.

583	90c. Type **373**	3·50	1·70
584	€4 Map of Antarctica and 1957 10f. Stamp (No. 20)	14·50	6·75

375 Building Facade

2007. Bicentenary of Court of Auditors.

586	**375**	90c. blue and vermilion	3·50	1·70

376 Ile Tromelin

2007. Eparses Islands. Multicoloured.

587	54c. Type **376**	2·10	1·20
588	54c. Iles Glorieuses	2·10	1·20
589	54c. Ile Juan de Nova	2·10	1·20
590	54c. Ile Bassas da India	2·10	1·20
591	54c. Ile Europa	2·10	1·20

377 'The Course of the Sun at Dumont d'Urville–21 June' (image scaled to 31% of original size)

2007

592	**377**	90c. multicoloured	4·00	1·90

377a Ilot des Apotres, Crozet Archipelago

2007. Antarctic Voyages. No value expressed. Multicoloured.

592a	(90c.) Type **377a**	4·00	1·90
592b	(90c.) Chamonix Lake, Kerguelen	4·00	1·90
592c	(90c.) Phylica wood, Amsterdam Island	4·00	1·90
592d	(90c.) Golfe du Morbihan, Kerguelen	4·00	1·90
592e	(90c.) Mount Cook, glacier and Chamonix Lake, Kerguelen	4·00	1·90
592f	(90c.) Tourbieres plateau, Amsterdam Island	4·00	1·90
592g	(90c.) Iles Nuageuses, Kerguelen	4·00	1·90
592h	(90c.) Caldera, Amsterdam Island	4·00	1·90
592i	(90c.) Mount Cook, Kerguelen	4·00	1·90
592j	(90c.) Central plateau, Kerguelen Penguin Island, Crozet Archipelago	4·00	1·90
592k	(90c.) Penguin Island, Crozet Archipelago	4·00	1·90
592l	(90c.) Antonelli crater, Amsterdam Island	4·00	1·90
592m	(90c.) Lake, Ile de la Possession, Crozet	4·00	1·90
592n	(90c.) Faraillous des Apotres, Crozet Archipelago	4·00	1·90
592o	(90c.) Presqu'ile de la Societe de Geographie, Kerguelen	4·00	1·90
592p	(90c.) Rock formation, Presquile Ronarch, Kerguelen	4·00	1·90

378 Flag

2008. Flag.

593	**378**	1c. multicoloured	25	25
594	**378**	2c. multicoloured	40	35
595	**378**	5c. multicoloured	55	50
596	**378**	10c. multicoloured	65	60
597	**378**	20c. multicoloured	95	85

379 Spinel

2008

598	**379**	15c. multicoloured	1·30	1·20

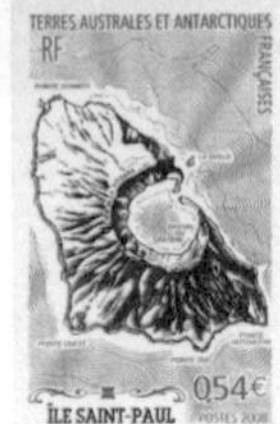

380 Ile Saint Paul

2008

599	**380**	54c. blue and olive	2·50	1·70

381 Samivel (self-portrait)

2008. Paul Gayet-Tancred (Samivel) (artist) Commemoration.

600	**381**	54c. chestnut and green	2·50	1·70

382 Female

2008. Elephant Seals. Sheet 190×140 mm containing T 382 and similar horiz designs. Multicoloured.

MS601	54c.×4, Type **382**; Alpha bull; Pup; Two males sparring	9·25	9·25

383 Rockhopper Penguin

2008

602	**383**	90c. multicoloured	4·00	2·00

384 *L'Espeerance*

2008. Ships.

603	**384**	90c. multicoloured	4·00	2·00

385 Port Jeanne d'Arc (image scaled to 62% of original size)

2008. Centenary of Port Jeanne d'Arc.

604	**385**	90c. multicoloured	4·00	2·00

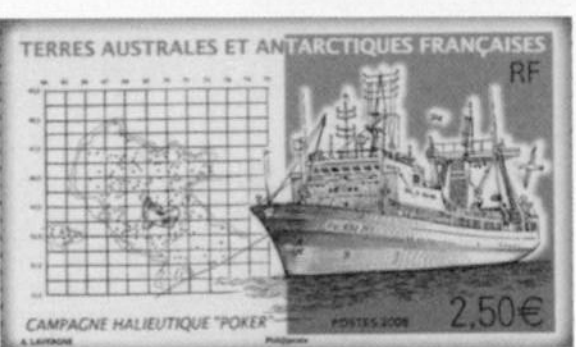

386 Map and Ship

2008. 'Poker' Fish Monitoring Campaign. Sheet 110×86 mm

MS605	**386** €2.50 multicoloured	10·50	10·50

387 *Macrourus carinatus*

2008

606	**387**	€4 multicoloured	14·50	7·25

388 *Galium antarcticum*

2008

607	**388**	€4.54 multicoloured	17·00	8·75

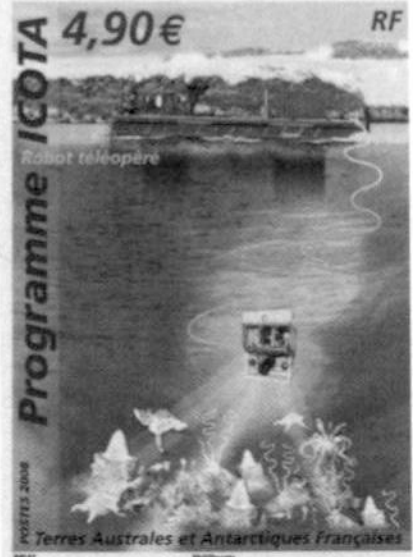

389 Ship and Robot

2008. ICOTA Programme.

608	**389**	€4.90 multicoloured	18·00	9·00

390 Gerard Megie

2008. Gerard Megie (research scientist) Commemoration.

609	**390**	54c. multicoloured	2·75	1·30

391 *Territoire infini ni grand ni petit à la dimension qu'on veut bien lui donner* (Michel Granger) (image scaled to 61% of original size)

2008

610	**391**	€4.54 multicoloured	17·00	9·25

392 Sooty Tern ('sterne fuligineuse')

2008. Sea Birds. Sheet 140×190 mm containing T 392 and similar multicoloured designs.

MS611	54c.×5, Type **392**; Red footed booby ('fou a pieds rouge') (vert); Masked booby ('fou masque') (vert); Pacific frigate bird ('frigate du Pacifique') (vert); Tropic bird ('paille en queue')	15·00	15·00

392a *Marion Dufresne*

2008. Ships. No value expressed.

611a	**392a**	(55c.) multicoloured	3·25	1·70

No. 611a is as Type **291** redrawn.

No. 611a was for use on mail weighing up to 20 grammes.

393 Pyrites

2009

612	**393**	15c. multicoloured	1·30	65

1959 Traité sur l'Antarctique 2009 RF 0,56€ 50e Anniversaire TERRES AUSTRALES ET ANTARCTIQUES FRANÇAISES

402a Penguins and Antarctica

2009. 50th Anniv of Antarctic Treaty

612a	**402a**	56c. deep blue, black and deep purple	3·25	1·70

394 Henri Paschal de Rochegude

2009. Henri Paschal de Rochegude (sailor, politician and scholar) Commemoration.

613	**394**	55c. multicoloured	3·25	1·70

395 Charles Rouillon

2009. Charles Gaston Rouillon (mountaineer and explorer) Commemoration.

614	**395**	55c. indigo and pink	3·25	1·70

396 Soft-plumaged Petrel (*pterodroma mollis*)

2009. Petrels. Sheet 190×80 mm containing T 396 and similar horiz designs. Multicoloured.
MS615 55c.×5, Type **396**; Wilson's storm petrel (*oceanites oceanicus*); Grey petrel (*procellaria cinerea*); Peruvian diving petrel (*pelecanoides urinatrix*); Snow petrel (*pagodroma nivea*) 15·00 15·00

397 1906 10c. Stamp of France (As Type **18**)

2009. Centenary of 'Residence de France–Kerguelen Islands' (stamps used by Bossière brothers (first letters from Kerguelen)).
616 **397** 90c. multicoloured 5·00 2·50

398 *Himanatothallus grandifolius*

2009. Marine Flora.
617 90c. green, brown and blue 5·00 2·50
618 €4 bright green, green and blue 21·00 10·50
DESIGNS: Type **398**; €4 *Laminaria pallida*.

399 Southern Lantern Shark ('requin a epines dorsales')

2009
619 **399** €2.50 multicoloured 13·50 6·75

400 *Jeanne d'Arc*

2009
620 **400** €4 multicoloured 21·00 10·50

401 Diver and Bivalve

2009. Macarbi Programme (environmental monitoring based on study of Bivalves).
621 **401** €4.55 multicoloured 24·00 12·00

402 Tourmaline

2010
622 **402** 28c. multicoloured 2·00 1·00

403 Jean Rivolier

2010. Jean Rivolier (doctor and Polar expedition member) Commemoration.
623 **403** 56c. multicoloured 3·25 1·70

404 Seabirds and Shoreline

2010. Ile du Lys, Glorieuses Archipelago.
624 **404** 56c. multicoloured 3·25 1·70

405 Maison Patureau

2010. Maison Patureau, Juan de Nova Island.
625 **405** 56c. multicoloured 3·25 1·70

406 Sea Lion

2010. Sea Lions of Amsterdam Island. Sheet 190×79 mm containing T 406 and similar multicoloured designs.
MS626 56c.×5, Type **406**; Mother and calf (horiz); Head (horiz); Head and adult scratching (horiz); Calf and adult sleeping (horiz) 15·00 15·00

407 Geodetic Receiver and Ice Field

2010. CRAC–ICE, Collaborative Research into Antarctic Iceberg Calving and Evolution.
627 **407** 90c. new blue, agate and blackish purple 5·00 2·50

408 Husky Team and Sled

2010. Evolution of Polar Transport. Sheet 146×104 mm containing T 408 and similar horiz designs.
MS628 90c.×6, Type **408**; Weasel M29C; Sno-Cat 743; HB40-Castor; Challenger 65; PB 330 30·00 30·00

409 *Ile St. Paul* (supply ship)

2010. Ships.
629 **409** €1.35 multicoloured 8·00 6·00

410 Orca

2010. Orcas of Crozet Island.
630 **410** €2.80 multicoloured 16·00 12·00

411 Terns

2010. Terns of Kerguelen Island.
631 **411** €4.30 multicoloured 22·00 12·00

413 Adult and Chick on Nest

2010. Endangered Species. Amsterdam Island Albatross (*Diomedea amsterdamensis*) . Multicoloured.
MS633 190×80 mm. 56c.×4, Type **413**; Close up of beak and eye; Head, facing right; Heads of two juveniles 11·50 11·50

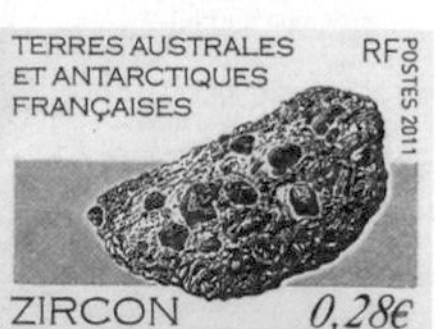

414 Stalls and Visitors

2010. Autumn Stamp Salon, Paris

(a) Ordinary gum
634 **414** 56c. multicoloured 3·25 1·70

(b) Self-adhesive
635 **414** 56c. multicoloured 3·25 1·70

415 Zircon in Natural State

2011. Minerals. Each deep carmine, new blue and agate.
636 28c. Type **415** 1·70 90
637 34c. Cut stone 2·10 1·00

416 Concordia Base and Constellation (image scaled to 62% of original size)

2011. Southern Cross at Concordia Antarctic Base
638 **416** 56c. multicoloured 3·00 1·70

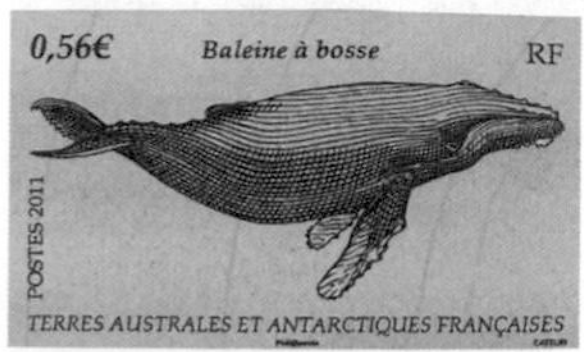

417 Humpback Whale ('Baleine à bosse')

2011. Baleen Whales. Multicoloured.
MS639 130×80 mm. 56c.×4, Type **417**; Southern right whale ('Baleine franche australe'); Sperm whale ('Cachalot'); Sei whale ('Rorqual de Rudolphi') 11·50 11·50

418 Farman F 190

2011. Aviation Accident of Madagascar to France Flight, Juan de Nova Island, 1929. Multicoloured.
640 56c. Type **418** 3·50 2·00
641 90c. Map of route 4·50 2·20
642 €1.35 Pilot, passengers and envelope overprinted with accident/interrupted mail details 7·00 5·50

419 Joseph Enzensperger

2011. Joseph Enzensperger (meteorologist) Commemoration
643 **419** 90c. crimson, black and ultramarine 4·75 2·50

420 Base and Environs (image scaled to 61% of original size)

2011. Martin de Viviès Base, Amsterdam Island
644 **420** 90c. multicoloured 4·75 2·50

421 André Chastain

2011. André Chastain (botanist) Commemoration
645 **421** €1.35 violet, black and blue 7·00 5·50

422 Black-faced Sheathbill (Le Chionis)

2011. Sub-Antarctic Birds
646 **422** €1.35 slate-lilac and black 7·00 5·50

423 *Artedidraco orianae*

2011. Antarctic Fish
647 **423** €1.35 multicoloured 7·00 5·50

424 Lapérouse (naval cruiser)

2011. Ships
648 **424** €4.30 violet, brown-olive and blue 23·00 13·00

Pt. 6

FRENCH SUDAN

A territory in central Africa. In 1899 parts of the colony were detached and added to neighbouring coastal colonies with the remainder becoming Senegambia and Niger (subsequently renamed Upper Senegal and Niger). In 1920 Niger became a separate colony and Upper Senegal reverted to the name of French Sudan.

From 1944 to 1959 French Sudan used the stamps of French West Africa. In 1959 French Sudan combined with Senegal to form the Mali Federation.

100 centimes = 1 franc.

1894. Stamps of French Colonies, "Commerce" type, surch SOUDAN Fais and value.
1 **J** 0.15 on 75c. red £4250 £2250
2 **J** 0.25 on 1f. olive £4500 £1600

1894. "Tablet" key-type inscr "SOUDAN FRANCAIS" in red (1, 5, 15, 25, 50 (No. 21), 75c., 1f.) or blue (others).
3 **D** 1c. black on blue 2·30 3·75
4 **D** 2c. brown on buff 3·00 3·00
5 **D** 4c. brown on grey 4·75 8·25
6 **D** 5c. green on light green 7·00 5·50
7 **D** 10c. black on lilac 14·00 29·00
18 **D** 10c. red 8·25 17·00
8 **D** 15c. blue 4·50 3·25
19 **D** 15c. grey 11·00 24·00
9 **D** 20c. red on green 24·00 23·00
10 **D** 25c. black on pink 32·00 30·00
20 **D** 25c. blue 12·00 21·00
11 **D** 30c. brown on drab 55·00 60·00
12 **D** 40c. red on yellow 35·00 28·00
13 **D** 50c. red on pink 70·00 65·00
21 **D** 50c. brown on blue 13·00 32·00
14 **D** 75c. brown on yellow 55·00 65·00
15 **D** 1f. green 8·25 20·00

1921. Stamps of Upper Senegal and Niger optd SOUDAN FRANCAIS.
85 **7** 1c. violet and purple 10 5·00
86 **7** 2c. purple and grey 10 4·50
87 **7** 4c. blue and black 20 4·75
88 **7** 5c. chocolate and brown 60 1·40
89 **7** 10c. green and light green 1·20 3·25
121 **7** 10c. blue and mauve 35 75
90 **7** 15c. orange and purple 1·60 4·75
122 **7** 15c. green and light green 20 4·25
123 **7** 15c. mauve and brown 1·20 3·75
91 **7** 20c. black and purple 1·30 1·00
92 **7** 25c. green and black 2·50 1·10
93 **7** 30c. carmine and red 3·25 6·75
124 **7** 30c. black and green 1·60 1·80
125 **7** 30c. green and olive 2·50 9·75
94 **7** 35c. violet and red 1·30 5·25
95 **7** 40c. red and grey 2·75 2·30
96 **7** 45c. brown and blue 2·50 5·25
97 **7** 50c. blue and ultramarine 1·20 3·00
126 **7** 50c. blue and orange 1·60 75
127 **7** 60c. violet on pink 1·50 6·25
128 **7** 65c. blue and brown 3·25 8·75
98 **7** 75c. brown and yellow 2·50 3·50
129 **7** 90c. carmine and red 9·75 19·00
99 **7** 1f. purple and brown 3·25 3·00
130 **7** 1f.10 mauve and blue 3·25 7·75
131 **7** 1f.50 blue 8·25 19·00
100 **7** 2f. blue and green 4·25 3·50
132 **7** 3f. mauve on pink 12·00 30·00
101 **7** 5f. black and violet 8·25 8·75

1922. Surch in figures and bars.
110 **7** 25c. on 45c. brown & blue 2·30 6·50
111 **7** 60 on 75c. violet on pink 1·60 2·10
112 **7** 65 on 75c. brown & yellow 2·30 6·50
113 **7** 85 on 2f. blue and green 1·80 9·25
114 **7** 85 on 5f. black and violet 2·00 10·00
115 **7** 90c. on 75c. red & carmine 2·75 4·50
116 **7** 1f.25 on 1f. lt bl & blue 1·40 8·50
117 **7** 1f.50 on 1f. ultram & bl 2·75 2·30
118 **7** 3f. on 5f. buff and pink 4·75 6·00
119 **7** 10f. on 5f. green and red 16·00 41·00
120 **7** 20f. on 5f. red and violet 21·00 60·00

14 Sudanese Woman marketing **15** Djenne Gateway

1931
135 **14** 1c. black and red 20 2·75
136 **14** 2c. red and blue 10 3·00
137 **14** 3c. black and red 20 7·00
138 **14** 4c. red and lilac 75 4·50
139 **14** 5c. green and blue 20 1·90
140 **14** 10c. red and green 20 1·50
141 **14** 15c. violet and black 30 70
142 **14** 20c. blue and brown 30 1·70
143 **14** 25c. pink and mauve 50 55
144 **15** 30c. light green and green 95 1·10
145 **15** 30c. red and blue 1·10 7·00
146 **15** 35c. green and olive 1·20 4·50
147 **15** 40c. red and green 40 1·70
148 **15** 45c. red and blue 2·75 2·50
149 **15** 45c. green and olive 1·40 7·25
150 **15** 50c. black and red 45 20
151 **15** 55c. red and blue 1·80 5·00
152 **15** 60c. brown and blue 90 6·25
153 **15** 65c. black and violet 1·20 1·40
154 **15** 70c. red and blue 2·50 7·00
155 **15** 75c. brown and blue 2·75 2·30
156 **15** 80c. brown and red 60 3·00
157 **15** 90c. orange and red 1·60 3·00
158 **15** 90c. black and violet 1·60 7·00
159 **15** 1f. green and blue 9·75 3·25
160 **15** 1f. red 6·25 2·75
161 **15** 1f. brown and red 55 2·75
162 - 1f.25 mauve and violet 3·25 3·50
163 - 1f.25 red and scarlet 1·60 4·75
164 - 1f.40 black and violet 1·90 5·00
165 - 1f.50 blue and indigo 1·70 2·30
166 - 1f.60 blue and brown 1·60 4·75
167 - 1f.70 blue and brown 3·25 2·30
168 - 1f.75 blue 1·60 7·25
169 - 2f. green and brown 1·20 1·10
170 - 2f.25 ultramarine & blue 1·40 6·00
171 - 2f.50 brown 2·75 5·00
172 - 3f. brown and green 1·00 75
173 - 5f. black and red 1·80 1·90
174 - 10f. green and blue 2·30 2·30
175 - 20f. brown and mauve 3·25 8·50
DESIGN: 1f.25 to 20f. Niger boatman.

1931. "Colonial Exhibition" key-types inscr "SOUDAN FRANCAIS".
186 **E** 40c. green and black 5·00 9·00
187 **F** 50c. mauve and black 3·75 9·00
188 **G** 90c. red and black 3·25 3·50
189 **H** 1f.50 blue and black 4·00 5·25

1937. International Exhibition, Paris. As T 58a of Guadeloupe.
190 20c. violet 1·40 5·00
191 30c. green 1·60 5·00
192 40c. red 90 3·50
193 50c. brown and agate 90 3·50
194 90c. red 90 2·00
195 1f.50 blue 90 3·75

1938. International Anti-cancer Fund. As T 58b of Guadeloupe.
197 1f.75+50c. blue 5·50 17·00

21 Rene Caillie

1939. Caillie.
198 **21** 90c. orange 55 2·10
199 **21** 2f. violet 85 1·40
200 **21** 2f.25 blue 65 5·25

1939. New York World's Fair. As T 58c of Guadeloupe.
201 1f.25 red 1·50 5·25
202 2f.25 blue 2·30 7·25

1939. 150th Anniv of French Revolution. As T 58d of Guadeloupe.
203 45c.+25c. green and black 10·00 23·00
204 70c.+30c. brown and black 10·00 23·00
205 90c.+35c. orange and black 10·00 23·00
206 1f.25+1f. red and black 10·00 23·00
207 2f.25+2f. blue and black 10·00 23·00

1940. Air. As T 6a of French Guinea.
208 1f.90 blue 85 5·75
209 2f.90 red 90 4·25
210 4f.50 green 1·00 3·50
211 4f.90 olive 1·00 3·00
212 6f.90 orange 1·20 5·25

1941. National Defence Fund. Surch SECOURS NATIONAL and value.
213 +1f. on 50c. (No. 150) 5·75 12·00
214 +2f. on 80c. (No. 156) 8·25 25·00
215 +2f. on 1f.50 (No. 165) 8·50 25·00
216 +3f. on 2f. (No. 169) 14·00 25·00

1941. Marshal Petain Issue. As T 16a of Ivory Coast.
217 1f. green 65 3·75
218 2f.50 blue 90 3·25
DESIGNS—VERT: Gate at Djenne and Marshal Petain.

1942. Air. Colonial Child Welfare Fund. As T 8 of French Guinea.
219 1f.50+3f.50 green 1·00 4·50
220 2f.+6f. brown 65 7·50
221 3f.+9f. red 1·10 6·00

1942. Air. Imperial Fortnight. As T 9a of French Guinea.
222 1f.20+1f.80 blue and red 90 5·50

27 Airplane over Camel Caravan

1942. Air.
223 **27** 50f. blue and green 2·50 6·25

POSTAGE DUE STAMPS

1921. Postage Due stamps of Upper Senegal and Niger optd SOUDAN FRANCAIS.
D102 **M** 5c. green 20 7·00
D103 **M** 10c. red 65 4·50
D104 **M** 15c. grey 1·40 5·25
D105 **M** 20c. brown 1·50 6·25
D106 **M** 30c. blue 1·40 8·00
D107 **M** 50c. black 3·25 8·75
D108 **M** 60c. orange 2·75 8·25
D109 **M** 1f. violet 2·40 8·75

1927. Postage Due stamps of Upper Senegal and Niger surch SOUDAN FRANCAIS and value.
D133 **M** "2F." on 1f. mauve 2·75 14·00
D134 **M** "3F." on 1f. brown 4·50 17·00

1931. "Figure" key-type inscr "SOUDAN FRANCAIS".
D176 **M** 5c. green 10 6·50
D177 **M** 10c. red 10 4·75
D178 **M** 15c. grey 20 7·00
D179 **M** 20c. brown 30 7·00
D180 **M** 30c. blue 35 5·75
D181 **M** 50c. black 45 7·50
D182 **M** 60c. orange 65 6·75
D183 **M** 1f. violet 85 2·50
D184 **M** 2f. mauve 1·50 4·50
D185 **M** 3f. brown 1·50 8·25

Pt. 6

FRENCH TERRITORY OF THE AFARS AND ISSAS

Formerly French Somali Coast. Became independent in 1977 as Djibouti Republic.

100 centimes = 1 franc.

66 Grey-headed Kingfisher

1967. Fauna.
504 **66** 10f. mult (postage) 4·50 6·00
505 - 15f. multicoloured 7·00 9·00
506 - 50f. purple, brown & grn 16·00 23·00
507 - 55f. blue, violet and grey 16·00 34·00
508 - 60f. orange, emer & grn 30·00 40·00
509 - 200f. sepia, bistre & bl (air) 50·00 50·00
DESIGNS—HORIZ: 15f. Oystercatcher; 50f. Common greenshank; 55f. Abyssinian roller. VERT: (22×36 mm); 60f. Unstriped ground squirrel. (27×48 mm): 200f. Tawny eagles.

67 Footballers

1967. Sports.
510 **67** 25f. brn, grn & bl (postage) 3·00 4·25
511 - 30f. brown, blue & purple 4·75 7·50
512 - 48f. pur, bl & bistre (air) 4·75 6·50
513 - 85f. brown, blue & bistre 3·25 19·00
DESIGNS—HORIZ: 30f. Basketball. VERT: (27×48 mm) 48f. Parachute-jumping; 85f. Aquatic sports.

1968. 20th Anniv of W.H.O. As T 34 of French Polynesia.
514 15f. multicoloured 2·75 4·50

68 Damerdjog Fort

1968. Administrative Outposts.
515 **68** 20f. blue, brown & green 2·00 4·00
516 - 25f. blue, green & brown 2·00 2·30
517 - 30f. blue, bistre & orange 2·30 4·25
518 - 40f. blue, brown & green 3·50 5·75
DESIGNS—FORTS: 25f. Ali Adde; 30f. Dorra; 40f. Assamo.

1968. Human Rights Year. As T 36 of French Polynesia.
519 10f. red, violet and yellow 2·50 4·50
520 70f. purple, green & orange 3·00 5·75

69 Broadcasting Station

70 Relief Map of Territory

1968. Buildings and Landmarks.
521 **69** 1f. bl, turq & red (postage) 1·50 2·75
522 - 2f. blue, green & lt blue 2·00 1·50
523 - 5f. brown, green & blue 2·20 1·90
524 - 8f. brown, blue & green 2·50 3·00
525 - 15f. brown, green & blue 4·50 6·25
526 - 40f. grey, brown & turq 4·00 6·25
527 - 60f. multicoloured 2·50 7·00
528 - 70f. brown, green & grey 4·50 8·75
529 - 85f. green, blue & brn 7·50 8·00
530 - 85f. grey, blue & green 10·00 12·00
531 - 100f. brown, grn & bl (air) 4·00 3·75
532 - 200f. blue, brown & purple 8·00 9·50
533 **70** 500f. orange, brown & bl 32·00 29·00
DESIGNS—As T **69**: HORIZ: 2f. Courts of Justice; 5f. Chamber of Deputies; 8f. Great Mosque; 40f. Post Office, Djibouti; 70f. Governor's Residence, Obock; 85f. (No. 529) Port Administration Building, Djibouti; 85f. (No. 530) Airport. VERT: 15f. Free French Forces' Monument. As T **70**: HORIZ: 60f. French High Commission, Djibouti. VERT: 100f. Djibouti Cathedral; 200f. Sayed Hassan Mosque.

1969. Air. 1st Flight of Concorde. As T 39 of French Polynesia.
534 100f. red and drab 38·00 42·00

71 Desert Locust

1969. Anti-Locust Campaign.

535	**71**	15f. brown, slate & green	6·00	5·75
536	-	50f. brn, green & blue	8·00	5·00
537	-	55f. brown, blue & lake	8·25	7·00

DESIGNS: 50f. Sud Aviation SE 3130 Alouette II helicopter spraying crops; 55f. Piper PA-18-A Super Cub spraying crops.

1969. 50th Anniv of International Labour Organization. As T 44 of French Polynesia.

538	30f. mauve, slate and red	2·75	5·50

73 Afar Dagger

1970

543	**73**	10f. brown, grn & myrtle	2·50	3·25
544	**73**	15f. brown, green & blue	2·50	3·25
545	**73**	20f. brown, green & red	2·50	3·50
546	**73**	25f. brown, green & violet	2·75	2·75

74 Ionospheric Station, Arta

1970. Air. Opening of Ionospheric Station, Arta.

547	**74**	70f. red, green and blue	5·00	10·00

1970. New U.P.U. Headquarters Building. As T 47 of French Polynesia.

548	25f. brown, green & bistre	3·75	5·25

75 Clay-pigeon Shooting

1970. Sports.

549	**75**	30f. brown, blue & green	4·50	4·75
550	-	48f. brown, purple & blue	5·00	6·75
551	-	50f. red, violet and blue	5·25	3·75
552	-	55f. brown, bistre & blue	5·00	7·00
553	-	60f. black, brown & green	7·50	7·75

DESIGNS—HORIZ: 48f. Speedboat racing; 50f. Show jumping; 60f. Pony-trekking. VERT: 55f. Yachting.

76 "Fish" Sword-guard

1970. Air "Expo 70" World Fair, Osaka, Japan.

554	**76**	100f. vio, bl & grn on gold	11·00	18·00
555	-	200f. vio, grn & red on gold	14·00	22·00

DESIGN: 200f. "Horse" sword-guard.

77 "Goubet"

1970. Inauguration of Car Ferry, Tajurah.

556	**77**	48f. brown, blue & green	5·25	7·00

78 Dolerite Basalt

1971. Geology. Multicoloured.

557	10f. Type **78**	4·25	4·75
558	15f. Olivine basalt	4·50	4·50
559	25f. Volcanic geode	7·25	3·75
560	40f. Diabase and chrysolite	8·25	7·25

79 Manta Rays

1971. Marine Fauna. Multicoloured. (a) Postage. As T 79.

561	4f. Type **79**	3·00	4·00
562	5f. Dolphin (fish)	3·50	4·25
563	9f. Small-toothed sawfish	3·75	5·25

(b) Air. Size 46×27 mm (30f.) or 48×27 mm (others).

564	30f. Queen parrotfish	5·50	5·75
565	40f. Long-armed octopus	5·00	6·50
566	60f. Dugong	9·25	8·00

1971. De Gaulle Commemoration. As Nos. 1937 and 1940 of France.

567	60f. black and blue	6·00	9·00
568	85f. black and blue	7·75	9·25

80 Aerial View of Port

1971. Air. New Harbour, Djibouti.

569	**80**	100f. multicoloured	6·50	10·00

81 Mantle Clanculus

1972. Sea Shells. Multicoloured.

570	4f. Type **81**	2·75	3·75
571	9f. Panther cowrie	3·00	5·00
572	20f. Bull-mouth helmet	5·25	6·00
573	50f. Melon shell	6·50	7·00

82 Lichtenstein's Sandgrouse

1972. Air. Birds. Multicoloured.

574	30f. Type **82**	5·50	8·00
575	49f. Hoopoe	7·00	8·25
576	66f. Great snipe	10·50	11·00
577	500f. Pale-bellied francolin	50·00	44·00

83 Swimming

1972. Air. Olympic Games, Munich.

578	-	5f. brown, green & violet	2·00	3·50
579	-	10f. brown, green & red	2·30	3·75
580	**83**	55f. brown, blue & green	3·75	5·25
581	-	60f. violet, red and green	4·00	5·75

DESIGNS—VERT: 5f. Running; 10f. Basketball. HORIZ: 60f. Olympic flame, rings and ancient frieze.

84 Pasteur and Equipment

1972. Air. "Famous Medical Scientists".

582	**84**	20f. brown, green & red	3·00	5·00
583	-	100f. brown, green & red	7·25	8·00

DESIGN: 100f. Calmette and Guerin (B.C.G. pioneers).

85 Mosque, Map and Transport

1973. Air. Visit of President Pompidou. Mult.

584	30f. Type **85**	18·00	13·00
585	200f. Mosque and street scene, Djibouti (vert)	20·00	22·00

86 Gemsbok

1973. Air. Wild Animals. Multicoloured.

587	30f. Type **86**	3·75	3·50
588	50f. Salt's dik-dik	6·75	7·00
590	66f. Caracal	8·25	9·50

See also Nos. 603/5, 641/3, 659/60 and 662/4.

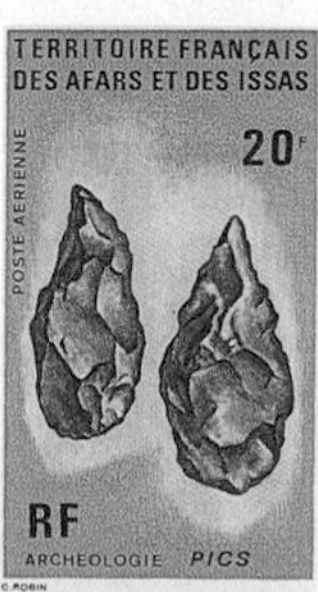

87 Flint Pick-heads

1973. Air. Archaeological Discoveries. Mult.

592	20f. Type **87**	4·50	6·00
593	40f. Arrow-heads and blade (horiz)	4·75	5·50
594	49f. Biface flint tool	9·00	8·00
595	60f. Flint axe-head and scraper (horiz)	6·50	8·00

88 Shepherd watering Sheep

1973. Pastoral Economy. Multicoloured.

596	9f. Type **88**	3·50	4·75
597	10f. Camel herd	4·00	5·00

89 Nicolas Copernicus (500th birth anniv)

1973. Air. Celebrities' Anniversaries.

598	**89**	8f. black, brown & purple	2·75	4·50
599	-	9f. purple, orange & brn	3·50	4·00
600	-	10f. purple, brown & red	2·75	4·25
601	-	49f. purple, grn & dp grn	5·75	6·50
602	-	85f. dp blue, blue & violet	7·75	7·00
607	-	100f. purple, blue & green	9·50	6·50
611	-	55f. indigo, brown & blue	4·25	7·00
615	-	10f. maroon, blue & pur	3·50	3·50
656	-	250f. brn, lt brn & grn	14·00	14·00
657	-	150f. turq, blue & brn	8·50	10·00
658	-	50f. brown, blue & green	7·00	5·50

DESIGNS: 9f. Wilhelm Rontgen (X-ray pioneer) (50th death anniv); 10f. (600) Edward Jenner (smallpox vaccination pioneer) (150th death anniv); 10f. (615) Marie Curie (physicist) (40th death anniv); 49f. Robert Koch (bacteriologist) (130th birth anniv); 50f. Clement Ader (aviation pioneer) (50th death anniv); 55f. Guglielmo Marconi (radio pioneer) (birth centenary); 85f. Moliere (playwright) (300th death anniv); 100f. Henri Farman (aviation pioneer) (birth centenary); 150f. Ampere (physicist) (birth bicentenary); 250f. Michelangelo (500th birth anniv).

1973. Air. Wild Animals (2nd series). As Type 86. Multicoloured.

603	20f. Olive baboon (vert)	4·25	5·50
604	50f. Large-spotted genet	5·00	5·00
605	66f. Abyssinian hare (vert)	8·75	8·25

90 Afar Dagger

1974

606	**90**	30f. purple and green	3·00	2·75

91 Greater Flamingos

1974. Lake Abbe. Multicoloured.

608	5f. Type **91**	4·50	2·75
609	15f. Two greater flamingos	4·25	4·50
610	50f. Greater flamingos in flight	6·50	5·75

92 Underwater Hunting

1974. Air. 3rd Underwater Hunting Trophy.

612	**92**	200f. blue, green & red	13·00	21·00

No. 612 has part of the original inscription blocked out.

93 Various Animals

1974. Air. Balho Rock Paintings.

613	**93**	200f. black and red	13·00	16·00

94 Football and Emblem

1974. World Cup Football Championship, West Germany.
614 **94** 25f. green and black 5·00 5·75

95 U.P.U. Emblem and Letters

1974. Centenary of Universal Postal Union.
616 **95** 20f. violet, blue & indigo 2·75 4·50
617 **95** 100f. brown, lt brn & red 5·00 6·25

96 Sunrise over Lake

1974. Air. Lake Assal. Multicoloured.
618 49f. Type **96** 4·25 6·00
619 50f. Rocky shore 4·50 6·00
620 85f. Crystallisation on dead wood 7·75 9·50

97 "Oleo chrysophylla"

1974. Forest Plants. Multicoloured.
621 10f. Type **97** 3·75 4·25
622 15f. "Ficus" (tree) 4·00 4·75
623 20f. "Solanum adoense" (shrub) 4·50 6·25

1975. Surch 40F.
624 **90** 40f. on 30f. purple & grn 3·50 3·75

99 Treasury Building

1975. Administrative Buildings, Djibouti.
625 **99** 8f. grey, blue and red 3·00 4·00
626 - 25f. grey, blue and red 3·25 5·25
DESIGN: 25f. "Government City" complex.

100 Textile Cone

1975. Sea Shells.
627 **100** 5f. brown and green 3·75 2·75
628 - 5f. brown and blue 4·00 4·50
629 - 5f. brown, mve & vio 3·75 5·00
630 - 10f. brown and purple 4·25 2·75
631 - 15f. brown and blue 4·75 4·00
632 - 20f. brown and violet 5·25 4·00
633 - 20f. brown and green 4·00 4·75
634 - 30f. brown, pur & grn 4·25 5·00
635 - 40f. brown and green 6·00 4·25
636 - 45f. brown, green & blue 4·75 3·50
637 - 55f. brown and blue 5·25 5·75
638 - 60f. black and brown 6·00 6·75
639 - 70f. brown, blue & black 8·00 7·50
640 - 85f. purple, blue & black 10·50 10·50
DESIGNS: 5f. (628) Rose-branch murex; 5f. (629) Tiger cowrie; 10f. Sumatran cone; 15f. Lovely cowrie; 20f. (632), 45f. Woodcock murex; 20f. (633) Burnt cowrie; 30f. Beech cowrie; 40f. Spiny frog shell; 55f. Red Sea cowrie; 60f. Ringed cone; 70f. Striate cone; 85f. Humpback cowrie.

1975. Wild Animals (3rd series). As T 86. Mult.
641 50f. White-tailed mongoose 5·50 6·75
642 60f. North African crested porcupine (vert) 6·75 7·75
643 70f. Zorilla 9·00 9·50

101 African Monarch

1975. Butterflies and Moths (1st series). Mult.
644 25f. Type **101** 3·50 5·75
645 40f. Narrow blue-banded swallowtail 4·75 6·00
646 70f. Citrus butterfly 7·25 7·50
647 100f. Mocker swallowtail 8·25 10·00
See also Nos. 666/7 and 675/6.

102 Speckled Pigeon

1975. Birds. Multicoloured.
648 20f. Pin-tailed whydah (postage) 3·25 5·25
649 25f. Rose-ringed parakeet 5·00 4·50
650 50f. Variable sunbird 4·75 6·75
651 60f. Goliath heron 6·75 8·00
652 100f. Hammerkop 11·00 9·25
653 100f. Namaqua dove 7·75 8·00
654 300f. African spoonbill 20·00 17·00
655 500f. Type **102** (air) 30·00 34·00

1975. Wild Animals (4th series). As T 86. Mult.
659 15f. Savanna monkeys (vert) 5·25 4·75
660 200f. Aardvarks 17·00 13·00

103 Palm Trees

1975
661 **103** 20f. multicoloured 4·00 4·00

1976. Wild Animals (5th series). As T 86. Multicoloured.
662 10f. Striped hyena 4·00 4·50
663 15f. African ass (vert) 4·25 4·75
664 30f. Beira antelope 4·75 5·25

104 Alexander Graham Bell and Satellite

1976. Telephone Centenary.
665 **104** 200f. blue, green & orge 11·00 8·50

1976. Butterflies and Moths (2nd series). As T 101. Multicoloured.
666 65f. Variable prince 5·00 7·00
667 100f. "Balachowsky gonimbrasia" 7·00 8·00

105 Basketball

1976. Olympic Games, Montreal. Mult.
668 10f. Type **105** 2·75 4·50
669 15f. Cycling 2·75 4·25
670 40f. Football 3·50 5·50
671 60f. Running 4·00 4·75

106 Radial Lionfish

1976. Marine Life.
672 **106** 45f. multicoloured 6·50 4·75

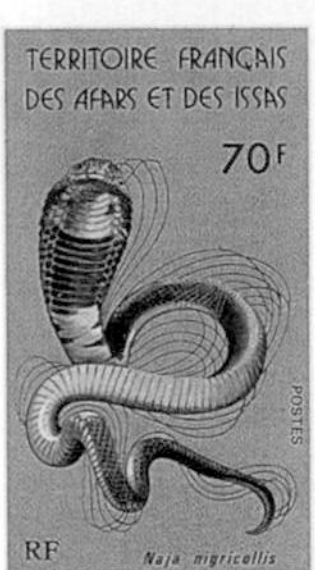

107 Black-necked Cobra

1976. Snakes. Multicoloured.
673 70f. Type **107** 5·50 7·75
674 80f. Elegant sand snake 6·50 8·25

1976. Butterflies and Moths (3rd series). As T 101. Multicoloured.
675 50f. Broad bordered acraea 4·75 7·00
676 150f. Painted lady 10·00 10·00

108 Motor Cyclist on Course

1977. Moto-Cross.
677 **108** 200f. multicoloured 14·50 11·00

109 Air Terminal

1977. Air. Inauguration of New Djibouti Airport.
678 **109** 500f. multicoloured 34·00 32·00

110 Black-spotted Sweetlips

1977. Fishes. Multicoloured.
679 15f. Type **110** 3·50 5·25
680 65f. Great barracuda 5·75 6·25

111 Edison and Phonograph

1977. Air. Celebrities.
681 **111** 55f. red, slate and green 7·75 7·75
682 - 75f. red, brown & green 16·00 14·00
DESIGN: 75f. Volta and TGV express train, France.

POSTAGE DUE STAMPS

D72 Nomadic Milk-Jug

1969
D539 **D72** 1f. slate, brn & pur 1·20 4·50
D540 **D72** 2f. slate, brn & grn 1·40 4·50
D541 **D72** 5f. slate, brn & blue 1·50 5·00
D542 **D72** 10f. slate, lake & brn 2·30 6·00

For later issues see **DJIBOUTI REPUBLIC**.

Pt. 6

FRENCH WEST AFRICA

The territory in north-west Africa comprising Senegal, French Guinea, Ivory Coast, Dahomey, French Sudan, Mauritania, Niger and Upper Volta. French Sudan and Senegal became the Mali Federation and the rest independent republics.

100 centimes = 1 franc.

1944. Mutual Aid and Red Cross Funds. As T 58e of Guadeloupe.

1	5f.+20f. purple	1·80	22·00

1945. Eboue. As T 58f of Guadeloupe.

2	2f. black	65	65
3	25f. green	1·00	9·50

1 Soldiers

1945

4	1	10c. blue and pink	1·00	2·75
5	1	30c. olive and cream	1·00	6·75
6	1	40c. blue and pink	90	5·00
7	1	50c. orange and grey	1·00	1·20
8	1	60c. olive and grey	1·00	5·75
9	1	70c. mauve and cream	1·80	7·50
10	1	80c. green and cream	1·00	5·75
11	1	1f. purple and olive	65	45
12	1	1f.20 brown and olive	2·75	8·25
13	1	1f.50 brown and red	90	90
14	1	2f. yellow and grey	1·50	90
15	1	2f.40 red and grey	1·40	5·50
16	1	3f. red and olive	75	45
17	1	4f. blue and red	1·30	90
18	1	4f.50 brown and olive	2·50	2·00
19	1	5f. violet and olive	1·40	45
20	1	10f. green and red	90	55
21	1	15f. brown and cream	2·30	1·60
22	1	20f. green and grey	2·50	2·20

1945. Stamp Day. As T 228 of France (Louis XI) but optd A O F.

23	2f.+3f. red	55	4·50

1945. Air. As T 63a of Guadeloupe.

24	5f.50 blue	90	2·10
25	50f. green	90	75
26	100f. red	90	1·30

1946. Air. Victory. As T 63b of Guadeloupe.

27	8f. mauve	90	1·00

1946. Air. From Chad to the Rhine. As T 63c of Guadeloupe.

28	5f. red	2·50	8·25
29	10f. blue	2·50	8·00
30	15f. mauve	1·80	8·75
31	20f. green	2·20	10·00
32	25f. brown	1·70	7·75
33	50f. brown	2·30	11·00

3 War Dance

6 Sudanese Carving

9 Natives and Airplane

1947

34	3	10c. blue (postage)	10	5·25
35	-	30c. brown	10	6·00
36	-	40c. green	75	5·75
37	-	50c. red	85	1·80
38	-	60c. grey	1·40	5·75
39	-	80c. lilac	1·40	3·25
40	-	1f. red	1·00	35
41	-	1f.20 green	1·80	5·75
42	-	1f.50 blue	3·00	6·75
43	6	2f. orange	90	20
68	-	3f. brown	1·80	55
45	-	3f.60 red	3·50	9·50
46	-	4f. blue	2·00	20
47	-	5f. green	2·30	35
48	-	6f. blue	2·00	45
49	-	10f. red	2·10	10
50	-	15f. brown	3·50	20
51	-	20f. brown	2·00	20
52	-	25f. black	2·75	65
53	-	8f. red (air)	3·25	75
54	-	50f. violet	5·50	1·30
55	-	100f. blue	10·00	2·75
56	9	200f. grey	6·50	3·25

DESIGNS—As Type **3/6**—HORIZ: 30c. Girl and bridge; 40c. Canoe; 50c. Niger landscape; 80c. Dahomey weaver; 1f. Donkey caravan; 1f.20, Crocodile and hippopotamus; 10f. Djenne Mosque; 15f. Renault model ABH railcar. VERT: 60c. Coconuts; 1f.50, Palm trees; 3f. Togo girl; 3f.60, Sudanese market; 4f. Dahomey labourer; 5f. Mauritanian woman; 6f. Guinea headdress; 20f. Ivory Coast girl; 25f. Niger washerwoman. As Type **9**—VERT: 8f. Antoine de Saint-Exupery. HORIZ: 50f. Caudron C-445 Goeland airplane over Dakar (Senegal); 100f. Flight of great egrets (Niger).

1949. 75th Anniv of U.P.U. As T 39 of French Equatorial Africa.

69	9	25f. multicoloured	2·75	7·25

1950. Colonial Welfare Fund. As T 40 of French Equatorial Africa.

70	10f.+2f. dp brown & brown	4·00	12·00

10 Medical Research

11 T. Laplene and Map of Ivory Coast

12 Logging Camp

1951

71	-	8f. blue & brown (postage)	2·75	1·70
72	10	15f. green, brown & sepia	1·30	10
73	-	20f. myrtle and turquoise	3·00	6·25
74	-	25f. sepia, blue and purple	1·80	20
75	11	40f. red	2·75	45
76	12	50f. brown and green (air)	3·00	90
77	-	100f. brown, blue & green	6·25	90
78	-	200f. green, turq & lake	23·00	3·00
79	-	500f. green, blue & orange	21·00	8·00

DESIGNS—As Type **11**: 8f. Governor-General Ballay; 20f. Houphouet-Boigny Bridge, Abidjan; 25f. Africans, animals and sailing canoe. As Type **12**: 100f. Telephonist, Lockheed Constellation airplane and pylons; 200f. Baobab trees; 500f. Vridi Canal, Abidjan.

1952. Centenary of Military Medal. As T 44 of French Equatorial Africa.

80	15f. sepia, yellow and green	4·50	2·00

1954. Air. 10th Anniv of Liberation. As T 46 of French Equatorial Africa.

81	15f. blue and indigo	7·50	4·50

13 Chimpanzee

1955. Nature Protection. Inscr as in T 13.

82	13	5f. sepia and grey	2·00	90
83	-	8f. sepia and green	2·00	1·60

DESIGN—HORIZ: 8f. Giant ground pangolin.

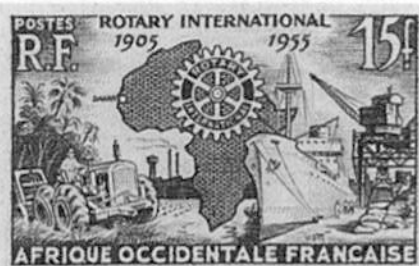

14

1955. 50th Anniv of Rotary International.

84	14	15f. blue	1·60	55

15 Mossi Railways

1955. Economic and Social Development Fund. Inscr "F.I.D.E.S.".

85	-	1f. green and myrtle	1·20	3·25
86	-	2f. myrtle and turquoise	2·50	3·25
87	15	3f. sepia and brown	3·25	3·50
88	-	4f. red	3·00	2·30
89	-	15f. blue and indigo	1·20	30
90	-	17f. blue and indigo	2·50	2·50
91	-	20f. purple	2·75	1·40
92	-	30f. purple and lilac	2·20	1·40

DESIGNS—HORIZ: 1f. Date palms; 2f. Milo River bridge; 4f. Herdsman and cattle; 15f. Combine harvester; 17f. Woman and aerial view; 20f. Palm oil factory; 30f. Abidjan-Abengourou road.

1956. Coffee. As T 51 of French Equatorial Africa.

93	15f. green and turquoise	2·00	20

16 Medical Station and Ambulance

1957. Order of Malta Leprosy Relief.

94	16	15f. claret, purple & red	1·40	2·00

1957. Air. Centenary of African Troops. As T 53 of French Equatorial Africa.

95	15f. blue and indigo	1·60	4·50

17 Map of Africa

1958. 6th African International Tourist Congress.

96	17	20f. red and green	1·50	4·75

18 "Communication"

1958. Stamp Day.

97	18	15f. brown, blue & orange	1·30	5·25

19 Isle of Goree and West African

1958. Air. Dakar Centenary. Inscr "CENTENAIRE DE DAKAR".

98	19	15f. multicoloured	1·10	1·80
99	-	20f. red, brown and blue	2·75	3·00
100	-	25f. multicoloured	1·00	1·00
101	-	40f. brown, green & blue	90	1·10
102	-	50f. violet, brown & green	1·50	1·40
103	-	100f. green, blue & brown	2·75	3·00

MS104 185×125 mm. Nos. 98/103 with view of Dakar	18·00	60·00

DESIGNS: 20f. Map of Dakar, liner, freighters and Lockheed Super Constellation and Douglas DC-6 aircraft; 25f. Town construction; 40f. Council house; 50f. Groundnuts, artisan and "L'Arachide" (freighter) at quayside; 100f. Bay of N'Gor.

20 Banana Plant and Fruit

1958. Banana Production.

105	20	20f. purple, green & olive	1·00	20

1958. Tropical Flora. As T 56 of French Equatorial Africa.

118	10f. multicoloured	75	30
119	25f. yellow, green and red	90	45
120	30f. brown, green and blue	1·40	75
121	40f. yellow, green & brown	1·60	2·00
122	65f. multicoloured	2·00	2·00

DESIGNS—VERT: 10f. "Gloriosa"; 25f. "Adenopus"; 30f. "Cyrtosperma"; 40f. "Cistanche"; 65f. "Crinum moorei".

22 Moro Naba Sagha and Map of Upper Volta

1958. 10th Anniv of Upper Volta Scheme.

123	22	20f. multicoloured	5·00	5·00

23 Native Chief and Musician

1958. Air. Inauguration of Nouakchott, Capital of Mauritania.

124	23	20f. sepia, brown & grey	2·75	4·75

1958. 10th Anniv of Declaration of Human Rights. As T 14 of French Polynesia.

125	20f. purple and blue	90	6·00

1959. Stamp Day. As T 18 but inscr "DAKAR-ABIDJAN" in place of "AFRIQUE OCCIDENTALE FRANCAISE".

126	20f. green, blue and red	2·50	11·00

No. 126 was for use in Ivory Coast and Senegal.

OFFICIAL STAMPS

O21

1958. Inscr "OFFICIEL".

O106	O21	1f. brown	2·50	2·30
O107	O21	3f. green	2·75	5·50
O108	O21	5f. red	2·00	1·00
O109	O21	10f. blue	3·25	2·50
O110	-	20f. red	3·25	1·70
O111	-	25f. violet	3·00	65
O112	-	30f. green	3·50	5·25
O113	-	45f. black	2·50	2·00
O114	-	50f. red	4·25	2·50
O115	-	65f. blue	3·00	3·75
O116	-	100f. olive	3·25	3·25
O117	-	200f. green	11·00	10·00

DESIGNS—VERT: 20f. to 45f. Head as Type O **21** but with female face; 50f. to 200f. Head as Type O **21** but with hooped headdress, portrait being diagonal on stamp.

POSTAGE DUE STAMPS

D10

1947

D57	D10	10c. red	45	6·50
D58	D10	30c. orange	45	5·50
D59	D10	50c. black	45	6·00
D60	D10	1f. red	1·40	6·75
D61	D10	2f. green	1·50	7·00
D62	D10	3f. mauve	2·30	7·00

D63	D10	4f. blue	2·75	7·50
D64	D10	5f. brown	2·30	7·00
D65	D10	10f. blue	2·30	8·50
D66	D10	20f. brown	4·25	12·00

Pt. 19

FUJEIRA

One of the Trucial States in the Persian Gulf. With six other sheikdoms formed the state of the United Arab Emirates on 18 July 1971. Fujiera stamps were replaced by issues of United Arab Emirates on 1 January 1973.

1964. 100 naye paise = 1 rupee.
1967. 100 dirhams = 1 riyal.

1 Shaikh Mohamed bin Hamad al Sharqi and Great Crested Grebe

1964. Multicoloured. (a) Size as T 1.

1	1n.p. Type **1**	20	20
2	2n.p. Arabian oryx	20	20
3	3n.p. Hoopoe	20	20
4	4n.p. Asiatic wild ass	20	20
5	5n.p. Great Egrets	20	20
6	10n.p. Arab horses	20	20
7	15n.p. Cheetah	20	20
8	20n.p. Dromedaries	20	20
9	30n.p. Lanner falcon	20	20

(b) Size 43½×28½ mm.

10	40n.p. Type **1**	45	20
11	50n.p. Arabian oryx	45	20
12	70n.p. Hoopoe	65	45
13	1r. Asiatic wild ass	75	65
14	1r.50 Great egrets	1·30	75
15	2r. Arab horses	1·60	1·20

(c) Size 53½×35½ mm.

16	3r. Leopard	2·40	2·40
17	5r. Dromedaries	4·00	4·00
18	10r. Lanner falcon	8·50	6·50

2 Shaikh Mohamed and Putting the Shot

1964. Olympic Games, Tokyo. Multicoloured. (a) Size as T 2.

19	25n.p. Type **2**	20	20
20	50n.p. Throwing the discus	50	50
21	75n.p. Fencing	65	65
22	1r. Boxing	75	75
23	1r.50 Relay-racing	1·30	1·30
24	2r. Football	1·70	1·70

(b) Size 53×35½ mm.

25	3r. High jumping	2·40	2·40
26	5r. Hurdling	3·75	3·75
27	7r.50 Horse-riding	6·00	6·00

3 Kennedy as a Boy

1965. Pres. Kennedy Commem. Each black and gold on coloured paper as given below.

28	3	5n.p. blue	20	15
29	-	10n.p. yellow	20	15
30	-	15n.p. pink	20	15
31	-	20n.p. green	20	20
32	-	25n.p. blue	30	20
33	-	50n.p. flesh	45	30
34	-	1r. lilac	1·40	1·20
35	-	2r. yellow	2·10	1·80
36	-	3r. blue	3·50	2·75
37	-	5r. buff	6·50	5·25

DESIGNS (Kennedy): 10n.p. As student. 15n.p. As cadet. 20n.p. As Senator. 25n.p. Sailing. 50n.p. As President. 33×51 mm: 1r. With Mrs. Kennedy and guest. 2r. With Pres. Eisenhower. 3r. With family. 5r. Full face portrait.

1965. Air. Designs similar to Nos. 1/9, but with "FUJEIRA" and value transposed, and inscr "AIR MAIL". Mult. (a) Size 43½×28½ mm.

39	15n.p. Type **1**	20	15
40	25n.p. Arabian oryx	30	15
41	35n.p. Hoopoe	55	15
42	50n.p. Asiatic wild ass	55	15
43	75n.p. Great egrets	85	15
44	1r. Arab horses	95	50

(b) Size 53½×35½ mm.

MS38	90×80 mm. Nos. 36/7 in new colours, but size 28½×44 mm	13·00	6·50
45	2r. Leopard	2·10	85
46	3r. Dromedaries	3·25	1·60
47	5r. Lanner falcon	5·25	1·90

4 Queen Nefertiti

1966. Stamp Centenary Exn, Cairo. Mult.

57	3n.p. Type **4**	10	10
58	5n.p. Colossi, Abu Simbel	10	10
59	10n.p. Tutankhamun's mask	10	10
60	15n.p. Sphinx, Gezir	10	10
61	25n.p. Statues of Prince Rahotep and his wife Nofret	20	15
62	50n.p. Ancient Church (horiz)	25	15
63	1r. Colonnade, Great Temple of Isis, Philae (horiz)	75	30
64	2r. Nile sphinxes (horiz)	1·60	75
65	5r. Pyramids, Giza (horiz)	3·75	1·80
MS66	120×75 mm. Nos. 64/5 but size 44×29 mm	8·00	8·00

5 Sir Winston Churchill as Harrow Schoolboy

1966. Churchill Commem. Each design black and gold; frame in colours given.

67	5	10n.p. yellow (postage)	10	10
68	-	15n.p. blue	10	10
69	-	25n.p. buff	20	15
70	-	50n.p. blue	30	20
71	-	75n.p. mauve	55	30
72	-	1r. blue	75	40
73	-	2r. gold (air)	1·60	65
74	-	3r. gold	2·40	1·40
MS75		105×75 mm. Nos. 73/4 in new colours but size 32×44 mm and inscr "POSTAGE" instead of "AIR MAIL"	5·25	5·25

DESIGNS—Churchill: 15n.p. Wearing Hussars' uniform; 25n.p. As Boer War correspondent; 50n.p. In morning dress; 75n.p. With Eisenhower; 1r. Painting; 2r. With grandson; 3r. Giving "V" sign.

6 Lunar Satellite

1966. Space Achievements. Multicoloured.

76	5n.p. Type **6**	10	15
77	10n.p. Satellite approaching Moon	10	15
78	15n.p. Satellite and planets	10	15
79	25n.p. Satellite and Solar System	30	15
80	50n.p. Communications satellite	45	15
81	75n.p. Venus probe	75	15
82	1r. "Telstar"	95	30
83	2r. "Relay"	2·10	85
MS84	130×90 mm. Nos. 82/3	3·75	3·75

1967. Various stamps with currency names changed by overprinting. (i) Nos. 1/18 (Definitives).

85	1d. on 1n.p.	30	10
86	2d. on 2n.p.	30	10
87	3d. on 3n.p.	30	10
88	4d. on 4n.p.	30	10
89	5d. on 5n.p.	30	10
90	10d. on 10n.p.	30	10
91	15d. on 15n.p.	30	10
92	20d. on 20n.p.	30	10
93	30d. on 30n.p.	20	20
94	40d. on 40n.p.	30	30
95	50d. on 50n.p.	30	30
96	70d. on 70n.p.	45	45
97	1r. on 1r.	65	65
98	1r.50 on 1r.50	1·10	1·10
99	2r. on 2r.	1·40	1·40
100	3r. on 3r. on 3r.	2·10	2·10
101	5r. on 5r.	3·50	3·50
102	10r. on 10r.	7·50	7·50

(ii) Air. Nos. 39/47 (Definitives).

123	15d. on 15n.p.	20	10
124	25d. on 25n.p.	20	10
125	35d. on 35n.p.	65	30
126	50d. on 50n.p.	65	30
127	75d. on 75n.p.	1·10	55
128	1r. on 1r.	1·30	65
129	2r. on 2r.	2·50	1·30
130	3r. on 3r.	4·25	2·10
131	5r. on 5r.	7·00	3·50

Nos. 19/37 and 57/83 were also surcharged in the new currency in limited quantities, but they had little local usage.

9 "Pararge felix"

1967. Butterflies. Multicoloured. (a) Postage. (i) Size 32×32 mm.

167	1d. Type **9**	10	10
168	2d. African clouded yellow (male)	10	10
169	3d. African clouded yellow (female)	10	10
170	4d. "Spindasis scotti"	10	10
171	5d. "Pararge felix" (different)	10	10
172	10d. "Lepidochrysops arabicus"	10	10
173	15d. "Eumenis tewfiki"	10	10
174	20d. "Euchrysops philbyi"	10	10
175	30d. "Mylothris arabicus"	15	10

(ii) Size 40×40 mm.

176	40d. Type **9**	15	10
177	50d. As No. 168	30	10
178	70d. As No. 169	30	20
179	1r. As No. 170	55	30
180	1r.50 As No. 171	85	50
181	2r. As No. 172	1·10	85

(iii) Size 42×42 mm.

182	3r. As No. 173	1·60	95
183	5r. As No. 174	2·75	1·60
184	10r. As No. 175	6·00	3·25

(b) Air. Size 45×45 mm.

185	15d. Type **9**	10	15
186	25d. As No. 168	10	15
187	35d. As No. 169	20	15
188	50d. As No. 170	30	15
189	75d. As No. 171	30	20
190	1r. As No. 172	55	30
191	2r. As No. 173	1·10	65
192	3r. As No. 174	1·60	85
193	5r. As No. 175	2·75	1·60

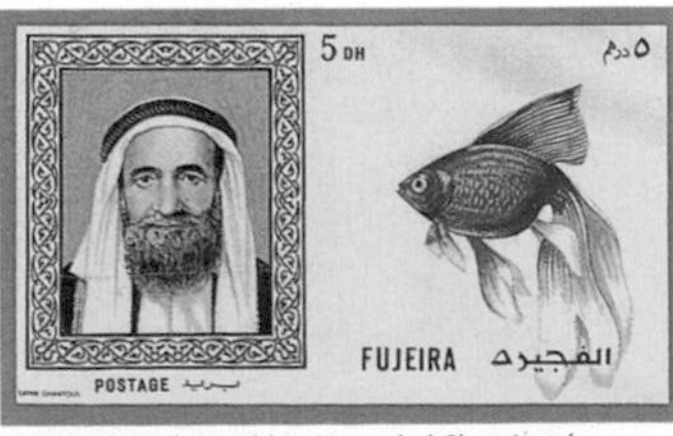

10 Shaikh Mohamed bin Hamad al Sharqi and Veil-tailed Goldfish

1971. Multicoloured.. Multicoloured..

194	5d. Type **10** (postage)	20	30
195	20d. Shaikh and semicircle angelfish (air)	10	15
196	35d. Shaikh and paradise fish	20	20
197	40d. Shaikh and moorish idol	20	20
198	60d. Shaikh and daisy	30	20
199	1r. Shaikh and rose	65	20
200	2r. Shaikh and gentian	1·30	55
201	3r. Shaikh and wild rose	1·80	85

OFFICIAL STAMPS

1965. Designs similar to Nos. 1/9, but with "FUJEIRA" and value transposed, additionally inscr "ON STATE'S SERVICE". Multicoloured. (a) Postage. Size 43½×28½ mm.

O48	25n.p. Type **1**	20	15
O49	40n.p. Arabian oryx	30	15
O50	50n.p. Hoopoe	45	20
O51	75n.p. Asiatic wild ass	75	30
O52	1r. Great egrets	95	55

(b) Air. (i) Size 43½×28½ mm.

O53	75n.p. Arab horses	65	30

(ii) Size 53½×35½ mm.

O54	2r. Leopard	1·90	85
O55	3r. Dromedaries	2·75	1·30
O56	5r. Lanner falcon	4·75	2·40

1967. Nos. 48/56 with currency name changed by overprinting.

O158	25d. on 25n.p. (postage)	20	20
O159	40d. on 40n.p.	30	30
O160	50d. on 50n.p.	45	45
O161	75d. on 75n.p.	65	65
O162	1r. on 1r.	95	95
O163	75d. on 75n.p. (air)	65	65
O164	2r. on 2r.	1·90	1·90
O165	3r. on 3r.	2·75	2·75
O166	5r. on 5r.	5·00	5·00

APPENDIX

The following stamps have either neen issued in excess of postal needs or have not been available to the public in reasonable quantities at face value. Such stamps may later be given full listing if there is evidence of regular postal use.

1967

"One Thousand and One Nights". Postage 10, 15, 30, 75d., 1r., 1r.50; Air 25, 50, 75d., 1r., 1r.25, 2r.
Famous Paintings. Postage 25, 50, 75d., 1, 1r.50; Air 2, 3, 5r.
Cats. Postage 10, 35, 50d., 1, 1r.50; Air 1r.25, 2r.75, 3r.50.

1968

Winter Olympic Games, Grenoble. 25, 50, 75d., 1, 1r.50, 2, 3r.
Famous Paintings (square designs). Postage 50, 75d., 1, 2, 3r.; Air 1r.50, 2r.50, 3r.50, 4, 5r.
Ships. Postage 15, 25, 50, 75d., 1r.; Air 2, 3, 4, 5r.
Olympic Games, Mexico. Optd on Nos. 22/6 and four values of 1968 Winter Olympics issue. Postage 1, 1r.50, 2, 3, 5r.; Air 1, 1r.50, 2, 3r.
Prehistoric Animals. Postage 15, 25, 50, 75d., 1r.50; Air 1, 2r.50, 3, 4, 5r.
Robert Kennedy Memorial issue. Optd on Nos. 34/7. 1, 2, 3, 5r.
Olympic Games, Mexico. Postage 15, 25, 35, 50, 75d., 1r.; Air 1r.50, 2, 3, 5r.
International Letter-writing Week. Paintings. Postage 25, 50, 75d., 1r.; Air 1r.50, 2, 3, 5r.
"EFIMEX" International Stamp Exhibition, Mexico. Optd on 1968 Letter-writing Week issue. Postage 25, 50, 75d.; 1r. Air 1r.50, 2, 3, 5r.
Gold Medal Winners, Olympic Games, Mexico. Optd on 1968 Olympic Games, Mexico issue. Postage 15, 25, 35, 50 75d., 1r.; Air 1r.50, 2, 3, 5r.

1969

Wild Animals of the World. Postage 15, 25, 50, 75d., 1r.; Air 1r.50, 2, 3, 5r.
Scenes from Shakespeare's Plays. Postage 25, 50, 75d., 1, 2r.; Air 1r.25, 2r.50, 3, 5r.
Olympic Games, Munich (1969). Optd on 1968 Olympic Games, Mexico issue. Postage 15, 25, 35, 50, 75d., 1r.; Air 1r.50, 2r.50, 3, 5r.
Famous Railway Locomotives. Postage 15, 25, 50, 75d., 1r.; Air 2, 3, 5r.
Moon Flight of "Apollo 8". Optd or surch on Nos. 76/83. 50, 75n.p., 1, 2, 2r.50 on 25n.p., 3r. on 15n.p., 4r. on 10n.p. 5r. on 5n.p.
Winter Olympic Games, Sapporo, Japan (1972). Optd on 1968 Winter Olympic Games, Grenoble issue. 25, 50, 75d., 1, 1r.50, 2, 3r.
Birds. Postage 25, 50d., 1r., 1r.50, 2r.; Air 1r.25, 2r.50, 3, 5r.
Pres. Eisenhower Memorial issue. Postage 25, 50d., 1r., 1r.50, 2r.; Air 1r.25, 2r.50, 3, 5r.
Champions of Peace. 25, 50, 75d., 1, 2, 3, 5r.
Human Rights Year. Optd on 1969 Champions of Peace issue. 25, 50, 75d., 1, 2, 3, 5r.
Flowers. Postage 25, 50d., 1, 1r.50, 2r.; Air 1r.25, 2r.50, 3, 5r.
"Apollo" Space Flights. Postage 10, 25, 50d., 1, 2r.; Air 2r.50, 3, 4, 5r.
Space Flight of "Apollo 10". Optd on 1969 "Apollo" Space Flights issue. Postage 10, 25, 50d., 1, 2r.; Air 2r.50, 3, 4, 5r.
Moon Landing. Optd on 1969 "Apollo" Space Flights issue. Postage 10, 25, 50d., 1, 2r.; Air 2r.50, 3, 4, 5r.
First Man on the Moon. 1969 "Apollo" Space Flights issue optd with various commemoration inscriptions. Postage 10, 25, 50d., 1, 2r.; Air 2r.50, 3, 4, 5r.

1970

Birth Bicentenary of Napoleon Bonaparte. 15, 25, 50, 75d., 1, 1r.50, 2r.

General De Gaulle Commemoration. Air 35, 60, 75d., 1r.25, 2r.50, 3, 5r.
Bible Stories. Postage 15d., 1r.; Air 35, 75d., 1r.25, 1r.50, 2r.50, 3r.
"Expo 70" World Fair, Osaka, Japan. Japanese Art. Postage 15, 25, 50, 75d., 1, 2r.; Air 75d., 1r.25, 2r.50, 4r.
Exploration of the Moon. 25, 50d., 1, 2, 3, 4, 5r.
Space Flight of "Apollo 13". Optd on 1970 Moon Exploration issue. 25, 50d., 1, 2, 3, 4, 5r.
Moon Mission of "Apollo 14". Optd on 1970 Moon Exploration issue. 25, 50d., 1, 2, 3, 4, 5r.
"Expo 70" World Fair, Osaka, Japan. Pavilions. 10, 20, 70d., 1r.×2, 2r.
World Football Cup, Mexico. 10, 20, 70d., 1r.×2, 2r.
Pres. Gamal Nasser Memorial issue. Postage 10, 20, 30, 40, 50d.; Air 5r.
Horses. Postage 10, 20d.; Air 70d., 1, 2r.
Cats. Postage 30, 70d.; Air 1, 2, 3r.
Dogs. Postage 30, 70d.; Air 1, 2, 3r.
Paintings of the Madonna. 30, 70d., 1, 2, 3r.
Stations of the Cross. 1r.×15.
Christmas. Paintings. Postage 30, 70d., 1r.; Air 2, 3r.

1971

American and European Cars. Postage 5, 20, 30d., 4r.; Air 30, 50, 70d., 1r.50, 2r.50, 4r.
Space Exploration. Air 40, 60d., 1, 2, 5r.
History of Railways. 10, 20, 70d., 2, 3r.
General De Gaulle Memorial issue. Air 30, 70d. 1, 2, 3r.
Moon Mission of "Apollo 14" Air 70d., 1, 2, 3, 4r.
Wild Animals. Air 20, 40, 60d., 1, 2, 3r.
Olympic Games, Munich (1972) (square designs). Postage 50d., 1r.; Air 2, 3, 4r.
Winter Olympic Games, Sapporo, Japan (1972). Postage 5, 10, 15, 20, 30, 50d.; Air 70d., 4r.
500th Birth Anniv of Durer. Paintings. Air 70d., 1, 2, 3, 4r.
Birth Bicentenary of Beethoven. Portraits and instruments. Postage 30, 70d.; Air 1, 3, 4r.
Mozart Commem. Postage 30, 70d.1r.; Air 3, 4r.
Frazier v Mohammed Ali World Heavyweight Boxing Championship Fight. Air 1, 2, 3r.
World Scout Jamboree, Asagiri, Japan. Postage 20, 30, 50, 70d., 1r.×2, 2r.×2; Air 3, 4r.
Butterflies. Air. 70d., 1, 2, 3, 5r.
Cats and Dogs. 10, 20, 30d., 1, 2, 3r.
Monkeys. 30, 70d., 1, 2, 3r.
Wild Animals. 30, 70d., 1, 2, 3r.
Horses. 70d., 1, 2, 3, 4r.
Olympic Games, Munich. Sports. 1, 2, 3, 4, 5, 6, 7, 8, 9, 10, 11, 12, 13, 14, 15, 16, 17, 18, 19, 20, 21, 22, 23, 24, 25, 26, 27, 28, 29, 30d.
Olympic Games, Munich. Sports and Arenas. Postage 35, 60d., 2, 3r.; Air 4r.
Christmas. Postage 40, 60d., 2r.; Air 3, 4r.
International Labour Day. Paintings. Postage 40, 60d., 2, 3r.; Air 2, 3, 4r.

During 1970 a number of other sets came onto the market, but their official status is in doublt

1972

400th Birth Anniv of Kepler. Postage 35, 75d., 1, 2r.; Air 3, 5r.
Moon Mission of "Apollo 15". Postage 30, 70d.; Air 1, 2, 5r.
2500th Anniv of The Persian Empire. Postage 35, 65, 75d.; Air 1r.25, 2, 3r.
Historical Costumes. 30, 70d., 1, 2, 3r.
Winter Olympic Games, Sapporo, Japan. Postage 25, 30, 70d.; Air 1r.25, 2, 3r.
Tropical Birds 30, 70d., 1, 2, 3r.
Children's Day. Paintings. Postage 10, 30, 60d.; Air 4, 5r.
Sculptures. Postage 30, 70d.; Air 1, 2, 6r.
Paintings of the Madonna. Postage 20, 30 50d.; Air 4, 5r.
Nude Paintings. 50d., 1, 2, 3, 4r.
Gold Medal Winners, Winter Olympic Games, Sapporo. Optd on 1972 Winter Olympic Games, Sapporo issue. Postage 25, 30, 70d.; Air 1r.25, 2, 3r.
Olympic Games, Munich. Discus-thrower. Air 8r.
Space Exploration. Postage 5, 10, 15, 20, 25, 30, 35, 40, 45, 50, 55, 60d.; Air 65, 70, 75d., 1, 2, 3, 4, 5r.
Walt Disney Cartoon Characters. Postage 1, 2, 3, 4, 5, 10, 15, 20, 25, 30d.; Air 45, 55, 65, 70d., 1, 1r.50, 2, 3, 4, 5r.
History of the Olympic Games Postage 1, 2, 3, 4, 5, 10, 15, 20, 25, 30, 45, 55d.; Air 65, 70d., 1, 1r.50, 2, 3, 5r.
Summit Meeting of Pres. Nixon and Mao Tse-tung. Air 2, 3, 5r.
Pres. Nixon's Visit of Russia. Optd on 1972 Nixon–Mao Tse-tung Meeting issue. Air 2, 3, 5r.
150th Death Anniv (1971) of Napoleon Bonaparte. Air 10r.
2nd Death Anniv of General De Gaulle. Air 10r.
Olympic Games, Munich, Javelin-thrower. Air 10r.
Gold Medal Winners, Olympic Games, Munich. Optd on 1972 Discus-thrower issue. Air 8r.
Moon Mission of "Apollo 16". Air 10r.
European Birds. 30, 70d., 1, 2, 3r.

A number of issues on gold and silver foil also exist, but it is understood that these were mainly for presentation purposes, although valid for postage.

During 1970 a number of other sets came on to the market, but their official status is in doubt.

The United Arab Emirates Ministry of Communications took over the Fujeira postal service on 1 August 1972. Further stamps were released without authority and had no validity.

Pt. 9

FUNCHAL

The District of Funchal (the chief town) was the administrative title of Madeira from 1892 to 1905. From 1905 the name reverted to Madeira.

1000 reis = 1 milreis.

4

1892

82	4	5r. yellow	3·25	2·00
86	4	10r. mauve	3·75	2·50
87	4	15r. brown	5·00	4·50
89	4	20r. lilac	5·50	3·75
83	4	25r. green	7·00	1·90
84	4	50r. blue	7·00	3·75
92	4	75r. pink	11·00	9·25
93	4	80r. green	21·00	16·00
95	4	100r. brown on buff	13·50	6·75
107	4	150r. red on pink	80·00	45·00
96	4	200r. blue on blue	90·00	65·00
97	4	300r. blue on brown	95·00	80·00

1897. "King Carlos" key-type inscr "FUNCHAL". Name and value in red (Nos. 123, 130) or black (others).

110	S	2½r. grey	75	50
111	S	5r. red	75	50
112	S	10r. green	75	50
113	S	15r. brown	8·75	6·75
126	S	15r. green	5·00	3·75
114	S	20r. lilac	2·10	1·20
115	S	25r. green	4·25	1·20
127	S	25r. red	2·10	95
128	S	50r. blue	2·10	1·50
129	S	65r. blue	1·80	1·50
117	S	75r. pink	2·20	1·60
130	S	75r. brown on yellow	2·75	1·70
118	S	80r. mauve	2·20	2·00
119	S	100r. blue on blue	2·20	2·00
131	S	115r. red on pink	3·50	2·30
132	S	130r. brown on cream	3·50	2·30
120	S	150r. brown on yellow	4·25	2·10
133	S	180r. grey on pink	3·50	2·30
121	S	200r. purple on pink	4·50	3·50
122	S	300r. blue on pink	4·50	3·50
123	S	500r. black on blue	4·75	4·00

Pt. 6, Pt. 13

GABON

A French colony on the W. coast of equatorial Africa. Became part of Fr. Equatorial Africa in 1937 and a republic within the French Community in 1958. Independence was declared in 1960.

100 centimes = 1 franc.

1886. Stamps of French Colonies, "Commerce" type, surch GAB surrounded by dots, and value in figures.

1	J	5c. on 20c. red on green	£400	£400
2	J	10c. on 20c. red on green	£400	£400
3	J	25c. on 20c. red on green	60·00	65·00
4	J	50c. on 15c. blue on light blue	£1300	£1400
5	J	75c. on 15c. blue on light blue	£1400	£1500

1888. Stamps of French Colonies, "Commerce" type, surch in figures.

6	15c. on 10c. black on lilac	£5000	£900
7	15c. on 1f. olive	£1900	£750
8	25c. on 5c. green	£1300	£200
9	25c. on 10c. black on lilac	£5000	£1400
10	25c. on 75c. red	£2750	£1200

1889. Postage Due stamps of French Colonies surch GABON TIMBRE and value in figures.

11	U	15c. on 5c. black	£200	£200
12	U	15c. on 30c. black	£4250	£3250
13	U	25c. on 20c. black	£110	90·00

6

1889. Imperf.

14	6	15c. black on pink	£1400	£850
15	6	25c. black on green	£850	£650

1904. "Tablet" key-type inscr "GABON" in red (1, 5, 15, 25, 35, 45, 75c., 1, 2f.) or blue (others).

16	D	1c. black on blue	90	1·10
17	D	2c. brown on buff	55	55
18	D	4c. brown on grey	1·30	1·00
19	D	5c. green	1·80	85
20	D	10c. red	2·75	65
21	D	15c. grey	5·25	2·00
22	D	20c. red on green	7·50	5·25
23	D	25c. blue	4·00	2·00
24	D	30c. brown on drab	10·00	9·25
25	D	35c. black on yellow	25·00	23·00
26	D	40c. red on yellow	16·00	13·00
27	D	45c. black on green	36·00	60·00
28	D	50c. brown on blue	7·25	6·50
29	D	75c. brown on orange	19·00	38·00
30	D	1f. green	50·00	60·00
31	D	2f. violet on pink	65·00	£100
32	D	5f. mauve on lilac	£120	£130

7 Gabon Warrior

9 Bantu Woman

8 View of Libreville

1910

33	7	1c. brown and orange	2·50	1·90
34	7	2c. black and brown	3·00	2·30
35	7	4c. violet and blue	1·40	1·30
36	7	5c. olive and green	1·20	1·20
37	7	10c. red and lake	2·75	1·80
38	7	20c. brown and violet	2·30	8·00
39	8	25c. brown and blue	3·25	5·00
40	8	30c. red and grey	21·00	37·00
41	8	35c. green and violet	18·00	20·00
42	8	40c. blue and brown	21·00	50·00
43	8	45c. violet and red	33·00	60·00
44	8	50c. grey and green	65·00	90·00
45	8	75c. brown and orange	£100	£120
46	9	1f. yellow and brown	£100	£120
47	9	2f. brown and red	£250	£275
48	9	5f. brown and blue	£250	£275

1910. As last but inscr "AFRIQUE EQUATORIALE GABON".

49	7	1c. brown and orange	20	50
50	7	2c. black and brown	35	50
51	7	4c. violet and blue	55	55
52	7	5c. grey and green	90	90
82	7	5c. black and yellow	1·20	5·00
53	7	10c. red and lake	1·50	90
83	7	10c. light green and green	55	4·25
54	7	15c. purple and pink	1·30	4·50
55	7	20c. brown and violet	12·00	11·00
56	8	25c. brown and blue	1·70	2·20
84	8	25c. black and green	2·10	4·00
57	8	30c. red and grey	2·10	4·25
65	9	5f. brown and blue	11·00	28·00
85	8	30c. red and carmine	1·80	3·50
58	8	35c. green and violet	3·25	3·00
59	8	40c. blue and brown	3·50	3·00
60	8	45c. violet and red	2·20	7·25
86	8	45c. red and black	2·75	4·25
61	8	50c. grey and green	2·75	5·25
87	8	50c. blue and deep blue	65	1·80
62	8	75c. brown and red	2·75	7·50
63	9	1f. bistre and brown	4·25	9·75
64	9	2f. brown and red	4·75	10·00

1912. "Tablet" key-type surch in figures.

66A	D	05 on 2c. brown on buff	55	1·70
67A	D	05 on 4c. brown on grey	45	2·50
68A	D	05 on 15c. grey	50	1·80
69A	D	05 on 20c. red on green	45	1·20
70A	D	05 on 25c. blue	45	65
71A	D	05 on 30c. brown on drab	50	5·25
72A	D	10 on 40c. red on yellow	40	55
73A	D	10 on 45c. black on green	65	75
74A	D	10 on 50c. brown on blue	30	1·80
75A	D	10 on 75c. brown on orange	75	2·75
76A	D	10 on 1f. green	50	2·75
77A	D	10 on 2f. violet on pink	40	2·30
78A	D	10 on 5f. mauve on lilac	2·00	6·50

1915. Surch with red cross and 5c.

79	7	10c.+5c. (No. 37)	16·00	40·00
81	7	10c.+5c. (No. 53)	90	4·50

1924. Inscr "AFRIQUE EQUATORIALE GABON" and optd AFRIQUE EQUATORIALE FRANCAISE.

88		1c. brown and orange	30	1·00
89		2c. black and brown	35	2·75
90		4c. violet and blue	70	3·75
91		5c. black and yellow	80	1·10
92		10c. light green and green	1·00	3·75
93		10c. blue and brown	85	1·20
94		15c. purple and pink	1·00	5·00
95		15c. pink and purple	2·00	3·25
96		20c. brown and violet	1·70	3·00
97	8	25c. black and green	1·00	90
98	8	30c. red and carmine	1·20	3·50
99	8	30c. yellow and black	35	2·30
100	8	30c. green	2·75	3·50
101	8	35c. green and violet	85	6·50
102	8	40c. blue and brown	1·30	45
103	8	45c. red and black	1·70	2·75
104	8	50c. blue and deep blue	1·60	3·50
105	8	50c. green and red	1·10	30
106	8	65c. red and blue	3·75	11·00
107	8	75c. brown and orange	1·70	2·20
108	8	90c. red and scarlet	5·00	6·75
109	9	1f. bistre and brown	1·70	1·40
110	9	1f.10 red and green	7·75	22·00
111	9	1f.50 blue and light blue	4·00	2·00
112	9	2f. brown and red	2·00	2·30
113	9	3f. mauve on pink	10·00	24·00
114	9	5f. brown and blue	7·50	20·00

1925. As last, surch in figures.

115		65 on 1f. brown and green	1·30	8·00
116		85 on 1f. brown and green	1·00	8·00
117	8	90c. on 75c. pink and red	90	8·50
118	9	1f.25 on 1f. ultram & bl	45	1·50
119	9	1f.50 on 1f. dp blue & blue	2·30	3·25
120	9	3f. on 5f. brown and mauve	3·25	24·00
121	9	10f. on 5f. green and brown	8·75	50·00
122	9	20f. on 5f. red and purple	12·00	46·00

1931. "Colonial Exn" key-type inscr "GABON".

123	E	40c. green	3·00	11·00
124	F	50c. mauve	90	5·00
125	G	90c. orange	2·75	9·25
126	H	1f.50 blue	6·00	10·00

21 Log Raft on the River Ogowe

22 Count de Brazza

1932

127	21	1c. red	35	5·50
128	21	2c. black on red	55	85
129	21	4c. green	85	6·50
130	21	5c. blue	1·10	6·25
131	21	10c. red on yellow	1·10	2·75
132	21	15c. red on green	3·00	7·50
133	21	20c. red	4·50	8·00
134	21	25c. brown	2·50	5·00
135	22	30c. green	4·00	8·50
136	22	40c. purple	3·75	7·50
137	22	45c. black on green	4·25	9·00
138	22	50c. brown	2·75	2·00
139	22	65c. blue	8·50	18·00
140	22	75c. black on orange	4·00	9·25
141	22	90c. red	5·50	10·00
142	22	1f. green on blue	9·25	29·00
143	-	1f.25 violet	5·00	4·25
144	-	1f.50 blue	6·75	5·75
145	-	1f.75 green	6·50	4·00
146	-	2f. red	19·00	50·00
147	-	3f. green on blue	7·25	7·50
148	-	5f. brown	10·00	25·00
149	-	10f. black on orange	16·00	65·00
150	-	20f. purple	55·00	75·00

DESIGN—HORIZ: 1f.25 to 20f. Gabon village.

25 Prime Minister Leon Mba

1959. 1st Anniv of Republic.

161	25	15f. brown	1·20	1·60
162	-	25f. green and sepia	1·60	85

PORTRAIT: 25f. Prime Minister Mba (profile).

26 CCTA Emblem

1960. 10th Anniv of African Technical Co-operation Commission.
163 **26** 50f. blue and purple 3·75 3·50

27 Dr. Albert Schweitzer (philosopher and missionary), Organ and View of Lambarene

1960. Air.
164 **27** 200f. brown, green and blue 6·50 2·00

1960. Air. Olympic Games. No. 192 of French Equatorial Africa surch with Olympic rings, XVIIe OLYMPIADE 1960 REPUBLIQUE GABONAISE 250F and bars.
165 250f. on 500f. blue, blk & grn 9·00 9·00

29 Tree Felling

1960. Air. 5th World Forestry Congress, Seattle.
166 **29** 100f. brown, black & green 4·00 1·80

30 Flag, Map and U.N. Emblem

1961. Admission into U.N.
167 **30** 15f. multicoloured 45 25
168 **30** 25f. multicoloured 45 40
169 **30** 85f. multicoloured 1·60 95

31 Lyre-tailed Honeyguide in flight

1961. Air. Birds. Multicoloured.
170 50f. Type **31** 3·25 1·30
171 100f. Madame Verreaux's sunbird 4·00 1·50
172 200f. Blue-headed bee eater (vert) 6·50 3·75
173 250f. Crowned eagle (vert) 10·00 5·00
174 500f. Narina's trogon (vert) 14·50 7·25

32 Combretum

1961
175 **32** 50c. red, purple and green 20 10
176 - 1f. red, turquoise and bistre 20 10
177 - 2f. yellow and green 25 20
178 - 3f. yellow, green and olive 45 35
179 - 5f. multicoloured 45 40
180 **32** 10f. red, green & turquoise 60 50

FLOWERS—VERT: 1f., 5f. Gabonese tulip (tree). HORIZ: 2f., 3f. Yellow cassia.

33 President Mba

1962
181 **33** 15f. blue, red and green 30 10
182 **33** 20f. sepia, red and green 45 10
183 **33** 25f. brown, red and green 50 25

34 Airliners, European and African

1962. Air. "Air Afrique" Airline.
184 **34** 500f. green, ochre & black 12·00 7·50

1962. Malaria Eradication. As T 55a of French Somali Coast.
185 25f.+5f. green 1·20 95

36 Start of Race

1962. Sports. Multicoloured.
186 20f. Type **36** (postage) 60 35
187 50f. Football 1·10 80
188 100f. Long jump (26×47 mm) (air) 3·50 1·70

37 Breguet 14 Biplane

1962. Air. Evolution of Air Transport.
189 **37** 10f. blue and red 60 25
190 - 20f. indigo, blue and brown 1·00 45
191 - 60f. blue, purple and green 2·20 1·00
192 - 85f. indigo, blue and orange 3·75 2·00
MS193 130×100 mm. Nos. 189/92 10·00 10·00

AIRCRAFT: 20f. De Havilland Dragon Rapide; 60f. Sud Aviation Caravelle; 85f. Rocket.

38 Union Flag

1962. 1st Anniv of Union of African and Malagasy States.
194 **38** 30f. green 1·50 90

39 Capt. Ntchorere and Flags

1962. Capt. Ntchorere Commemoration.
195 **39** 80f. multicoloured 1·40 95

41 Globe and Emblem

1963. Freedom from Hunger.
196 **41** 25f.+5f. green, brown and red 1·00 95

1963. Air. 50th Anniv of Arrival of Dr Schweitzer in Gabon. Surch 100F JUBILE GABONAIS 1913-1963.
197 **27** 100f. on 200f. brown, green and blue 3·50 1·60

43 Libreville Post Office

1963. Air. Cent of Gabon Postal Services.
198 **43** 100f. multicoloured 1·80 1·10

44 "Posts and Telecommunications"

1963. Air. African and Malagasy Posts and Telecommunications Union.
199 **44** 85f. multicoloured 1·80 90

45 "Telecommunications"

1963. Space Telecommunications.
200 **45** 25f. orange, blue and green 45 45
201 **45** 100f. brown, green & blue 2·00 1·60

46 Airline Emblem

1963. Air. 1st Anniv of "Air Afrique" and Inauguration of "DC-8" Service.
202 **46** 50f. multicoloured 1·30 80

47 "Europafrique"

1963. Air. European–African Economic Convention.
203 **47** 50f. multicoloured 1·50 85

48 UNESCO Emblem, Scales of Justice and Tree

1963. 15th Anniv of Declaration of Human Rights.
204 **48** 25f. slate, green and brown 55 40

49 Rameses and Gods, Wadi-es-Sebua

1964. Air. Nubian Monuments.
205 **49** 10f.+5f. brown and blue 1·00 1·00
206 **49** 25f.+5f. blue and red 1·20 1·20
207 **49** 50f.+5f. purple & myrtle 2·00 2·00

50 Barograph

1964. World Meteorological Day.
208 **50** 25f. green, blue and bistre 80 45

51 Arms of Gabon

1964
209 **51** 25f. multicoloured 80 45

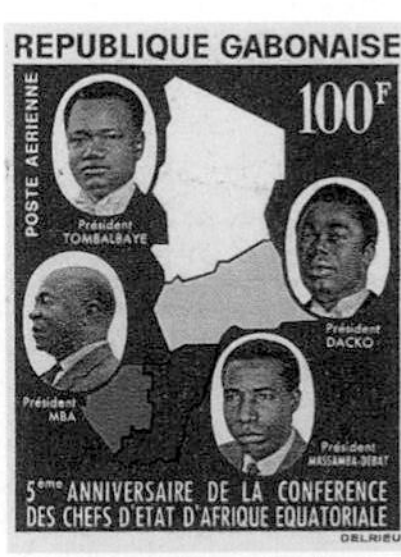

52 Map and African Heads of State

1964. Air. 5th Anniv of Equatorial African Heads of State Conf.
210 **52** 100f. multicoloured 2·00 1·20

53 Atlantic Tarpon

1964. Gabon Fauna.
211 **53** 30f. black, blue and brown 1·10 60
212 - 60f. brown, chestnut & grn 2·00 90
213 - 80f. brown, green and blue 2·50 1·20

DESIGNS—VERT: 60f. Gorilla. HORIZ: 80f. African buffalo.

54 Ear of Wheat, Cogwheel and Globe

1964. Air. 1st Anniv of "Europafrique".

214	**54**	50f. blue, olive and red	1·50	90

55 Start of Race

1964. Air. Olympic Games, Tokyo.

215	**55**	25f. green, brown & orange	85	45
216	-	50f. brown, orange & green	1·60	55
217	-	100f. violet, purple & olive	3·00	1·00
218	-	200f. brown, purple and red	5·00	3·00
MS219		191×100 mm. Nos. 215/18	13·00	13·00

DESIGNS—VERT: 50f. Massaging athlete; 100f. Anointing before the Games. HORIZ: 200f. Athletes.

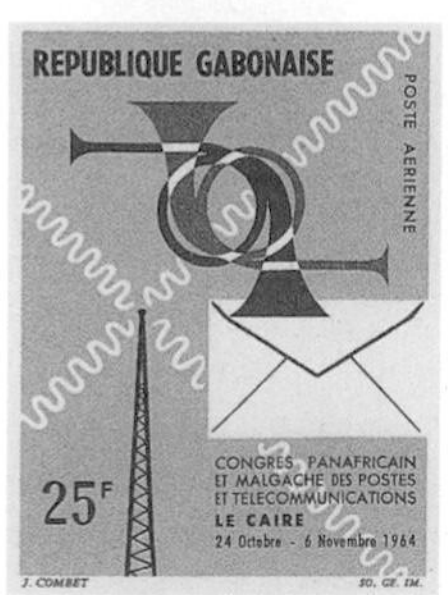

56 Posthorns, Envelope and Radio Mast

1964. Air. Pan-African and Malagasy Posts and Telecommunications Congress, Cairo.

220	**56**	25f. sepia, red and green	80	30

57 "Co-operation"

1964. French, African and Malagasy Co-operation.

221	**57**	25f. brown, blue and slate	80	45

58 "Dissotis rotundifolia"

1964. Flowers. Multicoloured.

222	3f. Type **58**	35	20
223	5f. "Gloriosa superba"	55	25
224	15f. "Eulophia horsfallii"	90	50

59 Pres. Kennedy

1964. Air. Pres. Kennedy Commem.

225	**59**	100f. black, orange & green	2·00	1·80
MS226		90×129 mm. No. 225×4	10·00	10·00

60 Women in Public Service

1964. Air. Social Evolution of Gabonese Women.

227	**60**	50f. brown, blue and red	1·30	60

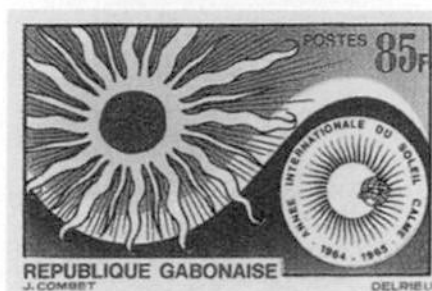

61 Sun and IQSY Emblem

1965. International Quiet Sun Year.

228	**61**	85f. multicoloured	1·50	90

62 Globe and ICY Emblem

1965. Air. International Co-operation Year.

229	**62**	50f. orange, turquoise & bl	1·30	60

63 17th-century Merchantman

1965. Air. Old Ships. Multicoloured.

230	25f. 16th-century galleon (vert)	1·30	80
231	50f. Type **63**	2·40	1·20
232	85f. 18th-century frigate (vert)	4·25	1·80
233	100f. 19th-century brig	6·00	2·20

64 Morse Telegraph Apparatus

1965. Centenary of ITU.

234	**64**	30f. green, orange and blue	80	45

65 Manganese Mine, Moanda

1965. "Mining Riches".

235	**65**	15f. red, violet and blue	55	25
236	-	60f. red and blue	1·80	80

DESIGN: 60f. Uranium mine, Mounana.

66 Nurse holding Child

1965. Air. Gabon Red Cross.

237	**66**	100f. brown, red and green	2·00	1·00

67 Football

1965. 1st African Games, Brazzaville.

238	**67**	25f. black, red & grn (post)	80	45
239	-	100f. purple, red and brown (air)	2·50	1·20

DESIGN (27×48½ mm): 100f. Basketball.

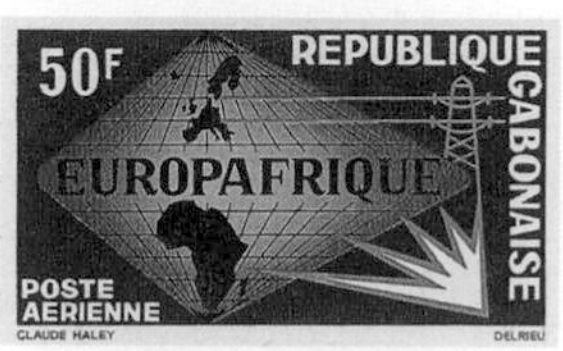

68 "Globe", Pylon and "Sun"

1965. Air. "Europafrique".

240	**68**	50f. multicoloured	1·80	75

69 President Mba

1965. Air. 5th Anniv of Independence.

241	**69**	25f. multicoloured	80	45

70 Okoukoue Dance

1965. Gabon Dances.

242	**70**	25f. yellow, brown & green	55	25
243	-	60f. black, red and brown	1·70	80

DESIGN: 60f. Makudji dance.

71 Abraham Lincoln

1965. Death Cent of Abraham Lincoln.

244	**71**	50f. multicoloured	95	80

72 Sir Winston Churchill

1965. Air. Churchill Commem.

245	**72**	100f. multicoloured	2·30	90

73 Dr. A. Schweitzer and Map

1965. Air. Schweitzer Commem.

246	**73**	1000f. gold	70·00	70·00

74 Pope John XXIII

1965. Air. Pope John Commem.

247	**74**	85f. multicoloured	1·50	90

75 Mail Carrier, Post Office and Van

1965. Stamp Day.

248	**75**	30f. brown, green and blue	80	60

76 Nurse and Patients

1966. Air. Red Cross. Multicoloured.

249	50f. Type **76**	1·30	80
250	100f. Bandaging patient	2·50	1·20
MS251	115×155 mm. No. 249×4	8·50	8·50
MS252	115×155 mm. No. 250×4	13·00	13·00

77 Balumbu Mask

1966. World Festival of Negro Arts, Dakar. Multicoloured.

253	5f. Type **77**	30	25
254	10f. Statuette—"Ancestor of the Fang (tribe), Byeri"	45	25
255	25f. Fang mask	95	30
256	30f. Okuyi Myene mask	1·20	75
257	85f. Bakota copper mask	2·75	1·40

78 WHO Building

1966. Inaug of WHO Headquarters, Geneva.

258	**78**	50f. black, yellow and blue	1·30	60

79 Satellite "A1" and Rocket

1966. Air. "Conquest of Space".
259 **79** 30f. lake, plum and blue 80 45
260 - 90f. plum, red and purple 1·80 80
DESIGN: 90f. Satellite "FR1" and rocket.

80 "Learning the Alphabet"

1966. UNESCO Literacy Campaign.
261 **80** 30f. multicoloured 80 45

81 Footballer

1966. World Cup Football Championship, England.
262 **81** 25f. bl, grn & lake (postage) 1·00 25
263 - 90f. purple and blue 2·00 1·00
264 - 100f. slate and red (air) 2·75 1·30
DESIGNS—VERT: 90f. Footballer (different). HORIZ: 100f. Footballers on world map (47½×27 mm).

82 Industrial Scenes within leaves of "Plant"

1966. Air. "Europafrique".
265 **82** 50f. multicoloured 1·30 65

83 Plywood Mill

1966. Economic Development.
266 **83** 20f. lake, purple and green 50 40
267 - 85f. brown, blue and green 3·50 1·60
DESIGN: 85f. "Roger Butin" (oil rig).

84 Aircraft and "Air Afrique" Emblem

1966. Air. Inauguration of Douglas DC-8F Air Services.
268 **84** 30f. grey, black and orange 85 50

85 Making Deposit

1966. Savings Bank.
269 **85** 25f. brown, green and blue 85 50

86 Scouts and Camp Fire

1966. Scouting.
270 **86** 30f. brown, red and slate 85 45
271 - 50f. brown, lake and blue 1·40 60
DESIGN—VERT: 50f. Scouts taking oath.

87 Gabonese Scholar

1966. Air. 20th Anniv of UNESCO.
272 **87** 100f. black, buff and blue 1·90 90

88 Libreville Airport

1966. Air.
273 **88** 200f. brown, red and blue 4·25 1·60

89 Sikorsky S-43 Amphibian, Map and Flag (Aeromaritime's First Airmail Service, 1937)

1966. Stamp Day.
274 **89** 30f. multicoloured 1·90 70

90 Hippopotami

1967. Gabon Fauna. Multicoloured.
275 1f. Type **90** 25 10
276 2f. Crocodiles 25 10
277 3f. Water chevrotains 50 10
278 5f. Chimpanzees 50 10
279 10f. African elephants 1·00 40
280 20f. Leopards 2·75 65

91 Lions Emblem and Anniversary Dates

1967. 50th Anniv of Lions Int. Mult.
281 30f. Type **91** 85 30
282 50f. Lions emblem, map and globe 1·00 60

92 Masked Faces

1967. Libreville Carnival.
283 **92** 30f. blue, brown and yellow 1·00 35

93 ITY Emblem and Transport

1967. Int Tourist Year.
284 **93** 30f. multicoloured 1·00 45

94 Diving-board (Mexico City)

1967. Publicity for 1968 Olympic Games, Mexico.
285 **94** 25f. turquoise, blue & violet 60 30
286 - 30f. purple, lake and green 1·00 50
287 - 50f. blue, green and purple 1·60 80
DESIGNS: 30f. Sun and snow crystal; 50f. Ice rink, Grenoble.

95 Farman F.190

1967. Air. Famous Aircraft.
288 **95** 200f. plum, blue & turq 4·25 1·60
289 - 300f. blue, purple & brown 7·75 2·10
290 - 500f. blue, purple and green 13·00 5·25
AIRCRAFT: 300f. De Havilland Heron 2; 500f. Potez 56.

96 Atomic Symbol, Dove and Globe

1967. International Atomic Energy Agency.
291 **96** 30f. red, blue and green 85 30

97 Aircraft on Flight-paths

1967. Air. ICAO Commem.
292 **97** 100f. purple, blue and green 2·20 1·10

98 Pope Paul VI

1967. Papal Encyclical "Populorum Progressio".
293 **98** 30f. black, blue and green 1·00 50

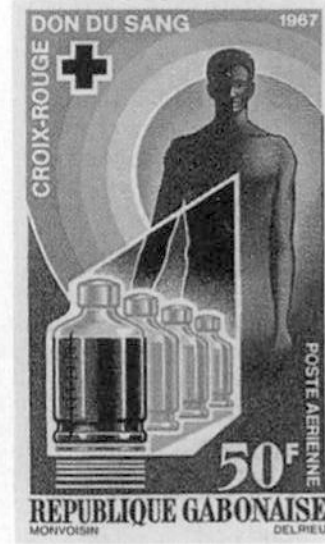

99 Blood Donor and Bank

1967. Air. Red Cross.
294 **99** 50f. multicoloured 1·60 60
295 - 100f. multicoloured 3·25 1·50
MS296 Two sheets each 115×155 mm. Nos. 294/5 in blocks of 4 20·00 20·00
DESIGN: 100f. Heart and blood-transfusion apparatus.

100 Indigenous Emblems

1967. World Fair, Montreal.
297 **100** 30f. brown, green and lake 85 50

101 "Europafrique"

1967. Europafrique.
298 **101** 50f. multicoloured 1·30 50

102 Orientation Diagram and Sun

1967. Air. World Scout Jamboree, Idaho.
299 **102** 50f. green, orange and blue 1·30 85
300 - 100f. red, green and blue 2·20 1·50
DESIGN: 100f. U.S. scout greeting Gabon scout on map.

103 U.N. Emblem, Gabon Women and Child

1967. U.N. Status of Women Commission.
301 **103** 75f. blue, green and brown 1·60 80

104 Map of Africa, Letters and Pylons

1967. Air. 5th Anniv of UAMPT.

302	**104**	100f. red, blue and olive	1·90	90

105 Baraka Mission, Libreville

1967. Air. 125th Anniv of American Missionaries Arrival.

303	**105**	100f. black, green and blue	3·00	1·30

106 U.N. Emblem and Book with Supporters

1967. Air. U.N. Int Rights Commission.

304	**106**	60f. multicoloured	1·00	75

107 "Draconea fragans"

1967. Gabon Trees.

305	**107**	5f. brown, green and blue (postage)	60	30
306	-	10f. green, bronze and blue	85	40
307	-	20f. red, green and brown	1·30	65
308	-	50f. green, bistre and blue (air)	1·70	90
309	-	100f. multicoloured	3·00	1·60
MS310 197×90 mm. Nos. 305/7 and 308/9			8·75	8·75

DESIGNS: 10f. "Pycnanthus angolensis"; 20f. "Disthemonanthus benthamianus". (27×48 mm): 50f. "Baillonella toxisperma"; 100f. "Aucoumea klaineana".

108 "Belgrano" and "Jean Guiton" (19th-century steam packets)

1967. Stamp Day. Multicoloured.

311	30f. Type **108**	1·60	85
312	30f. "Ango" and "Lucie Delmas" (modern mail carriers)	1·60	85

Nos. 311/12 were issued together, se-tenant, forming a composite design.

109 Chancellor Adenauer

1968. Air. Adenauer Commem.

313	**109**	100f. sepia, red and yellow	2·75	90
MS314 120×171 mm. No. 313×4			11·00	11·00

110 African WHO Building

1968. 20th Anniv of WHO.

315	**110**	20f. purple, blue and green	85	30

111 Dam and Power-station

1968. International Hydrological Decade.

316	**111**	15f. blue, orange and lake	60	30

112 President Bongo

1968

317	**112**	25f. black, yellow & green	65	35
318	-	30f. black, turquoise & pur	65	35

DESIGN: 30f. Pres. Bongo (half-length portrait).

113 "Madonna and Child with Rosary" (Murillo)

1968. Air. Religious Paintings. Multicoloured.

319	60f. Type **113**	1·40	60
320	90f. "Christ in Bonds" (Luis de Morales)	1·80	85
321	100f. "St. John at Patmos" (Juan Mates) (horiz)	2·20	1·30

114 Beribboned Rope

1968. Air. 5th Anniv of Europafrique.

322	**114**	50f. multicoloured	1·00	60

115 Refinery and Tanker

1968. Inauguration of Petroleum Refinery, Port Gentil, Gabon.

323	**115**	30f. multicoloured	85	30

116 Distribution to the Needy

1968. Air. Red Cross. Multicoloured.

324	50f. Type **116**	1·40	45
325	100f. "Support the Red Cross"	2·75	1·00
MS326 200×86 mm. Nos. 324/5		7·75	7·50

117 High-jumping

1968. Air. Olympic Games, Mexico.

327	**117**	25f. brown, slate and red	80	30
328	-	30f. brown, blue and red	90	50
329	-	100f. brown, yellow & blue	2·40	1·00
330	-	200f. brown, slate & green	4·75	2·10
MS331 237×103 mm. Nos. 327/30			11·00	11·00

DESIGNS—VERT: 30f. Cycling; 100f. Judo. HORIZ: 200f. Boxing.

118 Open Book

1968. Literacy Day.

332	**118**	25f. brown, red and blue	1·40	65

120 Coffee

1968. Agricultural Produce.

333	**120**	20f. red, myrtle and green	2·20	1·30
334	-	40f. orange, brown & grn	1·60	55

DESIGNS: 40f. Cocoa.

121 "Junon" (sail/steam warship)

1968. Stamp Day.

335	**121**	30f. violet, green & orange	1·80	85

122 President Mba and Flag

1968. Air. 1st Death Anniv of Pres. Mba.

336	**122**	1,000f. multicoloured	27·00	27·00

123 Advocate holding "Charter"

1968. Human Rights Year.

337	**123**	20f. black, green and red	60	30

124 President Bongo, Maps of Gabon and Owendo Port

1968. Air. "Laying of 1st Stone", Owendo Port. Multicoloured.

338	25f. Type **124**	1·40	50
339	30f. Harbour Project	1·40	50

125 "The Cloisters of Ste. Marie des Anges" (F. M. Granet)

1969. Air. "Philexafrique" Stamp Exhibition, Abidjan, Ivory Coast (1st issue).

340	**125**	100f. multicoloured	4·00	4·00

See also No. 346.

126 Mahatma Gandhi

1969. Air. "Apostles of Peace".

341	**126**	25f. black and pink	80	30
342	-	30f. black and green	80	45
343	-	50f. black and blue	1·30	55
344	-	100f. black and mauve	2·00	95
MS345 120×161 mm. Nos. 341/4			6·00	6·00

DESIGNS: 30f. J. F. Kennedy; 50f. R. F. Kennedy; 100f. Martin Luther King.

127 Oil Refinery. Port Gentil and Gabon Stamp of 1932

1969. Air. "Philexafrique" Stamp Exhibition, Abidjan, Ivory Coast (2nd issue).

346	**127**	50f. blue, red and green	2·00	2·00

128 View of Okanda Gates

1969. African Tourist Year.
347 **128** 10f. brown, green and blue 35 10
348 - 15f. blue, green and red 1·90 35
349 - 25f. purple, blue & brown 70 45
350 - 30f. brown, choc & blue 1·40 60
DESIGNS—HORIZ: 15f. Great barracuda. VERT: 25f. Kinguele Falls; 30f. Hunting trophies.

129 "Battle of Rivoli" (Philippoteaux)

1969. Air. Birth Bicentenary of Napoleon Bonaparte. Multicoloured.
351 50f. Type **129** 2·40 1·20
352 100f. "Oath of the Army" (J. L. David) 3·00 2·20
353 250f. "The Emperor Napoleon I on the Terrace at St. Cloud" (Ducis) 11·00 6·50

130 Mvet

1969. Traditional Musical Instruments from Folk Art Museum, Libreville.
354 **130** 25f. lake, drab and purple 45 25
355 - 30f. brown, drab and red 55 30
356 - 50f. lake, drab and purple 1·20 55
357 - 100f. brown, drab and red 2·30 95
MS358 130×100 mm. Nos. 354/7 6·00 6·00
DESIGNS: 30f. Ngombi harp; 50f. Ebele and Mbe drums; 100f. Medzang xylophone.

131 Refugees and Red Cross Plane

1969. Air. Red Cross. Aid for Biafra. Multicoloured.
359 15f. Type **131** 65 35
360 20f. Hospital and supplies van 80 30
361 25f. Doctor and nurse tending children 80 45
362 30f. Children and hospital 1·00 45
MS363 117×74 mm. Nos. 359/62 3·75 3·50

132 "Aframomum polyanthum"

1969. Flowers. Multicoloured.
364 1f. Type **132** 10 10
365 2f. "Chlamydocola chlamydantha" 40 25
366 5f. "Costus dinklagei" 40 25
367 10f. "Cola rostrata" 1·00 45
368 20f. "Dischistocalyx grandifolius" 1·40 80

133 Astronauts and Module on Moon

1969. Air. 1st Man on the Moon. Embossed on gold foil.
369 **133** 1000f. gold 25·00 25·00

134 Tree and Insignia

1969. "National Renovation".
370 **134** 25f. multicoloured 55 45

135 Oil Derrick

1969. 20th Anniv of Elf/Spafe Petroleum Consortium.
371 25f. Type **135** 75 25
372 50f. Oil rig 1·50 60

136 African Workers

1969. 50th Anniv of ILO.
373 **136** 30f. green, blue and red 80 30

137 Arms of Lambarene

1969. Town Arms (1st series).
374 **137** 20f. multicoloured 1·00 35
375 - 25f. gold, black and blue 1·30 25
376 - 30f. multicoloured 1·60 55
ARMS: 25f. Port-Gentil; 30f. Libreville.
See also Nos. 405/7, 460/2, 504/6, 510/12, 539/41, 596/8, 618/20, 669/71, 684/6, 729/31, 800/2, 898/900, 953/4, 1083 and 1128.

138 Adoumas Mail Pirogue

1969. Stamp Day.
377 **138** 30f. brown, emerald & grn 1·20 45

139 Satellite and Globe

1970. World Telecommunications Day.
378 **139** 25f. blue, black and lake 80 45

1970. New UPU Headquarters Building, Berne. As T 81 of New Caledonia.
379 30f. green, purple and brown 90 50

140 Japanese Geisha and African

1970. "EXPO 70" World Fair, Osaka, Japan.
380 **140** 30f. multicoloured 1·00 45

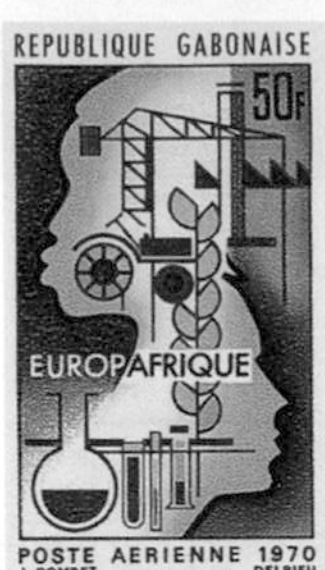

141 "Co-operation"

1970. Air. "Europafrique".
381 **141** 50f. multicoloured 1·20 60

142 Icarus and the Sun

1970. Air. History of Flight.
382 **142** 25f. blue, yellow and red 80 50
383 - 100f. green, brown & pur 1·80 75
384 - 200f. blue, red and slate 4·50 1·80
MS385 130×100 mm. Nos. 382/4 7·50 7·50
DESIGNS: 100f. Leonardo da Vinci's design for wings; 200f. Jules Verne's rocket approaching Moon.

143 UAMPT Emblem

1970. Air. UAMPT Conference, Libreville.
386 **143** 200f. gold, green and blue 3·75 1·60

144 Throwing-knives

1970. Air. Gabonaise Weapons, Folk Art Museum, Libreville. All values blue, red and green.
387 25f. Type **144** 60 30
388 30f. Assegai and crossbow (vert) 80 45
389 50f. War knives (vert) 1·00 55
390 90f. Dagger and sheath 2·10 85
MS391 170×100 mm. Nos. 387/90 6·00 6·00

145 Japanese Masks, Gateway and Mt. Fuji

1970. Air. "Expo 70" World Fair, Osaka, Japan. Embossed on gold foil.
392 **145** 1000f. red, black and green 23·00 23·00

146 President Bongo

1970. Air. 10th Anniv of Independence.
393 **146** 200f. multicoloured 4·50 2·20

147 Aircraft, Map and Airport

1970. 10th Anniv (1969) of Aerial Navigation Security Agency for Africa and Madagascar.
394 **147** 100f. green and blue 1·80 85

148 "Portrait of Young Man" (School of Raphael)

1970. Air. 450th Death Anniv of Raphael. Multicoloured.
395 50f. Type **148** 1·20 60
396 100f. "Jeanne d'Aragon" (Raphael) 2·30 95
397 200f. "The Virgin of the Blue Diadem" (Raphael) 4·50 2·40

149 U.N. Emblem, Globe, Dove and Wheat

1970. 25th Anniv of United Nations.
398 **149** 30f. multicoloured 80 45

150 Bushbucks

1970. Wild Fauna. Multicoloured.
399 5f. Type **150** 50 30
400 15f. Pel's flying squirrel 80 45
401 25f. White-cheeked mangabey (vert) 1·50 75
402 40f. African golden cat 3·00 1·50
403 60f. Servaline genet 4·50 2·20

151 Presidents Bongo and Pompidou

1971. Air. Visit of Pres. Pompidou of France to Gabon.

404	**151**	50f. multicoloured	2·20	1·10

1971. Town Arms (2nd series). As T 137. Multicoloured.

405	20f. multicoloured	90	35
406	25f. black, green and gold	90	35
407	30f. multicoloured	1·10	45

ARMS: 20f. Mouila; 25f. Bitam; 30f. Oyem.

152 Four Races and Emblem

1971. Racial Equality Year.

408	**152**	40f. black, orange & yell	85	35

153 Telecommunications Map

1971. Pan-African Telecommunications Network.

409	**153**	30f. multicoloured	80	30

154 Freesias

1971. Air. "Flowers by Air". Mult.

410	15f. Type **154**	45	25
411	25f. Carnations	60	25
412	40f. Roses	1·00	40
413	55f. Daffodils	1·50	55
414	75f. Orchids	2·50	80
415	120f. Tulips	3·00	1·10
MS416	129×74 mm. Nos. 414/15	7·00	7·00

155 Napoleon's Death Mask

1971. Air. 150th Death Anniv of Napoleon. Multicoloured.

417	100f. Type **155**	3·00	1·00
418	200f. "Longwood House" (after Marchand) (horiz)	4·25	2·00
419	500f. Napoleon's Tomb	11·00	5·00

156 "Charaxes smaragdalis"

1971. Butterflies. Multicoloured.

420	5f. Type **156**	1·70	40
421	10f. "Euxanthe crossleyi"	3·00	65
422	15f. "Epiphora rectifascia"	5·75	90
423	25f. "Imbrasia bouvieri"	6·75	1·20

157 Hertzian Communications Centre, Nkol Ogoum

1971. World Telecommunications Day.

424	**157**	40f. red, blue and green	1·00	45

158 De Gaulle as President of the Republic (1970)

1971. Air. 1st Death Anniv of General De Gaulle. Sheet 150×140 mm containing T 158 and similar vert designs. Multicoloured.

MS425	40f.×2 Type **158**; 80f.×2 De Gaulle in uniform (1940); 100f. De Gaulle quotation (26×76 mm)	10·00	10·00

159 Red Crosses

1971. Air. Red Cross.

426	**159**	50f. multicoloured	1·30	55

160 Uranium

1971. Air. Minerals. Multicoloured.

427	85f. Type **160**	5·75	2·75
428	90f. Manganese	7·00	3·50

161 Landing Module above Moon's Surface

1971. Air. Moon Flight of "Apollo 15". Embossed on gold foil.

429	**161**	1500f. multicoloured	28·00	28·00

162 Mother feeding Child

1971. 15th Anniv of Social Welfare Fund.

430	**162**	30f. brown, bistre & mve	80	30

163 U.N. Emblem and New York Headquarters

1971. 10th Anniv of Gabon's Admission to United Nations.

431	**163**	30f. multicoloured	80	35

164 Great Egret

1971. Birds. Multicoloured.

432	30f. Type **164**	1·40	65
433	40f. Grey parrot	2·20	95
434	50f. Woodland kingfisher	3·00	1·20
435	75f. Grey-necked bald crow	4·00	1·50
436	100f. Green turaco	5·50	1·70

166 UAMPT Building, Brazzaville and Bakota copper mask

1971. Air. 10th Anniv of African and Malagasy Posts and Telecommunications Union.

439	**166**	100f. multicoloured	1·80	85

167 Ski-jumping

1972. Air. Winter Olympic Games, Sapporo, Japan.

440	**167**	40f. violet, brown & green	1·80	85
441	-	130f. green, violet & brn	2·50	1·00
MS442		160×100 mm. Nos. 440/1	4·50	4·50

DESIGN: 130f. Speed-skating.

168 "Santa Maria della Salute" (Vanvitelli)

1972. Air. UNESCO "Save Venice" Campaign. Multicoloured.

443	60f. "The Basin and Grand Canal" (Vanvitelli) (horiz)	2·40	1·20
444	70f. "Rialto Bridge" (Canaletto)	3·75	1·80
445	140f. Type **168**	7·25	2·30

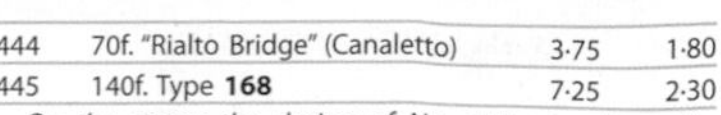

On the stamp the design of No. 445 wrongly attributed to Caffi.

1972. Air. General de Gaulle Monument. No. MS425 surch.

MS446	60f. on 40f.×2; 120f. on 80f.×2; 180f. on 100f	18·00	18·00

170 Hotel Intercontinental

1972. Air. Opening of Hotel Intercontinental.

447	**170**	40f. brown, green and blue	1·00	45

1972. Air. Visit of the Grand Master, Sovereign Order of Malta. No. 289 surch VISITE OFFICIELLE GRAND MAITRE ORDRE SOUVERAIN DE MALTE 3 MARS 1972 50F and emblem.

448	50f. on 300f. blue, pur & brn	95	40

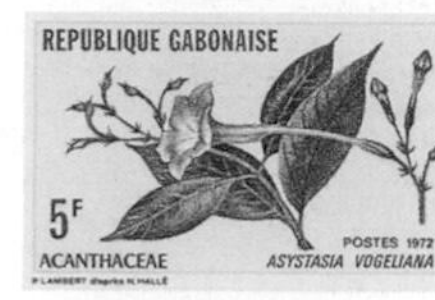
172 "Asystasia vogeliana"

1972. Flowers. Varieties of Acanthus. Multicoloured.

449	5f. Type **172**	30	25
450	10f. "Stenandriopsis guineensis"	45	25
451	20f. "Thomandersia hensii"	75	45
452	30f. "Thomandersia laurifolia"	1·00	60
453	40f. "Physacanthus batanganus"	2·00	90
454	65f. "Physacanthus nematosiphon"	3·00	1·30

173 "The Discus-thrower" (Alcamene)

1972. Air. Olympic Games, Munich. Ancient Sculptures.

455	**173**	30f. grey and red	80	60
456	-	100f. grey and red	2·00	1·00
457	-	140f. grey and red	2·50	1·30
MS458		131×101 mm. Nos. 455/7	6·00	6·00

DESIGNS: 100f. "Doryphoros" (Polyclete); 140f. "Gladiator" (Agasias).

174 Pasteur with Microscope

1972. 150th Anniv of Louis Pasteur (scientist).

459	**174**	80f. purple, green & red	1·20	45

1972. Town Arms (3rd series). Vert designs as T 137. Multicoloured.

460	30f. multicoloured	60	35
461	40f. multicoloured	1·00	35
462	60f. silver, black and green	1·30	60

ARMS: 30f. Franceville; 40f. Makokou; 60f. Tchibanga.

175 Global Emblem

1972. World Telecommunications Day.
463 **175** 40f. black, orange & yell 80 45

176 Nat King Cole

1972. Famous Negro Musicians. Mult.
464 40f. Type **176** 1·20 30
465 60f. Sidney Bechet 1·80 60
466 100f. Louis Armstrong 3·25 90

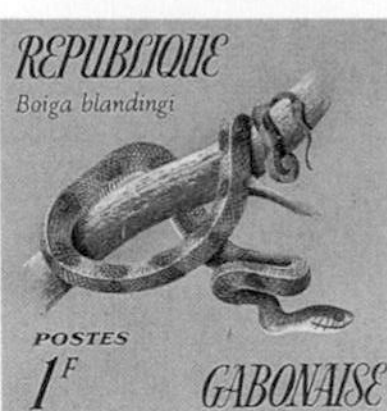

177 "Boiga blandingi"

1972. Reptiles. Multicoloured.
467 1f. Type **177** 20 10
468 2f. Sand snake 40 10
469 3f. Egg-eating snake 40 25
470 15f. Pit viper 2·10 45
471 25f. Jameson's tree asp 2·75 50
472 50f. Gabon viper 4·50 75

178 "The Adoration of the Magi" (Bruegel the Elder)

1972. Air. Christmas. Multicoloured.
473 30f. Type **178** 1·30 40
474 40f. "Madonna and Child" (Basaiti) (vert) 1·30 65

1972. Air. Olympic Gold Medal Winners. Nos. 455/7 surch as listed below.
475 **125** 40f. on 30f. grey and red 1·00 55
476 - 120f. on 100f. grey & red 2·00 1·00
477 - 170f. on 140f. grey & red 3·00 1·30
SURCHARGES: No. 475, **MORELON**; 476, **KEINO**; 477, **SPITZ**.

180 Dr. G. A. Hansen and Hospital, Lambarene

1973. Centenary of Dr. Hansen's Discovery of Leprosy Bacillus.
478 **180** 30f. brown, green and blue 1·20 60

181 "Thematic Collecting"

1973. Air. "PHILEXGABON 73" International Stamp Exhibition, Libreville.
479 **181** 100f. multicoloured 2·00 1·00
MS480 170×141 mm. No. 479×4 16·00 8·75

182 "Charaxes candiope"

1973. Butterflies. Multicoloured.
481 10f. Type **182** 1·20 20
482 15f. "Eunica pechueli" 1·90 25
483 20f. "Cyrestis camillus" 3·25 50
484 30f. "Charaxes castor" 3·75 70
485 40f. "Charaxes ameliae" 4·50 1·00
486 50f. "Pseudacrea boisduvali" 5·50 1·30

183 Douglas DC-10-30 over Libreville Airport

1973. Air. Libreville-Paris Air Service by "Air Afrique" "DC 10 Libreville". No gum.
487 **183** 40f. multicoloured 2·00 1·00

184 Montgolfier's Balloon, 1783

1973. History of Flight.
488 **184** 1f. green, myrtle & brown 30 10
489 - 2f. green and blue 30 10
490 - 3f. new blue, blue & orge 30 10
491 - 4f. violet & reddish violet 60 15
492 - 5f. green and orange 95 35
493 - 10f. purple and blue 1·10 35
493a - 10f. blue 2·40 1·10
DESIGNS—HORIZ: 2f. Santos-Dumont's airship "Ballon No. 6", 1901; 3f. Chanute's glider, 1896; 4f. Clement Ader's "Avion III" flying-machine, 1897; 5f. Bleriot's cross-Channel flight, 1909; 10f. (both) Fabre's seaplane "Hydravion", 1910.

185 Power Station

1973. Air. Kinguele Hydro-electric Project.
494 **185** 30f. green and brown 80 25
495 - 40f. blue, green and brown 1·00 45
DESIGN: 40f. Dam.

186 Interpol Emblem

1973. 50th Anniv of International Criminal Police Organization (Interpol).
496 **186** 40f. blue and red 80 45

187 Dish Aerial and Station

1973. Inauguration of "2 Decembre" Satellite Earth Station.
497 **187** 40f. brown, blue and green 80 45

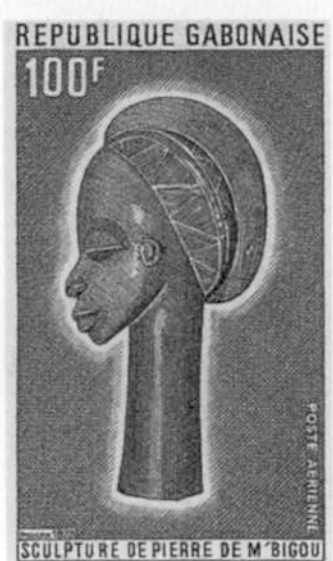

188 Gabon Woman

1973. Air. M'Bigou Stone Sculptures.
498 **188** 100f. brown, blue & black 2·00 1·00
499 - 200f. green and brown 3·75 1·90
DESIGN: 200f. Gabon man wearing head-dress.

1973. Air. Pan-African Drought Relief. No. 426 surch SECHERESSE SOLIDARITE AFRICAINE 100F.
500 **159** 100f. on 50f. mult 2·00 1·20

190 Party Headquarters

1973. Gabonaise Democratic Party Headquarters, Libreville.
501 **190** 30f. multicoloured 80 25

191 Astronauts and Lunar Rover

1973. Air. Moon Flight of "Apollo 17".
502 **191** 500f. multicoloured 9·00 4·50

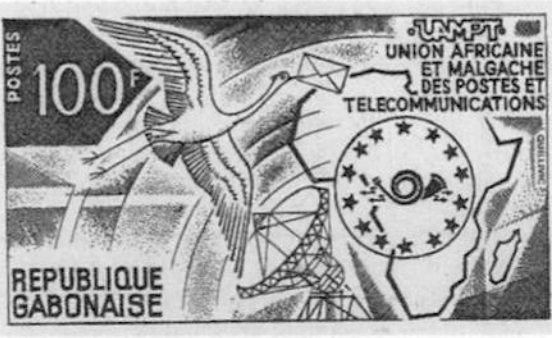

192 Crane with Letter and Telecommunications Emblem

1973. 12th Anniv of African and Malagasy Posts and Telecommunications Union.
503 **192** 100f. plum, purple & blue 1·20 80

1973. Town Arms (4th series). As T 137 dated "1973". Multicoloured.
504 30f. Kango 1·30 30
505 40f. Booue 1·70 50
506 60f. Koula-Moutou 2·40 55

193 St. Theresa of Lisieux

1973. Birth Cent of St. Theresa of Lisieux. Stained-glass windows in the Basilica at Lisieux. Multicoloured.
507 30f. Type **193** 80 25
508 40f. "St. Theresa with Saviour" 1·00 45

194 Flame Emblem

1973. 25th Anniv of Declaration of Human Rights.
509 **194** 20f. red, blue and green 55 25

1974. Town Arms (5th series). As T 137 dated "1974". Multicoloured.
510 5f. Gamba 45 10
511 10f. Ogooue-Lolo 50 20
512 15f. Fougamou 65 25

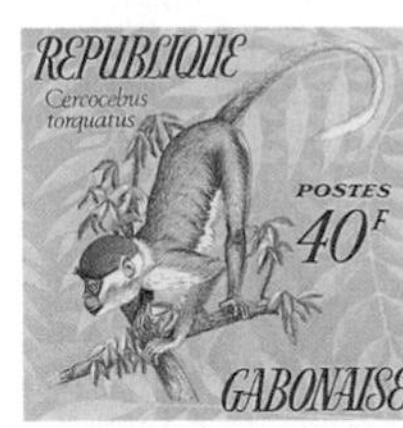

195 White-collared Mangabey

1974. Monkeys. Multicoloured.
513 40f. Type **195** 1·10 40
514 60f. Moustached monkey 1·80 55
515 80f. Mona monkey 3·00 85

196 De Gaulle and Houphouet-Boigny

1974. Air. 30th Anniv of Brazzaville Conference.
516 **196** 40f. blue and purple 2·00 80

197 "Pleasure Boats" (Monet)

1974. Air. Impressionist Paintings. Multicoloured.
517 40f. Type **197** 2·50 70
518 50f. "End of an Arabesque" (Degas) (vert) 4·00 1·00
519 130f. "Young Girl with Flowers" (Renoir) (vert) 6·00 1·80

198 American Bald Eagle, and Astronaut on Moon

1974. Air. 5th Anniv of First Manned Moon Landing.
520 **198** 200f. blue, brown & indigo 2·75 1·50

199 Ogooue River, Lambarene

1974. Gabon Views. Multicoloured.

521	30f. Type **199**	55	35
522	50f. Cape Esterias	80	55
523	75f. Rope bridge, Poubara	1·70	80

200 UPU Emblem and Letters

1974. Air. Centenary of UPU.

524	**200**	150f. turquoise and blue	2·50	1·10
525	-	300f. red and orange	4·50	2·40

DESIGN: 300f. Similar to Type **200**, but with design reversed.

201 "Apollo" and "Soyuz" Spacecraft, Flight Badge and Maps of U.S.A. and U.S.S.R.

1974. Air. Soviet-American Co-operation in Space.

526	**201**	1000f. green, red and blue	10·00	7·25

202 Ball and Footballers

1974. Air. World Cup Football Championship, West Germany.

527	**202**	40f. red, green and brown	60	45
528	-	65f. green, brown and red	95	65
529	-	100f. brown, red and green	1·50	85

MS530 170×100 mm. Nos. 527/9 4·00 4·00

DESIGNS: 65f., 100f. Football scenes similar to Type **202**.

203 Manioc Plantation

1974. Agriculture. Multicoloured.

531	40f. Type **203**	75	35
532	50f. Palm-tree grove	1·00	35

204 African Leaders, UDEAC Headquarters and Flags

1974. 10th Anniv of Central African Customs and Economic Union. Multicoloured.

533	40f. Type **204** (postage)	75	30
534	100f. African leaders, UDEAC Headquarters Building (air)	1·20	65

205 "The Visitation"

1974. Air. Christmas. Details from 15th-century tapestry of Notre Dame, Beaune. Multicoloured.

535	40f. Type **205**	1·00	40
536	50f. "The Annunciation" (horiz)	1·20	55

206 Dr. Schweitzer and Lambarene Hospital

1975. Air. Birth Centenary of Dr. Albert Schweitzer.

537	**206**	500f. green, lilac & brown	8·25	4·50

207 Dialogue Hotel

1975. Inauguration of "Hotel du Dialogue", Libreville.

538	**207**	50f. multicoloured	80	30

1975. Town Arms (6th series). As T 137 dated "1975". Multicoloured.

539	5f. Ogooue-Ivindo	25	10
540	10f. Moabi	25	10
541	15f. Moanda	65	10

208 "The Crucifixion" (Bellini)

1975. Air. Easter. Multicoloured.

542	140f. Type **208**	2·00	85
543	150f. "The Resurrection" (Burgundian School) (36×49 mm)	2·50	1·00

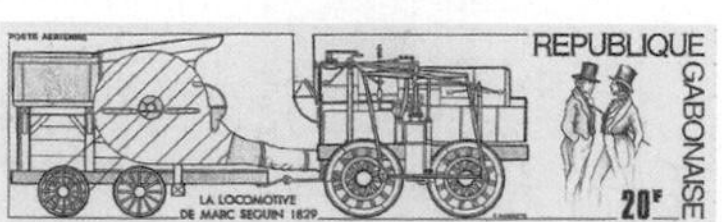

209 Marc Seguin Locomotive, 1829, France (image scaled to 46% of original size)

1975. Air. Scale Drawings of Steam Locomotives.

544	**209**	20f. blue, brown & brt bl	1·40	55
545	-	25f. red, yellow and blue	2·00	70
546	-	40f. blue, purple and green	2·40	1·00
547	-	50f. purple, blue and green	3·25	1·40

LOCOMOTIVES: 25f. "Iron Duke", 1847, Great Britain; 40f. "Thomas Rogers", 1855, U.S.A. (inscr "1895"); 50f. Class AA steam locomotive, 1934, Russia.

210 Congress Emblem

1975. 17th Lions Club Congress, Libreville.

548	**210**	50f. multicoloured	95	40

211 Aerial and Network Map

1975. Gabonese Development of Hertzian Wave Radio Links.

549	**211**	40f. green, brown and blue	80	45

212 Man and Woman and IWY Emblem

1975. International Women's Year.

550	**212**	50f. brown, red and blue	2·00	65

213 Ange M'ba (founder of Gabonaise Scouts)

1975. "Nordjamb 75" World Scout Jamboree, Norway.

551	**213**	40f. black, purple & green	60	40
552	-	50f. purple, green and red	90	45

DESIGN: 50f. Scout camp.

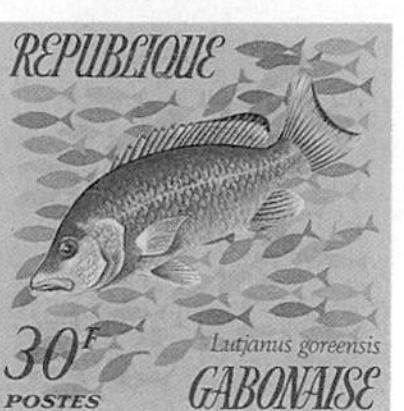

214 Pink Snapper

1975. Fishes. Multicoloured.

553	30f. Type **214**	65	35
554	40f. Guinean threadfin	1·10	50
555	50f. Round sardinella	1·80	55
556	120f. West African parrot-fish	3·00	1·10

215 Swimming Pool

1975. Air. Olympic Games, Montreal (1976) (1st issue). Multicoloured.

557	100f. Type **215**	1·30	60
558	150f. Boxing ring	2·00	90
559	300f. Aerial view of Games complex	3·50	1·80

MS560 170×100 mm. Nos. 557/9 7·50 7·50

See also Nos. 591/**MS**594.

1975. Air. "Apollo–Soyuz" Space Link. No. 526 optd JONCTION 17 Juillet 1975.

561	**201**	1000f. green, red and blue	10·00	5·25

217 "The Annunciation" (M. Denis)

1975. Air. Christmas. Multicoloured.

562	40f. Type **217**	1·30	45
563	50f. "Virgin and Child with Two Saints" (Fra Filippo Lippi)	1·30	60

218 Franceville Complex

1975. Inauguration of Agro-Industrial Complex, Franceville.

564	**218**	60f. multicoloured	95	45

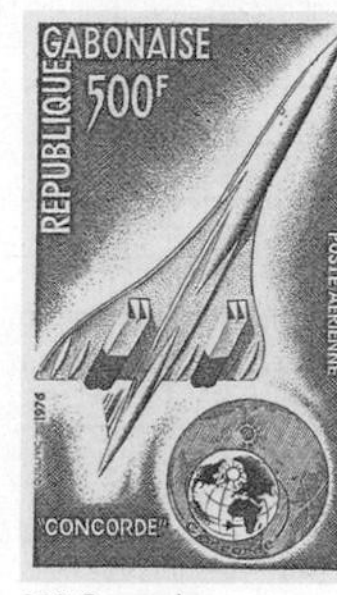

219 Concorde

1975. Air.

565	**219**	500f. ultramarine, bl & red	10·00	6·00

1975. Air. Concorde's First Commercial Flight. Surch 1000F 21 Janv. 1976 1er Vol Commercial de CONCORDE.

566	1000f. on 500f. ultram, blue and red	18·00	11·50

221 Tchibanga Bridge

1975. Gabon Bridges. Multicoloured.

567	5f. Type **221**	20	10
568	10f. Mouila Bridge	35	25
569	40f. Kango Bridges	85	35
570	50f. Lambarene Bridges (vert)	1·00	50

222 A. G. Bell and Early and Modern Telephones

1976. Telephone Centenary.

571	**222**	60f. grey, green and blue	95	45

223 Skiing (slalom)

1976. Air. Winter Olympic Games, Innsbruck.

572	**223**	100f. brown, blue & black	1·50	55
573	-	250f. brown, blue & black	3·00	1·70

MS574 170×90 mm. Nos. 572/3 5·75 5·75

DESIGN: 250f. Speed skating.

224 "The Crucifixion between Thieves" (wood-carving)

1976. Air. Easter. Multicoloured.
575 120f. Type **224** 1·50 90
576 130f. "Thomas placing finger in Jesus' wounds" (wood-carving) 2·10 1·20

225 Monseigneur Jean-Remy Bessieux

1976. Death Centenary of Bessieux.
577 **225** 50f. brown, blue & green 80 50

226 Boston Tea Party

1976. Air. Bicent of American Revolution.
578 **226** 100f. brown, orange & bl 1·20 75
579 - 150f. brown, orange & bl 2·00 1·00
580 - 200f. brown, orange & bl 2·75 1·30
DESIGNS: 150f. Battle scenes at Hudson Bay and New York; 200f. Wrecking of King George III's statue in New York.

227 Games Emblem

1976. 1st Central African Games.
581 **227** 50f. multicoloured 60 25
582 **227** 60f. multicoloured 85 25

1976. Air. U.S. Independence Day. Nos. 578/80 optd 4 JUILLET 1976.
583 **226** 100f. brown, orange & bl 1·20 75
584 - 150f. brown, orange & bl 2·00 1·10
585 - 200f. brown, orange & bl 2·75 1·30

229 Motobecane 125-LT3 (France)

1976. Motorcycles.
586 **229** 3f. black, green and blue 35 20
587 - 5f. black, mauve & yellow 35 20
588 - 10f. black, green and blue 55 30
589 - 20f. black, green and red 1·20 30
590 - 100f. black, blue and red 3·50 1·10
MOTORCYCLES: 5f. Bultaco 125 (Spain); 10f. Suzuki 125 (Japan); 20f. Kawasaki H2R (Japan); 100f. Harley-Davidson 750-TX (USA).

230 Running

1976. Air. Olympic Games, Montreal (2nd issue). Multicoloured.
591 **230** 100f. brown, blue & violet 1·30 60
592 - 200f. multicoloured 2·30 1·30
593 - 260f. brown, grn & myrtle 3·00 1·50
MS594 150×120 mm. Nos. 591/3 7·25 7·25
DESIGNS: 200f. Football; 260f. High Jumping.

231 Presidents Giscard d'Estaing and Bongo

1976. Air. Visit of Pres. Giscard d'Estaing to Gabon.
595 **231** 60f. multicoloured 1·20 60

1976. Town Arms (7th series). As T 137 dated "1976".
596 15f. multicoloured 50 25
597 25f. multicoloured 50 25
598 50f. black, gold and red 1·30 35
ARMS: 15f. Nyanga; 25f. Mandji; 50f. Mekambo.

232 Ricefield and Plant

1976. Agriculture. Multicoloured.
599 50f. Type **232** 80 30
600 60f. Pepper grove and plant 1·00 50

233 "Presentation at the Temple"

1976. Air. Christmas. Wood-carvings. Mult.
601 50f. Type **233** 85 45
602 60f. "The Nativity" 1·30 60

234 Photograph of Site

1976. Air. Discovery of Oklo Fossil Reactor.
603 **234** 60f. multicoloured 1·00 50

235 "The Last Supper" (Juste de Gand)

1977. Air. Easter. Multicoloured.
604 50f. Type **235** 1·00 60
605 100f. "The Deposition" (N. Poussin) 2·10 95

1977. Agriculture. As T 232 but dated "1977". Multicoloured.
606 50f. Banana plantation 80 30
607 60f. Groundnuts and market 1·10 50

236 Printed Circuit and Telephone

1977. 9th World Telecommunications Day.
608 **236** 60f. multicoloured 80 50

237 "Air Gabon" Insignia and Boeing 747

1977. Air. 1st "Air Gabon" Intercontinental Air Service.
609 **237** 60f. blue, yellow and green 1·00 50

238 Cap Lopez

1977. Gabon Views and Features. Mult.
610 50f. Type **238** 60 30
611 60f. Oyem 65 35
612 70f. Lebamba grotto 90 40

239 Beethoven and Musical Score

1977. Air. 150th Death Anniv of Beethoven.
613 **239** 260f. blue 3·00 1·80

240 Palais des Congres

1977. Organization of African Unity Conference.
614 **240** 100f. multicoloured 1·30 80

241 Gabon Coat of Arms

1977
615 **241** 50f. blue (22×36 mm) 1·30 45
616 **241** 60f. orange 1·00 50
617 **241** 80f. red 1·50 1·10

1977. Town Arms (8th series). As T 137 but dated "1977". Multicoloured.
618 50f. Omboue 1·00 45
619 60f. Minvoul 1·00 45
620 90f. Mayumba 1·60 60

242 Parliament Building, Libreville

1977. National Festival.
621 **242** 50f. multicoloured 80 25

243 Renault "Voiturette" of 1902

1977. Birth Centenary of Louis Renault (motor pioneer).
622 **243** 5f. blue, red and brown 65 35
623 - 10f. brown and red 65 35
624 - 30f. red, green and drab 1·70 55
625 - 40f. green, yellow & brown 2·50 55
626 - 100f. black, turquoise & bl 4·75 1·70
MS627 172×90 mm. 150f. violet and claret; 200f. violet, claret and brown 15·00 15·00
DESIGNS: 10f. Renault Type KH **12** coupe,1921; 30f. Renault Scaphandrier Torpedo, 1925; 40f. Renault Reinastella 40 CV saloon, 1929; 100f. Renault Nerva Grand Sport, 1937 150f. Renault 1 CV volturette, 1899; 200f. Renault A442 Alpine V-6 turbo racing car, 1977.

244 Lindbergh and "Spirit of St. Louis"

1977. Air. 50th Anniv of Lindbergh's Transatlantic Flight.
628 **244** 500f. blue, brown & lt bl 1·00 35

245 Footballer

1977. Air. World Cup Football Championship Qualifying Rounds.
629 **245** 250f. multicoloured 1·30 60

246 "Viking" on Mars

1977. Air. "Operation Viking".
630 **246** 1000f. multicoloured 12·00 10·50

1977. Air. 1st Commercial Paris–New York Flight by "Concorde". Optd PARIS NEW YORK PREMIER VOL 22.11.77.
631 **219** 500f. ultramarine, bl & red 10·00 6·50

248 "Study of a Head"

1977. Air. 400th Birth Anniv of Peter Paul Rubens. Multicoloured.

632	60f. "Lion Hunt" (horiz)	1·10	45
633	80f. "Hippopotamus Hunt" (horiz)	1·30	60
634	200f. Type **248**	3·25	1·60
MS635	176×136 mm. Nos. 632/4	7·25	7·25

249 "Adoration of the Magi" (Rubens)

1977. Air. Christmas. Multicoloured.

636	60f. Type **249**	1·00	40
637	80f. "The Flight into Egypt" (Rubens)	1·30	60

250 "Still Life and Maori Statue"

1978. Air. 75th Death Anniv of Paul Gauguin. Multicoloured.

638	150f. Type **250**	2·75	85
639	300f. "Self-Portrait"	5·50	2·00

251 Globe

1978. World Leprosy Day.

640	**251**	80f. green, blue and red	80	50

252 Boeing 747 Airplane, Diesel Locomotive and President

1978. 10th Anniv of National Renewal.

641	**252**	500f. multicoloured	6·25	2·50

253 Citroen "Cabriolet", 1922

1978. Birth Centenary of Andre Citroen (motor pioneer).

642	**253**	10f. purple, green and red	60	35
643	-	50f. green, blue & turq	1·40	60
644	-	60f. grey, brown and blue	2·00	75
645	-	80f. blue, slate and lilac	2·30	75
646	-	200f. brown, slate & orge	6·25	2·20
MS647		170×100 mm. 150f. green, deep brown and brown; 250f. deep brown, green and brown	16·00	16·00

DESIGNS: 50f. Citroen B 14 taxi, 1927; 60f. Citroen 8 CV Berline saloon, 1932; 80f. Citroen 7 CV Traction Avant Berline saloon. 1934 200f. Citroen 2 CV Berline saloon, 1948; 150f. Andre Citroen and Citroen Type A torpedo, 1919; 250f. Citroen CX 2400 Pallas saloon, 1975.

254 Ndjole and L'Ogooue

1978. Views of Gabon. Multicoloured.

648	30f. Type **254**	35	25
649	40f. Lambarene, Lake District	55	30
650	50f. Owendo Port	80	30

255 "Sternotomis mirabilis"

1978. Beetles. Multicoloured.

651	20f. Type **255**	80	25
652	60f. "Analeptes trifasciata"	2·10	55
653	75f. "Homoderus mellyi"	3·00	75
654	80f. "Stephanorrhina guttata"	3·25	90

257 Players heading Ball

1978. Air. World Cup Football Championship, Argentina.

660	**257**	100f. brown, red and green	1·00	50
661	-	120f. brown, red and green	1·30	80
662	-	200f. brown and red	2·30	95
MS663		180×99 mm. Nos. 660/2	5·75	5·75

DESIGNS: 120f. Players tackling. VERT: 200f. F.I.F.A. World Cup.

258 Anti-Apartheid Emblem

1978. International Anti-Apartheid Year.

664	**258**	80f. orange, brown & blue	80	45

1978. Air. Argentina's Victory in World Cup Football Championship. Nos. 660/2 optd.

665	**257**	100f. brown, red and green	1·00	50
666	-	120f. brown, red and green	1·30	80
667	-	200f. brown and red	2·00	1·00
MS668		180×99 mm. As Nos. 665/7 but optd in black	5·50	5·50

OVERPRINTS: 100f. **ARGENTINE HOLLAND 3 - 1**; 120f. **BRESIL ITALIE 2 - 1**; 200f. **CHAMPION DU MONDE 1978 ARGENTINE**.

1978. Town Arms (9th series). As T 137, but dated "1978".

669	5f. multicoloured	20	10
670	40f. multicoloured	50	20
671	60f. gold, black and blue	75	25

DESIGNS: 5f. Oyem; 40f. Okandja; 60f. Mimongo.

260 "Self-portrait at 13 years"

1978. Air. 450th Death Anniv of Albrecht Durer (artist).

672	**260**	100f. grey and red	1·30	60
673	-	250f. red and grey	3·50	1·30

DESIGN: 250f. "Lucas de Leyde".

261 Parthenon

1978. UNESCO Campaign for the Preservation of the Acropolis.

674	**261**	80f. brown, orange & blue	1·00	45

262 White Stork and Saxony 1850 3f. Stamp

1978. Air. "Philexafrique" Exhibitions, Libreville, Gabon and International Stamp Fair, Essen, W. Germany. Multicoloured.

675	100f. Type **262**	2·50	1·60
676	100f. Gorilla and Gabon 1971 40f. Grey Parrot stamp	2·50	1·60

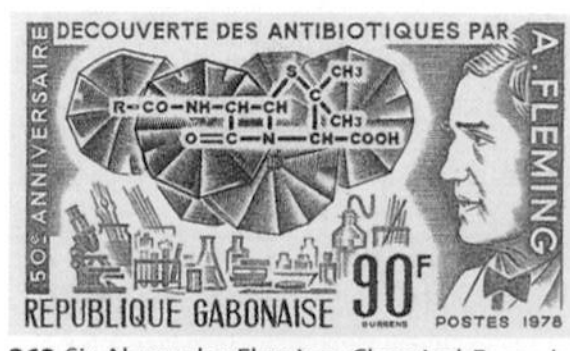
263 Sir Alexander Fleming, Chemical Formula and Laboratory Equipment

1978. 50th Anniv of Fleming's Discovery of Antibiotics.

677	**263**	90f. brown, orange & grn	2·20	1·00

264 "The Visitation"

1978. Christmas. Sculptures from the Church of St. Michel de Libreville. Multicoloured.

678	60f. Type **264**	80	30
679	80f. "Massacre of the Innocents"	1·00	50

265 Wright Brothers and Flyer I

1978. Air. 75th Anniv of First Powered Flight.

680	**265**	380f. brown, blue and red	4·50	1·80

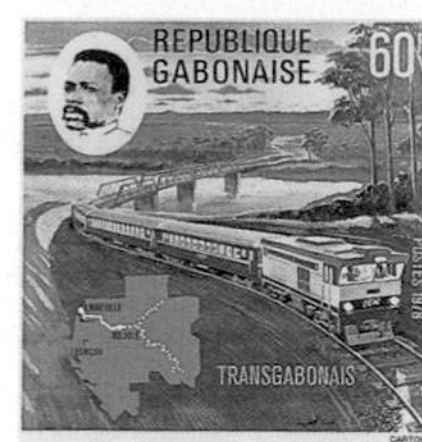
266 Diesel Train

1978. Inauguration of First Section of Trans-Gabon Railway, Libreville-Njole.

681	**266**	60f. multicoloured	1·20	55

267 Pope John Paul II

1979. Air. The Popes of 1978. Multicoloured.

682	100f. Type **267**	2·75	1·60
683	200f. Popes Paul VI and John Paul I with St. Peter's	5·00	1·70

1979. Town Arms (10th series). As T 137, but dated "1979". Multicoloured.

684	5f. Ogooue-Maritime	35	20
685	10f. Lastoursville	35	20
686	15f. M'Bigou	50	25

268 "The Two Disciples"

1979. Air. Easter. Wood-carvings from St. Michel de Libreville Church. Multicoloured.

687	100f. Type **268**	1·50	95
688	150f. "Jesus appearing to Mary Magdalene"	1·80	95

269 Long Jumping

1979. Pre-Olympic Year.
689 - 60f. red, brown & turq 55 30
690 **269** 80f. brown, turq & red 75 35
691 - 100f. turquoise, red & brn 95 50
MS692 179×99 mm Nos. 689/91 3·75 3·75
DESIGNS—Horiz: 60f. Horse riding; 100f. Yachting.
See also Nos. 725/**MS**728.

270 Sir Rowland Hill, Postal Messenger and Stamp

1979. "Philexafrique 2" Exhibition, Libreville.
693 **270** 50f. multicoloured 1·20 85
694 - 80f. multicoloured 2·00 1·40
695 - 150f. green, blue & brown 3·00 2·30
DESIGNS—VERT: 80f. Bakota mask and tulip flower. HORIZ: 150f. Canoeist, mail van, UPU emblem and stamps.

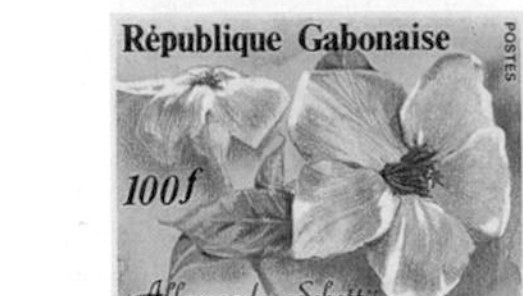

271 "Allamanda schottii"

1979. Philexafrique Stamp Exhibition, Libreville (3rd issue). Flowers. Sheet 150×110 mm containing T 271 and similar designs. Multicoloured.
MS696 100f. Type **271**; 100f. "Gloriosa superba"; 100f. "Phaeomeria magnifica" (vert); 100f. "Berlinia bracteosa" (vert) 9·00 9·00

272 Child holding Bird

1979. International Year of the Child.
697 **272** 100f. brown, violet & blue 1·30 50

273 Captain Cook

1979. Air. Death Bicent of Captain Cook.
698 **273** 500f. multicoloured 6·25 3·00

274 Louis Bleriot and Channel Flight Route

1979. Air. Aviation History. Multicoloured.
699 250f. Type **274** (First Channel Flight, 70th anniv) 3·00 1·80
700 1000f. Astronauts and module on Moon and Gabon S.G. 369 (Moon Landing, 10th anniv) 10·00 5·25

275 "Telecom 79"

1979. 3rd World Telecommunications Exhibition, Geneva.
701 **275** 80f. blue, orange & dp bl 85 35

276 Carved Head, Map and Rotary Emblem

1979. Air. 75th Anniv of Rotary International.
702 **276** 80f. multicoloured 1·00 45

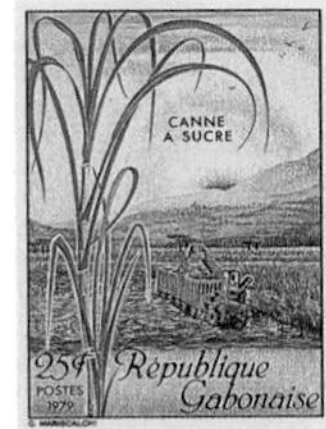

277 Harvesting Sugar Cane

1979. Agriculture. Multicoloured.
703 25f. Type **277** 45 10
704 30f. Igname 50 10

278 Judo

1979. World Judo Championships, Paris.
705 **278** 40f. olive, brown & orange 1·40 55

279 Eugene Jamot and Tsetse Fly

1979. Air. Birth Centenary of Eugene Jamot (discovery of sleeping sickness cure).
706 **279** 300f. black, brown & vio 4·50 2·50

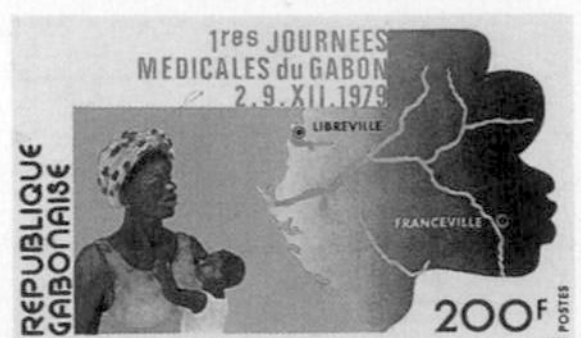

280 Mother with Child and Map of Gabon

1979. 1st Gabon Medical Days.
707 **280** 200f. multicoloured 2·30 85

281 "The Flight into Egypt"

1979. Christmas. Carvings from St. Michael's Church, Libreville. Multicoloured.
708 60f. Type **281** 80 45
709 80f. "The Circumcision" 1·00 40

282 Statue of President Bongo

1979. 44th Anniv of President Bongo.
710 **282** 60f. multicoloured 80 30
See also No. 714.

283 Bob Sleighing

1980. Air. Winter Olympic Games, Lake Placid. Multicoloured.
711 100f. Type **283** 1·00 60
712 200f. Ski jumping 2·00 1·10
MS713 150×100 mm. Nos. 711/12 3·75 3·75

1980. Investiture of President. As No. 710 but inscr "INVESTITURE 27 FEVRIER 1980".
714 80f. multicoloured 2·30 1·00

284 Oil Derrick

1980. 20th Anniv of OPEC.
715 **284** 50f. multicoloured 1·00 45

285 Donguila Church

1980. Easter. Multicoloured.
716 60f. Type **285** 55 25
717 80f. Bizangobibere Church 85 45

286 Dominique Ingres (artist)

1980. Air. Celebrities' Anniversaries.
718 **286** 100f. sepia, green & brown 1·30 55
719 - 200f. brown, pur & grey 3·25 1·40
720 - 360f. brown, green & sepia 3·50 1·80
DESIGNS: 100f. Type **286** (birth cent); 200f. Jacques Offenbach (composer, death cent); 360f. Gustave Flaubert (author, death cent).

287 Telephone

1980. Air. World Telecommunications Day.
721 **287** 80f. multicoloured 1·00 45

288 Savorgnan de Brazza and Map

1980. Centenary of Franceville.
722 **288** 165f. multicoloured 2·10 1·10

289 Dieudonne Costes, Maurice Bellonte and "Point d'Interrogation"

1980. Air. Aviation Anniversaries.
723 **289** 165f. red, blue and green 1·60 80
724 - 1000f. green, red and blue 10·00 5·00
DESIGNS: 165f. Type **289** (50th anniv of first North Atlantic flight); 1000f. Jean Mermoz and seaplane "Comte de la Vaulx" (50th anniv of first South Atlantic airmail).

290 Running

1980. Air. Olympic Games, Moscow.
725 **290** 50f. multicoloured 80 25
726 - 100f. black, red and green 1·00 50
727 - 250f. multicoloured 2·30 1·20
MS728 124×104 mm. As Nos. 725/7 but colours changed 6·75 6·75
DESIGNS: 100f. Pole vaulting; 250f. Boxing.

1980. District Arms (1st series). As T 137 but dated "1980".
729 10f. silver, black and gold 30 10
730 20f. multicoloured 40 10
731 30f. black, silver and red 40 20
DESIGNS: 10f. Haut-Ogooue; 20f. L'Estuaipe; 30f. Bitam.

291 Leon Mba and El Hadj Omar Bongo

1980. 20th Anniv of Independence.
732 **291** 60f. multicoloured 95 45

292 Peacock Emblem and Tourist Attractions

1980. World Tourism Conference, Manila.
733 **292** 80f. blue, violet and brown 95 45

293 Figures supporting OPEC Emblem

1980. 20th Anniv of Organization of Petroleum Exporting Countries. Multicoloured.
734 90f. Globe and OPEC Emblem (horiz) 1·20 50
735 120f. Type **293** 1·50 80

1980. Air. Olympic Medal Winners. Nos. 725/7 optd.
736 50f. **YIFTER (Eth.) NYAMBUI (Tanz.) MAANINKA (Finl.) 5000 Metres** 75 25
737 100f. **KOZIAKIEWICZ (Pol.) (record du monde) VOLKOV (Urss) et SLUSARSKI (Pol.)** 95 55
738 250f. **WELTERS ALDAMA (Cuba) MUGABI (Oug.) KRUBER (Rda) et SZCZERDA (Pol.)** 2·30 1·40
MS739 As Nos. 736/8 but colours changed 6·75 6·75

295 African River Martin

1980. Birds. Multicoloured.
740 50f. Type **295** 1·60 45
741 60f. White-fronted bee eater 2·10 70
742 80f. African pitta 2·75 90
743 150f. Pel's fishing owl 5·50 1·60

296 Charles de Gaulle

1980. Air. 10th Death Anniv of Charles de Gaulle. Multicoloured.
744 100f. Type **296** 1·30 90
745 200f. Charles and Mme. de Gaulle 2·75 1·30
MS746 160×131 mm. Nos. 744/5 with se-tenant label 6·00 6·00

297 St. Matthew

1980. Christmas. Carvings from Bizangobibere Church. Multicoloured.
747 60f. St. Luke 85 35
748 80f. Type **297** 1·10 50

298 Heinrich von Stephan

1981. 150th Birth Anniv of Heinrich von Stephan (founder of UPU).
749 **298** 90f. dp brn, lt brn & brn 95 45

299 Shooting at Goal

1981. Air. World Cup Football Championship Eliminators. Multicoloured.
750 60f. Type **299** 55 45
751 190f. Players with ball 2·00 1·00

300 Palais Renovation

1981. 13th Anniv of National Renewal.
752 **300** 60f. multicoloured 75 25

301 W. Herschel (Discovery of Uranus Bicent)

1981. Air. Space Anniversaries. Mult.
753 150f. Type **301** 1·50 80
754 250f. Yuri Gagarin, first man in space (20th anniv) 2·30 1·50
755 500f. Alan Shepard, first American in space (20th anniv) 4·50 2·50
MS756 130×115 mm. Nos. 753/5 7·25 7·25

302 Lion (St. Mark)

1981. Easter. Wood Carvings from Bizangobibere Church. Multicoloured.
757 75f. Type **302** 85 35
758 100f. Eagle (St. John) 1·10 50

303 Port Gentil

1981. 23rd Congress of Lions Club District 403 Libreville. Multicoloured.
759 60f. Type **303** 65 30
760 75f. District 403 85 30
761 80f. Libreville Cocotiers 90 35
762 100f. Libreville Hibiscus 1·20 50
763 165f. Ekwata 1·80 80
764 200f. Haute-Ogooue 2·20 1·00

304 Caduceus

1981. World Telecommunications Day.
765 **304** 125f. multicoloured 1·40 65

305 Map of Africa and Emblems of Gabon Electricity and Water Society and UPDEA

1981. Air. 7th Congress of African Electricity Producers and Suppliers.
766 **305** 100f. multicoloured 95 50

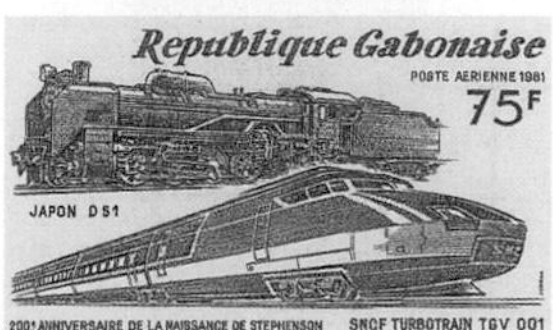

306 Japanese D-51 Locomotive and French Turbotrain TGV 001

1981. Air. Birth Bicent of George Stephenson.
767 **306** 75f. grey, orange & brown 1·00 35
768 - 100f. green, black & blue 1·50 50
769 - 350f. green, brown & red 4·25 1·80
MS770 190×100 mm. As Nos. 767/9 but colours changed 6·00 6·00
DESIGNS: 100f. Baltimore & Ohio Mallet 7100 and Prussian State Railway T-3 locomotives; 350f. George Stephenson, his locomotive "Rocket" (1829) and Alsthom diesel locomotive.

1981. Air. World Railway Speed Record. No. MS770 optd 26 fevrier 1981–Record du monde de vitesse 380km a l'heure.
MS771 190×100 mm. As Nos. 767/9 but colours changed 6·00 6·00

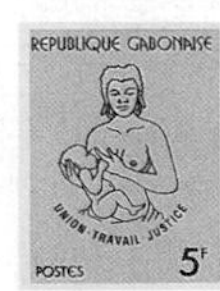

307 Mother Breast-feeding Child

1981
772 **307** 5f. brown and black 10 10
773 **307** 10f. mauve and black 10 10
774 **307** 15f. green and black 10 10
775 **307** 20f. pink and black 10 10
776 **307** 25f. blue and black 10 10
777 **307** 40f. pink and black 45 10
778 **307** 50f. green and black 50 10
779 **307** 75f. brown and black 70 30
779a **307** 90f. blue and black 85 25
780 **307** 100f. yellow and black 90 40
780a **307** 125f. green and black 1·30 45
780b **307** 150f. purple and black 1·70 65

308 R. P. Klaine (70th death anniv)

1981. Religious Personalities. Multicoloured.
781 70f. Type **308** 80 30
782 90f. Mgr. Walker (110th birth anniv) 1·10 45

309 Scout Badge on Map of Gabon

1981. 4th Pan-African Scout Congress, Abidjan.
783 **309** 75f. multicoloured 1·00 45

1981. 28th World Scout Conference, Dakar. Optd DAKAR 28e CONFERENCE MONDIALE DU SCOUTISME.
784 75f. multicoloured 1·20 60

311 "Helping the Disabled"

1981. International Year of Disabled People.
785 **311** 100f. red, dp green & grn 1·00 50

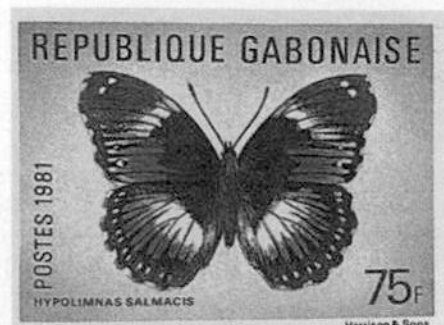

312 "Hypolimnas salmacis"

1981. Butterflies. Multicoloured.

786		75f. Type **312**	1·80	65
787		100f. "Euphaedra themis"	2·30	85
788		150f. "Amauris niavius"	3·00	1·30
789		250f. "Cymothoe lucasi"	4·75	2·00

313 "Paul as Harlequin"

1981. Birth Centenary of Pablo Picasso.

790	**313**	500f. multicoloured	6·50	2·75

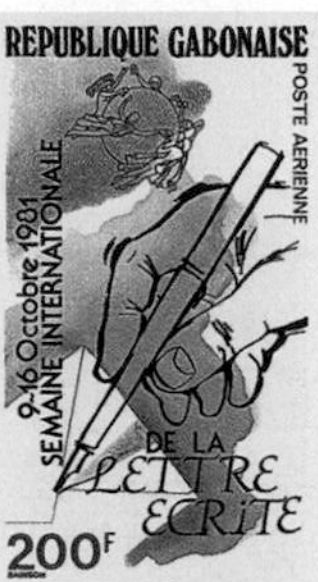

314 Hand holding Pen

1981. Air. International Letter-writing Week.

791	**314**	200f. multicoloured	2·00	95

315 Agricultural Scenes, Wheat and FAO Emblem

1981. World Food Day.

792	**315**	350f. brown, dp brn & bl	3·75	1·80

316 Traditional Hairstyle

1981. Traditional Hairstyles.

793	**316**	75f. red, yellow and black	1·00	50
794	-	100f. green, lilac and black	1·30	55
795	-	125f. lt green, green & blk	1·80	85
796	-	200f. pink, violet and black	2·75	1·30
MS797		108×133 mm. Nos. 793/6	7·00	7·00

DESIGNS: 100f. to 200f. Different hairstyles.

See also Nos. 964a and 1046.

317 Dancers around Fire

1981. Christmas. Multicoloured.

798		75f. Type **317**	75	25
799		100f. Christmas meal	1·30	45

1982. District Arms (2nd series). As T 137 but dated "1982". Multicoloured.

800		75f. Moyen-Ogooue	75	10
801		100f. Woleu-N'tem	1·00	20
802		150f. N'Gounie	1·50	45

318 Pope John Paul II

1982. Papal Visit.

803	**318**	100f. multicoloured	2·20	1·00

319 Alfred de Musset

1982. 125th Death Anniv of Alfred de Musset (writer).

804	**319**	75f. black	75	25

320 "Leonce Veilvieux" (freighter)

1982. Merchant Ships. Multicoloured.

805		75f. Type **320**	85	35
806		100f. "Correze" (container ship)	1·00	50
807		200f. Oil tanker	2·00	95

321 Dr. Robert Koch, Microscope, Bacillus and Guinea Pig

1982. Centenary of Discovery of Tubercle Bacillus.

808	**321**	100f. multicoloured	1·50	75

322 Rope Bridge, Poubara

1982. "Philexfrance 82" International Stamp Exhibition, Paris. Multicoloured.

809		100f. Type **322**	95	45
810		100f. Bapounou sculpture	1·90	80

323 Hexagonal Pattern

1982. World Telecommunications Day.

811	**323**	75f. multicoloured	95	50

324 Footballer (Brazil)

1982. World Cup Football Championship, Spain. Multicoloured.

812		100f. Type **324**	95	30
813		125f. Footballer (Argentina)	1·20	45
814		200f. Footballer (England)	1·80	75
MS815		102×120 mm. Nos. 812/14	4·50	4·50

325 "Caprice des Dames" (Morning)

1982. Flower "Caprice des Dames". Mult.

816		75f. Type **325**	1·00	45
817		100f. Midday	1·20	50
818		175f. Evening	1·80	90

326 Satellites

1982. Second U.N. Conference on Exploration and Peaceful Uses of Outer Space.

819	**326**	250f. blue, deep blue & red	2·75	1·50

1982. World Cup Football Championship Winners. Nos. 812/14 optd.

821	**324**	100f. multicoloured	95	50
822	-	125f. multicoloured	1·30	55
823	-	200f. multicoloured	1·80	80
MS824		102×120 mm. Nos. 812/14, sheet margin is inscribed **ITALIE CHAMPIONNE du MONDE**	4·50	4·50

OPTS: 100f. **DEMIE-FINALE POLOGNE 0—ITALIE 2**; 125f. **DEMIE-FINALE R. F. ALLEMAGNE 3—FRANCE 3**; 200f. **FINALE ITALIE 3—R. F. ALLEMAGNE 1**.

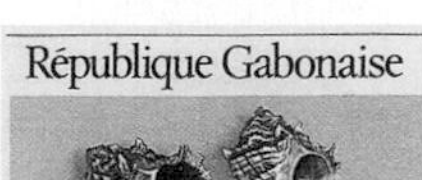

329 Duplex Murex

1982. Shells. Multicoloured.

825		75f. Type **329**	1·00	55
826		100f. "Chama crenulata"	1·50	65
827		125f. "Cardium hians"	2·30	1·10

330 "Still-life with Mandolin" (Braque, birth centenary)

1982. Painters' Anniversaries. Mult.

828		300f. Type **330**	3·25	1·10
829		350f. "Boy blowing Soap Bubbles" (Manet, death cent) (vert)	5·25	1·60

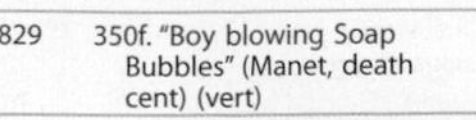

331 Okouyi Mask

1982. Artifacts. Multicoloured.

830		75f. Type **331**	60	25
831		100f. Ondoumbo reliquary	1·00	45
832		150f. Tsogho statuette	1·60	60
833		250f. Forge bellows	2·50	95

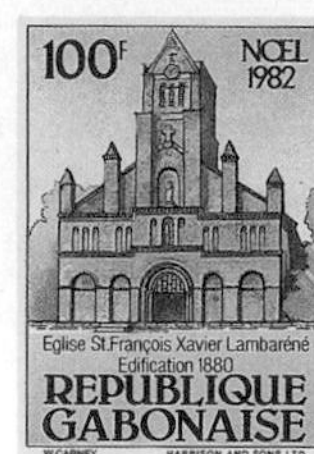

332 St. Francis Xavier Church, Lambarene

1982. Christmas.

834	**332**	100f. multicoloured	95	45

333 Presidents Bongo and Mitterand, Route Map and Diesel Train

1983. Inauguration of Second Stage of Trans-Gabon Railway.

835	**333**	75f. multicoloured	1·90	65

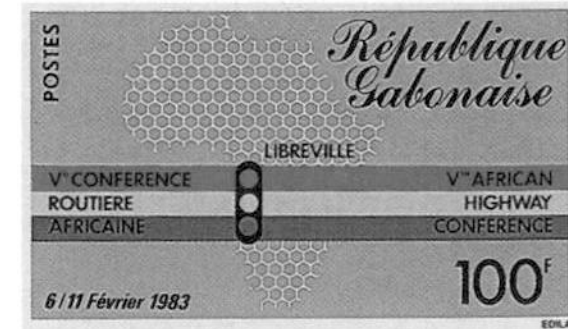

334 Stylized Highway and Map of Africa

1983. 5th African Highway Conference.

836	**334**	100f. multicoloured	95	45

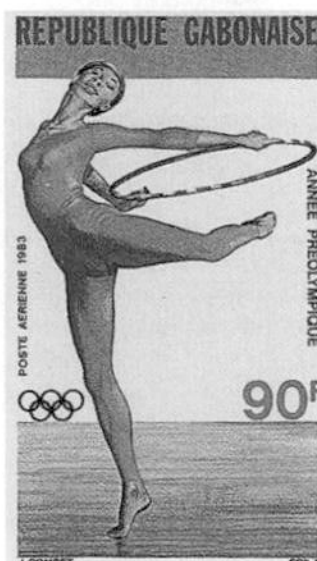

335 Gymnast with Hoop

1983. Air. Olympic Games, Los Angeles. Multicoloured.

837		90f. Type **335**	1·00	45
838		350f. Wind-surfing	3·50	1·40

336 "Epitorium trochiformis" (Estuaire)

1983. Provinces. Multicoloured.

839 75f. Bakota mask (Ogooue Ivindo) 1·00 50
840 90f. African buffalo (Nyanga) 1·20 50
841 90f. "Charaxes druceanus" (Ogooue Lolo) 1·20 50
842 100f. Isogho hairstyle (Ngounie) 1·20 65
843 125f. Manganese (Haut Ogooue) 1·70 70
844 125f. Crocodiles (Moyen Ogooue) 1·70 70
845 125f. Atlantic tarpon (Ogooue Maritime) 1·70 70
846 135f. Type **336** 1·80 85
847 135f. Coffee flowers (Woleu Ntem) 1·80 85

337 "Ville de Rouen" (container ship) and IMO Emblem

1983. 25th Anniv of International Maritime Organization.

848 **337** 125f. multicoloured 1·50 50

338 Water Chevrotain

1983. Fauna. Multicoloured.

849 90f. Type **338** 95 45
850 125f. Pink-backed pelican ("Pelican") 1·30 55
851 225f. African elephant 2·75 85
852 400f. Iguana 4·00 1·80
MS853 122×89 mm. Nos. 849/52 11·50 11·50

339 ECA Anniversary Emblem

1983. 25th Anniv of Economic Commission for Africa.

854 **339** 125f. multicoloured 1·20 55

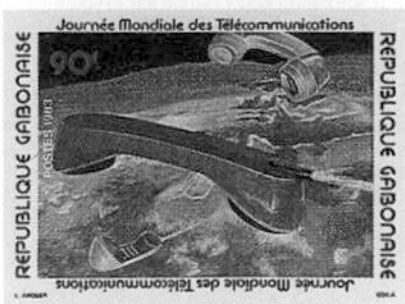

340 Telephones

1983. World Telecommunications Day. Mult.

855 90f. Type **340** 1·30 80
856 90f. As No. 855 but design inverted 1·30 80

341 "Double Eagle II" crossing Atlantic

1983. Air. Ballooning Anniversaries.

857 100f. grey, orange and blue 1·00 50
858 125f. green, purple and blue 1·30 75
859 350f. blue, green & light green 3·75 2·00

DESIGNS: 100f. Type **341** (5th anniv of first Atlantic crossing); 125f. Hot-air balloons (Bicentenary of Montgolfier Brothers' balloon); 350f. Pilatre de Rozier and Montgolfier balloon (Bicentenary of manned flight).

342 "Lady with Unicorn"

1983. Air. 150th Birth Anniv of Raphael.

860 **342** 1000f. multicoloured 11·00 5·00

343 Nkoltang Satellite Receiving Station

1983. World Communications Year.

861 **343** 125f. multicoloured 1·20 55

344 Rapids on the Ivindo River

1983. Tourism.

862 **344** 90f. blue, brown and green 85 40
863 - 125f. brown, green & grey 1·30 65
864 - 185f. grey, orange & green 1·90 75
865 - 350f. brown, green & blue 3·50 1·60

DESIGNS: 125f. Pirogue on the Ogooue River; 185f. Wonga Wongue Game Reserve; 350f. Coastal beach.

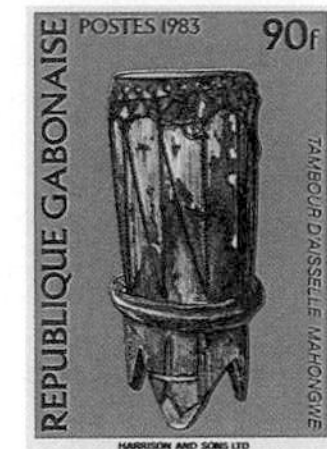

345 Mahongwe Drum

1983. Music and Dance. Multicoloured.

866 90f. Type **345** 95 40
867 125f. Okoukoue dance 1·30 60
868 135f. Ngomi bateke 1·50 80
869 260f. Ndoumou dancer 2·75 1·30

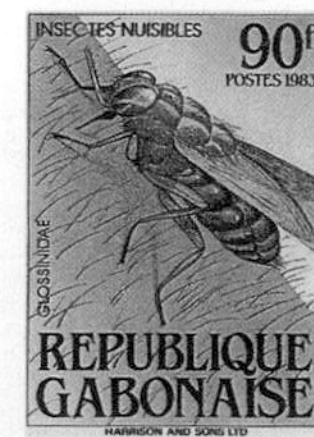

346 "Glossinidae"

1983. Harmful Insects. Multicoloured.

870 90f. Type **346** 1·40 65
871 125f. "Belonogaster junceus" 2·00 75
872 300f. "Aedes aegypti" 3·75 1·40
873 350f. "Mylabris" 5·00 1·80

347 "The Adulterous Woman"

1983. Christmas. Wood carvings from St. Michel Church, Libreville. Multicoloured.

874 90f. Type **347** 80 45
875 125f. "Parable of the Good Samaritan" 1·30 55

348 Boeing 747-200 Airliner and Gabon Stamp of 1966

1984. World Post Congress Stamp Exhibition, Hamburg. Multicoloured.

876 125f. Type **348** 1·50 55
877 225f. Douglas DC-10 and German airmail stamp of 1919 2·50 1·10

349 Pylons and Buildings

1984. 3rd Anniv of "Africa 1".

878 **349** 125f. multicoloured 1·20 45

350 Ice Hockey

1984. Air. Winter Olympic Games, Sarajevo.

879 **350** 125f. green, purple & blk 1·50 80
880 - 350f. blue, brown & black 3·75 1·50

DESIGN: 350f. Ice-dancing.

351 Coconut

1984. Fruit Trees. Multicoloured.

881 90f. Type **351** 1·10 45
882 100f. Pawpaw 1·20 55
883 125f. Mango 1·60 75
884 250f. Banana 3·25 1·30

352 Robin Dauphin and Piper Cherokee Six Aircraft

1984. Air. Paris–Libreville Air Rally.

885 **352** 500f. multicoloured 4·50 2·40

353 "Racehorses"

1984. Air. 150th Birth Anniv of Degas.

886 **353** 500f. multicoloured 7·25 3·25

354 Water Lily

1984. Flowers. Multicoloured.

887 90f. Type **354** 1·20 45
888 125f. Water hyacinth 1·50 65
889 135f. Hibiscus 1·90 80
890 350f. Bracteate orchid 4·00 2·10

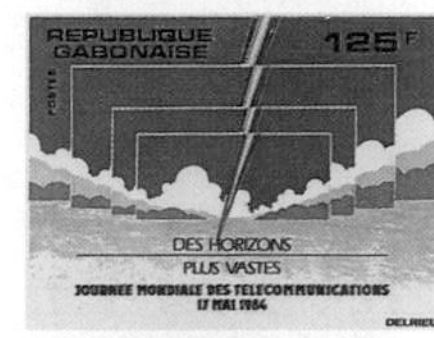

355 Spectrum

1984. World Telecommunications Day.

891 **355** 125f. multicoloured 1·20 50

356 Basketball

1984. Air. Olympic Games, Los Angeles. Multicoloured.

892 90f. Type **356** 80 45
893 125f. Steeplechase 1·30 55

357 Sikorsky S-43 Amphibian of Aeromartime

1984. Air. Universal Postal Union Congress, Hamburg. Sheet 130×108 mm.

MS894 **357** 1000f. multicoloured 20·00 20·00

358 Lionel Hampton

1984. Jazz Musicians. Multicoloured.

895 90f. Type **358** 1·80 75
896 125f. Charlie Parker 2·00 75
897 260f. Erroll Garner 4·00 2·20

1984. District Arms (3rd series). As T 137 but dated "1984". Multicoloured.

898 90f. Cocobeach 1·00 30
899 125f. Mouila 1·50 35

900 135f. N'Djole 1·50 40

359 Medouneu

1984. Tourism. Multicoloured.

901	90f. Type **359**	95	45
902	125f. Sunset over Ogooue	1·30	80
903	165f. Trans-Gabon train	2·50	1·40

1984. Air. Olympic Winners. Sheet 185×170 mm.
MS904 90f. multicoloured; 125f. multicoloured; 125f. emerald, magenta and black; 350f. blue, brown and black 7·00 7·00

DESIGNS: 90f. As Type **356**; 125f. As No. 893; 125f. as Type **350**; 359f. As No. 880, but all with additional inscriptions.

360 Globe, Post and Emblem

1984. Universal Postal Union Day.
905 **360** 125f. multicoloured 1·30 50

360a Kota Reliquary

1984. Traditional Art. Multicoloured.

905a	90f. Kouble mask
905b	125f. Pounou fan
905c	150f. Mahongoue reliquary
905d	250f. Type **360a**

361 "Icarus" (Hans Herni)

1984. 40th Anniv of International Civil Aviation Organization.
906 **361** 125f. dp blue, green & bl 1·30 50

362 Tympanum of Saint Michael's Church (left side)

1984. Christmas. Multicoloured.

907	90f. Type **362**	80	35
908	125f. Tympanum of Saint Michael's church (right side)	1·30	60

Nos. 907/8 were printed together, se-tenant, forming a composite design.

363 South African Crowned Cranes

1984. Birds. Multicoloured.

909	90f. Type **363**	1·10	70
910	125f. Snowy-breasted hummingbird	1·80	85
911	150f. Keel-billed toucan	2·20	1·00

364 Leper Colony, Libreville

1985. World Lepers' Day.
912 **364** 125f. multicoloured 1·30 50

365 I.Y.Y. Emblem

1985. International Youth Year.
913 **365** 125f. multicoloured 1·30 50

367 Profiles and Emblem

1985. 15th Anniv of Cultural and Technical Co-operation Agency.
914 **367** 125f. blue, red & dp blue 1·30 50

368 Water Rat

1985. Animals. Multicoloured.

915	90f. Type **368**	1·40	55
916	100f. Porcupine	1·50	55
917	125f. Giant pangolin	1·90	85
918	350f. Antelope	4·75	2·00
MS919	121×91 mm. Nos. 915/18	10·50	10·50

369 Score and Aleka

1985. Georges Damas Aleka (composer) Commemoration.
920 **369** 90f. multicoloured 1·00 45

370 Emblem and Coloured Lines

1985. World Telecommunications Day.
921 **370** 125f. multicoloured 1·30 50

371 Shield

1985. 30th Anniv of Christian Youth Workers' Movement in Gabon.
922 **371** 90f. multicoloured 1·00 50

372 "La Mpassa" (freighter)

1985
923 **372** 185f. multicoloured 2·00 80

373 Building and Dish Aerials

1985. 25th Anniv of Posts and Telecommunications Administration.
924 **373** 90f. multicoloured 1·00 50

374 President Bongo

1985. 25th Anniv of Independence.

925	**374**	250f. multicoloured	3·25	1·60
926	**374**	500f. multicoloured	6·50	4·00
MS927		120×89 mm. 1000f. Portraits as T **374** and Gabon seafront. Imperf	12·50	12·50

375 Dr. Albert Schweitzer

1985. Air. 20th Death Anniv of Dr. Albert Schweitzer.
928 **375** 350f. multicoloured 4·25 1·70

376 Hand holding U.N. and Gabon Flags

1985. Air. 20th Anniv of Membership of United Nations Organization.
929 **376** 225f. multicoloured 2·30 1·00

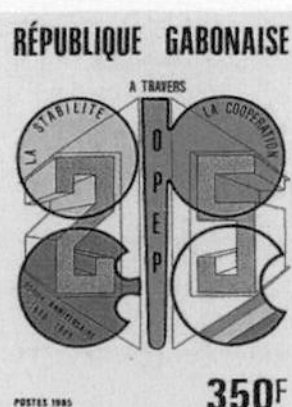

377 OPEC Emblem

1985. 25th Anniv of Organization of Petroleum Exporting Countries.
930 **377** 350f. multicoloured 3·75 1·90

378 Boy Scouts around Campfire and Elephant

1985. Air. "Philexafrique" Stamp Exhibition, Lome, Togo. Multicoloured.

931	100f. Type **378**	1·90	95
932	150f. Diesel train, satellite and dish aerial	3·25	1·20

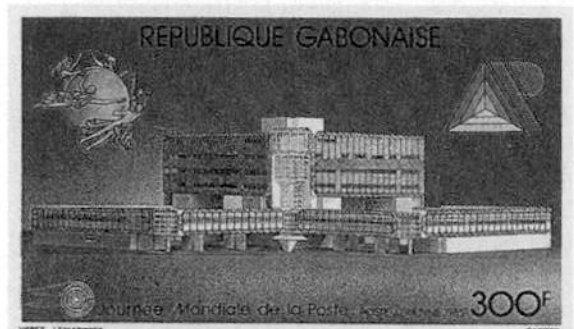

379 Central Post Office, Libreville, Gabon Posts and UPU Emblems

1985. Air. World Post Day.
933 **379** 300f. multicoloured 3·00 1·50

380 Hand holding Globe

1985. Air. 40th Anniv of UNO.
934 **380** 350f. multicoloured 3·75 1·60

381 Centre

1985. International Centre of Bantu Civilisations.
935 **381** 185f. multicoloured 1·80 85

381a Interior of Church

1985. Christmas. St. Andrew's Church, Libreville. Multicoloured.

935a	90f. Exterior of church
935b	125f. Type **381a**

382 Young People within Laurel Wreath

1986. 25th Anniv of UNESCO National Commission.
936 **382** 100f. multicoloured 1·00 50

383 "Mother and Child"

1986. Air. Gabon's Gift to United Nations Organization.
937 **383** 350f. multicoloured 3·75 1·60

384 Savorgnan de Brazza and Canoe

1986. Air. Centenary of Lastoursville.
938 **384** 100f. multicoloured 1·30 60

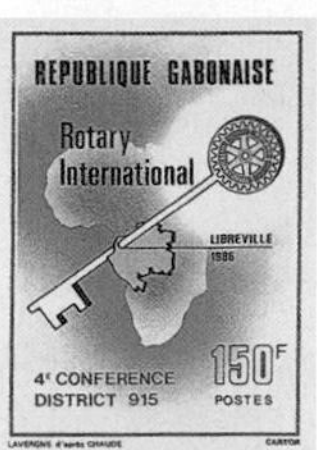

385 Key as Emblem and Map

1986. 4th Rotary International District 915 Conference, Libreville.
939 **385** 150f. multicoloured 1·60 80

386 Communications Equipment

1986. World Telecommunications Day.
940 **386** 300f. multicoloured 2·75 1·30

387 Goalkeeper saving Ball

1986. Air. World Cup Football Championship, Mexico. Multicoloured.
941 100f. Type **387** 1·00 45
942 150f. Footballers and Mexican statue 1·40 65
943 250f. World Cup trophy, footballers and map 2·30 1·00
944 350f. Flags, ball and stadium 3·00 1·50
MS945 140×110 mm. Nos. 941/4 9·00 9·00

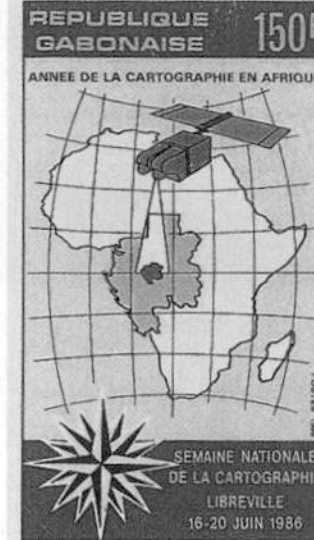

388 Map and Satellite

1986. African Cartography Year and National Cartography Week, Libreville.
946 **388** 150f. multicoloured 1·60 80

389 "L'Abanga" (container ship)

1986
947 **389** 250f. multicoloured 2·75 1·20

390 River and Gabon 1886 50c. Stamp

1986. Centenary of First Gabon Stamps.
948 **390** 500f. multicoloured 6·25 3·00

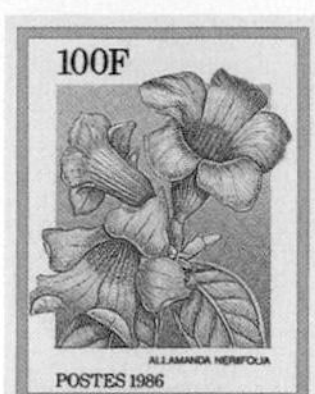

391 "Allamanda neriifolia"

1986. Flowers. Multicoloured.
949 100f. Type **391** 1·10 55
950 150f. "Musa cultivar" 1·60 75
951 350f. "Dissotis decumbens" 1·90 95
952 350f. "Campylospermum laeve" 4·25 1·90

392 Arms of Lambarn

1986. District Arms (4th series). Mult.
953 100f. Type **392** 1·00 40
954 160f. Leconi 1·70 60

393 Coffee Berries, Flowers and Beans

1986. 25th Anniv of African and Malagasy Coffee Producers Organization.
955 **393** 125f. multicoloured 1·70 80

394 "Machaon"

1986. Butterflies. Multicoloured.
956 150f. Type **394** 1·90 75
957 290f. "Urania" 4·00 1·50

395 Dove and UPU Emblem

1986. Air. World Post Day.
958 **395** 500f. multicoloured 4·50 2·20

1986. Air. World Cup Football Championship Winners. Nos 941/4 optd ARGENTINE 3-R.F.A. 2. Multicoloured.
959 100f. Type **387** 1·00 70
960 150f. Footballers and Mexican statue 1·40 85
961 250f. World Cup trophy, footballers and map 2·30 1·50
962 350f. Flags, ball and stadium 3·00 2·20

397 St. Peter's Church, Libreville

1986. Christmas.
963 **397** 500f. multicoloured 4·50 2·20

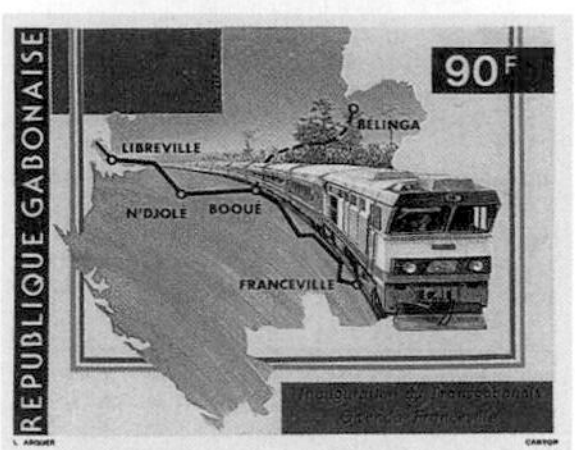

398 Diesel Train and Route Map

1986. Inauguration of Owendo–Franceville Trans-Gabon Railway.
964 **398** 90f. multicoloured 1·30 60

1986. Traditional Hairstyles. As T 316.
964a 150f. black, red and grey 5·25 1·50
MS965 105×80 mm. **398** 250f. multicoloured 3·75 3·50

399 West African Squirrelfish

1987. Fishes. Multicoloured.
966 90f. Type **399** 1·00 50
967 125f. West African parrotfish 1·40 70
968 225f. Flying gurnard 2·30 1·20
969 350f. Marbled stingray 3·50 1·60
MS970 121×91 mm. Nos. 966/9 11·00 11·00

400 Raoul Follereau (leprosy pioneer)

1987. World Leprosy Day.
971 **400** 125f. multicoloured 1·60 95

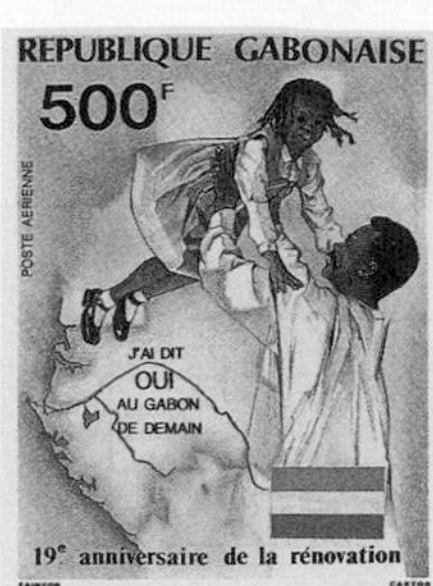

401 Man and Child in front of Map

1987. Air. 19th Anniv of National Renewal.
972 **401** 500f. multicoloured 5·75 2·20

402 Pres. Bongo receiving Prize

1987. Award of Dag Hammarskjold Peace Prize to Pres. Omar Bongo.
973 **402** 125f. multicoloured 1·20 75

403 Konrad Adenauer

1987. Air. 20th Death Anniv of Konrad Adenauer (German statesman).
974 **403** 300f. multicoloured 4·00 1·70

404 Symbols of Communication

1987. World Telecommunications Day.
975 **404** 90f. multicoloured 1·00 45

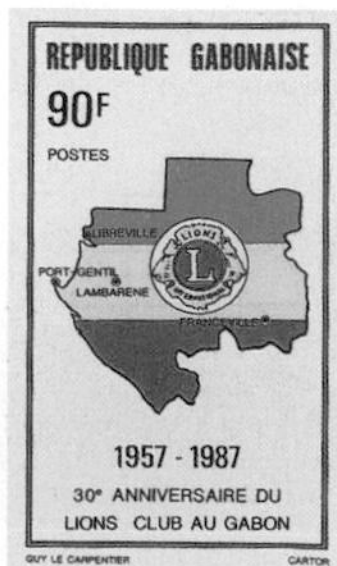

405 Emblem on Map

1987. 30th Anniv of Lions Club of Gabon.
976 **405** 90f. multicoloured 1·00 45

406 Coubertin and Runner with Torch

1987. 50th Death Anniv of Pierre de Coubertin (founder of modern Olympic Games).

977	**406**	200f. multicoloured	1·80	90

407 Map, Emblems and People

1987. 70th Anniv of Lions International.

978	**407**	165f. multicoloured	1·70	85

408 Globe in Envelope

1987. World Post Day.

979	**408**	125f. multicoloured	1·20	60

409 Pres. Bongo and Sam Nujoma

1987. Solidarity with South-West African Peoples' Organization.

980	**409**	225f. multicoloured	2·00	80

410 Fanel Moon

1987. Sea Shells. Multicoloured.

981	90f. Type **410**	1·30	60
982	125f. Lightning moon ("Natica fulminea cruentata")	1·70	60
MS983	72×92 mm. Nos. 981/2	5·00	5·00

See also Nos. 1018a/b.

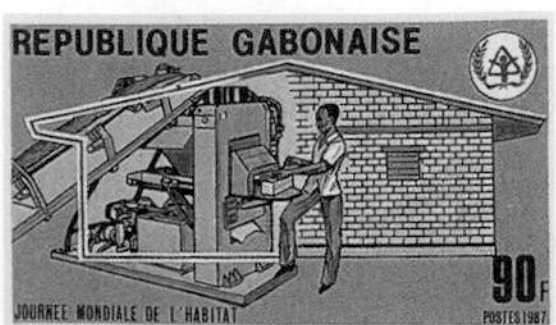

411 Man, House and Machinery

1987. International Year of Shelter for the Homeless. World Shelter Day.

984	**411**	90f. multicoloured	1·00	45

412 Mission

1987. Centenary of St. Anne of Odimba Mission.

985	**412**	90f. multicoloured	95	45

413 Nurse vaccinating Child

1987. Universal Vaccination for Children.

986	**413**	100f. multicoloured	1·20	45

414 President making Address

1987. 20th Anniv of Installation of President Omar Bongo.

987	**414**	1000f. multicoloured	9·00	5·50

415 St. Theresa's Church, Oyem

1987. Christmas.

988	**415**	90f. multicoloured	95	45

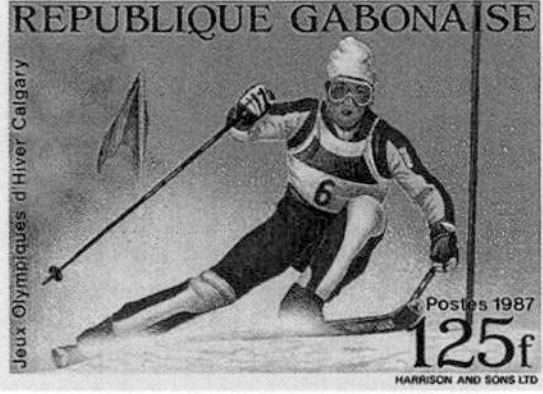

416 Skier

1987. Winter Olympic Games, Calgary (1988).

989	**416**	125f. multicoloured	1·20	60

417 "Cassia occidentalis"

1988. Medicinal Plants. Multicoloured.

990	90f. Type **417**	1·10	65
991	125f. "Tabernanthe iboga"	1·60	65
992	225f. "Cassia alata"	2·50	1·20
993	350f. "Anthocleista schweinfurthii"	4·50	2·50

418 Obamba Rattle

1988. Traditional Musical Instruments. Mult.

995	90f. Type **418**	1·00	60
996	100f. Fang sanza (vert)	1·30	70
997	125f. Mitsogho harp (vert)	1·50	85
998	165f. Fang xylophone	2·20	1·00
MS999	92×122 mm. Nos. 995/8	6·75	6·75

419 Elephant with raised Trunk

1988. Endangered Animals. African Elephant. Multicoloured.

1000	25f. Type **419**	1·50	55
1001	40f. Elephant family	2·40	1·00
1002	50f. Elephant in vegetation	3·75	1·10
1003	100f. Elephant	6·00	2·30

420 Postal Delta Building

1988. Inauguration of Postal Delta.

1004	**420**	90f. multicoloured	95	45

421 Village and Dr. Schweitzer

1988. Air. 75th Anniv of Arrival in Gabon of Dr. Albert Schweitzer.

1005	**421**	500f. multicoloured	6·00	2·20

422 Players

1988. World Cup Rugby Championship (1987).

1006	**422**	350f. multicoloured	3·75	2·20

423 Opposing Arrows

1988. World Telecommunications Day.

1007	**423**	125f. multicoloured	1·20	45

424 Storming the Bastille, 1789

1988. "Philexfrance 89" Stamp Exhibition, Paris.

1008	**424**	125f. multicoloured	1·50	80

425 Crops and Agricultural Activities

1988. 10th Anniv of International Agricultural Development Fund.

1009	**425**	350f. multicoloured	3·75	1·50

426 Emblem and Theatre Staff

1988. 125th Anniv of Red Cross.

1010	**426**	125f. multicoloured	1·20	45

427 Refinery

1988. Air. 20th Anniv of Port Gentil Oil Refinery.

1011	**427**	350f. multicoloured	3·50	1·50

428 Tennis

1988. Olympic Games, Seoul. Multicoloured.

1012	90f. Type **428**	1·00	45
1013	100f. Swimming	1·30	45
1014	350f. Running	3·75	1·50
1015	500f. Hurdling	5·50	1·90
MS1016	121×91 mm. Nos. 1012/15	12·00	12·00

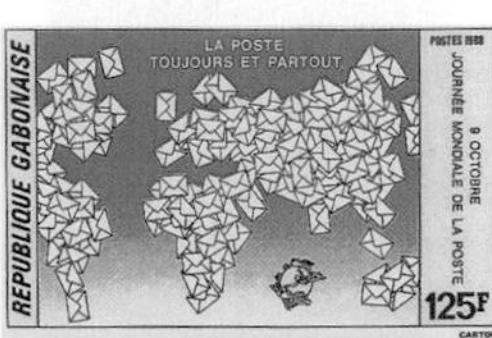

429 Envelopes forming World Map

1988. World Post Day.

1017	**429**	125f. black, blue & yell	1·20	45

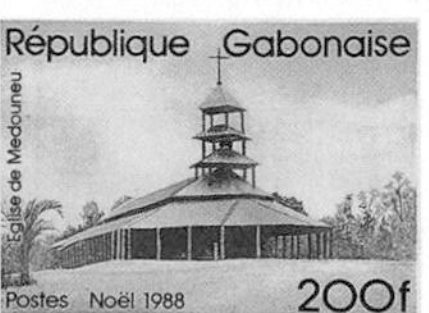

430 Medouneu Church

1988. Christmas.

1018	**430**	200f. multicoloured	1·80	85

1988. Sea Shells. As T 410. Multicoloured.

1018a	90f. Fanel moon ("Natica fanel var")	6·00	1·90
1018b	125f. "Natica variolaria" (inscr "Natica sp.")	8·75	2·40

431 Map and Emblem

1989. 10th Anniv of Chaine de Rotisseurs in Gabon.

1019 **431** 175f. multicoloured 1·50 85

432 Map

1989. Inauguration of Rabi Kounga Oil Field.

1020 **432** 125f. multicoloured 1·30 60

433 Boys playing

1989. Traditional Games.

1021 **433** 90f. multicoloured 1·00 50

434 White-crested Tiger Bittern

1989. Birds. Multicoloured.

1022 100f. Type **434** 1·00 45
1023 175f. Grey parrot 1·80 75
1024 200f. Red-billed dwarf hornbill 2·40 90
1025 500f. Blue-breasted kingfisher 5·00 2·20
MS1026 91×122 mm. Nos. 1022/5 10·50 10·50

435 Map and Emblem

1989. 8th Lions Club International Multidistrict 403 Convention, Libreville.

1027 **435** 125f. multicoloured 1·20 60

436 Arrows and Dish Aerials

1989. World Telecommunications Day.

1028 **436** 300f. multicoloured 3·00 1·50

437 Palm-nuts

1989. Fruits. Multicoloured.

1029 90f. Type **437** 1·00 45
1030 125f. Cabosse 1·30 50
1031 175f. Pineapple 2·00 80
1032 250f. Breadfruit 2·75 1·30
MS1033 89×122 mm. Nos. 1029/32 7·75 7·50

438 "Apples and Oranges"

1989. 150th Birth Anniv of Paul Cezanne (painter).

1034 **438** 500f. multicoloured 5·50 3·75

439 Phrygian Cap on Tree of Liberty and Sans-culotte

1989. "Philexfrance '89" International Stamp Exhibition, Paris.

1035 **439** 175f. multicoloured 2·00 95

440 Soldier and Sans-culotte

1989. Bicentenary of French Revolution.

1036 **440** 500f. multicoloured 6·00 3·75

441 Town Hall

1989. 10th Anniv of International Association of French-speaking Town Halls.

1037 **441** 100f. multicoloured 1·20 60

442 Emblem and Map showing Development Programmes

1989. 25th Anniv of African Development Bank.

1038 **442** 100f. multicoloured 95 50

443 Post Office

1989. 125th Anniv (1987) of Gabon Postal Service.

1039 **443** 90f. multicoloured 10·00 3·25

444 Footballers

1989. World Cup Football Championship, Italy (1990). Multicoloured.

1040 100f. Type **444** 1·00 45
1041 175f. Player tackling 1·80 80
1042 300f. Goalkeeper catching ball 3·00 1·20
1043 500f. Goalkeeper catching ball (different) 4·50 2·30
MS1044 122×91 mm. Nos. 1040/3 10·00 10·00

445 Woman and Child posting Letter

1989. World Post Day.

1045 **445** 175f. multicoloured 1·70 80

1989. Traditional Hairstyles. As T 316.

1046 175f. black, lilac and grey 1·80 80

447 St. Louis' Church, Port-Gentil

1989. Christmas.

1047 **447** 100f. multicoloured 95 45

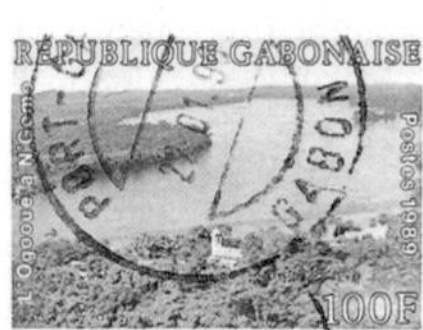

448 L'Ogooue, N'Gomo

1989

1048 **448** 100f. multicoloured

449 Axehead

1990. Prehistory. Stone Weapons. Mult.

1049 100f. Type **449** 1·30 60
1050 175f. Paring knife 2·40 1·10
1051 300f. Flint arrowhead 3·75 1·50
1052 400f. Double-edged knife 5·00 3·00
MS1053 120×89 mm. Nos. 1049/52 12·00 12·00

450 Arms of Libreville

1990. 22nd Anniv of National Renovation.

1054 **450** 100f. multicoloured 1·00 40

451 Penny Black and Beach

1990. 150th Anniv of the Penny Black.

1055 **451** 500f. multicoloured 6·25 3·75

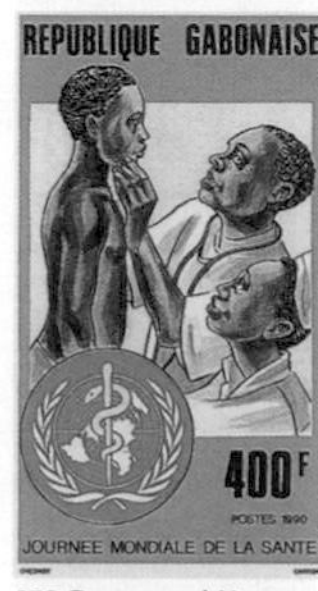

452 Doctor and Nurse examining Patient

1990. World Health Day.

1056 **452** 400f. multicoloured 4·25 2·20

453 Monkey

1990. Animals of Gabon. Multicoloured.

1057 100f. Type **453** 1·30 60
1058 175f. Bush pig (horiz) 2·00 1·10
1059 200f. Antelope (horiz) 2·75 1·50
1060 500f. Mandrill 6·75 3·75
MS1061 105×130 mm. Nos. 1057/60 12·50 12·50

454 De Gaulle and Map

1990. Air. 50th Anniv of De Gaulle's Call to Resist.

1062 **454** 500f. multicoloured 6·75 3·25

455 Map and Arms on Flag

1990. 30th Anniv of Independence.

1063 **455** 100f. multicoloured 1·00 65

456 "Phallus indusiatus"

1990. Fungi.

1064	100f. Type **456**	1·50	75
1065	175f. "Panaeolus sphinctrinus?"	3·00	1·70
1066	300f. "Agaricus bitorquis"	4·75	3·00
1067	500f. "Termitomyces" sp.	6·25	4·50

457 Flags of Member Countries

1990. 30th Anniv of Organization of Petroleum Exporting Countries.

1068	**457**	200f. multicoloured	1·80	1·00

458 Envelopes as World Map

1990. World Post Day.

1069	**458**	175f. blue, yellow & blk	1·80	95

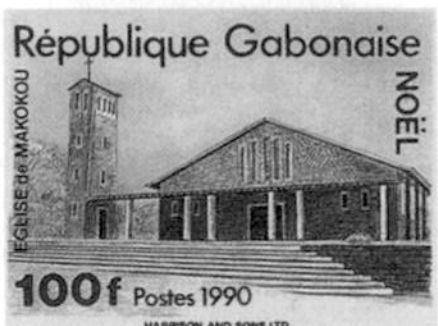

459 Makokou Church

1990. Christmas.

1070	**459**	100f. multicoloured	95	55

460 Frangipani

1991. Flowers. Multicoloured.

1071	100f. Type **460**	1·30	60
1072	175f. Burning bush	1·80	1·00
1073	200f. Flame tree	2·40	1·30
1074	300f. Porcelain rose	3·50	1·90
MS1075	123×93 mm. Nos. 1071/4	9·00	9·00

461 "Marseilles Harbour"

1991. Air. Death Centenary of Johan Barthold Jongkind (artist).

1076	**461**	500f. multicoloured	5·50	2·20

462 Lizard

1991. Prehistory. Petroglyphs. Multicoloured.

1077	100f. Type **462**	1·10	60
1078	175f. Triangular figure	1·80	1·10
1079	300f. Abstract pattern	3·50	1·50
1080	500f. Circles and chains	5·00	3·00
MS1081	118×88 mm. Nos. 1077/80	12·00	12·00

463 Collecting Resin from Rubber Trees

1991. Agriculture.

1082	**463**	100f. multicoloured	95	55

1991. District Arms (5th series). As T 392.

1083	100f. silver, black and green	95	35

DESIGN: 100f. Port-Gentil.

464 Couple and Arrows

1991. World Telecommunications Day.

1084	**464**	175f. multicoloured	1·70	80

465 Basket Weaving

1991. Arts and Crafts. Multicoloured.

1085	100f. Type **465**	1·00	70
1086	175f. Stone carving	2·00	1·10
1087	200f. Weaving	2·40	1·20
1088	500f. Straw plaiting	5·00	3·00

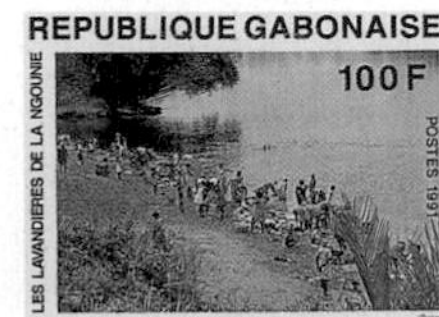

466 Women at Riverbank

1991. Washerwomen of the Ngounie.

1089	**466**	100f. multicoloured	95	55

467 Knight

1991. Order of the Equatorial Star. Mult.

1090	100f. Type **467**	1·00	60
1091	175f. Officer	1·80	95
1092	200f. Commander	2·00	1·20

468 Inspecting Fish Traps

1991. Fishing. Multicoloured.

1093	100f. Type **468**	1·00	55
1094	175f. Fishing from canoe	1·80	95
1095	200f. Casting net	2·00	1·20
1096	300f. Pulling in net	3·00	1·80
MS1097	120×90 mm. Nos. 1093/6	8·75	8·75

469 Post Box and Globe

1991. World Post Day.

1098	**469**	175f. blue, black and red	1·80	60

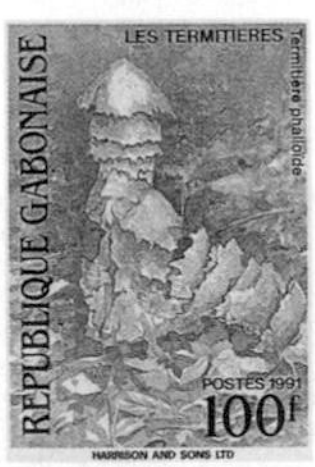

470 "Phalloid"

1991. Termitaries. Multicoloured.

1099	100f. Type **470**	1·00	80
1100	175f. "Cathedral"	2·20	1·00
1101	200f. "Mushroom"	3·00	1·50
1102	300f. "Treehouse"	3·50	2·75

471 Dibwangui Church

1991. Christmas.

1103	**471**	100f. multicoloured	95	55

472 Neolithic Ceramic Pot

1992. Prehistory. Pottery. Multicoloured.

1104	100f. Type **472**	1·00	70
1105	175f. Ceramic bottle (8th century)	1·70	95
1106	200f. Ceramic vase (late 8th century)	2·00	1·20
1107	300f. Ceramic vase (early 8th century)	3·25	1·80
MS1108	87×117 mm. Nos. 1104/7	9·00	9·00

473 Stripping Wood

1992. Arts and Crafts. Multicoloured.

1109	100f. Type **473**	1·00	70
1110	175f. Metalwork	1·70	95
1111	200f. Boat building	2·00	1·00
1112	300f. Hairdressing	3·25	2·10
MS1113	88×118 mm. Nos. 1109/12	8·75	8·75

474 Grand Officer of Order of Equatorial Star

1992. Gabonese Honours. Multicoloured.

1114	100f. Type **474**	1·00	60
1115	175f. Grand Cross of Order of Equatorial Star	1·80	95
1116	200f. Order of Merit	2·00	1·20

475 Konrad Adenauer

1992. 25th Death Anniv of Konrad Adenauer (German statesman).

1117	**475**	500f. black, stone & grn	5·50	3·75

476 Earth and Moon

1992. World Telecommunications Day.

1118	**476**	175f. multicoloured	1·80	60

477 Small Striped Swallowtail

1992. Butterflies. Multicoloured.

1119	100f. Type **477**	1·20	65
1120	175f. "Acraea egina"	2·10	1·00

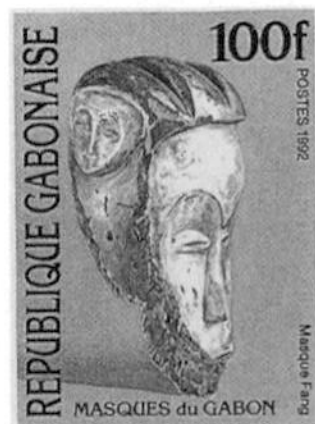

478 Fang Mask

1992. Gabonese Masks. Multicoloured.

1121	100f. Type **478**	1·00	55
1122	175f. Mpongwe mask	2·00	95
1123	200f. Kwele mask	2·00	1·20
1124	300f. Pounou mask	3·00	1·80

479 Cycling

1992. Olympic Games, Barcelona. Mult.

1125	100f. Type **479**		1·10	70
1126	175f. Boxing		2·00	95
1127	200f. Pole vaulting		2·30	1·30

1992. District Arms (6th series). As T 392.

1128	100f. silver, black and blue		95	25

DESIGN: 100f. Medouneu.

1992. World Post Day. As No. 1098 but dated "1992".

1129	**469**	175f. multicoloured	1·80	60

480 Columbus and Fleet

1992. Air. 500th Anniv of Discovery of America by Columbus.

1130	**480**	500f. multicoloured	5·00	2·75

481 African Owl

1992. Birds. Multicoloured.

1131	100f. Type **481**	1·80	65
1132	175f. Speckled mousebird	3·00	95
1133	200f. Palm-nut vulture	3·25	1·30
1134	300f. Giant kingfisher	5·75	1·70
MS1135	87×118 mm. Nos. 1131/4	18·00	18·00

482 Cattle

1992. Beef Production.

1136	**482**	100f. multicoloured	1·00	60
1137	-	175f. multicoloured	1·80	95
1138	-	200f. multicoloured	2·00	1·20

DESIGNS: 175, 200f. Cattle (different).

483 Tchibanga Church

1992. Christmas.

1139	**483**	100f. multicoloured	95	45

484 Emblems

1992. International Nutrition Conference, Rome.

1140	**484**	100f. multicoloured	95	55

485 "Giant Hairy Melongena"

1993. Shells. Multicoloured.

1141	100f. Type **485**	95	45
1142	175f. Butterfly cone	1·70	85
1143	200f. Carpat's spindle	1·90	1·00
1144	300f. "Cymatium linatella"	3·00	1·60
MS1145	117×87 mm. Nos. 1141/4	9·75	9·75

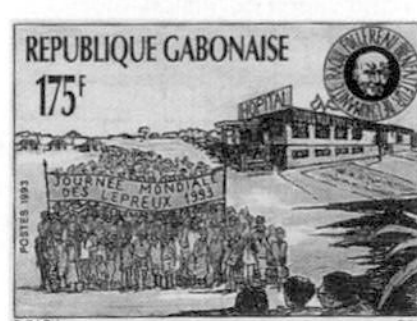

486 Crowd with Banner outside Hospital

1993. World Leprosy Day.

1146	**486**	175f. multicoloured	1·80	75

487 Fritz the Elephant

1993. Fernan-Vaz Mission.

1147	**487**	175f. multicoloured	2·00	1·30

488 Claude Chappe

1993. Bicentenary of Chappe's Optical Telegraph. Multicoloured.

1148	100f. Type **488**	1·00	45
1149	175f. Signals and table of signs	1·60	80
1150	200f. Emile Baudot (inventor of five-unit code telegraph printing system)	1·80	1·00
1151	300f. Satellite and fibre-optics	3·00	1·50
MS1152	90×111 mm. Nos. 1148/51	9·00	9·00

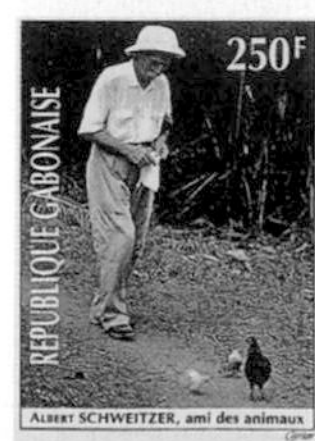

489 Schweitzer feeding Animals

1993. 80th Anniv of First Visit of Albert Schweitzer (medical missionary) to Lambarene. Multicoloured.

1153	250f. Type **489**	3·25	1·50
1154	250f. Schweitzer holding babies	3·25	1·50
1155	500f. Schweitzer (36×49 mm)	5·50	3·00

490 Copernicus (astronomer) and illustration from "De Revolutionibus"

1993. "Polska'93" International Stamp Exhibition, Poznan.

1156	**490**	175f. multicoloured	1·60	95

491 Emblem

1993. World Telecommunications Day.

1157	**491**	175f. multicoloured	1·60	75

492 Making Sugar-cane Wine

1993. Traditional Wine-making. Mult.

1158	100f. Type **492**	1·00	65
1159	175f. Filling bottle with palm wine	1·60	95
1160	200f. Gathering ingredients for palm wine	1·80	1·20
MS1161	114×85 mm. Nos. 1158/60	5·75	5·75

493 Lobster

1993. Crustaceans. Multicoloured.

1162	100f. Type **493**	1·10	55
1163	175f. Crab	1·70	80
1164	200f. Crayfish	2·00	1·00
1165	300f. Sea spider	3·00	1·60

494 Magnifying Glass, Flowers, Stamp and Emblem

1993. 1st European Stamp Salon, Flower Gardens, Paris.

1166	**494**	100f. multicoloured	1·00	55

495 Squirrel Trap

1993. Trapping. Multicoloured.

1167	100f. Type **495**	1·00	45
1168	175f. Small game trap	1·60	80
1169	200f. Large game trap	1·80	1·00
1170	300f. Palm squirrel trap	3·00	1·50

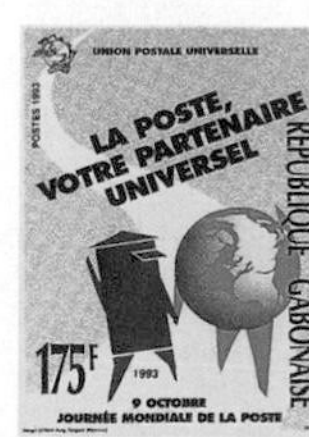

496 Post Box and Globe

1993. World Post Day.

1171	**496**	175f. multicoloured	1·60	75

497 Making Model Airplane

1993. Bamboo Toys.

1172	**497**	100f. multicoloured	1·00	65

498 Leconi Canyon

1993. Tourism. Multicoloured.

1173	100f. Type **498**	1·00	45
1174	175f. La Lope tourist site	1·60	75

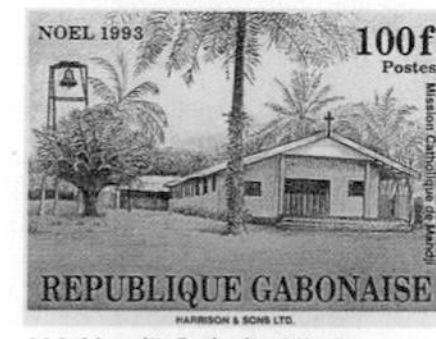

499 Mandji Catholic Mission

1993. Christmas.

1175	**499**	100f. multicoloured	1·00	65

OFFICIAL STAMPS

O119 Map of Gabon River

1968

O333	**O119**	1f. multicoloured	10	10
O334	**O119**	2f. multicoloured	10	10
O335	**O119**	5f. multicoloured	10	10
O336	**O119**	10f. multicoloured	35	10
O337	-	25f. multicoloured	55	25
O338	-	30f. multicoloured	55	30
O339	-	50f. multicoloured	1·00	65
O340	-	85f. multicoloured	1·60	60
O341	-	100f. multicoloured	2·00	75
O342	-	200f. multicoloured	3·75	1·50

DESIGNS: 25f., 30f. Gabon flag; 50f. to 200f. Gabon coat of arms.

O165 Gabon Flag

1971. Flag in actual colours; inscription in blue; background as below.

O436	**O165**	5f. blue	10	10
O437	**O165**	10f. grey	30	25
O437a	**O165**	20f. orange	30	10
O437b	**O165**	25f. yellow	30	25
O438	**O165**	30f. cobalt	45	10
O439	**O165**	40f. orange	75	45
O440	**O165**	50f. red	1·00	40
O441	**O165**	60f. brown	1·00	45
O441a	**O165**	75f. grey	75	30
O442	**O165**	80f. mauve	1·50	75
O443	**O165**	100f. mauve	1·00	40
O444	**O165**	500f. green	6·00	1·90

POSTAGE DUE STAMPS

1928. Postage Due type of French Colonies optd GABON A. E. F.

D123	**U**	5c. blue	35	4·25
D124	**U**	10c. brown	65	4·25
D125	**U**	20c. olive	90	4·75
D126	**U**	25c. red	1·00	5·25
D127	**U**	30c. red	1·20	4·75
D128	**U**	45c. green	1·50	5·25
D129	**U**	50c. red	2·30	4·25
D130	**U**	60c. brown	2·40	5·75
D131	**U**	1f. purple	2·50	5·00
D132	**U**	2f. red	3·25	5·25
D133	**U**	3f. violet	3·50	6·00

D19 Local Chief

1930

No.	Type	Description	Mint	Used
D134	**D19**	5c. drab and blue	1·70	4·75
D135	**D19**	10c. brown and red	1·40	5·00
D136	**D19**	20c. brown and green	2·75	5·50
D137	**D19**	25c. brown and blue	3·00	5·75
D138	**D19**	30c. green and brown	3·00	5·75
D139	**D19**	45c. drab and green	3·25	8·00
D140	**D19**	50c. brown and mauve	3·75	8·75
D141	**D19**	60c. black and violet	6·50	15·00
D142	-	1f. black and brown	7·75	22·00
D143	-	2f. brown and mauve	11·00	32·00
D144	-	3f. brown and red	12·00	36·00

DESIGN—VERT: 1f. to 3f. Count Savorgnan de Brazza.

D24 Pahquin Woman

1932

No.	Type	Description	Mint	Used
D151	**D24**	5c. blue on blue	55	3·75
D152	**D24**	10c. brown	90	4·75
D153	**D24**	20c. brown	3·75	6·00
D154	**D24**	25c. green on blue	2·50	5·25
D155	**D24**	30c. red	5·75	8·50
D156	**D24**	45c. red on yellow	9·25	14·50
D157	**D24**	50c. purple	6·50	10·50
D158	**D24**	60c. blue	8·00	11·00
D159	**D24**	1f. black on orange	8·00	10·00
D160	**D24**	2f. green	15·00	25·00
D161	**D24**	3f. red	14·50	26·00

D40 Pineapple

1962. Fruits.

No.	Type	Description	Mint	Used
D196		50c. red, yellow and green	10	10
D197		50c. red, yellow and green	10	10
D198		1f. mauve, yellow and green	10	10
D199		1f. mauve, yellow and green	10	10
D200		2f. yellow, brown and green	10	10
D201		2f. yellow, brown and green	10	10
D202		5f. yellow, green and brown	30	25
D203		5f. yellow, green and brown	30	25
D204		10f. multicoloured	75	75
D205		10f. multicoloured	75	75
D206		25f. yellow, green and purple	1·20	1·20
D207		25f. yellow, green and purple	1·20	1·20

FRUITS: No. D196, Type D **40**; D197, Mangoes; D198, Mandarin oranges; D199, Avocado pears; D200, Grapefruit; D201, Coconuts; D202. Oranges; D203, Papaws; D204, Breadfruit; D205, Guavas; D206, Lemons; D207, Bananas.

D256 "Charaxes candiope"

1978. Butterflies. Multicoloured.

No.	Type	Description	Mint	Used
D655		5f. Type D **256**	20	20
D656		10f. "Charaxes ameliae"	20	20
D657		25f. "Cyrestis camillus"	45	25
D658		50f. "Charaxes castor"	1·00	50
D659		100f. "Pseudacrea boisduvali"	1·80	90

Pt. 20

GALAPAGOS ISLANDS

These islands, noted for their fauna and flora, were annexed by Ecuador, and later (1973) became a province of that country.

100 centavos = 1 sucre.

1 Californian Sealions

1957. Inscr "ISLAS GALAPAGOS".

No.	Type	Description	Mint	Used
1	**1**	20c. brown (postage)	1·50	30
2	-	50c. violet	1·00	30
3	-	1s. green	5·00	85
4	-	1s. blue (air)	1·30	30
5	-	1s.80 purple	2·75	65
6	-	4s.20 black	8·25	1·30

DESIGNS—VERT: 50c. Map of Ecuador coastline. HORIZ: 1s. (No. 3) Iguana; 1s. (No. 4) Santa Cruz Island; 1s.80, Map of Galapagos Is; 4s.20, Giant tortoise.

1959. Air. United Nations Commem. Triangular design as T 316 of Ecuador but inscr "ISLAS GALAPAGOS".

No.	Type	Description	Mint	Used
7		2s. green	1·30	75

Pt. 1

GAMBIA

A British colony and protectorate on the West coast of Africa. Granted full internal self-government on 4 October 1963, and achieved indepedence on 18 February 1965. Became a republic within the Commonwealth on 24 April 1970.

1869. 12 pence = 1 shilling; 20 shillings = 1 pound.
1971. 100 butut = 1 dalasi.

1

1869. Imperf.

No.	Type	Description	Mint	Used
5	**1**	4d. brown	£400	£200
8	**1**	6d. blue	£350	£200

1880. Perf.

No.	Type	Description	Mint	Used
11B		½d. orange	14·00	21·00
12B		1d. purple	7·50	6·00
13B		2d. pink	45·00	11·00
14cB		3d. blue	70·00	32·00
30		4d. brown	13·00	2·00
17B		6d. blue	£120	45·00
19B		1s. green	£275	£150

1886

No.	Type	Description	Mint	Used
21		½d. green	5·50	2·25
23		1d. red	10·00	12·00
25		2d. orange	3·00	10·00
27		2½d. blue	9·00	1·25
29		3d. grey	9·00	15·00
34		6d. green	16·00	65·00
35		1s. violet	3·50	18·00

2

1898

No.	Type	Description	Mint	Used
37	**2**	½d. green	2·75	1·75
38	**2**	1d. red	2·50	75
39	**2**	2d. orange and mauve	6·00	3·50
40	**2**	2½d. blue	2·50	2·50
41	**2**	3d. purple and blue	38·00	12·00
42	**2**	4d. brown and blue	15·00	35·00
43	**2**	6d. green and red	13·00	40·00
44	**2**	1s. mauve and green	35·00	80·00

1902. As T 2, but portrait of King Edward VII.

No.	Type	Description	Mint	Used
57		½d. green	4·50	30
58		1d. red	4·50	15
47		2d. orange and mauve	3·25	2·00
74		2d. grey	2·00	11·00
60		2½d. blue	10·00	4·75
61		3d. purple and blue	12·00	2·00
75		3d. purple on yellow	5·50	1·00
50		4d. brown and blue	5·00	32·00
76		4d. black and red on yellow	2·25	65
63		5d. grey and black	14·00	27·00
77		5d. orange and purple	2·00	1·25
51		6d. green and red	11·00	12·00
78		6d. purple	2·25	2·25
65		7½d. green and red	15·00	60·00
79		7½d. brown and blue	3·25	2·50
80		10d. green and red	4·50	7·00
67		1s. mauve and green	32·00	60·00
81		1s. black on green	4·50	17·00
53		1s.6d. green and red on yellow	8·50	23·00
82		1s.6d. violet and green	25·00	75·00
54		2s. grey and orange	50·00	70·00
83		2s. purple and blue on blue	14·00	20·00
55		2s.6d. purple & brown on yell	15·00	70·00
84		2s.6d. black and red on blue	21·00	20·00
56		3s. red and green on yellow	20·00	70·00
85		3s. yellow and green	35·00	48·00

1906. Surch in words.

No.	Type	Description	Mint	Used
69		½d. on 2s.6d. (No. 55)	55·00	65·00
70		1d. on 3s. (No. 56)	60·00	30·00

1912. As T 2, but portrait of King George V.

No.	Type	Description	Mint	Used
86		½d. green	2·50	1·50
87		1d. red	2·50	80
88		1½d. olive and green	50	30
111		2d. grey	1·00	2·50
112		2½d. blue	50	9·50
91		3d. purple on yellow	50	30
92		4d. black and red on yellow	1·00	10·00
93		5d. orange and purple	1·00	2·00
94		6d. purple	1·50	2·50
95		7½d. brown and blue	3·50	10·00
96a		10d. green and red	4·25	15·00
97		1s. black on green	2·50	1·00
98		1s.6d. violet and green	15·00	10·00
99		2s. purple and blue on blue	5·50	6·00
100		2s.6d. black and red on blue	5·50	14·00
101		3s. yellow and green	12·00	40·00
117		4s. black and red	£100	£190
102		5s. green and red on yellow	£120	£190

9

10

1922

No.	Type	Description	Mint	Used
122	**9**	½d. black and green	55	55
124	**9**	1d. black and brown	1·00	30
125	**9**	1½d. black and red	1·00	30
126	**9**	2d. black and grey	1·00	4·50
127	**9**	2½d. black and orange	2·00	14·00
128	**9**	3d. black and blue	1·00	20
118	**9**	4d. black and red on yellow	4·75	5·00
130	**9**	5d. black and olive	3·75	13·00
131	**9**	6d. black and red	1·25	30
119	**9**	7½d. black & purple on yell	7·00	8·50
133	**9**	10d. black and blue	5·00	18·00
134	**10**	1s. black & purple on yell	3·00	2·25
135	**10**	1s.6d. black and blue	18·00	17·00
136	**10**	2s. black and purple on blue	10·00	7·00
137	**10**	2s.6d. black and green	10·00	9·50
138	**10**	3s. black and violet	23·00	80·00
140	**10**	4s. black and brown	14·00	21·00
141	**10**	5s. black and green on yellow	28·00	60·00
142	**10**	10s. black and olive	80·00	£130

10a Windsor Castle

1935. Silver Jubilee.

No.	Type	Description	Mint	Used
143	**10a**	1½d. blue and red	70	2·00
144	**10a**	3d. brown and blue	1·25	2·00
145	**10a**	6d. blue and olive	2·00	6·50
146	**10a**	1s. grey and purple	11·00	13·00

10b King George VI and Queen Elizabeth

1937. Coronation.

No.	Type	Description	Mint	Used
147	**10b**	1d. brown	30	1·25
148	**10b**	1½d. red	30	1·25
149	**10b**	3d. blue	55	2·00

11 Elephant (from Colony Badge)

1938

No.	Type	Description	Mint	Used
150	**11**	½d. black and green	15	70
151	**11**	1d. purple and brown	30	50
152b	**11**	1½d. lake and red	30	2·00
152c	**11**	1½d. blue and black	30	1·50
153	**11**	2d. blue and black	13·00	3·25
153a	**11**	2d. lake and red	1·25	2·25
154	**11**	3d. blue	30	10
154a	**11**	5d. green and purple	50	50
155	**11**	6d. olive and red	2·50	35
156	**11**	1s. blue and purple	4·50	20
156a	**11**	1s.3d. purple and blue	3·75	2·50
157	**11**	2s. red and blue	10·00	3·50
158	**11**	2s.6d. brown and green	14·00	2·75
159	**11**	4s. red and purple	30·00	2·75
160	**11**	5s. blue and red	30·00	4·25
161	**11**	10s. orange and black	30·00	7·00

11a Houses of Parliament, London

1946. Victory.

No.	Type	Description	Mint	Used
162	**11a**	1½d. black	10	50
163	**11a**	3d. blue	10	40

11b King George VI and Queen Elizabeth

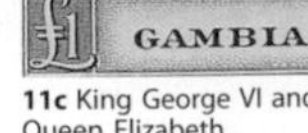

11c King George VI and Queen Elizabeth

1948. Silver Wedding.

No.	Type	Description	Mint	Used
164	**11b**	1½d. black	25	10
165	**11c**	£1 mauve	20·00	18·00

11d Hermes, Globe and Forms of Transport

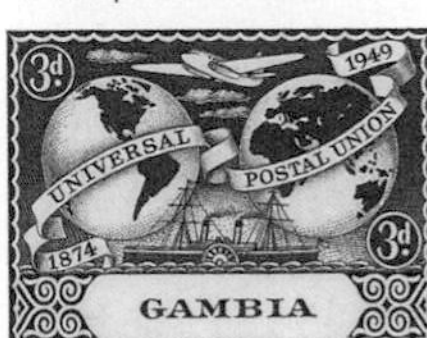

11e Hemispheres, Jet-powered Vickers Viking Airliner and Steamer

11f Hermes and Globe

11g UPU Monument

1949. UPU.

166	**11d**	1½d. black	30	1·50
167	**11e**	3d. blue	1·25	2·00
168	**11f**	6d. mauve	75	3·25
169	**11g**	1s. violet	45	60

11h Queen Elizabeth II

1953. Coronation.

170	**11h**	1½d. black and blue	80	1·25

12 Tapping for Palm Wine

1953. Queen Elizabeth II.

171	**12**	½d. red and green	40	30
172	-	1d. blue and brown	1·75	50
173	-	1½d. brown and black	20	1·00
174	-	2½d. black and red	45	70
175	-	3d. blue and lilac	35	10
176	-	4d. black and blue	60	3·00
177	**12**	6d. brown and purple	35	15
178	-	1s. brown and green	60	60
179	-	1s.3d. ultramarine and blue	11·00	60
180	-	2s. blue and red	7·00	4·00
181	-	2s.6d. green and brown	6·00	2·25
182	-	4s. blue and brown	14·00	3·75
183	-	5s. brown and blue	5·00	3·00
184	-	10s. blue and green	26·00	13·00
185	-	£1 green and black	26·00	13·00

DESIGNS—HORIZ: 1d., 1s.3d. Cutter (sailing ship); 1½d., 5s. Wollof woman; 2½d., 2s. Barra canoe; 3d., 10s. S.S. "Lady Wright"; 4d., 4s. James Island; 1s., 2s.6d. Woman hoeing; £1 As Type **11**.

20 Queen Elizabeth II and Palm

1961. Royal Visit.

186	**20**	2d. green and purple	30	40
187	-	3d. turquoise and sepia	75	15
188	-	6d. blue and red	75	70
189	**20**	1s.3d. violet and green	75	2·25

DESIGN: 3d., 6d. Queen Elizabeth II and West African map.

21a Protein Foods

1963. Freedom from Hunger.

190	**21a**	1s.3d. red	55	15

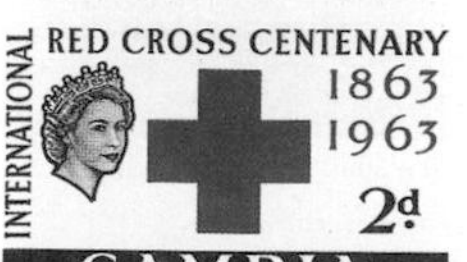

21b Red Cross Emblem

1963. Centenary of Red Cross.

191	**21b**	2d. red and black	20	50
192	**21b**	1s.3d. red and blue	40	1·00

22 Beautiful Sunbird

1963. Birds. Multicoloured.

193		½d. Type **22**	75	1·50
194		1d. Yellow-mantled whydah	75	30
195		1½d. Cattle egret	2·50	70
196		2d. Senegal parrot	2·50	70
197		3d. Rose-ringed parakeet	2·50	1·00
198		4d. Violet starling	2·50	80
199		6d. Village weaver	2·50	10
200		1s. Rufous-crowned roller	2·50	10
201		1s.3d. Red-eyed dove	14·00	3·00
202		2s.6d. Double-spurred francolin	9·00	2·50
203		5s. Palm-nut vulture	9·00	3·50
204		10s. Orange-cheeked waxbill	14·00	11·00
205		£1 African emerald cuckoo	29·00	14·00

1963. New Constitution. Nos. 194, 197 and 200/1 optd SELF GOVERNMENT 1963.

206		1d. multicoloured	15	50
207		3d. multicoloured	35	35
208		1s. multicoloured	35	10
209		1s.3d. multicoloured	35	45

35a Shakespeare and Memorial Theatre, Stratford-upon-Avon

1964. 400th Birth Anniv of Shakespeare.

210	**35a**	6d. blue	20	10

36 Gambia Flag and River

1965. Independence. Multicoloured.

211		½d. Type **36**	10	40
212		2d. Arms	15	10
213		7½d. Type **36**	40	35
214		1s.6d. Arms	50	30

1965. Nos 193/205 optd INDEPENDENCE 1965.

215		½d. Type **22**	30	1·00
216		1d. Yellow-mantled whydah	40	20
217		1½d. Cattle egret	60	1·00
218		2d. Senegal parrot	70	30
219		3d. Rose-ringed parakeet	70	15
220		4d. Violet starling	70	1·75
221		6d. Village weaver	70	10
222		1s. Rufous-crowned roller	70	10
223		1s.3d. Red-eyed dove	70	10
224		2s.6d. Double-spurred francolin	70	60
225		5s. Palm-nut vulture	70	75
226		10s. Orange-cheeked waxbill	1·75	5·00
227		£1 African emerald cuckoo	9·50	8·50

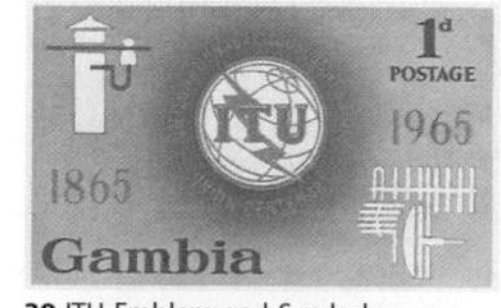

39 ITU Emblem and Symbols

1965. Centenary of ITU.

228	**39**	1d. silver and blue	25	10
229	**39**	1s.6d. gold and violet	1·00	40

40 Sir Winston Churchill and Houses of Parliament

1966. Churchill Commemoration.

230	**40**	1d. multicoloured	15	10
231	**40**	6d. multicoloured	35	15
232	**40**	1s.6d. multicoloured	60	75

41 Red-cheeked Cordon-bleu

1966. Birds. Multicoloured.

233		½d. Type **41**	90	40
234		1d. White-faced whistling duck	30	50
235		1½d. Red-throated bee eater	30	40
236		2d. Lesser pied kingfisher	4·75	75
237		3d. Golden bishop	30	10
238		4d. African fish eagle	50	30
239		6d. Yellow-bellied green pigeon	40	10
240		1s. Blue-bellied roller	40	10
241		1s.6d. African pygmy kingfisher	50	30
242		2s.6d. Spur-winged goose	50	70
243		5s. Cardinal woodpecker	50	75
244		10s. Violet turaco	50	2·75
245		£1 Pin-tailed whydah (25×39½ mm)	75	6·50

54 Arms, Early Settlement and Modern Buildings

1966. 150th Anniv of Bathurst.

246	**54**	1d. silver, brown and orange	10	10
247	**54**	2d. silver, brown and blue	10	10
248	**54**	6d. silver, brown and green	10	10
249	**54**	1s.6d. silver, brn & pur	15	15

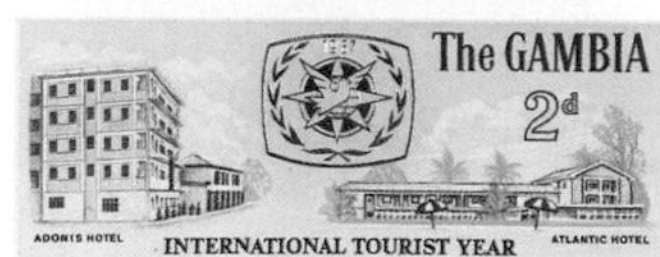

55 ITY Emblem and Hotels

1967. International Tourist Year.

250	**55**	2d. silver, brown and green	10	10
251	**55**	1s. silver, brown and orange	10	10
252	**55**	1s.6d. silver, brn & mve	15	35

56 Handcuffs

1968. Human Rights Year. Multicoloured.

253		1d. Type **56**	10	10
254		1s. Fort Bullen	10	10
255		5s. Methodist Church	30	1·00

59 Queen Victoria, Queen Elizabeth II and 4d. Stamp of 1869

1969. Gambia Stamp Centenary.

256	**59**	4d. sepia and ochre	20	10
257	**59**	6d. blue and green	20	10
258	-	2s.6d. multicoloured	70	1·60

DESIGN: 2s.6d. Queen Elizabeth II with 4d. and 6d. stamps of 1869.

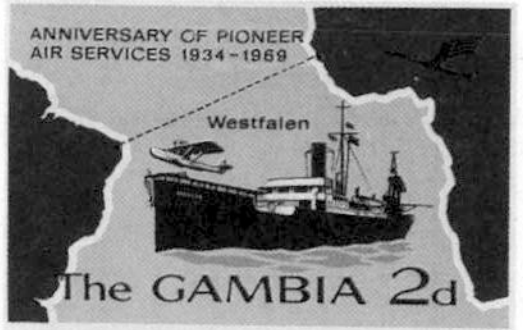

61 Catapult-ship "Westfalen" launching Dornier Wal

1969. 35th Anniv of Pioneer Air Service. Mult.

259		2d. Type **61**	50	20
260		1s. Dornier Wal flying boat "Boreas"	50	20
261		1s.6d. Airship "Graf Zeppelin"	60	1·60

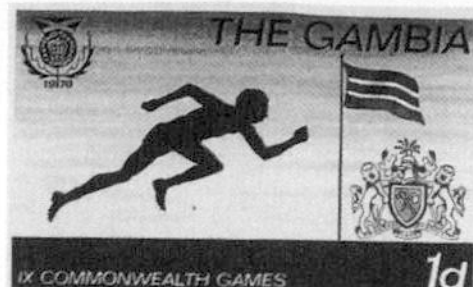

63 Athlete and Gambian Flag

1970. 9th British Commonwealth Games, Edinburgh.

262	**63**	1d. multicoloured	10	10
263	**63**	1s. multicoloured	10	10
264	**63**	5s. multicoloured	30	1·25

64 President Sir Dawda Kairaba Jawara and State House

1970. Republic Day. Multicoloured.

265		2d. Type **64**	10	10
266		1s. President Sir Dawda Jawara (vert)	15	10
267		1s.6d. President and flag of Gambia (vert)	50	60

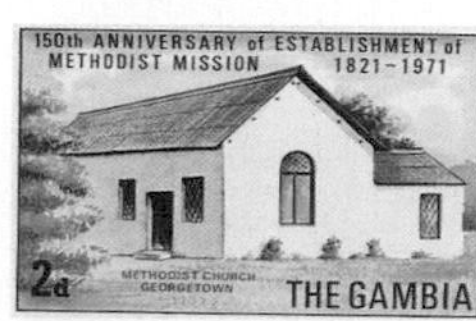

65 Methodist Church, Georgetown

1971. 150th Anniv of Establishment of Methodist Mission. Multicoloured.

268		2d. Type **65**	10	10
269		1s. Map of Africa and Gambian flag (vert)	15	15
270		1s.6d. John Wesley and scroll	15	1·00

66 Yellow-finned Tunny

1971. New Currency. Fishes. Multicoloured.

271		2b. Type **66**	10	75
272		4b. Peter's mormyrid	10	20
273		6b. Four-winged flyingfish	15	75
274		8b. African sleeper goby	15	75
275		10b. Yellow-tailed snapper	20	20
276		13b. Rock hind	20	60
277		25b. West African eel catfish	35	60
278		38b. Tiger shark	55	45
279		50b. Electric catfish	70	55
280		63b. Black swampeel	80	1·75
281		1d.25 Small-toothed sawfish	1·10	2·50
282		2d.50 Great barracuda	1·25	4·50
283		5d. Brown bullhead	1·50	7·00

67 Mungo Park in Scotland

1971. Birth Centenary of Mungo Park (explorer). Multicoloured.

284		4b. Type **67**	20	10
285		25b. Dug-out canoe	45	35
286		37b. Death of Mungo Park, Busa Rapids	75	1·50

68 Radio Gambia

1972. 10th Anniv of Radio Gambia.

287	**68**	4b. brown and black	10	10
288	-	25b. blue, orange and black	10	30
289	**68**	37b. green and black	20	1·25

DESIGN: 25b. Broadcast-area map.

69 High Jumping

1972. Olympic Games, Munich.

290	**69**	4b. multicoloured	10	10
291	**69**	25b. multicoloured	20	15
292	**69**	37b. multicoloured	25	20

70 Manding Woman

1972. International Conference on Manding Studies. Multicoloured.

293	2b. Type **70**	10	10
294	25b. Musician playing the Kora	15	15
295	37b. Map of Mail Empire	25	25

71 Children carrying Fanal

1972. Fanals (Model Boats). Multicoloured.

296	2b. Type **71**	10	10
297	1d.25 Fanal with lanterns	30	45

72 Groundnuts

1973. Freedom from Hunger Campaign.

298	**72**	2b. multicoloured	10	10
299	**72**	25b. multicoloured	15	10
300	**72**	37b. multicoloured	25	20

73 Planting and Drying Rice 74 Oil Palm

1973. Agriculture (1st series). Multicoloured.

301	2b. Type **73**	10	10
302	25b. Guinea corn	20	15
303	37b. Rice	25	25

1973. Agriculture (2nd series). Multicoloured.

304	2b. Type **74**	10	10
305	25b. Limes	30	30
306	37b. Oil palm (fruits)	40	40

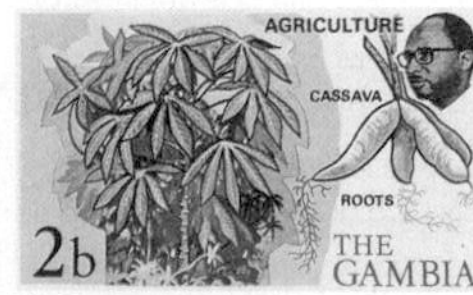

75 Cassava

1973. Agriculture (3rd series). Multicoloured.

307	2b. Type **75**	10	10
308	50b. Cotton	40	25

76 OAU Emblem

1973. 10th Anniv of OAU.

309	**76**	4b. multicoloured	10	10
310	**76**	25b. multicoloured	15	10
311	**76**	37b. multicoloured	15	20

77 Red Cross

1973. 25th Anniv of Gambian Red Cross.

312	**77**	4b. red and black	10	10
313	**77**	25b. red, black and blue	15	15
314	**77**	37b. red, black and green	20	20

78 Arms of Banjul

1973. Change of Bathurst's Name to Banjul.

315	**78**	4b. multicoloured	10	10
316	**78**	25b. multicoloured	15	15
317	**78**	37b. multicoloured	15	20

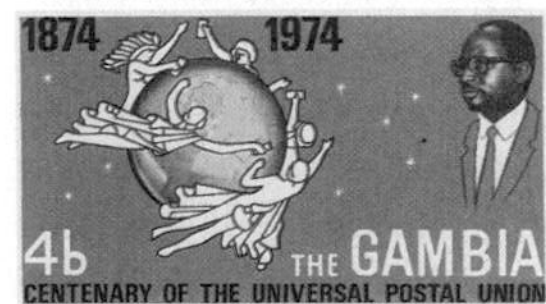

79 UPU Emblem

1974. Centenary of UPU.

318	**79**	4b. multicoloured	10	10
319	**79**	37b. multicoloured	20	30

80 Churchill as Harrow Schoolboy

1974. Birth Cent of Sir Winston Churchill. Mult.

320	4b. Type **80**	10	10
321	37b. Churchill as 4th Hussars officer	20	15
322	50b. Churchill as Prime Minister	30	60

81 "Different Races"

1974. World Population Year. Multicoloured.

323	4b. Type **81**	10	10
324	37b. "Multiplication and Division of Races"	15	15
325	50b. "World Population"	20	25

82 Dr. Schweitzer and River Scene

1975. Birth Centenary of Dr. Albert Schweitzer. Multicoloured.

326	10b. Type **82**	20	10
327	50b. Surgery scene	40	25
328	1d.25 River journey	75	55

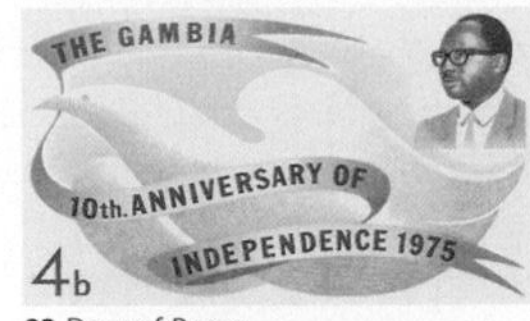

83 Dove of Peace

1975. 10th Anniv of Independence. Multicoloured.

329	4b. Type **83**	10	10
330	10b. Gambian flag	10	10
331	50b. Gambian arms	15	10
332	1d.25 Map of The Gambia	35	40

84 Development Graph 85 Statue of "David" (Michelangelo)

1975. 10th Anniv of African Development Bank. Multicoloured.

333	10b. Type **84**	10	10
334	50b. Symbolic plant	20	15
335	1d.25 Bank emblem and symbols	55	60

1975. 500th Birth Anniv of Michelangelo. Mult.

336	10b. Type **85**	15	10
337	50b. "Madonna of the Steps"	30	15
338	1d.25 "Battle of the Centaurs" (horiz)	50	1·25

86 School Building

1975. Centenary of Gambia High School. Mult.

339	10b. Type **86**	10	10
340	50b. Pupil with scientific apparatus	15	10
341	1d.50 School crest	35	35

87 "Teaching"

1975. International Women's Year. Multicoloured.

342	4b. Type **87**	10	10
343	10b. "Planting rice"	10	10
344	50b. "Nursing"	35	15
345	1d.50 "Directing traffic"	85	35

88 Woman playing Golf

1975. 11th Anniv of Independence. Mult.

346	10b. Type **88**	55	10
347	50b. Man playing golf	1·50	30
348	1d.50 President playing golf	2·25	70

89 American Militiaman

1976. Bicentenary of American Revolution. Mult.

349	25b. Type **89**	20	10
350	50b. Soldier of the Continental Army	30	20
351	1d.25 Independence Declaration	40	60
MS352	110×80 mm. Nos. 349/51	1·00	4·00

90 Mother and Child

1976. Christmas.

353	**90**	10b. multicoloured	10	10
354	**90**	50b. multicoloured	15	10
355	**90**	1d.25 multicoloured	50	45

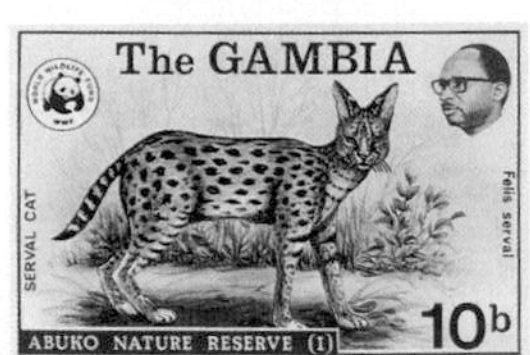

91 Serval Cat

1976. Abuko Nature Reserve (1st series). Mult.

356	10b. Type **91**	3·50	20
357	20b. Bushbuck	4·50	20
358	50b. Sitatunga (deer)	8·00	40
359	1d.25 Leopard	13·00	2·50
MS360	137×110 mm. Nos. 356/9	32·00	13·00

See also Nos. 400/3, 431/5 and 460/3.

92 Festival Emblem and Gambian Weaver

1977. 2nd World Black and African Festival of Arts and Culture, Nigeria.

361	**92**	25b. multicoloured	15	10
362	**92**	50b. multicoloured	20	15
363	**92**	1d.25 multicoloured	50	70
MS364		118×114 mm. Nos. 361/3	1·75	3·75

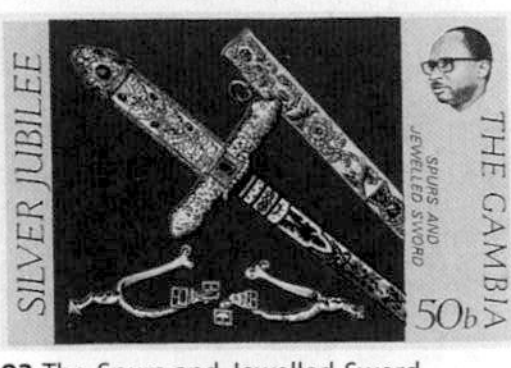

93 The Spurs and Jewelled Sword

1977. Silver Jubilee. Multicoloured.

365	25b. The Queen's visit, 1961	15	20
366	50b. Type **93**	15	20
367	1d.25 Oblation of the Sword	20	30

94 Stone Circles, Kuntaur

1977. Tourism. Multicoloured.

368	25b. Type **94**	10	10
369	50b. Ruined Fort, James Island	15	20

370	1d.25 Mungo Park Monument	40	80

95 Widow of Last Year

1977. Flowers and Shrubs. Multicoloured.

371	2b. Type **95**	10	15
372	4b. White water-lily	10	30
373	6b. Fireball lily (vert)	10	30
374	8b. Cocks-comb (vert)	10	15
375	10b. Broad leaved ground orchid (vert)	2·00	30
376	13b. Fibre plant (yellow background) (vert)	15	40
376a	13b. Fibre plant (grey background) (vert)	1·00	4·00
377	25b. False kapok (vert)	15	15
378	38b. Baobab (vert)	25	55
379	50b. Coral tree	35	35
380	63b. Gloriosa lily	40	70
381	1d.25 Bell-flowered mimosa (vert)	45	1·00
382	2d.50 Kindin dolo (vert)	50	1·00
383	5d. African tulip tree	60	2·00

96 Endangered Animals

1977. Banjul Declaration.

384	**96**	10b. black and blue	25	10
385	-	25b. multicoloured	30	10
386	-	50b. multicoloured	45	20
387	-	1d.25 black and red	1·50	75

DESIGNS: 25b. Extract from Declaration; 50b. Declaration in full; 1d.25, Endangered insects and flowers.

97 "Flight into Egypt"

1977. 400th Birth of Rubens. Multicoloured.

388	10b. Type **97**	15	10
389	25b. "The Education of the Virgin"	20	10
390	50b. "Clara Serena Rubens"	30	30
391	1d. "Madonna with Saints"	45	90

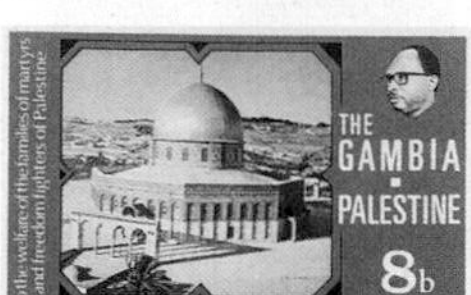

98 Dome of the Rock, Jerusalem

1978. Palestinian Welfare.

392	**98**	8b. multicoloured	50	15
393	**98**	25b. multicoloured	1·50	85

99 Walking on a Greasy Pole

1978. 13th Anniv of Independence. Multicoloured.

394	10b. Type **99**	10	10
395	50b. Pillow fighting	20	10
396	1d. Long boat rowing	45	45

100 Lion

1978. 25th Anniv of Coronation.

397	-	1d. black, brown and yellow	20	45
398	-	1d. multicoloured	20	45
399	**100**	1d. black, brown and yellow	20	45

DESIGNS: No. 397, White Greyhound of Richmond; 398, Queen Elizabeth II.

101 Verreaux's Eagle Owl

1978. Abuko Nature Reserve (2nd series). Multicoloured.

400	20b. Type **101**	10·00	65
401	25b. Lizard buzzard	10·00	65
402	50b. African harrier hawk	13·00	2·25
403	1d.25 Long-crested eagle	17·00	9·00

102 M.V. "Lady Wright"

1978. Launching of River Vessel "Lady Chilel Jawara". Multicoloured.

404	8b. Type **102**	15	10
405	25b. Sectional view of "Lady Chilel Jawara"	40	25
406	1d. "Lady Chilel Jawara"	1·25	1·40

103 Police Service

1979. 14th Anniv of Independence. Multicoloured.

407	10b. Type **103**	60	10
408	50b. Fire service	1·10	25
409	1d.25 Ambulance service	1·40	80

1979. Nos. 376 and 380/1 surch 25b.

410	25b. on 13b. Fibre plant	15	35
411	25b. on 63b. Gloriosa lily	10	20
412	25b. on 1d.25 Bell-flowered mimosa	10	20

105 "Ramsgate Sands" (detail showing children playing on beach)

1979. International Year of the Child. "Ramsgate Sands" (William Powell Frith). Multicoloured.

413	10b. Type **105**	10	10
414	25b. Detail showing child paddling (vert)	20	10
415	1d. Complete painting (60×23 mm)	60	60

106 1883 2½d. Stamp

1979. Death Centenary of Sir Rowland Hill. Multicoloured.

416	10b. Type **106**	10	10
417	25b. 1869 4d. stamp	10	10
418	50b. 1965 Independence 7½d. commemorative	15	20
419	1d.25 1935 Silver Jubilee 1½d. commemorative	35	50
MS420	109×83 mm. No. 419	65	1·00

107 Satellite Earth Station under Construction

1979. Abuko Satellite Earth Station. Multicoloured.

421	25b. Type **107**	20	10
422	50b. Satellite Earth Station (completed)	30	20
423	1d. "Intelsat" satellite	65	60

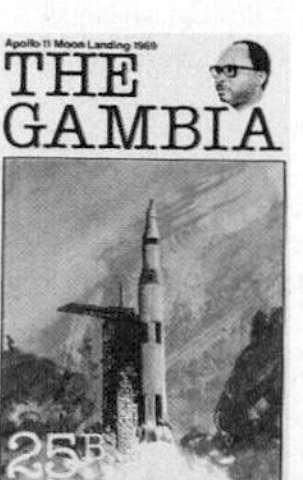

108 "Apollo 11" leaving Launch Pad

1979. 10th Anniv of Moon Landing. Multicoloured.

424	25b. Type **108**	20	10
425	38b. "Apollo 11" in Moon orbit	25	20
426	50b. Splashdown	30	40
430	2d. Lunar module on Moon	1·50	2·25

Nos. 424/6 also exist self-adhesive from booklet panes. No. 430 only exists in this form.

109 "Acraea zetes"

1980. Abuko Nature Reserve (3rd series). Butterflies. Multicoloured.

431	25b. Type **109**	5·00	20
432	50b. "Precis hierta"	6·00	50
433	1d. "Graphium leonidas"	8·50	1·40
434	1d.25 "Charaxes jasius"	8·50	2·00
MS435	145×122 mm. Nos. 431/4	42·00	9·50

110 Steam Launch "Vampire"

1980. "London 1980" International Stamp Exhibition. Multicoloured.

436	10b. Type **110**	20	10
437	25b. T.S.S. "Lady Denham"	25	10
438	50b. T.S.C.M.Y. "Mansa Kila Ba"	30	20
439	1d.25 T.S.S. "Prince of Wales"	50	60

Nos. 438 and 439 are larger, 49×26 mm.

111 Queen Elizabeth the Queen Mother

1980. 80th Birthday of Queen Elizabeth The Queen Mother.

440	**111**	67b. multicoloured	30	60

112 Phoenician Trading Vessel

1980. Early Sailing Vessels. Multicoloured.

441	8b. Type **112**	10	10
442	67b. Egyptian sea-going vessel	30	20
443	75b. Portuguese caravel	35	30
444	1d. Spanish galleon	40	50

113 "Madonna and Child" (Francesco de Mura)

1980. Christmas. Multicoloured.

445	8b. Type **113**	10	10
446	67b. "Praying Madonna with Crown of Stars" (workshop of Correggio)	25	25
447	75b. "La Zingarella" (workshop replica of Correggio painting)	25	30

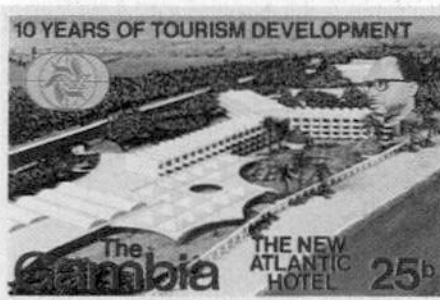

114 New Atlantic Hotel

1981. World Tourism Conference, Manila. Mult.

448	25b. Type **114**	15	10
449	75b. Ancient stone circles	20	40
450	85b. Conference emblem	30	60

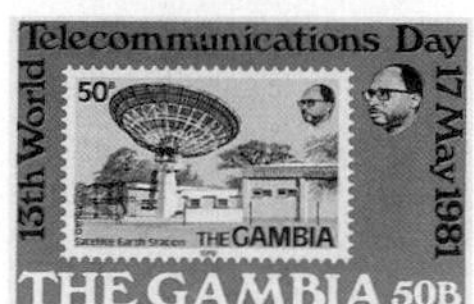

115 1979 Abuko Satellite Earth Station 50b. Commemorative

1981. World Telecommunications Day.

451	**115**	50b. multicoloured	45	20
452	-	50b. multicoloured	45	20
453	-	85b. black and brown	50	45

DESIGNS: No. 452, 1975 Birth centenary of Schweitzer 50b. commemorative; 453 ITU and WHO emblems.

116 Prince Charles in Naval Uniform

1981. Royal Wedding. Multicoloured.

454	75b. Wedding bouquet from Gambia	20	20
455	1d. Type **116**	25	30
456	1d.25 Prince Charles and Lady Diana Spencer	30	35

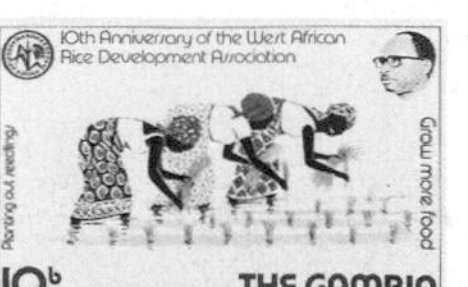

117 Planting-out Seedlings

1981. 10th Anniv of West African Rice Development Association. Multicoloured.

457	10b. Type **117**	10	10
458	50b. Care of the crops	25	35
459	85b. Winnowing and drying	40	55

118 Bosc's Monitor

1981. Abuko Nature Reserve (4th series). Reptiles. Multicoloured.

460	40b. Type **118**	7·00	30
461	60b. Dwarf crocodile	7·50	80
462	80b. Royal python	9·50	1·25
463	85b. Chameleon	9·50	1·25

119 Examination Room

1982. 30th Anniv of West African Examinations Council. Multicoloured.

464	60b. Type **119**	50	30
465	85b. First high school	65	45
466	1d.10 Council's office	85	55

1982. No. 454 surch 60B.

467	60b. on 75b. Wedding bouquet from Gambia	75	1·60

121 Tree-planting ("Conservation")

1982. 75th Anniv of Boy Scout Movement. Multicoloured.

468	85b. Type **121**	1·50	1·25
469	1d.25 Woodworking	1·75	2·50
470	1d.27 Lord Baden-Powell	2·00	3·25

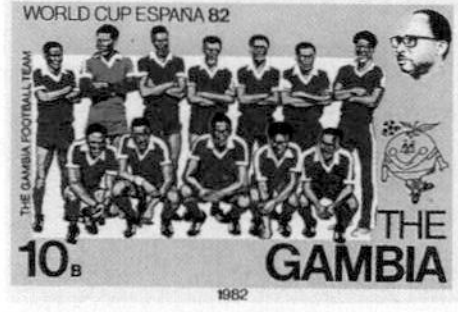

122 Gambia Football Team

1982. World Cup Football Championship, Spain. Multicoloured.

471	10b. Type **122**	20	10
472	1d.10 Gambian team practice	1·10	70
473	1d.25 Bernabeu Stadium, Madrid	1·10	75
474	1d.55 FIFA World Cup	1·25	80
MS475	114×85 mm. Nos. 471/4	4·00	4·50

123 Gambia Coat of Arms

1982. 21st Birthday of Princess of Wales. Multicoloured.

476	10b. Type **123**	10	10
477	85b. Princess at City Hall, Cardiff, October 1981	30	20
478	1d.10 Bride and groom returning to Buckingham Palace	35	35
479	2d.50 Formal portrait	1·25	1·00

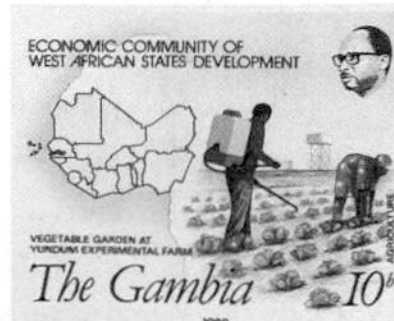

124 Vegetable Garden at Yundum Experimental Farm

1982. Economic Community of West African States Development. Multicoloured.

480	10b. Type **124**	30	15
481	60b. Banjul/Kaolack microwave tower	2·00	2·25
482	90b. Soap factory, Denton Bridge, Banjul	2·00	3·00
483	1d.25 Control tower, Yundum Airport	3·00	3·50

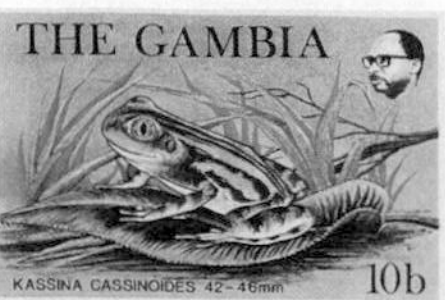

125 "Kassina cassinoides"

1982. Frogs. Multicoloured.

484	10b. Type **125**	2·00	20
485	20b. "Hylarana galamensis"	3·50	30
486	85b. "Euphlyctis occipitalis"	5·50	2·00
487	2d. "Kassina senegalensis"	7·50	12·00

126 Satellite View of Gambia

1983. Commonwealth Day. Multicoloured.

488	10b. Type **126**	10	10
489	60b. Batik cloth	20	45
490	1d.10 Bagging groundnuts	35	65
491	2d.10 Gambia flag	55	1·25

127 Blessed Anne Marie Javouhey (foundress of Order)

1983. Centenary of Sisters of St. Joseph of Cluny's Work in Gambia. Multicoloured.

492	10b. Type **127**	10	10
493	85b. Bathurst Hospital, nun and school children (horiz)	45	50

128 Canoes

1983. River Craft. Multicoloured.

494	1b. Type **128**	15	60
495	2b. Upstream ferry	20	60
496	3b. Dredger	20	60
497	4b. "Sir Dawda" (harbour launch)	30	60
498	5b. Cargo liner	30	60
499	10b. "Lady Dale" (60ft. launch)	30	20
500	20b. "Shonga" (container ship)	45	55
501	30b. Large sailing canoe	45	55
502	40b. "Lady Wright" (river steamer)	65	75
503	50b. Container ship (different)	65	75
504	75b. Fishing boats	75	1·00
505	1d. Tug with groundnut barges	90	1·00
506	1d.25 Groundnut canoe	1·00	1·50
507	2d.50 "Banjul" (car ferry)	1·75	2·50
508	5d. "Bintang Bolong" (freighter)	2·50	4·00
509	10d. "Lady Chilel Jawara" (river vessel)	4·00	6·50

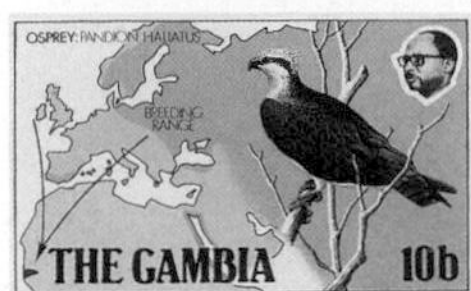

129 Osprey in Tree

1983. The Osprey. Multicoloured.

510	10b. Type **129**	1·50	50
511	60b. Osprey	2·75	2·50
512	85b. Osprey with catch	3·25	3·00
513	1d.10 In flight	3·50	5·00

130 Local Ferry

1983. World Communications Year. Multicoloured.

514	10b. Type **130**	10	10
515	85b. Telex operator	45	50
516	90b. Radio Gambia	45	50
517	1d.10 Loading mail onto Douglas DC-9-80 aircraft	1·50	65

131 "St. Paul preaching at Athens" (detail)

1983. 500th Birth Anniv of Raphael.

518	**131**	60b. multicoloured	35	40
519	-	85b. multicoloured	45	50
520	-	1d. multicoloured	50	55
MS521		105×83 mm. 2d. multicoloured (vert)	1·25	1·25

Nos. 519/20 show different details of "St. Paul preaching at Athens".

132 Montgolfier Balloon and Siege of Paris Cover

1983. Bicentenary of Manned Flight. Multicoloured.

522	60b. Type **132**	35	40
523	85b. Douglas DC-10 aircraft and flown cover	45	50
524	90b. Junkers seaplane "Atlantis" and Hans Bertram cover	45	50
525	1d.25 Lunar module and H. E. Sieger's space cover	50	70
526	4d. Airship "Graf Zeppelin"	2·25	3·00

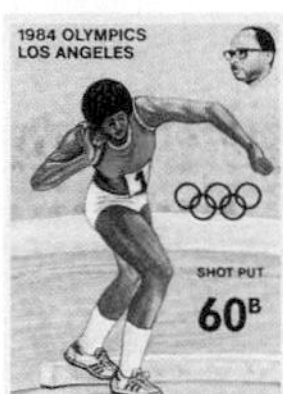

133 Shot-putting

1984. Olympic Games, Los Angeles (1st issue). Multicoloured.

527	60b. Type **133**	25	30
528	85b. High jumping (horiz)	35	40
529	90b. Wrestling	35	40
530	1d. Gymnastics	40	45
531	1d.25 Swimming (horiz)	50	55
532	2d. Diving	80	85
MS533	100×80 mm. 5d. Yachting	2·00	2·75

See also Nos. 555/8.

134 Goofy

1984. Easter. Multicoloured.

534	1b. Type **134**	10	10
535	2b. Mickey Mouse	10	10
536	3b. Huey, Dewey and Louie	10	10
537	4b. Goofy (different)	10	10
538	5b. Donald Duck	10	10
539	10b. Chip 'n' Dale	10	10
540	60b. Pluto	35	40
541	90b. Scrooge McDuck	50	60
542	5d. Morty and Ferdie	2·25	2·75
MS543	125×100 mm. 5d. Donald Duck (different)	3·50	3·50

Nos. 534/42 show Walt Disney cartoon characters painting eggs.

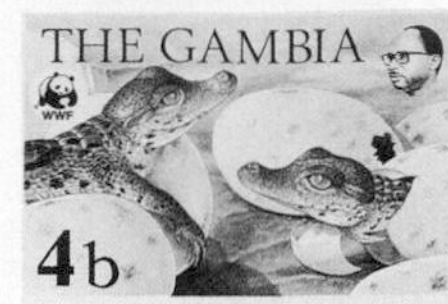

135 Young Crocodiles Hatching

1984. Endangered Species. The Nile Crocodile. Multicoloured.

544	4b. Type **135**	1·25	65
545	6b. Adult carrying young	1·25	65
546	90b. Adult	9·00	3·25
547	1d.50 Crocodile at riverbank	10·00	8·00
MS548	126×94 mm. As Nos. 544/7, but without W.W.F. logo	5·50	8·00

136 Port Banjul

1984. 250th Anniv of "Lloyd's List" (newspaper). Multicoloured.

549	60b. Type **136**	60	50
550	85b. Bulk carrier	75	80
551	90b. Sinking of the "Dagomba"	75	90
552	1d.25 19th-century frigate	1·25	1·60

1984. Universal Postal Union Congress, Hamburg. Nos. 507/8 optd 19th UPU CONGRESS HAMBURG.

553	2d.50 "Banjul" (car ferry)	1·00	1·50
554	5d. "Bintang Bolong" (ferry)	1·75	2·50

138 Sprinting

1984. Olympic Games, Los Angeles (2nd issue). Multicoloured.

555	60b. Type **138**	25	30
556	85b. Long jumping	35	40
557	90b. Long-distance running	35	40
558	1d.25 Triple jumping	50	55

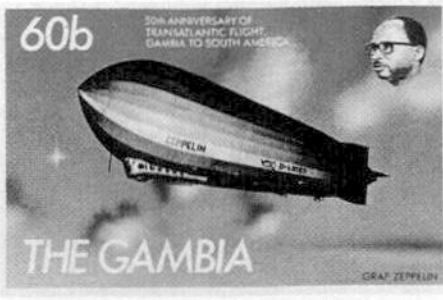

139 Airship "Graf Zeppelin"

1984. 50th Anniv of Gambia–South America Trans-Atlantic Flights. Multicoloured.

559	60b. Type **139**	1·10	1·00
560	85b. Dornier Wal on S.S. "Westfalen"	1·60	1·75
561	90b. Dornier Do-18	1·75	2·50
562	1d.25 Dornier Wal	1·75	2·75

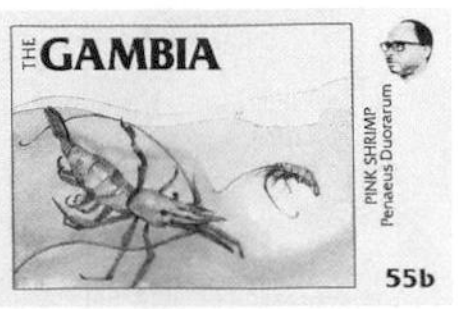

140 Pink Shrimp

1984. Marine Life. Multicoloured.

563	55b. Type **140**	35	30
564	75b. Atlantic loggerhead turtle	55	40
565	1d.50 Portuguese man-of-war	90	1·00
566	2d.35 Fiddler crab	1·40	1·60
MS567	105×70 mm. 5d. Cowrie snail	2·75	4·00

141 "Antanartia hippomene"

1984. Butterflies. Multicoloured.

568	10b. Type **141**	30	20
569	85b. "Pseudacraea eurytus"	80	90
570	90b. "Charaxes lactitinctus"	80	90
571	3d. "Graphium pylades"	2·00	3·75
MS572 105×75 mm. 5d. "Eurema hapale"		10·00	9·50

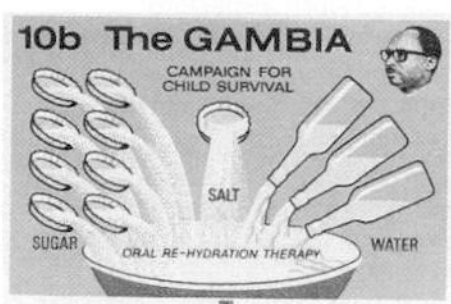

142 Oral Re-hydration Therapy

1985. Campaign for Child Survival.

573	**142**	10b. black, blue and brown	10	10
574	-	85b. multicoloured	35	45
575	-	1d.10 multicoloured	45	65
576	-	1d.50 multicoloured	60	80

DESIGNS: 85b. Growth monitoring; 1d.10, Health care worker with women and babies ("Promotion of breast feeding"); 1d.50, Universal immunization.

143 Women at Market

1985. Women and Development. Multicoloured.

577	60b. Type **143**	25	35
578	85b. Type **143**	35	50
579	1d. Woman office worker	40	60
580	1d.25 As 1d.	50	90

144 Turkey Vulture

1985. Birth Bicentenary of John J. Audubon (ornithologist). Designs showing original paintings. Multicoloured.

581	60b. Type **144**	1·40	75
582	85b. American darter ("American Anhinga")	1·60	1·50
583	1d.50 Green-backed heron ("Green Heron")	2·00	3·25
584	5d. Wood duck	3·25	5·50
MS585 100×70 mm. 10d. Great northern diver ("Common Loon")		6·50	4·00

145 The Queen Mother

1985. Life and Times of Queen Elizabeth the Queen Mother. Multicoloured.

586	85b. The Queen Mother and King George VI reviewing Home Guard	1·25	30
587	3d. Type **145**	1·75	1·50
588	5d. The Queen Mother with posy	2·50	2·25
MS589 56×85 mm. 10d. The Queen Mother in Garter robes		4·25	3·25

145a Mickey Mouse steering the "Calamity Jane"

1985. 150th Birth Anniv of Mark Twain (author). Designs showing Walt Disney cartoon characters in scenes from "Life on the Mississippi". Multicoloured.

590	1d.50 Type **145a**	2·00	2·00
591	2d. Mickey and Minnie Mouse at antebellum mansion	2·25	2·25
592	2d.50 Donald Duck and Goofy heaving the lead	2·50	2·50
593	3d. Poker game aboard the "Gold Dust"	2·75	2·75
MS594 126×101 mm. 10d. Mickey Mouse and riverboat		7·50	4·75

145b The King (Mickey Mouse) and Portrait of the Princess (Minnie Mouse)

1985. Birth Bicentenaries of Grimm Brothers (folklorists). Designs showing Walt Disney cartoon characters in scenes from "Faithful John". Multicoloured.

595	60b. Type **145b**	75	40
596	85b. The King showing the Princess his treasures	95	50
597	2d.35 Faithful John (Goofy) playing trumpet	2·25	1·40
598	5d. Faithful John turned to stone	3·25	2·50
MS599 126×101 mm. 10d. Faithful John after recovery		7·50	5·00

1985. Olympic Gold Medal Winners, Los Angeles. Nos. 527/32 optd.

600	60b. Type **133** (optd **GOLD MEDALLIST CLAUDIA LOCH WEST GERMANY**)	40	40
601	85b. High jumping (optd **GOLD MEDALLIST ULRIKE MEYFARTH WEST GERMANY**)	50	50
602	90b. Wrestling (optd **GOLD MEDALLIST PASQUALE PASSARELLI WEST GERMANY**)	50	50
603	1d. Gymnastics (optd **GOLD MEDALLIST LI NING CHINA**)	55	55
604	1d.25 Swimming (optd **GOLD MEDALLIST MICHAEL GROSS WEST GERMANY**)	70	70
605	2d. Diving (optd **GOLD MEDALLIST SYLVIE BERNIER CANADA**)	1·00	1·00
MS606 100×80 mm. 5d. Yachting (optd **GOLD MEDAL STAR CLASS U.S.A.**)		2·00	2·00

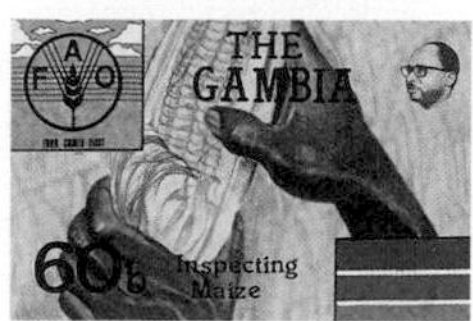

147 Inspecting Maize

1985. United Nations Anniversaries. Multicoloured.

607	60b. Type **147**	40	35
608	85b. Football match, Independence Stadium, Banjul	50	40
609	1d.10 Rice fields	60	60
610	2d. Central Bank of The Gambia	85	1·00
611	3d. Cow and calf	1·50	1·75
612	4d. Banjul harbour	2·00	2·25
613	5d. Gambian fruits	2·25	2·50
614	6d. Oyster Creek Bridge	2·50	3·00

Nos. 607, 609, 611 and 613 commemorate the 40th anniv of the Food and Agriculture Organization and Nos. 608, 610, 612 and 614 the 40th anniv of the United Nations Organization.

148 Fishermen in Fotoba, Guinea

1985. 50th Anniv of Diocese of The Gambia and Guinea. Multicoloured.

615	60b. Type **148**	40	30
616	85b. St. Mary's Primary School, Banjul	40	40
617	1d.10 St. Mary's Cathedral, Banjul	40	65
618	1d.50 Mobile dispensary at Christy Kunda	1·40	85

149 "Virgin and Child" (Dieric Bouts)

1985. Christmas. Religious Paintings. Multicoloured.

619	60b. Type **149**	20	25
620	85b. "The Annunciation" (Robert Campin)	25	30
621	1d.50 "Adoration of the Shepherds" (Gerard David)	45	50
622	5d. "The Nativity" (Gerard David)	1·60	1·75
MS623 106×84 mm. 10d. "Adoration of the Magi" (Hieronymus Bosch)		3·50	4·00

150 Enrolment Card

1985. 75th Anniv of Girl Guide Movement. Multicoloured.

624	60b. Type **150**	40	30
625	85b. 2nd Bathurst Company centre	50	35
626	1d.50 Lady Baden-Powell (vert)	70	1·00
627	5d. Miss Rosamond Fowlis (Gambian Guide Association leader) (vert)	2·00	3·75
MS628 97×67 mm. 10d. Gambian girl guides (vert)		4·50	6·00

151 Girl and Village Scene

1985. International Youth Year. Multicoloured.

629	60b. Type **151**	30	30
630	85b. Youth and wrestling bout	35	35
631	1d.10 Girl and Griot storyteller	45	1·25
632	1d.50 Youth and crocodile pool	1·00	1·75
MS633 106×76 mm. 5d. Herdsman with cattle		2·00	3·00

151a Maria Mitchell (astronomer) and Kitt Peak National Observatory, Arizona

1986. Appearance of Halley's Comet (1st issue). Multicoloured.

634	10b. Type **151a**	40	20
635	20b. Neil Armstrong, first man on Moon, 1969	55	25
636	75b. "Skylab 4" and Comet Kohoutek, 1973	85	65
637	1d. N.A.S.A.'s infra-red astronomical satellite and Halley's Comet	1·00	80
638	2d. Comet of 1577 from Turkish painting	1·50	1·50
639	10d. N.A.S.A.'s International Cometary Explorer	4·00	5·50

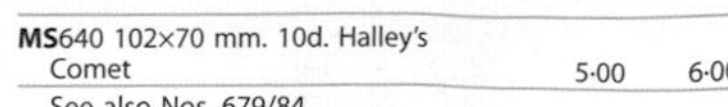

MS640 102×70 mm. 10d. Halley's Comet		5·00	6·00

See also Nos. 679/84.

151b Duke of York and Family, Royal Tournament, 1936

1986. 60th Birthday of Queen Elizabeth II.

641	**151b**	1d. black and yellow	35	30
642	-	2d.50 multicoloured	75	70
643	-	10d. multicoloured	3·00	3·50
MS644 120×85 mm. 10d. black and brown			3·25	3·00

DESIGNS: Nos. 642, Queen attending christening, 1983; 643, In West Germany, 1978; **MS**644, Duchess of York with her daughters, Balmoral, 1935.

152 Two Players competing for Ball

1986. World Cup Football Championship, Mexico. Multicoloured.

645	75b. Type **152**	75	60
646	1d. Player kicking ball	1·00	85
647	2d.50 Player kicking ball (different)	2·00	2·25
648	10d. Player heading ball	5·00	6·00
MS649 100×70 mm. 10d. Goalkeeper saving goal		7·50	7·00

153 Mercedes "500" (1986)

1986. "Ameripex" International Stamp Exhibition, Chicago. Centenary (1985) of First Benz Motor Car. Multicoloured.

650	25b. Type **153**	20	10
651	75b. Cord "810" (1935)	35	40
652	1d. Borgward "Isabella Coupe" (1957)	40	60
653	1d.25 Lamborghini "Countach" (1985/6)	50	70
654	2d. Ford "Thunderbird" (1955)	50	1·25
655	2d.25 Citroen "DS19" (1956)	50	1·60
656	5d. Bugatti "Atlante" (1936)	70	3·00
657	10d. Horch "853" (1936)	80	5·00
MS658 Two sheets, each 100×70 mm. (a) 12d. Benz "8/20" (1913). (b) 12d. Steiger "10/50" (1924) Set of 2 sheets		4·75	12·00

The 25b. value is inscribed "MECEDES" and the 10d. "LARL BENZ".

153a John Jacob Astor (financier)

1986. Centenary of Statue of Liberty (1st issue). Multicoloured. Designs showing Statue of Liberty and immigrants to the U.S.A.

659	20b. Type **153a**	10	10
660	1d. Jacob Riis (journalist)	40	50
661	1d.25 Igor Sikorsky (aeronautics engineer)	60	60
662	5d. Charles Boyer (actor)	2·50	2·50
MS663 114×80 mm. 10d. Statue of Liberty (vert)		4·00	4·50

See also Nos. 705/14.

153b Prince Andrew and Miss Sarah Ferguson

1986. Royal Wedding. Multicoloured.

664 1d. Type **153b** 40 45
665 2d.50 Prince Andrew 1·00 1·40
666 4d. Prince Andrew as helicopter pilot 2·50 2·00
MS667 88×88 mm. 7d. Prince Andrew and Miss Sarah Ferguson (different) 4·75 3·50

1986. World Cup Football Championship Winners, Mexico. Nos. 645/8 optd WINNERS Argentina 3 W.Germany 2.

668 75b. Type **152** 30 40
669 1d. Player kicking ball 40 55
670 2d.50 Player kicking ball (different) 1·00 1·25
671 10d. Player heading ball 4·25 4·75
MS672 100×70 mm. Goalkeeper saving goal 4·50 4·50

154 Minnie Mouse (Great Britain)

1986. Christmas. Designs showing Walt Disney cartoon characters posting letters in various countries. Multicoloured.

673 1d. Type **154** 75 60
674 1d.25 Huey (U.S.A.) 80 80
675 2d. Huey, Dewey and Louie (France) 1·25 1·40
676 2d.35 Kanga and Roo (Australia) 1·40 1·75
677 5d. Goofy (Germany) 2·25 3·00
MS678 127×101 mm. 10d. Goofy (Sweden) 8·00 6·00

Nos. 673/7 also show the "Stockholmia '86" International Stamp Exhibition emblem.

1986. Appearance of Halley's Comet (2nd issue). Nos. 634/9 optd HALLEYS COMET 1985-OFFICIAL-1986.

679 10b. Maria Mitchell (astronomer) and Kitt Peak National Observatory, Arizona 30 15
680 20b. Neil Armstrong, first man on Moon, 1969 50 20
681 75b. "Skylab 4" and Comet Kohoutek, 1973 75 50
682 1d. N.A.S.A.'s infra-red astronomical satellite and Halley's Comet 85 60
683 2d. Comet of 1577 from Turkish painting 1·10 1·75
684 10d. N.A.S.A.'s International Cometary Explorer 2·75 6·00
MS685 102×70 mm. 10d. Halley's Comet 3·00 4·25

155 Bugarab and Tabala

1987. Manding Musical Instruments. Multicoloured.

686 75b. Type **155** 15 20
687 1d. Balaphong and fiddle 15 25
688 1d.25 Bolongbato and konting (vert) 20 35
689 10d. Antique and modern koras (vert) 1·60 3·00
MS690 100×70 mm. 12d. Sabarr 1·90 2·50

156 "Snowing"

1987. Birth Centenary of Marc Chagall (artist). Multicoloured.

691 75b. Type **156** 40 40
692 85b. "The Boat" 50 50
693 1d. "Maternity" 65 65
694 1d.25 "The Flute Player" 75 75
695 2d.35 "Lovers and the Beast" 1·00 1·25
696 4d. "Fishes at Saint Jean" 1·25 2·00
697 5d. "Entering the Ring" 1·50 2·50
698 10d. "Three Acrobats" 2·25 3·75
MS699 Two sheets. (a) 110×68 mm. 12d. "The Cattle Driver" (104×61 mm). (b) 109×95 mm. 12d. "The Sabbath" (104×89 mm). Imperf Set of 2 sheets 7·50 8·50

157 "America", 1851

1987. America's Cup Yachting Championship. Multicoloured.

700 20b. Type **157** 20 15
701 1d. "Courageous", 1974 35 35
702 2d.50 "Volunteer", 1887 75 1·10
703 10d. "Intrepid", 1967 2·25 3·25
MS704 114×89 mm. 12d. "Australia II", 1983 4·00 3·00

158 Arm of Statue of Liberty

1987. Centenary of Statue of Liberty (1986) (2nd issue). Multicoloured.

705 1b. Type **158** 10 10
706 2b. Launch passing Statue (horiz) 10 10
707 3b. Schooner passing Statue (horiz) 10 10
708 5b. U.S.S. "John F. Kennedy" (aircraft carrier) and "Queen Elizabeth 2" (liner) (horiz) 10 10
709 50b. Checking Statue for damage 40 40
710 75b. Cleaning in progress 55 55
711 1d. Working on Statue 70 70
712 1d.25 Statue and fireworks 80 80
713 10d. Statue illuminated 4·25 4·75
714 12d. Statue and fireworks (different) 4·50 5·00

159 "Lantana camara"

1987. Flowers of Abuko Nature Reserve. Multicoloured.

715 75b. Type **159** 20 15
716 1d. "Clerodendrum thomsoniae" 20 20
717 1d.50 "Haemanthus multiflorus" 30 30
718 1d.70 "Gloriosa simplex" 30 35
719 1d.75 "Combretum microphyllum" 35 40
720 2d.25 "Eulophia quineensis" 50 60
721 5d. "Erythrina senegalensis" 1·10 1·25
722 15d. "Dichrostachys glomerata" 2·75 3·50
MS723 Two sheets, each 100×70 mm. (a) 15d. "Costus spectabilis". (b) 15d. "Strophanthus preussii" Set of 2 sheets 6·00 8·00

160 Front of Mail Bus

1987. "Capex '87" International Stamp Exhibition, Toronto and 10th Anniv of Gambia Public Transport Corporation. Mail Buses. Mult.

724 20b. Type **160** 60 20
725 75b. Bus in Banjul (horiz) 90 45
726 1d. Passengers queueing for bus (horiz) 90 45
727 10d. Two buses on rural road 3·50 6·50
MS728 77×70 mm. 12d. Parked bus fleet (horiz) 4·50 4·50

161 Basketball

1987. Olympic Games, Seoul (1988) (1st issue). Multicoloured.

729 50b. Type **161** 35 20
730 1d. Volleyball 50 35
731 3d. Hockey (horiz) 1·10 85
732 10d. Handball (horiz) 2·50 2·25
MS733 100×85 mm. 15d. Football (horiz) 3·00 2·75

See also Nos. 779/83.

162 "A Partridge in a Pear Tree"

1987. Christmas. Designs showing a Victorian couple in scenes from carol "The Twelve Days of Christmas". Multicoloured.

734 20b. Type **162** 70 60
735 40b. "Two turtle doves" 75 65
736 60b. "Three French hens" 80 70
737 75b. "Four calling birds" 80 70
738 1d. "Five golden rings" 80 70
739 1d.25 "Six geese a-laying" 90 75
740 1d.50 "Seven swans a-swimming" 90 75
741 2d. "Eight maids a-milking" 1·00 85
742 3d. "Nine ladies dancing" 1·10 1·00
743 5d. "Ten lords a-leaping" 1·40 1·40
744 10d. "Eleven pipers piping" 2·25 2·50
745 12d. "Twelve drummers drumming" 2·50 2·75
MS746 100×70 mm. 15d. Exchanging presents (horiz) 2·40 3·25

163 Campfire Singsong

1987. World Scout Jamboree, Australia. Multicoloured.

747 75b. Type **163** 50 30
748 1d. Scouts examining African katydid 70 40
749 1d.25 Scouts watching Red-tailed tropic bird 1·75 85
750 12d. Scouts helping bus passenger 4·25 5·00
MS751 72×98 mm. 15d. Scouts on field trip 7·00 8·00

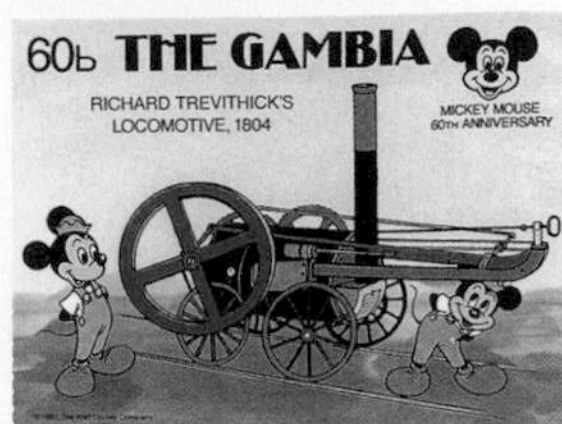

163a Morty and Ferdie examining Trevithick's Locomotive, 1804

1987. 60th Anniv of Mickey Mouse (Walt Disney cartoon character) (1st issue). Multicoloured.

752 60b. Type **163a** 35 25
753 75b. Clarabelle Cow in "Empire State Express", 1893 40 30
754 1d. Donald Duck inspecting Stephenson's "Rocket", 1829 50 40
755 1d.25 Piglet and Winnie the Pooh with Santa Fe Railroad locomotive, 1920 55 45
756 2d. Donald and Daisy Duck with Pennsylvania Railroad Class GG1 electric locomotive, 1933 80 70
757 5d. Mickey Mouse in "Stourbridge Lion", 1829 1·75 1·75
758 10d. Goofy in "Best Friend of Charleston", 1830 3·00 3·25
759 12d. Brer Bear and Brer Rabbit with Union Pacific diesel locomotive No. M10001, 1934 3·25 3·50
MS760 Two sheets, each 127×101 mm. (a) 15d. Chip n'Dale in "The General", 1855. (b) 15d. Donald Duck and Mickey Mouse in modern French "TGV" train Set of 2 sheets 7·50 8·00

See also Nos. 849/58.

164 Common Duiker and Acacia

1988. Flora and Fauna. Multicoloured.

761 50b. Type **164** 20 10
762 75b. Red-billed hornbill and casuarina (vert) 85 30
763 90b. West African dwarf crocodile and rice 30 20
764 1d. Leopard and papyrus (vert) 30 20
765 1d.25 Crowned crane ("Crested Crane") and millet 85 45
766 2d. Waterbuck and baobab tree (vert) 40 60
767 3d. Oribi and Senegal palm 50 1·25
768 5d. Hippopotamus and papaya (vert) 90 1·75
MS769 98×69 mm. (a) 12d. Red-throated bee eater and acacia (vert). (b) 12d. Eastern white pelican ("Great White Pelican") Set of 2 sheets 2·75 4·50

165 Wedding Portrait, 1947

1988. Royal Ruby Wedding.

770 **165** 75b. brown, black and orange 30 15
771 - 1d. brown, black and blue 40 20
772 - 3d. multicoloured 90 1·00
773 - 10d. multicoloured 2·25 3·25
MS774 100×75 mm. 15d. multicoloured 3·00 3·25

DESIGNS: 1d. Engagement photograph; 3d. Wedding portrait, 1947 (different); 10d. Queen Elizabeth II and Prince Philip (photo by Karsh), 1986; 15d. Wedding portrait with page, 1947.

1988. Stamp Exhibitions. Nos. 689, 703, 722 and 726 optd.

775 1d. Passengers queueing for bus (optd **Independence 40**, Israel) 25 25
776 10d. Antique and modern koras (optd **FINLANDIA 88**, Helsinki) 2·00 2·50
777 10d. "Intrepid" (yacht), 1967 (optd **Praga '88**, Prague) 2·00 2·50
778 15d. "Dichrostachys glomerata" (optd **OLYMPHILEX '88**, Seoul) 2·75 3·00

1988. Olympic Games, Seoul (2nd issue). As T 161. Multicoloured.

779	1d. Archery	50	20
780	1d.25 Boxing	50	25
781	5d. Gymnastics	1·25	1·10
782	10d. Start of 100 metre race (horiz)	2·00	2·25
MS783	74×102 mm. 15d. Medal winners on rostrum	2·40	3·25

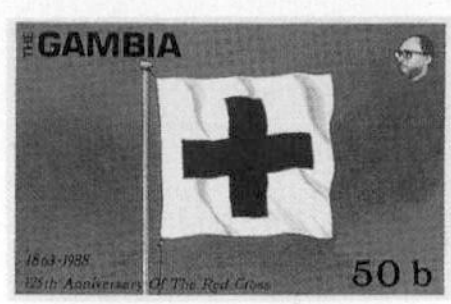

166 Red Cross Flag

1988. Anniversaries and Events. Multicoloured.

784	50b. Type **166** (125th anniv)	1·25	55
785	75b. "Friendship 7" spacecraft (25th anniv of first American manned Earth orbit)	85	60
786	1d. British Airways Concorde (10th anniv of Concorde London–New York service)	2·50	1·00
787	1d.25 "Spirit of St. Louis" (60th anniv of first solo transatlantic flight)	1·25	1·00
788	2d. North American X-15 (20th anniv of fastest aircraft flight)	1·60	1·40
789	3d. Bell "XS-1" rocket plane (40th anniv of first supersonic flight)	1·75	1·50
790	10d. English and Spanish galleons (400th anniv of Spanish Armada)	3·75	4·00
791	12d. "Titanic" (75th anniv of sinking)	6·50	5·00
MS792	Two sheets. (a) 113×85 mm. 15d. Kaiser Wilhelm Memorial Church, Berlin (vert) (750th anniv of Berlin). (b) 121×90 mm. 15d. Kangaroo (Bicentenary of Australian Settlement) Set of 2 sheets	4·75	7·00

166a "Emperor Charles V"

1988. 500th Birth Anniv of Titian (artist). Mult.

793	25b. Type **166a**	20	20
794	50b. "St. Margaret and the Dragon"	35	35
795	60b. "Ranuccio Farnese"	40	40
796	75b. "Tarquin and Lucretia"	55	55
797	1d. "The Knight of Malta"	70	70
798	5d. "Spain succouring Faith"	2·25	2·50
799	10d. Doge Francesco Venier"	3·50	3·50
800	12d. "Doge Grimani before the Faith" (detail)	3·75	3·75
MS801	110×95 mm. (a) 15d. "Jealous Husband" (detail). (b) 15d. "Venus blindfolding Cupid" Set of 2 sheets	4·75	7·00

167 John Kennedy sailing

1988. 25th Death Anniv of President John F. Kennedy. Multicoloured.

802	75b. Type **167**	15	15
803	1d. Kennedy signing Peace Corps legislation, 1962	15	20
804	1d.25 Speaking at U.N., New York (vert)	20	25
805	12d. Grave and eternal flame, Arlington National Cemetery (vert)	1·90	2·75
MS806	99×72 mm. 15d. John F. Kennedy (vert)	2·40	3·50

168 Airship "Graf Zeppelin" (first regular air passenger service), 1910

1988. Milestones of Transportation. Multicoloured.

807	25b. Type **168**	90	35
808	50b. Stephenson's "Locomotion" (first permanent public railway), 1825	2·00	50
809	75b. G.M. "Sun Racer" (first world solar challenge), 1987	1·50	65
810	1d. Sprague's "Premiere" (first operational electric tramway), 1888	1·75	80
811	1d.25 "Gold Rush" Bicycle (holder of man-powered land speed record), 1986	2·50	1·00
812	2d.50 Robert Goddard and rocket launcher (first liquid fuel rocket), 1925	2·25	1·25
813	10d. "Orukter Amphibolos" (first steam traction engine), 1805	4·50	3·50
814	12d. "Sovereign of the Seas" (largest cruise liner), 1988	4·50	4·00
MS815	Two sheets, each 71×92 mm. (a) 15d. U.S.S. "Nautilus" (first nuclear-powered submarine), 1954 (vert). (b) 15d. Fulton's "Nautilus" (first fish-shaped submarine), 1800's (vert) Set of 2 sheets	9·00	9·50

169 Emmett Kelley

1988. Entertainers. Multicoloured.

816	20b. Type **169**	10	10
817	1d. Gambia National Ensemble	25	25
818	1d.25 Jackie Gleason	30	30
819	1d.50 Laurel and Hardy	40	40
820	2d.50 Yul Brynner	75	75
821	3d. Cary Grant	95	95
822	10d. Danny Kaye	3·00	3·00
823	20d. Charlie Chaplin	5·50	5·50
MS824	Two sheets. (a) 110×77 mm. 15d. Marx Brothers (horiz). (b) 70×99 mm. 15d. Fred Astaire and Rita Hayworth (horiz) Set of 2 sheets	9·50	9·50

170 Prince Henry the Navigator and Caravel

1988. Exploration of West Africa. Multicoloured.

825	50b. Type **170**	80	60
826	75b. Jesse Ramsden's sextant, 1785	85	70
827	1d. 15th-century hourglass	90	80
828	1d.25 Prince Henry the Navigator and Vasco da Gama	1·40	95
829	2d.50 Vasco da Gama and ship	2·50	1·60
830	5d. Mungo Park and map of Gambia River (horiz)	4·00	2·50
831	10d. Map of West Africa, 1563 (horiz)	5·00	4·00
832	12d. Portuguese caravel (horiz)	5·00	4·50
MS833	Two sheets, each 65×100 mm. (a) 15d. Ship from Columbus's fleet off Gambia. (b) 15d. 15th-century ship moored off Gambia Set of 2 sheets	7·00	6·50

171 Projected Space Plane and Ernst Mach (physicist)

1988. 350th Anniv of Publications of Galileo's "Discourses". Space Achievements. Mult.

834	50b. Type **171**	70	30
835	75b. OAO III astronomical satellite and Niels Bohr (physicist)	80	40
836	1d. Space shuttle, projected space station and Robert Goddard (physicist) (horiz)	90	45
837	1d.25 Jupiter probe, 1979, and Edward Barnard (astronomer) (horiz)	1·25	60
838	2d. Hubble Space Telescope and George Hale (astronomer)	1·75	75
839	3d. Earth-to-Moon laser measurement and Albert Michaelson (physicist) (horiz)	1·75	85
840	10d. HEAO-2 "Einstein" orbital satellite and Albert Einstein "physicist"	3·25	2·75
841	20d. "Voyager" (first non-stop round-the-world flight), 1987, and Wright Brothers (aviation pioneers) (horiz)	5·50	5·00
MS842	Two sheets. (a) 99×75 mm. 15d. Great Red Spot on Jupiter (horiz). (b) 88×71 mm. 15d. Neil Armstrong (first man on Moon), 1969 Set of 2 sheets	6·00	8·00

172 Passing Out Parade

1989. Army Day. Multicoloured.

843	75b. Type **172**	25	25
844	1d. Standards of The Gambia Regiment	25	25
845	1d.25 Side drummer in ceremonial uniform (vert)	30	30
846	10d. Marksman with Atlantic Shooting Cup (vert)	2·00	2·00
847	15d. Soldiers on assault course (vert)	2·75	2·75
848	20d. Gunner with 105 mm field gun	3·00	3·00

173 Mickey Mouse, 1928

1989. 60th Birthday of Mickey Mouse (2nd issue). Multicoloured.

849	2d. Type **173**	1·10	90
850	2d. Mickey Mouse, 1931	1·10	90
851	2d. Mickey Mouse, 1936	1·10	90
852	2d. Mickey Mouse, 1955	1·10	90
853	2d. Mickey Mouse, 1947	1·10	90
854	2d. Mickey Mouse as magician, 1940	1·10	90
855	2d. Mickey Mouse with palette, 1960	1·10	90
856	2d. Mickey Mouse as Uncle Sam, 1976	1·10	90
857	2d. Mickey Mouse, 1988	1·10	90
MS858	138×109 mm. 15d. Mickey Mouse at 60th birthday party (132×103 mm) Imperf	4·25	4·00

Nos. 849/57 were printed together, se-tenant, forming a composite design.

174 "Le Coup de Lance" (detail)

1989. Easter. Religious Paintings by Rubens. Multicoloured.

859	50b. Type **174**	50	25
860	75b. "Flagellation of Christ"	60	35
861	1d. "Lamentation for Christ"	60	35
862	1d.25 "Descent from the Cross"	65	40
863	2d. "Holy Trinity"	1·10	70
864	5d. "Doubting Thomas"	2·00	1·75
865	10d. "Lamentation over Christ"	2·75	3·00
866	12d. "Lamentation with Virgin and St. John"	2·75	3·50
MS867	Two sheets, each 96×110 mm. (a) 15d. "The Last Supper". (b) 15d. "Raising of the Cross" Set of 2 sheets	4·50	6·00

175 African Emerald Cuckoo

1989. West African Birds. Multicoloured.

868	20b. Type **175**	90	30
869	60b. Grey-headed bush shrike	1·40	50
870	75b. South African crowned crane ("Crowned Crane")	1·40	55
871	1d. Secretary bird	1·60	60
872	2d. Red-billed hornbill	2·25	1·00
873	5d. Superb sunbird	3·00	3·00
874	10d. Pearl-spotted owlet ("Little owl")	4·00	4·25
875	12d. Bateleur ("Bateleur Eagle")	4·00	4·25
MS876	Two sheets, each 115×86 mm. (a) 15d. Ostrich. (b) 15d. Red-billed fire finch Set of 2 sheets	7·50	8·00

176 "Druryia antimachus"

1989. Butterflies of Gambia. Multicoloured.

877	50b. Type **176**	65	30
878	75b. "Euphaedra neophron"	75	45
879	1d. "Aterica rabena"	75	45
880	1d.25 "Salamis parhassus"	85	55
881	5d. "Precis rhadama"	2·25	2·25
882	10d. "Papilio demodocus"	3·00	3·00
883	12d. "Charaxes etesipe"	3·25	3·50
884	15d. "Danaus formosa"	3·25	3·75
MS885	Two sheets, each 99×68 mm. (a) 15d. "Euptera pluto". (b) 15d. "Euphaedra ceres" Set of 2 sheets	11·00	12·00

177 Class "River" Steam Locomotive No. 021, 1959, Nigeria

1989. African Steam Locomotive. Multicoloured.

886	50b. Type **177**	70	35
887	75b. Class 14A steam locomotive, Rhodesia	80	45
888	1d. British-built steam locomotive No. 120, Sudan	85	55
889	1d.25 Steam locomotive, 1925, U.S.A.	95	65
890	5d. North British steam locomotive, 1955	2·50	1·75
891	7d. Scottish-built steam locomotive No. 120, 1926	2·75	2·75
892	10d. East African Railways Class 1T steam tank locomotive	3·00	3·00
893	12d. American-built steam locomotive, Ghana	3·25	3·75
MS894	Two sheets, each 82×58 mm. (a) 15d. East African Railways Class 25 steam locomotive No. 2904 (vert). (b) 15d. East African Railways Class 25 steam locomotive No. 3700A (vert) Set of 2 sheets	10·50	11·00

1989. "Philexfrance '89" Int Stamp Exhibition, Paris. Nos. 686/9 optd PHILEXFRANCE '89.

895	75b. Type **155**	20	20
896	1d. Balaphong and fiddle	25	25
897	1d.25 Bolongbato and konting (vert)	30	30
898	10d. Antique and modern koras (vert)	2·00	2·75
MS899	100×70 mm. 12d. Sabarr	1·75	2·50

178a "Sparrow and Bamboo" (Hiroshige)

1989. Japanese Art. Multicoloured.

No.	Description	Mint	Used
900	50b. Type **178a**	65	30
901	75b. "Peonies and a Canary" (Hokusai)	80	40
902	1d. "Crane and Marsh Grasses" (Hiroshige)	1·00	45
903	1d.25 "Crossbill and Thistle" (Hokusai)	1·25	60
904	2d. "Cuckoo and Azalea" (Hokusai)	1·75	80
905	5d. "Parrot on a Pine Branch" (Hiroshige)	2·50	2·25
906	10d. "Mandarin Ducks in a Stream" (Hiroshige)	3·50	3·50
907	12d. "Bullfinch and Drooping Cherry" (Hokusai)	3·50	3·50
MS908	Two sheets, each 102×77 mm. (a) 15d. "Tit and Peony" (Hiroshige). (b) 15d. "Peony and Butterfly" (Shigenobou) Set of 2 sheets	10·00	11·00

179 Rialto Bridge, Venice

1989. World Cup Football Championship, Italy (1990) (1st issue). Designs showing landmarks and players. Multicoloured.

No.	Description	Mint	Used
909	75b. Type **179**	45	45
910	1d.25 The Baptistery, Pisa	60	60
911	7d. Casino, San Remo	2·25	2·75
912	12d. Colosseum, Rome	3·00	3·50
MS913	Two sheets, each 104×78 mm. (a) 15d. St. Mark's Cathedral, Venice. (b) 15d. Piazza Colonna, Rome Set of 2 sheets	10·50	11·00

See also Nos. 1064/8.

180 "Vitex doniana"

1989. Medicinal Plants. Multicoloured.

No.	Description	Mint	Used
914	20b. Type **180**	20	20
915	50b. "Ricinus communis"	30	30
916	75b. "Palisota hirsuta"	45	45
917	1d. "Smilax kraussiana"	55	55
918	1d.25 "Aspilia africana"	65	65
919	5d. "Newbouldia laevis"	1·75	2·00
920	8d. "Monodora tenuifolia"	1·90	2·50
921	10d. "Gossypium arboreum"	2·00	2·50
MS922	Two sheets, each 87×72 mm. (a) 15d. "Kigelia africana". (b) 15d. "Spathodea campanulata" Set of 2 sheets	11·00	11·00

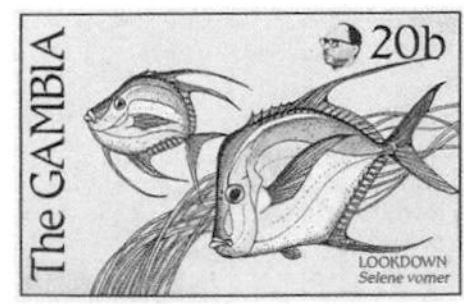

181 Lookdown Fish

1989. Fishes. Multicoloured.

No.	Description	Mint	Used
923	20b. Type **181**	25	25
924	75b. Boarfish	55	55
925	1d. Grey triggerfish	65	65
926	1d.25 Skipjack tuna	75	75
927	2d. Striped rudderfish	95	95
928	4d. Atlantic manta	1·60	1·75
929	5d. Flat-headed grey mullet	1·75	1·90
930	10d. Ladyfish	2·75	3·25
MS931	Two sheets, each 104×72 mm. (a) 15d. Porcupinefish. (b) 15d. Shortfin mako Set of 2 sheets	12·00	12·00

181a Little Hiawatha on Daniel Muller Indian Pony

1989. "World Stamp Expo '89" International Stamp Exhibition, Washington. Designs showing Walt Disney cartoon characters and American carousel horses. Multicoloured.

No.	Description	Mint	Used
932	20b. Type **181a**	70	30
933	50b. Morty on Herschell-Spillman stander	90	50
934	75b. Goofy on Gustav Dentzel stander	1·10	65
935	1d. Mickey Mouse on Daniel Muller armoured stander	1·25	70
936	1d.25 Minnie Mouse on jumper from Smithsonian Collection	1·40	80
937	2d. Webby on Illion "American Beauty"	2·00	1·25
938	8d. Donald Duck on Zalar jumper	4·25	4·50
939	10d. Mickey Mouse on Parker bucking horse	4·25	4·50
MS940	Two sheets, each 127×102 mm. (a) 12d. Donald, Mickey and Goofy in carousel car. (b) 12d. Donald's nephews on Roman chariot horses Set of 2 sheets	9·50	10·00

182 White House

1989. "World Stamp Expo '89" International Stamp Exhibition, Washington (2nd issue). Landmarks of Washington. Sheet 78×61 mm.

No.	Description	Mint	Used
MS941	10d. multicoloured	1·40	2·00

183 Mickey and Minnie Mouse in Pierce-Arrow, 1922

1989. Christmas. Designs showing Walt Disney cartoon characters with cars. Multicoloured.

No.	Description	Mint	Used
942	20b. Type **183**	80	25
943	50b. Goofy in Spyker, 1919	1·00	45
944	75b. Donald and Grandma Duck with Packard, 1929	1·10	55
945	1d. Mickey Mouse driving Daimler, 1920	1·25	65
946	1d.25 Mickey Mouse in Hispano "Suiza", 1924	1·40	90
947	2d. Mickey and Minnie Mouse in Opel "Laubfrosch", 1924	1·90	1·25
948	10d. Donald Duck driving Vauxhall "30/98", 1927	4·00	4·50
949	12d. Goofy with Peerless, 1923	4·00	4·50
MS950	Two sheets, each 127×102 mm. (a) 15d. Mickey and Minnie Mouse picnicking by Stutz "Blackhawk Speedster", 1928. (b) 15d. Donald Duck, Mickey and Minnie Mouse in Bentley "Supercharged", 1930 Set of 2 sheets	11·00	13·00

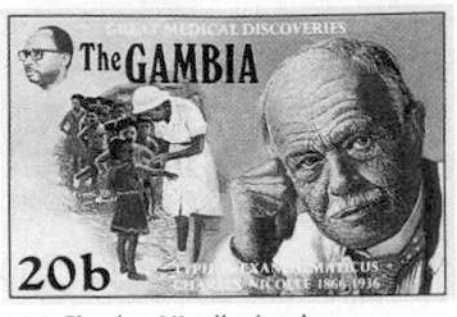

184 Charles Nicolle (typhus transmission) and Vaccination

1989. Great Medical Discoveries. Multicoloured.

No.	Description	Mint	Used
951	20b. Type **184**	1·00	30
952	50b. Paul Ehrlich (immunization pioneer) and medical examination	1·40	30
953	75b. Selman Waksman (discoverer of streptomycin) and T.B. clinic	1·60	40
954	1d. Edward Jenner (smallpox vaccination), and Jenner conducting experiment, 1796	1·75	50
955	1d.25 Robert Koch (developer of tuberculin test) and Gambian using vaccination gun	2·00	75
956	5d. Sir Alexander Fleming (discoverer of penicillin) and doctor giving injection	2·75	2·75
957	8d. Max Theiler (developer of yellow fever vaccine) and child clinic	3·50	4·00
958	10d. Louis Pasteur (bacteriologist) and health survey	3·50	4·00
MS959	Two sheets, each 121×86 mm. (a) 15d. Hughes 369 Viking medical helicopter. (b) 15d. B.A.C. One Eleven Nightingale C.9 medical relief plane Set of 2 sheets	8·00	8·50

No. **MS**959a is incorrectly inscribed "Vicking".

185 "Bulbophyllum lepidum"

1989. Orchids. Multicoloured.

No.	Description	Mint	Used
960	20b. Type **185**	45	30
961	75b. "Tridactyle tridactylites"	70	55
962	1d. "Vanilla imperialis"	90	70
963	1d.25 "Oeceoclades maculata"	1·10	90
964	2d. "Polystachya affinis"	1·40	1·25
965	4d. "Ancistrochilus rothschildianus"	2·25	2·50
966	5d. "Angraecum distichum"	2·40	2·50
967	10d. "Liparis guineensis"	3·75	4·50
MS968	Two sheets, each 99×67 mm. (a) 15d. "Plectrelminthus caudatus". (b) 15d. "Eulophia guineensis" Set of 2 sheets	8·50	8·50

186 John Newcombe

1990. Wimbledon Tennis Champions. Multicoloured.

No.	Description	Mint	Used
969	20b. Type **186**	20	20
970	20b. Mrs. G. W. Hillyard	20	20
971	50b. Roy Emerson	30	30
972	50b. Dorothy Chambers	30	30
973	75b. Donald Budge	40	40
974	75b. Suzanne Lenglen	40	40
975	1d. Laurence Doherty	45	45
976	1d. Helen Wills Moody	45	45
977	1d.25 Bjorn Borg	50	50
978	1d.25 Maureen Connolly	50	50
979	4d. Jean Borotra	1·25	1·25
980	4d. Maria Bueno	1·25	1·25
981	5d. Anthony Wilding	1·25	1·25
982	5d. Louise Brough	1·25	1·25
983	7d. Fred Perry	1·60	1·60
984	7d. Margaret Court	1·60	1·60
985	10d. Bill Tilden	2·00	2·00
986	10d. Billie Jean King	2·00	2·00
987	12d. Rod Laver	2·25	2·25
988	12d. Martina Navratilova	2·25	2·25
MS989	Two sheets, each 101×76 mm. (a) 15d. Rod Laver (different). (b) 15d. Martina Navratilova (different) Set of 2 sheets	8·50	9·50

187 Lunar Module "Eagle"

1990. 20th Anniv (1989) of First Manned Landing on Moon. Multicoloured.

No.	Description	Mint	Used
990	20b. Type **187**	85	20
991	50b. Lift-off of "Apollo 11" (vert)	1·10	30
992	75b. Neil Armstrong stepping on to Moon	1·25	45
993	1d. Buzz Aldrin and American flag	1·40	55
994	1d.25 "Apollo 11" emblem (vert)	1·60	60
995	1d.75 Crew of "Apollo 11"	1·90	1·40
996	8d. Lunar Module "Eagle" on Moon	3·50	4·00
997	12d. Recovery of "Apollo 11" after splashdown	3·75	4·50
MS998	Two sheets, each 110×89 mm. (a) 15d. Neil Armstrong (vert). (b) 15d. View of Earth from Moon (vert) Set of 2 sheets	7·00	7·50

188 Bristol Type 142 Blenheim Mk I

1990. R.A.F. Aircraft of Second World War. Multicoloured.

No.	Description	Mint	Used
999	10b. Type **188**	90	50
1000	20b. Fairey Battle	1·25	50
1001	50b. Bristol Type 142 Blenheim Mk IV	1·50	50
1002	60b. Vickers-Armstrong Wellington Mk 1c	1·60	50
1003	75b. Armstrong Whitworth Whitley Mk V	1·60	50
1004	1d. Handley Page Hampden Mk 1	1·60	50
1005	1d.25 Supermarine Spitfire Mk 1A and Hawker Hurricane Mk I	1·60	55
1006	2d. Avro Manchester	2·00	90
1007	3d. Short Stirling Mk I	2·00	1·90
1008	5d. Handley Page Halifax Mk I	2·50	2·50
1009	10d. Avro Lancaster Mk III	3·50	4·25
1010	12d. De Havilland Mosquito Mk IV	3·50	4·25
MS1011	Two sheets, each 107×77 mm. (a) 15d. Supermarine Spitfire Mk 1A. (b) 15d. Avro Type 683 Lancaster Mk III (different) Set of 2 sheets	8·50	9·00

189 White-faced Scops Owl

1990. African Birds. Multicoloured.

No.	Description	Mint	Used
1012	1d.25 Type **189**	70	70
1013	1d.25 Village weaver	70	70
1014	1d.25 Red-throated bee eater	70	70
1015	1d.25 Brown snake eagle ("Brown Harrier Eagle")	70	70
1016	1d.25 Red bishop	70	70
1017	1d.25 Scarlet-chested sunbird	70	70
1018	1d.25 Red-billed hornbill	70	70
1019	1d.25 Mosque swallow	70	70
1020	1d.25 White-faced whistling duck	70	70
1021	1d.25 African fish eagle	70	70
1022	1d.25 Eastern white pelican	70	70
1023	1d.25 Carmine bee eater	70	70
1024	1d.25 Hadada ibis	70	70
1025	1d.25 Egyptian plover	70	70
1026	1d.25 Variable sunbird	70	70
1027	1d.25 African skimmer	70	70
1028	1d.25 Woodland kingfisher	70	70
1029	1d.25 African jacana	70	70
1030	1d.25 African pygmy goose	70	70
1031	1d.25 Hammerkop	70	70

Nos. 1012/31 were printed together, se-tenant, forming a composite design of birds at a lake.

190 Penny Black

1990. 150th Anniv of the Penny Black.

No.	Type	Description	Mint	Used
1032	**190**	1d.25 black and blue	1·50	50
1033	**190**	12d. black and red	4·50	4·50
MS1034		79×73 mm. **190** 15d. black, silver and orange	6·00	7·00

The design of No. **MS**1034 is without the additional stamps behind the Penny Black as shown on Type **190**.

191 Flag and National Assembly Building

1990. 25th Anniv of Independence. Multicoloured.

1035 1d. Type **191** 50 25
1036 3d. President Sir Dawda Jawara 50 50
1037 12d. Map of Yundum airport and Boeing 707 airliner 6·50 6·50
MS1038 100×69 mm. 18d. State arms 5·00 6·50

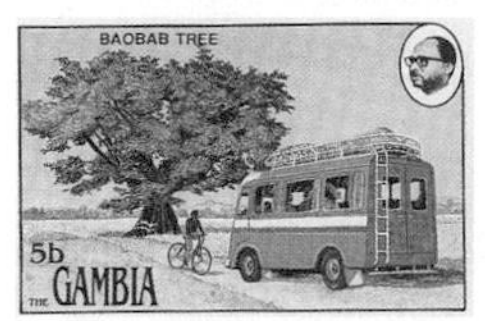

192 Baobab Tree

1990. Gambian Life. Multicoloured.

1039 5b. Type **192** 65 65
1040 10b. Woodcarving, Albert Market, Banjul 10 30
1041 20b. President Jawara planting seedling (vert) 10 10
1042 50b. Sailing canoe and map 1·50 25
1043 75b. Batik fabric 20 10
1044 1d. Hibiscus and Bakau beach 30 20
1045 1d.25 Bougainvillea and Tendaba Camp 30 20
1046 2d. Shrimp fishing and sorting 45 35
1047 5d. Groundnut oil mill, Denton Bridge 80 1·25
1048 10d. Handicraft pot and kora (musical instrument) 1·50 2·50
1049 15d. "Ansellia africana" (orchid) (vert) 7·00 8·00
1050 30d. "Euriphene gambiae" (butterfly) and ancient stone ring near Georgetown 9·00 12·00

193 Daisy Duck at 10 Downing Street

1990. "Stamp World London 90" International Stamp Exhibition. Walt Disney cartoon characters in England. Multicoloured.

1051 20b. Type **193** 70 30
1052 50b. Goofy in Trafalgar Square 90 35
1053 75b. Mickey Mouse on White Cliffs of Dover (horiz) 1·00 50
1054 1d. Mickey Mouse at Tower of London 1·00 50
1055 5d. Mickey Mouse and Goofy at Hampton Court Palace (horiz) 2·75 2·50
1056 8d. Mickey Mouse by Magdalen Tower, Oxford 3·25 3·50
1057 10d. Mickey Mouse on Old London Bridge (horiz) 3·25 3·50
1058 12d. Scrooge McDuck and Rosetta Stone, British Museum (horiz) 3·50 4·00
MS1059 Two sheets, each 125×100 mm. (a) 18d. Mickey Mouse and Donald Duck at Piccadilly Circus (horiz). (b) 18d. Mickey Mouse steering punt on River Thames (horiz) Set of 2 sheets 14·00 15·00

194 Lady Elizabeth Bowes-Lyon in High Chair

1990. 90th Birthday of Queen Elizabeth the Queen Mother.

1060 **194** 6d. black, mve & yell 1·40 1·75
1061 - 6d. black, mve & yell 1·40 1·75
1062 - 6d. black, mve & yell 1·40 1·75
MS1063 90×75 mm. 18d. mult 4·50 5·00

DESIGNS: No. 1061, **MS**1063, Lady Elizabeth Bowes-Lyon as a young girl; 1062, Lady Elizabeth Bowes-Lyon with wild flowers.

195 Vialli, Italy

1990. World Cup Football Championship, Italy (2nd issue). Multicoloured.

1064 1d. Type **195** 35 30
1065 1d.25 Cannegia, Argentina 40 35
1066 3d. Marchena, Costa Rica 90 1·00
1067 5d. Shaiba, United Arab Emirates 1·25 1·75
MS1068 Two sheets, each 75×92 mm. (a) 18d. Hagi, Rumania. (b) 18d. Van Basten, Netherlands Set of 2 sheets 14·00 14·00

195a Men's Discus

1990. Olympic Games, Barcelona (1992) (1st issue). Multicoloured.

1069 20b. Type **195a** 45 15
1070 50b. Men's 100 m 55 20
1071 75b. Women's 400 m 65 30
1072 1d. Men's 200 m 70 40
1073 1d.25 Women's rhythmic gymnastics 75 50
1074 3d. Football 1·25 1·50
1075 10d. Men's marathon 2·50 3·50
1076 12d. "Tornado" class yachting 2·50 3·50
MS1077 Two sheets, each 101×71 mm. (a) 15d. Parade of national flags (horiz). (b) 15d. Opening ceremony (horiz) Set of 2 sheets 13·00 13·00

See also Nos. 1289/97 and 1351/63.

195b "The Annunciation with St. Emidius" (detail) (Crivelli)

1990. Christmas. Paintings by Renaissance Masters. Multicoloured.

1078 20b. Type **195b** 45 10
1079 50b. "The Annunciation" (detail) (Campin) 65 10
1080 75b. "The Solly Madonna" (detail) (Raphael) 80 25
1081 1d.25 "The Tempi Madonna" (Raphael) 1·00 30
1082 2d. "Madonna of the Linen Window" (detail) (Raphael) 1·25 50
1083 7d. "The Annunciation, with St. Emidius" (different detail) (Crivelli) 2·75 3·50
1084 10d. "The Orleans Madonna" (Raphael) 3·00 3·50
1085 15d. "Madonna and Child" (detail) (Crivelli) 3·50 5·00
MS1086 72×101 mm. 15d. "Niccolini-Cowper Madonna" (Raphael) 6·00 7·00

195c "The Lion Hunt" (detail)

1990. 350th Death Anniv of Rubens. Multicoloured.

1087 20b. Type **195c** 20 15
1088 75b. "The Lion Hunt" (detail) 35 25
1089 1d. "The Tiger Hunt" (detail) 40 30
1090 1d.25 "The Tiger Hunt" (different detail) 40 35
1091 3d. "The Tiger Hunt" (different detail) 90 1·00
1092 5d. "The Boar Hunt" (detail) 1·40 1·75
1093 10d. "The Lion Hunt" (different detail) 2·00 2·50
1094 15d. "The Tiger Hunt" (different detail) 2·75 3·75
MS1095 Four sheets. (a) 100×71 mm. 15d. "The Boar Hunt". (b) 100×71 mm. 15d. "The Lion Hunt". (c) 100×71 mm. 15d. "The Crocodile and Hippopotomus Hunt". (d) 71×100 mm. 15d. "St. George slays the Dragon" (vert) Set of 4 sheets 12·00 13·00

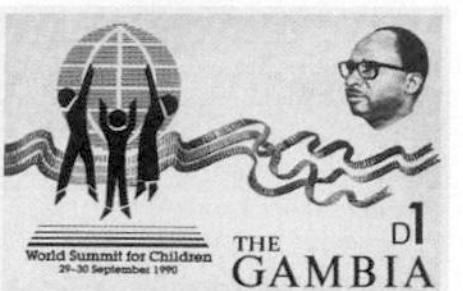

196 Summit Logo

1991. World Summit for Children, New York.

1096 **196** 1d. multicoloured 80 55

196a Sir Kay and Wart searching for Lost Arrow

1991. International Literacy Year (1990). Designs showing scenes from Disney cartoon film "The Sword in the Stone". Multicoloured.

1097 3d. Type **196a** 1·75 1·50
1098 3d. Merlin the Magician 1·75 1·50
1099 3d. Merlin teaching Wart 1·75 1·50
1100 3d. Wart writing on blackboard 1·75 1·50
1101 3d. Wart transformed into bird and Madame Mim 1·75 1·50
1102 3d. Merlin and Madame Mim 1·75 1·50
1103 3d. Madame Mim transformed into dragon 1·75 1·50
1104 3d. Wart pulling sword from stone 1·75 1·50
1105 3d. King Arthur on throne 1·75 1·50
MS1106 Two sheets, each 131×106 mm. (a) 20d. Sword in stone. (b) 20d. Merlin Set of 2 sheets 16·00 15·00

197 "Bebearia senegalensis"

1991. Wildlife. Multicoloured.

1107 1d. Type **197** 60 65
1108 1d. "Graphium ridleyanus" (butterfly) 60 65
1109 1d. "Precis antilope" (butterfly) 60 65
1110 1d. "Charaxes ameliae" (butterfly) 60 65
1111 1d. Addax 60 65
1112 1d. Sassaby 60 65
1113 1d. Civet 60 65
1114 1d. Green monkey 60 65
1115 1d. Spur-winged goose 60 65
1116 1d. Red-billed hornbill 60 65
1117 1d. Osprey 60 65
1118 1d. Glossy ibis 60 65
1119 1d. Egyptian plover 60 65
1120 1d. Golden-tailed woodpecker 60 65
1121 1d. Green wood hoopoe 60 65
1122 1d. Gaboon viper 60 65
1123 1d.50 Red-billed fire finch 60 65
1124 1d.50 Leaf-love 60 65
1125 1d.50 Piapiac 60 65
1126 1d.50 African emerald cuckoo 60 65
1127 1d.50 Red colobus monkey 60 65
1128 1d.50 African elephant 60 65
1129 1d.50 Duiker 60 65
1130 1d.50 Giant eland 60 65
1131 1d.50 Oribi 60 65
1132 1d.50 Western African dwarf crocodile 60 65
1133 1d.50 Crowned crane 60 65
1134 1d.50 Jackal 60 65
1135 1d.50 Yellow-throated longclaw 60 65
1136 1d.50 Abyssinian ground hornbill 60 65
1137 1d.50 "Papilio hesperus" 60 65
1138 1d.50 "Papilio antimachus" 60 65
1139 5d. Martial eagle 1·00 1·10
1140 5d. Red-cheeked cordon-bleu 1·00 1·10
1141 5d. Red bishop 1·00 1·10
1142 5d. Eastern white pelican 1·00 1·10
1143 5d. Patas monkey 1·00 1·10
1144 5d. Vervet monkey 1·00 1·10
1145 5d. Roan antelope 1·00 1·10
1146 5d. Western hartebeest 1·00 1·10
1147 5d. Waterbuck 1·00 1·10
1148 5d. Warthog 1·00 1·10
1149 5d. Spotted hyena 1·00 1·10
1150 5d. Olive baboon 1·00 1·10
1151 5d. "Palla decius" 1·00 1·10
1152 5d. "Acraea pharsalus" 1·00 1·10
1153 5d. "Neptidopsis ophione" 1·00 1·10
1154 5d. "Acraea caecilia" 1·00 1·10
MS1155 Three sheets, each 101×69 mm. (a) 18d. African spoonbill (vert). (b) 18d. White-billed buffalo weaver ("Buffalo Weaver") (vert). (c) 18d. Lion (vert) Set of 3 sheets 17·00 15·00

Nos. 1107/22, 1123/38 and 1139/54 respectively were issued together, se-tenant, forming composite designs.

198 "Papilio dardanus"

1991. Butterflies. Multicoloured.

1156 20b. Type **198** 60 30
1157 50b. "Bematistes poggei" 80 40
1158 1d. "Vanessa cardui" 90 55
1159 1d.50 "Amphicallia tigris" 1·00 85
1160 3d. "Hypolimnas dexithea" 1·75 1·25
1161 8d. "Acraea egina" 2·25 3·00
1162 10d. "Salamis temora" 2·25 3·00
1163 15d. "Precis octavia" 2·75 4·00
MS1164 Four sheets, each 100×70 mm. (a) 18d. "Danaus chrysippus". (b) 18d. "Charaxes jasius" (male). (c) 18d. "Papilio demodocus". (d) 18d. "Papilio nireus" Set of 4 sheets 16·00 15·00

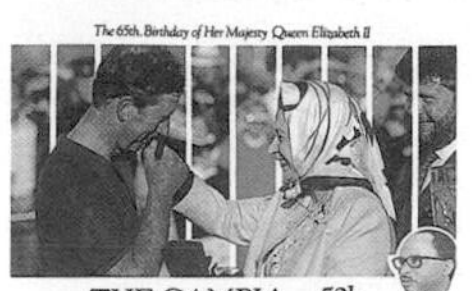

198a The Queen and Prince Charles at Windsor Polo Match

1991. 65th Birthday of Queen Elizabeth II. Mult.

1165 50b. Type **198a** 75 20
1166 1d. The Queen and Princess Anne at the Derby, 1988 1·00 35
1167 1d.25 The Queen at the Royal London Hospital, 1970 1·25 50
1168 12d. The Queen and Prince Philip at Balmoral, 1976 3·50 4·00
MS1169 68×90 mm. 18d. Separate photographs of The Queen and Prince Philip 4·75 5·50

198b Prince and Princess with Sons in June, 1989

1991. 10th Wedding Anniv of Prince and Princess of Wales. Multicoloured.

1170	20b. Type **198b**	70	25
1171	75b. Separate photographs of Prince, Princess and sons	1·25	50
1172	1d.50 Prince Henry on first day of school, 1987, and Prince William at polo match	1·50	85
1173	15d. Separate photographs of Prince and Princess of Wales	5·50	6·00

MS1174 68×90 mm. 18d. The family in Italy, 1985 6·50 7·00

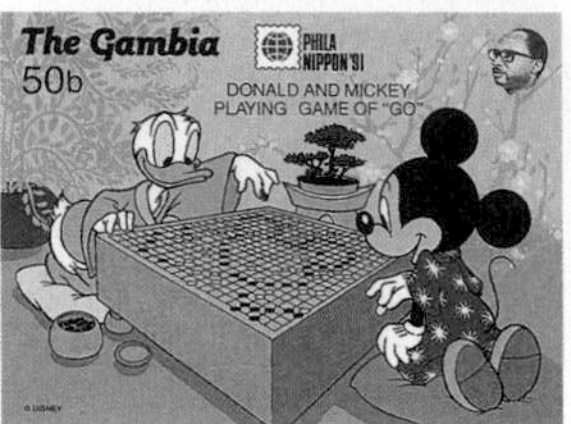

198c Donald Duck and Mickey Mouse playing "Go"

1991. "Phila Nippon '91" International Stamp Exhibition, Tokyo. Designs showing Walt Disney cartoon characters playing Japanese sports and games. Multicoloured.

1175	50b. Type **198c**	80	30
1176	75b. Morty, Ferdie and Pete as Sumo wrestlers	90	40
1177	1d. Minnie Mouse, Clarabelle Cow and Daisy Duck playing battledore and shuttlecock	1·00	45
1178	1d.25 Goofy and Mickey at Okinawa bullfight (vert)	1·10	55
1179	5d. Mickey flying hawk (vert)	2·75	2·50
1180	7d. Mickey, Minnie and Donald playing "jan-ken-pon" (vert)	2·75	3·25
1181	10d. Goofy as archer	3·00	3·25
1182	15d. Morty and Ferdie flying kites (vert)	4·00	4·50

MS1183 Four sheets, each 127×102 mm. (a) 20d. Mickey climbing Mt. Fuji. (b) 20d. Mickey fishing. (c) 20d. Scrooge McDuck and Mickey playing football. (d) 20d. Goofy playing baseball Set of 4 sheets 15·00 16·00

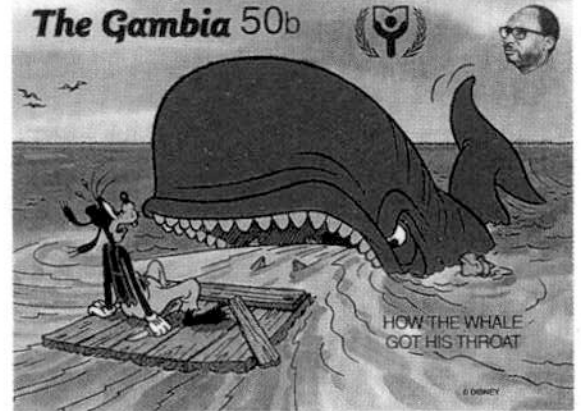

198d "How the Whale got his Throat"

1991. International Literacy Year (1990). Designs showing Walt Disney cartoon characters in Kipling's "Just So" stories. Multicoloured.

1184	50b. Type **198d**	85	30
1185	75b. "How the Camel got his Hump"	95	40
1186	1d. "How the Leopard got his Spots"	1·10	45
1187	1d.25 "The Elephant's Child"	1·40	55
1188	1d.50 "The Singsong of Old Man Kangaroo"	1·50	1·00
1189	7d. "The Crab that played with the Sea"	3·00	3·25
1190	10d. "The Cat that walked by Himself"	3·25	3·25
1191	15d. "The Butterfly that Stamped"	4·00	4·50

MS1192 Four sheets, each 127×102 mm. (a) 20d. Mickey Mouse reading story to Morte and Ferdie (horiz). (b) 20d. "How the Rhinoceros got his Skin" (horiz). (c) 20d. "How the Alphabet was made". (d) 20d. "How the first Letter was written" Set of 4 sheets 15·00 16·00

199 Canadian Pacific Steel Cupola Caboose

1991. Railway Brake-vans. Multicoloured.

1193	1d. Type **199**	65	65
1194	1d. Cumberland and Pennsylvania four-wheeled caboose, U.S.A.	65	65
1195	1d. Ferrocarril Interoceanico caboose, Mexico	65	65
1196	1d. Northern Pacific Railroad steel cupola caboose, U.S.A.	65	65
1197	1d. Morristown and Erie Railroad four-wheeled caboose, U.S.A.	65	65
1198	1d. Burlington Northern Railroad streamlined cupola caboose, U.S.A.	65	65
1199	1d. McCloud River Railroad caboose-coach, U.S.A.	65	65
1200	1d. Santa Fe Railroad wide-vision caboose, U.S.A.	65	65
1201	1d. Frisco Railroad wide-vision caboose, U.S.A.	65	65
1202	1d.50 Colorado and Southern Railroad four-wheeled caboose, U.S.A.	65	65
1203	1d.50 Santa Fe Railroad transfer caboose, U.S.A.	65	65
1204	1d.50 Canadian National wooden cupola caboose	65	65
1205	1d.50 Union Pacific steel transfer caboose, U.S.A.	65	65
1206	1d.50 Virginia and Truckee Railroad caboose-coach, U.S.A.	65	65
1207	1d.50 British Railways standard brake van	65	65
1208	1d.50 International Railways of Central America caboose	65	65
1209	1d.50 Northern Pacific Railroad steel cupola caboose, U.S.A.	65	65
1210	1d.50 Burlington Northern Railroad wooden caboose, U.S.A.	65	65
1211	2d. Oahu Railway caboose, Hawaii	65	65
1212	2d. British Railways standard brake van	65	65
1213	2d. Union Pacific steel wide-view caboose, U.S.A.	65	65
1214	2d. Belt Railway of Chicago four-wheeled caboose, U.S.A.	65	65
1215	2d. McCloud River Railroad four-wheeled caboose, U.S.A.	65	65
1216	2d. Angelina County Lumber Co caboose, U.S.A.	65	65
1217	2d. Coahuila Zacateca caboose, Mexico	65	65
1218	2d. United Railways of Yucatan caboose, Mexico	65	65
1219	2d. Rio Grande Railroad steel cupola caboose, U.S.A.	65	65

MS1220 Three sheets, each 79×56 mm. (a) 20d. Wooden caboose on steam goods train. (b) 20d. Pennsylvania Railroad steel caboose on electric goods train (vert). (c) 20d. Wooden caboose on passenger train and railwayman with flag (vert) Set of 3 sheets 13·00 14·00

200 Tiger Shark

1991. Fishes. Multicoloured.

1221	20b. Type **200**	25	15
1222	25b. Common jewelfish	25	15
1223	50b. Five-spotted cichlid	35	25
1224	75b. Small-toothed sawfish	35	25
1225	1d. Spotted tilapia	40	30
1226	1d.25 Dwarf jewelfish	40	35
1227	1d.50 Five-spotted jewelfish	45	40
1228	3d. Lion-headed cichlid	65	65
1229	10d. Egyptian mouthbrooder	2·00	2·50
1230	15d. Burton's mouthbrooder	2·75	3·50

MS1231 Two sheets, each 118×83 mm. (a) 18d. Great barracuda. (b) 18d. Yellow-tailed snapper Set of 2 sheets 12·00 13·00

200a Children waving

1991. Hummel Figurines. Multicoloured.

1232	20b. Type **200a**	10	10
1233	75b. Children under umbrella	15	15
1234	1d. Girl kissing friend	20	20
1235	1d.50 Children at window	30	30
1236	2d.50 Two girls in aprons	45	45
1237	5d. Two boys in bow ties	85	85
1238	10d. Two girls sitting on fence with birds	1·75	2·00
1239	15d. Boy and girl in Swiss costume	2·50	3·00

MS1240 Two sheets, each 98×128 mm. (a) 4d. × 4 As Nos. 1233/5 and 1239. (b) 5d. × 4 As Nos. 1232 and 1236/8 Set of 2 sheets 7·00 8·00

200b "The Old Cemetery Tower at Nuenen in the Snow"

1991. Death Centenary of Vincent van Gogh (artist). Multicoloured.

1241	20b. Type **200b**	50	25
1242	25b. "Head of Peasant Woman with White Cap" (vert)	50	25
1243	50b. "The Green Parrot" (vert)	60	25
1244	75b. "Vase with Carnations" (vert)	65	30
1245	1d. "Vase with Red Gladioli" (vert)	75	30
1246	1d.25 "Beach at Scheveningen in Calm Weather"	80	35
1247	1d.50 "Boy cutting Grass with Sickle"	90	40
1248	2d. "Coleus Plant in a Flower-pot" (detail) (vert)	1·00	40
1249	3d. "Self-portrait 1887" (vert)	1·25	60
1250	4d. "Self-portrait" (different) (vert)	1·50	90
1251	5d. "Self-portrait" (different) (vert)	1·75	1·25
1252	6d. "Self-portrait 1887" (different) (vert)	2·00	1·90
1253	8d. "Still Life with Bottle, Two Glasses, Cheese and Bread" (detail) (vert)	2·50	2·50
1254	10d. "Still Life with Cabbage, Clogs and Potatoes"	2·75	2·75
1255	12d. "Montmartre: The Street Lamps" (vert)	3·00	3·50
1256	15d. "Head of Peasant Woman with Brownish Cap" (vert)	3·25	4·00

MS1257 Four sheets, each 127×102 mm. (a) 20d. "The Potato Eaters" (horiz). (b) 20d. "Montmartre: Quarry and Mills" (horiz). (c) 20d. "Autumn Landscape" (horiz). (d) 20d. "Arles: View from the Wheat Fields" (detail) (horiz). Imperf Set of 4 sheets 20·00 21·00

200c "The Madonna of Humility"

1991. Christmas. Religious Paintings by Fra Angelico. Multicoloured.

1258	20b. Type **200c**	15	10
1259	50b. "Madonna and Child with Angels"	25	20
1260	75b. "Virgin and Child with Angels"	30	25
1261	1d. "The Annunciation"	35	30
1262	1d.25 "Presentation in the Temple"	40	35
1263	5d. "The Annunciation" (different)	1·50	1·50
1264	10d. "Madonna della Stella"	2·25	3·00
1265	15d. "Naming of St. John the Baptist"	2·75	4·00

MS1266 Two sheets, each 102×128 mm. (a) 20d. "Coronation of the Virgin". (b) 20d. "Annunciation and Adoration of the Magi" Set of 2 sheets 7·50 8·50

201 Son House

1992. Famous Blues Singers. Multicoloured.

1267	20b. Type **201**	15	15
1268	25b. W. C. Handy	15	15
1269	50b. Muddy Waters	30	30
1270	75b. Lightnin Hopkins	40	40
1271	1d. Ma Rainey	45	45
1272	1d.25 Mance Lipscomb	50	50
1273	1d.50 Mahalia Jackson	60	60
1274	2d. Ella Fizgerald	70	70
1275	3d. Howlin Wolf	85	85
1276	5d. Bessie Smith	1·25	1·25
1277	7d. Leadbelly	1·50	1·75
1278	10d. Joe Willie Wilkins	2·00	2·25

MS1279 Three sheets, each 110×78 mm. (a) 20d. String drum. (b) 20d. Elvis Presley. (c) 20d. Billie Holiday Set of 3 sheets 13·00 14·00

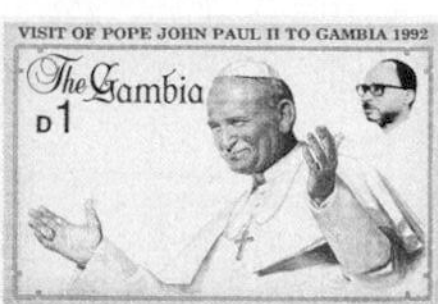

202 Pope John Paul II

1992. Papal Visit. Multicoloured.

1280	1d. Type **202**	60	40
1281	1d.25 Pope John Paul II and Pres. Sir Dawda Jawara	70	50
1282	20d. Gambian and Papal flags	5·50	7·00

MS1283 104×70 mm. 25d. Pope giving blessing 6·00 8·00

202a Pottery Market

1992. 40th Anniv of Queen Elizabeth II's Accession. Multicoloured.

1284	20b. Type **202a**	25	10
1285	50b. Ruins of early fort	35	20
1286	1d. Fishing boat	50	30
1287	15d. Canoes on beach	4·50	5·50

MS1288 Two sheets, each 75×97 mm. (a) 20d. "Lady Chilel Jawara" (river vessel). (b) 20d. River ferry being loaded Set of 2 sheets 9·50 10·00

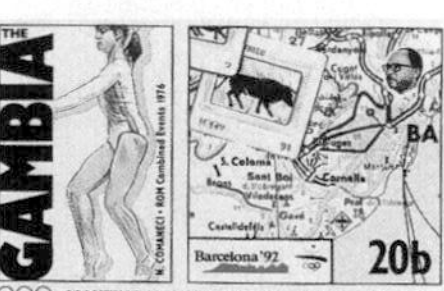

203 Nadia Comaneci (Rumania) (combined gymnastic events) and Map of Barcelona

1992. Olympic Games, Barcelona (2nd issue). Past Medal Winners. Multicoloured.

1289	20b. Type **203**	35	20
1290	50b. D. Moorcroft (G.B.) (5000 m) and map	45	20
1291	75b. M. Nemeth (Hungary) (javelin) and decorative tiles	45	25
1292	1d. J. Pedraza (Mexico) (20 km walk) and decorative plate	45	30
1293	1d.25 "Soling" class yachting (Brazil), state arms and flag	90	40
1294	1d.50 Women's hockey (G.D.R.) and Barcelona building	1·00	60
1295	12d. M. Jordan (U.S.A.) (basketball) and map	4·00	4·00
1296	15d. V. Borzov (U.S.S.R.) (100 m) and galleon	4·00	4·25

MS1297 Two sheets. (a) 82×112 mm. 20d. Silhouette of flamenco dancer on map (vert). (b) 112×82 mm. 20d. Silhouette of bull on map Set of 2 sheets 8·50 9·00

204 Mickey Mouse as Christopher Columbus

1992. International Stamp Exhibitions. Walt Disney cartoon characters. Multicoloured. (a) "Granada '92", Spain. Voyage of Columbus.

1298	20b. Type **204**	55	15
1299	75b. Mickey's plans derided	75	25
1300	1d.50 Mickey lands in America	1·00	60
1301	15d. Mickey presents treasure to Minnie	4·25	5·00
MS1302	127×102 mm. 18d. Mickey embarks for America	5·00	6·00

(b) World Columbian Stamp "Expo '92". Chicago Landmarks.

1303	50b. Navy Pier	60	10
1304	1d. Wrigley Building	75	25
1305	1d.25 University of Chicago	85	30
1306	12d. Alder Planetarium	4·00	4·75
MS1307	127×102 mm. 18d. Goofy hanging over Chicago (horiz)	5·00	6·00

204a "Christ presented to the People" (Rembrandt)

1992. Easter. Religious Paintings. Multicoloured.

1308	20b. Type **204a**	10	10
1309	50b. "Christ carrying the Cross" (Grunewald)	20	20
1310	75b. "The Crucifixion" (Grunewald)	25	25
1311	1d. "The Crucifixion" (Rubens)	30	30
1312	1d.25 "The Road to Calvary" (detail) (Tintoretto)	35	35
1313	1d.50 "The Road to Calvary" (Tintoretto) (different)	40	40
1314	15d. "The Crucifixion" (Masaccio)	2·75	3·75
1315	20d. "The Descent from the Cross" (Rembrandt)	3·50	4·50
MS1316	Two sheets, each 72×101 mm. (a) 25d. "The Crowning with Thorns" (detail) (Van Dyck). (b) 25d. "The Crowning with Thorns" (detail) (Titian) Set of 2 sheets	8·50	9·50

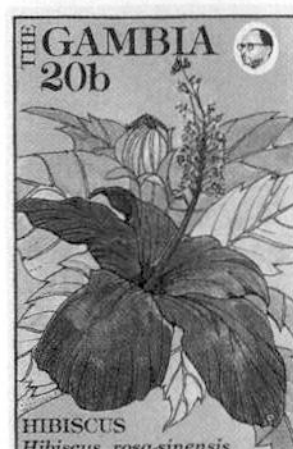

205 "Hibiscus rosa-sinensis"

1992. Flowers. Multicoloured.

1317	20b. Type **205**	10	10
1318	50b. "Monodora myristica"	20	20
1319	75b. "Bombax costatum"	25	25
1320	1d. "Oncoba spinosa"	30	30
1321	1d.25 "Combretum grandiflorum"	35	35
1322	1d.50 "Rothmannia longiflora"	40	40
1323	2d. "Clerodendrum splendens"	55	55
1324	5d. "Mussaenda erythrophylla"	1·10	1·25
1325	10d. "Nauclea latifolia"	1·75	2·00
1326	12d. "Clerodendrum capitatum"	1·90	2·50
1327	15d. "Costus spectabilis"	2·50	3·25
1328	18d. "Strophanthus preussii"	2·75	3·50
MS1329	Four sheeets, each 102×71 mm. (a) 20d. "Bougainvillea glabra". (b) 20d. "Nymphaea". (c) 20d. "Adansonia digitata". (d) 20d. "Clitoria ternatea" Set of 4 sheets	12·00	13·00

206 "Joven Antonia" (River Gambia)

1992. River Boats of the World. Multicoloured.

1330	20b. Type **206**	15	10
1331	50b. "Dresden" (River Elbe)	25	20
1332	75b. "Medway Queen" (River Medway)	30	25
1333	1d. "Lady Wright" (River Gambia)	35	30
1334	1d.25 "Devin" (River Vltava)	40	35
1335	1d.50 "Lady Chilel Jawara" (River Gambia)	45	50
1336	5d. "Robert Fulton" (River Hudson)	1·25	1·25
1337	10d. "Coonawarra" (River Murray)	2·00	2·25
1338	12d. "Nakusp" (River Columbia)	2·25	3·00
1339	15d. "Lucy Ashton" (Firth of Clyde)	2·75	3·50
MS1340	Two sheets, each 107×69 mm. (a) 20d. "City of Cairo" (Mississippi). (b) 20d. "Rüdesheim" (Rhine) Set of 2 sheets	9·00	10·00

206a U.S.S. "Pennsylvania" (battleship)

1992. 50th Anniv of Japanese Attack on Pearl Harbor. Multicoloured.

1341	2d. Type **206a**	1·75	1·25
1342	2d. Japanese Mitsubishi A6M Zero-Sen aircraft over Pearl Harbor	1·75	1·25
1343	2d. U.S.S. "Ward" (destroyer) sinking midget submarine	1·75	1·25
1344	2d. Ford Naval Station under attack	1·75	1·25
1345	2d. Agency report of Japanese attack	1·75	1·25
1346	2d. Newspaper headline	1·75	1·25
1347	2d. Japanese troops on Guam	1·75	1·25
1348	2d. U.S. forces regaining Wake Island	1·75	1·25
1349	2d. North American B-25B Mitchell bomber raid on Japan	1·75	1·25
1350	2d. American Douglas Dauntless dive bomber attacking Japanese carrier, Midway	1·75	1·25

207 Women's Double Sculls

1992. Winter Olympic Games, Albertville, and Olympic Games, Barcelona (3rd issue). Multicoloured.

1351	20b. Type **207**	25	15
1352	50b. Men's kayak (vert)	35	20
1353	75b. Women's rapid precision pistol shooting	50	30
1354	1d. Judo (vert)	55	30
1355	1d.25 Men's javelin (vert)	65	35
1356	1d.50 Men's vaulting horse (vert)	80	40
1357	2d. Men's downhill skiing (vert)	1·00	55
1358	3d. Windsurfing (vert)	1·10	90
1359	5d. Men's high jump	1·50	1·50
1360	10d. Four-man bobsled (vert)	2·50	2·75
1361	12d. 90 m ski-jump (vert)	2·75	3·00
1362	15d. Men's slalom skiing	3·00	4·00
MS1363	Four sheets, each 100×70 mm. (a) 18d. Table tennis (vert). (b) 18d. Men's 500 metre speed skating. (c) 18d. Women's 200 metre backstroke. (d) 18d. Pairs figure skating (vert) Set of 4 sheets	13·00	14·00

207a Dryosaurus

1992. "Genova '92" International Thematic Stamp Exhibition. Dinosaurs. Multicoloured.

1364	20b. Type **207a**	30	20
1365	25b. Saurolophus	30	20
1366	50b. Allosaurus	35	20
1367	75b. Fabrosaurus	40	25
1368	1d. Deinonychus	40	30
1369	1d.25 Cetiosaurus	50	35
1370	1d.50 Camptosaurus	50	35
1371	2d. Ornithosuchus	55	45
1372	3d. Spinosaurus	60	60
1373	5d. Ornithomimus	1·00	1·25
1374	10d. Kentrosaurus	1·75	2·25
1375	12d. Schlermochus	1·90	2·50
MS1376	Three sheets, each 104×75 mm. (a) 25d. As No. 1366. (b) 25d. As No. 1369. (c) 25d. As No. 1371 Set of 3 sheets	14·00	15·00

207b Immigration Centre, Ellis Island

1992. Postage Stamp Mega Event, New York. Sheet 100×70 mm.

MS1377	**207b** 18d. multicoloured	3·75	4·25

207c "The Holy Family" (Raphael)

1992. Christmas. Religious Paintings. Multicoloured.

1378	50b. Type **207c**	25	20
1379	75b. "The Little Holy Family" (Raphael)	30	25
1380	1d. "The Little Holy Family" (detail) (Raphael)	35	30
1381	1d.25 "Escape to Egypt" (Melchior Broederlam)	40	35
1382	1d.50 "Flight into Egypt" (Adriaen Isenbrant)	40	35
1383	2d. "The Holy Family" (El Greco)	55	55
1384	2d. "Flight into Egypt" (detail) (Cosimo Tura)	55	55
1385	2d. "Flight into Egypt" (detail) (Master of Hoogstraelen)	55	55
1386	4d. "The Holy Family" (Bernard van Orley)	90	1·00
1387	5d. "Holy Family with Infant Jesus Sleeping" (detail) (Charles Le Brun)	1·10	1·25
1388	10d. "Rest on The Flight to Egypt" (Orazio Gentileschi)	1·90	2·50
1389	12d. "Rest on The Flight to Egypt" (detail) (Orazio Gentileschi)	2·25	2·75
MS1390	Three sheets, each 102×77 mm. (a) 25d. "The Holy Family" (detail) (Giorgione). (b) 25d. "Flight into Egypt" (detail) (Vittore Carpaccio). (c) 25d. "Rest on The Flight to Egypt" (detail) (Simone Cantarino) Set of 3 sheets	11·00	12·00

207d Goofy in "Orphan's Benefit", 1934

1992. 60th Anniv of Goofy (Disney cartoon character). Multicoloured.

1391	50b. Type **207d**	30	20
1392	75b. Goofy and Donald Duck in "Moose Hunters", 1937	40	30
1393	1d. Goofy in "Mickey's Amateurs", 1937	50	40
1394	1d.25 Goofy, Donald and Mickey Mouse in "Lonesome Ghosts", 1937	55	55
1395	5d. Goofy, Donald and Mickey in "Boat Builders", 1938	1·40	1·40
1396	7d. Goofy, Donald and Mickey in "The Whalers", 1938	1·75	2·00
1397	10d. Goofy and Wilbur the grasshopper in "Goofy and Wilbur", 1939	2·00	2·25
1398	15d. Goofy in "Saludos Amigos", 1941	2·50	2·75
MS1399	Two sheets, each 127×102 mm. (a) 20d. Goofy in "The Band Concert", 1935 (vert). (b) 20d. Goofy today (vert) Set of 2 sheets	10·00	11·00

208 Pres. Jawara playing Golf and Map of Australia

209 Launch of European "Ariane 4"

1992. Open Golf Championships. Multicoloured.

1400	20b. Type **208**	65	20
1401	1d. Pres. Jawara and Gambia Open trophy	1·00	45
1402	1d.50 Pres. Jawara (winner of Gambia Open, 1985)	1·25	55
1403	2d. Pres. Jawara and map of Japan	1·75	70
1404	3d. Pres. Jawara and map of U.S.A.	2·00	1·25
1405	5d. Gambia Open trophy	2·25	1·75
1406	10d. Pres. Jawara and map of Scotland	3·50	4·00
1407	12d. Pres. Jawara and map of Italy	3·50	4·00
MS1408	Two sheets. (a) 106×71 mm. 10d. Pres. Jawara playing shot. (b) 67×99 mm. 18d. Flag of Gambia (horiz) Set of 2 sheets	11·00	12·00

1993. Anniversaries and Events. Multicoloured.

1409	2d. Type **209**	70	70
1410	2d. Konrad Adenauer and Berlin Airlift (horiz)	70	70
1411	2d. Airship "Hindenburg", 1928 (horiz)	70	70
1412	5d. "Santa Maria" (horiz)	2·00	1·25
1413	6d. Jentink's duiker (horiz)	1·40	1·40
1414	7d. World map and emblem (horiz)	2·50	1·60
1415	9d. Wolfgang Amadeus Mozart	3·50	2·75
1416	10d. Lions Club emblem	2·00	3·00
1417	10d. "Enterprise" (yacht), 1930	2·00	3·00
1418	10d. Imperial amazon (Imperial "Sisserou Parrot")	3·50	3·00
1419	12d. American space shuttle	3·25	3·50
1420	12d. Fleet of Columbus (horiz)	3·25	3·50
1421	15d. Adenauer and returning prisoners of war (horiz)	3·25	3·50
1422	18d. Airship LZ-1, 1900 (horiz)	3·75	4·25
MS1423	Six sheets. (a) 104×76 mm. 18d. Nose of projected European space station "Hermes". (b) 113×87 mm. 18d. Konrad Adenauer. (c) 85×65 mm. 18d. Count von Zeppelin. (d) 103×75 mm. 18d. Green-winged Macaw and bow of ship. (e) 85×65 mm. 18d. Globe. (f) 99×69 mm. 18d. Dancers from "The Marriage of Figaro". Set of 6 sheets	24·00	25·00

ANNIVERSARIES AND EVENTS: Nos. 1409, 1419, **MS**1423a, International Space Year; 1410, 1421, **MS**1423b, 25th death anniv of Konrad Adenauer (German statesman); 1411, 1422, **MS**1423c, 75th death anniv of Count Ferdinand von Zeppelin; 1412, 1420, **MS**1423d, 500th anniv of discovery of America by Columbus; 1413, 1418, **MS**1423e, Earth Summit '92, Rio; 1414, International Nutrition Conference, Rome; 1415, **MS**1423f, Death bicentenary of Mozart; 1416, 75th anniv of International Association of Lions Clubs; 1417, Americas Cup Yachting Championship.

209a Elvis Presley

1993. 15th Death Anniv (1992) of Elvis Presley (singer). Multicoloured.

1424	3d. Type **209a**	70	70
1425	3d. Elvis with guitar	70	70
1426	3d. Elvis with microphone	70	70

209b "St. John the Baptist" (Da Vinci)

1993. Bicentenary of the Louvre, Paris. Paintings. Multicoloured.

No.	Description	Unused	Used
1427	3d. Type **209b**	65	70
1428	3d. "Virgin of the Rocks" (Da Vinci)	65	70
1429	3d. "Bacchus" (Da Vinci)	65	70
1430	3d. "Lady of the Court, Milan" (Da Vinci)	65	70
1431	3d. "Virgin of the Rocks" (detail) (Da Vinci)	65	70
1432	3d. "Mona Lisa" (Da Vinci)	65	70
1433	3d. "Mona Lisa" (detail) (Da Vinci)	65	70
1434	3d. Sketches for "Two Horse-men" (Da Vinci)	65	70
1435	3d. "The Oath of Horatii" (left detail) (David)	65	70
1436	3d. "The Oath of Horatii" (right detail) (David)	65	70
1437	3d. "The Love of Paris and Helen" (detail) (David)	65	70
1438	3d. "The Sabine Women" (detail) (David)	65	70
1439	3d. "Leonidas at Thermopylae" (detail) (David)	65	70
1440	3d. "The Coronation of Napo-leon" (left detail) (David)	65	70
1441	3d. "The Coronation of Napo-leon" (centre detail) (David)	65	70
1442	3d. "The Coronation of Napo-leon" (right detail) (David)	65	70
1443	3d. "Peasant Family at Home" (detail) (L. le Nain)	65	70
1444	3d. "Smoking Room" (left detail) (L. le Nain)	65	70
1445	3d. "Smoking Room (right detail) (L. le Nain)	65	70
1446	3d. "The Cart" (detail) (L. le Nain)	65	70
1447	3d. "Peasants' Repast" (detail) (L. le Nain)	65	70
1448	3d. "Portrait in an Interior" (detail) (L. le Nain)	65	70
1449	3d. "Portrait in an Interior" (dif-ferent detail) (L. le Nain)	65	70
1450	3d. "The Forge" (L. le Nain)	65	70
MS1451	Two sheets, each 70×100 mm. (a) 20d. "Allegory of Victory" (M. le Nain) (52×86 mm). (b) 20d. "Madame Vigee-Le Brun and Daughter" (Le Brun) (52×86 mm) Set of 2 sheets	10·00	11·00

Nos. 1432/3 are incorrectly inscr "Monna Lisa".

210 Peace Corps and Gambian Flags

1993. 25th Anniv of U.S. Peace Corps.

No.	Type	Description	Unused	Used
1452	**210**	2d. multicoloured	1·00	1·00

211 Jackie Robinson and Ruby Dee ("The Jackie Robinson Story")

1993. Baseball Films. Multicoloured.

No.	Description	Unused	Used
1453	3d. Type **211**	75	80
1454	3d. Robert De Niro ("Bang the Drum Slowly")	75	80
1455	3d. James Earl Jones and Billy Dee Williams ("The Bingo Long Travelling All-Stars and Motor Kings")	75	80
1456	3d. Kevin Costner and Susan Sarandon ("Bull Durham")	75	80
1457	3d. Cast photograph ("Eight Men Out")	75	80
1458	3d. Ray Liotta ("Field of Dreams")	75	80
1459	3d. Charlie Sheen ("Major League")	75	80
1460	3d. Tom Selleck ("Mr. Baseball")	75	80
1461	3d. Wallace Beery, 1927, and Elliott Gould, 1986 ("Casey at the Bat")	75	80
1462	3d. Anna Nilsson and Babe Ruth ("Babe comes Home")	75	80
1463	3d. Joe Brown ("Elmer the Great")	75	80
1464	3d. Bud Abbott and Lou Costello ("The Naughty Nineties")	75	80
1465	3d. Frank Sinatra, Gene Kelly and Esther Williams ("Take Me Out to the Ball Game")	75	80
1466	3d. Tab Hunter and Gwen Verdon ("Damn Yankees")	75	80
1467	3d. Dan Dailey ("The Pride of St. Louis")	75	80
1468	3d. John Candy and Richard Pryor ("Brewster's Millions")	75	80
MS1469	Four sheets, each 132×107 mm. (a) 20d. John Goodman ("The Babe"). (b) 20d. Ronald Reagan ("The Winning Team"). (c) 20d. Tom Hanks and Madonna ("A League of Their Own") (vert). (d) 20d. Robert Redford ("The Natural") (vert) Set of 4 sheets	15·00	17·00

212 Giraffe

1993. Animals of West Africa. Multicoloured.

No.	Description	Unused	Used
1470	2d. Type **212**	55	60
1471	2d. Baboon	55	60
1472	2d. Caracal	55	60
1473	2d. Large-spotted genet	55	60
1474	2d. Bushbuck	55	60
1475	2d. Red-fronted gazelle	55	60
1476	2d. Red-flanked duiker	55	60
1477	2d. Cape buffalo	55	60
1478	2d. African civet	55	60
1479	2d. Side-striped jackal	55	60
1480	2d. Ratel	55	60
1481	2d. Striped polecat	55	60
1482	5d. Vervet	85	90
1483	5d. Blackish-green guenon	85	90
1484	5d. Long-tailed pangolin	85	90
1485	5d. Leopard	85	90
1486	5d. Elephant	85	90
1487	5d. Hunting dog	85	90
1488	5d. Spotted hyena	85	90
1489	5d. Lion	85	90
1490	5d. Hippopotamus	85	90
1491	5d. Nile crocodile	85	90
1492	5d. Aardvark	85	90
1493	5d. Warthog	85	90
MS1494	101×72 mm. 20d. As No. 1483	3·75	4·50

Nos. 1470/81 and 1482/93 were each printed together, se-tenant, with the backgrounds forming composite designs.

213 Long-tailed Pangolin hanging by Tail

1993. Endangered Species. Long-tailed Pangolin. Multicoloured.

No.	Description	Unused	Used
1495	1d.25 Type **213**	45	25
1496	1d.50 Sitting on branch	55	40
1497	2d. Climbing up branch	65	60
1498	5d. Climbing down branch	1·60	2·00
MS1499	72×100 mm. 20d. As No. 1496	4·00	4·50

214 Osprey

1993. Birds of Prey. Multicoloured.

No.	Description	Unused	Used
1500	1d.25 Type **214**	1·40	50
1501	1d.50 Egyptian vulture (horiz)	1·60	50
1502	2d. Martial eagle	1·75	55
1503	3d. Ruppell's griffon ("Ruppell's Griffon Vulture") (horiz)	2·25	75
1504	5d. Augur buzzard ("Auger Buzzard")	2·50	1·25
1505	8d. Greater kestrel	2·75	3·00
1506	10d. Secretary bird	2·75	3·00
1507	15d. Bateleur ("Bateleur Eagle") (horiz)	3·25	4·00
MS1508	Two sheets, each 108×80 mm. (a) 20d. Owl sp. ("Tawny Owl") (57×42½ mm). (b) 20d. Verreaux's eagle (57×42½ mm) Set of 2 sheets	14·00	14·00

215 Rose-ringed Parakeet

1993. African Birds. Multicoloured.

No.	Description	Unused	Used
1509	2d. Type **215**	1·25	1·25
1510	2d. Variable sunbird	1·25	1·25
1511	2d. Red-billed hornbill	1·25	1·25
1512	2d. Red-billed fire finch	1·25	1·25
1513	2d. Go-away bird ("Common Go-away Bird")	1·25	1·25
1514	2d. Burchell's gonolek ("Crim-son-breasted shrike")	1·25	1·25
1515	2d. Grey-headed bush shrike ("Gray-headed Bush shrike")	1·25	1·25
1516	2d. Western nicator ("Nicator")	1·25	1·25
1517	2d. Egyptian plover	1·25	1·25
1518	2d. Congo peafowl ("Congo Peacock")	1·25	1·25
1519	2d. Painted snipe ("Greater Painted Snipe")	1·25	1·25
1520	2d. South African crowned crane ("Crowned Crane")	1·25	1·25

215a Queen Elizabeth II (photograph by Cecil Beaton)

1993. 40th Anniv of Coronation.

No.	Type	Description	Unused	Used
1521	**215a**	2d. multicoloured	95	1·00
1522	-	5d. multicoloured	1·60	1·75
1523	-	8d. brown and black	1·75	1·90
1524	-	10d. multicoloured	1·90	2·00
MS1525		70×100 mm. 20d. mult	6·00	6·50

DESIGNS—(38×47 mm): 5d. Orb and sceptre; 8d. Sir Winston Churchill; 10d. Queen Elizabeth II at Trooping the Colour (28½×42½ mm); 20d. "Elizabeth II, 1972" (detail) (Joe King).

216 Hugo Eckener and "Graf Zeppelin"

1993. Aviation Anniversaries. Multicoloured.

No.	Description	Unused	Used
1526	2d. Type **216**	55	50
1527	2d. Guyot's balloon, 1785 (vert)	55	50
1528	5d. Airship "Luftschiffe 3" and crowd	1·00	1·00
1529	5d. Sopwith Snipe (fighter)	1·00	1·00
1530	8d. Eckener and "Graf Zeppelin"	1·60	1·75
1531	10d. "Comte d'Artois" (hot air balloon), 1785 (vert)	1·90	2·00
1532	15d. Royal Aircraft Factory S.E.5 (fighter)	2·40	3·00
MS1533	Three sheets. (a) 105×84 mm. 20d. Eckener and LZ-127 "Graf Zeppelin" (airship). (b) 84×105 mm. 20d. Blanchard's balloon, 1785 (vert). (c) 84×105 mm. 20d. Avro 504k (biplane) Set of 3 sheets	17·00	17·00

ANNIVERSARIES: Nos. 1526, 1528, 1530, **MS**1533a, Birth anniv of Hugo Eckener (airship pioneer); 1527, 1531, **MS**1533b, Bicentenary of first airmail flight; 1529, 1532, **MS**1533c, 75th anniv of Royal Air Force.

217 Henry Ford and "Model T", 1910

1993. Centenaries of Henry Ford's First Petrol Engine (Nos. 1534/45) and Karl Benz's First Four-wheeled Car (Nos. 1546/57). Multicoloured.

No.	Description	Unused	Used
1534	2d. Type **217**	45	50
1535	2d. Car of 1896	45	50
1536	2d. Henry Ford with Barney Oldfield and "999", 1902	45	50
1537	2d. Henry Ford, 1893, and car of 1896	45	50
1538	2d. "Model A", 1903	45	50
1539	2d. "Model T" with roof low-ered, 1908	45	50
1540	2d. "Model T" with roof raised, 1908	45	50
1541	2d. "Model K", 1906	45	50
1542	2d. "Model A", 1931	45	50
1543	2d. "Model A", 1906	45	50
1544	2d. "Model N", 1906	45	50
1545	2d. "Model F", 1905	45	50
1546	2d. Benz "Velo", 1894	45	50
1547	2d. Car of 1894	45	50
1548	2d. Three-wheeled car of 1885 from side	45	50
1549	2d. "Mannheim", 1905	45	50
1550	2d. Car of 1892	45	50
1551	2d. Car of 1900 from front	45	50
1552	2d. Racing car of 1911 from side	45	50
1553	2d. "Velo", 1893	45	50
1554	2d. Black car of 1900 from side	45	50
1555	2d. Red car of 1900 from side	45	50
1556	2d. Racing car of 1911 from front	45	50
1557	2d. Three-wheeled car of 1885 from back	45	50
MS1558	Two sheets, each 132×115 mm. (a) 20d. Ford car of 1896. (b) 20d. Benz car of 1900 Set of 2 sheets	8·50	9·00

Nos. 1534/45 and 1546/57 were each printed together, se-tenant, with the backgrounds forming composite designs.

218 Marilyn Monroe

1993. Musical Entertainers.

No.	Description	Unused	Used
1559-1593	3d.×35 multicoloured	38·00	32·00

Nos. 1559/93 were issued as four sheetlets, three of nine different designs (Nos. 1559/85) and one of eight (Nos. 1586/93), depicting Marilyn Monroe (Nos. 1559/67), Elvis Presley (Nos. 1568/76), Madonna (Nos. 1577/85) and Buddy Holly, Otis Redding, Bill Haley, Dinah Washington, musical instruments, Ritchie Valens, Clyde McPhatter, Elvis Presley (Nos. 1586/93).

219 Siamese

1993. Oriental Cats. Multicoloured.

No.	Description	Unused	Used
1594	2d. Type **219**	1·25	1·00
1595	2d. Colourpoint longhair sitting	1·25	1·00

1596 2d. Burmese 1·25 1·00
1597 2d. Birman 1·25 1·00
1598 2d. Snowshoe 1·25 1·00
1599 2d. Tonkinese 1·25 1·00
1600 2d. Foreign shorthair stretching 1·25 1·00
1601 2d. Balinese 1·25 1·00
1602 2d. Oriental shorthair 1·25 1·00
1603 2d. Foreign shorthair lying 1·25 1·00
1604 2d. Colourpoint longhair with black face standing 1·25 1·00
1605 2d. Colourpoint longhair with white face standing 1·25 1·00
MS1606 Two sheets, each 121×90 mm. (a) 20d. Colourpoint shorthair (vert). (b) 20d. Burmese (vert) Set of 2 sheets 9·00 9·50

Nos. 1594/1605 were printed together, se-tenant, with the background forming a composite design.

1993. Royal Dogs. As T 219. Multicoloured.

1607 2d. Shih tzu (Emperor of China) 1·25 1·00
1608 2d. Skye terrier (Queen Victoria) 1·25 1·00
1609 2d. Berner laufhund (King Louis XVI, France) 1·25 1·00
1610 2d. Boxer (King Francis I, France) 1·25 1·00
1611 2d. Welsh corgi (Queen Elizabeth II) 1·25 1·00
1612 2d. Dumfriesshire (Princess Anne) 1·25 1·00
1613 2d. Lurcher (King George VI) 1·25 1·00
1614 2d. Welsh corgi (Princess Anne) 1·25 1·00
1615 2d. Pekinese (Empress Ts'Eu-Hi, China) 1·25 1·00
1616 2d. Papillon (King Louis XIII, France) 1·25 1·00
1617 2d. Otterhound (King John) 1·25 1·00
1618 2d. Pug (Napoleon I, France) 1·25 1·00
MS1619 Two sheets, each 120×90 mm. (a) 20d. Cairn terrier (Mary, Queen of Scots). (b) 20d. Long-haired dachshund (Queen Victoria) Set of 2 sheets 9·00 9·50

Nos. 1607/18 were printed together, se-tenant, with the backgrounds forming a composite design.

219a National Monument and Statue, Jakarta

1993. Asian International Stamp Exhibitions. Multicoloured. (a) "Indopex '93", Surabaya, Indonesia.

1620 20b. Type **219a** 20 20
1621 20b. Pura Taman Ayun Temple, Bali 20 20
1622 2d. Guardian statue, Singosari Palace, Java 60 60
1623 2d. Candi Jawi, Java 60 60
1624 5d. Telek Luh mask 1·40 1·40
1625 5d. Jero Gde mask 1·40 1·40
1626 5d. Barong Macan mask 1·40 1·40
1627 5d. Monkey mask 1·40 1·40
1628 5d. Mata Gde mask 1·40 1·40
1629 5d. Jauk Kras mask 1·40 1·40
1630 5d. "Tree Mask" (Soedibio) 1·40 1·40
1631 5d. "Dry Lizard" (Hendra Gunawan) 1·40 1·40
1632 5d. "The Corn Eater" (Sudjana Kerton) 1·40 1·40
1633 5d. "Night Watchman" (Djoko Pekik) 1·40 1·40
1634 5d. "Hunger" (Kerton) 1·40 1·40
1635 5d. "Arje Player" (Soedjojono) 1·40 1·40
1636 5d. Central Temple, Lara Djonggrang 1·40 1·40
1637 5d. Irian Jaya Monument, Jakarta 1·40 1·40
1638 15d. Brahma and Siva Temples, Java 2·75 3·25
1639 15d. Date of the Year Temple, Java 2·75 3·25
MS1640 Two sheets, each 135×105 mm. (a) 18d. Tomb effigies, Torajaland (horiz). (b) 18d. Relief from Borobudur, Java (horiz) Set of 2 sheets 7·50 8·00

(b) "Taipei '93", Taiwan.

1641 20b. Fawang Si Pagoda, Henan 20 20
1642 20b. Wanshoubao Pagoda, Shashi 20 20
1643 2d. Red Pavilion, Shibaozhai 60 60
1644 2d. Songyue Si Pagoda, Henan 60 60
1645 5d. Pottery camel (walking) 1·40 1·40
1646 5d. Pottery horse and rider 1·40 1·40
1647 5d. Pottery camel (standing with mouth closed) 1·40 1·40
1648 5d. Yellow-glazed pottery horse 1·40 1·40
1649 5d. Pottery camel (standing with mouth open) 1·40 1·40
1650 5d. Pottery saddled horse 1·40 1·40
1651 5d. Qianlong vase 1·40 1·40
1652 5d. Small wine cup 1·40 1·40
1653 5d. Mei-ping vase 1·40 1·40
1654 5d. Urn vase 1·40 1·40
1655 5d. Tureen 1·40 1·40
1656 5d. Lidded potiche 1·40 1·40
1657 5d. Tianning Si Pagoda, Beijing 1·40 1·40
1658 5d. Bond Centre, Hong Kong 1·40 1·40
1659 15d. Forbidden City pavilion, Beijing 2·75 3·25
1660 15d. Xuanzhuang Pagoda, Shenxi 2·75 3·25
MS1661 Two sheets, each 135×105 mm. (a) 18d. Seated Buddha, Shanhua Temple, Shanxi. (b) 18d. Statues, Upper Huayan Si Temple, Datong (horiz) Set of 2 sheets 7·50 8·00

(c) "Bangkok '93", Thailand.

1662 20b. Sanctuary of Prasat Phanom Wan 20 20
1663 20b. Lai Kham Vihan, Chiang Mai 20 20
1664 2d. Upmarket spirit shrine, Bangkok 60 60
1665 2d. Walking Buddha statue, Wat Phra Si Ratana Mahathat 60 60
1666 5d. "Early Fruit Stand" 1·40 1·40
1667 5d. "Scene Rendered in Chinese Style" 1·40 1·40
1668 5d. "Buddha descends from Tauatimsa" 1·40 1·40
1669 5d. "Sang Thong Tales" (detail) 1·40 1·40
1670 5d. "The Damned in Hell" 1·40 1·40
1671 5d. "King Sanjaya travels on Elephant" 1·40 1·40
1672 5d. U Thong C Buddha (bronze) 1·40 1·40
1673 5d. Seated Buddha (bronze) 1·40 1·40
1674 5d. Phra Chai Buddha (ivory and gold) 1·40 1·40
1675 5d. Buddha (bronze) 1·40 1·40
1676 5d. U Thong A Buddha (bronze) 1·40 1·40
1677 5d. Crowned Buddha (bronze) 1·40 1·40
1678 5d. Statue of Buddha, Wat Mahathat 1·40 1·40
1679 5d. The Gopura of Prasat Phanom Rung 1·40 1·40
1680 15d. Slender Chedis, Mongkon 2·75 3·25
1681 15d. The Prang of Prasat Hin Phimai 2·75 3·25
MS1682 Two sheets, each 135×105 mm. (a) 18d. Khon (Thai dance drama). (b) 18d. Ceramics (horiz) Set of 2 sheets 7·50 8·00

220 "Woman with a Comb" (Picasso)

1993. Anniversaries and Events. Mult.

1683 2d. Type **220** 75 75
1684 2d. "Niedzica Castle" (horiz) 75 75
1685 5d. "The Mirror" (Picasso) 1·40 1·40
1686 5d. Early astronomical instrument 1·40 1·40
1687 7d. "Woman on a Pillow" (Picasso) 1·60 2·00
1688 10d. "Pont-Neuf in Paris" (Hanna Rudza-Cybisowa) (horiz) 2·50 3·00
1689 10d. "Honegger's Liturgical Symphony" (Marian Bogusz) (horiz) 2·50 3·00
1690 10d. Modern telescope 2·50 3·00
MS1691 Three sheets. (a) 75×105 mm. 18d. "The Three Dancers" (detail) (Picasso). P 14. (b) 105×75 mm. 18d. "When You enter here, Whisper my Name soundlessly" (detail) (Henryk Waniek) (horiz). P 14. (c) 102×74 mm. 18d. Copernicus Set of 3 sheets 14·00 14·00

ANNIVERSARIES AND EVENTS: Nos. 1683, 1685, 1687, **MS**1691a, 20th death anniv of Picasso (artist); 1684, 1688/9, **MS**1691b, "Polska '93" International Stamp Exhibition, Poznan; 1686, 1690, **MS**1691c, 450th death anniv of Copernicus (astronomer).

The captions on Nos. 1684 and 1689 are transposed in error.

No. **MS**1691b is inscribed "WHISPERT" in error.

221 Mudville Player at the Plate

1993. "Casey at the Bat". Scenes from Walt Disney's cartoon film. Multicoloured.

1692 2d. Type **221** 1·10 90
1693 2d. Mudville player out 1·10 90
1694 2d. Umpire and player arguing 1·10 90
1695 2d. Fans applauding 1·10 90
1696 2d. Casey reading newspaper at plate 1·10 90
1697 2d. Casey letting second pitch go by 1·10 90
1698 2d. Over-confident Casey 1·10 90
1699 2d. Casey striking out 1·10 90
1700 2d. Casey striking out at night 1·10 90
MS1701 Two sheets, each 129×103 mm. (a) 20d. Mudville manager. (b) 20d. Pitcher (vert) Set of 2 sheets 10·00 11·00

221a Hannich (Hungary) and Stopyra (France)

1993. World Cup Football Championship, 1994, U.S.A. (1st issue). Multicoloured.

1702 1d.25 Type **221a** 1·25 40
1703 1d.50 Labd (Morocco) and Gary Lineker (England) 1·40 50
1704 2d. Segota (Canada) and Morozov (Russia) 1·60 65
1705 3d. Roger Milla (Cameroun) 1·75 1·25
1706 5d. Rodax (Austria) and Weiss (Czechoslovakia) 2·25 1·75
1707 10d. Claesen (Belgium), Bossis and Amoros (France) 3·00 3·00
1708 12d. Candida (Brazil) and Ramirez (Costa Rica) 3·00 3·25
1709 15d. Silva (Brazil) and Michel Platini (France) 3·25 3·75
MS1710 Two sheets, each 100×70 mm. (a) 25d. Muller (Brazil) and McDonald (Ireland) (horiz). (b) 25d. Diego Maradona (Argentina) and Matthaeus (Germany) (horiz) Set of 2 sheets 12·00 13·00

See also Nos. 1882/90.

221b "The Adoration of the Magi" (detail) (Rubens)

1993. Christmas. Religious Paintings. Black, yellow and red (Nos. 1712/13 and 1715/17) or multicoloured (others).

1711 25b. Type **221b** 40 20
1712 1d. "The Holy Family with Joachim and Anna" (Durer) 80 20
1713 1d.50 "The Annunciation" (Durer) 1·10 30
1714 2d. "The Adoration of the Magi" (different detail) (Rubens) 1·25 70
1715 2d. "The Virgin Mary worshipped by Albrecht Bonstetten" (Durer) 1·25 70
1716 7d. "The Holy Family with Two Angels in a Portico" (detail) (Durer) 2·75 3·50
1717 10d. "Virgin on a Throne, crowned by an Angel" (Durer) 3·00 3·50
1718 15d. "The Adoration of the Magi" (different detail) (Rubens) 3·25 4·50
MS1719 Two sheets, each 102×127 mm. (a) 20d. "The Adoration of the Magi" (different detail) (Rubens). (b) 20d. "The Holy Family with Two Angels in a Portico" (different detail) (Durer) (horiz) Set of 2 sheets 9·00 10·00

221c "A Man in a Cap" (Rembrandt)

1993. Famous Paintings by Rembrandt and Matisse. Multicoloured.

1720 50b. Type **221c** 75 20
1721 1d.50 "Pierre Matisse" (Matisse) 1·25 40
1722 2d. "Man with a Gold Helmet" (Rembrandt) 1·50 85
1723 2d. "Auguste Pellerin" (Matisse) 1·50 85
1724 5d. "Andre Derain" (Matisse) 2·50 2·25
1725 7d. "A Franciscan Monk" (Rembrandt) 3·00 3·50
1726 12d. "The Young Sailor (II)" (Matisse) 3·50 4·25
1727 15d. "The Apostle Paul" (Rembrandt) 3·50 4·50
MS1728 Two sheets, each 127×102 mm. (a) 20d. "Dr. Tulp demonstrating the Anatomy of the Arm" (detail) (Rembrandt) (horiz). (b) 20d. "Pianist and Draughts Players" (detail) (Matisse) Set of 2 sheets 11·00 12·00

222 Mickey Mouse performing Ski Ballet

1993. Winter Sports. Walt Disney cartoon characters. Multicoloured.

1729 50b. Type **222** 50 15
1730 75b. Clarabelle and Horace ice dancing 60 15
1731 1d. Donald Duck and Dale speed skating 65 20
1732 1d.25 Donald in biathlon 70 20
1733 4d. Donald and nephews in bob-sled 1·75 1·60
1734 5d. Goofy on luge 2·00 1·75
1735 7d. Minnie Mouse figure skating 2·50 3·00
1736 10d. Goofy downhill skiing 2·75 3·00
1737 15d. Goofy playing ice hockey 3·00 3·50
MS1738 Two sheets, each 128×102 mm. (a) 20d. Minnie mogul skiing. (b) 20d. Goofy cross-country skiing Set of 2 sheets 9·50 11·00

222a Hong Kong 1979 $2 Butterflies Stamp and "Spring Garden" (M. Bruce)

1994. "Hong Kong '94" International Stamp Exhibition (1st issue). Multicoloured.

1739 1d.50 Type **222a** 65 75
1740 1d.50 Gambia 1990 50d. Gambian Life stamp and "Spring Garden" (M. Bruce) 65 75
MS1741 82×117 mm. 20d. Hong Kong 1970 Chinese New Year 10c. stamp 3·75 4·50

Nos. 1739/40 were printed together, se-tenant, forming the complete painting.

See also Nos. 1742/7.

222b Warriors and Horses

1994. "Hong Kong '94" International Stamp Exhibition (2nd issue). Qin Dynasty Terracotta Figures. Multicoloured.

1742	1d.50 Type **222b**	60	55
1743	1d.50 Head of warrior	60	55
1744	1d.50 Kneeling warrior	60	55
1745	1d.50 Chariot driver	60	55
1746	1d.50 Dog	60	55
1747	1d.50 Warriors as excavated	60	55

223 Pluto the Racer, 1934–35

1994. Chinese New Year ("Year of the Dog"). Walt Disney cartoon dogs. Multicoloured.

1748	25b. Type **223**	55	20
1749	50b. Fifi, 1933	70	30
1750	75b. Pluto Jnr, 1942	90	30
1751	1d.25 Goofy and Bowser	1·25	30
1752	1d.50 Butch, 1940	1·25	45
1753	2d. Toliver, 1936	1·50	60
1754	3d. Ronnie, 1946	1·75	1·00
1755	5d. Primo, 1950	2·00	1·40
1756	8d. Pluto's kid brother, 1946	2·25	2·25
1757	10d. The army mascot, 1942	2·25	2·50
1758	12d. Pluto and Fifi's puppies, 1937	2·25	3·00
1759	18d. Bent Tail Jnr, 1949	2·75	4·00
MS1760	Three sheets, each 127×102 mm. (a) 20d. Pluto and Fifi's puppies, 1937 (different). (b) 20d. Pluto and Dinah, 1950. (c) 20d. Pflip (horiz) Set of 3 sheets	12·00	13·00

Nos. 1758 and **MS**1760a are inscribed "Dinah's Pups" in error.

224 Ludwig von Drake and Easter Bunny

1994. Easter. Walt Disney cartoon characters. Multicoloured.

1761	25b. Type **224**	50	10
1762	50b. Minnie Mouse and Daisy Duck carrying banner	65	10
1763	3d. Mickey Mouse wearing top hat	1·75	85
1764	4d. Von Drake holding hatching egg	2·00	1·25
1765	5d. Donald Duck pushing trolley full of eggs	2·25	1·75
1766	8d. Bunny taking photograph of Von Drake	2·50	2·75
1767	10d. Goofy dressed as Easter Bunny	2·50	3·00
1768	12d. Von Drake holding dinosaur egg	2·75	3·50
MS1769	Two sheets. (a) 102×123 mm. 20d. Mickey and Minnie. (b) 123×102 mm. 20d. Ludwig von Drake Set of 2 sheets	8·50	9·50

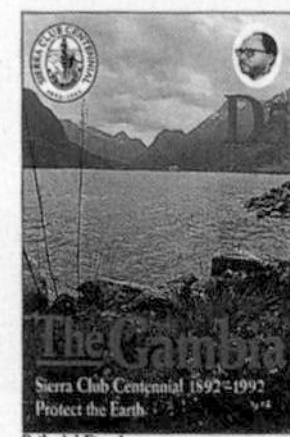

224a Briksdal Fjord

1994. Centenary (1992) of Sierra Club (environmental protection society). Endangered Environments. Multicoloured.

1770	5d. Type **224a**	1·00	1·10
1771	5d. Glacier, Briksdal Fjord	1·00	1·10
1772	5d. Waterfall, Briksdal Fjord	1·00	1·10
1773	5d. Frozen lake, Yosemite	1·00	1·10
1774	5d. Cliffs and river, Yosemite	1·00	1·10
1775	5d. Forest, Yosemite	80	90
1776	5d. Mother and child, Tibetan Plateau	80	90
1777	5d. Yellowstone in winter	80	90
1778	5d. Ross Island	80	90
1779	5d. Mount Erebus	80	90
1780	5d. Tibetan Plateau	80	90
1781	5d. Waterfall, Yellowstone	80	90
1782	5d. Sunset on the Serengeti	80	90
1783	5d. Dead trees, Ansel Adams Wilderness	80	90
1784	5d. Ansel Adams Wilderness in winter (horiz)	80	90
1785	5d. Ansel Adams Wilderness in summer (horiz)	80	90
1786	5d. Ridge on Mount Erebus (horiz)	80	90
1787	5d. Mount Erebus from a distance (horiz)	80	90
1788	5d. Prince William Sound (horiz)	80	90
1789	5d. Geysers, Yellowstone (horiz)	80	90
1790	5d. Local dwelling, Tibetan Plateau (horiz)	80	90
1791	5d. Sierra Club Centennial emblem (horiz)	80	90
1792	5d. Frozen lake, Prince William Sound (horiz)	1·00	1·10
1793	5d. Forest, Prince William Sound (horiz)	1·00	1·10
1794	5d. Baobab Tree, Serengeti (horiz)	1·00	1·10
1795	5d. Plains, Serengeti (horiz)	1·00	1·10
1796	5d. Volcano, Ross Island (horiz)	1·00	1·10
1797	5d. Mountains, Ross Island (horiz)	1·00	1·10

225 "Oeceoclades maculata"

1994. Orchids. Multicoloured.

1798	1d. Type **225**	35	20
1799	1d.25 "Angraecum distichum" (horiz)	45	30
1800	2d. "Plectrelminthus caudatus"	60	35
1801	5d. "Tridactyle tridactylites" (horiz)	1·25	1·25
1802	8d. "Bulbophyllum lepidum" (horiz)	1·40	1·50
1803	10d. "Angraecum eburneum"	1·60	1·90
1804	12d. "Eulophia guineensis"	1·75	2·00
1805	15d. "Angraecum eichleranum" (horiz)	2·00	2·50
MS1806	Two sheets, each 100×70 mm. (a) 25d. "Vanilla imperialis". (b) 25d. "Ancistrochilus rothschildianus" (horiz) Set of 2 sheets	9·00	10·00

226 "Girl with a Kitten" (Perronneau)

1994. Cats. Paintings of Cats. Multicoloured.

1807	5d. Type **226**	1·40	1·40
1808	5d. "Still Life with Cat and Fish" (Chardin)	1·40	1·40
1809	5d. "Tinkle a Cat"	1·40	1·40
1810	5d. "Naughty Puss!" (advertisement)	1·40	1·40
1811	5d. "Cats" (T.-A. Steinlen)	1·40	1·40
1812	5d. "Girl in Red with Cat and Dog" (Phillips)	1·40	1·40
1813	5d. "Cat, Butterfly and Begonia" (Harunobu)	1·40	1·40
1814	5d. "Cat and Kitten" (Pamela Higgins)	1·40	1·40
1815	5d. "Woman with a Cat" (Renoir)	1·40	1·40
1816	5d. "Minnie from Outskirts of the Village" (Thrall)	1·40	1·40
1817	5d. "The Fisher" (Raphael Tuck postcard)	1·40	1·40
1818	5d. "Artist and His Family" (detail) (Vaenius)	1·40	1·40
1819	5d. "The Arena" (Harold Weston) (horiz)	1·40	1·40
1820	5d. "Cat killing a Bird" (Picasso) (horiz)	1·40	1·40
1821	5d. "Cat and Butterfly" (Hokusai) (horiz)	1·40	1·40
1822	5d. "Winter: Cat on a Cushion" (Steinlen) (horiz)	1·40	1·40
1823	5d. "Rattown Tigers" (Prang) (horiz)	1·40	1·40
1824	5d. "Cat on the Floor" (Steinlen) (horiz)	1·40	1·40
1825	5d. "Cat and Kittens" (horiz)	1·40	1·40
1826	5d. "Cats looking over Fence" (Prang) (horiz)	1·40	1·40
1827	5d. "Little White Kittens into Mischief" (Ives) (horiz)	1·40	1·40
1828	5d. "Cat Bathing" (Hiroshige) (horiz)	1·40	1·40
1829	5d. "Playtime" (Tuck postcard) (horiz)	1·40	1·40
1830	5d. "Summer: Cat on a Balustrade" (Steinlen) (horiz)	1·40	1·40
MS1831	Two sheets, each 100×70 mm. (a) 20d. "The Graham Children" (detail) (William Hogarth). (b) 20d. "The Morning Rising" (detail) (Michel Lepicie) (horiz) Set of 2 sheets	9·00	10·00

227 Patas Monkey

1994. Monkeys. Multicoloured.

1832	1d. Type **227**	45	20
1833	1d.50 Collared mangabey	65	30
1834	2d. Black and white colobus	75	35
1835	5d. Mona monkey	1·25	1·10
1836	8d. Kirk's colobus	1·50	2·00
1837	10d. Vervet	1·75	2·25
1838	12d. Red colobus	2·00	2·50
1839	15d. Guinea baboon	2·25	2·75
MS1840	Two sheets, each 106×77 mm. (a) 25d. Head of Guinea baboon. (b) 25d. Head of Collared mangabey Set of 2 sheets	12·00	13·00

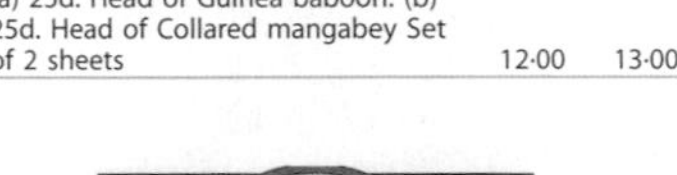

227a Yuri Gagarin (first cosmonaut)

1994. 25th Anniv of First Manned Moon Landing. Multicoloured.

1841	2d. Type **227a**	85	85
1842	2d. Valentina Tereshkova (first woman in Space)	85	85
1843	2d. Ham (first chimpanzee in Space)	85	85
1844	2d. Aleksei Leonov (first man to walk in Space)	85	85
1845	2d. Neil Armstrong (first man on Moon)	85	85
1846	2d. Svetlana Savitskaya (first woman to walk in Space)	85	85
1847	2d. Marc Garneau (first Canadian in Space)	85	85
1848	2d. Vladimir Komarov (first Soviet Space casualty)	85	85
1849	2d. Ulf Merbold (first German in Space)	85	85
MS1850	81×81 mm. 30d. "Apollo 11" crew at news conference	7·00	7·50

227b Daley Thompson (Great Britain) (decathlon), 1980 and 1984

1994. Centenary of International Olympic Committee. Gold Medal Winners. Multicoloured.

1851	1d.50 Type **227b**	50	40
1852	5d. Heide Marie Rosendohl (Germany) (long jump), 1972	1·25	1·50
MS1853	106×76 mm. 20d. Sweden (ice hockey), 1994	6·00	6·50

227c "Soema" (Dutch Sloop)

1994. 50th Anniv of D-Day. Multicoloured.

1854	50b. Type **227c**	90	50
1855	75b. H.M.S. "Belfast" (cruiser)	1·10	70
1856	1d. U.S.S. "Texas" (battleship)	1·25	80
1857	2d. "Georges Leygues" (French cruiser)	1·75	1·90
MS1858	105×76 mm. 20d. H.M.S. "Ramillies" (battleship) firing broadside	4·25	4·50

227d Soldiers on Horses

1994. "Philakorea '94" International Stamp Exhibition, Seoul. Screen paintings of the "Sanguozhi". Multicoloured.

1859	50b. Kungnakchon Hall (38×25 mm)	55	30
1860	1d. Type **227d**	65	75
1861	1d. Soldiers defending fort	65	75
1862	1d. Archers	65	75
1863	1d. General on horse	65	75
1864	1d. Three soldiers in battle	65	75
1865	1d. Army in retreat	65	75
1866	1d. Archers using fire arrows	65	75
1867	1d. Horsemen attacking fort	65	75
1868	1d. Women in summer house	65	75
1869	1d. Old man, child and house	65	75
1870	2d. Kettle of Popchusa (38×25 mm)	1·00	1·00
1871	3d. Pomun tourist resort (38×25 mm)	1·25	1·40
MS1872	98×68 mm. 20d. Tomb guardian, Taenung (38×25 mm)	5·00	6·00

228 "Mylothris rhodope"

1994. Butterflies. Multicoloured.

1873	1d. Type **228**	50	25
1874	1d.25 "Iolaphilus menas"	65	35
1875	2d. "Neptis nemetes"	75	40
1876	5d. "Antanartia delius"	1·25	1·10
1877	8d. "Acraea caecilia"	1·50	2·00
1878	10d. "Papilio nireus"	1·50	2·00
1879	12d. "Papilio menestheus"	1·75	2·50
1880	15d. "Iolaphilus julus"	2·00	2·75
MS1881	Two sheets, each 97×68 mm. (a) 25d. "Bematistes epaea". (b) 25d. "Colotis evippe" Set of 2 sheets	11·00	12·00

229 Bobby Charlton (England)

1994. World Cup Football Championship, U.S.A. (2nd issue). Multicoloured.

1882	50b. Type **229**	50	30
1883	75b. Ferenc Puskas (Hungary)	60	30
1884	1d. Paolo Rossi (Italy)	75	30
1885	2d. Biri Biri (Spain)	1·00	40
1886	3d. Diego Maradona (Argentina)	1·25	80
1887	8d. Johann Cruyff (Netherlands)	2·00	2·25
1888	10d. Franz Beckenbauer (Germany)	2·00	2·25
1889	15d. Thomas Dooley (U.S.A.)	2·25	3·25
MS1890	Two sheets, each 70×100 mm. (a) 25d. Pelé (Brazil). (b) 25d. Gordon Banks (England) Set of 2 sheets	12·00	12·00

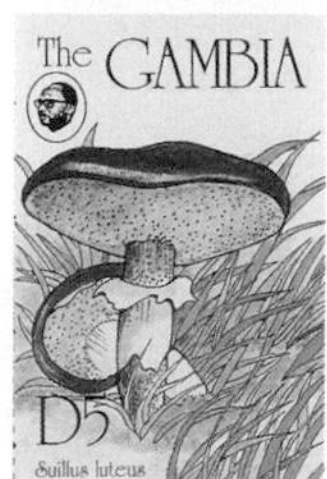

230 "Suillus luteus"

1994. Fungi. Multicoloured.

1891	5d. Type **230**	90	90
1892	5d. "Bolbitius vitellinus"	90	90
1893	5d. "Clitocybe nebularis"	90	90
1894	5d. "Omphalotus olearius"	90	90
1895	5d. "Auricularia auricula"	90	90
1896	5d. "Macrolepiota rhacodes"	90	90
1897	5d. "Volvariella volvacea"	90	90
1898	5d. "Psilocybe coprophila"	90	90
1899	5d. "Suillus granulatus"	90	90
1900	5d. "Agaricus campestris"	90	90
1901	5d. "Lepista nuda"	90	90
1902	5d. "Podaxis pistillaris"	90	90
1903	5d. "Oudemansiella radicata"	90	90
1904	5d. "Schizophyllum commune"	90	90
1905	5d. "Chlorophyllum molybdites"	90	90
1906	5d. "Hypholoma fasciculare"	90	90
1907	5d. "Mycena pura"	90	90
1908	5d. "Ganoderma lucidum"	90	90
MS1909	Two sheets, each 100×70 mm. (a) 20d. "Leucoagaricus naucinus". (b) 20d. "Cyathus striatus" Set of 2 sheets	11·00	11·00

Expectant Madonna with St. Joseph Anon., 15th Cent. French
Christmas 1994
THE GAMBIA 50b

230a "Expectant Madonna with St. Joseph" (French 15th-century)

1994. Christmas. Religious Paintings. Multicoloured.

1910	50b. Type **230a**	30	10
1911	75b. "Rest of the Holy Family" (Louis le Nain)	40	20
1912	1d. "Rest on the Flight into Egypt" (Antoine Watteau)	55	20
1913	2d. "Rest on the Flight into Egypt" (Jean-Honore Fragonard)	70	70
1914	2d. "Rest on the Flight into Egypt" (Francois Boucher)	70	70
1915	2d. "Noon" (Claude Lorrain)	70	70
1916	10d. "The Holy Family" (Nicolas Poussin)	2·50	3·25
1917	12d. "Mystical Marriage of St. Catherine" (Pierre-Francois Mignard)	2·50	3·50
MS1918	Two sheets, each 122×87 mm. (a) 25d. "Adoration of the Shepherds" (detail) (Mathieu le Nain). (b) 25d. "The Nativity by Torchlight" (detail) (Louis le Nain) Set of 2 sheets	10·00	11·00

231 Marilyn Monroe

1995. Marilyn Monroe (American entertainer) Commemoration. Multicoloured.

1919	4d. Type **231**	90	90
1920	4d. Wearing pendant necklace	90	90
1921	4d. In blue jacket	90	90
1922	4d. With sun-glasses on head	90	90
1923	4d. Looking over right arm	90	90
1924	4d. Wearing gold beret and jacket	90	90
1925	4d. Wearing hooped earrings	90	90
1926	4d. Smiling	90	90
1927	4d. Laughing	90	90
MS1928	Two sheets, each 70×100 mm. (a) 25d. Marilyn Monroe in red dress. (b) 25d. With pendant earrings Set of 2 sheets	8·50	9·00

232 Elvis as a Child

1995. 60th Birth Anniv of Elvis Presley (singer). Multicoloured.

1929	4d. Type **232**	1·10	90
1930	4d. Wearing white shirt	1·10	90
1931	4d. With his mother Gladys	1·10	90
1932	4d. With his wife Priscilla	1·10	90
1933	4d. With large gold medallion	1·10	90
1934	4d. In army uniform	1·10	90
1935	4d. In purple shirt	1·10	90
1936	4d. Wearing stetson	1·10	90
1937	4d. With his daughter Lisa-Marie	1·10	90

233 Pteranodon

1995. Prehistoric Animals. Multicoloured.

1938	2d. Type **233**	65	65
1939	2d. Archaeopteryx	65	65
1940	2d. Rhamphorhynchus	65	65
1941	2d. Ornithomimus	65	65
1942	2d. Stegosaurus	65	65
1943	2d. Heterodontosaurus	65	65
1944	2d. Lystrosaurus	65	65
1945	2d. Euoplocephalus	65	65
1946	2d. Coelophysis	65	65
1947	2d. Staurikosaurus	65	65
1948	2d. Giantoperis	65	65
1949	2d. Diarthrognathus	65	65
1950	3d. Archaeopteryx	65	65
1951	3d. Vangehuanosaurus	65	65
1952	3d. Celophysis	65	65
1953	3d. Plateosaurus	65	65
1954	3d. Baryonyx	65	65
1955	3d. Ornitholestes	65	65
1956	3d. Dryosaurus	65	65
1957	3d. Estemmenosuchus	65	65
1958	3d. Macroplata	65	65
1959	3d. Shonisaurus	65	65
1960	3d. Muraeonosaurus	65	65
1961	3d. Archelon	65	65
MS1962	Four sheets, each 100×70 mm. (a) 20d. Bactrosaurus. (b) 22d. Tyrannosaurus rex (vert). (c) 25d. Triceratops (vert). (d) 25d. Spinosaurus Set of 4 sheets	20·00	20·00

Nos. 1938/49 and 1950/61 respectively were printed together, se-tenant, forming composite designs.

234 Pig (Chinese characters in green)

1995. Chinese New Year ("Year of the Pig").

1963	**234**	3d. red, black and green	65	65
1964	-	3d. multicoloured (characters in blue)	65	65
1965	-	3d. orange, red and black (characters in white)	65	65
1966	-	3d. pink, red and black (characters in black)	65	65
MS1967		76×100 mm. 10d. mauve and red (three pigs)	2·25	2·50

DESIGNS: Nos. 1964/6, Different symbolic pigs.

235 Great Egret ("Great White Egret")

1995. Water Birds. Multicoloured.

1968	2d. Type **235**	80	60
1969	3d. Pintails	80	80
1970	3d. Fulvous whistling duck ("Fulvous Tree Duck")	80	80
1971	3d. Garganey	80	80
1972	3d. White-faced whistling duck ("White-faced Tree Duck")	80	80
1973	3d. White-backed duck	80	80
1974	3d. Egyptian goose	80	80
1975	3d. African pygmy geese ("Pygmy Goose")	80	80
1976	3d. Little bitterns	80	80
1977	3d. Common redshanks ("Redshank")	80	80
1978	3d. Ringed plovers	80	80
1979	3d. Black-winged stilt	80	80
1980	3d. Squacco herons	80	80
1981	8d. Hammerkop	2·00	2·50
1982	10d. Common shovelers ("Shoveler")	2·00	2·50
1983	12d. Crowned crane	2·25	2·75
MS1984	Two sheets, each 106×76 mm. (a) 25d. Ferruginous ducks. (b) 25d. Moorhen Set of 2 sheets	11·00	12·00

Nos. 1969/80 were printed together, se-tenant, forming a composite design.

236 Rural Road

1995. 20th Anniv of Economic Community of West African States (ECOWAS). Multicoloured.

1985	2d. Type **236**	50	25
1986	5d. Pres. Yayah Jammeh	1·25	1·50

237 Leather Back Turtle

1995. Marine Life. Multicoloured.

1987	3d. Type **237**	70	75
1988	3d. Tiger shark	70	75
1989	3d. Powder-blue surgeonfish	70	75
1990	3d. Emperor angelfish	70	75
1991	3d. Blue parrotfish	70	75
1992	3d. Clown triggerfish	70	75
1993	3d. Sea horses	70	75
1994	3d. Lionfish	70	75
1995	3d. Moray eel	70	75
1996	3d. Melon butterflyfish	70	75
1997	3d. Octopus	70	75
1998	3d. Common stingray	70	75
1999	8d. Stoplight parrotfish ("Multi-coloured Parrot Fish") (vert)	1·75	2·00
2000	8d. Stoplight parrotfish ("Sparisoma Viride") (vert)	1·75	2·00
2001	8d. Queen parrotfish (vert)	1·75	2·00
2002	8d. Bicoloured parrotfish (vert)	1·75	2·00
MS2003	Two sheets, each 98×68 mm. (a) 25d. Queen angelfish ("Angelicthys isabelita"). (b) 25d. Rock beauty ("Holacanthus ciliaris") Set of 2 sheets	13·00	13·00

Nos. 1987/98 and 1999/2002 respectively were printed together, se-tenant, forming composite designs.

No. 1991 is inscribed "BLUE PARRO FISH" in error.

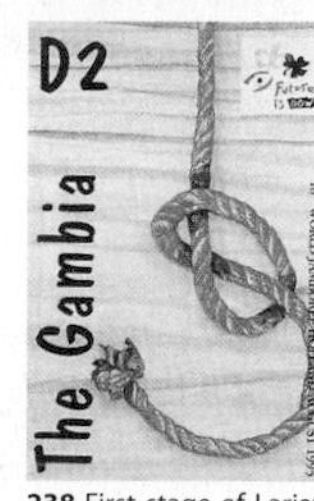

238 First stage of Lariat Knot

1995. 18th World Scout Jamboree, Netherlands. T 238 amd similar vert designs. Multicoloured.

MS2004	Two sheets, each 101×65 mm. (a) 2d. Type **238**; 2d. Second stage of knot with ropes end at right; 2d. Completed Lariat knot. (b) 5d. Completed Bowline knot; 10d. Second stage of knot; 12d. First stage of knot Set of 2 sheets	7·00	8·00
MS2005	Two sheets, each 72×102 mm. (a) 25d. Scout in rope using Hitch knot. (b) 25d. Injured scout supported by Bowline knot Set of 2 sheets	8·50	9·50

238a Peter Lawford

1995. 50th Anniv of End of Second World War in Europe. Film Stars. Black and red (Nos. 2008 and 2010) or multicoloured (others).

2006	3d. Type **238a**	1·25	1·00
2007	3d. Gene Tierney and Dana Andrews	1·25	1·00
2008	3d. Groucho and Harpo Marx	1·25	1·00
2009	3d. James Stewart	1·25	1·00
2010	3d. Chico and Zeppo Marx	1·25	1·00
2011	3d. Tyrone Power	1·25	1·00
2012	3d. Cary Grant and Ingrid Bergman	1·25	1·00
2013	3d. Veronica Lake	1·25	1·00
MS2014	105×75 mm. 25d. "A Lady Fights Back" film poster (vert)	7·50	8·50

No. 2012 is inscribed "BERMAN" in error.

238b Children in Class

1995. 50th Anniv of United Nations. Multicoloured.

2015	3d. Type **238b**	95	1·10
2016	3d. Teacher helping child	95	1·10
2017	3d. Child writing on blackboard	95	1·10
MS2018	104×74 mm. 25d. Nurse weighing baby	4·00	4·75

Nos. 2015/17 were printed together, se-tenant, forming a composite design.

238c Woman carrying Sack

1995. 50th Anniv of FAO Multicoloured.

No.	Description	Unused	Used
2019	3d. Type **238c**	95	1·10
2020	3d. Two men carrying sacks	95	1·10
2021	3d. Man carrying sack	95	1·10
MS2022	104×74 mm. 25d. Fisherman with net	3·75	4·75

Nos. 2019/21 were printed together, se-tenant, forming a composite design.

239 Paul Harris (founder) and Rotary Emblem

1995. 90th Anniv of Rotary International.

No.	Type	Description	Unused	Used
2023	**239**	15d. multicoloured	2·00	2·50
MS2024		75×105 mm. 20d. National flag and Rotary emblem	4·50	4·25

239a Queen Elizabeth the Queen Mother (pastel drawing)

1995. 95th Birthday of Queen Elizabeth the Queen Mother.

No.	Type	Description	Unused	Used
2025	**239a**	5d. brown, lt brn & blk	1·75	1·75
2026	-	5d. multicoloured	1·75	1·75
2027	-	5d. multicoloured	1·75	1·75
2028	-	5d. multicoloured	1·75	1·75
MS2029		102×126 mm. 25d. multicoloured	6·50	5·50

DESIGNS: Nos. 2026, Wearing blue hat and dress; 2027, At desk (oil painting); 2028, Wearing green hat and dress; **MS**2029 Wearing lavender hat and dress.

239b Fairey Firefly

1995. 50th Anniv of End of Second World War in the Pacific. Multicoloured.

No.	Description	Unused	Used
2030	5d. Type **239b**	1·25	1·25
2031	5d. Fairey Barracuda Mk III	1·25	1·25
2032	5d. Supermarine Seafire II	1·25	1·25
2033	5d. H.M.S. "Repulse" (battle cruiser)	1·25	1·25
2034	5d. H.M.S. "Illustrious" (aircraft carrier)	1·25	1·25
2035	5d. H.M.S. "Exeter" (cruiser)	1·25	1·25
MS2036	108×76 mm. 25d. Kamikaze aircraft heading for British "County" class cruiser	4·75	4·75

240 Kenichi Fukui (1981 Chemistry)

1995. Centenary of Nobel Prize Trust Fund. Past Prize Winners. Multicoloured.

No.	Description	Unused	Used
2037	2d. Type **240**	55	40
2038	3d. Gustav Stresemann (1929 Peace)	65	50
2039	5d. Thomas Mann (1929 Literature)	1·00	1·10
2040	5d. Marie Curie (1911 Chemistry)	1·00	1·10
2041	5d. Adolf Butenandt (1939 Chemistry)	1·00	1·10
2042	5d. Susumu Tonegwa (1987 Medicine)	1·00	1·10
2043	5d. Nelly Sachs (1966 Literature)	1·00	1·10
2044	5d. Yasunari Kawabata (1968 Literature)	1·00	1·10
2045	5d. Hideki Yukawa (1949 Physics)	1·00	1·10
2046	5d. Paul Ehrlich (1908 Medicine)	1·00	1·10
2047	5d. Bisaku Sato (1974 Peace)	1·00	1·10
2048	5d. Carl von Ossietsky (1935 Peace)	1·00	1·10
2049	8d. Albert Schweitzer (1952 Peace)	2·00	2·00
2050	12d. Leo Esaki (1973 Physics)	2·00	2·50
2051	15d. Lech Walesa (1983 Peace)	2·25	3·00
MS2052	75×105 mm. 25d. Willy Brandt (1971 Peace)	4·25	5·00

Nos. 2040/8 were printed together, se-tenant, forming a composite design.

No. 2048 is dated "1974" and No. 2051 inscribed "Lech Walsea", both in error.

241 Bruce Jenner (U.S.A.) (decathlon)

1995. Olympic Games, Atlanta (1996) (1st issue). Multicoloured.

No.	Description	Unused	Used
2053	1d. Type **241**	50	30
2054	1d.25 Greg Louganis (U.S.A.) (diving)	55	30
2055	1d.50 Michael Gross (Germany) (50 m butterfly)	55	30
2056	2d. Vasily Alexeev (Russia) (weightlifting)	60	30
2057	3d. Ewing (U.S.A.) and Corbalan (Spain) (basketball)	1·25	80
2058	3d. Stefano Cerioni (Italy) (fencing) (vert)	1·25	1·25
2059	3d. Alberto Cova (Italy) (10,000 m) (vert)	1·25	1·25
2060	3d. Mary Lou Retton (U.S.A.) (gymnastics) (vert)	1·25	1·25
2061	3d. Vladimir Artemov (Russia) (gymnastics) (vert)	1·25	1·25
2062	3d. Florence Griffith-Joyner (U.S.A.) (400 m relay) (vert)	1·25	1·25
2063	3d. Brazil (football) (vert)	1·25	1·25
2064	3d. Nelson Vails (U.S.A.) (sprint cycling) (vert)	1·25	1·25
2065	3d. Cheryl Miller (U.S.A.) (basketball) (vert)	1·25	1·25
2066	5d. U.S.A. v Brazil (men's volleyball)	1·50	1·75
2067	10d. Svenden (West Germany) and Fernandez (U.S.A.) (water polo)	2·00	2·25
2068	15d. Pertii Karppinen (Finland) (single sculls)	2·75	3·50
MS2069	Two sheets, each 71×101 mm. (a) 25d. Karen Stives (U.S.A.) (equestrian) (vert). (b) 25d. Edwin Moses (U.S.A.) (400 metre hurdles) (vert) Set of 2 sheets	10·00	11·00

No. 2059 is inscribed "Alberto Covo" and No. 2064 "Nelson Valis", both in error.

See also Nos. 2281/2303.

242 Rotary Emblem and Rotarians supporting School for the Deaf

1995. Local Rotary and Boy Scout Projects. Multicoloured.

No.	Description	Unused	Used
2070	2d. Type **242**	55	30
2071	5d. Scout wood badge course, 1980	1·25	1·40
2072	5d. Scout Commissioner M. J. E. Sambou (vert)	1·25	1·40

243 "Zantedeschia rehmannii"

1995. African Flowers. Multicoloured.

No.	Description	Unused	Used
2073	2d. Type **243**	55	45
2074	3d. "Kigelia africana"	60	65
2075	3d. "Hibiscus schizopelatus"	60	65
2076	3d. "Dombeya mastersii"	60	65
2077	3d. "Agapanthus orientalis"	60	65
2078	3d. "Strelitzia reginae"	60	65
2079	3d. "Spathodea campanulata"	60	65
2080	3d. "Rhodolaena bakeriana"	60	65
2081	3d. "Gazania rigens"	60	65
2082	3d. "Ixianthes retzioides"	60	65
2083	3d. "Canarina abyssinica"	60	65
2084	3d. "Nerine bowdenii"	60	65
2085	3d. "Zantedeschia aethiopica"	60	65
2086	3d. "Aframomum sceptrum"	60	65
2087	3d. "Schotia brachypetala"	60	65
2088	3d. "Catharanthus roseus"	60	65
2089	3d. "Protea grandiceps"	60	65
2090	3d. "Plumbago capensis"	60	65
2091	3d. "Uncarina grandidieri"	60	65
2092	5d. "Euadenia eminens"	1·10	1·25
2093	10d. "Passiflora vitifolia"	1·75	2·00
2094	15d. "Dietes grandiflora"	2·50	3·00
MS2095	Two sheets, each 106×75 mm. (a) 25d. "Eulophia quartiniana". (b) 25d. "Gloriosa simplex" Set of 2 sheets	9·50	10·00

Nos. 2074/82 and 2083/91 respectively were printed together, se-tenant, forming composite background designs.

244 Children outside Huts

1995. Kinderdorf International SOS Children's Villages. Multicoloured.

No.	Description	Unused	Used
2096	2d. Type **244**	50	50
2097	2d. Charity worker with children (vert)	50	50
2098	5d. Children at party	1·25	1·50

245 Roy Orbison

1995. History of Rock 'n' Roll Music. Multicoloured.

No.	Description	Unused	Used
2099	3d. Type **245**	1·00	85
2100	3d. Mick Jagger	1·00	85
2101	3d. Bruce Springsteen	1·00	85
2102	3d. Jimi Hendrix	1·00	85
2103	3d. Bill Haley	1·00	85
2104	3d. Gene Vincent	1·00	85
2105	3d. Buddy Holly	1·00	85
2106	3d. Jerry Lee Lewis	1·00	85
2107	3d. Chuck Berry	1·00	85
MS2108	116×86 mm. 25d. Elvis Presley	7·50	6·50

Nos. 2099/2107 were printed together, se-tenant, forming a composite design.

1995. Centenary of Cinema. As T 245 but depicting James Dean. Multicoloured.

No.	Description	Unused	Used
2109	3d. As a boy	85	75
2110	3d. On motorbike	85	75
2111	3d. With sports car and trophy	85	75
2112	3d. Close-up portrait	85	75
2113	3d. Facing left	85	75
2114	3d. Holding girl	85	75
2115	3d. "Rebel without a Cause" (film)	85	75
2116	3d. "Giant" (film)	85	75
2117	3d. "East of Eden" (film)	85	75
MS2118	116×86 mm. 25d. James Dean in "Rebel without a Cause"	4·50	4·50

Nos. 2109/17 were printed together, se-tenant, forming a composite design.

245a "Madonna and Child" (Maria della Vallicella)

1995. Christmas. Religious Paintings. Multicoloured.

No.	Description	Unused	Used
2119	75b. Type **245a**	55	15
2120	1d. "Madonna" (Giotto)	55	15
2121	2d. "The Flight into Egypt" (Luca Giordano)	75	25
2122	5d. "The Epiphany" (Bordone)	1·75	1·25
2123	8d. "Virgin and Child" (Burgkmair)	2·50	3·00
2124	12d. "Madonna" (Bellini)	2·75	3·75
MS2125	Two sheets, each 101×127 mm. (a) 25d. "Christ" (Carpaccio). (b) 25d. "Madonna and Child" (Rubens) Set of 2 sheets	12·00	13·00

246 Terminal Building

1995. Opening of New Terminal Building, Banjul International Airport.

No.	Type	Description	Unused	Used
2126	**246**	1d. multicoloured	55	10
2127	**246**	2d. multicoloured	70	25
2128	**246**	3d. multicoloured	90	75
2129	**246**	5d. multicoloured	1·40	1·60

247 UPU Emblem

1995. 121st Anniv of Universal Postal Union.

No.	Type	Description	Unused	Used
2130	**247**	1d. black and violet	40	10
2131	**247**	2d. black and blue	60	25
2132	**247**	3d. black and red	80	60
2133	**247**	7d. black and green	1·75	2·50

248 Commerson's Dolphin

1995. Whales and Dolphins. Multicoloured.

No.	Description	Unused	Used
2134	2d. Type **248**	50	25
2135	3d. Bryde's whale	75	75
2136	3d. Sperm whale	75	75
2137	3d. Humpback whale	75	75
2138	3d. Sei whale	75	75
2139	3d. Blue whale	75	75
2140	3d. Grey whale	75	75
2141	3d. Fin whale	75	75
2142	3d. Killer whale	75	75
2143	3d. Right whale	75	75
2144	3d. Northern right whale dolphin	75	75
2145	3d. Spotted dolphin	75	75
2146	3d. Common dolphin	75	75
2147	3d. Pacific white-sided dolphin	75	75
2148	3d. Atlantic humpbacked dolphin	75	75
2149	3d. Atlantic white-sided dolphin	75	75
2150	3d. White-beaked dolphin	75	75
2151	3d. Striped dolphin	75	75
2152	3d. Risso's dolphin	75	75
2153	5d. Narwhal	1·00	1·00
2154	8d. True's beaked whale	1·50	1·75
2155	10d. Rough-toothed dolphin	1·75	2·00
MS2156	Two sheets, each 110×80 mm. (a) 25d. Beluga and clymene dolphin. (b) 25d. Bowhead whale and blue shark (vert) Set of 2 sheets	11·00	12·00

Nos. 2135/43 and 2144/52 respectively were printed together, se-tenant, forming composite designs.

249 Big Pete as Seminole with Alligator

1995. Disney Cowboys and Indians. Walt Disney cartoon characters. Multicoloured.

No.	Description	Unused	Used
2157	15b. Type **249**	20	20
2158	20b. Donald Duck as Chinook fisherman	20	20
2159	25b. Huey, Dewey and Louie as Blackfoot braves	20	20

2160 30b. Minnie Mouse shooting bottles 20 20
2161 40b. Donald riding bull 20 20
2162 50b. Mickey Mouse branding steer 20 20
2163 2d. Donald in Tlingit mask 70 25
2164 3d. Mickey bronco-busting 80 40
2165 12d. Grandma Duck with lasso 2·75 2·75
2166 15d. Mickey in Pomo canoe 3·00 3·25
2167 15d. Goofy as ranch hand 3·00 3·25
2168 20d. Goofy and Minnie with Navaho weaving 3·25 3·50
MS2169 Four sheets, each 127×102 mm. (a) 25d. Minnie as Massachusetts squaw. (b) 25d. Minnie as Shoshoni squaw (vert). (c) 25d. Pluto singing to the Moon (vert). (d) 25d. Donald and steer (vert) Set of 4 sheets 19·00 20·00

250 Rat

1996. Chinese New Year ("Year of the Rat").
2170 **250** 63b. multicoloured 50 25
2171 - 75b. multicoloured 60 30
2172 - 1d.50 multicoloured 1·10 75
2173 - 4d. multicoloured 2·25 2·50
MS2174 84×88 mm. 3d. × 4 As Nos. 2170/3 2·75 3·00
MS2175 76×106 mm. 10d. red, violet and brown 1·75 2·25
DESIGNS: 75b. to 10d. Different stylized rats.

251 "Don Tiburcio Perez y Cuervo" (detail) (Goya)

1996. 125th Anniv of Metropolitan Museum of Art, New York. Multicoloured.
2176-2183 4d.×8 (Type **251**: "Jean Antoine Moltedo" (Ingres); "The Letter" (Corot); "General Etienne Gerard" (David); "Portrait of the Artist" (Van Gogh); "Joseph Henri Altes" (Degas); "Princess de Broglie" (Ingres); "Lady at the Table" (Cassatt)) 7·00 7·00
2184-2191 4d.×8 ("Broken Eggs" (Greuze); "Johann Joachim Winckleman" (Mengs); "Col. George Coussmaker" (Reynolds); "Self Portrait with Pupils" (Labille-Guiard); "Courtesan holding a Fan" (Utamaro); "The Woodgatherers" (Gainsborough); "Mrs Grace Elliott" (Gainsborough); "The Drummond Children" (Raeburn)) 7·00 7·00
2192-2199 4d.×8 ("Sunflowers" (Monet); "Still Life with Pansies" (Fantin-Latour); "Parisians enjoying the Parc" (Monet); "La Mere Larcheveque" (Pissarro); "Rue de L'Epicerie, Rouen" (Pissarro); "The Abduction of Rebecca" (Delacroix); "Daughter, Abraham- Ben-Chimol" (Delacroix); "Christ on Lake of Gennesaret" (Delacroix)) 7·00 7·00
2200-2207 4d.×8 ("Henry Prince of Wales" (Peake); "Saints Peter, Martha, Mary and Leonard" (Correggio); "Marriage Feast at Cana" (Juan de Flandes); "Portrait of One of Wedigh Family" (Holbein); "Guillaume Bude" (Clouet); "Portrait of a Cardinal" (El Greco); "St. Jerome as a Cardinal" (El Greco); "Portrait of a Man" (Titian)) 7·00 7·00
MS2208 Four sheets, each 95×70 mm, containing horiz designs, 81×53 mm. (a) 25d. "Israelites gathering Manna in the Desert" (Rubens). (b) 25d. "Henry IV at the Battle of Ivry" (Rubens). (c) 25d. "The Creation of the World and the Expulsion from Paradise" (Giovanni di Paolo). (d) 25d. "The Harvesters" (Bruegel) Set of 4 sheets 18·00 20·00

252 Fire-eater

1996. Fire-eating in the Gambia.
2209 **252** 1d. multicoloured 35 15
2210 - 2d. multicoloured 55 30
2211 - 3d. multicoloured 70 60
2212 - 7d. multicoloured 1·50 2·00
DESIGNS: 2d. to 7d. Various fire-eating scenes, the 2d. and 7d. being horiz.

253 Bruce Lee

1996. Bruce Lee (film star) Commemoration. Different portraits. Multicoloured.
2213 3d. Wearing cap and mask 70 60
2214 3d. Type **253** 70 60
2215 3d. Facing left 70 60
2216 3d. Wearing blue jumper and with hand to face 70 60
2217 3d. Wearing buff jacket 70 60
2218 3d. Wearing brown jacket (Chinese characters in brown) 70 60
2219 3d. Wearing black shirt (Chinese characters in lilac) 70 60
2220 3d. Wearing white shirt 70 60
2221 3d. Bare-chested 70 60
MS2222 Two sheets. (a) 140×85 mm. 5d. Deng Xiao Ping (Chinese leader) (78×51 mm). (b) 70×100 mm. 25d. Bruce Lee Set of 2 sheets 9·50 9·50

254 Donald Duck and Big Pete giving Blood

1996. Voluntary Activities. Walt Disney cartoon characters. Multicoloured.
2223 1d. Type **254** 35 30
2224 4d. Daisy Duck and Minnie Mouse adopting pets 1·00 75
2225 5d. Goofy as one-man band raising money for the needy 1·25 85
2226 10d. Goofy teaching outdoor skills 2·00 2·25
2227 15d. Minnie teaching reading 2·50 3·00
2228 20d. Donald, Mickey and Goofy as volunteer fire fighters 2·50 3·00
MS2229 Two sheets, each 127×102 mm. (a) 25d. Minnie counting whales. (b) 25d. Mickey planting roadside sapling Set of 2 sheets 8·50 9·00

255 Roan Antelope

1996. Wildlife. Multicoloured.
2230 3d. Type **255** 60 65
2231 3d. Lesser bushbaby 60 65
2232 3d. Black leopard 60 65
2233 3d. Guinea forest red colobus 60 65
2234 3d. Kobs 60 65
2235 3d. Common eland 60 65
2236 4d. African buffalo 65 70
2237 4d. Herd of topi 65 70
2238 4d. Vervet 65 70
2239 4d. Hippopotamuses 65 70
2240 4d. Waterbuck 65 70
2241 4d. Senegal chameleon 65 70
2242 4d. Western green mamba 65 70
2243 4d. Slender-snouted crocodile 65 70
2244 4d. Adanson's mud turtle 65 70
2245 15d. African civet 2·00 2·50
MS2246 Two sheets, each 98×68 mm. (a) 25d. Lion (vert). (b) 25d. Chimpanzee (vert) Set of 2 sheets 7·50 8·00
Nos. 2230/5 and 2236/44 respectively were printed together, se-tenant, Nos. 2236/44 forming a composite design.

255a Queen Elizabeth II

1996. 70th Birthday of Queen Elizabeth II. Mult.
2247 8d. Type **255a** 1·60 1·60
2248 8d. Wearing tiara facing right 1·60 1·60
2249 8d. Wearing tiara facing left 1·60 1·60
MS2250 125×104 mm. 25d. Buckingham Palace (horiz) 5·50 5·50

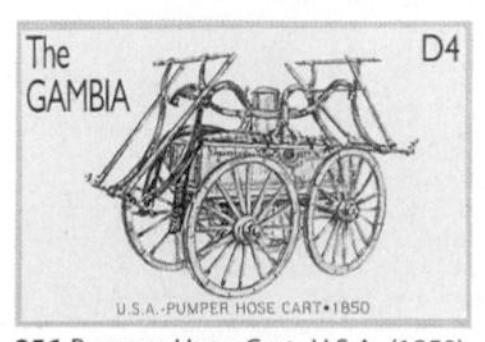

256 Pumper Hose Cart, U.S.A. (1850)

1996. Classic Road Transport. Fire Engines (Nos. 2251/6) or Cars (Nos. 2257/62). Multicoloured.
2251 4d. Type **256** 75 75
2252 4d. Steam fire engine, U.S.A. (1891) 75 75
2253 4d. Lausitzer engine, Germany (1864) 75 75
2254 4d. Chemical engine, Great Britain (1902) 75 75
2255 4d. Motor fire engine, Great Britain (1904) 75 75
2256 4d. Colonia No. 5 engine, Germany (1860) 75 75
2257 4d. Fiat Tipo 510, Italy (1912) 75 75
2258 4d. Toyota Model 4B Phaeton, Japan (1936) 75 75
2259 4d. Nag C4B, Germany (1924) 75 75
2260 4d. Cadillac, U.S.A. (1903) 75 75
2261 4d. Bentley, Great Britain (1925) 75 75
2262 4d. Renault Model AX, France (1909) 75 75
MS2263 Two sheets. (a) 76×58 mm. 25d. Amoskeag Steamer (fire engine), U.S.A. (1865). (b) 81×59 mm. 25d. Mitsubishi Model A, Japan (1917) Set of 2 sheets 8·00 8·50

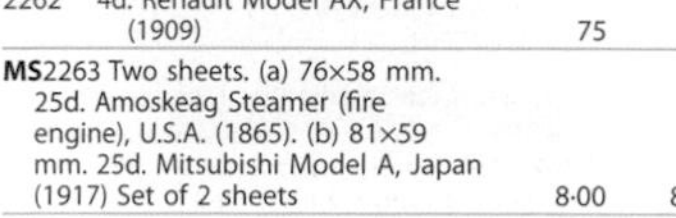
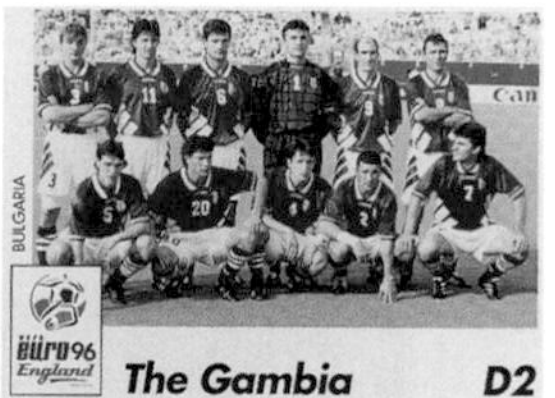

257 Bulgarian Team

1996. European Football Championship, England. Multicoloured.
2264 2d. Type **257** 45 45
2265 2d. Croatian team 45 45
2266 2d. Czech Republic team 45 45
2267 2d. Danish team 45 45
2268 2d. English team 45 45
2269 2d. French team 45 45
2270 2d. German team 45 45
2271 2d. Dutch team 45 45
2272 2d. Italian team 45 45
2273 2d. Portuguese team 45 45
2274 2d. Rumanian team 45 45
2275 2d. Russian team 45 45
2276 2d. Scottish team 45 45
2277 2d. Spanish team 45 45
2278 2d. Swiss team 45 45
2279 2d. Turkish team 45 45

MS2280 Sixteen sheets. (a) 115×85 mm. 25d. Danish team celebrating (43×28 mm). (b) 85×115 mm. 25d. Ruud Gullit (Netherlands) (28×43 mm). (c) 85×115 mm. 25d. Gary McAllister (Scotland) (28×43 mm). (d) 115×85 mm. 25d. Oleg Salenko (Russia) (28×43 mm). (e) 85×115 mm. 25d. Hami Mandirali (Turkey) (28×43 mm). (f) 85×115 mm. 25d. Hristo Stoitchkov (Bulgaria) (28×43 mm). (g) 115×85 mm. 25d. European Championship Trophy (28×43 mm). (h) 85×115 mm. 25d. Davor Suker (Croatia) (28×43 mm). (i) 115×85 mm. 25d. Jurgen Klinsmann (Germany) (43×28 mm). (j) 85×115 mm. 25d. Juan Goikoetxea (Spain) (28×43 mm). (k) 85×115 mm. 25d. Eusebio (Portugal) (28×43 mm). (l) 115×85 mm. 25d. Bryan Robson (England) (28×43 mm). (m) 85×115 mm. 25d. Roberto Baggio (Italy) (28×43 mm). (n) 85×115 mm. 25d. Christophe Ohrel (Switzerland) (28×43 mm). (o) 85×115 mm. 25d. Pavel Hapal (Czech Republic) (43×28 mm). (p) 85×115 mm. 25d. Gheorge Hagi (Rumania) (28×43 mm). P 14 Set of 16 sheets 65·00 65·00

258 Ray Ewry (U.S.A.) (standing high jump), 1912

1996. Olympic Games, Atlanta (2nd issue). Previous Gold Medal Winners. Multicoloured.
2281 1d. Type **258** 25 15
2282 2d. Fanny Durack (Australia) (100 m freestyle swimming), 1912 35 20
2283 3d. Fu Mingxia (China) (platform diving), 1992 40 45
2284 3d. H. Henkel (Germany) (high jump), 1992 40 45
2285 3d. Spanish team (soccer), 1992 40 45
2286 3d. Jackie Joyner-Kersee (U.S.A.) (heptathlon), 1988 and 1992 40 45
2287 3d. T. Gutsu (Russia) (gymnastics), 1992 40 45
2288 3d. M. Johnson (U.S.A.) (400 m running), 1992 40 45
2289 3d. Lin Li (China) (200 m medley swimming), 1992 40 45
2290 3d. G. Devers (U.S.A.) (100 m running), 1992 40 45
2291 3d. Michael Powell (U.S.A.) (long jump), 1992 40 45
2292 3d. Japanese volleyball team, 1964 40 45
2293 3d. Li Neng (China) (floor exercises), 1984 40 45
2294 3d. S. Bubka (U.S.S.R.) (pole vault), 1988 40 45
2295 3d. Nadia Comaneci (Romania) (gymnastics), 1976 40 45
2296 3d. Edwin Moses (U.S.A.) (400 m hurdles), 1984 40 45
2297 3d. Victor Scherbo (Russia) (gymnastics), 1992 40 45
2298 3d. Evelyn Ashford (U.S.A.) (100 m running), 1984 40 45
2299 3d. Mohammed Ali (U.S.A.) (light heavyweight boxing), 1960 40 45
2300 3d. Carl Lewis and C. Smith (U.S.A.) (400 m relay), 1984 40 45
2301 5d. Stockholm Olympic arena, 1912 70 75
2302 10d. Jim Thorpe (U.S.A.) (decathalon and pentathlon), 1912 1·25 1·40
MS2303 Two sheets, each 100×70 mm. 25d. Michael Gross (Germany) (butterfly swimming), 1984 and 1988 (horiz). 25d. Ulrike Meyfarth (Germany) (high jump), 1972 and 1984 Set of 2 sheets 9·50 10·00

258a Boy holding Shoes

1996. 50th Anniv of UNICEF Multicoloured.
2304 63b. Type **258a** 15 15

2305 3d. Girl being inoculated 40 35
2306 8d. Boy holding ladle 1·00 1·25
2307 10d. Child with blanket 1·25 1·40
MS2308 105×75 mm. 25d. Boy being inoculated (horiz) 3·25 3·75

259 Roman Officer and Pillar of Absalom

1996. 3000th Anniv of Jerusalem. Multicoloured.
2309 1d.50 Type **259** 45 25
2310 2d. Turk and Gate of Mercy 50 30
2311 3d. Ancient Greek and Church of the Holy Sepulchre 60 40
2312 10d. Modern Hasidic Jew at Wailing Wall 1·75 1·75
MS2313 100×70 mm. 25d. City coat of arms (vert) 4·25 4·25

259a Glenn Miller

1996. Centenary of Radio. Entertainers. Mult.
2314 1d. Type **259a** 20 20
2315 4d. Louis Armstrong 60 45
2316 5d. Nat "King" Cole 70 75
2317 10d. The Andrew Sisters 1·25 1·50
MS2318 105×74 mm. 25d. President Truman 3·25 3·75
No. 2314 is inscribed "Glen Miller" in error.

260 Jacqueline Kennedy Onassis in Wedding Dress

1996. Famous People of the 20th Century. Multicoloured.
2319 5d. Type **260** 75 75
2320 5d. Jaqueline Kennedy and White House 75 75
2321 5d. Jaqueline Kennedy wearing pink hat 75 75
2322 5d. Jaqueline Kennedy and motor yacht 75 75
2323 5d. Jacqueline Kennedy wearing red jumper 75 75
2324 5d. Jacqueline Kennedy and horse 75 75
2325 5d. Jacqueline Kennedy on book 75 75
2326 5d. Jacqueline Kennedy in blue dress and three rows of pearls 75 75
2327 5d. Jacqueline Kennedy and corner of fountain 75 75
2328 5d. President John Kennedy 75 75
2329 5d. Jacqueline Kennedy (inscr in capitals) 75 75
2330 5d. Willy Brandt 75 75
2331 5d. Marilyn Monroe 75 75
2332 5d. Mao Tse-tung 75 75
2333 5d. Sung Ching Ling 75 75
2334 5d. Charles De Gaulle 75 75
2335 5d. Marlene Dietrich 75 75
MS2336 105×74 mm. 25d. Jacqueline Kennedy (different) 3·25 3·75
No. 2330 is inscr "WILLIE BRANDT", No. 2331 "MARYLYN MONROE" and No. 2332 "MAO TSE TONG", all in error.

261 Richard Petty's 1969 Ford

1996. Richard Petty (stock car driver) Commem. Multicoloured.
2337 5d. Type **261** 90 80
2338 5d. Richard Petty 90 80
2339 5d. Dodge Magnum, 1978 90 80
2340 5d. Pontiac, 1987 90 80
2341 5d. Pontiac, 1989 90 80
2342 5d. Dodge Daytona, 1975 90 80
MS2343 104×74 mm. 25d. Plymouth, 1972 (84×27 mm) 4·00 4·25

1996. Results of European Football Championship, England. As Nos. 2265/6, 2268, 2270, 2272, 2275 and MS2280 (d, h, i, l, m, o), but each additionally inscribed with date and match result. Multicoloured.
2344 2d. Croatian team ("23/6/96 Germany 2, Croatia 1") 45 45
2345 2d. Czech Republic team ("9/6/96 Germany 2, Czech Rep. 0") 45 45
2346 2d. English team ("26/6/96 Germany 6, England 5") 45 45
2347 2d. German team ("30/6/96 Germany 2, Czech Rep. 1") 45 45
2348 2d. Italian team ("19/6/96 Germany 0, Italy 0") 45 45
2349 2d. Russian team ("16/6/96 Germany 3, Russia 0") 45 45
MS2350 Six sheets. (a) 114×84 mm. 25d. Oleg Salenko (Russia) (28×43 mm) ("16/6/96 Germany 3, Russia 0"). (b) 84×114 mm. 25d. Davor Suker (Croatia) (28×43 mm) ("23/6/96 Germany 2, Croatia 1"). (c) 114×84 mm. 25d. Jurgen Klinsmann (Germany) (43×28 mm) ("Final 30/6/96 Germany 2, Czech Republic 1"). (d) 114×84 mm. 25d. Bryan Robson (England) (28×43 mm) ("26/6/96 Germany 6 England 5"). (e) 84×114 mm. 25d. Roberto Baggio (Italy) (28×43 mm) ("19/6/96 Germany 0 Italy 0"). (f) 84×114 mm. 25d. Pavel Hapal (Czech Rep) (43×28 mm) ("9/6/96 Germany 2 Czech Republic 0") Set of 6 sheets 24·00 26·00

262 Elvis Presley with Microphone

1996. Elvis Presley Commemoration. Different Portraits. Multicoloured.
2351 5d. Type **262** 90 90
2352 5d. In dinner jacket 90 90
2353 5d. In Mexican outfit 90 90
2354 5d. Wearing blue jumper 90 90
2355 5d. In leather jacket 90 90
2356 5d. Wearing lei 90 90

263 Bob Dylan

1996. Rock and Roll Legends. Bob Dylan.
2357 **263** 5d. multicoloured 1·25 1·00

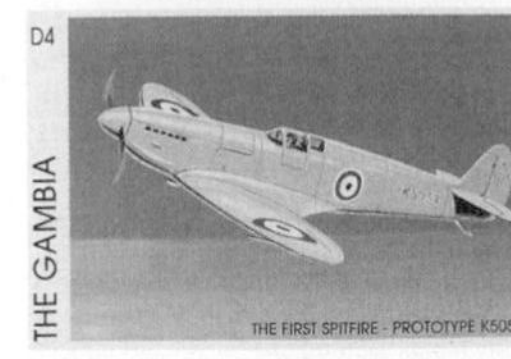

264 Supermarine Spitfire Prototype K5054

1996. 65th Anniv of Britain's Victory in Schneider Trophy Air Race. Multicoloured.
2358 4d. Type **264** 80 80
2359 4d. First production Spitfire K9787 80 80
2360 4d. Spitfire Mk 1A in Battle of Britain 80 80
2361 4d. Spitfire LF Mk IXE with D-Day markings 80 80
2362 4d. Spitfire Mk XII (first with "Griffon" engine) 80 80
2363 4d. Spitfire Mk XIVC with jungle markings 80 80
2364 4d. Spitfire XIX of Royal Swedish Air Force 80 80
2365 4d. Spitfire Mk XIX 80 80
2366 4d. Spitfire F Mk 22/24 (final variant) 80 80
2367 4d. Spitfire Mk XIX of Royal Swedish Air Force (from below) 80 80
2368 4d. Spitfire Mk VB of United States Army Air Corps 80 80
2369 4d. Spitfire Mk VC of French Air Force 80 80
2370 4d. Spitfire Mk VB of Soviet Air Force 80 80
2371 4d. Spitfire Mk IXE of Netherlands East Indies Air Force 80 80
2372 4d. Spitfire Mk IXE of Israeli Air Force 80 80
2373 4d. Spitfire Mk VIII of Royal Australian Air Force 80 80
2374 4d. Siptfire Mk VB of Turkish Air Force 80 80
2375 4d. Spitfire Mk XI of Royal Danish Air Force 80 80
MS2376 Two sheets, each 97×67 mm. (a) 25d. Supermarine S 6B S1595 seaplane taking off (42×29 mm). (b) 25d. Supermarine S 6B S1595 in flight (42×29 mm) Set of 2 sheets 10·00 10·00

265 Egyptian Plover

1996. Birds. Multicoloured.
2377 50b. Type **265** 30 20
2378 63b. Painted-snipe 35 20
2379 75b. Golden-breasted bunting 35 20
2380 1d. Bateleur 40 25
2381 1d.50 Didric cuckoo 50 30
2382 2d. Turtle dove ("European Turtle Dove") 55 30
2383 3d. Village weaver 65 35
2384 4d. European roller 75 50
2385 5d. Cut-throat weaver ("Cut-throat") 80 60
2386 10d. Hoopoe 1·75 1·50
2387 15d. White-faced scops owl 2·00 2·00
2388 20d. Narina's trogon 2·25 2·50
2389 25d. Lesser pied kingfisher 2·75 3·00
2390 30d. Common kestrel 3·25 3·50
2391 40d. Temminck's courser 3·75 4·25
2392 50d. European bee eater 4·50 5·00
2392a 100d. Green-winged teal 8·00 9·50
No. 2388 is inscribed "TROGAN" in error.

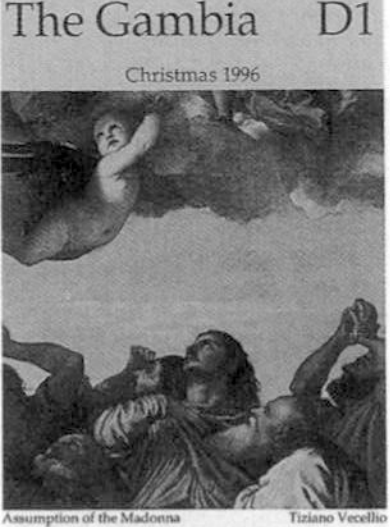

265a "Assumption of the Madonna" (detail)

1996. Christmas. Religious Paintings.
2393 **265a** 1d. multicoloured 25 10
2394 - 1d.50 multicoloured 30 15
2395 - 2d. multicoloured 35 20
2396 - 3d. multicoloured 50 30
2397 - 10d. multicoloured 1·50 1·75
2398 - 15d. multicoloured 2·00 2·50
MS2399 Two sheets, each 76×106 mm. (a) 25d. deep brown, black and brown ("Adoration of the Magi" (Filippo Lippi)) (horiz). (b) 25d. red, black and rose ("Virgin and Child with Infant St. John" (Raphael)) Set of 2 sheets 8·50 9·50
DESIGNS: 1d.50 to 15d. Different details of "Assumption of the Madonna" (Tiziano Vecellio).
No. **MS**2399a is inscribed "Flippo Lippi" in error.

266 Sylvester Stallone as Rocky Balboa

1996. 20th Anniv of Rocky (film). Sheet 143×182 mm.
MS2400 10d.×3 multicoloured 4·75 5·00

267 Ox

1997. Chinese New Year ("Year of the Ox").
2401 **267** 63b. multicoloured 40 25
2402 - 75b. multicoloured 40 25
2403 - 1d.50 multicoloured 60 50
2404 - 4d. multicoloured 1·25 1·50
MS2405 84×68 mm. 3d. × 4. As Nos. 2401/4 2·50 2·75
MS2406 76×106 mm. 10d. multicoloured (ox and sleeping peasant) (39½×24½ mm) 1·75 2·25
DESIGNS: 75b. to 4d. Symbolic oxen.

268 "Arch 22" Monument

1997. Economic Development. Multicoloured.
2407 63b. Type **268** 20 15
2408 1d. Tractor (horiz) 25 15
2409 1d.50 Man planting rice 30 20
2410 2d. As Type **268**, but with white panel at top 40 25
2411 3d. Model of Banjul International Airport terminal building (horiz) 75 60
2412 5d. Chamoi Bridge (horiz) 90 1·00
MS2413 Two sheets. (a) 106×76 mm. 20d. Workers in rice field (horiz). (b) 76×106 mm. 25d. As Type **268** Set of 2 sheets 7·00 8·00

269 Monkey King extinguishing Fire on Flame Mountain

1997. Mickey Mouse's Journey to the West. Disney cartoon characters. Multicoloured.
2414 2d. Type **269** 70 70
2415 2d. Demon Ox and Monkey King fighting 70 70
2416 2d. Mickey, Donald, Monkey King and Master San Tsang 70 70
2417 2d. Fighting the Spider Demon 70 70
2418 2d. Fighting the White Skeleton Demon 70 70
2419 2d. The real and the fake Monkey King 70 70
2420 3d. Monkey King trapped in furnace 70 70
2421 3d. Monkey King with magic weapon 70 70
2422 3d. Type **269** 70 70
2423 3d. At the Gate of South Heaven 70 70
2424 3d. Tasting the celestial peaches 70 70
2425 3d. Monkey King rescued from Five-Finger Mountain 70 70

MS2426	Four sheets, each 134×109 mm. (a) 5d. Mickey and Donald with Master San Tsang (vert). (b) 10d. Monkey King, Mickey and monkeys. (c) 10d. Monkey King, Mickey and tortoise (vert). (d) 15d. Mickey and Minnie with Buddhist scriptures Set of 4 sheets	14·00	14·00

270 Jackie Chan

1997. "HONG KONG '97" International Stamp Exhibition. Jackie Chan (film star). Multicoloured.

2427	4d. Type **270**	75	75
2428	4d. Wearing red jacket	75	75
2429	4d. In open-necked shirt	75	75
2430	4d. Bare-chested	75	75
2431	4d. Wearing black jacket	75	75
2432	4d. Wearing black and white spotted shirt	75	75
2433	4d. Wearing white T-shirt and red anorak	75	75
2434	4d. Wearing white sleeveless T-shirt	75	75
MS2435	76×106 mm. 25d. Jackie Chan in action (horiz)	4·50	4·75

271 Clouded Leopard

1997. Endangered Species. Multicoloured.

2436	1d.50 Type **271**	40	40
2437	1d.50 Audouin's gull	40	40
2438	1d.50 Leatherback turtle	40	40
2439	1d.50 White-eared pheasant	40	40
2440	1d.50 Kakapo	40	40
2441	1d.50 Right whale	40	40
2442	1d.50 Black-footed ferret	40	40
2443	1d.50 Dwarf lemur	40	40
2444	1d.50 Palawan peacock-pheasant ("Peacock-Pheasant")	40	40
2445	1d.50 Brown hyena	40	40
2446	1d.50 Cougar	40	40
2447	1d.50 Gharial	40	40
2448	1d.50 Monk seal	40	40
2449	1d.50 Mountain gorilla	40	40
2450	1d.50 Blyth's tragopan	40	40
2451	1d.50 Malayan tapir	40	40
2452	1d.50 Black rhinoceros	40	40
2453	1d.50 Polar bear	40	40
2454	1d.50 Red colobus	40	40
2455	1d.50 Tiger	40	40
2456	1d.50 Arabian oryx	40	40
2457	1d.50 Baiji	40	40
2458	1d.50 Ruffed lemur	40	40
2459	1d.50 California condor	40	40
2460	1d.50 Blue-headed quail dove	40	40
2461	1d.50 Numbat	40	40
2462	1d.50 Congo peafowl ("Congo Peacock")	40	40
2463	1d.50 White uakari	40	40
2464	1d.50 Eskimo curlew	40	40
2465	1d.50 Gouldian finch	40	40
2466	1d.50 Coelacanth	40	40
2467	1d.50 Toucan barbet	40	40
2468	1d.50 Snow leopard	40	40
2469	1d.50 Queen Alexandra's birdwing	40	40
2470	1d.50 Dalmatian pelican	40	40
2471	1d.50 Chaco tortoise	40	40
2472	1d.50 Mekong catfish	40	40
2473	1d.50 Helmeted hornbill	40	40
2474	1d.50 White-eyed river martin	40	40
2475	1d.50 Fluminense swallowtail	40	40
MS2476	Three sheets, each 103×72 mm. (a) 25d. Giant panda. (b) 25d. Humpback whale. (c) 25d. Manchurian crane ("Japanese Crane") Set of 3 sheets	13·00	13·00

272 Monkey

1997. "The Jungle Book" by Rudyard Kipling. Multicoloured.

2477	3d. Type **272**	60	60
2478	3d. Baloo (bear)	60	60
2479	3d. Elephant	60	60
2480	3d. Monkey and temple	60	60
2481	3d. Bagheera (panther)	60	60
2482	3d. Buffalo	60	60
2483	3d. Mandrill	60	60
2484	3d. Shere Khan (tiger)	60	60
2485	3d. Rama (wolf)	60	60
2486	3d. Kaa (cobra)	60	60
2487	3d. Mongoose	60	60
2488	3d. Mowgli	60	60

Nos. 2477/88 were printed together, se-tenant, with the backgrounds forming a composite design.

273 "Polyporus squamosus"

1997. Fungi. Multicoloured.

2489	1d. Type **273**	35	25
2490	3d. "Armillaria tabescens"	65	40
2491	4d. "Amanita caesarea" (vert)	75	80
2492	4d. "Lepiota procera" (vert)	75	80
2493	4d. "Hygrophorus psittacinus" (vert)	75	80
2494	4d. "Russula xerampelina" (vert)	75	80
2495	4d. "Laccaria amethystina" (vert)	75	80
2496	4d. "Coprinus micaceus" (vert)	75	80
2497	4d. "Boletus edulis" (vert)	75	80
2498	4d. "Morchella esculenta" (vert)	75	80
2499	4d. "Otidea auricula" (vert)	75	80
2500	5d. "Collybia velutipes"	85	85
2501	10d. "Sarcoscypha coccinea"	1·40	1·50
MS2502	76×106 mm. 25d. "Volvariella bombycina"	5·50	5·50

273a Cloister, Horyu-ji, Japan

1997. 50th Anniv of UNESCO Multicoloured.

2503	1d. Type **273a**	30	25
2504	2d. Great Wall, China	50	35
2505	3d. Statues, Ayutthaya, Thailand	55	40
2506	4d. Ascension Convent, Santa Maria, Philippines	60	65
2507	4d. Mount Nimba Nature Reserve, Guinea (vert)	60	65
2508	4d. Banc d'Argun National Park, Mauritania (vert)	60	65
2509	4d. Doorway, Marrakesh, Morocco (vert)	60	65
2510	4d. Ichkeul National Park, Tunisia (vert)	60	65
2511	4d. Village pottery, Mali (vert)	60	65
2512	4d. Hippopotamus, Salonga National Park, Zaire (vert)	60	65
2513	4d. Timgad Roman Ruins, Algeria (vert)	60	65
2514	4d. Wooden statue, Benin (vert)	60	65
2515	4d. Temple, Magao Caves, China (vert)	60	65
2516	4d. Statue, Magao Caves (vert)	60	65
2517	4d. Domes, Magao Caves (vert)	60	65
2518	4d. Great Wall from air, China (vert)	60	65
2519	4d. Statue, Great Wall (vert)	60	65
2520	4d. Bronze Bird, Imperial Palace, China (vert)	60	65
2521	4d. Temples, Imperial Palace, China (vert)	60	65
2522	4d. Dragon statue, Imperial Palace (vert)	60	65
2523	4d. Kyoto Gardens, Japan (vert)	60	65
2524	4d. Himeji Castle, Japan (vert)	60	65
2525	4d. Horyu-ji Temple, Japan (vert)	60	65
2526	4d. Buddha, Horyu-ji, Japan (vert)	60	65
2527	4d. Yakushima Forest, Japan (vert)	60	65
2528	4d. Ancient tree, Yakushima Forest, Japan (vert)	60	65
2529	4d. Temple, Kyoto, Japan (vert)	60	65
2530	4d. Pavilion, Kyoto, Japan (vert)	60	65
2531	5d. Riverside houses, Inselstadt, Germany	70	75
2532	5d. Rosaleda Gardens, Bamberg, Germany	70	75
2533	5d. Bamberg Cathedral, Germany	70	75
2534	5d. Timbered house, Maulbronn, Germany	70	75
2535	5d. Maulbronn Monastry, Germany	70	75
2536	5d. Ruins at Delphi, Greece	70	75
2537	5d. Rhodes waterfront, Greece	70	75
2538	5d. Knights' Hospital, Rhodes, Greece	70	75
2539	5d. Temple, Delphi, Greece	70	75
2540	5d. Delphi from air, Greece	70	75
2541	5d. Foliage, Shirakami-Sanchi, Japan	70	75
2542	5d. Notice board, Shirakami-Sanchi, Japan	70	75
2543	5d. Tower, Himeji Castle, Japan	70	75
2544	5d. Roof tops, Himeji Castle, Japan	70	75
2545	5d. Gateway, Himeji Castle, Japan	70	75
2546	10d. Komodo Dragons, Indonesia	1·40	1·50
2547	15d. Ancient hut, Timbuktu, Mali	1·90	2·25
MS2548	Four sheets, each 127×102 mm. (a) 25d. Plitvice Lakes National Park, Croatia. (b) 25d. Ruins of Kilwa Kisiwani, Tanzania. (c) 25d. Santa Maria de Alcobaca cloisters, Portugal. (d) 25d. Watergarden, Kyoto, Japan Set of 4 sheets	13·00	14·00

274 Minnie Mouse, 1928

1997. Minnie Mouse Through the Years. Designs showing Disney cartoon character in years stated. Multicoloured.

2549	4d. Type **274**	1·00	1·00
2550	4d. In 1933	1·00	1·00
2551	4d. In 1934	1·00	1·00
2552	4d. In 1937	1·00	1·00
2553	4d. In 1938	1·00	1·00
2554	4d. In 1941	1·00	1·00
2555	4d. In 1950	1·00	1·00
2556	4d. In 1990	1·00	1·00
2557	4d. In 1997	1·00	1·00
MS2558	133×108 mm. 25d. In 1987	6·50	7·00

275 Dipstick

1997. "101 Dalmatians". Disney cartoon characters. Multicoloured.

2559	50b. Type **275**	55	55
2560	50b. Fidget	55	55
2561	50b. Jewel	55	55
2562	50b. Lucky	55	55
2563	50b. Two-Tone	55	55
2564	50b. Wizzer	55	55
2565	2d. Two puppies playing (horiz)	65	65
2566	2d. Puppy and pig (horiz)	65	65
2567	2d. Two puppies with butterfly (horiz)	65	65
2568	2d. Puppy lying on back (horiz)	65	65
2569	2d. Puppy with ball (horiz)	65	65
2570	2d. Puppy with bone (horiz)	65	65
2571	2d. One puppy pulling another puppy's tail (horiz)	65	65
2572	2d. Two puppies pulling third puppy's ears (horiz)	65	65
2573	2d. Puppy with teddy bear (horiz)	65	65
2574	3d. Puppy asleep on biscuit box (horiz)	70	70
2575	3d. Puppy with hose (horiz)	70	70
2576	3d. Puppy and bottle (horiz)	70	70
2577	3d. Puppy and biscuit bowl (horiz)	70	70
2578	3d. Puppy wearing hat (horiz)	70	70
2579	3d. Three puppies with lipstick (horiz)	70	70
2580	3d. Puppy tying another up with string (horiz)	70	70
2581	3d. Two puppies and lunch box (horiz)	70	70
2582	3d. Three puppies and computer (horiz)	70	70
MS2583	Six sheets, each 127×103 mm. (a) 25d. Sheep and puppies (horiz). (b) 25d. Cruella de Vil (horiz). (c) 25d. Puppy looking at photograph (horiz). (d) 25d. Puppies in mail sack. (e) 25d. Two puppies covered in paint (horiz). (f) 25d. Two puppies playing computer game (horiz) Set of 6 sheets	32·00	30·00

276 Juventus Team, 1897

1997. Centenary of Juventus Football Team. Multicoloured.

2584	5d. Type **276**	80	80
2585	5d. Centenary emblem and player	80	80
2586	5d. Giampiero Boniperti	80	80
2587	5d. Roberto Bettega	80	80
2588	5d. Juventus team, 1996	80	80
2589	5d. Juventus '97 logo	80	80

276a Young Girl ("I'll Tell You a Story")

1997. 300th Anniv of Mother Goose Nursery Rhymes. Sheet 72×102 mm.

MS2590	**276a** 25d. multicoloured	3·75	4·00

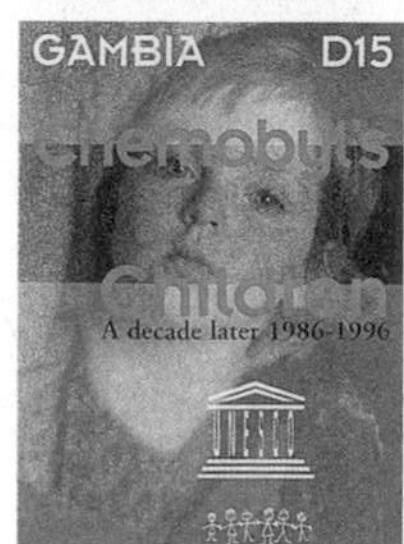

276b Child's Face and UNESCO Emblem

1997. 10th Anniv of Chernobyl Nuclear Disaster. Multicoloured.

2591	15d. Type **276b**	1·90	2·25
2592	15d. As No. 2591 but inscribed "CHABAD'S CHILDREN OF CHERNOBYL"	1·90	2·25

276c Rotary President Sydney Pascall planting Tree of Friendship

1997. 50th Death Anniv of Paul Harris (founder of Rotary International).

2593	10d. Type **276c**	1·40	1·75
MS2594	78×108 mm. 25d. Paul Harris and Preserve Planet Earth emblem	3·75	4·25

276d Queen Elizabeth II

1997. Golden Wedding of Queen Elizabeth and Prince Philip. Multicoloured.

2595	4d. Type **276d**	80	80
2596	4d. Royal coat of arms	80	80
2597	4d. Queen Elizabeth and Prince Philip applauding	80	80
2598	4d. Queen Elizabeth and Prince Philip taking the salute	80	80
2599	4d. Royal Yacht "Britannia"	80	80
2600	4d. Prince Philip	80	80
MS2601	100×70 mm. 20d. Princess Elizabeth, 1948	4·00	4·25

276e Von Stephan and Otto von Bismarck

1997. "Pacific '97" International Stamp Exhibition, San Francisco. Death Centenary of Henrich von Stephan (founder of UPU).

2602	**276e**	5d. mauve	90	1·00
2603	-	5d. brown	90	1·00
2604	-	5d. green and black	90	1·00
MS2605		82×118 mm. 25d. green and black	4·25	4·75

DESIGNS: Nos. 2603, Von Stephan and Mercury; 2604, Mail wagon, Boston, 1900; **MS**2605, Von Stephan and Hamburg–Lubeck postilion.

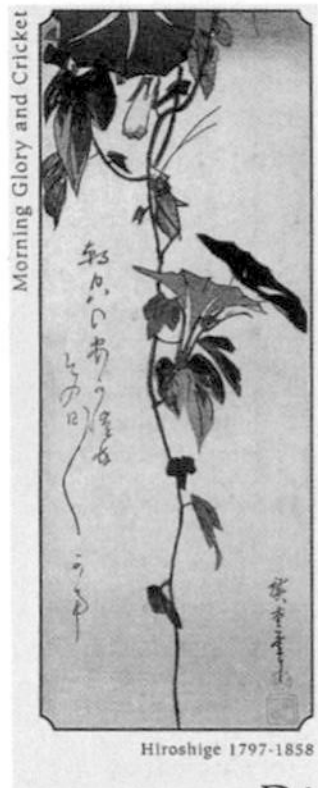

277 "Morning Glory and Cricket"

1997. Birth Bicentenary of Hiroshige (Japanese painter). Multicoloured.

2606-2611	4d.×6 (Type **277**: "Dragonfly and Begonia"; "Two Ducks swimming among Reeds"; "A Black-naped Oriole perched on a Stem of Rose Mallow"; "A Pheasant on a Snow-covered Pine"; "A Cuckoo flying through the Rain")	4·50	4·50
2612-2617	4d.×6 ("An Egret among Rushes"; "Peacock and Peonies"; "Three Wild Geese flying across the Moon"; "A Cock in the Snow"; "A Pheasant and Bracken"; "Peonies")	4·50	4·50
2618-2623	4d.×6 ("Sparrow and Bamboo"; "Mandarin Ducks on an Icy Pond with Brown Leaves falling"; "Blossoming Plum Tree"; "Java Sparrow and Magnolia"; "Chinese Bellflowers and Miscanthus"; "A Small Black Bird clinging to a Tendril of Ivy")	4·50	4·50
2624-2629	5d.×6 ("Sparrows and Camellia in Snow"; "Parrot on a Branch of Pine"; "A Long-tailed Blue Bird on a Branch of Flowering Plum"; "Sparrow and Bamboo"; "Bird in a Tree"; "A Wild Duck swimming beneath Snow-laden reeds")	4·50	4·50
2630-2635	5d.×6 ("Kingfisher above a Yellow-flowered Water Plant"; "Wagtail and Roses"; "A Mandarin Duck on a Snowy Bank"; "A Japanese White-eye on a Persimmon Branch"; "Sparrows and Camellia in Snow"; "Kingfisher and Moon above a Yellow- flowered Water Plant")	4·50	4·50
2636-2641	5d.×6 ("Sparrow and Bamboo by Night"; "Birds Flying over Waves"; "Blossoming Plum Tree with Full Moon"; "Kingfisher and Iris"; "A Blue-and-White Flycatcher on a Hibiscus Flower"; "Mandarin Ducks in Snowfall")	4·50	4·50
MS2642	Six sheets, each 95×120 mm. (a) 25d. Hawk on perch. (b) 25d. Two green birds on branch. (c) 25d. Kingfisher hovering. (d) 25d."Three Wild Geese flying across moon". (e) 25d. Red parrot on branch. (f) 25d. White bird on flowering bush Set of 6 sheets	35·00	38·00

277a Grandma's Cottage

1997. 175th Anniv of Brothers Grimm's Third Collection of Fairy Tales. Little Red Riding Hood. Multicoloured.

2643	10d. Type **277a**	1·75	1·90
2644	10d. Little Red Riding Hood	1·75	1·90
2645	10d. The Wolf	1·75	1·90
MS2646	126×96 mm. 10d. Little Red Riding Hood (horiz)	3·00	3·25

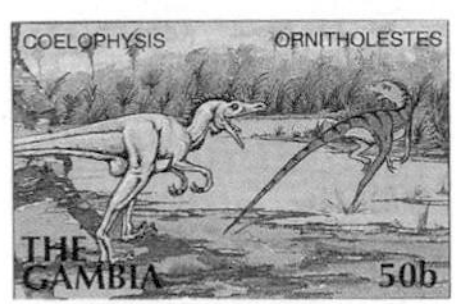

278 Coelophysis chasing Ornitholestes

1997. Dinosaurs. Multicoloured.

2647	50b. Type **278**	30	20
2648	63b. Spinosauru	35	20
2649	75b. Kentrosaurus	40	25
2650	1d. Ceratosaurus	40	25
2651	1d.50 Stygimoloch	50	35
2652	2d. Troodon	60	35
2653	3d. Velociraptor	70	45
2654	4d. Triceratops	80	80
2655	4d. Anurognathus	80	80
2656	4d. Pteranodon	80	80
2657	4d. Pterosaurus	80	80
2658	4d. Saltasaurus	80	80
2659	4d. Agathaumus	80	80
2660	4d. Stegosaurus	80	80
2661	4d. Albertosaurus libratus	80	80
2662	4d. Three Lesothosauruses running	80	80
2663	4d. Five Lesothosauruses running	80	80
2664	4d. Tarbosaurus bataar	80	80
2665	4d. Brachiosaurus	80	80
2666	4d. Styracosaurus	80	80
2667	4d. Baryonyx	80	80
2668	4d. Coelophysis	80	80
2669	4d. Carnotaurus	80	80
2670	4d. Compsognathus longipes	80	80
2671	4d. Compsognathus "Elegant Jaw"	80	80
2672	4d. Stenonychosaurus	80	80
2673	4d. Protoceratops	80	80
2674	10d. Ornithomimus	1·50	1·50
2675	15d. Stegosaurus	1·90	2·25
2676	20d. Ankylosaurus saichania	2·25	2·50
MS2677	Two sheets, each 106×81 mm. (a) 25d. Head of Deinonychus (50×37 mm). (b) 25d. Seismosaurus (88×27 mm) Set of 2 sheets	9·00	10·00

Nos. 2655/63 and 2664/72 respectively were printed together, se-tenant, with the backgrounds forming composite designs.

279 Margaret Thatcher and Deng Xiaoping toasting Joint Declaration, 1984

1997. Return of Hong Kong to China. Multicoloured.

2678	3d. Type **279**	60	60
2679	3d. Signing Joint Declaration on Hong Kong, 1984	60	60
2680	3d. Signing Joint Declaration on Macao, 1987	60	60
2681	3d. Deng Xiaoping toasting Prime Minister Anibal Silva of Portugal	60	60
2682	4d. Hong Kong in 1843 and Governor Sir Henry Pottinger	75	75
2683	4d. Kowloon in 1860 and Governor Sir Hercules Robinson	75	75
2684	4d. Reception in New Territories, 1898, and Governor Sir Henry Blake	75	75
2685	5d. Governor Sir Henry Pottinger and British warship	85	85
2686	5d. Governor Christopher Patten and Lantau Bridge	85	85
2687	5d. Chief Executive C. H. Tung and Hong Kong by night	85	85
2688	6d. Signing the Treaty of Nanking, 1842	1·00	1·10
2689	6d. Signing the Japanese Surrender of Hong Kong, 1945	1·00	1·10
2690	6d. Signing of the Sino-British Joint Declaration, 1984	1·00	1·10

280 Great Mosque, Samarra, Iran

1997. Natural and Man-made Wonders of the World. Multicoloured.

2691	63b. Type **280**	40	20
2692	75b. Moai statues, Easter Island (horiz)	50	20
2693	1d. Golden Gate Bridge, San Francisco (horiz)	50	20
2694	1d.50 The Statue of Liberty, New York	50	25
2695	2d. The Parthenon, Athens (horiz)	50	30
2696	3d. Pyramid of the Sun, Mexico (horiz)	60	40
2697	5d. The Rock of Gibraltar (horiz)	80	1·00
2698	5d. St. Peter's Basilica, Rome (horiz)	1·00	1·00
2699	5d. Santa Sophia, Istanbul (horiz)	80	1·00
2700	5d. "Gateway to the West" monument, St. Louis (horiz)	80	1·00
2701	5d. Great Wall of China (horiz)	80	1·00
2702	5d. City of Carcassonne, France (horiz)	80	1·00
2703	5d. Stonehenge, England (horiz)	1·00	1·00
2704	5d. Hughes HK-1 "Spruce Goose" flying boat (World's largest aircraft) (horiz)	1·00	1·00
2705	5d. Hoverspeed "Seacat" catamaran (fastest Atlantic crossing by a commercial catamaran) (horiz)	1·00	1·00
2706	5d. "Thrust 2" car (official land speed record) (horiz)	1·00	1·00
2707	5d. Stepped Pyramid, Egypt (horiz)	1·00	1·00
2708	5d. L.N.E.R. Clas A4 "Mallard" (fastest steam locomotive), 1938 (horiz)	1·00	1·00
MS2709	Three sheets, each 98×68 mm. (a) 5d. Mount Everest (42×28 mm). (b) 25d. The Grand Canyon, Colorado (42×28 mm). (c) 25d. Washington Monument (33×51 mm) Set of 3 sheets	12·00	13·00

No. 2702 is inscribed "CARCASSONNNE" in error.

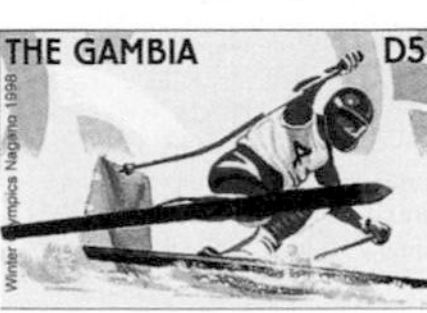

281 Downhill Skiing

1997. Winter Olympic Games, Nagano (1998). Multicoloured.

2710	5d. Type **281**	90	90
2711	5d. Two-man bobsleigh (vert)	90	90
2712	5d. Freestyle skiing (vert)	90	90
2713	5d. Speed skating (vert)	90	90
2714	5d. Slalom skiing (No. 8 on bib) (vert)	90	90
2715	5d. Womens figure skating (vert)	90	90
2716	5d. Downhill skiing (No. 4 on bib) (vert)	90	90
2717	5d. Pairs figure skating (vert)	90	90
2718	5d. Cross-country (vert)	90	90
2719	5d. Ski jumping (vert)	90	90
2720	5d. One-man luge	90	90
2721	5d. Ice hockey	90	90
2722	5d. Four-man bobsleigh	90	90
2723	5d. Ski-jumping	90	90
2724	5d. Curling	90	90
2725	5d. Figure skating	90	90
2726	5d. Speed skating	90	90
2727	5d. Biathlon	90	90
2728	5d. Downhill skiing (different)	90	90
2729	10d. One-man luge	1·60	1·75
2730	15d. Speed skating	2·25	2·50
2731	20d. Ice hockey	3·00	3·25
MS2732	Two sheets. (a) 97×67 mm. 25d. Bobsleigh. (b) 67×97 mm. 25d. Pairs figure skating (vert) Set of 2 sheets	9·50	10·00

282 Brown Pelican

1997. Sea Birds. Multicoloured.

2733	3d. Type **282**	85	85
2734	3d. Galapagos penguin	85	85
2735	3d. Red-billed tropic bird	85	85
2736	3d. Little tern	85	85
2737	3d. Dunlin	85	85
2738	3d. Black-legged kittiwake	85	85
2739	3d. Atlantic puffin	85	85
2740	3d. Wandering albatross	85	85
2741	3d. Blue-faced booby ("Masked Booby")	85	85
2742	3d. Glaucous-winged gull	85	85
2743	3d. Arctic tern	85	85
2744	3d. Piping plover	85	85
2745	5d. Roseate tern	1·00	1·00
2746	10d. Red-legged cormorant	1·50	1·60
2747	15d. Blue-footed booby	2·25	2·50
2748	20d. Sanderling	2·50	2·75
MS2749	Two sheets, each 106×76 mm. (a) 23d. Long-tailed skua (vert). (b) 23d. Osprey (vert) Set of 2 sheets	8·50	9·00

No. 2743 is inscribed "ARTIC TERN" and the captions on Nos. 2745/6 are transposed, both in error.

283 Scottish Fold Cat

1997. Cats and Dogs. Multicoloured.

2750	63b. Type **283**	30	20
2751	75b. Dalmatian	35	20
2752	1d. Rottweiler	35	20
2753	1d.50 American curl cat	45	25
2754	2d. British bi-colour cat	50	25
2755	3d. Newfoundland	60	35
2756	3d. Devon Rex cat	60	35
2757	4d. Great Dane	75	50
2758	5d. Burmilla cat	85	85
2759	5d. Blue Burmese cat	85	85
2760	5d. Korat cat	85	85
2761	5d. British tabby cat	85	85
2762	5d. Foreign white cat	85	85
2763	5d. Somali cat	85	85
2764	5d. Akita	85	85
2765	5d. Welsh corgi	85	85
2766	5d. German shepherd	85	85
2767	5d. Saint Bernard	85	85
2768	5d. Bullmastiff	85	85
2769	5d. Malamute	85	85
2770	6d. Silver tabby cat	95	95
2771	10d. Old English sheepdog	1·40	1·50
2772	15d. Queensland heeler	1·90	2·25
2773	20d. Abyssinian cat	2·25	2·50
MS2774	Four sheets, each 107×78 mm. (a) 25d. Cornish Rex cat. (b) 25d. Siamese cat. (c) 25d. Boxer. (d) Dobermann pinscher Set of 4 sheets	17·00	17·00

283a Uruguay Team, 1950

1997. World Cup Football Championship, France (1998).

2775	**283a**	1d. black	40	20
2776	-	1d.50 black	50	25
2777	-	2d. black	55	30
2778	-	3d. black	70	40

2779-2786 - 4d.×8 mult or brown (Nos. 2782/3) 5·00
2787-2794 - 4d.×8 mult or black (No. 2788) 5·00
2795-2802 - 4d.×8 brown (Nos. 2795/6, 2800 and 2802) or mult 5·00
2803-2810 - 4d.×8 mult 5·00
2811 - 5d. black 80 80
2812 - 10d. black 1·40 1·50
MS2813 Four sheets, each 102×127 mm. (a) 25d. multicoloured. (b) 25d. multicoloured. (c) 25d. black. (d) 25d. brown Set of 4 sheets 17·00 17·00

DESIGNS—HORIZ: No. 2776, West German team, 1954; 2777, Brazilian team, 1970; 2778, Brazilian team, 1962; 2779, Brazilian team, 1994; 2780, Argentine team, 1986; 2781, Brazilian team, 1970; 2782, Italian team, 1934; 2783, Uruguay team, 1958; 2784, English team, 1966; 2785, Brazilian team, 1962; 2786, West German team, 1990; 2787, Mario Kempes, Argentina (1978); 2788, Joseph Gaetjens, U.S.A. (1950) (inscr "ADEMIR BRAZIL" in error); 2789, Muller, West Germany (1970); 2790, Lineker, England (1986); 2791, Eusebio, Portugal (1966); 2792, Schillaci, Italy (1990); 2793, Lato, Poland (1974); 2794, Rossi, Italy (1982); 2811, Italian team, 1938; 2812, Uruguay team, 1930; **MS**2813a, Philippe Albert, Belgium; **MS**2813b, Juninho, Brazil; **MS**2813c, Eusebio, Portugal; **MS**2813d, Pele, Brazil. VERT: No. 2795, Moore, England (1966); 2796, Fritzwalter, West Germany (1954); 2797, Beckenbauer, West Germany (1974); 2798, Zoff, Italy (1982); 2799, Maradona, Argentina (1986); 2800, Passarella, Argentina (1978); 2801, Matthaus, West Germany (1990); 2802, Dunga, Brazil (1994); 2803, Kinkladze, Georgia; 2804, Shearer, England; 2805, Dani, Portugal; 2806, Weah, Portugal; 2807, Ravanelli, Italy; 2808, Raducioiu, Rumania; 2809, Schmeichel, Denmark; 2810, Bergkamp, Holland.

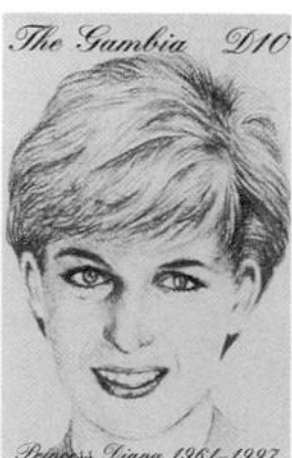

284 Diana, Princess of Wales

1997. Diana, Princess of Wales Commemoration. Each brown and black.
2814 10d. Type **284** 1·50 1·60
2815 10d. Wearing open-necked shirt 1·50 1·60
2816 10d. Wearing polo-neck jumper 1·50 1·60
2817 10d. Wearing diamond-drop earrings 1·50 1·60
MS2818 76×106 mm. 25d. Diana, Princess of Wales (multicoloured) 3·50 4·50

284a "Angel" (Rembrandt)

1997. Christmas. Paintings. Multicoloured.
2819 1d. Type **284a** 45 15
2820 1d.50 "Initiation into the Rites of Dionysus" at Villa dei Misteri 55 15
2821 2d. "Pair of Erotes with Purple Cloaks" 70 20
2822 3d. "The Ecstasy of Saint Theresa" (Gianlorenzo Bernini) 90 45
2823 5d. "Virgin and Child with Angels" (Matthias Grunewald) 1·25 1·00
2824 10d. "Angel playing the Organ" (Stefan Lochner) 2·00 2·75
MS2825 Two sheets, each 105×95 mm. (a) 25d. "The Rest on the Flight into Egypt" (Caravaggio). (b) 25d. "The Education of Cupid" (Titian) Set of 2 sheets 8·00 9·00

No. **MS**2825a is inscribed "THE REST OF THE FLIGHT INTO EGYPT" and No. **MS**2825b "TITAN", both in error.

285 Tiger

1998. Chinese New Year ("Year of the Tiger"). Multicoloured.
2826 3d. Type **285** ("GAMBIA" in green) 50 55
2827 3d. Tiger ("GAMBIA" in mauve) 50 55
2828 3d. Tiger ("GAMBIA" in lilac) 50 55
2829 3d. Tiger ("GAMBIA" in blue) 50 55
MS2830 73×100 mm. 10d. Tiger (42×28 mm) 1·75 1·90

286 Class 91 Electric Train, Great Britian

1998. Trains of the World. Multicoloured.
2831 5d. Type **286** 75 80
2832 5d. Class 26 steam locomotive No. 3450 "Red Devil", South Africa 75 80
2833 5d. TGV express train, France 75 80
2834 5d. People Mover railcar, Great Britain 75 80
2835 5d. ICE high speed train, Germany 75 80
2836 5d. Montmartre funicular car, France 75 80
2837 5d. Burlington Northern SD70 diesel locomotive No. 9716, U.S.A. 75 80
2838 5d. L.N.E.R. Class A4 steam locomotive "Mallard", 1938 75 80
2839 5d. Baldwin steam locomotive, Peru 75 80
2840 5d. Amtrak Class ARM-7 electric locomotive, U.S.A. 75 80
2841 5d. Rack steam locomotive No. B2503, Amberawa, Java 75 80
2842 5d. Beyer-Peacock steam locomotive No. 3108, Pakistan 75 80
MS2843 Two sheets, each 84×110 mm. (a) 25d. Futuristic monorail train, Great Britain. (b) 25d. Southern Pacific GS4 stream-lined steam locomotive, U.S.A. Set of 2 sheets 7·00 7·50

No. 2832 is inscribed "BEACONSFIELD CHINA", No. 2836 "MOUNTMAETRE FUNICULAR" and No. 2840 "SWEDEN RAIL 125 MPH", all in error.

287 Yellow Orchid

1998. African Flowers. Multicoloured.
2844 75b. Type **287** 25 15
2845 1d.50 Transvaal daisy 40 25
2846 3d. Torch lily 60 30
2847 4d. "Ancistrochilus rothschildianus" 70 40
2848 5d. "Adenium multiflorum" (horiz) 75 80
2849 5d. "Huernia namaquensis" (horiz) 75 80
2850 5d. "Gloriosa superba" (horiz) 75 80
2851 5d. "Strelitzia reginae" (horiz) 75 80
2852 5d. "Passiflora mollissima" (horiz) 75 80
2853 5d. "Bauhinia variegata" (horiz) 75 80
2854 10d. "Polystachya vulcanica" 1·75 1·90
2855 15d. Gladiolus 2·25 2·75
MS2856 Two sheets, each 106×76 mm. (a) 25d. "Aerangis rhodosticta". (b) 25d. "Ansella gigantea" Set of 2 sheets 7·00 8·00

Nos. 2848/53 were printed together, se-tenant, forming a composite background design.

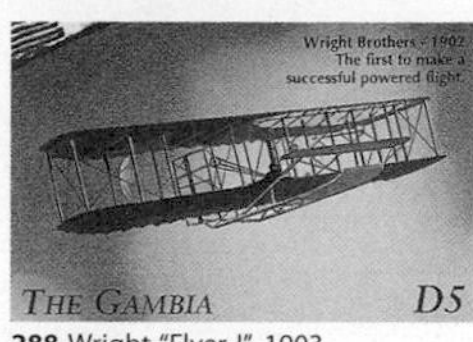

288 Wright "Flyer I", 1903

1998. History of Aviation. Multicoloured.
2857 5d. Type **288** 85 85
2858 5d. Curtiss A-1 seaplane, 1910 85 85
2859 5d. Farman biplane, 1907 85 85
2860 5d. Bristol monoplane, 1911 85 85
2861 5d. Antoinette IV, 1908 85 85
2862 5d. Sopwith "Bat Boat" amphibian, 1912 85 85
2863 5d. Short Type 38, 1913 85 85
2864 5d. Fokker F.VIIb/3m, 1925 85 85
2865 5d. Junkers J.13, 1919 85 85
2866 5d. Pitcairn "Mailwing", 1927 85 85
2867 5d. Douglas, 1920 85 85
2868 5d. Curtiss T-32 Condor II airliner, 1934 85 85
MS2869 Two sheets, each 106×76 mm. (a) 25d. Albatross, 1913 (84×28 mm). (b) 25d. Boeing 247 airliner, 1932 (84×28 mm) Set of 2 sheets 8·00 8·00

Nos. 2857/62 and 2863/8 respectively were printed together, se-tenant, forming composite background designs.
No. 2857 is dated "1902" in error.

289 Mulan

1998. "Mulan" (film). Multicoloured.
2870 4d. Type **289** 1·10 1·10
2871 4d. Mushu 1·10 1·10
2872 4d. Little Brother 1·10 1·10
2873 4d. Cri-kee 1·10 1·10
2874 4d. Grandmother Fa 1·10 1·10
2875 4d. Fa Li 1·10 1·10
2876 4d. Fa Zhou 1·10 1·10
2877 4d. Mulan and Khan 1·10 1·10
2878 5d. Mulan riding Khan 1·10 1·10
2879 5d. Shang 1·10 1·10
2880 5d. Chi-fu 1·10 1·10
2881 5d. Chien-po 1·10 1·10
2882 5d. Yao 1·10 1·10
2883 5d. Ling 1·10 1·10
2884 5d. Shan-yu 1·10 1·10
2885 5d. Mulan, Shang and Mushu 1·10 1·10
MS2886 Four sheets. (a) 102×127 mm. 25d. Mulan and Khan. (b) 127×102 mm. 25d. Mulan and firework. (c) 127×102 mm. 25d. Mulan in front of house. (d) 127×102 mm. 25d. Mulan performing karate kick Set of 4 sheets 20·00 22·00

289a Sidney Bechet

1998. Millennium Series. Famous People of the Twentieth Century. Multicoloured. (a) Famous Jazz Musicians.
2887 4d. Type **289a** 80 80
2888 4d. Sidney Bechet playing saxophone (53×38 mm) 80 80
2889 4d. Duke Ellington conducting (53×38 mm) 80 80
2890 4d. Duke Ellington 80 80
2891 4d. Louis Armstrong 80 80
2892 4d. Louis Armstrong playing trumpet (53×38 mm) 80 80
2893 4d. Charlie "Bird" Parker playing saxophone (53×38 mm) 80 80
2894 4d. Charlie "Bird" Parker 80 80

(b) Famous Theatrical Composers.
2895 4d. Cole Porter 80 80
2896 4d. "Born to Dance" (Cole Porter) (53×38 mm) 80 80
2897 4d. "Porgy and Bess" (George Gershwin) (53×38 mm) 80 80
2898 4d. George Gershwin 80 80
2899 4d. Rogers and Hammerstein 80 80
2900 4d. "The King and I" (Rogers and Hammerstein) (53×38 mm) 80 80
2901 4d. "West Side Story" (Leonard Bernstein) (53×38 mm) 80 80
2902 4d. Leonard Bernstein 80 80
MS2903 Two sheets, each 76×106 mm. (a) 25d. Ella Fitzgerald. (b) 25d. "Oh How I Hate to Get Up in the Morning" (Irving Berlin) Set of 2 sheets 7·50 8·00

290 Chinese Junk

1998. Ships. Multicoloured.
2904 2d. Type **290** 30 15
2905 3d. H.M.S. "Victory" (ship of the line, 1765) 1·00 65
2906 5d. "Santa Maria" (Columbus) 1·25 1·25
2907 5d. "Mary Rose" (galleon) 1·25 1·25
2908 5d. "Mayflower" (Pilgrim Fathers) 1·25 1·25
2909 5d. "Ark Royal" (galleon, 1587) 1·25 1·25
2910 5d. H.M.S. "Beagle" (Darwin) 1·25 1·25
2911 5d. H.M.S. "Bounty" (Bligh) 1·25 1·25
2912 5d. H.M.S. "Dreadnought" (battleship) 1·25 1·25
2913 5d. American "Truxton" Class cruiser 1·25 1·25
2914 5d. "Queen Mary" (liner) 1·25 1·25
2915 5d. "Canberra" (liner) 1·25 1·25
2916 5d. "Queen Elizabeth" (liner) 1·25 1·25
2917 5d. "Queen Elizabeth II" (liner) 1·25 1·25
2918 10d. British "County" Class destroyer 2·00 2·25
2919 15d. Viking longship 2·50 3·00
MS2920 Two sheets. (a) 70×100 mm. 25d. "Cutty Sark" (clipper) (41×56 mm). (b) 100×70 mm. 25d. "Sovereign of the Seas" (liner) (56×41 mm) Set of 2 sheets 8·00 8·50

291 Captain Edward Smith

1998. "Titanic" Commemoration.
2921 **291** 5d. brown, black and blue 1·25 1·25
2922 - 5d. brown, black and blue 1·25 1·25
2923 - 5d. brown and black 1·25 1·25
2924 - 5d. blue and black 1·25 1·25
2925 - 5d. mauve and black 1·25 1·25
2926 - 5d. mauve and black 1·25 1·25
MS2927 Three sheets, each 110×85 mm. (a) 25d. multicoloured. (b) 25d. sepia and black. (c) 25d. multicoloured Set of 3 sheets 12·00 12·00

DESIGNS—VERT: No. 2922, Mrs. J. J. "Molly" Brown (passenger); 2923, Newspaper boy with placard; 2924, Benjamin Guggenheim (passenger); 2925, Isidor Strauss (passenger); 2926, Ida Strauss (passenger). HORIZ: No. **MS**2927a, "Titanic" on postcard; **MS**2927b, "Titanic sinking"; **MS**2927c, Wreckage of "Titanic" on seabed.

291a "Death of Casagemas"

1998. 25th Death Anniv of Pablo Picasso (painter). Multicoloured.
2928 3d. Type **291a** 60 30
2929 5d. "Seated Woman" (vert) 90 75
2930 10d. "Mother and Child" (vert) 1·75 2·00
MS2931 102×126 mm. 25d. "Child playing with Toy Truck" (vert) 4·00 4·50

291b Scout Handshake

1998. 19th World Scout Jamboree, Chile. Mult.

2932	10d. Type **291b**	1·60	1·90
2933	10d. Dinghy sailing	1·60	1·90
2934	10d. Scout salute	1·60	1·90
MS2935	47×61 mm. 25d. Lord Baden-Powell (brown and black)	4·00	4·50

292 Mahatma Gandhi

1998. 50th Death Anniv of Mahatma Gandhi. Multicoloured.

2936	10d. Type **292**	2·00	2·00
2937	10d. Gandhi on Salt March with Mrs. Sarojini Naidu (53×38 mm)	2·00	2·00
2938	10d. Gandhi spinning yarn (53×38 mm)	2·00	2·00
2939	10d. Gandhi in 1916	2·00	2·00
MS2940	53×71 mm. 25d. Gandhi writing	5·50	5·50

292a Sepecat Jaguar GR1A

1998. 80th Anniv of Royal Air Force. Multicoloured.

2941	5d. Type **292a**	1·00	1·00
2942	5d. Panavia Tornado GR1A	1·00	1·00
2943	5d. Sepecat Jaguar GR1A (side view)	1·00	1·00
2944	5d. BAe Hawk 200	1·00	1·00
2945	5d. Sepecat Jaguar GR1A firing Sparrow missile	1·00	1·00
2946	5d. BAe Harrier GR7 firing SNEB rockets	1·00	1·00
2947	5d. Panavia Tornado GR1 firing AIM-9L missile	1·00	1·00
2948	5d. Panavia Tornado GR1 in low level flight	1·00	1·00
2949	7d. Panavia Tornado GR1 (facing left)	1·25	1·25
2950	7d. BAe Hawk T1A	1·25	1·25
2951	7d. Sepecat Jaguar GR1A	1·25	1·25
2952	7d. Panavia Tornado GR1 (facing right)	1·25	1·25
MS2953	Six sheets, each 90×68 mm. (a) 20d. EF-2000 Eurofighter. (b) 25d. Bristol F2B Fighter and bird of prey in flight. (c) 25d. Falcon's head and Bristol F2B Fighter. (d) 25d. Bristol F2B Fighter and Golden Eagle (bird). (e) 25d. Lancaster and EF-2000 Eurofighter. (f) 25d. Lightning and EF-2000 Eurofighter Set of 6 sheets	17·00	18·00

293 "Mule-drivers from Tetuan"

1998. Birth Bicentenary of Eugene Delacroix (painter). Multicoloured.

2954	4d. Type **293**	60	65
2955	4d. "Encampment of Arab Mule-drivers"	60	65
2956	4d. "An Orange Seller"	60	65
2957	4d. "The Banks of the River"	60	65
2958	4d. "View of Tangier from the Seashore"	60	65
2959	4d. "Arab Horses fighting in a Stable"	60	65
2960	4d. "Horses at the Trough"	60	65
2961	4d. "The Combat of Giaour and Hassan"	60	65
2962	4d. "Turk on a Sofa, Smoking"	60	65
2963	4d. "View of Tangier"	60	65
2964	4d. "The Spanish Coast at Salobrena"	60	65
2965	4d. "The Aissaouas"	60	65
2966	4d. "The Sea from the Cliffs of Dieppe"	60	65
2967	4d. "The Fanatics of Tangier"	60	65
2968	4d. "Arab Musicians"	60	65
2969	4d. "An Arab Camp at Night"	60	65
2970	4d. "Moroccan from Tangier, standing" (vert)	60	65
2971	4d. "A Man of Tangier" (vert)	60	65
2972	4d. "Young Arab standing with a Rifle" (vert)	60	65
2973	4d. "Moroccan Chieftain" (vert)	60	65
2974	4d. "Jewish Bride, Tangier" (vert)	60	65
2975	4d. "Seated Jewess from Morocco" (vert)	60	65
2976	4d. "Young Arab seated by a Wall" (vert)	60	65
2977	4d. "Arab Dancer" (vert)	60	65
MS2978	Three sheets. (a) 100×85 mm. 25d. "Massacre at Chios". (b) 100×85 mm. 25d. "Women of Algiers in their Apartment". (c) 85×100 mm. 25d. "Self-portrait" (vert) Set of 3 sheets	10·00	11·00

293a Diana, Princess of Wales

1998. 1st Death Anniv of Diana, Princess of Wales.

2979	**293a** 10d. multicoloured	1·75	1·90

294 Puppy in Stocking

295 Rabbit

1998. Christmas. Multicoloured.

2980	1d. Type **294**	25	10
2981	2d. Giraffe in Christmas wreath	40	15
2982	3d. Australian bee eater ("Rainbow Bee Eater") (bird) with bauble	55	25
2983	4d. Deer	75	50
2984	5d. Fawn	90	75
2985	10d. Puppy in gift box	1·75	2·00
MS2986	Two sheets, each 105×76 mm. (a) 25d. Brown classic tabby. (b) 25d. Basset hound and Rough collie Set of 2 sheets	4·50	5·00

1999. Chinese New Year ("Year of the Rabbit"). Multicoloured.

2987	3d. Type **295**	50	55
2988	3d. Rabbit looking over shoulder	50	55
2989	3d. Rabbit facing left	50	55
2990	3d. Rabbit running	50	55
MS2991	73×103 mm. 10d. Rabbit (42×28 mm)	1·75	2·00

296 Mowgli and Baloo (bear)

1999. "The Jungle Book" (film). Walt Disney cartoon characters. Multicoloured.

2992	5d. Type **296**	1·25	1·25
2993	5d. Kaa (snake) and Mowgli	1·25	1·25
2994	5d. King Louie at ruined temple	1·25	1·25
2995	5d. Monkey playing leaf "guitar"	1·25	1·25
2996	5d. Village girl collecting water	1·25	1·25
2997	5d. King Louie on throne with Mowgli	1·25	1·25
2998	5d. Mowgli and vultures	1·25	1·25
2999	5d. Shere Khan (tiger)	1·25	1·25
MS3000	Two sheets, each 127×102 mm. (a) 25d. Baloo (bear) (50×37 mm). (b) 25d. Baby elephant (50×37 mm) Set of 2 sheets	8·00	9·00

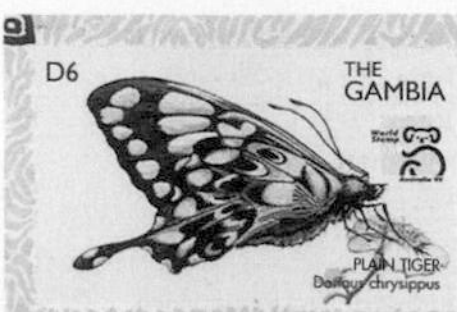

297 "Danaus chrysippus"

1999. "Australia '99" World Stamp Exhibition, Melbourne. African Butterflies. Multicoloured.

3001	6d. Type **297**	1·25	1·25
3002	6d. "Papilio zalmoxis"	1·25	1·25
3003	6d. "Papilio menestheus"	1·25	1·25
3004	6d. "Poecilmitis thysbe"	1·25	1·25
3005	6d. "Euxanthe wakefieldii"	1·25	1·25
3006	6d. "Pseudacraea boisduvali"	1·25	1·25
3007	6d. "Eurytela dryope"	1·25	1·25
3008	6d. "Papilio demodocus"	1·25	1·25
3009	6d. "Hemiolaus coeculus"	1·25	1·25
3010	6d. "Charaxes jasius"	1·25	1·25
3011	6d. "Junonia orithya"	1·25	1·25
3012	6d. "Kallimoides rumia"	1·25	1·25
MS3013	Two sheets, each 106×76 mm. (a) 25d. "Charaxes jasius" (vert). (b) 25d. "Catacroptera cloanthe" (vert) Set of 2 sheets	8·00	8·50

No. 3003 is inscribed "Papilio mnestheus" in error.

298 Prince Edward and Miss Sophie Rhys-Jones

1999. Royal Wedding. Multicoloured.

3014	10d. Type **298**	1·75	1·90
3015	10d. Prince Edward and Miss Sophie Rhys-Jones (with long hair)	1·75	1·90
3016	10d. Prince Edward and Miss Sophie Rhys-Jones (wearing a red jacket)	1·75	1·90
MS3017	78×78 mm. 25d. Prince Edward and Miss Sophie Rhys-Jones (39×29 mm)	4·00	4·25

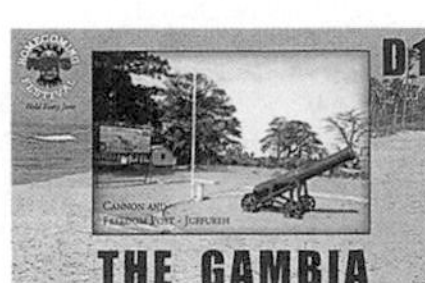

299 Cannon and Freedom Post, Jaffureh

1999. Roots Homecoming Festival. Multicoloured.

3018	1d. Type **299**	15	15
3019	2d. Fort Bullen	25	20
3020	3d. James Island	40	50

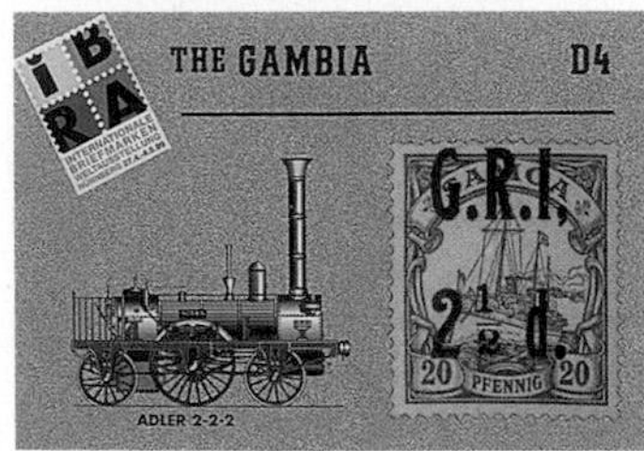

299a Railway locomotive "Adler", 1835, and Samoa 1914 G.R.I. 2½d. on 20pf. variety

1999. "iBRA '99" International Stamp Exhibition, Nuremberg. Multicoloured.

3021	4d. Type **299a**	85	45
3022	5d. Railway locomotive "Adler", 1835, and Samoa 1900 25pf. optd on Germany	1·00	75
3023	10d. "Friedrich August" (full-rigged ship) and Samoa 1900 Yacht type 50pf. and 80pf. stamps	1·75	1·90
3024	15d. "Friedrich August" (full-rigged ship) and Samoa 1900 Yacht type 2m. stamp	2·25	2·75
MS3025	162×107 mm. 25d. Samoa 1900 Yacht type 3m. stamp post-marked Palauli (60×40 mm)	4·00	4·25

299b "Exotic Beauty"

1999. 150th Death Anniv of Katsushika Hokusai (Japanese artist). Multicoloured.

3026	5d. Type **299b**	90	90
3027	5d. "Wind" (two people)	90	90
3028	5d. "Dancing Monkey"	90	90
3029	5d. "Lady and Maiden on an Outing"	90	90
3030	5d. "Wind" (three people)	90	90
3031	5d. "Courtesan with Fan"	90	90
3032	5d. "Bunshosei"	90	90
3033	5d. "Overthrower of Castles, Overthrower of Nations"	90	90
3034	5d. "Bee on Wild Rose"	90	90
3035	5d. "Sei Shonagon"	90	90
3036	5d. "Kuan-yu"	90	90
3037	5d. "The Fifth Month"	90	90
MS3038	Two sheets, each 72×103 mm. (a) 25d. "People on the Balcony of the Sazaido". (b) 25d. "Caocao before the Battle of Chibi" Set of 2 sheets	8·00	8·50

299c Child asleep

1999. 10th Anniv of United Nations Rights of the Child Convention. Multicoloured.

3039	10d. Type **299c**	1·60	1·90
3040	10d. Child drinking	1·60	1·90
3041	10d. Child drawing	1·60	1·90
MS3042	112×85 mm. 25d. Child laughing	4·00	4·25

Nos. 3039/41 were printed together, se-tenant, forming a composite design.

299d Road Carriage on Wagon

1999. "PhilexFrance 99" International Stamp Exhibition, Paris. Railway Transport. Two sheets, each 106×81 mm, containing T 299d and similar designs. Multicoloured.

MS3043	(a) 25d. Type **299d**. (b) 25d. Passenger locomotive, 1846 Set of 2 sheets	8·50	8·50

299e Faust quaffs the Spirit's Nectar

1999. 250th Birth Anniv of Johann von Goethe (German writer).

3044	**299e** 15d. violet, black & pur	2·00	2·25
3045	- 15d. blue and black	2·00	2·25
3046	- 15d. brown, blk & grn	2·00	2·25
MS3047	76×106 mm. 25d. blue, black and brown	4·00	4·25

DESIGNS—HORIZ: No. 3045, Goethe and Schiller; 3046, Faust contemplates mortality. VERT: No. **MS**3047, Johann von Goethe.

299f Bell X-14A VTOL Aircraft

1999. 30th Anniv of First Manned Landing on Moon. Multicoloured.

3048	6d. Type **299f**	1·00	1·10
3049	6d. Lunar landing practice rig	1·00	1·10
3050	6d. Early prototype lander	1·00	1·10
3051	6d. Astronaut during zero gravity training	1·00	1·10
3052	6d. Jet pack training	1·00	1·10
3053	6d. Lunar lander pilot training	1·00	1·10
MS3054	Two sheets. (a) 76×105 mm. 25d. "Apollo 11" splashdown. (b) 85×110 mm. 25d. Lunar module "Eagle" Set of 2 sheets	7·50	8·00

Nos. 3048/53 were printed together, se-tenant, forming a composite design.

300 Swallow-tailed Gull

1999. Marine Life of the Galapagos Islands. Multicoloured.

3055	1d.50 Type **300**	25	30
3056	1d.50 Magnificent frigate birds ("Frigate Bird")	25	30
3057	1d.50 Red-footed booby	25	30
3058	1d.50 Galapagos hawk	25	30
3059	1d.50 Great blue heron	25	30
3060	1d.50 Blue-faced booby ("Masked Booby")	25	30
3061	1d.50 Bottlenose dolphins	25	30
3062	1d.50 Black grunts	25	30
3063	1d.50 Surgeonfish	25	30
3064	1d.50 Stingray	25	30
3065	1d.50 Short-finned pilot whales	25	30
3066	1d.50 Pacific green sea turtle	25	30
3067	1d.50 Great white shark	25	30
3068	1d.50 Sealion	25	30
3069	1d.50 Marine iguana	25	30
3070	1d.50 Pacific manta ray	25	30
3071	1d.50 Moorish idol	25	30
3072	1d.50 Galapagos penguins	25	30
3073	1d.50 Silver grunts	25	30
3074	1d.50 Sea urchin	25	30
3075	1d.50 Wrasse	25	30
3076	1d.50 Almaco amber jack	25	30
3077	1d.50 Blue parrotfish	25	30
3078	1d.50 Yellow sea urchin	25	30
3079	1d.50 Lobster	25	30
3080	1d.50 Grouper	25	30
3081	1d.50 Scorpionfish	25	30
3082	1d.50 Squirrelfish	25	30
3083	1d.50 Octopus	25	30
3084	1d.50 King angelfish	25	30
3085	1d.50 Horned shark	25	30
3086	1d.50 Galapagos hogfish	25	30
3087	1d.50 Pufferfish	25	30
3088	1d.50 Moray eel	25	30
3089	1d.50 Orange tube coral	25	30
3090	1d.50 Whitestripe chromis	25	30
3091	1d.50 Long-nosed hawkfish	25	30
3092	1d.50 Sea cucumbers	25	30
3093	1d.50 Spotted hawkfish	25	30
3094	1d.50 Zebra moray eel	25	30
MS3095	106×76 mm. 25d. Emperor penguins	4·50	4·50

Nos. 3055/94 respectively were printed together, se-tenant, forming a composite design.

301 "Telstar 1" Satellite, 1962

1999. History of Space Exploration. Multicoloured.

3096	1d. Type **301**	20	15
3097	1d.50 "Skylab", 1973 (vert)	25	15
3098	2d. "Mars 3" spacecraft, 1971 (vert)	30	15
3099	3d. "Cobe", 1989 (vert)	45	20
3100	6d. "Mariner 4", 1964	90	90
3101	6d. "Viking" Mars Orbiter, 1975	90	90
3102	6d. Giotto, 1985	90	90
3103	6d. "Luna 9", 1966	90	90
3104	6d. "Voyager 1", 1977	90	90
3105	6d. Galileo, 1989	90	90
3106	6d. Soviet "Vostok 1", 1961	90	90
3107	6d. "Apollo" command and service module, 1968	90	90
3108	6d. "Mercury" capsule, 1961	90	90
3109	6d. "Apollo 16" lunar module, 1972	90	90
3110	6d. "Gemini 8", 1966	90	90
3111	6d. Soviet "Soyuz", 1975	90	90
3112	6d. German "V 2" rocket, 1942 (vert)	90	90
3113	6d. "Delta Straight 8", 1972 (vert)	90	90
3114	6d. "Ariane 4", 1988 (vert)	90	90
3115	6d. "Mercury MA-A Atlas", 1962 (vert)	90	90
3116	6d. "Saturn 1B", 1975 (vert)	90	90
3117	6d. "Cassini", 1997 (vert)	90	90
3118	10d. Bruce McCandless outside shuttle, 1984 (vert)	1·60	1·75
3119	15d. "Apollo 13" after splash-down, 1970 (vert)	2·00	2·50
MS3120	Two sheets. (a) 85×110 mm. 25d. "Mars Pathfinder", 1997 (56×41 mm). (b) 110×85 mm. 25d. "Apollo" and "Soyuz" joint mission, 1975 (56×41 mm) Set of 2 sheets	8·00	8·50

302 Carnotaurus

1999. Prehistoric Animals. Multicoloured.

3121	3d. Type **302**	45	45
3122	3d. Quetzalcoatlus	45	45
3123	3d. Peteinosaurus	45	45
3124	3d. Prenocephale	45	45
3125	3d. Hesperornis	45	45
3126	3d. Coelophysis	45	45
3127	3d. Camptosaurus	45	45
3128	3d. Panderichthys	45	45
3129	3d. Garudimimus	45	45
3130	3d. Cacops	45	45
3131	3d. Ichthyostega	45	45
3132	3d. Scutellosaurus	45	45
3133	3d. Diatryma	45	45
3134	3d. Pteranodon	45	45
3135	3d. Stegodon	45	45
3136	3d. Icaronycthris	45	45
3137	3d. Archaeopteryx	45	45
3138	3d. Chasmatosaurus	45	45
3139	3d. Tytthostonyx	45	45
3140	3d. Hyaenodon	45	45
3141	3d. Uintatherium	45	45
3142	3d. Hesperocyon	45	45
3143	3d. Ambelodon	45	45
3144	3d. Indricotherium	45	45
MS3145	Four sheets, each 110×85 mm. (a) 25d. Deinonychus. (b) 25d. Sabre-tooth Tiger. (c) 25d. Lepisosteus. (d) 25d. Microceratops Set of 4 sheets	14·00	15·00

Nos. 3121/32 and 3133/44 were printed together, se-tenant, forming composite designs.

303 Seagull

1999. Marine Life. Multicoloured.

3146	1d. Type **303**	20	15
3147	1d.50 Portuguese man-o-war	25	15
3148	3d. Whale shark	45	45
3149	3d. Grey reef shark	45	45
3150	3d. New England octopus	45	45
3151	3d. Pufferfish	45	45
3152	3d. Lionfish	45	45
3153	3d. Squid	45	45
3154	3d. Chambered nautilus	45	45
3155	3d. Clownfish	45	45
3156	3d. Moray eel	45	45
3157	3d. Spiny lobster	45	45
3158	3d. Spotted ray	45	45
3159	3d. Clown anemone	45	45
3160	3d. Angelfish	45	45
3161	3d. Leafy seadragon	45	45
3162	3d. Hawksbill turtle	45	45
3163	3d. Mandarinfish	45	45
3164	3d. Candy cane sea star	45	45
3165	3d. Plate coral	45	45
3166	3d. Butterflyfish	45	45
3167	3d. Coral polyp	45	45
3168	3d. Hermit crab	45	45
3169	3d. Strawberry shrimp	45	45
3170	3d. Giant blue clam	45	45
3171	3d. Sea cucumber	45	45
3172	5d. Walrus	75	75
3173	10d. Manatee	1·50	1·75
MS3174	110×85 mm. 25d. Common dolphin	4·00	4·25

Nos. 3148/59 and 3160/71 were printed together, se-tenant, forming composite designs.

304 "Sophrocattleya"

1999. Orchids of the World. Multicoloured.

3175	2d. Type **304**	50	25
3176	3d. "Cattleya" and butterfly	70	35
3177	4d. "Brassolaeliocattleya" (pink)	90	50
3178	5d. "Brassoepidendrum"	1·00	60
3179	6d. "Brassolaeliocattleya" (yellow)	1·00	1·00
3180	6d. "Cattleytonia"	1·00	1·00
3181	6d. "Lacliocattleya"	1·00	1·00
3182	6d. "Miltonia"	1·00	1·00
3183	6d. "Cattleya forbesii"	1·00	1·00
3184	6d. "Odontoglossum cervantesii"	1·00	1·00
3185	6d. "Lycaste macrobulbon"	1·00	1·00
3186	6d. "Laeliocattleya"	1·00	1·00
3187	6d. "Brassocattleya" (pink)	1·00	1·00
3188	6d. "Cattleya"	1·00	1·00
3189	6d. "Brassocattleya" (red spotted)	1·00	1·00
3190	6d. "Brassolaeliocattleya" (yellow and red)	1·00	1·00
3191	10d. "Sophrolaeliocattleya" and butterfly	1·75	1·90
3192	15d. "Iwanagaara" and butterfly	2·25	2·75
MS3193	Two sheets. (a) 81×106 mm. 25d. "Lycaste". (b) 85×110 mm. 25d. "Brassolaeliocattleya" (pink and white) Set of 2 sheets	8·50	8·50

305 American Black Oystercatcher

1999. Sea Birds. Multicoloured.

3194	2d. Type **305**	50	25
3195	3d. Blue-footed booby	70	35
3196	4d. Atlantic puffin	80	80
3197	4d. Red-billed tropic birds ("Red-tailed Tropic Bird")	80	80
3198	4d. Reddish egret	80	80
3199	4d. Laughing gull	80	80
3200	4d. Great egret	80	80
3201	4d. Northern gannet	80	80
3202	4d. Forster's tern	80	80
3203	4d. Common cormorant	80	80
3204	4d. Razorbill (perched on rocks)	80	80
3205	4d. Adelie penguin	80	80
3206	4d. Black skimmer	80	80
3207	4d. Big crested penguin ("Erect-crested Penguin")	80	80
3208	4d. Heermann's gull	80	80
3209	4d. Glaucous-winged gull	80	80
3210	4d. Laysan albatross	80	80
3211	4d. American white pelican	80	80
3212	4d. Tufted puffin	80	80
3213	4d. Black guillemot	80	80
3214	5d. Razorbill (in flight)	90	90
3215	5d. Common shelduck ("Shelduck")	90	90
3216	5d. Sandwich tern	90	90
3217	5d. Arctic skua	90	90
3218	5d. Northern gannet ("Gannet")	90	90
3219	5d. Mew gull ("Common Gull")	90	90
3220	10d. Western gull	1·75	1·90
3221	15d. Brown pelican	2·25	2·75
MS3222	Three sheets. (a) 110×85 mm. 25d. American white pelican ("Pelican"). (b) 105×76 mm. 25d. Gentoo penguin. (c) 106×76 mm. 25d. California gull Set of 3 sheets	11·00	12·00

Nos. 3196/3204, 3205/13 and 3214/19 were printed together, se-tenant, forming a composite design.

Nos. 3205 and 3210 are inscribed "ADELIES PENGUIN" or "LAYSON ALBATROSS", both in error.

305a Duchess of York and Princess Elizabeth, 1928

1999. "Queen Elizabeth the Queen Mother's Century".

3223	**305a**	10d. multicoloured	1·75	1·90
3224	-	10d. black and gold	1·75	1·90
3225	-	10d. black and gold	1·75	1·90
3226	-	10d. multicoloured	1·75	1·90
MS3227		153×155 mm. 25d. mult	4·25	4·50

DESIGNS: No. 3224, Lady Elizabeth Bowes-Lyon, 1923; 3225, Queen Elizabeth, 1946; 3226, Queen Mother and Prince Harry. (37×50 mm)—**MS**3227, Queen Mother on 89th Birthday, 1989.

306 Temple of A-Ma

1999. "China '99" International Stamp Exhibition, Beijing. Return of Macao to China. Multicoloured.

3228	7d. Type **306**	1·00	1·10
3229	7d. Border Gate	1·00	1·10
3230	7d. Ruins of St. Paul's	1·00	1·10

307 John F. Kennedy Jr. as Baby, 1961

1999. John F. Kennedy Jr. Commemoration. Each brown, blue and black.

3231	15d. Type **307**	2·00	2·50
3232	15d. John F. Kennedy Jr. as teenager	2·00	2·50
3233	15d. John F. Kennedy Jr. in 1997	2·00	2·50

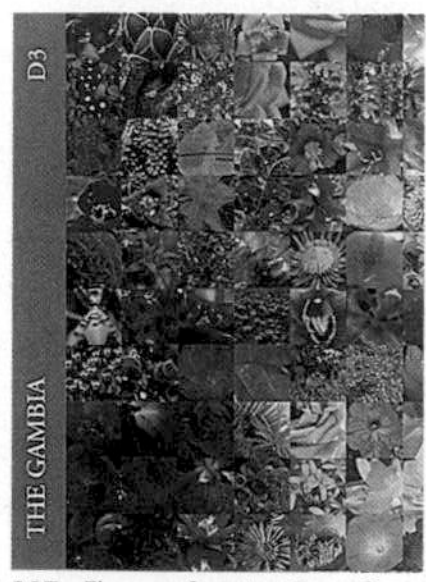

307a Flowers forming Top of Head

1999. Faces of the Millennium: Diana, Princess of Wales. Designs showing collage of miniature flower photographs. Multicoloured.

3234	3d. Type **307a** (face value at left)	50	50
3235	3d. Top of head (face value at right)	50	50
3236	3d. Ear (face value at left)	50	50
3237	3d. Eye and temple (face value at right)	50	50
3238	3d. Cheek (face value at left)	50	50
3239	3d. Cheek (face value at right)	50	50
3240	3d. Blue background (face value at left)	50	50
3241	3d. Chin (face value at right)	50	50

Nos. 3234/41 were printed together, se-tenant, so that the sheetlet forms a portrait of Diana, Princess of Wales.

308 Betty Boop

2000. Betty Boop (cartoon character). Mult.

3242 5d. Type **308** 75 80
3243 5d. In full-length gown 75 80
3244 5d. In T-shirt and dungarees 75 80
3245 5d. In cropped trousers, sleeveless shirt and tie 75 80
3246 5d. Sitting in wicker chair 75 80
3247 5d. In ripped purple trousers, orange T-shirt and gilet 75 80
3248 5d. In fur coat 75 80
3249 5d. In pink crinoline 75 80
3250 5d. In the gym 75 80
MS3251 Two sheets, each 140×89 mm. (a) 25d. In the bath. (b) 25d. With chin on hand Set of 2 sheets 8·00 8·50

309 Lucille Ball on Sofa

2000. Scenes from I Love Lucy (American T.V. comedy series). Multicoloured.

3252 5d. Type **309** 70 75
3253 5d. Lucy and Desi Arnaz talking 70 75
3254 5d. Lucy holding ball of string 70 75
3255 5d. Lucy in blue coat standing in front of lamp 70 75
3256 5d. Lucy and Desi kissing 70 75
3257 5d. Lucy in front of mirror 70 75
3258 5d. Lucy excited with hands clenched 70 75
3259 5d. Lucy sitting on Desi's knee 70 75
3260 5d. Lucy looking in purse 70 75
3261 5d. Lucy clutching shelf 70 75
3262 5d. Lucy leaning against wall with arms raised 70 75
3263 5d. Lucy with right fist in the air 70 75
3264 5d. Lucy sitting on shelf (front view) 70 75
3265 5d. Lucy smoothing hair with right hand 70 75
3266 5d. Lucy sitting on shelf (side view) 70 75
3267 5d. Desi Arnaz with Lucy bound 70 75
3268 5d. Lucy lying on sofa 70 75
3269 5d. Lucy being held by masked man 70 75
3270 5d. Lucy singing in Austrian costume 70 75
3271 5d. Lucy playing tambourine 70 75
3272 5d. Lucy and Desi in uniform singing 70 75
3273 5d. Lucy with stage trees 70 75
3274 5d. Lucy seated at organ with Desi 70 75
3275 5d. Desi with blonde girl sitting on bench 70 75
3276 5d. Lucy typing 70 75
3277 5d. Blonde girl with chorus 70 75
3278 5d. Lucy being carried off on bench 70 75
MS3279 Six sheets. (a) 100×140 mm. 25d. As No. 3256 (vert). (b) 100×140 mm. 25d. As No. 3257 (vert). (c) 103×130 mm. 25d. As No. 3269 (vert). (d) 130×98 mm. 25d. As No. 3270 (vert). (e) 130×100 mm. 25d. As No. 3273 (vert). (f) 130×100 mm. 25d. Lucy bound and gagged (vert) Set of 6 sheets 19·00 21·00

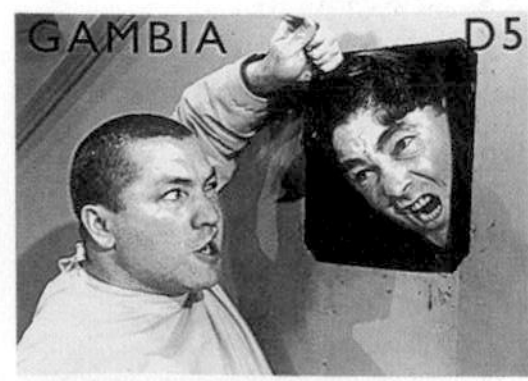

310 Curly pulling Moe through Hole

2000. Scenes from The Three Stooges (American T.V. comedy series). Multicoloured.

3280 5d. Type **310** 70 75
3281 5d. Curly with hands in mangle 70 75
3282 5d. Moe giving Curly a bottle 70 75
3283 5d. Larry having hair tugged 70 75
3284 5d. Moe with arms outstretched 70 75
3285 5d. Curly with finger up nose 70 75
3286 5d. Larry, Moe and Curly pointing 70 75
3287 5d. Moe biting Curly's nose with skull 70 75
3288 5d. Moe in yellow shirt and brown jacket 70 75
3289 5d. Moe in Heaven 70 75
3290 5d. Larry, Moe and Curly in Elizabethan costume 70 75
3291 5d. Larry, Moe and Curly in chemist shop 70 75
3292 5d. Moe with shotgun 70 75
3293 5d. With belly dancer 70 75
3294 5d. Larry and Moe in Scottish costume 70 75
3295 5d. Larry and Moe behind wheel 70 75
3296 5d. As postmen 70 75
3297 5d. Curly attacking Larry and Moe with stick 70 75
MS3298 Four sheets. (a) 89×140 mm. 25d. Larry wearing crown and leopard skin. (b) 140×89 mm. 25d. Curly using phone (inscr "GAMBIA") (vert). (c) 124×96 mm. 25d. Curly using phone (inscr "The Gambia") (vert). (d) 124×96 mm. 25d. Moe and Curly as postmen (vert) Set of 4 sheets 13·00 14·00

Nos. 3280/8 were printed together, se-tenant, forming a composite design.

310a Leonardo da Vinci's First Design for Flying Machine, 1480

2000. New Millennium. People and Events of Fifteenth Century (1450–1500). Multicoloured.

3299 2d. Type **310a** 30 30
3300 2d. Johannes Gutenberg (first printed Bible, 1455) 30 30
3301 2d. Capital "B" (first colour printing, 1457) 30 30
3302 2d. Ivan III ("the Great") becomes Grand Prince of Moscow, 1462 30 30
3303 2d. Walls under attack (Fall of Constantinople, 1453) 30 30
3304 2d. Great Wall of China rebuilt, 1488 30 30
3305 2d. Lorenzo de Medici (ruler of Florence) and "Pieta" (sculpture), 1479 30 30
3306 2d. King Henry VII of England (Foundation of Tudor dynasty, 1485) 30 30
3307 2d. Sailing ship and meeting with Indians (Vasco da Gama's voyage to India, 1497) 30 30
3308 2d. King Ferdinand V and Queen Isabella I (Union of Aragon and Castile, 1479) 30 30
3309 2d. Foetus (birth of Erasmus (Dutch scholar), 1466) 30 30
3310 2d. Sailing ship and Cross of St. George (John Cabot's voyage to North America, 1497) 30 30
3311 2d. King Henry VI and Richard, Duke of Gloucester (Wars of the Roses, 1455) 30 30
3312 2d. Bartolomeu Dias and map (Discovery of Cape of Good Hope, 1487) 30 30
3313 2d. Matthias Hunyadi (crowned King of Hungary, 1458) 30 30
3314 2d. Christopher Columbus (Discovery of the Americas, 1492) (59×39 mm) 30 30
3315 2d. Girolamo Savonarola (religious reformer) (executed 1498) 30 30

310b Max Planck (Quantum Theory of Energy, 1900)

2000. New Millennium. People and Events of Twentieth Century (1900–09). Multicoloured.

3316 3d. Type **310b** 45 45
3317 3d. Zeppelin in hangar (invention of rigid airship, 1900) 45 45
3318 3d. Guglielmo Marconi (first transatlantic radio message, 1901) 45 45
3319 3d. Funeral of Queen Victoria, 1901 45 45
3320 3d. Alfred Nobel (first Nobel Prizes awarded, 1901) 45 45
3321 3d. British infantry advancing (end of Boer War, 1902) 45 45
3322 3d. Wright Brothers and aircraft (first flight, 1903) 45 45
3323 3d. Early teddy bear, 1903 45 45
3324 3d. Panama Canal locks under construction, 1904 45 45
3325 3d. Albert Einstein (Theory of Relativity, 1905) 45 45
3326 3d. Crowd with flags (unrest in Russia, 1905) 45 45
3327 3d. Rescue squad and collapsed building, San Francisco earthquake, 1906 45 45
3328 3d. Louis Lumiere (development of colour photography, 1907) 45 45
3329 3d. "Les Demoiselles d'Avignon" (Pablo Picasso), 1907 45 45
3330 3d. Robert Peary (conquest of North Pole, 1909) 45 45
3331 3d. Henry Ford and first Model T, 1908 (59×39 mm) 45 45
3332 3d. Planting sapling (foundation of first Jewish kibbutz in Palestine, 1909) 45 45

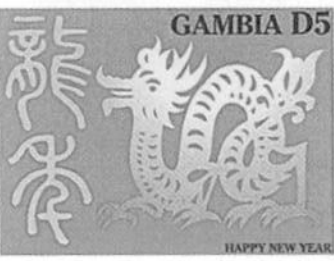

311 Dragon

2000. Chinese New Year ("Year of the Dragon"). Multicoloured.

3333 5d. Type **311** 70 75
3334 5d. Multicoloured dragon 70 75
3335 5d. Purple dragon 70 75
3336 5d. Brown dragon 70 75
MS3337 106×76 mm. 15d. Coiled dragon (39×24 mm) 2·00 2·25

312 Indris (lemur)

2000. Wildlife of Africa. Multicoloured.

3338 50b. Type **312** 20 15
3339 75b. Nubian ibex 20 15
3340 1d. Grevy's zebra (vert) 30 15
3341 2d. Bongo (vert) 40 20
3342 3d. White rhinoceros 80 50
3343 4d. Lesser galago 70 45
3344 5d. Okapi 75 75
3345 5d. Sable antelope 75 75
3346 5d. Greater kudu 75 75
3347 5d. African wild ass 75 75
3348 5d. Dorcas gazelle 75 75
3349 5d. Addax 75 75
3350 5d. Pelzeln's gazelle 75 75
3351 6d. Cheetah 90 90
3352 6d. Chimpanzee 90 90
3353 6d. Angwantibo 90 90
3354 6d. Black rhinoceros 90 90
3355 6d. Bontebok 90 90
3356 6d. Giant eland 90 90
3357 7d. Sacred ibis 1·00 1·00
3358 7d. Mauritius kestrel 1·00 1·00
3359 7d. Leopard 1·00 1·00
3360 7d. Radiated tortoise 1·00 1·00
3361 7d. Pygmy hippopotamus 1·00 1·00
3362 7d. Bald ibis 1·00 1·00
3363 7d. Mountain gorilla 1·00 1·00
3364 7d. Black-faced impala 1·00 1·00
3365 7d. Crowned lemur 1·00 1·00
3366 7d. Long-tailed ground roller 1·00 1·00
3367 7d. Brown hyena 1·00 1·00
3368 7d. Mountain zebra 1·00 1·00
3369 10d. Mhorr gazelle (vert) 1·60 1·75
MS3370 Four sheets, each 106×76 mm. (a) 25d. African elephant. (b) 25d. Aye-Aye. (c) 25d. Nile crocodile. (d) 25d. Black lechwe (vert) Set of 4 sheets 15·00 15·00

Nos. 3345/50, 3351/6, 3357/62 and 3363/8 were each printed together, se-tenant, with the backgrounds forming composite designs.

312a "A Genoese Senator" **312b** Prince William as Young Boy with Hands Clasped

2000. 400th Birth Anniv of Sir Anthony Van Dyck (Flemish painter). Multicoloured.

3371 5d. Type **312a** 70 70
3372 5d. "A Seated Gentlewoman" 70 70
3373 5d. "The Senator's Wife" 70 70
3374 5d. "Marchesa Balbi" 70 70
3375 5d. "Polyxena Spinola, Marchesa de Legones" 70 70
3376 5d. "Agostino Pallavicini" 70 70
3377 5d. "Anton Giulo Brignole-Sale" 70 70
3378 5d. "Paolina Adorno Brignole-Sale" 70 70
3379 5d. "Battina Balbi Durazzo" 70 70
3380 5d. "Man of the Cattaneo Family" 70 70
3381 5d. "Portrait of a Woman" 70 70
3382 5d. "Elena Grimaldi Cattaneo" 70 70
3383 5d. "Prince Rupert of the Palatinate" (1631–32) 70 70
3384 5d. "Prince William II of Orange-Nassau" 70 70
3385 5d. "Prince Charles Louis of the Palatinate" (1632) 70 70
3386 5d. "Prince Rupert, Count Palatinate" (1637) 70 70
3387 5d. "Princess Mary" 70 70
3388 5d. "Prince Charles Louis, Count Palatinate" (1637) 70 70
3389 5d. "Adoration of the Shepherds" (horiz) 70 70
3390 5d. "Rest on the Flight into Egypt" (Virgin of the Partridges) (horiz) 70 70
3391 5d. "Suffer the Little Children" (horiz) 70 70
3392 5d. "Christ and the Money-changers" (horiz) 70 70
3393 5d. "At the House of Simon the Pharisee" (horiz) 70 70
3394 5d. "Lamentation over the Dead Christ" (horiz) 70 70
3395 5d. "Samson and Delilah" (1619–20) (horiz) 70 70
3396 5d. Composition study for "Samson and Delilah" (horiz) 70 70
3397 5d. "Samson and Delilah" (1628–30) (horiz) 70 70
3398 5d. "Sir George Villiers and Lady Katherine Manners as Adonis and Venus" 70 70
3399 5d. "Lady Mary Villiers with Lord Arran as Cupid" 70 70
3400 5d. "Rachel de Ruvigney, Countess Southampton, as Fortune" 70 70
3401 5d. "Venus at Forge of Vulcan" 70 70
3402 5d. "Daedalus and Icarus" 70 70
3403 5d. "The Clipping of Cupid's Wings" 70 70
MS3404 Eight sheets. (a) 101×127 mm. 25d. "Portrait of Genoese Lady". (b) 101×127 mm. 25d. "Venetia, Lady Digby, as Prudence". (c) 101×127 mm. 25d. "Prince William II of Orange and his Bride". (d) 101×127 mm. 25d. "Prince Charles". (e) 127×101 mm. 25d. "Princes Charles Louis and Rupert of the Palatinate". (f) 127×101 mm. 25d. "The Three Eldest Children of Charles I". (g) 102×127 mm. 25d. "A Man with His Son" (horiz). (h) 102×127 mm. 25d. "Drunken Silenus" Set of 8 sheets 26·00 28·00

No. 3372 is inscribed "Getlewomen" and No. 3390 "Patridges", both in error.

2000. 18th Birthday of Prince William. Multicoloured.

3405 7d. Type **321b** 1·25 1·25

3406 7d. In blue checked shirt and blue jumper 1·25 1·25
3407 7d. With bouquet 1·25 1·25
3408 7d. Wearing suit 1·25 1·25
MS3409 100×80 mm. 25d. With Prince Harry in countryside 4·25 4·50

2000. "EXPO 2000" World Stamp Exhibition, Anaheim. Space Satellites. As T 582a of Ghana. Mult.
3410 7d. "Helios" (vert) 90 95
3411 7d. "Solar Max" (vert) 90 95
3412 7d. "SOHO" (vert) 90 95
3413 7d. "O.S.O." (vert) 90 95
3414 7d. Satellite rocket launch (vert) 90 95
3415 7d. "I.M.P." (vert) 90 95
3416 7d. "Uhuru" 90 95
3417 7d. "Rosat" 90 95
3418 7d. "I.U.E." 90 95
3419 7d. "Astro E" 90 95
3420 7d. "Exosat" 90 95
3421 7d. "Chandra" 90 95
MS3422 Two sheets, each 105×77 mm. (a) 25d. "Cassini Huygens". (b) 25d. "XMM" space telescope Set of 2 sheets 8·00 8·50
Nos. 3410/15 and 3416/21 were each printed together, se-tenant, with the backgrounds forming composite designs.

2000. 25th Anniv of "Apollo–Soyuz" Joint Project. As T 582b of Ghana. Multicoloured.
3423 15d. Donald Slayton ("Apollo 18" docking module pilot) 2·00 2·25
3424 15d. Thomas Stafford ("Apollo 18" Commander) 2·00 2·25
3425 15d. Vance Brand ("Apollo 18" command module pilot) 2·00 2·25
MS3426 70×87 mm. 25d. Diagram of docking tunnel (horiz) 4·00 4·25

2000. 50th Anniv of Berlin Film Festival. As T 582c of Ghana. Multicoloured.
3427 7d. Pane, *Amore e Fantasia*, 1954 90 95
3428 7d. Lord Olivier in *Richard III*, 1956 90 95
3429 7d. *Smultronstallet*, 1958 90 95
3430 7d. Sidney Poitier in *The Defiant Ones*, 1958 90 95
3431 7d. *The Living Desert*, 1954 90 95
3432 7d. *A Bout de Souffle*, 1960 90 95
MS3433 90×103 mm. 25d. Henry Fonda in "Twelve Angry Men", 1957 4·00 4·25

2000. 175th Anniv of Stockton and Darlington Line (first public railway). As T 582d of Ghana. Multicoloured.
3434 15d. As Type **582d** of Ghana 2·25 2·25
3435 15d. Septimus Norris' locomotive *Chesapeake*, 1846 2·25 2·25

312c Bach

2000. 250th Death Anniv of Johann Sebastian Bach (German composer). Sheet 105×100 mm.
MS3436 **312c** 25d. multicoloured 4·50 4·50

312d Albert Einstein

2000. Election of Albert Einstein (mathematical physicist) as Time Magazine "Man of The Century". Sheet 117×90 mm.
MS3437 **321d** 25d. multicoloured 4·00 4·25

2000. Centenary of First Zeppelin Flight. As T 582e of Ghana. Multicoloured.
3438 15d. LZ-10 *Schwaben*, 1911 2·00 2·25
3439 15d. LZ-127 *Graf Zeppelin*, 1928 2·00 2·25
3440 15d. LZ-129 *Hindenburg*, 1936 2·00 2·25
MS3441 92×66 mm. 25d. LZ-130 *Graf Zeppelin II* (50×36 mm) 4·00 4·25
Nos. 3438/40 were printed together, se-tenant, with the backgrounds forming a composite design.

2000. Olympic Games, Sydney. As T 582f of Ghana. Multicoloured.
3442 6d. P. Nurmi (cross-country runner), 1924 1·10 1·10
3443 6d. Basketball 1·10 1·10
3444 6d. Panathenian Stadium, Greece (1890) and Greek flag 1·10 1·10
3445 6d. Ancient Greek chariot racing 1·10 1·10

313 Pope John Paul II in Portugal, 1991

2000. Travels of Pope John Paul II.
3446-3455 6d.×10 (Type **313**: Poland, 1991; Hungary, 1991; Brazil, 1991; Senegal, 1992; Gambia, 1992; Guinea, 1992; Angola, 1992; St. Thomas and Prince Islands, 1992; Dominican Republic, 1992) 7·50 7·50
3456-3465 6d.×10 (Benin, 1993; Uganda, 1993; Sudan, 1993; Albania, 1993; Spain, 1993; Jamaica, 1993; Mexico, 1993; U.S.A., 1993; Lithuania, 1993; Latvia, 1993) 7·50 7·50
3466-3475 6d.×10 (Estonia, 1993; Croatia, 1994; Philippines, 1994; Papua New Guinea, 1995; Australia, 1995; Sri Lanka, 1995; Czech Republic, 1995; Belgium, 1995; Slovakia, 1995; Cameroon, 1995) 7·50 7·50
3476-3485 6d.×10 (South Africa, 1995; Kenya, 1995; U.S.A., 1995; United Nations, 1995; Guatemala, 1996; Nicaragua, 1996; El Salvador, 1996; Venezuela, 1996; Tunisia, 1996; Slovenia, 1996) 7·50 7·50
3486-3495 6d.×10 (Germany, 1996; Hungary, 1996; France, 1996; Bosnia, 1996; Czech Republic, 1997; Lebanon, 1997; Poland, 1997; France, 1997; Brazil, 1997; Cuba, 1998) 7·50 7·50
3496-3505 6d.×10 (Nigeria, 1998; Austria, 1998; Croatia, 1998; Mexico, 1999; U.S.A., 1999; Romania, 1999; Poland, 1999; Slovenia, 1999; India, 1999; Georgia, 1999) 7·50 7·50
MS3506 Eight sheets. (a) 80×75 mm. 25d. With Israeli children, 2000 (26×34 mm). (b) 75×80 mm. 25d. Rekindling "The Eternal Flame" at Yad Vashem Holocaust Museum, 2000 (26×34 mm). (c) 80×75 mm. 25d. Giving blessing from Mount Nebo, Jordan, 2000 (26×34 mm). (d) 80×75 mm. 25d. Looking down, Israel, 2000 (26×34 mm). (e) 80×75 mm. 25d. Praying at Western Wall, Jerusalem, 2000 (26×34 mm). (f) 80×75 mm. 25d. With Jewish bible, 2000 (26×34 mm). (g) 80×75 mm. 25d. Placing prayer in Western Wall, 2000 (26×34 mm). (h) 75×80 mm. 25d. Speaking at Yad Vashem Holocaust Memorial, 2000 (34×26 mm) Set of 8 sheets 24·00 26·00

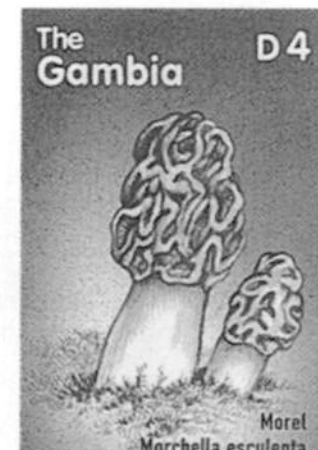

314 Morchella esculenta

2000. African Mushrooms. Multicoloured.
3507 4d. Type **314** 75 40
3508 5d. *Cantharellus cibarius* 85 45
3509 7d. *Leucocoprinus luteus* 1·00 1·00
3510 7d. *Panaeolus sphinctrinus* 1·00 1·00
3511 7d. *Agrocybe cylindracea* 1·00 1·00
3512 7d. *Amanita caesarea* 1·00 1·00
3513 7d. *Pluteus aurantiorugosus* 1·00 1·00
3514 7d. *Mycena pura* 1·00 1·00
3515 7d. *Lycoperdon perlatum* 1·00 1·00
3516 7d. *Astraeus hygrometricus* 1·00 1·00
3517 7d. *Volvariella bombycina* 1·00 1·00
3518 7d. *Lycoperdon pyriforme* 1·00 1·00
3519 7d. *Boletus appendiculatus* 1·00 1·00
3520 7d. *Cortinarius rubellus* 1·00 1·00
3521 15d. *Tricholoma ustale* 2·00 2·25
3522 20d. *Clavulinopsis helvola* 2·25 2·50
MS3523 Two sheets, each 106×76 mm. (a) 25d. "Collybia erythropus". (b) 25d. "Calocybe gambosa" Set of 2 sheets 8·00 8·50
No. 3516 is inscribed "Astracus" and No. 3519 "apendiculatus", both in error.

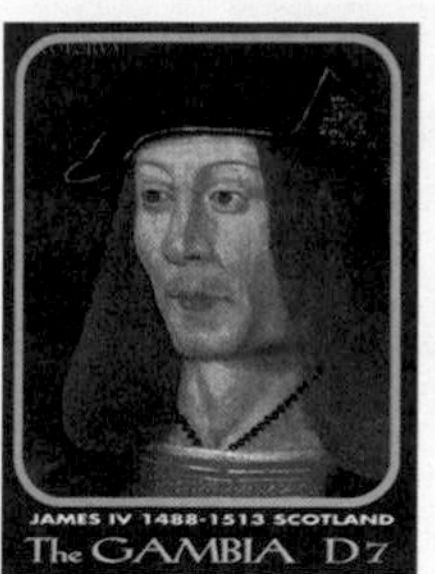

314a King James IV of Scotland

2000. Monarchs of the Millennium.
3524 **314a** 7d. multicoloured 1·00 1·00
3525 - 7d. multicoloured 1·00 1·00
3526 - 7d. multicoloured 1·00 1·00
3527 - 7d. multicoloured 1·00 1·00
3528 - 7d. multicoloured 1·00 1·00
3529 - 7d. multicoloured 1·00 1·00
3530 - 7d. black, stone and brown 1·00 1·00
3531 - 7d. multicoloured 1·00 1·00
3532 - 7d. multicoloured 1·00 1·00
3533 - 7d. black, stone and brown 1·00 1·00
3534 - 7d. multicoloured 1·00 1·00
3535 - 7d. black, stone and brown 1·00 1·00
3536 - 7d. multicoloured 1·00 1·00
3537 - 7d. multicoloured 1·00 1·00
MS3538 Three sheets, each 117×137 mm. (a) 25d. multicoloured. (b) 25d. multicoloured. (c) 25d. multicoloured Set of 3 sheets 11·00 12·00
DESIGNS: No. 3525, King James V of Scotland; 3526, King James VI of Scotland (I of England); 3527, Mary, Queen of Scots; 3528, Queen Mary II of England; 3529, Queen Elizabeth II of Great Britain (I of Scotland); 3530, King Charles II of France; 3531, Queen Catherine de Medici of France; 3532, Tsar Boris Godunov of Muscovy; 3533, Vasily III, Grand Prince of Moscow; 3534, Queen Anne of Great Britain; 3535, King Charles IX of France; 3536, King Charles I of England; 3537, Clovis IV, King of the Franks; **MS**3538a, King James IV of Scotland (*different*); **MS**3538b, Bahadur Shah II, King of Delhi; **MS**3538c, "King Robert I of Scotland".
No. 3537 is inscr "CLOVIS III", and No. **MS**3538a "JAMES IV OF ENGLAND"; both in error. No. **MS**3538c actually shows a portrait of Robert Walpole, first Prime Minister of Great Britain.

314b Felix IV

2000. Popes of the Millennium. Each black, yellow and olive.
3539 7d. Type **314b** 1·00 1·00
3540 7d. Gelasius I 1·00 1·00
3541 7d. Gregory I 1·00 1·00
3542 7d. Gregory IX 1·00 1·00
3543 7d. Gregory XII 1·00 1·00
3544 7d. Honorius III 1·00 1·00
3545 7d. Gregory XIII 1·00 1·00
3546 7d. Urban II 1·00 1·00
3547 7d. Sixtus I 1·00 1·00
3548 7d. Pius IX 1·00 1·00
3549 7d. Pius IV 1·00 1·00
3550 7d. Pascal I 1·00 1·00
3551 7d. Alexander VII 1·00 1·00
3552 7d. Benedict XI 1·00 1·00
3553 7d. Callistus III 1·00 1·00
3554 7d. Celestine V 1·00 1·00
3555 7d. Clement IX 1·00 1·00
3556 7d. Fabian 1·00 1·00
MS3557 Three sheets, each 115×135 mm. (a) 25d. Peter. (b) 25d. Damasus I. (c) 25d. John I. Each black, stone and brown Set of 3 sheets 12·00 12·00

315 *Amphicallia tigris*

2000. Butterflies. Multicoloured.
3558 1d.50 Type **315** 30 15
3559 2d. *Myrina silenus* 35 20
3560 3d. *Chrysiridia madagascariensis* 50 20
3560a 4d. *Amphicalia tigris* 15 20
3561 5d. *Papilionidae* 75 30
3562 7d. *Salamis temora* 90 40
3563 8d. *Cryestis camillus* 1·00 70
3564 10d. *Dasiothia medea* 1·25 75
3565 20d. *Papilio demodocus* 2·25 2·00
3566 25d. *Danaus chrysippus* 2·40 2·25
3567 50d. *Coeliades forestan* 4·50 4·50
3568 75d. *Ornithoptera alexandrae* 6·00 6·50
3568a 100d. *Morpho cypris* 7·50 8·50
No. 3558 is inscribed "Amphicalia", 3560 "madagascarensis" and 3563 "Cyrestis", all in error.

316 Pavel Nedved (Czech player)

2000. "Euro 2000" Football Championship. Multicoloured.
3569 7d. Type **316** 90 90
3570 7d. Czech Republic team 90 90
3571 7d. Ladislav Maier (Czech player) 90 90
3572 7d. Antonin Panenka (Czech player) 90 90
3573 7d. Selessin Stadium, Liege 90 90
3574 7d. Patrik Berger (Czech player) 90 90
3575 7d. Alan Shearer (English player) 90 90
3576 7d. English team 90 90
3577 7d. David Seaman (English player) 90 90
3578 7d. Sol Campbell (English player) 90 90
3579 7d. Philips Stadium, Eindhoven 90 90
3580 7d. Gareth Southgate (English player) 90 90
3581 7d. Oyvind Leonhardsen (Norwegian player) 90 90
3582 7d. Norwegian team 90 90
3583 7d. Erik Mykland (Norwegian player) 90 90
3584 7d. Stale Solbakken (Norwegian player) 90 90
3585 7d. Kjetil Rekdal (Norwegian player) 90 90
3586 7d. Sergen Yalcin (Turkish player) 90 90
3587 7d. Turkish team 90 90
3588 7d. Okan Buruk (Turkish player) 90 90
3589 7d. Arif Erdem (Turkish player) 90 90
3590 7d. Koning Boudewijn Stadium 90 90
3591 7d. Tayfun Korkut (Turkish player) 90 90
3592 7d. Fredrik Ljungberg (Swedish player) 90 90
3593 7d. Swedish team 90 90
3594 7d. Andersson (Swedish player) 90 90
3595 7d. Roland Nilsson (Swedish player) 90 90
3596 7d. Stefan Schwarz (Swedish player) 90 90
3597 7d. Aleksander Knavs (Slovene player) 90 90
3598 7d. Slovenian team 90 90
3599 7d. Alatko Zahovic (Slovene player) 90 90
3600 7d. Ales Ceh (Slovene player) 90 90
3601 7d. Stade Communal, Charleroi 90 90
3602 7d. Miran Pavlin (Slovene player) 90 90
MS3603 Six sheets, each 145×95 mm. (a) 25d. Jozef Chovanec (Czech trainer) (vert). (b) 25d. Kevin Keegan (English trainer) (vert). (c) 25d. Nils-Johan Semb (Norwegian trainer) (vert). (d) 25d. Mustafa Denizli (Turkish trainer) (vert). (e) 25d. Tommy Soderberg and Lars Lagerback (Swedish trainers) (vert). (f) 25d. Srecko Katanec (Slovene trainer) (vert) Set of 6 sheets 20·00 22·00
No. 3581 is inscribed "LEONARDSEN" in error.

317 West Highland White Terrier Puppy

2000. "The Stamp Show 2000" International Stamp Exhibition, London. Cats and Dogs of the World. (a) Dogs. Multicoloured.

3604	1d. Type **317**	20	20
3605	1d.50 Bernese mountain dog puppy	30	20
3606	3d. Yorkshire terrier puppy	50	25
3607	4d. Labrador (inscr "West Highland White Terrier Puppy")	65	40
3608	7d. Border collie puppy (brown)	1·00	1·00
3609	7d. Border collie puppy (black)	1·00	1·00
3610	7d. Yorkshire terrier puppies	1·00	1·00
3611	7d. German shepherd puppy	1·00	1·00
3612	7d. Beagle puppy	1·00	1·00
3613	7d. Spaniel puppy	1·00	1·00
3614	10d. Chow Chow puppy	1·75	1·90
3615	15d. Poodle puppy	2·25	2·50
MS3616	106×75 mm. 25d. Boxer puppy	4·25	4·50

(b) Cats. Designs as T 317, but horiz.

3617	4d. black, green and grey	65	70
3618	4d. black, green and grey	65	70
3619	4d. black, brown and grey	65	70
3620	4d. black, yellow and grey	65	70
3621	4d. black, blue and grey	65	70
3622	4d. black, orange and grey	65	70
3623	4d. black, blue and grey	65	70
3624	4d. black, yellow and grey	65	70
3625	5d. black, blue and grey	75	80
3626	5d. black, yellow and grey	75	80
3627	5d. black, green and grey	75	80
3628	5d. black, yellow and grey	75	80
3629	5d. black, yellow and grey	75	80
3630	5d. black, green and grey	75	80
3631	5d. black, yellow and grey	75	80
3632	5d. black, yellow and grey	75	80
MS3633	Two sheets, each 106×77 mm. (a) 25d. multicoloured. (b) 25d. multicoloured Set of 2 sheets	8·50	8·50

DESIGNS: No. 3617, Egyptian mau; 3618, Singapura; 3619, American shorthair; 3620, Cornish rex; 3621, Birman; 3622, Scottish fold; 3623, Turkish angora; 3624, Turkish van; 3625, Ragdoll; 3626, Bombay; 3627, Koral; 3628, Somali; 3629, British shorthair; 3630, American curl; 3631, Maine coon; 3632, Turkish van; **MS**3633a, Mother cat with kitten; **MS**3633b, Egyptian mau.

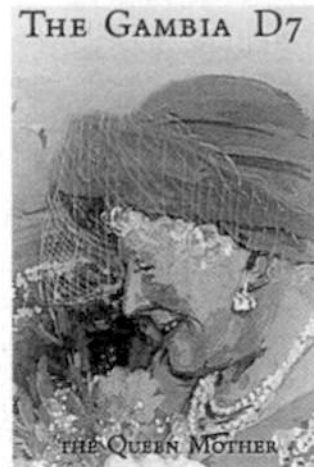

318 Queen Elizabeth the Queen Mother

2000. Queen Elizabeth the Queen Mother's 100th Birthday.

3634	**318**	7d. multicoloured	1·10	1·10

2000. Faces of the Millennium: Queen Elizabeth the Queen Mother's 100th Birthday. As T 307a showing collage of miniature flower photographs. Multicoloured.

3635	5d. Top of head (face value at left)	1·00	1·00
3636	5d. Top of head (face value at right)	1·00	1·00
3637	5d. Eye and temple (face value at left)	1·00	1·00
3638	5d. Temple (face value at right)	1·00	1·00
3639	5d. Cheek (face value at left)	1·00	1·00
3640	5d. Cheek (face value at right)	1·00	1·00
3641	5d. Chin (face value at left)	1·00	1·00
3642	5d. Neck (face value at right)	1·00	1·00

Nos. 3635/42 were printed together, se-tenant, in sheetlets of 8 with the stamps arranged in two vertical columns separated by a gutter also containing miniature photographs. When viewed as a whole, the sheetlet forms a portrait of the Queen Mother.

2000. Faces of the Millennium: 80th Birthday of Pope John Paul II. As T 307a showing collage of miniature religious photographs. Multicoloured.

3643	6d. Top of head (face value at left)	1·25	1·25
3644	6d. Top of head (face value at right)	1·25	1·25
3645	6d. Ear (face value at left)	1·25	1·25
3646	6d. Forehead (face value at right)	1·25	1·25
3647	6d. Neck (face value at left)	1·25	1·25
3648	6d. Cheek (face value at right)	1·25	1·25
3649	6d. Shoulder (face value at left)	1·25	1·25
3650	6d. Hands (face value at right)	1·25	1·25

Nos. 3643/50 were printed together, se-tenant, in sheetlets of 8 with the stamps arranged in two vertical columns separated by a gutter also containing miniature photographs. When viewed as a whole, the sheetlet forms a portrait of Pope John Paul II.

319 "A White Pheasant and other Fowl in a Classical Landscape" (Abraham Bisschop)

321 Antonio Vivaldi

320 Allard on Peking–Paris Rally

2000. Bird Paintings. Multicoloured.

3651	1d.50 Type **319**	40	25
3652	3d. "Salmon-crested Cockatoo" (Bartolomeo Bimbi)	60	30
3653	4d. "Great Bustard Cock and Other Birds" (Ludger Tom Ring)	70	45
3654	5d. "Still Life of Birds" (Caravaggio) (horiz)	75	75
3655	5d. "Turkeys with Young and Rock Doves" (Johan Wenzel Peter) (horiz)	75	75
3656	5d. "The Threatened Swan" (Jan Asselyn) (horiz)	75	75
3657	5d. "Still Life of Fruit and Birds in a Landscape" (Jokob Bogdani) (horiz)	75	75
3658	5d. "Mobbing the Owl" (Tobias Stranover) (horiz)	75	75
3659	5d. "Concert of Birds" (Melchior de Hondecoeter) (horiz)	75	75
3660	5d. "Owls and Young Ones" (William Tomkins) (horiz)	75	75
3661	5d. "Birds by a Stream" (Jean Baptiste Oudry) (horiz)	75	75
3662	5d. "Peacocks Hens and Mouse" (Tobias Stranover)	75	75
3663	5d. "Lady in a Red Jacket feeding a Parrot" (Frans van Mieris)	75	75
3664	5d. "Birds by a Pool" (Melchior de Hondecoeter)	75	75
3665	5d. "Ganymede and the Eagle" (Rubens)	75	75
3666	5d. "Leda and the Swan" (Cesare da Sesto)	75	75
3667	5d. "Ducks and Ducklings at the Foot of a Tree in a Mediterranean Landscape" (Adriaen van Oolen)	75	75
3668	5d. "Portrait of the Falconer Robert Cheseman carrying a Hooded Falcon" (Holbein)	75	75
3669	5d. "Golden Pheasant on a Stone Plinth, with other Birds" (Jacobus Vonck)	75	75
3670	15d. "Great Black-backed Gull and other Birds" (Jokob Bogdani)	2·25	2·50
MS3671	Two sheets, each 76×63 mm. (a) 25d. "Still Life of Birds" (Georg Flegel) (horiz). (b) 25d. "King Eagle pursued to the Sun" (Philip Reinagle) Set of 2 sheets	8·00	8·50

2000. 12th Classic Car Marathon. Showing cars from Himalayan Rally (No. MS3688a) or Peking–Paris Rally (others). Multicoloured.

3672	5d. Type **320**	75	75
3673	5d. Ford Coupe	75	75
3674	5d. Citroen Pilot	75	75
3675	5d. Packard (white)	75	75
3676	5d. Austin A90	75	75
3677	5d. Bentley	75	75
3678	5d. Packard (red)	75	75
3679	5d. Aston Martin	75	75
3680	5d. Morgan	75	75
3681	5d. Rover	75	75
3682	5d. Marmon	75	75
3683	5d. Rolls Royce Silver Cloud	75	75
3684	5d. Rolls Royce Phantom	75	75
3685	5d. Mercedes 680S	75	75
3686	5d. Mercedes saloon	75	75
3687	5d. Invicta	75	75
MS3688	Two sheets, each 86×59 mm. (a) 25d. Morris Minor. (b) 25d. Cadillac Set of 2 sheets	8·00	8·50

2000. Classical Opera and Oratorio Composers. Multicoloured.

3689	7d. Type **321**	1·25	1·25
3690	7d. Giacomo Puccini	1·25	1·25
3691	7d. Franz Joseph Haydn	1·25	1·25
3692	7d. Leopold Stokowski	1·25	1·25
3693	7d. Felix Mendelssohn	1·25	1·25
3694	7d. Gaetano Donizetti	1·25	1·25
3695	7d. Witold Lutoslawski	1·25	1·25
3696	7d. Sir William Sterndale Bennett	1·25	1·25
3697	7d. Wolfgang Amadeus Mozart	1·25	1·25
3698	7d. Ludwig van Beethoven	1·25	1·25
3699	7d. Sergei Rachmaninov	1·25	1·25
3700	7d. Pyotr Tchaikovsky	1·25	1·25
MS3701	Two sheets. (a) 95×72 mm. 25d. Frederic Chopin. (b) 67×95 mm. 25d. Manuel de Falla Set of 2 sheets	8·50	8·50

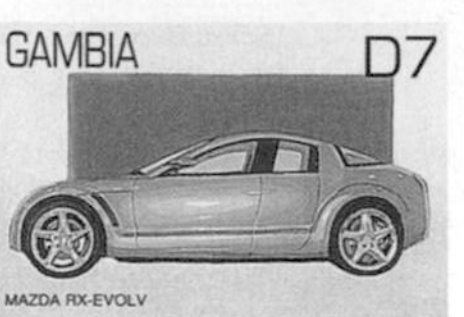

322 Mazda RX-Evolv

2000. Transport in the Next Millennium. Mult.

3702	7d. Type **322**	1·00	1·00
3703	7d. Isuzu Kai	1·00	1·00
3704	7d. Ford 021C	1·00	1·00
3705	7d. Pontiac GTO	1·00	1·00
3706	7d. Chevrolet Cerv III	1·00	1·00
3707	7d. Toyota Will VI	1·00	1·00
3708	7d. Blended-wing body BWB-1 aircraft	1·00	1·00
3709	7d. Boeing's 767-400ERX	1·00	1·00
3710	7d. New Lockheed concept fighter	1·00	1·00
3711	7d. Boeing "X" bomber	1·00	1·00
3712	7d. American National Aerospaceplane X30 concept	1·00	1·00
3713	7d. Hotol space plane separating from Antonov AN-225	1·00	1·00
3714	8d. Pendolare concept speedboat	1·10	1·10
3715	8d. Plansail catamaran	1·10	1·10
3716	8d. New Airfoil concept	1·10	1·10
3717	8d. Ferry Sea Coaster hydrofoil concept	1·10	1·10
3718	8d. *Shinaitoku Matu* (tanker) showing new sail technology	1·10	1·10
3719	8d. Supersport luxury yacht concept	1·10	1·10
3720	8d. Maglev MLU-002 train	1·10	1·10
3721	8d. Airport magnetic rail car system	1·10	1·10
3722	8d. Modern monorail train	1·10	1·10
3723	8d. Two-car monorail, Seattle	1·10	1·10
3724	8d. New "above cabin" monorail concept	1·10	1·10
3725	8d. Streamlined monorail concept	1·10	1·10
MS3726	Four sheets, each 110×85 mm. (a) 25d. Honda Sproket concept. (b) 25d. Nautic Air 400 flying boat concept. (c) 25d. Triton U.S. Coast Guard patrol vessel concept (58×43 mm). (d) 25d. Maglev train (58×43 mm) Set of 4 sheets	13·00	14·00

No. 3722 is inscribed "MONRAIL" in error.

323 Ships of the Spanish Armada, 1588

2000. Historic Ships of the World. Multicoloured.

3727	5d. Type **323**	1·00	50
3728	7d. 18th-century Chinese junks	1·10	1·10
3729	7d. 15th-century cog	1·10	1·10
3730	7d. *Henri Grace a Dieu* (galleon) at anchor	1·10	1·10
3731	7d. Tapestry of St. Brendan at sea	1·10	1·10
3732	7d. Figurehead by Grinling Gibbons	1·10	1·10
3733	7d. 16th-century British carrack	1·10	1·10
3734	7d. 18th-century British first-rate ship of the line	1·10	1·10
3735	7d. 16th-century Spanish galleon	1·10	1·10
3736	7d. Russian four-masted barque	1·10	1·10
3737	7d. *Henri Grace a Dieu* (galleon) at sea	1·10	1·10
3738	7d. Frontispiece from John Dee's *Arte of Navigation*	1·10	1·10
3739	7d. 19th-century British ironclad	1·10	1·10
3740	10d. *Colombo* (Brazilian river gunboat)	1·60	1·75
3741	15d. *Jenissel* (Russian minelayer)	2·00	2·25
3742	20d. *Yamato* (Japanese ironclad)	2·40	2·75
MS3743	Two sheets, each 102×115 mm. (a) 25d. H.M.S. *Challenger* (survey ship). (b) 25d. *Golden Hind* (Drake) Set of 2 sheets	8·50	8·50

Nos. 3728/33 and 3734/9 were each printed together, se-tenant, with the backgrounds forming composite designs.

324 Yellow-rumped Tinkerbird

326 Head of Akhal-Teke Horse

325 "At Full Stretch" (John Skeaping)

2000. Tropical Birds. Multicoloured.

3744	7d. Type **324**	1·10	1·10
3745	7d. Black-throated honeyguide ("Greater Honeyguide")	1·10	1·10
3746	7d. Hoopoe	1·10	1·10
3747	7d. European roller	1·10	1·10
3748	7d. Carmine bee eater	1·10	1·10
3749	7d. White-throated bee eater	1·10	1·10
3750	7d. Grey parrot	1·10	1·10
3751	7d. Great spotted cuckoo	1·10	1·10
3752	7d. Bar-tailed trogon	1·10	1·10
3753	7d. African hobby	1·10	1·10
3754	7d. Green turaco	1·10	1·10
3755	7d. Trumpeter hornbill	1·10	1·10
3756	7d. Pied flycatcher	1·10	1·10
3757	7d. Blackcap	1·10	1·10
3758	7d. Common stonechat	1·10	1·10
3759	7d. Nightingale	1·10	1·10
3760	7d. Black-headed tchagra	1·10	1·10
3761	7d. Yellow wagtail	1·10	1·10
MS3762	Three sheets, each 85×110 mm. (a) 25d. European bee eater (horiz). (b) 25d. Bateleur (horiz). (c) 25d. Secretary bird (horiz) Set of 3 sheets	12·00	12·00

Nos. 3744/9, 3750/5 and 3756/61 were each printed together, se-tenant, with the backgrounds forming composite designs.

2000. Horse Paintings. Multicoloured.

3763	4d. Type **325**	60	30
3764	5d. "The Burton" (Lionel Edwards)	75	40
3765	7d. "Horses emerging from the Sea" (Delacroix)	1·00	1·00
3766	7d. "The 9th Duke of Marlborough on a Grey Hunter" (Sir Alfred Munnings)	1·00	1·00
3767	7d. "Ovid in Exile amongst the Scythians" (Delacroix)	1·00	1·00
3768	7d. "Early Morning Gallop" (John Skeaping)	1·00	1·00
3769	7d. "Mare and Foal" (Sir Alfred Munnings)	1·00	1·00
3770	7d. "Three-a-side Polo at Simla" (Lionel Edwards)	1·00	1·00
3771	7d. "A Lady hawking" (E. Vernet) (vert)	1·00	1·00
3772	7d. "Captain Robert Orme" (Reynolds) (vert)	1·00	1·00
3773	7d. "Napoleon crossing the Alps" (David) (vert)	1·00	1·00
3774	7d. "Nobby Grey" (Sir Alfred Munnings) (vert)	1·00	1·00
3775	7d. "Amateur Jockeys near a Carriage" (Degas) (vert)	1·00	1·00
3776	7d. "Three-a-side Polo at Simla" (Lionel Edwards) (vert)	1·00	1·00
3777	10d. "Game of Polo" (Li-Lin)	1·60	1·75
3778	15d. "St. George and the Dragon" (Raphael)	2·00	2·50
MS3779	Two sheets, each 90×70 mm. (a) 25d. "The Reckoning" (George Morland). (b) 25d. "One of the Family" (Frederick Cotman) Set of 2 sheets	8·00	8·50

2000. Horses of the World. Multicoloured.

3780	7d. Type **326**	1·00	1·00
3781	7d. Palomino	1·00	1·00
3782	7d. Kladuber	1·00	1·00

3783	7d. Paint horse	1·00	1·00
3784	7d. Pinto	1·00	1·00
3785	7d. Kabaroin	1·00	1·00
3786	7d. Akhal-Teke (horiz)	1·00	1·00
3787	7d. Kladruber (horiz)	1·00	1·00
3788	7d. Palomino (horiz)	1·00	1·00
3789	7d. Pinto (horiz)	1·00	1·00
3790	7d. Paint horse (horiz)	1·00	1·00
3791	7d. Kabaroin (horiz)	1·00	1·00
MS3792	87×70 mm. 25d. Palomino	4·00	4·25

326a "The Madonna of the Fish" (Raphael)

2000. "Espana 2000". International Stamp Exhibition, Madrid. Paintings from the Prado Museum. Multicoloured.

3793	6d. Type **326a**	75	80
3794	6d. "The Holy Family with a Lamb" (Raphael)	75	80
3795	6d. "The Madonna of the Stair" (Andrea del Sarto)	75	80
3796	6d. Moneychanger from "The Moneychanger and his Wife" (Marinus van Reymerswaele)	75	80
3797	6d. "Madonna and Child" (Jan Gossaert)	75	80
3798	6d. Wife from "The Money-changer and his Wife" (Van Reymerswaele)	75	80
3799	6d. "St. Andrew" (Francisco Rizi)	75	80
3800	6d. "Christ Crucified" (Velazquez)	75	80
3801	6d. "St. Onuphrius" (Francisco Collantes)	75	80
3802	6d. "Charles II of Spain" (Juan de Miranda)	75	80
3803	6d. "St. Sebastian" (De Miranda)	75	80
3804	6d. "Peter Ivanovich Potemkin" (De Miranda)	75	80
3805	6d. St. Benedict from "St. Benedict's Supper" (Juan Ricci)	75	80
3806	6d. "Our Lady of the Immaculate Conception" (Zurbaran)	75	80
3807	6d. Monk with candle from "St. Benedict's Supper" (Ricci)	75	80
3808	6d. "The Penitent Magdalen" (Jose de Ribera)	75	80
3809	6d. "Christ as Man of Sorrows" (Antonio de Pereda)	75	80
3810	6d. "St. Jerome" (De Pereda)	75	80
3811	6d. "Children with a Shell" (Murillo)	75	80
3812	6d. "Our Lady of the Immaculate Conception" (Murillo)	75	80
3813	6d. "The Good Shepherd" (Murillo)	75	80
3814	6d. Young woman from "The Parasol" (Goya)	75	80
3815	6d. "A Rural Gift" (Ramon Bayeu)	75	80
3816	6d. Young man from "The Parasol" (Goya)	75	80
3817	6d. "Portrait of a Young Woman" (Velazquez)	75	80
3818	6d. "The Painter Francisco Goya" (Vicente Portana)	75	80
3819	6d. "Portrait of a Girl" (Raphael Diaz)	75	80
3820	6d. Virgin Mary from "The Nativity" (Frederico Barocci)	75	80
3821	6d. "Madonna and Child with St. John" (Correggio)	75	80
3822	6d. Holy Child from "The Nativity" (Barocci)	75	80
3823	6d. "Queen Isabelle Farnese" (Jean Ranc)	75	80
3824	6d. "Young Woman from Back" (Jean-Baptiste Greuze)	75	80
3825	6d. "Charles III of Spain as a Child" (Ranc)	75	80
3826	6d. "James Bordieu" (Reynolds)	75	80
3827	6d. "Dr. Isaac Henrique Sequeria" (Reynolds)	75	80
3828	6d. "Portrait of a Clergyman" (Reynolds)	75	80
MS3829	Six sheets, each 110×90 mm. (a) 25d. "The Defence of Cádiz against the English" (Zubarán). (b) 25d. "The Surrender of Juliers" (Jusepe Leonardo). (c) 25d. "The Holy Family with a Little Bird" (Murillo). (d) 25d. "Jacob's Dream" (De Ribera) (horiz). (e) 25d. "Venus and Adonis" (Veronese) (horiz). (f) 25d. "Danäe" (Titian) (horiz) Set of 6 sheets	20·00	22·00

327 Bristol Blenheim of 29 Squadron

2000. 60th Anniv of Battle of Britain. Mult.

3830	5d. Type **327**	1·00	1·00
3831	5d. Helmut Wick shooting down Hurricane	1·00	1·00
3832	5d. Spitfire of 65 Squadron attacking Dornier 217	1·00	1·00
3833	5d. Bristol Beaufighter IIF of 604 Squadron	1·00	1·00
3834	5d. Boulton Paul Defiants of 264 Squadron	1·00	1·00
3835	5d. Spitfire in dogfight with Stuka JU-87	1·00	1·00
3836	5d. British fighters over Tower Bridge	1·00	1·00
3837	5d. Gloster Gladiator of 615 Squadron	1·00	1·00
3838	5d. Hurricane attacking Messerschmitt Bf 109	1·00	1·00
3839	5d. Spitfire attacking two Messerschmitt Bf 109s	1·00	1·00
3840	5d. Flt.-Lt. Gilliam attacking Dornier 217s	1·00	1·00
3841	5d. Two Hurricanes of 610 Squadron	1·00	1·00
3842	5d. Hurricanes of 85 Squadron	1·00	1·00
3843	5d. G. A. Langley attacking Messerschmitt 109	1·00	1·00
3844	5d. Bristol Blenheim IV of 23 Squadron	1·00	1·00
3845	5d. Spitfires of 222 Squadron taking off	1·00	1·00
MS3846	Two sheets, each 110×85 mm. (a) 25d. Adolf Galland (commander of Group III of JG26). (b) 25d. Group Captain Frank Carey Set of 2 sheets	8·50	8·50

No. 3834 is inscribed "Bolton-Paul" in error.

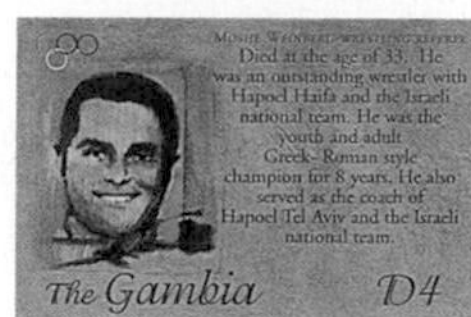

328 Moshe Weinberg (wrestling referee)

2000. Victims of Munich Olympics Massacre (1972) Commemoration. Showing Israeli athletes and officials. Multicoloured.

3847	4d. Type **328**	90	90
3848	4d. Eliezer Halffin (wrestler)	90	90
3849	4d. Mark Slavin (wrestler)	90	90
3850	4d. Ze'ev Friedman (weightlifter)	90	90
3851	4d. Joseph Romano (weightlifter)	90	90
3852	4d. Kahat Shor (shooting coach)	90	90
3853	4d. David Berger (weightlifter)	90	90
3854	4d. Joseph Gottfreund (wrestling referee)	90	90
3855	4d. Andrei Schpitzer (fencing referee)	90	90
3856	4d. Amitsur Shapira (athletics coach)	90	90
3857	4d. Yaakov Springer (weightlifting referee)	90	90
3858	4d. Munich Olympics emblem	90	90
MS3859	96×130 mm. 25d. Israeli athlete with Olympic torch (vert)	4·50	4·50

329 Ferrari 333SP Racing Car

2000. Ferrari Racing Cars. Multicoloured.

3860	4d. Type **329**	60	30
3861	5d. Ferrari 512S	75	40
3862	10d. Ferrari 312P	1·40	1·40
3863	25d. Ferrari 330P4	2·50	3·00

330 Symbolic Snake and Chinese Characters

2001. Chinese New Year ("Year of the Snake"). Showing different snakes. Multicoloured.

3864	4d. Type **330**	55	60
3865	4d. Orange and mauve snake	55	60
3866	4d. Blue and violet snake	55	60
3867	4d. Green and yellow snake	55	60
MS3868	71×100 mm. 15d. Snake in grass	2·00	2·25

330a "Vessels in a Strong Wind" (Jan Porcellis)

2001. Bicentenary of Rijksmuseum, Amsterdam. Dutch Paintings. Multicoloured.

3869	7d. Type **330a**	85	90
3870	7d. "Seascape in the Morning" (Simon de Vlieger)	85	90
3871	7d. "Travellers at a Country Inn" (Issack van Ostade)	85	90
3872	7d. "Orpheus with Animals in a Landscape" (Aelbert Cuyp)	85	90
3873	7d. "Italian with a Mountain Plateau" (Cornelis van Poelenburch)	85	90
3874	7d. Loading boat from "Boatman Moored on a Lake Shore" (Adam Pynacker)	85	90
3875	7d. Woman playing viol from "Gallant Company" (Pieter Codde)	85	90
3876	7d. Returning hunters from "Gallant Company" (Codde)	85	90
3877	7d. Kneeling man from "The Marriage of Willem van Loon and Margaretha Bas" (Jan Molenaer)	85	90
3878	7d. Bride's party from "The Marriage of Willem van Loon and Margaretha Bas" (Molenaer)	85	90
3879	7d. Man and two women from "The Marriage of Willem van Loon and Margaretha Bas" (Molenaer)	85	90
3880	7d. "Johanna Le Maire" (Nicolaes Pickenoy)	85	90
3881	7d. "The Meagre Company" (Hals and Codde)	85	90
3882	7d. "The Twins Clara and Aelbert de Bray" (Salomon de Bray)	85	90
3883	7d. "Self-portrait" (Ferdinand Bol)	85	90
3884	7d. "Ambulatory of the New Church in Delft" (Gerard Houckgeest)	85	90
3885	7d. "Tomb of Willem the Silent in New Church of Delft" (Emanuel de Witte)	85	90
3886	7d. "Mountainous Landscape" (Hercules Segers)	85	90
3887	7d. Pie and glass of wine from "Still Life with Turkey Pie" (Pieter Claesz)	85	90
3888	7d. "Still Life with Gilt Goblet" (Willem Heda)	85	90
3889	7d. "Still Life with Lobster and Nautilus Cup" (Jan de Heem)	85	90
3890	7d. "Bacchanal" (detail) (Moses van Uyttenbroeck)	85	90
3891	7d. "The Anatomy Lesson of Dr. Nicolaes Tulp" (Rembrandt)	85	90
3892	7d. "Johannes Lutma" (Jacob Backer)	85	90
3893	7d. Decanter from "Still Life with Turkey Pie" (Claesz)	85	90
3894	7d. "Bouquet of Flowers in a Vase" (Ambrosius Bosschaert)	85	90
3895	7d. Vase of flowers from "Still Life with Flowers, Fruit and Shells" (Balthasar van der Ast)	85	90
3896	7d. Basket of flowers and building from "Still Life with Flowers, Fruit and Shells" (Van der Ast)	85	90
3897	7d. "Tulips in a Vase" (Hans Boulenger)	85	90
3898	7d. "Laid Table with Cheese and Fruit" (Floris van Dijck)	85	90
3899	7d. Cows from "Boatman Moored on a Lake Shore" (Pynacker)	85	90
3900	7d. "The Ford in the River" (Jan Weenix)	85	90
3901	7d. "Two Horses near a Gate in a Meadow" (Paulus Potter)	85	90
3902	7d. "Cows and Sheep at a Stream" (Karel Dujardin)	85	90
3903	7d. Fiddler from "The Duet" (Cornelis Saftleven)	85	90
3904	7d. Viol player from "The Duet" (Saftleven)	85	90
MS3905	Six sheets. (a) 118×69 mm. 25d. "Meadow Landscape with Cattle" (Willem Roelofs) (horiz). (b) 118×69 mm. 25d. "Morning Ride on the Beach" (Anton Mauve) (horiz). (c) 118×96 mm. 25d. "The Spendthrift" (Cornelis Troost) (horiz). (d) 118×92 mm. 25d "View of New Church and Town Hall in Amsterdam" (Issak Outwater) (horiz). (e) 118×88 mm. 25d. "The Art Gallery of Jan Gildemeester Jansz" (Jan Ekels) (horiz). (f) 88×118 mm. 25d. "The Fall of Man" (Cornelis van Haarlem) (horiz) Set of 6 sheets	20·00	22·00

No. 3881 is inscribed "Frans Hal" and No. **MS**3905c "The Spendthrif", both in error.

331 Cowardly Lion

2001. Centenary of Publication of The Wizard of Oz (children's story by L. Frank Baum). Mult.

3906	7d. Type **331**	90	90
3907	7d. Land of Oz	90	90
3908	7d. Tin Man	90	90
3909	7d. Scarecrow	90	90
3910	7d. Toto	90	90
3911	7d. Munchkins	90	90
3912	7d. Witch of the North	90	90
3913	7d. Poppies of Oz	90	90
3914	7d. Dorothy's house	90	90
3915	7d. Witch of the East	90	90
3916	7d. Dorothy	90	90
3917	7d. Wizard of Oz	90	90
3918	7d. Witch's wolf	90	90
3919	7d. Witch's forest	90	90
3920	7d. Witch's monkey	90	90
3921	7d. Dorothy asleep in poppies	90	90
3922	7d. Queen Mouse	90	90
3923	7d. Witch and evil bees	90	90
MS3924	Three sheets. (a) 77×106 mm. 27d. Gatekeeper. (b) 106×77 mm. 27d. Dorothy at crossroads (horiz). (c) 77×106 mm. 27d. Green Maiden Set of 3 sheets	11·00	12·00

332 Head of Melpomene (Muse of Tragedy)

2001. The History of Drama. Multicoloured.

3925	6d. Type **332**	1·00	1·00
3926	6d. Ancient Greek masks	1·00	1·00
3927	6d. Bust of Euripides (Greek tragedian)	1·00	1·00
3928	6d. Figures of two actors playing drunks	1·00	1·00
3929	6d. Scene from a play by Tang Hsien-Tsu (Chinese dramatist)	1·00	1·00
3930	6d. Uday and Amala Shankar (Indian actors)	1·00	1·00
3931	6d. Scene from a Japanese Noh play	1·00	1·00
3932	6d. Scene from *Clytemnestra* (Alexandros Mastas)	1·00	1·00
3933	6d. William Shakespeare (English dramatist)	1·00	1·00
3934	6d. Johann von Goethe (German philosopher and author)	1·00	1·00
3935	6d. Moliere (French dramatist)	1·00	1·00
3936	6d. Henrik Ibsen (Norwegian playwright)	1·00	1·00
3937	6d. George Bernard Shaw (Irish playwright)	1·00	1·00
3938	6d. Anton Chekhov (Russian dramatist)	1·00	1·00
3939	6d. Sholom Aleichem (Jewish writer)	1·00	1·00
3940	6d. Tennessee Williams (American playwright)	1·00	1·00
MS3941	Two sheets, each 67×109 mm. (a) 25d. Sarah Bernhardt (French actress) as Phadera (vert). (b) 25d. John Barrymore (American actor) as Hamlet (vert) Set of 2 sheets	8·00	8·50

332a "Beedrill No. 15"

2001. Characters from "Pokemon" (children's cartoon series). Multicoloured.

3942	7d. Type **332a**	90	90
3943	7d. "Arbok No. 24"	90	90
3944	7d. "Machop No. 66"	90	90
3945	7d. "Vileplume No. 45"	90	90
3946	7d. "Clefairy No. 35"	90	90
3947	7d. "Poliwirl No. 61"	90	90
MS3948	74×115 mm. 25d. "Articuno No. 144"	4·00	4·25

333 Succory

334 *Encyclia alata*

2001. Medicinal Plants. Multicoloured.

3949	3d. Pokeweed (horiz)	50	25
3950	5d. Bay laurel (horiz)	75	40
3951	8d. Type **333**	1·10	1·10
3952	8d. Dandelion	1·10	1·10
3953	8d. Garlic	1·10	1·10
3954	8d. Hemp agrimony	1·10	1·10
3955	8d. Star thistle	1·10	1·10
3956	8d. Cypress	1·10	1·10
3957	8d. Restharrow	1·10	1·10
3958	8d. White willow	1·10	1·10
3959	8d. Sweet serge	1·10	1·10
3960	8d. Passion flower	1·10	1·10
3961	8d. Rosemary	1·10	1·10
3962	8d. Pepper	1·10	1·10
3963	10d. Coltsfoot (horiz)	1·10	1·10
3964	15d. Marsh mallow (horiz)	1·10	1·10
MS3965	Two sheets, each 83×108 mm. (a) 25d. Arbutus. (b) 25d. Olive Set of 2 sheets	8·00	8·50

2001. "Hong Kong 2001" Stamp Exhibition. Orchids. Multicoloured.

3966	1d.50 Type **334**	35	20
3967	2d. *Dendrobium lasianthera*	40	20
3968	3d. *Cymbidiella pardalina*	55	25
3969	4d. *Cymbidium lowianum*	65	65
3970	4d. *Epidendrum pseudepidendrum*	65	65
3971	4d. *Eriopsis biloba*	65	65
3972	4d. *Masdevallia coccinea*	65	65
3973	4d. *Odontoglossum lindleyanum*	65	65
3974	4d. *Oerstedella wallisii*	65	65
3975	4d. *Paphiopedilum acmodontum*	65	65
3976	4d. *Laelia rubescens*	65	65
3977	4d. *Huntleya wallisii*	65	65
3978	4d. *Lycaste longiscapia*	65	65
3979	4d. *Maxillaria variabilis*	65	65
3980	4d. *Mexicoa ghiesbrechtiana*	65	65
3981	4d. *Miltoniopsis phalaenopsis*	65	65
3982	5d. *Cypripedium irapeanum*	65	65
3983	7d. *Sobralia candida*	1·10	1·10
3984	7d. *Phragmipedium besseae*	1·10	1·10
3985	7d. *Phaius tankervilleae*	1·10	1·10
3986	7d. *Vanda rothchildiana*	1·10	1·10
3987	7d. *Telipogon pulcher*	1·10	1·10
3988	7d. *Rossioglossum insleayi*	1·10	1·10
3989	15d. *Doritis pulcherrima*	2·00	2·50
MS3990	Three sheets, each 72×98 mm. (a) 25d. *Cycnoches loddigesii*. (b) 25d. *Cattleya dowiana*. (c) 25d. *Chaubardia heteroclita* Set of 3 sheets	12·00	12·00

No. 3984 is inscribed "BASSEAE" and No. 3389 "DORITAS", both in error.

335 *Seutieama Steelei*

2001. Orchids of Africa. Multicoloured.

3991	7d. Type **335**	90	90
3992	7d. *Dendrobium inaequale*	90	90
3993	7d. *Dendrobium lasiothera* "sepik blue"	90	90
3994	7d. *Calypso bulbosa*	90	90
3995	7d. *Vanda hindsi*	90	90
3996	7d. *Dendrobium violaceflavens* (d.Comber)	90	90
3997	8d. *Phaleonpis rosenstomii* (horiz)	1·10	1·10
3998	8d. *Cypripedium guttatum* (horiz)	1·10	1·10
3999	8d. *Cypripedium reginae* (horiz)	1·10	1·10
4000	8d. *Dendrobium engae* (horiz)	1·10	1·10
4001	8d. *Diploculobium hydrophilum* (horiz)	1·10	1·10
4002	8d. *Dendrobium cuthbertsonii* (horiz)	1·10	1·10
4003	10d. *Eriopsis sceptrum*	1·40	1·40
4004	10d. *Sarcan thopis meullum*	1·40	1·40
4005	10d. *Dendrobium lineale* "Bougainville White"	1·40	1·40
4006	10d. *Telipogon klotzchianus*	1·40	1·40
MS4007	Two sheets, each 91×64 mm. (a) 25d. *Dendrobium spectabile*. (b) 25d. *Menadenium labiosum* Set of 2 sheets	7·50	8·00

Nos. 3991/6 printed together, se-tenant, with the background forming a composite design.

336 *Disa uniflora*

2001. African Flowers. Multicoloured.

4008	1d. Type **336**	20	25
4009	4d. *Monodora myristica*	60	30
4010	6d. *Clappertonia ficifolia*	80	45
4011	7d. *Canarina abyssinica* and european roller	90	90
4012	7d. *Amorphophallus abyssinicus*	90	90
4013	7d. *Calanthe rosea* and hoopoe	90	90
4014	7d. *Gloriosa simplex*	90	90
4015	7d. *Clappertonia ficifolia* (different)	90	90
4016	7d. *Ansellia gigantea*	90	90
4017	7d. *Vanilla planifolia* and antelope	90	90
4018	7d. *Strelitzia reginae* and antelope	90	90
4019	7d. *Spathiphyllum* ("Gladiolus cardinalis")	90	90
4020	7d. *Arctotis venusta* and antelope	90	90
4021	7d. *Protea obtusifolia* and antelope	90	90
4022	7d. *Geissorhiza rochensis*	90	90
4023	20d. *Calanthe rosea* (different)	2·40	2·75
MS4024	Two sheets. (a) 77×106 mm. 25d. *Arctotis venusta* (different). (b) 106×77 mm. 25d. *Geissorhiza rochensis* (horiz) Set of 2 sheets	8·00	8·50

Nos. 4011/16 and 4017/22 were each printed together, se-tenant, with the backgrounds forming composite designs.

Nos. 4008 and 4014 are inscribed "unifloria" or "Glorosa", both in error.

337 "Mount Fuji and Tea Fields" (Matsuoka Eikyu)

2001. "Philanippon '01" Internationl Stamp Exhibition, Tokyo. Japanese Art. Multicoloured.

4025	1d. Type **337**	20	25
4026	2d. "Herons and Flowers" (one heron) (Okamo Shuki)	30	25
4027	3d. "Herons and Flowers" (two herons) (Shuki)	50	50
4028	3d. "The Realm of the Gods in Yinzhou" (Timioka Tessai)	50	50
4029	4d. "Egret" (Takeuchi Seiho)	60	60
4030	4d. "Peach Blossom Spring in Wuling" (Tessai)	60	60
4031	5d. "Sparrows" (Seiho)	75	75
4032	5d. "Spring Colours of the Lake and Mountains" (Shoda Gyokan)	75	75
4033	5d. Peonies	75	75
4034	5d. Iris	75	75
4035	5d. Hollyhocks and hydrangea	75	75
4036	5d. Fruit and Japanese white-eye on branch	75	75
4037	5d. Little egret	75	75
4038	5d. Woodpecker in tree	75	75
4039	5d. Blossom and japonica flowers	75	75
4040	5d. Yellow flowers	75	75
4041	5d. Blossom and green pheasant in tree	75	75
4042	5d. Morning Glory	75	75
4043	5d. Blue and white flowers	75	75
4044	5d. White and red flowers	75	75
4045	7d. Workshop and man carrying pole (27×33 mm)	90	90
4046	7d. Two women and tree (27×33 mm)	90	90
4047	7d. Rocks and river (27×33 mm)	90	90
4048	7d. Two women on riverbank (27×33 mm)	90	90
4049	7d. Rocky landscape (27×33 mm)	90	90
4050	7d. Man by rocks (27×33 mm)	90	90
4051	7d. Couple by rocks (27×33 mm)	90	90
4052	7d. Women with scroll (27×33 mm)	90	90
4053	7d. White flowers and tree (27×33 mm)	90	90
4054	7d. Speckled cockerel by tree (27×33 mm)	90	90
4055	7d. Brown cockerel and red flowers (27×33 mm)	90	90
4056	7d. Cockerel and white flowers (27×33 mm)	90	90
4057	7d. Trees in stream (27×33 mm)	90	90
4058	7d. White cockerel and flowers (27×33 mm)	90	90
4059	7d. Cockerel and chicken (27×33 mm)	90	90
4060	7d. Black and white cockerel by tree (27×33 mm)	90	90
4061	10d. Branch with flower (27×33 mm)	1·40	1·40
4062	10d. European tree sparrows (27×33 mm)	1·40	1·40
4063	10d. Butterfly on blossom (27×33 mm)	1·40	1·40
4064	10d. Crayfish (27×33 mm)	1·40	1·40
4065	10d. "Ushiwakamaru" (Kano Osanobu)	1·40	1·40
4066	10d. "Red Lotus and White Goose" (Goun Saku)	1·40	1·40
4067	15d. "Woman selling Flowers" (Ito Shoha)	2·00	2·25
4068	20d. "The Sound of the Ocean" (Matsumoto Ichiyo)	2·40	2·75
MS4069	Five sheets, each 119×89 mm. (a) 30d. "Puppies and Morning Glories" (Yamaguchi Soken). (b) 30d. "Deep Pool" (Nishimura Goun). (c) 30d. "Poppies" (Tsuchida Bakusen). (d) 30d. "Spring Farming near a Riverside Village" (Mori Getsujō). (e) 30d. "Untitled" (couple and dogs by lake) (Utagawa Kuniyoshi). Imperf Set of 5 sheets	17·00	18·00

Nos. 4033/8 and 4039/44 ("Birds and Flowers of the Twelve Months" (Sakai Hoitsu)), 4045/52 (composite designs from "The Four Accomplishments" (Kaiho Yusho)), 4053/60 (composite designs from "Birds and Flowers" (Soga Chokuan)) and 4061/64 ("Book of Lacquer Paintings" (Shiban Zeshin)) were each printed together, se-tenant, in sheetlets of 4, 6 or 8.

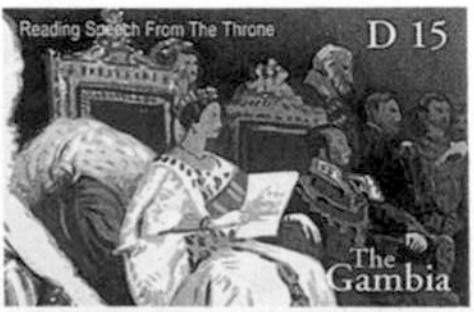
338 Queen Victoria reading Speech from the Throne

2001. Death Centenary of Queen Victoria. Multicoloured.

4070	15d. Type **338**	2·00	2·25
4071	15d. Prime Minister Benjamin Disraeli	2·00	2·25
4072	15d. Procession for State Opening of Parliament	2·00	2·25
MS4073	90×68 mm. 25d. Queen Victoria (vert)	4·00	4·25

339 Mao Tse-tung in 1935

2001. 25th Death Anniv of Mao Tse-tung (Chinese leader).

4074	**339**	15d. black, blue and light blue	2·00	2·25
4075	-	15d. multicoloured	2·00	2·25
4076	-	15d. black, deep blue and blue	2·00	2·25
MS4077		132×108 mm. 25d. multicoloured	4·00	4·25

DESIGNS: No. 4074, Type **339**; 4075, Mao in 1949; 4076, Mao in 1951; **MS**4077, Mao addressing meeting in 1928.

340 "Madame Monet on the Sofa", 1871

2001. 75th Death Anniv of Claude-Oscar Monet (French painter). Multicoloured.

4078	10d. Type **340**	1·40	1·50
4079	10d. "The Picnic", 1865	1·40	1·50
4080	10d. "The Luncheon", 1868	1·40	1·50
4081	10d. "Jean Monet on his Mechanical Horse", 1879	1·40	1·50
MS4082	137×110 mm. 25d. "La Japonaise", 1875 (vert)	4·00	4·25

341 Queen Elizabeth in Guards Uniform

2001. 75th Birthday of Queen Elizabeth II. Multicoloured.

4083	15d. Type **341**	2·00	2·25
4084	15d. Queen Elizabeth in pink suit and hat	2·00	2·25
4085	15d. Queen Elizabeth wearing ruby tiara	2·00	2·25
4086	15d. Queen Elizabeth wearing sapphire necklace	2·00	2·25
MS4087	80×110 mm. 25d. Princess Elizabeth on her wedding day (38×50 mm)	4·00	4·25

342 Queen Elizabeth II

2001. Golden Jubilee (1st issue).

4088	**342**	8d. multicoloured	1·25	1·25

See also Nos. 4295/**MS**4296.

No. 4088 was printed in sheetlets of 8, containing two vertical rows of four, separated by a large illustrated central gutter. Both the stamp and the illustration on the central gutter are made up of a collage of miniature flower photographs.

343 Verdi as an Old Man

2001. Death Centenary of Giuseppe Verdi (Italian composer). Multicoloured.

4089 10d. Type **343** 1·75 1·75
4090 10d. Singers and score for *La Traviata* (opera) 1·75 1·75
4091 10d. Singer and score for *Aida* (opera) 1·75 1·75
4092 10d. Verdi as a young man 1·75 1·75
MS4093 76×106 mm. 25d. Verdi as an old man 4·50 4·50

Nos. 4089/92 were printed together, se-tenant, with the backgrounds forming a composite design.

344 "At Le Rat Mort"

2001. Death Centenary of Henri de Toulouse-Lautrec (French painter). Multicoloured.

4094 7d. Type **344** 1·10 1·10
4095 7d. "The Milliner" 1·10 1·10
4096 7d. "Messaline" 1·10 1·10
MS4097 66×85 mm. 25d. "Napoleon" 4·00 4·25

345 Marlene Dietrich in Evening Dress

2001. Birth Centenary of Marlene Dietrich (actress and singer).

4098 **345** 10d. black, purple and claret 1·40 1·50
4099 - 10d. multicoloured 1·40 1·50
4100 - 10d. multicoloured 1·40 1·50
4101 - 10d. black, purple and claret 1·40 1·50

DESIGNS: No. 4099, Marlene Dietrich with roses; 4100, Marlene Dietrich with arms crossed; 4101, Marlene Dietrich wearing feathered hat.

346 *Orchis morio*

2001. "Belgica 2001" International Stamp Exhibition, Brussels. African Orchids. Multicoloured.

4102 3d. Type **346** 50 25
4103 4d. *Fulophia speciosa* 65 35
4104 5d. *Angraecum leonis* 75 45
4105 8d. *Ceratostylis retisquama* 1·10 1·10
4106 8d. *Rangaeris rhipsalisocia* 1·10 1·10
4107 8d. *Phaius hybrid* and baby chimpanzee 1·10 1·10
4108 8d. *Disa hybrid* 1·10 1·10
4109 8d. *Disa uniflora* 1·10 1·10
4110 8d. *Angraecum leonis* and chimpanzee 1·10 1·10
4111 8d. *Satyrium erectum* (horiz) 1·10 1·10
4112 8d. *Aeranthes grandiose* (horiz) 1·10 1·10
4113 8d. *Aerangis somasticta* (horiz) 1·10 1·10
4114 8d. *Polystachya bella* (horiz) 1·10 1·10
4115 8d. *Eulophia guineensis* (horiz) 1·10 1·10
4116 8d. *Disa blacki* (horiz) 1·10 1·10
4117 15d. *Oeceoclades maculata* 2·00 2·25
MS4118 78×97 mm. (a) 25d. *Disa kirstenbosch Pride.* 76×96 mm. (b) *Aerangis curnowiana* 4·25 4·50

Nos. 4105/4110 and 4111/16 were each printed together, se-tenant, with the backgrounds forming composite designs.

347 Children with Balloons

2001. S.O.S. Children's Villages (Kinderdorf International).

4119 **347** 10d. multicoloured 1·40 1·40

348 Hoopoe

2001. Animals of Africa. Multicoloured.

4120 2d. Type **348** 60 35
4121 3d. Great spotted cuckoo 70 40
4122 4d. Plain tiger (butterfly) 70 45
4123 5d. Zebra duiker 75 50
4124 10d. Sooty mangabey 1·40 1·40
4125 20d. Greater kudu 2·25 2·50
MS4126 145×82 mm. 8d. Grey parrot; 8d. Rachel's malimbe ("RACHEL'S WEAVER"); 8d. European bee-eater; 8d. River kingfisher; 8d. Red river hog; 8d. Bush buck 6·00 6·50
MS4127 145×82 mm. 8d. Blue diadem (butterfly); 8d. Fire-footed rope squirrel; 8d. *Clappertonia ficifolia* (flower); 8d. *Costus spectabilis* (flower); 8d. African migrant (butterfly); 8d. Giant African snail 6·00 6·50
MS4128 145×82 mm. 8d. Hippopotamus; 8d. Elephant; 8d. Parusta simplex (butterfly); 8d. Grey heron; 8d. *Charaxes imperialis* (butterfly); 8d. *Gloriosa simplex* (flower) 6·00 6·50
MS4129 145×82 mm. 8d. Alpine swift; 8d. Blotched genet; 8d. Thomas' galago; 8d. Carmine bee eater; 8d. Tree pangolin; 8d. Campbell's monkey 6·00 6·50
MS4130 Two sheets, each 85×110 mm. (a) 25d. Long-tailed pangolin (vert). (b) 25d. Common pestrel ("EURASIAN KESTREL") (vert) Set of 2 sheets 6·50 7·00

349 Blue-winged Teal

2001. Ducks of the World. Multicoloured.

4131 2d. Type **349** 50 20
4132 3d. Red-crested pochard 60 60
4133 3d. Wood duck (vert) 60 60
4134 4d. Mallard (vert) 75 75
4135 4d. Falcated teal 75 75
4136 5d. Mandarin duck 90 90
4137 5d. Barrow's goldeneye (head) (vert) 90 90
4138 10d. Bufflehead (head) (vert) 1·75 1·90
4139 10d. King eider 1·75 1·90
4140 15d. Hooded merganser 2·25 2·50
MS4141 116×131 mm. 7d. Barrow's goldeneye in flight; 7d. Harlequin duck; 7d. Northern pintail; 7d. Red-billed whistling duck ("Black-bellied Whistling Duck"); 7d. Cinnamon teal; 7d. Surf scoter 6·00 6·50
MS4142 116×131 mm. 7d. Black scoter; 7d. North American black duck; 7d. Green-winged teal; 7d. Bufflehead; 7d. Red-breasted merganser; 7d. Fulvous whistling duck 6·00 6·50
MS4143 123×123 mm. 8d. European wigeon; 8d. Mallard; 8d. Garganey; 8d. Northern pintail; 8d. Northern shoveler; 8d. Green-winged teal 6·00 6·50
MS4144 123×123 mm. 8d. North American black duck; 8d. Bufflehead; 8d. Cinnamon teal; 8d. Common goldeneye; 8d. Ruddy shelduck; 8d. Ferruginous duck 6·00 6·50
MS4145 123×123 mm. 8d. Masked duck; 8d. Long-tailed duck ("OLD SQUAW"); 8d. Ring-necked duck; 8d. Harlequin duck; 8d. Redhead; 8d. Canvasback 6·00 6·50
MS4146 Four sheets. (a) 70×98 mm. 25d. Wood duck. (b) 70×98 mm. 25d. American wigeon. (c) 70×98 mm. 25d. Baikal teal. (d) 105×76 mm. Green-winged teal Set of 4 sheets 12·00 13·00

350 Martial Eagle

2001. "The Gambia—A Wildlife Paradise". Multicoloured.

4147 2d. Type **350** 50 25
4148 4d. Lion 65 50
4149 5d. Aardvark 75 75
4150 10d. Lion cub 1·40 1·60
MS4151 149×96 mm. 7d. Lion cub; 7d. Water buffalo; 7d. Topi; 7d. Hyena; 7d. Secretary bird; 7d. Genet 6·00 6·50
MS4152 149×96 mm. 7d. Reedbuck; 7d. Hippopotamus; 7d. Waterbuck; 7d. Hoopoe; 7d. Eastern white pelican; 7d. Waterbuck 6·00 6·50
MS4153 Two sheets, each 92×66 mm. (a) 25d. Crocodile. (b) 25d. Hippopotamus Set of 2 sheets 8·50 9·00

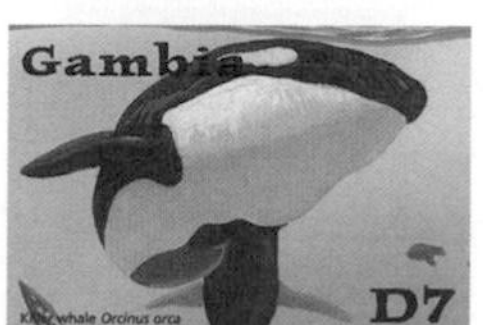

351 Killer Whale

2001. Whales. Multicoloured.

MS4154 149×96 mm. 7d. Type **351**; 7d. Two sperm whales; 7d. Narwhal; 7d. Grey whale; 7d. Blue whale; 7d. Northern right whale 6·00 6·50
MS4155 149×96 mm. 7d. Killer whale and tail fin of whale; 7d. Sperm whale; 7d. Strap-toothed whale; 7d. Humpback whale; 7d. Southern right whale; 7d. Beluga 6·00 6·50
MS4156 Two sheets, each 92×66 mm. (a) 25d. Killer whale. (b) 25d. Humpback whale 8·50 9·00

352 Seagull's Beaulu Queen

2001. Orchids. Multicoloured.

MS4157 152×127 mm. 6d.×6 *Spathoglottis portus-finschii; Dendrobium macrophyllum; Grammaneis ellisii; Stanhopea wardii; Dendrobium nindi var alba; Dendrobium williamsianum* 5·00 5·50
MS4158 Two sheets, each 160×95 mm.(a) 7d.×6 Type **352**; Hazel Boyd; Costa Rica; *Dendrobium infudibulum; Disa* hybrid; *Chysis.* (b) 7d.×6 Richard Mueller; Colmanara Wildcat; *Cycnoches chlorochilon; Vanda coerylea; Disa blackii;* Unnamed red and yellow orchid 11·00 12·00
MS4159 90×132 mm. 7d.×4 *Machu Piechu; Masdevallia* Copper Angel; *Masdevallia hirtzi;* Orchid (inscr "Tuakau canoy") (all vert) 4·25 4·50
MS4160 91×64 mm. 25d. *Dendrobium canaliculatum* 4·00 4·25
MS4161 105×94 mm. 25d. *Dendrobium nobile* 4·00 4·25
MS4162 99×86 mm. 25d. *Oncidium Alliance* (inscr "Ancidium") (vert) 4·00 4·25

The stamps within Nos. **MS**4158/9 form composite designs.

353 Black Crowned Crane

2001. Bird Photographs by Dr. Linda Barnett. Multicoloured.

4163 7d. Type **353** 1·10 1·10
4164 7d. Barn owl 1·10 1·10
4165 7d. African pygmy kingfisher 1·10 1·10
4166 7d. Audouin's gull 1·10 1·10
4167 7d. Flock of Royal terns on beach 1·10 1·10
4168 7d. Blue-bellied roller 1·10 1·10
MS4169 105×75 mm. 25d. Canada geese in flight 4·00 4·25

354 Rail Car in Snow, Paris, Lyons & Mediterranean Railway

2001. Trains. Multicoloured.

4170 2d. Type **354** 40 20
4171 2d. Rheingold Express, Netherlands Ports to Berne, Switzerland 40 20
4172 3d. Steam locomotive pulling Zugspitz Rack Train, Germany 50 20
4173 4d. Eurostar trains, France 65 40
4174 4d. Class A1 steam locomotive, Great Britain, 1922 65 40
4175 5d. Tee Four Car Train, Europe, 1957 75 40
4176 7d. Mallard, Great Britain 1·10 1·10
4177 7d. Rheingold Mitropa car, Germany, 1928 1·10 1·10
4178-4183 7d.×6 Steam locomotive, Siliguri to Darjeeling, India; California Zephyr train, USA; *Flying Scotsman*, UK; Trans Siberian Express; Indian-Pacific, Australia; Thunersee Interlaken to Berlin train 6·00 6·50
4184-4189 7d.×6 Eurostar London to Paris train; Flying Hamburger Berlin—Hamburgtrain; Coast Starlight train Seattle—Los Angeles; Trans Grande Vitesse Paris—Lyons; *Golden Arrow* London—Paris; Shinkanzen "Max", Japan 6·00 6·50
4190 8d. Steam locomotive Gerda, Germany, 1900 1·25 1·25
4191 10d. Amtrak train, USA 1·40 1·40
4192 10d. Stephenson's *Rocket* 1·40 1·40
4193 10d. Class 210 steam locomotive, Austrian State Railway 1·40 1·40
4194 15d. Blue Train, Cape Town to Pretoria, South Africa 2·00 2·25
4195 15d. TGV train, France 2·00 2·25
4196 15d. Steam locomotive, State Railway of Saxony 2·00 2·25
4197-4202 7d.×6 Royal Prussian Union Railway steam locomotive; Austrian Federal Railway; German Rugen steam locomotive; Rh B Ge electric locomotive; Panoramic Express, Switzerland; Brunig steam locomotive, Swiss National Railway 6·00 6·50
4203-4208 7d.×6 French National Railways Series 68 locomotive; French National Railway "Mistral"; Prussian State Railway steam locomotive; Austrian Southern Railway steam locomotive; Paris—Orleans Railway steam locomotive; German Federal Railway E 11 locomotive 6·00 6·50
4209-4212 10d.×4 Brother Jonathan, USA, 1832; Medoc Class, Germany—Switzerland, 1857; Class S 3/6, Germany, 1908; Class VT 11.5, Germany, 1959 5·00 5·50
4213-4216 10d.×4 Beuth, Germany, 1843; Crampton, France, 1852; Sut 877 Flying Hamburger, Germany, 1932; Class 103.1 Co-Co, Germany, 1970 5·00 5·50
4217-4220 10d.×4 *Puffing Billy*, Great Britain, 1813; *Adler*, Germany, 1836; Steam locomotive, Germany, 1906; Class 132 Co-Co, Germany 5·00 5·50
4221 20d. Cisalpino train, Milan to Geneva 2·25 2·50
MS4222 Two sheets, each 147×82 mm. (a) 8d.×6 No. 7029 *Clun Castle*, Britain; *Puffing Billy*, Britain; ICE electric locomotive, Germany; 4.4 2S locomotive, Belgium; 2.8.2 steam locomotive, Germany; PLM Coupe-Vents steam locomotive, France. (b) 8d.×6 *Le Shuttle*, France; Nord Express, France; 260 steam locomotive, Switzerland; *Duchess*, Britain; Balkan Express, Greece; Class 44 steam locomotive, Germany 11·00 12·00
MS4223 Two sheets, 100×70 mm. (a) 25d. *Flying Scotsman*, Scotland. (b) 25d. Stanier Class, Britain 7·50 8·00
MS4224 Two sheets, each 96×68 mm. (a) 25d. Cape Town to Victoria Falls train, South Africa. (b) 25d. *The Southerner*, New Zealand 7·50 8·00
MS4225 Two sheets, each 81×60 mm. (a) 25d. Class ET 403 Four-car electric train, Germany, 1973 (b) 25d. VT 10.5, Germany, 1953 7·50 8·00
MS4226 Two sheets, 106×58 mm. (a) 25d. German Federal Railway, V 200. (b) 25d. Germany Federal Railway Trans Europe Express 7·50 8·00

The stamps within Nos. **MS**4216a/b each form a composite background design.

355 Argentinian Player and Flag

356 St. Andrew (17th century)

2001. World Cup Football Championship, Japan and Korea (2002) (1st issue). Multicoloured.

4227 2d. Dutch player and flag 45 20
4228 3d. Type **355** 55 25
4229 4d. Ibaraki Kashima Football Stadium, Japan (horiz) 60 40
4230 5d. George Best and Northern Ireland flag 75 55
4231 10d. Dino Zoff and Italian flag 1·40 1·40
4232 15d. Poster for 1938 World Cup, France 2·00 2·25
MS4233 100×70 mm. 25d. Pat Bonner's penalty save for Ireland, 1990 (56×42 mm) 4·00 4·25

See also Nos. 4322/**MS**4370 and 4381/98.

2001. Royal Navy. Paintings. Multicoloured.

4234 3d. Type **356** 50 25
4235 4d. Fleet Manoeuvres, 1914 65 35
4236-4241 7d.×6 *Mary Rose*, 1512; The Attack off Quebec, 1759; The Armada Campaign,1588; Battle of Scheveningen, 1653; *Blanche* captures *La Pique*, 1795; Embarkation at Dover, 1520 (all horiz) 6·00 6·50
4242-4247 7d.×6 Battle of Navarino, 1827; The Sinking of *Eurydice*, 1878; HMS Pantaloon captures Borboleta, 1915; HMS *Pickle* captures *Bolodora*, 1829; HMS *Invincible & Inflexible*, Battle of the Falklands, 1914 (all horiz) 6·00 6·50
4248-4253 7d.×6 Battle of Quiberon Bay, 1759; Battle of Barfleur, 1692; Battle of the Nile, 1798; Battle of Trafalgar, 1805; Battle of Jutland, 1916; Battle of Camperdown, 1797 (all horiz) 6·00 6·50
4254 10d. HMS *Illustrious*, 1899 1·40 1·40
4255 15d. Battle of North Foreland, 1666 2·00 2·25
MS4256 Two sheets, each 127×63 mm. (a) 25d. *Ark Royal*, 1582. (b) 25d. *Sovereign of the Seas*, 1637 7·50 8·00

357 Kelly Chen

2001. "Operation Smile" China Medical Mission. Chinese Singers and Actors. T 356 and similar vert designs. Multicoloured.

MS4257 Five sheets, each 160×135 mm. (a) Kelly Chen: 15d.×4 Type **357**; As toddler; On swing; As young girl. (b) Jacky Cheung: 15d.×4 Laughing, head tilted to left; Looking at camera; Laughing, looking to left; Smiling, head tilted to left. (c) Andy Hui: 15d.×4 Wearing pink, bending forward; Wearing yellow, right arm raised; Wearing yellow, in close-up; Wearing pink, standing up. (d) Miriam Yeung: 15d.×4 Red roses at bottom right; Roses at bottom left; Roses at top right; Roses at top left. (e) 15d.×4 Alex Fong; William So; Flora Chan; Rain Li 28·00 30·00

The stamps within Nos. **MS**4257a and **MS**4257c/d form composite designs.

358 King Harald V and Queen Sonja, Norway

2001. European Royalty. Multicoloured.

4258 7d. Type **358** 1·00 1·00
4259 7d. Queen Margrethe II, Denmark 1·00 1·00
4260 7d. King Carl XVI Gustaf and Queen Silvia, Sweden 1·00 1·00
4261 7d. King Juan Carlos I and Queen Sofia, Spain 1·00 1·00
4262 7d. Queen Beatrix, Netherlands 1·00 1·00
4263 7d. King Albert I and Queen Paola, Belgium 1·00 1·00
MS4264 76×86 mm. 25d. King Juan Carlos I (vert) 4·00 4·25
MS4265 56×85 mm. 25d. Crown Prince Haakon and Princess Mette-Merit, Norway 4·00 4·25

2001. 101st Birthday of Queen Elizabeth the Queen Mother. As Nos. 3219/23, but new values.

4266 15d. multicoloured 2·00 2·25
4267 15d. black and gold 2·00 2·25
4268 15d. black and gold 2·00 2·25
4269 15d. multicoloured 2·00 2·25
MS4270 153×155 mm. 40d. multicoloured 7·00 6·00

DESIGNS: (As Nos. 3219/23): No. 4266, Duchess of York and Princess Elizabeth, 1928; 4267, Lady Elizabeth Bowes-Lyon, 1923; 4269, Queen Elizabeth, 1946; 4269, Queen Mother and Prince Harry. (37×50 mm)—No. **MS**4270, Queen Mother on 89th birthday, 1989.

359 Zebra

2001. Chinese New Year ("Year of the Horse").

MS4275 92×64 mm. **359** 20d. multicoloured 2·25 2·50

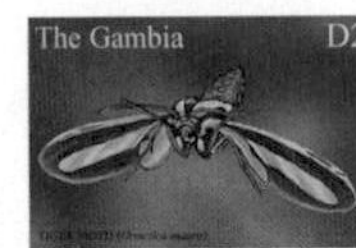

360 Tiger Moth (*Ormetica maura*)

2002. Moths of the World. Multicoloured.

4276 2d. Type **360** 40 20
4277 3d. Hawk moth (*Erinnyis ello*) 50 25
4278 10d. Pericopid moth (*Chetone angulosa*) 1·40 1·40
4279 15d. Spurge Hawk moth (*Celerio euphorbiae*) 2·00 2·25
MS4280 Two sheets, each 184×120 mm. (a) 10d.×6 Sloane's urania (*Uranus sloanus*); Saturnid moth (*Syssphinx Molina*); Black witch moth (*Ascalapha odorata*); Burnet moth (*Zygaena carniolica*); Day-flying moth (*Alcidis metaurus*); Lime hawk moth (*Mimas tiliae*) (all 50×38 mm). (b) 10d.×6 Emperor moth (*Saturnia pavonia*); Millar's tiger moth (*Calliोratis millari*); Hawk moth (*Amplyterus gamascus*); *Phrygionis privignara*; Burnet moth (*Zygaena carniolica*); *Urania leilus* (all 50×38 mm) 13·00 14·00
MS4281 Two sheets, each 93×68 mm. (a) 40d. Red under wing moth (*Catocala nupta*) (vert). (b) 40d. Emerald moth (*Geometra papilionaria*) 8·50 9·00

The stamps within Nos. **MS**4280a/b each form composite background designs showing forest landscapes.

361 Roosevelt as Lieut-Colone of "Rough Riders", Cuba

362 Jacqueline Kennedy as Baby, 1929

2002. Centenary (2001) of Theodore Roosevelt's Accession to Presidency of USA, 1901—9. Multicoloured.

4282 15d. Type **361** 2·00 2·25
4283 15d. Head and shoulders portrait 2·00 2·25
4284 15d. Three-quarter length portrait 2·00 2·25
4285 15d. Wearing hat, necktie and outdoor jacket 2·00 2·25
MS4286 79×105 mm. 40d. Facing right 4·75 5·50

2002. Jacqueline Kennedy Commemoration. Mult.

4287 7d. Type **362** 90 95
4288 7d. Aged 6, wearing riding hat 90 95
4289 7d. On her engagement to Senator John F Kennedy 90 95
4290 7d. On her wedding day, 1953 90 95
4291 7d. During Presidential campaign, 1960 90 95
4292 7d. In 1980 90 95
MS4293 66×88 mm. 30d. At wedding to Aristotle Onassis, 1968 4·00 4·50

363 Diana, Princess of Wales

2002. 40th Birth Anniv of Diana, Princess of Wales (2001). Multicoloured.

4294 15d. Type **362** 2·00 2·25
4295 15d. Wearing blue headscarf 2·00 2·25
4296 15d. Wearing tiara and yellow dress 2·00 2·25
4297 15d. Wearing mauve and white hat 2·00 2·25
MS4298 90×105 mm. 40d. Wearing red-brown and green dress 5·00 5·50

2002. Golden Jubilee (2nd issue). As T 507 of Grenada. Multicoloured.

4299 15d. Queen Elizabeth II (wearing fawn jacket) 2·00 2·25
4300 15d. Wearing red hat and coat with fur collar 2·00 2·25
4301 15d. Wearing blue and white check brimmed hat 2·00 2·25
4302 15d. Queen and Duke of Edinburgh watching event from Land Rover 2·00 2·25
MS4303 76×109 mm. 40d. Queen Elizabeth II in uniform 5·00 5·50

A 130d. gold stamp with a multicoloured centre illustration of Queen Elizabeth II at Trooping the Colour was also issued on the same date.

2002. "United We Stand". Support for Victims of 11 September 2001 Terrorist Attacks. As T 506 of Grenada. Multicoloured.

4304 20d. US flag around Statue of Liberty and Gambian flag 2·25 2·50

2002. Shirley Temple in Little Miss Broadway. Multicoloured designs as T 519 of Grenada showing film scenes.

4305 8d. With Roger Wendling (George Murphy) and Sarah Wendling (Edna May Oliver) 95 1·00
4306 8d. Betsy (Shirley Temple) smiling at camera 95 1·00
4307 8d. Waving from car 95 1·00
4308 8d. Holding man's tie 95 1·00
4309 8d. At hotel desk with Roger Wendling and others 95 1·00
4310 8d. With Barbara Shea (Phyllis Brooks), pointing to tooth 85 1·00
4311 10d. Dancing with Roger Wendling (vert) 1·25 1·40
4312 10d. Dancing with Jimmy Clayton (Jimmy Durante) (vert) 1·25 1·40
4313 10d. With boy (vert) 1·25 1·40
4314 10d. Holding hands with Jimmy Clayton (vert) 1·25 1·40
MS4315 106×76 mm. 30d. On platform dancing with Roger Wendling (vert) 3·75 4·25

364 Betty Boop

2002. Betty Boop (cartoon character). Multicoloured.

4316 7d. Type **364** 1·00 1·00
MS4317 Two sheets, each 96×146 mm. (a) 40d. Betty Boop carrying toy in basket (horiz). (b) 40d. Betty Boop in cafe with ice cream sundae (horiz) 7·50 8·50

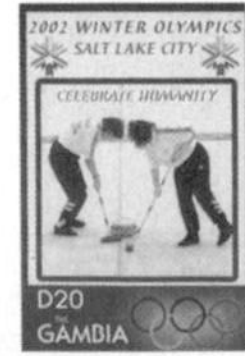

365 Curling

2002. Winter Olympic Games, Salt Lake City. Multicoloured.

4318 20d. Type **365** 2·75 3·25
4319 20d. Ski-jumping 2·75 3·25
MS4320 87×118 mm. Nos. 4318/19 5·50 6·50

2002. Chiune Sugihara (Japanese Consul-general in Lithuania who rescued Jews, 1939–40) Commemoration. As T 511 of Grenada.

4321 10d. Chiune Sugihara 2·00 2·00

366a Popeye skiing Cross-country

2002. Popeye (cartoon character). Designs showing Popeye and friends doing winter sports. Multicoloured.

MS4322 Two sheets, each 190×125 mm. (a) 10d. Type **366a**; 10d. Popeye ski-jumping; 10d. Popeye slalom skiing; 10d. Popeye snow-boarding. (b) 10d. Swee Pea on snow board; 10d. Olive Oyl on skis; 10d. Brutus on skis; 10d. Wimpy ice-skating 8·50 9·00
MS4323 Four sheets. (a) 115×82 mm. 25d. Popeye speed-skating (horiz). (b) 115×82 mm. 25d. Olive Oyl skating. (c) 82×115 mm. 25d. Popeye and Olive Oyl in bobsled. (d) 115×82 mm. 25d. Brutus as ice hockey goalkeeper 13·00 15·00

No. **MS**4322b has a composite background design showing a snowy mountain landscape.

2002. World Cup Football Championship, Japan and Korea (2nd issue). As T 524 of Grenada, showing matches from First Round (Nos. 4322/69) or stadiums in South Korea or Japan where the matches were played (No. MS4370).

4324-4329 9d.×6 First Round Group A: France v. Senegal; Uruguay v. Denmark; France v. Uruguay; Denmark v. Senegal; Denmark v. France; Senegal v. Uruguay 7·50 7·50
4330-4335 9d.×6 Group B: Paraguay v. South Africa; Spain v. Slovenia; Spain v. Paraguay; South Africa v. Slovenia; South Africa v. Spain; Slovenia v. Paraguay 7·50 7·50
4336-4341 9d.×6 Group C: Brazil v. Turkey; China v. Costa Rica; Brazil v. China; Costa Rica v. Turkey; Costa Rica v. Brazil; Turkey v. China 7·50 7·50
4342-4347 9d.×6 Group D: South Korea v. Poland; USA v. Portugal; South Korea v. USA; Portugal v. Poland; Portugal v. South Korea; Poland v. USA 7·50 7·50
4348-4353 9d.×6 Group E: Germany v. Saudi Arabia; Ireland v. Cameroon; Germany v. Ireland; Cameroon v. Saudi Arabia; Cameroon v. Germany; Saudi Arabia v. Ireland 7·50 7·50
4354-4359 9d.×6 Group F: England v. Sweden; Argentina v. Nigeria; Sweden v. Nigeria; Argentina v. England; Sweden v. Argentina; Nigeria v. England 7·50 7·50
4360-4365 9d.×6 Group G: Croatia v. Mexico; Italy v. Ecuador; Italy v. Croatia; Mexico v. Ecuador; Mexico v. Italy; Ecuador v. Croatia 7·50 7·50
4366-4371 9d.×6 Group H: Japan v. Belgium; Russia v. Tunisia; Japan v. Russia; Tunisia v. Belgium; Tunisia v. Japan; Belgium v. Russia 7·50 7·50
MS4372 Twenty-four sheets, each 82×82 mm. Group A: (a) 20d.×2. Seoul; Ulsan. (b) 20d.×2 Busan; Daegu. (c) 20d.×2 Inchon; Suwon. Group B: (d) 20d.×2 Busan; Gwangju. (e) 20d.×2 Jeonju; Daegu. (f) 20d.×2 Daejon; Seogwipo. Group C: (g) 20d.×2 Ulsan; Gwangju. (h) 20d.×2 Seogwipo; Inchon. (i) 20d.×2 Suwon; Seoul. Group D: (j) 20d.×2 Busan; Suwon. (k) 20d.×2 Daegu; Jeonju. (l) 20d.×2 Inchon; Daejon. Group E: (m) 20d.×2 Niigata; Sapporo. (n) 20d.×2 Ibaraki; Saitama. (o) 20d.×2 Shizuoka; Yokohama. Group F: (p) 20d.×2 Saitama; Ibaraki. (q) 20d.×2 Kobe; Sapporo. (r) 20d.×2 Miyagi; Osaka. Group G: (s) 20d.×2 Niigata; Sapporo. (t) 20d.×2 Ibaraki; Miyagi. (u) 20d.×2 Oita; Yokohama. Group H: (v) 20d.×2 Saitama; Kobe. (w) 20d.×2 Yokohama; Oita. (x) 20d.×2 Osaka; Shizuoka 60·00 70·00

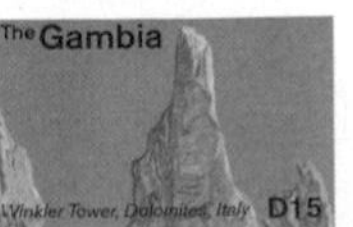

367 Winkler Tower, Dolomites, Italy

2002. International Year of Mountains. Mult.

MS4373 105×85 mm. 15d. Type **367**; 15d. Mt. Huanstan Chico, Peru; 15d. Hodaka Mountains, Japan; 15d. Mustagh Ata, Kashmir 7·50 8·00

MS4374	100×72 mm. 40d. Mt. Myoko, Japan	4·75	5·00

368 Bird-of-Paradise Flower

2002. UN Year of Ecotourism. Multicoloured.

MS4375	151×117 mm. 9d. Type **369**; 9d. Goliath heron; 9d. Baobab tree; 9d. Roan antelope; 9d. Red tip butterfly; 9d. Egyptian cobra	6·50	7·00
MS4376	82×97 mm. 9d. Yellow-bill stork in mangrove	1·25	1·50

369 Scout blowing Reveille on Cornet

2002. World Scout Jamboree, Thailand. Mult.

4377	15d. Type **369**	2·00	2·25
4378	15d. Scout lighting fire	2·00	2·25
4379	15d. Scout with fish and fishing rod	2·00	2·25
MS4380	×101 mm. 40d. Scout tying knot	4·75	5·00

2002. World Cup Football, Japan and Korea (3rd issue). Designs as Nos. 4339/50 and 4357/62 inscr with match scores.

4381-4386	9d.×6 Group E: Germany 8 Saudi Arabia 0; Ireland 1 Cameroon 1; Germany 1 Ireland 1; Cameroon 1 Saudi Arabia 0; Cameroon 0 Germany 2; Saudi Arabia 0 Ireland 3;	6·50	7·00
4387-4392	9d.×6 Group F: England 1 Sweden 1; Argentina 1 Nigeria 0; Sweden 2 Nigeria 1; Argentina 0 England 1; Sweden 1 Argentina 1; Nigeria 0 England 0	6·50	7·00
4393-4398	9d.×6 Group H: Japan 2 Belgium 2; Russia 2 Tunisia 0; Japan 1 Russia 0; Tunisia 1 Belgium 1; Japan 2 Tunisia 0; Belgium 3 Russia 2	6·50	7·00

Nos. 4381/6, 4387/92 and 4393/8 were printed together, se-tenant, in sheetlets of six stamps. The sheetlets have redrawn top margins and the additional inscriptions: "GERMANY AND IRELAND ADVANCE TO ROUND OF SIXTEEN" (No. 4383a), "ENGLAND AND SWEDEN ADVANCE TO ROUND OF SIXTEEN" (4387a) or "JAPAN AND BELGIUM ADVANCE TO ROUND OF SIXTEEN (4393a).

2002. 25th Death Anniv of Elvis Presley. As T 377a of Dominica. Multicoloured.

4399	5d. Elvis Presley	1·00	75

370 Den Helder Lighthouse

2002. "Amphilex '02" International Stamp Exhibition, Amsterdam. Mult. (a) Lighthouses of Holland.

MS4400	128×148 mm. 10d.×6 Type **370**; Terschelling; Maasvlakte; Ijmuiden; Westkapelle; Breskens	7·00	7·50

The stamps within **MS**4400 and **MS**4402 form composite background designs showing an aerial map of the Netherlands (**MS**4400) or Dutch stamps (**MS**4102).

(b) "Visions of Holland".

MS4001	130×130 mm.10d.×6 Aerial view of Dutch farmland; Dutch ceramics; Traditional Dutch town house; Skaters on frozen canal and watching crowd on footbridge; Hyacinth, daffodil and tulip; Crown Prince Willem-Alexander and Maxima Zorreguieta	6·50	7·00

(c) 150th Anniv of Postage Stamps in the Netherlands.

MS4002	160×90 mm. 10d.×6 1852 5c. Dutch stamp; 1934 6c. Anti-TB Fund stamp depicting Dowager Queen Emma; 1946 2½ g. Queen Wilhelmina stamp; 1979 55c. 70th Birthday of Queen Juliana stamp; 1981 65c. Queen Beatrix definitive; 2002 39c. Wedding of Prince Willem-Alexander and Maxima Zorreguieta stamp (all horiz)	6·50	7·00

(d) Traditional Costumes of the Netherlands.

MS4003	120×140 mm. 20d.×3 Hindeloopen, Friesland; Spakenburg, Utrecht; Huizen, Noord-Holland (all 37×51 mm)	7·00	7·50

371 Blue Whale

2002. Whales, Insects and Flowers of Africa and The Gambia. Multicoloured.

MS4404	Three sheets, each 152×108 mm. (a) 10d.×6 Type **371**; Pantropical spotted dolphin; Killer whale; Minke whale; Sperm whale; Pilot whale. (b) 10d.×6 Coloured shield-backed bug and *Waltheria indica* flowers; *Anax imperator* (dragonfly); Cotton stainer bug and *Baissea multiflora* flowers; *Harpagomantis* and *Mimosa pigra* flower; *Dioncomena ornate* (katydid) and *Cola cordifolia* (flower); African grasshopper and *Urena labata* flower. (c) 10d.×6 Juba-Jamba; Devil's tongue; Rattle box; *Vernonia purpurea*; Seaside purslane; Fireball lily	20·00	21·00
MS4405	Three sheets, each 105×75 mm. (a) 50d. Humpback whales. (b) 50d. African giant swallowtail. (c) 50d. Swamp arum (vert)	14·00	15·00
MS4406	149×110 mm. 60d. Gold-banded forester	5·50	6·00

The stamps within Nos. **MS**4404a/c form composite designs.

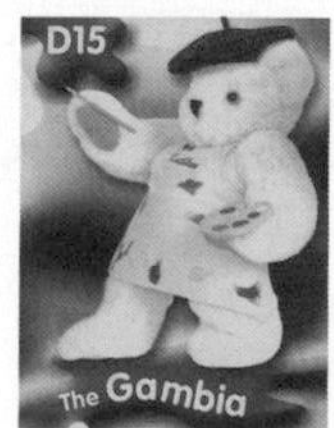

372 Artist Bear

2002. Centenary of the Teddy Bear (1st issue). T 372 and similar vert designs. Multicoloured (background colours given for MS4407).

MS4407	145×172 mm. 15d. Type **372**×4; scarlet; yellow; blue; magenta	7·00	7·00
MS4408	90×117 mm. 15d.×4 Teddy bear with cockaded hat; With mug of beer; With shawl and flowers; Wearing tall hat (all 28×42 mm)	7·00	7·50

The stamps within **MS**4407/8 form composite background designs.

See also Nos. 4488/**MS**4489 and 4499/**MS**4500.

373 "Madonna of Loreto" (detail) (Perugino)

2002. Christmas. Multicoloured.

4409	3d. Type **373**	50	20
4410	5d. "Madonna della Consolazione" (Perugino)	75	40
4411	7d. "Adoration of Shepherds" (detail) (Perugino)	90	60
4412	15d. "Transfiguration of Christ" (Giovanni Bellini)	2·00	2·25
4413	35d. "Adoration of the Magi" (Perugino)	4·00	4·50
MS4414	73×98 mm. 45d. "Christ Blessing" (Giovanni Bellini)	4·50	5·00

374 John F. Kennedy in Navy Uniform

2002. 40th Death Anniv (2003) of John F. Kennedy (President of USA, 1960–3). Multicoloured.

4415	15d. Type **374**	1·90	2·00
4416	15d. As young boy	1·90	2·00
4417	15d. Wearing open-necked shirt	1·90	2·00
4418	15d. At microphone	1·90	2·00
4419	15d. With daughter Caroline	1·90	2·00
4420	15d. As young man with book	1·90	2·00
4421	15d. With Jackie Kennedy on wedding day	1·90	2·00
4422	15d. With Jackie Kennedy	2·90	2·00

375 Charles Lindbergh as Boy

2002. Birth Centenary of Charles Lindbergh (aviator). Multicoloured.

4423	15d. Type **375**	1·90	2·00
4424	15d. As teenager	1·90	2·00
4425	15d. In army uniform	1·90	2·00
4426	15d. As young man	1·90	2·00
4427	15d. As boy with dog	1·90	2·00
4428	15d. Wearing flying jacket	1·90	2·00
4429	15d. Wearing suit and flying goggles	1·90	2·00
4430	15d. Anne Morrow Lindbergh	1·90	2·00

376 Diana Spencer as Young Girl

2002. Diana, Princess of Wales Commemoration. Multicoloured.

4431	15d. Type **376**	1·90	2·00
4432	15d. On wedding day	1·90	2·00
4433	15d. With baby Prince William	1·90	2·00
4434	15d. With Princes William and Harry	1·90	2·00
4435	15d. Wearing red hat and dress	1·90	2·00
4436	15d. Wearing red and white hat and jacket	1·90	2·00
4437	15d. Wearing white dress	1·90	2·00
4438	15d. Wearing black dress	1·90	2·00

377 James Cagney

2002. James Cagney (actor) Commemoration. Multicoloured.

4439	10d. Type **377**	1·25	1·40
4440	10d. In West Point Story, wearing hat and bow tie	1·25	1·40
4441	10d. With a gun in each hand	1·25	1·40
4442	10d. With pocket handkerchief	1·25	1·40
4443	10d. Looking to right	1·25	1·40
4444	10d. With woman	1·25	1·40

2002. Clark Gable (actor) Commemoration. As T 377. Multicoloured.

4445	10d. Wearing bow tie	1·25	1·40
4446	10d. In half-shadow	1·25	1·40
4447	10d. Wearing bow tie, looking right	1·25	1·40
4448	10d. Wearing pocket handkerchief, leaning on elbow	1·25	1·40
4449	10d. In close-up, looking down	1·25	1·40
4450	10d. In close-up, looking ahead	1·25	1·40

378 Ram

2003. Chinese New Year ("Year of the Ram"). Multicoloured.

4451	10d. Type **378**	1·25	1·40
4452	10d. As Type **378** (blue background)	1·25	1·40
4453	10d. Ram facing left (brown background)	1·25	1·40
4454	10d. As No. 4453 (yellow background)	1·25	1·40

379 "Concubine washing her Hands under an Ornate Faucet"

2003. Japanese Art. Paintings by Taiso Yoshitoshi. Multicoloured.

4455	5d. Type **379**	75	40
4456	10d. "Housewife in an Inner Chamber fanning a Fire"	1·25	1·25
4457	15d. "Geisha catching a Firefly"	2·00	2·25
4458	20d. "Music Teacher playing on a Shamisen"	2·25	2·50
4459	20d. "An 'Okamisan', or Proprietress of a Tea-House, at Work"	2·25	2·50
4460	20d. "A City Merchant's Widow absorbed in a Novelette"	2·25	2·50
4461	20d. "Busy Young Waitress preoccupied with her Responsibilities"	2·25	2·00
4462	25d. "A Young Geisha dressed as an Elegant Young Man while taking part in the Niwaka Celebration"	2·50	2·75
MS4463	67×96 mm. 45d. "A 'Saikun', or Wife of a Government Official, lighting an Oil Lamp"	4·50	5·00

380 "Composition X"

2003. Paintings by Wassily Kandinsky. Mult.

4464	2d. Type **380**	35	20
4465	4d. "Arrow towards the Circle"	60	65
4466	5d. "Yellow-Red-Blue"	75	45
4467	7d. "Accompanied Middle"	90	90
4468	10d. "In Blue"	1·25	1·25
4469	15d. "Picture with Archer" (vert)	2·00	2·25
4470	15d. "Light" (vert)	2·00	2·25
4471	15d. "Picture in the Picture" (vert)	2·00	2·25
4472	15d. "White Stroke" (vert)	2·00	2·25
4473	20d. "Round and Pointed"	2·25	2·50
MS4474	Two sheets, each 95×75 mm. (a) 45d. "On the Points". (b) 45d. "Improvisation XIX". Both imperf	8·50	9·50

2003. 450th Death Anniv of Lucas Cranach the Elder (artist). Paintings by Cranach the Elder and Cranach the Younger. As T 663 of Guyana. Multicoloured.

4475	5d. "Portrait of Johannes Scheyring" (Cranach the Elder)	75	45
4476	7d. "Rudolph Agricola" (Cranach the Elder)	90	90
4477	10d. "Portrait Head of a Gentleman" (Cranach the Younger)	1·25	1·25
4478	15d. "Margravine Elizabeth von Ansbach" (Cranach the Younger)	2·00	2·25
4479	15d. Elector Joachim II of Brandenburg" (Cranach the Younger)	2·00	2·25
4480	15d. "Portrait of a Nobleman" (Cranach the Younger)	2·00	2·25
4481	15d. "Portrait of a Noblewoman" (Cranach the Younger)	2·00	2·25
4482	20d. "Hans von Lindau" (detail) (Cranach the Younger)	2·25	2·50
MS4483	116×100 mm. 40d. "The Ill-Matched Couple" (detail) (Cranach the Elder)	4·25	4·50

2003. Columbia Space Shuttle Commemoration (1st issue). Sheet 184×145 mm containing vert designs as T 533 of Grenada showing crew members. Multicoloured.

MS4484 184×145 mm. 10d. David Brown; 10d. Commander Rick Husband; 10d. Laurel Clark; 10d. Kalpana Chawla; 10d. Michael Anderson; 10d. William McCool; 10d. Ilan Ramon 8·75 9·00

The stamps and margins of No. **MS**4484 form a composite design.

381 *Columbia* Crew

2003. Columbia Space Shuttle Commemoration (2nd issue). Sheets 177×113 mm, containing horiz designs as T 381. Multicoloured.

MS4485 (a) 15d.×4 Type **381**; Shuttle being transported by jet; Shuttle glowing on re-entry; Kalpana Shawla inside shuttle and astronaut space-walking. (b) 15d.×4 As Type **381** (dark background); Shuttle in orbit, Moon in background; Shuttle on launchpad; Laurel Clark. (c) 15d.×4 As Type **381** (blue background); Ilan Ramon; Shuttle on launch pad, engines firing; Shuttle in orbit above Cape Canaveral. (d) 15d.×4 As Type **381** ("THE GAMBIA" at top); Michael Anderson and jet; Shuttle lifting off; Shuttle in orbit and space station 28·00 29·00

2003. 50th Anniv of Coronation. As T 384 of Dominica. Multicoloured.

MS4486 147×85 mm. 20d. Queen Elizabeth II wearing tiara and blue dress; 20d. Wearing blue and white spotted hat and jacket; 20d. Wearing Garter robes 6·50 6·75

MS4487 68×98 mm. 45d. Young Queen wearing diadem 4·25 4·50

The stamps and margins of No. **MS**4486 form a composite background design.

2003. Centenary of the Teddy Bear (2nd issue). Embroidered Fabric Teddy Bears. As T 538 of Grenada. Self-adhesive.

4488 150d. ochre and blue 10·50 11·00

MS4489 126×158 mm. No. 4488×4 40·00 4·00

2003. 21st Birthday of Prince William. As T 385a of Dominica. Multicoloured.

MS4490 148×78 mm. 20d. As young boy (wearing blazer, no tie); 20d. As boy, wearing jacket and tie; 20d. As teenager, wearing blue shirt 6·50 6·75

MS4491 68×98 mm. 45d. As adult, wearing yellow polo shirt 4·25 5·50

The stamps and margins of No. **MS**4490 form a composite background design.

2003. Centenary of Tour de France Cycle Race. As T 623 of Ghana showing past winners. Multicoloured.

MS4492 160×100 mm. 15d. Henri Pelisser (1923); 15d. Ottavio Bottecchia (1924); 15d. Ottavio Bottechia (1925); 15d. Lucien Buysse (1926) 8·75 9·00

MS4493 160×100 mm. 15d. Nicolas Frantz (1927); 15d. Nicolas Frantz (1928); 15d. Maurice de Waele (1929); 15d. Andre Leducq (1930) 8·75 9·00

MS4494 160×100 mm. 15d. Antonin Magne (1931); 15d. Andre Leducq (1932); 15d. Georges Speicher (1933); 15d. Antonin Magne (1934) (wrongly inscr "ANTOMIN") 8·75 9·00

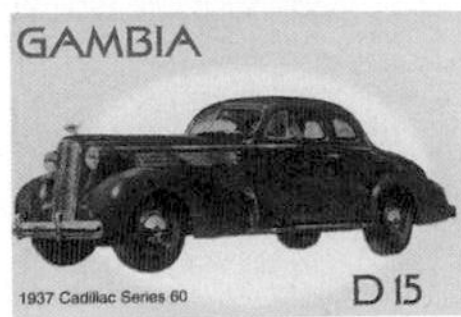

382 Cadillac Series 60 (1937)

2003. Centenary of General Motors Cadillac. Multicoloured.

MS4495 107×148 mm. 15d. Type **382**; 15d. Cadillac LaSalle (1927); 15d. Cadillac V-16 (1930); 15d. Cadillac V-16 Convertible (1931) 8·75 9·00

MS4496 100×75 mm. 45d. Cadillac Eldorado (1954) 4·25 4·50

383 Corvette Shark (1960)

2003. Centenary of General Motors Chevrolet Corvette. Multicoloured.

MS4497 107×150 mm. 15d. Type **383**; 15d. Corvette Sting Ray Convertible (1964); 15d. Corvette Convertible (1956); 15d. Corvette (1967) 8·75 9·00

MS4498 102×75 mm. 45d. Corvette Sting Ray (1964) 4·25 4·50

384 Schalke 04

2003. Centenary of the Teddy Bear (3rd issue). T 384 and similar multicoloured designs showing teddy bears as footballers. Multicoloured.

MS4499 Two sheets, each 178×102 mm. (a) 15d.×4 Type **384**; Bayer Munich; Baer Leaerkusen; Hertha Berlin. (b) 15d.×4 England; Brazil; Germany; Spain 17·50 18·00

MS4500 Two sheets, each 71×91 mm. (a) 45d. Bayern Munich (white). (b) 45d. Bayern Munich (red) (horiz) 8·50 9·00

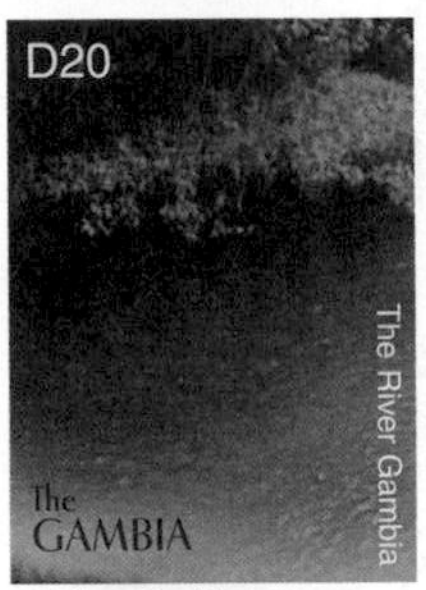

385 River Gambia

2003. International Year of Fresh Water. Mult.

MS4501 136×97 mm. 20d. Type **385**; 20d. River Gambia (floating vegetation in midstream); 20d. River Gambia (palm trees on bank) 2·25 2·50

MS4502 67×97 mm. 45d. Rapids on River Gambia 8·25 4·50

The stamps and margins of No. **MS**4501 form a composite design.

386 *Wright Flyer I*, 1903

2003. Centenary of Powered Flight. Multicoloured.

MS4503 176×107 mm. 15d. Type **386**; 15d. Goupy 1 (first full-size triplane), 1908; 15d. *Deutschland* LZ.7 (first commercial airship); 15d. Lt. Cdr. Richard Byrd's flight over North Pole, 1926 8·75 9·00

MS4504 176×107 mm. 15d. Granville Gee Bee (World Speed Record), 1932; 15d. Boeing 247D, 1933; 15d. Douglas DC-3, 1935; Amelia Earhart's solo Hawaii—California flight, 1935 8·75 9·00

MS4505 176×107 mm. 15d. MacCready *Solar Challenger* (solar powered flight), 1980; 15d. *Voyager 2* and Saturn's rings, 1981; 15d. *Columbia* space shuttle, 1981; 15d. *Voyager's* non-stop around the world flight, 1986 8·75 9·00

MS4506 Three sheets, each 105×75 mm. (a) 40d. Vought V-173 short takeoff and landing research airplane, 1942. (b) 40d. *Pioneer 10* leaving Solar System, 1983. (c) 40d. AD-1 Scissors-Wing SST aircraft, 1979 13·00 14·00

387 Ferrari 126 C2

2003. Ferrari Racing Cars. Multicoloured.

4507	2d. Type **387**	30	25
4508	3d. 313 T2	40	45
4509	5d. 312 T4	50	55
4510	7d. 126 C3	75	80
4511	10d. F399	1·00	1·10
4512	15d. F1-2000	2·00	2·25
4513	20d. F2001	2·25	2·50
4514	25d. F2002	2·40	2·50

2003. Centenary of Circus Clowns. As T 544 of Grenada. Multicoloured.

MS4515 115×200 mm. 15d. Francesco Caroli; 15d. Lou Jacobs; 15d. Frankie Saluto; 15d. Gingernut 8·00 8·25

MS4516 145×218 mm. 15d. Evgeny Maranogli (clown) with dog; 15d. Saby (acrobat); 15d. Colonel Joe with elephant; 15d. Puma 8·75 9·00

No. **MS**4515 shows clowns and is cut in the shape of a clown. No. **MS**4516 shows circus performers and is cut in the shape of an elephant.

388 Criorhynchus

2003. Prehistoric Animals. Multicoloured.

MS4517 136×115 mm. 30d. Type **388**; 30d. Seismosaurus; 30d. Triceratops; 30d. Stegosaurus 17·00 18·00

MS4518 115×136 mm. 30d. Petainosaurus; 30d. Pachycephalosaurus; 30d. Ichthyosaur; 30d. Anomalocaris (all vert) 17·00 18·00

MS4519 Two sheets. (a) 65×95 mm. 75d. Paradoxides (vert). (b) 75d. 95×75 mm. 75d. Edmontosaurus 15·00 16·00

The stamps and margins of Nos. **MS**4517/18 form composite designs.

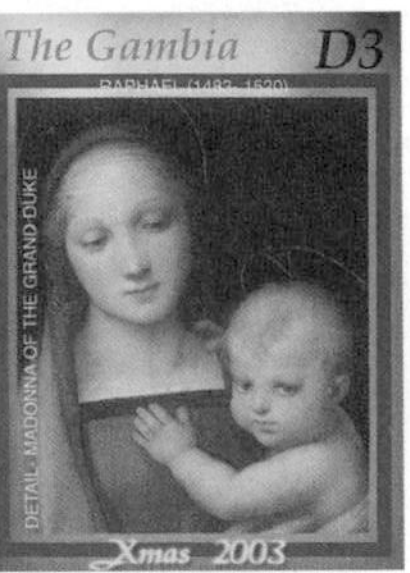

389 "Madonna of the Grand Duke" (detail) (Raphael)

2003. Christmas. Multicoloured.

4520	3d. Type **389**	40	45
4521	5d. "The Madonna dell' Impannata" (Raphael)	50	55
4522	7d. "Adoration of the Magi" (detail) (Filippo Lippi)	1·00	1·10
4523	60d. "Adoration in the Woods" (detail) (Filippo Lippi)	6·50	6·75

MS4524 114×80 mm. 75d. "Madonna del Carmelo" (Giambattista Tiepolo) 5·25 5·50

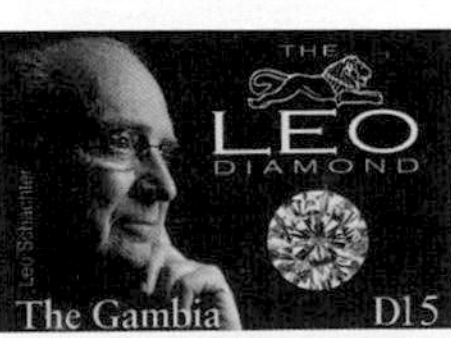

390 Leo Schachter (diamond dealer) and Leo Diamond

2003. Leo Diamonds.

4525 **390** 15d. multicoloured 2·00 2·25

MS4526 100×70 mm. **390** 60d. multicoloured 6·50 6·75

391 Rough Diamonds

2003. Diamonds. Multicoloured.

4527	20d. Type **391**	2·25	2·50
4528	20d. Yellow diamonds	2·25	2·50
4529	20d. Pink diamonds	2·25	2·50
4530	20d. Blue diamonds	2·25	2·50
4531	20d. White diamonds	2·25	2·50
4532	20d. Green diamonds	2·25	2·50

MS4533 82×75 mm. 75d. Champagne diamonds 5·25 5·50

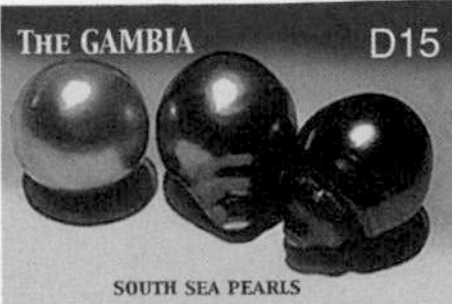

392 South Sea Pearls

2003. Pearls. Multicoloured.

4534	15d. Type **392**	2·00	2·25
4535	15d. Mabe pearls and oyster	2·00	2·25
4536	15d. Pinctada maxima (oyster) and pearls	2·00	2·25
4537	15d. Australian pearls and oyster	2·00	2·25
4538	15d. Pearls on ocean floor	2·00	2·50
4539	15d. South Sea white pearls and oyster	2·00	2·25

MS4540 81×75 mm. 60d. Champagne pearls 6·50 6·75

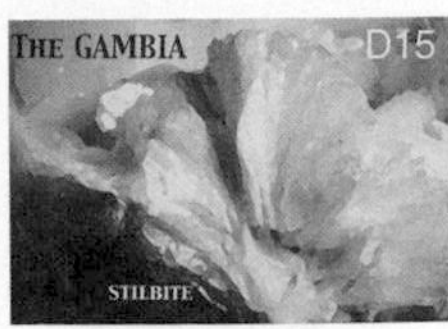

393 Stilbite

2003. Minerals. Multicoloured.

MS4541 182×120 mm. 15d. Type **393**; 15d. Smokey quartz; 15d. Lapis; 15d. Amethyst; 15d. Black opals; 15d. Ruby 10·00 10·25

MS4542 82×75 mm. 60d. Quartz 6·50 6·75

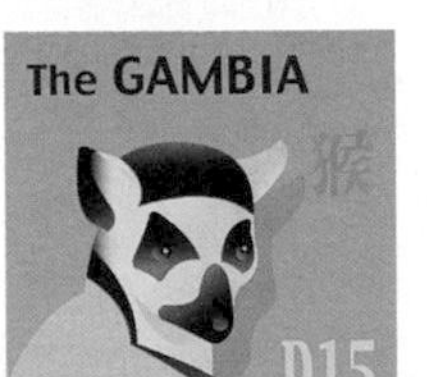

394 Ring-tailed Lemur

2004. Chinese New Year ("Year of the Monkey"). Multicoloured.

MS4543 152×153 mm. 15d. Type **394**; 15d. Grey monkey with white face; 15d. Colobus monkey; 15d. Orange-brown monkey 8·00 8·25

The stamps and margins of No. **MS**4543 form a composite design.

395 "Four Magpies"

2004. Hong Kong 2004 International Stamp Exhibition. Paintings by Xu Beihong. Multicoloured.

MS4544 185×104 mm. 10d. Type **395**; 10d. "Cormorants"; 10d. "Under the Banyan Tree"; 10d. "Citrus Tree"; 10d. "Double Happiness"; 10d. "Rooster in Bamboo Garden" 7·50 7·75

MS4545 118×117 mm. 25d. "Bird on the Kapok Tree" (50×37 mm); 25d. "Twin Pines" (50×37 mm) 4·75 5·00

396 Brain reading Book

2004. Arthur the Aardvark and Friends (created by Marc Brown). Multicoloured.

MS4546 150×184 mm. 20d. Type **396**; 20d. Sue Ellen reading "Kids" comic; 20d. Buster reading "Bionic Bunny magazine; 20d. Francine reading book; 20d. Muffy reading book; 20d. Binky reading "Football" book 12·00 12·50

MS4547	150×184 mm. 30d. Brain playing cello; 30d. Francine playing drums; 30d. Buster playing French horn; 30d. Sue Ellen playing saxophone	13·00	13·50
MS4548	150×184 mm. 30d. Brain playing clarinet; 30d. Francine playing banjo; 30d. Buster playing flute; 30d. Sue Ellen playing violin	13·00	13·50

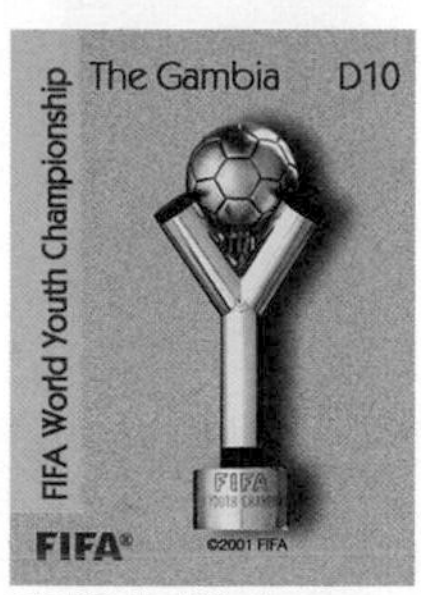

397 FIFA World Youth Championship Trophy

2004. Centenary of FIFA (Federation Internationale de Football Association) (1st issue). Football Trophies. Multicoloured.

4549	10d. Type **397**	1·25	1·25
4550	10d. FIFA Confederation's Cup	1·25	1·25
4551	10d. FIFA Club World Championship	1·25	1·25
4552	10d. FIFA Futsal World Championship	1·25	1·25
4553	10d. Jules Rimet Cup	1·25	1·25
4554	10d. FIFA U-19 Women's World Championship	1·25	1·25
4555	10d. FIFA World Cup	1·25	1·25
4556	10d. FIFA Women's World Cup	1·25	1·25
4557	10d. FIFA U-17 World Championship	1·25	1·25

398 "Portrait of a Gentleman" (Domenico Capriolo)

2004. 300th Anniv of St. Petersburg. "Treasures of the Hermitage". Multicoloured.

MS4558	110×130 mm. 30d. Type **398**; 30d. "Sybil" (Dosso Dossi); 30d. "A Woman in a Turban" (Anne-Louis Girodet-Trioson); 30d. "Portrait of a Gentleman" (Holbein)	12·00	14·00
MS4559	75×60 mm. 75d. "Husband and Wife" (Lorenzo Lotto). Imperf	9·00	10·00

399 Post Illustration (detail), 1937

2004. 25th Death Anniv (2003) of Norman Rockwell (artist). Multicoloured.

MS4560	150×180 mm. 30d. Type **399**; 30d. "Girl at Mirror"; 30d. "After the Prom"; 30d. "The Prom Dress"	14·00	15·00
MS4561	90×97 mm. 75d. "Losing the Game"	8·50	9·00

400 "Girl in Chemise"

2004. 30th Death Anniv (2003) of Pablo Picasso (artist). Multicoloured.

MS4562	132×170 mm. 30d. Type **400**; 30d. "Portrait of Jacinto Salvado as Harlequin"; 30d. "Tumblers"; 30d. "Woman with a Crow"	14·00	14·50
MS4563	100×75 mm. 75d. "The Siesta". Imperf	8·50	9·00

401 Concorde and Top of Eiffel Tower

2004. Last Flight of Concorde (2003). Mult.

MS4564	88×130 mm. 25d. Type **401**; 25d. Concorde, French flag and mid-section of Eiffel Tower; 25d. Concorde, French flag and lower section of Eiffel Tower	10·00	11·00
MS4565	88×128 mm. 25d. Concorde (39 mm long) and Australian flag; 25d. Concorde (38 mm long) and Australian flag; 25d. Concorde and clouds	10·00	11·00
MS4566	88×129 mm. 25d. Concorde and Statue of Liberty, New York; 25d. Concorde and US flag; 25d. Concorde, US flag and New York harbour sightseeing boat	10·00	11·00
MS4567	146×116 mm. 60d.×4 Concorde and Red Arrows flying over liner *Queen Elizabeth 2*	30·00	30·00

No. **MS**4564 depicts Concorde 213 F-BTSD and **MS**4565/6 Concorde 216 G-BOAF.

The stamps and margins of No. **MS**4564 form a composite background design showing the Eiffel Tower, Paris.

402 "Onoe Kikugoro V as Moronao with the Late Nakamura Sojuro I as Enya Hangan"

2004. Japanese Art. Famous Actors by Toyohara Kunichika. Multicoloured.

4568	10d. Type **402**	1·25	1·25
4569	15d. "Onoe Kikugoro V as Shinohara Kunimoto with Ichikawa Danjuro IV as Saigo Takamuri"	1·75	1·75
4570	20d. "Onoe Kikugoro V as Yamamoto Kansuke with Ichikawa Sadanji I as Ushikubo Daizo"	2·00	2·00
4571	35d. "Onoe Kikugoro V as the Ghost Seigen with Nakamura Fukusuke IV as Sakusahime"	3·25	3·75
MS4572	192×153 mm. 30d. "Ichikawa Sadanji as the Fishmonger Fukashichi"; 30d. "Ichikawa Sadanji I as Umeomaru"; 30d. "Ichikawa Kuzo III as Fujiwara Shihei"; 30d. Nakamura Shikan IV as Motome"	14·00	15·00
MS4573	120×80 mm. 15d. "Ichikawa Udanji as Koya Saihei" (horiz)	2·00	2·25

403 "Woman", (pastel on paper, 1934)

2004. 20th Death Anniv of Joan Miro (artist). Multicoloured.

4574	20d. Type **403**	2·00	2·25
4575	25d. "Woman" (pastel and pencil on emery paper, 1934)	2·40	2·25
4576	35d. "Self-portrait" (1937–60)	4·00	4·25
4577	75d. "Man with Pipe" (1934)	8·00	8·25
MS4578	180×140 mm. 30d. "Portrait IV" (1938); 30d. "Seated Woman" (1931); 30d. "Painting on Ingres Paper" (1932); 30d. "Portrait II" (1938)	14·00	14·50
MS4579	Two sheets, each 100×80 mm. (a) 75d. "Composition with Personages in the Burning Forest" (1931). (b) 75d. "Bird" (1960). Both imperf	16·00	19·00

404 Black and White Bicolour American Shorthair

405 *Hydrocybe conica*

2004. Cats and Dogs. Multicoloured.

MS4580	100×139 mm. 30d. Type **404**; 30d. Brown and white sphinx; 30d. Copper-eyed white Persian; 30d. Blue mackerel tabby oriental longhair	14·00	14·50
MS4581	102×140 mm. 30d. Bracco (Italian pointer); 30d. Shih tzu; 30d. Boston terrier; 30d. Chihuahua	14·00	14·50
MS4582	Two sheets. (a) 70×100 mm. 75d. Copper-eyed cameo Persian (horiz). (b) 100×70 mm. 75d. Borzoi (inscr "Borsoi") (horiz)	16·00	17·00

The stamps and margins of Nos. **MS**4580/1 form composite background designs showing Siamese cats (**MS**4580) or a Japanese chin dog (**MS**4581).

2004. Fungi. Multicoloured.

MS4583	100×139 mm. 30d. Type **405**; 30d. *Laccaria fraternal*; 30d. *Gomphus clavatus*; 30d. *Hydrocybe psittacina*	14·00	15·00
MS4584	218×134 mm. 30d. Steel-blue entoloma; 30d. Caged stinkhorn; 30d. Flowerpot depiota; 30d. Singeri Dodge (all horiz)	14·00	15·00
MS4585	100×70 mm. 75d. *Russula sanguinea*	8·00	8·50

The stamps and margins of No. **MS**4583 form a composite background design.

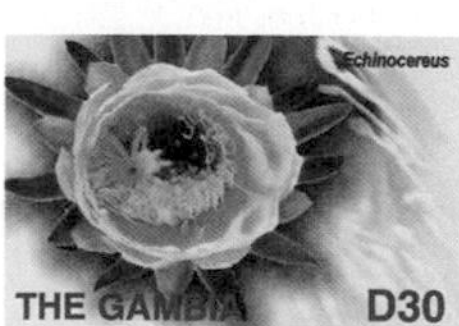

406 *Echinocereusi*

2004. Succulents ("The Orchid Cactus"). Mult.

MS4586	137×100 mm. 30d. Type **406**; 30d. *Harrisia*; 30d. *Stapelia*; 30d. *Matucana*	14·00	15·00
MS4587	208×139 mm. 30d. *Epiphyllum chichicastenango*; 30d. *Banksia ericifolia*; 30d. *Echinopsis*	14·00	15·00
MS4588	100×70 mm. 75d. *Epiphyllum*	8·00	8·50

The stamps and margins of No. **MS**4586 form a composite background design.

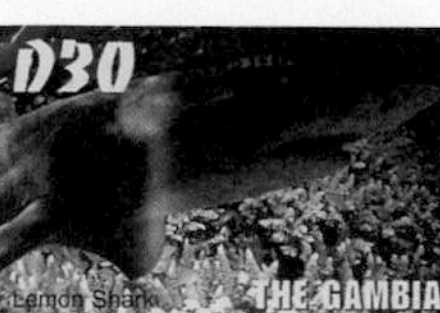

407 Lemon Shark

2004. Sharks. Multicoloured.

MS4589	129×130 mm. 30d. Type **407**; 30d. Nurse shark; 30d. Leopard shark; 30d. Starry smoothhound sharks	14·00	15·00
MS4590	90×90 mm. 75d. Basking shark	8·00	8·50

408 Bulgaria

2004. European Football Championship, Portugal. Multicoloured.

4591	6d. Type **408**	75	75
4592	6d. Croatia	75	75
4593	6d. Czech Republic	75	75
4594	6d. Denmark	75	75
4595	6d. England	75	75
4596	6d. France	75	75
4597	6d. Germany	75	75
4598	6d. Greece	75	75
4599	6d. Italy	75	75
4600	6d. Latvia	75	75
4601	6d. Netherlands	75	75
4602	6d. Portugal (no country name)	75	75
4603	6d. Russia	75	75
4604	6d. Spain	75	75
4605	6d. Sweden	75	75
4606	6d. Switzerland	75	75
MS4607	164×84 mm. 25d. Angelo Domenghini; 25d. Dragan Dzajic; 25d. Luigi Riva; 25d. Stadio Olimpico (all 27×41 mm)	9·50	9·75
MS4608	98×83 mm. 65d. Italian team, 1968	6·25	6·50

409 Steam Locomotive *City of Truro*

2004. Bicentenary of Steam Locomotives. Multicoloured.

4609–4617	12d.×9 Type **409**; Sharp Stewart steam locomotive; Indian Railways WT class; Charing Cross Station, London; Linlithgow Station, Scotland; Hellifield Station, England; Kings Cross Station, London; Paddington Station, London; Victoria Station, London	16·00	17·00
4618–4626	12d.×9 Steam locomotive *Mallard*; North British steam locomotive; Russian P36 steam locomotive; Forth Rail Bridge; Lune Viaduct; Lambley Viaduct; Alston Arches Viaduct; Royal Albert Bridge, Saltash; Blackfriars Bridge, London	16·00	17·00
4627–4635	12d.×9 Virgin Pendolino train; Mountain class Garratt steam locomotive; Steam locomotive No. 227; Kilsby Tunnel; Box Tunnel; Willersley Tunnel; Stansted Airport Tunnel; Clayton Tunnel; Severn Tunnel	16·00	17·00
MS4636	Three sheets, each 100×70 mm. (a) 65d. Steam locomotive, Darjeeling, India. 65d. Eurostar train. (c) 65d. Steam locomotive on West Highland line	7·00	7·50

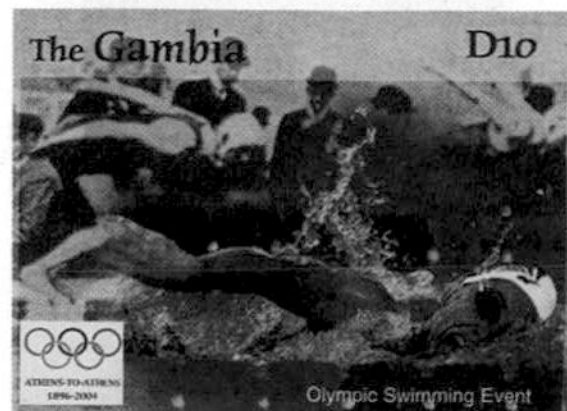

410 Swimming

2004. Olympic Games, Athens. Multicoloured.

4637	10d. Type **410**	1·25	70
4638	15d. Henri de Baillet-Latour (IOC President 1925–42) (vert)	2·00	2·25
4639	20d. Winner's medal from 1896 Olympic Games (vert)	2·25	2·50
4640	30d. Pentathlon (design on ancient Greek vase)	5·00	5·25

411 Marilyn Monroe

412 Deng Xiaoping

2004. Marilyn Monroe (actress) Commemoration. Multicoloured.

4641– 4656 7d.×16 Type **411** (background colours given); orange; emerald; magenta; yellow; blue; rosine; blue; green; turquoise; lemon; orange; violet; purple; blue; blue; cerise 17·00 18·00

MS4657 123×123 mm. Portraits with signature and initials "MM" in background: 25d.×2 Marilyn Monroe; 25d.×2 Wearing halter-neck dress 9·50 10·00

MS4658 120×110 mm. 25d.×4 With mouth open, wearing dress with jewelled straps; Wearing red and white necklace; Wearing dress with red shoestring straps; Wearing white blouse with collar 9·50 10·00

2004. 60th Anniv of D-Day Landings. As T 404 of Dominica. Multicoloured.

4659 7d. Jim Wallwork, 6th Airborne Division 1·10 70

4660 10d. Major Gen. Richard Gale 1·25 80

4661 15d. Winston Churchill 2·75 2·75

4662 30d. J. K. 'Paddy' Byrne, 197 Typhoon Squadron 5·50 6·50

MS4663 Two sheets, each 177×107 mm. (a) 25d. Heavy bombers over Normandy coast; 25d. RAF Mitchell bomber bombing German gun emplacements; 25d. British Horsa gliders on ground behind enemy lines; 25d. Paratroopers parachuting into Normandy and map. (b) 25d. British paratroopers and map showing Pegasus and Horsa Bridges; 25d. British paratroopers in control of Pegasus Bridge; 25d. American paratrooper and map showing Sainte Mere Eglise; 25d. American paratroopers and church at Sainte Mere Eglise 19·00 20·00

MS4664 Two sheets, each 100×70 mm. (a) 60d. Troops disembarking from landing craft. (b) 60d. RAF heavy bombers under construction 8·50 9·00

2004. Birth Centenary of Deng Xiaoping (Chinese leader). Sheet 98×68 mm.

MS4665 **412** 75d. multicoloured 4·25 4·50

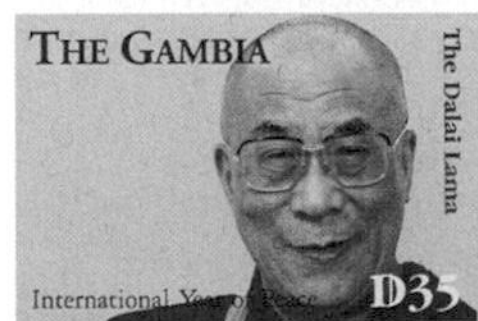

413 Dalai Lama

2004. United Nations International Year of Peace. Sheet 137×77 mm containing T 413 and similar horiz designs. Multicoloured.

MS4666 35d. Type **413**; 35d. "EUROPEAN NUCLEAR DISARMAMENT", peace doves and CND emblem; 35d. "3 DAYS of PEACE & MUSIC" notice and crowd at Woodstock Festival, Bethel, New York, 1969 8·00 8·50

414 Apsaroke Indians and Teepee

2004. American Indians. Multicoloured.

4667– 4672 12d. American Indian Women 15d.×6 Nakoaktok preparing bark; Papago cleaning wheat; Hopi fetching water; Hopi painting pottery; Tlaluit pounding fish; Arikara gathering rush (all 29×40 mm) 11·00 12·00

4673– 4676 12d. Indians of the Plains 30d.×4 Type **414**; Piegan Indians; Apsaroke Indians; Sioux Chiefs 10·00 10·50

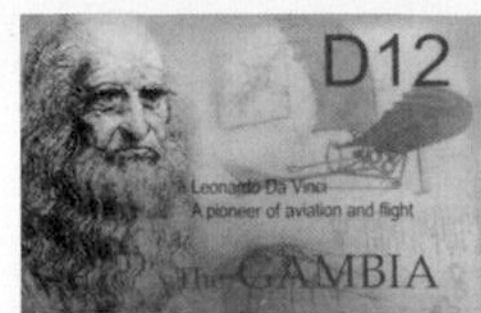

415 Leonardo da Vinci and Drawing

2004. Centenary of Powered Flight. Multicoloured.

4677 12d. Type **415** 1·50 1·50

4678 12d. Count Ferdinand von Zeppelin and airship 1·50 1·50

4679 12d. William Boeing and aircraft 1·50 1·50

4680 12d. Captain John Cunningham and aircraft 1·50 1·50

4681 12d. Captain Edwin Musick and first Transpacific airmail flight 1·50 1·50

4682 12d. Captain Jock Lowe and Concorde 1·50 1·50

4683 12d. William Lear (inventor of first autopilot for jet aircraft) and jet 1·50 1·50

4684 12d. Jenny Murray (pilot) and helicopter 1·50 1·50

MS4685 101×72 mm. 60d. Mars Rover Mission rocket 7·00 7·50

416 Pope John Paul II, St. Peter's Square, 1978

417 Isla de Flores Lighthouse, Uruguay

2004. 25th Anniv of Pontificate of Pope John Paul II. Multicoloured.

4686– 4695 10d.×10 Type **416**; In stadium with crowd, 1979; With Mother Teresa, 1980; In 1981; With Queen Elizabeth II, 1982; Reading speech, 1983; With Swiss Guards, 1984; With Prince and Princess of Wales, 1985; With koala, 1986; With President Reagan, 1987 15·00 15·00

4696– 4710 10d.×15 Pope seated, 1988; At microphone, 1989; With Mikhail Gorbachev, 1990; With mitre and staff, 1991; With Archbishop of Canterbury, 1992; Waving to crowd, 1993; With President Clinton, 1994; With children, 1995; With German Chancellor Helmut Kohl, 1996; With cardinals, 1997; Signing document, 1998; With Patriach Filaret of Kiev and Ukraine, 1999; At Wailing Wall, Jerusalem, 2000; Closing the Holy Door, St. Peter's Basilica, 2001; In 2002 24·00 25·00

2004. Lighthouses. Multicoloured.

4711 5d. Type **417** 1·25 60

4712 7d. Punta Brava Lighthouse, Uruguay 1·50 75

4713 15d. Boston Lighthouse, USA 2·50 2·50

4714 20d. Cabo Polonio Lighthouse, Uruguay 2·75 3·00

4715 20d. Bass Harbor Head Light, USA 2·75 3·00

4716 25d. Tybee Island Lighthouse, USA 2·75 3·00

4717 30d. Old Cape Henry Lighthouse, USA 3·75 4·00

4718 35d. Morris Island Lighthouse, USA 4·25 4·50

4719 40d. Hillsboro Inlet Lighthouse, USA 4·50 4·75

4720 45d. Punta del Este Lighthouse, USA 5·00 5·50

4721 50d. Cape Lookout Lighthouse, USA 6·00 6·50

4722 60d. Portland Head Lighthouse, USA 6·50 7·00

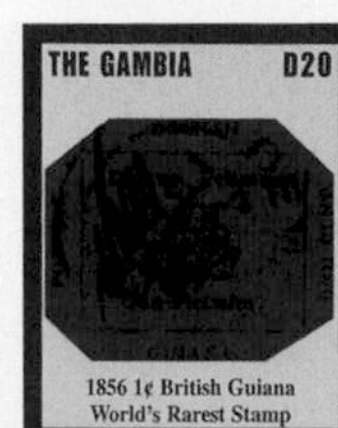

418 British Guiana 1856 1c. Stamp (world's rarest stamp)

2004. Rare and Famous Postage Stamps. Sheet 102×86 mm containing T 418 and similar vert designs. Multicoloured.

4723 20d. Type **418** 2·75 3·00

4724 20d. Penny Black (first stamp) 2·75 3·00

4725 20d. 1868 1c. Z Grill (rarest US stamp) 2·75 3·00

4726 20d. USA 1918 24c. inverted Curtis Jenny error 2·75 3·00

4727 20d. 1847 5c. Benjamin Franklin stamp (first US stamp) 2·75 3·00

419 *Babiana rubrocyanaea*

2004. Flowers. Multicoloured.

4728 1d. Type **419** 15 20

4729 2d. *Protea* 30 25

4730 3d. *Lithops bromfieldii* 40 45

4731 5d. *Saintpaulia ionantha* 50 55

4732 6d. *Monopsis lutea* 60 65

4733 7d. *Dudleya lancealata* 90 95

4734 9d. *Euphorbia punicea* 1·00 1·10

4735 10d. *Oxalis violacea* 1·25 1·00

4736 25d. *Helichrysum bracteatum* 2·40 2·50

4737 50d. *Senecio obovatus* 4·75 5·00

4738 75d. *Mesembryanthemum acinaciforme* 5·25 5·50

4739 100d. *Montbretia croscosmiiflora* 9·00 9·50

4740 200d. *Gladiolus colvillei* 18·00 19·00

420 Elvis Presley

2004. 50th Anniv of Elvis Presley's First Record. Multicoloured.

4741– 4749 12d.×9 Type **420**; With guitar, singing into microphone; Wearing black and yellow chevron-striped shirt; Singing, backing singer in left background; Wearing red and cream shirt; Singing into overhead microphone; Holding guitar; Seated, playing guitar; Leaning forward towards camera 18·00 19·00

4750– 4758 12d.×9 In black, standing on tiptoe with arm raised; At microphone playing guitar; Wearing white jacket and singing with backing musicians, guitar and drums in background; Wearing black, with guitar; Close-up portrait; With guitar, smiling for camera; Singing, wearing white; Wearing grey jacket, playing guitar; With guitar, backing musicians with drums in background 18·00 19·00

421 George Herman Ruth

2004. Centenary of Baseball World Series. Sheet 126×173 mm containing T 421 and similar vert designs showing George Herman Ruth Jr ("Babe Ruth"). Multicoloured.

MS4759 25d. Type **421**; 25d. Standing, with hand on hip; 25d. Holding bat over shoulders, facing forwards; 25d. Holding bat (half length portrait) 9·50 9·75

422 Pres. Reagan with Wife and Pope John Paul II

2004. Ronald Reagan (President of USA 1981–9) Commemoration. Multicoloured.

4760 15d. Type **422** 3·00 3·00

4761 15d. With Shimon Peres (Israeli Prime Minister) 3·00 3·00

4762 15d. In front of window 3·00 3·00

4763 15d. In front of microphone 3·00 3·00

4764 15d. Wearing bow tie, holding drink 3·00 3·00

4765 25d. Pres. Reagan with Margaret Thatcher, 1986 4·00 4·00

4766 25d. With Pope John Paul II 4·00 4·00

4767 25d. Signing Missing Children's Act and Victim Witness Protection Act, 1982 4·00 4·00

4768 25d. Pres. and Mrs. Reagan, 1987 4·00 4·00

4769 25d. The First Family, 1982 (horiz) 4·00 4·00

4770 25d. Signing INF Treaty with Mikhail Gorbachev, 1987 (horiz) 4·00 4·00

4771 25d. Assassination attempt, 1981 (horiz) 4·00 4·00

4772 25d. With Deng Xiaoping, finalizing Nuclear Agreement with China, 1984 (horiz) 4·00 4·00

MS4773 83×105 mm. 60d. Pres. Ronald Reagan 7·50 8·50

2004. Centenary of FIFA (Federation Internationale de Football Association) (2nd issue). Famous Players. As T 413 of Dominica. Multicoloured.

MS4774 192×97 mm. 25d. Dixie Dean, England; 25d. Ruud Gullit, Holland; 25d. Karl-Heinz Rummenigge, Germany; 25d. Luis Enrique Martinez, Spain 11·00 12·00

MS4775 108×87 mm. 65d. Pele, Brazil 7·50 8·50

423 Darko Milicic, Detroit Pistons

2004. US National Basketball Association Players. Multicoloured.

4776 10d. Type **423** 1·25 1·25

4777 10d. Andrei Kirilenko, Utah Jazz 1·25 1·25

4778 10d. Chris Kaman, Los Angeles Clippers 1·25 1·25

4779 10d. T. J. Ford, Milwaukee Bucks 13·50 13·50

424 *Bremen*

2004. Ocean Liners. Multicoloured.

4780 7d. Type **424** 1·40 70

4781 10d. RMS *Queen Mary* 1·60 85

4782 15d. *Queen Mary II* 2·25 2·25

4783 20d. RMS *Queen Elizabeth 2* 2·50 2·50

4784 25d. *Britanic* 2·75 2·75

4785 35d. RMS *Majestic* 4·00 5·00

MS4786 78×74 mm. 90d. RMS *Aquitania* 11·00 13·00

425 Elvis Presley

2004. Centenary of the Teddy Bear. Sheet 179×127 mm containing T 425 and similar vert designs. Multicoloured.

MS4787 20d. Type **425**; 20d. "Love Me Tender" teddy bear; 20d. Elvis Presley (in profile); 20d. "Love Me Tender" teddy bear (Elvis in background); 20d. Elvis Presley (wearing pale jacket); 20d. "Love Me Tender" teddy bear (guitar in background) 11·00 11·50

The stamps and margins of No. **MS**4787 form composite background designs.

426 "Greek Madonna" (detail) (Giovanni Bellini)

2004. Christmas. Multicoloured.

4788 7d. Type **426** 1·10 70
4789 10d. "Madonna in the Church" (detail) (Jan van Eyck) 1·25 75
4790 20d. "The Conestabile Madonna" (Raphael) 2·50 2·75
4791 25d. "Madonna and Child" (detail) (Sandro Botticelli) 2·75 3·25
MS4792 70×100 mm. 65d. "Madonna and Child with Chancellor Rolin" (Jan van Eyck) 8·00 9·00

427 Elvis Presley rehearsing "Love Me Tender", 1956

2005. 70th Birth Anniv of Elvis Presley. Multicoloured.

4793-4797 15d.×6 Type **427**; In "King Creole", 1958; In "Roustabout", 1964; Playing drums in "Spinout", 1966; Riding horse in "Stay Away Joe", 1968; On set of "The Trouble with Girls", 1969 12·00 13·00
4799-4804 15d.×6 On stage in the Ed Sullivan Show, 1956; Wearing army cap, 1957; Posing with guitar, 1968; Rehearsing "That's The Way It Is", 1970; On spring tour, 1972; In "Aloha from Hawaii" concert, 1973 12·00 13·00

428 "Rooster"

2005. Chinese New Year ("Year of the Rooster"). Paintings by Xu Beihong. Multicoloured.

4805 10d. Type **428** 1·50 1·50
MS4806 100×70 mm. 40d. "Black Rooster" (49×39 mm) 4·50 5·00

2005. US National Basketball Association Players (2nd series). As T 423. Multicoloured.

4807 25d. Steve Nash, Dallas Mavericks 2·40 2·50
4808 25d. Shaquille O'Neal, Los Angeles Lakers 2·40 2·50

429 Flooded Hillside Rice Terraces

2005. International Year of Rice (2004). Multicoloured.

MS4809 98×149 mm. 30d. Type **429**; 30d. Planting rice; 30d. Research workers with rice plants 6·50 6·75
MS4810 97×67 mm. 60d. People on embankment and harvested rice (horiz) 6·50 6·75

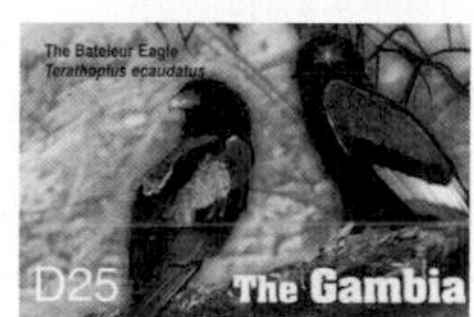

430 Bateleur Eagle

2005. "The Living World of Africa". Multicoloured.

MS4811 (a) 137×107 mm. 25d. Type **430**; 25d. Green mamba; 25d. Chimpanzee; 25d. Yellow pansy butterfly. (b) 137×107 mm. 25d. African fish eagle; 25d. Hummingbird hawk-moth; 25d. Nile crocodile; 25d. Blue wildebeest. (c) 137×107 mm. 25d. Jackass penguin; 25d. Leatherback turtle; 25d. Scaevola thunbergii; 25d. Cancrid crab. (d) 107×137 mm. 25d. Mediterranean monk seal; 25d. Horned boxfish; 25d. Scorpion fish; 25d. Cnidarians 17·00 19·00
MS4812 (a) 98×68 mm. 65d. Greater galago. (b) 68×98 mm. 65d. Burchell's zebra. (c) 98×68 mm. 65d. *Gerbera compositae* (vert). (d) 98×68 mm. 65d. Bottlenose dolphin (vert) 21·00 23·00

The stamps and margins of Nos. **MS**4811a/b form composite background designs showing a forest (**MS**4811a) or riverbank (**MS**4811b).

431 *Santisima Trinidad*

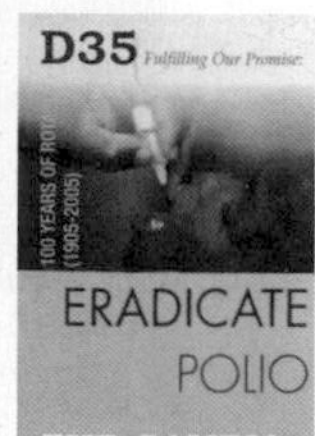

432 Young Child receiving Oral Polio Vaccine

2005. Bicentenary of the Battle of Trafalgar. Multicoloured.

4813 5d. Type **431** 90 60
4814 10d. HMS *Victory* firing on French flagship *Bucentaure* (horiz) 1·50 1·10
4815 15d. Horatio Nelson as young naval officer 2·25 2·25
4816 30d. French sailors from *Redoutable* boarding HMS *Victory* 4·00 4·50
MS4817 96×67 mm. 60d. Vice Admiral Nelson 8·00 8·50

2005. Centenary of Rotary International. Mult.

MS4818 149×70 mm. 35d. Type **432**; 35d. Child and vaccine dropper; 35d. Polio victim 21·00 23·00

433 "I Have a Date with Cookie"

2005. Blondie (cartoon) by Dean Young and Denis LeBrun. Multicoloured.

MS4819 Two sheets, each 127×100 mm. (a) 40d. Type **433**; 40d. "Wait one second please"; 40d. "Wow, Cookie! I didn't know your family was wealthy enough to have a chauffeur!". (b) 40d. "A potential major client is dropping by the office this morning! I want to see happy faces and busy hands!"; 40d. "Then after he leaves you can get back to normal"; 40d. "I want to see this place humming with activity and enthusiasm!" 23·00 24·00

The stamps within No. **MS**4819b form composite designs.

2005. 75th Anniv of First World Cup Football Championship, Uruguay. As T 420 of Dominica showing scenes from World Cup, Brazil, 1950. Multicoloured.

4820 25d. Winning Uruguay team (colour photo) 2·40 2·50
4821 25d. Final between Uruguay and Brazil 2·40 2·50
4822 25d. Maracana Stadium 2·40 2·50
4823 25d. Alcide Edgardo Ghiggia 2·40 2·50
MS4824 110×85 mm. 60d. Winning Uruguay team (black & white photo) 6·00 6·50

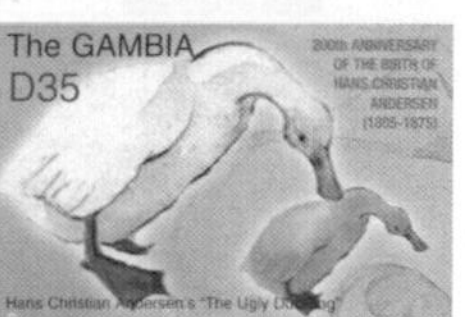

434 *The Ugly Duckling*

2005. Birth Bicentenary of Hans Christian Andersen (writer). Multicoloured.

MS4825 146×95 mm. 35d. Type **434**; 35d. The *Little Match Girl*; 35d. *The Rose Tree Regiment* 22·00 23·00
MS4826 95×67 mm. 60d. *The Emperor's New Clothes* (vert) 6·50 7·00

The stamps and margins of No. **MS**4825 have a composite background design showing Hans Christian Andersen and open book.

435 Statue of Schiller

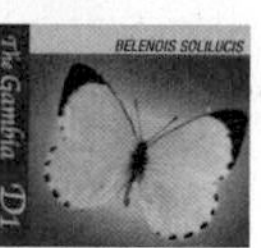

436 *Belenois solilucis*

2005. Death Bicentenary of Friedrich von Schiller (poet and dramatist). Multicoloured.

4827 35d. Type **435** 3·75 4·00
4828 35d. Portrait 3·75 4·00
4829 35d. Bust 3·75 4·00
MS4830 77×108 mm. 60d. Profile on medallion 6·50 7·00

2005. Butterflies. Multicoloured.

4831 1d. Type **436** 15 10
4832 2d. *Colotis evippe* 30 15
4833 3d. *Acraea cepheus* 40 25
4834 5d. *Bebearia senegalensis* (vert) 50 35
4835 6d. *Danaus chrysippus* (vert) 60 45
4836 7d. *Papilio dardanus* 75 50
4837 10d. *Graphium agamedes* 1·25 75
4838 15d. *Papilio Hesperus* 2·00 2·25
4839 25d. *Charaxes boueti* (vert) 2·40 2·50
4840 30d. *Cymothoe egesta* 3·00 3·25
4841 50d. *Amauris albimaculata* 4·75 5·00
4842 75d. *Charaxes lucreticus* 5·25 5·50
4843 100d. *Papilio zalmoxis* 9·00 9·50
4844 200d. *Papilio antimachus* (vert) 18·00 19·00

2005. Royal Wedding. As T 601 of Grenada but vert showing Prince Charles and Mrs. Camilla Parker-Bowles. Multicoloured.

4845 2d. Prince Charles and Mrs. Camilla Parker-Bowles (wearing red dress) 70 70
4846 2d. Embracing 70 70
4847 2d. Outdoors 70 70

437 Prince Bernhard and Prime Minister Gerbrandy

2005. 60th Anniv of the End of World War II (1st issue). Prince Bernhard of the Netherlands. Multicoloured.

4848 12d. Type **437** 1·50 1·50
4849 12d. Prince Bernhard and Queen Wilhelmina 1·50 1·50
4850 12d. Prince Bernhard and Generals Montgomery and Kruls 1·50 1·50
4851 12d. Prince Bernhard in liberated Nimwegen 1·50 1·50
4852 12d. German surrender 1·50 1·50
4853 12d. Return of Prince Bernhard and family 1·50 1·50

2005. 60th Anniv of the End of World War II (2nd issue). "The Route to Victory". As T 587 of Grenada. Multicoloured.

4854 20d. German troops in France 2·75 2·75
4855 20d. Anthony Bartley of 92nd Squadron 2·75 2·75
4856 20d. Fleet of ships and boats 2·75 2·75
4857 20d. Evacuated soldiers 2·75 2·75
4858 20d. Allied troops crossing Normandy beach 2·75 2·75
4859 20d. German guns blasting Sword Beach 2·75 2·75
4860 20d. Allied troops in French town 2·75 2·75
4861 20d. Surrender of German troops 2·75 2·75
MS4862 Two sheets, each 106×97 mm. (a) 80d. Troops awaiting evacuation from Dunkirk. (b) 80d. Royal Navy beach party ashore at Gold Beach 18·00 18·00

Nos. 4854/7 depict the evacuation from Dunkirk, 27th May to 4th June 1940, and Nos. 4858/61 D-Day, 6th June 1944.

2005. Pope John Paul II Commemoration. As T 600 of Grenada. Multicoloured.

4863 30d. Pope John Paul II and Mother Teresa 4·00 4·25

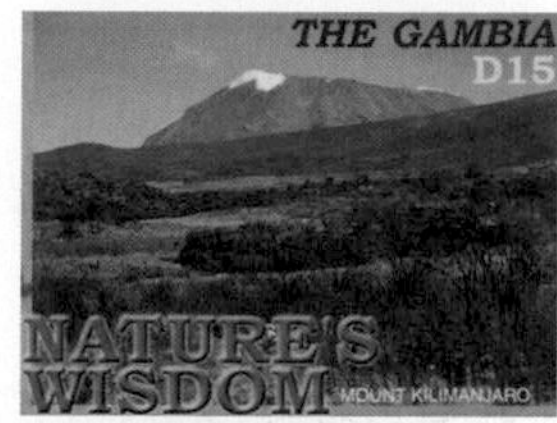

438 Mount Kilimanjaro

2005. EXPO 2005 World Exposition, Aichi, Japan. Multicoloured.

4864 15d. Type **438** 2·50 2·75
4865 15d. Lion 2·50 2·75
4866 15d. Red Sea parting for Moses 2·50 2·75
4867 15d. Astronaut on Moon with US flag 2·50 2·75

439 Moses Maimonides

2005. 800th Death Anniv of Moses Maimonides (Rabbi Moses ben Maimon). Multicoloured.

4868 25d. Type **439** 3·25 3·25
4869 25d. Moses Maimonides (line drawing) 3·25 3·25

440 Hungary 1969 40f. First Man on the Moon Stamp

2005. Death Centenary of Jules Verne (writer). Multicoloured.

4870 35d. Type **440** 3·25 3·50
4871 35d. Monaco 1978 25f. 150th birth anniv stamp 3·25 3·50
4872 35d. France 1955 30f. 50th death anniv stamp 3·25 3·50
MS4873 84×99 mm. 80d. Weightlessness in "From the Earth to the Moon" (vert) 6·50 7·00

No. 4871 is inscr "1955" and No. 4872 "1965", both in error.

441 "B-29 flies over the Missouri" (Jean Masterly)

2005. 60th Anniv of Victory in Japan Day. Multicoloured.

4874 25d. Type **441** 3·00 3·00
4875 25d. Boing B-29 Superfortress Enola Gay dropping atomic bomb, Hiroshima 3·00 3·00
4876 25d. Aerial dogfight over Pacific 3·00 3·00
4877 25d. Hellcat Fury fighter planes in battle 3·00 3·00
MS4878 109×83 mm. 80d. USS *Enterprise* (aircraft carrier) (42×56 mm) 6·50 7·00

442 Albert Einstein

2005. 50th Death Anniv of Albert Einstein (physicist). Multicoloured.

4879 35d. Type **442** 3·25 3·50
4880 35d. Albert Einstein (head and shoulders) 3·25 3·50
4881 35d. Einstein and equation 3·25 3·50

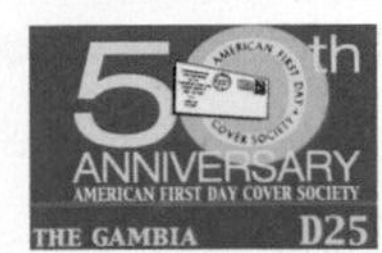

443 Emblem

2005. 50th Anniv of American First Day Cover Society.

4882 **443** 25d. multicoloured 2·75 3·00

444 Presidential Palace, Taipei

2005. TAIPEI 2005 International Stamp Exhibition. Multicoloured.

4883 35d. Type **444** 3·00 3·25
4884 35d. Chiang Kai-Shek Memorial Hall, Taipei 3·00 3·25
4885 35d. Queen's Head (rock formation), Yehliu 3·00 3·25
4886 35d. National Palace Museum, Taipei 3·00 3·25

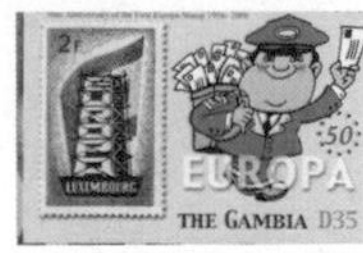

445 Luxembourg 2f. Stamp and Postman

2005. 50th Anniv of First Europa Stamp. All showing 1956 Europa stamps. Multicoloured.

4887 35d. Type **445** 3·00 3·25
4888 40d. French 30f. stamp, "50" and stars 3·25 3·50
4889 50d. French 15f. stamp and map showing EU member countries 3·50 3·75
MS4890 105×80 mm. Nos. 4887/9 and stamp-size label 8·75 9·25

446 Hiawatha

2005. Great American Indian Chiefs. Multicoloured.

4891 12d. Type **446** 1·25 1·40
4892 12d. Chief Joseph 1·25 1·40
4893 12d. Sitting Bull 1·25 1·40
4894 12d. Red Cloud 1·25 1·40
4895 12d. Powhatan 1·25 1·40
4896 12d. Sequoyah 1·25 1·40
4897 12d. Crazy Horse 1·25 1·40
4898 12d. Cochise 1·25 1·40
4899 12d. Geronimo 1·25 1·40
4900 12d. Tecumseh 1·25 1·40

447 Pope Benedict XVI

2005. Election of Pope Benedict XVI.

4901 **447** 35d. multicoloured 4·25 4·25

448 "The Annunciation" (detail) (Lorenzo di Credi)

2005. Christmas. Multicoloured.

4902 7d. Type **448** 70 30
4903 10d. "The Holy Family" (detail) (Lorenzo di Credi) 1·10 80
4904 25d. "The Adoration of the Magi" (detail) (Filippo Lippi) 2·75 3·25
4905 30d. "Marriage of St. Catherine" (detail) (Filippo Lippi) 3·00 3·50
MS4906 96×66 mm. 65d. "The Annunciation" (Beato Angelico) 6·00 7·00

449 Dog

2006. Chinese New Year ("Year of the Dog").

4907 **449** 15d. multicoloured 2·50 2·50

450 "Kitty" (Raquel Bobolia)

2006. "Kids-Did-It!" Designs. Children's paintings. Multicoloured.

4908 25d. Type **450** 2·50 2·50
4909 25d. "Jaguar" (Megan Albe) 2·50 2·50
4910 25d. "Quazy Jaguar" (Nick Abrams) 2·50 2·50
4911 25d. "Chelsy Cheetah" (Carly Bowerman) 2·50 2·50
4912 25d. "Three Flowers" (Lauren Van Woy) 2·50 2·50
4913 25d. "Blossoms" (Michelle Malachowski) 2·50 2·50
4914 25d. "Flower Pot" (Lauren Van Woy) 2·50 2·50
4915 25d. "Red Flower Pot" (Anne Wilks) 2·50 2·50
4916 25d. "Stripey" (Christopher Bowerman) 2·50 2·50
4917 25d. "Sea Turtle" (Tyler Overton) 2·50 2·50
4918 25d. "Hungry Lizard" (Jessica Shutt) 2·50 2·50
4919 25d. "Frogs" (Elyse Bobczynski) 2·50 2·50

451 Black-crowned Crane

2006. Endangered Species. Black-crowned Crane (Balearica pavonina). Multicoloured.

4920 30d. Type **451** 3·25 3·25
4921 30d. Adult crane, on ground 3·25 3·25
4922 30d. Chick 3·25 3·25
4923 30d. Three cranes, about to take-off 3·25 3·25
MS4924 153×100 mm. Nos. 4920/3, each ×2 23·00 24·00

2006. 80th Birthday of Queen Elizabeth II. As T 432 of Dominica. Multicoloured.

4925 30d. Princess Elizabeth in ATS uniform 3·50 3·50
4926 30d. Queen Elizabeth II at her Coronation, 1953 3·50 3·50
4927 30d. On cover of Time magazine 3·50 3·50
4928 30d. Princess Elizabeth on her wedding day, 1949 3·50 3·50
MS4929 120×120 mm. 75d. Portrait wearing diadem and Coronation robes 8·00 8·50

2006. Winter Olympic Games, Turin. As T 431 of Dominica but vert. Multicoloured.

4930 10d. Norway 1993 Winter Olympics 3k.50 torch bearer on skis stamp 1·50 1·50
4931 10d. Poster for Winter Olympic Games, Savoie, France 1·50 1·50
4932 15d. Norway 1993 Winter Olympics 3k.50 Lillehammer stamp 2·25 2·25
4933 20d. Flag of Salt Lake City 2002 Winter Olympic Games 2·50 2·50
4934 20d. France 1990 2f.30+20c. Albertville 92 emblem and ice skaters stamp (horiz) 2·50 2·50
4935 25d. Poster for Winter Olympic Games, Lillehammer, 1994 2·50 2·50

452 Marilyn Monroe

2006. 80th Birth Anniv of Marilyn Monroe (actress).

4936 **452** 30d. multicoloured 2·75 3·00

453 Martin Luther King

2006. Washington 2006 International Stamp Exhibition (1st issue).

4937 **453** 40d. multicoloured 3·25 3·50

454 1958 4c. Overland Mail Centenary Stamp

2006. Washington 2006 International Stamp Exhibition (2nd issue). 120th Anniv of American Philatelic Society. Sheet 178×124 mm containing T 454 and similar horiz designs showing United States stamps. Multicoloured.

MS4938 17d.×8 Type **454**; 1925 Special delivery 20c. mail truck stamp; 1869 3c. Baldwin steam locomotive stamp; 1918 air mail 24c. Curtiss "Jenny" stamp; 1940 3c. Pony Express stamp; 1888 Special delivery 10c. messenger running stamp; 1901 Pan-American Exposition 1c. Great Lakes steamship stamp; 1912 Parcel post 2c. city carrier stamp 13·00 15·00

The stamps and margins of No. **MS**4938 form a composite background design showing a map of the world.

455 Modern Zeppelin NT-2006

2006. 50th Death Anniv of Ludwig Durr (Zeppelin engineer). Multicoloured.

4939 40d. Type **455** 3·25 3·50
4940 40d. USS *Los Angeles* Zeppelin 2R-3 3·25 3·50
4941 40d. Zeppelin Z-R-S *Macon* 3·25 3·50

456 Mozart's Memorial, St. Mark's Cemetery, Vienna

2006. 250th Birth Anniv of Wolfgang Amadeus Mozart (composer). Multicoloured.

4942 30d. Type **456** 3·75 3·75
4943 30d. Posthumous portrait by Barbara Kraft, 1819 3·75 3·75
4944 30d. Named Chevalier of the Order of the Golden Spur, 1777 3·75 3·75
4945 30d. Mozart family graves, St. Sebastian Cemetery, Salzburg 3·75 3·75

457 Queen Juliana

2006. Queen Juliana of the Netherlands Commemoration.

4946 **457** 15d. multicoloured 2·25 2·25

458 "Jacob Blessing the Sons of Joseph" (detail, Joseph's wife Asenath)

2006. 400th Birth Anniv of Rembrandt Harmenszoon van Rijn (artist). Showing paintings. Multicoloured.

4947 10d. Type **458** 1·25 1·25
4948 12d. "Jacob Wrestling with the Angel" (detail, head of angel) 1·50 1·50
4949 15d. "Jacob Blessing the Sons of Joseph" (detail, Jacob and Joseph) 1·75 1·75
4950 25d. "Jacob Wrestling with the Angel" (detail, Jacob held by angel) 2·00 2·25
4951 25d. "Young Girl at Open Half-Door" (detail) 2·00 2·25
4952 25d. "Self-portrait", c. 1632–39 (detail) 2·00 2·25
4953 25d. "Self-portrait", c. 1640 (detail) 2·00 2·25
4954 25d. "Portrait of a Young Woman" 2·00 2·25
4955 25d. "A Married Couple with their Children" (detail of man) 2·00 2·25
4956 25d. "A Married Couple with their Children" (detail of girl) 2·00 2·25
4957 25d. "A Married Couple with their Children" (detail of boy) 2·00 2·25
4958 25d. "A Married Couple with their Children" (detail of woman) 2·00 2·25
4959 25d. "The Staalmeesters" (detail, man with hat, facing to right) 2·00 2·25
4960 25d. "The Staalmeesters" (detail, man with hat, head and shoulders) 2·00 2·25
4961 25d. "The Staalmeesters" (detail, man without hat) 2·00 2·25
4962 25d. "The Staalmeesters" (detail, man with hat, close-up) 2·00 2·25
MS4963 Three sheets, each 75×106 mm. (b) 65d. "The Knight with the Falcon" (detail). (c) 65d. "Portrait of a Lady with a Lap Dog" (detail). (d) 65d. "A Young Woman in Fancy Dress" (detail). All imperf 19·00 20·00

No. **MS**4963a is left for a miniature sheet not yet received.

459 Princess Maxima

2006. Princess Maxima of the Netherlands. Multicoloured.

4964 30d. Type **459** 2·00 2·25
4965 30d. Princess Maxima (half-length portrait) 2·00 2·25

460 Gingerbread Man

2006. Christmas. Multicoloured.

4966 25d. Type **460** 1·90 1·00
4967 30d. Christmas tree 2·00 1·60
4968 45d. Christmas bell 2·50 2·75
4969 50d. Mittens with snowflake pattern 2·50 2·75
MS4970 150×100 mm. 15d. As Type **460**; 18d. As No. 4967; 25d. As No. 4968; No. 4969 3·75 4·25

461 Australian Flag on Football

2006. World Cup Football Championship, Germany. Sheet 102×127 mm containing T 461 and similar vert designs each showing national flag on football. Multicoloured.

MS4971 10d. Type **461**; 20d. Germany; 25d. Sweden; 30d. Brazil 6·50 7·00

462 Andre Turcat (Concorde's first test pilot)

2006. Concorde. Multicoloured.

4972 15d. Type **462** 2·50 2·50
4973 15d. Take-off of Concorde, Toulouse, 1969 2·50 2·50
4974 15d. Arrival of Concorde, Filton, 2003 2·50 2·50
4975 15d. Concorde G-BOAF in flight, 2003 2·50 2·50

Nos. 4972/3 show the first Concorde flight on 2 March 1969 and Nos. 4974/5 the final flight on 26 November 2003.

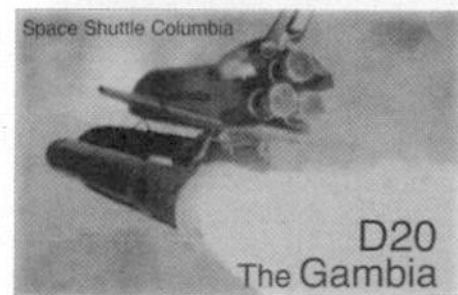

463 Space Shuttle *Columbia*

2006. Space Anniversaries. Multicoloured. (a) 25th Anniv of First Flight of Space Shuttle Columbia.

4976 20d. Type **463** 2·50 2·75
4977 20d. Lift-off of Space Shuttle *Columbia* 2·50 2·75
4978 20d. JSC Shuttle Mission Simulator (SMS) 2·50 2·75
4979 20d. Mission control during rollout of STS 1 2·50 2·75
4980 20d. Astronaut John Young 2·50 2·75
4981 20d. Astronaut Robert Crippen 2·50 2·75

(b) Mars Reconnaissance Orbiter, 2006.

4982 20d. *Mars Reconnaissance Orbiter* on surface of Mars 2·50 2·75
4983 20d. Orbiting Mars (antenna and solar panel seen from above) 2·50 2·75
4984 20d. On descent to Mars 2·50 2·75
4985 20d. Orbiting Mars (side view of antenna) 2·50 2·75
4986 20d. Orbiting Mars (underside of orbiter and solar panel) 2·50 2·75
4987 20d. Launch of *Mars Reconnaissance Orbiter* by Atlas V rocket 2·50 2·75

(c) 20th Anniv of Giotto Comet Probe.

4988 25d. Halley's Comet 2·75 3·00
4989 25d. *Giotto* Comet Probe (side view) 2·75 3·00
4990 25d. *Giotto* Comet Probe (seen from above) 2·75 3·00
4991 25d. Take-off of *Giotto* Comet Probe and Halley's Comet 2·75 3·00
MS4992 148×97 mm. 25d.×4 20th Anniv of Viking 1 First Mars Landing: In Mars orbit; Viking 1 Lander on surface (antenna boom at right); On surface (US flag on Lander base); On surface (meteorology boom at right) 10·00 11·00
MS4993 Three sheets, each 106×76 mm. (a) 65d. Space Shuttle *Discovery*, 2005 (vert). (b) 65d. Artist's conception of Japanese *Hayabusa* spacecraft above Asteroid Itokawa, 2005. (c) 65d. *Venus Express*, 2005 21·00 23·00

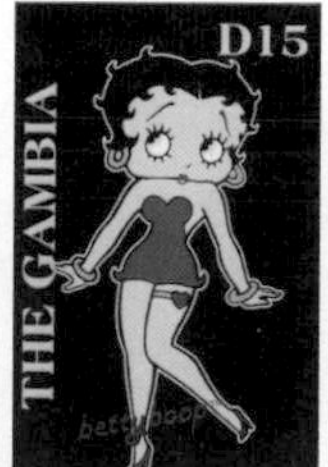

464 Betty Boop

2007. Betty Boop. Multicoloured.

4994 15d. Type **464** 2·00 2·25
4995 15d. With bouquet of red roses 2·00 2·25
4996 15d. With little dog tugging at dress 2·00 2·25
4997 15d. Lifting dress to show heart-shaped garter 2·00 2·25
4998 15d. With hands clasped 2·00 2·25
4999 15d. With hat and cane 2·00 2·25
MS5000 100×70 mm. 40d. Wearing flower-patterned dress (outline in rose); 40d. Wearing flower-patterned dress (outline in violet) 3·25 3·50

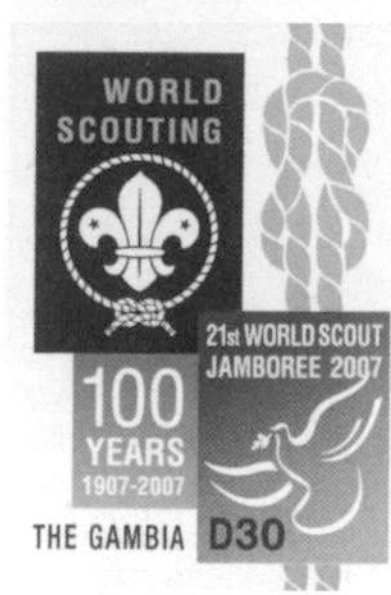

465 Scout Badge and 21st World Scout Jamboree Emblem

2007. Centenary of World Scouting and 21st World Scout Jamboree, England. Multicoloured.

5001 **465** 30d. multicoloured 2·25 2·25
MS5002 110×80 mm. **465** 65d. multicoloured 5·50 6·50

466 Pres. Kennedy greets Peace Corps Volunteers on White House Lawn, 1962

2007. 90th Birth Anniv of John F. Kennedy (President of USA 1960–3). Multicoloured.

5003 25d. Type **466** 2·50 2·75
5004 25d. R. Sargent Shriver, first Director of the Peace Corps 2·50 2·75
5005 25d. Pres. Kennedy issuing Executive Order creating Peace Corps, 1961 2·50 2·75
5006 25d. Pres. Kennedy greeting Peace Corps volunteers, 28 August 1962 2·50 2·75
5007 25d. Pres. Kennedy ready to announce Alliance for Progress plan 2·50 2·75
5008 25d. Pres. Kennedy meets with his Cabinet 2·50 2·75
5009 25d. Volunteer Ida Shoatz in Pisac Market in the Peruvian Andes 2·50 2·75
5010 25d. Pres. Kennedy arriving to speak to students at University of Michigan, 1960 2·50 2·75

467 Bronze Vessel of the Pig, Shang Dynasty, c. 1766–1122 BC

2007. Chinese New Year ("Year of the Pig").

5011 **467** 20d. multicoloured 2·50 2·50

468 Pope Benedict XVI

2007. 80th Birthday of Pope Benedict XVI.

5012 **468** 12d. multicoloured 1·75 1·75

469 Diana, Princess of Wales

2007. 10th Death Anniv of Diana, Princess of Wales. Multicoloured.

5013 15d. Type **469** 2·25 2·25
5014 15d. Wearing pale turquoise scarf 2·25 2·25
5015 15d. In close-up, wearing earring 2·25 2·25
5016 15d. Wearing white dress and jacket and tiara 2·25 2·25
5017 15d. Wearing pale turquoise strapless dress 2·25 2·25
5018 15d. Wearing black dress 2·25 2·25
5019 25d. Wearing turquoise and white dress and hat 3·25 3·25
5020 25d. Wearing pale pink and purple jacket and hat 3·25 3·25
5021 25d. Wearing black off-the-shoulder dress 3·25 3·25
5022 25d. Wearing red and white jacket and hat 3·25 3·25
MS5023 70×100 mm. 65d. Portrait, in profile (horiz) 9·00 9·00

470 Wedding of Princess Elizabeth

2007. Diamond Wedding of Queen Elizabeth II and Duke of Edinburgh. Multicoloured.

5024 15d. Type **470** 2·25 2·25
5025 15d. Queen Elizabeth and Duke of Edinburgh in evening dress, c. 2007 2·25 2·25
MS5026 100×70 mm. 65d. Queen Elizabeth and Duke of Edinburgh in uniform, c. 2007 (horiz) 9·00 9·00

471 Penguin playing drums and Duke of Edinburgh, 1947

2007. International Polar Year. Penguins. Designs showing stylized penguins. Multicoloured.

MS5027 150×115 mm. 15d.×6 Type **471**; Penguin in grass skirt, dancing; Playing drums and cymbals; Playing pink and purple guitar; With microphone, singing; Playing yellow and orange guitar 10·00 10·00
MS5028 100×70 mm. 65d. Penguin (seated in chair) and chick at table on beach 7·00 7·50

The stamps within **MS**5027 form a composite background design.

472 Ferrari 512 S, 1970

2007. 60th Anniv of Ferrari. Multicoloured.

5029 12d. Type **472** 1·50 1·50
5030 12d. F 310, 1996 1·50 1·50
5031 12d. 195 S, 1950 1·50 1·50
5032 12d. 275 P2, 1965 1·50 1·50
5033 12d. Mondial 8, 1980 1·50 1·50
5034 12d. 312 T, 1975 1·50 1·50
5035 12d. 500 F2, 1952 1·50 1·50
5036 12d. GTB Turbo, 1986 1·50 1·50

473 Halley's Comet Emblem

2007. Halley's Comet, 1986. Designs as T 473, background colours given. Multicoloured.

5037 **473** 20d. gold 2·25 2·50
5038 **473** 20d. azure 2·25 2·50
5039 **473** 20d. black 2·25 2·50
5040 **473** 20d. brown 2·25 2·50
MS5041 100×70 mm. 65d. Emblem as Type **473**, 'RETURNS 2062' and night sky 7·50 8·50

474 UH-1B/C Airborne Jeep

2007. Centenary of First Helicopter Flight. Multicoloured.

5042 15d. Type **474** 2·00 2·00
5043 15d. S-65/RH-53D heavy lift helicopter 2·00 2·00
5044 15d. UH-1 troop carrier helicopter 2·00 2·00
5045 15d. BK 117 air ambulance helicopter 2·00 2·00
5046 15d. Autogyro 2·00 2·00
5047 15d. AS-61 anti-ship missile carrying helicopter 2·00 2·00
MS5048 100×70 mm. 65d. AH-1 Huey Cobra helicopter gunship 9·00 9·00

475 'Autumn Leaves and Magpie'

2007. 50th Death Anniv of Qi Baishi (artist). Multicoloured.

5049 25d. Type **475** 2·75 3·00
5050 25d. Camellias 2·75 3·00
5051 25d. Pomegranates 2·75 3·00
5052 25d. Mynahs and Amaranthus 2·75 3·00
MS5053 60×125 mm. 65d. 'Magpie and Plum Blossoms' 7·50 8·00

476 Martha Washington

2007. The First Ladies of the United States of America. Multicoloured.

5054–5068 10d.×15 Type **476**; 10d. Abigail Adams; 10d. Dolley Madison; 10d. Elizabeth Monroe; Louisa Adams; Emily Donelson; Angelica Van Buren; Anna Harrison; Letitia Tyler; Julia Tyler; Sarah Polk; Margaret Taylor; Abigail Fillmore; Jane Pierce; The White House and Arms and flag of USA 16·00 16·00
5069–5082 10d.×14 Harriet Johnston; Mary Lincoln; Eliza Johnson; Julia Grant; Lucy Hayes; Lucretia Garfield; Mary Arthur Elroy; Frances Cleveland; Caroline Harrison; Ida McKinley; Edith Roosevelt; Helen Taft; Ellen Wilson; Edith Wilson 15·00 15·00
5083–5097 10d.×15 Florence Harding; Grace Coolidge; Lou Hoover; Eleanor Roosevelt; Bess Truman; Mamie Eisenhower; Jacqueline Kennedy; Lady Bird Johnson; Pat Nixon; Betty Ford; Rosalynn Carter; Nancy Reagan; Barbara Bush; Hillary Clinton; Laura Bush 16·00 16·00
5097a 65d. Martha Washington (facing to left) (37×50 mm) 6·75 6·75
MS5098 Fifty-two sheets, each 70×100 mm. (a) 65d. Martha Washington. (b) 65d. Abigail Adams. (c) 65d. Martha Jefferson. (d) 65d. Martha Washington Jefferson Randolph. (e) 65d. Dolley Madison. (f) 65d. Elizabeth Monroe. (g) 65d. Louisa Adams. (h) 65d. Rachael Jackson. (i) 65d. Emily Donelson. (j) 65d. Hannah Van Buren. (k) 65d. Angelica Van Buren. (l) 65d. Anna Harrison. (m) 65d. Letitia Tyler. (n) 65d. Julia Tyler. (o) 65d. Priscilla Tyler. (p) 65d. Sarah Polk. (q) 65d. Margaret Taylor. (r) 65d. Mary Taylor. (s) 65d. Abigail Fillmore. (t) 65d. Jane Pierce. (u) 65d. Harriet Johnston. (v) 65d. Mary Lincoln. (w) 65d. Eliza Johnson. (x) 65d. Julia Grant. (y) 65d. Lucy Hayes. (z) 65d. Lucretia Garfield. (za) 65d. Ellen Arthur. (zb) 65d. Mary Arthur McElroy. (zc) 65d. Frances Cleveland. (zd) 65d. Caroline Harrison. (ze) 65d. Mary Lord Harrison. (zf) 65d. Ida McKinley. (zg) 65d. Edith Roosevelt. (zh) 65d. Helen Taft. (zi) 65d. Ellen Wilson. (zj) 65d. Edith Wilson. (zk) 65d. Florence Harding. (zl) 65d. Grace Coolidge. (zm) 65d. Lou Hoover. (zn) 65d. Eleanor Roosevelt. (zo) 65d. Bess Truman. (zp) 65d. Mamie Eisenhower. Nos. (zq) 65d. Jacqueline Kennedy. (zr) 65d. Lady Bird Johnson. (zs) 65d. Pat Nixon. (zt) 65d. Betty Ford. (zu) 65d. Rosalynn Carter. (zv) 65d. Nancy Reagan. (zw) 65d. Barbara Bush. (zx) 65d. Hillary Clinton. (zy) 65d. Laura Bush (zz) Michelle Obama (8.6.2010) 23·00 23·00

No. **MS**5098 (a) to (r) and (zq) to (zy) all show portraits similar to T **476** but 37×50 mm with the White House in the background.

477 Mr. and Mrs. Ford

2007. Gerald Ford (US President 1974–7) Commemoration. Multicoloured.

5099 25d. Type **477** 2·60 2·75
5100 25d. Presidential inauguration ceremony 2·60 2·75
5101 25d. The Fords and the Nixons 2·60 2·75
5102 25d. Celebrating 90th birthday 2·60 2·75

478 Elvis Presley

2007. 30th Death Anniv of Elvis Presley. Multicoloured.

5103 15d. Type **478** 1·60 1·75
5104 15d. Wearing black suit 1·60 1·75
5105 15d. Wearing dark blue shirt 1·60 1·75
5106 15d. Wearing white 1·60 1·75
5107 15d. Wearing flecked jacket 1·60 1·75
5108 15d. Wearing black leather 1·60 1·75

479 Haya Rashed Al-Khalifa, President 61st UN GA

2007. Holocaust Remembrance. Multicoloured.

5109–5116 14d.×8 Type **479**; Denis Dangue Rewaka, Gabon; Crispin Grey-Johnson, The Gambia; Irakli Alasani, Georgia; Nana Effah-Apenteng, Ghana; Adamantios Th. Vassilakis, Greece; Jorge Skinner-Klee Arenales, Guatemala; Jean-Maurice Ripert, France 13·00 13·00
5117–5124 14d.×8 Ronaldo Mota Sardenberg, Brazil; Alisher Vohidov, Ukraine; Martin Belinga-Eboutou, Cameroon; Fernand Poukre-Kono, Central African Republic; Heraldo Munoz, Chile; Wang Guangya, China; Elbio O. Rosselli, Uruguay; Shashi Tharoor, Under Secretary-General 13·00 13·00
5125–5132 14d.×8 Basile Ikouebe, Republic of the Congo; Saul Weisleder, Costa Rica; Alcide Djedje, Ivory Coast; Andreas D. Mavroyiannis, Cyprus; Martin Palous, Czech Republic; Atoki Ileka, Dem. Republic of the Congo; Crispin S. Gregoire, Dominica; Parfait Onanga-Anyanga, Ambassador and Special Advisor of the 61st UN General Assembly 13·00 13·00
5133–5140 14d.×8 Hilario G. Davide Jr, Phillipines; Andrzej Towpik, Poland; Joao Manuel Guerra Salgueiro, Portugal; Alexei Tulbure, Republic of Moldova; Mihnea I. Motoc, Romania; Vitaly I. Churkin, Russian Federation; Joseph Nsengimana, Rwanda; Augustine P. Mahiga, Tanzania 13·00 13·00

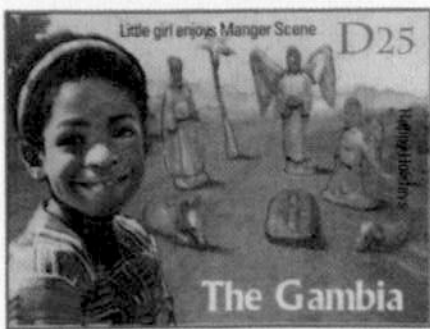

480 Girl and Manger Scene

2007. Christmas. Multicoloured.

5141 25d. Type **480** 2·60 2·75
5142 30d. Children eating holiday dishes 3·00 3·25
5143 45d. Boy and Madonna and Child sculpture 4·50 4·75
5144 50d. Three girls and drummers 5·25 5·50

481 Roman Goddess Diana reaching for Arrow

2007. Breast Cancer Research. Sheet 100×70 mm.

MS5145 65d. multicoloured 6·75 6·75

A similar stamp was issued by the USA on 29 July 1998 and by Belize on 26 October 2006.

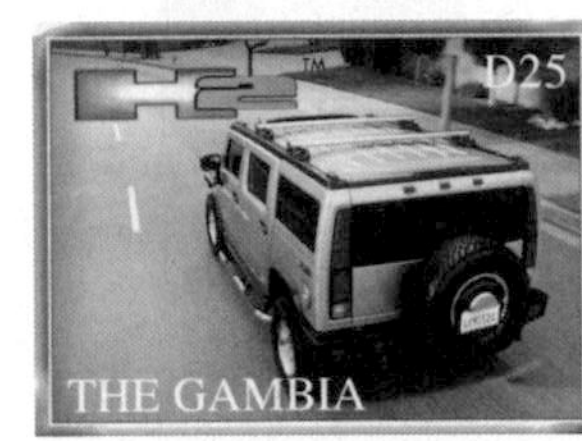

482 Rear View of Hummer H2

2007. General Motors Hummer H2. Multicoloured.

5146 25d. Type **482** 2·60 2·75
5147 25d. Front view of Hummer 2·60 2·75
5148 25d. Side view of silver Hummer 2·60 2·75
5149 25d. Side view of blue Hummer 2·60 2·75
MS5150 100×70 mm. 65d. Hummer 6·75 6·75

483 Carmelo Anthony, Denver Nuggets

2007. US National Basketball Association Players. Multicoloured.

5151 10d. Type **483** 1·25 1·25
5152 10d. Kobe Bryant, Los Angeles Lakers 1·25 1·25
5153 10d. Vince Carter, Nets 1·25 1·25
5154 10d. Allen Iverson, Denver Nuggets 1·25 1·25
5155 10d. LeBron James, Cleveland Cavaliers 1·25 1·25
5156 10d. Yao Ming, Rockets 1·25 1·25
5157 10d. Steve Nash, Phoenix Suns 1·25 1·25
5158 10d. Shaquille O'Neal, Miami Heat 1·25 1·25
5159 10d. Dwyane Wade, Miami Heat 1·25 1·25

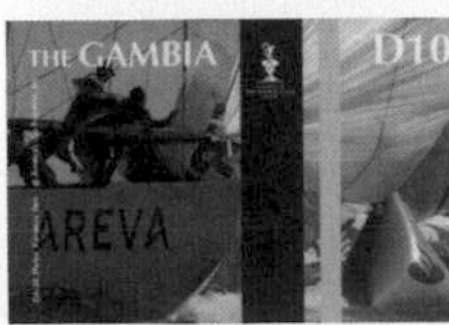

484 Yacht *Areva* and Buoy

2007. 32nd Americas Cup Yachting Championship, Valencia, Spain. Multicoloured.

5160 10d. Type **484** 1·00 1·10
5161 15d. Yacht '+39' 1·60 1·75
5162 20d. Yacht with multicoloured hull 2·00 2·10
5163 30d. Three yachts, 'Prada' at left 3·00 3·25

485 Rat

2008. Chinese New Year ('Year of the Rat'). Litho.

5164 **485** 30d. multicoloured 3·00 3·25

486 *Pioneer I* Satellite, 1958

2008. 50 Years of Space Exploration and Satellites. Multicoloured.

5165 15d. Type **486** 1·60 1·75
5166 15d. *Pioneer I* in storage casing 1·60 1·75
5167 15d. *Pioneer I* in flight 1·60 1·75
5168 15d. *Pioneer III* and laboratory technicians (horiz) 1·60 1·75
5169 15d. *Pioneer III* orbiting Earth (horiz) 1·60 1·75
5170 15d. Launch of *Pioneer III*, 6 December 1958 (horiz) 1·60 1·75
5171 20d. *Pioneer I* on launcher *Thor-Able I*, 11 October 1958 2·00 2·10
5172 20d. *Pioneer I* in orbit, Moon at left 2·00 2·10
5173 20d. *Pioneer III* (red background) 2·00 2·10
5174 20d. *Pioneer IIII* orbiting Earth, Moon at top left 2·00 2·10
MS5175 Two sheets. (a) 70×100 mm. 65d. *Pioneer I* above Earth's atmosphere, Moon in background (horiz). (b) 100×70 mm. 65d. *Pioneer III* casing and instruments (50×37 mm) 13·50 13·50

487 Temple Courtyard in Taipei

2008. Taipei 2008 International Stamp Exhibition. Multicoloured.

5176 12d. Type **487** 1·20 1·30
5177 12d. Dr. Sun Yat-sen Memorial Hall, Taipei 1·20 1·30
5178 12d. National Opera House, Taipei 1·20 1·30
5179 12d. Temple in Taipei 1·20 1·30
MS5180 100×70 mm. 45d. Lover's Bridge of Tamsui, Taipei (37×50 mm) 4·50 4·75

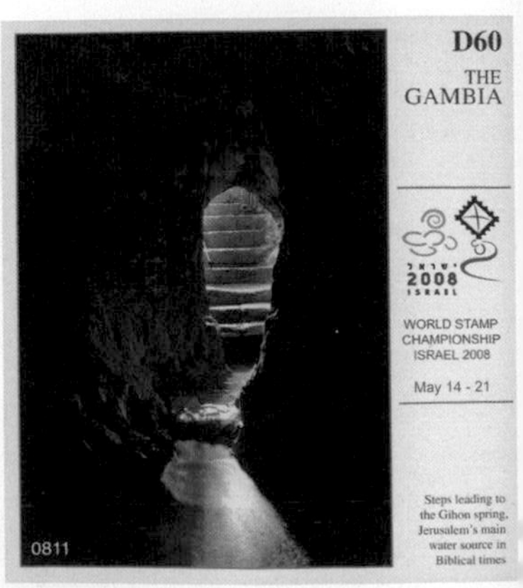

488 Steps leading to the Gihon Spring, Jerusalem (image scaled to 48% of original size)

2008. Israel 2008 World Stamp Championship, Tel-Aviv. Sheet 100×110 mm. Imperf.

MS5181 multicoloured 6·50 6·50

489 Mausoleum of Maussollos at Halicarnassus

2008. Seven Wonders of the Ancient World. Sheet 110×155 mm containing T 489 and similar horiz designs. Multicoloured.

MS5182	Type **489**; Colossus of Rhodes; Great Pyramid of Giza; Hanging Gardens of Babylon; Great Sphinx (inscr 'Great Pyramid of Giza'); Lighthouse of Alexandria; Statue of Zeus at Olympia; Temple of Artemis at Ephesus	9·50	9·50

490 Elvis Presley

2008. 40th Anniv of Film Speedway. Designs showing Elvis Presley.

5183	25d. Type **490**	2·60	2·75
5184	25d. Playing guitar (black and white photo)	2·60	2·75
5185	25d. With leg raised, arms on knee	2·60	2·75
5186	25d. Playing guitar (colour photo)	2·60	2·75

491 Sir Edmund Hillary

2008. Sir Edmund Hillary (first man to reach summit of Mount Everest) Commemoration. Multicoloured.

5187	25d. Type **491**	2·60	2·75
5188	25d. Mount Everest	2·60	2·75
5189	25d. Statue of Sir Edmund Hillary	2·60	2·75
5190	25d. Sir Edmund Hillary (as younger man)	2·60	2·75

492 Suzanne Lenglen (France) (tennis gold medallist), Antwerp, 1920

2008. Olympic Games, Beijing. Multicoloured.

5191	10d. Type **492**	1·00	1·10
5192	10d. Duke Kahanamoku (USA) (double swimming gold medallist), 1920	1·00	1·10
5193	10d. Nedo Nadi (Italy) winning fencing gold medal, 1920	1·00	1·10
5194	10d. OLYMPEX 2008	1·00	1·10

A 40d. gold stamp showing multicoloured Olympic rings and mascots was issued on 8 January 2008.

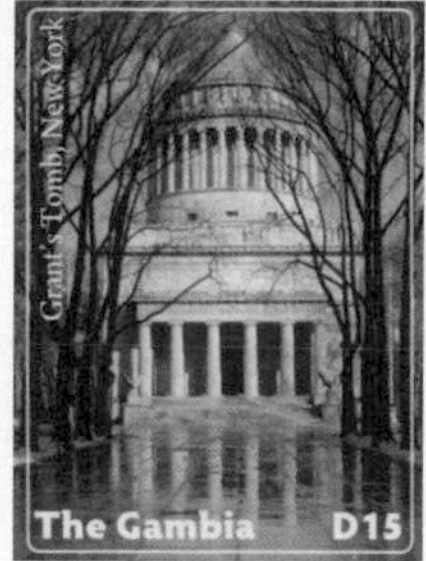

493 Grant's Tomb, New York

2008. Presidential Monuments. Multicoloured.

5195	15d. Type **493**	1·60	1·75
5196	15d. Jefferson Memorial, Washington DC	1·60	1·75
5197	15d. Kennedy Eternal Flame, Arlington, Virginia	1·60	1·75
5198	15d. Capitol Building, Washington DC	1·60	1·75
5199	15d. Lincoln Memorial, Washington DC	1·60	1·75
5200	15d. Washington Monument, Washington DC	1·60	1·75
MS5201	100×70 mm. 65d. Mount Rushmore, South Dakota	7·25	7·25

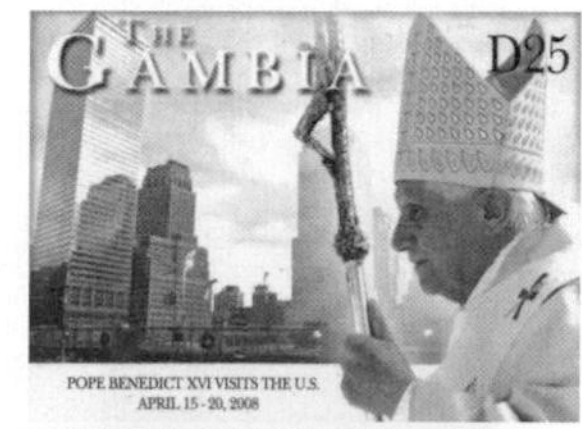

494 Pope Benedict XVI and New York

2008. 1st Visit of Pope Benedict XVI to the United States.

5202	**494** 25d. multicoloured	2·60	2·75

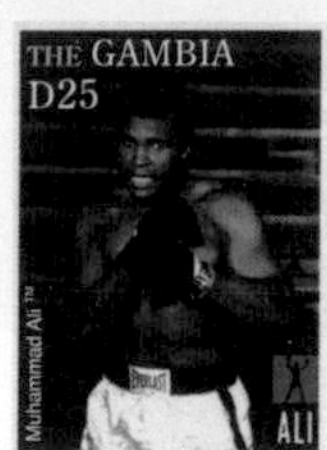

495 Muhammad Ali

2008. Muhammad Ali (world heavyweight boxing champion, 1964, 1974–8). Multicoloured.

5203	25d. Type **495**	2·60	2·75
5204	25d. Seated on logs	2·60	2·75
5205	25d. Hitting punchbag in gym	2·60	2·75
5206	25d. Skipping	2·60	2·75
5207	25d. Speaking into microphone (horiz)	2·60	2·75
5208	25d. With head resting on hand (horiz)	2·60	2·75
5209	25d. With fist raised (horiz)	2·60	2·75
5210	25d. Jogging along road (horiz)	2·60	2·75
MS5211	Two sheets, each 70×100 mm. (a) 65d. With arms raised in triumph. (b) 65d. Wearing white robe	13·50	13·50

496 Arms of Gambia

2008. Personalised Stamps.

5212	**496** 40d. grey and carmine	4·00	4·50

497 Marilyn Monroe

2008. Marilyn Monroe Commemoration. Multicoloured.

5213	25d. Type **497**	2·60	2·75
5214	25d. Laughing, looking towards left	2·60	2·75
5215	25d. Head turned to right	2·60	2·75

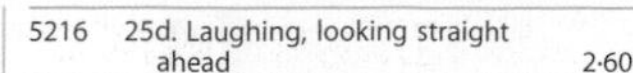

5216	25d. Laughing, looking straight ahead	2·60	2·75

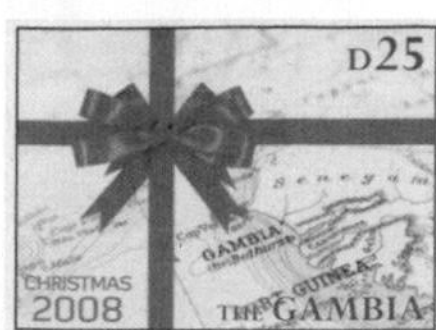

498 Map of West Africa as Parcel

2008. Christmas. Multicoloured.

5217	25d. Type **498**	2·60	2·75
5218	30d. Red, blue and green Christmas parcel decorations	3·00	3·25
5219	45d. Woman carrying Christmas parcel on head and national flag (vert)	4·75	5·00
5220	50d. Christmas presents, decorations and national flag	5·25	5·50

499 Abraham Lincoln and his Son Tad

2008. Birth Bicentenary of Abraham Lincoln (President of USA 1861–5). Multicoloured.

5221	25d. Type **499**	2·60	2·75
5222	25d. Abraham Lincoln in profile	2·60	2·75
5223	25d. Abraham Lincoln (as younger man)	2·60	2·75
5224	25d. Abraham Lincoln (older, with beard)	2·60	2·75

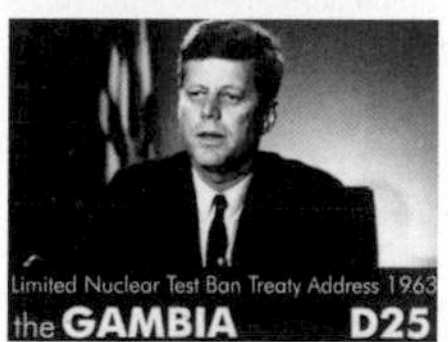

500 Limited Nuclear Test Ban Treaty Address, 1963

2008. 90th Birth Anniv (2007) of John F. Kennedy (President of USA 1960–3) (2nd issue). Multicoloured.

5225	25d. Type **500**	2·60	2·75
5226	25d. Meeting of Kennedy and Khrushchev, 1961	2·60	2·75
5227	25d. Commencement address, American University, 1963	2·60	2·75
5228	25d. Atomic testing, Bikini Atoll, 1946	2·60	2·75

501 *Calotropis procera*

2008. Flowers of the Gambia. Multicoloured.

5229	25d. Type **501**	2·60	2·75
5230	25d. *Calliandra surinamensis*	2·60	2·75
5231	25d. *Plumeria alba*	2·60	2·75
5232	25d. *Quisqualis indica*	2·60	2·75
5233	25d. *Adansonia digitata*	2·60	2·75
5234	25d. *Commelina benghalensis*	2·60	2·75
5235	25d. *Heliconia psittacorum*	2·60	2·75
5236	25d. *Tabebuia rosea*	2·60	2·75
MS5237	Two sheets, each 70×100 mm. (a) 65d. Flowers and leaves (38×50 mm). (b) 65d. *Tabebuia chrysotricha* (38×50 mm)	13·50	13·50

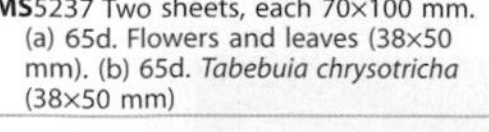

502 French Army Commander Petain

2008. 90th Anniv of End of First World War. Multicoloured.

MS5238	185×109 mm. 15d.×6 Type **502**; Soldier outside emplacement; Airman; Airman in cockpit; Soldier; Four officers	9·50	9·50
MS5239	190×163 mm. 25d.×4 Army unit; Tanks; Soldiers leaving trench; Artillery crew	10·50	10·50

503 Prince Charles

2008. 60th Birthday of Prince Charles. Sheet 150×100 mm containing T 503 and similar vert designs. Multicoloured.

MS5240	Type **503**; Wearing top hat; Smiling; Saluting	10·50	10·50

504 Ox

2009. Chinese New Year. Year of the Ox. Sheet 190×78 mm.

MS5241	25d. Type **504**×4 multicoloured	10·50	10·50

505 Pres. Barack Obama

2009. Inauguration of President Barack Obama. Multicoloured.

5242	16d. Type **505**	1·75	1·90
MS5243	132×93 mm. 60d. Type **505**; 60d. Vice President Joseph Biden	6·50	6·50

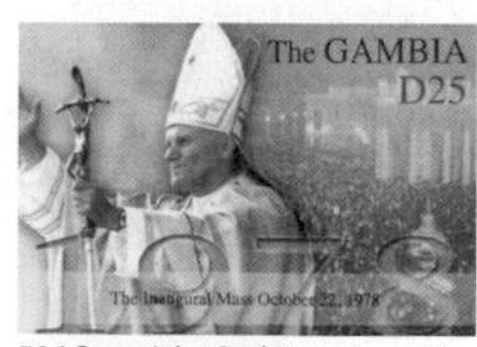

506 Pope John Paul II at Inaugural Mass, 22 October 1978

2009. Pope John Paul II Commemoration. Sheet 120×100 mm containing T 506 and similar horiz designs. Multicoloured.

MS5244	Type **506**; Addressing United Nations, New York, October 1979; In Warsaw, Poland, June 1983; World Youth Day, Denver, Colorado, USA, August 1993	10·50	10·50

507 Elvis Presley

2009. Elvis Presley in Jailhouse Rock (film). Multicoloured.

MS5245	125×90 mm. 60d. Type **507**	6·50	6·50
MS5246	90×125 mm. 60d. Playing guitar (vert)	6·50	6·50
MS5247	90×125 mm. 60d. Dancing in scene from *Jailhouse Rock* (vert)	6·50	6·50
MS5248	125×90 mm. 60d. Film poster for *Jailhouse Rock* (vert)	6·50	6·50

508 Elvis Presley

2009. Elvis Presley Commemoration. Sheet 190×127 mm containing T 508 and similar vert designs. Multicoloured.
MS5249 Type **508**; Wearing dark blue shirt and jacket; Wearing red; Wearing brown shirt and cream tie; Wearing denim shirt;Wearing white shirt and pale lilac jacket 12·00 12·00

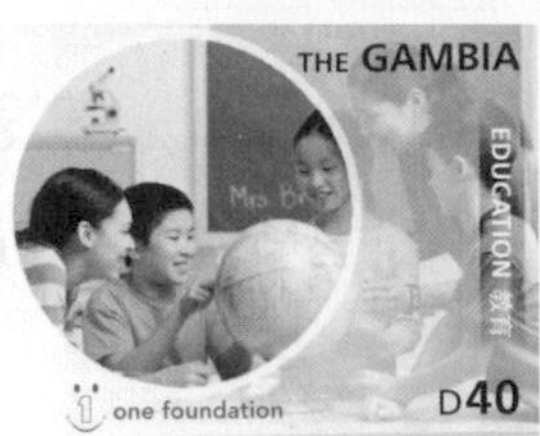

509 Teacher with Pupils and Globe ('EDUCATION')

2009. Jet Li One Foundation. Sheet 171×160 mm containing T 509 and similar horiz designs. Multicoloured.
MS5250 Type **509**; Jet Li (founder); Outstretched hands ('POVERTY'); 'HEALTH'; Mountain lake ('ENVIRONMENT'); 'DISASTER RELIEF' 22·00 22·00

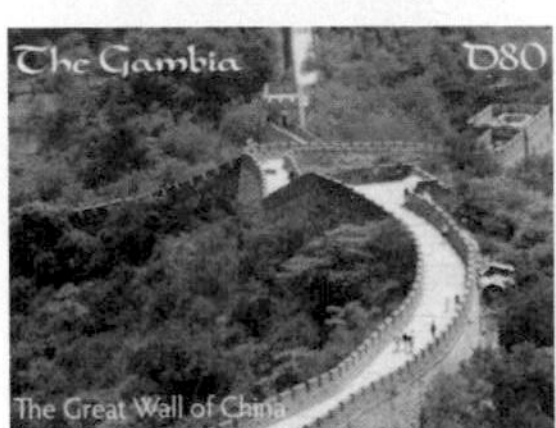

510 Great Wall of China

2009. China 2009 World Stamp Exhibition, Luoyang. Sheet 100×70 mm.
MS5251 multicoloured 7·75 8·00

511 Inaugural Speech of Pres. Barack Obama

2009. Birth Bicentenary of Abraham Lincoln (US President 1861–5) and Inauguration of President Barack Obama. Sheet 102×130 mm containing T 511 and similar vert designs. Multicoloured.
MS5252 Type **511**; Pres. Abraham Lincoln giving inaugural speech, 1861; Pres. Abraham Lincoln and train route of Whistle Stop Tour; Pres. Barack Obama in Wilmington, Delaware on Whistle Stop Tour 5·25 5·25

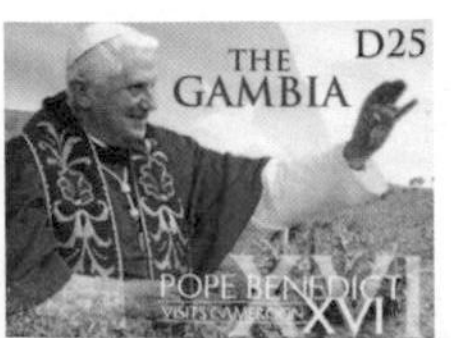

512 Pope Benedict XVI in Cameroon

2009. Visit of Pope Benedict XVI to Cameroon. Sheet 150×100 mm. Multicoloured.
MS5253 25d. Type **512**×4 10·50 10·50

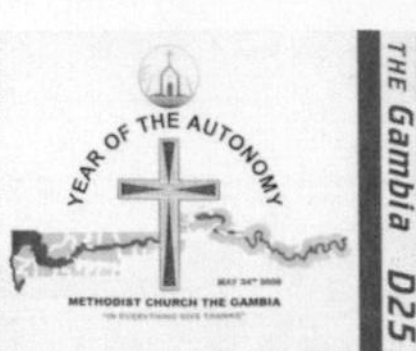

513 Cross and Map of Gambia River

2009. Independence of Methodist Church in Gambia. Multicoloured.
5254 25d. Type **513** (Autonomy of Methodist Church in Gambia) 2·60 2·75
5255 35d. Cross and map of Africa with colours of Cameroon flag (vert) (Inaugural Conference of Gambian Methodist Church) 3·25 3·50

514 *Rockin' thru the Rockies* (1940)

2009. The Three Stooges. Sheet 174×159 mm containing T 514 and similar vert designs showing scenes from films. Multicoloured.
MS5256 Type **514**; *The Sitter Downers* (1937); *Violent is the Word for Curly* (1938); *WeWant our Mummy* (1939) 10·50 10·50

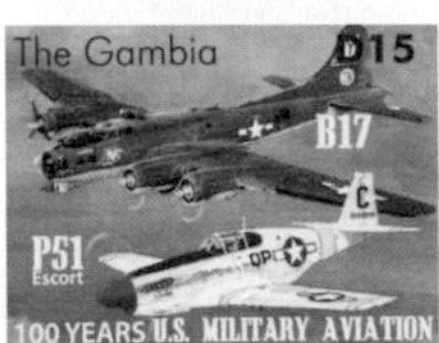

515 Boeing B17 Fortress and North American P51 Mustang Escort

2009. Centenary of US Military Aviation. T 515 and similar multicoloured designs.
MS5257 150×150 mm. 15d.×9 Type **515**; Doolittle's North American B25s; Consolidated B24; Republic P-47D Thunderbolt; North American F-86F Sabre; North American AT-6; Lockheed F80 Shooting Star; Boeing (McDonnell Douglas) F15 Eagle; Northrop T38 and Lockheed F117A Nighthawk 14·50 14·50
MS5258 95×119 mm. 80d. Lockheed P38 Lightening and Messerschmitt Me262 (37×50 mm) 7·50 7·50

516 Michael Jackson

2009. Michael Jackson Commemoration. T 516 and similar horiz designs. Multicoloured.
MS5259 130×100 mm. 20d. Type **516**; 20d. Wearing white jacket and white hat; 30d. As Type **516**; 30d. Wearing white jacket and white hat 12·00 12·00
MS5260 120×157 mm. 20d. Wearing dark blue jacket and hat; 20d. As teenager; 30d. Wearing dark blue jacket and hat; 30d. As teenager 12·00 12·00

517 Susan B. Anthony Dollar

2009. 40th Anniv of First Manned Moon Landing. Sheet 150×100 mm containing T 517 and similar vert designs. Multicoloured.
MS5261 20d.×6 Type **517**; Apollo 11 Lunar Module; Neil Armstrong; Apollo 11; Neil Armstrong statue; Apollo 11 Command Module 12·00 12·00

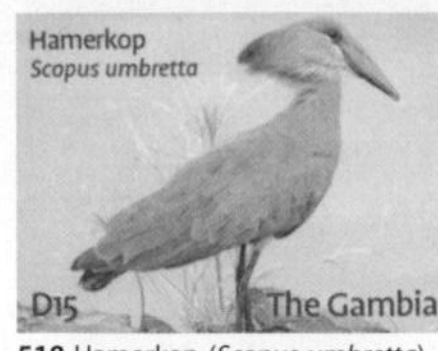

518 Hamerkop (*Scopus umbretta*)

2009. Birds of Gambia. Multicoloured.
5262 15d. Type **518** 1·60 1·75
5263 20d. Pied kingfisher (*Ceryle rudis*) 2·00 2·25
5264 25d. Black-capped babbler (*Pellorneum capistratum*) 2·60 2·75
5265 40d. African darter (*Anhinga rufa*) 4·00 4·00
MS5266 140×70 mm. 25d.×4 Malachite kingfisher (*Alcedo cristata*); Common bulbul (*Pycnonotus barbatus*); Black-crowned night heron (*Nycticorax nycticorax*); Wire-tailed swallow (*Hirundo smithii*) (all vert) 10·50 10·50
MS5267 70×100 mm. 40d.×2 Sacred ibis (*Threskiornis aethiopicus*); Little grebe (*Tachybaptus ruficollis*) 6·50 6·50

519 Raph

2009. 25th Anniv of Teenage Mutant Ninja Turtles. Sheet 170×200 mm containing T 519 and similar vert designs. Multicoloured.
MS5268 25d.×4 Type **519**; Leo; Mike; Don 10·50 10·50

520 Pembroke Welsh Corgi

2009. 125th Anniv of American Kennel Club. Two sheets, each 100×120 mm, containing T 520 and similar horiz designs showing Pembroke Welsh Corgi (MS5269) or West Highland White Terrier (MS5270).
MS5269 25d.×4 Type **520**; Corgi sat among pumpkins and flowers; Sat in front of baskets of flowers; Corgi in park 10·50 10·50
MS5270 25d.×4 Terrier in basket; With beach ball; Among Christmas presents; In basket (yellow flowers at right) 10·50 10·50

521 Pres. Barack Obama

2009. Visit of President Barack Obama to Buckingham Palace. Multicoloured.
MS5271 150×160 mm. 25d.×3 Type **521**; Queen Elizabeth II; Michelle Obama 7·50 7·50
MS5272 100×70 mm. 80d. Queen Elizabeth II at G20 World Leader Reception, Buckingham Palace (vert) 8·00 8·00

522 Pres. Obama, Bishop Jochen Bohl and German Chancellor Angela Merkel

2009. Visit of US Pres. Barack Obama to Germany, June 2009. Multicoloured.
MS5273 150×110 mm. 25d.×4 Type **522**; Pres. Barack Obama; Angela Merkel; Pres. Obama and Angela Merkel 10·50 10·50
MS5274 120×76 mm. 65d. Pres. Obama, Angela Merkel, Elie Wiesel (Holocaust survivor) and Bertrand Herz (International Buchenwald Committee President) at Buchenwald Concentration Camp (37×51 mm) 6·50 6·50

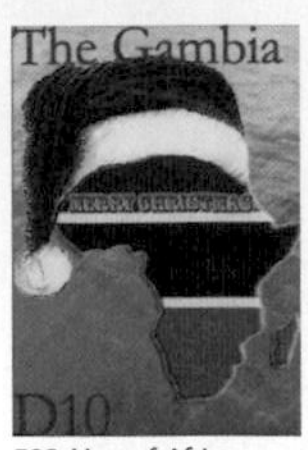

523 Map of Africa wearing Santa Hat

2009. Christmas. Multicoloured.
5275 10d. Type **523** 1·00 1·10
5276 15d. Candy canes 1·60 1·75
5277 25d. Christmas tree and star in lights 2·60 2·75
5278 30d. Candle 3·00 3·25

524 *Panaeolus bispora*

2009. Mushrooms. Multicoloured.
5279 10d. Type **524** 1·00 1·10
5280 15d. *Panaeolus tropicalis* 1·60 1·75
5281 25d. *Psilocybe mairei* 2·60 2·75
5282 30d. *Gymnopilus aeruginosus* 3·00 3·25
MS5283 110×140 mm. 15d.×6 *Panaeolus retirugis*; *Gymnopilus junionius*; *Psilocybe natalensis*; *Panaeolus africanus*; *Panaelous cinctulus*; *Panaeolus subbalteatus* (all horiz) 8·75 8·75

525 Elegant Acraea (*Acraea egina*)

2009. Butterflies of the Gambia. Multicoloured.
5284 10d. Type **525** 1·00 1·10
5285 15d. Bamboo charaxes (*Charaxes boueti*) 1·60 1·75
5286 25d. Green-veined charaxes (*Charaxes candiope*) 2·60 2·75
5287 30d. Pink acraea (*Acraea caecilia*) 3·00 3·25
MS5288 151×130 mm. 15d.×6 Abadima acraea (*Acraea pseudegina*); African common white (*Belenois creona*); Cream-bordered charaxes (*Charaxes epijasius*); African caper white (*Belenois aurota*); Large spotted acraea (*Acraea zetes*); Tiny orange tip (*Colotis evagore antigone*) (all horiz) 8·75 8·75

The stamps and margins of **MS**5288 form a composite design.

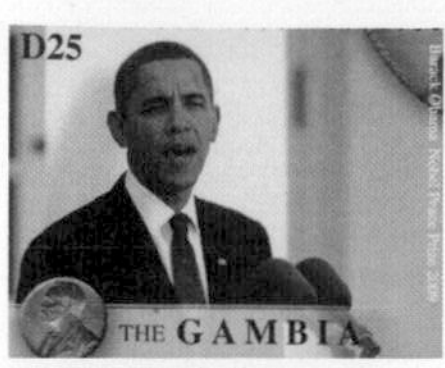

526 Pres. Barack Obama

2009. President Barack Obama's Nobel Peace Prize. Sheet 140×100 mm containing T 526 and simiilar horiz designs. Multicoloured.

MS5289 Type **526**; Pres. Obama (microphones at left); Pres. Obama (Bay leaves at right); Pres. Obama (in front of window) 10·50 10·50

527 Common Dolphin (*Delphinus delphis*)

2010. Whales and Dolphins. Multicoloured.. Multicoloured.

5290	10d. Type **527**	1·00	1·10
5291	15d. Pygmy killer whale (*Feresa attenuata*)	1·60	1·75
5292	25d. Short-finned pilot whale (*Globicephala macrorhynchus*)	2·60	2·75
5293	30d. Clymene dolphin (*Stenella clymene*)	3·00	3·25

MS5294 130×100 mm. 25d.×4 Southern bottlenose whale (*Hyperoodon planifrons*); Fraser's dolphin (*Lagenodelphis hosei*); Atlantic hump-backed dolphin (*Sousa teuszii*); Ginkgo-toothed beaked whale (*Mesoplodon ginkgodens*) 10·50 10·50

MS5295 70×100 mm. 35d.×2 Blainville's beaked whale (*Mesoplodon densirostris*); Atlantic spotted dolphin (*Stenella frontalis*) 3·75 3·75

528 Ferrari Superamerica, 2005

2010. Ferrari Cars. Multicoloured.

5296	12d. Type **528**	1·40	1·50
5297	12d. Yellow Ferrari Superamerica, 2005	1·40	1·50
5298	12d. Frame of Ferrari 360 Modena, 1999	1·40	1·50
5299	12d. Ferrari 360 Modena, 1999	1·40	1·50
5300	12d. Engine of Ferrari F2003-GA, 2003	1·40	1·50
5301	12d. Ferrari F2003-GA, 2003	1·40	1·50
5302	12d. Components of Ferrari California, 2008	1·40	1·50
5303	12d. Ferrari California, 2008	1·40	1·50

529 Warbler Finch

2010. Birth Bicentenary (2009) of Charles Darwin (naturalist and evolutionary theorist). Sheet 130×100 mm containing T 529 and similar vert designs. Multicoloured.

MS5304 Type **529**; Common cactus-finch; Large cactus-finch; Small ground-finch 10·50 10·50

529a Scout using Telescope

2010. Centenary of Boy Scouts of America. Multicoloured.

MS5304a 25d.×4 Type **529a** ×2; Archer in wheelchair ×2 21·00 21·00

MS5304b 25d.×4 First aid ×2; Scouts saluting US flag ×2 21·00 21·00

530 Abraham Lincoln, Peter Cooper and the Cooper Union, 1860

2010. Birth Bicentenary (2009) of Abraham Lincoln (US president, 1861–5). Two sheets each 150×96 mm. Multicoloured.

MS5305 25d.×4 Type **530**; Abraham Lincoln, Mathew Brady and the Brady Gallery, 1860; Abraham Lincoln, Abraham Cullen Bryant and the address at the Great Hall, Cooper Union, 1860; Abraham Lincoln and Horace Greeley and the Astor House, 1860 11·00 11·00

MS5306 25d.×4 Photograph of Lincoln by Mathew Brady, 1860, and portraits of Lincoln and Brady; Last photographs of Lincoln by Alexander Gardner, 1865, and portraits of Lincoln and Gardner; Lincoln centenary conceived by Pres. Roosevelt and Victor Brenner, and portraits of Lincoln and Brenner; Lincoln Memorial (dedicated 1923) and portraits of Lincoln and Daniel Chester French 11·00 11·00

531 John F. Kennedy

2010. 50th Anniversary of Election of Pres. John F. Kennedy. Sheet 145×93 mm containing T **531** and similar vert designs. Multicoloured.

MS5307 30d.×4 Type **531**; Inauguration; John F. Kennedy (US flag at right); With family 13·00 13·00

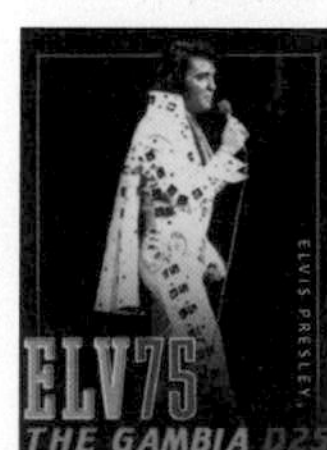

532 Elvis Presley

2010. 75th Birth Anniv of Elvis Presley. Multicoloured.

MS5308 181×140 mm. 25d.×4 Type **532**; Leaning forwards to right; Facing forwards, head turned to right; Stood with hands on hips, looking down (all inscr in blue) 11·00 11·00

MS5309 127×179 mm. 30d.×4 Holding guitar across body; Head and shoulders portrait, singing; Wearing white catsuit with bird emblem; Wearing white catsuit with black embroidery (all 51×37 mm, with mauve panel and inscriptions) 13·00 13·00

MS5310 173×112 mm. 30d.×4 Wearing check shirt; Wearing jacket; Wearing white top with two stripes; Wearing white T shirt (all 37×51 mm, with music score in stamp background) 13·00 13·00

533 Algeria

2010. World Cup Football Championship, South Africa. Multicoloured.

5311	20d. Type **533**	2·20	2·30
5312	20d. Argentina	2·20	2·30
5313	20d. Australia	2·20	2·30
5314	20d. Brazil	2·20	2·30
5315	20d. Cameroon	2·20	2·30
5316	20d. Chile	2·20	2·30
5317	20d. Denmark	2·20	2·30
5318	20d. England	2·20	2·30
5319	20d. France	2·20	2·30
5320	20d. Germany	2·30	2·30
5321	20d. Ghana	2·20	2·30
5322	20d. Greece	2·20	2·30
5323	20d. Honduras	2·20	2·30
5324	20d. Italy	2·30	2·30
5325	20d. Côte d'Ivoire	2·20	2·30
5326	20d. Japan	2·20	2·30
5327	20d. Korea DPR	2·20	2·30
5328	20d. Korea Republic	2·20	2·30
5329	20d. Mexico	2·20	2·30
5330	20d. Netherlands	2·20	2·30
5331	20d. New Zealand	2·20	2·30
5332	20d. Nigeria	2·20	2·30
5333	20d. Paraguay	2·20	2·30
5334	20d. Portugal	2·20	2·30
5335	20d. Serbia	2·20	2·30
5336	20d. Slovakia	2·20	2·30
5337	20d. Slovenia	2·20	2·30
5338	20d. South Africa	2·20	2·30
5339	20d. Spain	2·20	2·30
5340	20d. Switzerland	2·20	2·30
5341	20d. Uruguay	2·20	2·30
5342	20d. United States	2·20	2·20

534 David Ragan

2010. NASCAR (US National Association for Stock Car Racing). Sheet 110×141 mm containing T **534** and similar vert designs showing drivers. Multicoloured.

MS5343 25d.×4 Type **534**; Carl Edwards; Greg Biffle; Matt Kenseth 11·00 11·00

535 King George V sweeping away 'Made in Germany' in 1917 Cartoon

2010. Centenary of Accession of King George V. Multicoloured.

MS5344 20d.×6 Type **535**; King George V; King Edward VIII; Badge of the House of Windsor; King George VI; Coronation portrait of Queen Elizabeth II 13·00 13·00

536 Pres. Lech Kaczynski

2010. President Lech Kaczynski of Poland Commemoration

5345	**536**	30d. multicoloured	3·00	2·75

537 *Lamentation*

2010. 500th Death Anniv of Sandro Botticelli (artist). Multicoloured.

MS5346 20d.×6 Type **537**; *Madonna del Magnificat; The Return of Judith to Bethulia; Venus and Mars* (detail showing Venus); *Venus and Mars* (detail showing Mars); *The Punishment of Korah* 13·00 13·00

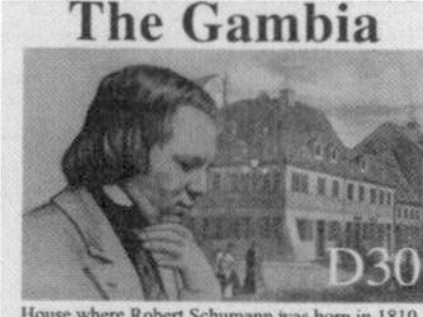

538 Robert Schumann and Birthplace

2010. Birth Bicentenary of Robert Schumann (composer). Multicoloured.

MS5347 150×100 mm. 30d.×4 Type **538**; Clara and Robert Schumann; Robert Schumann Monument, Zwickau, Germany; Grave, Bonn, Germany 12·00 12·00

MS5348 70×100 mm. 65d. Clara and Robert Schumann (vert) 6·25 6·25

539 Mother Teresa with Princess Diana

2010. Birth Centenary of Mother Teresa (Agnes Gonxha Bojaxhiu). Multicoloured.

MS5349 30d.×4 Type **539**; With Princess Diana: Standing side by side both with hands clasped); Walking hand in hand; Holding hands, Mother Teresa with hand raised 12·00 12·00

MS5350 30d.×4 With Pres. Ronald Reagan; With Desmond Tutu; With Pope John Paul II; With Queen Elizabeth II 12·00 12·00

540 Pope Benedict XVI in Malta, April 2010

2010. Visit of Pope Benedict XVI to Malta. Multicoloured.

5351	30d. Type **540**	3·00	2·75
5352	30d. Pope Benedict XVI (white and red background)	3·00	2·75

541 Scene from *Donzoko*

2010. Birth Centenary of Akira Kurosawa (film director). Multicoloured.

MS5353 153×133 mm. 30d.×4 Type **541**; *Hakuchi; Ikimono no kiroku; Ikiru* 12·00 12·00

MS5354 153×133 mm. 30d.×4 *Nora inu; Zoku Sugata Sanshirō; Shichinin no Samurai; Shizukanaru Ketto* 12·00 12·00

MS5355 100×70 mm. 80d. *Ichiban utsukushiku* (horiz) 12·00 12·00

Pt. 19

GAZA

1000 milliemes = £1 (Egyptian).

EGYPTIAN OCCUPATION

A strip of territory along the coast from Gaza to the Egyptian frontier, seized by Egypt when the British Mandate for Palestine ended in May 1948.

In 1967 Israeli troops seized the Gaza Strip and from that date Israeli stamps were used.

In May 1994 the area became autonomous under the Palestinian National Authority.

1948. Various stamps of Egypt optd PALESTINE in English and Arabic.

1	**91**	1m. brown (postage)	35	35
2	**91**	2m. red	35	35
3	**78**	3m. brown	35	35
4	**91**	4m. green	35	35
5	**91**	5m. brown	35	35
6	**78**	6m. green	35	35
7	**91**	10m. violet	35	35
8	**78**	13m. red	45	45
9	**91**	15m. purple	45	45
10	**91**	17m. green	45	45
11	**91**	20m. violet	45	45
12	**91**	22m. blue	60	60
13	-	30m. green (No. 340)	70	70
14	**106**	40m. brown	95	95
15	-	50m. blue (No. 342)	1·00	1·00
16	-	100m. purple (No. 280)	4·75	3·50
17	-	200m. violet (No. 281)	11·50	11·50
18	**86**	50p. brown and green	29·00	29·00
19	**87**	£E1 brown and blue	50·00	50·00
20	**101**	2m. red (air)	45	45
21	**101**	3m. brown	45	45
22	**101**	5m. red	45	45
23	**101**	7m. brown	70	70
24	**101**	8m. green	70	70
25	**101**	10m. violet	80	80
26	**101**	20m. blue	1·20	1·20
27	**101**	30m. purple	2·50	2·50
28	**101**	40m. red	1·70	1·70
29	**101**	50m. blue	2·50	2·50
30	**101**	100m. green	4·25	4·25
31	**101**	200m. grey	17·00	17·00

1953. As above but with portrait obliterated by three horiz bars. (a) Postage.

32	**91**	1m. brown	60	60
33	**91**	2m. red	60	60
34	**78**	3m. brown	60	60
35	**91**	4m. green	60	60
36	**91**	5m. brown	60	60
37	**78**	6m. green	60	60
38	**91**	10m. violet	70	70
39	**78**	13m. red	80	80
40	**91**	15m. purple	80	80
41	**91**	17m. green	85	85
42	**91**	20m. violet	95	95
43	**91**	22m. blue	1·20	1·20
44	-	30m. green	1·20	1·20
45	**106**	40m. brown	2·30	2·30
46	-	50m. blue	7·00	7·00
47	-	100m. purple	16·00	19·00
48	-	200m. violet	35·00	37·00
49	**86**	50p. brown and green	70·00	65·00
50	**87**	£E1 brown and blue	£150	£150

(b) Air.

51	**101**	2m. red	95	95
52	**101**	3m. brown	95	95
53	**101**	5m. red	16·00	19·00
54	**101**	7m. brown	95	1·20
55	**101**	8m. green	3·00	2·50
56	**101**	10m. violet	3·00	2·50
57	**101**	20m. blue	3·00	2·50
58	**101**	30m. purple	3·00	2·50
59	**101**	40m. red	5·75	5·75
60	**101**	50m. blue	23·00	23·00
61	**101**	100m. green	95·00	£100
62	**101**	200m. grey	9·25	9·25

1953. Air. Nos. 480/2, 485 and 489/90 of Egypt optd PALESTINE in English and Arabic.

63	2m. red	80	80
64	3m. brown	15·00	15·00
65	5m. red	2·30	2·50
66	10m. violet	22·00	23·00
67	50m. blue	7·00	9·25
68	100m. olive	50·00	50·00

1955. Stamps of Egypt, 1953/4, optd PALESTINE in English and Arabic.

69	**137**	1m. brown	45	45
70	**137**	2m. purple	45	45
71	**137**	3m. blue	45	45
72	**137**	4m. green	45	45
73	**137**	5m. red	45	45
74	**130**	10m. sepia (B)	45	45
75	**130**	15m. grey	45	45
76	**130**	17m. turquoise	45	45
77	**130**	20m. violet	60	60
78	**131**	30m. green	60	60
79	**131**	32m. blue	80	80
80	**131**	35m. violet	70	70
81	**131**	40m. brown	1·20	1·20
82	**131**	50m. purple	1·20	1·20
83	**132**	100m. brown	3·50	3·50
84	**132**	200m. turquoise	17·00	19·00
85	**132**	500m. violet	60·00	60·00
86	**132**	£E1 red and green	£100	£100

1955. Air. Nos. 433/4 of Egypt optd PALESTINE in English and Arabic.

86a	**133**	5m. brown	5·75	7·00
86b	**133**	15m. green	8·25	9·25

Types of Egypt (sometimes with colours changed) overprinted **PALESTINE** in English and Arabic.

1957. Re-occupation of Gaza Strip.

87	**152**	10m. green	5·00	5·25

1957. Stamps of 1957.

88	-	1m. turquoise (No. 538)	60	60
89	-	5m. sepia (No. 541)	60	60
90	**160**	10m. violet	60	60

UNITED ARAB REPUBLIC

1958. Stamps of 1958 (inscr "U A R EGYPT").

91	-	1m. red (No. 553)	35	35
92	-	2m. blue (No. 554)	35	35
93	**168**	3m. brown	35	35
94	-	4m. green (No. 556)	35	35
95	-	5m. sepia (No. 557)	35	35
96	**160**	10m. violet (No. 558)	45	35
96a	-	35m. blue (No. 559)	3·50	3·25

1958. 5th Anniv of Republic.

97	**172**	10m. brown	2·10	2·10

1958. 10th Anniv of Declaration of Human Rights.

98	**178**	10m. purple	3·00	4·75
99	**178**	35m. brown	8·75	9·25

1959. No. 588.

100	**132**	55m. on 100m. red	4·75	7·00

Types of Egypt with some colours changed and additionally inscribed "PALESTINE" in English and Arabic.

1960. As Nos. 603, etc.

101	**160**	1m. orange	35	35
104	-	4m. brown	35	35
105	-	5m. violet	35	35
106	-	10m. green	35	35

1960. World Refugee Year.

109	**205**	10m. brown	45	45
110	**205**	35m. black	1·70	1·50

1961. World Health Day.

111	**213**	10m. blue	1·20	95

1961. Palestine Day.

112	**215**	10m. violet	35	35

1961. U.N. Technical Co-operation Programme and 16th Anniv of UNO.

113	-	10m. blue and orange	35	35
114	**220**	35m. purple and red	80	80

1961. Education Day.

115	**223**	10m. brown	35	35

1961. Victory Day.

116	**224**	10m. brown and chestnut	35	35

1962. 5th Anniv of Egyptian Occupation of Gaza.

117	**229**	10m. brown	35	35

1962. Arab League Week.

118	**231**	10m. purple	35	35

1962. Malaria Eradication.

119	**235**	10m. red and brown	35	35
120	-	35m. yellow and black	1·20	95

1962. 17th Anniv of UNO and Hammarskjold Commemoration.

121	**245**	5m. blue and pink	35	35
122	**245**	10m. blue and brown	35	35
123	**245**	35m. indigo and blue	70	70

1963. As No. 739.

124	4m. blue, orange and black	35	35

1963. Freedom from Hunger.

125	**252**	5m. brown and green	35	35
126	-	10m. yellow and green	35	35
127	-	35m. yellow and purple	65	65

1963. Centenary of Red Cross.

128	**253**	10m. red, purple and blue	35	35
129	-	35m. ultram, blue & red	60	60

1963. UNESCO Campaign for Preservation of Nubian Monuments (4th issue).

130	**256**	5m. yellow and purple	35	35
131	-	10m. yellow and black	35	35
132	-	35m. yellow and violet	1·20	95

1963. Air. As Nos. 758, 760 and 761/2.

133	50m. purple and blue	1·20	1·20
134	80m. indigo and blue	2·50	2·50
135	115m. yellow and black	3·50	3·50
136	140m. red and blue	4·00	4·00

1963. 15th Anniv of Declaration of Human Rights.

137	**259a**	5m. yellow and sepia	35	35
138	-	10m. black, grey & pur	35	35
139	-	35m. black, green & turq	95	95

1964. As No. 769, etc.

140		1m. violet and green	40	40
141		2m. blue and orange	40	40
142		3m. blue, brown & lt blue	40	40
143		4m. green, brown & pink	40	40
144		5m. red, blue and pink	40	40
145		10m. red, brown and green	40	40
146		15m. yellow, violet & lilac	40	40
147		20m. green and violet	80	80
148	**261**	30m. blue and orange	1·70	1·70
149	-	35m. brown, green & orge	1·40	1·40
150	-	40m. blue and green	1·70	1·70
151	-	60m. brown and blue	2·50	2·50
152	**263**	100m. brown and blue	3·50	3·50

1964. Arab League Heads of State Congress, Cairo.

153	**266**	10m. black and olive	35	35

1964. Ramadan Festival.

154	**267**	4m. olive, red and lake	35	35

1964. 10th Anniv of Arab Postal Union's Permanent Office.

155	**271**	10m. blue and green	35	35

1964. World Health Day.

156	**272**	10m. purple and red	35	35

1965. Ramadan Festival. As No. 834.

157	4m. brown and green	35	35

1965. 20th Anniv of Arab League.

158	**289**	10m. green and red	35	35
159	-	20m. brown and green	35	35

1965. Air. World Meteorological Day.

160	**290**	80m. orange and blue	3·00	3·00

1965. World Health Day.

161	**291**	10m. red and green	35	35

1965. Deir Yassin Massacre.

162	**292**	10m. red and blue	35	35

1965. Centenary of I.T.U.

163	**293**	5m. blue, yellow and green	35	35
164	**293**	10m. rose, blue and red	35	35
165	**293**	35m. blue, yell & ultram	1·40	95

1965. Air. Re-establishment of Egyptian Civil Airlines "MISRAIR".

166	**295**	10m. green and orange	1·70	1·70

1966. U.N. Day.

167	**321**	5m. violet and red	35	35
168	-	10m. violet and brown	35	35
169	-	35m. violet and green	80	80

1966. Victory Day.

170	**324**	10m. red and olive	35	35

1967. Arab Publicity Week.

171	**328**	10m. brown and blue	35	35

1967. Labour Day.

172	**331**	10m. sepia and olive	35	35

EXPRESS LETTER STAMP

1948. Express Letter stamp of Egypt optd PALESTINE in English and Arabic.

E32	**E52**	40m. black and brown	13·00	12·50

POSTAGE DUE STAMPS

1948. Postage Due stamps of Egypt optd PALESTINE in English and Arabic.

D32	**D59**	2m. orange	2·10	2·30
D33	**D59**	4m. green	1·60	1·90
D34	**D59**	6m. green	1·60	1·90
D35	**D59**	8m. purple	1·60	1·90
D36	**D59**	10m. lake	1·60	1·90
D37	**D59**	12m. red	1·60	1·90
D38	**D59**	30m. violet	5·00	9·25

This area was occupied by Israel on 6 June 1967. Post Offices were opened in July 1967 and Israeli stamps are now used.

Pt. 10

GEORGIA

Formerly part of Russia, Georgia declared its independence after the Russian Revolution. In 1921 it became a Soviet Republic and in 1922 joined with Armenia and Azerbaijan to form the Transcaucasian Federation, whose stamps were used from September 1923. After absorption into the U.S.S.R. Russian stamps were used from 1924.

With the dissolution of the Soviet Union in 1991 Georgia again became an independent state.

1919. 100 kopeks = 1 rouble.
1993. kupon.
1995. 100 tetri = 1 lari.

1 St. George

3 Queen Tamara (A.D. 1184–1212)

1919. Imperf or perf.

1	**1**	40k. red	50	1·20
2	**1**	60k. red	50	1·20
3	**1**	70k. mauve	50	1·20
10	**1**	10k. blue	50	1·20
12	**1**	50k. green	50	1·20
15	-	1r. brown (20×25 mm)	50	1·20
16	**3**	2r. brown	60	1·00
17a	**3**	3r. blue	75	1·20
18	**3**	5r. yellow	1·30	1·60

4 Soldier

6 Industry and agriculture

1922. Perf.

28a	**4**	500r. red	3·75	5·75
29	-	1000r. brown (Sower)	4·75	5·25
30	**6**	2000r. grey	8·00	8·50
31	**6**	3000r. brown	7·50	8·50
32	**6**	5000r. green	7·50	8·50

7

1922. Famine Relief. Designs as T 7. Surch.

33	-	100r. on 50r. violet	1·00	3·25
34	-	3000r. on 100r. red	1·00	3·25
35	-	5000r. on 250r. green	1·00	3·25
36	**7**	10,000r. on 25r. blue	1·00	4·75

1923. Surch.

37	-	10,000r. on 1000r. (No. 29)	8·00	6·50
38	**6**	15,000r. on 2000r. grey	6·00	8·50
40a	**6**	40,000r. on 5000r. green	5·00	6·50
44	**4**	20,000r. on 500r. red	4·50	6·00
46	**6**	80,000r. on 3000r. brown	6·00	6·50

1923. Surch. (a) On Arms types of Russia.

47	**22**	10,000r. on 7k. blue	£100	95·00
48	**10**	15,000r. on 15k. blue & brn	7·25	9·50

(b) On No. 75B of Armenia.

49	1,5000r. on 5r. on 15k. blue and brown	£140	£200

1923. Arms types of Russia surch with hammer and sickle and value. Imperf or perf.

52	**22**	20,000r. on 5k. red	6·00	7·50
53	**14**	30,000r. on 20k. red & blue	6·75	6·75
54	**22**	35,000r. on 3k. red	7·50	9·00
50	**22**	75,000r. on 1k. orange	8·00	8·50
57	**22**	700,000r. on 2k. green	9·00	9·50

12 Map, National Flag and U.N. Emblem

1993. 1st Anniv of Admission to U.N.O.

58	**12**	25r. multicoloured	70	45
59	**12**	50r. multicoloured	1·20	95
60	**12**	100r. multicoloured	2·50	1·90
MS61 122×101 mm. Nos. 58/60			5·00	4·75

13 Arms and Flag

1993

62	**13**	0.50k. multicoloured	50	30

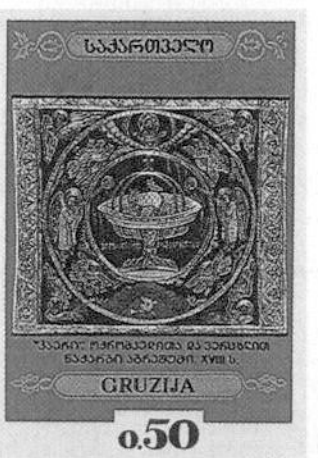

14 18th-century Fresco in gold

1993. Treasures of the National Museum.

63	**14**	0.50k. multicoloured	1·20	95

15 "Apostle Simon" (icon)

1993. Ancient Art.

64	**15**	1k. multicoloured	1·00	75

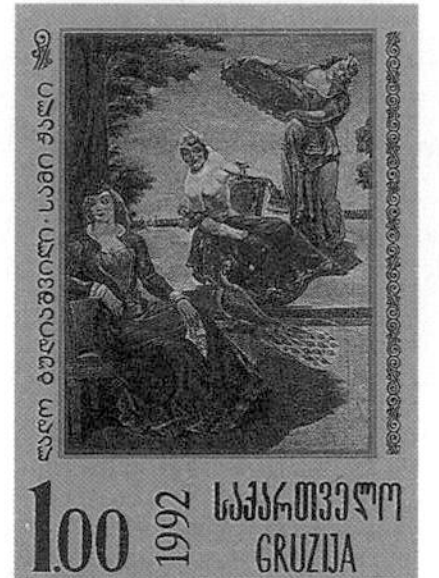

16 "Three Women" (Lado Gudiashvili)

1993. National Paintings.

65	**16**	1k. multicoloured	1·30	1·00

17 Juari Monastery, Mtskheta

1993. Places of Worship.

66	**17**	30k. blue	40	30
67	-	40k. brown	50	40
68	-	50k. brown	65	45
69	-	60k. red	80	65
70	-	70k. lilac	1·00	75
71	-	80k. green	1·10	85
72	-	90k. black	1·20	95

DESIGNS: 40k. Gelati Church; 50k. Nikortsminda Church; 60k. Ikorta Church; 70k. Samtavisi Church; 80k. Bolnisi Zion Synagogue; 90k. Gremi Citadel Church.

18 Emblem

1994. 2nd Anniv of International Olympic Committee Recognition of Georgian National Olympic Committee.

73	**18**	100k.+50k. multicoloured	1·00	75

19 Emblem

1994. Admission (1993) of Georgia to U.P.U.

74	**19**	200k. multicoloured	1·30	80

20 Window and Nikoladze

1994. 150th Birth Anniv (1993) of Niko Nikoladze (journalist).

75	**20**	150k. multicoloured	1·10	80

1994. Nos. 62/5 surch.

76	**13**	5000k. on 0.50k. mult	40	30
77	**14**	5000k. on 0.50k. mult	40	30
78	**15**	10000k. on 1k. mult	80	60
79	**16**	10000k. on 1k. mult	80	60

22 "Barba and the Lion" **24** Olympic Rings and Colours

1994. All-Georgian Congress.

80	**22**	100k. brown and pink	1·70	1·30
81	-	200k. deep blue and blue	3·50	2·75

DESIGN: 200k. Equestrian statue.

1994. Nos. 63/5 surch Georgia and new value.

82	**14**	200k. on 0.50k. mult	65	50
83	**15**	300k. on 1k. multicoloured	95	70
84	**16**	500k. on 1k. multicoloured	1·30	1·00

1995. Centenary of International Olympic Committee. Multicoloured.

85		10k. Type **24** (International Year of Sport)	1·10	85
86		15k. Emblem symbolizing founding congress	1·50	1·20
87		20k. Anniversary emblem	2·10	1·70
88		25k. Olympic rings and peace dove ("Olympic Truce")	2·50	2·10

25 "Giraffe"

1995. 77th Death Anniv of Niko Pirosmanashvili (painter). Multicoloured.

89		20k. Type **25**	1·60	1·30
90		20k. "Three Princes Carousing on the Grass" (horiz)	1·60	1·30
91		20k. "Brooder with Chicks" (horiz)	1·60	1·30
92		20k. "Boy on a Donkey"	1·60	1·30
93		20k. "Fisherman"	1·60	1·30
94		20k. "Woman with a Tankard of Beer"	1·60	1·30
95		20k. "Bear on a Moonlit Night"	1·60	1·30
96		20k. "Georgian woman with a Tambourine"	1·60	1·30
97		20k. "Still Life" (horiz)	1·60	1·30
98		20k. "Deer"	1·60	1·30
MS99 113×86 mm. 100k. "Family Picnicking" (horiz)			7·00	5·75

26 Alaverdi **27** Sveti-Zchoveli Cathedral, Mtskheta

28 Bitschvinta

1995. Monasteries. Value expressed by letter.

100	**26**	A blue and black	1·90	1·50
101	-	A green and black	1·90	1·50
102	**27**	I lilac and black	1·90	1·50
103	-	I brown and black	1·90	1·50
104	-	I green and black	1·90	1·50
105	**28**	U brown and black	1·90	1·50
106	-	U brown and black	1·90	1·50

DESIGNS: No. 101, Ananuri; 103, Kumurdo; 104, Dranda; 106, Metechi.

The stamps are inscribed with letters of the Georgian alphabet.

1995. Monasteries. As Nos. 106, 100 and 104 but with value expressed by figure.

107		1 purple and black	1·90	1·50
108		2 brown and black	1·90	1·50
109		3 brown and black	1·90	1·50

DESIGNS: No. 107, Metechi; 108, Alaverdi; 109, Dranda.

The numbers on Nos. 107/9 represent classes of postage rather than the face value of the stamps.

29 Iashvili and Family

1995. Birth Centenary (1994) of Paolo Iashvili (writer).

110	**29**	300k. brown and black	2·30	1·90

30 Brontosaurus

1995. Prehistoric Animals. Multicoloured.

111		15k. Type **30**	1·10	85
112		15k. Ceratosaurus	1·10	85
113		15k. Deinonichus	1·10	85
114		15k. Parasaurolophus	1·10	85
115		15k. Saurolophus	1·10	85
116		15k. Scolosaurus	1·10	85
117		15k. Stegosaurus	1·10	85
118		15k. Triceratops	1·10	85
119		15k. Tyrannosaurus	1·10	85
MS120 106×76 mm. 100k. Deinonychus			6·50	5·25

31 White-headed Stork, Bar-tailed Godwit, Mandarin Duck, Hyacinth Macaw and Deer

1995. Wildlife. Multicoloured.

121		15k. Heads of horse, monkey, eagle, deer, bird, lynx and elephant	70	55
122		15k. Dragonfly and butterfly at left, mosquitoes and fishes among heads of woolly-necked stork and greater flamingo	70	55
123		15k. Fishes and butterfly with heads of lioness, cow, parrot, monkey and owl with egret at right	70	55
124		15k. Fox's face at left, northern lapwing, skunk and fish	70	55
125		15k. Butterfly, scorpion, blue-throat, fishes and elephant's trunk at right	70	55
126		15k. Type **31**	70	55
127		15k. Fishes, shells, antelope, dogs, dolphin and silver pheasant	70	55
128		15k. Body of pipefish, Indian peacock and king eider, fox and fly	70	55
129		15k. Rhinoceros, seahorse and dolphin	70	55
130		15k. Zebra, hippopotamus, deer, fishes, spur-winged goose, northern bullfinch, common pheasant and moth	70	55
131		15k. Dog's head, Abyssinian ground hornbill, lobster, fishes and other mammals	70	55
132		15k. Seal, warthog, rabbits, fishes, beetle and red-breasted goose	70	55
133		15k. Ostrich, other birds, fish and lion's face	70	55
134		15k. Snake's head, fishes, slavonian grebe, beetle, giraffe's head and frog	70	55
135		15k. Sheep, antelope, fishes, ant and birds, including dove	70	55
136		15k. Whale, stoat, great crested grebe, killdeer plover, parrot, butterfly and lizard	70	55

Nos. 121/36 were issued together, se-tenant, forming a composite design.

32 Bagrati Cathedral

1995. UNESCO World Heritage Sites.

137	**32**	100k. multicoloured	1·20	95
MS138 75×105 mm. 500k. Jvari Monastery, Mtskhetha (28×42 mm)			6·50	5·25

33 Pterodactylus

1995. Prehistoric Animals. Multicoloured.

139		15t. Type **33**	95	75

140	15t. Rhamphorhynchus (inscr "Rhamphorhynghus")	95	75
141	15t. Pteranodon	95	75
142	15t. Spinosaurus	95	75
143	15t. Tyrannosaurus	95	75
144	15t. Velociraptor	95	75
145	15t. Monoklonius	95	75
146	15t. Ornithomimus	95	75
147	15t. Mastodon	95	75

Nos. 139/47 were issued together, se-tenant, forming a composite design.

34 Barn Swallows

1996. Birds. Multicoloured.

148	15t. Type **34**	60	45
149	15t. Redwing (spotted breast)	60	45
150	15t. Common starling (black with greenish wing)	60	45
151	15t. Hawfinch (brown with black patch on neck)	60	45
152	15t. Barred warbler (black and white bird on twig)	60	45
153	15t. Golden oriole (yellow with black wing)	60	45
154	15t. Collared flycatcher (black and white bird on trunk of tree)	60	45
155	15t. Chaffinch (chestnut front and back and small crest)	60	45
156	15t. Crested tit (brown body, black and white head and crest)	60	45
157	15t. Yellowhammer (speckled black and yellow)	60	45
158	15t. White wagtail (white with black chest, nape and wings)	60	45
159	15t. Blackbird (black with yellow beak)	60	45
160	15t. Common redstart (grey and black head, chestnut patch on front)	60	45
161	15t. European robin (red face and chest)	60	45
162	15t. Eurasian nuthatch (bird with black stripe across eye, on tree trunk)	60	45
163	15t. Blue tit (blue head, wings and tail and green back)	60	45
164	15t. White-tailed sea eagle (white tail)	60	45
165	15t. Osprey (black and white bird in flight)	60	45
166	15t. Short-toed eagle (speckled brown and white on tip of branch)	60	45
167	15t. Long-legged buzzard (chestnut)	60	45
168	15t. Red kite (red tail, in flight)	60	45
169	15t. Western marsh harrier (white tail and white wings tipped with brown, in flight)	60	45
170	15t. Northern goshawk (grey bird with black eye stripe, on branch)	60	45
171	15t. Tawny owl (on branch, tips of fir trees)	60	45
172	15t. Northern hobby (black and white bird on branch overhanging water)	60	45
173	15t. Common kestrel (black head and tail and brown body, valley in background)	60	45
174	15t. Long-eared owl (with large ears, sitting upright)	60	45
175	15t. Great grey owl (on top of tree stump, fir trees behind)	60	45
176	15t. Imperial eagle (both wings raised above body and flying over water)	60	45
177	15t. Imperial eagle (brown bird with white wing-tips, on branch overhanging water)	60	45
178	15t. Little owl (white owl on thick branch at water's edge)	60	45
179	15t. Northern eagle owl (brown bird with ears, spreading wings)	60	45
MS180	Two sheets, each 100×70 mm. (a) 100t. Screech Owl; (b) 100t. Barn Swallow at nest	14·50	11·50

Nos. 148/63 and 164/79 were issued respectively together, se-tenant, forming composite designs.

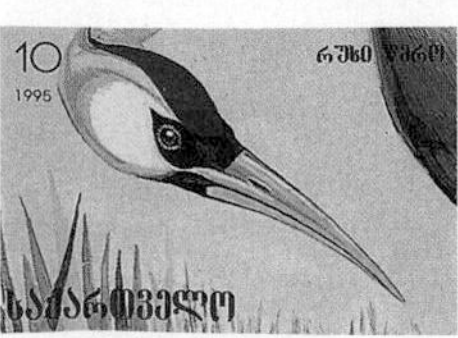

35 Head of Common Crane

1996. Animals. Multicoloured.

181	10t. Type **35**	75	55
182	10t. Body of common crane	75	55
183	10t. Head of snake	75	55
184	10t. Body of snake and moth	75	55
185	10t. Lizard	75	55
186	10t. Common crane and bearded reedling	75	55
187	10t. Dragonfly	75	55
188	10t. Bees on clover and body of snake	75	55
189	10t. Butterfly	75	55
190	10t. Frog	75	55
191	10t. Snail	75	55
192	10t. Turtle	75	55
193	10t. Crayfish	75	55
194	10t. Water plant and head of salamander	75	55
195	10t. Crested salamander and body of salamander	75	55
196	10t. Speckled salamander on trunk	75	55

Nos. 181/96 were issued together, se-tenant, forming a composite design of a pond.

36 Apatosaurus

1996. Prehistoric Animals. Multicoloured.

197	10t. Type **36**	80	70
198	10t. Archaeopteryx (bird)	80	70
199	10t. Leptoceratops (on rocks at entrance to cave)	80	70
200	10t. Parasaurolophus (pair) and body of apatosaurus	80	70
201	10t. Pentaceratops (with horns and neck flap)	80	70
202	10t. Hererasaurus (with mouth gaping, fronds in background)	80	70
203	10t. Hadrosaurus and nest with eggs	80	70
204	10t. Montanoceratops (green dinosaur with different dinosaur in background)	80	70
205	10t. Fulgoloterium (red dinosaur)	80	70

Nos. 197/205 were issued together, se-tenant, forming a composite design.

37 "Citizens of Paris" (Lado Gudiashvili)

1996. Paintings. Multicoloured.

206	10t. Type **37**	45	40
207	20t. "Abstract" (Wassily Kandinsky)	80	65
208	30t. "Still-life" (David Kakabadze)	1·20	95
209	50t. "Three Painters" (Shalva Kikodze)	1·60	1·30
MS210	83×100 mm. 80t. "Portrait of Niko Pirosmani" (Pablo Picasso) (black and gold). Imperf	3·00	2·30

38 Helsinki, 1952

1996. Cent of Modern Olympic Games. Mult.

211	1t. Type **38**	25	20
212	2t. Melbourne, 1956	35	30
213	3t. Rome, 1960	45	40
214	4t. Tokyo, 1964	60	45
215	5t. Mexico, 1968	70	55
216	6t. Munich, 1972	75	60
217	7t. Montreal, 1976	80	65
218	8t. Moscow, 1980	95	75
219	9t. Seoul, 1988	1·10	85
220	10t. Barcelona, 1992	1·20	95
MS221	Two sheets, each 99×70 mm. Each black and scarlet. (a) 50t. Wrestling; (b) 70t. Athletics	12·50	9·75

Each stamp is also inscribed with the names of Georgian gold medal winners at the relevant games.

39 Anniversary Emblem

1997. 50th Anniv of U.N.O.

222	**39**	30t. blue and purple	1·20	95
223	**39**	125t. blue and red	4·75	4·25

40 Javakhishvili and University

1997. 120th Birth Anniv (1996) of Ivane Javakhishvili (first director of Tbilisi University).

224	**40**	50t. multicoloured	1·90	1·50

41 Anton I

1997. 210th Death Anniv (1998) of Anton I (head of Georgian Orthodox Church).

225	**41**	30t. brown	1·60	1·30

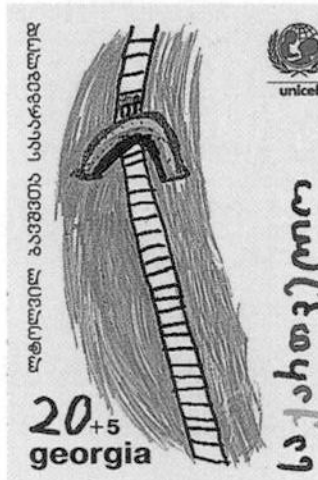

42 Railway Track and Tunnel

1997. 50th Anniv (1996) of UNICEF. Children's Paintings. Multicoloured.

226	20t.+5r. Type **42**	1·40	1·10
227	30t.+10r. Creature (horiz)	1·90	1·50

43 Rottweiler

1997. Dogs. Multicoloured.

228	10t. Type **43**	45	40
229	30t. Gordon setter	1·20	95
230	50t. St. Bernard	1·80	1·40
231	60t. English bulldog	1·90	1·50
232	70t. Caucasian sheepdog	2·30	1·90
233	125t. Caucasian sheepdog (different)	4·00	3·75
MS234	99×75 mm. No. 233	4·75	4·25

44 Two Mice

1997. Animated Cartoon Characters. Mult.

235	20t. Type **44**	70	55
236	30t. Man in bed	1·10	85
237	40t. Girl and rabbit on cloud with balloons	1·40	1·10

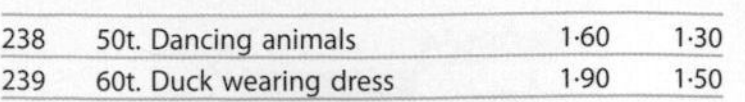

238	50t. Dancing animals	1·60	1·30
239	60t. Duck wearing dress	1·90	1·50

45 Nana Ioseliani (World Vice-Champion, 1988, 1993)

1997. Georgian Women Chess Players. Two sheets, each 90×90 mm, containing square design as T 45.

MS240	Two sheets (a) 20t. ochre, brown and silver (T **45**); 20t. ochre, brown and silver (Nana Alexandria (world vice-champion, 1975, 1981)); 40t. ochre, brown and gold (Maia Chiburdanidze (world champion, 1978, 1981, 1984, 1986, 1988)); 50t. ochre, brown and gold (Nona Gaprindashvili (world champion, 1962, 1965, 1969, 1972, 1975)). (b) Each ochre, brown and gold. Winning teams at chess Olympiads; 30t. Manila, 1992; 30t. Moscow, 1994; 30t. Yerevan, 1996	9·50	8·50

The dates for Maia Chiburdanidze are inaccurate.

46 Map of Caucasus, 1745

1997. 300th Birth Anniv (1996) of Prince Vakhushti Bagration. Multicoloured.

241	40t. Type **46**	1·40	1·10
242	80t. Prince Vakhushti Bagration (vert)	3·00	2·75

47 Tiflis Town Post

48 Congress and Cultural Emblems

1997. "Moscow '97" Int Stamp Exn.

243	**47**	80t. multicoloured	3·00	2·75
MS244		115×88 mm. 1l. As Type **47** but additionally dated "1857 1997". Imperf	4·75	4·25

1997. 1st World Junior (40t.) and Second World (80t.) Delphic Congresses, Tbilisi. Multicoloured.

245	40t. Type **48**	1·30	1·00
246	80t. Emblem and church, Mzcheta	3·00	2·75

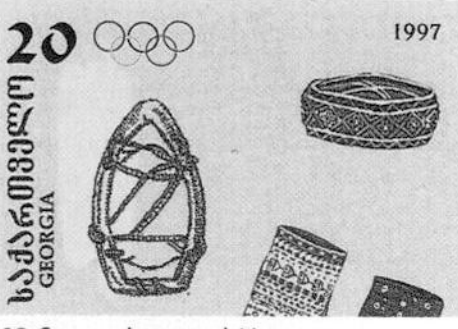

49 Snow-shoe and Hat

1998. Winter Olympic Games, Nagano, Japan. Mult. (a) Clothes and accessories.

247	20t. Type **49**	70	55
248	30t. Glove and snow-shoe	1·20	95
249	40t. Sledge and gloves	1·40	1·10
250	50t. Scarf and skates	1·90	1·70

(b) Ski Jumping.

251	20t. Ski jumper	70	55
252	30t. As No. 251	1·20	95
253	40t. As No. 251	1·40	1·10
254	50t. As No. 251	1·90	1·70
MS255	Two sheets (a) 76×106 mm. 70t. Georgian wearing snow-shoes; (b) 99×70 mm. 70t. Upper body of ski jumper	7·00	6·50

50 Greek Galley (terracotta plate)

1998. Voyage of the Argonauts (ancient Greek legend). Multicoloured.

256	30t. Type **50**	1·20	95
257	40t. Preparation for battle	1·50	1·20
258	50t. Boreads, Phineus (blind seer) and Harpy	2·00	1·70
259	60t. Punishment of King Amicus	2·30	2·10
260	70t. Argonauts in Colchis	2·75	2·50
261	80t. The dragon vomiting Jason	3·25	3·00

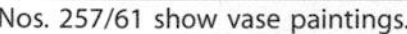
Nos. 257/61 show vase paintings.

51 Brown Horse

1998. Horses. Multicoloured.

262	10t. Type **51**	45	40
263	40t. Black horse	1·40	1·10
264	70t. Chestnut	2·30	2·10
265	80t. White horse	2·75	2·50
MS266	110×90 mm. 100t. Grey. Imperf	3·50	3·25

52 Pteranodon

1998. Prehistoric Animals. Multicoloured.

267	15t. Type **52** (inscr "Pterodactylus")	95	65
268	15t. Rhamphorhynchus facing right	95	65
269	15t. Pterodactyl (inscr "Pteranodon")	95	65
270	15t. Velociraptor (inscr "Spinosaurus")	95	65
271	15t. Tyrannosaurus facing right	95	65
272	15t. Spinosaurus (inscr "Velociraptor")	95	65
273	15t. Mastodon (inscr "Monoklonius")	95	65
274	15t. Ornithomimus facing left	95	65
275	15t. Monoklonius (inscr "Mastodon")	95	65

Nos. 267/75 were issued together, se-tenant, forming a composite design.

53 Class VL8 No. 888

1998. Electric Railway Locomotives built at Tbilisi. Multicoloured.

276	10t. Type **53**	45	40
277	30t. Class VL10 No. 580	1·20	95
278	40t. Class VL11 No. 500A	1·40	1·20
279	50t. Class VL11 No. 001B	1·80	1·60
280	80t. Class VL10u No. 591	2·30	2·10
MS281	107×73 mm. 100t. Class E13 No. 008. Imperf	3·50	3·25

54 Flag and "26 May"

1998. 80th Anniv of Declaration of National Republic.

282	**54**	80t. multicoloured	3·00	2·75

55 Berikaoba

1998. Europa. National Festivals. Value expressed by letter of Georgian alphabet.

283	A(80t.) Type **55**	1·80	1·60
284	B(100t.) Chiakokononba	2·30	2·10

56 Marbled Polecat

1999. Mammals. Multicoloured.

285	10t. Type **56**	45	40
286	40t. Striped hyena	1·40	1·20
287	80t. Brown bear	2·75	2·50
MS287	90×110 mm. 100t. Wild goat (*Capra aegagrus*). Imperf	1·75	1·75

57 Michael Bridge

1999. Bridges in Tbilisi. Multicoloured.

289	10t. Type **57**	45	40
290	40t. Saarbruken	1·20	95
291	50t. N. Baratashvili Bridge	1·80	1·60
292	60t. Mukhrani railway bridge	2·00	1·80
293	70t. Avlabari Bridge	2·30	2·10
294	80t. Metekhi Bridge	2·75	2·50

58 Mink

1999. The European Mink. Values expressed by letter of Georgian alphabet. Multicoloured.

295	A(10t.) Type **58**	1·20	95
296	B(20t.) Mink with fish	1·20	95
297	G(30t.) Two mink	1·20	95
298	D(60t.) Mink emerging from burrow	1·20	95

59 Batsara-Babaneury Reserve

1999. Europa. Parks and Gardens. Value indicated by letter of Georgian alphabet. Multicoloured.

299	A(80t.) Type **59**	1·80	1·60
300	B(100t.) Lagodekhy Reserve	2·30	2·10

60 Emblem and Athletes

1999. 10th Anniv of Georgian National Olympic Committee.

301	**60**	20t. red, black and gold	70	55
302	**60**	50t. red, black and gold	1·90	1·50

61 Writing Letter

1999. 125th Anniv of Universal Postal Union. Illustrations by Sergo Kobuladze from The Knight in the Tiger's Skin (poem). Multicoloured.

303	20t. Type **61**	70	55
304	80t. Woman writing letter	3·00	2·75

62 Georgian Script and Emblem

1999. Admission of Georgia to European Council. Multicoloured.

305	50t. Type **62**	2·00	1·90
306	80t. "EUROPA" and emblem	3·50	3·25

63 KAZ-585 Tipper Truck

1999. Kutaisi Automobile Factory. Trucks. Multicoloured.

307	20t. Type **63**	70	55
308	40t. KAZ-608-717	1·30	1·10
309	50t. KAZ-608-3	1·50	1·30
310	80t. KAZ-4530	2·50	2·30
MS311	110×73 mm. 100t. KAZ-4540. Imperf	3·50	3·25

64 Scarce Swallowtail (*Iphiclides podalirius*)

1999. Butterflies. Multicoloured.

312	10t. Type **64**	60	45
313	20t. Apollo (*Parnassius apollo*)	80	65
314	50t. Dawn clouded yellow (*Colias aurorina* Herrich-Schaffer)	1·80	1·60
315	80t. *Tomares romanovi*	3·50	3·25

65 Svanetia

1999. World Heritage Sites. Sheet 110×69 mm.

MS316	**65**	100t. multicoloured	4·00	3·75

66 "Building Europe" **67** Man kneeling (Mamuka Tavakarashvili)

2000. Europa.

317	**66**	80t. multicoloured	3·50	3·25
318	**66**	100t. multicoloured	4·75	4·50

2000. 800th Anniv of The Knight in a Tiger's Skin (poem by Shota Rustaveli). Showing illustrations by named artists of scenes from the poem. Multicoloured.

319	10t. Type **67**	35	30
320	20t. Horsemen (Sergio Kobuladze and Jacob Nikoladze)	80	70
321	30t. Man fighting tiger (Irakli Toidze and Ucha Japaridze)	1·20	1·00
322	50t. Man and horse (Levan Tsutskiridze and Teimuraz Gotsadze)	2·10	1·90
323	60t. Woman's head (Natela Iankoshvili and Temo Natsvlishvili)	2·50	2·30
MS324	85×110 mm. 80t. Man wearing headdress (Rusudan Petviashvili)	3·50	3·25

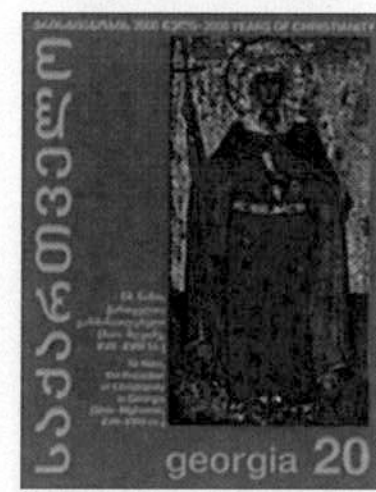

68 St. Nino, Shio Mghvime

2000. 2000th Birth Anniv of Jesus Christ. Icons. Multicoloured.

325	20t. Type **68**	60	45
326	50t. The Saviour, Alaverdi	1·30	1·00
327	80t. The Virgin Hodigitria, Tsilkani	2·10	1·90

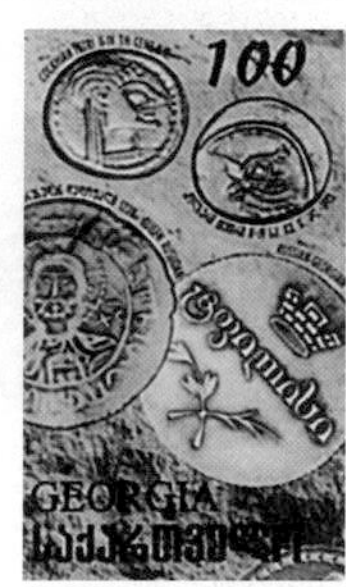

69 Coins

2000. 3000th Anniv of Georgia. Sheet 123×95 mm.

MS328	**69**	100t. multicoloured	4·00	3·75

70 Fish

2000. Fishes.

329	**70**	10t. multicoloured	60	45
330	-	20t. multicoloured	80	65
331	-	30t. multicoloured	95	80
332	-	50t. multicoloured	1·90	1·60
333	-	80t. multicoloured	3·00	2·50

DESIGNS: 20t. to 80t. Depicting fishes.

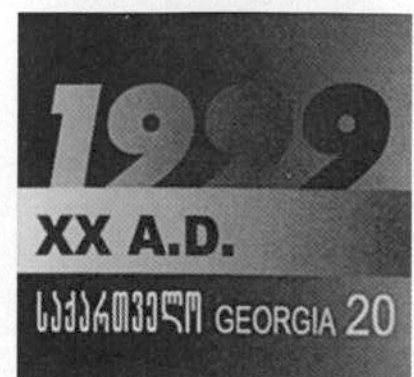

71 "1999"

2000. New Millennium. Each red and yellow.

334	20t. Type **71**	70	55
335	50t. "2000"	1·80	1·60
336	80t. "2001"	2·75	2·40

72 Athlete

2000. Olympic Games, Sydney. Multicoloured.

337	20t. Type **72**	70	55
338	50t. Athlete	1·80	1·60
339	80t. Athlete	2·75	2·40

73 Saradjishvili

2000. 89th Death Anniv of David Saradjishvili (first producer of brandy in Georgia).

340	**73**	80t. multicoloured	3·00	2·75

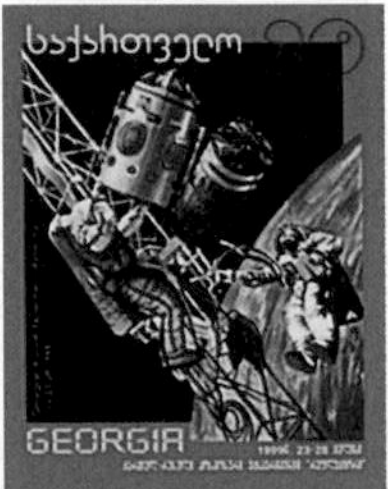

74 Cosmonauts working on Reflector

2000. Georgia–Russia Space Project. Multicoloured.

341	20t. Type **74**	45	40
342	80t. Antenna reflector in space	2·75	2·40

75 "hUMAN RighTS"

2000. Human Rights. Multicoloured.

343	50t. Type **75**	1·90	1·70
344	80t. "HuMAn RiGHtS"	2·75	2·40

76 Refugees

2000. 50th Anniv of United Nations High Commission for Refugees.

345	**76**	50t. multicoloured	1·90	1·70

77 Yellow Chanterelle (*Cantharellus cibarius*)

2000. Fungi. Multicoloured.

346	10t. Type **77**	45	40
347	20t. Field mushroom (*Agaricus campestris*)	70	65
348	30t. Boot-lace fungus (*Armillariella mella*)	1·20	1·00
349	50t. *Russula adusta*	1·80	1·60
350	80t. Violet cort (*Cortinarius violaceus*)	3·00	2·75

78 Church

2000. Churches.

351	**78**	10t. brown	45	40
352	-	50t. blue	1·40	1·30

DESIGN: 50t. Church.

79 Alexander Kazbegi

2000. Writers.

353	**79**	30t. black, red and pink	1·10	1·00
354	-	40t. black, brown and yellow	1·30	1·20
355	-	50t. black, deep green and green	1·60	1·50
356	-	70t. black, lavender and blue	2·30	2·20
357	-	80t. black, brown and chestnut	2·50	2·30

DESIGNS: 40t. Jakob Gogebashvili; 50t. Vadja Pshavela; 70t. Akaki Tsereteli; 80t. Ilia Chavchavadze.

80 Republic P-47 Thunderbolt

2000. 23rd Death Anniv of Alexander Kartveli (aircraft designer). Multicoloured.

358	10t. Type **80**	45	40
359	20t. Republic F-84	70	65
360	80t. Republic F-105D Thunderchief	2·50	2·30
MS361	75×115 mm. 100t. Kartveli (vert)	4·00	3·75

81 Emblem and Horse-drawn Vehicle

2000. 175th Anniv of Fire Service.

362	**81**	50t. multicoloured	1·80	1·70

82 Ritsa Lake

2001. Europa. Water Resources. Multicoloured.

363	40t. Type **82**	1·80	1·60
364	80t. Borjomi Spa	3·50	3·25

83 Synagogue, Kutaisi

2001

365	**83**	140t. multicoloured	4·00	3·75

84 Chess Pieces and Competition Emblem

2001. 1st Europe–Asia Intercontinental Chess Match, Batumi.

366	**84**	1l. multicoloured	3·50	3·25

85 "TRACEA" (transport corridor Europe–Caucasus–Asia) and Route

2001. The Great Silk Route. Multicoloured.

367	20t. Type **85**	80	65
MS368	74×76 mm. 80t. Map and route	3·25	3·00

86 Georgian and American Flags

2001. Support for America after Attacks on World Trade Buildings, New York. Multicoloured.

369	30t.+10t. Type **86**	1·50	1·40
MS370	135×77 mm. 120t.+10t. As No. 369	5·25	5·00

87 Taras Chevtchenko

2002. Poets. Multicoloured.

371	50t. Type **87**	2·10	1·90
372	50t. Akakii Tsereteli	2·10	1·90

Stamps of the same design were issued by Ukraine.

88 Passenger Ship

2002. 140th Anniv of Poti Port. Sheet 104×57 mm containing T **88** and similar horiz designs. Multicoloured.

MS373	30t. Type **88**; 30t. Container suspended from hoist; 30t. Tug guiding ship; 30t. Crane and rowboat; 30t. Steam tug; 30t. Tanker ship	7·00	6·75

89 Scenes from *Mtiuluri*

2002. National Ballet. Scenes from ballets by Soliko Virsaladze. Multicoloured.

374	30t. Type **89**	1·30	1·10
375	50t. *Samaya*	1·90	1·70
376	80t. *Jeirani*	2·50	2·20

90 Woman and Childrenn (statue)

2002

377	**90**	100t. blue	2·50	2·20

91 Man holding House (bas-relief)

2002

378	**91**	5l. brown	12·00	11·50

92 Acrobat

2002. Europa. Circus. Multicoloured.

379	40t. Type **92**	1·60	1·30
380	80t. Tbilisi circus	3·00	2·75

93 Refugees

2002. 50th Anniv of United Nations' Convention on the Status of Refugees.

381	**93**	50t. multicoloured	1·80	1·60

94 Crucifixion (10th-century) **95** The Annunciation

2002. Pectoral Crosses. Multicoloured.

382	10t. Type **94**	60	40
383	20t. Virgin and Child (Martvili, 7–9th century)	70	45
384	50t. Saints surrounding central stone (Martvili, 10th-century)	1·90	1·70
385	80t. Stone encrusted (King Tamari, 12th-century)	2·75	2·50

2002. Frescoes. Multicoloured.

386	10t. Type **95**	60	40
387	30t. Angel, Mary and Saints (horiz)	1·20	95
388	80t. Angel with upraised wings	2·75	2·50

96 Winning Football Team

2002. Dinamo Tbilisi. Winners of European Cup Winners Cup, 1981.

389	**96**	20t. multicoloured	80	65

97 Woman, House and Man holding Rifle

2002. Traditional Costumes. Multicoloured.

390 20t. Type **97** 95 75
391 30t. Woman, round tower and man holding dagger 1·20 95
392 50t. Woman, fortress and man holding sword and shield 1·90 1·70

98 Bell Flower

2002. Flowers. Multicoloured.

393 20t. Type **98** 80 65
394 30t. Caucasia rhododendron 1·20 95
395 50t. Anemone 1·90 1·70
396 80t. Marsh marigold 2·75 2·50

99 SU 25 Scorpio

2002. Aircraft. Multicoloured.

397 30t. Type **99** 1·20 95
398 80t. MIG 21U 2·75 2·50

100 Children encircling Globe

2002. United Nations Year of Dialogue among Civilizations.

399 **100** 40t. multicoloured 1·60 1·30

101 First Georgian Stamp and Ifsda Emblem

2002. 50th Anniv of Ifsda (international federation of stamp dealers' association).

400 **101** 100t. multicoloured 3·00 2·30

102 Alexandre Dumas

103 Three men, Donkey and Dog

2002. Birth Bicentenary of Alexandre Dumas (writer). Sheet 124×104 mm.

MS401 **102** 120t. multicoloured 4·00 3·75

2003. Europa. Poster Art. Multicoloured.

402 40t. Type **103** 1·60 1·30
403 80t. Boy and men 3·00 2·75

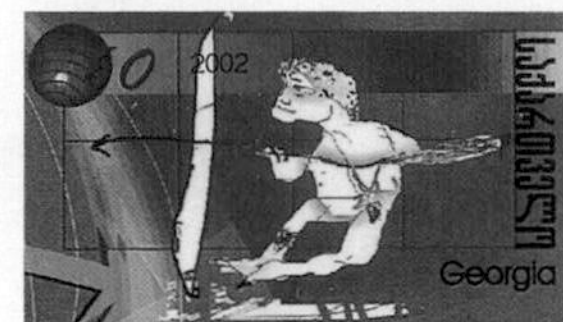

104 Figure

2003. Pre-historic Man. Sheet 130×76 mm containing T 104 and similar horiz design. Multicoloured.

MS404 60t. Type **104**; 60t. Skull 3·75 3·50

105 Players

2003. World Cup Football Championship, Japan and South Korea. Sheet 82×105 mm.

MS405 **105** 1l. black, red and salmon 3·50 3·25

106 Rainbow, Boy and Girl on Horseback

2003. Youth.

406 **106** 50t. multicoloured 1·70 1·50

107 Women holding Globe and Doves

2003. United Nations Development Fund for Women.

407 **107** 50t. multicoloured 1·70 1·50

108 Sloe (*Prunus spinosa*) **109** Elephant

2003. Fruits. Multicoloured.

408 10t. Type **108** 45 40
409 20t. Cherry laurel (*Laurocerasus officinalis*) 75 60
410 30t. Quince (*Cydonia oblonga*) 1·10 95
411 50t. Pomegranate (*Punica granatum*) 1·60 1·50
412 80t. Pear (*Pyrus caucasica*) 2·75 2·50

2003. Tbilisi Zoological Park. Multicoloured.

413 20t. Type **109** 80 65
414 30t. Wolf 1·10 95
415 40t. Ostrich 1·40 1·30
416 50t. Bear 1·80 1·60

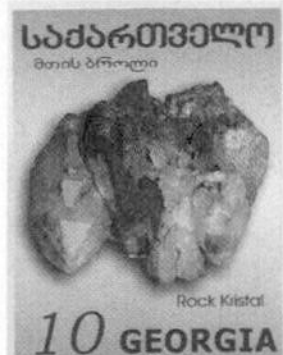

110 Rock Crystal

2003. Minerals. Multicoloured.

417 10t. Type **110** 55 40
418 20t. Agate with amethyst 80 65
419 30t. Orpiment rose (*Arsenic Sulfide*) 1·10 95
420 50t. Realgar (*Arsenic Sulfide*) 1·60 1·50

111 "Old Tbilisi" and Elene Akhvlediani

2003. Birth Centenary (2001) of Elene Akhvlediani (artist). Sheet 170×75 mm.

MS421 **111** 80t. multicoloured 3·00 3·25

112 Self-portrait with Grey Felt Hat

2003. 150th Birth Anniv of Vincent Van Gogh (artist). Sheet 132×65 mm.

MS422 **112** 100t. multicoloured 4·00 3·75

(113)

2003. 10th Anniv of Georgia. No. 58 and MS61 optd with T 113.

423 25t. multicoloured 95 80
MS424 122×101 mm. 25, 50, 100t. multicoloured 5·25 5·00

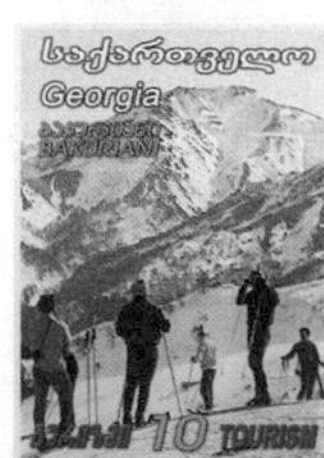

114 Snow Slopes, Bakuriani

2003. Tourism. Multicoloured.

425 10t. Type **114** 55 40
426 20t. Caves, Vardzia 80 75
427 30t. Coastline and ship, Batumi 1·10 95
428 50t. Mountains and Lake Ritsa 1·60 1·40

115 Aladasturi

2003. Grapes. Multicoloured.

429 10t. Type **115** 55 40
430 20t. Rkhatsiteli 80 65
431 30t. Ojaleshi 1·20 95
432 50t. Goruli Mtsvane 1·80 1·60
433 80t. Aleksandrouli (Khvanchkhara) 2·75 2·50

116 Association Emblem

2003. 10th Anniv of International Association of Academies of Sciences.

434 **116** 30t. multicoloured 1·50 1·40

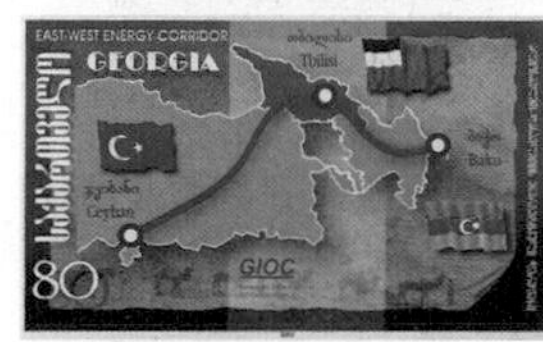

117 Map of Route

2003. Baku—Tbilisi—Ceyhan Oil Pipeline.

435 **117** 80t. multicoloured 3·00 2·75

118 Snowman and Snow-covered House

2004. Europa. Holidays. Multicoloured.

436 40t. Type **118** ("Happy Christmas") 2·10 1·90
437 80t. Child carrying lantern and bowl of eggs ("Happy Easter") 4·00 3·75

119 Belt and Buckle (Ureki) (3rd—4th century)

2004. Jewellery. Multicoloured.

438 20t. Type **119** 95 80
439 30t. Belt buckle and necklace (Aragvispri) (3rd—4th century) 1·40 1·20
440 40t. Necklace and pins (Trialeti) (2000—1500 BC) 1·90 1·70
441 80t. Necklace (Vani) (5th century) and pin (Urbnisi) (3000 BC) 3·50 3·25

120 Towers (Ushguli) (12th—13th century)

2004. World Heritage Sites. Multicoloured.

442	20t. Type **120**	95	75
443	30t. Bagrati Cathedral (11th century)	1·40	1·20
444	50t. Gelati Monastery (12th century)	2·30	2·10
445	60t. Samtavro Monastery (11th century)	2·75	2·50
446	70t. Svetitskhoveli Cathedral (11th century)	3·25	3·00
447	80t. Jvari Monastery (6th century)	3·50	3·25

121 Fencer (sculpture) (B. Skhulukhia)

2004. Olympic Games, Athens. Multicoloured.

448	20t. Type **121**	95	80
449	30t. Athlete (sculpture) (V. Cherkezishvilli)	1·40	1·20
450	50t. Runners (sculpture) (N. Jikia)	2·30	2·10
451	80t. Judo competitor (painting) (L. Vardosanidze)	3·50	3·25

122 Boris Paichadze

2004. Centenary of FIFA (Federation Internationale de Football Association). Caricatures of players. Multicoloured.

452	20t. Type **122**	95	80
453	30t. Avtandil Gogoberidze	1·40	1·20
454	50t. Mikhail Meskhi	2·30	2·10
455	80t. David Kipiani	3·50	3·25

123 Giorgi Tsereteli

2004. Birth Centenary of Giorgi Tsereteli (linguist).

456	**123**	30t. multicoloured	1·40	1·20

124 Crowd waving New Flag, Tbilisi

2004. Rose Revolution. Sheet 91×77 mm containing T 124 and similar horiz designs. Multicoloured.

MS457 50t.×2, Type **124**; Protestors, Batumi	4·75	4·50

125 State Flag

2005

458	**125**	50t. multicoloured	2·10	2·10

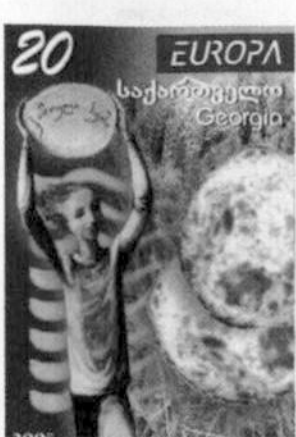

126 Girl and Lavash (flat breads)

2005. Europa. Gastronomy. Multicoloured.

459	20t. Type **126**	1·40	1·20
460	80t. Bread and bakers	7·75	7·50

127 Rabi Abraam Khvoles

2005. Rabi Abraam Khvoles (chief Rabbi) Commemoration.

461	**127**	1l. multicoloured	4·25	4·00

128 Speed Skating

2005. Winter Olympic Games, Turin. Multicoloured.

462	10t. Type **128**	70	55
463	20t. Biathalon	95	80
464	30t. Ski jumping	1·40	1·20
465	40t. Figure skating	1·90	1·70
466	80t. Slalom	3·50	3·25

129 *Dactylorhiza euxina*

130 Georgian Theatre, Kutaisi

2005. Orchids. Multicoloured.

467	20t. Type **129**	95	80
468	40t. *Dactylorhiza* (inscr "ibezica")	1·90	1·70
469	50t. *Ophrys caucasica* (inscr "Oprys")	2·30	2·00
470	80t. *Orchis caucasica*	3·50	3·25

2005. Theatres. Multicoloured.

471	30t. Type **130**	1·40	1·20
472	30t. Georgian Academic Theatre, Tbilisi	1·40	1·20
473	30t. Georgian Theatre, Batumi	1·40	1·20
474	30t. Georgian Opera and Ballet Theatre, Tbilisi	1·40	1·20
475	30t. Ossetian Theatre, Tskhinvali	1·40	1·20
476	30t. Armenian Theatre, Tbilisi	1·40	1·20
477	30t. Abkhazian Theatre, Sukhumi	1·40	1·20
478	30t. Georgian Theatre, Tbilisi	1·40	1·20

131 Vera Tsignadze (ballerina)

2005. Ballet. Multicoloured.

479	40t. Type **131**	1·90	1·70
480	50t. Vakhtang Chabukiani	2·30	2·10

132 Wrestling

2005. Olympic Games, Beijing—2008.

481	**132**	80t. vermilion, grey and black	3·50	3·25

133 Emblem

134 Railway, Mountain and Tower

2005. World Cup Football Championships, Germany—2006.

482	**133**	100t. multicoloured	4·00	3·75

2005. Tbilisi Funicular Railway. Sheet 87×85 mm.

MS483 **134** 100t. multicoloured	9·50	9·50

135 Georgian Europa Stamps

2006. 50th Anniv of Europa Stamps. Multicoloured.

484	10t. Type **135**	45	35
485	20t. Postcard	95	80
486	30t. Magnifying glass and Europa stamps	1·40	1·20
487	40t. Globe enclosed in paper	1·90	1·70
MS488	Four sheets, each 102×76 mm. (a) 80t. As. No. 484. (b) 80t. As No. 485. (c) 80t. As No. 486. (d) 80t. As No. 487	14·00	14·00

136 Stylized Children and Flags

2006. Europa. Integration. Multicoloured.

489	20t. Type **136**	1·20	1·00
490	80t. Stars, globe and Georgia flag	3·50	3·25

(138)

2006. No. 65 surch as T 138.

493	10t. on 1k. multicoloured	60	40

139 Nikola Tesla

2006. 150th Birth Anniv of Nikola Tesla.

494	**139**	50t. multicoloured	2·00	1·60

140 University Building

2007. Centenary of State University, Tbilisi.

495	**140**	40t. multicoloured	1·50	1·30

141 Rider

2007. Georgian Trick Riders in Buffalo Bill's Wild West Show. Sheet 87×78 mm.

MS496 1l. multicoloured	4·00	3·75

142 *Aquila rapax*

2007. Eagles. Multicoloured.

497	10t. Type **142**	80	60
498	30t. *Haliaeetus albicilla*	1·40	1·40
499	50t. *Circaetus gallicus*	1·90	1·70
500	70t. *Aquila chrysaetus* (inscr 'chryaetus')	2·50	2·30

143 Tanks

2007. Armed Forces. Multicoloured.

501	20t. Type **143**	85	65
502	30t. Soldiers	1·40	1·20
503	40t. Cruiser	1·50	1·30
504	50t. Helicopter	1·70	1·50

144 Caravel

2007. Ships. Multicoloured.

505	20t. Type **144**	85	65
506	30t. Crusader ship	1·40	1·20
507	50t. Trireme	1·70	1·50
508	70t. Egyptian sail ship	2·10	1·90

145 In Flight

2007. Greater Spotted Eagle (Aquila clanga). Multicoloured.

509	30t. Type **145**	1·40	1·20
510	40t. Perching	1·50	1·30
511	50t. With wings raised on prey	1·70	1·50
512	60t. Head	2·10	1·90

146 David Guramishvili

2007. 300th Birth Anniv of David Guramishvili (poet).

513	**146**	50t. bistre and black	1·60	1·40

147 Rifle firing Mechanism

2007. Museum Exhibits. Two sheets, each 121×81 mm containing T 147 and similar multicoloured designs.

MS514 (a) 50t.×4, Type **147**; Long barrelled pistol firing mechanism; Blunderbuss firing mechanism; Flintlock pistol. (b) 1l. Wine toast master (7th century bronze statue) (vert)		9·75	9·25

No. 514a and Type **147a** have been left for 'Cradle of Wine Making', issued on 11 July 2007, not yet received.

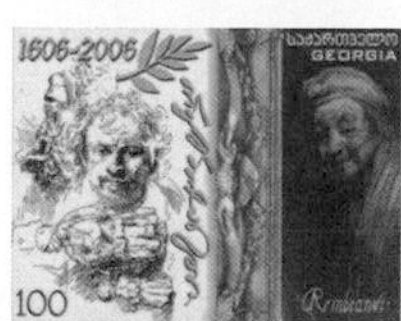

148 Etchings and Portrait (Rembrandt)

2007. Birth Anniversaries in 2006. Multicoloured.

515	100t. Type **148** (Rembrandt Harmenszoon van Rijn) (400th)	3·00	2·50
516	100t. Score and Mozart (Wolfgang Amadeus Mozart) (250th) (41×27 mm)	3·00	2·50

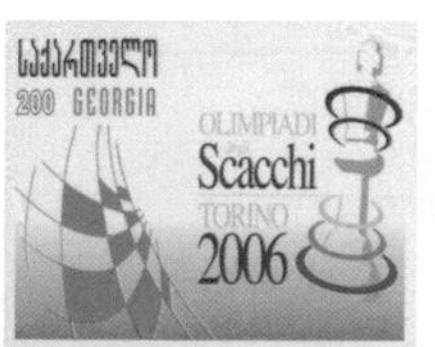

149 Emblems

2007. Chess Olympiad, Turin.

517	**149**	200t. multicoloured	6·75	6·25

149a Ushba

2008. Mountains. Multicoloured.

518s	20t. Type **149**	85	65
519	50t. Kazbeg	1·70	1·50
520	70t. Shkhara	2·10	1·90

150 Castle, River and Scouts

2008. Europa. Centenary (2007) of Scouting. Multicoloured.

521	90t. Type **150**	3·75	3·50
522	1l. Campfire in forest	4·00	3·75

151 Georgian and Japanese Flags and Children

2008. 15th Anniv of Georgia—Japan Diplomatic Relations.

523	**151**	1l. multicoloured	4·00	3·75

152 Magician

2008. Georgian Art of Illusion. Sheet 80×70 mm.

524	**152**	1l. multicoloured	4·00	3·75

2008. Mountains. As T 149a.

525	30t. Ushba (different)	1·40	1·20

153 Pistol shooting

2008. Olympic Games, Beijing. Multicoloured.

526	10t. Type **153**	65	55
527	30t. Wrestling	1·70	1·40
528	60t. Weightlifting	2·50	2·20
529	80t. Judo	3·75	3·25

153a King David IV (11th-century fresco)

2008. King David IV (Bagrationi dynasty, king of Georgia 1089–1125) Commemoration.

529a	**153a**	50t. multicoloured	7·50	7·00

154 2006 20t. Stamp (As Type **136**), Dove and envelopes

2008. Europa. The Letter. Multicoloured.

530	90t. Type **154**	3·75	3·50
531	1l. 2006 80t. Stamp (As No. 490), dove and letter	4·00	3·75

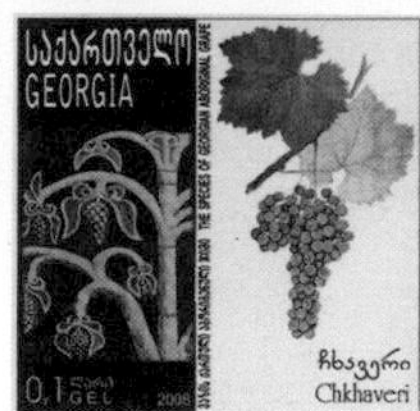

155 Chkhaveri Grapes

2009. Grapes. Designs showing grapes. Multicoloured.

532	10t. Type **155**	35	25
533	20t. Aleksandrouli	75	50
534	30t. Rkatsiteli	1·30	1·00
535	40t. Ojaleshi	1·40	1·10
536	50t. Tsolikouri	1·60	1·20
537	70t. Tavkveri	2·10	1·90
538	90t. Saperavi	3·50	3·00

156 Red and White Flowers

2009. United Georgia. Sheet 125×117 mm containing T 156 and similar horiz designs. Multicoloured.

MS539 30t. Type **156**; 50t. Hands and flags (live chain); 70t. Pro-Georgian demonstration		8·25	8·25

157 Sulkhan-Saba Orbeliani

2009. 350th (2008) Birth Anniv of Prince Sulkhan-Saba Orbeliani (prince, writer, monk and convert to Roman Catholicism).

540	**157**	60t. multicoloured	2·25	1·90

158 Kakutsa Cholokhashvili

2009. Kaikhosro (Kakutsa) Cholokhashvili (Georgian nobleman, military commander and National Hero) Commemoration.

541	**158**	80t. multicoloured	3·00	2·50

159 Early View of Port

2009. 150th Anniv of Poti Sea Port.

542	**159**	1l. multicoloured	3·75	3·25

160 Buildings

2009. 50th Anniv of European Court of Human Rights.

543	**160**	1l. multicoloured	3·75	3·25

161 '60' and Emblem

2009. 60th Anniv of Council of Europe.

544	**161**	2l. multicoloured	7·00	6·50

Index